College Edition

HARPER COLLINS
RUSSIAN
DICTIONARY

College Edition

HARPER COLLINS
RUSSIAN
DICTIONARY

RUSSIAN • ENGLISH ENGLISH • RUSSIAN

HarperCollins*Publishers*

First published in this edition 1994

© Copyright 1994 HarperCollins Publishers

HarperCollins Publishers
P.O. Box, Glasgow G4 ONB, Great Britain

ISBN 0 00 433388-8

10 East 53rd Street, New York, NY 10022

ISBN 0-06-276528-0 (paperback)

First HarperCollins edition published 1995

Library of Congress Cataloging-in-Publication Data

Ozieva, Albina.
    Collins Russian English English Russian dictionary / Albina
Ozieva, Olga Stott, Marina Hepburn.
        p.   cm.
    ISBN 0-06-276528-0 :
        1. Russian language–Dictionaries–English. 2. English language–
Dictionaries–Russian.   I. Stott, Olga.   II. Hepburn, Marina.
III. Title.
PG2640.098 1994
491.73'21–dc20   94-13824
                                                               CIP

94 95 96 97 98 HCM 10 9 8 7 6 5 4 3 2 1

Typeset by / Набор текста произведён
Tradespools Ltd, Somerset, Great Britain

Printed in Great Britain by HarperCollins Manufacturing, Glasgow

АВТОРСКИЙ КОЛЛЕКТИВ/MAIN CONTRIBUTORS

Albina Ozieva • Olga Stott • Marina Hepburn • Katya Butler
Maria Marquise • Elena Cook • Irina Moore • Dr Lara Ryazanova
Dr Natasha Vasilyeva McGrath • Tanya Herries • Fatima Eloyeva
Daniel Brennan • Rose France • Rebecca Brown
Michael Cowan-Young • Sheila Bentley
Professor D. Ward

РЕДАКТОР СЕРИИ/SERIES EDITOR

Lorna Sinclair Knight

ЗАВЕДУЮЩИЙ РЕДАКЦИЕЙ/EDITORIAL MANAGEMENT

Jeremy Butterfield

ВЕДУЩИЙ РЕДАКТОР/EDITOR

Maree Airlie

РЕДАКТОРЫ/EDITORIAL STAFF

Judith Turtle • Andrew Knox • Isobel Gordon
Sandra Harper • Elspeth Anderson
Mary Steele • Merle Read

КОМПЬЮТЕРНОЕ ОБСЛУЖИВАНИЕ/COMPUTING

André Gautier • Colette Clenaghan

Содержание

Contents

Введение	ix	Introduction	ix
О пользовании словарём	x	Using the dictionary	xiii
Грамматическая характеристика	xv	Style and layout	xv
Условные сокращения	xix	Abbreviations used in this dictionary	xix
Таблица русского произношения	xxiv	Russian pronunciation guide	xxiv
Таблица английского произношения	xxix	English pronunciation guide	xxix
		Russian alphabet	
		English alphabet	
РУССКО-АНГЛИЙСКИЙ	1–572	RUSSIAN-ENGLISH	1–572
Грамматическое приложение к русской части	1–9	Guide to Russian Grammar	1–9
АНГЛО-РУССКИЙ	1–564	ENGLISH-RUSSIAN	1–564
Английские неправильные глаголы	2	English irregular verbs	2
Таблицы неправильных форм к русской части	4	Tables of Russian irregular forms	4
Числительные	14	Numbers	14
Даты	17	Time	17
Время	18	Date	18
		English alphabet	
		Russian alphabet	

ТОВАРНЫЕ ЗНАКИ ®

Слова, которые по нашему мнению, являются товарными знаками, получили соответствующее обозначение. Наличие или отсутствие обозначения не влияет на юридический статус того или иного товарного знака.

TRADEMARKS ®

Words which we have reason to believe constitute trademarks have been designated as such. However, neither the presence or the absence of such designation should be regarded as affecting the legal status of any trademark.

ВВЕДЕНИЕ

INTRODUCTION

Мы рады, что Вы выбрали словарь, подготовленный издательством Коллинз. Мы надеемся, что он окажется Вам полезен, где бы Вы им ни пользовались – дома, на отдыхе или на работе.

В настоящем введении излагаются некоторые советы по эффективному использованию данного издания: его обширного словника и сведений, содержащихся в каждой словарной статье. Правильное и максимально полное использование приводимой информации поможет Вам не только читать и понимать современный английский, но также овладеть устной речью.

В начале словаря Коллинз помещён список условных сокращений, используемых в корпусе словаря. Далее следуют произносительные таблицы для русского и английского языков. Между двумя частями словаря помещён раздел, посвящённый русской грамматике. В конце англо-русской части даётся список английских неправильных глаголов а также таблицы русских неправильных форм. Некоторые словарные статьи отсылают читателя к данным таблицам для получения нужной грамматической информации. Числительные и фразы, обозначающие даты и время находятся в самом конце словаря.

We are delighted that you have decided to use the Collins Russian Dictionary and hope that you will enjoy it and benefit from using it at home, on holiday or at work.

This introduction gives you a few tips on how to get the most out of your dictionary – not simply from its comprehensive wordlist but also from the information provided in each entry. This will help you to read and understand modern Russian, as well as communicate and express yourself in the language.

The Collins Russian Dictionary begins by listing the abbreviations used in the text, follwed by a guide to Russian and English pronunciation. Between the two sides of the dictionary you will find a section on Russian grammar, and at the end of the English-Russian text are listed English irregular verbs, plus the tables of irregular Russian forms to which entries in the text are referred. Numbers and expressions using time and date are situated at the very back of the dictionary.

О Пользовании Словарём

Заглавные слова

Заглавными называются слова, начинающие словарную статью. Они напечатаны жирным шрифтом и расположены в строго алфавитном порядке. При многих из них приводятся словосочетания и сращения, частью которых выступает данное заглавное слово. Они напечатаны жирным шрифтом меньшего размера. Два заглавных слова в верхней части страницы указывают на первое и последнее слово, отрезка словника, представленного на данной странице.

Перевод

Перевод заглавных слов напечатан обычным шрифтом. Как правило, варианты перевода рассматриваемого слова разделяются запятой, если они синонимичны и взаимозаменяемы в значении, обозначенном пометой. Различные значения много-значного слова разделены точкой с запятой. Более подробно о пометах см. ниже.

Переводы для различных значений многозначных производных слов часто разделены только точкой с запятой и перед ними даётся одна помета типа (*см прил*). Это означает, что последовательное разделение значений рассматриваемого слова и их переводов даётся при слове, от которого данное производное слово образовано. Например, **annul/annulment**.

В некоторых случаях точный эквивалент перевода невозможен, например, когда английское слово обозначает явление или учреждение, не существующие в России, или же существующие в несколько иной форме. Если возможен приблизительный эквивалент перевода, то он обозначается знаком (≈). Если же культурный эквивалент в языке перевода отсутствует, то вместо него приводится толкование.

Пометы

Пометы, служат для разделения значений многозначного слова. Они приводятся на языке-источнике. Их цель – помочь читателю выбрать перевод, наиболее подходящий в том или ином контексте. Пометы являют собой либо синоним, либо слово, указывающее на характерную для данного значения слова лексическую сочетаемость. Пометы также обозначают переносные значения. Пометы напечат-аны курсивом и заключены в круглые скобки.

При многих заглавных словах даны необходимые стилистические пометы, обозначающие разговорное или просторечное использование этих слов. Эмоционально – стилистическая окраска перевода обычно совпадает с окраской переводимого слова. Нецензурные или грубые слова помечены восклицательным знаком (!).

Произношение

В англо-русской части словаря все заглавные слова снабжены фонетической транскрипцией, которая заключена в квадратные скобки. В тех случаях, где в роли заглавного слова выступает словосочетание, состоящее из двух или более слов, которые, в свою очередь, приводятся в словаре по отдельности, их произношение указывается только там, где они даны как одиночные слова в алфавитном порядке. Список фонетических знаков приводится на страницах xxix–xxx.

В русско-английской части словаря все русские слова снабжены знаком ударения, поскольку их произношение большей частью достаточно ясно, если указано место ударения. В тех словах, где возможно двоякое ударение, обычно указывается только одно, наиболее часто употребляющееся. Омографы (слова, имеющие одинаковое написание, но различное ударение и значение) приводятся как самостоятельные заглавные слова в том порядке, в котором в них проставлено ударение, например, первым даётся слово **за́мок**, затем - **замо́к**. Более подробную информацию о принципах русского произношения читатель может найти в разделе на страницах xxiv-xxviii.

Служебные слова

В словаре уделяется особое внимание тем русским и английским словам, которые обладают сложной грамматической или семантической структурой. Таковыми являются в первую очередь служебные слова, вспомогательные глаголы, местоимения, частицы итп. Они обозначены пометой KEYWORD.

Английские фразовые глаголы

Фразовыми глаголами называются устойчивые сочетания глагола с элементами **in**, **out**, **up** итп, типа **blow up**, **cut down** итп. Они приводятся в словарной статье базовых глаголов, таких как **blow**, **cut**, и сгруппированы в алфавитном порядке.

Аббревиатуры и собственные имена существительные

Аббревиатуры, сложносокращённые слова и собственные имена существительные включены в общий словник словаря в алфавитном порядке.

Употребление "Вы/ты" при переводе "You"

При переводе на русский язык английских фраз, содержащих местоимения "you/your", даются две формы местоимения:одна в ед. числе, а другая во мн. числе --» "ты/твой", "Вы/Ваш". Если в состав фразы входит глагол в форме повелительного наклонения, то он также переводится двумя формами: 2-го лица ед. числа / 2-го лица мн. числа. В тех случаях, где эмоционально-стилистическая окраска фразы является явно неформальной, для местоимения даётся только форма "ты/твой", а для глаголов в повелительном наклонении форма 2-го лица ед. числа, например, "get lost!" переводится как "отстань!"

Употребление or/или, косой черты и скобок

В англо-русской части словаря между взаимозаменяемыми вариантами перевода, а также частями фразы на языке-источнике употребляется союз "*or*". В русско-английской части словаря ему соответствует союз "*или*". Косая черта (/) означает, что приведённые варианты перевода или фразы в языке-источнике не являются взаимозаменяемыми. В круглые скобки заключаются необязательные но возможные в данном выражении слова, как в переводе, так и во фразе на языке-источнике.

Употребление тильды (~)

Тильда в англо-русской части заменяет заглавное слово в словосочетаниях. Например, если в качестве заглавного выступает слово "**order**", то фраза "**out of order**" будет представлена следующим образом: **out of ~**. В русско-английской части тильда заменяет: 1) целое заглавное слово: например, в статье "**до́бр|ый**" фраза "**до́брый день**" показана следующим образом: **~ день**. 2) тильда заменяет часть заглавного слова, предшествующую вертикальной черте: например, в статье "**до́бр|ый**" фраза "**до́брое у́тро**" показана следующим образом: **~ое у́тро**.

Употребление звёздочки (*)

При переводе звёздочкой (*) отмечаются те существительные, в склонении которых наблюдаются те или иные отклонения от нормы. В русско-английской части даётся дополнительная информация относительно отклонений от правил склонения и спряжения.

Headwords

The **headword** is the word you look up in a dictionary. Headwords are listed in alphabetical order, and printed in bold type so that they stand out on the page. Each headword may contain other references such as **phrases** and **compounds**, which are in smaller bold type. The two headwords appearing at the top of each page indicate the first and last word dealt with on the page in question.

Translations

The translations of the headword are printed in ordinary roman type. As a rule, translations separated by a comma can be regarded as interchangeable for the meaning indicated. Translations separated by a semi-colon are not interchangeable, though the different meaning splits are generally marked by an indicator (see below). Where a semi-colon separates translations and the indicator refers to a different part of speech eg. (*see adj*), the translations mirror the splits shown at the other part of speech eg. **annul/annulment**.

It is not always possible to give an exact translation equivalent, for instance when the English word denotes an object or institution which does not exist or exists in a different form in Russia or in the Republics. If an approximate equivalent exists, it is given preceded by ≈. If there is no cultural equivalent, a *gloss* is given to explain the source item.

Indicators

An *indicator* is a piece of information in the source language about the usage of the headword to guide you to the most appropriate translation. Indicators give some idea of the contexts in which the headword might appear, or they provide synonyms for the headword. They are printed in italic type and shown in brackets.

Colloquial and informal language in the dictionary is marked at the headword. You should assume that the translations will match the source language in register, and rude or offensive translations are also marked with (!).

Pronunciation

On the English-Russian side of the dictionary you will find the phonetic spelling of the word in square brackets after the headword. Where the entry is composed of two or more unhyphenated words, each of which is given elsewhere in this dictionary, you will find the pronunciation of each word in its alphabetical position. A list of the symbols used is given on pages xxix-xxx.

For Russian-English, stress is given on all Russian words as a guide to pronunciation. Where stress can be placed over either of two vowels, the most common or correct stress position is shown for the purpose of this dictionary. Words which are spelt in the same way, but have different stress positions are treated as separate entries, the order following the order of the stress eg. **за́мок** comes before **замо́к**. The section on pages xxiv-xxviii explains Russian pronunciation in more detail.

Keywords

In this dictionary we have given special status to "key" Russian and English words. As these words can be grammatically complex and often have many different usages, they have been given special attention in the dictionary, and are labelled with KEYWORD.

Abbreviations and proper names

Abbreviations, acronyms and proper names have been included in the word list in alphabetical order.

"You" in phrases

In translations of English phrases containing "you/your" or the imperative, "Вы/Ваш" and the formal form is given, unless the phrase is very colloquial eg. "get lost!" where it would be more natural to give the familiar form of the imperative.

Use of or/или, oblique and brackets

The words "*or*" on the English-Russian side, and "*или*" on the Russian-English side are used between interchangeable parts of a translation or source phrase. The oblique (/) is used between non-interchangeable alternatives in the translation or source phrase. Round brackets are used to show optional parts of the translation or source phrase.

Use of the swung dash (~)

The swung dash (~) is used on the English-Russian side of the dictionary to stand for the headword in phrases eg. at "order" the phrase "**out of order**" is shown as "**out of** ~". On the Russian- English side of the dictionary the swung dash can either stand for the full headword eg. at "**добрый**" the phrase "**добрый день**" is shown as "~ **день**", or it can stand for the part of the word before the hairline eg. at "**добрый**" the phrase "**доброе утро**" appears as "**~ое утро**".

Use of the superior asterisk (*)

The asterisk (*) is used to mark translations which are in some way irregular in their declension. The Russian-English side of the dictionary contains further information on irregularities.

American variants

American spelling variants are generally shown at the British headword eg. **colour/color** and also as a separate entry if they are not alphabetically adjacent to the British form. Variant forms are generally shown as headwords in their own right eg. **trousers/pants**, unless the British and American forms are alphabetically adjacent, in which case the American form is only shown separately if phonetics are required eg. **jump leads/jumper cables**.

Russian reflexive verbs

Russian reflexive verbs eg. **мыться, краситься** are listed under the basic verb eg. **мыть, красить**.

STYLE AND LAYOUT OF THE DICTIONARY

RUSSIAN-ENGLISH

Inflectional and grammatical information

Inflectional information is shown in the dictionary in brackets immediately after the headword and before the part of speech eg. **стол (-á)** *м*.

Grammatical information is shown after the part of speech and refers to the whole entry eg. **завйд|овать (-ую**; *perf* **позавйдовать)** *несов неперех* (+*dat*).

Where grammatical information eg. *no perf* is given in the middle of the entry, it then governs all the following senses.

Use of hairline (|)

The hairline is used in headwords to show where the inflection adds on eg. **кнйг|а (-и)**. It is also used for swung dash relacement where the swung dash stands for the part of the word before the hairline in phrases.

Stress

Stress changes are shown where they occur, the last form given being indicative of the rest of the pattern eg. **игр|á (-ы**; *nom pl* **-ы)**. In this example the stress is on the last syllable for the singular declension, moves to the first syllable for the plural and remains there for the rest of the plural declension.

Tables

Some headwords which have particularly irregular inflections are declined in full in tables at the back of the dictionary. Shown in these tables are a small group of nouns, verbs, all cardinal and collective numerals, and personal, interrogative and negative pronouns.

Nouns

In order to help you determine the declension and stress pattern of nouns, we have shown the genitive singular for all singular nouns, and the genitive plural for all plural nouns. This is given as the first piece of information after the headword and is not labelled eg. **стол (-á)**.

Where the noun has further irregularities in declension such as irregular plural forms, partitive genitive, locative singular in "у/ю" or change in stress throughout the declension these are shown at the headword and labelled eg. **яблок|о (-а**; *nom pl* **-и)**.

Adjectives

As the declension of a large number of adjectives in the long form is governed by regular rules, we have not shown the long form endings for these adjectives.

Long form endings have been shown for adjectives which may cause problems in declension in the long form such as adjectives ending in **-ий**, where you might be unsure whether the adjective is "soft" or not, and adjectives ending in **-ин** and **-ов**.

Short form endings have been shown for all adjectives where they exist.

Numerals and pronouns

The genitive as been shown for all numerals and pronouns.

Verbs

Where to look:

The majority of verbs are dealt with in aspectual pairs, and we have chosen to show the translation of the verb at the base form of the pair.

Where the perfective is formed by adding a prefix to the imperfective, the imperfective is considered to be the base form and the translation is shown there. The corresponding perfective aspect can also be found in the dictionary in its alphabetical position, cross-referred to the imperfective aspect.

Where the aspect to be cross-referred is alphabetically adjacent to the aspect to which it will be referred, it is not shown separately unless there is some irregularity in its declension. With the pair **завинчивать/завинтить, завинчивать** is not shown separately.

Where the imperfective is formed by adding a suffix to the perfective, the perfective is considered to be the base form and the translation is shown there. The corresponding imperfective aspect can also be found in the dictionary in its alphabetical position, cross-referred to the perfective aspect.

Verbs which do not occur in aspectual pairs are dealt with at their individual headwords.

In phrases both aspects are shown if both work in the context.

To help you see how a verb conjugates, inflections are shown immediately after the verb headword for all verbs according to the following rules:

- for regular 1st conjugation verbs the 1st person singular only is shown eg. **работа|ть (-ю)**

- for 1st conjugation verbs which contain vowel/consonant mutation the 1st and 2nd person singular
   are shown eg. **жд|ать (-у, -ёшь)**
   пи|сáть (-шý, -шешь)

- for regular 2nd conjugation verbs the 1st and 2nd person singular are shown eg. **говор|йть (-ю, -йшь)**

- for 2nd conjugation verbs which contain vowel/consonant mutation, insert "л", or where the stress changes throughout the declension the 1st and 2nd person singular are shown eg. **люб|йть (-лю, -ишь)**

- for verbs where the verb form changes more than once throughout the conjugation, the 1st, 2nd person singular and 3rd person plural are shown. *umn* is inserted after the 2nd person singular to show that the pattern continues until the next form shown eg. **тол|óчь (-кý, -чёшь** *umn*, **-кýт)**

- for verbs which are not used in the 1st person singular, the inflections are shown for their usual usage eg. **темне|ть** (*3sg* **-ет**) Where the restriction applies to one of the senses, the inflections are shown at the sense itself only if they are irregular.

The imperative mood is shown at the headword where it is irregularly formed.

The past tense is shown at the headword where it is irregularly formed or contains a change in stress.

Inflections given as separate entries

Irregular inflected forms are also shown at their alphabetical position and cross-referred to the base headword. In places an inflected form appears as a separate entry and is followed by *umn*, meaning that there are other inflected forms of the same headword which follow the same pattern eg. **отца́** *umn* means that the other inflections of **отец** follow the same pattern by dropping a vowel in oblique cases.

Spelling rules

Russian has the following spelling rules which we have not taken as irregular when showing inflection information:

- after ж,ч,ш,щ,г,к and х, ы is replaced by и, я by a and ю by у.
- after ж,ч,ш,щ and ц, e replaces an unstressed o.
- the letter и is replaced by ы following a prefix ending in a consonant.

ENGLISH-RUSSIAN

Gender

The gender of Russian nouns given as translations is not shown for:

- masculine nouns which end in a hard consonant eg. труд, in -й eg. музе́й or in a hard or soft sibilant eg. нож, плащ
- feminine nouns which end in -a eg. страна́ or in -я eg. земля́
- neuter nouns which end in -o eg. окно́, in -e eg. мо́ре or in -ё eg. ружьё.

Nouns for which the gender is shown are:

- those ending in -ь which can be either masculine or feminine eg. дождь
- neuter nouns ending in -я
- masculine nouns ending in -a eg. па́па or -я eg. дя́дя

Nouns which have a common gender eg. сирота́ are labelled *m/f*.

Indeclinable nouns are labelled with gender followed by the abbreviation *ind* eg. кино́ *nt ind*.

Adjectives used as nouns are labelled with gender followed by the abbreviation *adj* eg. столо́вая *f adj*.

Where the feminine form of a masculine noun is also given as a translation, and the gender of the masculine noun is shown according to the guidelines given above, the gender of the feminine is shown as follows: учи́тель(ница) *m(f)*.

Plural noun translations are always labelled with the abbreviation *pl*, eg. кани́кулы *pl*, and the gender is shown if a singular form exists.

Noun translations are only marked with *sg* where a plural noun headword has a singular translation.

The label *no pl* is used for nouns which do not have a plural form and are only used in the singular eg. лу́ковица, unless the English is also not used in the plural.

Feminine forms

The following conventions are used in this dictionary to show feminine forms of masculine nouns.

- If the feminine ending adds on to the masculine form, the feminine ending is bracketed eg. учи́тель(ница).

- If the feminine ending substitutes part of the masculine form, the last common letter of the masculine and feminine form is shown before the feminine ending, preceded by a dash and enclosed in brackets eg. актёр(-три́са). Where an adjective is used as a noun and has a feminine form, the last common letter does not have to be given eg. безрабо́тный(- ая).

- If the feminine form is given in full, it is bracketed and separated from the masculine form by a character space eg. чех (че́шка).

Adjectives

Russian translations of adjectives are always given in the masculine, unless the adjective relates only to a feminine noun eg. бере́менная.

The masculine short form (or feminine if the adjective only applies to a feminine noun) is also given where it is appropriate.

Verbs

In translation of the headword, imperfective and perfective aspects are shown in full where they both apply eg. **to do** де́лать (сде́лать *perf*). If only one aspect is shown, it means that only one aspect works for this sense.

In infinitve phrases, if the two aspects apply they are shown and labelled eg. **to buy sth** покупа́ть (купи́ть *perf*) что-н.

Where the English phrase contains the construction "to do" standing for any verb, it has been replaced by +*infin*/+*impf infin*/+*perf infin* in the Russian translation, depending on which aspects of the Russian verb work in the given context.

Where the English phrase contains the past tense of a verb in the 1st person singular, the Russian translation gives only the masculine form eg. **I was glad** я был рад

Where both the present tense and the past tense of the verb "to be" are given in a phrase, eg. **he is/was** ..., it means that the Russian translation will govern the nominative case in either tense. If, however, only the present tense is shown, it can be assumed that the past tense of the Russian translation will govern the instrumental case.

Prepositions

Unless they are bracketed, prepositions and cases which follow verbs, adjectives etc are obligatory as part of the translation eg. **to inundate with** зава́ливать (завали́ть *perf*) +*instr*

Where they are separated by *or* they are interchangeable.

An oblique (/) is used to separate prepositions when the preposition depends on the following noun rather than on the preceding verb eg. идти́ в/на.

Условные Сокращения в Англо-Русской Части

сокращение	**abbr**	abbreviation
винительный падеж	**acc**	accusative
имя прилагательное	**adj**	adjective
администрация	**ADMIN**	administration
наречие	**adv**	adverb
сельское хозяйство	**AGR**	agriculture
анатомия	**ANAT**	anatomy
архитектура	**ARCHIT**	architecture
автомобильное дело	**AUT**	automobiles
вспомогательный глагол	**aux vb**	auxiliary verb
авиация	**AVIAT**	aviation
биология	**BIO**	biology
ботаника	**BOT**	botany
британский английский	**BRIT**	British English
химия	**CHEM**	chemistry
коммерция	**COMM**	commerce
компьютер	**COMPUT**	computing
союз	**conj**	conjunction
строительство	**CONSTR**	construction
сращение	**cpd**	compound
кулинария	**CULIN**	culinary
дательный падеж	**dat**	dative
сколняется	**decl**	declines
определённый артикль	**def art**	definite article
уменьшительное	**dimin**	diminutive
экономика	**ECON**	economics
электроника	**ELEC**	electricity
особенно	**esp**	especially
и тому подобное	**etc**	et cetera
междометие	**excl**	exclamation
женский род	**f**	feminine
в переносном значении	**fig**	figurative
родительный падеж	**gen**	genitive
география	**GEO**	geography
геометрия	**GEOM**	geometry
безличный	**impers**	impersonal
несовершенный вид	**impf**	imperfective verb
несклоняемое	**ind**	indeclinable
неопределённый артикль	**indef art**	indefinite article
разговорное	**inf**	informal
грубо	**inf!**	offensive
инфинитив	**infin**	infinitive
творительный падеж	**instr**	instrumental
неизменяемое	**inv**	invariable
неправильный	**irreg**	irregular
лингвистика	**LING**	linguistics

Условные Сокращения в Англо-Русской Части

местный падеж	*loc*	locative
мужской род	*m*	masculine
субстантивированное прилагательное	*m/f/nt adj*	adjectival noun
математика	*MATH*	mathematics
медицина	*MED*	medicine
военный термин	*MIL*	military
музыка	*MUS*	music
имя существительное	*n*	noun
морской термин	*NAUT*	nautical
именительный падеж	*nom*	nominative
существительное во множественном числе	*npl*	plural noun
средний род	*nt*	neuter
числительное	*num*	numeral
себя	*o.s.*	oneself
разделительный	*part*	partitive
пренебрежительное	*pej*	pejorative
совершенный вид	*perf*	perfective verb
фотография	*PHOT*	photography
физика	*PHYS*	physics
физиология	*PHYSIOL*	physiology
множественное число	*pl*	plural
политика	*POL*	politics
страдательное причастие	*pp*	past participle
предлог	*prep*	preposition
местоимение	*pron*	pronoun
предложный падеж	*prp*	prepositional
психология	*PSYCH*	psychiatry
прошедшее время	*pt*	past tense
железнодорожный термин	*RAIL*	railways
религия	*REL*	religion
кто-нибудь	*sb*	somebody
просвещение	*SCOL*	school
единственное число	*sg*	singular
что-нибудь	*sth*	something
подлежащее	*subj*	subject
превосходная степень	*superl*	superlative
техника	*TECH*	technology
теле(связь)	*TEL*	telecommunications
театр	*THEAT*	theatre
телевидение	*TV*	television
типографский термин	*TYP*	printing

Условные Сокращения в Англо-Русской Части

американский английский	**US**	American English
обычно	**usu**	usually
глагол	**vb**	verb
непереходный глагол	**vi**	intransitive verb
глагольное слобосочетание	**vt fus**	inseparable verb
переходный глагол	**vt**	transitive verb
зоология	**ZOOL**	zoology
зарегистрированный товарный знак	®	registered trademark
вводит культурный эквивалент	≈	introduces a cultural equivalent

Abbreviations Used in Russian-English

aviation	**АВИА**	авиация
automobiles	**АВТ**	автомобильное дело
administration	**АДМИН**	администрация
anatomy	**АНАТ**	анатомия
architecture	**АРХИТ**	архитектура
impersonal	**безл**	безличный
biology	**БИО**	биология
botany	**БОТ**	ботаника
parenthesis	**вводн сл**	вводное слово
military	**ВОЕН**	военный термин
reflexive	**возв**	возвратный глагол
geography	**ГЕО**	география
geometry	**ГЕОМ**	геометрия
verb	**глаг**	глагол
offensive	**груб!**	грубо
singular	**ед**	единственное число
feminine	**ж**	женский род
zoology	**ЗООЛ**	зоология
history	**ИСТ**	история
et cetera	**итп**	и тому подобное
predicate	**как сказ**	как сказуемое
commercial	**КОММ**	коммерция
computing	**КОМП**	компьютер
somebody	**кто-н**	кто-нибудь
culinary	**КУЛИН**	кулинария
linguistics	**ЛИНГ**	лингвистика
masculine	**м**	мужской род
mathematics	**МАТ**	математика
medicine	**МЕД**	медицина
exclamation	**межд**	междометие
pronoun	**мест**	местоимение
plural	**мн**	множественное число
nautical	**МОР**	морской термин
music	**МУЗ**	музыка
adverb	**нареч**	наречие
invariable	**неизм**	неизменяемое
intransitive	**неперех**	непереходный глагол
indeclinable	**нескл**	несклоняемое
imperfective	**несов**	несовершенный вид
attributive	**опред**	определение
figurative	**перен**	в переносном значении
transitive	**перех**	переходный
subject	**подлеж**	подлежащее
politics	**ПОЛИТ**	политика
superlative	**превос**	превосходная степень
preposition	**предл**	предлог

ABBREVIATIONS USED IN RUSSIAN-ENGLISH

pejorative	*пренебр*	пренебрежительное
adjective	*прил*	имя прилагательное
possessive	*притяж*	притяжательный
school	*ПРОСВЕЩ*	просвещение
psychology	*ПСИХОЛ*	психология
informal	*разг*	разговорное
religion	*РЕЛ*	религия
see	*см*	смотри
collective	*собир*	собирательное
perfective	*сов*	совершенный вид
abbreviation	*сокр*	сокращение
neuter	*ср*	средний род
comparative	*сравн*	сравнительная степень
construction	*СТРОИТ*	строительство
noun	*сущ*	имя существительное
agriculture	*С.-Х.*	сельское хозяйство
television	*ТЕЛ*	телевидение
technology	*ТЕХ*	техника
printing	*ТИПОГ*	типографский термин
diminutive	*уменьш*	уменьшительное
physics	*ФИЗ*	физика
photography	*ФОТО*	фотография
chemistry	*ХИМ*	химия
particle	*част*	частица
somebody's	*чей-н*	чей-нибудь
numeral	*чис*	числительное
something	*что-н*	что-нибудь
economics	*ЭКОН*	экономика
eletricity	*ЭЛЕК*	электроника
law	*ЮР*	юридический термин
registered trademark	®	зарегистрированный товарный знак
introduces a cultural equivalent	≈	вводит культурный эквивалент

GUIDE TO RUSSIAN PRONUNCIATION

Vowels

1. Russian vowels are inherently short, whereas in English some vowels are inherently long (eg. **beat**) while others are inherently short (eg. **bit**). Russian stressed vowels, however, tend to be slightly longer than unstressed vowels. In unstressed positions all vowels are "reduced" ie. their individual characteristics are not as definite as those of their stressed counterparts.

2. In unstressed positions the letter **o** has the same value as the letter **a** eg. **города́** [gərʌ'da]. Some loanwords and acronyms are exceptions eg. **ра́дио** ['raḍio], **госба́нк** [goz'bank].

3. In unstressed positions the letter **e** is pronounced like **bit** eg. **село́** [ṣi'lo]. The same is true of **я** before stressed syllables eg. **пяти́** [pi'ṭi], and of **a** when it follows **ч** or **щ** eg. **щади́ть** [ɰi'ḍiṭ]. After **ж, ц** and **ш** unstressed **e** is pronounced as [+] eg. **жена́** [ʒ+'na].

4. All Russian diphthongs end in [j], which in diphthongs is pronounced as [i] (eg. **sheet**) with the tongue very close to the roof of the mouth.

N.B. The letter **ë**, always stressed, is not an independent letter of the alphabet, being used only in grammar books, dictionaries etc. to avoid ambiguity eg. **нéбо** and **нёбо**.

Consonants

1. The consonants **п, б, м, ф, в, т, д, н, с, з, л, р, к, г, x** have "soft" or "palatalised" consonants, which are indicated by a "softening" vowel letter **e, ë, и, ю, я** or the soft sign **ь** following the consonant letter: **те** [ṭɛ], **ни́ва** ['ɲvə], **ся́ду** ['ṣadu], **мать** [maṭ]. Consonants preceding a "soft" consonant may also be pronounced soft, usually if they are pronounced in the same place in the mouth (ie. are "homorganic") eg. **стих** [ṣṭix], though this is not always the case eg. **свет** [sᶌɛt].

2. The "soft" consonants **п, б, м, ф, в, г** are pronounced like their "hard" counterparts with simultaneous [j] (as in **yet**).

3. In pronouncing "soft" **т, д, н** the tip of the tongue is drawn back slightly from the position for **т, д, н** and in these "soft" consonants, togther with "soft" **с, з**, the front of the tongue is arched up towards the [j] position.

4. "Soft" **л** is very different from **л**. The front of the tongue is raised to the [j] position, while the back of the tongue must not be raised at all, cf. **лот** [lot] and **лёт** [ļot], **по́лка** ['polkə] and **по́лька** ['poļkə].

5. In "soft" **к, г, x** the back of the tongue is raised somewhat further forward in the mouth than in **к, г, x** and a good portion of the middle of the tongue touches or approaches the roof of the mouth eg. **руки́** [ru'ḳi], **ноги́** [nʌ'gi].

6. The consonants **т, д, н** eg. **ток** [tok], **дом** [dom], **нас** [nas] are pronounced with the tongue-tip slightly further forward in the mouth than in the English counterparts.

7. The consonants **п, т, к** eg. **пасть** [paṣt], **ток** [tok] and **кот** [tok] are pronounced without the slight puff of air which follows them in English before stressed vowels.

8. **л** eg. **ло́дка** ['lotkə] is pronounced with the tongue-tip in the same position as in English [l], but the back of the tongue is raised as if one were pronouncing [u], while the middle of the

tongue is depressed. The result is an л which is even "darker" than that at the end of English **wall**.

9. There are pairs of voiced and voiceless consonants –

Voiced: б, в, д, з, г and their "soft" counterparts
Voiceless: п, ф, т, с, к and their "soft" counterparts

a) At the end of a word a voiced consonant is replaced by the corresponding voiceless consonant eg. **го́род** ['gorət] (cf. **го́рода** ['gorədə]).

b) When a voiced consonant occurs before a voiceless consonant in the same word or at the close juncture of two words it is replaced by the corresponding voiceless consonant eg. **городка́** [gərʌt'ka], **из того́** [is tʌ'vo] (cf. **из э́того** [l'zɛtəvə]).

c) When a voiceless consonant occurs before one of the voiced members of the pairs (except **в** and its "soft" counterpart), the converse happens, and the voicless consonant is replaced by a voiced consonant eg. **сдава́ть** [zd 'vaṱ] (cf. **сойти́** [śʌj'ṱi]), but **свой** [svoj], **свет** [ʂɣɛt].

N.B. The spelling does not reflect these consonant changes except that the prefixes **воз-/вз-**, **из-**, **(с)низ-** and **раз-/роз-** change to **вос-/вс-**, **ис-**, **(с)нис-** and **рас-/рос-** respectively in the appropriate circumstances eg. **изойти́** [ɪzʌj'ṱi] to **исходи́ть** [isxʌ'ḍiṱ].

RUSSIAN PRONUNCIATION

Vowels and Diphthongs

Symbol	Russian Example	English Example/Explanation
[ɑ]	д*а*ть	pronounced like the beginning of diphthong in "eye"
[æ]	ч*а*сть	c*a*t
[ʌ]	дав*а*л, *а*двок*а*т	c*u*p
[ə]	сту́л*а*	*a*long
[ɪ]	ч*а*сы́, щ*а*ди́ть	b*i*t
[ɛ]	с*е*л	g*e*t
[e]	с*е́*ли	pronounced like the beginning of diphthong in "eight"
[jɛ]	*е*л	*ye*t
[je]	*е*сть	only before "soft" consonants
[ɪ]	с*е*ло́	b*i*t
[ji]	*е*го́	*yi*p
[ɨ]	ж*е*на́	*see note 3 under Vowels*
[o]	д*ё*сны, ч*ё*рный	*aw*e
[jo]	*ё*лка, мо*ё*	*yaw*n
[i]	*и*х, н*и́*ва	sh*ee*t
[ɪ]	*и*гра́	b*i*t
[ɨ]	ж*и*ть	after "ж, ц, ш"
[j]	*й*од, мо*й*	*y*ield
[o]	к*о*т	*aw*e
[ʌ]	*но*га́, *о*ткрыва́ть	c*u*p
[ə]	к*о*лбаса́, я́бл*око*	*a*long
[u]	*у*м	sh*oo*t
[ɨ]	с*ы*н	pronounced like "ee", but with the tongue arched further back in the mouth
[ɛ]	*э*то	g*e*t
[e]	*э*то	pronounced like the beginning of diphthong in "eight"
[ɨ]	съ*э*коно́мить	not after "soft" consonants
[u]	ут*ю*г	n*oo*n
[ju]	*ю*г, обо*ю*дный	*you*, *you*th
[a]	т*я́*жкий	pronounced like the beginning of diphthong in "eye"

[ja]	<u>я</u>сно	initially and after vowels
[æ]	с<u>я</u>дь	c<u>a</u>t
[jæ]	<u>я</u>сень	<u>ya</u>k
[ɪ]	п<u>я</u>ти́	b<u>i</u>t
[jɪ]	<u>я</u>зы́к, по<u>я</u>са́	<u>yi</u>p
[ə]	ды́н<u>я</u>	<u>a</u>long
[jə]	сча́сть<u>я</u>	"y" + <u>a</u>long

Consonants

Symbol	Russian Example	English Example/Explanation
[b]	<u>б</u>анк	<u>b</u>ut
[b̦]	о<u>б</u>е́д	see note 2 under Consonants
[p]	зу<u>б</u>, ю́<u>б</u>ка	<u>p</u>ut
[p̦]	го́лу<u>б</u>ь	see note 2 under Consonants
[v]	<u>в</u>от	<u>v</u>at
[ɣ]	<u>в</u>е́тка	see note 2 under Consonants
[f]	ле<u>в</u>	<u>f</u>at
[f̦]	бро<u>в</u>ь	see note 2 under Consonants
[g]	<u>г</u>од	<u>g</u>ot
[g̦]	но<u>г</u>и́	see note 5 under Consonants
[k]	но<u>г</u>, но́<u>г</u>ти	<u>c</u>at
[d]	<u>д</u>ом	<u>d</u>og
[d̦]	<u>д</u>е́вушка	see note 3 under Consonants
[t]	са<u>д</u>	<u>t</u>op
[ț]	ло́ша<u>д</u>ь	see note 3 under Consonants
[ʒ]	<u>ж</u>ена́	mea<u>s</u>ure
[ʃ]	ё<u>ж</u>, ло́<u>ж</u>ка	<u>sh</u>oot
[z]	<u>з</u>а́втра	do<u>z</u>e
[z̦]	га<u>з</u>е́та	see note 3 under Consonants
[s]	га<u>з</u>	ga<u>s</u>
[ș]	гря<u>з</u>ь	at end of word or before voiceless consonant
[ʒ]	и<u>зж</u>о́га	mea<u>s</u>ure
[k]	<u>к</u>от	<u>c</u>ot
[k̦]	ру<u>к</u>и́	see note 5 under Consonants

xxvii

[ʃ]	и**з** шёлка	**sh**oot
[ɹ]	и**з** чего́	**sh**eet
[l]	**л**о́дка	wa**ll**
[ļ]	**л**ес	*see note 4 under Consonants*
[m]	**м**ать	**m**at
[m̩]	**м**ять	*see note 2 under Consonants*
[n]	**н**ас	**n**o
[ņ]	**н**ет	*see note 3 under Consonants*
[p]	**п**асть	**p**ut
[p̦]	**п**еть	*see note 2 under Consonants*
[b]	ослё**н**	**b**ut
[r]	**р**от	pronounced like rolled Scots "r"
[ɾ]	**р**яд	*see note 2 under Consonants*
[s]	**с**ад	**s**at
[ş]	**с**ел	*see note 3 under Consonants*
[z]	**с**дава́ть	do**z**e
[ʐ]	**с**де́лать	before some voiced consonants
[ɹ]	**с**шить	**sh**oot
[ʒ]	**с**жать	mea**s**ure
[ɹ]	**с**чи́стить	**sh**eet
[t]	**т**ок	**t**op
[ḓ]	**т**е	*see note 3 under Consonants*
[d]	о**т**говори́ть	**d**og
[ţ]	о**т**де́лать	before "soft" "д"
[f]	**ф**о́рма	**f**at
[f̦]	бу**ф**е́т	*see note 2 under Consonants*
[v]	а**ф**га́нец	**v**at
[x]	**х**од	pronounced like Scots "ch" in "loch"
[χ]	**х**и́мик	*see note 5 under Consonants*
[ts]	**ц**ель	bi**ts**
[dz]	оте́**ц** **б**ы	a**dz**e
[tʃ]	**ч**а́сто	**ch**ip
[dʒ]	до**чь** **б**ы	**j**ig
[ʃ]	**ш**у́тка	**sh**oot
[ɯ]	**щ**ит	fre**sh sh**eets

Английское Произношение

Гласные и дифтонги

Знак	Английский Пример	Русское Соответствие/Описание
[ɑ:]	f*a*ther	м*á*ма
[ʌ]	b*u*t, c*o*me	*а*лья́нс
[æ]	m*a*n, c*a*t	*э́*тот
[ə]	fath*e*r, *a*go	рáн*а*, п*а*рохóд
[ə:]	b*i*rd, h*ea*rd	ф*ё*дор
[ε]	g*e*t, b*e*d	ж*е*ст
[ɪ]	*i*t, b*i*g	к*и*т
[i:]	t*ea*, s*ea*	*и́*ва
[ɔ]	h*o*t, w*a*sh	х*о*д
[ɔ:]	s*a*w, *a*ll	*ó*чень
[u]	p*u*t, b*oo*k	б*у*к
[u:]	t*oo*, y*ou*	*ý*лица
[aɪ]	fl*y*, h*i*gh	л*áй*
[au]	h*ow*, h*ou*se	*á*ут
[εə]	th*ere*, b*ear*	произнóсится как сочетáние звýков "э" и крáткого "а"
[eɪ]	d*ay*, ob*ey*	*эй*
[ɪə]	h*ere*, h*ear*	произнóсится как сочетáние звýков "и" и крáткого "а"
[əu]	g*o*, n*o*te	*óу*
[ɔɪ]	b*oy*, *oi*l	б*óй*
[uə]	p*oo*r, s*ure*	произнóсится как сочетáние звýков "у" и крáткого "а"
[juə]	p*ure*	произнóситься как сочетáние звýков "ю" и крáткого "а"

Согласные

Знак	Английский Пример	Русское Соответствие/Описание
[b]	*b*ut	*б*ал
[d]	men*ded*	аре́н*д*а
[g]	*g*o, *g*et, bi*g*	*г*ол, ми*г*
[dʒ]	*g*in, *j*ud*ge*	*дж*и́нсы, и́ми*дж*
[ŋ]	si*ng*	произно́сится как ру́сский "н", но не ко́нчиком языка́, а за́дней ча́стью его́ спи́нки
[h]	*h*ouse, *h*e	*х*а́ос, *х*и́мия
[j]	*y*oung, *y*es	*й*од, *й*е́мен
[k]	*c*ome, mo*ck*	*к*а́мень, ро*к*
[r]	*r*ed, t*r*ead	*р*от, т*р*ава́
[s]	*s*and, ye*s*	*с*ад, ри*с*
[z]	ro*s*e, *z*ebra	ро́*з*а, *з*е́бра
[ʃ]	*sh*e, ma*ch*ine	*ш*и́на, ма*ш*и́на
[tʃ]	*ch*in, ri*ch*	*ч*ин, кули́*ч*
[v]	*v*alley	*в*альс
[w]	*w*ater, *wh*ich	*у́*отергейт, *у*ик-э́нд
[ʒ]	vi*s*ion	ва́*ж*ный
[θ]	*th*ink, my*th*	произно́сится как ру́сский "с", но ко́нчик языка́ нахо́дится ме́жду зуба́ми
[ð]	*th*is, *th*e	произно́сится как ру́сский "з", но ко́нчик языка́ нахо́дится ме́жду зуба́ми
[f]	*f*ace	*ф*акт
[l]	*l*ake, *l*ick	*л*ай, *л*ом
[m]	*m*ust	*м*ат
[n]	*n*ut	*н*ет
[p]	*p*at, *p*ond	*п*арохо́д
[t]	*t*ake, ha*t*	э́*т*о*т*, не*т*
[x]	lo*ch*	*х*од

[ɑʒ]	А, а
[be]	Б, б
[ve]	В, в
[ge]	Г, г
[de]	Д, д
[je]	Е, е
[jɔ]	Ё, ё
[ʒe]	Ж, ж
[ze]	З, з
[i]	И, и
[iˈkratkɔje]	Й, й
[ka]	К, к
[ɛl]	Л, л
[ɛm]	М, м
[ɛn]	Н, н
[ɔ]	О, о
[pe]	П, п
[ɛr]	Р, р
[ɛs]	С, с
[te]	Т, т
[u]	У, у
[ɛf]	Ф, ф
[xa]	Х, х
[tse]	Ц, ц
[tʃe]	Ч, ч
[ʃa]	Ш, ш
[ʃta]	Щ, щ
[ˈtɣɔrd+ znak]	Ъ, ъ
[+]	Ы, ы
[ˈm̩akk+ znak]	Ь, ь
[ɛ]	Э, э
[ju]	Ю, ю
[ja]	Я, я

A, a [eɪ]
B, b [biː]
C, c [siː]
D, d [diː]
E, e [iː]
F, f [ɛf]
G, g [dʒiː]
H, h [eɪtʃ]
I, i [aɪ]
J, j [dʒeɪ]
K, k [keɪ]
L, l [ɛl]
M, m [ɛm]
N, n [ɛn]
O, o [əu]
P, p [piː]
Q, q [kjuː]
R, r [ɑː*]
S, s [ɛs]
T, t [tiː]
U, u [juː]
V, v [viː]
W, w ['dʌblju]
X, x [ɛks]
Y, y [waɪ]
Z, z [zɛd, (US) ziː]

~ A, a ~

A, a *сущ нескл* (*буква*) *the 1st letter of the Russian alphabet*; **от ~ до я** from A to Z.

KEYWORD

а *союз* **1** (*выражает противопоставление*) but; **он согласи́лся, а я отказа́лся** he agreed, but I refused; **я чита́л, а он рисова́л** I was reading and he was drawing
2 (*выражает присоединение*) and; **снача́ла говори́л он, а пото́м мы** first he spoke, and then we did
3 (*перед перечислением*) namely; (*перед уточнением*) to be exact *или* precise; **пришли́ дво́е, а и́менно: Ивано́в и Петро́в** two people came, namely Ivanov and Petrov; **я до́лжен встать ра́но, а и́менно в 6 утра́** I have to get up early, at 6 am to be exact *или* precise
4 (*во фразах*): **а (не) то** or (else); **спеши́, а (не) то опозда́ешь** hurry, or (else) you'll be late; **а и́менно** (*то есть*) that is; **а вот** but
♦ *част* **1** (*усиливает обращение*) hey; **Ма́ша, а Ма́ша!** hey, Masha!
2 (*обозначает отклик*): **иди́ сюда́! – а, что тако́е!** come here! – yes? what is it?; **а как же** (*разг*) of course; **ты обе́дал? а как же** have you had lunch? of course
♦ *межд* (*выражает припоминание, догадку*) ah; (*выражает ужас, боль*) oh; **а ну** (*разг*) go on; **а ну, беги́ в дом!** go on, run along in!; **а ну́ его́!** (*разг*) stuff him!

А- *сокр*: **~72, ~76** *different grades of petrol.*
абажу́р (**-а**) *м* lampshade.
абба́т (**-а**) *м* (*в монастыре*) abbot.
абба́ти́с|а (**-ы**) *ж* abbess.
абба́тств|о (**-а**) *ср* abbey.
аббревиату́р|а (**-ы**) *ж* abbreviation.
Аберди́н (**-а**) *м* Aberdeen.
абза́ц (**-а**) *м* paragraph.
абитурие́нт (**-а**) *м entrant to university, college etc.*
абитурие́нт|ка (**-ки**; *gen pl* **-ок**) *ж см* **абитурие́нт**.
абонеме́нт (**-а**) *м* season ticket.
абонеме́нтный *прил* (*концерт, лекция*) for season-ticket holders.
абоне́нт (**-а**) *м* subscriber.

абориге́н (**-а**) *м* aborigine.
або́рт (**-а**) *м* abortion; **де́лать (сде́лать** *perf*) **~** to have an abortion.
абрази́в (**-а**) *м* abrasive.
абракада́бр|а (**-ы**) *ж* gobbledegook.
абрико́с (**-а**) *м* (*плод*) apricot; (*дерево*) apricot tree.
абсолю́тен *прил см* **абсолю́тный**.
абсолюти́зм (**-а**) *м* absolutism.
абсолю́тно *нареч* absolutely.
абсолю́тный (**-ен, -на, -но**) *прил* absolute; **~ная монопо́лия** absolute monopoly; **абсолю́тный слух** perfect pitch.
абсорби́р|овать (**-ую**) (*не*)*сов перех* to absorb.
абстраги́р|оваться (**-уюсь**) (*не*)*сов возв*: **~ (от** +*gen*) to detach o.s. (from).
абстра́кт|ный (**-ен, -на, -но**) *прил* abstract; **абстра́ктное** (*и́мя*) **существи́тельное** abstract noun.
абстра́кци|я (**-и**) *ж* abstraction.
абсу́рд (**-а**) *м* absurdity; **доводи́ть (довести́** *perf*) **что-н до ~а** to take sth to the point of absurdity.
абсу́рд|ный (**-ен, -на, -но**) *прил* absurd.
абсце́сс (**-а**) *м* abscess.
аванга́рд (**-а**) *м* (*также* ВОЕН) vanguard; (*ИСКУССТВО*) avant-garde; **в ~е** (+*gen*) in the vanguard (of).
авангарди́зм (**-а**) *м* the avant-garde.
ава́нс (**-а**) *м* (*КОММ*) advance; **в счёт платеже́й** advance against payments.
аванси́р|овать (**-ую**) (*не*)*сов перех*: **~ что-н кому́-н** to advance sb sth; (*КОММ*) to make sb an advance payment of sth.
ава́нсом *нареч* in advance.
авансце́н|а (**-ы**) *ж* proscenium.
авантю́р|а (**-ы**) *ж* adventurism; **втя́гивать** (**втяну́ть** *perf*) **кого́-н в ~у** to involve sb in a risky undertaking.
авантюри́ст (**-а**) *м* adventurist.
авантюри́ст|ка (**-ки**; *gen pl* **-ок**) *ж см* **авантюри́ст**.
авари́йный *прил* (*служба, машина*) emergency *опред*; (*дом, состояние техники*) unsafe; **авари́йный сигна́л** alarm signal.
ава́ри|я (**-и**) *ж* accident; (*повреждение*:

механизма, аппаратуры) breakdown; **терпе́ть** (**потерпе́ть** *perf*) ~**ю** (*машина, самолёт итп*) to crash; **попа́сть** (*perf*) **в** ~**ю** to have an accident.

а́вгуст (-а) *м* August; *см также* **октя́брь**.

а́вгустовский (-ая, -ое, -ие) *прил* August *опред*.

а́виа *нескл* (*авиапочта*) air mail.

авиали́ни|я (-и) *ж* flight path.

авиано́с|ец (-ца) *м* aircraft carrier.

авиацио́нный *прил* aviation *опред*.

авиа́ци|я (-и) *ж* aviation; **гражда́нская** ~ civil aviation.

ави́зо *ср нескл* (*КОММ*) advice note.

авитамино́з (-а) *м* vitamin deficiency, avitaminosis.

аво́сек *сущ см* **аво́ська**.

аво́сь *част* (*разг*) perhaps; **на** ~ (*разг*) on the off chance; (: *наугад*) by guesswork; **наде́яться** (*impf*) **на** ~ to trust to luck.

аво́сь|ка (-ьки; *gen pl* -ек) *ж* (*разг*) (string) bag.

авра́л (-а) *м* (*МОР*) emergency task; (*перен*: *разг*) rush job.

австрали́ек *сущ см* **австрали́йка**.

австрали́|ец (-йца) *м* Australian.

австрали́йка (-йки; *gen pl* -ек) *ж см* **австрали́ец**.

австрали́йский (-ая, -ое, -ие) *прил* Australian.

австрали́йца *итп сущ см* **австрали́ец**.

Австра́ли|я (-и) *ж* Australia.

австри́ек *сущ см* **австри́йка**.

австри́|ец (-йца) *м* Austrian.

австри́йка (-йки; *gen pl* -ек) *ж см* **австри́ец**.

австри́йский (-ая, -ое, -ие) *прил* Austrian.

австри́йца *итп сущ см* **австри́ец**.

А́встри|я (-и) *ж* Austria.

авт. *сокр* (= *автомоби́льный*) auto. (= *automobile*); = **автоно́мный, а́вторский, а́втор**.

авто- *часть сложных слов* (*со значением автоматический*) indicating sth done automatically *eg*. *автопило́т*; (*со значением автомобильный*) indicating a connection with vehicles *eg*. *автозаво́д*; (*со значением свой, само-*) self- or auto-, indicating a connection with oneself *eg*. *автобиогра́фия*.

автоба́з|а (-ы) *ж* depot (*where a company's vehicles are kept and maintained*).

автобиографи́ческ|ий (-ая, -ое, -ие) *прил* autobiographical.

автобиогра́фи|я (-и) *ж* autobiography.

авто́бус (-а) *м* bus; (*на дальние расстояния*) coach (*BRIT*), bus (*US*).

авто́бусный *прил* (*см сущ*) bus *опред*; coach *опред* (*BRIT*).

автовокза́л (-а) *м* bus *или* coach (*BRIT*) station.

авто́граф (-а) *м* autograph.

автодоро́жный *прил* (*происшествие*) road *опред*; (*инспекция*) traffic *опред*.

автозаво́д (-а) *м* car (*BRIT*) *или* automobile (*US*) plant.

автозапра́вочн|ая (-ой; *decl like adj*) *ж* (*также*: ~ **ста́нция**) filling station.

автока́р (-а) *м* fork-lift truck.

автола́в|ка (-ки; *gen pl* -ок) *ж* mobile shop.

автомагистра́л|ь (-и) *ж* motorway (*BRIT*), expressway (*US*).

автома́т (-а) *м* automatic machine; (*ВОЕН*) sub-machine-gun.

автоматиза́ци|я (-и) *ж* automation.

автоматизи́р|овать (-ую) (*не*)*сов перех* to automate.

автома́тик|а (-и) *ж* automatic equipment.

автомати́ческ|ий (-ая, -ое, -ие) *прил* automatic.

автомаши́н|а (-ы) *ж* (motor)car, automobile (*US*).

автомоби́л|ь (-я) *м* (motor)car, automobile (*US*); **легково́й** ~ (passenger) car.

автоно́мен *прил см* **автоно́мный**.

автоно́ми|я (-и) *ж* autonomy.

автоно́м|ный (-ен, -на, -но) *прил* autonomous; (*ТЕХ*) independent; (*КОМП*) off-line, stand-alone.

автоотве́тчик (-а) *м* answering machine.

автопило́т (-а) *м* automatic pilot.

автопортре́т (-а) *м* self-portrait.

а́втор (-а) *м* author.

авторефера́т (-а) *м* abstract (*of dissertation*).

авториз|ова́ть (-у́ю) (*не*)*сов перех* to authorize.

авторита́р|ный (-ен, -на, -но) *прил* authoritarian.

авторите́т (-а) *м* authority; **по́льзоваться** (*impf*) ~**ом** to enjoy authority; **завоёвывать** (**завоева́ть** *perf*) ~ to gain authority.

авторите́т|ный (-ен, -на, -но) *прил* authoritative.

а́вторск|ий (-ая, -ое, -ие) *прил* author's; **а́вторский ве́чер** (*поэта итп*) reading; (*композитора*) recital (*given by the composer*); **а́вторское пра́во** copyright; **а́вторское свиде́тельство** patent.

авторуч́|ка (-ки; *gen pl* -ек) *ж* fountain pen.

автосто́п (-а) *м* (*способ путешествия*) hitchhiking.

автостра́д|а (-ы) *ж* motorway (*BRIT*), expressway (*US*).

автотра́нспорт (-а) *м* road transport.

авуа́р|ы (-ов) *мн* (*КОММ*) assets *мн*.

ага́ *межд* aha ♦ *част* (*разг*: *выражает согласие*) uh huh.

ага́т (-а) *м* agate.

аге́нт (-а) *м* agent.

аге́нтств|о (-а) *ср* agency; **телегра́фное** ~ news agency; **аге́нтство печа́ти** press agency.

агенту́р|а (-ы) *ж* intelligence service ♦ *собир* agents *мн*.

агита́тор (-а) *м* (political) campaigner; (*на выборах*) canvasser.

агитацио́нный *прил* (political) promotional.

агита́ци|я (-и) *ж* campaigning.

агити́р|овать (-ую) *несов неперех*: ~ (**за** +*acc*) to campaign (for).

аго́ни|я (-и) *ж* death throes *мн*.

агра́рный *прил* agrarian.

агрега́т (-а) *м* machine; (*узел*) unit (*of machine*).

агресси́в|ный (-ен, -на, -но) *прил* aggressive.

агре́сси|я (-и) *ж* aggression.

агроно́м (-а) *м* agronomist.

агрономи́чес|кий (-ая, -ое, -ие) *прил* agronomic.

агроно́ми|я (-и) *ж* agronomy.

ад (-а) *м* hell.

ада́жио *ср нескл, нареч* adagio.

ада́мово *прил*: A~ я́блоко Adam's apple.

адапта́ци|я (-и) *ж* adaptation.

ада́птер (-а) *м* adaptor.

адапти́р|овать (-ую) *(не)сов перех* to adapt
▸ **адапти́роваться** *(не)сов возв* to adapt.

адвока́т (-а) *м* (*ЮР*) ≈ barrister (*BRIT*), ≈ attorney (*US*); (*консультант*) solicitor; **колле́гия ~ов** ≈ the Bar (*BRIT*).

адвокату́р|а (-ы) *ж собир* ≈ the Bar (*BRIT*).

АДД *м сокр* (= *авторефера́т диссерта́ции на соиска́ние учёной сте́пени до́ктора нау́к*) abstract of doctoral thesis.

Адди́с-Абе́б|а (-ы) *ж* Addis Ababa.

адеква́т|ный (-ен, -на, -но) *прил* adequate; (*совпадающий*) identical.

адено́ид|ы (-ов) *мн* (*МЕД*) adenoids *мн*.

адм. *сокр* (= **администра́ция**) admin (= *administration*).

администрати́в|ный *прил* administrative; (*способности*) managerial, management *опред*; **в ~ом поря́дке** by authority; **~ тон** an official tone of voice.

администра́тор (-а) *м* administrator; (*в театре, гостинице, кино*) manager.

администра́ци|я (-и) *ж, собир* administration; (*гостиницы*) management.

администри́р|овать (-ую) *несов неперех* (+*instr*) to administrate.

адмира́л (-а) *м* admiral.

АДМП *ж сокр* = *Агра́рно-демократи́ческая па́ртия*.

а́дрес (-а; *nom pl* **-а́)** *м* address; **в ~** +*gen* (addressed) to; **Ва́ше обвине́ние не по ~у** (*разг*) you've got the wrong person; **по ~у кого́-н** concerning *или* about sb; **абсолю́тный/относи́тельный ~** (*КОМП*) absolute/relative address.

а́дресный *прил*: **стол** address bureau.

адрес|ова́ть (-у́ю) *(не)сов перех*: **~ что-н кому́-н** to address sth to sb; (*критику*) to direct sth at sb.

адриати́чес|кий (-ая, -ое, -ие) *прил*: **А~ое мо́ре** the Adriatic (Sea).

а́дс|кий (-ая, -ое, -ие) *прил* (*РЕЛ*) infernal; (*разг*: *холод, условия*) diabolical; (: *терпение, выносливость*) fantastic; (*замысел*) cunning.

адъюта́нт (-а) *м* aide-de-camp.

аж *част, союз* (*разг*) even; **он ~ вскри́кнул от удивле́ния** he even cried out in surprise.

ажиота́ж (-а) *м* (*перен*) commotion; (*КОММ*) stockjobbing.

ажу́р (-а) *м keeping of books up to date*; **в ~е** (*разг*) in cracking order.

ажу́рный *прил* lace; **ажу́рная рабо́та** fine *или* delicate work.

АЗС *ж сокр* (= *автозапра́вочная ста́нция*) filling station.

аз|ы́ (-о́в) *мн* (*перен*) basics *мн*; **начина́ть (нача́ть** *perf*) **с ~о́в** to start from scratch.

аза́ли|я (-и) *м* azalea.

аза́рт (-а) *м* ardour (*BRIT*), ardor (*US*); **с ~ом** with zest; **входи́ть (войти́** *perf*) **в ~** to get carried away.

аза́рт|ный (-ен, -на, -но) *прил* ardent; **аза́ртная игра́** game of chance.

а́збу|ка (-и) *м* alphabet; (*букварь*) first reading book; (*перен*: *основные начала*) rudiments *мн*; **но́тная ~** *the system of musical notation*; **а́збука Мо́рзе** Morse code.

а́збучный *прил* alphabetical; **а́збучная и́стина** truism.

Азербайджа́н (-а) *м* Azerbaijan.

азербайджа́н|ец (-ца) *м* Azerbaijani.

азербайджа́н|ка (-ки; *gen pl* **-ок)** *ж см* **азербайджа́нец**.

азербайджа́нс|кий (-ая, -ое, -ие) *прил* Azerbaijani.

азербайджа́нца *итп сущ см* **азербайджа́нец**.

азиа́т (-а) *м* Asian.

азиа́т|ка (-ки; *gen pl* **-ок)** *ж см* **азиа́т**.

азиа́тс|кий (-ая, -ое, -ие) *прил* Asian.

а́зимут (-а) *м* azimuth.

А́зи|я (-и) *ж* Asia.

азо́вс|кий (-ая, -ое, -ие) *прил*: **А~ое мо́ре** the Sea of Azov.

азо́рс|кий (-ая, -ое, -ие) *прил*: **А~ие острова́** the Azores.

азо́т (-а) *м* nitrogen.

азо́тный *прил* nitric.

а́ист (-а) *м* stork.

ай *межд* (*выражает боль*) ow, ouch; (*выражет испуг, страх*) oh; **~ да Мари́я!** good for Maria!

айв|а́ (-ы́) *м* (*плод*) quince; (*дерево*) quince tree.

айда́ *межд* (*разг*) let's go; **~ купа́ться!** let's go for a swim!

а́йсберг (-а) *м* iceberg.

акад. *сокр* = **акаде́мик**.

акаде́мик (-а) *м* academician.

академи́чес|кий (-ая, -ое, -ие) *прил* (*также перен*) academic; **академи́ческий теа́тр** *honorary title given to theatres*.

акаде́ми|я (-и) *ж* academy; **акаде́мия нау́к** Academy of Sciences; **акаде́мия худо́жеств** the Academy of Arts.

а́ка|ть (-ю) *несов неперех to pronounce unstressed "o" as "a" in Russian*.

ака́ци|я (-и) *м* acacia.

аквала́нг (-а) *м* aqualung.

аквамари́н (-а) *м* aquamarine.

аквамари́новый *прил* aquamarine.

акваре́л|ь (-и) *ж* watercolours *мн* (*BRIT*), watercolors *мн* (*US*); (*картина*) watercolo(u)r.

акваре́льный *прил* watercolour *опред* (*BRIT*), watercolor *опред* (*US*).

аква́риум (-а) *м* aquarium, fish tank.

аквато́ри|я (-и) *ж*: ~ по́рта area of water near the port.

акведу́к (-а) *м* aqueduct.

АКД *м сокр* (= авторефера́т диссерта́ции на соиска́ние учёной сте́пени кандида́та нау́к) abstract of dissertation for first level of postgraduate degree.

акклиматиза́ци|я (-и) *м* acclimatization, acclimation (*US*).

акклиматизи́р|оваться (-у́юсь) (*не*)*сов возв* to acclimatize, acclimate (*US*).

аккомпанеме́нт (-а) *м* (*МУЗ, перен*) accompaniment.

аккомпани́р|овать (-ую) *несов неперех* (+*dat*; *МУЗ*) to accompany.

акко́рд (-а) *м* chord; **брать** (**взять** *perf*) ~ to play a chord; **заключи́тельный** ~ (*перен*) climax.

аккордео́н (-а) *м* accordion.

акко́рдн|ый *прил*: ~**ая рабо́та** piecework; **он на** ~**ой опла́те** he is on piecework.

аккредити́в (-а) *м* letter of credit.

аккредити́вный *прил* credit *опред*.

аккредито́ванный *прил*: ~ **аге́нт** accredited agent.

аккредит|ова́ть (-у́ю) (*не*)*сов перех* to accredit.

аккумули́р|овать (-ую) (*не*)*сов перех* (*ТЕХ, перен*) to accumulate.

аккумуля́тор (-а) *м* accumulator.

аккура́тен *прил см* **аккура́тный**.

аккура́тно *нареч* (*регулярно*) regularly; (*старательно*) carefully; (*опрятно*) neatly.

аккура́тност|ь (-и) *ж* (*см прил*) regularity; meticulousness; accuracy; neatness.

аккура́т|ный (-ен, -на, -но) *прил* (*посещение*) regular; (*работник*) meticulous; (*работа*) accurate; (*костюм*) neat.

акр (-а) *м* acre.

акри́л (-а) *м* acrylic.

акри́ловый *прил* acrylic.

акроба́т (-а) *м* acrobat.

акроба́тик|а (-и) *ж* acrobatics.

акселера́т (-а) *м* early developer (*physically*).

акселера́тор (-а) *м* accelerator.

акселера́ци|я (-и) *м* early physical maturity.

аксессуа́р (-а) *м* (*одежды*) accessory; *см также* **аксессуа́ры**.

аксессуа́р|ы (-ов) *мн* (*перен*: *в живописи итп*) details *мн*; (: *в театре*) props *мн* (= *properties*).

аксио́м|а (-ы) *ж* axiom.

акт (-а) *м* act; (*торжественное собрание*) ceremony; **составля́ть** (**соста́вить** *perf*) ~ to draw up a formal document; **а́кты** гражда́нского состоя́ния register (*of births, marriages, deaths*).

актёр (-а) *м* actor.

акти́в (-а) *м* activists *мн* (*in organization*); (*КОММ*) assets *мн*; **запи́сывать** (**записа́ть** *perf*) **что-н в** ~ to count sth as an asset; **заморо́женные** ~**ы** (*КОММ*) frozen assets.

акти́вен *прил см* **акти́вный**.

активизи́р|овать (-ую) (*не*)*сов перех* to enliven.

акти́вно *нареч* (*участвовать*) actively; (*работать*) energetically.

акти́в|ный (-ен, -на, -но) *прил* active; **акти́вный бала́нс** balance of assets; **акти́вный слова́рь** *или* **запа́с слов** active vocabulary.

актри́с|а (-ы) *ж* actress.

актуа́лен *прил см* **актуа́льный**.

актуа́льност|ь (-и) *ж* topicality.

актуа́л|ьный (-ен, -ьна, -ьно) *прил* topical.

аку́л|а (-ы) *ж* shark.

акупункту́р|а (-ы) *ж* acupuncture.

акусти́к|а (-и) *ж* acoustics *ед*; (*в зале, в студии*) acoustics *мн*.

акусти́ческ|ий (-ая, -ое, -ие) *прил* acoustic(al); ~ **соедини́тель** (*КОМП*) acoustic coupler.

акуше́р (-а) *м* obstetrician.

акуше́р|ка (-ки; *gen pl* -ок) *ж см* **акуше́р**.

акуше́рск|ий (-ая, -ое, -ие) *прил* obstetric(al).

акце́нт (-а) *м* accent; **де́лать** (**сде́лать** *perf*) ~ **на** +*prp* (*перен*) to emphasize; **расставля́ть** (**расста́вить** *perf*) **все** ~**ы** (*перен*) to draw attention to the most important things.

акценти́р|овать (-ую) (*не*)*сов перех* (*перен*) to accentuate.

акце́пт (-а) *м* (*КОММ, ЮР*) acceptance.

акце́птный *прил* (*КОММ*): ~ **банк** accepting house.

акцепт|ова́ть (-у́ю) (*не*)*сов перех* (*КОММ*) to accept.

акци́з (-а) *м* (*КОММ*) excise (tax).

акци́зный *прил* (*КОММ*) excise *опред*.

акционе́р (-а) *м* shareholder.

акционе́рный *прил* joint-stock *опред*; **акционе́рное о́бщество** joint-stock company; **акционе́рный капита́л** share capital.

акционе́рск|ий (-ая, -ое, -ие) *прил* (*права, доля*) shareholders'.

а́кци|я (-и) *ж* (*КОММ*) share; (*действие*) action; **именна́я/обыкнове́нная** ~ registered/ordinary share; **паке́т** ~**й** block of shares; **по́лностью опла́ченная** ~ fully-paid share; ~**и без пра́ва го́лоса** non-voting shares; **дипломати́ческая** ~ diplomatic move.

алба́н|ец (-ца) *м* Albanian.

Алба́ни|я (-и) *ж* Albania.

алба́н|ка (-ки; *gen pl* -ок) *ж см* **алба́нец**.

алба́нск|ий (-ая, -ое, -ие) *прил* Albanian.

алба́нца *итп сущ см* **алба́нец**.

а́лгебр|а (-ы) *ж* algebra.

алгори́тм (-а) *м* algorithm.

алеба́стр (-а) *м* alabaster.
алеба́стровый *прил* alabaster *опред*.
александри́т (-а) *м* (ГЕО) alexandrite.
Александри́я (-и) *ж* Alexandria.
але́|ть (-ю) *несов неперех* (*флаг, мак*) to show scarlet; (*закат*) to glow scarlet; (*perf* **заале́ть**; *закат, небо*) to turn scarlet.
Алжи́р (-а) *м* Algeria.
алжи́р|ец (-ца) *м* Algerian.
алжи́р|ка (-ки; *gen pl* -ок) *ж см* **алжи́рец**.
алжи́рск|ий (-ая, -ое, -ие) *прил* Algerian.
алжи́рца *итп сущ см* **алжи́рец**.
а́либи *ср нескл* alibi.
алиме́нтщик (-а) *м* (*разг: пренебр*) *man paying alimony or maintenance*.
алиме́нт|ы (-ов) *мн* alimony *ед*, maintenance *ед*.
алка́ш (-а́) *м* (*разг: пренебр*) alky.
алкоголи́зм (-а) *м* alcoholism.
алкого́лик (-а) *м* alcoholic.
алкоголи́|чка (-ки; *gen pl* -ек) *ж* (*разг*) *см* **алкого́лик**.
алкого́л|ь (-я) *м* alcohol.
Алла́х (-а) *м* Allah.
аллего́ри|я (-и) *ж* allegory.
алле́гро *ср нескл, нареч* allegro.
аллерге́н (-а) *м* allergen.
аллерги́ческ|ий (-ая, -ое, -ие) *прил* allergic.
аллерги́|я (-и) *ж* allergy.
алле́|я (-и) *ж* alley.
аллига́тор (-а) *м* alligator.
аллилу́йя *межд* hallelujah.
алло́ *межд* hello (*on answering phone*).
аллю́р (-а) *м* gait (*of horses*).
А́лма-Ата́ (-ы́) *ж* Alma-Ata.
алма́з (-а) *м* diamond.
алма́зный *прил* diamond *опред*; (*инструмент*) diamond-tipped.
ало́э *ср нескл* aloe.
алта́р|ь (-я́) *м* (*в церкви*) chancel; (*жертвенник*) altar; **возлага́ть** (**возложи́ть** *perf*) **что-н на ~ чего́-н** to sacrifice sth on the altar of sth.
алфави́т (-а) *м* alphabet; **по ~у** in alphabetical order.
а́лчен *прил см* **а́лчный**.
а́лчност|ь (-и) *ж* greed.
а́лч|ный (-ен, -на, -но) *прил* greedy.
а́л|ый (-, -а, -о) *прил* scarlet.
алыч|а́ (-и́) *ж* cherry plum.
альбо́м (-а) *м* album; (*по искусству*) *book of art reproductions*.
альмана́х (-а) *м* anthology.
альпи́йск|ий (-ая, -ое, -ие) *прил* alpine; (*в Альпах*) Alpine.
альпини́зм (-а) *м* mountaineering.
А́льп|ы (-) *мн* the Alps.
альт (-а́) *м* (*голос*) alto; (*инструмент*) viola.
альтернати́в|а (-ы) *ж* alternative.
альтернати́вный *прил* alternative.

альтруи́зм (-а) *м* altruism.
алья́нс (-а) *м* alliance.
Аля́ск|а (-и) *ж* Alaska.
алюми́ниевый *прил* aluminium *опред* (*BRIT*), aluminum *опред* (*US*).
алюми́ний (-я) *м* aluminium (*BRIT*), aluminum (*US*).
аляпова́т|ый (-, -а, -о) *прил* gaudy.
амазо́н|ка (-ки; *gen pl* -ок) *ж* (*всадница*) horsewoman (*мн* horsewomen); (*платье*) riding habit.
амальга́м|а (-ы) *ж* (*хим, перен*) amalgam.
амба́р (-а) *м* barn.
амбицио́з|ный (-ен, -на, -но) *прил* (*человек*) arrogant; (*планы*) presumptuous.
амби́ци|я (-и) *ж* (*самолюбие*) pride, arrogance; (*обычно мн: притязания*) ambition; **ударя́ться** (**уда́риться** *perf*) **в ~ю** (*разг*) to go into a huff.
амбулато́ри|я (-и) *ж* doctor's surgery (*BRIT*) *или* office (*US*).
амво́н (-а) *м* (*РЕЛ*) ≈ pulpit.
амёб|а (-ы) *ж* amoeba (*BRIT*), ameba (*US*).
Аме́рик|а (-и) *ж* America.
америка́н|ец (-ца) *м* American.
американиза́ци|я (-и) *ж* Americanization.
американизи́р|овать (-ую) (*не*)*сов перех* to Americanize.
америка́н|ки (-ки; *gen pl* -ок) *ж см* **америка́нец**.
америка́нск|ий (-ая, -ое, -ие) *прил* American.
америка́нца *итп сущ см* **америка́нец**.
амети́ст (-а) *м* amethyst.
аминокисл|ота́ (-оты́; *nom pl* -о́ты) *ж* amino acid.
ами́н|ь *част* (*РЕЛ*) amen.
аммиа́к (-а) *м* ammonia.
АМН *ж сокр* (= *Акаде́мия медици́нских нау́к*) Academy of Medical Sciences.
амнисти́р|овать (-ую) (*не*)*сов перех* to grant (an) amnesty to.
амни́сти|я (-и) *ж* amnesty; **попада́ть** (**попа́сть** *perf*) **под ~ю** to be granted (an) amnesty.
амора́лен *прил см* **амора́льный**.
амора́льност|ь (-и) *ж* (*см прил*) immorality; amorality.
амора́л|ьный (-ен, -ьна, -ьно) *прил* (*поступок*) immoral; (*человек*) amoral.
амортиза́тор (-а) *м* (*ТЕХ*) shock absorber.
амортизацио́нный *прил* (*ТЕХ*) shock-absorbing; (*ЭКОН*) depreciation *опред*; **амортизацио́нные отчисле́ния** (*ЭКОН*) depreciation deductions *мн*; **амортизацио́нный срок** (*ЭКОН*) period of depreciation.
амортиза́ци|я (-и) *ж* (*ТЕХ*) shock absorption; (*ЭКОН*) depreciation; (*КОММ*) amortization.
амо́рф|ный (-ен, -на, -но) *прил* amorphous.
ампе́р (-а) *м* amp (= *ampère*).
амплиту́д|а (-ы) *ж* amplitude.
амплуа́ *ср нескл* (*актёра*) speciality; **э́то не**

моё ~ (*разг*) that's not (in) my line.

áмпул|а (-ы) *ж* ampoule (*BRIT*), ampule (*US*).

ампутáци|я (-и) *ж* amputation.

ампути́р|овать (-ую) (*не*)*сов перех* to amputate.

АМТС *ж сокр* (= *автомат́ическая междугорóдная телефóнная связь*) ≈ STD (*BRIT*) (= *subscriber trunk dialling*).

амуни́ци|я (-и) *ж собир* ammunition.

Амýр (-а) *м* Cupid; *см также* **амýры**.

амýр|ы (-ов) *мн* (*разг: любовные дела*) intrigues *мн*, love affairs *мн*.

амфи́би|я (-и) *ж* amphibian.

амфитеáтр (-а) *м* amphitheatre (*BRIT*), amphitheater (*US*).

АН *ж сокр* (= *Акадéмия наýк*) Academy of Sciences ♦ *м сокр* = *самолёт констрýкции О. К. Антонóва*.

Ан *м сокр* = **АН**.

анáлиз (-а) *м* analysis; **сдавáть (сдать** *perf*) **кровь/мочý на** ~ to give a blood/urine sample; **подвергáть (подвéргнуть** *perf*) ~**y** to analyse (*BRIT*), analyze (*US*); ~ **издéржек и при́были** (*КОММ*) cost-benefit analysis; ~ **эффекти́вности рабóты** time and motion study; **анáлиз крóви** blood test.

анализи́р|овать (-ую; *perf* **проанализи́ровать**) *несов перех* to analyse (*BRIT*), analyze (*US*).

анали́тик (-а) *м* (*специалист*) analyst; **он хорóший** ~ (*склонный к анализу*) he has a very analytical mind.

анáлог (-а) *м* analogue (*BRIT*), analog (*US*).

аналоги́ч|ный (-ен, -на, -но) *прил* analogous.

аналóги|я (-и) *ж* analogy; **по** ~**и (с** +*instr*) in a similar way (to); **проводи́ть (провести́** *perf*) ~**ю мéжду** +*instr* to draw an analogy between.

аналó|й (-я) *м* lectern.

анáмнез (-а) *м* (*МЕД*) case history.

ананáс (-а) *м* pineapple.

анархи́зм (-а) *м* anarchism.

анархи́стск|ий (-ая, -ое, -ие) *прил* anarchist *опред*.

анáрхи|я (-и) *ж* anarchy.

анатóми|я (-и) *ж* anatomy.

анáфем|а (-ы) *ж* anathema; **предавáть (предáть** *perf*) ~**е** to anathematize.

анахрони́зм (-а) *м* anachronism.

анахрони́ч|ный (-ен, -на, -но) *прил* anachronistic.

ангáр (-а) *м* hangar.

áнгел (-а) *м* (*также разг*) angel.

áнгельск|ий (-ая, -ое, -ие) *прил* angelic; **áнгельское терпéние** the patience of a saint.

анги́н|а (-ы) *ж* tonsillitis, quinsy.

англи́йск|ий (-ая, -ое, -ие) *прил* English; (*британский*) British; ~ **язы́к** English; **англи́йская булáвка** safety pin; **англи́йский газóн** lawn.

англикáнск|ий (-ая, -ое, -ие) *прил* Anglican; **англикáнская цéрковь** the Anglican church.

англичáн|ин (-ина; *nom pl* -е, *gen pl* -) *м* Englishman (*мн* Englishmen).

англичáн|ка (-ки; *gen pl* -ок) *ж* Englishwoman (*мн* Englishwomen).

Áнгли|я (-и) *ж* England.

Ангóл|а (-ы) *ж* Angola.

ангóл|ец (-ьца) *м* Angolan.

ангóл|ка (-ки; *gen pl* -ок) *ж см* **ангóлец**.

ангóльск|ий (-ая, -ое, -ие) *прил* Angolan.

ангóльца *итп сущ см* **ангóлец**.

ангóрск|ий (-ая, -ое, -ие) *прил* angora *опред*; **ангóрская шерсть** angora (wool).

Áнд|ы (-) *мн* the Andes.

анекдóт (-а) *м* joke; **со мной случи́лся** ~ (*разг*) something funny happened to me.

анекдоти́ч|ный (-ен, -на, -но) *прил* (*смешной и странный*) funny.

анеми́ч|ный (-ен, -на, -но) *прил* anaemic (*BRIT*), anemic (*US*).

анеми́|я (-и) *ж* anaemia (*BRIT*), anemia (*US*).

анестезиóлог (-а) *м* anaesthetist (*BRIT*), anesthiologist (*US*).

анестези́р|овать (-ую) (*не*)*сов перех* to anaesthetize (*BRIT*), anesthetize (*US*).

анестези́|я (-и) *ж* anaesthesia (*BRIT*), anesthesia (*US*); **мéстная/óбщая** ~ local/general ana(e)sthesia.

анили́н (-а) *м* aniline.

анили́новый *прил* aniline *опред*.

ани́совый *прил* aniseed *опред*; **ани́совая вóдка** aniseed vodka.

АНК *м сокр* (= *Африкáнский национáльный конгрéсс*) ANC (= *African National Congress*).

Анкар|á (-ы́) *м* Ankara.

анкéт|а (-ы) *ж* (*опросный лист*) questionnaire; (*бланк для сведений*) form; (*сбор сведений*) survey; **проводи́ть (провести́** *perf*) ~**у** to carry out a survey.

анкéтн|ый *прил*: ~**ые дáнные** personal details *мн*; **анкéтный лист** questionnaire.

аннáл|ы (-ов) *мн* annals *мн*; **в** ~**ах истóрии** in the annals of history.

аннéкси|я (-и) *ж* annexation.

аннотáци|я (-и) *ж* précis.

анноти́р|овать (-ую; *perf* **проанноти́ровать**) *несов перех* to summarize.

аннуитéт (-а) *м* (*КОММ*) annuity; **пожи́зненный** ~ life annuity.

аннули́рование (-я) *ср* (*см глаг*) annulment; repeal; cancellation.

аннули́р|овать (-ую) (*не*)*сов перех* (*брак, договор*) to annul; (*закон*) to repeal; (*долг*) to cancel.

анóд (-а) *м* anode.

аномáль|ный (-ен, -ьна, -ьно) *прил* anomalous.

анони́м (-а) *м* anonymous author.

анони́мен *прил см* **анони́мный**.

анони́м|ка (-ки; *gen pl* -ок) *ж* (*разг: пренебр*) poison-pen letter.

анони́м|ный (-ен, -на, -но) *прил* anonymous.

анони́мок *сущ см* **анони́мка**.

анóнс (-а) *м* announcement.

анорекси|я (-и) *ж* anorexia; **она страдает ~ей** she is anorexic.

ансамбль (-я) *м* ensemble; *(танцоров)* troupe; *(эстрадный)* group.

АНТ *м сокр* = **самолёт конструкции А. Н. Туполева.**

антагони́зм (-а) *м* antagonism.

Антаркти́д|а (-ы) *ж* Antarctica.

Анта́ркти|ка (-и) *ж* Antarctica, the Antarctic.

антаркти́чес|кий (-ая, -ое, -ие) *прил* Antarctic.

Антве́рпен (-а) *ж* Antwerp.

анте́нн|а (-ы) *ж* aerial (*BRIT*), antenna (*US*).

антибио́тик (-а) *м* antibiotic.

антивое́нный *прил* antiwar.

антидемократи́ческ|ий (-ая, -ое, -ие) *прил* antidemocratic.

антиква́р (-а) *м* antiquary.

антиква́рен *прил см* **антиква́рный.**

антиквариа́т (-а) *м собир* antiques *мн.*

антиква́р|ный (-ен, -на, -но) *прил* antique *опред*; **антиква́рный магази́н** antique shop.

антило́п|а (-ы) *ж* antelope.

антинау́ч|ный (-ен, -на, -но) *прил* antiscientific.

антипати́ч|ный (-ен, -на, -но) *прил* unlikable.

антипа́ти|я (-и) *ж* antipathy.

антипо́д (-а) *м* antithesis.

антирелигио́зный *прил* antireligious.

антисанита́рен *прил см* **антисанита́рный.**

антисанитари́|я (-и) *ж* unhygienic *или* insanitary conditions *мн.*

антисанита́р|ный (-ен, -на, -но) *прил* unhygienic, insanitary.

антисеми́т (-а) *м* anti-Semite.

антисемити́зм (-а) *м* anti-Semitism.

антисеми́т|ка (-ки; *gen pl* -ок) *ж см* **антисеми́т.**

антисеми́ток *сущ см* **антисеми́тка.**

антисеми́тск|ий (-ая, -ое, -ие) *прил* anti-Semitic.

антисе́птик (-а) *м* antiseptic.

антисепти́ческ|ий (-ая, -ое, -ие) *прил* antiseptic.

антите́з|а (-ы) *ж* antithesis.

антите́л|о (-а; *nom pl* -а́) *ср* (*обычно мн*) antibody.

антифаши́стск|ий (-ая, -ое, -ие) *прил* antifascist.

антифри́з (-а) *м* antifreeze.

анти́христ (-а) *м* Antichrist.

антицикло́н (-а) *м* anticyclone.

анти́чность (-и) *ж* antiquity.

анти́чный *прил* classical; **анти́чный мир** the Ancient World.

антоло́ги|я (-и) *ж* anthology.

анто́ним (-а) *м* antonym.

анто́нов|ка (-ки; *gen pl* -ок) *ж* antonovka (*apple*).

антра́кт (-а) *м* interval.

антраци́т (-а) *м* anthracite.

антреко́т (-а) *м* entrecôte.

антрепренёр (-а) *м* impresario.

антресо́л|и (-ей) *мн* (*полуэтаж*) mezzanine *ед*; (*балкон*) gallery *ед*; (*под потолком*) cupboard *ед.*

антрополо́ги|я (-и) *ж* anthropology.

анфа́с *нареч* full face.

анфила́д|а (-ы) *ж* suite (*of rooms*).

анчо́ус (-а) *м* anchovy.

аншла́г (-а) *м* (*объявление*) sellout; (*заголовок*) banner headline; **проходи́ть** (**пройти́** *perf*) **с ~ом** to be a sellout.

аню́тины (-х) *мн*: **~ гла́зки** pansy *ед.*

АО *ж сокр* = **автоно́мная о́бласть** ◆ *м сокр* = **автоно́мный о́круг.**

А/О *ср сокр* (= **акционе́рное о́бщество**) joint-stock company.

ао́рт|а (-ы) *ж* aorta.

АП *м сокр* (= **Ассо́шиэйтед пресс**) AP (= *Associated Press*).

апарте́йд (-а) *м* apartheid.

апати́ч|ный (-ен, -на, -но) *прил* apathetic.

апа́ти|я (-и) *ж* apathy.

апелли́р|овать (-ую) (*не*)*сов неперех* (*ЮР*) to appeal; **~** (*impf/perf*) **к** +*dat* to appeal to.

апелляцио́нный *прил* (*ЮР*) appeal *опред*; **апелляцио́нный суд** court of appeal.

апелля́ци|я (-и) *ж* (*ЮР*) appeal; **~ к** +*dat* appeal to.

апельси́н (-а) *м* orange.

апельси́нный *прил* = **апельси́новый.**

апельси́новый *прил* orange.

аперити́в (-а) *м* aperitif.

АПК *м сокр* = **агра́рно-промы́шленный ко́мплекс.**

аплоди́р|овать (-ую) *несов неперех* (+*dat*) to applaud.

аплодисме́нт|ы (-ов) *мн* applause *ед.*

апло́мб (-а) *м* assurance; **с ~ом** with aplomb.

АПН *ср сокр* (= **аге́нтство печа́ти „Но́вости"**) "Novosti" Press Agency ◆ *ж сокр* (= **Акаде́мия педагоги́ческих нау́к**) Academy of Pedagogical Sciences *шиенный ко́мпиекс.*

апоге́|й (-я) *м* (*также перен*) apogee; **он в ~е сла́вы** he is at the height of his fame.

апока́липсис (-а) *м* (*РЕЛ*) (the Book of) Revelation, the Apocalypse.

аполити́ч|ный (-ен, -на, -но) *прил* apolitical.

апологе́т (-а) *м* apologist.

апо́стол (-а) *м* apostle; (*книга*) the Acts of the Apostles and the Epistles.

апо́стольск|ий (-ая, -ое, -ие) *прил* apostolic.

апостро́ф (-а) *м* apostrophe.

апофео́з (-а) *м* (*восхваление*) apotheosis; (*ТЕАТР*) grand finale.

аппара́т (-а) *м* apparatus; (*ФИЗИОЛОГИЯ*) system; (*штат*) staff; **телефо́нный ~** telephone; **госуда́рственный ~** state apparatus.

аппара́т|ная (-ой; *decl like adj*) *ж* equipment room.

аппарату́р|а (-ы) *ж собир* apparatus, equipment;

(*прибо́ры*) instruments мн.
аппара́тчик (-а) м operative; (*разг: рабо́тник аппара́та*) apparatchik.
аппе́ндикс (-а) м appendix.
аппендици́т (-а) м appendicitis.
аппети́т (-а) м appetite; (*обы́чно мн: перен: разг*) craving; **прия́тного ~а!** bon appétit!; **перебива́ть (переби́ть** *perf*) **~** to spoil one's appetite; **во́лчий ~** a voracious appetite.
аппети́тный (-ен, -на, -но) прил appetizing.
апплика́ция (-и) ж appliqué.
апре́ль (-я) м April; *см та́кже* **октя́брь**.
апроби́р|овать (-ую) (*не*)*сов перех* to approve.
апте́к|а (-и) ж dispensing chemist's (*BRIT*), pharmacy.
апте́карск|ий (-ая, -ое, -ие) прил (*това́ры*) pharmaceutical.
апте́кар|ь (-я) м chemist (*BRIT*), pharmacist.
апте́чк|а (-ки; *gen pl* -ек) ж medicine chest; (*пе́рвой по́мощи*) first-aid kit.
апте́чный прил chemist's.
апчхи́ межд: **~!** atishoo!
ара́б (-а) м Arab.
арабе́ск|а (-ки; *gen pl* -ок) ж arabesque (*ART*).
ара́б|ка (-ки; *gen pl* -ок) ж см **ара́б**.
ара́бск|ий (-ая, -ое, -ие) прил (*страны́*) Arab; **~ язы́к** Arabic; **ара́бские ци́фры** Arabic numerals.
арави́ек сущ см **арави́йка**.
арави́|ец (-йца) м Arabian.
арави́|йка (-йки; *gen pl* -ек) ж см **арави́ец**.
арави́йск|ий (-ая, -ое, -ие) прил Arabian опред.
арави́йца итп сущ см **арави́ец**.
Ара́ви|я (-и) ж Arabia.
ара́льск|ий (-ая, -ое, -ие) прил: **А~ое мо́ре** Aral Sea.
аранжи́р|овать (-ую) (*не*)*сов перех* to arrange.
аранжиро́в|ка (-ки; *gen pl* -ок) ж arrangement.
ара́хис (-а) м peanut.
ара́хисовый прил peanut опред.
АРБ ж сокр (= *Ассоциа́ция росси́йских ба́нков*) *association of Russian banks*.
арби́тр (-а) м (*в спо́рах*) arbitrator; (*в футбо́ле*) referee; (*в бейсбо́ле, те́ннисе*) umpire.
арбитра́ж (-а) м arbitration; (*о́рган*) arbitration service.
арбитра́жный прил arbitration опред.
арбу́з (-а) м watermelon.
Аргенти́н|а (-ы) ж Argentina.
аргенти́н|ец (-ца) м Argentinian.
аргенти́н|ка (-ки; *gen pl* -ок) ж см **аргенти́нец**.
аргенти́нск|ий (-ая, -ое, -ие) прил Argentinian.
аргенти́нца итп сущ см **аргенти́нец**.
арго́н (-а) м argon.
аргуме́нт (-а) м (*та́кже МАТ*) argument.
аргумента́ци|я (-и) ж argument.
аргументи́р|овать (-ую) (*не*)*сов перех* to argue.
аре́н|а (-ы) ж (*в ци́рке*) ring; (*часть стадио́на, перен*) arena.
аре́нд|а (-ы) ж (*наём*) lease; (*пла́та*) rent; **сдава́ть (сдать** *perf*) **в ~у** to lease.

аренда́тор (-а) м leaseholder.
аре́ндн|ый прил lease опред; **на ~ых нача́лах** on a rental basis; **аре́ндная пла́та** rent; **аре́ндный подря́д** rental agreement, lease.
аренд|ова́ть (-у́ю) (*не*)*сов перех* to lease.
аре́ст (-а) м (*престу́пника*) arrest; (*иму́щества*) sequestration; **брать (взять** *perf*) **кого́-н под ~** to place sb under arrest; **налага́ть (наложи́ть** *perf*) **~ на** +*acc* to sequester; **находи́ться** (*impf*) **под ~ом** to be under arrest.
аресто́ванн|ая (-ой; *decl like adj*) ж см **аресто́ванный**.
аресто́ванн|ый (-ого; *decl like adj*) м *person held in custody*.
арест|ова́ть (-у́ю; *impf* **аресто́вывать**) *сов перех* (*престу́пника*) to arrest; (*иму́щество*) to sequestrate.
аристокра́т (-а) м aristocrat.
аристократи́ческ|ий (-ая, -ое, -ие) прил aristocratic.
аристокра́ти|я (-и) ж aristocracy.
аритми́|я (-и) ж arrhythmia (*irregular heartbeat*).
арифме́тик|а (-и) ж arithmetic.
арифмети́ческ|ий (-ая, -ое, -ие) прил arithmetic(al).
а́ри|я (-и) ж aria.
АРКА м сокр (= *Америка́но-Росси́йский комме́рческий алья́нс*) *American-Russian commercial alliance*.
а́р|ка (-ки; *gen pl* -ок) ж arch.
арка́д|а (-ы) ж (*АРХИТ*) arcade.
арка́н (-а) м lasso.
арка́н|ить (-ю, -ишь; *perf* **заарка́нить**) *несов перех* to lasso.
А́рктик|а (-и) ж the Arctic.
аркти́ческ|ий (-ая, -ое, -ие) прил Arctic.
арлеки́н (-а) м harlequin.
армату́р|а (-ы) ж собир (*СТРОИТ*) steel framework; (*вспомога́тельные устро́йства*) fittings мн.
арме́йск|ий (-ая, -ое, -ие) прил army опред.
Арме́ни|я (-и) ж Armenia.
а́рми|я (-и) ж army; (*перен*): **~** +*gen* (*помо́щников, чита́телей*) army of.
армяни́н (-а; *nom pl* **армя́не**, *gen pl* **армя́н**) м Armenian.
армя́н|ка (-ки; *gen pl* -ок) ж см **армяни́н**.
армя́нск|ий (-ая, -ое, -ие) прил Armenian опред; **~ язы́к** Armenian.
а́рок сущ см **а́рка**.
арома́т (-а) м (*цвето́в*) fragrance; (*ко́фе итп*) aroma; (*перен: мо́лодости*) spirit.
арома́тен сущ см **арома́тный**.
аромат́и́ческ|ий (-ая, -ое, -ие) прил aromatic.
арома́тный (-ен, -на, -но) прил fragrant.
арсена́л (-а) м (*склад*) arsenal; (*заво́д*) munitions factory; **в ~е** (*перен*) at one's disposal.
арта́ч|иться (-усь, -ишься) *несов возв* (*разг*) to be pig-headed.

артезиа́нск|ий (-ая, -ое, -ие) *прил* artesian.
арте́л|ь (-и) *ж* worker's or peasant's cooperative.
арте́льный *прил* collective *опред*; **на ~ых нача́лах** on a collective basis.
артериа́льн|ый *прил*: **~ое давле́ние** blood pressure.
арте́ри|я (-и) *ж* (*также перен*) artery; **со́нная ~** carotid artery.
арти́кл|ь (-я) *м* (*линг*) article.
артиллери́йск|ий (-ая, -ое, -ие) *прил* artillery *опред*.
артиллери́ст (-а) *м* artilleryman (*мн* artillerymen), gunner (*BRIT*).
артилле́ри|я (-и) *ж* artillery.
арти́ст (-а) *м* artist(e); (*КИНО*) actor; **он ~ расска́зывать исто́рии** he's ace at telling stories.
артисти́ческ|ий (-ая, -ое, -ие) *прил* artistic; **~ая убо́рная** dressing room.
арти́ст|ка (-ки; *gen pl* -ок) *ж* (*см м*) artist(e); actress.
артишо́к (-а) *м* (globe) artichoke.
артри́т (-а) *м* arthritis.
а́рф|а (-ы) *ж* harp.
арфи́ст (-а) *м* harpist.
арфи́ст|ка (-ки; *gen pl* -ок) *ж см* **арфи́ст**.
архаи́зм (-а) *м* archaism.
арха́и́чный (-ен, -на, -но) *прил* archaic.
арха́нгел (-а) *м* archangel.
Арха́нгельск (-а) *м* Archangel.
архео́лог (-а) *м* archaeologist (*BRIT*), archeologist.
археологи́ческ|ий (-ая, -ое, -ие) *прил* archaeological.
археоло́ги|я (-и) *ж* archaeology.
архи́в (-а) *м* (*учрежде́ние, отде́л*) archive; (*собра́ние ру́кописей итп*) archives *мн*; **сдава́ть (сдать** *perf*) **что-н в ~** (*перен*) to consign sth to history.
архива́риус (-а) *м* archivist.
архи́вный *прил* archival; **~ файл** (*КОМП*) archive file.
архиепи́скоп (-а) *м* archbishop.
архиере́|й (-я) *м* general term for upper orders of the church.
архимандри́т (-а) *м* archimandrite.
архипела́г (-а) *м* archipelago.
архите́ктор (-а) *м* architect.
архитекту́р|а (-ы) *ж* architecture.
архитекту́рный *прил* architectural.
арши́н (-а; *gen pl* -или -ов) *м* (*устаре́вший*) arshin (*unit of measurement equal to 0.71 m*); **ме́рить** (*impf*) **кого́-н на свой ~** (*перен*) to judge sb by one's own standards.
арши́нный *прил* (*разг*) very big, tall, high or long.
ас (-а) *м* (*лётчик*) ace; (*перен*) expert.
асбе́ст (-а) *м* asbestos.
АСЕА́Н *ж сокр* ASEAN (= *Association of South-East Asian Nations*).

асепти́ческ|ий (-ая, -ое, -ие) *прил* aseptic.
асимметри́чн|ый (-ен, -на, -но) *прил* asymmetric(al).
асимме́три|я (-и) *ж* asymmetry.
аске́т (-а) *м* ascetic.
аскети́зм (-а) *м* asceticism.
аскети́ческ|ий (-ая, -ое, -ие) *прил* ascetic *опред*.
аскорби́нов|ый *прил*: **~ая кислота́** ascorbic acid.
аспе́кт (-а) *м* aspect; **в ~е** + *gen* in (the) light of.
аспира́нт (-а) *м* postgraduate (*doing a PhD*).
аспиранту́р|а (-ы) *ж* postgraduate studies *мн* (*leading to a PhD*).
аспири́н (-а) *м* aspirin.
ассамбле́|я (-и) *ж* assembly; **Генера́льная А~ Организа́ции Объединённых На́ций** General Assembly of the United Nations.
ассе́мблер (-а) *м* (*КОМП*) assembler.
ассениза́ци|я (-и) *ж* sewage disposal system.
ассигнова́ни|е (-я) *ср* allocation.
ассигн|ова́ть (-у́ю) (*не*)*сов перех* to allocate.
ассимили́р|овать (-ую) (*не*)*сов перех* to assimilate.
▶ **ассимили́роваться** (*не*)*сов возв* to become assimilated.
ассимиля́ци|я (-и) *ж* assimilation.
ассисте́нт (-а) *м* assistant; (*в вузе*) assistant lecturer.
ассисти́р|овать (-ую) *несов неперех* (+*dat*) to assist.
ассорти́ *ср нескл* assortment.
ассортиме́нт (-а) *м* assortment.
ассоциати́вный (-ен, -на, -но) *прил* based on association.
ассоциа́ци|я (-и) *ж* association.
ассоции́р|овать (-ую) (*не*)*сов перех*: **~ что-н с кем-н/чем-н** to associate sth with sb/sth
▶ **ассоции́роваться** (*не*)*сов возв*: **~ся с** +*instr* to be associated with.
АССР *ж сокр* (*ист*: = *автоно́мная сове́тская социалисти́ческая респу́блика*) ASSR (= *Autonomous Soviet Socialist Republic*).
астеро́ид (-а) *м* asteroid.
астигмати́зм (-а) *м* astigmatism.
а́стм|а (-ы) *ж* asthma.
астма́тик (-а) *м* asthmatic.
астмати́ческ|ий (-ая, -ое, -ие) *прил* asthmatic.
а́стр|а (-ы) *ж* aster.
астро́лог (-а) *м* astrologer.
астроло́ги|я (-и) *ж* astrology.
астрона́вт (-а) *м* astronaut.
астрона́втик|а (-и) *ж* astronautics.
астроно́м (-а) *м* astronomer.
астрономи́ческ|ий (-ая, -ое, -ие) *прил* (*также перен*) astronomic(al).
астроно́ми|я (-и) *ж* astronomy.

АСУ ж сокр (= автоматизи́рованная систе́ма управле́ния) automatic control system.

асфа́льт (-а) м asphalt.

асфальти́р|овать (-ую; perf **заасфальти́ровать**) (не)сов перех to asphalt.

асфикси́|я (-и) ж asphyxia.

ата́к|а (-и) ж (также перен) attack; **идти́ (пойти́** perf) **в ~у** to launch an attack; ~ **на кого́-н/что-н** an attack on sb/sth.

атак|ова́ть (-у́ю) (не)сов перех (также перен) to attack.

атама́н (-а) м ataman (*Cossack leader*); (перен: банды) leader.

атеи́зм (-а) м atheism.

атеи́ст (-а) м atheist.

атеи́ст|ка (-ки; gen pl -ок) ж см **атеи́ст**.

атеисти́ческ|ий (-ая, -ое, -ие) прил atheist опред.

атеи́сток сущ см **атеи́стка**.

ателье́ ср нескл (художника, фотографа) studio; (мод) tailor's shop; **телевизио́нное ~** television repair shop; **ателье́ прока́та** rental shop.

атланти́ческ|ий (-ая, -ое, -ие) прил: **А~ океа́н** Atlantic Ocean.

а́тлас (-а) м atlas.

атла́с (-а) м satin.

атла́сный прил satin; (шелковистый) satiny; **атла́сная ко́жа** (перен) skin like satin.

атле́т (-а) м athlete; (крепкий человек) muscleman.

атлети́зм (-а) м (телосложение) athletic build; (культуризм) body building.

атле́тик|а (-и) ж athletics; **лёгкая ~** track and field events; **тяжёлая ~** weightlifting.

атлети́ческ|ий (-ая, -ое, -ие) прил athletic.

АТМ ж сокр (= автомати́ческая ка́ссовая маши́на) ATM (= *automated telling machine*).

атмосфе́р|а (-ы) ж (также перен) atmosphere.

атмосфе́рный прил atmospheric.

а́том (-а) м atom.

а́томный прил atomic; **а́томный вес** atomic weight.

а́томщик (-а) м (разг) atomic scientist.

атрибу́т (-а) м attribute.

атрибути́вный прил (линг) attributive.

атрофи́рованный прил atrophied.

атрофи́р|оваться (3sg -уется, 3pl -уются) (не)сов возв to atrophy.

атрофи́|я (-и) ж atrophy.

АТС ж сокр (= автомати́ческая телефо́нная ста́нция) automatic telephone exchange.

атташе́ м нескл attaché.

аттеста́т (-а) м certificate; **аттеста́т зре́лости** *certificate attained for passing school-leaving examinations.*

аттеста́ци|я (-и) ж certification; (отзыв) recommendation.

аттест|ова́ть (-у́ю) (не)сов перех (давать характеристику) to recommend; (оценивать знания) to give a mark.

аттракцио́н (-а) м (цирковой номер) attraction; (качели, карусель итп) amusement.

ау́ межд hallo (*cry for attention*).

аудие́нци|я (-и) ж (приём) audience.

ауди́т (-а) м (комм) audit; **о́бщий ~** general audit.

аудито́ри|я (-и) ж (помещение) lecture hall ♦ собир (слушатели) audience.

аукцио́н (-а) м auction; **продава́ть (прода́ть** perf) **что-н с ~а** to sell sth by auction; **покупа́ть (купи́ть** perf) **что-н на ~е** to buy sth at an auction.

аукционе́р (-а) м person attending an auction.

аукциони́ст (-а) м auctioneer.

ау́л (-а) м aul (*mountain village in the Caucasus and Middle Asia*).

а́ут (-а) м (в теннисе) out; (в футболе): **мяч в а́уте** the ball is out of play; (в боксе): ~! knockout!

аутенти́ч|ный (-ен, -на, -но) прил authentic.

аутоге́нн|ый прил: **~ая трениро́вка** autogenic training.

аутса́йдер (-а) м outsider.

афга́н|ец (-ца) м Afghan; (ветеран) Afghan war veteran.

Афганиста́н (-а) м Afghanistan.

афга́н|ка (-ки; gen pl -ок) ж см **афга́нец**.

афга́нца итп сущ см **афга́нец**.

афе́р|а (-ы) ж swindle.

афери́ст (-а) м swindler.

афери́ст|ка (-ки; gen pl -ок) ж см **афери́ст**.

Афи́н|ы (-) мн Athens.

афи́ш|а (-и) ж poster.

афиши́р|овать (-ую) (не)сов перех to parade.

афори́зм (-а) м aphorism.

А́фрик|а (-и) ж Africa.

африка́н|ец (-ца) м African.

африка́н|ка (-ки; gen pl -ок) ж см **африка́нец**.

африка́нск|ий (-ая, -ое, -ие) прил African.

африка́нца итп сущ см **африка́нец**.

аффе́кт (-а) м fit of passion.

ах межд: ~! oh!, ah!; ~ **да!** (разг) ah yes!; **не ~** (разг) not up to much.

а́ха|ть (-ю; perf **а́хнуть**) несов неперех (разг) *to express surprise, regret etc.*

ахиле́сова прил: ~ **пята́** Achilles' heel.

ахине́|я (-и) ж (разг) rubbish; **нести́** (impf) ~**ю** to talk rubbish.

а́хн|уть (-у, -ешь) сов от **а́хать** ♦ неперех (разг: орудие итп) to bang ♦ перех (разг: сломать) to smash; (: выпить) to knock back; **он и ~ не успе́л, как они́ убежа́ли** (разг) before he could get a word out, they ran away.

АХО м сокр (= администрати́вно-хозя́йственный отде́л) department concerned with property and maintenance.

ахти́ межд (разг): **не ~ как** not specially; **не ~ (како́й)** (разг) not specially good.

ацето́н (-а) м acetone.

Ашхаба́д (-а) м Ashkhabad.

аэро́бик|а (-и) ж aerobics.

аэро́бус (-а) м airbus.

аэровокза́л (-а) м air terminal (*BRIT*).
аэродина́мик|**а** (-и) ж aerodynamics.
аэродинами́ческ|**ий** (-ая, -ое, -ие) *прил*
　aerodynamic; **аэродинами́ческая труба́** wind
　tunnel.
аэродро́м (-а) м aerodrome.
аэрозо́л|**ь** (-я) м aerosol.
аэро́н (-а) м air-sickness tablets *мн*.

аэропла́н (-а) м aeroplane (*BRIT*), airplane (*US*).
аэропо́рт (-а; *loc sg* -ý) м airport.
аэроста́т (-а) м aerostat.
аэрофотосъём|**ка** (-ки; *gen pl* -ок) ж aerial
　photography.
АЭС ж *сокр* (= *а́томная электроста́нция*)
　atomic power station.
аятолл|**а́** (-ы́) м ayatollah.

~ Б, б ~

Б, б *сущ нескл* (*буква*) the 2nd letter of the Russian alphabet.

б *част см* **бы**.

ба *межд* well, well!; ~! **кого́ я ви́жу!** gosh! look who it is!

ба́б|а (-ы) *ж* (*разг*) woman; (: *пренебр: мужчина*) old woman.

ба́б|а-яг|а́ (-ы, -и́) *ж* Baba Yaga (*old witch in Russian folk-tales*); (*разг*) old witch (*fig*).

ба́б|ий (-ья, -ье, -ьи) *прил* (*разг: пренебр*) womanish; **ба́бье ле́то** Indian summer; **ба́бьи разгово́ры** women's talk; **ба́бьи ска́зки** old wives' tales.

ба́б|ка (-ки; *gen pl* -ок) *ж* (*бабушка*) grandmother; (*разг: старуха*) old woman.

ба́боч|ка (-ки; *gen pl* -ек) *ж* butterfly; (*галстук*) bow tie.

ба́буш|ка (-ки; *gen pl* -ек) *ж* grandma, granny; (*разг*) old woman; ~ **на́двое сказа́ла** we shall see (what we shall see).

Бава́ри|я (-и) *ж* Bavaria.

бава́рск|ий (-ая, -ое, -ие) *прил* Bavarian.

бага́ж (-а́) *м* luggage (*BRIT*), baggage (*US*); **сдава́ть** (**сдать** *perf*) **ве́щи в** ~ to check in one's luggage (*BRIT*) *или* bags (*US*); **отправля́ть** (**отпра́вить** *perf*) **багажо́м** to send as unaccompanied baggage; **бага́ж зна́ний** knowledge.

бага́жник (-а) *м* (*в автомобиле*) boot (*BRIT*), trunk (*US*); (*на крыше автомобиля*) roof rack; (*на велосипеде*) carrier.

бага́жный *прил* luggage *опред* (*BRIT*), baggage *опред* (*US*).

бага́мск|ий (-ая, -ое, -ие) *прил*: **Б~ие острова́** Bahama Islands, Bahamas.

Багда́д (-а) *м* Baghdad.

багрове́|ть (-ю; *perf* **побагрове́ть**) *несов неперех* to turn crimson; (*no perf; цветы*) to show crimson.

багро́в|ый (-, -а, -о) *прил* crimson.

багря́н|ый (-, -а, -о) *прил* crimson.

бадминто́н (-а) *м* badminton.

бадминтони́ст (-а) *м* badminton player.

бадминтони́ст|ка (-ки; *gen pl* -ок) *ж см* **бадминтони́ст**.

ба́з|а (-ы) *ж* basis; (*ВОЕН, АРХИТ*) base; (*для туристов, спортсменов*) centre (*BRIT*), center (*US*); (*продовольствия, товаров*) warehouse; **на** ~**е** +*gen* on the basis of; **ба́за да́нных** database.

база́льт (-а) *м* basalt.

база́р (-а) *м* market; (*новогодний, книжный итп*) fair; (*перен: разг*) racket; **пти́чий** ~ bird colony.

база́рный *прил* market *опред*; **база́рная ба́ба** (*разг*) fishwife.

базили́к|а (-и) *ж* basilica.

бази́р|овать (-ую) *несов перех*: ~ **что-н на** +*prp* to base sth on
► **бази́роваться** *несов возв* to be based; ~**ся** (*impf*) **на** +*prp* (*на фактах итп*) to be based on.

ба́зис (-а) *м* basis.

байда́р|ка (-ки; *gen pl* -ок) *ж* canoe.

ба́йк|а (-и) *ж* flannelette.

Байка́л (-а) *м* Lake Baikal.

ба́йковый *прил* flannelette.

байт (-а; *gen pl* -) *м* byte.

бак (-а; *МОР*) forecastle, fo'c'sle.

бакале́йн|ый *прил*: ~ **магази́н** grocer's shop (*BRIT*), grocery store (*US*); ~**ые това́ры** groceries.

бакале́|я (-и) *ж* (*в магазине*) grocery section; (*товары*) groceries *мн*.

ба́кен (-а) *м* buoy.

бакенба́рд|ы (-) *мн* sideburns *мн*.

баклажа́н (-а; *gen pl* - *или* -ов) *м* aubergine (*BRIT*), eggplant (*US*).

баклу́ши *мн*: **бить** ~ (*разг*) to idle away one's time.

бактериологи́ческ|ий (-ая, -ое, -ие) *прил* bacteriological; **бактериологи́ческая война́** germ *или* bacteriological warfare.

бактерици́дный *прил* bactericidal, germicidal.

бакте́ри|я (-и) *ж* bacterium (*мн* bacteria).

Баку́ *м нескл* Baku.

бал (-а; *loc sg* -ý, *nom pl* -ы́) *м* (*вечер*) ball.

балага́н (-а) *м* (*перен: разг*) farce.

балала́йк|а (-йки; *gen pl* -ек) *ж* balalaika.

бала́нс (-а) *м* (*также КОММ*) balance; (*ведомость*) balance sheet; **расчётный** ~ balance of claims and liabilities; **бухга́лтерский** ~ balance sheet; **платёжный/торго́вый** ~ balance of payments/trade.

баланси́р|овать (-ую) *несов неперех*: ~ (**на** +*prp*) to balance (on) ♦ (*perf* **сбаланси́ровать**) *перех* (*КОММ*) to balance; ~ (*impf*) **на гра́ни чего́-н** (*перен*) to be poised on the verge *или* brink of sth.

бала́нсовый *прил* balance *опред*; **бала́нсовый**

отчёт balance sheet.
балахо́н (-а) м (*разг*) sack (*baggy, shapeless garment*).
балд|а́ (-ы́) м/ж chump.
балери́н|а (-ы) ж ballerina.
бале́т (-а) м ballet.
балетме́йстер (-а) м ballet master.
ба́л|ка (-ки; *gen pl* -ок) ж (*железобетонная, деревянная*) beam; (*металлическая*) girder; (*овраг*) gully.
Балка́н|ы (-) *мн* the Balkans.
балко́н (-а) м (*АРХИТ*) balcony; (*ТЕАТР*) circle (*BRIT*), balcony (*US*).
балл (-а) м (*на экзамене*) mark; (*на соревновании*) point; **проходно́й ~** pass mark; **ве́тер си́лой в 5 ба́ллов** a force 5 wind.
балла́д|а (-ы) ж ballad.
балла́ст (-а) м ballast; (*перен*) dead weight.
балли́сти|ка (-и) ж ballistics.
баллисти́ческ|ий (-ая, -ое, -ие) *прил* ballistic *опред*; **баллисти́ческая раке́та** ballistic missile.
балло́н (-а) м (*газовый*) cylinder; (*с жидкостью*) jar; (*с кислотой, щёлочью*) carboy; (*АВТ*) balloon tyre.
баллоти́р|овать (-ую) *несов перех* to vote for
▸ **баллоти́роваться** *несов возв*: **~ся в** +*acc или* **на пост** +*gen* to stand (*BRIT*) *или* run (*US*) for.
баллотиро́вочный *прил*: **~ бюллете́нь** ballot paper.
ба́л|овать (-ую; *perf* **изба́ловать**) *несов перех* to spoil
▸ **ба́ловаться** *несов возв* to fool around.
ба́лок *сущ см* **ба́лка**.
балти́йск|ий (-ая, -ое, -ие) *прил*: **Б~ое мо́ре** the Baltic (Sea).
бальза́м (-а) м balsam; (*перен*) balm.
бальзами́р|овать (-ую) (*не*)*сов перех* to embalm.
ба́льн|ый *прил*: **~ое пла́тье** ball gown; **ба́льные та́нцы** ballroom dancing.
балюстра́д|а (-ы) ж balustrade.
БАМ (-а) м *сокр* (= *Байка́ло-Аму́рская (железнодоро́жная) магистра́ль*) Baikal-Amur Railway.
бамбу́к (-а) м bamboo.
ба́мпер (-а) м bumper.
БАН м *сокр* (= *Библиоте́ка Акаде́мии нау́к*) *library of the Academy of Sciences*.
бана́лен *прил см* **бана́льный**.
бана́льность (-и) ж banality, platitude.
бана́льный (-ен, -ьна, -ьно) *прил* banal, trite.
бана́н (-а) м banana.
Бангладе́ш (-а) м Bangladesh.
бангладе́шск|ий (-ая, -ое, -ие) *прил* Bangladeshi.
ба́нд|а (-ы) ж gang.
банда́ж (-а́) м support bandage.

бандеро́л|ь (-и) ж package; **я посла́л кни́гу ~ю** I packaged the book and sent it.
банди́т (-а) м bandit.
банк (-а) м bank; **сберега́тельный ~** savings bank; **акционе́рный ~** joint-stock bank; **э́кспортно-и́мпортный ~** export-import bank.
ба́н|ка (-ки; *gen pl* -ок) ж (*стеклянная*) jar; (*жестяная*) tin (*BRIT*), can (*US*); (*обычно мн*: *мед*) cupping glass.
банке́т (-а) м banquet.
банки́р (-а) м banker.
банкно́т (-а; *gen pl* -) м banknote.
ба́нковск|ий (-ая, -ое, -ие) *прил* bank *опред*.
банкро́т (-а) м bankrupt; **объявля́ть (объяви́ть** *perf*) **кого́-н ~ом** to declare sb bankrupt.
банкро́тств|о (-а) *ср* bankruptcy.
ба́нный *прил* bath *опред*.
ба́нок *сущ см* **ба́нка**.
бант (-а) м bow.
ба́н|я (-и; *gen pl* -ь) ж bathhouse; (*разг*: *мытьё*) bath; **фи́нская ~** sauna; **ру́сская/туре́цкая ~** Russian/Turkish baths; **задава́ть (зада́ть** *perf*) **кому́-н ~ю** (*разг*) to give sb what for.
бапти́зм (-а) м baptism.
бапти́ст (-а) м Baptist.
бар (-а) м bar; (*gen pl* -; *физ*) bar.
бараба́н (-а) м drum.
бараба́н|ить (-ю, -ишь) *несов неперех* to drum.
бараба́нн|ый *прил*: **~ая перепо́нка** eardrum.
бара́к (-а) м barracks *мн*.
бара́н (-а) м sheep; **смотре́ть** (*impf*) **на кого́-н/что-н как ~ на но́вые воро́та** (*разг*) to gawk at sb/sth; **ста́до ~ов** (*также перен*: *пренебр*) flock of sheep.
бара́н|ий (-ья, -ье, -ьи) *прил* (*суп, котлета*) lamb; (*тулуп*) sheepskin.
бара́нин|а (-ы) ж mutton; (*молодая*) lamb.
бара́н|ка (-ки; *gen pl* -ок) ж *small, hard bread ring*; (*перен*: *разг*) wheel.
барахл|о́ (-а́) *ср собир* junk; (*разг*: *человек, вещь*) trash.
барахо́л|ка (-ки; *gen pl* -ок) ж flea market.
бара́хта|ться (-юсь) *несов возв* (*разг*) to flounder; (*играя*) to wallow.
бара́ш|ек (-ка) м (*разг*) lamb; (*шкура*) lambskin; *см также* **бара́шки**.
бара́шк|и (-ов) *мн* (*облака*) fleecy clouds *мн*; (*волны*) white horses *мн*, whitecaps *мн*.
барбари́с (-а) м barberry.
бард (-а) м singer-songwriter.
барда́к (-а́) м (*груб!*: *беспорядок*) hell broke loose (*!*)
барелье́ф (-а) м bas-relief.
ба́ренцев (-а, -о, -ы) *прил*: **Б~о мо́ре** Barents Sea.
ба́рж|а (-и) ж barge.
ба́рин (-а; *nom pl* **господа́**, *gen pl* **госпо́д**) м (*ист*) ≈ lord (*member of the landowning gentry*);

жить *(impf)* как ~ to live like a king.
баритóн (-а) *м* baritone.
бáрмен (-а) *м* barman (*мн* barmen), bartender (*US*).
барокáмер|а (-ы) *ж* pressure chamber.
барóкко *ср нескл* baroque.
барóметр (-а) *м* barometer.
баррéл|ь (-я) *м* barrel (*unit of measurement*).
баррикáд|а (-ы) *ж* barricade; **быть** *(impf)* по рáзные стóроны баррикáд to be on opposite sides of the fence.
баррикади́р|овать (-ую; *perf* забаррикади́ровать) *несов перех* to barricade.
барс (-а) *м* snow leopard.
Барселóн|а (-ы) *ж* Barcelona.
бáрск|ий (-ая, -ое, -ие) *прил* (*перен*) lordly, haughty; **бáрская усáдьба** manor house.
барсýк (-á) *м* badger.
бáртер (-а) *м* barter; **по** ~**у** on a barter basis.
бáртерн|ый *прил*: ~**ая торгóвля** goods *мн* for barter; **на** ~**ой оснóве** on a barter basis.
бáрхат (-а) *м* velvet.
бáрхатный *прил* velvet; (*перен: кожа, голос*) velvety; **бáрхатный сезóн** *warm autumn days by the sea.*
барьéр (-а) *м* (*в беге*) hurdle; (*на скачках*) fence; (*перен*) barrier; **тари́фный** ~ tariff barrier.
бас (-а; *nom pl* -ы́) *м* bass.
бáсен *сущ см* **бáсня**.
баскетбóл (-а) *м* basketball.
баскетболи́ст (-а) *м* basketball player.
баскетболи́ст|ка (-ки; *gen pl* -ок) *ж см* **баскетболи́ст**.
баснослóв|ный (-ен, -на, -но) *прил* fabulous.
бá|сня (-ни; *gen pl* -ен) *ж* fable; (*обычно мн: перен: разг*) fairy story.
басóвый *прил* bass *опред*.
бассéйн (-а) *м* (swimming) pool; (*реки, озера итп*) basin; **каменноугóльный** ~ coalfield.
бастовáть (-ýю) *несов неперех* to be on strike.
батальóн (-а) *м* batallion.
батарé|йка (-йки; *gen pl* -ек) *ж* (*ЭЛЕК*) battery.
батарé|я (-и) *ж* (*отопительная*) radiator; (*ВОЕН, ЭЛЕК*) battery.
бати́ст (-а) *м* cambric, lawn.
батóн (-а) *м* (white) loaf (*long or oval*).
батрáк (-á) *м* farm hand.
батрá|чка (-ки; *gen pl* -ек) *ж см* **батрáк**.
баттерфля́|й (-я) *м* butterfly (stroke).
бáтю|шка (-ки; *gen pl* -ек) *м* (*также РЕЛ*) father; *см также* **бáтюшки**.
бáтюшки *межд*: ~ (**мой**)! good heavens!
бах *межд* bang.
бáхн|уть (-у, -ешь; *impf* бáхать) *сов (не)перех* to bang.
Бахрéйн (-а) *м* Bahrain.
бахром|á (-ы́) *ж* fringe.
бахчá (-и́) *ж melon or pumpkin patch.*
бахчевы́е *прил*: ~ **культýры** *melons or pumpkins.*
баци́лл|а (-ы) *ж* bacillus (*мн* bacilli).

бáшен *сущ см* **бáшня**.
башк|á (-и́) *ж* (*разг*) head.
башмáк (-á) *м* (*туфель*) shoe; (*ботинок*) boot; **деревя́нный** ~ clog; **быть** *(impf)* под башмакóм у когó-н to be under sb's thumb.
бá|шня (-ни; *gen pl* -ен) *ж* tower; (*ВОЕН*) gun turret; (*разг*) tower block.
баю-бáй *межд* refrain (*in lullaby*).
баю́ка|ть (-ю) *несов перех* to lull to sleep.
бáюшки-баю́ *межд см* **баю-бáй**.
бая́н (-а) *м* bayan (*kind of concertina*).
БВЛ *ж сокр* (= Библиотéка всеми́рной литератýры) *series of books on world literature.*
бди́тел|ьный (-ен, -ьна, -ьно) *прил* vigilant.
бег (-а) *м* running; (*СПОРТ*) race; ~ **на дли́нные диста́нции** long-distance race; ~ **на корóткие диста́нции** sprint; *см также* **бегá**.
бег|á (-óв) *мн* the races *мн*; **быть** *(impf)* в ~**х** (*разг*) to be on the run *или* go.
бéга|ть (-ю) *несов неперех* to run; (*челнок*) to fly to and fro; ~ *(impf)* **от** +*gen* (*разг*) to avoid; ~ *(impf)* **за кем-н** (*разг*) to chase *или* run after sb; **у негó глазá** ~**ли** he looked shifty.
бегемóт (-а) *м* hippopotamus.
беги́(те) *несов см* **бежáть**.
беглéц (-á) *м* fugitive.
бéгло *нареч* (*читать, говори́ть*) fluently; (*просмотрéть, ознакóмиться*) cursorily.
бéглый *прил* (*каторжник, преступник*) escaped; (*крепостнóй*) runaway *опред*; (*речь, чтéние*) fluent; (*обзор*) cursory; **бéглые глáсные** fleeting vowels; **бéглый огóнь** (*ВОЕН*) rapid fire.
бегля́н|ка (-ки; *gen pl* -ок) *ж см* **беглéц**.
бегов|óй *прил* (*лошадь*) race *опред*; (*лыжи*) racing; ~**áя дорóжка** running track.
бегóм *нареч* quickly; (*перен: разг*) in a rush; **бежáть** *(impf)* ~ to race, fly.
бегóни|я (-и) *ж* begonia.
бéгств|о (-а) *ср* (*из плена*) escape; (*из дома*) flight; (*с поля боя*) rout; **обращáть** (**обрати́ть** *perf*) **в** ~ to rout; **спасáться** (**спасти́сь** *perf*) ~**м** to escape.
бегý *итп несов см* **бежáть**.
бегýн (-á) *м* runner.
бегýн|ья (-и) *ж см* **бегýн**.
бед|á (-ы́; *nom pl* -ы) *ж* tragedy; (*личная*) misfortune; **прóсто** ~! it's just awful!; **попадáть** (**попáсть** *perf*) **в** ~**ý** to get into trouble; **быть** *(impf)* **в** ~**é** to be in trouble; ~ **в том, что** ... the trouble is (that) ...; ~ (**мне**) **с ним** (*разг*) he's nothing but trouble (to me); **на** ~**ý** (*разг*) unfortunately; **не** ~! (*it's*) nothing!; **лихá** ~ **начáло** (*разг*) the first step is always the hardest.
бéден *прил см* **бéдный**.
бéдер *сущ см* **бедрó**.
беднé|ть (-ю; *perf* обеднéть) *несов неперех* to become poor.
бéдност|ь (-и) *ж* (*также перен*) poverty.

бе́д|ный (-ен, -на́, -но) *прил* poor.
бедня́г|а (-и) *м/ж* (*разг*) poor thing.
бедня́к (-а́) *м* poor man.
бе́дренный *прил* (*см сущ*) thigh *опред*; hip *опред*.
бедр|о́ (-а́; *nom pl* **бёдра**, *gen pl* **бёдер**) *ср* (*верхняя часть ноги*) thigh; (*таз*) hip.
бе́дствен|ный (-, -на, -но) *прил* disastrous.
бе́дстви|е (-я) *ср* disaster.
бе́дств|овать (-ую) *несов неперех* to live in poverty.
бе|жа́ть (*см* **Table 20**) *несов неперех* to run; (*время*) to fly; (*облака*) to scud ◆ (*не*)*сов* (*из плена, из тюрьмы*) to escape.
бе́жевый *прил* beige.
бе́жен|ец (-ца) *м* refugee.
бе́жен|ка (-ки; *gen pl* -ок) *ж см* **бе́женец**.
бе́женца *итп сущ см* **бе́женец**.
бежи́шь *итп несов см* **бежа́ть**.
без *предл* (+*gen*) without; ~ **пяти́/десяти́ мину́т шесть** five to/ten to six; **не** ~ +*gen* (*труда, осложений*) not without; **и** ~ **того́** (*и так уже*) already; **не** ~ **того́** (*разг*) sort of; ~ **у́стали** tirelessly; ~ **тебя́ проблём хвата́ет** there are enough problems without you adding to them *.
безава́рийный *прил* accident-free.
безала́бер|ный (-ен, -на, -но) *прил* (*разг*) sloppy.
безалкого́льный *прил* nonalcoholic, alcohol-free; **безалкого́льный напи́ток** soft drink.
безапелляцио́н|ный (-ен, -на, -но) *прил* (*тон, ответ*) peremptory; (*юр: решение*) final; ~**ый пригово́р** *a sentence without the right of appeal*.
безбе́д|ный (-ен, -на, -но) *прил* comfortable.
безбиле́тник (-а) *м* (*разг: пассажир*) fare dodger.
безбиле́тниц|а (-ы) *ж см* **безбиле́тник**.
безбо́жен *прил см* **безбо́жный**.
безбо́жник (-а) *м* (*разг*) heathen.
безбо́жно *нареч* (*разг*) shamelessly.
безбо́ж|ный (-ен, -на, -но) *прил* (*разг*) shameless.
безболе́знен|ный (-, -на, -но) *прил* (*также перен*) painless.
безбоя́знен|ный (-, -на, -но) *прил* fearless.
безбра́чи|е (-я) *ср* celibacy.
безбре́ж|ный (-ен, -на, -но) *прил* (*также перен*) boundless.
безве́ст|ный (-ен, -на, -но) *прил* unknown.
безве́трен|ный (-, -на, -но) *прил* calm.
безвку́сен *прил см* **безвку́сный**.
безвку́сиц|а (-ы) *ж* bad taste.
безвку́с|ный (-ен, -на, -но) *прил* tasteless.
безвла́сти|е (-я) *ср* anarchy.
безво́д|ный (-ен, -на, -но) *прил* (*среда, почва*) arid.
безвозвра́т|ный (-ен, -на, -но) *прил* irretrievable; **безвозвра́тная ссу́да**

nonrepayable subsidy.
безвозме́здно *нареч* for free.
безвозме́зд|ный *прил* free.
безво́л|ьный (-ен, -ьна, -ьно) *прил* weak-willed.
безвре́д|ный (-ен, -на, -но) *прил* harmless.
безвре́мен|ный (-ен, -на, -но) *прил* untimely.
безвы́ездно *нареч* continuously.
безвы́ход|ный (-ен, -на, -но) *прил* hopeless.
безгла́сный *прил* (*перен*) silent.
безголо́в|ый (-, -а, -о) *прил* (*перен: разг*) brainless.
безголо́с|ый (-, -а, -о) *прил*: ~ **пе́вец** singer with a weak voice.
безгра́мот|ный (-ен, -на, -но) *прил* illiterate; (*работник*) incompetent.
безграни́ч|ный (-ен, -на, -но) *прил* (*также перен*) boundless.
безгре́ш|ный (-ен, -на, -но) *прил* sinless.
безда́р|ный (-ен, -на, -но) *прил* (*писатель, музыкант*) talentless; (*произведение, роман*) mediocre.
безда́р|ь (-и) *ж* (*разг*) nobody.
бездейств|овать (-ую) *несов неперех* (*машина, предприятие*) to be out of action; (*человек*) to take no action.
безделу́ш|ка (-ки; *gen pl* -ек) *ж* (*разг*) trinket, knick-knack.
безде́ль|е (-я) *ср* idleness.
безде́льник (-а) *м* (*разг*) loafer.
безде́льниц|а (-ы) *ж см* **безде́льник**.
безде́льнича|ть (-ю) *несов неперех* (*разг*) to loaf *или* lounge about.
безде́нежный *прил* (*расчёт, перевод*) noncash; (*разг: человек*) hard up.
безде́т|ный (-ен, -на, -но) *прил* childless.
безде́ятел|ьный (-ен, -ьна, -ьно) *прил* inactive.
бе́здн|а (-ы) *ж* abyss; **у меня́** ~ **дел** (*разг*) I've got heaps of things to do.
бездоказа́тел|ьный (-ен, -ьна, -ьно) *прил* unsubstantiated.
бездо́м|ный (-ен, -на, -но) *прил* (*человек*) homeless; (*собака*) stray *опред*.
бездо́н|ный (-ен, -на, -но) *прил* bottomless; **бездо́нная бо́чка** (*разг*) bottomless pit; (: *человек*) (old) soak.
безду́м|ный (-ен, -на, -но) *прил* thoughtless.
безду́ш|ный (-ен, -на, -но) *прил* (*человек*) heartless; (*игра актёра*) soulless.
безе́ *ср нескл* meringue.
безжа́лост|ный (-ен, -на, -но) *прил* ruthless.
безжи́знен|ный (-, -на, -но) *прил* lifeless; (*взгляд, лицо*) expressionless.
беззабо́т|ный (-ен, -на, -но) *прил* carefree.
беззако́нен *прил см* **беззако́нный**.
беззако́ни|е (-я) *ср* lawlessness; (*поступок*) unlawful act.

беззако́н|ный (-ен, -на, -но) *прил* unlawful.
беззасте́нчив|ый (-, -а, -о) *прил* shameless; ~
лгун barefaced liar.
беззащи́т|ный (-ен, -на, -но) *прил* defenceless
(*BRIT*), defenseless (*US*).
беззву́ч|ный (-ен, -на, -но) *прил* inaudible.
беззло́б|ный (-ен, -на, -но) *прил* good-natured.
беззу́б|ый (-, -а, -о) *прил* toothless; (*перен*)
feeble.
безли́к|ий (-ая, -ое, -ие; -, -а, -о) *прил*
nondescript.
безли́чный *прил* (*линг*) impersonal.
безлю́д|ный (-ен, -на, -но) *прил* (*улица, место*)
deserted, empty; **безлю́дная техноло́гия**
automated technology; **безлю́дный фонд** *funds
for employees not on regular staff*.
безме́р|ный (-ен, -на, -но) *прил* (*счастье,
любовь*) boundless; (*требования*) unlimited.
безмо́зглый *прил* (*разг*) brainless.
безмо́лв|ный (-ен, -на, -но) *прил* (*также
перен*) silent; **~ное согла́сие** tacit agreement.
безмяте́ж|ный (-ен, -на, -но) *прил* tranquil.
безнадёж|ный (-ен, -на, -но) *прил* hopeless; ~
больно́й hopeless case (*MED*).
безнака́зан|ный (-, -на, -но) *прил* unpunished.
безнали́чный *прил* noncash; **безнали́чный
расчёт** clearing settlement.
безно́г|ий (-ая, -ое, -ие) *прил* one-legged; (*без
двух ног*) legless.
безнра́вствен|ный (-, -на, -но) *прил* immoral.
безо *предл см* **без**.
безоби́д|ный (-ен, -на, -но) *прил* harmless;
(*шутка, высказывание*) inoffensive, innocuous.
безо́блач|ный (-ен, -на, -но) *прил* cloudless;
(*перен: жизнь, детство*) carefree; (: *счастье*)
unclouded.
безобра́зен *прил см* **безобра́зный**.
безобра́зи|е (-я) *ср* (*физическое уродство*)
ugliness; (*поступок*) outrage; ~! it's
outrageous!, it's a disgrace!
безобра́зник (-а) *м* (*разг*) (little) horror.
безобра́зниц|а (-ы) *ж см* **безобра́зник**.
безобра́знича|ть (-ю; *perf* **набезобра́зничать**)
несов неперех (*разг*) to carry on.
безобра́з|ный (-ен, -на, -но) *прил* ugly;
(*поступок, действие*) outrageous, disgraceful.
безогово́роч|ный (-ен, -на, -но) *прил*
unconditional.
безопа́сен *прил см* **безопа́сный**.
безопа́сност|ь (-и) *ж* safety; (*международная*)
security; **в ~и** out of danger; **Сове́т Б~и**
Security Council; **те́хника ~и** health and safety;
безопа́сность движе́ния road safety.
безопа́с|ный (-ен, -на, -но) *прил* safe.
безору́ж|ный (-ен, -на, -но) *прил* unarmed;
(*перен: в споре*) defenceless (*BRIT*), defenseless
(*US*).
безостано́вочно *нареч* incessantly.
безотве́т|ный (-ен, -на, -но) *прил* (*любовь*)
unrequited; (*существо*) meek.
безотве́тственност|ь (-и) *ж* irresponsibility.

безотве́тствен|ный (-, -на, -но) *прил*
irresponsible.
безотка́з|ный (-ен, -на, -но) *прил* reliable.
безотлага́тел|ьный (-ен, -ьна, -ьно) *прил*
urgent.
безотноси́тельно *нареч*: ~ **к** +*dat* irrespective
of.
безотра́д|ный (-ен, -на, -но) *прил* (*жизнь*)
dreary; (*положение*) bleak.
безотхо́д|ный (-ен, -на, -но) *прил*: **~ное
произво́дство** *production process which
recycles waste*.
безотчёт|ный (-ен, -на, -но) *прил* (*чувство*)
irrational; (*поведение*) unaccountable.
безоши́боч|ный (-ен, -на, -но) *прил* (*решение,
догадка*) correct; (*судья, ценитель*) infallible.
безрабо́тиц|а (-ы) *ж* unemployment.
безрабо́тн|ая (-ой; *decl like adj*) *ж см*
безрабо́тный.
безрабо́т|ный *прил* unemployed ◆ (-ого; *decl
like adj*) *м* unemployed person; **~ые** the
unemployed.
безра́дост|ный (-ен, -на, -но) *прил* (*жизнь,
детство*) cheerless, joyless; (*голос, взгляд*)
dull.
безразде́л|ьный (-ен, -ьна, -ьно) *прил*
(*господство, владение*) absolute; (*внимание*)
undivided.
безразли́чен *прил см* **безразли́чный**.
безразли́чно *нареч* indifferently ◆ *как сказ*:
мне ~ it doesn't matter to me, it makes no
difference to me; ~, **придёт он и́ли нет** it makes
no difference whether he comes or not; ~
кто/что no matter who/what.
безразли́ч|ный (-ен, -на, -но) *прил* indifferent.
безразме́р|ный *прил*: **~ые носки́/чулки́** one-
size socks/stockings.
безрассу́д|ный (-ен, -на, -но) *прил*
(*поведение*) reckless; (*любовь*) impulsive.
безрезульта́т|ный (-ен, -на, -но) *прил*
fruitless.
безро́пот|ный (-ен, -на, -но) *прил*
uncomplaining.
безрука́в|ка (-ки; *gen pl* -ок) *ж* (*кофта*)
sleeveless top; (*куртка*) sleeveless jacket.
безру́к|ий (-ая, -ое, -ие; -, -а, -о) *прил* one-
armed; (*без двух рук*) with no arms; (*перен:
разг*) ham-fisted.
безры́бь|е (-я) *ср*: **на ~ и рак ры́ба** something
is better than nothing.
безубы́точ|ный (-ен, -на, -но) *прил*: **~ное
предприя́тие** *business which is not making a
loss*.
безуда́р|ный (-ен, -на, -но) *прил* (*линг*)
unstressed.
безукори́знен|ный (-, -на, -но) *прил*
(*поведение, человек*) irreproachable; (*работа*)
flawless.
безу́мен *прил см* **безу́мный**.
безу́м|ец (-ца) *м* madman (*мн* madmen).
безу́ми|е (-я) *ср* madness; **до ~я** madly.

безу́мно *нареч* (*любить*) madly; (*устать*) terribly.

безу́м|ный (-ен, -на, -но) *прил* (*план, намерение*) mad; (*счастье, ярость итп*) wild; **он зараба́тывает ~ные де́ньги** (*разг*) he earns crazy money; **~ная ро́скошь** unbelievable luxury.

безу́мца *итп сущ см* **безу́мец**.

безупре́ч|ный (-ен, -на, -но) *прил* (*поведение, человек*) irreproachable; (*работа*) flawless.

безусло́вен *прил см* **безусло́вный**.

безусло́вно *нареч* (*повиноваться, доверить*) unconditionally ♦ *част* (*несомненно*) without a doubt; **~, я бу́ду рад помо́чь Вам** naturally, I'll be happy to help you.

безусло́в|ный (-ен, -на, -но) *прил* (*повиновение, доверие*) unconditional, absolute; (*успех, превосходство*) indisputable.

безуспе́ш|ный (-ен, -на, -но) *прил* unsuccessful.

безуча́ст|ный (-ен, -на, -но) *прил* disinterested.

безъя́дерный *прил* nuclear-free.

безымя́н|ный (-ен, -на, -но) *прил* (*река, гора*) unnamed; (*герой, автор*) anonymous; **безымя́нный па́лец** ring finger.

безысхо́д|ный (-ен, -на, -но) *прил* hopeless.

бей(ся) *несов см* **би́ть(ся)**.

Бейру́т (-а) *м* Beirut.

бе́йте(сь) *несов см* **би́ть(ся)**.

беко́н (-а) *м* bacon.

БелА́З (-а) *м сокр = Белору́сский автомоби́льный заво́д*; (*автомобиль*) *vehicle manufactured at the Belorussian car factory*.

белару́с (-а) *м* Belorussian.

белару́с|ка (-ки; *gen pl* -ок) *ж см* **белару́с**.

белару́сск|ий (-ая, -ое, -ие) *прил* Belorussian.

Белару́с|ь (-и) *ж* Belarus.

Белгра́д (-а) *м* Belgrade.

беле́|ть (-ю; *perf* **побеле́ть**) *несов неперех* (*лицо*) to go *или* turn white; (*no perf*; *цветы*) to show white.

белиберд|а́ (-ы́) *ж* (*разг*) gobbledegook.

Бели́з (-а) *м* Belize.

бели́л|а (-) *мн* emulsion *ед*.

бел|и́ть (-ю́, -ишь; *perf* **побели́ть**) *несов перех* to whitewash.

бе́личий (-ья, -ье, -ьи) *прил* squirrel's; (*шуба*) squirrel (fur).

бе́л|ка (-ки; *gen pl* -ок) *ж* squirrel; **верте́ться** (*impf*) **как ~ в колесе́** to run round in circles.

белка́ *итп сущ см* **бело́к**.

белко́вый *прил* proteinous.

беллетри́стик|а (-и) *ж* fiction; (*лёгкое чтение*) light reading.

белови́к (-а́) *м* fair copy.

белогварде́|ец (-йца) *м* (*ИСТ*) White Guardsman (*мн* Guardsmen).

бе́лок *сущ см* **бе́лка**.

бел|о́к (-ка́) *м* protein; (*яйца*) (egg) white; (*АНАТ*) white (of the eye).

белокро́ви|е (-я) *ср* (*МЕД*) leukaemia (*BRIT*), leukemia (*US*).

белоку́р|ый (-, -а, -о) *прил* (*человек*) fair(-haired); (*волосы*) fair.

белору́ч|ка (-ки; *gen pl* -ек) *м/ж* (*разг: пренебр*) shirker.

белосне́ж|ный (-ен, -на, -но) *прил* snow-white.

белу́г|а (-и) *ж* beluga (*sturgeon*).

белу́ж|ий (-ья, -ье, -ьи) *прил* beluga *опред*.

Бе́лфаст (-а) *м* Belfast.

бе́л|ые (-ых; *decl like adj*) *мн* (*ШАХМАТЫ*) white *ед*.

бе́л|ый (-, -а́, -о) *прил* white; (*гриб*) сер ♦ (-ого; *decl like adj*) *м* (*человек*) white (person); **средь ~а дня** (*разг*) in broad daylight; **бе́лая воро́на** the odd one out; **бе́лая гва́рдия** (*ИСТ*) the White Guard; **бе́лая горя́чка** the DT's (= *delirium tremens*); **бе́лое духове́нство** secular clergy; **бе́лый медве́дь** polar bear; *см также* **бе́лые**.

бельги́ек *сущ см* **бельги́йка**.

бельги́|ец (-йца) *м* Belgian.

бельги́|йка (-йки; *gen pl* -ек) *ж см* **бельги́ец**.

бельги́йск|ий (-ая, -ое, -ие) *прил* Belgian.

бельги́йца *итп сущ см* **бельги́ец**.

Бе́льги|я (-и) *ж* Belgium.

бель|ё (-я́) *ср собир* linen; (*стиранное*) washing; **ни́жнее ~** underwear; **посте́льное ~** bedclothes, bed linen.

бельэта́ж (-а) *м* (*ТЕАТР*) dress circle; (*АРХИТ*) first floor, second floor (*US*).

беля́ш (-а́) *м* meat pie.

бемо́л|ь (-я) *м* (*МУЗ*) flat.

бенефи́с (-а) *м performance commemorating and featuring an actor*.

бензи́н (-а) *м* petrol (*BRIT*), gas (*US*).

бензи́новый *прил* petrol (*BRIT*), gas (*US*); **~ дви́гатель** petrol engine.

бензоба́к (-а) *м* petrol (*BRIT*) *или* gas (*US*) tank.

бензоколо́н|ка (-ки; *gen pl* -ок) *ж* petrol (*BRIT*) *или* gas (*US*) pump.

Бенилю́кс (-а) *м* Benelux.

бенуа́р (-а) *м* (*ТЕАТР*) boxes *мн*.

бе́рег (-а; *loc sg* -у́, *nom pl* -а́) *м* (*моря, озера*) shore; (*реки*) bank.

берёг(ся) *итп несов см* **бере́чь(ся)**.

берегов|о́й *прил* (*см сущ*) coastal; riverside; **береговая ли́ния** coastline; **береговая слу́жба** coastguard.

берегу́(сь) *итп несов см* **бере́чь(ся)**.

бере́жен *прил см* **бе́режный**.

бережёшь(ся) *итп несов см* **бере́чь(ся)**.

бережли́вост|ь (-и) *ж* economy, thrift.

бережли́в|ый (-, -а, -о) *прил* economical, thrifty.

бе́режност|ь (-и) *ж* care.

бе́реж|ный (-ен, -на, -но) *прил* (*заботливый*)

caring; (*осторожный*) careful.
берёз|а (-ы) *ж* birch (tree).
Берёз|ка (-ки; *gen pl* -ок) *ж* Beriozka (*hard-currency shop in the USSR*).
берёзовый *прил* birch.
Берёзок *сущ см* **Берёзка**.
берём *несов см* **брать**.
бере́мене|ть (-ю; *perf* забере́менеть) *сов неперех* to get pregnant.
бере́менн|ая (-а) *прил* pregnant ◆ (-ой; *decl like adj*) *ж* pregnant woman.
бере́менност|ь (-и) *ж* pregnancy.
бере́т (-а) *м* beret.
берёт *итп несов см* **брать**.
бере́|чь (-гу́, -жёшь *итп*, -гу́т; *pt* -ёг, -егла́, -егло́) *несов перех* (*документы*) to keep; (*де́ньги*) to be careful with; (*время*) to make good use of; (*здоровье, детей*) to look after, take care of; ~ (*impf*) **как зени́цу о́ка** to guard with one's life
► **бере́чься** (*perf* побере́чься) *несов возв* (+*gen*) to watch out for; ~**еги́тесь просту́ды** take care you don't catch a cold; ~**еги́тесь!** watch out!
бе́рингов (-а, -о, -ы) *прил*: **Б~ проли́в** Bering Strait.
Берли́н (-а) *м* Berlin.
берму́дск|ий (-ая, -ое, -ие) *прил*: **Б~ие острова́** Bermuda, the Bermudas.
Берн (-а) *м* Berne.
беру́(сь) *итп несов см* **брать(ся)**.
берцо́в|ый *прил*: ~**ая кость** shinbone.
бес (-а) *м* demon, devil; (*перен*) devil.
бесе́д|а (-ы) *ж* conversation; (*не официальная*) chat; (*популярный доклад*) discussion.
бесе́д|ка (-ки; *gen pl* -ок) *ж* pavilion.
бесе́д|овать (-ую) *несов неперех*: ~ (*с* +*instr*) to talk (to); (*не официально*) to chat (to).
бесе́док *сущ см* **бесе́дка**.
бе|си́ть (-шу́, -сишь; *perf* взбеси́ть) *несов перех* to infuriate
► **беси́ться** *несов возв* (*разг*) to run wild; (*perf* взбеси́ться; *раздражаться*) to become furious; **с жи́ру** ~**ся** (*impf*) (*разг*) to become spoilt and fussy.
бескла́ссовый *прил* classless.
бескомпроми́сс|ный (-ен, -на, -но) *прил* uncompromising.
бесконе́чен *прил см* **бесконе́чный**.
бесконе́чно *нареч* (*очень долго*) endlessly; (*чрезвычайно*) infinitely.
бесконе́чност|ь (-и) *ж* infinity; **до** ~**и** (*очень долго*) endlessly; (*очень сильно*) infinitely.
бесконе́ч|ный (-ен, -на, -но) *прил* (*пространство, дорога*) endless; (*время, удовольствие*) endless, infinite; (*число*) infinite; (*вечер, песня*) interminable; (*любовь, ненависть*) undying.
бесконтро́л|ьный (-ен, -ьна, -ьно) *прил* uncontrolled.
бескоры́стен *прил см* **бескоры́стный**.

бескоры́сти|е (-я) *ср* unselfishness.
бескоры́ст|ный (-ен, -на, -но) *прил* unselfish.
бескро́в|ный (-ен, -на, -но) *прил* bloodless.
беспардо́н|ный (-ен, -на, -но) *прил* shameless, brazen.
беспереба́|йный (-ен, -йна, -йно) *прил* uninterrupted.
бесперспекти́в|ный (-ен, -на, -но) *прил* (*работа*) without prospects; (*отношения*) with no future.
беспе́чен *прил см* **беспе́чный**.
беспе́чност|ь (-и) *ж* carefreeness.
беспе́ч|ный (-ен, -на, -но) *прил* carefree.
беспла́т|ный (-ен, -на, -но) *прил* free.
беспло́д|ный *прил см* **беспло́дный**.
беспло́ди|е (-я) *ср* (*женщины*) infertility; (*земли*) barrenness, infertility.
беспло́д|ный (-ен, -на, -но) *прил* (*женщина*) infertile; (*брак*) childless; (*почва*) barren, infertile; (*попытки, дискуссии*) fruitless.
бесповоро́т|ный (-ен, -на, -но) *прил* irrevocable.
беспадо́б|ный (-ен, -на, -но) *прил* (*разг*) fantastic.
беспоко́ен *прил см* **беспоко́йный**.
беспоко́|ить (-ю, -ишь) *несов перех* (*причинять боль*) to trouble; (*perf* побеспоко́ить; *мешать*) to disturb; (*perf* обеспоко́ить; *тревожить*) to bother, worry
► **беспоко́иться** *несов возв* (*утруждать себя*) to put o.s. out, trouble o.s.; (*тревожиться*): ~**ся о** +*prp или* **за** +*acc* to worry about; **не** ~**йтесь, я сде́лаю всё сам** don't put yourself out, I'll do it myself.
беспоко́|йный (-ен, -йна, -йно) *прил* (*человек*) anxious; (*взгляд*) uneasy, anxious; (*поездка*) uncomfortable; (*ребёнок*) fidgety, restless; (*море, сон, время*) troubled; **э́то о́чень** ~**йная рабо́та** this is a very stressful job.
беспоко́йств|о (-а) *ср* anxiety, unease; (*заботы, хлопоты*) trouble; **прости́те за** ~**!** sorry to trouble you!
бесполе́з|ный (-ен, -на, -но) *прил* useless.
беспо́мощен *прил см* **беспо́мощный**.
беспо́мощност|ь (-и) *ж* (*см прил*) helplessness; weakness.
беспо́мощ|ный (-ен, -на, -но) *прил* helpless; (*перен*) weak.
беспоря́д|ки (-ов) *мн* disturbances *мн*.
беспоря́д|ок (-ка) *м* disorder; **в** ~**ке** (*комната, дела*) in a mess; *см также* **беспоря́дки**.
беспоря́доч|ный (-ен, -на, -но) *прил* (*груда бумаг*) disorderly, untidy; (*рассказ, записи*) confused.
бесеса́дочный *прил* nonstop.
беспо́чвен|ный (-, -на, -но) *прил* groundless.
беспо́шлинный *прил* duty-free.
беспоща́д|ный (-ен, -на, -но) *прил* (*наказание, удар*) merciless; (*критика, сатира*) ruthless; ~ **к** +*dat* ruthless *или* merciless towards.
беспра́вен *прил см* **беспра́вный**.

беспра́ви|е (-я) *ср* (*беззако́ние*) lawlessness.
беспра́в|ный (-ен, -на, -но) *прил* without (civil)
rights.
беспреде́л|ьный (-ен, -ьна, -ьно) *прил*
(*простра́нство, мо́ре*) boundless; (*любо́вь,
не́нависть*) immeasurable.
беспрекосло́в|ный (-ен, -на, -но) *прил*
unquestioning.
беспрепя́тственно *нареч* without difficulty.
беспрепя́тствен|ный (-, -на, -но) *прил*
unimpeded.
беспрецеде́нт|ный (-ен, -на, -но) *прил*
unprecedented.
беспри́был|ьный (-ен, -ьна, -ьно) *прил*
unprofitable.
беспризо́рен *прил см* беспризо́рный.
беспризо́рник (-а) *м* (street) urchin.
беспризо́рниц|а (-ы) *ж см* беспризо́рник.
беспризо́р|ный (-ен, -на, -но) *прил* (*ребёнок*)
homeless; (*дом, хозя́йство*) neglected.
беспринци́п|ный (-ен, -на, -но) *прил*
unscrupulous.
беспристра́ст|ный (-ен, -на, -но) *прил*
unbias(s)ed.
беспричи́н|ный (-ен, -на, -но) *прил* irrational.
беспросве́т|ный (-ен, -на, -но) *прил* (*нужда́*)
desperate; (*грусть*) hopeless; (*ночь, мгла*)
impenetrable.
беспроце́нтный *прил* interest-free.
Бессара́би|я (-и) *ж* Bessarabia.
бессвя́з|ный (-ен, -на, -но) *прил* disjointed.
бессерде́чен *прил см* бессерде́чный.
бессерде́чность (-и) *ж* heartlessness.
бессерде́ч|ный (-ен, -на, -но) *прил* heartless.
бесси́лен *прил см* бесси́льный.
бесси́ли|е (-я) *ср* (*больно́го, старика́*) debility;
(*чу́вства*) impotence.
бесси́л|ьный (-ен, -ьна, -ьно) *прил* (*больно́й,
стари́к*) feeble, weak; (*гнев, не́нависть*)
impotent; (*он/президе́нт* ~ен (*измени́ть
ситуа́цию*) he/the president is powerless (to
change the situation).
бессме́ртен *прил см* бессме́ртный.
бессме́рти|е (-я) *ср* immortality.
бессме́рт|ный (-ен, -на, -но) *прил* immortal.
бессмы́сленность (-и) *ж* (*слов*)
meaninglessness; (*посту́пка*) senselessness,
pointlessness.
бессмы́слен|ный (-, -на, -но) *прил* (*слова́*)
meaningless; (*посту́пок*) senseless, pointless;
(*взгляд, улы́бка*) inane.
бессо́вест|ный (-ен, -на, -но) *прил*
(*нече́стный*) unscrupulous; (*на́глый*)
shameless.
бессодержа́тел|ьный (-ен, -ьна, -ьно) *прил*
(*слова́*) empty; (*статья́*) thin.
бессозна́тел|ьный (-ен, -ьна, -ьно) *прил*
(*страх, де́йствия*) instinctive; **быть** (*impf*) **в**

~ьном состоя́нии to be unconscious.
бессо́нниц|а (-ы) *ж* insomnia.
бессо́нный *прил* (*ночь*) sleepless; (*страж,
сиде́лка*) wakeful.
бесспо́рен *прил см* бесспо́рный.
бесспо́рно *нареч* indisputably ♦ *част*
(*несомне́нно*) absolutely; **он, ~, умён** he is
indisputably clever.
бесспо́р|ный (-ен, -на, -но) *прил* indisputable.
бессро́ч|ный (-ен, -на, -но) *прил* indefinite.
бесстра́ш|ный (-ен, -на, -но) *прил* fearless.
бессты́д|ный (-ен, -на, -но) *прил* shameless,
brazen; (*ложь*) barefaced.
беста́кт|ный (-ен, -на, -но) *прил* tactless.
бе́сти|я (-и) *м/ж* (*разг*) rogue.
бестолко́в|ый (-, -а, -о) *прил* (*глу́пый*) stupid;
(*невразуми́тельный*) incoherent.
бестсе́ллер (-а) *м* best seller.
бесхи́трост|ный (-ен, -на, -но) *прил* simple.
бесхо́зный *прил* ownerless.
бесхозя́йствен|ный (-, -на, -но) *прил*
(*руководи́тель*) inefficient; (*поли́тика*)
uneconomic; ~ная же́нщина a bad
housekeeper.
бесцве́т|ный (-ен, -на, -но) *прил* colourless
(*BRIT*), colorless (*US*).
бесце́л|ьный (-ен, -ьна, -ьно) *прил* pointless,
futile.
бесце́н|ный (-ен, -на, -но) *прил* (*колле́кция,
сокро́вища*) priceless; (*друг, жена́*) invaluable.
бесце́нок *м*: **за** ~ dirt cheap, for next to nothing.
бесцеремо́н|ный (-ен, -на, -но) *прил*
unceremonious, familiar.
бесчелове́ч|ный (-ен, -на, -но) *прил* inhuman.
бесче́|стить (-щу, -стишь; *perf* обесче́стить)
несов перех (*де́вушку*) to violate.
бесчи́слен|ный (-, -на, -но) *прил* numerous.
бесчу́вствен|ный (-, -на, -но) *прил*
(*жесто́кий*) unfeeling; (*лишённый созна́ния*)
senseless.
бето́н (-а; *part gen* -у) *м* concrete.
бетони́р|овать (-ую; *perf* забетони́ровать)
несов перех to concrete.
бефстро́ганов *м нескл* boeuf *или* beef
stroganoff.
бе́шенств|о (-а) *ср* (*перен*) rage; (*МЕД*) rabies;
приходи́ть (прийти́ *perf*) **в** ~ to fly into a rage.
бе́шен|ый *прил* (*взгляд*) furious; (*хара́ктер,
темпера́мент, урага́н*) violent; (*МЕД*) rabid;
(*разг: де́ньги, це́ны*) crazy; **э́то сто́ит ~ых
де́нег** (*разг*) it costs a bomb.
бешу́(сь) *несов см* беси́ть(ся).
биатло́н (-а) *м* biathlon.
биатлони́ст (-а) *м* biathlete.
биатлони́ст|ка (-ки; *gen pl* -ок) *ж см*
биатлони́ст.
Би-би-си *ж сокр* (= Брита́нская
радиовеща́тельная корпора́ция) BBC (=

British Broadcasting Corporation).

библе́йск|ий (**-ая, -ое, -ие**) *прил* biblical.

библиографи́ческ|ий (**-ая, -ое, -ие**) *прил* bibliographical; **библиографи́ческая ре́дкость** rare edition.

библиогра́фи|я (**-и**) *ж* bibliography.

библиоте́к|а (**-и**) *ж* library.

библиоте́кар|ь (**-я**) *м* librarian.

библиоте́чный *прил* library *опред*.

Би́бли|я (**-и**) *ж* the Bible.

бигуди́ *ср/мн нескл* curlers *мн*; **накру́чивать** (**накрути́ть** *perf*) **во́лосы на ~** to put one's hair in curlers.

бидо́н (**-а**) *м* (*для молока*) churn; (*маленький*) can.

бижуте́ри|я (**-и**) *ж* costume jewellery.

би́знес (**-а**) *м* business; **де́лать** (**сде́лать** *perf*) **~ на** +*prp* to make a living from.

бизнесме́н (**-а**) *м* businessman (*мн* businessmen).

бики́ни *ср нескл* bikini.

биле́т (**-а**) *м* ticket; (*члена организации*) (membership) ticket; **обра́тный ~** (*BRIT*) *или* roundtrip (*US*) ticket; **казначе́йский ~** banknote; **входно́й ~** ticket (*for standing room*).

биллио́н (**-а**) *м* billion (*one thousand million*).

билья́рд (**-а**) *м* (*игра*) billiards; (*стол*) billiard table.

бино́кл|ь (**-я**) *м* binoculars *мн*.

бинт (**-а́**) *м* bandage; **накла́дывать** (**наложи́ть** *perf*) **~ы на** +*acc* to put a bandage on.

бинт|ова́ть (**-у́ю**; *perf* **забинтова́ть**) *несов перех* to bandage.

био́граф (**-а**) *м* biographer.

биогра́фи|я (**-и**) *ж* biography.

био́лог (**-а**) *м* biologist.

биоло́ги|я (**-и**) *ж* biology.

би́рж|а (**-и**) *ж* (*комм*) exchange; **валю́тная ~** exchange market; **~ це́нных бума́г** securities exchange; **това́рная ~** commodity exchange; **фо́ндовая ~** stock exchange *или* market; **игра́ть** (*impf*) **на ~е** to play the stock exchange.

биржеви́к (**-а́**) *м* stockbroker.

биржево́й *прил* (*сделка*) stock-exchange; **биржево́й бро́кер** stockbroker.

би́рк|а (**-ки**; *gen pl* **-ок**) *ж* tag.

Бирминге́м (**-а**) *м* Birmingham.

би́рок *сущ см* **би́рка**.

бирюз|а́ (**-ы́**) *ж* (*ГЕО*) turquoise.

бис *межд*: **Б~!** encore!; **исполня́ть** (**испо́лнить** *perf*) **что-н на ~** to do sth as an encore.

би́сер (**-а**; *part gen* **-у**) *м собир* glass beads *мн*; **мета́ть** (*impf*) **~ пе́ред сви́ньями** to cast pearls before swine.

бискви́т (**-а**) *м* sponge (cake).

бистро́ *ср нескл* bistro.

бит (**-а**) *м* (*комп*) bit.

би́тв|а (**-ы**) *ж* battle.

битко́м *нареч*: **~** (**наби́т**) (*разг*) chock-a-block, jam-packed.

би́тый *прил* broken; **би́тый час** (*разг*) a good hour.

бить (**бью, бьёшь**; *imper* **бей(те)**, *perf* **поби́ть**) *несов перех* (*также перен*) to beat; (*стёкла*) to break ♦ (*perf* **проби́ть**) *неперех* (*часы*) to strike; **~** (*impf*) **в** +*acc* (*в дверь*) to bang at; (*дождь, ветер*) to beat against; (*орудие*) to hit; **~** (*impf*) **на** +*acc* (*стремиться к*) to aim for; **~** (*impf*) **по столу́** to bang on the table; **~** (*impf*) **в бараба́н** to beat a drum; **свет бьёт мне в глаза́** the light is blinding me; **~** (*impf*) **по чьим-н недоста́ткам** to severely criticize sb's failings; **~** (*impf*) **по карма́ну** to hit one's pocket; **э́то бьёт по мои́м интере́сам** it conflicts with my interests; **его́ бьёт озно́б** he's got a fit of the shivers

▶ **би́ться** *несов возв* (*сердце, пульс*) to beat; (*стекло, фарфор*) to be breakable; (*сражаться*) to fight; **би́ться** (*impf*) **о** +*acc* to bang against; **би́ться** (*impf*) **над** +*instr* (*над задачей, над решением*) to struggle with; **хоть голово́й об сте́ну бе́йся** you might as well bang your head against a brick wall.

бифште́кс (**-а**) *м* steak.

бич (**-а́**) *м* (*плеть*) whip; (*перен*) scourge.

Бишке́к (**-а**) *м* Bishkek.

б-ка *сокр* = **библиоте́ка**.

бла́г|а (**-**) *мн* rewards *мн*; **всех благ!** all the best!

бла́г|о (**-а**) *ср* benefit; **на ~** +*gen* for the benefit of; *см также* **бла́га**.

благови́д|ный (**-ен, -на, -но**) *прил* (*предлог*) plausible; (*стремления, поступки*) seemingly well-intentioned.

благодар|и́ть (**-ю́, -и́шь**; *perf* **поблагодари́ть**) *несов перех* to thank.

благода́рност|ь (**-и**) *ж* gratitude, thanks; **приноси́ть** (**принести́** *perf*) **~ кому́-н** to express one's gratitude to sb.

благодаря́ *предл* (+*dat*) thanks to ♦ *союз*: **~ тому́, что** owing to the fact that; **здоро́в, ~ тому́, что занима́юсь спо́ртом** I'm healthy thanks to *или* owing to the fact that I play sport.

благоде́тел|ь (**-я**) *м* benefactor.

благоде́тельниц|а (**-ы**) *ж* benefactress.

благо́й *прил*: **~ие наме́рения** good intentions *мн*; **крича́ть** (*impf*) **~им ма́том** (*разг*) to shout at the top of one's voice.

благонадёж|ный (**-ен, -на, -но**) *прил* trustworthy.

благополу́чи|е (**-я**) *ср* (*в семье, в отношениях*) wellbeing; (*материальная обеспеченность*) prosperity; **жела́ю Вам вся́кого ~я** I wish you all the very best.

благополу́ч|ный (**-ен, -на, -но**) *прил* successful.

благоприя́т|ный (**-ен, -на, -но**) *прил* favourable (*BRIT*), favorable (*US*).

благоприя́тствовани|е (**-я**) *ср*: **усло́вия/поли́тика наибо́льшего ~я** the most favourable (*BRIT*) *или* favorable (*US*) conditions/policy.

благоразу́ми|е (**-я**) *ср* prudence.

благоразу́м|ный (-ен, -на, -но) *прил* prudent.
благоро́д|ный (-ен, -на, -но) *прил* noble; **он ~ного происхожде́ния** he is of noble birth; **благоро́дные га́зы** the noble gases; **благоро́дные мета́ллы** precious metals.
благоро́дств|о (-а) *ср* nobility.
благослов|и́ть (-лю́, -и́шь; *impf* **благословля́ть**) *сов перех* to bless; ~ *(perf)* **кого́-н (на что-н)** to give sb one's blessing (for sth).
благосостоя́ни|е (-я) *ср* wellbeing.
благотвори́тел|ь (-я) *м* philanthropist.
благотвори́тельниц|а (-ы) *ж см* **благотвори́тель**.
благотвори́тельност|ь (-и) *ж* charity.
благотвори́тельн|ый *прил* charitable; **~ая организа́ция** charity (organization); **~ конце́рт** charity concert.
благоустро́ен|ный (-, -на, -но) *прил* (*кварти́ра, дом*) *with all modern conveniences*; **~ го́род** a city with every amenity; **~ная ку́хня** a well-equipped kitchen.
блаже́н|ный (-, -на, -но) *прил* blissful; (*no short form*; *РЕЛ*) Blessed.
блаже́нств|о (-а) *ср* bliss; **быть** (*impf*) **на верху́ ~а** to be in seventh heaven.
бланк (-а) *м* form.
блат (-а) *м* (*разг*) connections *мн*; **по бла́ту** (*разг*) through (one's) connections.
блатно́й *прил* criminal.
бле́ден *прил см* **бле́дный**.
бледне́|ть (-ю; *perf* **побледне́ть**) *несов неперех* to (grow) pale; (*перен*): ~ (*перед* +*instr*) to pale (beside).
бле́дност|ь (-и) *ж* (*см прил*) pallor, paleness; dullness.
бле́дный (-ен, -на́, -но) *прил* pale; (*перен*) dull.
блёкн|уть (-у, -ешь; *perf* **поблёкнуть**) *несов неперех* to fade.
блеск (-а; *part gen* -у) *м* (*огне́й, мо́лнии*) brilliance, brightness; (*мета́лла*) shine; (*перен*) brilliance; **во всём бле́ске** in full splendour (*BRIT*) *или* splendor (*US*); **с бле́ском** brilliantly; **сдать** (*perf*) **экза́мен с бле́ском** to pass an exam with flying colours.
блесн|у́ть (-у́, -ёшь) *сов неперех* to flash; **у него́ ~у́ла мысль** a thought flashed through his mind; **~у́ла наде́жда** there was a ray of hope.
бле|сте́ть (-щу́, -сти́шь *или*, -щешь) *несов неперех* (*звёзды, мета́лл*) to shine; (*ка́мни, глаза́*) to sparkle; **она́ бле́щет красото́й** she is dazzling; **он бле́щет умо́м** he shines intellectually.
блестя́ще *нареч* brilliantly; **дела́ иду́т ~** everything's going brilliantly.
блестя́щ|ий (-ая, -ее, -ие; -, -а́, -е) *прил* (*звезда́*) bright; (*мета́лл*) shining; (*глаза́*) sparkling; (*перен*) brilliant.

блещу́ *итп несов см* **блесте́ть**.
бле́|ять (-ю) *несов неперех* to bleat.
ближа́йш|ий (-ая, -ее, -ие) *прил* (*го́род, дом*) the nearest; (*год*) the next; (*пла́ны*) immediate; (*друг*) closest; **в ~ем бу́дущем** in the near future; **при ~ем уча́стии** +*gen* with the close cooperation of; **при ~ем рассмотре́нии** on closer inspection; **ближа́йший ро́дственник** next of kin.
бли́же *сравн прил от* **бли́зкий**.
бли́жн|ий (-яя, -ее, -ие) *прил* (*го́род, дере́вня*) neighbouring (*BRIT*), neighboring (*US*); **éхать** (**пое́хать** *perf*) **~им путём** to take the shortest route; **Б~ Восто́к** Middle East.
бли́зк|ие (-их; *decl like adj*) *мн* (*ро́дственники*) relatives *мн*.
бли́з|кий (-кая, -кое, -кие; -ок, -ка́, -ко) *прил* (*го́род*) nearby; (*коне́ц*) imminent; (*друг, отноше́ния*) close; -, -*dat* (*интере́сы, те́ма*) similar *или* close to; **~ по** +*dat* (*по содержа́нию, по цели*) similar *или* close in; **они́ близки́ во мне́ниях** they think alike; **бли́зкий ро́дственник** close relative.
бли́зко *нареч* near *или* close by ♦ *как сказ* not far off; **~ от** +*gen* near, close to; **го́род ~** the town isn't far off; **~ узна́ть** (*perf*) **кого́-н** to get to know sb well; **принима́ть (приня́ть** *perf*) **что-н ~ к се́рдцу** to take sth to heart.
близне́ц (-а́) *м* (*обы́чно мн*) twin; **бра́тья/сёстры-близнецы́** twin brothers/sisters; *см та́кже* **Близнецы́**.
Близнецы́ (-о́в) *мн* (*созве́здие*) Gemini.
бли́зок *прил см* **бли́зкий**.
близору́к|ий (-ая, -ое, -ие; -, -а, -о) *прил* short-sighted (*BRIT*), nearsighted (*US*).
близору́кост|ь (-и) *ж* (*см прил*) short-sightedness, nearsightedness.
бли́зост|ь (-и) *ж* proximity; (*интере́сов, мне́ний*) closeness; (*бли́зкие отноше́ния*) intimacy.
блин (-а́) *м* pancake.
бли́нчик (-а) *м уменьш от* **блин**.
блок (-а) *м* (*ПОЛИТ*) bloc; (*ТЕХ*) unit.
блока́д|а (-ы) *ж* (*ВОЕН*) siege; (*ЭКОН*) blockade; **устана́вливать (установи́ть** *perf*)**/снима́ть** (**снять** *perf*) **~у** to impose/lift a blockade.
блоки́р|овать (-ую) (*не*)*сов перех* to blockade; (*СПОРТ, КОМП*) to block.
блокно́т (-а) *м* notebook.
блонди́н (-а) *м*: **он – ~** he is blond.
блонди́н|ка (-ки; *gen pl* -ок) *ж* blonde.
блох|а́ (-и́; *nom pl* -и) *ж* flea.
блужда́|ть (-ю) *несов неперех* to wander *или* roam (around); (*перен: мы́сли*) to wander; (: *взгляд*) to rove.
блу́з|ка (-ки; *gen pl* -ок) *ж* blouse.
блю́д|о (-а) *ср* dish.
блю|сти́ (-ду́, -дёшь; *pt* -л, -ла́-ло́, *perf*

соблюсти) *несов перех* (*интересы*) to guard; (*чистоту*) to maintain.

блядь (**-и**) *ж* (*груб!: проститутка*) whore (*!*) ◆ *м/ж* (*груб!: женщина*) bitch (*!*); (: *мужчина*) bastard (*!*)

бляха (**-и**) *ж* (*на форме*) badge; (*на ремне*) buckle.

БМП *ж сокр* (= *боевáя машúна пехóты*) *armoured car for infantry.*

БМР *м сокр* (= *Банк междунарóдных расчётов*) BIS (= *Bank for International Settlements*).

боб (**-á**) *м* bean; **на ~áх остáться** (*perf*) to be left high and dry.

бобр (**-á**) *м* beaver.

Бог (**-а**; *voc* **Бóже**) *м* God; **вéрить** (*impf*) **в Бóга** to believe in God; **~ знáет** *или* **весть что** God knows what; **благословú Вас ~!** God bless you!; **не дай ~!** God forbid!; **рáди Бóга!** for God's sake!; **слáва Бóгу** (*к счáстью*) thank God.

богатéть (**-ю**; *perf* **разбогатéть**) *несов неперех* to become rich.

богáтства (**-**) *мн* resources *мн*.

богáтство (**-а**) *ср* wealth, riches *мн*; (*обстанóвки, одéжды*) richness; *см также* **богáтства**.

богáтый (**-, -а, -о**) *прил* rich; **~ урожáй** bumper harvest; **~ +instr** (*ископáемыми, событиями*) rich in; **чем ~ы, тем и рáды** what's ours is yours.

богатырь (**-я**) *м warrior hero of Russian folk epics*; (*перен*) Hercules.

богáч (**-á**) *м* rich man (*мн* men).

богáче *сравн прил от* **богáтый**.

богéма (**-ы**) *ж собир* bohemians *мн*; (*образ жúзни*) bohemian lifestyle.

богúня (**-и**) *ж* goddess.

богорóдица (**-ы**) *ж* the Virgin Mary.

богослóвие (**-я**) *ср* theology.

богослужéние (**-я**) *ср* service; **совершáть** (**совершúть** *perf*) **~** to take a service.

боготворúть (**-ю, -úшь**) *несов перех* to worship, idolize.

богоугóдный *прил*: **~ое заведéние** *charitable institution.*

богохýльный *прил* blasphemous.

бод (**-а**) *м* (*КОМП*) baud.

бодáть (**-ю**; *perf* **забодáть**) *несов перех* to butt.

бóдрость (**-и**) *ж* (*см прил*) energy, liveliness; cheerfulness.

бóдрый (**-, -á, -о**) *прил* (*человéк, похóдка*) energetic, lively; (*настроéние, мýзыка*) cheerful.

боевúк (**-á**) *м* (*солдáт*) fighter; (*фильм*) action movie.

боевóй *прил* military; (*настроéние, дух*) fighting *опред*.

боеголóвка (**-ки**; *gen pl* **-ок**) *ж* warhead.

бóек *прил см* **бóйкий**.

бóен *сущ см* **бóйня**.

боеприпáсы (**-ов**) *мн* ammunition *ед*.

боéц (**-йцá**) *м* (*солдáт*) soldier; (*учáстник бóя*) fighter.

Бóже *сущ см* **Бог** ◆ *межд*: **~ (ты мой)!** good Lord *или* God!; **~!** **какáя красотá!** God, it's beautiful!; **~ сохранú** *или* **упасú** *или* **избáви** (*разг*) God forbid.

бóжеский (**-ая, -ое, -ие**) *прил* (*РЕЛ*) divine; (*разг: цéны, услóвия*) half-decent; **приводúть** (**привестú** *perf*) **когó-н/что-н в ~ вид** to make sb/sth look decent.

божéственный (**-ен, -на, -но**) *прил* divine.

бóжий (**-ья, -ье, -ьи**) *прил* God's; **кáждый ~ день** every single day; **бóжий дар** God-given talent; **бóжья корóвка** ladybird.

бой (**-я**; *loc sg* **-ю**, *nom pl* **-ú**, *gen pl* **-ёв**) *м* battle; (*боксёров, быкóв*) fight; (*барабáнов*) beating; (*часóв*) striking.

бóйкий (**-йкая, -йкое, -йкие; -ек, -йкá, -йко**) *прил* (*распорядúтель, продавéц*) smart; (*движéния*) brisk; (*речь, отвéт*) quick; (*no short form; мéсто, базáр*) busy.

бойкóт (**-а**) *м* boycott.

бойкотúровать (**-ую**) (*не*)*сов перех* to boycott.

бóйлер (**-а**) *м* boiler.

бóйня (**-йни**; *gen pl* **-ен**) *ж* slaughterhouse, abattoir.

бойцá *итп сущ см* **боéц**.

бóйче *сравн прил от* **бóйкий**.

бок (**-а**; *part gen* **-у**, *loc sg* **-ý**, *nom pl* **-á**) *м* side; **под бóком** (*разг*) right nearby; **ó ~** side by side.

бокáл (**-а**) *м* (*wine*)glass, goblet; **поднимáть** (**поднять** *perf*) **~ за когó-н/что-н** to raise one's glass to sb/sth.

бóком *нареч* (*выйти, пройти*) sideways; **это ему́ ~ вышло** (*разг*) it was all screwed up for him.

бокс (**-а**) *м* (*СПОРТ*) boxing; (*МЕД*) cubicle.

боксёр (**-а**) *м* boxer.

болвáн (**-а**) *м* (*разг*) blockhead.

болгáрин (**-ина**; *nom pl* **-ы**, *gen pl* **-**) *м* Bulgarian.

Болгáрия (**-и**) *ж* Bulgaria.

болгáрка (**-ки**; *gen pl* **-ок**) *ж см* **болгáрин**.

болгáрский (**-ая, -ое, -ие**) *прил* Bulgarian; **~ язык** Bulgarian.

бóлее *нареч* more; **~ или мéнее** more or less; **~ тогó** what's more; **тем ~** all the more so; **~ чем** more than.

болéзненный (**-, -на, -но**) *прил* sickly; (*укóл, перевязка*) painful; (*перен: подозрúтельность*) unhealthy; **у негó ~ое самолюбие** he's ultra-sensitive.

болéзнь (**-и**) *ж* illness; (*зарáзная*) disease; **~и рóста** growing pains.

болéльщик (**-а**) *м* fan.

болéльщица (**-ы**) *ж см* **болéльщик**.

бóлен *прил см* **больнóй**.

болéть (**-éю**) *несов неперех*: **~ (+instr**) to be ill (with); (*3sg* **-úт**, *3pl* **-ят**; *подлеж: рýки итп*) to ache; **~** (*impf*) **за +acc** to be a fan of; **у меня душá ~ит за них** (*перен*) I'm very worried about them.

болеутоля́ющ|ий (-ая, -ее, -ие) *прил*: ~ее сре́дство painkiller.
боло́н|ка (-ки; *gen pl* -ок) *ж* lapdog.
боло́нь|я (-и) *ж* (*ткань*) *lightweight waterproof material.*
боло́т|о (-а) *ср* marsh, bog; (*перен*) backwater.
болт (-á) *м* bolt.
болта́|ть (-ю) *несов перех* (*разг*) to talk ♦ *неперех* (*разговаривать*) to chat; (: *много*) to chatter; (*без толку*) to drivel; (*лишнее*) to blab; ~ (*impf*) **по-англи́йски** to chatter away in English; ~ (*impf*) **нога́ми** to dangle one's legs
► **болта́ться** *несов возв* (*разг*) to dangle; ~ся (*impf*) **без де́ла** to hang around with nothing to do.
болтовн|я́ (-и́) *ж* (*разг*) waffle.
болту́н (-á) *м* chatterbox.
болту́ш|ка (-ки; *gen pl* -ек) *ж см* **болту́н**.
бол|ь (-и) *ж* pain, ache; **зубна́я** ~ toothache; **головна́я** ~ headache; ~ **в груди́/животе́** chest/abdominal pain.
больни́ц|а (-ы) *ж* hospital; **ложи́ться (лечь** *perf*) **в** ~**у** to go into hospital; **выпи́сываться (вы́писаться** *perf*) **из** ~**ы** to be discharged from hospital.
больни́чный *прил* hospital *опред*; **больни́чный лист** medical certificate.
бо́льно *нареч* (*ударúться, упáсть*) badly, painfully; (*обидеть*) deeply; ~! that hurts!; **мне** ~ I am in pain; **де́лать (сде́лать** *perf*) ~ **кому́-н** to hurt sb; **мне** ~ **поду́мать об э́том** it hurts me to think about it.
больн|о́й *прил* (*рука итп*) sore; (*воображе́ние*) unhealthy; (-ен, -ьна́, -ьно́; *нездоро́в*) ill, sick ♦ (-**ьно́го**; *decl like adj*) *м* (*тот, кто боле́ет*) sick person; (*пацие́нт*) patient; **у неё** ~ **вид** she doesn't look very well; **де́ти** ~**ьны́** the children are ill *или* sick; **больно́е се́рдце** a bad heart; **больно́й вопро́с** a sore point.
бо́льше *сравн прил от* **большо́й** ♦ *сравн нареч от* **мно́го** ♦ *нареч*: ~ +*gen* (*часа, килограмма итп*) more than; ~ **не бу́ду** (*разг*) I won't do it again; ~ **так не де́лай** don't do that again; ~ **того́** what's more; ~ **всего́** most of all; **ни** ~ **ни ме́ньше (чем** *или* **как)** no more, no less (than); **она́ здесь** ~ **не живёт** she doesn't live here any more.
большеви́к (-á) *м* Bolshevik.
большинств|о́ (-á) *ср* majority; **в** ~**é (слу́чаев)** in most cases; **подавля́ющее** ~ an overwhelming majority.
больш|о́й *прил* (*дом, река, де́рево*) big, large; (*ра́дость*) great; (*де́ти*) grown-up; **бо́льшей ча́стью, по бо́льшей ча́сти** for the most part; **я не** ~ **люби́тель бале́та** I'm not a great ballet fan; **я не** ~ **знато́к э́того де́ла** I'm no expert in this matter; **больша́я бу́ква** capital letter; **большо́й па́лец** (*руки́*) thumb; (*ноги́*) big toe.

боля́ч|ка (-ки; *gen pl* -ек) *ж* sore.
бо́мб|а (-ы) *ж* bomb.
бомб|и́ть (-лю́, -и́шь) *несов перех* to bomb.
бомбоубе́жище (-а) *ср* bomb shelter.
бо́н|а (-ы) *ж* (*обычно мн: комм*) bond; (*временные деньги*) voucher.
бордо́вый *прил* dark red.
бордю́р (-а) *м* border; (*тротуа́ра*) kerb (*вRIT*), curb (*US*).
бор|е́ц (-ца́) *м* (*за свобо́ду итп*) fighter; (*СПОРТ*) wrestler.
бормо|та́ть (-чу́, -чешь) *несов перех* to mutter.
бо́рн|ый *прил*: ~**ая кислота́** boric acid.
борови́к (-á) *м* сер.
бор|ода́ (*acc sg* -оду, *gen sg* -оды́, *nom pl* -оды, *gen pl* -о́д, *dat pl* -ода́м) *ж* beard; **отпуска́ть (отпусти́ть** *perf*) **бо́роду** to grow a beard; **с** ~**одо́й** (*перен: разг*) ancient; **анекдо́т с** ~**одо́й** an old chestnut.
борода́в|ка (-ки; *gen pl* -ок) *ж* (*на па́льцах итп*) wart.
борозд|и́ть (-жу́, -ди́шь; *perf* **изборозди́ть**) *несов перех* to furrow; (*кора́бль*) to leave a wake.
бор|о́ться (-ю́сь, -ешься) *несов возв* (*СПОРТ*) to wrestle; ~ (*impf*) (**с** +*instr*) to fight (with *или* against); ~ (*impf*) **с** +*instr или* **про́тив** +*gen* (*с конкуре́нтами*) to compete with *или* against; (*с предрассу́дками, с нарко́тиками*) to fight (against); ~ (*impf*) **за** +*acc* (*за мир*) to fight for.
борт (-а; *acc sg* **за́ борт** *или* **за бо́рт**, *instr sg* **за бо́ртом** *или* **за борто́м**, *loc sg* -**у́**, *nom pl* -**á**) *м* side; **на** ~**у́** *или* ~ on board, aboard; **челове́к за** ~**ом!** man overboard!; **остава́ться (оста́ться** *perf*) **за** ~**ом** (*перен*) to be left behind.
бортпроводни́к (-á) *м* steward (*on plane*).
бортпроводни́ц|а (-ы) *ж* air hostess, stewardess (*on plane*).
борца́ *итп сущ см* **боре́ц**.
борщ (-á) *м* borsch (*beetroot-based soup*).
борьб|á (-ы́) *ж* fight; (*СПОРТ*) wrestling.
босико́м *нареч* barefoot.
бос|о́й (-, -á, -о) *прил* barefoot.
босоно́ж|ка (-и) *ж* (*обычно мн*) sandal; (: *закры́тым но́сом*) slingback.
босс (-а) *м* boss.
Босфо́р (-а) *м* Bosphorus.
бося́к (-á) *м* tramp.
бося́ч|ка (-ки; *gen pl* -ек) *ж см* **бося́к**.
бота́ник|а (-и) *ж* botany.
боти́н|ок (-ка) *м* (*обычно мн*) ankle boot.
бо́цман (-а) *м* boatswain, bosun.
бо́ч|ка (-ки; *gen pl* -ек) *ж* (*сосуд*) barrel.
бо|я́ться (-ю́сь, -и́шься) *несов возв*: ~ (+*gen*) to be afraid (of); ~ (*impf*) +*infin* to be afraid of doing *или* to do; **я** ~**ю́сь ходи́ть** (*impf*) **но́чью** I'm afraid of being out *или* to be out at night; ~**ю́сь сказа́ть** I wouldn't like to say.

бра́во *межд* bravo.
брази́л|ец (**-ьца**) *м* Brazilian.
Брази́ли|я (**-и**) *ж* Brazil.
брази́льск|ий (**-ая, -ое, -ие**) *прил* Brazilian.
брази́льца *итп сущ см* **брази́лец**.
бразилья́н|ка (**-ки**; *gen pl* **-ок**) *ж см* **брази́лец**.
бразды́ *мн:* ~ **правле́ния** the reins of power *или* government.
брак (**-а**) *м* (*супружество*) marriage; (*продукция*) rejects *мн*; (*дефект*) flaw; **вступа́ть** (**вступи́ть** *perf*) **в** ~ to get married; **расторга́ть** (**расто́ргнуть** *perf*) ~ to dissolve a marriage.
брако́ванн|ый *прил* reject *опред*.
бракова́ть (**-у́ю**; *perf* **забракова́ть**) *несов перех* to reject.
браконье́р (**-а**) *м* poacher.
браконье́рств|о (**-а**) *ср* poaching.
бракосочета́ни|е (**-я**) *ср* marriage ceremony.
браслет (**-а**) *м* bracelet; (*кольцо из металла, кости итп*) bangle.
брасс (**-а**) *м* breaststroke.
брат (**-а**; *nom pl* **-ья**, *gen pl* **-ьев**) *м* brother; **сво́дный** ~ stepbrother; **двою́родный** ~ cousin.
Братисла́в|а (**-ы**) *ж* Bratislava.
бра́ти|я (**-и**) *ср* brotherhood.
бра́тск|ий (**-ая, -ое, -ие**) *прил* brotherly, fraternal; **бра́тская моги́ла** communal grave.
бра́тств|о (**-а**) *ср* (*содружество*) brotherhood.
бра|ть (**беру́, берёшь**; *pt* **-л, -ла́, -ло́**, *perf* **взять**) *несов перех* to take; (*билет*) to get; (*ня́ню*) to take on; (*крепость, город*) to take, seize; (*высоту*) to conquer; (*барьер*) to clear; ~ (*impf*) **нало́г у кого́-н/за что-н** to tax sb/sth; ~ (**взять** *perf*) **что-н в расчёт** *или* **во внима́ние** to take sth into account *или* consideration
▸ **бра́ться** (*perf* **взя́ться**) *несов возв*: **бра́ться за** +*acc* (*дотронуться*) to touch; (*хватать рукой*) to get hold of; (*за учёбу, за работу*) to get down to; (*за перо*) to take up; (*за книгу*) to begin; (*решение проблемы*) to take on, undertake; **отку́да у тебя́ вре́мя берётся?** where do you find the time?; **отку́да у него́ де́ньги беру́тся?** where does he get the money?; **бра́ться** (**взя́ться** *perf*) **за ум** to come to one's senses.
бра́тья *итп сущ см* **брат**.
бра́чн|ый *прил* (*контракт*) marriage *опред*; (*союз*) conjugal.
бревн|о́ (**-а́**; *nom pl* **брёвна**, *gen pl* **брёвен**) *ср* log; (*СПОРТ*) the beam; (*перен*) oaf.
бред (**-а**; *loc pl* **-у́**) *м* delirium; (*перен*) nonsense; ~ **сумасше́дшего** the ravings of a madman.
бре́дить (**-жу, -дишь**) *несов неперех* to be delirious; ~ (*impf*) **кем-н/чем-н** to be mad about sb/sth.
бредо́в|ый *прил* (*разг*) crazy.
бреду́ *итп несов см* **брести́**.
бре́жу *несов см* **бре́дить**.
бре́зга|ть (**-ю**) *несов* = **бре́зговать**.

брезгли́в|ый (**-, -а, -о**) *прил* (*человек*) fastidious; (*взгляд*) disgusted.
бре́зг|овать (**-ую**; *perf* **побре́зговать**) *несов неперех* (+*instr*) to be fastidious about.
брезе́нт (**-а**; *part gen* **-у**) *м* tarpaulin.
брёл *итп несов см* **брести́**.
бре́м|я (**-ени**; *как* **вре́мя**; *см* **Table 4**) *ср* burden.
бр|ести́ (**-еду́, -едёшь**; *pt* **-ёл, -ела́, -ело́**) *несов неперех* (*человек*) to trudge; (*лошадь*) to plod.
брета́нск|ий (**-ая, -ое, -ие**) *прил* Breton.
Брета́н|ь (**-и**) *ж* Brittany.
брето́нск|ий (**-ая, -ое, -ие**) *прил* = **брета́нский**.
Брето́н|ь (**-и**) *ж* = **Брета́нь**.
бреш|ь (**-и**) *ж* (*пролом*) breach.
бре́ю(сь) *итп несов см* **брить(ся)**.
брига́д|а (**-ы**) *ж* (*ВОЕН*) brigade; (*в поезде*) crew; (*на производстве*) (work) team.
бригади́р (**-а**) *м* (*в поезде*) ≈ chief guard (*BRIT*), ≈ senior conductor (*US*); (*на производстве*) team leader.
бриз (**-а**) *м* sea breeze.
бриллиа́нт (**-а**) *м* (*cut*) diamond.
бриллиа́нтовый *прил* diamond *опред*.
брита́н|ец (**-ца**) *м* Briton; ~**цы** the British.
Брита́ни|я (**-и**) *ж* Britain.
брита́н|ка (**-ки**; *gen pl* **-ок**) *ж см* **брита́нец**.
брита́нск|ий (**-ая, -ое, -ие**) *прил* British.
брита́нца *итп сущ см* **брита́нец**.
бри́тв|а (**-ы**) *ж* razor; **безопа́сная** ~ safety razor.
бр|ить (**-е́ю, -е́ешь**; *perf* **побри́ть**) *несов перех* (*человека*) to shave; (*бороду*) to shave off
▸ **бри́ться** (*perf* **побри́ться**) *несов возв* to shave.
бри́финг (**-а**) *м* briefing.
бров|ь (**-и**; *gen pl* **-е́й**) *ж* eyebrow; **попа́сть** (*perf*) **не в** ~, **а в глаз** to hit the nail on the head; **он и бро́вью не повёл** he didn't bat an eyelid.
бро|ди́ть (**-жу́, -дишь**) *несов неперех* to wander; (*perf* **выбродить**; *вино, пиво*) to ferment.
бродя́г|а (**-и**) *м/ж* tramp; (*любящий странствовать*) drifter.
броже́ни|е (**-я**) *ср* fermentation; (*перен*) ferment.
брожу́ *несов см* **броди́ть**.
бро́йлер (**-а**) *м* broiler.
бро́кер (**-а**) *м* broker; **биржево́й** ~ stockbroker.
бро́керск|ий (**-ая, -ое, -ие**) *прил* broker's.
бром (**-а**) *м* bromine.
бронемаши́н|а (**-ы**) *ж* armoured (*BRIT*) *или* armored (*US*) car.
бронетранспортёр (**-а**) *м* armoured (*BRIT*) *или* armored (*US*) personnel carrier.
бро́нз|а (**-ы**) *ж* bronze.
бро́нзовый *прил* bronze; **бро́нзовый век** the Bronze Age; **бро́нзовый призёр** bronze medallist (*BRIT*) *или* medalist (*US*).
брони́ровани|е (**-я**) *ср* reservation.
брони́р|овать (**-ую**; *perf* **заброни́ровать**) (*не*)*сов перех* to reserve.
бронх (**-а**) *м* (*обычно мн*) bronchial tube.
бронхи́т (**-а**) *м* bronchitis.
брон|ь (**-и**) *ж* (*разг*) reservation.

бро́н|я (-и) ж reservation.
брон|я́ (-и́) ж armour (BRIT) или armor (US) plating.
броса́|ть (-ю) несов от **бро́сить**
▶ **броса́ться** несов от **бро́ситься** ♦ возв: ~**ся** снежка́ми/камня́ми to throw snowballs/stones at each other; ~**ся** (impf) деньга́ми to throw one's money around; ~**ся** (impf) друзья́ми to abandon one's friends.
бро́|сить (-шу, -сишь; impf **броса́ть**) сов перех (камень, мяч итп) to throw; (семью, друга) to abandon; (войска, отряд) to dispatch; (спорт) to give up; **броса́ть** (~ perf) замеча́ние to pass comment; меня́ ~**сило в жар** I broke out in a (cold) sweat; **броса́ть** (~ perf) +infin to give up doing; ~**сьте!** stop it!
▶ **бро́ситься** (impf **броса́ться**) сов возв: ~**ся на** +acc (на врага, на обидчика) to throw o.s. at; **броса́ться** (~**ся** perf) в дра́ку/ата́ку to rush into the fray/to the attack; **броса́ться** (~**ся** perf) кому́-н на по́мощь to rush to sb's aid; ~**ся** (perf) по ле́стнице вниз to rush downstairs; ~**ся** (perf) кому́-н в объя́тия to fall into sb's arms; **кра́ска** ~**силась ему́ в лицо́** the colour rushed to his face.
бро́совый прил (разг) trashy; **бро́совая цена́** giveaway price; **бро́совый э́кспорт** (КОММ) dumping.
бро́ш|ка (-ки; gen pl -ек) ж brooch.
бро́шу(сь) сов см **бро́сить(ся)**.
брошь (-и) ж см **бро́шка**.
брошю́р|а (-ы) ж (небольшая книжка) pamphlet; (рекламный буклет) brochure.
брус (-а; nom pl -ья, gen pl -ьев) м beam; см также **бру́сья**.
бруска́ итп сущ см **брусо́к**.
брусни́к|а (-и) ж cowberry.
брусо́к (-ка́) м (камень для точки) whetstone; (мыла) bar.
бру́сь|я (-ев) мн parallel bars мн.
бру́тто прил неизм gross опред.
бры́з|гать (-жу, -жешь) несов неперех (фонтан, грязь) to splash; (~гаю) опрыскивать): ~ **на** +acc to splash.
бры́зг|и (-) мн splashes мн; (мелкие) spray ед; (стекла, камня) fragments мн, splinters мн.
бры́зжу итп несов см **бры́згать**.
бры́нз|а (-ы) ж brynza (sheep's milk cheese).
брысь межд shoo.
брю́кв|а (-ы) ж swede.
брю́к|и (-) мн trousers мн, pants мн (US).
брюне́т (-а) м: он ~ he has dark hair.
брюне́т|ка (-ки; gen pl -ок) ж brunette.
Блрюссе́л|ь (-и) ж Brussels.
брю́х|о (-а) ср (также разг) belly; (разг: толстяк) pot.
брюшно́й прил abdominal; **брюшно́й тиф**

typhoid fever.
БСЭ ж сокр = Больша́я Сове́тская Энциклопе́дия.
бубён сущ см **бу́бны**.
бу́блик (-а) м ≈ bagel.
бу́бн|ы (-ён; dat pl -нам) мн (КАРТЫ) diamonds мн.
буго́р (-ра́) м mound; (на коже) lump.
Будапе́шт (-а) м Budapest.
будди́зм (-а) м Buddhism.
будди́ст (-а) м Buddhist.
будди́ст|ка (-ки; gen pl -ок) ж см **будди́ст**.
бу́дем несов см **быть**.
бу́дет несов см **быть** ♦ част that's enough; **попла́кали и** ~ that's enough crying; ~ **тебе́!** that's enough from you!
бу́дешь итп несов см **быть**.
буди́льник (-а) м alarm clock; **заводи́ть** (завести́ perf) ~ **на** +acc to set the alarm (clock) for.
буди́ть (-жу́, -дишь; perf **разбуди́ть**) несов перех to wake (up), awaken; (perf **пробуди́ть**; перен) to awaken.
бу́д|ка (-ки; gen pl -ок) ж (сторожа) hut; (для собаки) kennel; **часова́я** ~ sentry box; **телефо́нная** ~ telephone booth или box.
бу́док сущ см **бу́дка**.
будора́ж|ить (-ю, -ишь) несов от **взбудора́жить**.
бу́дто союз (якобы) apparently; (словно): **(как)** ~ **(бы)** as if; **уверя́ет,** ~ **сам её ви́дел** he claims to have seen her himself; **он** ~ **бы до́лжен е́хать в Москву́** apparently he has to go to Moscow; **он улыба́лся,** ~ **(бы) был рад ви́деть нас** he smiled as if he were glad to see us.
бу́ду итп несов см **быть**.
бу́дущ|ее (-его; decl like adj) ср the future; **в** ~**ем** in the future; **на** ~ for the future; **не де́лайте э́того в** ~**ем** don't do it in future.
бу́дущ|ий (-ая, -ее, -ие) прил (следующий) next; (предстоящий) future; **бу́дущее вре́мя** future tense.
бу́дь(те) несов см **быть** ♦ союз: **будь то** be it.
бу́ен прил см **бу́йный**.
буженин|а (-ы) ж cooked and seasoned pork, served cold.
бужу́ несов см **буди́ть**.
бу́|й (-я; nom pl -и́) м buoy.
бу́йвол (-а) м buffalo.
бу́йволиц|а (-ы) ж см **бу́йвол**.
бу́йный (-ен, -йна́, -йно) прил wild; (обильный: растительность) luxuriant, lush.
бук (-а) м beech.
бу́кв|а (-ы) ж letter; (перен): ~ +gen (закона, документа) the letter of; **прописна́я/строчна́я**

~ capital/small letter; ~ в бvкву word for word.

бvква́льно *нареч* literally.

бvква́льный *прил* literal.

бvква́рь (-я́) *м* first reading book.

буке́т (-а) *м* (*цветов, вина*) bouquet; (*перен: разг: болезней, недостатков*) range.

букини́ст (-а) *м* second-hand bookseller.

букинисти́ческий (-ая, -ое, -ие) *прил*: ~ **магази́н** second-hand bookshop.

букле́т (-а) *м* booklet.

букси́р (-а) *м* tug; (*трос*) towrope; **тяну́ть** (*impf*) *или* **вести́** (*impf*) **на** ~**е** to give sb a tow.

була́в|ка (-ки; *gen pl* -ок) *ж* pin; **англи́йская** ~ safety pin.

була́ный (-ого; *decl like adj*) *м* dun.

була́т (-а) *м* Damascus *или* damask steel.

бvл|ка (-ки; *gen pl* -ок) *ж* roll; (*белый хлеб*) loaf.

бvлоч|ка (-ки; *gen pl* -ек) *ж см* **бvлка**.

бvлочн|ая (-ой; *decl like adj*) *ж* baker, baker's (shop).

булы́жник (-а) *м* cobblestone.

булы́жн|ый *прил*: ~**ая мостова́я** cobbled street.

бульва́р (-а) *м* boulevard.

бульва́рный *прил* boulevard *опред*; ~ **рома́н** trashy novel; **бульва́рная пре́сса** gutter press.

бульдо́г (-а) *м* bulldog.

бульдо́зер (-а) *м* bulldozer.

бульо́н (-а; *part gen* -у) *м* stock.

бум (-а) *м* (*оживление*) boom.

бума́г|а (-и) *ж* paper; ~ **за по́дписью кого́-н** a document signed by sb; **це́нные** ~**и** securities; **ге́рбовая** ~ headed paper; *см также* **бума́ги**.

бума́г|и (-) *мн* papers *мн*.

бума́ж|ка (-ки; *gen pl* -ек) *ж* piece of paper.

бума́жник (-а) *м* wallet, pocketbook (*US*).

бума́жный *прил* paper; (*бюрократический*) bureaucratic; **бума́жная волоки́та** red tape.

бумера́нг (-а) *м* boomerang.

бvнгало *ср нескл* bungalow.

бvнкер (-а) *м* bunker.

бунт (-а) *м* (*мятеж*) riot; (: *на корабле*) mutiny.

бунт|ова́ть (-у́ю) *несов неперех* (*см сущ*) to riot; to mutiny.

бура́в|ить (-лю, -ишь; *perf* **пробура́вить**) *несов перех* to drill.

бура́к (-а́) *м* beetroot.

бура́н (-а) *м* blizzard, snowstorm.

бvргер (-а) *м* burger.

бурд|а́ (-ы́) *ж* (*разг*): **э́тот чай про́сто** ~ the tea is just like dishwater.

бvрен *прил см* **бvрный**.

буре́ни|е (-я) *ср* boring, drilling.

буржуази́|я (-и) *ж* bourgeoisie; **ме́лкая** ~ petty bourgeoisie.

буржуа́зный *прил* bourgeois.

буржу́|й (-я) *м* (*разг*) bourgeois.

бур|и́ть (-ю́, -и́шь; *perf* **пробури́ть**) *несов перех* to bore, drill.

бу́ркн|уть (-у, -ешь) *сов перех* (*разг*) to grunt.

бурл|и́ть (-ю́, -и́шь) *несов неперех* (*вода*) to boil; (*ручей*) to bubble; (*толпа*) to seethe (*with*

---

excitement).

бvр|ный (-ен, -на́, -но) *прил* (*погода, океан*) stormy, rough; (*река*) turbulent; (*чувство, порыв*) wild; (*спор*) heated; (*рост*) rapid.

буровик (-а́) *м* driller.

бурово́й *прил* boring, drilling; **бурова́я вы́шка** derrick; **бурова́я сква́жина** bore(hole).

бурч|а́ть (-у́, -и́шь; *perf* **пробурча́ть**) *несов неперех* (*разг: ворчать*) to mutter; ~ (**пробурча́ть** *perf*) **себе́ под нос** to mutter *или* grumble to o.s.

бvр|ый (-, -а́, -о) *прил* brown; **бvрый у́голь** (*ГЕО*) brown coal, lignite.

бvр|я (-и) *ж* storm; (*перен*) burst; ~ **в стака́не воды́** storm in a teacup.

бурят (-а; *gen pl* -) *м* Buryat.

Буря́ти|я (-и) *ж* Buryatia.

буря́т|ка (-ки; *gen pl* -ок) *ж см* **буря́т**.

бvс|ы (-) *мн* beads *мн*.

бутафо́ри|я (-и) *ж* (*ТЕАТР*) props *мн* (= *properties;*) (*перен*) sham.

бутербро́д (-а) *м* sandwich.

бутон (-а) *м* bud.

бvтс|а (-ы) *ж* (*обычно мн*) football boot.

буты́л|ка (-ки; *gen pl* -ок) *ж* bottle.

буты́лочный *прил* bottle *опред*; (*цвет*) bottle-green.

бvфер (-а; *nom pl* -а́) *м* (*также перен, КОМП*) buffer.

буфериза́ци|я (-и) *ж* (*КОМП*) buffering.

бvферный *прил* (*также перен*) buffer *опред*.

буфе́т (-а) *м* (*для продажи закусок*) snack bar; (*шкаф*) sideboard.

буфе́тчик (-а) *м* assistant (*in snack bar*).

буфе́тчиц|а (-ы) *ж см* **буфе́тчик**.

бух *межд*: ~**!** bang!; (*разг: упал*) whoops!

буха́н|ка (-ки; *gen pl* -ок) *ж* loaf.

Бухаре́ст (-а) *м* Bucharest.

бvха|ть (-ю) *несов от* **бvхнуть**.

бухга́лтер (-а) *м* accountant, book-keeper; ~**-ревизо́р** auditor.

бухгалте́ри|я (-и) *ж* accountancy, book-keeping; (*отдел*) accounts office.

бухга́лтерск|ий (-ая, -ое, -ие) *прил* book-keeping *опред*, accountancy *опред*; **бухга́лтерские кни́ги** books; **бухга́лтерский учёт** book-keeping, accountancy.

бvхн|уть (-у, -ешь; *impf* **бvхать**) *сов неперех* (*дверь*) to bang; (*пушка*) to thunder ♦ *несов неперех* to swell.

бvхт|а (-ы) *ж* bay.

бvхты-бара́хты *нареч*: **с** ~ just like that; (*внезапно*) out of the blue.

буш|ева́ть (-у́ю) *несов неперех* (*пожар, ураган*) to rage.

Буэ́нос-А́йрес (-а) *м* Buenos Aires.

БЦЖ *ж сокр* BCG (= *Bacillus Calmette-Guérin*).

┌─────────────┐
│ **KEYWORD** │
└─────────────┘

бы *част* **1** (*выражает предположительную возможность*): **купи́л бы, е́сли бы бы́ли де́ньги** I would buy it if I had the money; **я бы**

давно уже купил эту книгу, если бы у меня были деньги I would have bought this book long ago if I had had the money
2 (*выражает пожелание*): я бы хотел поговорить с тобой I would like to speak to you; я бы не хотел об этом говорить I would rather not talk about it; чаю бы I could do with some tea
3 (*выражает совет*): ты бы написал ей you should write to her
4 (*выражает опасение*): не захватил бы нас дождь I hope we don't get caught in the rain; отдохнуть/погулять бы it would be nice to have a rest/walk; не опоздать бы better not be late.

бывало *част* expresses a repeated action in the past; ~ сидим и разговариваем we used to sit and talk.
быва|ть (-ю) *несов неперех* (*приходить, посещать*) to be; (*случаться, происходить*) to happen, take place; он ~ет у нас часто he often comes to see us; ~ют странные случаи strange things happen; как не ~ло (*разг*) as if it had never been; как ни в чём не ~ло (*разг*) as if nothing had happened; с кем не ~ет it happens to the best of us.
бы́вш|ий (-ая, -ее, -ие) *прил* former; (*жена, муж*) ex-, former.
бык (-а) *м* bull; (*рабочий*) ox; **брать (взять** *perf*) ~а за рога to take the bull by the horns.
был *итп несов см* быть.
былин|а (-ы) *ж* bylina (*Russian folk epic*).
было *част* expresses non-fulfilment of an intended action; он начал ~ говорить, но остановился he was about to say something, but stopped; мы начали ~ уходить, но пошёл дождь we were about to leave, but it began to rain.
быль (-и) *ж* (*рассказ*) true story.
быстро *нареч* quickly.
быстрот|а (-ы) *ж* speed; (*ума, рук*) quickness.
быстроход|ный (-ен, -на, -но) *прил* fast.
быстр|ый (-, -а, -о) *прил* fast; (*лошадь*) swift, fast; (*проворный, беглый*) quick.
быт (-а; *loc sg* -у) *м* life; (*повседневная жизнь*) everyday life; это вошло в ~ this has become a part of our everyday life; служба быта consumer services *мн*.

бытов|ой *прил* everyday *опред*; **бытовая живопись** genre painting; **бытовое обслуживание населения** consumer services *мн*; **бытовое явление** everyday occurrence.

┌─ **KEYWORD** ─────────────────────────────┐

быть (*см* **Table 21**) *несов* **1** (*omitted in present tense*) to be; **книга на столе** the book is on the table; **завтра я буду в школе** I will be at school tomorrow; **дом был на краю города** the house stood on the edge of the town; **на ней красивое платье** she is wearing a beautiful dress; **вчера был дождь** it rained yesterday
2 (*часть составного сказ*) to be; **я хочу быть учителем** I want to be a teacher; **я был рад видеть тебя** I was happy to see you; **так и быть!** so be it!; **как быть?** what is to be done?; **этого не может быть** that's impossible; **кто/какой бы то ни был** whoever/whatever it might be; **будьте добры!** excuse me, please!; **будьте добры – позовите его!** would you be so good *или* kind as to call him?; **будьте здоровы!** take care!
3 (*образует будущее время*: +*impf vb*): **вечером я буду писать письма** I'll be writing letters this evening; **я буду любить тебя всегда** I'll love you forever.

└──┘

бью(сь) *итп несов см* бить(ся).
Бэйсик (-а) *м* (*комп*) BASIC.
бюджет (-а) *м* budget; **доходный** ~ income, revenue; **расходный** ~ expenditure.
бюджетный *прил* budgetary.
бюллетен|ь (-я) *м* bulletin; (*листок: для голосования*) ballot paper; (*нетрудоспособности*) medical certificate; **быть** (*impf*) **на** ~**e** to be off sick (*from work*).
бюро *ср нескл* office, agency; **справочное** ~ inquiry office; **бюро (добрых) услуг** domestic help agency; **бюро находок** lost property office; **бюро по трудоустройству** employment agency.
бюрократ (-а) *м* bureaucrat.
бюрократизм (-а) *м* bureaucracy.
бюрократическ|ий (-ая, -ое, -ие) *прил* bureaucratic.
бюрократи|я (-и) *ж* bureaucracy.
бюст (-а) *м* bust.
бюстгальтер (-а) *м* bra (= *brassiere*).
бязь (-и) *ж* calico.

~ В, в ~

В, в *сущ нескл (буква)* the 3rd letter of the Russian alphabet.
В *сокр* (= *вольт*) v. (= *volt*).

KEYWORD

в *предл* (+*acc*) **1** (*о месте направления*) in(to); **я положи́л кни́гу в портфе́ль** I put the book in(to) my briefcase; **я сел в маши́ну** I got in(to) the car

2 (*уехать, пойти*) to; **он уе́хал в Москву́** he went to Moscow; **идти́ (пойти́** *perf*) **в учителя́** to become a teacher; **выбира́ть (вы́брать** *perf*) **кого́-н в комите́т** to elect sb to a committee

3 (*об изменении состояния*): **погружа́ться в рабо́ту** to be absorbed in one's work; **погружа́ться** (*impf*) **в разду́мья** to be deep in thought

4 (*об объекте физического действия*): **он постуча́л в дверь** he knocked on the door; **он посмотре́л мне в глаза́/в лицо́** he looked me in the eyes/face; **мать поцелова́ла меня́ в щёку** mother kissed me on the cheek

5 (*обозначает форму, вид*): **брю́ки в кле́тку** checked trousers; **лека́рство в табле́тках** medicine in tablet form; **разрыва́ть (разорва́ть** *perf*) **что-н в кло́чья** to tear sth to shreds; **растира́ть (растере́ть** *perf*) **что-н в порошо́к** to grind sth to a powder

6 (*о размере, количестве*): **ве́сом в 3 то́нны** 3 tons *или* tonnes in weight; (: +*prp*): **дра́ма в трёх частя́х** a drama in three acts; **отря́д в десяти́ челове́к** a detachment of ten men; **в пяти́ ме́трах от доро́ги** five metres (*BRIT*) *или* meters (*US*) from the road

7 (*о соотношении величин*): **в два ра́за бо́льше/длинне́е/то́лще** twice as big/long/thick; **во мно́го раз лу́чше/умне́е** much better/cleverer; **во мно́го раз поле́знее/краси́вее** much more useful/beautiful

8 (*о времени совершения чего-н*): **он пришёл в понеде́льник** he came on Monday; **я ви́дел его́ в про́шлом году́** I saw him last year; **я встре́тил его́ в два часа́** I met him at two o'clock; **э́то случи́лось в ма́рте/в двадца́том ве́ке** it happened in March/in the twentieth century

9 (+*prp*; *о месте*) in; **ко́шка сиди́т в корзи́не** the cat is sitting in the basket; **я живу́ в дере́вне** I live in the country; **сын у́чится в шко́ле/ университе́те** my son is at school/university; **в отдале́нии/сосе́дстве** in the distance/the neighbourhood

10 (*о чём-н облегающем, покрывающем*): **ру́ки в кра́ске/са́же** hands covered in paint/soot; **това́р в упако́вке** packaged goods; **не́бо в ту́чах** the sky is overcast

11 (*об одежде*) in; **мужчи́на в очка́х/в ша́пке** a man in *или* wearing glasses/a hat

12 (*о состоянии*): **быть в у́жасе/негодова́нии** to be terrified/indignant.

в. *сокр* (= *век*) с (= *century*); (= *восто́к*) E (= *East*); (= *восто́чный*) E (= *East*).

ва-ба́нк *нареч (также перен)*: **идти́ ~** to stake everything.

ваго́н (**-а**) *м* (*пассажирский*) carriage (*BRIT*), coach (*BRIT*), car (*US*); (*товарный*) wagon (*BRIT*), truck (*BRIT*); **спа́льный ~** couchette car; **мя́гкий ~** ≈ sleeping car; **ваго́н-рестора́н** dining (*BRIT*) *или* club (*US*) car.

вагоне́т|ка (**-ки**; *gen pl* **-ок**) *ж* trolley (*RAIL*).

ваго́нный *прил* carriage *опред* (*BRIT*), car *опред* (*US*); **ваго́нный парк** train depot.

вагоноремо́нтный *прил* (*завод*) coach (*BRIT*) *или* car (*US*) reparation *опред*.

вагонострои́тельный *прил* (*завод*) coach (*BRIT*) *или* car (*US*) building *опред*.

ва́жен *прил см* **ва́жный**.

ва́жнича|ть (**-ю**) *несов неперех* to act in a self-important manner.

ва́жност|ь (**-и**) *ж* importance; (*надменность*) self-importance; **(не) велика́ ~** what does it matter.

ва́ж|ный (**-ен, -на́, -но**) *прил* important; (*гордый*) pompous.

ВАЗ (**-а**) *м сокр* = **В**о́лжский автомоби́льный заво́д; (*автомобиль*) *vehicle manufactured at the Volga car factory*.

ва́з|а (**-ы**) *ж* vase.

вазели́н (**-а**; *part gen* **-у**) *м* Vaseline®.

вака́нси|я (**-и**) *ж* vacancy; **откры́лась ~ в бухгалте́рии** a vacancy has now arisen in accounts.

вака́нт|ный (**-ен, -на, -но**) *прил* vacant; **~ная до́лжность** vacancy.

ва́кс|а (**-ы**) *ж* black shoe polish.

ва́куум (**-а**) *м (также перен)* vacuum.

вакци́н|а (**-ы**) *ж* vaccine.

вакцини́р|овать (-ую) *(не)сов перех* to vaccinate.

вал (-а; *loc sg* -ý, *nom pl* -ы́) *м* (*насыпь*) bank; (: *крепости*) rampart; (*стержень*) shaft; (*волна*) breaker; (*экон*) gross product.

вале́жник (-а) *м собир* dead wood.

ва́лен|ок (-ка) *м* (*обычно мн*) felt boot.

валериа́н|а (-ы) *ж* valerian.

валериа́нк|а (-и) *ж* valerian drops *мн*.

валериа́нов|ый *прил*: ~ые ка́пли valerian drops.

валерья́н|а (-ы) *ж* = валериа́на.

вале́т (-а) *м* (*КАРТЫ*) jack.

валидо́л (-а) *м type of mild sedative*.

ва́лик (-а) *м* (*в механизме*) cylinder; (*для краски*) roller; (*подушка*) bolster.

вал|и́ть (-ю́, -ишь; *perf* свали́ть *или* повали́ть) *несов перех* (*заставить падать*) to knock over; (*рубить*) to fell; (*perf* свали́ть; *разг: бросать*) to dump ♦ *неперех* (*no perf; народ*) to flock; (*дым, пар*) to pour out; ~ (свали́ть *perf*) вину́ на +*acc* (*разг*) to point the finger at; ва́лит снег it's snowing heavily; толпа́ ~и́ла на конце́рт the crowd flocked to the concert

► **вали́ться** (*perf* свали́ться *или* повали́ться) *несов возв* (*падать*) to fall; (*разг: опускаться*) to flake out; все бе́ды ва́лятся на него́ he attracts misfortune; у него́ всё ва́лится из рук everything he does fails; ~ся (*impf*) с ног (*разг*) to be dead on one's feet.

валово́й *прил* (*доход*) gross *опред*; **валово́й вну́тренний проду́кт** gross domestic product; **валово́й национа́льный проду́кт** gross national product; **валова́я при́быль** gross profit; ~ **объём прода́жи** gross sales *мн*.

ва́лом *нареч*: ~ вали́ть (*разг: народ*) to flock.

валто́рн|а (-ы) *ж* French horn.

валу́н (-а́) *м* boulder.

вальс (-а) *м* waltz.

вальц|ева́ть (-ую) *несов перех* to roll.

вальц|ы́ (-о́в) *мн* (*станок*) rolling press *ед*.

валю́т|а (-ы) *ж* currency ♦ *собир* foreign currency; **твёрдая** ~ hard currency.

валю́тно-фина́нсовый *прил* monetary.

валю́тный *прил* currency *опред*; ~ **контро́ль** exchange control; **валю́тный курс** rate of exchange; **валю́тный фонд** currency reserves *мн*.

валю́тчик (-а) *м* (*разг*) *person illegally dealing in foreign currency*.

валю́тчиц|а (-ы) *ж см* валю́тчик.

валя́|ть (-ю) *несов перех* (*катать*) to roll; (*perf* сваля́ть; *скатывать*) to shape

► **валя́ться** *несов возв* (*кататься*) to roll about; (*разг: человек, бумаги итп*) to lie about; (: *с гриппом итп*) to be laid up; **де́ньги на земле́** *или* **на доро́ге не** ~ются (*разг*) money doesn't grow on trees.

вам *итп мест см* **вы**.

вампи́р (-а) *м* vampire.

ВАН *м сокр* (= Ве́стник Акаде́мии нау́к Росси́и) Bulletin of the Russian Academy of Science.

вандали́зм (-а) *м* vandalism.

ванили́н (-а; *part gen* -у) *м* vanillin.

вани́л|ь (-и) *ж* vanilla.

ва́нн|а (-ы) *ж* bath; **принима́ть (приня́ть** *perf*) ~у to wash *или* have a bath.

ва́нн|ая (-ой; *decl like adj*) *ж* bathroom.

ва́рвар (-а) *м* barbarian.

ва́рварск|ий (-ая, -ое, -ие) *прил* barbaric.

ва́рварств|о (-а) *ср* (*бескультурие*) barbarism; (*жестокость*) barbarity.

ва́реж|ка (-ки; *gen pl* -ек) *ж* (*обычно мн*) mitten.

варе́ник (-а) *м* (*обычно мн*) sweet dumpling (*with curd or fruit filling*).

варёный *прил* boiled.

варе́нь|е (-я) *ср* jam.

вариа́нт (-а) *м* version; (*возможность*) option; (*разновидность*) variant.

вариа́ци|я (-и) *ж* variation.

вар|и́ть (-ю́, -ишь; *perf* свари́ть) *несов перех* (*обед*) to cook; (*суп, кофе*) to make; (*картофель, мясо*) to boil; (*ТЕХ*) to weld; (*сталь*) to found; **у него́ голова́** *или* **котело́к ва́рит** (*разг*) he has a good head on his shoulders

► **вари́ться** (*perf* свари́ться) *несов возв* (*приготовляться*) to be cooking; ~ся (*impf*) в со́бственном соку́ (*перен*) to live in a world of one's own; **до́лго/бы́стро** ~ся (*impf*) to cook slowly/quickly.

Варша́в|а (-ы) *ж* Warsaw.

варьете́ *ср нескл* variety show.

варьи́р|овать (-ую) *несов (не)перех* to vary.

вас *мест см* **вы**.

василёк (-ька́) *м* cornflower.

ВАТА *ж сокр* (= Всеми́рная ассоциа́ция тури́стических аге́нтств) IATA (= *International Association of Travel Agencies*).

ва́т|а (-ы) *ж* cotton wool (*BRIT*), (absorbent) cotton (*US*).

вата́г|а (-и) *ж* (*ребят*) gang.

ватерли́ни|я (-и) *ж* water line.

ватерпа́с (-а) *м* spirit level.

ватерполи́ст (-а) *м* water-polo player.

ватерпо́ло *ср нескл* water polo.

вати́н (-а) *м* padding.

ва́тк|а (-и) *ж* cotton wool ball.

ва́тман (-а) *м heavy paper for drawing etc*.

ва́тник (-а) *м* quilted jacket.

ва́тный *прил* cotton-wool (*BRIT*), absorbent cotton *опред* (*US*); **ва́тное одея́ло** quilt.

ватру́шк|а (-ки; *gen pl* -ек) *ж* curd tart.

ватт (-а) *м* watt.

ва́учер (-а) *м* voucher.

ва́фельный *прил*: ~ **торт** waffle.

ва́фл|я (-ли; *gen pl* -ель) *ж* wafer.

The spelling rules for Russian are shown on page xvii.

ва́хт|а (-ы) ж watch; **стоя́ть** (impf) **на ~e** to keep watch.

ва́хтенный прил (служба) watch опред; **ва́хтенный журна́л** log(book).

вахтёр (-а) м caretaker, janitor.

Ваш мест см ваш.

ваш (-его; f -a, nt -e, pl -и; как наш; см Table 9) притяж мест your; **э́то ва́ше** this is yours; **наш дом бо́льше ва́шего** our house is bigger than yours; см также **ва́ши**.

ва́ш|и (-их; decl like adj) мн your nearest and dearest мн; **и на́шим и ~м** (разг: пренебр) all things to all people.

Вашингто́н (-а) м Washington.

вбе|жа́ть (как бежа́ть; см Table 20; impf **вбега́ть)** сов неперех: **~ (в** +acc) to run in(to).

вберу́ итп сов см **вобра́ть**.

вбива́|ть (-ю) несов от **вбить**.

вбира́|ть (-ю) несов от **вобра́ть**.

вбить (вобью́, вобьёшь; impf **вбива́ть)** сов перех: **~ (в** +acc) to drive или hammer in(to); **я не могу́ ~ э́то ей в го́лову** (разг) I can't seem to get it into her thick skull.

вблизи́ нареч nearby ♦ предл: **~** +gen или **от** +gen near (to).

вбок нареч sideways.

вбра́сыва|ть (-ю) несов от **вбро́сить**.

вброд нареч: **переходи́ть (перейти́** perf) **~** to ford.

вбро́|сить (-шу, -сишь; impf **вбра́сывать)** сов перех to throw in; **вбра́сывать (~** perf) **мяч** (СПОРТ) to take a throw-in.

ввали́|ться (-юсь, -ишься; impf **вва́ливаться)** сов возв (разг): **~ (в** +acc) to burst in(to); (щёки, глаза) to become sunken.

введе́ни|е (-я) ср introduction; (войск) sending in; (данных) input.

вве|зти́ (-у́, -ёшь; pt ввёз, -ла́, -ло́, impf **ввози́ть)** сов перех (в дом итп) to take in; (в страну) to import.

вве́ргн|уть (-у, -ешь; impf **ввергáть)** сов перех (перен): **~ в** +acc to reduce to; **он вверга́ет меня́ в тоску́** he depresses me.

ввернúть (-у́, -ёшь; impf **вве́ртывать)** сов перех to screw in; (перен: разг: слово) to put in.

вверх нареч up ♦ предл: **~ по** +dat up; **~ по тече́нию** upstream; **всё в до́ме/в ко́мнате ~ дном** (разг) everything in the house/room is topsy-turvy; **~ нога́ми** (разг) upside down.

вверху́ нареч up ♦ предл (+gen) at the top of.

вв|ести́ (-еду́, -едёшь; pt -ёл, -ела́, -ело́, impf **вводи́ть)** сов перех to take in; (машину: в гара́ж) to put in; (иглу́: в ве́ну итп) to slip in; (лека́рство, раство́р) to inject; (в компью́тер) to enter; (установи́ть: зако́н, по́шлины итп) to introduce; (сде́лать де́йствующим): **~ что-н в** +acc to put sth into; **вводи́ть (~** perf) **кого́-н в заблужде́ние/искуще́ние** to mislead/tempt sb; **вводи́ть (~** perf) **кого́-н в расхо́ды** to cause sb expense; **вводи́ть (~** perf) **что-н в мо́ду** to bring sth into fashion; **вводи́ть (~** perf) **кого́-н в курс**

собы́тий to bring sb up-to-date with events.

ввиду́ предл (+gen) in view of ♦ союз: **~ того́, что** in view of the fact that; **~ плохо́й пого́ды рейс отло́жен** the flight has been delayed because of the bad weather.

ввин|ти́ть (-чу́, -ти́шь; impf **ввинчивать)** сов перех to screw in.

ввод (-а) м bringing in; (данных) input, feeding in; (электри́ческий, телефо́нный) lead-in.

вво|ди́ть (-жу́, -дишь) несов от **ввести́**.

вво́дн|ый прил (статья́) introductory; (устро́йство) lead-in опред; **вво́дное отве́рстие** input; **вво́дное сло́во** parenthesis.

ввожу́ несов см **ввози́ть**.

ввоз (-а) м (проце́сс) importation; (и́мпорт) imports мн; **беспо́шлинный ~** duty-free imports.

вво|зи́ть (-жу́, -зишь) несов от **ввезти́**.

ввозн|о́й прил imported; **ввозны́е по́шлины** import duty ед.

вво́лю нареч to one's heart's content.

ввосьмеро́м нареч in a group of eight; **они́ живу́т там ~** there are eight of them living there.

ВВП м сокр (= валово́й вну́тренний проду́кт) GDP (= gross domestic product).

ВВС мн сокр (= вое́нно-возду́шные си́лы) ≈ RAF (= Royal Air Force ед).

ВВФ м сокр (= Вое́нно-возду́шный флот) ≈ RAF (= Royal Air Force).

ввысь нареч upwards.

ввя|за́ться (-жу́сь, -жешься; impf **ввя́зываться)** сов возв (разг) to get involved.

вгиба́|ть (-ю) несов от **вогну́ть**.

вглубь нареч (down) into the depths ♦ предл (+gen; вниз) into the depths of; (внутрь) into the heart of.

вгля|де́ться (-жу́сь, -ди́шься; impf **вгля́дываться)** сов возв: **~ в** +acc to peer at.

вгоню́ итп сов см **вогна́ть**.

вгоня́|ть (-ю) несов от **вогна́ть**.

вда|ва́ться (-ю́сь) несов от **вда́ться**.

вдав|и́ть (-лю́, -ишь; impf **вда́вливать)** сов перех: **~ (в** +acc) to press in(to).

вдади́мся итп сов см **вда́ться**.

вдалеке́ нареч in the distance; **~ от** +gen a long way from.

вдали́ нареч = вдалеке́.

вдаль нареч into the distance.

вда́ться (как дать; см Table 14; impf **вдава́ться)** сов возв: **~ в** +acc to jut out into; (перен: в рассужде́ния) to get caught up in; **вдава́ться** (impf) **в подро́бности** to go into details.

вдво́е нареч (сложи́ть) in two; **~ сильне́е/ умне́е** twice as strong/clever.

вдвоём нареч: **они́ живу́т/рабо́тают ~** the two of them live/work together.

вдвойне́ нареч (получи́ть, заплати́ть) double (the amount).

вде́ла|ть (-ю; impf **вде́лывать)** сов перех: **~ в** +acc (вста́вить) to set into.

вде|ть (-ну, -нешь; *impf* **вдева́ть**) *сов перех* to put in; **вдева́ть** (~ *perf*) **ни́тку в иго́лку** to thread a needle.

ВДНХ *ж сокр* (= **Вы́ставка достиже́ний наро́дного хозя́йства СССР**) *exhibition of economic achievements of the USSR*.

вдоба́вок *нареч* (*разг*) in addition ♦ *предл*: ~ **к** +*dat* in addition to.

вдов|а́ (-ы́; *nom pl* **-ы**) *ж* widow.

вдове́ц (-ца́) *м* widower.

вдо́воль *нареч* to one's heart's content; (**в до́ме) всего́** ~ there is plenty of everything (in the house).

вдовца́ *итп сущ см* **вдове́ц**.

вдо́вый *прил* widowed.

вдого́нку *нареч* (*бежа́ть*) behind ♦ *предл*: ~ **за** +*instr* after.

вдоль *нареч* (*слома́ться, расколо́ться*) lengthways ♦ *предл* (+*gen*) along; ~ **и поперёк** here, there and everywhere; (*перен*) inside out.

вдох (-а) *м*: **де́лать** (**сде́лать** *perf*) ~ to breathe in.

вдохнове́ни|е (-я) *ср* inspiration.

вдохнове́н|ный (-ен, -на, -но) *прил* inspired.

вдохнов|и́ть (-лю́, -и́шь; *impf* **вдохновля́ть**) *сов перех* to inspire; ~ (*perf*) **кого́-н на что-н** to inspire sb to sth

▸ **вдохнови́ться** (*impf* **вдохновля́ться**) *сов возв* (+*instr*) to be inspired by.

вдохн|у́ть (-у́, -ёшь; *impf* **вдыха́ть**) *сов перех* (*воздух*) to breathe in; (*дым, лекарство*) to inhale; **вдыха́ть** (~ *perf*) **уве́ренность/ве́ру в кого́-н** to inspire confidence/faith in sb.

вдре́безги *нареч* to smithereens.

вдруг *нареч* suddenly; (*а если*) what if; ~ **он не придёт** what if he doesn't come.

вду́ма|ться (-юсь; *impf* **вду́мываться**) *сов возв*: ~ **в** +*acc* to think over.

вду́мчив|ый (-, -а, -о) *прил* contemplative.

вду́мыва|ться (-юсь) *несов от* **вду́маться**.

вдыха́ни|е (-я) *ср* inhalation.

вдыха́|ть (-ю) *несов от* **вдохну́ть**.

вегетариа́н|ец (-ца) *м* vegetarian.

вегетариа́н|ка (-ки; *gen pl* **-ок**) *ж см* **вегетариа́нец**.

вегетариа́нск|ий (-ая, -ое, -ие) *прил* vegetarian.

вегетариа́нца *сущ см* **вегетариа́нец**.

вегета́ци|я (-и) *ж* vegetation.

ве́да|ть (-ю) *несов перех* (*знать*) to know ♦ *неперех*: ~ +*instr* (*управля́ть*) to be in charge of.

ведём *несов см* **вести́**.

ве́дени|е (-я) *ср* authority; **принима́ть** (**приня́ть** *perf*) **в своё** ~ to take charge of; **быть** (*impf*) **в** ~**и кого́-н** to be under sb's authority.

веде́ни|е (-я) *ср* (*урока, сле́дствия*) conducting; (*войны́*) waging; ~ **хозя́йства** housekeeping.

вёдер *сущ см* **ведро́**.

ведёт(ся) *итп несов см* **вести́(сь)**.

ве́домо *ср*: **с/без ве́дома кого́-н** (*согла́сие*) with/without sb's consent; (*уведомле́ние*) with/without sb's knowledge.

ве́домост|и (-е́й) *мн* gazette *ед*.

ве́домост|ь (-и; *gen pl* **-е́й**) *ж* register; **расчётная** *или* **платёжная** ~ payroll; *см также* **ве́домости**.

ве́домственный *прил* departmental; (*подхо́д*) narrow-minded.

ве́домств|о (-а) *ср* department.

ведр|о́ (-а́; *nom pl* **вёдра**, *gen pl* **вёдер**) *ср* bucket, pail; (**дождь) льёт, как из** ~**а́** it's pouring *или* bucketing (with rain).

веду́(сь) *итп несов см* **вести́(сь)**.

веду́щ|ая (-ей; *decl like adj*) *ж см* **веду́щий**.

веду́щ|ий (-ая, -ее, -ие) *прил* leading ♦ (-его; *decl like adj*) *м* presenter.

ведь *нареч* (*в вопро́се*): ~ **ты хо́чешь пое́хать?** you do want to go, don't you?; (*в утвержде́нии*): ~ **она́ не спра́вится одна́!** she can surely manage alone! ♦ *союз* (*ука́зывает на причи́ну*) seeing as; ~ **она́ ра́да?** she is glad, isn't she?; **пое́шь,** ~ **ты го́лоден** you should eat, seeing as you're hungry; ~ **я проси́л тебя́!** I'm asking YOU!

ве́дьм|а (-ы) *ж* (*также перен*) witch; **охо́та за** ~**ми** *или* **на ведьм** witch-hunt.

ве́ер (-а; *nom pl* **-á**) *м* fan.

ве́жливо *нареч* politely.

ве́жливост|ь (-и) *ж* politeness.

ве́жлив|ый (-, -а, -о) *прил* polite.

вёз *итп несов см* **везти́**.

везде́ *нареч* everywhere; ~ **и всю́ду** everywhere you go.

вездесу́щ|ий (-ая, -ее, -ие; -, -а, -е) *прил* (*Бог*) omnipresent; (*челове́к*) ubiquitous.

вездехо́д (-а) *м* ≈ Landrover®.

везе́ни|е (-я) *ср* luck.

вез|ти́ (-у́, -ёшь; *pt* **вёз**, **-ла́**, **-ло́**) *несов перех* to transport, take; (*дви́гать: за собо́й*) to pull; (: *перед собо́й*) to push ♦ (*perf* **повезти́**) *безл* (+*dat*; *разг*) to be lucky; **ему́ (ча́сто)** ~**ёт** he is (often) lucky.

Везу́вий (-я) *м* Vesuvius.

везу́ч|ий (-ая, -ее, -ие; -, -а, -е) *прил* lucky.

вей(те) *несов см* **вить**.

век (-а; *loc sg* **-у́**, *nom pl* **-á**) *м* century; (*истори́ческий пери́од*) age; (*чья-н жизнь*) lifetime; **це́лый** ~ **тебя́ не ви́дел** I haven't seen you for ages; **на** ~**á** forever; **в ко́и-то ве́ки** (*разг*) for the first time in ages; **жить** (*impf*) **в** ~**áх** to live on forever; **во ве́ки** ~**о́в** forever.

ве́к|о (-а) *ср* eyelid.

веково́й *прил* (*тради́ция, де́рево*) ancient.

ве́ксел|ь (-я; *nom pl* **-я́**) *м* promissory note; **переводно́й** ~ bill of exchange; **казначе́йский**

~ treasury bill; **плати́ть (заплати́ть** *perf*) **по ~ю** to settle an account.

вёл(ся) *итп несов см* **вести́(сь).**

вел|е́ть (-ю́, -и́шь) (*не)сов неперех* (+*dat*) to order; **он ~е́л мне прийти́, он ~е́л что́бы я пришёл** he ordered me to come.

велика́н (-а) *м* giant.

вели́к|ий (-ая, -ое, -ие; -, -а́, -о́) *прил* great; (*no full form*; *обувь, одежда*) too big; **сапоги́ велики́** the boots are too big; **вели́кие держа́вы** the Great Powers.

Великобрита́ни|я (-и) *ж* Great Britain.

великоду́ш|ный (-ен, -на, -но) *прил* magnanimous, big-hearted.

великоле́п|ный (-ен, -на, -но) *прил* (*роскошный*) magnificent, splendid; (*разг*) fantastic.

великому́ченик (-а) *м* holy martyr.

великоро́сс (-а) *м* (*ИСТ: обычно мн*) Great Russian (*old name for a Russian*).

вели́чествен|ный (-, -на, -но) *прил* majestic.

вели́честв|о (-а) *ср*: **Ва́ше** *итп* **~** Your *итп* Majesty.

вели́чи|е (-я) *ср* grandeur.

величин|а́ (-ы́) *ж* size; (*МАТ*) quantity; (*КОМП: значение*) value.

вело́(сь) *несов см* **вести́(сь).**

велого́н|ка (-ки; *gen pl* -ок) *ж* (*СПОРТ: обычно мн*) cycle race.

велодро́м (-а) *м* velodrome.

велосипе́д (-а) *м* bicycle; **го́ночный ~** racing bicycle, racer.

велосипеди́ст (-а) *м* cyclist.

велосипеди́ст|ка (-ки; *gen pl* -ок) *ж см* **велосипеди́ст.**

вельве́т (-а) *м* corduroy.

вельмо́ж|а (-и) *м* dignitary.

велю́р (-а) *м* velours.

Ве́н|а (-ы) *ж* Vienna.

ве́н|а (-ы) *ж* vein.

венге́р|ка (-ки; *gen pl* -ок) *ж см* **венгр.**

венге́рск|ий (-ая, -ое, -ие) *прил* Hungarian; **~ язы́к** Hungarian.

венгр (-а) *м* Hungarian.

Ве́нгри|я (-и) *ж* Hungary.

Вене́р|а (-ы) *ж* Venus.

венери́ческ|ий (-ая, -ое, -ие) *прил*: **~ая боле́знь** venereal disease.

венероло́ги|я (-и) *ж* venereology.

Венесуэ́л|а (-ы) *ж* Venezuela.

венесуэ́л|ец (-ьца) *м* Venezuelan.

венесуэ́л|ка (-ки; *gen pl* -ок) *ж см* **венесуэ́лец.**

венесуэ́льск|ий (-ая, -ое, -ие) *прил* Venezuelan.

венесуэ́льца *итп сущ см* **венесуэ́лец.**

вен|е́ц (-ца́) *м* crown; (*АСТРОНОМИЯ*) corona; **идти́ (пойти́** *perf*) **под ~ с кем-н** to walk down the aisle with sb.

венециа́нский (-ая, -ое, -ие) *прил* Venetian.

Вене́ци|я (-и) *ж* Venice.

ве́нзел|ь (-я; *nom pl* -я́) *м* monogram.

ве́ник (-а) *м* broom, besom.

венка́ *итп сущ см* **вено́к.**

вено́зный *прил* venous.

вен|о́к (-ка́) *м* wreath.

вентили́р|овать (-ую; *perf* **провентили́ровать**) *несов перех* (*помещение*) to ventilate.

ве́нтил|ь (-я) *м* valve.

вентиля́тор (-а) *м* (ventilator) fan.

вентиля́ци|я (-и) *ж* ventilation.

венца́ *итп сущ см* **вене́ц.**

венча́ни|е (-я) *ср* (*коронование*) coronation; (*бракосочетание*) church wedding.

венча́|ть (-ю; *perf* **обвенча́ть** *или* **повенча́ть**) *несов перех* (*соединять браком*) to marry; (*находиться наверху*) to crown; **~ (***impf***) на ца́рство кого́-н** to crown sb

▶ **венча́ться** (*perf* **обвенча́ться**) *несов возв* to be married (*in church*).

ве́нчик (-а) *м* (*БОТ*) corolla.

венчу́р|ный *прил*: **~ое предприя́тие** venture; **~ капита́л** venture capital.

ве́р|а (-ы) *ж* faith; (*в бога*) belief; **~ в кого́-н/что-н** faith in sb/sth; **~ой и пра́вдой служи́ть** (*impf*) **кому́-н/чему́-н** to serve sb/sth faithfully; **на ~у принима́ть (приня́ть** *perf*) **что-н** to take sth on trust.

вера́нд|а (-ы) *ж* verandah.

ве́рб|а (-ы) *ж* pussy willow.

верба́льный *прил* verbal.

верблю́д (-а) *м* camel.

верблю́диц|а (-ы) *ж см* **верблю́д.**

ве́рбн|ый *прил*: **~ое воскресе́нье** ≈ Palm Sunday.

верб|ова́ть (-у́ю; *perf* **завербова́ть**) *несов перех* to recruit.

вербо́в|ка (-ки; *gen pl* -ок) *ж* recruitment.

верди́кт (-а) *м* verdict; **выноси́ть (вы́нести** *perf*) **обвини́тельный/оправда́тельный ~** to pronounce a verdict of guilty/not guilty.

верёв|ка (-ки; *gen pl* -ок) *ж* (*толстая*) rope; (*тонкая*) string; (*для белья*) line; **вить** (*impf*) **~ки из кого́-н** to twist sb round one's little finger.

ве́рен *прил см* **ве́рный.**

верени́ц|а (-ы) *ж* (*предметов*) line; (*людей*) file; (*перен: мыслей итп*) series.

ве́реск (-а) *м* heather.

верет|ено́ (-ена́; *nom pl* -ёна) *ср* spindle.

верещ|а́ть (-у́, -и́шь) *несов неперех* (*женщина*) to chatter.

верзи́л|а (-ы) *м/ж* (*разг*) beanpole.

вери́г|а (-и) *ж* (*обычно мн*) chain (*worn for religious reasons*).

вери́тельн|ый *прил*: **~ая гра́мота** credentials *мн*.

ве́р|ить (-ю, -ишь; *perf* **пове́рить**) *несов неперех* (+*dat*) to believe; (*доверять*) to trust; **~ (пове́рить** *perf*) **в кого́-н/что-н** to believe *или* have faith in sb/sth; **~** (*impf*) **(в Бо́га)** to believe (in God); **~ (пове́рить** *perf*) **на́ слово кому́-н** to take sb at his *итп* word; **я не ~ю свои́м**

глаза́м/уша́м I don't believe my eyes/ears
- **ве́риться** *несов безл*: **не ~ится, что э́то пра́вда** it's hard to believe it's true.

вермише́л|ь (-и) *ж* vermicelli.

ве́рмут (-а) *м* vermouth.

верне́е *вводн сл* or rather; **~ всего́** most likely.

верниса́ж (-а) *м* private view (*of art exhibition etc*).

ве́рно *нареч* (*преданно*) faithfully; (*правильно*) correctly ♦ *как сказ* that's right ♦ *вводн сл* probably; **она́, ~, больна́** she must be или is probably ill.

веронодда́нн|ая (-ой; *decl like adj*) *ж см* **веронодда́нный**.

веронодда́нн|ый (-ого; *decl like adj*) *м* loyal subject.

ве́рность (-и) *ж* (*преданность*) faithfulness, loyalty; (*правильность*) correctness; **для ~и** just to make sure.

верну́ть (-у́, -ёшь) *сов перех* to return, give back; (*долг*) to pay back; (*здоровье, надежду итп*) to restore; **~ (*perf*) кого́-н к действи́тельности** to bring sb back (down) to earth; **~ (*perf*) кого́-н про́шлому** to take sb back
- **верну́ться** *сов возв*: **~ся (к +dat)** to return (to).

ве́р|ный (-ен, -на́, -но) *прил* (*преданный*) faithful; (*надёжный*) sure; (*правильный*) correct; (*no short form*; *неизбежный*) certain; **~ сло́ву** true to one's word; **она́ верна́ самой себе́** she acts true to form.

ве́ровани|е (-я) *ср* (*обычно мн*) belief.

ве́р|овать (-ую) *несов неперех* to believe (in God).

вероисповеда́ни|е (-я) *ср* faith.

вероло́м|ный (-ен, -на, -но) *прил* (*друг*) treacherous; (*нападение*) deceitful.

вероотсту́пник (-а) *м* apostate.

вероотерпи́мост|ь (-и) *ж* (*РЕЛ*) tolerance.

вероуче́ни|е (-я) *ср* teachings *мн*.

вероя́тен *прил см* **вероя́тный**.

вероя́тно *как сказ* it is likely или probable ♦ *вводн сл* probably.

вероя́тност|ь (-и) *ж* probability; **по всей ~и** in all probability.

вероя́т|ный (-ен, -на, -но) *прил* likely, probable; **~нее всего́** most likely или probably.

ве́рси|я (-и) *ж* version.

верст|а́ (-ы́; *nom pl* **вёрсты**) *ж* verst (*former Russian unit of measurement equal to 1.06 km*); **ви́дно за ~у́** it is visible from a long way away.

верста́к (-а́) *м* (*ТЕХ*) (work)bench.

верста́|ть (-ю; *perf* **сверста́ть**) *несов перех* to set.

ве́рстк|а (-и) *ж* (page)proof.

ве́ртел (-а; *nom pl* -а́) *м* spit (*for roasting*).

верт|е́ть (-чу́, -ишь) *несов перех* (*руль*) to turn; **~ (*impf*) +instr** (*зонтиком, тростью*) to twirl;

как ни ~ти́, а он прав (*разг*) no matter which way you look at it, he's right; **~ (*impf*) в рука́х что-н** to fiddle with sth
- **верте́ться** *несов возв* (*колесо*) to spin; (*человек*) to fidget; (: *хлопотать*) to be kept busy; **~ся** (*impf*) **в голове́** (*разг*: *мысль*) to go round and round in one's head; **его́ и́мя ве́ртится у меня́ на языке́** his name is on the tip of my tongue; **~ся** (*impf*) **под нога́ми** (*разг*) to get under one's feet.

вертика́л|ьный (-ен, -ьна, -ьно) *прил* vertical.

вертихво́ст|ка (-ки; *gen pl* -ок) *ж* flirt.

вертолёт (-а) *м* helicopter.

вертолётчик (-а) *м* helicopter pilot.

верту́ш|ка (-ки; *gen pl* -ек) *ж* revolving object; (*разг*: *о человеке*) featherbrain; **дверь-~** revolving door.

ве́рующ|ая (-ей; *decl like adj*) *ж см* **ве́рующий**.

ве́рующ|ий (-его; *decl like adj*) *м* believer.

верф|ь (-и) *ж* shipyard; (*военная*) dockyard.

верх (-а; *loc sg* -у́, *nom pl* -и́) *м* (*дома, стола*) top; (*экипажа, коляски*) hood; (*шубы*) outer layer; (*обуви*) upper; **~ соверше́нства/глу́пости** the height of perfection/stupidity; **оде́рживать (одержа́ть *perf*) или брать (взять *perf*) ~ над кем-н** to get the upper hand over sb; *см также* **верхи́**.

верх|и́ (-о́в) *мн*: **в ~а́х** at the top; **встре́ча/перегово́ры в ~а́х** summit meeting/talks.

ве́рхн|ий (-яя, -ее, -ие) *прил* top; **ве́рхняя оде́жда** outer clothing или garments *мн*.

верхо́вный *прил* (*главный*) supreme; **Верхо́вный Сове́т** Supreme Soviet; **Верхо́вный Суд** High Court (*BRIT*), Supreme Court (*US*).

верхов|о́й *прил*: **~а́я езда́** riding, horseback riding (*US*); **~а́я ло́шадь** mount.

верхо́вь|е (-я) *ср* upper reaches *мн*.

верхола́з (-а) *м* steeplejack.

верхо́м *нареч* astride; **~ на ло́шади** on horseback.

верху́ш|ка (-ки; *gen pl* -ек) *ж* (*дерева, насыпи*) top; (*перен*: *правящая*) elite.

верчу́(сь) *несов см* **верте́ть(ся)**.

верши́н|а (-ы) *ж* (*холма, дерева*) top; (*горы*) summit, peak; **на ~е сла́вы** at the height of his *итп* fame; **на ~е сча́стья** in seventh heaven.

верш|и́ть (-у́, -и́шь) *несов перех* (*суд*) to conduct ♦ *неперех*: **~ +instr** (*судьбами*) to control.

вес (-а; *part gen* -у, *nom pl* -а́) *м* weight; (*перен*: *влияние*) authority; **ве́сом в 5 килогра́мм** weighing 5 kilogrammes; **закрепля́ть (закрепи́ть *perf*) что-н на ~у́** to suspend sth; **прибавля́ть (приба́вить *perf*) в ве́се** to put on weight; **боре́ц лёгкого/тяжёлого ве́са** light-/heavyweight wrestler; **цени́ться** (*impf*) или **быть** (*impf*) **на ~ зо́лота** to be worth one's weight in gold.

ве́сел *прил см* **весёлый**.

ве́сел *сущ см* **весло́**.

веселе́|ть (-ю; *perf* **повеселе́ть**) *несов неперех* to cheer up.

весел|и́ть (-ю, -и́шь; *perf* **развесели́ть**) *несов перех* to amuse.

► **весели́ться** *несов возв* to have fun.

ве́село *нареч* (*сказать*) cheerfully ♦ *как сказ*: **здесь ~** it's fun here; **мне ~** I'm having fun.

весёлый (-ел, -ла́, -ло) *прил* cheerful.

весе́лье (-я) *ср* (*настроение*) cheerfulness; (*времяпровождение*) merriment.

весе́нн|ий (-яя, -ее, -ие) *прил* spring *опред*.

ве́с|ить (-шу, -сишь) *несов неперех* to weigh.

ве́с|кий (-кая, -кое, -кие; -ок, -ка, -ко) *прил*: **~ аргуме́нт** an argument that carries a lot of weight.

весл|о́ (-а́; *nom pl* **вёсла**, *gen pl* **вёсел**) *ср* oar.

весн|а́ (-ы́; *nom pl* **вёсны**, *gen pl* **вёсен**) *ж* spring.

весно́й *нареч* in (the) spring.

весно́ю *нареч* = **весно́й**.

весну́ш|ка (-ки; *gen pl* -ек) *ж* (*обычно мн*) freckle.

весово́й *прил* (*хлеб, конфеты итп*) *sold or bought by weight*; **весова́я катего́рия** (weight) category (*in boxing etc*).

ве́сок *прил см* **ве́ский**.

весо́м|ый (-, -а, -о) *прил* (*перен*) substantial.

вест (-а) *м* (*МОР*) west; (*ветер*) west wind.

ве́стерн (-а) *м* western.

ве|сти́ (-ду́, -дёшь; *pt* **вёл, -ла́, -ло́**) *несов перех* to take; (*машину, поезд*) to drive; (*корабль*) to navigate; (*войско, отряд*) to lead; (*собрание, заседание*) to chair; (*работу, исследования*) to conduct; (*хозяйство*) to run; (*дневник, записи*) to keep ♦ (*perf* **привести́**) *неперех*: **~ к** +*dat* to lead to; (*impf*) **себя́** to behave; (*impf*) **речь о** +*prep* to talk about; (*impf*) **нача́ло от** +*gen* to originate from

► **вести́сь** *несов возв* (*расследование*) to be carried out; (*переговоры*) to go on.

вестибю́ль (-я) *м* (*в гостинице*) lobby; (*в метро*) entrance hall.

ве́стник (-а) *м* messenger; (*перен*) herald; (*издание*) bulletin.

весть (-и) *ж* news; **пропада́ть** (**пропа́сть** *perf*) **без ~и** (*ВОЕН*) to go missing; **без ~и пропа́вший** (*ВОЕН*) missing feared dead; **Бог ~ кто/что** (*разг*) God knows who/what; **пье́са была́ не Бог ~ кака́я** (*разг*) the play wasn't up to much.

вес|ы́ (-о́в) *мн* scales *мн*; (*созвездие*): **В~** Libra.

весь (**всего́**; *см* **Table 13**; *f* **вся**, *nt* **всё**, *pl* **все**) *мест* (*целый, полностью*) all; **~ день** all day; **я стара́лась со всех сил** I tried with all my might; **он появи́лся ~ мо́крый/гря́зный** he appeared all wet/dirty; **при всём жела́нии я не смогу́ тебе́ помо́чь** with the best will in the world, I can't help you; **всего́ хоро́шего** или **до́брого!** all the best!; **без всего́** with nothing;

по всему́ (*по всем призна́кам*) by all the signs.

весьма́ *нареч* quite; **~ непло́хо** not bad.

ветв|ь (-и; *gen pl* -е́й) *ж* branch.

ве́т|ер (-ра) *м* wind; **каки́м ~ром его́ сюда́ занесло́?** (*разг*) what brought him here?; **у него́ ~ в голове́** (*разг*) he hasn't a serious thought in his head.

ветера́н (-а) *м* veteran.

ветерина́р (-а) *м* vet (*inf*) (= *veterinary surgeon*,) veterinarian (*US*).

ве́т|ка (-ки; *gen pl* -ок) *ж* branch; **железнодоро́жная ве́тка** branch line.

ве́то *ср нескл* veto; **накла́дывать** (**наложи́ть** *perf*) **~ на что-н** to veto sth.

ве́ток *сущ см* **ве́тка**.

ве́тра *сущ см* **ве́тер**.

ве́треный *прил* windy; (*де́вушка*) empty-headed.

ветро́в|ка (-и) *ж* windcheater.

ветрово́й *прил* wind *опред*; **ветрово́е стекло́** windscreen (*BRIT*), windshield (*US*).

ветря́нка (-и) *ж* (*МЕД*) chickenpox.

ветряно́й *прил* (*двигатель*) wind-powered; **~а́я ме́льница** windmill.

ве́тх|ий (-ая, -ое, -ие; -, -а́, -о) *прил* (*старик*) decrepit; (*дом*) dilapidated; (*одежда*) shabby; **Ве́тхий заве́т** the Old Testament.

ветхозаве́тный *прил* Old Testament *опред*; (*перен*) antediluvian.

ветчин|а́ (-ы́; *nom pl* -и́ны) *ж* ham.

ве́х|а (-и) *ж* (*обычно мн*) landmark.

ве́ч|е (-а) *ср* (*ИСТ*) *town assembly in medieval Russia*.

ве́чен *прил см* **ве́чный**.

ве́чер (-а; *nom pl* -а́) *м* evening; (*праздник*) party; **на ~е** at a party.

вечере́|ть (*3sg* -ет) *несов безл* to grow dark.

вечери́н|ка (-ки; *gen pl* -ок) *ж* party.

вече́рн|ий (-яя, -ее, -ие) *прил* evening *опред*; **~ие ку́рсы** evening classes.

вече́рник (-а) *м* (*разг*) part-timer (*studying in the evening*).

ве́чером *нареч* in the evening.

ве́чно *нареч* eternally; (*разг: жаловаться*) perpetually.

вечнозелёный *прил* evergreen.

ве́чность (-и) *ж* eternity; **не ви́дел тебя́ це́лую ~** (*разг*) I haven't seen you for ages.

ве́чн|ый (-ен, -на, -но) *прил* eternal, everlasting; (*бессрочный*) indefinite; (*no short form; разг: непрестанный*) perpetual; **ве́чная мерзлота́** permafrost; **ве́чные снега́** everlasting snows.

ве́шал|ка (-ки; *gen pl* -ок) *ж* (*планка*) rack; (*стойка*) hatstand; (*плечики*) coat hanger; (*гардероб*) cloakroom; (*петля*) loop.

ве́ша|ть (-ю; *perf* **пове́сить**) *несов перех* to hang; (*perf* **све́шать**; *товар*) to weigh; **~ (пове́сить** *perf*) **го́лову** to look downcast

► **ве́шаться** (*perf* **пове́ситься**) *несов возв* to hang o.s.; **~ся** (*impf*) **на ше́ю кому́-н** (*разг: пренебр*) to throw o.s. at sb.

вешу *несов см* **весить**.

вещ|ать (*3sg* -ет, *3pl* -ют) *несов неперех* to broadcast; ~ (*impf*) **на Москву** to broadcast to Moscow.

веществ|енный *прил* material; **вещественное доказательство** material evidence.

веществ|о (-á) *ср* substance.

вещ|ий (-ая, -ее, -ие) *прил* prophetic.

вещь (-и; *gen pl* -éй) *ж* thing; (книга, фильм) piece; **она оставила вещи в машине** she left her things in the car; **называть** (**назвать** *perf*) **вещи своими именами** to call a spade a spade.

вéяни|е (-я) *ср* breath; (перен: в искусстве) trend.

вé|ять (-ю, -ешь) *несов неперех* (ветер) to blow lightly; (флаг, парус) to flutter; **в воздухе ~ет весной** spring is in the air.

вжи|ться (-вусь, -вёшься; *pt* -лся, -лась, -лось, *impf* **вживаться**) *сов возв*: ~ **в роль** to get into a role.

взад *нареч*: **~-вперёд** (разг) back and forth; **он не двигался ни ~ ни вперёд** he didn't budge (an inch).

взаймен *прил см* **взаимный**.

взаймность (-и) *ж* mutual feeling; **любовь без ~и** unrequited love; **отвечать** (*impf*) **кому-н ~ю** to reciprocate sb's feelings; **пользоваться** (*impf*) **~ю** to be loved in return.

взаймн|ый (-ен, -на, -но) *прил* mutual.

взаимовы́руч|ка (-ки; *gen pl* -ек) *ж* team spirit.

взаимодействи|е (-я) *ср* (связь) interaction; (поддержка) cooperation.

взаимообусловленность (-и) *ж* interdependence.

взаимоотношéни|е (-я) *ср* (обычно мн) (inter)relationship.

взаимопомощь (-и) *ж* mutual assistance *или* aid.

взаимопонимáни|е (-я) *ср* mutual understanding; **достигáть** (**достигнуть** *или* **достичь** *perf*) **~я** to come to *или* reach a mutual understanding.

взаимосвя́з|ь (-и) *ж* interconnection.

взаймы *нареч*: **давáть/брать дéньги ~** to lend/borrow money.

взамéн *нареч* in exchange ♦ *предл* (+*gen*; вмéсто) instead of; (в обмéн) in exchange for; **он ничегó не прóсит ~** he doesn't want anything in return.

взаперти *нареч* under lock and key; **сидéть** (*impf*) **~** (перен) to stay indoors.

взахлёб *нареч* (разг) eagerly; **~ хвали́ть** (*impf*) **что-н** to gush over sth.

взбáдрива|ть (-ю) *несов от* **взбодри́ть**.

взбáлмош|ный (-ен, -на, -но) *прил* (разг) hysterical.

взбáлтыва|ть (-ю) *несов перех от* **взболтáть**.

взбéй(те) *сов см* **взбить**.

взберýсь *сов см* **взобрáться**.

взбе|си́ть(ся) (-шý(сь), -сишь(ся)) *сов от* **беси́ть(ся)**.

взбивá|ть (-ю) *несов от* **взбить**.

взбирá|ться (-юсь) *несов от* **взобрáться**.

взбить (**взобью, взобьёшь**; *imper* **взбей(те)**) *сов перех* (яйца) to beat; (сливки) to whip; (вóлосы) to fluff up; (подýшки) to plump up.

взбодри́|ть (-ю, -йшь; *impf* **взбáдривать**) *сов перех* (эмоционáльно) to hearten, cheer; (физи́чески) to invigorate.

взбол|тáть (-ю; *impf* **взбáлтывать**) *сов перех* to shake.

взбре|сти́ (-дý, -дёшь; *pt* **взбрёл, -лá, -ло́**) *сов неперех*: ~ **нá гору** to slog up a hill; **емý ~ло́ в гóлову** +*infin* ... (разг) he took it into his head to ....

взбудорá|жить (-у, -ишь; *impf* **взбудорáживать** *или* **будорáжить**) *сов перех* to agitate.

взбунт|овáться (-ýю(сь)) *сов возв* to rebel.

взбýч|ка (-ки; *gen pl* -ек) *ж* (разг) dressing-down.

взвал|и́ть (-ю́, -ишь; *impf* **взвáливать**) *сов перех*: ~ **что-н на** +*acc* to haul sth up onto; **взвáливать** (~ *perf*) **отвéтственность на когó-н** (перен: разг) to burden sb with responsibility.

взведý *итп сов см* **взвести́**.

взвёл *сов см* **взвести́**.

взвé|сить (-шу, -сишь; *impf* **взвéшивать**) *сов перех* (товáр) to weigh; (перен: фáкты) to weigh up, consider.

взве|сти́ (-дý, -дёшь; *pt* **взвёл, -лá, -ло́**, *impf* **взводи́ть**) *сов перех*: **взводи́ть курóк** to cock a gun.

взвéшен|ный (-, -на, -но) *прил* (обдýманный) considered; **во ~ном состоя́нии** (перен: разг) in suspense.

взвéшива|ть (-ю) *несов от* **взвéсить**.

взвéшу *сов см* **взвéсить**.

взвивá|ться (-юсь) *несов от* **взви́ться**.

взви́згн|уть (-у, -ешь; *impf* **взви́згивать**) *сов неперех* to let out a squeal.

взвин|ти́ть (-чý, -ти́шь; *impf* **взви́нчивать**) *сов перех* (разг: цéны) to jack up.

взви́нчен|ный (-, -на, -но) *прил* (состоя́ние) agitated; **он взви́нчен** he is worked up.

взви́|ться (-овью́сь, -овьёшься; *impf* **взвивáться**) *сов возв* to shoot up; (перен) to fly off the handle.

взвод (-а) *м* platoon; **на взвóде** (курóк) cocked; (разг: человéк) on edge.

взвóди́ть (-жý, -ди́шь) *несов от* **взвести́**.

взволнóван|ный (-, -на, -но) *прил* (в трево́ге) agitated; (рáдостный) excited.

взволн|овáть(ся) (-ýю(сь)) *сов от* **волновáть(ся)**.

взв|ыть (-óю, -óешь) *сов неперех* (живóтное,

человек) to howl; (*сирена*) to wail; ~ (*perf*) **от бóли** to howl in *или* with pain.

взгляд (-а) *м* glance; (*выражение*) look; (*перен*: *мнение*) view; **с пéрвого взгля́да, на пéрвый** ~ at first sight *или* glance; **обмéниваться** (**обменя́ться** *perf*) **взгля́дами** to exchange glances; **на мой/твой** ~ in my/your view; **остана́вливать** (**останови́ть** *perf*) ~ **на** +*acc* to rest one's gaze on.

взгляну́ть (-ý, -ешь; *impf* **взгля́дывать**) *сов неперех*: ~ **на** +*acc* to look at; (*кратко*) to glance at; (*no impf*; *обратить внимание*) to look at.

взгромозди́ть (-жý, -ди́шь; *impf* **взгромождáть**) *сов перех*: ~ (**на** +*prp*) to haul up (onto).

взгрустну́ться (*3sg* -ётся) *сов безл* (+*dat*; *разг*) to feel sad.

вздёрну́ть (-у, -ешь; *impf* **вздёргивать**) *сов перех* to jerk up; (*руку*) to throw up; ~ (*perf*) **когó-н на ви́селицу** (*разг*) to string sb up.

вздор (-а) *м* (*разг*) rubbish; **нести́** (*impf*) *или* **молóть** (*impf*) ~ (*разг*) to talk rubbish.

вздóрен *прил см* **вздóрный**.

вздóрить (-ю, -ишь; *perf* **повздóрить**) *несов неперех* to squabble.

вздóрный (-ен, -на, -но) *прил* (*нелепый*) absurd; (*сварливый*) crotchety.

вздорожáть (-ю) *сов от* **дорожáть**.

вздох (-а) *м* (*облегчения итп*) sigh; (*ужаса*) gasp.

вздохну́ть (-ý, -нёшь) *сов неперех* to sigh; (*разг*: *отдохнуть*) to have a breather; **мне** ~ **нéкогда** I'm rushed off my feet.

вздрáгивать (-ю) *несов от* **вздрóгнуть**.

вздремну́ть (-ý, -ёшь) *сов неперех* (*разг*) to have a nap *или* snooze.

вздрóгнуть (-у, -ешь) *сов неперех* to shudder.

вздувáться (-юсь) *несов от* **вздýться**.

взду́мать (-ю) *сов неперех* (*разг*): **он** ~**л заня́ться рýсским языкóм** he took it into his head to learn Russian; **не** ~**йте лгать!** don't even think of lying!

взду́ть (-ю, -ешь) *сов перех* (*разг*: *цены*) to inflate; **у негó вздýло живóт** his stomach became bloated

▸ **вздýться** (*impf* **вздувáться**) *сов возв* (*щека*, *живот*) to swell up; (*разг*: *цены*) to shoot up.

вздымáться (*3sg* -ется, *3pl* -ются) *несов возв* (*грудь*) to heave; (*волны*) to rise.

вздыхáть (-ю) *несов неперех* to sigh; (*тосковать*): ~ **о** +*prp* (*о молодости*) to yearn for; ~ (*impf*) **по** +*dat* to pine for.

взимáние (-я) *ср* collecting.

взимáть (-ю) *несов перех* to collect.

взлáмывать (-ю) *несов от* **взломáть**.

взлеле́ять (-ю) *сов от* **лелéять**.

взлёт (-а) *м* (*самолёта*) takeoff; (*перен*: *мысли*) flight.

взлетéть (-чý, -ти́шь; *impf* **взлетáть**) *сов неперех* (*птица*) to soar; (*самолёт*) to take off;

взлетáть (~ *perf*) **на вóздух** to explode.

взлётно-посáдочный *прил*: **взлётно-посáдочная полосá** runway.

взлётный *прил*: ~**ая полосá** *или* **дорóжка** runway, airstrip.

взлечу́ *сов см* **взлетéть**.

взломáть (-ю; *impf* **взлáмывать**) *сов перех* to break open, force.

взлóмщик (-а) *м* burglar.

взлохмáтить (-чу, -тишь) *сов от* **лохмáтить**.

взмáливаться (-юсь) *несов от* **взмоли́ться**.

взмахну́ть (-ý, -ёшь; *impf* **взмáхивать**) *сов неперех* (+*instr*, *рукóй*) to wave; (*крылом*) to flap.

взметну́ться (-ýсь, -ёшься) *сов возв* (*пыль*, *искры*) to fly up; (*пламя*, *конь*) to leap up.

взмоли́ться (-ю́сь, -ишься; *impf* **взмáливаться**) *сов возв* to beg.

взмóрье (-я) *ср* seashore.

взмы́ть (-óю, -óешь; *impf* **взмывáть**) *сов неперех* to soar.

взнос (-а) *м* (*страховóй*) payment; (*в фонд*) contribution; (*членский, вступительный*) fee; **ежемéсячный** ~ monthly instalment.

взобрáться (**взберýсь**, **взберёшься**; *pt* -лся, -лáсь, -лóсь, *impf* **взбирáться**) *сов возв*: ~ **на** +*acc* to climb (up) onto; **взбирáться** (~ *perf*) **нá гóру** to climb (up) a hill.

взобью́ *итп сов см* **взбить**.

взовью́сь *итп сов см* **взвиться**.

взойти́ (*как* **идти́**; *см* **Table 18**; *impf* **всходи́ть** *или* **восходи́ть**) *сов неперех* (*солнце*, *луна*) to rise; (*семена*) to come up; (*на гору, на престол*) to ascend.

взор (-а) *м* glance; (*выражение*) look.

взорвáть (-ý, -ёшь; *pt* -áл, -алá, -áло, *impf* **взрывáть**) *сов перех* (*бóмбу*) to detonate; (*дом, мост*) to blow up

▸ **взорвáться** (*impf* **взрывáться**) *сов возв* (*гранáта, бóмба*) to explode; (*мост, дом*) to be blown up; (*разг*: *не сдержаться*) to blow up.

взошёл *итп сов см* **взойти́**.

взрасти́ть (-щý, -сти́шь; *impf* **взрáщивать**) *сов перех* to cultivate, grow; (*перен*) to nurture.

взревéть (-ý, -ёшь) *сов неперех* to roar.

взрóслая (-ой; *decl like adj*) *ж см* **взрóслый**.

взрослéть (-ю; *perf* **повзрослéть**) *несов неперех* to grow up; (*духовно*) to mature.

взрóслый *прил* (*человек*) grown-up *опред*; (*фильм, билет, животное*) adult *опред* ♦ (-ого; *decl like adj*) *м* adult.

взрыв (-а) *м* explosion; (*дома*) blowing up; (+*gen*; *возмущения*) outburst of; **раздáлся** ~ there was an explosion; ~ **смéха** a burst of laughter.

взрывáть(ся) (-ю(сь)) *несов от* **взорвáть(ся)**.

взрывнóй *прил*: ~**ая волнá** blast.

взрывоопáсный (-ен, -на, -но) *прил* (*также перен*) explosive.

взрывчáтка (-ки; *gen pl* -ок) *ж* explosive

(substance); **закла́дывать (заложи́ть** *perf*) **~ку**
to plant an explosive.

взры́вчатый *прил* explosive.

взрыхл|и́ть (-ю, -и́шь) *сов от* **рыхли́ть** ♦ (*impf*
взрыхля́ть) *перех* to break up.

взъеро́ш|ить (-ю, -ишь) *сов от* **еро́шить.**

взыва́|ть (-ю; *perf* **воззва́ть**) *несов неперех*: **~ к
кому́-н** +*prp* to appeal to sb for; **~ (воззва́ть**
perf) **к чьему́-н милосе́рдию/ра́зуму** to appeal
to sb's sense of compassion/reason.

взыска́ни|е (-я) *ср* (*долга*) recovery; (*штрафа*)
exaction; (*выговор*) reprimand; **накла́дывать
(наложи́ть** *perf*) **~ на кого́-н** to reprimand sb.

взыска́тел|ьный (-ен, -ьна, -ьно) *прил*
(*публика*) demanding; (*начальник*) exacting;
(*критика*) severe.

взы|ска́ть (-щу́, -щешь; *impf* **взы́скивать**) *сов
перех* (*доля*) to recover; (*штраф*) to exact ♦
неперех: **~ с кого́-н** to call sb to account; **не
~щи́те!** I'm sorry!

взя́ти|е (-я) *ср* (*власти, территории*) seizure;
(*города, крепости*) capture.

взя́т|ка (-ки; *gen pl* **-ок**) *ж* (*подкуп*) bribe; (*КАРТЫ*)
trick; **дава́ть (дать** *perf*) **кому́-н ~ку** to bribe sb;
брать (*impf*) **~ку** to take a bribe.

взя́точник (-а) *м* bribe-taker.

взя́точниц|а (-ы) *ж см* **взя́точник.**

взя|ть (возьму́, возьмёшь; *pt* **-л, -ла́, -ло**) *сов
от* **брать** ♦ *перех* (*разг*) to nick; **возьму́ и или
да и откажу́сь** (*разг*) I could refuse just like
that; **~л да и пое́хал** (*разг*) he upped and left; **~
или возьми́те хотя́ бы тако́й приме́р** let's take
this example; **с чего́ или отку́да ты ~л** (*разг:
пренебр*) whatever gave you that idea?

▶ **взя́ться** *сов от* **бра́ться** ♦ *возв*: **отку́да ни
возьми́сь, появи́лась Ма́ша** Masha appeared
from out of the blue *или* as if from nowhere.

вибри́р|овать (-ую) *несов неперех* to vibrate.

вивисе́кци|я (-и) *ж* vivisection.

вид (-а; *part gen* **-у,** *loc sg* **-ý**) *м* (*внешность*)
appearance; (*состояние: предмета*) form;
(*панорама*) view; (*разновидность: растений,
животных*) species; (: *спорта*) type;
(: *искусства*) form; (*линг*) aspect;
(*состояние*): **у него́ больно́й/серди́тый ~** he
looks ill/angry; **в ви́де** +*gen* in the form of; **на
~ý у** +*gen* in full view of; **под ви́дом** +*gen* in the
guise of; **~ на о́зеро/го́ры/пло́щадь** a view of
the lake/hills/square; **в ви́де шу́тки** as a joke;
име́ть (*impf*) **в ~ý** to mean; (*учитывать*) to bear
in mind; **скрыва́ться (скры́ться** *perf*)**/исчеза́ть
(исче́знуть** *perf*) **из ви́да** to hide/disappear from
view; **де́лать (сде́лать** *perf*) **~** to pretend;
упуска́ть (упусти́ть *perf*) **из ви́ду что-н**
(*перен*) to lose sight of sth; **теря́ть (потеря́ть**
perf) **кого́-н из ви́ду** to lose sight of sb; **вид на
жи́тельство** residence permit; *см также* **ви́ды.**

вида́|ть (-ю; *perf* **повида́ть**) *несов перех* to see;

(*испытать*) to know ♦ *вводн сл* obviously; **где
э́то ви́дано!** (*разг*) whatever next!

▶ **вида́ться** (*perf* **повида́ться**) *несов возв*
(*разг*) to see each other.

ви́ден *прил см* **ви́дный.**

ви́дени|е (-я) *ср* vision.

виде́ни|е (-я) *ср* (*во сне*) vision; (*призрак*)
apparition.

видеоза́пис|ь (-и) *ж* video (recording).

видеоигр|а́ (-ы; *nom pl* **-ы**) *ж* video game.

видеока́мер|а (-ы) *ж* camcorder, videocamera.

видеокассе́т|а (-ы) *ж* video cassette.

видеомагнитофо́н (-а) *м* video (recorder).

видеоплёнк|а (-ки; *gen pl* **-ок**) *ж* (video) tape.

видеофи́льм (-а) *м* video (film).

ви́|деть (-жу, -дишь) *несов неперех* to see ♦
(*perf* **уви́деть**) *перех* to see; (*испытать*) to
know; **рад Вас ~** it's good to see you; **~дите ли
you** see; **(там) уви́дим** (*разг*) we'll see.

▶ **ви́деться** *несов от* **приви́деться** ♦ (*perf*
уви́деться) *возв* to see each other; **вы́ход
~дится в эконо́мии средств** economizing is
viewed as the solution; **мы с ним ча́сто
~димся** we see a lot of each other.

ви́димо *вводн сл* it looks like; **он, ~, не придёт**
it looks like he's not coming.

ви́димо-неви́димо *нареч* (*разг*): **наро́ду на
пло́щади ~** there are masses of people in the
square.

ви́димост|ь (-и) *ж* visibility; (*подобие*) outward
appearance; **по всей ~и** seemingly; **для ~и** for
the sake of appearances.

ви́дим|ый (-, -а, -о) *прил* visible; (*no short form*;
кажущийся) superficial; **~ э́кспорт/и́мпорт**
visible exports/imports *мн.*

видне́|ться (3sg -ется, 3pl -ются) *несов возв* to
be visible.

ви́дно *как сказ* (*можно видеть*) one can see;
(*можно понять*) clearly ♦ *вводн сл* probably; **из
окна́ ~ го́ры** you can see the hills from the
window; **~, что он волну́ется** clearly he is
worried; **~, он уста́л** he is probably tired; **тебе́
видне́е** you know best; **как ~** as it happens; **там
~ бу́дет** we'll see.

ви́дн|ый (-ен, -на́, -но, -ны́) *прил* (*заметный*)
visible; (*no short form*; *известный*) prominent;
(*привлекательный*) fine; **~ мужчи́на** he's a fine
figure of a man; **~ен успе́х** success is in sight.

видоизмен|и́ть (-ю, -и́шь; *impf* **видоизменя́ть**)
сов перех to modify

▶ **видоизмени́ться** (*impf* **видоизменя́ться**)
сов возв to alter.

ви́д|ы (-ов) *мн* prospects *мн*; **име́ть** (*impf*) **~ на
что-н** to have one's sights set on sth.

ви́жу(сь) *несов см* **ви́деть(ся).**

ви́з|а (-ы) *ж* visa; (*директора, редактора*)
official stamp.

византи́йск|ий (-ая, -ое, -ие) *ж* Byzantine.

Визáнти|я (-и) ж Byzantine Empire.
визг (-а) м (собаки) yelp; (ребёнка, поросёнка) squeal; (человека) shriek; (металла, тормозов итп) screech.
визжáть (-ý, -ишь) несов неперех (см сущ) to yelp; to squeal; to shriek; to screech.
визи́р|овать (-ую; perf завизи́ровать) несов перех (документ) to stamp; **емý ~овáли пáспорт** he was issued with a visa.
визи́т (-а) м visit; **прибывáть (прибы́ть** perf) **с ~ом** to arrive on an official visit; **дéлать (сдéлать** perf) или **наноси́ть (нанести́** perf) **~ комý-н** to visit sb.
визи́тн|ый прил: **~ая кáрточка** (business) card.
визуáл|ьный (-ен, -ьна, -ьно) прил visual.
викáри|й (-я) м vicar.
виктори́н|а (-ы) ж quiz game.
ви́л|ка (-ки; gen pl -ок) ж fork; **штéпсельная ~** two-pin plug.
ви́лл|а (-ы) ж villa.
ви́лок сущ см **ви́лка**.
ви́л|ы (-) мн pitchfork ед; **~ами на водé пи́сано** (разг) it's pie in the sky.
вильнýть (-ý, -ёшь) сов неперех: **~** +instr (хвостом) to wag; (бёдрами) to wiggle; (дорога, река итп) to bend sharply.
Ви́льнюс (-а) м Vilnius.
виля́|ть (-ю) несов неперех: **~** +instr (хвостом) to wag; (бёдрами) to wiggle; (дорога, река итп) to wind (along); (перен: разг: человек) to be shifty.
вин|á (-ы́; nom pl -ы) м (чувство) guilt; (ответственность) blame; **возлагáть (возложи́ть** perf) **~ý на** +acc to place the blame on; **авáрия произошлá по егó ~é** the accident was his fault, he was to blame for the accident.
винегрéт (-а) м beetroot salad.
вини́тельный прил: **~ падéж** accusative (case).
вин|и́ть (-ю́, -и́шь) несов перех to blame sb for; (упрекать): **~ когó-н в** +prp **когó-н за** +acc to accuse sb of.
вин|ó (-á; nom pl -а) ср wine.
виновáт|ый прил (взгляд итп) guilty; (-, -а, -о): **~ (в** +prp) (в проигрыше, неудаче) responsible (for), to blame (for); **~!** sorry!, excuse me!; **чýвствовать** (impf) **себя́ ~ым** to feel guilty; **он виновáт пéред дрýгом** he has failed his friend; **он виновáт в том, что ...** it is his fault that ....
винóвен прил см **винóвный**.
винóвн|ая (-ой; decl like adj) ж см **винóвный**.
винóвник (-а) м culprit; **он ~ ~ трагéдии** he is to blame for the tragedy.
винóвниц|а (-ы) ж см **винóвник**.
винóвност|ь (-и) ж guilt; **устанáвливать (установи́ть** perf) **~** to establish guilt.
винóвн|ый (-ен, -на, -но) прил guilty ♦ (-ного; decl like adj) м guilty party; **признавáть (призна́ть** perf) **себя́ ~ым** to plead guilty.
виногрáд (-а) м (растение) (grape)vine; (ягоды) grapes мн.
виногрáдник (-а) м vineyard.

винодéли|е (-я) ср wine-making.
винт (-á) м screw; (самолёта) propeller.
ви́нтик (-а) м screw.
винтóв|ка (-ки; gen pl -ок) ж rifle.
виньéт|ка (-ки; gen pl -ок) ж vignette.
виóл|а (-ы) ж (МУЗ) viol.
виолончели́ст (-а) м cellist.
виолончели́ст|ка (-ки; gen pl -ок) ж см **виолончели́ст**.
виолончéл|ь (-и) ж cello.
ви́р|а межд: **~!** lift!
виráж (-á) м (поворот) turn; (СПОРТ) bend.
виртуáльный прил (КОМП) virtual.
виртуóз (-а) м virtuoso.
виртуóзн|ый (-ен, -на, -но) прил masterly; **~ное исполнéние** a virtuoso performance.
ви́рус (-а) м virus.
вис итп несов см **ви́снуть**.
ви́селиц|а (-ы) ж gallows ед.
ви|сéть (-шý, -си́шь) несов неперех to hang; (угрожать): **~ над** +instr to hang over; **~** (impf) **в вóздухе** (перен) to be up in the air; **у негó на шéе ~ся́т рóдственники жены́** (разг) his wife's relatives are a burden to him; **~** (impf) **на телефóне** (разг) to spend ages on the phone.
вискá сущ см **висóк**.
ви́ски ср нескл whisky (BRIT), whiskey (US, IRELAND).
вискóз|а (-ы) ж viscose.
Ви́сл|а (-ы) ж Vistula (river).
ви́снуть (-ну, -нешь; pt -, -ла, -ло, perf повы́снуть) несов неперех (цветы) to droop; (волосы) to hang limply; **~** (impf) **у когó-н на шéе** (перен) to cling to sb.
вис|óк (-ка́) м (АНАТ) temple.
високóсный прил: **~ год** leap year.
вист (-а) м whist.
вися́ч|ий (-ая, -ее, -ие) прил: **~ мост** suspension bridge; **закрепля́ть (закрепи́ть** perf) **что-н в ~ем положéнии** to suspend sth.
витами́н (-а) м vitamin.
вит|áть (-ю) несов неперех (запах) to hang in the air; **~** perf **над** +instr (опасность, смерть) to hang или hover over; **~** (impf) **в облакáх** (перен) to have one's head in the clouds.
витиевáт|ый (-, -а, -о) прил flowery.
виткá сущ см **витóк**.
витóй прил twisted; (лестница) spiral.
вит|óк (-ка́) м (спирали) twist; (перен: этап) stage.
витрáж (-á) м stained-glass window.
витри́н|а (-ы) ж (в магазине) shop window; (в музее) display case.
витри́но-вы́ставочн|ый прил: **~ая реклáма** display advertising.
ви|ть (вью, вьёшь; pt -л, -лá, -ло, imper вей(те), perf сви́ть) несов перех (венок, верёвку) to weave; (гнездо) to build.
▶ **ви́ться** несов возв (растения) to trail; (волосы) to curl; (флаг, лента) to flutter; (дым) to spiral up.
вих|óр (-рá) м forelock.

вихр|ь (-я) *м* whirlwind; (*перен: революции*) maelstrom; (: *развлечений*) whirl.
ви́це-председа́тел|ь (-я) *м* vice-chairman.
ви́це-президе́нт (-а) *м* vice president.
ВИЧ *м сокр* (= *ви́рус иммунодефици́та челове́ка*) HIV (= *human immunodeficiency virus*); **~-инфици́рованный** HIV-positive.
ви́шен *сущ см* **ви́шня**.
вишнёвый *прил* cherry.
ви́ш|ня (-ни; *gen pl* -ен) *ж* (*дерево*) cherry (tree); (*плод*) cherry.
вишу́ *несов см* **висе́ть**.
вишь *част* (*разг*) (just) look (*used sarcastically*); ~ (**ты**), **како́й он сме́лый** look how brave he is, what a hero.
вка́лыва|ть (-ю) *несов от* **вколо́ть** ♦ *неперех* (*no perf*; *разг*) to slog.
вка́пыва|ть (-ю) *несов от* **вкопа́ть**.
вкати́ть (-чу́, -тишь; *impf* **вка́тывать**) *сов перех* (*тачку, коляску*) to wheel in; (*бочку*) to roll in; (*перен: разг*): ~ **кому́-н пощёчину/вы́говор** to give sb a slap across the face/a dressing-down.
вклад (-а) *м* (*действие*) investment; (*в банке*) deposit; (*в нау́ку, в литерату́ру*) contribution; **вноси́ть** (**внести́** *perf*) ~ **в** +*acc* to make a contribution to.
вкла́дчик (-а) *м* investor.
вкла́дчиц|а (-ы) *ж см* **вкла́дчик**.
вкла́дыва|ть (-ю) *несов от* **вложи́ть**.
вкла́дыш (-а) *м* (*в кни́ге, в альбо́ме*) insert; (*в детали*) inlay.
включа́|ть (-ю) *несов от* **включи́ть** ♦ *перех*: ~ (**в себя́**) to include
▸ **включа́ться** *несов от* **включи́ться**.
включа́я *предл* (+*acc*) including; **пришли́ все ~ дире́ктора** everybody came including the director.
включи́тельно *нареч* inclusive; **с 1-го по 5-ое ма́я ~** from (the) 1st to (the) 5th of May inclusive.
включ|и́ть (-у́, -и́шь; *impf* **включа́ть**) *сов перех* to turn *или* switch on; **включа́ть** (~ *perf*) **кого́-н в что-н** to include sb in sth
▸ **включи́ться** (*impf* **включа́ться**) *сов возв* to come on; (*присоедини́ться*): ~**ся в** +*acc* to join in.
вкол|о́ть (-ю́, -ёшь; *impf* **вка́лывать**) *сов перех* to stick in.
вконе́ц *нареч* completely and utterly.
вкопа́|ть (-ю; *impf* **вка́пывать**) *сов перех*: ~ **что-н в** +*acc* to sink sth into.
вкось *нареч* at an angle; **смотре́ть** (**посмотре́ть** *perf*) ~ **на кого́-н** to look at sb out of the corner of one's eye.
вкраду́сь *итп сов см* **вкра́сться**.
вкра́дчив|ый (-, -а, -о) *прил* ingratiating.
вкра́дыва|ться (-юсь) *несов от* **вкра́сться**.
вкрапле́ни|е (-я) *ср* (*обычно мн: в го́рных*

поро́дах) fragment; (*в те́ксте*) interspersion.
вкра́|сться (-ду́сь, -дёшься; *impf* **вкра́дываться**) *сов возв* to creep in; **вкра́дываться** (~ *perf*) **в дове́рие к кому́-н** to worm one's way into sb's confidence.
вкра́тце *нареч* briefly.
вкривь *нареч*: ~ **и вкось** (*разг*) squint.
вкругову́ю *нареч*: **ходи́ть ~** to go the long way round.
вкру|ти́ть (-чу́, -ти́шь; *impf* **вкру́чивать**) *сов перех* to screw in.
вкруту́ю *нареч* hard-boiled; **вари́ть** (**свари́ть** *perf*) **яйцо́ ~** to hard-boil an egg.
вкру́чива|ть (-ю) *несов от* **вкрути́ть**.
вкручу́ *сов см* **вкрути́ть**.
вку́пе *нареч*: ~ **с** +*instr* together with.
вкус (-а; *part gen* -у) *м* taste; **про́бовать** (**попро́бовать** *perf*) **что-н на** (~ *еду*) to taste sth; **на чей-н** ~, **в чьём-н вку́се** to sb's taste; **приходи́ться** (**прийти́сь** *perf*) **кому́-н по вку́су** to be to sb's taste *или* liking; **она́ оде́та со вку́сом** she is tastefully dressed; **входи́ть** (**войти́** *perf*) **во** ~ to start to enjoy o.s.; **о вку́сах не спо́рят** there is no accounting for taste.
вку́сен *прил см* **вку́сный**.
вку́сно *нареч* tastily ♦ *как сказ*: **о́чень** ~ it's delicious; **она́ ~ гото́вит** she is a good cook; **здесь ~ ко́рмят** the food here is very good.
вку́с|ный (-ен, -на́, -но) *прил* tasty; **обе́д был о́чень** ~ the lunch was delicious.
вла́г|а (-и) *ж* moisture.
влага́лищ|е (-а) *ср* vagina.
владе́л|ец (-ьца) *м* (*магази́на, заво́да*) owner, proprietor; (*кни́ги, карти́ны*) owner.
владе́лиц|а (-ы) *ж см* **владе́лец**.
владе́льца *сущ см* **владе́лец**.
владе́ни|е (-я) *ср* estate; (*заво́дом*) ownership; (*обы́чно мн: брита́нские итп*) possession; **вступа́ть** (**вступи́ть** *perf*) **во** ~ **чем-н** to assume ownership *или* possession of sth.
владе́|ть (-ю) *несов неперех* (+*instr*; *обладать*) to own, possess; (*уме́ть по́льзоваться*): **хорошо́** ~ **шпа́гой** to be a proficient *или* skilful swordsman; ~ (*impf*) **собо́й** to control o.s.; ~ (*impf*) **рука́ми/нога́ми** to have the use of one's arms/legs; **она́ в соверше́нстве ~ет англи́йским** she has a perfect command of English.
Владивосто́к (-а) *м* Vladivostok.
Владикавка́з (-а) *м* Vladikavkaz.
вла́жность (-и) *ж* humidity.
вла́ж|ный (-ен, -на́, -но) *прил* (*земля́, во́здух*) damp; (*глаза́, ко́жа*) moist.
вла́ств|овать (-ую) *несов неперех*: ~ **над** +*instr* to rule; (*перен*) to hold sway over.
вла́стен *прил см* **вла́стный**.
вла́ст|и (-е́й) *мн* authorities *мн*.
вла́ст|ный (-ен, -на, -но) *прил* (*челове́к,*

характер) imperious; **он не ~ен** +*infin* ... it's not within his power to ....

власт|ь (-и; *gen pl* -**е́й**) *ж* (*политическая*) power; (*родительская*) authority; **быть** (*impf*) **у вла́сти** to be in power; **приходи́ть** (**прийти́** *perf*) **к вла́сти** to come to power; **теря́ть** (**потеря́ть** *perf*) ~ **над собо́й** to lose one's self-control; *см также* **вла́сти**.

вле́во *нареч* (to the) left; ~ **от доро́ги** to the left of the road.

влез|ть (-у, -ешь; *pt* -, -ла, -ло, *impf* **влеза́ть**) *сов непереx*: ~ **на** +*acc* (*на дерево*) to climb (up); (*на крышу, на стул итп*) to climb onto; **влеза́ть** (~ *perf*) **в** +*acc* (*забраться*) to climb into; (*разг: в трамвай, в автобус итп*) to get on; (*пренебр: в разговор*) to butt in on; (: *в дело*) to meddle in; **ешь ско́лько влезет** (*разг*) eat as much as you want *или* like.

вле́й(те) *сов см* **влить**.

влёк *итп несов см* **влечь**.

влеку́ *итп несов см* **влечь**.

вле|те́ть (-чу́, -ти́шь; *impf* **влета́ть**) *сов непереx*: ~ **в** +*acc* to fly into ◆ *безл* (+*dat*; *разг*) to be told off; **ему́ ~те́ло от учи́теля за опозда́ние** he was told off by his teacher for being late.

влече́ни|е (-я) *ср*: ~ (**к** +*dat*) (*к человеку*) attraction (to); (*к искусству итп*) liking (for); (*к науке, к политике*) interest (in).

влечу́ *сов см* **влете́ть**.

вле|чь (-ку́, -чёшь итп, -ку́т; *pt* влёк, -кла́, -кло́, *perf* **повле́чь**) *несов переx*: ~ **за собо́й** to lead to; (*no perf*): **его́ ~чёт нау́ка** he is drawn to science.

влива́ни|е (-я) *ср* injection.

влива́|ть (-ю) *несов от* **влить**.

вли́п|нуть (-ну, -нешь; *pt* -, -ла, -ло) *сов непереx* (*в мёд*) to get stuck; (*перен: разг*) to get into a mess.

вли|ть (**волью́, вольёшь**; *pt* -л, -ла́, -ло, *imper* **вле́й(те)**, *impf* **влива́ть**) *сов переx* to pour in; (*перен: средства*) to inject

▶ **вли́ться** *сов возв*: **вли́ться в** +*acc* to flow into.

влия́ни|е (-я) *ср* influence; **ока́зывать** (**оказа́ть** *perf*) ~ **на** +*acc* to influence, have an influence on; **под ~м** +*gen* under the influence of.

влия́тель|ный (-ен, -ьна, -ьно) *прил* influential.

влия́|ть (-ю) *несов непереx*: ~ **на** +*acc* (*на людей, на события*) to influence; (*на организм, на климат*) to affect; **хорошо́/пло́хо** ~ (*impf*) **на** +*acc* to have a good/bad influence on.

ВЛКСМ *м сокр* (*ист*: = **Всесою́зный Ле́нинский Коммунисти́ческий Сою́з Молодёжи**) Leninist Communist Youth League.

вложе́ни|е (-я) *ср* (*обычно мн: экон*) investment.

вло|жи́ть (-у́, -ишь; *impf* **вкла́дывать**) *сов переx* (*средства, деньги*) to invest; (*положить внутрь*) to insert.

влюби́|ться (-лю́сь, -ишься; *impf* **влюбля́ться**) *сов возв*: ~ **в** +*acc* to fall in love with; **влюбля́ться** (~ *perf*) **в кого́-н с пе́рвого взгля́да** to fall in love with sb at first sight.

влюблён|ный (-, -а, -о) *прил* in love; (*no short form*: *взгляд, глаза*) loving ◆ (-**ного**; *decl like adj*) *м*: ~**ные** lovers; **смотре́ть** (*impf*) **на кого́-н ~ными глаза́ми** to look lovingly at sb.

влюблю́сь *сов см* **влюби́ться**.

влюбля́|ться (-юсь) *несов от* **влюби́ться**.

вмен|и́ть (-ю́, -и́шь; *impf* **вменя́ть**) *сов переx*: ~ **что-н кому́-н в вину́** to lay the blame for sth on sb; **вменя́ть** (~ *perf*) **кому́-н в обя́занность** +*infin* to charge sb to do.

вменя́емы|й (-, -а, -о) *прил* (*ЮР*) of sound mind.

вменя́|ть (-ю) *несов от* **вмени́ть**.

вме́сте *нареч* together; ~ **с** +*instr* together with; ~ **с тем** at the same time.

вмести́тель|ный (-ен, -ьна, -ьно) *прил* (*помещение, автобус*) spacious; **э́тот чемода́н о́чень** ~ this suitcase holds a lot.

вме|сти́ть (-щу́, -сти́шь; *impf* **вмеща́ть**) *сов переx* (*подлеж: зал*) to hold; (: *гостиница*) to accommodate; (*уместить*): ~ **что-н/кого́-н в** +*acc* to fit sth/sb into

▶ **вмести́ться** (*impf* **вмеща́ться**) *несов возв* to fit in.

вме́сто *предл* (+*gen*; *взамен*) instead of; (*замещая*) in place *или* instead of ◆ *союз*: ~ **того́ что́бы** instead of, rather than; **пошли́ в теа́тр** ~ **конце́рта** let's go to the theatre instead of the concert; **он рабо́тает** ~ **отца́** he's standing in for his father; ~ **того́ что́бы критикова́ть, постара́йтесь поня́ть** try and understand instead of just criticizing.

вмеша́тельств|о (-а) *ср* (*в разговор, в спор*) interference; (*ВОЕН, ЭКОН*) intervention.

вмеша́|ть (-ю; *impf* **вме́шивать**) *сов переx* (*добавить*) to mix in; (*перен*): ~ **кого́-н в** +*acc* to get sb mixed up in

▶ **вмеша́ться** (*impf* **вме́шиваться**) *сов возв* (*вторгнуться*) to interfere; (*присоединиться*: *в прегово́ры итп*) to intervene.

вмеща́|ть(ся) (-ю(сь)) *несов от* **вмести́ть(ся)**.

вмещу́(сь) *сов см* **вмести́ть(ся)**.

вмиг *нареч* instantly.

вмонти́р|овать (-ую) *сов переx*: ~ **что-н в** +*acc* to fix sth to.

вмя́тин|а (-ы) *ж* dent.

внаём *нареч*: **отдава́ть** ~ to let, rent out; „**сдаётся** ~" (*объявление*) "to let (*BRIT*) *или* rent (*US*)".

внайм|ы́ *нареч* = **внаём**.

внакла́де *как сказ* (*разг*): **остава́ться** ~ to come out worse off.

внача́ле *нареч* at first; ~ **она́ испуга́лась** at first she was scared.

вне *предл* (+*gen*) outside; (*чьих-н обязанностей*) outwith; (*сверх: плана*) over and above; ~ **о́череди** out of turn; **он был** ~ **себя́** he was beside himself; **э́то** ~ **вся́кого сомне́ния** that is beyond any doubt.

внебра́чный *прил* (*отношения*) extramarital;

(*ребёнок*) illegitimate.
внедре́ни|е (-я) *ср* introduction.
внедр|и́ть (-ю́, -и́шь; *impf* **внедря́ть**) *сов перех*
(*ввести*) to introduce
▶ **внедри́ться** (*impf* **внедря́ться**) *сов возв*
(*методы*) to become established; (*идеи,*
традиции) to take root.
внеза́п|ный (-ен, -на, -но) *прил* sudden.
внекла́ссный *прил* extracurricular.
внема́точ|ный *прил*: ~**ная бере́менность**
ectopic pregnancy.
внеочередно́й *прил* unscheduled; (*заседание*)
extraordinary.
внес|ти́ (-у́, -ёшь; *pt* **внёс, -сла́, -сло́**, *impf*
вноси́ть) *сов перех* (*вещи, мебель итп*) to
carry *или* bring in; (*взнос, сумму*) to pay;
(*законопроект*) to bring in; (*поправку,*
параграф) to insert; (*раздор, путаницу*) to
cause; **вноси́ть** (~ *perf*) **предложе́ние/пла́ту** to
make a proposal/payment; **он внёс оживле́ние**
в вечери́нку he livened up the party; **вноси́ть**
(~ *perf*) **я́сность в де́ло** to shed light on the
proceedings.
внешко́льный *прил* extracurricular.
вне́шне *нареч* outwardly.
внешнеполити́ческ|ий (-ая, -ое, -ие) *прил*
foreign-policy.
внешнеторго́в|ый *прил* (*связи, оборот*)
foreign-trade.
вне́шн|ий (-яя, -ее, -ие) *прил* (*стена*) exterior
орпед; (*спокойствие*) outward; (*связи*)
external; ~**яя охра́на** outer guard; ~ **мир**
outside world; ~**яя сторона́** +*gen* the outside of;
вне́шний вид appearance; **вне́шняя поли́тика**
foreign policy; **вне́шняя торго́вля** foreign
trade.
вне́шност|ь (-и) *ж* appearance; **у неё прия́тная**
~ she is good-looking.
внешта́тный *прил* freelance.
Внешторгба́нк (-а) *м сокр* (= *Банк для*
вне́шней торго́вли) foreign trade bank.
вниз *нареч*; ~ (**по** +*dat*) down; ~ **по тече́нию**
downstream.
внизу́ *нареч* below; (*в здании*) downstairs ◆
предл (+*gen*): ~ **страни́цы** at the foot *или*
bottom of the page; **доро́га прохо́дит** ~ the
road runs down below; ~ **магази́н нахо́дится**
there is a shop on the ground (*BRIT*) *или* first (*US*)
floor.
вни́к|нуть (-ну, -нешь; *pt* -, -ла, -ло, *impf*
вника́ть) *сов неперех*: ~ **в** +*acc* to understand
well.
внима́ни|е (-я) *ср* attention; ~**ю покупа́телей/**
пассажи́ров! attention all shoppers/
passengers!; **привлека́ть** (**привле́чь** *perf*) ~ **к**
+*dat* to draw attention to; **принима́ть** (**приня́ть**
perf) **во** ~ **что-н** to take sth into account *или*
consideration; **ока́зывать** (**оказа́ть** *perf*) ~

кому́-н to pay attention to sb.
внима́тельност|ь (-и) *ж* (*в работе*) care;
(*заботливость*) attentiveness.
внима́тел|ьный (-ен, -ьна, -ьно) *прил*
(*сосредоточенный*) attentive; (*тщательный*)
careful; (*заботливый*): ~ **к** +*dat* attentive to.
внима́|ть (-ю) *несов от* **внять**.
вничью́ *нареч* (*СПОРТ*): **сыгра́ть** ~ to draw.
вновь *нареч* again.
вно|си́ть (-шу́, -сишь) *несов от* **внести́**.
ВНП *м сокр* (= *валово́й национа́льный проду́кт*)
GNP (= *gross national product*).
вну|к (-ка; *nom pl* -ки *или* -ча́та) *м* grandson; *см*
также **вну́ки**.
вну́к|и (-ов) *мн* grandchildren *мн*.
вну́тренне *нареч* inwardly.
вну́тренн|ий (-яя, -ее, -ие) *прил* (*поверхность,*
стенка) interior; (*побуждение, голос*) inner;
(*политика, рынок*) domestic; (*рана,*
кровотечение) internal; **Министе́рство**
вну́тренних дел ≈ the Home Office (*BRIT*), ≈ the
Department of the Interior (*US*); **вну́тренние**
о́рганы internal organs *мн*.
вну́тренност|и (-ей) *мн* (*АНАТ*) insides *мн*;
(*КУЛИН*) offal *ед*.
вну́тренност|ь (-и) *ж*: ~ (+*gen*) interior (of); *см*
также **вну́тренности**.
внутри́ *нареч* inside; (*в пределах, в рамках*)
within ◆ *предл*: ~ +*gen* (*дома, ящика*) inside;
(*организации*) within.
внутриве́нный *прил* intravenous.
внутриполити́ческ|ий (-ая, -ое, -ие) *прил*
(*кризис*) internal political *опред*; ~**ая борьба́**
political infighting.
внутрь *нареч* inside ◆ *предл* (+*gen*) inside;
принима́ть (*impf*) **лека́рство** ~ to be taken
internally.
внуча́та *сущ см* **внук**.
внуча́т(н)ый *прил*: ~ **племя́нник** great-
nephew.
вну́ч|ка (-ки; *gen pl* -ек) *ж* granddaughter.
внуша́|ть (-ю) *несов от* **внуши́ть**.
внуши́тел|ьный (-ен, -ьна, -ьно) *прил*
(*внешность*) imposing; (*сумма, успех*)
impressive.
внуш|и́ть (-у́, -и́шь; *impf* **внуша́ть**) *сов перех*
(*вызвать*) to inspire; **внуша́ть** (~ *perf*) **что-н**
кому́-н to instil (*BRIT*) *или* instill (*US*) sth in sb.
вня́т|ный (-ен, -на, -но) *прил* (*отчётливый*)
clear; (*вразумительный*) intelligible.
вня́|ть (*pt* -л, -ла́, -ло, *impf* **внима́ть**) *сов неперех*
(+*dat*: *просьбам*) to heed.
В.О. *м сокр* = *Васи́льевский о́стров* (*Петербу́рг*).
ВО *м сокр* = *вое́нный о́круг*.
во *предл см* **в** ◆ *част* (*разг*: *вот*) there;
(: *выражает согласие*) that's it; (: *выражает*
оценку) great.
во́бл|а (-ы) *ж* Caspian roach.

вобра́|ть (вберу́, вберёшь; *pt* -л, -ла́, -ло, *impf* **вбира́ть**) *сов перех* (*воздух, воду*) to take in; **вбира́ть** (~ *perf*) **в себя́** to incorporate; **вбира́ть** (~ *perf*) **го́лову в пле́чи** to hunch one's shoulders.

вове́к(и) *нареч* (*навек*) forever; (*никогда*) never; ~ **его́ не прощу́** I will never forgive him.

вовле́|чь (-еку́, -ечёшь *итп* -еку́т; *pt* -ёк, -екла́, -екло́, *impf* **вовлека́ть**) *сов перех*: ~ **кого́-н в** +*acc* (*в разговор, в спор*) to draw sb into; (*в рабо́ту*) to involve sb in.

во́время *нареч* on time.

во́все *нареч* (*разг*) completely; ~ **нет** not at all; **она́ на тебя́** ~ **не се́рдится** she's not angry with you at all.

вовсю́ *нареч* (*разг*): **бежа́ть/гнать (маши́ну)** ~ to run/drive as fast as one can; **он стара́ется** ~ he is giving it his all.

во-вторы́х *вводн сл* secondly, in the second place.

вогна́|ть (вгоню́, вго́нишь; *pt* -л, -ла́, -ло, *impf* **вгоня́ть**) *сов перех*: ~ (**во что-н**) to drive in(to sth); **вгоня́ть** (~ *perf*) **кого́-н в отча́яние** to drive sb to despair; **вгоня́ть** (~ *perf*) **в кра́ску кого́-н** to make sb blush.

во́гну́т|ый (-, -а, -о) *прил* concave.

вогну́|ть (-у́, -ёшь; *impf* **вгиба́ть**) *сов перех* to bend *или* curve inwards.

вод|а́ (*acc sg* -у, *gen sg* -ы́, *nom pl* -ы) *ж* water; (*no pl*; *перен: в докладе*) padding; **что ты как** ~**ы́ в рот набра́л?** (*разг*) has the cat got your tongue?; **как в во́ду опу́щенный** (*разг*) down in the dumps; **похо́жи как две ка́пли** ~**ы́** as like as two peas in a pod; **выходи́ть (вы́йти** *perf*) **сухи́м из** ~**ы́** (*разг*) to get off scot-free; **выводи́ть (вы́вести** *perf*) **на чи́стую во́ду кого́-н** (*разг*) to force sb to come clean; *см также* **во́ды**.

водвор|и́ть (-ю́, -и́шь) *сов перех* (*поселить*) to settle; (*тишину*) to establish.

▶ **водвори́ться** *возв* (*тишина*) to be established.

водеви́л|ь (-и) *ж* musical comedy.

води́тел|ь (-я) *м* driver.

води́тельск|ий (-ая, -ое, -ие) *прил*: ~**ие права́** driving licence (*BRIT*), driver's license (*US*).

вод|и́ть (-жу́, -дишь) *несов перех* (*ребёнка, собаку*) to take; (*лошадь, войско*) to lead; (*машину, поезд*) to drive; (*самолёт*) to fly; (*корабль*) to sail; ~ (*impf*) **дру́жбу/знако́мство с кем-н** to be friends/acquainted with sb; ~ (*impf*) **за́ нос кого́-н** to lead sb on

▶ **води́ться** *несов возв* (*рыба итп*) to be (found); ~**ся** (*impf*) **с** +*instr* (*разг*) to be pals with; **у него́ во́дятся де́ньги** (*разг*) he's got money; **как во́дится** (*разг*) as is usually the way.

во́дк|а (-и) *ж* vodka.

во́дный *прил* water *опред*; **во́дные лы́жи** water-skiing; **во́дное по́ло** water polo; **во́дные процеду́ры** hydrotherapy.

водоворо́т (-а) *м* whirlpool; (*перен*) whirlpool, maelstrom.

водоём (-а) *м* reservoir.

водоизмеще́ни|е (-я) *ср* displacement; **су́дно** ~**м в 10 ты́сяч тонн** a vessel of 10 thousand tons displacement.

водока́ч|ка (-ки; *gen pl* -ек) *ж* (*ТЕХ*) waterworks.

водола́з (-а) *м* (*человек*) diver.

Водоле́|й (-я) *м* (*созвездие*) Aquarius.

водолече́бниц|а (-ы) *ж* hydrotherapy clinic.

водолюби́вый *прил* (*растение*) water-loving.

водонапо́рн|ый *прил*: ~**ая ба́шня** water tower.

водонепроница́емый *прил* waterproof.

водоотта́лкивающ|ий (-ая, -ее, -ие) *прил* water-repellent.

водоочистно́й *прил* water-purifying.

водопа́|д (-а) *м* waterfall.

водопо́|й (-я) *м* (*для животных*) (water) trough.

водопрово́д (-а) *м* water supply system; **у них в до́ме** ~ their house has running water.

водопрово́дн|ый *прил* (*труба, кран*) water *опред*; (*система*) plumbing *опред*.

водопрово́дчик (-а) *м* plumber.

водоразде́л (-а) *м* (*также перен*) watershed.

водоро́д (-а) *м* hydrogen.

водоро́дный *прил* hydrogen *опред*; **водоро́дная бо́мба** hydrogen bomb.

во́доросл|ь (-и) *ж* (*обычно мн*) algae *мн*; (*разг: в реке*) waterweed; (*в море*) seaweed.

водосбро́с (-а) *м* floodgate.

водосто́чн|ый *прил*: ~**ая труба́** drainpipe; ~**ая кана́ва** gutter.

водохрани́лищ|е (-а) *ср* reservoir.

водру|зи́ть (-жу́, -зи́шь; *impf* **водружа́ть**) *сов перех* to raise.

во́д|ы (-) *мн* (*государственные, нейтральные*) waters *мн*; (*минеральные источники*) spa *ед*.

водяни́стый *прил* watery.

водяно́й *прил* water *опред*; **водяно́й знак** watermark; **водяно́й пар** steam.

во|ева́ть (-ю́ю) *несов неперех* (*страна*) to be at war; (*человек*) to fight; ~ (*impf*) **с бюрокра́тами** *или* **про́тив бюрокра́тов** (*перен*) to wage war on *или* against bureaucracy.

воеди́но *нареч* together.

военача́льник (-а) *м* (*military*) commander.

военизи́р|овать (-ую) (*не*)*сов перех* to militarize.

военкома́т (-а) *м сокр* (= **вое́нный комиссариа́т**) ministry for war.

военно-возду́шн|ый *прил*: **военно-возду́шные си́лы** (the) air force.

вое́нно-морско́й *прил*: ~ **флот** (the) navy.

военнообя́занн|ый (-ого; *decl like adj*) *м* person eligible for compulsory military service.

военноплённ|ый (-ого; *decl like adj*) *м* prisoner of war.

вое́нно-полево́й *прил* (*госпиталь*) field *опред*; **вое́нно-полево́й суд** court martial.

вое́нно-промы́шленный *прил*: ~ **ко́мплекс** military-industrial complex.

военнослу́жащ|ий (-его; *decl like adj*) *м*

serviceman (*мн* servicemen).

воённые (**-ых**; *decl like adj*) *мн собир* the military.

воённ|**ый** *прил* military; (*врач*) army *опред* ♦ (**-ого**; *decl like adj*) *м* serviceman (*мн* servicemen); **воённое положёние** martial law; **воённая промышленность** military-related industry; *см также* **воённые**.

воёнщин|**а** (**-ы**) *ж собир* (*пренебр*) warmongers *мн*.

вожа́к (**-а́**) *м* leader.

вожа́т|**ый** (**-ого**; *decl like adj*) *м* (*в горах*) guide.

вожделё́ни|**е** (**-я**) *ср* (*к женщине*) lust; (*к власти, к пище*) craving.

вождё́ни|**е** (**-я**) *ср* (*машины, поезда*) driving; (*судна*) steering; (*яхты*) sailing; (*самолёта*) flying.

вожд|**ь** (**-я́**) *м* (*племени*) chief, chieftain; (*движения, партии*) leader.

вожж|**а́** (**-и́**; *nom pl* **-и**, *gen pl* **-ей**) *ж* (*обычно мн*) rein.

вожу́(**сь**) *несов см* **води́ть**(**ся**), **вози́ть**(**ся**).

ВОЗ *м сокр* (= *Всеми́рная организа́ция здравоохранёния*) WHO (= *World Health Organization*).

воз (**-а**; *loc sg* **-у́**, *nom pl* **-ы́**) *м* loaded cart; (*перен: раза*) loads *мн*, heaps *мн*.

возбраня́|ться (*3sg* **-ется**, *3pl* **-ются**) *несов возв* (*запрещается*) to be prohibited.

возбуди́м|**ый** (**-**, **-а**, **-о**) *прил* excitable.

возбуди́тель (**-я**) *м* (*МЕД*) pathogen.

возбу|**ди́ть** (**-ужу́**, **-у́дишь**; *impf* **возбужда́ть**) *сов перех* (*вызвать*) to arouse; (*взволновать*) to excite; **возбужда́ть** (**~** *perf*) **дёло** *или* **процёсс про́тив** +*gen* to bring a case *или* institute proceedings against; **возбужда́ть** (**~** *perf*) **иск** to begin legal proceedings; **возбужда́ть** (**~** *perf*) **хода́тайство о** +*prp* to submit a petition for; **возбужда́ть** (**~** *perf*) **нё́нависть** to incite hatred

▸ **возбуди́ться** *сов возв* (*возникнуть*) to be aroused; (*взволноваться*) to become excited.

возбужда́ющ|**ий** (**-ая**, **-ее**, **-ие**) *прил*: **~ее срё́дство** stimulant.

возбуждё́ни|**е** (**-я**) *ср* (*волнение*) agitation; (*: радостное*) excitement.

возбуждё́нный *прил* (*см сущ*) agitated; excited.

возбужу́(**сь**) *сов см* **возбуди́ть**(**ся**).

возведё́ни|**е** (**-я**) *ср* (*здания, стены итп*) elevation.

возвели́ч|**ить** (**-у**, **-ишь**; *impf* **возвели́чивать**) *сов перех* to extol.

возве|**сти́** (**-ду́**, **-дёшь**; *pt* **возвёл**, **-ла́**, **-ло́**, *impf* **возводи́ть**) *сов перех* to erect; **возводи́ть** (**~** *perf*) **что́-н в при́нцип** to adopt sth as a fundamental principle; **э́то бы́ло ~денó в закóн** it was enshrined in law; **возводи́ть** (**~**

perf) **обвинё́ние на когó-н** to level an accusation against sb; **возводи́ть** (**~** *perf*) **клевету́ на когó-н** to slander sb; **возводи́ть** (**~** *perf*) **что́-н к** +*dat* to trace sth back to.

возве|**сти́ть** (**-щу́**, **-сти́шь**; *impf* **возвеща́ть**) *сов перех* to proclaim.

возво|**ди́ть** (**-жу́**, **-дишь**) *несов от* **возвести́**.

возвра́т (**-а**) *м* return; (*долга, займа*) repayment; **без ~а** irrevocably; **подлежа́щий ~у** returnable; **не подлежа́щий ~у** nonreturnable; **бозвра́т нало́га** tax refund.

возвра|**ти́ть** (**-щу́**, **-ти́шь**; *impf* **возвраща́ть**) *сов перех* (*книгу, покупку*) to return; (*долг, ссуду*) to repay; (*свободу, здоровье, счастье*) to restore; **возвраща́ть** (**~** *perf*) **когó-н к жи́зни** (*больного*) to bring sb back from the brink of death

▸ **возврати́ться** (*impf* **возвраща́ться**) *сов возв*: **~ся (к** +*dat*) to return *или* come back (to).

возвра́тный *прил* (*КОММ*) repayable; (*ЛИНГ*) reflexive.

возвраща́|ть(**ся**) (**-ю**(**сь**)) *несов от* **возврати́ть**(**ся**).

возвращё́ни|**е** (**-я**) *ср* return.

возвращу́(**сь**) *сов см* **возврати́ть**(**ся**).

возвы́|сить (**-шу**, **-сишь**; *impf* **возвыша́ть**) *сов перех* (*работника итп*) to elevate; **возвыша́ть** (**~** *perf*) **когó-н в чьих-н глаза́х** to raise sb in sb's estimation

▸ **возвы́ситься** (*impf* **возвыша́ться**) *сов возв* to be elevated.

возвыша́|ться (**-юсь**) *несов возв* to tower.

возвышё́ни|**е** (**-я**) *ср* elevation.

возвы́шен|ный (**-**, **-на**, **-но**) *прил* (*перен: идея, цель*) lofty; (*натура, музыка*) sublime; (*берег*) high.

возвы́шу(**сь**) *сов см* **возвы́сить**(**ся**).

возгла́в|ить (**-лю**, **-ишь**; *impf* **возглавля́ть**) *сов перех* to head.

во́зглас (**-а**) *м* exclamation.

возда|ва́ть (**-ю́**) *несов от* **возда́ть**.

возда́ть (*как дать; см* Table 14; *impf* **воздава́ть**) *сов перех*: **~ хвалу́** *или* **по́чести комý-н** to eulogize sb, pay homage to sb; **воздава́ть** (**~** *perf*) **комý-н по заслу́гам** (*в награду*) to reward sb for their services; (*в наказание*) to give sb what they deserve; **воздава́ть** (**~** *perf*) **до́лжное комý-н** to give sb their due.

воздви́г *итп сов см* **воздви́гнуть**.

воздвига́|ть (**-ю**; *perf* **воздви́гнуть**) *несов перех* to erect.

воздви́г|нуть (**-ну**, **-нешь**; *pt* **-**, **-ла**, **-ло**) *несов от* **воздвига́ть**.

воздё́йстви|**е** (**-я**) *ср* effect; (*идеологическое, педагогическое*) influence; **ока́зывать** (**оказа́ть** *perf*) **~ на** +*acc* to influence; **под ~м** +*gen* under the influence of.

воздё́йств|овать (**-ую**) (*не*)*сов неперех*: **~ на**

+*acc* ((*по*)*влиять*) to have an effect on;
(*оказа́ть де́йствие*) to influence.

возде́ла|ть (-ю; *impf* **возде́лывать**) *сов перех*
(*обрабатывать*) to cultivate; (*растить*) to
grow.

воздержа́вш|аяся (-ейся; *decl like adj*) *ж см*
воздержа́вшийся.

воздержа́вш|ийся (-егося; *decl like adj*) *м*
(*полит*) abstainer.

воздержан|ный (-, -на, -но) *прил* frugal; (*в*
напитках, еде) abstemious; **он возде́ржан в**
оце́нках/в сужде́ниях he is cautious in his
evaluations/judgements.

возд|ержа́ться (-ержу́сь, -е́ржишься; *impf*
возде́рживаться) *сов возв*: ~ **от** +*gen* (*от*
комментариев, от курения) to refrain from;
(*от голосования*) to abstain from; **~ержа́лось**
10 челове́к there were 10 abstentions.

во́здух (-а) *м* air; (*перен*) atmosphere; **на**
(**откры́том**) **~е** outside, outdoors; **в ~е но́сится**
опа́сность there is danger in the air.

возду́шн|ый *прил* air *опред*; (*десант*) airborne;
посыла́ть (**посла́ть** *perf*) **кому́-н ~ поцелу́й** to
blow sb a kiss; **возду́шная трево́га** air-raid
warning; **возду́шная я́ма** air pocket;
возду́шный флот air force.

воззва́ни|е (-я) *ср* appeal.

возз|ва́ть (-ову́, -вёшь) *сов от* **взыва́ть**.

воззре́ни|е (-я) *ср* view.

во|зи́ть (-жу́, -зишь) *несов перех* to take; **нас**
~зи́ли по Ло́ндону на авто́бусе we were taken
round London on a bus; **ка́ждый день она́**
во́зит дете́й в шко́лу на маши́не every day she
takes *или* drives the children to school; **~** (*impf*)
во́ду на ком-н (*разг*) to work sb into the ground

▶ **вози́ться** *несов возв* to potter about; (*дети*) to
romp around *или* about; **~ся** (*impf*) **с** +*instr* (*разг*:
с работой итп) to make heavy weather of; (*с*
детьми итп) to spend a lot of time with.

возлага́ть (-ю) *несов от* **возложи́ть**.

во́зле *нареч* nearby ♦ *предл* (+*gen*) near; **де́ти**
игра́ли ~ the children were playing nearby; **дом**
был ~ реки́ the house stood near the river.

возлож|и́ть (-у́, -ишь; *impf* **возлага́ть**) *сов*
перех (*положить*) to lay, place; (*поручить*) to
entrust; **возлага́ть** (**~** *perf*) **вину́ на кого́-н** to lay
the blame on sb; **возлага́ть** (**~** *perf*)
отве́тственность на кого́-н to hold sb
responsible; **возлага́ть** (**~** *perf*) **наде́жды на**
кого́-н to pin one's hopes on sb.

возлю́бленн|ая (-ой) *ж см* **возлю́бленный**.

возлю́бленный (-ого; *decl like adj*) *м* beloved.

возме́зди|е (-я) *ср* retribution.

возме|сти́ть (-щу́, -сти́шь; *impf* **возмеща́ть**)
сов перех (*ущерб, убытки*) to compensate for;
(*затраты*) to refund, reimburse.

возмеще́ни|е (-я) *ср*: **~ убы́тков** compensation;
~ затра́т reimbursement; **изде́ржки ~я**
replacement cost; **сто́имость страхово́го ~я**
(*комм*) replacement value.

возмещу́ *сов см* **возмести́ть**.

возмо́жен *прил см* **возмо́жный**.

возмо́жно *как сказ* it is possible ♦ *вводн сл*
(*может быть*) possibly ♦ *нареч*: **~ лу́чше/**
бы́стрее as well/quickly as possible; **~ ему́**
помо́чь it is possible to help him; **~, он**
согласи́тся he may possibly agree.

возмо́жност|и (-ей) *мн* (*творческие*) potential;
фина́нсовые *или* **материа́льные ~** financial
resources.

возмо́жност|ь (-и) *ж* opportunity;
(*допустимость*) possibility; **по (ме́ре) ~и** as
far as possible; **име́ть** (*impf*) **~** +*infin* to be able to
do; **при пе́рвой ~и** at the first opportunity; *см*
также **возмо́жности**.

возмо́жн|ый (-ен, -на, -но) *прил* possible.

возмужа́|ть (-ю) *сов от* **мужа́ть**.

возмути́тел|ьный (-ен, -ьна, -ьно) *прил*
appalling.

возму|ти́ть (-щу́, -ти́шь; *impf* **возмуща́ть**) *сов*
перех to appal (*BRIT*), appall (*US*)

▶ **возмути́ться** (*impf* **возмуща́ться**) *сов возв* to
be appalled.

возмуще́ни|е (-я) *ср* indignation.

возмущённо *нареч* indignantly.

возмущённый *прил* indignant.

возмущу́(сь) *сов см* **возмути́ть(ся)**.

вознагра|ди́ть (-жу́, -ди́шь; *impf*
вознагражда́ть) *сов перех* to reward; (*комм*) to
remunerate.

вознагражде́ни|е (-я) *ср* reward.

вознагражу́ *сов см* **вознагради́ть**.

возненави́|деть (-жу, -дишь) *сов перех* to
come to hate.

Вознесе́ни|е (-я) *ср* Ascension Day.

вознес|ти́ (-у́, -ёшь; *pt* **вознёс, -ла́, -ло́**, *impf*
возноси́ть) *сов перех* (*хвалить*) to exalt;
возноси́ть (**~** *perf*) **чьи-н досто́инства** to extol
(*BRIT*) *или* extoll (*US*) sb's virtues

▶ **вознести́сь** (*impf* **возноси́ться**) *сов возв* to
rise (up).

возни́к *итп сов см* **возни́кнуть**.

возника́|ть (-ю) *несов от* **возни́кнуть**.

возникнове́ни|е (-я) *ср* emergence.

возни́к|нуть (-ну, -нешь; *pt* **-, -ла, -ло**, *impf*
возника́ть) *сов неперех* to arise.

возно|си́ть (-шу́, -сишь) *несов от* **вознести́**.

возн|я́ (-и́) *ж* (*при игре*) frolicking; (*перен*:
интриги) intrigue; **~ с** +*instr* (*хлопоты*) bother
with; **мыши́ная ~** (*перен*) a lot of fuss about
nothing.

возоблада́|ть (*3sg* **-ет**, *3pl* **-ют**) *сов неперех*: **~**
над +*instr* to prevail over.

возобнов|и́ть (-лю́, -и́шь; *impf* **возобновля́ть**)
сов перех (*начать снова*) to resume;
возобновля́ть (**~** *perf*) **контра́кт** to renew a
contract

▶ **возобнови́ться** (*impf* **возобновля́ться**) *сов*
возв to resume.

возомн|и́ть (-ю́, -и́шь) *сов перех*: **~ себя́**
ге́нием/поэ́том to consider o.s. a genius/poet.

возража́|ть (-ю) *несов от* **возрази́ть**.

возражéни|е (-я) *ср* objection; **предложéние встрéтило ~я** the proposal met with opposition.

возра|зи́ть (-жу́, -зи́шь; *impf* **возража́ть**) *сов неперех*: ~ (+*dat*) to object (to); **возража́ть** (~ *perf*) **на замеча́ние/обвинéние** to object to a remark/an allegation.

во́зраст (-а) *м* age; **ребёнок в ~е десяти́ лет** a ten-year-old child; **он был ужé в ~е** he was getting on in years; **вы́йти** (*perf*) **из ~а** to be over the age limit.

возр|асти́ (*3sg* -астёт, *3pl* -асту́т, *pt* -óс, -осла́, -осло́, *impf* **возраста́ть**) *сов неперех* to grow.

возрастно́й *прил* age *опред*.

возро|ди́ть (-жу́, -ди́шь; *impf* **возрожда́ть**) *сов перех* to revive.

▸ **возроди́ться** (*impf* **возрожда́ться**) *сов возв* to revive.

возрождéни|е (-я) *ср* (*хозяйства, традиции*) revival; (*нации, веры*) rebirth; (*территории, демократии*) regeneration; **В~** Renaissance.

возро́с *итп сов см* **возрасти́**.

возымé|ть (-ю) *сов перех*: ~ **дéйствие** to take effect.

возьму́(сь) *итп сов см* **взя́ть(ся)**.

во́ин (-а) *м* warrior.

во́инск|ий (-ая, -ое, -ие) *прил* military; **во́инская повѝнность** conscription.

во́инствен|ный (-ен, -на, -но) *прил* (*племена*) warlike; (*вид, тон, намéрения*) belligerent; (*воинствующий*) militant.

во́истину *нареч* in truth.

во|й (-я) *м* howl.

войду́ *итп сов см* **войти́**.

во́йлок (-а) *м* felt.

войн|а́ (-ы́; *nom pl* -ы) *ж* war; **вести́** (*impf*) **~у́** wage war; **идти́** (**пойти́** *perf*) **на ~у́** to go to war.

во́йск|о (-а; *nom pl* -á) *ср* (*обычно мн*) (the) forces *мн*.

войти́ (*как* **идти́**; см **Table 18**; *impf* **входи́ть**) *сов неперех*: ~ (**в** +*acc*) to enter, go in(to); (*включиться*) to become a member (of); (*уместиться*) to fit in(to); **в шкаф вхо́дит мно́го книг** the cupboard holds a lot of books; **э́та статья́ не вошла́ в сбо́рник** this article was not included in the collection; **входи́ть** (~ *perf*) **в спи́сок** to be added to the list; **входи́ть** (~ *perf*) **в систéму** (*комп*) to log in.

вокали́ст (-а) *м* vocalist.

вока́льн|ый *прил* vocal; (*конкурс*) singing *опред*; **она́ у́чится на ~ом отделéнии** she is studying singing.

вокза́л (-а) *м* station.

вокру́г *нареч* around, round ◆ *предл*: ~ +*gen* (*кругом*) around; round; (*по поводу*) about, over; ~ **го́рода лес** the town is surrounded by a forest; (*реформы бы́ло мно́го спо́ров* there was a lot of controversy surrounding *или* over the reforms; **ходи́ть** (*impf*) ~ **да о́коло** (*разг*) to beat about the bush.

вол (-á) *м* ox (*мн* oxen), bullock.

вола́н (-а) *м* (*на одéжде*) flounce; (*в бадминто́не*) shuttlecock.

Во́лг|а (-и) *ж* Volga.

Волгогра́д (-а) *м* Volgograd.

волды́р|ь (-я́) *м* blister.

волево́й *прил* (*человéк, характер*) strong-willed; (*усилие, нату́ра*) determined.

волейбо́л (-а) *м* volleyball.

волейболи́ст (-а) *м* volleyball player.

волейболи́ст|ка (-ки; *gen pl* -ок) *ж см* **волейболи́ст**.

во́лей-нево́лей *нареч* (*без желания*) like it or not; **ему́ ~ пришло́сь э́то сдéлать** he had no choice but to do it.

во́лен *прил см* **во́льный**.

во́лжск|ий (-ая, -ое, -ие) *прил* Volga *опред*, of the Volga.

волк (-а; *gen pl* -о́в) *м* wolf (*мн* wolves); **во́лком смотрéть** (*impf*) **на кого́-н** to look daggers at sb.

волкода́в (-а) *м* wolfhound.

волн|а́ (-ы́; *nom pl* **во́лны**) *ж* (*также перен*) wave; **на коро́тких/срéдних/дли́нных во́лнах** on short/medium/long wave.

волнéни|е (-я) *ср* (*на мо́ре*) choppiness; (*человéка: радостное*) excitement; (: *нéрвное*) agitation; (*обычно мн: в массах*) disturbance, unrest *ед*.

волни́ст|ый (-, -а, -о) *прил* (*во́лосы*) wavy.

волн|ова́ть (-у́ю; *perf* **взволнова́ть**) *несов перех* (*общество, человéка*) to trouble; (*мо́ре*) to agitate

▸ **волнова́ться** (*perf* **взволнова́ться**) *несов возв* (*мо́ре*) to be rough *или* choppy; (*человéк*) to worry.

волоки́т|а (-ы) *ж* red tape.

вол|окно́ (-окна́; *nom pl* -о́кна, *gen pl* -о́кон) *ср* fibre (*BRIT*), fiber (*US*).

во́лос (-а; *gen pl* **воло́с**, *dat pl* -а́м) *м* hair *только ед*; **~ы рвать** (*impf*) **на себé** (*перен*) to kick o.s.; **э́то притя́нуто за́ волосы** that's a bit far-fetched.

волоса́т|ый (-, -а, -о) *прил* (*грудь*) hairy.

волос|о́к (-ка́) *м* hair; (*лампочки*) filament; **быть** (*impf*) *или* **находи́ться** (*impf*) **на ~** *или* **на волоскé от** +*gen* to be within a hair's-breadth of; **висéть** (*impf*) *или* **держа́ться** (*impf*) **на ~кé** to hang by a thread.

во́лост|ь (-и) *ж* volost (*administrative division*).

волосяно́й *прил* (*покро́в*) hair *опред*.

воло|чи́ть (-у́, -́чишь) *несов перех* to drag; **едва́** *или* **éле но́ги ~** (*impf*) to drag o.s. along.

волча́та *итп сущ см* **волчо́нок**.

во́лч|ий (-ья, -ье, -ьи) *прил* wolf *опред*; ~ **зако́н** the law of the jungle; ~ **аппети́т** voracious appetite.

волчи́ц|а (-ы) *ж* she-wolf.

волчо́нок (-о́нка; *nom pl* -я́та, *gen pl* -я́т) *м* wolf cub.

волше́бник (-а) *м* wizard.

волше́бница (-ы) *ж* (good *или* white) witch.

волше́бный *прил* magic *опред*; (*перен: чарующий*) magical.

волшебство́ (-а́) *ср* (*также перен*) magic.

волы́н|ка (-ки; *gen pl* -ок) *ж* bagpipes *мн*; (*разг: канитель*) palaver.

вольго́т|ный (-ен, -на, -но) *прил* free and easy.

вольер (-а) *м* enclosure.

вольнича|ть (-ю) *несов неперех* (*разг*) to take liberties.

во́льно *нареч* freely; ~! (*ВОЕН*) at ease!; ~ **или невольно** willing or not.

вольноду́м|ец (-ца) *м* freethinker.

вольнолюби́в|ый (-, -а, -о) *прил* freedom-loving.

вольнонаёмный *прил* (*рабочий, труд*) casual.

во́льност|ь (-и) *ж* (*нескромность*) licence (*BRIT*), license (*US*).

во́ль|ный (-ен, -ьна́, -ьно) *прил* (*свободный*) free; (*нескромный*) familiar ◆ *как сказ* (*no full form*): ~**ен** +*infin* he is free to do; **во́льная борьба́** freestyle wrestling; **во́льные упражне́ния** free floor routine; **во́льный перево́д** free translation.

вольт (-а; *gen pl* -) *м* volt.

вольтме́тр (-а) *м* voltmeter.

волью́ *итп сов см* **влить**.

во́л|я (-и) *ж* will; (*стремление*) ~ **к побе́де/ достиже́нию чего́-н** the will to win/to achieve sth; **дава́ть (дать** *perf***) ~ю слеза́м/языку́** to cry/speak without restraint; **дава́ть (дать** *perf***) ~ю чу́вствам** to give free rein to one's feelings; **де́лать (сде́лать** *perf***) что-н по свое́й ~е** to do sth of one's own volition *или* free will; **это не в мое́й ~е** it's not in *или* within my power.

вон *нареч* (*разг: прочь*) out; (: *там*) (over) there ◆ *част*: ~ **туда́ иди́те** you need to go THAT way; ~ **отсю́да!** get lost!; **вы́йди** ~! get out!; ~ **она́ идёт** look, there she is; ~ **(оно́) что** so that's it!

вонз|и́ть (-жу́, -зи́шь; *impf* **вонза́ть**) *сов перех*: ~ **в** +*acc* (*иголка, кинжал*) to stick in(to); (*зубы, когти*) to sink in(to)

▶ **вонзи́ться** (*impf* **вонза́ться**) *сов возв* (*иголка, кинжал*) to stick out; (*когти, зубы*) to sink in.

вонь (-и) *ж* (*разг*) pong.

воню́ч|ий (-ая, -ее, -ие; -, -а, -е) *прил* (*разг*) pongy.

воня́|ть (-ю) *несов неперех* (*разг*) to pong.

вообража́|ть (-ю) *несов от* **вообрази́ть** ◆ *неперех* (*разг: гордиться*) to think a lot of o.s.

вообраз|и́ть (-жу́, -зи́шь; *impf* **вообража́ть**) *сов перех* to imagine; **он ~зи́л, что все про́тив него́** he imagined that everyone was against him; **он ~зи́л себя́ ге́нием** he fancied himself as a genius; ~**зи́те!** (just) imagine!

KEYWORD

вообще́ *нареч* **1** (*в общем*) on the whole; **она́ вообще́ до́брая** on the whole she is kind **2** (*при любых обстоя́тельствах*) absolutely; **ходи́ть в кино́ он вообще́ запрети́л** he absolutely forbade us to go to the cinema; **это нам вообще́ не подхо́дит** that does not suit us at all **3** (+*noun*; *не каса́ясь частностей*) in general; **мы говори́ли о поли́тике вообще́** we talked about politics in general; **вообще́ говоря́** generally speaking.

воодушев|и́ть (-лю́, -и́шь; *impf* **воодушевля́ть**) *сов перех* to inspire; ~ (*perf*) **кого́-н на то, что́бы** +*infin* to inspire sb to do

▶ **воодушеви́ться** *сов возв* (+*instr*) to be inspired by.

воодушевле́ни|е (-я) *ср* enthusiasm.

воодушевлю́ *сов см* **воодушеви́ть**.

воодушевля́|ть (-ю) *несов от* **воодушеви́ть**.

вооружа́|ть(ся) (-ю(сь)) *сов см* **вооружи́ть(ся)**.

вооруже́ни|е (-я) *ср* (*процесс*) arming; (*оружие*) arms *мн*; (*техника*) armament equipment; **брать (взять** *perf***) на** ~ (*перен*) to make use of.

вооружённост|ь (-и) *ж* (*оснащённость*) armed capability; **техни́ческая** ~ technical capability.

вооружённый *прил* armed; **вооружённые си́лы** (the) armed forces.

вооруж|и́ть (-у́, -и́шь; *impf* **вооружа́ть**) *сов перех* to arm; (*перен*) to equip

▶ **вооружи́ться** (*impf* **вооружа́ться**) *сов возв* (*человек, полиция*) to arm o.s.; (*население*) to take up arms; **вооружа́ться** (~**ся** *perf*) **терпе́нием** to arm o.s. with patience.

воо́чию *нареч* with one's own eyes.

во-пе́рвых *нареч* firstly, first of all.

воп|и́ть (-лю́, -и́шь) *несов неперех* (*разг: кричать*) to shriek; (*громко плакать*) to keen.

вопию́щ|ий (-ая, -ее, -ие) *прил* (*ошибка, несправедливость*) glaring; (*безобразие, обман*) brazen ◆ (-его; *decl like adj*) *м*: **глас** ~**его в пусты́не** a voice in the wilderness.

вопло|ти́ть (-щу́, -ти́шь; *impf* **воплоща́ть**) *сов перех* to embody; **воплоща́ть** (~ *perf*) **в себе́** to be the embodiment of; **воплоща́ть** (~ *perf*) **в жизнь** to realize

▶ **воплоти́ться** (*impf* **воплоща́ться**) *сов возв*: ~**ся в** +*prp* to be embodied in; **воплоща́ться** (~**ся** *perf*) **в жизнь** to be realized.

воплоще́ни|е (-я) *ср* embodiment.

воплощу́ *сов см* **воплоти́ть**.

вопль (-я) *м* scream.

воплю́ *несов см* **вопи́ть**.

вопреки́ *предл* (+*dat*; *ожиданию, прогнозу*) contrary to; (*желанию, приказу*) against.

вопро́с (-а) *м* question; (*проблема*) question, issue; **задава́ть (зада́ть** *perf***)** ~ to ask a question; **ста́вить (поста́вить** *perf***) под** ~ to call into question; **быть** (*impf*) *или* **находи́ться**

(*impf*) **под** ~**ом** to be in question; **поднима́ть** (**подня́ть** *perf*) ~ to raise an issue; **э́то** – ~ **де́нег/вре́мени** it's a question of money/time; ~ **по поря́дку веде́ния** (*ЮР*) point of order.

вопроси́тельный *прил* (*взгляд, интонация*) questioning; (*ЛИНГ*) interrogative; **вопроси́тельный знак** question mark.

вопью́сь *итп сов см* **впи́ться**.

вор (-**а**; *gen pl* -**о́в**) *м* thief.

ворва́|ться (-**у́сь, -ёшься**; *pt* -**а́лся, -ала́сь, -ало́сь**, *impf* **врыва́ться**) *сов возв* to burst in; (*звуки*) to flood in.

ворк|ова́ть (-**у́ю**) *несов неперех* (*также перен*) to coo.

вороб|е́й (-**ья́**) *м* sparrow.

воро́ванный *прил* stolen.

вор|ова́ть (-**у́ю**) *несов перех* to steal.

воро́в|ка (-**ки**; *gen pl* -**ок**) *ж см* **вор**.

воровств|о́ (-**а́**) *ср* theft.

во́рон (-**а**) *м* raven.

воро́н|а (-**ы**) *ж* crow; (*перен: разг*) scatterbrain.

ворон|и́ть (-**ю́, -и́шь**; *perf* **проворони́ть**) *сов перех* (*разг*) to miss.

воро́н|ка (-**ки**; *gen pl* -**ок**) *ж* (*для переливания*) funnel; (*после взрыва*) crater.

ворон|о́й *прил* black ◆ (-**о́го**; *decl like adj*) *м* black horse.

воро́нок *сущ см* **воро́нка**.

во́рот (-**а**) *м* neck (*of clothes*).

воро́т|а (-) *мн* gates *мн*; (*вход*) gateway *ед*; (*СПОРТ*) goal *ед*; **э́то ни в каки́е** ~ **не ле́зет** (*разг*) this is daft.

вороти́л|а (-**ы**) *м* (*разг*) big shot.

воротни́к (-**á**) *м* collar.

во́рох (-**а**; *nom pl* -**á**) *м* heap.

воро́ча|ть (-**ю**) *несов перех* to shift ◆ *неперех* (+*instr*; *разг*) to have control of

▶ **воро́чаться** *несов возв* to toss and turn.

вороши́|ть (-**ý, -и́шь**) *несов перех* (*листья, пепел*) to stir up; ~ (*impf*) **се́но** to toss hay; ~ (*impf*) **про́шлое** to stir up the past.

ворс (-**а**) *м* (*на ткани*) nap.

ворча́ни|е (-**я**) *ср* (*животного*) growling; (*человека*) grumbling.

ворча́|ть (-**ý, -и́шь**) *несов неперех* (*см сущ*) to growl; to grumble.

ворчли́в|ый (-, -**а**, -**о**) *прил* querulous.

ворчу́н (-**á**) *м* (*разг*) whinger.

восемна́дцати *чис см* **восемна́дцать**.

восемна́дцат|ый (-**ая, -ое, -ые**) *чис* eighteenth; *см также* **пя́тый**.

восемна́дцат|ь (-**и**; *как* **пять**; *см* **Table 27**) *чис* eighteen; *см также* **пять**.

во́с|емь (-**ьми**; *как* **пять**; *см* **Table 27**) *чис* eight; *см также* **пять**.

во́с|емьдесят (-**ьми́десяти**; *как* **пятьдеся́т**; *см* **Table 29**) *чис* eighty; *см также* **пятьдеся́т**.

восемьсо́т (-**ьмисо́т**; *как* **пятьсо́т**; *см* **Table**

34) *чис* eight hundred; *см также* **сто**.

воск (-**а**; *part gen* -**у**) *м* wax.

воскли́кн|уть (-**у, -ешь**; *impf* **восклица́ть**) *сов неперех* to exclaim.

восклица́ни|е (-**я**) *ср* exclamation.

восклица́тельный *прил* (*интонация*) exclamatory; **восклица́тельный знак** exclamation mark (*BRIT*) *или* point (*US*).

восклица́|ть (-**ю**) *несов от* **воскли́кнуть**.

восково́й *прил* wax; (*цвет*) waxen.

воскре́с *итп сов см* **воскре́снуть**.

воскреса́|ть (-**ю**) *несов от* **воскре́снуть**.

воскресе́ни|е (-**я**) *ср* (*РЕЛ*) resurrection; (*перен: обновление*) regeneration; (: *идеи, движения*) revival.

воскресе́нь|е (-**я**) *ср* Sunday; **в** ~ on Sunday; **по** ~**ям** on Sundays; **в сле́дующее/про́шлое** ~ next/last Sunday; **сего́дня** ~ **деся́тое ма́я** today is Sunday (the) 10th (of) May.

воскре|си́ть (-**шý, -си́шь**; *impf* **воскреша́ть**) *сов перех* to resurrect, raise from the dead; (*перен*) to revive.

воскре́с|нуть (-**ну, -нешь**; *pt* -, -**ла, -ло**, *impf* **воскреса́ть**) *сов неперех* to be resurrected, rise from the dead; (*перен*) to be revived.

воскре́сный *прил* Sunday *опред*.

воскреша́|ть (-**ю**) *несов от* **воскреси́ть**.

воскреше́ни|е (-**я**) *ср* resurrection.

воскрешý *сов см* **воскреси́ть**.

воспале́ни|е (-**я**) *ср* inflammation; **воспале́ние лёгких** pneumonia.

воспал|и́ться (-**ю́сь, -и́шься**; *impf* **воспаля́ться**) *сов возв* to become inflamed.

восп|е́ть (-**о́ю, -оёшь**; *impf* **воспева́ть**) *сов перех* to extol (*BRIT*), extoll (*US*).

воспита́ни|е (-**я**) *ср* upbringing; (*школьников, граждан*) education; ~ **че́стности** instilling of honesty; **брать** (**взять** *perf*) **на** ~ to adopt.

воспи́танник (-**а**) *м* (*учителя, тренера*) pupil; (*вуза*) student; (*приёмный ребёнок*) adopted child.

воспи́танниц|а (-**ы**) *ж см* **воспи́танник**.

воспи́тан|ный (-, -**на, -но**) *прил* well-brought-up.

воспита́тел|ь (-**я**) *м* teacher; (*в лагере, в колонии*) instructor.

воспита́|ть (-**ю**; *impf* **воспи́тывать**) *сов перех* (*ребёнка*) to bring up; (*трудолюбие, честность итп*) to foster, cultivate; **воспи́тывать** (~ *perf*) **из кого́-н специали́ста/спортсме́на** to make a specialist/sportsman of sb.

воспламен|и́ться (-**ю́сь, -и́шься**; *impf* **воспламеня́ться**) *сов возв* to ignite.

восполн|и́ть (-**ю, -ишь**; *impf* **восполня́ть**) *сов перех* (*недостатки*) to make up *или* compensate for; (*пробелы*) to fill in.

воспо́льз|оваться (-**уюсь**) *сов от*

по́льзоваться.

воспомина́ни|**е** (-я) *ср* memory, recollection; *см также* **воспомина́ния**.

воспомина́ни|**я** (-й) *мн* memoirs *мн*, reminiscences *мн.*

воспою́ *итп сов см* **воспе́ть**.

воспрепя́тств|**овать** (-ую) *сов от* **препя́тствовать**.

воспре|**ти́ть** (-щу́, -ти́шь) *impf* **воспреща́ть**) *сов перех* to forbid.

воспреща́|**ться** (*3sg* -ется, *3pl* -ются) *несов возв* to be forbidden; **посторо́нним вход** **~ется** no entry to unauthorized persons.

воспрещу́ *сов см* **воспрети́ть**.

восприи́мчив|**ый** (-, -а, -о) *прил* (*легко усва́ивающий*) receptive; (*подве́рженный*) susceptible.

восприня́ть (-иму́, -и́мешь; *impf* **воспринима́ть**) *сов перех* to perceive; (*иде́ю, смысл*) to comprehend.

восприя́ти|**е** (-я) *ср* perception.

воспроизведе́ни|**е** (-я) *ср* (*зву́ка, мело́дии*) reproduction; (*собы́тий, пейза́жа*) re-creation.

воспроизв|**ести́** (-еду́, -еде́шь; *pt* -ёл, -ла́, -ло́, *impf* **воспроизводи́ть**) *сов перех* to reproduce; (*капита́л*) to restore.

воспроизв|**оди́ть** (-ожу́, -о́дишь) *несов от* **воспроизвести́**.

воспроти́в|**иться** (-люсь, -ишься) *сов от* **проти́виться**.

воспря́н|**уть** (-у, -ешь) *сов неперех*: ~ ду́хом to take heart.

воссозда|**ва́ть** (-ю́) *несов от* **воссозда́ть**.

воссозда́ть (*как* **дать**; *см* **Table 14**; *impf* **воссоздава́ть**) *сов перех* (*о́браз, собы́тия*) to re-create.

восста|**ва́ть** (-ю́, -ёшь) *несов от* **восста́ть**.

восстана́влива|**ть(ся)** (-ю(сь)) *несов от* **восстанови́ть(ся)**.

восста́ни|**е** (-я) *ср* uprising.

восстанови́тельный *прил* (*рабо́ты*) restoration *опред*; ~ пери́од period of restoration.

восстан|**ови́ть** (-овлю́, -о́вишь; *impf* **восстана́вливать**) *сов перех* to restore; **восстана́вливать** (~ *perf*) **кого́-н в до́лжности** to reinstate sb; **восстана́вливать** (~ *perf*) **кого́-н в права́х** to restore sb's rights; **восстана́вливать** (~ *perf*) **кого́-н про́тив кого́-н/чего́-н** to turn *или* set sb against sb/sth

► **восстанови́ться** (*impf* **восстана́вливаться**) *сов возв* to be restored.

восста́ть (-ну, -нешь; *impf* **восстава́ть**) *сов неперех*: ~ (про́тив +*gen*) to rise up (against); (*перен*) to take a stand (against).

восто́к (-а) *м* east; **В~** the East, the Orient; **éхать** (*impf*) **на ~** to travel east; **лежа́ть** (*impf*)/ **находи́ться** (*impf*) **к ~у от** +*gen* to lie/be situated to the east of.

восто́рг (-а) *м* rapture; **быть** (*impf*) **в ~е от** +*gen* to be enraptured by; **приходи́ть** (**прийти́** *perf*) **в**

~ **от** +*gen* to be thrilled by.

восторга́|**ть** (-ю) *несов перех* to delight, enrapture

► **восторга́ться** *несов возв* (+*instr*) to be delighted *или* enraptured by.

восто́ржен|**ный** (-, -на, -но) *прил* (*зри́тель, покло́нник итп*) ecstatic; (*слова́, похвала́*) rapturous.

восторжеств|**ова́ть** (-у́ю) *сов неперех*: ~ (**над** +*instr*) to triumph (over).

восто́чный *прил* eastern; ~ **ве́тер** east wind.

востре́бовани|**е** (-я) *ср* (*багажа́, гру́за*) claim; **письмо́ до** ~**я** a letter sent poste restante (*BRIT*) *или* general delivery (*US*).

востре́б|**овать** (-ую) *сов перех* to claim.

востро́ *наре́ч*: **держа́ть у́хо** ~ (*разг*) to keep an ear to the ground.

восхити́тельный (-ен, -на, -но) *прил* (*му́зыка, стихи́ итп*) delightful; (*краса́вица*) ravishing.

восхи|**ти́ть** (-щу́, -ти́шь; *impf* **восхища́ть**) *сов перех*: **меня́** ~**ща́ет он/его́ хра́брость** I admire him/his courage

► **восхити́ться** (*impf* **восхища́ться**) *сов возв* (+*instr*) to be delighted with.

восхище́ни|**е** (-я) *ср* admiration; (*восто́рг*) delight; **приходи́ть** (**прийти́** *perf*) **в** ~ **от** +*gen* to be enraptured *или* delighted by; **приводи́ть** (**привести́** *perf*) **в** ~ **кого́-н** to delight sb.

восхищу́|**(сь)** *сов см* **восхити́ть(ся)**.

восхо́д (-а) *м*: ~ **со́лнца** sunrise; ~ **луны́** moonrise.

восх|**оди́ть** (-ожу́, -о́дишь) *несов от* **взойти́** ♦ *неперех*: ~ **к** +*dat* (*к пери́оду вре́мени*) to date back to; (*к тради́ции*) to be based on.

восходя́щ|**ий** (-ая, -ее, -ие) *прил* rising.

восхожу́ *несов см* **восходи́ть**.

восьм|**а́я** (-о́й; *decl like adj*) *ж*: **одна́** ~ one eighth.

восьмёр|**ка** (-ки; *gen pl* -ок) *ж* (*разг*: *ци́фра*) eight; (*гру́ппа из восьми́*) group of eight; (*разг*: *авто́бус, трамва́й итп*) (number) eight (*bus, tram etc*); **ло́дка-**~ eight (*ROWING*).

во́сьмер|**о** (-ы́х; *как* **че́тверо**; *см* **Table 36a**) *чис* eight; *см также* **дво́е**.

восьми́ *чис см* **во́семь**.

восьми́десяти *чис см* **во́семьдесят**.

восьмидесятиле́ти|**е** (-я) *ср* (*срок*) eighty years *мн*; (*годовщи́на*) eightieth anniversary; (*день рожде́ния*) eightieth birthday.

восьмидесятиле́тн|**ий** (-яя, -ее, -ие) *прил* (*пери́од*) eighty-year; (*стари́к*) eighty-year-old.

восьмидеся́т|**ый** (-ая, -ое, -ые) *чис* eightieth; *см также* **пятидеся́тый**.

восьмидне́вный *прил* eight-day.

восьмикла́ссник (-а) *м* pupil *in eighth year at school (usually 14 years old)*.

восьмикла́ссни|**ца** (-ы) *ж см* **восьмикла́ссник**.

восьмикра́тн|**ый** *прил*: ~ **чемпио́н** eight-times champion; **в** ~**ом разме́ре** eightfold.

восьмиле́ти|**е** (-я) *ср* (*срок*) eight years; (*годовщи́на*) eighth anniversary.

восьмиле́тн|ий (**-яя, -ее, -ие**) прил (период) eight-year; (ребёнок) eight-year-old.
восьмиме́сячный прил eight-month; (ребёнок) eight-month-old.
восьминеде́льный прил eight-week; (ребёнок) eight-week-old.
восьмисо́т чис см **восемьсо́т.**
восьмисотле́ти|е (**-я**) ср (срок) eight hundred years мн; (годовщина) eight-hundredth anniversary, octocentenary.
восьмисотле́тн|ий (**-яя, -ее, -ие**) прил (период) eight hundred-year; (дерево) eight hundred-year-old.
восьмисо́т|ый (**-ая, -ое, -ые**) чис eight-hundredth.
восьмиуго́льник (**-а**) м octagon.
восьмичасово́й прил (рабочий день) eight-hour; (поезд) eight-o'clock.
восьм|о́й (**-а́я, -о́е, -ы́е**) чис eighth; см также **пя́тый.**

KEYWORD

вот част **1** (при указании): **вот моя́ ма́ма** there is my mother; **вот мои́ де́ти** here are my children; **вот он идёт** here he comes
2 (выражает указание) this; **вот в чём де́ло** this is what it's about; **вот где ну́жно иска́ть** this is where we need to look
3 (при эмфатике): **вот посмотри́, како́е безобра́зие** just look at the mess; **вот ты и сде́лай э́то** YOU do this; **вот него́дяй!** what a rascal!
4 (как часть сказ): **но́вая кни́га – вот моя́ цель** a new book – that's my goal; **вот-во́т** (разг: вот именно) you've got it; **он вот-во́т ля́жет спать** he is just about to go to bed; **вот ещё!** (разг) not likely!; **вот (оно́) как или что!** is that so или right?; **вот тебе́ (и) погуля́ли!** (разг) so much for the walk!; **вот тебе́ и на** или **те раз!** (разг) well I never!

воткн|у́ть (**-у́, -ёшь**; impf **втыка́ть**) сов перех (иголку, нож) to stick in; **втыка́ть** (**~** perf) **кол в зе́млю** to drive a stake into the ground.
вотру́(сь) итп сов см **втере́ть(ся).**
во́тум (**-а**) м: **~ дове́рия/недове́рия** vote of confidence/no confidence.
вошёл итп сов см **войти́.**
вошь (**вши**; instr sg **во́шью**, nom pl **вши**) ж louse (мн lice).
вошью́ итп сов см **вшить.**
вощёный прил waxed.
вою́ итп несов см **выть.**
впада́|ть (**-ю**) несов от **впасть ♦** неперех: **~ в** +acc to flow into.
впа́дин|а (**-ы**) ж (в земле) gully; (на дне моря) trench; **глазна́я ~** eye socket.
впа|сть (**-ду́, -дёшь**; impf **впада́ть**) сов неперех (щёки, глаза) to become sunken; **впада́ть** (**~**

perf) **в отча́яние** to fall into despair; **впада́ть** (**~** perf) **в исте́рику** to go into hysterics; **впада́ть** (**~** perf) **в па́нику** to get into a panic; **впада́ть** (**~** perf) **в оши́бку** to err; **впада́ть** (**~** perf) **в кра́йности** to go to extremes; **впада́ть** (**~** perf) **в заблужде́ние** to be deluded.
впервы́е нареч for the first time.
вперёд нареч (идти, смотреть итп) (straight) ahead, forward; (заплати́ть, тре́бовать) in advance.
впереди́ нареч in front; (в будущем) ahead ♦ предл (+gen) in front of; **у Вас вся жизнь ~** you have your whole life in front of you.
вперемешку нареч higgledy-piggledy.
впечатле́ни|е (**-я**) ср impression; **находи́ться** (impf) **под ~м чего-н** to be impressed by sth; **производи́ть** (**произвести́** perf) **~ на** +acc to make an impression on; **тако́е ~, что** или **бу́дто** it looks as if.
впечатли́тельный (**-ен, -ьна, -ьно**) прил impressionable.
впечатля́|ть (**-ю**) несов неперех to be impressive.
впива́|ться (**-юсь**) несов от **впи́ться.**
впи|са́ть (**-шу́, -шешь**; impf **впи́сывать**) сов перех to insert, include
► **впиcа́ться** (impf **впи́сываться**) сов возв (перен) to fit in well.
впита́|ть (**-ю**; impf **впи́тывать**) сов перех to absorb; (перен) to absorb, take in
► **впита́ться** сов возв to be absorbed.
впи́|ться (**вопью́сь, вопьёшься**; impf **впива́ться**) сов возв: **~ в** +acc (комар) to bite; **впива́ться** (**~** perf) **глаза́ми в** +acc to fix или fasten one's eyes on; **впива́ться** (**~** perf) **когтя́ми/зуба́ми в** +acc to sink one's claws/teeth into.
впишу́(сь) итп сов см **вписа́ть(ся).**
ВПК сокр (= вое́нно-промы́шленный ко́мплекс) ≈ military-industrial complex.
вплавь нареч by swimming.
вплотну́ю нареч (близко) close (by) ♦ предл: **~ к** +dat (близко: к городу) right up close to; (: к стене) right up against; **занима́ться** (**заня́ться** perf) **чем-н** или **бра́ться** (**взя́ться** perf) **за что-н ~** to get down to sth in earnest.
вплоть предл: **~ до** +gen (вечера, зимы) right up till; (включая) right up to; **~ до того́, что ...** to the extent that ....
вполго́лоса нареч (говорить, спросить) in hushed tones; (петь) softly.
впо́ру как сказ: **~** +infin there is nothing for it but to do; **пла́тье/шля́па ~** the dress/hat fits nicely.
впосле́дствии нареч subsequently.
впотьма́х нареч in the dark.
впп ж сокр (= взлётно-поса́дочная полоса́) landing strip.
впра́ве как сказ: **~** +infin to do rightly или justly;

он не ~ так поступа́ть he's got no right to behave like that.

впра́в|ить (-лю, -ишь; *impf* **вправля́ть**) *сов перех* to set.

впра́во *нареч* to the right; ~ **от до́ма** to the right of the house.

впредь *нареч* in future ♦ *предл*: ~ **до** +*gen* pending.

впритъ́к *нареч* (*разг*) right up close.

впро́голодь *нареч*: **жить** ~ to live hand to mouth.

впрок *нареч* for future use ♦ *как сказ*: **идти́ ~ кому́-н** to do sb good.

впроса́к *нареч*: **попа́сть(ся)** ~ (*разг*) to get (o.s.) into a fix.

впро́чем *союз* however, though ♦ *вводн сл* but then again; **пого́да здесь хоро́шая, ~ не всегда́** the weather's good here, though not always; ~, **я не уве́рен** but then again, I'm not sure.

впряг *итп сов см* **впрячь**.

впряга́|ть (-ю) *несов от* **впрячь**.

впрягу́ *итп сов см* **впрячь**.

впрямь *част*: **и ~** (*разг*) really; **он и ~ испуга́лся** he really got a fright.

впря́|чь (-гу́, -жёшь *итп*, -гут; *pt* -г, -гла́, -гло́, *impf* **впряга́ть**) *сов перех* to harness.

впу|сти́ть (-щу́, -стишь; *impf* **впуска́ть**) *сов перех* (*в дом, в зал*) to admit, let in.

впу́та|ть (-ю) *сов от* **пу́тать** ♦ (*impf* **впу́тывать**) *перех* (*разг*): ~ **кого́-н** (**в** +*acc*) to get sb mixed up (in)

▶ **впу́таться** *сов от* **пу́таться** ♦ (*impf* **впу́тываться**) *возв* to get involved.

впущу́ *сов см* **впусти́ть**.

впя́теро *нареч* (*больше, меньше*) five times; (*увеличить*) fivefold.

впятеро́м *нареч* in a group of five.

в-пя́тых *вводн сл* fifthly, in the fifth place.

враг (-а́) *м* enemy ♦ *собир* (*ВОЕН*) the enemy.

вражда́ (-ы́) *ж* enmity, hostility; **пита́ть** (*impf*) ~**у́ к** +*dat* to harbour enmity towards.

вражде́б|ный (-ен, -на, -но) *прил* (*отношение, тон*) hostile; (*лагерь, сторона*) enemy *опред*.

вражд|ова́ть (-у́ю) *несов неперех*: ~ (**с** +*instr*) to be on hostile terms (with).

враз *нареч* (*разг*) at once.

вразбро́д *нареч* separately.

вразбро́с *нареч* (*разг*) scattered about.

вразва́лку *нареч* (*разг*): **ходи́ть** ~ to waddle.

вразнобо́й *нареч* (*разг*) in a muddled way.

вразно́с *нареч*: **торгова́ть** ~ to peddle.

вразре́з *нареч*: ~ **с** +*instr* in contravention of.

вразуми́тельный (-ен, -ьна, -ьно) *прил* comprehensible.

вразум|и́ть (-лю, -и́шь; *impf* **вразумля́ть**) *сов перех*: ~ **кого́-н** to make sb understand.

вранье́ (-я́) *ср* (*разг*) lies *мн*.

враспло́х *нареч* unawares.

врассыпну́ю *нареч* in all directions.

врата́р|ь (-я́) *м* goalkeeper.

вр|ать (-у́, -ёшь; *pt* -ал, -ла́, -ло, *perf* **навра́ть** *или* **совра́ть**) *несов неперех* (*разг: человек*) to fib; (: *часы*) to be wrong.

врач (-а́) *м* doctor.

враче́бный *прил* medical.

враща́|ть (-ю) *несов перех* (*колесо*) to turn

▶ **враща́ться** *несов возв* (*колесо, планета*) to revolve, rotate; ~**ся** (*impf*) **в полити́ческих круга́х** to move in political circles; **разгово́р** ~**ся вокру́г теа́тра** the conversation revolved around the theatre.

враще́ни|е (-я) *ср* revolution, rotation.

вред (-а́) *м* (*делу, здоро́вью*) damage; (*челове́ку*) harm, injury ♦ *предл*: **во** ~ +*dat* to the detriment of; **его́ де́йствия бы́ли во ~ интере́сам фи́рмы** his actions were against the company's interests; **причиня́ть** (**причини́ть** *perf*) *или* **приноси́ть** (**принести́** *perf*) ~ **кому́-н** to harm sb, do sb harm; **причиня́ть** (**причини́ть** *perf*) *или* **приноси́ть** (**принести́** *perf*) ~ **чему́-н** to damage *или* cause damage to sth.

вре́ден *прил см* **вре́дный**.

вреди́тел|ь (-я) *м* (*насекомое*) pest; (*человек*) saboteur.

вре|ди́ть (-жу́, -ди́шь; *perf* **навреди́ть**) *несов неперех* (+*dat*) to harm, hurt; (*здоро́вью*) to damage; (*врагу́*) to inflict damage on.

вре́дно *нареч*: ~ **влия́ть на** +*acc* to have a harmful effect on ♦ *как сказ*: **кури́ть** ~ smoking is bad for you; **ему́** ~ **есть жи́рное** fatty foods are bad for him.

вре́дный (-ен, -на́, -но) *прил* harmful; (*no short form*; *разг*) nasty.

вре́|зать (-жу, -жешь) *сов перех* (*замок*) to fit ♦ *неперех* (*разг*): ~ **кому́-н** to bash sb.

врежу́ *несов см* **вреди́ть**.

вре́|заться (-жусь, -жешься; *impf* **вреза́ться**) *сов возв*: ~ **в** +*acc* (*пила, верёвка*) to cut into; (*ворва́ться*) to plough (*BRIT*) *или* plow (*US*) into; (*в сердце, в па́мять*) to engrave itself on.

времен|а́ (-ён; *dat pl* -ена́м) *мн* (*эпоха*) the time *ед*; ~ **Петра́ Пе́рвого** the time of Peter the First.

времена́ми *нареч* at times.

вре́мени *итп сущ см* **вре́мя**.

вре́мен|ный (-ен, -на, -но) *прил* temporary.

вре́м|я (-ени; *см* **Table 4**) *ср* time; (*линг*) tense ♦ *предл*: **во** ~ +*gen* during ♦ *союз*: **в то** ~ **как** *или* **когда́** while; (**а**) **в то же** ~ (but) at the same time; **во́ время** on time; ~ **от вре́мени** from time to time; **в после́днее** ~ recently; **в своё** ~ (*когда необходимо*) in due course; **в своё** ~ **она́ была́ краса́вицей** she was a real beauty in her day; **на** ~ for a while; **со** ~**енем** with *или* in time; **тем** ~**енем** meanwhile; **ско́лько** ~**ени?** what time is it?; **в 8 часо́в по моско́вскому** ~**ени** at 8 o'clock (by) Moscow time; ~ **до́ступа** (*КОМП*) access time; ~ **реализа́ции зака́за** (*КОММ*) lead time; **лу́чшее эфи́рное** ~ prime time; **хорошо́ проводи́ть** (**провести́** *perf*) ~ to have a good time; **вре́мя го́да** season; *см также* **времена́**.

времяисчисле́ни|е (-я) *ср* calendar.
времяпрепровожде́ни|е (-я) *ср* way of
spending time.
время́н|ка (-ки; *gen pl* -ок) *ж* (*печка*) makeshift
stove; (*жилище*) makeshift hut (*next to new
rural dwelling*).
вро́вень *нареч*: ~ с +*instr* level with.
вро́де *предл* (+*gen*) like ♦ *част* it looks as if; **он
у меня́ ~ сове́тника** he's like an advisor to me;
он ~ уе́хал it looks as if he's gone.
врождённый *прил* (*способности*) innate;
(*уродство, болезнь*) congenital.
врозь *нареч* (*жить*) apart; (*работать, ехать*)
separately ♦ *предл*: ~ с +*instr или от* +*gen* (*разг*)
separate from.
вро́ю *итп сов см* **врыть**.
вру *несов см* **врать**.
вруб|и́ть (-лю́, -ишь; *impf* **вруба́ть**) *сов перех*
(*разг: включить*) to turn on.
врун (-а́) *м* (*разг*) fibber.
вру́нь|я (-и) *ж см* **врун**.
вруч|и́ть (-у́, -и́шь; *impf* **вруча́ть**) *сов перех*: ~
что-н кому́-н to hand sth (over) to sb; (*орден,
премию*) to present sb with sth.
вручну́ю *нареч* (*разг*) by hand.
врыва́|ться (-юсь) *несов от* **ворва́ться**.
вр|ыть (-о́ю, -о́ешь; *impf* **врыва́ть**) *сов перех*
(*столб*) to sink in; (*дерево*) to plant firmly.
вряд *част*: ~ **ли** hardly; ~ **ли он согласи́тся**
he's hardly likely to agree.
ВС *мн сокр* (= *Вооружённые Си́лы*) armed forces
мн; (= *Верхо́вный Сове́т*) Supreme Soviet.
вса|ди́ть (-жу́, -дишь; *impf* **вса́живать**) *сов
перех*: ~ **в** +*acc* (*нож, стрелу*) to sink into;
вса́живать (~ *perf*) **пу́лю в лоб кому́-н** (*разг*)
to put a bullet in sb's head.
вса́дник (-а) *м* rider, horseman (*мн* horsemen).
вса́дниц|а (-ы) *ж* rider, horsewoman (*мн*
horsewomen).
вса́жива|ть (-ю) *несов от* **всади́ть**.
всажу́ *сов см* **всади́ть**.
вса́сыва|ть (-ю) *несов от* **всоса́ть**.
все *мест см* **весь**.

KEYWORD

всё (**всего́**) *мест см* **весь**
    ♦ *ср* (*как сущ: без исключения*) everything; **вот
и всё** that's all; **ча́ще всего́** most
often; **лу́чше всего́ написа́ть ей письмо́** it
would be best to write to her; **меня́ э́то волну́ет
ме́ньше всего́** that is the least of my worries;
мне всё равно́ it's all the same to me; **Вы
хоти́те чай и́ли ко́фе? – всё равно́** do you
want tea or coffee? – I don't mind; **я всё равно́
пойду́ туда́** I'll go there all the same
    ♦ *нареч* **1** (*разг: всё время*) all the time
2 (*разг: до сих пор*) still
3 (*только*) all; **э́то всё он винова́т** it's all his
fault

4 (*о нарастании признака*): **шум всё
уси́ливается** the noise keeps getting louder
5 (*о постоянстве признака*): **всё так же** still
the same; **всё там же** still there; **всё же** all the
same; **всё ещё** still.

всевла́сти|е (-я) *ср* absolute power.
всевозмо́ж|ный (-ен, -на, -но) *прил* all sorts of.
всегда́ *нареч* always.
всего́ *мест см* **весь**, **всё** ♦ *нареч* in all ♦ *част*
only; ~ **лишь** (*разг*) only; ~-**на́всего** (*разг*) all
in all.
вселе́нн|ая (-ой; *decl like adj*) *ж* the whole world;
В~ universe.
всел|и́ть (-ю́, -и́шь; *impf* **вселя́ть**) *сов перех*
(*жильцов*) to install; (*перен*) to instil (*BRIT*),
instill (*US*)
► **всели́ться** (*impf* **вселя́ться**) *сов возв*
(*жильцы*) to move in; (*перен*) to be instilled.
всем *мест см* **весь**, **всё**, **все**.
всеме́р|ный *прил* (*помощь*) all possible.
всемеро́м *нареч* in a group of seven.
все́ми *мест см* **все**.
всеми́рный *прил* worldwide; (*конгресс*) world
опред.
всемогу́щ|ий (-ая, -ее, -ие; -, -а, -е) *прил*
omnipotent, all-powerful.
всему́ *мест см* **весь**, **всё**.
всенаро́ден *прил см* **всенаро́дный**.
всенаро́дно *нареч* publicly.
всенаро́д|ный (-ен, -на, -но) *прил* national.
всено́щн|ая (-ой; *decl like adj*) *ж* (*РЕЛ*) vespers.
всео́буч (-а) *м сокр* (= *всео́бщее обуче́ние*)
general education.
всео́бщ|ий (-ая, -ее, -ие; -, -а, -е) *прил* universal;
всео́бщая забасто́вка/пе́репись general
strike/census.
всеобъе́млющ|ий (-ая, -ее, -ие; -, -а, -о) *прил*
comprehensive.
всеору́жи|е (-я) *ср*: **во** ~**и зна́ний** armed with
knowledge; (**встреча́ть** (**встре́тить** *perf*) **врага́
во** ~**и** to be primed for battle.
всеросси́йск|ий (-ая, -ое, -ие) *прил* All-Russia.
всерьёз *нареч* in earnest; **ты э́то говори́шь** ~?
are you serious?
всеси́ль|ный (-ен, -ьна, -ьно) *прил* all-
powerful.
всесторо́нн|ий (-яя, -нее, -ние; -ен, -ня, -не)
прил comprehensive.
всё-таки *част* still, all the same ♦ *союз*: **а** ~ all
the same, nevertheless; **мо́жет,** ~ **пое́дем?** can
we not still go?; **бы́ло ску́чно, и** ~ **я не ушёл** I
was bored, but all the same I didn't leave.
всеуслы́шание *ср*: **во** ~ publicly.
всех *мест см* **все**.
всеце́ло *нареч* completely.
всея́дный *прил* omnivorous.
вска́кива|ть (-ю) *несов от* **вскочи́ть**.
вска́пыва|ть (-ю) *несов от* **вскопа́ть**.

вскара́бка|ться (-юсь) *сов от* **кара́бкаться**.

вскачь *нареч* at a gallop; **пуска́ть** (**пусти́ть** *perf*) **коня́** ~ to break into a gallop.

вски́н|уть (-у, -ешь; *impf* **вски́дывать**) *сов перех* (*на плечи*) to shoulder; (*голову*) to jerk up; (*руки*) to throw up; **вски́дывать** (~ *perf*) **что-н на что-н** to throw sth on(to) sth; **вски́дывать** (~ *perf*) **глаза́ на кого́-н** to glance up at sb.

вскип|е́ть (-лю́, -и́шь; *impf* **кипе́ть**) *сов неперех* to boil; (*перен*) to flare up; ~ (*perf*) **от гне́ва** to fly into a rage.

вскипя|ти́ть(ся) (-чу́(сь), -ти́шь(ся)) *сов от* **кипяти́ть(ся)**.

вcклоко́ченный *прил* (*разг*) tousled.

всколыхн|у́ть (-у́, -ёшь) *сов перех* (*подлеж: ветер*) to stir; (*перен: массы*) to stir up.

▶ **всколыхну́ться** *сов возв* (*перен*) to become stirred up.

вскользь *нареч* in passing.

вскоп|а́ть (-ю; *impf* **вска́пывать**) *сов перех* to dig (over).

вско́ре *нареч* soon ◆ *предл*: ~ **по́сле** +*gen* soon *или* shortly after.

вскоч|и́ть (-у́, -ишь; *impf* **вска́кивать**) *сов неперех*: ~ **в/на** +*acc* (*на коня, в седло*) to leap up onto; **вска́кивать** (~ *perf*) (**на́ ноги**) to leap to one's feet.

вскри́кн|уть (-у, -ешь; *impf* **вскри́кивать**) *сов неперех* to cry out.

вскро́ю(сь) *итп сов см* **вскры́ть(ся)**.

вскруж|и́ть (-у́, -ишь) *сов перех*: ~ **го́лову кому́-н** to turn sb's head (*fig*).

вскрыва́|ть (-ю) *несов от* **вскрыть**.

вскры́ти|е (-я) *ср* (*трупа*) postmortem (examination); (*сейфа итп*) opening.

вскры́|ть (-о́ю, -о́ешь; *impf* **вскрыва́ть**) *сов перех* (*открыть*) to open; (: с силой) to force open; (*выявить*) to reveal; (*нарыв*) to lance; (*труп*) to carry out a postmortem on

▶ **вскры́ться** *сов возв* (*перен: выявиться*) to come to light, be revealed; **река́ ~ы́лась** the ice on the river cracked.

всласть *нареч* to one's heart's content.

вслед *нареч* (*бежать*) behind ◆ *предл*: ~ (**за** +*instr*) after; ~ +*dat* (*другу, поезду*) after.

всле́дстви|е *предл* (+*gen*) as a result of, because of ◆ *союз*: ~ **того́ что** because; ~ **чего́** as a result of which.

вслепу́ю *нареч* blindly; **печа́тать** (*impf*) **на маши́нке** ~ to touch-type.

вслух *нареч* aloud; **сказа́ть** (*perf*) **что-н** ~ to say sth out loud.

вслу́ша|ться (-юсь; *impf* **вслу́шиваться**) *сов возв*: ~ **в** +*acc* to listen carefully to.

ВСМ *м сокр* (= *Всеми́рный Сове́т Ми́ра*) World Peace Council.

всмотр|е́ться (-ю́сь, -ишься; *impf* **всма́триваться**) *сов возв*: ~ **в** +*acc* to peer at.

всмя́тку *нареч*: **яйцо́** ~ soft-boiled egg.

всо́выва|ть (-ю) *несов от* **всу́нуть**.

всос|а́ть (-у́, -ёшь; *impf* **вса́сывать**) *сов перех* (*втянуть*) to suck; (*впитать*) to absorb.

вспа́рхива|ть (-ю) *несов от* **вспорхну́ть**.

вспа|ха́ть (-шу́, -шешь) *сов от* **паха́ть**.

вспе́н|иться (-юсь, -ишься) *сов от* **пе́ниться**.

всплеск (-а) *м* (*волны*) splash.

всплесн|у́ть (-у́, -ёшь; *impf* **всплёскивать**) *сов неперех* (*рыба, пловец*) to splash; ~ (*perf*) **рука́ми** to throw up one's hands.

всплыва́|ть (-ю) *несов от* **всплыть**.

всплыву́ *итп сов см* **всплыть**.

всплы́ти|е (-я) *ср* surfacing.

всплы́|ть (-ву́, -вёшь; *pt* -л, -ла́, -ло, *impf* **всплыва́ть**) *сов неперех* to surface, come to the surface; (*перен*) to come to light; **всплыва́ть** (~ *perf*) **в па́мяти** to pop into one's head; **всплыва́ть** (~ *perf*) **в созна́нии** to appear before one.

всполош|и́ть(ся) (-у́(сь), -и́шь(ся)) *сов от* **полоши́ть(ся)**.

вспо́мн|ить (-ю, -ишь; *impf* **вспомина́ть**) *сов перех* to remember ◆ *неперех*: ~ **о** +*prp* to remember about.

вспомога́тельный *прил* (*материал, литература*) supplementary; (*судно, отряд*) auxiliary; **вспомога́тельный глаго́л** auxiliary verb.

вспорхн|у́ть (-у́, -ёшь; *impf* **вспа́рхивать**) *сов неперех* to fly off.

вспоте́|ть (-ю) *сов от* **поте́ть**.

вспры́сн|уть (-у, -ешь; *impf* **вспры́скивать**) *сов перех* to spray.

вспугн|у́ть (-у́, -ёшь; *impf* **вспу́гивать**) *сов перех* to scare away *или* off.

вспу́хн|уть (-у, -ешь) *сов от* **пу́хнуть** ◆ (*impf* **вспуха́ть**) *неперех* to swell up.

вспу́ч|иться (3*sg* -ится, 3*pl* -атся) *несов от* **пу́читься**.

вспыл|и́ть (-ю́, -и́шь) *сов неперех* to lose one's temper.

вспы́льчивост|ь (-и) *ж* short-temperedness.

вспы́льчив|ый (-, -а, -о) *прил* short-tempered.

вспы́хн|уть (-у, -ешь; *impf* **вспы́хивать**) *сов неперех* (*солома, бумага*) to burst into flames; (*спичка, конфликт, страсть*) to flare up; (*покраснеть: человек*) to blush; **в окне́ ~ул свет** the window lit up.

вспы́ш|ка (-ки; *gen pl* -ек) *ж* flash; (*энтузиазма*) burst; (*гнева*) outburst; (*болезни*) outbreak.

вспять *нареч* back.

ВСРФ *мн сокр* = **вооружённые си́лы росси́йской федера́ции**.

встава́|ть (-ю; *imper* -ва́й(те)) *несов от* **встать** ◆ *неперех*: **рабо́тать/писа́ть не** ~**ва́я** to work/write without a break.

вста́в|ить (-лю, -ишь; *impf* **вставля́ть**) *сов перех* to insert, put in; **вставля́ть** (~ *perf*) **зу́бы** to have a set of dentures *или* false teeth made; **вставля́ть** (~ *perf*) **ка́мень в опра́ву** to set a stone.

вста́в|ка (-ки; *gen pl* -ок) *ж* insertion; (*в одежде*) inset.

вста́влю *сов см* **вста́вить**.

вставля́ть (-ю) *несов от* **вста́вить**.

вставн|о́й *прил* (*рамы*) removable; **~ы́е зу́бы** dentures, false teeth.

вста́вок *сущ см* **вста́вка**.

вста|ть (-ну, -нешь; *impf* **встава́ть**) *сов неперех* (*на ноги*) to stand up; (*с постели*) to get up; (*солнце*) to rise; (*трудности, вопрос*) to arise; (*no impf; разг*: *часы, мотор*) to stop; **пе́ред на́ми вста́ли но́вые тру́дности** we were faced with new difficulties.

встопо́рщ|ить(ся) (-у(сь), -ишь(ся)) *сов от* **топо́рщить(ся)**.

встрева́|ть (-ю) *несов неперех* (*разг*: *вмешиваться*) to stick one's oar in.

встрево́жен|ный (-, -а, -о) *прил* anxious.

встрево́ж|ить(ся) (-у(сь), -ишь(ся)) *несов от* **трево́жить(ся)**.

встрепену́ться (-у́сь, -ёшься) *сов возв* to give a start.

встре́|тить (-чу, -тишь; *impf* **встреча́ть**) *сов перех* to meet; (*гостей, делега́цию итп*) to meet, welcome; (*обнаружить: слово, цита́ту*) to come across; (*оппози́цию, сопротивле́ние*) to meet with, encounter; (*праздник итп*) to celebrate.

▸ **встре́|титься** (*impf* **встреча́ться**) *сов возв*: **~ся** (**с** +*instr*) to meet; (*перен: с сопротивле́нием итп*) to meet with, encounter; **мне ~тились друзья́/интере́сные фа́кты** I came across some friends/interesting facts.

встре́ч|а (-и) *ж* meeting; (*поеди́нок*) match.

встреча́|ть (-ю) *несов от* **встре́тить**

▸ **встреча́ться** *несов от* **встре́титься** ♦ *возв* (*регуля́рно ви́деться*) to meet; (*попада́ться*) to be found.

встре́чн|ый *прил* (*маши́на, по́езд итп*) oncoming; (*ме́ра*) counter *опред* ♦ (**-ого**; *decl like adj*) *м someone coming from the opposite direction*; **~ ве́тер** head wind; **пе́рвый ~** (*разг*) anyone; **встре́чная ата́ка** counterattack; **встре́чный иск** counterclaim.

встре́чу(сь) *сов см* **встре́тить(ся)**.

встря́с|ка (-ки; *gen pl* -ок) *ж* (*потрясе́ние*) shock; (*систе́мы*) upheaval.

встряхн|у́ть (-у́, -ёшь; *impf* **встря́хивать**) *сов перех* to shake (out); (*перен: о́бщество*) to shake (up).

вступа́|ть(ся) (-ю(сь)) *несов от* **вступи́ть(ся)**.

вступи́тельный *прил* (*речь, статья́*) introductory; **вступи́тельный взнос** subscription fee; **вступи́тельный экза́мен** entrance exam.

вступ|и́ть (-лю́, -ишь; *impf* **вступа́ть**) *сов неперех*: **~ в** +*acc* to enter; (*в па́ртию, в о́бщество*) to join; (*в спор, в перегово́ры*) to enter into; **вступа́ть** (**~** *perf*) **на** +*acc* to mount;

вступа́ть (**~** *perf*) **в бой** to join battle

▸ **вступи́ться** (*impf* **вступа́ться**) *сов возв*: **~ся за** +*acc* to stand up for.

вступле́ни|е (-я) *ср* (*войск: в го́род*) entry; (*в па́ртию*) joining; (*в ста́дию*) entering; (*в кни́ге, в статье́*) introduction; (*в бесе́де*) preamble.

вступлю́ *сов см* **вступи́ть**.

всу́н|уть (-у, -ешь; *impf* **всо́вывать**) *сов перех*: **~** (**в** +*acc*) to stick *или* put in(to).

всухомя́тку *нареч*: **пита́ться ~** *to live off cold snacks*; **есть** (*impf*) **хлеб ~** to eat dry bread.

всуч|и́ть (-у́, -ишь; *impf* **всу́чивать**) *сов перех* (*навяза́ть*) to palm off.

всхлип (-а) *м* sob.

всхли́пыва|ть (-ю) *несов неперех* to sob.

всходи́ть (-жу́, -дишь) *несов от* **взойти́**.

всхо́д|ы (-ов) *мн* shoots *мн*.

всхожу́ *сов см* **всходи́ть**.

всы́п|ать (-лю, -лешь; *impf* **всыпа́ть**) *сов перех*: **~ в** +*acc* to pour into ♦ *неперех*: **~ кому́-н** (*разг*: *отчита́ть*) to give sb what for.

всю *мест см* **вся**.

всю́ду *нареч* everywhere.

вс|я (**-ей**) *мест см* **весь**.

вся́к|ий (**-ая, -ое, -ие**) *мест* (*ка́ждый*) every; (*разнообра́зный*) all kinds of; (*любо́й*) any ♦ (**-ого**; *decl like adj*) *м* (*любо́й*) anyone; (*ка́ждый*) everyone; **здесь продаю́т ~ие това́ры** all kinds of goods are sold here; **у меня́ пропа́ло ~ое жела́ние помо́чь** I have lost all desire to help; **без ~ого сомне́ния/интере́са/жела́ния** without the slightest doubt/interest/desire; **безо ~ого** *или* **~их согласи́ться** (*perf*)/**приня́ть** (*perf*) (*разг*) to agree/accept without a second thought.

вся́ко *нареч* (*разг*) all sorts of things.

вся́чески *нареч* in every possible way.

вся́ческ|ий (**-ая, -ое, -ие**) *мест* (*подде́ржка, сопротивле́ние*) all possible; (*това́ры*) all kinds of.

вся́чин|а (-ы) *ж* (*разг*): **вся́кая ~** all sorts of things.

Вт *сокр* (= *ватт*) W (= *watt*).

вта́йне *нареч* secretly, in secret.

вта́лкива|ть (-ю) *несов от* **втолкну́ть**.

вта́птыва|ть (-ю) *несов от* **втопта́ть**.

втащ|и́ть (-у́, -ишь; *impf* **вта́скивать**) *сов перех*: **~** (**в** +*acc*) to drag in(to).

втёк *итп сов см* **втечь**.

втека́|ть (*3sg* -ет, *3pl* -ют) *несов от* **втечь**.

втеку́т *сов см* **втечь**.

втере́ть (вотру́, вотрёшь; *pt* втёр, втёрла, втёрло, *impf* **втира́ть**) *сов перех*: **~** (**в** +*acc*) to rub in(to)

▸ **втере́ться** (*impf* **втира́ться**) *сов возв* to be absorbed; (*разг*: *пренебр*) to worm one's way in; **~ся** (*perf*) **в дове́рие кому́-н** to worm one's way into sb's confidence.

вте|чь (*3sg* -чёт, *3pl* -кут, *pt* втёк, -кла, -кло, *impf* **втекать**) *сов неперех*: ~ **в** +*acc* to flow into.

втира́ть(ся) (-ю(сь)) *несов от* **втере́ть(ся)**.

вти́сн|уть (-у, -ешь; *impf* **вти́скивать**) *сов перех*: ~ **(в** +*acc*) to cram in(to)

▸ **вти́снуться** *сов возв* (*разг*) (*impf* **вти́скиваться**): ~**ся (в** +*acc*) (*человек*) to squeeze in(to).

втихомо́лку *нареч* (*разг*) on the quiet.

втолкн|у́ть (-у́, -ёшь; *impf* **вта́лкивать**) *сов перех*: ~ **(в** +*acc*) to push in(to).

втолк|ова́ть (-у́ю; *impf* **втолко́вывать**) *сов перех* (*разг*): ~ **что-н кому́-н** to get sth through to sb.

втоп|та́ть (-чу́, -чешь; *impf* **вта́птывать**) *сов перех*: ~ **(в** +*acc*) to trample in(to); **вта́птывать** (~ *perf*) **кого́-н в грязь** (*перен*) to humiliate sb.

втор|а́я (-о́й; *decl like adj*) *ж*: **одна́** ~ one half.

вто́рг|нуться (-усь, -ешься; *impf* **вторга́ться**) *сов возв*: ~ **в** +*acc* (*в страну*) to invade; (*вмешаться*) to interfere with *или* in.

вто́р|ить (-ю, -ишь) *несов неперех* (+*dat*; *петь*) to sing the second part to; (*разг*: *поддакивать*) to parrot.

вто́рник (-а) *м* Tuesday; **во** ~ on Tuesday; **по** ~**ам** on Tuesdays; **в сле́дующий/про́шлый** ~ next/last Tuesday; **сего́дня** ~, **деся́тое ма́я** today is Tuesday (the) 10th (of) May.

второго́дник (-а) *м pupil repeating a year at school*.

второго́дниц|а (-ы) *ж см* **второго́дник**.

втор|о́е (-о́го; *decl like adj*) *ср* main course; **на** ~ – **бифште́кс** the main course is steak.

втор|о́й (-а́я, -о́е, -ы́е) *прил* second; (*роль*) secondary; **быть** (*impf*) **на** ~**о́м пла́не** to stay in the background; **сейча́с** ~**час** it's after one; **сейча́с полови́на** ~**о́го** it's half past one; **второ́е дыха́ние** second wind; **втора́я мо́лодость** second wind; **второ́й сорт** second class; *см также* **пя́тый**.

второкла́ссник (-а) *м pupil in second year at school* (*usually eight years old*).

второкла́ссниц|а (-ы) *ж см* **второкла́ссник**.

второпя́х *нареч* in a hurry.

второсо́рт|ный (-ен, -на, -но) *прил* second-class; (*посредственный*) second-rate.

второстепе́н|ный (-ен, -на, -но) *прил* secondary.

в-тре́тьих *вводн сл* thirdly, in the third place.

втри́дорога *нареч* (*разг*): **плати́ть** ~ to pay a mint *или* bomb.

втро́е *нареч* (*больше, меньше*) three times; (*увеличить*) threefold.

втроём *нареч* in a group of three.

втройне́ *нареч* three times as much.

втул|ка (-ки; *gen pl* -ок) *ж* (*пробка*) plug; (*тех*) bush.

втыка́|ть (-ю) *несов от* **воткну́ть**.

втян|у́ть (-у́, -ешь; *impf* **втя́гивать**) *сов перех* (*втащить*) to pull in; (*вобрать*) to take in; **втя́гивать** (~ *perf*) **кого́-н в** +*acc* (*перен*: *в дело*) to involve sb in; (: *в конфликт итп*) to draw sb into

▸ **втяну́ться** (*impf* **втя́гиваться**) *сов возв*: ~**ся в** +*acc* to get involved in; (*привыкнуть*) to settle into.

вуали́р|овать (-ую; *perf* **завуали́ровать**) *несов перех* to veil.

вуа́л|ь (-и) *ж* veil.

вуз (-а) *м сокр* (= *вы́сшее уче́бное заведе́ние*) institution of higher education.

ву́зовск|ий (-ая, -ое, -ие) *прил* university *опред*; ~**ая систе́ма** higher education system.

вулка́н (-а) *м* volcano; **де́йствующий/поту́хший** ~ active/extinct volcano.

вульга́рен *прил см* **вульга́рный**.

вульга́рность (-и) *ж* vulgarity.

вульга́р|ный (-ен, -на, -но) *прил* (*человек, слова*) vulgar.

вундерки́нд (-а) *м* child prodigy.

вход (-а) *м* (*движение*) entry; (*место*) entrance; (*тех*) inlet; (*комп*) input.

вхо|ди́ть (-жу́, -дишь) *несов от* **войти́**.

входно́й *прил* (*дверь*) entrance *опред*; (*комп*) input *опред*; **входно́й биле́т** entrance ticket.

входя́щий (-ая, -ее, -ие) *прил* incoming.

вхожу́ *сов см* **входи́ть**.

вхолосту́ю *нареч*: **рабо́тать** ~ to idle.

вцеп|и́ться (-лю́сь, -ишься; *impf* **вцепля́ться**) *сов возв*: ~ **в** +*acc* to seize.

ВЦСПС *м сокр* (= *Всеросси́йский Центра́льный Сове́т профессиона́льных сою́зов*) *central trade-union council*.

ВЧ *ж сокр* (= *высо́кая частота́*) HF (= *high frequency*) ◆ *прил* (*высокочасто́тный*) HF (= *high-frequency*).

вчера́ *нареч, м нескл* yesterday.

вчера́шн|ий (-яя, -ее, -ие) *прил* (*также перен*) yesterday's; **жить** (*impf*) ~**им днём** to live in the past.

вчерне́ *нареч* in rough.

вче́тверо *нареч* (*больше, меньше*) four times; (*увеличить*) fourfold.

вчетверо́м *нареч* in a group of four.

в-четвёртых *нареч* fourthly, in the fourth place.

вчита́|ться (-юсь; *impf* **вчи́тываться**) *сов возв*: ~ **(в** +*acc*) to get the gist (of).

вшей(те) *сов см* **вшить**.

вше́стеро *нареч* (*больше, меньше*) six times; (*увеличить*) sixfold.

вшестеро́м *нареч* in a group of six.

вши *итп сущ см* **вошь**.

вшива́|ть (-ю) *несов от* **вшить**.

вши́ве|ть (-ю; *perf* **завши́веть**) *несов неперех* to become lice-ridden.

вши́вый *прил* lice-ridden.

вширь *нареч* in breadth; **раздава́ться** (**разда́ться** *perf*) ~ to put on weight.

вшить (**вошью́, вошьёшь**; *imper* **вшей(те)**, *impf*

вшива́ть) *сов перех* to sew in.
въеда́ться (-юсь) *несов сов от* въе́сться.
въе́дешь *итп сов см* въе́хать.
въе́дливый (-, -а, -о) *прил* meticulous.
въе́ду *итп сов см* въе́хать.
въедя́тся *сов см* въе́сться.
въезд (-а) *м (движение)* entry; *(место)* entrance.
въездно́й *прил* entry *опред*.
въезжа́ть (-ю) *несов от* въе́хать.
въе́сться (*3sg* -стся, *3pl* -дя́тся, *impf* въеда́ться) *сов возв*: ~ в +*acc (кислота, ржавчина)* to eat into; *(краска, грязь)* to become ingrained in.
въе́хать (*как* е́хать; *см* **Table 19**; *impf* въезжа́ть) *сов неперех* to enter; *(в новый дом)* to move in; *(наверх: на машине)* to drive up; *(: на коне, велосипеде)* to ride up.
вы- *префикс (in verbs; об исчерпанности действия) indicating completion of action eg.* вы́яснить, вы́спаться; *(о движении ианутри) indicating movement outwards eg.* вы́бежать.
Вы (Вас; *см* **Table 5b**) *мест* you; быть *(impf)* на ~ с кем-н to be on formal terms with sb.
вы (вас; *см* **Table 5b**) *мест* you *(plural)*.
вы́бежать (*как* бежа́ть; *см* **Table 20**; *impf* выбега́ть) *сов неперех* to run out.
вы́бей(те) *сов см* вы́бить.
вы́бел|ить (-ю, -ишь) *сов от* бели́ть.
вы́беру(сь) *итп сов см* вы́брать(ся).
выбива́|ть(ся) (-ю(сь)) *несов от* вы́бить(ся).
выбира́|ть (-ю) *несов от* вы́брать ♦ *перех*: ~ слова́ to choose one's words
▸ выбира́ться *несов от* вы́браться.
вы́би|ть (-ью, -ьешь; *imper* вы́бей(те), *impf* выбива́ть) *сов перех* to knock out; *(противника)* to oust; *(ковер)* to beat; *(надпись)* to carve; *(разг: деньги, контракт)* to manage to get; выбива́ть *(~ perf)* чек *(кассир)* to ring up the total; выбива́ть *(~ perf)* чек в ка́ссе *(покупатель)* to get a ticket from the cashier *(to claim purchase)*
▸ вы́биться (*impf* выбива́ться) *сов возв*: ~ся из +*gen (освободиться)* to get out of; выбива́ться *(~ся perf)* из сил to wear o.s. out; выбива́ться *(~ся perf)* из гра́фика to fall behind schedule; *(~ся perf)* в лю́ди to make one's way up in the world.
вы́боин|а (-ы) *ж (на дороге)* pothole; *(на металле, в стене)* dent.
вы́бор (-а) *м* choice; *(ассортимент)* choice, selection; предлага́ть (предложи́ть *perf)* что-н на ~ to offer a selection of sth; по чьему́-н ~у of sb's choice.
вы́бор|ка (-ки; *gen pl* -ок) *ж (обычно мн: из текста)* extract; *(статистическая)* sample.
вы́борный *прил (собрание, кампания)* election

опред; *(бюллетень)* ballot *опред*; *(должность, орган)* elective.
вы́борок *сущ см* вы́борка.
вы́бороч|ный (-ен, -на, -но) *прил* selective.
вы́борщик (-а) *м (полит)* ≈ elector *(US)*, *elected representative taking part in elections on a higher level.*
вы́бор|ы (-ов) *мн* election *ед*.
выбра́сыва|ть(ся) (-ю(сь)) *несов от* вы́бросить(ся).
вы́б|рать (-еру, -ерешь; *impf* выбира́ть) *сов перех* to choose; *(отобрать)* to pick; *(голосованием)* to elect
▸ вы́браться (*impf* выбира́ться) *сов возв* to manage to get out; *(разг: в театр)* to find time to go.
вы́бр|ить (-ею, -еешь; *impf* выбрива́ть) *сов перех* to shave.
вы́бро|дить (-жу, -дишь) *сов от* броди́ть.
вы́брос (-а) *м (газа, радиации)* emission; *(отходов)* discharge; *(нефти)* spillage; *(десанта)* landing.
вы́бро|сить (-шу, -сишь; *impf* выбра́сывать) *сов перех* to throw out; *(разг: с работы)* to sack; *(отходы)* to discharge; *(газы)* to emit; *(десант)* to land; выбра́сывать *(~ perf)* на ры́нок to bring onto the market
▸ вы́броситься (*impf* выбра́сываться) *сов возв (из окна)* to throw o.s. out; выбра́сываться *(~ся perf)* с балко́на to throw o.s. off the balcony; выбра́сываться *(~ся perf)* с парашю́том to bale out.
вы́быть (*как* быть; *см* **Table 21**; *impf* выбыва́ть) *сов неперех*: ~ из +*gen* to leave.
вы́бью *итп сов см* вы́бить.
вы́вал|ить (-ю, -ишь; *impf* выва́ливать) *перех*: ~ *(из +gen)* to empty (out of)
▸ вы́валиться (*impf* выва́ливаться) *сов возв (выпасть)* to fall out; *(разг: толпа)* to pour out.
выведе́ни|е (-я) *ср (формулы)* deduction; *(цыплят, птенцов)* hatching; *(сорта, породы)* breeding; *(вредителей)* extermination.
вы́веду(сь) *итп сов см* вы́вести(сь).
вы́ве|зти (-зу, -зешь; *impf* вывози́ть) *сов перех* to take; *(товар: из страны)* to take out.
вы́вер|ить (-ю, -ишь; *impf* выверя́ть) *сов перех* to check; *(часы)* to set *(to the right time).*
вы́верн|уть (-у, -ешь; *impf* выверя́ть или вывора́чивать) *сов перех (винт, лампу)* to unscrew; *(пробку)* to pull out; *(карманы, рукава)* to turn inside out
▸ вы́вернуться (*impf* вывёртываться или вывора́чиваться) *сов возв (винт, лампа)* to come unscrewed; *(пробка)* to come out; *(человек: из беды)* to get out.
выверя́|ть (-ю) *несов от* вы́верить.
вы́ве|сить (-шу, -сишь; *impf* выве́шивать) *сов перех (флаг, лозунг)* to put up; *(бельё)* to hang

out; (*объявление*) to post (up).

вы́вес|ка (-ки; *gen pl* -ок) ж sign; (*перен*) front; **под⊝кой чего́-н** under the guise of sth.

вы́ве|сти (-ду, -дешь; *impf* **выводи́ть**) *сов перех* to take out; (*войска: из го́рода*) to pull out; (: *на пара́д*) to bring out; (*форму́лу*) to deduce; (*заключе́ние*) to draw; (*птенцо́в*) to hatch; (*сорт, поро́ду*) to breed; (*вреди́телей*) to exterminate; (*КОМП*) to output; (*изобрази́ть*) to portray; (*исключи́ть*): ~ **кого́-н из** +*gen* (*из па́ртии, из комите́та*) to expel sb from; (*из игры́*) to take sb off; **выводи́ть** (~ *perf*) **кого́-н из шо́ка/из тра́нса** to bring sb out of a shock/trance; **выводи́ть** (~ *perf*) **кого́-н из терпе́ния** to exasperate sb; **выводи́ть** (~ *perf*) **кого́-н из равнове́сия** to disturb sb's equilibrium; **выводи́ть** (~ *perf*) **кого́-н в лю́ди** to help sb on in life; **выводи́ть** (~ *perf*) **кого́-н из себя́** to drive sb mad.

▸ **вы́вестись** (*impf* **выводи́ться**) *сов возв* (*цыпля́та*) to hatch (out); (*исче́знуть*) to be eradicated.

вы́ветр|иться (*3sg* -ится, *3pl* -ятся, *impf* **выве́триваться**) *сов возв* (*запах, дым*) to disperse; (*бе́рег, го́рные поро́ды*) to weather.

выве́шива|ть (-ю) *несов см* **вы́весить**.

вы́вешу *сов см* **вы́весить**.

вы́вих (-а) *м* dislocation.

вы́вихн|уть (-у, -ешь; *impf* **вы́вихивать**) *сов перех* to dislocate.

вы́вод (-а) *м* (*войск: из го́рода*) withdrawal; (*форму́лы*) deduction; (*умозаключе́ние*) conclusion; (*ЭЛЕК*) outlet; (*КОМП*) output; **приходи́ть** (**прийти́** *perf*) **к** ~**у** to come to a conclusion.

выводи́ть(ся) (-вожу́(сь), -во́дишь(ся)) *несов от* **вы́вести(сь)**.

вы́вод|ок (-ка) *м* brood.

вывожу́(сь) *несов см* **выводи́ть(ся)**, **вы́возить**.

вы́воз (-а) *м* removal; (*дете́й: на да́чу*) taking out; (*това́ров*) export.

вы́воз|ить (-вожу́, -во́зишь) *несов от* **вы́везти**.

вывозно́й *прил* export *опред*.

вывора́чива|ть(ся) (-ю(сь)) *несов от* **вы́вернуть(ся)**.

вы́гада|ть (-ю; *impf* **выга́дывать**) *сов перех* (*получи́ть преиму́щество*) to gain; (*сэконо́мить*) to save.

вы́гиб (-а) *м* curve.

выгиба́|ть (-ю) *несов от* **вы́гнуть**.

вы́глад|ить (-жу, -дишь) *сов от* **гла́дить**.

выгля|де́ть (-жу, -дишь) *несов неперех* to look; **она́ хорошо́** ~**дит сего́дня** she looks nice today; **он** ~**дит печа́льным** he looks sad.

выгля́дыва|ть (-ю) *несов от* **вы́глянуть**.

вы́гляжу *несов см* **вы́глядеть**.

вы́глян|уть (-у, -ешь; *impf* **выгля́дывать**) *сов неперех* to look out.

вы́г|нать (-оню, -онешь; *impf* **выгоня́ть**) *сов*

out; (*из страны́*) to banish; (*разг: с рабо́ты*) to sack; (*ста́до, табу́н*) to drive out.

вы́гн|уть (-у, -ешь; *impf* **выгиба́ть**) *сов перех* to bend; (*спи́ну*) to arch.

выгова́рива|ть (-ю) *несов от* **вы́говорить**.

вы́говор (-а) *м* (*произноше́ние*) accent; (*за прови́нность*) reprimand; **де́лать** (**сде́лать** *perf*) ~ **кому́-н за что́-н** to tell sb off for sth; **выноси́ть** (**вы́нести** *perf*) ~ **кому́-н** to issue sb with a reprimand.

вы́говор|ить (-ю, -ишь; *impf* **выгова́ривать**) *сов перех* (*произнести́*) to pronounce; (*сказа́ть*) to say

▸ **вы́говориться** *сов возв* (*разг*) to say what's on one's mind.

вы́год|а (-ы) *ж* advantage, benefit; (*при́быль*) profit; **кака́я ему́ от э́того** ~? what does he hope to gain from this?

вы́годно *нареч* (*прода́ть*) at a profit ◆ *как сказ* it is profitable; **мне э́то** ~ this is to my advantage; (*фина́нсово*) this is profitable for me.

вы́год|ный (-ен, -на, -но) *прил* (*сде́лка*) profitable; (*усло́вия*) advantageous; (*впечатле́ние*) favourable (*BRIT*), favorable (*US*); **выставля́ть** (**вы́ставить** *perf*) **и́ли представля́ть** (**предста́вить** *perf*) **что́-н в** ~**ном све́те** to show sth to (the) best advantage.

вы́гоню *итп сов см* **вы́гнать**.

выгоня́|ть (-ю) *несов от* **вы́гнать**.

вы́гор|еть (*3sg* -ит, *3pl* -ят, *impf* **выгора́ть**) *сов неперех* (*сгоре́ть*) to burn down; (*вы́сохнуть*) to be scorched; (*вы́цвести*) to fade; (*разг: удава́ться*) to come off.

вы́горо|дить (-жу, -дишь; *impf* **выгора́живать**) *сов перех* (*разг*) to fence off.

вы́гравир|овать (-ую) *несов от* **гравирова́ть**.

вы́гре|сти (-бу, -бешь; *pt* -б, -ла, -ло, *impf* **выгреба́ть**) *сов перех* to rake out.

вы́гру|зить (-жу, -зишь; *impf* **выгружа́ть**) *сов перех* to unload; (*КОМП*) to dump

▸ **вы́грузиться** (*impf* **выгружа́ться**) *сов возв* to unload; (*вы́садиться*) to disembark; (: *из по́езда*) to get off.

выдава́|ть (-ю) *несов от* **вы́дать**

▸ **выдава́ться** *несов от* **вы́даться** ◆ *возв*: ~**ся чем-н** to stand out by virtue of sth.

вы́дав|ить (-лю, -ишь; *impf* **выда́вливать**) *сов перех* (*лимо́н*) to squeeze; (*я́годы*) to press; (*дверь*) to break down; **выда́вливать** (~ *perf*) **что́-н из чего́-н** to squeeze sth out of sth.

вы́да|ть (*как* **дать**; *см* **Table 14**; *impf* **выдава́ть**) *сов перех* to give out; (*свиде́тельство, пате́нт итп*) to issue; (*проду́кцию*) to produce; (*та́йну, соо́бщников*) to give away; **выдава́ть** (~ *perf*) **кого́-н/что́-н за** +*acc* to pass sb/sth off as; **выдава́ть** (~ *perf*) **де́вушку за́муж** to marry a girl off

▸ **вы́даться** (*impf* **выдава́ться**) *сов возв* (*бе́рег*) to jut out; **сего́дня** ~**лся хоро́ший день** (*разг*) it's turned out fine today.

вы́дач|а (-и) *ж* (*справки*) issue; (*зарплаты*) payment; (*продукции*) output; (*заложников*) release.

вы́дашь(ся) *сов см* **вы́дать(ся)**.

выдаю́щийся (-аяся, -ееся, -иеся) *прил* outstanding.

выдвига́ть(ся) (-ю(сь)) *несов от* **вы́двинуть(ся)**.

выдвиже́ни|е (-я) *ср* (*кандидата*) nomination; (*предложения*) proposal.

выдвижно́й *прил* sliding.

вы́двин|уть (-у, -ешь; *impf* **выдвига́ть**) *сов перех* to pull out; (*предложение, гипотезу, человека*) to put forward; (*обвинение*) to level

▶ **вы́двинуться** (*impf* **выдвига́ться**) *сов возв* to slide out; (*работник*) to get ahead, advance; **выдвига́ться** (~**ся** *perf*) **на руководя́щую рабо́ту** to be promoted to a management position.

выдвор|и́ть (-ю, -ишь; *impf* **выдворя́ть**) *сов перех* (*разг*) to kick out.

вы́дела|ть (-ю; *impf* **вы́делывать**) *сов перех* to treat.

выделе́ни|е (-я) *ср* (*средств*) allocation; (*ФИЗИОЛОГИЯ*) secretion; (*обычно мн: в гинекологии*) discharge.

выдел|и́ть (-ю, -ишь; *impf* **выделя́ть**) *сов перех* to assign, allocate; (*время*) to allot; (*отличить: ученика, цитату*) to pick out; (*пот*) to secrete; (*газы, вредные вещества*) to emit

▶ **вы́делиться** (*impf* **выделя́ться**) *сов возв* (*в отдельное предприятие*) to split off; (*пот*) to be secreted; (*газ, вредные вещества*) to be emitted; **выделя́ться** (~**ся** *perf*) **чем-н** to stand out by virtue of sth.

вы́дел|ка (-и) *ж* treatment.

вы́де́лыва|ть (-ю) *несов от* **вы́делать** ◆ *перех* (*разг: вытворять*) to get up to; **что э́то он там** ~**ет?** what is he up to?

выделя́ть(ся) (-ю(сь)) *несов от* **вы́делить(ся)**.

выдёргива|ть (-ю) *несов от* **вы́дернуть**.

вы́держан|ный (-, -на, -но) *прил* (*человек*) self-possessed; (*no short form; изложение, теория*) consistent; (*вино, сыр*) mature; (*древесина*) seasoned.

вы́держ|ать (-у, -ишь; *impf* **выде́рживать**) *сов перех* (*давление, тяжесть*) to withstand; (*боль*) to bear; (*экзамен, испытание*) to get through; (*график, параметры*) to keep to; (*вино, сыр*) to let mature; (*древесину*) to season ◆ *неперех*: **он не** ~**ал и рассмея́лся** he couldn't contain his laughter; **кни́га** ~**ала мно́го изда́ний** the book has been published in several editions; **выде́рживать** (~ *perf*) **хара́ктер** to hold one's ground.

вы́держек *сущ см* **вы́держка**.

выде́ржива|ть (-ю) *несов от* **вы́держать**.

вы́держ|ка (-ки; *gen pl* -ек) *ж* (*самообладание*) self-control; (*из текста*) excerpt; (*вина*) maturing; (*древесины*) seasoning; (*ФОТО*) exposure.

вы́дерн|уть (-у, -ешь; *impf* **выдёргивать**) *сов перех* to pull out.

вы́деру *итп сов см* **вы́драть**.

выдира́|ть (-ю) *несов от* **вы́драть**.

вы́долб|ить (-лю, -ишь) *сов от* **долби́ть**.

вы́дох (-а) *м* exhalation; **де́лать** (**сде́лать** *perf*) ~ to breathe out.

вы́дохн|уть (-у, -ешь; *impf* **выдыха́ть**) *сов перех* to exhale, breathe out

▶ **вы́дохнуться** (*impf* **выдыха́ться**) *сов возв* (*вино, духи*) to lose all smell; (*разг*) to be washed out.

вы́др|а (-ы) *ж* otter.

вы́дра|ить (-ю, -ишь) *сов от* **дра́ить**.

вы́др|ать (-еру, -ерешь) *сов от* **драть** ◆ (*impf* **выдира́ть**) *перех* (*разг: вырвать*) to tear out.

вы́дрессир|овать (-ую) *сов от* **дрессирова́ть**.

вы́дуб|ить (-лю, -ишь) *несов от* **дуби́ть**.

выдува́|ть (-ю) *несов от* **вы́дуть**.

вы́думанный *прил* made-up.

вы́дума|ть (-ю; *impf* **выду́мывать**) *сов перех* (*историю*) to make up, invent; (*игру*) to invent.

вы́дум|ка (-ки; *gen pl* -ок) *ж* invention.

выду́мыва|ть (-ю) *несов от* **вы́думать**.

вы́ду|ть (-ю; *impf* **выдува́ть**) *сов перех* to blow out; (*разг: водку итп*) to knock back; (*impf* **выдува́ть** *или* **дуть**, *ТЕХ*) to blow.

выдыха́ни|е (-я) *ср* exhalation.

выдыха́|ть(ся) (-ю(сь)) *несов от* **вы́дохнуть(ся)**.

выеда́|ть (-ю) *несов от* **вы́есть**.

вы́еду *итп сов см* **вы́ехать**.

вы́езд (-а) *м* (*отъезд*) departure; (*место*) way out.

вы́езд|ить (-жу, -дишь; *impf* **выезжа́ть**) *сов перех* (*лошадь*) to break in.

вы́езд|ка (-и) *ж* (*СПОРТ*) dressage.

выездно́й *прил* (*виза, документ*) exit *опред*; (*сессия суда*) in temporary premises; (*спектакль*) travelling (*BRIT*), traveling (*US*); ~ **матч** away match.

выезжа́|ть (-ю) *несов от* **вы́ехать**.

вы́езжу *сов см* **вы́ездить**.

вы́ем|ка (-ки; *gen pl* -ок) *ж* (*писем*) collection; (*грунта*) excavation; (*углубление*) hollow.

вы́есть (*как* **есть**; *см* **Table 15**; *impf* **выеда́ть**) *сов перех* (*съесть*) to eat; (*испортить*) to eat through.

вы́е|хать (*как* **е́хать**; *см* **Table 19**; *impf* **выезжа́ть**) *сов непeрех* (*уехать*) to leave; (*машина, танк*) to drive out; (*всадник*) to ride out; **выезжа́ть** (~ *perf*) **на ком-н/чём-н** (*перен: разг*) to use sb/sth.

вы́ж|ать (-му, -мешь; *impf* **выжима́ть**) *сов перех* (*лимон*) to squeeze; (*ягоды*) to press; (*бельё*) to wring (out); **выжима́ть** (~ *perf*) **что-н из чего-н** to squeeze sth out of sth; **выжима́ть** (~ *perf*) **что-н из кого-н** (*перен*) to wring sth out of sb.

вы́жгу *итп сов см* **вы́жечь.**

вы́жд|ать (-у, -ёшь; *impf* **выжида́ть**) *сов перех*: ~ **подходя́щий моме́нт** to pick one's moment.

вы́ж|ечь (-гу, -жешь *итп* -гут; *pt* -ег, -гла, -гло, *impf* **выжига́ть**) *сов перех* (*подлеж*: *солнце*) to scorch; **выжига́ть** (~ *perf*) **клеймо́** to brand; **выжига́ть** (*impf*) **по де́реву** to do pokerwork.

выжива́ни|е (-я) *ср* survival.

выжива́|ть (-ю) *несов от* **вы́жить.**

вы́живу *итп сов см* **вы́жить.**

выжига́|ть (-ю) *несов от* **вы́жечь.**

выжида́|тельный (-ен, -ьна, -ьно) *прил* (*тактика, политика*) delaying; **занима́ть** (**заня́ть** *perf*) ~**ьную пози́цию** to play a waiting game.

выжида́|ть (-ю) *несов от* **вы́ждать.**

выжима́|ть (-ю) *несов от* **вы́жать.**

вы́жи|ть (-ву, -вешь; *impf* **выжива́ть**) *сов неперех* to survive ♦ *перех* (*разг*) to drive out; ~ (*perf*) **из ума́** to become senile.

вы́жму *итп сов см* **вы́жать.**

вы́з|вать (-ову, -овешь; *impf* **вызыва́ть**) *сов перех* to call; (*гнев, критику*) to provoke; (*восторг*) to arouse; (*пожар*) to cause; **вызыва́ть** (~ *perf*) **кого-н на что-н** to challenge sb to sth; **вызыва́ть** (~ *perf*) **что-н к жи́зни** to give rise to sth; **вызыва́ть** (~ *perf*) **врача́ на́ дом** to call out a doctor

▸ **вы́з|ваться** (*impf* **вызыва́ться**) *сов возв*: ~**ся** +*infin* to volunteer to do.

вы́зво|лить (-ю, -ишь; *impf* **вызволя́ть**) *сов перех* (*разг*) to bale out.

вы́здорове|ть (-ю, -ишь; *impf* **выздора́вливать**) *сов неперех* to recover.

вы́зов (-а) *м* call; (*в суд, к дире́ктору*) summons; ~ +*dat* (*обществу, роди́телям итп*) challenge to; **броса́ть** (**бро́сить** *perf*) ~ **кому́-н/чему́-н** to challenge sb/sth.

вы́зову(сь) *сов см* **вы́звать(ся).**

вы́зубр|ить (-ю, -ишь) *сов от* **зубри́ть.**

вызыва́|ть(ся) (-ю(сь)) *несов от* **вы́звать(ся).**

вызыва́|ющий (-ая, -ее, -ее) *прил* provocative.

вы́игра|ть (-ю; *impf* **выи́грывать**) *сов перех* to win ♦ *неперех* (*получи́ть вы́году*) to gain, benefit.

вы́игрыш (-а) *м* (*ма́тча*) winning; (*кру́пный, де́нежный*) winnings *мн*; (*вы́года*) advantage; ~ **пал на но́мер 10** number 10 wins.

вы́игрыш|ный (-ен, -на, -но) *прил* (*вы́годный*) advantageous; ~ **вклад** ≈ premium bonds.

вы́йти (*как* **идти́;** *см* **Table 18;** *impf* **выходи́ть**) *сов неперех* to leave; (*из игры́*) to drop out; (*сойти́*) to get off; (*появи́ться*) to come out; (*случи́ться*) to ensue; (*КОМП*) to exit; (*исся́кнуть*) to run out; (*оказа́ться*): ~ +*instr* to

come out; **выходи́ть** (~ *perf*) **из** +*gen* (*из затрудне́ния*) to get out of; (*из употребле́ния, из мо́ды*) to go out of; (*из крестья́н*) to be descended from; (*из гра́фика, из расписа́ния*) to fall behind; **выходи́ть** (~ *perf*) **на** +*acc* (*разг*) to get in with; **выходи́ть** (~ *perf*) **за́муж за** +*acc* to marry (*of woman*), get married to; **выходи́ть** (~ *perf*) **из больни́цы** to leave hospital; **выходи́ть** (~ *perf*) **из себя́** to lose one's temper; **выходи́ть** (~ *perf*) **из систе́мы** (*КОМП*) to log off; **из него́** ~**шел хоро́ший врач** he has turned out to be a good doctor; **из э́того ничего́ не** ~**шло** nothing came of it.

выка́пыва|ть (-ю) *несов от* **вы́колоть.**

выка́пыва|ть (-ю) *несов от* **вы́копать.**

вы́карабка|ться (-юсь; *impf* **выкара́бкиваться**) *сов возв*: ~ (**из** +*gen*) to clamber out (of); (*разг: из тру́дностей*) to get o.s. out (of); (: *из боле́зни*) to pull through.

выка́рмлива|ть (-ю) *несов от* **вы́кормить.**

вы́ка|тить (-чу, -тишь; *impf* **выка́тывать**) *сов перех* (*что-н кру́глое*) to roll out; (*что-н на колеса́х*) to wheel out; **выка́тывать** (~ *perf*) **глаза́** (*разг*) to open one's eyes wide.

вы́кача|ть (-ю; *impf* **выка́чивать**) *сов перех* to pump out; (*перен: разг: де́ньги*) to squeeze *или* wring out.

вы́качу *сов см* **вы́катить.**

выка́шива|ть (-ю) *несов от* **вы́косить.**

выки́дыва|ть (-ю) *несов от* **вы́кинуть.**

вы́кидыш (-а) *м* miscarriage.

вы́кин|уть (-у, -ешь; *impf* **выки́дывать**) *сов перех* (*му́сор*) to throw out; (*пропусти́ть*) to omit; (*разг: това́р*) to put on sale; **выки́дывать** (~ *perf*) **шу́тку** *или* **фо́кус** (*разг*) to play a trick.

вы́кип|еть (*3sg* -ит, *3pl* -ят, *impf* **выкипа́ть**) *сов неперех* to boil away.

вы́клад|ка (-ки; *gen pl* -ок) *ж* (*облицо́вка*) facing; (*обы́чно мн: расчёты*) calculation.

выкла́дыва|ть(ся) (-ю(сь)) *несов от* **вы́ложить(ся).**

выключа́тел|ь (-я) *м* switch.

вы́ключ|ить (-у, -ишь; *impf* **выключа́ть**) *сов перех* to turn off; (*исключи́ть*) to expel

▸ **вы́ключ|иться** (*impf* **выключа́ться**) *сов возв* (*мо́тор, телеви́зор итп*) to go off; (*свет*) to go out; (*перен*) to switch off.

выкля́нчи|ть (-у, -ишь) *сов от* **кля́нчить.**

вы́к|овать (-ую; *impf* **выко́вывать**) *сов перех* (*мета́лл*) to forge.

выкола́чива|ть (-ю) *несов от* **вы́колотить.**

вы́коло|тить (-чу, -тишь; *impf* **выкола́чивать**) *сов перех* (*ковёр*) to beat; (*нало́ги*) to wring out.

вы́кол|оть (-ю, -ешь; *impf* **выка́пывать**) *сов перех* to poke out.

вы́колочу *сов см* **вы́колотить.**

вы́копа|ть (-ю; *impf* **выка́пывать** *или* **копа́ть**) *сов перех* (*я́му*) to dig; (*коло́дец*) to sink; (*о́вощи*) to dig up.

вы́корм|ить (-лю, -ишь; *impf* **выка́рмливать**) *сов перех* to rear.

вы́корч|евать (-ую; *impf* **выкорчёвывать** *или* **корчева́ть**) *сов перех* to uproot; *(перен)* to root out.

вы́ко|сить (-шу, -сишь; *impf* **выка́шивать**) *сов перех* to mow.

выкра́дыва|ть (-ю) *несов от* **вы́красть**.

выкра́ива|ть (-ю) *несов перех* to cut out.

вы́кра|сить(ся) (-шу(сь), -сишь(ся)) *сов от* **кра́сить(ся)**.

вы́кра|сть (-ду, -дешь; *impf* **выкра́дывать**) *сов перех* to steal.

вы́крик (-а) *м* shout.

вы́крикн|уть (-у, -ешь; *impf* **выкри́кивать**) *сов перех* to shout *или* cry out.

вы́кристаллиз|ова́ться (*3sg* -уется, *3pl* -уются) *сов от* **кристаллизова́ться**.

вы́кроек *сущ см* **вы́кройка**.

вы́кро|ить (-ю, -ишь) *сов от* **крои́ть** ♦ (*impf* **выкра́ивать**) *перех* (*перен*): ~ **вре́мя на** +*acc* to find time for; ~ (*perf*) **де́ньги на** +*acc* to scrape together money for.

вы́кройка (-йки; *gen pl* -ек) *ж* pattern.

выкрута́с|ы (-ов) *мн* (*разг: в танце*) fancy footwork *ед*; (*перен: в речи*) fancy turns *мн* of phrase; (: *в поведении*) foibles *мн*.

вы́кру|тить (-чу, -тишь; *impf* **выкру́чивать**) *сов перех* to unscrew; **выкру́чивать** (~ *perf*) **ру́ки кому́-н** (*также перен*) to twist sb's arm

▶ **вы́крутиться** *сов возв* to come unscrewed; (*перен*) to get o.s. out.

вы́куп (-а) *м* (*действие: заложника*) ransoming; (: *вещей*) redemption; (*плата*) ransom.

вы́купа|ть(ся) (-ю(сь)) *несов от* **купа́ть(ся)**.

вы́куп|ить (-лю, -ишь; *impf* **выкупа́ть**) *сов перех* (*заложника*) to ransom; (*вещи*) to redeem.

вы́кур|ить (-ю, -ишь; *impf* **выку́ривать**) *сов перех* (*трубку*) to smoke; (*зверя*) to smoke out.

выла́влива|ть (-ю) *несов от* **вы́ловить**.

вы́лаз|ка (-ки; *gen pl* -ок) *ж* (*воен*) sortie.

выла́мыва|ть (-ю) *несов от* **вы́ломать**.

вылеза́|ть (-ю) *несов от* **вы́лезти**.

вы́лез|ти (-у, -ешь; *pt* -, -ла, -ло, *impf* **вылеза́ть**) *сов неперех* (*волосы, шерсть*) to fall out; **вылеза́ть** (~ *perf*) (**из** +*gen*) to climb out (of); (*разг: из долгов*) to get o.s. out (of); (: *из болезней*) to pull through; (: *рубашка*) to hang out.

вы́леп|ить (-лю, -ишь) *сов от* **лепи́ть**.

вы́лет (-а) *м* departure.

вы́ле|теть (-чу, -тишь; *impf* **вылета́ть**) *сов неперех* to fly out; (*машина*) to hurtle out; **его́ и́мя ~тело у меня́ из головы́** his name has slipped my mind.

вы́леч|ить (-у, -ишь; *impf* **вылечивать** *или* **лечи́ть**) *сов перех* to cure

▶ **вы́лечиться** (*impf* **вылечиваться** *или* **лечи́ться**) *несов возв* to be cured.

вы́лечу *сов см* **вы́лететь**.

вылива́|ть(ся) (-ю(сь)) *несов от* **вы́лить(ся)**.

вы́ли|зать (-жу, -жешь; *impf* **выли́зывать**) *сов перех* (*тарелку*) to lick clean; (*разг: дом*) to spring-clean.

вы́л|ить (-ью, -ьешь; *impf* **вылива́ть**) *сов перех* to pour out; (*impf* **лить**; *деталь, статую*) to cast

▶ **вы́литься** (*impf* **вылива́ться**) *сов возв* (*также перен*) to pour out; **вылива́ться** (~*ся perf*) **в** +*acc* to turn into.

вы́лов|ить (-лю, -ишь; *impf* **выла́вливать**) *сов перех* to catch.

вы́лож|ить (-у, -ишь; *impf* **выкла́дывать**) *сов перех* to lay out; (*перен: правду*) to lay bare; **выкла́дывать** (~ *perf*) **что-н чем-н** (*кирпичом, плиткой*) to face sth with sth

▶ **вы́ложиться** (*impf* **выкла́дываться**) *сов возв* to apply o.s.

вы́лома|ть (-ю) *impf* **выла́мывать**) *сов перех* to break open.

вы́луп|иться (*3sg* -ится, *3pl* -ятся, *impf* **вылу́пливаться**) *сов возв* (*птенцы*) to hatch (out).

вы́лью(сь) *итп сов см* **вы́лить(ся)**.

вы́ма|зать (-жу, -жешь) *сов от* **ма́зать** ♦ (*impf* **выма́зывать**) *перех* (*покрыть*) to coat; (*разг: запачкать*) to smear

▶ **вы́мазаться** *сов от* **ма́заться**.

выма́лива|ть (-ю) *несов от* **вы́молить**.

выма́нива|ть (-ю, -ешь; *impf* **вы́манить**) *сов перех* (*зверя*) to lure out; **выма́нивать** (~ *perf*) **что-н у кого́-н** to cheat sb out of sth.

вы́мара|ть(ся) (-ю(сь)) *сов от* **мара́ть(ся)**.

выма́чива|ть (-ю) *несов от* **вы́мочить**.

вы́мени *итп сущ см* **вы́мя**.

вы́м|ереть (*3sg* -рет, *3pl* -рут, *impf* **вымира́ть**) *сов неперех* (*динозавры*) to die out, become extinct; (*город, селение*) to be dead.

вы́ме|сти (-ту, -тешь; *pt* -л, -ла, -ло, *impf* **вымета́ть**) *сов перех* to sweep out.

вы́ме|стить (-щу, -стишь; *impf* **вымеща́ть**) *сов перех*: ~ **что-н на ком-н** to take sth out on sb.

вымета́|ть (-ю) *несов от* **вы́мести**.

вы́мету *итп сов см* **вы́мести**.

вымеща́|ть (-ю) *несов от* **вы́местить**.

вымещу́ *сов см* **вы́местить**.

вымира́|ть (*3sg* -ет, *3pl* -ют) *несов от* **вы́мереть**.

вымога́тел|ь (-я) *м* extortionist.

вымога́тельств|о (-а) *ср* extortion.

вымога́|ть (-ю) *несов перех* to extort.

вы́мок|нуть (-ну, -нешь; *pt* -, -ла, -ло) *сов неперех* to get soaked through.

вы́молв|ить (-лю, -ишь) *сов перех* to utter.

вы́мол|ить (-ю, -ишь; *impf* **выма́ливать**) *сов перех* to successfully plead for.

вы́мо|стить (-щу, -стишь) *сов от* **мости́ть**.

вы́моч|ить (-у, -ишь; *impf* **выма́чивать**) *сов*

перех to soak.

вы́мощу *сов см* **вы́мостить**.

вы́мою *итп сов см* **вы́мыть**.

вы́мпел (-а) *м* (*на мачте корабля*) pennant; (*награда*) award (*in the form of a pennant*).

вы́мрет *итп сов см* **вы́мереть**.

вы́муштр|овать (-ую) *сов от* **муштрова́ть**.

вымыва́ть (-ю) *несов от* **вы́мыть**.

вы́мыс|ел (-ла) *м* fantasy; (*ложь*) fabrication.

вы́м|ыть (-ою, -оешь; *impf* **мыть**) *сов перех* to wash; (*impf* **вымыва́ть**; *яму*) to hollow out; (*русло*) to channel out.

вы́мышлен|ный (-, -на, -но) *прил* fictitious.

вы́м|я (-ени; *как* **вре́мя**; *см* **Table 4**) *ср* udder.

вына́шива|ть (-ю) *несов от* **вы́носить**.

вы́нес|ти (-у, -ешь; *pt* -, -ла, -ло, *impf* **выноси́ть**) *сов перех* to carry *или* take out; (*приговор, вердикт*) to pass, pronounce; (*впечатления, знания*) to gain; (*боль, оскорбление*) to bear; **выноси́ть** (~ *perf*) **кому́-н благода́рность** to officially thank sb; **выноси́ть** (~ *perf*) **кому́-н вы́говор** to issue sb with a reprimand

▶ **вы́нестись** (*impf* **выноси́ться**) *сов возв* to fly *или* rush out.

вынима́|ть (-ю) *несов от* **вы́нуть**.

вы́нос (-а) *м* (*тела*) bearing out (*of coffin*); **продава́ть** (*impf*) **на** ~ to do take-aways.

вы́но|сить (-шу, -сишь; *impf* **вына́шивать**) *сов перех* (*перен*) to nurture; (*младенца*) to carry to term.

вын|оси́ть (-ошу, -о́сишь) *несов от* **вы́нести** ◆ *перех*: **я его́ не** ~**ошу́** I can't bear *или* stand him

▶ **выноси́ться** *несов от* **вы́нестись**.

выносли́в|ый (-, -а, -о) *прил* hardy.

вы́ношу *сов см* **вы́носить**.

выношу́(сь) *несов см* **выноси́ть(ся)**.

вы́ну|дить (-жу, -дишь; *impf* **вынужда́ть**) *сов перех*: ~ **кого́-н/что-н к чему́-н** to force sb/sth into sth; **вынужда́ть** (~ *perf*) **кого́-н/что-н** +*infin* to force sb/sth into doing.

вы́нужденный *прил* forced; **вы́нужденная поса́дка** emergency landing.

вы́нужу *сов см* **вы́нудить**.

вы́н|уть (-у, -ешь; *impf* **вынима́ть**) *сов перех* to take out.

вы́нырн|уть (-у, -ешь; *impf* **выны́ривать**) *сов неперех* (*из воды*) to surface; (*разг: из-за угла*) to pop up.

вы́пад (-а) *м* (*враждебное действие*) attack; (*СПОРТ*) lunge (*in fencing*).

выпада́|ть (-ю) *несов от* **вы́пасть**.

выпаде́ни|е (-я) *ср* (*осадков*) fall; (*зубов, волос*) falling out.

вы́паду *итп сов см* **вы́пасть**.

вы́пал|ить (-ю, -ишь) *сов* **пали́ть** ◆ (*impf* **выпа́ливать**) *перех* (*перен: разг*) to blurt out.

вы́пар|иться (*3sg* -ится, *3pl* -ятся, *impf* **выпа́риваться**) *сов возв* to evaporate.

вы́па|сть (-ду, -дешь; *impf* **выпада́ть**) *сов неперех* to fall out; (*осадки*) to fall; (+*dat*;

задание, задача итп) to fall to; **мне** ~**л слу́чай/сча́стье встре́тить его́** I chanced to/ had the luck to meet him.

вы́пачка|ть(ся) (-ю(сь)) *сов от* **па́чкать(ся)**.

вы́пей(те) *сов см* **вы́пить**.

выпека́|ть (-ю) *несов от* **вы́печь**.

вы́пеку *итп сов см* **вы́печь**.

вы́п|ереть (-ру, -решь; *pt* -ер, -ерла, -ерло, *impf* **выпира́ть**) *сов перех* (*разг*) to chuck out.

вы́пест|овать (-ую) *сов от* **пе́стовать**.

вы́печк|а (-и) *ж* baking.

выпечн|о́й *прил*: ~**ые изде́лия** bakery products *мн*.

вы́печь (-ку, -чешь *итп*, -кут; *impf* **выпека́ть**) *сов перех* to bake.

вы́пивк|а (-и) *ж* (*разг: попойка*) boozing ◆ *собир* (*спиртное*) booze.

выпира́|ть (-ю) *несов от* **вы́переть** ◆ *неперех* (*разг: выпячиваться*) to stick out.

вы́пи|сать (-шу, -шешь; *impf* **выпи́сывать**) *сов перех* (*цитату, данные*) to copy *или* write out; (*пропуск, счёт, рецепт*) to make out; (*газету, журнал*) to subscribe to; (*пациента*) to discharge; (*с местопроживания*) to change sb's residence permit

▶ **вы́писаться** (*impf* **выпи́сываться**) *несов возв* (*из больницы*) to be discharged; (*с место-проживания*) to change one's residence permit.

вы́пис|ка (-ки; *gen pl* -ок) *ж* (*действие*) copying *или* writing out; (*цитата*) extract; ~ **с ба́нковского счёта** bank statement.

выпи́сыва|ть(ся) (-ю(сь)) *несов от* **вы́писать(ся)**.

вы́п|ить (-ью, -ьешь; *imper* -ей(те)) *сов от* **пить**.

вы́пишу(сь) *итп сов см* **вы́писать(ся)**.

вы́плав|ить (-лю, -ишь; *impf* **выплавля́ть**) *сов перех* to smelt.

вы́плав|ка (-ки; *gen pl* -ок) *ж* (*действие*) smelting; (*продукция*) smelted metal.

вы́плавлю *сов см* **вы́плавить**.

выплавля́|ть (-ю) *несов от* **вы́плавить**.

вы́плавок *сущ см* **вы́плавка**.

вы́плат|а (-ы) *ж* payment.

вы́пла|тить (-чу, -тишь; *impf* **выпла́чивать**) *сов перех* to pay; (*долг*) to pay off.

выплёвыва|ть (-ю) *несов от* **вы́плюнуть**.

вы́плесн|уть (-у, -ешь; *impf* **выплёскивать**) *сов перех* to pour out.

вы́пл|ыть (-ву, -вешь; *impf* **выплыва́ть**) *сов неперех* to swim out; (*всплыть*) to surface; (*перен*) to emerge, come to light.

вы́плюн|уть (-у, -ешь; *impf* **выплёвывать**) *сов перех* to spit out.

вы́полз|ти (-у, -ешь; *pt* -, -ла, -ло, *impf* **выполза́ть**) *сов неперех* to crawl out.

выполни́м|ый (-, -а, -о) *прил* practicable, feasible.

вы́полн|ить (-ю, -ишь; *impf* **выполня́ть**) *сов перех* (*задание, заказ*) to carry out; (*план, условие*) to fulfil (*BRIT*), fulfill (*US*); (*рисунок,*

чертёж) to execute; (*КОМП*) to run.
вы́полоскать (-ю) *сов от* полоска́ть.
вы́пол|оть (-ю, -ешь) *сов от* поло́ть.
вы́пор|оть (-ю, -ешь) *сов от* поро́ть.
вы́порхн|уть (-у, -ешь) *сов неперех* to dart out.
вы́потрош|ить (-у, -ишь) *сов от* потроши́ть.
вы́прав|ить (-лю, -ишь; *impf* выправля́ть) *сов перех* (*расспрямить*) to straighten (up); (*текст, чертёж*) to correct; (*положение, ситуацию*) to rectify, put right
▶ **вы́правиться** (*impf* выправля́ться) *несов возв* (*что-н кривое*) to straighten (out); (*положение, ситуация*) to be rectified.
вы́прав|ка (-ки; *gen pl* -ок) *ж* bearing.
вы́правлю(сь) *сов см* вы́править(ся).
вы́правля́|ть(ся) (-ю(сь)) *несов от* вы́править(ся).
вы́правок *сущ см* вы́правка.
выпра́шива|ть (-ю) *несов перех* to beg for.
вы́про|сить (-шу, -сишь) *сов перех*: **он ~сил у отца́ маши́ну** he persuaded his father to give him the car.
вы́пру *итп сов см* вы́переть.
вы́прыгн|уть (-у, -ешь; *impf* выпры́гивать) *сов неперех* to jump out.
вы́прям|ить (-лю, -ишь; *impf* выпрямля́ть) *сов перех* to straighten (out)
▶ **вы́прямиться** (*impf* выпрямля́ться) *несов возв* to straighten (up).
выпрямля́|ть(ся) (-ю(сь)) *несов от* вы́прямить(ся).
вы́пуклый *прил* (*лоб, глаза итп*) bulging; (*стекло, линза*) convex; (*буква*) embossed.
вы́пуск (-а) *м* (*продукции*) output; (*газа, воздуха*) emission, release; (*книги*) instalment (*BRIT*), installment (*US*); (*денег, марок, акций*) issue; (*учащиеся*) school leavers *мн* (*BRIT*), graduates *мн* (*US*).
выпуска́|ть (-ю) *несов от* вы́пустить.
выпускни́к (-а́) *м* final-year student; (*окончивший вуз*) graduate.
выпускни́ца (-ы) *ж см* выпускни́к.
выпускн|о́й *прил* (*класс*) final-year; (*ТЕХ*): ~ **кла́пан** exhaust valve; ~**о́е отве́рстие** outlet; **выпускно́й ве́чер** graduation; **выпускно́й экза́мен** final exam, finals *мн*.
вы́пу|стить (-щу, -стишь; *impf* выпуска́ть) *сов перех* to let out; (*дым*) to exhale; (*заключённого, заложника*) to release; (*специалистов*) to turn out; (*продукцию*) to produce; (*книгу, газету итп*) to publish; (*заём, марки*) to issue; (*деньги*) to put into circulation; (*исключить: часть текста, параграф*) to omit; **выпуска́ть** (~ *perf*) (**из рук**) to let go of; **выпуска́ть** (~ *perf*) **в свет** (*книгу, журнал*) to publish; **выпуска́ть** (~ *perf*) **возмо́жность/шанс** to miss an opportunity/a chance; **выпуска́ть** (~ *perf*) **кого́-н/что-н из**

ви́ду to let sb/sth out of sight.
выпу́та|ться (-юсь; *impf* выпу́тываться) *сов возв* (*также перен*) to extricate o.s.
выпу́тыва|ться (-юсь) *несов от* вы́путаться.
вы́пущу *сов см* вы́пустить.
вы́пью *итп сов см* вы́пить.
вы́пя|тить (-чу, -тишь; *impf* выпя́чивать) *сов перех* (*разг: грудь*) to stick out; **выпя́чивать** (~ *perf*) **губу́** to pout.
вы́работа|ть (-ю; *impf* выраба́тывать) *сов перех* to produce; (*план*) to work out; (*характер, стиль, привычку*) to develop.
вы́работ|ка (-ки; *gen pl* -ок) *ж* (*действие*) production; (*годовая, промышленная*) output, production; (*продукты*) yield.
выра́внива|ть(ся) (-ю(сь)) *несов от* вы́ровнять(ся).
выража́|ть (-ю) *несов от* вы́разить
▶ **выража́ться** *несов от* вы́разиться ◆ *возв* (*разг*) to swear.
выраже́ни|е (-я) *ср* expression.
вы́ражу(сь) *сов см* вы́разить(ся).
вырази́тельно *нареч* (*читать*) expressively.
вырази́тел|ьный (-ен, -ьна, -ьно) *прил* expressive.
вы́ра|зить (-жу, -зишь; *impf* выража́ть) *сов перех* to express
▶ **вы́разиться** (*impf* выража́ться) *сов возв* (*чувство, состояние*) to manifest *или* express itself; (*человек*) to express o.s.
выраста́|ть (-ю) *несов от* вы́расти.
вы́р|асти (-асту, -астешь; *pt* -ос, -осла, -осли) *сов от* расти́ ◆ (*impf* выраста́ть) *неперех* (*горы, башня*) to rise up; **выраста́ть** (~ *perf*) **в** +*acc* to become; **выраста́ть** (~ *perf*) **из оде́жды** to grow out of one's clothes.
вы́раст|ить (-у, -ишь; *impf* выра́щивать) *сов перех* (*детей*) to raise; (*растение*) to grow; (*животных*) to rear.
выра́щивани|е (-я) *ср* (*растений*) cultivation; (*животных*) rearing.
выра́щива|ть (-ю) *несов от* вы́растить.
вы́ращу *сов см* вы́растить.
вы́рв|ать (-у, -ешь; *impf* вырыва́ть) *сов перех* to pull out; (*отнять*): ~ **что-н у кого́-н** to snatch sth from sb; (*перен*) to wring sth from sb ◆ (*impf* рвать) *безл* (*разг*): **её ~ало** she threw up; **ему́ ~али зуб** he had his tooth taken out
▶ **вы́рваться** (*impf* вырыва́ться) *сов возв* (*из объятий*) to free o.s.; (*из рук, из пут*) to break free, escape; (*из тюрьмы*) to make a break; (*перен: в театр, на концерт*) to manage to get away; (*пламя*) to shoot out; (*дым*) to pour out.
вы́режу *итп сов см* вы́резать.
вы́рез (-а) *м*: **пла́тье с больши́м ~ом** a low-cut dress.
вы́ре|зать (-жу, -жешь; *impf* выреза́ть) *сов перех* (*фотографию итп*) to cut out; (*опухоль,*

гно́йник) to remove; (*из де́рева, из ко́сти итп*) to carve; (*на ка́мне, на мета́лле итп*) to engrave; (*население, живо́тных*) to slaughter.

вы́рез|ка (-ки; *gen pl* -ок) ж (*газе́тная*) cutting, clipping; (*мясна́я*) fillet.

вы́рис|ова́ться (3sg -у́ется, 3pl -у́ются, *impf* **вырисо́вываться**) *сов возв* (*стать ви́дным*) to stand out; (*стать я́вным*) to appear; (*перен: ситуа́ция*) to emerge.

вы́ровня́ть (-ю) *сов от* **ровня́ть** ♦ (*impf* **выра́внивать**) *перех* to level

▶ **вы́ровня́ться** (*impf* **выра́вниваться**) *сов возв* (*отря́д*) to form ranks; (*перен: хара́ктер*) to improve.

вы́род|иться (3sg -ится, 3pl -ятся, *impf* **вырожда́ться**) *сов возв* (*та́кже перен*) to degenerate.

вы́род|ок (-ка) м (*разг*) degenerate.

вырожда́|ться (-юсь) *несов от* **вы́родиться**.

вырожде́ни|е (-я) *ср* degeneration.

вы́рон|ить (-ю, -ишь) *сов перех* to drop.

вы́рос *итп сов см* **вы́расти**.

вы́рост (-а) м: **шить/покупа́ть оде́жду на ~** (*разг*) to make/buy clothes with room for growth.

вы́рою *итп сов см* **вы́рыть**.

выруба́|ть (-ю) *несов от* **вы́рубить**.

вы́руб|ить (-лю, -ишь; *impf* **выруба́ть**) *сов перех* (*лес, дере́вья*) to cut down; (*я́му, углубле́ние*) to hew out; (*свет, сигнализа́цию*) to cut off.

вы́руга|ть(ся) (-ю(сь)) *сов от* **руга́ть(ся)**.

вы́руч|ить (-у, -ишь; *impf* **выруча́ть**) *сов перех* to rescue, help out; (*де́ньги*) to make; **выруча́ть** (~ *perf*) **кого́-н из беды́** to help sb out of trouble.

вы́руч|ка (-и) ж rescue; (*де́ньги*) takings мн; **приходи́ть** (**прийти́** *perf*) **на ~у кому́-н** to come to sb's rescue.

вырыва́|ть(ся) (-ю(сь)) *несов от* **вы́рвать(ся)**, **вы́рыть**.

вы́р|ыть (-ою, -оешь) *сов от* **рыть** ♦ (*impf* **вырыва́ть**) *перех* (*карто́фель, ка́мень итп*) to dig up.

вы́са|дить (-жу, -дишь; *impf* **выса́живать**) *сов перех* (*расте́ние*) to plant out; (*пассажи́ра: дать вы́йти*) to drop off; (: *заста́вить вы́йти*) to throw out; (*войска́, отря́д*) to land; ~ (*perf*) **деса́нт** to make a landing

▶ **вы́садиться** (*impf* **выса́живаться**) *сов возв*: ~**ся (из** +*gen*) to get off.

выса́сыва|ть (-ю) *несов от* **вы́сосать**.

высве́чивани|е (-я) *ср* (*КОМП*) highlighting.

вы́свобо|дить (-жу, -дишь; *impf* **высвобожда́ть**) *сов перех* (*но́гу, ру́ку*) to free; (*рабо́чую си́лу, сре́дства*) to release; (*вре́мя*) to set aside.

вы́сек *итп сов см* **вы́сечь**.

высека́|ть (-ю) *несов от* **вы́сечь**.

вы́секу *итп сов см* **вы́сечь**.

вы́сел|ить (-ю, -ишь; *impf* **выселя́ть**) *сов перех* to evict.

вы́се|чь (-ку, -чешь итп, -кут; *pt* -к, -кла, -кло) *сов от* **сечь** ♦ (*impf* **высека́ть**) *перех* (*фигу́ру*) to carve, sculpt; (*на́дпись*) to engrave.

вы́си|деть (-жу, -дишь; *impf* **выси́живать**) *сов перех* to hatch; (*перен: ле́кцию*) to sit out.

вы́с|иться (3sg -ится, 3pl -ятся) *несов возв* to tower.

выска́блива|ть (-ю) *несов от* **вы́скоблить**.

вы́ска|зать (-жу, -жешь; *impf* **выска́зывать**) *сов перех* to express; **я ему́ всё ~зал** I told him exactly what I thought

▶ **вы́сказаться** (*impf* **выска́зываться**) *сов возв* to speak one's mind; **выска́зываться** (~**ся** *perf*) **про́тив** +*gen*/**за** +*acc* to speak out against/in favour of.

выска́зывани|е (-я) *ср* (*мне́ния*) expression; (*сужде́ние*) statement.

выска́зыва|ть(ся) (-ю(сь)) *несов от* **вы́сказать(ся)**.

выска́кива|ть (-ю) *несов от* **вы́скочить**.

выска́льзыва|ть (-ю) *несов от* **вы́скользнуть**.

вы́скоб|лить (-ю, -ишь; *impf* **выска́бливать**) *сов перех* (*очи́стить*) to scrape; (*удали́ть скобле́нием*) to remove.

вы́скользн|уть (-у, -ешь; *impf* **выска́льзывать**) *сов непере́х* (*та́кже перен*) to slip out.

вы́скоч|ить (-у, -ишь; *impf* **выска́кивать**) *сов непере́х* to jump out; **его́ и́мя ~ило у меня́ из головы́** (*разг*) his name has slipped my mind.

вы́скоч|ка (-ки; *gen pl* -ек) м/ж (*разг: пренебр*) upstart.

вы́сла|ть (-шлю, -шлешь; *impf* **высыла́ть**) *сов перех* (*посы́лку, де́ньги*) to send off; (*полит*) to exile; (*шпио́на*) to deport.

вы́сле|дить (-жу, -дишь; *impf* **высле́живать**) *сов перех* to track down.

вы́слуг|а (-и) ж: **за ~у лет** for long service.

вы́служ|ить (-у, -ишь; *impf* **высл́уживать**) *сов перех* (*пе́нсию, повыше́ние*) to qualify for; (*о́рден, награ́ду*) to earn

▶ **вы́служиться** *сов возв* to work one's way up.

вы́слуша|ть (-ю; *impf* **выслу́шивать**) *сов перех* to hear out.

вы́сме|ять (-ю; *impf* **высме́ивать**) *сов перех* to ridicule.

вы́сморка|ть (-ю) *сов от* **сморка́ть** ♦ *перех*: ~ **нос** to blow one's nose

▶ **вы́сморкаться** *сов от* **сморка́ться**.

высо́выва|ть(ся) (-ю(сь)) *несов от* **вы́сунуть(ся)**.

высо́к|ий (-ая, -ое, -ие; -, -а́, -о́) *прил* high; (*челове́к*) tall; (*честь, отве́тственность*) great; (*гость*) distinguished; **быть** (*impf*) **~ого мне́ния о** +*prp* to have a high opinion of; **высо́кая вода́** high tide.

высоко́ *нареч* high (up) ♦ *как сказ* it's high (up), it's a long way up; **до верши́ны ~** it is a long way to the top.

высокого́рный *прил* alpine.

высококáчественный *прил* high-quality.
высококвалифици́рованный *прил* (*учитель, юрист*) highly qualified; (*слесарь, токарь*) highly skilled.
высокомéрен *прил см* **высокомéрный**.
высокомéри|**е** (-я) *ср* haughtiness, arrogance.
высокомéр|**ный** (-ен, -на, -но) *прил* haughty, arrogant.
высокоопла́чиваемый *прил* highly paid.
высокопа́р|**ный** (-ен, -на, -но) *прил* (*речь*) high-flown, pompous.
высокопоста́вленный *прил* high-ranking.
высокопроизводи́тельный (-ен, -ьна, -ьно) *прил* highly productive.
вы́сос|**ать** (-у, -ешь; *impf* **выса́сывать**) *сов перех* to suck out; (*насосом*) to pump out.
высот|**а́** (-оты́; *nom pl* -о́ты) *ж* height; (*ГЕО*) altitude; (*звука*) pitch; (*давления, температуры*) level; **набира́ть** (**набра́ть** *perf*) ~**оту́** to climb, gain height; **на большо́й** ~**оте́** at a high altitude *или* great height; **быть** (*impf*) *или* **оказа́ться** (*perf*) **на** ~**оте́** (**положéния**) to be equal to the occasion.
высо́тный *прил* (*полёт*) high-altitude; (*здание*) high-rise.
высо́х|**нуть** (-ну, -нешь; *pt* -, -ла, -ло) *сов от* **со́хнуть** ♦ (*impf* **высыха́ть**) *неперех* (*бельё, дрова*) to dry out; (*лужа, река*) to dry up.
высо́честв|**о** (-а) *ср*: **Ва́ше** *итп* **В**~ Your *итп* Highness.
вы́сп|**аться** (-люсь, -ишься; *impf* **высыпа́ться**) *сов возв* to sleep well.
вы́став|**ить** (-лю, -ишь; *impf* **выставля́ть**) *сов перех* (*поставить наружу*) to put out; (*грудь*) to stick out; (*кандидату́ру*) to put forward; (*требования*) to lay down; (*картину*) to exhibit; (*товар*) to display; (*часовых, охрану*) to post; (*разг: выгнать*) to chuck out; **выставля́ть** (~ *perf*) **кого́-н в дурно́м свéте** to show sb in an unfavourable light
▶ **вы́ставиться** (*impf* **выставля́ться**) *сов возв* (*на выставке*) to exhibit.
вы́став|**ка** (-ки; *gen pl* -ок) *ж* exhibition, show; ~**-прода́жа книг** book fair.
вы́ставлю(сь) *сов см* **вы́ставить(ся)**.
выставля́|**ть(ся)** (-ю(сь)) *несов от* **вы́ставить(ся)**.
вы́ставок *сущ см* **вы́ставка**.
выста́ива|**ть** (-ю) *несов от* **вы́стоять**.
вы́стега|**ть** (-ю) *сов от* **стега́ть**.
вы́ст|**лать** (-елю, -елешь; *impf* **выстила́ть**) *сов перех*: ~ **что-н чем-н** to line sth with sth.
вы́сто|**ять** (-ю, -ишь; *impf* **выста́ивать**) *сов неперех* (*долго простоять*) to stand; (*удержаться*) to remain standing; (*не сдаться*) to stand one's ground.
вы́страда|**ть** (-ю) *сов перех* to suffer; (*счастье, свободу*) *to achieve through much suffering*.

выстра́ива|**ть(ся)** (-ю(сь)) *несов* = **стро́ить(ся)**.
вы́стрел (-а) *м* shot; **разда́лся** ~ a shot rang out.
вы́стрел|**ить** (-ю, -ишь) *сов неперех* to fire; ~ (*perf*) **из ружья́/из пу́шки** to fire a gun/cannon.
вы́строга|**ть** (-ю) *сов от* **строга́ть**.
вы́стро|**ить(ся)** (-ю(сь), -ишь(ся)) *сов от* **стро́ить(ся)**.
вы́ступ (-а) *м* ledge.
выступа́|**ть** (-ю) *несов от* **вы́ступить** ♦ *неперех* (*берег*) to jut out; (*скулы*) to protrude.
вы́ступ|**ить** (-лю, -ишь; *impf* **выступа́ть**) *сов неперех* (*против закона, в защиту друга*) to come out; (*из толпы́, из рядо́в*) to step out; (*оркестр, актёр*) to perform; (*пот, сыпь*) to break out; (*в поход, на по́иски*) to set off *или* out; **выступа́ть** (~ *perf*) **рéчью** to make a speech.
выступлéни|**е** (-я) *ср* (*МУЗ*) performance; (*в поход*) departure; (*в печати*) article; (*речь*) speech.
выступлю́ *сов см* **вы́ступить**.
вы́сун|**уть** (-у, -ешь; *impf* **высо́вывать**) *сов перех* to stick out; **бежа́ть** (*impf*), ~**ув язы́к** (*перен: разг*) to run flat out
▶ **вы́сунуться** (*impf* **высо́вываться**) *сов возв* to lean out; (*рука, нога*) to stick out; (*перен: разг*): ~**ся с** +*instr* to come out with.
вы́суш|**ить(ся)** (-у(сь), -ишь(ся)) *сов от* **суши́ть(ся)**.
вы́счита|**ть** (-ю; *impf* **высчи́тывать**) *сов перех* to calculate.
вы́сш|**ий** (-ая, -ее, -ие) *прил* (*орган власти, начальство*) highest, supreme; **в** ~**ей стéпени** extremely; **товáры** ~**его со́рта** goods of the highest quality; **вы́сшая мéра наказа́ния** capital punishment; **вы́сшая шко́ла** university; **вы́сшее образова́ние** higher education; **вы́сшее учéбное заведéние** higher education establishment.
высыла́|**ть** (-ю) *несов от* **вы́слать**.
высы́л|**ка** (-ки; *gen pl* -ок) *ж* (*посылки, денег*) sending; (*осуждённого*) exile; (*шпио́на*) deportation.
высы́п|**ать** (-лю, -лешь; *impf* **высыпа́ть**) *сов перех* to pour out ♦ *неперех* (*сыпь, пры́щи*) to break out; (*разг: толпа, народ итп*) to pour out
▶ **высы́паться** (*impf* **высыпа́ться**) *сов возв* to pour out.
высыха́|**ть** (-ю) *несов от* **вы́сохнуть**.
высь (-и) *ж* height.
выта́лкива|**ть** (-ю) *несов от* **вы́толкнуть**.
выта́птыва|**ть** (-ю) *несов от* **вы́топтать**.
вы́таращ|**ить(ся)** (-у(сь), -ишь(ся)) *сов от* **тара́щить(ся)**.
выта́скива|**ть** (-ю) *несов см* **вы́тащить**.
вы́тащ|**ить** (-у, -ишь) *сов от* **тащи́ть** ♦ (*impf* **выта́скивать**) *перех* (*мебель*) to drag out.

вы́твер|дить (-жу, -дишь) *сов от* **тверди́ть**.

вытворя́|ть (-ю) *сов перех (разг)* to get up to.

вы́тек *итп сов см* **вы́течь**.

вытека́|ть (*3sg* -ет, *3pl* -ют) *несов от* **вы́течь** ♦ *неперех (вывод)* to follow; *(река)* to flow out.

вы́тер|еть (-ру, -решь; *pt* -ер, -ерла, -ерло, *impf* **вытира́ть**) *сов перех (грязь, лужу)* to wipe up; *(посуду)* to dry (up); *(руки, глаза)* to wipe; **вытира́ть** (~ *perf*) **пыль** to dust

▸ **вы́тереться** (*impf* **вытира́ться**) *сов возв (человек)* to dry o.s.

вы́терп|еть (-лю, -ишь) *сов перех* to bear, endure.

вы́тесн|ить (-ю, -ишь; *impf* **вытесня́ть**) *сов перех (удалить)* to oust; *(заменить собой)* to supplant.

вы́те|чь (*3sg* -чет, *3pl* -кут, *pt* -к, -кла, -кло, *impf* **вытека́ть**) *сов неперех* to flow out.

вытира́|ть(ся) (-ю(сь)) *несов от* **вы́тереть(ся)**.

вы́тк|ать (-у, -ешь) *сов перех* to weave.

вы́толкн|уть (-у, -ешь; *impf* **выта́лкивать**) *сов перех* to push out.

вы́топ|тать (-чу, -чешь; *impf* **выта́птывать**) *сов перех* to trample down.

вы́точ|ить (-у, -ишь) *сов от* **точи́ть**.

вы́трав|ить (-лю, -ишь; *impf* **вытравля́ть** *или* **вытра́вливать**) *сов перех (пятно)* to remove; *(крыс, тараканов)* to exterminate; *(рисунок)* to etch.

вытрезви́тел|ь (-я) *м overnight police cell for drunks*.

вы́тру(сь) *итп сов см* **вы́тереть(ся)**.

вы́тряс|ти (-у, -ешь; *pt* -, -ла, -ло) *сов от* **трясти́**.

вы́тряхн|уть (-у, -ешь; *impf* **вытря́хивать**) *сов перех* to shake out.

выть (**во́ю, во́ешь**) *несов неперех (зверь, ветер, вьюга)* to howl; *(сирена)* to wail; *(разг: плакать)* to howl, wail.

вытя́гива|ть(ся) (-ю(сь)) *несов от* **вы́тянуть(ся)**.

вы́тяж|ка (-ки; *gen pl* -ек) *ж (действие: дыма, вредных частиц)* extraction; *(экстракт)* extract.

вы́тян|уть (-у, -ешь; *impf* **вытя́гивать**) *сов перех* to pull out; *(дым, вредные вещества)* to extract; *(руки, ноги, ткань)* to stretch ♦ *неперех (разг: выдержать)* to last out; ~ *(perf)* **(всю) ду́шу из кого́-н** *(разг)* to wear sb out; **из него́ сло́ва не** ~**ешь** *(разг)* you won't get a word out of him

▸ **вы́тянуться** (*impf* **вытя́гиваться**) *сов возв (дым, газ)* to escape; *(одежда)* to stretch; *(на диване, вдоль берега)* to stretch out; *(разг: вырасти)* to shoot up; *(встать смирно)* to stand at attention; **у него́** ~**улось лицо́** *(перен)* his face fell.

вы́у|дить (-жу, -дишь; *impf* **выу́живать**) *сов перех (рыбу)* to catch; *(перен: разг: сведения)* to wheedle out.

вы́тюж|ить (-у, -ишь) *сов от* **утю́жить**.

выучива́|ть (-ю) *несов* to learn.

вы́учи|ть(ся) (-у(сь), -ишь(сь)) *сов от* **учи́ть(ся)**.

выха́жива|ть (-ю) *несов от* **вы́ходить**.

вы́хва|тить (-чу, -тишь; *impf* **выхва́тывать**) *сов перех (вырвать)* to snatch; *(пистолет)* to draw.

выхлопно́й *прил* exhaust *опред*; **выхлопны́е га́зы** exhaust fumes.

вы́ход (-а) *м (войск)* withdrawal; *(из партии, из комиссии)* departure; *(из кризиса)* way out; *(на сцену)* appearance; *(в море)* sailing; *(книги)* publication; *(на экран)* showing; *(место, комп)* exit; **дава́ть (дать** *perf*) ~ **чему́-н** to give vent to sth.

вы́ходец (-ца) *м*: **он** ~ **из Росси́и** he is of Russian origin *или* is Russian by birth.

выхо́дит *вводн сл (разг)* it turns out.

вы́ходить (-жу, -дишь; *impf* **выха́живать**) *сов перех (больного)* to nurse (back to health).

выхо́дить (-ожу, -о́дишь) *несов от* **вы́йти** ♦ *неперех*: ~ **на** +*acc (юг, север)* to face; **окно́** ~**о́дит в парк** the window looks out onto the park; **дверь** ~**о́дит в коридо́р** the door opens onto the corridor.

вы́ход|ка (-ки) *ж* prank.

выходно́й *прил* exit *опред*; *(платье, костюм)* best ♦ (-о́го; *decl like adj*) *м (также:* ~ **день**) day off (work); ~**о́е отве́рстие** outlet; **сего́дня** ~ *(разг)* today is a holiday; **я сего́дня** ~ *(разг)* I have a day off today; ~**ы́е** weekend *ед*; **выходна́я дверь** exit; **выходно́е посо́бие** redundancy payment; **выходны́е да́нные** imprint.

вы́ходца *итп сущ см* **вы́ходец**.

вы́хожу *сов см* **вы́ходить**.

выхожу́ *несов см* **выходи́ть**.

вы́цара|пать (-ю; *impf* **выцара́пывать**) *сов перех* to scratch out; *(перен: деньги, путёвку)* to wring out.

вы́цве|сти (*3sg* -тет, *3pl* -тут, *impf* **выцвета́ть**) *сов неперех* to fade.

вы́черкн|уть (-у, -ешь; *impf* **вычёркивать**) *сов перех* to cross *или* score out.

вы́черпа|ть (-ю; *impf* **вычёрпывать**) *сов перех (извлечь)* to scoop out; *(опорожнить)* to drain; **вычёрпывать** (~ *perf*) **во́ду из ло́дки** to bail out a boat.

вы́чест|ь (-ту, -тешь; *impf* **вычита́ть**) *сов перех (мат)* to subtract; *(долг, налог)* to deduct.

вы́чет (-а) *м* deduction ♦ *предл*: **за** ~**ом** +*gen* minus; **до** ~**а нало́гов** pre-tax.

вычисле́ни|е (-я) *ср* calculation.

вычисли́тельный *прил (операция, функция)* computing; **вычисли́тельная маши́на** computer; **вычисли́тельная те́хника** computers *мн*; **вычисли́тельный центр** computer centre (*BRIT*) *или* center (*US*).

вы́числ|ить (-ю, -ишь; *impf* **вычисля́ть**) *сов перех* to calculate.

вы́чи|стить (-щу, -стишь) *сов от* **чи́стить**.

вычита́ни|е (-я) *ср* subtraction.
вычита́ть (-ю; *impf* **вычи́тывать**) *сов перех* (*разг: узна́ть*) to find out (*by reading*).
вычита́|ть (-ю) *несов от* **вы́честь**.
вы́чту *сов см* **вы́честь**.
вычи́тыва|ть (-ю) *несов от* **вы́читать**.
вы́чур|ный (-ен, -на, -но) *прил* elaborate.
вы́швырн|уть (-у, -ешь; *impf* **вышвы́ривать**) *сов перех* (*также перен: разг*) to chuck out.
вы́ше *сравн прил от* **высо́кий** ◆ *нареч* higher; (*в те́ксте*) above ◆ *предл* (+*gen*) above; **мы подняли́сь** ~ we went further up, we climbed higher; ~ **мы привели́ но́вые да́нные** we have cited new data above; **самолёт лете́л** ~ **облако́в** the plane was flying above the clouds; **э́то** ~ **моего́ понима́ния** it is beyond me *или* my comprehension.
вы́шек *сущ см* **вы́шка**.
вы́шел *сов см* **вы́йти**.
вышестоя́щ|ий (-ая, -ее, -ие) *прил* higher; ~**ее лицо́** superior.
вы́шиб|ить (-у, -ешь; *pt* -, -ла, -ло, *impf* **вышиба́ть**) *сов перех* (*выбить*) to knock out; (*разг: прогна́ть*) to chuck out.
вышива́ни|е (-я) *ср* needlework.
вышива́|ть (-ю) *несов от* **вы́шить**.
вы́шив|ка (-ки; *gen pl* -ок) *ж* embroidery.
вышин|а́ (-ы́) *ж* (*высота́*) height.
вы́ш|ить (-ью, -ьешь; *impf* **вышива́ть**) *сов перех* to embroider.
вы́ш|ка (-ки; *gen pl* -ек) *ж* (*высо́кое строе́ние*) tower; (*разг: престу́пнику*) death penalty; (*СПОРТ*) diving board; **бурова́я** *или* **нефтяна́я** ~ derrick; **прыжки́ в во́ду с** ~**ки** high diving.
вы́школ|ить (-ю, -ишь) *сов перех* to train.
вы́шла *итп сов см* **вы́йти**.
вы́шлю *итп сов см* **вы́слать**.
вы́шью *итп сов см* **вы́шить**.
вы́щипа|ть (-ю; *impf* **выщи́пывать**) *сов перех* to pluck.
вы́яв|ить (-лю, -ишь; *impf* **выявля́ть**) *сов перех* (*тала́нт*) to discover; (*недоста́тки*) to expose

▶ **вы́явиться** (*impf* **выявля́ться**) *сов возв* to come to light, be revealed.
вы́ясн|ить (-ю, -ишь; *impf* **выясня́ть**) *сов перех* (*обнару́жить*) to find out; (*сде́лать я́сным*) to clarify; **нам ну́жно** ~ **отноше́ния** we have to sort things out between us
▶ **вы́ясниться** (*impf* **выясня́ться**) *сов возв* to become clear.
Вьетна́м (-а) *м* Vietnam.
вьетна́м|ец (-ца) *м* Vietnamese.
вьетна́м|ка (-ки; *gen pl* -ок) *ж см* **вьетна́мец**.
вьетна́мск|ий (-ая, -ое, -ие) *прил* Vietnamese.
вьетна́мца *итп сущ см* **вьетна́мец**.
выо́г|а (-и) *ж* snowstorm, blizzard.
выо́чн|ый *прил*: ~**ое живо́тное** beast of burden.
вяжу́ *сов см* **вяза́ть**.
вя́жущ|ий (-ая, -ее, -ие) *прил* (*вкус*) acerbic; (*материа́л, соста́в*) binding, cementing.
вяз *итп несов см* **вя́знуть** ◆ (-а) *м* elm.
вяза́ни|е (-я) *ср* (*сно́пов*) tying, binding; (*рукоде́лие*) knitting.
вя́заный *прил* knitted.
вяза́|ть (-жу́, -жешь; *perf* **связа́ть**) *несов перех* to tie up, bind; (*ко́фту, носки́*) to knit ◆ *безл* (*по perf*): **э́то лека́рство вя́жет во рту** this medicine burns the inside of your mouth.
вя́зк|ий (-ая, -ое, -ие; -ок, -ка́, -ко) *прил* (*тягу́чий*) viscous; (*то́пкий*) boggy.
вя́з|нуть (-ну, -нешь; *pt* -, -ла, -ло, *perf* **завя́знуть** *или* **увя́знуть**) *несов неперех*: ~ (**в** +*prp*) to get stuck (in).
вя́зок *прил см* **вя́зкий**.
вя́леный *прил* dried.
вя́л|ить (-ю, -ишь) *несов перех* to dry.
вя́ло *нареч* (*говори́ть*) dully.
вя́лост|ь (-и) *ж* sluggishness.
вя́л|ый (-, -а, -о) *прил* (*ли́стья, цветы́*) wilted, withered; (*челове́к, речь*) sluggish.
вя́|нуть (-ну, -нешь; *perf* **завя́нуть** *или* **увя́нуть**) *несов неперех* (*цветы́*) to wilt, wither; (*перен: красота́*) to fade; **его́ слу́шать – у́ши** ~**нут** (*разг*) it makes you sick to listen to him.

~ Г, г ~

Г, г *сущ нескл* (*буква*) the 4th letter of the Russian alphabet.

г *сокр* (= **грамм**) g, gm (= *gram*).

г. *сокр* = **год, го́род**.

га *м сокр* (= **гекта́р**) ha (= *hectare*).

Гаа́га (**-и**) *ж* The Hague.

габари́т (**-а**) *м* (*обычно мн: ТЕХ*) dimension; *см также* **габари́ты**.

габари́ты (**-ов**) *мн* (*разг: человека*) size *ед*.

ГАБТ (**-а**) *м сокр* (= *Госуда́рственный академи́ческий Большо́й теа́тр*) (State Academic) Bolshoi Theatre (*BRIT*) *или* Theater (*US*).

Гава́йи *м нескл* Hawaii.

Гава́н|а (**-ы**) *ж* Havana.

га́ван|ь (**-и**) *ж* harbour (*BRIT*), harbor (*US*).

га́вка|ть (**-ю**) *несов неперех* (*разг: также перен*) to yap.

гага́р|а (**-ы**) *ж* diver (*BRIT*), loon (*US*).

гага́т (**-а**) *м* (*ГЕО*) jet.

гад (**-а**) *м* (*разг*) rat.

гада́л|ка (**-ки**; *gen pl* **-ок**) *ж* fortune-teller.

гада́ть (**-ю**) *несов неперех* (*строить предположения*) to guess; (*perf* **погада́ть**): **~ кому́-н** to tell sb's fortune; **~ (погада́ть** *perf*) **на ка́ртах** to read the cards; **~** (*impf*) **на кофе́йной гу́ще** ≈ to read the tea leaves.

га́дин|а (**-ы**) *ж* (*разг*) rat.

га́дить (**-жу, -дишь**; *perf* **нага́дить**) *несов неперех* (*разг: животное*) to defecate; **~ (нага́дить** *perf*) +*dat* (*разг*) to do the dirty on.

га́дкий (**-кая, -кое, -кие; -ок, -ка́, -ко**) *прил* loathsome.

га́дко *нареч* (*поступить*) terribly ♦ *как сказ*: **э́то ~** it's disgusting.

га́дост|ь (**-и**) *ж* (*поступка, слов*) nastiness; (*разг*) filth; **де́лать (сде́лать** *perf*)/**говори́ть (сказа́ть** *perf*) **~и** to do/say nasty things; **э́то ~** it's disgusting.

гадю́к|а (**-и**) *ж* viper.

га́ек *сущ см* **га́йка**.

га́ечный *прил*: **~ ключ** spanner.

га́же *сравн прил от* **га́дкий** ♦ *сравн нареч от* **га́дко**.

га́жу *несов см* **га́дить**.

ГАЗ (**-а**) *м сокр* (*автомобиль*) vehicle manufactured at the Gorky car factory.

газ (**-а**; *part gen* **-у**) *м* gas; **гото́вить (пригото́вить** *perf*) **на га́зе** to cook with gas; **дава́ть (дать** *perf*) **~** (*разг*) to put one's foot down (*BRIT*), step on the gas (*US*); *см также* **га́зы**.

газе́т|а (**-ы**) *ж* newspaper.

газе́тный *прил* newspaper *опред*.

газе́тчик (**-а**) *м* (*разг: сотрудник*) journalist; (*продавец*) newspaper vendor.

га́зик (**-а**) *м* (*разг*) car manufactured at the Gorky car plant.

газиро́ванный *прил*: **~ая вода́** carbonated water.

газиро́в|ка (**-ки**; *gen pl* **-ок**) *ж* (*разг*) soda.

газо́вщик (**-а́**) *м* (*разг*) gasman (*мн* gasmen).

га́зовый *прил* gas; **га́зовая ка́мера** gas chamber.

газо́н (**-а**) *м* lawn.

газопрово́д (**-а**) *м* gas pipeline.

га́з|ы (**-ов**) *мн* (*МЕД*) wind *ед*.

ГАИ *ж сокр* (= *Госуда́рственная автомоби́льная инспе́кция*) *state motor vehicle inspectorate*.

Гаи́ти *м нескл* Haiti.

гаитя́нский (**-ая, -ое, -ие**) *прил* Haitian.

гаи́шник (**-а**) *м* (*разг*) ≈ traffic cop.

га́й|ка (**-йки**; *gen pl* **-ек**) *ж* nut; **закру́чивать (закрути́ть** *perf*) **~йки** (*разг*) to put the screws on.

гаймори́т (**-а**) *м* sinusitis.

гала́ *прил неизм* gala *опред*.

галакти́к|а (**-и**) *ж* galaxy; **На́ша Г~** the Galaxy.

гала́нтен *прил см* **гала́нтный**.

галантере́|я (**-и**) *ж* haberdashery (*BRIT*), notions store (*US*).

гала́нт|ный (**-ен, -на, -но**) *прил* gallant.

галере́|я (**-и**) *ж* gallery.

гале́т|а (**-ы**) *ж* sort of biscuit.

галимать|я́ (**-и́**) *ж* (*разг*) gobbledygook.

галифе́ *мн/ср нескл* riding breeches *мн* ♦ *прил неизм*: **брю́ки ~** jodhpurs.

га́л|ка (**-ки**; *gen pl* **-ок**) *ж* jackdaw.

галло́н (**-а**) *м* gallon.

галлюцина́ци|я (**-и**) *ж* hallucination.

га́лок *сущ см* **га́лка**.

гало́п (**-а**) *м* (*бег лошади*) gallop; (*танец*) galop.

гало́пом *нареч* at a gallop; **я прочита́л кни́гу ~** (*разг*) I raced through the book.

га́лоч|ка (**-ки**; *gen pl* **-ек**) *ж* (*в тексте*) tick, check (*US*).

гало́ш|а (**-и**) *ж* (*обычно мн: обувь*) galosh; **сажа́ть (посади́ть** *perf*) **кого́-н в ~у** (*разг*) to

put sb on the spot; **сади́ться (сесть** *perf*) **в ~у**
(*разг*) to get into a jam.
га́лстук (-а) *м* tie, necktie (*US*); **завя́зывать**
(**завяза́ть** *perf*) ~ to tie a tie.
гальваниза́ци|я (-и) *ж* galvanization.
гальванизи́р|овать (-ую) (*не*)*сов перех* to
galvanize.
га́льк|а (-и) *ж, собир* pebble.
гам (-а) *м* uproar.
гама́к (-а́) *м* hammock.
гама́ш|а (-и) *ж* (*обычно мн*) gaiter.
Га́мбург (-а) *м* Hamburg.
га́мбургер (-а) *м* hamburger.
га́мм|а (-ы) *ж* (*муз*) scale; (*чувств, красок*)
range.
га́мма-глобули́н (-а) *м* gamma globulin.
га́мма-излуче́ни|е (-я) *ср* gamma radiation.
Га́н|а (-ы) *ж* Ghana.
гангре́н|а (-ы) *ж* gangrene.
га́нгстер (-а) *м* gangster.
гандбо́л (-а) *м* handball.
гандболи́ст (-а) *м* handball player.
гандболи́ст|ка (-ки; *gen pl* **-ок)** *ж см*
гандболи́ст.
ганте́л|ь (-и) *ж* dumbbell.
гара́ж (-а́) *м* garage.
гара́нт (-а) *м* guarantor.
гаранти́йный *прил* guarantee *опред*, warranty
опред; **гаранти́йное письмо́** letter of guarantee.
гаранти́р|овать (-ую) (*не*)*сов перех* to
guarantee; ~ (*impf/perf*) **кого́-н от** +*gen* to protect
sb against.
гара́нти|я (-и) *ж* guarantee; ~ **от убы́тков**
guarantee against damage; **това́р с ~ей** item
under guarantee; **ба́нковская** ~ bank's letter of
guarantee; **авари́йная** ~ warranty; ~ **за́нятости**
job security.
гардеро́б (-а) *м* wardrobe; (*в общественном
здании*) cloakroom.
гардеро́бщик (-а) *м* cloakroom attendant.
гардеро́бщиц|а (-ы) *ж см* **гардеро́бщик.**
гарди́н|а (-ы) *ж* curtain.
га́рев|ый *прил*: **~ая доро́жка** cinder track.
гаре́м (-а) *м* harem.
гармо́ник|а (-и) *ж* concertina; **губна́я** ~ mouth
organ.
гармони́р|овать (-ую) *несов неперех*: ~ **с**
+*instr* (*со средой*) to be in harmony with;
(*одежда*) to go with.
гармони́ст (-а) *м* concertina player.
гармони́чный (-ен, -на, -но) *прил* harmonious.
гармо́ни|я (-и) *ж* harmony.
гармо́шк|а (-ки; *gen pl* **-ек)** *ж* (*разг*) ≈ squeeze-
box; (*одежда*): **в ~ку** creased; **при уда́ре
маши́на смя́лась в ~ку** the car concertinaed on
impact.
гарнизо́н (-а) *м* garrison.
гарни́р (-а) *м* side dish.

гарниту́р (-а) *м* (*одежды*) outfit; (*украшения*)
set; (*мебели*) suite.
гарпу́н (-а́) *м* harpoon.
гар|ь (-и) *ж* (*угля*) cinders *мн*; **па́хнет га́рью**
there's a smell of burning.
гас *итп несов см* **га́снуть.**
га|си́ть (-шу́, -сишь; *perf* **погаси́ть)** *несов перех*
(*лампу, свет*) to put out; (*пожар*) to extinguish,
put out; (*скорость*) to reduce; (*звук*) to deaden;
(*марку*) to frank; (*no perf*; *перен: инициативу*) to
stifle, suppress; ~ (**погаси́ть** *perf*)
задо́лженность to settle one's debts; ~
(**погаси́ть** *perf*) **и́звесть** to slake lime.
га́|снуть (-ну, -нешь; *pt* - или **-нул, -ла, -ло,** *perf*
пога́снуть или **уга́снуть)** *несов неперех* (*огни*)
to go out; (*звёзды, чувства, надежда*) to fade.
гастри́т (-а) *м* gastritis.
гастро́л|и (-ей) *мн performances of a touring
company*; **е́здить/е́хать (пое́хать** *perf*) **на** ~ to
go on tour.
гастроли́р|овать (-ую) *несов неперех* to be on
tour.
гастроно́м (-а) *м* food store.
гастрономи́ческ|ий (-ая, -ое, ие) *прил*: ~
магази́н = **гастроно́м.**
гастроно́ми|я (-и) *ж* delicatessen.
ГАТТ *м сокр* (= *Генера́льное соглаше́ние о
тари́фах и торго́вле*) GATT (= *General
Agreement on Tariffs and Trade*).
гауптва́хт|а (-ы) *ж* (*воен*) guardroom (*as a
place of detention*); **сажа́ть (посади́ть** *perf*)
кого́-н на ~у to confine sb to the guardroom.
гашёны|й *прил* (*марка*) franked; **~ая и́звесть**
slaked lime.
гаши́ш (-а) *м* hashish.
гашу́ *несов см* **гаси́ть.**
ГБ *ж сокр* = **госбезопа́сность.**
гвалт (-а) *м* (*разг*) row.
гварде́|ец (-йца) *м* (*воен*) guardsman (*мн*
guardsmen).
гва́рди|я (-и) *ж* (*воен*) Guards *мн*; **Кра́сная/
Бе́лая** ~ (*ист*) the Red/White Guard.
Гватема́л|а (-ы) *ж* Guatemala.
Гвине́|я (-и) *ж* Guinea.
гвозди́к|а (-и) *ж* (*цветок*) carnation; (*пряность*)
cloves *мн*.
гвозд|ь (-я́; *nom pl* **-и,** *gen pl* **-е́й)** *м* nail; ~
програ́ммы the highlight of the show; **и
никаки́х ~е́й!** (*разг*) and that's that!
гг *сокр* = **го́ды**; (= *господа́*) Messrs (= *messieurs*).
ГД *ж сокр* = **Госуда́рственная Ду́ма.**
Гда́ньск (-а) *м* Gdansk.
где *нареч* where; (*разг: где-нибудь*) somewhere,
anywhere ♦ *союз* where; ~ **Вы живёте?** where
do you live?; **поду́майте, не забы́ли ли** ~ try
and think whether you left it anywhere *или*
somewhere; **го́род,** ~ **я жил** the town where I
lived; **ты ско́ро бу́дешь бога́тым** – ~ **уж там!**

(*разг*) you'll soon be rich – hardly!

гдé-либо *нареч* = **гдé-нибудь**.

гдé-нибудь *нареч* somewhere; (*в вопросе*) anywhere.

гдé-то *нареч* somewhere.

ГДР *ж сокр* (*ист*: = **Герма́нская Демократи́ческая Респу́блика**) GDR (= *German Democratic Republic*).

гегемони́зм (-а) *м* hegemony.

гéйзер (-а) *м* geyser.

гейм (-а) *м* (*СПОРТ*) game.

гекта́р (-а) *м* hectare.

гель (-я) *м* gel (*for hair*).

гемоглоби́н (-а) *м* haemoglobin (*BRIT*), hemoglobin (*US*).

геморро́й (-я) *м* haemorrhoids *мн* (*BRIT*), hemorrhoids *мн* (*US*), piles *мн*.

гемофили́я (-и) *ж* haemophilia (*BRIT*), hemophilia (*US*).

ген (-а) *м* gene.

генеалоги́ческий (-ая, -ое, -ие) *прил*: ~ое **дéрево** genealogical chart; (*семьи*) family tree.

генеало́гия (-и) *ж* genealogy.

гéнезис (-а) *м* genesis.

генера́л (-а) *м* (*ВОЕН*) general; **генера́л а́рмии** general (*BRIT*), General of the Army (*US*).

генера́льный *прил* general; (*главный*) main; ~**ая убо́рка** spring-clean; **генера́льная репети́ция** dress rehearsal; **генера́льное сраже́ние** decisive battle; **генера́льный штаб** chief headquarters.

генера́тор (-а) *м* generator.

генéтик (-а) *м* geneticist.

генéтика (-и) *ж* genetics.

генети́ческий (-ая, -ое, -ие) *прил* genetic.

гениа́льно *нареч* (*написанный*) superbly ♦ *как сказ* it's great.

гениа́льный (-ен, -ьна, -ьно) *прил* great.

гéний (-я) *м* genius.

геноци́д (-а) *м* genocide.

генсéк (-а) *м сокр* = *генера́льный секрета́рь*; (*ПОЛИТ*) General Secretary (*of the Communist Party*).

Гéнуя (-и) *ж* Genoa.

гео́граф (-а) *м* geographer.

геогра́фия (-и) *ж* geography.

геодéзия (-и) *ж* geodesy.

гео́лог (-а) *м* geologist.

геоло́гия (-и) *ж* geology.

геомéтрия (-и) *ж* geometry.

геополи́тика (-и) *ж* geopolitics.

георги́н (-а) *м* dahlia.

георги́на (-ы) *ж* = **георги́н**.

гепа́рд (-а) *м* cheetah.

гепати́т (-а) *м* hepatitis.

гера́льдика (-и) *ж* heraldry.

гера́нь (-и) *ж* geranium.

герб (-á) *м* coat of arms; **госуда́рственный** ~ national emblem.

герба́рий (-я) *м* herbarium.

гербици́д (-а) *м* herbicide.

гéрбовый *прил* heraldic; (*с гербом*) bearing a

coat of arms; **гéрбовая бума́га** headed paper; **гéрбовая ма́рка** official stamp (*relating to stamp duty*); **гéрбовый сбор** stamp duty.

геркулéс (-а) *м* (*человек*) Hercules; (*кулин*) porridge oats *мн*.

герма́нец (-ца) *м* (*обычно мн*: *ист*) Teuton.

Герма́ния (-и) *ж* Germany.

герма́нский (-ая, -ое, -ие) *прил* German.

герма́нца *итп сущ см* **герма́нец**.

герметизи́ровать (-ую; *perf* **загерметизи́ровать**) *несов неперех* to make airtight.

гермети́чный (-ен, -на, -но) *прил* hermetic.

геро́изм (-а) *м* heroism.

герои́н (-а) *м* heroin.

герои́ня (-и) *ж* heroine.

герои́ческий (-ая, -ое, -ие) *прил* heroic; **герои́ческий эпос** heroic epic.

геро́й (-я) *м* hero.

герц (-а) *м* hertz.

гéрцог (-а) *м* duke.

герцоги́ня (-и) *ж* duchess.

геста́по *ср нескл* the Gestapo.

геста́повец (-ца) *м* member of the Gestapo.

гетероге́нный *прил* heterogeneous.

гéтра (-ы) *ж* (*обычно мн*) legwarmer.

гéтто *ср нескл* ghetto.

г-жа *м сокр* = **госпожа́**.

гжель (-и) *ж type of ceramic made in Gzhel*.

гиаци́нт (-а) *м* hyacinth.

гиб *итп несов см* **ги́бнуть**.

ги́белен *прил см* **ги́бельный**.

ги́бель (-и) *ж* (*человека*) death; (*армии*) destruction; (*самолёта, надежды, ценностей*) loss; (*карьеры*) ruin; **они́ бы́ли обречены́ на** ~ they were doomed; **на краю́** ~**и** (*дело*) on the brink of disaster; (*человек*) on the verge of death.

ги́бельный (-ен, -ьна, -ьно) *прил* disastrous.

ги́бкий (-кая, -кое, -кие; -ок, -ка́, -ко) *прил* flexible; **ги́бкий диск** (*КОМП*) floppy disk; **ги́бкое произво́дство** (*ТЕХ*) flexible production methods.

ги́бкость (-и) *ж* flexibility.

ги́бнуть (-ну, -нешь; *pt* -, -ла, -ло, *perf* **поги́бнуть**) *несов неперех* to perish; (*растения*) to die; (*перен*) to come to nothing; ~ (**поги́бнуть** *perf*) **от** +*gen* to die of.

ги́бок *прил см* **ги́бкий**.

Гибралта́р (-а) *м* Gibraltar.

гибри́д (-а) *м* hybrid.

ги́бче *сравн прил от* **ги́бкий**.

гига́нт (-а) *м* giant; **пласти́нка-**~, **диск-**~ twelve-inch record.

гига́нтский (-ая, -ое, -ие) *прил* gigantic.

гигиéна (-ы) *ж* hygiene.

гигиени́ческий (-ая, -ое, -ие) *прил* sanitary; **гигиени́ческий тампо́н** tampon.

гигиени́чный (-ен, -на, -но) *прил* hygienic.

гигроскопи́чный *прил* absorbent.

гид (-а) *м* guide.

гидравли́ческий (-ая, -ое, -ие) *прил*

hydraulic.

гидрокостю́м (-а) *м* diving suit.

гидрометце́нтр (-а) *м сокр* =
Гидрометеорологи́ческий центр.

гидроста́нци|я (-и) *ж см*
гидроэлектроста́нция.

гидроэлектроста́нци|я (-и) *ж* hydroelectric
power station.

гие́н|а (-ы) *ж* hyena.

ги́льди|я (-и) *ж* guild.

ги́льз|а (-ы) *ж* cartridge case.

гильоти́н|а (-ы) *ж* guillotine.

Гимала́|и (-ев) *мн* the Himalayas.

гимн (-а) *м* (*государственный*) anthem;
(*хвалебная песня*) hymn.

гимнази́ст (-а) *м* ≈ grammar school student.

гимнази́ст|ка (-ки; *gen pl* -ок) *ж см* **гимнази́ст.**

гимна́зи|я (-и) *ж* ≈ grammar school.

гимна́ст (-а) *м* gymnast.

гимнастёр|ка (-ки; *gen pl* -ок) *ж* soldier's blouse.

гимна́стик|а (-и) *ж* exercises *мн*; (*спортивная*)
~ gymnastics *мн*; **худо́жественная** ~ modern
rhythmic gymnastics; **де́лать (сде́лать** *perf*) ~**у**
to do one's exercises.

гимна́ст|ка (-ки; *gen pl* -ок) *ж см* **гимна́ст.**

гинеко́лог (-а) *м* gynaecologist (*BRIT*),
gynecologist (*US*).

гинеколо́ги|я (-и) *ж* gynaecology (*BRIT*),
gynecology (*US*).

гипе́рбол|а (-ы) *ж* hyperbole.

гиперто́ник (-а) *м person suffering from high
blood pressure.*

гипертони́|я (-и) *ж* high blood pressure.

гипертрофи́рованный *прил* (*МЕД*)
hypertrophied; (*перен*) excessive.

гипно́з (-а) *м* hypnosis.

гипнотизи́р|овать (-ую; *perf*
загипнотизи́ровать) *несов перех* to hypnotize.

гипо́тез|а (-ы) *ж* hypothesis; **выдвига́ть
(вы́двинуть** *perf*) ~**у** to put forward a
hypothesis.

гипотети́ческий (-ая, -ое, -ие) *прил*
hypothetical.

гипото́ник (-а) *м person suffering from low
blood pressure.*

гипотони́|я (-и) *ж* low blood pressure.

гиппопота́м (-а) *м* hippopotamus.

гипс (-а) *м* (*ГЕО*) gypsum; (*ИСКУССТВО*) plaster of
Paris; (*МЕД*) plaster; **накла́дывать (наложи́ть**
perf) ~ **на что-н** to put sth in plaster.

гипю́р (-а) *м* (guipure) lace.

гирля́нд|а (-ы) *ж* garland.

ги́р|я (-и) *ж* (*весов*) weight; (*СПОРТ*) dumbbell.

гита́р|а (-ы) *ж* guitar.

гитари́ст (-а) *м* guitarist.

гитари́ст|ка (-ки; *gen pl* -ок) *ж см* **гитари́ст.**

ГК *м сокр* (= Гражда́нский Ко́декс) civil code.

гл. *сокр* (= глава́) ch. (= *chapter*).

глав|а́ (-ы́; *nom pl* -ы) *ж* (*делегации, семьи*) head;
(*церкви*) dome; (*книги, статьи*) chapter; **во** ~**é
с** +*instr* headed by; **во** ~**é** +*gen* at the head of; **во**
~**у́ угла́ ста́вить (поста́вить** *perf*) **что-н** to give
top priority to sth.

глава́р|ь (-я́) *м* (*банды*) leader.

гла́венств|о (-а) *ср* leading role.

гла́венств|овать (-ую) *несов неперех*: ~ **над**
+*instr* to hold sway over.

главк (-а) *м сокр* (= гла́вный комите́т) *chief
administrative body within a ministry.*

гла́вное *вводн сл* the main thing; **он,** ~**, все
отрица́ет** the main thing is, he denies
everything.

главнокома́ндующ|ий (-его; *decl like adj*) *м*
commander in chief.

гла́вн|ый *прил* main; (*старший по положению*)
senior, head *опред*; ~**ым о́бразом** chiefly,
mainly; **гла́вная кни́га** (*КОММ*) general ledger.

глаго́л (-а) *м* verb.

глади́л|ьный (-ен, -ьна, -ьно) *прил*: ~**ьная
доска́** ironing board.

гладио́л|ус (-а) *м* gladiolus.

гла́|дить (-жу, -дишь; *perf* погла́дить) *несов
перех* to iron; (*волосы*) to stroke; **они́ тебя́ не
погла́дят по голо́вке за э́то** they won't be best
pleased with you for this.

гла́д|кий (-кая, -кое, -кие; -ок, -ка́, -ко) *прил*
(*ровный*) smooth; (*одноцветный*) plain,
unpatterned; (*плавный*) flowing; (*прямой*)
straight.

гла́дко *нареч* (*ровно*) smoothly; (*причёсанный*)
tightly; ~ **вы́бритый** clean-shaven.

гла́же *сравн прил от* **гла́дкий** ♦ *сравн нареч от*
гла́дко.

гла́жу *несов см* **гла́дить.**

глаз (-а; *loc sg* -у́, *nom pl* -а́, *gen pl* -) *м* (*также
перен*) eye; (*зрение*) eyesight; **в** ~**áх** +*gen* in the
eyes of; **на** ~**áх у кого́-н** before sb's eyes; **с
гла́зу на** ~ tête à tête; **на** ~ roughly; **она́ всегда́
говори́т о нём за** ~**á** (*разг*) she is always
talking about him behind his back; **за ним
ну́жен** ~ **да** ~ you need to keep your eye on
him; **куда́** ~**á́ гляди́т идти́ (пойти́** *perf*) (*разг*) to
go where one's fancy takes one; **де́лать
(сде́лать** *perf*) **больши́е** ~**á** to look amazed.

глаза́стый *прил* (*разг*) with big eyes; (*зоркий*)
sharp-eyed.

Гла́зго *м нескл* Glasgow.

глазе́|ть (-ю) *несов неперех*: ~ **на** +*acc* to stare
at.

глазир|ова́ть (-у́ю) (*не)сов перех* (*также ТЕХ*)
to glaze; (*торт*) to ice, frost (*US*).

глазка́ *сущ см* **глазо́к.**

глазни́к (-а́) *м* (*разг*) eye doctor.

глазни́ц|а (-ы) *ж* eyeball.

глазно́й *прил eye опред.*

глаз|о́к (-ка́) *м* peephole.

глазоме́р (-а) м: **у него́ хоро́ший ~** he has a good eye.

глазу́нь|я (-и) м fried egg.

глазу́р|ь (-и) ж (*на кера́мике итп*) glaze; (*на торте*) icing, frosting (*US*).

гла́нд|а (-ы) ж (*обычно мн*) gland.

глас|и́ть (*3sg* -и́т, *3pl* -я́т) *несов перех* to state; **зако́н/пра́вило ~и́т, что** ... the law/rule states that ...; **уста́в ~и́т, что** the regulations stipulate that.

гла́сность (-и) ж openness; (*ИСТ*) glasnost; **предава́ть (преда́ть** *perf*) **~и** to make public.

гла́сн|ый *прил* (*суд, процесс*) public; (*линг*) voiced ♦ (**-ого**; *decl like adj*) м vowel.

глауко́м|а (-ы) ж glaucoma.

гли́н|а (-ы) ж clay.

глинтве́йн (-а; *part gen* -у) м mulled wine.

гли́няный *прил* clay.

глист (-á) м (*обычно мн*) (intestinal) worm.

глицери́н (-а) м glycerin(e).

глици́нь|я (-и) ж wisteria.

глоба́л|ьный (-ен, -ьна, -ьно) *прил* (*перен*) thorough; (*no short form*; *климат, политика*) global.

гло́бус (-а) м globe.

глода́|ть (-ю) *несов перех* to gnaw at.

глота́|ть (-ю; *perf* **проглоти́ть**) *несов перех* to swallow; (*разг: обед*) to scoff; (*перен: книгу*) to devour; **~ (проглоти́ть** *perf*) **слёзы** to choke back one's tears.

гло́т|ка (-ки; *gen pl* -ок) ж gullet.

глото́к (-ка́) м gulp, swallow; (*воды, чая*) drop.

гло́х|нуть (-ну, -нешь; *pt* -, -ла, -ло, *perf* **огло́хнуть**) *несов неперех* to grow deaf; (*perf* **загло́хнуть**; *шум*) to die away; (*мотор*) to stall.

глу́бже *сравн прил от* **глубо́кий** ♦ *сравн нареч от* **глубоко́**.

глубин|а́ (-ы́; *nom pl* -ы) ж depth; (*дно*) depths мн; (*леса*) heart; (*зала, сада*) middle; (*перен*): **~** +*gen* (*иде́и итп*) profundity of; **на ~ине́ 10 ме́тров** at a depth of 10 metres (*BRIT*) *или* meters (*US*); **в ~ине́ души́** in one's heart of hearts; **до ~ины́ души́ тро́нут** deeply moved; **до ~ины́ души́ удивлён** astounded; **до ~ины́ души́ огорчён** cut to the quick.

глубо́к|ий (-ая, -ое, -ие; -, -á, -ó) *прил* deep; (*провинция*) remote; (*мысль, интерес*) profound; (*зима, осень*) late; **~ая ста́рость** ripe old age; **~ая ночь** the dead of night; **~ снег** deep snow; **~ покло́н** deep bow; **~ая та́йна** deep secret.

глубоко́ *нареч* deeply ♦ *как сказ*: **здесь ~** it's deep here.

глубоково́д|ный (-ен, -на, -но) *прил* deep; (*no short form*; *иссле́дования*) deep-sea.

глубокомы́слен|ный (-, -на, -но) *прил* (*речь, замеча́ние*) profound; (*взгляд, вид*) thoughtful.

глубокоуважа́емый *прил* dear.

глуб|ь (-и) ж (*леса*) heart; (*океа́на*) depths мн.

глуми́ться (-лю́сь, -и́шься) *несов возв*: **~ над** +*instr* to mock.

глупе́|ть (-ю; *perf* **поглупе́ть**) *несов неперех* to grow stupid.

глуп|и́ть (-лю́, -и́шь; *perf* **сглупи́ть**) *несов неперех* to be silly *или* stupid.

глу́по *нареч* stupidly ♦ *как сказ* it's stupid *или* silly.

глу́пост|ь (-и) ж stupidity, silliness; (*посту́пок*) stupid *или* silly thing; (*слова́*) nonsense; **де́лать** (*impf*) **~и** to do silly things; **написа́ть ей письмо́ бы́ло ~ю** it was foolish *или* stupid to write to her; **име́ть** (*impf*) **~** +*infin* to be foolish enough to do; **~и! никуда́ не пойдёшь** nonsense! you're not going anywhere.

глу́п|ый (-, -á, -о) *прил* stupid, silly.

глуха́р|ь (-я́) м (*ЗООЛ*) capercaillie.

глух|о́й (-, -á, -о) *прил* deaf; (*волне́ние, недово́льство*) suppressed, pent-up; (*звук*) muffled; (*no short form*; *пора́*) dead; **~ лес** dense forest; **~а́я стена́** blank wall; **он глух к про́сьбам/жа́лобам** he is deaf to requests/complaints.

глухонем|о́й *прил* deaf-and-dumb ♦ (**-о́го**; *decl like adj*) м deaf-mute; **а́збука для ~ы́х** deaf-and-dumb alphabet.

глухот|а́ (-ы́) ж deafness.

глуши́тел|ь (-я) м (*ТЕХ*) silencer; (*АВТ*) silencer (*BRIT*), muffler (*US*); (*перен*) suppressor.

глуш|и́ть (-у́, -и́шь; *perf* **заглуши́ть**) *несов перех* (*зву́ки, шум итп*) to muffle; (*мотор*) to turn off; (*перен: инициати́ву*) to stifle, suppress; (*perf* **оглуши́ть**; *рыбу*) to stun; **~** (*impf*) **во́дку/вино́** to hit the vodka/wine.

глуш|ь (-и́; *instr sg* -ью, *loc sg* -и́) ж wilderness; (*леса*) deepest part; (*перен*) backwoods мн.

глы́б|а (-ы) ж (*ледяна́я*) block; **ка́менная ~** boulder.

глюко́з|а (-ы) ж glucose.

гля|де́ть (-жу́, -ди́шь; *perf* **погляде́ть**) *несов неперех* to look; (*забо́титься*): **~ за** +*instr* to look after; (*оце́нивать*): **~ на** +*acc* to look at; **на ночь гля́дя** (so) late at night; **на́ зиму гля́дя** just before winter; **я захоте́л есть, гля́дя на тебя́** seeing you eat has made me hungry; **того́ и ~ди́ дождь пойдёт** (*разг*) it looks like it could rain any minute; **того́ и ~ди́ де́ньги зако́нчатся** the money might run out at any time; **там погляди́м** (*разг*) we'll see

▶ **гляде́ться** *несов возв*: **~ся в** +*acc* to look at o.s. in.

гля́н|ец (-ца) м lustre (*BRIT*), luster (*US*), sheen; **наводи́ть (навести́** *perf*) **~ на что-н** (*перен*) to add the finishing touches to sth.

гля́нцевый *прил* glossy.

гм *межд* h'm.

гна|ть (гоню́, го́нишь; *pt* -л, -ла́, -ло) *несов перех* (*ста́до*) to drive; (*зве́ря*) to chase; (*удаля́ть: челове́ка*) to throw out; (*ло́шадь*) to drive *или* urge on; (*маши́ну*) to drive fast; (*во́дку итп*) to distil (*BRIT*), distill (*US*); (*разг: проду́кцию*) to churn out; **~** (*impf*) **от себя́** to drive off *или* away; **~** (*impf*) **кого́-н с** +*instr* to rush sb with; **гони́те де́ньги/еду́!** (*разг*) give us your money/some food!

▶ **гна́|ться** *несов возв*: **гна́ться за** +*instr* (*преследовать*) to pursue; (*добиваться*) to strive after.

гнев (-а) *м* wrath; **быть** (*impf*) **в гне́ве** to be in a rage.

гне́ва|ться (-юсь) *несов возв* to be angry.

гне́вен *прил см* **гне́вный**.

гнев|и́ть (-лю́, -и́шь) *несов перех* to anger; **не ~й Бо́га!** ≈ you should count your blessings!

гне́в|ный (-ен, -на́, -но) *прил* wrathful.

гнедо́й *прил* (*масть лошади*) bay.

гнезди́ться (*3sg* -и́тся, *3pl* -я́тся) *несов возв* (*птицы*) to nest; (*мысль, чувство*) to take root.

гнезд|о́ (-а́; *nom pl* **гнёзда**, *gen pl* **гнёзд**) *м* (*у птиц*) nest; (*для патронов*) socket, pocket; (*для посуды*) compartment; (*линг*) word family; **вить** (**свить** *perf*) ~ to build a nest.

гнездо́вье (-я) *ср* nesting.

гне|сти́ (-ту́, -тёшь) *несов перех* to gnaw.

гнёт (-а) *м* (*бедности итп*) yoke; **под ~ом** under the yoke.

гнету́щий (-ая, -ее, -ие) *прил* depressing.

гни́д|а (-ы) *ж* nit; (*разг: пренебр*) louse.

гнил|о́й (-, -а́, -о) *прил* (*продукты, ткань итп*) rotten; (*климат*) unhealthy; (*перен: настроения, теория*) decadent.

гни́л|ь (-и) *ж* rotten stuff.

гни|ть (-ю́, -ёшь; *perf* **сгнить**) *несов неперех* to rot.

гно|и́ть (-ю́, -и́шь; *perf* **сгнои́ть**) *несов перех* to let rot.

▶ **гнои́ться** *несов возв* (*рана*) to discharge.

гно|й (-я) *м* pus.

гнойни́к (-а́) *м* boil.

гном (-а) *м* gnome.

гнуса́в|ить (-лю, -ишь) *несов неперех* to talk through one's nose.

гнуса́в|ый (-, -а, -о) *прил* (*голос, тон*) affected and nasal.

гну́сен *прил см* **гну́сный**.

гну́сност|ь (-и) *ж* (*клеветы, поведения*) vileness; (*поступок*) vile thing.

гну́с|ный (-ен, -на́, -но) *прил* vile.

гн|уть (-у, -ёшь; *perf* **согну́ть**) *несов перех* to bend; ~ (*impf*) **свою́ ли́нию** (*разг*) to have things one's own way; **куда́** *или* **к чему́ он ~ёт?** (*разг*) what's he driving at?; ~ (*impf*) **спи́ну на кого́-н** to slave away for sb

▶ **гну́ться** *несов возв* (*ветка, полка*) to bend.

гнуша́|ться (-юсь; *perf* **погнуша́ться**) *несов возв* (+*gen*) to abhor; **ничем не** ~ to have no scruples whatsoever.

гобеле́н (-а) *м* tapestry.

гобо́|й (-я) *м* oboe.

гове́|ть (-ю) *несов неперех to fast and attend church in preparation for confession and*

Communion.

говн|о́ (-а́) *ср* (*груб!*) shit (*!*)

го́вор (-а) *м* (*линг*) dialect; (*звуки разговора*) voices *мн*.

говор|и́ть (-ю́, -и́шь; *perf* **сказа́ть**) *несов перех* to say; (*правду*) to tell ◆ *неперех* to speak, talk; (*обсуждать*): ~ **о** +*prp* to discuss, talk about; (*общаться*): ~ **с** +*instr* to talk to *или* with; **~я́т** it's said, they say; ~ (*impf*) **по-ру́сски** to speak Russian; **что вы ~и́те?** you don't say!, really?; **не ~я́** (**уже́**) **о** +*prp* not to mention; **что и ~!** (*разг*) what else is there to say?; **что ни ~й!** (*разг*) say what you like!; **коро́че** *или* **коро́тко ~я́** in short; **стро́го ~я́** strictly speaking; **открове́нно ~я́** to be frank; **по пра́вде ~я́** to tell (you) the truth; **ина́че ~я́** in other words

▶ **говори́ться** *несов возв* (*произноситься*) to be said; **как ~ится** as they say.

говорли́в|ый (-, -а, -о) *прил* talkative.

говя́дин|а (-ы) *ж* beef.

го́гот (-а) *м* (*гусей*) honking; (*разг: пренебр*) guffaw.

гого|та́ть (-чу́, -чешь; *perf* **прогогота́ть**) *несов неперех* (*см сущ*) to honk; to guffaw.

год (-а; *part gen* -у, *loc sg* -у́, *nom pl* -ы, *gen pl* -о́в/ **лет**) *м* year; **прошло́ 3 го́да/5 лет** 3/5 years passed; **из го́да в** ~ year in year out; **кру́глый** ~ all year round; **с ~а́ми** with the years; **от го́да** from year to year; *см также* **го́ды**.

года́ми *нареч* for years.

го́ден *прил см* **го́дный**.

год|и́ться (-жу́сь, -ди́шься) *несов возв* (+*dat*) to suit; ~ (*impf*) **в** +*nom pl* to be (well) suited to be; ~ (*impf*) **для** +*gen* to be suitable for; **куда́ э́то ~ди́тся?** (*разг*) what good is this?; ~ (*impf*) **в отцы́/в ма́тери кому́-н** to be old enough to be sb's father/mother; ~ (*impf*) **в сыновья́ кому́-н** to be young enough to be sb's son.

го́дност|ь (-и) *ж* suitability; (*билета*) validity; **срок ~и** shelf life.

го́д|ный (-ен, -на́, -но) *прил*: ~ **к** +*dat или* **для** +*gen* fit *или* suitable for; **биле́т ~ен до ...** the ticket is valid until ....

годовщи́н|а (-ы) *ж* anniversary; ~ **со дня сме́рти кого́-н** the anniversary of sb's death.

го́ды (-о́в) *мн*: **де́тские/вое́нные** ~ childhood/ war years; **он уже́ в года́х** he's getting on (in years) now; **пятидеся́тые** ~ the Fifties *или* 1950s.

гожу́сь *несов см* **годи́ться**.

Гозна́к (-а) *м сокр* = **Гла́вное управле́ние** *произво́дства госуда́рственных зна́ков, моне́т и ордено́в*.

гол (-а; *nom pl* -ы́) *м* goal; **забива́ть** (**заби́ть** *perf*) ~ to score a goal.

голеносто́пный *прил*: ~ **суста́в** ankle.

го́лен|ь (-и) *ж* shin; (*у животного*) shank.

голки́пер (-а) *м* goalkeeper.

голла́нд|ец (-ца) *м* Dutchman (*мн* Dutchmen).

Голла́нди|я (-и) *ж* Holland.

голла́нд|ка (-ки; *gen pl* -ок) *ж* Dutchwoman (*мн* Dutchwomen).

голла́ндск|ий (-ая, -ое, -ие) *прил* Dutch; ~ язы́к Dutch; „Г~ аукцио́н" (*КОММ*) Dutch auction.

голла́ндца *итп сущ см* **голла́ндец**.

Голливу́д (-а) *м* Hollywood.

гол|ова́ (-овы́; *acc sg* -ову, *dat sg* -ове́, *nom pl* -овы, *gen pl* -о́в, *dat pl* -ова́м) *ж* head; **с ~овы́ до ног** from head to foot; **его́ имя́ вы́летало у меня́ из ~овы́** his name slipped my mind; **на ~ову вы́ше кого́-н** head and shoulders above sb; **де́лать (сде́лать** *perf*) **что-н на свою́/чью́-н го́лову** (*разг*) to make matters worse for o.s./sb; **они́ де́йствовали че́рез мою́/его́ го́лову** they acted over my/his head.

голове́ш|ка (-ки; *gen pl* -ок) *ж* smouldering (*BRIT*) *или* smoldering (*US*) log.

голо́в|ка (-ки; *gen pl* -ок) *ж* (*гвоздя́*) head; (*чесно́ка*) bulb; **~ лу́ка** onion.

головно́й *прил* (*платок итп*) head *опред*; (*отря́д*) front *опред*; (*предприятие*) main; **головно́й мозг** brain.

голово́к *сущ см* **голо́вка**.

головокруже́ни|е (-я) *ср* giddiness.

головокружи́тельный *прил* (*высота́*) dizzy; (*карье́ра*) breath-taking.

головоло́м|ка (-ки; *gen pl* -ок) *ж* (*также перен*) puzzle; **задава́ть (зада́ть** *perf*) **(кому́-н) ~ку** (*перен*) to pose a problem (to sb).

головомо́йк|а (-и) *ж* (*разг*) telling off.

головоре́з (-а) *м* (*бандит*) cutthroat.

го́лод (-а) *м* hunger; (*дли́тельное недоеда́ние*) starvation; (*массовое бе́дствие*) famine; (*перен*): **кни́жный/бума́жный ~** severe shortage of books/paper; **умира́ть (умере́ть** *perf*) **с ~у** *или* **от ~а** to die of hunger.

голода́ни|е (-я) *ср* starvation; (*воздержа́ние*) fasting; **кислоро́дное ~** oxygen deficiency.

голода́|ть (-ю) *несов неперех* to starve; (*воздержива́ться от пищи*) to fast.

гол|о́дный (-оден, -одна́, -одно) *прил* hungry; (*год, время*) hunger-stricken; (*край*) barren; **~о́дные бо́ли** hunger pangs; **~о́дная смерть** death from starvation.

голодо́в|ка (-ки; *gen pl* -ок) *ж* hunger strike; (*разг*) famine; **объявля́ть (объяви́ть** *perf*) **~ку** to go on hunger strike.

гололёд (-а) *м* (*на дорогах*) black ice.

гололе́диц|а (-ы) *ж* (*на дере́вьях*) ice; (*на дорогах*) black ice.

го́лос (-а; *part gen* -у, *nom pl* -а́) *м* voice; (*в хо́ре*) part; (*крови*) the call; (*полит*) vote; **~ рассу́дка/со́вести** the voice of reason/conscience; **подава́ть (пода́ть** *perf*) **~** to vote; **пра́во ~а** the right to vote; **в оди́н ~** with one voice; **во весь ~** at the top of one's voice; *см также* **голоса́**.

голос|а́ (-о́в) *мн foreign-controlled radio*

stations broadcasting to the Soviet Union.

голоси́ст|ый (-, -а, -о) *прил* loud.

голосло́в|ный (-ен, -на, -но) *прил* unsubstantiated.

голосова́ни|е (-я) *ср* ballot, vote; **откры́тое/та́йное ~** open/secret ballot; **манда́тное** *или* **представи́тельное ~** card *или* block vote.

голос|ова́ть (-у́ю; *perf* **проголосова́ть**) *несов неперех* to vote; (*разг*) to hitch (a lift); **~ (проголосова́ть** *perf*) **за** +*acc*/**про́тив** +*gen* to vote for/against.

голосов|о́й *прил* vocal; **~ы́е свя́зки** vocal chords.

голубе́|ть (-ю) *несов неперех* to show blue; (*perf* **поголубе́ть**) to turn blue.

голубе́|ц (-ца́) *м* (*обычно мн*) stuffed cabbage leaf.

голуби́к|а (-и) *ж* great bilberry.

голу́бк|а (-и) *ж* (*обраще́ние*) pet.

голуб|о́й *прил* light blue ♦ (-о́го; *decl like adj*) *м* (*разг: гомосексуали́ст*) gay; **голуба́я мечта́** pipe dream; **голубо́й экра́н** small screen.

голу́бушк|а (-и) *ж см* **голу́бчик**.

голубца́ *итп сущ см* **голубе́ц**.

голу́бчик (-а) *м* (*разг*) (my) dear.

го́луб|ь (-я; *gen pl* -е́й) *м* pigeon; dove; **~ ми́ра** dove of peace.

голубя́тн|я (-ни; *gen pl* -ен) *ж* pigeon loft; dovecot.

го́л|ый (-, -а́, -о) *прил* (*челове́к*) naked; (*че́реп*) bald; (*дерево, стены*) bare; (*no short form*; *правда*) naked; (*ци́фры, факты*) bare; **~ыми рука́ми** with one's bare hands; **его́ ~ыми рука́ми не возьмёшь** (*перен*) he's a slippery character; **го́лый про́вод** bare wire.

голышо́м *нареч* starkers.

гол|ь (-и) *ж собир* rabble; **~ на вы́думки хитра́** ≈ necessity is the mother of invention.

гольф (-а) *м* golf; (*обычно мн: чулки́*) knee sock; *см также* **го́льфы**.

го́льф|ы (-ов) *мн* (*брю́ки*) plus-fours *мн*.

гомеопа́т (-а) *м* homoeopath (*BRIT*), homeopath (*US*).

гомеопати́ческ|ий (-ая, -ое, -ие) *прил* homoeopathic (*BRIT*), homeopathic (*US*); **~ая до́за** (*перен*) tiny amount.

гомеопа́ти|я (-и) *ж* homoeopathy (*BRIT*), homeopathy (*US*).

гомери́ческ|ий (-ая, -ое, -ие) *прил*: **смех** *или* **хо́хот** roar of laughter.

гомоге́нный *прил* homogenous.

го́мон (-а) *м* (*толпы́*) hubbub; (*пти́чий*) ~ chorus of birdsong; **поднима́ть (подня́ть** *perf*) **~** to make a din.

гомосексуали́зм (-а) *м* homosexuality.

гомосексуали́ст (-а) *м* homosexual.

гонг (-а) *м* gong; **уда́рить** (*perf*) **в ~** to beat a gong.

гондо́л|а (-ы) *ж* gondola; (*дирижабля*) car (*of airship*).

Гондура́с (-а) *м* Honduras.

гоне́ни|е (-я) *ср* persecution; **подверга́ться (подве́ргнуться** *perf*) **~ям** to be persecuted; **~я на кого́-н/что-н** persecution of sb/sth.

гоне́ц (-ца́) *м* messenger.

го́н|ка (-ки; *gen pl* **-ок**) *ж* (*разг: спешка*) rush; (*обычно мн: соревнования*) racing; **го́нка вооруже́ний** arms race.

Гонко́нг (-а) *м* Hong Kong.

го́нок *итп сущ см* **го́нка**.

го́нор (-а) *м* arrogance.

гонора́р (-а) *м* fee; **а́вторский ~** royalty.

гонор́е|я (-и) *ж* gonorrhoea (*BRIT*), gonorrhea (*US*).

го́ночный *прил* racing *опред*; **го́ночный велосипе́д** racer.

гонт (-а) *м* (*СТРОИТ*) shingles *мн*.

гонца́ *итп сущ см* **гоне́ц**.

гонча́р (-а́) *м* potter.

го́нча|я (-ей; *decl like adj*) *ж* hound.

го́нщик (-а) *м* (*автомобиля*) racing (*BRIT*) *или* race car (*US*) driver; (*велосипеда*) racing cyclist.

гоню́(сь) *итп несов см* **гнать(ся)**.

гоня́|ть (-ю, -ешь) *несов перех* (*стадо*) to drive; (*птиц, поклонников*) to chase off *или* away; (*разг: курьера*) to keep on the go; (: *мяч*) to knock about; (: *ученика*) to grill ♦ *неперех* to race; **~** (*impf*) **голубе́й** (*СПОРТ*) to race pigeons; **~** (*перен: разг*) to loaf around; **~** (*impf*) **чай** (*разг*) to lounge around drinking tea

▶ **гоня́ться** *несов возв*: **~ся за** +*instr* (*преследовать*) to chase (after); (*перен*) to pursue.

гоп-компа́ни|я (-и) *ж* (*разг*) rowdy bunch.

гор. *сокр* = **го́род, городско́й**.

гор|а́ (*acc sg* **-у**, *gen sg* **-ы́**, *nom pl* **-ы**, *dat pl* **-а́м**) *ж* mountain; (*небольшая*) hill; (*перен: разг*) heap; **идти́** (**пойти́** *perf*) **в го́ру** to go uphill; (*перен: разг: улучшаться*) to be looking up; (: *делать карьеру*) to go up in the world; **идти́** (**пойти́** *perf*) **под ~у** (*также перен: разг*) to go downhill; **у меня́ ~ с плеч свали́лась** (*разг*) that's a weight off my mind; **обеща́ть** (*impf*) **золоты́е го́ры** to promise the earth; **стоя́ть** (*impf*) **~о́й за кого́-н** (*разг*) to stand up for sb; **пир ~о́й** (*разг*) celebratory blowout; *см также* **го́ры**.

гора́зд (-а, -о) *как сказ* (*разг*): **~ на что́-н/**+*infin* very good at sth/at doing; **кто во что ~** (*разг: пренебр*) everyone doing his own thing.

гора́здо *нареч* much.

горб (-а́; *loc sg* **-у́**) *м* hump; **тащи́ть** (*impf*) **всё на ~у́** (*перен: разг*) to take everything upon o.s.; **испы́тывать** (**испыта́ть** *perf*) **что-н на своём ~у́** (*разг*) to learn sth the hard way; **он зарабо́тал всё свои́м ~о́м** (*разг*) he earned everything through his own hard graft.

горба́т|ый (-, -а, -о) *прил* (*человек*) hunchbacked; (*нос*) hooked; **~ого моги́ла испра́вит** he *итп* will never change, ≈ a leopard can't change his spots.

горби́н|ка (-ки; *gen pl* **-ок**) *ж*: **нос с ~кой** Roman nose.

го́рб|ить (-лю, -ишь; *perf* **сго́рбить**) *несов перех*: **~ спи́ну** to stoop.

▶ **го́рбиться** (*perf* **сго́рбиться**) *несов возв* to stoop; (*от старости*) to develop a stoop.

горбоно́с|ый (-, -а, -о) *прил* hooknosed.

горбу́н (-а́) *м* hunchback.

горбу́нь|я (-и) *ж см* **горбу́н**.

горбу́ш|а (-и) *ж* (hunchback) salmon.

горбу́ш|ка (-ки; *gen pl* **-ек**) *ж* crust.

горде́ли́в|ый (-, -а, -о) *прил* proud.

горди́ться (-жу́сь, -ди́шься) *несов возв* (+*instr*) to be proud of.

го́рдост|ь (-и) *ж* pride; (+*instr*; *победой, успехами*) pride in; **он – ~ на́шей семьи́** he's the pride and joy of the family.

го́рд|ый (-, -а́, -о, -ы́) *прил* proud; (+*instr*; *победой, успехами*) proud of.

го́р|е (-я) *ср* (*скорбь*) grief, sorrow; (*несчастье*) misfortune; **хлебну́ть** (*perf*) **~я** (*разг*) to suffer one's share of misfortune; **помога́ть** (**помо́чь** *perf*) **~ю** to help out in times of trouble; **с ~я** with *или* from grief; **в ~** in (one's) grief; **как на ~** (*разг*) as ill luck would have it; **~ ты моё!** you'll be the death of me!; **ему́ и ~я ма́ло** (*разг*) he couldn't care less.

гор|ева́ть (-ю́ю) *несов неперех* to grieve; **~** (*impf*) **о** +*prp* to grieve for; **не ~ю́й!** cheer up!

го́рек *прил см* **го́рький**.

горе́л|ка (-ки; *gen pl* **-ок**) *ж* burner; **пая́льная ~** blowtorch.

горе́лый *прил* burnt.

горелье́ф (-а) *м* high relief.

горемы́к|а (-и) *м/ж* (*разг*) poor soul.

го́рест|ный (-ен, -на, -но) *прил* sorrowful.

го́рест|ь (-и) *ж* grief, sorrow; (*обычно мн: несчастье*) trouble.

гор|е́ть (-ю́, -и́шь; *perf* **сгоре́ть**) *несов неперех* to burn; (*no perf*; *дом, лес*) to be on fire; (*больной, лоб*) to be burning hot; (*рана*) to smart; (+*instr*; *ненавистью, нетерпением*) to burn with; **зака́т ~е́л** there was a blazing sunset; **~** (*impf*) **от стыда́/ любопы́тсва** to burn with shame/curiosity; **он ~и́т на рабо́те** he puts everything into his work; **план/спекта́кль ~и́т!** the plan/play is in danger of being a complete failure!; **~и́ всё си́ним огнём** *или* **пла́менем!** (*разг*) to hell with it!; **не ~и́т** (*разг*) there's no hurry; **у меня́ душа́ ~и́т** I'm bursting with enthusiasm.

го́р|ец (-ца) *м* mountain dweller.

го́реч|ь (-и) *ж* bitter taste; (*потери*) bitterness.

горже́т|ка (-ки; *gen pl* **-ок**) *ж* boa.

горжу́сь *несов см* **горди́ться**.

горизо́нт (-а) *м* horizon; **появля́ться (появи́ться** *perf*) **на чьём-н ~е** to come into sb's life.

горизонта́лен *прил см* **горизонта́льный.**

горизонта́ль (-и) *ж* horizontal; (*на ка́рте*) contour; (*на ша́хматной доске́*) rank.

горизонта́льный (-ен, -ьна, -ьно) *прил* horizontal.

гори́лл|**а** (-ы) *ж* gorilla.

горисполко́м (-а) *м сокр* (*ИСТ: = городско́й исполни́тельный комите́т*) town *или* city executive committee.

гори́стый *прил* mountainous.

го́р|**ка** (-ки; *gen pl* -ок) *ж* hill; (*склон*) slope; (*шкаф*) cabinet; (*ку́чка*) small pile; (*АВИА*) steep climb.

го́ркн|**уть** (*3sg* -ет, *perf* **прого́ркнуть**) *несов неперех* (*ма́сло*) to go rancid.

горко́м (-а) *м сокр* (*ИСТ: = городско́й комите́т*) town *или* city committee.

горла́н|**ить** (-ю, -ишь) *несов неперех* (*разг*) to bawl.

горла́стый (-, -а, -о) *прил* (*разг*) noisy.

го́рлиц|**а** (-ы) *ж* turtledove.

го́рл|**о** (-а) *ср* throat; (*у сосу́да*) neck; **стать** (*perf*) **поперёк ~а кому́-н** (*перен: разг*) to stick in sb's throat; **во всё ~** (*разг*) at the top of one's voice; **пристава́ть** (**приста́ть** *perf*) **к кому́-н с ножо́м к ~у** (*разг: пренебр*) to pester the life out of sb; **у меня́ рабо́ты по ~** (*разг*) I'm up to my ears in work; **я сыт по ~** (*разг*) I'm stuffed; (: *перен: обеща́ниями, упрёками*) I've had it up to here.

го́рлыш|**ко** (-ка; *nom pl* -ки, *gen pl* -ек) *ср* (*буты́лки, сосу́да*) neck.

гормо́н (-а) *м* hormone.

гормона́льный *прил* hormonal.

горн (-а) *м* (*для перепла́вки*) furnace; (*для обжи́га*) kiln; (*МУЗ*) bugle.

горни́ст (-а) *м* bugler.

го́рничн|**ая** (-ой; *decl like adj*) *ж* chambermaid.

горно-бурово́й *прил* mining *опред*, mine-excavation *опред*.

горнодобыва́ющий (-ая, -ее, -ие) *прил* mining *опред*.

горнозаво́дск|**ий** (-ая, -ое, -ие) *прил* mining *опред*.

горноль́жный *прил* ski *опред*.

горнопромы́шленный *прил* = **горнозаво́дский.**

горнопрохо́дческ|**ий** (-ая, -ое, -ие) *прил*: **~ие рабо́ты** tunnelling work *ед*.

горнорабо́ч|**ий** (-его; *decl like adj*) *м* miner.

горноспаса́тельный *прил* mountain-rescue *опред*.

горноста́|**й** (-я) *м* stoat; (*мех*) ermine.

го́рн|**ый** *прил* mountain *опред*; (*лы́жи*) downhill *опред*; (*страна́*) mountainous; (*бога́тства*) mineral *опред*; (*промы́шленность*) mining *опред*; **~ые поро́ды** rocks; **~ хруста́ль** rock crystal; **го́рная боле́знь** altitude sickness;

го́рный хребе́т mountain range.

горня́к (-а́) *м* (*рабо́чий*) miner; (*инжене́р*) mining engineer.

го́род (-а; *nom pl* -а́) *м* (*большо́й*) city; (*небольшо́й*) town; **е́хать** (**пое́хать** *perf*) **за́ город** to go out of town; **жить** (*impf*) **за́ городом** to live out of town.

горо́д|**ить** (-жу́, -ди́шь) *несов перех*: **~ ерунду́** *или* **вздор** *или* **чушь** (*разг: пренебр*) to talk rubbish.

городо́к (-ка́) *м* small town; **спорти́вный ~** sports complex; **вое́нный ~** military settlement; **университе́тский ~** (university) campus; **де́тский ~** playground.

городско́й *прил* urban; (*сад*) municipal; **~ жи́тель** town dweller; (*большо́го го́рода*) city dweller.

горожа́н|**ин** (-ина; *nom pl* -е, *gen pl* -) *м* city dweller.

горожа́н|**ка** (-ки; *gen pl* -ок) *ж см* **горожа́нин.**

горожу́ *несов см* **городи́ть.**

го́рок *сущ см* **го́рка.**

гороско́п (-а) *м* horoscope.

горо́х (-а; *part gen* -у) *м собир* peas *мн*; (*на пла́тье итп*) polka dots *мн*; **как об сте́ну ~** like talking to a brick wall.

горо́ховый *прил* (*суп*) pea; **шут ~** (*разг: пренебр*) buffoon.

горо́ш|**ек** (-ка) *м собир* peas *мн*; (*на пла́тье итп*) polka dots *мн*; **ткань в ~** spotted material; **зелёный ~** garden peas *мн*; **души́стый ~** sweet pea.

горо́шин|**а** (-ы) *ж* pea.

горо́шка *итп сущ см* **горо́шек.**

горсове́т (-а) *м сокр* (= **городско́й сове́т**) ≈ town *или* city council.

го́рст|**ка** (-ки; *gen pl* -ок) *ж* (*также перен*) handful.

горст|**ь** (-и; *gen pl* -е́й) *ж* (*руки́*) cupped hand; (*также перен*) handful.

горта́нный *прил* guttural.

горта́н|**ь** (-и) *ж* larynx.

горте́нзи|**я** (-и) *ж* hydrangea.

го́рц|**а** *итп сущ см* **го́рец.**

го́рче *сравн прил от* **го́рький ♦** *сравн нареч от* **го́рько.**

горч|**и́ть** (*3sg* -и́т, *3pl* -а́т) *несов неперех* to taste bitter.

горчи́ц|**а** (-ы) *ж* mustard.

горчи́чник (-а) *м* mustard plaster.

горчи́чный *прил* mustard.

го́рше *сравн прил от* **го́рький ♦** *сравн нареч от* **го́рько.**

горшо́к (-ка́) *м* pot; (*также:* **ночно́й ~**) chamber pot; **цвето́чный ~** flowerpot.

го́р|**ы** (-; *dat pl* -а́м) *мн* mountains *мн*.

го́рьк|**ий** (-ькая, -ькое, -ькие; -ек, -ька́, -ько) *прил* (*вкус, разочарова́ние*) bitter; (*оби́да, собы́тие*) painful; **го́рькая и́стина** the painful truth; **го́рький пья́ница** (*разг*) a hopeless drunkard; **го́рькие слёзы** bitter tears; **го́рький**

смех bitter laughter.

го́рько *нареч* (*пла́кать*) bitterly ♦ *как сказ:* **во рту** ~ I have a bitter taste in my mouth; **мне** ~, **что меня́ не понима́ют** I feel bitter that nobody understands me.

горю́ч|ее (-его; *decl like adj*) *ср* fuel.

горю́ч|ий (-ая, -ее, -ие) *прил* flammable; ~**ие слёзы** bitter tears.

горя́чек *сущ см* **горя́чка**.

горя́ч|ий (-ая, -ее, -ие; -, -а́, -о́) *прил* hot; (*перен: любо́вь*) passionate; (: *спор*) heated; (: *жела́ние*) burning; (: *челове́к*) hot-tempered; (*день итп*) hectic; ~ **хара́ктер** hot temper; **де́лать (сде́лать** *perf*) **что-н по** ~**им следа́м** to do sth without delay; **я попа́л ему́ под** ~**ую ру́ку** I caught him while he was in a bad mood; **горя́чая то́чка** trouble spot.

горя́ч|и́ться (-у́сь, -и́шься; *perf* **разгорячи́ться**) *несов возв* to get worked up.

горя́ч|ка (-ки; *gen pl* -ек) *ж* (*разг*) frenzy; **поро́ть** (*impf*) ~**ку** to rush.

горя́чность (-и) *ж* irascibility.

горячо́ *нареч* (*спо́рить, люби́ть*) passionately ♦ *как сказ* it's hot.

Госба́нк (-а) *м сокр* (= *госуда́рственный банк*) state bank.

госбезопа́сность (-и) *ж сокр* (ИСТ: = *госуда́рственная безопа́сность*) national security.

госбюдже́т (-а) *м сокр* (= *госуда́рственный бюдже́т*) state budget.

госдепарта́мент (-а) *м сокр* (= *госуда́рственный департа́мент*) State Department.

Госкомизда́т *м сокр* = *Госуда́рственный комите́т Сове́та Мини́стров по дела́м изда́тельства полигра́фии и кни́жной торго́вли*.

госкомите́т (-а) *м сокр* (= *госуда́рственный комите́т*) state committee.

госкреди́т (-а) *м сокр* (= *госуда́рственный креди́т*) state credit.

госпитализи́р|овать (-ую) (*не*)*сов перех* to hospitalize.

го́спиталь (-я) *м* army hospital.

Госпла́н *м сокр* (ИСТ: = *Госуда́рственная пла́новая коми́ссия*) state planning committee.

господа́ *итп сущ см* **господи́н**.

го́споди *межд:* Г~! good Lord!

госп|оди́н (-оди́на; *nom pl* -ода́, *gen pl* -о́д) *м* gentleman (*мн* gentlemen); (*хозя́ин*) master; (*при обраще́нии*) sir; (*при фами́лии, зва́нии*) Mr (= *Mister*).

госпо́дств|о (-а) *ср* supremacy; (*над страно́й*) dominion; (*иде́й*) predominance.

госпо́дств|овать (-ую) *несов непере́х* to rule; (*мне́ние*) to prevail; ~ (*impf*) **на мо́ре** to rule the seas; ~ (*impf*) **над** +*instr* (*ме́стностью*) to tower above, dominate.

госпо́дствующ|ий (-ая, -ее, -ие) *прил* (*па́ртия, класс*) ruling; (*взгля́ды*) prevailing; (*гора́, ба́шня итп*) imposing.

Госпо́дь (Го́спода; *voc* Го́споди) *м* (*та́кже:* ~ **Бог**) the Lord; **не дай Го́споди!** God forbid!; **сла́ва тебе́ Го́споди!** Glory be to God!; (*разг*) thank God!

госпож|а́ (-и́) *ж* lady; (*хозя́йка*) mistress; (*при обраще́нии, зва́нии*) Madam; (*при фами́лии: заму́жняя*) Mrs; (: *незаму́жняя*) Miss; (: *заму́жняя или незаму́жняя*) Ms.

Госстра́х (-а) *м сокр* (= *Гла́вное управле́ние госуда́рственного страхова́ния Министе́рства фина́нсов Росси́и*) *department dealing with national insurance*.

госстра́х (-а) *м сокр* (= *госуда́рственное страхова́ние*) ≈ national insurance.

ГОСТ (-а) *м сокр* (= *госуда́рственный общесою́зный станда́рт*) *standard manufacturing specifications under the Soviet system*.

гост (-а) *м сокр* = **ГОСТ**.

гостеприи́м|ный (-ен, -на, -но) *прил* hospitable.

гости́н|ая (-ой; *decl like adj*) *ж* living *или* sitting room, lounge (BRIT); (*ме́бель*) living-room suite.

гости́ниц|а (-ы) *ж* hotel.

го|сти́ть (-щу́, -сти́шь) *несов непере́х* to stay.

гост|ь (-я; *gen pl* -е́й) *м* guest; **идти́ (пойти́** *perf*) **в го́сти к кому́-н** to go to see sb; **быть** (*impf*) **в** ~**я́х у кого́-н** to be at sb's house; **в** ~**я́х хорошо́, а до́ма лу́чше** there's no place like home.

го́сть|я (-и; *gen pl* -ий) *ж см* **гость**.

госуда́рственн|ый *прил* state *опред;* ~ **язы́к** official language; ~ **строй** government system; **госуда́рственное пра́во** public law; **госуда́рственный экза́мен** Finals *мн*.

госэкза́мен (-а) *м сокр* (= *госуда́рственный экза́мен*) ≈ finals *мн*.

госуда́рств|о (-а) *ср* state.

госуда́рын|я (-и; *gen pl* -ь) *ж* sovereign; (*при обраще́нии*) Your Majesty; **ми́лостивая** ~ Madam.

госуда́р|ь (-я) *м* sovereign; (*при обраще́нии*) Your Majesty; **ми́лостивый** ~ Sir.

го́тик|а (-и) *ж* Gothic.

готи́ческ|ий (-ая, -ое, -ие) *прил* Gothic.

готова́|льня (-ьни; *gen pl* -ен) *ж* (*архите́ктора*) drawing instruments *мн*; (*шко́льника*) geometry set.

гото́в|ить (-лю, -ишь; *perf* **пригото́вить**) *несов перех* to get ready; (*уро́ки*) to prepare; (*обе́д*) to prepare, make; (*perf* **подгото́вить**; *специали́ста*) to train; (*ученика́*) to coach ♦ *непере́х* to cook; **она́ хорошо́** ~**ит** she's a good cook

▶ **готóвить|ся** (*perf* **приготóвиться**) *несов возв*: ~**ся к** +*dat* (*к отъéзду*) to get ready for; ~**ся** (**подготóвиться** *perf*) **к** +*dat* (*к экзáмену*) to prepare for; ~**ятся больши́е собы́тия/ измене́ния** great events/changes are in the offing.

готóвност|ь (**-и**) *ж* readiness; ~ +*infin* readiness *или* willingness to do; **в боево́й** ~**и** ready for action.

готóво *как сказ* that's it.

готóв|ый (**-**, **-а**, **-о**) *прил* (*обéд*) ready; (*no short form*; *издéлие*) ready-made; ~ **к** +*dat*/+*infin* prepared for/to do; ~ **на перегово́ры** prepared *или* willing to negotiate; ~ **на всё** ready for anything; **она́ живёт на всём** ~**ом** her every need is catered for; **готóвое плáтье** off-the-peg (*BRIT*) *или* off-the -rack (*US*) dress.

гофриро́ванный *прил* (*юбка*) pleated; (*жесть*) corrugated.

гофри́р|овáть (**-ýю**) *несов перех* (*см прил*) to pleat; to corrugate.

гощý *несов см* **гости́ть**.

ГПТУ *ср сокр* (= *городскóе профессионáльно-техни́ческое учи́лище*) ≈ CTC (= city technology college).

гр. *сокр* (= **грáдус**) d. (= *degree*); (= **граждани́н**) Mr (= *Mister*); (= **граждáнка**) Mrs; (= **грýппа**).

граб (**-а**) *м* hornbeam.

грабёж (**-ежá**) *м* (*также перен*) robbery; (*дóма*) burglary; ~ **среди́ бéла дня** (*разг*) daylight robbery.

грáбель *сущ см* **грáбли**.

граби́тель (**-я**) *м* (*см сущ*) robber; burglar.

граби́тельск|ий (**-ая**, **-ое**, **-ие**) *прил* (*война*) predatory; (*цены*) extortionate; ~**ое нападéние** (*на дом*) burglary; (*на банк*) robbery; (*на странý*) pillage.

грáб|ить (**-лю**, **-ишь**; *perf* **огрáбить**) *несов перех* (*также перен*: *человéка*) to rob; (*дом*) to burgle; (*гóрод*) to pillage.

грáбл|и (**-ель** *или* **-лей**) *мн* rake *ед*.

грáблю *несов см* **грáбить**.

гравёр (**-а**) *м* engraver.

грáви|й (**-я**) *м* gravel.

гравир|овáть (**-ýю**; *perf* **вы́гравировать**) *несов перех* to engrave ♦ *неперех* to etch.

гравитáци|я (**-и**) *ж* gravitation.

гравю́р|а (**-ы**) *ж* (*оттиск*) engraving; (*офорт*) etching.

град (**-а**) *м* (*также перен*) hail; (*перен*): ~ +*gen* (*пуль*) hail of; (*упрёков*) stream of.

градáци|я (**-и**) *ж* gradation.

грáдин|а (**-ы**) *ж* hailstone.

гради́р|ня (**-ни**; *gen pl* **-ен**) *ж* cooling tower.

грáдом *нареч* thick and fast; **кати́ться** (*impf*) ~ (*слёзы*) to stream down.

градострои́тел|ь (**-я**) *м* town (*BRIT*) *или* city (*US*) planner.

градострои́тельств|о (**-а**) *ср* town (*BRIT*) *или* city (*US*) planning.

грáдус (**-а**) *м* degree; **под** ~**ом** (*разг*) tiddly.

грáдусник (**-а**) *м* thermometer.

граждани́н (**-а**; *nom pl* **грáждане**, *gen pl* **грáждан**) *м* citizen.

граждáн|ка (**-ки**; *gen pl* **-ок**) *ж см* **граждани́н**.

граждáнск|ий (**-ая**, **-ое**, **-ие**) *прил* civil; (*долг*) civic; (*плáтье*) civilian; **граждáнская война́** civil war; **граждáнская панихи́да** civil funeral service; **граждáнский кóдекс** civil code.

граждáнств|о (**-а**) *ср* citizenship; **получáть** (**получи́ть** *perf*) ~ *или* **правá граждáнства** to be granted citizenship.

грамзáпис|ь (**-и**) *ж* recording; **óпера в** ~**и** recording of an opera.

грамм (**-а**; *gen pl* **-ов**) *м* gramme (*BRIT*), gram (*US*); **у негó (нет) ни грáмма сóвести** (*разг*) he doesn't have an ounce of conscience.

граммáтик|а (**-и**) *ж* grammar.

граммати́ческ|ий (**-ая**, **-ое**, **-ие**) *прил* (*ошибка*) grammatical; (*упражнéние*) grammar *опрéд*.

грáмот|а (**-ы**) *ж* reading and writing; (*докумéнт*) certificate; **для меня́ э́то кита́йская** ~ (*разг*) it's Greek *или* double Dutch (*BRIT*) to me; **почётная** ~ certificate of merit.

грáмотн|ый (**-ен**, **-на**, **-но**) *прил* (*человéк*) literate; (*текст*) properly *или* correctly written; (*специали́ст*, *план*) competent.

грампласти́нк|а (**-и**) *ж* gramophone (*BRIT*) *или* phonograph (*US*) record.

гранáт (**-а**) *м* (*плод*) pomegranate; (*дéрево*) pomegranate (tree); (*минерáл*) garnet.

гранáт|а (**-ы**) *ж* grenade.

гранáтовый *прил* (*сок*) pomegranate *опрéд*; (*браслéт*) garnet *опрéд*; (*цвет*) deep red.

гранатомёт (**-а**) *м* grenade launcher.

грандиóзн|ый (**-ен**, **-на**, **-но**) *прил* (*сооружéние*) grand; (*масштáбы*, *плáны*) grandiose.

гранёный *прил* (*стакáн*) cut-glass *опрéд*; (*алмáз*) cut *опрéд*.

грани́т (**-а**) *м* granite.

грани́тный *прил* (*плита́*) granite.

гран|и́ть (**-ю́**, **-и́шь**) *несов перех* to cut.

грани́ц|а (**-ы**) *ж* (*госудáрства*) border; (*учáстка*) boundary; (*обычно мн*: *перен*) limit; **éхать** (**поéхать** *perf*) **за** ~**y** to go abroad; **жить** (*impf*) **за** ~**ей** to live abroad; **из-за** ~**ы** from abroad; **в** ~**х прили́чия/закóна** within the bounds of decency/the law; **егó поведéние перехóдит все** ~**ы!** he's gone too far!

грани́ч|ить (**-у**, **-ишь**) *несов неперех*: ~ **с** +*instr* to border on; (*перен*) to verge on.

грáн|ка (**-ки**; *gen pl* **-ок**) *ж* (*ТИПОГ*) proof.

грáнул|а (**-ы**) *ж* granule.

гран|ь (**-и**) *ж* (*ГЕОМ*) face; (*алмáза*) facet; (*перен*) bounds *мн*; **переступáть** (**переступи́ть** *perf*) ~ to overstep the mark; **на грáни** +*gen* on the brink *или* verge of.

граф (**-а**) *м* count, earl (*BRIT*).

граф|á (**-ы́**) *ж* column.

грáфик (**-а**) *м* (*МАТ*) graph; (*план*) schedule,

timetable; (*художник*) graphic artist; **работать** (*impf*) **по ~у** to work to schedule; **поезд идёт по ~у** the train is running to time; ~ **расчёта точки „нулевой" прибыли** (*комм*) break-even chart.

график|а (-и) *ж* graphic art; (*буквы*) script ♦ *собир* (*рисунки*) graphics *мн*.

графин (-а) *м* (*для воды*) water jug; (*для вина*) decanter; (: *открытый*) carafe.

графин|я (-и) *ж* countess.

графит (-а) *м* (*минерал*) graphite; (*грифель*) (pencil) lead.

графи́ть (-лю, -ишь; *perf* **разграфить**) *несов перех* to rule (*lines*).

графи́ческий (-ая, -ое, -ие) *прил* graphic.

графлю *несов см* **графить**.

графство (-а) *ср* county.

грациозный (-ен, -на, -но) *прил* graceful.

граци|я (-и) *ж* grace; (*корсет*) corset.

грач (-а́) *м* rook.

грёб *итп несов см* **грести**.

гребён|ка (-ки; *gen pl* -ок) *ж* (*также тех*) comb; **стричь** (*impf*) **всех под одну ~ку** to lump everyone together.

греб|ень (-ня) *м* comb; (*волны, горы*) crest.

греб|е́ц (-ца́) *м* oarsman (*мн* oarsmen), rower.

гребеш|о́к (-ка́) *м* comb; (*также:* **морской ~**) scallop.

гребл|я (-и) *ж* rowing.

гребной *прил:* ~ **спорт** rowing.

гребня *итп сущ см* **гребень**.

греб|о́к (-ка) *м* stroke.

гребу *итп несов см* **грести**.

гребца *итп сущ см* **гребец**.

грёжу(сь) *несов см* **грезить(ся)**.

грёз|а (-ы) *ж* (*обычно мн*) daydream.

грё|зить (-жу, -зишь) *несов неперех* to (day)dream, fantasize

▶ **грёзиться** (*perf* **пригрёзиться**) *несов возв:* **ему ~зится...** he dreams of ....

грейдер (-а) *м* grader; (*разг: дорога*) dirt road.

грейпфрут (-а) *м* grapefruit.

грек (-а) *м* Greek (man) (*мн* men).

грел|ка (-ки; *gen pl* -ок) *ж* hot-water bottle; **электрическая ~** electric blanket.

грем|е́ть (-лю, -ишь; *perf* **прогреметь**) *несов неперех* (*поезд*) to thunder by; (*выстрелы*) to thunder out; (*гром*) to rumble; (*перен*) to resound; ~ (**прогреметь** *perf*) +*instr* (*ведром, кастрюлями*) to clatter; (*ключами*) to jangle.

грему́чий (-ая, -ее, -ие) *прил:* ~**ая змея** rattlesnake; ~ **газ** firedamp.

Гренад|а (-ы) *ж* Grenada.

гренадёр (-а; *gen pl* -или -ов) *м* (*солдат*) grenadier; **он настоящий ~** (*разг*) he's a real hulk.

гренка *итп сущ см* **гренок**.

Гренланди|я (-и) *ж* Greenland.

гренландск|ий (-ая, -ое, -ие) *прил* Greenlandic.

грен|о́к (-ка́; *nom pl* -ки) *м* (*обычно мн*) crouton.

гре|сти́ (-бу́, -бёшь; *pt* **грёб, -бла, -бло**) *несов неперех* to row; (*веслом, руками*) to paddle ♦ *перех* to rake.

гре|ть (-ю) *несов перех* (*подлеж: солнце, печь*) to heat, warm; (: *шуба*) to keep warm; (*воду*) to heat (up); (*руки*) to warm; ~ (*impf*) **руки на чём-н** (*разг*) to line one's pockets with sth

▶ **гре́ться** *несов возв* (*человек*) to warm o.s.; (*вода*) to warm *или* heat up.

грех (-а́) *м* sin ♦ *как сказ:* ~ +*infin* (*разг*) it's a sin to do; **как на ~** (*разг*) as ill luck would have it; **от ~а́ пода́льше** just to be on the safe side; **уйди от ~а́ пода́льше!** go away and stay out of trouble!; **с ~о́м попола́м** (*разг*) by a hair('s breadth).

грехо́вный (-ен, -на, -но) *прил* sinful.

грехопаде́ни|е (-я) *ж* the Fall.

Гре́ци|я (-и) *ж* Greece.

гре́цк|ий (-ая, -ое, -ие) *прил:* ~ **оре́х** walnut.

греча́н|ка (-ки; *gen pl* -ок) *ж* Greek (woman) (*мн* women).

гре́ческ|ий (-ая, -ое, -ие) *прил* Greek; (*культура*) (Ancient) Greek; ~ **язы́к** Greek.

гречи́х|а (-и) *ж* buckwheat.

гре́чк|а (-и) *ж* buckwheat.

гре́чневый *прил* buckwheat.

гре́шен *прил см* **гре́шный**.

греш|и́ть (-у́, -ишь; *perf* **согреши́ть**) *несов неперех* to sin; (*perf* **погреши́ть**; *противоречить*): ~ **про́тив** +*gen* to sin against.

гре́шник (-а) *м* sinner.

гре́шниц|а (-ы) *ж см* **гре́шник**.

гре́шн|ый (-ен, -на́, -но) *прил* sinful.

гриб (-а́) *м* fungus (*мн* fungi); (*съедобный*) (edible) mushroom; **несъедо́бный ~** toadstool.

грибка́ *итп сущ см* **грибо́к**.

грибни́к (-а́) *м* mushroom picker.

грибни́ц|а (-ы) *ж* mushroom spore.

грибн|о́й *прил* (*суп*) mushroom; ~**о́е ме́сто** a good place for mushrooms; **грибно́й дождь** *rain during sunshine*.

гриб|о́к (-ка́) *м* (*на коже*) fungal infection; (*на дереве*) fungus; (*на хлебе итп*) mould; (*укрытие*) *mushroom-shaped shelter in a playground, on the beach etc.*

гри́в|а (-ы) *ж* mane.

гри́венник (-а) *м* (*разг*) ten-kopeck piece.

грим (-а) *м* stage make-up, greasepaint.

грима́с|а (-ы) *ж* grimace; **строить** (**состроить** *perf*) **или ко́рчить** (**ско́рчить** *perf*) ~**ы** to make *или* pull faces.

грима́снича|ть (-ю) *несов неперех* to make *или* pull faces.

гримёр (-а) *м* make-up artist.

гримёрн|ая (-ой; *decl like adj*) *ж* dressing room.

гримир|ова́ть (-у́ю; *perf* **загримирова́ть**) *несов перех:* ~ **кого́-н** to make sb up

▶ **гримирова́ться** (*perf* **загримирова́ться** *или* **нагримирова́ться**) *несов возв* to put on one's make-up.

грипп (-а) *м* flu.

гриппо́зн|ый *прил* flu *опред;* **у больно́го ~ое состоя́ние** the patient has influenza.

гриф (-а) *м* (*ЗООЛ*) vulture; (*МИФОЛОГИЯ*) griffin; (*МУЗ*) fingerboard; (*штемпель*) stamp.

гри́фел|ь (-я) *м* (pencil)lead.

гроб (-а; *loc sg* -ý, *nom pl* -ы́) *м* coffin; **вгоня́ть** (**вогна́ть** *perf*) **кого́-н в ~** (*разг*) to drive sb to their grave; **в ~ý я э́то ви́дел!** (*разг*) I don't give a damn about it!

гро́б|ить (-лю, -ишь; *perf* **угро́бить**) *несов перех* (*разг*) to screw up.

гробни́ц|а (-ы) *ж* tomb.

гробов|о́й *прил:* **~ го́лос** sepulchral tones *мн;* **гробово́е молча́ние** deathly silence; **гробова́я тишина́** deathly hush.

грог (-а; *part gen* -у) *м* grog.

грожу́(сь) *несов см* **грози́ть(ся)**.

гр|оза́ (-озы́; *nom pl* -о́зы) *ж* thunderstorm; (*перен*): **~ +gen** (*садов, зверей*) threat to.

гроздь (-и; *gen pl* -éй) *ж* (*виногра́да*) bunch; (*сирени*) cluster.

гро́зен *прил см* **гро́зный**.

гро|зи́ть (-жý, -зи́шь) *несов неперех* (*no perf;* *опасность*) to loom; (*+instr: катастрофой*) to be threatened by; (*perf* **погрози́ть**): **~ кому́-н чем-н** to threaten sb with sth; **~** (**пригрози́ть** *perf*) **кому́-н разво́дом** to threaten sb with divorce; **он пригрози́л нача́льнику уйти́** he threatened the boss that he would resign

▶ **грози́ться** (*perf* **пригрози́ться**) *несов возв* to threaten.

гро́з|ный (-ен, -на́, -но) *прил* (*взгляд, письмо́*) threatening; (*проти́вник, ору́жие*) formidable; (*царь*) severe, harsh; (*учитель*) strict.

грозов|о́й *прил:* **~а́я ту́ча** storm cloud.

гром (-а; *gen pl* -о́в) *м* thunder; (*перен*) din; **пока́ ~ не гря́нет** (*разг*) until it's too late; **мета́ть** (*impf*) **гро́мы и мо́лнии** (*перен: разг*) to rant and rave.

грома́д|а (-ы) *ж* bulk.

грома́ден *прил см* **грома́дный**.

грома́дин|а (-ы) *ж* (*разг*) whopper, monster.

грома́дный *прил* enormous, huge.

гром|и́ть (-лю́, -и́шь) *несов перех* to destroy; (*перен: разг*) to slag (off).

гро́м|кий (-кая, -кое, -кие; -ок, -ка́, -ко) *прил* (*голос*) loud; (*no short form; скандал*) big; (*имя, дело*) famous; (*слова*) high-flown.

гро́мко *нареч* loudly.

громкоговори́тел|ь (-я) *м* (loud)speaker.

громлю́ *несов см* **громи́ть**.

громов|о́й *прил* (*голос*) thunderous; **~ые раска́ты** thunderclaps *мн*.

громогла́с|ный (-ен, -на, -но) *прил* very loud; **~ное заявле́ние** public announcement.

громозди́ть (-жý, -ди́шь; *perf* **нагромозди́ть**) *несов перех* to pile up

▶ **громозди́ться** (*perf* **нагромозди́ться**) *несов возв* (*скалы*) to loom; **~ся** (**взгромозди́ться** *perf*) **на +acc** (*разг*) to clamber up onto.

громо́здкий (-кая, -кое, -кие; -ок, -ка, -ко) *прил* cumbersome; (*перен*) clumsy.

громозжу́(сь) *несов см* **громозди́ть(ся)**.

гро́мок *прил см* **гро́мкий**.

громоотво́д (-а) *м* lightning conductor.

гро́мче *сравн прил от* **гро́мкий** ♦ *сравн нареч от* **гро́мко**.

громыха́|ть (-ю; *perf* **прогромыха́ть**) *несов неперех* (*разг: гром*) to rumble; (*колёса*) to rattle; **~** (**прогромыха́ть** *perf*) **+instr** (*кастрю́лями, ведро́м*) to clatter.

гроссме́йстер (-а) *м* grandmaster.

грот (-а) *м* (*пеще́ра*) grotto; (*парус*) mainsail.

гроте́ск (-а) *м* grotesque.

гро́хн|уть (-у, -ешь) *сов неперех* (*разг: вы́стрел*) to ring out; (*: рассмея́ться*) to go into stitches ♦ *перех* (*разг: ва́зу итп*) to smash; (*: мешо́к*) to bang down

▶ **гро́хнуться** (*impf* **гро́хаться**) *сов возв* (*разг*) to come crashing down.

гро́хот (-а) *м* racket.

грох|ота́ть (-очý, -о́чешь; *perf* **прогрохота́ть**) *несов неперех* to rumble.

грош (-á) *м* half-kopeck coin; **э́то сто́ит ~й** it costs next to nothing; **у меня́ нет ни ~á** (*разг*) I'm stony broke; **~á ло́маного не сто́ит** (*разг*) it's not worth a brass farthing (*BRIT*) *или* a plugged nickel (*US*).

грошо́вый *прил* (*разг: вещь*) dirt-cheap; (*сумма*) paltry; (*расчёты*) petty.

груб|е́ть (-ю; *perf* **огрубе́ть**) *несов неперех* (*челове́к*) to grow rude; (*душа́*) to grow hard; (*perf* **загрубе́ть**; *ко́жа*) to become rough; (*perf* **погрубе́ть**; *черты́*) to harden.

груб|и́ть (-лю́, -и́шь; *perf* **нагруби́ть**) *несов неперех* (*+dat*) to be rude to.

грубия́н (-а) *м* rude person (*мн* people).

грубия́н|ка (-ки; *gen pl* -ок) *ж см* **грубия́н**.

грублю́ *несов см* **груби́ть**.

гру́бо *нареч* (*отвеча́ть*) rudely; (*разгова́ривать*) crudely; (*обточи́ть, подсчита́ть*) roughly; **~ говоря́** roughly speaking.

гру́бост|ь (-и) *ж* (*выраже́ние*) crudeness, coarseness; (*посту́пок*) rudeness.

гру́б|ый (-, -á, -о) *прил* (*челове́к, поведе́ние*) rude; (*ткань, пища*) coarse; (*ко́жа, подсчёт*) rough; (*голос*) gruff; (*оши́бка, шу́тка*) crude; (*наруше́ние пра́вил*) gross.

гру́д|а (-ы) *ж* pile, heap.

груди́н|ка (-и) *ж* (*говя́дина*) brisket; (*копчёная свинина́*) bacon; **бара́нья ~** breast of lamb; **свина́я ~** pork fillet.

грудни́ц|а (-ы) *ж* mastitis.

грудн|о́й *прил* (*молоко́*) breast *опред;* (*кашель*) chest *опред;* (*младе́нец*): **~ ребёнок** baby; **грудно́й го́лос** chest voice; **грудны́е же́лезы** mammary glands *мн;* **грудна́я кле́тка** thorax;

груднóе **кормлéние** breast-feeding.
грудь (-уди́; *instr sg* -**ý**дью, *nom pl* -**ý**ди) ж (*АНАТ*) chest; (: женщины) breasts *мн*; ~ **рубáшки** shirt front; **вставáть** (**встать** *perf*) ~**ý**дью **на защи́ту когó-н/чегó-н** to stake one's life in defence (*BRIT*) *или* defense (*US*) of sb/sth; **корми́ть** (*impf*) ~**ý**дью to breast-feed.
гружёный *прил* loaded.
гружý(**сь**) *несов см* **грузи́ть**(**ся**).
груз (-а) *м* (*тяжесть*) weight; (*товар*) cargo, freight.
груздь (-я́) *м* milk agaric.
грýзен *прил см* **грýзный**.
грузи́л|о (-а) *ср* sinker, weight.
грузи́н (-а) *м* Georgian.
грузи́н|ка (-ки; *gen pl* -ок) ж *см* **грузи́н**.
грузи́нск|ий (-ая, -ое, -ие) *прил* Georgian.
грузи́ть (-ужý, -ýзишь; *perf* **загрузи́ть** *или* **нагрузи́ть**) *несов перех* (*корабль итп*) to load (up); ~ (**погрузи́ть** *perf*) (**в/на** +*acc*) (*товар*) to load (onto)
▶ **грузи́ться** (*perf* **погрузи́ться**) *несов возв* (*люди*) to board; (*судно*) to take on cargo; (*машина*) to be loaded up.
Грýзия (-и) ж Georgia.
грýз|ный (-ен, -нá, -но) *прил* (*человек*) hefty; (*походка*) lumbering.
грузови́к (-á) *м* lorry (*BRIT*), truck (*US*).
грузов|**óй** *прил* (*судно, самолёт*) cargo *опред*; **грузовáя маши́на** goods vehicle; **грузовóе такси́** removal (*BRIT*) *или* moving (*US*) van.
грузооборóт (-а) *м* turnover of goods.
грузоотправи́тел|ь (-я) *м* consignor of goods.
грузоподъёмност|ь (-и) ж freight *или* cargo capacity.
грузополучáтел|ь (-я) *м* consignee.
грýзчик (-а) *м* (*на складе*) warehouse porter; (*в магазине*) stockroom worker; (*в порту*) docker (*BRIT*), stevedore (*US*); (*на вокзале*) porter.
грунт (-а) *м* soil, earth; (*дно водоёма*) bottom; (*краска*) primer.
грунт|**овáть** (-ýю; *perf* **загрунтовáть**) *несов перех* to prime.
грунтóв|ка (-и) ж undercoat.
грунтов|**óй** *прил*: ~**ая дорóга** dirt road; ~**ая крáска** primer.
грýпп|а (-ы) ж group; **грýппа крóви** blood group.
группир|**овáть** (-ýю; *perf* **сгруппировáть**) *несов перех* (*людей*) to group; (*отдел*) to establish, set up; (*данные, цифры*) to group, classify
▶ **группировáться** (*perf* **сгруппировáться**) *несов возв* (*объединяться*) to form groups; (*классифицироваться*) to be grouped *или* classified.
группирóв|ка (-ки; *gen pl* -ок) ж grouping; (*религиозная*) group.
группов|**óй** *прил* group *опред*.

грýстен *прил см* **грýстный**.
грусти́ть (-щý, -сти́шь) *несов неперех* to be melancholy, feel very sad; ~ (*impf*) **по** +*dat или* **о** +*prp* (*семье, дому*) to pine for.
грýстно *нареч* sadly ◆ *как сказ* (+*dat*): **мне** ~ I feel sad.
грýст|ный (-ен, -нá, -но) *прил* (*настроение*) sad, melancholy; (*no short form; конец*) sad.
грусть (-и) ж sadness, melancholy.
грýш|а (-и) ж (*плод*) pear; (*дерево*) pear (tree).
грущý *несов см* **грусти́ть**.
грýж|а (-и) ж hernia.
грыз *итп несов см* **грызть**.
грызн|я (-и) ж (*разг: собак итп*) scrap; (*перен: пренебр*) squabble.
грыз|ть (-ý, -ёшь; *pt* -, -ла, -ло) *несов перех* (*печенье, яблоки*) to nibble (at); (*perf* **разгры́зть**; *кость*) to gnaw (on); (*орехи*) to nibble; (*перен: разг: человека*) to get at; ~ (*impf*) **нóгти** to bite one's nails; **меня́ гры́зло раскáяние/сомнéние** I was consumed by remorse/doubt
▶ **гры́зться** *несов возв* (*собаки итп*) to fight; (*перен: разг*) to squabble.
грызýн (-á) *м* rodent.
гряд|á (-ы́; *nom pl* -ы) ж row (*of flowers, vegetables*); (*гор*) range; (*волн*) series; ~ **облакóв** bank of cloud.
грядёт *итп несов см* **грясти́**.
грýд|ка (-ки; *gen pl* -ок) ж row.
грядýщ|ее (-его; *decl like adj*) *ср* the future.
грядýщ|ий (-ая, -ее, -ие) *прил* (*год*) coming; **на сон** ~ before going to bed.
грязелечéни|е (-я) *ср* mud cure.
гря́зен *прил см* **гря́зный**.
гря́з|и (-ей) *мн* mud cure; (*место*) mud baths *мн*.
грязн|и́ть (-ю́, -и́шь; *perf* **загрязни́ть**) *несов перех* (*платье*) to get dirty; (*пол*) to make dirty; (*перен: репутацию*) to tarnish ◆ (*perf* **нагрязни́ть**) *неперех* (*в доме*) to make a mess; (*на улице*) to drop litter
▶ **грязни́ться** (*perf* **загрязни́ться**) *несов возв* to become dirty.
гря́зно *как сказ безл*: **дóма/на ýлице** ~ the street/house is filthy.
грязнýл|я (-и) *м/ж* (*разг*) pig; (: *ребёнок*) mucky kid.
гря́з|ный (-ен, -нá, -но) *прил* dirty; (*ребёнок, платье*) dirty, grubby; (*перен: анекдот, личность*) sordid; (*цвет*) murky; ~**ное дéло** dirty business; ~**ная войнá** dirty war.
грязь (-и; *loc sg* -и́) ж dirt; (*на дороге*) mud; (*перен*) filth; **обливáть** (**обли́ть** *perf*) **когó-н гря́зью**, **мешáть** (**смешáть** *perf*) **когó-н с гря́зью** (*перен*) to sling mud at sb; *см также* **гря́зи**.
грян|уть (-у, -ешь) *сов перех* (*марш*) to strike up ◆ *неперех* (*выстрел*) to ring out; (*война*) to

break out; ~ *(perf)* **пе́сню** to burst into song; ~**ул гром** there was a clap of thunder.

гря|сти́ *(3sg* -**дёт**, *3pl* -**ду́т)** *несов неперех* to draw near.

гуа́ш|ь (-**и)** *ж* gouache.

губ|а́ (-**ы́;** *nom pl* -**ы**, *dat pl* -**а́м)** *ж* lip; *(обычно мн: тиско́в)* jaw *(of pliers etc)*; *(зали́в)* bay *(in North Russia)*; **дуть (наду́ть** *perf)* **гу́бы** *(перен: разг)* to be in a huff; **у него́ ~ не ду́ра** *(разг)* he knows what's good for him.

губе́рни|я (-**и)** *ж* gubernia *(administrative region)*.

губерна́тор (-**а)** *м* governor.

губи́тел|ьный (-**ен**, -**ьна**, -**ьно)** *прил (кли́мат)* unhealthy; *(влия́ние)* pernicious; *(после́дствия)* ruinous; *(привы́чка)* harmful; *(моро́з):* ~ **(для** +*gen)* disastrous (for).

губи́ть (-**лю́**, -**ишь;** *perf* **погуби́ть)** *несов перех* to kill; *(урожа́й, здоро́вье)* to ruin; **он её погу́бит** he'll be the ruin of her.

гу́б|ка (-**ки;** *gen pl* -**ок)** *ж* sponge.

гублю́ *несов см* **губи́ть**.

губн|о́й *прил:* ~**а́я пома́да** lipstick; ~**а́я гармо́шка** harmonica.

гу́бок *сущ см* **гу́бка**.

гуверна́нт|ка (-**ки;** *gen pl* -**ок)** *ж* governess.

гуверне́р (-**а)** *м* (private) tutor.

гугу́ *как сказ:* **она́ ни** ~ *(разг)* she doesn't say a word; **ни** ~! *(разг)* not a word!

гуде́ни|е (-**я)** *ж (жуко́в)* drone; *(про́водов)* hum; *(ве́тра)* moan.

гу|де́ть (-**жу́**, -**ди́шь)** *несов неперех (шмель, провода́)* to hum; *(ве́тер)* to moan; *(толпа́)* to murmur; *(маши́на)* to hoot; *(разг: но́ги итп)* to throb.

гуд|о́к (-**ка́)** *м (устро́йство: автомоби́ля)* horn; *(: парохо́да, заво́да)* siren; *(звук)* hoot.

гудро́н (-**а)** *м* tar.

гужу́ *несов см* **гуде́ть**.

гул (-**а)** *м (маши́н, голосо́в)* drone; *(мо́ре)* murmur.

гу́л|кий (-**кая**, -**кое**, -**кие;** -**ок**, -**ка́**, -**ко)** *прил (уда́р, шаги́)* resounding; *(свод)* echoing.

гу́лькин *прил:* **с** ~ **нос** *(разг)* next to nothing.

гуля́нье (-**ья;** *nom pl* -**ий)** *ср:* **наро́дное** ~ *outdoor merrymaking on a public holiday.*

гуля́|ть (-**ю)** *perf* **погуля́ть)** *несов неперех (прогу́ливаться)* to stroll; *(быть на у́лице)* to be out; *(на сва́дьбе)* to have a good time, enjoy o.s.; **идти́ (пойти́** *perf)* ~ to go for a walk; **я сего́дня** ~**ю** *(разг)* we're taking the day off

today.

гуля́ш (-**а́)** *м* goulash.

ГУМ (-**а)** *м сокр* (= *Госуда́рственный универса́льный магази́н) state department store.*

гуманита́рн|ый *прил (по́мощь)* humanitarian; *(образова́ние, факульте́т)* arts *опред*; **гуманита́рные нау́ки** the humanities *или* arts.

гума́нность (-**и)** *ж* humaneness, humanity.

гума́н|ный (-**ен**, -**на**, -**но)** *прил* humane.

гумн|о́ (-**а́)** *ср (сара́й)* barn; *(площа́дка)* threshing floor.

гурма́н (-**а)** *м* gourmet.

гурт (-**а́)** *м (коро́в)* herd.

гурто́м *нареч (разг: отпра́виться)* en masse; *(: прода́ть, купи́ть)* in bulk.

гурьб|а́ (-**ы́)** *ж* crowd; **ходи́ть** *(impf) или* **гуля́ть** *(impf)* ~**о́й** to go about in a gang.

гуса́к (-**а́)** *м* gander.

гу́сениц|а (-**ы)** *ж* caterpillar; *(тра́ктора)* caterpillar track.

гус|ёнок (-**ёнка;** *nom pl* -**я́та**, *gen pl* -**я́т)** *м* gosling.

гуси́н|ый *прил (яйцо́)* goose; ~**ое ста́до** gaggle of geese; ~**ая ко́жа** goose flesh, goose pimples *(BRIT) или* bumps *(US)*.

гус|те́ть *(3sg* -**ет**, *3pl* -**ют**, *perf* **погусте́ть)** *несов неперех (тума́н)* to grow *или* become denser; *(perf* **загусте́ть;** *ка́ша)* to thicken.

густ|о́й (-, -**а́**, -**о)** *прил (лес, облака́)* dense; *(бро́ви)* bushy; *(суп, во́лосы)* thick; *(цвет, бас)* deep, rich.

густонаселённый *прил* densely-populated.

густот|а́ (-**ы́)** *ж (во́лос, ка́ши)* thickness; *(заро́слей, ды́ма)* density; *(голоса́, цве́та)* richness, deepness.

гусы́н|я (-**и)** *ж* goose *(female)*.

гус|ь (-**я;** *gen pl* -**е́й)** *м* goose; **как с гу́ся вода́** *(разг)* like water off a duck's back; **хоро́ш** ~! *(разг: пренебр)* a fine one!

гусько́м *нареч* in single file.

гуся́та *итп сущ см* **гусёнок**.

гуся́тниц|а (-**ы)** *ж* casserole (dish).

гута́лин (-**а)** *м* shoe polish.

гу́щ|а (-**и)** *ж (ко́фейная)* grounds *мн*; *(пивна́я)* lees *мн*, dregs *мн*; *(су́па)* solids *(in soup etc)*; *(ле́са)* thicket; **в** ~**е собы́тий/толпы́** in the thick of things/the crowd.

гу́ще *сравн прил от* **густо́й**.

Гц *сокр* (= **герц)** Hz (= *hertz)*.

ГЭС *ж сокр* (= *гидроэлектроста́нция)* hydroelectric power station.

~ Д, д ~

Д, д *сущ нескл (буква)* the 5th letter of the Russian alphabet.

д. *сокр* = **дере́вня, дом.**

да *част* **1** *(выражает утверждение, согласие)* yes

2 *(не так ли)*: **ты придёшь, да?** you're coming, aren't you?; **ты меня́ лю́бишь, да?** you love me, don't you?; **я получи́л письмо́ от ма́мы – да?** I got a letter from my mum – really?

3 *(при воспоминании, размышлении)* oh, yes

4 *(пусть: в лозунгах, призывах)*: **да – ми́ру!** yes to peace!; **да здра́вствует демокра́тия!** long live democracy!; **вот э́то да!** *(разг)* cool!; **ну да!** *(разг)* sure!; *(выражает недоверие)* I'll bet!; **да ну!** *(разг)* no way!

♦ *союз (и)* and; *(но, однако)* but; **помога́ет ма́ло, да и то неохо́тно** he doesn't help much, and then only unwillingly; **у неё то́лько одно́ пла́тье, да и то ста́рое** she has one dress and even that's old; **пла́чет, да и то́лько** he does nothing but cry.

да́бы *союз*: ~ +*infin* in order to do; **он спря́тал де́ньги, ~ никто́ не нашёл** he hid the money in order that it wouldn't be found.

дава́й(те) *несов см* **дава́ть** ♦ *част* let's; ~ **пить чай** let's have some tea; ~ **помоги́(те) мне!** come on, give me a hand!; **дава́й-дава́й!** *(разг)* come on!, get on with it!

дава́ть (-ю; *imper* **дава́й(те)**) *несов от* **дать** ♦ *перех (no perf, разг: продавать)* to sell; **вот (во) ~ёт!** *(разг)* that's incredible!; **в магази́не ~ют мя́со** *(разг)* they sell meat in the shop

▶ **дава́ться** *несов от* **да́ться** ♦ *возв (иметь место)* to take place.

дави́ть (-лю́, -ишь) *несов перех (подлеж: обувь)* to pinch; *(perf* **задави́ть**; *калечить)* to crush, trample; *(подлеж: машина)* to run over; *(perf* **раздави́ть**; *насекомых)* to squash; *(подлеж: чувства)* to oppress; ~ *(impf)* **на** +*acc* *(налегать тяжестью)* to press *или* weigh down on; ~ *(impf)* **кого́-н свои́м авторите́том** *(разг)* to intimidate sb; **воротни́к да́вит** the collar feels tight

▶ **дави́ться** *несов возв (разг: в автобусе, в*

тесной комнате) to be crushed *или* squashed; ~**ся (подави́ться** *perf)* +*instr (костью, словами)* to choke (on).

да́вка (-ки; *gen pl* -ок) *ж* crush.

давле́ние (-я) *ср (газа, жидкости, воздуха)* pressure; **кровяно́е** ~ blood pressure; **атмосфе́рное** ~ atmospheric pressure; **под** ~**м** +*gen* under the pressure of; **ока́зывать (оказа́ть** *perf)* ~ **на** +*acc* to put pressure on.

давлю́(сь) *несов см* **дави́ть(ся).**

да́вн|ий (-яя, -ее, -ие) *прил*: **в** ~**ие времена́** a long time ago; **с** ~**их пор** for a long time; **э́то** ~ **слу́чай** it happened a long time ago.

давно́ *нареч (случиться, встретиться)* a long time ago; *(ждать)* for a long time; ~ **бы так!** about time too!

да́вность (-и) *ж (ЮР: срок)* prescription; *(длительное существование)*: **дру́жба/ вражда́ име́ет большу́ю** ~ the friendship/feud is of long standing; **за** ~**ю лет** due to the number of years which have elapsed.

давны́м-давно́ *нареч (разг)* ages ago.

да́вок *сущ см* **да́вка.**

дади́м(ся) *итп сов см* **дать(ся).**

да́же *част* even; **так испуга́лся,** ~ **вскри́кнул** I was so frightened, I even screamed; ~ **я согласи́лся** even I agreed.

да́йджест (-а) *м* newspaper rubric.

да́й(те) *сов см* **дать** ♦ *част (разг)*: ~ **я поду́маю** let me think.

дактилоскопи́я (-и) *ж* fingerprinting.

дал *итп сов см* **дать.**

да́лее *нареч* further; **и так** ~ and so on; **не** ~ **как** *или* **чем вчера́** only yesterday.

далёк|ий (-ая, -ое, -ие; -, -а́, -о́) *прил (страна, звуки)* distant, far-off; *(прошлое, будущее)* distant; *(путь, путешествие)* long; **в** ~**ие го́ды** in the distant past; **они́ далеки́ друг от дру́га лю́ди** they are very different (from one another); ~ **от реа́льности** far removed from reality; **она́ – челове́к** ~ **от нау́ки** she's far from being an expert when it comes to science.

далеко́ *нареч (о расстоянии)* far (away); *(о времени)* a long way off ♦ *как сказ (располагаться)* it's a long way away; **го́род ещё** ~ the town is still a long way off; **до ле́та** ~

summer is a long way off; ~ **от** +*gen* far (away)
from; ~ **за** +*acc* long after; **ему́ ~ за 50** he's well
over 50; ~ **не** far from, by no means; ~ **пойти́**
(*perf*) (*перен*) to go far; **мне ~ до него́** I'm no
match for him.

да́ло *итп см* **дать**.

дал|ь (**-и**; *loc sg* **-й**) *ж* faraway place; **э́то така́я ~**
(*разг*) it's such a long way (away).

дальне́йш|ий (**-ая, -ее, -ие**) *прил* further; **в ~ем**
in the future.

да́льн|ий (**-яя, -ее, -ие**) *прил* distant; **Д~ Восто́к**
the Far East; **раке́та ~его де́йствия** long-range
missile; **по́езд/авто́бус ~его сле́дования**
long-distance train/bus.

дальнобо́йный *прил* (*ВОЕН*) long-range.

дальнови́д|ный (**-ен, -на, -но**) *прил* far-
sighted.

дальнозо́рк|ий (**-ая, -ое, -кие, -ок, -ка, -ко**)
прил long-sighted (*BRIT*), far-sighted (*US*);
(*дальновидный*) far-sighted.

да́льше *сравн прил от* **далёкий** ♦ *сравн нареч*
от **далеко** ♦ *нареч* next; **так пло́хо, ~ не́куда**
(*разг*) things couldn't be any worse; **не ~ как**
или **чем вчера́/у́тром** only yesterday/this
morning.

дам(ся) *сов см* **дать(ся)**.

да́м|а (**-ы**) *ж* lady; (*КАРТЫ*) queen.

Дама́ск (**-а**) *м* Damascus.

дама́сск|ий (**-ая, -ое, -ие**) *прил*: ~**ая сталь**
Damascus steel, damask.

да́мб|а (**-ы**) *ж* dam.

да́м|ка (**-ки**; *gen pl* **-ок**) *ж* king (*in draughts or
checkers*).

да́мск|ий (**-ая, -ое, -ие**) *прил* ladylike; (*одежда,
парикмахер*) ladies'.

Да́ни|я (**-и**) *ж* Denmark.

да́нность (**-и**) *ж* actuality.

да́нн|ые (**-ых**; *decl like adj*) *мн* (*сведения*) data *ед*,
information *ед*; (*способности*) talent *ед*.

да́нн|ый *прил* this, the given; **в ~ом слу́чае** in
this case; **в ~ момéнт** at present.

дан|ь (**-и**) *ж* tribute; (*перен: моде, традиции*)
concession; **отдава́ть** (**отда́ть** *perf*) ~
кому́-н/чему́-н to pay tribute to sb/sth.

дар (**-а**; *nom pl* **-ы́**) *м* (*также перен*) gift;
получа́ть (**получи́ть** *perf*) **что-н в ~** to be given
sth as a present.

дар|и́ть (**-ю́, -ишь**; *perf* **подари́ть**) *несов перех*
to give; ~ (*impf*) **что-н кому́-н** to give sb sth as a
present.

дармов|о́й (**-а́я, -о́е, -ы́е**) *прил* (*разг*) free.

дармое́д (**-а**) *м* (*разг*) sponger.

дарова́ни|е (**-я**) *ср* gift.

дарови́тый (**-, -а, -о**) *прил* gifted.

да́ром *нареч* (*бесплатно*) free, for nothing;
(*бесполезно*) in vain; **теря́ть** (**потеря́ть** *perf*)
вре́мя ~ to waste time; **э́то ему́ ~ не пройдёт**
he'll pay for this; ~ **пропада́ть** (**пропа́сть** *perf*)
to be wasted, go to waste.

да́рственн|ый *прил*: ~**ая на́дпись** dedication.

даст(ся) *сов см* **дать(ся)**.

да́т|а (**-ы**) *ж* date; **кру́глая ~** *anniversary which is
a multiple of ten years*; ~ **вступле́ния в си́лу**
effective date.

да́тельный *прил*: ~ **паде́ж** dative case.

дати́р|овать (**-ую**) (*не*)*сов перех* to date.

да́тск|ий (**-ая, -ое, -ие**) *прил* Danish; ~ **язы́к**
Danish.

датча́н|ин (**-ина**; *nom pl* **-е**, *gen pl* **-**) *м* Dane.

датча́н|ка (**-ки**; *gen pl* **-ок**) *ж см* **датча́нин**.

да́тчик (**-а**) *м* sensor.

дать (*см* Table 14; *impf* **дава́ть**) *сов* to give;
(*разг: ударить*) to clout; (*устроить: концерт,
спектакль*) to put on; (*позволить*): ~ **кому́-н**
+*infin* to allow sb to do, let sb do; **дава́ть** (~ *perf*)
кому́-н что-н to give sb sth, give sth to sb;
дава́ть (~ *perf*) **себя́ знать** to make itself felt;
зима́ даёт себя́ знать winter is making its
presence felt; **ни ~ ни взять** (*разг*) no more, no
less; **я тебе́ дам!** (*угроза*) I'll get you!; ~
(**дава́ть** *impf*) **кому́-н знать о чём-н**
(*сообщить*) to let sb know about sth

▶ **да́|ться** (*impf* **дава́ться**) *сов возв* (*разг*): **я не
да́мся им в ру́ки** I won't let them catch me; **ей
легко́ даю́тся языки́** languages come easily to
her; **дала́сь тебе́ э́та те́ма!** (*разг*) you're
obsessed with the subject!

да́ч|а (**-и**) *ж* (*дом*) dacha (*holiday cottage in the
country*); (*корма*) portion; (*показаний,
консультаций*) provision; **они́ всё ле́то живу́т
на ~е** they are spending the whole of the
summer at their dacha.

да́чник (**-а**) *м* person who spends time at his or
her dacha.

да́чниц|а (**-ы**) *ж см* **да́чник**.

дашь(ся) *сов см* **дать(ся)**.

ДВ *сокр* (= *дли́нные во́лны*) LW= *long wave ед* ♦
прил сокр (= *длинноволново́й*) LW (= *long-
wave*).

дв|а (**-ух**; *см* Table 23; *f* **две**, *nt* **два**) *м чис* two ♦
м нескл (*ПРОСВЕЩ*) ≈ poor (*school mark*); **ей ~
го́да** she is two (years old); **они́ живу́т в до́ме
но́мер ~** they live at number two; **о́коло ~ух**
about two; **кни́га сто́ит ~ рубля́** the book costs
two roubles; ~ **с полови́ной часа́** two and a
half hours; ~**е с полови́ной мину́ты** two and a
half minutes; **сейча́с ~ часа́** it's two o'clock;
я́блоки продаю́тся по ~е шту́ки the apples are
sold in twos; **дели́ть** (**раздели́ть** *perf*) **что-н на
~** to divide sth into two; **в ~ух шага́х** (**от** +*gen*)
within a stone's throw (of *или* from); **в ~ух
слова́х** in a few words; **в ~ух счёта** (*разг*) in a
jiffy.

двадцати́ *чис см* **два́дцать**.

двадцатиле́ти|е (**-я**) *ср* (*срок*) twenty years;
(*годовщина*) twenty years anniversary.

двадцатиле́тн|ий (**-яя, -ее, -ие**) *прил* (*период*)
twenty-year; (*человек*) twenty-year-old.

двадцатипятиле́ти|е (**-я**) *ср* (*срок*) twenty-five
years; (*годовщина*) twenty-fifth anniversary.

двадца́т|ый (**-ая, -ое, -ые**) *чис* twentieth; *см
также* **пятидеся́тый**.

двáдцат|ь (-и; *как* **пять**; *см* **Table 27**) *чис* twenty; *см также* **пятьдесят**.

двáжды *нареч* twice; **он приходи́л сюда́** ~ he has come here twice; ~ **три – шесть** two times three is six; **я́сно как** ~ **два** (*разг*) as plain as day.

две *ж чис см* **два**.

двенáдцати *чис см* **двенáдцать**.

двенадцатиперéстн|ый *прил*: ~**ая кишка́** duodenum.

двенадцатичасово́й *прил* (*рабочий день*) twelve-hour; (*отправление*) twelve-o'clock.

двенáдцат|ый (-ая, -ое, -ые) *чис* twelfth; *см также* **пя́тый**.

двенáдцат|ь (-и; *как* **пять**; *см* **Table 27**) *чис* twelve; *см также* **пять**.

двéр|ца (-цы; *gen pl* -ец) *ж* door.

двер|ь (-и; *loc sg* -и́, *gen pl* -éй) *ж* door; **при закры́тых** ~**я́х** behind closed doors; **стоя́ть** (*impf*) **в** ~**я́х** to stand in the doorway; **показа́ть** (*perf*) **на** ~ **кому́-н** (*перен*) to show sb the door; **день откры́тых** ~**éй** open day.

дв|ести (-ухсо́т; *см* **Table 31**) *чис* two hundred; *см также* **сто**.

дви́гател|ь (-я) *м* engine, motor; (*перен*) driving force; ~ **вну́треннего сгора́ния** internal-combustion engine.

дви́|гать (-гаю; *perf* **дви́нуть**) *несов перех* to move; (*3sg* -**жет**, *3pl* -**жут**; *перен*) to further; (*no perf*; *механизм*) to drive; **им** ~**жет за́висть/любо́вь** he is motivated by envy/love; ~ (**дви́нуть** *perf*) **па́льцами/руко́й** to move one's fingers/hand

▸ **дви́|гаться** (*perf* **дви́нуться**) *несов возв* to move; (*направляться*): ~**ся в/на** +*acc* to set off *или* start out for; ~**ся** (**дви́нуться** *perf*) **в путь** to set off on a journey; **дéло не** ~**гается** we are making no progress.

движéни|е (-я) *ср* movement; (*дорожное*) traffic; (*перен*) impulse; **приводи́ть** (**привести́** *perf*) **что-н в** ~ to set sth in motion; **пра́вила доро́жного** *или* **у́личного** ~**я** ≈ the Highway Code; ~ **в защи́ту ми́ра** the peace movement.

дви́жимост|ь (-и) *ж* movables *мн*.

дви́жим|ый (-, -а, -о) *прил*: ~ +*instr* motivated by; **дви́жимое иму́щество** movables.

движ|о́к (-ка́) *м* (*ТЕХ*) *sliding part of a mechanism*.

дви́н|уть(ся) (-у(сь), -ешь(ся)) *сов от* **дви́гать(ся)**.

дво|е (-и́х; *см* **Table 36а**) *м чис* two; ~ **часо́в/сане́й** two watches/sledges; ~ **брюк/но́жниц** two pairs of trousers/scissors; **их бы́ло** ~ there were two of them; **он не спал** ~ **су́ток** he didn't sleep for forty-eight hours; **есть** (*impf*) **за двои́х** to eat enough for two; **на свои́х двои́х** (*разг*) on foot.

двоебо́рь|е (-я) *ср* biathlon.

двоебра́чи|е (-я) *ср* bigamy.

двоевла́сти|е (-я) *ср* dual power, diarchy.

дво́ек *сущ см* **дво́йка**.

дво́ен *сущ см* **дво́йня**.

двоето́чи|е (-я) *ср* (*ЛИНГ*) colon.

дво́ечник (-а) *м* (*разг*) dimwit.

дво́ечни|ца (-ы) *ж см* **дво́ечник**.

двои́м *итп чис см* **дво́е**.

дво|и́ться (*3sg* -и́тся) *несов возв*: **у него́ в глаза́х** ~и́тся he is seeing double.

двои́х *чис см* **дво́е**.

дво́ичный *прил* binary.

дво́|йка (-йки; *gen pl* -ек) *ж* (*цифра, карта*) two; (*ПРОСВЕЩ*) ≈ D (*school mark*); (*разг*: *автобус, трамвай итп*) (*number*) two (*bus, tram etc*).

двойн|о́й (-а́я, -о́е, -ы́е) *прил* double; **двойна́я игра́** double-dealing.

дво́йн|я (-йни; *gen pl* -ен) *ж* twins *мн*.

дво́йствен|ный (-, -на, -но) *прил* ambiguous.

двор (-а́) *м* (*между домами*) courtyard, yard; (*при отдельном доме*) yard; (*крестьянское хозяйство*) homestead; (*королевский*) court; **моне́тный** ~ mint; **при** ~**é** at court; **на** ~**é темно́** (*разг*) it's dark outside; **не ко** ~**у́ оказа́ться** (*perf*) *или* **прийти́сь** (*perf*) (*разг*) to be like a fish out of water.

двор|е́ц (-ца́) *м* palace; **дворе́ц бракосочета́ния** wedding palace (*venue for wedding ceremonies*), ≈ registry office (*BRIT*); **дворе́ц спо́рта** sports centre (*BRIT*) *или* center (*US*).

дво́рник (-а) *м* (*работник*) road sweeper; (*АВТ*) windscreen (*BRIT*) *или* windshield (*US*) wiper.

дворня́|га (-и) *ж* mongrel.

дворня́|жка (-ки; *gen pl* -ек) *ж* = **дворня́га**.

дворца́ *сущ см* **дворе́ц**.

дворцо́вый *прил* palace *опред*.

двор|яни́н (-яни́на; *nom pl* -я́не, *gen pl* -я́н) *м* nobleman (*мн* noblemen).

двор|я́нка (-я́нки; *gen pl* -ок) *ж* noblewoman (*мн* noblewomen).

дворя́нств|о (-а) *ср* nobility.

двою́родн|ый *прил*: ~ **брат** (first) cousin (*male*); ~**ая сестра́** (first) cousin (*female*).

двоя́к|ий (-ая, -ое, -ие; -, -ка, -ко) *прил* dual.

двубо́ртный *прил* double-breasted.

двузна́чный *прил* (*число*) two-digit; (*слово, выражение*) ambiguous.

двукра́тн|ый *прил*: ~ **чемпио́н** two-times champion; **в** ~**ом разме́ре** twofold.

двули́чный (-ен, -на, -но) *прил* two-faced.

двум *итп чис см* **два**.

двумста́м *итп чис см* **две́сти**.

двунапра́вленный *прил* (*КОМП*) bidirectional.

двуно́гий (-ая, -ое, -ие) *прил* two-legged.

двусло́жный *прил* two-syllable.

двусмы́слен|ный (-, -на, -но) *прил* ambiguous; ~**ная шу́тка** double entendre.

двуспа́льн|ый *прил*: ~**ая крова́ть** double bed;

двуспа́льная пала́тка two-person tent.

двуство́льн|ый *прил*: ~ое ружьё double-barrelled (*BRIT*) *или* double-barreled (*US*) shotgun.

двусторо́н|ний (-няя, -нее, -ние; -ен, -ня, -не) *прил (движение)* two-way; *(соглашение, переговоры)* bilateral; ~нее воспале́ние лёгких double pneumonia.

двух *чис см* два.

двухгоди́чный *прил* two-year.

двухдне́вный *прил* two-day.

двухкопе́еч|ный *прил*: ~ная моне́та two-kopeck coin.

двухле́ти|е (-я) *ср (срок)* two years; *(годовщина)* second anniversary.

двухле́т|ний (-яя, -ее, -ие) *прил (период)* two-year; *(ребёнок)* two-year old; *(БОТ)* biennial.

двухме́стный *прил (номер)* double; *(купе, каюта)* two-berth.

двухме́сячный *прил* two-month; *(ребёнок)* two-year-old; *(издание)* bimonthly.

двухнеде́льный *прил* two-week; *(ребёнок)* two-week-old; *(издание)* fortnightly.

двухпала́тный *прил (ПОЛИТ)* two-chamber.

двухсме́н|ка (-ки; *gen pl* -ок) *ж (разг) two shift working pattern*.

двухсо́т *чис см* две́сти.

двухсотле́тие (-я) *ср (срок)* two hundred years; *(годовщина)* bicentenary (*BRIT*), bicentennial (*US*).

двухсотле́т|ний (-яя, -ее, -ие) *прил (период)* two-hundred-year; *(дерево)* two-hundred-year-old.

двухсо́т|ый (-ая, -ое, -ые) *чис* two hundredth.

двухста́х *чис см* две́сти.

двухто́мник (-а) *м* two-volume edition.

двухцве́тный *прил* two-coloured (*BRIT*), two-colored (*US*).

двухчасов|о́й (-а́я, -о́е, -ы́е) *прил (фильм)* two-hour; *(отправление)* two-o'clock.

двухэта́жный *прил* two-storey (*BRIT*), two-story (*US*).

дву́ш|ка (-ки; *gen pl* -ек) *ж (разг)* two-kopeck coin.

двуязы́ч|ный (-ен, -на, -но) *прил* bilingual.

дебарка́дер (-а) *м* landing stage.

дебати́р|овать (-ую) *несов перех* to debate.

деба́т|ы (-ов) *мн* debate *ед*.

де́бет (-а) *м* debit; заноси́ть (занести́ *perf*) что-н в ~ to debit sth.

дебетова́ни|е (-я) *ср*: прямо́е ~ direct debit.

дебет|ова́ть (-у́ю) *(не)сов перех* to debit.

дебето́вый *прил*: ~ оста́ток debit balance; дебето́вое ави́зо debit note.

дебя́л (-а) *м (разг: пренебр)* moron.

дебито́р (-а) *м* debtor.

де́бр|и (-ей) *мн (в лесу)* thicket *ед*; *(перен)*: ~ +*gen (науки, техники)* maze of.

дебю́т (-а) *м* debut; *(в шахматах)* opening.

дебюта́нт (-а) *м person making his debut*.

дебюта́нт|ка (-ки; *gen pl* -ок) *ж см* дебюта́нт.

де́в|а (-ы) *ж*: ста́рая ~ spinster; *(созвездие)*: Д~ Virgo.

девальва́ци|я (-и) *ж* devaluation.

девальви́р|овать (-ую) *(не)сов перех* to devalue.

дева́|ть (-ю) *несов от* деть ♦ *сов перех (разг)* to put; мне не́куда ~ де́ньги/вре́мя I've got more money/time than I know what to do with

▸ дева́|ться *несов от* де́ться ♦ *сов возв (разг)*: куда́ она́ ~лась? where has she got to?; куда́ ~ся it can't be helped.

де́вер|ь (-я) *м* brother-in-law (*wife's brother*).

деви́з (-а) *м* motto.

деви́ца (-ы) *ж (ФОЛЬКЛОР)* maiden.

деви́ца (-ы) *ж (девушка)* girl.

деви́честв|о (-а) *ср (до замужества)* girlhood; в ~е Петро́ва née Petrova.

де́вич|ий (-ья, -ье, -ьи) *прил*: ~ья фами́лия maiden name.

де́в|ка (-ки; *gen pl* -ок) *ж (разг: девушка)* girl.

де́воч|ка (-ки; *gen pl* -ек) *ж (ребёнок)* little girl; *(разг: девушка)* girl.

де́вуш|ка (-ки; *gen pl* -ек) *ж* girl; *(разг: обращение)* miss.

девчо́н|ка (-ки; *gen pl* -ок) *ж (разг: девочка)* little girl, kid.

девяно́ст|о (-а; *как сто; см* Table 30) *чис* ninety; *см также* пятьдеся́т.

девяностоле́ти|е (-я) *ср (срок)* ninety years; *(годовщина)* ninetieth anniversary.

девяностоле́т|ний (-яя, -ее, -ие) *прил (период)* ninety-year; *(человек)* ninety-year-old.

девяно́ст|ый (-ая, -ое, -ые) *чис* ninetieth; *см также* пятидеся́тый.

девя́т|ая (-ой; *decl like adj*) *ж*: одна́ ~ one ninth.

де́вятер|о (-ы́х; *как че́тверо; см* Table 36a) *чис* nine; *(ботинок, перчаток)* nine pairs; *см также* дво́е.

девя́т|и *чис см* де́вять.

девятидне́вный *прил* nine-day.

девятикла́ссник (-а) *м pupil in ninth year at school (usually 15 years old)*.

девятикла́ссни|ца (-ы) *ж см* девятикла́ссник.

девятикра́тн|ый *прил*: ~ чемпио́н nine-times champion; в ~ом разме́ре ninefold.

девятиле́ти|е (-я) *ср (срок)* nine years; *(годовщина)* ninth anniversary.

девятиле́т|ний (-яя, -ее, -ие) *прил (период)* nine-year; *(ребёнок)* nine-year-old.

девятиме́сячный *прил* nine-month; *(ребёнок)* nine-week-old.

девятинеде́льный *прил* nine-week; *(ребёнок)* nine-week-old.

девятисо́т *чис см* девятьсо́т.

девятисотле́ти|е (-я) *ср (срок)* nine hundred years *мн*; *(годовщина)* nine-hundredth anniversary.

девятисотле́т|ний (-яя, -ее, -ие) *прил (период)* nine hundred-year; *(дерево)* nine hundred-year-old.

девятисо́т|ый (-ая, -ое, -ые) *чис* nine-hundredth.

девятиста́м *итп чис см* **девятьсо́т.**

девятичасов|о́й (-а́я, -о́е, -ы́е) *прил* (*опера́ция*) nine-hour; (*отправле́ние*) nine o'clock.

девя́т|ка (-ки; *gen pl* -ок) *ж* (*ци́фра, ка́рта*) nine; (*гру́ппа из девяти́*) group of nine; (*разг: авто́бус, трамва́й итп*) (number) nine (*bus, tram etc*).

девятна́дцати *чис см* **девятна́дцать.**

девятна́дцат|ый (-ая, -ое, -ые) *чис* nineteenth; *см также* **пя́тый.**

девятна́дцат|ь (-и; *как* **пять;** *см* **Table 27**) *чис* nineteen; *см также* **пять.**

девя́ток *сущ см* **девя́тка.**

девя́т|ый (-ая, -ое, -ые) *чис* ninth; *см также* **пя́тый.**

де́вят|ь (-и́; *как* **пять;** *см* **Table 27**) *чис* nine; *см также* **пять.**

девятьс́о́т (-исо́т; *как* **пятьсо́т;** *см* **Table 34**) *чис* nine hundred; *см также* **сто.**

де́вятью *чис см* **де́вять** ♦ *нареч* nine times; ~ **пять – со́рок пять** nine times five is forty-five.

девятьюста́ми *чис см* **девятьсо́т.**

дегенерати́в|ный (-ен, -на, -но) *прил* degenerate.

дегенера́ци|я (-и) *ж* degeneration.

дёг|оть (-тя) *м* tar.

деград́и́р|овать (-ую) (*не*)*сов неперех* to degenerate.

дёгтя *сущ см* **дёготь.**

дегусти́р|овать (-ую) (*не*)*сов перех* to taste, sample.

дед (-а) *м* grandfather; (*разг*) old man; **Дед Моро́з** ≈ Father Christmas; *см также* **деды́.**

де́довск|ий (-ая, -ое, -ие) *прил* grandfather's; (*перен*) old-fashioned.

дедовщи́н|а (-ы) *ж the abuse of new conscripts by older soldiers.*

деду́кци|я (-и) *ж* deduction.

дед|ы́ (-о́в) *мн* (*разг*) *final-year conscripts.*

дееприча́сти|е (-я) *ср* gerund.

дееспосо́б|ный (-ен, -на, -но) *прил* (*войска́*) functional; (*ЮР*) responsible.

дежу́р|ить (-ю, -ишь) *несов неперех* (*в поря́дке о́череди*) to be on duty; ~ (*impf*) **у чего́-н** to guard sth; ~ (*impf*) **у посте́ли больно́го** to sit at a patient's bedside.

дежу́рн|ая (-ой; *decl like adj*) *ж см* **дежу́рный.**

дежу́рн|ый *прил* (*пренебр: цита́ты, остро́ты*) hackneyed; ~ **врач/милиционе́р** doctor/(police) officer on duty ♦ (-ого; *decl like adj*) *м* person on duty; (*по ста́нции*) assistant station master; **дежу́рный магази́н** late-night shop; **дежу́рное блю́до** dish of the day.

дезерти́р (-а) *м* deserter.

дезерти́р|овать (-ую) (*не*)*сов неперех* to desert.

дезинсе́кци|я (-и) *ж* pest control (*of insects*).

дезинфе́кци|я (-и) *ж* disinfection.

дезинфици́р|овать (-ую) (*не*)*сов перех* to disinfect.

дезинформа́ци|я (-и) *ж* misinformation.

дезинформи́р|овать (-ую) (*не*)*сов перех* to misinform.

дезодора́нт (-а) *м* antiperspirant.

дезорганиза́ци|я (-и) *ж* disorganization.

дезорганиз|ова́ть (-у́ю) (*не*)*сов перех* to disorganize.

дезориенти́р|овать (-ую) (*не*)*сов перех* to disorientate.

де́йствен|ный (-, -на, -но) *прил* effective.

де́йстви|е (-я) *ср* (*механи́зма, зако́на*) functioning; (*рома́на итп*) action; (*часть пье́сы*) act; (*лека́рства, предупрежде́ния*) effect; **вводи́ть** (**ввести́** *perf*) **в** ~ (*фа́брику*) to open; (*турби́ну*) to activate; (*зако́н*) to introduce; **приводи́ть** (**привести́** *perf*) **в** ~ to carry out, implement; **под** ~**м** +*gen* under the influence of; *см также* **де́йствия.**

действи́телен *прил см* **действи́тельный.**

действи́тельно *нареч, вводн сл* really; **она́** ~ **краси́ва** she is really beautiful; ~, **уже́ пора́ идти́** it really is time to go.

действи́тельност|ь (-и) *ж* reality; **в** ~**и** in reality.

действи́тел|ьный *прил* (*факт, по́льза*) real, actual; (-ен, -ьна, -ьно; *про́пуск, удостовере́ние*) valid; **действи́тельный зало́г** active voice; **действи́тельная (вое́нная) слу́жба** active service (*BRIT*) *или* duty (*esp US*).

де́йстви|я (-й) *мн* (*посту́пки*) actions *мн*; (*ВОЕН*) operations *мн*.

де́йств|овать (-ую) *несов неперех* (*челове́к*) to act; (*механи́змы, зако́н*) to operate, work; (*perf* **поде́йствовать;** *влия́ть*): ~ **на** +*acc* (*лека́рство, угово́ры*) to have an effect on.

де́йствующ|ий (-ая, -ее, -ие) *прил:* ~**ие ли́ца** (*персона́жи*) characters *мн*; (*уча́стники собы́тий*) protagonists *мн*; **де́йствующая а́рмия** standing army; **де́йствующий вулка́н** active volcano.

декабри́ст (-а) *м* (*ИСТ*) Decembrist.

дека́бр|ь (-я́) *м* December; *см также* **октя́брь.**

дека́д|а (-ы) *ж* ten-day period; ~ **францу́зского кино́** ten-day festival of French cinema.

декаде́нт (-а) *м* decadent.

декаде́нтск|ий (-ая, -ое, -ие) *прил* decadent.

декаде́нтств|о (-а) *ср* decadence.

дека́н (-а) *м* dean.

декана́т (-а) *м* faculty office.

деклами́р|овать (-ую; *perf* **продеклами́ровать**) *несов перех* to recite.

деклара́ци|я (-и) *ж* declaration; **таможенная** ~ customs declaration; ~ **судово́го гру́за** ship's manifest.

деклари́р|овать (-ую) *(не)сов перех* to declare.
деклассирован|ный *прил*: ~ые элеме́нты social outcasts.
деко́дер (-а) *м (КОМП)* decoder.
декоди́р|овать (-ую) *(не)сов перех* to decode.
декольте́ *ср нескл, прил неизм* décolleté.
декорати́вный *прил (растения)* ornamental; *(искусство)* decorative.
декора́ци|я (-и) *ж (ТЕАТР)* set.
декре́т (-а) *м (постановление)* decree; *(разг: отпуск)* maternity leave; **издава́ть (изда́ть** *perf)* ~ о +*prp* to issue a decree on; **уходи́ть (уйти́** *perf)* в ~ *(разг)* to take maternity leave.
декре́тный *прил*: ~ о́тпуск maternity leave.
де́ланный *прил (смех)* false.
де́ла|ть (-ю; *perf* **сде́лать)** *сов перех* to make; *(упражнения, опыты, подлость итп)* to do; ~ **(сде́лать** *perf)* **уро́ки** to do one's homework; ~ **(сде́лать** *perf)* **прыжо́к** to jump; ~ **(сде́лать** *perf)* **из кого́-н что-н** to make sth out of sb; ~ *(impf)* **не́чего** ~ there is nothing to be done; **от не́чего** ~ for want of something better to do; **что** ~? what can be done?
▶ **де́латься** *(perf* **сде́латься)** *несов возв (происходить)* to happen; ~**ся (сде́латься** *perf)* +*instr* to become.
делега́т (-а) *м* delegate.
делега́т|ка (-ки; *gen pl* **-ок)** *ж см* **делега́т**.
делега́ци|я (-и) *ж* delegation.
де́лен *прил см* **де́льный**.
деле́ни|е (-я) *ср* division; *(на линейке, в термо́метре)* point.
дел|е́ц (-ьца́) *м* dealer.
Де́ли *м нескл* Delhi.
деликате́с (-а) *м* delicacy.
делика́тно *нареч* tactfully.
делика́тный *прил* delicate.
дел|и́ть (-ю́, -ишь; *perf* **подели́ть** или **раздели́ть)** *несов перех (также МАТ)* to divide; ~ **(раздели́ть** *perf)* **что-н на** +*acc* to divide sth by; ~ **(раздели́ть** *perf)* **что-н с** +*instr* to share sth with; ~ **(раздели́ть** *perf)* **ра́дость/го́ре (с кем-н)** to share one's joy/grief (with sb)
▶ **дели́ться** *(perf* **раздели́ться)** *несов возв*: ~**ся (на** +*acc)* (*отряд*) to divide или split up (into); ~**ся** *(impf)* **на** +*acc (книга, статья)* to be divided into; *(МАТ)* to be divisible by; ~**ся (подели́ться** *perf)* **чем-н с кем-н** to share sth with sb.
де́л|о (-а) *ср* matter; *(надобность, также КОММ)* business; *(положение)* situation; *(поступок)* act; *(ЮР)* case; *(АДМИН)* file; **э́то моё** ~ that's my business; **э́то не твоё** ~ it's none of your business; **я пришёл по** ~у I've come on business; **у меня́ к Вам** ~ I have something to discuss with you; **как дела́?** how are things?; **в чём** ~? what's wrong?; ~ **в том, что ...** the thing is that ...; **не в э́том** ~ this isn't the issue; **на (са́мом)** ~е in (actual) fact; **на** ~е in practise; **пе́рвым** ~м in the first case или instance; **за** ~ fairly; **ме́жду** ~м in between times; **то и** ~ every

now and then.
делови́тост|ь (-и) *ж* businesslike manner.
делови́тый (-, -а, -о) *прил* businesslike.
делов|о́й (-а́я, -о́е, -ы́е) *прил (встреча, круги)* business *опред*; *(человек)* efficient; *(вид, тон)* businesslike.
делопроизводи́тел|ь (-я) *м* clerk.
делопроизво́дств|о (-а) *ср* clerical work.
де́л|ьный (-ен, -ьна, -ьно) *прил (человек)* businesslike, efficient; *(совет, предложение)* practical.
де́льт|а (-ы) *ж* delta.
дельтапла́н (-а) *м* hang-glider.
дельфи́н (-а) *м* dolphin.
дельца́ *итп сущ см* **деле́ц**.
деля́|га (-и) *м (разг: пренебр)* wheeler-dealer.
демаго́г (-а) *м* demagogue.
демаго́ги|я (-и) *ж* demagogy; **разводи́ть (развести́** *perf)* ~ю *(разг)* to talk a lot of hot air.
демаркацио́нн|ый *прил*: ~ая ли́ния demarcation line.
демилитариза́ци|я (-и) *ж* demilitarization.
демисезо́нн|ый *прил*: ~ое пальто́ *coat for spring and autumn wear*.
демобилиза́ци|я (-и) *ж* demobilization.
демобилиз|ова́ться (-у́юсь) *(не)сов возв* to be demobilized.
демографи́ческ|ий (-ая, -ое, -ие) *прил (исследование)* population *опред*, demographic; **демографи́ческий взрыв** population explosion.
демогра́фи|я (-и) *ж* demography.
демокра́т (-а) *м* democrat.
демократи́зм (-а) *м* democracy.
демократи́ческ|ий (-ая, -ое, -ие) *прил* democratic.
демокра́ти|я (-и) *ж* democracy.
де́мон (-а) *м* demon.
демонстра́нт (-а) *м* demonstrator.
демонстра́нт|ка (-ки; *gen pl* **-ок)** *ж см* **демонстра́нт**.
демонстрати́в|ный (-ен, -на, -но) *прил (поведение, уход)* theatrical.
демонстра́ци|я (-и) *ж* demonstration; *(показ: фильма)* showing; (*: экспона́тов)* show.
демонстри́р|овать (-ую) *(не)сов неперех (полит)* to demonstrate ♦ *несов перех* to show.
демонти́р|овать (-ую) *(не)сов перех* to dismantle.
деморализа́ци|я (-и) *ж* demoralization.
де́мпинг (-а) *м (КОММ)* dumping.
де́мпинговый|ый *прил*: ~ые це́ны artificially lowered prices.
денатура́т (-а) *м* meths.
денационализа́ци|я (-и) *ж* denationalization.
денационализи́р|овать (-ую) *(не)сов перех* to denationalize.
дендра́ри|й (-я) *м* arboretum.
де́нег *сущ см* **де́ньги**.
де́нежный *прил (реформа)* monetary; *(рынок)* money *опред*; *(разг)* well-off; **де́нежный знак**

banknote; **де́нежный штраф** fine.
деномина́ци|я (**-и**) *ж (ЭКОН)* denomination.
де́ну(сь) *итп сов см* **де́ть(ся)**.
день (дня) *м* day; **Д~ Побе́ды** ≈ V-E Day,
Victory Day (*the anniversary of the USSR's
victory over Germany in World War 2*);
светово́й ~ daylight; **~ ото дня́** day by day;
изо дня́ в ~ day in, day out; **че́рез ~** every
other day; **со дня на́ ~** (*постепенно*) from one
day to the next; (*скоро*) in the next few days; **на
друго́й ~** the next day; **на днях** (*скоро*) in the
next few days; (*недавно*) the other day; **день
рожде́ния** birthday.
де́нь|ги (-ег; *dat pl* **-ьга́м)** *мн* money *ед*; **броса́ть**
(*impf*) *или* **швыря́ть** (*impf*) **~ на ве́тер** to throw
money down the drain; **бума́жные ~** paper
money, banknotes; **нали́чные ~** (ready) cash.
департа́мент (-а) *м* department.
депе́ш|а (-и) *ж* dispatch.
депо́ *ср нескл* depot.
депози́т (-а) *м* deposit.
депози́тный *прил* deposit *опред*.
депози́тор (-а) *м* depositor.
депоне́нт (-а) *м* = **депози́тор**.
депони́р|овать (-ую) (*не*)*сов перех* to deposit.
депорта́ци|я (-и) *ж* deportation.
депорти́р|овать (-ую) (*не*)*сов перех* to deport.
депре́сси|я (-и) *ж* depression.
депута́т (-а) *м* deputy (*POL*).
депута́тск|ий (-ая, -ое, -ие) *прил* deputies'.
дёрга|ть (-ю) *несов перех* to tug *или* pull (at);
(*перен: разг*) to hassle ♦ *неперех* (+*instr*;
плечом, головой) to jerk
▶ **дёргаться** *несов возв* (*машина, лошадь*) to
jerk; (*лицо, губы*) to twitch; (*перен: разг*) to
(make a) fuss.
деревене́|ть (-ю; *perf* **одеревене́ть)** *несов
неперех* to grow *или* go numb.
дереве́нск|ий (-ая, -ое, -ие) *прил* (*дом,
житель*) country *опред*; (*тишина, пейзаж*)
rural; (*площадь, колодец*) village *опред*.
дере́в|ня (-ни; *gen pl* **-е́нь,** *dat* **-ня́м)** *ж* (*селение*)
village; (*местность*) the country;
олимпи́йская ~ Olympic Village.
де́рев|о (-ева; *nom pl* **-е́вья,** *gen pl* **-е́вьев)** *ср*
tree; (*древесина*) wood; **родосло́вное ~** family
tree; **кра́сное ~** mahogany.
деревообрабо́т|ка (-ки; *gen pl* **-ок)** *ж* timber
processing.
дере́вья *итп сущ см* **де́рево**.
деревя́нный *прил* (*также перен*) wooden.
держа́в|а (-ы) *ж* (*государство*) power;
(*эмблема*) orb; **вели́кие ~ы** The Great (World)
Powers.
держа́тел|ь (-я) *м* holder.
держа́|ть (-у, -ишь) *сов перех* to keep; (*в руках,
во рту, в зубах*) to hold; (*не отпускать*) to
keep hold of; (*поддерживать*) to hold up;

(*нанимать*) to take on; **~** (*impf*) **речь** to make a
speech; **~** (*impf*) **экза́мен** to sit an exam; **~** (*impf*)
отве́т to be responsible; **~** (*impf*) **сло́во** to keep
one's word; **~** (*impf*) **себя́ про́сто/
высокоме́рно** to behave simply/haughtily; **~**
(*impf*) **себя́ в рука́х** to keep one's head
▶ **держа́ться** *несов возв* to stay; (*на колоннах,
на сваях*) to be supported; (*иметь осанку*) to
stand; (*вести себя*) to behave; **~ся** (*impf*) +*gen*
(*берега, стены итп*) to keep to; (*перен*) to
adhere to; **~ся** (*impf*) **за** +*acc* (*за сумку, за
стену*) to hold onto; **~ся** (*impf*) **за го́лову** to
hold one's head.
дерз|и́ть (2sg -и́шь, 3sg -и́т) *несов неперех*: **~
кому́-н** to be rude to sb.
де́рз|кий (-кая, -кое, -кие; -ок, -ка́, -ко) *прил*
(*грубый*) impertinent; (*смелый*) audacious.
де́рзост|ь (-и) *ж* (*см прил*) impertinence;
audacity; **говори́ть** (*сказа́ть perf*) **~и** to be
impertinent; **име́ть** (*impf*) **~** +*infin* to have the
cheek to do.
дерива́т (-а) *м* (*ЛИНГ*) derivative.
дерматин (-а) *м* leatherette.
дерматоло́ги|я (-и) *ж* dermatology.
дёрн (-а) *м* turf.
дёрн|уть (-у, -ешь) *несов перех* to tug (at) ♦
неперех (+*instr*; *плечом, головой*) to jerk; **~уло
меня́** *или* **чёрт ~ул меня́ сде́лать э́то** (*разг*) I
don't know what possessed me to do it
▶ **дёрнуться** *несов возв* (*машина*) to start with a
jerk; (*лошадь*) to shy; (*лицо, губы*) to twitch.
деру́(сь) *несов перех см* **дра́ть(ся)**.
дерьм|о́ (-а́) *ср* (*груб!: также перен*) shit (*!*),
crap (*!*)
деса́нт (-а) *м* landing troops *мн*; (*высадка войск*)
landing; **выса́живать** (**вы́садить** *perf*) **~** to
make a landing.
деса́нтник (-а) *м* (*ВОЕН*) paratrooper.
десе́н *сущ см* **десна́**.
десе́рт (-а) *м* dessert.
де́скать *част*: **она́, ~, ничего́ не зна́ет** she
claims she doesn't know anything.
десн|а́ (-ы́; *nom pl* **дёсны,** *gen pl* **дёсен)** *ж* (*АНАТ*)
gum.
деспоти́ческ|ий (-ая, -ое, -ие) *прил* despotic.
деся́т|ая (-ой; *decl like adj*) *ж*: **одна́ ~** one tenth.
деся́тер|о (-ы́х; *как* **че́тверо;** *см* Table 36a) *чис*
ten; (*десять пар*) ten pairs; *см также* **дво́е**.
десяти́ *сущ см* **де́сять**.
десятибо́р|ец (-ца) *м* decathlete.
десятибо́рь|е (-я) *ср* decathlon.
десятидне́вный *прил* ten-day.
десятикла́ссник (-а) *м* pupil in tenth year at
school (*usually 17 years old*).
десятикла́ссниц|а (-ы) *ж см* **десятикла́ссник**.
десятикопе́ечн|ый *прил*: **~ая моне́та** ten-
kopeck coin.
десятикра́тн|ый *прил*: **~ чемпио́н** ten-times

champion; **в ~ом разме́ре** tenfold.
десятиле́ти|е (**-я**) *ср* (*срок*) decade; (*годовщина*) tenth anniversary.
десятиле́т|ка (**-ки**; *gen pl* **-ок**) *ж* (*разг*) ≈ secondary school (*BRIT*), ≈ high school (*US*).
десятиле́тн|ий (**-яя, -ее, -ие**) *прил* (*период*) ten-year; (*ребёнок*) ten-year-old.
десятиле́ток *сущ см* **десятиле́тка**.
десятиме́сячный *прил* ten-month; (*ребёнок*) ten-month-old.
десятин|а (**-ы**) *ж old unit of measurement approximately equal to 2.7 acres.*
десятинеде́льный *прил* ten-week; (*ребёнок*) ten-week-old.
десятирублёв|ка (**-ки**; *gen pl* **-ок**) *ж* (*разг*) ten-rouble note.
десятичасов|о́й (**-а́я, -о́е, -ы́е**) *прил* (*операция*) ten-hour; (*отправление*) ten o'clock *опред*.
деся́ти́чный *прил* decimal.
деся́т|ка (**-ки**; *gen pl* **-ок**) *ж* (*цифра*) ten; (*группа из десяти*) group of ten; (*разг: денежный знак*) tenner; (: *автобус, трамвай итп*) (number) ten (*bus, tram etc*).
деся́тк|и (**-ов**) *мн*: ~ **люде́й/книг** scores of people/books.
деся́т|ок (**-ка**) *м* ten; **он не ро́бкого ~ка** he's not afraid of anything; **ему́ пошёл шесто́й ~** he has turned fifty; *см также* **деся́тки**.
деся́т|ый (**-ая, -ое, -ые**) *прил* tenth; *см также* **пя́тый**.
де́сять (**-и́**; *как* **пять**; *см* **Table 27**) *чис* ten; *см также* **пять**.
дета́лен *прил см* **дета́льный**.
детализи́р|овать (**-ую**) (*не*)*сов перех* to work out in detail.
дета́л|ь (**-и**) *ж* detail; (*механизма, прибора*) component, part.
дета́льно *нареч* (*обсудить*) in detail.
дета́л|ьный (**-ен, -ьна, -ьно**) *прил* detailed.
детвор|а́ (**-ы́**) *ж собир* little children *мн*.
детдо́м (**-а**; *nom pl* **-а́**) *м сокр* (= **де́тский дом**) children's home.
детдо́мов|ец (**-ца**) *м child in care.*
детдо́мов|ка (**-ки**; *gen pl* **-ок**) *ж см* **детдо́мовец**.
детдо́мовца *сущ см* **детдо́мовец**.
детекти́в (**-а**) *м* (*следователь*) detective; (*фильм*) detective film; (*книга*) detective novel.
детекти́вный *прил* detective *опред*.
дете́ктор (**-а**) *м* detector.
детёныш (**-а**) *м* cub.
де́т|и (**-е́й**; *dat pl* **-ям**, *instr pl* **-ьми́**, *prp pl* **-ях**, *nom sg* **ребёнок**) *мн* children *мн*.
дети́н|а (**-ы**) *м* (*разг*) hulk.
дети́ще (**-а**) *ср* creation.
де́тка (**-и**) *ж* (*в обращении*) sweetheart.
детона́тор (**-а**) *м* detonator.
детса́д (**-а**; *nom pl* **-ы́**) *м сокр* (= **де́тский сад**) kindergarten.
де́тск|ая (**-ой**; *decl like adj*) *ж* nursery.
де́тск|ий (**-ая, -ое, -ие**) *прил* (*годы, болезнь*)

childhood; (*книга, игра*) children's; (*рассуждение, затея*) childish; **де́тская площа́дка** playground; **де́тский дом** children's home; **де́тский сад** kindergarten.
де́тств|о (**-а**) *ср* childhood; **впада́ть (впасть** *perf*) **в ~** to go senile.
де|ть (**-ну, -нешь**; *impf* **дева́ть**) *сов перех* (*разг*) to put; (*время, деньги*) to do with; **куда́ же я ~л э́ту кни́гу?** what on earth have I done with that book?; **э́того никуда́ не де́нешь** there's no arguing with that
▶ **де́ться** (*impf* **дева́ться**) *сов возв* (*разг*) to get to; **куда́ она́/кни́га де́лась?** where has she/the book got to?; **не́куда ~ва́ться** (*impf*) (*разг*) there's nothing else for it.
де-фа́кто *нареч* de facto.
дефе́кт (**-а**) *м* defect.
дефекти́вный (**-ен, -на, -но**) *прил* (*умственно*) mentally defective; (*физически*) physically handicapped.
дефе́ктный *прил* defective.
дефектоскопи́|я (**-и**) *ж* (*ТЕХ*) detection of flaws.
дефи́с (**-а**) *м* hyphen.
дефици́т (**-а**) *м* (*экон*) deficit; (*нехватка*): ~ **+gen** или **в +prp** shortage of; ~ **платёжного бала́нса** (*экон*) balance of payments deficit.
дефици́тный *прил* (*предприятие, производство*) unprofitable; (*товар, сырьё*) scarce, in short supply.
дефля́ци|я (**-и**) *ж* (*экон*) deflation.
деформа́ци|я (**-и**) *ж* deformation.
деформи́р|овать (**-ую**) (*не*)*сов перех* to deform
▶ **деформи́роваться** (*не*)*сов возв* to be deformed.
децентрализа́ци|я (**-и**) *ж* decentralization.
децентрализ|ова́ть (**-у́ю**) (*не*)*сов перех* to decentralize.
媒цибе́л (**-а**) *м* decibel.
дециме́тр (**-а**) *м* decimetre (*BRIT*), decimeter (*US*).
дешеве́|ть (*3sg* **-ет**, *3pl* **-ют**, *perf* **подешеве́ть**) *несов неперех* to go down in price.
дешёв|ка (**-ки**; *gen pl* **-ок**) *ж* (*перен: пренебр*): **э́та карти́на ~** this picture is tacky; **купи́ть** (*perf*)**/прода́ть** (*perf*) **что-н по ~ке** to buy/sell sth dirt-cheap.
деше́вле *сравн прил от* **дешёвый** ♦ *сравн нареч от* **дёшево**.
дёшево *нареч* (*купить*) cheaply.
дешёвое *сущ см* **дешёвка**.
дешёвый (**дёшев, дешева́, дёшево**) *прил* (*также разг*) cheap.
дешифр|ова́ть (**-у́ю**) (*не*)*сов перех* to decipher.
де-ю́ре *нареч* de jure.
де́ятелен *прил см* **де́ятельный**.
де́ятел|ь (**-я**) *м*: **госуда́рственный ~** statesman; **полити́ческий ~** politician; ~ **культу́ры** *person involved in the arts.*
де́ятельность (**-и**) *ж* (*научная, педагогическая*) work, activity; (*сердца, мозга*)

activity.

де́ятельный (**-ен, -ьна, -ьно**) *прил* active, energetic.

джаз (**-а**) *м* jazz.

джем (**-а**) *м* jam.

дже́мпер (**-а**) *м* jumper.

джентльме́н (**-а**) *м* gentleman (*мн* gentlemen).

джин (**-а**) *м* gin.

джи́нсов|ый *прил* denim; **джи́нсовая ткань** denim.

джи́нс|ы (**-ов**) *мн* jeans *мн*.

джо́йстик (**-а**) *м* (*КОМП*) joystick.

джо́кер (**-а**) *м* (*КАРТЫ*) joker.

джу́нгл|и (**-ей**) *мн* jungle *ед*.

джут (**-а**) *м* jute.

дзюдо́ *ср нескл* judo.

дзюдои́ст (**-а**) *м* judoist.

диабе́т (**-а**) *м*: **са́харный ~** diabetes.

диабе́тик (**-а**) *м* diabetic.

диа́гноз (**-а**) *м* diagnosis; **ста́вить (поста́вить** *perf*) **~** to make a diagnosis.

диагности́р|овать (**-ую**) (*не*)*сов перех* (*МЕД*) to diagnose; (*ТЕХ*) to check.

диагона́л|ь (**-и**) *ж* diagonal.

диагра́мм|а (**-ы**) *ж* diagram.

диакрити́ческ|ий (**-ая, -ое, -ие**) *прил*: **~ знак** diacritical mark.

диале́кт (**-а**) *м* dialect.

диале́ктик|а (**-и**) *ж* dialectics; (*событий, процесса*) dialectic.

диало́г (**-а**) *м* dialogue.

диало́говый *прил* (*КОМП*) conversational.

диа́метр (**-а**) *м* diameter.

диапазо́н (**-а**) *м* range; (*частот*) waveband; (*голоса, звука*) range, diapason.

диапозити́в (**-а**) *м* (*ФОТО*) slide.

диате́з (**-а**) *м* diathesis.

диафи́льм (**-а**) *м* (*ФОТО*) slide film.

диафра́гм|а (**-ы**) *ж* diaphragm.

дива́н (**-а**) *м* sofa.

дива́н-крова́т|ь (**-и**) *ж* sofa bed.

ди́вен *прил см* **ди́вный**.

диверса́нт (**-а**) *м* saboteur.

диверсифика́ци|я (**-и**) *ж* diversification.

диве́рси|я (**-и**) *ж* sabotage; **соверша́ть (соверши́ть** *perf*) **~ю** to commit sabotage.

дивертисме́нт (**-а**) *м* divertissement.

дивиде́нд (**-а**) *м* dividend; **приноси́ть (принести́** *perf*) **~ы** to pay dividends.

дивизио́н (**-а**) *м* unit; (*военных кораблей*) division.

диви́зи|я (**-и**) *ж* division.

ди́в|ный (**-ен, -на, -но**) *прил* marvellous.

дидакти́ческ|ий (**-ая, -ое, -ие**) *прил* didactic.

дие́з (**-а**) *м* (*МУЗ*) sharp.

дие́т|а (**-ы**) *ж* diet; **быть** (*impf*) **на ~е** to be on a diet; **соблюда́ть** (*impf*) **~у** to keep to a diet.

диети́ческ|ий (**-ая, -ое, -ие**) *прил* dietetic.

диза́йн (**-а**) *м* design.

диза́йнер (**-а**) *м* designer.

ди́зел|ь (**-я**) *м* diesel engine.

дизентери́|я (**-и**) *ж* dysentery.

дика́р|ка (**-ки**; *gen pl* **-ок**) *ж* savage; (*перен*) shy, unsociable woman or girl.

дика́р|ь (**-я́**) *м* savage; (*перен*) shy, unsociable man or boy; (: *разг*) independent holidaymaker; **е́хать (пое́хать** *perf*) **дикарём на юг/на мо́ре** to go off on spec to the South/the seaside.

ди́к|ий (**-ая, -ое, -ие**; **-, -а́, -о**) *прил* wild; (*человек*) savage; (*ребёнок*) shy and unsociable; (*голод, холод*) terrible.

дикобра́з (**-а**) *м* porcupine.

дико́вин|а (**-ы**) *ж* (*разг*) marvel; **э́то мне в ~у** this is all too new.

дико́вин|ка (**-ки**; *gen pl* **-ок**) *ж* = **дико́вина**.

дикорасту́щ|ий (**-ая, -ее, -ие**) *прил* wild.

ди́кост|ь (**-и**) *ж* wildness; (*поступка, мысли*) absurdity.

дикта́нт (**-а**) *м* dictation.

дикта́тор (**-а**) *м* dictator.

диктату́р|а (**-ы**) *ж* dictatorship.

дикт|ова́ть (**-у́ю**; *perf* **продиктова́ть**) *несов перех* to dictate.

дикто́в|ка (**-ки**; *gen pl* **-ок**) *ж* dictation; **под чью-н ~ку** (*записывать*) from sb's dictation; (*действовать*) at sb's bidding.

ди́ктор (**-а**) *м* announcer; (*читающий новости*) newsreader.

диктофо́н (**-а**) *м* Dictaphone®.

ди́кци|я (**-и**) *ж* diction.

диле́мм|а (**-ы**) *ж* dilemma.

ди́лер (**-а**) *м*: **~ (по** +*prp*) dealer (in).

дина́мик (**-а**) *м* (loud)speaker.

дина́мик|а (**-и**) *ж* (*ФИЗ*) dynamics; (*развития, процесса*) dynamics *мн*.

динами́т (**-а**) *м* dynamite.

динами́ч|ный (**-ен, -на, -но**) *прил* dynamic.

дина́сти|я (**-и**) *ж* dynasty.

диноза́вр (**-а**) *м* dinosaur.

дио́д (**-а**) *м* diode.

дио́птри|я (**-и**) *ж* dioptre (*BRIT*), diopter (*US*).

дипко́рпус (**-а**) *м сокр* (= **дипломати́ческий ко́рпус**) CD (= *Corps Diplomatique*).

дипло́м (**-а**) *м* (*ПРОСВЕЩ: свидетельство*) degree certificate; (: *на конкурсе*) certificate, diploma; (*научная работа*) dissertation (*for undergraduate degree*); **защища́ть (защити́ть** *perf*) **~** to have a viva (*for undergraduate degree*).

диплома́нт (**-а**) *м* award winner.

диплома́т (**-а**) *м* diplomat; (*разг: портфель*) briefcase.

дипломати́ческ|ий (**-ая, -ое, -ие**) *прил* diplomatic.

диплома́ти|я (**-и**) *ж* diplomacy.

дипломи́рованный *прил* qualified.

дир. *сокр* (= **дире́ктор**) dir. (= *director*).

директи́в|а (-ы) *ж* directive.

дире́ктор (-а; *nom pl* -á) *м* director; ~ **шко́лы** headmaster; ~-**распоряди́тель** managing director; **гла́вный исполни́тельный** ~ chief executive.

дире́кци|я (-и) *ж* (*завода, фабрики*) management; (*школы*) ≈ board (of governors); (*фирмы*) board (of directors).

дирижа́бл|ь (-я) *м* airship, dirigible.

дирижёр (-а) *м* (*МУЗ*) conductor.

дирижёрск|ий (-ая, -ое, -ие) *прил*: ~**ая па́лочка** (conductor's) baton.

дирижи́р|овать (-ую) *несов неперех* (+*instr*) to conduct.

дисгармо́ни|я (-и) *ж* discord.

диск (-а) *м* (*также КОМП*) disk; (*СПОРТ*) discus; (*МУЗ*) record; **ги́бкий/жёсткий** ~ floppy/hard disk; ~ **с удво́енной пло́тностью** double-density floppy disk.

дисквалифици́р|овать (-ую) (*не*)*сов перех* (*врача, юриста*) to strike off; (*спортсмена*) to disqualify.

диске́т (-а) *м* diskette.

диске́т|а (-ы) *ж* = **диске́т**.

диск-жоке́|й (-я) *м* disc jockey.

ди́ско *ср нескл* disco.

диско́нт (-а) *м* (*КОММ*) discount.

дискоте́к|а (-и) *ж* (*собрание пластинок*) record collection; (*танцы*) discotheque.

дискредити́р|овать (-ую) (*не*)*сов перех* to discredit.

дискримина́ци|я (-и) *ж* discrimination.

дискримини́р|овать (-ую) (*не*)*сов перех* to discriminate against.

дискуссио́нный *прил* (*спорный*) debat(e)able.

диску́сси|я (-и) *ж* discussion.

дискути́р|овать (-ую) *несов перех* to discuss.

дислока́ци|я (-и) *ж* (*ВОЕН*) deployment; (*МЕД*) dislocation.

дислоци́р|овать (-ую) (*не*)*сов перех* (*ВОЕН*) to deploy.

диспансе́р (-а) *м* dispensary.

диспе́тчер (-а) *м* controller; **авиацио́нный** ~ air-traffic controller.

диспе́тчерск|ая (-ой; *decl like adj*) *ж* controller's office; (*АВИА*) control tower.

диспе́тчерск|ий (-ая, -ое, -ие) *прил*: ~**ая слу́жба** control section; ~**ая вы́шка** control tower.

дисппле́|й (-я) *м* (*КОМП*) display.

диспропо́рци|я (-и) *ж* disproportion.

ди́спут (-а) *м* debate.

диссерта́нт (-а) *м* (*post-graduate*) *student defending a PhD thesis*.

диссерта́ци|я (-и) *ж* ≈ PhD thesis; **защища́ть** (*impf*) ~**ю** to be examined on one's thesis; **защити́ть** (*perf*) ~**ю** to pass a viva.

диссиде́нт (-а) *м* dissident.

диссона́нс (-а) *м* (*МУЗ*) dissonance; (*перен*) discord; **вноси́ть** (**внести́** *perf*) ~ **во что-н** (*перен*) to bring a note of discord into sth.

дистанцио́нн|ый *прил*: ~**ое управле́ние** remote control.

диста́нци|я (-и) *ж* distance; **сохраня́ть** (**сохрани́ть** *perf*) ~**ю** (*перен*) to keep one's distance; **он сошёл с** ~**и** (*СПОРТ*) he didn't last the distance.

дистилли́р|овать (-ую) (*не*)*сов перех* to distil (*BRIT*), distill (*US*).

дистрибью́тор (-а) *м* distributor.

дистрофи́|я (-и) *ж* dystrophy.

дисципли́н|а (-ы) *ж* discipline.

дисциплини́рован|ный (-, -на, -но) *прил* disciplined.

дит|я́ (-я́; *nom pl* **де́ти**) *ср* child; *см также* **де́ти**.

дифтери́т (-а) *м* diphtheria.

дифто́нг (-а) *м* diphthong.

дифференциа́льный *прил* (*ЭКОН*) differential *опред*.

дифференци́рованн|ый *прил*: ~**ая зарпла́та** differential.

дифференци́р|овать (-ую) (*не*)*сов перех* to differentiate.

дича́|ть (-ю; *perf* **одича́ть**) *несов неперех* to grow wild.

дич|ь (-и) *ж собир* game; (*разг*) rubbish.

диэле́ктрик (-а) *м* dielectric.

ДК *м сокр* (= *Дворе́ц культу́ры, Дом культу́ры*) *centre for social and cultural activities*.

длин|а́ (-ы́) *ж* length; **в** ~**у́** lengthways; ~**ой 10 ме́тров** 10 metres (*BRIT*) *или* meters (*US*) long; ~ **тка́ни – 10 метро́в** the cloth is 10 metres long.

дли́нен *прил см* **дли́нный**.

длинноволново́й *прил* long-wave.

длинноволо́сый *прил* long-haired.

длинноно́г|ий (-ая, -ое, -ие) *прил* long-legged.

длиннору́к|ий (-ая, -ое, -ие) *прил* with long arms.

дли́нно *нареч* (*рассужда́ть*) at length ◆ *как сказ*: **пла́тье мне** ~ the dress is too long for me.

дли́нн|ый (-ен, -на́, -но) *прил* long; (*разг: челове́к*) tall; **у него́** ~ **язы́к** (*разг*) he's got a big mouth; **дли́нный рубль** (*разг*) easy money.

дли́тельност|ь (-и) *ж* length.

дли́тельный *прил* lengthy.

дли́ться (3sg **-и́тся**, 3pl **-я́тся**, *perf* **продли́ться**) *несов возв* (*урок, бесе́да*) to last.

KEYWORD

для *предл* (+*gen*) **1** for; **для о́бщего бла́га** for the general good; **ме́сто для по́дписи** space for a signature; **крем для лица́** face cream; **альбо́м для рисова́ния** sketch pad

2 (*в отношении кого-н/чего-н*): **для меня́ э́то име́ет большо́е значе́ние** this is very important to me; **для того́ что́бы** in order to; **для него́ э́то про́сто рабо́та** this is just work to him; **э́то поле́зно для здоро́вья** this is good for one's health; **для своего́ во́зраста он о́чень развито́й** he is very advanced for his age

дм *сокр* (= **дециме́тр**) dm= *decimetre* (*BRIT*) *или* *decimeter* (*US*).

дн|ева́ть (-ю́ю, -ю́ешь) *несов неперех*: ~ **и**

ночева́ть где́-нибудь (*разг*) to be somewhere day and night.

дневни́к (-а́) *м* diary; (*ПРОСВЕЩ*) register; вести́ (*impf*) ~ to keep a diary.

дневн|о́й *прил* (*выработка, заработок*) daily; ~а́я фо́рма обуче́ния full-time education; ~ свет daylight; ~о́е вре́мя daytime; дневно́й спекта́кль matinee.

днём *сущ см* день ♦ *нареч*: ~ in the daytime; (*после обеда*) in the afternoon; его́ ~ с огнём не найти́ he is absolutely nowhere to be found.

Днепр (-а) *м* Dnieper.

Днестр (-а) *м* Dniester.

дни *итп сущ см* день.

дни́ще (-а) *ср* bottom.

ДНК *ж сокр* (= *дезоксирибонуклеи́новая кислота́*) DNA (= *deoxyribonucleic acid*).

дн|о (-а) *ср* (*моря, реки*) bottom, bed; (*ямы, оврага*) bottom; (*nom pl* до́нья, *gen pl* до́ньев; *бочки, ящика*) bottom; идти́ (пойти́ *perf*) ко ~у to sink to the bottom; (*перен: предприятие*) to go under; (: *человек*) to sink.

дня *итп сущ см* день.

KEYWORD

до *предл* (+*gen*) **1** (*о пределе движения*) as far as, to; мы дое́хали до реки́ we went as far as *или* to the river; я проводи́л его́ до ста́нции I saw him off at the station

2 (*о расстоянии*) to; до го́рода 3 киломе́тра it is 3 kilometres (*BRIT*) *или* kilometers (*US*) to the town

3 (*о временно́м пределе*) till, until; я отложи́л заседа́ние до утра́ I postponed the meeting till *или* until morning; я рабо́таю с восьми́ до пяти́ I work from eight to five; до свида́ния! goodbye!

4 (*перед*) before; мы зако́нчили до переры́ва we finished before the break

5 (*о пределе состояния*): мне бы́ло оби́дно до слёз I was so hurt I cried; он крича́л до хрипоты́ he shouted himself hoarse; на́до нагре́ть во́ду до кипе́ния the water must be heated until it boils

6 (*полностью*): я отда́л ей всё до копе́йки I gave her everything down to my last kopeck; он вы́пил буты́лку до дна́ he drank the bottle dry

7 (*направление действия*): ребёнок дотро́нулся до игру́шки the child touched the toy; мне до него́ нет никако́го де́ла (*разг*) I have no truck with him

♦ *ср нескл* (*МУЗ*) doh.

до- *префикс* (*in verbs*; *доведеине действия до конца*) indicating completion of action eg. *добежа́ть*; (*о достижении какого-нибудь результата*) indicating achievement of a certain goal eg. *дозвони́ться*; (*in adverbs*;

доведе́ние ка́чества до како́го-нибудь преде́ла) indicating attainment of a quality to a certain degree eg. *докрасна́*; (*о дополнительном де́йствии*) indicating supplement to an action eg. *доба́ть*; (*in adjectives*; бы́вший пре́жде чего-н) pre-.

доба́в|ить (-лю, -ишь; *impf* добавля́ть) *сов перех* to add.

доба́в|ка (-ки; *gen pl* -ок) *ж* (*к обеду*) additional helping; (*пищевая, бетонная*) additive.

добавле́ни|е (-я) *ср* addition; де́лать (сде́лать *perf*) ~я к +*dat* to make an addition to; в ~ к +*dat* in addition to.

доба́влю *сов см* доба́вить.

добавля́|ть (-ю) *несов от* доба́вить.

доба́вок *сущ см* доба́вка.

доба́вочн|ый *прил* additional ♦ (-ого; *decl like adj*) *м* (*также*: ~ телефо́н) extension number.

добе|жа́ть (*как* бежа́ть; *см* **Table 20**; *impf* добега́ть) *сов неперех*: ~ до +*gen* to run to *или* as far as; (*звуки, волны*) to reach.

добела́ *нареч*: отмы́ть что-н ~ to wash sth clean; раскали́ть (*perf*) что-н ~ to heat sth until it's white-hot.

доберу́сь *итп сов см* добра́ться.

добива́|ть(ся) (-ю(сь)) *несов от* доби́ть(ся).

добира́|ться (-юсь) *несов от* добра́ться.

доби́|ть (-ью, -ьешь; *impf* добива́ть) *сов перех* (*убить*) to finish off; (*разбить*) to break

▶ доби́|ться (*impf* добива́ться) *сов возв* (+*gen*) to achieve; добива́ться (~ся *perf*) своего́ to get what one wants.

до́блест|ный (-ен, -на, -но) *прил* valiant.

до́блесть (-и) *ж* valour (*BRIT*), valor (*US*).

добр|а́ться (-еру́сь, -ерёшься; *impf* добира́ться) *сов возв*: ~ до +*gen* to get to, reach; (*решения*) to reach; добира́ться (~ *perf*) до су́ти (де́ла) to get to the heart of the matter; я до тебя́ ~еру́сь! (*разг*) I'll get you!

добр|е́ть (-ю; *perf* подобре́ть) *несов неперех* to become kinder; (*perf* раздобре́ть; *разг*) to fill out.

добр|о́ (-а́) *ср* good; (*разг: имущество*) things *мн* ♦ *част* (*разг: ладно*) fine; жела́ть (пожела́ть *perf*) кому́-н ~а́ to wish sb well; ~ пожа́ловать (в Москву́)! welcome (to Moscow)!; дава́ть (дать *perf*) кому́-н ~ на что-н to give sb the go-ahead for sth; получа́ть (получи́ть *perf*) ~ (на что-н) to get the go-ahead (for sth).

доброво́л|ец (-ьца) *м* volunteer; идти́ (пойти́ *perf*) ~ьцем to volunteer.

доброво́л|ьный (-ен, -ьна, -ьно) *прил* voluntary; на ~ьных нача́лах on a voluntary basis.

доброво́льца *итп сущ см* доброво́лец.

доброде́тел|ь (-и) *ж* virtue.

доброде́тельный *прил* virtuous.

добродуш|ный (-ен, -на, -но) *прил* good-natured.

доброжелательность (-и) *ж* benevolence.

доброжелательный *прил* benevolent.

доброка́чествен|ный (-, -на, -но) *прил* (*продукт, изделие*) quality *опред*; (*no short form*; *опухоль*) benign.

добропоря́доч|ный (-ен, -на, -но) *прил* respectable.

добросерде́ч|ный (-ен, -на, -но) *прил* (*человек*) kind-hearted; (*слова*) kind.

добросо́вест|ный (-ен, -на, -но) *прил* conscientious.

добрососе́дств|о (-а) *ср* neighbourliness (*BRIT*), neighborliness (*US*).

доброта́ (-ы́) *ж* kindness.

добро́т|ный (-ен, -на, -но) *прил* good-quality.

до́бр|ый (-, -á, -о, -ы) *прил* kind; (*совет, имя*) good; (*милый: друг итп*) dear; **бу́дьте добры́!** excuse me!; **бу́дьте добры́, позвони́те нам за́втра!** would you be so good as to phone us tomorrow?; **всего́ ~oro!** all the best!; **~oro здоро́вья!** take care!; **~ день/ве́чер!** good afternoon/evening!; **~oe у́тро!** good morning!; **по ~ой во́ле** of one's own free will; **чего́ ~oro** (*разг*) it's not impossible.

добу́ду *итп сов см* **добы́ть**.

добыва́|ть (-ю) *несов от* **добы́ть**.

добыва́|ющий (-ая, -ее, -ие) *прил*: **~ая промы́шленность** mining, gas and oil industries.

добы́тчик (-а) *м* (*золота*) miner; (*нефти*) oil worker.

добы́ть (*как* **быть**; *см* **Table 21**; *impf* **добыва́ть**) *сов перех* (*денег, машину*) to get; (*нефть*) to extract; (*руду, золото*) to mine.

добы́ч|а (-и) *ж* (*процесс: нефти*) extraction; (: *руды*) mining, extraction; (*то, что добыто*) output; (: *на охоте, ловле*) catch.

добью́(сь) *итп сов см* **добы́ть(ся)**.

доведу́(сь) *итп сов см* **довести́(сь)**.

довез|ти́ (-у́; *pt* **довёз, -ла́, -ло́**, *impf* **довози́ть**) *сов перех*: **~ кого́-н до** +*gen* to take sb to *или* as far as.

довёл(ся) *итп сов см* **довести́(сь)**.

дове́ренность (-и) *ж* power of attorney; **де́йствовать** (*impf*) **по ~и** to act by proxy.

дове́ренн|ый (-ого; *decl like adj*) *м* (*также:* **~oe лицо́**) proxy.

дове́ри|е (-я) *ср* confidence, trust; **по́льзоваться** (*impf*) **чьим-н ~м** to enjoy sb's confidence; **входи́ть** (**войти́** *perf*) **в чьё-н ~** to gain sb's confidence; **выходи́ть** (**вы́йти** *perf*) **из чье́го-н ~я** to lose sb's confidence.

довери́телен *прил см* **довери́тельный**.

довери́тель (-я) *м* person who empowers another to act on his or her behalf.

довери́тель|ный (-ен, -ьна, -ьно) *прил* trusting.

дове́р|ить (-ю, -ишь; *impf* **доверя́ть**) *сов перех*: **~ что-н кому́-н** to entrust sb with sth

▸ **дове́риться** (*impf* **доверя́ться**) *сов возв*: **~ся** +*dat* to confide in; (*положиться*) to trust.

до́верху *нареч* (up) to the top; **напо́лненный ~** full to the brim.

дове́рчивость (-и) *ж* trustingness.

дове́рчив|ый (-, -а, -о) *прил* trusting.

доверша́|ть (-ю) *несов от* **доверши́ть**.

доверше́ни|е (-я) *ср* completion; **в ~ или к доверше́нию всего́** on top of everything else.

доверш|и́ть (-у́, -и́шь; *impf* **доверша́ть**) *сов перех* to complete.

доверя́|ть (-ю) *несов от* **дове́рить** ♦ *неперех*: **~** +*dat* to trust.

дове|сти́ (-ду́, -дёшь; *pt* **довёл, -ла́, -ло́**, *impf* **доводи́ть**) *сов перех*: **~ кого́-н/что-н до** +*gen* to take sb/sth to *или* as far as; **доводи́ть** (**~** *perf*) **что-н до конца́** to see sth through to the end; **доводи́ть** (**~** *perf*) **кого́-н до слёз** to reduce sb to tears; **доводи́ть** (**~** *perf*) **кого́-н до отча́яния** to drive sb to despair; **доводи́ть** (**~** *perf*) **что-н до соверше́нства** to perfect sth; **доводи́ть** (**~** *perf*) **ско́рость до преде́ла** to reach the speed limit; **доводи́ть** (**~** *perf*) **что-н до све́дения кого́-н** to inform sb of sth

▸ **довести́сь** *сов безл*: **мне не ~дётся верну́ться туда́** I won't get the opportunity *или* chance to go back there; **переда́йте приве́т, е́сли Вам ~дётся встре́тить её** say hello if you happen to see her.

до́вод (-а) *м* argument; **приводи́ть** (**привести́** *perf*) **~** to put forward an argument.

доводи́ть (-жу́, -дишь) *несов от* **довести́**

▸ **доводи́ться** *несов от* **довести́сь** ♦ *возв*: **он дово́дится ей бра́том/вну́ком** (*разг*) he is her brother/grandson.

довое́нный *прил* prewar.

довожу́(сь) *несов см* **доводи́ть(ся)**.

дово|зи́ть (-жу́, -зишь) *несов от* **довезти́**.

дово́лен *прил см* **дово́льный**.

дово́льно *нареч* (*известный, сильный*) quite; (*улыбаться, сказать*) with satisfaction ♦ *как сказ* it's enough; **~ спо́ров или спо́рить!** that's enough arguing!

дово́ль|ный (-ен, -ьна, -ьно) *прил* satisfied, contented; **он ~ен рабо́той/жи́знью** he's satisfied *или* happy with his work/life.

дово́льств|оваться (-уюсь) *несов возв*: **~** +*instr* to be happy *или* content with; **он ~уется ма́лым или немно́гим** it doesn't take much to make him happy.

довооруж|и́ть (-у́, -и́шь; *impf* **довооружа́ть**) *сов перех* (*окончательно*) to arm; (*дополнительно*) to provide with additional arms.

довы́бор|ы (-ов) *мн* ≈ by-election *ед*.

дог (-а) *м* (*зоол*) Great Dane.

догада́|ться (-юсь; *impf* **дога́дываться**) *сов возв* to guess.

дога́д|ка (-ки; *gen pl* **-ок**) *ж* guess; **стро́ить** (*impf*) **~ки о** +*prp* to speculate about; **теря́ться** (*impf*) **в ~х** to be baffled *или* at a loss.

догáдлив|ый (-, -а, -о) *прил* quick-witted.
догáдок *сущ см* **догáдка**.
догáдыва|ться (-юсь) *несов от* **догадáться**.
дóгм|а (-ы) *ж* dogma.
догмáт (-а) *м* (*РЕЛ*) dogma.
догматúческ|ий (-ая, -ое, -ие) *прил* dogmatic.
дог|нáть (-онþ, -óнишь; *impf* **догонять**) *сов перех* to catch up with; ~ (*perf*) **когó-н/чтó-н до** +*gen* to drive sb/sth to.
договáрива|ться (-юсь) *несов от* **договорúться**.
договóр (-а) *м* (*ПОЛИТ*) treaty; (*КОММ*) agreement; ~ **о** +*prp*/**на** +*acc* agreement on *или* about; **заключáть (заключúть** *perf*)/ **расторгáть (растóргнуть** *perf*) ~ to sign/annul a treaty.
договорённост|ь (-и) *ж* agreement; **достигáть (достúгнуть** *perf*) ~**и в чём-н** to reach an agreement on *или* about sth; **по ~и** by agreement.
договоренó *как сказ*: ~ **о** +*prp* ... there's been an agreement on ....
договор|úться (-þсь, -úшься; *impf* **договáриваться**) *сов возв*: ~ **с кем-н о чём-н** (*о встрече*) to arrange sth with sb; (*о цене*) to agree sth with sb; **мы ~úлись до глýпостей/грýбостей** we ended up talking nonsense/insulting each other; **мы ~úлись встрéтиться** we agreed to meet.
договóрник (-а) *м* (*разг*) contract worker.
договóрн|ый *прил* (*цена*) agreed; (*обязáтельство*) contractual; **на ~ых начáлах** on a contractual basis.
доголá *нареч*: **раздéться** ~ to strip bare; **пострúчься** (*perf*) ~ to have all one's hair cut off.
догонþ *итп сов см* **догнáть**.
догоня|ть (-ю) *несов от* **догнáть**.
догор|éть (-þ, -úшь; *impf* **догорáть**) *сов непéрех* to burn out.
догру|зúть (-жý, -зишь) *сов перех* to finish loading.
дод|áть (*как* **дать**; *см* **Table 14**; *impf* **додавáть**) *сов перех*: ~ **комý-н 10 рублéй** to give sb an extra 10 roubles.
додéла|ть (-ю; *impf* **додéлывать**) *сов перех* to finish.
додýма|ться (-юсь; *impf* **додýмываться**) *сов возв*: ~ **до** +*gen* to hit on; **как ты мог до такóго** ~? what on earth gave you that idea?
доедá|ть (-ю) *несов от* **доéсть**.
доéдешь *итп сов см* **доéсть**.
доедúм *итп сов см* **доéсть**.
доéду *итп сов см* **доéхать**.
доезжáй(те) *сов см* **доéхать**.
доезжá|ть (-ю) *несов от* **доéхать**.
доéсть (*как* **есть**; *см* **Table 15**; *impf* **доедáть**) *сов перех* to finish off, eat up.

доéхать (*как* **éхать**; *см* **Table 19**; *impf* **доезжáть**) *сов непéрех*: ~ **до** +*gen* to reach.
доéшь *сов см* **доéсть**.
дожд|áться (-ýсь, -ёшься; *pt* -áлся, -алáсь, -алóсь, *imper* -ú(те)сь) *сов непéрех*: ~ **когó-н/чегó-н** to wait until sb/sth comes; ~ (*perf*) **пóезда** to wait until the train arrives; **он ~ётся выговора** (*разг*) he'll end up getting told off; **ты у меня ~ёшься!** (*разг*) just you wait!; **он ждёт не ~ётся** (*разг*) he can't wait.
дождлúв|ый (-, -а, -о) *прил* rainy.
дожд|ь (-я) *м* rain; (*перен*) cascade; **гулять** (*impf*) **в** ~ to go for a walk in the rain; ~ **идёт** it's raining; ~ **пошёл** it has started to rain; **попадáть (попáсть** *perf*) **под** ~ to get caught in the rain; ~ **льёт как из ведрá** it's bucketing (with rain).
дожива|ть (-ю) *несов от* **дожúть** ♦ *непéрех* (*жизнь, годы*) to live out.
дожидá|ться (-юсь) *несов возв* (+*gen*) to wait for.
дож|úть (-вý, -вёшь; *impf* **доживáть**) *несов непéрех*: ~ **до** +*gen* (*до стáрости*) to live to; (*до концá года*) to live until.
дóз|а (-ы) *ж* dose; ~ **облучéния** dose of radiation.
дозвáнива|ться (-юсь) *несов от* **дозвонúться**.
дозвóленный *прил* permitted.
дозвон|úться (-юсь, -úшься; *impf* **дозвáниваться**) *сов возв* to get through.
дозúметр (-а) *м* dosimetre (*BRIT*), dosimeter (*US*).
дозúр|овать (-ую) (*не*)*сов перех* to measure out.
дозóр (-а) *м* patrol; **быть** (*impf*) **в** ~**е** to be on patrol.
доигрá|ть (-ю; *impf* **доúгрывать**) *сов перех* to finish (playing).
доúгрывани|е (-я) *ср* (*СПОРТ*) playing to a finish.
доúгрыва|ть (-ю) *несов от* **доигрáть**.
доисторúческ|ий (-ая, -ое, -ие) *прил* prehistoric.
до|úть (-ю, -ишь; *perf* **подоúть**) *несов перех* to milk.
дóйн|ый *прил*: ~**ая корóва** dairy cow.
доймý *итп сов см* **донять**.
дойтú (*как* **идтú**; *см* **Table 18**; *impf* **доходúть**) *сов непéрех*: ~ **до** +*gen* to reach; (*традúции, предáния*) to be passed down to; (*словá, смысл*) to get through to; **доходúть** (~ *perf*) **до отчáяния/истощéния** to reach the point of desperation/exhaustion; **до моегó свéдения дошлó, что** ... it has been brought to my attention that ....
док (-а) *м* dock.
докажý *итп сов см* **доказáть**.

доказа́тельств|о (-а) *ср* (*правоты, дружбы*) proof, evidence; (*теории*) demonstration; **служи́ть (послужи́ть** *perf*) **~м** +*gen* to be evidence of.

дока|за́ть (-жу́, -жешь; *impf* **дока́зывать**) *сов перех* (*правду, вино́вность*) to prove; (*теоре́му*) to demonstrate.

дока́нчива|ть (-ю) *несов от* **доко́нчить**.

дока́ныва|ть (-ю) *несов от* **докона́ть**.

дока́пыва|ться (-юсь) *несов от* **докопа́ться**.

дока|ти́ться (-чу́сь, -ти́шься; *impf* **дока́тываться**) *сов возв* (*звуки, шум*) to reach; **дока́тываться** (**~** *perf*) **до** +*gen* (*мяч, волны*) to roll in to; **дока́тываться** (**~** *perf*) **до преступле́ния** to stoop to crime.

до́кер (-а) *м* docker.

докла́д (-а) *м* (*на съе́зде итп*) paper; (*дире́ктору итп*) report.

докладн|а́я (-о́й; *decl like adj*) *ж* (*также:* **~ запи́ска**) memo.

докла́дчик (-а) *м* speaker.

докла́дчиц|а (-ы) *ж см* **докла́дчик**.

докла́дыва|ть (-ю) *несов от* **доложи́ть**.

докона́|ть (-ю; *impf* **дока́нывать**) *сов перех* (*разг*): **~ кого́-н** to do sb in.

докон́ч|ить (-у, -ишь; *impf* **дока́нчивать**) *сов перех* to finish off.

докопа́|ться (-юсь; *impf* **дока́пываться**) *сов возв*: **~ до** +*gen* (*перен: разг*: *до фа́ктов, и́стины*) to dig up; (*до кла́да, воды́*) to dig down to.

до́ктор (-а; *nom pl* -**á**) *м* doctor; **~ нау́к** Doctor of Sciences (*postdoctoral research degree in Russia*).

до́кторск|ий (-ая, -ое, -ие) *прил* (*МЕД*) doctor's; (*ПРОСВЕЩ*) postdoctoral.

доктри́н|а (-ы) *ж* doctrine.

докуме́нт (-а) *м* document.

докуча́|ть (-ю) *несов неперех*: **~ кому́-н чем-н** to pester sb with sth.

документа́льный (-ен, -ьна, -ьно) *прил* documentary; **документа́льный фильм** documentary.

документа́ци|я (-и) *ж собир* documentation.

документи́р|овать (-ую) (*не*)*сов перех* to document.

долб|и́ть (-лю́, -и́шь; *perf* **продолби́ть**) *несов перех* to hollow out; (*no perf*; *разг*: **зубри́ть**) to learn by rote; **~** (*impf*) **в дверь** (*разг*) to hammer on the door.

долг (-а; *loc sg* -**ý**, *nom pl* -**и́**) *м* debt; **вне́шний/ госуда́рственный ~** (*ЭКОН*) foreign/national debt; **дава́ть (дать** *perf*)/**брать (взять** *perf*) **что-н в ~** to lend/borrow sth; **входи́ть (войти́** *perf*)/**залеза́ть (зале́зть** *perf*) **в ~и** to get/fall into debt; **быть** (*impf*) **в ~у́ пе́ред кем-н** *или* **кого́-н** to be indebted to sb; **по до́лгу слу́жбы** in the course of duty; **пе́рвым до́лгом** (*разг*) first of all.

до́лг|ий (-гая, -гое, -гие; -ог, -га́, -го) *прил* long; **в ~ я́щик откла́дывать (отложи́ть** *perf*) **что-н**

to put sth off, postpone sth; **до́лгий гла́сный** long vowel.

до́лго *нареч* for a long time; **как ~ продли́тся фильм?** how long will the film last?

долгове́ч|ный (-ен, -на, -но) *прил* (*материа́л*) durable, long-lasting; (*дру́жба*) lasting.

долгов|о́й *прил*: **~а́я распи́ска** IOU; **~о́е обяза́тельство** promissory note.

долговре́менный *прил* prolonged.

долгожда́нный *прил* long-awaited.

долгожи́тел|ь (-я) *м* long-lived person.

долгожи́тельниц|а (-ы) *ж см* **долгожи́тель**.

долгоигра́ющ|ий (-ая, -ее, -ие) *прил*: **~ая пласти́нка** L.P. (= *long-playing record*).

долголе́тн|ий (-яя, -ее, -ие) *прил*: **~ее сотру́дничество** long-standing cooperation.

долгосро́чный *прил* long-term.

долгот|а́ (-ы́) *ж* length; (*ГЕО*) longitude.

до́лее *сравн прил от* **до́лгий** ♦ *сравн нареч от* **до́лго**.

до́лек *сущ см* **до́лька**.

доле|те́ть (-чу́, -ти́шь; *impf* **долета́ть**) *сов неперех*: **~ до** +*gen* to fly to, reach; (*звук, слу́хи*) to reach.

KEYWORD

до́лж|ен (-на́, -но́, -ны́) *часть сказуемого* (+*infin*) **1** (*обязан*): **я до́лжен уйти́** I must go; **я до́лжен бу́ду уйти́** I will have to go; **она́ должна́ была́ уйти́** she had to go

2 (*выража́ет предположе́ние*): **он до́лжен ско́ро прийти́** he should arrive soon

3 (+*dat*; *о до́лге*): **ты до́лжен мне 5 рубле́й** you owe me 5 roubles

4: **должно́ быть** (*вероя́тно*) probably; **кто́-то, должно́ быть сто́рож, закры́л дверь** somebody, probably the night watchman, closed the door; **должно́ быть, она́ о́чень уста́ла** she must have been very tired.

должни́к (-**á**) *м* debtor.

должни́ц|а (-ы) *ж см* **должни́к**.

до́лжн|ое (-ого; *decl like adj*) *ср* due; **отдава́ть (отда́ть** *perf*) *или* **воздава́ть (возда́ть** *perf*) **~ кому́-н** to give sb his *итп* due.

должностн|о́й *прил* official; **~о́е преступле́ние** malfeasance; **должностно́е лицо́** official.

до́лжност|ь (-и; *gen pl* -**е́й**) *ж* (*пост*) post; (*обя́занность*) duties *мн*; **вступа́ть (вступи́ть** *perf*) **в ~ кого́-н** to assume sb's post; **по ~и** ex officio.

до́лжный *прил* (*у́ровень*) required; (*внима́ние*) sufficient.

доли́н|а (-ы) *ж* valley.

до́ллар (-а) *м* dollar.

до́лларов|ый *прил* dollar *опред*; **~ счёт** dollar account.

доложи́ть (-у́, -ишь; *impf* **докла́дывать**) *сов перех* to report ♦ *неперех*: **~ о** +*prp* to give a report on; **~** (*perf*) **о прихо́де кого́-н** to announce sb.

доло́й *нареч* away with; **~ апартеи́д!** down

with apartheid!

доло|то́ (-ота́; *nom pl* **-о́та**) *ср* chisel; (*для бурения*) drill.

до́льше *сравн прил от* **до́лгий** ♦ *сравн нареч от* **до́лго**.

до́лька (-ьки; *gen pl* **-ек**) *ж* (*апельсина*) segment.

до́л|я (-и; *gen pl* **-е́й**) *ж* share; (*пирога*) portion; (*судьба*) lot, fate; ~ **секу́нды/сантиме́тра** a fraction of a second/centimetre (*BRIT*) *или* centimeter (*US*); **входи́ть** (**войти́** *perf*) **в** ~**ю с кем-н** to go shares with sb; **выпада́ть** (**вы́пасть** *perf*) **на чью-н** ~**ю** to fall to sb's lot.

дом (-а; *nom pl* **-а́**) *м* house; (*многоэтажный*) block of flats (*BRIT*), apartment building (*US*); (*свое жильё*) home; (*семья*) household; ~ **Рома́новых** the house of Romanov; ~ **культу́ры** *centre for social and cultural activities*; **рабо́тать** (*impf*) **на** ~**у́** to work from home; **рабо́тать** (*impf*) **по до́му** to do the housework; **дом моде́лей** fashion house; **дом о́тдыха** ≈ holiday centre (*BRIT*) *или* center (*US*).

до́ма *нареч* at home; **быть** (*impf*) *или* **чу́вствовать** (*impf*) **себя́ как** ~ to feel at home; **его́ нет** ~ he's out *или* not at home; **сиде́ть** (*impf*) ~ to stay in *или* at home; **у него́ не все** ~ (*разг*) he's not all there.

дома́шн|ий (-яя, -ее, -ие) *прил* (*адрес, телефон*) home *опред*; (*еда*) home-made; (*животное*) domestic; ~**ие ту́фли** (carpet) slippers; ~**ее пла́тье** housecoat; **дома́шняя хозя́йка** housewife; **дома́шняя рабо́тница** domestic help (*BRIT*), maid (*US*); **дома́шнее зада́ние** homework.

до́менн|ый *прил* (*цех*) smelting *опред*; ~**ая печь** blast furnace.

доминика́нск|ий (-ая, -ое, -ие) *прил*: **Д**~**ая Респу́блика** Dominican Republic.

доминио́н (-а) *м* dominion.

домини́р|овать (-ую) *несов неперех* (*идея, мелодия*) to predominate; ~ (*impf*) **над** +*instr* to dominate.

домино́ *ср нескл* (*игра*) dominoes *ед*; (*фишка, костюм*) domino.

домко́м (-а) *м сокр* (= *домово́й комите́т*) ≈ residents' association.

домкра́т (-а) *м* (*TEX*) jack.

домовладе́л|ец (-ьца) *м* home owner.

домовладе́ни|е (-я) *ср* (*дом с участком*) *house with grounds attached*; (*владение домом*) home ownership.

домово́дств|о (-а) *ср* home economics.

домов|о́й (о́го; *decl like adj*) *м* (*ФОЛЬКЛОР*) house spirit.

домо́вый *прил* (*ворота*) house *опред*; **домо́вая кни́га** property register.

домога́|ться (-юсь) *несов возв*: ~ +*gen* (*власти*) to strive for; ~ (*impf*) **чьей-н руки́** to court *или* woo sb.

домо́й *нареч* home; **мне пора́** ~ it's time for me to go home.

доморо́щенный *прил* (*разг: пренебр*) homespun.

домосе́д (-а) *м* stay-at-home.

домоуправле́ни|е (-я) *ср* ≈ housing department.

домофо́н (-а) *м* intercom.

домохозя́й|ка (-йки; *gen pl* **-ек**) *ж* (= **дома́шняя хозя́йка**) housewife.

домоча́|дец (-ца) *м* (*обычно мн*) member of the household.

домрабо́тниц|а (-ы) *ж* (= **дома́шняя рабо́тница**) domestic help (*BRIT*), maid (*US*).

домча́|ться (-у́сь, -и́шься) *сов возв*: ~ (**до** +*gen*) to rush (to).

до́мысе|л (-ла) *м* conjecture.

донага́ *нареч*: **разде́ть кого́-н** ~ to strip sb naked.

дона́шива|ть (-ю) *несов от* **доноси́ть**.

доне́льзя *нареч* (*разг*) terribly.

донёс *итп сов см* **донести́**.

донесе́ни|е (-я) *ср* report.

донес|ти́ (-у́, -ёшь; *pt* **донёс**, -ла́, -ло́, *impf* **доноси́ть**) *сов перех* to carry ♦ *неперех*: ~ **на** +*acc* to inform on; ~ (*perf*) **о** +*prp* to report on

▸ **донести́сь** (*impf* **доноси́ться**) *сов возв*: ~**сь до** +*gen* to reach.

до́низу *нареч* to the bottom; **све́рху** ~ from top to bottom.

донима́|ть (-ю) *несов от* **доня́ть**.

до́нор (-а) *м* donor.

до́норск|ий (-ая, -ое, -ие) *прил* donor *опред*.

доно́с (-а) *м*: ~ (**на** +*acc*) denunciation (of); **де́лать** (**сде́лать** *perf*) ~ **на кого́-н** to inform on sb.

доно|си́ть (-шу́, -сишь) *несов от* **донести́** ♦ (*impf* **дона́шивать**) *сов перех* (*одежду*) to wear out; (*ребёнка*) to carry to term; **дона́шивать** (~ *perf*) **ве́щи за кем-н** to wear sb's hand-me-downs

▸ **доноси́ться** *несов от* **донести́сь**.

доно́счик (-а) *м* informer.

доно́счиц|а (-ы) *ж см* **доно́счик**.

доношу́(сь) *сов см* **доноси́ть(ся)**.

до́нья *итп сущ см* **дно**.

до|ня́ть (-йму́, -ймёшь; *impf* **донима́ть**) *сов перех* (*разг*) to exasperate.

доп. *сокр* = **дополни́тельный**.

допе́й(те) *сов см* **допи́ть**.

допива́|ть (-ю) *несов от* **допи́ть**.

до́пинг (-а) *м* drugs *мн*.

допи|са́ть (-шу́, -шешь; *impf* **допи́сывать**) *сов перех* (*письмо*) to finish (writing); (*картину*) to finish (painting); (*написать дополнительно*) to add.

допи́ть (**допью́**, **допьёшь**; *pt* -, -ла́, -ло, *imper* **допе́й(те)**, *impf* **допива́ть**) *сов перех* to drink up.

допишу́ *итп сов см* **дописа́ть**.

допла́т|а (-ы) *ж* additional payment; **~ за бага́ж** excess baggage (charge).

доплы́|ть (-ву́, -вёшь; *pt* -л, -ла́, -ло, *impf* **доплыва́ть**) *сов неперех*: **~ до** +*gen* (*на корабле́*) to sail to; (*вплавь*) to swim to.

допо́длинно *нареч*: **~ изве́стно** for certain.

допоздна́ *нареч* (*разг*) till late.

дополне́ни|е (-я) *ср* supplement; (*линг*) object; **в ~ (к** +*dat*) in addition (to); **прямо́е/ко́свенное ~** direct/indirect object.

дополни́тельно *нареч* in addition.

дополни́тельный *прил* additional.

допо́лн|ить (-ю, -ишь; *impf* **дополня́ть**) *сов перех* to supplement; **дополня́ть** (**~** *perf*) **кого́-н** to add to what sb has said; **дополня́ть** (*impf*) **друг дру́га** to complement one another.

допото́пный *прил* (*разг*) ancient.

допра́шива|ть (-ю) *несов от* **допроси́ть**.

допро́с (-а) *м* interrogation; **подверга́ть** (**подве́ргнуть** *perf*) **кого́-н ~у** to subject sb to an interrogation.

допро|си́ть (-шу́, -сишь; *impf* **допра́шивать**) *сов перех* to interrogate, question.

до́пуск (-а) *м* (*к зда́нию*) admittance; (*к докуме́нтам*) access; (*тех*) tolerance.

допуска́|ть (-ю; *perf* **допусти́ть**) *несов перех* to admit, allow in; (*предположи́ть*) to assume; **~** (**допусти́ть** *perf*) **оши́бку** (*де́лать*) to make a mistake; (*позволя́ть*) to allow for a mistake; **~** (**допусти́ть** *perf*) **кого́-н до уча́стия/ соревнова́ния** to allow sb to participate/ compete.

допу́стим *вводн сл* let us assume.

допусти́м|ый (-, -а, -о) *прил* permissible, acceptable; (*мысль*) feasible.

допу|сти́ть (-щу́, -стишь) *несов от* **допуска́ть**.

допуще́ни|е (-я) *ср* (*см глаг*) admittance; assumption.

допущу́ *сов см* **допусти́ть**.

допью́ *итп сов см* **допи́ть**.

дорабо́та|ть (-ю; *impf* **дораба́тывать**) *сов неперех*: **~ до** +*gen* to work until ♦ *перех* to finish.

дораст|и́ (-у́, -ёшь; *pt* **доро́с, доросла́, доросло́**, *impf* **дораста́ть**) *сов неперех*: **~ до** +*gen* (*до потолка́*) to grow to; (*до како́го-н во́зраста*) to reach; **он доро́с до дире́ктора** he rose to become a director.

дорв|а́ться (-у́сь, -ёшься; *pt* -а́лся, -ала́сь, -ало́сь, *impf* **дорыва́ться**) *сов неперех*: **~ до** +*gen* (*разг*: *до вла́сти*) to grab; (: *до еды́*) to fall (up)on.

дореволюцио́нный *прил* pre-revolutionary.

доро́г|а (-и) *ж* way; (*путь сообще́ния*) road; по **~е** on the way; **мне с тобо́й** *или* **нам по ~е** we're going the same way; **сбива́ться (сби́ться** *perf*) **с ~и** (*также перен*) to lose one's way; **желе́зная ~** railway (*BRIT*), railroad (*US*).

до́рого *нареч* (*купи́ть, прода́ть*) at a high price

♦ *как сказ* it's expensive; **заплати́ть** (*perf*) **~ за что́-н** (*перен*) to pay dearly for sth; **~ бы дал** *или* **заплати́л** *итп* would give anything; **э́то ~ сто́ит** it's expensive.

дорогови́зн|а (-ы) *ж* high prices *мн*.

доро́гой *нареч* on the way.

дор|ого́й (-ог, -ога́, -ого) *прил* (*кни́га, дом*) expensive; (*цена́*) high; (*no short form*; *друг, мать*) dear; (*no full form*; *воспомина́ния, пода́рок*) cherished ♦ (-ого́; *decl like adj*) *м* dear, darling; **~ цено́й плати́ть (заплати́ть** *perf*) **за что́-н** (*перен*) to pay dearly for sth.

дорожа́|ть (*3sg* -ет, *3pl* -ют, *perf* **вздорожа́ть** *или* **подорожа́ть**) *несов неперех* to rise *или* go up in price.

доро́же *сравн прил от* **дорого́й** ♦ *сравн нареч от* **до́рого**.

доро́жек *сущ см* **доро́жка**.

дорож|и́ть (-у́, -и́шь) *несов неперех*: **~** +*instr* to value.

доро́|жка (-ки; *gen pl* -ек) *ж* pathway; (*для пла́вания*) lane; (*для бе́га, на магнитофо́не*) track; (*ковёр*) runner; (*в аэропорту́*) runway.

доро́жный *прил* (*знак, строи́тельство*) road *опред*; (*костю́м, расхо́ды*) travelling (*BRIT*), traveling (*US*); (*су́мка*) travel; **доро́жный чек** traveller's cheque (*BRIT*), traveler's check (*US*).

доро́с *итп сов см* **дорасти́**.

дорыва́|ться (-юсь) *несов от* **дорва́ться**.

ДОС *ж сокр* (= **ди́сковая операцио́нная систе́ма**) DOS (= *disk operating system*).

ДОСА́АФ *м сокр* = **Доброво́льное о́бщество соде́йствия а́рмии, авиа́ции и фло́ту**.

Доса́аф *м сокр* = **ДОСА́АФ**.

доса́д|а (-ы) *ж* annoyance; **с ~ы** out of annoyance; **~ берёт меня́** I am annoyed.

доса́дный (-ен, -на, -но) *прил* annoying.

доск|а́ (-ки́; *nom pl* -ки, *gen pl* -о́к) *ж* board; (*мра́морная*) slab; (*чугу́нная*) plate; **их нельзя́ ста́вить на одну́ до́ску** they're not in the same league; **доска́ объявле́ний** notice (*BRIT*) *или* bulletin (*US*) board.

доска|за́ть (-жу́, -жешь; *impf* **доска́зывать**) *сов перех* to finish (telling).

доскона́льный (-ен, -ьна, -ьно) *прил* thorough.

доследовани|е (-я) *ср* (*ЮР*) further examination *или* inquiry.

досло́вно *нареч* verbatim, word for word.

досло́вный *прил* literal, word-for-word.

дослуж|и́ться (-у́сь, -ишься; *impf* **дослу́живаться**) *сов возв*: **~ до** +*gen* to rise to the rank of.

дослу́ша|ть (-ю; *impf* **дослу́шивать**) *сов перех* to listen to.

досма́трива|ть (-ю) *несов от* **досмотре́ть**.

досмо́тр (-а) *м*: **тамо́женный ~** customs examination.

досмотр|е́ть (-ю́, -ишь; *impf* **досма́тривать**) *сов перех* to watch the end of; (*бага́ж*) to check; **~** (*perf*) **до** +*gen* to watch until.

досо́к *сущ см* **доска́**.

доспе́х|и (**-ов**) *мн* (*рыцаря*) armour *ед* (*BRIT*), armor *ед* (*US*); (*перен: разг*) gear *ед*.

досро́чно *нареч* early, ahead of time.

досро́чный *прил* early.

достава́ть(ся) (**-ю(сь)**) *несов от* **доста́ть(ся)**.

доста́в|ить (**-лю, -ишь**; *impf* **доставля́ть**) *сов перех* (*груз*) to deliver; (*пассажиров*) to carry, transport; (*удовольствие, возможность*) to give; (*трудности*) cause.

доста́в|ка (**-ки**; *gen pl* **-ок**) *ж* delivery; **с ~кой на́ дом** ≈ recorded delivery (*BRIT*), ≈ certified mail (*US*).

доста́влю *сов см* **доста́вить**.

доставля́|ть (**-ю**) *несов от* **доста́вить**.

доста́вок *сущ см* **доста́вка**.

доста́ну(сь) *итп сов см* **доста́ть(ся)**.

доста́н(те) *сов см* **доста́ть**.

доста́т|ок (**-ка**) *м*: **жить в ~ке** to be well provided for.

доста́точно *нареч*: **~ хорошо́/подро́бно** good/detailed enough ♦ *как сказ* that's enough; **~ де́нег/хле́ба** enough money/bread; **~ шепта́ться/болта́ть!** that's enough whispering/chattering!; **~ уви́деть, что́бы поня́ть** one only has to see to understand; **~ сказа́ть, что ...** suffice it to say, that ....

доста́|ть (**-ну, -нешь**; *imper* **доста́нь(те)**, *impf* **достава́ть**) *сов перех* to take; (*раздобыть*) to get ♦ *неперех*: **~ до** +*gen* to reach

▶ **доста́|ться** (*impf* **достава́ться**) *сов возв* (+*dat*; *при разделе*): **мне ~лся дом** I got the house; **мно́го забо́т ему́ ~лось** he was burdened down with a lot of worries; **мне ~лось** (*разг*) I got it in the neck.

дости́г *итп сов см* **дости́чь**.

достига́|ть (**-ю**) *несов от* **дости́гнуть**, **дости́чь**.

дости́гну *итп сов см* **дости́чь**.

дости́гн|уть (**-у, -ёшь**) *сов от* **дости́чь**.

достиже́ни|е (**-я**) *ср* achievement; (*предела, возраста*) reaching.

достижи́м|ый (**-, -а, -о**) *прил* achievable, attainable.

дости́|чь (**-гну, -гнешь**; *pt* **-г, -гла, -гло**, *impf* **достига́ть**) *сов неперех* (+*gen*) to reach; (*результата, цели*) to achieve; (*положения*) to attain.

достове́р|ный (**-ен, -на, -но**) *прил* reliable; **из ~ных исто́чников** from reliable sources.

досто́ен *прил см* **досто́йный**.

досто́инств|о (**-а**) *ср* (*книги, плана*) merit; (*моральные качества*) virtue; (*уважение к себе*) dignity; (*КОММ*) value; **чу́вство со́бственного ~а** self-respect; **счита́ть** (**посчита́ть** *perf*) **что-н ни́же своего́ ~а** to consider sth beneath one's dignity; **ба́нковский биле́т ~м в 100 рубле́й** a banknote to the value

of 100 roubles; **оце́нивать** (**оцени́ть** *perf*) **по ~у кого́-н/что-н** to judge sb/sth on his/its merits.

досто́йно *нареч* with dignity.

досто́йный *прил* (*награда, кара*) fitting; (*человек*) worthy; (**-ен, -йна, -йно**; +*gen*): **~ любви́/уваже́ния** worthy of love/respect.

достопримеча́тельност|ь (**-и**) *ж* sight; (*музея*) interesting exhibit; **осма́тривать** (**осмотре́ть** *perf*) **~и** to go sightseeing.

достопримеча́тель|ный (**-ен, -ьна, -ьно**) *прил* noteworthy.

достоя́ни|е (**-я**) *ср* property; **стать** (*perf*) **или сде́латься** (*perf*) **~м наро́да** to become public property.

до́ступ (**-а**) *м* admittance; (*к документам итп*) access; **открыва́ть** (**откры́ть** *perf*) **~ кому́-н куда́-нибудь** to give sb access to somewhere; **нет ~а во́здуха/кислоро́да** there is no way for air/oxygen to get in.

досту́п|ный (**-ен, -на, -но**) *прил* (*место*) accessible; (*цены*) affordable; (*объяснение, изложение*) comprehensible; (*человека*) approachable.

досу́г (**-а**) *м* leisure (time); **на ~е** in one's spare *или* free time.

до́суха *нареч*: **вы́тереть ~** to dry.

до́сыта *нареч*: **их накорми́ли ~** they were fed until they could eat no more.

досье́ *ср нескл* dossier, file; **заводи́ть** (**завести́** *perf*) **~ на кого́-н** to open a file on sb.

досяга́емост|ь (**-и**) *ж*: **вне ~и** unattainable; **в преде́лах ~и** attainable.

досяга́ем|ый (**-, -а, -о**) *прил* (*задача, цель*) attainable; (*место*) accessible.

дота́скива|ть(ся) (**-ю(сь)**) *несов от* **дотащи́ть(ся)**.

дота́ци|я (**-и**) *ж* subsidy.

дотащ|и́ть (**-у́, -ишь**; *impf* **дота́скивать**) *сов перех* to lug; **е́ле дота́скивать** (**~** *perf*) **но́ги** to drag one's feet

▶ **дотащ|и́ться** (*impf* **дота́скиваться**) *сов возв* (*разг*): **~ся до** +*gen* to drag o.s. to.

дотемна́ *нареч* until dark.

дотла́ *нареч*: **сгоре́ть ~** to burn down (to the ground).

дото́ш|ный (**-ен, -на, -но**) *прил* (*разг*) meticulous.

дотро́н|уться (**-усь, -ёшься**; *impf* **дотра́гиваться**) *сов возв*: **~ до** +*gen* to touch.

дотян|у́ть (**-у́, -ешь**; *impf* **дотя́гивать**) *сов перех*: **~ что-н до** +*gen* to extend sth as far as; **он ~у́л рабо́ту до ве́чера** he dragged the work out until the evening

▶ **дотян|у́ться** (*impf* **дотя́гиваться**) *сов возв*: **~ся до** +*gen* to reach.

доучи́|ться (**-усь, -ишься**; *impf* **доу́чиваться**) *сов возв* to complete one's education; **~** (*perf*) **до конца́ го́да/пя́того кла́сса** to study up until the end of the year/of fifth form.

до́хл|ый *прил* dead; (*разг: слабосильный*) wimpish.

до́х|нуть (-ну, -нешь; *pt* -, -ла, -ло, *perf* **подо́хнуть**) *несов неперех (животное)* to die; (*разг: человек*) to snuff it.

дохну́ть (-у́, -ёшь) *сов неперех (разг: человек)* to breathe; **мне ~ не́когда** (*разг*) I don't get a moment's rest.

дохо́д (-а) *м (предприятия)* income, revenue; (*человека*) income; **национа́льный ~** the national income; **дава́ть (дать** *perf*) *или* **приноси́ть (принести́** *perf*) **~** to generate income; **извлека́ть (извле́чь** *perf*) **~ из чего́-н** to make a profit from sth.

дохо́ден *прил см* **дохо́дный**.

доходи́ть *несов от* **дойти́**.

дохо́д|ный (-ен, -на, -но) *прил* profitable.

дохо́дчив|ый (-, -а, -о) *прил* clear, easy to understand.

доце́нт (-а) *м* ≈ reader (*BRIT*), ≈ associate professor (*US*).

до́чек *сущ см* **до́чка**.

до́чери *итп сущ см* **дочь**.

доче́рн|ий (-яя, -ее, -ие) *прил* daughter's; **~яя компа́ния/фи́рма** subsidiary company/firm.

до́черью *итп сущ см* **дочь**.

до́чиста *нареч* clean.

дочита́|ть (-ю; *impf* **дочи́тывать**) *сов перех* to finish (reading); **~** (*perf*) **до +***gen* to read until.

до́ч|ка (-ки; *gen pl* -ек) *ж* daughter.

дочь (-ери; *см* **Table 2**) *ж* daughter.

дошёл *сов см* **дойти́**.

дошко́льник (-а) *м* preschool child.

дошко́льни|ца (-ы) *ж см* **дошко́льник**.

дошко́льный *прил* preschool.

дошла́ *сов см* **дойти́**.

доща́тый *прил* made of boards.

доя́р|ка (-ки; *gen pl* -ок) *ж* milkmaid.

ДПР *ж сокр* = **Демократи́ческая па́ртия Росси́и**.

др. *сокр* = **друго́й**, **други́е**.

драгоце́нность (-и) *ж* jewel; (*перен*) gem, treasure.

драгоце́нный *прил (камень, металл)* precious; (*время, сведения, мех*) valuable.

драже́ *ср нескл* dragée.

дразн|и́ть (-ю́, -ишь) *несов перех* to tease; (*аппетит, воображение*) to stimulate.

дра́|ить (-ю, -ишь; *perf* **надра́ить**) *несов перех* to scrub.

дра́|ка (-и) *ж* fight; (*битва*) battle; **лезть (поле́зть** *perf*) *или* **ввя́зываться (ввяза́ться** *perf*) **в ~у** to get into a fight.

драко́н (-а) *м* dragon; (*ЗООЛ*) draco *или* flying lizard.

драко́новск|ий (-ая, -ое, -ие) *прил*: **~ие ме́ры** Draconian measures.

дра́м|а (-ы) *ж* drama; (*событие*) crisis; **пережива́ть (пережи́ть** *perf*) **тяжёлую ~у** to go through a crisis.

драматизи́р|овать (-ую) *(не)сов перех* to

dramatize.

драмати́ческ|ий (-ая, -ое, -ие) *прил* dramatic; (*актёр*) stage *опред*; **драмати́ческий кружо́к** drama group; **драмати́ческий теа́тр** theatre, theater (*US*).

драмату́рг (-а) *м* playwright.

драматурги́|я (-и) *ж* drama ◆ *собир* plays.

драмкруж|о́к (-ка́) *м сокр* (= **драмати́ческий кружо́к**) drama group.

дра́ный *прил (разг)* ragged.

драп (-а) *м* *thick woollen cloth.*

драпир|ова́ть (-у́ю; *perf* **задрапирова́ть**) *несов перех*: **~** (**чем-н**) to drape (with sth).

драпиро́в|ка (-ки; *gen pl* -ок) *ж* drapery.

драть (**деру́, дерёшь**; *perf* **разодра́ть**) *несов перех (бумагу, одежду)* to tear *или* rip up; (*perf* **задра́ть**; *подлеж: волк, лиса*) to tear to pieces; (*perf* **вы́драть**; *разг: побить*) to thrash; (*perf* **содра́ть**; *кору, обои*) to strip; **~** (**содра́ть** *perf*) **шку́ру с живо́тного** to skin an animal; **~** (**содра́ть** *perf*) **де́ньги с кого́-н** (*разг*) to rip sb off; **он с меня́ шку́ру сдерёт** (*разг*) he'll have my guts for garters; **~** (*impf*) **го́рло** (*разг*) to bawl

▶ **дра́ться** *несов возв*: **дра́ться (с +***instr*) to fight (with); (*perf* **подра́ться**; *дети*) to fight.

дребеде́нь (-и) *ж (разг)* rubbish.

дре́безг (-а) *м*: **разби́ться с ~ом** to shatter; **разбива́ть (разби́ть** *perf*) **в ме́лкие ~и** to smash to smithereens.

дребезж|а́ть (*3sg* -и́т, *3pl* -а́т) *несов неперех* to jingle.

древеси́н|а (-ы) *ж собир* wood.

древе́сный *прил* wood; **древе́сные поро́ды** species of tree; **древе́сный у́голь** charcoal.

дре́вк|о (-а) *ср (копья)* shaft; **~ фла́га** flagpole.

дре́вн|ий (-яя, -ее, -ие) *прил* ancient; **дре́вняя исто́рия** ancient history.

дре́вность (-и) *ж* antiquity.

дрези́н|а (-ы) *ж* trolley (*BRIT*), handcar (*US*).

дрейф (-а) *м* drift; **снима́ться (сня́ться** *perf*) **с дре́йфа** to regain course; **лежа́ть** (*impf*) **в дре́йфе** to heave to.

дрейф|ова́ть (-у́ю) *несов неперех* to drift.

дрель (-и) *ж* drill.

дрем|а́ть (-лю́, -лешь) *несов неперех* to doze; **враг не дре́млет** (*перен*) the enemy never sleeps.

дремота́ (-ы́) *ж* drowsiness.

дрему́ч|ий (-ая, -ее, -ие; -, -а, -е) *прил* dense; (*перен: невежда*) absolute.

дрена́ж (-а́) *м (почвы)* drainage; (*раны*) draining.

дрессир|ова́ть (-у́ю; *perf* **вы́дрессировать**) *несов перех* to train.

дро́бен *прил см* **дро́бный**.

дроб|и́ть (-лю́, -йшь; *perf* **раздроби́ть**) *несов перех (камень, кость)* to crush; (*силы, отряд*) to divide.

дроблёный *прил (орехи)* crushed.

дро́б|ный (-ен, -на, -но) *прил (перечень,*

список) itemized; (*стук, шаг*) staccato; (*no short form*; *мат*) fractional.

дроб|ь (-и; *gen pl* -**ей**) ж fraction; (*дождя, шагов*) patter; (*барабана*) beat.

дров|á (-; *dat pl* -**áм**) *мн* firewood *ед*; **он наломáл** ~! (*перен: разг*) he made a hash of it!; **кто в лес, кто по** ~ at sixes and sevens.

дрóгн|уть (-у, -ешь) *сов неперех* (*стёкла, руки, голос*) to shake, tremble; (*лицо*) to quiver; (*свет, огонь*) to flicker; (*человек*) to waver; **у меня рукá не** ~**ет** +*infin* ... I won't hesitate to ....

дрожáни|е (-я) *ср* (*стёкол*) vibration; (*колен, голоса*) trembling; (*лица*) quivering; (*света, огня*) flickering.

дрож|áть (-ý, -**йшь**) *несов неперех* (*стёкла*) to vibrate; (*руки, голос*) to shake, tremble; (*лицо*) to quiver; (*свет, огонь*) to flicker; ~ (*impf*) **за** +*acc или* **над** +*instr* (*разг*) to fuss over; ~ (*impf*) **над** (*каждой*) **копéйкой** to grudge every penny; ~ (*impf*) **пéред кем-н** to tremble before sb.

дрóжж|и (-ей) *мн* yeast *ед*.

дрож|ь (-и) ж (*от холода*) shiver; (*от страха*) shudder; **егó бросáет в** ~ he is shuddering.

дрозд (-á) *м* thrush; **чёрный** ~ blackbird.

друг (-га; *nom pl* -**зья́**, *gen pl* -**зéй**) *м* friend; (*разг: обращение*) mate; ~ **дрýга** one another, each other; ~ **дрýгу** (*говорить*) to one another *или* each other; ~ **за дрýгом** one after another; ~ **о дрýге** (*говорить*) about one another *или* each other.

другóй|е (-**йх**; *decl like adj*) *мн* others *мн*.

другóй *прил* (*иной*) another; (*второй*) the other; (*не такой, как этот*) different ♦ (-**óго**; *decl like adj*) *м* (*кто-то иной*) another (person); (*второй*) the other (one); ~**óе мнéние** different opinion; **в** ~ **раз** another time; **и тот и** ~ both; **чтó-то** ~**óе** something else; ~**ими словáми** in other words; **на** ~ **день** the next day; **э́то** ~**óе дéло** that's a different matter; *см также* **другúе**.

дрýжб|а (-ы) ж friendship.

дружелю́би|е (-я) *ср* friendliness.

дружелю́б|ный (-ен, -на, -но) *прил* friendly, amicable.

дрýжен *прил см* **дрýжный**.

дрýжески *нареч* in a friendly manner, amicably.

дрýжеск|ий (-ая, -ое, -ие) *прил* friendly.

дрýжествен|ный (-ен, -на, -но) *прил* friendly.

дружúн|а (-ы) ж (*ист, воен*) host.

друж|úть (-ý, -ишь) *несов неперех*: ~ **с** +*instr* to be friends with

▶ **дружúться** (*perf* **подружúться**) *несов возв*: ~**ся с** +*instr* to make friends with.

дрýжищ|е (-а) *м* (*разг*) mate.

дрýж|ный (-ен, -нá, -но, -ны) *прил* (*семья, коллектив*) close-knit; (*апплодисменты, смех*) general; (*усилия*) concerted.

друж|óк (-кá) *м* (*друг*) friend; (*обращение*) love.

друзья́ *итп сущ см* **друг**.

дры́га|ть (-ю) *несов неперех*: ~ **ногáми** to kick.

дры́хн|уть (-у, -ешь) *несов неперех* (*разг*) to kip, sleep.

дря́бл|ый (-, -á, -о) *прил* (*кожа*) sagging; (*человек, тело*) flabby.

дря́зг|и (-) *мн* (*разг*) squabbles *мн*.

дрянн|óй *прил* (*разг: товар, работа*) trashy; (*: характер*) rotten.

дрян|ь (-и) ж (*разг*) rubbish (*BRIT*), trash (*US*).

дряхлé|ть (-ю; *perf* **одряхлéть**) *несов неперех* to become infirm.

дря́хл|ый (-, -á, -о) *прил* (*человек*) infirm; (*здание*) dilapidated, decrepit.

ДСО *ср сокр* (= **добровóльное спортúвное óбщество**) amateur sports association.

дуб (-а; *loc sg* -ý, *nom pl* -**ы́**) *м* (*бот*) oak (tree); (*древесина*) oak; (*перен: разг*) blockhead.

дубúн|а (-ы) ж club ♦ *м/ж* (*разг*) blockhead.

дубúн|ка (-ки; *gen pl* -**ок**) ж cudgel; **резúновая** ~ truncheon.

дуб|úть (-лю́, -ишь; *perf* **вы́дубить**) *несов перех* to tan.

дублён|ка (-ки; *gen pl* -**ок**) ж sheepskin coat.

дублёный *прил* (*мех*) tanned.

дублёр (-а) *м* backup; (*театр*) understudy; (*кино*) double.

дубликáт (-а) *м* duplicate.

Дýблин (-а) *м* Dublin.

дублúр|овать (-ую) *несов перех* (*деятельность*) to duplicate; (*театр*) to understudy; (*кино*) to dub; (*комп*) to back up.

дубл|ь (-я) *м* (*кино*) take.

дублю́ *несов см* **дубúть**.

дубóвый *прил* oak; (*перен: стиль, язык*) ponderous.

Дувр (-а) *м* Dover.

дуг|á (-и; *nom pl* -**и**) ж (*геом*) arc.

дуд|éть (2sg -**ишь**, 3sg -**úт**) *несов неперех* to play the pipe.

дýд|ка (-ки; *gen pl* -**ок**) ж (*муз*) pipe; **пляса́ть** (*impf*) **под чью-н** ~**ку** (*перен*) to dance to sb's tune.

дýж|ка (-ки; *gen pl* -**ек**) ж (*серёг*) hoop; (*ведра*) handle.

дýл|о (-а) *ср* (*отверстие ствола*) muzzle; (*сам ствол*) barrel.

дýм|а (-ы; *размышление*) meditation, thought; **Д**~ (*полит*) the Duma (*lower house of the Russian parliament*); **Госудáрственная Д**~ the State Duma.

дýма|ть (-ю) *несов неперех*: ~ (**о чём-н**) to think (about sth); ~ (*impf*) **над чем-н** to think sth over; **он** ~**ет купúть машúну** he is thinking of buying a car; **я** ~**ю, что да/нет** I think/don't think so; **и не** ~**йте** (*разг*) don't even think of it!

▶ **дýматься** (*perf* **подýматься**) *несов безл* (+*dat*) to seem; **мне** ~**ется, он прав** I think he's right.

Дуна|й (-я) *м* Danube.

дунове́ни|е (-я) *ср* breath.

ду́нуть (-у, -ешь) *сов неперех* to blow.

дупл|о́ (-á; *nom pl* **-а,** *gen pl* **-ел)** *ср (дерева)* hollow; *(зуба)* cavity.

ду́р|а (-ы) *ж (разг)* fool, idiot.

дура́к (-á) *м (разг)* fool, idiot; **игра́ть** *(impf)* **в дурака́** to play "durak" *(Russian card game)*; **он не ~ вы́пить/пое́сть** *(разг)* he loves his drink/food; **дурака́ валя́ть** *(impf)* *(разг: дура́читься)* to clown about, play the fool; *(: безде́льничать)* to lounge about; **остава́ться (оста́ться** *perf)* **в дурака́х** *(перен: разг)* to be made a fool of.

дура́ц|кий (-ая, -ое, -ие) *прил (разг)* stupid, idiotic.

дура́честв|о (-а) *ср* stupidity, idiocy.

дура́ч|ить (-у, -ишь; *perf* **одура́чить)** *несов перех (разг)* to con

▶ **дура́читься** *несов возв (разг)* to play the fool.

дурачь|ё (-я́) *ср собир (разг)* bunch of idiots.

дурён *сущ см* **дурно́й.**

дур|е́нь (-ня) *м (разг)* dimwit, fool.

дуре́|ть (-ю; *perf* **одуре́ть)** *несов неперех (разг)*: **~ от** +*gen* to grow stupid from.

ду́р|ий (-ья, -ье, -ьи) *прил*: **~ья голова́** *или* **башка́** *(разг)* dope, fool.

дур|и́ть (-ю́, -и́шь) *несов неперех (разг: челове́к)* to fool around; *(живо́тное)* to be stubborn; **(задури́ть** *perf)* **го́лову кому́-н** *(разг)* to mix sb up.

дурма́н (-а) *м* thorn apple, jimson weed (*US*); *(опьяня́юще сре́дство)* intoxicant; *(: перен)* drug.

дурма́н|ить (-ю, -ишь; *perf* **одурма́нить)** *несов перех* to intoxicate.

дурне́|ть (-ю; *perf* **подурне́ть)** *несов неперех* to lose one's looks.

ду́рно *нареч (па́хнуть, вы́глядеть)* bad; *(вести́ себя́)* badly ♦ *как сказ*: **мне ~** I don't feel well; **ему́ сде́лалось ~** he felt faint.

дур|но́й (-ён, -на́, -но) *прил* nasty; *(пита́ние)* bad; **она́ ~на́ собо́й** she is very plain; **дурно́й при́знак** bad omen.

дурнот|а́ (-ы́) *ж* faintness.

ду́рня *итп сущ см* **ду́рень.**

ду́роч|ка (-ки; *gen pl* **-ек)** *ж (разг)* silly girl.

дуршла́г (-а) *м* colander.

дур|ь (-и) *ж (разг)* rubbish, nonsense; **вы́брось э́ту ~ из головы́!** *(разг)* get that foolish idea out of your head!; **ду́рью ма́яться** *(impf)* *или* **му́читься** *(impf)* *(разг)* to muck around.

ду́тый *прил* hollow; *(перен)* exaggerated, inflated.

ду|ть (-ю, -ешь) *несов неперех* to blow ♦ *(perf* **вы́дуть)** *перех* to blow; **здесь ду́ет** it's draughty (*BRIT*) *или* drafty (*US*) in here.

дух (-а; *part* **ген -у)** *м* spirit; *(разг)*: **перевести́ ~** to get one's breath back; **в ду́хе** +*gen* in the spirit of; **па́дать** *(impf)* **ду́хом** to lose heart; **быть** *(impf)* **в ду́хе/не в ду́хе** to be in high/low spirits;

сохраня́ть (сохрани́ть *perf)* **прису́тствие ду́ха** to retain one's presence of mind; **у меня́ не хва́тит ду́ху на э́то** *(разг)* I don't have the heart to do this; **во весь ~** *(разг)* at full *или* top speed; **чтоб ду́ху твоего́ здесь не́ было!** *(разг)* get out of my sight!

дух|и́ (-о́в) *мн* perfume *ед*, scent *ед*.

духове́нств|о (-а) *ср собир* clergy; *(правосла́вное, католи́ческое)* priesthood.

духо́вк|а (-и) *ж* oven.

духо́вник (-а) *м* confessor.

духо́вност|ь (-и) *ж* spirituality.

духо́вный *прил (интере́сы, запро́сы)* spiritual; *(си́ла, мир, жизнь)* inner; *(му́зыка)* sacred, church *опред*; **духо́вная акаде́мия** seminary; **духо́вное зва́ние** ecclesiastical rank; **духо́вное лицо́** ecclesiastic, cleric; **духо́вный сан** holy orders *мн*.

духово́й *прил (МУЗ)* wind *опред*.

духот|а́ (-ы́) *ж* stuffiness; *(жара́)* closeness.

душ (-а) *м* shower; **принима́ть (приня́ть** *perf)* **~** to have *или* take a shower.

душ|а́ (-и́; *nom pl* **-и)** *ж* soul; *(ИСТ: крестья́нин)* serf; **до́брая ~** kind heart; **ни́зкая/по́длая ~** mean/ignoble spirit; **~ моя́** my dear; **рабо́тать** *(impf)* **с ~о́й** to put one's heart into one's work; **в ~é** at heart; **на ду́шу (населе́ния)** per head (of the population); **он в ней ~й не ча́ет** she's the apple of his eye; **быть** *(impf)* **~о́й** +*gen (о́бщества, де́ла)* to be the life and soul of; **не име́ть** *(impf)* **гроша́ за ~о́й** to be without a penny to one's name; **говори́ть** *(impf)*/**бесе́довать** *(impf)* **по ~м** to have a heart-to-heart talk/chat; **отводи́ть (отвести́** *perf)* **ду́шу** to pour out one's heart; **как Бог на́ ~ у поло́жит** *(разг)* any old way; **у меня́ ~ в пя́тки ушла́** *(разг)* I was scared to death; **от всей ~й** from the bottom of one's heart; **в глубине́ ~й** in one's heart of hearts.

Душанбе́ *м нескл* Dushanbe.

душевнобольн|а́я (-о́й; *decl like adj)* *ж см* **душевнобольно́й.**

душевнобольн|о́й (-о́го; *decl like adj)* *м* mentally-ill person.

душе́вный *прил (си́лы, подъём)* inner; *(разгово́р)* sincere, heartfelt; *(челове́к)* kindly; **~ое потрясе́ние** shock.

душегре́йк|а (-и; *разг)* *ж* body warmer.

душегу́б (-а) *ж (разг)* butcher.

душегу́б|ка (-ки; *gen pl* **-ок)** *ж см* **душегу́б;** *(автомаши́на)* mobile gas chamber.

душе́н *сущ см* **ду́шный.**

душеразд|ира́ющий (-ая, -ее, -ие; -, -а, -е) *прил (крик)* bloodcurdling; *(плач)* heart-rending.

души́стый *прил (цвето́к)* fragrant; *(мы́ло)* perfumed.

души́тел|ь (-я) *м (перен)* suppressor.

душ|и́ть (-у́, -ишь; *perf* **задуши́ть** *или* **удуши́ть)** *несов перех* to strangle; *(свобо́ду, прогре́сс)* to stifle, suppress; *(perf* **надуши́ть;** *плато́к)* to scent; **его́ ду́шит смех** he is choking with laughter; ~ *(impf)* **в объя́тиях кого́-н** to smother sb in one's embrace.

души́ц|а (-ы) *ж* marjoram.

ду́шно *как сказ* it's stuffy *или* close; **в ко́мнате** ~ the room is very stuffy; **мне ~, откро́йте окно́** I find it very stuffy *или* close, open the window.

ду́ш|ный (-ен, -на́, -но) *прил* stuffy; *(жаркий)* sultry.

дуэ́л|ь (-и) *ж* duel; **вызыва́ть (вы́звать** *perf)* **кого́-н на** ~ to challenge sb to a duel.

дуэ́т (-а) *м (произведение)* duet, duo; *(исполнители)* duo.

ды́бом *нареч*: **встава́ть ~** *(волосы, шерсть)* to stand on end.

дыб|ы́ (-о́в) *мн*: **на ~ станови́ться** *(лошадь)* to rear up; *(перен: разг)* to kick up a fuss.

дым (-а; *part gen* **-у,** *loc sg* **-у́,** *nom pl* **-ы́)** *м* smoke; **поруга́ться** *(perf)* **в ~** to fall out completely.

дым|и́ть (-лю́, -и́шь; *perf* **надыми́ть)** *несов неперех (печь, дрова)* to smoulder (*BRIT*), smolder (*US*); *(разг):* ~ +*instr* to puff on

▸ **дыми́ться** *несов возв (труба)* to be smoking.

ды́мк|а (-и) *ж* haze.

ды́мно *как сказ*: **(здесь)** ~ it's smoky (in here).

ды́мный *прил (дрова, головешка)* smouldering (*BRIT*), smoldering (*US*); *(комната, помещение)* smoky, smoke-filled.

дымохо́д (-а) *м* flue.

ды́мчатый *прил (кот)* smoky; **ды́мчатые очки́** tinted glasses.

ды́н|я (-и) *ж* melon.

дыр|а́ (-ы́; *nom pl* **-ы)** *ж* hole; **в ды́рах** full of holes.

ды́р|ка (-ки; *gen pl* **-ок)** *ж* hole.

дыроко́л (-а) *м* punch.

дыря́в|ый (-, -а, -о) *прил (разг)* holey; **у него́** ~**ая голова́** *(разг)* he has a head like a sieve.

дыха́ни|е (-я) *ср* breathing, respiration; ~ **весны́** a breath of spring; **с затаённым** ~**м** with bated breath; **второ́е** ~ second wind; **иску́сственное** ~ artificial respiration.

дыха́тельный *прил (упражнения)* breathing *опред*; *(процесс)* respiratory; **дыха́тельное го́рло** windpipe; **дыха́тельные пути́** respiratory tract *ед*.

дыш|а́ть (-у́, -ишь) *несов неперех* to breathe; ~ *(impf)* +*instr (ненавистью)* to exude; *(любовью)* to radiate

▸ **дыша́ться** *несов возв* (+*dat*): **мне здесь ле́гче ды́шится** I can breathe more easily here.

дья́вол (-а) *м* devil; **за каки́м** ~**ом я до́лжен идти́ туда́!** *(разг)* why the devil should I go there!; **како́го** ~**а ...!** what the devil ...!

дья́вольск|ий (-ая, -ое, -ие) *прил* diabolic(al); *(разг: холод)* devilish; ~**ое терпе́ние** ≈ the patience of Job.

дья́кон (-а) *м* deacon.

дю́жин|а (-ы) *ж* dozen; **чёртова** ~ baker's dozen.

дюйм (-а) *м* inch.

дю́н|а (-ы; *gen pl* **-)** *ж (обычно мн)* dune.

дюралюми́ний (-я) *м* Duralumin®.

дюше́с (-а) *м (БОТ)* Duchess pear.

дя́гиль (-я) *м* angelica.

дя́д|ька (-ьки; *gen pl* **-ек)** *м* uncle; *(разг)* guy.

дя́д|я (-и) *м* uncle; *(разг)* man; (: *обращение)* mister.

дя́тел (-ла) *м* woodpecker.

~ E, е ~

E, е *сущ нескл (буква)* the 6th letter of the Russian alphabet.

ЕАСТ *ж сокр* (= *Европейская ассоциа́ция свобо́дной торго́вли*) EFTA (= *European Free Trade Association*).

ЕБРР *м сокр* (= *Европейский банк реконстру́кции и разви́тия*) EBRD (= *European Bank for Reconstruction and Development*).

ева́нгели|е (-я) *ср* the Gospels *мн*; (*одна из книг*) gospel.

евангели́ст (-а) *м* evangelist.

евангели́ческ|ий (-ая, -ое, -ие) *прил* evangelical.

ева́нгельск|ий (-ая, -ое, -ие) *прил*: ~ текст gospel.

е́внух (-а) *м* eunuch.

Евра́зи|я (-и) *ж* Eurasia.

евре́|ек *сущ см* **евре́йка**.

евре́|й (-я) *м* Jew.

евре́|йка (-йки; *gen pl* -ек) *ж* Jewess.

евре́йск|ий (-ая, -ое, -ие) *прил (народ, обычаи)* Jewish; ~ язы́к Hebrew.

евроазиа́тск|ий (-ая, -ое, -ие) *прил* Eurasian.

Еврови́дени|е (-я) *ср* Eurovision.

Евро́п|а (-ы) *ж* Europe.

европе́|ец (-йца) *м* European.

европе́й|ка (-и) *ж см* **европе́ец**.

европе́йск|ий (-ая, -ое, -ие) *прил* European; **европейский сове́т** Council of Europe; **европейский суд** European Court of Justice; **европейское соо́бщество** European Community.

европе́йца *итп сущ см* **европе́ец**.

ЕВС *ж сокр* (= *Европейская валю́тная систе́ма*) EMS (= *European Monetary System*).

ЕВФ *м сокр* (= *Европейский валю́тный фонд*) (= *European monetary fund*).

е́гер|ь (-я) *м (на охоте)* huntsman (*мн* huntsmen).

Еги́п|ет (-та) *м* Egypt.

еги́петск|ий (-ая, -ое, -ие) *прил* Egyptian.

Еги́пта *итп сущ см* **Еги́пет**.

египтя́н|ин (-ина; *nom pl* -е, *gen pl* -) *м* Egyptian.

египтя́н|ка (-ки; *gen pl* -ок) *ж см* **египтя́нин**.

его́ *мест см* **он, оно́** ♦ *притяж мест (относительно мужчины итп)* his; (*относительно предмета итп*) its.

егожу́ *несов см* **егози́ть**.

егоз|а́ (-ы́) *м/ж (разг)* fidget.

егози́ть (-жу́, -зи́шь) *несов неперех (разг)* to fidget; ~ (*impf*) **пе́ред** +*instr (перен)* to fawn on.

ед|а́ (-ы́) *ж (пища)* food; (*процесс*): **за** ~**о́й, во вре́мя** ~**ы́** at mealtimes; **мо́йте ру́ки пе́ред** ~**о́й** wash your hands before eating.

KEYWORD

едва́ *нареч* **1** (*с трудом: нашёл, достал, доехал итп*) only just

2 (*только, немного*) barely, hardly; **больно́й едва́ ды́шит** the patient is barely *или* hardly breathing; **едва́ созре́вший плод** a barely ripe fruit

3 (*только что*) just; **ему́ едва́ испо́лнилось 20 лет** he has just turned 20

♦ *союз (как только)* as soon as; **едва́ он пришёл, на́чал рабо́тать** as soon as he arrived, he set to work; **едва́ ли** hardly; **уже́ по́здно, едва́ ли он придёт** it's late, he's hardly likely to come now; **едва́ ли не** almost; **он едва́ ли не са́мый лу́чший учени́к** he is almost the best pupil.

е́дем *итп сов см* **е́хать**.

еди́м *несов см* **есть**.

едине́ни|е (-я) *ср* unity.

едини́|ца (-ы) *ж (цифра)* one; (*изображение*) the figure 1; (*ПРОСВЕЩ*) ≈ very poor (*school mark*); (*измерения, часть целого*) unit; **де́нежная** ~ monetary unit; **шта́тная** ~ member of staff; *см также* **едини́цы**.

едини́цы (-) *мн* a few; **оста́лись в живы́х** ~ only a few people survived.

едини́чн|ый (-ен, -на, -но) *прил (редкий: экземпляр)* single; (*случай*) isolated.

единобо́рств|о (-а) *ср* single combat; **вступа́ть (вступи́ть** *perf*) **в** ~ **с** +*instr* to enter into combat with.

единобра́чи|е (-я) *ср* monogamy.

единовла́стен *прил см* **единовла́стный**.

единовла́сти|е (-я) *ср* autocracy.

единовла́стн|ый (-ен, -на, -но) *прил* autocratic.

единовре́мен|ный (-ен, -на, -но) *прил* one-off; ~**ное посо́бие** one-off benefit payment.

единогла́сен *прил см* **единогла́сный**.

единогла́си|е (-я) *ср* unanimity.

единогла́сно *нареч* unanimously; **при́нято** ~ carried unanimously.

единогла́с|ный (-ен, -на, -но) *прил* unanimous.
единоду́ши|е (-я) *ср* unanimity.
единоду́шно *нареч* unanimously.
единоду́шный *прил* unanimous.
единокро́вный *прил*: ~ **брат** half-brother (*with the same father*).
единоли́чник (-а) *м* (*ист*) peasant smallholder; (*пренебр*) maverick.
единоли́чный *прил* (*индивидуальный: власть, решение*) individual.
единомы́сли|е (-я) *ср* like-mindedness.
единомы́шленник (-а) *м* like-minded person; (*сообщник*) confederate.
единонача́ли|е (-я) *ср* one-man rule.
единообра́з|ный (-ен, -на, -но) *прил* unified.
единоро́г (-а) *м* unicorn.
единоутро́бный *прил*: ~ **брат** half-brother (*with the same mother*).
еди́нственен *прил см* **еди́нственный**.
еди́нственно *част* (*только*) only ♦ *нареч*: ~ **пра́вильный/возмо́жный путь** the only correct/possible way; ~, **о чём я прошу́** the only thing I ask.
еди́нствен|ный (-ен, -на, -но) *прил* (the) only; ~ **в своём ро́де** one of a kind; ~**ная наде́жда** the only hope; **он – ~ ребёнок** he is an only child; **еди́нственное число́** (*линг*) singular.
еди́нств|о (-а) *ср* unity.
еди́н|ый *прил* (*цельный*) united; (*общий*) common; (*только один*) one, single; ~**ое це́лое** a unified whole; **все до ~ого** to a man; **еди́ный (проездно́й) биле́т** travel pass (*for use on all forms of transport*).
еди́те *несов см* **есть**.
е́д|кий (-кая, -кое, -кие; -ок, -ка́, -ко) *прил* (*также перен*) caustic; (*запах, дым*) acrid.
е́дкость (-и) *ж* (*хим*) causticity; (*перен*) acerbity.
едо́к *прил см* **е́дкий**.
едо́к (-а́) *м*: **у него́ в семье́ пять едоко́в** he has five mouths to feed.
е́ду *итп несов см* **е́хать**.
едя́т *несов см* **есть**.
её *мест от* **она́** ♦ *притяж мест* (*относительно женщины итп*) her; (*относительно предмета итп*) its.
ёж (-а́) *м* hedgehog; **морско́й** ~ sea urchin; **ежу́ поня́тно** (*разг*) it's as plain as the nose on your face.
ежеви́к|а (-и) *ж* (*растение*) bramble; (*ягода*) blackberry; (*собир*) blackberries *мн*, brambles *мн*.
ежеви́чный *прил* (*варенье, куст*) blackberry *опред*, bramble *опред*.
ежего́дник (-а) *м* annual (publication).
ежего́дно *нареч* annually.
ежего́дный *прил* annual *опред*.
ежедне́вен *прил см* **ежедне́вный**.

ежедне́вник (-а) *м* (*блокнот-дневник*) diary.
ежедне́вно *нареч* daily, every day.
ежедне́в|ный (-ен, -на, -но) *прил* daily; (*повседневный*) everyday.
ежеме́сячник (-а) *м* (*периодическое издание*) monthly.
ежеме́сячно *нареч* monthly.
ежеме́сячный *прил* monthly *опред*.
ежемину́тен *прил см* **ежемину́тный**.
ежемину́тно *нареч* every minute; (*постоянно*) constantly.
ежемину́т|ный (-ен, -на, -но) *прил*: ~**ная прове́рка** checks at one-minute intervals; (*очень частый*) constant.
еженеде́льник (-а) *м* weekly.
еженеде́льно *нареч* weekly.
еженеде́льный *прил* weekly *опред*.
ежесеку́нд|ный (-ен, -на, -но) *прил* occurring every second; (*чрезвычайно частый*) incessant.
ёжик (-а) *м* hedgehog; (*причёска*) crew cut; **стри́чься (постри́чься** *perf*) ~**ом** to have a crew cut.
ёж|иться (-усь, -ишься; *perf* **съёжиться**) *несов возв*: ~ **от** +*gen* (*от холода*) to huddle up from; (*от страха, от стыда*) to cringe with.
ежо́вый *прил*: **держа́ть кого́-н в ежо́вых рукави́цах** to rule sb with a rod of iron.
езд|а́ (-ы́) *ж* (*перемещение: на велосипеде, верхом*) riding; (: *на машине*) driving; (*мера: на машине*) drive; **в двадцати́ мину́тах** ~**ы́ от** +*gen* a twenty-minute drive from.
е́з|дить (-жу, -дишь) *несов неперех* to go; ~ (*impf*) **на** +*prp* (*на лошади, на велосипеде*) to ride; (*на поезде, на автобусе итп*) to travel *или* go by; (*перен: эксплуатировать*) to make use of.
ездово́й *прил*: **ездова́я соба́ка** sled dog; **ездова́я ло́шадь** draught horse.
ездо́к (-а́) *м* rider; **туда́ я бо́льше не** ~ I'm not going there again.
е́зжу *несов см* **е́здить**.
ей *мест см* **она́**.
ей-бо́гу *межд* (*разг*) really, truly.
ЕКА *ср сокр* (= *Европе́йское косми́ческое аге́нтство*) ESA (= *European Space Agency*).
Екатеринбу́рг (-а) *м* Ekaterinburg.
ёка|ть (*3sg* -ет, *3pl* -ют, *perf* **ёкнуть**) *несов неперех* (*сердце*) to miss a beat.
ёкн|уть (*3sg* -ет, *3pl* -ут) *сов от* **ёкать**.
ел *итп несов см* **есть**.
е́ле *нареч* (*с трудом*) only just; (*едва*) barely, hardly.
е́ле-е́ле *нареч*: **он** ~ **спа́сся** he had a narrow escape; **ло́шадь** ~ **плетётся** the horse is on its last legs.
еле́|йный (-ен, -йна, -йно) *прил* (*перен: слащавый*) unctuous.
ёл|ка (-ки; *gen pl* -ок) *ж* fir (tree); (*бот*) spruce; (*праздник*) New Year party for children;

(рожде́ственская *или* новогодняя) ~ ≈ Christmas tree.

ело́вый *прил* fir; (*БОТ*) spruce.

ёлок *сущ см* **ёлка**.

ёлочн|ый *прил*: ~ые украше́ния *или* игру́шки Christmas-tree decorations *мн*.

ель (-и) *ж* fir (tree); (*БОТ*) spruce.

е́льник (-а) *м* (*лес*) fir grove; (*плантация*) fir plantation; (*ветки*) fir branches *мн*.

ем *несов см* **есть**.

ём|кий (-кая, -кое, -кие; -ок, -ка, -ко) *прил* (*вместительный*) capacious; (*перен: содержательный*) meaningful.

ёмкост|ь (-и) *ж* (*вместимость*) capacity; (*вместилище*) container; **ме́ры** ~и units of volume.

ёмок *прил см* **ёмкий**.

ему́ *мест см* **он, оно́**.

ено́т (-а) *м* raccoon.

ено́товый *прил* raccoon.

епа́рхи|я (-и) *ж* diocese; (*в православной церкви*) eparchy.

епи́скоп (-а) *м* bishop.

ерала́ш (-а) *м* (*разг: беспорядок*) mess.

Ерева́н (-а) *м* Yerevan.

е́рес|ь (-и) *ж* heresy; (*перен*) nonsense.

ерети́к (-á) *м* heretic.

ерети́ческ|ий (-ая, -ое, -ие) *прил* heretical.

ёрза|ть (-ю) *несов неперех* (*разг: беспокойно сидеть*) to fidget.

еро́ш|ить (-у, -ишь; *perf* **взъеро́шить**) *несов перех* (*разг: волосы*) to ruffle.

ерунд|а́ (-ы́) *ж* (*разг: чепуха*) rubbish, nonsense; **э́то** ~ (*пустяк*) it's a mere trifle, it's nothing.

ёрш (-á) *м* (*рыба*) ruff(e); (*щётка*) brush.

ерши́ться (-у́сь, -и́шься) *несов возв* (*о волосах*) to stick up; (*разг: горячиться*) to fly off the handle.

ЕС *ср сокр* (= Европе́йское соо́бщество) EC (= *European Community*) ♦ *м сокр* (= Европе́йский сове́т) Council of Europe.

есау́л (-а) *м* esaul (*rank equivalent to captain in Cossack army*).

KEYWORD

е́сли *союз* **1** (*в том случае когда*) if; **е́сли она́ придёт, дай ей э́то письмо́** if she comes, give her this letter; **е́сли ..., то ...** (*если*) if ..., then ...; **е́сли он опозда́ет, то иди́ оди́н** if he is late, (then) go alone

2 (*об условном действии*): **е́сли бы(, то/тогда́)** if; **е́сли бы я мог, (то) помо́г бы тебе́** if I could, I would help you

3 (*выражает сильное желание*): (**ах** *или* **о**) **е́сли бы** if only; **ах е́сли бы он позвони́л!** oh, if only he would phone (*BRIT*) *или* call (*US*)!

4 (*выражает противопоставление*) if; **е́сли с ма́мой я ча́сто спо́рю, с отцо́м мне легко́** if I argue with Mum, I get on all the better with Dad; **е́сли не ..., то ...** if not ..., then ...; **е́сли не ка́ждый день, то ча́сто** often, if not every day; **е́сли уж на то пошло́** if it comes to it; **е́сли**

хоти́те *или* **уго́дно** (*возможно*) perhaps; **что е́сли...?** (*а вдруг*) what if...?

ест *несов см* **есть**.

есте́ственен *прил см* **есте́ственный**.

есте́ственно *нареч* naturally ♦ *вводн сл* (*конечно*) of course.

есте́ственност|ь (-и) *ж* (*нормальность*) naturalness; (*непринуждённость*) spontaneity.

есте́ствен|ный (-ен, -на, -но) *прил* natural; ~ные нау́ки natural sciences; ~ная смерть death from natural causes.

естествозна́ни|е (-я) *ср* natural sciences *мн*.

естествоиспыта́тел|ь (-я) *м* (natural) scientist.

есть (*см* **Table 15**; *perf* **пое́сть** *или* **съесть**) *несов перех* (*питаться*) to eat; (*perf* **съесть**; *разрушать химически: металл*) to corrode; (*no perf*; *раздражать*) to sting, irritate; **мне хо́чется** ~ I'm hungry; ~ (*impf*) **кого́-н глаза́ми** (*разг*) to gaze at sb.

есть *несов* (*один предмет*) there is; (*много предметов*) there are ♦ *межд*: ~! (*ВОЕН*) yes, sir!; ~ **мно́го возмо́жностей** there are many possibilities; **на столе́** ~ **я́блоки** there are apples on the table; **у меня́** ~ **друг** I have a friend.

ЕФР *м сокр* (= Европе́йский фонд разви́тия) EDF (= *European Development Fund*).

ефре́йтор (-а) *м* (*ВОЕН*) lance corporal.

е́хать (*см* **Table 19**) *несов неперех* to go; (*поезд, автомобиль: приближаться*) to come; (: *двигаться*) to go, travel; (*разг: скользить*) to slide; ~ (*impf*) **на** +*prp* (*на лошади, на велосипеде*) to ride; ~ (*impf*) +*instr* *или* **на** +*prp* (*на поезде, на автобусом*) to travel *или* go by.

ехи́ден *прил см* **ехи́дный**.

ехи́дн|а (-ы) *ж* echidna, spiny anteater.

ехи́днича|ть (-ю; *perf* **съехи́дничать**) *несов неперех* (*разг: язвить*) to make spiteful remarks.

ехи́дный (-ен, -на, -но) *прил* malicious, spiteful.

ехи́дств|о (-а) *ср* (*язвительность*) spite.

ешь *несов см* **есть**.

KEYWORD

ещё *нареч* **1** (*дополнительно*) more; **хочу́ ещё ко́фе** I want more coffee; **купи́ ещё 3 кни́ги** buy 3 more books; **на́до ещё порабо́тать** we must do some more work

2 (*опять: приеду, позвоню итп*) again; **позвоню́ ещё за́втра** I'll phone again tomorrow

3 (*до сих пор*) still; **ты ещё не зна́ешь, что случи́лось?** do you still not know what happened?; **нет ещё** not yet

4 (*уже*): **он зако́нчил рабо́ту ещё вчера́** he had already finished the work the day before; **она́ уе́хала ещё три го́да наза́д** she left as long as three years ago; **ещё студе́нтом он сде́лал ва́жное откры́тие** while still a student he made an important discovery

5 (*о наличии возможности*) still; **ещё успéю на
самолёт** I can still catch the plane
6 (*+comparative*; *лучше, красивее итп*) even; **в
результáте он стал ещё богáче** as a result he
became even richer
♦ *част* (*усиливает выразительность*): **ещё
как рассердúлся/испугáлся** boy, did he get
angry/frightened; **дай мне кнúгу! какýю ещё
кнúгу!** give me the book! what book for

goodness sake!; **всё ещё** still; **онú всё ещё не
помирúлись** they still haven't made up; **ещё
бы!** (*разг*) you bet!; **вот ещё!** (*разг*) not likely!;
ещё чегó! (*разг*) not likely!

ЕЭС *ср сокр* (= *Европéйское экономúческое
сообщество*) EEC (= *European Economic
Community*).
éю *мест см* **онá**.

~ Ж, ж ~

Ж, ж *сущ нескл (буква)* the 7th letter of the Russian alphabet.

ж *союз, част см* **же**.

жа́б|а (-ы) *ж (зоол)* toad.

жабо́ *ср нескл* jabot.

жа́бр|а (-ы) *ж (зоол: обычно мн)* gill; **брать (взять** *perf***) за ~ы кого́-н** *(разг)* to twist sb's arm.

жа́ворон|ок (-ка) *м (зоол)* lark.

жа́ден *прил см* **жа́дный**.

жа́дин|а (-ы) *м/ж (разг: пренебр)* meanie.

жа́днича|ть (-ю; *perf* **пожа́дничать**) *несов неперех (разг)* to be mingy.

жа́дность (-и) *ж:* **~ (к** +*dat*) *(к вещам, к деньгам)* greed (for); *(к жизни)* lust (for); *(к развлечениям)* desire (for); **~ к еде́** greed; **с ~ю** *(есть)* greedily; *(слушать, смотреть)* avidly.

жа́дный (-ен, -на́, -но) *прил* greedy; *(на работу)* eager.

жа́жд|а (-ы) *ж* thirst; **~ зна́ний** *(перен)* thirst for knowledge; **~** +*infin* eagerness to do; **утоля́ть (утоли́ть** *perf***) ~у** to quench one's thirst.

жа́жда|ть (-у, -ешь) *несов неперех:* **~** +*gen (перен: мира)* to long for; **~** *(impf)* +*infin (познавать)* to long to do.

жаке́т (-а) *м* (woman's) jacket.

жал(ся) *итп несов см* **жать(ся)**.

жале́|ть (-ю; *perf* **пожале́ть**) *несов перех* to feel sorry for; *(скупиться)* to grudge ♦ *неперех:* **~ о** +*prp* to regret; **не ~я сил** sparing no effort; **~ (пожале́ть** *perf***), что ...** to regret that ....

жа́л|ить (-ю, -ишь; *perf* **ужа́лить**) *несов перех (подлеж: оса)* to sting; *(: змея)* to bite.

жа́лкий (-кая, -кое, -кие; -ок, -ка, -ко) *прил (вид)* pitiful, pathetic; *(одежда)* shabby; *(трус)* abject.

жа́лко *как сказ* = **жаль**.

жа́л|о (-а) *ср (пчелы́)* sting; *(змеи́)* forked tongue.

жа́лоб|а (-ы) *ж* complaint; **подава́ть (пода́ть** *perf***) ~у на кого́-н** to lodge a complaint against sb.

жа́лоб|ный (-ен, -на, -но) *прил (голос, песня)* plaintive; *(лицо)* sorrowful; **жа́лобная кни́га** complaints book *(in shop, post office etc)*.

жа́лованье (-я) *ср* salary.

жа́л|овать (-ую) *несов перех (разг):* **колле́ги его́ не ~уют** he is not very popular with his colleagues

▶ **жа́ловаться** *(perf* **пожа́ловаться***) несов возв:* **~ся на** +*acc* to complain about; *(разг:* ябедничать*)* to tell on.

жа́лок *прил см* **жа́лкий**.

жа́лостен *прил см* **жа́лостный**.

жа́лостлив|ый (-, -а, -о) *прил* sympathetic.

жа́лост|ный (-ен, -на, -но) *прил* mournful; **~ фильм** tear-jerker.

жа́лость (-и) *ж:* **~ к** +*dat* sympathy for; **кака́я ~** what a shame; **де́лать (сде́лать** *perf***) что-н из ~и** to do sth out of pity.

KEYWORD

жаль *как сказ* **1** (+*acc; о сострадании):* **(мне) жаль дру́га** I am sorry for my friend
2 (+*acc или* +*gen; о сожалении, о досаде):* **(мне) жаль вре́мени/де́нег** I grudge the time/money
3 (+*infin):* **жаль уезжа́ть так бы́стро** it's a pity *или* shame to leave so soon; **жаль, что ты меня́ не понима́ешь** it's a pity *или* shame you don't understand me

♦ *вводн сл (к сожалению)* unfortunately; **хоте́л пое́хать в Ло́ндон, да, жаль, нет вре́мени** I wanted to go to London, but unfortunately I didn't have time.

жанр (-а) *м (лирический)* genre; *(перен)* style.

жар (-а; *part gen* -у, *loc sg* -у́) *м (тепло)* heat; *(перен)* fervour *(BRIT)*, fervor *(US)*; *(мед)* fever; **его́ бро́сило в ~** *(перен)* he broke out in a sweat.

жар|а́ (-ы́) *ж* heat.

жарго́н (-а) *м* slang; *(профессиональный)* jargon.

жа́реный *прил (на сковороде)* fried; *(в духовке)* roast.

жа́р|ить (-ю, -ишь; *perf* **зажа́рить**) *несов перех (на сковороде)* to fry; *(в духовке)* to roast

▶ **жа́риться** *(perf* **зажа́риться***) несов возв* to fry; **~ся** *(impf)* **на со́лнце** *(разг)* to bask in the sun.

жа́р|ка (-и) *ж* frying.

жа́р|кий (-кая, -кое, -кие; -ок, -ка́, -ко) *прил* hot; *(перен)* heated; **жа́ркие стра́ны** tropical countries.

жа́рко *нареч (спорить)* heatedly; *(целовать)* passionately ♦ *как сказ* it's hot; **мне ~** I'm hot; **ему́ ни хо́лодно ни ~** *(разг)* it's all the same to him.

жарко́е (-о́го; *decl like adj*) *ср* meat *(fried)*.

жа́рок *прил см* **жа́ркий**.

жаропонижа́ющий (-ая, -ее, -ие) *прил* febrifugal.

жаропро́ч|ный (-ен, -на, -но) *прил* (*материал*) heat-resistant; (*посуда*) ovenproof.
жар-пти́ц|а (-ы) *ж* Firebird.
жа́рче *сравн прил от* **жа́ркий**.
жасми́н (-а) *м* jasmine.
жа́тв|а (-ы) *ж* harvest.
жать (**жму, жмёшь**) *несов перех* (*руку*) to shake; (*лимон, сок*) to squeeze;; (**жну, жнёшь**; *perf* **сжать**; to harvest; **сапоги́ мне жмут**; my boots are pinching (my feet); **э́то пла́тье жмёт в та́лии**; this dress is too tight at the waist;
▶ **жа́ться**; **жмусь, жмёшься**) ♦ *несов возв* (*от холода*) to huddle up; (*разг:* **колеба́ться**) to dither; (*:* **скупи́ться**) to be stingy.
жва́ч|ка (-ки; *gen pl* **-ек**) *ж* cud; (*разг:* **жева́тельная рези́нка**) chewing gum.
жгу(сь) *итп несов см* **жечь(ся)**.
жгут (-а́) *м* (*из соломы*) rope; (*МЕД*) tourniquet.
жгу́ч|ий (-ая, -ее, -ие; -, -а, -е) *прил* (*также* **перен**) burning; (*мороз*) biting; **жгу́чий брюне́т** man with jet-black hair.
ж.д. *сокр* (= **желе́зная доро́га**) R., r. (= railway), RR (*US*) (= railroad).
ж/д *сокр* = **ж.д.**
ж.-д. *сокр* = **ж.д.**
жд|ать (-у, -ёшь; *pt* -ал, -ала́, -а́ло) *несов перех* (*also* +*gen*; *письмо, дождя, госте́й*) to expect; (*друга, поезда*) to wait for; (*наде́яться:* **награды, пощады**) to hope for; **что нас ~ёт?** what's in store for us?; **~а́ли, что он извини́тся** they hoped that he would apologize; **вре́мя не ~ёт** there's no time to lose; **я ~у не дожду́сь кани́кул** (*разг*) I can't wait for the holidays.

┌─────────────────┐
│ **KEYWORD** │
└─────────────────┘

же *союз* **1** (*при противопоставлении*) but; **я не люблю́ матема́тику, литерату́ру же обожа́ю** I don't like mathematics, but I love literature
2 (*вводит дополнительные сведения*) and; **успе́х зави́сит от нали́чия ресу́рсов, ресу́рсов же ма́ло** success depends on the presence of resources, and the resources are insufficient
♦ *част* **1** (*ведь*): **вы́пей ещё ча́ю, хо́чешь же!** have more tea, you want some, don't you?
2 (*именно*): **приду́ сейча́с же** I'll come right now; **когда́ же ты уйдёшь?** when will you go then?
3 (*выражает сходство*): **тако́й же** the same; **тако́й же дом** the same (kind of) house; **в э́том же году́** this very year; **те же лю́ди** the same (kind of) people.

жева́ть (-ую́) *несов перех* to chew.
жёг(ся) *итп несов см* **жечь(ся)**.
жезл (-а) *м* baton.
жела́нен *прил см* **жела́нный**.
жела́ни|е (-я) *ср* (*просьба*) request; **~** +*gen*/+*infin* desire for/to do; **горе́ть** (*impf*) **~м** +*infin* to be

eager to do.
жела́н|ный (-ен, -на, -но) *прил* (*гость, весть*) welcome.
жела́телен *прил см* **жела́тельный**.
жела́тельно *как сказ:* **~** +*infin* it is desirable to do; **~, что́бы Вы пришли́** it would be preferable if you could come.
жела́тел|ьный (-ен, -ьна, -ьно) *прил* desirable.
жела́|ть (-ю; *perf* **пожела́ть**) *несов неперех* (+*gen*) to desire; **~** (**пожела́ть** *perf*) +*infin* to wish *или* want to do; **~** (**пожела́ть** *perf*) **кому́-н сча́стья/всего́ хоро́шего** to wish sb happiness/all the best; **Ва́ша рабо́та оставля́ет ~ лу́чшего** your work leaves much to be desired.
жела́ющ|ий (-его; *decl like adj*) *м* (*обычно мн*): **~ие пое́хать/порабо́тать** those interested in going/working; **~ие есть?** is anybody interested?
желва́к (-а́) *м* (*разг*) lump.
желе́ *ср нескл* jelly.
желез|а́ (-ы́; *nom pl* **-ы**, *gen pl* **-ёз**, *dat pl* **-еза́м**) *ж* gland.
железнодоро́жник (-а) *м* rail(way) (*BRIT*) *или* railroad (*US*) worker.
железнодоро́жный *прил* (*вокзал*) railway *опред* (*BRIT*), railroad *опред* (*US*); (*транспорт*) rail *опред*.
желе́зн|ый *прил* (*также перен*) iron; (*: логика*) cast-iron; **~ые не́рвы** nerves of steel; **желе́зная доро́га** railway (*BRIT*), railroad (*US*).
желе́з|о (-а) *ср* iron.
железобето́н (-а) *м* reinforced concrete.
жёлоб (-а; *nom pl* **-а́**) *м* (*водосто́чный*) gutter.
желте́|ть (-ю; *perf* **пожелте́ть**) *несов неперех* to turn yellow; (*no perf*; **видне́ться**) to show yellow.
желт|о́к (-ка́) *м* yolk.
желторо́т|ый (-, -а, -о) *прил* yellow-beaked (*of young birds*); (*разг: пренебр*): **он ещё ~ юне́ц** he's still wet behind the ears.
желту́х|а (-и) *ж* jaundice.
жёлт|ый (-, -а́, -о) *прил* yellow; **жёлтая пре́сса** the gutter press.
желу́д|ок (-ка) *м* (*АНАТ*) stomach; **расстро́йство ~ка** stomach upset.
желу́дочный *прил* (*боль*) stomach *опред*; (*сок*) gastric.
жёлудь (-я) *м* acorn.
жёлч|ный *прил:* **~ пузы́рь** gall bladder; (-ен, -на, -но; *перен*) bilious.
жёлчь (-и) *ж* (*также перен*) bile.
жема́н|ный (-ен, -на, -но) *прил* affected.
же́мчуг (-а; *nom pl* **-а́**) *м* pearls *мн*; **бу́сы из ~а** pearl necklace.
жемчу́жин|а (-ы) *ж* pearl; (*перен*) treasure.
жемчу́жный *прил* pearl; (*перен: зубы*) pearly.
жен|а́ (-ы́; *nom pl* **жёны**, *gen pl* **жён**) *ж* wife.
жена́т|ый (-, -ы) *прил* married (*of man*); **он**

жена́т на +*prp* he is married to; **они́ ~ы** they are married.

Жене́в|а (-ы) *ж* Geneva.

жени́ть (-ю́, -ишь) *(не)сов перех (сына, внука)*: ~ **(на** +*prp*) to marry (off) (to); *(perf* **пожени́ть**; *разг)* to marry

▶ **жени́ться** *(не)сов возв*: **~ся на** +*prp* to marry *(of man)*; *(perf* **пожени́ться**; *разг)* to get hitched.

жени́х (-а́) *м (до свадьбы)* fiancé; *(на свадьбе)* (bride)groom.

женонена́ви́стник (-а) *м* misogynist, woman-hater.

женоподо́бный (-ен) *прил* effeminate.

же́нск|ий (-ая, -ое, -ие) *прил (одежда, раздева́лка)* women's; *(логика, органы)* female; **же́нская консульта́ция** ≈ gynaecological and antenatal *(BRIT) или* gynecological and prenatal *(US)* clinic; **же́нский пол** the female sex; **же́нский род** feminine gender.

же́нственный *прил* feminine.

же́нщин|а (-ы) *ж* woman.

женьше́н|ь (-я) *м* ginseng.

жердь (-и; *gen pl* -е́й) *ж* pole.

жереб|ёнок (-ёнка; *nom pl* -я́та, *gen pl* -я́т) *м* foal.

жереб|е́ц (-ца́) *м* stallion.

жереб|и́ться *(3sg* -и́тся, *3pl* -я́тся, *perf* **ожереби́ться**) *несов возв* to foal.

жеребца́ *итп сущ см* **жереб|е́ц**.

жереб|ёвка (-ки; *gen pl* -ок) *ж* casting *или* drawing of lots.

жеребя́та *итп сущ см* **жереб|ёнок**.

жерл|о́ (-а́; *nom pl* -а) *ср (пушки, вулкана)* mouth.

жёрнов (-а; *nom pl* -а́) *м* millstone.

же́ртв|а (-ы) *ж* victim; *(РЕЛ)* sacrifice; **приноси́ть (принести́** *perf)* **кого́-н/что-н в ~у кому́-н/чему́-н** to sacrifice sb/sth for sb/sth; **челове́ческие ~ы** casualties; **пасть** *(perf)* **~ой чего́-н** to fall victim to sth.

же́ртв|овать (-ую; *perf* **поже́ртвовать**) *несов непере́х* (+*instr*) to sacrifice ◆ *перех* to donate.

жертвоприноше́ни|е (-я) *ср (РЕЛ)* sacrifice; **соверша́ть (соверши́ть** *perf)* ~ to offer up a sacrifice.

жест (-а) *м* gesture; **язы́к же́стов** sign language.

жестикули́р|овать (-ую) *несов непере́х* to gesticulate.

жёст|кий (-кая, -кое, -кие; -ок, -ка́, -ко) *прил (кровать, человек)* hard; *(мясо)* tough; *(волосы)* coarse; *(условия)* strict; **жёсткий ваго́н** railway carriage with hard seats; **жёсткая вода́** hard water; **жёсткий диск** hard disk.

жесто́к|ий (-ая, -ое, -ие; -, -а́, -о) *прил* cruel; *(перен)* severe; **~ая необходи́мость** cruel necessity.

жесто́ко *нареч (распра́виться)* cruelly.

жесто́кост|ь (-и) *ж* cruelty.

жёстче *сравн прил от* **жёст|кий**.

жест|ь (-и) *ж* tin-plated sheet metal.

жестя́н|ка (-ки; *gen pl* -ок) *ж* tin box.

жето́н (-а) *м* tag; *(в метро)* token.

жечь (жгу, жжёшь *итп*, жгут; *pt* жёг, жгла, жгло, *perf* **сжечь**) *несов перех* to burn

▶ **же́чься** *несов возв (утюг)* to be very hot; *(крапи́ва)* to sting; *(perf* **обже́чься**; *разг)* to burn o.s.

жже́ни|е (-я) *ср* burning sensation.

жжёшь(ся) *итп несов см* **жечь(ся)**.

живи́тел|ьный (-ен, -ьна, -ьно) *прил (воздух)* invigorating.

жи́во *нареч (предста́вить себе́)* vividly; *(откли́кнуться)* animatedly.

жив|о́й (-, -а́, -о) *прил* alive; *(no short form; организм)* living; *(живо́тное)* live; *(человек: энерги́чный)* lively; *(вырази́тельный)* vivid; **~ приме́р** a living example; **он ~ наде́ждой/воспомина́ниями** he lives in hope/for his memories; **он ещё ~?** is he still alive?; **жив – здоро́в** *(разг)* alive and well; **в нём ещё ~а́ оби́да** the insult still rankles with him; **ни жив ни мёртв** *(разг)* petrified; **задева́ть (заде́ть** *perf)* **кого́-н за ~о́е** to cut sb to the quick; **оста́ться** *(perf)* **в ~ы́х** to survive; **жива́я и́згородь** hedge; **живо́й уголо́к** area in school where pets are kept for pupils to look after; **живо́й язы́к** living language; **живы́е цветы́** fresh flowers.

живопи́сен *прил см* **живопи́сный**.

живопи́с|ец (-ца) *м* painter.

живопи́сный (-ен, -на, -но) *прил* picturesque.

живопи́сца *итп сущ см* **живопи́с|ец**.

жи́вопис|ь (-и) *ж (иску́сство)* painting.

живо́т (-а́) *м* stomach, abdomen; *(разг)* belly, tummy.

животново́д (-а) *м* farmer specializing in animal husbandry.

животново́дств|о (-а) *ср* animal husbandry.

живо́тн|ое (-ого; *decl like adj) ср (также перен)* animal.

живо́тный *прил* animal *опред*; *(перен)* bestial.

животрепе́щущ|ий (-ая, -ее, -ие) *прил* topical.

живу́(сь) *итп несов см* **жить(ся)**.

живу́ч|ий (-ая, -ее, -ие; -, -а, -е) *прил* hardy; *(обычай, представле́ние)* enduring; *(предрассу́дки)* deep-rooted; **он ~ как ко́шка** he has nine lives.

живьём *нареч* alive.

жи́д|кий (-кая, -кое, -кие) *прил* liquid; *(-ок, -ка́, -ко; молоко́, суп)* watery; *(состоя́ние, му́скулы, го́лос)* weak; *(во́лосы)* sparse, thin; **жи́дкое то́пливо** liquid fuel.

жи́дкост|ь (-и) *ж* liquid.

жи́док *прил см* **жи́дкий**.

жи́ж|а (-и) *ж* slurry.

жи́же *сравн прил от* **жи́дкий**.

жизнедея́тельност|ь (-и) *ж (органи́зма, кле́тки)* (vital) activity.

жи́знен|ный (-, -на, -но) *прил (вопрос, интере́сы)* vital; *(необходи́мость)* basic; **~ у́ровень** standard of living; **~ о́пыт** experience;

~ **путь** journey through life.
жизнерáдост|ный (-ен, -на, -но) *прил* cheerful.
жизнеспосóб|ный (-ен, -на, -но) *прил* (*также перен*) viable.
жизн|ь (-и) *ж* life; **óбраз жи́зни** way of life; **ýровень жи́зни** standard of living; **как ~?** (*разг*) how's life?
жи́л|а (-ы) *ж* (*также ГЕО*) vein; (*сухожилие*) tendon, sinew; **золотáя ~** (*перен: разг*) gold mine.
жилéт (-а) *м* waistcoat (*BRIT*), vest (*US*); **спасáтельный ~** life jacket.
жил|éц (-ьцá) *м* (*квартиросъёмщик*) tenant; (*квартирант*) lodger; **он не ~** (*разг*) he's not long for this world.
жи́листый (-, -а, -о) *прил* (*мясо*) stringy; (*старик*) sinewy; (*рука*) veiny.
жили́щ|е (-а) *ср* (*дом*) dwelling.
жили́щный *прил* housing *опред*.
жи́л|ка (-ки; *gen pl* -ок) *ж* vein; (*перен: склонность*) streak.
жилóй *прил* (*дом, здание*) residential; (*комната, помещение*) inhabited; **жилáя плóщадь** accommodation.
жи́лок *сущ см* **жи́лка**.
жилплóщадь (-и) *ж сокр* = **жилáя плóщадь**.
жиль|ё (-я́) *ср* (*человеческое*) habitation; (*жилище*) accommodation (*BRIT*), lodgings *мн*.
жильцá *итп сущ см* **жилéц**.
жи́молост|ь (-и) *ж* honeysuckle.
жир (-а; *part gen* -у, *loc sg* -ý, *nom pl* -ы́) *м* (*животный*) fat; (*растительный*) oil; **с жи́ру беси́ться** (*impf*) (*разг*) to become spoilt; **ры́бий ~** (*МЕД*) cod-liver oil.
жирáф (-а) *м* giraffe.
жи́рен *прил см* **жи́рный**.
жирé|ть (-ю; *perf* **разжирéть** *или* **ожирéть**) *несов неперех* to grow fat.
жи́р|ный (-ен, -нá, -но) *прил* (*пища*) fatty; (*человек*) fat; (*no short form; волосы*) greasy; (*чернозём, известь*) rich; **жи́рный шрифт** bold type.
жирови́к (-á) *м* lipoma.
жирорасчёт (-а) *м* Giro.
житéйск|ий (-ая, -ое, -ие) *прил* (*мудрость*) worldly; (*проблемы*) everyday; **дéло ~ое!** (*разг*) that's nothing unusual!
жи́тел|ь (-я) *м* resident; **городскóй ~** city dweller.
жи́тельниц|а (-ы) *ж см* **жи́тель**.
жи́тельств|о (-а) *ср* residence; **мéсто постоя́нного ~а** a permanent place of residence.
жи́тниц|а (-ы) *ж* (*перен*) breadbasket.
жи|ть (-вý, -вёшь; *pt* -л, -лá, -ло) *несов неперех* to live; (*также перен*): **~ в** +*prp* to live in; **~** (*impf*) +*instr* (*детьми, наукой*) to live on/with; **~** (*impf*) **на** +*acc*/**с** +*instr* to live on/with; **~** (*impf*) **на свои́ срéдства** to support o.s.; **~л-был** there once

was, once upon a time there was
▸ **жи́ться** *несов возв* (*разг*): **емý вéсело/ тоскли́во ~вётся** he's having a good/miserable time; **как Вам ~вётся?** how's life?
жмот (-а) *м* (*разг*) skinflint.
жму(сь) *итп несов см* **жáть(ся)**
жмýр|ить (-ю, -ишь; *perf* **зажмýрить**) *несов неперех*: ~ **глазá** to screw up one's eyes
▸ **жмýриться** (*perf* **зажмýриться**) *несов возв* to squint; ~**ся** (**зажмýриться** *perf*) **от свéта** to squint in the light.
жмýр|ки (-ок) *мн* blind man's buff *ед*; **игрáть** (*impf*) **в ~** to play blind man's buff.
жнец (-á) *м* reaper.
жни́ц|а (-ы) *ж см* **жнец**.
жну *итп несов см* **жать**.
жокé|й (-я) *м* jockey.
жонглёр (-а) *м* juggler.
жонгли́р|овать (-ую) *несов неперех*: ~ +*instr* to juggle (with).
жóп|а (-ы) *ж* (*груб!*) arse (*BRIT*) (*!*), ass (*US*) (*!*)
жр|ать (-у, -ёшь; *pt* -ал, -алá, -áло, *perf* **сожрáть**) *несов перех* (*разг*) to scoff.
жрéбий (-я) *м*: **бросáть ~** to cast lots.
жрец (-á) *м* (*РЕЛ*) (pagan) priest; (*перен*) devotee.
жри́ц|а (-ы) *ж* (*РЕЛ*) (pagan) priestess.
ЖСК *м сокр* (= *жили́щно-строи́тельный кооперати́в*) housing cooperative.
жýжелиц|а (-ы) *ж* ground beetle.
жужж|áть (-ý, -и́шь) *несов неперех* to buzz.
жук (-á) *м* beetle.
жýлик (-а) *м* swindler; (*в игре*) cheat.
жýльнича|ть (-ю; *perf* **сжýльничать**) *несов неперех* (*разг*) to cheat.
жýльничеств|о (-а) *ср* underhandedness; (*в игре*) cheating.
журáвл|ь (-я́) *м* crane.
жур|и́ть (-ю́, -и́шь) *несов перех* (*разг*) to chide.
журнáл (-а) *м* magazine; (*судовой*) journal; (*классный*) register; (*КИНО*) short; ~ **протокóлов** minute book.
журнали́ст (-а) *м* journalist.
журнали́ст|ка (-ки; *gen pl* -ок) *ж см* **журнали́ст**.
журнали́стик|а (-и) *ж* journalism.
журнали́сток *сущ см* **журнали́стка**.
журч|áть (-ý, -и́шь) *несов неперех* (*ручей итп*) to babble, murmur.
жýт|кий (-кая, -кое, -кие; -ок, -кá, -ко) *прил* terrible.
жýтко *нареч* (*неприятный*) terribly ♦ *как сказ*: **здесь ~** it's terrifying here; **мне ~** I am terrified.
жýток *прил см* **жýткий**.
жут|ь (-и) *ж* (*разг*) terror ♦ *как сказ* it's terrible; **какáя ~!** (*разг*) how terrible!
жýхлый *прил* faded.
ЖЭК (-а) *м сокр* (= *жили́щно-эксплуатацио́нная конто́ра*) ≈ housing office.
жюри́ *ср нескл* panel of judges.

~ З, з ~

З, з *сущ нескл (буква)* the 8th letter of the Russian alphabet.

з. *сокр* (= за́пад) W (= West); (= за́падный) W (= West).

KEYWORD

за *предл* (+*acc*) **1** out (of); **вы́йти** *(perf)* **за дверь** to go out (of) the door

2 *(позади)* behind; **спря́таться** *(perf)* **за де́рево** to hide behind a tree

3 *(около: сесть, встать)* at; **сесть** *(perf)* **за стол** to sit down at the table

4 *(свыше какого-н предела)* over; **ему́ за со́рок** he is over forty; **моро́з за два́дцать гра́дусов** over twenty degrees of frost

5 *(при указании на расстояние, на время)*: **за пять киломе́тров отсю́да** five kilometres (*BRIT*) *или* kilometers (*US*) from here; **за три часа́ до нача́ла спекта́кля** three hours before the beginning of the show; **за э́ти де́сять лет он постаре́л** he has aged over the last ten years

6 *(при указании объекта действия)*: **держа́ться за** +*acc* to hold onto; **ухвати́ться** *(perf)* **за** +*acc* to take hold of; **взять** *(perf)* **кого́-н за́ руку** to take sb by the hand; **взя́ться** *(perf)* **за рабо́ту** to start work

7 *(об объекте чувств)* for; **ра́доваться** *(impf)* **за сы́на** to be happy for one's son; **отвеча́ть** *(impf)* **за успе́х предприя́тия** to be responsible for the success of an enterprise; **беспоко́иться** *(impf)* **за му́жа** to worry about one's husband

8 *(о цели)* for; **сража́ться** *(impf)* **за побе́ду** to fight for victory

9 *(в пользу)* for, in favour (*BRIT*) *или* favor (*US*) of; **голосова́ть** *(impf)* **за предложе́ние** to vote for *или* in favour (*BRIT*) *или* favor (*US*) of a proposal

10 *(по причине, в обмен)* for; **благодарю́ Вас за по́мощь** thank you for your help; **плати́ть** (**заплати́ть** *perf*) **за что-н** to pay for sth; **быть** *(impf)* **нака́занным за воровство́** to be punished for stealing; **я сде́лал э́то за де́ньги** I did it for money

11 *(вместо кого-н)* for; **рабо́тать** *(impf)* **за дру́га** to fill in for a friend

♦ *предл* (+*instr*) **1** *(по другую сторону)* on the other side of; **жить** *(impf)* **за реко́й** to live on the other side of the river

2 *(вне)* outside; **жить** *(impf)* **за́ городом** to live outside the town; **за грани́цей** abroad

3 *(позади)* behind; **стоя́ть** *(impf)* **за две́рью** to stand behind the door; **я шёл за ним** I walked behind him; **бежа́ть** *(impf/perf)* **за престу́пником** to run after a criminal

4 *(около: стоять, сидеть)* at; **сиде́ть** *(impf)* **за столо́м** to sit at the table

5 *(о смене событий)* after; **год за го́дом** year after year; **за зимо́й идёт весна́** spring comes after winter

6 *(во время чего-н)* over; **поговори́ть** *(perf)* **за за́втраком** to talk over breakfast

7 *(о объекте внимания)*: **смотре́ть** *или* **уха́живать за** +*instr* to look after; **моя́ сестра́ за́мужем за врачо́м** my sister is married to a doctor

8 *(с целью получить, достать что-н)* for; **я посла́л его́ за газе́той** I sent him out for a paper; **он пошёл за врачо́м** he went to fetch the doctor

9 *(по причине)* owing to; **за отсу́тствием доказа́тельств** in the absence of proof

♦ *как сказ (согласен)* in favour (*BRIT*) *или* favor (*US*); **кто за?** who is in favour (*BRIT*) *или* favor (*US*)?

♦ *ср нескл* pro; **взве́сить** *(perf)* **все за и про́тив** to weigh up all the pros and cons.

за- *префикс (in verbs; о начале действия) indicating beginning of an action eg.* **зааплоди́ровать**; *(о доведении действия до крайней степени) indicating taking sth to an extreme degree eg.* **завра́ться**; *(образует совершенный вид) used in the formation of some perfective aspects eg.* **заасфальти́ровать**; *(in nouns and adjectives) находящийся по ту сторону чего-н* trans-.

заале́|ть *(3sg* -**ет**, *3pl* -**ют**) *сов неперех* to turn scarlet.

заарка́н|ить (-**ю**, -**ишь**; *impf* **заарка́нивать**) *сов неперех* to lasso.

заарта́ч|иться (-**усь**, -**ишься**) *сов возв (разг)* to become obstinate.

заасфальти́р|овать (-**ую**) *сов от* **асфальти́ровать**.

заба́в|а (-**ы**) *ж* amusement.

заба́вен *прил см* **заба́вный**.

забавля́|ть (-**ю**) *несов перех* to amuse

▶ **забавля́ться** *несов возв* to amuse o.s.

забáвно *нареч* (*рассказывать*) in an amusing
way ♦ *как сказ* it's funny.
забáв|ный (-ен, -на, -но) *прил* amusing.
забаллоти́р|овать (-ую) *сов перех* to reject.
забальзами́р|овать (-ую) *сов от*
бальзами́ровать.
забарахл|и́ть (*3sg* -и́т, *3pl* -я́т) *сов неперех*
(*разг: мотор, компьютер итп*) to go on the
blink.
забаррикади́р|овать (-ую) *сов от*
баррикади́ровать.
забаст|овáть (-у́ю) *сов неперех* to go on strike.
забастóв|ка (-ки; *gen pl* -ок) *ж* strike; **всеóбщая**
~ general strike; **сидя́чая** ~ sit-in.
забастóвочный *прил* strike *опред*.
забастóвщик (-а) *м* striker.
забастóвщиц|а (-ы) *ж см* **забастóвщик**.
забвéни|е (-я) *ср* (*забытьё*) oblivion;
предавáть (**предáть** *perf*) **что-н ~ю** to consign
sth to oblivion.
забéг (-а) *м* (*СПОРТ*) race; **предвари́тельный** ~
preliminary heat; ~ **на стó мéтров** the hundred
metres.
забегáть (-ю) *сов неперех* (*люди*) to start
running; (*глаза*) to roam about.
забе|жáть (*как* **бежáть**; *см* **Table 20**; *impf*
забегáть) *сов неперех*: ~ (**в** +*acc*) (*в дом, в
деревню*) to run in(to); (*разг: в музей*) to drop
in(to); **забегáть** (~ *perf*) **к знакóмым** (*разг*) to
drop in on one's friends; **забегáть** (~ *perf*) **со
сторонý** (*разг*) to come up from the side;
забегáть (~ *perf*) **вперёд** to run ahead; (*перен*)
to race ahead.
заберéмене|ть (-ю) *сов от* **берéменеть**.
заберý(сь) *итп сов см* **забрáть(ся)**.
забеспокó|иться (-юсь, -ишься) *сов возв* to
start to worry.
забетони́р|овать (-ую) *сов от* **бетони́ровать**.
забивáть(ся) (-ю(сь)) *несов от* **заби́ть(ся)**.
забинт|овáть (-у́ю; *impf* **бинтовáть** *или*
забинтóвывать) *сов перех* to bandage.
забирá|ть(ся) (-ю(сь)) *несов от* **забрáть(ся)**.
заби́тый (-, -а, -о) *прил* cowed.
заб|и́ть (-ью, -ьёшь) *сов неперех* (*часы*) to
begin to strike; (*орудие, пушка*) to start firing;
(*озноб, лихорадка*) to begin to spread; (*вода*) to
begin to flow; (*фонтан*) to start up ♦ (*impf*
забивáть) *перех* (*гвоздь, сваю*) to drive in;
(*СПОРТ: гол*) to score; (: *мяч, шар*) to drive
home; (*окно, дом*) to board up; (*наполнить:
склад, холодильник*) to overfill; (*засорить:
трубу, сток*) to clog (up); (*скот, зверя*) to
slaughter; (*перен: человека*) to knock flat; ~
(*perf*) **в барабáн/кóлокол** to start drumming/
ringing a bell; **забивáть** (~ *perf*) **гóлову чем-н**
to fill one's head with sth
▸ **заби́ться** *сов возв* (*сердце, пульс*) to start
beating; (*impf* **забивáться**; *спрятаться*) to hide

(away); (*засориться: труба, сток*) to clog up;
~**ся** (*perf*) **в сýдорогах** to have a fit; ~**ся** (*perf*) **в
истéрике** to have a fit of hysterics.
забия́|ка (-и) *м/ж* (*разг*) bully.
заблаговрéменно *нареч* in good time.
заблагорассýд|иться (*3sg* -ится) *сов безл*
(*вздуматься*): **поступáйте, как Вам** ~**ится** act
as you see fit.
заблес|тéть (-щý, -ти́шь) *сов неперех* (*река,
слёзы*) to glisten; (*глаза*) to light up; (*металл*)
to gleam.
заблуд|и́ться (-ужýсь, -ýдишься) *сов возв* to
get lost.
заблýдш|ий (-ая, -ее, -ие) *прил*: ~ **человéк**
person who has lost his or her way; **заблýдшая
овцá** (*перен*) a lost sheep.
заблуждá|ться (-юсь) *несов возв* to be
mistaken.
заблуждéни|е (-я) *ср* error, delusion; **вводи́ть**
(**ввести́** *perf*) **когó-н в** ~ to delude sb;
выводи́ть (**вывести** *perf*) **когó-н из** ~**я** to open
sb's eyes.
заблужýсь *сов см* **заблуди́ться**.
забодá|ть (*3sg* -ет, *3pl* -ют) *сов от* **бодáть**.
забó|й (-я) *м* (*ГЕО*) (working) face; (*действие:
скотá*) slaughtering.
забóйщик (-а) *м* face worker.
заболевáемост|ь (-и) *ж* (*по стране*) incidence
(*of illness*).
заболевáни|е (-я) *ср* illness.
заболé|ть (-ю; *impf* **заболевáть**) *сов неперех*: ~
+*instr* (*ветрянкой, гриппом*) to fall ill with;
(*разг: компьютерами, театром итп*) to get
hooked on; (*нога, горло*) to begin to hurt.
заболóченный (-, -а, -о) *прил* marshy, boggy.
забóр (-а) *м* fence.
забóт|а (-ы) *ж* (*беспокойство*) worry; (*уход*)
concern; (*обычно мн: хлопоты*) trouble.
забó|тить (-чу, -тишь) *несов перех* to worry,
trouble
▸ **забóтиться** (*perf* **позабóтиться**) *несов возв*:
~**ся о** +*prp* to take care of.
забóтлив|ый (-, -а, -о) *прил* (*человек*) caring,
thoughtful.
забóчу(сь) *несов см* **забóтить(ся)**.
забрак|овáть (-ýю; *impf* **браковáть** *или*
забракóвывать) *сов перех* to reject.
забрáл|о (-а) *ср* (*у шлема*) visor; (*ТЕХ*) screen.
забрá|сывать (-ю) *несов от* **забросáть**,
забрóсить.
заб|рáть (-ерý, -ерёшь; *pt* -рáл, -ралá, -рáло,
impf **забирáть**) *сов перех* to take; (*разг:
захватить*) to nick; (*перен: подляж: страх,
тоска*) to grip; **забирáть** (~ *perf*) **впрáво/
влéво** to veer off to the right/left
▸ **забрáться** (*impf* **забирáться**) *сов возв*
(*спрятаться*) to hide (o.s.) away; (*разг:
уехать*) to go off; **забирáться** (~**ся** *perf*) **в/на**

+*acc* (*в шкаф, в дом*) to get inside *или* into; (*на дереве*) to climb up; (*в скважину*) to go down; **забира́ться** (*~ся perf*) **под одея́ло** to crawl under the blanket; **забира́ться** (*~ся perf*) **внутрь/наве́рх** to get inside/to the top.

забреда́|ть (-ю) *несов от* **забрести́**.

забреду́ *итп сов см* **забрести́**.

забре́зж|ить (*3sg* **-ит**) *сов неперех* (*огонь*) to flicker; (*рассвет, утро*) to break.

забр|ести́ (-еду́, -едёшь; *pt* -ёл, -ела́, -ело́, *impf* **забреда́ть**) *сов неперех* (*разг: в лес*) to saunter off; (: *в гости*) to drop in.

заброни́р|овать (-ую) *сов от* **брони́ровать**.

заброса́|ть (-ю; *impf* **забра́сывать**) *сов перех*: ~ **что-н чем-н** (*канаву, яму*) to fill with; (*камнями*) to pelt with; (*цветами*) to shower with; (*перен: фактами, вопросами*) to bombard with.

забро́|сить (-шу, -сишь; *impf* **забра́сывать**) *сов перех* (*мяч, камень*) to fling; (*десант*) to drop; (*шпиона*) to plant; (*разг: доставить*) to drop off; (*не заниматься*) to neglect.

забро́шен|ный (-, -а, -о) *прил* (*дом*) derelict; (*шахта*) disused; (*вид, сад, ребёнок*) neglected.

забро́шу *сов см* **забро́сить**.

забры́зга|ть (-ю; *impf* **забры́згивать**) *сов перех* to splash.

забу́ду(сь) *итп сов см* **забы́ть(ся)**.

забыва́|ть(ся) (-ю(сь)) *несов от* **забы́ть(ся)**.

заб|ы́ть (*как* **быть**; *см* **Table 21**; *impf* **забыва́ть**) *сов перех* to forget; ~**удь туда́/сюда́ доро́гу!** don't go there/come here any more!; **себя́ не забыва́ть** (*~ perf*) to look out for o.s.

▶ **забы́ться** (*impf* **забыва́ться**) *сов возв* (*задремать*) to doze off; (*в мечтах*) to lose o.s.; (*сорваться*) to forget o.s.; (*события, факты*) to be forgotten.

забы́ть|ё (-я́) *ср* (*беспамятство*) oblivion; (*полусон*) drowsiness; (*задумчивость*) pensiveness; **впада́ть** (**впасть** *perf*) **в** ~ to lose consciousness; (*уснуть*) to doze off.

забью́(сь) *итп сов см* **забить(ся)**.

зав (-а) *м сокр* (*разг* = **заве́дующий**) boss.

зав. *сокр* = **заве́дующий**.

завал (-а) *м* obstruction; (*искусственный*) barrier; **у нас сейча́с** ~ **с рабо́той** we have a backlog of work.

зава|ли́ть (-лю́, -лишь; *impf* **зава́ливать**) *сов перех* (*вход, дверь*) to block off; (*дом, стену*) to knock down; (*разг: экзамен, мероприятие*) to mess up; **зава́ливать** (*~ perf*) +*instr* (*дорогу: снегом*) to cover with; (*яму: землёй*) to fill with; (*разг: магазины: товарами*) to cram with; (*перен: разг: поручениями*) to saddle with

▶ **завали́ться** (*impf* **зава́ливаться**) *сов возв* (*упасть*) to fall; (*стена, забор*) to collapse; (*разг: дело*) to go to the wall; (: *на экзамене*) to come a cropper; **зава́ливаться** (*~ся perf*) **в го́сти к кому́-н** (*разг*) to turn up on sb's doorstep; (**хоть**) ~**ли́сь!** (*разг: очень много*)

you can't move for them!

заваля́|ться (*3sg* **-ется**, *3pl* **-ются**) *сов возв* (*разг*) to be kicking about.

зава|ри́ть (-рю́, -ришь; *impf* **зава́ривать**) *сов перех* (*чай, кофе*) to brew; (*тех*) to weld; **зава́ривать** (*~ perf*) **ка́шу** (*разг*) to stir up trouble

▶ **завари́ться** (*impf* **зава́риваться**) *сов возв* (*чай, кофе*) to brew; (*разг: дело, кутерьма*) to start.

зава́рк|а (-и) *ж* (*действие*: *чая, кофе*) brewing; (*разг: сухой чай*) char; (*заваренный чай*) brew.

заварн|о́й *прил* (*кулин*): ~**о́е те́сто** choux pastry; ~ **крем** custard filling.

заведе́ни|е (-я) *ср* (*учреждение*) establishment; **уче́бное** ~ educational establishment.

заве́д|овать (-ую) *несов неперех* (+*instr*) to be in charge of.

заве́домый *прил* (*обманщик, лжец*) notorious; (*обман, ложь*) blatant.

заведу́(сь) *итп сов см* **завести́(сь)**.

заве́дующ|ая (-ей) *ж см* **заве́дующий**.

заве́дующий (-его; *decl like adj*) *м* (*складом, редакцией*) manager; (*лабораторией, кафедрой*) head.

зав|езти́ (-езу́, -езёшь; *pt* -ёз, -езла́, -езло́, *impf* **завози́ть**) *сов перех* to drop off; (*увезти*) to take.

заверб|ова́ть (-у́ю) *сов от* **вербова́ть**.

заваре́ни|е (-я) *ср* assurance.

заве́ренный *прил* (*копия, подпись*) authenticated, certified.

завери́тел|ь (-я) *м* (*документа, копии*) witness, attestant.

заве́р|ить (-ю, -ишь; *impf* **заверя́ть**) *сов перех* (*копию, подпись*) to witness; **заверя́ть** (*~ perf*) **кого́-н в чём-н** to assure sb of sth.

заверн|у́ть (-у́, -ёшь; *impf* **завёртывать** *или* **завора́чивать**) *сов перех* (*рукав*) to roll up; (*кран*) to turn up; (*гайку*) to tighten up; (*налево, направо, за угол*) to turn; (*разг: в гости, к другу*) to drop by *или* round; **завёртывать** *или* **завора́чивать** (*~ perf*) (**в** +*acc*) (*посылку, книгу, ребёнка*) to wrap (in)

▶ **заверну́ться** (*impf* **завёртываться** *или* **завора́чиваться**) *сов возв* (*рукав*) to roll up; **завёртываться** *или* **завора́чиваться** (*~ся perf*) **в** +*acc* (*в полотенце, в плед*) to wrap o.s. up in.

заве́р|теть (-ерчу́, -е́ртишь) *сов неперех* (+*instr*; *верёвкой*) to twirl; (*глазами*) to roll

▶ **заверте́ться** *сов возв* (*колесо, карусель*) to start turning; (*разг: захлопотаться*) to be run off one's feet.

завёртыва|ть(ся) (-ю(сь)) *несов см* **заверну́ть(ся)**.

заверчу́(сь) *сов см* **заверте́ть(ся)**.

заверша́|ть(ся) (-ю(сь)) *несов от* **заверши́ть(ся)**.

заверша́ющий (-ая, -ее, -ие) *прил* final.

заверше́ни|е (-я) *ср* (*работы*) completion;

(*разговора, лекции*) conclusion; **в ~** +*gen* at the conclusion of.

заверш|и́ть (**-у́, -и́шь;** *impf* **заверша́ть**) *сов перех* to complete; (*разговор*) to end

▶ **заверши́ться** (*impf* **заверша́ться**) *сов возв* to be completed; (*разговор*) to end.

заверя́|ть (**-ю**) *несов от* **заве́рить**.

заве́с|а (**-ы**) *ж* (*перен*) veil; **дымова́|я ~** (*перен*) smoke screen.

заве́|сить (**-шу, -сишь;** *impf* **заве́шивать**) *сов перех* (*окно*) to curtain; (*картину, лампу*) to cover.

зав|ести́ (**-еду́, -едёшь;** *pt* **-ёл, -ела́, -ело́**, *impf* **заводи́ть**) *сов перех* to take; (*увести далеко*) to lead; (*приобрести*) to get; (*установить*) to introduce; (*переписку, разговор*) to initiate; (*часы*) to wind up; (*машину*) to start; (*разг: разозлить*): **~ кого́-н** to wind sb up

▶ **завести́сь** (*impf* **заводи́ться**) *сов возв* to appear; (*мотор, часы*) to start working; (*разг: разозлиться*) to get (all) wound up.

заве́т (**-а**) *м* (*наставление*) precept; (*РЕЛ*): **Ве́тхий/Но́вый ~** the Old/New Testament.

заве́т|ный (**-ен, -на, -но**) *прил* treasured.

заве́ша|ть (**-ю**; *impf* **заве́шивать**) *сов перех* to hang; **заве́шивать** (**~** *perf*) **сте́ны карти́нами** to hang pictures on the walls.

заве́шива|ть (**-ю**) *несов от* **заве́сить**, **заве́шать**.

заве́шу *сов см* **заве́сить**.

завеща́ни|е (**-я**) *ср* (*документ*) will; (*наставление*) precept.

завеща́|ть (**-ю**) (*не*)*сов перех*: **~ что-н кому́-н** (*наследство*) to bequeath sth to sb; **~** (*impf/perf*) **кому́-н** +*infin* to call upon sb to do.

завзя́тый *прил* (*разг: курильщик*) inveterate; **он ~ футболи́ст/охо́тник** he is a football/hunting fanatic.

завива́|ть(ся) (**-ю(сь)**) *несов от* **зави́ть(ся)**.

зави́вк|а (**-и**) *ж* (*волос*) curling; (*причёска*) curly hair.

зави́ден *прил см* **зави́дный**.

зави́дно *нареч*: **он ~ краси́в/умён** he has enviable good looks/intelligence ◆ *как сказ*: **~ как она́ говори́т по-англи́йски** her English is enviable; **ему́ ~** he feels envious.

зави́д|ный (**-ен, -на, -но**) *прил* enviable.

зави́д|овать (**-ую**; *perf* **позави́довать**) *несов неперех* (+*dat*) to envy, be jealous of.

завизжа́|ть (**-у́, -и́шь**) *сов неперех* to begin to yelp.

завизи́р|овать (**-ую**) *сов от* **визи́ровать**.

завин|ти́ть (**-чу́, -ти́шь;** *impf* **зави́нчивать**) *сов перех* to tighten (up).

завира́|ться (**-юсь**) *несов от* **завра́ться**.

зави́|сеть (**-шу, -сишь**) *несов неперех*: **~ от** +*gen* to depend on.

зави́симост|ь (**-и**) *ж* (*отношение*) correlation; **~** (**от** +*gen*) dependence (on); **в ~и от** +*gen* depending on.

зави́сим|ый (**-, -а, -о**) *прил* (*человек, страна*) dependent; **~ от** +*gen* (*погоды, обстоятельств*) dependent on.

зави́стлив|ый (**-, -а, -о**) *прил* envious.

за́вист|ь (**-и**) *ж* envy, jealousy; **она́ вы́глядит на ~ хорошо́** (*разг*) it makes you sick how well she looks.

завитка́ *сущ см* **завито́к**.

завито́й *прил* (*волосы*) curly; (*девушка*) curly-haired; (*проволока, шнур*) coiled.

завит|о́к (**-ка́**) *м* (*локон*) curl; (*спирали*) twist; (*орнамента*) flourish, whorl.

зав|и́ть (**-ью, -ьёшь;** *pt* **-и́л, -ила́, -и́ло**, *impf* **завива́ть**) *сов перех* (*волосы, усы*) to curl; (*проволоку, шнур*) to twist

▶ **зави́ться** (*impf* **завива́ться**) *сов возв* (*волосы, усы*) to curl; (*проволока, шнур*) to get twisted; (*сделать завивку*) to curl one's hair.

завихре́ни|е (**-я**) *ср* whirl; (*перен*) peculiarity.

зави́шу *несов см* **зави́сеть**.

завладе́|ть (**-ю**; *impf* **завладева́ть**) *сов неперех* (+*instr*; *имуществом*) to take possession of; (*ВОЕН, вниманием*) to capture.

завл|е́чь (**-еку́, -ечёшь** *итп*, **-еку́т;** *pt* **-ёк, -екла́, -екло́**, *impf* **завлека́ть**) *сов перех* (*зверя, врага*) to lure; (*перен*) to captivate.

заво́д (**-а**) *м* factory; (*в часах, у игрушки*) clockwork; (*действие*) winding up; **ко́нный ~** stud farm.

завод|и́ть(ся) (**-ожу́(сь), -о́дишь(ся)**) *несов от* **завести́(сь)**.

заводно́й *прил* (*механизм, игрушка*) clockwork *опред*; (*ключ, ручка*) winding *опред*; (*разг: человек*) easily excitable.

заводско́й *прил* factory *опред*.

за́вод|ь (**-и**) *ж* backwater.

завоева́ни|е (**-я**) *ср* (*земель, страны*) conquest; (*обычно мн: достижения*) achievement.

завоева́тел|ь (**-я**) *м* conqueror.

завоева́тельн|ый *прил* (*политика*) aggressive; (*набеги*) offensive; **~ые во́йны** wars of conquest.

заво|ева́ть (**-ю́ю**; *impf* **завоёвывать**) *сов перех* to conquer; (*перен: доверие*) to win.

завожу́ *несов см* **заводи́ть**, **завози́ть**.

завожу́сь *несов см* **заводи́ться**.

заво́з (**-а**) *м* delivery.

завоз|и́ть (**-ожу́, -о́зишь**) *несов от* **завезти́**.

заволн|ова́ться (**-у́юсь**) *сов возв* to become agitated.

завора́чива|ть(ся) (**-ю(сь)**) *несов от* **заверну́ть(ся)**.

за́ворот (**-а**) *м*: **~ кишо́к** (*МЕД*) acute intestinal illness.

заворо́т (**-а**) *м* (*реки, дороги*) bend; (*движение*) turn.

заворч|а́ть (-у́, -и́шь) *сов неперех* to start grumbling.

заво́ю *итп сов см* **завы́ть**.

завр|а́ться (-у́сь, -ёшься; *pt* -а́лся, -ала́сь, -а́лось, *impf* **завира́ться**) *сов возв* (*разг*) to get tied (up) in knots (*by lying*).

завсегда́та|й (-я) *м* (*разг*) regular.

за́втра *нареч, ср нескл* tomorrow; **до ~!** see you tomorrow!; **откла́дывать** (**отложи́ть** *perf*) **что-н на** или **до ~** to put sth off until tomorrow.

за́втрак (-а) *м* breakfast.

за́втрака|ть (-ю; *impf* **поза́втракать**) *несов неперех* to have breakfast.

за́втрашн|ий (-яя, -ее, -ие) *прил* tomorrow's; **за́втрашний день** tomorrow.

завуали́ровать (-ую) *сов от* **вуали́ровать**.

за́вуч (-а) *м сокр* = **заве́дующий уче́бной ча́стью**; (*в школе, в училище*) ≈ deputy head.

завхо́з (-а) *м сокр* = **заве́дующий хозя́йством**; (*в школе, в институте*) bursar; (*на заводе*) *person in charge of supplies*.

завши́ве|ть (-ю) *сов от* **вши́веть**.

завыва́ни|е (-я) *ср* (*собак, метели*) howling; (*сирены*) wail; (*самолёта*) shriek.

завыва́|ть (-ю) *несов неперех* (*собака, метель*) to howl; (*сирена*) to wail; (*самолёт*) to shriek.

завы́|сить (-шу, -сишь; *impf* **завыша́ть**) *сов перех* (*нормы, цены*) to increase excessively; ~ (*perf*) **план** to set unreasonable targets.

завы́|ть (-о́ю, -о́ешь) *сов неперех* (*собака*) to begin to howl; (*сирена*) to start to wail.

завыша́|ть (-ю) *несов от* **завы́сить**.

завыше́ни|е (-я) *ср* excessive increase.

завы́шен|ный (-, -а, -о) *прил* excessively increased.

завы́шу *сов см* **завы́сить**.

завью́(сь) *итп сов см* **зави́ть(ся)**.

завяз|а́ть (-яза́ю, -яза́ешь) *несов от* **завя́знуть** ♦ (-яжу́, -я́жешь; *impf* **завя́зывать**) *сов перех* (*верёвку, ленту*) to tie; (*руку, посылку*) to bind; (*разговор*) to start (up); (*дружбу*) to form; (*отношение*) to establish; (*разг: пить, воровать*) to quit; **завя́зывать** (~ *perf*) **глаза́ кому́-н** to blindfold sb

▶ **завяз|а́ться** (*impf* **завя́зываться**) *сов возв* (*шнурки, бант*) to be tied; (*разговор*) to start (up); (*дружба*) to form; (*отношения*) to become established; (*бот*) to set.

завя́з|ка (-ки; *gen pl* -ок) *ж* (*тесьма*) band; (*лента*) ribbon; (*разговора, событий*) beginning; (*боя*) onset; (*романа, рассказа*) opening.

завя́зн|уть (-у, -ешь; *impf* **завяза́ть** или **вя́знуть**) *сов неперех* (*в снегу, в грязи*) to get stuck; (*перен: разг*): ~ **в** +*prp* (*в трудностях, в долгах*) to be up to one's neck in.

завя́зок *сущ см* **завя́зка**.

завя́зыва|ть(ся) (-ю(сь)) *несов от* **завяза́ть(ся)**.

завя́н|уть (-у, -ешь) *сов от* **вя́нуть**.

загад|а́ть (-ю; *impf* **зага́дывать**) *сов перех* (*зага́дку*) to set; (*шараду*) to act out; (*число, слово*) to think of; (*желание*) to make ♦ *неперех* (*разг*) to guess.

зага́|дить (-жу, -дишь) *сов перех* (*разг*) to mess up.

зага́д|ка (-ки; *gen pl* -ок) *ж* riddle; (*перен*) puzzle, mystery.

зага́доч|ный (-ен, -на, -но) *прил* (*явление, событие*) puzzling, mysterious; (*выражение лица, слова*) enigmatic.

зага́дыва|ть (-ю) *несов от* **загада́ть**.

зага́жу *сов см* **зага́дить**.

загазо́ван|ный (-, -а, -о) *прил* (*атмосфера*) polluted.

зага́р (-а) *м* (sun)tan.

загво́зд|ка (-и) *ж* (*разг*) obstacle; **в э́том вся ~** (*разг*) that's the whole problem.

загерметизи́р|овать (-ую) *сов от* **герметизи́ровать**.

заги́б (-а) *м* (*на бумаге*) crease; (*перен: разг*) twist.

загиба́|ть(ся) (-ю(сь)) *несов от* **загну́ть(ся)**.

загипнотизи́р|овать (-ую) *сов от* **гипнотизи́ровать**.

загла́ви|е (-я) *ср* title.

загла́вный *прил*: **~ая бу́ква** capital letter; **загла́вная роль** title role.

загла́|дить (-жу, -дишь; *impf* **загла́живать**) *сов перех* (*складки*) to iron; (*лист*) to fold; (*сгиб*) to make; (*перен: ошибки*) to put right; (: *обиду*) to make up for; **загла́живать** (~ *perf*) **вину́** to make amends.

загло́хн|уть (-у, -ешь) *сов от* **гло́хнуть** ♦ *неперех* (*сад, тропинка*) to become overgrown; (*перен: разг: стройка, дело*) to die a death.

загло́хш|ий (-ая, -ее, -ие) *прил* overgrown.

заглуша́|ть (-ю; *perf* **заглуши́ть**) *несов перех* = **глуши́ть**.

заглуш|и́ть (-у́, -и́шь) *сов от* **глуши́ть**, **заглуша́ть**.

загляде́нь|е (-я) *ср* (*разг*) feast for the eyes.

загля|де́ться (-жу́сь, -ди́шься; *impf* **загля́дываться**) *сов возв* to gaze.

загля|ну́ть (-яну́, -я́нешь; *impf* **загля́дывать**) *сов неперех* (*в окно, в спальню*) to peep; (*в книгу, в словарь*) to glance; (*разг: к соседу, к друзьям*) to pop in; **загля́дывать** (~ *perf*) **вперёд** to take a brief look ahead.

загна́ива|ться (-юсь) *несов от* **загнои́ться**.

заг|на́ть (-оню́, -о́нишь; *pt* -на́л, -нала́, -на́ло, *impf* **загоня́ть**) *сов перех* (*коров, детей*) to drive; (*разг: гвоздь, нож*) to ram in; (: *продать*) to flog (*BRIT*), sell; (*изнурить: лошадь*) to ride too hard; (: *рабочих*) to drive into the ground.

загн|и́ть (-ию́, -иёшь; *pt* -и́л, -ила́, -и́ло, *impf* **загнива́ть**) *сов неперех* to begin to rot.

загно|и́ться (-ю́сь, -и́шься; *impf* **загна́иваться**) *сов возв* (*рана*) to fester; (*глаз*) to become inflamed.

за́гнут|ый (-, -а, -о) *прил* bent.

загн|у́ть (-у́, -ёшь; *impf* **загиба́ть**) *сов перех* (*гвоздь*) to bend; (*край*) to fold; (*страницу*) to dog-ear; (*разг: сказать*) to spout; **загиба́ть (~** *perf*) **рука́в вверх/вниз** to pull a sleeve up/down
► **загну́ться** (*impf* **загиба́ться**) *сов возв* (*гвоздь*) to bend; (*край*) to fold; (*страница*) to become dog-eared; (*воротник*) to twist; (*разг: умереть*) to kick the bucket.

загова́рива|ть (-ю) *несов от* **заговори́ть ♦** *неперех*: **зу́бы ~ кому́-н** (*разг*) to steer sb off a subject
► **загова́риваться** *несов возв* (*говорить бессвязно*) to rave.

за́говень|е (-я) *ср* (*РЕЛ*) eve of fast, ≈ Shrove Tuesday.

за́говор (-а) *м* conspiracy; (*от болезни*) spell.

заговор|и́ть (-ю́, -и́шь) *сов неперех* (*начать говорить*) to begin to speak; (*по-английски, по-русски*) to be able to speak; (*перен: совесть, гордость итп*) to stir ♦ (*impf* **загова́ривать**) *перех* (*болезнь, боль*) to magic away; **загова́ривать (~** *perf*) **кого́-н** to wear sb out through constant talk; **в нём ~и́ла со́весть** his conscience stirred in him.

загово́рщик (-а) *м* conspirator.

загово́рщиц|а (-ы) *ж см* **загово́рщик**.

заголо́в|ок (-ка) *м* headline.

заго́н (-а) *м* (*скота, овец*) driving in; (*для скота*) enclosure; (*для овец*) pen; **быть** (*impf*) **в ~е** (*разг*) to be pushed to one side.

загоню́ *итп сов см* **загна́ть**.

загоня́|ть (-ю) *несов от* **загна́ть**.

загора́жива|ть(ся) (-ю(сь)) *несов от* **загороди́ть(ся)**.

загора́|ть(ся) (-ю(сь)) *несов от* **загоре́ть(ся)**.

загоре́л|ый (-, -а, -о) *прил* tanned.

загор|е́ть (-ю́, -и́шь; *impf* **загора́ть**) *сов неперех* to go brown, get a tan
► **загоре́ться** (*impf* **загора́ться**) *сов возв* (*дрова, костёр*) to light; (*здание итп*) to catch fire; (*лампочка, глаза*) to light up; **загора́ться (~ся** *perf*) **жела́нием** +*infin* to have a burning desire to do; **он ~е́лся э́той иде́ей** the idea fired his imagination.

за́город (-а) *м* (*разг*) the country.

загор|оди́ть (-ожу́, -о́дишь; *impf* **загора́живать**) *сов перех* (*улицу, вход*) to block off; (*свет*) to block out; **загора́живать (~** *perf*) **кого́-н собо́й** to shield sb; **загора́живать (~** *perf*) **кому́-н доро́гу** (*перен*) to stand on sb's way
► **загороди́ться** (*impf* **загора́живаться**) *сов возв*: **~ся (от** +*gen*) (*от солнца, от удара*) to shield o.s. (from).

загоро́д|ка (-ки; *gen pl* -ок) *ж* barrier; (*в комнате*) partition.

за́городн|ый *прил* (*экскурсия*) out-of-town; (*дом*) country *опред*; **~ая пое́здка** a trip out of town *или* into the country.

загоро́док *сущ см* **загоро́дка**.

загорожу́(сь) *сов см* **загороди́ть(ся)**.

загота́влива|ть (-ю) *несов от* **заготовить**.

заготови́тел|ь (-я) *м person responsible for state procurements of timber, grain etc.*

заготови́тельный *прил*: **~ пункт** collection point; **заготови́тельная цена́** state procurement price.

загото́в|ить (-лю, -ишь; *impf* **загота́вливать** *или* **заготовля́ть**) *сов перех* (*сено, корм итп*) to lay in; (*билеты, документы итп*) to prepare.

загото́в|ка (-ки; *gen pl* -ок) *ж* (*действие: кормов, леса итп*) laying in; (*закупка государством*) procurement; (*полуфабрикат*) component; (: *для туфель*) upper.

загото́влю *сов см* **заготовить**.

заготовля́|ть (-ю) *несов от* **заготовить**.

загото́вок *сущ см* **загото́вка**.

загради́тельный *прил*: **~ое сооруже́ние** barrier; **загради́тельный ого́нь** (*ВОЕН*) defensive fire; **загради́тельный патру́ль** roadblock.

загра|ди́ть (-жу́, -ди́шь; *impf* **загражда́ть**) *сов перех* to obstruct.

загражде́ни|е (-я) *ср* barrier.

загражу́ *сов см* **загради́ть**.

загра́ниц|а (-ы) *ж* (*разг*) foreign countries *мн*.

заграни́чный *прил* foreign; **заграни́чный па́спорт** passport (*issued specifically for travel abroad*).

За́греб (-а) *м* Zagreb.

загрёб *итп сов см* **загрести́**.

загреба́|ть (-ю) *несов от* **загрести́ ♦** *неперех* (*вёслами*) to row; (*руками, лапами*) to paddle ♦ *перех*: **~ де́ньги** (*разг*) to rake in the money.

загребу́ *итп сов см* **загрести́**.

загрем|е́ть (-лю́, -и́шь) *сов неперех* (*гром*) to crash out; (*голос*) to thunder; (*тарелки итп*) to start to rattle.

загр|ести́ (-ебу́, -ебёшь; *pt* -ёб, -ебла́, -ебло́, *impf* **загреба́ть**) *сов перех* (*мусор, листья итп*) to rake up.

загри́в|ок (-ка) *м* (*у лошади*) withers *мн*; **взять** (*perf*) **кого́-н за ~** (*разг*) to grab sb by the scruff of the neck.

загримиров|а́ть (-у́ю; *impf* **загримиро́вывать** *или* **гримирова́ть**) *сов перех* to make up
► **загримирова́ться** (*impf* **загримиро́вываться** *или* **гримирова́ться**) *сов возв* to make o.s. up.

загро́бный *прил*: **~ мир** the next world; (*перен: голос*) gloomy; **загро́бная жизнь** the afterlife.

загромозд|и́ть (-жу́, -ди́шь; *impf* **загроможда́ть**) *сов перех* to clutter (up).

загрубе́л|ый (-, -а, -о) *прил* (*кожа, руки*) calloused, rough; (*лицо*) coarse; (*голос*) gruff; (*перен: человек, душа*) hardened.

загрубе́|ть (-ю) *сов от* **грубе́ть.**

загру|зи́ть (-ужу́, -у́зишь) *сов от* **грузи́ть ♦** (*impf* **загружа́ть**) *перех* (*машину, судно*) to load up; (*комп*) to boot, load up; (*перен: сотрудников, учеников*) to load with work; (: *день*) to fill up; (: *печь, домну*) to load.

загру́з|ка (-и) *ж* (*машины, судна*) loading; (*предприятия, станка*) capacity.

загрунт|ова́ть (-у́ю; *impf* **загрунто́вывать** *или* **грунтова́ть**) *сов перех* to prime.

загру|сти́ть (-щу́, -сти́шь) *сов неперех* to become sad; **~** (*perf*) **по до́му** to start to feel homesick.

загры́|зть (-зу́, -зёшь; *impf* **загрыза́ть**) *сов перех* (*овцу, петуха*) to kill; (*no impf; перен: разг: замучить*) to nag to death; **её ~ы́зла со́весть** she was tormented by her conscience.

загрязне́ни|е (-я) *ср* pollution; **загрязне́ние окружа́ющей среды́** (environmental) pollution.

загрязнё́нн|ый (-ён, -ена́, -ено́) *прил* polluted.

загрязн|и́ть (-ю́, -и́шь) *сов от* **грязни́ть ♦** (*impf* **загрязня́ть**) *перех* (*воздух, водоём*) to pollute; **загрязня́ть** (**~** *perf*) **что-н** (*сапоги, платье итп*) to get sth dirty.

▶ **загрязни́ться** *сов от* **грязни́ться ♦** (*impf* **загрязня́ться**) *возв* (*см перех*) to become polluted; to get dirty.

ЗАГС (-а) *м сокр* (= *за́пись а́ктов гражда́нского состоя́ния*) ≈ registry office.

загуб|и́ть (-ублю́, -у́бишь) *сов от* **губи́ть ♦** *перех* (*человека*) to destroy; (*растение*) to kill; (*жизнь, вечер*) to ruin; (*разг: деньги, средства*) to waste.

загуде́|ть (-жу́, -ди́шь) *сов неперех* (*машина*) to honk; (*гудок*) to sound.

загу́л (-а) *м* (*разг*) drinking session; **уда́риться** (*perf*) **в ~** to go on a bender.

загуля́|ть (-ю; *impf* **загу́ливать**) *сов неперех* (*разг: кутить*) to booze.

загусте́|ть (*3sg* -ет, *3pl* -ют) *сов от* **густе́ть.**

зад (-а; *part gen* -у, *loc sg* -у́, *nom pl* -ы́, *gen pl* -о́в) *м* (*человека*) behind, rear; (*животного*) rump; (*машины, дома*) rear.

зада́брива|ть (-ю) *несов от* **задо́брить.**

задава́|ть (-ю́, -ёшь) *несов от* **зада́ть**

▶ **задава́ться** *несов от* **зада́ться ♦** *возв* (*разг: важничать*) to be cocky.

зада|ви́ть (-авлю́, -а́вишь) *сов от* **дави́ть ♦** *перех* to crush; **её ~ави́ло де́ревом** she was crushed under a tree; **его́ ~ави́ла маши́на** he was run over by a car.

зада́м(ся) *итп сов см* **зада́ть(ся).**

зада́ни|е (-я) *ср* (*поручение*) task; (*упражнение*) exercise; (*воен*) mission; **дома́шнее ~** homework.

задар|и́ть (-рю́, -а́ришь; *impf* **зада́ривать**) *сов перех*: **~ кого́-н пода́рками** to shower sb with presents.

зада́ром *нареч* (*разг: дёшево*) for next to nothing; (: *зря*) for nothing.

зада́ст(ся) *сов см* **зада́ть(ся).**

зада́тка *сущ см* **зада́ток.**

зада́тк|и (-ов) *мн* (*о способностях*) ability *ед*.

зада́т|ок (-ка) *м* deposit; **дава́ть** (**дать** *perf*) **~** to put down a deposit; *см также* **зада́тки.**

зада́|ть (*как* **дать**; *см* **Table 14**; *impf* **задава́ть**) *сов перех* to set; **задава́ть** (**~** *perf*) **кому́-н вопро́с** to ask sb a question; **задава́ть** (**~** *perf*) **пир** (*разг*) to lay on a spread; **я тебе́ ~а́м!** (*разг*) just you wait!

▶ **зада́ться** (*impf* **задава́ться**) *сов возв*: **~ся це́лью** +*infin* (*сделать, написать итп*) to set o.s. the task of doing; **~ся** (*perf*) **вопро́сом** to ask o.s.

зада́ч|а (-и) *ж* task; (*мат*) problem; **ста́вить** (**поста́вить** *perf*) **пе́ред собо́й ~у** to set o.s. a task; **реша́ть** (**реши́ть** *perf*) **~у** to solve a problem.

зада́чник (-а) *м* book of problems.

зада́шь(ся) *сов см* **зада́ть(ся).**

задвига́|ть (-ю) *сов неперех* (+*instr*) to begin to move

▶ **задви́гаться** *сов возв* to begin to move.

задвига́|ть(ся) (-ю(сь)) *несов от* **задви́нуть(ся).**

задви́жк|а (-и) *ж* bolt; **закрыва́ть** (**закры́ть** *perf*) **дверь на ~у** to bolt the door.

задвижн|о́й *прил*: **~а́я дверь** sliding door.

задви́|нуть (-у, -ешь; *impf* **задвига́ть**) *сов перех* to push; (*ящик, занавеску*) to close

▶ **задви́нуться** (*impf* **задвига́ться**) *сов возв* to close.

задво́р|ки (-ок) *мн* backyard *ед*; **на ~ках о́бщества** (*перен*) on the margins of society; **на ~ках исто́рии** (*перен*) in the footnotes of history.

задева́|ть (-ю) *несов от* **заде́ть ♦** *сов перех* (*разг: положить*) to put; **куда́ ты ~л мою́ су́мку?** where have you put my bag?

▶ **задева́ться** *сов возв* (*разг*) to go missing; **куда́ ~лась моя́ ру́чка?** what's happened to my pen?

задде́йств|овать (-ую) *сов перех* (*оборудование*) to render operational; (*полк, дивизию*) to mobilize ♦ *неперех* (*взяться за дело*) to get busy.

заде́л (-а) *м* groundwork; **создава́ть** (**созда́ть** *perf*) **~ на бу́дущее** to create foundations for the future.

заде́ла|ть (-ю; *impf* **заде́лывать**) *сов перех* to seal up.

заде́ну *итп сов см* **заде́ть.**

задёрга|ть (-ю) *сов неперех* (+*instr*; *ногой, вожжами*) to jerk ♦ *перех* (*разг: измучить*) to wear out

▶ **задёргаться** *сов возв* (*тело, глаз, губы*) to twitch; (*начать нервничать*) to become twitchy; (*разг: измучиться*) to reach the end of one's tether.

задёргива|ть (-ю) *несов от* **задёрнуть.**

задеревене́|ть (-ю) *сов неперех* to go stiff.

задержа́ни|е (-я) *ср* (*юр*) detention.

зад|ержа́ть (-ержу́, -е́ржишь; *impf* **заде́рживать**) *сов перех (самолёт, поезд итп)* to delay, hold up; *(зарплату, уплату долгов)* to withhold; *(преступника)* to detain; *(школьников)* to keep back; **я не хочу́ Вас ~е́рживать** I don't want to hold you back; **заде́рживать (~** *perf)* **дыха́ние** to hold one's breath; **заде́рживать (~** *perf)* **взгляд на** +*prp* to stare at; **заде́рживать (~** *perf)* **шаг** to slow up

▸ **задержа́ться** (*impf* **заде́рживаться**) *сов возв* to be delayed *или* held up; *(у двери, перед домом итп)* to pause; **заде́рживаться (~ся** *perf)* **с отве́том/рабо́той** to be late in answering/finishing the work.

задер́ж|ка (-ки; *gen pl* -ек) *ж* delay, hold-up; **без ~ек** without further delay.

задёрн|уть (-у, -ешь; *impf* **задёргивать**) *сов перех (шторы)* to pull shut; **задёргивать (~** *perf)* **окно́ занаве́ской/што́рой** to shut the curtains/blind.

задеру́(сь) *итп сов см* **задра́ть(ся)**.

заде́|ть (-ну, -нешь; *impf* **задева́ть**) *сов перех*: **~ (за** +*acc)* *(стол итп)* to brush against; *(кость, лёгкое)* to graze; *(перен: самолюбие, человека)* to wound; **его́ тон меня́ ~л** I found his tone offensive; **~ (** *perf)* **кого́-н за живо́е** to cut sb to the quick.

задир́|а (-ы) *м/ж (разг)* troublemaker.

задира́|ть(ся) (-ю(сь)) *несов от* **задра́ть(ся)**.

задир́ист|ый (-, -а, -о) *прил* quarrelsome.

за́дн|ий (-яя, -ее, -ие) *прил* back *опред*; **помеча́ть (поме́тить** *perf)* **~им число́м** to backdate; **опла́чивать (оплати́ть** *perf)* **~им число́м** to make a back payment; **она́ ~им умо́м крепка́** she's simply being wise after the event; **он был без ~их ног** *(разг)* he was dead on his feet; **~яя мысль** ulterior motive; **~ие но́ги** hind legs; **за́дний прохо́д** (АНАТ) rectum; **за́дний ход** back entrance.

за́дник (-а) *м (ботинка)* back; *(ТЕАТР)* backdrop.

за́дниц|а (-ы) *ж (разг)* backside.

задо́бр|ить (-ю, -ишь; *impf* **задабривать**) *сов перех* to soften up.

задо́лго *нареч*: **~ до** +*gen* long before.

задолжа́|ть (-ю) *сов перех* to owe.

задо́лженность (-и) *ж* debts *мн; (по работе,в учёбе)* work outstanding.

за́дом *нареч* backwards; **~ наперёд** back to front; **повора́чиваться (поверну́ться** *perf)* **~ к кому́-н** to turn one's back to sb; **стоя́ть** (*impf)* **~ к кому́-н** to stand with one's back to sb.

задо́р (-а) *м* enthusiasm.

задо́р|ный (-ен, -на, -но) *прил* lively.

задохну́|ться (-у́сь, -ёшься; *impf* **задыха́ться**) *сов возв (в дыму)* to suffocate; *(от бега, при ходьбе)* to be out of breath; *(от злости, от смеха)* to choke.

задра́|ить (-ю, -ишь; *impf* **задра́ивать**) *сов*

перех (МОР) to batten down.

задрапир|ова́ть (-у́ю) *сов от* **драпирова́ть**.

задр|а́ть (-еру́, -ерёшь; *pt* -ра́л, -рала́, -ра́ло, *impf* **драть** *или* **задира́ть**) *сов перех (платье, юбка)* to hitch *или* hike up; *(растерзать)* to savage; **задира́ть (~** *perf)* **го́лову** to tip one's head back; **задира́ть (~** *perf)* **нос** *(разг)* to be stuck-up

▸ **задра́ться** (*impf* **задира́ться**) *сов возв (разг: платье, рубашка)* to hitch itself up; *(рукав)* to ruck.

задрем|а́ть (-емлю́, -е́млешь) *сов неперех* to doze off.

задрож|а́ть (-у́, -и́шь) *сов неперех (человек, голос)* to begin to tremble; *(здание, стекло)* to begin to shake.

задува́|ть (-ю) *несов от* **заду́ть**.

заду́ма|ть (-ю; *impf* **заду́мывать**) *сов перех (повесть, план)* to think up; *(карту, число)* to think of; *(+infin: уехать итп)* to think of doing

▸ **заду́маться** (*impf* **заду́мываться**) *сов возв (погрузиться в раздумье)* to be deep in thought; **заду́мываться (~ся** *perf)* **над** +*instr/***о** +*prp (над задачей, над жизнью)* to ponder; **о чём Вы ~лись?** what are you thinking about?; **он отве́тил, не заду́мываясь** he answered without hesitation; **она́ на мину́ту ~лась** she reflected for a moment.

заду́мчивост|ь (-и) *ж* pensiveness; **быть** (*impf)* **в глубо́кой ~и** to be deep in thought.

заду́мчив|ый (-, -а, -о) *прил* pensive, thoughtful.

заду́мыва|ть(ся) (-ю(сь)) *несов от* **заду́мать(ся)**.

заду́|ть (-ю, -ешь; *impf* **задува́ть**) *сов перех (огонь, свечу итп)* to blow out ♦ *неперех (ветер)* to get up; **ве́тром ~ло песо́к в ко́мнату** the wind blew sand into the room.

задуше́в|ный (-ен, -на, -но) *прил (мысли, тайна, разговор)* intimate; *(песня, рассказ)* soulful; *(друг, человек)* genial.

заду́ш|ить (-у́, -у́шишь) *сов от* **души́ть**.

задым|и́ть (-лю́, -и́шь) *сов неперех* to begin to smoulder (*BRIT)* *или* smolder (*US)*

▸ **задыми́ться** *сов возв* to begin to give off smoke.

задыха́|ться (-юсь) *несов от* **задохну́ться**.

зае́д|им *итп сов см* **зае́сть**.

зае́дешь *итп сов см* **зае́хать**.

заеди́м *итп сов см* **зае́сть**.

зае́ду *итп сов см* **зае́хать**.

заедя́т *итп сов см* **зае́сть**.

заéзд (-а) *м (СПОРТ)* race *(in horse-racing, motor-racing)*; *(: отборочный)* heat; *(туристов, отдыхающих)* arrival; **с ~ом/без заéзда в Москву́** with/without a stopoff in Moscow.

заéз|дить (-жу, -дишь) *сов перех (перен: разг)*:

~ кого́-н to drive sb too hard.
заезжа́|ть (-ю) *несов от* **зае́хать**.
зае́зжу *сов см* **зае́здить**.
зае́л *итп сов см* **зае́сть**.
зае́м *итп сов см* **зае́сть**.
заём (за́йма) *м* loan.
заёмщик (-а) *м* borrower.
зае́сть (*как* **есть**; *см* **Table 15**; *impf* **заеда́ть**) *сов перех* (*подлеж: комары*) to eat; (*разг: подлеж: жена, начальник, среда*) to get to ◆ *безл* (*разг: ружьё*) to jam; **пласти́нку зае́ло** (*разг*) the record is stuck; **заеда́ть** (~ *perf*) **лека́рство/во́дку чем-н** to eat sth to take away the taste of the medicine/vodka.
зае́хать (*как* **е́хать**; *см* **Table 19**; *impf* **заезжа́ть**) *сов неперех*: ~ **за кем-н** to go to fetch sb; **заезжа́ть** (~ *perf*) **в** +*acc* (*в канаву, во двор*) to drive into; (*в Москву, в магазин итп*) to stop off at; ~ (*perf*) **к друзья́м** to stop off at friends; ~ (*perf*) **кому́-н в лицо́** (*разг*) to smash sb in the face; ~ (*perf*) **кому́-н в у́хо** (*разг*) to box sb's ears.
зажа́рить (-ю, -ишь) *сов от* **жа́рить** ◆ (*impf* **зажа́ривать**) *перех* (*на сковоро́дке*) to fry; (*в духо́вке*) to roast
▶ **зажа́риться** *сов от* **жа́риться** ◆ (*impf* **зажа́риваться**) *возв* (*см перех*) to fry; to roast.
зажа́|ть (-му́, -мёшь; *impf* **зажима́ть**) *сов перех* to squeeze; (*рот, уши*) to cover; (*перен: инициативу, проект*) to stifle, suppress; (*разг: деньги*) to pocket; **зажима́ть** (~ *perf*) **нос** to hold one's nose; **зажима́ть** (~ *perf*) **рот кому́-н** (*перен*) to silence sb.
зажгу́(сь) *итп сов см* **заже́чь(ся)**.
зажда́|ться (-у́сь, -ёшься) *сов возв* (+*gen*; *разг*) to be sick of waiting for.
заже́|чь (-гу́, -жёшь *итп*, -гу́т; *pt* -ёг, -гла, -гло, *impf* **зажига́ть**) *сов перех* (*свечу, спичку итп*) to light; (*свет*) to turn on; (*перен: аудиторию*) to inflame; (: *интерес, любовь*) to spark (off)
▶ **заже́чься** (*impf* **зажига́ться**) *сов возв* (*свеча, спичка итп*) to light; (*свет*) to go on; (*перен: интерес, любовь*) to be sparked off.
зажива́|ть (-ю) *несов от* **зажи́ть**.
заживу́ *итп сов от* **зажи́ть**.
зажига́лк|а (-и) *ж* (*cigarette*) lighter; (*разг: бомба*) firebomb.
зажига́ни|е (-я) *ср* (*действие*) lighting; (*АВТ*) ignition; **включа́ть** (**включи́ть** *perf*) ~ to turn on the ignition.
зажига́тел|ьный (-ен, -ьна, -ьно) *прил* (*также перен*) inflammatory; (*снаряд*) incendiary; **зажига́тельный шнур** fuse wire.
зажига́|ть(ся) (-ю(сь)) *несов от* **заже́чь(ся)**.
зажи́м (-а) *м* (*ТЕХ*) clamp; (*ЭЛЕК*) terminal; (*перен: инициативы, критики*) stifling, suppression.
зажима́|ть (-ю) *несов от* **зажа́ть**.
зажи́точ|ный (-ен, -на, -но) *прил* prosperous.
зажи́|ть (-иву́, -ивёшь; *pt* -ил, -ила́, -ило, *impf* **зажива́ть**) *сов неперех* (*рана*) to heal (up); (*по*

impf; начать жить) to start to live; ~ (*perf*) **по-но́вому** to change one's lifestyle.
зажму́ *итп сов см* **зажа́ть**.
зажму́р|ить (-ю, -ишь) *сов от* **жму́рить** ◆ (*impf* **зажму́ривать**) *перех*: ~ **глаза́** to screw up one's eyes
▶ **зажму́риться** *сов от* **жму́риться** ◆ (*impf* **зажму́риваться**) *возв* to screw up one's eyes.
зажужжа́|ть (-у́, -и́шь) *сов неперех* to start buzzing.
зазва́|ть (-ову́, -овёшь; *pt* -ва́л, -вала́, -ва́ло, *impf* **зазыва́ть**) *сов перех* (*разг*): ~ **кого́-н в го́сти** to invite sb over.
зазвене́|ть (-ю, -ишь) *сов неперех* to start ringing; **у меня́** ~**ло в уша́х** my ears started ringing.
зазвон|и́ть (-ю́, -и́шь) *сов неперех* to start ringing.
зазвуча́|ть (*3sg* -и́т, *3pl* -а́т) *сов неперех* to be heard.
заздра́вный *прил* congratulatory.
зазелене́|ть (*3sg* -ет) *сов неперех* to turn green.
заземле́ни|е (-я) *ср* (*ЭЛЕК: действие*) earthing (*BRIT*), grounding (*US*); (: *устройство*) earth (*BRIT*), ground (*US*).
заземл|и́ть (-ю́, -и́шь; *impf* **заземля́ть**) *сов перех* to earth (*BRIT*), ground (*US*).
зазна|ва́ться (-ю́сь) *несов от* **зазна́ться**.
зазна́|йка (-йки; *gen pl* -ек) *м/ж* (*разг*) bighead.
зазна́|ться (-ю́сь; *impf* **зазнава́ться**) *сов возв* (*разг*) to think a lot of o.s.
зазову́ *итп сов см* **зазва́ть**.
зазо́р (-а) *м* gap.
зазре́ни|е (-я) *ср*: **без** ~**я со́вести** without a twinge of conscience.
зазу́брен|ный (-, -а, -о) *прил* serrated, jagged.
зазу́брива|ть (-ю) *несов от* **зазубри́ть**.
зазу́брин|а (-ы) *ж* serration.
зазубр|и́ть (-ю́, -и́шь; *impf* **зазу́бривать**) *сов перех* (*разг*): ~ **что-н** to learn sth parrot-fashion.
зазыва́|ть (-ю) *несов от* **зазва́ть**.
заигра́|ть (-ю) *сов* (*не)перех* (*музыкант, оркестр*) to begin to play ◆ *неперех* (*музыка*) to begin ◆ (*impf* **заи́грывать**) *перех* (*пластинку, колоду карт*) to wear out
▶ **заигра́ться** (*impf* **заи́грываться**) *сов возв* to be absorbed in one's games.
заи́грыва|ть (-ю) *несов от* **заигра́ть** ◆ *неперех*: ~ **с** +*instr* (*разг: любезничать*) to flirt with; (: *заискивать*) to suck up to
▶ **заи́грываться** *несов от* **заигра́ться**.
за́йк|а (-и) *м/ж* stutterer.
заика́ни|е (-я) *ср* (*действие*) stuttering; (*порок речи*) stutter.
заика́|ться (-ю́сь) *несов возв* to have a stutter; (*разг: от испуга, от волнения*) to stammer; (*perf* **заикну́ться**) ~ **о** +*prp* (*поездке, приглашении*) to drop hints about.
заимообра́зно *нареч* on loan.
заи́мствовани|е (-я) *ср* borrowing.
заи́мств|овать (-ую; *impf* **позаи́мствовать**)

(не)сов перех (слова, сюжет) to borrow;
(опыт) to benefit from.

заиндеве́вш|ий (-ая, -ое, -ие) *прил* frost-
covered.

за́йндеве|ть (-ю) *сов от* **йндеветь.**

заинтересо́ван|ный (-, -а, -о) *прил* interested;
я заинтересо́ван в э́том де́ле I have an interest
in the matter; **заинтересо́ванная сторона́**
interested party.

заинтерес|ова́ть (-у́ю; *impf* **заинтерес-**
о́вывать) *сов перех* to interest

▶ **заинтересова́ться (** *impf* **заинтерес-**
о́вываться) *сов возв* (*+instr*) to become
interested in.

заинтриг|ова́ть (-у́ю; *impf* **заинтриго́вывать)**
сов перех to intrigue.

Заи́р (-а) *м* Zaire.

заи́рск|ий (-ая, -ое, -ие) *прил* Zairean.

заи́скива|ть (-ю) *несов неперех:* ~ **пе́ред** *+instr*
to ingratiate o.s. with.

заи́скивающ|ий (-ая, -ее, -ие) *прил*
ingratiating.

зайду́ *итп сов см* **зайти́.**

за́йма *сущ см* **заём.**

за́ймов|ый *прил:* ~**ая опера́ция** loan
transaction; ~ **проце́нт** interest (*on loan*).

займу́(сь) *итп сов см* **заня́ть(ся).**

зайти́ (*как* **идти́;** *см* **Table 18;** *impf* **заходи́ть)**
сов неперех (солнце, луна) to go down; *(спор,*
разговор) to start up; *(посетить):* ~ **(в/на**
*+acc)***/к** *+dat)* to call in (at); *(попасть):* ~ **в/на**
+acc to stray into; **заходи́ть (~** *perf)* **за кем-н** to
go to fetch sb; **заходи́ть (~** *perf)* **за хле́бом/**
молоко́м to pop in for bread/milk; **заходи́ть (~**
perf) **на рабо́ту/к дру́гу** to call in at work/a
friend's; **заходи́ть (~** *perf)* **спра́ва/сле́ва** to
come in from the right/left; **мы зашли́ в**
незнако́мую часть го́рода we strayed into an
unfamiliar part of town; **заходи́ть (~** *perf)* **в**
тупи́к *(перен)* to reach a dead end; **де́ло зашло́**
сли́шком далеко́ things have gone too far.

за́йца *сущ см* **за́яц.**

зайча́та *итп сущ см* **зайчо́нок.**

за́йчик (-а) *м уменьш от* **за́яц;** *(разг: также:*
со́лнечный ~*)* reflection of the sun.

зайчи́х|а (-и) *ж* doe, female hare.

зайчо́нок (-о́нка; *nom pl* **-а́та,** *gen pl* **-а́т)** *м*
leveret.

закабал|и́ть (-ю́, -и́шь; *impf* **закабаля́ть)** *сов*
перех to enslave.

закавка́зск|ий (-ая, -ое, -ие) *прил*
Transcaucasian.

закады́чн|ый *прил:* ~ **друг** bosom friend.

закажу́ *итп сов от* **заказа́ть.**

зака́з (-а) *м (действие: платья, обеда итп)*
ordering; *(: телефонного разговора)* booking;
(: портрета) commissioning; *(заказанный*
предмет) order; **де́лать (сде́лать** *perf)* **что-н**

на ~ to make sth to order; **по** ~**у** *(также перен)*
to order.

зак|аза́ть (-ажу́, -а́жешь; *impf* **зака́зывать)** *сов*
перех (см сущ) to order; to book; to
commission.

заказн|о́й *прил:* ~**о́е письмо́** registered letter.

зака́зчик (-а) *м* customer.

зака́зчиц|а (-ы) *ж см* **зака́зчик.**

зака́зыва|ть (-ю) *несов от* **заказа́ть.**

закал|ённый (-ён, -ена́, -ено́) *прил (физически)*
resistant; *(нравственно)* resilient.

зака́ливани|е (-я) *ср (ребёнка, организма)*
toughening up.

закал|и́ть (-ю́, -и́шь; *impf* **зака́ливать** *или*
закаля́ть) *сов перех (сталь)* to harden, temper;
(ребёнка, организм) to toughen up; *(волю,*
характер) to toughen

▶ **закали́ться (** *impf* **зака́ливаться** *или*
закаля́ться) *сов возв (сталь)* to be hardened
или tempered; *(ребёнок, организм)* to build up
one's resistance; *(воля, характер)* to toughen.

зака́лк|а (-и) *ж (см глаг)* hardening, tempering;
toughening up; toughening; *(стойкость)*
toughness.

зака́лыва|ть (-ю) *несов от* **заколо́ть.**

закаля́ть(ся) (-ю(сь)) *несов от* **закали́ть(ся).**

закамуфли́р|овать (-ую) *сов от*
камуфли́ровать.

зака́нчива|ть(ся) (-ю(сь)) *несов от*
зако́нчить(ся).

зака́па|ть (-ю; *impf* **зака́пывать)** *сов перех*
(платье, тетрадь итп) to splatter;
(лекарство, капли) to apply ◆ *неперех (no impf):*
дождь ~**л** it started spitting (with rain).

зака́пыва|ть (-ю) *несов от* **зака́пать,** **закопа́ть**

▶ **зака́пываться** *несов от* **закопа́ться.**

зака́т (-а) *м:* ~ **(со́лнца)** sunset; *(перен: жизни,*
карьеры) twilight; **на** ~**е дней** in the twilight of
one's years.

заката́|ть (-ю; *impf* **зака́тывать)** *сов перех* to roll
up.

зак|ати́ть (-ачу́, -а́тишь; *impf* **зака́тывать)** *сов*
перех to roll; **зака́тывать (~** *perf)* **сканда́л**
(разг) to create a scandal; **зака́тывать (~** *perf)*
исте́рику *(разг)* to get hysterical; **зака́тывать**
(~ *perf)* **глаза́** to roll one's eyes

▶ **закати́ться (** *impf* **зака́тываться)** *сов возв* to
roll; *(солнце)* to set.

закача́|ться (-юсь) *сов возв* to begin to sway.

закачу́(сь) *сов см* **закати́ть(ся).**

зака́шля|ть (-ю) *сов неперех* to start coughing

▶ **зака́шляться** *сов возв* to have a coughing fit.

заква́|сить (-шу, -сишь; *impf* **заква́шивать)** *сов*
перех (капусту) to pickle; *(молоко)* to sour

▶ **заква́ситься (** *impf* **заква́шиваться)** *сов возв*
(см перех) to be pickled; to be soured.

заква́ск|а (-и) *ж (для теста)* leaven; *(для*
кефира) culture.

The spelling rules for Russian are shown on page xvii.

заква́шива|ть(ся) (-ю(сь)) несов от
заква́сить(ся).

заква́шу(сь) сов см **заква́сить(ся).**

закида́ть (-ю; impf **заки́дывать)** сов перех =
заброса́ть.

заки́н|уть (-у, -ешь; impf **заки́дывать)** сов перех
to throw; **судьба́ ~ула меня́ в Шотла́ндию**
fate has brought me to Scotland; **заки́дывать (~**
perf) **у́дочку** to cast a line; (перен: разг) to put
out feelers.

закипе́ть (3sg **-и́т,** 3pl **-я́т,** impf **закипа́ть)** сов
непрех to start to boil; (перен: работа) to
increase.

заки́с|нуть (-ну, -нешь; pt **-, -ла, -ло,** impf
закиса́ть) сов непрех (тесто, квас) to turn
sour; (перен) to stagnate.

за́кис|ь (-и) ж oxide.

закла́д (-а) м: **в ~е** in pawn; **би́ться** (impf) **об ~**
(разг) to bet.

закла́д|ка (-и) ж (сада, фундамента) laying; (в
книге) bookmark.

закладн|а́я (-о́й; decl like adj) ж mortgage deed.

закла́дыва|ть (-ю) несов от **заложи́ть.**

закл|ева́ть (-юю, -юёшь; impf **заклёвывать)**
сов перех to peek at; (перен: разг) to harass.

закле́|ить (-ю, -ишь; impf **закле́ивать)** сов
перех to seal (up)

▸ **закле́иться** (impf **закле́иваться)** сов возв to
seal.

заклейм|и́ть (-лю́, -и́шь) сов от **клейми́ть.**

заклепа́|ть (-ю; impf **заклёпывать)** сов перех to
rivet.

заклёп|ка (-и) ж (стержень) rivet.

заклёпыва|ть (-ю) несов от **заклепа́ть.**

заклина́ни|е (-я) ср (магические слова)
incantation; (перен: мольба) plea.

заклина́|ть (-ю) несов перех (духов, змея) to
charm; (перен: умолять) to plead with.

заклин|и́ть (-ю, -ишь; impf **закли́нивать)** сов
перех (дверь итп) to jam; **руль ~ило** the wheel
has jammed.

заключа́|ть (-ю) несов от **заключи́ть.**

заключа́|ться (3sg **-ется,** 3pl **-ются)** несов возв:
~ в +prp (состоять в) to lie in; (содержаться
в) to be contained in; (заканчиваться): **~** +instr
to conclude with; **дело́/пробле́ма ~ется в
том, что ...** the point/problem is that ...; **на́ша
цель ~ется в том, что́бы привле́чь
инвести́ции в го́род** our aim is to attract
investment into the city.

заключе́ни|е (-я) ср conclusion; (в тюрьме)
imprisonment, confinement; **в ~** in conclusion;
тюре́мное ~ imprisonment; **находи́ться** (impf)
в ~и to be held in confinement.

заключённ|ая (-ой; decl like adj) ж см
заключённый.

заключённ|ый (-ого; decl like adj) м prisoner.

заключи́тельный прил concluding, final.

заключ|и́ть (-у́, -и́шь; impf **заключа́ть)** сов
перех (соглашение, договор, сделку) to
conclude, seal; **заключа́ть (~** perf) **в себе́** to

compromise; **заключа́ть (~** perf) **контра́кт** to
conclude a contract; **заключа́ть (~** perf) **кого́-н
в тюрьму́** to put sb in prison; **заключа́ть (~** perf)
кого́-н под стра́жу to take sb into custody;
заключа́ть (~ perf) **кого́-н в объя́тия** to
embrace sb.

закля́тый прил: **~ враг** sworn enemy.

зак|ова́ть (-у́ю; impf **зако́вывать)** сов перех to
chain up; (подлеж: лёд) to cover.

закоди́рова|ть (-ую) сов от **коди́ровать.**

закола́чива|ть (-ю) несов от **заколоти́ть.**

заколдо́ван|ный (-, -а, -о) прил enchanted;
заколдо́ванный круг vicious circle.

заколд|ова́ть (-у́ю; impf **заколдо́вывать)** сов
перех to bewitch.

зако́л|ка (-и) ж (для волос) hairpin, hairclip.

закол|оти́ть (-очу́, -о́тишь; impf **закола́чивать)**
сов перех (окна, дом) to board up; (ящик) to nail
up.

зак|оло́ть (-олю́, -о́лешь) сов от **коло́ть** ◆ (impf
зака́лывать) перех (свинью, индейку) to
slaughter; (волосы) to pin up; (галстук,
воротник) to pin back; **у меня́ ~оло́ло в боку́**
I've got a stitch.

заколочу́ сов см **заколоти́ть.**

закомпости́рова|ть (-ую) сов от
компости́ровать.

зако́н (-а) м law; **вне ~а** outside the law;
объявля́ть (объяви́ть perf) **кого́-н вне ~а** to
outlaw sb; **Зако́н Бо́жий** religious education.

зако́нен прил см **зако́нный.**

зако́нность (-и) ж (документа, завещания)
legality; (в стране) law and order.

зако́н|ный (-ен, -на, -но) прил legitimate,
lawful; (право, приём) legal; (документ) valid;
на ~ном основа́нии on a legal basis; **~ным
о́бразом** legally, lawfully; **зако́нный брак/муж**
lawful wedlock/wedded husband.

законода́тел|ь (-я) м legislator; (перен: вкусов,
мнений) arbiter; **~ мод** trendsetter.

законода́тельни|ца (-ы) ж см **законода́тель.**

законода́тельный прил legislative.

законода́тельств|о (-а) ср legislation.

закономе́р|ный (-ен, -на, -но) прил
(результат, явление) predictable; (понятный)
legitimate.

законопа́|тить (-а́чу, -а́тишь; impf
законопа́чивать) сов перех to patch up.

законоположе́ни|е (-я) ср statute.

законопрое́кт (-а) м (полит) bill.

законсерви́р|овать (-ую) сов от
консерви́ровать.

законспекти́р|овать (-ую) сов от
конспекти́ровать.

законтракт|ова́ть (-у́ю; impf
законтракто́вывать) сов перех to sign a
contract for.

зако́нчен|ный (-, -на, -но) прил (мысль,
рассказ) complete; (негодяй, мерзавец) utter.

зако́нч|ить (-у, -ишь; impf **зака́нчивать)** сов
перех to finish, end

▶ **зако́нчиться** (*impf* **зака́нчиваться**) *сов возв* to finish, end.

закопа́ть (**-ю**; *impf* **зака́пывать**) *сов перех* (*деньги, золото итп*) to bury; (*канаву, яму*) to fill in

▶ **закопа́ться** (*impf* **зака́пываться**) *сов возв* (*в землю итп*) to bury o.s.

закоп|ти́ть (**-чу́, -ти́шь**) *сов от* **копти́ть**

▶ **закопти́ться** *сов возв* to be covered in smoke.

закопчённый *прил* (*чайник итп*) charred; (*потолок*) smoke-stained.

закопчу́(сь) *сов см* **закопти́ть(ся)**.

закорене́лый *прил* (*традиции, предрассудки итп*) deep-rooted; (*дурак, кокетка итп*) incorrigible; ~ **престу́пник** hardened criminal.

закорене́|ть (**-ю**) *сов неперех*: ~ **в** +*prp* (*мнении, предрассудках*) to be entrenched in.

зако́р|ки (**-ок**) *мн* (*разг*): **посади́ть кого́-н на** ~ to lift sb onto one's back; **нести́** (*impf*) **кого́-н на** ~**ках** to give sb a piggyback.

закорю́ч|ка (**-ки**; *gen pl* **-ек**) *ж* squiggle.

закосне́|ть (**-ю**) *сов от* **коснеть**.

закостене́лый *прил* stiff.

закостене́|ть (**-ю**) *сов от* **костенеть**.

закоу́л|ок (**-ка**) *м* (*города*) back street *или* alley; (*дома, замка, двора*) nook; **обы́скивать** (**обыска́ть** *perf*) **все** ~**ки** to look in all the nooks and crannies.

закочене́лый *прил* numb.

закочене́|ть (**-ю**) *сов неперех* to go numb.

закрадётся *итп сов см* **закра́сться**.

закра́дыва|ться (*3sg* **-ется**, *3pl* **-ются**) *несов от* **закра́сться**.

закра́|сить (**-шу, -сишь**; *impf* **закра́шивать**) *сов перех* to paint over.

закра́|сться (*3sg* **-адётся**, *3pl* **-аду́тся**, *pt* **-а́лся, -а́лась, -а́лось**, *impf* **закра́дываться**) *сов возв* to creep in.

закра́шива|ть (**-ю**) *несов от* **закра́сить**.

закра́шу *сов см* **закра́сить**.

закрепи́тел|ь (**-я**) *м* (*ФОТО*) fixative.

закреп|и́ть (**-лю́, -и́шь**; *impf* **закрепля́ть**) *сов перех* (*деталь, грунт*) to fasten; (*победу, позицию*) to consolidate; (*ФОТО*) to fix; **закрепля́ть** (~ *perf*) **что-н за кем-н** to secure sth for sb; **закрепля́ть** (~ *perf*) **кого́-н за кем-н** to assign sb to sb

▶ **закрепи́ться** (*impf* **закрепля́ться**) *сов возв* (*деталь, грунт*) to be fastened; (*успехи*) to be consolidated; (*слово, привычка*) to become established; (*ВОЕН*): ~**ся на** +*acc* (*на высоте*) to consolidate one's position on.

закрёп|ка (**-и**) *ж* fastener.

закреплю́(сь) *сов см* **закрепи́ть(ся)**.

закрепля́|ть(ся) (**-ю(сь)**) *несов от* **закрепи́ть(ся)**.

закрепо|сти́ть (**-щу́, -сти́шь**; *impf* **закрепоща́ть**) *сов перех* to enslave.

закрепоще́ни|е (**-я**) *ср* enslavement.

закрепощу́ *сов см* **закрепости́ть**.

закрич|а́ть (**-у́, -и́шь**) *сов неперех* to start shouting.

закро́йщик (**-а**) *м* cutter (*DRESSMAKING*).

закро́йщиц|а (**-ы**) *ж см* **закро́йщик**.

за́кром (**-а**; *nom pl* **-а́**) *м* (*в амбаре*) grain store; *см также* **закрома́**.

закром|а́ (**-о́в**) *мн* (*перен*) breadbasket *ед* (*esp US*), granary *ед*.

закро́ю(сь) *итп сов см* **закры́ть(ся)**.

закругле́ни|е (**-я**) *ср* curve.

закруглён|ный (**-, -на, -но**) *прил* curved, rounded.

закругл|и́ть (**-ю́, -и́шь**; *impf* **закругля́ть**) *сов перех* (*край*) to round off; (*поверхность*) to make round

▶ **закругли́ться** (*impf* **закругля́ться**) *сов возв* to become rounded; (*перен: разг: закончить*) to round off.

закр|ужи́ть (**-ужу́, -у́жишь**) *сов перех*: ~ **кого́-н** (*начать кружить*) (to start) to spin sb round; (*довести до головокружения*) to make sb dizzy

▶ **закружи́ться** *сов возв* (*начать кружиться*) to start spinning; (*ослабеть*) to start to feel dizzy; (*перен: разг: захлопотаться*) to get o.s. into a tizzy; **у меня́** ~**ужи́лась голова́** my head has started spinning.

закр|ути́ть (**-учу́, -у́тишь**; *impf* **закру́чивать**) *сов перех* (*волосы, усы*) to twist; (*верёвку, ленту*) to wind; (*кран*) to turn off; (*гайку*) to screw in

▶ **закрути́ться** (*impf* **закру́чиваться**) *сов возв* (*верёвка, лента*) to wind up; (*перен: разг: захлопотаться*) to get o.s. into a flap.

закрыва́|ть(ся) (**-ю(сь)**) *несов от* **закры́ть(ся)**.

закры́ти|е (**-я**) *ср* (*магазина итп*) closing (time); (*сезона, конкурса*) close.

закры́тый (**-, -а, -о**) *прил* shut, closed; (*no short form; терраса, машина*) enclosed; (*стадион, бассейн*) indoor; (*собрание, заседание*) closed, private; (*перелом, рана*) internal; **в** ~**ом помеще́нии** indoors; **при** ~**ых дверя́х** behind closed doors; **вопро́с закры́т** the matter is closed; **закры́тое голосова́ние** secret vote *или* ballot; **закры́тое мо́ре** inland sea; **закры́тое пла́тье** dress with a high neck; **закры́тый ко́нкурс** closed competition.

закр|ы́ть (**-о́ю, -о́ешь**; *impf* **закрыва́ть**) *сов перех* to close, shut; (*заслонить, накрыть*) to cover (up); (*проход, проезд, границу*) to close (off); (*воду, газ итп*) to shut off; **закрыва́ть** (~ *perf*) **кого́-н в ко́мнате** to shut sb in a room; **закрыва́ть** (~ *perf*) **счёт** to close an account; **закрыва́ть** (~ *perf*) **глаза́ на что-н** to close one's eyes to sth

▶ **закр|ы́ться** (*impf* **закрыва́ться**) *сов возв* to close, shut; (*магазин, предприятие*) to close *или* shut down; (*накрыться*) to cover o.s. up; (*запереться: в доме итп*) to shut o.s. up; (*рана*) to close up.

закули́сн|ый *прил* backstage *опред*; (*перен: интриги, борьба*) behind-the-scenes; **~ая жизнь** off-stage life.

закупи́ть (**-уплю́, -у́пишь**; *impf* **закупа́ть**) *сов перех* (*купить оптом*) to buy up; (*запастись*) to stock up with.

заку́пк|а (**-и**) *ж* purchase.

закуплю́ *сов см* **закупи́ть**.

заку́пор|ить (**-ю, -ишь**; *impf* **заку́поривать**) *сов перех* (*бутылку*) to cork (up); (*бочку*) to seal up.

заку́порк|а (**-и**) *ж* (*см перех*) corking; sealing; (*МЕД: кишечника, сосудов*) blockage; **заку́порка вен** (*МЕД*) embolism.

заку́почн|ый *прил*: **~ая цена́** purchase price.

заку́пщик (**-а**) *м* buyer.

закур|и́ть (**-урю́, -у́ришь**; *impf* **заку́ривать**) *сов перех* to light (up) ♦ *неперех* to start smoking.

закуса́|ть (**-ю**) *сов перех* (*разг*) to bite; **меня́ ~ли комары́** I've been bitten to death by mosquitoes.

закус|и́ть (**-ушу́, -у́сишь**; *impf* **заку́сывать**) *неперех* (*поесть*) to have a bite to eat ♦ *перех*: **~ во́дку/лека́рство** *итп* to have sth to eat with the vodka/medicine; **заку́сывать** (**~** *perf*) **губу́** to bite one's lip; **заку́сывать** (**~** *perf*) **удила́** (*перен*) to take the bit between one's teeth.

заку́ск|а (**-и**) *ж* snack; (*обычно мн: для водки*) zakuska (*мн* zakuski), nibbles *мн*; (*в начале обеда*) hors d'oeuvre; **на~у** (*перен: разг*) for the finale.

заку́сочн|ая (**-ой**; *decl like adj*) *ж* snack bar.

заку́сыва|ть (**-ю**) *несов от* **закуси́ть**.

закута́|ть (**-ю**) *сов от* **ку́тать** ♦ (*impf* **заку́тывать**) *перех* (*ребёнка*) to wrap up; (*ноги итп*) to cover

▶ **закута́ться** *сов от* **ку́таться** ♦ (*impf* **заку́тываться**) *возв* to wrap (o.s.) up.

закуто́к (**-ка́**) *м* (*разг*) dark corner.

заку́тыва|ть(ся) (**-ю(сь)**) *несов от* **закута́ть(ся)**.

закушу́ *сов см* **закуси́ть**.

зал (**-а**) *м* hall; (*в музее, в библиотеке*) room; **зал ожида́ния** waiting room.

зала́|дить (**-жу, -дишь**) *сов* (*не)перех* (*разг*) to harp on (about); (+*infin*) to take to doing.

зала́мыва|ть (**-ю**) *несов от* **заломи́ть**.

залата́|ть (**-ю**) *сов от* **лата́ть**.

зала́я|ть (**-ю**) *сов неперех* to start barking, start to bark.

залёг *итп сов см* **зале́чь**.

залега́|ть (**-ю**) *несов от* **зале́чь**.

заледене́лый *прил* covered in ice; (*пальцы, руки*) icy.

заледене́|ть (**-ю**) *сов неперех* (*дорога*) to ice over; (*перен: пальцы, руки*) to freeze.

залежа́л|ый (**-, -а, -о**) *прил* (*разг*) old.

залежа́|ться (**-у́сь, -и́шься**; *impf* **залёживаться**) *сов возв*: **~ в магази́не/в**

посте́ли to lie in the shop/in bed for too long.

за́леж|ь (**-и**) *ж* (*угля, золота*) seam; (*с.-х.*) fallow land.

зале́з|ть (**-у, -ешь**; *impf* **залеза́ть**) *сов неперех*: **~ на** +*acc* (*на крышу*) to climb onto; (*на дерево, на лестницу*) to climb (up); (*разг*): **~ в** +*acc* (*в квартиру, в магазин*) to break into; **залеза́ть** (**~** *perf*) **кому́-н в карма́н** to pick sb's pockets; **залеза́ть** (**~** *perf*) **в долги́** to get into debt.

зал|епи́ть (**-еплю́, -е́пишь**; *impf* **залепля́ть**) *сов перех* (*дыру, трещину*) to seal up; (*подлеж: снег, грязь*) to plaster; **~** (*perf*) **кому́-н пощёчину** (*разг*) to give sb a slap round the face.

зале|те́ть (**-чу́, -ти́шь**; *impf* **залета́ть**) *сов неперех*: **~ (в** +*acc*) to fly in(to); **залета́ть** (**~** *perf*) **за** +*acc* (*за море, за облака итп*) to fly over; **залета́ть** (**~** *perf*) **далеко́** to fly a long way; (*перен*) to go far; **самолёт ~те́л в Москву́ за горю́чим** the plane stopped off in Moscow for refuelling.

зал|ечи́ть (**-ечу́, -е́чишь**; *impf* **зале́чивать**) *сов перех* (*язву, рану*) to heal; **~** (*perf*) **кого́-н** (*разг*) to make sb feel worse (*by excessive medication*).

▶ **залечи́ться** (*impf* **зале́чиваться**) *сов возв* to heal (up).

залечу́ *сов см* **залете́ть**.

зал|е́чь (**-я́гу, -я́жешь** *итп*, **-я́гут**; *pt* **-ёг, -егла́, -егло́**, *impf* **залега́ть**) *сов неперех* (*в постель*) to lie down; (*в нору*) to retreat; (*укрыться*) to lie low; (*ГЕО: уголь, золото*) to be deposited; **залега́ть** (**~** *perf*) **в заса́де** to lie in wait.

зали́в (**-а**) *м* bay; (*длинный*) gulf.

залива́|ть(ся) (**-ю(сь)**) *несов от* **зали́ть(ся)**.

заливн|о́е (**-о́го**; *decl like adj*) *ср* (*КУЛИН*) fish or meat in aspic.

заливно́й *прил* (*рыба, мясо*) jellied; **заливно́й луг** water meadow.

зал|и́ть (**-ью́, -ьёшь**; *pt* **-и́л, -ила́, -и́ло**, *impf* **залива́ть**) *сов перех* to flood; (*костёр, огонь*) to extinguish; **залива́ть** (**~** *perf*) **руба́шку пи́вом** to spill beer on one's shirt; **залива́ть** (**~** *perf*) **бензи́н в маши́ну** to fill a car with petrol; **залива́ть** (**~** *perf*) **доро́гу асфа́льтом** to cover a road with asphalt; **залива́ть** (**~** *perf*) **го́ре** to drown one's sorrows; **слёзы ~и́ли его́ лицо́** the tears poured down her face

▶ **зали́ться** (*impf* **залива́ться**) *сов возв* (*луг, пол*) to be flooded; (*вода*) to seep; **залива́ться** (**~ся** *perf*) **слеза́ми/сме́хом** to burst into tears/ out laughing; **её лицо́ ~и́лось румя́нцем** the colour flooded into her cheeks.

зало́г (**-а**) *м* (*действие: вещей*) pawning; (*: квартиры*) mortgaging; (*заложенная вещь*) security; (*линг: активный, пассивный*) voice; (*перен: знак*) token.

зал|ожи́ть (**-ожу́, -о́жишь**; *impf* **закла́дывать**) *сов перех* (*покрыть*) to clutter up; (*отметить*) to mark; (*отдать в залог: кольцо, шубу*) to pawn; (*: дом*) to mortgage; (*заполнить: трубу, дыру*) to block up; **закла́дывать** (**~** *perf*) **что-н**

за что-н to put sth behind sth; **заклáдывать (~** *perf)* **гóрод** to lay the foundations of a city; **у менá ~ожúло нóс/гóрло** *(разг)* my nose/throat is all bunged up.

залóжник (-а) *м* hostage.

залóжниц|а (-ы) *ж см* **залóжник.**

зал|омúть (-омлю́, -óмишь; *impf* **залáмывать)** *сов перех* to tear off; **залáмывать (~** *perf)* **рýки** to throw up one's hands; **залáмывать (~** *perf)* **высóкую цéну** to ask too high a price.

залп (-а) *м* salvo *(мн* salvoes), volley.

зáлпом *нареч (разг: проглотить, проговорить)* all in one go; **вы́стрелить** *(perf)* **~** to fire a volley *или* salvo of bullets.

залы́син|а (-ы) *ж* bald patch.

залью́(сь) *итп сов см* **залúть(ся).**

залюб|овáться (-у́юсь) *сов возв (+instr; картиной, девушкой)* to be transfixed by.

заля́гу *итп сов см* **залéчь.**

заля́жешь *итп сов см* **залéчь.**

заля́п|ать (-ю; *impf* **заля́пывать)** *сов перех (разг)* to mess up.

зам (-а) *м сокр (разг:* = **заместúтель)** number two.

зам. *м сокр (* = **заместúтель)** dep. (= *deputy).*

зам- *префикс* deputy.

замá|зать (-жу, -жешь; *impf* **замáзывать)** *сов перех (пятно, рисунок)* to paint over; *(окна, щели)* to fill with putty; *(запачкать)* to smear

▶ **замáзаться** *(impf* **замáзываться)** *сов возв:* **~ся** *(+instr)* to become smeared (with).

замáзк|а (-и) *ж* putty.

замáзыва|ть(ся) (-ю(сь)) *несов от* **замáзать(ся).**

замáлчива|ть (-ю) *несов от* **замолчáть.**

зам|áнить (-аню́, -áнишь; *impf* **замáнивать)** *сов перех* to lure, entice.

замáнчив|ый (-, -а, -о) *прил* tempting.

замарá|ть(ся) (-ю(сь)) *сов от* **марáть(ся).**

замарин|овáть (-у́ю) *сов от* **маринóвать.**

замаскирóван|ный (-, -а, -о) *прил* disguised; *(намёк, угроза)* veiled.

замаскир|овáть (-у́ю; *impf* **замаскирóвывать** *или* **маскировáть)** *сов перех* to disguise; *(самолёт, танк)* to camouflage

▶ **замаскировáться** *(impf* **замаскирóвываться** *или* **маскировáться)** *сов возв* to disguise o.s.; *(солдаты)* to camouflage o.s.

замáтыва|ть(ся) (-ю(сь)) *несов от* **замотáть(ся).**

зам|ахáть (-ашу́, -áшешь) *сов неперех (+instr; палкой, газетой итп)* to brandish; **~** *(perf)* **рукóй** to start waving.

замахн|у́ться (-у́сь, -ёшься; *impf* **замáхиваться)** *сов возв:* **~ на** *+acc (на собаку, на ребёнка)* to raise one's hand to; *(перен)* to set one's sights on; **он ~у́лся на бóльшее** he has

set his sights on bigger and better things.

замáчива|ть (-ю) *несов от* **замочúть.**

замáшк|и (-ек) *мн* manners *мн.*

замбúйск|ий (-ая, -ое, -ие) *прил* Zambian.

Зáмби|я (-и) *ж* Zambia.

замедлéни|е (-я) *ср* slowing down; **без ~я** without delay.

замéдленный *прил* retarded; **~ ход** reduced speed.

замéдл|ить (-ю, -ишь; *impf* **замедля́ть)** *сов перех* to slow down; *(no impf; задержаться):* **~ с** *+instr* to be slow with; **не ~** *(perf)* +*infin* to be quick to do

▶ **замéдлиться** *(impf* **замедля́ться)** *сов возв* to slow down.

замёл *итп сов см* **заместú.**

замéн|а (-ы) *ж* replacement; *(СПОРТ)* substitution.

заменúм|ый (-, -а, -о) *прил* replaceable.

заменúтел|ь (-я) *м (суррогат)* substitute.

зам|енúть (-еню́, -éнишь; *impf* **заменя́ть)** *сов перех* to replace; **онá ~енúла им мать** she was like a mother to them.

зам|ерéть (-ру́, -рёшь; *pt* **-ер, -ерлá, -ерло,** *impf* **замирáть)** *сов неперех (человек, животное)* to stop dead; *(перен: душа, сердце)* to stand still; *(: работа, страна)* to come to a standstill; *(звук)* to die away; *(шум, стрельба)* to die down; **~** *(perf)* **на мéсте** to stop dead in one's tracks.

замерзáни|е (-я) *ср* freezing; **тóчка ~я** freezing point.

замёрз|нуть (-ну, -нешь; *pt* **-, -ла, -ло,** *impf* **замерзáть)** *сов неперех* to freeze; *(река)* to freeze (up); *(окно)* to ice up; **я совсéм замёрз** I'm completely frozen.

замéр|ить (-ю, -ишь; *impf* **замеря́ть)** *сов перех* to measure.

зáмертво *нареч:* **упáсть** *или* **рýхнуть ~** to collapse in a heap.

замеря́|ть (-ю) *несов от* **замéрить.**

зам|есúть (-ешу́, -éсишь; *impf* **замéшивать)** *сов перех (бетон, глину)* to mix up; *(тесто)* to knead.

зам|естú (-ету́, -етёшь; *pt* **-ёл, -елá, -елó,** *impf* **заметáть)** *сов перех (мусор, листья)* to sweep up; *(подлеж: метель: дорогу итп)* to cover; **заметáть (~** *perf)* **следы́** *(также перен)* to cover one's tracks.

заместúтел|ь (-я) *м* replacement; *(должность)* deputy; **~ дирéктора/премьéр-минúстра** deputy director/prime minister.

заместúтельниц|а (-ы) *ж см* **заместúтель.**

заме|стúть (-щу́, -стúшь) *сов от* **замещáть.**

заметá|ть (-ю) *несов от* **заместú.**

заметá|ться (-чу́сь, -чешься) *сов возв (в кровати, в бреду)* to start tossing and turning; *(в отчаянии)* to get into a state; **он ~тáлся по**

ко́мнате he began to rush about the room.
заме́тен *прил см* **заме́тный**.
заме́|тить (-чу, -тишь; *impf* **замеча́ть**) *сов перех* to notice; (*запомнить*) to take note of; (*сказать*) to remark.
заме́т|ка (-ки; *gen pl* -ок) *ж* (*на дереве итп*) mark, notch; (*в записной книжке итп*) note; (*в газете итп*) short piece *или* article; **брать** (**взять** *perf*) **что-н на ~ку** to make a (mental) note of sth; **он на ~ке у мили́ции** (*разг*) the police have got their eye on him.
заме́тно *нареч* noticeably ♦ *как сказ* (*видно*) it is obvious.
заме́т|ный (-ен, -на, -но) *прил* noticeable; (*личность, человек*) prominent.
замету́ *итп сов см* **замести́**.
замеча́ни|е (-я) *ср* comment, remark; (*выговор*) reprimand.
замеча́телен *прил см* **замеча́тельный**.
замеча́тельно *нареч* (*красив, умён*) extremely; (*писать*) wonderfully, brilliantly ♦ *как сказ*: ~! that's brilliant *или* wonderful!
замеча́тельный (-ен, -ьна, -ьно) *прил* (*очень хороший*) wonderful, brilliant; (*необыкновенный*) remarkable; (*выдающийся*) outstanding.
замеча́|ть (-ю) *несов от* **заме́тить**.
замеча́ться (-юсь) *сов возв* to start daydreaming.
замечу́ *сов см* **заме́тить**.
замечу́сь *итп сов см* **замета́ться**.
замеша́тельств|о (-а) *ср* confusion; **приводи́ть** (**привести́** *perf*) **кого́-н в ~** to throw sb into confusion; **приходи́ть** (**прийти́** *perf*) **в ~** to become confused.
замеша́|ть (-ю; *impf* **заме́шивать**) *сов перех*: ~ **кого́-н во что-н** to get sb mixed up in sth
▸ **замеша́ться** (*impf* **заме́шиваться**) *сов возв*: ~**ся в** +*acc* (*в историю, в преступление*) to get mixed up in; (*скрыться: в толпе*) to mingle with.
заме́шива|ть (-ю) *несов от* **замеси́ть**, **замеша́ть**
▸ **заме́шиваться** *несов от* **замеша́ться**.
заме́шка|ть (-ю) *сов от* **ме́шкать**
▸ **заме́шкаться** *сов возв* (*разг: с работой, с ответом*) to drag one's heels; (: *пробыть дольше*) to faff about.
замещу́ *сов см* **замести́ть**.
замеща́|ть (-ю) *несов перех* (*начальника итп*) to stand in *или* deputize for; (*perf* **замести́ть**; *заменять: работника итп*) to replace; (: *игрока*) to substitute; (*вакантную должность*) to fill.
замеще́ни|е (-я) *ср* (*работника, директора*) replacement; (*игрока*) substitution; ~ **вака́нтной до́лжности** filling of a vacancy.
замещу́ *сов см* **замести́ть**.
замина́|ть(ся) (-ю(сь)) *несов от* **замя́ть(ся)**.
замини́р|овать (-ую) *сов от* **мини́ровать**.
зами́нк|а (-и) *ж* (*в работе*) hitch; (*в речи*)

stumble.
замира́|ть (-ю) *несов от* **замере́ть**.
за́мка *сущ см* **за́мок**.
замка́ *сущ см* **замо́к**.
за́мкнут|ый (-, -а, -о) *прил* (*среда, жизнь*) cloistered; (*человек, характер*) reclusive; **за́мкнутая цепь** (*ЭЛЕК*) closed circuit; **за́мкнутый круг** vicious circle.
замкн|у́ть (-у́, -ёшь; *impf* **замыка́ть**) *сов перех* to close
▸ **замкну́ться** (*impf* **замыка́ться**) *сов возв* to close; (*перен: обособиться*) to shut o.s. off; **замыка́ться** (~**ся** *perf*) **в себе́** to withdraw into o.s.
замну́(сь) *итп сов см* **замя́ть(ся)**.
замоги́льный *прил*: ~ **го́лос** ghostly voice.
за́м|ок (-ка) *м* castle.
зам|о́к (-ка́) *м* lock; (*также: вися́чий* ~) padlock; (*браслета, цепочки*) clasp; **на** ~ке́ locked; **под** ~**ко́м** under lock and key; **храни́ть** (*impf*) **что-н за семью́** ~**ка́ми** to keep sth very closely guarded.
замо́к|нуть (*3sg* -нет, *pt* -, -ла, -ло, *impf* **замока́ть**) *сов неперех* to get soaked.
замо́лв|ить (-лю, -ишь) *сов перех*: ~ **сло́во за кого́-н** (**пе́ред кем-н**) (*разг*) to put in a word for sb (with sb).
замо́лк|нуть (-ну, -нешь; *pt* -, -ла, -ло, *impf* **замолка́ть**) *сов неперех* to fall silent; (*звук, песня, спор итп*) to stop.
замолч|а́ть (-у́, -и́шь) *сов неперех* (*человек*) to go quiet; (*перестать писать*): **он ~а́л ещё два го́да наза́д** I haven't heard from him for two years ♦ (*impf* **зама́лчивать**) *перех* (*разг: факты, происшествие*) to hush up; ~**й!** be quiet!, shut up!
заморáживани|е (-я) *ср* (*продуктов, овощей*) refrigeration; **заморáживание цен/зáработной плáты** price/wage freeze.
заморáжива|ть (-ю) *несов от* **заморóзить**.
замор|и́ть (-ю́, -и́шь) *сов от* **мори́ть**.
заморó|зить (-жу, -зишь; *impf* **заморáживать**) *сов перех* (*продукты, овощи*) to freeze; (*десну, палец*) to freeze, numb; (*строительство*) to put on hold; **заморáживать** (~ *perf*) **цéны/зарплáту/счёт** to freeze prices/wages/an account.
за́морозк|и (-ов) *мн* frosts *мн*.
заморóч|ить (-у, -ишь) *сов от* **морóчить**.
замóрск|ий (-ая, -ое, -ие) *прил* (*разг*) foreign.
замóрыш (-а) *м* (*разг*) weed, wimp.
замо|сти́ть (-щу́, -сти́шь) *сов от* **мости́ть**.
замóтан|ный (-, -а, -о) *прил* (*разг*) knackered, whacked.
замота́|ть (-ю; *impf* **замáтывать**) *сов перех* (*разг: утомить*) to knacker out; (*верёвку, канат*): ~ **что-н во что-н** to wind sth around sth
▸ **замота́ться** (*impf* **замáтываться**) *сов возв* (*в платок, шарфом*) to bundle o.s. up; (*разг: утомиться*) to be knackered (out).
замощу́ *сов см* **замости́ть**.

зам|очи́ть (**-очу́, -о́чишь**; *impf* **зама́чивать**) *сов перех*: ~ **кого́-н/что-н** to get sb/sth wet; (*бельё, кожу*) to soak.

замру́ *итп сов см* **замере́ть**.

за́муж *нареч*: **выходи́ть** ~ (**за** +*acc*) to get married (to), marry; **выдава́ть** (**вы́дать** *perf*) **кого́-н** ~ (**за** +*acc*) to marry sb off (to).

за́мужем *нареч* married; **быть** (*impf*) ~ **за кем-н** to be married to sb.

заму́жеств|о (**-а**) *ср* marriage.

заму́жн|яя *прил* married ♦ (**-ей**; *decl like adj*) *ж* married woman (*мн* women).

замур|ова́ть (**-у́ю**; *impf* **замуро́вывать**) *сов перех* (*отверстие, окно*) to brick up; (*человека, ценности*) to brick in.

замути́ть(ся) (**-чу́(сь), -ти́шь(ся)**) *сов от* **мути́ть(ся)**.

заму́ч|ить (**-у, -ишь**) *сов от* **му́чить** ♦ *перех* (*заставить страдать*) to torment; (*утомить*) to exhaust; (*до смерти*) to torture to death

▸ **заму́читься** *сов от* **му́читься** ♦ *возв* (*утомиться*) to exhaust o.s.

замучу́(сь) *сов см* **замути́ть(ся)**.

за́мш|а (**-и**) *ж* suede.

за́мшевый *прил* suede.

замше́лый *прил* mossy, moss-covered.

замыва́|ть (**-ю**) *несов от* **замы́ть**.

замыка́ни|е (**-я**) *ср* (*также*: **коро́ткое** ~) short circuit.

замыка́|ть (**-ю**) *несов от* **замкну́ть** ♦ *перех* (*колонну, шествие*) to bring up the rear of

▸ **замыка́ться** *несов от* **замкну́ться**.

за́мыс|ел (**-ла**) *м* (*человека, правительства*) scheme; (*картины, произведения*) idea.

замы́сл|ить (**-ю, -ишь**; *impf* **замышля́ть**) *сов перех* (*план, побег*) to think up; (+*infin*) to think about doing; **он ~ил купи́ть себе́ дом** he is thinking about buying a house.

замыслова́т|ый (**-, -а, -о**) *прил* intricate.

зам|ы́ть (**-о́ю, -о́ешь**; *impf* **замыва́ть**) *сов перех* to wash out.

замышля́|ть (**-ю**) *несов от* **замы́слить**.

зам|я́ть (**-ну́, -нёшь**; *impf* **замина́ть**) *сов перех* (*разг: сделать незаметным: вопрос*) to hush up; (: *приостановить: разговор*) to put an end *или* a stop to

▸ **замя́ться** (*impf* **замина́ться**) *сов возв* to clam up; (*разг: замолчать*) to stop short.

за́навес (**-а**) *м* (*ТЕАТР*) curtain; **желе́зный** ~ (*ИСТ*) the Iron Curtain.

занаве́|сить (**-шу, -сишь**; *impf* **занаве́шивать**) *сов перех* to hang a curtain over.

занаве́с|ка (**-ки**; *gen pl* **-ок**) *ж* curtain.

занаве́шива|ть (**-ю**) *несов от* **занаве́сить**.

занаве́шу *сов см* **занаве́сить**.

зана́шива|ть (**-ю**) *несов от* **заноси́ть**.

зан|ести́ (**-есу́, -есёшь**; *pt* **-ёс, -есла́, -есло́**, *impf* **заноси́ть**) *сов перех* (*принести*) to bring;

(*поднять: ногу, руку*) to lift; (*записать*) to take down; (*доставить*): ~ **что-н кому́-н** to drop sth off to sb; (*отнести*): ~ **за** +*acc* to take behind; **доро́гу ~есло́ сне́гом** the road is covered over with snow; **судьба́ ~есла́ меня́ сюда́ мно́го лет наза́д** fate brought me here many years ago.

зани|зить (**-жу, -зишь**; *impf* **занижа́ть**) *сов перех* to lower; **занижа́ть** (**занизи́ть** *perf*) **отме́тки кому́-н** to undermark sb.

занима́тельный (**-ен, -ьна, -ьно**) *прил* engaging.

занима́|ть (**-ю**) *несов от* **заня́ть**

▸ **занима́ться** *несов возв*: ~**ся** (+*instr*) (*учиться*) to study; (*работать*) to work (in); (*на рояле итп*) to practise (*BRIT*), practice (*US*); ~**ся** (*impf*) **англи́йским (языко́м)** to study English; ~**ся** (*impf*) **спо́ртом/му́зыкой** to play sports/music; **чем ~ется Ваш оте́ц?** what does your father do (for a living)?; **он ~ется би́знесом/поли́тикой** he's a businessman/politician; **чем ты сейча́с ~ешься?** what are you doing at the moment?

за́ново *нареч* again.

заножу́ *сов см* **занози́ть**.

зано́з|а (**-ы**) *ж* splinter.

зано|зи́ть (**-жу́, -зи́шь**) *сов перех* to get a splinter in.

зано́с (**-а**) *м* (*обычно мн*) drift; **сне́жные ~ы** snowdrift.

зан|оси́ть (**-ошу́, -о́сишь**) *несов от* **занести́** ♦ (*impf* **зана́шивать**) *сов перех* (*платье, пальто итп*) to wear out.

зано́счив|ый (**-, -а, -о**) *прил* arrogant.

заноче|ва́ть (**-у́ю**) *сов неперех* to spend the night.

заношу́ (*не*)*сов см* **заноси́ть**.

зану́д|а (**-ы**) *м/ж* bore.

зану́д|ный (**-ен, -на, -но**) *прил* tiresome, tedious.

зан|ы́ть (**-о́ю, -о́ешь**) *сов неперех* (*ребёнок*) to start whinging; (*сердце, зуб*) to begin to ache.

за́нят (**-, -á, -о**) *прил* busy; **он был о́чень** ~ he was very busy; **телефо́н** ~ the phone *или* line is engaged.

за́нятен *прил см* **заня́тный**.

заня́ти|е (**-я**) *ср* occupation; (*обычно мн: в школе, в институте*) lesson, class; (*времяпрепровождение*) pastime, pursuit; **нача́ло шко́льных ~й** (*начало учебного года*) the beginning of the school year; (*утром*) the beginning of the school day.

заня́т|ный (**-ен, -на, -но**) *прил* entertaining.

занято́й *прил* busy; **он - ~ челове́к** he is a busy man.

за́нятост|ь (**-и**) *ж* (*ЭКОН*) employment; **по́лная** ~ full employment.

зан|я́ть (**займу́, займёшь**; *pt* **-я́л, -яла́, -я́ло**, *impf* **занима́ть**) *сов перех* (*квартиру, город*) to occupy; (*должность, позицию*) to take up;

(*де́ньги*) to borrow; (*вре́мя*) to take; (*развле́чь*)
to occupy; ~ (*perf*) **ме́сто кому́-н** to keep a place
for sb; **все ~яли́ свои́ места́** everyone took
their places; ~ (*perf*) **пе́рвое/второ́е ме́сто** to
take first/second place; **э́та рабо́та ~яла́ (у
меня́) два часа́** the work took (me) two hours;
э́то займёт всего́ одну́ мину́тку it will only
take a minute
▸ **заня́ться** *сов возв*: **~ся** +*instr* (*языко́м,
предме́том, спо́ртом*) to go into; (*би́знесом,
поли́тикой*) to go into; (*помо́чь*): **~ся с кем-н
(чем-н)** to assist sb with sth; **~ся** (*perf*)
собо́й/детьми́ to devote time to o.s./one's
children; **~ся** (*perf*) **убо́ркой** to do the cleaning;
ему́ пора́ ~ся де́лом it's time that he did
something serious with his life.
заобла́чный *прил* lofty.
заодно́ *нареч* (*вме́сте*) as one; (*попу́тно*) at the
same time; **де́йствовать** (*impf*) ~ to act as one
или with one accord; **мы с ни́ми** ~ we are in
total accord.
заостри́ть (**-ю́, -и́шь**; *impf* **заостря́ть**) *сов
перех* (*копьё, каранда́ш*) to sharpen; (*перен:
мысль, вопро́с*) to define; **заостря́ть** (~ *perf*)
внима́ние на чём-н to focus one's attention on
sth
▸ **заостри́ться** (*impf* **заостря́ться**) *сов возв*
(*черты́ лица́*) to become more pointed.
зао́чник (**-а**) *м* part-time student (*studying by
correspondence*).
зао́чни|ца (**-ы**) *ж см* **зао́чник**.
зао́чно *нареч*: **учи́ться** ~ to study part-time (*by
correspondence*); **обсужда́ть** (*impf*) **кого́-н** ~ to
discuss sb in his *отп* absence.
зао́чный *прил* part-time; **зао́чное обуче́ние**
distance learning; **зао́чный институ́т**
correspondence school.
за́пад (**-а**) *м* west; **З~** (*ПОЛИТ*) the West.
запада́ть (*3sg* **-ет**, *3pl* **-ют**) *несов от* **запа́сть**.
западёт *итп сов см* **запа́сть**.
за́падник (**-а**) *м* westernizer.
западноевропе́йск|ий (**-ая, -ое, -ие**) *прил*
West European.
за́падный *прил* western; (*ве́тер*) westerly.
западн|я́ (**-и́**) *ж* snare; (*перен*) trap.
запа́ива|ть (**-ю**) *несов от* **запая́ть**.
запак|ова́ть (**-у́ю**) *сов от* **пакова́ть** ♦ (*impf*
запако́вывать) *перех* to wrap up.
запа́ко|стить (**-щу, -стишь**) *сов от* **па́костить**.
запа́л (**-а**) *м* (*заря́да*) fuse; (*разг: пыл*) fire (*fig*).
запа́льчив|ый (**-, -а, -о**) *прил* (*челове́к,
хара́ктер*) quick-tempered; (*отве́т, тон*)
impatient.
запанибра́та *нареч* (*разг*): **обраща́ться** ~ **с
кем-н** to be overly familiar with sb.
запаник|ова́ть (**-у́ю**) *сов неперех* (*разг*) to
panic.
запа́рк|а (**-и**) *ж* (*разг*) mad rush.
запа́рыва|ть (**-ю**) *несов от* **запоро́ть**.
запа́с (**-а**) *м* (*проду́ктов, то́плива итп*) store,
supply; (*руды́, поле́зных ископа́емых*) deposit;

(*перен: зна́ний*) store; (*на брю́ках, на пла́тье*)
hem; (*ВОЕН*) the reserves *мн*; **у меня́ два часа́ в
~е** I've got two hours to spare; **оставля́ть
(оста́вить** *perf*) **себе́ что-н про** ~ to put sth by;
золото́й ~ gold reserves *мн*; **запа́с слов**
vocabulary.
запаса́|ть(ся) (**-ю(сь)**) *несов от* **запасти́(сь)**.
запа́сливый (**-, -а, -о**) *прил* thrifty.
запа́сник (**-а**) *м* (*в музе́е*) storage room; (*разг:
ВОЕН*) reserve.
запасн|о́й *прил* spare ♦ (**-о́го**; *decl like adj*) *м*
(*СПОРТ: та́кже:* ~ **игро́к**) substitute; (*ВОЕН*)
reservist; **запасно́й вы́ход** emergency exit;
запасно́й путь siding; **запасно́й соста́в** (*ВОЕН*)
the reserves.
запа́сный *прил* = **запасно́й**.
запа|сти́ (**-су́, -сёшь**; *pt* **-с, -сла́, -сло́**, *impf*
запаса́ть) *сов перех* (*дрова́, то́пливо*) to lay in
▸ **запасти́сь** (*impf* **запаса́ться**) *сов возв*: **~сь**
(+*instr*) (*хле́бом, молоко́м*) to stock up (on);
запаса́ться (**~сь** *perf*) **терпе́нием** to arm o.s.
with patience.
запа́|сть (*3sg* **-дёт**, *3pl* **-ду́т**, *pt* **-л, -ла, -ло**, *impf*
запада́ть) *сов неперех* (*глаза́, щёки*) to become
sunken; (*перен: фра́за, слова́*) to be imprinted;
его́ слова́ ~ли мне в па́мять his words remain
imprinted on my memory.
запатент|ова́ть (**-у́ю**) *сов от* **патентова́ть** ♦
(*impf* **запатенто́вывать**) *перех* to patent.
за́пах (**-а**; *part gen* **-у**) *м* smell.
запа́х (**-а**) *м* (*хала́та, пальто́*) fold.
запа́хива|ть (**-ю**) *несов от* **запахну́ть**.
запа́х|нуть (**-ну, -нешь**; *pt* **-, -ла, -ло**) *сов
неперех*: ~ (+*instr*) to start to smell (of).
запахну́ть (**-у́, -ёшь**; *impf* **запа́хивать**) *сов
перех* to wrap round.
запа́чка|ть (**-ю**) *сов от* **па́чкать** ♦ *перех* to soil,
dirty; (*перен: со́весть, и́мя*) to tarnish, sully
▸ **запа́чкаться** *сов от* **па́чкаться** ♦ *возв* to get
dirty.
запая́|ть (**-ю**; *impf* **запа́ивать**) *сов перех* to
solder.
запева́л|а (**-ы**) *м/ж* (*МУЗ*) leader (*of a song*).
запева́|ть (**-ю**) *несов неперех* to lead off ♦
перех: ~ **пе́сню** to start up a song.
запе́й(те) *сов см* **запи́ть**.
запёк|ся итп *сов см* **запе́чь(ся)**.
запека́нк|а (**-и**) *ж* (*карто́фельная итп*) bake;
(*сла́дкая*) baked pudding.
запека́|ть(ся) (**-ю(сь)**) *несов от* **запе́чь(ся)**.
запеку́(сь) итп сов см **запе́чь(ся)**.
запелена́|ть (**-ю**) *сов от* **пелена́ть**.
запеленг|ова́ть (**-у́ю**) *сов от* **пеленгова́ть**.
запе|ре́ть (**-ру́, -рёшь**; *pt* **-ер, -ерла́, -ерло́**, *impf*
запира́ть) *сов перех* (*дверь, шкаф, замо́к*) to
lock; (*дом, челове́ка, де́ньги*) to lock up
▸ **запере́ться** (*impf* **запира́ться**) *сов возв*
(*дверь, шкаф, замо́к*) to lock; (*челове́к*) to lock
o.s. up; (*разг: не призна́ться*) to clam up.
запе́|ть (**-о́ю, -о́ешь**) *сов перех*: ~ **пе́сню** to start
singing a song.

запеча́та|ть (-ю; *impf* **запеча́тывать**) *сов перех*
to seal up.

запечатле́|ть (-ю; *impf* **запечатлева́ть**) *сов
перех* (*на картине, в повести итп*) to capture;
(*в памяти*) to impress

▶ **запечатле́ться** (*impf* **запечатлева́ться**) *сов
возв*: **~ся в па́мяти** to be imprinted on one's
memory.

запеча́тыва|ть (-ю) *несов от* **запеча́тать**.

запе́|чь (-еку́, -ечёшь итп, -еку́т; *pt* -ёк, -екла́,
-екло́, *impf* **запека́ть**) *сов перех* to bake

▶ **запе́чься** (*impf* **запека́ться**) *сов возв* to bake;
(*кровь*) to congeal; (*губы, рот*) to become
parched.

запива́|ть (-ю) *несов от* **запи́ть**.

запина́|ться (-юсь) *несов от* **запну́ться**.

запи́н|ка (-ки; *gen pl* -ок) *ж* hesitation; **без ~ки**
smoothly.

запира́тельств|о (-а) *ср* obstinacy.

запира́|ть(ся) (-ю(сь)) *несов от* **запере́ть(ся)**.

запи|са́ть (-ишу́, -и́шешь; *impf* **запи́сывать**) *сов
перех* (*адрес, имя итп*) to write down;
(*концерт, пластинку*) to record; (*в кружок, на
курсы*) to enrol; **запи́сывать (~** *perf*) **ле́кцию** to
take notes (*in a lecture*); **~** (*perf*) **кого́-н (на
приём) к врачу́** to make a doctor's appointment
for sb

▶ **записа́ться** (*impf* **запи́сываться**) *сов возв* (*в
кружок, на курсы*) to enrol (o.s.); (*музыкант: на
плёнку*) to make a recording; **~ся** (*perf*) **(на
приём) к врачу́** to make a doctor's appointment.

за́пис|и (-ей) *мн* (*лекции итп*) notes *мн*.

запи́ск|а (-и) *ж* note; (*служебная*) memo; *см
также* **запи́ски**.

запи́ск|и (-ок) *мн* (*короткие записи*) jottings *мн*;
(*ЛИТЕРАТУРА*) notes *мн*, sketches *мн*.

записн|о́й *прил*: **~а́я кни́жка** notebook.

запи́сок *сущ см* **запи́ски**.

запи́сыва|ть(ся) (-ю(сь)) *несов от*
записа́ть(ся).

за́пис|ь (-и) *ж* (*событий, КОМП*) record; (*в
дневнике*) entry; (*МУЗ*) recording; (*в кружок, на
курсы*) enrolment (*BRIT*), enrollment (*US*); (*на
приём к врачу*) registration; *см также* **за́писи**.

запи́|ть (-ью́, -ьёшь; *pt* -и́л, -ила́, -и́ло, *imper*
-е́й(те), *impf* **запива́ть**) *сов перех* (*лекарство,
обед*): **~ что-н (чем-н)** to wash sth down (with
sth) ◆ (*pt* -ил,-ила́,-ило) *неперех* (*начать
пить*) to take to drink.

запиха́|ть (-ю; *impf* **запи́хивать**) *сов перех*: **~
что-н в** +*acc* (*разг*) to stuff sth into.

запихн|у́ть (-у́, -ёшь) *сов* = **запиха́ть**.

запишу́(сь) *итп сов см* **записа́ть(ся)**.

запла́кан|ный (-, -а, -о) *прил* tearful; (*глаза*)
puffy.

запла́|кать (-чу, -чешь) *сов неперех* to start
crying *или* to cry.

заплани́р|овать (-ую) *сов перех* to plan.

запла́т|а (-ы) *ж* patch.

запла|ти́ть (-чу́, -а́тишь) *сов от* **плати́ть**.

запла́т|ка (-ки; *gen pl* -ок) *ж* = **запла́та**.

заплачу́ *итп сов см* **запла́кать**.

заплачу́ *сов см* **заплати́ть**.

заппл|ева́ть (-юю́; *impf* **заплёвывать**) *сов перех*
(*пол итп*) to spit on; (*человека*) to spit at.

заплёл *итп сов см* **заплести́**.

заплесневе́лый *прил* mouldy (*BRIT*), moldy
(*US*).

заплесневе́|ть (*3sg* -ет, *3pl* -ют) *сов от*
пле́сневеть.

запл|ести́ (-ету́, -етёшь; *pt* -ёл, -ела́, -ело́, *impf*
заплета́ть) *сов перех* (*волосы, косу*) to plait.

заплета́|ться (*3sg* -ется, *3pl* -ются) *несов возв*:
у него́ но́ги ~ются he keeps tripping over his
feet; **у неё язы́к ~ется** she is muddling her
words.

заплету́ *итп сов см* **заплести́**.

запломбир|ова́ть (-у́ю) *сов от*
пломбирова́ть.

заплы́в (-а) *м* (*СПОРТ*) race (*in swimming*);
(: *отборочный*) heat.

заплы́|ть (-ву́, -вёшь; *impf* **заплыва́ть**) *сов
неперех* (*человек*) to swim off; (*корабль*) to sail
off; (*бревно*) to float off; (*глаза*) to become
swollen.

запн|у́ться (-у́сь, -ёшься; *impf* **запина́ться**) *сов
возв* to falter, stumble.

запове́дник (-а) *м* (*природный*) nature reserve;
пти́чий ~ bird reserve.

запове́дный *прил* (*лес, территория*)
protected.

за́повед|ь (-и) *ж* (*РЕЛ*) commandment; (*перен*)
cardinal rule; **де́сять ~ей** the Ten
Commandments.

заподо́зр|ить (-ю, -ишь) *сов перех* to suspect;
~ (*perf*) **кого́-н в** +*acc* to suspect sb of.

запо́ем *нареч*: **пить ~** to drink heavily; **он
чита́ет ~** (*разг*) he's an avid reader.

запозда́лый *прил* (*помощь, тревога итп*)
belated; (*гость, весна*) late.

запо́|й (-я) *м* binge.

заполз|ти́ (-у́, -ёшь; *impf* **заполза́ть**) *сов
неперех* to crawl.

заполне́ни|е (-я) *ср* (*бака, резервуара*) filling;
(*анкеты, бланка*) completion.

заполн|ить (-ю, -ишь; *impf* **заполня́ть**) *сов
перех* (*бак, комнату*) to fill (up); (*анкету,
бланк*) to fill in *или* out

▶ **запо́лниться** (*impf* **заполня́ться**) *сов возв* to
fill up.

заполя́рный *прил* polar.

запомина́|ть (-ю) *несов от* **запо́мнить**

▶ **запомина́ться** *несов от* **запо́мниться**;
легко́/тру́дно ~ся (*impf*) to be easy/difficult to
remember.

запомина́ющий (-ая, -ее, -ие) *прил* (*КОМП*):

~ее устро́йство memory; ~ее устро́йство с произво́льной вы́боркой random access memory.

запо́мн|ить (-ю, -ишь; *impf* запомина́ть) *сов перех* to remember

▶ **запо́мниться** (*impf* запомина́ться) *сов возв*: мне ~ились его́ слова́ I remembered his words.

за́понк|а (-и) *ж* cuff link.

запо́р (-а) *м* (МЕД) constipation; (*замок*) lock; **быть** (*impf*) **на** ~**е** to be locked.

запор|о́ть (-орю́, -о́решь; *impf* запа́рывать) *сов перех* (*разг: испо́ртить*) to botch up.

запоро́ш|ить (*3sg* -ит) *сов перех безл* to sprinkle; **доро́гу** ~**и́ло сне́гом** a sprinkling of snow covered the road.

запотева́|ть (-ю) *несов от* запоте́ть.

запоте́вш|ий (-ая, -ее, -ие) *прил* misty.

запоте́|ть (-ю; *impf* запотева́ть) *сов неперех* to steam up.

запою́ *итп сов см* запе́ть.

запра́в|ить (-лю, -ишь; *impf* заправля́ть) *сов перех* (*руба́шку*) to tuck in; (*ла́мпу*) to fill; (*сала́т*) to dress; **заправля́ть** (~ *perf*) **маши́ну** to fill up the engine

▶ **запра́виться** (*impf* заправля́ться) *сов возв* (*разг: горю́чим*) to tank up; (: *пое́сть*) to fuel up.

запра́в|ка (-ки; *gen pl* -ок) *ж* (*маши́ны, самолёта итп*) refuelling; (*КУЛИН*) dressing; (*разг: также*: ~**очная ста́нция**) filling station.

запра́влю(сь) *сов см* запра́вить(ся).

заправля́|ть (-ю) *несов от* запра́вить ♦ *неперех*: ~ (+*instr*) (*разг: дела́ми итп*) to be in charge (of)

▶ **заправля́ться** *несов возв от* запра́виться.

запра́вок *сущ см* запра́вка.

запра́вск|ий (-ая, -ое, -ие) *прил* true, real.

запра́шива|ть (-ю) *несов от* запроси́ть.

запре́т (-а) *м*: ~ (**на** +*acc*/+*infin*) ban (on/on doing); **быть** (*impf*) **под** ~**ом** to be banned.

запре́тен *прил см* запре́тный.

запре|ти́ть (-щу́, -ти́шь; *impf* запреща́ть) *сов перех* to ban.

запре́т|ный (-ен, -на, -но) *прил* forbidden; ~**ная те́ма** taboo subject; **запре́тная зо́на** restricted area *или* zone; **запре́тный плод** forbidden fruit.

запреща́|ть (-ю) *несов от* запрети́ть

▶ **запреща́ться** *несов возв* to be forbidden *или* prohibited.

запреще́ни|е (-я) *ср* banning.

запрещённ|ый (-, -а, -о) *прил* banned; **запрещённый приём** (*СПОРТ*) foul; (*перен*) underhand tactic.

запрещу́ *сов см* запрети́ть.

запрограмми́р|овать (-ую) *сов от* программи́ровать.

запроекти́р|овать (-ую) *сов от* проекти́ровать.

запроки́н|уть (-у, -ешь; *impf* запроки́дывать) *сов перех*: ~ **го́лову** to throw one's head back

▶ **запроки́нуться** (*impf* запроки́дываться) *сов возв* to jerk backwards.

запропа|сти́ться (-щу́сь, -сти́шься) *сов неперех* (*разг*) to disappear.

запро́с (-а) *м* inquiry; (*обычно мн: тре́бования*) need, requirement; (*стремле́ния*) expectation.

запр|оси́ть (-ошу́, -о́сишь; *impf* запра́шивать) *сов перех* (*мне́ние, отве́т итп*) to request; (*це́ну*) to ask.

за́просто *нареч* (*разг: без уси́лий*) easily; (*без церемо́ний*) without making a fuss; **он обы́чно захо́дит к нам** ~ he usually just drops in.

запротест|ова́ть (-у́ю) *сов неперех* to start protesting.

запротоколи́р|овать (-ую) *сов от* протоколи́ровать.

запрошу́ *сов см* запроси́ть.

запру́(сь) *итп сов см* запере́ть(ся).

запру́д|а (-ы) *ж* (*плоти́на*) weir; (*водоём*) millpond.

запр|уди́ть (-ужу́, -у́дишь; *impf* запру́живать *или* пруди́ть) *сов перех* (*ре́ку, руче́й*) to dam; (*impf* запру́живать; *перен: пло́щадь итп*) to pack.

запры́га|ть (-ю) *сов неперех* to start jumping.

запр|я́чь (-ягу́, -яжёшь итп, -ягу́т; *pt* -я́г, -ягла́, -ягло́, *impf* запряга́ть) *сов перех* (*ло́шадь*) to harness, hitch up; (*разг: нагрузи́ть рабо́той*) to weigh down.

запу́ганн|ый (-, -на, -но) *прил* frightened, scared.

запуга́|ть (-ю; *impf* запу́гивать) *сов перех* to frighten, scare.

за́пуск (-а) *м* (*мото́ра, станка́*) starting; (*раке́ты, спу́тника*) launch.

запуска́|ть (-ю) *несов от* запусти́ть.

запусте́ни|е (-я) *ср* neglect.

запу|сти́ть (-щу́, -у́стишь; *impf* запуска́ть) *сов перех* (*бро́сить*) to hurl; (*мото́р, стано́к*) to start (up); (*раке́ту, спу́тник*) to launch; (*хозя́йство, рабо́ту, боле́знь*) to neglect; (*разг: ру́ку, ко́гти*) to plunge; (: *впусти́ть*) to let in ♦ *неперех*: ~ **чем-н в кого́-н** to hurl sth at sb; **запуска́ть** (~ *perf*) **что-н в произво́дство** to launch production of sth.

запу́танн|ый (-, -на, -но) *прил* (*ни́тки, во́лосы*) tangled, entangled; (*де́ло, вопро́с*) confused; (*фра́за*) muddled.

запу́та|ть (-ю) *сов от* пу́тать ♦ (*impf* запу́тывать) *перех* (*ни́тки, во́лосы*) to tangle; (*вопро́с, челове́ка*) to confuse

▶ **запу́таться** *сов от* пу́таться ♦ (*impf* запу́тываться) *возв* (*ни́тки, во́лосы*) to become tangled (up); (*челове́к: в верёвках*) to get tangled *или* caught up; (*де́ло, вопро́с*) to become confused; (*разг: сби́ться с то́лку*) to get o.s. in a tangle; (: *сби́ться с пути́*) to get lost; **запу́тываться** (~**ся** *perf*) **в долга́х** to become trapped in debt; **запу́тываться** (~**ся** *perf*) **в отве́те** to get muddled up.

запу́щенн|ый (-, -на, -но) *прил* neglected.

запущу́ *сов см* **запусти́ть.**

запча́ст|ь (**-и**) *ж сокр* = **запасна́я часть;** (*обычно мн*) spare (part).

запыла́ть (**-ю**) *сов неперех* (*костёр, камин*) to flare up; (*щёки, человек*) to flush.

запыл|и́ть(ся) (**-ю́(сь), -и́шь(ся)**) *сов от* **пыли́ть(ся).**

запыха́ться (**-юсь**) *сов возв* to be out of breath.

запью́ *итп сов см* **запи́ть.**

запя́сть|е (**-ья;** *gen pl* **-ий**) *ср* wrist.

запята́|я (**-ой;** *decl like adj*) *ж* comma.

запятна́ть (**-ю**) *сов от* **пятна́ть.**

зарабо́та|ть (**-ю;** *impf* **зараба́тывать**) *сов перех* to earn ♦ *неперех* (*no impf*; *начать работать*) to start up

▶ **зарабо́таться** (*impf* **зараба́тываться**) *сов возв* (*разг*) to work o.s. into the ground.

за́работка *сущ см* **за́работок.**

за́работн|ый *прил:* **~ая пла́та** pay, wages *мн.*

за́работ|ок (**-ка**) *м* earnings *мн.*

зара́внива|ть (**-ю**) *несов от* **заровня́ть.**

заража́|ть(ся) (**-ю(сь)**) *несов от* **зарази́ть(ся).**

зараже́ни|е (**-я**) *ср* (*организма, крови итп*) infection; (*местности, водоёма итп*) contamination.

заражённ|ый (**-, -а, -о**) *прил* (*см сущ*) infected; contaminated.

заражу́(сь) *сов см* **зарази́ть(ся).**

зара́з|а (**-ы**) *ж* infection ♦ *м/ж* (*разг: мерзавец*) pain, pest.

зара́зен *прил см* **зара́зный.**

зарази́тел|ьный (**-ен, -ьна, -ьно**) *прил* (*перен*) infectious.

зара|зи́ть (**-жу́, -зи́шь;** *impf* **заража́ть**) *сов перех* (*человека: также перен*) to infect; (*воду, местность*) to contaminate

▶ **зарази́ться** (*impf* **заража́ться**) *сов возв* (**+instr;** *гриппом, корью итп*) to catch; (*перен: страхом, весельем*) to be infected by.

зара́з|ный (**-ен, -на, -но**) *прил* infectious.

зара́нее *нареч* in advance.

зар|асти́ (**-асту́, -астёшь;** *pt* **-о́с, -осла́, -осло́,** *impf* **зараста́ть**) *сов неперех* (*рана, порез*) to close up; **зараста́ть** (**~ perf**) (**+instr**) (*травой итп*) to be overgrown (with); **он ~о́с щети́ной** he has let his beard grow.

зарв|а́ться (**-у́сь, -ёшься;** *impf* **зарыва́ться**) *сов неперех* (*разг*) to go too far; **зарыва́ться** (**~ perf**) **в тре́бованиях** to demand too much.

зарёван|ный (**-, -а, -о**) *прил* (*разг*) = **запла́канный.**

зарев|е́ть (**-у́, -ёшь**) *сов неперех* (*медведь, лев*) to start roaring; (*бык*) to start bellowing; (*разг: заплакать*) to start bawling.

за́рев|о (**-а**) *ср* glow.

зарегистри́рованный *прил* registered; **~ торго́вый знак** registered trademark.

зарегистри́р|овать (**-ую**) *сов от* регистри́ровать.

заре́жу(сь) *итп сов см* **заре́зать(ся).**

заре́з (**-а**) *м:* **по ~, до ~у** (*разг*) badly; **мне по ~ нужна́ твоя́ по́мощь** I badly need your help.

заре́|зать (**-жу, -жешь**) *сов от* **ре́зать** ♦ *перех* (*человека*) to knife; (*impf* **ре́зать;** *козу, поросёнка*) to slaughter; (*разг: книгу, проект*) to axe (*BRIT*), ax (*US*)

▶ **заре́заться** *сов возв* (*разг*) to knife o.s.

зарека́|ться (**-юсь**) *несов от* **заре́чься.**

зарекоменд|ова́ть (**-у́ю;** *impf* **зарекомендо́вывать**) *сов перех:* **~ себя́ +instr** to prove *или* show o.s. to be; **он хорошо́ себя́ ~ова́л** he proved to be good.

зар|е́чься (**-еку́сь, -ечёшься** *итп*, **-еку́тся;** *pt* **-ёкся, -екла́сь, -екло́сь,** *impf* **зарека́ться**) *сов возв* (**+infin**) to swear *или* vow never to do; **она́ ~екла́сь ходи́ть туда́** she vowed never to go there.

заржа́ве|ть (**3sg -ет**) *сов от* **ржа́веть.**

заржа́влен|ный (**-, -а, -о**) *прил* rusty.

заржа́|ть (**-у́, -ёшь**) *сов неперех* (*лошадь*) to neigh; (*разг: человек*) to roar with laughter.

зарис|ова́ть (**-у́ю;** *impf* **зари́совывать**) *сов перех* (*дом, лодку*) to sketch; **они́ ~ова́ли всю сте́ну** (*разг*) they drew all over the wall.

зарисо́в|ка (**-ки;** *gen pl* **-ок**) *ж* (*действие*) sketching; (*обычно мн: рисунок*) sketch.

зари́совыва|ть (**-ю**) *несов от* **зарисова́ть.**

зарни́ц|а (**-ы**) *ж* sheet lightning.

заровня́|ть (**-ю;** *impf* **зара́внивать**) *сов перех* (*поверхность*) to level; (*яму, канаву*) to fill up.

зарод|и́ться (**3sg -и́тся, 3pl -я́тся,** *impf* **зарожда́ться**) *сов возв* (*явление*) to emerge; (*перен: идея*) to be born; (: *чувство, сомнения*) to arise.

заро́дыш (**-а**) *м* (*био*) embryo; (*растения, также перен*) germ; **в ~е** (*перен*) in embryo; **подавля́ть** (**подави́ть** *perf*) **что-н в ~е** to nip sth in the bud.

зарожда́|ться (**3sg -ется, 3pl -ются**) *несов от* **зароди́ться.**

зарожде́ни|е (**-я**) *ср* (*жизни*) emergence; (*идеи, чувства*) conception.

заро́к (**-а**) *м* pledge, vow.

заро́с *итп сов см* **зарасти́.**

за́росл|ь (**-и**) *ж* (*обычно мн*) thicket.

зарпла́т|а (**-ы**) *ж* pay.

заруба́|ть (**-ю**) *несов от* **заруби́ть.**

зарубе́жный *прил* foreign.

зарубе́жь|е (**-я**) *ср* overseas; **стра́ны бли́жнего ~я** "near abroad" (*the republics of the former USSR*).

зар|уби́ть (**-ублю́, -у́бишь;** *impf* **заруба́ть**) *сов перех* to hack down; **~уби́ себе́ на носу́** *или* **лбу** (*разг*) mark my words.

зару́б|ка (**-и**) *ж* notch.

зарублю́ *сов см* **заруби́ть.**

зарубцева́ться (*3sg* -у́ется, *3pl* -у́ются) *сов от* рубцева́ться ♦ (*impf* зарубцо́вываться) *возв* to cicatrize.

заруми́н|иться (-юсь, -ишься; *impf* заруми́ниваться) *сов возв* (лицо, щёки) to colour (*BRIT*), color (*US*); (пирог, мясо) to brown.

заруч|и́ться (-у́сь, -и́шься; *impf* заруча́ться) *сов возв* (+*instr*; помощью, согласием) to secure.

зарыва́|ть (-ю) *несов от* зары́ть
▸ **зарыва́ться** *несов от* зары́ться, зарва́ться.

зарыда́|ть (-ю) *сов неперех* to begin to weep.

зар|ы́ть (-о́ю, -о́ешь; *impf* зарыва́ть) *сов перех* to bury; (яму, канаву) to fill
▸ **зары́ться** (*impf* зарыва́ться) *сов возв*: ~ся в +*acc* (в землю, в песок) to bury o.s. in; **зарыва́ться** (~ся *perf*) **в рабо́ту/учёбу** to bury o.s. in one's work/books; **она́ ~ы́лась голово́й в поду́шку** she buried her head in the pillow.

зар|я́ (-и́; *nom pl* зо́ри, *gen pl* зорь, *dat pl* зо́рям) ж (утренняя, также перен) dawn; (вечерняя) sundown; (*ВОЕН*) reveille; **ни свет ни** ~ at the crack of dawn; **от** ~**й до** ~**й** from dawn to dusk.

заря́д (-а) м (*ВОЕН, ЭЛЕК*) charge; (перен: бодрости, энергии) charge.

заря|ди́ть (-жу́, -ди́шь; *impf* заряжа́ть) *сов перех* (пистолет, пушку, фотоаппарат) to load; (батарейку, аккумулятор) to charge; **он** ~**ди́л одно́ и то же** (разг) he keeps going on about it; **дождь** ~**ди́л** (разг) it started pouring
▸ **заряди́ться** (*impf* заряжа́ться) *сов возв* (батарейка, аккумулятор) to recharge; **заряжа́ться** (~ся *perf*) **эне́ргией** (перен) to recharge one's batteries.

заря́д|ка (-и) ж (упражнения) exercises мн.

заряжа́|ть(ся) (-ю(сь)) *несов от* заряди́ть(ся).

заряжу́(сь) *сов см* заряди́ть(ся).

заса́д|а (-ы) ж ambush; (отряд) ambush party; **устра́ивать** (**устро́ить** *perf*) ~**у** to set up an ambush; **сиде́ть** (*impf*) **в** ~**е** to lie in ambush.

заса|ди́ть (-ажу́, -а́дишь; *impf* заса́живать) *сов перех* (грядку, клумбу): ~ (+*instr*) to plant (with); (разг: нож, топор): ~ **в** +*acc* to sink into; ~ (*perf*) **кого́-н за решётку** (разг) to stick sb behind bars; **заса́живать** (~ *perf*) **кого́-н за рабо́ту** to set sb to work.

заса́ленный прил greasy.

заса́лива|ть (-ю) *несов от* засоли́ть, заса́лить
▸ **заса́ливаться** *несов от* заса́литься.

заса́л|ить (-ю, -ишь; *impf* заса́ливать) *сов перех* to soil
▸ **заса́литься** (*impf* заса́ливаться) *сов возв* to get greasy.

засасыва|ть (*3sg* -ет, *3pl* -ют) *несов от* засоса́ть.

заса́харенн|ый прил: ~**ые фру́кты** crystallized fruits мн.

заса́хар|ить (-ю, -ишь; *impf* заса́харивать) *сов перех* to crystallize
▸ **заса́хариться** (*impf* заса́хариваться) *сов*

возв (мёд, варенье) to crystallize.

засверка́|ть (-ю) *сов неперех* (молния, глаза) to flash.

засве|ти́ть (-чу́, -тишь; *impf* засве́чивать) *сов перех* (ФОТО) to expose
▸ **засвети́ться** (*impf* засве́чиваться) *сов возв* to be exposed.

за́светло нареч before nightfall или dark.

засве́чива|ть(ся) (-ю(сь)) *несов от* засвети́ть(ся).

засвечу́(сь) *сов см* засвети́ть(ся).

засвиде́тельств|овать (-ую) *сов перех* (факт) to testify to; (документ, копию) to certify.

засева́|ть (-ю) *несов от* засе́ять.

заседа́ни|е (-я) ср (собрание) meeting; (парламента, суда) session, sitting.

заседа́тель (-я) м: **прися́жный** ~ member of the jury.

заседа́|ть (-ю) *несов неперех* (на совещании) to meet; (в парламенте, в суде) to sit; (парламент, суд) to be in session.

засе́ива|ть (-ю) *несов от* засе́ять.

засе́к итп *сов см* засе́чь.

засека́|ть (-ю) *несов от* засе́чь.

засекре́|тить (-чу, -тишь; *impf* засекре́чивать) *сов перех* (сведения, документы) to restrict access to.

засекре́ченный прил (сведения, документы) classified; (завод итп) secret.

засекре́чива|ть (-ю) *несов от* засекре́тить.

засекре́чу *сов см* засекре́тить.

засеку́ итп *сов см* засе́чь.

засе́л итп *сов см* засе́сть.

заселе́ни|е (-я) ср (земель) settlement; (дома) occupation.

заселённый (-ён, -ена́, -ено́) прил (область, район) settled; (дом, квартира) occupied.

засел|и́ть (-ю́, -и́шь; *impf* заселя́ть) *сов перех* (земли) to settle; (дом) to take up occupancy of.

засе́сть (-я́ду, -я́дешь; *pt* -е́л, -е́ла, -е́ло) *сов неперех* (надолго остаться: дома) to ensconce o.s.; (спрятаться) to sit tight; (застрять) to lodge; ~ (*perf*) **за что-н/**+*infin* to get down to sth/down to doing.

засе́ч|ка (-ки; *gen pl* -ек) ж notch.

засе́|чь (-ку́, -чёшь итп, -ку́т; *pt* -ёк, -екла́, -екло́, *impf* засека́ть) *сов перех* (место) to locate; (разг: заметить) to nail down; (выпороть) to flog; **засека́ть** (~ *perf*) **вре́мя** to record the time.

засе́|ять (-ю; *impf* засева́ть или засе́ивать) *сов перех* to sow.

засиде́ться (-жу́сь, -ди́шься; *impf* заси́живаться) *сов неперех* to stay for a long time; **мы вчера́** ~**де́лись в гостя́х** we stayed late at friends yesterday.

заси́ль|е (-я) ср dominance.

заси|я́ть (-ю) *сов неперех* to begin to shine.

заско́к (-а) м (разг: в мыслях) peculiarity.

заскору́зл|ый (-, -а, -о) прил (кожа, руки)

calloused.

заск|очи́ть (**-очу́, -о́чишь**) *сов неперех* (*разг: в гости*) to drop in.

заскреж|ета́ть (**-ещу́, -е́щешь**) *сов неперех*: ~ **зуба́ми** to grind one's teeth.

заскуча́|ть (**-ю**) *сов неперех* to get bored; ~ (*perf*) **по кому́-н/чему́-н** to start to miss sb/sth.

за|сла́ть (**-шлю, -шлёшь**; *impf* **засыла́ть**) *сов перех* to send out.

засло́н (**-а**) *м* screen, shield.

заслон|и́ть (**-ю́, -и́шь**; *impf* **заслоня́ть**) *сов перех* to block out; (*от ветра, от пули*) to shield, screen.

засло́н|ка (**-ки**; *gen pl* **-ок**) *ж* (*печи*) vent; (*шлюза*) gate.

заслоня́|ть (**-ю**) *несов от* **заслони́ть**.

заслу́г|а (**-и**) *ж* (*обычно мн*) service; **~и пе́ред страно́й** services to one's country; **награди́ть** (*perf*) **кого́-н по ~м** to fully reward sb; **его́ наказа́ли по ~м** he got what he deserved.

заслу́женный *прил* well-deserved, well-merited; (*врач, учёный итп*) renowned; **Заслу́женный арти́ст Росси́и/ма́стер спо́рта** *title awarded by the state in honour of cultural/sporting achievement.*

заслу́жива|ть (**-ю**) *несов от* **заслужи́ть** ♦ *неперех* (*доверия, внимания итп*) to deserve.

заслуж|и́ть (**-ужу́, -у́жишь**; *impf* **заслу́живать**) *сов перех* to earn.

заслу́ша|ть (**-ю**; *impf* **заслу́шивать**) *сов перех* to listen to

▶ **заслу́шаться** (*impf* **заслу́шиваться**) *сов возв*: ~**ся** (+*instr*) (*музыкой, рассказом*) to be captivated (by).

засма́трива|ться (**-юсь**) *несов от* **засмотре́ться**.

засме|я́ть (**-ю́, -ёшь**; *impf* **засме́ивать**) *сов перех* to taunt

▶ **засмея́ться** *сов возв* to start laughing.

засм|отре́ться (**-отрю́сь, -о́тришься**; *impf* **засма́триваться**) *сов неперех*: ~ **на** +*acc* to be transfixed by.

заснё́жен|ный (**-, -а, -о**) *прил* snow-covered.

засн|у́ть (**-у́, -ёшь**; *impf* **засыпа́ть**) *сов неперех* to go to sleep, fall asleep.

засо́в (**-а**) *м* bolt.

засо́выва|ть (**-ю**) *несов от* **засу́нуть**.

засо́л (**-а**) *м* (*рыбы*) salting.

засол|и́ть (**-олю́, -о́лишь**; *impf* **заса́ливать**) *сов перех* to salt.

засоре́ни|е (**-я**) *ср* (*рек*) pollution; (*раковины, туалета*) blockage; **засоре́ние желу́дка** stomach upset.

засор|и́ть (**-ю́, -и́шь**; *impf* **засоря́ть**) *сов перех* (*комнату, поляну*) to litter; (*раковину, туалет*) to block *или* clog up; (*перен: мысли, речь*) to contaminate; ~ (*perf*) **глаза́** to get grit in one's eyes; ~ (*perf*) **желу́док** to get a stomach upset

▶ **засори́ться** (*impf* **засоря́ться**) *сов возв* (*раковина, туалет*) to become clogged up.

засос|а́ть (**-у́, -ёшь**; *impf* **заса́сывать**) *сов перех* to suck in ♦ *неперех* (*no impf*; *подлеж: младенец*) to start feeding.

засо́хн|уть (**-у, -ешь**) *сов от* **со́хнуть** ♦ (*impf* **засыха́ть**) *неперех* (*грязь*) to dry up; (*растение*) to wither.

за́спан|ный (**-, -на, -но**) *прил* sleepy.

заспо́р|ить (**-ю, -ишь**) *сов неперех* to start arguing.

заста́в|а (**-ы**) *ж* (*также*: **пограни́чная ~**) frontier post; (*ВОЕН: отряд*) party, detachment.

застава́|ть (**-ю́, -ёшь**) *несов от* **заста́ть**.

заста́в|ить (**-лю, -ишь**; *impf* **заставля́ть**) *сов перех* (*занять*) to clutter up; (*закрыть*) to block off; **заставля́ть** (~ *perf*) **кого́-н** +*infin* to force sb to do, make sb do; **он ~ил меня́ помо́чь ему́** he made me help him.

заста́ива|ться (*3sg* **-ется**, *3pl* **-ются**) *несов от* **застоя́ться**.

заста́ну *итп сов см* **заста́ть**.

застаре́лый *прил* old.

заста́|ть (**-ну, -нешь**; *impf* **застава́ть**) *сов перех* to catch, find; **я его́ не ~л до́ма** I didn't manage to catch him at home; **я ~л её за рабо́той** I found her at work.

застегн|у́ть (**-у́, -ёшь**; *impf* **застёгивать**) *сов перех* to do up

▶ **застегну́ться** (*impf* **застёгиваться**) *сов возв* (*человек: на пуговицы*) to button o.s. up; (: *на молнию*) to zip o.s. up; (*пуговицы, молния*) to do up.

застё́ж|ка (**-ки**; *gen pl* **-ек**) *ж* fastener.

застекл|и́ть (**-ю́, -и́шь**; *impf* **застекля́ть**) *сов перех* to glaze.

застел|и́ть (**-ю́, -ишь**; *impf* **застила́ть**) *сов перех* (*кровать*) to make up; (*стол, пол*) to cover.

застелю́ *итп сов см* **застла́ть**.

засте́нка *сущ см* **засте́нок**.

застеногра́фи́р|овать (**-ую**) *сов от* **стенографи́ровать**.

засте́н|ок (**-ка**; *nom pl* **-ки**) *м* torture chamber.

засте́нчив|ый (**-, -а, -о**) *прил* shy.

застесня́|ться (**-юсь**) *сов возв* (*разг*) to go all shy.

засти́г *итп сов см* **засти́чь**.

застига́|ть (**-ю**) *несов от* **засти́гнуть, засти́чь**.

засти́гну *итп сов см* **засти́чь**.

засти́гн|уть (**-у, -ешь**; *pt* ~ *или* **-нул, -ла, -ло**, *impf* **застига́ть**) *сов = засти́чь*.

застила́|ть (**-ю**) *несов от* **застели́ть, застла́ть**.

застира́|ть (**-ю**; *impf* **засти́рывать**) *сов перех* (*бельё, оде́жду*) to overwash; (*пятно*) to wash off *или* out.

засти́|чь (**-гну, -гнешь**; *pt* **-г, -гла, -гло**, *impf* **застига́ть**) *сов перех* to catch.

заст|ла́ть (-елю́, -е́лешь; *impf* застила́ть) *сов перех* (*подлеж: облака, туман*) to cover; (: *слёзы, дым*) to blur.

засто́|й (-я) *м* (*в делах, в работе*) standstill; (*в жизни, в мыслях*) stagnation.

засто́йный *прил* (*также перен*) stagnant.

засто́льн|ый *прил*: ~ые разгово́ры table talk; ~ая пе́сня drinking song.

заст|она́ть (-ону́, -о́нешь) *сов неперех* to groan.

засто́пор|ить (-ю, -ишь) *сов от* сто́порить

▶ засто́пориться *сов возв* (*машина, станок*) to come to a halt; (*дело, работа*) to be held up.

засто|я́ться (3sg -и́тся, 3pl -я́ться, *impf* заста́иваться) *сов перех* (*вода*) to go stagnant.

застра́ива|ть (-ю) *несов от* застро́ить.

застрахо́ван|ный (-, -а, -о) *прил* insured.

застрах|ова́ть (-у́ю; *impf* застрахо́вывать) *сов перех*: ~ (от +*gen*) (*также перен*) to insure (against)

▶ застрахова́ться (*impf* застрахо́вываться) *сов возв*: ~ся (от +*gen*) to insure o.s. (against).

застра́чива|ть (-ю) *несов от* застрочи́ть.

застрева́|ть (-ю) *несов от* застря́ть.

застрел|и́ть (-елю́, -е́лишь; *impf* застре́ливать) *сов перех* to shoot

▶ застрели́ться (*impf* застре́ливаться) *сов возв* to shoot o.s.

застро́енный *прил* built-up.

застро́|ить (-ю, -ишь; *impf* застра́ивать) *сов перех* to build on, develop.

застро́йк|а (-и) *ж* development.

застроч|и́ть (-у́, -и́шь; *impf* застра́чивать) *сов перех* (*выточки, складки*) to stitch ♦ *неперех* (*по impf, пулемёт*) to spray bullets; (*начать писать*) to start scribbling away.

застр|я́ть (-ну, -нешь; *impf* застрева́ть) *сов неперех* to get stuck.

заст|уди́ть (-ужу́, -у́дишь; *impf* засту́живать) *сов перех* (*разг*): ~ го́рло/у́ши to get a sore throat/sore ears.

заступ|и́ться (-уплю́сь, -у́пишься; *impf* заступа́ться) *сов возв*: ~ за +*acc* to stand up for.

засту́пник (-а) *м* defender.

засту́пниц|а (-ы) *ж см* засту́пник.

застыва́|ть (-ю) *несов от* засты́ть.

засты́вш|ий (-ая, -ее, -ие) *прил* (*также перен*) frozen; (*лава*) solidified; (*цемент, желе*) set.

засты́|ть (-ну, -нешь; *impf* застыва́ть) *сов неперех* to freeze; (*лава*) to solidify; (*цемент*) to set; застыва́ть (~ *perf*) на ме́сте to freeze, stop dead; (*perf*) от стра́ха to be paralysed with fear.

засуе|ти́ться (-чу́сь, -ти́шься) *сов возв* to start bustling about.

засу́н|уть (-у, -ешь; *impf* засо́вывать) *сов перех*: ~ что-н в +*acc* to thrust sth into.

за́сух|а (-и) *ж* drought.

засухоусто́йчив|ый (-, -а, -о) *прил* drought-resistant.

засуч|и́ть (-у́, -у́чишь; *impf* засу́чивать) *сов*
перех (*штанину, рукав*) to roll up; ~чи́в рукава́ (*перен*) in earnest.

засуш|и́ть (-ушу́, -у́шишь; *impf* засу́шивать) *сов перех* to dry up.

засу́шлив|ый (-, -а, -о) *прил* dry.

засчита́|ть (-ю; *impf* засчи́тывать) *сов перех* to take into account; (*гол, результат*) to allow (to stand).

засыла́|ть (-ю) *несов от* засла́ть.

засы́п|ать (-лю, -лешь; *impf* засыпа́ть) *сов перех* (*яму, канаву*) to fill (up); (*покрыть*) to cover; (*разг: студента*) to flunk; (*муку, крупу итп*) to pour; засыпа́ть (~ *perf*) кого́-н вопро́сами/пода́рками to bombard sb with questions/gifts; его́ ~ало песко́м he was buried under the sand

▶ засы́паться (*impf* засыпа́ться) *сов возв*: ~ся +*instr* (*песком, землёй*) to be covered with; (*разг: попасться*) to cock up; (: на экза́мене) to flunk; засыпа́ться (~ся *perf*) в +*acc*/за +*acc* to get into/behind.

засыпа́|ть (-ю) *несов от* засну́ть, засы́пать

▶ засыпа́ться (-ю) *несов от* засы́паться.

засы́плю(сь) *итп сов см* засы́пать(ся).

засыха́|ть (-ю) *несов от* засо́хнуть.

зася́ду *итп сов см* засе́сть.

зата|и́ть (-ю́, -и́шь; *impf* зата́ивать) *сов перех* (*неприязнь, мечту*) to harbour (*BRIT*), harbor (*US*); зата́ивать (~ *perf*) оби́ду to harbour a grudge; зата́ивать (~ *perf*) дыха́ние to hold one's breath

▶ затаи́ться *сов возв* to hide.

зата́лкива|ть (-ю) *несов от* затолка́ть, затолкну́ть.

зата́плива|ть (-ю) *несов от* затопи́ть.

зата́птыва|ть (-ю) *несов от* затопта́ть.

зата́скан|ный (-, -на, -но) *прил* worn-out.

затаска́|ть (-ю; *impf* зата́скивать) *сов перех* (*разг: одежду, шутку*) to wear out; зата́скивать (~ *perf*) кого́-н по магази́нам (*разг*) to drag sb round the shops; ~ (*perf*) кого́-н по суда́м (*разг*) to drag sb through the courts.

зата́скива|ть (-ю) *несов от* затаска́ть, затащи́ть.

зата́чива|ть (-ю) *несов от* заточи́ть.

зат|ащи́ть (-ащу́, -а́щишь; *impf* зата́скивать) *сов перех* to drag; ~ (*perf*) кого́-н в кино́ (*разг*) to drag sb off to the cinema.

затвердева́|ть (3sg -ет, 3pl -ют) *несов от* затверде́ть.

затверде́лый *прил* hardened.

затверде́ни|е (-я) *ср* (*МЕД*) callus.

затверде́|ть (3sg -ет, 3pl -ют, *impf* затвердева́ть) *сов неперех* (*земля, цемент*) to harden; (*жидкость*) to solidify.

затверд|и́ть (-жу́, -ди́шь) *сов от* тверди́ть ♦ (*impf* затве́рживать) *перех* to learn by rote.

затво́р (-а) *м* (*плотины*) floodgate; (*фотоаппарата*) shutter; (*винтовки*) breech.

затво́рник *м* (*РЕЛ*) hermit; (*перен*) hermit, recluse.

затво́рниц|**а** (-ы) *ж см* **затво́рник**.
затева́ть (-ю) *несов от* **зате́ять**.
зате́йлив|**ый** (-, -а, -о) *прил* intricate.
зате́йник (-а) *м* entertainer.
затёк *итп сов см* **зате́чь**.
затека́ть (-ю) *несов от* **зате́чь**.
затеку́т *сов см* **зате́чь**.
зате́м *нареч* (*потом*) then; (*для того*) for that reason; ~ **что́бы** in order to.
затемне́ни|**е** (-я) *ср* (*перен: рассудка*) obscuring; (*ВОЕН*) blackout.
затемнённый *прил* (*очки, стекло*) tinted.
затемн|**и́ть** (-ю́, -и́шь; *impf* **затемня́ть**) *сов перех* to darken; (*перен: рассудок*) to obscure; (*город, окна*) to black out.
за́темно *нареч* (*разг: до рассвета*) before light; (: *когда стемнело*) after dark.
затемня́ть (-ю) *несов от* **затемни́ть**.
затен|**и́ть** (-ю́, -и́шь; *impf* **затеня́ть**) *сов перех* to shade; (*комнату*) to darken.
зате́пл|**иться** (*3sg* -ится, *3pl* -ятся) *сов неперех* (*огонёк*) to begin to flicker; (*надежда*) to appear.
зат|**ере́ть** (-ру́, -рёшь; *pt* -ёр, -ёрла, -ёрло, *impf* **затира́ть**) *сов перех* (*пятно, надпись*) to rub out; (*перен: разг: работника*) to shackle; **её** ~**ёрли в толпе́** she got caught up in the crowd; **кора́бль** ~**ёрло льда́ми** the ship was icebound.
зате́рянный *прил* (*человек*) forgotten; (*место, дом*) forsaken.
затеря́|**ться** (-юсь) *сов от* **теря́ться** ♦ *возв* (*разг*) to go missing, disappear; (*в дали, в толпе*) to disappear.
зате́чь (*3sg* -ечёт, *3pl* -еку́т, *pt* -ёк, -екла́, -екло́, *impf* **затека́ть**) *сов неперех* (*опухнуть*) to swell up; (*онеметь*) to go numb; (*вода*): ~ **за** +*acc*/**в** +*acc* to seep behind/into.
затещу́сь *итп сов см* **затеса́ться**.
зате́|**я** (-и) *ж* (*замысел*) idea, scheme; (*забава*) escapade; **без** ~**й** without frills.
зате́|**ять** (-ю; *impf* **затева́ть**) *сов перех* (*разговор, игру*) to start (up); **он, ка́жется, что́-то затева́ет** (*разг*) he's got something up his sleeve.
затира́ть (-ю) *несов от* **затере́ть**.
затих|**нуть** (-ну, -нешь; *pt* -, -ла, -ло, *impf* **затиха́ть**) *сов неперех* (*люди, место*) to quieten (*BRIT*) *или* quiet (*US*) down; (*шум, ветер, буря*) to die down.
зати́шь|**е** (-я) *ср* lull.
заткн|**у́ть** (-у́, -ёшь; *impf* **затыка́ть**) *сов перех* to stop up, plug; ~ (*perf*) **что́-н за** +*acc*/**в** +*acc* to stuff sth behind/into; **затыка́ть** (~ *perf*) **кого́-н** *или* **рот кому́-н** (*разг*) to shut sb up; **затыка́ть** (~ *perf*) **кого́-н за по́яс** (*перен: разг*) to outdo sb
▶ **заткну́ться** (*impf* **затыка́ться**) *сов возв* (*разг: замолчать*) to shut up; ~**и́сь!** (*разг: пренебр*) shut it!
затмева́ть (-ю) *несов от* **затми́ть**.

затме́ни|**е** (-я) *ср* (*солнца, луны*) eclipse; (*разг: ума*) blackout; **на меня́ нашло́** ~ my mind went blank.
затм|**и́ть** (-и́шь; *impf* **затмева́ть**) *сов перех* (*также перен*) to eclipse.
зато́ *союз* (*также:* **но** ~: *однако*) but then (again); (*поэтому*) but (to make up for it); **кварти́ра ма́ленькая, (но)** ~ **в хоро́шем райо́не** the flat is small, but then again it's in a nice district.
затова́ривани|**е** (-я) *ср* (*КОММ: скопление товаров*) stockpiling; (*склада, магазина*) overstocking.
затова́р|**ить** (-ю, -ишь; *impf* **затова́ривать**) *сов перех* (*см сущ*) to stockpile; to overstock.
затолка́ть (-ю; *impf* **зата́лкивать**) *сов перех* (*разг*) to shove; (*в автобусе, в толпе*) to squash.
затолкн|**у́ть** (-у́, -ёшь; *impf* **зата́лкивать**) *сов перех* to shove.
зат|**ону́ть** (-ону́, -о́нешь) *сов неперех* to sink.
затоп|**и́ть** (-оплю́, -о́пишь; *impf* **зата́пливать**) *сов перех* (*печь, камин*) to light; (*impf* **затопля́ть**; *остров, деревню*) to flood; (*судно*) to sink.
затопта́ть (-опчу́, -о́пчешь; *impf* **зата́птывать**) *сов перех* (*цветы, газон*) to trample on; (*огонь, следы*) to stamp out; (*убить*) to trample to death.
зато́р (-а) *м* congestion; (*на улице*) traffic jam; (*на реке*) log jam.
затормо|**зи́ть(ся)** (-жу́, -зи́шь) *сов от* **тормози́ть(ся)**.
затор|**опи́ться** (-оплю́сь, -о́пишься) *сов возв* to hasten.
затоск|**ова́ть** (-у́ю) *сов неперех* to begin to feel melancholic; ~ (*perf*) **по** +*dat* to start to miss.
заточа́ть (-ю) *несов от* **заточи́ть**.
заточе́ни|**е** (-я) *ср* incarceration.
зато|**чи́ть** (-чу́, -́чишь; *impf* **зата́чивать**) *сов перех* to sharpen; (*impf* **заточа́ть**; *в тюрьму*) to incarcerate.
затошн|**и́ть** (*3sg* -и́т) *сов безл*: **меня́** ~**и́ло** I began to feel sick.
затр|**ави́ть** (-влю́, -́авишь) *сов от* **трави́ть** ♦ (*impf* **затра́вливать**) *перех* (*зайца, утку*) to hunt; (*перен: человека*) to harass.
затра́гива|**ть** (-ю) *несов от* **затро́нуть**.
затрапе́з|**ный** (-ен, -на, -но) *прил* (*разг*) shabby.
затра́т|**а** (-ы) *ж* expenditure.
затра́т|**ить** (-чу, -тишь; *impf* **затра́чивать**) *сов перех* to expend.
затре́б|**овать** (-ую) *сов перех* to request.
затрепе|**та́ть** (-щу́, -́щешь) *сов неперех* to begin to tremble.
затреща́ть (-у́, -и́шь) *сов неперех* (*стул, дерево*) to start to split.

The spelling rules for Russian are shown on page xvii.

затрéщин|а (-ы) ж whack.

затрóн|уть (-у, -ешь; *impf* **затрáгивать**) *сов перех* (*подлеж:* *пуля*) to graze; (*перен: вопрос, тему*) to touch on; (: *душу, человека*) to affect; **затрáгивать** (~ *perf*) **чьё-н самолюбие** to dent sb's ego.

затрý *итп сов см* **затерéть**.

затруднéни|е (-я) *ср* difficulty.

затруднённый (-ён, -енá, -енó) *прил* laboured (*BRIT*), labored (*US*).

затрудни́тел|ьный (-ен, -ьна, -ьно) *прил* difficult, awkward.

затрудни́|ть (-ю, -и́шь; *impf* **затрудня́ть**) *сов перех:* ~ **что-н** to make sth difficult; **éсли Вас не** ~**и́т** if it isn't too much trouble

▸ **затрудни́ться** (*impf* **затрудня́ться**) *сов возв:* ~**ся с** +*instr*/+*infin* to have difficulty with/doing; **я** ~**я́юсь** (**Вам**) **сказáть** that is difficult to say.

затр|ясти́сь (-ясу́сь, -ясёшься; *pt* -я́сся, -ясла́сь, -ясло́сь) *сов возв* (to start) to shake.

затумáн|ить (-ю, -ишь) *сов от* **тумáнить**

▸ **затумáниться** *сов от* **тумáниться** ◆ (*impf* **затумáниваться**) *возв* (*небо*) to cloud over; (*глазá*) to mist over; (*перен: сознáние*) to become blurred.

затуп|и́ть (-уплю́, -у́пишь) *сов от* **тупи́ть** ◆ (*impf* **затупля́ть**) *перех* to blunt

▸ **затупи́ться** *сов от* **тупи́ться** ◆ (*impf* **затупля́ться**) *возв* to become blunt.

зату́х|нуть (3sg -нет, 3pl -нут, *pt* -, -ла, -ло, *impf* **затухáть**) *сов неперех* (*огонь*) to die out; (*сигнáл*) to die away; (*колебáния*) to die down.

затуш|евáть (-у́ю; *impf* **затушёвывать**) *сов перех* to shade (in); (*перен: сглáдить*) to brush over.

зату́ш|ить (-ушу́, -у́шишь) *сов от* **туши́ть**.

зáтхл|ый (-, -а, -о) *прил* stale; (*зáпах*) musty.

затыкáть(ся) (-ю(сь)) *несов от* **заткну́ть(ся)**.

заты́л|ок (-ка) *м* the back of the head.

заты́ч|ка (-ки; *gen pl* -ек) ж (*разг*) stopper.

затю́ка|ть (-ю) *сов перех* (*разг*) to bug.

затя́гива|ть(ся) (-ю(сь)) *несов от* **затяну́ть(ся)**.

затя́ж|ка (-ки; *gen pl* -ек) ж (*промедлéние*) delay; (*при курéнии*) drag, puff.

затяжнóй *прил* protracted, prolonged; **затяжны́е дожди́** long periods of rain; **затяжнóй прыжóк** delayed drop.

затяну́|ть (-яну́, -я́нешь; *impf* **затя́гивать**) *сов перех* (*шнурки́, гáйку*) to tighten; (*замéдлить*) to drag out; (*вовлéчь*): ~ **когó-н в** +*acc* to drag sb into; **онá** ~**яну́ла тáлию пóясом** she pulled the belt tight around her waist; **нéбо** ~**яну́ло ту́чами** storm clouds gathered in the sky; **затя́гивать** (~ *perf*) **пéсню** to strike up a song

▸ **затяну́ться** (*impf* **затя́гиваться**) *сов возв* (*пéтля, у́зел*) to tighten; (*рáна*) to close up; (*дéло, переговóры итп*) to drag on; (*при курéнии*) to inhale; **затя́гиваться** (~**ся** *perf*) +*instr* (*пóясом, корсéтом*) to tighten.

зау́м|ный (-ен, -на, -но) *прил* unintelligible.

зауны́в|ный (-ен, -на, -но) *прил* mournful.

заупокóй|ный *прил:* ~**ая моли́тва** prayer for the dead; **заупокóйная слу́жба** funeral service.

заупря́м|иться (-люсь, -ишься) *сов возв* to become stubborn.

заури́дный (-ен, -на, -но) *прил* unexceptional, mediocre.

заусéн|ец (-ца; *nom pl* -цы) *м* (*на метáлле*) burr; (*у нóгтя*) hangnail.

зáутрен|я (-и) ж (*РЕЛ*) dawn mass, ≈ matins.

зау́чен|ный (-, -на, -но) *прил* (*отвéт, жест*) (pre)rehearsed.

зау́ч|ить (-учу́, -у́чишь; *impf* **зау́чивать**) *сов перех* to memorize, learn

▸ **заучи́ться** (*impf* **зау́чиваться**) *сов возв* (*разг*) to study too hard.

зафарширова́ть (-у́ю) *сов от* **фарширова́ть**.

зафикси́р|овать (-ую) *сов от* **фикси́ровать**.

зафрахт|ова́ть (-у́ю; *impf* **зафрахтóвывать** или **фрахтова́ть**) *сов перех* to charter.

захвал|и́ть (-ю́, -ишь; *impf* **захвáливать**) *сов перех* to overpraise.

захвáт (-а) *м* seizure, capture; (*СПОРТ*) hold; (*ТЕХ*) clamp.

захв|ати́ть (-ачу́, -áтишь; *impf* **захвáтывать**) *сов перех* to seize, capture; (*взять с собóй*) to take; (*подлеж: му́зыка, рабóта*) to captivate; (*болéзнь, пожáр*) to catch (in time); **дух** ~**áтывает** it takes your breath away; **у меня́ дух** ~**ати́ло от волнéния** I was breathless with excitement.

захвáтническ|ий (-ая, -ое, -ие) *прил* (*намéрения, поли́тика*) aggressive; ~**ая войнá** war of aggression.

захвáтчик (-а) *м* invader.

захвáтываю|щий (-ая, -ее, -ие) *прил* (*кни́га, заня́тие*) gripping, absorbing; (*вид*) breathtaking.

захвáтыва|ть (-ю) *несов от* **захвати́ть**.

захвачу́ *итп сов см* **захвати́ть**.

захвора́|ть (-ю) *сов неперех* (*разг*) to be taken ill.

захирé|ть (-ю) *сов от* **хирéть**.

захлам|и́ть (-лю́, -и́шь; *impf* **захламля́ть**) *сов перех* to clutter up.

захламлённый (-ён, -енá, -енó) *прил* cluttered.

захламлю́ *сов см* **захлами́ть**.

захламля́|ть (-ю) *несов от* **захлами́ть**.

захлебн|у́ться (-у́сь, -ёшься; *impf* **захлёбываться**) *сов возв* to choke; (*перен: атáка, наступлéние*) to be stopped in its tracks; (: *мотóр*) to fail to start; **захлёбываться** (~ *perf*) **от смéха/слёз** to choke with laughter/on one's tears; **захлёбываться** (~ *perf*) **от счáстья/востóрга** to gasp in joy/elation.

захлестн|у́ть (-у́, -ёшь; *impf* **захлёстывать**) *сов перех* (*подлеж: волнá*) to swallow; (*перен: подлеж: чу́вство*) to overwhelm ◆ *неперех* (*водá*) to wash over.

захлóпа|ть (-ю) *сов неперех* (*двéри*) to slam;

(*выстрелы*) to crash out; (*слушатели, зрители*): ~ **(в ладо́ши)** to start clapping.
захло́пн|уть (-у, -ешь; *impf* **захло́пывать**) *сов перех*: ~ **что-н** to slam sth shut
▶ **захло́пнуться** (*impf* **захло́пываться**) *сов возв* to slam shut.
захо́д (-а) *м* (*также:* ~ **со́лнца**) sundown; (*в порт*) call; (*попытка*) go; **с пе́рвого/второ́го** ~**а** at the first/second attempt; **с** ~**ом/без захо́да в** +*acc* stopping off/without stopping off at.
зах|оди́ть (-ожу́, -о́дишь) *несов от* **зайти́** ♦ *сов непepex* to start pacing.
захолу́сть|е (-я) *ср* provincial backwater.
захороне́ни|е (-я) *ср* (*действие*) burial; (*могила, могильник*) burial ground.
захор|они́ть (-оню́, -о́нишь) *сов перех* to bury.
зах|оте́ть (*как* **хоте́ть**; *см* **Table 16**) *сов (не)перех* to want
▶ **захоте́ться** *сов безл* (+*dat*): **мне** ~**оте́лось есть/пить** I started to feel hungry/thirsty.
захуда́л|ый *прил* wretched.
зацв|ести́ (*3sg* -етёт, *3pl* -ету́т, *pt* -ёл, -ела́, -ело́, *impf* **зацвета́ть**) *сов непepex* (*цветы*) to blossom, bloom; (*разг: сыр, хлеб*) to go mouldy (*BRIT*) *или* moldy (*US*).
зацел|ова́ть (-у́ю) *сов перех*: ~ **кого́-н** to smother sb with kisses.
зацементи́р|овать (-ую) *сов от* **цементи́ровать**.
зацеп|и́ть (-еплю́, -е́пишь; *impf* **зацепля́ть**) *сов перех* (*поддеть*) to hook up; (*разг: случайно задеть*) to catch against
▶ **зацепи́ться** (*impf* **зацепля́ться**) *сов возв*: ~**ся за** +*acc* (*задеть за*) to catch *или* get caught on; (*ухватиться за*) to grab hold of; **я** ~**епи́лся рука́вом за гвоздь** I caught my sleeve on a nail.
заце́п|ка (-ки; *gen pl* -ок) *ж* (*перен*) pretext.
зацеплю́(сь) *сов см* **зацепи́ть(ся)**.
зацепля́|ть(ся) (-ю(сь)) *несов от* **зацепи́ть(ся)**.
заци́кл|иться (-юсь, -ишься; *impf* **заци́кливаться**) *сов возв*: ~ **на** +*acc* (*разг*) to be crazy about.
зачар|ова́ть (-у́ю; *impf* **зачаро́вывать**) *сов перех* to enthral (*BRIT*), enthrall (*US*).
зача|сти́ть (-щу́, -сти́шь) *сов непepex* to come more often; **дождь** ~**сти́л** the rain got heavier.
зачасту́ю *нареч* often.
зача́ти|е (-я) *ср* conception.
зача́т|ок (-ка; *nom pl* -ки) *м* (*обычно мн: любви, иде́и итп*) beginning, germ *только ед*; **в** ~**ке** (*перен*) in embryo.
зача́точ|ный (-ен, -на, -но) *прил* (*также перен*) embryonic; **в** ~**ном состоя́нии** in an embryonic state.
зач|а́ть (-ну́, -нёшь; *pt* -а́л, -ала́, -а́ло, *impf* **зачина́ть**) *сов (не)перех* to conceive.

зача́х|нуть (-ну, -нешь; *pt* -, -ла, -ло) *сов от* **ча́хнуть**.
зачащу́ *сов см* **зачасти́ть**.
заче́м *нареч* why; ~ **он э́то сде́лал?** why did he do it?; **ей ста́ло поня́тно,** ~ **он э́то сде́лал** it became clear to her why he had done it.
заче́м-нибудь *нареч* for any reason.
заче́м-то *нареч* for some reason.
зачеркн|у́ть (-у́, -ёшь; *impf* **зачёркивать**) *сов перех* to cross out; (*перен: прошлое*) to blot out.
зачерпн|у́ть (-у́, -ёшь; *impf* **заче́рпывать**) *сов перех* to scoop up.
зачерстве́|ть (-ю) *сов от* **черстве́ть**.
зач|еса́ть (-ешу́, -е́шешь; *impf* **зачёсывать**) *сов перех* to comb.
зач|е́сть (-ту́, -тёшь; *pt* -ёл, -ла́, -ло́, *impf* **зачи́тывать**) *сов перех* (*одобрить*) to pass; (*засчитать: диплом, опыт*) to take into account; **ему́** ~**ли отрабо́танные дни в счёт о́тпуска** he was given time off in lieu
▶ **заче́сться** (*impf* **зачи́тываться**) *сов возв* to be taken into account.
зачёсыва|ть (-ю) *несов от* **зачеса́ть**.
зачёт (-а) *м* (*ПРОСВЕЩ*) test; **сдава́ть** (*impf*)/**сдать** (*perf*) ~ **по фи́зике** to sit (*BRIT*) *или* take/pass a physics test.
зачётный *прил*: **зачётная рабо́та** assessed essay (*BRIT*), term paper (*US*); **зачётная кни́жка** assessment record book.
зачешу́ *сов см* **зачеса́ть**.
зачина́тел|ь (-я) *м* originator.
зачина́|ть (-ю) *несов от* **зача́ть**.
зачи́нщик (-а) *м* instigator.
зачи́сл|ить (-ю, -ишь; *impf* **зачисля́ть**) *сов перех* (*в институт*) to enrol; (*на работу*) to take on; (*на счёт*) to enter; **зачисля́ть** (~ *perf*) **расхо́ды** to keep a record of expenditure
▶ **зачи́слиться** (*impf* **зачисля́ться**) *сов возв* (*в институт*) to enrol; (*на работу*) to be taken on.
зачита́|ть (-ю; *impf* **зачи́тывать**) *сов перех* (*прочесть вслух*) to read out; ~ (*perf*) **у кого́-н кни́гу** to borrow a book from sb and not give it back
▶ **зачита́ться** (*impf* **зачи́тываться**) *сов возв*: ~**ся** +*instr* (*кни́гой*) to be engrossed in; **я** ~**лся до утра́** I read until morning.
зачи́тыва|ть(ся) (-ю(сь)) *несов от* **заче́сть(ся), зачита́ть(ся)**.
зачну́ *итп сов см* **зача́ть**.
зачту́(сь) *итп сов см* **заче́сть(ся)**.
зашага́|ть (-ю) *сов непepex* to start walking.
зашата́|ться (-юсь) *сов возв* (*здание*) to start to shake; (*дерево, пьяница*) to begin to sway.
зашвырн|у́ть (-у́, -нёшь; *impf* **зашвы́ривать**) *сов перех* to hurl.
зашвыря́|ть (-ю) *сов перех*: ~ **кого́-н чем-н** to pelt sb with sth.

зашевел|и́ть (-ю́, -и́шь) *сов неперех* (+*instr*) to move

▶ **зашевели́ться** *сов возв* to move.

зашёл *сов см* **зайти́**.

заш|и́ть (-ью́, -ьёшь; *impf* **зашива́ть**) *сов перех* (*дырку, носки*) to mend; (*шов, рану*) to stitch.

зашифр|ова́ть (-у́ю; *impf* **зашифро́вывать**) *сов перех* to encode, put into code.

зашла́ *итп сов см* **зайти́**.

зашлю́ *итп сов см* **засла́ть**.

зашнур|ова́ть (-у́ю; *impf* **зашнуро́вывать**) *сов перех* to lace up.

зашпакл|ева́ть (-ю́ю) *сов от* **шпаклева́ть**.

зашто́па|ть (-ю; *impf* **што́пать**) *сов перех* to darn.

заштрих|ова́ть (-у́ю; *impf* **заштрихо́вывать**) *сов перех* to shade (in).

зашум|е́ть (-лю́, -и́шь) *сов неперех* (*люди, толпа*) to become noisy; **внизу́ ~е́ли голоса́** from downstairs came the sound of voices.

зашью́ *итп сов см* **заши́ть**.

защёлк|а (-и) *ж* (*на двери*) latch; (*на шкатулке, у замка*) catch.

защёлкн|уть (-у, -ешь; *impf* **защёлкивать**) *сов перех* to shut

▶ **защёлкнуться** (*impf* **защёлкиваться**) *сов возв* to click shut.

защем|и́ть (-лю́, -и́шь; *impf* **защемля́ть**) *сов перех* to clamp.

защи́т|а (-ы) *ж* (*также юр, спорт*) defence (*BRIT*), defense (*US*); (*от комаров, пыли*) protection; (*диплома, диссертации*) viva (*open to the public*); **брать** (**взять** *perf*) **под ~у** to defend.

защи|ти́ть (-щу́, -ти́шь; *impf* **защища́ть**) *сов перех* to defend; (*от солнца, от комаров итп*) to protect; **защища́ть** (**~** *perf*) **диссерта́цию** to defend one's thesis (*at public viva*)

▶ **защити́ться** (*impf* **защища́ться**) *сов возв* to defend o.s.; (*диссертант, студент*) to defend one's thesis.

защи́тник (-а) *м* (*также спорт*) defender; (*ЮР*) defence counsel (*BRIT*), defense attorney (*US*); **ле́вый/пра́вый ~** (*футбол*) left/right back.

защи́тный *прил* protective; **защи́тный цвет** khaki.

защища́|ть (-ю) *несов от* **защити́ть** ♦ *перех* (*подсудимого, преступника*) to defend

▶ **защища́ться** *несов от* **защити́ться**.

защищу́(сь) *сов см* **защити́ть(ся)**.

за|яви́ть (-явлю́, -я́вишь; *impf* **заявля́ть**) *сов перех* (*претензию, протест*) to declare ♦ *неперех:* **~ о** +*prp* to announce; **заявля́ть** (**~** *perf*) **о свои́х права́х** (**на** +*acc*) to claim one's rights (to); **заявля́ть** (**~** *perf*) **на кого́-н в мили́цию** to report sb to the police

▶ **заяви́ться** (*impf* **заявля́ться**) *сов возв* (*разг*) to turn up.

за|я́вка (-ки; *gen pl* -ок) *ж:* **~** (**на** +*acc*) application (for); (*на билеты*) order (for); **~ на изобрете́ние** patent application; **присыла́йте**

ва́ши ~ки по а́дресу ... please apply to the following address ....

заявле́ни|е (-я) *ср* (*правительства*) statement; (*просьба*): **~** (**о** +*prp*) application (for); **де́лать** (**сде́лать** *perf*) **~** to make a statement; **подава́ть** (**пода́ть** *perf*) **~ на рабо́ту/об о́тпуске** to apply for a job/leave.

заявлю́(сь) *сов см* **заяви́ть(ся)**.

заявля́|ть(ся) (-ю(сь)) *несов от* **заяви́ть(ся)**.

за́|ядлый *прил* (*разг: курильщик*) inveterate; **он ~ футболи́ст/охо́тник** he is a football/hunting fanatic.

за́|яц (-йца) *м* (*зоол*) hare; (*разг: безбилетник*) fare dodger.

за́яч|ий (-ья, -ье, -ьи) *прил* (*мех, хвост*) hare's; **за́ячья губа́** harelip.

зва́ни|е (-я) *ср* (*воинское*) rank; (*учёное, почётное*) title; **присва́ивать** (**присво́ить** *perf*) **кому́ ~** to award sb a title.

зва́ный *прил:* **~ гость** welcome guest; **зва́ный обе́д** dinner party.

зв|ать (зову́, зовёшь; *pt* -ал, -ала́, -а́ло, *perf* **позва́ть**) *несов перех* to call; (*приглашать*) to ask; (*no perf;* +*instr;* *называть*): **~ кого́-н кем-н** to call sb sth; **как Вас зову́т?** what is your name?; **меня́/его́ зову́т Алекса́ндр** my/his name is Alexander; **~** (**позва́ть** *perf*) **кого́-н в го́сти/в кино́** to ask sb over/to the cinema

▶ **зва́ться** *несов возв* (+*instr*) to be called.

звезд|а́ (-ы́; *nom pl* **звёзды**) *ж* (*также перен*) star; **морска́я ~** starfish.

звёздный *прил* (*ночь, небо*) starry, starlit; **э́то был его́ ~ час** that was his finest hour; **звёздные во́йны** Star Wars; **Звёздный городо́к** Star City (*training centre for Russian cosmonauts*).

звёздоч|ка (-ки; *gen pl* -ек) *ж уменьш от* **звезда́**; (*типог*) asterisk.

звен|е́ть (-ю́, -и́шь) *несов неперех* (*звонок*) to ring; (*колокольчик*) to jingle; (*голос*) to chime; (*стаканы*) to clink; (*монеты*) to jangle.

звен|о́ (-а́; *nom pl* -ья, *gen pl* -ьев) *ср* (*цепи, также перен*) link; (*конструкции*) section; (*воен: самолётов*) flight; (*в школе*) group; (*на работе*) team.

звер|е́ть (-ю; *perf* **озвере́ть**) *несов неперех* to go wild.

звери́н|ец (-ца) *м* menagerie.

звери́ный *прил* (*вой, тропа, шкура*) (wild) animal *опред*; (*перен: законы*) bestial; (: *страх, инстинкт*) animal *опред*.

зверово́дств|о (-а) *ср breeding of animals for their fur*.

звероло́в (-а) *м* trapper.

зве́рск|ий (-ая, -ое, -ие) *прил* (*убийство, поступок*) brutal, savage; (*разг: жара, аппетит*) wicked; (: *скука*) severe.

зве́рств|о (-а) *ср* (*жестокость*) brutality; (*обычно мн: ужас*) atrocity.

зве́рств|овать (-ую) *несов неперех* to commit atrocities.

зверь (-я; *gen pl* **-е́й**) *м* beast, wild animal; (*перен*) beast, animal.

звон (-а) *м* clinking; (*ко́локола*) peal, chime.

звона́рь (-я) *м* bell-ringer.

звон|и́ть (-ю́, -и́шь; *perf* **позвони́ть**) *несов непереx* to ring; (*по телефо́ну*): ~ **кому́** to ring *или* phone *или* call (*US*) sb; ~ (*impf*) **в звоно́к** to ring the bell.

звонка́ *сущ см* **звоно́к**.

зво́нкий (-о́нок, -онка́, -о́нко) *прил* (*го́лос, пе́сня*) sonorous; (*дно, свод*) resonant; **зво́нкий согла́сный** (*линг*) voiced consonant.

звон|о́к (-ка́; *nom pl* -ки́) *м* (*на две́ри, на велосипе́де*) bell; (*звук*) ring; (*по телефо́ну*) (telephone) call; **отсиде́ть** (*perf*) **от ~ка́ до ~ка́** ≈ to work from nine to five.

зво́нче *сравн прил от* **зво́нкий**.

звук (-а) *м* sound; **он не произнёс ни зву́ка** he didn't utter a sound; **без зву́ка** (*сде́лать, согласи́ться*) without so much as a word.

звуково́й *прил* sound *опред*, audio; **звукова́я волна́** sound wave; **звукова́я доро́жка** track (*on audio tape*); **звукова́я аппарату́ра** hi-fi equipment.

звукоза́пис|ь (-и) *ж* sound recording; **сту́дия ~и** recording studio.

звукоизоля́ци|я (-и) *ж* soundproofing.

звуконепроница́ем|ый (-, -а, -о) *прил* soundproof.

звукоопера́тор (-а) *м* sound technician.

звукоподража́ни|е (-я) *ср* onomatopoeia.

звукоподража́тельн|ый *прил*: ~**ое сло́во** onomatopoeic word.

звукопрово́дност|ь (-и) *ж* conductivity (*of sound*).

звукопроводя́щий (-яя, -ее, -ие) *прил* conductive (*of sound*).

звукорежиссёр (-а) *м* sound engineer.

звукоснима́тел|ь (-я) *м* pick-up.

звуча́ни|е (-я) *ср* sound; (*перен: полити́ческое итп*) resonance.

звуч|а́ть (*3sg* -и́т, *3pl* -а́т) *несов непереx* (*издава́ть зву́ки*) to sound; (*раздава́ться*) to be heard; ~**и́т убеди́тельно** it sounds convincing; **в её го́лосе** ~**а́ла оби́да** she sounded hurt.

зву́чный (-учен, -учна́, -учно) *прил* (*смех, го́лос*) deep, resounding; (*инструме́нт*) rich-sounding.

звя́кн|уть (-у, -ешь; *impf* **звя́кать**) *сов непереx* (*звоно́к*) to ring; (*стака́н*) to clink; (*стекло́*) to tinkle; (+*instr*; *стака́нами*) to clink; (*ключа́ми*) to jangle.

зги: **ни ~ не ви́дно** it's pitch-black.

з-д *сокр* = **заво́д**.

зда́ни|е (-я) *ср* building.

здесь *наре́ч* here; **есть ~ кто́-нибудь?** is (there) anyone here?; ~ **нет ничего́ смешно́го** there's nothing funny about it.

зде́шн|ий (-яя, -ее, -ие) *прил* (*разг*) local.

здоро́ва|ться (-юсь; *perf* **поздоро́ваться**) *несов возв* ~ **с** +*instr* to say hello to; ~ (**поздоро́ваться** *perf*) **друг с дру́гом** to greet each other; ~ (**поздоро́ваться** *perf*) **за́ руку** to shake hands.

здо́рово *наре́ч* (*разг: отли́чно*) really well; (: *о́чень си́льно*) terribly ♦ *как сказ* (*разг*) it's great.

здоро́в|ый (-о́в, -о́ва, -о́во) *прил* healthy; (*пита́ние*) wholesome; (*перен: иде́я*) sound; (-о́в, -ова́, -ово́; *разг: большо́й*) hefty; **бу́дьте ~о́вы!** (*при чиха́нии*) take care!; (*при чиха́нии*) bless you!

здоро́вь|е (-я) *ср* health; **как Ва́ше ~?** how are you keeping?; **за Ва́ше ~!** (to) your good health!; **на ~!** enjoy it!

здра́вниц|а (-ы) *ж* convalescent home.

здра́во *наре́ч* sensibly.

здравомы́слящ|ий (-ая, -ее, -ие) *прил* sensible.

здравоохране́ни|е (-я) *ср* health care; **систе́ма ~я** ≈ the Health Service (*BRIT*), ≈ Medicaid (*US*); **министе́рство ~я** ≈ Department of Health.

здравоохрани́тельный *прил* health-care.

здра́вств|овать (-ую) *несов непереx* to thrive; ~**уйте** hello; **да ~ует...!** long live ...!

здра́в|ый (-, -а, -о) *прил* (*поли́тика, мысль*) sound.

зе́бр|а (-ы) *ж* zebra; (*пешехо́дный перехо́д*) zebra crossing (*BRIT*).

зев (-а) *м* pharynx.

зева́к|а (-и) *м/ж* (*разг*) idler.

зева́|ть (-ю) *несов непереx* to yawn; (*разг: глазе́ть*) to gawp; (*perf* **прозева́ть**; *разг*) to miss out; **не ~й!** (*разг*) keep your wits about you!

зевка́ *итп сущ см* **зево́к**.

зевн|у́ть (-у́, -ёшь) *сов непереx* to yawn.

зев|о́к (-ка́; *nom pl* -ки́) *м* yawn.

зево́т|а (-ы) *ж* yawning.

зелене́|ть (-ю; *perf* **позелене́ть**) *несов непереx* to go *или* turn green; **на горизо́нте ~л лес** the green of the forest could be seen on the horizon.

зелён|ый (-зёлен, -зелена́, -зелено) *прил* (*также перен*) green; **"3~ые"** (*полит*) the Greens; **дать** (*perf*) **чему́-н ~ую у́лицу** to give sth the green light; **зелёные насажде́ния** trees and shrubs; **зелёный лук** spring onion.

зе́лен|ь (-и) *ж* (*цвет*) green ♦ *собир* (*расти́тельность*) greenery; (*о́вощи и тра́вы*) greens *мн*.

земе́ль *сущ см* **земля́**.

земе́льн|ый *прил* land *опред*; ~ **наде́л** *или* **уча́сток** plot of land.

землевладе́л|ец (-ьца) *м* landowner.

землевладе́ни|е (-я) *ср* landownership.

земледе́л|ец (-ьца) *м* arable farmer.
земледе́ли|е (-я) *ср (возде́лывание земли)* arable farming.
земледе́льца *сущ см* **земледе́лец.**
земледе́льческ|ий (-ая, -ое, -ие) *прил (райо́н)* agricultural; *(маши́ны)* farming *опред.*
землеме́рный *прил* surveying *опред.*
землепо́льзовани|е (-я) *ср* land tenure.
землеро́йный *прил*: **~ые рабо́ты** dredging; **~ая маши́на** dredger.
землетрясе́ни|е (-я) *ср* earthquake.
землечерпа́лк|а (-и) *ж* dredger.
земли́ст|ый (-, -а, -о) *прил (цвет лица́)* sallow; *(песо́к, торф)* earthy.
зем|ля́ (-ли́; *acc sg* **-лю́,** *nom pl* **-ли,** *gen pl* **-éль)** *ж* land; *(плане́та)* earth; *(пове́рхность)* ground; *(по́чва)* earth, soil.
земля́к (-á) *м* compatriot.
земля́н|е (-) *мн* earth dwellers *мн.*
земляни́к|а (-и) *ж (расте́ние)* wild strawberry; *(собир: я́годы)* wild stawberries *мн.*
земля́н|ка (-ки; *gen pl* **-ок)** *ж* dugout *(shelter).*
земляно́й *прил (вал, пол)* earthen; **~ые рабо́ты** excavations; **земляно́й червь** earthworm.
земля́ч|ка (-ки; *gen pl* **-ек)** *ж см* **земля́к.**
земново́дн|ые (-ых; *decl like adj) мн* amphibians *мн.*
земново́дный *прил* amphibious.
земно́й *прил (пове́рхность, кора́)* earth's; *(перен: бла́га, жела́ния)* earthly; **земно́й шар** the globe.
зени́т (-а) *м (также перен)* zenith.
зени́т|ка (-ки; *gen pl* **-ок)** *ж* anti-aircraft gun.
зени́тный *прил (АСТРОНОМИЯ)* zenithal; *(ВОЕН)* anti-aircraft.
зёрен *сущ см* **зерно́.**
зерка́лен *прил см* **зерка́льный.**
зе́рк|ало (-ала; *nom pl* **-ала́,** *gen pl* **-а́л,** *dat pl* **-ала́м)** *ср* mirror; *(перен: во́ды, зали́ва)* glassy surface.
зерка́льный (-ен, -ьна, -ьно) *прил (произво́дство)* mirror *опред;* *(пове́рхность)* glassy; **его́ пье́са – э́то ~ьное отображе́ние действи́тельности** his play is a true reflection of real life; **~ шкаф** mirror wardrobe; **зерка́льный карп** mirror carp.
зерни́ст|ый (-, -а, -о) *прил (ма́сса, снег)* granular; *(пове́рхность)* grainy; **зерни́стая икра́** unpressed caviar.
зерно́ (зерна́; *nom pl* **зёрна,** *gen pl* **зёрен)** *ср* *(пшени́цы)* grain; *(ко́фе)* bean; *(ма́ка)* seed; *(по́роха)* granule ◆ *собир (семенно́е, на хлеб)* grain; **~ и́стины** a grain of truth; **жемчу́жное ~** pearl.
зернов́ой *прил (торго́вля, запа́с)* grain *опред;* **зернов́ые культу́ры** cereals *мн.*
зернов́|ые (-ых; *decl like adj) мн* cereals *мн.*
зерносуши́лк|а (-и) *ж* grain drier.
зерноубо́рочный *прил* harvesting *опред;* **~ комба́йн** combine harvester.

зернохрани́лищ|е (-а) *ср* granary.
зефи́р (-а) *м* ≈ marshmallow.
зигза́г (-а) *м* zigzag.
зи́жд|иться (3sg **-ится,** *3pl* **-утся)** *несов возв:* **~ на** *+prp* to be based on.
ЗИЛ *м сокр =* **Моско́вский автомоби́льный заво́д и́мени И.А. Лихачёва;** *(автомоби́ль) vehicle manufactured at the Moscow car factory.*
зим|á (-ы́; *acc sg* **-у,** *dat sg* **-е́,** *nom pl* **-ы)** *ж* winter.
Зимба́бве *ср нескл* Zimbabwe.
зимбабви́йск|ий (-ая, -ое, -ие) *прил* Zimbabwean.
зи́мн|ий (-яя, -ее, -ие) *прил (день)* winter's; *(пого́да)* wintry; *(лес, оде́жда)* winter *опред.*
зим|ова́ть (-у́ю; *perf* **прозимова́ть)** *несов непере́х (челове́к)* to spend the winter; *(пти́цы)* to winter.
зимо́в|ка (-ки; *gen pl* **-ок)** *ж* wintering place; *(для птиц)* wintering ground; **остава́ться (оста́ться** *perf)* **на ~ку** to spend the winter.
зимо́вь|е (-я) *ср (для люде́й)* winter hut; *(звере́й, птиц)* wintering ground.
зимо́й *нареч* in the winter.
зи|я́ть (3sg **-ет,** *3pl* **-ют)** *несов непере́х* to gape.
злак (-а) *м* grass; **зернов́ой ~** cereal.
зла́чный *прил*: **~ое ме́сто** *(разг)* den of iniquity.
зле́йш|ий (-ая, -ее, -ие) *превос прил*: **~ враг** worst enemy.
зл|ить (-ю, -ишь; *perf* **разозли́ть)** *несов перех* to annoy
▶ **зли́ться** *(perf* **разозли́ться)** *несов возв* to get angry.
зло (зла; *gen pl* **зол)** *ср* evil; *(неприя́тность)* harm ◆ *нареч (посмотре́ть, сказа́ть)* spitefully; **со зла** out of spite; **причиня́ть (причини́ть** *perf)* **кому́-н ~** to cause sb harm; **меня́ ~ берёт** *(разг)* it makes me angry; **у меня́ на неё зла не хвата́ет** *(разг)* she annoys me no end; **из двух зол выбира́ть (вы́брать** *perf)* **ме́ньшее** to choose the lesser of two evils.
зло́б|а (-ы) *ж* malice; **статья́ на ~у дня** an article tackling the burning issue of the moment.
зло́бный (-ен, -на, -но) *прил (хара́ктер, челове́к)* mean; *(улы́бка)* hateful, wicked; *(тон, го́лос)* nasty.
злободне́в|ный (-ен, -на, -но) *прил* topical.
зло́бств|овать (-ую) *несов непере́х* to rage.
злове́щий (-ая, -ее, -ие; -, -а, -е) *прил (улы́бка, вид, слу́хи)* sinister; *(тишина́)* ominous.
злово́нный *прил см* **злово́нный.**
злово́ни|е (-я) *ср* noxious odour *(BRIT)* или odor *(US).*
злово́нный (-ен, -на, -но) *прил* rank, fetid.
зловре́дный (-ен, -на, -но) *прил* mean, horrid.
злоде́й (-я) *м* villain.
злоде́й|ка (-и) *ж см* **злоде́й.**
злоде́йск|ий (-ая, -ое, -ие) *прил* wicked.
злоде́йств|о (-а) *ср* act of evil.
злодея́ни|е (-я) *ср* evil deed, crime.
злой (зол, зла, зло) *прил (челове́к, жена́)* mean,

bad-tempered; (*собака*) vicious; (*глаза, лицо*) mean; (*мысли*) evil; (*карикатура, замечание*) scathing; (*перен: разг: мороз*) cruel; (: *перец, горчица*) lethal; **я зол на тебя́** I'm angry with you; **без зло́го у́мысла** no harm meant; **зла́я судьба́** cruel fate; **злы́е языки́** malicious talk.

злока́чествен|ный (-, -на, -но) *прил* malignant.

злоключе́ни|е (-я) *ср* misadventure.

злонаме́рен|ный (-, -на, -но) *прил* ill-intentioned.

злопа́мят|ный (-ен, -на, -но) *прил* (*человек*) unforgiving.

злополу́ч|ный (-ен, -на, -но) *прил* (*охотник*) ill-fated; (*день, час*) fateful.

злопыха́тел|ь (-я) *м* malevolent person (*мн* people).

злопыха́|ть (-ю) *несов неперех* to rant.

злора́дный (-ен, -на, -но) *прил* gloating.

злора́дств|о (-а) *ср* malicious pleasure.

злора́дств|овать (-ую) *несов неперех* to gloat.

злосло́ви|е (-я) *ср* abuse, ridicule.

злосло́в|ить (-лю, -ишь) *несов неперех* to indulge in ridicule.

зло́ст|ный (-ен, -на, -но) *прил* (*намерение*) malicious; (*правонарушитель*) persistent.

злост|ь (-и) *ж* malice; **сказа́ть** *(perf)* **что-н со зло́стью** to say sth angrily.

злосча́ст|ный (-ен, -на, -но) *прил* ill-fated.

злоумы́шленник (-а) *м* conspirator.

злоумы́шленный *прил* (*поступок*) malicious.

злоупотреб|и́ть (-лю́, -и́шь; *impf* **злоупотребля́ть)** *сов неперех* (+*instr*) to abuse; (*доверием*) to breach; (*сладким*) to indulge in.

злоупотребле́ни|е (-я) *ср* (+*instr*) abuse of; (*обычно мн: незаконные действия*) malpractise; ~ **дове́рием** breach of confidence.

злоупотреблю́ *сов см* **злоупотреби́ть**.

злоупотребля́|ть (-ю) *несов от* **злоупотреби́ть**.

злю́к|а (-и) *м/ж* crosspatch.

змееви́к (-а́) *м* coil.

змее́ныш (-а) *м* (*перен*) little sneak.

змеи́ный *прил* (*кожа*) snake опред; (*нора, питомник*) snake's; (*перен: улыбка, усмешка*) venomous; ~ **яд** venom.

зме́|й (-я; *gen pl* -ев) *м* serpent; (*также:* **возду́шный** ~) kite; **змей-горы́ныч** many-headed dragon.

зме|я́ (-и́; *nom pl* -е́и, *gen pl* -е́й) *ж* (*также перен*) snake; **змея́ подколо́дная** (*разг*) snake in the grass.

знак (-а) *м* sign; (*МАТ, МУЗ, ТИПОГ*) symbol; (*КОМП*) character; **в** ~ +*gen* as a sign of; **под зна́ком** +*gen* in an atmosphere of; **знак ра́венства** equals sign; **зна́ки препина́ния** punctuation marks; **зна́ки разли́чия** (*ВОЕН*) stripes; **зна́ки отли́чия** decorations; **зна́ки зодиа́ка** signs of the Zodiac.

знако́м|ая (-ой; *decl like adj*) *ж см* **знако́мый**.

знако́м|ить (-лю, -ишь; *perf* **познако́мить)** *несов перех*: ~ **кого́-н с** +*instr* to introduce sb to; (*perf* **ознако́мить;** *с приказом, с документом*) to acquaint sb with

▶ **знако́миться** (*perf* **познако́миться)** *несов возв*: ~**ся с** +*instr* (*с человеком*) to meet; (*perf* **ознако́миться;** *с приказом, с документом*) to acquaint o.s. with.

знако́мств|о (-а) *ср* (*отношения*) acquaintance; ~**а** (*круг знакомых*) acquaintances; ~ **с** +*instr* acquaintance with; **пе́рвое** ~ **с** +*instr* first introduction to; **завя́зывать (завяза́ть** *perf*) ~ **с кем-н** to make sb's acquaintance.

знако́м|ый (-, -а, -о) *прил*: ~ (**с** +*instr*) familiar (with) ◆ **(-ого;** *decl like adj*) *м* acquaintance.

знамена́телен *прил см* **знамена́тельный**.

знамена́тел|ь (-я) *м* denominator; **приводи́ть (привести́** *perf*) **к о́бщему** ~**ю** to reduce to a common denominator.

знамена́тель|ный (-ен, -ьна, -ьно) *прил* momentous.

зна́мени *итп сущ см* **зна́мя**.

зна́мени|е (-я) *ср* (*предзнаменование*) omen; **зна́мение вре́мени** sign of the times.

знамени́тост|ь (-и) *ж* celebrity.

знамени́т|ый (-, -а, -о) *прил* famous.

знамен|ова́ть (-у́ю) *несов перех* to mark.

знамено́с|ец (-ца) *м* standard-bearer.

зна́м|я (-ени; *как* вре́мя; *см* Table 4) *ср* banner; (*перен: руководящая идея*) flag; **под** ~**енем** +*gen* (*перен*) under the banner of.

зна́ни|е (-я) *ср* knowledge *только ед*; **со** ~**м де́ла** knowledgeably.

зна́|тный (-а́тен, -атна́, -а́тно) *прил* (*род, человек*) noble; (*учёный*) prominent.

знато́к (-а́) *м* (*литературы*) expert; (*вина*) connoisseur.

зна|ть (-ти) *ж* nobility; ◆ **(-ю)** *несов перех* to know; **она́ не зна́ет ме́ры** she doesn't know when to stop; ~ (*impf*) **своё ме́сто** to know one's place; **кто (его́) зна́ет?** (*разг*) who knows?; **так и** ~**й** (*разг*) mark my words; ~ (*impf*) **це́ну** +*dat* to appreciate; **дава́ть (дать** *perf*) **себя́** ~ to make itself known; **как** ~ maybe; **как зна́ешь** as you wish; **он не** ~**л пораже́ний** he had never known defeat; **он не зна́ет уста́лости** he never tires; **я не зна́ю поко́я** I don't have a moment's peace

▶ **зна́ться** *несов возв*: **зна́ться с** +*instr* (*разг*) to associate with.

значе́ни|е (-я) *ср* (*слова, взгляда*) meaning; (*решения, победы*) importance; **э́то не име́ет** ~**я** it's not important; **придава́ть (прида́ть** *perf*) **осо́бое/большо́е** ~ **чему́-н** to attach special/ great importance to sth.

зна́чимост|ь (-и) *ж* (*важность*) significance; (*наличие смысла*) meaningfulness.

зна́чим|ый (-, -а, -о) *прил* important; ~**ая часть**

сло́ва unit of meaning.

зна́чит *вводн сл (разг)* so ♦ **союз** (*следовательно*) that means; ~, **ты не зна́ешь** so, you don't know then; **идёт снег, ~, сего́дня бу́дет хо́лодно** it's snowing, that means it's going to be cold today.

значи́тельный (-ен, -на, -ьно) *прил* significant; (*вид, взгляд*) meaningful; **в ~ьной сте́пени** to a significant degree.

зна́ч|ить (-у, -ишь) *несов (не)перех* to mean; **что э́то ~ит?** what does it mean?; **э́то ничего́ не ~ит** it doesn't mean anything

▸ зна́читься *несов возв* (*состоять*) to appear; (*числиться*): **~ся больны́м** to be considered ill; **его́ и́мя ~ится в спи́ске** his name appears on the list.

знач|о́к (-ка́) *м* badge; (*пометка*) mark.

зна́ющ|ий (-ая, -ее, -ие; -, -а, -е) *прил* competent.

зноб|и́ть (*3sg* -и́т) *несов безл*: **его́ ~и́т** he's shivery.

зно́ен *прил см* зно́йный.

зно|й (-я) *м* intense heat.

зно́йный (-ен, -йна, -йно) *прил* (*день, лето*) scorching; (*перен: взгляд*) intense; (: *чувство*) burning.

зоб (-а; *loc sg* -у́, *nom pl* -ы́) *м* (*у птицы*) crop; (*МЕД*) goitre (*BRIT*), goiter (*US*).

зов (-а) *м* (*о помощи, громкий*) call; **приходи́ть** (**прийти́** *perf*) **по пе́рвому зо́ву** to come at the first call.

зову́ *итп несов см* звать.

зодиа́к (-а) *м* zodiac.

зо́дчеств|о (-а) *ср* architecture.

зо́дч|ий (-его; *decl like adj*) *м* architect.

зол *сущ см* зло ♦ *прил см* злой.

зол|а́ (-ы́) *ж* cinders *мн.*

золо́в|ка (-ки; *gen pl* -ок) *ж* sister-in-law, husband's sister.

золоти́ст|ый (-, -а, -о) *прил* golden.

золо|ти́ть (-чу́, -ти́шь; *perf* позолоти́ть) *несов перех* to gild; **со́лнце позолоти́ло верху́шки дере́вьев** the sun cast a golden light over the tree tops.

золотни́к (-а) *м* slide valve.

зо́лот|о (-а) *ср* gold; (*золотые нити*) gold thread; **она́ про́сто ~** (*перен*) she's a real gem.

золотоиска́тель (-я) *м* gold-digger.

золот|о́й *прил* gold; (*рубль, локоны, лучи солнца итп*) golden; (*перен: человек, время*) wonderful; (: *работник*) priceless ♦ (-о́го; *decl like adj*) *м* gold coin; (*дорогой*) precious; **золота́я сва́дьба** golden wedding *или* anniversary; **золота́я середи́на** the golden mean; **золото́е дно** gold mine; **золото́е се́рдце** heart of gold; **золото́е пра́вило** golden rule; **золото́й век** golden age; **золото́й фонд** gold reserves.

золотоно́с|ный (-ен, -на, -но) *прил*: ~ **райо́н** goldfield.

золотопромы́шленность (-и) *ж* gold-

mining.

золочёный *прил* gilt.

золочу́ *несов см* золоти́ть.

Зо́лушк|а (-и) *ж* Cinderella.

зо́н|а (-ы) *ж* zone; (*лесная*) area; (*для заключённых*) prison; **при́городная** ~ suburb; ~ **о́тдыха** holiday area; ~ **обстре́ла** field of fire.

зона́льный (-ен, -ьна, -ьно) *прил* (*граница, деление*) zone *опред*; (*особенности, соревнование*) regional.

зонд (-а) *м* (*МЕД, ТЕХ*) probe.

зонди́р|овать (-ую; *perf* прозонди́ровать) *несов перех* to probe; ~ (**прозонди́ровать** *perf*) **по́чву** *или* **обстано́вку** (*перен*) to test the water.

зонт (-а́) *м* (*от дождя*) umbrella; (*от солнца*) parasol; (*над дверью, над ветриной*) awning.

зо́нтик (-а) *м* (*от дождя*) umbrella; (*от солнца*) parasol.

зоо́лог (-а) *м* zoologist.

зоологи́ческ|ий (-ая, -ое, -ие) *прил* zoological.

зооло́ги|я (-и) *ж* zoology.

зоомагази́н (-а) *м* pet shop.

зоопа́рк (-а) *м* zoo.

зооте́хник (-а) *м* animal geneticist.

зо́р|и *итп сущ см* заря́.

зо́р|кий (-кая, -кое, -кие; -ок, -ка, -ко) *прил* (*человек*) sharp-eyed; (*глаза, ум*) sharp; (*перен: наблюдатель*) observant.

зрач|о́к (-ка́) *м* (*АНАТ*) pupil.

зре́лищ|е (-а) *ср* (*предмет обозрения*) sight, spectacle; (*представление*) show.

зре́лищн|ый *прил*: ~ые **предприя́тия** entertainment venues *мн.*

зре́лость (-и; *ж*) (*плода, яблока*) ripeness; (*организма, человека*) maturity.

зре́л|ый (-, -а, -о) *прил* mature; (*плод, зерно*) ripe.

зре́ни|е (-я) *ср* (eye)sight.

зре|ть (-ю; *perf* созре́ть) *несов неперех* to mature; (*плод, яблоко*) to ripen; (*решение, мысль*) to develop; (*обида*) to grow.

зри́тель (-я) *м* (*в театре, в кино*) member of the audience; (*на стадионе*) spectator; (*наблюдатель*) onlooker.

зри́тельный *прил* (*память, восприятие*) visual; **зри́тельный зал** auditorium; **зри́тельный нерв** optic nerve.

зря *нареч* (*разг: без пользы*) for nothing, in vain; ~ **тра́тить** (*impf*) **де́ньги/вре́мя** to waste money/time; ~ **ты ему́ э́то сказа́л** you shouldn't have told him about it; **ты ~ купи́л э́ту кни́гу** there was no need to buy this book.

зря́ч|ий (-ая, -ее, -ие) *прил* sighted.

зуб (-а; *nom pl* -ы, *gen pl* -о́в) *м* tooth (*мн* teeth); (*nom pl* -ья, *gen pl* -ьев; *пилы, шестерни*) tooth (*мн* teeth); (*грабель, вилки*) prong; **у неё ~ на́ ~ не попада́ет** her teeth are chattering; **говори́ть** (*impf*) **сквозь зу́бы** (*разг*) to talk through one's teeth; **э́то мне не по ~ам** (*перен*) it's too much for me; **он вооружён до ~о́в** he's armed to the teeth; **онá на негó ~ имéет** (*разг*) she bears a grudge against him; **ни в ~ ногóй** (*разг*) he *итп* doesn't have a clue; **зуб мýдрости** wisdom tooth.

зубáст|ый (-, -а, -о) *прил* (*разг: щука, собака*) with big sharp teeth; (*перен: разг*) sharp-tongued.

зуб|éц (-цá; *nom pl* -цы́) *м* (*пилы, шестерни*) tooth (*мн* teeth); (*грабель, вилки*) prong.

зуби́л|о (-а) *ср* chisel.

зубкá *итп сущ см* **зубóк**.

зубнóй *прил* dental; **зубнáя боль** toothache; **зубнáя пáста** toothpaste; **зубнáя щётка** toothbrush; **зубнóй врач** dentist; **зубнóй протéз** dentures.

зубоврачéбный *прил*: ~ **кабинéт** dental surgery (*BRIT*), dentist's office (*US*).

зубоскáл (-а) *м* (*разг*) scoffer.

зубоскáл|ить (-ю, -ишь) *несов неперех* (*разг*) to scoff.

зубочи́ст|ка (-ки; *gen pl* -ок) *ж* toothpick.

зубр (-а) *м* bison; (*перен: ретроград*) die-hard; (*разг: опытный специалист*) boffin.

зубри́л|а (-ы) *м/ж* (*разг*) swot (*BRIT*), grind (*US*).

зубри́ть (-ю́, -йшь; *impf* **вы́зубрить**) *несов перех* (*разг*) to swot (*BRIT*), grind (*US*).

зубцá *итп сущ см* **зубéц**.

зубчáт|ый *прил* (*стена, башня*) castellated; ~**ое колесó** cog(wheel); ~**ая передáча** toothed gear; ~ **край** serrated edge.

зуд (-а) *м* (*также перен*) itch.

зу|дéть (*3sg* **-ди́т**, *3pl* **-дя́т**) *несов неперех* (*разг: чесаться*) to itch; (**-жý**, **-ди́шь**; *комар, пчела*) to buzz; (*перен: нудиться*) to nag.

ЗУПВ *сокр* (= *запоминáющее устрóйство с произвóльной вы́боркой*) RAM (= *random access memory*).

зы́б|кий (-кая, -кое, -кие; -ок, -ка, -ко) *прил* (*поверхность озера*) ripply; (*грунт, болото*) swampy; (*основание*) shaky; (*перен: положение*) unstable.

зыбý́ч|ий (-ая, -ее, -ие; -, -а, -е) *прил*: ~**ие пески́** quicksands *мн*.

зыб|ь (-и) *ж* ripple.

зы́ч|ный (-ен, -на, -но) *прил* (*голос*) booming; (*хохот*) thunderous.

зя́бко *как сказ* (*разг: холодно*): **мне ~** I feel chilly.

зя́блик (-а) *м* chaffinch.

зя́бн|уть (-у, -ешь; *perf* **озя́бнуть**) *несов неперех* to be cold.

зябь (-и) *ж* field *ploughed in autumn ready for sowing in the spring*.

зять (-я) *м* (*муж дочери*) son-in-law; (*муж сестры*) brother-in-law, sister's husband; (*муж золовки*) brother-in-law (*husband's sister's husband*).

~ И, и ~

И, и *сущ нескл (буква)* the 9th letter of the Russian alphabet.

KEYWORD

и *союз* **1** and; **я и мой друг** my friend and I; **и вот показа́лся лес** and then a forest appeared

2 *(тоже)*: **и он пошёл в теа́тр** he went to the theatre too; **и он не пришёл** he didn't come either

3 *(даже)* even; **и сам не рад** even he himself is not pleased

4 *(именно)*: **о том и речь!** that's just it!

5 *(во фразах)*: **ну и нагле́ц же ты!** what a cheek you have!; **туда́ и сюда́** here and there; **и ... и ...** both ... and ....

и́бо *союз (так как)* for, because.

и́в|а (**-ы**) *ж* willow.

ива́н-ча́й (**-я**) *м (no pl)* rosebay willowherb.

и́вовый *прил* willow.

и́вол|га (**-ги**; *gen pl* **-**) *ж* oriole.

игл|а́ (**-ы́**; *nom pl* **-ы**) *ж* needle; *(у ежа)* spine; *(проигрывателя)* needle, stylus.

иглодержа́тел|ь (**-я**) *м (МЕД)* needleholder; *(проигрывателя)* cartridge.

иглоука́лывани|е (**-я**) *ср* acupuncture.

игнори́р|овать (**-ую**; *perf* **игнори́ровать** *или* **проигнори́ровать**) *несов перех* to ignore.

и́г|о (**-а**) *ср (рабства итп)* yoke.

иго́л|ка (**-ки**; *gen pl* **-ок**) *ж* = **игла́**; **сиде́ть** *(impf)* **как на ~х** to be on tenterhooks.

иго́льный *прил*: **~ое у́шко** eye of a needle.

иго́льчатый *прил (мех)* spiky; *(подшипник)* needle *опред*.

иго́рный *прил*: **~ дом** gaming club.

игр|а́ (**-ы́**; *nom pl* **-ы**) *ж* game; *(на скрипке итп)* playing; *(актёра)* performance; **~ воображе́ния** fantasy; **~ слов** play on words.

игра́льн|ый *прил*: **~ые ка́рты** playing cards *мн*.

игра́|ть (**-ю**) *несов неперех* to play ♦ *(perf* **сыгра́ть)** *перех* to play; *(пьесу)* to perform; **~** *(сыгра́ть perf)* **в** +*acc (СПОРТ)* to play; **~** *(impf)* **в пря́тки** to play hide-and-seek *(ВRIT)* **или** hide-and-go-seek *(US)*; **~** *(impf)* **людьми́/в демокра́тию** *(перен)* to play with people/at democracy; **~** *(impf)* **на** +*prp (МУЗ)* to play; **~** *(сыгра́ть perf)* **конём/королём** to play one's knight/king; **~** *(сыгра́ть perf)* **на чьих-н сла́бостях** to play on sb's weaknesses; **~** *(impf)* **на чьих-н не́рвах** to irritate sb; **~** *(сыгра́ть perf)*

сва́дьбу to celebrate a wedding; **вино́ ~ло в бока́ле** the wine sparkled in the glass.

игра́ючи *нареч (разг: легко)* with one's eyes closed.

игри́вый (**-**, **-а**, **-о**) *прил* playful.

игри́стый *прил* sparkling.

игров|о́й *прил*: **~а́я ко́мната** playroom; **~ы́е ви́ды спо́рта** team sports; **игрово́й автома́т** fruit machine.

игро́к (**-á**) *м* player; *(в азартные игры)* gambler.

игроте́к|а (**-и**) *ж (собрание игр)* compendium *(ВRIT)*; *(комната)* games room.

игру́шек *сущ см* **игру́шка**.

игру́шечный *прил* toy *опред*; *(перен)* tiny.

игру́ш|ка (**-ки**; *gen pl* **-ек**) *ж* puppet; **ёлочные ~ки** Christmas tree decorations.

идеа́л (**-а**) *м* ideal; **~ демокра́тии** democratic ideal; **он – мой ~** he's someone I look up to.

идеа́лен *прил см* **идеа́льный**.

идеализи́р|овать (**-ую**) *(не)сов перех* to idealize.

идеали́зм (**-а**) *м* idealism.

идеали́ст (**-а**) *м* idealist.

идеалисти́ческ|ий (**-ая**, **-ое**, **-ие**) *прил* idealistic.

идеалисти́чный *прил* idealistic.

идеа́льн|ый (**-ен**, **-ьна**, **-ьно**) *прил* ideal.

иде́йн|ый (**-ен**, **-йна**, **-йно**) *прил (идеологический)* ideological; *(прогрессивный)* radical; **~йная осно́ва рома́на** the main theme of the novel.

идём *несов см* **идти́**.

идентифици́р|овать (**-ую**) *(не)сов перех* to identify.

иденти́чн|ый (**-ен**, **-на**, **-но**) *прил* identical.

идео́лог (**-а**) *м* ideologist.

идеологи́ческ|ий (**-ая**, **-ое**, **-ие**) *прил* ideological.

идеоло́ги|я (**-и**) *ж* ideology.

иде́|я (**-и**) *ж* idea; **по ~е** *(разг)* supposedly; **по ~е** +*gen* in accordance with; **подава́ть (пода́ть** *perf)* **кому́-н ~ю** to give sb an idea.

идилли́ческ|ий (**-ая**, **-ое**, **-ие**) *прил* idyllic.

иди́лли|я (**-и**) *ж* idyll.

идио́м|а (**-ы**) *ж* idiom.

идио́т (**-а**) *м (также МЕД)* idiot.

идиоти́зм (**-а**) *м (МЕД)* mental retardation; *(разг: глупость)* idiocy.

идио́тск|ий (-ая, -ое, -ие) *прил* idiotic.
и́дол (-а) *м* idol.
идти́ (*см* **Table 18)** *несов непереx* to go;
(*пешком*) to walk; (*дни, годы*) to go by; (*фильм, спектакль итп*) to be on; (*часы*) to work; (*товар*) to sell; (*подходить: одежда*): ~ **к** +*dat* to go with; ~ **(пойти́** *perf*) **(в/на** +*acc*) to go (to); ~ **(пойти́** *perf*) +*instr* (*конём, тузом итп*) to play; **я шёл 3 часа́** I walked for 3 hours; **иди́ сюда́!** come here!; **иду́!** (I'm) coming!; **идёт по́езд/авто́бус** the train/bus is coming; **по́езд идёт до Москвы́** the train goes as far as Moscow; **маши́на идёт со ско́ростью 100км в час** the car is going at *или* doing 100km per hour; **идёт дождь/снег** it's raining/snowing; **идёт зима́** winter is coming; **идёт гроза́** there is a storm coming; **дела́ иду́т хорошо́/пло́хо** things are going well/badly; **сейча́с иду́т перегово́ры/экза́мены** the talks/exams are in progress; **что сейча́с идёт в кино́?** what's on at the cinema just now?; **спекта́кль идёт 2 часа́** the play goes on for 2 hours; **мой часы́ иду́т ме́дленно/бы́стро** my watch is slow/fast; **Вам идёт э́та шля́па** the hat suits you; **из трубы́ идёт дым** there is smoke coming from the chimney; **у меня́ идёт кровь из но́са** my nose is bleeding; **ему́ идёт пя́тый год** he was four on his last birthday; ~ **(пойти́** *perf*) **пешко́м** to walk, go on foot; ~ **(пойти́** *perf*) **на рабо́ту/в теа́тр** to go to work/the theatre; ~ **(пойти́** *perf*) **на э́кспорт/прода́жу** to be for export/sale; **э́ти я́блоки пойду́т на варе́нье** these apples will do for making jam; ~ **(пойти́** *perf*) **на у́быль** to decrease; ~ **(пойти́** *perf*) **на сниже́ние** to descend; ~ **(пойти́** *perf*) **на риск** to take a risk; ~ **(пойти́** *perf*) **на компроми́сс** to go for a compromise; ~ **(пойти́** *perf*) **на хи́трость/обма́н** to resort to cunning/deception; **идёт!** (*разг*) fine!
иезуи́т (-а) *м* Jesuit.
ие́н|а (-ы) *ж* yen.
иера́рхи|я (-и) *ж* hierarchy.
иеро́глиф (-а) *м* (*китайский, японский*) character; (*египетский*) hieroglyph (*мн* hieroglyphics).
Иерусали́м (-а) *м* Jerusalem.
ИЖ *м сокр* = *Иже́вский мотоцикле́тный заво́д*; (*мотоцикл*) *motorcycle manufactured at the Izhevsk motorcycle factory*.
иждиве́н|ец (-ца) *м* (*ребёнок, престарелые*) dependant; (*бездельник*) sponger.
иждиве́ни|е (-я) *ср* maintenance; **состоя́ть** (*impf*) *или* **быть** (*impf*) **на** ~**и у** +*gen* to be dependent on.
иждиве́нца *итп сущ см* **иждиве́нец**.
иждиве́нчеств|о (-а) *ср* dependence.

The spelling rules for Russian are shown on page xvii.

KEYWORD

из *предл* (+*gen*) **1** (*о направлении действия откуда-нибудь*) out of; **он вы́шел из ко́мнаты** he went out of the room; **она́ доста́ла из карма́на плато́к** she took a handkerchief out of her pocket
2 (*при обозначении происхождения, источника*) from; **све́дения из кни́ги** information from a book; **из достове́рных исто́чников** from reliable sources; **я из Москвы́** I am from Moscow
3 (*при выделении части из целого*) of; **вот оди́н из приме́ров** here is one of the examples
4 (*при обозначении компонентов целого*) made of; **э́тот стол сде́лан из сосны́** this table is made of pine; **ва́за из стекла́** a glass vase; **варе́нье из я́блок** apple jam; **блу́за из нейло́на** nylon blouse
5 (*при указании причины*) out of; **из осторо́жности/за́висти** out of wariness/envy; **из эконо́мии** in order to save money
6 (*во фразах*): **из го́да в год** year in, year out; **я бежа́л изо всех сил** I ran at top speed

---

изб|а́ (-ы́; *nom pl* **-ы)** *ж* hut.
избави́тел|ь (-я) *м* saviour.
избави́тельниц|а (-ы) *ж см* **избави́тель**.
изба́в|ить (-лю, -ишь; *impf* **избавля́ть)** *сов переx*: ~ **кого́-н от** +*gen* (*от проблем, от забот*) to relieve sb of; (*от врагов*) to deliver sb from
▸ **изба́виться (** *impf* **избавля́ться)** *сов возв*: ~**ся от** +*gen* (*от проблем, от посетителей*) to get rid of; (*от страха, от предрассудков*) to get over.
избало́ван|ный (-, -на, -но) *прил* spoilt.
избало́в|ать (-ую) *сов см* **бало́вать**.
избало́в|аться (-у́юсь; *impf* **избало́вываться)** *сов возв* (*разг*) to become spoilt.
избе́га|ть (-ю) *сов переx* (*разг*) to run around.
избега́|ть (-ю) *несов от* **избежа́ть, избе́гнуть** ♦ *непереx*: ~ **чего́-н/** +*infin* to avoid sth/doing.
избе́г|нуть (-ну, -нешь; *pt* **-, -ла, -ло,** *impf* **избега́ть)** *сов непереx* = **избежа́ть**.
избегу́ *итп сов см* **избежа́ть**.
избежа́ни|е (-я) *ср*: **во** ~ +*gen* (in order to) to avoid.
избежа́ть (*как* **бежа́ть;** *см* **Table 20;** *impf* **избега́ть)** *сов непереx*: ~ +*gen* to avoid.
изберу́ *итп сов см* **избра́ть**.
избива́|ть (-ю) *несов от* **изби́ть**.
избие́ни|е (-я) *ср* beating; (*массовое убийство*) massacre.
избира́телен *прил см* **избира́тельный**.
избира́тел|ь (-я) *м* voter.
избира́тельниц|а (-ы) *ж см* **избира́тель**.
избира́тел|ьный *прил* (*система*) electoral; (-**ен, -ьна, -ьно;** *эффект*) selective; ~**ная кампа́ния** election campaign; **избира́тельный**

уча́сток polling station; **избира́тельный бюллете́нь** ballot paper.

избира́|ть (-ю) *несов от* **избра́ть ♦** *перех* to elect.

изби́т|ый (-, -а, -о) *прил* clichéd, hackneyed.

из|би́ть (-обью, -обьёшь; *impf* **избива́ть)** *сов перех (человека)* to beat; *(обувь)* to wear out.

изборозди́ть (-жу́, -ди́шь) *сов от* **борозди́ть.**

избра́ни|е (-я) *ср* election.

избра́нник (-а) *м* chosen one; ~ **судьбы́** fate's darling; **наро́дные ~и** deputies.

избра́нниц|а (-ы) *ж см* **избра́нник.**

и́збранн|ые (-ых; *decl like adj)* *мн* select *или* chosen few *мн.*

и́збранный *прил (рассказы, стихи)* selected; *(люди, круга)* select; *см также* **и́збранные.**

изб|ра́ть (-еру́, -ерёшь; *pt* **-ра́л, -рала́, -ра́ло,** *impf* **избира́ть)** *сов перех (профессию)* to choose; *(президента)* to elect; **избира́ть (~** *perf)* **кого́-н в парла́мент** to elect sb to parliament.

избы́т|ок (-ка) *м (излишек)* surplus; *(обилие)* excess; **име́ть** *(impf)* **что-н в ~ке** to have plenty of sth; **э́того хва́тит с ~ком** it is more than enough; **она́ запла́кала от ~ка чувств** overwhelmed by emotion, she burst into tears.

избы́точ|ный (-ен, -на, -но) *прил (вес, влага)* excess *опред; (информация)* abundant; **~ное предложе́ние (ЭКОН)** excess supply.

изва́яни|е (-я) *ср* effigy.

изве́да|ть (-ю; *impf* **изве́дывать)** *сов перех* to come to know.

изведу́(сь) *итп сов см* **извести́(сь).**

изве́дыва|ть (-ю) *несов от* **изве́дать.**

и́зверг (-а) *м* monster *(fig).*

изве́рг|нуть (-у, -ешь; *impf* **изверга́ть)** *сов перех* to spew (out).

изверже́ни|е (-я) *ср* eruption.

изве́р|иться (-юсь, -ишься) *сов возв:* ~ **в** *+prp* to lose faith in.

изверну́|ться (-у́сь, -ёшься; *impf* **изве́ртываться** *или* **извора́чиваться)** *сов возв* to twist around; *(перен)* to pull through.

изве́стен *прил см* **изве́стный.**

изв|ести́ (-еду́, -едёшь; *pt* **-ёл, -ела́, -ело́,** *impf* **изводи́ть)** *сов перех (разг: истратить)* to fritter away; (: *измучить)* to exasperate; *(истребить)* to exterminate

▸ **извести́сь** *(impf* **изводи́ться)** *сов возв* to torment o.s.

изве́сти|е (-я) *ср* news; *см также* **изве́стия.**

изве|сти́ть (-щу́, -сти́шь; *impf* **извеща́ть)** *сов перех:* ~ **кого́-н о** *+prp* to inform sb of.

изве́сти|я (-й) *мн (издание)* bulletin *ед.*

изве́стк|а (-и) *ж* slaked lime.

изве́стно *как сказ:* ~, **что ...** it is well known that ...; **мне э́то ~** I know about it; **наско́лько мне ~** as far as I know; **как ~** as is well known.

изве́стност|ь (-и) *ж* fame; **по́льзоваться** *(impf)* **~ю** to be well known; **ста́вить (поста́вить** *perf)* **кого́-н в ~** to inform sb.

изве́ст|ный (-ен, -на, -но) *прил* famous, well-known; *(no short form; разг:* **лентяй, бабник)** notorious; *(условия)* certain; ~ **+instr** famous *или* well-known for; **он ~ен как тала́нтливый руководи́тель** he is known to be a talented leader; **~ное де́ло!** *(разг)* that's no surprise!

известня́к (-а́) *м* limestone.

и́звест|ь (-и) *ж* lime.

изве́ч|ный (-ен, -на, -но) *прил (проблема, спор)* perpetual.

извеща́|ть (-ю) *несов от* **извести́ть.**

извеще́ни|е (-я) *ср* notification; *(КОММ)* advice note; **почто́вое ~** signed receipt of delivery.

извещу́ *сов см* **извести́ть.**

извива́|ться (-юсь) *несов возв (змея)* to slither; *(человек)* to writhe; *(дорога, река)* to wind.

извили́н|а (-ы) *ж* bend; ~ **мо́зга** convolution.

изви́листый (-, -а, -о) *прил* winding, twisting.

извине́ни|е (-я) *ср* apology; *(оправдание)* excuse; **проси́ть (попроси́ть** *perf)* **~я (у кого́-н)** to apologize (to sb).

извини́тельный *прил (тон, улыбка)* apologetic; *(-ен, -ьна, -ьно; ошибка, слабость)* excusable, forgivable.

извин|и́ть (-ю́, -и́шь; *impf* **извиня́ть)** *сов перех (простить):* ~ **что-н (кому́-н)** to excuse (sb for) sth; **~и́те!** excuse me!; **~и́те, Вы не ска́жете где вокза́л?** excuse me, could you tell me where the station is?; **в э́том, ~и́те, я с Ва́ми не согла́сен** sorry, but I cannot agree with you on that

▸ **извини́ться** *(impf* **извиня́ться)** *сов возв:* **~ся (за** *+acc)* to apologize (for); **он ~и́лся, что не позвони́л** he apologized for not phoning *(BRIT)* *или* calling *(US).*

извиня́ющийся (-аяся, -ееся, -иеся) *прил* apologetic.

извлёк *итп сов см* **извле́чь.**

извлека́|ть (-ю) *несов от* **извле́чь.**

извлеку́ *итп сов см* **извле́чь.**

извлече́ни|е (-я) *ср (золота, пользы итп)* extraction; *(из документа)* extract, excerpt.

извл|е́чь (-еку́, -ечёшь итп, -еку́т; *pt* **-ёк, -екла́, -екло́,** *impf* **извлека́ть)** *сов перех (занозу, осколок)* to remove, take out; *(золото)* to extract; *(перен: пользу, выгоду итп)* to derive; **извлека́ть (~** *perf)* **уро́к** to learn a lesson; **извлека́ть (~** *perf)* **ко́рень (МАТ)** to find the root.

извне́ *нареч* from outside.

изво|ди́ть(ся) (-жу́(сь), -о́дишь(ся)) *несов от* **извести́(сь).**

изво́зчик (-а) *м (кучер)* coachman *(мн* coachmen); *(экипаж)* cab *(coach).*

изво́л|ить (-ю, -ишь) *несов неперех:* ~ **+infin** to condescend to do; **~ьте не крича́ть** would you mind not shouting.

извора́чива|ться (-юсь) *несов от* **изверну́ться.**

изворо́тлив|ый (-, -а, -о) *прил (человек)* wily; *(ум, делец)* shrewd.

извра|ти́ть (-щу́, -ти́шь; *impf* **извраща́ть**) *сов перех* to distort.

извраще́ни|е (-я) *ср* distortion; **полово́е** ~ sexual perversion.

извращён|ный (-, -на, -но) *прил* perverted.

извращу́ *сов см* **извратить**.

изга́|дить (-жу, -дишь) *сов перех* (*разг*) to mess up.

изги́б (-а) *м* bend.

изгиба́|ть(ся) (-ю(сь)) *несов от* **изогну́ть(ся)**.

изгла́|дить (-жу, -дишь; *impf* **изгла́живать**) *сов перех*: ~ **что-н из па́мяти** to blot sth out of one's memory

▶ **изгла́диться** (*impf* **изгла́живаться**) *сов возв* to be blotted out.

изгна́ни|е (-я) *ср* (*ссылка*) exile; (*врага*) expulsion; (*злых духов*) exorcism.

изгна́нник (-а) *м* exile.

изгна́нниц|а (-ы) *ж см* **изгна́нник**.

изг|на́ть (-оню́, -о́нишь; *pt* -на́л, -нала́, -на́ло, *impf* **изгоня́ть**) *сов перех* to drive out; (*сослать*) to exile.

изго́|й (-я) *м* outcast.

изголо́вь|е (-я) *ср*: **у** ~**я** at the head of the bed.

изголода́|ться (-юсь) *сов возв* to be starving; (*перен*): ~ **по** +*dat* (*по книгам*) to long *или* yearn for; ~ (*perf*) **по ла́ске** to crave affection.

изгоню́ *итп сов см* **изгнать**.

изгоня́|ть (-ю) *несов от* **изгна́ть**.

и́згород|ь (-и) *ж* fence; **жива́я** ~ hedge.

изгото́в|ить (-лю, -ишь; *impf* **изготовля́ть**) *сов перех* to manufacture.

изготовле́ни|е (-я) *ср* manufacture.

изгото́влю *сов см* **изгото́вить**.

изготовля́|ть (-ю) *несов см* **изгото́вить**.

изгры́з|ть (-у́, -ёшь; *pt* -, -ла, -ло) *сов перех* to gnaw (away) at.

изд. *сокр* (= **изда́ние**) ed. (= *edition*).

изда|ва́ть (-ю́, -ёшь) *несов от* **изда́ть**.

и́здавна *нареч* for a long time.

издади́м *итп сов см* **изда́ть**.

издалека́ *нареч* from a long way off *или* away; **начина́ть (нача́ть** *perf*) **разгово́р** ~ (*перен*) to start a conversation in a roundabout way.

и́здали *нареч* = **издалека́**.

изда́м *итп сов см* **изда́ть**.

изда́ни|е (-я) *ср* (*действие*) publication; (*изданная вещь*) edition.

изда́ст *сов см* **изда́ть**.

изда́тел|ь (-я) *м* publisher.

изда́тельск|ий (-ая, -ое, -ие) *прил* publishing *опред*.

изда́тельств|о (-а) *ср* publisher, publishing house.

изда́ть (*как* **дать**; *см* **Table 14**; *impf* **издава́ть**) *сов перех* (*книгу*) to publish; (*закон, постановление*) to issue; (*крик, стон*) to let out; (*запах*) to give off.

изд-во *сокр* (= **изда́тельство**) pub(l). (= *publisher*).

издева́тельск|ий (-ая, -ое, -ие) *прил* (*насмешливый*) mocking, scoffing; (*оскорбительный*) abusive.

издева́тельств|о (-а) *ср* mockery; (*наглое*) jibe; (*жестокое*) abuse.

издева́|ться (-юсь) *несов возв*: ~ **над** +*instr* (*над подчинёнными*) to make a mockery of; (*над книгой*) to pour scorn on; (*над чьей-н одеждой*) to mock, ridicule.

издёв|ка (-ки; *gen pl* -ок) *ж* (*разг*) jibe.

изде́ли|е (-я) *ср* (*товар*) article; **ювели́рные** ~**я** jewellery (*BRIT*), jewelery (*US*); **стекля́нные** ~**я** glassware; **игру́шка куста́рного** ~**я** handmade toy.

издёрган|ный (-, -на, -но) *прил* (*разг*) edgy.

издёрга|ть (-ю) *сов перех* (*разг*) to put on edge

▶ **издёргаться** *сов возв* (*разг*) to become edgy.

издер|жа́ть (-ержу́, -е́ржишь; *impf* **изде́рживать**) *сов перех* (*деньги*) to use up; (*ресурсы*) to exhaust.

изде́рж|ки (-ек) *мн* (*производственные*) expenses *мн*; **суде́бные** ~ legal costs; **э́то всё** – ~ **плохо́го воспита́ния** it's all the result of bad upbringing.

издеру́ *итп сов см* **изодра́ть**.

издыха́ни|е (-я) *ср*: **при после́днем** ~**и** on one's deathbed.

изжи́|ть (-ву́, -вёшь; *pt* -л, -ла́, -ло, *impf* **изжива́ть**) *сов перех* (*плохую привычку*) to overcome; (*преступность*) to eliminate; **изжива́ть** (~ *perf*) **себя́** to outlive its usefulness.

изжо́г|а (-и) *ж* heartburn.

из-за *предл*: ~ +*gen* (*занавески*) from behind; (*угла*) from around; (*по вине*) because of; **встава́ть (встать** *perf*) ~ **стола́** to get up from the table; ~ **того́ что** because; ~ **тебя́ мы пропусти́ли по́езд** we missed the train because of you.

иззя́б|нуть (-ну, -нешь; *pt* -, -ла, -ло) *сов неперех* (*разг*) to be frozen stiff.

излага́|ть (-ю) *несов от* **изложи́ть**.

изла́мыва|ть (-ю) *несов от* **излома́ть**.

излече́ни|е (-я) *ср* (*лечение*) treatment; (*выздоровление*) recovery; **быть** (*impf*) **на** ~**и** to undergo treatment.

изле́чива|ть (-ю) *несов от* **излечи́ть**

▶ **изле́чиваться** *несов от* **излечи́ться** ♦ *возв* (*болезнь*) to be curable.

излечи́м|ый (-, -а, -о) *прил* curable.

изле́ч|ить (-ечу́, -е́чишь; *impf* **изле́чивать**) *сов перех*: ~ **кого́-н (от** +*gen*) to cure sb (of)

▶ **излечи́ться** *сов возв*: ~**ся от** +*gen* (*от болезни*) to recover from; (*от наркомании, от алкоголизма*) to be cured of.

изли́|ть (**изолью́, изолье́шь**; *pt* -л, -ла́, -ло, *impf* **излива́ть**) *сов перех* (*перен: тоску*) to pour out; **изливать** (~ *perf*) **душу** to pour one's heart out; **изливать** (~ *perf*) **гнев** to vent one's anger

▶ **излиться** (*impf* **изливаться**) *сов возв* to pour one's heart out; **изливаться** (*impf*) **в благодарностях** to express one's great appreciation.

излиш|ек (-ка) *м* (*остаток*) remainder; ~ +*gen* (*влаги, веса*) excess of.

излишество (-а) *ср* overindulgence.

излишка *итп сущ см* **излишек**.

излиш|ний (-няя, -нее, -ние; -ен, -ня, -не) *прил* unnecessary; **комментарии ~ни** there is nothing to add.

излияни|е (-я) *ср* (*чувств*) gush; (*обычно мн*: *дружеские, любовные*) outburst.

изловч|иться (-усь, -ишься) *сов возв* (*приспособиться*) to manage.

изложени|е (-я) *ср* presentation.

изл|ожить (-ожу, -ожишь; *impf* **излагать**) *сов перех* (*события*) to recount; (*просьбу, решение итп*) to state.

изломан|ный (-, -на, -но) *прил* (*судьба, жизнь*) ruined; (*характер*) unbalanced.

излома|ть (-ю; *impf* **изламывать**) *сов перех* (*забор, игрушку*) to smash; (*перен: жизнь*) to ruin; (: *характер*) to unbalance.

излуча|ть (-ю) *несов перех* (*также перен*) to radiate.

▶ **излучаться** *несов возв* to radiate.

излучени|е (-я) *ср* radiation.

излучин|а (-ы) *ж* bend.

излюбленный *прил* favourite (*BRIT*), favorite (*US*).

измаза|ть(ся) (-жу(сь), -жешь(ся)) *сов от* **мазать(ся)**.

измара|ть(ся) (-ю(сь)) *сов от* **марать(ся)**.

изматыва|ть(ся) (-ю(сь)) *несов от* **измотать(ся)**.

измельча|ть (-ю) *сов от* **мельчать**.

измельч|ить (-у, -ишь) *сов от* **мельчить**.

▶ **измельчиться** *сов возв* to crumble.

измен|а (-ы) *ж* (*родине*) treason; (*другу*) betrayal; **государственная** ~ high treason; **супружеская** ~ adultery.

изменени|е (-я) *ср* change; (*поправка*) alteration.

изм|енить (-еню, -енишь; *impf* **изменять**) *сов перех* to change ♦ *неперех:* ~ +*dat* (*родине, другу*) to betray; (*супругу*) to be unfaithful to; (*память*) to fail; **силы ему ~енили** his strength failed him

▶ **измениться** (*impf* **изменяться**) *сов возв* to change.

изменник (-а) *м* (*родине*) traitor.

изменниц|а (-ы) *ж см* **изменник**.

изменчивый (-, -а, -о) *прил* changeable.

изменяем|ый (-, -а, -о) *прил* (*линг*): **~ое окончание** variable ending.

изменя|ть(ся) (-ю(сь)) *несов от* **изменить(ся)**.

измерени|е (-я) *ср* (*действие: площади*) measurement; (*величина*) dimension.

измерительный *прил* measuring *опред*.

измер|ить (-ю, -ишь; *impf* **измерять**) *сов перех* to measure; **измерять** (~ *perf*) **температуру кому-н** to take sb's temperature; ~ (*perf*) **кого-н взглядом** to look sb up and down.

измеря|ться (3sg -ется, 3pl -ются) *несов возв* (+*instr*): ~ **килограммами/метрами** to be measured in kilogrammes/metres (*BRIT*) *или* meters (*US*).

изможлени|е (-я) *ср* exhaustion.

изможлён|ный (-, -а, -о) *прил* (*человек*) worn out; (-, -на, -но; *вид, лицо*) haggard.

измок|нуть (-ну, -нешь; *pt* -, -ла, -ло) *сов неперех* to get soaked.

измор (-а) *м:* **взять кого-н/что-н ~ом** (*город*) to wage a war of attrition against sb/sth; (*перен: разг*) to wear down.

изморозь (-и) *ж* hoarfrost.

изморось (-и) *ж* drizzle.

измота|ть (-ю; *impf* **изматывать**) *сов перех* to wear out

▶ **измотаться** (*impf* **изматываться**) *сов возв* (*разг*) to be worn out.

измучен|ный (-, -а, -о) *прил* (*человек*) worn out; (-, -на, -но; *лицо*) haggard.

измуч|ить (-у, -ишь) *сов от* **мучить**.

измыва|ться (-юсь) *несов возв:* ~ **над** +*instr* (*разг*) to taunt.

измышлени|е (-я) *ср* fabrication.

из|мять(ся) (-омну(сь), -омнёшь(ся)) *сов от* **мять(ся)**.

изнанк|а (-и) *ж* (*одежды*) inside; (*ткани*) wrong side; (*перен: жизни, событий*) dark side.

изнасил|овать (-ую) *сов от* **насиловать**.

изначаль|ный (-ен, -ьна, -ьно) *прил* initial.

изнашива|ть(ся) (-ю(сь)) *несов от* **износить(ся)**.

изнежен|ный (-, -а, -о) *прил* pampered.

изнеж|ить (-у, -ишь) *сов перех* to pamper

▶ **изнежиться** *сов возв* to be pampered.

изнемог *итп сов см* **изнемочь**.

изнемога|ть (-ю) *несов от* **изнемочь**.

изнемогу *итп сов см* **изнемочь**.

изнеможени|е (-я) *ср* exhaustion; **до ~я** to the point of exhaustion.

изнеможён|ный (-, -а, -о) *прил* (*человек*) worn out; (-, -на, -но; *вид, лицо*) haggard.

изнемо|чь (-гу, -жешь *итп*, **-гут;** *pt* -г, -гла, -гло, *impf* **изнемогать**) *сов неперех* to be exhausted.

износ (-а) *м* (*механизмов*) wear; (*перен: организма*) ageing; **работать** (*impf*) **на** ~ (*перен*) to work o.s. into the ground.

изн|осить (-ошу, -осишь; *impf* **изнашивать**) *сов перех* to wear out

▶ **износиться** (*impf* **изнашиваться**) *сов возв* to wear out.

изношен|ный (-, -а, -о) *прил* worn-out.

изношу(сь) *сов см* **износить(ся)**.

изнурён|ный (-, -а, -о) *прил* (*человек*) exhausted; (-, -на, -но; *лицо, вид*) haggard.

изнури|тельный (-ен, -ьна, -ьно) *прил*

exhausting.

изнури́ть (-ю́, -и́шь; *impf* **изнуря́ть**) *сов перех* to exhaust.

изнутри́ *нареч* from inside.

изныва́|ть (-ю) *несов неперех* to languish.

изо *предл* = **из**.

изоби́ли|е (-я) *ср* abundance; **в ~и** in abundance.

изоби́л|овать (*3sg* -**ует**, *3pl* -**уют**) *несов неперех* (+*instr*) to abound in.

изоби́л|ьный (-ен, -ьна, -ьно) *прил* abundant.

изоблича́|ть (-ю) *несов от* **изобличи́ть** ◆ *перех* (*обнаружить*): ~ **кого́-н в** +*prp* (*подлеж: одежда, акцент итп*) to give sb away as.

изоблич|и́ть (-у́, -и́шь; *impf* **изоблича́ть**) *сов перех* (*шпиона, взяточника итп*) to expose; **изоблича́ть** (~ *perf*) **кого́-н во лжи/в моше́нничестве** to expose sb's lies/deception.

изобража́|ть(ся) (-ю(сь)) *несов от* **изобрази́ть(ся)**.

изображе́ни|е (-я) *ср* image; (*действие: событиия*) depiction, representation.

изображу́(сь) *сов см* **изобрази́ть(ся)**.

изобрази́тел|ьный (-ен, -ьна, -ьно) *прил* descriptive; **изобрази́тельное иску́сство** fine art.

изобра|зи́ть (-жу́, -зи́шь; *impf* **изобража́ть**) *сов перех* (*на картине, в романе итп*) to depict, portray; (*подлеж: лицо*) to show; (*копировать*) to impersonate; **изобража́ть** (~ *perf*) **из себя́ наи́вного/знатока́** to make o.s. out to be naive/an expert

▶ **изобрази́ться** (*impf* **изобража́ться**) *сов возв* to show; **на его́ лице́ ~зи́лся у́жас** a look of horror came over his face.

изобр|ести́ (-ету́, -ете́шь; *pt* -ёл, -ела́, -ело́, *impf* **изобрета́ть**) *сов перех* to invent.

изобрета́тел|ь (-я) *м* inventor.

изобрета́тельниц|а (-ы) *ж см* **изобрета́тель**.

изобрета́тельность (-и) *ж* inventiveness.

изобрета́тельств|о (-а) *ср* innovation.

изобрета́|ть (-ю) *несов от* **изобрести́**.

изобрете́ни|е (-я) *ср* invention.

изобью́ *итп сов см* **изби́ть**.

изогну́ть (-у́, -ёшь; *impf* **изгиба́ть**) *сов перех* to bend

▶ **изогну́ться** (*impf* **изгиба́ться**) *сов возв* to bend.

из|одра́ть (-деру́, -дерёшь; *pt* -одра́л, -одрала́, -одра́ло) *сов перех* (*разг*) to rip to shreds.

изойти́ (*как* **идти́**; *см* **Table 18**; *impf* **исходи́ть**) *сов неперех*: ~ **слеза́ми** to cry one's eyes out; **она́ ~шла́ го́рем** she was completely grief-stricken.

изоли́рованный *прил* (*случай, явление итп*) isolated; (*комната, провод*) insulated.

изоли́р|овать (-ую) (*не*)*сов перех* (*больного, преступника*) to isolate; (*вход*) to cut off; (*ТЕХ,*

ЭЛЕК) to insulate

▶ **изоли́роваться** (*не*)*сов возв* (*человек*) to isolate o.s.

изолью́(сь) *итп сов см* **изли́ть(ся)**.

изоля́тор (-а) *м* (*ТЕХ, ЭЛЕК*) insulator; (*в больни́це*) isolation unit; (*в тюрьме́*) solitary confinement.

изоляцио́нн|ый *прил*: ~**ая ле́нта** insulating tape.

изоля́ци|я (-и) *ж* (*см глаг*) isolation; insulation; **жить** (*impf*) **в ~и** to live in isolation.

изомну́(сь) *итп сов см* **измя́ть(ся)**.

изопью́ *итп сов см* **испи́ть**.

изорв|а́ть (-у́, -ёшь; *pt* -а́л, -ала́, -а́ло) *сов перех* to rip up; ~ (*perf*) **в кло́чья** to tear to shreds.

изото́п (-а) *м* isotope.

изотрётся *итп сов см* **истере́ться**.

изошёл *итп сов см* **изойти́**.

изощрён|ный (-, -на, -но) *прил* sophisticated.

изощр|и́ться (-ю́сь, -и́шься; *impf* **изощря́ться**) *сов возв* (*отличи́ться*) to surpass o.s.; (*вкус, ум*) to become more sophisticated.

изощр|я́ться (-ю́сь) *несов от* **изощри́ться** ◆ *неперех*: ~ **в** +*prp* to excel in.

из-под *предл* (+*gen*) from under(neath); (*около*) from outside; ~ **стола́ вы́ползла ко́шка** a cat crawled from under the table; **он прие́хал ~ Ки́ева** he comes from outside Kiev; **вы́ходи́ть** (**вы́йти** *perf*) ~ **чьего́-н влия́ния** to free o.s. from sb's influence; **бежа́ть** (*impf*) ~ **стра́жи** to escape from custody; **ба́нка ~ варе́нья** jam jar; **буты́лка ~ во́дки** vodka bottle.

изразе́ц (-ца́) *м* tile.

изразцо́вый *прил* tiled.

Изра́ил|ь (-я) *м* Israel.

изра́ильск|ий (-ая, -ое, -ие) *прил* Israeli.

израильтя́н|ин (-ина; *nom pl* -е, *gen pl* -) *м* Israeli.

израильтя́н|ка (-ки; *gen pl* -ок) *ж см* **израильтя́нин**.

изра́н|ить (-ю, -ишь) *сов перех* to injure badly.

израсхо́д|овать (-ую) *сов от* **расхо́довать**.

и́зредка *нареч* now and then *или* again.

изре́|зать (-жу, -жешь; *impf* **изреза́ть**) *сов перех* to cut up; (*подлеж: дороги, каналы*) to crisscross.

изрёк *итп сов см* **изре́чь**.

изрека́|ть (-ю) *несов от* **изре́чь**.

изреку́ *итп сов см* **изре́чь**.

изрече́ни|е (-я) *ср* utterance.

изре́|чь (-ку́, -че́шь *итп*, -ку́т; *pt* -ёк, -екла́, -екло́, *impf* **изрека́ть**) *сов перех* to utter.

изреше|ти́ть (-чу́, -ти́шь) *сов перех*: ~ **кого́-н пу́лями** to pepper sb with bullets.

изр|уби́ть (-убло́, -у́бишь; *impf* **изруба́ть**) *сов перех* (*убить*) to hack to pieces.

изрыга́|ть (-ю) *несов перех* (*лаву*) to spew (out); (*перен: проклятия*) to let out a torrent of.

изры́т|ый (-, -а, -о) *прил (поверхность)* pitted; ~ **о́спой** pockmarked.

изры́|ть (-о́ю, -о́ешь) *сов перех* to riddle.

изря́д|ный (-ен, -на, -но) *прил (сумма, доход)* fair; *(раза: мошенник, пьяница итп)* real.

изуве́р (-а) *м* monster.

изуве́рск|ий (-ая, -ое, -ие) *прил* monstrous.

изуве́рств|о (-а) *ср* monstrosity.

изуве́ч|ить (-у, -ишь; *impf* **изуве́чивать**) *сов перех* to maim

▶ **изуве́читься** (*impf* **изуве́чиваться**) *сов возв* to be maimed.

изукра́|сить (-шу, -сишь; *impf* **изукра́шивать**) *сов перех* to adorn; *(разг: избить)* to beat black and blue.

изуми́тел|ьный (-ен, -ьна, -ьно) *прил* marvellous (*BRIT*), marvelous (*US*), wonderful.

изуми́|ть (-лю́, -и́шь; *impf* **изумля́ть**) *сов перех* to amaze, astound

▶ **изуми́ться** (*impf* **изумля́ться**) *сов возв* to be amazed.

изумле́ни|е (-я) *ср* amazement; **приходи́ть (прийти́** *perf*) **в ~** to be amazed; **с ~м** *(слушать, рассматривать)* in amazement; **я с ~м обнару́жил, что ...** to my great amazement I discovered that ....

изумлю́(сь) *сов см* **изуми́ть(ся)**.

изумля́|ть(ся) (-ю(сь)) *несов от* **изуми́ть(ся)**.

изумру́д (-а) *м* emerald.

изумру́дный *прил (кольцо итп)* emerald; *(цвет)* emerald-green.

изуро́д|овать (-ую) *сов от* **уро́довать**.

изуча́|ть (-ю) *несов от* **изучи́ть** ◆ *перех (о процессе)* to study.

изуче́ни|е (-я) *ср* study.

из|учи́ть (-учу́, -у́чишь; *impf* **изуча́ть**) *сов перех (язык, предмет)* to learn; *(понять)* to get to know; *(исследовать)* to study.

изъеда́|ть (*3sg* -ет, *3pl* -ют) *несов от* **изъе́сть**.

изъе́ден|ный (-, -а, -о) *прил:* ~ **мо́лью** moth-eaten; ~ **кислото́й** eaten away by acid.

изъеди́м *итп сов см* **изъе́сть**.

изъе́з|дить (-жу, -дишь) *сов перех* to travel (round).

изъ|е́сть (*как есть; см* **Table 15**; *impf* **изъеда́ть**) *сов перех (мех, ткань)* to eat away; *(металл)* to corrode.

изъяви́тел|ьный *прил (линг):* ~**ое наклоне́ние** the indicative mood.

изъяв|и́ть (-явлю́, -я́вишь; *impf* **изъявля́ть**) *сов перех* to indicate.

изъя́н (-а) *м* flaw.

изъясн|и́ть (-ю́, -и́шь; *impf* **изъясня́ть**) *сов перех* to clarify.

изъя́ти|е (-я) *ср (см глаг)* withdrawal; removal.

изъя́|ть (изыму́, изы́мешь; *impf* **изыма́ть**) *сов перех (из обращения, из продажи)* to withdraw; *(отобрать)* to remove.

изыска́ни|е (-я) *ср* investigation; *(геологические)* exploration.

изы́сканность (-и) *ж* refinement.

изы́скан|ный (-, -на, -но) *прил* refined.

изыска́тель (-я) *ср* surveyor.

изыска́тельск|ий (-ая, -ое, -ие) *прил* exploratory.

изыска́|ть (-ыщу́, -ы́щешь; *impf* **изы́скивать**) *сов перех* to find.

изы́скива|ть (-ю) *несов от* **изыска́ть** ◆ *перех (искать)* to seek out.

изыщу́ *итп сов см* **изыска́ть**.

изю́м (-а) *м собир* raisins *мн*.

изю́мин|а (-ы) *ж* raisin.

изю́мин|ка (-ки; *gen pl* -ок) *ж уменьш от* **изю́мина**; *(перен)* highlight; **без** ~**ки** lacklustre.

изя́щен *прил см* **изя́щный**.

изя́ществ|о (-а) *ср* elegance.

изя́щ|ный (-ен, -на, -но) *прил* elegant.

ика́|ть (-ю) *несов неперех* to hiccup.

икн|у́ть (-у́, -ёшь) *сов неперех* to hiccup.

ико́н|а (-ы) *ж (РЕЛ)* icon.

иконопи́с|ец (-ца) *м* icon painter.

и́конопис|ь (-и) *ж* icon painting.

иконоста́с (-а) *м* iconostasis.

ико́т|а (-ы) *ж* hiccups *мн*.

икр|а́ (-ы́) *ж (рыбы)* roe; *(чёрная, красная)* caviar; *(кабачковая, баклажанная)* pâté; *(nom pl* -ы; *АНАТ)* calf *(мн* calves)*.

икри́н|ка (-ки; *gen pl* -ок) *ж* grain of caviar.

икс (-а) *м (МАТ)* X; **ми́стер И**~ Mr X.

ИЛ (-а) *м сокр* = **самолёт констру́кции С.В. Илью́шина**.

ил (-а) *м* silt.

и́ли *союз* or; **чай** ~ **ко́фе** tea or coffee; ~ **...** ~ **...** either ... or ...; ~ **ты не понима́ешь?** *(разг)* don't you understand or something?

и́лист|ый (-, -а, -о) *прил* silt *опред*.

иллюзиони́ст (-а) *м* conjurer.

иллю́зи|я (-и) *ж (также перен)* illusion.

иллюзо́р|ный (-ен, -на, -но) *прил* illusory.

иллюмина́тор (-а) *м (корабля)* porthole; *(самолёта)* window.

иллюмина́ци|я (-и) *ж* illuminations *мн*.

иллюстра́тор (-а) *м* illustrator.

иллюстра́ци|я (-и) *ж* illustration.

иллюстри́р|овать (-ую; *perf* **иллюстри́ровать** *или* **проиллюстри́ровать**) *несов перех* to illustrate.

ильм (-а) *м* elm.

им *мест см* **он, оно́, они́**.

им. *сокр* = **и́мени**.

имби́р|ь (-я) *м* ginger.

и́мени *итп сущ см* **и́мя**.

име́ни|е (-я) *ср* estate.

имени́нник (-а) *м person who is celebrating his name day or birthday*.

имени́нниц|а (-ы) *ж см* **имени́нник**.

имени́н|ы (-) *мн (РЕЛ)* name day *ед*.

имени́тельный *прил (линг):* ~ **паде́ж** the nominative case.

имени́т|ый (-, -а, -о) *прил* renowned.

и́менно *част* exactly, precisely ◆ *союз (перед перечислением):* **а** ~ namely; **э́то на́до сде́лать** ~ **сего́дня** it has to be done today; ~ **в**

э́том до́ме я роди́лся it was in this house that I was born; ~ так я и поступи́л that is exactly what I did; вот ~! exactly!, precisely!; на собра́нии прису́тствовало 6 челове́к а ~: Ивано́в, Петро́в ... there were 6 people present at the meeting, namely Ivanov, Petrov ....

именно́й прил (оружие, часы) personalized; (акции, чек) nontransferable; **именно́й про́пуск** pass (issued in somebody's name); **именно́й спи́сок** nominal roll.

имен|ова́ть (-у́ю; perf **наименова́ть**) несов перех to name.

име́|ть (-ю) несов перех to have; ~ (impf) **ме́сто** (совершаться) to take place; ~ (impf) **де́ло с** +instr to deal with; **я не хочу́ ~ с ним де́ло** I don't want anything to do with him; ~ (impf) **в виду́** to bear in mind; (подразумевать) to mean; **я ~ю зада́чу/цель** или **зада́чей/це́лью** +infin my task/aim is to do; ~ (impf) **что́-нибудь про́тив** +gen to have something against; **ничего́ не ~** (impf) **про́тив** +gen to have nothing against

▸ **име́ться** несов возв (сведения, средства) to be available; **у нас ~ются ну́жные сре́дства** we have the necessary resources available.

и́ми мест см **они́**.

и́мидж (-а) м image.

имита́ци|я (-и) ж imitation.

имити́р|овать (-ую; perf **сымити́ровать**) несов перех to imitate.

иммигра́нт (-а) м immigrant.

иммигра́нт|ка (-ки; gen pl -ок) ж см **иммигра́нт**.

иммиграцио́нный прил immigration.

иммигра́ци|я (-и) ж immigration ♦ собир immigrants мн.

иммигри́р|овать (-ую) (не)сов неперех to immigrate.

иммуните́т (-а) м (МЕД, перен): ~ **(к** +dat) immunity (to); **выраба́тывать (вы́работать** perf) ~ **к** +dat to develop an immunity to; **у меня́** ~ **к шу́му/кри́тике** I'm immune to noise/criticism; **дипломати́ческий** ~ diplomatic immunity.

имму́нн|ый прил (МЕД): ~**ая систе́ма** immune system.

иммуноло́ги|я (-и) ж immunology.

императи́в (-а) м (также линг) imperative.

импера́тор (-а) м emperor.

импера́торск|ий (-ая, -ое, -ие) прил imperial.

императри́ц|а (-ы) ж empress.

империали́зм (-а) м imperialism.

империали́ст (-а) м imperialist.

империалисти́ческ|ий (-ая, -ое, -ие) прил imperialistic.

импе́ри|я (-и) ж empire.

импе́рск|ий (-ая, -ое, -ие) прил imperial.

импи́чмент (-а) м (ПОЛИТ) impeachment.

импланта́т (-а) м (МЕД) implant.

импланта́ци|я (-и) ж implantation.

импланти́р|овать (-ую) (не)сов перех to implant.

импони́р|овать (-ую) несов неперех (+dat) to appeal to.

и́мпорт (-а) м (ввоз) importation ♦ собир (товары) imports мн; (раз: о заграничных товарах) foreign goods мн; **по́шлины/нало́г на** ~ import duty/tax; **и́мпорт капита́ла** capital investment from abroad.

импортёр (-а) м importer.

импорти́р|овать (-ую) (не)сов перех to import.

и́мпортный прил imported; **и́мпортная кво́та** import quota.

импоте́нт (-а) м impotent male.

импоте́нт|ный (-ен, -на, -но) прил (МЕД) impotent.

импоте́нци|я (-и) ж (МЕД) impotence.

импреса́рио м нескл (музыканта) agent; (устроитель концертов итп) impresario.

импрессиони́зм (-а) м impressionism.

импрессионисти́ческ|ий (-ая, -ое, -ие) прил impressionist.

импровиза́тор (-а) м improviser.

импровиза́ци|я (-и) ж improvisation.

импровизи́р|овать (-ую; perf **импровизи́ровать** или **сымпровизи́ровать**) (не)сов перех to improvise.

и́мпульс (-а) м (ФИЗ, БИО) impulse; (перен): ~ **(к** +dat) (к работе, к реформам итп) impetus (for).

импульси́вный (-ен, -на, -но) прил impulsive.

иму́щественный прил property опред.

иму́ществ|о (-а) ср property; (принадлежности) belongings мн; **дви́жимое** ~ (ЮР) movables; **недви́жимое** ~ (ЮР) property.

иму́щий (-ая, -ее, -ие) прил (классы) propertied; **власть ~ие** the powers that be.

и́м|я (-ени; как вре́мя; см Table 4) ср (также перен) name; (также: ли́чное ~) first или Christian name; (знаменитый человек) famous name; **во** ~ +gen (ради) in the name of; **на** ~ +gen (письмо) addressed to; **биле́ты оста́влены на Ва́ше** ~ the tickets have been left under your name; **от ~ени** +gen on behalf of; **моё** ~ – **Мари́я** my name is Maria; **Теа́тр ~ени Че́хова** the Chekhov Theatre; **~енем зако́на** in the name of the law; **называ́ть** (impf) **ве́щи свои́ми имена́ми** to call a spade a spade; **и́мя прилага́тельное** adjective; **и́мя существи́тельное** noun.

инакомы́слящ|ий (-его; decl like adj) м dissident.

ина́че нареч (по-другому) differently ♦ союз otherwise, or else; **вы́глядеть** (impf) ~ to look different; **так и́ли** ~ one way or another; **а как же ~?** how else?

инвали́д (-а) м disabled person (мн people).

инвали́дн|ый *прил:* ~ая коля́ска wheelchair; **инвали́дный дом** home for the disabled.
инвали́дност|ь (-и) *ж* disability; **пе́нсия по ~и** disablement benefit; **получа́ть** (**получи́ть** *perf*) ~ to be registered as disabled.
инвалю́т|а (-ы) *ж сокр* (= **иностра́нная валю́та**) foreign currency.
инвалю́тный *прил* (*поступле́ния, счёт*) foreign-currency.
инвентариза́ци|я (-и) *ж* stocktaking.
инвента́р|ь (-я́) *м* (*предме́ты*) equipment; (*опись*) inventory.
инве́рси|я (-и) *ж* (*линг*) inversion.
инвести́р|овать (-ую) (*не*)*сов* (*не*)*перех* (*экон*) to invest.
инвестицио́нный *прил* investment *опред*; **инвестицио́нный банк** investment bank.
инвести́ци|я (-и) *ж* (*обычно мн*) investment; **иностра́нные ~и** foreign investment; **дохо́д от ~й** investment income.
инве́стор (-а) *м* investor.
ингаля́тор (-а) *м* (*мед*) inhaler.
ингаля́ци|я (-и) *ж* inhalation.
ингредие́нт (-а) *м* ingredient.
ингу́ш (-а́) *м* Ingush.
Ингуше́ти|я (-и) *ж* Ingushetia.
ингу́ш|ка (-ки; *gen pl* -ек) *ж см* **ингу́ш**.
и́ндеве|ть (-ю; *perf* **зай́ндеветь**) *несов неперех* to become covered in frost.
инде́ек *сущ см* **инде́йка**.
инде́|ец (-йца) *м* Native American, North American Indian.
инде́йка (-йки; *gen pl* -ек) *ж* turkey.
инде́|йца *итп сущ см* **инде́ец**.
и́ндекс (-а) *м* (*цен, книг*) index (*мн* indexes); (*также:* **почто́вый ~**) post (*BRIT*) *или* zip (*US*) code; **фо́ндовый ~** share index; **и́ндекс** (**ро́зничных/потреби́тельных**) цен (retail/consumer) price index.
индекса́ци|я (-и) *ж* (*экон*) index-linking (*BRIT*), indexing (*US*).
индекси́р|овать (-ую) *несов перех* (*экон*: *зарпла́ту*) to index, index-link (*BRIT*).
индиа́н|ка (-ки; *gen pl* -ок) *ж см* **инди́ец, инде́ец**.
индиви́д (-а) *м* individual.
индивидуа́лен *прил см* **индивидуа́льный**.
индивидуали́зм (-а) *м* individualism.
индивидуали́ст (-а) *м* individualist.
индивидуа́льност|ь (-и) *ж* (*совоку́пность черт*) individuality; (*ли́чность*) individual.
индивидуа́л|ьный (-ен, -ьна, -ьно) *прил* individual.
индиви́дуум (-а) *м* individual.
инди́го *ср нескл* indigo.
инди́|ец (-йца) *м* Indian.
инди́йск|ий (-ая, -ое, -ие) *прил* Indian; **Инди́йский океа́н** the Indian Ocean.
инди́|йца *итп сущ см* **инди́ец**.
И́нди|я (-и) *ж* India.
индонези́ек *сущ см* **индонези́йка**.
индонези́|ец (-йца) *м* Indonesian.
индонези́|йка (-йки; *gen pl* -ек) *ж см*

индонези́ец.
индонези́йск|ий (-ая, -ое, -ие) *прил* Indonesian.
индонези́|йца *итп сущ см* **индонези́ец**.
Индоне́зи|я (-и) *ж* Indonesia.
индосса́нт (-а) *м* (*комм*) endorser.
индосса́т (-а) *м* (*комм*) endorsee.
индуи́зм (-а) *м* Hinduism.
инду́кци|я (-и) *ж* (*физ*) induction.
инду́с (-а) *м* Hindu.
индустриализа́ци|я (-и) *ж* industrialization.
индустриализи́р|овать (-ую) (*не*)*сов перех* to industrialize.
индустриа́льный *прил* industrial.
индустри́|я (-и) *ж* industry; ~ **мо́ды/ кино́/тури́зма** the fashion/film/tourist industry.
индю́к (-а́) *м* turkey cock.
индю́шка (-ки; *gen pl* -ек) *ж* (*разг*) = **инде́йка**.
и́не|й (-я) *м* hoarfrost.
ине́ртный (-ен, -на, -но) *прил* (*физ, хим*) inert; (*перен*) inactive.
ине́рци|я (-и) *ж* (*физ, перен*) inertia; **дви́гаться** (*impf*) **по ~и** (*физ*) to move by inertia; **де́лать** (*impf*) **что-н по ~и** to do sth out of habit; **я по ~и дал ему́ ста́рый телефо́н** I gave him my old telephone number automatically.
инжене́р (-а) *м* engineer; ~ **по те́хнике безопа́сности** health and safety officer; **инжене́р-меха́ник/-констру́ктор/-строи́тель** mechanical/design/construction engineer.
инжене́рный *прил:* ~ая нау́ка engineering (*science*); ~ое де́ло engineering (*profession*).
инжи́р (-а) *м* (*де́рево*) fig ◆ *собир* (*плоды́*) figs *мн*.
ИНИО́Н (-а) *м сокр* = Институ́т нау́чной информа́ции по обще́ственным нау́кам.
инициализи́р|овать (-ую) (*не*)*сов перех* (*комп*) to initialize.
инициа́л|ы (-ов) *мн* initials *мн*.
инициати́в|а (-ы) *ж* initiative; **по со́бственной ~e** on one's own initiative.
инициати́в|ный (-ен, -на, -но) *прил* enterprising; **он о́чень ~ челове́к** he has a lot of initiative; **инициати́вная гру́ппа** action group.
инициа́тор (-а) *м* initiator.
инкасса́тор (-а) *м* security guard (*employed to collect and deliver money*).
инкасси́р|овать (-ую) (*не*)*сов перех* (*комм*) to encash.
инка́ссо *ср нескл* (*комм*) encashment.
инквизи́тор (-а) *м* (*перен*) inquisitor.
инквизи́ци|я (-и) *ж* (*перен*) inquisition.
инко́гнито *нареч, м/ж нескл* incognito.
Инкомба́нк (-а) *м сокр* (= **Иностра́нный комме́рческий банк**) foreign commercial bank.
инкримини́р|овать (-ую) (*не*)*сов перех:* ~ **что-н кому́-н** to charge sb with sth.
инкруста́ци|я (-и) *ж* inlay.
инкрусти́р|овать (-ую) (*не*)*сов перех* to inlay.
инкуба́тор (-а) *м* incubator.

инкубацио́нный *прил*: ~ пери́од (*БИО, МЕД*) incubation period.
инкуба́ци|я (-и) *ж* incubation.
иногда́ *нареч* sometimes.
иногоро́дн|ий (-яя, -ее, -ие) *прил* from another town ♦ **(-его**; *decl like adj*) *м person from another town*.
иноэе́мный *прил* foreign.
ин|о́й *прил* different ♦ *мест* (*некоторый*) some (people); ~ **раз** at times; ~**ы́ми слова́ми** in other words; **не что** ~**о́е, как ..., не кто** ~**, как ...** none other than ...; ~**ы́е счита́ют, что ...** some (people) think (that) ....
и́нок (-а) *м* monk (*in the Orthodox Church*).
инопланетя́н|ин (-ина; *nom pl* -**е**, *gen pl* -**)** *м* alien.
иноро́д|ный (-ен, -на, -но) *прил* alien; **иноро́дное те́ло** (*МЕД*) foreign body.
иносказа́ни|е (-я) *ср* allegory.
иносказа́тел|ьный (-ен, -ьна, -ьно) *прил* allegorical.
иностра́н|ец (-ца) *м* foreigner.
иностра́н|ка (-ки; *gen pl* -**ок)** *ж см* **иностра́нец**.
иностра́нн|ый *прил* foreign; **Министе́рство** ~**ых дел** Ministry of Foreign Affairs, ≈ Foreign Office (*BRIT*), ≈ State Department (*US*).
иностра́нок *сущ см* **иностра́нка**.
иностра́нца *итп сущ см* **иностра́нец**.
иноязы́чн|ый *прил* (*слово*) foreign; ~**ое населе́ние** foreign-language-speaking population.
инсинуа́ци|я (-и) *ж* insinuation.
инспекти́р|овать (-ую; *perf* **проинспекти́ровать)** *несов перех* to inspect.
инспе́ктор (-а) *м* inspector.
инспе́кци|я (-и) *ж* inspection; (*организация*) inspectorate.
инста́нци|я (-и) *ж* (*ПОЛИТ*) body, authority.
инсти́нкт (-а) *м* instinct.
инстинкти́в|ный (-ен, -на, -но) *прил* instinctive.
институ́т (-а) *м* institute; (*семьи, брака*) institution.
институ́тск|ий (-ая, -ое, -ие) *прил* institute *опред*.
инструкти́р|овать (-ую; *perf* **проинструкти́ровать)** (*не)сов перех* to instruct.
инстру́ктор (-а) *м* instructor; ~ **по пла́ванию/лы́жам** swimming/ski instructor.
инстру́кци|я (-и) *ж* instructions *мн*; (*также:* ~ **по эксплуата́ции**) instructions (for use).
инструме́нт (-а) *м* (*МУЗ, ТЕХ, перен*) instrument ♦ *собир* instruments *мн*.
инструмента́льный *прил* (*МУЗ*) instrumental; **инструмента́льная му́зыка** instrumental music; **инструмента́льный анса́мбль** instrumental ensemble; **инструмента́льный**

цех tool workshop.
инсули́н (-а) *м* insulin.
инсу́льт (-а) *м* (*МЕД*) stroke.
инсцени́р|овать (-ую) (*не)сов перех* (*перен*: *обморок, ограбление*) to stage; (*роман*) to adapt.
инсцениро́вк|а (-и) *ж* adaptation.
ин-т *сокр* = **институ́т**.
интегра́л (-а) *м* (*МАТ*) integral.
интегра́льн|ый *прил*: ~**ое исчисле́ние** integral calculus.
интегри́р|овать (-ую) (*не)сов перех* (*также МАТ*) to integrate.
интегра́ци|я (-и) *ж* (*также МАТ*) integration.
интелле́кт (-а) *м* intellect.
интеллектуа́л (-а) *м* intellectual.
интеллектуа́л|ьный (-ен, -ьна, -ьно) *прил* intellectual; **интеллектуа́льная со́бственность** intellectual property.
интеллиге́нт (-а) *м* member of the intelligentsia.
интеллиге́нт|ный (-ен, -на, -но) *прил* cultured and educated.
интеллиге́нци|я (-и) *ж собир* the intelligentsia; **техни́ческая/тво́рческая** ~ the science/arts community.
интенда́нт (-а) *м* (*ВОЕН*) quartermaster.
интенси́в|ный (-ен, -на, -но) *прил* intensive; (*окраска*) intense.
интенсифика́ци|я (-и) *ж* intensification.
интенсифици́р|овать (-ую) (*не)сов перех* to intensify.
интеракти́вный *прил* (*КОМП*) interactive.
интерва́л (-а) *м* interval; (*ТИПОГ*) spacing; **с** ~**ом в 10 мину́т** with a 10 minute interval.
интервент (-а) *м* interventionist.
интерве́нци|я (-и) *ж* intervention.
интервью́ *ср нескл* interview; **брать (взять** *perf*)/**дава́ть (дать** *perf*) ~ to do/give an interview.
интервьюи́р|овать (-ую; *perf* **проинтервьюи́ровать)** (*не)сов перех* to interview.
интере́с (-а) *м*: ~ **(к** +*dat*) interest (in); **представля́ть (предста́вить** *perf*) ~ **(для** +*gen*) to be of interest (to); *см также* **интере́сы**.
интере́сен *прил см* **интере́сный**.
интере́сно *нареч*: **он о́чень** ~ **расска́зывает** he is very interesting to listen to ♦ *как сказ*: ~**(, что ...)** it's interesting (that ...); **мне э́то о́чень** ~ I find it very interesting; **э́то никому́ не** ~ that is of no interest to anyone; ~**, где он э́то нашёл** I wonder where he found that; ~ **знать, где он был** I'd be interested to know where he was; **как** ~**!** that's really interesting!; ~**! (***разг*: *выража́ет недово́льство, возраже́ние*) so!; **она́** ~ **мы́слит** she has an interesting way of thinking.

интере́с|ный (-ен, -на, -но) *прил* interesting; (*вне́шность, же́нщина*) attractive.

интерес|ова́ть (-у́ю) *несов перех* to interest
▶ **интересова́ться** *несов возв* (+*instr*) to be interested in; (*осведомля́ться*) to inquire after; **он ~ова́лся, когда́ ты приезжа́ешь/где ты бу́дешь жить** he was asking when you would be arriving/where you would be living.

интере́с|ы (-ов) *мн* (*госуда́рства, фи́рмы итп*) interests *мн*; (*духо́вные*) concerns *мн*; **в ~ах** +*gen* in the interests of; **затра́гивать** (**затро́нуть** *perf*) *или* **задева́ть** (**заде́ть** *perf*) **чьи-н ~** to touch on sb's interests.

интерлю́ди|я (-и) *ж* (*МУЗ*) interlude.

интерме́ди|я (-и) *ж* (*ТЕАТР*) interlude.

инте́рн (-а) *м* (*МЕД*) ≈ houseman (*BRIT*) (*мн* housemen), ≈ intern (*US*).

интерна́т (-а) *м* boarding school.

Интернациона́л (-а) *м* (*ИСТ*) the International.

интернационализа́ци|я (-и) *ср* internationalization.

интернационали́зм (-а) *м* internationalism.

интернационали́ст (-а) *м* internationalist.

интернациона́льный *прил* international.

ИНТЕРПО́Л (-а) *м сокр* (= *Междунаро́дная организа́ция уголо́вной поли́ции*) Interpol (= *International Criminal Police Organization*).

интерпрета́тор (-а) *м* interpreter.

интерпрета́ци|я (-и) *ж* interpretation.

интерпрети́р|овать (-ую) (*не*)*сов перех* to interpret.

интерфе́йс (-а) *м* (*КОМП*) interface.

интерье́р (-а) *м* (*зда́ния*) interior.

инти́м|ный (-ен, -на, -но) *прил* intimate.

интоксика́ци|я (-и) *ж* intoxication.

интона́ци|я (-и) *ж* (*ЛИНГ, МУЗ*) intonation; (*недово́льная, трево́жная итп*) note.

интри́г|а (-и) *ж* (*полити́ческая*) intrigue; (*любо́вная*) affair; (*рома́на*) plot.

интрига́н (-а) *м* intriguer.

интрига́н|ка (-ки; *gen pl* -ок) *ж см* **интрига́н**.

интриг|ова́ть (-у́ю; *perf* **заинтригова́ть**) *несов перех* to intrigue ◆ *несов неперех* (*no perf*): **~ про́тив** +*gen* to intrigue against.

интрове́рт (-а) *м* introvert.

интуити́в|ный (-ен, -на, -но) *прил* intuitive.

интуи́ци|я (-и) *ж* intuition.

Интури́ст (-а) *м сокр* (= *Гла́вное управле́ние по иностра́нному тури́зму*) *Russian tourist agency dealing with foreign tourism.*

инфа́ркт (-а) *м* (*та́кже:~ миока́рда*) heart attack; **обши́рный ~** (**миока́рда**) massive heart attack.

инфекцио́нный *прил* infectious; **инфекцио́нная больни́ца** hospital for infectious diseases.

инфе́кци|я (-и) *ж* infection.

инфинити́в (-а) *м* infinitive.

инфици́рован|ный (-, -на, -но) *прил* infected.

инфля́ци|я (-и) *ж* (*ЭКОН*) inflation.

инфляцио́нный *прил* inflationary.

информати́в|ный (-ен, -на, -но) *прил* informative.

информа́тик|а (-и) *ж* information technology.

информа́тор (-а) *м* informant.

информацио́нный *прил* information *опред*; **информацио́нная програ́мма** news programme (*BRIT*) *или* program (*US*).

информа́ци|я (-и) *ж* information.

информи́рованный *прил* well-informed.

информи́р|овать (-ую; *perf* **информи́ровать** *или* **проинформи́ровать**) *несов перех* to inform.

инфракра́сный *прил* infrared.

инфраструкту́р|а (-ы) *ж* infrastructure.

инциде́нт (-а) *м* incident.

инъе́кци|я (-и) *ж* injection.

иня́з (-а) *м сокр* = **институ́т иностра́нных языко́в**; **факульте́т иностра́нных языко́в**.

и.о. *сокр* = **исполня́ющий обя́занности** acting.

ио́н (-а) *м* ion.

иорда́н|ец (-ца) *м* Jordanian.

Иорда́ни|я (-и) *ж* Jordan.

иорда́н|ка (-ки; *gen pl* -ок) *ж см* **иорда́нец**.

иорда́нск|ий (-ая, -ое, -ие) *прил* Jordanian.

иорда́нца *сущ см* **иорда́нец**.

ипоста́с|ь (-и) *ж* (*РЕЛ*) hypostasis; **в ~и** +*gen* (*перен*) in the role of.

ипоте́к|а (-и) *ж* (*КОММ*) mortgage.

ипоте́чн|ый *прил* mortgage; **~ая ссу́да** mortgage; **~ банк** ≈ building society.

ипохо́ндрик (-а) *м* hypochondriac.

ипохо́ндри|я (-и) *ж* hypochondria.

ипподро́м (-а) *м* racecourse (*BRIT*), racetrack (*US*).

ипри́т (-а) *м* mustard gas.

Ира́к (-а) *м* Iraq.

ира́к|ец (-ца) *м* Iraqi.

ира́кск|ий (-ая, -ое, -ие) *прил* Iraqi.

ира́кца *итп сущ см* **ира́кец**.

Ира́н (-а) *м* Iran.

ира́н|ец (-ца) *м* Iranian.

ира́н|ка (-ки; *gen pl* -ок) *ж см* **ира́нец**.

ира́нск|ий (-ая, -ое, -ие) *прил* Iranian.

ира́нца *итп сущ см* **ира́нец**.

и́рис (-а) *м* (*БОТ*) iris; (*ни́тки*) thread (*for embroidery etc*).

ири́с (-а) *м* (*конфе́та*) toffee.

ири́с|ка (-ки; *gen pl* -ок) *ж* (*ра́зг*) toffee.

ирла́нд|ец (-ца) *м* Irishman (*мн* Irishmen).

Ирла́нди|я (-и) *ж* Ireland.

ирла́нд|ка (-ки; *gen pl* -ок) *ж* Irishwoman (*мн* Irishwomen).

ирла́ндск|ий (-ая, -ое, -ие) *прил* Irish.

ирла́ндца *итп сущ см* **ирла́ндец**.

ИРЛИ *м сокр* = **Институ́т ру́сской литерату́ры**.

иронизи́р|овать (-ую) *несов неперех*: **~ (над** +*instr*) to be ironic (about).

ирони́ч|ный (-ен, -на, -но) *прил* ironic.

иро́ни|я (-и) *ж* irony; **~ судьбы́** the irony of fate.

иррациона́л|ьный (-ен, -ьна, -ьно) *прил* irrational.

иррегуля́рн|ый *прил*: ~ые войска́ irregular forces *мн*, irregulars *мн*.

иррига́ци|я (-и) *ж* irrigation.

иск (-а) *м* lawsuit; **встре́чный ~** counterclaim; **де́нежный ~** damages; **предъявля́ть (предъяви́ть** *perf*) **кому́-н ~** to take legal action against sb.

искажа́|ть(ся) (-ю(сь)) *несов от* **исказить(ся)**.

искаже́ни|е (-я) *ср* (*фактов*) distortion; (*в тексте*) error.

иска|зи́ть (-жу́, -зи́шь; *impf* **искажа́ть)** *сов перех* (*факты, смысл*) to distort; (*лицо*) to contort; (*КОМП*) to corrupt; **зло́ба ~зи́ла его́ лицо́** his face contorted with malice

▶ **исказ|и́ться (** *impf* **искажа́ться)** *сов возв* (*изображение, смысл*) to be distorted; (*выражение лица, голос*) to contort.

искале́ч|ить (-у, -ишь) *сов от* **кале́чить**.

иска́ни|е (-я) *ср* (*обычно мн: творческие, научные*) quest.

иска́тел|ь (-я) *м* (*золота*) prospector; (*стремящийся к новому*) explorer; **~ приключе́ний** adventure seeker.

иска́тельниц|а (-ы) *ж см* **иска́тель**.

иска́ть (ищу́, и́щешь) *несов перех* to look *или* search for.

исключа́|ть (-ю) *несов от* **исключи́ть**.

исключа́|я *предл* (+*acc*) excluding; **не ~** +*gen* including.

исключе́ни|е (-я) *ср* (*из списка, из очереди*) exclusion; (*из института*) expulsion; (*отклонение от нормы*) exception; **за ~м** +*gen* with the exception of; **де́лать (сде́лать** *perf*) **что-н в ви́де ~я** to make an exception of sth.

исключи́телен *прил см* **исключи́тельный**.

исключи́тельно *нареч* (*особенно*) exceptionally; (*только*) exclusively.

исключи́тел|ьный (-ен, -ьна, -ьно) *прил* exceptional; (*no short form*; *право*) exclusive.

исключ|и́ть (-у́, -и́шь; *impf* **исключа́ть)** *сов перех* (*удалить: из списка*) to exclude; (: *из института*) to expel; (*ошибку, случайность*) to exclude the possibility of; **э́то ~ено́** that is out of the question; **компроми́сс ~ён** a compromise is out of the question.

исковерка|ть (-ю) *сов от* **коверкать**.

исколе|си́ть (-шу́, -си́шь) *сов перех* (*разг*) to travel; **он ~сил весь мир** he's been all over the world.

иско́мка|ть (-ю) *сов от* **комкать**.

иско́м|ый *прил* (*МАТ*): ~**ая величина́** unknown value ♦ **(-ого;** *decl like adj*) *ср* (*МАТ*) unknown.

иско́н|ный (-ен, -на, -но) *прил* (*население*) original; (*право*) intrinsic; **~ язы́к** the vernacular.

ископа́ем|ое (-ого; *decl like adj*) *ср* fossil; (*также: поле́зное* ~: *обычно мн*) mineral.

ископа́емый *прил* (*животное, растение*) fossilized.

искоре́ж|ить (-у, -ишь) *сов от* **коре́жить**.

искорен|и́ть (-ю́, -и́шь; *impf* **искореня́ть)** *сов перех* to eradicate.

и́скоса *нареч* (*взгляну́ть, смотре́ть*) sideways; **смотре́ть** (*impf*) ~ **на кого́-н** (*перен*) to look askance at sb.

и́скр|а (-ы) *ж* (*огня, также перен*) spark; (*снега, бриллианта*) glint, glistening; **у меня́ ~ы из глаз посы́пались** I began to see stars; **зарони́ть** (*perf*) **в ком-н ~у наде́жды** to give sb a glimmer of hope.

и́скренне *нареч* sincerely; **~ Ваш** Yours sincerely.

и́скрен|ний (-няя, -нее, -ние; -ен, -на, -но *или* **-не)** *прил* sincere.

и́скренност|ь (-и) *ж* sincerity.

искрив|и́ть (-лю́, -и́шь; *impf* **искривля́ть)** *сов перех* to bend.

искривле́ни|е (-я) *ср* bend; **искривле́ние позвоно́чника** (*МЕД*) curvature of the spine.

искривлю́ *сов см* **искриви́ть**.

искривля́|ть (-ю) *несов от* **искриви́ть**.

искри́ст|ый (-, -а, -о) *прил* glistening, sparkling.

искр|и́ться (-ю́сь, -и́шься) *несов возв* to glisten, sparkle.

искроме́т|ный (-ен, -на, -но) *прил* (*перен*: *взгляд*) fiery; (: *остроумие*) sparkling.

искромса́|ть (-ю) *сов от* **кромса́ть**.

искрош|и́ть (-у́, -и́шь) *сов от* **кроши́ть**.

искупа́|ть(ся) (-ю(сь)) *сов от* **купа́ть(ся)**.

иску|пи́ть (-плю́, -́пишь; *impf* **искупа́ть)** *сов перех* (*перен*: *вину, проступок*) to atone for, expiate; (*возмещать, также РЕЛ*) to redeem.

искупле́ни|е (-я) *ср* (*вины, проступка*) atonement, expiation; (*РЕЛ*) redemption.

искуплю́ *сов см* **искупи́ть**.

искуса́|ть (-ю; *impf* **иску́сывать)** *сов перех* (*подлеж: комары*) to bite all over; (: *пчёлы*) to sting all over.

иску́сен *прил см* **иску́сный**.

искуси́тел|ь (-я) *м* tempter.

иску́сник (-а) *м* master.

иску́сниц|а (-ы) *ж см* **иску́сник**.

иску́с|ный (-ен, -на, -но) *прил* (*работник*) skilful (*BRIT*), skillful (*US*); (*работа*) fine.

иску́ственник (-а) *м* bottle-fed baby.

иску́ственниц|а (-ы) *ж см* **иску́ственник**.

иску́ствен|ный *прил* artificial; (*волокно, ткань, камин*) synthetic; (*мех*) fake; (-, -на, -но; *притворный: смех*) faked; **иску́ственное дыха́ние** artificial respiration; **иску́ственный интелле́кт** artificial intelligence; **иску́ственный спу́тник Земли́** artificial satellite.

иску́ств|о (-а) *ср* art; **де́лать** (*impf*) **что-н из любви́ к ~у** (*разг*) to do sth for its own sake.

искусствовéд (-а) *м* art historian.
искусствовéдени|е (-я) *ср* art history.
иску́сыва|ть (-ю) *несов от* искуса́ть.
искуша́|ть (-ю) *несов перех* to tempt; ~ *(impf)*
судьбу́ to tempt fate.
искуше́ни|е (-я) *ср* temptation; **поддава́ться**
(подда́ться *perf*) ~ю to give in to temptation.
искушён|ный (-, -á, -ó) *прил* (*зритель*,
публика) sophisticated; (*политик*) seasoned;
(*женщина*) worldly; **он искушён в таки́х дела́х**
he is well versed in such matters.
исла́м (-а) *м* Islam.
исла́мск|ий (-ая, -ое, -ие) *прил* Islamic.
исла́нд|ец (-ца) *м* Icelander.
Исла́нди|я (-и) *ж* Iceland.
исла́нд|ка (-ки; *gen pl* -ок) *ж см* исла́ндец.
исла́ндск|ий (-ая, -ое, -ие) *прил* Icelandic; ~
язы́к Icelandic.
исла́ндца *итп сущ см* исла́ндец.
испа́ко|стить (-щу, -стишь) *сов от* па́костить.
испа́н|ец (-ца) *м* Spaniard.
Испа́ни|я (-и) *ж* Spain.
испа́н|ка (-ки; *gen pl* -ок) *ж см* испа́нец.
испа́нск|ий (-ая, -ое, -ие) *прил* Spanish; ~ **язы́к**
Spanish.
испа́нца *итп сущ см* испа́нец.
испаре́ни|е (-я) *ср* (*действие: воды*)
evaporation; (*обычно мн: продукт*) vapour
(*BRIT*), vapor (*US*).
испа́рин|а (-ы) *ж* perspiration.
испар|и́ть (-ю́, -и́шь; *impf* испаря́ть) *сов перех*
to evaporate
▸ **испари́ться** (*impf* испаря́ться) *сов возв*
(*также перен*) to evaporate.
испа́чка|ть(ся) (-ю(сь)) *сов от* па́чкать(ся).
испеку́(сь) *итп сов см* испе́чь(ся).
испепел|и́ть (-ю́, -и́шь; *impf* испепеля́ть) *сов*
перех to reduce to ashes; **испепеля́ть** (~ *perf*)
кого́-н взгля́дом to give sb a withering look.
испе́|чь(ся) (-ку́(сь), -чёшь(ся) *итп*, -ку́т(ся))
сов от печь(ся).
испещр|и́ть (-ю́, -и́шь; *impf* испещря́ть) *сов*
перех to speckle.
исп|иса́ть (-ишу́, -и́шешь; *impf* испи́сывать)
сов перех (*тетрадь, дневник*) to fill up;
(*карандаш, ручку*) to wear out; (*бумагу*) to use
up
▸ **исписа́ться** (*impf* испи́сываться) *несов возв*
(*карандаш*) to wear out; (*ручка*) to run out;
(*разг: писатель*) to lose one's touch.
исп|и́ть (изопью́, изопьёшь; *pt* -л, -ла́, -ло) *сов*
неперех (+*gen*; *перен: горя, разочарований*) to
suffer; (*воды*) to sup.
испишу́(сь) *итп сов см* исписа́ть(ся).
испове́да|льня (-льни; *gen pl* -ен) *ж* (*РЕЛ*)
confessional.
испове́дани|е (-я) *ср* denomination.
испове́да|ть(ся) (-ю(сь)) (*не*)*сов* =
испове́довать(ся).
испове́дник (-а) *м* (*РЕЛ*) confessor.
испове́д|овать (-ую) *несов перех* (*религию*,

мораль, идею) to profess ◆ (*не*)*сов перех* (*РЕЛ*):
~ **кого́-н** to hear sb's confession
▸ **испове́доваться** (*не*)*сов возв*: ~**ся кому́-н**
или **у кого́-н** to confess to sb.
и́споведь (-и) *ж* (*РЕЛ, перен*) confession.
и́сподволь *нареч* unbeknown to all.
исподло́бья *нареч*: **гляде́ть на кого́-н** ~ to
look at sb with mistrust.
исподтишка́ *нареч* (*разг: действовать*) on the
sly *или* quiet.
испоко́н *предл*: ~ **веко́в** from time immemorial.
исполи́н (-а) *м* giant.
исполи́нск|ий (-ая, -ое, -ие) *прил* gargantuan.
исполко́м (-а) *м сокр* (= *исполни́тельный*
комите́т) executive committee.
исполне́ни|е (-я) *ср* (*приказа, указа*) execution;
(*обещания, желания*) fulfilment (*BRIT*),
fulfillment (*US*); (*симфонии, роли итп*)
performance; **в** ~**и** +*gen* performed by;
приводи́ть (привести́ *perf*) **что-н в** ~ to carry
sth out; **э́кспортное** ~ (*КОММ*) export version.
испо́лненный (-, -а, -о) *прил* (+*gen*) full of,
filled with.
исполни́м|ый (-, -а, -о) *прил* (*просьба*,
желание) realizable.
исполни́телен *прил см* исполни́тельный.
исполни́тел|ь (-я) *м* (*пьесы, роли*) performer;
(*приказа, политики*) executive; **суде́бный** ~
bailiff.
исполни́тельниц|а (-ы) *ж см* исполни́тель.
исполни́тельный *прил* (*комитет, власть*)
executive; (*-ен, -ьна, -ьно: старательный*)
efficient; **исполни́тельный дире́ктор**
executive director; **исполни́тельный лист** (*ЮР*)
court order.
испо́лн|ить (-ю, -ишь; *impf* исполня́ть) *сов*
перех (*приказ*) to carry out; (*обещание, долг*,
желание) to fulfil (*BRIT*), fulfill (*US*); (*танец*,
симфонию, роль итп) to perform; ~ (*perf*)
кого́-н наде́ждой/ра́достью *итп* to fill sb with
hope/joy *итп*
▸ **испо́лниться** (*impf* исполня́ться) *сов возв*
(*желание*) to be fulfilled; (+*instr*; *надеждой*,
радостью итп) to be filled with; **ему́** ~**илось**
10 лет he is 10.
испо́льзовани|е (-я) *ср* use.
испо́льз|овать (-ую) (*не*)*сов перех* to use.
испо́р|тить(ся) (-чу(сь), -тишь(ся)) *сов от*
по́ртить(ся).
испо́рченный *прил* (*замок*) broken;
(*настроение*) bad; (*ребёнок*) spoilt; (*КОМП*)
corrupt.
испра́вен *прил см* испра́вный.
исправи́м|ый (-, -а, -о) *прил* correctable.
исправи́тельный *прил* (*меры*) corrective;
исправи́тельные рабо́ты (*ЮР*) corrective
labour.
исправи́тельно-трудово́й *прил*:
исправи́тельно-трудова́я коло́ния labour
(*BRIT*) *или* labor (*US*) colony.
испра́в|ить (-лю, -ишь; *impf* исправля́ть) *сов*

перех (повреждение, телефон) to repair;
(ошибку) to correct; *(характер, дисциплину)* to
improve
► **испра́виться** (*impf* **исправля́ться**) *сов возв*
(характер, человек) to change (for the better).
исправле́ни|е (*-я*) *ср (повреждения)* repairing;
(: *характера*) reforming; *(текста,*
преступника) correction; **вноси́ть (внести́** *perf*)
~**я в** +*acc* to make corrections to.
испра́влю(сь) *сов см* **испра́вить(ся)**.
исправля́ть(ся) (*-ю(сь)*) *несов от*
испра́вить(ся).
испра́вность (*-и*) *ж*: **в (по́лной)** ~**и** in (full)
working order; **всё в** ~**и** everything's in order.
испра́в|ный (*-ен, -на, -но*) *прил (механизм)* in
good working order; *(работник)* diligent.
испражне́ни|е (*-я*) *ср* faeces *мн*.
испражня́|ться (*-юсь*) *несов возв* to defecate.
испро́б|овать (*-ую*) *сов от* **про́бовать**.
испу́г (*-а*; *part gen* *-у*) *м* fright; **в** ~**е, с** ~**у** in *или*
with fright.
испу́ган|ный (*-, -а, -о*) *прил (человек)*
frightened; (*-, -на, -но*; *вид, взгляд*) frightened.
испуга́|ть(ся) (*-ю(сь)*) *сов от* **пуга́ть(ся)**.
испусти́ть (*-ущу́, -у́стишь*; *impf* **испуска́ть**) *сов*
перех (крик, стон) to let out; *(свет)* to give off,
emit.
испыта́ни|е (*-я*) *ср (машины, прибора итп)*
testing; *(нового работника)* trial; *(обычно мн:*
экзамен) test; *(несчастье)* ordeal.
испы́тан|ный (*-, -на, -но*) *прил (приём)* tried
and tested; *(друг)* proven.
испыта́тел|ь (*-я*) *м* tester; **лётчик-испыта́тель**
test pilot.
испыта́тельный *прил*: ~ **срок** trial period,
probation; **испыта́тельная тра́сса** test circuit;
испыта́тельный полёт test flight.
испыта́|ть (*-ю*; *impf* **испы́тывать**) *сов перех*
(механизм) to test; *(работника)* to try out;
(нужду, трудности, радость итп) to
experience.
испыту́ющ|ий (*-ая, -ее, -ие*; *-, -а, -е*) *прил*: ~
взгляд searching look.
испы́тыва|ть (*-ю*) *несов от* **испыта́ть**.
исс|е́чь (*-еку́, -ечёшь итп, -еку́т*; *pt -ёк, -екла́,*
-екло́) *сов перех* (*кнутом*) to flog.
и́ссиня- *префикс*: ~**чёрный** blue-black.
иссле́довани|е (*-я*) *ср (см глаг)* research;
examination; *(научный труд)* study;
занима́ться (*impf*) ~**ями в о́бласти** +*gen* to
conduct research into.
иссле́дователь (*-я*) *м* researcher.
иссле́довательск|ий (*-ая, -ое, -ие*) *прил*: ~**ая**
рабо́та research; ~ **институ́т** research institute.
иссле́д|овать (*-ую*) *(не)сов перех* to research;
(больного) to examine.
иссо́х|нуть (*-ну, -нешь*; *pt -, -ла, -ло*, *impf*
иссыха́ть) *сов неперех (водоём)* to dry up;

(трава) to dry out; *(исхудать)* to wither away.
исстари *нареч* since days of old.
исстрада́|ться (*-юсь*) *сов возв* to suffer a great
deal.
исстреля́|ть (*-ю*; *impf* **исстре́ливать**) *сов перех*
(патроны) to use up.
исступле́ни|е (*-я*) *ср* frenzy; **приходи́ть**
(прийти́ *perf*) **в** ~ to go into a frenzy.
исступлён|ный (*-, -на, -но*) *прил* frenzied.
иссыха́|ть (*-ю*) *несов от* **иссо́хнуть**.
исся́к|нуть (*3sg* *-нет*, *3pl -нут*, *pt -, -ла, -ло*, *impf*
иссяка́ть) *сов неперех (источник, запасы)* to
run dry; *(перен: терпение, силы)* to run out.
иста́плива|ть (*-ю*) *несов от* **истопи́ть**.
иста́птыва|ть (*-ю*) *несов от* **истопта́ть**.
иста́скан|ный (*-, -на, -но*) *прил (разг: вид)*
bedraggled.
иста́ска|ть (*-ю*; *impf* **иста́скивать**) *сов перех*
(разг) to wear out
► **иста́ска|ться** (*impf* **иста́скиваться**) *сов возв*
(разг) to wear out.
исте́блишмент (*-а*) *м* the Establishment.
истёк *итп сов см* **исте́чь**.
истека́|ть (*-ю*) *несов от* **исте́чь**.
истеку́т *итп сов см* **исте́чь**.
исте́кш|ий (*-ая, -ее, -ие*) *прил* past, previous.
ист|ере́ться (*3sg* изотрётся, *3pl* изотру́тся, *pt*
-ёрся, -ёрлась, -ёрлось, *impf* **истира́ться**) *сов*
возв (подошвы, канат) to wear down.
исте́рзан|ный (*-, -на, -но*) *прил (душа, вид)*
tortured.
истерза́|ть (*-ю*) *сов от* **терза́ть**.
исте́рик (*-а*) *м* hysterical man *(мн* men).
исте́рик|а (*-и*) *ж* hysterics *мн*; **устра́ивать**
(устро́ить *perf*) ~**у** *или* **зака́тывать (закати́ть** *perf*)
~**у** to become hysterical.
истери́чек *сущ см* **истери́чка**.
истери́чен *прил см* **истери́чный**.
истери́ческ|ий (*-ая, -ое, -ие*) *прил (больной,*
смех, плач) hysterical; ~ **припа́док** a fit of
hysterics.
истери́чк|а (*-и*; *gen pl -ек*) *ж* hysterical woman
(мн women).
истери́чный (*-ен, -на, -но*) *прил* hysterical.
истери́|я (*-и*) *ж (МЕД, перен)* hysteria.
исте́ц (*-ца́*) *м* plaintiff.
истече́ни|е (*-я*) *ср*: **по** ~**и** +*gen (года, месяца*
итп) after a period of; **по** ~**и э́того сро́ка** once
this period has elapsed; **за** ~**м сро́ка Ва́шего**
па́спорта due to expiry of your passport.
ист|е́чь (*3sg* -ечёт, *3pl* -еку́т, *pt -ёк, -екла́, -екло́*,
impf **истека́ть**) *сов неперех (срок)* to expire;
(время) to run out; **истека́ть** (~ *perf*) **кро́вью** to
bleed.
и́стин|а (*-ы*) *ж* truth.
и́стинен *прил см* **и́стинный**.
и́стинност|ь (*-и*) *ж* truthfulness.
и́стин|ный (*-ен, -на, -но*) *прил* true.

истира́|ться (3sg -ется, 3pl -ются) несов от
истере́ться.

истле́|ть (-ю; impf истлева́ть) сов неперех
(са́нить) to decompose; (сгоре́ть) to turn to
ash.

исто́к (-а) м (обычно мн: реки) source то́лько
ед; (: перен) source.

истолк|ова́ть (-у́ю; impf истолко́вывать) сов
перех to interpret.

истол|о́чь (-ку́, -чёшь итп, -ку́т; pt -о́к, -кла́,
-кло́) сов от толо́чь.

исто́м|а (-ы) ж languor.

истом|и́ть(ся) (-лю́(сь), -и́шь(ся)) сов от
томи́ть(ся).

истоп|и́ть (-оплю́, -о́пишь; impf иста́пливать)
сов перех to heat up.

истоп|та́ть (-опчу́, -о́пчешь; impf иста́птывать)
сов перех to trample all over; (разг: о́бувь) to
wear out.

исто́рик (-а) м historian.

истори́ческ|ий (-ая, -ое, -ие) прил historical;
(ва́жный: собы́тие, реше́ние итп) historic.

исто́ри|я (-и) ж (нау́ка, предмет) history;
(расска́з, происше́ствие) story; попада́ть
(попа́сть perf) в ~ю (разг) to get into a tricky
situation; со мной произошла́ стра́нная/
заба́вная ~ a strange/funny thing happened to
me; ве́чная ~! (разг) it's the same old story!;
исто́рия боле́зни (МЕД) case history.

истоск|ова́ться (-у́юсь) сов возв: ~ по +dat to
yearn for.

источа́|ть (-ю) несов перех (арома́т, свет,
тепло́) to emit; (не́нависть, доброту́ итп) to
exude.

исто́чник (-а) м (во́дный) source, spring.

исто́ш|ный (-ен, -на, -но) прил (крик) desperate.

истоща́|ть(ся) (-ю(сь)) несов от
истощи́ть(ся).

истоще́ни|е (-я) ср (органи́зма) depletion;
(средств, запа́сов) exhaustion; ~ не́рвной
систе́мы nervous exhaustion; доводи́ть
(довести́ perf) себя́ до по́лного ~ to run o.s.
into the ground.

истощённый (-ён, -ена́, -ено́) прил (челове́к)
malnourished; (-ён, -енна, -енно; вид, лицо́)
drained.

истощ|и́ть (-у́, -и́шь; impf истоща́ть) сов перех
(органи́зм) to run down; (по́чву, ресу́рсы) to
deplete

▸ истощ|и́ться (impf истоща́ться) сов возв
(си́лы, органи́зм, по́чва) to become depleted;
(запа́сы, терпе́ние) to run out.

истра́|тить(ся) (-чу(сь), -тишь(ся)) сов от
тра́тить(ся).

истреби́тел|ь (-я) м (ВОЕН: самолёт) fighter
(plane); (: лётчик) fighter pilot; (тарака́нов,
мыше́й итп) exterminator.

истреби́тельн|ый прил (ого́нь) destructive;
~ая война́ war of destruction; ~ая авиа́ция
fighter planes.

истреб|и́ть (-лю́, -и́шь; impf истребля́ть) сов

перех (лес, посе́вы итп) to destroy; (крыс,
тарака́нов) to exterminate.

истребле́ни|е (-я) ср (см глаг) destruction;
extermination.

истреблю́ сов см истреби́ть.

истребля́|ть (-ю) несов от истреби́ть.

истр|епа́ть(ся) (-еплю́(сь), -е́плешь(ся)) сов
от трепа́ть(ся).

истре́ска|ться (3sg -ется, 3pl -ются, impf
истре́скиваться) сов возв to crack.

истука́н (-а) м idol.

истца́ итп сущ см исте́ц.

и́стый прил genuine.

истяза́ни|е (-я) ср torture.

истяза́|ть (-ю) несов перех to torture.

исхл|еста́ть (-ещу́, -е́щешь; impf
исхлёстывать) сов перех to whip.

исхо́д (-а) м outcome; у меня́ де́ньги/терпе́ние
на ~е my money/patience is running out; на ~е
дня at the end of the day; с лета́льным ~ом
resulting in death.

исх|оди́ть (-ожу́, -о́дишь) несов от изойти́ ♦
сов перех (обойти́) to walk all over ♦ несов
неперех: ~ из +gen (све́дения, слу́хи) to
emanate from; (осно́вываться: из да́нных) to be
derived from; ~одя́ из/от +gen on the basis of; я
~ожу́ из того́, что... I am working on the
premise that ....

исхо́дный прил (иде́я, да́нные) primary; ~
те́зис premise; исхо́дное положе́ние (СПОРТ)
starting position; исхо́дный пункт starting
point.

исходя́щ|ий (-ая, -ее, -ие) прил
(корреспонде́нция) outgoing; исходя́щий
но́мер (АДМИН) reference number.

исхожу́ (не)сов см исходи́ть.

исхуда́лый прил emaciated.

исхуда́|ть (-ю) сов неперех to become
emaciated.

исцара́па|ть (-ю; impf исцара́пывать) сов
перех to scratch all over.

исцеле́ни|е (-я) ср healing.

исцел|и́ть (-ю́, -и́шь; impf исцеля́ть) сов перех
to heal

▸ исцел|и́ться (impf исцеля́ться) сов возв to
recover.

исча́ди|е (-я) ср: ~ а́да the devil incarnate.

исчеза́|ть (-ю) несов от исче́знуть.

исчезнове́ни|е (-я) ср disappearance.

исче́з|нуть (-ну, -нешь; pt -, -ла, -ло, impf
исчеза́ть) сов неперех to disappear.

исчёрка|ть (-ю; impf исчёркивать) сов перех to
scribble over.

исче́рпа|ть (-ю; impf исче́рпывать) сов перех
to exhaust; инциде́нт ~н the matter is closed

▸ исче́рпа|ться (impf исче́рпываться) несов
возв (запа́сы, терпе́ние) to be exhausted.

исче́рпыва|ться (3sg -ется, 3pl -ются) несов
от исчерпа́ться ♦ возв (разреша́ться) to end;
э́тим де́ло не ~ется the matter does not end
here.

исчёрпывающ|ий (-ая, -ее, -ие; -, -а, -е) *прил* exhaustive.
исчислёни|е (-я) *ср* (*расходов, стоимости итп*) calculation; (*МАТ*) calculus.
исчисл|ить (-ю, -ишь; *impf* **исчислять**) *сов перех* to calculate.
исчисля́|ться (*3pl* **-ются**) *несов возв* (+*instr*; *тысячами*) to amount to.
ита́к *союз* thus, hence; ~, **мо́жно заключи́ть, что** ... thus it can be concluded that ....
Ита́ли|я (-и) *ж* Italy.
италья́н|ец (-ца) *м* Italian.
италья́н|ка (-ки; *gen pl* -ок) *ж см* **италья́нец**.
италья́нск|ий (-ая, -ое, -ие) *прил* Italian; ~ **язы́к** Italian.
италья́нца *итп сущ см* **италья́нец**.
ИТАР *м сокр* (= Информацио́нное телегра́фное аге́нтство Росси́и) *Russian telegraph agency*.
и т.д. *сокр* (= **и так да́лее**) etc. (= *et cetera*).
ИТК *м сокр* (= исправи́тельно-трудова́я коло́ния) labour (*BRIT*) *или* labor (*US*) colony.
ито́г (-а) *м* (*работы, переговоров итп*) result; (*общая сумма*) total; **в** ~**е** (*при подсчёте*) in total; **в** (**коне́чном**) ~**е** in the end; **подводи́ть** (**подвести́** *perf*) ~**и** to sum up.
итого́ *нареч* in total, altogether; ~, **мы зарабо́тали 100 рубле́й** in total *или* altogether we made 100 roubles.
ито́говый *прил* (*сумма, ци́фры*) total; (*результат*) final; **ито́говый отчёт** (*КОММ*) financial report.
и т.п. *сокр* (= **и тому́ подо́бное**) etc. (= *et cetera*).
иудаи́зм (-а) *м* Judaism.
их *мест см* **они́** ◆ *притяж мест* their; ~ **дом бо́льше на́шего** their house is bigger than ours; **чья э́та маши́на? –** ~ whose car is this? – it's theirs.
и́хн|ий (-яя, -ее, -ие) *притяж мест* (*разг*) = **их**.
иша́к (-а́) *м* (*ЗООЛ*) donkey; (*перен: работя́га*) dogsbody.
иша́ч|ить (-у, -ишь) *несов неперех* (*разг*) to slog away.
и́шиас (-а) *м* sciatica.
ишь *част* (*разг*): ~ **чего́ захоте́л!** you're asking a lot, aren't you?; ~ **како́й он на́глый!** how cheeky can he get!
ище́|йка (-йки; *gen pl* -ек) *ж* bloodhound; **полице́йская** ~ sniffer dog.
ищу́ *итп несов см* **иска́ть**.
ию́л|ь (-я) *м* July; *см также* **октя́брь**.
ию́льск|ий (-ая, -ое, -ие) *прил* July *опред*.
ию́н|ь (-я) *м* June; *см также* **октя́брь**.
ию́ньск|ий (-ая, -ое, -ие) *прил* June *опред*.

~ Й, й ~

Й, й *сущ нескл (буква) the 10th letter of the Russian alphabet.*

Йе́мен (-а) *м* Yemen.

йе́мен|ец (-ца) *м* Yemeni.

йе́мен|ка (-ки; *gen pl* -ок) *ж см* йе́менец.

йе́менск|ий (-ая, -ое, -ие) *прил* Yemeni.

йог (-и) *ж* yogi.

йо́г|а (-и) *ж* yoga; **занима́ться** (*impf*) ~ой to do yoga.

йо́гурт (-а) *м* yoghurt.

йод (-а) *м* iodine.

йо́дистый *прил* = **йо́дный**.

йо́дный *прил* iodine *опред*.

Йорк (-а) *м* York.

йо́т|а (-ы) *ж*: **ни на** ~**у** not one iota.

йота́ци|я (-и) *ж* vowel softening.

Йоха́ннесбург (-а) *м* Johannesburg.

~ К, к ~

К, к *сущ нескл (буква)* the 11th letter of the Russian alphabet.

к *предл (+dat)* **1** *(обозначает направление)* towards; **я пошёл к дому/вокзалу** I went towards the house/station; **звать (позвать** *perf*) **кого-н к телефону** to call sb to the phone; **мы поехали к друзьям** we went to see friends; **поставь лестницу к стене** put the ladder against the wall
2 *(обозначает добавление, включение)* to; **к уже существующим проблемам прибавились новые осложнения** new complications were added to the existing problems; **эта бабочка относится к очень редкому виду** this butterfly belongs to a very rare species
3 *(обозначает отношение)* of; **любовь к музыке/порядку** love of music/order; **он привык к хорошей еде** he is used to good food; **к моему удивлению** to my surprise
4 *(обозначает назначение)* with; **Вы хотите печенья к чаю?** would you like biscuits (*BRIT*) *или* cookies (*US*) with your tea?; **приправы к мясу** seasonings for meat.

к. *сокр* = **копейка.**

-ка *част (разг)* used to moderate imperative or indicate indecision; **иди-ка сюда** could you come here; **пойду-ка я домой** I think I'll maybe be off home.

кабак (-á) *м* tavern; *(разг)* pub.

кабал|á (-ы) *ж (перен)* slavery; **быть** *(impf)* **в ~é у кого-н** to be at sb's mercy.

кабальн|ый *прил*: **~ труд** slave labour (*BRIT*) *или* labor (*US*); **~ая зависимость** slavery (*fig*).

кабан (-á) *м* boar; *(дикий)* wild boar.

кабаре *ср нескл* cabaret.

кабач|ок (-ка́) *м уменьш от* **кабак**; *(БОТ, КУЛИН)* marrow (*BRIT*), squash (*US*).

кабел|ь (-я) *м* cable.

кабельный *прил* cable *опред*; **кабельное телевидение** cable television.

кабин|а (-ы) *ж (телефонная)* booth; *(грузовика)* cab; *(самолёта)* cabin; *(лифта)* cage; *(для голосования)* voting booth; **пляжная ~** beach

---

hut.

кабинет (-а) *м (в доме)* study; *(на работе)* office; *(ПРОСВЕЩ)* classroom; *(врача)* surgery (*BRIT*), office (*US*); *(ПОЛИТ: также:* **~ министров)** cabinet.

каблограмм|а (-ы) *ж* cablegram.

каблу́к (-á) *м* heel; **быть** *(impf)* **под каблуком у кого-н** *(разг)* to be under sb's thumb.

каботаж (-а) *м* coastal shipping.

Кабул (-а) *м* Kabul.

кавалер (-а) *м (в танце)* partner; *(поклонник)* suitor; *(награждённый орденом):* **~ +gen** knight of; **Георгиевский ~** knight of St George.

кавалерийск|ий (-ая, -ое, -ие) *прил* cavalry *опред*.

кавалерист (-а) *м* cavalryman (*мн* cavalrymen).

кавалери|я (-и) *ж* cavalry.

кавалькад|а (-ы) *ж* cavalcade.

кавардак (-á) *м (разг)* mess.

каверз|а (-ы) *ж* dirty trick; **подстро́ить** *(perf)* **кому-н ~у** to play a dirty trick on sb.

каверзн|ый (-ен, -на, -но) *прил* tricky.

Кавказ (-а) *м* Caucasus.

кавказск|ий (-ая, -ое, -ие) *прил* Caucasian.

кавы́чк|и (-ек; *dat pl* **-кам)** *мн* inverted commas *мн*, quotation marks *мн*; **открыва́ть (откры́ть** *perf*)**/закрыва́ть (закры́ть** *perf*) **~** to open/close inverted commas; **в ~ках** *(также перен)* in inverted commas.

кагор (-а) *м* red dessert wine.

каденци|я (-и) *ж* cadence.

кадет (-а) *м (ВОЕН)* cadet; *(ИСТ:* = *конституционный демократ)* Cadet *(Constitutional Democrat)*.

кадетск|ий (-ая, -ое, -ие) *прил (форма)* cadet's; **кадетский корпус** officer training corps.

кади́л|о (-а) *ср (РЕЛ)* censer.

кади́ть (-жу́, -ди́шь) *несов неперех (РЕЛ)* to burn incense.

кадк|а (-и; *gen pl* **-ок)** *ж* vat.

кадмий (-я) *м* cadmium.

кадок *сущ см* **кадка.**

кадочный *прил (огурцы, капуста итп)* preserved in vats.

кадр (-а) *м (ФОТО, КИНО)* shot; *(разг: работник)* worker; *см также* **кадры.**

ка́дров|ый *прил (офицер, войска)* regular опред; *(АДМИН)*: ~ая полúтика staffing policy.
ка́др|ы (-ов) *мн (работники)* personnel *ед*, staff *ед*; *(ВОЕН)* regular army personnel *ед*; *(партийные)* cadres *мн*; отдéл ~ов personnel department.
кады́к (-á) *м* Adam's apple.
каём *сущ см* кайма́.
каём|ка (-ки; *gen pl* -ок) *ж* = кайма́.
каждоднéвный *прил* daily.
ка́ждый *прил* each, every.
кажу́ *несов см* кадúть.
кажу́сь *итп несов см* каза́ться.
каза́к (-á; *nom pl* каза́ки) *м* Cossack.
каза́н (-á) *м large round copper cooking vessel.*
Каза́н|ь (-и) *ж* Kazan.
каза́рм|а (-ы) *ж* barracks *мн*.
каза́рменный *прил*: ~ поря́док barracks regime; каза́рменное положéние confinement to barracks.
ка|за́ться (-жу́сь, -жешься; *perf* показа́ться) *несов возв* (+*instr*) to look; (мне) ка́жется/каза́лось, что ... it seems/seemed (to me) that ...; он ~за́лся ста́рше свои́х лет he looked older than his years.
каза́х (-а) *м* Kazakh.
каза́хск|ий (-ая, -ое, -ие) *прил* Kazakh.
Казахста́н (-а) *м* Kazakhstan.
каза́цк|ий (-ая, -ое, -ие) *прил* = каза́чий.
каза́чек *сущ см* каза́чка.
каза́честв|о (-а) *ср* собир the Cossacks *мн*.
каза́чий (-ья, -ье, -ьи) *прил* Cossack.
каза́ч|ка (-ки; *gen pl* -ек) *ж см* каза́к.
каземáт (-а) *м* cell.
казённый *прил* public; *(отношение, язык)* officious; на ~ счёт at public expense; казённая кварти́ра tied accommodation; казённое иму́щество government property.
казинó *ср нескл* casino.
казн|á (-ы́) *ж* treasury.
казначéй (-я) *м* treasurer.
казнú|ть (-ю, -йшь) *несов перех* to execute; *(перен)* to punish
▶ **казнú́ться** *несов возв (разг)* to torture o.s.
казн|ь (-и) *ж* execution; смéртная ~ the death penalty; приговорú́ть *(perf)* когó-н к смéртной ка́зни to sentence sb to death.
Каи́р (-а) *м* Cairo.
каймá (-ймы́; *nom pl* -ймы́, *gen pl* -ём) *ж* hem.
кайф (-а) *м (разг)* high, kick.
кайф|ова́ть (-у́ю) *несов неперех (разг: на пляже, в отпуске)* to chill out; *(: от наркотиков, от вина)* to get high.

как *местоимённое нареч* **1** *(вопросительное)* how; как Вы себя́ чу́вствуете? how do you feel?; как делá/дéти? how are things/the children?; как тебя́ зову́т? what's your name?
2 *(относительное)*: я сдéлал, как ты просú́ла I did as you asked; я не зна́ю, как э́то моглó случи́ться I don't know how that could have happened
3 *(насколько)*: как бы́стро/тóчно/давнó how quickly/accurately/long ago
4 *(до какой степени)*: как краси́во/пóдло! how beautiful/mean!; как жаль! what a pity *или* shame!
5 *(выражает возмущение)* what; как! он опя́ть напú́лся! what! he's drunk again!
6 *(о внезапном действии)*: онá как закричú́т/запла́чет she suddenly cried out/burst into tears
♦ *союз* **1** *(подобно)* as; мя́гкий, как ва́та as soft as cotton wool; как мóжно скорéе/грóмче as soon/loud as possible; он одéт, как бродя́га he is dressed like a tramp
2 *(в качестве)* as; как консульта́нт он óчень полéзен as a consultant he is very useful
3 *(о временных отношениях: о будущем, об одновременности)* when; (: о прошлом) since; как закóнчишь, позвонú́ мне phone *(BRIT)* *или* call *(US)* me when you finish; как вспóмню об э́том, хóчется пла́кать when I remember it I feel like crying; прошлó два гóда, как онá исчéзла two years have passed since she disappeared:
4: как бу́дто, как бы as if; он согласú́лся как бы нéхотя he agreed as if unwillingly; как же of course; как говоря́т *или* говоря́т as it were; как ни however; как никáк after all; как раз вóвремя/то, что нáдо just in time/what we need; э́то пла́тье/пальтó мне как раз this dress/coat is just my size; как ..., так и ... both ... and ...; как тóлько as soon as.

какаду́ *м нескл* cockatoo.
какáо *ср нескл* cocoa.
ка́ка|ть (-ю; *perf* покáкать) *несов неперех (разг)* to do a pooh.
ка́к-либо *нареч* = ка́к-нибудь.
ка́к-нибудь *нареч (так или иначе)* somehow; *(когда-нибудь)* sometime; *(кое-как)* anyhow; уговорú́те егó ~ try to convince him somehow; зайдú́ ~ pop in sometime; ты всё дéлаешь ~ you're doing everything just anyhow.
какóв (-á, -ó, -ы́) *мест* what; ~ наглéц! what a cheek!; ~ он собóй? what does he look like?

как|óй (-а́я, -óе, -ие) *мест* **1** *(вопросительное)* what; какóй тебé нрáвится цвет? what colour do you like?; какáя сегóдня погóда? what's the weather like today?; в какóм году́ э́то бы́ло? in what year was that?
2 *(относительное)* which; скажú́, какáя кни́га интерéснее tell me which book is more interesting; скажú́, в какóм гóроде нахóдится Колизéй tell me in which city the Coliseum is
3 *(выражает оценку)* what; какóй подлéц! what a rascal!; какáя неожú́данность! what a surprise!
4 *(в риторических вопросах: совсем не)* what kind of; какóй он дирéктор? what kind of

director is he?
5 (*разг*: *неопределённое*) any; **нет ли каки́х вопро́сов?** are there any questions?; **какой ни на есть** any you like; **ни в каку́ю** not for anything; **каки́м о́бразом** in what way; **како́е там!** no way!

как|о́й-либо (-**а́я**, -**о́е**, -**и́е**) *мест* = **како́й-нибудь**.

как|о́й-нибудь (-**а́я**, -**о́е**, -**и́е**) *мест* (*тот или иной*) any; (*приблизительно*) some; **он и́щет ~ рабо́ты** he's looking for any kind of work; **~и́х-нибудь два-три ме́сяца** in some two or three months.

как|о́й-то (-**а́я**, -**о́е**, -**и́е**) *мест*: **Вам ~о́е-то письмо́** there's a letter for you; (*напоминающий*): **она́ ~а́я-то стра́нная сего́дня** she's acting a bit oddly today; **э́то не ко́мната, а свина́рник ~** it's more like a pigsty than a room.

какофони́ческий (-**ая**, -**ое**, -**ие**) *прил* cacophonous.

какофони|я (-**и**) *ж* cacophony.

ка́к-то *мест* (*каким-то образом*) somehow; (*в некоторой степени*) somewhat; (*разг*): **~ (раз)** once; **мне бы́ло ~ не по себе́** I was feeling somewhat *или* a little out of sorts; **я ~ встре́тил его́ на у́лице** I bumped into him once in the street.

ка́ктус (-**а**) *м* cactus (*мн* cacti).

кал (-**а**) *м* excrement.

каламбу́р (-**а**) *м* pun.

каламбу́р|ить (-**ю**, -**ишь**; *perf* **скаламбу́рить**) *несов неперех* to pun, make puns.

каланч|а́ (-**и́**; *gen pl* -**е́й**) *ж* watchtower; (*разг*: *человек*) beanpole.

кала́ч (-**а́**) *м* ≈ cottage loaf; **его́ калачо́м не зама́нишь** nothing will persuade him.

кала́чиком *нареч*: **сверну́ться ~** to curl up in a ball.

калейдоско́п (-**а**) *м* (*также перен*) kaleidoscope.

ка́лек *сущ см* **ка́лька**.

кале́к|а (-**и**) *м/ж* cripple.

календа́рный *прил*: **~ ме́сяц/год** calendar month/year.

календа́р|ь (-**я́**) *м* calendar.

кале́ни|е (-**я**) *ср* incandescence; **довести́** (*perf*) **кого́-н до бе́лого ~я** to send sb into a blind rage.

кале́ный *прил* red-hot; **выжига́ть (вы́жечь** *perf*) **~ым желе́зом** to brand.

кале́ч|ить (-**у**, -**ишь**; *perf* **покале́чить** *или* **искале́чить**) *несов перех* to cripple.

кали́бр (-**а**) *м* (*ВОЕН, перен*) calibre (*BRIT*), caliber (*US*); (*ТЕХ*) gauge.

калибр|ова́ть (-**у́ю**) (*не*)*сов перех* to calibrate.

калибро́вк|а (-**и**) *ж* calibration.

ка́ли|й (-**я**) *м* potassium.

кали́н|а (-**ы**) *ж* guelder-rose.

кали́т|ка (-**и**; *gen pl* -**ок**) *ж* gate.

Калифо́рни|я (-**и**) *ж* California.

каллиграфи́ческий (-**ая**, -**ое**, -**ие**) *прил*: **~ по́черк** beautiful handwriting.

каллигра́фи|я (-**и**) *ж* calligraphy.

калмы́к (-**а**) *м* Kalmyk.

Калмы́ки|я (-**и**) *ж* Kalmykia.

калмы́ч|ка (-**ки**; *gen pl* -**ек**) *ж см* **калмы́к**.

калори́йност|ь (-**и**) *ж* (*пищи*) calorie content; (*ФИЗ*) calorific value.

кало́ри|я (-**и**) *ж* calorie.

ка́л|ька (-**ьки**; *gen pl* -**ек**) *ж* (*бумага*) tracing paper; (*копия*) traced copy; (*ЛИНГ*) calque.

кальки́р|овать (-**ую**; *perf* **скальки́ровать**) *несов перех* (*чертёж*) to trace.

калькуля́тор (-**а**) *м* calculator.

кальма́р (-**а**) *м* squid.

кальсо́н|ы (-) *мн* long johns *мн*.

ка́льци|й (-**я**) *м* calcium.

КамА́З (-**а**) *м сокр* = **Ка́мский автомоби́льный заво́д**; (*автомобиль*) *vehicle manufactured at the Kamskiy car factory*.

ка́мбал|а (-**ы**) *ж* flatfish.

Камбо́дж|а (-**и**) *ж* Cambodia.

камбоджи́йский (-**ая**, -**ое**, -**ие**) *прил* Cambodian.

ка́мбуз (-**а**) *м* galley.

каме́ли|я (-**и**) *ж* camelia.

камене́|ть (-**ю**) *несов от* **окамене́ть**.

камени́ст|ый (-, -**а**, -**о**) *прил* (*почва*) stony.

каменноу́гольный *прил* coal *опред*; **~ бассе́йн** coalfield.

ка́менн|ый *прил* stone; (*перен*) stony; **у неё ~ое се́рдце** she has a heart of stone; **ка́менный век** the Stone Age.

каменоло́мн|я (-**и**; *gen pl* -**ен**) *ж* quarry.

каменотёс (-**а**) *м* stonemason.

ка́менщик (-**а**) *м* bricklayer; **во́льный ~** Freemason.

ка́м|ень (-**ня**; *gen pl* -**ней**) *м* stone; **драгоце́нный ~** precious stone; **краеуго́льный ~** (*перен*) cornerstone; **~ в по́чках** kidney stone; **~ преткнове́ния** stumbling block; **у него́ ~ на се́рдце лежи́т** there's a weight lying heavy on his heart; **у меня́ ~ с души́ свали́лся** it was a great weight off my mind; **держа́ть** (*impf*) **~ за па́зухой** to bear a grudge.

ка́мер|а (-**ы**) *ж* (*тюремная*) cell; (*АВТ*) inner tube; (*также*: **телека́мера, кинока́мера**) camera; (*ТЕХ, АНАТ*) chamber; **снима́ть (снять** *perf*) **что-н скры́той ~ой** to film sth secretly; **ка́мера хране́ния** (*на вокзале*) left-luggage office (*BRIT*), checkroom (*US*); (*в музее*) cloakroom.

камерди́нер (-**а**) *м* (*ИСТ*) valet.

ка́мерный *прил* (*обстановка*) cosy; **ка́мерная му́зыка** chamber music; **ка́мерный орке́стр** chamber orchestra.

камертóн (-а) м tuning fork.
кáмеш|ек (-ка; *nom pl* -**ки**, *gen pl* -**ков**) м stone.
камéя (-и) ж cameo (*in jewellery*).
камзóл (-а) м frock coat.
камúн (-а) м fireplace.
камнепáд (-а) м avalanche (*of rocks, stones*).
кáмня *итп сущ см* **кáмень**.
камóрк|а (-и) ж (*разг*) cubbyhole.
кампáни|я (-и) ж campaign.
кампучúйск|ий (-ая, -ое, -ие) *прил* Kampuchean.
Кампучúя (-и) ж Kampuchea.
камуфлúр|овать (-ую; *perf* **закамуфлúровать**) *несов перех* to camouflage.
камуфля́ж (-а) м camouflage.
кáмфор|а (-ы) ж camphor.
камфóрк|а (-и) ж ring (*on stove*).
кáмфорн|ый *прил*: ~**ое мáсло** camphorated oil.
камы́ш (-á) м rushes *мн*.
канáв|а (-ы) ж ditch; **стóчная** ~ gutter.
Канáд|а (-ы) ж Canada.
канáд|ец (-ца) м Canadian.
канáдк|а (-ки; *gen pl* -**ок**) *см* **канáдец**.
канáдск|ий (-ая, -ое, -ие) *прил* Canadian.
канáдца *итп сущ см* **канáдец**.
канáл (-а) м (*также* АНАТ) canal; (*связь, тел, перен*) channel; **я бýду дéйствовать по своúм** ~**ам** I shall use the means available to me.
канализациóнн|ый *прил*: ~**ая трубá** sewer pipe; **канализациóнная сеть** the sewers.
канализáци|я (-и) ж sewerage.
канáль|я (-ьи; *gen pl* -**ий**) м/ж rogue.
канарéйк|а (-йки; *gen pl* -**ек**) ж canary.
канáрск|ий (-ая, -ое, -ие) *прил*: **К**~**ие островá** the Canary Islands, the Canaries.
канáт (-а) м cable.
канáтн|ый *прил*: ~**ая дорóга** cable car.
канатохóд|ец (-ца) м tightrope walker.
канв|á (-ы́) ж (*в вышивании*) sampler; (*перен: рассказа*) outline.
кандал|ы́ (-óв) *мн* shackles *мн*.
канделя́бр (-а) м candelabra (*мн* candelabra).
кандидáт (-а) м candidate; (*ПРОСВЕЩ*): ~ **наýк** ≈ Doctor.
кандидáтск|ий (-ая, -ое, -ие) *прил* candidate's; **кандидáтская диссертáция** ≈ doctoral thesis; **кандидáтский экзáмен** *entrance exam for postgraduate study*.
кандидатýр|а (-ы) ж candidacy; **выставля́ть (выставить** *perf*) **чью-н** ~**у** to nominate sb.
каникул|ы (-) *мн* holidays *мн* (*BRIT*), vacation *ед* (*US*); **парлáментские** ~ parliamentary recess.
каникуля́рный *прил* holiday *опред* (*BRIT*), vacation *опред* (*US*).
канúстр|а (-ы) ж jerry can.
канитéл|иться (-юсь, -ишься) *несов возв* (*разг*): ~ (**с** +*instr*) to waste one's time (over).
канитéл|ь (-и) ж (*золотая итп*) thread; (*перен*) bore, drag; **тянýть** (*impf*) ~ (*перен: разг*) to drag things out.
канифóл|ь (-и) ж (*ХИМ*) resin; (*МУЗ*) rosin.
канкáн (-а) м cancan.

каннибáл (-а) м cannibal.
каннибалúзм (-а) м cannibalism.
канойст (-а) м canoeist.
канóн (-а) м canon.
канонáд|а (-ы) ж cannonade.
канонизáци|я (-и) ж (*также перен*) canonization.
канонизúр|овать (-ую) (*не)сов перех* (*также перен*) to canonize.
канóник (-а) м canon (*REL*).
каноníческ|ий (-ая, -ое, -ие) *прил* (*РЕЛ*) canonical; (*перен: правила, образец*) definitive; ~**ое прáво** canon law.
канóэ *ср нескл* canoe.
кантáт|а (-ы) ж cantata.
кант|овáть (-ýю; *perf* **окантовáть**) *несов перех* (**окаймлять**) to mount; (*no perf; переворáчивать*) to tilt; „**не** ~!" "keep upright!"
канýн (-а) м eve; **в** ~ +*gen* on the eve of; ~ **Нóвого гóда** New Year's Eve.
кáн|уть (-у, -ешь) *сов неперех* (**исчéзнуть**) to vanish; ~ (*perf*) **в Лéту** *или* **вéчность** to fade into obscurity; **он слóвно в вóду** ~**ул** he vanished into thin air.
канцеляри́зм (-а) м official jargon.
канцеля́ри|я (-и) ж office.
канцеля́рск|ий (-ая, -ое, -ие) *прил* office *опред*; ~ **слог** *или* **язы́к** officialese.
канцеля́рщин|а (-ы) ж (*формализм*) red tape.
кáнцлер (-а) м (*глава госудáрства*) chancellor.
каньóн (-а) м canyon.
каню́к (-á) м buzzard.
каню́ч|ить (-у, -ишь) *несов неперех* (*разг*) to whinge.
каолúн (-а) м kaolin.
кáпа|ть (-ю) *несов неперех* (*вода*) to drip ♦ (*perf* **накáпать**) *перех* (*микстуру*) to pour out drop by drop; **дождь** ~**ет** it's spotting with rain.
кáпелек *сущ см* **кáпелька**.
капéлл|а (-ы) ж (*МУЗ*) choir; (*РЕЛ*) chapel.
капеллáн (-а) м chaplain.
кáпел|ь *сущ см* **кáпля**.
кáпел|ь (-и) ж thaw.
кáпел|ька (-ьки; *gen pl* -**ек**) ж droplet; ~ +*gen* (*молока итп*) a drop of; (*счáстья, прáвды*) a grain of; **всё до послéдней** ~**ьки** every last little bit.
кáпельку *нареч* (*разг*) a tad *или* touch; **ну ещё** ~ a little bit more; **почитáй хоть** ~ read for just a little while at least.
капельмéйстер (-а) м bandmaster.
кáпел|ьница (-ы) ж (*МЕД*) drip(-feed); **стáвить (постáвить** *perf*) **комý-н** ~**у** to put sb on a drip.
кáперс|ы (-ов) *мн* (*КУЛИН*) capers *мн*.
капилля́р (-а) м capillary.
капитáл (-а) м (*КОММ*) capital; (*перен: политический*) power; **вы́пущенный акционéрный** ~ (*КОММ*) issued capital.
капитáлен *прил см* **капитáльный**.
капитализáци|я (-и) ж capitalization.
капитализúр|овать (-ую) (*не)сов перех*

катара́кт|а (-ы) ж (МЕД) cataract.

катастро́ф|а (-ы) ж (авиационная, железнодорожная) disaster; (перен) catastrophe.

катастрофи́ческий (-ая, -ое, -ие) прил catastrophic, disastrous.

ката́|ть (-ю) несов перех (что-н круглое) to roll; (что-н на колёсах) to wheel; ~ (impf) кого́-н на маши́не to take sb for a drive

▸ ката́ться несов возв: ~ся на маши́не/велосипе́де to go for a drive/cycle; ~ся (impf) на конька́х/ло́шади to go skating/horse (BRIT) или horseback (US) riding; ~ся (impf) от бо́ли to roll about in pain; ~ся (impf) со́ смеху to fall about laughing; как сыр в ма́сле ~ся (impf) to be in clover.

катафа́лк (-а) м hearse.

катего́ричен прил см катего́ричный.

категори́ческий (-ая, -ое, -ие) прил categoric.

категори́ч|ный (-ен, -на, -но) прил categorical.

катего́ри|я (-и) ж category.

ка́тер (-а) м boat; сторожево́й/торпе́дный ~ patrol/torpedo boat.

катехи́зис (-а) м catechism.

кати́|ть (-чу́, -тишь) несов перех (что-н круглое) to roll; (что-н на колёсах) to wheel ♦ неперех (разг: в автомобиле) to bomb along; ~ (impf) бо́чки на кого́-н (перен) to snipe at sb.

катка́ сущ см като́к.

като́д (-а) м cathode.

кат|о́к (-ка́) м ice или skating rink; (ТЕХ: также: асфа́льтовый ~) steamroller.

като́лик (-а) м Catholic.

католици́зм (-а) м Catholicism.

католи́чек сущ см католи́чка.

католи́ческий (-ая, -ое, -ие) прил Catholic.

католи́ч|ка (-ки; gen pl -ек) ж см като́лик.

ка́торг|а (-и) ж hard labour (BRIT) или labor (US).

каторжа́н|ин (-ина; nom pl -е, gen pl -) м convict (in a labour camp).

каторжа́н|ка (-ки; gen pl -ек) ж см каторжа́нин.

ка́торжник (-а) м см каторжа́нин.

кату́ш|ка (-ки; gen pl -ек) ж spool.

каучу́к (-а) м rubber.

каучу́ковый прил rubber.

КАФ м сокр CAF (= cost and freight).

кафе́ ср нескл café.

ка́федр|а (-ы) ж (ПРОСВЕЩ) department; (РЕЛ) pulpit; (лекторская) rostrum; заве́дующий ~ой chair; он получи́л ~у he obtained a chair.

кафедра́льный прил: ~ собо́р cathedral.

ка́фел|ь (-я) м собир tiles мн.

ка́фельный прил tiled.

кафете́ри|й (-я) м cafeteria.

кафта́н (-а) м caftan.

кача́л|ка (-ки; gen pl -ок) ж rocking chair.

кача́ни|е (-я) ср (на качелях) swinging; (на волнах) rocking, roll.

кача́|ть (-ю) несов перех (колыбель) to rock; (подбрасывать) to throw into the air; (нефть) to pump; ~ (impf) голово́й to shake one's head; кора́бль си́льно ~ло the ship was rocking violently

▸ кача́ться несов возв to swing; (на волнах) to rock, roll; (от усталости) to sway.

каче́л|и (-ей) мн swing ед.

ка́чественно нареч (другой) essentially; (делать, работать) to a high standard.

ка́чествен|ный прил qualitative; (-, -на, -но; товар, изделие) high-quality; ка́чественное прилага́тельное qualitative adjective.

ка́честв|о (-а) ср quality ♦ предл: в ~е +gen as; в ~е приме́ра by way of example; я рабо́таю в ~е меха́ника I work as a mechanic.

ка́ч|ка (-и) ж: бортова́я ~ rolling; килева́я ~ pitching.

качн|у́ть (-у́, -ёшь) сов перех to swing

▸ качну́ться сов возв to swing.

ка́ш|а (-и) ж ≈ porridge; у него́ в голове́ ~ he's totally mixed up.

кашало́т (-а) м sperm whale.

ка́шел|ь (-ля) м cough.

кашеми́р (-а) м cashmere.

ка́шля сущ см ка́шель.

ка́шлян|уть (-у, -ешь) сов неперех to cough.

ка́шля|ть (-ю) несов неперех to cough.

Кашми́р (-а) м Kashmir.

кашне́ ср нескл narrow scarf, usually worn under a coat.

кашта́н (-а) м (дерево) chestnut (tree); (плод) chestnut; (: несъедобный) conker; таска́ть (impf) ~ы из огня́ to do the dirty work; ко́нский ~ horse chestnut.

кашта́новый прил (аллея, волосы) chestnut.

ка|ю́к (-юка́ как сказ (разг): ему́ ~ he's finished.

каю́т|а (-ы) ж (МОР) cabin.

каю́т-компа́ни|я (-и) ж naval officers' lounge.

ка́|яться (-юсь; perf пока́яться) несов возв: ~ (в чём-н пе́ред кем-н) to confess (sth to sb); я хочу́ тебе́ пока́яться в чём-то I must tell you something; до́лжен пока́яться, я никогда́ не люби́л её I must confess, I never loved her.

кБт сокр (= килоба́йт) KB, kbyte (= kilobyte); = килоби́т.

КВ мн сокр (= коро́ткие во́лны) SW = short wave ед.

кв. сокр (= квадра́тный) sq. (= square); (= кварти́ра) Apt. (= apartment).

квадра́т (-а) м square; возводи́ть (возвести́ perf) что-н в ~ to square sth.

квадра́т|ный (-ен, -на, -но) прил square; ~ ко́рень square root; квадра́тные ско́бки square brackets.

ква́канье (-я) ср croaking.

ква́кн|уть (3sg -ет, 3pl -ут) сов неперех to croak.

квалификацио́нный прил: ~ экза́мен

professional exam.

квалифика́ци|я (-и) ж qualification; (*профессия*) profession.

квалифици́рованно *нареч* competently.

квалифици́рован|ный (-, -на, -но) *прил* (*работник*) qualified; (*труд*) skilled.

квалифици́р|овать (-ую) (не)сов перех (*спортсмена*) to rank; (*преступление, поведение*) to categorize.

квант (-а) м quantum.

ква́нтов|ый *прил:* ~**ая меха́ника/фи́зика** quantum mechanics/physics.

кварта́л (-а) м quarter.

кварта́льный *прил* (*отчёт, план*) quarterly.

кварте́т (-а) м quartet.

кварти́р|а (-ы) ж flat (*BRIT*), apartment (*US*); (*снимаемое жильё*) lodgings мн; **жить** (*impf*) **на** ~**е** to rent a flat *или* apartment; **съезжа́ть (съе́хать** *perf*) **с** ~**ы** to move out of lodgings.

кварти́ра́нт (-а) м lodger.

кварти́ра́нт|ка (-ки; *gen pl* **-ок)** ж см **кварти́ра́нт.**

кварти́р|ова́ть (-у́ю) *несов неперех* (*разг: снимать жильё*) to rent a flat (*BRIT*) *или* apartment (*US*).

кварти́росъёмщик (-а) м leaseholder.

квартпла́т|а (-ы) ж *сокр* (= **кварти́рная пла́та**) rent (*for a flat*).

кварц (-а) м quartz.

ква́рцев|ый *прил* (*порода, руда*) quartz; ~**ая ла́мпа** quartz lamp.

квас (-а; *nom pl* **-ы́)** м kvass (*mildly alcoholic drink made from fermented rye bread, yeast or berries*).

ква́|сить (-шу, -сишь; *perf* **заква́сить)** *несов перех* to pickle; (*молоко*) to sour.

ква́шен|ый *прил* (*молоко*) sour; ~**ая капу́ста** sauerkraut, pickled cabbage.

квашн|я́ (-и́; *gen pl* **-е́й)** ж (*кадушка*) fermenting bucket (*for dough*); (*разг: человек*) clodhopper.

ква́шу *несов см* **ква́сить.**

Квебе́к (-а) м Quebec.

квинте́т (-а) м quintet.

квинтэссе́нци|я (-и) ж quintessence.

квита́нци|я (-и) ж receipt.

кви́ты *как сказ* (*разг*): **мы** ~ we're quits.

КВН м *сокр* (= **клуб весёлых и нахо́дчивых**) *contest in which teams compete in various activities.*

кво́рум (-а) м quorum.

кво́т|а (-ы) ж quota; **и́мпортная** ~ import quota.

кВт *сокр* (= **килова́тт**) kW (= *kilowatt*).

кг *сокр* (= **килогра́мм**) kg (= *kilogram(me)*).

КГБ м *сокр* (*ист:* = **Комите́т госуда́рственной безопа́сности**) KGB.

ке́гл|и (-ей) мн skittles мн; (*игра*) skittles ед.

кедр (-а) м cedar (tree).

ке́д|ы (-) мн pumps мн.

Кейпта́ун (-а) м Cape Town.

кейф (-а) м = **кайф.**

кейф|ова́ть (-у́ю) *несов* = **кайфова́ть.**

кекс (-а) м (fruit)cake.

келе́ен *прил см* **келе́йный.**

келе́йно *нареч* secretly.

келе́йный *прил* (*жизнь*) reclusive; (*тишина*) sublime; (**-ен, -йна, -йно**; *перен: переговоры, совещания*) secret.

Кёльн (-а) м Cologne.

кельт (-а) м Celt.

ке́льтск|ий (-ая, -ое, -ие) *прил* Celtic.

ке́л|ья (-ьи; *gen pl* **-ий)** ж (*монашеская*) cell.

кем *мест см* **кто.**

Ке́мбридж (-а) м Cambridge.

ке́мпинг (-а) м camping site, campsite.

кенгуру́ *ср нескл* kangaroo.

кени́йск|ий (-ая, -ое, -ие) *прил* Kenyan.

Ке́ни|я (-и) ж Kenya.

ке́пи *ср нескл* peaked cap.

ке́п|ка (-ки; *gen pl* **-ок)** ж cap.

кера́мик|а (-и) ж *собир* ceramics мн.

керами́ческ|ий (-ая, -ое, -ие) *прил* ceramic.

кероси́н (-а) м paraffin, kerosene (*US*).

кероси́н|ка (-ки; *gen pl* **-ок)** ж paraffin stove.

ке́сарев *прил:* ~**о сече́ние** Caesarean (*BRIT*) *или* Cesarean (*US*) section.

кессо́нн|ый *прил:* ~**ая боле́знь** decompression sickness, the bends мн.

ке́т|а (-ы) ж Keta salmon.

кефа́л|ь (-и) ж grey mullet.

кефи́р (-а) м kefir (*yoghurt drink*).

киберне́тик (-а) м specialist in cybernetics.

киберне́тик|а (-и) ж cybernetics.

кибернети́ческ|ий (-ая, -ое, -ие) *прил* cybernetic.

киби́т|ка (-и) ж carriage.

кива́|ть (-ю) *несов неперех* (+*dat*) to nod; ~ (*impf*) **на кого́-н** (*разг*) to pin the blame on sb.

кивка́ *сущ см* **киво́к.**

кивн|у́ть (-у́, -ёшь) *сов неперех* to nod.

киво́к (-ка́) м nod.

кида́|ть (-ю) *несов от* **ки́нуть.**

▶ **кида́ться** *несов от* **ки́нуться** ♦ *возв:* ~**ся камня́ми** to throw stones at each other; ~**ся** (*impf*) **деньга́ми** to throw money around.

Ки́ев (-а) м Kiev.

кизи́л (-а) м cornel.

кизи́ловый *прил* cornel *опред.*

ки|й (-я; *nom pl* **-и,** *gen pl* **-ёв)** м (*СПОРТ*) cue.

кики́мор|а (-ы) ж *female goblin in Russian mythology*; (*пренебр: человек*) fright.

килоба́йт (-а) м kilobyte.

килова́тт (-а) м kilowatt.

килогра́мм (-а) м kilogram(me).

килограммо́вый *прил* of one kilogram(me).

киломе́тр (-а) м kilometre (*BRIT*), kilometer (*US*).

километро́вый *прил* (*расстояние*) of one kilometre (*BRIT*) *или* kilometer (*US*); (*гонка*) one-kilometre.

кил|ь (-я) м keel.

кильва́тер (-а) м wake.

ки́льк|а (-и) ж sprat.

кимоно́ *ср нескл* kimono.

кинематóграф (-а) *м* (*киноиндустрия*) cinematography; (*кинотеатр*) cinema.
кинематографи́ст (-а) *м* cinematographer.
кинематографи́ческ|ий (-ая, -ое, -ие) *прил* cinematographic.
кинематогра́фи|я (-и) *ж* cinematography.
кинéтик|а (-и) *ж* kinetics.
кинети́ческ|ий (-ая, -ое, -ие) *прил* kinetic.
кинжáл (-а) *м* dagger.
кинó *ср нескл* cinema; (*разг: фильм*) film, movie (*US*); **идти́ (пойти́** *perf*) **в ~** (*разг*) to go to the pictures (*BRIT*) *или* movies (*US*); **э́то прóсто ~** (*разг*) it's an absolute joke.
киноактёр (-а) *м* (film) actor.
киноактри́с|а (-ы) *ж* (film) actress.
киноарти́ст (-а) *м* = **киноактёр**.
киноарти́ст|ка (-ки; *gen pl* -ок) *ж* = **киноактри́са**.
кинокарти́н|а (-ы) *ж* film.
кинооперáтор (-а) *м* cameraman (*мн* cameramen).
кинорежиссёр (-а) *м* (film) director.
киносту́ди|я (-и) *ж* film studio.
киносъёмк|а (-и) *ж* filming, shooting.
кинотеáтр (-а) *м* cinema.
кинофи́льм (-а) *м* film.
ки́н|уть (-у, -ешь; *impf* **кидáть**) *сов перех* (*дрова, камень*) to throw; (*взгляд*) to cast; (*друзей*) to desert; (*силы, ресурсы*) to channel
▸ **ки́нуться** (*impf* **кидáться**) *сов возв*: **~ся на** +*acc* (*на врага*) to attack; (*на еду*) to fall upon; **кидáться** (**~ся** *perf*) **комý-н на шéю** to fall on sb; **кидáться** (**~ся** *perf*) **к комý-н** to throw o.s. at sb; **кидáться** (**~ся** *perf*) **со скáлы** to throw o.s. off a cliff.
киóск (-а) *м* kiosk.
киóт (-а) *м* icon case.
ки́п|а (-ы) *ж* bundle.
кипари́с (-а) *м* cypress.
кипари́совый *прил* cypress *опред*.
кипéни|е (-я) *ср* boiling; **температу́ра** *или* **тóчка ~я** boiling point.
кип|éть (-лю́, -и́шь; *perf* **вскипéть**) *несов неперех* (*вода, чайник*) to boil; **рабóта ~и́т** work is in full swing; **жизнь ~и́т** life is busy; **~** (**вскипéть** *perf*) **негодовáнием/злóбой** to seethe with indignation/anger.
Кипр (-а) *м* Cyprus.
киприóт (-а) *м* Cypriot.
киприóт|ка (-ки; *gen pl* -ок) *ж см* **киприóт**.
кипу́ч|ий (-ая, -ее, -ие; -, -а, -о) *прил* bubbling; (*перен*) busy.
кипяти́льник (-а) *м* element (*for heating water*).
кипя|ти́ть (-чу́, -ти́шь; *perf* **вскипяти́ть**) *несов перех* to boil
▸ **кипяти́ться** *несов возв* (*овощи*) to boil; (*шприцы, бельё*) to be boiled; (*перен: разг: горячиться*) to get shirty.

кипят|óк (-кá) *м* boiling water.
кипячёный *прил* boiled.
кипячу́(сь) *несов см* **кипяти́ть(ся)**.
кирги́з (-а) *м* Kirghiz.
Кирги́зи|я (-и) *ж* Kirghizia.
кирги́з|ка (-ки; *gen pl* -ок) *ж см* **кирги́з**.
кирги́зск|ий (-ая, -ое, -ие) *прил* Kirghiz.
кири́ллиц|а (-ы) *ж* the Cyrillic alphabet.
киркá (-и́) *ж* pick(axe).
кирпи́ч (-á) *м* (*СТРОИТ*) brick.
кирпи́чный *прил* brick; **кирпи́чный завóд** brickworks.
кисéйн|ый *прил* muslin; **~ая бáрышня** *prim young miss*.
ки́сел *прил см* **ки́слый**.
кисéл|ь (-я) *м* fruit jelly; **седьмáя водá на киселé** distant relative.
кисéт (-а) *м* tobacco pouch.
кисе|я́ (-и́) *ж* muslin.
кисли́нк|а (-и) *ж* sour taste.
кислорóд (-а) *м* oxygen.
ки́сло-слáд|кий (-кая, -кое, -кие; -ок, -ка, -ко) *прил* (*хлеб*) sweet with a bitter aftertaste; (*ягоды*) bittersweet.
кислотá (-оты́; *nom pl* -óты) *ж* acid.
кислóтност|ь (-и) *ж* acidity.
кислóтный *прил* acid; **~ дождь** acid rain.
ки́с|лый (-ел, -лá, -ло) *прил* (*также перен*) sour; **ки́слая капу́ста** sauerkraut; **ки́слое молокó** soured milk.
ки́с|нуть (-ну, -нешь; *pt* -, -ла, -ло, *perf* **проки́снуть** *или* **ски́снуть**) *несов неперех* to go off; (*no perf; перен: разг*) to mope (about).
кист|á (-ы́) *ж* cyst.
ки́сточ|ка (-ки; *gen pl* -ек) *ж* (paint)brush; (*винограда*) bunch; (*на берете, на скатерти итп*) tassel.
кист|ь (-и) *ж* (*АНАТ*) hand; (*гроздь: рябины*) cluster; (: *винограда*) bunch; (*на скатерти, на одежде итп*) tassel; (*художника, маляра*) (paint) brush; **он хорошó владéет ки́стью** he's a good painter; **полотнó ки́сти Мати́сса** painting by Matisse.
кит (-á) *м* whale.
китá|ец (-йца) *м* Chinese.
Китáй (-я) *м* China.
китáйск|ий (-ая, -ое, -ие) *прил* Chinese; **~ язы́к** Chinese; **~ая грáмота** double Dutch.
китáйца *итп сущ см* **китáец**.
китая́н|ка (-ки; *gen pl* -ок) *ж см* **китáец**.
ки́тел|ь (-я; *nom pl* -и, *gen pl* -ей) *м military jacket*.
китобóйный *прил* whaling *опред*.
китóвый *прил* whale *опред*.
кич|и́ться (-у́сь, -и́шься) *несов возв*: **~** +*instr* to preen o.s. on.
кичли́в|ый (-, -а, -о) *прил* conceited.
киш|éть (*3sg* -и́т, *3pl* -áт) *несов неперех* (*мошкара, черви*) to swarm; **~** (*impf*) +*instr* (*людьми, рыбой*) to teem with.

кише́чник (-а) *м* intestines *мн.*
кише́чный *прил* intestinal.
Кишинёв (-а) *м* Kishinev.
киш|ка́ (-ки́; *gen pl* -о́к, *dat pl* -ка́м) *ж* gut, intestine; **пряма́я** ~ rectum; **то́лстая** ~ large intestine.
кишла́к (-а́) *м village in Central Asia.*
кишми́ш (-а) *м собир* seedless grapes *мн*; (*изюм*) currants *мн.*
кишмя́ *нареч* (*разг*): ~ **кише́ть** to swarm.
кишо́к *сущ см* кишка́.
кл. *сокр* = класс.
клавеси́н (-а) *м* harpsichord.
клавиату́р|а (-ы) *ж* keyboard; **(ма́лая)** ~ (*комп*) keypad.
кла́виш|а (-и) *ж* key; ~ **„возвра́т каре́тки"/вы́хода** (*комп*) return/escape key.
кла́вишный *прил*: ~ **инструме́нт** keyboard instrument.
клад (-а) *м* treasure.
кла́дбище (-а) *ср* cemetery; (*возле церкви*) graveyard.
кладби́щенск|ий (-ая, -ое, -ие) *прил* (*см сущ*) cemetery *опред*; graveyard *опред*; ~ **сто́рож** sexton.
кла́дез|ь (-я) *м* (*перен*): ~ **зна́ний или прему́дрости** mine of information.
кла́дк|а (-и) *ж* (*действие*) laying; **кирпи́чная** ~ brickwork; **ка́менная** ~ masonry.
кладова́|я (-о́й; *decl like adj*) *ж* store.
кладо́в|ка (-ки; *gen pl* -ок) *ж* (*разг*) cubby-hole.
кладовщи́к (-а́) *м* storeman (*мн* storemen).
кладовщи́|ца (-ы) *ж* storewoman (*мн* storewomen).
кладу́ *итп несов см* класть.
клад|ь (-и) *ж* load; **ручна́я** ~ hand luggage.
кла́ксон (-а) *м* horn.
клан (-а) *м* clan.
кла́ня|ться (-юсь; *perf* поклони́ться) *несов возв* to bow; (*свидетельствовать уважение*) to send one's regards; (*перен: униженно просить*) to beg.
кла́пан (-а) *м* valve.
кларне́т (-а) *м* clarinet.
кларнети́ст (-а) *м* clarinetist.
класс (-а) *м* class; (*комната*) classroom ♦ *как сказ* (*выражает восхищение*) it's great; **он вёл** ~ **фортепья́но в консервато́рии** he taught the piano at the conservatory; **специали́ст высо́кого кла́сса** highly-qualified specialist; **пока́зывать** (**показа́ть** *perf*) ~ (*разг*) to show one's class.
кла́ссен *прил см* кла́ссный.
кла́ссик (-а) *м* (*литературы, музыки*) classic; (*учёный*) classical scholar.
кла́ссик|а (-и) *ж* classics *мн.*
классификацио́нный *прил* (*экзамен*) assessment *опред*; (*таблица*) classification *опред.*
классифика́ци|я (-и) *ж* classification.
классифици́р|овать (-ую) (*не)сов перех* to

classify.
классици́зм (-а) *м* classicism.
класси́ческ|ий (-ая, -ое, -ие) *прил* (*пример, работа*) classic; (*музыка, литература*) classical; (*разг: жулик, политикан итп*) typical; ~**ая гимна́зия** *grammar school specializing in Latin and Ancient Greek*; ~**ое образова́ние** classical education.
кла́сс|ный *прил* (*сочинение, собрание*) class *опред*; (-ен, -на, -но; *разг: водитель, обед*) great; **кла́ссный руководи́тель** form teacher.
кла́ссовый *прил* class *опред.*
кла|сть (-ду́, -дёшь; *pt* -л, -ла, -ло, *perf* **положи́ть**) *несов перех* to put; (*perf* **сложи́ть**; *фундамент*) to lay; ~ (**положи́ть** *perf*) **основа́ние** to lay down the foundations; ~ (**положи́ть** *perf*) **жизнь за кого́-н/что-н** to lay down one's life for sb/sth; ~ (**положи́ть** *perf*) **что-н на му́зыку** to put sth to music; ~ (*impf*) **я́йца** to lay eggs.
кла́цань|е (-я) *ср* (*разг*) chattering.
кла́ца|ть (-ю) *несов неперех* (*разг*) to chatter.
клёв (-а) *м* bite; **сего́дня хоро́ший** ~ the fish are biting today.
кл|ева́ть (-юю́) *несов перех* (*подлеж: птица*) to peck ♦ *неперех* (*рыба*) to bite; ~ (*impf*) **но́сом** to nod; **у меня́** ~**юёт** I've got a bite
► **клева́ться** *несов возв* to peck.
кле́вер (-а) *м* clover.
клевет|а́ (-ы́) *ж* (*устная*) slander; (*письменная*) libel.
клеве|та́ть (-щу́, -щешь; *perf* наклевета́ть) *несов неперех*: ~ **на** +*acc* (*см сущ*) to slander; to libel.
клеветни́к (-а́) *м* slanderer.
клеветни́ческ|ий (-ая, -ое, -ие) *прил* (*см сущ*) slanderous; libellous.
клевещу́ *итп несов см* клевета́ть.
кле́ек *прил см* кле́йкий.
клеён|ка (-ки; *gen pl* -ок) *ж* oilcloth.
клеёнчатый *прил* oilskin *опред.*
кле́|ить (-ю, -ишь; *perf* скле́ить) *несов перех* to glue
► **кле́иться** *несов возв* to stick; (*перен: работа*) to come together; (: *разговор*) to go smoothly.
кле|й (-я) *м* glue.
кле́|йкий (-йкая, -йкое, -йкие; -ек, -йка, -йко) *прил* sticky; **кле́йкая ле́нта** sticky tape.
клеймёный *прил* (*товар*) stamped; (*скот*) branded.
клейм|и́ть (-лю́, -и́шь; *perf* заклейми́ть) *несов перех* (*товар, груз*) to stamp; (*скот, преступление*) to brand; (*перен: человека, поведение*) to stigmatize; ~ (**заклейми́ть** *perf*) **кого́-н позо́ром** to hold sb up to shame; **его́ заклейми́ли преда́телем** he was branded a traitor.
клейм|о́ (-а́; *nom pl* -а, *gen pl* -) *ср* stamp; (*на теле скота, осуждённого*) brand; ~ **позо́ра** stigma.
кле́йстер (-а; *part gen* -у) *м* paste.

кле́мм|а (-ы) ж (ЭЛЕК) terminal.
клён (-а) м maple.
клено́вый прил maple.
клепа́ть (-а́ю; perf **склепа́ть**) несов перех to rivet; ♦ (-лю́, -лешь; perf **наклепа́ть**) неперех (разг): ~ **на** +acc to snitch on.
клептома́н (-а) м kleptomaniac.
клептома́ни|я (-и) ж kleptomania.
клептома́н|ка (-ки; gen pl -ок) ж см **клептома́н**.
клерк (-а) м clerk.
кле́т|ка (-ки; gen pl -ок) ж (для птиц, животных) cage; (на ткани) check; (на бумаге) square; (БИО) cell; **бума́га в ~ку** squared paper; **ткань в ~ку** checked material; **грудна́я** ~ chest; **ле́стничная** ~ landing.
кле́точный прил (БИО) cell опред.
клетча́тк|а (-и) ж (no pl; БОТ) cellulose; (АНАТ) cell tissue.
кле́тчатый прил (ткань, шарф итп) chequered, checked.
клёц|ка (-ки; gen pl -ек) ж (обычно мн) dumpling.
клёш (-а) м flare ♦ прил неизм: **брю́ки** ~ flares; **ю́бка** ~ flared skirt.
клешн|я́ (-и́; gen pl -е́й) ж claw, pincer.
клещ (-а́) м (ЗООЛ) tick.
кле́щ|и (-е́й) мн tongs мн.
клие́нт (-а) м client.
клие́нт|ка (-ки; gen pl -ок) ж см **клие́нт**.
клиенту́р|а (-ы) ж собир clientèle.
кли́зм|а (-ы) ж enema.
клик (-а) м (человека) cry; (птицы) call.
кли́к|а (-и) ж clique.
клику́ш|а (-и) ж hysterical woman (мн women) ♦ м/ж panicmonger.
кли́макс (-а) м (БИО) menopause.
климактери́ческ|ий (-ая, -ое, -ие) прил menopausal; **климактери́ческий пери́од** menopause.
кли́мат (-а) м (также перен) climate.
климати́ческ|ий (-ая, -ое, -ие) прил climatic.
клин (-а; nom pl -ья или -ы́, gen pl -ьев или -о́в) м wedge; (солдат, журавлей) V-formation; **борода́ кли́ном** goatee; ~ **кли́ном вышиба́ть** (impf) to fight fire with fire.
кли́ник|а (-и) ж clinic.
клини́ческ|ий (-ая, -ое, -ие) прил clinical; **клини́ческая больни́ца** training hospital; **клини́ческая смерть** (МЕД) clinical death.
клин|о́к (-ка́) м blade.
кли́пс|ы (-ов) мн clip-on earrings мн.
клир (-а) м собир (РЕЛ) the clergy.
кли́рик (-а) м clergyman (мн clergymen).
кли́ринг (-а) м (КОММ) clearing.
кли́рос (-а) м choir (part of church).
клич (-а) м cry; **боево́й** ~ battle cry.
кли́ч|ка (-ки; gen pl -ек) ж (собаки, кошки итп) name; (человека) nickname.
клише́ ср нескл (перен) cliché; (ТИПОГ) plate.
клоа́к|а (-и) ж (перен: загрязнённое место)

cesspit; (: безнравственная среда) cesspool.
клобу́к (-а́) м (РЕЛ) cowl.
кло|к (-ка́; nom pl -чья, gen pl -чьев) м (волос) tuft; (ваты) wad.
клокота́ни|е (-я) ср (воды) gurgling.
клок|ота́ть (-очу́, -о́чешь) несов неперех (вода, поток) to gurgle; (перен: негодовать) to seethe.
клон|и́ть (-ю́, -ишь) несов перех to bow, bend ♦ неперех: ~ **к** +dat to drive at; **его́ ~и́ло ко сну** he was drifting off (to sleep); **ло́дку кло́нит на́ бок** the boat is tilting; **к чему́ ты кло́нишь?** what are you getting или driving at?
▶ **клони́ться** несов возв (пригибаться) to bend; (близиться): ~**ся к** +dat to approach; **день ~и́лся к ве́черу** evening was drawing near.
клоп (-а́) м bedbug.
кло́ун (-а) м clown.
кло́унск|ий (-ая, -ое, -ие) прил clown's; (перен) clownish.
клоч|о́к (-ка́) м уменьш от **клок**; (земли) plot; (бумаги) scrap.
кло́чья итп сущ см **клок**.
клуб (-а) м (общество, здание) club; (обычно мн: дыма, пыли) cloud.
клу́б|ень (-ня) м (картофеля) tuber.
клуб|и́ться (3sg -и́тся, 3pl -я́тся) несов возв to swirl.
клубка́ сущ см **клубо́к**.
клубни́к|а (-и) ж strawberry ♦ собир strawberries мн.
клубни́чный прил strawberry.
клуб|о́к (-ка́) м (ниток, шерсти) ball; (перен: противоречий) tangle, knot; **сверну́ться** (perf) ~**ко́м** to curl up in a ball.
клу́мб|а (-ы) ж flowerbed.
клу́ш|а (-и) ж (разг: пренебр) clumsy woman.
клык (-а́) м (человека) canine (tooth); (животного) fang.
клюв (-а) м beak.
клюк|а́ (-и́) ж walking stick.
клю́кв|а (-ы) ж cranberry ♦ собир cranberries мн; **разве́систая** ~ tall story.
клю́квенный прил: ~ **морс/кисе́ль** cranberry juice/jelly.
клю́н|уть (-у, -ешь) сов перех to peck.
ключ (-а́) м (также перен) key; (родник) spring; (МУЗ): **скрипи́чный/басо́вый** ~ treble/bass clef; **га́ечный** ~ spanner; ~ **от входно́й две́ри** front-door key; **бить** (impf) или **кипе́ть** (impf) ~**о́м** (вода) to jet, spout; **жизнь бьёт** или **кипи́т** ~**о́м** life is really buzzing; **в пре́жнем** ~**é** (перен) as before; **сдава́ть** (**сдать** perf) **что-н под** ~ (здание) to hand over sth ready for immediate entry; **ключ зажига́ния** ignition key.
ключево́й прил (позиция, проблемы итп) key опред; **ключева́я вода́** spring water.
ключи́ц|а (-ы) ж collarbone.

клю́ш|ка (-ки; *gen pl* -ек) ж (*ХОККЕЙ*) hockey stick; (*ГОЛЬФ*) club.

кля́кс|а (-ы) ж smudge.

кляну́(сь) *итп несов см* **кля́сть(ся)**.

кля́нч|ить (-у, -ишь; *perf* **вы́клянчить**) *несов перех* (*разг*): ~ что-н у кого́-н to pester sb for sth.

кляп (-а) м gag; **засу́нуть** (*perf*) **кому́-н** ~ **в рот** to gag sb.

кля́|сть (-ну́, -нёшь; *pt* -л, -ла́, -ло) *несов перех* to curse

▸ **кля́сться** (*perf* **покля́сться**) *несов возв* to swear; **кля́сться** (**покля́сться** *perf*) **в ве́чной любви́** to swear eternal love; **кля́сться** (**покля́сться** *perf*) **жи́знью/Бо́гу** to swear on one's life/to God.

кля́тв|а (-ы) ж oath; **дава́ть** (**дать** *perf*)/ **сде́рживать** (**сдержа́ть** *perf*) ~у to take *или* swear/keep an oath; **наруша́ть** (**нару́шить** *perf*) ~у to break one's oath.

кля́уз|а (-ы) ж backbiting.

кля́узен *прил см* **кля́узный**.

кля́узник (-а) м (*пренебр*) scandalmonger.

кля́узнича|ть (-ю; *perf* **накля́узничать**) *несов непєрєх*: ~ (на +*acc*) to spread gossip (about).

кля́уз|ный (-ен, -на, -но) *прил*: ~ное письмо́ slanderous letter.

кля́ч|а (-и) ж (*разг: пренебр: лошадь*) old nag.

км. *сокр* (= **киломе́тр**) km (= *kilometre* (*BRIT*) *или kilometer* (*US*)).

км/ч *сокр* (= **киломе́тров в час**) km/h (= *kilometres per hour*).

КНДР ж *сокр* (= **Коре́йская Наро́дно-Демократи́ческая Респу́блика**) DPRK (= *Democratic People's Republic of Korea*).

кне́л|и (-ей) *мн* quenelles *мн*.

кни́г|а (-и) ж book; **ка́ссовая** ~ cash-book; **телефо́нная** ~ telephone book *или* directory; ~ **зака́зов** order book; ~ **учёта** day book; **кни́га жа́лоб и предложе́ний** suggestions book.

книголю́б (-а) м book-lover.

книгопеча́тани|е (-я) *ср* book printing.

кни́ж|ка (-ки; *gen pl* -ек) ж book; **записна́я** ~ notebook; **зачётная** ~ (*ПРОСВЕЩ*) register; **трудова́я** ~ employment record book; **че́ковая** ~ chequebook (*BRIT*), checkbook (*US*).

кни́жник (-а) м (*знаток книг*) bibliophile.

кни́жный *прил* (*перен: знания, стиль*) bookish; **кни́жный магази́н** bookshop; **кни́жный шкаф** bookcase; **кни́жный червь** bookworm.

кни́зу *нареч* downwards.

кно́п|ка (-ки; *gen pl* -ок) ж (*звонка, лифта*) button; (*канцелярская*) drawing pin (*BRIT*), thumbtack (*US*); (*застёжка*) press stud, popper (*BRIT*).

КНР ж *сокр* (= **Кита́йская Наро́дная Респу́блика**) PRC (= *People's Republic of China*).

кнут (-а́) м whip; **поли́тика** ~а́ **и пря́ника** the carrot and the stick policy.

княги́н|я (-и) ж princess (*wife of a prince*).

кня́ж|ить (-у, -ишь) *несов непєрєх* to reign.

княжн|а́ (-ны́; *gen pl* -о́н) ж princess (*daughter of a prince*).

князь (-я; *nom pl* -ья́, *gen pl* -е́й) м prince (*in Russia*); **вели́кий** ~ (*ИСТ*) grand prince (*son or brother of the tsar*).

ко *предл см* **к**.

коагули́р|овать (*3sg* -ует, *3pl* -уют) *несов перех* to coagulate.

коагуля́ци|я (-и) ж coagulation.

коа́л|а (-ы) ж koala (*bear*).

коалицио́нн|ый *прил*: ~ое прави́тельство coalition government; ~ **догово́р** coalition pact.

коали́ци|я (-и) ж coalition.

ко́бальт (-а) м cobalt.

кобе́л|ь (-я́) м dog (*male*).

ко́бр|а (-ы) ж cobra.

кобур|а́ (-ы́) ж holster.

кобы́л|а (-ы) ж mare; (*перен: разг*) strapping lass.

ко́ван|ый (-, -а, -о) *прил* (*меч, решётка итп*) forged; (*обитый железом*) metal-bound.

кова́рен *прил см* **кова́рный**.

кова́рность (-и) ж treachery.

кова́р|ный (-ен, -на, -но) *прил* devious.

кова́рств|о (-а) *ср* deviousness.

кова́|ть (кую́, куёшь; *imper* **куй(те)**, *perf* **скова́ть**) *несов перех* to forge; **куй желе́зо пока́ горячо́** strike while the iron's hot.

ковбо́|й (-я) м cowboy.

ковёр (-ра́) м carpet; **вызыва́ть** (**вы́звать** *perf*) **на** ~ **кого́-н** to call sb to account.

ковёрканье (-я) *ср* mangling.

ковёрка|ть (-ю; *perf* **исковёркать**) *несов перех* (*произношение, слова*) to mangle; (*язык*) to butcher; (*душу*) to twist; **коверка́ть** (**исковерка́ть** *perf*) **чью-н мысль/чьи-н слова́** to twist sb's ideas/words.

ко́вк|а (-и) ж forging.

ковра́ *итп сущ см* **ковёр**.

коври́г|а (-и) ж loaf (*мн* loaves).

коври́ж|ка (-ки; *gen pl* -ек) ж ≈ gingerbread.

ко́врик (-а) м rug; (*дверной*) mat.

ковро́в|ый *прил*: ~ая доро́жка runner.

ковроде́ли|е (-я) *ср* carpet weaving.

ковче́г (-а) м: **Но́ев** ~ Noah's Ark.

ковш (-а́) м ladle; (*экскаватора*) shovel.

ковы́ль (-я́) м (*БОТ*) feather grass.

ковыля́|ть (-ю) *несов непєрєх* to hobble.

ковыря́|ть (-ю) *несов перех* to dig up; ~ (*impf*) **в зуба́х/носу́** to pick one's teeth/nose

▸ **ковыря́ться** *несов возв* (*медлить*) to faff about; ~**ся** (*impf*) (**в** +*prp*) (*копаться: в земле*) to root *или* poke about (in).

когда́ *нареч* when; (*иногда*) sometimes; ~ **ты зако́нчишь?** when will you finish?; **мы не зна́ем,** ~ **э́то произошло́** we don't know when it happened; ~ **пью ко́фе,** ~ **чай** sometimes I drink coffee, sometimes tea.

когда́-либо *нареч* = **когда́-нибудь**.

когда́-нибудь *нареч* (*в вопросительных предложениях*) ever; (*в утвердительных предложениях*)

предложениях) some *или* one day; **Вы ~ там бы́ли?** have you ever been there?; **я ~ туда́ пое́ду** I'll go there some *или* one day.

когда́-то *нареч* once; **он был ~ бога́т** he was once a rich man; **~ ещё я туда́ пое́ду** just when will I have another chance to go there?

кого́ *мест от* **кто**.

когóрт|а (-ы) *ж* (*перен*) cohort.

кóг|оть (-тя; *gen pl* -тéй) *м* (*кошки, льва итп*) claw; (*орла*) talon; **пока́зывать (показа́ть** *perf*) **~ти** (*перен*) to bare one's teeth.

код (-а) *м* code; **передава́ть (переда́ть** *perf*) **сообще́ние по ко́ду** to send a message in code; **~ си́мвола** (*КОМП*) character code.

кодеи́н (-а) *м* codeine.

кóдекс (-а) *м* code; **гражда́нский/уголо́вный ~** (*ЮР*) civil/criminal code.

коди́р|овать (-ую; *perf* **закоди́ровать**) *несов перех* to encode, code.

кодиро́вк|а (-и) *ж* coding.

кодиро́вщик (-а) *м* coder.

коди́рующий (-ая, -ее, -ие) *прил*: **~ее устро́йство** (*КОМП*) encoder.

кодифика́ци|я (-и) *ж* (*ЮР*) codification.

кодифици́р|овать (-ую) (*не*)*сов перех* (*ЮР*) to codify.

кóдов|ый *прил*: **~ые зна́ки** code symbols *мн*; **кóдовое назва́ние** codename.

ко́е-где́ *нареч* here and there.

ко́ек *сущ см* **ко́йка**.

ко́е-ка́к *нареч* (*небрежно*) any old how; (*с трудом*) somehow.

ко́е-како́й (**ко́е-како́го**) *мест* some; **нам нужна́ ко́е-кака́я по́мощь** we need some sort of help.

ко́е-когда́ *нареч* now and then, now and again.

ко́е-кто́ (**ко́е-кого́**) *мест* (*некоторые*) some (people).

ко́е-куда́ *нареч* (*разг*) this place and that.

ко́е-что́ (**ко́е-чего́**) *мест* (*нечто*) something; (*немногое*) a little.

ко́ж|а (-и) *ж* skin; (*материал*) leather; (*апельсина, яблока*) peel; **гуси́ная ~** goose bumps *мн или* pimples *мн*; **~ да ко́сти** (*разг*) all skin and bone; **из ~и вон лезть** (*impf*) to sweat blood.

кóжаный *прил* leather.

кожéвенный *прил* leather; **кожéвенный заво́д** tannery.

кóжник (-а) *м* (*МЕД*) dermatologist.

кóжн|ый *прил*: **~ые боле́зни** skin diseases; **ко́жный врач** dermatologist; **ко́жный покро́в** skin.

кожур|а́ (-ы́) *ж* (*апельсина*) peel; (*ореха*) skin.

коз|а́ (-ы́; *nom pl* -ы) *ж* (nanny) goat.

кóзел *сущ см* **ко́злы**.

козёл (-ла́; *nom pl* -лы́) *м* (billy) goat; (*в гимнастике*) horse; (*разг: игра*) dominoes; **от него́ как от ~ла́ молока́** (*разг*) he's worse than

useless; **забива́ть** (*impf*) **~ла́** to play dominoes; **козёл отпуще́ния** scapegoat.

Козеро́г (-а) *м* (*созвездие*) Capricorn.

ко́з|ий (-ья, -ье, -ьи) *прил* goat *опред*; **~ье молоко́** goat's milk.

козла́ *итп сущ см* **козёл**.

козлёнок (-ёнка; *nom pl* -я́та, *gen pl* -я́т) *м* (*ЗООЛ*) kid.

козли́н|ый *прил* (*голос*) reedy; **~ая боро́дка** goatee.

ко́з|лы (-ел) *мн* (*сиденье*) coach box *ед*; (*опора*) trestle *ед*.

козля́та *итп сущ см* **козлёнок**.

кóзн|и (-ей) *мн* intrigues *мн*; **стро́ить** (*impf*) **~** to scheme.

козырёк (-ька́) *м* (*картуза, фуражки*) peak; (*навес*) lintel; **брать (взять** *perf*) **под ~** to salute.

козырн|о́й *прил*: **~а́я ка́рта** trump.

козырн|у́ть (-у́, -нёшь) *сов от* **козыря́ть**.

ко́зыр|ь (-я) *м* (*КАРТЫ*) trump; (*перен*) trump card.

козырька́ *сущ см* **козырёк**.

козыря́ть (-ю; *perf* **козырну́ть**) *несов неперех* (*разг: в картах*) to play a trump; (*хвастаться*): **~ +instr** to show off about; (: *отдавать честь*): **~ть +dat** to salute.

козя́в|ка (-ки; *gen pl* -ок) *ж* (*разг: букашка*) bug; (: *пренебр: человек*) small fry *только ед*.

ко́|йка (-йки; *gen pl* -ек) *ж* (*на судне*) berth; (*в казарме*) bunk; (*в больнице, общежитии*) bed.

кок (-а) *м* (*повар*) ship's cook; (*вихор*) quiff.

кока́ин (-а) *м* cocaine.

кокаини́ст (-а) *м* cocaine addict.

кокаини́ст|ка (-ки; *gen pl* -ок) *ж см* **кокаини́ст**.

кока́рд|а (-ы) *ж* cockade.

коке́т|ка (-ки; *gen pl* -ок) *ж* flirt, coquette.

коке́тливост|ь (-и) *ж* flirtatiousness.

коке́тлив|ый (-, -а, -о) *прил* (*девушка, взгляд, смех*) flirtatious; (*шапочка, платье итп*) pretty.

коке́тнича|ть (-ю) *несов неперех* to flirt.

коке́ток *сущ см* **коке́тка**.

коке́тств|о (-а) *ср* flirting.

коклю́ш (-а) *м* whooping cough.

КОКО́М *сокр* COCOM.

ко́кон (-а) *м* cocoon.

коко́с (-а) *м* coconut.

коко́сов|ый *прил*: **~ая па́льма** coconut palm; **коко́совое молоко́** coconut milk; **коко́совый оре́х** coconut.

кокс (-а) *м* coke.

ко́кс|овать (-у́ю) *несов перех* (*ТЕХ*) to coke.

кокте́йл|ь (-я) *м* cocktail.

кол (-а́; *loc sg* -у́, *nom pl* -ья, *gen pl* -ьев) *м* stake; (*nom pl* -ы́; *разг: ПРОСВЕЩ*) ≈ E (*school mark*); **у меня́ нет ни ~а́ ни двора́** I don't have a thing to my name; (**ему́** *итп*) **хоть ~ на голове́ чеши́** it's like talking to a brick wall.

The spelling rules for Russian are shown on page xvii.

ко́лб|а (-ы) ж (хим) flask.
колбас|а́ (-ы́) ж sausage.
кол-во сокр (= коли́чество) amt (= amount).
колго́т|ки (-ок) мн tights мн (BRIT), panty hose мн (US).
колдо́бин|а (-ы) ж (на доро́ге) pothole.
колд|ова́ть (-у́ю) несов неперех to practise (BRIT) или practice (US) witchcraft; (перен): ~ **над** +instr (над карти́ной, над у́жином итп) to conjure up.
колдовско́й прил magical; (перен) bewitching.
колдовств|о́ (-а́) ср sorcery, witchcraft.
колду́н (-а́) м wizard, sorcerer.
колду́нь|я (-и; gen pl -ий, dat pl -ьям) ж sorceress.
колеба́ни|е (-я) ср (физ) oscillation; (маятника) swing; (почвы, зда́ния) vibration; (перен: цен, температу́ры) fluctuation; (: обычно мн: нереши́тельность) wavering, vacillation.
колеба́тельный прил (физ) oscillatory.
кол|еба́ть (-е́блю, -е́блешь) несов перех to rock, swing; (perf **поколеба́ть**; авторите́т) to shake
▶ **колеба́ться** (perf **поколеба́ться**) несов возв (физ) to oscillate; (ли́стья, пла́мя итп) to flicker; (це́ны, пого́да) to fluctuate; (сомнева́ться) to waver, vacillate.
колеблющийся (-аяся, -ееся, -иеся) прил (свет, те́ни) flickering; (челове́к) vacillating.
коленко́р (-а) м calico.
коленко́ровый прил calico.
коле́нн|ый прил: ~**ая ча́шка** kneecap.
коле́н|о (-а; nom pl -и, gen pl -ей) ср knee; (nom pl -а; трубы́) joint; (разг: муз) phrase; (поколе́ние) generation; **встава́ть** (**встать** perf) **на** ~**и** to kneel (down); **стоя́ть** (impf) **на** ~**ях** to be kneeling (down); **опуска́ться** (**опусти́ться** perf) **на** ~**и** to go down on one's knees; **сиде́ть** (impf) **у кого́-н на** ~**ях** to sit on sb's knee или lap; **поста́вить** (perf) **кого́-н на** ~**и** (перен) to bring sb to his итп knees; **ей мо́ре по** ~ everything washes straight over her.
коленопреклонённый прил kneeling.
коле́нчатый прил: ~ **вал** crankshaft.
ко́лер (-а) м colour (BRIT), color (US).
колёсик|о (-а) ср уменьш от колесо́; (часово́е) wheel.
коле|си́ть (-шу́, -си́шь) несов неперех to get around; **я** ~**си́л по всему́ го́роду** I've been all over town.
колесни́ц|а (-ы) ж chariot.
кол|есо́ (-еса́; nom pl -ёса) ср wheel; **пя́тое** ~ (перен) fifth wheel (fig); **жизнь на** ~**ёсах** life on the road; **жить** (impf) **на** ~**ёсах** to live out of a suitcase.
коле́ц сущ см кольцо́.
колешу́ несов см колеси́ть.
коле|я́ (-и́) ж (на доро́ге) rut; (для поездо́в) track; (перен) routine; **выбива́ть** (**вы́бить** perf) **из** ~**й** to get out of a rut.

ко́лик|и (-) мн colic ед.
коли́чественный прил quantitative.
коли́честв|о (-а) ср quantity.
ко́лк|а (-и) ж (дров) chopping; (льда) breaking up.
ко́лк|ий (-ая, -ое, -ие; -ок, -ка́, -ко) прил (хво́я, трава́) prickly; (перен: шу́тка, замеча́ния) biting.
ко́лкост|ь (-и) ж (нра́ва, замеча́ний) abrasiveness; (насме́шка) biting remark.
коллаборациони́зм (-а) м collaborationism.
коллаборациони́ст (-а) м collaborator.
колла́ж (-а) м collage.
колле́г|а (-и) м/ж colleague.
коллегиа́лен прил см коллегиа́льный.
коллегиа́льност|ь (-и) ж: **при́нцип** ~**и** collective responsibility.
коллегиа́льный (-ен, -ьна, -ьно) прил collective.
колле́ги|я (-и) ж (поли́т) collegium (executive body in charge of government ministry); **адвока́тская** ~ ≈ the Bar; **редакцио́нная** ~ editorial board.
ко́лледж (-а) м college.
коллекти́в (-а) м collective; **а́вторский** ~ (team of) contributors.
коллекти́вен прил см коллекти́вный.
коллективиза́ци|я (-и) ж (ист) collectivization (creation of collective farms in the late 1920's and 1930's).
коллекти́вный (-ен, -на, -но) прил collective.
колле́ктор (-а) м (библиоте́чный) book depository; (канализацио́нный) manifold; (элек) collector.
коллекционе́р (-а) м collector.
коллекциони́рование (-я) ср collecting.
коллекциони́р|овать (-ую) несов перех to collect.
коллекцио́нный прил collectable.
колле́кци|я (-и) ж collection.
ко́лли ж нескл collie.
колли́зи|я (-и) ж clash.
колло́квиум (-а) м (просвещ) seminar; (совеща́ние специали́стов) colloquium.
коловоро́т (-а) м (водоворо́т) eddy; (тех) ice drill; (перен: столпотворе́ние) hurly-burly; ~ **собы́тий** the vortex of events.
коло́д|а (-ы) ж (бревно́) block; (карт) pack, deck; **че́рез пень** ~**у** half-heartedly.
коло́дезн|ый прил: ~**ая вода́** water from the well.
коло́дец (-ца) м well; (в ша́хте) shaft.
коло́дк|а (-ки; gen pl -ок) ж (обувна́я) shoetree; (орде́нская) strip.
коло́дцы итп сущ см коло́дец.
ко́лок прил сущ см ко́лкий.
ко́локол (-а; nom pl -а́) м bell; **звони́ть** (impf) **в** ~ to ring a bell.
колоко́льн|я (-ьни; gen pl -ен) ж bell tower; **смотре́ть** (impf) **со свое́й** ~**ьни на что-н** to take a narrow view of sth.
колоко́льчик (-а) м bell; (бот) bluebell.

колониали́зм (-а) м colonialism.
колониа́льный прил colonial.
колониза́тор (-а) м colonizer.
колонизи́р|овать (-ую) (не)сов перех to colonize.
колониз|ова́ть (-у́ю) (не)сов = **колонизи́ровать**.
колони́ст (-а) м colonist.
колони́ст|ка (-ки; gen pl -ок) ж см **колони́ст**.
коло́ни|я (-и) ж colony; **исправи́тельно-трудова́я** ~ penal colony; ~ **для малоле́тних престу́пников** или **несовершенноле́тних** young offenders' institution.
коло́н|ка (-ки; gen pl -ок) ж column; (газовая) geyser (BRIT), water heater; (для воды, для бензина) pump.
колонка́ сущ см **коло́нок**.
коло́нко́вый прил polecat опред.
коло́нн|а (-ы) ж (АРХИТ) column; (ряд): ~ **солда́т/демонстра́нтов** column of soldiers/demonstrators.
колонна́д|а (-ы) ж colonnade.
коло́нок сущ см **коло́нка**.
колоно́к (-ка́) м polecat.
колорату́рн|ый прил: ~**ое сопра́но** coloratura (soprano).
колори́т (-а) м (перен: эпохи, страны итп) colour (BRIT), color (US); (ИСКУССТВО) use of colour; **ме́стный** ~ local colour.
колори́т|ный (-ен, -на, -но) прил colourful (BRIT), colorful (US).
ко́л|ос (-оса; nom pl -о́сья, gen pl -о́сьев) м ear (of corn, wheat).
коло́сс (-а) м (также перен) colossus; ~ **на гли́няных нога́х** a giant with feet of clay.
колосса́льн|ый (-ен, -ьна, -ьно) прил colossal; ~**ьно!** that's fantastic!
кол|оти́ть (-очу́, -о́тишь) несов неперех (по столу, в дверь) to thump ◆ перех (разг: бить) to whack; **меня́** ~**о́тит (дрожь)** I'm shaking all over
▶ **колоти́ться** несов возв (сердце) to thump; ~**ся** (impf) **в дверь** to thump on the door.
ко́лот|ый прил: ~ **са́хар** lump sugar; ~**ая ра́на** stab wound.
кол|о́ть (-ю́, -ешь; perf **расколо́ть**) несов перех (дрова) to chop (up); (орехи) to crack; (perf **заколо́ть**; штыком итп) to spear; (perf **уколо́ть**; иголкой) to prick; (разг: делать укол): ~ **кого́-н** to give sb an injection; ~ (impf) **кому́-н что-н** (разг) to inject sb with sth; **у меня́ ко́лет в боку́** I've got a stitch; **пра́вда глаза́ ко́лет** the truth is hard to swallow
▶ **коло́ться** несов возв (ёж, шиповник) to be prickly; (орех) to crack; (наркоман) to be on drugs.
колочу́(сь) несов см **колоти́ть(ся)**.

колпа́к (-а́) м (шутовской, поварской) hat; (лампы) lampshade.
колпач|о́к (-ка́) м уменьш от **колпа́к**; (контрацептив) (Dutch) cap.
колумби́йск|ий (-ая, -ое, -ие) прил Columbian.
Колу́мби|я (-и) ж Columbia.
колупа́|ть (-ю) несов перех (разг) to scratch.
колхо́з (-а) м kolkhoz, collective farm.
колхо́зник (-а) м kolkhoznik, collective farmer.
колхо́зный прил kolkhoz опред, collective farm опред.
колча́н (-а) м quiver.
колчеда́н (-а) м pyrite.
колыбе́л|ь (-и) ж (также перен) cradle; **с** ~**и** (перен) from the cradle.
колыбе́льн|ая (-ой; decl like adj) ж (также: ~ **пе́сня**) lullaby.
колыма́г|а (-и) ж (разг: машина) old banger.
колыха́ни|е (-я) ср rocking, swaying.
кол|ыха́ть (-ы́шу, -ы́шешь) несов перех to rock
▶ **колыха́ться** несов возв (море, грудь) to heave; (трава, дерево) to sway.
ко́лыш|ек (-ка) м уменьш от **кол**; (для палатки) (tent) peg.
колы́шу(сь) итп несов см **колыха́ть(ся)**.
колье́ ср нескл necklace.
кольн|у́ть (-у́, -ёшь) сов перех (иголкой) to prick; (перен: обидным намёком) to sting; **у меня́** ~**у́ло в спине́** a pain shot up my back.
кольра́би ж нескл kohlrabi.
кольт (-а) м automatic (revolver).
кольцева́|ть (-ю) несов перех to ring.
кольцево́й прил round, circular; **кольцева́я доро́га** ring road; **кольцева́я ли́ния** circle line.
коль|цо́ (-ца́; nom pl -ьца, gen pl -е́ц) ср ring; (в маршруте автобуса итп) circle.
кольчу́г|а (-и) ж (ИСТ) chain-mail shirt.
ко́лья сущ см **кол**.
колю́чек сущ см **колю́чка**.
колю́ч|ий (-ая, -ее, -ие; -, -а, -е) прил (куст, усы, мороз) prickly; (перен: насмешка, замечание, юмор) barbed; **колю́чая про́волока** barbed wire.
колю́ч|ка (-ки; gen pl -ек) ж (чертополоха, розы) thorn; (проволоки) barb.
коля́д|ка (-ки; gen pl -ок) ж ≈ Christmas carol (sung in rural Russia).
коляд|ова́ть (-у́ю) несов неперех ≈ to go carol singing.
коля́док сущ см **коля́дка**.
коля́с|ка (-ки; gen pl -ок) ж (экипаж) carriage; (детская) pram (BRIT), baby carriage (US); (инвалидная) wheelchair.
ком мест см **кто** ◆ (-а; nom pl -ья, gen pl -ьев) м lump; **у меня́** ~ **к го́рлу подкати́л** I felt a lump in my throat; **пе́рвый блин ко́мом ...** (перен) ≈ if at first you don't succeed ....
ко́м|а (-ы) ж coma.

кома́нд|а (-ы) ж command; (*судна*) crew; (*СПОРТ*) team; **пожа́рная** ~ fire brigade; ~ **президе́нта** presidential team; **быть** (*impf*) **под** ~**ой кого́-н** to be under sb.

команди́р (-а) м commander, commanding officer.

командиро́ванн|ый (-ого; *decl like adj*) м = **командиро́вочный**.

командир|ова́ть (-у́ю) (*не*)*сов перех* to post; **его́** ~**ова́ли в Москву́** he has been posted to Moscow.

командиро́в|ка (-ки; *gen pl* -ок) ж (*коро́ткая*) business trip; (*дли́тельная*) secondment (*BRIT*), posting; **е́хать** (**пое́хать** *perf*) **в** ~**ку** to go away on business; **получа́ть** (**получи́ть** *perf*) ~**ку** to be seconded (*BRIT*) *или* posted.

командиро́вочн|ые (-ых; *decl like adj*) мн (*де́ньги*) subsistence allowance *ед*.

командиро́вочный *прил*: ~**ое удостовере́ние** *permit issued to employee travelling on official business* ♦ (-**ого**; *decl like adj*) м person on business.

кома́ндн|ый *прил* command *опред*; (*до́лжность*) managerial; (*СПОРТ*): ~**ое состяза́ние** team event; ~**ые высо́ты** (*ВОЕН, перен*) key positions; **кома́ндный соста́в** (*ВОЕН*) command personnel.

кома́ндовани|е (-я) *ср*: ~ (+*instr*) (*судно́м, во́йском*) command (of) ♦ *собир* (*ВОЕН*) command.

кома́нд|овать (-ую; *perf* **скома́ндовать**) *несов непе́рех* to give orders; (*no perf*; +*instr*; *а́рмией*) to command; (*му́жем*) to order around.

кома́ндующ|ий (-его; *decl like adj*) м commanding officer, commander.

кома́р (-а́) м mosquito (*мн* mosquitoes); ~ **но́са не подто́чит** you can't fault it.

комато́зный *прил* comatose.

комба́йн (-а) м (*С.-Х.*) combine (harvester); **кухо́нный** ~ food processor.

комбайнёр (-а) м combine operator.

комбико́рм (-а) м *сокр* (= **комбини́рованный корм**) mixed fodder.

комбина́т (-а) м plant; **моло́чный/пищево́й** ~ dairy-/food-processing plant.

комбина́ци|я (-и) ж combination; (*разг: план*) scheme; (*ШАХМАТЫ*) position; (*же́нское бельё*) slip.

комбинезо́н (-а) м overalls мн; (*де́тский*) dungarees мн.

комбини́рованный *прил* (*ме́тод, подхо́д*) integrated.

комбини́р|овать (-ую; *perf* **скомбини́ровать**) *несов перех* (*блю́да*) to combine; (*оде́жду*) to match up ♦ *непе́рех* (*разг*) to scheme.

комедиа́нт (-а) м (*также перен*) comedian.

комедиа́нт|ка (-ки; *gen pl* -ок) ж comedienne.

комеди́йный (-ен, -йна, -йно) *прил* comic; (*актёр*) comedy *опред*.

коме́ди|я (-и) ж comedy; (*перен: смешно́е собы́тие*) farce; **лома́ть** (*impf*) ~**ю** to play-act.

коменда́нт (-а) м (*общежи́тия, тюрьмы́*) warden; (*ВОЕН*) commandant.

коменда́нтск|ий (-ая, -ое, -ие) *прил*: ~ **час** curfew.

комендату́р|а (-ы) ж (*ВОЕН*) commandant's office.

коме́т|а (-ы) ж comet.

коми́зм (-а) м comedy; ~ **ситуа́ции** the funny side of the situation.

ко́мик (-а) м (*актёр*) comedian, comic; (*разг: смешно́й челове́к*) comedian.

Коминте́рн (-а) м *сокр* (*ИСТ*: = **Коммунисти́ческий Интернациона́л**) Comintern.

комисса́р (-а) м (*ИСТ*: *также*: **Наро́дный К**~) People's Commissar; (*мили́ции ООН*) commissioner.

комиссионе́р (-а) м agent.

комиссио́н|ка (-ки; *gen pl* -ок) ж (*разг*) *second-hand shop which sells goods on a commission basis*.

комиссио́нн|ые (-ых; *decl like adj*) мн commission.

комиссио́нный *прил*: ~ **магази́н** = **комиссио́нка**.

комиссио́нок *сущ см* **комиссио́нка**.

коми́сси|я (-и) ж (*ПОЛИТ, КОММ*) commission; **брать** (**взять** *perf*) **что-н на** ~**ю** to take sth on commission; **постоя́нная** ~ standing committee.

комите́т (-а) м committee; **Комите́т Госуда́рственной Безопа́сности** (*ИСТ*) the KGB.

коми́чен *прил см* **коми́чный**.

коми́ческий (-ая, -ое, -ие) *прил* comic; ~ **актёр** comic actor.

коми́чный (-ен, -на, -но) *прил* comical.

комка́ *сущ см* **комо́к**.

ко́мка|ть (-ю; *perf* **скомка́ть**) *несов перех* (*письмо́, бельё итп*) to crumple; (*перен*: *ле́кцию итп*) to make a mess of.

коммента́ри|й (-я) м (*поясне́ние, репорта́ж*) commentary; **дава́ть** (**дать** *perf*) ~ **к чему́-н** to provide a commentary on sth; ~**и изли́шни** it speaks for itself.

коммента́тор (-а) м commentator.

коммента́р|овать (-ую) (*не*)*сов перех* (*текст*) to comment on; (*собы́тия, матч*) to commentate on.

коммерса́нт (-а) м businessman (*мн* businessmen).

комме́рческий (-ая, -ое, -ие) *прил* commercial; **комме́рческий банк** commercial bank; **комме́рческий дире́ктор** sales and finance director; **комме́рческий магази́н** privately-run shop.

коммивояжёр (-а) м travelling (*BRIT*) *или* traveling (*US*) salesman (*мн* salesmen).

комму́н|а (-ы) ж commune.

коммуна́л|ка (-ки; *gen pl* -ек) ж (*разг*) communal flat (*BRIT*) *или* apartment (*US*).

коммунáльный *прил* communal;
коммунáльная квартúра communal flat (*BRIT*)
или apartment (*US*); **коммунáльные платежú**
bills; **коммунáльные услýги** utilities.
коммунáр (-а) *м* (*ИСТ*) member of a commune.
коммунúзм (-а) *м* communism.
коммуникáбел|**ьный** (-ен, -ьна, -ьно) *прил*
sociable.
коммуникатúвный *прил* (*методы*)
communicative.
коммуникациóнн|**ый** *прил*: ~**ая лúния** line of
communication.
коммуникáци|**я** (-и) *ж* communication.
коммунúст (-а) *м* communist.
коммунистúческ|**ий** (-ая, -ое, -ие) *прил*
communist.
коммунúст|**ка** (-ки; *gen pl* -ок) *ж см* **коммунúст**.
коммутáтор (-а) *м* (*ТЕЛ*) switchboard; (*ЭЛЕК*)
commutator.
коммутациóнн|**ый** *прил*: ~**ая доскá**
switchboard.
коммутáци|**я** (-и) *ж*: ~ **пакéтов/сообщéний**
(*КОМП*) packet/message switching.
коммюникé *ср нескл* communiqué.
кóмнат|**а** (-ы) *ж* room; **кóмната мáтери и**
ребёнка *room for mothers with young children*.
кóмнатный *прил* indoor *опред*; **кóмнатная**
температýра room temperature; **кóмнатное**
растéние house plant.
комóд (-а) *м* chest of drawers.
ком|**óк** (-кá) *м уменьш от* **ком**; (*ваты*) ~
бумáги crumpled-up piece of paper; **он – ~**
нéрвов he's a bag *или* bundle of nerves.
компáкт-дúск (-а) *м* compact disc.
компáкт|**ный** (-ен, -на, -но) *прил* compact;
(*изложение, доклад*) concise.
компанéйск|**ий** (-ая, -ое, -ие) *прил* (*разг*): **он ~**
пáрень he's good company.
компáни|**я** (-и) *ж* (*друзья*) group of friends;
(*КОММ*) company; **выпей со мной за** ~**ю** have a
drink, to keep me company; **он тебé не** ~ he's
not the right company for you.
компаньóн (-а) *м* companion; (*КОММ*) partner.
компаньóн|**ка** (-ки; *gen pl* -ок) *ж* (*старой дамы*)
companion.
компáрти|**я** (-и) *ж* Communist party.
кóмпас (-а) *м* compass.
компенсациóнный *прил* compensatory.
компенсáци|**я** (-и) *ж* compensation.
компенсú|**ровать** (-ую) (*не*)*сов перех* to
compensate.
компетéнтен *прил см* **компетéнтный**.
компетéнтность (-и) *ж* competence.
компетéнтный (-ен, -на, -но) *прил* competent;
(*соответствующий*) appropriate.
компетéнци|**я** (-и) *ж* jurisdiction; **это не вхóдит**
в нáшу ~**ю** that is outside our jurisdiction.
компилú|**ровать** (-ую; *perf* **скомпилú**|**ровать**)

несов перех (*пренебр*) to cobble together.
компилятú|**вный** (-ен, -на, -но) *прил*: ~ **труд**
compilation.
компилятор (-а) *м* hack (writer).
компиляци|**я** (-и) *ж* rehash.
кóмплекс (-а) *м* (*упражнений, мер, знаний итп*)
range; **спортúвный** ~ sports complex;
кóмплекс неполноцéнности inferiority
complex.
кóмплексный *прил* integrated; (*соединение,*
число) complex.
комплéкт (-а) *м* set.
комплектáци|**я** (-и) *ж* assembly; **отдéл** ~**и** (*в*
библиотеке) acquisitions (department).
комплект|**овáть** (-ýю; *perf* **укомплектовáть**)
несов перех to build up.
комплéкци|**я** (-и) *ж* build (*of person*).
комплимéнт (-а) *м* compliment; **дéлать**
(**сдéлать** *perf*) **комý-н** ~ to pay sb a compliment;
говорúть (*impf*) ~**ы** (**комý-н**) to pay (sb)
compliments.
композúтор (-а) *м* composer.
композициóнный *прил* compositional.
композúци|**я** (-и) *ж* composition.
компонéнт (-а) *м* component.
компон|**овáть** (-ýю; *perf* **скомпоновáть**) несов
перех to arrange, set out.
компонóвк|**а** (-и) *ж* (*материалов*) arranging.
компóст (-а) *м* compost.
компóстер (-а) *м* ticket punch.
компости́р|**овать** (-ую; *perf*
закомпости́ровать) *сов перех* to punch *или*
clip (*ticket*).
компóстн|**ый** *прил*: ~**ая яма** compost pit.
компóт (-а) *м* compote.
компрéсс (-а) *м* (*МЕД*) compress.
компрéссор (-а) *м* (*ТЕХ*) compressor.
компрометú|**ровать** (-ую; *perf*
скомпрометúровать) несов перех to
compromise.
компрометúрующ|**ий** (-ая, -ое, -ие) *прил*
(*поступок, слова*) damaging.
компромúсс (-а) *м* (*соглашение*) compromise;
идтú (**пойтú** *perf*) **на** ~ to (make a) compromise;
приходúть (**прийтú** *perf*) **к** ~**у** to come to a
compromise.
компромúссный *прил* compromise *опред*.
компью́тер (-а) *м* computer.
компью́терный *прил* computer *опред*.
комсомóл (-а) *м* Komsomol (*communist youth*
organization).
комсомóл|**ец** (-ьца) *м* komsomol member.
комсомóл|**ка** (-ки; *gen pl* -ок) *ж см*
комсомóлец.
комсомóльск|**ий** (-ая, -ое, -ие) *прил* komsomol
опред.
комсомóльца *сущ см* **комсомóлец**.
комý *мест см* **кто**.

The spelling rules for Russian are shown on page xvii.

комфо́рт (-а) м comfort.

комфорта́бел|ьный (-ен, -ьна, -ьно) прил comfortable.

комье́в итп сущ см ком.

кон (-а; nom pl -ы, gen pl -о́в) м (партия) round; (для ставки) kitty; (место: в городках) wicket.

конве́йер (-а) м conveyor (belt); **поста́вить** (perf) что-н на ~ to mass-produce sth; (перен) to churn sth out.

конве́йерн|ый прил: ~ая ле́нта conveyor belt.

конве́нци|я (-и) ж convention.

конверге́нци|я (-и) ж convergence.

конве́рси|я (-и) ж conversion.

конве́рт (-а) м (почтовый) envelope; (для младенца) baby nest.

конверти́р|овать (-ую) (не)сов перех to convert.

конверти́руемый прил convertible.

конво́йр (-а) м escort.

конвои́р|овать (-ую) несов перех to escort.

конво́|й (-я) м escort; **под ~ем** under escort.

конво́йный прил escort опред ♦ (-ого; decl like adj) м escort.

конву́льси|я (-и) ж convulsion.

конгломера́т (-а) м conglomerate.

Ко́нго ср нескл Congo (river and state).

конголе́зск|ий (-ая, -ое, -ие) прил Congolese.

конгре́сс (-а) м (съезд) congress; (в США) Congress.

конгрессме́н (-а) м Congressman (мн Congressmen).

конденса́тор (-а) м condenser.

конденса́ци|я (-и) ж condensation.

конденси́р|оваться (3sg -уется, 3pl -уются) (не)сов возв to condense.

конди́тер (-а) м confectioner.

конди́терск|ая (-ой; decl like adj) ж confectioner's.

конди́терск|ий (-ая, -ое, -ие) прил confectionery опред; **конди́терский магази́н** confectioner's.

кондиционе́р (-а) м air conditioner.

кондицио́нный прил (условия поставки) conditional; (продукт, овощи итп) up to standard.

конди́ци|я (-и) ж standard; **я сейча́с не в ~и** (разг) I'm not in good shape at the moment; **доводи́ть (довести́ perf) что-н до ~и** to bring sth up to scratch.

кондо́вый прил diehard опред.

кондра́шк|а (-и) ж: **его́ хвати́ла ~** (разг) he had a fit.

конду́ктор (-а) м (автобуса) conductor; (поезда) guard.

конево́д (-а) м horse-breeder.

конево́дство (-а) ср horse-breeding.

конё|к (-ька́) м уменьш от конь; (обычно мн: СПОРТ) skate; (перен: любимая тема) hobbyhorse; **ката́ться** (impf) **на ~ька́х** to skate; **сади́ться** (impf) **на своего́ ~ька́** to get on(to) one's hobbyhorse; **морско́й ~** sea horse; см

также **конёк**.

кон|е́ц (-ца́) м end; **без ~ца́** endlessly; **из конца́ в ~** from end to end; **и де́ло с ~цо́м** (разг) and that's the end of it; **в ~це́ концо́в** in the end; **биле́т в оди́н ~** single (BRIT) или one-way ticket; **мне ~** (разг) I'm done for; **своди́ть** (impf) **~цы́ с ~ца́ми** to make ends meet; **на худо́й ~** (разг) if the worst comes to the worst; **под ~** towards the end; **отда́ть** (perf) **~цы́** (разг) to kick the bucket.

коне́чно вводн сл of course, certainly; **мне мо́жно закури́ть? – ~** may I smoke? – of course.

коне́чность (-и) ж (обычно мн) limb.

коне́ч|ный (-ен, -на, -но) прил (цель, итог) final; (станция, остановка) last; **в ~ном счёте** или **ито́ге** in the final analysis; **коне́чный по́льзователь** (КОМП) end user.

кони́н|а (-ы) ж horse meat.

кони́ческий (-ая, -ое, -ие) прил conical.

конкре́тен прил см конкре́тный.

конкретизи́р|овать (-ую) (не)сов перех: ~ что-н to make sth more concrete.

конкре́тно нареч (говорить) specifically.

конкре́т|ный (-ен, -на, -но) прил (реальный) concrete; (факт) actual.

конкуре́нт (-а) м competitor.

конкуре́нтк|а (-и) ж см конкуре́нт.

конкуре́нтный прил: ~ая борьба́ competition.

конкурентоспосо́б|ный (-ен, -на, -но) прил competitive.

конкуре́нци|я (-и) ж competition; **наш това́р вне ~и** our product is in a class of its own.

конкури́р|овать (-ую) несов неперех: ~ с +instr to compete with.

ко́нкурс (-а) м competition; **проходи́ть (пройти́ perf) вне ~а** to be admitted to university etc under special provisions; **проходи́ть (пройти́ perf) по ~у** to attain the pass mark.

ко́нкурсн|ый прил competition опред; ~ая коми́ссия (в университете) examining committee; (в состязании) judging panel; **ко́нкурсный экза́мен** entrance examination.

ко́нниц|а (-ы) ж cavalry.

конногварде́|ец (-йца) м cavalryman (мн cavalrymen).

коннозаво́дчик (-а) м stud-farm owner.

ко́нный прил (двор, сбруя) horse опред; **ко́нная а́рмия** cavalry; **ко́нный заво́д** stud farm; **ко́нная мили́ция** mounted police.

конопа́тить (-чу, -тишь; perf законопа́тить) несов перех (сруб, лодку, пол итп) to patch up.

конопа́т|ый (-, -а, -о) прил (разг: веснушчатый) freckled.

конопа́чу несов см конопа́тить.

конопл|я́ (-и́) ж hemp.

конопля́ный прил hemp.

коноса́мент (-а) м bill of lading.

консервати́вность (-и) ж conservatism.

консервати́в|ный (-ен, -на, -но) прил conservative.

консерва́тор (-а) м conservative; (полит) Conservative.

консервато́ри|я (-и) ж (муз) conservatoire (BRIT), conservatory (US).

консерва́ци|я (-и) ж (стройки) suspension; (продуктов, здания) preservation.

консерви́ровани|е (-я) ср (в жестяных банках) canning; (в стеклянных банках) bottling.

консерви́рованный прил (см сущ) canned; bottled.

консерви́р|овать (-ую) (не)сов перех to preserve; (в жестяных банках) to can; (в стеклянных банках) to bottle; (стройку) to suspend.

консе́рвный прил: ~ заво́д canned-food factory; консе́рвная ба́нка can.

консе́рв|ы (-ов) мн canned food ед.

конси́лиум (-а) м consultation between doctors about a patient.

консисте́нци|я (-и) ж consistency.

ко́нск|ий (-ая, -ое, -ие) прил horse's.

консолида́ци|я (-и) ж consolidation.

консолиди́р|овать (-ую) (не)сов перех to consolidate.

консо́л|ь (-и) ж cantilever.

консо́рциум (-а) м consortium.

конспе́кт (-а) м notes мн.

конспекти́в|ный (-ен, -на, -но) прил: в ~ной фо́рме in note form.

конспекти́р|овать (-ую); perf законспекти́ровать) несов перех to take notes on.

конспирати́вный прил conspiratorial; конспирати́вная кварти́ра safe house.

конспира́тор (-а) м conspirator.

конспира́ци|я (-и) ж conspiracy.

констата́ци|я (-и) ж: ~ фа́ктов stating of the facts.

констати́р|овать (-ую) (не)сов перех to certify; (факты) to state.

конституцио́нный прил constitutional.

конститу́ци|я (-и) ж constitution.

конструи́р|овать (-ую); perf сконструи́ровать) несов перех to construct.

констру́ктивен прил см конструкти́вный.

конструкти́вность (-и) ж constructiveness.

конструкти́в|ный прил construction опред; (-ен, -на, -но; замысл, идея) constructive.

констру́ктор (-а) м designer; (детская игра) construction set; инжене́р-~ mechanical engineer.

констру́кторск|ий (-ая, -ое, -ие) прил: ~ое бюро́ design studio.

констру́кци|я (-и) ж construction.

ко́нсул (-а) м consul.

ко́нсульск|ий (-ая, -ое, -ие) прил consular.

ко́нсульств|о (-а) ср consulate.

консульта́нт (-а) м consultant.

консультацио́нный прил consultative.

консульта́ци|я (-и) ж (у врача, у юриста) consultation; (учреждение) consultancy; же́нская ~ ≈ gynaecological and antenatal (BRIT) или gynecological and prenatal (US) clinic; дава́ть (дать perf) ~ю кому́-н to give professional advice to sb.

консульти́р|овать (-ую; perf проконсульти́ровать) несов перех to give professional advice to

▶ **консульти́роваться** (impf проконсульти́роваться) несов возв: ~ся с кем-н to consult sb.

конта́кт (-а) м contact.

конта́кт|ный (-ен, -на, -но) прил (человек) approachable; конта́ктные ли́нзы contact lenses; конта́ктный телефо́н contact number.

конте́йнер (-а) м container.

конте́кст (-а) м context; в ~е +gen in the context of.

континге́нт (-а) м contingent.

контине́нт (-а) м continent.

континента́льный прил continental.

конто́р|а (-ы) ж office.

конто́рск|ий (-ая, -ое, -ие) прил office опред; конто́рская кни́га account book.

ко́нтр|а (-ы) ж (разг): быть в ~х с кем-н to be at odds with sb.

контраба́нд|а (-ы) ж smuggling; (товары) contraband.

контрабанди́ст (-а) м smuggler.

контрабанди́ст|ка (-ки; gen pl -ок) ж см контрабанди́ст.

контраба́ндный прил contraband.

контраба́с (-а) м double bass.

контрабаси́ст (-а) м double-bass player.

контрадмира́л (-а) м rear admiral.

контра́кт (-а) м contract; фо́рвардный ~ (КОММ) forward contract.

контра́льто ср нескл contralto.

контрама́р|ка (-ки; gen pl -ок) ж ≈ complimentary ticket.

контрапу́нкт (-а) м counterpoint.

контра́ст (-а) м contrast.

контра́стен прил см контра́стный.

контрасти́р|овать (-ую) несов неперех: ~ с +instr to contrast with.

контра́ст|ный (-ен, -на, -но) прил contrasting.

контрата́|ка (-и) ж counterattack.

контрацепти́в (-а) м contraceptive.

контрацепти́вный прил contraceptive опред.

контрибу́ци|я (-и) ж reparations мн; налага́ть (наложи́ть perf) ~ю to exact reparations.

контрнаступле́ни|е (-я) ср counteroffensive.

контролёр (-а) м (железнодорожный) (ticket) inspector; (театральный) ≈ usher; (сберкассы) cashier.

контроли́р|овать (-ую) *несов перех* to control.
контро́л|ь (-я) *м* (*наблюдение*) monitoring; (*проверка*) testing, checking; (*в транспорте*) ticket inspection; (*в магазине*) checkout ◆ *собир* (*проверяющие*) inspectors *мн*; **па́спортный ~** passport control; **~ за це́нами** price control; **~ ка́чества** quality control.
контро́льн|ая (-ой; *decl like adj*) *ж* (*также:~* **рабо́та**) class test.
контро́льн|ый *прил*: **~ая коми́ссия** inspection team; **~ая рабо́та по** +*prp* class test in; **контро́льные ци́фры** control figures.
контрразве́дк|а (-и) *ж* counterespionage.
контрреволюционе́р (-а) *м* counter-revolutionary.
контрреволю́ци|я (-и) *ж* counter-revolution.
контрфо́рс (-а) *м* buttress.
конту́|зить (-жу, -зишь) *сов безл*: **его́ ~зило** he was contused.
конту́зи|я (-и) *ж* (*МЕД*) contusion.
ко́нтур (-а) *м* contour.
ко́нтурный *прил* contour *опред*; **ко́нтурная ка́рта** contour map.
конур|а́ (-ы́) *ж* (*собачья*) kennel; (*перен*: *комната*) shoe box.
ко́нус (-а) *м* cone.
конусообра́з|ный (-ен, -на, -но) *прил* conical.
конферансье́ *ср нескл* compère.
конфере́нц-за́л (-а) *м* conference room.
конфере́нци|я (-и) *ж* conference.
конфе́т|а (-ы) *ж* sweet.
конфетти́ *ср нескл* confetti.
конфигура́ци|я (-и) *ж* configuration.
конфиденциа́льный (-ен, -ьна, -ьно) *прил* confidential.
конфиска́ци|я (-и) *ж* confiscation.
конфиск|ова́ть (-у́ю) (*не*)*сов перех* to confiscate.
конфли́кт (-а) *м* (*военный*) conflict; (*в семье, на работе*) tension.
конфли́ктный *прил* (*ситуация*) conflict *опред*.
конфликт|ова́ть (-у́ю) *несов неперех*: **~ с** +*instr* (*разг*) to be at loggerheads with.
конфо́рк|а (-ки; *gen pl* -ок) *ж* ring (*on cooker*).
конфронта́ци|я (-и) *ж* confrontation.
конфу́жу(сь) *несов см* **конфу́зить(ся)**.
конфу́з (-а) *м* embarrassment.
конфу́|зить (-жу, -зишь) (*perf* **сконфу́зить**) *несов перех* to embarrass
▶ **конфу́зиться** (*perf* **сконфу́зиться**) *несов возв* to get embarrassed.
конца́ *итп сущ см* **коне́ц**.
концентра́т (-а) *м* (*о корме*) concentrate; (*о руде*) concentration.
концентрацио́нный *прил*: **~ ла́герь** concentration camp.
концентра́ци|я (-и) *ж* concentration.
концентри́рованный *прил* concentrated.
концентри́р|овать (-ую; *perf* **сконцентри́ровать**) *несов перех* to concentrate
▶ **концентри́роваться** (*perf* **сконцентри́роваться**) *несов возв* (*капитал*) to

be concentrated; (*ученик*) to concentrate.
концентри́ческ|ий (-ая, -ое, -ие) *прил* concentric.
конце́пци|я (-и) *ж* concept.
конце́рн (-а) *м* (*ЭКОН*) concern.
конце́рт (-а) *м* concert; **дава́ть (дать** *perf*) **~** to give a concert; **~ для фортепья́но с орке́стром** piano concerto.
концерти́р|овать (-ую) *несов неперех* to give concerts.
концертме́йстер (-а) *м* (*МУЗ*) leader, concertmaster (*US*); (*аккомпаниатор*) accompanist.
конце́ртный *прил* concert *опред*.
конце́сси|я (-и) *ж* concession; **отдава́ть (отда́ть** *perf*) **что-н на ~ю** to grant sth as a concession.
концла́гер|ь (-я; *nom pl* -я́) *м* concentration camp.
концо́вк|а (-ки; *gen pl* -ок) *ж* ending.
конча́|ть (-ю) *несов от* **ко́нчить**
▶ **конча́ться** *несов от* **ко́нчиться** ◆ *возв*: **~ся на** +*acc* to end in; **всё хорошо́, что хорошо́ ~ется** all's well that ends well.
конча́я *предл* (+*instr*) to; **начина́я с кого́-н/чего́-н и ~ кем-н/чем-н** from sb/sth to sb/sth; **яви́лись все, ~ са́мыми да́льними ро́дственниками** everyone turned up, including the most distant relatives.
ко́нченый *прил*: **он ~ челове́к** he's a lost cause.
ко́нчик (-а) *м* tip.
ко́нчин|а (-ы) *ж* end.
ко́нч|ить (-у, -ишь; *impf* **конча́ть**) *сов перех* (*жизнь, представление, отношения*) to end; (*университет, игру, книгу, работу*) to finish; **конча́ть (~** *perf*) +*instr* (*бандитом*) to end up as; (*пьесой, словами*) to finish with; **конча́ть (~** *perf*) **рабо́ту** *или* **рабо́тать** to finish work; **он пло́хо ~ил** he ended up in a bad way
▶ **ко́нчиться** (*impf* **конча́ться**) *сов возв* (*разговор, книга, игра*) to end, finish; (*запасы, де́ньги*) to run out; (*пустыня, лес итп*) to end.
конъюнктиви́т (-а) *м* conjunctivitis.
конъюнкту́р|а (-ы) *ж* climate; **~ ры́нка** state of the market; **понижа́тельная ры́ночная ~** (*КОММ*) falling market; **пониже́ние/повыше́ние ~** downturn/upturn of the market; **он хорошо́ чу́вствует ~у** he is good at gauging the climate.
конъюнкту́рн|ый *прил* (*соображения*) tactical; **~ые це́ны** market prices *мн*.
конъюнкту́рщик (-а) *м* opportunist.
кон|ь (-я́; *nom pl* -и, *gen pl* -е́й) *м* (*лошадь*) horse; (*ШАХМАТЫ*) knight; **быть** (*impf*) **на ~е́** to be on the ball.
конька́ *итп сущ см* **конёк**.
конь|ки́ (-о́в) *мн* skates *мн*; (*разг*: *вид спорта*) skating *ед*.
конькобе́ж|ец (-ца) *м* speed skater.
конькобе́жный *прил* speed-skating; **конькобе́жный спорт** speed skating.

конькобе́жца *итп сущ см* **конькобе́жец**.
конья́к (-а́) *м* brandy, cognac.
ко́нюх (-а) *м* groom (*at stable*).
коню́ш|ня (-ни; *gen pl* -ен) *ж* stable.
кооперати́в (-а) *м* cooperative; (*разг:* **кварти́ра**) *flat in housing cooperative;* **жили́щный** ~ *form of house or flat ownership.*
кооперати́вный *прил* cooperative; ~ **магази́н** *или* **ларёк** co-op; ~ **дом** cooperative (*form of house or flat ownership*).
коопера́тор (-а) *м member of a private enterprise.*
коопера́ци|я (-и) *ж* cooperative enterprise; (*труда́*) co-operation; **потреби́тельская** ~ cooperative (society).
коопери́р|овать (-ую) (*не*)*сов перех* (*труд, сре́дства*) to organize through a cooperative.
коопти́р|овать (-ую) (*не*)*сов перех* to coopt.
координа́т|а (-ы) *ж* (*ГЕОМ: обы́чно мн*) coordinate; (*разг: местонахожде́ние*) number (and address).
координа́ци|я (-и) *ж* (*уси́лий*) coordination.
координи́р|овать (-ую) (*не*)*сов перех* (*де́йствия, уси́лия, движе́ния*) to coordinate; ~ (*impf/perf*) **произво́дство с тре́бованиями ры́нка** to adjust production to meet the demands of the market.
коп. *сокр* = **копе́йка**.
копа́|ть (-ю) *несов от* **вы́копать** ◆ *перех* to dig; (*выка́пывать*) to dig up; ~ (*impf*) **под** +*acc* (*разг*) to cook up a scheme against.
► **копа́ться** *несов возв* (*в огоро́де*) to potter about; (*в чужи́х веща́х*) to snoop about; (*разг: в душе́*) to search; (: *до́лго вози́ться*) to dawdle.
копе́ек *сущ см* **копе́йка**.
копе́ечк|а (-и) *ж*: **э́то тебе́ вста́нет в** ~у it'll cost you a pretty penny.
копе́йк|а (-йки; *gen pl* -ек) *ж* kopeck; **остава́ться** (**оста́ться** *perf*) **без** ~йки to be left without a penny.
Копенга́ген (-а) *м* Copenhagen.
копи́л|ка (-ки; *gen pl* -ок) *ж* piggy bank.
копира́|йт (-а) *м* copyright.
копи́рк|а (-и) *ж* (*разг*) carbon paper; **писа́ть** (*impf*) **под** ~у to make a carbon copy of.
копирова́льно-мно́жительный *прил* copying *опред*.
копирова́льный *прил*: ~**ая маши́на** photocopying machine, photocopier; **копирова́льная бума́га** carbon paper.
копи́р|овать (-ую; *perf* **скопи́ровать**) *несов перех* to copy.
коп|и́ть (-лю́, -ишь; *perf* **накопи́ть** *или* **скопи́ть**) *несов перех* to save; (*перен: оби́ды*) to harbour (*BRIT*), harbor (*US*)
► **копи́ться** (*perf* **накопи́ться** *или* **скопи́ться**) *несов возв* to accumulate.
ко́пи|я (-и) *ж* copy; (*перен*) spitting image; **он** – ~

своего́ отца́! he's the spitting image of his father; **снима́ть** (**снять** *perf*) ~**ю с чего́-н** to make a copy of sth.
коплю́(сь) *несов см* **копи́ть(ся)**.
копн|а́ (-ы́; *nom pl* -ы) *ж* (*се́на*) stack; (*во́лос*) thatch.
копн|у́ть (-у́, -ёшь) *несов перех* to dig; (*перен*): **е́сли** ~ **поглу́бже** ... if you dig deeper ....
ко́пот|ь (-и) *ж* layer of soot.
копош|и́ться (-у́сь, -и́шься) *несов возв* (*мышь*) to busy itself; (*перен: подозре́ния*) to stir; (*вози́ться*) to dawdle.
коп|те́ть (-чу́, -ти́шь) *несов непере́х* to give off black smoke; (*корпе́ть*): ~ **над** +*instr* to pore over.
коп|ти́ть (-чу́, -ти́шь) *несов непере́х* (*ла́мпа*) to give off soot ◆ (*perf* **закопти́ть**) *перех* (*мя́со, ры́бу*) to smoke; ~ (*impf*) **не́бо** to fritter one's life away.
копу́ш|а (-и) *м/ж* (*разг*) slowcoach (*BRIT*), slowpoke (*US*).
копчёни|е (-я) *ср* (*ветчины́*) smoking; **ры́ба горя́чего/холо́дного** ~**я** *fish smoked at a high/low temperature; см также* **копчёнья**.
копчёност|и (-ей) *мн* smoked food *ед*.
копчёный *прил* smoked.
копчён|ья (-ий) *мн* = **копчёности**.
ко́пчик (-а) *м* соссух (*мн* соссухes).
копы́т|о (-а) *ср* hoof (*мн* hooves).
копь|ё (-я́; *nom pl* -я, *gen pl* -ий) *ср* spear; (*СПОРТ*) javelin; **мета́ние** ~**я́** javelin.
кор. *сокр* (= **корреспонде́нт**) corr. (= correspondent).
кор|а́ (-ы́) *ж* (*де́рева*) bark; (*АНАТ*) cortex; **земна́я** ~ the earth's crust; ~ **головно́го мо́зга** cerebral cortex.
корабе́льный *прил* ship's.
кораблестрое́ни|е (-я) *ср* shipbuilding.
кораблестрои́тель (-я) *м* shipbuilder.
кораблестрои́тельный *прил* shipbuilding *опред*.
кора́бл|ь (-я́) *м* ship; **сжига́|ть** (**сжечь** *perf*) **свой корабли́** to burn one's boats.
кора́лл (-а) *м* coral.
кора́лловый *прил* (*также цвет*) coral; **кора́лловый риф** coral reef.
Кора́н (-а) *м* the Koran.
кордебале́т (-а) *м* corps de ballet.
кордо́н (-а) *м* cordon; **за** ~**ом** (*разг*) abroad.
коре́|ец (-йца) *м* Korean.
корёж|ить (-у, -ишь; *perf* **искорёжить** *или* **покорёжить**) *несов перех* (*разг*) to twist; (*no perf; перен*): **его́ поведе́ние меня́** ~**ит** his behaviour makes me cringe.
коре́йк|а (-и) *ж* smoked brisket of pork.
коре́йский (-ая, -ое, -ие) *прил* Korean.
корена́стый (-, -а, -о) *прил* stocky.
корен|и́ться (*3sg* -и́тся, *3pl* -я́тся) *несов возв*: ~

в +*prp* to be rooted in.
коренн|о́й *прил (население, традиции)* indigenous; *(вопрос, преобразования)* fundamental; **~ым о́бразом** fundamentally; **коренно́й зуб** molar.
ко́р|ень (-ня; *nom pl* -ни, *gen pl* -не́й) *м* root; **в ~не** fundamentally; **пресека́ть (пресе́чь** *perf*) **что-н в ~не** to nip sth in the bud; **пуска́ть (пусти́ть** *perf*) **~ни** to put down roots; **подруба́ть (подруби́ть** *perf*) **под ~** to uproot; **смотре́ть** (*impf*) **в ~ вопро́са/де́ла** to examine the root of the problem/matter.
коре́нь|я (-ев) *мн (БОТ)* roots *мн.*
ко́реш (-а) *м (разг)* mate, pal.
корешо́к (-ка́) *м уменьш от* **ко́рень**; *(чековой книжки)* counterfoil; *(переплёта)* spine.
коре́йца *итп сущ см* **коре́ец.**
Коре́я (-и) *ж* Korea.
коре́ян|ка (-ки; *gen pl* -ок) *ж см* **коре́ец.**
корж (-а́) *м* layer (*of a cake*).
ко́ржик (-а) *м уменьш от* **корж**; *(пряник)* ≈ shortbread.
корзи́н|а (-ы) *ж* basket; **валю́тная ~** *(ЭКОН)* basket of currencies.
корзи́н|ка (-ки; *gen pl* -ок) *ж* (small) basket.
корзи́ночк|а (-ки; *gen pl* -ек) *ж (КУЛИН)* tart.
корзи́нщик (-а) *м* basket weaver.
кориа́ндр (-а) *м* coriander.
коридо́р (-а) *м* corridor.
коридо́рн|ая (-ой; *decl like adj*) *ж* chambermaid.
коридо́рн|ый (-ого; *decl like adj*) *м* room attendant (*in hotel*).
кори́ть (-ю́, -и́шь) *несов перех* to chastise.
корифе́й (-я) *м* luminary.
кори́ц|а (-ы) *ж* cinnamon.
кори́чневый *прил* brown.
ко́р|ка (-ки; *gen pl* -ок) *ж уменьш от* **кора́**; *(апельсинная)* peel; *(на коже)* scab; **прочита́ть** (*perf*) **что-н от ~ки до ~ки** to read sth from cover to cover.
корм (-а; *nom pl* -а́) *м (для скота)* fodder, feed; *(диких животных)* food.
корм|а́ (-ы́) *ж* stern.
кормёжк|а (-и) *ж (разг: скота)* feeding; (: *еда*) grub.
корми́л|ец (-ьца) *м* breadwinner.
корми́лиц|а (-ы) *ж* breadwinner; *(грудного ребёнка)* wet nurse.
корми́л|о (-а) *ср:* **стоя́ть** *или* **быть у ~а вла́сти** to be at the helm.
корми́льца *сущ см* **корми́лец.**
корми́|ть (-лю́, -ишь) *несов перех* to feed; (*perf* **прокорми́ть**; *содержать*) to feed, keep; (*perf* **накорми́ть**): **~ кого́-н (чем-н)** to feed sb (sth); **~** (*impf*) **гру́дью** to breast-feed; **его́ хле́бом не ~й, то́лько дай в футбо́л поигра́ть** he's never happier than when he's playing football
▶ **корми́ться** (*perf* **прокорми́ться**) *несов возв (животное)* to feed; (+*instr*; *человек*) to live on.
кормле́ни|е (-я) *ср* feeding.
кормлю́(сь) *несов см* **корми́ть(ся).**

кормов|о́й *прил (с.-х.):* **~ые сорта́** fodder crops; **кормова́я свёкла** beet; **кормово́е весло́** rudder.
корму́шк|а (-и) *ж (для скота)* trough; *(для птиц)* bird table; *(перен: разг)* slush fund.
корневи́щ|е (-а) *ср* rhizome.
корнепло́д (-а) *м* root vegetable.
корнепло́дн|ый *прил:* **~ое расте́ние** root plant.
корне́т (-а) *м* cornet.
ко́рн|я *итп сущ см* **ко́рень.**
ко́роб (-а) *м* rectangular basket; **с три ~а наговори́ть** (*perf*) to talk through one's hat; **с три ~а наобеща́ть** (*perf*) **кому́-н** to promise sb the earth.
короб|и́ть (-лю, -ишь; *perf* **покоро́бить**) *несов перех* to warp; **меня́ ~ит от его́ шу́ток** his jokes make me cringe
▶ **короби́ться** (*perf* **покоро́биться**) *несов возв* to warp.
коро́б|ка (-ки; *gen pl* -ок) *ж* box; *(остов дома)* frame; **коро́бка скоросте́й** gearbox.
коро́бка *сущ см* **коробо́к.**
коро́блю(сь) *несов см* **коро́бить(ся).**
коробо́к *сущ см* **коро́бка.**
коробо́к (-ка́) *м:* **~ спи́чек** box of matches.
коробо́чк|а (-ки; *gen pl* -ек) *ж уменьш от* **коро́бка**; *(БОТ)* boll.
коро́в|а (-ы) *ж* cow; *(разг: пренебр)* silly cow; **до́йная ~** dairy cow.
коро́в|ий (-ья, -ье, -ьи) *прил:* **~ье молоко́** cow's milk.
коро́вник (-а) *м* cowshed.
коро́вниц|а (-ы) *ж* milkmaid.
ко́рок *сущ см* **ко́рка.**
короле́в|а (-ы) *ж (также ШАХМАТЫ, перен)* queen; **короле́ва красоты́** beauty queen.
короле́вск|ий (-ая, -ое, -ие) *прил* royal.
короле́вств|о (-а) *ср* kingdom.
короле́к (-ька́) *м (апельсин)* blood orange; *(хурма)* sharon fruit; *(ЗООЛ)* goldcrest.
коро́л|ь (-я) *м (также ШАХМАТЫ, КАРТЫ)* king.
король́ка *сущ см* **короле́к.**
коро́н|а (-ы) *ж* crown.
корона́рный *прил* coronary *опред.*
корона́ци|я (-и) *ж* coronation.
коро́нный *прил (разг)* best, favourite; **~ но́мер** party piece.
коронова́ни|е (-я) *ср* crowning.
коронова́ть (-у́ю) *(не)сов перех* to crown.
коро́ст|а (-ы) *ж* scab.
коросте́л|ь (-я) *м* corncrake.
корота́ть (-ю; *perf* **скорота́ть**) *несов перех (вечер, время итп)* to while away; *(свои дни, жизнь)* to live out.
коро́тк|ий (-ая, -ое, -ие; *короток, коротка́, коротко, коротки*) *прил* short; *(отношения)* close; **у него́ ~ая па́мять** he has a short memory; **у него́ ру́ки ко́ротки** he's not up to it; **мы с ним на ~ой ноге́** we're on good terms; **коро́ткие во́лны** short wave; **коро́ткое**

замыка́ние short circuit.
ко́ротко *нареч* briefly; *(стричься)* short; *(узнать)* intimately ♦ *как сказ:* **э́то пла́тье мне ~** this dress is too short for me.
коротково́лновый *прил* short-wave *опред.*
коротметра́жный *прил:* **~ фильм** short (film).
коротконо́гий (-**ая**, -**ое**, -**ие**) *прил* short-legged.
коро́ток *прил см* **коро́ткий.**
короты́ш (-**а́**) *м (разг)* shorty.
коро́че *сравн прил от* **коро́ткий** ♦ *сравн нареч от* **ко́ротко; ~ говоря́** to put it briefly.
коро́чк|а (-**и**) *ж уменьш от* **ко́рка;** *(на пироге итп)* crust.
корп|е́ть (-**лю́**, -**йшь**) *несов неперех:* **~ над** +*instr* to slave away at.
корпорати́вный *прил* corporate.
корпора́ци|я (-**и**) *ж* corporation.
ко́рпус (-**а**; *nom pl* -**ы**) *м* body; *(самолёта)* fuselage; *(nom pl* -**а́**; *остов: судна, здания)* frame; *(здание)* block; *(ист: учебное заведение)* academy; *(дипломатический, офицерский)* corps.
корре́ктен *прил см* **корре́ктный.**
корректи́в (-**а**) *м (поправка: обычно мн)* amendment; **вноси́ть (внести́** *perf)* **~ы в план** to amend a plan.
корректи́ровать (-**ую**; *perf* **скорректи́ровать)** *несов перех (ошибку)* to correct; *(perf* **откорректи́ровать;** *рукопись, статью)* to proofread.
корректиро́в|ка (-**ки**; *gen pl* -**ок**) *ж (комп: обновление)* update.
корре́кт|ный (-**ен**, -**на**, -**но**) *прил* correct.
корре́ктор (-**а**) *м* proofreader.
корректу́р|а (-**ы**) *ж (исправление ошибок)* proofreading; *(оттиск с набора)* proofs *мн.*
корре́кци|я (-**и**) *ж* correction.
корреля́ци|я (-**и**) *ж* correlation.
корреспонде́нт (-**а**) *м* correspondent.
корреспонде́нт|ка (-**ки**; *gen pl* -**ок**) *ж см* **корреспонде́нт.**
корреспонде́нци|я (-**и**) *ж* correspondence.
корри́д|а (-**ы**) *ж* bullfight.
корроди́р|овать (*3sg* -**ует**, *3pl* -**уют**) *(не)сов неперех* to corrode.
коррози́йный *прил* corrosive.
корро́зи|я (-**и**) *ж* corrosion.
коррумпи́рован|ный (-, -**а**, -**о**) *прил* corrupt.
корру́пци|я (-**и**) *ж* corruption.
корса́ж (-**а**) *м* bodice.
корсе́т (-**а**) *м* corset.
корт (-**а**) *м* (tennis) court.
корте́ж (-**а**) *м (траурный)* cortege; *(свадебный)* procession.
ко́ртик (-**а**) *м* dagger, knife (*мн* knives).
ко́рточ|ки (-**ек**) *мн:* **присе́сть на ~** to squat down; **сиде́ть** *(impf)* **на ~ках** to squat.

корч|ева́ть (-**у́ю**) *несов от* **вы́корчевать** ♦ *перех* to uproot.
корч|ить (-**у**, -**ишь**; *perf* **скорчить**) *несов перех* to contort ♦ *безл:* **его́ всего́ ~ило от бо́ли** he was doubled up in pain; **~ (скорчить** *perf)* **ро́жу** to pull a face; **~** *(impf)* **из себя́ дурака́/свято́го** *(разг)* to act the fool/saint
▸ **ко́рчиться** (*perf* **ско́рчиться**) *несов возв (от боли, от смеха)* to writhe about.
ко́ршун (-**а**) *м (зоол)* kite.
коры́ст|ный (-**ен**, -**на**, -**но**) *прил (интерес, цель)* mercenary; *(любовь)* selfish.
корыстолюби́в|ый (-, -**а**, -**о**) *прил* mercenary.
корыстолю́би|е (-**я**) *ср* greed.
коры́ст|ь (-**и**) *ж (выгода)* gain; *(корыстолюбие)* greed.
коры́т|о (-**а**) *ср* tub; **оста́ться** *(perf)* **у разби́того ~а** to end up with nothing.
кор|ь (-**и**) *ж* measles *мн.*
ко́рюш|ка (-**ки**; *gen pl* -**ек**) *ж* smelt *(fish).*
коря́в|ый (-, -**а**, -**о**) *прил (дерево, пальцы)* gnarled; *(почерк)* squiggly; *(перен: фразы, стиль)* clumsy.
коря́г|а (-**и**) *ж* dead branch (*мн* branches).
кос|а́ (-**ы́**; *acc sg* -**у**, *dat sg* -**е́**, *nom pl* -**ы**) *ж (волосы)* plait; *(орудие)* scythe; **заплета́ть** *(perf)* **ко́сы кому́-н** to plait sb's hair; **носи́ть** *(impf)* **ко́сы** to wear one's hair in plaits; **нашла́ ~ на ка́мень** they are an equal match for each other.
коса́р|ь (-**я́**) *м* mower *(person).*
коса́т|ка (-**и**) *ж* killer whale.
ко́свенный *прил* indirect; *(дополнение, падеж)* oblique; **ко́свенная речь** indirect speech.
ко́сен *прил см* **ко́сный.**
коси́л|ка (-**ки**; *gen pl* -**ок**) *ж* mower *(machine).*
ко́синус (-**а**) *м* cosine.
ко|си́ть (-**шу́**, -**сишь**; *perf* **скоси́ть**) *несов перех (газон, сено)* to mow; *(перен: подлеж: эпидемия, болезнь)* to wipe out; *(рот, глаза)* to twist; *(глаза)* to slant; **у него́ ~ся́т глаза́** he has a slight squint
▸ **коси́ться** (*perf* **скоси́ться**) *несов возв (здание)* to lean to one side; **~ся** *(impf)* **на кого́-н** *(смотреть искоса)* to give sb a sidelong glance; *(перен)* to look askance at sb.
коси́чк|а (-**ки**; *gen pl* -**ек**) *ж* pigtail.
косма́т|ый (-, -**а**, -**о**) *прил* shaggy.
косме́тик|а (-**и**) *ж* make-up ♦ *собир* cosmetics *мн.*
космети́чек *сущ см* **космети́чка.**
космети́ческ|ий (-**ая**, -**ое**, -**ие**) *прил* cosmetic; **~ ремо́нт** decorating; **космети́ческий кабине́т** beauty salon.
космети́ч|ка (-**ки**; *gen pl* -**ек**) *ж (человек)* beautician; *(сумочка)* make-up bag.
космето́лог (-**а**) *м (также:* **врач-~)** cosmetic surgeon.
космет|оло́ги|я (-**и**) *ж* cosmetic surgery.

косми́ческ|ий (**-ая, -ое, -ие**) *прил* (*полёт, раке́та*) space *опред*; (*тео́рия*) cosmic; **~ая ско́рость** (*перен*) terrific speed; **косми́ческий кора́бль** spaceship; **косми́ческое простра́нство** (outer) space.

космодро́м (**-а**) *м* spaceport.

космоло́ги|я (**-и**) *ж* cosmology.

космона́вт (**-а**) *м* cosmonaut; (*в США итп*) astronaut.

космона́втик|а (**-и**) *ж* space technology and exploration.

космополи́т (**-а**) *м* cosmopolitan.

космополити́зм (**-а**) *м* cosmopolitanism.

ко́смос (**-а**) *м* the cosmos.

ко́см|ы (**-**) *мн* (*разг*) tousled locks *мн*.

косне́|ть (**-ю**; *perf* **закосне́ть**) *несов неперех*: **~ (в** +*prp*) to stagnate (in).

ко́сность (**-и**) *ж* intransigence.

косн|у́ться (**-у́сь, -ёшься**) *сов от* **каса́ться**.

ко́с|ный (**-ен, -на, -но**) *прил* (*ум, челове́к*) inflexible; (*среда́, о́бщество*) stagnant.

ко́со *нареч* (*расположи́ть*) squint; **~ смотре́ть** (*impf*) **на** +*acc* (*перен*) to look askance at.

кособо́к|ий (**-ая, -ое, -ие**; **-, -а, -о**) *прил* lopsided.

косоворо́т|ка (**-ки**; *gen pl* **-ок**) *ж* *traditional Russian shirt with a collar fastening at the side.*

косогла́зи|е (**-я**) *ср* squint.

косогла́з|ый (**-, -а, -о**) *прил* cross-eyed.

косого́р (**-а**) *м* hillside.

кос|о́й (**-, -а́, -о**) *прил* (*глаза́*) squinty; (*дождь, лучи́*) slanting; **броса́ть** (*impf*) **~ы́е взгля́ды (на** +*acc*) to look askance (at); **у него́ ~а́я са́жень в плеча́х** (*разг*) he's built like an ox.

косола́п|ый (**-, -а, -о**) *прил* (*челове́к*) pigeon-toed.

костене́|ть (**-ю**; *perf* **закостене́ть**) *несов неперех* to go stiff.

кост|ёр (**-ра́**) *м* campfire.

кости́ст|ый (**-, -а, -о**) *прил* bony.

костля́в|ый (**-, -а, -о**) *прил* bony.

ко́стный *прил* (*АНАТ*): **~ мозг** (bone) marrow.

ко́сточ|ка (**-ки**; *gen pl* **-ек**) *ж уменьш от* **кость**; (*абрико́совая, вишнёвая*) stone; (*виногра́да*) seed; (*лимо́на*) pip; **перемыва́ть** (*impf*) **~ки кому́-н** (*разг*) to bitch about sb.

костра́ *сущ см* **костёр**.

костыл|ь (**-я́**) *м* (*инвали́да*) crutch (*мн* crutches); (*гвоздь*) spike.

кост|ь (**-и**; *prp sg* **-и́**, *gen pl* **-е́й**) *ж* bone; (*игра́льная*) dice (*мн* die); **лечь** (*perf*) **~ми́** (*поги́бнуть*) to lay down one's life; (*перен*) to do everything possible; **промока́ть** (**промо́кнуть** *perf*) **до ~е́й** to get soaked to the skin.

костю́м (**-а**) *м* outfit; (*маскара́дный, на сце́не*) costume; (*пиджа́к и брю́ки/ю́бка*) suit; **брю́чный ~** trouser (*BRIT*) *или* pant (*US*) suit.

костюме́р (**-а**) *м* wardrobe assistant.

костюми́рованный *прил*: **~ бал** costume ball.

костя́к (**-а́**) *м* skeleton; (*перен*) backbone.

костян|о́й *прил* (*нож, украше́ние*) bone; **~а́я**

му́ка bone meal.

костя́ш|ка (**-ки**; *gen pl* **-ек**) *ж* (*па́льцев*) knuckle; (*на счётах*) bead; (*домино́*) domino.

косу́л|я (**-и**) *ж* (*ЗООЛ*) roe deer.

косы́н|ка (**-ки**; *gen pl* **-ок**) *ж* (triangular) scarf.

кося́к (**-а**) *м* (*две́ри*) jamb; (*рыб*) school, shoal; (*птиц*) flock.

кот (**-а́**) *м* tomcat; **там хле́ба ~ напла́кал** (*разг*) there's hardly any bread left; **вся рабо́та пошла́ ко́ту под хвост** (*разг*) all the work has gone down the plughole; **~ в мешке́** a pig in a poke.

кот|ёл (**-ла́**) *м* (*сосу́д*) pot; (*парово́й*) boiler; **о́бщий ~** kitty; **вари́ться** (*impf*) **в одно́м ~ле́** to live in each other's pockets.

котел|о́к (**-ка́**) *м уменьш от* **котёл**; (*похо́дная кастрю́ля*) billycan; (*шля́па*) bowler (hat) (*BRIT*), derby (*US*).

коте́льн|ая (**-ой**; *decl like adj*) *ж* boilerhouse.

кот|ёнок (**-ёнка**; *nom pl* **-я́та**, *gen pl* **-я́т**) *м* kitten.

ко́тик (**-а**) *м уменьш от* **кот**; (*тюле́нь*) fur seal; (*мех*) sealskin.

ко́тиковый *прил* sealskin.

коти́р|овать (**-ую**) (*не)сов перех* (*КОММ*) to quote

▶ **коти́роваться** *несов возв* (*КОММ*): **~ся (в** +*acc*) to be quoted (at); (*также перен*) to have a high value.

котиро́в|ка (**-и**) *ж* (*КОММ*) quotation.

коти́ться (*3sg* **-и́тся**, *perf* **окоти́ться**) *несов возв* (*ко́шка*) to have kittens; (*за́йцы, кро́лики итп*) to give birth.

котла́ *сущ см* **котёл**.

котле́т|а (**-ы**) *ж* rissole; (*также*: **отбивна́я ~**) chop.

котлова́н (**-а**) *м* pit.

котлови́н|а (**-ы**) *ж* (*ГЕО*) basin.

кото́м|ка (**-ки**; *gen pl* **-ок**) *ж* knapsack; (*разг*) bag.

┌─────────────────┐
│ **KEYWORD** │
└─────────────────

кото́р|ый (**-ая, -ое, -ые**) *мест* **1** (*вопроси́тельное*) which; **в кото́рый день он пришёл?** which day did he come?; **кото́рый час?** what time is it?

2 (*относи́тельное*: *о предме́те*) which; (: *о челове́ке*) who; **собы́тие, кото́рое нас потрясло́** an event which shook us; **ребёнок, кото́рого моро́женое** the child who has the ice-cream; **челове́к, с кото́рым я говори́л** the person with whom I was speaking; **же́нщина, сы́на кото́рой я зна́ю** the woman whose son I know; **же́нщина, кото́рую я люблю́** the woman I love

3 (*не пе́рвый*): **кото́рый день/год мы не ви́делись** we haven't seen each other for many days/years.

котте́дж (**-а**) *м* cottage.

котя́та *итп сущ см* **котёнок**.

ко́фе (*м нескл*) coffee; **~ в зёрнах** coffee beans.

кофева́р|ка (**-ки**; *gen pl* **-ок**) *ж* percolator.

кофе́ен *сущ см* **кофе́йня**.

кофеи́н (**-а**) *м* caffeine.

кофе́йник (**-а**) *м* coffeepot.

кофе́йн|ый *прил* coffee *мн*; **~ого цве́та** coffee-coloured; **кофе́йный серви́з** coffee service.
кофе́йня (**-йни**; *gen pl* **-ен**) *ж* coffee shop.
кофемо́л|ка (**-ки**; *gen pl* **-ок**) *ж* coffee grinder.
ко́фт|а (**-ы**) *ж* blouse; (*шерстяная*) cardigan.
коча́н (**-á**) *м*: **~ капу́сты** cabbage.
коч|ева́ть (**-у́ю**) *несов неперех* (*также перен*) to lead a nomadic life; (*животные*) to roam.
коче́вник (**-а**) *м* nomad.
кочево́й *прил* nomadic.
коче́в|ье (**-ья**; *gen pl* **-ий**) *ср* nomad camp.
кочега́р (**-а**) *м* stoker.
кочега́р|ка (**-ки**; *gen pl* **-ок**) *ж* furnace room.
ко́чек *сущ см* **ко́чка**.
кочене́|ть (**-ю**; *perf* **окочене́ть**) *несов неперех* (*руки, труп*) to go stiff; (*человек*) to get stiff.
кочер|га́ (**-ги́**; *gen pl* **-ёг**) *ж* poker.
кочеры́ж|ка (**-ки**; *gen pl* **-ек**) *ж* heart (*of cabbage*).
ко́ч|ка (**-ки**; *gen pl* **-ек**) *ж* tussock.
коша́р|а (**-ы**) *ж* sheepfold.
коша́тник (**-а**) *м* cat-lover.
коша́тниц|а (**-ы**) *ж см* **коша́тник**.
коша́чий (**-ья, -ье, -ьи**) *прил* (*также перен*) feline; (*мех, лапа*) cat's.
ко́шек *сущ см* **ко́шка**.
кошел|ёк (**-ька́**) *м* purse.
кошёл|ка (**-ки**; *gen pl* **-ок**) *ж* basket.
кошелька́ *сущ см* **кошелёк**.
ко́ш|ка (**-ки**; *gen pl* **-ек**) *ж* cat; (*скалолаза: обычно мн*) crampon; **~ки-мы́шки** (*игра*) tag; **игра́ть** (*impf*) **в ~ки-мы́шки с кем-н** (*перен*) to play cat and mouse with sb.
кошма́р (**-а**) *м* (*также перен*) nightmare.
кошма́р|ный (**-ен, -на, -но**) *прил* (*сон*) nightmarish; (*перен*) dreadful, nightmarish.
кошу́(сь) *несов см* **коси́ть(ся)**.
кощ|е́й (**-я**) *м*: **~ бессме́ртный** *evil spirit in Russian fairytales*.
кощу́нствен|ный (**-, -на, -но**) *прил* blasphemous.
кощу́нств|о (**-а**) *ср* blasphemy.
кощу́нств|овать (**-ую**) *несов неперех* to blaspheme.
коэффицие́нт (**-а**) *м* coefficient; **коэффицие́нт поле́зного де́йствия** efficiency.
КПСС *ж сокр* (*ист*: = **Коммунисти́ческая па́ртия Сове́тского Сою́за**) CPSU (= *Communist Party of the Soviet Union*).
краб (**-а**) *м* crab.
кра́деный *прил* stolen.
краду́(сь) *итп несов см* **кра́сть(ся)**.
кра́дучись *нареч* stealthily.
краеве́д (**-а**) *м* local historian.
краеве́ден|ие (**-я**) *ср* local studies *мн*.
краеве́дческ|ий (**-ая, -ое, -ие**) *прил*: **~ музе́й** local-history museum.
краево́й *прил* regional.
краеуго́льный *прил* fundamental;

краеуго́льный ка́мень cornerstone.
кра́ж|а (**-и**) *ж* theft; **~ со взло́мом** burglary.
кра|й (**-я**; *loc sg* **-ю́**, *nom pl* **-я́**, *gen pl* **-ёв**) *м* edge; (*чашки, коробки*) rim; (*местность*) region; (*полит*) krai (*regional administrative unit*); **непоча́тый ~ рабо́ты** an endless amount of work; **на ~ све́та** to the ends of the earth; **на ~ю́ све́та** at the ends of the earth; **да́льние/тёплые ~я́** far-off/warm climes; **родно́й ~** native country; **находи́ться** (*impf*) **на ~ю́ ги́бели** to be on the verge of disaster; **кра́ем у́ха слу́шать** (*impf*) to half listen; **кра́ем у́ха слы́шать** (*impf*) to overhear; **хвати́ть** (*perf*) **че́рез ~** to go too far; **бить** (*impf*) **че́рез ~** to overflow.
кра́йне *нареч* extremely.
кра́йн|ий (**-яя, -ее, -ие**) *прил* extreme; (*дом*) end *опред*; (*пункт, маршрута*) last, final; **в ~ем слу́чае** as a last resort; **по ~ей ме́ре** at least; **кра́йний напада́ющий** winger; **Кра́йний Се́вер** the Arctic; **кра́йний срок** (final) deadline.
кра́йность (**-и**) *ж* (*крайняя степень*) extremity; (*противоположное*) extreme; **броса́ться** (*impf*) **в ~и** to go from one extreme to the other; **твоё поведе́ние надое́ло мне до ~и** I find your behaviour tedious in the extreme.
кра́л|я (**-и**) *ж* (*разг: подруга*) chick; (: *красотка*) queen bee.
крамо́л|а (**-ы**) *ж* subversion; **говори́ть** (*impf*)/**писа́ть** (*impf*) **~у** to say/write subversive things.
крамо́льный *прил* subversive.
кран (**-а**) *м* tap, faucet (*US*); (*строит*) crane.
крановщи́к (**-а́**) *м* crane operator.
крановщи́ц|а (**-ы**) *ж см* **крановщи́к**.
крапи́в|а (**-ы**) *ж* nettle.
крапи́вниц|а (**-ы**) *ж* (*мед*) nettle rash.
крапи́вный *прил*: **~ щи** nettle soup.
кра́пин|а (**-ы**) *ж* = **кра́пинка**.
кра́пин|ка (**-ки**; *gen pl* **-ок**) *ж* fleck, speck.
краплёный *прил* (*карты*) marked.
кра́пчатый (**-, -а, -о**) *прил* speckled.
крас|а́ (**-ы́**) *ж* beauty; (*перен*): **~ +gen** (*школы итп*) the pride of.
краса́в|ец (**-ца**) *м* handsome *или* good-looking man (*мн* men).
краса́виц|а (**-ы**) *ж* beautiful woman (*мн* women).
краса́в|ка (**-и**) *ж* deadly nightshade.
краса́вца *итп сущ см* **краса́вец**.
кра́сен *прил см* **кра́сный**.
краси́вость (**-и**) *ж* superficial beauty.
краси́в|ый (**-, -а, -о**) *прил* beautiful; (*мужчина*) handsome; (*решение, фраза, слова*) fine.
краси́льный *прил* dye *опред*; **краси́льные вещества́** dyestuffs.
краси́тел|ь (**-я**) *м* dye.
кра́|сить (**-шу, -сишь**; *perf* **покра́сить**) *несов перех* to paint; (*волосы*) to dye; (*perf* **накра́сить**; *щёки, губы итп*) to paint; (*no perf*;

перен: украшать) to adorn; **тако́е поведе́ние тебя́ не ~сит** such behaviour does not become you

▶ **кра́|ситься** (*perf* **покра́ситься**) *несов возв* to be covered in paint; (*разг: пачкать*) to run; (*perf* **накра́ситься**) to wear make-up.

кра́с|ка (-ки; *gen pl* -ок) *ж* paint; (*обычно мн: нежные, весенние итп*) colour (*BRIT*), color (*US*); (*стыда*) blush; **опи́сывать (описа́ть** *perf*) **что-н чёрными ~ми** to paint a gloomy picture of sth.

красне́|ть (-ю; *perf* **покрасне́ть**) *несов неперех* to turn red; (*от стыда*) to blush, flush; (*от гнева*) to go red; (*перен*): **~ пе́ред кем-н за кого́-н** to be ashamed of sb in front of sb; **~** (*impf*) **до корне́й воло́с** to blush to the roots of one's hair.

красноарме́|ец (-йца) *м* (*ИСТ*) Red-Army soldier.

красноба́|й (-я) *м* (*разг*) waffler.

красногварде́|ец (-йца) *м* (*ИСТ*) Red Guardsman (*мн* Guardsmen).

краснодере́вщик (-а) *м* cabinet-maker.

красноречи́в|ый (-, -а, -о) *прил* (*оратор, письмо*) eloquent; (*взгляд, жест*) expressive; (*цифры, факты*) revealing.

красноре́чи|е (-я) *ср* eloquence.

краснот|а́ (-ы́) *ж* (*лица*) redness; (*в горле*) inflammation.

краснощёк|ий (-ая, -ое, -ие) *прил* rosy-cheeked.

красну́х|а (-и) *ж* German measles.

кра́сн|ый (-ен, -на́, -но) *прил* red; **проходи́ть** (*impf*) **~ной ни́тью** *или* **ли́нией** to run through; **кра́сная а́рмия** Red Army; **кра́сная ры́ба** salmon; **кра́сная строка́** new paragraph; **кра́сное вино́** red wine; **кра́сное де́рево** mahogany; **кра́сный пе́рец** paprika.

крас|ова́ться (-у́юсь) *несов возв* (*перед зеркалом, людьми*) to parade.

кра́сок *сущ см* **кра́ска.**

крас|ота́ (-оты́; *nom pl* -о́ты) *ж* beauty; **~!** wonderful!; *см также* **красо́ты.**

красо́тк|а (-и) *ж* pretty girl.

красо́т|ы (-) *мн* (*природы*) beautiful scenery *ед*.

кра́соч|ный (-ен, -на, -но) *прил* (*язык, расцветка*) colourful (*BRIT*), colorful (*US*).

кра|сть (-ду́, -дёшь; *perf* **укра́сть**) *несов перех* to steal

▶ **кра́сться** *несов возв* (*человек*) to creep, steal.

кра́сящ|ий (-ая, -ее, -ие) *прил*: **~ее вещество́** dye.

крат *нареч*: **во́ сто ~** a hundred times.

кра́тер (-а) *м* crater.

кра́т|кий (-кая, -кое, -кие; -ок, -ка́, -ко) *прил* short; (*беседа*) brief, short; (*словарь, отчёт*) concise; **~кое прилага́тельное** short-form adjective; **„и“ ~кое** the 10th letter of the Russian alphabet.

кратковре́мен|ный (-ен, -на, -но) *прил* short.

краткосро́ч|ный (-ен, -на, -но) *прил* (*отпуск,*

командировка) short; (*заём, ссуда*) short-term.

кра́ткост|ь (-и) *ж* brevity.

кра́тный *прил* divisible.

кра́ток *прил см* **кра́ткий.**

кра́тче *сравн прил см* **кра́ткий.**

крах (-а) *м* collapse; (*перен*) destruction.

крахма́л (-а) *м* starch.

крахма́л|ить (-ю, -ишь; *perf* **накрахма́лить**) *несов перех* to starch.

крахма́льный *прил* starched.

кра́ше *сравн прил от* **краси́вый.**

краше́ни|е (-я) *ср* dyeing.

кра́шен|ый *прил* (*мех, ткань*) dyed; (*стол, дверь*) painted; **~ая блонди́нка** (*разг*) peroxide blonde.

крашу́(сь) *несов см* **кра́сить(ся).**

краю́х|а (-и) *ж* (*разг: хлеба*) doorstep.

креве́тк|а (-и) *ж* shrimp.

креди́т (-а) *м* credit; (*политический*) credibility; **в ~** on credit; **превыша́ть (превы́сить** *perf*) **~** to overdraw; **брать (взять** *perf*) **~ в ба́нке** to arrange an overdraft.

креди́тный *прил* credit *опред*; **~ оста́ток на счёте** credit balance; **креди́тная ка́рточка** credit card; **креди́тный счёт** credit account.

кредит|ова́ть (-у́ю) (*не)сов перех* to grant credit to.

кредито́р (-а) *м* creditor; **незастрахо́ванный ~** unsecured creditor.

кредито́рск|ий (-ая, -ое, -ие) *прил* creditor's.

кредитоспосо́бност|ь (-и) *ж* solvency.

кредитоспосо́бный *прил* solvent.

кре́до *ср нескл* credo.

кре́йсер (-а) *м* (*ВОЕН*) battleship, cruiser.

крейси́р|овать (-ую) *несов неперех* to sail (*along a specific route*); (*ВОЕН*) to patrol.

кре́кинг (-а) *м* (*нефти*) cracking.

крем (-а) *м* cream; **сапо́жный ~** shoe polish.

кремато́ри|й (-я) *м* crematorium.

крема́ци|я (-и) *ж* cremation.

креме́н|ь (-ня́) *м* flint.

креми́р|овать (-ую) (*не)сов перех* to cremate.

кремл|ь (-я́) *м* citadel; **К~** the Kremlin.

кремнёвый *прил* flint.

кремни́|й (-я) *м* silicon.

кремня́ *итп сущ см* **креме́нь.**

кре́мовый *прил* cream.

крен (-а) *м* (*судна*) list; (*самолёта*) bank; **~ в сто́рону чего́-н** (*перен*) a move towards sth.

кре́ндел|ь (-я; *nom pl* -я) *м* krendel (*sweet pastry*).

крен|и́ть (-ю́, -и́шь; *perf* **накрени́ть**) *несов перех* (*судно*) to list; (*самолёт*) to bank

▶ **крени́ться** (*perf* **накрени́ться**) *несов возв* (*судно*) to list; (*самолёт*) to bank.

креозо́т (-а) *м* creosote.

креп (-а) *м* crêpe.

крепдеши́н (-а) *м* crêpe de chine.

крепёжный *прил* reinforcing *опред*.

крепи́тельн|ый *прил* (*ТЕХ*) reinforcing *опред*; **~ое сре́дство** anti-diarrhoea tablets.

крепи́|ть (-лю́, -и́шь) *несов перех* to fix;

(*делать прочным*) to reinforce; **меня́ ~йт** I'm constipated.

кре́п|кий (**-кая, -кое, -кие; -ок, -ка́, -ко**) *прил* strong; (*мороз, удар*) hard; ~ **оре́шек** (*перен*) tough nut; **кре́пкие напи́тки** spirits.

кре́пко *нареч* strongly; (*спать, любить*) deeply; (*завязать*) tightly.

кре́пко-на́крепко *нареч* (*связать, закрыть*) as tightly as possible.

крепле́ни|е (**-я**) *ср* (*свай*) reinforcement; (*обычно мн: лыжные*) binding.

крепл|ёный *прил*: ~**ое вино́** fortified wine.

крепл́ю *несов см* **крепи́ть**.

кре́п|нуть (**-ну, -нешь;** *pt* **-, -ла, -ло,** *perf* **окре́пнуть**) *несов неперех* to get stronger; (*уверенность*) to grow.

кре́пок *прил см* **кре́пкий**.

крепостни́к (**-á**) *м* (*ИСТ*) serf owner.

крепостни́чество (**-а**) *ср* (*ИСТ*) serfdom.

крепостн|о́й *прил* (*ИСТ: отношения*) serf *опред*; (*башня, сооружение*) fortress *опред* ♦ (**-о́го;** *decl like adj*) *м* (*ИСТ: также:* ~ **крестья́нин**) serf; **крепостно́е пра́во** (*ИСТ*) serfdom.

кре́пост|ь (**-и**) *ж* strength; (*ВОЕН*) fortress.

крепча́|ть (*3sg* **-ет,** *3pl* **-ют**) *несов неперех* (*мороз*) to harden; (*ветер*) to get stronger.

кре́пче *сравн прил от* **кре́пкий** ♦ *сравн нареч от* **кре́пко**.

крепы́ш (**-а́**) *м* (*разг: ребёнок*) chubby chops.

кре́сл|о (**-а;** *gen pl* **-ел**) *ср* armchair; (*в театре*) seat.

кре́сл|о-крова́ть (**-а, -и**) *ж* ≈ sofa bed.

крест (**-а́**) *м* cross; **поста́вить** (*perf*) ~ **на ком-н/чём-н** to give sb/sth up for lost.

крестец́ (**-ца́**) *м* sacrum.

кре́ст|и (**-**) *мн* (*разг: КАРТЫ*) clubs *мн*.

крест|и́ть (**-щу́, -сти́шь;** *perf* **окрести́ть**) *несов перех* to christen, baptize; ~ (**перекрести́ть** *perf*) **кого́-н** to make the sign of the cross over sb; ~ (**окрести́ть** *perf*) **кого́-н кем-н** to christen sb sth

▸ **крести́ться** (*не*)*сов возв* to be christened *или* baptized; (*perf* **перекрести́ться;** *крестить себя*) to cross o.s.

крест-на́крест *нареч* crosswise.

кре́стник (**-а**) *м* godson.

кре́стниц|а (**-ы**) *ж* goddaughter.

кре́стн|ый *прил*: ~**ое зна́мение** sign of the cross; ~ **ход** religious procession.

крёстн|ый *прил*: ~**ая мать** godmother; ~ **отец** godfather.

кресто́в|ый *прил*: ~ **похо́д** crusade; ~**ая да́ма/деся́тка** (*разг*) the queen/ten of clubs.

крестоно́с|ец (**-ца**) *м* crusader.

крестца́ *итп сущ см* **крестец́**.

крестья́н|ин (**-ина;** *nom pl* **-е,** *gen pl* **-**) *м* peasant.

крестья́н|ка (**-ки;** *gen pl* **-ок**) *ж см* **крестья́нин**.

крестья́нский (**-ая, -ое, -ие**) *прил* peasant *опред*.

крестья́нств|о (**-а**) *ср* peasantry.

крети́н (**-а**) *м* imbecile.

кре́чет (**-а**) *м* gerfalcon.

креще́ндо *нареч, ср нескл* crescendo.

креще́ни|е (**-я**) *ср* (*обряд*) christening, baptism; (*праздник*) ≈ the Epiphany; **он получи́л боево́е** ~ (*перен*) he fought his first battle.

креще́нский (**-ая, -ое, -ие**) *прил*: ~ **пра́здник** the Epiphany; ~**ие моро́зы** *coldest time of the year, traditionally following the Epiphany*.

крещу́(сь) (*не*)*сов см* **крести́ть(ся)**.

крив|а́я (**-о́й;** *decl like adj*) *ж* (*МАТ*) curve.

криве́|ть (**-ю;** *perf* **окриве́ть**) *несов неперех* to become cockeyed.

кривизн|а́ (**-ы́**) *ж* (*пола, потолка*) unevenness; (*линии, позвоночника*) curvature.

крив|и́ть (**-лю́, -и́шь;** *perf* **скриви́ть** *или* **покриви́ть**) *несов перех* to curve; (*лицо, губы*) to twist; ~ (**покриви́ть** *perf*) **душо́й** to be insincere

▸ **криви́ться** (*perf* **скриви́ться**) *несов возв* (*забор, стена итп*) to lean; (*лицо, губы*) to twist; (*человек*) to slouch.

кривля́|ться (**-юсь**) *несов возв* (*гримасничать*) to squirm; (*манерничать*) to show off.

крив|о́й (**-, -а́, -о**) *прил* (*линия, палка, улыбка*) crooked; (*ноги*) bandy; (*разг: человек*) cockeyed; ~**о́е зе́ркало** (*перен*) distorting mirror.

криволине́йный *прил* (*движение*) curvilinear.

кривоно́г|ий (**-ая, -ое, -ие**) *прил* bow-legged.

кривото́лк|и (**-ов**) *мн* gossip *ед*.

кри́зис (**-а**) *м* crisis; (*болезни*) critical point, crisis.

кри́зисный *прил* crisis *опред*.

крик (**-а;** *part gen* **-у**) *м* cry; (*человека*) shout, cry; (*птиц*) call, cry; **после́дний ~ мо́ды** (*разг*) the last word in fashion.

кри́кет (**-а**) *м* (*СПОРТ*) cricket.

крикли́в|ый (**-, -а, -о**) *прил* (*женщина, платье*) loud; (*голос*) yapping.

кри́кн|уть (**-у, -ешь**) *сов неперех* to shout.

крику́н (**-а́**) *м* (*разг*) bawler.

крику́н|ья (**-ьи;** *gen pl* **-ий**) *ж см* **крику́н**.

кримина́л (**-а**) *м* (*разг*) criminal case; **я не ви́жу здесь** ~**а** I don't see anything criminal in it.

криминали́ст (**-а**) *м* specialist in crime detection.

криминали́стик|а (**-и**) *ж* crime detection.

кримина́льный *прил* (*случай*) criminal; (*история, хроника*) crime *опред*.

криминоло́г (**-а**) *м* criminologist.

криминоло́ги|я (**-и**) *ж* criminology.

кри́н|ка (**-ки;** *gen pl* **-ок**) *ж* *ceramic container for milk*.

криста́лен прил см **криста́льный**.

криста́лл (-а) м crystal.

кристаллиза́ци|я (-и) ж crystallization.

кристаллиз|ова́ться (3sg -у́ется, 3pl -у́ются, perf **вы́кристаллизоваться**) (не)сов возв to crystallize.

криста́л|ьный (-ен, -ьна, -ьно) прил (светлый) crystal-clear; (безупречный) pure.

Крит (-а) м Crete.

крите́ри|й (-я) м criterion (мн criteria).

кри́тик (-а) м critic.

кри́тик|а (-и) ж criticism; **литерату́рная ~** literary criticism; **это не выде́рживает никако́й ~и** it doesn't stand up to criticism; **подверга́ть** (подве́ргнуть perf) **кого́-н/что-н ~е** to subject sb/sth to criticism.

критика́н (-а) м (разг: пренебр) nit-picker.

критик|ова́ть (-у́ю) несов перех to criticize.

критици́зм (-а) м criticism.

крити́чен прил см **крити́чный**.

крити́ческ|ий (-ая, -ое, -ие) прил critical; **~ отде́л** review section; **~ая статья́** critique.

крити́ч|ный (-ен, -на, -но) прил critical.

крич|а́ть (-у́, -и́шь) несов неперех (птица) to cry; (человек: от боли, от гнева) to cry (out); (: говорить громко) to shout; **~** (impf) **на** +acc (бранить) to shout at.

крича́щий (-ая, -ее, -ие) прил (перен: наряды) loud; (: реклама) eye-catching.

кров (-а) м shelter; **остава́ться** (оста́ться perf) **без кро́ва** to have no roof over one's head.

крова́в|ый прил (руки, одежда) bloodied; (нож) bloodstained; (рана, битва) bloody; (диктатура) ruthless; **~ая ба́ня** blood bath; **~ бифште́кс** rare steak.

крова́т|ка (-ки; gen pl -ок) ж cot (BRIT), crib (US).

крова́т|ь (-и) ж bed.

кро́вель сущ см **кро́вля**.

кро́вельный прил roofing опред.

кро́вельщик (-а) м roofer.

кровено́сный прил blood опред.

кро́в|ля (-ли; gen pl -ель) ж roof; **жить** (impf) **под одно́й ~лей** to live under one roof.

кро́вн|ый прил (родство) blood опред; (обида) grave; **~ые интере́сы** vested interests; **~ враг** deadly enemy; **~ые де́ньги** blood money; **кро́вная месть** blood feud.

кровожа́ден прил см **кровожа́дный**.

кровожа́дность (-и) ж bloodthirstiness.

кровожа́д|ный (-ен, -на, -но) прил bloodthirsty.

кровоизлия́ни|е (-я) ср haemorrhage (BRIT), hemorrhage (US).

кровообраще́ни|е (-я) ср (МЕД) circulation.

кровоостана́вливающ|ий (-ая, -ее, -ие) прил (средства) clotting опред.

кровопи́йц|а (-ы) м/ж bloodsucker.

кровоподте́к (-а) м blood blister.

кровопроли́тен прил см **кровопроли́тный**.

кровопроли́ти|е (-я) ср bloodshed.

кровопроли́т|ный (-ен, -на, -но) прил bloody.

кровопуска́ни|е (-я) ср (также МЕД) blood-letting.

кровосмеше́ни|е (-я) ср incest.

кровотече́ни|е (-я) ср bleeding.

кровоточ|и́ть (3sg -и́т, 3pl -а́т) несов неперех to bleed.

кров|ь (-и; loc sg -и́) ж blood; **го́лос кро́ви** call of the blood; **по́ртить** (impf) **~ кому́-н** (разг) to make sb's blood boil; **пролива́ть** (проли́ть perf) **(свою́) ~ за кого́-н/что-н** to sacrifice o.s. for sb/sth; **пролива́ть** (проли́ть perf) **чью-н ~** to spill sb's blood; **пить** (impf) **чью-н ~** to suck the lifeblood out of sb; **~ с молоко́м** about a healthy, ruddy-faced person; **плоть и ~** (чья) (sb's) flesh and blood; **у меня́ се́рдце кро́вью облива́ется** my heart bleeds.

кровян|о́й прил blood опред; **кровяна́я колбаса́** black pudding; **кровяно́е давле́ние** blood pressure.

кро|и́ть (-ю́, -и́шь) несов перех to cut out.

крокоди́л (-а) м crocodile.

крокоди́л|ов (-а, -о, -ы) прил: **~ы слёзы** crocodile tears мн.

крокоди́ловый прил crocodile опред.

кро́лик (-а) м rabbit; (мех) rabbit fur; **ша́пка из ~а** rabbit-fur hat.

кро́лич|ий (-ья, -ье, -ьи) прил rabbit опред.

крольча́тник (-а) м rabbit hutch.

крольчи́х|а (-и) ж doe (rabbit).

кро́ме предл: **~** +gen (за исключением) except; (сверх чего-н) as well as; **~ того́** besides; **~ него́ я никого́ не ви́дел** I haven't seen anyone except for или apart from him; **~ соба́ки у них есть ещё и ко́шка** as well as a dog, they also have a cat; **~ шу́ток** (разг) joking apart; **ему́ ничего́ оста́лось ~ как уйти́** (разг) he had no choice but to leave; **~ как от тебя́, ни от кого́ не́ было пи́сем** I didn't get a letter from anyone except (for) you; **~ того́, мне на́до идти́ на собра́ние** apart from that или besides I have to go to a meeting.

кроме́шн|ый прил: **ад ~** hell on earth; **здесь тьма ~ая** it's pitch-black in here.

кро́м|ка (-и) ж (ткани) trim; (льда, поля) edge.

кромса́|ть (-ю; perf **искромса́ть**) несов перех (хлеб, материал) to hack off; (перен: рукопись, пьесу) to chop.

кро́н|а (-ы) ж (дерева) crown; (деньги) krona.

кронште́йн (-а) м (балкона) support; (лампы, полки) bracket.

кропа́|ть (-ю; perf **накропать**) несов перех (разг) to scribble.

кроп|и́ть (-лю́, -и́шь; perf **окропи́ть**) несов перех (РЕЛ) to sprinkle (with holy water).

кропотли́в|ый (-, -а, -о) прил (работа) painstaking; (человек) fastidious.

кросс (-а) м (бег) cross-country; (гонки) cross-country race.

кроссво́рд (-а) м crossword.

кроссо́в|ка (-ки; gen pl -ок) ж (обычно мн) trainer.

крот (-а́) м mole.

кро́т|кий (-кая, -кое, -кие; -ок, -ка́, -ко) прил

meek.
крото́вый *прил* moleskin.
кро́ток *прил см* **кро́ткий**.
кро́тост|ь (**-и**) *ж* meekness.
кро́х|а (**-и**) *ж* (*обычно мн*) scrap ♦ *м/ж* (*ребёнок*) little one.
крохобо́р (**-а**) *м* miser.
крохобо́рств|о (**-а**) *ср* (*пренебр*) stinginess.
кро́хотный (**-ен, -на, -но**) *прил* tiny.
кро́шек *сущ см* **кро́шка**.
кро́шечн|ый (**-ен, -на, -но**) *прил* (*разг*) teeny-weeny, tiny.
кроши́ть (**-у́, -ишь**) *несов перех* (*хлеб*) to crumble; (*кулин*) to dice ♦ *неперех* (*сорить*) to drop crumbs
▸ **кроши́ться** *несов возв* (*хлеб, мел*) to crumble.
кро́ш|ка (**-ки**; *gen pl* **-ек**) *ж* (*кусочек*) crumb; (*малютка*) little one.
крою́(сь) *итп несов см* **крыть(ся)**.
круг (**-а**; *nom pl* **-и́**) *м* circle; (*СПОРТ*) lap; (*сыра, хлеба*) round; (*loc sg* **-у́**; *перен: знакомых*) circle; (: *обязанностей, интересов, вопросов*) range; **у меня́ голова́ кру́гом идёт** my head is spinning; **ходи́ть** (*impf*) **по кру́гу** to go round and round; **бегово́й ~** racing track; **поля́рный ~** polar circle; *см также* **круги́**.
круги́ (**-о́в**) *мн* (*литерату́рные, полити́ческие*) circles *мн*.
кругле́|ть (**-ю**; *perf* **округле́ть**) *несов неперех* (*полнеть*) to fill out; (*становиться круглым*) to become round.
круглогоди́чный *прил* all-year-round.
круглоли́ц|ый (**-, -а, -о**) *прил* round-faced.
круглосу́точный *прил* (*работа*) round-the-clock; (*детский сад*) twenty-four-hour.
кру́гл|ый (**-, -а́, -о**) *прил* round; (*no short form; идио́т, дура́к*) complete, total; (*цифра*) round; **~ год** all year (round); **~ые су́тки** twenty-four hours; **~ая су́мма** hefty sum.
кругово́й *прил* circular; **кругова́я пору́ка** mutual dependence; (*у преступников*) mutual cover-up.
кругово́рот (**-а**) *м* cycle; (*событий*) turmoil.
кругозо́р (**-а**) *м*: **он челове́к широ́кого ~а** he is knowledgeable.
круго́м *нареч* around; (*разг: совершенно*) entirely; **идти́ (пойти́** *perf*) **~** to make a detour; **~!** about turn! (*BRIT*), about face! (*US*).
кругооборо́т (**-а**) *м* (*КОММ*) turnover.
кругосве́тный *прил* round-the-world.
кружевни́ц|а (**-ы**) *ж* lace-maker.
кружевно́й *прил* lace.
кру́жев|о (**-а**; *nom pl* **-а́**, *gen pl* **-**) *ср* lace.
кру́жек *сущ см* **кру́жка**.
кружи́ть (**-у́, -ишь**) *несов перех* to spin ♦ *неперех* (*птица*) to circle; (*по лесу итп*) to go round in circles
▸ **кружи́ться** *несов возв* (*в хороводе*) to move

in a circle; (*в танце*) to spin (around); **у меня́ голова́ кру́жится** my head's spinning.
кру́ж|ка (**-ки**; *gen pl* **-ек**) *ж* (*жестяная, глиняная*) mug; (*для пожертвований*) collection box.
кружка́ *сущ см* **кружо́к**.
кружко́в|ый *прил*: **~ые заня́тия** extracurricular activities.
кружо́к (**-ка́**) *м* circle; (*организация*) club.
круи́з (**-а**) *м* cruise.
круп (**-а**) *м* (*лошади*) crupper; (*МЕД*) croup.
круп|а́ (**-ы́**; *nom pl* **-ы**) *ж* grain.
кру́пен *прил см* **кру́пный**.
крупи́н|ка (**-ки**; *gen pl* **-ок**) *ж* (*разг*) grain.
крупи́ц|а (**-ы**) *ж* (*таланта, здравого смысла*) ounce; (*истины*) grain.
крупне́|ть (**-ю**; *perf* **покрупне́ть**) *несов неперех* to grow larger.
кру́пно *нареч* (*нарезать*) coarsely; **писа́ть (написа́ть** *perf*) **~** to write in big letters; **~ поссо́риться** (*perf*) **с кем-н** to have a big row with sb.
крупномасшта́бный *прил* large-scale.
кру́п|ный (**-ен, -на́, -но**) *прил* (*песок, соль*) coarse; (*размеры, ребёнок, фирма*) large; (*талант*) great; (*учёный, дело, фабрикант*) prominent; (*ссора, событие, успех*) major; **у меня́ бу́дут ~ые неприя́тности** I'll be in serious trouble; **~ разгово́р** (*разг*) serious talk; **кру́пный го́род** major city; **кру́пный план** close-up; **кру́пный рога́тый скот** (*С.-Х.*) cattle.
крупо́зн|ый *прил*: **~ое воспале́ние лёгких** pneumonia with croup.
крутизн|а́ (**-ы́**) *ж* steepness.
крути́ть (**-чу́, -тишь**) *несов перех* (*руль*) to turn; (*perf* **скрути́ть**; *руки*) to twist; (*верёвку*) to splice; (*папиросу*) to roll; **~** (*impf*) **ке́м-н** (*разг*) to manipulate sb; **~** (*impf*) **рома́н с кем-н** (*разг*) to have an affair with sb; **как ни ~ти́, нам придётся ..** (*разг*) we've no choice but to ...
▸ **крути́ться** *несов возв* (*вертеться*) to turn around; (: *колесо*) to spin; (: *дети*) to fidget; (*перен: хлопотать*) to be kept busy.
кру́то *нареч* (*поднима́ться*) steeply; (*поворачивать*) sharply; **~ обходи́ться (обойти́сь** *perf*) **с кем-н** to give sb a hard time.
крут|о́й (**-, -а́, -о**) *прил* (*берег, подъём*) steep; (*поворот, перемены*) sharp; (*нрав, меры*) harsh; (*no short form; те́сто*) stiff; (*каша*) thick; **~ кипято́к** fiercely boiling water; **~ па́рень** (*разг*) cool guy; **круто́е яйцо́** hard-boiled egg.
кру́ч|а (**-и**) *ж* steep slope.
кру́че *сравн прил от* **круто́й** ♦ *сравн нареч от* **кру́то**.
кручёный *прил* (*нитки*) twisted; **кручёный уда́р** (*в те́ннисе*) spin shot.
кручу́(сь) *несов см* **крути́ть(ся)**.
круше́ни|е (**-я**) *ср* (*поезда*) crash; (*перен: надежд, планов*) shattering; **терпе́ть**

(потерпéть *perf*) ~ **(корáбль)** to be wrecked; **(поезд)** to crash.

крушйн|а (-ы) ж buckthorn (*used as a laxative*).

круш|йть (-ý, -йшь) *несов перех* **(врагóв)** to crush; **(дерéвья, домá)** to wreck.

крыжóвник (-а) м **(кустáрник)** gooseberry (bush); **(ягода)** gooseberry.

крылáт|ый *прил* **(насекóмые)** winged; **~ые словá** proverbial expressions; **крылáтая ракéта** (*ВОЕН*) cruise missile.

крыл|ó (-á; *nom pl* **-ья**, *gen pl* **-ьев**) *ср* wing; **(ветряной мéльницы)** sail; **подрезáть (подрéзать** *perf*) **крылья комý-н (перен)** to clip sb's wings; **расправлять (распрáвить** *perf*) **крылья (перен)** to spread one's wings.

крылышк|о (-а) *ср* wing; **под ~м у когó-н** under sb's wing.

крыльц|ó (-á) *ср* porch.

Крым (-а) м Crimea.

крымск|ий (-ая, -ое, -ие) *прил* Crimean.

крын|ка (-ки; *gen pl* **-ок**) ж = **крйнка**.

крыс|а (-ы) ж rat.

крысйный *прил* **(норá, хвост)** rat's; ~ **яд** rat poison.

крытый *прил* covered.

крыть (-óю, -óешь; *perf* **покрыть**) *несов перех* to cover; **(кáрту)** to trump; ~ **(impf)** **мáтом** (*разг*) to turn the air blue (*with bad language*)

▸ **крыться** *несов возв:* ~**ыться в** +*prp* **(причйна)** to lie; **в расчётах ~ылась ошйбка** the calculations contained a mistake; **причйна э́того явлéния ~óется в том, что ...** the reason for this lies in the fact that ....

крыш|а (-и) ж roof.

крыш|ка (-ки; *gen pl* **-ек**) ж **(ящика, чáйника)** lid; **тут емý и ~ (разг)** that was the end of him.

крэк (-а) м crack (*drug*).

крю|к (-кá; *nom pl* **-чья**, *gen pl* **-чьев**) м **(в стенé)** hook; **(разг: лишнее расстояние)** detour.

крюч|ить (*3sg* **-ит**, *perf* **скрючить**) *несов безл:* **егó ~ит от бóли** he is bent double in pain

▸ **крючиться** (*perf* **скрючиться**) *несов возв* to be bent double.

крючкóва|тый (-, -а, -о) *прил* hooked.

крюч|óк (-кá) м hook; ~ **для вязáния** crochet hook.

крючья *итп сущ см* **крюк**.

крюшóн (-а) м **(кулин)** punch.

кряду *нареч:* **дождь шёл пять дней** ~ it rained for five whole days.

кряж (-а) м **(горный)** ridge.

кряжист|ый (-, -а, -о) *прил* (*также перен*) stumpy.

крякани|е (-я) *ср* quacking.

кряка|ть (-ю) *несов от* **крякнуть**.

крякн|уть (-у, -ешь) *сов* **перех (утка)** to quack; **(перен: человек)** to grunt.

кряхт|éть (-чý, -тйшь) *несов неперех* to groan.

ксерокóпи|я (-и) ж photocopy, Xerox®.

ксéрокс (-а) м **(автомáт)** photocopier; **(кóпия)** photocopy, Xerox®.

ксилофóн (-а) м xylophone.

ксилогрáфи|я (-и) ж **(образéц рабóты)** woodcut; **(процéсс)** wood engraving.

кстáти *вводн сл* **(мéжду прóчим)** incidentally, by the way; **(случáйно)** by any chance ♦ *нареч* **(к мéсту)** relevant; ~, **ты слышал, что ...?** by the way, did you hear that ...?; **Вы, ~, не знáете, что случйлось?** you don't, by any chance, know what happened?; **дéньги пришлйсь как нельзя** ~ the money came just at the right time.

кто (**когó;** *см* **Table 6)** *мест* **1** **(вопросйтельное, относйтельное)** who; **кто там?** who is there?; **нáдо узнáть, кто приходйл** we must find out who has come

2 **(разг: кто-нибудь)** anyone; **éсли кто позвонйт, позовй меня** if anyone phones, please call me

3: **мáло ли кто** many (people); **мáло кто** few (people); **мáло кто пошёл в кинó** only a few of us went to the cinema; **кто-кто, а он всегдá прáвду говорйт** I don't know about anyone else, but he always tells the truth; **кто из вас ...** which of you ...; **кто (егó) знáет!** who knows!

кто́-либо (**когó-либо;** *как* **кто;** *см* **Table 6)** *мест* = **кто́-нибудь.**

кто́-нибудь (**когó-нибудь;** *как* **кто;** *см* **Table 6)** *мест* **(в вопросйтельных предложéниях)** anybody, anyone; **(в утвердйтельных предложéниях)** somebody, someone; **мне** ~ **звонйл?** did anybody *или* anyone phone for me?; ~ **дóлжен емý помóчь** somebody *или* someone should help him.

кто́-то (**когó-то;** *как* **кто;** *см* **Table 6)** *мест* somebody, someone; ~ **Вам звонйл** somebody *или* someone phoned for you.

куб (-а) м **(ГЕОМ, МАТ)** cube; **3 в кýбе** 3 cubed.

куб. *сокр* (= **кубйческий**) cu. (= *cubic*).

Кýб|а (-ы) ж Cuba.

кýбарем *нареч* (*разг*) headfirst.

кубйзм (-а) м cubism.

кýбик (-а) м **(игрушка)** building brick *или* block.

кубйн|ец (-ца) м Cuban.

кубйн|ка (-ки; *gen pl* **-ок**) ж *см* **кубйнец.**

кубйнск|ий (-ая, -ое, -ие) *прил* Cuban.

кубйнца *итп сущ см* **кубйнец.**

кубйст (-а) м cubist.

кубйческ|ий (-ая, -ое, -ие) *прил* cubic; **кубйческий кóрень** cube root.

кýб|ок (-ка) м goblet; **(СПОРТ)** cup.

кубомéтр (-а) м cubic metre (*BRIT*) *или* meter (*US*).

кýбрик (-а) м crew's quarters *мн.*

кувáлд|а (-ы) ж sledgehammer.

Кувéйт (-а) м Kuwait.

кувшйн (-а) м jug (*BRIT*), pitcher (*US*).

кувшйн|ка (-и) ж water lily.

кувыркá|ться (-юсь) *несов возв* to somersault.

кувыркн|ýться (-ýсь, -ёшься) *сов возв* to turn a somersault.

кувырко́м *нареч* head over heels; **жизнь у меня́ пошла́** ~ my life has been turned on its head.
кувыр|о́к (**-ка́**) *м* somersault.

KEYWORD

куда́ *нареч* **1** (*вопросительное, относительное*) where; **куда́ ты положи́л мою́ ру́чку?** where did you put my pen?; **скажи́, куда́ ты идёшь** tell me where you are going **2** (*разг: для чего*) why; **куда́ мне сто́лько де́нег?** why would I want so much money? **3** (*+dat, разг: о невозможности чего-н*): **куда́ мне с ни́ми состяза́ться?** how can I compare with them? **4** (*+comparative; разг: гораздо*) much; **мой дом куда́ бо́льше** my house is much bigger.

куда́-либо *нареч* = **куда́-нибудь**.
куда́-нибудь *нареч* (*в вопросительных предложениях*) anywhere; (*в утвердительных предложениях*) somewhere; **Вы ~ съе́здили ле́том?** did you go anywhere in the summer?; **дава́й ~ пойдём** let's go somewhere.
куда́-то *нареч* somewhere; **он ~ ушёл** he has gone off somewhere.
куда́хтанье (**-я**) *ср* clucking.
куда́х|тать (**-чу, -чешь**) *несов неперех* to cluck.
куде́сник (**-а**) *м* sorcerer.
ку́др|и (**-е́й**) *мн* curls *мн*.
кудря́в|ый (**-, -а, -о**) *прил* (*волосы*) curly; (*человек*) curly-haired; (*дерево*) bushy; (*перен: слог*) flowery.
кузне́ц (**-а́**) *м* blacksmith.
кузне́чик (**-а**) *м* grasshopper.
кузне́чный *прил* blacksmith's; **кузне́чные меха́** bellows *мн*.
ку́зниц|а (**-ы**) *ж* smithy, forge.
ку́зов (**-а;** *nom pl* **-а́**) *м* (*АВТ*) back (*of a van, lorry etc*).
куй(те) *несов см* **кова́ть**.
кукаре́ка|ть (**-ю**) *несов неперех* to crow.
кукареку́ *межд* (*крик петуха*) cock-a-doodle-doo.
ку́киш (**-а**) *м* fig; **он показа́л мне ~** (*перен: разг*) ≈ he told me to get lost.
ку́к|ла (**-лы;** *gen pl* **-ол**) *ж* (*также перен*) doll; (*в театре*) puppet; **теа́тр ~ол** puppet theatre (*BRIT*) *или* theater (*US*).
кук|ова́ть (**-у́ю**) *несов неперех* to cuckoo; (*перен: разг*) to twiddle one's thumbs.
ку́кол *сущ см* **ку́кла**.
ку́кол|ка (**-ки;** *gen pl* **-ок**) *ж уменьш от* **ку́кла**; (*ЗООЛ*) pupa (*мн* pupae).
ку́кольный *прил* (*игрушечный*): ~ **до́мик** doll's house; **ку́кольный теа́тр** puppet theatre (*BRIT*) *или* theater (*US*).
ку́к|ситься (**-шусь, -сишься**) *несов возв* (*разг*) to sulk.
кукуру́з|а (**-ы**) *ж* (*БОТ*) maize; (*КУЛИН*) (sweet) corn.

кукуру́зный *прил* (*см сущ*) maize; corn.
куку́шк|а (**-и**) *ж* cuckoo.
ку́кшусь *несов см* **ку́кситься**.
кула́к (**-а́**) *м* fist; (*ИСТ*) kulak (*member of the land-owning peasant class, eradicated during collectivization*).
кула́чный *прил*: ~ **бой** fist fight.
кулебя́к|а (**-и**) *ж* pie made with meat, fish or rice.
кул|ёк (**-ька́**) *м* paper bag.
кули́к (**-а́**) *м* (*ЗООЛ*) wader.
кулина́р (**-а**) *м* master chef.
кулинари́|я (**-и**) *ж* (*приготовление пищи*) cookery; (*магазин*) ≈ delicatessen ♦ *собир* (*продукты*) cooked foods and groceries.
кулина́рный *прил* (*искусство*) culinary.
кули́с|а (**-ы**) *ж* (*обычно мн: ТЕАТР*) wing; **за ~ми** (*также перен*) backstage, behind the scenes.
кули́ч (**-а́**) *м* kulich (*Easter cake*).
кули́чки *нареч* (*разг*): **у чёрта на кули́чках** in the middle of nowhere; **к чёрту на ~** to the back of beyond.
куло́н (**-а**) *м* (*украшение*) pendant; (*ФИЗ*) coulomb.
кулуа́рный *прил* (*встречи, сделки*) backstage.
кулуа́р|ы (**-ов**) *мн* (*ПОЛИТ*) lobby *ед*; **в ~ах бесе́ды иду́т** behind-the-scene talks are currently in progress.
куль (**-я́**) *м* sack.
кулька́ *итп сущ см* **кулёк**.
кульминацио́нный *прил* climactic.
кульмина́ци|я (**-и**) *ж* (*АСТРОНОМИЯ*) culmination; (*перен*) high point, climax.
культ (**-а**) *м* (*служение божеству*) cult; (*совокупность обрядов: православной*) religion; (*перен: красоты, денег*) cult worship; **служи́тели ку́льта** church officials; **культ ли́чности** personality cult.
культиви́ровани|е (**-я**) *ср* cultivation.
культиви́р|овать (**-ую**) *несов перех* to cultivate.
ку́льтовый *прил* religious.
культу́р|а (**-ы**) *ж* (*также с.-х., БИО*) culture; (*разведение: льна итп*) cultivation, culture; (*быта*) high quality; ~ **труда́** work ethic.
культу́рен *прил см* **культу́рный**.
культури́зм (**-а**) *м* body building.
культури́ст (**-а**) *м* body builder.
культу́р|ный (**-ен, -на, -но**) *прил* cultural; (*no short form; растение*) cultivated.
кум (**-а;** *nom pl* **-овья́,** *gen pl* **-овьёв**) *м* godfather.
кум|а́ (**-ы́**) *ж* godmother.
кумачо́вый *прил* calico.
куми́р (**-а**) *м* (*также перен*) idol.
кумовство́ (**-а**) *ср* nepotism.
кумовь|я́ (**-ёв**) *мн от* **кум**.
кумы́с (**-а**) *м* fermented horse's milk.
куни́ц|а (**-ы**) *ж* marten.
купа́льник (**-а**) *м* swimming *или* bathing costume (*BRIT*), bathing suit (*US*).

купа́льный *прил*: ~ **костю́м** swimming *или* bathing costume (*BRIT*), bathing suit (*US*); ~ **сезо́н** swimming season.

купа́нь|е (-я) *ср* bathing; (*плавание*) swimming.

купа́ть (-ю; *perf* **вы́купать** *или* **искупа́ть)** *несов перех* to bath.

▶ **купа́ться** (*perf* **вы́купаться** *или* **искупа́ться)** *несов возв* to bathe; (*плавать*) to swim; (*в ванне*) to have a bath; **~ся** (*impf*) **в зо́лоте** to be rolling in money.

купе́ *ср нескл* compartment (*in railway carriage*).

купе́йный *прил*: ~ **ваго́н** Pullman (car).

купе́л|ь (-и) *ж* (*РЕЛ*) font.

купе́|ц (-ца́) *м* merchant.

купе́ческий (-ая, -ое, -ие) *прил* (*сословие*) merchant *опред*; (*перен: нравы*) vulgar.

купе́честв|о (-а) *ср собир* the merchants *мн*.

купи́рованный *прил* = **купе́йный**.

купи́ть (-лю́, -ишь; *impf* **покупа́ть)** *сов перех* to buy.

купле́т (-а) *м* couplet; *см также* **купле́ты**.

купле́т|ы (-ов) *мн* satirical song in couplet form.

куплю́ *сов см* **купи́ть**.

ку́пл|я (-и) *ж* purchase; **~-прода́жа** buying and selling.

ку́пол (-а; *nom pl* **-а́)** *м* cupola.

купо́н (-а) *м* (*ценных бумаг*) ticket; (*денежный знак*) coupon (*used as the Ukrainian currency*); **стричь** (*impf*) **~ы** to make easy money; **пода́рочный** ~ gift voucher.

купца́ *итп сущ см* **купе́ц**.

ку́пчий (-ая, -ее, -ие) *прил* (*также:* **~ая кре́пость**: *ЮР*) deed of purchase.

купчи́х|а (-и) *ж см* **купе́ц**.

купю́р|а (-ы) *ж* (*сокращение*) cut; (*ЭКОН*) denomination; **статья́ печа́тается без купю́р** the article is printed in full.

ку́р|а (-ы) *ж* (*разг*) chicken.

курага́ (-и́) *ж собир* dried apricots *мн*.

кура́ж|иться (-усь, -ишься) *несов возв*: ~ **над кем-н** to bully sb.

кура́нт|ы (-ов) *мн* chiming clock *ед*.

кура́тор (-а) *м* supervisor.

курга́н (-а) *м* (*могильник*) (burial) mound.

ку́рев|о (-а) *ср* (*разг*) smokes *мн*, fags *мн*.

куре́ни|е (-я) *ср* smoking.

кури́л|ка (-ки; *gen pl* **-ок)** *ж* (*разг*) smoking room.

кури́льщик (-а) *м* smoker.

кури́льщиц|а (-ы) *ж см* **кури́льщик**.

кури́ный *прил* (*яйцо*) hen's; (*бульон, перья*) chicken; **кури́ная слепота́** (*МЕД*) night blindness.

кури́тельный *прил*: ~ **таба́к** rolling tobacco; **кури́тельная ко́мната** smoking room.

кури́ть (-ю́, -ишь) *несов (не)перех* to smoke; **„~ запреща́ется"**, **„не ~"** "no smoking"; **„у нас не ку́рят"** "kindly refrain from smoking"

▶ **кури́ться** *несов возв* (*вулкан*) to smoke; (*вершины гор*) to be shrouded in mist.

ку́р|ица (-ицы; *nom pl* **ку́ры)** *ж* hen, chicken; (*мясо*) chicken; **~ам на смех** (*разг*) it's a

complete joke; **де́нег у неё ~ы не клюю́т** (*разг*) she's absolutely loaded.

ку́рка *сущ см* **куро́к**.

курно́с|ый (-, -а, -о) *прил* snub-nosed.

куро́к (-ка́) *м* hammer (*on gun*); **взводи́ть** (**взвести́** *perf*) ~ to cock a gun.

куроле́|сить (-шу, -сишь) *несов неперех* to play up.

куропа́т|ка (-ки; *gen pl* **-ок)** *ж* grouse.

куро́рт (-а) *м* (holiday) resort.

куро́ртный *прил* (*зона, город*) resort *опред*; **куро́ртный сезо́н** the holiday season.

курс (-а) *м* course; (*ПОЛИТ*) policy; (*КОММ*) exchange rate; (*ПРОСВЕЩ*) year (*of university studies*); **брать** (**взять** *perf*) ~ **на** +*acc* to set a course for; **идти́** (*impf*) **по ку́рсу** to be on (the right) course; **переходи́ть** (**перейти́** *perf*) **на четвёртый** ~ to go into the fourth year (*of university*); **быть** (*impf*) **в ку́рсе де́ла** to be up on what's going on; **входи́ть** (**войти́** *perf*) **в** ~ **чего́-н** to put o.s. in the picture about sth; **вводи́ть** (**ввести́** *perf*) **кого́-н в** ~ (**чего́-н**) to put sb in the picture about sth).

курса́нт (-а) *м* (*ВОЕН*) cadet.

курси́в (-а) *м* italics *мн*; **„~ мой"** "the italics are mine".

курси́вный *прил*: ~ **шрифт** italic font.

курси́р|овать (-ую) *несов неперех*: ~ **ме́жду** +*instr* ... **и** +*instr* ... (*самолёт, автобус*) to shuttle between ... and ...; (*судно*) to sail between ... and ...

курсов|о́й *прил*: **~а́я рабо́та** project; **~о́е собра́ние** student's year meeting; **~а́я ра́зница** (*КОММ*) difference in exchange rates.

ку́рсор (-а) *м* cursor.

ку́рт|ка (-ки; *gen pl* **-ок)** *ж* jacket.

курча́в|ый (-, -а, -о) *прил* (*волосы*) curly; (*человек, животное*) curly-haired.

ку́р|ы (-) *мн от* **ку́рица**.

курьёз (-а) *м* curious thing.

курьёзный (-ен, -на, -но) *прил* curious.

курье́р (-а) *м* messenger; (*дипломатический*) courier.

курье́рский (-ая, -ое, -ие) *прил*: ~ **отде́л** dispatch department; **курье́рский по́езд** express train.

куря́тин|а (-ы) *ж* chicken (*meat*).

куря́тник (-а) *м* chicken coop.

куса́ть (-ю) *несов перех* to bite; (*сахар, конфеты*) to crunch

▶ **куса́ться** *несов возв* (*животное*) to bite; (*растение*) to sting; (*разг: цены, налоги*) to hurt.

куса́ч|ки (-ек) *мн* wire cutters *мн*.

куска́ *итп сущ см* **кусо́к**.

кусков́ой *прил*: ~ **са́хар** lump sugar.

кусо́к (-ка́) *м* piece; ~ **са́хара** sugar lump; ~ **мы́ла** bar of soap; ~ **хле́ба** (*перен*) daily bread.

куст (-а́) *м* (*БОТ*) bush; **пря́таться** (**спря́таться** *perf*) **в ~ы́** (*перен*) to run for cover.

куста́рник (-а) *м* shrubbery ◆ *собир* bushes *мн*.

куста́рный *прил* handicraft *опред*; *(перен: методы, оборудование)* crude, primitive; ~ труд craftwork; **куста́рные изде́лия** handicrafts.

куста́р|ь (-я́) *м* craftsman *(мн* craftsmen).

кусти́ст|ый (-, -а, -о) *прил* bushy.

ку́та|ть (-ю; *perf* закута́ть) *несов перех (плечи, ноги итп)* to cover up; *(ребёнка)* to bundle up

▸ ку́таться *(perf* закута́ться) *несов возв:* ~ся в +*acc* to wrap o.s. up in.

кутёж (-а́) *м* drinking spree.

кутерьм|а́ (-ы́) *ж (разг)* mayhem, chaos.

ку|ти́ть (-чу́, -тишь) *несов неперех* to go on a drinking spree.

кату́з|ка (-ки; *gen pl* -ок) *ж (разг)* the slammer, the clink *(BRIT)*.

куха́р|ка (-ки; *gen pl* -ок) *ж* cook.

ку́х|ня (-ни; *gen pl* -онь) *ж (помещение)* kitchen; *(еда)* cooking; **ру́сская** ~ Russian cuisine.

кухо́нный *прил* kitchen *опред*.

ку́хонь *сущ см* ку́хня.

ку́ц|ый (-, -а, -о) *прил (собака)* with no tail; *(перен: программа, права)* limited.

ку́ч|а (-и) *ж (песка, листьев)* pile, heap; (+*gen*; *разг: денег, проблем)* heaps *или* loads of; **вали́ть** *(impf)* **всё в одну́** ~у to lump everything together.

кучев|о́й *прил:* ~ы́е облака́ cumulus (clouds *мн*).

ку́чер (-а; *nom pl* -а́) *м* coachman *(мн* coachmen).

кучу́ *несов см* кути́ть.

куш (-а) *м* jackpot; **срыва́ть (сорва́ть** *perf*) ~ to hit the jackpot.

куша́к (-а́) *м* sash.

ку́шанье (-ья; *gen pl* -ий) *ср* food.

ку́ша|ть (-ю; *perf* поку́шать *или* ску́шать) *несов перех* to eat; ~йте, пожа́луйста have something to eat.

кушё́т|ка (-ки; *gen pl* -ок) *ж* couch.

кюве́т (-а) *м* gutter.

~ Л, л ~

Л, л *сущ нескл* (*буква*) the 12th letter of the Russian alphabet.

л. *сокр* (= **лист**) f. (= *folio*).

лабири́нт (-а) *м* maze; (*перен*) labyrinth.

лабора́нт (-а) *м* (*в лаборатории*) lab technician; (*на кафедре*) secretary.

лабора́нт|ка (-ки; *gen pl* -ок) *ж см* **лабора́нт**.

лаборато́ри|я (-и) *ж* laboratory.

ла́в|а (-ы) *ж* lava; (*забой*) drift.

лава́нд|а (-ы) *ж* lavender.

лава́ш (-а) *м* lavash (*Caucasian flat bread*).

лави́н|а (-ы) *ж* (*также перен*) avalanche.

лави́р|овать (-ую; *perf* **слави́ровать**) *несов неперех* (*МОР*) to tack; (*перен*) to manoeuvre (*BRIT*), maneuver (*US*).

ла́в|ка (-ки; *gen pl* -ок) *ж* (*скамья*) bench; (*магазин*) shop.

ла́воч|ка (-ки; *gen pl* -ек) *ж уменьш от* **ла́вка**; (*перен: разг*) shady business.

ла́вочник (-а) *м* shopkeeper.

лавр (-а) *м* laurel; *см также* **ла́вры**.

ла́вр|а (-ы) *ж* monastery.

лавро́вый *прил* laurel; **лавро́вый лист** bay leaf.

ла́вр|ы (-ов) *мн* (*венок*) laurels *мн*; **пожина́ть** (*impf*) ~ to be crowned with laurels; **почи́ть** (*perf*) **на ~ах** to rest on one's laurels.

лавса́н (-а) *м* lavsan (*synthetic polyester fibre or fabric*).

ЛАГ *м сокр* (= **Ли́га ара́бских госуда́рств**) Arab League.

ла́герный *прил* camp *опред*.

ла́гер|ь (-я; *nom pl* -я́) *м* camp; (*nom pl* -и; *перен*) camp.

лагу́н|а (-ы) *ж* lagoon.

лад (-а; *loc sg* -у́, *nom pl* -ы́) *м* (*разг: гармония*) harmony; (*МУЗ: обычно мн: деление на грифе*) fret; (: *клавиша*) key; (: *строй*) mode; **быть** (*impf*) **не в ~а́х с** +*instr* to be at odds with; **на свой** ~ in one's own way; **на все ~ы** in all sorts of ways, every which way (*US*); **руга́ть** (*impf*) **кого́-н на все ~ы́** to call sb every name under the sun; **де́ло идёт на** ~ things are getting better.

ла́дан (-а) *м* incense; **дыша́ть** (*impf*) **на** ~ (*разг*) to be on one's last legs.

ла́ден *прил см* **ла́дный**.

ла́|дить (-жу, -дишь; *perf* **пола́дить**) *несов неперех*: ~ **с** +*instr* to get on (well) with

ла́|диться *несов возв* to go well.

ла́дно *част* (*разг*) O.K., all right; **пойдём в кино́ – ~** let's go to the cinema – O.K. *или* all right; ~ **тебе́!** (*разг: не стоит, не надо*) don't be silly!; ~ **тебе́ жа́ловаться/крича́ть** that's enough of your complaining/shouting; **да ~!** you don't say!

ла́д|ный (-ен, -на́, -но) *прил* (*разг: хорошо сложенный*) well-built; **у него́ ~ная фигу́ра** he's a fine figure of a man.

ла́дожск|ий (-ая, -ое, -ие) *прил*: **Л~ое о́зеро** Lake Ladoga.

ладо́н|ь (-и) *ж* (*АНАТ*) palm; **отсю́да Москва́ видна́ как на ~и** from here you can see Moscow clearly.

ладо́ш|и (-) *мн*: **бить в** ~ to clap one's hands; **хло́пать** (*impf*) **в** ~ to clap.

ладь|я́ (-и́; *gen pl* -е́й) *ж* (*ШАХМАТЫ*) rook, castle.

ЛАЗ (-а) *м сокр* = **Льво́вский авто́бусный заво́д**; (*автобус*) bus manufactured at the Lvov bus factory.

лаз (-а) *м* gap.

лазаре́т (-а) *м* (*ВОЕН*) field hospital.

ла́за|ть (-ю) *несов* = **ла́зить**.

лазе́й|ка (-йки; *gen pl* -ек) *ж* gap; (*перен: в правилах*) loophole.

ла́зер (-а) *м* laser.

ла́зерный *прил* laser *опред*; **ла́зерный при́нтер** laser printer.

ла́|зить (-жу, -зишь) *несов неперех* to climb; (*под стол, под кровать итп*) to crawl.

лазури́т (-а) *м* lapis lazuli.

лазу́рный *прил* azure, sky-blue.

лазу́р|ь (-и) *ж* azure.

ла́|й (-я) *м* barking.

ла́й|ка (-и) *ж* husky; (*кожа*) kid.

ла́йковый *прил* kid *опред*.

ла́йнер (-а) *м* liner.

лак (-а) *м* (*для ногтей, для пола*) varnish; (*для волос*) lacquer; **покрыва́ть** (**покры́ть** *perf*) **что-н ла́ком** to varnish sth.

лака́|ть (-ю) *несов перех* to lap up.

лаке́|й (-я) *м* (*слуга*) footman (*мн* footmen); (*подхалим*) lackey.

лакиро́ванный *прил* (*шкатулка*) lacquered; (*туфли*) patent-leather.

лакир|ова́ть (-у́ю; *perf* **отлакирова́ть**) *несов перех* (*изделие*) to lacquer; (*кожу*) to patent.

лакиро́в|ка (-и) *ж* (*изделия*) lacquer.

ла́кмусов|ый *прил*: ~**ая бума́га** litmus paper.
ла́ковый *прил* (*изделия*) lacquered; (*раствор, краски*) lacquer *опред*; **ла́ковая ко́жа** patent leather.
ла́ком|иться (-**люсь, -ишься**; *perf* **пола́комиться**) *несов неперех* (+*instr*) to feast on.
ла́ком|ка (-**ки**; *gen pl* -**ок**) *м/ж* (*любящий вкусное*) gourmet; **она́ настоя́щая ~а** (*сладкоежка*) she has a sweet tooth.
ла́комлюсь *несов см* **ла́комиться**.
ла́комок *сущ см* **ла́комка**.
ла́комый *прил* delicious; **ла́комый кусо́к** titbit (*BRIT*), tidbit (*US*).
лакони́зм (-**а**) *м* succinctness.
лакони́чно *нареч* laconically, succinctly.
лакони́чный *прил* (*речь*) laconic, succinct; (*формы здания, рисунок*) spare, austere.
лакто́з|а (-**ы**) *ж* lactose.
ла́м|а (-**ы**) *ж* (*ЗООЛ*) llama ♦ *м* (*РЕЛ*) lama.
Ла-Ма́нш (-**а**) *м* the (English) Channel.
ла́мп|а (-**ы**) *ж* (*осветительная, керосиновая*) lamp; (*ТЕХ*) tube; **ла́мпа дневно́го све́та** fluorescent light.
лампа́д|а (-**ы**) *ж* icon lamp.
лампа́с (-**а**) *м* (*обычно мн*) stripe (*down trouser leg*).
ла́мпоч|ка (-**ки**; *gen pl* -**ек**) *ж* lamp; (*для освещения*) light bulb; **ему́ всё до ~ки** (*разг*) he couldn't care less.
ланге́т (-**а**) *м* fillet steak.
ландша́фт (-**а**) *м* landscape.
ла́ндыш (-**а**) *м* lily of the valley.
ланоли́н (-**а**) *м* lanolin.
ланце́т (-**а**) *м* (*МЕД*) lancet.
лан|ь (-**и**) *ж* fallow deer.
Лао́с (-**а**) *м* Laos.
лао́сск|ий (-**ая, -ое, -ие**) *прил* Laotian.
ла́п|а (-**ы**) *ж* (*зверя*) paw; (*птицы*) foot; (*сосны, ёлки*) bough; (*якоря*) fluke; **попада́ть** (**попа́сть** *perf*) **кому́-н в ~ы** (*разг*) to fall into sb's clutches; **дава́ть** (**дать** *perf*) **кому́ в ~у** (*разг*) to give sb a backhander; **ходи́ть** (*impf*) **на за́дних ~х пе́ред кем-н** (*перен*: *разг*) to dance attendance on sb.
ла́п|оть (-**тя**; *nom pl* -**ти**, *gen pl* -**те́й**) *м* (*обычно мн*) bast shoe.
ла́поч|ка (-**ки**; *gen pl* -**ек**) *м/ж* (*разг*) dear, darling.
лапт|а́ (-**ы́**) *ж* lapta (*traditional Russian ball game*).
ла́птя *итп сущ см* **ла́поть**.
ла́пушк|а (-**и**) *ж* dear, darling.
лапш|а́ (-**и́**) *ж* noodles *мн*; (*суп*) noodle soup.
ларёк (-**ька́**) *м* stall.
лар|е́ц (-**ца́**) *м* (*шкатулка*) casket.
ларинги́т (-**а**) *м* laryngitis.
ларинголо́ги|я (-**и**) *ж* laryngology.
ларца́ *итп сущ см* **ларе́ц**.
лар|ь (-**я́**) *м* bin.
ларька́ *итп сущ см* **ларёк**.
ла́с|ка (-**ки**) *ж* tenderness; (*gen pl* -**ок**; *ЗООЛ*) weasel.
ласка́тельный *прил*: ~ **су́ффикс** (*ЛИНГ*) diminutive suffix (*denoting affection*).
ласка́|ть (-**ю**) *несов перех* (*ребёнка, девушку*) to caress; (*собаку*) to pet; ~ (*impf*) **слух/взор** to be pleasing to the ear/eye
▶ **ласка́ться** (*perf* **прилáска́ться**) *несов возв*: ~**ся к** +*dat* (*ребёнок*) to snuggle up to; (*кошка*) to rub up against; (*собака*) to fawn on.
ла́сков|ый (-, -**а, -о**) *прил* affectionate; (*перен*: *ветер, солнце итп*) gentle.
ла́сок *сущ см* **ла́ска**.
ласт (-**а**) *м* (*ЗООЛ, СПОРТ*: *обычно мн*) flipper.
ла́стик (-**а**) *м* (*разг*) rubber (*BRIT*), eraser.
ла́сточ|ка (-**ки**; *gen pl* -**ек**) *ж* swallow; **городска́я/берегова́я** ~ house/sand martin.
лат (-**а**) *м* lat (*Latvian currency unit*).
лата́|ть (-**ю**; *perf* **залата́ть**) *несов перех* to patch.
латви́йск|ий (-**ая, -ое, -ие**) *прил* Latvian.
Ла́тви|я (-**и**) *ж* Latvia.
лати́нск|ий (-**ая, -ое, -ие**) *прил* Latin; ~ **язы́к** Latin.
ла́т|ка (-**ки**; *gen pl* -**ок**) *ж* (*разг*) patch.
лату́н|ь (-**и**) *ж* brass.
ла́т|ы (-) *мн* armour *ед* (*BRIT*), armor *ед* (*US*).
латы́н|ь (-**и**) *ж* Latin.
латы́ш (-**á**) *м* Latvian.
латы́ш|ка (-**ки**; *gen pl* -**ек**) *ж см* **латы́ш**.
латы́шск|ий (-**ая, -ое, -ие**) *прил* Latvian; ~ **язы́к** Latvian.
лауреа́т (-**а**) *м* winner (*of an award*).
лафа́ *как сказ* (*разг*): **нам здесь** ~ we've got it easy here.
ла́цкан (-**а**) *м* lapel.
лачу́г|а (-**и**) *ж* hovel.
ла́я|ть (-**ю**; *perf* **проля́ять**) *несов неперех* to bark.
лба *итп сущ см* **лоб**.
ЛГ *ж сокр* (= „Литерату́рная газе́та") "Literary Gazette".
лгать (**лгу, лжёшь** *итп*, **лгут**; *perf* **солга́ть** или **налга́ть**) *несов неперех* to lie.
лгун (-**á**) *м* liar.
лгу́нь|я (-**и**; *gen pl* -**ий**) *ж см* **лгун**.
ЛДПР *ж сокр* = Либера́льно-демократи́ческая па́ртия Росси́и.
лебед|а́ (-**ы́**) *ж* (*БОТ*) orache.
лебедёнок (-**ёнка**; *nom pl* -**я́та**, *gen pl* -**я́т**) *м* cygnet.
лебеди́н|ый *прил* swan *опред*; (*перен*: *шея*) swanlike; (: *поступь*) graceful; ~**ая ста́я** flock of swans; **лебеди́ная пе́сня** swan song.
лебёд|ка (-**ки**; *gen pl* -**ок**) *ж* winch.
лебед|ь (-**я**; *gen pl* -**ей**) *м* swan.
лебедя́та *итп сущ см* **лебедёнок**.
лебези́ть (-**жу́, -зи́шь**) *несов неперех*: ~ (**пе́ред**

+*instr*) (*разг*) to fawn (on).

лебя́ж|ий (-ья, -ье, -ьи) *прил*: ~ **пух** swan's-down.

лев (**льва**) *м* lion; (*созвездие*): **Л~** Leo.

левко́|й (-я) *м* (*БОТ*) stock.

левосторо́нн|ий (-яя, -ее, -ие) *прил* on the left; **в Великобрита́нии ~ее движе́ние** in Britain they drive on the left.

левш|а́ (-и́; *gen pl* -е́й) *м/ж* left-handed person; **он/она́** ~ he/she is left-handed.

ле́в|ый *прил* left, left-hand; (*партия, взгляды*) left-wing; **~ая рабо́та** (*разг*) moonlighting.

лёг *итп сов см* **лечь**.

лега́в|ый (-ого; *decl like adj*) *м type of gun dog.*

лега́лен *прил см* **лега́льный**.

легализи́р|овать (-ую) (*не*)*сов перех* to legalize.

лега́л|ьный (-ен, -ьна, -ьно) *прил* legal.

леге́нд|а (-ы) *ж* legend; (*перен*) fairy story.

легенда́р|ный (-ен, -на, -но) *прил* legendary.

легио́н (-а) *м* legion.

леги́рованн|ый *прил*: **~ая сталь** steel alloy.

лёг|кий (-кая, -кое, -кие; -ок, -ка́, -ко́) *прил* (*нетяжёлый*) light; (*нетрудный, несерьёзный*) easy; (*боль, насморк*) slight; (*фигура*) graceful; (*характер, человек*) easy-going; **у него́ сли́шком ~кое отноше́ние к жи́зни** he doesn't take life seriously enough; **у него́ ~кая рука́** he brings good luck; **он нашёл рабо́ту с мое́й ~кой руки́** he found work thanks to me; **он ~ок на подъём** (*разг*) he doesn't take much persuading; **~ок на поми́не!** (*разг*) talk of the devil!; **лёгкая атле́тика** athletics (*BRIT*), track-and-field (*US*); **лёгкая промы́шленность** light industry.

легко́ *нареч* easily; ~ **сказа́ть** (*разг*) easier said than done; **мне здесь ~** I feel at ease here; **это ~** it's easy.

легкоатле́т (-а) *м* athlete (*in track and field events*).

легкоатле́т|ка (-ки; *gen pl* -ок) *ж см* **легкоатле́т**.

легкове́р|ный (-ен, -на, -но) *прил* gullible, credulous.

легкове́с|ный (-ен, -на, -но) *прил* superficial.

легков|о́й *прил*: **~а́я маши́на, ~ автомоби́ль** car, automobile (*US*).

легкову́ш|ка (-ки; *gen pl* -ек) *ж* (*разг*) motor (*BRIT*), auto (*US*).

лёгк|ое (-ого; *decl like adj*) *ср* (*обычно мн*) lung.

легкомы́слен|ный (-, -на, -но) *прил* (*человек*) frivolous; (*поступок*) thoughtless; (*отношение*) frivolous, flippant.

легкомы́сли|е (-я) *ср* (*человека*) frivolity; (*поступка*) thoughtlessness.

легкопла́в|кий (-кая, -кое, -кие; -ок, -ка, -ко) *прил* fusible.

лёгкост|ь (-и) *ж* (*походки, веса*) lightness; (*задания*) simplicity, easiness; (*характера*) easy-going nature; **у него́ мно́го друзе́й благодаря́ ~и его́ хара́ктеру** he has many friends thanks to his easy-going nature.

лёгок *прил см* **лёгкий**.

лёгочный *прил* pulmonary, lung *опред*; ~ **больно́й** patient with a pulmonary *или* lung condition.

ле́гче *сравн прил от* **лёгкий** ♦ *сравн нареч от* **легко́** ♦ *как сказ*: **больно́му сего́дня ~** the patient is feeling better today.

лёд (**льда**; *loc sg* **льду**) *м* ice; ~ **тро́нулся** (*перен*) things are moving now.

ледене́|ть (-ю; *perf* **заледене́ть** *или* **оледене́ть**) *несов неперех* to freeze; (*человек, руки*) to be freezing; **он оледене́л от стра́ха** fear made his blood run cold.

ледене́|ц (-ца́) *м* fruit drop.

ледене́|ть (*3sg* -́йт, *3pl* -́ят) *несов перех* to freeze; **у́жас ~йт** (**его́**) **кровь** terror makes his blood run cold.

леденца́ *итп сущ см* **ледене́ц**.

ледене́|щий (-щая, -ее, -ие) *прил* (*ветер, вода*) icy; (*перен: ужас, страх*) chilling.

ле́ди *ж нескл* lady.

ледни́к (-а́) *м* glacier.

ледняко́вый *прил* glacial.

ледо́вый *прил* ice *опред*.

ледоко́л (-а) *м* icebreaker.

ледору́б (-а) *м* ice axe.

ледохо́д (-а) *м breaking up and drifting of ice on rivers in spring.*

ледян́о́й *прил* (*глыба, покров*) ice *опред*; (*ветер, вода, взгляд*) icy.

ле́ек *сущ см* **ле́йка**.

лежа́к (-а́) *м* lounger.

лежа́лый *прил* (*хлеб*) stale; (*товар*) old.

лежа́|ть (-у́, -́ишь) *несов неперех* (*человек, животное*) to lie; (*предмет, вещи: на столе, на полке*) to be (lying); (: **в я́щике, в шкафу** *итп*) to be; ~ (*impf*) **в больни́це** to be in hospital; **на нём ~ат забо́ты о семье́** he is responsible for looking after his family; (**у меня́**) **душа́ не ~йт к э́той рабо́те** my heart's not in this work; (**у меня́**) **душа́ не ~йт к нему́** I don't feel very well disposed towards him.

лежа́|чий (-ая, -ее, -ие) *прил* lying; ~ **больно́й** bedridden patient; **рабо́та – не бей ~его** (*разг*) it's a cushy job.

ле́жбище (-а) *ср* rookery (*of seals etc*).

лежебо́к|а (-и) *м/ж* (*разг*) couch potato.

лез *итп несов см* **лезть**.

ле́зви|е (-я) *ср* blade.

лез|ть (-у, -ешь; *pt* -, -ла, -ло) *несов неперех* (*выпадать: волосы, шерсть*) to fall out; (*проникать куда-н*): ~ **в** +*acc* to climb in(to); ~ (*impf*) **на** +*acc* to climb (up); ~ (*impf*) **в карма́н** (*разг*) to reach into one's pocket; ~ (*impf*) **в чужи́е дела́** (*разг*) to poke one's nose into other people's business; ~ (*impf*) **в разгово́р** (*разг*) to butt into a conversation; ~ (*impf*) **кому́-н на глаза́** (*разг*) to hang around sb.

лей *несов см* **лить** ♦ (**ле́я**) *м* lay (*Moldavian currency unit*).

лейбори́ст (-а) *м* Labour party member.

лейбори́ст|**кий** (-ая, -ое, -ие) *прил* Labour.
ле́й|**ка** (-йки; *gen pl* -ек) *ж* watering can.
лейко́з (-а) *м* leukaemia (*BRIT*), leukemia (*US*).
лейкопла́стыр|**ь** (-я) *м* sticking plaster (*BRIT*), adhesive tape (*US*).
лейкоци́т (-а) *м* (*обычно мн*) leucocyte.
Ле́йпциг (-а) *м* Leipzig.
ле́йте *несов см* лить.
лейтена́нт (-а) *м* lieutenant.
лейтмоти́в (-а) *м* (*также перен*) leitmotif.
лека́л|**о** (-а) *ср* French curve.
лека́рственный *прил* medicinal;
лека́рственная фо́рма medicine.
лека́рств|**о** (-а) *ср* medicine; ~ **от** +*gen* medicine for; ~ **от ка́шля** cough medicine; **принима́ть** (**приня́ть** *perf*)/**прописывать** (**прописа́ть** *perf*) ~ to take/prescribe medicine.
ле́кси|**ка** (-и) *ж* vocabulary.
лексико́граф (-а) *м* lexicographer.
лексикографи́ческ|**ий** (-ая, -ое, -ие) *прил* lexicographical.
лексикогра́фи|**я** (-и) *ж* lexicography.
лексиколо́ги|**я** (-и) *ж* lexicology.
лексико́н (-а) *м* vocabulary.
ле́ктор (-а) *м* lecturer.
лекцио́нный *прил* lecture *опред*; ~ **курс** course of lectures.
ле́кци|**я** (-и) *ж* lecture.
леле́|**ять** (-ю; *perf* **взлеле́ять**) *несов перех* (*также перен*) to cherish.
ле́мех (-а) *м* ploughshare (*BRIT*), plowshare (*US*).
лему́р (-а) *м* lemur.
лён (**льна**) *м* (*БОТ*) flax; (*ткань*) linen.
лени́вый (-, -а, -о) *прил* lazy.
Ленингра́д (-а) *м* Leningrad.
ленини́зм (-а) *м* Leninism.
лен|**и́ться** (-ю́сь, -ишься; *perf* **полени́ться**) *несов возв* to be lazy; ~ (**полени́ться** *perf*) +*infin* to be too lazy to do.
ле́нт|**а** (-ы) *ж* (*в косе, на шляпе*) ribbon; (*изоляционная, магнитная*) tape; (*фильм*) film.
ле́нточный *прил*: ~ **червь** tapeworm; ~ **транспортёр** conveyor belt.
лентя́ек *сущ см* **лентя́йка**.
лентя́|**й** (-я) *м* lazybones.
лентя́|**йка** (-йки; *gen pl* -ек) *ж см* **лентя́й**.
лентя́йнича|**ть** (-ю) *несов неперех* (*разг*) to lounge about.
лен|**ь** (-и) *ж* laziness ◆ *как сказ*: **ему́** ~ **учи́ться/рабо́тать** he can't be bothered studying/working; (**все**) **кому́ не** ~ (*разг*) anyone who feels like it.
леопа́рд (-а) *м* leopard.
лепест|**о́к** (-ка́) *м* petal.
ле́пет (-а) *м* babble; **де́тский** ~ (*перен*) drivel.
лепёш|**ка** (-ки; *gen pl* -ек) *ж* flat bread.
леп|**и́ть** (-лю́, -ишь; *perf* **вы́лепить**) *несов перех* (*из глины, из пластилина*) to model; (*perf* **слепи́ть**; *соты, гнёзда*) to build

▶ **леп**|**и́ться** *несов возв* (*на деревьях, на склонах*) to cling.
ле́п|**ка** (-и) *ж* modelling (*BRIT*), modeling (*US*).
лепл|**ю́**(**сь**) *несов см* **лепи́ть**(**ся**).
лепно́й *прил* modelled (*BRIT*), modeled (*US*); (*потолок*) moulded (*BRIT*), molded (*US*).
ле́пт|**а** (-ы) *ж* contribution; **вноси́ть** (**внести́** *perf*) **свою́** ~**у** (**во что-н**) to do one's bit (for sth); (*внести деньги*) to make a contribution (to sth).
лес (-а; *loc sg* -**у́**, *nom pl* -**а́**) *м* (*большой*) forest; (*небольшой*) wood ◆ **собир** (*материал*) timber (*BRIT*), lumber (*US*); **кто в** ~, **кто по дрова́** at sixes and sevens; *см также* **леса́**.
лес|**а́** (-о́в) *мн* (*СТРОИТ*) scaffolding *ед*.
лесбия́н|**ка** (-ки; *gen pl* -ок) *ж* lesbian.
леси́стый (-, -а, -о) *прил* wooded.
ле́ск|**а** (-и) *ж* fishing line.
лесни́к (-а́) *м* forester.
лесни́честв|**о** (-а) *ср* (*участок леса*) area of forest; (*учреждение*) ≈ forestry commission.
лесни́чий (-его; *decl like adj*) *м* forest ranger.
лесно́й *прил* (*см сущ*) forest *опред*; woodland *опред*.
лесово́дств|**о** (-а) *ср* forestry.
лесозагото́в|**ка** (-ки; *gen pl* -ок) *ж* (*обычно мн*) logging *ед*.
лесозащи́тн|**ый** *прил*: ~**ая зо́на** shelter belt (*of trees*).
лесоматериа́л (-а) *м* (*обычно мн*) timber *только ед* (*BRIT*), lumber *только ед* (*US*).
лесонасажде́ни|**е** (-я) *ср* (*искусственный лес*) plantation; (*разведение леса*) afforestation.
лесопа́рк (-а) *м* woodland park.
лесопи́л|**ка** (-и) *ж* (*разг*) sawmill.
лесопромы́шленност|**ь** (-и) *ж сокр* (= *лесна́я промы́шленность*) timber (*BRIT*) *или* lumber (*US*) industry.
лесопромы́шленный *прил* timber-industry *опред* (*BRIT*), lumber-industry *орпед* (*US*).
лесоразрабо́т|**ки** (-ок) *мн* timber (*BRIT*) *или* lumber (*US*) processing.
лесору́б (-а) *м* lumberjack.
лесосе́|**ка** (-и) *ж* felling area.
лесоспла́в (-а) *м* timber rafting.
лесосте́п|**ь** (-и) *ж* forest-steppe (*area in which forest and steppe are mixed*).
ле́стен *прил см* **ле́стный**.
ле́стни|**ца** (-ы) *ж* (*лестничная клетка*) staircase; (*ступени*) stairs *мн*; (*переносная*) ladder; (*стремянка*) stepladder; **служе́бная** ~ career ladder.
ле́стнич|**ный** *прил*: ~**ая площа́дка** landing; ~ **пролёт** stairway; ~**ая кле́тка** stairwell.
ле́ст|**ный** (-ен, -на, -но) *прил* flattering.
лест|**ь** (-и) *ж* flattery.
лёт (-а) *м*: **на лету́** in flight; (*перен: понима́ть, усва́ивать*) very quickly; **он по́нял всё с** ~**у** (*разг*) he understood everything in a flash.

летá (лет) *мн см* **год**; (*возраст*): **скóлько Вам лет?** how old are you?; **емý 16 лет** he is 16 (years old); **он в ~х** he is getting on; **он одни́х лет со мной** he is the same age as me.

летáльный (-ен, -ьна, -ьно) *прил* fatal; **~ьная дóза** lethal dose.

летарги́ческий (-ая, -ое, -ие) *прил* lethargic.

летáтельный *прил* flying *опред*.

летáть (-ю) *несов неперех* to fly.

летéть (-чý, -ти́шь) *несов неперех* to fly; (*перен: мчаться*) to fly, rush; (*perf* **полетéть**; *разг*): **~ с** +*gen* (*со стула*) to fall off; (*с лестницы*) to fall down; **врéмя ~ти́т** time flies; **все нáши плáны полетéли** (*разг*) all our plans were dashed.

лéтний (-яя, -ее, -ие) *прил* summer *опред*.

лéтный *прил*: **~ая погóда** good weather for flying; **лёное пóле** airfield; **лёная шкóла** flying school.

лéто (-а) *ср* summer; **скóлько лет, скóлько зим!** it's been ages!

летопи́сец (-ца) *м* chronicler.

лéтопись (-и) *ж* chronicle.

летосчислéние (-я) *ср* calendar.

летýчек *сущ см* **летýчка**.

летýчий (-ая, -ее, -ие) *прил* (*газ, масло*) volatile; (*семена*) winged; (*песок*) shifting; (*перен: собрание, разговор*) brief; **летýчая мышь** bat.

летýчка (-ки; *gen pl* -ек) *ж* (*разг: собрание*) brief meeting; (: *листок*) leaflet.

лётчик (-а) *м* pilot; **~-испытáтель** test pilot; **~-истреби́тель** fighter pilot.

лётчица (-ы) *ж см* **лётчик**.

лéчащий (-ая, -ее, -ие) *прил*: **~ врач** ≈ consultant-in-charge (*BRIT*), ≈ attending physician (*US*).

лечéбница (-ы) *ж* clinic.

лечéбный *прил* (*учреждение*) medical; (*свойства, трава*) medicinal; (*грязь*) medicated; **у негó богáтая ~ая прáктика** he has extensive clinical experience; **~ая гимнáстика** therapeutic exercise; **лечéбное срéдство** medication.

лечéние (-я) *ср* (*раненных, детей*) treatment; (*от простуды, от туберкулёза итп*) cure.

лечи́ть (-ý, -ишь) *несов от* **вы́лечить** ♦ *перех* to treat; (*больного*): **~ когó-н от** +*gen* to treat sb for

▶ **лечи́ться** *несов от* **вы́лечиться** ♦ *возв* to undergo treatment.

лечý *несов см* **летéть**.

лечь (*ля́гу, ля́жешь итп, ля́гут; pt* **лёг, леглá, легло́**, *imper* **ля́г(те)**, *impf* **ложи́ться**) *сов неперех* (*на землю, на диван итп*) to lie down; (*пойти спать*) to go to bed; (*снег*) to fall; (*перен*): **~ на** +*acc* (*ответственность, заботы*) to fall on; **ложи́ться** (**~** *perf*) **в больни́цу** to be in hospital; **ложи́ться** (**~** *perf*) **в дрейф** to drift.

лéший (-его; *decl like adj*) *м* wood goblin.

лещ (-á) *м* bream.

лженаýка (-и) *ж* pseudoscience.

лжесвидéтель (-я) *м* perjurer.

лжесвидéтельница (-ы) *ж см* **лжесвидéтель**.

лжесвидéтельство (-а) *ср* perjury.

лжесвидéтельствовать (-ую) *несов неперех* to commit perjury.

лжец (-á) *м* liar.

лжи *итп сущ см* **ложь**.

лжи́вость (-и) *ж* falseness.

лжи́вый (-, -а, -о) *прил* (*человек*) deceitful; (*улыбка, заверения*) false.

ли *част* (*в вопросе*) **зна́ешь ~ ты, что ...** do you know that ...; (*в косвенном вопросе*): **спроси́, смóжет ~ он нам помóчь** ask if he can help us ♦ *союз*: **придёт ~, не придёт, не вáжно** it's not important if he comes or not; **онá краси́ва, не так ~?** she's beautiful, isn't she?; **они́ бы́ли прáвы, не так ~?** they were right, weren't they?

лиáна (-ы) *ж* (*БОТ: растение*) liana.

либерáл (-а) *м* Liberal; (*о терпимом человеке*) liberal.

либерáлен *прил см* **либерáльный**.

либерализáция (-и) *ж* liberalization.

либерали́зм (-а) *м* liberalism; (*с бездельниками, с подчинёнными итп*) tolerance.

либерáльничать (-ю) *несов неперех*: **~ с** +*instr* (*с подчинёнными*) to fraternize with; (*с бездельниками*) to connive at.

либерáльный (-ен, -ьна, -ьно) *прил* liberal; (*no short form; партия*) Liberal.

ли́бо *союз* (*или*) or; **~ я, ~ он** it's either me or him.

либретти́ст (-а) *м* librettist.

либрéтто *ср нескл* libretto.

Ливáн (-а) *м* (the) Lebanon.

ливáнский (-ая, -ое, -ие) *прил* Lebanese.

ли́вень (-ня) *м* (*дождь*) downpour; (*перен: огня, свинца*) shower.

ли́вер (-а) *м* offal.

ли́верный *прил*: **~ая колбасá** *sausage made with offal*.

Ливерпýль (-я) *м* Liverpool.

ли́вневый *прил*: **~ дождь** downpour; **~ые вóды** rainwater.

ли́вня *итп сущ см* **ли́вень**.

ливрéя (-и) *ж* livery.

ли́га (-и) *ж* (*ПОЛИТ, СПОРТ*) league.

лигатýра (-ы) *ж* (*МЕД, ЛИНГ*) ligature.

ли́дер (-а) *м* leader.

ли́дерство (-а) *ср* leadership.

лиди́ровать (-ую) *несов неперех* to be in the lead, lead.

лизáть (-жý, -жешь) *несов перех* (*тарелку, мороженое*) to lick; (*подлеж: пламя, волны*) to lap.

ли́зинг (-а) *м* leasing.

лизнýть (-ý, -ёшь) *сов перех* to lick.

лик (-а) *м* countenance.

ликбéз (-а) *м сокр* (*ист*: = **ликвидáция**

безгра́мотности) campaign against illiteracy; (*перен: обучение элементарному*) basic teaching.

ликвида́тор (**-а**) *м* (*пожара, последствий аварии*) relief worker; (*комм*) liquidator.

ликвида́ци|я (**-и**) *ж* (*также экон*) liquidation; (*оружия*) destruction; **доброво́льная ~** (*экон*) voluntary liquidation.

ликвиди́р|овать (**-ую**) (*не*)*сов перех* (*оружие*) to destroy; (*фирму, дела*) to liquidate

▶ **ликвиди́роваться** (*не*)*сов возв* (*экон*: *фирма, трест итп*) to be liquidated.

ликви́дност|ь (**-и**) *ж* liquidity.

ликви́дны|й *прил*: **~ые акти́вы** или **сре́дства** liquid assets.

ликви́ды (**-ов**) *мн* liquid assets *мн*.

ликёр (**-а**) *м* liqueur.

ликёро-во́дочный *прил*: **~ заво́д** distillery.

ликова́ни|е (**-я**) *ср* rejoicing.

лик|ова́ть (**-у́ю**) *несов неперех* to be elated.

лилипу́т (**-а**) *м* midget.

лилипу́т|ка (**-ки**; *gen pl* **-ок**) *ж см* **лилипу́т**.

ли́ли|я (**-и**) *ж* lily.

лило́вый *прил* purple.

лима́н (**-а**) *м* mud flats *мн*.

лими́т (**-а**) *м* (*на электроэнергию, на бензин*) quota; (*цен*) limit.

лимити́р|овать (**-ую**) (*не*)*сов перех* (*потребление, импорт*) to limit; (*цены*) to cap.

лими́тчик (**-а**) *м* (*разг*) *person who holds a temporary residence permit issued in connection with work.*

лимо́н (**-а**) *м* (*дерево*) lemon tree; (*плод*) lemon; **он как вы́жатый ~** he's completely washed out.

лимона́д (**-а**) *м* lemonade; (*разг: любой газированный напиток*) fizzy drink.

лимо́нный *прил* lemon; **лимо́нная кислота́** citric acid.

лимузи́н (**-а**) *м* limousine.

лимфати́ческ|ий (**-ая, -ое, -ие**) *прил* lymphatic.

лингафо́нный *прил*: **~ кабине́т** language laboratory.

лингви́ст (**-а**) *м* linguist.

лингви́стик|а (**-и**) *ж* linguistics.

лингвисти́ческ|ий (**-ая, -ое, -ие**) *прил* linguistic.

лине́|йка (**-йки**; *gen pl* **-ек**) *ж* (*линия*) line; (*инструмент*) ruler; (*шеренга*) ≈ assembly; **тетра́дь в ~йку** lined notebook.

лине́йны|й *прил* (*расположение, построение*) linear; **~ солда́т** soldier of the line; **~ые ме́ры** linear measures; **лине́йные войска́** regular forces; **лине́йный кре́йсер** battle cruiser.

ли́нз|а (**-ы**) *ж* lens.

ли́ни|я (**-и**) *ж* line; (*перен: партийная, профсоюзная*) policy, line; **по ~и** +*gen* in the line of; **вести́** (*impf*) или **проводи́ть** (*impf*) **~ю**

на +*acc* to pursue a policy of; **проводи́ть** (**провести́** *perf*) **~ю** to draw a line; **вести́** (*impf*) или **гнуть** (*impf*) **свою́ ~ю** (*разг*) to have one's own way; **желе́знодоро́жная ~** railway (*BRIT*) или railroad (*US*) track; **возду́шная ~** airway; **морска́я ~** sea route; **трамва́йная ~** tramway; **ли́ния фро́нта** (*ВОЕН*) front line; **ли́ния воро́т** goal line.

линко́р (**-а**) *м сокр* (= **лине́йный кора́бль**) destroyer.

лино́ванный *прил* lined, ruled.

лин|ова́ть (**-у́ю**; *perf* **разлинова́ть**) *несов перех* to rule.

лино́леум (**-а**) *м* linoleum.

линч|ева́ть (**-у́ю**) (*не*)*сов перех* to lynch.

линя́лый *прил* discoloured (*BRIT*), discolored (*US*).

линя́|ть (*3sg* **-ет**, *3pl* **-ют**, *perf* **полиня́ть**) *несов неперех* to run (*colour*); (*perf* **облиня́ть**; *животные*) to moult (*BRIT*), molt (*US*).

Лио́н (**-а**) *м* Lyon.

ли́п|а (**-ы**) *ж* (*дерево*) lime (tree); (*разг*: *фальшивка*) fake.

ли́п|кий (**-кая, -кое, -кие; -ок, -ка́, -ко**) *прил* sticky.

ли́п|нуть (**-ну, -нешь**; *pt* **-, -ла, -ло**, *perf* **прили́пнуть**) *несов неперех* (*грязь, тесто*) to stick; (*перен: человеку*) to cling.

ли́повый *прил* (*цвет, лист*) lime; (*из липы*) lime-blossom *опред*; (*разг: фальшивый*) forged.

ли́пок *прил см* **ли́пкий**.

липу́ч|ка (**-ки**; *gen pl* **-ек**) *ж* (*разг: липкая лента*) sticky tape; (: *застёжка*) Velcro® fastening.

ли́р|а (**-ы**) *ж* (*МУЗ*) lyre; (*денежная единица*) lira.

лири́зм (**-а**) *м* lyricism.

ли́рик (**-а**) *м* lyric poet.

ли́рик|а (**-и**) *ж* lyric poetry.

лири́чен *прил см* **лири́чный**.

лири́ческ|ий (**-ая, -ое, -ие**) *прил* lyrical.

лири́чны|й (**-ен, -на, -но**) *прил* lyrical.

лис (**-а**) *м* (male) fox, dog fox.

лис|а́ (**-ы́**; *nom pl* **-ы**) *ж* fox; (*перен: хитрый человек*) sly fox.

лис|ёнок (**-ёнка**; *nom pl* **-я́та**, *gen pl* **-я́т**) *м* fox cub.

ли́с|ий (**-ья, -ье, -ьи**) *прил* (*след, нора*) fox's; (*шуба, воротник, горжетка*) fox-fur.

лиси́ц|а (**-ы**) *ж* vixen.

лиси́ч|ка (**-ки**; *gen pl* **-ек**) *ж уменьш от* **лиса́**; (*гриб*) chanterelle.

лист (**-а́**; *nom pl* **-ья**) *м* (*растения, дерева*) leaf; (*nom pl* **-ы́**; *бумаги, железа*) sheet; **исполни́тельный ~** writ of execution; **опро́сный ~** questionnaire.

листа́|ть (**-ю**) *несов перех* (*страницы*) to turn; **~** (*impf*) **кни́гу** to leaf through a book.

листв|а́ (**-ы́**) *ж собир* foliage, leaves *мн*.

ли́ственниц|**а** (-ы) *ж* larch.
ли́ственный *прил* deciduous.
листка́ *итп сущ см* **листо́к**.
листо́в|**ка** (-ки; *gen pl* -ок) *ж* leaflet.
листово́й *прил* (сталь, железо) sheet *опред*;
(табак) leaf *опред*.
листо́вок *сущ см* **листо́вка**.
лист|**о́к** (-ка́) *м* (бумаги) sheet; (бланк:
контрольный, техосмотра) certificate; **листо́к
нетрудоспосо́бности** disability certificate.
листопа́д (-а) *м* fall of leaves.
ли́стья *итп сущ см* **лист**.
лися́та *итп сущ см* **лисёнок**.
лит (-а) *м* lit (*Lithuanian currency unit*).
лита́вр|**ы** (-) *мн* kettledrum *ед*; **бить** (*impf*) **в ~**
(перен: торжествовать) to sound the
trumpets.
Литв|**а́** (-ы́) *ж* Lithuania.
лите́йный *прил*: **~ цех** foundry.
лите́йщик (-а) *м* foundry worker.
ли́тер|**а** (-ы) *ж* (*типог*) type.
литера́тор (-а) *м* literary man.
литерату́р|**а** (-ы) *ж* literature; (также:
худо́жественная **~**) fiction.
литерату́рный *прил* literary; **литерату́рный
язы́к** literary language.
литературове́д (-а) *м* literary critic.
литературове́дени|**е** (-я) *ср* literary criticism.
литературове́дческ|**ий** (-ая, -ое, -ие) *прил*
literary.
ли́терный *прил* (с цифрой) lettered; **~ набо́р**
typesetting.
ли́тий (-я) *м* lithium.
лито́в|**ец** (-ца) *м* Lithuanian.
лито́в|**ка** (-ки; *gen pl* -ок) *ж см* **лито́вец**.
лито́вск|**ий** (-ая, -ое, -ие) *прил* Lithuanian; **~
язы́к** Lithuanian.
лито́вца *итп сущ см* **лито́вец**.
литографи́ческ|**ий** (-ая, -ое, -ие) *прил*
lithographic.
литогра́фи|**я** (-и) *ж* (*искусство*) lithograph;
(*типог*) lithography.
литой *прил* (*ТЕХ*) moulded (*BRIT*), molded (*US*),
cast; **литое изде́лие** cast.
литр (-а) *м* litre (*BRIT*), liter (*US*).
литро́вый *прил* (бутылка, фляга итп) (one-)
litre (*BRIT*), (one-)liter (*US*).
литурги́|**я** (-и) *ж* liturgy.
лить (лью, льёшь; *pt* лил, лила́, ли́ло) *несов
перех* (воду) to pour; (слёзы) to shed; (*ТЕХ*:
детали, изделия) to cast, mould (*BRIT*), mold
(*US*) ♦ *неперех* (вода, дождь) to pour; **дождь
льёт как из ведра́** it's pouring (down)
▶ **ли́ться** *несов возв* (вода) to pour; (перен:
звуки) to float; (: свет) to flood.
лить|**ё** (-я́) *ср* (действие: деталей) casting,
moulding (*BRIT*), molding (*US*) ♦ *собир* (литые
изделия) casts *мн*.
лиф (-а) *м* bodice.
лифт (-а) *м* lift.
лифтёр (-а) *м* lift operator.
лифтёрш|**а** (-и) *ж см* **лифтёр**.

ли́фчик (-а) *м* bra.
лиха́ч (-а́) *м* (*разг*) reckless driver.
лиха́честв|**о** (-а) *ср* (при вождении) reckless
driving; (в поведении) recklessness.
лихв|**а́** (-ы́) *ж*: **он отплати́л мне с ~о́й за мо́ю
доброту́** he more than repaid me for my
kindness; **тебе́ вре́мени/де́нег хва́тит с ~о́й**
you've got more than enough time/money.
ли́х|**о** (-а) *ср*: **не помина́й(те) ~м** (*разг*)
remember me kindly.
лих|**о́й** (-, -а́, -о) *прил* (наездник) dashing;
(скакун) swift; (пора, враг) evil; **~а́ беда́
нача́ло** the first step is the hardest.
лихора́д|**ить** (*3sg* -ит) *несов безл*: **меня́ ~ит** I
feel feverish; **эконо́мику ~ит** the economy is
ailing.
лихора́д|**ка** (-и) *ж* (*МЕД, также перен*) fever;
(: на губа́х) cold sore; **золота́я ~** gold fever.
лихора́доч|**ный** (-ен, -на, -но) *прил* (также
перен) feverish.
Лихтенште́йн (-а) *м* Liechtenstein.
лицево́й *прил* (нерв) facial; **~а́я сторона́
матери́и** the right side of the material; **лицево́й
счёт** personal account.
лицезре́|**ть** (-ю, -ишь) *несов перех* to behold.
лице́ист (-а) *м* lycée pupil, ≈ secondary school
pupil.
лице́|**й** (-я) *м* lycée, ≈ secondary school.
лицеме́р (-а) *м* hypocrite.
лицеме́рен *прил см* **лицеме́рный**.
лицеме́ри|**е** (-я) *ср* hypocrisy.
лицеме́р|**ить** (-ю, -ишь) *несов неперех* to be
hypocritical or a hypocrite.
лицеме́р|**ный** (-ен, -на, -но) *прил* hypocritical.
лицензи́ровани|**е** (-я) *ср* licensing.
лицензи|**я** (-и) *ж* licence (*BRIT*), license (*US*).
лиц|**о́** (-а́; *nom pl* -ца) *ср* face; (перен:
индивидуа́льность) image; (ткани итп) right
side; (*ЛИНГ*) person; **от ~ца́** +*gen* in the name of,
on behalf of; **пе́ред ~м** +*gen* in the face of; **э́та
блу́за тебе́ к ~цу́** that blouse suits you; **тебе́ не
к ~цу́ безде́льничать** shame on you for being
so lazy; **знать** (*impf*) **кого́-н в ~** to know sb's
face; **на ней ~ца́ нет** she looks dreadful; **они́ не
удари́ли в грязь ~м** they didn't disgrace
themselves; **стира́ть** (**стере́ть** *perf*) **с ~ца́
земли́** to wipe from или off the face of the earth;
пе́рвое/тре́тье ~ (*ЛИНГ*) first/third person;
показа́ть (*perf*) **това́р ~м** to show sth to
advantage; **~ к лицу́** face to face;
официа́льное ~ official; **физи́ческое ~** (*ЮР*)
natural person, individual.
личи́н|**а** (-ы) *ж* mask; **под ~ой** +*gen* under the
guise of.
личи́н|**ка** (-ки; *gen pl* -ок) *ж* maggot.
ли́чно *нареч* (знать) personally; (встретить)
in person; **~ я ...** (*разг*) as for me ...; **~ мне всё
равно́** (*разг*) personally, I don't care; **он всё
проверя́ет ~** he checks everything personally
или himself.
ли́чность (-и) *ж* (выдающаяся, зага́дочная)

individual; (*обычно мн: обидные замечания*) personal remark; **устана́вливать (установи́ть** *perf*) **чью-н** ~ to establish sb's identity.

ли́чн|ый *прил* (*персональный*) personal; (*частный*) private; **ли́чная ссу́да** (*КОММ*) personal loan; **ли́чное де́ло** personal records; **ли́чный соста́в** staff.

лиша́|й (-я) *м* herpes.

лиша́йник (-а) *м* lichen.

лиша́|ть (-ю) *несов от* **лиши́ть**.

лишён (-а́, -о́, -ы́) *как сказ*: **он ~ та́кта/чу́вства ю́мора** he is devoid of tact/a sense of humour; **э́то не лишено́ основа́ния/смы́сла** this is not totally lacking in reason/sense.

лише́ни|е (-я) *ср* (*прав, привилегий*) deprivation; (*большое, горькое*) loss; (*обычно мн: нужда*) privation; ~ **свобо́ды** imprisonment; **терпе́ть** (*impf*) ~**я** to suffer privation; ~ **пра́ва со́бственности** (*ЮР*) foreclosure.

лиши́|ть (-у́, -ишь; *impf* **лиша́ть)** *сов перех*: ~ **кого́-н/что-н** +*gen* (*отнять: прав, привилегий*) to deprive sb/sth of; (*покоя, счастья*) to rob sb/sth of; **лиша́ть** (~ *perf*) **кого́-н насле́дства** to disinherit sb; **лиша́ть** (~ *perf*) **жи́зни кого́-н** to take sb's life; **лиша́ть** (~ *perf*) **кого́-н сло́ва** to deny sb the right to speak.

ли́шн|ий (-яя, -ее, -ие) *прил* (*вес*) extra; (*деньги, билет*) spare; (*расходы, вещи*) unnecessary; ~ **раз** once again *или* more; **не** ~**ее** *или* ~**е** +*infin* ... it would not be a bad idea to ...; **сказа́ть** (*perf*) ~**ее** to say the wrong thing; **три килогра́мма с** ~**им** over three kilogrammes; **тре́тий** ~ three's a crowd.

лишь *част* (*только*) only ◆ *союз* (*как только*) as soon as; ~ **бы она́ согласи́лась!** if only she would agree!; **ему́ не ва́жно что де́лать,** ~ **бы не рабо́тать** he doesn't care what he does, as long as he doesn't have to work; **ему́** ~ **бы уйти́** he just wants to leave.

лоб (лба; *loc sg* **лбу)** *м* forehead; **сказа́ть** (*perf*) **кому́-н в** ~ (*перен*) to tell sb straight; **у него́ на лбу напи́сано, что он врёт** (*разг*) it's written all over his face that he's lying.

ло́бби *ср нескл* lobby.

лобби́ст (-а) *м* lobbyist.

ло́бзик (-а) *м* fret saw.

ло́бный *прил* (*АНАТ*) frontal.

лобово́й *прил* frontal; **лобово́е стекло́** windscreen (*BRIT*), windshield (*US*).

лоботря́с (-а) *м* (*разг*) lazybones.

лов (-а) *м* catching.

лов|е́ц (-ца́) *м* catcher; ~ **жёмчуга** pearl diver.

лов|и́ть (-лю́, -ишь; *perf* **пойма́ть)** *несов перех* to catch; (*случай, момент*) to seize; (*impf*) **ры́бу** to fish; ~ (*impf*) **кого́-н на лжи** to catch sb out; **пойма́ть** (*perf*) **кого́-н на сло́ве** to take sb at their word; ~ (**пойма́ть** *perf*) **на себе́ чей-н**

взгляд to catch sb's eye; ~ (**пойма́ть** *perf*) **себя́ на мы́сли, что** ... to catch o.s. thinking that ....

лова́ч (-а́) *м* (*разг*) dodgy character.

ло́в|кий (-кая, -кое, -кие; -ок, -ка́, -ко) *прил* (*человек*) agile; (*прыжок, движение*) nimble; (*удар*) swift; (*разг: торговец*) sharp.

ло́вко *нареч* (*прыгнуть*) nimbly; (*придумать*) smartly; (*придумано, сделано*) smartly ◆ *как сказ* that's smart.

ловлю́ *несов см* **лови́ть**.

ло́вл|я (-и) *ж* (*действие*) catching; **ры́бная** ~ fishing.

лов|о́к *прил см* **ло́вкий**.

лову́ш|ка (-ки; *gen pl* **-ек)** *ж* (*также перен*) trap.

ловца́ *итп сущ см* **ловец**.

логари́фм (-а) *м* logarithm.

логарифми́ческ|ий (-ая, -ое, -ие) *прил*: ~**ая лине́йка** slide rule.

ло́гик|а (-и) *ж* logic.

логи́чен *прил см* **логи́чный**.

логи́ческ|ий (-ая, -ое, -ие) *прил* logical.

логи́чн|ый (-ен, -на, -но) *прил* logical.

ло́говищ|е (-а) *ср* (*также перен*) den, lair.

ло́гов|о (-а) *ср* = **ло́говище**.

ло́дж|ия (-и) *ж* recess balcony.

ло́д|ка (-ки; *gen pl* **-ок)** *ж* boat; **подво́дная** ~ submarine.

ло́доч|ка (-ки; *gen pl* **-ек)** *ж уменьш от* **ло́дка**; (*обычно мн: открытые туфли*) court shoe.

ло́дочный *прил* (*вёсла*) boat's; **ло́дочная ста́нция** boat-hire place.

лоды́ж|ка (-ки; *gen pl* **-ек)** *ж* ankle.

ло́дырнича|ть (-ю) *несов неперех* (*разг*) to idle.

ло́дыр|ь (-я) *м* (*разг*) idler.

ло́ж|а (-и) *ж* (*в театре, в зале*) box; (*массонская*) lodge; **ло́жа пре́ссы** press gallery.

ложби́н|а (-ы) *ж* dip (*in the ground*).

ло́ж|е (-а) *ср* bed.

ло́жек *сущ см* **ло́жка**.

ло́жен *прил см* **ло́жный**.

ложи́|ться (-у́сь, -и́шься) *несов от* **лечь**.

ло́ж|ка (-ки; *gen pl* **-ек)** *ж* spoon.

ло́жн|ый (-ен, -на, -но) *прил* false; (*вывод*) wrong; **представля́ть (предста́вить** *perf*) **что-н в** ~**ном све́те** to show sth in a false light; **ло́жные показа́ния** false evidence; **ло́жная трево́га** false alarm.

ложь (лжи; *instr sg* **ло́жью)** *ж* lie.

лоз|а́ (-ы́; *nom pl* **-ы)** *ж* (*ивы итп*) cane; (*винограда*) vine.

ло́зунг (-а) *м* (*призыв*) slogan; (*плакат*) banner.

лока́лен *прил см* **лока́льный**.

локализа́ци|я (-и) *ж* localization.

локализ|ова́ть (-у́ю) *(не)сов перех* to localize.

лока́льн|ый (-ен, -ьна, -ьно) *прил* local.

лока́тор (-а) *м*: **опти́ческий** ~ radar; **звуково́й** ~ sonar.

локомоти́в (-а) *м* locomotive.

ло́кон (-а) *м* singlet.

ло́к|оть (-тя; *gen pl* **-те́й**, *dat pl* **-тя́м**) *м* elbow; **куса́ть** (*impf*) ~**ти** (*разг*) to kick o.s.; **чу́вство** ~**тя** team spirit.

ло́ктя *итп сущ см* **ло́коть**.

лом (-а) *м* crowbar ♦ *собир* (*для переработки*) scrap; **металли́ческий** ~ scrap metal.

ло́ман|ый *прил* broken; ~**ая ли́ния** zigzag.

лома́|ть (-ю; *perf* **слома́ть** *или* **разлома́ть**) *несов перех* (*разделять на куски*) to break; (*perf* **слома́ть** *или* **полома́ть**; *приводить в негодность*) to break; (*perf* **полома́ть**; *устои, традиции*) to challenge; (*планы*) to frustrate; ~ (*impf*) **го́лову над чем-то** to rack one's brains over sth; ~ (*impf*) **привы́чки** to force o.s. to change one's habits; **жизнь слома́ла его́** life dealt him a cruel blow

▶ **лома́ться** (*perf* **полома́ться** *или* **слома́ться**) *несов возв* to break; (*no perf*; *перен: обычаи, устои*) to be challenged; (*: человек*) to show off; (*: заставлять себя просить*) to be fussy.

ломба́рд (-а) *м* pawnshop; **закла́дывать** (**заложи́ть** *perf*) **что-н в** ~ to pawn sth.

ломба́рдный *прил* pawn *опред*.

лом|и́ть (-лю́, -ишь) *несов безл*: **у меня́ ло́мит ко́сти** my bones are aching; **наро́д ло́мит туда́** (*разг*) the people are flocking there

▶ **ломи́ться** *несов возв* (*ветви, деревья*) to groan; (*разг: идти насильно*) to pour in; **стол** ~**и́лся от еды́** (*перен*) the table groaned under the food.

ло́мк|а (-и) *ж* breaking.

ло́м|кий (-кая, -кое, -кие; -ок, -ка́, -ко) *прил* (*хрупкий: стекло*) fragile; (*: лёд*) brittle.

ломлю́(сь) *несов см* **ломи́ть(ся)**.

ломово́й *прил*: ~**ая ло́шадь** carthorse; (*перен: разг*) dogsbody.

ло́мок *прил см* **ло́мкий**.

ломо́т|а (-ы) *ж* ache.

ломо́|ть (-тя) *м* slice.

ло́мтик (-а) *м* = **ломо́ть**.

ломтя́ *итп сущ см* **ломо́ть**.

Ло́ндон (-а) *м* London.

ло́ндон|ец (-ца) *м* Londoner.

ло́ндон|ка (-ки; *gen pl* -**ок**) *ж см* **ло́ндонец**.

ло́ндонца *итп сущ см* **ло́ндонец**.

ло́н|о (-а) *ср* (*женщины*) bosom; (*перен*): **на** ~**е приро́ды** in the open air.

лопа́сть (-и; *gen pl* -**е́й**) *ж* (*также тех*) blade.

лопа́т|а (-ы) *ж* spade.

лопа́т|ка (-ки; *gen pl* -**ок**) *ж уменьш от* **лопа́та**; (*АНАТ*) shoulder blade; **класть** (**положи́ть** *perf*) **кого́-н на о́бе** ~**ки** (*перен*) to beat sb hands down.

ло́па|ть (-ю; *perf* **сло́пать**) *несов перех* (*разг*) to gobble (up).

ло́па|ться (-юсь) *сов от* **ло́пнуть**.

ло́пн|уть (-у, -ешь; *perf* **ло́паться**) *сов непрех* (*разрываться: шар*) to burst; (*стекло*) to shatter; (*верёвка, струна*) to snap; (*разг:*

банк, предприятие) to go bust; **у меня́ терпе́ние** ~**уло** (*разг*) I've run out of patience.

лопу́х (-а́) *м* burdock; (*перен: разг: простак*) simpleton.

ЛОР (-а) *м сокр* (= *оториноларинголо́гия*) ORL (= *otorhinolaryngology*), ENT (= *ear-nose-throat*).

лорд (-а) *м* lord.

лорне́т (-а) *ж* lorgnette.

Лос-А́нджелес (-а) *м* Los Angeles.

лоси́н|а (-ы) *ж* (*кожа лося*) elkskin; (*мясо лося*) elk (*meat*); *см также* **лоси́ны**.

лоси́н|ы (-) *мн* leggings *мн*.

лоси́х|а (-и) *ж* female elk *или* moose (*мн* moose).

лоск (-а) *м* (*глянец*) shine; (*перен: в доме*) spotlessness; (*: в одежде*) flair; **наводи́ть** (**навести́** *perf*) ~ **на что-н** to give sth a polish.

лоску́т (-а́) *м* (*материи, кожи*) scrap.

лоску́тн|ый *прил*: ~**ое одея́ло** patchwork quilt.

лосни́ться (-ю́сь, -и́шься) *несов возв* (*от жира, от крема*) to shine.

лососёвый *прил* salmon.

лососи́н|а (-ы) *ж* salmon (*meat*).

лосо́с|ь (-я) *м* salmon.

лос|ь (-я; *gen pl* -**е́й**) *м* elk, moose (*мн* moose).

лосьо́н (-а) *м* lotion.

лот (-а) *м* (*МОР*) lead line; (*КОММ: на аукционе, на торгах*) lot.

лоте́рейный *прил* lottery *опред*.

лотере́|я (-и) *ж* lottery.

лотка́ *итп сущ см* **лото́к**.

лото́ *ср нескл* lotto.

лот|о́к (-ка́) *м* (*прилавок*) stall; (*ящик для торговли*) trader's tray; (*жёлоб*) trough.

ло́тос (-а) *м* lotus.

лото́чник (-а) *м* stallholder.

лохма́|тить (-чу, -тишь; *perf* **взлохма́тить**) *несов перех* to fluff up.

лохма́т|ый (-, -а, -о) *прил* (*животное*) shaggy; (*волосы*) straggly; (*человек*) dishevelled.

лохма́чу *сов см* **лохма́тить**.

лохмо́т|ья (-ев) *мн* rags *мн*.

ло́цман (-а) *м* pilot (*on ship*).

лошади́ный *прил* (*седло, упряжь*) horse's; (*лицо*) equine; **лошади́ная си́ла** horsepower.

лоша́дник (-а) *м* (*разг: любитель лошадей*) horse-lover; (*торговец лошадьми*) horse-trader.

ло́шад|ь (-и; *gen pl* -**е́й**) *ж* horse.

лощёный *прил* (*бумага*) glossy; (*перен: человек, внешность*) polished.

лощи́н|а (-ы) *ж* dell.

лоя́льный (-ен, -ьна, -ьно) *прил* loyal (*to a state*).

л.с. *сокр* (= *лошади́ная си́ла*) h.p. (= *horsepower*).

ЛСД *м сокр* LSD (= *lysergic acid diethylamide*).

Луа́р|а (-ы) *ж* the Loire.

луб|о́к (-ка́) *м* (*кора*) bast; (*повязка*) splint; **ру́сский** ~ (*ФОЛЬКЛОР*) lubok (*popular colour print*).

лубрика́тор (-a) *м* lubricant.
луг (-a; *loc sg* -ý, *nom pl* -á) *м* meadow.
луди́ть (-жý, -дишь; *несов перех* to tin.
лу́ж|а (-и) *ж* (*на улице, на доро́ге*) puddle; (*на полу, на столе́*) pool; **сади́ться** (**сесть** *perf*) **в ~у** (*перен: разг*) to get o.s. into a mess.
лужа́йка (-йки; *gen pl* -ек) *ж* (*поля́нка*) glade; (*газо́н*) lawn.
лужёный *прил* (*самова́р, ча́йник итп*) tin-plated; **у него́ ~ая гло́тка** (*перен: разг*) he has iron lungs.
лужу́ *несов см* **луди́ть**.
лу́з|а (-ы) *ж* pocket (*on a billiard table*).
лук (-a) *м собир* onions *мн* ♦ (*ору́жие*) bow; **зелёный ~** spring onion (*BRIT*), scallion; **ре́пчатый ~** onion bulbs.
лука́в|ить (-лю, -ишь; *perf* **слука́вить**) *несов непeрex* to be deceitful; **ты, ка́жется, ~ишь** you're being a bit vague.
лука́вый (-, -а, -о) *прил* (*челове́к, посту́пок*) crafty; (*взгляд, улы́бка*) sly; (*де́вушка*) coquettish.
лу́ковиц|а (-ы) *ж* bulb; (*во́лоса*) follicle.
лукошко (-ка; *gen pl* -ек) *ср* basket.
лун|а́ (-ы́) *ж* moon; **ты что, с ~ы́ свали́лся?** where've you been all this time?
лу́на-парк (-a) *м* funfair (*BRIT*), amusement park (*US*).
луна́тик (-a) *м* sleepwalker.
лу́н|ка (-ки; *gen pl* -ок) *ж* hole.
лу́нный *прил*: **~ые фа́зы** phases of the moon; **лу́нный свет** moonlight.
лу́нок *сущ см* **лу́нка**.
лунохо́д (-a) *м* lunar research module.
лун|ь (-я) *м* harrier.
лу́п|а (-ы) *ж* magnifying glass.
лупи́ть (-лю́, -ишь; *perf* **облупи́ть**) *несов перех* (*яйцо́*) to shell; (*perf* **отлупи́ть**; *разг: бить*) to thrash; (*no perf*; *разг: си́льно ударя́ть*) to hammer on
► **лупи́ться** (*perf* **облупи́ться**) *несов возв* (*шелуши́ться*) to peel (off).
луч (-á) *м* ray; (*проже́ктора, фонаря́*) beam; **рентге́новские ~и** X-ray; **~ наде́жды** a ray of hope; **ла́зерный ~** laser beam.
лучев|о́й *прил* (*физ: эне́ргия*) beamed; **~а́я кость** radius (*bone*); **лучева́я боле́знь** radiation sickness.
лучеза́р|ный (-ен, -на, -но) *прил* (*бу́дущее*) glorious; (*улы́бка*) radiant.
лучи́н|а (-ы) *ж* (*ще́пка*) splinter ♦ *собир* (*ще́пки*) kindling wood *собир*.
лучи́стый (-, -а, -о) *прил* (*улы́бка, лицо́*) beaming; (*глаза́*) shining.
лу́чник (-a) *м* archer.
лу́чниц|а (-ы) *ж см* **лу́чник**.
лу́чше *сравн прил от* **хоро́ший** ♦ *сравн нареч от* **хорошо́** ♦ *как сказ*: **больно́му ~** the patient

is feeling better ♦ *част*: **~ не опра́вдывайся** don't try and justify yourself ♦ *вводн сл*: **~ (всего́) е́сли ты позвони́шь ве́чером** it would be better if you phone in the evening; **от э́того никому́ не ~** it doesn't do anyone any good; **нам ~ чем им** we're better off than them; **будь осторо́жен и́ли, ~, вообще́ не ходи́ туда́** take care, or better still, don't go there at all; **~ возьми́ маши́ну** you'd better take the car; **как нельзя́ ~** couldn't be better; **~ не спра́шивай** don't ask.
лу́чш|ий (-ая, -ее, -ие) *прил* (*са́мый хоро́ший*) best; **э́то ~ая рабо́та в кла́ссе** it's the best work in the class; **в ~ем слу́чае нам уда́стся зако́нчить рабо́ту за́втра** if we're lucky we'll finish the work tomorrow; **за неиме́нием ~его** for want of something better; **э́то (всё) к ~ему** it's (all) for the best.
лущи́ть (-у́, -и́шь; *perf* **облущи́ть**) *несов перех* (*се́мечки, оре́хи*) to crack (open); (*горо́х*) to shell.
лы́ж|а (-и) *ж* (*обы́чно мн*) ski; *см также* **лы́жи**.
лы́ж|и (-) *мн* (*вид спо́рта*) skiing; **во́дные ~** (*сами лы́жи*) water-skis; (*вид спо́рта*) water-skiing; **го́рные ~** downhill skis; **ходи́ть** (*impf*) **на ~ах** to go cross-country skiing.
лы́жник (-a) *м* skier.
лы́жниц|а (-ы) *ж см* **лы́жник**.
лы́жный *прил* (*крепле́ния, мазь итп*) ski *опред*; (*соревнова́ния*) skiing *опред*; **лы́жный костю́м** ski suit; **лы́жные па́лки** ski poles.
лыжн|я́ (-и́) *ж* ski track.
лы́к|о (-a) *ср* (*ли́пы, и́вы*) bast; **он ~а не вя́жет** (*разг*) he's roaring drunk; **он не ~м шит** (*разг*) he's someone to be reckoned with.
лысе́ть (-ю; *perf* **облысе́ть** *или* **полысе́ть**) *несов непeрex* to go bald.
лы́син|а (-ы) *ж* bald patch.
лы́с|ый (-, -á, -о) *прил* (*голова́, челове́к*) bald; (*гора́, холм*) bare.
ль *част = ли*.
львёнок (-ёнка; *nom pl* -я́та, *gen pl* -я́т) *м* lion cub.
льви́ный *прил* (*шку́ра, гри́ва итп*) lion's; **~ая ста́я** pride of lions; **~ая до́ля** the lion's share; **льви́ный зев** (*БОТ*) snapdragon.
льви́ц|а (-ы) *ж* lioness.
Льво́в (-a) *м* Lvov.
льв|я́та *итп сущ см* **львёнок**.
льго́т|а (-ы) *ж* (*инвали́дам, бере́менным итп*) benefit; (*обы́чно мн: предприя́тиям, экспортёрам итп*) special term; (*эли́те, ветера́нам*) privilege; **нало́говые ~ы** tax relief.
льго́тный *прил* (*тари́ф*) concessionary; (*усло́вия*) privileged; (*заём*) special-rate; **льго́тный биле́т** concessionary ticket.
льд|а *итп сущ см* **лёд**.
льди́н|а (-ы) *ж* ice floe.

льди́н|ка (-ки; *gen pl* -ок) ж piece of ice.
льна *итп сущ см* **лён**.
льново́дств|о (-а) *ср* flax-growing.
льн|у́ть (-у́, -ёшь; *perf* **прильну́ть**) *несов*
неперех: ~ **к** +*dat* (**к ма́тери**) to cling to;
(*перен*: **к богача́м, к влия́тельным лю́дям**) to
try to get in with.
льня|но́й *прил* (*полоте́нце, пла́тье*) linen;
(*цвет*) flaxen; **~о́е полотно́** linen; **льняно́е
ма́сло** linseed oil.
льсте́ц (-а́) *м* flatterer.
льсти́в|ый (-, -а, -о) *прил* (*челове́к*) smarmy;
(*улы́бка*) unctuous; (*завере́ния, речь*) flattering.
ль|сти́ть (-щу, -стишь; *perf* **польсти́ть**) *несов*
неперех (+*dat*; *хвали́ть из коры́сти*) to flatter;
(*доставля́ть удовлетворе́ние*) to gratify; ~
(*impf*) **себя́ наде́ждой** to live in hope.
лью(сь) *итп несов см* **лить(ся)**.
любвеоби́л|ьный (-ен, -ьна, -ьно) *прил*
loving.
любви́ *итп сущ см* **любо́вь**.
любе́зен *прил см* **любе́зный**.
любе́знича|ть (-ю) *несов неперех*: ~ **с** +*instr*
(*разг*) to pay compliments to.
любе́зность (-и) ж (*одолже́ние*) favour (*BRIT*),
favor (*US*); (*комплиме́нт*) compliment; (*в
поведе́нии*) courtesy; **ока́зывать (оказа́ть** *perf*)
~ **кому́-н** to do sb a favour; **не откажи́те в** ~**и?**
would you do me a favour?
любе́з|ный (-ен, -на, -но) *прил* polite; **бу́дьте**
~**ны!** excuse me, please!; **бу́дьте** ~**ны,
принеси́те нам ко́фе?** could you be so kind as
to bring us some coffee?
люби́м|ая (-ой; *decl like adj*) ж beloved.
люби́м|ец (-ца) *м* (*челове́к, живо́тное*)
favourite (*BRIT*), favorite (*US*).
люби́миц|а (-ы) ж см **люби́мец**.
люби́мца *итп сущ см* **люби́мец**.
люби́мчик (-а) *м* (*разг*) pet; **быть** (*impf*) **в** ~**ах у
кого́-н** to be sb's pet.
люби́м|ый (-, -а, -о) *прил* (*же́нщина, брат*)
beloved; (*писа́тель, заня́тие итп*) favourite
(*BRIT*), favorite (*US*) ◆ (-ого; *decl like adj*) *м*
beloved.
люби́тел|ь (-я) *м* (*непрофессиона́л*) amateur; ~
му́зыки/спо́рта music-/sports-lover.
люби́тельниц|а (-ы) ж: ~ **му́зыки/чте́ния**
music-/book-lover.
люби́тельск|ий (-ая, -ое, -ие) *прил* (*спорт,
теа́тр итп*) amateur; **люби́тельские права́**
driving licence (*BRIT*) *или* driver's license (*US*).
люб|и́ть (-лю́, -ишь) *несов перех* (*ро́дину,
мать, му́жа итп*) to love; (*му́зыку, спорт итп*)
to like; **я** ~**лю́ его́ всем се́рдцем** I love him
with all my heart; **цветы́ лю́бят тепло́** plants
like the warmth; **я** ~**лю́, когда́ мне говоря́т
комплиме́нты** I like it when people pay me
compliments; **я** ~**лю́, когда́ лю́ди прихо́дят
во́время** I like it when people come on time.
люб|ова́ться (-у́юсь; *perf* **полюбова́ться**)
несов возв (+*instr*) to admire; **полюбу́йтесь на**

него́! take a look at him!
любо́вник (-а) *м* lover.
любо́вниц|а (-ы) ж см **любо́вник**.
любо́вный *прил* (*дела́, похожде́ния*) lover's;
(*пе́сня, письмо́*) love *опред*; (*отноше́ние,
подхо́д*) loving.
люб|о́вь (-ви́) ж love; (*привя́занность*): ~ **к** +*dat*
(*к ро́дине, к ма́тери итп*) love for; (*к чте́нию, к
иску́сству итп*) love of; **занима́ться** (*impf*) ~**ю́**
to make love.
любозна́телен *прил см* **любозна́тельный**.
любозна́тельность (-и) ж inquisitiveness.
любозна́тел|ьный (-ен, -ьна, -ьно) *прил*
inquisitive.
люб|о́й *мест* (*вся́кий*) any ◆ (-о́го; *decl like adj*) *м*
(*любо́й челове́к*) anyone; **в** ~**о́е вре́мя** at any
time; ~ **цено́й** at any price.
любопы́тен *прил см* **любопы́тный**.
любопы́тно *нареч* curiously ◆ *как сказ*: ~!
that's interesting!; (*мне*) ~ **узна́ть** I'm intrigued
или curious to know.
любопы́т|ный (-ен, -на, -но) *прил* (*приме́р,
кни́га итп*) interesting; (*челове́к, толпа́*)
curious.
любопы́тств|о (-а) *ср* curiosity; **из** ~**а** out of
curiosity.
лю́бящ|ий (-ая, -ее, -ие) *прил* loving.
люд (-а) *м собир* (*разг*) folk.
лю́ден *прил см* **лю́дный**.
лю́д|и (-е́й; *dat pl* -ям, *instr pl* -ьми́, *prp pl* -ях) *мн*
people *мн*; (*солда́ты и офице́ры*) men *мн*;
(*ка́дры*) staff *ед*; **выходи́ть** (**вы́йти** *perf*) **в** ~ to
get on in life; **на** ~**ях** (*разг*) in public; **молоды́е**
~ young men; (*молодёжь*) young people; *см
также* **челове́к**.
лю́д|ный (-ен, -на, -но) *прил* (*у́лица итп*) busy;
(*го́род*) lively; (*сбо́рище*) crowded.
людое́д (-а) *м* (*челове́к*) cannibal; (*живо́тное*)
man-eater; (*в ска́зке*) ogre.
людое́дств|о (-а) *ср* cannibalism.
людско́й *прил* human; **род** ~ humankind.
люк (-а) *м* (*та́нка, самолёта*) hatch; (*на доро́ге*)
manhole; (*на сце́не*) trap door.
люкс (-а) *м* (*о ваго́не*) first-class carriage; (*о
каю́те*) first-class cabin ◆ *прил неизм* (*вы́сшего
кла́сса*) first-class; **мы живём в лю́ксе** we've
got a luxury suite.
Люксембу́рг (-а) *м* Luxembourg.
лю́л|ька (-ьки; *gen pl* -ек) ж (*та́кже СТРОИТ*)
cradle; (*мотоци́кла*) sidecar.
лю́мпен (-а) *м* member of the lumpen proletariat.
люпи́н (-а) *м* lupin.
лю́рекс (-а) *м* lurex.
лю́стр|а (-ы) ж chandelier.
лю́тен *сущ см* **лю́тня**.
лютера́н|ин (-ина; *nom pl* -е, *gen pl* -) *м* Lutheran.
лютера́н|ка (-ки; *gen pl* -ок) ж см **лютера́нин**.
лютера́нск|ий (-ая, -ое, -ие) *прил* Lutheran.
лю́тик (-а) *м* buttercup.
лю́т|ня (-ни; *gen pl* -ен) ж lute.
лю́т|ый (-, -а́, -о) *прил* (*враг, зверь*) fierce;

лю́церн|а (-ы) *ж* lucerne.

ля *ср нескл* (*муз*) lah.

ляга́|ть (-ю) *несов перех* (*подлеж: лошадь, корова*) to kick

▸ **ляга́ться** *несов возв* (*лошадь, корова*) to kick.

лягн|у́ть (-у́, -ёшь) *сов перех* to kick.

ля́г(те) *сов см* **лечь**.

ля́гу *итп сов см* **лечь**.

лягуша́та *итп сущ см* **лягушо́нок**.

лягуша́тник (-а) *м* (*разг*) shallow end.

лягу́ш|ка (-ки; *gen pl* **-ек**) *ж* frog.

лягушо́н|ок (-онка; *nom pl* **-а́та**, *gen pl* **-а́т**) *м* young frog.

ля́жек *сущ см* **ля́жка**.

ля́жешь *итп сов см* **лечь**.

ля́ж|ка (-ки; *gen pl* **-ек**) *ж* thigh.

лязг (-а) *м* (*звук: цепей, оружия*) clanging; (: *зубов*) gnash; (: *подков*) clatter.

ля́зга|ть (-ю) *несов неперех* (*засов, цепь*) to clang; (+*instr*; *зубами*) to gnash; (*ключами*) to rattle.

ля́м|ка (-ки; *gen pl* **-ок**) *ж* strap; **тяну́ть** (*impf*) **~ку** (*разг*) to toil away.

ля́па|ть (-ю) *несов от* **ля́пнуть** ◆ (*perf* **сля́пать**) *перех* (*разг: делать наспех*) to slap together ◆ (*perf* **наля́пать**) *перех* to make a mess of ◆ *неперех* to make a mess.

ля́пн|уть (-у, -ешь; *impf* **ля́пать**) *сов перех*: **~ глу́пость** to make a blunder.

ля́псус (-а) *м* blunder.

~ М, м ~

М, м *сущ нескл* (*буква*) the 13th letter of the Russian alphabet.

М *сокр* = метро́; (= мегаба́йт) МВ (= *megabyte*).

м *сокр* (= метр) m= *metre* (*BRIT*) *или* meter (*US*); (= мину́та) m (= *minute*).

мавзоле́й (-я) *м* mausoleum.

маг (-а) *м* magician, wizard; (*разг*) tape recorder.

магази́н (-а) *м* shop; (*ружья́*) magazine.

МАГАТЭ *ср сокр* (= Междунаро́дное аге́нтство по а́томной эне́ргии) IAEA (= *International Atomic Energy Agency*).

маги́стр (-а) *м* (*учёная сте́пень*) master's degree; ~ **гуманита́рных нау́к** Master of Arts.

магистра́л|ь (-и) *ж* (*железнодоро́жная*) main line; (*доро́жная*) arterial road; **во́дная** ~ main waterway.

магистра́льный *прил* main.

маги́ческ|ий (-ая, -ое, -ие) *прил* (*перен*) magic *опред*.

ма́ги|я (-и) *ж* magic.

магна́т (-а) *м* magnate.

магне́зи|я (-и) *ж* magnesia.

магнети́зм (-а) *м* magnetism.

ма́гни|й (-я) *м* magnesium.

магни́т (-а) *м* magnet.

магни́тный *прил* magnetic; ~ **диск** (*КОМП*) magnetic disk.

магнито́л|а (-ы) *ж* radio cassette player.

магнитофо́н (-а) *м* tape recorder; (*кассе́тный*) tape *или* cassette recorder.

магнитофо́нн|ый *прил*: ~**ая за́пись** tape recording; ~**ая кассе́та** (audio)cassette.

магно́ли|я (-и) *ж* magnolia.

Мадагаска́р (-а) *м* Madagascar.

мада́м *ж нескл* madame.

мадемуазе́л|ь (-и) *ж* mademoiselle.

мадо́нн|а (-ы) *ж* madonna.

Мадри́д (-а) *м* Madrid.

ма́ек *сущ см* ма́йка.

мает|а́ (-ы́) *ж* (*разг*) bother.

мажо́р (-а) *м* (*МУЗ*) major key.

мажорита́рн|ый *прил*: ~**ая систе́ма** (*ПОЛИТ*) system of majority rule.

мажо́рный *прил* (*МУЗ*) major; (*перен*: *настрое́ние*) cheerful.

МАЗ (-а) *м сокр* = Ми́нский автомоби́льный заво́д; (*автомоби́ль*) *vehicle manufactured at the Minsk car factory*.

ма́зать (-жу, -жешь; *perf* нама́зать *или* помазать) *несов перех* to spread; (*perf* изма́зать; *разг*: *па́чкать*) to get dirty; (: *рисова́ть*) to daub ◆ (*perf* прома́зать) *неперех* (*разг*) to miss; ~ (**нама́зать** *perf*) **что-н** to spread sth with sth; ~ (**нама́зать** *perf*) **гу́бы пома́дой** to put on lipstick

▶ **ма́заться** (*perf* нама́заться) *несов возв* (*разг*: *де́лать макия́ж*) to put on make-up; (*perf* **вы́мазаться** *или* изма́заться; *разг*: *па́чкаться*) to get dirty; ~**ся** (**нама́заться** *perf*) **кре́мом/ма́зью** to apply cream/ointment.

мазка́ *сущ см* мазо́к.

мазн|я́ (-и́) *ж* (*разг*: *о рисова́нии*) daub; (: *о письме́*) scribble.

мазо́к (-ка́) *м* (*ки́сти*) stroke; (*МЕД*) smear.

мазу́рк|а (-и) *ж* mazurka.

мазу́т (-а) *м* fuel oil.

маз|ь (-и) *ж* (*МЕД*) ointment; (*лы́жная*) wax; (*колёсная*) grease; **де́ло на** ~**й** (*разг*) things are going smoothly.

маи́с (-а) *м* maize (*BRIT*), corn (*US*).

маи́совый *прил* maize (*BRIT*), corn (*US*).

ма|й (-я) *м* May; *см та́кже* октя́брь.

ма́|йка (-йки; *gen pl* -ек) *ж* vest (*BRIT*), sleeveless undershirt (*US*).

майо́лик|а (-и) *ж собир* majolica.

майоне́з (-а) *м* mayonnaise.

майо́р (-а) *м* (*ВОЕН*) major.

ма́йск|ий (-ая, -ое, -ие) *прил* May *опред*; **ма́йский жук** May beetle, cockchafer.

мак (-а) *м* poppy; (*кули́н*) poppy seeds *мн*.

мака́к|а (-и) *ж* macaque.

макаро́нник (-а) *м* pasta bake.

макаро́н|ы (-) *мн* pasta *ед*.

макаро́нный *прил* (*КУЛИН*) pasta *опред*; **макаро́нные изде́лия** pasta.

мака́|ть (-ю) *несов перех* to dip.

македо́н|ец (-ца) *м* Macedonian.

Македо́ни|я (-и) *ж* Macedonia.

македо́н|ка (-ки; *gen pl* -ок) *ж см* македо́нец.

македо́нск|ий (-ая, -ое, -ие) *прил* Macedonian.

македо́нца *сущ см* македо́нец.

маке́т (-а) *м* (*моде́ль*) model; (*КОМП*) breadboard.

макинто́ш (-а) *м* mackintosh.

ма́клер (-а) *м* (*КОММ*) broker.

макн|у́ть (-у́, -ёшь) *сов перех* (*перо́, кисть*) to dip.

ма́ковк|а (-и) *ж* poppyhead; (*разг*: *ку́пол це́ркви*) (onion) dome.

ма́ков|ый (-, -а, -о) *прил* poppy-seed *опред*; **с ~о зёрнышко** as small as a pinhead; **у него́ с утра́ во рту́ ~ой роси́нки не́ было́** he hasn't had a bite to eat since morning.

макраме́ *ср нескл* macramé.

макре́л|ь (-и) *ж* mackerel.

макроэконо́мик|а (-и) *ж* macroeconomics *мн*.

ма́кси *ср нескл* maxi ◆ *прил неизм* maxi *опред*.

макс(им) *сокр* (= максима́льный) max. (= *maximum*).

максима́лен *прил см* максима́льный.

максимали́ст (-а) *м* maximalist.

максима́льный (-ен, -ьна, -ьно) *прил* maximum *опред*.

ма́ксимум (-а) *м* maximum ◆ *нареч* at most, maximum.

макулату́р|а (-ы) *ж собир* wastepaper (*for recycling*); (*перен: пренебр*) pulp literature.

маку́шк|а (-ки; *gen pl* -ек) *ж* (*разг: дерева, горы*) top; (*головы*) crown; **у него́ у́шки на ~ке** he's keeping his ear to the ground.

Мала́ви *ср нескл* Malawi.

мала́г|а (-и) *ж* (*вино*) Malaga (wine).

мала́|ец (-йца) *м* Malay.

Мала́йзи|я (-и) *ж* Malaysia.

мала́|йка (-йки; *gen pl* -ек) *ж см* мала́ец.

мала́йский (-ая, -ое, -ие) *прил* Malaysian.

мала́йца *сущ см* мала́ец.

малахи́т (-а) *м* malachite.

мал|ева́ть (-ю́ю, -ю́ешь; *perf* намалева́ть) *несов перех* (*разг*) to daub.

мале́йший (-ая, -ее, -ие) *прил* (*ошибка, промах*) the slightest; **не име́ть** (*impf*) **ни ~его представле́ния о чём-н** to not have the slightest idea about sth.

мал|ёк (-ька́) *м* young (fish), fry.

ма́леньк|ий (-ая, -ое, -ие) *прил* small, little; (*незначительный*) slight; (*малолетний*) little ◆ (-ого; *decl like adj*) *м* little one; **моё де́ло ~ое** (*разг*) it's none of my business; **ма́ленькая бу́ква** small letter.

Мали́ *ср нескл* Mali.

мали́н|а (-ы) *ж* (*кустарник*) raspberry cane *или* bush; (*ягода*) raspberries *мн*; **не жизнь, а ~!** (*разг*) it's a cushy life!

мали́нник (-а) *м собир* raspberry canes *мн*.

мали́новк|а (-и) *ж* robin (redbreast).

мали́новый *прил* (*варенье, куст*) raspberry; (*цвет*) crimson.

KEYWORD

ма́ло *чис* (+*gen*; *друзей, книг*) only a few; (*работы, денег*) not much; **нам да́ли ма́ло книг** they only gave us a few books; **я ви́дел ма́ло друзе́й** I only saw a few friends; **у меня́ ма́ло де́нег** I don't have much money; **ма́ло ра́дости** little joy

◆ *нареч* not much; **она́ ма́ло измени́лась** she hasn't changed much; **они́ ма́ло рабо́тают** they don't work much

◆ *как сказ*: **критикова́ть ма́ло, на́до помо́чь** it's not enough to criticize, you have to help; **мне э́того ма́ло** this is not enough for me; **ему́ всё ма́ло** it is impossible to satisfy him; **ма́ло ли что so** what?; **ма́ло ли кто/где/когда́** it doesn't matter who/where/when; **ма́ло того́** (and) what's more; **ма́ло того́, она́ ещё груби́ла** (and) what's more, she was rude; **ма́ло того́ что not** only; **ма́ло того́ что бы́ло хо́лодно, нам ещё не да́ли у́жин** not only was it cold, but they didn't give us any supper.

малова́жный (-ен, -на, -но) *прил* of little importance.

малова́т *как сказ* (*разг: о размере*) on the small side.

малова́то *нареч* (*разг*) not quite enough.

малове́р (-а) *м* sceptic.

маловероя́тный (-ен, -на, -но) *прил* improbable.

малово́дь|е (-ья; *gen pl* -ий) *ср* low water level; (*недостаток воды*) drought.

малові́годный (-ен, -на, -но) *прил* unprofitable.

малогабари́тный (-ен, -на, -но) *прил* small.

малоговоря́щий (-ая, -ее, -ие) *прил* unimpressive.

малогра́мотный (-ен, -на, -но) *прил* semiliterate; (*руководитель*) incompetent.

малодосту́пный (-ен, -на, -но) *прил* (*место*) inaccessible.

малоду́шен *прил см* малоду́шный.

малоду́шнича|ть (-ю; *perf* смалоду́шничать) *несов неперех* (*разг*) to be yellow (*fig*).

малоду́шный (-ен, -на, -но) *прил* cowardly.

малозаме́тный (-ен, -на, -но) *прил* (*пятно, окраска*) hardly noticeable; (*человек, событие*) insignificant.

малознако́мый (-, -а, -о) *прил* unfamiliar.

малокали́берный *прил* small-bore, small-calibre (*BRIT*), small-caliber (*US*).

малокро́ви|е (-я) *ср* (sickle-cell) anaemia (*BRIT*) *или* anemia (*US*).

малоле́тк|а (-и) *м/ж* (*разг*) kid.

малоле́тний (-яя, -ее, -ие) *прил* young.

малолитра́|жка (-ки; *gen pl* -ек) *ж* (*разг*) small car (*with small cylinder capacity*).

малолитра́жный *прил*: **~ автомоби́ль** small car (*with small cylinder capacity*).

малолю́дный (-ен, -на, -но) *прил* (*улица*) unfrequented; (*район, село*) sparsely populated.

ма́ло-ма́льски *нареч* (*разг*) quite.

малома́льский (-ая, -ое, ие) *прил* (*разг*) the slightest.

малому́щный (-ен, -на, -но) *прил* weak.

малонаселён|ный *прил* sparsely populated.

малообеспе́ченный *прил* disadvantaged.

малообла́ч|ный (-ен, -на, -но) *прил* (*небо*,

пого́да) slightly cloudy.

малообразо́ван|ный (-, -на, -но) *прил* undereducated.

малоподви́ж|ный (-ен, -на, -но) *прил* (*образ жи́зни*) sedentary.

ма́ло-пома́лу *нареч* (*разг*) little by little.

малора́звит|ый (-, -а, -о) *прил* underdeveloped.

малоро́слый *прил* undersized.

малосеме́йный (-ен, -йна, -йно) *прил* with a small family.

малоси́л|ьный (-ен, -ьна, -ьно) *прил* (*дви́гатель*) low-powered; (*ло́шадь*) weak.

малосо́л|ьный (-ен, -ьна, -ьно) *прил* pickled (*in weak brine*).

ма́лост|ь (-и) *ж* (*разг*) trifle ♦ *нареч* (*разг*) a bit.

малотира́жный *прил* (*газе́та, журна́л*) with a low circulation; (*кни́га*) *published in a small edition*.

малочи́слен|ный (-, -на, -но) *прил* small; (*поселе́ния*) scarce.

ма́л|ый (-, -а́, -о́) *прил* small, little; (*дохо́д, ско́рость*) low ♦ (-ого; *decl like adj*) *м* (*разг*) chap; (*молодо́й челове́к*) lad ♦ **как сказ** (*no full form*): **пла́тье/пальто́ мало́** the dress/coat is too small; **дово́льствоваться** (*impf*) **~ым** to have modest needs; **с ~ых лет** from childhood; **у него́ семья́ мал мала́ ме́ньше** he has a very large family of small children; **он мал да уда́л** (*разг*) he's a smart little guy; **без ~ого два часа́** (*разг*) just before two o'clock; **са́мое ~ое** at the very least; **Ма́лая А́зия** Asia Minor.

малы́ш (-а́) *м* little boy.

малы́ш|ка (-ки; *gen pl* -ек) *ж* little girl.

малышня́ (-й) *ж собир* (*разг*) little kids *мн.*

ма́льв|а (-ы) *ж* mallow.

мальди́вск|ий (-ая, -ое, -ие) *прил*: **М~ие острова́** Maldives, Maldive Islands.

малька́ *сущ см* **малёк.**

Ма́льт|а (-ы) *ж* Malta.

мальти́|ец (-йца) *м* Maltese.

мальти́й|ка (-йки; *gen pl* -ек) *ж см* **мальти́ец.**

мальти́йск|ий (-ая, -ое, -ие) *прил* Maltese.

мальти́йца *сущ см* **мальти́ец.**

ма́льчик (-а) *м* boy.

мальчи́шек *сущ см* **мальчи́шка.**

мальчи́шеск|ий (-ая, -ое, -ие) *прил* (*задо́р, вид*) boyish; (*несерьёзный*) childish, puerile.

мальчи́шеств|о (-а) *ср* childishness.

мальчи́ш|ка (-ки; *gen pl* -ек) *м* (*разг*) boy; (*нео́пытный мужчи́на*) child.

мальчи́шник (-а) *м* stag night *или* party (*BRIT*), stag (*US*).

малю́сеньк|ий (-ая, -ое, -ие) *прил* (*разг*) tiny, wee (*esp SCOTTISH*).

малю́т|ка (-ки; *gen pl* -ок) *м/ж* baby; **кни́жка/фотоаппара́т~** miniature book/camera.

маля́в|ка (-ки; *gen pl* -ок) *ж* small fish ♦ *м/ж* (*разг: пренебр*) shrimp.

маля́р (-а́) *м* painter (and decorator).

маляри́йный *прил* malarial.

маляри́|я (-и) *ж* malaria.

маля́рный *прил* painter's; **~ая кисть** paintbrush.

ма́м|а (-ы) *ж* mummy (*BRIT*), mommy (*US*).

мамалы́г|а (-и) *ж* polenta, maize porridge.

мама́ш|а (-и) *ж* (*разг: мать*) mummy (*BRIT*), mommy (*US*); (: *обраще́ние к пожило́й же́нщине*) missus.

ма́менькин (-а, -о, -ы) *прил*: **~ сыно́к** (*разг: пренебр*) mummy's boy; **~а до́чка** (*разг*) mummy's girl.

ма́монт (-а) *м* mammoth.

мана́т|ки (-ок) *мн* (*разг*) stuff *ед.*

ма́нго *ср нескл* mango.

мангу́ст|а (-ы) *ж* mongoose.

мандари́н (-а) *м* tangerine.

мандари́новый *прил* tangerine.

манда́т (-а) *м* mandate.

мандоли́н|а (-ы) *ж* mandoline.

манёвр (-а) *м* (*также перен*) manoeuvre (*BRIT*), maneuver (*US*); *см также* **манёвры.**

маневри́р|овать (-ую; *perf* **сманеври́ровать**) *несов неперех* (*войска́, диплома́т итп*) to manoeuvre (*BRIT*), maneuver (*US*); (*перен*): **~ +instr** (*ресу́рсами, фина́нсами*) to make full use of.

манёвр|ы (-ов) *мн* manoeuvres *мн* (*BRIT*), maneuvers *мн* (*US*); (*на желе́зной доро́ге*) shunting *ед.*

мане́ж (-а) *м* (*для верхово́й езды́*) manège (*ци́рка*) ring; (*для младе́нцев*) playpen; (*также*: **легкоатлети́ческий ~**) indoor stadium (*мн* stadia).

манеке́н (-а) *м* (*портно́го*) dummy; (*в витри́не*) dummy, mannequin.

манеке́нщик (-а) *м* model.

манеке́нщиц|а (-ы) *ж см* **манеке́нщик.**

мане́р (-а) *м* (*разг*): **таки́м ~ом** like this ♦ *предл*: **на ~ +gen** like.

мане́р|а (-ы) *ж* manner; (*худо́жника, поэ́та*) style; *см также* **мане́ры.**

мане́рен *прил см* **мане́рный.**

мане́рнича|ть (-ю) *несов неперех* to put on airs.

мане́р|ный (-ен, -на, -но) *прил* affected.

мане́р|ы (-) *мн* manners *мн.*

манже́т|а (-ы) *ж* cuff.

маниака́льный *прил* maniacal.

маникю́р (-а) *м* manicure.

маникю́рный *прил* manicure *опред.*

маникю́рш|а (-и) *ж* manicurist.

Мани́л|а (-ы) *ж* Manila.

манипули́р|овать (-ую) *несов неперех* (*+instr*; *также перен*) to manipulate.

манипуля́ци|я (-и) *ж* (*также перен*) manipulation.

мани́|ть (-ю́, -ишь; *perf* **помани́ть**) *несов перех* to beckon; (*no perf*; *перен*: *привлека́ть*) to attract.

манифе́ст (-а) *м* manifesto.

манифеста́ци|я (-и) *ж* demonstration.

мани́ш|ка (-ки; *gen pl* -ек) *ж* (*часть руба́шки*) shirt front; (*нагру́дник*) dicky.

ма́ни|я (**-и**) ж mania.
ма́нк|а (**-и**) ж (*разг*) semolina.
ма́нн|а (**-ы**) ж manna; **ждать** (*impf*) **как ~ы небе́сной** to await impatiently.
ма́нн|ый *прил*: **~ая ка́ша**, **~ая крупа́** semolina.
маноме́тр (**-а**) м manometer.
манса́рд|а (**-ы**) ж garret.
ма́нти|я (**-и**) ж robe.
манто́ *ср нескл* (ladies') fur coat.
мануфакту́р|а (**-ы**) ж (*ист: фабрика*) (textile) mill.
Манче́стер (**-а**) м Manchester.
Маньчжу́ри|я (**-и**) ж Manchuria.
манья́к (**-а**) м maniac.
мара́зм (**-а**) м (*мед*) dementia; (*перен: разг*) idiocy; **ста́рческий ~** senility, senile dementia.
мара́л (**-а**) м Siberian deer.
мара́|ть (**-ю**; *perf* **вы́марать** *или* **измара́ть**) *несов перех* (*разг: пачкать*) to get dirty; (*perf* **замара́ть**; *перен: разг*) to drag through the dirt; (*perf* **намара́ть**; *разг: рисовать, писать*) to scribble; **~** (*impf*) **ру́ки** (*перен: разг*) to get one's hands dirty
▶ **мара́ться** (*perf* **вы́мараться** *или* **измара́ться**) *несов возв* (*разг: пачкаться*) to get dirty; (*perf* **замара́ться**; *разг: портить репутацию*) to ruin one's reputation.
марафе́т (**-а**) м (*разг*): **навести́ ~** to tidy up; (*: прихорашиваться*) to smarten (o.s.) up.
марафо́н (**-а**) м marathon.
марафо́н|ец (**-ца**) м marathon runner.
ма́рган|ец (**-ца**) м manganese.
марганцо́вк|а (**-и**) ж (*разг*) potassium permanganate.
маргари́н (**-а**) м margarine.
маргари́т|ка (**-ки**; *gen pl* **-ок**) ж daisy.
маргина́льный *прил* marginal.
ма́рж|а (**-и**) ж (*комм*) margin.
марина́д (**-а**) м (*соус*) marinade; (*обычно мн: маринованные овощи*) pickle.
марин|ова́ть (**-у́ю**; *perf* **замаринова́ть**) *несов перех* (*грибы, овощи*) to pickle; (*мясо, рыбу*) to marinate, marinade; (*no perf*; *разг: дело*) to put off.
марионе́т|ка (**-ки**; *gen pl* **-ок**) ж (*также перен*) puppet.
марионе́точный *прил* (*также перен*) puppet *опред*.
Мариу́пол|ь (**-я**) м Mariupol.
ма́р|ка (**-ки**; *gen pl* **-ок**) ж (*почтовая*) stamp; (*торговая*) trademark; (*сорт*) brand; (*качество*) grade; (*модель*) make; (*денежная единица*) mark; **держа́ть** (*impf*) **~ку** to keep up one's reputation; **держи́те ~ку шко́лы/фи́рмы** don't let your school/the firm down.
ма́ркетинг (**-а**) м marketing.
ма́ркий (**-кая, -кое, -кие; -ок, -ка, -ко**) *прил*: **э́то пальто́ о́чень ~кое** this coat shows the dirt easily.
маркир|ова́ть (**-у́ю**) *несов перех* (*продукцию*) to trademark.
маркси́зм (**-а**) м Marxism.
маркси́ст (**-а**) м Marxist.
ма́рлевый *прил* gauze.
ма́рл|я (**-и**) ж gauze.
мармела́д (**-а**; *part gen* **-у**) м fruit jellies *мн*.
мароде́р (**-а**) м looter; (*разг: спекулянт*) profiteer.
мароде́рств|о (**-а**) *ср* looting.
ма́рок *сущ см* **ма́рка** ♦ *прил см* **ма́ркий**.
Маро́кко *ср нескл* Morocco.
ма́рочный *прил* (*изделие*) branded; (*вино*) vintage.
Марс (**-а**) м Mars.
Марсе́л|ь (**-я**) м Marseilles.
март (**-а**) м March; *см также* **октя́брь**.
марты́шк|а (**-и**) ж marmoset ♦ *м/ж* (*перен: разг*) monkey.
марципа́н (**-а**) м marzipan.
марш (**-а**) м (*также перен*) march ♦ *межд* (*воен*): **~!** forward march!; **ле́стничный ~** flight of stairs; **~ домо́й!** (*разг*) off you go home!
ма́ршал (**-а**) м marshal.
маршир|ова́ть (**-у́ю**; *perf* **промаршировать**) *несов неперех* to march.
маршру́т (**-а**) м route.
маршру́т|ка (**-ки**; *gen pl* **-ок**) ж (*разг*) fixed-route taxi.
маршру́тный *прил*: **~ое такси́** fixed-route taxi.
маршру́ток *сущ см* **маршру́тка**.
ма́сел *сущ см* **ма́сло**.
ма́с|ка (**-ки**; *gen pl* **-ок**) ж (*также перен*) mask; (*косметическая*) face pack.
маскара́д (**-а**) м masked ball; (*перен*) masquerade.
маскир|ова́ть (**-у́ю**; *perf* **замаскирова́ть**) *несов перех* (*также перен*) to camouflage
▶ **маскирова́ться** (*perf* **замаскирова́ться**) *несов возв* to camouflage o.s.
маскиро́вк|а (**-и**) ж (*воен*) camouflage; (*перен*) disguise.
маскиро́вочный *прил* camouflage *опред*.
ма́сленица (**-ы**) ж ≈ Shrovetide.
маслён|ка (**-ки**; *gen pl* **-ок**) ж butter dish; (*тех*) oilcan.
маслён|ок (**-ёнка**; *nom pl* **-я́та**, *gen pl* **-я́т**) м annulated *или* yellow boletus (*edible mushroom*).
ма́сленый *прил* (*в масле*) buttery; (*запачканный маслом*) oily; (*перен: разг*): **льсти́вый**) slick; (*: сластолюбивый*) voluptuous; **ма́сленая неде́ля** ≈ Shrovetide.
масли́н|а (**-ы**) ж (*дерево*) olive (tree); (*плод*) olive.
ма́сл|ить (**-ю, -ишь**; *perf* **нама́слить** *или*

помаслить) *несов перех* to butter.
масличный *прил* oil-yielding.
масло (-ла; *nom pl* -ла, *gen pl* -ел) *ср* (*сливочное*) butter; (*растительное, смазочное*) oil; (*ИСКУССТВО*) oils *мн*; **дело идёт как по ~лу** (*разг*) things are going smoothly; **подливать** (**подлить** *perf*) **~ла в огонь** to add fuel to the fire; **~ масляное** (*разг*) tautology.
маслобойня (-йни; *gen pl* -ен) *ж* creamery.
маслозавод (-а) *м* creamery.
маслянистый (-, -а, -о) *прил* oily.
масляный *прил* (*краска, фильтр*) oil *опред*; (*пятно*) oily.
маслята *итп сущ см* **маслёнок**.
масок *прил см* **маска**.
масон (-а) *м* Freemason, Mason.
масонский (-ая, -ое, -ие) *прил* Masonic.
масса (-ы) *ж* (*также ФИЗ*) mass; (*керамическая*) paste; (*древесная*) pulp; (*no pl; много*) loads *мн*; **денежная ~** money supply; *см также* **массы**.
массаж (-а) *м* massage; **~ сердца** cardiac massage.
массажист (-а) *м* masseur.
массажистка (-ки; *gen pl* -ок) *ж* masseuse.
массив (-а) *м* (*водный*) expanse; (*земельный, лесной*) tract; (*КОМП*) array; **горный ~** massif; **жилой** *или* **жилищный ~** housing estate (*BRIT*) *или* project (*US*).
массивный (-ен, -на, -но) *прил* massive.
массированный *прил* (*атака*) all-out.
массировать (-ую) *несов перех* to massage.
массовик (-а) *м* organizer of group activities.
массовка (-ки; *gen pl* -ок) *ж* (*КИНО, ТЕАТР: массовая сцена*) crowd scene; (: *статисты*) extras *мн*; (*разг*) group outing.
массовый *прил* mass production; (*поставка*) bulk *опред*; **товары ~ого спроса** mass-market goods; **массовое производство** (*ЭКОН*) mass production.
массы (-) *мн* (*народ*) the masses *мн*.
мастак (-а) *м* (*разг*): **~ на** +*acc*/**в** +*prp* a dab hand at.
мастер (-а; *nom pl* -а) *м* master; (*на производстве*) foreman (*мн* foremen); (*ремесленник*) craftsman (*мн* craftsmen); **часовой ~** watchmaker; **~ на** +*acc* expert at; **~ на все руки** handyman (*мн* handymen); **мастер спорта** master sportsman (*title awarded to sportsmen*).
мастерить (-ю, -ишь; *perf* **смастерить**) *несов перех* to make (by hand).
мастерок (-ка) *м* trowel.
мастерская (-ой; *decl like adj*) *ж* (*часовая, столярная*) workshop; (*художника, скульптора*) studio; (*на заводе*) shop.
мастерство (-а) *ср* (*квалификация*) skill; (*ремесло*) trade.
мастика (-и) *ж* mastic; (*для натирания полов*) floor polish.
маститит (-а) *м* mastitis.
маститый (-, -а, -о) *прил* eminent.

масть (-и; *gen pl* -ей) *ж* (*лошади*) colour (*BRIT*), color (*US*); (*КАРТЫ*) suit.
масштаб (-а) *м* scale.
масштабный *прил* scale *опред*; (-ен, -на, -но; *произведение, стройка*) large-scale; **масштабная линейка** scale.
мат (-а) *м* (*ШАХМАТЫ*) checkmate; (*половик, также СПОРТ*) mat; (*ругательства*) bad language; **ругаться** (*impf*) **матом** (*разг*) to use bad language.
матадор (-а) *м* matador.
математик (-а) *м* mathematician.
математика (-и) *ж* mathematics.
математический (-ая, -ое, -ие) *прил* mathematical; (*факультет*) mathematics *опред*.
матери *итп сущ см* **мать**.
материал (-а) *м* material; (*обычно мн: служебные, следствия*) document.
материален *прил см* **материальный**.
материализм (-а) *м* materialism.
материалист (-а) *м* materialist.
материальный (-ен, -ьна, -ьно) *прил* material *опред*; (*no short form; финансовый*) financial, material *опред*; **~ ущерб** material damage; **материальная помощь** financial assistance.
материк (-а) *м* continent; (*суша*) mainland.
материковый *прил* mainland *опред*.
материнский (-ая, -ое, -ие) *прил* maternal; (*БИО, БОТ*) parent *опред*.
материнство (-а) *ср* maternity, motherhood; (*чувство*) motherliness.
материться (-юсь, -ишься) *несов возв* (*разг*) to swear.
материя (-и) *ж* matter; (*разг: ткань*) cloth; **говорить** (*impf*) **о высоких ~х** to speak about elevated matters.
матерный *прил* (*разг*) obscene.
матерчатый *прил* cloth.
матёрый *прил* (*волк, медведь*) mature, full-grown; (*перен: преступник*) hardened.
матерь (-и) *ж*: **М~ Божья** Mother of God.
матерью *итп сущ см* **мать**.
матка (-ки; *gen pl* -ок) *ж* uterus, womb; (*ЗООЛ: также: пчелиная ~*) queen bee.
матовый (-, -а, -о) *прил* (*без блеска*) mat(t); **матовое стекло** frosted glass.
маток *сущ см* **матка**.
матрас (-а) *м* mattress.
матрац (-а) *м* = **матрас**.
матрёшка (-ки; *gen pl* -ек) *ж* Russian doll.
матриархат (-а) *м* (*ИСТ*) matriarchy.
матричный *прил*: **~ принтер** (*КОМП*) dot-matrix printer.
матрос (-а) *м* sailor.
матроска (-и) *ж* sailor top *или* shirt.
матросский (-ая, -ое, -ие) *прил* sailor's.
матушка (-ки; *gen pl* -ек) *ж* (*мать*) mother; (*РЕЛ*) priest's wife.
матч (-а) *м* (*СПОРТ*) match.
мать (-ери; *см* **Table 1**) *ж* mother; (*разг: как обращение*) missus; **в чём ~ родила** (*разг*) in

one's birthday suit; **мать-одино́чка** single mother.

мать-и-ма́чех|а (**-и**) *ж* coltsfoot.

мафио́зный *прил* mafia *опред*.

мафио́зи *м нескл* mafioso.

ма́фи|я (**-и**) *ж* the Mafia; (*перен*) Mafia.

мах (**-а**; *part gen* **-у**) *м* (*крыла*) flap; (*колеса*) turn; (*ногой*) swing; (*рукой*) swing, stroke; **дать** (*perf*) **ма́ху** (*разг: ошиби́ться*) to boob.

ма|ха́ть (**-шу́**, **-шешь**) *несов неперех* (+*instr*) to wave; (*крыльями*) to flap; ~ (*impf*) **кому́-н руко́й** to wave to sb.

махи́н|а (**-ы**) *ж* (*разг*) monster (*fig*).

махина́тор (**-а**) *м* machinator, schemer.

махина́ци|я (**-и**) *ж* machination, scheme.

махн|у́ть (**-у́**, **-ёшь**) *сов неперех* to give a wave; (*разг: поехать*) to go; (*через забор*) to jump; ~ (*perf*) **на кого́-н/что-н руко́й** to give sb/sth up as a bad job

▸ **махну́ться** *сов возв* (*разг*: +*instr*) to swap.

махо́рк|а (**-и**) *ж* ≈ shag, coarse tobacco.

махро́в|ый *прил* (*халат*) towelling; (*цветок*) double; (*перен: отъя́вленный*) out-and-out; ~**ая ткань** terry towelling.

ма́чех|а (**-и**) *ж* stepmother.

ма́чт|а (**-ы**) *ж* mast.

машбюро́ *ср нескл сокр* (= *машинопи́сное бюро́*) typing pool.

маши́н|а (**-ы**) *ж* (*также перен*) machine; (*автомобиль*) car.

машина́лен *прил см* **машина́льный**.

машина́льно *нареч* mechanically.

машина́льный (**-ен**, **-на**, **-но**) *прил* mechanical.

машини́ст (**-а**) *м* (*комбайна, экскаватора*) driver, operator; ~ **локомоти́ва** engine driver (*esp BRIT*), engineer (*US*).

машини́ст|ка (**-ки**; *gen pl* **-ок**) *ж* typist.

маши́н|ка (**-ки**; *gen pl* **-ок**) *ж* machine; **пишу́щая** ~ typewriter.

маши́нный *прил* (*производство, части, масло*) machine *опред*; (*счёт, обработка*) mechanical; **маши́нное отделе́ние** engine room; **маши́нный код/язы́к** (*КОМП*) machine code/language.

маши́нок *сущ см* **маши́нка**.

машинопи́сный *прил* (*текст*) typewritten; **машинопи́сное бюро́** typing pool.

машинопи́с|ь (**-и**) *ж* (*печатание*) typing; (*текст*) typescript.

машинострое́ни|е (**-я**) *ср* mechanical engineering.

машу́ *итп несов см* **маха́ть**.

мая́к (**-а́**) *м* lighthouse.

ма́ятник (**-а**) *м* (*часов*) pendulum.

ма́|яться (**-юсь**; *perf* **ума́яться**) *несов возв* (*разг: томи́ться*) to suffer.

мая́|чить (**-у**, **-ишь**) *несов неперех* (*разг: виднеться*) to be visible; (: *надоедливо*

возникать) to hang around.

МБ *м сокр* (= *Министе́рство безопа́сности*) *ministry for security*.

МБР *м сокр* (= *Министе́рство безопа́сности Росси́и*) *Russian Ministry for security*; (= *межконтинента́льная баллисти́ческая раке́та*) ICBM (= *intercontinental ballistic missile*).

МБРР *м сокр* (= *Междунаро́дный банк реконстру́кции и разви́тия*) IBRD (= *International Bank for Reconstruction and Development*).

МВД *ср сокр* (= *Министе́рство вну́тренних дел*) ≈ the Home Office (*BRIT*), ≈ the Department of the Interior (*US*).

МВК *м сокр* (= *механи́зм валю́тных ку́рсов*) ERM (= *Exchange Rate Mechanism*).

МВФ *м сокр* (= *Междунаро́дный валю́тный фонд*) IMF (= *International Monetary Fund*).

МВЭС *ср сокр* (= *Министе́рство внешнеэкономи́ческих свя́зей*) *ministry of foreign economic links*.

мг. *сокр* (= *миллигра́мм*) mg (= *milligram(me)*).

МГц *сокр* (= *мегаге́рц*) MHz (= *megahertz*).

мгл|а (**-ы**) *ж* haze; (*вечерняя*) gloom.

мгнове́нен *прил см* **мгнове́нный**.

мгнове́ни|е (**-я**) *ср* moment; **в одно́** ~ right away.

мгнове́н|ный (**-ен**, **-на**, **-но**) *прил* (*решение, реакция, фотография*) instant; (*смерть*) instantaneous; (*злость, раздраже́ние*) momentary; (*вспышка*) lightning *опред*.

МГУ *м сокр* (= *Моско́вский госуда́рственный университе́т*) Moscow State University.

ме́бел|ь (**-и**) *ж собир* furniture; **мя́гкая** ~ three-piece suite.

ме́бельный *прил* furniture *опред*.

ме́бельщик (**-а**) *м* furniture-maker.

мегаба́йт (**-а**) *м* megabyte.

мегава́тт (**-а**) *м* megawatt.

мегафо́н (**-а**) *м* megaphone.

меге́р|а (**-ы**) *ж* (*разг*) dragon.

мёд (**-а**; *part gen* **-у**, *loc sg* **-у́**, *nom pl* **-ы́**) *м* honey.

медали́ст (**-а**) *м* (*человек*) medallist (*BRIT*), medalist (*US*).

медали́ст|ка (**-ки**; *gen pl* **-ок**) *ж* medallist (*BRIT*), medalist (*US*).

меда́л|ь (**-и**) *ж* medal; **оборо́тная сторона́** ~**и** (*перен*) the other side of the coin.

медальо́н (**-а**) *м* medallion.

медбра́т (**-а**) *м сокр* (= *медици́нский брат*) nurse (*male*).

медве́диц|а (**-ы**) *ж* she-bear; **Больша́я М**~ the Great Bear.

медве́д|ь (**-я**) *м* (*также перен*) bear.

медвежа́та *итп сущ см* **медвежо́нок**.

медве́ж|ий (**-ья**, **-ье**, **-ьи**) *прил* bear *опред*; **медве́жья услу́га** ≈ more of a hindrance than a help.

медвежо́нок (-о́нка; *nom pl* -а́та, *gen pl* -а́т) *м* bear cub.

ме́дик (-а) *м* medic.

медикаме́нт (-а) *м* (*обычно мн*) medicine.

медици́н|а (-ы) *ж* medicine.

медици́нск|ий (-ая, -ое, -ие) *прил* medical.

ме́дленно *нареч* slowly.

ме́дленный *прил* slow.

медли́тельный (-ен, -ьна, -ьно) *прил* slow.

ме́дл|ить (-ю, -ишь) *несов неперех* to delay; ~ (*impf*) **с реше́нием/отве́том** to be slow in deciding/answering.

ме́дный *прил* copper; (*муз*) brass.

медо́вый *прил* honey *опред*; ~ **вкус/арома́т** taste/smell of honey; **медо́вый ме́сяц** honeymoon.

медпу́нкт (-а) *м сокр* (= **медици́нский пункт**) ≈ first-aid post.

медсестр|а́ (-ы́) *ж сокр* (= **медици́нская сестра́**) nurse.

меду́з|а (-ы) *ж* jellyfish.

медь (-и) *ж* copper ◆ *собир* coppers *мн*.

медя́к (-а́) *м* (*разг*) copper (*coin*).

меж|а́ (-и́; *nom pl* -и) *ж* boundary.

междоме́ти|е (-я) *ср* interjection.

KEYWORD

ме́жду *предл* (+*instr*) **1** between; **ме́жду дома́ми/города́ми** between the houses/towns; **ме́жду заседа́ниями/ле́кциями** between the meetings/lectures; **ме́жду оро́га ~ Москво́й и Петербу́ргом** the road between Moscow and St. Petersburg

2: **они́ договори́лись ме́жду собо́й** they agreed among themselves; **ме́жду на́ми (говоря́)** between ourselves

3 (+*gen*; *в окружении*) amongst; **ме́жду домо́в росло́ большо́е де́рево** a big tree grew in amongst the houses

4: **ме́жду про́чим** (*попутно*) in passing; (*кстати*) by the way; **ме́жду про́чим, мы ви́дели Ма́шу** by the way, we saw Masha; **ме́жду тем** meanwhile; **ме́жду тем как** while.

междуве́домственный *прил* interdepartmental.

междугоро́дный *прил* intercity.

междунаро́дный *прил* international.

мезони́н (-а) *м* attic.

Ме́кк|а (-и) *ж* Mecca.

Ме́ксик|а (-и) *ж* Mexico.

мексика́н|ец (-ца) *м* Mexican.

мексика́н|ка (-ки; *gen pl* -ок) *ж см* **мексика́нец**.

мексика́нск|ий (-ая, -ое, -ие) *прил* Mexican.

мексика́нца *сущ см* **мексика́нец**.

мел (-а; *part gen* -у, *loc sg* -у́) *м* chalk.

меланхо́лик (-а) *м* melancholic.

меланхоли́чный *прил* melancholic *опред*.

меланхо́ли|я (-и) *ж* melancholy.

мел|е́ть (*3sg* -ет, *3pl* -ют, *perf* **обмеле́ть**) *несов неперех* to become shallower.

мелиора́ци|я (-и) *ж* soil improvement.

мелка́ *сущ см* **мело́к**.

ме́л|кий (-кая, -кое, -кие; -лок, -лка́, -лко) *прил* (*почерк*) small; (*песок, дождь*) fine; (*неглубокий*) shallow; (*малозначительный*) petty; (*no short form*; *собственник*) small; (*несущественный*) minor; ~**кие де́ньги** (*мелочь*) small change; **ме́лкая буржуази́я** petty bourgeoisie.

ме́лко *нареч* (*резать, дробить*) finely; (*писать*) small ◆ *как сказ* (*у берега итп*) it's shallow.

мелкобуржуа́з|ный (-ен, -на, -но) *прил* petty-bourgeois.

мелково́д|ный (-ен, -на, -но) *прил* shallow.

мелкокали́берный *прил* small-bore, small-calibre (*BRIT*), small-caliber (*US*).

мелоди́чный (-ен, -на, -но) *прил* melodious.

мело́ди|я (-и) *ж* tune, melody.

мелодра́м|а (-ы) *ж* (*также перен*) melodrama.

ме́лок *прил см* **ме́лкий**.

мел|о́к (-ка́) *м* piece of chalk.

мелома́н (-а) *м* music-lover.

ме́лочен *прил см* **ме́лочный**.

мело́ч|иться (-усь, -ишься) *несов возв* (*разг*) to be petty.

ме́лочный (-ен, -на, -но) *прил* petty; (*человек*) small-minded, petty.

ме́лочь (-и; *gen pl* -е́й) *ж* (*пустяк*) triviality; (*подробность*) detail ◆ *ж собир* little things *мн*; (*мелкие монеты*) small change; „**Ты́сяча мелоче́й**" *name of shops selling household goods*; **разме́ниваться** (*impf*) **по мелоча́м** to waste one's talents.

мель (-и; *loc sg* -и́) *ж* shallows *мн*, shoal; **сади́ться (сесть** *perf*) **на** ~ (*МОР*) to run aground; **быть** (*impf*) **на мели́** (*перен*: *разг*) to be (stony (*BRIT*) *или* stone (*US*)) broke.

Ме́льбурн (-а) *м* Melbourne.

мелька́|ть (-ю) *несов неперех* (*появиться и исчезнуть*) to flash past; (*мерцать*) to twinkle; ~ (*impf*) **в уме́** *или* **голове́** to flash through one's mind.

мелькн|у́ть (-у́, -ёшь) *сов неперех* to flash.

ме́льком *нареч* in passing.

ме́льник (-а) *м* miller.

ме́льниц|а (-ы) *ж* mill.

ме́льничный *прил* mill *опред*.

мельхио́р (-а) *м* nickel silver.

мельча́|ть (-ю; *perf* **измельча́ть**) *несов неперех* (*река, залив*) to get shallower; (*интересы, люди*) to become petty; (*хозяйство итп*) to become smaller.

ме́льче *сравн прил от* **ме́лкий** ◆ *сравн нареч от* **ме́лко**.

мельч|и́ть (-у́, -и́шь; *perf* **измельчи́ть** *или* **размельчи́ть**) *несов перех* (*ножом*) to cut up small; (*в ступке*) to crush.

мелю́ *итп несов см* **моло́ть**.

мелюзга́ (-и́) *ж собир* (*разг*: *пренебр*) small fry.

мембра́н|а (-ы) *ж* (*ТЕХ*) diaphragm.

мемора́ндум (-а) *м* memorandum.

мемориа́л (**-а**) *м* memorial.
мемориа́льный *прил* memorial *опред*.
мемуа́ры (**-ов**) *мн* memoirs *мн*.
ме́неджер (**-а**) *м* manager; ~ **по ма́ркетингу** marketing manager.
менеджме́нт (**-а**) *м* management.
ме́нее *сравн нареч нареч* less; **тем не** ~ nevertheless; ~ **всего́** least of all; ~ **всего́ удо́бный** least convenient of all.
мензу́р|ка (**-ки**; *gen pl* **-ок**) *ж* measuring glass.
менинги́т (**-а**) *м* meningitis.
менструа́ци|я (**-и**) *ж* menstruation.
менто́л (**-а**) *м* menthol.
ме́ньше *сравн прил от* **ма́лый, ма́ленький** ♦ *сравн нареч от* **ма́ло** ♦ *нареч* less than; ~ **всего́** least of all.
ме́ньш|ий (**-ая, -ее, -ие**) *сравн прил от* **ма́лый, ма́ленький** ♦ *прил* (*младший*) younger; **по ~ей ме́ре** at least; **са́мое ~ее** no less than.
меньшинств|о́ (**-а́**) *ср собир* minority; **национа́льное** ~ ethnic minority.
меню́ *ср нескл* menu.
меня́ *мест см* **я**.
меня́ть (**-ю**; *perf* **поменя́ть**) *несов перех* to change; ~ (**поменя́ть** *perf*) **что-н на** +*acc* to exchange sth for
▸ **меня́ться** (*perf* **поменя́ться**) *несов возв* to change; (*жилплощадью*) to swap; (*perf* **измени́ться**; *погода, вкусы*) to change; ~**ся** (**поменя́ться** *perf*) **чем-н с кем-н** to exchange sth with sb.
ме́р|а (**-ы**) *ж* measure; (*предел*) limit; **без ~ы** extremely; **сверх ~ы** excessively; **в по́лной ~е** fully; **по ~е** +*gen* with; **по ~е того́ как** as; **по ~е сил** as much as one can; **по ~е возмо́жности** as far as possible; **принима́ть** (**приня́ть** *perf*) **~ы по** +*prp* to take measures as regards; **вы́сшая ~ наказа́ния** capital punishment.
ме́рен *прил см* **ме́рный**.
мере́ть (*3sg* **мрёт**, *3pl* **мрут**, *pt* **мёр, -ла, -ло**) *несов неперех* (*разг: умирать*) to snuff it.
мере́щ|иться (**-усь, -ишься**; *perf* **помере́щиться**) *несов возв* (+*dat*) to appear; **ему́ ~ился о́браз** he thought he saw a figure.
мёрз *итп несов см* **мёрзнуть**.
мерза́в|ец (**-ца**) *м* (*разг*) nasty piece of work.
мерза́в|ка (**-ки**; *gen pl* **-ок**) *ж см* **мерза́вец**.
мерза́вца *сущ см* **мерза́вец**.
ме́рз|кий (**-кая, -кое, -кие**; *сотр* **-ка́, -ко**) *прил* (*слова, личность, посту́пок*) disgusting; (*погода, настроение*) foul.
мерзлот|а́ (**-ы́**) *ж*: **ве́чная** ~ permafrost.
мёрзлый *прил* (*земля*) frozen; (*овощи*) frost-damaged.
мёрз|нуть (**-ну, -нешь**; *pt* **-, -ла, -ло**, *perf* **замё́рзнуть**) *несов неперех* to freeze.
мёрзок *прил см* **ме́рзкий**.
ме́рзост|ь (**-и**) *ж* disgusting thing; (*посту́пка*)

baseness; **кака́я** ~! how disgusting!
меридиа́н (**-а**) *м* meridian.
мери́л|о (**-а**) *ср* criterion (*мн* criteria).
ме́рин (**-а**) *м* gelding.
ме́р|ить (**-ю, -ишь**; *perf* **сме́рить** *или* **изме́рить**) *несов перех* to measure; (*perf* **поме́рить**; *примерять*) to try on; ~ (**сме́рить** *perf*) **взгля́дом кого́-н** (*перен*) to look sb up and down
▸ **ме́риться** (*perf* **поме́риться**) *несов возв* (+*instr*): ~**ся зна́ниями/си́лами с кем-н** to measure one's knowledge/strengths against sb.
мерк *итп несов см* **ме́ркнуть**.
ме́р|ка (**-ки**; *gen pl* **-ок**) *ж* measurements *мн*; (*перен: критерий*) standard; (*мерило*) measure; **снима́ть** (**снять** *perf*) ~**ку с кого́-н** to take sb's measurements.
ме́рк|нуть (*3sg* **-нет**, *3pl* **-нут**, *pt* **-, -ла, -ло**, *perf* **поме́ркнуть**) *несов неперех* (*также перен*) to fade.
Мерку́ри|й (**-я**) *м* Mercury.
ме́р|ный (**-ен, -на, -но**) *прил* (*размеренный*) measured; (*no short form*; *ТЕХ*) measuring.
ме́рок *сущ см* **ме́рка**.
мероприя́ти|е (**-я**) *ср* measure; **культу́рное** ~ cultural event.
мертве́|ть (**-ю**; *perf* **омертве́ть**) *несов неперех* (*от холода*) to go numb; (*perf* **помертве́ть**; *от страха, от го́ря*) to be numb.
мертве́ц (**-а́**) *м* dead person (*мн* people).
мёртв|ый (**-, -а́, -о́**) *прил* dead; (*взгляд, улица*) lifeless; **спать** (*impf*) ~**ым сном** to sleep the sleep of the dead; **лежа́ть** (*impf*) ~**ым гру́зом** to lie unused; **мёртвый сезо́н** dead season; **мёртвая хва́тка** mortal grip; **мёртвый язы́к** dead language.
мертвя́щ|ий (**ая, -ое, -ие**) *прил* (*обстано́вка*) lifeless.
мерца́|ть (*3sg* **-ет**, *3pl* **-ют**) *несов неперех* to glimmer, flicker; (*звёзды*) to twinkle.
ме́сив|о (**-а**) *ср* mush; (*на доро́ге*) slush.
ме|си́ть (**-шу́, -сишь**; *perf* **смеси́ть**) *несов перех* (*тесто, гли́ну*) to knead; ~ (*impf*) **грязь** (*перен*) to wade through the mud.
ме́сс|а (**-ы**) *ж* (*РЕЛ*) Mass.
мест|а́ (**-**) *мн* provinces *мн*.
места́ми *нареч* in places.
ме|сти́ (**-ту́, -тёшь**; *pt* **мёл, -ла́, -ло́**, *perf* **подмести́**) *несов перех* (*пол, ко́мнату итп*) to sweep; (*мусор, ли́стья итп*) to sweep up; (*подлеж: мете́ль*) to whirl; **на дворе́** ~**тёт** it's a blizzard outside.
местко́м (**-а**) *м сокр* (= **ме́стный комите́т**) *local trade-union committee*.
ме́стность (**-и**) *ж* (*холми́стая, ро́вная*) terrain; (*се́льская, да́чная*) area, district.
ме́стный *прил* local ♦ (**-ого**; *decl like adj*) *м* local (inhabitant); **ме́стные вла́сти** local authorities

мн; **ме́стный нарко́з** (МЕД) local anaesthetic (BRIT) или anaesthetic (US).

ме́ст|о (-а; nom pl -á) ср place; (для постройки) site; (действия, происшествия) scene; (работа) job; (: вакантное) post; (в театре, поезде итп) seat; (багажа, груза) item; (в книге, в пьесе) part; **сла́бое** ~ weak spot; **здесь не** ~ **говори́ть о деньга́х** this is not the place to talk about money; **реши́ть** (perf) **на** ~**е** to decide on the spot; ~**а себе́ не находи́ть** (impf) to worry; **к** ~**у** to the point; **спа́льное** ~ berth; **на Ва́шем** ~**е я бы** ... in your place или if I were you, I would ...; **ни с** ~**а!** don't move!; **у меня́ душа́** или **се́рдце не на** ~**е** I'm worried; см также **места́**.

местожи́тельств|о (-а) ср place of residence.

местоимени́е (-я) ср pronoun.

местонахожде́ни|е (-я) ср location.

местопребыва́ни|е (-я) ср residence.

месторожде́ни|е (-я) ср (скопление) deposit; (угля, нефти, золота) field.

месть (-и) ж vengeance, revenge.

ме́сяц (-а; nom pl -ы) м month; (часть луны) crescent moon; (диск луны) moon.

ме́сячн|ые (-ых; decl like adj) мн (разг) (menstrual) period ед.

ме́сячный прил monthly.

мета́лл (-а) м metal.

металли́ческий (-ая, -ое, -ие) прил metal; (блеск, скрежет) metallic.

металлоло́м (-а) м scrap metal.

металлу́рги|я (-и) ж metallurgy.

метаморфо́з|а (-ы) ж metamorphosis.

мета́тель (-я) м thrower; ~ **ди́ска** discus thrower.

мета́|ть (-чу́, -чешь) несов перех (гранату, диск итп) to throw; (perf **намета́ть**; шов) to tack, baste; (perf **промета́ть** или **смета́ть**; для примерки) to tack; ~ (impf) **жре́бий** to draw lots; ~ (**смета́ть** perf) **стог се́на** to stack hay; ~ (**вы́метать** perf) **икру́** to spawn; **рвать** (impf) **и** ~ (impf) (разг) to storm and rage

▸ **мета́ться** несов возв (в постели, в бреду) to toss and turn; (по комнате) to rush about.

мета́фор|а (-ы) ж metaphor.

мётел сущ см **метла́**.

мете́л|ь (-и) ж snowstorm, blizzard.

метео́р (-а) м meteor.

метеори́т (-а) м meteorite.

метеоро́лог (-а) м meteorologist.

метеороло́ги|я (-и) ж meteorology.

метеосво́д|ка (-ки; gen pl -ок) ж сокр (= метеорологи́ческая сво́дка) weather forecast или report.

метеоста́нци|я (-и) ж сокр (= метеорологи́ческая ста́нция) weather station.

ме́ти|ть (-чу, -тишь; perf **поме́тить**) несов перех to mark ♦ неперех: ~ **в** +acc (в противника, в цель) to aim at; **он** ~**тил в профессора́/нача́льники** his ambition was to become a professor/manager

▸ **ме́титься** (perf **наме́титься**) несов возв: ~**ся в** +acc to aim at.

ме́т|ка (-ки; gen pl -ок) ж mark.

ме́ткий (-кая, -кое, -кие; -ок, -ка́, -ко) прил (точный) accurate; (перен) apt; **име́ть** (impf) ~ **глаз** to have a good aim.

метл|а́ (-ы́; nom pl **мётлы**, gen pl **мётел**) ж broom; **но́вая** ~ (разг) new broom (fig).

метн|у́ть (-у́, -ёшь) сов перех (диск, камень) to throw

▸ **метну́ться** сов возв (разг: устремиться) to rush.

ме́тод (-а) м method.

мето́дик|а (-и) ж (преподавания) teaching methodology; (исследований, работы) methods мн.

методи́ческий (-ая, -ое, -ие) прил systematic.

ме́ток прил см **ме́ткий**.

метр (-а) м metre (BRIT), meter (US); (линейка) measure.

метра́ж (-á) м (квартиры, помещения) (metric) area; (ткани) length.

метрдоте́л|ь (-я) м head waiter.

ме́трик|а (-и) ж birth certificate.

метри́ческий (-ая, -ое, -ие) прил metric; ~**ая систе́ма мер** metric system; ~**ая то́нна** metric ton.

метро́ ср нескл metro, tube (BRIT).

мету́ итп несов см **мести́**.

мех (-а; loc sg -ý, nom pl -á) м fur; см также **меха́**.

мех|á (-о́в) мн (кузнечный, аккордеона) bellows мн.

механиза́тор (-а) м (С.-Х.) machine operator.

механизи́р|овать (-ую) (не)сов перех to mechanize.

механи́зм (-а) м mechanism; (перен: бюрократический) machinery.

меха́ник (-а) м mechanic.

меха́ник|а (-и) ж mechanics.

механи́ческий (-ая, -ое, -ие) прил mechanical; (цех) machine опред.

Ме́хико (нескл) м Mexico City.

мехово́й прил fur; ~ **магази́н** furrier's.

меч (-á) м sword.

ме́ченый прил marked.

мече́т|ь (-и) ж mosque.

мечт|а́ (-ы́; gen pl -а́ний) ж dream; **не о́тдых, а** ~**!** (разг) it's a dream holiday!

мечта́ни|е (-я) ср (обычно мн) daydream; **преде́л** ~**й** ultimate dream.

мечта́тельный прил dreamy.

мечта́тел|ь (-я) м dreamer.

мечта́тельниц|а (-ы) ж см **мечта́тель**.

мечта́|ть (-ю) несов неперех: ~ (**о** +prp) to dream (of); ~ (impf) **стать врачо́м/учи́ться** to dream of becoming a doctor/studying.

ме́чу(сь) сов см **ме́тить(ся)**.

мечу́(сь) итп несов см **мета́ть(ся)**.

мешани́н|а (-ы) ж (разг) jumble.

меша́|ть (-ю; perf **помеша́ть**) несов перех (суп, чай) to stir; (perf **смеша́ть**; напитки, краски) to mix ♦ *неперех* (+*dat*; *быть помехой*) to disturb, bother; (*создавать затруднения*) to hinder; **не ~ло бы пое́сть** (*разг*) it wouldn't hurt to eat; **~ (помеша́ть** *perf*) **кому́-н** +*infin* (*препятствовать*) to make it difficult for sb to do

▸ **меша́ться** *несов возв* (*разг: ребёнок, вещи*) to be a pain; (*perf* **смеша́ться**; *путаться*) to get mixed up; **~ся** (*impf*) **в** +*acc* (*вмешиваться*) to meddle *или* interfere in.

мешка́ *сущ см* **мешо́к**.

ме́шка|ть (**-ю**; *perf* **заме́шкать**) *несов неперех* (*разг*) to dawdle; **~ (заме́шкать** *perf*) **с отве́том/ отъе́здом** to be slow in answering/leaving.

мешкова́т|ый (**-, -а, -о**) *прил* (*пальто, платье*) baggy; (*фигура*) clumsy.

мешкови́н|а (**-ы**) *ж* sacking.

мешо́к (**-ка́**) *м* sack; (*спальный, вещевой*) bag; (*разг: человек*) lump; **~** +*gen* sack(ful) of; **де́нежный ~** moneybags; **у него́ ~ки под глаза́ми** he has bags under his eyes; **костю́м сиди́т на нём ~ко́м** his suit hangs like a sack on him.

мешо́ч|ек (**-ка**) *м*: **в ~** (*яйцо*) soft-boiled.

мешу́ *несов см* **меси́ть**.

меща́ни|н (**-ани́на**; *nom pl* **-а́не**, *gen pl* **-а́н**) *м* petty bourgeois.

меща́нк|а (**-и**) *ж см* **меща́нин**.

меща́нск|ий (**-ая, -ое, -ие**) *прил* (*взгляды*) petty-bourgeois; (*вкусы*) philistine.

меща́нств|о (**-а**) *ср* petty-bourgeois mentality; (*вкусы*) vulgarity; (*сословие*) petty bourgeoisie.

ми *ср нескл* (*муз*) mi.

МИГ (**-а**) *м сокр* = самолёт констру́кции А.И. Микоя́на и М.И. Гуре́вича.

миг (**-а**) *м* moment.

мига́|ть (**-ю**) *несов неперех* to wink; (*перен*) to twinkle.

мигн|у́ть (**-у́, -ёшь**) *сов неперех* to wink.

ми́гом *нареч* (*разг*) as quick as a flash; **приду́ ~!** I'll be there in a jiffy!

мигра́ци|я (**-и**) *ж* migration.

мигре́н|ь (**-и**) *ж* migraine.

МИД (**-а**) *м сокр* (= Министе́рство иностра́нных дел) ≈ the Foreign Office (*BRIT*), ≈ the State Department (*US*).

ми́ди *ср нескл* midi ♦ *прил неизм* midi *опред*.

ми́ди|я (**-и**) *ж* mussel.

ми́зер|ный (**-ен, -на, -но**) *прил* meagre (*BRIT*), meager (*US*).

мизи́н|ец (**-ца**) *м* (*на руке*) little finger; (*на ноге*) little toe.

микроавто́бус (**-а**) *м* minibus.

микро́б (**-а**) *м* microbe.

микробио́лог (**-а**) *м* microbiologist.

микробиоло́ги|я (**-и**) *ж* microbiology.

микрокли́мат (**-а**) *м* microclimate; (*перен*) atmosphere.

микро́н (**-а**) *м* micron.

микроорганизм (**-а**) *м* microorganism.

микропроце́ссор (**-а**) *м* microprocessor.

микрорайо́н (**-а**) *м* ≈ catchment area (*administrative subdivision of urban region in Russia*).

микроско́п (**-а**) *м* microscope.

микроскопи́ческ|ий (**-ая, -ое, -ие**) *прил* (*также перен*) microscopic.

микросхе́м|а (**-ы**) *ж* (micro)chip.

микрофи́льм (**-а**) *м* microfilm.

микрофи́ш|а (**-и**) *ж* microfiche.

микрофо́н (**-а**) *м* microphone.

микрохирурги́|я (**-и**) *ж* microsurgery.

микроэконо́мик|а (**-и**) *ж* microeconomics *мн*.

ми́ксер (**-а**) *м* mixer.

миксту́р|а (**-ы**) *ж* mixture; **~ от ка́шля** cough mixture *или* linctus.

Мила́н (**-а**) *м* Milan.

ми́леньк|ий (**-ая, -ое, -ие**) *прил* (*хорошенький*) pretty *или* sweet little; (*: любимый*) darling; **он сде́лает э́то как ~** he'll do it or else.

милитари́зм (**-а**) *м* militarism.

милитаризова́ть (**-ую**) (*не*)*сов перех* to militarize.

милитари́ст (**-а**) *м* militarist.

милиционе́р (**-а**) *м* policeman (*in Russia*) (*мн* policemen).

мили́ци|я (**-и**) *ж, собир* police (*in Russia*); (*разг: участок*) police station.

миллиа́рд (**-а**) *м* billion.

миллиарде́р (**-а**) *м* billionaire.

миллигра́мм (**-а**) *м* milligram(me).

миллиме́тр (**-а**) *м* millimetre (*BRIT*), millimeter (*US*).

миллиметро́вк|а (**-и**) *ж* (*разг*) graph paper.

миллио́н (**-а**) *м* million.

миллионе́р (**-а**) *м* millionaire.

миллио́нн|ый (**-ая, -ое, -ые**) *чис* (*посетитель, автомоби́ль итп*) millionth; (*исчисляемый миллионами*) million-strong; **у него́ ~ое состоя́ние** he is worth millions.

ми́ло *нареч* (*улыбнуться*) sweetly ♦ *как сказ*: **как ~!** how sweet!

ми́л|овать (**-ую**; *perf* **поми́ловать**) *несов перех* to have mercy on.

милови́д|ный (**-ен, -на, -но**) *прил* pleasing; **она́ ~на** she has a pleasing appearance.

милосе́рден *прил см* **милосе́рдный**.

милосе́рди|е (**-я**) *ср* compassion; **сестра́ ~я** nurse.

милосе́рд|ный (**-ен, -на, -но**) *прил* compassionate.

ми́лостын|я (**-и**) *ж* alms.

ми́лост|ь (**-и**) *ж* (*доброта*) kind-heartedness; **де́лать (сде́лать** *perf*) **что-н из ~а** to do sth out of the kindness of one's heart; **~и про́сим!**

welcome!; **по твое́й ~и опозда́ли** thanks to you we are late; **скажи́те на ~** you don't say.

ми́лочк|а (-и) ж (разг: обращение) dearest.

ми́л|ый (-, -а, -о) прил (симпатичный) pleasant, nice; (дорогой) dear ◆ **(-ого;** decl like adj) м (возлюбленный) darling.

ми́л|я (-и) ж mile; **морска́я ~** nautical mile.

мим (-а) м mime (artist).

ми́мик|а (-и) ж expression.

ми́мо нареч past ◆ предл (+gen) past.

мимо́з|а (-ы) ж (БОТ) mimosa.

мимолёт|ный (-ен, -на, -но) прил fleeting.

мимохо́дом нареч on the way; (перен: упомянуть) in passing.

мин. сокр (= **мину́та**) min. (= minute); (= **минима́льный**) min. (= minimum).

ми́н|а (-ы) ж (ВОЕН) mine; (выражение лица) expression.

минаре́т (-а) м minaret.

миндале́ви́дный прил almond-shaped; **у него́ миндалеви́дные глаза́** he is almond-eyed.

минда́лин|а (-ы) ж (МЕД: обычно мн) tonsil.

минда́л|ь (-я) м almond.

минда́льный прил almond.

мине́р (-а) м (ВОЕН) person who lays mines.

минера́л (-а) м mineral.

минера́лк|а (-и) ж (разг) mineral water.

минера́льный прил mineral.

ми́ни ср нескл mini; **~ ю́бка** miniskirt; **~ пла́тье** minidress.

миниатю́р|а (-ы) ж (ИСКУССТВО) miniature; (ТЕАТР) short play; **в ~е** in miniature.

миниатю́р|ный (-ен, -на, -но) прил (статуэтка) miniature опред; (перен: женщина) dainty.

минима́льный (-ен, -на, -но) прил minimum опред.

ми́нимум (-а) м minimum ◆ нареч minimum; **прожи́точный ми́нимум** minimum living wage.

мини́р|овать (-ую; perf **замини́ровать) (не)**сов перех (ВОЕН) to mine.

минисериа́л (-а) м mini-series.

министе́рск|ий (-ая, -ое, -ие) прил ministerial.

министе́рств|о (-а) ср ministry.

мини́стр (-а) м (ПОЛИТ) minister.

минздра́в (-а) м сокр (= **министе́рство здравоохране́ния**) Ministry of Health.

мин|ова́ть (-у́ю) (не)сов перех to pass; (no impf; +gen; избежать) to escape, avoid ◆ неперех to pass, be over.

мино́г|а (-и) ж lamprey.

миноиска́тел|ь (-я) м mine detector.

миномёт (-а) м mortar.

минно́с|ец (-ца) м destroyer.

мино́р (-а) м minor key.

мино́рный прил (МУЗ) minor; (перен) subdued.

Минск (-а) м Minsk.

мину́вше|е (-его; decl like adj) ср the past.

мину́вш|ий (-ая, -ее, -ие) прил past.

ми́нус (-а) м (также МАТ) minus; (перен: недостаток) drawback ◆ м нескл minus; **пять ~ два – три** five minus two equals three.

ми́нусовый прил (температура) subzero.

мину́т|а (-ы) ж minute; **(одну́) ~у!** (просьба подождать) just a minute!; **~ в мину́ту** to the minute; **он без пяти́ мину́т врач/юри́ст** (разг) he's a step away from qualifying as a doctor/ lawyer; **она́ придёт с ~ы на ~у** she will be here any minute.

мину́тный прил (стрелка) minute опред; (дело, разговор) brief; (порыв, увлечение) momentary.

мин|у́ть (3sg **-ет,** 3pl **-ут)** сов неперех (+dat; исполниться): **ей ~уло 16 лет** she has turned 16.

мин|у́ть (-у́, -ёшь) сов (не)перех to pass.

мир (-а; nom pl **-ы́)** м world; (Вселенная) universe; (loc sg **-у́;** РЕЛ) (secular) world; (состояние без войны) peace; **~ те́сен** it's a small world; **он не от ми́ра сего́** he has his head in the clouds; **заключа́ть (заключи́ть** perf) **~** to make peace; **чемпио́н ми́ра** world champion.

мира́ж (-а́) м (также перен) mirage.

ми́рен прил см **ми́рный**.

мир|и́ть (-ю́, -и́шь; perf **помири́ть** или **примири́ть)** несов перех to reconcile.

▶ **мир|и́ться (**perf **помири́ться)** несов возв: **~ся с** +instr to make up или be reconciled with; (perf **примири́ться**; с недостатками, с положением) to come to terms with, reconcile o.s to.

ми́р|ный (-ен, -на, -но) прил peaceful; **ми́рное вре́мя** peacetime; **ми́рное населе́ние** civilian population; **ми́рные перегово́ры** peace talks или negotiations.

мировоззре́ни|е (-я) ср (писателя, общества) philosophy of life.

мирово́й прил world опред; (перен: разг: хороший) fantastic.

мирозда́ни|е (-я) ср universe.

миролюби́в|ый (-, -а, -о) прил peaceable.

миропонима́ни|е (-я) ср conception of the world.

миротво́р|ец (-ца) м peacemaker.

миротво́рческ|ий (-ая, -ое, -ие) прил peacemaking; **миротво́рческие войска́** peacekeeping force ед.

мирско́й прил (РЕЛ) worldly.

ми́ск|а (-ки; gen pl **-ок)** ж bowl.

мисс ж нескл Miss.

миссионе́р (-а) м missionary.

ми́ссис ж нескл Mrs.

Миссиси́пи ср нескл Mississippi.

ми́сси|я (-и) ж mission.

ми́стер (-а) м Mr.

ми́стик|а (-и) ж mysticism; (разг: о чем-н загадочном) mystery.

мистифика́ци|я (-и) ж hoax.

мисти́ческ|ий (-ая, -ое, -ие) прил mystical.

ми́тинг (-а) м mass meeting, rally.

митингов|а́ть (-у́ю) несов неперех to hold a mass meeting или rally.

митрополи́т (-а) м (РЕЛ) metropolitan.

миф (-а) *м* (*также перен*) myth.
мифи́ческий (-ая, -ое, -ие) *прил* mythical.
мифоло́ги|я (-и) *ж* mythology.
мише́н|ь (-и) *ж* (*также перен*) target.
ми́шк|а (-и) *м* (*разг*) bear; (*игрушка*) teddy (bear).
мишур|а́ (-ы́) *м* tinsel.
МКК *м сокр* (= *Междунаро́дный Кра́сный Крест*) IRC (= *International Red Cross*).
мл. *сокр* (= **мла́дший**) Junr (= *junior*).
младе́н|ец (-ца) *м* infant, baby.
младе́нческ|ий (-ая, -ое, -ие) *прил*: ~ие го́ды infancy.
младе́нчеств|о (-а) *ср* infancy, babyhood.
мла́дше *сравн прил от* **молодо́й**.
мла́дш|ий (-ая, -ее, -ие) *прил* younger; (*самый младший*) (the) youngest; (*сотрудник, класс*) junior; ~ **лейтена́нт** second lieutenant.
млекопита́ющ|ее (-его; *decl like adj*) *ср* mammal.
мле|ть (-ю) *несов неперех*: ~ (**от** +*gen*) (*от счастья, от любви*) to be overcome (with).
мле́чный *прил* milky; **М~ Путь** the Milky Way; **мле́чный сок** latex.
млн. *сокр* = **миллио́н**.
мм *сокр* (= **миллиме́тр**) mm= *millimetre* (BRIT) *или millimeter* (US).
мне *мест см* **я**.
мне́ни|е (-я) *ср* opinion.
мни́мый *прил* (*кажущийся*) imaginary; (*ложный*) fake.
мни́телен *прил см* **мни́тельный**.
мни́тельност|ь (-и) *ж* suspiciousness.
мни́тел|ьный (-ен, -ьна, -ьно) *прил* suspicious.
мно́г|ие *прил* many ♦ (-их; *decl like adj*) мн (**много** людей) many (people).

KEYWORD

мно́го *чис* (+*gen*) a lot of; **они́ созда́ли нам мно́го пробле́м** they created a lot of problems for us; **мно́го книг тебе́ да́ли?** did they give you many *или* a lot of books?; **мно́го рабо́ты тебе́ да́ли?** did they give you much *или* a lot of work?
♦ *нареч* **1** (*разговаривать, пить итп*) a lot; **он мно́го рабо́тает** he works a lot
2 (+*comparative*; *гораздо*) much
♦ *как сказ*: **у него́ мно́го враго́в** he has a lot of enemies; **у него́ мно́го друзе́й?** does he have many friends?; **по мно́гу** +*gen* many; **они́ приходи́ли по мно́гу раз** they came many times.

многобо́р|ец (-ца) *м competitor in multi-event competition*.
многобо́рь|е (-я) *ср multi-event competition*.
многогра́нен *прил см* **многогра́нный**.
многогра́нник (-а) *м* polyhedron.
многогра́н|ный (-ен, -на, -но) *прил* (*талант,*

камень, личность) multifaceted; (*фигура*) polyhedral.
многоде́т|ный (-ен, -на, -но) *прил* with many children.
мно́гое (-ого; *decl like adj*) *ср* a great deal.
многожёнств|о (-а) *ср* polygamy.
многозна́чен *прил см* **многозна́чный**.
многозначи́тел|ьный (-ен, -ьна, -ьно) *прил* significant.
многозна́ч|ный (-ен, -на, -но) *прил* (*число, номер*) multi-digit; (*слово, глагол*) polysemantic.
многокра́т|ный (-ен, -на, -но) *прил* (*визиты*) repeated; (*виза*) multiple(-entry); ~ **чемпио́н/ призёр** many-times champion/prizewinner.
многоле́т|ний (-яя, -ее, -ие) *прил* (*планы*) long-term; (*труд, усилия*) of many years; (*растения*) perennial.
многолю́д|ный (-ен, -на, -но) *прил* (*улица*) crowded; (*митинг*) well-attended.
многонациона́л|ьный (-ен, -ьна, -ьно) *прил* multinational.
многопо́льзовательск|ий (-ая, -ое, -ие) *прил* (*КОМП*) multiaccess.
многообеща́ющ|ий (-ая, -ее, -ие) *прил* promising.
многообра́зен *прил см* **многообра́зный**.
многообра́зи|е (-я) *ср* (*жизни*) variety; (*растений, животных*) diversity.
многообра́з|ный (-ен, -на, -но) *прил* diverse, varied.
многосеме́й|ный (-ен, -йна, -йно) *прил* with a large family.
многосло́в|ный (-ен, -на, -но) *прил* verbose, long-winded.
многосло́жный *прил* polysyllabic.
многосторо́н|ний (-няя, -нее, -ние) *прил* (*ГЕОМ*) polygonal; (*переговоры, встреча*) multilateral; (*вопрос, личность*) many-sided; (-ен, -ня, -не; *интересы*) diverse.
многотира́жк|а (-и; *gen pl* -ек) *ж* (*разг*) factory news sheet.
многотира́жный *прил* with a large circulation.
многото́чи|е (-я) *ср* (*линг*) ellipsis.
многоуважа́емый *прил* esteemed; (*в письме*) Dear.
многоуго́льник (-а) *м* polygon.
многочи́слен|ный (-, -на, -но) *прил* numerous.
многочле́н (-а) *м* (*МАТ*) multinomial.
многоэта́жный *прил* multistorey (BRIT), multistory (US).
мно́жествен|ный *прил*: ~ое число́ (*линг*) the plural (number).
мно́жеств|о (-а) *ср* (*МАТ*) set; ~ +*gen* a great number of.
мно́жительн|ый *прил*: ~ая те́хника photocopying equipment.
мно́|жить (-у, -ишь; *perf* **умно́жить**) *несов перех* (*увеличивать*) to multiply; (*perf* **помно́жить**;

мат): ~ (**на** +*acc*) to multiply (by)
▶ **мно́житься** (*perf* **умно́житься**) *несов возв* to multiply.
мной *мест см* **я**.
мнс *м сокр* (= *мла́дший нау́чный сотру́дник*) junior researcher.
мну (**сь**) *итп несов см* **мять**(**ся**).
моби́лен *прил см* **моби́льный**.
мобилиза́ци|я (**-и**) *ж* mobilization.
мобилиз|ова́ть (**-у́ю**) (*не*)*сов перех* to mobilize; ~ (*impf*/*perf*) **кого́-н на что-н** to mobilize sb for sth.
моби́л|ьный (**-ен, -ьна, -ьно**) *прил* (*войска́, дом*) mobile; (*ум, руково́дство*) active.
мог *несов см* **мочь**.
моги́л|а (**-ы**) *ж* grave; **стоя́ть** (*impf*) **одно́й ного́й в** ~**е** (*разг*) to have one foot in the grave.
моги́льник (**-а**) *м* burial ground; (*для радиоакти́вных отхо́дов*) dumping ground.
моги́льный *прил* (*плита́*) grave *опред*; (*холм, уча́сток*) burial *опред*.
моги́льщик (**-а**) *м* grave digger.
могла́ *итп несов см* **мочь**.
могу́ *итп несов см* **мочь**.
могу́ч|ий (**-ая, -ее, -ие; -, -а, -е**) *прил* mighty; (*тала́нт, ум*) great.
могу́ществен|ный (**-, -на, -но**) *прил* mighty, powerful.
могу́ществ|о (**-а**) *ср* might, power.
мо́д|а (**-ы**) *ж* fashion; (*разг*: *мане́ра поведе́ния*) habit; **по** ~**е** fashionably; **быть** (*impf*) **в** ~**е** to be in fashion; **входи́ть** (**войти́** *perf*) **в** ~**у** to come into fashion; **выходи́ть** (**вы́йти** *perf*) **из** ~**ы** to go out of fashion; *см та́кже* **мо́ды**.
модели́р|овать (**-ую**) (*не*)*сов перех* (*оде́жду*) to design; (*perf* **смодели́ровать**; *проце́сс, поведе́ние*) to simulate.
моде́л|ь (**-и**) *ж* model.
модель́ер (**-а**) *м* fashion designer.
моде́льный *прил* (*о́бувь, оде́жда*) high-fashion.
моде́м (**-а**) *м* (*КОМП*) modem.
мо́ден *прил см* **мо́дный**.
модерниза́ци|я (**-и**) *ж* modernization.
моде́рн (**-а**) *м* (*ИСКУССТВО*) art nouveau.
модернизи́р|овать (**-ую**) (*не*)*сов перех* to modernize.
модифика́ци|я (**-и**) *ж* modification.
мо́дник (**-а**) *м* (*разг*) snappy dresser.
мо́дниц|а (**-ы**) *ж см* **мо́дник**.
мо́днича|ть (**-ю**) *несов неперех* (*разг*) to be a snappy dresser.
мо́дно *нареч* (*одева́ться, стри́чься*) fashionably ◆ *как сказ*: ~ **носи́ть ми́ни** miniskirts are in fashion.
мо́дный (**-ен, -на, -но**) *прил* fashionable; (*no short form*; *журна́л*) fashion *опред*.
мо́д|ы (**-**) *мн* fashions *мн*; **журна́л мод** fashion magazine.
мое́ (**-его́**) *притяж мест см* **мой**.
мо́жет *несов см* **мочь** ◆ *вводн сл* (*разг*) maybe, perhaps.

мо́жешь *итп несов см* **мочь**.
можжеве́льник (**-а**) *м* juniper.
мо́жно *как сказ* (*возмо́жно*): ~ +*infin* it is possible to do; ~ **кури́ть** smoking is allowed *или* permitted; ~ (**войти́**)**?** may I (come in)?; **как** ~ (*разг*: *выража́ет осужде́ние*) how could he *итп*; **как** ~ **лу́чше/быстре́е** as well/quickly as possible.
моза́ик|а (**-и**) *ж* (*узо́р*) mosaic; (*иску́сство*) mosaic work.
мозаи́чный (**-ен, -на, -но**) *прил* mosaic.
Мозамби́к (**-а**) *м* Mozambique.
мозг (**-а**; *loc sg* **-у́**, *nom sg* **-и́**) *м* brain; (*перен*: *центр*) nerve centre (*BRIT*) *или* center (*US*); **спинно́й** ~ spinal cord; **ко́стный** ~ (bone) marrow; **до мо́зга косте́й** through and through; **шевели́ть** (**пошевели́ть** *perf*) ~**а́ми** (*разг*) to use one's head; *см та́кже* **мозги́**.
мозг|и́ (**-о́в**) *мн* (*КУЛИН*) brains *мн*.
мозг|ова́ть (**-у́ю**) *несов неперех* (*разг*) to think.
мозгови́тый *прил* (*разг*) brainy.
мозгово́й *прил* cerebral; (*интеллектуа́льный*) intellectual; ~ **центр** nerve centre (*BRIT*) *или* center (*US*).
мозо́листый (**-, -а, -о**) *прил* calloused.
мозо́л|ить (**-ю, -ишь**) *несов перех*: ~ **глаза́ кому́-н** (*разг*) to bug sb by one's very presence.
мозо́л|ь (**-и**) *ж* corn, callus.
мозо́льный *прил*: ~ **пла́стырь** corn plaster.
мой (**моего́**; *см* **Table 8**; *f* **моя́**, *nt* **моё**, *pl* **мой**) *притяж мест* my; **по-мо́ему** my way; (*по моему́ мне́нию*) in my opinion.
мо́йк|а (**-и**) *ж* (*мытьё*) washing; (*ра́ковина*) sink.
МОК (**-а**) *м сокр* (= *Междунаро́дный олимпи́йский комите́т*) IOC (= *International Olympic Committee*)
мо́к|нуть (**-ну, -нешь**; *pt* **-, -ла, -ло**) *несов неперех* to get wet; (*лежа́ть в воде́*) to be soaking.
мо́кро *как сказ* it's wet.
мокро́т|а (**-ы**) *ж* phlegm.
мокрот|а́ (**-ы́**) *ж* (*разг*) dampness.
мо́крый (**-, -а́, -о**) *прил* wet.
мол (**-а**; *loc sg* **-у́**) *м* breakwater, mole ◆ *част* (*разг*): **он, ~, ничего́ не зна́ет** he says he knows nothing.
молв|а́ (**-ы́**) *ж* rumour (*BRIT*), rumor (*US*).
молда́вс|кий (**-ая, -ое, -ие**) *прил* Moldavian.
Молдо́в|а (**-ы**) *ж* Moldova.
молдова́н|ин (**-ина**; *nom pl* **-е**) *м* Moldavian.
молдова́н|ка (**-ки**; *gen pl* **-ок**) *ж см* **молдова́нин**.
моле́б|ен (**-на**) *м* (*РЕЛ*) service.
моле́кул|а (**-ы**) *ж* molecule.
молекуля́рный *прил* molecular.
моле́ни|е (**-я**) *ср* praying; (*мольба́*) entreaty.
моли́тв|а (**-ы**) *ж* prayer.
моли́твенник (**-а**) *м* prayer book.
моли́ться (**-ю́сь, -ишься**; *perf* **помоли́ться**) *несов возв*: ~ +*dat* to pray to; (*no perf*; *перен*): ~ **на** +*acc* to idolize.

моллю́ск (-а) *м* mollusc.

молниено́с|ный (-ен, -на, -но) *прил* lightning *опред*.

мо́лни|я (-и) *ж* lightning; (*застёжка*) zip (fastener) (*BRIT*), zipper (*US*); **телегра́мма-~** express telegram.

молодёжный *прил* (*клуб, театр*) youth *опред*; (*мода, газета*) for young people.

молодёж|ь (-и) *ж собир* young people *мн*.

молоде́|ть (-ю; *perf* **помолоде́ть**) *несов неперех* (*выглядеть моложе*) to look younger; (*чувствовать себя моложе*) to feel younger; (*население*) to become younger.

мо́лод|ец (-ца) *м* (*ФОЛЬКЛОР*) brave lad, fine young man.

молод|е́ц (-ца́) *м* strong fellow; **~!** (*разг*) well done!; **она́/он ~!** (*разг*) she/he has done well!; **держа́ться** (*impf*) **~цо́м** to put up a good show.

молоде́цк|ий (-ая, -ое, -ие) *прил* (*вид*) dashing; (*поступок*) valiant.

молод|и́ть (-жу́, -ди́шь) *несов перех*: **~ кого́-н** to make sb look younger

▶ **молоди́ться** *несов возв* to try to look younger.

молодня́|к (-á) *м собир* (*ЗООЛ*) young (*of animals*); (*БОТ*) saplings *мн*.

молодожён (-а) *м* (*обычно мн*) newlywed.

молодо́й (**мо́лод, молода́, мо́лодо**) *прил* young; (*картофель, листва*) new; (*задор, отвага*) youthful; (*no short form*; *вино, пиво*) young; (*сыр*) unripe.

мо́лодост|ь (-и) *ж* youth; **он не пе́рвой ~и** he's getting on in years.

мо́лодца *итп сущ см* **мо́лодец**.

молодца́ *итп сущ см* **молоде́ц**.

молодцева́тый *прил* sprightly.

моло́дчик (-а) *м* thug.

моложа́в|ый (-, -а, -о) *прил* (*человек*) young-looking; (*вид, лицо*) youthful.

моло́же *сравн прил от* **молодо́й**.

моложу́(сь) *несов см* **молоди́ть(ся)**.

молоко́ (-á) *ср* milk.

молокосо́с (-а) *м* (*разг: пренебр*) greenhorn.

мо́лот (-а) *м* hammer.

молоти́л|ка (-ки; *gen pl* -ок) *ж* threshing machine.

мол|оти́ть (-очу́, -о́тишь) *несов перех* (*пшеницу*) to thresh; (*разг: колотить*) to hammer.

молот|о́к (-ка́) *м* hammer; **продава́ть** (**прода́ть** *perf*) **что́-н с ~ка́** to sell sth by auction, auction sth.

мо́лотый *прил* (*кофе, перец*) ground.

мол|о́ть (мелю́, ме́лешь; *perf* **смоло́ть** *или* **помоло́ть**) *несов перех* (*зерно, кофе*) to grind; **~** (*impf*) **вздор** *или* **чепуху́** (*разг*) to talk rubbish.

молочк|о́ (-á) *ср* (*жидкий крем*) lotion.

моло́чник (-а) *м* (*посуда*) milk jug; (*разносчик молока*) milkman (*мн* milkmen).

моло́чниц|а (-ы) *ж* milklady.

моло́чный *прил* (*продукты, скот*) dairy *опред*; (*каша, коктейль*) milk *опред*; (*поросёнок, телёнок*) sucking; (*железа*) mammary; (*хим*) lactic; **моло́чная ку́хня** *place where baby food is prepared*; **моло́чная сестра́** foster sister; **моло́чный брат** foster brother; **моло́чный зуб** milk tooth.

молочу́ *несов см* **молоти́ть**.

мо́лча *нареч* (*кивнуть, уйти*) silently; (*согласиться*) tacitly.

молчали́в|ый (-, -а, -о) *прил* silent; (*no short form*; *согласие, одобрение*) tacit; **~ мужчи́на** a man of few words.

молча́ни|е (-я) *ср* (*безмолвие*) silence; **~ – знак согла́сия** silence can be taken to mean approval.

молч|а́ть (-у́, -и́шь) *несов неперех* to be silent; **~** (*impf*) **о** +*prp* to keep silent *или* quiet about.

мол|ь (-и) *ж* moth.

мольб|а́ (-ы́) *ж* entreaty.

мольбе́рт (-а) *м* easel.

моме́нт (-а) *м* moment; (*в фильме*) episode; (*доклада, исследования*) point; **теку́щий ~** the current situation.

момента́лен *прил см* **момента́льный**.

момента́льно *нареч* instantly.

момента́льный (-ен, -ьна, -ьно) *прил* instant.

мона́рх (-а) *м* monarch.

мона́рхи|я (-и) *ж* monarchy.

монасты́р|ь (-я́) *м* (*мужской*) monastery; (*женский*) convent.

мона́х (-а) *м* monk.

мона́хин|я (-и; *gen pl* -ь) *ж* nun.

мона́шеск|ий (-ая, -ое, -ие) *прил* (*также перен*) monastic.

мона́шеств|о (-а) *ср* monastic life.

Монбла́н (-а) *м* Mont Blanc.

монго́л (-а) *м* Mongol, Mongolian.

монго́л|ка (-ки; *gen pl* -ок) *ж см* **монго́л**.

монго́льск|ий (-ая, -ое, -ие) *прил* Mongolian.

Монго́ли|я (-и) *ж* Mongolia.

моне́т|а (-ы) *ж* coin; **плати́ть** (**отплати́ть** *perf*) **кому́-н той же ~ой** (*отомстить*) to pay sb back in kind; **принима́ть** (**приня́ть** *perf*) **что́-н за чи́стую ~у** to take sth at face value.

монетари́ст (-а) *м* monetarist.

монета́рный *прил* monetary.

моне́тный *прил*: **~ двор** mint.

монито́р (-а) *м* monitor.

моногра́мм|а (-ы) *ж* monogram.

монографи|я (-и) *ж* monograph.

моноли́т (-а) *м* monolith.

моноли́т|ный (-ен, -на, -но) *прил* (*глыба, колонна*) monolithic; (*перен*) united.

моноло́г (-а) *м* monologue.

монополиза́ци|я (-и) *ж* monopolization.

монополизи́р|овать (-ую) (*не*)*сов перех* to

monopolize.

монополи́ст (**-а**) *м* monopolist.

монопо́ли|я (**-и**) *ж* monopoly.

монопо́льный *прил* monopoly *опред*.

моното́н|ный (**-ен, -на, -но**) *прил* (*также перен*) monotonous.

монохро́мный *прил* (*комп*) monochrome.

Монреа́л|ь (**-я**) *м* Montreal.

монта́ж (**-а́**) *ж* (*сооружения*) erection; (*оборудования*) mounting, assembly; (*кадров, фильма*) editing.

монта́жник (**-а**) *м* (*на стройке*) rigger; (*на фабрике*) fitter.

монта́жниц|а (**-ы**) *ж см* **монта́жник**.

монтёр (**-а**) *м* fitter; (*электромонтёр*) electrician.

монти́р|овать (**-ую**; *perf* **смонти́ровать**) *несов перех* (*оборудование, схему*) to assemble; (*фильм, передачу*) to edit.

монуме́нт (**-а**) *м* monument.

монумента́л|ьный (**-ен, -ьна, -ьно**) *прил* monumental.

мопе́д (**-а**) *м* moped (*with movable pedals*).

мор (**-а**) *м* pestilence, plague.

мора́лен *прил см* **мора́льный**.

морализи́р|овать (**-ую**) *несов неперех* to moralize.

мора́л|ь (**-и**) *ж* (*этика поведения*) morals *мн*, ethics *мн*; (*басни, сказки*) moral; (*разг: нравоучение*) moralizing.

мора́л|ьный (**-ен, -ьна, -ьно**) *прил* moral; (*no short form*; *кодекс, нормы*) moral, ethical; **мора́льный изно́с, мора́льное устарева́ние** obsolescence.

морато́ри|й (**-я**) *м* moratorium.

морг (**-а**) *м* morgue.

морга́|ть (**-ю**) *несов неперех* to blink; (*подмигивать*): **~** (+*dat*) to wink (at).

моргн|у́ть (**-у́, -ёшь**) *сов неперех* to blink; (*подмигнуть*): **~** (+*dat*) to wink (at); **не ~у́в гла́зом** (*разг*) without batting an eyelid.

мо́рд|а (**-ы**) *ж* (*животного*) muzzle; (*разг: лицо*) mug.

мордви́н (**-а**) *м* Mordvin.

мордви́н|ка (**-ки**; *gen pl* **-ок**) *ж см* **мордви́н**.

Мо́рдви|я (**-и**) *ж* Mordvia.

мо́р|е (**-я**; *nom pl* **-я́**, *gen pl* **-е́й**) *ср* (*также перен*) sea; **откры́тое ~** open sea; **ему́ ~ по коле́но** (*разг*) he's afraid of nothing.

морепла́вани|е (**-я**) *ср* (*плавание*) seafaring; (*вождение судов*) navigation.

морепла́вател|ь (**-я**) *м* seafarer.

морехо́дк|а (**-и**) *ж* (*разг*) naval college.

морехо́дный *прил* (*училище, испытания*) naval; (*инструменты*) navigational.

морж (**-а́**) *м* walrus; (*перен*) *wintertime open-air bather*.

моржи́х|а (**-и**) *ж см* **морж**.

моржо́вый *прил* walrus *опред*.

мори́лк|а (**-и**) *ж* (*разг: краска*) stain; (*от насекомых*) insecticide.

мор|и́ть (**-ю́, -и́шь**; *perf* **помори́ть**) *несов перех* (*насекомых*) to exterminate; (*дерево*) to stain; (*дуб*) to fume; (*perf* **размори́ть**; *подлеж: сон, жара*) to exhaust, drain; **~** (**замори́ть** *perf*) **го́лодом кого́-н** to starve sb; **~** (**умори́ть** *perf*) **шу́тками кого́-н** (*разг*) to have sb in stitches with one's jokes.

морко́в|ка (**-ки**; *gen pl* **-ок**) *ж* (*разг: одна штука*) carrot; (*морковь*) carrots *мн*.

морко́вный *прил* carrot *опред*.

морко́в|ь (**-и**) *ж* carrots *мн*.

моро́жениц|а (**-ы**) *ж* (*аппарат*) ice-cream maker; (*кафе*) ice-cream parlour (*BRIT*) или parlor (*US*).

моро́жен|ое (**-ого**; *decl like adj*) *ср* ice cream.

моро́женый *прил* frozen; (*испорченный морозом*) frost-damaged.

моро́жу *несов см* **моро́зить**.

моро́з (**-а**) *м* frost; **у нас стоя́т ~ы** we're having a spell of freezing (cold) weather; **Дед М~** ≈ Father Christmas.

моро́зен *прил см* **моро́зный**.

морози́льник (**-а**) *м* freezer.

морози́льный *прил* freezing; **морози́льная ка́мера** deepfreeze.

моро́|зить (**-жу, -зишь**) *несов перех* to freeze ♦ *безл*; **на у́лице ~зит** it's freezing outside.

моро́з|ный (**-ен, -на, -но**) *прил* frosty.

морозосто́йкий (**-йкая, -йкое, -йкие; -ек, -йка, -йко**) *прил* frost-resistant.

морос|и́ть (*3sg* **-и́т**, *3pl* **-я́т**) *несов неперех* to drizzle.

моро́ч|ить (**-у, -ишь**; *perf* **заморо́чить**) *несов перех* (*разг*) to fool; **~** (**заморо́чить** *perf*) **го́лову кому́-н** (*разг*) to pull sb's leg.

моро́шк|а (**-и**) *ж* cloudberry.

морс (**-а**; *part gen* **-у**) *м* (fruit) drink.

морск|о́й (**-а́я, -о́е, -и́е**) *прил* sea *опред*; (*био, воен*) marine; (*курорт, лечебница*) seaside *опред*; **~о́е страхова́ние** marine insurance; **~о́е пра́во** maritime law; **морска́я боле́знь** seasickness; **морско́й волк** sea dog; **морска́я сви́нка** guinea pig.

мо́рфи|й (**-я**) *м* morphine, morphia.

морфоло́ги|я (**-и**) *ж* morphology.

морщи́н|а (**-ы**) *ж* (*на лице*) wrinkle; (*на ткани*) crease.

морщи́нист|ый (**-, -а, -о**) *прил* (*лицо*) wrinkled.

мо́рщ|ить (**-у, -ишь**; *perf* **намо́рщить**) *несов перех* (*брови*) to knit; (*perf* **смо́рщить**; *нос, лоб*) to wrinkle; (*лицо*) to screw up.

▶ **мо́рщиться** (*perf* **намо́рщиться**) *несов возв* to screw up one's face; (*одежда, ткань*) to crease; **~ся** (**смо́рщиться** *perf*) **от** +*gen* (*от старости, от солнца*) to become wrinkled from; (*от боли*) to wince in.

морщ|и́ть (*3sg* **-и́т**, *3pl* **-а́т**) *несов неперех* (*разг*) to be wrinkled.

моря́к (**-а́**) *м* sailor.

Москв|а́ (**-ы́**) *ж* Moscow.

москви́ч (**-а́**) *м* Muscovite.

москви́ч|ка (-ки; *gen pl* -ек) *ж см* **москви́ч**.

мост (-а́; *loc sg* -у́) *м* bridge; (*телевизионный, космический*) link; (*АВТ*) axle.

мо́стик (-а) *м* bridge; **капита́нский ~** bridge (*NAUT*).

мо|сти́ть (-щу́, -сти́шь; *perf* **вы́мостить**) *несов перех* (*площадь, улицу*) to pave; (*perf* **намости́ть**; *пол*) to lay.

мостки́ (-о́в) *мн* (*через лужу*) duckboard *ед*; (*у реки, у пруда*) wooden platform *ед*.

мостов|а́я (-о́й; *decl like adj*) *ж* road.

МОТ *ж сокр* (= междунаро́дная организа́ция труда́) ILO (= *International Labour Organization*).

мота́|ть (-ю; *perf* **намота́ть**) *несов перех* (*нитки*) to wind ♦ (*perf* **умота́ть**) *неперех* (*разг: уехать*) to go off; (*perf* **помота́ть**): **~ +instr** (*головой*) to shake; **~й отсю́да!** get lost!; **~** (*impf*) **кому́-н не́рвы** (*разг*) to get on sb's nerves

▶ **мота́ться** *несов возв* to swing; (*разг: хлопотать*) to rush about.

моте́л|ь (-я) *м* motel.

моти́в (-а) *м* (*преступления*) motive; (*для развода*) grounds *мн*; (*мелодия*) motif.

мотиви́р|овать (-ую) (*не)сов перех* to justify.

мотка́ *сущ см* **мото́к**.

мотого́н|ка (-ки; *gen pl* -ок) *ж* (*обычно мн*) motorcycle race.

мотого́нщик (-а) *м* motorcycle racer.

мото́|к (-ка́) *м* skein.

мото́р (-а) *м* motor; (*автомобиля, лодки*) engine.

мотори́ст (-а) *м* motor mechanic.

мото́рный *прил* motor *опред*; **мото́рная ло́дка** motorboat.

моторо́ллер (-а) *м* (motor) scooter.

мотоци́кл (-а) *м* motorcycle.

моты́г|а (-и) *ж* hoe.

мотыл|ёк (-ька́) *м* moth.

м|ох (мха; *loc sg* мху, *nom pl* мхи) *м* moss.

мохе́р (-а) *м* mohair.

мохе́ровый *прил* mohair.

мохна́тый (-, -а, -о) *прил* (*животное*) shaggy; (*ель, сосна*) bushy; (*no short form*; *плед, шапка*) fluffy.

моховик (-а́) *м* (*БОТ*) variegated boletus.

моцио́н (-а) *м* (*прогулка*) constitutional.

моча́ (-и́) *ж* urine.

моча́л|ка (-ки; *gen pl* -ок) *ж* sponge.

мочево́й *прил*: **~ пузы́рь** bladder.

мочего́нный *прил* diuretic.

мо́чек *сущ см* **мо́чка**.

мочёный *прил* (*яблоко, брусника*) preserved (*in sugar solution*).

моч|и́ть (-у́, -ишь; *perf* **намочи́ть**) *несов перех* (*ноги, волосы, одежду*) to wet; (*perf* **замочи́ть**; *бельё*) to soak; (*яблоки*) to preserve

▶ **мочи́ться** (*perf* **помочи́ться**) *несов возв* to urinate.

мо́ч|ка (-ки; *gen pl* -ек) *ж* ear lobe.

мо|чь (-гу́, -жешь *итп*, -гут; *pt* -г, -гла́, -гло́, *perf* **смочь**) *несов неперех*: **~ +infin** to be able to do ♦ (-чи) *ж*: **йзо всей мо́чи** with all one's might; **я ~гу́ игра́ть на гита́ре/говори́ть по-англи́йски** I can play the guitar/talk English; **он мо́жет прийти́** he can come *или* is able to come; **она́ не ~гла́ купи́ть дом** she couldn't buy *или* wasn't able to buy the house; **я сде́лаю всё, что ~гу́** I will do all I can; **за́втра мо́жешь не приходи́ть** you don't have to come tomorrow; **он мо́жет оби́деться** he may well be offended; **не ~гу́ поня́ть э́того** I can't understand this; **мо́жешь бо́льше не извиня́ться** don't bother apologising any more; **мо́жет быть** maybe; **не мо́жет быть!** (*выражение сомнения*) it's impossible!

мо́шек *сущ см* **мо́шка**.

моше́нник (-а) *м* swindler, crook.

моше́нничa|ть (-ю; *perf* **смоше́нничать**) *несов неперех* to swindle.

моше́нническ|ий (-ая, -ое, -ие) *прил* devious.

моше́нничеств|о (-а) *ср* deviousness.

мо́ш|ка (-ки; *gen pl* -ек) *ж* midge.

мошкар|а́ (-ы́) *ж собир* midges *мн*.

мо́щен *прил см* **мо́щный**.

мощёный *прил* paved.

мо́щност|и (-ей) *мн* facilities *мн*.

мо́щност|ь (-и) *ж* power; (*воздействие*) force; **неиспо́льзуемая произво́дственная ~** idle capacity; *см также* **мо́щности**.

мо́щ|ный (-ен, -на́, -но) *прил* (*взрыв, выступление*) powerful; (*организм, дуб*) mighty; (*рост, подъем*) vigorous; (*массивный*) massive; (*no short form*; *двигатель, агрегат*) powerful.

мощу́ *несов см* **мости́ть**.

мощь (-и) *ж* power, might.

мо́ю(сь) *итп несов см* **мы́ть(ся)**.

мо́|я (-е́й) *притяж мест см* **мой**.

м.п. *сокр* = **ме́сто печа́ти**.

МП *м сокр* (= маши́нный перево́д) MT (= *machine translation*).

мрак (-а) *м* (*темнота*) darkness; (*перен*) gloom.

мракобе́с (-а) *м* obscurantist.

мра́мор (-а) *м* marble.

мра́морный *прил* (*также перен*) marble; (*узор, линолеум*) marbled; **Мра́морное мо́ре** Sea of Marmara.

мра́чен *прил см* **мра́чный**.

мрачне́|ть (-ю; *perf* **помрачне́ть**) *несов неперех* (*небо, горизонт*) to grow dark; (*взгляд, лицо*) to darken.

мра́ч|ный (-ен, -на́, -но) *прил* (*небо, мысли, взгляд*) gloomy; (*времена, годы, период*) dark.

мсти́тел|ь (-я) *м* avenger.

мсти́тельниц|а (-ы) *ж см* **мсти́тель**.

мсти́тель|ный (-ен, -ьна, -ьно) *прил* vindictive.
мсти́ть (мщу, мсти́шь; *perf* **отомсти́ть**) *несов неперех*: ~ **кому́-н** to take revenge on sb.
МТП *ж сокр* (= *междунаро́дная торго́вая пала́та*) ICC (= *International Chamber of Commerce*).
МТС *ж сокр* (= *междугоро́дная телефо́нная ста́нция*) ≈ international telephone exchange.
мудрё|ный (-ён, -ена́, -ено́) *прил* (*непоня́тный*) strange; (*сло́жный*) tricky, complicated; **не ~ено́, что ...** it's no wonder that ....
мудре́ц (-а́) *м* wise man (*мн* men).
мудри́|ть (-ю́, -и́шь; *perf* **намудри́ть**) *несов неперех* to try to be clever.
му́дрост|ь (-и) *ж* wisdom; **зуб ~и** wisdom tooth.
му́др|ый (-, -а́, -о) *прил* wise.
муж (-а; *nom pl* -ья́, *gen pl* -е́й) *м* husband; (*nom pl* -и́): **госуда́рственный ~** elder statesman (*мн* statesmen); **учёный ~** man of science.
мужа́|ть (-ю; *perf* **возмужа́ть**) *несов неперех* to mature
▶ **мужа́ться** *несов возв* to take heart, have courage.
мужеподо́б|ный (-ен, -на, -но) *прил* masculine.
му́жествен|ный (-, -на, -но) *прил* (*лицо́, нату́ра*) strong; (*посту́пок, шаг*) courageous.
му́жеств|о (-а) *ср* courage.
мужи́к (-а́) *м* (*разг: мужчи́на*) man (*мн* men); (*крестья́нин*) muzhik.
мужикова́тый *прил* boorish.
мужск|о́й (-а́я, -о́е, -и́е) *прил* (*боти́нки, туале́т, парикма́хер*) men's; (*хара́ктер, рукопожа́тие*) masculine; (*о́рганы, кле́тка*) male; **мужско́й пол** male sex; **мужско́й род** masculine gender.
мужчи́н|а (-ы) *м* man (*мн* men).
мужья́ *сущ см* **муж**.
му́з|а (-ы) *ж* muse.
музе́|й (-я) *м* museum.
музе́йный *прил* museum *опред*.
му́зык|а (-и) *ж* (*та́кже перен*) music.
музыка́л|ьный (-ен, -ьна, -ьно) *прил* musical; **музыка́льная шко́ла** music school.
музыка́нт (-а) *м* musician.
му́к|а (-и) *ж* torment.
мук|а́ (-и́) *ж* flour; (*гру́бого помо́ла*) meal; **ко́стная ~** bone meal; **карто́фельная ~** (*крахма́л*) potato starch.
мул (-а) *м* mule.
мулл|а́ (-ы́) *м* mullah.
му́льтик (-а) *м* (*разг*) cartoon.
мультиплика́тор (-а) *м* multiplier.
мультипликацио́нный *прил*: ~ **фильм** cartoon.
мультиплика́ци|я (-и) *ж* cartoon.
мультфи́льм (-а) *м сокр* (= *мультипликацио́нный фильм*) cartoon, animation film.
му́ми|я (-и) *ж* mummy.
мунди́р (-а) *м* uniform; **карто́фель в ~е** jacket potatoes.

мундшту́к (-а́) *м* cigarette holder; (*муз*) mouthpiece.
муниципалите́т (-а) *м* municipality, city council.
муниципа́льный *прил* municipal.
МУР (-а) *м сокр* (= *Моско́вский уголо́вный ро́зыск*) Moscow Criminal Investigation Department.
мур|а́ (-ы́) *ж* (*разг*) rubbish.
мураве́|й (-ья́) *м* ant.
мураве́йник (-а) *м* ant hill.
муравья́ *итп сущ см* **мураве́й**.
мура́ш|ки (-ек) *мн*: **у меня́ ~ по спине́ бе́гают** shivers are running down my spine; **покрыва́ться (покры́ться** *perf*) **~ками** to come out in goose pimples (*BRIT*) *или* goose bumps (*US*).
мурлы́|кать (-чу, -чешь) *несов неперех* to purr
◆ (*perf* **промурлы́кать**) *перех* to hum.
муска́т (-а) *м* (*оре́х*) nutmeg; (*сорт виногра́да*) muscat; (*сорт вина́*) muscat(el).
му́скул (-а) *м* muscle.
мускулату́р|а (-ы) *ж собир* musculature.
мускули́ст|ый (-, -а, -о) *прил* muscular.
му́сор (-а) *м* rubbish (*BRIT*), garbage (*US*).
му́сор|ить (-ю, -ишь; *perf* **наму́сорить**) *несов неперех* to make a mess.
му́сорный *прил* rubbish *опред* (*BRIT*), garbage *опред* (*US*); **му́сорное ведро́** dustbin.
мусоропрово́д (-а) *м* refuse *или* garbage (*US*) chute.
мусс (-а) *м* (*кули́н*) mousse.
мусульма́нин (-а) *м* Muslim.
мусульма́н|ка (-ки; *gen pl* -ок) *ж см* **мусульма́нин**.
мусульма́нск|ий (-ая, -ое, -ие) *прил* Muslim.
мусульма́нств|о (-а) *ср* Islam.
му́тен *прил см* **му́тный**.
му|ти́ть (-чу́, -ти́шь; *perf* **взмути́ть** *или* **замути́ть**) *несов перех* (*жи́дкость*) to muddy; (*perf* **помути́ть**; *перен: рассудок*) to cloud; (*no perf; разг: народ, толпу́*) to work up ◆ *несов безл* (*разг*): **меня́ му́тит** I feel sick
▶ **мути́ться** (*perf* **замути́ться**) *несов возв* (*вода́, раство́р*) to become cloudy; (*perf* **помути́ться**; *перен: рассу́док*) to become clouded ◆ *безл* (*разг*): **у меня́ в глаза́х** *или* **в голове́ помути́лось** I felt giddy.
мутне́|ть (*3sg* -ет, *3pl* -ют, *perf* **помутне́ть**) *несов неперех* (*жи́дкость*) to become cloudy; (*взор, глаза́*) to grow dull; **он так уста́л, что у него́ созна́ние ~ет** he is so tired, he can't think straight.
му́т|ный (-ен, -на́, -но) *прил* (*жи́дкость*) cloudy; (*стекло́, взор, глаза́*) dull; (*взор, глаза́*) glazed; (*перен: голова́, рассу́док*) confused.
мут|ь (-и) *ж* sediment; (*разг: фильм, кни́га итп*) rubbish; (*перен: на душе́*) ache.
му́фт|а (-ы) *ж* (*ТЕХ*) sleeve; (*же́нская оде́жда*) muff.
му́х|а (-и) *ж* fly; **де́лать (сде́лать** *perf*) **из ~и**

слонá ≈ to make a mountain out of a molehill; под ~**ой** (раза) legless.

мухомóр (-а) *м* (*БОТ*) fly agaric.

мучéни|**е** (-я) *ср* torment, torture.

мýченик (-а) *м* martyr.

мýчениц|**а** (-ы) *ж см* **мýченик**.

мучи́телен *прил см* **мучи́тельный**.

мучи́тел|**ь** (-я) *м* tormentor.

мучи́тельниц|**а** (-ы) *ж см* **мучи́тель**.

мучи́тельн|**ый** (-ен, -ьна, -ьно) *прил* agonizing.

мýч|**ить** (-у, -ишь; *perf* **замýчить** *или* **измýчить**) *несов перех* to torment

▸ **мýчиться** (*perf* **замýчиться**) *несов возв*: ~**ся** +*instr* (сомнéниями, угрызéниями сóвести) to be tormented by; ~**ся** (**замýчиться** *perf*) **от** +*gen* (от болéй, от при́ступов) to suffer from; ~**ся** (**замýчиться** *perf*) **с** +*instr* (*разг*) to have a lot of hassle with; ~**ся** (*impf*) **над** +*instr* to agonize over.

мучн|**óе** (-óго; *decl like adj*) *ср* starchy foods *мн*.

мýш|**ка** (-ки; *gen pl* -**ек**) *ж* (для прицéла) sight; (на лицé) beauty spot; **брать** (**взять** *perf*) **когó-н/что-н на ~ку** (прицéлиться) to take aim at sb/sth; (*перен*) to keep a close eye on sb/sth.

муштр|**овáть** (-ýю; *perf* **вы́муштровать**) *несов перех* (солдáт) to drill.

мха *итп сущ см* **мох**.

МХАТ (-а) *м сокр* (= Москóвский Худóжественный академи́ческий теáтр) Moscow Arts Theatre (*BRIT*) *или* Theater (*US*).

мч|**ать** (-у, -ишь) *несов неперех* (пóезд, автомоби́ль) to speed along; (лóшадь) to race along ♦ *перех* to rush

▸ **мчáться** *несов возв* (пóезд, автомоби́ль) to speed along; (лóшадь) to race along; (*перен*: гóды, врéмя) to fly past.

мщéни|**е** (-я) *ср* revenge, vengeance.

мщу *несов см* **мстить**.

мы (нас; *см* Table 5b) *мест* we; ~ **с тобóй/женóй** you/my wife and I; **кто закóнчил рабóту?** – ~ who finished the job? – we did; **кто винови́т?** – ~ who is to blame? – we are.

мы́л|**ить** (-ю, -ишь; *perf* **намы́лить**) *несов перех* to soap

▸ **мы́литься** (*perf* **намы́литься**) *несов возв* to soap o.s.; (мы́ло, шампýнь) to lather.

мы́л|**о** (-а) *ср* soap; **он весь в ~е** (*перен*: *разг*: в потý) he's in a lather.

мы́льниц|**а** (-ы) *ж* soap dish.

мы́льный *прил* soap *опред*.

мыс (-а; *loc sg* -**ý**, *nom pl* -**ы**) *м* cape, promontory.

мы́сленно *нареч* mentally.

мы́сленный *прил* mental.

мысли́тел|**ь** (-я) *м* thinker.

мысли́тельный *прил* (процéсс) thought *опред*; (спосóбности, ýровень) intellectual.

мы́сл|**ить** (-ю, -ишь) *несов неперех* to think, reason ♦ *перех* to imagine; **я не ~ю жи́зни без рабóты** I can't imagine life without work.

мысл|**ь** (-и) *ж* thought; (идéя) idea; **зáдняя ~** ulterior motive; **óбраз мы́слей** way of thinking; **собирáться** (**собрáться** *perf*) **с мы́слями** to collect one's thoughts; **э́то ~**! that's a thought!

мысля́щ|**ий** (-ая, -ее, -ие) *прил* thinking *опред*.

мыть (**мóю, мóешь**; *perf* **вы́мыть** *или* **помы́ть**) *несов перех* to wash; **рукá рýку мóет** *partners in crime will always cover for each other*

▸ **мы́ться** (*perf* **вы́мыться** *или* **помы́ться**) *несов возв* to wash o.s.

мыч|**áть** (-ý, -и́шь; *perf* **промычáть**) *несов неперех* (корóва) to moo; (бык) to bellow; (*разг*: человéк) to mumble.

мы́шек *сущ см* **мы́шка**.

мышелó|**вка** (-ки; *gen pl* -**ок**) *ж* mousetrap.

мы́шечный *прил* muscular.

мыши́н|**ый** *прил* (цвет) grey (*BRIT*), gray (*US*); ~**ая норá** mouse hole; **мыши́ная возня́** (*перен*) intrigue.

мы́ш|**ка** (-ки; *gen pl* -**ек**) *ж уменьш от* **мышь**; **под ~кой** under one's arm.

мышлéни|**е** (-я) *ср* thought, thinking.

мы́шц|**а** (-ы) *ж* muscle.

мыш|**ь** (-и) *ж* (*ЗООЛ, КОМП*) mouse.

мышья́к (-á; *part gen* -**ý**) *м* arsenic.

мэр (-а) *м* mayor.

мэ́ри|**я** (-и) *ж* city hall.

мя́гкий (-кая, -кое, -кие; -ок, -ка́, -ко) *прил* soft; (движéния, похóдка) smooth; (харáктер, человéк) mild, gentle; (пригово́р, вы́говор, наказáние) lenient; (климáт, зима́, погóда) mild; **мя́гкий вагóн** railway carriage with soft seats; **мя́гкий знак** soft sign (Russian letter).

мя́гко *нареч* gently; (отругáть) mildly; ~ **выражáясь** to put it mildly.

мягкосердéч|**ный** (-ен, -на, -но) *прил* kind-hearted.

мя́гкое *прил см* **мя́гкий**.

мя́гче *сравн прил от* **мя́гкий** ♦ *сравн нареч от* **мя́гко**.

мя́киш (-а) *м* crumb.

мя́кот|**ь** (-и) *ж* flesh; (мя́со без костéй) meat off the bone.

мя́мл|**ить** (-ю, -ишь; *perf* **промя́млить**) *несов перех* (*разг*) to mumble.

мяси́ст|**ый** (-, -а, -о) *прил* meaty; (плéчи, лицó, плод) fleshy.

мясни́к (-á) *м* butcher.

мясн|**óй** *прил* (из мя́са) meat; (корóва, скот) beef; (отдéл, магази́н) butcher's; ~**ы́е консéрвы** tinned meat.

мя́с|**о** (-а) *ср* meat; (*разг*: говя́дина) beef.

мясорý|**бка** (-ки; *gen pl* -**ок**) *ж* mincer (*BRIT*), grinder (*US*).

мя́т|**а** (-ы) *ж* mint.

мятéж (-á) *м* revolt.

мятéжный *прил* rebellious; (душá, харáктер)

restless.

МЯ́ТНЫЙ *прил* mint.

МЯ́ТЫЙ *прил* (*одежда*) creased; (*бумага*) crumpled.

МЯТЬ (мну, мнёшь; *perf* **размя́ть**) *несов перех* (*глину*) to knead; (*кожу*) to work; (*perf* **измя́ть** *или* **смять**; *одежду*) to crease; (*бумагу*) to rumple; (*волосы*) to ruffle

▶ **МЯ́ТЬСЯ** *несов возв* (*разг*: *человек*) to shilly-shally; (*perf* **измя́ться** *или* **помя́ться** *или* **смя́ться**; *одежда*) to get creased; (*бумага*) to get rumpled.

МЯУ́КА|ТЬ (**-ю**; *perf* **промяу́кать**) *несов неперех* to miaow, mew.

МЯЧ (**-а́**) *м* ball; **ручно́й** ~ (*СПОРТ*) handball; **футбо́льный** ~ football.

~ Н, н ~

Н, н *сущ нескл (буква)* the 14th letter of the Russian alphabet.

┌─────────────┐
│ **KEYWORD** │
└─────────────┘

на *предл (+acc)* **1** *(направление на поверхность)* on; **положи тарéлку на стол** put the plate on the table; **я повéсил картину на стéну** I hung the picture on the wall; **надо наклéить мáрку на конвéрт** you need to stick the stamp on the envelope

2 *(направление в какое-н мéсто)* to; **на Юг/Украйну** to the South/Ukraine; **éздить** *(impf)* **на мóре/рабóту/конферéнции** to go to the seaside/to work/to a conference; **сесть** *(perf)* **на пóезд** to get on(to) the train

3 *(об объéкте воздéйствия)*: **обрати внимáние на этого человéка** pay attention to this man; **нажми на педáль/кнóпку** press the pedal/button; **я люблю смотрéть на детéй/на звёзды** I love watching the children/the stars

4 *(о врéмени, срóке)* for; **назначáть (назнáчить** *perf)* **на зáвтра/на 5 часóв** to arrange sth for tomorrow/for 5 o'clock; **он уéхал на час/мéсяц** he has gone away for an hour/a month

5 *(о цéли, о назначéнии)* for; **дéньги на книги** money for books; **ткань на плáтье** material for a dress; **на написáние доклáда ушлó мнóго врéмени** much time was spent writing the report; **провéрка на сообразительность** intelligence test

6 *(о мéре)* into; **дели́ть** *(impf)* **что-н на чáсти/парáграфы** to divide sth into parts/paragraphs

7 *(при сравнéнии)*: **я получáю на сто рублéй мéньше** I get one hundred roubles less

8 *(об изменéнии состояния)* into; **надо перевести́ текст на англи́йский** the text must be translated into English; **мы перешли́ на рýсский язы́к** we switched (in)to Russian; **я обменя́л маши́ну на я́хту** I exchanged the car for a yacht ♦ *предл (+prp)* **1** *(нахождéние на повéрхности)* on; **книга на пóлке** the book is on the shelf; **я сижý на дивáне** I am sitting on the sofa; **на дéвочке шáпка/шýба** the girl has a hat/fur coat on

2 *(о пребывáнии где-н)* in; **на Украи́не/Кавкáзе** in the Ukraine/Caucasus; **на ýлице** in the street;

быть *(impf)* **на рабóте/заседáнии** to be at work/at a meeting

3 *(о врéмени осуществлéния чего-н)*: **встрéтимся на слéдующей недéле** let's meet next week; **на пéрвых порáх** at first; **на ходý** *(сказáть, брóсить итп)* in passing; *(поймáть)* without stopping

4 *(об объéкте воздéйствия)* on; **сосредотóчиться** *(perf)*/**остановиться** *(perf)* **на чём-н** to concentrate/dwell on sth; **сойти́** *(perf)* **с умá на чём-н** to go mad about sth

5 *(о срéдстве осуществлéния чего-н)*: **éздить на пóезде/велосипéде** to travel by train/bicycle; **игрáть** *(impf)* **на роя́ле/скри́пке** to play the piano/violin; **катáться** *(impf)* **на лы́жах/конькáх** to go skiing/skating; **говори́ть** *(impf)* **на рýсском/англи́йском языкé** to speak (in) English/Russian

6 *(о состáвной чáсти предмéта)*: **раствóр на йóде** iodine solution; **кáша на водé** porridge made with water

7 *(разг: о большóм коли́честве чего-н)*: **оши́бка на оши́бке** mistake upon mistake.

на (**нáте**) *част (разг)* here (you are).

наб. *сокр* = **нáбережная**.

набáв|ить (-лю, -ишь; *impf* **набавля́ть)** *сов перех* to increase.

набалдáшник (-а) *м* knob *(of walking stick)*.

набáлтыва|ть (-ю) *несов от* **наболтáть**.

набáт (-а) *м* alarm bell; **бить** *(impf)* **в ~** *(перен)* to sound the alarm.

набéг (-а) *м* raid.

набегáть (-ю) *сов перех (километрá итп)* to run; **~** *(perf)* **инфáркт** *(разг)* to give o.s. a heart attack *(by running)*.

набегáть (-ю) *несов от* **набежáть**.

набегáться (-юсь) *сов возв* to wear o.s. out running.

набегý *итп сов см* **набежáть**.

набéдренн|ый *прил*: **~ая повя́зка** loincloth.

набежáть (*как* **бежáть**; *см* **Table 20**; *impf* **набегáть)** *сов непéрех (разг: тýчи)* to gather; *(: толпá, букáшки)* to come running; *(: водá)* to well up; *(процéнты, выходны́е итп)* to mount up; *(наскочи́ть)*: **~ на** *+acc* to run into; *(вóлны: на бéрег)* to lap against.

набезобра́знича|ть (-ю) *сов от*
безобра́зничать.
набекре́нь *нареч* (*шапка*) tilted to one side; **у**
него́ мозги́ ~ (*разг*) he's not with it.
на́бело *нареч*: **переписа́ть что-н ~** to write sth
out in neat.
на́бережн|ая (-ой; *decl like adj*) *ж* embankment.
наберу́(сь) *итп сов см* **набра́ть(ся).**
набива́|ть(ся) (-ю(сь)) *несов от* **наби́ть(ся).**
наби́вк|а (-и) *ж* stuffing.
набивно́й *прил* (*матрас, подушка*) stuffed;
(*ткань*) printed.
набира́|ть(ся) (-ю(сь)) *несов от* **набра́ть(ся).**
наб|и́ть (-ью, -ьёшь; *impf* **набива́ть**) *сов перех*
(*прикрепить гвоздями*) to nail; (*полотно,
ситец*) to print; (*разг: тарелок, чашек*) to
smash; (: *настрелять*) to bag; **набива́ть** (~
perf) (+*instr*) (*матрас, чемодан итп*) to stuff
(with); ~ (*perf*) **ши́шку/синя́к** (*разг*) to get a
bump/bruise; ~ (*perf*) **оско́мину** (*перен*) to reach
saturation point; ~ (*perf*) **ру́ку** (**на** +*prp*) (*разг*) to
get the knack (of); **набива́ть** (~ *perf*) **це́ну**
(*разг*) to talk up the price
▶ **наби́ться** (*impf* **набива́ться**) *сов возв* (*разг*):
~**ся в** +*acc* (*в комнату, в автобус*) to pack; **она́**
всё вре́мя ~ива́ется к нам в го́сти she's
always inviting herself round.
наблюда́телен *прил см* **наблюда́тельный.**
наблюда́тел|ь (-я) *м* observer.
наблюда́тельный (-ен, -ьна, -ьно) *прил*
(*человек*) observant; ~ **пункт** observation point.
наблюда́|ть (-ю) *несов перех* to observe;
(*пациента*) to treat ♦ *непepex*: ~ **за** +*instr* to
monitor; (*за порядком, за детьми*) to watch
over
▶ **наблюда́ться** *несов возв* (*случаться*) to be;
~**ся** (*impf*) **у** +*gen* (*лечиться*) to be treated by; **в**
стране́ ~ется рост престу́пности there has
been an increase in crime across the country.
на́божный (-ен, -на, -но) *прил* devout.
набо́йк|а (-йки; *gen pl* -ек) *ж* (*ткани, узора*)
printing; (*ткань*) printed fabric; (*на каблуке*)
heel.
на́бок *нареч* to one side.
наболева́|ть (3sg -ет) *несов от* **наболе́ть.**
наболе́вший (-ая, -ее, -ие) *прил* (*перен:
проблема, тема*) sensitive; ~ **вопро́с** sore
point.
наболе́|ть (3sg -ет, *impf* **наболева́ть**) *сов
непepex* to become sore; (*проблема*) to become
acute; **у неё ~ло на душе́** she has suffered a
great deal.
наболта́|ть (-ю; *impf* **набалтывать**) *сов перех*
(*разг*): ~ **глу́постей** to talk a lot of rubbish ♦
непepex: ~ **кому́-н про кого́-н** to tell sb stories
about sb.
набо́р (-а) *м* (*совокупность*) set; (*студентов*)
selection; (*армии, штата*) recruitment; (*типог*)
typesetting; ~ **слов** (*перен*) gibberish.
набо́рный *прил* (*типог*): ~ **цех** typesetter's;
набо́рный стано́к galley.

набо́рщик (-а) *м* (*типог*) typesetter.
набо́рщиц|а (-ы) *ж см* **набо́рщик.**
набра́сыва|ть (-ю) *несов от* **наброса́ть,
набро́сить.**
▶ **набра́сываться** *несов от* **набро́ситься.**
наб|ра́ть (-еру́, -ерёшь; *pt* -ра́л, -рала́, -ра́ло,
impf **набира́ть**) *сов* (*не*)*перех* (+*acc или* +*gen*;
грибов, цветов) to pick; (*воды*) to fetch;
(*работы, студентов, работников*) to take on;
(*армию, труппу*) to assemble; (*скорость,
высоту, баллы*) to gain; (*код, номер
телефона*) to dial; (*статью, текст*) to
typeset; **набира́ть** (~ *perf*) **о́пыт** to gain
experience
▶ **набра́ться** (*impf* **набира́ться**) *сов возв* (+*gen*;
много народу) to gather; (*сумма денег*) to
accumulate; (*разг: напиться*) to get sloshed;
~**ся** (*perf*) +*gen* (*предрассудков итп*) to acquire;
набира́ться (~**ся** *perf*) **сил** to build up one's
strength; **набира́ться** (~**ся** *perf*) **хра́брости** to
muster up courage; **набира́ться** (~**ся** *perf*)
терпе́ния to arm o.s. with patience.
набр|ести́ (-еду́, -едёшь; *pt* -ёл, -ела́, -ело́, *impf*
набреда́ть) *сов непepex* (*разг*): ~ **на** +*acc*
(*перен*) to come across; ~ (*perf*) **на мысль**
(*перен*) to hit upon an idea.
наброса́|ть (-ю; *impf* **набра́сывать**) *сов перех*
(*план, текст*) to sketch out ♦ (*не*)*перех* (+*acc
или* +*gen; вещей, окурков*) to throw about.
набро́|сить (-шу, -сишь; *impf* **набра́сывать**)
сов перех (*пальто, платок*) to throw on;
(*покрывало*) to throw over
▶ **набро́ситься** (*impf* **набра́сываться**) *сов
возв*: ~**ся на** +*acc* (*на добычу, на жертву*) to
fall upon; (*разг: на еду, на работу*) to get stuck
into; ~**ся** (*perf*) **на кого́-н** (*разг: с упрёками*) to
lay into sb.
набро́с|ок (-ка) *м* (*плана*) sketch; (*статьи,
письма*) draft.
набро́шу(сь) *итп сов см* **набро́сить(ся).**
набры́зга|ть (-ю) *сов* (*не*)*перех*: ~ +*acc или*
+*gen или* +*instr* to splash.
набу́х|нуть (3sg -нет, 3pl -нут, *pt* -, -ла, -ло, *impf*
набуха́ть) *сов непepex* to swell up.
набью́(сь) *итп сов см* **наби́ть(ся).**
нава́г|а (-и) *ж* (*зоол*) *type of cod.*
наважде́ни|е (-я) *ср* apparition.
нава́л|ить (-алю́, -а́лишь; *impf* **нава́ливать**) *сов*
(*не*)*перех* (+*acc или* +*gen; мусору, кирпичей
итп*) to pile up ♦ *непepex* (*no impf; толпа*) to
flock; **нава́ливать** (~ *perf*) (**на** +*acc*) to pile
on(to); **нава́ливать** (~ *perf*) **на кого́-н
рабо́ту/обя́занности** to load sb with work/
responsibilities; **в э́том году́ ~а́ли́ло мно́го
сне́гу** there was a lot of snow this year
▶ **навали́ться** (*impf* **нава́ливаться**) *сов возв*:
~**ся на** +*acc* (*на дверь итп*) to lean into;
(*насыпаться: земля*) to pile up on; (*разг:
наброситься: на еду*) to get stuck into; **на меня́
~а́ли́лось мно́го рабо́ты** (*разг*) I'm swamped
with work.

нава́лом *нареч*: **грузи́ть** ~ to pile up ♦ *как сказ*: ~ +*gen* (*разг*: *фру́ктов, де́нег итп*) there's loads of.

нава́р (-а) *м* (*бульон*) broth; (*жир*) fat; (*разг*: *прибыль*) take-in.

нава́ривать (-ю) *несов от* **навари́ть**.

нава́рист|ый (-, -а, -о) *прил* rich.

нав|ари́ть (-арю́, -а́ришь; *impf* **нава́ривать**) *сов перех* (*ТЕХ*: *стали*) to weld; (: *кусо́к мета́лла*) to weld on ♦ (*не*)*перех* (+*acc или* +*gen*; *супа, варенья*) to make a lot of.

навева́ть (-ю) *несов от* **навея́ть**.

наве́да|ться (-юсь; *impf* **наве́дываться**) *сов возв* (*разг*): ~ **к** +*dat* to call in on.

наведе́ни|е (-я) *ср* (*порядка*) establishment; (*справки*) making; (*орудия*) aiming.

наведу́ *итп сов см* **навести́**.

наве́дыва|ться (-юсь) *несов от* **наве́даться**.

нав|езти́ (-езу́, -езёшь; *pt* -ёз, -езла́, -езло́, *impf* **навози́ть**) *сов перех* to bring a lot of.

наве́к *нареч* (*навсегда*) for good, forever.

наве́ки *нареч* = **наве́к**.

навёл *итп сов см* **навести́**.

наве́рно *вводн сл* probably ♦ *нареч* (*точно*) for sure.

наве́рное *нареч* = **наве́рно**.

наверн|у́ть (-у́, -ёшь; *impf* **навёртывать**) *сов перех*: ~ (**на** +*acc*) (*навинтить*) to screw on(to); (*намотать*) to wrap (around).

▶ **наверну́ться** (*impf* **навёртываться**) *сов возв* (*слёзы*) to well up.

наверняка́ *вводн сл* (*конечно*) certainly ♦ *нареч* (*несомненно*) definitely, for sure; **он де́йствует** ~ he doesn't take any chances.

наверста́|ть (-ю; *impf* **навёрстывать**) *сов перех* (*типог*) to typeset; **навёрстывать** (~ *perf*) **упу́щенное** *или* **поте́рянное вре́мя** to make up for lost time.

нав|ерте́ть (-ерчу́, -е́ртишь; *impf* **навёртывать**) *сов перех*: ~ (**на** +*acc*) to twist (around).

навёртыва|ть (-ю) *несов от* **наверну́ть**, **наверте́ть**

▶ **навёртываться** *несов от* **наверну́ться**.

наве́рх *нареч* up; (*на верхний этаж*) upstairs; (*на поверхность*) to the top; **посмотре́ть** (*perf*) ~ to look up; **обраща́ться** (**обрати́ться** *perf*) ~ (*перен*) to go to the top.

наверху́ *нареч* (*также перен*) at the top; (*в верхнем этаже*) upstairs; (*на поверхности*) on (the) top ♦ *предл* (+*gen*) at the top of.

наверчу́ *сов см* **наверте́ть**.

наве́с (-а) *м* (*над прилавком, у подъезда*) canopy; (*скалы, берега*) overhang.

навеселе́ *нареч* (*разг*): **быть** ~ to be merry *или* tipsy.

наве́|сить (-шу, -сишь; *impf* **наве́шивать**) *сов перех* (*дверь, замок*) to hang; (*разг*: *картин,*

плакатов) to hang up; (*СПОРТ*) to lob.

нав|ести́ (-еду́, -едёшь; *pt* ёл, -ела́, -ело́, *impf* **наводи́ть**) *сов перех* (*вызвать*: *ужас, грусть итп*) to cause; (*бинокль, объектив*) to focus; (*орудие*) to aim; (*мост*) to lay; (*лак, краску*) to apply; (*разг*: *гостей, прия́телей, друзей*) to bring; (*порядок*) to establish; **наводи́ть** (~ *perf*) **кого́-н на** +*acc* (*на место, на след*) to lead sb to; **наводи́ть** (~ *perf*) **спра́вки** to make inquiries; **наводи́ть** (~ *perf*) **чистоту́** to clean up; **наводи́ть** (~ *perf*) **красоту́** (*разг*) to tart o.s. up; **э́та му́зыка** ~**о́дит на меня́ тоску́** this music makes me sad; **наводи́ть** (~ *perf*) **кого́-н на мысль** to give sb an idea; **его́ расска́з** ~**ёл меня́ на размышле́ния** his story started me thinking.

наве|сти́ть (-щу́, -сти́шь; *impf* **навеща́ть**) *сов перех* to visit.

наве́чно *нареч* for evermore.

наве́ша|ть (-ю; *impf* **наве́шивать**) *сов* (*не*)*перех* (+*acc или* +*gen*; *белья, картин, украшения*) to hang up; (*муки, печений*) to weigh out.

наве́шива|ть (-ю) *несов от* **наве́сить**, **наве́шать**.

наве́шу *сов см* **наве́сить**.

навеща́|ть (-ю) *несов от* **навести́ть**.

навещу́ *сов см* **навести́ть**.

наве́|ять (-ю, -ешь; *impf* **навева́ть**) *сов перех* (*перен*: *тоску итп*) to evoke.

на́взничь *нареч* on one's back.

навзры́д *нареч*: **пла́кать** ~ to sob loudly.

навига́тор (-а) *м* navigator.

навига́ци|я (-и) *ж* navigation.

навин|ти́ть (-чу́, -ти́шь; *impf* **нави́нчивать**) *сов перех* (*гайку, пробку*) to screw in; (*крышку*) to screw on.

нави́с|нуть (-ну, -нешь; *pt* -, -ла, -ло, *impf* **нависа́ть**) *сов неперех*: ~ **на** +*acc* (*волосы: на лоб*) to hang down over; **нависа́ть** (~ *perf*) **на** +*prp* (*сосульки: на ветках*) to hang from; **нависа́ть** (~ *perf*) **над** +*instr* (*скалы*) to overhang; (*тучи, опасность*) to loom over.

нави́сш|ий (-ая, -ее, -ие) *прил* (*берег, скала*) overhanging.

навл|е́чь (-еку́, -ечёшь итп, -еку́т; *pt* -ёк, -екла́, -екло́, *impf* **навлека́ть**) *сов перех* (*подозрения, несчастье*) to attract; **навлека́ть** (~ *perf*) **на кого́-н беду́** to bring sb bad luck; **навлека́ть** (~ *perf*) **на себя́ чей-н гнев** to incur sb's wrath.

нав|оди́ть (-ожу́, -о́дишь) *несов от* **навести́**.

наво́дк|а (-и) *ж* (*объектива*) focusing; (*оружия*) aiming.

наводне́ни|е (-я) *ср* flood; (*рынков товаром*) flooding.

наводн|и́ть (-ю́, -и́шь; *impf* **наводня́ть**) *сов перех*: ~ **что-н** +*instr* (*товарами, продуктами*) to flood sth with.

наво́дчик (-а) *м* (*сообщник*) *informant who tips*

thieves off.

наводя́щий (-ая, -ее, -ие) *прил*: ~ **вопро́с** pointer, hint.

навожу́ *несов см* **навози́ть**.

навожу́ *несов см* **наводи́ть, навози́ть**.

наво́з (-а) *м* manure.

наво́зить (-жу, -зишь; *perf* **унаво́зить**) *несов перех* to fertilize.

навози́ть (-ожу́, -о́зишь) *несов от* **навезти́**.

на́волочка (-ки; *gen pl* -ек) *ж* pillowcase.

навостри́ть (-ю́, -и́шь; *сов перех* (*разг*): ~ **у́ши** to prick up one's ears; ~ (*perf*) **лы́жи** (*разг*) to be ready to shoot off.

навра́ть (-у́, -ёшь; *pt* -а́л, -ала́, -а́ло) *сов от* **врать**.

навреди́ть (-жу́, -ди́шь) *сов от* **вреди́ть**.

навсегда́ *нареч* forever; **раз и** ~ once and for all.

навстре́чу *предл* (+*dat*) towards ♦ *нареч*: **бежа́ть** ~ **к кому́-н** to run towards sb; **она́ вы́шла** ~ **гостя́м** she came out to meet the guests; **идти́ (пойти́** *perf*) ~ **кому́-н** (*перен*) to give sb a hand.

навы́ворот *нареч* (*разг*: наизнанку) inside out; (*перен*: наоборот) the wrong way round.

на́вык (-а) *м* skill.

навы́кат(е) *нареч*: **глаза́** ~ bulging eyes.

навы́лет *нареч* right through; **его́ ра́нило пуле́й** ~ the bullet went right through him.

навы́нос *нареч* to take away (*BRIT*), to go (*US*); **мы не продаём** ~ we don't do takeaways (*BRIT*) *или* takeouts (*US*).

навы́пуск *нареч* outside, over; **он но́сит руба́шку** ~ he wears his shirt outside his trousers.

навы́тяжку *нареч*: **стоя́ть** ~ to stand to attention.

навью́чить (-у, -ишь; *impf* **навью́чивать**) *сов перех* to load.

навяза́ть (-жу́, -я́жешь; *impf* **навя́зывать**) *сов перех*: ~ (**на** +*acc*) (на шею, на удочку) to tie on(to); **навя́зывать** (~ *perf*) +*gen* (*связать*) to knit a lot of; (*снопов, веников*) to tie a lot of; (*венков*) to weave a lot of; **навя́зывать** (~ *perf*) **что-н кому́-н** (*перен*) to impose sth on sb

▶ **навяза́ться** (*impf* **навя́зываться**) *сов возв* (*разг*): ~**ся кому́-н в друзья́** to impose o.s. on sb; ~**ся** (*perf*) **в го́сти** to invite o.s. round.

навя́зчивый (-, -а, -о) *прил* (*мысль*) persistent; (*человек*) bothersome; **она́ ужа́сно** ~**ая** she's a real pest.

навя́зывать(ся) (-ю(сь)) *несов от* **навяза́ть(ся)**.

нагада́ть (-ю; *impf* **нага́дывать**) *сов перех* (*разг*) to predict.

нага́дить (-жу, -дишь) *сов от* **га́дить**.

нага́дывать (-ю) *несов от* **нагада́ть**.

нага́жу *сов см* **нага́дить**.

нага́йка (-йки; *gen pl* -ек) *ж* whip.

нага́н (-а) *м* revolver.

нага́р (-а) *м* snuff (*of candle*).

нагиба́ть(ся) (-ю(сь)) *несов от* **нагну́ть(ся)**.

нагишо́м *нареч* (*разг*) stark-naked.

нагла́дить (-жу, -дишь; *impf* **нагла́живать**) *сов перех* to iron.

нагле́ть (-ю; *perf* **обнагле́ть**) *несов неперех* to get impudent.

нагле́ц (-а́) *м* impudent upstart.

на́гло *нареч* impudently.

на́глость (-и) *ж* impudence, impertinence.

наглота́ться (-ю́сь) *сов возв* (+*gen*) to swallow.

на́глухо *нареч* tight, securely; **застёгиваться** (**застегну́ться** *perf*) ~ to do one's coat right up.

на́глый (-, -а́, -о) *прил* insolent, impudent; ~**ая ложь** brazen lie.

нагля́ден *прил см* **нагля́дный**.

нагляде́ться (-жу́сь, -ди́шься) *сов возв*: ~ **на** +*acc* to tire of looking at; **дай мне на тебя́** ~ let me take a good look at you.

нагля́дный (-ен, -на, -но) *прил* (*пример, случай*) clear; (*no short form*; *метод обучения*) visual; **нагля́дные посо́бия** visual aids.

нагляжу́сь *сов см* **нагляде́ться**.

нагна́ть (-оню́, -о́нишь; *pt* -на́л, -нала́, -на́ло, *impf* **нагоня́ть**) *сов перех* (*беглеца*) to catch up with; (*упущенное, пройденное*) to make up for; (*подлеж: ветер: грозу, тучи*) to blow; (*спирта, самогона*) to distil (*BRIT*), distill (*US*); **нагоня́ть** (~ *perf*) **страх на кого́-н** to strike fear into sb; **нагоня́ть** (~ *perf*) **тоску́ на кого́-н** to fill sb with sadness.

нагнести́ (-ту́, -тёшь; *impf* **нагнета́ть**) *сов перех* to pump.

нагнета́ть (-ю) *несов от* **нагнести́** ♦ *перех* (*перен: напряжение*) to heighten.

нагное́ние (-я) *ср* festering.

нагно́иться (*3sg* -и́тся, *3pl* -я́тся) *сов возв* to fester.

нагну́ть (-у́, -ёшь; *impf* **нагиба́ть**) *сов перех* (*ветку, человека*) to pull down; (*шею, голову*) to bend

▶ **нагну́ться** (*impf* **нагиба́ться**) *сов возв* to bend down.

нагова́ривать(ся) (-ю(сь)) *несов от* **наговори́ть(ся)**.

наговор (-а) *м* (*разг: клевета*) slander; (*колдовской*) spell.

наговори́ть (-ю́, -и́шь; *impf* **нагова́ривать**) *сов перех* (*текст: на плёнку*) to record ♦ *неперех* (*разг: наклеветать*): ~ **на** +*acc* to slander; ~ (*perf*) **чепухи́** to talk a lot of nonsense; ~ (*perf*) **кому́-н комплиме́нтов** to shower sb with compliments

▶ **наговори́ться** (*impf* **нагова́риваться**) *сов возв* to talk one's fill.

наго́й (-, -а́, -о) *прил* (*человек*) naked, nude; (*руки, ноги, лес*) bare.

на́голо *нареч*: **остри́чься** ~ to shave one's head; **обри́ть** (*perf*) **кого́-н** ~ to shave sb's head.

нагopо́ *нареч*: **ша́шки** ~ drawn swords.

на́голову *нареч*: **разби́ть** *или* **разгроми́ть** ~ to rout.

нагоню́ *итп сов см* **нагна́ть**.

нагоня́|й (-я) *м* (*разг*): **получи́ть** ~ **(от кого́-н)** to get a ticking off (from sb).

нагоня́ть (-ю) *несов от* **нагна́ть**.

нагоре́|ть (*3sg* -и́т, *impf* **нагора́ть**) *сов безл* (*+gen*; *израсходоваться*) to be used up.

наго́рный *прил* (*пастбище, растительность*) alpine, mountain *опред*; (*гористый*) hilly.

нагоро|ди́ть (-ожу́, -о́дишь) *сов (не)перех* (*+acc или +gen*; *разг*: *построек*) to put up; **он** ~**оди́л ерунды́** (*разг*) he came out with a load of nonsense.

наго́рь|е (-я) *ср* plateau.

нагот|а́ (-ы́) *ж* nudity, nakedness.

нагота́влива|ть (-ю) *несов от* **нагото́вить**.

нагото́ве *нареч* at the ready.

нагото́в|ить (-лю, -ишь; *impf* **нагота́вливать**) *сов перех* (*запасти*) to stock up with; (*сварить*) to cook.

награб|ить (-лю, -ишь) *сов перех* to plunder.

награ́д|а (-ы) *ж* reward; (*за учёбу, за работу*) prize; (*ВОЕН*) decoration; **дать** (*perf*) **что-н кому́-н в** ~**у** to give sb sth as a reward.

награ|ди́ть (-жу́, -ди́шь; *impf* **награжда́ть**) *сов перех*: ~ **кого́-н чем-н** (*орденом*) to award sb sth, award sth to sb; (*перен: способностями*) to endow sb with sth; (: *поцелуем, улыбкой*) to reward sb with sth.

награжде́ни|е (-я) *ср* awards ceremony.

награжу́ *сов см* **наградить**.

нагреба́|ть (-ю) *несов от* **нагрести́**.

нагребу́ *итп сов см* **нагрести́**.

нагрева́ни|е (-я) *ср* heating.

нагрева́тельный *прил*: ~ **прибо́р** heating appliance.

нагрева́|ть(ся) (-ю(сь)) *несов от* **нагре́ть(ся)**.

нагрес|ти́ (-ебу́, -ебёшь; *pt* -ёб, -ебла́, -ебло́, *impf* **нагреба́ть**) *сов перех* to rake together.

нагре́|ть (-ю; *impf* **нагрева́ть**) *сов перех* to heat, warm; ~ (*perf*) **ру́ки (на** +*prp*) (*перен*) to line one's pockets (with)

► **нагре́ться** (*pt* нагрева́ться) *сов возв* to warm up.

награмир|ова́ться (-у́юсь) *сов от* **гримирова́ться**.

нагроможда́|ть (-ю) *несов от* **громозди́ть**.

нагроможде́ни|е (-я) *ср* (*предметов*) pile; (*фактов*) mound.

нагромозд|и́ть (-жу́, -ди́шь) *сов от* **громозди́ть**.

награб|и́ть (-лю, -и́шь) *сов от* **грубить**.

нагру́дник (-а) *м* bib; (*рыцарский*) breastplate.

нагру́дный *прил*: ~ **карма́н** breast pocket.

нагру|зи́ть (-ужу́, -у́зишь) *сов от* **грузи́ть** ♦ (*impf* **нагружа́ть**) *перех* to load up; **нагружа́ть** (~ *perf*) **кого́-н рабо́той** to load sb with work.

нагру́зк|а (-и) *ж* (*действие*) loading; (*груз, также* ЭЛЕК, ТЕХ) load; (*занятость*) workload;

(*общественная*) responsibilities *мн*.

нагрязни́ть (-ю́, -и́шь) *сов от* **грязни́ть**.

нагря́н|уть (-у, -ешь) *сов неперех* (*гости, полиция*) to descend on; (*холода*) to set in; ~**ула беда́** tragedy struck.

нагуля́|ть (-ю; *impf* **нагу́ливать**) *сов перех* (*разг*): ~ **аппети́т** to work up an appetite; **нагу́ливать** (~ *perf*) **румя́нец** to get some colour in one's cheeks

► **нагуля́ться** *сов возв* to have a good walk.

над *предл* (+*instr*) above; **рабо́тать** (*impf*) ~ **прое́ктом** to work on a project; **ду́мать** (*impf*) ~ **зада́чей** to think about a problem; **смея́ться** (*impf*) ~ **ребёнком** to laugh at a child; **сиде́ть** (*impf*) ~ **кни́гой** to sit over a book.

над- *префикс* (*in verbs*; *об увеличении чего-н*) *indicating an increase in sth eg.* **надстро́ить**; (*о неполном действии*) *indicating an incomplete action eg.* **надку́сить**; (*in nouns and adjectives*; *поверх чего-н*) *indicating position above sth eg.* **надзе́мный**.

нада|ва́ть (-ю́, -ёшь) *сов перех* (*разг*): ~ **кому́-н чего́-н** (*подарков, советов, обещаний*) to give sb lots of sth ♦ *неперех*: ~ **кому́-н** (*разг*) to thrash sb.

нада́ви|ть (-авлю́, -а́вишь; *impf* **нада́вливать**) *сов (не)перех* (*+acc или +gen*; *разг*: *тараканов итп*) to squash ♦ *неперех*: ~ **на** +*acc* (*на дверь итп*) to lean against; (*на кнопку*) to press.

нада́влива|ть (-ю) *несов от* **надавить**.

нада́рю *сов см* **надоить**.

надар|и́ть (-ю́, -ишь; *impf* **нада́ривать**) *сов перех* (*разг*): ~ **кому́-н пода́рков** to give sb lots of presents.

надба́в|ить (-лю, -ишь; *impf* **надбавля́ть**) *сов перех* (*разг*) = **наба́вить**.

надба́вк|а (-и) *ж* (*к зарплате*) rise; (*к пенсии*) supplement; (*к цене*) surcharge; **надба́вка за вре́дность** danger money (*BRIT*), hazard pay (*US*).

надба́влю *сов см* **надба́вить**.

надбавля́|ть (-ю) *несов от* **надба́вить**.

надви́н|уть (-у, -ешь; *impf* **надвига́ть**) *сов перех*: ~ **что-н (на** +*acc*) to pull down sth (over)

► **надви́нуться** (*impf* **надвига́ться**) *сов возв* (*гроза, опасность, старость*) to approach; **надвига́ться** (~**ся** *perf*) **(на** +*acc*) (*на лоб, на уши*) to slide down (over).

надво́дный *прил* above water; (*корабль*) surface *опред*.

на́двое *нареч* in(to) two.

надво́рный *прил*: ~**ые постро́йки** outbuildings *мн*.

надвя|за́ть (-жу́, -я́жешь; *impf* **надвя́зывать**) *сов перех* (*свитер, рукава*) to lengthen (*knitted garment*); (*верёвку, нитку*) to tie on.

надгро́би|е (-я) *ср* gravestone, tombstone.

надгро́бный *прил* (*речь*) at the graveside;

(*надпись*) gravestone *опред*; **надгро́бный ка́мень** headstone; **надгро́бный па́мятник** memorial.

надёванный *прил* (*разг*) worn.

надева́|ть (-ю) *несов от* **наде́ть**.

наде́жд|а (-ы) *ж* hope; **в ~е на** +*acc* in the hope of; **пита́ть** (*impf*) **~у на что-н** to hope for sth; **подава́ть** (*impf*) **~ы** to show promise.

надёжен *прил см* **надёжный**.

надёжно *нареч* securely.

надёжность (-и) *ж* reliability.

надёж|ный (-ен, -на, -но) *прил* reliable; (*дверь, механизм*) secure; (*средство, путь*) safe.

наде́ла|ть (-ю) *сов (не)перех* (+*acc или* +*gen*; *ошибок, салатов*) to make lots of; (*неприятностей, вреда*) to cause a lot of; **не ~й глу́постей** don't do anything stupid; **что ты ~л?** what have you done?

надел|и́ть (-ю́, -и́шь; *impf* **наделя́ть**) *сов перех*: **~ кого́-н чем-н** (*землёй, участком*) to grant sb sth; (*перен*: *талантом, умом*) to endow sb with sth.

наде́ну *итп сов см* **наде́ть**.

надёрга|ть (-ю; *impf* **надёргивать**) *сов (не)перех* (+*acc или* +*gen*; *перьев, сорняков*) to pull out; (*разг*: *цитат, примеров*) to choose carefully.

надёрн|уть (-у, -ешь; *impf* **надёргивать**) *сов перех* to pull over.

наде́|ть (-ну, -нешь; *impf* **надева́ть**) *сов перех* to put on.

наде́я|ться (-юсь) *несов возв*: **~** +*infin* (*отдохнуть, успеть итп*) to hope to do; (*perf* **понаде́яться**): **~ на** +*acc* (*на друга, на семью*) to rely on; (*на улучшение*) to hope for; **я наде́юсь, что ...** I hope that ....

надзе́мный *прил* (*сооружение*) overground; (*часть растения*) above ground.

надзира́тел|ь (-я) *м* guard.

надзо́р (-а) *м* control.

надира́|ться (-юсь) *несов от* **надра́ться**.

надку|си́ть (-шу́, -́сишь; *impf* **надку́сывать**) *сов перех* to take a bite of.

надла́мыва|ть(ся) (-ю(сь)) *несов от* **надломи́ть(ся)**.

надлежа́щий (-ая, -ее, -ие) *прил* appropriate, suitable; **~им о́бразом** in the appropriate manner.

надлежи́т (*pt* -а́ло) *несов безл*: **ему́ ~ яви́ться в 9 часо́в** he is required to make an appearance at 9 o'clock.

надло́м (-а) *м* (*на ветке*) crack; (*угнетение*) breakdown.

надл|оми́ть (-омлю́, -о́мишь; *impf* **надла́мывать**) *сов перех* (*также перен*) to break; (*здоровье, психику*) to damage

▸ **надломи́ться** (*impf* **надла́мываться**) *сов возв* to break; (*перен*: *здоровье*) to suffer; (: *человек*) to damage one's health.

надме́нный (-ен, -на, -но) *прил* haughty.

на́до *как сказ* **1** (*о долженствовании*): **на́до ему́ помо́чь** it is necessary to help him; **на́до, что́бы он пришёл во́время** he must come on time; **на́до всегда́ говори́ть пра́вду** one must always speak the truth; **мне/ему́ на́до зако́нчить рабо́ту** I/he must finish the job; **помо́чь тебе́? – не на́до!** can I help you? – there's no need!; **не на́до!** (*не делай этого*) don't!

2 (*о потребности*): **на́до мно́го лет** it takes many years; **на варе́нье на́до мно́го са́хара** you need a lot of sugar to make jam; **им на́до 5 рубле́й** they need 5 roubles; **мне на́до спать** I need to sleep; **что тебе́ на́до?** what do you want?; **так ему́/ей и на́до** (*разг*) it serves him/her right; **на́до же!** (*разг*) of all things!; **на́до ду́мать** (*вероятно*) probably; (*конечно*) of course; **что на́до** (*разг*) excellent; **фильм что на́до!** it's an excellent film!

на́до *предл см* **над**.

на́добность (-и) *ж* necessity.

надоеда́|ть (-ю) *несов от* **надое́сть**.

надое́|м *итп сов см* **надое́сть**.

надое́дливый (-, -а, -о) *прил* tedious, tiresome.

надое́сть (*как* **есть**; *см* **Table 15**; *impf* **надоеда́ть**) *сов неперех*: **~ кому́-н** (+*instr*) (*разговорами, упрёками*) to bore sb (with); **мне ~ло ждать** I'm tired of waiting; **он мне ~л** I've had enough of him; **переста́нь мне надоеда́ть!** stop bothering me!

надо|и́ть (-ю́, -и́шь; *impf* **нада́ивать**) *сов (не)перех* (+*acc или* +*gen*; *молока*) to get.

надо́лго *нареч* for a long time; **Вы здесь ~?** are you here for long?

надо́мник (-а) *м* homeworker.

надо́мниц|а (-ы) *ж см* **надо́мник**.

надорв|а́ть (-у́, -ёшь; *impf* **надрыва́ть**) *сов перех* (*лист, материю*) to make a tear in; (*пакет*) to start to tear open; (*перен*: *голос*) to strain; (: *силы, здоровье*) to tax

▸ **надорва́ться** (*impf* **надрыва́ться**) *сов возв* (*конверт, воротник*) to tear slightly; (*перенапрячься*) to do o.s. an injury; (*перен*) to overexhaust o.s.

надоу́м|ить (-лю, -ишь) *сов перех*: **~ кого́-н** +*infin* (*разг*) to advise sb to do; **э́то он меня́ ~ил** he was the one who gave me the idea.

надпи|са́ть (-ишу́, -и́шешь; *impf* **надпи́сывать**) *сов перех* (*книгу, фотогра́фию*) to inscribe; (*посылку, конверт*) to address; **надпи́сывать** (**~** *perf*) **а́дрес на** +*acc* to address.

на́дпис|ь (-и) *ж* inscription.

надпишу́ *итп сов см* **надписа́ть**.

надра́|ить (-ю, -ишь) *сов от* **дра́ить**.

надра́|ться (-еру́сь, -ерёшься; *impf* **надира́ться**) *сов возв* (*разг*) to get sozzled.

надре́жу *итп сов см* **надре́зать**.

надре́з (-а) *м* cut.

надре́з|ать (-́ежу, -́ежешь; *impf* **надреза́ть**) *сов перех* to cut into.

надруга́тельств|о (-а) *ср*: ~ **(над** +*instr*) (*над памятью, над честью*) violation (of); (*над человеком*) abuse (of).
надруга́|ться (-юсь) *(не)сов возв*: ~ **над** +*instr* to abuse.
надры́в (-а) *м* (*надорванное место*) tear, rip; (*перен: физический*) strain; (: *в пении итп*) hysterical streak; **с ~ом в го́лосе** with a trembling voice.
надрыва́|ть (-ю) *несов от* **надорва́ть**
▶ **надрыва́ться** *несов от* **надорва́ться** ◆ *возв* (*кричать*) to scream away; (*разг*): **~ся (над** +*instr*) to break one's back (over) (*fig*); **у меня́ се́рдце** *или* **душа́ ~ется** my heart bleeds.
надры́в|ный (-ен, -на, -но) *прил* hysterical.
надсмо́трщик (-а) *м* (*тюремный*) warden; (*на плантации*) overseer.
надсмо́трщиц|а (-ы) *ж см* **надсмо́трщик**.
надста́в|ить (-лю, -ишь; *impf* **надставля́ть**) *сов перех* to lengthen (*by adding extra material*).
надстра́ива|ть (-ю) *несов от* **надстро́ить**.
надстро́ек *сущ см* **надстро́йка**.
надстро́|ить (-ю, -ишь; *impf* **надстра́ивать**) *сов перех* (*стену, дом*) to build onto; (*этаж*) to add.
надстро́йка (-йки; *gen pl* -ек) *ж* (*здания*) additional floor; (*ФИЛОСОФИЯ*) superstructure.
надува́тельств|о (-а) *ср* (*разг*) con.
надува́|ть(ся) (-ю(сь)) *несов от* **наду́ть(ся)**.
надувно́й *прил* inflatable.
наду́манный *прил* contrived.
наду́ма|ть (-ю; *impf* **наду́мывать**) *сов неперех* (+*infin*; *разг*) to take it into one's head to do.
наду́т|ый (-, -а, -о) *прил* (*почки, вена*) swollen; (*разг: высокомерный*) puffed-up; (: *обиженный*) sulky.
наду́|ть (-ю, -ешь; *impf* **надува́ть**) *сов перех* (*мяч, колесо*) to inflate, blow up; (*разг: обмануть*) to con ◆ *безл* (+*gen*; *пыли, холоду итп*) to blow; (*в ухо, в шею итп*) to catch a chill; **мне ~ло в грудь** I've caught a chill (on my chest).
▶ **наду́ться** (*impf* **надува́ться**) *сов возв* (*матрас, мяч*) to inflate; (*парус*) to billow; (*почка, вена, река*) to swell up; (*перен: от важности*) to swell up; (: *разг: обидеться*) to sulk; ~ (*perf*) **гу́бы** (*разг*) to go into a sulk.
надым|и́ть (-лю́, -и́шь) *сов от* **дыми́ть**.
надыша́|ть (-у́, -ишь) *сов неперех* (*в комнате, в купе*) to get warm (*from body heat*); ~ (*perf*) **на** +*acc* (*на стекло, на очки*) to breathe on
▶ **надыша́ться** *сов возв* (+*instr*; *дымом, газом*) to breathe in; **~ся** (*perf*) **во́здухом** to get plenty of fresh air; **пе́ред сме́ртью не нады́шишься** it's too late to do anything about it now.
наеда́|ться (-юсь) *несов от* **нае́сться**.
нае́дешь *итп сов см* **нае́хать**.
наеди́мся *сов см* **нае́сться**.
наедине́ *нареч*: ~ **(с** +*instr*) alone (with); **они́**

оста́лись ~ they were left on their own; **я до́лжен оста́ться** ~ **с собо́й** I need time to be by myself.
наеди́те(сь) *сов см* **нае́сть(ся)**.
нае́ду *сов см* **нае́хать**.
наедя́тся *сов см* **нае́сться**.
нае́зд (-а) *м* (*визит*) visit.
нае́|здить (-зжу, -здишь; *impf* **наезжа́ть**) *сов перех* (*сто километров*) to clock up; (*дорогу*) to flatten; (*лошадь*) to break in
▶ **нае́здиться** *сов возв* to travel a lot; **я ~здился в командиро́вки** I'm tired of going away on business.
нае́здник (-а) *м* rider.
нае́здниц|а (-ы) *ж см* **нае́здник**.
наезжа́|ть (-ю) *несов от* **нае́здить, нае́хать** ◆ *неперех*: ~ **(в го́сти) к кому́-н** to pay sb visits.
нае́зженный *прил* well-used.
нае́зжу(сь) *сов см* **нае́здить(ся)**.
нае́лся *итп сов см* **нае́сться**.
нае́мся *сов см* **нае́сться**.
наём (-йма) *м* hiring; (*кварти́ры*) renting.
наёмник (-а) *м* (*ВОЕН, также перен*) mercenary; (*наёмный работник*) casual worker.
наёмный *прил* (*труд, работник*) hired; (*помещение*) rented, leased; (*земля*) leased; ~ **уби́йца** hitman.
нае́сться (*как* **есть**; *см* Table 15; *impf* **наеда́ться**) *сов возв* (+*gen*; *сладкого, овощей*) to eat a lot of; (+*instr*; *супом*) to fill o.s. up on; **я нае́лся** I'm full.
нае́хать (*как* **е́хать**; *см* Table 19; *impf* **наезжа́ть**) *сов неперех* (*разг: туристы, гости*) to arrive in droves; **наезжа́ть** (~ *perf*) **на** +*acc* to drive into.
нае́шься *сов см* **нае́сться**.
нажа́л|оваться (-уюсь) *сов возв* (*разг*): ~ **(кому́-н на** +*acc*) to complain (to sb about).
нажа́р|ить (-ю, -ишь; *impf* **нажа́ривать**) *сов перех* to fry.
нажа́|ть (-му́, -мёшь; *impf* **нажима́ть**) *сов* (*не*)*перех* (+*acc или* +*gen*; *соку*) to squeeze; (*снопов, хлеба*) to reap ◆ *неперех* (*перен*): ~ **на** +*acc* (*на работников, на руководство*) to put pressure on; (*разг: на работу, на учёбу*) to get moving with; **нажима́ть** (~ *perf*) **на** +*acc* (*на кнопку*) to press; (*на рычаг*) to press (down).
нажгу́ *итп сов см* **наже́чь**.
нажда́к (-а) *м* emery.
наждачн|ый *прил*: ~**ая бума́га** emery paper.
наж|е́чь (-гу́, -жёшь *итп*, -гу́т; *pt* -ёг, -гла́, -гло́, *impf* **нажига́ть**) *сов* (*не*)*перех* (+*acc или* +*gen*; *дров, угля, керосина*) to burn a lot of; (*разг: лицо, спину итп*) to burn.
нажи́в|а (-ы) *ж* gain.
нажива́|ть(ся) (-ю(сь)) *несов от* **нажи́ть(ся)**.
наживи́|ть (-лю́, -и́шь; *impf* **наживля́ть**) *сов перех* to bait.

нажи́вк|а (-и) ж bait.

наживлю́ сов см **наживи́ть**.

наживля́|ть (-ю) несов от **наживи́ть**.

наживно́й прил: **де́ньги – де́ло** ~**о́е** money will start to roll in given time.

наживу́(сь) итп сов см **нажи́ть**.

нажига́|ть (-ю) несов от **нажечь**.

нажи́м (-а) м (также перен) pressure; **сде́лать** (perf) **что-н под** ~**ом** to do sth under pressure.

нажима́|ть (-ю) несов от **нажа́ть**.

нажира́|ться (-юсь) несов от **нажра́ться**.

нажи́|ть (-ву́, -вёшь; impf **нажива́ть**) сов перех (состояние, миллионы) to acquire; ~ (perf) (себе) **враго́в** to make enemies; ~ (perf) (себе) **неприя́тность** to get o.s. into trouble; **наживёшь себе́ радикули́т** you'll end up with backache

▶ **нажи́ться** (impf **нажива́ться**) сов возв: ~**ся** (**на** +prp) (на войне, на спекуля́ции) to gain (from).

нажму́ итп сов см **нажа́ть**.

нажра́ться (-у́сь, -ёшься; impf **нажира́ться**) сов возв (животное) to eat its fill; (разг: человек) to stuff o.s.; (: напи́ться) to get plastered.

наза́втра нареч (разг) next day.

наза́д нареч back; (нагну́ться, кати́ться итп) backwards; (тому́) ~ ago; **де́сять лет/неде́лю** (тому́) ~ ten years/one week ago.

назва́нива|ть (-ю) несов неперех (разг) to keep ringing.

назва́ни|е (-я) ср name; (отдельное издание) title; **под** ~**м** +gen named, called; **э́то не велосипе́д, а одно́** ~ you can hardly call it a proper bicycle; **торго́вое** ~ trade name.

наз|ва́ть (-ову́, -овёшь; pt -ва́л, -вала́, -ва́ло, impf **называ́ть**) сов перех to call; (ребёнка, соба́ку) to name, call; (назна́чить: кандида́тов, день, це́ну) to name; **называ́ть** (~ perf) **ве́щи свои́ми имена́ми** to call a spade a spade

▶ **назва́ться** (impf **называ́ться**) сов возв (+instr; предста́виться) to call o.s.

назе́мный прил surface опред; **назе́мные войска́** ground troops.

на́земь нареч (упа́сть, бро́сить) to the ground.

назида́ни|е (-я) ср edification.

назида́тельный (-ен, -ьна, -ьно) прил edifying.

назло́ нареч out of spite; ~ **кому́-н** to spite sb; **как** ~ to make things worse.

назнача́|ть (-ю) несов от **назна́чить**.

назначе́ни|е (-я) ср (времени, цены итп) setting; (на работу) appointment; (лекарства) prescription; (функция) function; **пункт или ме́сто** ~**я** destination.

назна́ч|ить (-у, -ишь; impf **назнача́ть**) сов перех (нача́льником) to appoint; (время, цену) to set; (встречу) to arrange; (лекарство, курс лечения) to prescribe; **он** ~**ил ей свида́ние** he asked her to meet him.

назову́(сь) итп сов см **назва́ть(ся)**.

назо́йлив|ый (-, -а, -о) прил (человек) tiresome; (вопрос, мысль) persistent.

назре́ть (3sg -ет, 3pl -ют, impf **назрева́ть**) сов неперех to come to a head; (перен: вопрос, разговор) to become unavoidable.

назубо́к нареч (разг): **вы́учить/знать** ~ to learn/know off by heart.

называ́емый прил: **так** ~ so-called.

называ́|ть (-ю) несов от **назва́ть**

▶ **называ́ться** несов от **назва́ться** ♦ возв (носить название) to be called; **как** ~**ется э́то ме́сто?** what is this place called?; **ситуа́ция, что** ~**ется, крити́ческая** the situation is what you might call critical.

наибо́лее нареч: ~ **интере́сный/краси́вый** the most interesting/beautiful.

наибо́льш|ий (-ая, -ее, -ие) прил the greatest.

наи́вный (-ен, -на, -но) прил naive.

наивы́сш|ий (-ая, -ее, -ие) прил the highest.

наи́гранный прил artificial, false.

наигра́|ть (-ю; impf **наи́грывать**) сов перех (мелодию) to play; (для записи) to record

▶ **наигра́ться** сов возв to play for a long time.

наи́грыва|ть (-ю) несов от **наигра́ть** ♦ неперех: ~ **на** +prp (на флейте) to play quietly on.

наи́грыш (-а) м tune.

наизна́нку нареч inside out.

наизу́сть нареч: **знать/вы́учить** ~ to know/learn by heart.

наилу́чш|ий (-ая, -ее, -ие) прил the best.

наиме́нее нареч: ~ **уда́чный/спосо́бный** the least successful/capable.

наименова́ни|е (-я) ср name; (проекта, книги) title, name.

наименов|а́ть (-у́ю) сов от **именова́ть**.

наиме́ньш|ий (-ая, -ее, -ие) прил (длина, высота итп) the smallest; (усилие) the least.

наискосо́к нареч (разг: разрезать) crosswise; (: идти́) diagonally.

на́искось нареч diagonally.

наиху́дш|ий (-ая, -ее, -ие) прил the worst.

найдёныш (-а) м foundling.

найду́(сь) итп сов см **найти́(сь)**.

на́йма итп сущ см **наём**.

найми́т (-а) м hireling.

найму́(сь) итп сов см **наня́ть(ся)**.

найти́ (-йду́, -йдёшь; pt -шёл, -шла́, -шло́, impf **находи́ть**) сов перех to find ♦ неперех (толпа, гости, тучи) to gather; (натолкну́ться): ~ **на** +acc to stumble into; **на него́** ~**шла́ тоска́** he was overcome with sadness; **на меня́** ~**шёл смех** I couldn't help laughing; ~**шёл чем горди́ться!** (разг) is that all you've got to be proud of?; **находи́ть** (~ perf) **о́бщий язы́к** to find a common language; ~ (perf) **себя́** to find o.s.

▶ **найти́сь** (impf **находи́ться**) сов возв (ключи, ребёнок итп) to turn up; (доброво́льцы, жела́ющие) to come forward; (не растеря́ться) to come up with an answer.

накажу́ *итп сов см* **наказа́ть.**

нака́з (-a) *м* (*полит*) mandate (*to govern*); (*наставление*) wish.

наказа́ни|е (-я) *ср* punishment; (*перен: разг*) pain, hassle.

наказа́ть (-ажу́, -а́жешь; *impf* **нака́зывать**) *сов перех* (*за проступок итп*) to punish; (*приказать*) to order.

нака́л (-a) *м* (*борьбы*) heat.

накал|и́ть (-ю́, -и́шь; *impf* **нака́ливать** *или* **накаля́ть**) *сов перех* to heat up; (*перен: обстано́вку*) to hot up

▶ **накали́ться** (*impf* **нака́ливаться** *или* **накаля́ться**) *сов возв* to heat; (*перен: обстано́вка*) to become heated; (: *стра́сти*) to become inflamed; **~ся** (*perf*) **докрасна́/добела́** to become red-/white-hot.

нака́пыва|ть(ся) (-ю(сь)) *несов от* **наколо́ть(ся).**

накаля́|ть(ся) (-ю(сь)) *несов от* **накали́ть(ся).**

накану́не *нареч* the day before, the previous day ◆ *предл* (+*gen*) on the eve of.

нака́па|ть (-ю) *сов от* **ка́пать.**

нака́плива|ть(ся) (-ю(сь)) *несов от* **накопи́ть(ся).**

нака́пыва|ть (-ю) *несов от* **накопа́ть.**

нака́рка|ть (-ю) *сов от* **ка́ркать** ◆ *перех* (*разг*): **~ кому́-н беду́** to bring sb bad luck.

наката́|ть (-ю; *impf* **нака́тывать**) *сов перех* to roll; (*доро́гу, колею́*) to flatten out; (*разг: написа́ть*) to rattle off

▶ **наката́ться** *сов возв* (*на конька́х*) to have a good time skating; (*на лы́жах*) to have a good time skiing.

накат|и́ть (-ачу́, -а́тишь; *impf* **нака́тывать**) *сов непере* (*разг: толпа́, го́сти*) to descend; (*тоска́*) to be overwhelming ◆ *перех*: **~ что-н на** +*acc* to roll sth onto; **нака́тывать** (**~** *perf*) (**на** +*acc*) (*волна́*) to roll up (onto)

▶ **накати́ться** (*impf* **нака́тываться**) *сов возв*: **~ся на** +*acc* (*волна́, лави́на*) to roll up onto.

нака́тыва|ть (-ю) *несов от* **наката́ть, накати́ть**

▶ **нака́тываться** *несов от* **накати́ться.**

накача́|ть (-ю; *impf* **нака́чивать**) *сов (не)перех* (+*acc или* +*gen*: *воды́, во́здуха*) to pump; (*ка́меру, ши́ну*) to pump up.

накида́|ть (-ю; *impf* **наки́дывать**) *сов перех* to throw.

наки́д|ка (-ки; *gen pl* -ок) *ж* (*оде́жда*) wrap; (*покрыва́ло*) bedspread, thrower.

наки́дыва|ть (-ю) *несов от* **накида́ть, наки́нуть**

▶ **наки́дываться** *несов от* **наки́нуться.**

наки́|нуть (-у, -ешь; *impf* **наки́дывать**) *сов перех* (*плато́к*) to throw on; (*разг: наба́вить*) to add on

▶ **наки́нуться** (*impf* **наки́дываться**) *сов возв*: **~ся на** +*acc* (*на челове́ка*) to hurl o.s. at; (*разг:*

на еду, на книгу) to get stuck into; **наки́дываться** (**~ся** *perf*) **на кого́-н с вопро́сами/жа́лобами** (*разг*) to bombard sb with questions/complaints.

накип|е́ть (*3sg* -и́т, *impf* **накипа́ть**) *сов непере* (*на́кипь, пе́на*) to form ◆ *безл* (*перен: зло́ба, оби́да*) to build up.

на́кип|ь (-и) *ж* (*на бульо́не*) scum; (*в ча́йнике*) fur (*BRIT*), scale (*US*).

накла́д|ка (-ки; *gen pl* -ок) *ж* (*шиньо́н*) hairpiece; (*разг: недоразуме́ние*) mix-up.

накладн|а́я (-о́й; *decl like adj*) *ж* (*КОММ*) bill of lading (*BRIT*), waybill (*US*); **грузова́я ~** consignment note.

накладно́й *прил* (*во́лосы, борода́*) false; (*карма́н*) sewn-on; **накладно́е зо́лото** rolled gold; **накладны́е расхо́ды** (*ЭКОН*) overheads *мн* (*BRIT*), overhead (*US*).

накла́д|ок *сущ см* **накла́дка.**

накла́дыва|ть (-ю) *несов от* **наложи́ть.**

наклевета́|ть (-ещу́, -е́щешь) *сов от* **клевета́ть.**

наклёвыва|ться (*3sg* -ется, *3pl* -ются) *несов от* **наклю́нуться.**

накле́ек *сущ см* **накле́йка.**

накле́|ить (-ю, -ишь; *impf* **накле́ивать**) *сов перех* (*афи́шу, ма́рку итп*) to stick on; (*фона́риков, украше́ний итп*) to make (*with glue and paper*).

накле́й|ка (-йка; *gen pl* -ек) *ж* label.

наклёпа|ть (-ю) *сов от* **клепа́ть** ◆ (*impf* **наклёпывать**) *перех* to rivet on.

наклёп|ка (-и) *ж* stud.

наклёпыва|ть (-ю) *несов от* **наклепа́ть.**

накли́к|ать (-чу, -чешь; *impf* **наклика́ть**) *сов перех*: **~ кому́-н несча́стье** to bring misfortune on sb.

накло́н (-a) *м* incline, slope; (*головы́*) tilt; (*по́черка*) slope.

наклоне́ни|е (-я) *ср* (*линг*) mood.

накл|они́ть (-оню́, -о́нишь; *impf* **наклоня́ть**) *сов перех* to tilt

▶ **наклони́ться** (*impf* **наклоня́ться**) *сов возв* to bend down.

накло́нност|ь (-и) *ж*: **~ к** +*dat* (*к му́зыке итп*) aptitude for; (*к меланхо́лии итп*) tendency toward; **дурны́е/хоро́шие наскло́нности** bad/good habits.

накло́нный *прил* slanting.

наклоня́|ть(ся) (-ю(сь)) *несов от* **наклони́ть(ся).**

наклю́|нуться (*3sg* -ется, *3pl* -утся, *impf* **наклё́вываться**) *сов возв* (*цыплёнок*) to peck its way out of the shell; (*перен: по́чки, росто́к*) to form; (: *вы́годное де́ло*) to turn up.

накля́узнича|ть (-ю) *сов от* **кля́узничать.**

накова́льн|я (-ьни; *gen pl* -ен) *ж* anvil.

нако́жный *прил* skin *опред*.

наколе́нник (-а) *м* (*СПОРТ*) kneepad.

нако́лк|а (-и) *ж* (*разг: татуировка*) tattoo.

нако|ло́ть (-олю́, -о́лешь; *impf* **нака́лывать**) *сов перех* (*руку, палец*) to prick; (*татуировку*) to apply; (*прикрепить*): ~ **(на** +*acc*) (*на шляпу, на дверь*) to pin on(to) ◆ **(не)***перех* (+*acc или* +*gen*; *дров*) to chop; (*сахару*) to break up

▸ **наколо́ться** (*impf* **нака́лываться**) *сов возв*: ~**ся (на** +*acc*) to prick o.s. (on).

наконе́ц *нареч* at last, finally ◆ *вводн сл* after all; ~**то!** at long last!; **он ~ по́нял** he finally understood; **ты мог бы, ~, позвони́ть** if nothing else, you could have phoned; **ну, иди́ же ~!** come on, it really is time for you to go!

наконе́чник (-а) *м* tip, end.

накопа́|ть (-ю; *impf* **нака́пывать**) *сов перех* to dig up.

накопи́тельств|о (-а) *ср* acquisitiveness.

накоп|и́ть (-лю́, -ишь) *сов от* **копи́ть** ◆ (*impf* **нака́пливать**) *перех* (*силы, информацию*) to store up; (*средства*) to accumulate

▸ **накопи́ться** *сов от* **копи́ться** ◆ (*impf* **нака́пливаться**) *возв* (*силы, толпа*) to build up; (*средства*) to accumulate; (*раздражение*) to mount.

накопле́ни|е (-я) *ср* (*действие*) accumulation; ~ **да́нных** (*КОМП*) data storage; *см также* **накопле́ния**.

накопле́ни|я (-й) *мн* (*сбережения*) savings *мн*.

накоплю́(сь) *сов см* **накопи́ть(ся)**.

накоп|ти́ть (-чу́, -ти́шь) *сов от* **копти́ть** ◆ *перех* (*рыбы, колбасы*) to smoke.

накорм|и́ть (-лю́, -ишь) *сов от* **корми́ть**.

накра́пыва|ть (*3sg* -ет) *несов неперех* to drizzle.

накра́|сить (-шу, -сишь) *сов от* **кра́сить** ◆ (*impf* **накра́шивать**) *перех* to paint

▸ **накра́ситься** *сов от* **кра́ситься** ◆ (*impf* **накра́шиваться**) *возв* to put on make-up.

накрахма́л|ить (-ю, -ишь) *сов от* **крахма́лить**.

накра́шива|ть(ся) (-ю(сь)) *несов от* **накра́сить(ся)**.

накра́шу(сь) *сов см* **накра́сить(ся)**.

накрен|и́ть(ся) (-ю́(сь), -и́шь(ся)) *сов от* **крени́ть(ся)**.

на́крепко *нареч* (*запереть, забить*) tight; (*также*: **кре́пко-~**: *запретить, наказать*) strictly; **~ запо́мни** ~ be sure to remember.

на́крест *нареч* (*также*: **крест-~**) crosswise.

накрич|а́ть (-у́, -и́шь) *сов неперех*: ~ **на** +*acc* (*на ребёнка, на подчинённого*) to shout at

▸ **накрича́ться** *сов возв* (*разг*) to shout a lot; **ну что, ~а́лся?** are you through shouting?

накропа́|ть (-ю) *сов от* **кропа́ть**.

накрош|и́ть (-у́, -и́шь) *сов от* **кроши́ть**.

накру́|ить *итп сов см* **крои́ть**.

накр|ути́ть (-учу́, -у́тишь; *impf* **накру́чивать**) *сов перех* (*веревок, пряжи*) to twist; (*разг: ерунды, небылиц*) to spin; **накру́чивать** (~ *perf*) **(на** +*acc*) (*гайку: на болт*) to screw on(to); (*канат: на столб*) to wind (round)

▸ **накрути́ться** (*impf* **накру́чиваться**) *сов возв* (*разг: завить*) to put one's hair in rollers; **накру́чиваться** (~**ся** *perf*) **на** +*acc* to wind around.

накр|ы́ть (-о́ю, -о́ешь; *impf* **накрыва́ть**) *сов перех* to cover; (*разг: преступника, вора*) to nail, nab; **накрыва́ть** (~ *perf*) **(на) стол** to lay the table

▸ **накры́ться** (*impf* **накрыва́ться**) *сов возв* (*разг: мероприятие, прогулка*) to fall through; **накрыва́ться** (~**ся** *perf*) (+*instr*) (*пледом, одеялом*) to cover o.s. up (with).

накуп|и́ть (-лю́, -ишь; *impf* **накупа́ть**) *сов перех* to buy lots of.

наку́ренный *прил* (*помещение, вагон*) smoke-filled; (*воздух*) smoky.

накур|и́ть (-урю́, -у́ришь; *impf* **наку́ривать**) *сов неперех*: ~ **в ко́мнате** to fill a room with smoke

▸ **накури́ться** (*impf* **наку́риваться**) *сов возв* to smoke too much.

налага́|ть (-ю) *несов от* **наложи́ть**.

нала́|дить (-жу, -дишь; *impf* **нала́живать**) *сов перех* (*мотор, станок*) to repair, fix; (*сотрудничество*) to initiate; (*хозяйство*) to sort out; (*порядок*) to establish; (*разг: гитару, рояль*) to tune

▸ **нала́диться** (*impf* **нала́живаться**) *сов возв* (*работа*) to go well; (*отношения, здоровье*) to improve.

нала́мыва|ть (-ю) *несов от* **наломáть**.

нал|га́ть (-гу́, -жёшь) *сов от* **лгать**.

нале́во *нареч* (*повернуть, посмотреть*) to the) left; (*разг: продать, сбыть*) on the side.

налёг *итп сов см* **нале́чь**.

налега́|ть (-ю) *несов от* **нале́чь**.

налегке́ *нареч* (*ехать*) without luggage; (*в лёгкой одежде*) lightly-clad; **путеше́ствовать** (*impf*) ~ to travel light.

нале́з|ть (-у, -ешь; *impf* **налеза́ть**) *сов неперех* (*разг: насекомые, дети*) to accumulate; (*надеться*) to fit; (*шапка*): ~ **на** +*acc* (*на глаза*) to slide over.

налеп|и́ть (-лю́, -ишь) *сов от* **лепи́ть** ◆ (*не*) *перех* (+*acc или* +*gen*; *фигурок, птиц*) to model.

налёт (-а) *м* (*птиц, авиации*) flying in, approach; (*на врага, на город*) raid; (*на банк, на квартиру*) robbery; (*пыли, плесени*) thin coating *или* layer; (*МЕД*) spot, patch; **с ~а(-у)** (*на полном ходу*) at full pelt; (*перен: сразу*) in a flash.

нале|те́ть (-чу́, -ти́шь; *impf* **налета́ть**) *сов неперех*: ~ **на** +*acc* (*натолкнуться*) to fly against; (*перен: разг: на приятеля, на столб*) to run into; (*напасть*) to swoop down on; (*перен: разг: с бранью, с упрёками*) to lay into; (*буря, ветер*) to spring up; (*саранча, стая*) to fly in; (*пыль, листва*) to drift in.

налётчик (-а) *м* burglar.

налечу́ *сов см* **налете́ть**.

нал|е́чь (-я́гу, -я́жешь *итп*, -я́гут; *pt* -ёг, -егла́, -егло́, *impf* **налега́ть**) *сов неперех*: ~ **на** +*acc* (*на стол*) to lean on; (*плечом: на дверь*) to press against; (*перен: на работников*) to exert pressure on; (: *на учёбу, на работу*) to apply o.s. to; (*роса, снег*) to settle on; **налега́ть** (~ *perf*) **на вёсла** to ply one's oars.

налива́|ть(ся) (-ю(сь)) *несов от* **нали́ть(ся)**.

нали́в|ка (-ки; *gen pl* -ок) *ж* fruit liquor.

наливн|о́й *прил*: ~о́е су́дно tanker; (*яблоко, хлеба*) ripe.

нали́вок *сущ см* **нали́вка**.

нали́м (-а) *м* (*ЗООЛ*) burbot, eelpout.

нали́п|нуть (*3sg* -ет, *3pl* -ут, *impf* **налипа́ть**) *сов неперех*: ~ **на** +*acc* to stick to.

налито́й *прил* (*колос, яблоко*) ripe; (*мускулы, щёки итп*) fleshy.

нал|и́ть (-ью́, -ьёшь; *impf* **налива́ть**) *сов перех* to pour (out); **налива́ть** (~ *perf*) **стака́н вина́** to pour a glass of wine

▶ **нали́ться** (*impf* **налива́ться**) *сов возв* (*натечь во что-н*): ~**ся в** +*acc* to pour into; (*наполниться*): ~**ся** +*instr* to fill with; (*рожь, плоды*) to ripen; (*перен: злобой*) to brim over; ~**ся** (*perf*) **кро́вью** to turn red.

налицо́ *как сказ*: **фа́кты** ~ the facts are obvious; **доказа́тельство** ~ there is proof; **свиде́тели** ~ there are witnesses on hand.

нали́чи|е (-я) *ср* presence.

нали́чник (-а) *м* casing, jambs and lintel (*of door or window*).

нали́чност|ь (-и) *ж* cash.

нали́чн|ые (-ых; *decl like adj*) *мн* cash *ед*; **платёж** ~**ыми при доста́вке гру́за** cash on delivery.

нали́чн|ый *прил*: ~**ые де́ньги** cash; ~ **расчёт** cash payment; ~ **счёт** cash account.

наловч|и́ться (-у́сь, -и́шься) *сов возв* (*разг*: +*infin*) to get the hang of doing.

нало́г (-а) *м* (*ЭКОН*) tax; **подохо́дный** ~ income tax; **поиму́щественный** ~ property tax; ~ **на ввоз** +*gen* import duty on; ~ **на при́быль** profits tax; ~ **на предме́ты ро́скоши** luxury tax; ~ **на перево́д капита́ла** capital transfer tax; **ко́свенный** ~ hidden tax.

нало́говый *прил тж опред*.

налогоплате́льщик (-а) *м* taxpayer.

налогоплате́льщиц|а (-ы) *ж см* **налогоплате́льщик**.

нало́женн|ый *прил*: ~**ым платежо́м** cash on delivery.

нал|ожи́ть (-ожу́, -о́жишь; *impf* **накла́дывать**) *сов перех* to put *или* place on; (*кальку*) to superimpose; (*МЕД: шину*) to fasten; (: *компресс, бинт*) to apply; (*лак, позолоту*) to apply; (*печать*) to affix; (*резолюцию*) to append; (*кашу итп*) to dish up; (*дров: в печку*) to put on; (*impf* **налага́ть**; *штраф*) to impose; (*запрет*) to place.

налома́|ть (-ю; *impf* **нала́мывать**) *сов перех* (+*gen*) to break; ~ (*perf*) **дров** (*разг*) to do

something stupid.

налью́(сь) *итп сов см* **нали́ть(ся)**.

налюб|ова́ться (-у́юсь) *сов возв* to gaze one's fill; **не могу́** ~ **са́дом** I am lost in admiration for the garden.

наля́гу *итп сов см* **нале́чь**.

наля́па|ть (-ю) *сов от* **ля́пать**.

нам *мест см* **мы**.

нама́жу(сь) *итп сов см* **нама́зать(ся)**.

нама́з (-а) *м* (*РЕЛ*) (*Mohammedan*) prayer.

нама́|зать(ся) (-жу(сь), -жешь(ся)) *сов от* **ма́зать(ся)**.

намалева́|ть (-ю) *сов от* **малева́ть**.

нама́лыва|ть (-ю) *несов от* **намоло́ть**.

намара́|ть (-ю) *сов от* **мара́ть**.

нама́сл|ить (-ю, -ишь) *сов от* **ма́слить**.

нама́тыва|ть(ся) (-ю(сь)) *несов от* **намота́ть(ся)**.

намёк (-а) *м* (*также перен*) hint.

намека́|ть (-ю; *perf* **намекну́ть**) *несов неперех*: ~ **на** +*acc* to hint at.

намелю́ *итп сов см* **намоло́ть**.

наменя́|ть (-ю) *сов см* (*не*)*перех* (+*acc или* +*gen*; *денег, марок, значков*) to get *или* obtain by exchange.

намерева́|ться (-юсь) *несов возв*: ~ +*infin* to intend to.

наме́рен (-а, -о) *как сказ*: **он** ~ **уе́хать** he intends to leave.

наме́рени|е (-я) *ср* intention.

наме́ренн|ый (-, -на, -но) *прил* intentional, deliberate.

на́мертво *нареч* (*разг*) tightly, fast.

намётанн|ый *прил*: ~ **глаз** trained eye; **у него́ глаз намётан** he has a good eye.

намета́|ть (-ю) *сов от* **мета́ть**.

наме́|тить (-чу, -тишь) *сов от* **ме́тить** ◆ (*impf* **намеча́ть**) *перех* to plan; (*план*) to project; (*контуры*) to outline

▶ **наме́титься** *сов от* **ме́титься** ◆ (*impf* **намеча́ться**) *возв* (*маршрут*) to take shape; (*разногласия, усы*) to begin to show.

намёт|ка (-и) *ж* (*юбки, платья*) tacking (*BRIT*), basting; (*нитка*) tacking (*BRIT*) *или* basting thread; (*плана*) rough draft; (*маршрута*) preliminary outline.

намеча́|ть(ся) (-ю(сь)) *несов от* **наме́тить(ся)**.

наме́чу(сь) *сов см* **наме́тить(ся)**.

на́ми *мест см* **мы**.

намина́|ть (-ю) *несов от* **намя́ть**.

намно́го *нареч* much, far; ~ **ху́же/интере́снее** much worse/more interesting.

намну́ *итп сов см* **намя́ть**.

намо́к|нуть (-у, -ешь; *impf* **намока́ть**) *сов неперех* to get wet.

нам|оло́ть (-елю́, -е́лешь; *impf* **нама́лывать**) *сов перех* to grind, mill.

намо́рдник (-а) *м* muzzle.

намо́рщ|ить (-у(сь), -ишь(ся)) *сов от* **мо́рщить(ся)**.

намо|сти́ть (-щу́, -сти́шь) *сов от* **мости́ть**.

намота́|ть (-ю) *сов от* **мота́ть** ♦ (*impf* **нама́тывать**) *перех* to wind
▶ **намота́ться** (*impf* **нама́тываться**) *сов возв* (*нитка на шпульку*) to be wound; (*разг: устать*) to run o.s. ragged.

нам|очи́ть (-очу́, -о́чишь) *сов от* **мочи́ть**.

намощу́ *сов см* **намости́ть**.

намо́ю *итп сов см* **намы́ть**.

намудр|и́ть (-ю́, -и́шь) *сов от* **мудри́ть**.

наму́сор|ить (-ю, -ишь) *сов от* **му́сорить**.

наму́ч|иться (-усь, -ишься) *сов возв* (*разг*) to wear o.s. out.

намы́лива|ть (-ю; *perf* **намы́лить**) *несов перех* = **мы́лить**.

намы́л|ить(ся) (-ю(сь), -ишь(ся)) *сов от* **мы́лить(ся)**.

нам|ы́ть (-о́ю, -о́ишь) *сов перех* to wash; (*плотину*) to deposit; (*зо́лота*) to pan out.

нам|я́ть (-ну́, -нёшь; *impf* **намина́ть**) *сов* (*не*)*перех* (+*acc или* +*gen*; *льна, кож, глины*) to mash; (*траву, солому*) to trample.

нан|ести́ (-есу́, -есёшь; *pt* -ёс, -есла́, -есло́, *impf* **наноси́ть**) *сов* (*не*)*перех* (+*acc или* +*gen*; *подарков, продуктов*) to bring; (*снегу, песку*) to heap, pile up; (*лак, мазь, краску*) to apply; (*узор, рисунок, резьбу*) to draw; (*на карту, на схему*) to plot; (*удар*) to deliver; (*урон*) to inflict; **наноси́ть** (~ *perf*) **кому́-н оскорбле́ние** to insult; **наноси́ть** (~ *perf*) **кому́-н пораже́ние** to defeat sb; ~ (*perf*) **кому́-н визи́т** to pay sb a visit.

нани́зыва|ть (-ю) *несов перех* (*жемчуг, бусины*) to string, thread; (*перен: слова, фразы*) to string.

нанима́тел|ь (-я) *м* tenant; (*рабочей силы*) employer.

нанима́тельни|ца (-ы) *ж см* **нанима́тель**.

нанима́|ть(ся) (-ю(сь)) *несов от* **наня́ть(ся)**.

нано́с (-а) *м* (*речной*) alluvium; (*ледниковый, снежный*) drift.

нан|оси́ть (-ошу́, -о́сишь) *сов от* **нанести́** ♦ *перех* (*воды, песку, камней*) to bring.

нано́сный *прил* (*ил*) alluvial; (*перен: увлечения*) alien.

на|ня́ть (-йму́, -ймёшь; *pt* -нял, -няла́, -няло, *impf* **нанима́ть**) *сов перех* (*работника*) to hire; (*лодку, машину*) to hire, rent
▶ **наня́ться** (*impf* **нанима́ться**) *сов возв* to get a job; **нанима́ться** (~ся *perf*) **секретарём/редактором** to get a job as a secretary/editor.

наоборо́т *нареч* (*прочитать слово*) backwards; (*поступать, делать*) the wrong way (round) ♦ *вводн сл, част* (*при противопоставлении*) on the contrary.

наобу́м *нареч* (*разг: делать, отвечать*) without thinking; (*стрелять*) at random.

на́отмашь *нареч* with a bold swipe.

наотре́з *нареч* flatly, point-blank.

напада́|ть (-ю) *несов от* **напа́сть**.

напада́ющ|ий (-его; *decl like adj*) *м* (СПОРТ) forward.

нападе́ни|е (-я) *ср* attack; (СПОРТ) forwards *мн*.

напа́д|ки (-ок) *мн* attacks *мн*.

нападу́ *итп сов см* **напа́сть**.

напа́ко|стить (-щу, -стишь) *сов от* **па́костить**.

напа́лм (-а) *м* napalm.

напа́рник (-а) *м* fellow worker.

напа́рни|ца (-ы) *ж см* **напа́рник**.

напа́рыва|ться (-юсь) *несов от* **напоро́ться**.

напа|сти́сь (-у́сь, -ёшься) *сов возв*: **на тебя́ са́хара не ~ёшься** you haven't got in enough sugar.

напа́|сть (-сти) *ж* (*разг: беда*) calamity; ♦ (-аду́, -адёшь; *pt* -а́л, -а́ла, -а́ло, *impf* **напада́ть**) *сов неперех*: ~ **на** +*acc* to attack; (*на золотую жилу*) to come across, stumble (up)on; (*перен: на идею*) to have; (*тоска, грусть, страх*) to grip, seize.

напе́в (-а) *м* tune, melody.

напева́|ть (-ю) *несов от* **напе́ть** ♦ *перех* (*песенку*) to hum.

напе́в|ный (-ен, -на, -но) *прил* melodious.

напёк *итп сов см* **напе́чь**.

напека́|ть (-ю) *несов от* **напе́чь**.

напеку́ *итп сов см* **напе́чь**.

наперебо́й *нареч* vying with each other.

напереве́с *нареч*: **держа́ть ружьё** ~ to hold one's gun at the ready.

наперего́нки *нареч* (*разг*) racing each other.

наперёд *нареч* (*знать, угадать*) in advance; **за́дом** ~ back to front.

напереко́р *нареч* (*говорить, поступать, идти́*) defiantly ♦ *предл* (+*dat*; *судьбе, врагу, здравому смыслу*) in defiance of.

наперере́з *нареч* (*бежать, идти, плыть итп*) in order to intercept.

напе|ре́ть (-ру́, -рёшь; *pt* -ёр, -ёрла, -ёрло, *impf* **напира́ть**) *сов неперех*: ~ **на** +*acc* (*разг: на дверь*) to push against.

наперечёт *нареч* (*знать, помнить*) without exception.

напёрсток (-а) *м* thimble.

наперч|и́ть (-у́, -и́шь) *сов от* **перчи́ть**.

напе́|ть (-ою, -оёшь; *impf* **напева́ть**) *сов перех* (*мотив, песню, мелодию*) to sing; **напева́ть** (~ *perf*) **пласти́нку** to make a recording of one's singing.

напеча́та|ть(ся) (-ю(сь)) *сов от* **печа́тать(ся)**.

напе́|чь (-ку́, -чёшь *итп*, -ку́т; *pt* -ёк, -екла́, -екло́, *impf* **напека́ть**) *сов перех* (*блинов, пирогов*) to bake ♦ *безл* (*разг: голову, плечи*) to burn.

напива́|ться (-юсь) *несов от* **напи́ться**.

напи́льник (-а) *м* file.

напира́|ть (-ю) *несов от* **напере́ть** ♦ *неперех*: ~ **на** +*acc* (*теснить*) to push against; (*перен*) to stress.

написа́ни|е (-я) *ср* writing; (*буквы*) spelling.

напи|са́ть (-шу́, -шешь) *сов от* **писа́ть**.

напи́т|ок (-ка) *м* drink.

напи́|ться (-ью́сь, -ьёшься; *impf* **напива́ться**) *сов возв* (*воды, сока, чаю*) to have a drink; (*квасом, лимонадом*) to quench one's thirst; (*разг: опьянеть*) to get drunk.

напиха́|ть (-ю; *impf* **напи́хивать**) *сов перех* (*разг*): ~ **в** +*acc* to stuff into.

напи́чка|ть (-ю) *сов от* **пи́чкать**.

напишу́ *итп сов см* **написа́ть**.

напла́кать *сов перех*: **кот напла́кал** (*разг*) very little; **у нас де́нег – кот напла́кал** we have very little money

▸ **напла́|каться** ◆ (-чусь, -чешься) *сов возв* (*ребёнок*) to cry one's eyes out; **напла́чешься ты с ней** (*перен*) you'll have nothing but problems with her.

напл|ева́ть (-юю́) *сов от* **плева́ть** ◆ *неперех* to spit; ~! (*разг*) to hell with it!

наплева́тельск|ий (-ая, -ое, -ие) *прил* (*разг: отношение*) harum-scarum.

напль́в (-а) *м* (*перен: туристов*) influx; (: *заявлений, чувств*) flood.

наплы́|ть (-ву́, -вёшь; *impf* **наплыва́ть**) *сов неперех*: ~ **на** +*acc* (*на мель, на камень*) to run against; (*облако, туча*) to drift over *или* in front of; (*тина, водоросли*) to be washed up; (*перен: воспоминания*) to come flooding back.

напова́л *нареч* outright.

наподо́бие *предл* (+*gen*) like, resembling.

нап|ои́ть (-ою́, -о́ишь) *сов от* **пои́ть**.

напока́з *нареч* for show.

наполз|ти́ (-у́, -ёшь; *impf* **наполза́ть**) *сов неперех*: ~ **на** +*acc* (*на преграду*) to crawl onto; (*туча*) to creep up; (*муравьи*) to crawl in.

наполн|ить (-ю, -ишь; *impf* **наполня́ть**) *сов перех*: ~ +*instr* to fill with

▸ **напо́лниться** (*impf* **наполня́ться**) *сов возв*: ~**ся** +*instr* to fill with.

наполови́ну *нареч* (*уменьшить, увеличить*) by half; (*наполнить, налить*) half.

напо́льн|ый *прил* floor *орпед*; ~**ые часы́** grandfather clock.

напомина́ни|е (-я) *ср* reminder.

напомина́|ть (-ю) *несов от* **напо́мнить** ◆ *перех* (*иметь сходство*) to resemble; **он ~ет мне моего́ отца́** he resembles my father.

напо́мн|ить (-ю, -ишь; *impf* **напомина́ть**) *сов перех*: ~ +*acc или* **о** +*prp* to remind of.

напо́р (-а) *м* (*воды, воздуха*) pressure; (*ветра*) force; (*войск*) onslaught; (*разг: настойчивость*) push, go.

напо́рист|ый (-, -а, -о) *прил* forceful.

напор|о́ть (-ю́, -ешь) *сов от* **поро́ть** ◆ *перех* (*разг: руку, ногу*) to cut

▸ **напоро́ться** (*impf* **напа́рываться**) *сов возв*: ~**ся на** +*acc* (*разг: на гвоздь, на сучок*) to cut o.s. on; (: *на беду, на скандал*) to run up against.

напо́р|тить (-чу, -тишь) *сов* (*не*)*перех* (+*acc или* +*gen*; *бумаги, материала*) to spoil ◆ *неперех* (+*dat*; *разг: делу*) to wreck; (: *другу*) to harm.

напосле́док *нареч* (*разг*) in the end, finally.

напою́ *итп сов см* **напе́ть**.

напра́в|ить (-лю, -ишь; *impf* **направля́ть**) *сов перех* (*взгляд, внимание, разговор*) to direct; (*в госпиталь, к врачу*) to refer; (*на завод*) to assign; (*телеграмму, послание*) to send; **направля́ть** (~ *perf*) **свой путь куда́-нибудь** to make one's way somewhere

▸ **напра́виться** (*impf* **направля́ться**) *сов возв*: ~**ся в** +*acc*/**к** +*dat* (*в город, к острову*) to make for.

направле́ни|е (-я) *ср* direction; (*специалистов*) sending; (*деятельности, также воен*) line; (*политики*) orientation; (*течение*) school; (*документ: в больницу*) referral; (: *на работу, на учёбу*) directive; **по** ~**ю к** +*dat* towards.

напра́вленност|ь (-и) *ж* focus.

напра́влю(сь) *сов см* **напра́вить(ся)**.

направля́|ть(ся) (-ю(сь)) *несов от* **напра́вить(ся)**.

напра́во *нареч* (*идти, повернуть*) (to the) right; (*от дороги, от дома*) to the right.

напра́сен *прил см* **напра́сный**.

напра́сно *нареч* in vain.

напра́сн|ый (-ен, -на, -но) *прил* (*труд, усилия*) vain; (*тревога, страх*) unfounded.

напра́шива|ться (-юсь) *несов от* **напроси́ться**.

наприме́р *вводн сл* for example *или* instance.

напроказни|чать (-ю) *сов от* **прока́зничать**.

напрока́т *нареч*: **взять** ~ to hire; **отдава́ть** (**отда́ть** *perf*) ~ to hire out.

напролёт *нареч* without a break.

напроло́м *нареч* stopping at nothing.

напроро́ч|ить (-у, -ишь) *сов от* **проро́чить**.

напр|оси́ться (-ошу́сь, -о́сишься; *impf* **напра́шиваться**) *сов возв* (*разг: в гости, на до́лжность*) to force o.s.; **напра́шиваться** (~ *perf*) **на** +*acc* (*на комплимент, на оскорбле́ние*) to invite.

напро́тив *нареч* opposite ◆ *вводн сл* on the contrary ◆ *предл* (+*gen*) opposite.

на́прочь *нареч* (*разг*) completely.

напрошу́сь *сов см* **напроси́ться**.

напря́г(ся) *итп сов см* **напря́чь(ся)**.

напряга́|ть(ся) (-ю(сь)) *несов от* **напря́чь(ся)**.

напрягу́(сь) *итп сов см* **напря́чь(ся)**.

напряже́ни|е (-я) *ср* tension; (*внимания, с ресурсами*) strain; (*физ: механическое*) strain, stress; (: *электрическое*) voltage.

напряжённ|ый (-, -на, -но) *прил* tense; (*отношения, голос, встреча*) strained.

напрями́к *нареч* (*идти, ехать*) straight; (*перен: сказать*) straight out.

напря́|чь (-гу́, -жёшь *итп*, -гу́т; *pt* -́г, -гла́,

-ягло́, *impf* напряга́ть) *сов перех* to strain
▶ напря́чься (*impf* напряга́ться) *сов возв* (*мускулы, леска*) to become tense; (*внутренне*) to strain o.s.
напуга́ть(ся) (-ю(сь)) *сов от* пуга́ть(ся).
напу́др|ить(ся) (-ю(сь), -ишь(ся)) *сов от* пу́дрить(ся).
напуска́|ть(ся) (-ю(сь)) *несов от* напусти́ть(ся).
напускно́й *прил* (*грубость*) affected; (*спокойствие*) feigned.
нап|усти́ть (-ущу́, -у́стишь; *impf* напуска́ть) *сов перех*: ~ +*gen* (*дыму, воды, рыбы*) to fill with; (*разг*): ~ на +*acc* to put on; (*разг: собак*) to let loose; напуска́ть (~ *perf*) на себя́ что-н to assume sth
▶ напусти́ться (*impf* напуска́ться) *сов возв* (*разг*): ~ся на +*acc* to attach.
напу́та|ть (-ю; *impf* напу́тывать) *сов (не)перех* (+*acc или* +*gen*; *ниток, пряжи*) to tangle; напу́тывать (~ *perf*) в +*prp* (*в делах итп*) to make a mess of.
напу́тственн|ый *прил* (*речь*) farewell *опред*; ~ое сло́во parting words *мн*.
напу́тстви|е (-я) *ср* parting words *мн или* wishes *мн*, farewell speech.
напу́тыва|ть (-ю) *несов от* напу́тать.
напущу́(сь) *сов см* напусти́ть(ся).
напы́ж|иться (-усь, -ишься) *сов от* пы́житься.
напыл|и́ть (-ю́, -и́шь) *сов от* пыли́ть.
напы́щен|ный (-, -на, -но) *прил* (*вид, человек*) pompous; (*речь, рассказ*) high-flown, bombastic.
напью́сь *итп сов см* напи́ться.
наравне́ *нареч*: ~ с +*instr* (*по одной линии*) on a level with; (*на равных правах*) on an equal footing with.
нара́д|оваться (-уюсь) *сов возв*: ~ на +*acc* to fully enjoy.
нараспа́шку *нареч* (*разг: одежда*) unbuttoned; душа́ ~ у неё she is very open.
нараспе́в *нареч* drawlingly.
нараст|и́ (3sg -тёт, 3pl -ту́т, *impf* нараста́ть) *сов неперех* (*много грибов, трава*) to spring up; (*долги, проценты*) to accumulate; (*волнение, сопротивление*) to grow; нараста́ть (~ *perf*) на +*prp* (*мох*) to grow on; (*плесень*) to form on; (*водоросли*) to build up on.
нара|сти́ть (-щу́, -сти́шь; *impf* нара́щивать) *сов перех* (*мускулы*) to develop; (*канат, трубу*) to lengthen.
нарасхва́т *нареч* (*продаваться, покупаться*) like hot cakes; таки́е специали́сты сейча́с ~ such specialists are in great demand nowadays.
нара́щива|ть (-ю) *несов от* нарасти́ть ♦ *перех* (*темпы, объём итп*) to increase.
наращу́ *сов см* нарасти́ть.
нарв|а́ть (-у́, -ёшь; *impf* нарыва́ть) *сов (не)перех* (+*acc или* +*gen*; *травы, цветов, земляники*) to pick; (*бумаги*) to tear
▶ нарва́ться (*impf* нарыва́ться) *сов возв*

(*разг*): ~ся на +*acc* (*на хулигана, грубияна*) to run up against; (*на оскорбление*) to have to take *или* наро́ваться; нарыва́ться (~ся *perf*) на неприя́тность to run into some trouble.
наре́зать (-жу, -жешь; *impf* нареза́ть) *сов (не)перех* (+*acc или* +*gen*; *колбасы, хлеба, сыр*) to slice, cut; (*веток, цветов*) to cut; (*земли, участки*) to allot; (*ТЕХ*) to thread.
наре́зк|а (-и) *ж* (*винта*) thread.
нарека́ни|е (-я) *ср* reprimand, censure.
наре́чи|е (-я) *ср* (*линг: говоры*) dialect; (: *часть речи*) adverb.
нарза́н (-а) *м* Narzan (*kind of mineral water*).
нарис|ова́ть (-у́ю) *сов от* рисова́ть.
нарица́тельн|ый *прил*: и́мя ~ое (*линг*) common noun; ~ая сто́имость (*ЭКОН*) nominal cost.
нарко́з (-а) *м* (*МЕД*) narcosis, anaesthesia (*BRIT*), anesthesia (*US*).
нарко́лог (-а) *м* (*МЕД*) expert in narcotics.
наркологи́ческ|ий (-ая, -ое, -ие) *прил*: ~ диспансе́р drug-abuse clinic.
наркома́н (-а) *м* drug addict *или* abuser.
наркома́ни|я (-и) *ж* (*МЕД*) drug addiction *или* abuse.
наркома́н|ка (-ки; *gen pl* -ок) *ж см* наркома́н.
нарко́тик (-а) *м* narcotic, drug.
наро́д (-а; *part gen* -у) *м* people *мн*; ру́сский ~ the Russian people; мно́го ~у many people.
наро́ден *прил см* наро́дный.
наро́дность (-и) *ж* nationality; (*литературы*) national character.
наро́дн|ый (-ен, -на, -но) *прил* national; (*фронт*) popular; (*искусство*) folk *опред*; ~ поэ́т national poet *или* bard; ~ худо́жник/ арти́ст artist/actor who has received an official honour from the state.
народонаселе́ни|е (-я) *ср* population.
нарожа́ть (-ю) *сов перех* (*разг*) to give birth to.
наро́ст (-а) *м* (*наслоение*) covering; (*утолщение: на дереве*) outgrowth; (: на суставах) growth.
нарочи́т|ый (-, -а, -о) *прил* deliberate, intentional.
наро́чно *нареч* (*опоздать, отверну́ться*) purposely, on purpose; (*разг: сказать, заплакать*) for fun; как ~ (*разг*) to make things worse; ~ не приду́маешь! (*разг*) this is quite something!
наро́чн|ый (-ого; *decl like adj*) *м* courier.
на́рт|а (-ы) *ж* sledge (*BRIT*) *или* sled (*US*) (*drawn by reindeer or dogs*).
наруб|и́ть (-лю́, -ишь; *impf* наруба́ть) *сов (не)перех* (+*acc или* +*gen*; *дров, капусты*) to chop.
нару́жен *прил см* нару́жный.
нару́жность (-и) *ж* exterior; (*строения, города*) outward appearance.
нару́жн|ый (-ен, -на, -но) *прил* (*дверь, стена*) exterior; (*лекарство*) for external application; (*спокойствие, сдержанность*) outward.

нару́жу *нареч* out.
наружя́н|ить(ся) (-ю(сь), -ишь(ся)) *сов от*
　румя́нить(ся).
нару́чник (-а) *м* (*обычно мн*) handcuff.
нару́чн|ый *прил*: ~ые часы́ wristwatch.
наруша́ть(ся) (-ю(сь)) *несов от*
　нару́шить(ся).
наруши́тель (-я) *м* (*закона*) transgressor,
　infringer; (*границы*) trespasser; (*ЮР: порядка*)
　offender; ~ дисципли́ны troublemaker.
наруши́тельниц|а (-ы) *ж см* **наруши́тель**.
нару́ш|ить (-у, -ишь; *impf* **наруша́ть**) *сов перех*
　(*покой, тишину*) to break, disturb; (*связь*) to
　break; (*правила, договор*) to break, violate;
　(*дисциплину*) to breach; **наруша́ть** (~ *perf*)
　грани́цу to illegally cross a border
▶ **нару́шиться** (*impf* **наруша́ться**) *сов возв* to
　be broken *или* disturbed.
нарци́сс (-а) *м* daffodil, narcissus.
на́р|ы (-) *мн* plank bed *ед*.
нары́в (-а) *м* (*МЕД*) abscess, boil.
нарыва́ть (-ю) *несов от* **нарва́ть** ◆ *неперех*
　(*рана*) to fester; **у меня́ па́лец** ~**ет** I have a boil
　on my finger
▶ **нарыва́ться** *несов от* **нарва́ться**.
наря́д (-а) *м* (*одежда*) outfit; (*красивая одежда*)
　attire; (*распоряжение*) directive; (*КОММ*) order;
　(*ВОЕН: подразделение*) division; (*: задание*)
　assignment.
наря́ден *прил см* **наря́дный**.
наря́д|ить (-жу́, -я́дишь; *impf* **наряжа́ть**) *сов*
　перех (*невесту итп*) to dress; (*в караул, на*
　кухню итп) to assign; **наряжа́ть** (~ *perf*) **ёлку** ≈
　to decorate (*BRIT*) *или* trim (*US*) the Christmas
　tree; **наряжа́ть** (~ *perf*) **кого́-н** +*instr*/**в** +*acc* to
　dress sb as/in
▶ **наряди́ться** (*impf* **наряжа́ться**) *сов возв*: ~**ся**
　(**в** +*acc*) to dress o.s. (in).
наря́дный (-ен, -на, -но) *прил* (*человек*) well-
　dressed; (*комната, улица*) well-decorated;
　(*шляпа, платье*) fancy.
наряду́ *нареч*: ~ **с** +*instr* at the same time as;
　(*наравне*) on an equal footing with.
наряжа́ть(ся) (-ю(сь)) *несов от* **наряди́ть(ся)**.
наряжу́(сь) *сов см* **наряди́ть(ся)**.
нас *мест см* **мы**.
НА́СА *ср сокр* NASA (= *National Aeronautics*
　and Space Administration).
насад|и́ть (-ажу́, -а́дишь; *impf* **наса́живать**) *сов*
　перех (*надеть*) to put.
наса́дк|а (-ки; *gen pl* -ок) *ж* (*для рыбы*) bait; (*ТЕХ*)
　nozzle.
насажде́ни|е (-я) *ср* (*БОТ*) plantation.
наса́жива|ть (-ю) *несов от* **насади́ть**.
насажу́ *сов см* **насади́ть**.
насви́стыва|ть (-ю) *несов перех*: ~ **мело́дию**
　to whistle a tune under one's breath.
наседа́|ть (-ю) *несов от* **насе́сть** ◆ *неперех*

(*разг: толпа*) to press forward.
насе́д|ка (-ки; *gen pl* -ок) *ж* broody hen.
насеко́м|ое (-ого; *decl like adj*) *ср* insect.
населе́ни|е (-я) *ср* population.
населённый *прил* (*район, область*) populated,
　inhabited; (*квартира*) inhabited; ~ **пункт**
　locality.
насел|и́ть (-ю́, -и́шь; *impf* **населя́ть**) *сов перех*
　(*край*) to settle; (*дом*) to move into.
населя́|ть (-ю) *несов от* **насели́ть** ◆ *перех*
　(*лес, страну*) to inhabit.
насе́ст (-а) *м* (*для кур итп*) roost.
насе́с|ть (-я́ду, -я́дешь; *impf* **наседа́ть**) *сов*
　неперех (*пыль, копоть*) to settle; **наседа́ть** (~
　perf) **на** +*acc* (*перен: разг: с просьбами, в*
　вопросами) to pester; (*на противника*) to fall
　upon.
насе́ч|ка (-ки; *gen pl* -ек) *ж* notch.
наси́женный *прил*: ~**ое ме́сто** (*разг*) familiar
　surroundings *мн*.
наси́ли|е (-я) *ср* (*физическое*) violence; (*над*
　личностью) suppression.
наси́л|овать (-ую; *perf* **изнаси́ловать**) *несов*
　перех (*женщину, девушку*) to rape; (*no perf*;
　личность) to suppress.
наси́лу *нареч* (*разг: успеть, догнать*) only just.
наси́льник (-а) *м person who commits an act of*
　violence; (*над женщиной*) rapist.
наси́льно *нареч* forcibly; ~ **заста́вить** (*perf*)
　кого́-н +*infin* to force sb to do.
наси́льственный *прил* (*меры*) violent;
　наси́льственная смерть violent death.
наска́кива|ть (-ю) *несов от* **наскочи́ть**.
наскво́зь *нареч* through; **ви́деть** (*impf*) ~ **кого́-н**
　to see (right) through sb.
наско́к (-а) *м* (*разг*) slagging; **с** ~**а** (*разг*)
　impromptu.
наско́лько *нареч* so much.
на́скоро *нареч* (*разг*) on the double.
наск|очи́ть (-очу́, -о́чишь; *impf* **наска́кивать**)
　сов неперех: ~ **на** +*acc* to run into; (*перен: разг:*
　на обидчика, на оппонента) to attack; (*: на*
　неприятность) to get into.
наскрес|ти́ (-у́, -ёшь; *pt* -ёб, -ебла́, -ебло́,
　impf **наскреба́ть**) *сов перех* (*крошек, муки*) to
　collect; (*перен: мелочи, денег*) to scrape
　together.
наску́ч|ить (-у, -ишь) *сов неперех*: ~ **кому́-н** to
　bore sb.
наслад|и́ться (-жу́сь, -ди́шься; *impf*
　наслажда́ться) *сов возв*: ~ +*instr* to enjoy.
наслажде́ни|е (-я) *ср* enjoyment.
наслажу́сь *сов см* **наслади́ться**.
насла́ива|ться (*3sg* -ется, *3pl* -ются) *несов от*
　наслои́ться.
насле́ди|е (-я) *ср* (*культурное*) heritage;
　(*идеологическое*) legacy.
насле|ди́ть (-жу́, -ди́шь) *сов от* **следи́ть**.

насле́дник (-а) *м* (*престо́ла, состоя́ния*) heir; (*перен: преемник*) inheritor.

насле́дниц|а (-ы) *ж* (*см м*) heiress; inheritor.

насле́дный *прил:* ~ **принц** prince next in line (to the throne).

насле́довани|е (-я) *ср* inheritance; (*престо́ла*) succession.

насле́д|овать (-ую) (*не)сов перех* to inherit; (*престо́л*) to succeed.

насле́дственный *прил* inherited; (*черты́, боле́знь*) hereditary.

насле́дств|о (-а) *ср* (*иму́щество*) inheritance; (*культу́рное*) heritage; (*идеологи́ческое*) legacy; **получа́ть** (**получи́ть** *perf*) **что-н** в ~ to inherit sth.

наслежу́ *сов см* **насле́дить**.

наслое́ни|е (-я) *ср* (*ГЕО*) stratification.

насло|и́ться (*3sg* -и́тся, *3pl* -я́тся, *impf* **насла́иваться**) *сов возв:* ~ **на** +*acc* to settle on; (*перен*) to add to.

наслу́ша|ться (-юсь) *сов возв:* ~ +*gen* to hear a lot of; (*вдо́воль послу́шать*) to hear enough of.

наслы́шан *как сказ:* **я** ~ **об э́том/о нём** I have heard a lot about it/him.

наслы́ш|аться (-усь, -ишься) *сов возв* (*разг*): ~ **о** +*prp* to hear a lot about.

насма́рку *нареч* (*разг*): **идти́** ~ to be wasted.

на́смерть *нареч* (*сража́ться*) to the death; (*разби́ться, ра́нить*) fatally; (*перен: разг: перепуга́ться*) to death; (: *поруга́ться*) strongly.

насмеха́|ться (-юсь) *несов возв:* ~ **над** +*instr* to mock.

насме́шек *сущ см* **насме́шка**.

насмеш|и́ть (-у́, -и́шь) *сов от* **смеши́ть**.

насме́ш|ка (-ки; *gen pl* -ек) *ж* (*оби́дная шу́тка*) jibe; **сказа́ть** (*perf*) **что-н** в ~**ку** to say sth mockingly.

насме́шлив|ый (-, -а, -о) *прил* mocking.

насмея́|ться (-юсь) *сов возв:* ~ **над** +*instr* to offend.

на́сморк (-а) *м* runny nose.

насм|отре́ться (-отрю́сь, -о́тришься) *сов возв:* ~ (**на** +*acc*) to see enough (of); (+*gen*: *чуде́с, люде́й*) to see a lot of.

насовсе́м *нареч* (*разг*) for good.

насол|и́ть (-ю́, -ишь) *сов перех* to preserve (*in brine*) ♦ *неперех* (+*dat*; *перен: разг:* сде́лать неприя́тность) to be nasty to.

насор|и́ть (-ю́, -и́шь) *сов от* **сори́ть**.

насо́с (-а) *м* pump.

на́спех *нареч* hurriedly.

наста|ва́ть (*3sg* -ёт, *3pl* -ю́т) *несов от* **наста́ть**.

наста́ви|тельный (-ен, -ьна, -ьно) *прил* (*тон*) preaching.

наста́в|ить (-лю, -ишь) *сов неперех* (+*gen*; *поста́вить*) to put; (*синяко́в, ши́шек*) to cause ♦ (*impf* **наставля́ть**) *перех* (*пла́тье, рука́в*) to lengthen; (*револьве́р, ружьё*) to aim; **наставля́ть** (~ *perf*) **кого́-н на путь и́стинный** to set sb on the right path.

наставле́ни|е (-я) *ср* (*поуче́ние*) lecture; (*руково́дство*) instructions *мн*.

наста́влю *сов см* **наста́вить**.

наставля́|ть (-ю) *несов от* **наста́вить** ♦ *перех* (*ученико́в*) to teach.

наста́вник (-а) *м* mentor.

наста́ива|ть(ся) (-ю(сь)) *несов от* **настоя́ть(ся)**.

наста́|ть (*3sg* -нет, *3pl* -нут, *impf* **настава́ть**) *сов неперех* (*ле́то*) to begin; (*молча́ние, ночь*) to fall; (*день отъе́зда*) to come.

на́стежь *нареч* (*откры́ть*) wide; (*окно́, дверь итп*) wide open; **распахну́ть** (*perf*) ~ to fling wide open.

насте́л|ить (-ю́, -ешь) *сов от* **стели́ть**.

насте́нный *прил* wall *опред*.

настига́|ть (-ю) *несов от* **насти́чь**.

настигн|у́ть (-у, -ешь; *impf* **настига́ть**) *сов перех* = **насти́чь**.

насти́л (-а) *м* (*из се́на*) bedding; (*деревя́нный*) boarding.

насти́|чь (-гну, -гнешь; *pt* -г, -гла, -гло, *impf* **настига́ть**) *сов перех* to catch up with.

насто́ек *сущ см* **насто́йка**.

насто́|й (-я) *м* infusion.

насто́й|ка (-йки; *gen pl* -ек) *ж* (*экстра́кт*) tincture; (*алкого́ль*) liqueur.

насто́йчив|ый (-, -а, -о) *прил* (*челове́к, хара́ктер*) persistent; (*про́сьба, взгляд итп*) insistent.

насто́лько *нареч* so.

насто́льн|ый *прил* (*ла́мпа, часы́*) table *опред*; (*календа́рь*) desk *опред*; ~**ая кни́га** (*перен*) bible; **насто́льный те́ннис** table tennis.

настора́жива|ть(ся) (-ю(сь)) *несов от* **насторожи́ть(ся)**.

насторожё *нареч* on the alert ♦ *как сказ:* **он всегда́** ~ he is always on the alert.

насторо́женно *нареч* intently.

насторо́жен|ный (-, -на, -но) *прил* alert.

насторожё|нный (-, -на, -но) *прил* = **насторо́женный**.

насторож|и́ть (-у́, -и́шь; *impf* **настора́живать**) *сов перех* to alert

▸ **насторожи́ться** (*impf* **настора́живаться**) *сов возв* to become more alert.

настоя́ни|е (-я) *ср:* **по** ~**ю кого́-н** on sb's insistence.

настоя́тельн|ый (-ен, -ьна, -ьно) *прил* (*про́сьба*) persistent; (*зада́ча*) urgent.

насто|я́ть (-ю́, -и́шь; *impf* **наста́ивать**) *сов неперех:* ~ **на** +*prp* to insist on ♦ *перех* (*рома́шку*) to infuse; **наста́ивать** (~ *perf*) **на своём** to insist on having one's own way

▸ **настоя́ться** (*impf* **наста́иваться**) *сов возв* (*чай, лека́рство*) to infuse.

настоя́щее (-его; *decl like adj*) *ср* the present.

настоя́щий (-ая, -ее, -ие) *прил* real; (*моме́нт, вре́мя*) present; (*да́нный: статья́*) this; **по-**~**ему** (*как на́до*) properly; (*пре́данный*) really; **настоя́щее вре́мя** (*линг*) the present tense.

настрадá|ться (-ю́сь) *сов возв* to suffer a lot.

настрáива|ть(ся) (-ю(сь)) *несов от* **настрóить(ся)**.

нáстрого *нареч* (*разг*) strictly.

настроéни|е (-я) *ср* mood; (*антивоенное*) feeling; **не в ~и** in a bad mood; **общéственное ~** the mood in society.

настрó|ить (-ю, -ишь; *impf* **настрáивать**) *сов* (*не*)*перех* (+*acc или* +*gen*; *домов, мостов, больниц*) to build ♦ *перех* (*гитару, пианино итп*) to tune; (*приёмник*) to tune in; (*механизм*) to adjust; **настрáивать** (~ *perf*) **когó-н на** +*acc* to put sb in the right frame of mind for; **настрáивать** (~ *perf*) **когó-н прóтив** +*gen* to incite sb against

▸ **настрóиться** (*impf* **настрáиваться**) *сов возв* (*приёмник*) to be tuned in; (*дружелюбно, враждебно*) to be disposed; **~ся** (*perf*) +*infin* to be disposed to do.

настрó|й (-я) *м* mood.

настрó|йщик (-а) *м*: **~ роя́ля** piano tuner.

наступáтел|ьный (-ен, -ьна, -ьно) *прил* (*бой, действие*) offensive.

наступá|ть (-ю) *несов от* **наступúть** ♦ *неперех* (*ВОЕН*) to go on the offensive.

наступ|úть (-уплю́, -у́пишь; *impf* **наступáть**) *сов неперех*: **~ на** +*acc* (*на камень, на ногу итп*) to step on; (*ночь, тишина*) to fall; (*утро, лето*) to begin; (*день отъезда*) to come.

наступлéни|е (-я) *ср* (*ВОЕН*) offensive; (*весны, старости*) beginning; (*темноты*) fall; **с ~м зимы́** at the beginning of winter; **с ~м темноты́** at nightfall.

наступлю́ *сов см* **наступúть**.

настýрци|я (-и) *ж* nasturtium.

насты́р|ный (-ен, -на, -но) *прил* (*разг*) persistent.

насýп|иться (-люсь, -ишься) *сов возв* (*разг*) to frown.

нáсухо *нареч*: **вы́тереть что-н ~** to dry sth thoroughly.

насýщ|ный (-ен, -на, -но) *прил* vital.

насчёт *предл* (+*gen*) regarding.

насчитá|ть (-ю; *impf* **насчúтывать**) *сов перех* to count.

насчúтыва|ть (-ю) *несов от* **насчитáть** ♦ *неперех* to have; **деревня ~ет ты́сячу жúтелей** the village has a thousand inhabitants

▸ **насчúтываться** *несов возв безл* to have.

насы́п|ать (-лю, -лешь; *impf* **насыпáть**) *сов перех* to pour; (*набросать*) to strew.

нáсып|ь (-и) *ж* embankment.

насы́|тить (-щу, -тишь; *impf* **насыщáть**) *сов перех* (*голодного, ребёнка*) to satiate; (*запахом, водой, радостью*) to fill; (*раствор, рынок*) to saturate

▸ **насы́титься** (*impf* **насыщáться**) *сов возв* (*наесться*) to eat one's fill; (*земля*) to be saturated.

насы́щенный *прил* (*хим*) saturated; (*перен*: *жизнь*) rich.

насы́щу(сь) *сов см* **насы́тить(ся)**.

нася́ду *итп сов см* **насéсть**.

натáлкива|ть(ся) (-ю(сь)) *несов от* **натолкнýть(ся)**.

натаскá|ть (-ю; *impf* **натáскивать**) *сов* (*не*)*перех* (+*acc или* +*gen*; *дров, сучьев итп*) to bring; (*разг*: *перен*: *цитат, отрывков*) to fish out; (: *студента, ученика*) to coach (*for examination*).

натащ|úть (-ý, -ишь) *сов* (*не*)*перех* (+*acc или* +*gen*; *разг*: *камней, сучьев, грязи*) to bring in.

натвор|úть (-ю́, -úшь) *сов* (*не*)*перех* (+*acc или* +*gen*; *разг*) to get up to.

нат|ерéть (-рý, -рёшь; *pt* -ёр, -ёрла, -ёрло, *impf* **натирáть**) *сов перех* (*ботинки, полы*) to polish; (*руку, шею итп*) to chafe; (*морковь, сыр итп*) to grate; **натирáть** (~ *perf*) **что-н чем-н** (*руки итп*: *мазью, кремом*) to rub sth into sth; **натирáть** (~ *perf*) **себé мозóли** to get a callus

▸ **натерéться** (*impf* **натирáться**) *сов возв*: **~ся** (+*instr*; *мазью, кремом*) to rub o.s. (with).

натерп|éться (-лю́сь, -ишься) *сов возв*: **~** +*gen* (*разг*: *горя, беды*) to experience a lot of.

натирá|ть(ся) (-ю(сь)) *несов от* **натерéть(ся)**.

нáтиск (-а) *м* pressure.

наткн|ýться (-ýсь, -ёшься; *impf* **натыкáться**) *сов возв*: **~ýться на** +*acc* (*разг*: *на пень, на преграду*) to bump into; (*перен*: *на непонимание, на сопротивление*) to come up against.

НАТО *ср сокр* NATO (= *North Atlantic Treaty Organization*).

натолкн|ýть (-ý, -ёшь; *impf* **натáлкивать**) *сов перех*: **~ когó-н на** +*acc* (*разг*: *на идею*) to lead sb to; **натáлкивать** (~ *perf*) **когó-н на мысль** to put a thought into sb's head

▸ **натолкнýться** (*impf* **натáлкиваться**) *сов возв*: **~ся на** +*acc* (*также перен*) to bump into.

натоп|úть (-лю́, -ишь) *сов перех* (*избу, печь*) to heat; (*жир, воск*) to melt.

натоп|тáть (-чý, -чешь) *сов перех* (*разг*) to make dirty footmarks across.

наточ|úть (-очý, -óчишь) *сов от* **точúть**.

натощáк *нареч* on an empty stomach.

натрав|úть (-лю́, -ишь; *impf* **натрáвливать**) *сов перех*: **~ когó-н на** +*acc* to set sb on; (*перен*) to incite sb against.

натренирóван|ный (-, -а, -о) *прил* trained.

натренир|овáть(ся) (-ýю(сь)) *сов от* **тренировáть(ся)**.

нáтри|й (-я) *м* sodium.

нáтрое *нареч* in(to) three.

натрý(сь) *итп сов см* **натерéть(ся)**.

натруд|úться (-ужýсь, -ýдишься) *сов возв* (*разг*) to work hard.

нату́г|а (-и) ж (разг) effort.
на́туго нареч (разг) tightly.
нату́ж|иться (-усь, -ишься; impf
нату́живаться) сов возв (разг) to strain.
нату́р|а (-ы) ж (характер) nature; (натурщик)
model (ART); **увиде́ть** (perf) **что-н/кого́-н ~е** to
see sth/sb in real life; **рисова́ть** (impf) **с ~ы** to
paint from nature; **~ой, в ~е** (ЭКОН) in kind.
натура́лен прил см **натура́льный**.
натурализа́ци|я (-и) ж naturalization.
натурали́зм (-а) м naturalism.
натурали́ст (-а) м naturalist.
натура́льный (-ен, -ьна, -ьно) прил natural;
(мех, кожа, слёзы) real; (обмен, доходы, налог)
in kind; **~ьная величина́** life-sized.
нату́рщик (-а) м model (ART).
нату́рщиц|а (-ы) ж см **нату́рщик**.
натыка́ться (-юсь) несов от **наткну́ться**.
натюрмо́рт (-а) м still life.
натя́гива|ть(ся) (-ю(сь)) несов от
натяну́ть(ся).
натя́ж|ка (-ки; gen pl -ек) ж (в аргументах)
distortion; **с ~кой** at a pinch.
натя́нут|ый (-, -а, -о) прил strained.
натяну́ть (-у́, -ешь; impf **натя́гивать**) сов перех
(струны, вожжи, холст) to pull tight; (разг:
сапоги, перчатки) to pull on; (: одеяло) to pull
over; **он ~у́л ему́ пятёрку** (разг) he stretched
his mark to an A
▸ **натяну́ться** (impf **натя́гиваться**) сов возв to
tighten.
науга́д нареч (идти, взять) at random;
отвеча́ть (impf) **~** to guess.
нау́к|а (-и) ж science; (разг: урок) lesson;
есте́ственные ~и science; **гуманита́рные ~и**
arts.
науте́к нареч (разг: пуститься, броситься) at
full tilt.
нау́тро нареч next morning.
нау́чен прил см **нау́чный**.
науч|и́ть(ся) (-учу́(сь), -у́чишь(ся)) сов от
учи́ть(ся).
нау́чно-популя́рный прил (программа)
science опред; (литература) scientific.
нау́чно-техни́ческ|ий (-ая, -ое, -ие) прил
scientific.
нау́чн|ый (-ен, -на, -но) прил scientific; **нау́чная
фанта́стика** science fiction.
нау́шник (-а) м (обычно мн: на шапке) earflap;
магнитофо́нные ~и headphones.
нафтали́н (-а; part gen -у) м naphthalene.
наха́л (-а) м (разг) cheeky beggar.
наха́лен прил см **наха́льный**.
наха́лк|а (-и) ж см **наха́л**.
наха́льный (-ен, -ьна, -ьно) прил cheeky.
наха́льств|о (-а) ср cheek.
нахам|и́ть (-лю́, -и́шь) сов от **хами́ть**.
нахвата́|ть (-ю) сов неперех (+gen; разг:
товаров, знаний) to pick up
▸ **нахвата́ться** сов возв (+gen; разг: знаний,
привычек) to pick up; (: воды) to gulp.

нахле́бник (-а) м (разг) sponger.
нахлобу́ч|ить (-у, -ишь; impf **нахлобу́чивать**)
сов перех (разг) to pull down.
нахлы́н|уть (3sg -ет, 3pl -ут) сов неперех
(поток) to surge; (перен: толпа) to surge
forward; (: мысли) to surge up; **~ули
воспомина́ния** memories came flooding back.
нахму́р|ить(ся) (-ю(сь), -ишь(ся)) несов от
хму́рить(ся).
нах|оди́ть (-ожу́, -о́дишь) несов от **найти́**
▸ **находи́ться** несов от **найти́сь** ♦ возв (дом,
город) to be situated; (человек) to be.
нахо́д|ка (-ки; gen pl -ок) ж (потерянного)
discovery; (приём: писателя, актёра)
innovation; **он ~ для нас** he is a real find for
us; **Бюро́ ~ок** lost property office (BRIT), lost
and found (US).
нахо́дчив|ый (-, -а, -о) прил (человек)
resourceful; (ответ) apt.
нахожде́ни|е (-я) ср (преступника)
whereabouts.
нахо́жен|ный (-, -а, -о) прил (тропа) well-
trodden.
нахожу́(сь) несов см **находи́ть(ся)**.
нахох|ота́ться (-очу́сь, -о́чешься) сов возв to
have a good laugh.
нахра́пист|ый (-, -а, -о) прил (разг: продавец,
посетитель) pushy.
нахра́пом нареч (разг): **де́йствовать ~** to be
pushy.
нахулига́н|ить (-ю, -ишь) сов от **хулига́нить**.
нацара́па|ть (-ю) сов от **цара́пать**.
наце|ди́ть (-жу́, -́дишь; impf **наце́живать**) сов
перех to strain.
наце́лен|ный (-, -а, -о) прил: **~ на** +acc (на
побе́ду) aiming for.
наце́л|ить (-ю, -ишь) сов от **це́лить** ♦ (impf
наце́ливать) перех: **~ кого́-н на** +acc to push
sb towards
▸ **наце́литься** сов от **це́литься**.
наце́н|ка (-ки; gen pl -ок) ж (на товар) surcharge;
(ресторанная) cover charge.
нацеп|и́ть (-лю́, -ишь; impf **нацепля́ть**) сов
перех (повесить) to hang on; (разг: украшения,
шляпу) to doll o.s. up in.
наци́зм (-а) м Nazism.
национализа́ци|я (-и) ж nationalization.
национализи́р|овать (-ую) (не)сов перех to
nationalize.
национали́зм (-а) м nationalism.
национали́ст (-а) м nationalist.
национали́ст|ка (-ки; gen pl -ок) ж см
национали́ст.
национали́стск|ий (-ая, -ое, -ие) прил
(политика, лозунга) nationalistic.
национа́льность (-и) ж (нация) nation;
(принадлежность к нации) nationality.
национа́льный прил national; **национа́льный
о́круг** administrative division of minor
nationalities.
наци́ст (-а) м Nazi.

наци́ст|ский (-ая, -ое, -ие) *прил* Nazi.
на́ци|я (-и) *ж* nation; **Организа́ция Объединённых Н~й** United Nations Organization.
нацме́н (-а) *м сокр* = *представи́тель национа́льного меньшинства́*.
нач. *сокр* = **нача́льник**.
нача|ди́ть (-жу́, -ди́шь) *сов от* **чади́ть**.
нача́л|а (-) *мн* (*методы*) basis *ед*; (*принципы*) fundamentals *мн*; **на коллекти́вных/ комме́рческих ~х** on a collective/commercial basis.
нача́л|о (-а) *ср* beginning, start; (*основа: организующее, сдерживающее*) foundation; (: *волевое, поэтическое*) nature; **быть** (*impf*) **под ~м кого́-н** *или* **у кого́-н** to be under sb; **брать** (*impf*) ~ to start; **вести́** (*impf*) **своё ~ от** +*gen* to have its origins in; **положи́ть** (*perf*) *или* **дать** (*perf*) ~ **чему́-н** to make a start on sth; *см также* **нача́ла**.
нача́льник (-а) *м* (*цеха*) floor manager; (*управления*) head; (*экспедиции*) leader.
нача́льническ|ий (-ая, -ое, -ие) *прил* (*тон*) authoritative.
нача́льный *прил* (*период, этап*) initial; (*глава книги*) first; (*первоначальный: сведения, уроки*) very first; **нача́льная шко́ла** (*ПРОСВЕЩ*) primary (*BRIT*) *или* elementary (*US*) school; **нача́льное образова́ние** (*ПРОСВЕЩ*) primary (*BRIT*) *или* elementary (*US*) education; **нача́льные кла́ссы** (*ПРОСВЕЩ*) *the first three classes of primary school*.
нача́льственный *прил* superior.
нача́льств|о (-а) *ср* (*власть*) authority ♦ *собир* (*руководители*) management; **под ~м кого́-н** (*служить, находиться*) under sb.
нача́льствующ|ий (-ая, -ее, -ие) *прил* managing *опред*.
нача́тк|и (-ов) *мн* fundamentals *мн*.
нача́|ть (-ну́, -нёшь; *pt* -ал, -ала́, -ало, *impf* **начина́ть**) *сов перех* to begin, start; (*начать использовать*) to start; **начина́ть** (~ *perf*) +*infin* to start doing
▶ **нача́ться** (*impf* **начина́ться**) *сов возв* to begin, start.
начеку́ *нареч*: **быть** ~ to be on one's guard.
начерка́|ть (-ю) *сов от* **черка́ть** ♦ *перех* (*разг: линии, штрихи итп*) to draw (*randomly*); (*записку*) to scribble.
начерн|и́ть (-ю́, -и́шь) *сов от* **черни́ть**.
на́черно *нареч* (*написать, подготовить*) roughly.
начерта́ни|е (-я) *ср* (*букв*) outline.
начер|ти́ть (-чу́, -тишь) *сов от* **черти́ть**.
начёс (-а) *м* (*на шерсти, на ткани*) nap; (*вид причёски*) bouffant.
начёт (-а) *м* (*денежное взыскание*) penalty.
начина́ни|е (-я) *ср* initiative.

начина́тел|ь (-я) *м* initiator.
начина́|ть(ся) (-ю(сь)) *несов от* **нача́ть(ся)**.
начина́юща|я (-ей; *decl like adj*) *ж см* **начина́ющий**.
начина́ющий (-ая, -ее, -ие) *прил* (*писатель, учитель*) novice *опред* ♦ (-его; *decl like adj*) *м* beginner.
начина́я *предл* (+*instr*) including; ~ **с** +*gen* from; ~ **от** +*gen или* **с** +*gen* (*включая*) including.
начин|и́ть (-ю́, -и́шь; *impf* **начиня́ть**) *сов перех* (*пирог*) to fill.
начи́нк|а (-и; *gen pl* -ок) *ж* filling.
начиня́|ть (-ю) *несов от* **начини́ть**.
начисле́ни|е (-я) *ср* (*действие*) addition; (*начисленная сумма*) surcharge.
начи́сл|ить (-ю, -ишь; *impf* **начисля́ть**) *сов перех* (*проценты*) to add on.
начи́|стить (-щу, -стишь; *impf* **начища́ть**) *сов перех* (*туфли*) to clean ♦ *неперех* (+*gen*; *картошки*) to peel.
на́чисто *нареч* (*набело*) cleanly; (*разг: совершенно*) absolutely.
начистоту́ *нареч* (*разг*) straight.
начи́тан|ный (-, -на, -но) *прил* well-read.
начита́|ть (-ю; *impf* **начи́тывать**) *сов перех* to read
▶ **начита́ться** *сов возв* (+*gen*) to read a lot of.
начи́тыва|ть (-ю) *несов от* **начита́ть**.
начиха́|ть (-ю) *сов неперех* (*перен: разг*): **ему́** ~ **на сове́ты** he doesn't give a toss about taking people's advice.
начища́|ть (-ю) *несов от* **начи́стить**.
начи́щу *сов см* **начи́стить**.
начме́д (-а) *м сокр* SG (= *Surgeon General*).
начну́(сь) *сов см* **нача́ть(ся)**.
наш (-его; *см* Table 9; *f* -а, *nt* -е, *pl* -и) *притяж мест* our; ~ **го́род о́чень ста́рый** our city is very old; **чей э́то дом?** – ~ whose is this house? – ours; **чьи э́то кни́ги?** – **на́ши** whose are these books? – ours; **по-на́шему** our way; (*по нашему мнению*) in our opinion; **на́ша взяла́!** (*разг*) we won!; *см также* **на́ши**.
нашаты́рный *прил*: ~ **спирт** (*МЕД*) liquid ammonia.
нашаты́р|ь (-я́) *м* (*ХИМ*) ammonium chloride; (*разг: нашатырный спирт*) liquid ammonia.
на́ше (-го) *притяж мест см* **наш**.
наше́стви|е (-я) *ср* invasion.
на́ш|и (-их) *притяж мест см* **наш**; ♦ *decl like adj мн* (*о членах семьи*) relatives *мн*; (*о соотечественниках*) compatriots *мн*; **и ~м и ва́шим** (*разг*) all things to all people; ~ **вы́играли** we won.
нашива́|ть (-ю) *несов от* **наши́ть**.
наши́в|ка (-ки; *gen pl* -ок) *ж* (*на погонах*) stripe (*showing rank*).
на́шим *притяж мест см* **наш, на́ше, на́ши**.
на́шими *притяж мест см* **на́ши**.

нашинк|ова́ть (-у́ю) *сов от* **шинкова́ть**.

наши́|ть (-ью, -ьёшь; *impf* **нашива́ть**) *сов перех* (тесьму, эмблему) to sew on ◆ *неперех* (*no perf*): ~ +*gen* (нарядов) to sew.

на́ших *притяж мест см* **наш**.

нашлёпа|ть (-ю) *сов перех* (разг) to smack.

нашпиг|ова́ть (-у́ю) *сов от* **шпигова́ть**.

нашуме́|ть (-лю, -и́шь) *сов неперех* to make a lot of noise; (*фильм, книга*) to cause a stir.

нашью́ *итп сов см* **наши́ть**.

нащу́па|ть (-ю; *impf* **нащу́пывать**) *сов перех* (также перен) to find.

наэлектриз|ова́ть (-у́ю) *сов от* **электризова́ть**.

най|бедни́ча|ть (-ю) *сов от* **я́бедничать**.

наяву́ *нареч* in reality; **как** ~ distinctly.

НДС *м сокр* (= нало́г на доба́вленную сто́имость) VAT (= *value-added tax*).

не *част* not; ~ **я написа́л э́то письмо́** I didn't write this letter; **я** ~ **рабо́таю** I don't work; ~ **пла́чьте/опозда́йте** don't cry/be late; ~ **могу́** ~ **согласи́ться/не возрази́ть** I can't help agreeing/objecting; ~ **я на́до помо́чь, а ему́** I am not the one who needs help, he is; **слу́шаю** ~ **без удово́льствия/удивле́ния** I listen not without pleasure/surprise; ~ **до** +*gen* no time for; **мне** ~ **до тебя́** I have no time for you; ~ **без того́** (разг: *в положительных ответах*) that's about it; ~ **то** (разг: *в противном случае*) or else; **откро́й дверь,** ~ **то я её слома́ю** open the door or else I'll break it down.

неадеква́т|ный (-ен, -на, -но) *прил* inadequate.

неаккура́т|ный (-ен, -на, -но) *прил* (*человек*) untidy; (*подсчёт*) inaccurate; (*работа*) sloppy.

неактуа́л|ьный (-ен, -ьна, -ьно) *прил* irrelevant.

неаполита́нск|ий (-ая, -ое, -ие) *прил* Neapolitan.

Неа́пол|ь (-я) *м* Naples.

небезопа́с|ный (-ен, -на, -но) *прил* somewhat dangerous.

небезоснова́тел|ьный (-ен, -ьна, -ьно) *прил* not unreasonable.

небезызве́ст|ный (-ен, -на, -но) *прил* (*факты*) reasonably well-known; (*сплетник, интриган*) notorious.

небезынтере́с|ный (-ен, -на, -но) *прил* reasonably interesting.

небеса́ *итп сущ см* **не́бо**.

небе́сный *прил* (*небосвод, сфера*) celestial; (*перен*) heavenly; **небе́сные тела́** heavenly bodies; **небе́сные си́лы** (*РЕЛ*) the heavenly host; **небе́сный цвет** sky blue.

небесполе́з|ный (-ен, -на, -но) *прил* reasonably useful.

неблагови́д|ный (-ен, -на, -но) *прил* unseemly.

неблагода́рен *прил см* **неблагода́рный**.

неблагода́рность (-и) *ж* ingratitude.

неблагода́р|ный (-ен, -на, -но) *прил* (*человек*) ungrateful; (*занятие, работа*) thankless.

неблагозву́ч|ный (-ен, -на, -но) *прил* dissonant.

неблагополу́ч|ный (-ен, -на, -но) *прил* unsuccessful.

не́б|о (-а; *nom pl* **небеса́**, *gen pl* **небе́с**) *ср* sky; (*РЕЛ*) Heaven; **на седьмо́м** ~**е** in seventh heaven; **под откры́тым** ~**м** out in the open; **с** ~**а свали́ться** (*perf*) (разг: *неожиданно появиться*) to appear out of nowhere; **я был ме́жду** ~**м и землёй** I didn't know whether I was coming or going; **превозноси́ть** (*impf*) **кого́-н до небе́с** to praise sb to the skies.

не́б|о (-а) *ср* (*АНАТ*) palate.

небога́т|ый (-, -а, -о) *прил* (*страна*) not wealthy; (*выбор, улов*) fairly poor; **он челове́к** ~ he has a modest income.

небольш|о́й *прил* small; (*расстояние, промежуток времени*) short; (*должность, звание*) minor; (*польза, авторитет*) limited; **на** ~ **глубине́/высоте́** not very deep/high; **ей три́дцать (лет) с** ~**им** she is a little over thirty.

небосво́д (-а) *м* the heavens *мн*.

небоскрёб (-а) *м* skyscraper.

небо́сь *вводн сл* (разг) I dare say.

небре́жен *прил см* **небре́жный**.

небре́жность (-и) *ж* (*в работе, подсчётов*) carelessness; (*родителей, работников*) negligence; (*тона, в обращении*) offhandedness.

небре́ж|ный (-ен, -на, -но) *прил* (*человек, работа, подсчёт*) careless; (*причёска, почерк*) untidy; (*тон, отношение*) offhand(ed).

небыва́л|ый (-, -а, -о) *прил* (*чувство, ощущение*) unknown; (*случай*) unprecedented.

небыли́ц|а (-ы) *ж* tall story.

небыти́|е́ (-я́) *ср* nonexistence.

Нев|а́ (-ы́) *ж* the Neva.

неважен *прил см* **нева́жный**.

нева́жно *нареч* (*работать, делать что-н*) not very well ◆ *как сказ* it's not important; **я чу́вствую себя́** ~ I'm not feeling too good; **он** ~ **у́чится в шко́ле** he isn't doing very well at school.

нева́ж|ный (-ен, -на, -но) *прил* unimportant; (*не очень хороший*) poor; **обе́д был нава́жный** dinner wasn't great; **у неё** ~**ное здоро́вье** her health isn't very good.

невдалеке́ *нареч* (*слышаться, видеться*) not far off; ~ **от** +*gen* not far from.

невдомёк *как сказ* (+*dat*): **ей** ~, **что** ... (разг) she doesn't realize that ....

неве́дени|е (-я) *ср* ignorance; **сде́лать** (*perf*)/ **сказа́ть** (*perf*) **что-н по** ~**ю** to do/say sth out of ignorance; **он пребыва́ет в по́лном** ~**и** he doesn't know anything (about it).

неве́домо *нареч*: ~ **кто/что/как** *итп* (разг) God knows who/what/how *итп*.

неве́дом|ый (-, -а, -о) *прил* unknown.

неве́ж|а (-и) *м/ж* boor.

неве́жд|а (-ы) *м/ж* ignoramus.

неве́жествен|ный (-, -на, -но) *прил* ignorant.

неве́жеств|о (-а) *ср* ignorance.

неве́жлив|ый (-, -а, -о) *прил* impolite.
невезе́ни|е (-я) *ср* (*разг*) bad luck.
невели́к|ий (-ая, -ое, -ие; -, -а́, -о́) *прил* (*по размеру*) small; (*по длине*) short; (*убытки, ущерб*) minor; **он ро́стом невели́к** he's not very tall; **невелика́ беда́!** (*разг*) it's no big deal!
неве́рен *прил см* **неве́рный**.
неве́ри|е (-я) *ср* lack of faith.
неве́рно *нареч* incorrectly ♦ *как сказ*: (**э́то**) ~ that's not right.
неве́рность (-и) *ж* (*рассуждений, понятия*) incorrectness; (*друга, союзника*) disloyalty; (*жены, мужа*) infidelity.
неве́р|ный (-ен, -на, -но) *прил* (*см сущ*) incorrect; disloyal; unfaithful; (*шаги, движения*) unsteady; (*голос, звук*) faltering; (*нота*) false.
невероя́тен *прил см* **невероя́тный**.
невероя́тно *нареч* incredibly ♦ *как сказ* it's incredible.
невероя́тность (-и) *ж* (*сообщения, результатов*) improbability; **до** ~**и** incredibly.
невероя́т|ный (-ен, -на, -но) *прил* (*неправдоподобный*) improbable; (*чрезвычайный*) incredible.
неве́рующий (-ая, -ее, -ие) *прил* (*РЕЛ*) faithless ♦ (-**его**; *decl like adj*) *м* unbeliever.
неве|сёлый (-сел, -села́, -село) *прил* gloomy.
невесо́мость (-и) *ж* (*ФИЗ*) weightlessness.
невесо́м|ый (-, -а, -о) *прил* weightless; (*перен*: *преимущество, превосходство*) negligible.
неве́ст|а (-ы) *ж* (*после помолвки*) fiancée; (*на свадьбе*) bride.
неве́ст|ка (-ки; *gen pl* -ок) *ж* (*жена сына*) daughter-in-law; (*жена брата*) sister-in-law.
неве́сть *нареч*: ~ **кто/что/куда́** *итп* (*разг*) goodness knows who/what/where *итп*.
невзго́д|а (-ы) *ж* (*обычно мн*) adversity.
невзира́я *предл*: ~ **на** +*acc* in spite of.
невз|люби́ть (-юблю́, -ю́бишь) *сов перех* to take a dislike to.
невзнача́й *нареч* (*разг*) by accident.
невзра́ч|ный (-ен, -на, -но) *прил* ordinary-looking.
невзыска́тельный (-ен, -ьна, -ьно) *прил* undemanding.
неви́дал|ь (-и) *ж* (*разг*) oddity; ~ **кака́я!** now there's a surprise!
неви́дан|ный (-, -на, -но) *прил* unprecedented.
невиди́м|ка (-ки; *gen pl* -ок) *м/ж* (*человек*) invisible being ♦ *ж* (*шпилька*) hairpin.
неви́дим|ый (-, -а, -о) *прил* invisible.
неви́дящий (-ая, -ее, -ие) *прил* unseeing.
неви́нен *прил см* **неви́нный**.
неви́нность (-и) *ж* innocence.
неви́н|ный (-ен, -на, -но) *прил* innocent.
невино́вен *прил см* **невино́вный**.

невино́вность (-и) *ж* innocence.
невино́в|ный (-ен, -на, -но) *прил* innocent.
невку́сен *прил см* **невку́сный**.
невку́сно *нареч*: **она́** ~ **гото́вит** she is a bad cook; **здесь** ~ **ко́рмят** the food here is not very nice.
невку́с|ный (-ен, -на́, -но) *прил* (*суп, салат, пища*) tasteless.
невменя́емость (-и) *ж* derangement; **в состоя́нии** ~**и** (*ЮР*) non compos mentis.
невменя́ем|ый (-, -а, -о) *прил* deranged.
невмеша́тельств|о (-а) *ср* non interference; (*ЭКОН*) laissez faire.
невнима́ни|е (-я) *ср* (*невнимательность*) lack of attention; (*равнодушие*) lack of concern.
невнима́телен *прил см* **невнима́тельный**.
невнима́тельность (-и) *ж* (*см прил*) inattention; lack of consideration; carelessness.
невнима́тел|ьный (-ен, -ьна, -ьно) *прил* (*ученик, слушатель*) inattentive; (*незаботливый: сын, дочь*) inconsiderate; (: *отношение, обращение*) careless.
невня́т|ный (-ен, -на, -но) *прил* muffled.
не́вод (-а) *м* fishing net.
невозвра́тен *прил см* **невозвра́тный**.
невозврати́м|ый (-, -а, -о) *прил* irretrievable.
невозвра́т|ный (-ен, на, -но) *прил* = **невозврати́мый**.
невозвраще́н|ец (-ца) *м* defector.
невозвраще́н|ка (-ки; *gen pl* -ок) *ж см* **невозвраще́нец**.
невозвраще́нца *итп сущ см* **невозвраще́нец**.
невозде́ржан|ный (-, -на, -но) *прил* highly strung (*BRIT*), high-strung (*US*).
невозмо́жен *прил см* **невозмо́жный**.
невозмо́жно *как сказ*: ~ +*infin* (*сделать, найти итп*) it is impossible to do ♦ *нареч* (*большой, трудный*) impossibly; (**э́то**) ~ that's impossible.
невозмо́жность (-и) *ж*: **до** ~**и** exceedingly.
невозмо́ж|ный (-ен, -на, -но) *прил* impossible; (*боль, жара*) unbearable; (*тон, поведение, вид*) insufferable.
невозмути́м|ый (-, -а, -о) *прил* (*человек*) unflappable; (*тон, ответ*) unruffled; (*тишина, спокойствие*) undisturbed.
нево́лен *прил см* **нево́льный**.
нево́л|ить (-ю, -ишь) *несов перех* (*разг*): ~ **кого́-н** +*infin* (*согласиться, отказаться итп*) to force sb to do.
нево́льник (-а) *м* slave.
нево́льниц|а (-ы) *ж см* **нево́льник**.
нево́льный (-ен, -ьна, -ьно) *прил* (*ложь, вина*) unintentional; (*движение, улыбка, свидетель*) involuntary.
нево́л|я (-и) *ж* captivity; **в** ~**е** in captivity.
невообрази́м|ый (-, -а, -о) *прил* unimaginable.
невооружён|ный *прил* unarmed; ~**ым гла́зом**

(*без оптических приборов*) with the naked eye; **э́то ви́дно ~ым глазо́м** (*перен*) it's plain for all to see.

невоспи́тан|ный (-, -на, -но) *прил* ill-bred.

невоспри|и́мчив|ый (-, -а, -о) *прил*: ~ **к** +*dat* (*к знаниям*) unreceptive (to); (*к болезням*) immune (to).

невостре́бованный *прил* unclaimed.

невпопа́д *нареч* (*разг*) out of turn.

невразуми́тел|ьный (-ен, -ьна, -ьно) *прил* unintelligible.

невралги́ческ|ий (-ая, -ое, -ие) *прил* neuralgic.

невралги́|я (-и) *ж* neuralgia.

неврасте́ник (-а) *м* neurotic.

неврастени́ч|ный (-ен, -на, -но) *прил* neurotic.

неврастени́|я (-и) *ж* (*МЕД*) nervous tension.

невреди́м|ый (-, -а, -о) *прил* (*лодка, машина*) undamaged; (*человек*) unharmed.

невро́з (-а) *м* neurosis (*мн* neuroses).

невропато́лог (-а) *м* neurologist.

невтерпёж *как сказ* (+*dat*): **ей ~ пойти́/узна́ть** she can't wait to go/find out; **ему́ всё ~** he is always in a hurry.

невы́год|ный (-ен, -на, -но) *прил* unprofitable; (*условия, ситуация, впечатление*) unfavourable (*BRIT*), unfavorable (*US*); (*внешность*) unattractive.

невы́держан|ный (-, -на, -но) *прил* (*человек, поведение*) uncontrolled; (*стиль*) erratic.

невыноси́м|ый (-, -а, -о) *прил* unbearable, intolerable.

невыполне́ни|е (-я) *ср* (*обязательства, плана*) failure to carry out; (*обещания*) failure to keep.

невыполни́м|ый (-, -а, -о) *прил* not feasible.

невырази́м|ый (-, -а, -о) *прил* inexpressible.

невырази́тельный (-ен, -ьна, -ьно) *прил* (*лицо, глаза*) expressionless; (*рассказ, исполнение*) bland.

невысо́к|ий (-ая, -ое, -ие; -, -а́, -о) *прил* low; (*человек*) short.

не́г|а (-и) *ж* bliss.

негати́в (-а) *м* (*ФОТО*) negative.

негати́в|ный (-ен, -на, -но) *прил* negative.

негашёный *прил*: **негашёная ма́рка** unused stamp; **негашёная и́звесть** quicklime.

не́где *как сказ* (+*infin*) there is nowhere to do; **мне ~ жить** I don't have anywhere to live; **здесь ~ купи́ть еды́** there is nowhere to buy food around here.

неги́б|кий (-ая, -ое, -ие; -ок, -ка́, -ко) *прил* (*также перен*) inflexible.

негла́с|ный (-ен, -на, -но) *прил* secret.

неглубо́к|ий (-ая, -ое, -ие; -, -а́, -о́) *прил* (*яма, река*) shallow; (*знания, человек, чувство*) superficial; (*сон*) light.

неглу́п|ый (-, -а́, -о) *прил* fairly clever; **он о́чень неглу́п** he's by no means stupid.

него́ *мест от* **он, оно́**.

него́ден *прил см* **него́дный**.

него́дность (-и) *ж* worthlessness; **приходи́ть**

(**прийти́** *perf*) **в ~** (*оборудование*) to become defunct; (*одежда*) to be worn out.

него́д|ный (-ен, -на, -но) *прил* (*непригодный*) unusable; (*скверный*) good-for-nothing.

негодова́ни|е (-я) *ср* indignation.

негодова́ть (-ую) *несов неперех* to be indignant.

негоду́ющий (-ая, -ее, -ие) *прил* indignant.

негодя́|й (-я) *м* scoundrel.

негр (-а) *м* black man (*мн* men).

негра́мот|ный (-ен, -на, -но) *прил* (*человек, ученик*) illiterate; (*содержащий ошибки: речь*) ungrammatical; (*специалист, работа*) incompetent.

негритёнок (-ёнка, *nom pl* -я́та, *gen pl* -я́т) *м* black child (*мн* children).

негритя́н|ка (-ки; *gen pl* -ок) *ж* black woman (*мн* women).

негритя́нск|ий (-ая, -ое, -ие) *прил* black.

негритя́та *итп сущ см* **негритёнок**.

негро́м|кий (-кая, -кое, -кие; -ок, -ка́, -ко) *прил* quiet.

не́гры (-ов) *мн* black people *мн*.

неда́вн|ий (-яя, -ее, -ие) *прил* recent; **до ~его вре́мени** until recently.

неда́вно *нареч* recently.

недалёк|ий (-ая, -ое, -ие; -, -а́, -о́) *прил* (*место*) nearby; (*расстояние, путь*) short; (*недавний*) near; (-, -а, -о; *перен: человек, ум*) limited; **в ~ом бу́дущем** in the near future; **она́ недалека́ от и́стины** she is not far from the truth.

недалеко́ *нареч* (*жить, находиться*) nearby; (*идти, ехать*) not far ♦ *как сказ*: ~ (**до** +*gen*) it isn't far (to); ~ **от** +*gen* not far from; **до утра́ ~** it will soon be morning.

недальнови́д|ный (-ен, -на, -но) *прил* short-sighted.

неда́ром *нареч* (*не напрасно*) not in vain; (*не без цели*) for a reason; **я ~ сто́лько учи́лся** all of that studying has paid off; **я ~ прие́хал сего́дня** I do have a reason for coming today.

недви́жимость (-и) *ж* property.

недви́жимый *прил*: **недви́жимое иму́щество** = **недви́жимость**.

недвижи́м|ый (-, -а, -о) *прил* (*неподвижный*) motionless; (*не способный двигаться: больно́й*) immobile.

недвусмы́слен|ный (-, -на, -но) *прил* unambiguous.

недееспосо́б|ный (-ен, -на, -но) *прил* (*ЮР: человек*) incapacitated; (: *организация, структура*) impotent, ineffective.

недействи́тел|ьный (-ен, -ьна, -ьно) *прил* invalid.

неделика́т|ный (-ен, -на, -но) *прил* (*человек*) tactless; (*замечание, вопрос*) indelicate, tactless.

недели́м|ый (-, -а, -о) *прил* indivisible; **недели́мое число́** prime number.

неде́льный *прил* (*срок, отпуск*) one-week; (*запас, заработок итп*) *а или* one week's.

неде́л|я (-и) ж week; **че́рез ~ю** in a week; **на про́шлой/э́той/сле́дующей ~е** last/this/next week.

недобо́р (-а) м shortage.

недоброжела́тель|ный (-ен, -ьна, -ьно) *прил* hostile.

недоброка́чествен|ный (-, -на, -но) *прил* poor-quality.

недобросо́вест|ный (-ен, -на, -но) *прил* (*небре́жный*) unconscientious; (*нече́стный*) unscrupulous.

недо́бр|ый (-, -á, -о) *прил* unkind; (*чу́вства, наме́рения*) ill; (*вре́мя, сон, предчу́вствие*) bad; **~ые ве́сти** ill tidings.

недова́р|и́ть (-арю́, -а́ришь; *impf* **недова́ривать**) *сов перех* to undercook.

недове́ри|е (-я) *ср* mistrust, distrust; **относи́ться (отнести́сь** *perf*) **к кому́-н/чему́-н с ~м** to be mistrustful *или* distrustful of sb/sth.

недове́рчивост|ь (-и) ж mistrust, distrust.

недове́рчив|ый (-, -а, -о) *прил* mistrustful, distrustful.

недове́с (-а) м shortfall (*in weight*).

недове́|сить (-шу, -сишь; *impf* **недове́шивать**) *сов перех*: **~ кому́-н чего́-н** to give sb too little of sth.

недово́ль|ный (-ен, -ьна, -ьно) *прил* discontented, dissatisfied; **она́ всем ~ьна** she is never satisfied.

недово́льств|о (-а) *ср*: **~** (+*instr*) dissatisfaction (with).

недога́длив|ый (-, -а, -о) *прил* inscrutable.

недогля|де́ть (-жу́, -ди́шь) *сов перех* (*оши́бки, опеча́тки*) to overlook ♦ *неперех*: **~ за** +*acc* to fail to keep an eye on.

недогово́р|и́ть (-ю́, -и́шь; *impf* **недогова́ривать**) *сов перех* to leave unsaid; **он что́-то недогова́ривает** there is something that he's not saying.

недоде́лан|ный (-, -на, -но) *прил* unfinished.

недоде́л|ка (-ки; *gen pl* -ок) ж loose end.

недоеда́|ть *несов неперех* to eat badly; **они́ постоя́нно ~ют** they never eat enough.

недозре́лый *прил* unripe.

недойм|ка (-ки; *gen pl* -ок) ж arrears мн.

недока́зан|ный (-, -на, -но) *прил* unproven.

недо́лгий (-гая, -гое, -гие; -ог, -гá, -го) *прил* short.

недо́лго *нареч* for a short time, not for long ♦ *как сказ* (*разг*): **мне ~ э́то сде́лать** it won't take me long (to do); **~ по́сле** +*gen* not long after; **я там бу́ду ~** I won't be there for long; **ему́ оста́лось ~ (жить)** he hasn't got long (to live).

недолгове́ч|ный (-ен, -на, -но) *прил* short-lived.

недо́лог *прил см* **недо́лгий**.

недолю́блива|ть (-ю) *несов перех* to dislike.

недомога́ни|е (-я) *ср* queasiness; **чу́вствовать** (*impf*) **~** to feel queasy.

недомога́|ть (-ю) *несов неперех* to feel unwell.

недомо́лв|ка (-ки; *gen pl* -ок) ж indirect reference; **говори́ть** (*impf*) **о чём-н ~ми** to refer to sth indirectly.

недомы́сли|е (-я) *ср*: **по ~ю** without thinking.

недоно́шен|ный (-, -а, -о) *прил*: **~ ребёнок** premature baby.

недооц|ени́ть (-еню́, -е́нишь; *impf* **недооце́нивать**) *сов перех* to underestimate.

недооце́н|ка (-и) ж underestimation.

недопусти́м|ый (-, -а, -о) *прил* not permissible.

недорабо́т|ка (-и) ж = **недоде́лка**.

недора́звит|ый (-, -а, -о) *прил* underdeveloped; (*разг*) dumb.

недоразуме́ни|е (-я) *ср* misunderstanding.

недо́рого *нареч* cheaply.

недорог|о́й (-а́я, -о́е) *прил* inexpensive.

недоса́лива|ть (-ю) *несов от* **недосоли́ть**.

недосмо́тр (-а) м oversight; **по ~у** through lack of attention.

недосмо́|тре́ть (-отрю́, -о́тришь) *сов неперех* = **недогляде́ть**.

недосо́л|и́ть (-олю́, -о́лишь; *impf* **недоса́ливать**) *сов перех*: **ты ~оли́л суп** you haven't put enough salt in the soup.

недосп|а́ть (-лю́, -и́шь; *impf* **недосыпа́ть**) *сов неперех* to not get enough sleep.

недоста|ва́ть (*3sg* -ёт) *несов безл* (+*gen*; *не хвата́ть*) to lack; (*быть ну́жным*) to need; **ей ~ёт терпе́ния** she lacks patience; **нам о́чень тебя́ ~ва́ло** we really needed you; **э́того ещё ~ва́ло!** as if that were not enough!

недоста́т|ок (-ка; *nom pl* -ки) м shortage, lack; (*в хара́ктере, в рабо́те*) shortcoming.

недоста́точен *прил см* **недоста́точный**.

недоста́точно *нареч* insufficiently ♦ *как сказ* (+*gen*): **у нас ~ еды́/де́нег** we don't have enough food/money; **я ~ зна́ю об э́том** I don't know enough about it; **~ критикова́ть, на́до помо́чь** it's not enough to criticize, you need to help.

недоста́точност|ь (-и) ж inadequacy; **серде́чная ~** heart failure.

недоста́точ|ный (-ен, -на, -но) *прил* insufficient.

недоста́ч|а (-и) ж (*разг*: *материа́лов, обору́дования*) lack; (*де́нег*: *при прове́рке*) shortfall; **у нас в ка́ссе ~ де́нег** the till is short.

недостаю́щий (-ая, -ое, -ие) *прил* missing.

недостижи́м|ый (-, -а, -о) *прил* (*высота́, у́ровень*) unreachable; (*мечта́, идеа́л*) unattainable.

недостове́р|ный (-ен, -на, -но) *прил* unreliable.

недосто́й|ный (-ен, -йна, -йно) *прил*: **~** (+*gen*) unworthy (of).

недосту́п|ный (-ен, -на, -но) *прил* (также *перен*) inaccessible; (*цена*) unaffordable; (*человек*) unapproachable; **э́то ~но моему́ понима́нию** it is beyond my understanding.

недосу́г *как сказ*: **ему́ ~** (+*infin* ...) (*разг*) he can never find the time (to ...).

недосчита́|ться (-юсь; *impf* **недосчи́тываться**) *сов возв* (+*gen*) to be short; **я ~лся пяти́ до́лларов** I'm five dollars short; **мы ~ли́сь двух челове́к** we are missing two people.

недосыпа́|ть (-ю) *несов от* **недоспа́ть**.

недосяга́ем|ый (-, -а, -о) *прил* unattainable.

недотро́г|а (-и) *м/ж* (*разг*): **он тако́й ~** he's very touchy.

недоумева́|ть (-ю) *несов неперех* to be perplexed *или* bewildered.

недоумева́ющий (-ая, -ее, -ие) *прил* perplexed, bewildered.

недоуме́ни|е (-я) *ср* perplexity, bewilderment.

недоуме́нный *прил* perplexed, bewildered.

недоу́ч|ка (-ки; *gen pl* -ек) *м/ж* (*разг*): **он/она́ ~** he/she is badly educated.

недочёт (-а) *м* (*в подсчётах*) shortfall; (*обычно мн*: *в работе*) deficiency.

не́др|а (-) *мн* depths *мн*; **в ~х земли́** in the bowels of the earth; **в ~х души́** in the depths of one's soul; **в ~х о́бщества** at the heart of society.

недре́млющий (-ая, -ее, -ие) *прил* vigilant.

не́друг (-а) *м* foe.

недружелю́б|ный (-ен, -на, -но) *прил* unfriendly.

неду́г (-а) *м* ailment.

неду́рно *нареч* not badly.

недур|но́й (-ён, -на́, -но́) *прил* not bad; **он ~ён собо́й** he's not bad-looking.

неё *мест см* **она́**.

неесте́ствен|ный (-, -на, -но) *прил* unnatural.

нежда́н|ный (-ен, -на, -но) *прил* unexpected.

нежела́ни|е (-я) *ср* unwillingness.

нежела́тел|ьный (-ен, -ьна, -ьно) *прил* undesirable.

не́жен *прил см* **не́жный**.

нежена́т|ый *прил* unmarried.

не́жен|ка (-ки; *gen pl* -ок) *м/ж* (*разг*) softy.

неживо́й *прил* dead; (*природа, мир*) inorganic; (*перен*: *взгляд, голос*) lifeless.

нежизнеспосо́б|ный (-ен, -на, -но) *прил* (*организм, растение*) incapable of surviving; (*перен*: *теория*) impractical.

нежило́й *прил* nonresidential.

не́ж|иться (-усь, -ишься) *несов возв* to laze about; **~** (*impf*) **на со́лнце** to bask in the sun.

нежнича́|ть (-ю) *несов неперех* (*разг*): **~ с** +*instr* to make a fuss of.

не́жност|ь (-и) *ж* tenderness; **шепта́ть** (*impf*) **~и кому́-н на́ ухо** to whisper sweet nothings in sb's ear.

не́жно *нареч* gently.

не́ж|ный (-ен, -на́, -но) *прил* tender, gentle;

(*кожа, пух*) soft; (*запах*) subtle; (*сложение, здоровье*) fragile.

незабве́н|ный (-ен, -на, -но) *прил* beloved.

незабу́д|ка (-ки; *gen pl* -ок) *ж* forget-me-not.

незабыва́ем|ый (-, -а, -о) *прил* unforgettable.

незави́д|ный (-ен, -на, -но) *прил* unenviable.

незави́симо *нареч* independently; **~ от** +*gen* (*условий, времени*) regardless of.

незави́симост|ь (-и) *ж* independence.

незави́сим|ый (-, -а, -о) *прил* independent.

независя́щий (-ая, -ее, -ие) *прил*: **по ~им от нас обстоя́тельствам** due to circumstances beyond our control.

незада́ч|а (-и) *ж* (*разг*) pain.

незада́чливый (-, -а, -о) *прил* (*разг*) unlucky.

незадо́лго *нареч*: **~ до** +*gen или* **пе́ред** +*instr* shortly before.

незаинтересо́ван|ный (-, -на, -но) *прил* (*ученик, слушатели итп*) indifferent; (*лицо, сторона*) disinterested.

незако́нност|ь (-и) *ж* illegality.

незако́н|ный (-ен, -на, -но) *прил* illegal; (*ребёнок*) illegitimate.

незако́нчен|ный (-, -на, -но) *прил* unfinished, incomplete.

незамедли́тел|ьный (-ен, -ьна, -ьно) *прил* immediate.

незамени́м|ый (-, -а, -о) *прил* irreplaceable.

незаме́тен *прил см* **незаме́тный**.

незаме́тно *нареч* (*изменяться*) imperceptibly
♦ *как сказ* it isn't noticeable; **он ~ подошёл/ушёл** he approached/left unnoticed; **~, что ты всю ночь не спал** you may not have slept all night, but it doesn't show.

незаме́т|ный (-ен, -на, -но) *прил* not noticeable; (*перемены, изменения*) imperceptible; (*перен*: *человек, внешность*) unremarkable.

незаме́чен|ный (-, -на, -но) *прил* unnoticed.

незаму́жняя *прил* unmarried.

незамыслова́т|ый (-, -а, -о) *прил* uncomplicated.

неза́нят|ый *прил* (*дом, помещение*) unoccupied; (*человек, работник*) not occupied; (*вечер, утро*) free; **~ая часть населе́ния** the non-working population.

незапа́мят|ный *прил*: **с ~ых времён** from time immemorial; **в ~ые времена́** in the days of yore.

незара́з|ный (-ен, -на, -но) *прил* noncontagious.

незаслу́жен|ный (-, -на, -но) *прил* undeserved.

незауря́д|ный (-ен, -на, -но) *прил* exceptional.

не́зачем *как сказ* (*разг*): **~ ходи́ть/э́то де́лать** there's no reason to go/do it.

незва́ный *прил* uninvited.

нездоро́в|иться (*3sg* -ится) *несов безл*: **мне ~ится** I feel unwell, I don't feel well.

нездоро́в|ый (-, -а, -о) *прил* unhealthy; **он нездоро́в** he isn't well; **у него́ ~ цвет лица́** his face is an unhealthy colour; **у неё ~ вид** she doesn't look well.

неземно́й *прил* (*тело, объект итп*) alien;

(*силы, красота*) unearthly.
незнако́м|ец (**-ца**) *м* stranger.
незнако́м|ка (**-ки**; *gen pl* **-ок**) *ж см* **незнако́мец**.
незнако́мца *итп сущ см* **незнако́мец**.
незнако́м|ый (**-**, **-а**, **-о**) *прил* unfamiliar; **я незнако́м с ним** I am not acquainted with him; **я незнако́м с э́тими фа́ктами** I am not familiar with these facts.
незна́ни|е (**-я**) *ср* ignorance.
незнача́щий (**-ая**, **-ее**, **-ие**) *прил* meaningless.
незначи́тел|ьный (**-ен**, **-ьна**, **-ьно**) *прил* (*небольшой*) insignificant; (*несущественный*) trivial.
незре́л|ый (**-**, **-а**, **-о**) *прил* (*яблоко итп*) unripe; (*человек, книга*) immature; (*мысль*) half-formed.
незри́м|ый (**-**, **-а**, **-о**) *прил* anonymous; (*бой*) hidden.
незы́блем|ый (**-**, **-а**, **-о**) *прил* unshakable.
неизбе́жен *прил см* **неизбе́жный**.
неизбе́жно *как сказ:* **э́то ~** it's inevitable.
неизбе́ж|ный (**-ен**, **-на**, **-но**) *прил* inescapable, inevitable.
неизве́дан|ный (**-**, **-на**, **-но**) *прил* (*путь, пространство*) unexplored; (*счастье, чувство*) new.
неизве́стен *прил см* **неизве́стный**.
неизве́стно *как сказ* it's not known; **никому́ ~** nobody knows; **~ кто/что/почему́** Heaven (only) knows who/what/why.
неизве́стн|ое (**-ого**; *decl like adj*) *ср* (*МАТ*) unknown.
неизве́стность (**-и**) *ж* uncertainty; (*незаметное существование*) obscurity.
неизве́ст|ный (**-ен**, **-на**, **-но**) *прил* unknown ♦ (**-ного**; *decl like adj*) *м* stranger.
неизглади́м|ый (**-**, **-а**, **-о**) *прил* indelible.
неизлечи́м|ый (**-**, **-а**, **-о**) *прил* (*болезнь*) incurable; (*больной*) terminally ill.
неизме́н|ный (**-ен**, **-на**, **-но**) *прил* (*постоянный*) unchanging; (*верный*) steadfast.
неизменя́ем|ый (**-**, **-а**, **-о**) *прил* invariable.
неизмери́мо *нареч* immeasurably.
неизмери́м|ый (**-**, **-а**, **-о**) *прил* immeasurable.
неизу́ченный *прил* (*вопрос, проблема*) unexplored.
неиме́ни|е (**-я**) *ср:* **за ~м** +*gen* for want of; **за ~м лу́чшего** for want of something better.
неиме́рный (**-ен**, **-на**, **-но**) *прил* extreme.
неиму́щий (**-ая**, **-ее**, **-ие**) *прил* deprived.
неинтере́с|ный (**-ен**, **-на**, **-но**) *прил* boring, uninteresting; (*некрасивый*) plain.
неискорени́м|ый (**-**, **-а**, **-о**) *прил* deep-rooted.
неи́скрен|ний (**-няя**, **-нее**, **-ние**; **-ен**, **-на**, **-но** *или* **не**) *прил* insincere.
неискушённый *прил* unsophisticated.
неисполне́ни|е (**-я**) *ср* failure to carry out.
неисполни́м|ый (**-**, **-а**, **-о**) *прил* unrealizable.

неиспо́льзованный *прил* unused.
неиспо́рченный *прил* (*человек*) innocent.
неиспра́вен *прил см* **неиспра́вный**.
неисправи́м|ый (**-**, **-а**, **-о**) *прил* (*ошибка*) irreversible; (*пьяница*) incorrigible.
неиспра́вность (**-и**) *ж* (*механизма, станка*) fault.
неиспра́в|ный (**-ен**, **-на**, **-но**) *прил* (*механизм, станок*) faulty; (*плательщик, поставщик*) unreliable.
неиспы́танный *прил* (*самолёт, машина*) untested; (*чувство, счастье*) unexperienced.
неиссле́дованный *прил* (*вопрос, район*) unexplored.
неиссяка́ем|ый (**-**, **-а**, **-о**) *прил* inexhaustible.
нейстовств|о (**-а**) *ср* (*исступление*) frenzy; (*жестокость*) atrocity; **приходи́ть (прийти́** *perf*) **в ~** to go into a frenzy.
нейстовств|овать (**-ую**) *несов неперех* to be in a frenzy; (*перен: буря, метель*) to rage; (: *каратели*) to commit atrocities.
нейстов|ый (**-**, **-а**, **-о**) *прил* (*ужас, радость*) intense; (*крики*) frenzied; (*аплодисменты, буря*) wild; (*грохот*) crashing.
неистощи́м|ый (**-**, **-а**, **-о**) *прил* inexhaustible.
неисчерпа́ем|ый (**-**, **-а**, **-о**) *прил* inexhaustible.
неисчисли́м|ый (**-**, **-а**, **-о**) *прил* (*силы*) countless; (*неприятности*) innumerable.
ней *мест см* **она́**.
нейло́н (**-а**) *м* nylon.
нейло́новый *прил* nylon *опред*.
нейрохиру́рг (**-а**) *м* neurosurgeon.
нейрохирурги́|я (**-и**) *ж* neurosurgery.
нейтра́лен *прил см* **нейтра́льный**.
нейтрализа́ци|я (**-и**) *ж* neutrality.
нейтрализ|ова́ть (**-ую**) (*не*)*сов перех* to neutralize.
нейтралите́т (**-а**) *м* neutrality.
нейтра́л|ьный (**-ен**, **-ьна**, **-ьно**) *прил* neutral.
нейтро́н (**-а**) *м* neutron.
неказ|и́стый (**-**, **-а**, **-о**) *прил* unsightly.
нека́чественно *нареч:* **~ сде́ланный** badly made.
нека́чествен|ный (**-ен**, **-на**, **-но**) *прил* poor-quality.
неквалифици́рован|ный (**-**, **-на**, **-но**) *прил* (*работник*) unqualified, unskilled; (*работа*) unskilled.
не́кем *мест см* **не́кого**.
не́к|ий (**-ого**; *f* **-ая**, *nt* **-ое**, *pl* **-ие**) *мест* a certain; (*момент, время*) some.
не́когда *как сказ* (*читать, гулять*) there is no time; **ей ~** she is busy; **ей ~** +*infin* ... she has no time to ....
не́к|ого (*как кто; см* **Table 6**) *мест:* **~ спроси́ть/позва́ть** there is nobody to ask/call.
некомпете́нт|ный (**-ен**, **-на**, **-но**) *прил* (*человек*) incompetent; (*суждение*)

inappropriate.

не́кому *мест см* **не́кого.**

не́которые (**-ых**) *мест* (*отдельные*) several.

не́который (**-ого**; *f* **-ая**, *nt* **-ое**, *pl* **-ые**) *мест* some; **с ~ых пор** for some time; **в ~ой сте́пени** to a certain degree; **в ~ом ро́де** somewhat; **~ым о́бразом** somehow; *см также* **не́которые.**

некраси́вый (**-**, **-а**, **-о**) *прил* (*человек, лицо*) unattractive, ugly; (*поступок, поведение*) ugly.

некроло́г (**-а**) *м* obituary.

некста́ти *нареч* (*сказать, явиться итп*) at the wrong time ♦ *как сказ*: **э́то ~** this is untimely.

некта́р (**-а**) *м* nectar.

не́кто *мест* a certain person (*мн* certain people).

не́куда *как сказ* (*идти, поехать*) there is nowhere; **да́льше** *или* **хуже́/лу́чше ~** (*разг*) it can't get any worse/better.

некульту́рный (**-ен**, **-на**, **-но**) *прил* (*растение*) uncultivated; (*человек, поведение*) uncivilized.

некуря́щий (**-его**; *decl like adj*) *м* non-smoker; ♦ (**-ая**, **-ее**, **-ие**) *прил*: **~ мужчи́на, некуря́щая же́нщина** non-smoker.

нела́дно *как сказ* (*в семье, на душе*) there's unease.

нела́ды (**-ов**) *мн* (*разг: в семье, в коллективе*) tension *ед*; (: *с учёбой, с работой*) problems *мн*.

нелега́льный (**-ен**, **-ьна**, **-ьно**) *прил* (*газета, въезд*) illegal.

нелегити́мный (**-ен**, **-на**, **-но**) *прил* illegitimate.

нелёгкий (**-кая**, **-кое**, **-кие**; **-ок**, **-ка́**, **-ко́**) *прил* (*ноша, груз*) heavy; (*задание, работа*) difficult.

нелегко́ *как сказ* it's not easy; **мне нелегко́ согласи́ться на э́то** it's not easy for me to agree to this.

неле́пость (**-и**) *ж* stupidity; **говори́ть** (*impf*)/ **де́лать** (*impf*) **~и** to say/do stupid things.

неле́пый (**-**, **-а**, **-о**) *прил* stupid.

неле́стный (**-ен**, **-на**, **-но**) *прил* (*высказывание, характеристика*) unflattering.

нелётный *прил*: **~ая пого́да** poor weather for flying; **~ое вре́мя** not a good time to fly.

нело́вкий (**-кая**, **-кое**, **-кие**; **-ок**, **-ка́**, **-ко**) *прил* awkward; **нело́вкое положе́ние** awkward situation.

нело́вко *нареч* awkwardly ♦ *как сказ* (*говорить, просить*) it's awkward; **мне ~ (пе́ред ней)** I feel awkward (with her).

нело́вкость (**-и**) *ж* awkwardness; **чу́вствовать** (**почу́вствовать** *perf*) **~** to feel awkward.

нело́вок *прил см* **нело́вкий.**

нелоги́чный (**-ен**, **-на**, **-но**) *прил* (*довод, доказательство*) illogical.

нельзя́ *как сказ* (*невозможно*) it is impossible; (*не разрешается*) it is forbidden; **~ ли?** would it be possible?; **~ сказа́ть, что она́ умна́** she can hardly be described as clever; **как ~ лу́чше** as well as could be expected.

нелюби́мый (**-**, **-а**, **-о**) *прил* unloved.

нелюди́мый (**-**, **-а**, **-о**) *прил* (*человек, сосед*) unsociable.

нём *мест см* **он, оно́.**

нема́ло *нареч* (+*gen*; *денег*) a good deal of; (*идей, люде́й, книг*) a good few.

немалова́жный (**-ен**, **-на**, **-но**) *прил* significant.

нема́лый *прил* (*доход*) reasonable; (*труд*) much; (*успех*) considerable; (*чин, должность*) important; **~ые де́ньги** a sizeable sum of money.

неме́дленен *прил см* **неме́дленный.**

неме́дленно *нареч* immediately.

неме́дленный (**-ен**, **-на**, **-но**) *прил* immediate.

неме́ркнущий (**-ая**, **-ее**, **-ие**) *прил* (*также перен*) unfading.

немета́лл (**-а**) *м* (*хим*) nonmetal.

неме́ть (**-ю**; *perf* **онеме́ть**) *несов неперех* (*от ужаса, от восторга*) to be struck dumb; (*нога, руки*) to go numb.

не́мец (**-ца**) *м* German.

неме́цкий (**-ая**, **-ое**, **-ие**) *прил* German; **~ язы́к** German.

немило́сть (**-и**) *ж* disfavour; **впада́ть** (**впасть** *perf*) **в ~** to fall out of favour (*BRIT*) *или* favor (*US*).

неминуе́мый (**-**, **-а**, **-о**) *прил* (*беда, события*) unavoidable.

не́мка (**-ки**; *gen pl* **-ок**) *ж см* **не́мец.**

немно́гие (**-их**; *decl like adj*) *мн* few.

немно́гий (**-ая**, **-ое**, **-ие**) *прил* (*части, слова, люди*) a few; **~им ху́же/лу́чше/бо́льше/ме́ньше** a little worse/better/more/less; **за ~им исключе́нием** with few exceptions.

немно́го *нареч* (*отдохну́ть, ста́рше*) a little, a bit; (*друзе́й, слов*) a few.

немно́гое (**-ого**; *decl like adj*) *ср* (*можно сказа́ть, уви́деть*) little.

немногосло́вный (**-ен**, **-на**, **-но**) *прил* (*отзыв, изложе́ние*) brief; (*человек*) laconic.

немногочи́сленный (**-**, **-на**, **-но**) *прил* (*ошибки*) few; **на дипломати́ческом приёме бы́ло ~ное о́бщество** there weren't many (people present) at the diplomatic reception.

немно́жко *нареч* (*разг*) = **немно́го.**

немну́щийся (**-аяся**, **-ееся**, **-иеся**) *прил* (*брюки, мате́рия, ю́бка*) crease-resistant.

немо́й (**-**, **-а́**, **-о**) *прил* (*человек*) dumb; (*перен: ночь, лес, глубина́*) silent; (: *вопро́с, упрёк*) implied ♦ (**-о́го**; *decl like adj*) *м* mute; **нема́я сце́на** situation in which somebody freezes in surprise, shock etc; **немо́й фильм** silent film.

немолодо́й (**-о́лод**, **-олода́**, **-о́лодо**) *прил* old.

немота́ (**-ы́**) *ж* (*ребёнка, мужчи́ны*) dumbness.

немо́щный (**-ен**, **-на**, **-но**) *прил* (*стари́к, человек*) sick, ailing.

нему́ *мест от* **он, оно́.**

немудрёный (**-**, **-а**, **-о**) *прил* (*разг*) simple.

не́мца *итп сущ см* **не́мец.**

немы́слимый (**-**, **-а**, **-о**) *прил* unthinkable.

ненави́деть (**-жу**, **-дишь**) *несов перех* to hate.

ненави́стный (**-ен**, **-на**, **-но**) *прил* (*человек, работа*) hateful.

не́нависть (-и) ж hatred.
ненагля́дный *прил* (*разг*) beloved.
ненадёж|ный (-ен, -на, -но) *прил* (*человек, сведения*) unreliable; (*механизм*) unsafe.
ненадобность (-и) ж: **вы́бросить что-н за** ~**ю** to throw sth out *или* away because it is not needed.
ненадо́лго *нареч* for a short while.
ненападе́ни|е (-я) *ср* nonaggression.
ненаро́ком *нареч* (*разг: случайно*) without meaning to.
ненас́т|ный (-ен, -на, -но) *прил* (*день, осень*) wet and dismal.
ненастоя́щий (-ая, -ее, -ие) *прил* (*мех, золото*) artificial; (*дружба, любовь*) contrived.
ненасть|е (-я) *ср* awful weather.
ненасы́т|ный (-ен, -на, -но) *прил* (*также перен*) insatiable.
ненатура́л|ьный (-ен, -ьна, -ьно) *прил* (*мех, свет*) artificial; (*смех*) forced; (*поведение*) affected.
ненорма́лен *прил см* **ненорма́льный**.
ненорма́льность (-и) ж abnormality.
ненорма́л|ьный (-ен, -ьна, -ьно) *прил* abnormal; (*разг: сумасшедший*) mad ♦ (-ьного; *decl like adj*) *м* (*разг*) crackpot.
нену́ж|ный (-ен, -на́, -но) *прил* (*осторожность*) unnecessary; (*человек*) dispensable; (*инструмент*) inessential.
необду́манно *нареч* (*поступить*) rashly.
необду́ман|ный (-, -на, -но) *прил* ill-considered.
необеспе́ченный *прил* poor.
необита́ем|ый (-, -а, -о) *прил* (*место*) uninhabited; ~ **о́стров** desert island.
необозри́м|ый (-, -а, -о) *прил* (*просторы, дали*) vast.
необосно́ван|ный (-, -на, -но) *прил* unfounded.
необрабо́танный *прил* (*земля*) uncultivated; (*деталь*) unfinished; (*металл, дерево*) untreated.
необразо́ван|ный (-, -на, -но) *прил* uneducated.
необу́здан|ный (-, -на, -но) *прил* (*страсть*) unbridled; (*человек, характер*) ungovernable.
необходи́мо *как сказ* it is necessary; **мне** ~ **с Ва́ми поговори́ть** I really need to talk to you.
необходи́мость (-и) *ж* (*увидеть, сделать*) need, necessity; ~ **в** +*prp* need for; **по ме́ре** ~**и** as (far as is) necessary; **по** ~**и** out of necessity; **предме́ты пе́рвой** ~**и** bare essentials.
необходи́м|ый (-, -а, -о) *прил* necessary.
необщи́тел|ьный (-ен, -ьна, -ьно) *прил* unsociable.
необъекти́в|ный (-ен, -на, -но) *прил* (*отношение, критика*) not objective, bias(s)ed.
необъясни́м|ый (-, -а, -о) *прил* inexplicable.

необъя́т|ный (-ен, -на, -но) *прил* (*просторы, дали, познания*) vast.
необыкнове́н|ный (-ен, -на, -но) *прил* exceptional.
необыча́й|ный (-ен, -йна, -йно) *прил* = **необыкнове́нный**.
необы́ч|ный (-ен, -на, -но) *прил* (*человек, явление*) unusual.
необяза́тел|ьный (-ен, -ьна, -ьно) *прил* (*предмет, лекция*) optional; (*факты*) nonessential; (*человек*) unreliable.
неограни́чен|ный (-, -на, -но) *прил* unlimited; **неограни́ченная мона́рхия** absolute monarchy.
неодина́ков|ый (-, -а, -о) *прил* (*размер*) different.
неоднокра́тен *прил см* **неоднокра́тный**.
неоднокра́тно *нареч* (*говорить*) repeatedly; (*повторять*) time after time.
неоднокра́т|ный (-ен, -на, -но) *прил* repeated.
неодноро́д|ный (-ен, -на, -но) *прил* (*масса*) heterogeneous; (*тесто*) mixed; (*явления*) dissimilar.
неодобре́ни|е (-я) *ср* disapproval.
неодобри́тел|ьный (-ен, -ьна, -ьно) *прил* disapproving.
неодоли́м|ый (-, -а, -о) *прил* (*упорство, страх*) insurmountable; (*сила*) invincible.
неодушевлённый *прил* inanimate.
неожи́данно *нареч* unexpectedly.
неожи́данность (-и) ж (*атаки*) unexpectedness; (*приятная, большая*) surprise; **вздра́гивать** (**вздро́гнуть** *perf*) **от** ~**и** to start in surprise.
неожи́дан|ный (-, -на, -но) *прил* unexpected.
неоконча́тел|ьный (-ен, -ьна, -ьно) *прил* (*вариант, решение*) not final.
неоко́нченный *прил* unfinished.
неоли́т (-а) *м* Neolithic.
неологи́зм (-а) *м* neologism.
нео́н (-а) *м* (*хим*) neon.
неонаци́зм (-а) *м* Neo-Nazism.
нео́новый *прил* neon *опред*.
неопа́сен *прил см* **неопа́сный**.
неопа́сно *нареч* safely ♦ *как сказ* it's safe, it's not dangerous.
неопа́с|ный (-ен, -на, -но) *прил* (*путешествие, место*) safe; (*противник, заболевание*) harmless.
неописуем|ый (-, -а, -о) *прил* indescribable.
неопла́т|ный (-ен, -на, -но) *прил*: ~ **долг** debt that cannot be repaid; **я твой** ~ **должни́к** I'm greatly indebted to you.
неопла́ченный *прил* unpaid.
неопо́знан|ный (-, -на, -но) *прил* unidentified.
неопра́вданный *прил* (*вывод, обвинение*) unjustified; (*траты, потери*) unwarranted.
неопределённость (-и) ж uncertainty.

неопределён|ный (-, -на, -но) *прил* (*время, срок*) indefinite; (*путь*) undecided; (*ответ, выражение, жест*) vague; (*звук*) indistinct.
неопровержи́м|ый (-, -а, -о) *прил* irrefutable.
неопря́т|ный (-ен, -на, -но) *прил* untidy.
неопублико́ванный *прил* unpublished.
нео́пытен *прил см* **нео́пытный**.
нео́пытност|ь (-и) *ж* inexperience.
нео́пыт|ный (-ен, -на, -но) *прил* inexperienced.
неорганизо́ванный *прил* disorganized; (*массы*) unorganized.
неоргани́ческий (-ая, -ое, -ие) *прил* inorganic.
неосведомлённый *прил* ill-informed.
неосла́б|ный (-ен, -на, -но) *прил* (*надзор*) constant; (*контроль*) unrelenting.
неосмотри́тел|ьный (-ен, -ьна, -ьно) *прил* (*человек*) careless; (*поступок*) imprudent.
неоспори́м|ый (-, -а, -о) *прил* (*преимущество*) unquestionable; (*доказательство*) incontrovertible.
неосторо́жен *прил см* **неосторо́жный**.
неосторо́жност|ь (-и) *ж* carelessness.
неосторо́ж|ный (-ен, -на, -но) *прил* (*поступок*) careless; (*поведение, высказывание*) imprudent.
неосуществи́м|ый (-, -а, -о) *прил* unrealizable, unattainable.
неотврати́м|ый (-, -а, -о) *прил* inevitable.
неотдели́м|ый (-, -а, -о) *прил*: ~ (**от** +*gen*) inseparable (from).
неотёсан|ный (-, -а, -о) *прил* unpolished; (*перен: разг*) crude.
не́откуда *как сказ*: мне *итп* де́нег взять ~ I *итп* can't get money from anywhere.
неотло́жен *прил см* **неотло́жный**.
неотло́жк|а (-и) *ж* (*разг: учреждение*) ambulance service; (: *машина*) emergency medical care.
неотло́ж|ный (-ен, -на, -но) *прил* urgent; **неотло́жная медици́нская по́мощь** emergency medical service.
неотрази́м|ый (-, -а, -о) *прил* (*атака, красота*) irresistible; (*перен: довод*) compelling; (*удар, впечатление*) powerful.
неотсту́п|ный (-ен, -на, -но) *прил* (*мечта, мысль*) constant; (*преследование*) relentless.
неотъе́млем|ый (-, -а, -о) *прил* (*право*) inalienable; (*часть*) integral.
неофаши́зм (-а) *м* Neo-fascism.
неофаши́ст (-а) *м* Neo-fascist.
неофаши́стск|ий (-ая, -ое, -ие) *прил* Neo-fascist.
неофициа́л|ьный (-ен, -ьна, -ьно) *прил* unofficial.
неохо́т|а (-ы) *ж* (*разг: нежелание*) reluctance ◆ *как сказ*: мне ~ спо́рить I don't feel like arguing.
неохо́тно *нареч* reluctantly.
неохо́тный *прил* reluctant.
неоцени́м|ый (-, -а, -о) *прил* invaluable.
неощути́м|ый (-, -а, -о) *прил* (*незаметный*) imperceptible.
Непа́л (-а) *м* Nepal.
непа́льск|ий (-ая, -ое, -ие) *прил* Nepalese.
непа́рный *прил* (*перчатки, ботинки*) odd.
непереводи́м|ый (-, -а, -о) *прил* untranslatable.
непередава́ем|ый (-, -а, -о) *прил* (*страх, впечатление*) inexpressible.
непереходный *прил*: ~ **глаго́л** (*линг*) intransitive verb.
непеча́тный *прил* (*разг*) unprintable.
непи́саный *прил* unwritten.
неплатёж (-ежа́) *м* nonpayment.
неплатёжеспосо́б|ный (-ен, -на, -но) *прил* (*человек*) unable to pay; (*предприятие*) insolvent.
неплате́льщик (-а) *м* (*налогов, алиментов*) defaulter.
неплате́льщиц|а (-ы) *ж см* **неплате́льщик**.
неплодоро́д|ный (-ен, -на, -но) *прил* infertile, barren.
непло́тно *нареч* not tightly *или* firmly.
непло́хо *нареч* not badly, quite well ◆ *как сказ* it's not bad.
непло́х|ой (-о́х, -оха́, -о́хо) *прил* not bad, quite good.
непобеди́м|ый (-, -а, -о) *прил* invincible.
неповинове́ни|е (-я) *ср* disobedience, insubordination.
неповоро́тлив|ый (-, -а, -о) *прил* (*неуклюжий*) clumsy; (*медлительный*) slow.
неповтори́м|ый (-, -а, -о) *прил* unique.
непого́д|а (-ы) *ж* bad weather.
непогреши́м|ый (-, -а, -о) *прил* infallible.
неподалёку *нареч* (*разг*) not far off ◆ *предл*: ~ **от** +*gen* not far from.
неподви́жен *прил см* **неподви́жный**.
неподви́жно *нареч* without moving.
неподви́ж|ный (-ен, -на, -но) *прил* (*больной, рука, туман*) motionless; (*взгляд*) fixed; (*лицо*) rigid; (*медлительный*) slow.
неподда́|ющийся (-ается, -еется, -ется) *прил* (*разг: перевоспитанию, лечению*) resistant, unresponsive.
неподде́л|ьный (-ен, -ьна, -ьно) *прил* (*также перен*) genuine.
неподку́п|ный (-ен, -на, -но) *прил* (*человек, ревизор*) incorruptible; (*совесть, принципы*) honourable (*BRIT*), honorable (*US*).
неподража́ем|ый (-, -а, -о) *прил* inimitable.
неподходя́щий (-ая, -ее, -ие) *прил* (*место*) unsuitable; (*время*) inappropriate.
неподчине́ни|е (-я) *ср* (*закону, властям*) insubordination.
неподъём|ный (-ен, -на, -но) *прил* (*разг*) very heavy.
непозволи́тел|ьный (-ен, -ьна, -ьно) *прил* inadmissible.
непоколеби́м|ый (-, -а, -о) *прил* unshakable.
непоко́р|ный (-ен, -на, -но) *прил* (*конь, слуга*) recalcitrant; (*характер, нрав*) rebellious.
непокры́т|ый *прил*: **с** ~**ой голово́й**

непола́дки (-ок) *мн* fault *ед*, defect *ед*; (*разг: в семье*) quarrel *ед*.

неполноправ|ный (-ен, -на, -но) *прил* not possessing full rights.

неполнота́ (-ы́) *ж* incompleteness.

неполноце́нность (-и) *ж* lack; **ко́мплекс ~и** inferiority complex.

неполноце́н|ный (-ен, -на, -но) *прил* insufficient.

непо́л|ный (-он, -на́, -но) *прил* (*чашка, мешок*) not full; (*список, перечень, данные*) incomplete.

непоме́р|ный (-ен, -на, -но) *прил* excessive.

непонима́ни|е (-я) *ср* (*задачи, происходящее*) incomprehension; (*равнодушие*) indifference.

непоня́тен *прил см* **непоня́тный**.

непоня́тлив|ый (-, -а, -о) *прил* (*ученик, студент*) slow on the uptake, dull.

непоня́тно *нареч* incomprehensibly ♦ *как сказ* it is incomprehensible; **мне ~, что происхо́дит** I cannot understand what is going on.

непоня́тный (-ен, -на, -но) *прил* incomprehensible.

непоправи́м|ый (-, -а, -о) *прил* (*ошибка*) irreparable; (*шаг, несчастье*) irreversible.

непоро́ч|ный (-ен, -на, -но) *прил* pure, chaste.

непоря́д|ок (-ка; *nom pl* -ки) *м* disorder.

непоря́доч|ный (-ен, -на, -но) *прил* (*человек, поведение*) dishonourable (*BRIT*), dishonorable (*US*).

непосе́да (-ы) *м/ж* (*разг*) fidget.

непосе́длив|ый (-, -а, -о) *прил* restless.

непоси́льный (-ен, -ьна, -ьно) *прил* (*труд, задача*) beyond one's strength.

непосле́довательность (-и) *ж* inconsistency.

непосле́довательный (-ен, -ьна, -ьно) *прил* inconsistent.

непослуша́ни|е (-я) *ср* (*детей, подчинённых*) disobedience.

непослу́ш|ный (-ен, -на, -но) *прил* (*ребёнок, собака*) disobedient; (*перен: волосы, кудри*) unmanageable.

непосре́дственность (-и) *ж* spontaneity.

непосре́дствен|ный *прил* (*начальник*) immediate; (*результат, свидетель, участник*) direct; (-ен, -на, -но; *натура, тон*) spontaneous.

непостижи́м|ый (-, -а, -о) *прил* (*загадка, сила*) incomprehensible; **уму́ ~о** it's incomprehensible.

непостоя́н|ный (-ен, -на, -но) *прил* changeable.

непостоя́нств|о (-а) *ж* inconstancy, changeability.

непотре́б|ный (-ен, -на, -но) *прил* (*разг*) indecent.

непохо́ж|ий (-ая, -ее, -ие; -, -а, -е) *прил* dissimilar.

непоча́т|ый (-, -а, -о) *прил* (*бутылка, пачка*) unopened; (*чашка кофе*) full, untouched; (*перен: силы*) unused; (: *запас, энергии*)

untapped; **непоча́тый край** no end, a great deal.

непочте́ни|е (-я) *ср* disrespect.

непочти́тельно *нареч* disrespectfully.

непра́в (-á, -о, -ы) *как сказ*: **ты ~** you are wrong.

непра́вд|а (-ы) *ж* lie, untruth ♦ *как сказ* it's not true; **э́то ~!** it's *или* this is a lie!

неправдоподо́б|ный (-ен, -на, -но) *прил* (*история, рассказ*) improbable, implausible.

непра́вилен *прил см* **непра́вильный**.

непра́вильно *нареч* (*решить*) incorrectly, wrongly ♦ *как сказ*: **э́то ~** it's wrong; **~ ду́мать, что ...** it's wrong to think that ...; **~ поня́ть** (*perf*) to misunderstand; **~ написа́ть** (*perf*) to misspell.

непра́вил|ьный (-ен, -ьна, -ьно) *прил* (*решение, произношение, идея*) wrong; (*черты лица, форма*) irregular; **непра́вильная дробь** (*МАТ*) improper fraction.

неправоме́р|ный (-ен, -на, -но) *прил* unjustifiable.

неправомо́ч|ный (-ен, -на, -но) *прил* (*неправомо́чная организа́ция*) *organization without legal authority*.

непревзойдён|ный (-, -на, -но) *прил* (*рекорд, мастерство*) unsurpassed; (*тупость, жестокость*) unprecedented.

непредви́денный *прил* unforeseen.

непреднаме́рен|ный (-, -на, -но) *прил* unpremeditated.

непредсказу́ем|ый (-, -а, -о) *прил* unpredictable.

непредубеждён|ный *прил* unbias(s)ed.

непредусмо́тренный *прил* unforeseen, unanticipated.

непредусмотри́тел|ьный (-ен, -ьна, -ьно) *прил* short-sighted.

непрекло́н|ный (-ен, -на, -но) *прил* (*человек*) unbending; (*противник*) uncompromising; (*воля*) unshakable; (*характер*) strong, firm; (*решение*) firm.

непрекраща́ющийся (-аяся, -ееся, -иеся) *прил* (*дождь*) persistent; (*ссора*) endless; (*стрельба*) continuous.

непрело́ж|ный (-ен, -на, -но) *прил* (*правило, закон*) immutable; **непрело́жная и́стина** unquestionable truth.

непреме́нен *прил см* **непреме́нный**.

непреме́нно *нареч* (*обязательно*) by all means.

непреме́н|ный (-ен, -на, -но) *прил* (*условие*) necessary; (*следствие*) unavoidable; (*деталь, черта*) indispensable.

непреодоли́м|ый (-, -а, -о) *прил* (*препятствие*) insurmountable; (*желание, смущение*) overwhelming.

непререка́ем|ый (-, -а, -о) *прил* (*авторитет*) unquestionable; (*интонация*) peremptory.

непреры́вен *прил см* **непреры́вный**.

непреры́вно *нареч* (*спрашивать, меняться*) uninterruptedly, continuously.

непреры́в|**ный** (**-ен, -на, -но**) *прил* uninterrupted, continuous.

неприве́тлив|**ый** (**-, -а, -о**) *прил* (*человек, тон*) unfriendly; (*перен: лес, место*) bleak.

непривлека́тел|**ьный** (**-ен, -ьна, -ьно**) *прил* unattractive.

непривы́чен *прил см* **непривы́чный**.

непривы́чк|**а** (**-и**) *ж*: **с ~и к физи́ческому труду́ он бы́стро уста́л** (*разг*) not being used to physical work, he got tired quickly.

непривы́чно *как сказ*: **мне ~** +*infin* I'm not used to doing.

непривы́ч|**ный** (**-ен, -на, -но**) *прил* (*мысль*) unusual; (*обстановка*) not the usual; (*человек*) unaccustomed.

непригля́д|**ный** (**-ен, -на, -но**) *прил* (*вид, внешность*) unsightly, unattractive; (*поступок, поведение*) unseemly.

неприго́д|**ный** (**-ен, -на, -но**) *прил* unsuitable.

неприе́млем|**ый** (**-, -а, -о**) *прил* unacceptable.

непри́знанный *прил* (*писатель, художник*) unrecognized, unacknowledged.

неприка́ян|**ный** (**-, -на, -но**) *прил* (*разг*) restless and drifting.

неприкоснове́нность (**-и**) *ж* inviolability; **дипломати́ческая ~** diplomatic immunity.

неприкоснове́н|**ный** (**-ен, -на, -но**) *прил* (*фонд*) reserve *опред*; (*ценность*) inviolable; (*лицо, личность*) protected by law; **неприкоснове́нный запа́с** emergency ration.

неприкра́шенный *прил* (*действительность*) plain, unvarnished; (*вид*) plain.

неприкры́т|**ый** (**-, -а, -о**) *прил* (*дверь*) open; (*отряд, батальон*) open, exposed; (*перен: правда*) plain; (: *ложь*) barefaced, blatant; (: *грубость*) undisguised.

неприли́чен *прил см* **неприли́чный**.

неприли́чи|**е** (**-я**) *ср*: **до ~я** extremely.

неприли́чно *нареч* indecently, improperly.

неприли́ч|**ный** (**-ен, -на, -но**) *прил* (*вид, анекдот, рисунок*) indecent; (*платье*) outrageous.

неприме́т|**ный** (**-ен, -на, -но**) *прил* (*незаметный*) imperceptible; (*непримечательный*) unremarkable.

непримири́м|**ый** (**-, -а, -о**) *прил* (*спорщики, противоречия*) irreconcilable; (*характер*) uncompromising.

непринуждённость (**-и**) *ж* (*беседы*) informality; (*движений*) freeness, casualness.

непринуждён|**ный** (**-, -на, -но**) *прил* informal, relaxed.

неприсоедине́ни|**е** (**-я**) *ср* (*полит*) nonalignment.

непристо́ен *прил см* **непристо́йный**.

непристо́йность (**-и**) *ж* obscenity.

непристо́йный (**-ен, -йна, -йно**) *прил* obscene.

непристу́п|**ный** (**-ен, -на, -но**) *прил* (*крепость*) impregnable; (*высота*) inaccessible; (*человек*) unapproachable; (*характер, вид*) unfriendly.

непритво́р|**ный** (**-ен, -на, -но**) *прил* unfeigned.

непритяза́тел|**ьный** (**-ен, -ьна, -ьно**) *прил* (*читатель, зритель, вкус*) undiscriminating; (*острота, стихи*) unsubtle.

неприхотли́в|**ый** (**-, -а, -о**) *прил* (*человек, студент*) unpretentious; (*вкус, требования*) modest; (*растение, цветок*) undemanding; (*простой: пища*) frugal; (: *рисунок*) simple.

неприя́знен|**ный** (**-ен, -на, -но**) *прил* hostile.

неприя́знь (**-и**) *ж* hostility.

неприя́тел|**ь** (**-я**) *м собир* the enemy.

неприя́тен *прил см* **неприя́тный**.

неприя́ти|**е** (**-я**) *ср* rejection.

неприя́тно *как сказ*: **~** +*infin* (*думать, слушать*) it's unpleasant *или* disagreeable to do; **мне ~ говори́ть об э́том** I don't enjoy talking about it.

неприя́тность (**-и**) *ж* (*обычно мн: на работе, в семье*) trouble.

неприя́т|**ный** (**-ен, -на, -но**) *прил* unpleasant, disagreeable.

непробива́ем|**ый** (**-, -а, -о**) *прил* (*броня, борт*) impregnable; (*перен: спокойствие*) imperturbable; (: *разг: дурак*) utter.

непробу́д|**ный** (**-ен, -на, -но**) *прил* (*пьяница*) inveterate; **~ сон** deep sleep; **~ное пья́нство** drunken stupor.

непроводни́к (**-а́**) *м* (*физ*) nonconductor, dielectric.

непрогля́д|**ный** (**-ен, -на, -но**) *прил* (*ночь*) pitch-dark; (*тьма*) impenetrable.

непродолжи́тельный (**-ен, -ьна, -ьно**) *прил* short.

непродукти́в|**ный** (**-ен, -на, -но**) *прил* unproductive.

непроду́манный *прил* ill-considered.

непрое́зж|**ий** (**-ая, -ее, -ие**) *прил* impassable.

непрозра́ч|**ный** (**-ен, -на, -но**) *прил* opaque.

непроизводи́тел|**ьный** (**-ен, -ьна, -ьно**) *прил* (*труд*) unproductive; (*расходы*) wasteful.

непроизво́л|**ьный** (**-ен, -ьна, -ьно**) *прил* involuntary.

непрола́з|**ный** (**-ен, -на, -но**) *прил* (*разг*) impassable.

непромока́ем|**ый** (**-, -а, -о**) *прил* (*куртка, сапоги*) waterproof.

непроница́ем|**ый** (**-, -а, -о**) *прил* (*мрак, туман*) impenetrable; (*перен: вид, лицо*) inscrutable; **~ для** +*gen* impervious to.

непропорциона́л|**ьный** (**-ен, -ьна, -ьно**) *прил* disproportionate.

непрости́тел|**ьный** (**-ен, -ьна, -ьно**) *прил* unforgivable, inexcusable.

непроходи́мость (**-и**) *ж* (*мед*) blockage.

непроходи́м|**ый** (**-, -а, -о**) *прил* (*чаща, болото*) impassable; (*no short form; перен: разг: дурак*) utter.

непро́ч|**ный** (**-ен, -на́, -но**) *прил* (*дом*) unstable; (*материал*) flimsy; (*перен: чувства*) questionable; (: *привязанность*) precarious.

непрóшеный *прил* (*разг*) uninvited.

непрямóй *прил* (*путь*) indirect; (*ответ*) evasive.

Непту́н (**-а**) *м* Neptune.

непью́щий (**-ая, -ее, -ие**) *прил* (*человек*) teetotal.

неработоспосóб|ный (**-ен, -на, -но**) *прил* unable to work.

нерабóч|ий (**-ая, -ее, -ие**) *прил*: ~**ее врéмя** time off; ~**ая обстанóвка** atmosphere which is not conducive to work.

нерáвен *прил см* **нерáвный**.

нерáвенств|о (**-а**) *ср* inequality; **знак** ~**а** (*МАТ*) inequality sign.

неравноду́ш|ный (**-ен, -на, -но**) *прил*: ~ (**к** +*dat*) not indifferent (to); **он к ней** ~**ен** he finds her attractive.

неравномéр|ный (**-ен, -на, -но**) *прил* (*развитие, глубина*) uneven; (*движения*) irregular.

неравноправен *прил см* **неравноправный**.

неравноправи|е (**-я**) *ср* inequality (of rights).

неравноправ|ный (**-ен, -на, -но**) *прил* unequal.

нерáв|ный (**-ен, -нá, -но**) *прил* unequal.

нерадúв|ый (**-, -а, -о**) *прил* careless, negligent.

неразберú|х|а (**-и**) *ж* (*разг*) muddle.

неразбóрчив|ый (**-, -а, -о**) *прил* (*буквы, почерк*) illegible; (*читатель, вкус*) undiscriminating; ~ **в срéдствах** unscrupulous.

неразвит|óй (**-, -а, -о**) *прил* undeveloped.

неразгáданный *прил* unsolved.

неразговóрчив|ый (**-, -а, -о**) *прил* taciturn.

нераздéль|ный (**-ен, -ьна, -ьно**) *прил* inseparable, indivisible.

неразличú|м|ый (**-, -а, -о**) *прил* (*схожий*) indistinguishable; (*úздали, в темнотé*) indiscernible.

неразлу́ч|ный (**-ен, -на, -но**) *прил* inseparable.

неразрешённый *прил* (*запрещённый*) prohibited; (*оставшийся неясным*) unsolved.

неразрешú|м|ый (**-, -а, -о**) *прил* insoluble.

неразры́в|ный (**-ен, -на, -но**) *прил* indissoluble.

неразу́м|ный (**-ен, -на, -но**) *прил* (*поведение, поступок*) foolish; (*разг: малыш, ребёнок*) silly.

нераспространéни|е (**-я**) *ср* nonproliferation; ~ **я́дерного ору́жия** nonproliferation of nuclear weapons.

нерассудú|тель|ный (**-ен, -ьна, -ьно**) *прил* lacking (in) common sense.

нерасторжú|м|ый (**-, -а, -о**) *прил* indissoluble.

нерасторóп|ный (**-ен, -на, -но**) *прил* slow, sluggish.

нерасчётлив|ый (**-, -а, -о**) *прил* wasteful.

нерв (**-а**) *м* (*АНАТ*) nerve; **больны́е нéрвы** nervous disorder; **он всем дéйствует на нéрвы** he gets on everyone's nerves; **перестáнь трепáть мне нéрвы!** (*разг*) stop getting on my nerves!

нервú|р|овать (**-ую**) *несов перех* to make nervous.

нéрвнича|ть (**-ю**) *несов неперех* to fret.

нéрвно *нареч* nervously.

нервнобольн|óй (**-óго**; *decl like adj*) *м person suffering from a nervous disorder*.

нéрвный *прил* nervous; (*работа, занятие*) nerve-racking; (*окончания, клéтки*) nerve *опред*; **нéрвная систéма** the nervous system.

нервóзен *прил см* **нервóзный**.

нервóзност|ь (**-и**) *ж* nervousness.

нервóз|ный (**-ен, -на, -но**) *прил* (*человек*) nervous, highly (*BRIT*) *или* high (*US*) strung; (*тон, характер*) nervous; (*обстановка*) nerve-racking.

нервотрёпк|а (**-и**) *ж* (*разг*) hassle.

нереáлен *прил см* **нереáльный**.

нереáльност|ь (**-и**) *ж* (*событий, обстановки*) unreality; (*неосуществимость*) impracticality.

нереáль|ный (**-ен, -ьна, -ьно**) *прил* (*мир, события*) unreal; (*неосуществимый*) impractical.

нерегуля́р|ный (**-ен, -на, -но**) *прил* irregular.

нерéдко *нареч* (*часто*) not infrequently, quite often.

нерентáбелен *прил см* **нерентáбельный**.

нерентáбельност|ь (**-и**) *ж* unprofitability.

нерентáбель|ный (**-ен, -на, -но**) *прил* unprofitable.

нéрест (**-а**) *м* spawning.

нерешú|мост|ь (**-и**) *ж* indecision.

нерешú|телен *прил см* **нерешú|тельный**.

нерешú|тельно *нареч* indecisively.

нерешú|тельност|ь (**-и**) *ж* indecision, indecisiveness; **быть** (*impf*) **в** ~**и** to be undecided.

нерешú|тель|ный (**-ен, -ьна, -ьно**) *прил* indecisive.

нержавé|йк|а (**-йки**; *gen pl* **-ек**) *ж* (*разг*) stainless steel.

нержавé|ющий (**-ая, -ее, -ие**) *прил* (*крыша, бочка*) rustproof; **нержавé|ющая стáль** stainless steel.

нерóвно *нареч* (*порéзать*) unevenly.

нерóвный *прил* (*поверхность, край*) uneven; (*местность*) rough, rugged; (*линия*) crooked; (*пульс*) irregular; (*характер, поведение*) unbalanced.

нéрп|а (**-ы**) *ж* (*ЗООЛ*) seal.

нерушú|мый *прил* (*союз*) indestructible.

неря́х|а (**-и**) *м/ж* (*разг*) scruff.

неря́шлив|ый (**-, -а, -о**) *прил* (*человек, одежда*) scruffy; (*работа*) careless.

несамостоя́тель|ный (**-ен, -ьна, -ьно**) *прил* dependent; **Вáша рабóта** ~**на** this is not all your own work.

несбы́точ|ный (**-ен, -на, -но**) *прил* unrealizable;

~ные ме́чты pipe dreams.
несваре́ни|е (-я) *ср:* ~ желу́дка indigestion.
несве́дущ|ий (-ая, -ее, -ие; -, -а, -е, -и) *прил* ignorant.
несве́ж|ий (-ая, -ее, -ие; -, -а́, -о) *прил* (*руба́шка*) dirty; **о́вощи** ~**ие** the vegetables are not very fresh; **у тебя́** ~ **вид** you look weary.
несвоевре́мен|ный (-ен, -на, -но) *прил* untimely.
несвя́зный *прил* disjointed.
несгиба́емый *прил* staunch.
несгово́рчив|ый (-, -а, -о) *прил* pig-headed.
несгора́емый *прил* fireproof.
несде́ржанност|ь (-и) *ж* fieriness.
несде́ржан|ный (-, -на, -но) *прил* (*хара́ктер, челове́к*) fiery; (*тон, поведе́ние*) passionate.
несдоброва́ть *как сказ:* **ему́** ~ (*разг*) he's in trouble.
несе́ни|е (-я) *ср* (*охра́ны, слу́жбы*) carrying out; (*наказа́ния*) taking.
несери́йный *прил* (*изде́лие*) custom-made.
несерьёз|ный (-ен, -на, -но) *прил* (*челове́к*) frivolous; (*предложе́ние*) flippant; (*боле́знь*) mild; ~**ная ра́на** flesh wound.
несимметри́ч|ный (-ен, -на, -но) *прил* asymmetrical.
несказа́н|ный (-ен, -на, -но) *прил* inexpressive.
несклад|ный (-ен, -на, -но) *прил* (*расска́з, жизнь*) disjointed; (*челове́к, фигу́ра*) ungainly.
несклоня́емый *прил* (*линг*) indeclinable.
не́сколько (-их) *чис* (+*gen*) a few ♦ *нареч* (*немно́го: оби́деться*) somewhat; **в** ~**их слова́х** in a few words, briefly.
несконча́ем|ый (-, -а, -о) *прил* unending.
нескро́м|ный (-ен, -на, -но) *прил* (*челове́к, поведе́ние*) immodest; (*вопро́с*) indelicate; (*жест, предложе́ние*) brazen.
нескрыва́ем|ый (-, -а, -о) *прил* undisguised.
несло́ж|ный (-ен, -на́, -но) *прил* simple.
неслы́хан|ный (-, -на, -но) *прил* unheard of.
неслы́шно *нареч* (*сказа́ть, прое́хать*) quietly ♦ *как сказ:* **мне** ~ I can't hear.
неслы́ш|ный (-ен, -на, -но) *прил* inaudible.
несме́тный (-ен, -на, -но) *прил* infinite.
несмолка́ем|ый (-, -а, -о) *прил* unceasing.
несмотря́ *предл:* ~ **на** +*acc* (*тру́дности, уста́лость*) in spite of, despite; ~ **на то что** ... in spite of *или* despite the fact that ...; ~ **ни на что** no matter what.
несмыва́емый *прил* (*пятно́*) indelible; (*позо́р*) ineradicable.
несмышлён|ный *прил* (*ребёнок*) innocent.
несно́с|ный (-ен, -на, -но) *прил* (*челове́к, поведе́ние итп*) insufferable; (*жара́, хо́лод*) unbearable.
несоблюде́ни|е (-я) *ср* nonobservance.
несоверше́нен *прил см* **несоверше́нный**.
несовершенноле́т|ний (-его; *decl like adj*) *м* minor; ♦ (-яя, -ее, -ие) *прил:* ~ **ребёнок** minor.
несовершенноле́т|няя (-ей; *decl like adj*) *ж см* **несовершенноле́тний**.

несоверше́н|ный (-ен, -на, -но) *прил* flawed; **несоверше́нный вид** (*линг*) imperfective (aspect).
несоверше́нств|о (-а) *ср* (*о́бщества, систе́мы*) imperfect nature.
несовмести́мост|ь (-и) *ж* incompatibility; **несовмести́мость тка́ней** (*мед*) antagonism.
несовмести́м|ый (-, -а, -о) *прил* incompatible.
несогла́си|е (-я) *ср* (*отка́з*) refusal; (*в семье́*) disagreement.
несогласо́ванност|ь (-и) *ж* lack of coordination.
несогласо́ван|ный (-, -на, -но) *прил* (*де́йствия*) uncoordinated.
несозна́телен *прил см* **несозна́тельный**.
несозна́тельност|ь (-и) *ж* irresponsibility.
несозна́тел|ьный (-ен, -ьна, -ьно) *прил* irresponsible.
несоизмери́м|ый (-, -а, -о) *прил* (*поня́тия*) disproportionate.
несокруши́м|ый (-, -а, -о) *прил* indestructible.
несомне́нен *прил см* **несомне́нный**.
несомне́нно *нареч* (*пра́вильный, хоро́ший итп*) indisputably ♦ *вводн сл* without a doubt ♦ *как сказ:* **э́то** ~ this is indisputable; ~, **что он придёт** there is no doubt that he will come.
несомне́нност|ь (-и) *ж* indisputability.
несомне́н|ный (-ен, -на, -но) *прил* (*факт, успе́х*) indisputable.
несообра́зен *прил см* **несообра́зный**.
несообрази́тел|ьный (-ен, -ьна, -ьно) *прил* (*челове́к*) slow, thick.
несообра́зност|ь (-и) *ж* (*поведе́ния*) foolishness; **говори́ть** (*impf*)/**де́лать** (*impf*) ~**и** to say/do foolish things.
несообра́з|ный (-ен, -на, -но) *прил* (*поведе́ние*) foolish; ~ **с** +*instr* (*с возмо́жностями, с обстоя́тельствами*) out of line with.
несоотве́тстви|е (-я) *ср:* ~ +*dat* (*пра́вилам, зако́ну*) nonconformity with; (*возмо́жностям, обстоя́тельствам*) discrepancy with.
несоразме́р|ный (-ен, -на, -но) *прил* unbalanced.
несостоя́телен *прил см* **несостоя́тельный**.
несостоя́тельност|ь (-и) *ж* (*до́вода*) lack of substantiation; (*комм*) insolvency; **обнару́живать** (**обнару́жить** *perf*) **свою́** ~ to prove to be worthless.
несостоя́тел|ьный (-ен, -на, -но) *прил* (*до́вод*) unsubstantiated; (*комм: компа́ния, должни́к*) insolvent; (*руководи́тель*) incompetent.
неспе́ш|ный (-ен, -на, -но) *прил* unhurried.
несподру́чно *как сказ* (*разг*) it is inconvenient; **мне** ~ **де́лать э́то** it's inconvenient for me to do this.
несподру́чный *прил* (*разг*) inconvenient.
неспоко́ен *прил см* **неспоко́йный**.
неспоко́йно *как сказ* (*в до́ме, в стране́*) there's unease; **у меня́ на душе́** ~ I feel uneasy.
неспоко́й|ный (-ен, -йна, -йно) *прил* (*сон*)

uneasy; (жизнь) troubled.
неспосо́бен прил см **неспосо́бный**.
неспосо́бность (-и) ж inability; ~ на +acc (на жертвы, на уступки итп) inability to make.
неспосо́б|ный (-ен, -на, -но) прил: ~ к +dat incapable of; ~ к языка́м/матема́тике incapable of learning languages/doing maths; ~ на +acc (на жертвы, на уступки) incapable of making.
несправедли́во нареч unfairly, unjustly ◆ как сказ: э́то ~ this is unfair или unjust.
несправедли́вость (-и) ж injustice.
несправедли́в|ый (-, -а, -о) прил (человек, суд, упрёк) unfair, unjust; (сообщение) unfounded.
неспроста́ нареч (разг) for a reason.
неспряга́емый прил (линг) inconjugable.
несрабо́танность (-и) ж lack of harmony at work.
несравне́нен прил см **несравне́нный**.
несравне́нно нареч (лучшее, красивее итп) incomparably.
несравне́н|ный (-ен, -на, -но) прил incomparable.
несравни́мый (-, -а, -о) прил incomparable.
нестанда́рт|ный (-ен, -на, -но) прил (подход) original; (товар) substandard.
нестерпи́м|ый (-, -а, -о) прил intolerable.
нес|ти́ (-у́, -ёшь; pt нёс, -ла́, -ло́) несов от **носи́ть** ◆ перех to carry; (влечь: хаос, разруху, неприятности) to bring; (разг: чепуху, вздор) to spout; (perf понести́; службу, охрану) to carry out; (perf снести́; яйцо) to lay ◆ безл: ~ёт бензи́ном/во́дкой there's a smell of petrol (BRIT) или gas (US)/of vodka; с мо́ря ~ёт прохла́дой coolness wafted in from the sea; ~ (понести́ perf) наказа́ние to take punishment; ~ (понести́ perf) поте́ри to suffer losses; ~ (понести́ perf) уще́рб to be damaged; куда́ тебя́ ~ёт? (разг) where on earth are you going?; кого́ э́то ~ёт? (разг) who on earth is that?
▶ **нес|ти́сь** несов возв (человек, машина) to race; (перен: сплетни) to spread; (: музыка) to carry; (perf снести́сь; курица) to lay eggs.
несто́ящий (-ая, -ее, -ие) прил (человек) worthless; (дело) valueless.
нестро́йный (-ен, -йна, -йно) прил shapeless; (ряды) ragged.
несудохо́дный прил not navigable.
несура́зен прил см **несура́зный**.
несура́зность (-и) ж silliness; говори́ть (impf)/де́лать (impf) ~и to say/do silly things.
несура́з|ный (-ен, -на, -но) прил silly; (характер) idiotic.
несуще́ственный прил inconsequential.
несхо́д|ный (-ен, -на, -но) прил dissimilar.
несча́стен прил см **несча́стный**.
несчастли́вый (несча́стлив, несча́стлива,

несча́стливо) прил (человек) unhappy; (попытка) unfortunate.
несча́ст|ный (-ен, -на, -но) прил (человек, лицо) unhappy; (день) sad; (no short form; разг: жалкий) wretched; у него́ о́чень ~ вид he looks very unhappy; несча́стная любо́вь unrequited love; несча́стный слу́чай accident.
несча́сть|е (-я) ср (беда) misfortune; к ~ю unfortunately.
несчётный прил incalculable.
несъедо́б|ный (-ен, -на, -но) прил inedible.

KEYWORD

нет част **1** (при отрицании, несогласии) no; ты согла́сен? – нет do you agree? – no; нет, э́то не то no, that's not right; тебе́ не нра́вится мой суп? – нет, нра́вится don't you like my soup? – yes, I do
2 (для привлечения внимания): нет, ты то́лько посмотри́ на него́! would you just look at him!
3 (выражает недоверие): нет, ты действи́тельно не се́рдишься? so you are really not angry?
◆ как сказ (+gen; не имеется: об одном предмете) there is no; (: о нескольких предметах) there are no; нет вре́мени there is no time; нет биле́тов или биле́тов нет there are no tickets; у меня́ нет де́нег I have no money; его́ нет в го́роде he is not in town
◆ союз **1**: (так) нет (же) (разг: однако) but; я помога́л ему́ три дня, (так) нет (же) ему́ всё ма́ло I helped him for three days, but it still wasn't enough; своди́ть (свести́ perf) что-н на нет to bring sth to nothing; сойти́ (perf) на нет to come to nothing
2 (во фразах): нет – так нет it can't be helped; нет-нет да и зайдёт/ска́жет every now and then he called in/said; чего́ то́лько нет? what don't they have?; нет чтобы извини́ться/сказа́ть пра́вду (разг) instead of saying sorry/ telling the truth.

нетакти́чен прил см **нетакти́чный**.
нетакти́чность (-и) ж tactlessness.
нетакти́ч|ный (-ен, -на, -но) прил tactless.
нетвёрдый прил (походка) unsteady; (решение) shaky.
нетерпели́во нареч impatiently.
нетерпели́в|ый (-, -а, -о) прил impatient.
нетерпе́ни|е (-я) ср impatience; с ~м ждать (impf)/слу́шать (impf) to wait/listen impatiently.
нетерпи́мость (-и) ж intolerance.
нетерпи́м|ый (-, -а, -о) прил (недопустимый) intolerant; (непримиримый): ~ к +dat (ко лжи) intolerant of.
нетороп́ли́во нареч unhurriedly.
нетороп́ли́в|ый (-, -а, -о) прил unhurried.
нето́чность (-и) ж (данных, описания) inexactness; (в работе, в описании)

inexactitude.

нето́ч|ный (-ен, -но, -на) *прил* inexact.

нетре́бова́тел|ьный (-ен, -ьна, -ьно) *прил* (*нача́льник*) undemanding; (*вкус, пу́блика*) unsophisticated; (*челове́к*) unassuming.

нетре́звый *прил* drunk; **в нетре́звом состоя́нии** drunk.

нетро́нут|ый (-, -а, -о) *прил* (*снег*) virgin; (*обед*) untouched.

нетру́ден *прил см* **нетру́дный**.

нетру́дно *как сказ*: **э́то ~** it's easy *или* not difficult; **~ поня́ть** it's easy *или* not difficult to understand.

нетру́д|ный (-ен, -но, -на) *прил* easy.

нетрудово́й *прил*: **~ дохо́д** unearned income.

нетрудоспосо́бен *прил см* **нетрудоспосо́бный**.

нетрудоспосо́бност|ь (-и) *ж* disability; **посо́бие по ~и** disability living allowance.

нетрудоспосо́б|ный (-ен, -на, -но) *прил* *unable to work through disability*.

не́тто *прил неизм* (*о ве́се*) net *опред*; **вес ~** net weight; **~-акти́вы** (*комм*) net assets.

неубеди́тел|ьный (-ен, -ьна, -ьно) *прил* unconvincing.

неу́бранный *прил* (*урожа́й*) ungathered; (*поля́*) unharvested; (*посте́ль*) unmade; (*ко́мната*) untidy.

неуваже́ни|е (-я) *ср* disrespect.

неуве́ренно *нареч* uncertainly.

неуве́ренный *прил* (*челове́к*) unsure; (*тон*) uncertain; **~ в себе́** unsure of o.s.

неувяда́ем|ый (-, -а, -о) *прил* (*тала́нт, сла́ва*) enduring; (*красота́*) unfading.

неувя́з|ка (-ки; *gen pl* **-ок)** *ж* (*разг: в описа́нии, в аргумента́ции*) discrepancy; (*недоразуме́ние*) misunderstanding.

неугаси́м|ый (-, -а, -о) *прил* inextinguishable.

неугомо́н|ный (-ен, -на, -но) *прил* unruly.

неуда́ч|а (-и) *ж* (*в дела́х*) failure; **терпе́ть (потерпе́ть** *perf*) **~у** to meet with failure.

неуда́чен *прил см* **неуда́чный**.

неуда́члив|ый (-, -а, -о) *прил* (*челове́к*) unlucky.

неуда́чно *нареч* unsuccessfully; **её жизнь сложи́лась ~** her life was a failure.

неуда́ч|ный (-ен, -на, -но) *прил* (*попы́тка*) unsuccessful; (*фильм, стихи́*) bad.

неудержи́м|ый (-, -а, -о) *прил* (*пото́к, бег*) uncontrollable; (*слёзы, ра́дость*) unrestrained.

неудиви́тельно *как сказ* it's not surprising.

неудо́бен *прил см* **неудо́бный**.

неудо́бно *нареч* (*располо́женный, сиде́ть*) uncomfortably ◆ *как сказ* it's uncomfortable; (*неприли́чно*) it's awkward; **мне ~** I am uncomfortable; **~ задава́ть лю́дям таки́е вопро́сы** it's awkward to ask people such questions; (**мне**) **~ сказа́ть ему́ об э́том** I feel uncomfortable telling him that.

неудо́б|ный (-ен, -на, -но) *прил* uncomfortable.

неудобовари́м|ый (-, -а, -о) *прил* (*та́кже*

перен) indigestible.

неудо́бств|о (-а) *ср* (*нело́вкость*) discomfort; (*в по́езде итп*) lack of comfort.

неудовлетворённост|ь (-и) *ж*: **~ +instr** (*рабо́той, жи́знью*) dissatisfaction with.

неудовлетворённый *прил* (*любопы́тство*) unsatisfied; (*чита́тель, зри́тель*) dissatisfied.

неудовлетвори́телен *прил см* **неудовлетвори́тельный**.

неудовлетвори́тельно *нареч* (*сде́лать*) unsatisfactorily ◆ *ср нескл* (*ПРОСВЕЩ*) ≈ D (*school mark*).

неудовлетвори́тел|ьный (-ен, -ьна, -ьно) *прил* unsatisfactory.

неудово́льстви|е (-я) *ср* dissatisfaction.

неуём|ный (-ен, -на, -но) *прил* (*эне́ргия*) irrepressible; (*тоска́*) unrestrained.

неуже́ли *част* really; **~ она́ так ду́мает?** does she really think that?

неужи́вчив|ый (-, -а, -о) *прил* unaccommodating.

неузнава́емост|ь (-и) *ж*: **до ~и** beyond (all) recognition.

неузнава́ем|ый (-, -а, -о) *прил* unrecognizable.

неукло́нно *нареч* steadily.

неукло́н|ный (-ен, -на, -но) *прил* steady.

неуклю́жий (-ая, -ее, -ие; -, -а, -е) *прил* clumsy.

неукосни́телен *прил см* **неукосни́тельный**.

неукосни́тельно *нареч* strictly.

неукосни́тел|ьный (-ен, -ьна, -ьно) *прил* strict.

неукроти́м|ый (-, -а, -о) *прил* (*гнев*) unrestrained; (*эне́ргия*) irrepressible.

неулови́м|ый (-, -а, -о) *прил* imperceptible; (*челове́к*) elusive.

неуме́лый *прил* inept.

неуме́ни|е (-я) *ср* incapability.

неуме́рен|ный (-, -на, -но) *прил* (*восто́рг*) boundless; (*потре́бности*) unlimited.

неуме́ст|ный (-ен, -на, -но) *прил* inappropriate; **шу́тка была́ соверше́нно ~на** the joke was completely out of place.

неу́мный *прил* (*поли́тика*) unintelligent.

неумоли́м|ый (-, -а, -о) *прил* (*мсти́тель*) relentless; (*зако́н*) stringent.

неумо́лч|ный (-ен, -на, -но) *прил* unremitting.

неумы́шленный *прил* (*посту́пок*) unintentional; (*уби́йство*) unpremeditated.

неупла́т|а (-ы) *ж* nonpayment.

неупоря́доченный *прил* disorderly.

неупотреби́тел|ьный (-ен, -ьна, -ьно) *прил*: **э́то сло́во сейча́с ~ьно** this word is not in use any more.

неуправля́ем|ый (-, -а, -о) *прил* (*недисциплини́рованный*) unruly.

неуравнове́шенност|ь (-и) *ж* irascibility.

неуравнове́шен|ный (-, -на, -но) *прил* unbalanced.

неурожа́|й (-я) *м* poor harvest.

неурожа́йный *прил*: **~ год** year with a poor harvest.

неуро́чный *прил* (*вре́мя, час*) unearthly.

неуря́диц|а (-ы) ж (разг: обычно мн: в семье, на работе) squabble.
неуспева́емость (-и) ж poor performance.
неуспева́ющий (-ая, -ее, -ие) прил (ученик) poor.
неуста́нен прил см **неуста́нный**.
неуста́нно нареч indefatigably.
неуста́н|ный (-ен, -на, -но) прил indefatigable.
неусто́йка (-йки; gen pl -ек) ж (КОММ) penalty; (разг: неудача) flop.
неусто́йчивость (-и) ж (цен) instability.
неусто́йчив|ый (-, -а, -о) прил (стул, цены) unstable; (погода) unsettled.
неустрани́м|ый (-, -а, -о) прил insurmountable.
неустраши́м|ый (-, -а, -о) прил fearless.
неустро́ен|ный (-, -на, -но) прил (жизнь, быт) uncomfortable.
неусы́п|ный (-ен, -на, -но) прил vigilant.
неуте́шен прил см **неуте́шный**.
неутеши́тельный (-ен, -ьна, -ьно) прил upsetting.
неуте́ш|ный (-ен, -на, -но) прил inconsolable.
неутоли́м|ый (-, -а, -о) прил (жажда) unquenchable; (голод, также перен) insatiable.
неутоми́м|ый (-, -а, -о) прил untiring.
не́уч (-а) м (разг) dunce.
неучти́вость (-и) ж lack of civility; **говори́ть** (impf) ~и to be uncivil.
неучти́в|ый (-, -а, -о) прил uncivil.
неую́тно нареч (сидеть) uncomfortably ◆ как сказ it's uncomfortable; **мне ~ с чужи́ми людьми́** I don't feel at ease with strangers.
неуязви́м|ый (-, -а, -о) прил (противник, позиция) impregnable; (аргумент) unassailable.
неформа́л (-а) м (разг) member of a nonconformist organization.
неформа́льный прил (отношение) relaxed; (организация) nonconformist.
нефри́т (-а) м (МЕД) nephritis; (ГЕО) jade.
нефтедобыва́ющий (-ая, -ее, -ие) прил (промышленность) oil опред.
нефтедобы́ч|а (-и) ж drilling for oil.
нефтедо́ллар|ы (-ов) мн petrodollars мн.
нефтено́сный прил: ~ пласт oilfield.
нефтеперерабо́тк|а (-и) ж oil-processing plant.
нефтепрово́д (-а) м oil pipeline.
нефтепроду́кт (-а) м (обычно мн) oil product.
нефтехрани́лище (-а) ср oil storage tank.
нефт|ь (-и) ж oil, petroleum.
нефтя́ник (-а) м worker in the oil industry.
нефтян|о́й прил: ~а́я платфо́рма oil rig; **нефтяна́я вы́шка** (oil) derrick.
нехва́тк|а (-и) ж: ~ +gen (разг) shortage of.
нехи́трый прил (простой) simple.
нехо́жен|ый (-, -а, -о) прил little-used.
нехоро́ш|ий (-ая, -ее, -ие) прил bad.
нехорошо́ нареч (поступить) badly ◆ как сказ it's bad; **мне ~** I'm not well; ~ **на душе́** I feel uneasy; **он нехоро́ш собо́й** he isn't good-looking.
не́хотя нареч unwillingly.
нецензу́р|ный (-ен, -на, -но) прил unprintable; ~**ное сло́во** swearword.
неча́янно нареч unintentionally.
неча́ян|ный (-на, -но) прил (неумышленный) unintentional; (неожиданный) chance опред.
не́чего как сказ: ~ **рассказа́ть** there is nothing to tell; (разг: не следует) there's no need to do; **не́ для чего стара́ться** there's nothing to try for; **не́ к чему придра́ться** there is nothing to find fault with; **мне не́ с чем идти́** I have nothing to take; **не́ о чем говори́ть** there is nothing to talk about; **не́чему серди́ться** there is nothing to be angry about; **не́ за что!** (в ответ на благодарность) not at all!, you're welcome! (US); ~ **(и) говори́ть** (разг: конечно) no buts about it; ~ **сказа́ть!** (разг) would you credit it!; **от ~ де́лать** (разг) for want of something better to do; **де́лать ~** there's nothing else to be done.
нечелове́ческий (-ая, -ое, -ие) прил inhuman; (колоссальный: усилия) superhuman.
нечёсаный прил unkempt.
нече́стен прил см **нече́стный**.
нече́стно нареч dishonestly ◆ как сказ: э́то ~ this is dishonest.
нече́стность (-и) ж dishonesty.
нече́ст|ный (-ен, -на, -но) прил dishonest.
нечётный прил (число) odd.
нечи́сто как сказ: **в ко́мнате** ~ the room is untidy; **здесь что́-то** ~ (разг) there's something fishy here.
нечистопло́т|ный (-ен, -на, -но) прил (неопрятный) untidy; (неразборчивый) unscrupulous.
нечисто́т|ы (-) мн sewage ед; (отбросы) waste ед.
нечи́ст|ый (-, -а, -о) прил (одежда, комната) dirty; (произношение) indistinct; (приёмы, игра) unscrupulous; **у него́** ~**ая со́весть** he has a guilty conscience; **он нечи́ст на́ руку** (нечестен) he is dishonest; (вороват) he is light-fingered; **нечи́стая си́ла** evil spirit.
нечист|ь (-и) ж собир (нечистая сила) evil spirit; (перен: преступная, нацистская) scum.
нечленоразде́л|ный (-ен, -ьна, -ьно) прил inarticulate.
не́что мест something.
нечувстви́телен прил см **нечувстви́тельный**.
нечувстви́тельность (-и) ж insensitivity.
нечувстви́тельный (-ен, -ьна, -ьно) прил insensitive.
нечу́тк|ий (-ая, -ое, -ие) прил (человек) unsympathetic.
нешу́точ|ный (-ен, -на, -но) прил (серьёзный)

serious; (*значительный*) large; **это ~ное дело**
it's no laughing matter.
нещаден *прил см* **нещадный**.
нещадно *нареч* unmercifully.
нещадный (-ен, -на, -но) *прил* (*критика,
наказание*) merciless; (*перен: жара*) relentless.
неэкономичен *прил см* **неэкономичный**.
неэкономичность (-и) *ж* (*методов,
технологии*) inefficiency.
неэкономичный (-ен, -на, -но) *прил*
(*технология, отрасль*) inefficient; (*мотор*)
uneconomical.
неэтичный *прил* (*поведение*) unethical.
неэффективный (-ен, -на, -но) *прил*
ineffective.
неявка (-ки; *gen pl* -ок) *ж* (*на работу*) absence;
(*на суд*) failure to appear; **за ~кой, по ~ке** by
default.
неясен *прил см* **неясный**.
неясно *нареч*: **он ~ объяснил положение** he
didn't explain the situation clearly ♦ *как сказ* it's
not clear; **мне ~, почему он отказался** I'm not
clear *или* it's not clear to me why he refused.
неясность (-и) *ж* vagueness; (*в тексте*)
ambiguity.
неясный (-ен, -на, -но) *прил* (*очертания, звук*)
indistinct; (*мысль, вопрос*) vague.
НЗ *м сокр* = **неприкосновенный запас**.

KEYWORD

ни *част* **1** (*усиливает отрицание*) not a; **ни
один** not one, not a single; **она не произнесла
ни слова** she didn't say a word; **она ни разу не
пришла** she didn't come once; **у меня не
осталось ни рубля** I don't have a single rouble
left;
2: **кто/что/как ни** who/what/however; **сколько
ни** however much; **что ни говори, а ей
приходится трудно** whatever you say, it is hard
for her; **как ни старайся, не убедишь его**
however hard you try, you will not convince
him; **куда ни посмотри, везде бедность**
wherever you look, there is poverty
♦ *союз* (*in negative sentences; при перечислении*):
ни ..., ни ... neither ... nor ...; **ни денег, ни еды у
неё нет** she had neither money nor food; **ни за
что** no way; **ни за какие деньги** not for any
money; **ни-ни!** (*разг*) no way!

нива (-ы) *ж* field (*of crops*).
нивелировать (-ую) (*не*)*сов перех* (*перен*) to
even out.
нигде *нареч* nowhere; **его ~ не было** he was
nowhere to be found; **~ нет моей книги** I can't
find my book anywhere, my book is nowhere to
be found; **~ не мог поесть** I couldn't find
anywhere to get something to eat.
нигерийский (-ая, -ое, -ие) *ж* Nigerian.
Нигерия (-и) *ж* Nigeria.
нигилизм (-а) *м* nihilism.
нигилист (-а) *м* nihilist.
нидерландский (-ая, -ое, -ие) *прил* Dutch.

Нидерланды (-ов) *мн* the Netherlands.
ниже *сравн прил от* **низкий** ♦ *сравн нареч от*
низко ♦ *нареч* (*далее*) late ♦ *предл* (+*gen*)
below; **~ речь пойдёт о ...** later (on) we will
deal with ...; **он выступил ~ своих
возможностей** he performed below his
capabilities.
нижеизложенный *прил*: **~ые данные/
аргументы** the facts/arguments given below.
нижеподписавшийся (-аяся, -ееся, -иеся)
прил undersigned.
нижесказанное (-ого; *decl like adj*) *ср* what has
been said below.
нижестоящий (-ая, -ее, -ие) *прил* lower.
нижеуказанный *прил* undermentioned.
нижеупомянутый *прил* = **нижеуказанный**.
нижний (-яя, -ее, -ие) *прил* (*ступенька, ящик*)
bottom; (*течение реки*) lower reaches *мн*;
(*регистр*) low; **~ этаж** ground (*BRIT*) *или* first
(*US*) floor; **Н~ Новгород** Nizhni Novgorod;
нижнее бельё underwear; **нижняя юбка**
underskirt.
низ (-а; *loc sg* -у, *nom pl* -ы) *м* (*стола, ящика итп*)
bottom; (*дома*) ground (*BRIT*) *или* first (*US*) floor;
по ~у along the bottom; *см также* **низы**.
низвергнуть (-у, -ешь; *impf* **низвергать**) *сов
перех* to overthrow
▸ **низвергнуться** *сов возв* to hurtle down.
низина (-ы) *ж* low-lying land.
низкий (-кая, -кое, -кие; -ок, -ка, -ко) *прил* low;
(*no short form; происхождение*) lowly; **этот стол
мне ~ок** this table is too low for me; **~ лоб**
narrow forehead; **~кое место** (*низменность*)
low-lying area; **~ поклон** low bow; (*перен*)
forelock tugging.
низко *нареч* low.
низкооплачиваемый *прил* low-paid.
низкопоклонник (-а) *м* sycophant.
низкопоклонство (-а) *ср* sycophancy.
низкопробный (-ен, -на, -но) *прил* (*золото,
серебро*) low-grade; (*книга, газета*) trashy;
(*делец*) amoral.
низкорослый *прил* (*человек*) small; (*дерево,
кустарник*) stunted.
низкосортный (-ен, -на, -но) *прил* low-quality.
низкокачественный *прил* low-quality.
низложить (-ожу, -ожишь; *impf* **низлагать**) *сов
перех* to depose.
низменность (-и) *ж* (*ГЕО*) low-lying area;
(*интересов*) baseness.
низменный *прил* (*местность, болота*) low-
lying; (-, -на, -но; *интересы, мысли*) base;
(*инстинкты*) basic.
низовой *прил* (*организация*) grass-roots;
низовые работники the grass roots.
низовье (-ья; *gen pl* -ьев) *ср* lower reaches *мн*.
низок *прил см* **низкий**.
низом *нареч* along the bottom.
низость (-и) *ж* baseness; **говорить** (*impf*) **~и** to
say base things; **делать** (*impf*) **~и** to behave
basely.

нúзш|ий (**-ая, -ее, -ие**) *сравн прил от* **нúзкий**; (*звание*) junior; **~ие чинь́** the lowest ranks.

низь́ (**-óв**) *мн* (*нúзший классы*) lowest classes *мн*; (*широкие массы*) masses *мн*; **он вь́шел из ~óв** he came from the lowest classes of society; **опирáться** (*impf*) **на ~** to rely for support on the masses.

никáк *нареч* (*никаким образом*) no way; **~ не могý запóмнить э́то слóво** I can't remember this word at all; **дверь ~ не открывáлась** the door just wouldn't open; **емý ~ не удавáлось её встрéтить** there's no way he could have managed to meet her; **~ нельзя́** +*infin* ... one can't do ....

никак|óй (**-áя, -óе, -úе**) *мест*: **~úе дéньги не помоглú** no amount of money would have helped; (*разг*): **~ он не врач** he's not a doctor at all; (: *плохой*): **писáтель он ~** he can't be called a writer; **ни у какóго человéка не бýдет сомнéния** nobody will have any doubt about it; **ни к какóму дéлу он не спосóбен** he is not capable of anything; **он не соглашáлся ни с какúм аргумéнтном** he didn't agree with any of the arguments; **нет ~óго сомнéния** there is absolutely no doubt (at all); **у меня нет ~óго сомнéния** I have absolutely no doubts; **и ~úх!** and that's that!

Никарáгуа *ж нескл* Nicaragua.

никарагуáнск|ий (**-ая, -ое, -ие**) *прил* Nicaraguan.

никелир|овáть (**-ýю**) *perf* **отникелировáть**) *несов перех* to nickel.

никелирóвк|а (**-и**) *ж* (*действие*) nickelling (*BRIT*), nickeling (*US*); (*покрытие*) nickel plate.

нúкел|ь (**-я**) *м* (*хим*) nickel.

нúкн|уть (**-у, -ешь**) *несов от* **понúкнуть** ◆ *неперех* (*трава, цветы*) to droop.

никогдá *нареч* never; **как ~** as never before.

никогó *мест см* **никтó**.

никóй *нареч*: **никóим óбразом** not at all; **ни в кóем слýчае** under no circumstances.

ни|ктó (**-когó**; *как кто; см* **Table 6**) *мест* nobody ◆ *м*: **онá мне ~** (*разг: не родственник*) she's not a relative of mine; (*не друг*) she's nothing to me; **ни у когó нет сомнéния** nobody has any doubts; **ни к комý не подходúл** I didn't approach anyone; **ни с кем не говорúл** I didn't speak to anyone; **ни о ком не знáю** I don't know anything about anyone.

никудá *местоимённое нареч* nowhere ◆ *как сказ* (*разг*): **обслýживание здесь – ~** the service here is terrible; **я ~ не поéду** I'm not going anywhere; **~ я не поéду** I'm going nowhere; **э́то ~ не годúтся** that just won't do.

никудь́ш|ный (**-ен, -на, -но**) *прил* (*разг*) good-for-nothing.

никчём|ный (**-ен, -на, -но**) *прил* no good for anything.

Нил (**-а**) *м* the Nile.

НИИ *м сокр* (= *научно-исслéдовательский инститýт*) scientific research institute.

нимб (**-а**) *м* nimbus.

ниоткýда *местоимённое нареч* from nowhere; **~ нет пóмощи** I get no help from anywhere.

нипочём *как сказ*: **бéдность емý ~** (*разг*) being poor doesn't bother him; **емý всё ~** (*разг*) nothing hassles him.

нúппел|ь (**-я**) *м* (*TEX*) nipple.

нискóлько *местоимённое нареч* not at all; (*не лучше, не полезнее*) no; (*не рад, не удивлён*) at all; **ты рад? – ~** are you pleased? – not at all *или* in the slightest.

ниспадá|ть (*3sg* **-ет**, *3pl* **-ют**) *несов неперех* to fall.

ниспровéрг|нуть (**-ну, -нешь**; *pt* **-**, **-ла, -ло**, *impf* **ниспровергáть**) *сов перех* to overthrow.

нисходя́щий (**-ая, -ее, -ие**) *прил* (*линия*) descending; (*интонация*) falling.

нитевúд|ный (**-ен, -на, -но**) *прил* long and thin.

нúт|ка (**-ки**; *gen pl* **-ок**) *ж* (*обычно мн: для шитья*) thread *ед*; (*для вязания*) yarn; **~ жéмчуга** string of pearls; **~ газопровóда** gas pipeline; **промóкнуть** (*perf*) **до ~ки** to get soaked right through; **вдевáть** (**вдеть** *perf*) **~ку в игóлку** to thread a needle.

нитрáт (**-а**) *м* nitrate.

нит|ь (**-и**) *ж* thread; (*для вязания*) yarn; (*повествования, воспоминаний*) thread of; **нúти зáговора** strands of a plot; **нúти дрýжбы** threads of friendship.

них *мест см* **онú**.

ниц *м*: **пáдать ~** to prostrate o.s.

Нúцц|а (**-ы**) *ж* Nice.

ничегó *мест см* **ничтó** ◆ *нареч* fairly well; (*это*) **~, что ...** it's all right that ...; **извинúте, я Вас побеспокóю – ~!** sorry to disturb you – it's all right!; **как живёшь? – ~** how are you? – all right; **~ себé** (*сносно*) fairly well; **~ себé!** (*выражает удивление*) well, I never!

нич|éй (**-ьегó**; *f* **-ья́**, *nt* **-ьё**, *pl* **-ьú**; *как чей; см* **Table 7**) *мест* nobody's; **он не слýшает ~ьúх совéтов** he doesn't follow anybody's advice; **ни к чьемý совéту не прислýшивается** he doesn't listen to anybody's advice; **ни с чьим мнéнием не считáется** he doesn't consider anyone's views; **ни о чьём благополýчии не беспокóится** he doesn't worry about anyone's wellbeing.

ничéй|ный *прил* (*полоса, зона*) no man's; **~ая земля** no-man's-land; **~ результáт, ничéйная пáртия** draw.

ничкóм *нареч* face down.

нич|тó (**-егó**; *как что; см* **Table 6**) *мест, ср* nothing; **ни для чегó не пригóдный** not suitable for anything; **ни с чем не соглáсен** I don't agree with anything; **ни о чём не прошý** I don't ask for anything; ~ мне не интере́сно nothing interests me; ~его́ с ним не случи́тся nothing happens to him; ~его́ подо́бного не ви́дел I've never seen anything like it; ~его́ подо́бного! (*разг: совсем не так*) nothing like it!; всего́ ~его́ (*разг*) next to nothing; ни за что! (*ни в коем случае*) no way!; ни за что не соглаша́йся whatever you do, don't agree; ни за что ни про что for nothing; я здесь ни при чём it has nothing to do with me; ~его́ не поде́лаешь there's nothing to be done.

ничто́жен *прил см* **ничто́жный**.

ничто́жеств|о (-а) *ср* nonentity.

ничто́ж|ный (-ен, -на, -но) *прил* paltry.

ничу́ть *местоимённое нареч* (*нисколько*) not at all; (*не лучше, не больше*) no; (*не испугался, не огорчился*) at all; ~ не быва́ло not at all.

ничь|я́ (-е́й) *ж* (*СПОРТ*) draw; **сыгра́ть** (*perf*) в ~ю́ to draw (*BRIT*), tie (*US*).

ни́ш|а (-и) *ж* niche.

нища́|ть (-ю; *perf* **обнища́ть**) *несов неперех* to become impoverished.

ни́щ|ая (-ей; *decl like adj*) *ж* beggar.

ни́щен|ка (-ки; *gen pl* -ок) *ж* = **ни́щая**.

ни́щенский (-ая, -ое, -ие) *прил* (*ничтожный*) beggarly; ~ая жизнь life of begging.

нищет|а́ (-ы́) *ж* poverty.

ни́щий (-ая, -ее, -ие) *прил* poverty-stricken ♦ (-его; *decl like adj*) *м* beggar.

НЛО *м сокр* (= неопо́знанный лета́ющий объе́кт) UFO (= *unidentified flying object*).

но *союз* but ♦ *ср нескл* (*препятствие*) setback ♦ *межд* gee up; **я предложи́л ему́ по́мощь**, ~ **он отказа́лся** I offered to help him, but he refused; ~ **вдруг** then suddenly; ~ **то́лько** only; ~**-но, осторо́жнее!** now then, be more careful!

нова́тор (-а) *м* innovator.

нова́торств|о (-а) *ср* innovation.

нова́ция (-и) *ж* innovation.

нове́лл|а (-ы) *ж* novella.

новелли́ст (-а) *м* writer of novellas.

новелли́ст|ка (-ки; *gen pl* -ок) *ж см* **новелли́ст**.

но́веньк|ая (-ой; *decl like adj*) *ж* newcomer; (*в классе*) new pupil.

но́веньк|ий (-ая, -ое, -ие) *прил* (*разг*) new ♦ (-ого; *decl like adj*) *м* newcomer; (*в классе*) new pupil; **что** ~**ого?** what's new?

новизн|а́ (-ы́) *ж* (*идей, подхода*) novelty.

нови́н|ка (-ки; *gen pl* -ок) *ж* new product; ~ **мо́ды** new fashion item; **кни́жная** ~ new book; **мне э́то в** ~**ку** it's new to me.

новичо́к (-ка́) *м* newcomer; (*в классе*) new pupil; **я** ~ **в** +*prp* I am a newcomer to.

но́во *как сказ*: **здесь мне всё** ~ it's all new to me here.

новобра́н|ец (-ца) *м* new recruit.

новобра́чн|ая (-ой; *decl like adj*) *ж см* **новобра́чный**.

новобра́чн|ый (-ого; *decl like adj*) *м* newlywed.

нововведе́ни|е (-я) *ср* innovation.

нового́дн|ий (-яя, -ее, -ие) *прил* New Year

опре́д; **нового́дняя ёлка** ≈ Christmas tree.

новозела́ндск|ий (-ая, -ое, -ие) *прил* New Zealand опре́д.

новоиспечённый *прил* (*разг*) new.

новокаи́н (-а) *м* (*МЕД*) Novocaine ®.

новолу́ни|е (-я) *ср* new moon.

новорождённ|ая (-ой; *decl like adj*) *ж* newborn girl.

новорождённ|ый *прил* newborn ♦ (-ого; *decl like adj*) *м* newborn boy.

новосёл (-а) *м* (*дома*) new owner.

новосе́ль|е (-ья; *gen pl* -ий) *ср* house-warming.

Новосиби́рск (-а) *м* Novosibirsk.

новостро́|йка (-йки; *gen pl* -ек) *ж* (*строительство*) construction of new buildings; (*новое здание*) new building; **больни́ца-**~ newly-built hospital.

но́вост|ь (-и; *gen pl* -е́й) *ж* (*известие*) news; (*медицины, техники*) innovation.

новоя́вленный *прил* new.

но́вшеств|о (-а) *ср* (*в жизни, в обществе*) novelty; (*техническое*) innovation.

но́в|ый (-, -а́, -о) *прил* new; **но́вая исто́рия** modern history; **Но́вый заве́т** the New Testament; **Но́вая Зела́ндия** New Zealand; **Но́вая Земля́** Novaya Zemlya.

нов|ь (-и) *ж* new era.

ног|а́ (-и́; *acc sg* -у, *nom pl* -и, *gen pl* -, *dat pl* -а́м) *ж* (*ступня*) foot; (*выше ступни*) leg; **переступа́ть** (*impf*) *или* **перемина́ться** (*impf*) с ~й на́ ~у to shift from one foot to the other; **идти́** (*impf*) в но́гу со вре́менем (*перен*) to move with the times; **он бежа́л со всех ног** he ran as fast as his legs would carry him; **сби́ться** (*perf*) **с ног** to be run off one's feet; **поста́вить** (*perf*) **кого́-н на́** ~**и** (*перен: больного*) to get sb back on his *итп* feet; (*детей*) to make sb stand on his *итп* own two feet; **с ног на́ голову перевора́чивать** (**переверну́ть** *perf*) *или* **ста́вить** (**поста́вить** *perf*) **что-н** to turn *или* put sth on its head; **е́ле но́ги унести́** (*perf*) to escape by the skin of one's teeth; ~**й мое́й там не бу́дет** (*разг*) I won't step foot there again; **в** ~**х** (*постели*) at the foot of the bed; **вверх** ~**ми** upside down; **в до́ме все вверх** ~**ми** the house is completely topsy turvy; **жить** (*impf*) **на широ́кую но́гу** to live lavishly; **на коро́ткой** *или* **дру́жеской** ~**é с** +*instr* on friendly terms with.

ноготк|и́ (-о́в) *мн* marigold.

но́гот|ь (-тя; *gen pl* -те́й) *м* nail; **до ко́нчиков ногте́й** (*перен: совершенно*) from top to toe.

нож (-а́) *м* knife; **быть** (*impf*) **с кем-н на** ~**а́х** (*враждебно*) to be at daggers drawn with sb; **твои́ посту́пки мне** – ~ **о́стрый** (*перен: разг*) your behaviour gives me a lot of grief.

ножево́й *прил* (*рана*) knife опре́д.

но́жек *сущ см* **но́жка**.

но́жен *сущ см* **но́жны**.

но́жик (-а) *м*: **перочи́нный** ~ penknife; **складно́й** ~ flick knife (*BRIT*), switchblade (*US*).

но́ж|ка (-ки; *gen pl* -ек) *ж уменьш от* **нога́**; (*стула, стола итп*) leg; (*циркуля*) arm; **подставля́ть** (**подста́вить** *perf*) **~ку кому́-н** (*также перен*) to trip sb up.

но́жницы (-) *мн* (*инструмент*) scissors *мн*, pair *ед* of scissors (*мн* pairs of scissors); (*расхождение*) disproportion.

ножно́й *прил* foot *опред*.

но́ж|ны (-ен) *мн* (*для кинжала*) sheath *ед*; (*для шпаги, сабли итп*) scabbard *ед*.

ножо́в|ка (-ки; *gen pl* -ок) *ж* hacksaw.

ноздрева́т|ый (-, -а, -о) *прил* (*сыр*) holey.

ноздр|я́ (-и́; *nom pl* -и, *gen pl* -е́й) *ж* (*обычно мн*) nostril.

нока́ут (-а) *м* knockout.

нокаути́р|овать (-ую) (*не*)*сов перех* to knock out.

нокда́ун (-а) *м* knockdown.

нол|ь (-я́) *м* (*МАТ*) zero, nought; (*при исчислении температуры*) zero; (*перен: человек*) nothing; **~ це́лых пять деся́тых, 0.5** zero *или* nought point five, 0.5; **встре́титься** (*perf*) **в де́сять ~-ноль** to meet at exactly ten o'clock.

номенклату́р|а (-ы) *ж* (*товаров, услуг*) list ♦ *собир* (*номенклатурные работники*) nomenklatura.

номенклату́рный *прил* (*единица*) listed; **номенклату́рный рабо́тник** nomenklatura.

но́мер (-а; *nom pl* -а́) *м* number; (*журнала, газеты*) issue; (*перчаток*) size; (*в гостинице*) room; (*концерта*) number, turn; **но́мер маши́ны** registration (number).

номерка́ *сущ см* **номеро́к**.

номерно́й *прил* (*завод*) *identified only by a number*; **номерно́й знак** (**автомоби́ля**) (car) number (*BRIT*) *или* license (*US*) plate; **номерно́й счёт** (**в ба́нке**) numbered account.

номеро́к (-ка́) *ж* (*для пальто*) ≈ ticket.

номина́л (-а) *м* (*КОММ*) face value.

номина́льный (-ен, -ьна, -ьно) *прил* (*зарплата*) nominal; **~ьная цена́** face value.

но́нсенс (-а) *м* nonsense.

нор|а́ (-ы́; *nom pl* -ы) *ж* (*зайца*) burrow; (*лисы*) den; (*барсука*) set; (*перен*) hole.

Норве́ги|я (-и) *ж* Norway.

норве́ж|ец (-ца) *м* Norwegian.

норве́ж|ка (-ки; *gen pl* -ек) *ж см* **норве́жец**.

норве́жск|ий (-ая, -ое, -ие) *прил* Norwegian; **~ язы́к** Norwegian.

норве́жца *итп сущ см* **норве́жец**.

но́р|ка (-ки; *gen pl* -ок) *ж* mink.

но́рковый *прил* mink *опред*.

но́рм|а (-ы) *ж* standard; (*выработки, прибыли*) rate; **~ поведе́ния** behavioural norm; **войти́** (*perf*) *или* **прийти́** (*perf*) **в ~у** (*в обычное состояние*) to return to normal; **он сего́дня в ~е** (*разг*) he's fine today.

норма́лен *прил см* **норма́льный**.

нормализа́ци|я (-и) *ж* normalization.

нормализ|ова́ть (-ую) (*не*)*сов перех* (*обстановку, отношения*) to normalize

▸ **нормализова́ться** (*не*)*сов возв* to stabilize.

норма́льно *нареч* normally ♦ *как сказ*: **э́то вполне́ ~** this is quite normal; **как дела́? – ~** how are things? – not bad; **у нас всё ~** everything's fine with us.

норма́льность (-и) *ж* normality.

норма́льный (-ен, -ьна, -ьно) *прил* normal; (*психически*) of sound mind.

Норма́нди|я (-и) *ж* Normandy.

нормати́в (-а) *м* norm.

нормати́вный *прил* normative.

норми́ровани|е (-я) *ср* (*цен*) standardization; (*мяса*) rationing.

норми́р|овать (-ую) (*не*)*сов перех* to standardize.

норов|и́ть (-лю́, -и́шь) *несов неперех* (*разг*): **~ +infin** to take pains to do.

но́рок *сущ см* **но́рка**.

нос (-а; *part gen* -у, *loc sg* -у́, *nom pl* -ы́) *м* nose; (*корабля*) bow; (*птицы*) beak, bill; (*ботинка*) toe; **из-под но́са у** +*gen* from under the nose of; **отъе́зд/экза́мен на ~у́** (*разг*) the departure/ exam is imminent; **под но́сом** (*разг: близко*) under one's (very) nose; **с но́сом оста́ться** (*perf*) to be left with nothing; **води́ть** (*impf*) **кого́-н за ~** to lead sb by the nose; **он не ви́дит да́льше со́бственного но́са** (*разг*) he can't see further than his own nose; **сова́ть** (*impf*) **~ в** +*acc* (*разг*) to poke *или* stick one's nose into.

носа́т|ый (-, -а, -о) *прил* with a big nose.

но́сик (-а) *м* (*человека*) small nose; (*чайника*) spout.

носи́л|ки (-ок) *мн* (*для раненых*) stretcher.

носи́льщик (-а) *м* porter.

носи́тел|ь (-я) *м* (*идей, прогресса*) bearer; (*инфекции*) carrier; (*данных, информации*) transmitter; **носи́тель языка́** native speaker.

носи́тельниц|а (-ы) *ж* (*идей, прогресса*) bearer.

нос|и́ть (-шу́, -сишь) *несов перех* (*вещи, камни*) to carry; (*платье, очки*) to wear; (*усы, бороду, причёску*) to sport; (*фамилию мужа*) to use; (*отличаться: подлеж: предложение, спор,*) to be characterized by; **на́ши отноше́ния но́сят делово́й хара́ктер** our relations are of a business nature; **~** (*impf*) **на рука́х** to carry; (*перен: любить*) to adore

▸ **носи́ться** *несов возв* (*человек*) to rush; (*слухи*) to spread; (*одежда*) to wear; (*разг: увлекаться*): **~ся с** +*instr* (*с идеей*) to be preoccupied with; (*с человеком*) to make a fuss of; **~ся** (*impf*) **в во́здухе** (*настроения*) to be in the air; (*идея*) to be widespread.

но́ск|а (-и) *ж* (*одежды, обуви*) wearing; **удо́бный в ~е** comfortable (to wear).

носка́ итп сущ см **носо́к**.

но́с|кий (-кая, -кое, -кие; -ок, -ка́, -ко) прил (туфли, ткань) hard-wearing.

носов|о́й прил (звук) nasal; ~**а́я часть** bow; **носово́й плато́к** handkerchief.

но́сок прил см **но́ский**.

нос|о́к (-ка́; gen pl -о́к) м (обычно мн: чулок) sock; (gen pl -ко́в; боти́нка, чулка́, ноги́) toe; **встава́ть** (**встать** perf) **на** ~**ки́** to stand on tiptoe.

носоро́г (-а) м rhinoceros, rhino (inf).

ностальги́ческ|ий (-ая, -ое, -ие) прил nostalgic.

ностальги́|я (-и) ж (по до́му) homesickness, nostalgia; (по утра́ченному) nostalgia.

но́т|а (-ы) ж note; см также **но́ты**.

нотариа́льный прил (услуги) notarial; **нотариа́льная конто́ра** notarial office.

нота́риус (-а) м notary (public).

нота́ци|я (-и) ж (выговор) lecture.

но́тн|ый прил: ~**ое письмо́** musical notation.

но́ты (-) мн (муз) sheet music; **как по** ~**ам** (перен) smoothly.

но́у-ха́у ср нескл know-how.

ноч|ева́ть (-у́ю; perf **переночева́ть**) несов неперех to spend the night.

ночёв|ка (-ки; gen pl -ок) ж: **останови́ться на** ~**ку** to spend the night; **они́ прие́хали с** ~**кой** they came and stayed the night.

ночле́г (-а) м (место) somewhere to spend the night; **останови́ться** (perf) **на** ~ to spend the night.

ночле́жный прил: ~ **дом** hostel.

ночни́к (-á) м night-light.

ночн|о́й прил (час, холод) night опред; **ночна́я руба́шка** nightshirt; **ночна́я сме́на** night shift.

ноч|ь (-и; loc sg -и́, nom pl -и, gen pl -е́й) ж night; **с утра́ до** ~**и** from dawn to dusk; **на** ~ before bed; **споко́йной но́чи!** good night!

но́чью нареч at night; **и днём и** ~ day and night.

но́ш|а (-и) ж burden.

ноше́ни|е (-я) ср (действие) wearing; ~ **ору́жия** (ЮР) carrying of offensive weapons.

но́шеный прил (одежда, туфли) second-hand.

ношу́(сь) несов см **носи́ть(ся)**.

но́ю итп несов см **ныть**.

ноя́бр|ь (-я́) м November; см также **октя́брь**.

ноя́брьск|ий (-ая, -ое, -ие) прил November опред.

нрав (-а) м (человека) temperament; **э́то мне по нра́ву** this is to my liking; см также **нра́вы**.

нра́в|иться (-люсь, -ишься; perf **понра́виться**) несов возв (+dat): **мне** ~**ится э́тот фильм** I like this film; **мне** ~**ится чита́ть/гуля́ть** I like to read/go for a walk.

нравоуче́ни|е (-я) ср lecture on morals; (в ба́сне) moral; **чита́ть** (impf) **кому́-н** ~**я** to give sb a lecture on morals.

нравоучи́тельный (-ен, -ьна, -ьно) прил (рассказ, история) with a moral; (тон) moralizing.

нра́вственность (-и) ж morals мн.

нра́вствен|ный (-, -на, -но) прил moral.

нра́в|ы (-ов) мн (обычаи) customs мн.

н.с. сокр (= но́вого сти́ля) NS (New Style).

НТР ж сокр = нау́чно-техни́ческая револю́ция.

KEYWORD

ну межд **1** (выражает побуждение) come on; **ну, начина́й!** come on, get started!
2 (выражает восхищение) what; **ну и си́ла!** what strength!
3 (выражает иронию) well (well); **ну и у́мник же ты!** well (well), what a clever fellow you are!
♦ част **1** (неужели): (**да**) **ну?!** not really?!; **я женю́сь – да ну?!** I'm getting married – not really?!
2 (усиливает выразительность): **ну коне́чно!** why of course!; **ну, я тебе́ покажу́!** why, I'll show you!
3 (допустим): **ты говори́шь по-англи́йски?-** **ну, говорю́** do you speak English? – what if I do
4 (во фразах): **ну и ну!** (разг) well well!; **ну-ка!** (разг) come on!; **ну тебя́/его́!** (разг) to hell with you/him!

нувори́ш (-а) м nouveau riche.

нуга́ (-и́) ж nougat.

ну́ден прил см **ну́дный**.

нуди́ст (-а) м nudist.

нуди́ст|ка (-и) ж см **нуди́ст**.

ну́дно нареч tediously.

ну́д|ный (-ен, -на́, -но) прил tedious.

нужд|а́ (-ы́; nom pl -ы) ж (no pl: бе́дность) poverty; (потре́бность): ~ (**в** +prp) need (for); **ну́жды населе́ния** the needs of the population; **в э́том нет** ~**ы́** there is no need for it.

нужда́|ться (-юсь) несов возв (бе́дствовать) to be needy; ~ (impf) **в** +prp to need, be in need of.

ну́жен прил см **ну́жный**.

ну́жно как сказ (необходимо): ~ **им помо́чь** или ~, **что́бы им помогли́** it is necessary to help them; ~ **хоро́шего специали́ста** a good specialist is needed; **мне** ~ **идти́** I have to go, I must go; **мне** ~ **10 рубле́й** I need 10 roubles; **о́чень** ~**!** (разг) my foot!

ну́ж|ный (-ен, -на́, -но, -ны́) прил necessary.

нулев|о́й прил: ~**а́я температу́ра** temperature of zero; ~**а́я отме́тка** (mark of) zero; ~ **результа́т** no result.

нул|ь (-я́) м (МАТ) zero, nought; (при исчислении т.эмперату́ры) zero; (перен: человек) nothing; **начина́ть** (**нача́ть** perf) **с** ~**я́** to start from scratch; **своди́ться** (**свести́сь** perf) **к** ~**ю́** to come to nothing.

нумера́ци|я (-и) ж numbering.

нумер|ова́ть (-у́ю; perf **пронумерова́ть**) несов перех to number.

нумизма́т (-а) м numismatist.

нумизма́тик|а (-и) ж numismatics.

ну́три|я (-и) ж (ЗООЛ) coypu.

нутр|о́ (-á) ср (разг: интуиция) instincts мн; **это**

мне не по ~ý I'm not too keen on this.
НФ м сокр (= национа́льный фронт) NF (=
National Front;) (= нау́чная фанта́стика)
sci-fi, SF (= *science fiction*).
НХЛ ж сокр (= Национа́льная хокке́йная ли́га)
NHL (= *National Hockey League*).
НЧ сокр (= ни́зкая частота́) LF (= *low
frequency*) ♦ прил (низкочасто́тный) LF (=
low-frequency).
ны́не нареч today.
ны́нешн|ий (-яя, -ее, -ие) прил (собы́тия,
правительство) the present; (молодёжь)
today's; ~ее ле́то this summer.
ны́нче нареч (разг: сего́дня) today; (: теперь)
nowadays.
нырн|у́ть (-ý, -ёшь) сов неперех (также перен)
to dive.
ныря́льщик (-а) м diver.
ныря́льщиц|а (-ы) ж см ныря́льщик.
ныря́|ть (-ю) несов неперех (также перен) to
dive.
ныть (но́ю, но́ешь) несов неперех (рана, зуб) to
ache; (жа́ловаться) to moan.

Нью-Йо́рк (-а) м New York.
н.э. сокр (= на́шей э́ры) AD (= *anno Domini*).
НЭП м сокр (ист: = но́вая экономи́ческая
поли́тика) NEP (= *New Economic Policy*).
нюа́нс (-а) м nuance.
Ню́рнберг (-а) м Nuremberg.
нюх (-а) м (собаки) nose; (перен: разг): ~ на
+acc nose for.
ню́ха|ть (-ю; perf поню́хать) несов перех
(цветы, воздух) to smell; (спирт) to sniff; ~
(impf) таба́к to take snuff.
ня́нек сущ см ня́нька.
ня́неч|ка (-ки; gen pl -ек) ж (разг) = ня́ня.
ня́нч|ить (-у, -ишь) несов перех to mind
▸ **ня́нчиться** несов возв: ~ся с +instr (с
младе́нцем) to mind; (разг: с ленты́ем, с
му́жем) to fuss over.
ня́нь|ка (-ьки; gen pl -ек) ж (разг: ребёнка)
nanny.
ня́н|я (-и; gen pl -ь) ж nanny; (работающая на
дому́) child minder; (в больни́це) auxiliary
nurse; (в де́тском саду́) cleaner; приходя́щая
~ babysitter.

~ О, о ~

О, о *сущ нескл (буква)* the 15th letter of the Russian alphabet.

о *предл (+prp)* about; *(+acc; опереться, удариться)* against; *(споткнуться)* over ♦ *межд* oh; **кни́га ~ Росси́и** a book on *или* about Russia; **мы́сли ~ до́ме** thoughts of home; **во́лны бью́тся ~ ска́лы** the waves are beating against the cliffs; **~ да/нет!** oh yes/no!; **~, е́сли бы ты знал!** oh, if only you knew!

о. *сокр* (= **о́стров**) I (= *island*); (= **о́зеро**) L (= *lake*).

о- *префикс (in verbs; сделать каким-нибудь) indicating change of state eg.* округли́ть; *(снабдить чем-н) indicating suppy of sth eg.* озагла́вить; *(распространить действие на всю поверхность) indicating covering of a surface with sth eg.* охвати́ть; *(распространить действие на многих) indicating action involving many people eg.* одари́ть.

оа́зис (**-а**) *м (также перен)* oasis.

ОАЕ *ж сокр* (= **Организа́ция африка́нского еди́нства**) OAU (= *Organization of African Unity*).

ОАПЕК *ж сокр* (= **Организа́ция ара́бских стран-экспортёров не́фти**) OAPEC (= *Organization of Arab Petroleum-Exporting Countries*).

об *предл* = **о**.

об- *префикс см* **о-**.

о́б|а (**-о́их**; *см* **Table 26**; *f* **о́бе**, *nt* **о́ба**) *м чис* both; **смотре́ть** *(impf)* **в ~** *(разг: быть осторожным)* to watch out; *(: быть внимательным)* to keep one's eyes peeled.

обалде́ть (**-ю**; *impf* **обалдева́ть**) *сов неперех (разг)* to go crazy.

обанкро́|титься (**-чусь, -тишься**) *сов возв* to go bankrupt; *(перен: идея, политика)* to prove (to be) bankrupt.

обая́ни|е (**-я**) *ср* charm.

обая́тел|ьный (**-ен, -ьна, -ьно**) *прил* charming.

обва́л (**-а**) *м (в шахте, в штольне)* rock fall; *(снежный)* avalanche; *(здания, этажа)* collapse.

обва́лива|ть (**-ю**) *несов от* **обваля́ть**.

обвал|и́ться (*3sg* **-ится**, *3pl* **-ятся**, *impf* **обва́ливаться**) *сов возв* to collapse; *(потолок, крыша)* to cave in, collapse.

обваля́|ть (**-ю**; *impf* **обва́ливать**) *сов перех*: **~ кого́-н/что-н в** +*prp* to roll sb/sth in.

обв|ари́ть (**-арю́, -а́ришь**; *impf* **обва́ривать**) *сов перех* to pour boiling water over; *(кулин)* to blanch; *(обжечь)* to scald

► **обвари́ться** (*impf* **обва́риваться**) *сов возв (обжечься)* to scald o.s.

обведу́ *итп сов см* **обвести́**.

обвенча́|ть (**-ю**; *impf* **венча́ть**) *сов перех* to marry

► **обвенча́ться** (*impf* **венча́ться**) *сов возв* to get married, marry.

обв|ести́ (**-еду́, -едёшь**; *pt* **-ёл, -ела́, -ело́**, *impf* **обводи́ть**) *сов перех (букву, чертёж)* to go over *(drawing, outline etc)*; *(окаймить: заголовок, рисунок)* to edge; *(футболиста)* to pass *(while keeping possession of the ball/puck etc)*; **обводи́ть** (**~** *perf*) **вокру́г** +*gen (стола, дома)* to lead *или* take round; **обводи́ть** (**~** *perf*) **что-н/кого́-н глаза́ми** to run one's eye over sth/sb; **~** *(perf)* **кого́-н вокру́г па́льца** *(разг)* to twist sb round one's little finger.

обве́тренный *прил* weather-beaten.

обве́тр|иться (**-юсь, -ишься**; *impf* **обве́триваться**) *сов возв* to become weather-beaten.

обветша́лый *прил* dilapidated.

обвива́|ть(ся) (**-ю(сь)**) *несов от* **обви́ть(ся)**.

обвине́ни|е (**-я**) *ср*: **~ (в** +*prp*) accusation (of); *(юр)* charge (of) ♦ *собир (обвиняющая сторона)* the prosecution; **свиде́тели ~я** witnesses for the prosecution.

обвини́тель (**-я**) *м* accuser; *(юр)* prosecutor.

обвини́тельный *прил (речь, выступление)* accusatory; **~ пригово́р** *(юр)* verdict of guilty; **~ акт** *(юр)* indictment.

обвин|и́ть (**-ю́, -и́шь**; *impf* **обвиня́ть**) *сов перех*: **~ кого́-н (в** +*prp*) to accuse sb (of); *(юр)* to charge sb (with).

обвиня́ем|ая (**-ой**; *decl like adj*) *ж см* **обвиня́емый**.

обвиня́емый (**-ого**; *decl like adj*) *м* the accused *или* defendant.

обвиня́|ть (**-ю**) *несов от* **обвини́ть** ♦ *перех (юр)* to prosecute.

обвиса́|ть (*3sg* **-ет**, *3pl* **-ют**, *perf* **обви́снуть**) *несов неперех* to droop.

обви́слый *прил (разг: кожа)* sagging; *(: усы)* drooping; *(: тело)* flabby.

обви́с|нуть (*3sg* **-нет**, *3pl* **-нут**, *pt* **-, -ла, -ло**) *сов от* **обвиса́ть**.

об|ви́ть (-овью́, -овьёшь; *impf* **обвива́ть**) *сов перех* (*подлеж: плющ, вьюн*) to twine around; **обвива́ть** (~ *perf*) кого́-н/что-н чем-н to wind sth round sb/sth; **обвива́ть** (~ *perf*) чью-н ше́ю рука́ми to wrap one's arms around sb's neck

▸ **обви́ться** (*impf* **обвива́ться**) *сов возв*: ~ся вокру́г +*gen* to twine around.

обв|оди́ть (-ожу́, -о́дишь) *несов от* **обвести́**.

обводн|и́ть (-ю́, -и́шь; *impf* **обводня́ть**) *перех* to irrigate.

обво́дный *прил*: ~ кана́л *canal encircling a town*.

обводня́|ть (-ю) *несов от* **обводни́ть**.

обвожу́ *несов см* **обводи́ть**.

обвора́жива|ть (-ю) *несов от* **обворожи́ть**.

обвор|ова́ть (-у́ю; *impf* **обворо́вывать**) *сов перех* (*разг: кварти́ру*) to do over; (: *сосе́да*) to rob.

обворожи́тельный (-ен, -ьна, -ьно) *прил* captivating.

обворож|и́ть (-у́, -и́шь; *impf* **обвора́живать**) *сов перех* to captivate.

обв|яза́ть (-яжу́, -я́жешь; *impf* **обвя́зывать**) *сов перех*: ~ кого́-н/что-н чем-н (*верёвкой, платком*) to tie sth round sb/sth; ~ (*perf*) что-н спи́цами/крючко́м to knit/crochet a border on sth

▸ **обвяза́ться** (*impf* **обвя́зываться**) *сов возв*: ~ся чем-н to tie sth round o.s.

обгл|ода́ть (-ожу́, -о́жешь; *impf* **обгла́дывать**) *сов перех* to pick clean.

обговор|и́ть (-ю́, -и́шь; *impf* **обгова́ривать**) *сов перех* (*разг*) to discuss.

обго́н (-а) *м* overtaking.

обгоню́ *итп сов см* **обогна́ть**.

обгоня́|ть (-ю) *несов от* **обогна́ть**.

обгора́|ть (-ю) *несов от* **обгоре́ть**.

обгоре́лый *прил* (*дом, де́рево*) burnt; (*разг: спина́, пле́чи*) sunburnt.

обгор|е́ть (-ю́, -и́шь; *impf* **обгора́ть**) *неперех* (*дом*) to be burnt; (*разг: на пожа́ре*) to get burnt; (: *на со́лнце*) to get sunburnt.

обгры́з|ть (-у́, -ёшь; *impf* **обгрыза́ть**) *сов перех* (*я́блоко, кость*) to gnaw; **обгрыза́ть** (~ *perf*) но́гти to bite one's nails right down.

обдел|и́ть (-елю́, -е́лишь; *impf* **обделя́ть**) *сов перех*: он ~ели́л её деньга́ми he didn't give her the money; приро́да ~ели́ла его́ умо́м/си́лой he is not blessed with intelligence/strength; всем да́ли пода́рки, а его́ ~ели́ли everybody got a present but he was left out.

обдеру́ *итп сов см* **ободра́ть**.

обдира́|ть (-ю) *несов от* **ободра́ть**.

обду́ман|ный (-, -на, -но) *прил* considered.

обду́ма|ть (-ю; *impf* **обду́мывать**) *сов перех* to consider, think over.

обдур|и́ть (-ю́, -и́шь; *impf* **обдуря́ть**) *сов перех*: ~ кого́-н (*разг: обману́ть*) to pull the wool over

sb's eyes; (: *смоше́нничать*) to rip sb off.

о́б|е (-е́их) *ж чис см* **о́ба**.

обега́|ть (-ю; *impf* **обега́ть**) *сов перех* (*разг*) to rush round.

обега́|ть (-ю) *несов от* **обега́ть, обежа́ть**.

обегу́ *итп сов см* **обежа́ть**.

обе́д (-а) *м* lunch, dinner; (*вре́мя*) lunch *или* dinner time; (*разг: переры́в*) lunch break; **за** ~ом at lunch *или* dinner; **по́сле** ~а after lunch *или* dinner; (*по́сле 12 часо́в дня*) in the afternoon; (*по́сле 12 часо́в дня*) ~ closed for lunch.

обе́да|ть (-ю; *perf* **пообе́дать**) *несов неперех* to have lunch *или* dinner; (*разг: уходи́ть на переры́в*) to take a lunch break.

обе́ден *сущ см* **обе́дня**.

обе́денный *прил* (*стол, серви́з*) dinner *опред*; (*часы́, вре́мя*) lunch *опред*, dinner *опред*.

обедне́вший (-ая, -ее, -ие) *прил* impoverished.

обедне́|ть (-ю) *сов от* **бедне́ть**.

обе́д|ня (-ни; *gen pl* -ен) *ж* (*РЕЛ*) Mass; **идти́** (**пойти́** *perf*) **к** ~не to go to Mass; **служи́ть** (*impf*) ~ню to hear Mass.

обежа́ть (*как* **бежа́ть**; *см* **Table 20**; *impf* **обега́ть**) *сов перех* (*разг: магази́ны*) to rush round ◆ *неперех*: ~ **вокру́г** +*gen* to run round.

обезбо́ливани|е (-я) *ж* anaesthetization (*BRIT*), anesthetization (*US*).

обезбо́лива|ть (-ю) *несов от* **обезбо́лить**.

обезбо́ливающ|ее (-его; *decl like adj*) *ср* (*разг*) painkiller.

обезбо́ливающий (-ая, -ее, -ие) *прил* anaesthetic *опред* (*BRIT*), anesthetic *опред* (*US*).

обезбо́л|ить (-ю, -ишь; *impf* **обезбо́ливать**) *сов перех* to anaesthetize (*BRIT*), anesthetize (*US*); **обезбо́ливать** (~ *perf*) кому́-н ро́ды to give sb an anaesthetic (*BRIT*) *или* anesthetic (*US*) during childbirth.

обезво́|дить (-жу, -дишь; *impf* **обезво́живать**) *сов перех* (*зе́млю*) to drain; (*органи́зм*) to dehydrate.

обезво́жу *сов см* **обезво́дить**.

обезвре́|дить (-жу, -дишь; *impf* **обезвре́живать**) *сов перех* (*бо́мбу*) to defuse; (*во́ду*) to purify; (*престу́пника*) to make powerless.

обезгла́в|ить (-лю, -ишь; *impf* **обезгла́вливать**) *сов перех* to behead; (*перен: восста́ние*) to leave without a leader.

обездо́лен|ный (-, -на, -но) *прил* deprived.

обездо́л|ить (-ю, -ишь) *сов перех* to deprive.

обезжи́ренный *прил* fat-free.

обезжи́р|ить (-ю, -ишь; *impf* **обезжи́ривать**) *сов перех* (*молоко́, творо́г*) to skim; (*шерсть*) to remove fat from.

обезли́ч|ить (-у, -ишь; *impf* **обезли́чивать**) *сов перех* to depersonalize; (*рабо́ту, руково́дство*) to remove individual responsibility from.

обезобра́|зить (-жу, -зишь; *impf*

обезобра́живать) *сов перех* to disfigure.

обезопа́|сить (-шу, -сишь) *сов перех* (*себя, друга*) to protect

▶ **обезопа́ситься** *сов возв* to protect o.s.

обезору́ж|ить (-у, -ишь; *impf* **обезору́живать**) *сов перех* (*также перен*) to disarm.

обезу́ме|ть (-ю) *сов неперех*: ~ **от** +*gen* (*страха, горя итп*) to go out of one's mind with.

обезья́н|а (-ы) *ж* (*с хвостом*) monkey; (*без хвоста*) ape; (*перен: разг*) copycat.

обезья́н|ий (-ья, -ье, -ьи) *прил* (*хвост*) monkey's; (*повадки*) apelike.

обезья́ннича|ть (-ю; *impf* **собезья́нничать**) *несов неперех* (*разг*) to be a copycat.

обе́их *чис см* **о́бе**.

обе́й(те) *сов см* **оби́ть**.

обели́ск (-а) *м* obelisk.

обел|и́ть (-ю́, -и́шь; *impf* **обеля́ть**) *сов перех* to whitewash.

оберега́|ть (-ю) *несов перех* (*человека*) to protect; (*имущество*) to guard.

оберн|у́ть (-у́, -ёшь; *impf* **обёртывать** *или* **обора́чивать**) *сов перех* (*книгу, посылку*) to wrap (up); (*impf* **обора́чивать**; *капитал*) to turn over; **обёртывать** *или* **обора́чивать** (~ *perf*) **что-н вокру́г** +*gen* (*талии, головы*) to wrap sth round; **обора́чивать** (~ *perf*) **де́ло в свою́ по́льзу** (*перен*) to turn things to one's own advantage

▶ **оберну́ться** (*impf* **обора́чиваться**) *сов возв* (*поверну́ться назад*) to turn (round); (*капитал, деньги*) to be recovered; **обора́чиваться** (~*ся perf*) +*instr* (*неприятностями, сюрпризом*) to turn out to be; (*лебедем, волком*) to turn into.

обёрт|ка (-ки; *gen pl* -ок) *ж* (*книжная, конфетная*) wrapper; (*на посылке*) wrapping.

обёрточн|ый *прил*: ~**ая бума́га** wrapping paper.

обёртыва|ть (-ю) *несов от* **оберну́ть**.

оберу́(сь) *итп сов см* **обобра́ть(ся)**.

обескро́в|ить (-лю, -ишь) *сов перех* (*перен*) to sap the strength of.

обескура́жен|ный (-, -на, -но) *прил* baffled.

обескура́ж|ить (-у, -ишь; *impf* **обескура́живать**) *сов перех* (*озадачить*) to baffle.

обеспе́чени|е (-я) *ср* (*мира, безопасности, договора*) guarantee; ~ +*instr* (*сырьём, продуктами*) provision of; **материа́льное** ~ financial security.

обеспе́ченность (-и) *ж* (material) comfort; (*школ, завода итп*) provision; **фина́нсовая** ~ financial security.

обеспе́ченн|ый (-, -на, -но) *прил* well-off, well-to-do.

обеспе́ч|ить (-у, -ишь; *impf* **обеспе́чивать**) *сов перех* (*семью*) to provide for; (*мир, успех*) to guarantee, ensure; **обеспе́чивать** (~ *perf*) **кого́-н/что-н чем-н** to provide *или* supply sb/sth with sth, provide *или* supply sth for sb/sth.

обеспоко́|ить (-ю, -ишь) *сов от* **беспоко́ить**.

обесси́ле|ть (-ю; *impf* **обесси́левать**) *сов неперех* to become *или* grow weak.

обесси́л|ить (-ю, -ишь; *impf* **обесси́ливать**) *сов перех* to weaken.

обессла́в|ить (-лю, -ишь) *сов перех* to besmirch.

обессме́р|тить (-чу, -тишь) *сов перех* to immortalize.

обесто́ч|ить (-у, -ишь; *impf* **обесто́чивать**) *сов перех* (*тех*) to cut off the power to.

обесцве́|тить (-чу, -тишь; *impf* **обесцве́чивать**) *несов перех* to bleach; (*перен: рассказ*) to tone down

▶ **обесцве́титься** (*impf* **обесцве́чиваться**) *сов возв* to be bleached; (*ткань: от времени*) to fade; (*перен: рассказ*) to become flat.

обесце́нивани|е (-я) *ср* (*валюты*) depreciation; (: *намеренное*) devaluation.

обесце́н|ить (-ю, -ишь; *impf* **обесце́нивать**) *сов перех* (*также перен*) to devalue

▶ **обесце́ниться** (*impf* **обесце́ниваться**) *сов возв* to be devalued; (*вещь*) to depreciate.

обесче́|стить (-щу, -стишь) *сов от* **бесче́стить**.

обе́т (-а) *м* vow.

обетова́нн|ый *прил*: ~**ая земля́** the Promised Land.

обеща́ни|е (-я) *ср* promise.

обеща́|ть (-ю; *perf* **обеща́ть** *или* **пообеща́ть**) *несов (не)перех* to promise.

обжа́ловани|е (-я) *ср* appeal.

обжа́л|овать (-ую) *сов перех* to appeal against.

обжа́р|ить (-ю, -ишь; *impf* **обжа́ривать**) *сов перех* to brown.

обж|е́чь (-огу́, -ожжёшь итп, -огу́т; *pt* -жёг, -огла́, -огло́) *сов от* **жечь** ◆ (*impf* **обжига́ть**) *перех* to burn; (*кирпич итп*) to fire; (*дерево итп*) to scorch; (*подлеж: крапива*) to sting

▶ **обже́чься** *сов от* **же́чься** ◆ (*impf* **обжига́ться**) *возв* to burn o.s.; (*перен: потерпеть неудачу*) to get one's fingers burnt.

обжира́|ться (-юсь) *несов от* **обожра́ться**.

обжито́й *прил* (*дом*) lived-in.

обжо́р|а (-ы) *м/ж* (*разг*) pig, greedy guts.

обжо́рств|о (-а) *ср* (*разг*) greediness.

обжу́л|ить (-ю, -ишь; *impf* **обжу́ливать**) *сов перех* (*разг*) to con.

обзаве|сти́сь (-ду́сь, -дёшься; *impf* **обзаводи́ться**) *сов возв* (+*instr*; *разг*) to get o.s.

обзвон|и́ть (-ю́, -и́шь; *impf* **обзва́нивать**) *сов перех* (*разг*) to phone round.

обзову́ *итп сов см* **обозва́ть**.

обзо́р (-а) *м* view; (*статьи, новостей*) review.

обзо́рн|ый *прил* general; ~**ая статья́** review.

обзыва́|ть (-ю) *несов от* **обозва́ть**

▶ **обзыва́ться** *несов возв* (*разг*) to call people names.

обива́|ть (-ю) *несов от* **оби́ть**.

оби́в|ка (-и) *ж* upholstery.

оби́д|а (-ы) *ж* (*несправедливость*) insult;

(*горечь*) grievance; **кака́я ~!** what a pity!;
наноси́ть (нанести́ *perf*) **~y кому́-н** to hurt *или*
offend sb; **не дава́ть (дать** *perf*) **кого́-н в ~у**
(*разг*) to stand *или* stick up for sb; **быть** (*impf*) **в**
~е на кого́-н to be in a huff with sb.

оби́ден *прил см* **оби́дный**.

оби́деть (-жу, -дишь; *impf* **обижа́ть**) *сов перех*
to hurt, offend; **он ~жен умо́м/красото́й** (*разг*)
he's not too smart/good-looking

▸ **оби́деться** (*impf* **обижа́ться**) *сов возв*: **~ся**
(на +*acc*) to be hurt *или* offended (by).

оби́дно *как сказ* (*см прил*) it's offensive; it's
annoying; **мне ~ слы́шать э́то** it hurts me to
hear this; **~, что мы не встре́тились** it's
annoying that we didn't meet.

оби́д|ный (-ен, -на, -но) *прил*
(*оскорби́тельный*) offensive; (*разг: досадный*)
annoying.

оби́дчив|ый (-, -а, -о) *прил* touchy.

обижа́|ть(ся) (-ю(сь)) *несов от* **оби́деть(ся)**.

оби́жен|ный (-, -на, -но) *прил* aggrieved.

оби́жу(сь) *сов см* **оби́деть(ся)**.

оби́лен *прил см* **оби́льный**.

оби́ли|е (-я) *ср* abundance.

оби́л|ьный (-ен, -ьна, -ьно) *прил* abundant;
(+*instr*; *рыбой, талантами*) rich in; **~ьная еда́**
food in abundance.

обиня́к (-а́) *м*: **без обиняко́в** plainly.

обира́|ть (-ю) *несов от* **обобра́ть**.

обита́ем|ый (-, -а, -о) *прил* inhabited.

обита́тель (-я) *м* inhabitant.

обита́|ть (-ю) *несов неперех* to live.

оби́|ть (-обью, -обьёшь; *imper* **обе́й(те)**, *impf*
обива́ть) *сов перех*: **~** (+*instr*) to cover (with);
обива́ть (~ *perf*) **поро́ги у кого́-н** to camp on
sb's doorstep.

обихо́д (-а) *м*: **быть в ~е** to be in use; **входи́ть**
(**войти́** *perf*) **в ~** to come into use; **выходи́ть**
(**вы́йти** *perf*) **из ~a** to go out of use.

обихо́дный (-ен, -на, -но) *прил* everyday.

обка́та|ть (-ю; *impf* **обка́тывать**) *сов перех*
(*поверхность, дорогу*) to flatten (out);
(*машину*) to run in; (*станок итп*) to test (out).

обка́тк|а (-и) *ж* (*дороги*) flattening; (*машины,*
станка) testing.

обка́тыва|ть (-ю) *несов от* **обката́ть**.

обкла́дыва|ть(ся) (-ю(сь)) *несов от*
обложи́ть(ся).

обкле́|ить (-ю, -ишь; *impf* **обкле́ивать**) *сов*
перех (*плакатами, бумагой*) to cover; (*обоями*)
to (wall)paper.

обко́м (-а) *м сокр* = **областно́й комите́т**;
(*профсоюза, партии*) ≈ regional committee.

обкраду́ *итп сов см* **обокра́сть**.

обкра́дыва|ть (-ю) *несов от* **обокра́сть**.

обку́р|ить (-урю́, -у́ришь; *impf* **обку́ривать**) *сов*
перех (*разг: комнату*) to fill with smoke; **ты**
меня́ совсе́м ~и́л your smoke is suffocating

me.

обкуса́|ть (-ю; *impf* **обку́сывать**) *сов перех* to
nibble; **обку́сывать (~** *perf*) **но́гти** to bite one's
nails.

обл. *сокр* = **о́бласть**.

обла́в|а (-ы) *ж* (*на преступников*) roundup;
устро́ить (*perf*) **~у на** +*acc* (*на зверя*) to close in
on.

облага́|ть (-ю) *несов от* **обложи́ть**.

облагоде́тельств|овать (-ую) *сов перех*: **~**
кого́-н to do sb a great favour (*BRIT*) *или* favor
(*US*).

облада́тель (-я) *м* possessor.

облада́|ть (-ю) *несов неперех* (+*instr*) to
possess; (*женщиной*) to have; **~** (*impf*)
здоро́вьем to enjoy good health; **~** (*impf*)
красото́й to be beautiful.

обла́|зить (-жу, -зишь) *сов перех* (*разг*) to go
round.

обла́ива|ть (-ю) *несов от* **обла́ять**.

о́блак|о (-а; *nom pl* **-á**, *gen pl* **-о́в**) *ср* (*также*
перен) cloud; **вита́ть** (*impf*) **в облака́х** to have
one's head in the clouds.

обла́мыва|ть(ся) (-ю(сь)) *несов от*
обломи́ть(ся).

обласка́|ть (-ю) *сов перех* to be kind to.

областно́й *прил* (*центр, театр*) ≈ regional,
oblast *опред*; (*выражение, слово*) regional.

о́бласт|ь (-и; *gen pl* **-е́й**) *ж* region; (*админ*) ≈
region, oblast; (*науки, искусства*) field; **в ~и**
+*gen* (*в сфере*) in the field of.

о́блачен *прил см* **о́блачный**.

о́блачность (-и) *ж* cloud.

о́блач|ный (-ен, -на, -но) *прил* cloudy.

обла́|ять (-ю; *impf* **обла́ивать**) *сов перех* to bark
at; (*перен: разг*) to swear at.

облёг *итп сов см* **обле́чь**.

облега́|ть (-ю) *несов от* **обле́чь** ♦ *перех* to fit.

облега́ющий (-ая, -ее, -ие) *прил* close-fitting.

облегче́ни|е (-я) *ср* (*условий труда, жизни*)
improvement; (*успокоение*) relief.

облегчённо *нареч* with relief.

облегчённый *прил* (*ткань, инструмент*)
light; (*труд, экзамен*) easier; (*ответ, улыбка*)
relieved.

облегч|и́ть (-у́, -и́шь; *impf* **облегча́ть**) *сов перех*
(*вес*) to lighten; (*экзамен, жизнь*) to make
easier; (*боль, страдание*) to relieve; **облегча́ть**
(**~** *perf*) **ду́шу** to ease one's mind.

обледене́л|ый *прил* (*ступени, горка*) icy;
(*борода*) frozen.

обледене́|ть (-ю) *сов неперех* (*см прил*) to
become icy; to freeze.

облеза́|ть (-ю) *несов от* **обле́зть**.

обле́зл|ый *прил* (*разг: собака, птица*) mangy;
(*вид, внешность*) scruffy; (*стены*) peeling.

обле́з|ть (-у, -ешь; *impf* **облеза́ть**) *сов неперех* (*разг*) to grow mangy; (*краска, обои*) to peel (off); (*стены*) to peel.

облёк *итп сов см* **облечь**.

облека́ть (-ю) *несов от* **облечь**.

облеку́ *сов см* **облечь**.

облен|и́ться (-ю́сь, -е́нишься) *сов возв* to grow lazy.

обл|епи́ть (-еплю́, -е́пишь; *impf* **облепля́ть**) *сов перех* (*подлеж: грязь, глина*) to stick to; (*перен: подлеж: люди, мухи*) to surround; (*разг: покрыть*): ~ **что-н чем-н** to plaster sth with sth.

облете́ть (-чу́, -ти́шь; *impf* **облета́ть**) *сов перех* to fly round; (*новость*) to spread; (*листья*) to fall off.

обл|е́чь (-еку́, -ече́шь *итп*, -еку́т; *pt* -ёк, -екла́, -екло́, *impf* **облека́ть**) *сов перех*: ~ **кого́-н/что́-н чем-н** (*властью, доверием*) to vest sb/sth with sth; (*тайной*) to shroud sb/sth in sth; (*impf* **облега́ть**, *3sg* -я́жет, *3pl* -я́гут, *pt* -ёг, -егла́, -егло́) to envelop; **облека́ть** (~ *perf*) **что-н в** +*acc* to express sth in.

облива́ть (-ю) *несов от* **обли́ть**

▸ **облива́ться** *несов от* **обли́ться ♦** *возв*: ~**ся слеза́ми** to be in floods of tears; **у меня́ се́рдце кро́вью** ~**ется** my heart bleeds.

облига́ци|я (-и) *ж* (*комм*) debenture (bond); **премиа́льные** ~**и** premium bond; **прави́тельственные** ~**и** government stock.

обл|иза́ть (-ижу́, -и́жешь; *impf* **обли́зывать**) *сов перех* (*губы, ложку*) to lick; **пиро́г – па́льчики** ~**и́жешь** (*разг*) the pie is scrumptious

▸ **облиза́ться** (*impf* **обли́зываться**) *сов возв* (*человек*) to lick one's lips; (*собака, кошка*) to lick itself.

о́блик (-а) *м* (*внешний вид*) appearance; (*характер, также перен*) character.

облиня́|ть (-ю) *сов от* **линя́ть**.

об|ли́ть (-олью́, -ольёшь; *impf* **облива́ть**) *сов перех*: ~ **кого́-н/что́-н чем-н** (*намеренно*) to pour sth over sb/sth; (*случайно*) to spill sth over sb/sth; **облива́ть** (~ *perf*) **кого́-н гря́зью** (*перен*) to throw mud at sb; **облива́ть** (~ *perf*) **кого́-н презре́нием** to pour scorn on sb; **облива́ть** (~ *perf*) **что-н слеза́ми** to shed tears over sth

▸ **обли́ться** (*impf* **облива́ться**) *сов возв*: ~**ся** +*instr* (*водо́й*) to sluice o.s. with; (*соком*) to spill over o.s.; **облива́ться** (~**ся** *perf*) **по́том** to be bathed in sweat.

облицева́ть (-у́ю; *impf* **облицо́вывать**) *сов перех*: ~ **что-н чем-н** to face sth with sth.

облицо́вк|а (-и) *ж* facing.

облицо́выва|ть (-ю) *несов от* **облицева́ть**.

обличи́|ть (-ю) *несов от* **обличи́ть**.

обличи́тел|ьный (-ен, -ьна, -ьно) *прил* damning.

облич|и́ть (-у́, -и́шь; *impf* **облича́ть**) *сов перех* to expose.

обло́жек *сущ см* **обло́жка**.

обложе́ни|е (-я) *ср* (*действие: налогом итп*) imposition; (*сбор*) levy.

обл|ожи́ть (-ожу́, -о́жишь; *impf* **обкла́дывать**) *сов перех* to surround; (*печь*) to face; (*подлеж: тучи, облака*) to cover; (*разг: обругать*) to swear at; **облага́ть** (~ *perf*) **кого́-н/что́-н чем-н** to impose sth on sb/sth; **го́рло** ~**ожи́ло** my throat is furred

▸ **обложи́ться** (*impf* **обкла́дываться**) *сов возв*: ~**ся** +*instr* to surround o.s. with.

обло́жк|а (-ки; *gen pl* -ек) *ж* (*книги, тетради*) cover; (*для паспорта итп*) holder.

облок|оти́ться (-очу́сь, -о́тишься; *impf* **облока́чиваться**) *сов возв*: ~ **на** +*acc* to lean on (*with elbows*).

облома́|ть (-ю; *impf* **обла́мывать**) *сов перех* (*ветки, ногти итп*) to break off; (*перен: разг*): ~ **кого́-н** to talk sb round

▸ **облома́ться** (*impf* **обла́мываться**) *сов возв* (*ветка, ногти итп*) to break off.

обло́м|ок (-ка) *м* fragment.

обл|упи́ть (-уплю́, -у́пишь) *сов от* **лупи́ть ♦** (*impf* **облу́пливать**) *перех* to peel

▸ **облупи́ться** *сов от* **лупи́ться ♦** (*impf* **облу́пливаться**) *возв* (*разг*) to peel.

облу́пленн|ый *прил* (*разг*) peeling; **знать** (*impf*) **кого́-н как** ~**ого** (*разг*) to know sb inside out.

облу́плива|ть(ся) (-ю(сь)) *несов от* **облупи́ть(ся)**.

облупи́ть(ся) *сов см* **облупи́ть(ся)**.

облуча́|ть(ся) (-ю(сь)) *несов от* **облучи́ть(ся)**.

облуче́ни|е (-я) *ср* irradiation.

облуч|и́ть (-у́, -и́шь; *impf* **облуча́ть**) *сов перех* to irradiate

▸ **облучи́ться** (*impf* **облуча́ться**) *сов возв* to be irradiated.

облущ|и́ть (-у́, -и́шь) *сов от* **лущи́ть**.

облысе́|ть (-ю) *сов от* **лысе́ть**.

облюб|ова́ть (-у́ю; *impf* **облюбо́вывать**) *сов перех* to choose.

обля́жет *итп сов см* **облечь**.

обма́|зать (-жу, -жешь; *impf* **обма́зывать**) *сов перех*: ~ **кого́-н/что́-н чем-н** to coat sb/sth with sth; (*разг: испачкать*) to get sb/sth covered in sth.

обмакну́|ть (-у́, -ёшь; *impf* **обма́кивать**) *сов перех*: ~ **что-н в** +*acc* to dip sth into.

обма́н (-а) *м* deception; ~ **зре́ния** optical illusion.

обма́нный *прил* fraudulent; **обма́нным путём** fraudulently.

обм|ану́ть (-ану́, -а́нешь; *impf* **обма́нывать**) *сов перех* to deceive; (*поступить нечестно*) to cheat; (*не выполнить обещание*) to fail

▸ **обману́ться** (*impf* **обма́нываться**) *сов возв*: ~**ся в** +*prp* to be disappointed in.

обма́нчив|ый (-, -а, -о) *прил* deceptive.

обма́нщик (-а) *м* cheat.

обма́нщиц|а (-ы) *ж см* **обма́нщик**.

обма́ныва|ть(ся) (-ю(сь)) *несов от* **обману́ть(ся)**.

обма́тыва|ть(ся) (-ю(сь)) *несов от* **обмота́ть(ся)**.

обмахну́ть (-у́, -ёшь; *impf* **обма́хивать**) *сов перех* (*пыль*) to brush off; (*стол*) to wipe down; **обма́хивать** (~ *perf*) **лицо́ ве́ером** to fan one's face *или* o.s.
▶ **обмахну́ться** (*impf* **обма́хиваться**) *сов возв*: ~**ся ве́ером** to fan o.s.
обмеле́ть (-ю) *сов от* **меле́ть**.
обме́н (-а) *м* (*также экон*) exchange; (*документов*) renewal; (*также*: ~ **веще́ств**: БИО) metabolism; (*также*: ~ **жилпло́щадью**) exchange (*of flats etc*); **в ~ на** +*acc* in exchange for.
обменя́ть (-ю; *impf* **обме́нивать**) *сов перех* (*вещи, билеты*) to change
▶ **обменя́ться** (*impf* **обме́ниваться**) *сов возв*: ~**ся** +*instr* to exchange.
обме́р|ить (-ю, -ишь; *impf* **обме́ривать**) *сов перех* (*участок итп*) to measure.
обме|сти́ (-ту́, -тёшь; *impf* **обмета́ть**) *сов перех* (*песок, паутину*) to brush away.
обм|ета́ть (-ечу́, -е́тишь; *impf* **обмётывать**) *сов перех* to oversew ♦ *безл* (*разг*): **гу́бы ~ета́ло** my lips are chapped.
обмету́ *итп сов см* **обмести́**.
обмётыва|ть (-ю) *несов от* **обмета́ть**.
обмечу́ *сов см* **обмета́ть**.
обмола́чива|ть (-ю) *несов от* **обмолоти́ть**.
обмо́лв|иться (-люсь, -ишься) *сов возв* (*разг*: *сказать невзначай*) to slip in; (: *оговориться*) to slip up; **сло́вом не ~** (*perf*) (*разг*) to keep mum.
обмоло́т (-а) *м* (*действие*) threshing; (*количество*) yield (*from threshing*).
обмоло|ти́ть (-очу́, -о́тишь; *impf* **обмола́чивать**) *сов перех* to thresh.
обморо́|зить (-жу, -зишь; *impf* **обмора́живать**) *сов перех*: ~ **но́гу/ру́ку** to get frostbite in one's foot/hand
▶ **обморо́зиться** (*impf* **обмора́живаться**) *сов возв* to suffer from frostbite.
о́бморок (-а) *м* faint; **па́дать** (**упа́сть** *perf*) **в ~** to faint.
обмота́|ть (-ю; *impf* **обма́тывать**) *сов перех*: ~ **кого́-н/что-н чем-н** to wrap sth round sb/sth; (*обвить*): ~ **что-н вокру́г** +*gen* (*пальца, столба*) to wind sth round
▶ **обмота́ться** (*impf* **обма́тываться**) *сов возв*: ~**ся вокру́г** +*gen* to be wound round; **обма́тываться** (~**ся** *perf*) +*instr* (*разг: шарфом, одеялом*) to wrap o.s. in.
обмо́тк|а (-и) *ж* (*ЭЛЕК*) winding.
обмо́ю *итп сов см* **обмы́ть**.
обмундирова́ни|е (-я) *ср* (*ВОЕН: действие*) fitting out; (*комплект одежды*) uniform.
обмундир|ова́ть (-у́ю) *impf* **обмундиро́вывать**) *сов перех* to fit out.
обмы́|ть (-о́ю, -о́ешь; *impf* **обмыва́ть**) *сов перех* (*рану*) to bathe; (*разг: событие, премию*) to celebrate (*by drinking*).
обнагле́ть (-ю) *сов от* **нагле́ть**.
обнадёж|ить (-у, -ишь; *impf* **обнадёживать**) *сов перех* to reassure; (*обещать*) to assure.
обнажа́|ть(ся) (-ю(сь)) *несов от* **обнажи́ть(ся)**.
обнаж|ённый (-ён, -ена́, -ено́) *прил* bare; (*корни*) exposed.
обнаж|и́ть (-у́, -и́шь; *impf* **обнажа́ть**) *сов перех* to expose; (*руки, ноги*) to bare; (*ветки*) to strip bare; (*шпагу, мечь*) to draw
▶ **обнажи́ться** (*impf* **обнажа́ться**) *сов возв* to be exposed; (*человек*) to strip; (*рука, нога итп*) to be bared; (*лес, дерево*) to become bare.
обнаро́довани|е (-я) *ср* (*см глаг*) publication; promulgation.
обнаро́д|овать (-ую) *сов перех* (*факты, статью*) to make public; (*закон, указ*) to promulgate.
обнару́ж|ить (-у, -ишь; *impf* **обнару́живать**) *сов перех* (*найти*) to find; (*проявить*) to show; (*раскрыть*) to reveal
▶ **обнару́житься** (*impf* **обнару́живаться**) *сов возв* (*найтись*) to be found; (*проявиться*) to show; (*стать явным*) to become evident.
обна́шива|ться (-юсь) *несов от* **обноси́ться**.
обн|ести́ (-есу́, -есёшь; *pt* -ёс, -есла́, -есло́, *impf* **обноси́ть**) *сов перех*: ~ **что-н/кого́-н вокру́г** +*gen* to carry sth/sb round; (*огородить*): ~ **что-н чем-н** to surround sth with sth; **обноси́ть** (~**ся** *perf*) **кого́-н чем-н** (*вином*) to serve sb with sth.
обнима́|ть(ся) (-ю(сь)) *несов от* **обня́ть(ся)**.
обни́мк|а *ж*: **в ~у** (*разг*) with their arms around each other.
обниму́(сь) *итп сов см* **обня́ть(ся)**.
обнища́|ть (-ю) *сов от* **нища́ть**.
обнов|и́ть (-лю́, -и́шь; *impf* **обновля́ть**) *сов перех* (*оборудование, гардероб*) to replenish; (*репертуар, знания*) to refresh; (*памятник, дом*) to renovate; (*жизнь, искусство*) to revitalize; (*разг: платье*) to christen
▶ **обнови́ться** (*impf* **обновля́ться**) *сов возв* (*оборудование, гардероб*) to be replenished; (*репертуар*) to be refreshed; (*организм, природа*) to be regenerated; (*жизнь, искусство*) to be revitalized.
обновле́ни|е (-я) *ср* (*см возв*) replenishment; refreshment; regeneration; revitalization.
обновлю́(сь) *сов см* **обнови́ть(ся)**.
обновля́|ть(ся) (-ю(сь)) *несов от* **обнови́ть(ся)**.
обн|оси́ть (-ошу́, -о́сишь) *несов от* **обнести́**.
обн|оси́ться (-ошу́сь, -о́сишься; *impf* **обна́шиваться**) *сов возв* (*разг: старик, ребёнок*) to wear out one's clothes; (: *одежда*) to become worn to bits.
обно́ск|и (-ов) *мн* old clothes *мн*.

обношу́(сь) *несов см* **обноси́ть(ся)**.
обню́ха|ть (-ю; *impf* **обню́хивать**) *сов перех* to sniff.
обня́|ть (-иму́, -и́мешь; *pt* -ял, -яла́, -яло, *impf* **обнима́ть**) *сов перех* to embrace
▸ **обня́ться** (*impf* **обнима́ться**) *сов возв* to embrace (each other).
обо *предл см* **о**.
об|обра́ть (-еру́, -ерёшь; *impf* **обира́ть**) *сов перех* (*смородину, черешню*) to pick; (*разг: прохожего, клиента*) to fleece
▸ **обобра́ться** *сов возв*: **забо́т не ~ерёшься** (*разг*) no end of worries.
обобща́|ть (-ю) *несов от* **обобщи́ть**.
обобще́ни|е (-я) *ср* generalization.
обобщё́нный (-, -на́, -но) *прил* general.
обобществ|и́ть (-лю́, -и́шь; *impf* **обобществля́ть**) *сов перех* (*производство, хозяйство*) to socialize; (*землю, труд*) to collectivize.
обобществле́ни|е (-я) *ср* socialization.
обобществлю́ *сов см* **обобществи́ть**.
обобществля́|ть (-ю) *несов от* **обобществи́ть**.
обобщ|и́ть (-у́, -и́шь; *impf* **обобща́ть**) *сов перех* (*результаты, факты*) to generalize from; (*статью, выступление*) to summarize.
обобью́ *итп сов см* **обби́ть**.
обовью́(сь) *итп сов см* **обви́ть(ся)**.
обога|ти́ть (-щу́, -ти́шь; *impf* **обогаща́ть**) *сов перех* to enrich; (*руду*) to concentrate
▸ **обогати́ться** (*impf* **обогаща́ться**) *сов возв* (*человек, страна*) to be enriched; (*почва, руда*) to be concentrated.
об|огна́ть (-гоню́, -го́нишь; *impf* **обгоня́ть**) *сов перех* to overtake; (*перен*) to outstrip.
обогн|у́ть (-у́, -ёшь; *impf* **огиба́ть**) *сов перех* (*стол, дом*) to go round.
обогре́в (-а) *м* heating.
обогре́|ть (-ю; *impf* **обогрева́ть**) *сов перех* (*помещение*) to heat; (*замёрзших*) to warm; (*перен: приласкать*) to be kind to
▸ **обогре́ться** (*impf* **обогрева́ться**) *сов возв* (*согреться: человек*) to warm o.s.; (*помещение*) to heat up; (*душа*) to be warmed.
о́б|од (-ода; *nom pl* -о́дья, *gen pl* -о́дьев) *м* rim; (*ракетки*) frame.
обод|о́к (-ка́) *м уменьш от* **о́бод**; (*на рисунке, платье*) border.
обо́дран|ный (-, -а, -о) *прил* (*стена*) stripped; (*дом, одежда*) shabby; (*руки*) scratched; (*колени*) skinned.
об|одра́ть (-деру́, -дерёшь; *impf* **обдира́ть**) *сов перех* (*кору, шкуру*) to strip; (*руки*) to scratch; (*колени*) to skin; (*перен: разг: покупателя, клиента*) to fleece.
ободре́ни|е (-я) *ср* encouragement.
ободри́тел|ьный (-ен, -ьна, -ьно) *прил* encouraging.
ободр|и́ть (-ю́, -и́шь; *impf* **ободря́ть**) *сов перех* to encourage.

обожа́|ть (-ю) *несов перех* to adore; ~ (*impf*) **что-н/+infin** (*разг*) to adore sth/doing.
обожгу́(сь) *итп сов см* **обже́чь(ся)**.
обожеств|и́ть (-лю́, -и́шь; *impf* **обожествля́ть**) *сов перех* to worship.
обожествле́ни|е (-я) *ср* worship.
обожествлю́ *сов см* **обожестви́ть**.
обожествля́|ть (-ю) *несов от* **обожестви́ть**.
обожжёшь(ся) *итп сов см* **обже́чь(ся)**.
обожр|а́ться (-у́сь, -ёшься; *pt* -а́лся, -ала́сь, -ало́сь, *impf* **обжира́ться**) *сов возв* (*разг*) to stuff o.s.
обо́з (-а) *м* convoy.
об|озва́ть (-зову́, -зовёшь; *impf* **обзыва́ть**) *сов перех*: ~ **кого́-н кем-н** (*разг*) to call sb sth.
обозли́ть(ся) (-ю́(сь), -и́шь(ся)) *сов от* **злить(ся)**.
обозна́|ться (-юсь) *сов возв* (*разг*) to be mistaken.
обознача́|ть (-ю) *несов от* **обозна́чить** ◆ *перех* (*о знаках*) to signify
▸ **обознача́ться** *несов от* **обозна́читься**.
обозначе́ни|е (-я) *ср* (*границы, направления*) marking; (*на карте, в тексте итп*) symbol.
обозна́ч|ить (-у, -ишь; *impf* **обознача́ть**) *сов перех* (*границу, направление*) to mark; (*no impf*): ~ **что-н** (*нос, черты лица*) to make sth stand out
▸ **обозна́читься** (*impf* **обознача́ться**) *сов возв* to appear; (*становиться ощутимым*) to become noticeable.
обозрева́тел|ь (-я) *м* (*событий*) observer; (*на радио и телевидении*) editor; **междунаро́дный/полити́ческий** ~ international/political editor.
обозре́ни|е (-я) *ср* review; (*представление*) revue.
обозри́м|ый (-, -а, -о) *прил* (*пространство*) visible; (*события*) observable; ~**ое бу́дущее** the foreseeable future.
обо́|и (-ев) *мн* wallpaper *ед*.
обо́их *чис см* **о́ба**.
обойду́(сь) *итп сов см* **обойти́(сь)**.
обо́йм|а (-ы) *ж* (*ВОЕН*) (cartridge) clip; (*ТЕХ*) ring, hoop; (*перен: вопросов, аргументов*) round.
обо|йти́ (*как* **идти́**; *см* **Table 18**; *impf* **обходи́ть**) *сов перех* to go round; (*пройти стороной: лужу, канаву*) to skirt, go round; (*перен: вопрос, тему*) to skirt; (: *закон, указ*) to get round; (*обогнать*) to pass; (*перен: обмануть*) to take in; **обходи́ть** (~ *perf*) **что-н молча́нием** to ignore
▸ **обойти́сь** (*impf* **обходи́ться**) *сов возв* (*уладиться*) to turn out; (*стоить*): ~**сь в** +*acc* to cost; **обходи́ться** (~**сь** *perf*) **с кем-н/чем-н** to treat sb/sth; **обходи́ться** (~**сь** *perf*) +*instr* (*разг*) to get by with; **обходи́ться** (~**сь** *perf*) **без** +*gen* (*разг*) to get by without; (*без скандала*) to be settled without.
об|окра́сть (-краду́, -крадёшь; *impf*

обкра́дывать) *сов перех* to rob.
оболг|а́ть (-гу́, -жёшь; *pt* -га́л, -гала́, -га́ло) *сов перех* (*разг: человека*) to slander.
оболо́ч|ка (-ки; *gen pl* -ек) *ж* (*плода*) pericarp; (*зерна*) testa, (seed) coat; (*Земли*) crust; (*перен: человека*) shell; (: *вопроса*) surface; (*аэростата*) hull; **сли́зистая ~** mucous membrane.
обо́лтус (-а) *м* (*разг*) waster.
оболь|сти́ть (-щу́, -сти́шь; *impf* **обольща́ть**) *сов перех* (*соблазнить*) to seduce; (*увлечь*) to captivate.
обольща́|ться (-юсь) *несов возв* to be under a delusion.
обольщу́ *сов см* **обольсти́ть**.
оболью́(сь) *итп сов см* **обли́ть(ся)**.
обомле́|ть (-ю) *сов неперех* (*разг*) to freeze.
обоня́ни|е (-я) *ср* sense of smell.
обопру́сь *итп сов см* **опере́ться**.
обора́чиваемост|ь (-и) *ж* (*КОММ*) turnover.
обора́чива|ть(ся) (-ю(сь)) *несов от* **оберну́ть(ся)**.
оборва́н|ец (-ца) *м* (*разг*) scruff.
обо́рван|ный (-, -а, -о) *прил* (*разг: одежда*) tattered; (: *рассказ, мысли*) fragmented.
оборва́нца *итп сущ см* **оборва́нец**.
оборв|а́ть (-у́, -ёшь; *pt* -а́л, -ала́, -а́ло) *impf* **обрыва́ть**) *сов перех* (*верёвку, нитку*) to break, snap; (*ягоды, цветы*) to pick; (*перен: разговор, дружбу*) to break off; (: *разг: говорящего*) to cut short
▶ **оборва́ться** (*impf* **обрыва́ться**) *сов возв* (*верёвка, нитка*) to break, snap; (*со скалы*) to fall; (*перен: жизнь, разговор, дружба*) to be cut short suddenly.
обо́р|ка (-ки; *gen pl* -ок) *ж* frill.
оборо́н|а (-ы) *ж* defence (*BRIT*), defense (*US*); (*линия сооружений*) defences *мн* (*BRIT*), defenses *мн* (*US*); **занима́ть (заня́ть** *perf*) **~y** to take up a defensive position; **держа́ть** (*impf*) **~y** to hold the defence.
оборо́нный *прил* (*промышленность*) defence опред (*BRIT*), defense опред (*US*).
обороноспосо́бност|ь (-и) *ж* defence (*BRIT*) или defense (*US*) capacity.
обороня́|ть (-ю) *несов перех* to defend
▶ **обороня́ться** *несов возв* (*защищаться*) to defend o.s.
оборо́т (-а) *м* (*полный круг*) revolution; (*КОММ*) turnover; (*обратная сторона*) back; (*перен: поворот событий*) turn; (*судов, вагонов*) turnaround; (*словесное выражение*) turn of phrase; **в ~e** in use; **входи́ть (войти́** *perf*) **в ~** to come into use; **пуска́ть (пусти́ть** *perf*) **в ~** (*деньги*) to put into circulation; (*средства, сбережения*) to invest; **брать (взять** *perf*) **кого́-н в ~** (*разг*) to take sb in hand.
оборо́тлив|ый (-, -а, -о) *прил* resourceful.

оборо́тный *прил* (*КОММ*) working опред.
обору́довани|е (-я) *ср* (*действие: завода*) equipping; (*предметы*) equipment; (*КОМП*) hardware.
обору́д|овать (-ую) (*не*)*сов перех* to equip.
обоснова́ни|е (-я) *ср* (*действие: теории*) substantiation; (*довод*) basis.
обосно́ван|ный (-, -на, -но) *прил* substantiated; **~ изно́с** (*КОММ*) fair wear and tear.
обосно́в|ать (-у́ю; *impf* **обосно́вывать**) *сов перех* (*теорию, вывод*) to substantiate
▶ **обоснова́ться** (*impf* **обосно́вываться**) *сов возв* (*расположиться*) to be (situated); (*разг: прочно устроиться*) to settle.
обосо́б|ить (-лю, -ишь; *impf* **обособля́ть**) *сов перех* to set apart; (*предложение*) to detach
▶ **обосо́биться** (*impf* **обособля́ться**) *сов возв* (*от коллектива, от семьи*) to alienate o.s.
обосо́блен|ный (-, -на, -но) *прил* (*дом, также ЛИНГ*) detached; (*комната*) separate; (*жизнь*) solitary.
обосо́блю(сь) *сов см* **обосо́бить(ся)**.
обособля́|ть(ся) (-ю(сь)) *несов от* **обосо́бить(ся)**.
обостре́ни|е (-я) *ср* (*см глаг*) sharpening; intensification; aggravation; straining.
обостр|и́ть (-ю́, -и́шь; *impf* **обостря́ть**) *сов перех* (*желания, конфликт*) to intensify; (*боль, какое-нибудь чувство*) to aggravate; (*отношения*) to strain
▶ **обостри́ться** (*impf* **обостря́ться**) *сов возв* to sharpen; (*желание, разногласия*) to intensify; (*боль, какое-нибудь чувство*) to become more acute; (*отношения*) to become strained.
оботру́(сь) *итп сов см* **обтере́ть(ся)**.
обо́чин|а (-ы) *ж* verge.
обошёл(ся) *итп сов см* **обойти́(сь)**.
обошью́ *итп сов см* **обши́ть**.
обою́дный (-ен, -на, -но) *прил* mutual.
обрабо́та|ть (-ю; *impf* **обраба́тывать**) *сов перех* (*камень*) to cut; (*кожу*) to cure; (*деталь: на станке*) to turn; (*статью, песню*) to polish up; (*землю, поле*) to till; (*перен: разг: человека*) to work on.
обрабо́т|ка (-ки; *gen pl* -ок) *ж* (*см глаг*) cutting; curing; turning; polishing up; tilling; (*перен: человека*) influencing; **~ да́нных** (*КОМП*) computing; **пла́та за ~ку** (*КОММ*) handling charge.
обра́д|овать(ся) (-ую(сь)) *сов от* **ра́довать(ся)**.
о́браз (-а) *м* image; (*человека, зверя*) appearance; (*ЛИТЕРАТУРА*) figure; (*жизни, мыслей*) way; (*икона*) icon; **каки́м ~ом?** in what way?; **таки́м ~ом** in this way; (*следовательно*) consequently; **гла́вным ~ом** mainly; **ра́вным ~ом** similarly; **не́которым ~ом** to some extent.

óбразен *прил см* **óбразный**.

образ|éц (-ца́) *м* (*ткани, изделий, оружия*) sample; (*скромности, мужества, также ТЕХ*) model.

óбраз|ный (-ен, -на, -но) *прил* vivid; **óбразное выраже́ние** (*линг*) figure of speech.

образова́ни|е (-я) *ср* formation; (*получение знаний*) education.

образо́ван|ный (-, -на, -но) *прил* educated.

образ|ова́ть (-у́ю; *impf* **образова́ть** *или* **образо́вывать**) *сов перех* to form

► **образова́ться** (*impf* **образова́ться** *или* **образо́вываться**) *сов возв* (*трещина, опухоль*) to form; (*группа, комиссия*) to be formed; (*разг: уладиться*) to turn out all right.

образу́м|ить (-лю, -ишь) *сов перех*: ~ **кого́-н** to make sb see sense

► **образу́миться** *сов возв* (*стать благоразумным*) to come to one's senses.

образца́ *итп сущ см* **образе́ц**.

образцо́в|ый (-, -а, -о) *прил* exemplary.

обраст|и́ (-у́, -ёшь; *pt* **обро́с, обросла́, обросло́,** *impf* **обраста́ть**) *сов неперех*: ~ +*instr* (*травой, деревьями*) to become overgrown with; (*разг: волосами, грязью*) to be covered in; (: *хозяйством, барахлом*) to surround o.s. with.

обрати́м|ый (-, -а, -о) *прил* reversible.

обра|ти́ть (-щу́, -ти́шь; *impf* **обраща́ть**) *сов перех* (*взгляд, мысли*) to turn; **обраща́ть** (~ *perf*) **кого́-н/что-н в** +*acc* to turn sb/sth into; **обраща́ть** (~ *perf*) **внима́ние на** +*acc* to pay attention to; **обраща́ть** (~ *perf*) **кого́-н в бе́гство** to force sb to take flight; **обраща́ть** (~ *perf*) **кого́-н в свою́ ве́ру** to convert sb to one's own faith

► **обрати́ться** (*impf* **обраща́ться**) *сов возв* (*подлеж: взгляд*) to turn; (*с вопросом*) to inquire; (*превратиться*): ~**ся в** +*acc* to turn into; **обраща́ться** (~**ся** *perf*) **к** +*dat* (*к врачу итп*) to consult; (*к зрителям*) to address; **обраща́ться** (~**ся** *perf*) **в суд** to go to court; **обраща́ться** (~**ся** *perf*) **в бе́гство** to take flight.

обра́тно *нареч* back; **туда́ и** ~ there and back; **биле́т туда́ и** ~ return ticket (*BRIT*), round-trip ticket (*US*).

обра́тн|ое (-ого; *decl like adj*) *ср* the opposite; **убежда́ть** (**убеди́ть** *perf*) **кого́-н в** ~**ом** to convince sb of the opposite.

обра́тн|ый *прил* (*порядок, движение, мысль*) reverse; (*дорога, путь*) return *опред*; **на** ~**ом пути́** on the way back; **в** ~**ую сто́рону** in the opposite direction; **в** ~**ом направле́нии** the other way; **обра́тная сторона́** reverse (side); **обра́тный а́дрес** return address; **обра́тный биле́т** return (*BRIT*) *или* round-trip (*US*) ticket.

обраща́|ть (-ю) *несов от* **обрати́ть**

► **обраща́ться** *несов от* **обрати́ться** ♦ *возв* (*деньги, товар*) to circulate; ~**ся** (*impf*) **с** +*instr* (*применять*) to use; (*уметь справляться*) to handle; (*с человеком*) to treat.

обраще́ни|е (-я) *ср* address; (*ЭКОН*) circulation;

~ **к** +*dat* (*к народу итп*) address to; ~ **с** +*instr* (*с прибором, с огнём*) handling of; (*с животными, с больным*) treatment of; **находи́ться** (*impf*) **в** ~**и** to be in circulation.

обращу́(сь) *сов см* **обрати́ть(ся)**.

обре́жу *итп сов см* **обре́зать**.

обре́з (-а) *м* (*книги, альбома*) edge; (*оружие*) sawn-off (*BRIT*) *или* sawed-off (*US*) shotgun; **вре́мени/де́нег в** ~ (*разг*) there's just enough time/money.

обре́|зать (-жу, -жешь; *impf* **обреза́ть**) *сов перех* to trim; (*разг: прервать*) to cut short; (*РЕЛ*) to circumcise.

обре́з|ок (-ка) *м* scrap.

обрёк *итп сов см* **обре́чь**.

обрека́|ть (-ю) *несов от* **обре́чь**.

обреку́ *итп сов см* **обре́чь**.

обремени́тел|ьный (-ен, -ьна, -ьно) *прил* onerous.

обремен|и́ть (-ю́, -и́шь; *impf* **обременя́ть**) *сов перех*: ~ **кого́-н чем-н** to load sb down with sth.

обр|ести́ (-ету́, -етёшь; *pt* **-ёл, -ела́, -ело́,** *impf* **обрета́ть**) *сов перех* to find.

обречённый (-ён, -ена́, -ено́) *прил* doomed.

обре́|чь (-ку́, -чёшь *итп*, -ку́т; *pt* **-ёк, -екла́, -екло́,** *impf* **обрека́ть**) *сов перех*: ~ **кого́-н на что-н** to condemn sb to sth.

обрис|ова́ть (-у́ю; *impf* **обрисо́вывать**) *сов перех* (*перен*) to describe.

обр|они́ть (-оню́, -о́нишь) *сов перех* to drop; (*замечание, фразу*) to let drop.

обро́с *итп сов см* **обрасти́**.

обр|уби́ть (-ублю́, -у́бишь; *impf* **обруба́ть**) *сов перех* to lop off.

обру́б|ок (-ка) *м* (*пень, хвоста*) stump; (*дерева*) chunk.

обруга́|ть (-ю) *сов перех* (*выбранить*) to curse; (*обозвать*) to swear at; (*разг: раскритиковать*) to pan, slate (*BRIT*).

óбруч (-а) *м* hoop; (*для волос*) (Alice) band.

обруча́льн|ый *прил*: ~**ое кольцо́** wedding ring.

обруча́|ть(ся) (-ю(сь)) *несов от* **обручи́ть(ся)**.

обруче́ни|е (-я) *ср* betrothal.

обруч|и́ть (-у́, -и́шь; *impf* **обруча́ть**) *сов перех* to betroth

► **обручи́ться** (*impf* **обруча́ться**) *сов возв* to get betrothed.

обру́ш|ить (-у, -ишь; *impf* **обру́шивать**) *сов перех* (*стену, крышу*) to bring down; **обру́шивать** (~ *perf*) **что-н на** +*acc* to bring sth down onto; ~ (*perf*) **обвине́ния/угро́зы на кого́-н** to bombard sb with accusations/threats

► **обру́шиться** (*impf* **обру́шиваться**) *сов возв* (*крыша, здание*) to collapse; **обру́шиваться** (~**ся** *perf*) **на** +*acc* (*на голову*) to crash down onto; (*на врага*) to fall upon; (*на человека: с упрёками*) to come down on; **на него́** ~**илась беда́** he was struck down by misfortune.

обры́в (-а) *м* (*ГЕО*) precipice; (*на линии*) break.

обрыва́|ть(ся) (-ю(сь)) *несов от*

оборва́ть(ся).

обры́вист|**ый** (-, -а, -о) *прил* (*склон, берег*) steep; (*мысли, фразы*) fragmentary.

обры́в|**ок** (-ка) *м* (*верёвки*) piece; (*бумаги*) scrap; (*обычно мн: мыслей, воспоминаний*) fragment; (*: разговора*) snatch.

обры́воч|**ный** (-ен, -на, -но) *прил* fragmentary.

обры́зга|**ть** (-ю; *impf* **обры́згивать**) *сов перех*: ~ **кого́-н/что-н** +*instr* (*водой*) to splash sb/sth with; (*грязью, краской*) to splatter sb/sth with

▸ **обры́згаться** (*impf* **обры́згиваться**) *сов возв*: ~**ся** +*instr* (*см перех*) to get splashed with; to get splattered with.

обря́д (-а) *м* ritual.

обря́довый *прил* (*песни*) ceremonial; (*действия*) ritual.

обса́сыва|**ть** (-ю) *несов от* **обсоса́ть**.

обсервато́ри|**я** (-и) *ж* observatory.

обсле́довани|**е** (-я) *ср* (*см глаг*) inspection; examination.

обсле́д|**овать** (-ую) (*не*)*сов перех* to inspect; (*больного*) to examine.

обслу́живани|**е** (-я) *ср* service; **медици́нское** ~ health care; **сфе́ра** ~**я** service industry.

обслу́жива|**ть** (-ю) *несов от* **обслужи́ть** ♦ *перех* (*подлеж: магазин*) to supply; (*: поликлиника*) to see to.

обслу́жива|**ющий** (-ая, -ее, -ие) *прил*: ~ **персона́л** ancilliary staff.

обслу́жи́ть (-ужу́, -у́жишь; *impf* **обслу́живать**) *сов перех* (*покупателей*) to serve; (*клиентов*) to attend to; (*подлеж: поликлиника, магазин*) to see to; (*станки*) to operate.

обсос|**а́ть** (-у́, -ёшь; *impf* **обса́сывать**) *сов перех* to suck.

обста́в|**ить** (-лю, -ишь; *impf* **обставля́ть**) *сов перех* (*квартиру, кабинет*) to furnish; **обставля́ть** (~ *perf*) **стол сту́льями** to put chairs around the table.

обстано́в|**ка** (-ки; *gen pl* -ок) *ж* (*квартиры, кабинета*) furnishings *мн*; (*в мире, в семье*) situation; **междунаро́дная** ~ the international situation.

обстоя́тельно *нареч* in detail.

обстоя́тель|**ный** (-ен, -ьна, -ьно) *прил* detailed; (*разг: человек*) solid.

обстоя́тельств|**о** (-а) *ср* circumstance; (*линг*) adverbial modifier; **ни при каки́х** ~**ах** under no circumstances; **стече́ние обстоя́тельств** coincidence; **смотря́ по** ~**ам** depending on the circumstances; (*как ответ на вопрос*) it depends.

обсто|**я́ть** (*3sg* -и́т, *3pl* -я́т) *несов неперех* (*дела, работа, учёба*) to be; **как** ~**я́т дела́?** how are things going?; **всё** ~**и́т хорошо́** everything is going well.

обстра́гива|**ть** (-ю) *несов от* **обстрога́ть**.

обстре́л (-а) *м* fire; **артиллери́йский** ~ artillery fire.

обстреля́|**ть** (-ю; *impf* **обстре́ливать**) *сов перех* to fire at.

обстри́|**чь** (-гу́, -жёшь *итп*, -гу́т) *сов от* **стричь**.

обстрога́|**ть** (-ю; *impf* **обстра́гивать**) *сов перех* to plane.

обстру́кци|**я** (-и) *ж* obstruction.

обсту|**пи́ть** (*3sg* -у́пит, *3pl* -у́пят, *impf* **обступа́ть**) *сов перех* to surround.

обс|**уди́ть** (-ужу́, -у́дишь; *impf* **обсужда́ть**) *сов перех* to discuss.

обсужде́ни|**е** (-я) *ср* discussion; **предложи́ть** (**предлага́ть** *impf*) **что-н на** ~ to bring sth up for discussion.

обсужу́ *сов см* **обсуди́ть**.

обсчита́|**ть** (-ю; *impf* **обсчи́тывать**) *сов перех* to overcharge; (*результат, параметры*) to calculate

▸ **обсчита́ться** (*impf* **обсчи́тываться**) *сов возв* (*разг*) to miscalculate.

обсы́па|**ть** (-лю, -лешь; *impf* **обсыпа́ть**) *сов перех*: ~ **что-н чем-н** to sprinkle sth with sth

▸ **обсы́паться** (*impf* **обсыпа́ться**) *сов возв*: ~**ся** +*instr* to get covered in.

обта́чива|**ть** (-ю) *несов от* **обточи́ть**.

обтека́ем|**ый** (-, -а, -о) *прил* (*поверхность, форма*) streamlined; (*разг: ответ, объяснение*) ambiguous.

об|**тере́ть** (-отру́, -отрёшь; *impf* **обтира́ть**) *сов перех* to wipe

▸ **обтере́ться** (*impf* **обтира́ться**) *сов возв* to sponge o.s. down.

обт|**еса́ть** (-ешу́, -е́шешь; *impf* **обтёсывать**) *сов перех* (*бревно*) to trim; (*разг: манеры, человека*) to bring up to scratch.

обтира́|**ть(ся)** (-ю(сь)) *несов от* **обтере́ть(ся)**.

обт|**очи́ть** (-очу́, -о́чишь; *impf* **обта́чивать**) *сов перех* (*на станке*) to turn; (*на точильном камне*) to sharpen.

обто́чк|**а** (-и) *ж* (*см глаг*) turning; sharpening.

обтрёпан|**ный** (-, -на, -но) *прил* shabby.

обтреп|**а́ть** (-еплю́, -е́плешь) *сов перех* to wear out

▸ **обтрепа́ться** *сов возв* (*износиться*) to wear out.

обтя́гива|**ть** (-ю) *несов от* **обтяну́ть**.

обтя́жк|**а** (-и) *ж*: в ~**у** skintight.

обтя|**ну́ть** (-ну́, -нешь; *impf* **обтя́гивать**) *сов перех* (*кресло, диван*) to cover; (*фигуру*) to fit tightly.

обува́|**ть(ся)** (-ю(сь)) *несов от* **обу́ть(ся)**.

обувно́й *прил* shoe *опред*.

о́був|**ь** (-и) *ж* footwear.

обу́гл|**иться** (*3sg* -ится, *3pl* -ятся, *impf* **обу́гливаться**) *сов возв* to become charred.

обу́жива|**ть** (-ю) *несов от* **обу́зить**.

обу́жу *сов см* **обу́зить**.

обу́з|**а** (-ы) *ж* burden; **быть** (*impf*) ~**ой для**

кого́-н (разг) to be a burden to sb.

обу́|зить (-жу, -зишь; impf обу́живать) сов перех to make too tight.

обусло́в|ить (-лю, -ишь; impf обусла́вливать) сов перех (яви́ться причи́ной) to lead to; обусла́вливать (~ perf) что-н чем-н to make sth conditional on sth.

обу́т|ый (-, -а, -о) прил: ~ в ту́фли/сапоги́ wearing shoes/boots; (no full form; обеспе́ченный обу́вью) provided with shoes or boots.

обу́|ть (-ю; impf обува́ть) сов перех (ту́фли, сапоги́) to put on; (разг: снабди́ть обу́вью) to provide with shoes or boots; (ребёнка) to put shoes on

► обу́|ться (impf обува́ться) сов возв to put on one's shoes or boots; (разг: обеспе́чить себя́ обу́вью) to provide o.s. with shoes or boots.

о́бух (-а) м (топора́) blunt end; как ~ом по голове́ like a bolt from the blue.

обуча́|ть(ся) (-ю(сь)) несов от обучи́ть(ся).

обуче́ни|е (-я) ср: ~ +dat (преподава́ние) teaching of, instruction in; (изуче́ние) education in.

обу|чи́ть (-учу́, -у́чишь; impf обуча́ть) сов перех: ~ кого́-н чему́-н/+infin to teach sb sth/to do

► обучи́|ться (impf обуча́ться) сов возв: ~ся чему́-н/+infin to learn sth/to do.

обу́я|ть (3sg -ет, 3pl -ют) сов перех to overcome.

обхам|и́ть (-лю́, -и́шь) сов перех (разг) to be rude to.

обхва́т (-а) м circumference (measured by putting arms around object); в ~е in circumference.

обхва|ти́ть (-чу́, -а́тишь; impf обхва́тывать) сов перех: ~ что-н (рука́ми) to put one's arms round sth.

обхо́д (-а) м (путь) way round; (в больни́це, на предприя́тии) round; (ВОЕН) turning movement; в ~ +gen (о́зера, зако́на) bypassing; идти́ (impf) в ~ чего́-н to go round sth; (зако́на, пра́вил) to evade sth.

обходи́тел|ьный (-ен, -ьна, -ьно) прил courteous.

обх|оди́ть(ся) (-ожу́(сь), -о́дишь(ся)) несов от обойти́(сь).

обходно́й прил (путь) detour опред; (мане́вр, движе́ние) turning; обходно́й лист a certificate which must be signed on leaving job to prove that all property has been returned.

обхожде́ни|е (-я) ср manners мн.

обхожу́(сь) несов см обходи́ть(ся).

обхохо|та́ться (-чу́сь, -о́чешься) сов возв (разг) to kill o.s. laughing.

обчи́|стить (-щу, -стишь) сов от чи́стить.

обша́р|ить (-ю, -ишь; impf обша́ривать) сов перех (разг) to ransack.

обшива́|ть (-ю) несов от обши́ть.

обши́в|ка (-ки; gen pl -ок) ж (пла́тья, пальто́) trim; (корабля́) plating; (до́ма) cladding.

обши́р|ный (-ен, -на, -но) прил extensive;

(ко́мната) spacious.

обши́т|ый (-, -а, -о) прил: ~ +instr (бахромо́й, ме́хом) trimmed with; (доска́ми) faced with; (мета́ллом) plated with.

об|ши́ть (-ошью́, -ошьёшь; impf обшива́ть) сов перех (разг: семью́ итп) to make clothes for; обшива́ть (~ perf) (+instr) (ме́хом, бахромо́й) to trim (with); (де́ревом) to face (with); (мета́ллом) to plate или cover (with).

обшла́г (-ага́; nom pl -ага́) м cuff.

обща́|ться (-юсь) несов возв: ~ с +instr (с друзья́ми, с ро́дственниками) to spend time with; (с поли́тиками, с престу́пниками итп) to associate with; я бо́льше с ним не ~юсь I don't see him any more.

общевойсково́й прил military.

общегородско́й прил town опред, city опред.

общегосуда́рственный прил state опред.

общедосту́пный прил (сре́дства, спо́соб) available to everyone; (це́ны) affordable; (изложе́ние, ле́кция) accessible.

о́бщее (-его; decl like adj) ср similarity; в ~ем (разг) on the whole; в ~ем и це́лом by and large; у них мно́го/нет ничего́ ~его they have a lot/nothing in common.

общежи́ти|е (-я) ср (рабо́чее) hostel; (студе́нческое) hall of residence (BRIT), dormitory или hall (US); (сосуществова́ние) communal living.

общеизве́ст|ный (-ен, -на, -но) прил well-known.

общенаро́дный прил national опред.

общенациона́льный прил national опред.

обще́ни|е (-я) ср (делов́ые, дру́жеские) relations мн; (с приро́дой, с друзья́ми) communication.

общеобразова́тельный прил comprehensive.

общепи́т (-а) м сокр (= обще́ственное пита́ние) public catering.

общепри́знанный прил universally recognized.

общепри́нят|ый прил generally accepted; в ~ом смы́сле сло́ва in the accepted sense of the word.

общераспространённый прил widespread.

обще́ственност|ь (-и) ж собир community.

обще́ственный прил social; (призна́ние, со́бственность, жизнь) public; (организа́ция) civic; обще́ственное мне́ние public opinion; обще́ственные нау́ки social sciences.

о́бществ|о (-а) ср society; (компа́ния) company; в ~е +gen in the company of.

обществове́дени|е (-я) ср social science.

общеупотреби́тел|ьный (ен, -ьна, -ьно) прил commonly-used.

общечелове́ческ|ий (-ая, -ое, -ие) прил universal.

о́бщ|ий (-ая, -ее, -ие) прил general; (труд) communal; (дом, кни́ги) shared; (друзья́) mutual; (интере́сы, увлече́ния, не́нависть) common; (сто́имость, коли́чество) total; (-, -а́,

-ó; *картина, описание*) general; **~ими**
уси́лиями together; **в ~ей сло́жности**
altogether; **на ~их основа́ниях** on equal terms;
в ~их черта́х in general terms; **находи́ть**
(**найти́** *perf*) ~ **язы́к** to find a common language;
~ие слова́ waffle; **о́бщее образова́ние**
general education.

общи́н|а (-ы) *ж* community.

общипа́ть (-иплю́, -и́плешь; *impf*
общи́пывать) *сов перех* to pluck.

общи́телен *прил см* **общи́тельный**.

общи́тельность (-и) *ж* sociability.

общи́тельный (-ен, -ьна, -ьно) *прил* sociable.

о́бщность (-и) *ж* (*взглядов, целей*) similarity;
(*историческая, социальная*: community).

объеда́|ть(ся) (-ю(сь)) *несов от* **объе́сть(ся)**.

объе́дешь *итп сов см* **объе́хать**.

объеди́м(ся) *сов см* **объе́сть(ся)**.

объедине́ние (-я) *ср* (*сил, усилий, талантов*)
concentration; (*литераторов,
производственное*) association; (*воен*) unit.

объединённый *прил* (*заседание, собрание*)
joint; (*усилия, ресурсы*) joint, united; **О~ые**
Ара́бские Эмира́ты United Arab Emirates.

объедини́ть (-ю́, -йшь; *impf* **объединя́ть**) *сов*
перех to join, unite; (*ресурсы*) to pool;
(*компании*) to amalgamate

▶ **объедини́ться** (*impf* **объединя́ться**) *сов*
возв (*люди*) to unite; (*компании*) to amalgamate.

объеди́те(сь) *сов см* **объе́сть(ся)**.

объе́дки (-ов) *мн* (*разг*) leftovers *мн*.

объе́ду *итп сов см* **объе́хать**.

объедя́т(ся) *сов см* **объе́сть(ся)**.

объе́зд (-а) *м* detour; (*с целью осмотра*) tour;
е́хать (**пое́хать** *perf*) **в ~** to make a detour.

объе́здить (-жу, -дишь; *impf* **объезжа́ть**) *сов*
перех (*место*) to travel round; (*лошадь*) to
break in; (*друзей*) to visit.

объезжа́|ть (-ю) *несов от* **объе́здить,
объе́хать**.

объе́зжу *сов см* **объе́здить**.

объе́кт (-а) *м* (*изучения, наблюдения*) subject;
(*строит, воен*) site.

объекти́в (-а) *м* lens.

объекти́вен *прил см* **объекти́вный**.

объекти́вность (-и) *ж* objectivity.

объекти́вный (-ен, -на, -но) *прил* objective.

объе́л(ся) *итп сов см* **объе́сть(ся)**.

объе́м(ся) *сов см* **объе́сть(ся)**.

объём (-а) *м* (*геом*) volume; (*ведра, чашки*)
capacity; (*работы, знаний*) amount.

объёмен *прил см* **объёмный**.

объёмистый (-, -а, -о) *прил* bulky.

объёмный (-ен, -на, -но) *прил* (*геом*)
volumetric; (*изображение, кино*) three-
dimensional; (*книга, папка*) bulky.

объе́сть (*как* **есть**; *см* **Table 15**; *impf*
объеда́ть) *сов перех* (*кость, яблоко*) to nibble

(at); ~ (*perf*) **кого́-н** (*разг*) to eat sb out of house
and home

▶ **объе́сться** (*impf* **объеда́ться**) *сов возв* to
overeat.

объе́хать (*как* **е́хать**; *см* **Table 19**; *impf*
объезжа́ть) *сов перех* (*камень, яму*) to go *или*
drive round; (*с велью осмотра*) to travel round;
(*друзей, страны*) to visit.

объе́шь(ся) *сов см* **объе́сть(ся)**.

объяви́ть (-явлю́, -я́вишь; *impf* **объявля́ть**)
сов перех to announce; (*войну*) to declare ♦
неперех: ~ **о** +*prp* (*о решении, о случившемся*)
to announce; **объявля́ть** (~ *perf*) **собра́ние
закры́тым/кого́-н победи́телем** to declare the
meeting closed/sb the winner

▶ **объяви́ться** (*impf* **объявля́ться**) *сов возв*
(*разг*) to turn up.

объявле́ни|е (-я) *ср* announcement; (*войны*)
declaration; (*рекламное сообщение*)
advertisement; (*извещение*) notice.

объявлю́(сь) *сов см* **объяви́ть(ся)**.

объявля́|ть(ся) (-ю(сь)) *несов от*
объяви́ть(ся).

объясне́ни|е (-я) *ср* explanation; ~ **в любви́**
declaration of love.

объясни́мый (-, -а, -о) *прил* explicable.

объясни́ть (-ю́, -йшь; *impf* **объясня́ть**) *сов*
перех to explain

▶ **объясни́ться** (*impf* **объясня́ться**) *сов возв*:
~ся (**с** +*instr*) to clear things up (with); **всё
~йлось** everything became clear; **объясня́ться**
(**~ся** *perf*) (**кому́-н**) **в любви́** to declare one's
love (to sb).

объясня́|ться (-юсь) *несов от* **объясни́ться** ♦
возв (*жестами, на английском языке*) to
communicate; ~ (*impf*) +*instr* (*трудностями,
усталостью*) to be explained by.

объя́ти|е (-я) *ср* embrace; **встреча́ть**
(**встре́тить** *perf*) **кого́-н с распростёртыми
~ями** to welcome sb with open arms.

обыва́тел|ь (-я) *м* (*пренебр*) philistine; (*ист*)
resident.

обыва́тельск|ий (-ая, -ое, -ие) *прил* philistine.

обыгра́ть (-ю; *impf* **обы́грывать**) *сов перех*
(*команду, соперника*) to beat; (*разг: ошибку,
оговорку*) to turn to one's advantage.

обы́ден|ный (-, -на, -но) *прил* mundane.

обыкнове́ни|е (-я) *ср* habit; **име́ть** (*impf*) ~
+*infin* to be in the habit of doing; **по ~ю** as usual;
про́тив ~я against the norm; **по своему́ ~ю** as
is his *итп* wont.

обыкнове́нно *нареч* usually.

обыкнове́нный (-ен, -на, -но) *прил*
(*заурядный: человек, явление*) ordinary;
(*частый*) common.

о́быск (-а) *м* search; **производи́ть** (**произвести́**
perf) ~ to carry out a search.

обы́ска́ть (-ыщу́, -ы́щешь; *impf* **обы́скивать**)

сов перех to search.

обы́чай (-я) *м* custom.

обы́чен *прил см* **обы́чный**.

обы́чно *нареч* usually.

обы́ч|ный (-ен, -на, -но) *прил* usual; (*заурядный*) ordinary.

обыщу́ *итп сов см* **обыска́ть**.

обяжу́(сь) *итп сов см* **обяза́ть(ся)**.

обя́занност|и (-ей) *мн* (*директора итп*) duties *мн*, responsibilities *мн*; **исполня́ть** (*impf*) ~ +*gen* to act as; **он исполня́ет** ~ **дире́ктора** he is the acting director.

обя́занност|ь (-и) *ж* duty; *см также* **обя́занности**.

обя́зан|ный (-, -а, -о) *прил*: ~ +*infin* (*помочь, сделать итп*) obliged to do; ~ +*dat* obliged *или* indebted to; **я Вам о́чень обя́зан** I am greatly obliged to you.

обя́зателен *прил см* **обяза́тельный**.

обяза́тельно *нареч* definitely, without fail; **не** ~ not necessarily.

обяза́тель|ный (-ен, -ьна, -ьно) *прил* (*правило, условие*) binding; (*исполнение, обучение*) compulsory, obligatory; (*человек, работник*) reliable; **в ~ьном поря́дке** as a compulsory measure.

обяза́тельств|о (-а) *ср* commitment, obligation; (*обычно мн: комм*) liability; **долгово́е** ~ (*комм*) promissory note; **брать (взять** *perf*) **на себя́** ~ to take on some commitment.

об|яза́ть (-яжу́, -я́жешь; *impf* **обя́зывать)** *сов перех*: ~ **кого́-н** +*infin* to oblige sb to do; **Вы меня́ ~я́жите, е́сли сде́лаете э́то** I would be very much obliged if you would do this; **он ~яза́л меня́ свое́й доброто́й** I am obliged to him for his kindness

▶ **обяза́ться (impf обя́зываться)** *сов возв* to pledge.

обя́зыва|ть (-ю) *несов от* **обяза́ть ♦** *перех* (*подлеж: правила, закон, факты*) to oblige; **положе́ние ~ет** his *итп* position demands it

▶ **обя́зываться** *несов от* **обяза́ться**.

ова́л (-а) *м* oval; **у неё краси́вый** ~ **лица́** her face is a lovely shape.

ова́льный (-ен, -ьна, -ьно) *прил* oval.

ова́ци|я (-и) *ж* ovation.

ОВД *м сокр* = **отде́л вну́тренних дел**.

овдове́|ть (-ю) *сов неперех* (*женщина*) to become a widow, be widowed; (*мужчина*) to become a widower, be widowed.

Ове́н (-на́) *м* (*созвездие*) Aries.

ов|ёс (-са́) *м собир* oats *мн*.

ове́ц *сущ см* **овца́**.

ове́ч|ий (-ья, -ье, -ьи) *прил* (*шерсть, сыр*) sheep's; (*молоко*) ewe's.

ОВИР *м сокр* = **Отде́л виз и регистра́ции иностра́нных гра́ждан**.

овладе́|ть (-ю, -ешь; *impf* **овладева́ть)** *сов неперех*: ~ +*instr* (*городом, высото́й*) to capture, seize; (*перен: разговором*) to take

control of; (: *вниманием*) to capture; (: *языком, профессией*) to master; **им ~ла ра́дость** he was overcome with joy.

Овна́ *сущ см* **Ове́н**.

о́вод (-а) *м* gadfly.

о́вощ (-а) *м* vegetable; *см также* **о́вощи**.

о́вощ|и (-ей) *мн* vegetables *мн*.

овощно́й *прил* (*суп, блюдо*) vegetable *опред*; **овощно́й магази́н** greengrocer's (*BRIT*), fruit and vegetable shop.

овра́г (-а) *м* ravine.

овса́ *итп сущ см* **овёс**.

овся́нк|а (-и) *ж собир* (*разг: крупа*) oats *мн*; (*каша*) porridge (*BRIT*), oatmeal (*US*).

овся́ный *прил* oat *опред*.

овуля́ци|я (-и) *ж* ovulation.

ов|ца́ (-цы́; *nom pl* **-цы,** *gen pl* **-е́ц)** *ж* sheep (*мн* sheep); (*самка*) ewe.

овцево́дств|о (-а) *ср* sheep-farming.

ОВЧ *сокр* (= **о́чень высо́кая частота́**) VHF (= *very high frequency*).

овча́р|ка (-ки; *gen pl* **-ок)** *ж* sheepdog.

овча́рн|я (-и) *ж* sheepfold.

овчи́н|а (-ы) *ж* sheepskin.

ога́р|ок (-ка) *м* candle end.

огиба́|ть (-ю) *несов от* **обогну́ть**.

оглавле́ни|е (-я) *ср* (table of) contents.

огла|си́ть (-шу́, -си́шь; *impf* **оглаша́ть)** *сов перех* (*решение, проект*) to announce; (*приказ, закон*) to proclaim; (*телеграмму*) to read out; ~ (*perf*) **что-н чем-н** to fill sth with sth

▶ **огласи́ться (impf оглаша́ться)** *сов возв*: ~**ся** +*instr* to resound with.

огла́ск|а (-и) *ж* publicity; **предава́ть (преда́ть** *perf*) **что-н** ~**е** to make sth public.

оглаша́|ть(ся) (-ю(сь)) *несов от* **огласи́ть(ся)**.

оглашу́(сь) *сов см* **огласи́ть(ся)**.

огло́бл|я (-ли; *gen pl* **-ель)** *ж* shaft (*on cart*).

огло́хн|уть (-у, -ешь) *сов от* **гло́хнуть**.

оглуша́|ть (-ю) *несов от* **оглуши́ть**.

оглуши́тель|ный (-ен, -ьна, -ьно) *прил* deafening.

оглу|ши́ть (-шу́, -ши́шь; *impf* **оглуша́ть)** *сов перех*: ~ **кого́-н чем-н** (*звуками, криками*) to deafen sb with sth; (*ударом*) to stun sb with sth.

огля|де́ть (-жу́, -ди́шь; *impf* **огля́дывать)** *сов перех* to look round

▶ **огляде́ться (impf огля́дываться)** *сов возв* to look around.

огля́д|ка (-ки) *ж*: **с ~ой** with caution; **де́лать (сде́лать** *perf*) **что-н без ~и** to do sth resolutely; **он бежа́л без ~и** (*разг*) he ran as fast as his legs would carry him.

огля́дыва|ть (-ю) *несов от* **огляде́ть**

▶ **огля́дываться** *несов от* **огляде́ться, огляну́ться**.

огляжу́(сь) *сов см* **огляде́ть(ся)**.

огля|ну́ться (-ну́сь, -нешься; *impf* **огля́дываться)** *сов возв* to look back; (*я*) **не успе́л** ~, **как** ... before I knew it ....

огнево́й *прил* (*характер, взгляд*) fiery; **огнева́я**

заве́са (ВОЕН) curtain of fire; **огнева́я пози́ция** firing position; **огнева́я то́чка** (ВОЕН) emplacement.

огнеды́шащ|ий (-ая, -ее, -ие) *прил* (*дракон*) fire-breathing; (*вулкан*) erupting.

огнемёт (-а) *м* flame-thrower.

о́гненный *прил* (*цвет, глаза, характер*) fiery; (*поцелуй*) passionate; ~ **столб** burst of flames.

огнеопа́с|ный (-ен, -на, -но) *прил* (in)flammable.

огнесто́йкий (-йкая, -йкое, -йкие; -ек, -йка, -йко) *прил* fireproof.

огнестре́льн|ый *прил*: ~ое ору́жие firearms *мн*; **огнестре́льная ра́на** bullet wound.

огнетуши́тел|ь (-я) *м* fire-extinguisher.

огнеупо́р|ный (-ен, -на, -но) *прил* (*материал*) fire-proof; **огнеупо́рная гли́на** fire clay; **огнеупо́рный кирпи́ч** firebrick.

огня́ *итп сущ см* **ого́нь.**

ого́ *межд*: ~! well!; ~, каки́м ты стал взро́слым! my, how you've grown!

оговор|и́ть (-ю́, -и́шь; *impf* огова́ривать) *сов перех* to slander; (*условия, срок*) to agree (on); (*подлеж: правила*) to stipulate

▶ **оговори́ться** (*impf* огова́риваться) *сов возв*: я ~и́лся it was a slip of the tongue.

огово́р|ка (-ки; *gen pl* -ок) *ж* (*обмолвка*) slip of the tongue; (*условие*) proviso; **я могу́ сказа́ть без ~ок, что** ... I can say without reservation that ....

оголённый (-ён, -ена́, -ено́) *прил* bare.

огол|и́ть (-ю́, -и́шь; *impf* оголя́ть) *сов перех* to bare, expose; (*деревья, провод, землю*) to strip; (*меч, кинжал*) to draw; (*фронт, участок*) to expose

▶ **оголи́ться** (*impf* оголя́ться) *сов возв* (*шея, плечо итп*) to become uncovered; (*деревья, земля*) to become bare; (*провод*) to be exposed; (*фронт, участок*) to become exposed.

оголте́л|ый (-, -а, -о) *прил* mad.

оголя́ть(ся) (-ю(сь)) *несов перех от* **оголи́ть(ся).**

огон|ёк (-ька́) *м* (*блеск глаз*) twinkle; **рабо́тать** (*impf*) **с ~ько́м** to work enthusiastically *или* with enthusiasm; **заходи́ть** (**зайти́** *perf*) **на ~** to drop in.

ого́н|ь (-ня́) *м* fire; (*фонарей, в окне*) light; (*перен: любви, негодования*) flame; **разводи́ть** (**развести́** *perf*) ~ to light a fire; **зажига́ть** (**заже́чь** *perf*) ~ to turn on the light; **открыва́ть** (**откры́ть** *perf*) ~ to open fire; **в ~не́ сраже́ния** in the heat of battle; **боя́ться** (*impf*) **чего́-н/кого́-н как ~ня́** to be terrified by sb/sth; **игра́ть** (*impf*) **с ~нём** (*перен*) to play with fire; **ме́жду двух ~не́й** between two fires.

огонёк *итп сущ см* **огон|ёк.**

огора́жива|ть (-ю) *несов перех от* **огороди́ть.**

огоро́д (-а) *м* vegetable *или* kitchen garden.

огор|оди́ть (-ожу́, -о́дишь; *impf* огора́живать) *сов перех*: ~ что-н (чем-н) to fence sth in (with sth).

огоро́ш|ить (-у, -ишь; *impf* огоро́шивать) *сов перех* (*разг*) to astound.

огорча́|ть(ся) (-ю(сь)) *несов от* **огорчи́ть(ся).**

огорче́ни|е (-я) *ср* distress; **к моему́ ~ю** to my dismay.

огорчённый (-ён, -ена́, -ено́) *прил* distressed; **у него́ был огорочённый вид** he looked upset.

огорчи́тельный (-ен, -ьна, -ьно) *прил* distressing.

огорч|и́ть (-у́, -и́шь; *impf* огорча́ть) *сов перех* to distress

▶ **огорчи́ться** (*impf* огорча́ться) *сов возв* to be upset *или* distressed.

огра́б|ить (-лю, -ишь) *сов от* **гра́бить.**

ограбле́ни|е (-я) *ср* robbery.

огра́блю *сов см* **огра́бить.**

огра́д|а (-ы) *ж* (*стена*) wall; (*забор*) fence; (*решётка*) railings *мн*.

оград|и́ть (-жу́, -ди́шь; *impf* огражда́ть) *сов перех* (*перен*) to defend, protect.

огражде́ни|е (-я) *ср* barrier.

огражу́ *сов см* **огради́ть.**

огран|и́ть (-ю́, -и́шь; *impf* огра́нивать) *сов перех* to cut.

ограниче́ни|е (-я) *ср* restriction, limitation; (*правило*) restriction.

ограни́чен|ный (-, -на, -но) *прил* limited; (*человек*) narrow-minded.

ограни́чива|ть(ся) (-ю(сь)) *несов от* **ограни́чить(ся).**

ограничи́тельный (-ен, -ьна, -ьно) *прил*: ~ьные ме́ры restrictive measures *мн*.

ограни́ч|ить (-у, -ишь; *impf* ограни́чивать) *сов перех* to limit, restrict

▶ **ограни́читься** (*impf* ограни́чиваться) *сов возв*: ~ся +*instr* (*удовлетвориться*) to content o.s with; (*свестись*) to become limited to.

огре́|ть (-ю) *сов перех* (*разг*) to whack.

огро́м|ный (-ен, -на, -но) *прил* enormous.

огрубе́лый *прил* (*руки, кожа*) coarse; (*сердце, душа*) hardened.

огрубе́|ть (-ю) *сов от* **грубе́ть.**

огрыза́|ться (-юсь) *несов возв* to snap.

огрызн|у́ться (-у́сь, -ёшься) *сов возв* to snap.

огры́з|ок (-ка) *м* (*огурца, яблока*) half-eaten bit; (*карандаша, ластика*) stub; (*бумажки*) scrap.

огу́л|ьный (-ен, -ьна, -ьно) *прил* unfounded.

огур|е́ц (-ца́) *м* cucumber; (*маринованный*) gherkin.

о́д|а (-ы) *ж* ode.

ода́лжива|ть (-ю) *несов от* **одолжи́ть.**

одарён|ный (-, -на, -но) *прил* gifted.

одар|и́ть (-ю́, -и́шь; *impf* ода́ривать *или* одаря́ть) *сов перех*: ~ кого́-н чем-н to give sb sth; **приро́да ~и́ла её красото́й** she is blessed

with good looks.
одева́ть (-ю) *несов от* **одеть**
▶ **одева́ться** *несов от* **оде́ться** ♦ *возв* (*носить одежду*) to dress.
оде́жд|а (-ы) *ж* clothes *мн*.
одеколо́н (-а) *м* eau de Cologne.
одели́ть (-ю, -йшь; *impf* **оделя́ть**) *сов перех*: ~ кого́-н чем-н to give sth out to sb.
оде́ну(сь) *итп сов см* **оде́ть(ся)**.
одёргива|ть (-ю) *несов от* **одёрнуть**.
одеревене́лый *прил* (*руки, пальцы*) numb; (*человек*) paralysed (*BRIT*), paralyzed (*US*).
одеревене́ть (-ю) *сов от* **деревене́ть**.
одерж|а́ть (-ержу́, -е́ржишь; *impf* **оде́рживать**) *сов перех*: ~ побе́ду to be victorious; **оде́рживать** (~ *perf*) **верх на соревнова́нии/в спо́ре** to win a competition/argument.
одержи́м|ый (-, -а, -о) *прил*: ~ +*instr* (*эмоциями*) possessed by; (*мыслью*) obsessed by.
одёрн|уть (-у, -ешь; *impf* **одёргивать**) *сов перех* (*одежду*) to straighten; (*разг: человека*) to check.
Оде́сс|а (-ы) *ж* Odessa.
оде́т|ый (-, -а, -о) *прил* dressed; (*разг: обеспеченный одеждой*) clothed; (*покрытый*): ~ +*instr* (*снегом итп*) covered with.
оде́|ть (-ну, -нешь; *impf* **одева́ть**) *сов перех* to dress; (*разг: снабдить одеждой*) to clothe; (*перен: снегом*) to cover
▶ **оде́ться** (*impf* **одева́ться**) *сов возв* to get dressed; (*также разг: тепло, легко, приобретать одежду*) to dress; (*покрываться*): ~ся +*instr* to be covered with.
одея́л|о (-а) *ср* (*шерстяное*) blanket; (*стёганое*) quilt; (*пуховое*) eiderdown.

KEYWORD

оди́н (-но́го; *см* Table 22; *f* **одна́**, *nt* **одно́**, *pl* **одни́**) *м чис* one; **одна́ кни́га** one book; **одни́ брю́ки** one pair of trousers; **ей оди́н год** she is one (year old); **они́ живу́т в до́ме но́мер оди́н** they live at number one; **кни́га сто́ит оди́н рубль** the book costs one rouble; **я́блоки продаю́тся по одно́й шту́ке** the apples are sold singly
♦ *прил* alone; (*единственный, единый*) one; (*одинаковый, тот же самый*) the same; **он идёт в кино́ оди́н** he goes to the cinema alone; **есть то́лько оди́н вы́ход** there is only one way out; **у них одни́ взгля́ды** they hold similar views; **я оди́н** (*без супруги*) I am single
♦ *мест* **1** (*какой-то*): **оди́н мой знако́мый** a friend; **одни́ неприя́тности** nothing but problems
2 (*во фразах*): **оди́н из** +*gen pl* one of; **оди́н и тот же** the same; **одно́ и то́ же** the same thing; **оди́н раз** once; **оди́н на оди́н** one to one; **все до одного́** all to a man; **ни оди́н** not one; **оди́н за други́м** one after the other; **по одному́** one by one; **одно́ к одному́** (*разг*) one thing after another; **оди́н к одному́** one as good as another;

одно́ из двух one of two things; **одно́ вре́мя** for some time; **в оди́н го́лос** with one voice; **оди́н-еди́нственный** only one; **оди́н-одинёшенек** (*разг*) all alone.

одина́ково *нареч* in the same way.
одина́ков|ый (-, -а, -о) *прил* similar.
одина́рный *прил* single.
одиннадцатичасово́й *прил* eleven-hour; (*отправление*) eleven-o'clock.
оди́ннадцат|ый (-ая, -ое, -ые) *чис* eleventh; *см также* **пя́тый**.
оди́ннадцать (-и; *как* **пять**; *см* Table 27) *чис* eleven; *см также* **пять**.
одино́к|ий (-ая, -ое, -ие; -, -а, -о) *прил* (*дом, дерево*) solitary; (*жизнь, человек*) lonely; (*без семьи: женщина, мужчина*) single.
одино́чек *сущ см* **одино́чка**.
одино́честв|о (-а) *ср* loneliness.
одино́|чка (-ки; *gen pl* -ек) *ж* (*человек*): **жить ~кой** to live alone; **ба́йдарка-~** one-man canoe; **в ~ку** on one's own; **сиде́ть** (*impf*) **в ~ке** (*разг*) to be in solitary confinement.
одино́чн|ый *прил* (*стук, выстрел*) single, lone; (*проживание, дома*) solitary; **~ полёт** solo flight; **~ое заключе́ние** solitary confinement; **одино́чное ката́ние (на конька́х)** (*СПОРТ*) singles figure skating.
одио́з|ный (-ен, -на, -но) *прил* odious.
одича́лый *прил* wild.
одича́ть (-ю) *сов от* **дича́ть**.
одн|а́ (-о́й) *ж чис см* **оди́н**.
одна́жды *нареч* once.
одна́ко *союз, вводн сл* however; **его́ повы́сили – ~!** he's been promoted – no, really!; **~ же** even so.
одни́ (-х) *мн чис см* **оди́н**.
одн|о́ (-ого́) *ср чис см* **оди́н**.
одноа́ктный *прил* one-act, in one act.
однобо́ртный *прил* single-breasted.
одновреме́нно *нареч*: ~ (с +*instr*) at the same time (as).
одновреме́нный *прил* simultaneous.
одного́ *итп чис см* **оди́н**, **одно́**.
одного́д|ок (-ка) *м* (*разг*): **он мой ~** he was born in the same year as me.
однодне́вн|ый *прил* (*зарплата, работа*) one day's; **~ая пое́здка** day trip.
однозву́чный (-ен, -на, -но) *прил* monotonous.
однозна́чный (-ен, -на, -но) *прил* (*тождественный*) synonymous; (*с одним значением: слово*) monosemantic; (: *выражение, ответ*) unambiguous; (*МАТ*) single-figure; **однозна́чное число́** single-digit number.
одноимённый *прил* of the same name.
однокла́ссник (-а) *м* classmate.
однокла́ссни|ца (-ы) *ж см* **однокла́ссник**.
однокле́точный *прил* single-cell.
однаколе́йный *прил* single-lane.
однокра́тный *прил* single.
однолетний (-яя, -ее, -ие) *прил* annual.

одноме́стный *прил* (*купе, номер*) single; (*каюта*) single-berth.

однообра́зи|**е** (-**я**) *ср* monotony.

однообра́зный *прил* monotonous.

однопо́лый *прил* unisexual.

однора́зовый *прил* disposable; ~ **про́пуск** temporary pass (*valid only once*).

однора́дный (-**ен, -на, -но**) *прил* (*явления, понятия*) similar; (*жидкость, масса*) homogenous.

односло́ж|**ный** (-**ен, -на, -но**) *прил* (*также перен*) monosyllabic.

односторо́н|**ний** (-**няя, -нее, -ние**) *прил* (*ткань*) one-sided; (*разоружение*) unilateral; (*движение, связь*) one-way; (-**ен, -ня, -не**; *перен: воспитание, развитие*) narrow; (: *мышление*) parochial; **у него́ ~ парали́ч** he is paralysed (*BRIT*) *или* paralyzed (*US*) down one side.

одноти́п|**ный** (-**ен, -на, -но**) *прил* of the same type *или* kind.

однотом́ный *прил* one-volume.

однофами́л|**ец** (-**ьца**) *м* namesake (*with same surname*).

однофами́лиц|**а** (-**ы**) *ж см* **однофами́лец**.

однофами́льца *итп сущ см* **однофами́лец**.

одноцве́т|**ный** (-**ен, -на, -но**) *прил* plain.

одночле́н (-**а**) *м* monomial.

одноэта́жный *прил* single-storey (*BRIT*), single-story (*US*), one-storey (*BRIT*), one-story (*US*).

одобре́ни|**е** (-**я**) *ср* approval.

одобри́телен *прил см* **одобри́тельный**.

одобри́тельно *нареч* favourably.

одобри́тель|**ный** (-**ен, -ьна, -ьно**) *прил* (*отзыв, реакция*) favourable (*BRIT*), favorable (*US*); (*восклицание, взгляд*) of approval; (*статья*) positive.

одо́бр|**ить** (-**ю, -ишь**; *impf* **одобря́ть**) *сов перех* to approve.

одоле́ть (-**ю**; *impf* **одолева́ть**) *сов перех* (*врага*) to overpower; (*смущение, неприязнь*) to overcome; (*разг: книгу, задачу*) to get through; (: *подлеж: жара, комары*) to bug; (*науку*) to master; **его́ ~ла грусть/лень** he was overwhelmed by sadness/a feeling of laziness.

одолже́ни|**е** (-**я**) *ср* favour (*BRIT*), favor (*US*); **сде́лайте ~** would you do me a favour?; (*ответ*) be my guest.

одолж|**и́ть** (-**у́, -и́шь**; *impf* **ода́лживать**) *сов перех*: ~ **что-н кому́-н** to lend sth to sb; **ода́лживать** (~ *perf*) **что-н у кого́-н** (*разг*) to borrow sth from sb.

одряхле́ть (-**ю**) *сов от* **дряхле́ть**.

одува́нчик (-**а**) *м* dandelion.

оду́ма|**ться** (-**юсь**; *impf* **оду́мываться**) *сов возв* to think again.

одура́ч|**ить** (-**у, -ишь**) *сов от* **дура́чить**.

одуре́лый *прил* (*разг*) befuddled.

одуре́ть (-**ю**) *сов от* **дуре́ть**.

одурма́н|**ить** (-**ю, -ишь**) *сов от* **дурма́нить**.

о́дур|**ь** (-**и**) *ж*: **напи́ться до ~и** (*разг*) to drink o.s. silly; **набе́гаться** (*perf*) **до ~и** (*разг*) to run until one is ready to drop; **я насмотре́лся дете́ктивов до ~и** (*разг*) I've watched thrillers until I'm sick of them.

одутлова́тый (-, -**а, -о**) *прил* puffed up, puffy.

одухотворён|**ный** (-, -**на, -но**) *прил* (*вид, лицо*) spiritual; (*речь*) inspired.

одухотвор|**и́ть** (-**ю́, -и́шь**; *impf* **одухотворя́ть**) *сов перех* to inspire.

оды́шк|**а** (-**и**) *ж*: **у него́ ~** he is short of breath; **страда́ть** (*impf*) **~ой** to be short-winded.

ОЕЭС *ж сокр* (= **Организа́ция европе́йского экономи́ческого сотру́дничества**) OEEC (= *Organization for European Economic Cooperation*).

ожереб|**и́ться** (*3sg* -**и́тся**, *3pl* -**я́тся**) *сов от* **жереби́ться**.

ожере́ль|**е** (-**я**) *ср* necklace.

ожесточа́|**ть(ся)** (-**ю(сь)**) *несов от* **ожесточи́ть(ся)**.

ожесточе́ни|**е** (-**я**) *ср* bitterness; **с ~м** furiously.

ожесточён|**ный** (-, -**на, -но**) *прил* (*человек*) hardened, embittered; (*спор, сражение*) fierce.

ожесточ|**и́ть** (-**у́, -и́шь**; *impf* **ожесточа́ть**) *сов перех* (*человека*) to harden, embitter

► **ожесточи́ться** (*impf* **ожесточа́ться**) *сов возв* to become hardened *или* embittered.

ожива́|**ть** (-**ю**) *несов от* **ожи́ть**.

ожив|**и́ть** (-**лю́, -и́шь**; *impf* **оживля́ть**) *сов перех* to revive; (*глаза, лицо*) to light up; (*улицу, долину*) to bring to life; (*торговлю, работу*) to revitalize

► **оживи́ться** (*impf* **оживля́ться**) *сов возв* to liven up; (*лицо*) to brighten; (*улица, школа*) to come to life.

оживле́ни|**е** (-**я**) *ср* (*на улице, в доме*) bustle; (*организма, растения*) revival.

оживлён|**ный** (-, -**на, -но**) *прил* (*беседа, спор*) animated; (*улица, место, деятельность*) lively; (*торговля*) brisk; (-, -**а́, -о́**; *человек*) lively.

оживлю́(сь) *сов см* **оживи́ть(ся)**.

оживля́|**ть(ся)** (-**ю(сь)**) *несов от* **оживи́ть(ся)**.

оживу́ *итп сов см* **ожи́ть**.

ожида́ни|**е** (-**я**) *ср* anticipation; (*обычно мн: надежды*) expectation; **в ~и чего́-н** in anticipation of sth; **обма́нывать** (**обману́ть** *perf*) **чьи-н ~я** to fail to come up to sb's expectations.

ожида́ть (-**ю**) *несов перех* (*ждать*) to expect; (+*gen; надеяться*) to expect; **его́ ~ет блестя́щая карье́ра** he has a brilliant career ahead of him; **э́того мо́жно бы́ло ~** that was to be expected

► **ожида́ться** *несов возв* to be expected.

ожире́ни|е (-я) *ср* obesity.

ожире́|ть (-ю) *сов от* **жире́ть**.

ож|и́ть (-иву́, -ивёшь; *impf* **ожива́ть**) *сов неперех* to come to life; (*перен: чувства, человек*) to revive.

ожо́г (-а) *м* burn.

озабо́|тить (-чу, -тишь) *сов перех* to worry, trouble.

озабо́чен|ный (-, -на, -но) *прил* worried.

озабо́чу *сов см* **озабо́тить**.

озагла́в|ить (-лю, -ишь; *impf* **озагла́вливать**) *сов перех* to entitle.

озада́чен|ный (-, -на, -но) *прил* puzzled.

озада́ч|ить (-у, -ишь; *impf* **озада́чивать**) *сов перех* to puzzle, perplex.

озар|и́ть (-ю́, -и́шь; *impf* **озаря́ть**) *сов перех* (*подлеж: солнце, улыбка*) to light up; (: *идея, догадка*) to dawn on

▶ **озари́ться** (*impf* **озаря́ться**) *сов возв*: ~**ся** +*instr* (*также перен*) to be lit up by.

озвере́|ть (-ю) *сов от* **звере́ть** ◆ *неперех* to become violent.

озву́ч|ить (-у, -ишь; *impf* **озву́чивать**) *сов перех*: ~ **фильм** to record the soundtrack for a film.

оздорови́тельн|ый *прил*: ~**ые мероприя́тия** health-improving measures; **оздорови́тельный ко́мплекс** ≈ health farm.

оздоров|и́ть (-лю́, -и́шь; *impf* **оздоровля́ть**) *сов перех* (*перен: коллектив, обстановку*) to clean up; **оздоровля́ть** (~ *perf*) **органи́зм** to improve one's health; ~ (*perf*) **ме́стность** to improve the ecology of an area.

озелен|и́ть (-ю́, -и́шь; *impf* **озеленя́ть**) *несов перех* to green.

о́з|еро (-ера; *nom pl* -ёра) *ср* lake.

ози́м|ые (-ых; *decl like adj*) *мн* winter crops *мн*.

ози́м|ый *прил*: ~**ая пшени́ца/рожь** winter wheat/rye; *см также* **ози́мые**.

озира́|ться (-юсь) *несов возв*: ~ (**по сторона́м**) to glance about *или* around.

озло́б|ить (-лю, -ишь; *impf* **озлобля́ть**) *сов перех* to anger

▶ **озло́биться** (*impf* **озлобля́ться**) *сов возв* to become angry.

озлобле́ни|е (-я) *ср* anger.

озло́блен|ный (-, -на, -но) *прил* angry.

озлоблю́(сь) *сов см* **озло́бить(ся)**.

озлобля́|ть(ся) (-ю(сь)) *несов от* **озло́бить(ся)**.

ознако́м|ить (-лю, -ишь) *сов от* **знако́мить** ◆ (*impf* **ознакомля́ть**) *перех*: ~ **кого́-н с** +*instr* to familiarize sb with

▶ **ознако́миться** *сов от* **знако́миться** ◆ (*impf* **ознакомля́ться**) *возв*: ~**ся с** +*instr* to familiarize o.s. with.

ознаменова́ни|е (-я) *ср*: **в** ~ +*gen* (*в память*) in commemoration of.

ознамен|ова́ть (-у́ю; *impf* **ознамено́вывать**) *сов перех* to commemorate, mark; **его́ побе́да** ~**ова́ла э́тот год** his victory made this a

memorable year

▶ **ознаменова́ться** (*impf* **ознамено́вываться**) *сов возв* (+*instr*) to be remembered for.

означа́|ть (-ю) *несов перех* to mean.

озно́б (-а) *м* shivering.

ОЗО *ср сокр* (= **отделе́ние зао́чного обуче́ния**) extra-mural department.

озо́н (-а) *м* ozone.

озо́новый *прил*: ~ **слой** ozone layer; **озо́новая дыра́** hole in the ozone layer.

озорни́|к (-а́) *м* (*разг*) scallywag.

озорно́й *прил* mischievous.

озорств|о́ (-а́) *ср* mischief.

озя́бн|уть (-у, -ешь) *сов от* **зя́бнуть**.

ой *межд*: ~! (*выражает испуг*) argh!; (*выражает удивление, восхищение*) oh!; (*выражает боль*) ouch!, ow!; **им жило́сь** ~ **как тру́дно** their life was ever so difficult.

ОК *м сокр* (= **отде́л ка́дров**) personnel department.

ок|аза́ть (-ажу́, -а́жешь; *impf* **ока́зывать**) *сов перех*: ~ **по́мощь/соде́йствие кому́-н** to provide help/assistance for sb; **ока́зывать** (~ *perf*) **влия́ние на** +*acc* to exercise influence over *или* on; **ока́зывать** (~ *perf*) **давле́ние на** +*acc* to put pressure on *или* upon; **ока́зывать** (~ *perf*) **внима́ние кому́-н** to pay attention to sb; **ока́зывать** (~ *perf*) **предпочте́ние кому́-н** to give preference to sb; **ока́зывать** (~ *perf*) **сопротивле́ние (кому́-н)** to offer resistance (to sb); **ока́зывать** (~ *perf*) **услу́гу кому́-н** to do sb a service

▶ **оказа́ться** (*impf* **ока́зываться**) *сов возв* (*найтись: на столе итп*) to appear; (*очути́ться: на острове итп*) to find o.s.; **ока́зываться** (~**ся** *perf*) +*instr* (*вором, шпио́ном*) to turn out to be; ~**а́зывается, она́ была́ права́** it turns out that she was right; **у него́ не** ~**аза́лось де́нег** it turned out that he didn't have any money.

ока́зи|я (-и) *ж* opportunity; **посыла́ть (посла́ть** *perf*) **что-н с** ~**ей** to send sth with somebody.

ока́з|ыва|ть(ся) (-ю(сь)) *несов от* **оказа́ть(ся)**.

окайм|и́ть (-лю́, -и́шь; *impf* **окаймля́ть**) *сов перех* (*рисунок*) to frame; (*плато́к*) to border.

окамени́ва|ть (-ю) *сов от* **камене́ть**.

окамене́лый *прил* (*де́рево, расте́ние*) fossilized; (*хлеб, сыр*) rock-hard; (*перен: челове́к, взгляд, лицо́*) motionless.

окамене́|ть (-ю; *impf* **окаменева́ть** *или* **камене́ть**) *сов неперех* (*де́рево, расте́ние*) to fossilize; (*хлеб, сыр*) to go stale; (*перен: лицо́, взгляд*) to freeze; (: *душа́, се́рдце*) to turn to stone; ~ (*perf*) **от стра́ха** to turn rigid with fear; ~ (*perf*) **от го́ря** to be numb with grief.

окант|ова́ть (-у́ю; *impf* **оканто́вывать**) *сов перех* (*карти́ну, фотогра́фию*) to frame; (*воротни́к, плато́к*) to border.

ока́нчива|ть (-ю) *несов от* **око́нчить**

▶ **ока́нчиваться** *несов от* **око́нчиться** ◆ *возв*: ~**ся на гла́сную/согла́сную** to end in a vowel/

consonant; **э́та у́лица ~ется тупико́м** this
(street) is a dead end.
ока́пыва|ть(ся) (-ю(сь)) *несов от* **окопа́ть(ся)**.
окати́ть (-ачу́, -а́тишь; *impf* **ока́чивать**) *сов
перех*: ~ **кого́-н/что-н чем-н** to pour sth over
sb/sth.
океа́н (-а) *м (также перен)* ocean.
Океа́ни|я (-и) *ж* Oceania.
океаноло́ги|я (-и) *ж* oceanography.
оки́н|уть (-у, -ешь; *impf* **оки́дывать**) *сов перех*:
~ **кого́-н/что-н взгля́дом** to glance over at
sb/sth.
о́кис|ел (-ла) *м* oxide.
окисле́ни|е (-я) *ср* oxidation.
окисли́ть (*3sg* -и́т, *3pl* -я́т, *impf* **окисля́ть**) *сов
перех* to oxidize
▶ **окисли́ться** (*impf* **окисля́ться**) *сов возв* to
oxidize.
о́кис|ь (-и) *ж* oxide.
оккупа́нт (-а) *м (захватчик)* occupier.
оккупацио́нный *прил* occupation *опред*.
оккупа́ци|я (-и) *ж* occupation.
оккупи́р|овать (-ую) *(не)сов перех* to occupy.
окла́д (-а) *м (зарплата)* salary; *(на иконе)*
overlay.
оклеве|та́ть (-щу́, -́щешь) *сов перех* to
slander.
окле́|ить (-ю, -ишь; *impf* **окле́ивать**) *сов перех*:
~ **что-н чем-н** to cover sth with sth; **окле́ивать**
(~ *perf*) **сте́ны обо́ями** to paper the walls.
оклик|ну́ть (-у, -ешь; *impf* **оклика́ть**) *сов перех*
to call out to.
окн|о́ (-а́; *nom pl* -на, *gen pl* -он) *ср* window;
(подоконник) windowsill; *(разг: между
уроками)* gap.
око́в|ы (-) *мн (также перен)* fetters *мн*.
окола́чива|ться (-юсь) *несов возв (разг)* to
hang about.
околд|ова́ть (-у́ю; *impf* **околдо́вывать**) *сов
перех (также перен)* to bewitch.
околева́|ть (-ю) *несов от* **околе́ть**.
околе́сиц|а (-ы) *ж (разг)* claptrap, tripe; **нести́**
(impf) ~**у** to talk tripe.
околе́|ть (-ю; *impf* **околева́ть**) *сов неперех
(животное)* to die.
о́коло *нареч* nearby ♦ *предл (+gen; рядом с)*
near; *(приблизительно)* about.
околозе́мн|ый *прил* around the earth; ~**ая
орби́та** the earth's orbit.
око́льн|ый *прил* roundabout *опред*; *(перен:
метод)* devious; **мы пошли́** ~**ым путём** we
took a roundabout route.
окольц|ева́ть (-у́ю) *сов от* **кольцева́ть**.
о́кон *сущ см* **окно́**.
оконе́чност|ь (-и) *ж* tip.
око́нн|ый *прил*: ~**ая ра́ма** window frame; ~**ое
стекло́** windowpane.
оконча́ни|е (-я) *ср* end; *(линг)* ending.

оконча́телен *прил см* **оконча́тельный**.
оконча́тельно *нареч (решить, ответить)*
definitely; *(разбить, победить, влюбиться)*
completely; *(отредактировать, проверить)*
finally.
оконча́тельн|ый (-ен, -ьна, -ьно) *прил (вывод,
редакция, ответ)* final; *(победа, свержение)*
complete.
око́нч|ить (-у, -ишь; *impf* **ока́нчивать**) *сов
перех* to finish; *(вуз)* to graduate from
▶ **око́нчиться** (*impf* **ока́нчиваться**) *сов возв* to
finish; ~**ся** *(perf)* +*instr (скандалом, свадьбой)* to
result in.
око́п (-а) *м* trench.
окопа́ть (-ю; *impf* **ока́пывать**) *сов перех*: ~
расте́ние to loosen the soil around a plant
▶ **окопа́ться** (*impf* **ока́пываться**) *сов возв
(воен)* to dig (o.s.) in; *(разг: в библиотеке, в
кабинете)* to bury o.s.
о́корок (-а; *nom pl* -а́) *м* gammon.
окосе́|ть (-ю) *сов перех (разг: косить)* to
squint; (: *ослепнуть*) to lose an eye; (:
опьянеть) to get drunk.
окостенева́|ть (-ю) *несов от* **окостене́ть**.
окостене́лый *прил* ossified; *(руки, ноги)* stiff;
(ум, жизнь) fossilized.
окостене́|ть (-ю; *impf* **окостенева́ть**) *сов
неперех* to ossify; *(руки, ноги)* to stiffen; *(ум)* to
fossilize.
око́т (-а) *м (кошки)* birth of kittens; *(овцы)*
lambing.
окоти́ться (*3sg* -и́тся, *3pl* -я́тся) *сов от*
коти́ться.
окочене́лый *прил* stiff with cold.
окочене́|ть (-ю) *сов от* **кочене́ть**.
окра́ин|а (-ы) *ж (поля, леса)* edge; *(города)*
outskirts *мн*; *(страны)* remote parts *мн*.
окра́|сить (-шу, -сишь; *impf* **окра́шивать**) *сов
перех (ткань, волосы)* to dye; *(рассказ, жизнь)*
to colour *(brit)*, color *(us)*
▶ **окра́ситься** (*impf* **окра́шиваться**) *сов возв*:
~**ся в чёрный/кра́сный цвет** to come out
black/red; **облака́** ~**сились в ро́зовый цвет**
the clouds were tinged with pink.
окра́с|ка (-ки; *gen pl* -ок) *ж (ткани, волос)*
dyeing; *(животного, выражения)* colouring
(brit), coloring *(us)*; **принима́ть (приня́ть** *perf)*
совсе́м другу́ю ~**ку** *(перен)* to take on a
different complexion.
окра́шива|ть(ся) (-ю(сь)) *несов от*
окра́сить(ся).
окра́шу(сь) *сов см* **окра́сить(ся)**.
окре́пн|уть (-у, -ешь) *сов от* **кре́пнуть**.
окре|сти́ть (-щу́, -́стишь) *сов от* **крести́ть** ♦
сов перех: ~ **кого́-н/что-н чем-н** *(разг)* to
nickname sb/sth sth
▶ **окрести́ться** *сов от* **крести́ться**.
окре́стност|ь (-и) *ж (города, деревни)* environs

мн; в ~и +*gen* in the vicinity of.

окре́стн|ый *прил* (*города́, дере́вни*) neighbouring (*BRIT*), neighboring (*US*); ~**ое населе́ние** the population of the surrounding area.

окрещу́(сь) *сов см* **окрести́ть(ся)**.

окриве́ть (**-ю**) *сов от* **криве́ть**.

о́крик (**-а**) *м* shout.

окри́кн|уть (**-у, -ешь**; *impf* **окри́кивать**) *сов перех*: ~ **кого́-н** to shout to sb.

окрова́вленн|ый (**-, -а, -о**) *прил* bloodstained.

окроп|и́ть (**-лю́, -и́шь**) *сов от* **кропи́ть**.

окро́шк|а (**-и**) *ж* okroshka (*cold kvass soup with vegetables and cooked meat*).

о́круг (**-а**) *м* (*административный, военный*) district; (*избирательный*) ward; (*национальный*) territory; (*города*) area.

окру́г|а (**-и**) *ж* (*разг*) neighbourhood (*BRIT*), neighborhood (*US*).

округле́|ть (**-ю**) *сов от* **кругле́ть**.

округл|и́ть (**-ю́, -и́шь**; *impf* **округля́ть**) *сов перех* (*форму, заготовку*) to round off; (*цифру, результат*) to round up *или* down; (*разг: сумму, капитал*) to increase; **округля́ть** (~ *perf*) **глаза́** (*от удивления, от страха*) to open one's eyes wide

▸ **округл|и́ться** (*impf* **округля́ться**) *сов возв* (*фигура, лицо*) to fill out; (*перен: разг: капитал, сумма*) to increase; **у неё** ~**и́лись глаза́** her eyes widened.

окру́глый *прил* rounded; (*лицо*) round.

округля́|ть(ся) (**-ю(сь)**) *несов от* **округли́ть(ся)**.

окружа́|ть (**-ю**) *несов от* **окружи́ть** ◆ *перех* to surround.

окружа́ющее (**-его**; *decl like adj*) *ср* environment.

окружа́ющие (**-их**; *decl like adj*) *мн* (*также:* ~ **лю́ди**) the people around one; **ничего́ нельзя́ скрыть от** ~**их** you can't hide anything from (other) people.

окружа́ющий (**-ая, -ее, -ие**) *прил* surrounding; **окружа́ющая среда́** environment.

окруже́ни|е (**-я**) *ср* (*среда*) environment; (*компания*) company; (*ВОЕН*) encirclement; **в** ~**и** +*gen* (*в сопровождении*) in the company of; (*среди*) surrounded by.

окруж|и́ть (**-у́, -и́шь**; *impf* **окружа́ть**) *сов перех* to surround; **окружа́ть** (~ *perf*) **что-н** +*instr* to surround sth by; **окружа́ть** (~ *perf*) **кого́-н** +*instr* to surround sb with.

окружно́й *прил* (*центр, конференция*) regional; **окружна́я доро́га** bypass; **окружна́я избира́тельная коми́ссия** constituency electoral committee.

окру́жность (**-и**) *ж* circle; **на три киломе́тра в** ~**и** three kilometres (*BRIT*) *или* kilometers (*US*) in circumference.

О́ксфорд (**-а**) *м* Oxford.

окта́в|а (**-ы**) *ж* octave.

октя́бр|ь (**-я́**) *м* October; **прие́ду пе́рвого**

октября́ I shall arrive on the first of October; **в про́шлом/бу́дущем октябре́** last/next October; **в конце́/нача́ле/середи́не октября́** at the end of/beginning of/in the middle of October.

октя́брьск|ий (**-ая, -ое, -ие**) *прил* October опред.

окули́ст (**-а**) *м* ophthalmologist.

окун|у́ть (**-у́, -ёшь**; *impf* **окуна́ть**) *сов перех* to dip

▸ **окун|у́ться** (*impf* **окуна́ться**) *сов возв* to plunge.

о́кун|ь (**-я**) *м* (*ЗООЛ*) perch.

окупа́емост|ь (**-и**) *ж* viability.

окуп|и́ть (**-лю́, -у́пишь**; *impf* **окупа́ть**) *сов перех* (*расходы*) to cover; (*поездку, проект*) to cover the cost of

▸ **окуп|и́ться** (*impf* **окупа́ться**) *сов возв* to pay for itself; (*перен: усилия, работа*) to be rewarded.

оку́р|ок (**-ка**; *nom pl* **-ки**) *м* stub, butt.

оку́та|ть (**-ю**; *impf* **оку́тывать**) *сов перех* (*подлеж: туман, дым*) to envelop; **оку́тывать** (~ *perf*) **что-н/кого́-н чем-н** to wrap sth/sb (up) in sth

▸ **оку́та|ться** (*impf* **оку́тываться**) *сов возв*: ~**ся** +*instr* to wrap up in; (*перен: земля итп*) to be enveloped in.

оку́ч|ить (**-у, -ишь**; *impf* **оку́чивать**) *сов перех* to earth up.

ола́дь|я (**-и**; *gen pl* **-ий**) *ж* ≈ drop scone, ≈ (Scotch) pancake.

оледене́ни|е (**-я**) *ср* freezing.

оледене́|ть (**-ю**) *сов от* **ледене́ть**.

олен|ёнок (**-ёнка**; *nom pl* **-я́та**, *gen pl* **-я́т**) *м* fawn.

оле́н|ий (**-ья, -ье, -ьи**) *прил* deer's; ~**ьи рога́** antlers.

олени́н|а (**-ы**) *ж* venison.

оле́н|ь (**-я**) *м* deer (*мн* deer).

оленя́та *итп сущ см* **оленёнок**.

оли́вк|а (**-и**) *ж* olive.

оли́вковый *прил* olive опред; (*цвет*) olive-green.

олимпиа́д|а (**-ы**) *ж* (*СПОРТ*) the Olympics мн; (*по физике итп*) Olympiad; **Бе́лая/Ле́тняя О~** the Winter/Summer Olympics.

олимпи́йск|ий (**-ая, -ое, -ие**) *прил* Olympic опред; ~**ое споко́йствие** superhuman calm; **олимпи́йские и́гры** the Olympic Games.

оли́ф|а (**-ы**) *ж* drying oil.

олицетвор|и́ть (**-ю́, -и́шь**; *impf* **олицетворя́ть**) *сов перех* to personify.

о́лов|о (**-а**) *ср* (*ХИМ*) tin.

оловя́нный *прил* tin.

о́лух (**-а**) *м* (*разг*) oaf.

О́льстер (**-а**) *м* Ulster.

ольх|а́ (**-и́**) *ж* alder.

ом (**-а**) *м* ohm.

Ома́н (**-а**) *м* Oman.

ома́р (**-а**) *м* lobster.

оме́г|а (**-и**) *ж* omega.

омерзе́ни|е (**-я**) *ср* disgust.

омерзи́тел|ьный (-ен, -ьна, -ьно) *прил* disgusting.

омертве́лый *прил* dead.

омертве́|ть (-ю) *сов от* **мертве́ть**.

омле́т (-а) *м* omelette.

омоло|ди́ть (-жу́, -ди́шь; *impf* **омола́живать**) *сов перех* to rejuvenate

▶ **омолоди́ться** (*impf* **омола́живаться**) *сов возв* to be rejuvenated.

ОМОН *м сокр* (= отря́д мили́ции осо́бого назначе́ния) *special police force*.

омо́ним (-а) *м* homonym.

омоно́в|ец (-ца) *м member of* ОМОН.

омо́ю *итп сов см* **омы́ть**.

омрач|и́ть (-у́, -и́шь; *impf* **омрача́ть**) *сов перех* (*настрое́ние, ра́дость, лицо́*) to cloud; (*пра́здник, встре́чу*) to cast a cloud over

▶ **омрачи́ться** (*impf* **омрача́ться**) *сов возв* (*взгляд, лицо́, настрое́ние*) to darken.

о́мут (-а) *м* (*водоворо́т*) whirlpool.

омыва́|ть (-ю) *несов от* **омы́ть** ♦ *перех* (*подлеж: мо́ре, океа́н*) to wash.

ом|ы́ть (-о́ю, -о́ешь; *impf* **омыва́ть**) *сов перех* to wash.

он (его́; *см* Table 5a) *мест* (*челове́к*) he; (*живо́тное, предме́т*) it.

она́ (её; *см* Table 5a) *мест* (*челове́к*) she; (*живо́тное, предме́т*) it.

онани́зм (-а) *м* masturbation.

онда́тр|а (-ы) *ж* musquash, muskrat.

онеме́лый *прил* numb.

онеме́|ть (-ю) *сов от* **неме́ть**.

они́ (их; *см* Table 5b) *мест* they.

онко́лог (-а) *м* oncologist.

онкологи́ческ|ий (-ая, -ое, -ие) *прил* oncological; **~ая кли́ника** cancer clinic.

оно́ (его́; *см* Table 5a) *мест* it; **~ и ви́дно!** (*разг*) sure! (*used ironically*); **я хоте́л помо́чь Вам – ~ и ви́дно** I was only trying to help you – sure you were; **вот ~ что** *или* **как!** (*разг*) so that's what it is!

ОНЧ *сокр* (= о́чень ни́зкая частота́) VLF (= *very low frequency*).

ООН *ж сокр* (= Организа́ция Объединённых На́ций) UNO (= *United Nations Organization*).

ООП *ж сокр* (= Организа́ция освобожде́ния Палести́ны) PLO (= *Palestine Liberation Organization*).

опада́|ть (*3sg* -ет, *3pl* -ют) *несов от* **опа́сть**.

опаду́т *итп сов см* **опа́сть**.

опа́здыва|ть (-ю) *несов от* **опозда́ть**.

опа́л (-а) *м* opal.

опа́л|а (-ы) *ж* (*перен*) disfavour (*BRIT*), disfavor (*US*); **быть** (*impf*) **в ~е** (**у** +*gen*) to be out of favour (with).

опал|и́ть (-ю́, -и́шь; *impf* **опа́ливать** *или* **опаля́ть**) *сов перех* (*во́лосы, кры́лья, де́рево итп*) to singe; (*ко́жу, лицо́*) to burn; (*impf*

опа́ливать; *ку́рицу, у́тку*) to singe.

опа́р|а (-ы) *ж* leaven.

опаса́|ться (-юсь) *несов возв*: **~** +*gen* (*неприя́теля, рецензе́нта*) to be afraid of; (*сквозняка́, просту́ды*) to avoid; **~** (*impf*) **за** +*acc* to be worried about.

опа́сен *прил см* **опа́сный**.

опасе́ни|е (-я) *ср* apprehension.

опа́ск|а (-и) *ж*: **с ~ой** cautiously; **без ~и** fearlessly.

опа́сно *нареч* dangerously ♦ *как сказ* it's dangerous; **э́то ~ для жи́зни** it's life-threatening.

опа́сност|ь (-и) *ж* danger; **в ~и** in danger; **с ~ю для жи́зни** endangering one's life.

опа́с|ный (-ен, -на, -но) *прил* dangerous.

опа́|сть (*3sg* -дёт, *3pl* -ду́т, *impf* **опада́ть**) *сов неперех* (*цветы́, ли́стья*) to fall; (*о́пухоль, ши́шка*) to go down; (*разг: щёки, бока́*) to get thinner.

ОПЕК *м/ж сокр* (= Организа́ция стран-экспортёров не́фти) OPEC (= *Organization of Petroleum-Exporting Countries*).

опе́к|а (-и) *ж* (*попечи́тельство: госуда́рства*) guardianship; (: *ма́тери, отца́*) custody; (*забо́та*) care ♦ *собир* guardians *мн*; **брать** (**взять** *perf*) **кого́-н под ~у** to take sb into one's care; **она́ рабо́тает под мое́й ~ой** she works under my supervision.

опека́|ть (-ю) *несов перех* to take care of; (*сироту́*) to be guardian to.

опеку́н (-а́) *м* (*сироты́*) guardian; (*насле́дника, насле́дства*) trustee.

опеку́нш|а (-и) *ж* (*сироты́*) guardian.

оп|ёнок (-ёнка; *nom pl* -я́та, *gen pl* -я́т) *м* (БОТ) honey agaric.

о́пер|а (-ы) *ж* opera.

операти́вен *прил см* **операти́вный**.

операти́вност|ь (-и) *ж* efficiency.

операти́в|ный (-ен, -на, -но) *прил* (*рабо́та, гру́ппа, штаб*) executive *опред*; (*ме́ры, де́йствия, руково́дство*) efficient; (*хирурги́ческий*) surgical; **операти́вное вмеша́тельство** surgical intervention.

опера́тор (-а) *м* operator.

операцио́нн|ая (-ой; *decl like adj*) *ж* (МЕД) operating theatre (*BRIT*), operating room (*US*).

операцио́нный *прил* (*инструме́нты, отделе́ние*) surgical; **операцио́нный стол** operating table.

опера́ци|я (-и) *ж* operation.

опере|ди́ть (-жу́, -ди́шь; *impf* **опережа́ть**) *сов перех* (*в бе́ге, в учёбе, в разви́тии*) to outstrip; **~** (*perf*) **кого́-н** (*в разгово́ре*) to beat sb to it.

опере́ни|е (-я) *ср* (ЗООЛ) plumage; (АВИА): **хвостово́е ~** tail.

опере́тт|а (-ы) *ж* operetta.

опере́ться (обопру́сь, обопрёшься; *pt* опёрся, оперла́сь, оперло́сь, *impf* опира́ться) *сов неперех*: ~ **на** +*acc* (*дерево, трость*) to lean on; (*перен: на това́рища, на коллекти́в*) to rely on; (*перен: на фа́кты, на тео́рию*) to be supported *или* backed up by.

опери́р|овать (-ую; *perf* опери́ровать *или* проопери́ровать) *несов перех* (*больно́го*) to operate on ◆ *неперех* (*no perf*; ВОЕН) to operate; ~ (*impf*) +*instr* (*а́кциями, це́нными бума́гами*) to deal in; (*перен: ци́фрами, фа́ктами*) to use.

опери́ться (*3sg* -и́тся, *3pl* -я́тся, *impf* оперя́ться) *сов возв* to become fully fledged.

о́перный *прил* (*а́рия, партиту́ра*) operatic; (*певе́ц*) opera *опред*; ~ **теа́тр** opera house.

оперя́|ться (*3sg* -ется, *3pl* -ются) *несов от* **опери́ться**.

опеча́л|иться (-юсь) *сов от* **печа́литься**.

опеча́та|ть (-ю; *impf* опеча́тывать) *сов перех* to seal.

опеча́т|ка (-ки; *gen pl* -ок) *ж* misprint; **спи́сок** ~**ок** errata.

опеча́тыва|ть (-ю) *несов от* **опеча́тать**.

опе́ш|ить (-у, -ишь) *сов неперех* (*разг*) to be taken aback.

опи́л|ки (-ок) *мн* (*древе́сные*) sawdust *ед*; (*металли́ческие*) filings *мн*.

опира́|ться (-юсь) *несов от* **опере́ться**.

описа́ни|е (-я) *ср* description.

описа́тельный (-ен, -ьна, -ьно) *прил* descriptive.

оп|иса́ть (-ишу́, -и́шешь; *impf* опи́сывать) *сов перех* to describe; (*соста́вить пере́чень*) to make a list *или* an inventory of; (*наложи́ть аре́ст*) to distrain.

опи́са|ться (-юсь) *сов возв* (*разг*) to wet o.s.

опи́сыва|ть (-ю) *несов от* **описа́ть**.

о́пис|ь (-и) *ж* (*спи́сок*) list, inventory; (*аре́ст*) distraint.

о́пиум (-а) *м* opium.

опишу́ *итп сов см* **описа́ть**.

опла́|кать (-чу, -чешь; *impf* опла́кивать) *сов перех* to mourn.

опла́т|а (-ы) *ж* payment.

опл|ати́ть (-ачу́, -а́тишь; *impf* опла́чивать) *сов перех* (*рабо́ту, труд*) to pay for; (*счёт*) to pay.

опла́чу *итп сов см* **опла́кать**.

оплачу́ *сов см* **оплати́ть**.

оплеу́х|а (-и) *ж* (*разг*) clout; (*перен: оскорбле́ние*) slap in the face.

оплодотворе́ни|е (-я) *ср* fertilization.

оплодотвор|и́ть (-ю́, -и́шь; *impf* оплодотворя́ть) *сов перех* to fertilize.

опломбир|ова́ть (-у́ю) *сов от* **пломбирова́ть**.

оплот (-а) *м* stronghold, bastion.

оплоша́|ть (-ю) *сов неперех* (*разг*) to boob.

опло́шност|ь (-и) *ж* mistake; **допуска́ть** (**допусти́ть** *perf*) ~ to make a mistake.

опове|сти́ть (-щу́, -сти́шь; *impf* опоеща́ть) *сов перех* to notify.

оповеще́ни|е (-я) *ср* notification.

оповещу́ *сов см* **оповести́ть**.

опога́н|ить (-ю) *сов от* **пога́нить**.

опозда́вш|ий (-его; *decl like adj*) *м* latecomer.

опозда́ни|е (-я) *ср* lateness; (*по́езда, самолёта*) late arrival; **приходи́ть** (**прийти́** *perf*) **с** ~**м/без опозда́ния** to arrive late/on time.

опозда́|ть (-ю; *impf* опа́здывать) *сов неперех*: **опа́здывать** (**в/на** +*acc*) (*в шко́лу, на рабо́ту итп*) to be late (for); **опа́здывать** (~ *perf*) **с чем-н** to be late with sth; ~ (*perf*) **на по́езд/самолёт** to miss the train/plane.

опознава́тельный *прил* (*знак*) identifying; (*огни́*) distinguishing.

опознава́|ть (-ю́) *несов от* **опозна́ть**.

опозна́ни|е (-я) *ср* identification.

опозна́|ть (-ю; *impf* опознава́ть) *сов перех* to identify.

опозо́р|ить(ся) (-ю(сь)) *сов от* **позо́рить(ся)**.

ополо́скива|ть (-ю) *несов от* **ополосну́ть**.

о́полз|ень (-ня) *м* landslide.

ополосн|у́ть (-у́, -ёшь; *impf* опола́скивать) *сов перех* (*посу́ду*) to rinse; (*лицо́, ру́ки*) to wash.

ополоуме|ть (-ю) *сов неперех* (*разг*) to go wild.

ополча́|ться (-юсь) *несов от* **ополчи́ться**.

ополче́н|ец (-ца) *м* member of the home guard.

ополче́ни|е (-я) *ср* home guard.

ополче́нца *итп сущ см* **ополче́нец**.

ополч|и́ться (-у́сь, -и́шься; *impf* ополча́ться) *сов возв*: ~ **на** +*acc или* **про́тив** +*gen* (*челове́ка*) to turn against; (*тео́рию, недоста́тки*) to attack.

опо́мн|иться (-юсь, -ишься) *сов возв* (*прийти́ в созна́ние*) to come round; (*оду́маться*) to come to one's senses; ~**ись, что ты де́лаешь!** think what you're doing!

опо́р (-а) *м*: **во весь** ~ at top speed.

опо́р|а (-ы) *ж* (*та́кже перен*) support; (*СТРОИТ*) pile; **то́чка** ~**ы** fulcrum; **опо́ра электропереда́ч** (*обы́чно мн*) electricity pylon.

опо́рный *прил* supporting *опред*; **опо́рный прыжо́к** vault; **опо́рный пункт** base; (*ВОЕН*) strongpoint.

опорожн|и́ть (-ю́, -и́шь; *impf* опорожня́ть) *сов перех* to drain, empty.

опоро́с (-а) *м* farrowing.

опоро́ч|ить (-у, -ишь) *сов от* **поро́чить**.

опохмел|и́ться (-ю́сь, -и́шься; *impf* опохмеля́ться) *сов возв* (*разг*) to take the hair of the dog (*to cure a hangover*).

опо́шл|ить (-ю, -ишь; *impf* опошля́ть) *сов перех* (*мысль, челове́ка, иде́ю*) to debase, demean; (*сло́во, пе́сню*) to vulgarize.

опоэтизи́р|овать (-ую) *сов от* **поэтизи́ровать**.

оппозицио́нный (-ен, -на, -но) *прил* (*па́ртия, блок*) opposition; ~**ные настрое́ния** mood of opposition.

оппози́ци|я (-и) *ж* opposition; **быть** (*impf*) **в** ~ (*ПОЛИТ*) to be in opposition; **быть** (*impf*) **в** ~ **к** +*dat* to oppose.

оппонéнт (-а) *м* external examiner (*for doctoral thesis*); (*в споре*) opponent.

опрáв|а (-ы) *ж* frame.

оправдáни|е (-я) *ср* justification; (*ЮР*) acquittal; (*извинение*) excuse; **говори́ть (сказáть** *perf*) **что-н в своё ~** to say sth in one's defence (*BRIT*) *или* defense (*US*).

опрáвдан|ный (-, -на, -но) *прил* justified.

оправдá|ть (-ю; *impf* **опрáвдывать**) *сов перех* to justify; (*ЮР*) to acquit, find not guilty

▶ **оправдá|ться** (*impf* **опрáвдываться**) *сов возв* to justify o.s.; (*надежды, опасения, расходы*) to be justified.

опрáв|ить (-лю, -ишь; *impf* **оправлять**) *сов перех* (*платье, постель*) to straighten; (*драгоценный камень, зеркало*) to mount; (*линзы*) to frame

▶ **опрáв|иться** (*impf* **оправля́ться**) *сов возв*: **~ся от** +*gen* to recover from.

опрáшива|ть (-ю) *несов от* **опроси́ть**.

определéни|е (-я) *ср* determination; (*понятия, значения*) definition; (*линг*) attribute; (*ЮР*) ruling.

определён|ный (-ен, -на, -но) *прил* (*установленный*) definite; (*некоторый*) certain; (*явный: успех, способности*) unqualified; **при ~ных обстоя́тельствах** under certain circumstances.

определ|и́ть (-ю́, -и́шь; *impf* **определя́ть**) *сов перех* to determine; (*явление, понятие*) to define

▶ **определи́ться** (*impf* **определя́ться**) *сов возв* (*болезнь*) to be diagnosed; (*задачи*) to become clear; (*разг: характер*) to take shape; (*пилот*) to get one's bearings.

опрéлост|ь (-и) *ж* rash; (*у младенца*) nappy (*BRIT*) *или* diaper (*US*) rash.

опресн|и́ть (-ю́, -и́шь; *impf* **опресня́ть**) *сов перех* to desalinate.

оприхо́д|овать (-ую) *сов от* **прихо́довать**.

опро́б|овать (-ую) (*не*)*сов перех* to test.

опроверг|ну́ть (-у, -ешь; *impf* **опроверга́ть**) *сов перех* to refute.

опроверже́ни|е (-я) *ср* refutation.

опроки́|нуть (-у, -ешь; *impf* **опроки́дывать**) *сов перех* (*стакан, стул*) to knock over; (*лодку*) to capsize, overturn; (*прохожего, ребёнка*) to knock down *или* over; (*перен: войска, наступление*) to repel; (: *взгляды, представления*) to demolish

▶ **опроки́нуться** (*impf* **опроки́дываться**) *сов возв* (*стакан, стул, человек*) to fall over; (*лодка*) to capsize.

опроме́тчив|ый (-, -а, -о) *прил* precipitate, hasty.

о́прометью *нареч* headlong.

опро́с (-а) *м* (*свидетелей*) questioning; (*населения*) survey; **опро́с обще́ственного**

мне́ния opinion poll.

опр|оси́ть (-ошу́, -о́сишь; *impf* **опра́шивать**) *сов перех* (*свидетелей*) to question; (*население*) to survey.

опро́сный *прил*: **~ лист** questionnaire.

опротест|овать (-у́ю; *impf* **опротесто́вывать**) *сов перех* (*ЮР*) to appeal against; (*вексель*) to protest.

опроти́ве|ть (-ю) *сов неперех*: **мне э́то ~ло** I am sick of it.

опрошу́ *сов см* **опроси́ть**.

опры́ска|ть (-ю; *impf* **опры́скивать**) *сов перех* to spray.

опры́скиватель (-я) *м* sprayer; (*садовый*) sprinkler.

опры́скива|ть (-ю) *несов от* **опры́скать**.

опря́т|ный (-ен, -на, -но) *прил* neat, tidy.

о́птик|а (-и) *ж* (*раздел физики*) optics ♦ *собир* optical instruments *мн*.

оптимáль|ный (-ен, -ьна, -ьно) *прил* optimum.

оптими́зм (-а) *м* optimism.

оптими́ст (-а) *м* optimist.

оптимисти́ч|ный (-ен, -на, -но) *прил* optimistic.

опти́ческ|ий (-ая, -ое, -ие) *прил* optical.

оптови́к (-á) *м* wholesaler.

опто́в|ый *прил* wholesale; **~ые заку́пки** (*КОММ*) bulk buying.

о́птом *нареч*: **купи́ть/прода́ть ~** to buy/sell wholesale.

опубликова́ни|е (-я) *ср* (*статьи, книги*) publication; (*закона*) promulgation.

опублик|ова́ть (-у́ю; *impf* **опублико́вывать** *или* **публикова́ть**) *сов перех* (*статью, книгу*) to publish; (*закон*) to promulgate.

опуска́|ть(ся) (-ю(сь)) *несов от* **опусти́ть(ся)**.

опусте́л|ый *прил* (*дом, сад*) empty; (*улица*) deserted.

опусте́|ть (3*sg* -ет, 3*pl* -ют) *сов от* **пусте́ть**.

опу|сти́ть (-щу́, -́стишь; *impf* **опуска́ть**) *сов перех* to lower; (*голову*) to bow; (*воротник*) to turn down; (*слово, параграф*) to miss out; **опуска́ть** (**~** *perf*) **в** +*acc* (*в стакан, в ящик*) to drop *или* put in(to); (*человека: в яму*) to lower into; **опуска́ть** (**~** *perf*) **ру́ки** (*перен*) to give up

▶ **опусти́ться** (*impf* **опуска́ться**) *сов возв* (*человек: на диван, на землю*) to sit (down); (*солнце*) to sink; (*мост, шлагбаум*) to be lowered; (*перен: человек*) to let o.s. go.

опустоша́|ть (-ю) *несов от* **опустоши́ть**.

опустошён|ный (-, -а, -о) *прил* (*человек, душа*) empty.

опустоши́тель|ный (-ен, -ьна, -ьно) *прил* devastating.

опустош|и́ть (-у́, -и́шь; *impf* **опустоша́ть**) *сов перех* (*страну, поле*) to devastate; (*разг: бутылку, ящик*) to empty; (*перен: жизнь, человека*) to ruin.

опу́та|ть (-ю; *impf* **опу́тывать**) *сов перех* (*подлеж: ветки, плющ*) to entangle; **опу́тывать** (~ *perf*) **чем-н** (*верёвками, интригами*) to enmesh in sth.

опу́хн|уть (-у, -ешь) *сов от* **пу́хнуть** ♦ (*impf* **опуха́ть**) *неперех* to swell (up).

о́пухол|ь (-и) *ж* (*на руке, на ноге*) swelling; (*внутренняя*) tumour (*BRIT*), tumor (*US*).

опу́хш|ий (-ая, -ее, -ие) *прил* swollen.

опу́шк|а (-и) *ж* (*леса*) edge; (*шапки, воротника*) trim(ming).

опуще́ни|е (-я) *ср* (*деталей, слов*) omission; (*желудка, матки*) prolapse.

опущу́(сь) *сов см* **опусти́ть(ся)**.

опыле́ни|е (-я) *ср* pollination.

опыл|и́ть (-ю́, -и́шь; *impf* **опыля́ть**) *сов перех* to pollinate; (*от вредителей*) to spray (*with insecticide*).

о́пыт (-а) *м* (*знания*) experience; (*эксперимент*) experiment; (*попытка*) attempt; **на со́бственном ~е** from (one's own) experience.

о́пыт|ный (-ен, -на, -но) *прил* (*врач, рабочий*) experienced; (*лаборатория, отдел*) experimental; (*экземпляр*) sample *опред*; (*полёт*) test *опред*; **~ экземпля́р** (test) sample; **~ образе́ц** trail sample; **дока́зывать (доказа́ть** *perf*) **что-н ~ным путём** to prove sth by experiment; **~ный образе́ц** sample.

опьяне́ни|е (-я) *ср* intoxication.

опьяне́|ть (-ю) *сов от* **пьяне́ть**.

опьян|и́ть (-ю́, -и́шь; *impf* **опьяня́ть** *или* **пьяни́ть**) *сов перех* (*также перен*) to intoxicate.

опя́та *итп сущ см* **опёнок**.

опя́ть *нареч* again; **~ же** (*разг*) yet again; **~ два́дцать пять!** (*разг*) not again!

ора́в|а (-ы) *ж* (*разг*) gang.

орангута́н(г) (-а) *м* orang-utan.

ора́нжевый *прил* orange.

оранжере́йный *прил* hothouse *опред*.

оранжере́|я (-и) *ж* hothouse.

ора́тор (-а) *м* orator; (*выступающий*) speaker.

орато́ри|я (-и) *ж* oratorio.

орато́рск|ий (-ая, -ое, -ие) *прил* oratorical.

ор|а́ть (-у́, -ёшь) *несов неперех* (*разг*) to yell; (: *ребёнок*) to bawl, howl; **~** (*impf*) **во всё го́рло** (*разг*) to yell at the top of one's voice.

орби́т|а (-ы) *ж* orbit.

орбита́льный *прил* orbital.

о́рган (-а) *м* (*также АНАТ*) organ; (*здравоохранения*) body; (*орудие*): **~ +gen** (*пропаганды*) vehicle for; **ме́стные ~ы вла́сти** local authorities (*BRIT*) *или* government (*US*); **половы́е ~ы** genitals; *см также* **о́рганы**.

орга́н (-а) *м* (*МУЗ*) organ.

организа́тор (-а) *м* organizer.

организа́торск|ий (-ая, -ое, -ие) *прил* organizational.

организацио́нный *прил* organizational.

организа́ци|я (-и) *ж* organization; (*устройство*) system; **Организа́ция Объединённых На́ций** United Nations Organization.

органи́зм (-а) *м* organism.

организо́ван|ный (-, -на, -но) *прил* organized; **организо́ванная престу́пность** organized crime.

организ|ова́ть (-у́ю) (*не*)*сов перех* (*создать*) to organize

▶ **организова́ться** (*не*)*сов возв* to be organized; (*в отряд, в ансамбль*) to organize o.s.; (*разг: жизнь*) to sort o.s. out.

органи́ст (-а) *м* organist.

органи́ческ|ий (-ая, -ое, -ие) *прил* organic; (*перен: неприязнь, отвращение*) natural; **~ поро́к се́рдца** heart defect.

о́рган|ы (-ов) *мн* (*разг*) *the Ministry of Internal Affairs and the KGB*.

о́рги|я (-и) *ж* orgy.

оргкомите́т (-а) *м сокр* (= *организацио́нный комите́т*) organizational committee.

орграбо́т|а (-ы) *ж сокр* (= *организацио́нная рабо́та*) organizational work.

оргте́хник|а (-и) *ж* office automation equipment.

орд|а́ (-ы́; *nom pl* **о́рды**) *ж* horde.

о́рден (-а; *nom pl* -а́) *м* order; (*nom pl* -ы; *рыцарский, масонский*) order.

орденоно́сный *прил* (*батальон, театр*) order-bearing.

орденоно́сца *итп сущ см* **орденоно́сец**.

о́рдер (-а) *м* (*на арест, на обыск*) warrant; (*на кварти́ру*) authorization.

ордина́р|ный (-ен, -на, -но) *прил* ordinary.

ордина́тор (-а) *м* (*МЕД*) ≈ registrar (*BRIT*), ≈ resident (*US*).

ординату́р|а (-ы) *ж* two-year period in which junior doctor specializes in particular field.

орёл (орла́; *nom pl* **орлы́**) *м* eagle; (*перен: человек*) hero; **~ и́ли ре́шка?** (*разг*) heads or tails?

Оренбу́рг (-а) *м* Orenburg.

орео́л (-а) *м* halo; (*перен: славы, таинственности*) aura.

оре́х (-а) *м* nut; (*древесина*) walnut; **мне доста́лось на ~е** (*разг*) I got it in the neck.

оре́ховый *прил* nut; (*мебель*) walnut.

оре́шник (-а) *м* (*кустарник*) hazel; (*собир: заросль*) hazel grove.

ОРЗ *ср сокр* (= *о́строе респира́торное заболева́ние*) ARD (= *acute respiratory disease*).

оригина́л (-а) *м* original; (*разг: чудак*) eccentric.

оригина́льный (-ен, -ьна, -ьно) *прил* original.

ориента́ци|я (-и) *ж* orientation; **име́ть** (*impf*) **хоро́шую ~ю в чём-н** to have a good grasp of sth.

ориенти́р (-а) *м* landmark.

ориенти́р|овать (-ую) (*не*)*сов перех* to orient, orientate; (*перен*): **~ кого́-н на +acc** to orient *или* orientate sb towards

▶ **ориенти́роваться** (*perf* **ориенти́роваться**

или **сориенти́роваться**) *несов возв* to find или get one's bearings; (*перен: в ситуации*) to find one's feet; (*разбира́ться*) to be versed; **~ся** (*impf/perf*) **на** +*acc* (*перен*) to be oriented или orientated towards; (*на мая́к, на со́лнце*) to find one's bearings by.

ориенти́ро|вочный (**-ен, -на, -но**) *прил* provisional; ~ **пункт** landmark.

орке́стр (**-а**) *м* orchestra.

оркестра́нт (**-а**) *м* member of an orchestra.

оркестро́в|ка (**-ки**; *gen pl* **-ок**) *ж* orchestration.

оркне́йск|ий (**-ая, -ое, -ие**) *прил*: **О́-ие острова́** Orkney Islands, Orkneys.

орла́ *итп сущ см* **орёл**.

орли́|ный *прил* (*клюв, гнездо*) eagle's; ~ **взгляд** proud look.

орна́мент (**-а**) *м* (decorative) pattern.

орнито́лог (**-а**) *м* ornithologist.

орнитоло́ги|я (**-и**) *ж* ornithology.

оробе́|ть (**-ю**) *сов от* **робе́ть**.

ороси́тельный *прил* irrigation *опред*.

оро|си́ть (**-шу́, -си́шь**; *impf* **ороша́ть**) *сов перех* to irrigate; (*подлеж: дождь*) to water.

ороше́ни|е (**-я**) *ср* irrigation.

орошу́ *сов см* **ороси́ть**.

ортодокса́л|ьный (**-ен, -ьна, -ьно**) *прил* orthodox.

ортопе́д (**-а**) *м* orthopaedic (*BRIT*) или orthopedic (*US*) surgeon.

ортопеди́ческ|ий (**-ая, -ое, -ие**) *прил* orthopaedic (*BRIT*), orthopedic (*US*).

ору́ди|е (**-я**) *ср* (*также перен*) tool; (*ВОЕН*) gun (*used of artillery*).

ору́д|овать (**-ую**) *несов неперех* (+*instr*; *разг*: *вёслами, лопатой*) to work away with; (: *вор, браконьер*) to be at work.

оруже́йный *прил*: ~ **заво́д** arsenal; ~ **ма́стер** armourer (*BRIT*), armorer (*US*); **Оруже́йная пала́та** The Armoury Palace.

ору́жи|е (**-я**) *ж* (*также перен*) weapon; (*собир*) arms *мн*.

орфографи́ческ|ий (**-ая, -ое, -ие**) *прил* orthographical.

орфогра́фи|я (**-и**) *ж* (*правописание*) spelling; (*правила*) orthography.

орхиде́|я (**-и**) *ж* orchid.

ос|а́ (**-ы́**; *nom pl* **о́сы**) *ж* wasp.

оса́д|а (**-ы**) *ж* siege; **снима́ть** (**снять** *perf*) **~у** to lift a siege.

оса|ди́ть (**-жу́, -ди́шь**; *impf* **осажда́ть**) *сов перех* to besiege; (*хим*) to precipitate; (*impf* **оса́живать**; *коня, лошадь*) to rein in; **осажда́ть** (~ *perf*) **кого́-н чем-н** (*перен*) to besiege sb with sth; ~ (*perf*) **кого́-н** (*разг*) to put sb in his *итп* place.

оса́дка *сущ см* **оса́док**.

оса́дк|и (**-ов**) *мн* precipitation *ед*.

оса́д|ный *прил*: ~**ое положе́ние** state of siege.

оса́д|ок (**-ка**) *м* sediment; **у меня́ оста́лся неприя́тный ~ от э́той встре́чи** the meeting left me with an unpleasant aftertaste.

оса́дочный *прил* sedimentary.

осажда́|ть (**-ю**) *несов от* **осади́ть**

▶ **осажда́ться** *несов возв* to precipitate.

оса́жива|ть (**-ю**) *несов от* **осади́ть**.

осажу́ *сов см* **осади́ть**.

оса́нист|ый (**-, -а, -о**) *прил* imposing.

оса́н|ка (**-и**) *ж* posture.

осатане́|ть (**-ю**) *несов от* **осатане́ть**.

осатане́лый *прил* (*разг*) frenzied; (: *человек*) furious.

осатане́|ть (**-ю**; *impf* **осатанева́ть**) *сов неперех* (*разг*) to go wild; (: *надоедать*): ~ **кому́-н** to drive sb mad.

ОСВ *сокр* = **ограниче́ние стратеги́ческих наступа́тельных вооруже́ний**: **перегово́ры/догово́р** ~ SALT (= *Strategic Arms Limitation Talks/Treaty*).

осва́ива|ть(ся) (**-ю(сь)**) *несов от* **осво́ить(ся)**.

осведоми́тел|ь (**-я**) *м* informer.

осведоми́тельниц|а (**-ы**) *ж см* **осведоми́тель**.

осведом|ить (**-лю́, -и́шь**; *impf* **осведомля́ть**) *сов перех* to inform

▶ **осведоми́ться** (*impf* **осведомля́ться**) *сов возв*: ~**ся о** +*prp* to inquire about; **осведомля́ться** (~**ся** *perf*) **о чьём-н здоро́вье** to inquire after sb's health.

осведомлён|ный (**-, -на, -но**) *прил* knowledgeable.

осведомлю́|(сь) *сов см* **осве́домить(ся)**.

осведомля́|ть(ся) (**-ю(сь)**) *несов от* **осве́домить(ся)**.

освеж|и́ть (**-у́, -и́шь**; *impf* **освежа́ть**) *сов перех* (*воздух*) to freshen; (*комнату, платье*) to freshen up; (*краски*) to liven up; (*воспоминания, знания*) to refresh; **о́тдых ~и́л меня́** I feel refreshed after my rest

▶ **освежи́ться** (*impf* **освежа́ться**) *сов возв* (*воздух*) to freshen; (*человек: под душем итп*) to freshen up; (*краски*) to brighten up; (*воспоминания, знания*) to be refreshed.

освети́тел|ь (**-я**) *м* (*ТЕАТР*) lighting technician.

освети́тельный *прил*: ~ **прибо́р** light; **освети́тельная раке́та** flare.

осве|ти́ть (**-щу́, -ти́шь**; *impf* **освеща́ть**) *сов перех* (*также перен*) to light up; (*вопрос, проблему, дело*) to highlight

▶ **освети́ться** (*impf* **освеща́ться**) *сов возв* (*также перен*) to be lit up; (*лицо*) to light up.

освеще́ни|е (**-я**) *ср* lighting; (*вопроса, проблемы, дела*) coverage.

освещу́(сь) *сов см* **освети́ть(ся)**.

осв|иста́ть (**-ищу́, -и́щешь**; *impf* **освистывать**) *сов перех* to boo.

освободи́тел|ь (**-я**) *м* liberator.

освободи́тельниц|а (-ы) *ж см* **освободи́тель**.

освободи́тельн|ый *прил* liberation *опред*; **~ая война́** war of liberation.

освобо|**ди́ть** (-жу́, -ди́шь; *impf* **освобожда́ть**) *сов перех* to release; (*из капкана*) to free; (*город, деревню*) to liberate; (*полку, комнату*) to clear; (*дом, квартиру*) to vacate; (*время, день*) to leave free; **~** (*perf*) **кого́-н от хлопо́т/наказа́ния** to spare sb the trouble/from punishment; **~** (*perf*) **кого́-н от эксплуата́ции** to liberate sb from exploitation; **~** (*perf*) **кого́-н от до́лжности** to dismiss sb

▶ **освободи́ться** (*impf* **освобожда́ться**) *сов возв* (*из тюрьмы́*) to be released; (*из капкана: зверь*) to free itself; (: *человек*) to free o.s.; (*квартира, дом*) to be vacated; (*место, полка*) to be cleared; **~ся** (*perf*) **от наказа́ния** to escape punishment; **~ся** (*perf*) **от рабо́ты** to finish work.

освобожде́ни|е (-я) *ср* release, freeing; (*города, деревни*) liberation; **~ от до́лжности** dismissal; **~ от нало́гов** tax exemption.

освобожу́(сь) *сов см* **освободи́ть(ся)**.

ОСВОД *м сокр* = Всеросси́йское о́бщество спасе́ния на во́дах.

освое́ни|е (-я) *ср* (*см глаг*) mastering; cultivation.

осво́|**ить** (-ю, -ишь; *impf* **осва́ивать**) *сов перех* (*технику, язык*) to master; (*земли, пустыню*) to cultivate

▶ **осво́иться** (*impf* **осва́иваться**) *сов возв* (*на новой рабо́те*) to find one's feet.

освя|**ти́ть** (-щу́, -ти́шь; *impf* **освяща́ть** *или* **святи́ть**) *сов перех* (*РЕЛ*) to bless.

осед|**а́ть** (-ю) *несов от* **осе́сть**.

оседла́|**ть** (-ю) *сов от* **седла́ть** ♦ (*impf* **осёдлывать**) *несов перех* (*разг: стул, бревно*) to straddle; (: *родственников, знакомых*) to take advantage of.

осе́длый *прил* settled.

осека́|**ться** (-юсь) *несов от* **осе́чься**.

осёкся *итп сов см* **осе́чься**.

осеку́сь *итп сов см* **осе́чься**.

осёл (-ла́) *м* donkey; (*перен: разг*) ass.

осен|**и́ть** (*3sg* **-и́т**, *3pl* **-я́т**, *impf* **осеня́ть**) *сов перех* (*подлеж: мысль*) to strike; **меня́ ~и́ло, что ...** it struck me that ...; **осеня́ть** (**~** *perf*) **кресто́м** to bless.

осе́нн|ий (-яя, -ее, -ие) *прил* autumn *опред*, fall *опред* (*US*); (*похожий на осень: погода, день*) autumnal, fall.

о́сен|ь (-и) *ж* autumn, fall (*US*).

о́сенью *нареч* in autumn, in the fall (*US*).

осеня́|**ть** (-ю) *несов от* **осени́ть**.

ос|**е́сть** (-я́ду, -я́дешь; *impf* **оседа́ть**) *сов непepex* (*пол, дом*) to settle; (*пыль, осадок*) to settle; **они́ ~е́ли в го́роде** they settled in the city.

осети́н (-а; *gen pl* -) *м* Ossetian.

осети́н|**ка** (-ки; *gen pl* -ок) *ж см* **осети́н**.

Осе́ти|я (-и) *ж*: **Се́верная/Ю́жная ~** North/South Ossetia.

ос|**ётр** (-етра́) *м* sturgeon (*ZOOL*).

осетри́н|а (-ы) *ж* sturgeon (*CULIN*).

осе́|**чка** (-чки; *gen pl* -ек) *ж* (*перен: разг*) cockup (*BRIT*), mess (*US*); **дава́ть** (**дать** *perf*) **~ку** to misfire.

ос|**е́чься** (-еку́сь, -ечёшься *итп*, -еку́тся; *pt* ёкся, -е́клась, -е́клось, *impf* **осека́ться**) *сов непepex* to stop short.

оси́л|**ить** (-ю, -ишь; *impf* **оси́ливать**) *сов перех* (*противника*) to overpower; (*разг: книгу*) to get through; (: *физику, упражнение*) to get to grips with.

оси́н|а (-ы) *ж* aspen.

оси́новый *прил* aspen *опред*.

оси́н|ый *прил*: **~ое гнездо́** wasp's nest; (*перен*) hornet's nest.

оси́пн|**уть** (-у, -ешь) *сов от* **си́пнуть**.

осироте́вш|ий (-ая, -ее, -ие) *прил* (*ребёнок*) orphaned; (*перен: дом, сад*) abandoned.

осироте́лый *прил* = **осироте́вший**.

осироте́|**ть** (-ю) *сов от* **сироте́ть**.

оска́л|**ить** (-ю, -ишь; *impf* **оска́ливать** *или* **ска́лить**) *сов перех*: **~ зу́бы** (*также перен*) to bare one's teeth

▶ **оска́литься** (*impf* **оска́ливаться** *или* **ска́литься**) *сов возв* (*также перен*) to bare one's teeth; (*разг: осклабиться*) to smirk.

осканда́л|**иться** (-юсь, -ишься) *сов возв* (*разг*) to show o.s. up.

оскверн|**и́ть** (-ю, -и́шь; *impf* **оскверня́ть**) *сов перех* to defile; (*чувства, идеи*) to debase.

оскла́б|**иться** (-люсь, -ишся) *сов непepex* to grin.

оско́л|**ок** (-ка) *м* (*стекла, чашки*) piece; (: *мелкий*) sliver; (*бомбы, снаряда*) shrapnel *только ед*; (*перен: прошлого*) fragment.

оско́лочный *прил* (*рана, бомба*) shrapnel *опред*.

оско́мин|а (-ы) *ж* acidic taste; **наби́ть** (*perf*) **кому́-н ~у** (*перен*) to bore sb stupid.

оскоп|**и́ть** (-лю́, -и́шь; *impf* **оскопля́ть**) *сов перех* to castrate.

оскорби́тельн|ый (-ен, -ьна, -ьно) *прил* offensive.

оскорб|**и́ть** (-лю́, -и́шь; *impf* **оскорбля́ть**) *сов перех* to insult, offend; **оскорбля́ть** (**~** *perf*) **кого́-н в лу́чших чу́вствах** to offend sb's finer feelings; **оскорбля́ть** (**~** *perf*) **слух** to offend the ear

▶ **оскорби́ться** (*impf* **оскорбля́ться**) *сов возв* to be offended, take offence *или* offense (*US*).

оскорбле́ни|е (-я) *ср* insult.

оскорблю́(сь) *сов см* **оскорби́ть(ся)**.

оскорбля́ть(ся) (-ю(сь)) *несов от* **оскорби́ть(ся)**.

оскуде́|**ть** (-ю; *impf* **оскудева́ть** *или* **скуде́ть**) *сов непepex* (*страна*) to become impoverished; (*запасы итп*) to become depleted.

осла́ *итп сущ см* **осёл**.

ослабе́|ть (-ю; *impf* ослабева́ть *или* слабе́ть) *сов неперех* to weaken; (*давление, ветер*) to drop; (*внимание*) to wander; (*дождь*) to slacken *или* ease off; (*шум*) to die down; (*ремень*) to loosen; (*дисциплина*) to slacken.

осла́б|ить (-лю, -ишь; *impf* ослабля́ть) *сов перех* to weaken; (*внимание*) to let wander; (*ремень*) to loosen; (*дисциплина*) to relax.

ослабле́ни|е (-я) *ср* weakening; (*давления, шума*) reduction; (*внимания*) slackening; (*дисциплины*) decline; **за́втра ожида́ется ~ ве́тра/дождя́** the wind/rain should ease off by tomorrow.

ослабл́ю *сов см* осла́бить.

ослабля́|ть (-ю) *несов от* осла́бить.

ослабн|уть (-у, -ешь) *сов от* сла́бнуть.

осла́в|ить (-лю, -ишь) *сов перех* (*разг*) to smear

▸ осла́виться *сов возв* (*разг*) to get o.s. a bad name.

осл|ёнок (-ёнка; *nom pl* -я́та, *gen pl* -я́т) *м* foal (*of donkey*).

ослепи́тельный (-ен, -ьна, -ьно) *прил* dazzling.

ослеп|и́ть (-лю́, -и́шь; *impf* ослепля́ть) *сов перех* (*также перен*) to blind; (*подлеж: солнце, красота*) to dazzle.

ослепле́ни|е (-я) *ср* (*перен*) blindness.

ослеплю́ *сов см* ослепи́ть.

ослепля́|ть (-ю) *несов от* ослепи́ть.

осле́п|нуть (-ну, -нешь; *pt* -, -ла, -ло) *сов от* сле́пнуть ♦ *неперех* (*перен*): **~ от не́нависти/любви́** to be blinded by hatred/love.

осли́н|ый *прил* donkey's; **~ое упря́мство** pig-headedness.

осли́ц|а (-ы) *ж* female donkey.

О́сло *м нескл* Oslo.

осложне́ни|е (-я) *ср* complication.

осложн|и́ть (-ю́, -и́шь; *impf* осложня́ть) *сов перех* to complicate

▸ осложни́ться (*impf* осложня́ться) *сов возв* to become complicated; (*болезнь*) to develop complications.

ослы́ш|аться (-усь, -ишься) *сов возв* to mishear.

осля́та *итп сущ см* ослёнок.

осма́трива|ть(ся) (-ю(сь)) *несов от* осмотре́ть(ся).

осме́ива|ть (-ю) *несов от* осмея́ть.

осмеле́|ть (-ю) *несов от* смеле́ть.

осме́л|иться (-юсь, -ишься) *сов возв* to dare.

осме́|ять (-ю́; *impf* осме́ивать) *сов перех* (*поведение, человека*) to mock; (*теорию*) to ridicule.

осмо́тр (-а) *м* inspection; (*больного*) examination; (*выставки, музея*) visit.

осм|отре́ть (-отрю́, -о́тришь; *impf* осма́тривать) *сов перех* (*см сущ*) to inspect; to examine; to visit

▸ осмотре́ться (*impf* осма́триваться) *сов возв* (*по сторонам*) to look around; (*перен: на но́вом месте*) to settle in.

осмотри́тельность (-и) *ж* circumspection.

осмотри́тельный *прил* prudent, cautious.

осмысле́ни|е (-я) *ср* comprehension.

осмы́слен|ный (-, -на, -но) *прил* (*взгляд*) intelligent; (*поступок, поведение*) premeditated.

осмы́сл|ить (-ю, -ишь; *impf* осмы́сливать *или* осмысля́ть) *сов перех* to comprehend.

осна|сти́ть (-щу́, -сти́шь; *impf* оснаща́ть) *сов перех* (*предприятие, лаборато́рию*) to equip; (*судно*) to rig.

оснаще́ни|е (-я) *ср* (*предприятия, лаборато́рии, армии*) equipment; (*судна*) rigging.

оснащённость (-и) *ж* equipping.

оснащу́ *сов см* оснасти́ть.

осно́в|а (-ы) *ж* (*сооружения*) foundation; (*общества, развития*) basis; (*ткани, материи*) warp; (*линг*) stem; **на ~е** +*gen* on the basis of; **класть** (положи́ть *perf*) **в ~у чего́-н** to use as a basis for sth; **быть** (*impf*) *или* **лежа́ть** (*impf*) **в ~е чего́-н** to be the basis of sth; *см также* осно́вы.

основа́ни|е (-я) *ср* (*также мат, хим*) base; (*города, общества*) founding; (*теории, науки*) basis; (*опозда́ния, поступка*) grounds *мн*; (*здания*) foundation; **без вся́ких ~й** without any reason; **до ~я** completely; **на ~и** +*gen* on the grounds of; **на како́м ~и?** on what grounds?; **на о́бщем ~и** on an equal basis; **с по́лным ~м** with good reason.

основа́телен *прил см* основа́тельный.

основа́тел|ь (-я) *м* founder.

основа́тельниц|а (-ы) *ж см* основа́тель.

основа́тельный (-ен, -ьна, -ьно) *прил* (*причины, до́вод*) good; (*сооружение, человек*) solid; (*разг: вес, сумма*) fair; (*прове́рка, осмотр*) thorough.

основ|а́ть (*pt* -л, -ла, -ло, *impf* осно́вывать) *сов перех* to found; осно́вывать (**~** *perf*) **что-н на** +*prp* to base sth on *или* upon

▸ основа́ться (*impf* осно́вываться) *сов возв* (*общество, компания*) to be founded; (*разг: в Москве́, на но́вом ме́сте*) to settle down.

основн|о́й *прил* (*цель, зада́ча*) main; (*закон, при́нцип*) fundamental, basic; **в ~о́м** on the whole.

основополо́жник (-а) *м* founder.

осно́выва|ть (-ю) *несов от* основа́ть

▸ осно́вываться *несов от* основа́ться ♦ *возв*: **~ся на** +*prp* to be based on.

осно́в|ы (-) *мн* (*физики итп*) basics *мн*, rudiments *мн*.

осо́б|а (-ы) *ж* individual.

осо́бенен *прил см* осо́бенный.

осо́бенно *нареч* particularly; (*смотреть, вести себя*) in an unusual way; (*приятно, хорошо*) especially, particularly; **не ~** (*разг*) not particularly.

осо́бенност|ь (-и) *ж* (*не обыкновенность*) uniqueness; (*свойство*) peculiarity; **в ~и** in particular.

осо́бен|ный (-ен, -на, -но) *прил* special; **ничего́ ~ного** (*разг*) nothing special.

особня́к (-á) *м* mansion.

особняко́м *нареч* by oneself.

осо́б|ый *прил* (*вид, случай*) special, particular; (*вход, помещение*) separate; **у него́ ~ое мне́ние на э́тот счёт** he has his own opinion about this.

о́соб|ь (-и) *ж* individual.

осовреме́н|ить (-ю, -ишь; *impf* **осовреме́нивать**) *сов перех* to update.

осозна|ва́ть (-ю́, -ёшь) *несов от* **осозна́ть**.

осо́знанный *прил* (*риск, поступок*) calculated; (*необходимость*) acknowledged.

осозна́|ть (-ю; *impf* **осознава́ть**) *сов перех* to realize.

осо́к|а (-и) *ж* sedge.

осолове́|ть (-ю) *сов от* **солове́ть**.

о́сп|а (-ы) *ж* smallpox; (*разг: шрам*) pockmarks *мн*.

оспа́рива|ть (-ю) *несов от* **оспо́рить** ◆ *перех* (*первенство*) to contend *или* compete for.

о́спин|а (-ы) *ж* pockmark.

оспо́р|ить (-ю, -ишь; *impf* **оспа́ривать**) *сов перех* (*мнение, решение*) to question.

осрам|и́ть(ся) (-лю́(сь), -и́шь(ся)) *сов от* **срами́ть(ся)**.

оста|ва́ться (-ю́сь, -ёшься) *несов от* **оста́ться** ◆ *возв*: **счастли́во ~!** good luck!, all the best!

оста́в|ить (-лю, -ишь; *impf* **оставля́ть**) *сов перех* to leave; (*сохранить*) to keep; (*задержать: после уроков*) to keep in; (*работу, занятие, разговор*) to stop; (*мысли, мечты, надежды*) to give up; **~ь!** stop it!; **оставля́ть** (**~** *perf*) **кого́-н позади́** (*перен*) to leave sb standing; **оставля́ть** (**~** *perf*) **кого́-н/что-н в поко́е** to leave sb/sth in peace *или* alone; **оставля́ть** (**~** *perf*) **кого́-н на второ́й год** (*ПРОСВЕЩ*) to make sb repeat a year; **оставля́ть** (**~** *perf*) **кого́-н в дурака́х** to make a fool of sb; **мы ~или госте́й ночева́ть** we asked our guests to stay overnight; **созна́ние ~ило его́** he lost consciousness.

остальн|о́е (-о́го; *decl like adj*) *ср* the rest; **в ~ом** in other respects.

остальн|о́й *прил* (*часть*) the remaining; **~ые де́ньги/де́ти** the rest of the money/children; **~ое вре́мя** the rest of the time.

остальн|ы́е (-ы́х; *decl like adj*) *мн* the others; **все ~** all the others; (*вещи*) all the rest.

остана́влива|ть(ся) (-ю(сь)) *несов от* **останови́ть(ся)**.

оста́нк|и (-ов) *мн* remains *мн*.

остан|ови́ть (-овлю́, -о́вишь; *impf*

остана́вливать) *сов перех* to stop; **остана́вливать** (**~** *perf*) **взгляд/внима́ние на чём-н** to let one's gaze/attention rest on sth; **остана́вливать** (**~** *perf*) **свой вы́бор на** +*acc* to choose

▶ **останов|и́ться** (*impf* **остана́вливаться**) *сов возв* to stop; (*в гостинице, у друзей*) to stay; **~ся** (*perf*) **на** +*prp* (*на вопросе, на описании*) to dwell on; (*на решении, на заключении*) to come to; (*взгляд*) to rest on; **не остана́вливаться** (**~ся** *perf*) **ни перед чем** to stop at nothing.

остано́вк|а (-и) *ж* (*мотора, часов, эксперимента*) stopping; (*в речи, в работе*) pause; (*автобусная, поезда, в пути*) stop; **за кем/чем ~?** (*разг*) who/what is holding us up?

остановлю́(сь) *сов см* **останови́ть(ся)**.

оста́нусь *итп сов см* **оста́ться**.

оста́т|ок (-ка) *м* (*пищи, дня*) the remainder, the rest; (*материи*) remnant; (*МАТ*) remainder; **~ки** (*дома, стены*) remains *мн*; (*еды*) leftovers *мн*; (*красоты, чувства*) traces *мн*; **всё без ~ка** absolutely everything.

оста́|ться (-нусь, -нешься; *impf* **остава́ться**) *сов неперех* to stay; (*сохраниться: дом, чувство*) to remain; (*оказаться*) to be left; (*разг: проиграть*) to lose; **остава́ться** (**~** *perf*) **сиде́ть/стоя́ть** to remain sitting/standing; **мне ~лось дочита́ть 2 страни́цы** I have 2 pages left to read; **остава́ться** (**~** *perf*) **на второ́й год** (*ПРОСВЕЩ*) to repeat a year; **остава́ться** (**~** *perf*) **при своём мне́нии** to stick to one's opinion; **остава́ться** (**~** *perf*) **ни с чем** to end up with nothing; **остава́ться** (**~** *perf*) **ни при чём** to be left out; **остава́ться** (**~** *perf*) **в живы́х** to survive; **не остаётся ничего́ друго́го как ...** there is nothing for it but ....

остеклене́|ть (-ю) *сов от* **стеклене́ть**.

остепен|и́ться (-ю́сь, -и́шься; *impf* **остепеня́ться**) *сов неперех* to settle down.

остервене́лый *прил* frenzied, furious.

остервене́|ть (-ю) *сов от* **стервене́ть**.

остерега́|ть (-ю; *perf* **остере́чь**) *несов перех* to warn

▶ **остерега́|ться** (*perf* **остере́чься**) *несов возв*: **~ся** +*gen* to be wary of; **~йтесь просту́ды!** mind you don't catch cold!

о́стов (-а) *м* (*здания, корабля*) frame; (*зверя*) skeleton; (*словаря, романа*) framework.

остолбене́|ть (-ю) *сов от* **столбене́ть**.

остоло́п (-а) *м* (*разг*) dimwit.

осторо́жен *прил см* **осторо́жный**.

осторо́жно *нареч* (*взять, подня́ть*) carefully; (*ходить, выступать, говорить*) cautiously; **~!** look out!

осторо́жност|ь (-и) *ж* (*обращения, ухода*) care; (*поступка, поведения*) caution; **забыва́ть (забы́ть** *perf*) **о вся́кой ~и** to throw caution to the winds.

осторо́жный (-ен, -на, -но) *прил* careful; (*осмотрительный*) cautious.

осточерте́|ть (-ю; *impf* **осточертева́ть**) *сов*

*непере*х (+*dat*; *разг*) to bore rigid.
острёр *прил см* **óстрый**.
остригý(сь) *сов см* **острúчь(ся)**.
острие́ (-я́) *ср* (*пера, иглы, шпиля*) point; (*ножа, меча, бритвы*) edge; (*критики, сатиры*) cutting edge.
острúть (-ю́, -úшь) *несов перех* (*нож, меч*) to sharpen ♦ (*perf* **сострúть**) *неперех* (*шутить*) to make witty remarks.
острú|чь(ся) (-игý(сь), -ижёшь(ся) *итп*, -игýт(ся)) *сов от* **стрúчь(ся)**.
óстров (-а; *nom pl* -á) *м* (*также перен*) island.
островó|к (-ка́) *м* island; **островóк безопáсности** traffic island.
остроконéч|ный (-ен, -на, -но) *прил* pointed.
остронóс|ый (-, -а, -о) *прил* (*человек*) sharp-nosed; (*туфли*) pointed.
острослóв|ить (-лю, -ишь) *несов неперех* to be witty.
остросовремéн|ный (-ен, -на, -но) *прил* (*пьеса*) extremely topical.
остросюжéт|ный (-ен, -на, -но) *прил* (*фильм, пьеса*) gripping; ~ **фильм**, ~ **ромáн** thriller.
острóт|а (-ы) *ж* witticism.
остротá (-ы́) *ж* (*ножа*) sharpness; (*зрения, слуха*) sharpness, keenness; (*шутки, слова*) wit; (*запаха, вкуса*) pungency; (*пищи*) spiciness; (*желания, радости*) poignancy; (*положения, ситуации*) acuteness; (*игры*) tension.
остроугóль|ный (-ен, -ьна, -ьно) *прил* acute-angled.
остроýмен *прил см* **остроýмный**.
остроýми|е (-я) *ср* wit; (*рассказа*) wittiness.
остроýм|ный (-ен, -на, -но) *прил* witty.
óстр|ый (-р *или* -ёр, -ра́, -ро́ *или* -ро) *прил* (*нож, память, вкус*) sharp; (*борода, нос, носок*) pointed; (*зрение, слух*) keen; (*шутка, слово*) witty; (*запах*) pungent; (*блюдо, еда*) spicy; (*сыр*) strong; (*желание*) burning; (*боль*) acute; (*ситуация*) critical; (*игра*) tense; (*no short form*; *аппендицит, воспаление лёгких*) acute; **óстрый ýгол** acute angle; **óстрый язы́к** sharp tongue.
остря́к (-а́) *м* (*разг*) wit.
остря́ч|ка (-ки; *gen pl* -ек) *ж* (*разг*) *см* **остря́к**.
ост|удúть (-ужý, -ýдишь; *impf* **остужáть** *или* **студúть**) *сов перех* (*молоко, чай, суп*) to cool; (*перен: желания*) to curb; (: *чувства*) to restrain.
оступ|úться (-люсь, -úшься; *impf* **оступáться**) *сов возв* to trip, stumble; (*разг: совершить ошибку*) to trip up.
осты́|ть (-ну, -нешь; *impf* **остывáть**) *сов неперех* (*также перен*) to cool down; (*чувства, желание*) to cool; (*суп*) to get cold; **остывáть** (~ *perf*) **к** +*dat* (*перен*) to lose interest in.
ос|удúть (-ужý, -ýдишь; *impf* **осуждáть**) *сов перех* to condemn; (*приговорить*) to convict.

осуждéни|е (-я) *ср* (*см глаг*) condemnation; conviction.
осуждён|ая (-ой; *decl like adj*) *ж см* **осуждённый**.
осуждён|ый (-ого; *decl like adj*) *м* convict.
осужý *сов см* **осудúть**.
осýн|уться (-усь, -ешься) *сов возв* to look drawn.
осушá|ть (-ю) *несов от* **осушúть**.
осушúтельный *прил* drainage *опред*.
ос|ушúть (-ушý, -ýшишь; *impf* **осушáть**) *сов перех* to drain.
осуществú|мый (-, -а, -о) *прил* (*мечты, желания*) realizable.
осуществлéни|е (-я) *ср* (*мечты, идеи, намерения*) realization; (*плана, реорганизации*) implementation.
осуществ|úть (-лю́, -úшь; *impf* **осуществля́ть**) *сов перех* (*мечту, намерение*) to realize; (*идею*) to put into practice; (*план, реорганизацию*) to implement
► **осуществ|úться** (*impf* **осуществля́ться**) *сов возв* (*мечты*) to come true; (*идея*) to materialize; (*надежды*) to be fulfilled.
осчастлú|вить (-лю, -ишь) *сов перех* to make happy.
осы́п|ать (-лю, -лешь; *impf* **осыпáть**) *сов перех* (*кучу песка, землю*) to knock down; **осыпáть** (~ *perf*) **когó-н/что-н чем-н** to scatter sth over sb/sth; (*перен: подарками, поцелуями*) to shower sb/sth with sth; (*оскорблениями*) to heap sth on sb/sth
► **осы́|паться** (*impf* **осыпáться**) *сов возв* (*земля, насыпь, песок*) to subside; (*штукатурка, потолок*) to crumble; (*листья, цветы*) to fall.
ос|ь (-и; *loc sg* -й) *ж* (*колеса, механизма*) axle; (*ГЕОМ*) axis (*мн* axes); (*перен: событий, происходящего*) centre (*BRIT*), center (*US*), hub.
осьминóг (-а) *м* octopus (*мн* octopuses).
ося́ду *итп сов см* **осéсть**.
осязá|емый (-, -а, -о) *прил* (*перен: результат*) tangible.
осязáни|е (-я) *ср* touch.
осязáтельный *прил* (*нервные окончания, органы*) tactile; (*перен: результат, разница, успех*) tangible.

KEYWORD

от *предл* (+*gen*) **1** from; **он отошёл от стола́** he moved away from the table; **недалекó от меня́** not far from me; **он узнáл об э́том от дрýга** he found out about it from a friend; **у негó есть сын от пéрвого брáка** he has a son from his first marriage; **от ча́са до двух** from one (o'clock) to two (o'clock); **он ушёл от семьи́** he left his family
2 (*указывает на причину*): **бумáга размóкла**

от дождя́ the paper got wet with rain; **от зло́сти** with anger; **от ра́дости** for *или* in joy; **от удивле́ния** in surprise; **от разочарова́ния/ стра́ха** out of disappointment/fear

3 (*о подлежащем устранении*): **отмо́й лицо́ от гря́зи** wash the dirt off your face

4 (*указывает на что-н, против чего направлено действие*) for; **лека́рство от ка́шля** medicine for a cough, cough medicine

5 (*о части целого*): **ру́чка/ключ от две́ри** door handle/key; **я потеря́л пу́говицу от пальто́** I lost the button off my coat

6 (*при противопоставлении*) from; **они́ не мо́гут отличи́ть добро́ от зла** they can't tell right from wrong

7 (*в датах*): **письмо́ от пе́рвого февраля́** a letter of *или* dated the first of February

8 (*о временной последовательности*): **год от го́да** from year to year; **вре́мя от вре́мени** from time to time.

от- *префикс* (*in verbs*; *прекращение действия*) *indictaing cessation of action eg.* отзвуча́ть; (*удаление от чего-н*) *indictaing removal from sth eg.* откле́ить; (*об уклонении от чего-н*) *indicating avoidance of sth eg.* отшути́ться.

ота́плива|ть (**-ю**) *несов перех* to heat

▶ **ота́пливаться** *несов возв* to be heated.

ота́р|а (**-ы**) *ж* flock (*of sheep*).

отба́в|ить (**-лю, -ишь;** *impf* **отбавля́ть**) *сов перех* (*сахар, порцию*) to take away; (*молоко, воду*) to pour off; **хоть отбавля́й** (*разг*) more than enough.

отбараба́н|ить (**-ю, -ишь;** *impf* **отбараба́нивать**) *сов перех* (*мелодию*) to tap out; (*разг: ответ, вопрос*) to rattle off.

отбежа́ть (*как* бежа́ть; *см* **Table 20**; *impf* **отбега́ть**) *сов непepex* to run off.

отбе́ливател|ь (**-я**) *м* bleach.

отбел|и́ть (**-елю́, -е́лишь;** *impf* **отбе́ливать**) *сов перех* to bleach.

отберу́ *итп сов см* **отобра́ть**.

отбива́|ть(ся) (**-ю**) *несов от* **отби́ть(ся)**.

отбивн|а́я (**-о́й;** *decl like adj*) *ж* tenderized steak; (*также:* **~ котле́та**) chop.

отбира́|ть (**-ю**) *несов от* **отобра́ть**.

отб|и́ть (**-обью, -обьёшь;** *impf* **отбива́ть**) *сов перех* (*отколоть*) to break off; (*мяч, удар*) to parry; (*атаку, нападение*) to repulse; (*город, пленных*) to recapture; (*разг: жениха, невесту*) to pinch; (*такт, мелодию*) to beat out; (*мясо*) to tenderize; **за́пах ~би́л у меня́ жела́ние есть** the smell put me off my food; **я ~би́л себе́ но́ги** my feet are sore

▶ **отби́ться** (*impf* **отбива́ться**) *сов возв* (*отколоться*) to break off; **~ся** (*perf*) (**от** +*gen*) (*от нападающих, от собак*) to defend o.s. (against); (*от компании, от стада*) to fall behind; **~ся** (*perf*) **от рук** to get out of hand.

отблагодар|и́ть (**-ю́, -и́шь**) *сов перех* to show one's gratitude to.

о́тблеск (**-а**) *м* reflection.

отбо́|й (**-я**) *м* (*ВОЕН: ко сну*) the last post; (: *после воздушной тревоги*) all-clear (signal); (: *к отступлению*) retreat; **у неё ~ю нет от покло́нников** (*разг*) she has an endless stream of admirers.

отбо́йный *прил*: **~ молото́к** pickaxe (*BRIT*), pickax (*US*).

отбо́р (**-а**) *м* selection.

отбо́рн|ый *прил* (*картофель, семена*) selected; (*ругань, выражения*) well-chosen; **~ые войска́** crack troops.

отбо́рочн|ый *прил* (*СПОРТ*) qualifying; **~ая коми́ссия** selection committee.

отбро́|сить (**-шу, -сишь;** *impf* **отбра́сывать**) *сов перех* to throw aside; (*противника, войска*) to repel; (*перен: сомнения, тревоги итп*) to cast aside; (*тень, свет*) to cast.

отбро́с|ы (**-ов**) *мн* (*производства*) waste *ед*; (*пищевые*) scraps *мн*.

отбро́шу *сов см* **отбро́сить**.

отб|ы́ть (*как* быть; *см* **Table 21**; *impf* **отбыва́ть**) *сов непepex*: **~** (**из** +*gen*/**в** +*acc*) to depart (from/ for) ◆ (*pt* **-ы́л, -ыла́, -ыло**) *перех*: **~ наказа́ние** to serve a sentence.

отва́г|а (**-и**) *ж* bravery.

отва́|дить (**-жу, -дишь;** *impf* **отва́живать**) *сов перех* (*разг*): **~ кого́-н от чего́-н** (*от вредных привычек*) to wean sb off sth; (*от дома*) to drive sb away from sth.

отва́жен *прил см* **отва́жный**.

отва́жива|ть (**-ю**) *несов от* **отва́дить**.

отва́ж|иться (**-усь, -ишься;** *impf* **отва́живаться**) *сов возв*: **~** +*infin* (*пойти, сказать итп*) to find the courage to do; **~** (*perf*) **на** +*acc* to venture on.

отва́жн|ый (**-ен, -на, -но**) *прил* brave.

отва́жу *сов см* **отва́дить**.

отва́жусь *сов см* **отва́житься**.

отва́л (**-а**) *м* (*породы, земли*) heap; **нае́сться** (*perf*) **до ~а** (*разг*) to eat one's fill; **накорми́ть** (*perf*) **кого́-н до ~а** to stuff sb with food.

отва́л|ить (**-алю́, -а́лишь;** *impf* **отва́ливать**) *сов перех* (*камень, бревно*) to push aside; (*разг: кучу денег*) to fork out

▶ **отвали́ться** (*impf* **отва́ливаться**) *сов возв* (*обои, штукатурка*) to fall off; (*разг: откинуться назад*) to slump.

отва́р (**-а**; *part gen* **-у**) *м* (*из трав*) decoction; **мясно́й ~** meat broth.

отва́р|ить (**-арю́, -а́ришь;** *impf* **отва́ривать**) *сов перех* to boil

▶ **отвари́ться** (*impf* **отва́риваться**) *сов возв* to boil.

отварно́й *прил* boiled.

отведу́ *итп сов см* **отвести́**.

отвез|ти́ (**-у́, -ёшь;** *pt* **-ёз, -езла́, -езло́,** *impf* **отвози́ть**) *сов перех* (*увезти*) to take away; **отвози́ть** (**~** *perf*) **кого́-н/что-н в го́род/на да́чу** to take sb/sth off to town/the dacha.

отве́ргн|уть (**-у, -ешь;** *impf* **отверга́ть**) *сов* перех (*решение, помощь*) to reject; (*жениха*) to spurn.

отверде|ть (*3sg* -ет, *3pl* -ют, *impf* **отвердевать**) *сов неперех* to harden.

отверженн|ая (-ой; *decl like adj*) *ж см* **отверженный**.

отверженн|ый (-, -на, -но) *прил* outcast *опред* ♦ (-ого; *decl like adj*) *м* outcast.

отверн|уть (-у́, -ёшь; *impf* **отвёртывать**) *сов перех* (*гайку, пробку*) to unscrew; (*кран*) to turn on; (*поля, рукав*) to turn back; (*impf* **отворачивать**; *лицо, голову*) to turn aside; (*разг: отломать: ручку*) to twist off

▶ **отверн|уться** (*impf* **отвёртываться**) *сов возв* (*гайка, пробка*) to come unscrewed; (*кран*) to turn on; (*поля, рукав*) to be turned back; (*impf* **отворачиваться**; *человек*) to turn away; ~**ся** (*perf*) **от кого-н** to ostracize sb.

отверсти|е (-я) *ср* opening.

отвёрт|ка (-ки; *gen pl* -ок) *ж* screwdriver.

отвёртывать(ся) (ю(сь)) *несов от* **отвернуть(ся)**.

отвес (-а) *м* (*груз*) plumb; ~ **скалы** cliff face.

отвесен *прил см* **отвесный**.

отве́|сить (-шу, -сишь; *impf* **отвешивать**) *сов перех* to weigh out; ~ (*perf*) **кому-н пощёчину** (*разг*) to give sb a slap in the face.

отвес|ный (-ен, -на, -но) *прил* (*склон, берег, стена*) vertical.

отве|сти (-еду, -едёшь; *pt* -ёл, -ела́, -ело́, *impf* **отводить**) *сов перех* (*человека: домой, к врачу*) to take (off); (: *от окна*) to lead away; (*войска, полк*) to relocate, move; (*воду, реку*) to divert; (*ветки*) to push aside; (*глаза, взгляд*) to avert, turn away; (*перен: беду, удар*) to avert; (*заявление, кандидатуру*) to reject; (*участок, сад*) to allot; (*средства*) to allocate; **отводить** (~ *perf*) **кого-н в сторону** to take *или* lead sb aside; **отводить** (~ *perf*) **время на что-н** (*себе*) to set aside time for sth; (*другим*) to allocate time for sth; **отводить** (~ *perf*) **ду́шу** to unburden one's soul.

ответ (-а) *м* (*на вопрос*) answer; (*реакция*) response; (*на письмо, на приглашение*) reply; **в** ~ (**на** +*acc*) in response (to); **быть** (*impf*) **в** ~**е за** +*acc* to be answerable for; **призывать** (**призвать** *perf*) **к** ~**у** to call to account.

ответв|иться (*3sg* -ится, *3pl* -я́тся, *impf* **ответвляться**) *сов возв* to branch.

ответвле́ни|е (-я) *ср* (*дерева, дороги*) branch; (*перен: движения, религии*) branch, offshoot.

ответвля́|ться (*3sg* -ется, *3pl* -ются) *несов от* **ответвиться**.

отве́|тить (-чу, -тишь; *impf* **отвеча́ть**) *сов неперех*: ~ (**на** +*acc*) to answer, reply (to); (*на увольнение, на грубость*) to retaliate (against); ~ (*perf*) **за** +*acc* (*за преступление, за поступок*) to answer for; **отвеча́ть** (~ *perf*) **любо́вью на**

(**чью-н**) **любо́вь** to return sb's love.

отве́тственност|ь (-и) *ж* (*задания, заказа*) importance; (*за поступки, за действия*) responsibility; **нести** (**понести** *perf*) ~ **за** +*acc* to be responsible for; **привлека́ть** (**привле́чь** *perf*) **кого-н к** ~**и** to call sb to account.

отве́тствен|ный (-, -на, -но) *прил* responsible; (*работа, поручение, момент*) important; **отве́тственный квартиросъёмщик** responsible tenant; **отве́тственный рабо́тник** executive.

отве́тчик (-а) *м* (*ЮР*) defendant.

отве́тчиц|а (-ы) *ж см* **отве́тчик**.

отвеча́|ть (-ю) *несов от* **отве́тить** ♦ *неперех*: ~ +*dat* (*требованиям*) to meet; (*описанию*) to answer; (*интересам итп*) to suit; ~ (*impf*) **за кого-н/что-н** to be responsible for sb/sth.

отве́чу *сов см* **отве́тить**.

отве́шива|ть (-ю) *несов от* **отве́сить**.

отве́шу *сов см* **отве́сить**.

отви́лива|ть (-ю; *perf* **отвильну́ть**) *несов неперех*: ~ **от** +*gen* (*разг: от работы итп*) to dodge.

отвин|ти́ть (-чу́, -ти́шь; *impf* **отви́нчивать**) *сов перех* to unscrew.

▶ **отвин|ти́ться** (*impf* **отви́нчиваться**) *сов возв* to come unscrewed.

отвиса́|ть (*3sg* -ет, *3pl* -ют) *несов от* **отви́снуть**.

отви́слый *прил* (*щёки*) sagging; (*уши*) droopy.

отви́с|нуть (*3sg* -ет, *3pl* -ут, *impf* **отвиса́ть**) *сов неперех* to sag.

отвлёк(ся) *сов см* **отвле́чь(ся)**.

отвлека́|ть(ся) (-ю(сь)) *несов от* **отвле́чь(ся)**.

отвлеку́(сь) *итп сов см* **отвле́чь(ся)**.

отвлече́ни|е (-я) *ср* (*внимания, интереса*) distraction; (*абстракция*) abstraction.

отвлечён|ный (-, -на, -но) *прил* abstract.

отвл|е́чь (-еку́, -ечёшь *итп*, -еку́т; *pt* -ёк, -екла́, -екло́, *impf* **отвлека́ть**) *сов перех*: ~ (**от** +*gen*) (*противника*) to divert (from); (*от дел*) to distract (from); **отвлека́ть** (~ *perf*) **чьё-н внима́ние** to distract sb's attention

▶ **отвл|е́чься** (*impf* **отвлека́ться**) *сов возв*: ~**ся** (**от** +*gen*) to be distracted (from); (*от темы*) to digress (from); (*абстрагироваться*) to abstract o.s. (from).

отво́д (-а) *м* (*воды, газа*) diversion; (*войск*) relocation; (*кандидатуры, судьи*) rejection; **для** ~**а глаз** (*разг*) as a distraction.

отво|ди́ть (-ожу́, -о́дишь) *несов от* **отвести́**.

отводно́й *прил* drainage *опред*.

отво|ева́ть (-ю́ю; *impf* **отвоёвывать**) *сов перех* (*также перен*) to win back ♦ *неперех* (*разг: кончить воевать*) to finish fighting

▶ **отвоева́ться** *сов возв* (*разг: солдат, полк*) to finish fighting.

отвожу́ *несов см* **отводи́ть**.

отв|озить (-ожý, -óзишь) *несов от* **отвезти́**.

отворáчива|ть(ся) (-ю(сь)) *несов от* **отверну́ть(ся)**.

отвор|и́ть (-ю́, -и́шь; *impf* **отворя́ть**) *сов перех* to open.

отврáтен *прил см* **отврáтный**.

отврати́телен *прил см* **орвратительный**.

отврати́тельно *нареч* (*пахнуть*) disgusting; (*поступить*) abominably ◆ *как сказ* it's disgusting.

отврати́тел|ьный (-ен, -ьна, -ьно) *прил* disgusting.

отвра|ти́ть (-щу́, -ти́шь; *impf* **отвращáть**) *сов перех* to avert.

отврáт|ный (-ен, -на, -но) *прил* (*разг*) revolting.

отвращá|ть (-ю) *несов от* **отврати́ть**.

отвращéни|е (-я) *ср* disgust, repulsion.

отвращу́ *сов см* **отврати́ть**.

отвы́к|нуть (-ну, -нешь; *pt* -, -ла, -ло, *impf* **отвыкáть**) *сов неперех*: ~ **от** (*от наркотиков*) to give up; (*от людей, от дома, от работы*) to become unaccustomed to; **отвыкáть** (~ *perf*) **от кypéния** to give up smoking; **он отвы́к от дóма/рабóты** he is not used to living at home/working any more.

отв|язáть (-яжу́, -я́жешь; *impf* **отвя́зывать**) *сов перех* (*верёвку*) to untie; (*собаку, коня*) to untie, untether

▶ **отвязá|ться** (*impf* **отвя́зываться**) *сов возв* (*верёвка*) to come undone; (*собака, конь*) to break loose; (*разг*): ~**ся от** +*gen* (*от человека*) to leave in peace; (*отделаться*) to get rid of; ~**яжи́сь (от меня́)!** (*разг*) get lost!

отгадá|ть (-ю; *impf* **отгáдывать**) *сов перех* to guess.

отгáд|ка (-ки; *gen pl* -ок) ж answer (*to riddle*).

отгáдыва|ть (-ю) *несов от* **отгадáть**.

отгибá|ть(ся) (-ю(сь)) *несов от* **отогну́ть(ся)**.

отглагóльный *прил* verbal.

отгла́|дить (-жу, -дишь; *impf* **отгла́живать**) *сов перех* to iron.

▶ **отгла́|диться** (*impf* **отгла́живаться**) *сов возв* to be ironed.

отговор|и́ть (-ю́, -и́шь; *impf* **отговáривать**) *сов перех*: ~ **когó-н от чегó-н/**+*infin* to dissuade sb from sth/from doing

▶ **отговори́ться** (*impf* **отговáриваться**) *сов возв* (+*instr*; *разг*: *незнанием, болезнью*) to plead; (~ *perf*) **незнáнием** to plead ignorance; **он ~и́лся болéзнью** he gave the excuse that he was ill.

отговóр|ка (-ки; *gen pl* -ок) ж excuse.

отголóс|ок (-ка; *nom pl* -ки) м (*также перен*) echo.

отгоню́ *итп сов см* **отогнáть**.

отгоня́|ть (-ю) *несов от* **отогнáть**.

отгор|оди́ть (-ожу́, -óдишь; *impf* **отгорáживать**) *сов перех* (*дом, участок*) to fence off; (*часть комнаты*) to partition off; (*от жизни*) to isolate; (*от забот*) to shelter

▶ **отгороди́ться** (*impf* **отгорáживаться**) *сов*

возв (*забором*) to fence o.s. off; (*ширмой*) to screen o.s. off; (*от жизни, от забот*) to cut o.s. off.

отгрёб *итп сов см* **отгрести́**.

отгребá|ть (-ю) *несов от* **отгрести́**.

отгребу́ *итп сов см* **отгрести́**.

отгрем|éть (*3sg* -и́т, *3pl* -я́т) *сов неперех* (*гром, аплодисменты*) to stop; **егó слáва ~éла** he is no longer famous; **бой ~éл** the battle is over.

отгр|ести́ (-ебу́, -ебёшь; *pt* -ёб, -ебла́, -ебло́, *impf* **отгребáть**) *сов перех* (*листья, снег*) to rake away ◆ *неперех* (*от берега*) to row away.

отгр|узи́ть (-ужу́, -у́зишь; *impf* **отгружáть**) *сов перех* (*отправить*) to ship.

отгрýз|ка (-и) ж shipment.

отгры́з|ть (-у́, -ёшь; *pt* -, -ла, -ло, *impf* **отгрызáть**) *сов перех* to bite off.

отгýл (-а) м day off.

отгуля́|ть (-ю; *impf* **отгýливать**) *сов перех* (*разг*: *отпуск, праздники*) to finish (*one's holidays etc*); (: *за дежурство, за сверхуро́чные*) to have time off; **мы ~ли óтпуск** our holidays are over.

отдавá|ть (-ю́, -ёшь) *несов от* **отдáть** ◆ *неперех*: ~ +*instr* (*разг*: *пахнуть*) to reek of

▶ **отдавá|ться** *несов от* **отдáться**.

отдав|и́ть (-авлю́, -а́вишь; *impf* **отдáвливать**) *сов перех* to crush.

отдади́м(ся) *итп сов см* **отдáть(ся)**.

отдáй(ся) *сов см* **отдáть(ся)**.

отдáйте(сь) *сов см* **отдáть(ся)**.

отдалéни|е (-и) *ср*: **в ~и, на ~и** in the distance; **в ~и от** +*gen* some way away from.

отдалён|ный (-, -на, -но) *прил* distant; (*место, сходство*) remote.

отдал|и́ть (-ю́, -и́шь; *impf* **отдаля́ть**) *сов перех* (*смерть, разлуку*) to postpone; (*сына, друзей*) to alienate

▶ **отдали́ться** (*impf* **отдаля́ться**) *сов возв*: ~**ся от** +*gen* (*от берега, от города*) to move away from; (*от темы, от дел*) to digress from; (*от друзей, от семьи*) to become alienated from.

отдá|ть (*как* **дать**; *см* Table 14; *impf* **отдавáть**) *сов перех* (*возвратить*) to return; (*дать*) to give; (*дать*: *город, крепость*) to surrender; (*ребёнка*: *в школу, в детский сад*) to send; (*разг*: *заплатить*) to pay; (*подлеж*: *ружьё*) to kick; (: *боль*) to spread; **он ~л жизнь наýке** he devoted his life to science; **отдавáть** (~ *perf*) **тýфли в ремóнт** to put one's shoes in for repair; **отдавáть** (~ *perf*) **что-н за бесцéнок** to give sth away; **отдавáть** (~ *perf*) **дочь зáмуж** to give one's daughter away (*in marriage*); **отдавáть** (~ *perf*) **(комý-н) распоряжéние/прикáз** to give (sb) instructions/an order; **отдавáть** (~ *perf*) **когó-н под суд** to prosecute sb; **отдавáть** (~ *perf*) **комý-н честь** to salute sb; **отдавáть** (~ *perf*) **себé отчёт** to realize; **отдавáть** (~ *perf*) **дóлжное** *или* **справедли́вость комý-н** to give

sb his итп due; **отдава́ть** (~ *perf*) **кому́-н**
после́дний долг to pay one's last respects to sb;
отдава́ть (~ *perf*) **концы́** (*разг: умере́ть*) to
kick the bucket
▶ **отда́ться** (*impf* **отдава́ться**) *сов возв* (*голос,*
эхо) to resound, reverberate; **отдава́ться** (~**ся**
perf) +*dat* to give o.s. up *или* surrender to;
(*воспомина́ниям*) to lose o.s. in; (*иску́сству*) to
devote o.s. to; (*любо́внику*) to give o.s. to; **боль**
отдава́лась в спине́ the pain spread to his
back.
отда́ч|а (-**и**) *ж* (*при вы́стреле*) recoil; (*СПОРТ*)
return; **рабо́тать** (*impf*) **с по́лной** ~**ей** to put a
lot into one's work.
отда́шь(ся) *сов см* **отда́ть(ся)**.
отде́л (-**а**) *м* (*учрежде́ния, универма́га*)
department; (*кни́ги, газе́ты*) section; (*исто́рии,*
нау́ки) branch; **отде́л здравоохране́ния** health
department; **отде́л ка́дров** personnel
department; **отде́л отпра́вки** dispatch
department.
отде́ла|ть (-**ю**; *impf* **отде́лывать**) *сов перех*
(*кварти́ру*) to do up; (*разг: поколоти́ть*) to do
over; **отде́лывать** (~ *perf*) **что-н чем-н**
(*пальто́: ме́хом*) to trim sth with sth; (*ко́мнату:*
де́ревом) to do sth out with sth
▶ **отде́латься** (*impf* **отде́лываться**) *сов возв:*
~**ся от** +*gen* (*разг: от рабо́ты, от дел*) to get
away from; (: *от челове́ка*) to get rid of; ~**ся**
(*perf*) +*instr* (*разг: лёгким уши́бом*) to get away
with; **легко́** ~**ся** (*perf*) he got off lightly; **он**
~**лся обеща́ниями** he did no more than make a
few promises; **он** ~**лся испу́гом** more than
anything he got a fright.
отделе́ни|е (-**я**) *ср* (*де́йствие: от семьи́ итп*)
separation; (*пена́ла, стола́*) section; (*су́мки*)
compartment; (*уче́бного заведе́ния, больни́цы*)
department; (*ба́нка*) branch; (*конце́рта*) part;
(*ВОЕН*) section; **отделе́ние свя́зи** post office;
отделе́ние мили́ции police station.
отдел|и́ть (-**елю́**, -**е́лишь**; *impf* **отделя́ть**) *сов*
перех: ~ (**от** +*gen*) to separate (from); (*уча́сток,*
часть ко́мнаты) to separate *или* divide off
▶ **отдели́ться** (*impf* **отделя́ться**) *сов возв:* ~**ся**
(**от** +*gen*) to separate (from); ~**ся** (*perf*) **от**
роди́телей to alienate o.s. from one's parents.
отде́л|ка (-**ки**; *gen pl* -**ок**) *ж* decoration; (*в*
кварти́ре) decor; (*на пла́тье*) trimmings *мн*.
отде́лочный *прил* (*материа́лы, тесьма́,*
пу́говицы) decorative; **отде́лочные рабо́ты**
decorating.
отде́лыва|ть(ся) (-**ю(сь)**) *несов от*
отде́лать(ся).
отде́льно *нареч* separately.
отде́льност|ь (-**и**) *ж*: **в** ~**и** separately.
отде́льный *прил* separate; (*едини́чный:*
приме́ры, возраже́ния) isolated.
отделя́|ть(ся) (-**ю(сь)**) *несов от* **отдели́ть(ся)**.

отдёрн|уть (-**у**, -**ешь**; *impf* **отдёргивать**) *сов*
перех to pull back.
отдеру́ *итп сов см* **отодра́ть(ся)**.
отдира́|ть (-**ю**) *несов от* **отодра́ть**.
отдохн|у́ть (-**у́**, -**ёшь**; *impf* **отдыха́ть**) *сов*
непе́рех to (have a) rest; (*на мо́ре*) to have a
holiday; **я хорошо́** ~**у́л** I had a good rest.
отдува́|ться (-**юсь**) *несов непе́рех* (*разг*) to
pant; (: *за оши́бки, за други́х*) to carry the can.
отду́шин|а (-**ы**) *ж* vent; (*перен*) escape.
о́тдых (-**а**) *м* rest; (*о́тпуск*) holiday; **на** ~**е** (*в*
о́тпуске) on holiday; **он на заслу́женном** ~**е**
(*на пе́нсии*) he is having a well-earned rest; **дом**
~**а** holiday centre; **без** ~**а** without a moment's
rest.
отдыха́|ть (-**ю**) *несов от* **отдохну́ть**.
отдыха́ющ|ая (-**ей**; *decl like adj*) *ж см*
отдыха́ющий.
отдыха́ющ|ий (-**его**; *decl like adj*) *м*
holidaymaker (*BRIT*).
отдыш|а́ться (-**усь**, -**ишься**) *сов возв* to
get one's breath back.
отёк (-**а**) *м* swelling; **отёк лёгких** (*МЕД*)
emphysema.
отёк *итп сов см* **оте́чь**.
отека́|ть (-**ю**) *несов от* **оте́чь**.
отеку́ *итп сов см* **оте́чь**.
отёл (-**а**) *м* calving.
от|ели́ться (*3sg* -**е́лится**, *3pl* -**е́лятся**) *сов от*
тели́ться.
оте́л|ь (-**я**) *м* hotel.
от|е́ц (-**ца́**) *м* (*та́кже РЕЛ, перен*) father.
оте́ческ|ий (-**ая**, -**ое**, -**ие**) *прил* fatherly, paternal.
оте́чественн|ый *прил* (*не иностра́нный:*
промы́шленность) domestic; **това́р** ~**ого**
произво́дства home-produced goods; **Вели́кая**
О~**ая Война́** Great Patriotic War (*World War*
II); **Оте́чественная Война́** patriotic war (*fought*
in defence of one's country).
оте́честв|о (-**а**) *ср* fatherland.
оте́чный *прил* swollen.
от|е́чь (-**еку́**, -**ечёшь** итп, -**еку́т**; *pt* **отёк**, -**екла́**,
-**екло́**, *impf* **отека́ть**) *сов непе́рех* to swell up.
от|жа́ть (-**ожму́**, -**ожмёшь**; *impf* **отжима́ть**) *сов*
перех (*рука́ми*) to wring out; (*в стира́льной*
маши́не) to spin dry.
отзвен|е́ть (*3sg* -**и́т**, *3pl* -**я́т**) *сов непе́рех* to stop
ringing.
отзвон|и́ть (-**ю́**, -**и́шь**) *сов перех* (*подлеж:*
ко́локол) to ring out; **часы́** ~**и́ли по́лночь** the
clock struck midnight.
о́тзвук (-**а**) *м* (*та́кже перен*) echo.
отзвуч|а́ть (*3sg* -**и́т**, *3pl* -**а́т**) *сов непе́рех* to come
to an end (*of music, speeches etc*).
отзову́(сь) *итп сов см* **отозва́ть(ся)**.
о́тзыв (-**а**) *м* (*мне́ние*) impression; (*реце́нзия*)
review; (*перен: в душе́*) echo; (*ВОЕН*) reply (*to a*
password).

The spelling rules for Russian are shown on page xvii.

отзы́в (-а) м (*представителя, посла*) recall.
отзыва́ть(ся) (-ю(сь)) *несов от* **отозва́ть(ся)**.
отзы́вчив|ый (-, -а, -о) *прил* ready to help.
оти́т (-а) м (*МЕД*) otitis (*ear infection*).
ОТК м *сокр* = **отде́л техни́ческого контро́ля**.
откажу́(сь) *итп сов см* **отказа́ть(ся)**.
отка́з (-а) м refusal; (*на заявление, от решения*) rejection; (*механизма*) failure; **закру́чивать** (**закрути́ть** *perf*) **до** ~**а** to turn full on; **рабо́тать** (*impf*) **без** ~**а** to operate smoothly; **набива́ть** (**наби́ть** *perf*) **до** ~**а** to cram.
отк|аза́ть (-ажу́, -а́жешь; *impf* **отка́зывать**) *сов непepex*: ~ **кому́-н в чём-н** to refuse sb sth; (*лишить кого-н чего-н*) to deny sb sth; (*мотор, нервы*) to fail; **ему́ не** ~**а́жешь в тала́нте** you can't deny that he's talented
▶ **отказа́ться** (*impf* **отка́зываться**) *сов возв*: ~**ся** (**от** +*gen*) to refuse; **отка́зываться** (~**ся** *perf*) **от свои́х слов** to retract one's words; **отка́зываться** (~**ся** *perf*) **от мы́сли** to give up on an idea; **не** ~**ажу́сь** I wouldn't say no.
отка́лыва|ть(ся) (-ю(сь)) *несов от* **отколо́ть(ся)**.
отка́пыва|ть (-ю) *несов от* **откопа́ть**.
отка́рмлива|ть (-ю) *несов от* **откорми́ть**.
отк|ати́ть (-ачу́, -а́тишь; *impf* **отка́тывать**) *перех* (*что-н круглое*) to roll away; (*что-н на колёсах*) to wheel away ♦ *непepex* (*разг: быстро отъехать*) to speed off
▶ **откати́ться** (*impf* **отка́тываться**) *сов возв* to roll away.
отка́ча|ть (-ю; *impf* **отка́чивать**) *сов перех* (*жидкость, газ*) to pump (out); (*привести в чувство*) to resuscitate.
откачу́(сь) *сов см* **откати́ть(ся)**.
отка́шлива|ться (-юсь) *несов от* **отка́шляться**.
отка́шлян|уть (-у, -ешь; *impf* **отка́шливать**) *сов перех* to cough up.
отка́шля|ться (-юсь; *impf* **отка́шливаться**) *сов возв* to clear one's throat.
откидно́й *прил* foldaway.
отки́н|уть (-у, -ешь; *impf* **отки́дывать**) *сов перех* to throw; (*перен: тревоги, сомнения*) to cast aside; (*верх, сиденье*) to open; (*руку*) to throw back; (*волосы, голову*) to toss back; (*в дуршлаг: макароны, рис*) to tip out; (*разг: войска, противника*) to push back
▶ **отки́нуться** (*impf* **отки́дываться**) *сов возв*: ~**ся на** +*acc* to lean back against; **отки́дываться** (~**ся** *perf*) **наза́д** to lean backwards.
откла́дыва|ть (-ю) *несов от* **отложи́ть**.
откле́|ить (-ю, -ишь; *impf* **откле́ивать**) *сов перех* to peel off
▶ **откле́иться** (*impf* **откле́иваться**) *сов возв* to come off.
о́тклик (-а) м response; (*перен*) echo; (*обычно мн: в печати*) comment.
откли́кн|уться (-усь, -ешься; *impf* **откли́каться**) *сов возв*: ~ (**на** +*acc*) to answer;

(*на события, на просьбу*) to respond (to).
отклоне́ни|е (-я) *ср* deflection; (*перен: просьбы*) rejection; (*от курса*) deviation; (*МЕД*) abnormality; ~ **от те́мы** digression.
откло|ни́ть (-оню́, -о́нишь; *impf* **отклоня́ть**) *сов перех* (*стрелку*) to deflect; (*перен: предложение, просьбу*) to reject
▶ **отклони́ться** (*impf* **отклоня́ться**) *сов возв* (*стрелка*) to deflect; (*перен: в сторону, от удара*) to dodge; (*от курса, на север*) to be deflected; **отклоня́ться** (~**ся** *perf*) **от те́мы** to digress.
отключ|и́ть (-у́, -и́шь; *impf* **отключа́ть**) *сов перех* to switch off; (*телефон*) to cut off
▶ **отключи́ться** (*impf* **отключа́ться**) *сов возв* (*также перен*) to switch off.
отковыря́|ть (-ю; *impf* **отковы́ривать**) *сов перех* to pick off.
откозыря́|ть (-ю) *сов от* **козыря́ть**.
откол|оти́ть (-очу́, -о́тишь) *сов перех* (*разг*): ~ **кого́-н** to give sb a thrashing.
отк|оло́ть (-олю́, -о́лешь; *impf* **отка́лывать**) *сов перех* (*кусок*) to break off; (*бант, булавку*) to unpin; ~ (*perf*) **но́мер** (*разг*) to pull a fast one
▶ **отколо́ться** (*impf* **отка́лываться**) *сов возв* (*также перен*) to break off; (*бант, булавка*) to come unpinned.
отколочу́ *сов см* **отколоти́ть**.
откомандир|ова́ть (-у́ю; *impf* **откомандиро́вывать**) *сов перех* to post, second.
отк|опа́ть (-опа́ю; *impf* **отка́пывать**) *сов перех* to dig up; (*перен: книгу, сведения*) to unearth.
отк|орми́ть (-ормлю́, -о́рмишь; *impf* **отка́рмливать**) *сов перех* to fatten (up).
откорректи́р|овать (-ую) *сов от* **корректи́ровать**.
отко́с (-а) м (*горы, берега*) slope; (*железной дороги*) embankment; **пуска́ть** (**пусти́ть** *perf*) **по́езд под** ~ to derail a train.
открепи́ть (-лю́, -и́шь; *impf* **открепля́ть**) *сов перех* (*значок, вывеску*) to unfasten; (*снять с учёта*) to take off the register
▶ **открепи́ться** (*impf* **открепля́ться**) *сов возв* (*вывеска*) to come unfastened; (*сняться с учёта*) to sign o.s. off the register.
открове́нен *прил см* **открове́нный**.
открове́ни|е (-я) *ср* revelation.
открове́нничать (-ю) *несов непepex*: ~ (**с** +*instr*) to bare one's soul (to).
открове́нно *нареч* frankly; ~ **говоря́** frankly speaking.
открове́нность (-и) ж frankness.
открове́н|ный (-ен, -на, -но) *прил* frank; (*хамство, обман*) blatant; (*разг: платье, туалет*) revealing.
откро́ю(сь) *итп сов см* **откры́ть(ся)**.
открут|и́ть (-учу́, -у́тишь; *impf* **откру́чивать**) *сов перех* to unscrew.
открыва́л|ка (-ки; *gen pl* -ок) ж (*для консервов*) tin-opener; (*для бутылок*) bottle-opener.

открыва́|ть(ся) (-ю(сь)) *несов от* **откры́ть(ся)**.

откры́ти|е (-я) *ср* (*также перен*) discovery; (*сезона, выставки, клуба*) opening.

откры́т|ка (-ки; *gen pl* -ок) *ж* postcard.

откры́т|ый (-, -а, -о) *прил* open; (*голова, шея*) bare; (*лицо, взгляд, человек*) frank; **в ~ую** openly; **на ~ом во́здухе** outside, outdoors; **музе́й под ~ым не́бом** open-air museum; **~ая маши́на** open-top car; **~ое пла́тье** low-cut dress; **откры́тая ра́на** open wound; **откры́тое голосова́ние/письмо́** open vote/letter; **откры́тый вопро́с** open question.

откры́|ть (-о́ю, -о́ешь; *impf* **открыва́ть**) *сов перех* to open; (*лицо итп*) to uncover; (*намерения, правду итп*) to reveal; (*воду, кран*) to turn on; (*возможность, путь, позицию*) to open up; (*явление, закон*) to discover; **открыва́ть (~ *perf*) торго́влю чем-н** to start selling sth; **открыва́ть (~ *perf*) Аме́рику** (*перен*) to reinvent the wheel; **открыва́ть (~ *perf*) счёт** (*КОММ*) to open an account; (*СПОРТ*) to open the scoring; **открыва́ть (~ *perf*) ого́нь** to open fire

▶ **откры́ться** (*impf* **открыва́ться**) *сов возв* to open; (*возможность, путь, позиция*) to open up; (*тайна*) to be revealed; (*пейзаж, река*) to open out; **~ (*perf*) кому́-н** to open up to sb; **у него́ глаза́ ~ылись** (*перен*) he has begun to see things clearly.

отку́да *нареч* where from ◆ *союз* whence, from where; **Вы ~?** where are you from?; **~ Вы прие́хали?** where have you come from?; **~ ты э́то зна́ешь?** how do you know about that?; **он не мог поня́ть, ~ слы́шался звук** he couldn't work out where the sound was coming from; **~ сле́дует...** hence ...; **~ ни возьми́сь** out of nowhere; **~ я зна́ю?** (*разг*) how do I know?

отку́да-нибудь *нареч* from somewhere (or other).

отку́да-то *нареч* from somewhere.

откуп|и́ться (-лю́сь, -ишься; *impf* **откупа́ться**) *сов возв*: **~ от** +*gen* to buy one's way out of.

отку́пор|ить (-ю, -ишь; *impf* **отку́поривать**) *сов перех* to unseal.

отку|си́ть (-шу́, -усишь; *impf* **отку́сывать**) *сов перех* (*зубами*) to bite off; (*кусачками*) to snip off.

отл. *сокр* (= *отли́чно*) ≈ O (*US*) (= *outstanding*), ≈ A (*BRIT*).

отлага́тельств|о (-а) *ср* delay.

отла́д|ка (-и) *ж* (*КОМП*) debugging.

отлакир|ова́ть (-у́ю) *сов от* **лакирова́ть**.

отла́мыва|ть(ся) (-ю) *несов от* **отлома́ть(ся)**, **отломи́ть(ся)**.

отлежа́|ть (-у́, -и́шь) *сов перех*: **я ~а́л но́гу/ру́ку** my leg/arm has gone dead

▶ **отлежа́ться** (*impf* **отлёживаться**) *сов возв* (*разг*) to rest up.

отлеп|и́ть (-еплю́, -е́пишь; *impf* **отлепля́ть**) *сов перех* to peel off

▶ **отлепи́ться** (*impf* **отлепля́ться**) *сов возв* to peel off.

отлёт (-а) *м* (*птиц*) flight; (*самолёта*) departure; **на ~е** (*жить*) on the outskirts; (*держать*) in one's outstretched hand.

отле|те́ть (-чу́, -ти́шь; *impf* **отлета́ть**) *сов неперех* to fly off; (*мяч*) to fly back; (*человек: от удара*) to be sent flying back.

отл|е́чь (*3sg* -я́жет, *3pl* -я́гут, *pt* -ёг, -егла́, -егло́) *сов безл*: **у меня́ ~егло́ от се́рдца** a weight has been lifted from my mind.

отли́в (-а) *м* (*в море*) ebb; (*оттенок*) sheen.

отлива́|ть (-ю) *несов от* **отли́ть** ◆ *неперех* (+*instr*; *серебром, лиловым*) to be tinted with.

отли́в|ка (-и) *ж* (*деталей, форм*) casting.

отл|и́ть (-олью́, -ольёшь; *pt* -ил, -ила́, -и́ло, *impf* **отлива́ть**) *сов перех* (*воду, вино*) to pour off; (*ТЕХ: деталь, форму*) to cast; **у него́ кровь ~ила́ от лица́** the blood drained from his face.

отлича́|ть (-ю) *несов от* **отличи́ть** ◆ *перех* (*подлеж: красота, новизна*) to be a feature of

▶ **отлича́ться** *несов от* **отличи́ться** ◆ *возв* (*не походить*): **~ся (от** +*gen*) to be different (from); **~ся** (*impf*) +*instr* (*оригинальностью, красотой итп*) to be distinguished by; **она́ ~ется умо́м** she has a distinguished mind.

отли́чен *прил см* **отли́чный**.

отли́чи|е (-я) *ср* distinction; **зна́ки ~я** decorations; **дипло́м с ~м** ≈ first-class degree with distinction; **в ~ от** +*gen* unlike.

отличи́тельный *прил* distinguishing.

отлич|и́ть (-у́, -и́шь; *impf* **отлича́ть**) *сов перех*: **~ кого́-н/что-н от** +*gen* to tell sb/sth from; (*наградить*) to honour (*BRIT*), honor (*US*); **отлича́ть (~ *perf*) плохо́е от хоро́шего** to tell the difference between good and bad; **я не могу́ ~ их (друг от дру́га)** I can't tell them apart

▶ **отличи́ться** (*impf* **отлича́ться**) *сов возв* to distinguish o.s.; (*разг: сделать что-н необычное*) to outdo o.s.

отли́чник (-а) *м* 'A'grade pupil.

отли́чниц|а (-ы) *ж см* **отли́чник**.

отли́чно *нареч* extremely well ◆ *как сказ* it's great ◆ *ср нескл* (*ПРОСВЕЩ*) ≈ excellent *или* outstanding (*school mark*); **он ~ зна́ет, что он винова́т** he knows perfectly well that he's wrong; **здесь ~** it's great here; **учи́ться** (*impf*) **на ~** to get top marks; **~!** (that's) excellent!

отли́чный (-ен, -на, -но) *прил* excellent; (*иной*): **~ от** +*gen* distinct from.

отло́г|ий (-ая, -ое, -ие; -, -а, -о) *прил* sloping.

отложе́ни|е (-я) *ср* (*ГЕО, МЕД*) deposit.

отл|ожи́ть (-ожу́, -о́жишь; *impf* **откла́дывать**) *сов перех* to put aside; (*отсрочить*) to postpone; (*яйцо*) to lay.

отложнóй *прил* (*воротник, манжеты*) turndown.

отломá|ть (-ю; *impf* **отлáмывать**) *сов перех* to break off.

▸ **отломáться** (*impf* **отлáмываться**) *сов возв* to break off.

отл|оми́ть (-омлю́, -óмишь; *impf* **отлáмывать**) *сов перех* to break off

▸ **отломи́ться** (*impf* **отлáмываться**) *сов возв* to break off.

отл|упи́ть (-уплю́, -у́пишь) *сов от* **лупи́ть**.

отлуч|и́ть (-у́, -и́шь; *impf* **отлучáть**) *сов перех*: ~ когó-н от +*gen* (*от дома, от семьи*) to take sb from; **отлучáть** (~ *perf*) когó-н от цéркви to excommunicate sb

▸ **отлучи́ться** (*impf* **отлучáться**) *сов возв*; я дóлжен ~ся на полчасá I'll have to go out for half an hour.

отлы́нива|ть (-ю) *несов неперех*: ~ от +*gen* to try to get out of.

отмáлчива|ться (-юсь) *несов от* **отмолчáться**.

отмáтыва|ть (-ю) *несов от* **отмотáть**.

отмахн|у́ться (-у́сь, -ёшься; *impf* **отмáхиваться**) *сов возв*: ~ от +*gen* (*от мухи*) to brush away; (*от человека, от предложения*) to brush *или* wave aside.

отмáчива|ть (-ю) *несов от* **отмочи́ть**.

отмеж|евáться (-у́юсь; *impf* **отмежёвываться**) *сов возв*: ~ от +*gen* (*перен*) to distance o.s. from.

óтмел|ь (-и) *ж*: песчáная ~ sandbank.

отмéн|а (-ы) *ж* (*см глаг*) repeal; reversal; abolition; cancellation.

отм|ени́ть (-еню́, -éнишь; *impf* **отменя́ть**) *сов перех* (*закон*) to repeal; (*решение, приговор*) to reverse; (*налог*) to abolish; (*лекцию*) to cancel.

от|мерéть (*3sg* -омрёт, *3pl* -омру́т, *pt* -мер, -мерлá, -мерло, *impf* **отмирáть**) *сов неперех* (*ткань, ветка*) to die; (*перен: обычаи, привычки*) to die (out).

отмёрз|нуть (*3sg* -нет, *3pl* -нут, *pt* -, -ла, -ло, *impf* **отмерзáть**) *сов неперех* (*ветки, побеги*) to freeze; (*разг: руки, ноги*) to be frozen.

отмéр|ить (-ю, -ишь; *impf* **отмеря́ть**) *сов перех* to measure out.

отм|ести́ (-ету́, -етёшь; *pt* -ёл, -елá, -елó, *impf* **отметáть**) *сов перех* (*мусор, снег*) to sweep away; (*перен: доводы, возражения*) to sweep aside.

отмéстк|а (-и) *ж*: в ~у за +*acc* in revenge for.

отметá|ть (-ю) *несов от* **отмести́**.

отмéтин|а (-ы) *ж* mark.

отмé|тить (-чу, -тишь; *impf* **отмечáть**) *сов перех* (*на карте, в книге*) to mark; (*затраты, расходы*) to record; (*присутствующих, отсутствующих*) to take a note of; (*достоинства, недостатки, успехи*) to recognise; (*юбилей, день рождения*) to celebrate; нýжно ~, что ... it should be noted that ...

▸ **отмéтиться** (*impf* **отмечáться**) *сов возв* to register.

отмéт|ка (-ки; *gen pl* -ок) *ж* mark; (*в документе, в паспорте*) note.

отмету́ *итп сов см* **отмести́**.

отмечá|ть (-ю) *несов от* **отмéтить**

▸ **отмечáться** *несов от* **отмéтиться** ♦ *возв* (*успехи, талант*) to be apparent.

отмирá|ть (*3sg* -ет, *3pl* -ют) *несов от* **отмерéть**.

отмóк|нуть (*3sg* -нет, *3pl* -нут, *pt* -, -ла, -ло, *impf* **отмокáть**) *сов неперех* to get damp; (*бельё*) to soak; (*отклеиться*) to come off (*as a result of soaking*).

отмолчá|ться (-у́сь, -и́шься; *impf* **отмáлчиваться**) *сов неперех* to keep silent.

отморó|зить (-жу, -зишь; *impf* **отморáживать**) *сов перех*: ~ рýки/нóги to get frostbite in one's hands/feet.

отмотá|ть (-ю; *impf* **отмáтывать**) *сов перех* to unwind.

отм|очи́ть (-очу́, -óчишь; *impf* **отмáчивать**) *сов перех* (*наклейку, бинт*) to soak off; (*разг: глупость*) to come out with.

отмóю(сь) *итп сов см* **отмы́ть(ся)**.

отму́ч|иться (-усь, -ишься) *сов возв*: он наконéц ~ился his suffering has finally come to an end.

отм|ы́ть (-óю, -óешь; *impf* **отмывáть**) *сов перех*: ~ что-н to get sth clean; (*грязь, пятно*) to wash out

▸ **отмы́ться** (*impf* **отмывáться**) *сов возв* (*см перех*) to wash out; у меня́ рýки не ~ывáются I can't get my hands clean.

отмы́чк|а (-и) *ж* skeleton key.

отнéкива|ться (-юсь) *несов неперех* (*разг: отказываться*) to keep saying no; (*не признаваться*) to refuse to own up.

отн|ести́ (-есу́, -есёшь; *pt* -ёс, -еслá, -еслó, *impf* **относи́ть**) *сов перех* to take (off); (*подлеж: течение, ветер*) to carry off; (*причислить к*): ~ что-н к +*dat* (*к периоду, к году*) to date sth back to; (*к разряду, к категории*) to classify sth as; **относи́ть** (~ *perf*) что-н за *или* на счёт +*gen* to put sth down to, attribute sth to

▸ **отнести́сь** (*impf* **относи́ться**) *сов возв*: ~сь +*dat* (*к человеку*) to treat; (*к предложению, к событию*) to take; как он ~ёсся к Вáшему предложéнию? what did he think of your suggestion?

отникели|ровáть (-рую) *сов от* **никелировáть**.

отнимá|ть(ся) (-ю(сь)) *несов от* **отня́ть(ся)**.

отниму́(сь) *итп сов см* **отня́ть(ся)**.

относи́тельно *прил см* **относи́тельный**.

относи́тельно *нареч* relatively ♦ *предл* (+*gen*; *в отношении*) regarding, with regard to.

относи́тельн|ый (-ен, -ьна, -ьно) *прил* relative; **относи́тельное местоимéние/ прилагáтельное** (*линг*) relative pronoun/ adjective.

отн|оси́ть (-ошу́, -óсишь) *несов перех см* **отнести́**

▶ **относи́ться** *несов от* **отнести́сь** ♦ *возв:* ~**ся к** +*dat* to relate to; (*к классу, к категории*) to belong to; (*к году, к эпохе*) to date from; **он к ней хорошо́** ~**о́сится** he likes her; **как ты** ~**о́сишься к нему́?** what do you think about him?; **э́то к нам не** ~**о́сится** it has nothing to do with us.

отноше́ни|**е** (-**я**) *ср:* ~ **к** +*dat* attitude (to); (*связь*) relation (to); (*МАТ*) ratio; (*документ*) letter; **в** ~**и** +*gen* with regard to; **по** ~**ю к** +*dat* towards; **в э́том** ~**и** in this respect *или* regard; **в не́котором** ~**и** in certain respects *или* regards; **во всех** ~**ях** in all respects *или* regards; **име́ть** (*impf*) ~ **к** +*dat* to be connected with; **не име́ть** (*impf*) ~**я к** +*dat* to have nothing to do with; *см также* **отноше́ния**.

отноше́ни|**я** (-**й**) *мн* (*политические, семейные итп*) relations *мн*.

отношу́(**сь**) *сов см* **относи́ть**(**ся**).

отны́не *нареч* henceforth.

отню́дь *нареч:* ~ **не** by no means, far from; ~ **нет** absolutely not.

отня́ть (-**иму́**, -**и́мешь**; *pt* -**я́л**, -**яла́**, -**я́ло**, *impf* **отнима́ть**) *сов перех* to take away; (*силы, время*) to take up; (*ногу, руку*) to take off; **отнима́ть** (~ *perf*) **от груди́** to wean; **э́того у него́ не** ~**и́мешь** (*перен*) you can't take that away from him

▶ **отня́ться** (*impf* **отнима́ться**) *сов возв:* **у него́** ~**яли́сь но́ги/ру́ки** he has lost the use of his legs/arms; **у меня́ язы́к** ~**я́лся** (*перен: разг*) I was left speechless.

ото *предл см* **от**.

отобража́|**ть** (-**ю**) *несов от* **отобрази́ть**.

отображе́ни|**е** (-**я**) *ср* representation.

отобра|**зи́ть** (-**жу́**, -**зи́шь**; *impf* **отобража́ть**) *сов перех* to represent.

ото|**бра́ть** (-**беру́**, -**берёшь**; *pt* -**обра́л**, -**обрала́**, -**обра́ло**, *impf* **отбира́ть**) *сов перех* (*отнять*) to take away; (*выбрать*) to select.

отобью́(**сь**) *итп сов см* **отби́ть**(**ся**).

отовсю́ду *нареч* from all around.

ото|**гна́ть** (-**гоню́**, -**го́нишь**; *impf* **отгоня́ть**) *сов перех* to chase away; (*перен: мысли, сомнения*) to drive out.

отогну́ть (-**у́**, -**ёшь**; *impf* **отгиба́ть**) *сов перех* (*металл*) to bend back; (*скатерть, страницу*) to fold back

▶ **отогну́ться** (*impf* **отгиба́ться**) *сов возв* to bend back.

отогре́|**ть** (-**ю**; *impf* **отогрева́ть**) *сов перех* to warm

▶ **отогре́ться** (*impf* **отогрева́ться**) *сов возв* to get warm.

отодви́н|**уть** (-**у**, -**ешь**; *impf* **отодвига́ть**) *сов перех* (*шкаф*) to move; (*щеколду, засов*) to slide back; (*срок, экзамен*) to put back

▶ **отодви́нуться** (*impf* **отодвига́ться**) *сов возв*

(*человек*) to move; (*срок, экзамен*) to be put back.

ото|**дра́ть** (-**деру́**, -**дерёшь**; *impf* **отдира́ть**) *сов перех* (*разг: оторвать*) to rip off; (: *высечь*) to thrash

▶ **отодра́ться** *сов возв* (*разг*) to come off.

отождеств|**и́ть** (-**лю́**, -**и́шь**; *impf* **отождествля́ть**) *сов перех* to equate.

отождествле́ни|**е** (-**я**) *ср* equating.

отождествлю́ *сов см* **отождестви́ть**.

отождествля́|**ть** (-**ю**) *несов от* **отождестви́ть**.

отожму́ *итп сов см* **отжа́ть**.

ото|**зва́ть** (-**зову́**, -**зовёшь**; *impf* **отзыва́ть**) *сов перех* to call back; (*посла, представителя, документы*) to recall; **отзыва́ть** (~ *perf*) **кого́-н в сто́рону** to take sb aside; **отзыва́ть** (~ *perf*) **иск** (*ЮР*) to drop a case

▶ **отозва́ться** (*impf* **отзыва́ться**) *сов возв:* ~**ся** (**на** +*acc*) to respond (to); **хорошо́/пло́хо** ~**ся** (*perf*) **о** +*prp* to speak well/badly of; ~**ся** (*perf*) **о** +*prp* (*о книге*) to voice one's opinion about.

ото|**йти́** (*как* **идти́**; *см* **Table 18**; *impf* **отходи́ть**) *сов неперех:* ~ **от** +*gen* to move away from; (*перен: от друзей, от взглядов*) to distance o.s. from; (*от темы, от оригинала*) to depart from; (*поезд, автобус*) to leave; (*войска, полк*) to withdraw; (*обои, краска*) to come off; (*пятно, грязь*) to come out; (*отлучиться*) to go off; (*оттаять*) to thaw; (*перестать сердиться*) to calm down; **я** ~**йду́ на 5 мину́т** I'll be back in 5 minutes.

отолью́ *итп сов см* **отли́ть**.

отоларинго́лог (-**а**) *м* ear, nose and throat specialist.

отомрёт *итп сов см* **отмере́ть**.

отом|**сти́ть** (-**щу́**, -**сти́шь**) *сов от* **мстить**.

отопи́тельный *прил* (*прибор*) heating *опред*; ~ **сезо́н** the cold season.

отопле́ни|**е** (-**я**) *ср* heating.

отопру́(**сь**) *итп сов см* **отпере́ть**(**ся**).

отопью́ *итп сов см* **отпи́ть**.

ото́рван|**ный** (-, -**а**, -**о**) *прил:* ~ **от** +*gen* (*от жизни, от друзей*) cut off from; (*воротник, пуговица*) torn-off.

оторв|**а́ть** (-**у́**, -**ёшь**; *impf* **отрыва́ть**) *сов перех:* ~ (**от** +*gen*) to tear away (from); (*воротник, пуговицу*) to tear off; **ему́** ~**а́ло но́гу** his leg was blown off; **отрыва́ть** (~ *perf*) **что-н от себя́** to sacrifice sth

▶ **оторва́ться** (*impf* **отрыва́ться**) *сов возв:* ~**ся** (**от** +*gen*) (*от работы*) to tear o.s. away (from); (*от отряда, от бегунов, от преследователей*) to break away (from); (*от семьи, от друзей, от жизни*) to lose touch (with); (*воротник, штанина*) to tear; (*пуговица*) to come off; **отрыва́ться** (~**ся** *perf*) **от земли́** to take off.

оторопе́лый *прил* (*разг*) dumbstruck.

оторопе́|ть (-ю) *сов неперех (разг)* to be dumbstruck.

ото|сла́ть (-шлю́, -шлёшь; *impf* **отсыла́ть**) *сов перех:* ~ **кого́-н к** +*dat* to refer sb to; (*письмо, посы́лку*) to send (off); (*челове́ка, маши́ну*) to send back.

отоспа́|ться (-лю́сь, -и́шься; *impf* **отсыпа́ться**) *сов перех (разг)* to have a good sleep.

ототру́ *итп сов см* **оттере́ть**.

от|очи́ть (-очу́, -о́чишь) *сов перех* to sharpen.

отоше́л *итп сов см* **отойти́**.

отошлю́ *итп сов см* **отосла́ть**.

отоща́|ть (-ю) *сов от* **тоща́ть**.

отпада́|ет *итп сов см* **отпа́сть**.

отпада́|ть (-ю) *несов от* **отпа́сть**.

отпа́ива|ть (-ю) *несов от* **отпая́ть, отпои́ть**.

отпа́рива|ть (-ю) *несов от* **отпа́рить**.

отпари́р|овать (-ую) *сов от* **пари́ровать**.

отпа́р|ить (-ю, -ишь; *impf* **отпа́ривать**) *сов перех* (*брю́ки, ю́бку*) to steam press.

отпа́рыва|ть(ся) (-ю(сь)) *несов от* **отпоро́ть(ся)**.

отпа́|сть (*3sg* -дёт, *3pl* -ду́т, *impf* **отпада́ть**) *сов неперех* (*обо́и, штукату́рка*) to come off; (*жела́ние, необходи́мость*) to pass; **у меня́ ~ла охо́та идти́ туда́** I don't feel like going there any more.

отпая́|ть (-ю; *impf* **отпа́ивать**) *сов перех* to melt off.

отпева́ни|е (-я) *ср* funeral service.

отпева́|ть (-ю) *несов от* **отпе́ть**.

от|пере́ть (-опру́, -опрёшь; *pt* -пер, -перла́, -перло, *impf* **отпира́ть**) *сов перех* to unlock

▸ **отпере́ться** (*impf* **отпира́ться**) *сов возв* (*дверь, воро́та, шкаф*) to unlock.

отпе́тый *прил (разг)* out-and-out.

отпе́|ть (-о́ю, -о́ешь; *impf* **отпева́ть**) *сов перех* (*РЕЛ*) to read a service for.

отпеча́та|ть (-ю; *impf* **отпеча́тывать**) *сов перех* (*та́кже* ФОТО) to print; (*на компью́тере*) to finish typing; (*следы́*) to leave; (*помеще́ние*) to open up

▸ **отпеча́таться** (*impf* **отпеча́тываться**) *сов возв* (*на земле́, на песке́*) to leave a print; (*перен: в па́мяти, в созна́нии*) to imprint itself.

отпеча́т|ок (-ка) *м* (*та́кже перен*) imprint; **отпеча́тки па́льцев** fingerprints.

отпеча́тыва|ть(ся) (-ю(сь)) *несов от* **отпеча́тать(ся)**.

отпива́|ть (-ю) *несов от* **отпи́ть**.

отпил|и́ть (-ю́, -и́лишь; *impf* **отпи́ливать**) *сов перех* to saw off.

отпира́тельств|о (-а) *ср* denial.

отпира́|ть (-ю) *несов от* **отпере́ть**

▸ **отпира́ться** *несов от* **отпере́ться** ♦ *возв:* ~**ся (от** +*gen*) (*от слов итп*) to deny.

отпи|са́ться (-шу́сь, -шешься; *impf* **отпи́сываться**) *сов неперех (разг)* to send a formal reply.

отпи́с|ка (-ки; *gen pl* -ок) *ж* formal reply.

отпи́сыва|ться (-юсь) *несов от* **отписа́ться**.

от|пи́ть (-опью́, -опьёшь; *impf* **отпива́ть**) *сов*
перех (*полстака́на итп*) to drink; ~ (*perf*) **глото́к** to take a sip.

отпихну́|ть (-у́, -ёшь; *impf* **отпи́хивать**) *сов перех (разг)* to shove

▸ **отпихну́ться** (*impf* **отпи́хиваться**) *сов возв* (*разг*): ~**ся (от** +*gen*) (*от бе́рега*) to push off (from).

отпишу́сь *итп сов см* **отписа́ться**.

отпла́т|а (-ы) *ж* repayment (*fig*); **в ~у за** +*acc* in repayment *или* as a reward for.

отпла|ти́ть (-чу́, -а́тишь; *impf* **отпла́чивать**) *сов неперех* (+*dat; награди́ть*) to repay; (*отомсти́ть*) to pay back.

отплыва́|ть (-ю) *несов от* **отплы́ть**.

отплыву́ *итп сов см* **отплы́ть**.

отплы́ти|е (-я) *ср* (*отправле́ние*) departure.

отплы́|ть (-ву́, -вёшь; *impf* **отплыва́ть**) *сов неперех* (*челове́к*) to swim off; (*кора́бль*) to set sail.

о́тповед|ь (-и) *ж* rebuke.

отпо́|ить (-ю́, -и́шь; *impf* **отпа́ивать**) *сов перех:* ~ **кого́-н чем-н** (*разг*) to give sb sth (to drink).

отполз|ти́ (-у́, -ёшь; *impf* **отполза́ть**) *сов неперех* to crawl away.

отполир|ова́ть (-у́ю) *сов от* **полирова́ть**.

отпо́р (-а) *м:* **дать** ~ +*dat* (*врагу́*) to repel, repulse; (*иде́е*) to rebuff; **получа́ть** (**получи́ть** *perf*) **реши́тельный** ~ to be rebuffed.

отп|оро́ть (-орю́, -о́решь; *impf* **отпа́рывать**) *сов перех* (*рука́в, пу́говицу*) to unstitch

▸ **отпоро́ться** (*impf* **отпа́рываться**) *сов возв* (*рука́в*) to come unstitched; (*пу́говица*) to come off.

отпою́ *итп сов см* **отпои́ть**.

отправи́тел|ь (-я) *м* sender.

отпра́в|ить (-лю, -ишь; *impf* **отправля́ть**) *сов перех* to send; **отправля́ть** (~ *perf*) **кого́-н на тот свет** to do away with sb

▸ **отпра́виться** (*impf* **отправля́ться**) *сов возв* (*челове́к*) to set off; (*по́езд, теплохо́д*) to depart.

отпра́в|ка (-ки; *gen pl* -ок) *ж* (*письма́, посы́лки*) posting; (*гру́за*) dispatch; (*по́езда, теплохо́да*) departure.

отправле́ни|е (-я) *ср* (*письма́, посы́лки*) dispatch; (*по́езда, теплохо́да*) departure; (*обя́занностей, правосу́дия*) administration; (*зака́зное, почто́вое*) item; **отправле́ния органи́зма** bodily function.

отправлю́(сь) *сов см* **отпра́вить(ся)**.

отправля́|ть (-ю) *несов от* **отпра́вить** ♦ *перех* (*обя́занности*) to exercise; (*правосу́дие*) to administer

▸ **отправля́ться** *несов от* **отпра́виться**.

отправн|о́й *прил:* ~ **пункт** point of departure; ~**а́я цена́** (*КОММ*) reserve price (*BRIT*), upset price (*US*); **отправна́я то́чка** (*перен*) starting point.

отпра́здн|овать (-ую) *сов от* **пра́здновать**.

отпра́шива|ться (-юсь) *несов от* **отпроси́ться**.

отпресс|ова́ть (-у́ю) *сов от* прессова́ть.
отпр|оси́ться (-ошу́сь, -о́сишься; *impf* **отпра́шиваться**) *сов возв* to ask to be let off; **он ~оси́лся домо́й** he asked to be allowed to go home.
отпры́гн|уть (-у, -ешь; *impf* **отпры́гивать**) *сов неперех* to jump.
о́тпрыск (-а) *м* shoot; *(перен)* offspring.
отпря́г *итп сов см* **отпря́чь**.
отпряга́|ть (-ю) *несов от* **отпря́чь**.
отпрягу́ *итп сов см* **отпря́чь**.
отпря́н|уть (-у, -ешь) *сов неперех* to recoil.
отпря́|чь (-гу́, -жёшь *итп*, -гу́т; *pt* -г, -гла́, -гло́, *impf* **отпряга́ть**) *сов перех* to unharness.
отпугн|у́ть (-у́, -ёшь; *impf* **отпу́гивать**) *сов перех* to scare off.
о́тпуск (-а) *м* leave, holiday *(BRIT)*, vacation *(US)*; *(ВОЕН)* leave; *(товаров)* sale; **ежего́дный ~** annual leave; **быть** *(impf)* **в ~е** to be on holiday; **идти́ (пойти́** *perf*) **в ~** to go on holiday; **брать (взять** *perf*) **~** to take leave.
отпуска́|ть (-ю) *несов от* **отпусти́ть**.
отпускни́к (-а́) *м* holiday-maker; *(ВОЕН)* soldier on leave.
отпускни́ц|а (-ы) *ж (разг) см* **отпускни́к**.
отпускны́|е (-х; *decl like adj*) *мн (также:~* **де́ньги**) holiday pay *ед*.
отп|усти́ть (-ущу́, -у́стишь; *impf* **отпуска́ть**) *сов перех* to let out; *(из рук)* to let go of ♦ **безл** *(разг: боль)* to ease off; *(товар, проду́кты)* to sell; *(де́ньги, сре́дства)* to release; *(бо́роду, во́лосы)* to grow; **отпуска́ть (~** *perf*) **кому́-н грехи́** *(РЕЛ)* to absolve sb of his sins; **отпуска́ть (~** *perf*) **комплиме́нт** *(разг)* to compliment sb; **отпуска́ть (~** *perf*) **шу́тку** *(разг)* to crack a joke.
отраба́тыва|ть (-ю) *несов от* **отрабо́тать**.
отраба́танный *прил (поро́да)* worked out; *(газ)* waste *опред*.
отрабо́та|ть (-ю; *impf* **отраба́тывать**) *сов перех (долги́)* to work off; *(како́е-то вре́мя)* to work ♦ *неперех (ко́нчить рабо́тать)* to finish work; *(осво́ить)* to work on, polish.
отра́в|а (-ы) *ж* poison.
отрави́тел|ь (-я) *м* poisoner.
отрави́тельниц|а (-ы) *ж см* **отрави́тель**.
отр|ави́ть (-авлю́, -а́вишь; *impf* **отравля́ть**) *сов перех* to poison; *(перен: удово́льствие, пра́здник итп)* to spoil
▶ **отрави́ться** *сов от* трави́ться ♦ *(impf* **отравля́ться**) *возв* to poison o.s.; *(едо́й)* to get food-poisoning; *(га́зом итп)* to be poisoned.
отравле́ни|е (-я) *ср* poisoning.
отравлю́(сь) *сов см* **отрави́ть(ся)**.
отравля́|ть(ся) (-ю(сь)) *несов от* **отрави́ть(ся)**.
отравля́ющий (-ая, -ее, -ие) *прил* poisonous, toxic.
отра́д|а (-ы) *ж* joy.

отра́д|ный (-ен, -на, -но) *прил* satisfying.
отража́тел|ь (-я) *м* reflector.
отража́|ть(ся) (-ю(сь)) *несов от* **отрази́ть(ся)**.
отраже́ни|е (-я) *ср (см глаг)* reflection; deflection.
отра|зи́ть (-жу́, -зи́шь; *impf* **отража́ть**) *сов перех (также перен)* to reflect; *(нападе́ние, уда́р)* to deflect
▶ **отрази́ться** *(impf* **отража́ться**) *сов возв (также перен)* to be reflected; **отража́ться (~ся** *perf*) **на** +*prp (на здоро́вье, на успе́хах итп)* to have an effect on.
отрапорт|ова́ть (-у́ю) *сов от* рапортова́ть.
отраслево́й *прил related to a particular branch of industry*.
о́трасл|ь (-и) *ж* branch *(of research, industry)*.
отра|сти́ (*3sg* -стёт, *3pl* -сту́т, *pt* -о́с, -осла́, -осло́, *impf* **отраста́ть**) *сов неперех* to grow.
отра|сти́ть (-щу́, -сти́шь; *impf* **отра́щивать**) *сов перех* to grow.
отреаги́р|овать (-ую) *сов от* реаги́ровать.
отре́бь|е (-я) *ср собир (пренебр)* scum.
отрегули́р|овать (-ую) *сов от* регули́ровать.
отредакти́р|овать (-ую) *сов от* редакти́ровать.
отре́жу *итп сов см* **отре́зать**.
отре́з (-а) *м* piece of fabric; **ли́ния ~а** dotted line.
отре́зать (-жу, -жешь; *impf* **отреза́ть**) *сов перех* to cut off ♦ *несов перех (разг: ре́зко отве́тить)* to cut short.
отрезве́|ть (-ю) *сов от* трезве́ть.
отрезв|и́ть (-лю́, -и́шь; *impf* **отрезвля́ть**) *сов перех (также перен)* to sober up.
отре́зка *итп сущ см* **отре́зок**.
отрезно́й *прил (тало́н)* tear-off; *(рука́в)* detachable.
отре́з|ок (-ка) *м (тка́ни)* piece; *(пути́)* section; *(вре́мени)* period; *(ГЕОМ)* segment.
отрека́|ться (-юсь) *несов от* **отре́чься**.
отрекоменд|ова́ть (-у́ю) *сов от* рекомендова́ть.
отрёкся *итп сов см* **отре́чься**.
отреку́сь *итп сов от* **отре́чься**.
отремонти́р|овать (-ую) *сов от* ремонти́ровать.
отрепети́р|овать (-ую) *сов от* репети́ровать.
отреставри́р|овать (-ую) *сов от* реставри́ровать.
отрецензи́р|овать (-ую) *сов от* рецензи́ровать.
отрече́ни|е (-я) *ср*: **~ от** +*gen* reununciation of; **отрече́ние от престо́ла** abdication.
отре́|чься (-ку́сь, -чёшься *итп*, -ку́тся; *pt* -ёкся, -екла́сь, -екло́сь, *impf* **отрека́ться**) *сов возв*: **~ от** +*gen* to renounce; **отрека́ться (~** *perf*) **от престо́ла** to abdicate.
отреша́|ться (-юсь) *несов от* **отреши́ться**.

отрешён|ный (-, -а, -о) *прил* resolute.
отреш|и́ться (-у́сь, -и́шься; *impf* **отреша́ться**) *сов возв*: ~ **от** +*gen* to reject.
отрица́ни|е (-я) *ср* denial; (*линг*) negation.
отрица́тел|ьный (-ен, -ьна, -ьно) *прил* (*также* МАТ, ЭЛЕК) negative.
отрица́|ть (-ю) *несов перех* to deny; (*литературу, моду итп*) to reject.
отро́г (-а) *м* (*ГЕО*) spur.
о́троду *нареч*: ~ **не** +*pt* (*разг*) never; **я ~ тако́го не ви́дел** I've never ever seen anything like it.
отро́дь|е (-я) *ср* (*разг: пренебр*) scum.
отро́с *итп сов см* **отрасти́**.
отро́ст|ок (-ка) *м* (*побег*) shoot; (*ответвление*) branch; ~ **слепо́й кишки́** appendix.
о́трочеств|о (-а) *ср* adolescence.
отро́|ю *итп сов см* **отры́ть**.
отруба́|ть (-ю) *несов от* **отруби́ть**.
о́труб|и (-ей) *мн* bran *ед*.
отруб|и́ть (-ублю́, -у́бишь; *impf* **отруба́ть**) *сов перех* (*ветку, го́лову*) to chop off ♦ *неперех* (*разг: резко ответить*) to cut short.
отруга́|ть (-ю) *сов от* **руга́ть**.
отры́в (-а) *м*: ~ **от** +*gen* (*отряда, семьи*) separation from; **ли́ния ~а** a perforated line; **учи́ться** (*impf*) **без ~а от произво́дства** *to study without giving up work*; **быть** (*impf*) **в ~е от** +*gen* to be cut off from.
отрыва́|ть (-ю) *несов от* **оторва́ть**, **отры́ть**.
▶ **отрыва́ться** *несов от* **оторва́ться**.
отры́вист|ый (-, -а, -о) *прил* (*смех*) spasmodic; (*сигнал*) interrupted; (*речь, замечания*) disjointed.
отры́вка *итп сущ см* **отры́вок**.
отрывно́й *прил* (*блокнот, талоны*) tear-off.
отры́в|ок (-ка) *м* excerpt.
отры́воч|ный (-ен, -на, -но) *прил* fragmented; disjointed.
отрыгн|у́ть (-у́, -ёшь; *impf* **отры́гивать**) *сов* (*не*)*перех* to burp (*inf*).
отры́жк|а (-и) *ж* burp (*inf*).
отры́|ть (-ю, -ёшь; *impf* **отрыва́ть**) *сов перех* (*также перен*) to dig up.
отря́д (-а) *м* party, group; (*ВОЕН*) detachment; (*ЗООЛ*) order; **поиско́вый ~** search party.
отряхн|у́ть (-у́, -ёшь; *impf* **отря́хивать**) *сов перех* (*снег, пыль*) to shake off; (*пальто, сапоги*) to shake down
▶ **отряхну́ться** (*impf* **отря́хиваться**) *сов возв* to shake o.s. down.
отса|ди́ть (-жу́, -а́дишь; *impf* **отса́живать**) *сов перех* (*ученика, болтуна*) to move; (*растение, цветок*) to add new soil to.
отса́жива|ться (-юсь) *несов от* **отсе́сть**.
отсажу́ *сов см* **отсади́ть**.
отсалют|ова́ть (-у́ю) *сов от* **салютова́ть**.
отса́сыва|ть (-ю) *несов от* **отсоса́ть**.
о́тсвет (-а) *м* reflection.
отсве́чива|ть (*3sg* -ет, *3pl* -ют) *несов неперех* to reflect the light.
отсебя́тин|а (-ы) *ж* (*разг: пренебр*): **нести́ ~у** to say whatever comes into one's head; **занима́ться** (*impf*) **~ой** to do whatever comes into one's head.
отсе́в (-а) *м* (*действие: шелухи*) separation; (*то, что отсеяно*) siftings *мн*; (*кандидатов*) elimination; (*студентов*) expulsion.
отсе́ива|ть(ся) (-ю(сь)) *несов от* **отсе́ять(ся)**.
отсе́к (-а) *м* (*судна, помещения*) compartment; (*ракеты*) module.
отсёк *итп сов см* **отсе́чь**.
отсека́|ть (-ю) *несов от* **отсе́чь**.
отсеку́ *итп сов см* **отсе́чь**.
отс|е́сть (-я́ду, -я́дешь; *impf* **отса́живаться**) *сов неперех*: ~ (**от** +*gen*) to move away (from); ~ (*impf*) **пода́льше** to sit further away.
отс|е́чь (-еку́, -ечёшь *итп*, -ку́т; *pt* -ёк, -екла́, -екло́, *impf* **отсека́ть**) *сов перех* to cut off.
отсе́|ять (-ю; *impf* **отсе́ивать**) *сов перех* (*семена, шелуху*) to sift out; (*перен: кандидатов*) to eliminate; (: *учеников*) to expel
▶ **отсе́яться** (*impf* **отсе́иваться**) *сов возв* (*см перех*) to be separated; to be eliminated; to drop out.
отси|де́ть (-жу́, -ди́шь; *impf* **отси́живать**) *сов неперех* (*просидеть*) to wait; (*лекцию*) to sit through; (*разг: в тюрьме́*) to do time ♦ *перех*: **я ~де́л но́гу** my leg has gone dead; **я ~де́л там два часа́** I sat (and waited) there for two hours
▶ **отсиде́ться** (*impf* **отси́живаться**) *сов возв* (*разг*) to sit tight.
отска́блива|ть (-ю) *несов от* **отскобли́ть**.
отска́кива|ть (-ю) *несов от* **отскочи́ть**.
отскобл|и́ть (-ю́, -и́шь; *impf* **отска́бливать**) *сов перех* to scrub off.
отск|очи́ть (-очу́, -о́чишь; *impf* **отска́кивать**) *сов неперех*: ~ **от** +*gen* (*мяч*) to bounce off; (*человек*) to jump off; (*в сторону, назад*) to jump; (*разг: пуговица, кнопка*) to come off; **отска́кивать** (~ *perf*) **в сто́рону/наза́д** to jump to the side/back.
отскре|сти́ (-бу́, -бёшь; *impf* **отскреба́ть**) *сов перех* to scratch off.
отсло|и́ть (-ю́, -и́шь; *impf* **отсла́ивать**) *сов перех* to strip away.
отслу|жи́ть (-жу́, -у́жишь) *сов неперех* (*какое-то время*) to serve ♦ *перех* (*военную службу*) to serve out; (*панихиду, молебен*) to conduct.
отсн|я́ть (-иму́, -и́мешь) *сов перех* (*плёнку*) to finish off, use up; (*фильм, серию*) to finish shooting.
отсове́т|овать (-ую) *сов неперех*: ~ **кому́-н** +*infin* (*делать, ездить итп*) to advise sb not to do *или* against doing.
отсоедин|и́ть (-ю́, -и́шь; *impf* **отсоединя́ть**) *сов перех* to disconnect.
отсо́с (-а) *м* (*действие*) suction; (*устройство*) suction pump.
отсос|а́ть (-у́, -ёшь; *impf* **отса́сывать**) *сов перех* to draw off.
отсо́хн|уть (-у, -ешь; *impf* **отсыха́ть**) *сов*

неперех to wither.
отсро́ч|ить (-у, -ишь; *impf* **отсро́чивать**) *сов перех* to defer.
отсро́чк|а (-и) *ж* deferral.
отстава́ни|е (-я) *ср* (*в работе, в учёбе*) falling behind; (*в развитии*) retardation.
отста|ва́ть (-ю́, -ёшь) *несов от* **отста́ть**.
отста́в|ить (-лю, -ишь; *impf* **отставля́ть**) *сов перех* to move aside; **~!** (*ВОЕН*) as you were!
отста́в|ка (-ки; *gen pl* -ок) *ж* (*ВОЕН*) retirement; (*с государственной службы*) resignation; **подава́ть** (**пода́ть** *perf*) **в ~ку** to offer one's resignation; **уходи́ть** (**уйти́** *perf*) **в ~ку** to resign one's commission; **офице́р в ~ке** retired officer; **~ прави́тельства/кабине́та** resignation of the government/cabinet.
отста́влю *сов см* **отста́вить**.
отставля́|ть (-ю) *несов от* **отста́вить**.
отста́вок *сущ см* **отста́вка**.
отста́ива|ть(ся) (-ю) *несов от* **отстоя́ть(ся)**.
отста́лост|ь (-и) *ж* backwardness.
отста́лый *прил* backward.
отста́|ть (-ну, -нешь; *impf* **отстава́ть**) *сов неперех*: **~** (**от** +*gen*) (*от группы, от друзей*) to fall behind; (*от поезда, от автобуса*) to be left behind; (*перен: в учёбе, в работе, в развитии*) to fall behind; (*обои, пластырь*) to come off; (*часы*) to be slow; **~нь от меня́!** stop pestering me!; **часы́ отстаю́т на 5 мину́т** the clock is 5 minutes slow; **отстава́ть** (**~** *perf*) **от вре́мени** (*перен*) to be behind the times; **отстава́ть** (**~** *perf*) **от жи́зни** to be out of touch.
отстега́|ть (-ю) *сов от* **стега́ть**.
отстегн|у́ть (-у́, -ёшь; *impf* **отстёгивать**) *сов перех* (*крючок*) to unfasten; (*капюшон, рукава*) to detach
▶ **отстегну́ться** (*impf* **отстёгиваться**) *сов возв* (*крючок*) to come unfastened.
отстира́|ть (-ю; *impf* **отсти́рывать**) *сов перех* (*пятно, грязь*) to wash out; (*рубашку, юбку*) to wash clean
▶ **отстира́ться** (*impf* **отсти́рываться**) *сов возв* (*см перех*) to wash out; to wash clean.
отсто́й (-я) *м* sediment.
отсто́йник (-а) *м* (*ТЕХ*) settling tank.
отсто|я́ть (-ю́, -и́шь; *impf* **отста́ивать**) *сов перех* (*город, своё мнение*) to defend; (*воду, раствор*) to allow to stand; (*службу, концерт*) to stand through; (*два часа итп*) to wait; **мы ~я́ли всю слу́жбу** we stood through the whole service; **я ~я́л два часа́ в о́череди** I stood (and waited) for two hours in the queue ♦ *несов неперех* (*no perf*): **~ от** +*gen* to be situated away from; **их дом ~и́т на 3 киломе́тра от го́рода** their house is situated 3 kilometres from the town
▶ **отстоя́ться** (*impf* **отста́иваться**) *сов возв* to settle.
отстра́ива|ть (-ю) *несов от* **отстро́ить**.

отстран|и́ть (-ю́, -и́шь; *impf* **отстраня́ть**) *сов перех* (*уволить*): **~ от** +*gen* (*от должности*) to relieve of; (*отодвинуть*) to push away
▶ **отстрани́ться** (*impf* **отстраня́ться**) *сов возв*: **~ся от** +*gen* (*от должности*) to relinquish; (*отодвинуться*) to draw back.
отстреля́|ться (-юсь; *impf* **отстре́ливаться**) *сов возв*: **~ от** +*gen* to drive back (*with gunfire*); (*разг: кончить дела*) to do one's bit.
отстри|чь (-гу́, -ижёшь *итп*, -гу́т; *impf* **отстрига́ть**) *сов перех* to cut off.
отстро́|ить (-ю, -ишь; *impf* **отстра́ивать**) *сов перех* to finish building.
о́тступ (-а) *м* (*в начале строки*) indentation.
отступ|и́ть (-лю́, -у́пишь; *impf* **отступа́ть**) *сов неперех* to step back; (*ВОЕН*) to retreat; (*перен: перед трудностями, перед опасностью*) to give up; (*морозы, холода*) to abate; **отступа́ть** (**~** *perf*) **наза́д** to step back; **он ~упи́л на 2 шага́** he took 2 steps back; **отступа́ть** (**~** *perf*) **от свои́х взгля́дов** to retreat from one's beliefs; **отступа́ть** (**~** *perf*) **от те́мы** to digress
▶ **отступи́ться** (*impf* **отступа́ться**) *сов возв*: **~ся от** +*gen* (*от взглядов, от требований итп*) to abandon.
отступле́ни|е (-я) *ср* (*также ВОЕН*) retreat; (*от темы*) digression.
отступлю́(сь) *сов см* **отступи́ть(ся)**.
отсту́пник (-а) *м* apostate.
отсту́пниц|а (-ы) *ж см* **отсту́пник**.
отсту́пничеств|о (-а) *ср* apostasy.
отступя́ *нареч* away, off; **немно́го от** +*gen* away from.
отсу́тстви|е (-я) *ср* (*человека*) absence; (*денег, вкуса*) lack; **в ~** +*gen* in the absence of.
отсу́тств|овать (-ую) *несов неперех* (*в классе итп*) to be absent; (*желание, аппетит*) to be lacking.
отсу́тствующ|ий (-ая, -ее, -ие) *прил* (*взгляд, вид*) absent ♦ (-его; *decl like adj*) *м* absentee.
отсчёт (-а) *м* (*шагов, минут*) calculation; **~ вре́мени** time-keeping.
отсчи́та|ть (-ю; *impf* **отсчи́тывать**) *сов перех* (*шаги, минуты*) to count; (*деньги*) to count out.
отсыла́|ть (-ю) *несов от* **отосла́ть**.
отсы́лк|а (-и) *ж* cross-reference.
отсы́п|ать (-лю, -лешь; *impf* **отсыпа́ть**) *сов перех* (+*gen*) to pour off; **отсыпа́ть** (**~** *perf*) **кому́-н чего́-н** to give sb sth.
отсыпа́|ться (-юсь) *несов от* **отоспа́ться**.
отсы́п|лю *сов см* **отсы́пать**.
отсыре́|ть (-ю; *impf* **отсырева́ть**) *сов неперех* to get damp.
отсыха́|ть (*3sg* -ет, *3pl* -ют) *несов от* **отсо́хнуть**.
отсю́да *нареч* from here; **~ мо́жно заключи́ть, что** ... from this we can conclude that ....

отся́ду *итп сов см* **отсе́сть.**
Отта́в|а (-ы) *ж* Ottawa.
отта́ива|ть (-ю) *несов от* **отта́ять.**
отта́лкива|ть(ся) (-ю(сь)) *несов от*
оттолкну́ть(ся).
отта́лкивающ|ий (-ая, -ее, -ие) *прил* repellent.
отт|ащи́ть (-ащу́, -а́щишь; *impf* отта́скивать)
сов перех: ~ (от +*gen*) (от огня́, от окна́) to
drag away (from); (в сто́рону, наза́д) to drag.
отта́|ять (-ю; *impf* отта́ивать) *сов неперех*
(земля́); (мя́со, ры́ба) to thaw out;
(перен: челове́к) to soften ♦ *перех*
(разморо́зить) to defrost.
оттен|и́ть (-ю́, -и́шь; *impf* оттеня́ть) *сов перех*
(рису́нок, ко́нтур) to shade in; (перен: гла́вное,
подро́бности) to highlight.
отте́н|ок (-ка) *м* (также перен) shade.
оттеня́|ть (-ю) *несов от* **оттени́ть.**
о́ттепел|ь (-и) *ж* thaw; (полит) the Thaw (*the
period of political liberalization*).
от|тере́ть (-отру́, -отрёшь; *pt* -тёр, -тёрла,
-тёрло, *impf* оттира́ть) *сов перех* (гря́зь,
пятно́) to rub out; (щёки, ру́ки) to rub.
оттесн|и́ть (-ю́, -и́шь; *impf* оттесня́ть) *сов
перех* to drive back.
оттира́|ть (-ю) *несов от* **оттере́ть.**
о́ттиск (-а) *м* (ступни́, ладо́ни) impression;
(рису́нок, гравю́ры) print; (также:
корректу́рный ~) proof; (статьи́) offprint.
оттого́ *нареч* that is why; ~ что because.
оттолкн|у́ть (-у́, -ёшь; *impf* отта́лкивать) *сов
перех* to push away; (перен: друзе́й) to shun
► оттолкн|у́ться (*impf* отта́лкиваться) *сов
возв*: ~ся от +*gen* (от бе́рега) to push o.s. away
или back from; (перен: от како́го-н положе́ния,
от да́нных) to take as one's starting point.
оттопы́ренн|ый *прил* (карма́ны) bulging;
(губа́) pouting; (у́ши) protruding.
оттопы́р|иться (*3sg* -ится, *3pl* -ятся, *impf*
оттопы́риваться) *сов возв* to stick out;
(карма́н) to bulge.
отто́ргн|уть (-у, -ешь; *impf* оттерга́ть) *сов
перех* (МЕД: о́рган, ткань) to reject; (зе́мли,
иму́щество) to seize.
отторже́ни|е (-я) *ср* (см глаг) rejection; seizure.
отту́да *нареч* from there.
оття́гива|ть (-ю) *несов от* **оттяну́ть.**
оття́ж|ка (-ки; *gen pl* -ок) *ж* delay.
оттян|у́ть (-яну́, -я́нешь; *impf* оття́гивать) *сов
перех* to pull back; (разг: челове́ка) to pull
away; (карма́н) to stretch; (разг: выполне́ние,
реше́ние) to delay; **оття́гивать** (~ *impf*) **вре́мя**
to play for time.
отупе́лый *прил* glazed, dazed.
отупе́ни|е (-я) *ср* stupor.
отупе́|ть (-ю) *сов от* **тупе́ть.**
отутю́ж|ить (-у, -ишь) *сов от* **утюжи́ть.**
от|учи́ть (-учу́, -у́чишь; *impf* отуча́ть) *сов
перех*: ~ от +*gen* (от куре́ния, от буты́лки) to
wean sb off; (+*infin*; ворова́ть, врать) to teach
sb not to do

► отучи́ться (*impf* отуча́ться) *сов возв* (+*infin*)
to get out of the habit of doing; отуча́ться (~ся
perf) от плохи́х привы́чек to get out of bad
habits.
отфильтр|ова́ть (-у́ю; *impf*
отфильтро́вывать) *сов перех* to filter off.
отфутбо́л|ить (-ю, -ишь; *impf* отфутбо́ливать)
сов перех (разг): ~ кого́-н to send sb packing.
отха́ркивающ|ий (-ая, -ее, -ие) *прил* (МЕД):
~ее сре́дство expectorant.
отхв|ати́ть (-ачу́, -а́тишь; *impf* охва́тывать) *сов
перех* (разг: отруби́ть) to cut off; (: доста́ть)
to get.
отхлебн|у́ть (-у́, -ёшь; *impf* отхлёбывать) *сов
перех* (разг) to take a swig of.
отхлест|а́ть (-ю; *impf* отхлёстывать) *сов перех*
(разг): ~ кого́-н to give sb a hiding.
отхлы́н|уть (*3sg* -ет, *3pl* -ут) *сов неперех*
(во́лны) to roll back; (кровь от лица́) to drain;
(перен: толпа́) to draw back.
отхо́д (-а) *м* departure; (ВОЕН) withdrawal; ~ от
тради́ций/действи́тельности departure from
tradition/reality; *см также* **отхо́ды.**
отхо|ди́ть (-жу́, -дишь) *несов от* **отойти́.**
отхо́дн|ая (-ой; *decl like adj*) *ж* (РЕЛ) prayer for
the dying.
отхо́дчив|ый (-, -а, -о) *прил*: он ~ he doesn't
stay angry for long.
отхо́д|ы (-ов) *мн* (промы́шленности итп) waste
мн.
отхожу́ *несов см* **отходи́ть.**
отца́ *итп сущ см* **оте́ц.**
отцве|сти́ (-ту́, -тёшь; *impf* отцвета́ть) *сов
неперех* to finish blossoming.
отце|ди́ть (-жу́, -дишь; *impf* отце́живать) *сов
перех* to strain off.
отцеп|и́ть (-лю́, -ишь; *impf* отцепля́ть) *сов
перех* (ваго́н, парово́з) to uncouple; (колю́чку)
to unsnag
► отцеп|и́ться (*impf* отцепля́ться) *сов возв*
(ваго́н, парово́з) to come uncoupled; ~и́сь от
меня́! (разг) leave me alone!
отцо́вск|ий (-ая, -ое, -ие) *прил* father's; (перен)
paternal, fatherly.
отцо́вств|о (-а) *ср* fatherhood.
отча́ива|ться (-юсь) *несов от* **отча́яться.**
отча́л|ить (-ю, -ишь; *impf* отча́ливать) *сов
неперех* to set sail.
отча́сти *нареч* partially.
отча́яни|е (-я) *ср* despair.
отча́янно *нареч* (пыта́ться) desperately;
(крича́ть) in despair; (спо́рить) terribly.
отча́янн|ый (-, -на, -но) *прил* desperate;
(сме́лый) daring; (разг: врун, болту́н итп)
terrible.
отча́|яться (-юсь; *impf* отча́иваться) *сов возв*:
~ (+*infin*) to despair (of doing).
отчего́ *нареч* (почему́) why ♦ *союз* (всле́дствие
чего́) which is why; ~ же? (разг) what for?
отчего́-либо *нареч* = **отчего́-нибудь.**
отчего́-нибудь *нареч* for any reason.

отчего́-то *нареч* for some reason.
отчека́н|ить (-ю, -ишь; *impf* **отчека́нивать**) *сов перех* (*монету*) to mint; (*изделие*) to emboss; (*перен: слово*) to pronounce distinctly; **отчека́нивать** (~ *perf*) **отве́т** to answer distinctly.
о́тчеств|о (-a) *ср* patronymic.
отчёт (-a) *м* account; **фина́нсовый** ~ financial report; **годово́й** ~ annual report; **отдава́ть** (**отда́ть** *perf*) **себе́** ~ **в чём-н** to realize sth.
отчётлив|ый (-, -a, -o) *прил* (*звук, отпечаток*) distinct; (*объяснение, повествование*) clear.
отчётность (-и) *ж* accountability ◆ *собир* (*финансовая, административная*) records *мн*.
отчётный *прил* (*собрание*) review *опред*; (*год*) current; ~ **докла́д** report; **отчётный пери́од** accounting period.
отчи́зн|а (-ы) *ж* mother country.
о́тч|ий (-ая, -ее, -ие) *прил* (*ласка, совет*) fatherly; ~ **дом** one's father's house.
о́тчим (-a) *м* stepfather.
отчисле́ни|е (-я) *ср* (*работника*) dismissal; (*студента*) expulsion; (*обычно мн: на строительство*) allocation *ед*; (: *денежные: удержание*) deduction; (: *выделение*) assignment.
отчи́сл|ить (-ю, -ишь; *impf* **отчисля́ть**) *сов перех* (*работника*) to dismiss; (*студента*) to expel; (*деньги: удержать*) to deduct; (: *выделить*) to assign
▸ **отчи́слиться** (*impf* **отчисля́ться**) *сов возв:* ~**ся** (**из** +*gen*) to leave.
отчи́|стить (-щу, -стишь; *impf* **отчища́ть**) *сов перех* (*грязь*) to clean off; (*пятно*) to remove; (*пальто, туфли*) to clean
▸ **отчи́ститься** (*impf* **отчища́ться**) *сов возв* (*грязь*) to come off; (*пятно*) to come out; (*пальто, туфли*) to come clean.
отчита́|ть (-ю; *impf* **отчи́тывать**) *сов перех* (*ребёнка*) to tell off
▸ **отчита́ться** (*impf* **отчи́тываться**) *сов возв* to report; **отчи́тываться** (~**ся** *perf*) **пе́ред** +*instr*/**o** +*prp* to report to/on.
отчища́|ть(ся) (-ю(сь)) *несов от* **отчи́стить(ся)**.
отчи́щу(сь) *сов см* **отчи́стить(ся)**.
отчуди́ть (-ишь) *сов перех* (*разг*): **он сего́дня тако́е** ~**и́л!** he did something really weird today!
отчужда́|ть (-ю) *несов перех* (*также ЮР*) to alienate.
отчужде́ни|е (-я) *ср* (*прекращение отношений*) estrangement; (*ЮР*) alienation.
отчуждённость (-и) *ж* alienation.
отчуждён|ный (-, -на, -но) *прил* (*взгляд, вид*) indifferent.
отшатн|у́ться (-у́сь, -ёшься; *impf* **отша́тываться**) *сов возв* (*от удара*) to recoil;

(*назад, в сторону*) to move; **отша́тываться** (~ *perf*) **от** +*gen* (*разг: от друзей итп*) to ditch.
отшвырн|у́ть (-у́, -ёшь; *impf* **отшвы́ривать**) *сов перех* (*разг: предмет*) to toss away; (: *человека*) to shove aside.
отше́льник (-a) *м* (*также перен*) hermit.
отше́льниц|а (-ы) *ж см* **отше́льник**.
отши́б (-a) *м*: **на** ~**е** (*разг: жить*) alone, on one's tod (*BRIT*); (*стоять: дом итп*) on its own.
отшиб|и́ть (-у́, -ёшь; *impf* **отшиба́ть**) *сов перех* (*разг: руку, ногу*) to hurt; **у меня́ па́мять отши́бло** my memory's gone.
отшлёпа|ть (-ю; *impf* **отшлёпывать**) *сов перех* (*разг*): ~ **кого́-н** (*ребёнка*) to give sb a walloping.
отшлиф|ова́ть (-у́ю; *impf* **отшлифо́вывать**) *сов перех* (*деталь, поверхность*) to grind; (*рассказ, пьесу*) to put the finishing touches to.
отштамп|ова́ть (-у́ю) *сов от* **штампова́ть**.
отштукату́р|ить (-ю, -ишь) *сов от* **штукату́рить**.
отшу|ти́ться (-чу́сь, -́тишься; *impf* **отшу́чиваться**) *сов возв* to reply with a joke.
отщеп|и́ть (-лю́, -ишь; *impf* **отщепля́ть**) *сов перех* (*кусочек дерева итп*) to chip off
▸ **отщепи́ться** (*impf* **отщепля́ться**) *сов возв* (*кусочек дерева итп*) to split off.
отъеда́|ться (-юсь) *несов от* **отъе́сться**.
отъе́дешь *итп сов см* **отъе́хать**.
отъеди́мся *итп сов см* **отъе́сться**.
отъе́ду *итп сов см* **отъе́хать**.
отъедя́тся *итп сов см* **отъе́сться**.
отъе́зд (-a) *м* departure; **быть** (*impf*) **в** ~**е** to be away.
отъезжа́|ть (-ю) *несов от* **отъе́хать**.
отъе́сться (*как* **есть**; *см* **Table 15**; *impf* **отъеда́ться**) *сов возв* (*после голода*) to eat one's fill; (*потолстеть*) to grow fat.
отъе́хать (*как* **е́хать**; *см* **Table 19**; *impf* **отъезжа́ть**) *сов неперех* to travel; **отъезжа́ть** (~ *perf*) **от** +*gen* to move away from.
отъе́шься *сов см* **отъе́сться**.
отъя́вленный *прил* (*мошенник итп*) absolute.
отыгра́|ть (-ю; *impf* **оты́грывать**) *сов перех* to win back
▸ **отыгра́ться** (*impf* **оты́грываться**) *сов возв* (*в карты, в шахматы*) to win again; (*перен*) to get one's own back.
отыс|ка́ть (-щу́, -́щешь; *impf* **оты́скивать**) *сов перех* to hunt out; (*КОМП*) to retrieve
▸ **отыска́ться** (*impf* **оты́скиваться**) *сов возв* to turn up.
отяго|ти́ть (-щу́, -ти́шь; *impf* **отягоща́ть**) *сов перех*: ~ **кого́-н чем-н** to burden sb with sth.
отягча́|ющий (-ая, -ее, -ие) *прил*: ~**ие обстоя́тельства** (*ЮР*) aggravating circumstances.
отягч|и́ть (-у́, -и́шь; *impf* **отягча́ть**) *сов перех*

(*вину, положение*) to aggravate.

отяжеле́ть (-ю) *сов от* **тяжеле́ть**.

о́фис (-а) *м* office.

офице́р (-а) *м* (*ВОЕН*) officer; (*разг: ШАХМАТЫ*) bishop.

офице́рск|ий (-ая, -ое, -ие) *прил* (*звание, форма*) officer's; (*комната, столовая*) officers'.

офице́рств|о (-а) *ср собир* officers *мн*.

официа́льный (-ен, -ьна, -ьно) *прил* official; **официа́льное лицо́** official.

официа́нт (-а) *м* waiter.

официа́нт|ка (-ки; *gen pl* -ок) *ж* waitress.

официо́зный (-ен, -на, -но) *прил:* ~**ная газе́та** *newspaper which supports the government.*

оформи́тель (-я) *м:* ~ **интерье́ра/спекта́кля** interior/set designer; ~ **витри́ны** window-dresser.

оформи́тельниц|а (-ы) *ж см* **оформи́тель**.

офо́рм|ить (-лю, -ишь; *impf* **оформля́ть**) *сов перех* (*книгу*) to design the layout of; (*витрину*) to dress; (*спектакль*) to design the sets for; (*документы, договор*) to draw up; **оформля́ть** (~ *perf*) **кого́-н на рабо́ту** (+*instr*) to take sb on (as)

▶ **офо́рмиться** (*impf* **оформля́ться**) *сов возв* (*мнение, взгляды*) to form; **оформля́ться** (~**ся** *perf*) **на рабо́ту** (+*instr*) to be taken on (as).

оформле́ни|е (-я) *ср* design; (*документов, договора*) drawing up; (*на работу*) taking on; **музыка́льное** ~ music.

офо́рмлю(сь) *сов см* **офо́рмить(ся)**.

оформля́|ть(ся) (-ю(сь)) *несов от* **офо́рмить(ся)**.

офо́рт (-а) *м* etching.

офсе́т (-а) *м* offset (process).

офтальмо́лог (-а) *м* ophthalmologist.

ох *межд* oh.

оха́ива|ть (-ю) *несов от* **оха́ять**.

оха́п|ка (-ки; *gen pl* -ок) *ж* armful; **схвати́ть** (*perf*) **что-н в** ~**ку** to grab sth in one's arms.

охарактеризова́ть (-у́ю) *сов от* **характеризова́ть**.

о́ха|ть (-ю) *несов неперех* (*от боли*) to groan; (*от сожаления, печали*) to sigh.

оха́|ять (-ю; *impf* **оха́ивать**) *сов перех* (*разг*) to slate (*BRIT*), to slag (off).

охва|ти́ть (-чу́, -а́тишь; *impf* **охва́тывать**) *сов перех* (*подлеж: пламя, чувства, темнота*) to engulf; (*подписчиков, население*) to cover; (*ВОЕН*) to envelop; **охва́тывать** (~ *perf*) **что-н чем-н** (*руками, лентой*) to put sth round sth; **охва́тывать** (~ *perf*) **взгля́дом** to take in; **охва́тывать** (~ *perf*) **умо́м** to grasp.

охладе́|ть (-ю; *impf* **охладева́ть**) *сов неперех* (*отношения*) to cool; **охладева́ть** (~ *perf*) **к** +*dat* (*к мужу, к невесте*) to grow cool towards; (*к футболу, к сладкому*) to go off.

охлади́ть (-жу́, -ди́шь; *impf* **охлажда́ть**) *сов перех* (*воду, чувства*) to cool; (*забияку*) to cool down

▶ **охлади́ться** (*impf* **охлажда́ться**) *сов возв* (*печка, вода*) to cool down; (*человек: водой*) to cool off.

охлажде́ни|е (-я) *ср* (*также перен*) cooling.

охлажу́(сь) *сов см* **охлади́ть(ся)**.

охламо́н (-а) *м* (*разг: пренебр*) loafer.

охмур|и́ть (-ю́, -и́шь; *impf* **охмуря́ть**) *сов перех* (*разг*) to lead on.

о́хн|уть (-у, -ешь) *сов неперех* to gasp.

охо́т|а (-ы) *ж* hunt; (*желание*) ~ **к чему́-н/**+*infin* desire for sth/to do; ~ **на лис** fox hunting (*to kill*); ~ **за лисо́й** fox hunting (*to catch*); **ходи́ть/идти́** (**пойти́** *perf*) **на** ~**у** to go hunting; ~ **за престу́пником/уби́йцей** the hunt for a criminal/murderer; **мне** ~ **посмотре́ть э́ту переда́чу** (*разг*) I fancy watching that programme; **что Вам за** ~ **спо́рить с ней?** (*разг*) what do you get out of arguing with her?; ~ **тебе́ спо́рить!** (*разг*) do you really have to argue?

охо́|титься (-чусь, -тишься) *несов возв:* ~ **на** +*acc* to hunt (*to kill*); ~ (*impf*) **за** +*instr* to hunt (*to catch*); (*перен: разг*) to hunt for.

охо́тник (-а) *м* hunter; ~ +*infin* volunteer to do; **быть** (*impf*) **больши́м** ~**ом до** +*gen* (*разг: до женщин, сладкого*) to be crazy about.

охо́тничий (-ья, -ье, -ьи) *прил* hunting *опред*.

охо́тно *нареч* gladly.

охо́чусь *несов см* **охо́титься**.

о́хр|а (-ы) *ж* ochre, ocher (*US*).

охра́н|а (-ы) *ж* (*защита: помещения, президента*) security; (*группа людей: президента*) bodyguard; (: *помещения*) guard; (*здоровья, растений, животных*) protection; **под** ~**ой зако́на** protected by law; **охра́на поря́дка** maintenance of law and order; **охра́на приро́ды** nature conservation; **охра́на труда́** health and safety regulations *мн*.

охране́ни|е (-я) *ср* (*также ВОЕН*) protection.

охра́нник (-а) *м* guard.

охра́нниц|а (-ы) *ж см* **охра́нник**.

охра́нн|ый *прил* (*зона, территория*) guarded; ~**ая ро́та** security company.

охран|я́ть (-ю) *несов перех* (*помещение, президента*) to guard; (*здоровье*) to look after; (*природу*) to protect.

охри́плый *прил* (*разг: голос, крик*) hoarse.

охри́пн|уть (-у, -ешь) *сов от* **хри́пнуть**.

охри́пший (-ая, -ее, -ие) *прил* hoarse.

охроме́|ть (-ю) *сов неперех* to go lame.

оцара́па|ть(ся) (-ю(сь)) *сов от* **цара́пать(ся)**.

оцен|и́ть (-ю́, -ишь; *impf* **оце́нивать**) *сов перех* (*определить цену*) to value; (*определить уровень*) to assess; (*признать достоинства*) to appreciate; **оце́нивать** (~ *perf*) **что-н по досто́инству** to appreciate the true value of sth.

оце́н|ка (-ки; *gen pl* -ок) *ж* (*вещи*) valuation; (*работника, поступка*) assessment; (*отметка*) mark.

оце́нщик (-а) *м* valuer.

оцепене́лый *прил* (*взгляд, человек*) stunned; **оцепене́лое состоя́ние** stupor.

оцепене́ни|е (-я) *ср* numbness; (*БИО*) dormancy.

оцепене́|ть (-ю) *сов от* **цепене́ть**.

оцепи́ть (-еплю́, -е́пишь; *impf* **оцепля́ть**) *сов перех* to cordon off.

оцепле́ни|е (-я) *ср* (*действие*) cordoning off; (*группа*) cordon.

оцеплю́ *сов см* **оцепи́ть**.

оцепля́|ть (-ю) *несов от* **оцепи́ть**.

оцинк|ова́ть (-у́ю; *impf* **оцинко́вывать**) *сов перех* (*ТЕХ*) to galvanize.

оча́г (-а́) *м* hearth; (*перен: заболевания*) source; (: *культуры*) heart; ~ **войны́** flash point; **дома́шний** ~ hearth and home.

очарова́ни|е (-я) *ср* charm.

очарова́тельный (-ен, -ьна, -ьно) *прил* charming.

очар|ова́ть (-у́ю; *impf* **очаро́вывать**) *сов перех* to charm.

очеви́ден *прил см* **очеви́дный**.

очеви́д|ец (-ца) *м* eyewitness.

очеви́дно *нареч, част* obviously ♦ *как сказ*: ~, **что он винова́т** it's obvious that he is guilty ♦ *вводн сл*: ~, **он не придёт** apparently he's not coming; **э́то соверше́нно** ~! it is perfectly obvious!; **он винова́т? –** ~! is he guilty? – obviously!

очеви́д|ный (-ен, -но, -на) *прил* (*факт, истина*) plain; (*желание, намерение*) obvious.

очеви́дца *итп сущ см* **очеви́дец**.

о́чень *нареч* (+*adv*, +*adj*) very; (+*vb*) very much; ~ **удо́бный/удо́бно** very comfortable/comfortably; **мы** ~ **хоти́м, что́бы она́ пришла́** we would very much like her to come.

очередн|о́й *прил* next; (*ближайший: задача*) immediate; (: *номер газеты*) latest; (*следующий по порядку: собрание, отпуск*) regular; (*повторяющийся: ссора, глупость*) usual.

о́черед|ь (-и) *ж* (*порядок*) order; (*место в порядке*) turn; (*группа людей*) queue (*BRIT*), line (*US*); (*тоннеля, завода итп*) section; **в пе́рвую** ~ in the first instance; **в поря́дке** ~**и** when one's turn comes; **в свою́** ~ in turn; ~ **за ни́ми** it is their turn; **по** ~**и** in turn; **стоя́ть** (*impf*) **на** ~**и на** +*acc* (*на квартиру итп*) to be on the waiting list for; **пулемётная** ~ (*ВОЕН*) burst of automatic rifle fire; **на** ~**и стои́т вопро́с/зада́ча** this is the next question/task.

о́черк (-а) *м* (*литературный*) essay; (*газетный*) sketch.

очерн|и́ть (-ю́, -и́шь) *сов от* **черни́ть**.

очерстве́|ть (-ю) *сов от* **черстве́ть**.

очерта́ни|е (-я) *ср* (*обычно мн*) outline *ед*.

оч|ерти́ть (-ерчу́, -е́ртишь; *impf* **оче́рчивать**) *сов перех* to outline.

оче́чник (-а) *м* spectacle case.

оч|ини́ть (-иню́, -и́нишь; *impf* **очиня́ть**) *сов перех* to sharpen.

очисти́тельный *прил* purifying, purification *опред*.

очи́|стить (-щу, -стишь; *impf* **очища́ть**) *сов перех* to clean; (*газ, воду*) to purify; (*совесть, город, квартиру*) to clear; (*душу*) to cleanse; (*разг: обокрасть: дом итп*) to clean out; (*impf* **очища́ть** *или* **чи́стить**; *яблоко, картошку*) to peel; (*рыбу*) to clean

▶ **очи́ститься** (*impf* **очища́ться**) *сов возв* (*газ, вода*) to be purified; (*перен: совесть*) to be cleared; (: *душа*) to be cleansed; **не́бо** ~**стилось от туч** the sky cleared.

очи́стк|а (-и) *ж* purification; **для** ~**и со́вести** to ease one's conscience; *см также* **очи́стки**.

очи́стк|и (-ов) *мн* peelings *мн*.

очистн|о́й *прил*: ~**ые сооруже́ния** purification plant *ед*.

очи́щенный *прил* (*хим*) purified; (*яблоко, картошка*) peeled; (*рыба*) cleaned.

очи́щу(сь) *сов см* **очи́стить(ся)**.

очк|и́ (-о́в) *мн* (*для чтения*) glasses *мн*, spectacles *мн*; (*для плавания*) goggles *мн*; **со́лнечные** ~ sunglasses; **защи́тные** ~ safety specs.

очк|о́ (-а) *ср* (*СПОРТ*) point; (*КАРТЫ*) pip; **дать** (*perf*) **сто** ~**в вперёд** to be miles better.

очковтира́тел|ь (-я) *м* deceiver.

очковтира́тельств|о (-а) *ср* deception.

очко́в|ый *прил*: ~**ая змея́** cobra.

очн|у́ться (-у́сь, -ёшься) *сов возв* (*после сна*) to wake up; (*после обморока*) to come to; (*после испуга*) to steady o.s.

о́чный *прил* (*обучение, институт итп*) *with direct contact between students and teachers*; **о́чная ста́вка** (*ЮР*) confrontation.

очуме́|ть (-ю) *сов неперех* (*разг*) to go off one's head.

оч|ути́ться (2*sg* -у́тишься, 3*sg* -у́тится) *сов возв* to find o.s.

ошара́ш|ить (-у, -ишь; *impf* **ошара́шивать**) *сов перех* (*разг: вопросом, поведением*) to dumbfound.

оше́йник (-а) *м* collar.

ошеломи́тельный (-ен, -ьна, -ьно) *прил* stunning.

ошелом|и́ть (-лю́, -и́шь; *impf* **ошеломля́ть**) *сов перех* to stun.

ошеломля́ющ|ий (-ая, -ее, -ие; -, -а, -е) *прил* = **ошеломи́тельный**.

ошиб|и́ться (-у́сь, -ёшься; *pt* -и́бся, -и́блась, -и́блось, *impf* **ошиба́ться**) *сов возв* to make a mistake; **ошиба́ться** (~ *perf*) **в ком-н** to misjudge sb.

оши́б|ка (-ки; *gen pl* -ок) *ж* mistake, error; (*КОМП*) bug; **по ~ке** by mistake.

оши́боч|ный (**-ен, -на, -но**) *прил* (*мнение, представление*) mistaken, erroneous; (*суждение, вывод*) wrong.

ошива́|ться (**-юсь**) *несов возв* (*разг: пренебр*) to hang about.

ошпа́р|ить (**-ю, -ишь;** *impf* **ошпа́ривать**) *сов перех* (*разг: ногу, палец, помидор*) to scald

▸ **ошпа́риться** (*impf* **ошпа́риваться**) *сов возв* (*разг*) to scald o.s.

оштраф|ова́ть (**-у́ю**) *сов от* **штрафова́ть**.

оштукату́р|ить (**-ю, -ишь**) *сов от* штукату́рить.

ощени́|ться (*3sg* **-йтся,** *3pl* **-ятся**) *сов от* щени́ться.

ощети́нива|ться (*3sg* **-ется,** *3pl* **-ются**) *несов* = щети́ниться.

ощети́н|иться (*3sg* **-ится,** *3pl* **-ятся**) *сов от* щети́ниться.

ощипа́|ть (**-иплю́, -и́плешь**) *сов от* щипа́ть.

ощи́пыва|ть (**-ю**) *несов перех* = щипа́ть.

ощу́па|ть (**-ю;** *impf* **ощу́пывать**) *сов перех* (*стол*) to feel for; (*лицо*) to feel.

о́щуп|ь (**-и**) *ж:* **на ~** by touch; **пробира́ться** (*impf*) **на ~** to grope one's way through.

о́щупью *нареч* by touch; (*перен*) blindly; **пробира́ться** (*impf*) **~** to grope one's way through.

ощути́м|ый (**-, -а, -о**) *прил* (*потепление, запах*) noticeable; (*успех, расходы*) appreciable.

ощути́тельный (**-ен, -ьна, -ьно**) *прил* = ощути́мый.

ощути́|ть (**-щу́, -ти́шь;** *impf* **ощуща́ть**) *сов перех* (*запах*) to notice; (*радость, желание, боль*) to feel.

ощуща́|ть (**-ю**) *несов от* **ощути́ть**.

ощуще́ни|е (**-я**) *ср* (*прикосновения, запаха*) sense; (*радости, боли*) feeling.

ощущу́ *сов см* ощути́ть.

ОЭСР *ж сокр* (= Организа́ция экономи́ческого сотру́дничества и разви́тия) OECD (= *Organization for Economic Cooperation and Development*).

оягни́|ться (*3sg* **-йтся,** *3pl* **-я́тся**) *сов от* ягни́ться.

~ П, п ~

П, п *сущ нескл* (*буква*) *the 16th letter of the Russian alphabet*.

п. *сокр* (= **пара́граф**) par. (= *paragraph*); = **посёлок**.

па *ср нескл* (dance) step.

п.а. *сокр* (= *почто́вый а́дрес*) postal address.

павиа́н (-а) *м* baboon.

павильо́н (-а) *м* pavilion; (*кино́*) studio.

павли́н (-а) *м* peacock.

па́водок (-ка) *м* flood.

па́губный (-ен, -на, -но) *прил* (*после́дствия*) ruinous; (*влия́ние, привы́чка*) pernicious.

па́даль (-и) *ж собир* carrion.

па́дать (-ю; *perf* упа́сть *или* пасть) *несов непeрex* to fall; (*настрое́ние*) to sink; (*дисципли́на, нра́вы*) to decline; (*умира́ть: живо́тное*) to die; (*no perf; снег*) to fall; ~ **(упа́сть** *perf*) **на** +*acc* (*ложи́ться: тень*) to fall on; ~ **(пасть** *perf*) **на** +*acc* (*подозре́ние*) to fall on; (*отве́тственность*) to fall to *или* on; ~ **(упа́сть** *perf*) **ду́хом** to lose heart; **у неё упа́ло настрое́ние** her spirits sank; ~ **(упа́сть** *perf*) **в чьих-н глаза́х** to fall in sb's estimation; ~ **(упа́сть** *perf*) **в о́бморок** to faint.

паде́ж (-а́) *м* (*линг*) case.

паде́жный *прил* (*линг*) case *опред*.

Па-де-Кале́ *м нескл* Pas de Calais.

паде́ние (-я) *ср* (*также перен*) fall; (*нра́вов, дисципли́ны*) decline.

па́дкий (-кая, -кое, -кие; -ок, -ка, -ко) *прил*: ~ **на** +*acc* greedy for.

паду́ *итп сов см* пасть.

па́дчерица (-ы) *ж* stepdaughter.

па́дший (-ая, -ее, -ие) *прил* fallen.

паево́й *прил* (*экон*) share *опред*; **на** ~**ы́х нача́лах** on a shareholder basis.

паёк (-йка́) *м* ration; **сухо́й** ~ dry ration.

паж (-а́) *м* page(boy).

ПАЗ *м сокр* = Па́вловский авто́бусный заво́д; (*авто́бус*) *vehicle manufactured at the Pavlovsk car factory*.

паз (-а; *loc sg* -у́, *nom pl* -ы́) *м* (*тех*) groove.

па́зуха (-и) *ж* bosom; **держа́ть** (*impf*) **ка́мень за** ~**ой на кого́-н** to bear a grudge against sb, bear sb a grudge; **жить** (*impf*) **как у Христа́ за** ~**ой** (*разг*) to be without a care in the world.

пай (-я; *nom pl* -и́) *м* (*экон*) share; **на** ~**я́х** jointly.

пайка́ *итп сущ см* паёк.

па́йщик (-а) *м* shareholder.

пакга́уз (-а) *м* warehouse.

паке́т (-а) *м* (*бума́жный свёрток, комп*) package; (*мешо́к*) (paper *или* plastic) bag; (*конве́рт*) official envelope (*containing important or secret documents*); (*комм*): (*контро́льный*) ~ **а́кций** (controlling) shareholding; ~ **програ́мм** (*комп*) software package; ~ **прикладны́х програ́мм** (*комп*) applications package.

паке́тный *прил*: ~**ая обрабо́тка** (*комп*) batch processing.

Пакиста́н (-а) *м* Pakistan.

пакиста́нец (-ца) *м* Pakistani.

пакиста́нка (-ки; *gen pl* -ок) *ж см* пакиста́нец.

пакиста́нский (-ая, -ое, -ие) *прил* Pakistani.

пакиста́нца *сущ см* пакиста́нец.

пако́вать (-ю; *perf* запакова́ть *или* упакова́ть) *несов перех* to pack.

па́костен *прил см* па́костный.

па́костить (-щу, -стишь; *perf* запа́костить) *несов перех* (*раз*) to soil, dirty ◆ (*perf* напа́костить) *непeрex*: ~ (*кому́-н*) to play a dirty trick (on sb).

па́костный (-ен, -на, -но) *прил* (*разг*) vile, nasty.

па́кощу *несов см* па́костить.

пакт (-а) *м* pact.

ПАЛ *сокр* PAL (= *phase alternation line*).

пала́с (-а) *м* double-sided woven rug.

пала́та (-ы) *ж* (*в больни́це*) ward; (*полит*) chamber, house; **ве́рхняя/ни́жняя** ~ (*полит*) Upper/Lower Chamber; ~ **общи́н/ло́рдов** House of Commons/Lords; **Кни́жная** ~ Book Chamber (*Bibliographical centre in Moscow*); **Торго́вая** ~ Chamber of Commerce.

пала́тка (-ки; *gen pl* -ок) *ж* (*туристи́ческая*) tent; (*ларёк*) stall.

пала́ч (-а́) *м* executioner.

Палести́на (-ы) *ж* Palestine.

палести́нский (-ая, -ое, -ие) *прил* Palestinian.

па́лец (-ьца) *м* (*руки́*) finger; (*ноги́*) toe; **безымя́нный** ~ fourth *или* ring finger; **большо́й** ~ (*руки́*) thumb; (*ноги́*) big toe;

сре́дний ~ middle finger; **указа́тельный** ~ index finger; **знать** *(impf)* **что-н как свой пять** ~**ьцев** to know sth like the back of one's hand; **он** ~ **о** ~ **не уда́рил, он па́льцем не шевельну́л** he didn't lift a finger; **смотре́ть** *(impf)* **сквозь** ~**ьцы на что-н** to shut one's eyes to sth.

палиса́дник (-а) *м* (small) front garden (*BRIT*) *или* yard (*US*).

пали́тр|а (-ы) *ж (также перен)* palette.

пали́|ть (-ю, -йшь; *perf* **опали́ть**) *несов перех (волосы)* to singe; (*perf* **спали́ть**; *подлеж: солнце*) to scorch; (*perf* **вы́палить**; *разг: стреля́ть*) to fire.

па́л|ка (-ки; *gen pl* -**ок**) *ж* stick; **лы́жные** ~**ки** ski poles; **де́лать (сде́лать** *perf*) **что-н из-под** ~**ки** (*разг*) to be bludgeoned into doing sth; **э́то** ~ **о двух конца́х** it cuts both ways; ~**ки в колёса вставля́ть** *(impf)* **кому́-н** to put a spoke in sb's wheel.

пало́мник (-а) *м* pilgrim.

пало́мничеств|о (-а) *ср* pilgrimage.

па́лоч|ка (-ки; *gen pl* -**ек**) *ж уменьш от* **па́лка**; *(мед)* bacillus (*мн* bacilli); **дирижёрская** ~ (conductor's) baton; **волше́бная** ~ magic wand.

па́лочн|ый *прил:* ~**ая дисципли́на** *(перен)* heavy-handed discipline.

па́луб|а (-ы) *ж (мор)* deck.

па́льм|а (-ы) *ж* palm (tree).

пальто́ *ср нескл* overcoat.

па́льца *итп сущ см* **па́лец**.

памфле́т (-а) *м* lampoon.

па́мятен *прил см* **па́мятный**.

па́мят|ка (-ки; *gen pl* -**ок**) *ж (туриста, отдыхающих)* guidelines *мн*; *(на работе)* memorandum (*мн* memoranda).

па́мятник (-а) *м* monument; *(на могиле)* tombstone; *(археологический)* relic; ~**и старины́** ancient monuments; **па́мятники пи́сьменности** ancient manuscripts.

па́мятн|ый (-ен, -на, -но) *прил (незабываемый)* memorable; (*no short form*; *сделанный в память*) commemorative.

па́мяток *сущ см* **па́мятка**.

па́мят|ь (-и) *ж (также комп)* memory; *(воспоминание)* memories *мн*; **в чью-н** ~, **в** ~ **о ком-н** in memory of sb; **на** ~ *(читать стихи)* from memory; *(подарить, взять)* as a memento; **быть** *(impf)* **без** ~**и** to be unconscious; **он лю́бит её без** ~**и** *(разг)* he is crazy about her; **она́ без** ~**и от э́того актёра** *(разг)* she's mad about that actor.

Пана́м|а (-ы) *ж* Panama.

пана́м|а (-ы) *ж* Panama (hat).

пана́мск|ий (-ая, -ое, -ие) *прил:* **П~ кана́л** Panamanian Canal.

панаце́|я (-и) *ж* panacea.

па́нд|а (-ы) *ж* panda.

пандеми́|я (-и) *ж* pandemia.

пане́л|ь (-и) *ж (тротуар)* pavement (*BRIT*), sidewalk (*US*); *(строит)* panel; *(тех)* control panel.

панибра́тств|о (-а) *ср* familiarity.

па́ник|а (-и) *ж* panic.

паник|ова́ть (-у́ю) *несов неперех (разг)* to panic.

панихи́д|а (-ы) *ж (рел)* funeral service; **гражда́нская** ~ civil funeral.

пани́ческ|ий (-ая, -ое, -ие) *прил (состояние, бегство итп)* panic-stricken; *(слухи)* alarming.

панно́ *ср нескл* decorative panel.

панора́м|а (-ы) *ж* panorama.

пансио́н (-а) *м (школа)* boarding school; *(полное содержание)* (full) board and lodging.

пансиона́т (-а) *м* boarding house.

пантео́н (-а) *м* pantheon.

панте́р|а (-ы) *ж* panther.

пантоми́м|а (-ы) *ж* mime.

па́нцир|ь (-я) *м (черепахи)* shell; *(рыцаря)* coat of armour (*BRIT*) *или* armor (*US*).

па́п|а (-ы) *м* dad; *(также:* **Ри́мский** ~) the Pope.

папа́х|а (-и) *ж* papakha *(tall fur cap)*.

папа́ш|а (-и) *м (разг: папа)* old man; (: *как обращение*) grandad.

па́перт|ь (-и) *ж* church porch.

папиро́с|а (-ы) *ж type of cheap Russian cigarette with cardboard filter.*

папиро́сн|ый *прил:* ~**ая бума́га** *(для курения)* cigarette paper; *(тонкая бумага)* tissue paper.

папи́рус (-а) *м* papyrus.

па́п|ка (-ки; *gen pl* -**ок**) *ж* folder (*BRIT*), file (*US*).

па́поротник (-а) *м* fern.

папье́-маше́ *ср нескл* papier-mâché.

пар (-а; *loc sg* -**у́**, *nom pl* -**ы́**) *м* steam; *(с.-х.)* fallow land; **на всех** ~**а́х** *(перен)* full steam ahead; *см также* **пары́**.

па́р|а (-ы) *ж (туфель итп)* pair; *(супружеская)* couple; *(просвещ)* poor *(school mark)*; ~ **слов/мину́т** *(разг)* a couple of words/minutes; **рабо́тать** *(impf)*/**игра́ть** *(impf)* **в** ~**е с кем-н** to work/play with sb; **э́то** ~ **пустяко́в** *(разг)* it's child's play; **они́ два сапога́** ~ *(разг)* they are as bad as each other.

Парагва́|й (-я) *м* Paraguay.

пара́граф (-а) *м* paragraph.

пара́д (-а) *м* parade; **в по́лном** *или* **при всём** ~**е** *(разг)* dressed up to the nines.

пара́дн|ая (-ой; *decl like adj*) *ж* = **пара́дное**.

пара́дн|ое (-ого; *decl like adj*) *ср* entrance.

пара́дн|ый *прил (обед)* formal; *(стол)* festive; *(вид)* smart (*BRIT*), stylish (*US*); *(вход, лестница)* front *опред*, main; **пара́дный костю́м, пара́дная фо́рма** full dress.

парадо́кс (-а) *м* paradox.

парадокса́льн|ый (-ен, -ьна, -ьно) *прил* paradoxical.

парази́т (-а) *м* parasite.

парализ|ова́ть (-у́ю) *(не)сов перех (также перен)* to paralyze; **у́жас** ~**ова́л его́** he was paralyzed with fear.

парали́ч (-а́) *м* paralysis.

паралле́лен *прил см* **паралле́льный**.

параллéл|ь (-и) ж (*также перен*) parallel.
параллéл|ьный (-ен, -ьна, -ьно) *прил* parallel.
парамéдик (-а) *м* paramedic.
парáметр (-а) *м* (*также перен*) parameter; (*комп*) default option.
паранджá|á (-й) ж yashmak.
паранóй|я (-и) ж paranoia.
парапéт (-а) *м* parapet.
парапсихолóги|я (-и) ж parapsychology.
парафи́н (-а) *м* paraffin (wax).
парафи́новый *прил* paraffin *опред*.
парашю́т (-а) *м* parachute.
парашюти́ст (-а) *м* parachutist.
парашюти́ст|ка (-ки; *gen pl* -ок) ж *см* **парашюти́ст**.
пáр|ень (-ня; *gen pl* -нéй) *м* (*разг: юноша*) lad, boy; (*: мужчина*) chap *или* fellow (*BRIT*), guy (*US*); **он свóй ~** (*разг*) he's an easy-going guy.
пари́ *ср нескл* bet; **держáть** (*impf*) ~, **что** ... to bet that ...; **заключáть** (**заключи́ть** *perf*) ~ **с кем-н** (**на что-н**) to make a bet with sb (about sth).
Пари́|ж (-а) *м* Paris.
парижá́н|ин (-ина; *nom pl* -е, *gen pl* -) *м* Parisian.
пари́жá́н|ка (-ки; *gen pl* -ок) ж Parisienne.
пари́|жский (-ая, -ое, -ие) *прил* Parisian.
пари́к (-á) *м* wig.
парикмáхер (-а) *м* hairdresser.
парикмáхерск|ая (-ой; *decl like adj*) ж hairdresser's (*BRIT*), beauty salon (*US*).
пари́л|ка (-ки; *gen pl* -ок) ж steam room (*in sauna*).
пари́р|овать (-ую; *perf* **пари́ровать** *или* **отпари́ровать**) *несов перех* (*также перен*) to parry.
паритéт (-а) *м* parity.
пáр|ить (-ю, -ишь) *несов перех* (*овощи*) to steam
▶ **пáриться** *несов возв* (*овощи*) to be steamed; (*в бане*) to have a sauna; (*разг: в тёплой одежде*) to sweat.
пар|и́ть (-ю́, -и́шь) *несов непeрех* to glide; ~ (*impf*) **в облакáх** (*перен*) to have one's head in the clouds.
парк (-а) *м* park; (*трамвáйный*) depot; **вагóнный ~** rolling stock; **автомоби́льный ~** fleet of cars.
паркéт (-а) *м* parquet.
парк|овáть (-у́ю) *несов перех* to park.
парлáмент (-а) *м* parliament.
парламентáри|й (-я) *м* parliamentarian.
парлáментск|ий (-ая, -ое, -ие) *прил* parliamentary.
парни́к (-á) *м* (*из стеклá*) greenhouse; (*из полиэтилéна*) (poly)tunnel.
парникóв|ый *прил* (*растéние*) hothouse *опред*; ~**ое хозя́йство** glasshouse nursery; **парникóвый эффéкт** greenhouse effect.
парнóй *прил* fresh.
пáрн|ый *прил*: ~ **боти́нок/носóк** one of a pair of boots/socks; ~**ое кáтанье (на конькáх)** pairs' ice-skating; **где ~ боти́нок?** where is the other boot?
пáрня *итп сущ см* **пáрень**.
паровóз (-а) *м* steam engine *или* locomotive.
паровóй *прил* steam *опред*.
пароди́р|овать (-ую) (*не*)*сов перех* to parody.
парóди|я (-и) ж (*также перен*): ~ (**на** +*acc*) parody (of).
парóл|ь (-я) *м* password.
парóм (-а) *м* ferry.
парохóд (-а) *м* steamer, steamship.
парохóдств|о (-а) *ср* shipping; (*учреждéния*) ≈ port and navigation authority; (*фирма*) shipping company.
пáрт|а (-ы) ж desk.
партбилéт (-а) *м сокр* (= *партийный билéт*) (Party) membership card (*of the Communist Party*).
партéр (-а) *м* the stalls *мн*.
партизáн (-а; *gen pl* -) *м* partisan, guerrilla.
парти́йн|ый *прил* (*съезд*) party *опред* ◆ (-ого; *decl like adj*) *м* Party member.
партиту́р|а (-ы) ж score.
пáрти|я (-и) ж (*полит*) party; (*: в СССР*) the (Communist) Party; (*муз*) part; (*грýза*) consignment; (*издéлий: в произвóдстве*) batch, lot; (*грýппа*): **пóисковая ~** search party; (*спорт*): ~ **в шáхматы/волейбóл** a game of chess/volleyball.
парткóм (-а) *м сокр* (= *партийный комитéт*) (Communist) Party committee.
партнёр (-а) *м* partner.
партнёрств|о (-а) *ср* (*экон*) partnership.
парторганизáци|я (-и) ж *сокр* (= *партийная организáция*) (Communist) Party organization.
пáрус (-а; *nom pl* -á) *м* sail; **на всех парусáх** (*перен*) at full speed.
паруси́н|а (-ы) ж canvas.
паруси́новый *прил* canvas *опред*.
пáрусник (-а) *м* sailing vessel.
парфюмéри|я (-и) ж *собир* perfume and cosmetic goods.
парчá|á (-й) ж brocade.
парши́в|ый (-, -а, -о) *прил* (*разг*) lousy, rotten.
пар|ы́ (-óв) *мн* vapour *ед* (*BRIT*), vapor *ед* (*US*).
пас (-а) *м* (*спорт*) pass.
пас(ся) *итп несов см* **пасти́(сь)**.
пáсек|а (-и) ж apiary.
пáсечник (-а) *м* bee keeper.
пáсквил|ь (-я) *м* send-up (*inf*).
паску́дный (-ен, -на, -но) *прил* (*разг*) nasty.
пáсмурен *прил см* **пáсмурный**.
пáсмурно *как сказ*: **сегóдня ~** it is overcast today.
пáсмур|ный (-ен, -на, -но) *прил* overcast, dull; (*перен*) gloomy.
пас|овáть (-у́ю) *несов перех* (*мяч*) to pass ◆

(*perf* **спасова́ть**) *неперех*: ~ **пе́ред** +*instr* to give in to.

па́спорт (-а; *nom pl* -а́) *м* passport; (*автомобиля, станка*) registration document; **заграни́чный** ~ passport (*for foreign travel*).

пасса́ж (-а) *м* arcade; (*муз*) passage.

пассажи́р (-а) *м* passenger.

пассажи́р|ка (-ки; *gen pl* -ок) *ж см* **пассажи́р**.

пассажи́рск|ий (-ая, -ое, -ие) *прил* passenger *опред*.

пасси́в (-а) *м* (*комм*) liabilities *мн*; (*линг*) passive (voice).

пасси́в|ный (-ен, -на, -но) *прил* (*также линг*) passive; (*no short form*; *комм*): ~ **бала́нс** unfavourable (*брит*) *или* unfavorable (*US*) balance; ~ **партнёр** (*комм*) silent partner.

па́ст|а (-ы) *ж* (*томатная*) purée; (*в ручке*) ink; **зубна́я** ~ toothpaste.

па́стбищ|е (-а) *ср* pasture.

пасте́л|ь (-и) *ж* pastel.

пасте́льный *прил* pastel *опред*.

пастеризо́ванный *прил* pasteurized.

пастериз|ова́ть (-у́ю) (*не*)*сов перех* to pasteurize.

пастерна́к (-а) *м* parsnip.

пас|ти́ (-у́, -ёшь; *pt* -, ла́, -ло́) *несов перех* (*скот*) to graze

▶ **пасти́сь** *несов возв* to graze.

пастила́ (-и́лы; *nom pl* -и́лы) *ж* ≈ marshmallow.

па́стор (-а) *м* minister, pastor.

пасту́х (-а́) *м* (*коров*) herdsman (*мн* herdsmen); (*овец*) shepherd.

па́стыр|ь (-я) *м* pastor.

па|сть (-ду́, -дёшь; *pt* -л, -ла, -ло) *сов от* **па́дать** ◆ *неперех* (*no impf*; *крепость, правительство*) to fall ◆ (-сти) *ж* (*зверя*) mouth.

па́сх|а (-и) *ж* (*в иудаизме*) Passover; (*в христианстве*) ≈ Easter; (*кушанье*) paskha (*sweet dish made with cream cheese at Easter*).

па́сын|ок (-ка) *м* stepson.

пат (-а) *м* (*в шахматах*) stalemate.

пате́нт (-а) *м* (*на изобретение*) patent; (*торговый*) licence (*брит*), license (*US*).

пате́нтный *прил* patent *опред*; **пате́нтное бюро́/пра́во** patent office/rights.

патент|ова́ть (-у́ю; *perf* **запатентова́ть**) *несов перех* to patent.

патети́ческ|ий (-ая, -ое, -ие) *прил* (*страстный*) passionate, emotional.

па́ток|а (-и) *ж* treacle.

патологи́ческ|ий (-ая, -ое, -ие) *прил* (*также перен*) pathological.

патоло́ги|я (-и) *ж* pathology.

патриа́рх (-а) *м* patriarch.

патриарха́льный *прил* patriarchal.

патриа́рхи|я (-и) *ж* patriarchate.

патрио́т (-а) *м* patriot.

патриоти́зм (-а) *м* patriotism.

патрио́т|ка (-ки; *gen pl* -ок) *ж см* **патрио́т**.

патро́н (-а) *м* (*воен*) cartridge; (*дрели*) chuck; (*лампы*) socket; (*покровитель*) patron.

патрона́ж (-а) *м* (*мед*) home visiting by a district nurse for newborn babies or the chronically ill.

патрона́ж|ный *прил*: ~**ая сестра́** (*мед*) ≈ district (*брит*) *или* visiting (*US*) nurse.

па́труб|ок (-ка) *м* branch pipe.

патрули́р|овать (-ую) *несов* (*не*)*перех* to patrol.

патру́л|ь (-я́) *м* patrol.

па́уз|а (-ы) *ж* (*также муз*) pause.

пау́к (-а́) *м* spider.

паути́н|а (-ы) *ж* spider's web, spiderweb (*US*); (*в помещении*) cobweb; (*перен*) web.

па́фос (-а) *м* zeal, fervour (*брит*), fervor (*US*).

пах (-а; *loc sg* -у́) *м* groin.

пах *итп несов см* **па́хнуть**.

па́хар|ь (-я) *м* ploughman (*брит*), plowman (*US*) (*мн* ploughmen *или* plowmen).

пах|а́ть (-шу́, -шешь; *perf* **вспаха́ть**) *несов перех* to plough (*брит*), plow (*US*).

па́х|нуть (-ну, -нешь; *pt* -, -ла, -ло) *несов неперех*: ~ (+*instr*) to smell (of); (*разг*): ~ +*instr* (*скандалом*) to smack of; **от неё** ~**нет духа́ми** she smells of perfume.

пахн|у́ть (*3sg* -ёт, *3pl* -у́т) *сов неперех* (+*instr*): ~**уло ро́зами** the scent of roses wafted by.

па́хот|а (-ы) *ж* ploughing (*брит*), plowing (*US*).

паху́ч|ий (-ая, -ее, -ие; -, -а, -е) *прил* strong-smelling.

паца́н (-а́) *м* (*разг*) boy, lad.

пацие́нт (-а) *м* patient.

пацие́нт|ка (-ки; *gen pl* -ок) *ж см* **пацие́нт**.

пацифи́ст (-а) *м* pacifist.

па́ч|ка (-ки; *gen pl* -ек) *ж* (*бумаг, денег итп*) bundle; (*чая, сигарет итп*) packet; (*балерины*) tutu.

па́чка|ть (-ю; *perf* **запа́чкать** *или* **испа́чкать**) *несов перех*: ~ **что-н** to get sth dirty; (*perf* **запа́чкать**; *перен*: *репутацию*) to sully, tarnish

▶ **па́чкаться** (*perf* **запа́чкаться** *или* **испа́чкаться**) *несов возв* to get dirty.

па́ш|ня (-ни; *gen pl* -ен) *ж* ploughed (*брит*) *или* plowed (*US*) field.

пашту́т (-а) *м* pâté.

пашу́ *итп несов см* **паха́ть**.

па́юсн|ый *прил*: ~**ая икра́** pressed caviar(e).

пая́льник (-а) *м* soldering iron.

пая́сничаі|ть (-ю) *несов неперех* (*разг*) to play the fool.

пая́|ть (-ю) *несов перех* to solder.

пая́ц (-а) *м* clown.

ПВО *ж сокр* (= *противовозду́шная оборо́на*) anti-aircraft defence (*брит*) *или* defense (*US*) system.

ПДВ *м сокр* (= *преде́льно допусти́мый вы́брос*) maximum permitted discharge.

пев|е́ц (-ца́) *м* singer.

певи́ц|а (-ы) *ж см* **певе́ц**.

певи́ца *итп см* **певе́ц**.

пе́вч|ий (-ая, -ее, -ие) *прил*: ~**ая пти́ца** songbird ◆ (-его; *decl like adj*) *м* chorister.

пе́г|ий (-ая, -ое, -ие) *прил* piebald *опред*.

педагóг (-а) *м* (*учитель*) teacher.

педагóгик|а (-и) *ж* education science.

педагоги́ческ|ий (-ая, -ое, -ие) *прил* (*коллектив*) teaching *опред*; ~ **институ́т** teacher-training (*BRIT*) *или* teachers' (*US*) college; **у неё** ~ **тала́нт** she has a talent for teaching; **у него́** ~**ое образова́ние** he trained as a teacher.

педáл|ь (-и) *ж* pedal.

педáнт (-а) *м* pedant.

педиáтр (-а) *м* paediatrician (*BRIT*), pediatrician (*US*).

педиатри́|я (-и) *ж* paediatrics (*BRIT*), pediatrics (*US*).

педикю́р (-а) *м* pedicure.

пединститу́т (-а) *м сокр* (= *педагоги́ческий институ́т*) teacher-training college.

педсовéт (-а) *м сокр* (= *педагоги́ческий совéт*) staff meeting.

педучи́лищ|е (-а) *ср сокр* (= *педагоги́ческое учи́лище*) teacher-training college (*for nursery and primary level*).

пей *несов см* **пить**.

пейзáж (-а) *м* (*также ИСКУССТВО*) landscape; **морско́й** ~ (*ИСКУССТВО*) seascape.

пейзажи́ст (-а) *м* landscape painter.

пéйте *несов см* **пить**.

пёк(ся) *итп несов см* **печь(ся)**.

пекáр|ня (-ни; *gen pl* -ен) *ж* bakery.

пéкар|ь (-я) *м* baker.

Пеки́н (-а) *м* Beijing, Peking.

пéкл|о (-а) *ср* (*зной*) scorching heat; (*перен: ад*) hell.

пеку́(сь) *итп несов см* **печь(ся)**.

пелен|á (-ы́) *ж* (*тумана, облаков*) veil, shroud; **у него́ сло́вно** ~ **с глаз упáла** the scales fell from his eyes.

пеленá|ть (-ю; *perf* **запеленáть**) *несов перех* to swaddle.

пеленг|овáть (-у́ю; *perf* **запеленговáть**) *несов перех* (*ТЕХ*) to take the bearings of.

пелёнк|а (-ки; *gen pl* -ок) *ж* swaddling clothes *мн*; **с** ~**ок** (*перен*) from a very early age.

пеликáн (-а) *м* pelican.

пельмéн|ь (-я; *nom pl* -и) *м* (*обычно мн*) ≈ ravioli *только ед*.

пéмз|а (-ы) *ж* pumice (stone).

пéн|а (-ы) *ж* (*мыльная*) suds *мн*; (*морская*) foam; (*бульонная*) froth; **говори́ть** (*impf*) **с** ~**ой у ртá** to foam at the mouth.

пенáл (-а) *м* pencil case.

пенáльти *ср нескл* penalty.

Пенджáб (-а) *м* Punjab.

пенджáбск|ий (-ая, -ое, -ие) *прил* Punjabi.

пéней *сущ см* **пéня**.

пéн|и (-ей) *мн* = **пéня**.

пéни|е (-я) *ср* singing.

пéнистый *прил* frothy.

пéн|иться (*3sg* -ится, *3pl* -ятся, *perf* **вспéниться**) *несов возв* to foam, froth.

пеницилли́н (-а) *м* penicillin.

пéнк|а (-и) *ж* (*на молоке*) skin; **снимáть** (*impf*) ~**и** (*перен*) to cream off the best for o.s.

пéнни *ср нескл* penny.

пеноплáст (-а) *м* foam plastic.

пенс (-а) *м* pence *мн*.

пенсионéр (-а) *м* pensioner.

пенсионéр|ка (-ки; *gen pl* -ок) *ж см* **пенсионéр**.

пенсио́нный *прил* (*фонд*) pension *опред*; **пенсио́нный во́зраст** pension age.

пéнси|я (-и) *ж* pension; ~ **по инвали́дности** ≈ invalidity benefit; **выходи́ть** (**вы́йти** *perf*) **на** ~**ю** to retire.

пенснé *ср нескл* pince-nez.

пень (**пня**) *м* (tree) stump; (*разг: пренебр: о человеке*) dolt, blockhead.

пенькá (-и́) *ж* hemp (*fibre*).

пенью́áр (-а) *м* negligee.

пéн|я (-и; *gen pl* -ей) *ж* fine.

пеня́|ть (-ю) *несов неперех*: ~ **на себя́** (*разг*) to blame *или* reproach o.s.; **пусть он** ~**ет на себя́** he has only himself to blame.

пéп|ел (-ла) *м* ash; (*хлопья*) ashes *мн*.

пепели́щ|е (-а) *ср* site of a fire.

пéпельниц|а (-ы) *ж* ashtray.

пéпла *итп сущ см* **пéпел**.

пер. *сокр* = **переу́лок**.

пёр *итп несов см* **перéть**.

первéйш|ий (-ая, -ее, -ие) *прил* primary.

пéрвенец (-ца) *м* first-born.

пéрвенств|о (-а) *ср* (*положение*) first place; (*соревнование*) championship.

пéрвенств|овать (-ую) *несов неперех* to take first place, come first.

пéрвенца *итп сущ см* **пéрвенец**.

перви́чный *прил* (*самый ранний*) initial *опред*, primary; (*низовой*) grass root.

первобы́т|ный *прил* primeval; (-ен, -на, -но; *перен: методы*) primitive.

пéрв|ое (-ого; *decl like adj*) *ср* first course.

первоздá|нный *прил* primordial.

первоисто́чник (-а) *м* primary source.

первоклáссник (-а) *м pupil in first year at school (usually seven years old)*.

первоклáссниц|а (-ы) *ж см* **первоклáссник**.

первоклáсс|ный *прил*: ~**ые инвести́ции** (*КОММ*) blue-chip investment.

пéрво-нáперво *нареч* (*разг*) first of all.

первонача́л|ьный (-ен, -ьна, -ьно) *прил* (*исходный*) original, initial *опред*.

первообрáз (-а) *м* prototype.

первооткрывáтел|ь (-я) *м* discoverer.

первоочередно́й *прил* (*неотложный*) immediate.

первоочерёдный *прил* = **первоочередно́й**.

первопрохо́д|ец (-ца) *м* (*поселенец*) pioneer; (*исследователь*) explorer.

перворазря́дный *прил* first-class, top-class.

первосо́рт|ный (-ен, -на, -но) *прил* top-quality, top-grade, first-rate.

первостепе́н|ный (-ен, -на, -но) *прил* (*задача, значение*) paramount.

первоцве́т (-а) *м* primrose.

пе́рв|ый (-ая, -ое, -ые) *чис* first; (*по времени*) first, earliest; **~ эта́ж** ground (*BRIT*) *или* first (*US*) floor; **~ое вре́мя** at first; **в ~ую о́чередь** in the first place *или* instance; **~ час дня/но́чи** after midday/midnight; **из ~ых рук** first-hand; **он ~ учени́к** he is top of the class; **~ым де́лом** *или* **до́лгом** first of all; **това́р ~ого со́рта** top grade product (*on a scale of 1-3*); **пе́рвая по́мощь** first aid; *см также* **пя́тый**.

перга́мент (-а) *м* parchment.

пере- *префикс* (*in verbs; о направлении действия через что-н*) *indicating movement over or across sth eg.* переходи́ть; (*о направлении действия из одного места в другое*) *indicating movement from one place to another eg.* передви́нуть; (*разделение что-н на две части*) *indicating division of sth into two parts eg.* перепили́ть; (*изменение направленности действия*) *indicating redirection of sth eg.* передове́рить; (*повторение действия*) *indicating repetition of sth eg.* переде́лать; (*обозначает превосходство в чём-н*) *indicating superiority in sth eg.* переспо́рить; (*чрезмерность действия*) *indicating excessive action eg.* перепи́ть; (*прекращение действия после длительного проявления*) *indicating cessation of action after certain length of time eg.* переволнова́ться; (*распространение действия на много лиц или предметов*) *indicating action involving of many people or objects eg.* перечита́ть; (*обозначает взаимность действия*) *indicating reciprocal nature of action eg.* перепи́сываться; (*in nouns; обозначает промежуточность*) *indicating intermediate stage of sth eg.* переми́рие.

переадрес|ова́ть (-у́ю; *impf* **переадресо́вывать)** *сов перех* to readdress.

перебази́р|овать (-ую) *сов перех* to relocate.

перебарщива|ть (-ю) *несов от* **переборщи́ть.**

перебежа́|ть (*как* **бежа́ть;** *см* **Table 20;** *impf* **перебега́ть**) *сов неперех:* **~** (*через +acc*) to run across; **перебега́ть** (**~** *perf*) **к** +*dat* (*разг: к противнику итп*) to go over to.

перебе́й(те) *сов см* **переби́ть.**

переберу́(сь) *итп сов см* **перебра́ть(ся).**

переб|еси́ться (-еш́усь, -е́сишься) *сов возв* to run riot; (*разг*) to sow one's wild oats.

перебива́|ть(ся) (-ю(сь)) *несов от* **переби́ть(ся).**

перебира́|ть (-ю) *несов от* **перебра́ть** ◆ *перех:* **~ кла́виши** to run one's fingers over the keys

▸ **перебира́ться** *несов от* **перебра́ться.**

переб|и́ть (-ью, -ьёшь; *impf* **перебива́ть)** *сов*
перех to interrupt; (*убить*) to kill; (*разбить*) to break; (*обить*) to reupholster; **перебива́ть (~** *perf*) **аппети́т** to spoil *или* ruin one's appetite; **перебива́ть (~** *perf*) **мысль** to interrupt one's train of thought; **перебива́ть (~** *perf*) **за́пах чего-н** to conceal the smell of sth

▸ **переби́ться** (*impf* **перебива́ться**) *сов возв* to make ends meet, get by; (*no impf*; **обойти́сь**): **~ся (без** +*gen*) (*разг*) to do without; **они́ с трудо́м ~и́лись до зарпла́ты** they managed to get by till payday; **он ~ьётся!** he'll survive *или* manage!

перебо́|й (-я) *м* (*сердца*) irregularity; (*двигателя*) misfire; (*задержка*) interruption, break.

переболе́|ть (-ю) *сов неперех:* **~** +*instr* to recover from; (*дети, люди: корью, гриппом*) to come down with; **у него́ душа́ ~ла** he is over the heartache.

перебо́р (-а) *м* (*муз*) strumming; (*излишнее*): **э́то уже́ ~** that's too much.

переб|оро́ть (-орю́, -о́решь) *сов перех* to overcome.

переборщ|и́ть (-у́, -и́шь; *impf* **переба́рщивать**) *сов неперех:* **~ в** +*prp* (*разг*) to go over the top with.

перебра́сыва|ть(ся) (-ю(сь)) *несов от* **перебро́сить(ся).**

переб|ра́ть (-еру́, -ерёшь; *impf* **перебира́ть**) *сов перех* (*пересмотреть: бумаги*) to sort out; (: *крупу, ягоды*) to sort; (*мысленно воспроизвести*) to go over *или* through (in one's mind); (*взять слишком много*) to take too much; (*выпить лишнее*) to drink too much; (*струны*) to pluck (*BRIT*), pick (*US*)

▸ **перебра́ться** (*impf* **перебира́ться**) *сов возв* (*разг: через реку*) to manage to get across; (*на новую кварти́ру*) to move.

перебро́|сить (-шу, -сишь; *impf* **перебра́сывать**) *сов перех* (*мяч, мешок*) to throw over; (*войска*) to transfer, move

▸ **перебро́ситься** (*impf* **перебра́сываться**) *сов возв* (*войска*) to be transferred; **перебра́сываться (~ся** *perf*) +*instr* (*мячом*) to throw (to each other); (*словами*) to exchange (with one another).

перебыва́|ть (-ю) *сов неперех* (*у многих людей*) to call on; (*во многих местах*): **он везде́ ~л** he has been all over the world.

перебью́(сь) *итп сов см* **переби́ть(ся).**

перева́л (-а) *м* (*в горах*) pass.

перева́л|ить (-ю́, -ишь; *impf* **перева́ливать**) *сов неперех:* **~** (*через* +*acc*) to cross; **перева́ливать (~** *perf*) **за** +*acc* (*разг*) to top.

перева́лочный *прил:* **~ пункт/ла́герь** transit area/camp.

перева́р|ить (-ю́, -ишь; *impf* **перева́ривать**) *сов перех* to overcook (*by boiling*); (*пищу, информацию*) to digest

▸ **перевари́ться** (*impf* **перева́риваться**) *сов*

возе to be overdone *или* overcooked; *(пища)* to be digested.

переведу́(сь) *итп сов см* **перевести́(сь)**.

переве|зти́ (-езу́, -езёшь; *pt* -ёз, -езла́, -езло́, *impf* **перевози́ть**) *сов перех (переместить)* to take *или* transport across; *(доставить)* to transport, take.

переверн|у́ть (-у́, -ёшь; *impf* **переверётывать** *или* **перевора́чивать**) *сов перех* to turn over; *(изменить)* to change (completely); *(no impf; комнату)* to turn upside down

▸ **переверну́ться** (*impf* **перевёртываться** *или* **перевора́чиваться**) *сов возе (человек)* to turn over; *(лодка, машина)* to overturn.

переве́с (-а) *м (преимущество)* advantage.

переве́|сить (-шу, -сишь; *impf* **переве́шивать**) *сов перех (товар)* to reweigh; *(подлеж: аргумент)* to outweigh.

переве|сти́ (-еду́, -едёшь; *pt* -ёл, -ела́, -ело́, *impf* **переводи́ть**) *сов перех (помочь перейти)* to take across; *(часы, учреждение, сотрудника)* to transfer, move; *(текст)* to translate; *(: устно)* to interpret; *(переслать: деньги)* to send, transfer; *(доллары, метры итп)* to convert; *(разг: израсходовать)* to waste; **переводи́ть** (*~ perf*) **разгово́р** to change the subject; **переводи́ть** (*~ perf*) **текст с ру́сского языка́ на англи́йский** to translate a text from Russian into English; **переводи́ть** (*~ perf*) **дух** *или* **дыха́ние** to take a (deep) breath

▸ **перевести́сь** (*impf* **переводи́ться**) *сов возе* to move; *(разг: исчезнуть)* to die out.

переве́шива|ть (-ю) *несов от* **переве́сить**.

переве́шу *сов см* **переве́сить**.

перевида́|ть (-ю) *сов перех* to see.

перевира́|ть (-ю) *несов от* **переврать**.

перево́д (-а) *м (на другую должность)* transfer; *(стрелки часов)* resetting; *(текст)* translation; *(деньги)* remittance; *~* **строки́** *(КОМП)* line feed; **креди́тный** *~ (КОММ)* credit transfer, bank giro.

перево|ди́ть(ся) (-ожу́(сь), -о́дишь(ся)) *несов от* **перевести́(сь)**.

перево́дный *прил* in translation.

перево́дчик (-а) *м* translator; *(устный)* interpreter.

перево́дчиц|а (-ы) *ж см* **перево́дчик**.

перевожу́ *несов см* **перевози́ть**.

перевожу́(сь) *несов см* **переводи́ть(ся)**.

перево́з (-а) *м (груза)* transportation.

перево|зи́ть (-ожу́, -о́зишь) *несов от* **перевезти́**.

перево́з|ка (-ки; *gen pl* -ок) *ж* transportation, conveyance.

переволн|ова́ться (-у́юсь) *сов возе* to be worried sick.

перевоору́ж|ить (-у́, -и́шь; *impf* **перевооружа́ть**) *сов перех (армию)* to rearm; *(промышленность)* to re-equip.

перевопло|ти́ться (-щу́сь, -ти́шься; *impf* **перевоплоща́ться**) *сов возе (актёр)* to be transformed.

перевора́чива|ть(ся) (-ю(сь)) *несов от* **переверну́ться(ся)**.

переворо́т (-а) *м (полит)* coup (d'état); *(в судьбе)* upheaval.

перевоспита́|ть (-ю; *impf* **перевоспи́тывать**) *сов перех* to re-educate.

перевр|а́ть (-у́, -ёшь; *impf* **перевира́ть**) *сов перех (разг: содержание)* to muddle.

перевы́|боры (-ов) *мн* election *ед (occurring at regular intervals)*.

перевы́полн|ить (-ю, -ишь; *impf* **перевыполня́ть**) *сов перех (задание, план)* to overfulfil; *(норму)* to exceed.

перевя|за́ть (-жу́, -я́жешь; *impf* **перевя́зывать**) *сов перех (руку, раненого)* to bandage; *(рану)* to dress, bandage; *(коробку)* to tie up; *(чулки, свитер)* to reknit.

перевя́з|ка (-ки; *gen pl* -ок) *ж (раны, раненых)* bandaging.

перевя́зочный *прил: ~* **материа́л** bandage.

перевя́зыва|ть (-ю) *несов от* **перевяза́ть**.

перевя́з|ь (-и) *ж* shoulder-belt; *(для руки)* sling.

перега́р (-а) *м* smell or taste of (stale) alcohol; **от него́ несёт** *~***ом** he reeks of alcohol.

переги́б (-а) *м (страницы, ткани)* fold; *(перен: крайность)* excess мн.

перегиба́|ть (-ю) *несов от* **перегну́ть**.

перегля|ну́ться (-ну́сь, -я́нешься; *impf* **перегля́дываться**) *сов возе: ~ (с +instr)* to exchange glances (with).

перег|на́ть (-оню́, -о́нишь; *pt* -на́л,-нала́,-на́ло, *impf* **перегоня́ть**) *сов перех (переместить: скот, машину)* to drive; *(обогнать: бегуна, конкурента)* to overtake; *(нефть)* to refine; *(спирт)* to distil *(BRIT)*, distill *(US)*.

перегно́|й (-я) *м* humus.

перегн|у́ть (-у́, -ёшь; *impf* **перегиба́ть**) *сов перех (бумагу)* to fold (over) ♦ *неперех (с критикой)* to go too far; **перегиба́ть** *(~ perf)* **па́лку** *(перен)* to go too far.

перегова́рива|ться (-юсь) *несов возе: ~ (с +instr)* to exchange remarks (with).

переговор|и́ть (-ю́, -и́шь) *сов неперех: ~ +instr (обсудить)* to have a talk with ♦ *перех (разг)* to outtalk.

переговор́ный *прил: ~* **пункт** telephone office *(for long-distance calls)*.

перегово́р|ы (-ов) *мн* negotiations мн, talks мн; *(по телефону)* call *ед*; **зака́зывать (заказа́ть** *perf) ~* **с** *+instr* to book a call to.

перего́н (-а) *м (на железной дороге)* stage *(between two railway stations)*.

перего́н|ка (-ки; *gen pl* -ок) *ж (нефти)* refining; *(спирта)* distillation.

перегоню́ *итп сов см* **перегна́ть**.

перегоня́|ть (-ю) *несов от* **перегна́ть.**

перегора́|жива|ть (-ю) *несов от* **перегороди́ть.**

перегор|е́ть (*3sg* -**и́т**, *3pl* -**я́т**, *impf* **перегора́ть**) *сов неперех* (*лампочка*) to fuse; (*двигатель*) to burn out.

перегоро|ди́ть (-жу́, -ди́шь; *impf* **перегора́живать**) *сов перех* (*комнату*) to partition (off); (*дорогу*) to block.

перегоро́д|ка (-ки; *gen pl* -**ок**) *ж* partition.

перегорожу́ *сов см* **перегороди́ть.**

перегре́|ть (-ю; *impf* **перегрева́ть**) *сов перех* to overheat

▸ **перегре́ться** (*impf* **перегрева́ться**) *сов возв* to overheat; **он ~лся на со́лнце** he got a touch of sunstroke.

перегру|зи́ть (-ужу́, -у́зишь; *impf* **перегружа́ть**) *сов перех* to overload.

перегру́з|ка (-ки; *gen pl* -**ок**) *ж* overload; (*обычно мн: нервные*) strain.

перегры́з|ть (-у́, -ёшь; *impf* **перегрыза́ть**) *сов перех* to gnaw through

▸ **перегры́зться** (*impf* **перегрыза́ться**) *сов возв* to fight.

KEYWORD

пе́ред *предл* (+*instr*) **1** (*о положении, в присутствии*): *in front of*); **пе́ред до́мом/ зе́ркалом** in front of the house/mirror; **он робе́л пе́ред де́вушками** he was shy in front of girls; **моли́ться** (*impf*) **пе́ред ико́ной** to pray before an icon

2 (*раньше чего-н: ужином, войной, концом итп*) before; **я говори́л с ним пе́ред уро́ком** I spoke to him before the lesson

3 (*об объекте воздействия*): **устоя́ть пе́ред тру́дностями** to stand one's ground in the face of difficulties; **извиня́ться** (**извини́ться** *perf*) **пе́ред кем-н** to apologize to sb; **я винова́т пе́ред тобо́й** I am guilty in your eyes; **отчи́тываться** (**отчита́ться** *perf*) **пе́ред** +*instr* to report to

4 (*по сравнению*) compared to; **пе́ред ним ты челове́к ничто́жный** compared to him, you are a nonentity

5 (*как союз*): **пе́ред тем как** before; **пе́ред тем как уйти́/зако́нчить** before leaving/finishing.

перёд (**пе́реда**) *м* front.

переда|ва́ть(ся) (-ю́(сь); *imper* **передава́й(те)**) *несов от* **переда́ть(ся).**

переда́м(ся) *итп сов см* **переда́ть(ся).**

переда́тчик (-а) *м* (*TEX*) transmitter.

переда́|ть (*как* **дать**; *см* **Table 14**; *impf* **передава́ть**) *сов перех*: **~ что-л** (**кому́-н**) (*письмо, подарок*) to pass *или* hand sth (over) (to sb); (*известие, любовь, интерес*) to pass sth on (to sb); (*идеи, эмоции*) to convey sth *или* get sth across (to sb); **~йте ему́ (мой) приве́т** give him my regards; **~йте ей, что я не приду́** tell her I am not coming; **передава́ть** (**~** *perf*) **что-н по телеви́дению/ра́дио** to televise/broadcast sth; **передава́ть** (**~** *perf*) **де́ло в суд** to take a case to court

▸ **переда́ться** (*impf* **передава́ться**) *сов возв* (+*dat*; *эмоция*): **его́ страх ~лся други́м** his fear communicated itself to the others; **ему́ ~лся тала́нт отца́** he has inherited his father's talent.

переда́ч|а (-и) *ж* (*известия*) passing on; (*концерта, новостей*) transmission; (*ТЕЛ, РАДИО: интересная*) programme (*BRIT*), program (*US*); (*больному, заключённому*) parcel; **програ́мма переда́ч** television and radio guide.

переда́шь(ся) *сов см* **переда́ть(ся).**

передвига́|ть (-ю) *несов от* **передви́нуть**

▸ **передвига́ться** *несов от* **передви́нуться** ♦ *возв* (*на машине, на танке итп*) to move.

передвиже́ни|е (-я) *ср* (*предмета, войск*) movement; (*срока*) alteration, change; **сре́дства ~я** means of transport.

передвижно́й *прил* (*выставка, цирк*) travelling (*BRIT*), traveling (*US*); (*лаборатория, библиотека*) mobile.

передви́|нуть (-у, -ешь; *impf* **передвига́ть**) *сов перех* to move

▸ **передви́нуться** (*impf* **передвига́ться**) *сов возв* to move.

переде́ла|ть (-ю; *impf* **переде́лывать**) *сов перех* (*работу*) to redo; (*характер*) to change; (*рассказ*) to rewrite; **~** (*perf*) **все дела́** to get everything done.

переде́л|ка (-ки; *gen pl* -**ок**) *ж* (*одежды*) alteration; (*характера*) change; **попада́ть** (**попа́сть** *perf*) **в ~ку** (*разг*) to get into a fix; **побыва́ть** (*perf*) **в ~х** (*разг*) to be in a fix.

переде́лыва|ть (-ю) *несов от* **переде́лать.**

передёргива|ть (-ю) *несов от* **передёрнуть.**

переде́рж|ать (-у́, -ишь; *impf* **переде́рживать**) *сов перех*: **он ~а́л мя́со в духо́вке** he left the meat in the oven for too long.

передёрн|уть (-у, -ешь; *impf* **передёргивать**) *сов перех* (*разг: факты, цифры*) to massage ♦ *безл* (+*acc*): **его́ ~уло от хо́лода** he convulsed from the cold; **его́ ~уло от отвраще́ния** he shuddered in disgust.

пере́дн|ий (-яя, -ее, -ие) *прил* front; **П~яя А́зия** the Middle East; **~ план** (*КОМП*) foreground; **пере́дний край** (*ВОЕН, перен*) front line.

пере́дник (-а) *м* apron.

пере́дн|яя (-ей; *decl like adj*) *ж* (entrance) hall.

пе́редо *предл*: **~ мной** in front of me; = **пе́ред.**

передов|а́я (-о́й; *decl like adj*) *ж* (*также: ~ статья́*) editorial; (*также: ~ пози́ция*: *ВОЕН*) vanguard.

передово́й *прил* (*отряд*) advance, forward; (*машина*) front *опред*; (*технология*) advanced; (*писатель, взгляды*) progressive.

передохн|у́ть (-у́, -ёшь) *сов неперех* (*разг*) to take a breather (*BRIT*) *или* break (*US*).

передра́з|ни́ть (-азню́, -а́знишь; *impf* **передра́знивать**) *сов перех* to mimic.

передýма|ть (-ю; *impf* **передýмывать**) *сов неперех* to change one's mind.

передý|ш|ка (-ки; *gen pl* **-ек**) *ж* rest; *(перерыв)* (short) break.

переéду *итп сов см* **переéхать**.

переéзд (-а) *м (в новый дом)* move; *(на железной дороге)* level crossing.

переé|хать (*как* **éхать**; *см* **Table 19**; *impf* **переезжáть**) *сов неперех (переселиться)* to move; **переезжáть** (~ *perf*) *(чéрез +acc)* to cross.

пережгý *итп сов см* **пережéчь**.

переждá|ть (-ý, -ёшь; *impf* **пережидáть**) *сов перех*: ~ дождь to wait for the rain to pass.

пережé|чь (-гý, -жёшь *итп*, -гýт; *pt* -ёг, -глá, -глó, *impf* **пережигáть**) *сов перех (зерна кофе)* to burn; *(глину)* to overfire.

пережива́ни|е (-я) *ср (обычно мн)* feeling.

пережива́|ть (-ю) *несов от* **пережи́ть ♦** *неперех*: ~ **(за** +acc) *(разг)* to worry (about).

переживý *итп сов см* **пережи́ть**.

пережига́|ть (-ю) *несов от* **пережéчь**.

пережида́|ть (-ю) *несов от* **переждáть**.

пережи́т|ок (-ка) *м* relic.

пережи́|ть (-вý, -вёшь; *impf* **пережива́ть**) *сов перех (прожить дольше)* to outlive; *(выжить)* to survive; *(испытать)* to experience; *(вытерпеть)* to suffer.

перезаря|ди́ть (-жý, -ди́шь; *impf* **перезаряжáть**) *сов перех (аккумулятор)* to recharge; *(ружьё)* to reload.

перезвон|и́ть (-ю́, -и́шь; *impf* **перезвáнивать**) *сов неперех* to phone *(BRIT)* *или* call *(US)* back.

перезим|овáть (-ýю) *сов от* **зимовáть**.

перезрé|ть (-ю; *impf* **перезревáть**) *сов неперех* to become overripe.

переигрá|ть (-ю; *impf* **переи́грывать**) *сов перех (играть снова)* to replay ♦ *неперех (разг)* to overact; **э́то дéло нáдо** ~ *(разг)* this will have to be looked at again.

переизбрá|ть (-ерý, -ерёшь; *pt* -рáл, -ралá, -рáло, *impf* **переизбирáть**) *сов перех* to re-elect.

переиздава́|ть (-ю; *imper* **переиздáй(те)**) *несов от* **переиздáть**.

переиздáм *итп сов см* **переиздáть**.

переиздáни|е (-я) *ср (действие)* republication; *(исправленное, дополненное)* new edition.

переиздá|ть (*как* **дать**; *см* **Table 14**; *impf* **переиздавáть**) *сов перех* to republish.

переимен|овáть (-ýю; *impf* **переименóвывать**) *сов перех* to rename.

перейдý *итп сов см* **перейти́**.

переймý *итп сов см* **перенять**.

перейти́ (*как* **идти́**; *см* **Table 18**; *impf* **переходи́ть**) *сов перех*: ~ **(чéрез** +acc) to cross ♦ *неперех*: ~ **в/на** +acc *(поменять место)* to go to; *(на другую работу)* to move to;

переходи́ть (~ *perf*) **к** +dat *(к сыну итп)* to pass to; *(к делу, к обсуждению)* to turn to; **переходи́ть** (~ *perf*) **в атáку** to launch an attack; **переходи́ть** (~ *perf*) **на** +acc to switch to; **переходи́ть** (~ *perf*) **грани́цу** to cross the frontier *или* border; *(перен)* to overstep the bounds *или* mark; **переходи́ть** (~ *perf*) **из рук в рýки** to change hands; **переходи́ть** (~ *perf*) **на грýбости** to resort to bad language; **дрýжба** ~**шлá в любóвь** friendship turned *или* developed into love.

перекáпыва|ть (-ю) *несов от* **перекопáть**.

перекáрмлива|ть (-ю) *несов от* **перекорми́ть**.

перек|ати́ть (-ачý, -áтишь; *impf* **перекáтывать**) *сов перех (что-н круглое)* to roll; *(что-н на колёсах)* to wheel.

перекáшива|ть(ся) (-ю(сь)) *несов от* **перекоси́ть(ся)**.

переквалифици́р|оваться (-уюсь) *сов возв* to retrain.

перекиднóй *прил*: ~ **мост** gangplank; ~ **календáрь** desk calendar.

переки́н|уть (-у, -ешь; *impf* **переки́дывать**) *сов перех* to throw over

► **переки́нуться** (*impf* **переки́дываться**) *сов возв (мячом)* to throw to each other.

переклáдин|а (-ы) *ж* crossbeam; *(СПОРТ)* (horizontal *или* high) bar.

переклáдн|ые (-ых; *decl like adj*) *мн* stagecoach *ед*.

переклáдыва|ть (-ю) *несов от* **переложи́ть**.

переклика́|ться (-юсь) *несов возв (люди, животные)* to call to each other; ~ (*impf*) **(с** +instr) *(перен: образы, идеи)* to have something in common (with).

перекли́ч|ка (-ки; *gen pl* **-ек**) *ж* roll call.

переключа́тел|ь (-я) *м* switch.

переключа́|ть(ся) (-ю(сь)) *несов от* **переключи́ть(ся)**.

переключéни|е (-я) *ср* switching; *(скорости)* changing *(BRIT)*, shifting *(US)*.

переключ|и́ть (-ý, -и́шь; *impf* **переключа́ть**) *сов перех* to switch; **переключáть** (~ *perf*) **скóрость** to change *(BRIT)* *или* shift *(US)* gear; **переключáть** (~ *perf*) **разговóр** to change the subject

► **переключи́ться** (*impf* **переключáться**) *сов возв*: ~**ся (на** +acc) *(внимание)* to shift (to).

перек|овáть (-ýю; *impf* **перекóвывать**) *сов перех (коня)* to reshoe; *(изделие, деталь)* to reforge.

перекопá|ть (-ю; *impf* **перекáпывать**) *сов перех (огород)* to dig up; *(разг: чемодан, шкаф)* to rummage through.

перекорм|и́ть (-лю́, -ишь; *impf* **перекáрмливать**) *сов перех* to overfeed.

перекос|и́ть (-шý, -си́шь; *impf* **перекáшивать**)

сов *перех* (*рисуя*) to draw crooked; (*вырезая*) to cut crooked

► **перекоси́ться** (*impf* **перека́шиваться**) сов **возв** (*деталь, рисунок*) to come out crooked; (*лицо, тело*) to become distorted.

перекоч|ева́ть (-у́ю; *impf* **перекочёвывать**) сов *неперех* (*стадо, табор*) to move on.

перекошу́(сь) сов см **перекоси́ть(ся)**.

перекра́ива|ть (-ю) *несов от* **перекро́йть**.

перекр|ести́ть (-ещу́, -е́стишь) сов *от* **крести́ть**

► **перекрести́ться** сов *от* **крести́ться** ♦ (*impf* **перекре́щиваться**) возв (*также перен*) to cross.

перекрёстка *сущ см* **перекрёсток**.

перекрёстный *прил* intersecting; **перекрёстный допро́с** cross-examination; **перекрёстный ого́нь** crossfire.

перекрёст|ок (-ка) м crossroads.

перекре́щива|ться (-юсь) *несов от* **перекрести́ться**.

перекрещу́(сь) сов см **перекрести́ть(ся)**.

перекрич|а́ть (-у́, -и́шь; *impf* **перекри́кивать**) сов *перех* (*в споре*) to shout down; (*шум, музыку*) to shout above.

перекро́|йть (-ю́, -и́шь; *impf* **перекра́ивать**) сов *перех* (*платье*) to cut differently; (*карту*) to redraw.

перекро́ю *итп* сов см **перекры́ть**.

перекр|ути́ть (-учу́, -у́тишь; *impf* **перекру́чивать**) сов *перех* (*гайку, кран*) to overtighten

► **перекрути́ться** (*impf* **перекру́чиваться**) сов **возв** to get tangled up.

перекрыва́|ть (-ю) *несов от* **перекры́ть**.

перекры́|тие (-я) *ср* ceiling; (*реки*) damming.

перекры́|ть (-о́ю, -о́ешь; *impf* **перекрыва́ть**) сов *перех* (*покрыть заново*) to re-cover; (*реку*) to dam; (*дорогу, улицу*) to close off; (*воду, газ*) to cut off; (*разг: план*) to exceed.

перек|упи́ть (-уплю́, -у́пишь; *impf* **перекупа́ть**) сов *перех* to buy.

переку́пщик (-а) м dealer.

переку́р (-а) м (*разг*) cigarette break.

перек|ури́ть (-урю́, -у́ришь; *impf* **переку́ривать**) сов *перех* (*разг*) to break for a cigarette; (: *сделать перерыв*) to take a break.

перек|уси́ть (-ушу́, -у́сишь; *impf* **переку́сывать**) сов *перех* to bite through ♦ *неперех* (*разг*) to have a snack.

перела́влива|ть (-ю) *несов от* **перелови́ть**.

перелага́|ть (-ю) *несов от* **переложи́ть**.

перела́мыва|ть (-ю) *несов от* **переломи́ть**.

перелез|ть (-у, -ешь; *pt* -, -ла, -ло, *impf* **перелеза́ть**) сов (*не*)*перех*: ~ (*че́рез* +*acc*) (*забор, канаву*) to climb (over); **перелеза́ть** (~ *perf*) **в/на** +*acc* to get *или* climb into.

переле́с|ок (-ка) м (*небольшой лес*) copse, coppice; (*редкий лес*) sparsely wooded area.

перелёт (-а) м flight; (*птиц*) migration.

переле|те́ть (-чу́, -ти́шь; *impf* **перелета́ть**) сов

(*не*)*перех*: ~ (*че́рез* +*acc*) to fly over.

перелётный *прил* (*птицы*) migratory.

перелечу́ сов см **перелете́ть**.

перели́в (-а) м (*красок, звуков*) (subtle) gradation; (*голоса*) modulation.

перелива́ни|е (-я) *ср*: ~ **кро́ви** blood transfusion.

перелива́|ть (-ю) *несов от* **перели́ть** ♦ *неперех* (*блестеть*): ~ +*instr* to shimmer with; ~ (*impf*) **все́ми цвета́ми ра́дуги** to be iridescent.

перелиста́|ть (-ю; *impf* **перели́стывать**) сов *перех* (*просмотреть*) to leaf through; (*быстро перебрать*) to flick through.

перел|и́ть (-ью́, -ьёшь; *impf* **перелива́ть**) сов *перех* to pour (*from one container to another*); **перелива́ть** (~ *perf*) **кровь кому́-н** to give sb a blood transfusion.

перел|ови́ть (-овлю́, -о́вишь) *impf* **перела́вливать**) сов *перех* to catch.

переложе́ни|е (-я) *ср* (*пьесы, повести*) adaptation; (*музыкального произведения*) arrangement.

перел|ожи́ть (-ожу́, -о́жишь) *impf* **перекла́дывать**) сов *перех* to move, shift; (*impf* **перекла́дывать** *или* **перелага́ть**; *повесть, пьесу*) to adapt; **перекла́дывать** (~ *perf*) **что-н на кого́-н** (*ответственность, работу итп*) to pass sth onto sb; ~ (*perf*) **со́ли в суп** to put too much salt in the soup.

перело́м (-а) м (*МЕД*) fracture; (*перен*) turning point.

перелома́|ть (-ю) сов *перех* to break.

перел|оми́ть (-омлю́, -о́мишь; *impf* **перела́мывать**) сов *перех* (*палку*) to break in two; (*перен: ход событий*) to change dramatically.

перело́мный *прил* critical.

перелью́ *итп* сов см **перели́ть**.

перема́|зать (-жу, -жешь; *impf* **перема́зывать**) сов *перех* to cover.

перема́лыва|ть (-ю) *несов от* **перемоло́ть**.

перем|ани́ть (-аню́, -а́нишь; *impf* **перема́нивать**) сов *перех* (*разг*) to entice.

перема́тыва|ть (-ю) *несов от* **перемота́ть**.

перемежа́|ть (-ю) *несов перех*: ~ **что-н с чем-н** to alternate sth with sth

► **перемежа́|ться** *несов возв*: ~**ся с** +*instr* to alternate with.

перемелю́ *итп* сов см **перемоло́ть**.

переме́н|а (-ы) *ж* change; (*в школе*) break (*BRIT*), recess (*US*).

перем|ени́ть (-еню́, -е́нишь) сов *перех* to change

► **перемени́ться** сов *возв* (*жизнь, погода*) to change; **он ~ени́лся в лице́** (*от волнения итп*) his expression changed.

переме́нный *прил* (*погода*) changeable; (*успех, ветер*) variable; **переме́нный ток** alternating current.

переме́р|ить (-ю, -ишь; *impf* **переме́ривать**)

сов перех (*измерить снова*) to remeasure; (*примерить*) to try on.

переме|сти́ть (-щу́, -сти́шь; *impf* **перемеща́ть**) *сов перех* (*предмет*) to move, shift; (*людей*) to transfer

▶ **перемести́ться** (*impf* **перемеща́ться**) *сов возв* to move.

переметну́ть (-у́, -ёшь) *сов* (*не*)*перех*: ~ (**че́рез** +*acc*) to throw over

▶ **переметну́ться** *сов возв* (*на сторону противника итп*) to go over; ~**ся** (*perf*) **че́рез** +*acc* to leap over.

перемеша́|ть (-ю; *impf* **переме́шивать**) *сов перех* (*кашу*) to stir; (*угли, дрова*) to poke; (*вещи, бумаги*) to mix up

▶ **перемеша́ться** (*impf* **переме́шиваться**) *сов возв* to get mixed up.

перемеща́|ть(ся) (-ю(сь)) *несов от* **перемести́ть(ся)**.

перемеще́ни|е (-я) *ср* reshuffle (*in government, of jobs*); (*передвижение*) transfer.

перемещённ|ый *прил*: ~**ое лицо́** (*обычно мн*) displaced person (*мн* people).

перемещу́(сь) *сов см* **перемести́ть(ся)**.

перемигну́ться (-у́сь, -ёшься; *impf* **переми́гиваться**) *сов возв* (*разг*) to wink at each other; **он** ~**у́лся с де́вушкой** he winked at the girl and she winked back.

перемина́|ться (-юсь) *несов возв*: ~ **с ноги́ на́ ногу** to shift from one foot to the other.

переми́ри|е (-я) *ср* truce.

перемно́ж|ить (-у, -ишь; *impf* **перемножа́ть**) *сов перех* (*числа*) to multiply.

перемо́лв|иться (-люсь, -ишься) *сов возв*: ~ (**сло́вом**) **с кем-н** (*разг*) to pass the time of day with sb.

перемо́л|оть (-елю́, -е́лешь; *impf* **перема́лывать**) *сов перех* to grind.

перемота́|ть (-ю; *impf* **перема́тывать**) *сов перех* (*нитку, шерсть*) to wind; (*магнитофонную плёнку*) to rewind.

перемы́|ть (-о́ю, -о́ешь; *impf* **перемыва́ть**) *сов перех* to wash; (*вымыть заново*) to wash again, rewash; **перемыва́ть** (~ *perf*) **ко́сточки кому́-н** (*разг*) to gossip about sb.

перемы́|чка (-ки; *gen pl* -ек) *ж* (*соединение*) crosspiece; (*перекрытие: окна, двери*) lintel.

перенапря́г *итп сов см* **перенапря́чь**.

перенапряга́|ть (-ю) *несов от* **перенапря́чь**.

перенапрягу́ *итп сов см* **перенапря́чь**.

перенапряже́ни|е (-я) *ср* (*физическое, умственное*) overexertion.

перенапря́|чь (-гу́, -жёшь *итп*, -гу́т; *pt* -г, -гла́, -гло́, *impf* **перенапряга́ть**) *сов перех* to overstrain, overexert.

перенаселённ|ый (-, -а́, -о́) *прил* overpopulated.

перенасы́|тить (-щу, -тишь; *impf*

перенасыща́ть) *сов перех* to oversaturate; **он** ~**тил свою́ речь цита́тами** his speech was riddled with quotations.

перен|ести́ (-есу́, -есёшь; *pt* -ёс, -есла́, -есло́, *impf* **переноси́ть**) *сов перех*: ~ **что-н че́рез** +*acc* to carry sth over *или* across; (*поменять место*) to move; (*встречу, заседание*) to reschedule; (*болезнь*) to suffer from; (*несчастье, голод, холод итп*) to endure; **переноси́ть** (~ *perf*) **сло́во на другу́ю стро́ку** to carry a word over to the next line

▶ **перенести́сь** (*impf* **переноси́ться**) *сов возв* (*также перен*) to be transported.

перенима́|ть (-ю) *несов от* **переня́ть**.

перено́с (-а) *м* (*вещей, предметов*) transfer; (*заседания*) rescheduling; (*линг*) hyphen.

перен|оси́ть (-ошу́, -о́сишь) *несов от* **перенести́** ♦ *перех*: **не** ~ **антибио́тиков/ самолёта** to react badly to antibiotics/flying; **он хорошо́** ~**ёс доро́гу** he coped well with the journey; **она́ не** ~**о́сит его́** she can't stand him

▶ **переноси́ться** *несов от* **перенести́сь**.

перено́сиц|а (-ы) *ж* bridge of the nose.

переносно́й *прил* portable.

перено́сный *прил* (*значение*) figurative.

перено́счик (-а) *м* (*мед*) carrier.

переночева́|ть (-ю) *сов от* **ночева́ть**.

переношу́(сь) *несов см* **переноси́ть(ся)**.

перен|я́ть (-йму́, -ймёшь; *pt* -ня́л, -няла́, -ня́ло, *impf* **перенима́ть**) *сов перех* (*опыт, идеи*) to assimilate; (*обычаи, привычки*) to adopt.

переобору́д|овать (-ую) *сов перех* to re-equip.

переобу́|ть (-ю, -ешь; *impf* **переобува́ть**) *сов перех* (*туфли*) to change (out of); **переобува́ть** (~ *perf*) **кого́-н** to change sb's shoes.

переоде́|ть (-ну, -нешь; *impf* **переодева́ть**) *сов перех* (*одежду*) to change (out of); **переодева́ть** (~ *perf*) **кого́-н** to change sb's clothes

▶ **переоде́ться** (*impf* **переодева́ться**) *сов возв* to change, get changed.

переосмы́сл|ить (-ю, -ишь; *impf* **переосмы́сливать**) *сов перех* (*осмыслить заново*) to reassess.

переоцен|и́ть (-ю́, -е́нишь; *impf* **переоце́нивать**) *сов перех* (*дать новую цену*) to re-evaluate, revalue; (*оценить слишком высоко*) to overestimate.

переоце́н|ка (-ки; *gen pl* -ок) *ж* (*см глаг*) re-evaluation, revaluation; overestimation; ~ **це́нностей** (*перен*) reappraisal *или* reassessment of values.

перепа́д (-а) *м*: ~ +*gen* drop in.

перепада́|ть (*3sg* -ет, *3pl* -ют) *несов от* **перепа́сть**.

перепадёт *итп сов см* **перепа́сть**.

перепа́л|ка (-ки; *gen pl* -ок) *ж* (*разг*) row.

перепа́|сть (*3sg* -дёт, *3pl* -ду́т, *impf* **перепада́ть**) *сов неперех* (+*dat*; *достаться*) to come one's way; мне ~ла ко́е-кака́я ме́бель some furniture has come my way.

перепа́чка|ть (-ю) *сов перех* (*разг*) to get filthy.

перепева́|ть (-ю) *несов перех* (*перен*) to rehash.

пе́репел (-а; *nom pl* -а́) *м* quail.

перепёл|ка (-ки; *gen pl* -ок) *ж см* **пе́репел**.

перепеча́та|ть (-ю) *сов перех* (*статью*) to reprint; (*рукопись*) to type.

перепи|ли́ть (-илю́, -и́лишь; *impf* **перепи́ливать**) *сов перех* (*много дров*) to saw; (*доску*) to saw in two.

перепис|а́ть (-ишу́, -и́шешь; *impf* **перепи́сывать**) *сов перех* (*написать заново*) to rewrite; (*скопировать*) to copy; (*сделать список*) to list, make a list of; (*КОМП*) to overwrite.

перепи́с|ка (-ки; *gen pl* -ок) *ж* (*см глаг*) rewriting; copying; listing; (*деловая*) correspondence ♦ *собир* (*письма*) letters *мн*; быть (*impf*) в ~ке с +*instr* to be in correspondence with.

▶ **перепи́сываться** *несов возв*: ~ся (с +*instr*) to correspond (with).

пе́репис|ь (-и) *ж* (*населения*) census; (*имущества*) inventory.

перепишу́ *итп сов см* **переписа́ть**.

перепла|ти́ть (-ачу́, -а́тишь; *impf* **перепла́чивать**) *сов неперех* to pay too much.

перепле|сти́ (-ту́, -тёшь; *pt* -ёл, -ела́, -ело́, *impf* **переплета́ть**) *сов перех* (*книгу, диссертацию*) to bind; (*верёвки, пальцы*) to interlace.

▶ **переплести́сь** (*impf* **переплета́ться**) *сов возв* to intertwine; (*перен: события*) to become interwoven.

переплёт (-а) *м* (*обложка*) binding; **попа́дать** (**попа́сть** *perf*) **в** ~ (*перен: разг*) to get into a fix; **отдава́ть** (**отда́ть** *perf*) **кни́гу/диссерта́цию в** ~ to have a book/thesis bound; **око́нный** ~ window sash.

переплета́|ть(ся) (-ю(сь)) *несов от* **переплести́(сь)**.

переплётн|ая (-ой; *decl like adj*) *ж* (book) bindery.

переплету́(сь) *итп сов см* **переплести́(сь)**.

переплы́|ть (-ву́, -вёшь; *pt* -л, -ла́, -ло, *impf* **переплыва́ть**) *сов (не)перех*: ~ (**че́рез** +*acc*) (*вплавь*) to swim (across); (*на лодке, на корабле*) to sail (across).

переплю́н|уть (-у, -ешь) *сов перех* (*перен: разг*) to go one up on.

переподгото́в|ка (-ки; *gen pl* -ок) *ж* retraining.

переполз|ти́ (-у́, -ёшь; *pt* -, -ла́, -ло́, *impf* **переполза́ть**) *сов (не)перех* to crawl; **переполза́ть** (~ *perf*) (**че́рез** +*acc*) (*дорогу, поле итп*) to crawl across.

перепо́лн|ить (-ю, -ишь; *impf* **переполня́ть**) *сов перех* (*сосуд, контейнер*) to overfill; (*вагон, автобус итп*) to overcrowd; **моё се́рдце** ~**ено любо́вью** my heart is overflowing with love

▶ **перепо́лниться** (*impf* **переполня́ться**) *сов возв* (*сосуд*) to be overfilled; (*душа, сердце*) to overflow.

переполо́х (-а) *м* hullabaloo.

переполоши́|ть (-у́, -и́шь) *сов перех* (*разг*) to alarm

▶ **переполоши́ться** *сов возв* (*разг*) to become alarmed.

перепо́н|ка (-ки; *gen pl* -ок) *ж* membrane; **бараба́нная** ~ eardrum.

перепра́в|а (-ы) *ж* crossing.

перепра́в|ить (-лю, -ишь; *impf* **переправля́ть**) *сов перех* (*через реку, границу*) to take across; (*посылку, письмо*) to forward; (*ошибку, фразу*) to correct

▶ **перепра́виться** (*impf* **переправля́ться**) *сов возв* (*через реку, горы итп*) to cross.

перепро́б|овать (-ую) *сов перех* (*еду*) to taste; (*способы*) to try (out).

перепрода|ва́ть (-ю́; *imper* **перепродава́й(те)**) *несов от* **перепрода́ть**.

перепрода́ть (*как* **дать**; *см* **Table 14**; *impf* **перепродава́ть**) *сов перех* to resell.

перепроизво́дств|о (-а) *ср* overproduction.

перепры́гн|уть (-у, -ешь; *impf* **перепры́гивать**) *сов (не)перех*: ~ (**че́рез** +*acc*) to jump (over).

перепу́г (-а) *м* (*разг*): **с** ~**у** in fright.

перепуга́|ть (-ю) *сов перех*: ~ **кого́-н** to scare the life out of sb.

перепу́та|ть (-ю; *impf* **перепу́тывать** *или* **пу́тать**) *сов перех* (*нитки, провода*) to tangle (up); (*факты*) to confuse; (*имена, адреса*) to mix up

▶ **перепу́таться** (*impf* **перепу́тываться** *или* **пу́таться**) *сов возв* (*нитки, провода*) to get tangled up; (*перен: мысли, воспоминания*) to get confused.

перепу́ть|е (-я) *ср* crossroads; **на** ~ (*перен*) at a crossroads.

перерабо́та|ть (-ю; *impf* **перераба́тывать**) *сов перех* (*сырьё, нефть*) to process; (*идеи, статью, теорию*) to rework ♦ *неперех* (*переутомиться*) to be overworked.

перераспредел|и́ть (-ю́, -и́шь; *impf* **перераспределя́ть**) *сов перех* to redistribute.

перер|асти́ (-асту́, -астёшь; *pt* -о́с, -осла́, -осло́, *impf* **перераста́ть**) *сов перех* (*также перен*) to outgrow; **перераста́ть** (~ *perf*) **в** +*acc* (*превратиться*) to escalate into.

перерасхо́д (-а) *м* (*энергии, денег*) overexpenditure; (*комм*) overdraft.

перерасхо́д|овать (-ую) *сов перех*: ~ **эне́ргию/де́ньги** to expend too much energy/money.

перерасчёт (-а) *м* (*счёт заново*) recalculation; (*комм: в другие единицы*) conversion.

перере́|зать (-жу, -жешь; *impf* **перереза́ть**) *сов перех* (*провод*) to cut in two; (*перен:*

преградить) to cut off.

перерис|овáть (-ýю; *impf* **перерисóвывать**) *сов перех* to copy.

переро|дúться (-жýсь, -дúшься; *impf* **перерождáться**) *сов возв* (*природа, общество*) to be regenerated; (*человек*) to be transformed.

перерождéни|е (-я) *ср* (*см глаг*) regeneration; transformation.

перерожýсь *сов см* **переродúться**.

перерóс *итп сов см* **перерастú**.

перерóю *итп сов см* **перерúть**.

переругá|ться (-юсь) *сов возв* to quarrel.

перерýв (-а) *м* break; **обéденный ~** lunch break; **дéлать** (**сдéлать** *perf*) **~** to take a break.

перер|ýть (-óю, -óешь) *сов перех* (*перекопать*) to dig up; (*разг: вещи, книги*) to rummage through.

перес|адúть (-ажý, -áдишь; *impf* **пересáживать**) *сов перех* to move; (*на другой поезд, самолёт итп*) to transfer; (*дерево, цветок, сердце*) to transplant; (*кость, кожу*) to graft; (**~** *perf*) **когó-н на другóе мéсто** to move sb to another seat.

пересáд|ка (-ки; *gen pl* -ок) *ж* (*растения*) transplantation; (*на поезд итп*) change; (*МЕД: сердца*) transplant; (*: кожи*) graft; **дéлать** (**сдéлать** *perf*) **~ку в Москвé** to change in Moscow.

пересáжива|ть (-ю) *несов от* **пересадúть**.

пересáжива|ться (-юсь) *несов от* **пересéсть**.

пересажý *сов см* **пересадúть**.

пересáлива|ть (-ю) *несов от* **пересолúть**.

пересда|вáть (-ю; *imper* **пересдавáй(те)**) *несов перех* to resit.

пересдá|ть (*как* **дать**; *см* **Table 14**) *сов перех* (*экзамен, зачёт*) to pass (*after resit*).

пересёк(ся) *итп сов см* **пересéчь(ся)**.

пересекá|ть(ся) (-ю(сь)) *несов от* **пересéчь(ся)**.

пересекý(сь) *итп сов см* **пересéчь(ся)**.

переселéн|ец (-ца) *м* (*на новую территорию*) settler; (*временно переселяемый*) *person having to move to temporary accommodation*.

переселéн|ка (-ки; *gen pl* -ок) *ж см* **переселéнец**.

переселéнца *итп сущ см* **переселéнец**.

пересел|úть (-ю, -úшь; *impf* **переселя́ть**) *сов перех* (*на новые земли*) to settle; (*в новую квартиру*) to move

▶ **пересел**ú**ться** (*impf* **переселя́ться**) *сов возв* (*в другую страну*) to emigrate; (*в новый дом*) to move.

перес|éсть (-я́ду, -я́дешь; *impf* **пересáживаться**) *сов неперех* (*на другое место*) to move; **пересáживаться** (**~** *perf*) **на другóе мéсто** to move to another seat; **пересáживаться** (**~** *perf*) **на другóй пóезд/**

самолёт to change trains/planes.

пересечéни|е (-я) *ср* (*действие*) crossing; (*место*) intersection.

пересечённый *прил* (*ГЕО: местность итп*) broken.

перес|éчь (-екý, -ечёшь *итп*, -екýт; *pt* -ёк, -еклá, -еклó, *impf* **пересекáть**) *сов перех* to cross

▶ **пересéчься** (*impf* **пересекáться**) *сов возв* to intersect; (*интересы*) to cross.

пересú|лить (-ю, -ишь; *impf* **пересúливать**) *сов перех* (*человека*) to overpower; (*чувство*) to overcome.

перескажý *итп сов см* **пересказáть**.

пересказ (-а) *м* (*содержания фильма*) retelling; (*изложение*) exposition.

переск|азáть (-ажý, -áжешь; *impf* **пересказывать**) *сов перех* to tell.

переск|очúть (-очý, -óчишь; *impf* **перескáкивать**) *сов* (*не*)*перех*: **~** (**чéрез** +*acc*) to jump (over); (*перен*): **~ на** +*acc* (*на другую тему*) to jump to.

переспа|стúть (-щý, -стúшь; *impf* **переслáщивать**) *сов перех*: **~ что-н** to put too much sugar in sth.

пере|слáть (-шлю, -шлёшь; *impf* **пересылáть**) *сов перех* (*отослать*) to send; (*по другому адресу*) to forward.

переслáщива|ть (-ю) *несов от* **пересластúть**.

переслащý *сов см* **пересластúть**.

пересмáтрива|ть (-ю) *несов от* **пересмотрéть**.

пересмéива|ться (-юсь) *несов возв* to smile at each other.

пересмéн|а (-ы) *ж* (*на заводе, на вахте*) change of shift.

пересмéшник (-а) *м* mockingbird.

пересм|отрéть (-отрю́, -óтришь; *impf* **пересмáтривать**) *сов перех* (*книги, вещи*) to look through; (*решение, вопрос, позицию*) to reconsider.

пересн|я́ть (-имý, -úмешь; *pt* -я́л, -ялá, -я́ло, *impf* **переснимáть**) *сов перех* (*документ*) to make a copy of; (*сцену в фильме*) to reshoot; (*фотографию*) to take again.

перес|олúть (-олю́, -óлишь; *impf* **пересáливать**) *сов перех*: **~ что-н** to put too much salt in sth.

пересóх|нуть (*3sg* -нет, *3pl* -нут, *pt* -, -ла, -ло, *impf* **пересыхáть**) *сов неперех* (*почва, бельё*) to dry out; (*река, ручей*) to dry up.

переспá|ть (-лю́, -úшь; *impf* **пересыпáть**) *сов неперех* (*спать слишком долго*) to oversleep; **~** (*perf*) **с кем-н** (*разг*) to sleep with sb.

переспéлый *прил* overripe.

переспé|ть (*3sg* -ет, *3pl* -ют) *сов неперех* to become overripe.

пересплю́ *сов см* **переспáть**.

переспо́р|ить (-ю, -ишь) *сов перех:* ~ **кого́-н** to defeat sb in an argument.

переспр|оси́ть (-ошу́, -о́сишь; *impf* **переспра́шивать**) *сов перех* to ask again.

пересс́о́р|иться (-юсь, -ишься) *сов возв:* ~ (с +*instr*) to quarrel *или* fall out (with).

переста|ва́ть (-ю́; *imper* **переставай(те)**) *несов от* **переста́ть**.

переста́в|ить (-лю, -ишь; *impf* **переставля́ть**) *сов перех* to move; (*изменить порядок*) to rearrange.

переста́ну *итп сов см* **переста́ть**.

перестара́|ться (-юсь) *сов возв* to overdo it.

переста́ть (-ну, -нешь; *impf* **переставать**) *сов непepex* to stop; **переставать** (~ *perf*) +*infin* to stop doing; ~**ньте!** stop it!

перестира́|ть (-ю; *impf* **перести́рывать**) *сов перех* (*все вещи*) to wash; (*постирать заново*) to wash again, rewash.

пересто|я́ть (*3sg* -и́т, *3pl* -я́т) *сов непepex* (*квас, суп*) to stand too long; (*молоко*) to go off.

перестрада́|ть (-ю) *сов* (*не)перех* to suffer.

перестра́ива|ть(ся) (-ю(сь)) *несов от* **перестро́ить(ся)**.

перестрах|ова́ться (-у́юсь; *impf* **перестрахо́вываться**) *сов возв* (КОММ) to reinsure; (*перен*) to play safe.

перестрахо́в|ка (-ки; *gen pl* -ок) *ж* (*см глаг*) reinsurance; playing safe.

перестрахо́выва|ться (-юсь) *несов от* **перестрахова́ться**.

перестре́л|ка (-ки; *gen pl* -ок) *ж* exchange of fire.

перестро́ек *сущ см* **перестро́йка**.

перестро́ечный *прил* (*процессы, явления*) perestroika *опред*.

перестро́|ить (-ю, -ишь; *impf* **перестра́ивать**) *сов перех* (*дом, мост*) to rebuild, reconstruct; (*программу, экономику*) to reorganize; (*ряды, колонны*) to re-form; (*музыкальный инструмент*) to retune

▶ **перестро́иться** (*impf* **перестра́иваться**) *сов возв* (*человек*) to reorganize o.s.; (*фабрика, коллектив*) to restructure; (*солдаты, шеренги*) to re-form.

перестро́|йка (-йки; *gen pl* -ек) *ж* (*дома*) rebuilding, reconstruction; (*расписания, экономики*) reorganization; (МУЗ) retuning; (ИСТ) perestroika.

пересту|пи́ть (-плю́, -́пишь; *impf* **переступа́ть**) *сов* (*не)перех* (*перен*) to overstep; **переступа́ть** (~ *perf*) (**че́рез** +*acc*) (*порог, предмет*) to step over.

пересу́д|ы (-ов) *мн* (*разг*) gossip *ед*.

пересчёт (-а) *м* count; (*повторный*) re-count; **ско́лько э́то в** ~**е на рубли́?** how much is it when converted into roubles?

пересчита́|ть (-ю; *impf* **пересчи́тывать**) *сов перех* to count; (*повторно*) to re-count, count again; (*в других единицах*) to convert.

пересыла́|ть (-ю) *несов от* **пересла́ть**.

пересы́л|ка (-ки; *gen pl* -ок) *ж* sending;

(*тюрьма*) transit prison (*where prisoners stay temporarily*).

пересы́п|ать (-лю, -лешь; *impf* **пересыпа́ть**) *сов перех* (*насыпать*) to pour; (*перен: речь, рассказ*) to intersperse.

пересыпа́|ть (-ю) *несов от* **переспа́ть**.

пересы́плю *итп сов см* **пересы́пать**.

пересыха́|ть (*3sg* -ет, *3pl* -ют) *несов от* **пересо́хнуть**.

переся́ду *итп сов см* **пересе́сть**.

перета́скива|ть (-ю) *несов от* **перетащи́ть**.

перетас|ова́ть (-у́ю; *impf* **перетасо́вывать**) *сов перех* (*карты*) to shuffle; (*перен: министров*) to reshuffle.

перета́щ|ить (-ащу́, -́ащишь; *impf* **перета́скивать**) *сов перех* (*мешок*) to drag over.

перетр|уди́ться (-ужу́сь, -у́дишься; *impf* **перетружда́ться**) *сов возв* (*разг*) to be burnt out.

перетру́|сить (-шу, -сишь) *сов непepex* (*разг*) to be scared out of one's wits.

перетряс|ти́ (-у́, -ёшь; *pt* -, -ла́, -ло́) *сов перех* to shake out.

пере́|ть (**пру, прёшь;** *pt* **пёр, пёрла, пёрло**) *несов непepex* (*разг: идти*) to trudge; (*ломиться*) to barge through; (*perf* **спере́ть**) (*красть*) to pinch

▶ **пере́ться** *несов возв* (*разг: идти*) to trudge.

перетя|ну́ть (-ну́, -́нешь; *impf* **перетя́гивать**) *сов перех* (*передвинуть*) to pull, tow; (*быть более тяжёлым*) to outweigh; (*стянуть*): ~ **что-н чем-н** to tie sth tightly round sth.

переубе|ди́ть (-жу́, -ди́шь; *impf* **переубежда́ть**) *сов перех:* ~ **кого́-н** to make sb change his mind.

переу́л|ок (-ка) *м* lane, alley.

переустро́йство (-а) *ср* reconstruction.

переутом|и́ться (-лю́сь, -и́шься; *impf* **переутомля́ться**) *сов возв* to tire o.s. out.

переутомле́ни|е (-я) *ср* exhaustion.

переутомлю́сь *сов см* **переутоми́ться**.

переутомля́|ться (-юсь) *несов от* **переутоми́ться**.

переучёт (-а) *м* stocktaking.

переучи́|ть (-учу́, -́учишь; *impf* **переу́чивать**) *сов перех* to retrain

▶ **переучи́ться** (*impf* **переу́чиваться**) *сов возв* to undergo retraining.

переформати́р|овать (-ую) (*не)сов перех* (КОМП) to reformat.

перефрази́р|овать (-ую) (*не)сов перех* to paraphrase.

перехва|ти́ть (-чу́, -́тишь; *impf* **перехва́тывать**) *сов перех* (*захватить на пути*) to intercept; (*разг: переборщить*) to go too far; (*обвязать*): ~ **что-н чем-н** to tie sth round sth; **у него́** ~**ати́ло дыха́ние** he caught his breath; **перехва́тывать** (~ *perf*) **бутербро́д** (*разг*) to grab a sandwich; **перехва́тывать** (~ *perf*) **чей-н взгляд** (*перен*) to catch sb's eye.

перехитр|и́ть (-ю́, -и́шь) *сов перех* to outwit.
перехо́д (-а) *м* crossing; (*к друго́й систе́ме*) transition; (*в зда́нии, между зда́ниями*) passage.
перех|оди́ть (-ожу́, -о́дишь) *несов от* **перейти́**.
перехо́дный *прил* (*промежу́точный*) transitional; **перехо́дный глаго́л** transitive verb.
переходя́щ|ий (-ая, -ее, -ие) *прил*: ~ **ку́бок** (*СПОРТ*) challenge cup.
перехожу́ *несов см* **переходи́ть**.
пе́р|ец (-ца) *м* pepper; (*зёрнышко*) peppercorn; **жгу́чий** ~ chilli pepper; **болга́рский** ~ capsicum.
пе́реч|ень (-ня) *м* list; ~ **служе́бных обя́занностей** job specification.
перечеркн|у́ть (-у́, -ёшь; *impf* **перечёркивать**) *сов перех* to cross out; (*перен: наде́жды*) shatter.
переч|ерти́ть (-ерчу́, -е́ртишь; *impf* **перече́рчивать**) *сов перех* (*начерти́ть сно́ва*) to draw again; (*скопи́ровать*) to copy.
переч|е́сть (-ту́, -тёшь; *pt* -ёл, -ла́, -ло́) *сов перех* (*пересчита́ть*) to re-count, count again; (*перечита́ть*) to reread, read again.
перечисле́ни|е (-я) *ср* transfer; **плати́ть** (*заплати́ть perf*) по ~ю to pay by transfer.
перечи́сл|ить (-ю, -ишь; *impf* **перечисля́ть**) *сов перех* (*упомяну́ть*) to list; (*КОММ*) to transfer.
перечита́|ть (-ю; *impf* **перечи́тывать**) *сов перех* to read; (*чита́ть за́ново*) to reread, read again.
пе́речня *итп сущ см* **пе́речень**.
перечту́ *итп сов см* **перече́сть**.
перешагн|у́ть (-у́, -ёшь; *impf* **переша́гивать**) *сов (не)перех*: ~ (*че́рез +acc*) to step over.
переше́|ек (-йка) *м* isthmus.
перешёл *итп сов см* **перейти́**.
перешёптыва|ться (-юсь) *несов возв* to whisper to each other.
переш|и́ть (-ью, -ьёшь; *impf* **перешива́ть**) *сов перех* (*пла́тье, костю́м*) to alter; (*пу́говицу, крючо́к*) to move (*by sewing on somewhere else*).
перешлю́ *сов см* **пересла́ть**.
перещеголя́|ть (-ю) *сов перех* (*разг*) to outshine.
переэкзамено́в|ка (-ки; *gen pl* -ок) *ж* resit.
пери́л|а (-) *мн* railing *ед*; (*ле́стницы*) banisters *мн*.
пери́метр (-а) *м* perimeter.
пери́н|а (-ы) *ж* feather bed.
пери́од (-а) *м* period; **пе́рвый/второ́й** ~ **игры́** (*СПОРТ*) first/second half (of the game).
периоди́к|а (-и) *ж собир* periodicals *мн*.
периоди́чески *нареч* periodically.
периоди́ческ|ий (-ая, -ое, -ие) *прил* periodical

опред; **периоди́ческая печа́ть** the periodical press.
периоди́чност|ь (-и) *ж* regularity.
перипети́|я (-и) *ж* (*обычно мн*) upheaval.
перитони́т (-а) *м* peritonitis.
перифери́йный *прил* peripheral.
перифери́|я (-и) *ж* the provinces *мн* ♦ *собир* (*КОМП*) peripherals *мн*, peripheral devices *мн*.
перифрази́р|овать (-ую) (*не*)*сов перех* to paraphrase.
перл (-а) *м* (*та́кже перен*) pearl.
перламу́тр (-а) *м* mother-of-pearl.
перламу́тровый *прил* mother-of-pearl *опред*; (*цвет*) pearly.
перло́в|ка (-ки; *gen pl* -ок) *ж* (*разг*) pearl barley.
перло́в|ый *прил* (*суп, ка́ша*) barley *опред*; ~**ая крупа́** pearl barley.
перлюстри́р|овать (-ую) *сов перех* to censor.
переме́нт (-а) *м* perm (= *permanent wave*).
перма́нентный (-ен, -на, -но) *прил* permanent.
перна́т|ый (-ого; *decl like adj*) *м* (*обычно мн*) bird.
пе́рн|уть (-у, -ешь) *сов непере́х* (*груб!*) to fart (!)
пер|о́ (-а́; *nom pl* -ья, *gen pl* -ьев) *ср* (*пти́цы*) feather; (*для письма́: гуси́ное*) quill; (: *стально́е, золото́е*) nib.
перочи́нный *прил*: ~ **нож** penknife (*мн* penknives).
перпендикуля́р|ный (-ен, -на, -но) *прил* perpendicular.
перро́н (-а) *м* platform (*RAIL*).
перс (-а) *м* Persian.
перси́дск|ий (-ая, -ое, -ие) *прил* Persian; **Перси́дский зали́в** Persian Gulf.
пе́рсик (-а) *м* (*де́рево*) peach tree; (*плод*) peach.
Пе́рси|я (-и) *ж* Persia.
персия́н|ка (-ки; *gen pl* -ок) *ж см* **перс**.
персо́н|а (-ы) *ж* person; **со́бственной** ~**ой** in person.
персона́ж (-а) *м* character.
персона́л (-а) *м* (*АДМИН*) personnel, staff.
персона́льный *прил* personal; **персона́льная вы́ставка** one-man exhibition; **персона́льный компью́тер** PC (= *personal computer*).
перспекти́в|а (-ы) *ж* (*ГЕОМ*) perspective; (*вид*) view; ~**ы** (*пла́ны*) prospects *мн*; **в** ~**е** (*в бу́дущем*) in store.
перспекти́вный *прил* (*изображе́ние*) in perspective; (*плани́рование*) long-term; (*многообеща́ющий*) promising; ~ **план** plan of future developments.
пе́рст|ень (-ня) *м* ring.
Перу́ *ж нескл* Peru.
перуа́нск|ий (-ая, -ое, -ие) *прил* Peruvian.
перфока́рт|а (-ы) *ж сокр* (= *перфораци́онная ка́рта*) punched *или* punch (*BRIT*) card.
перфоле́нт|а (-ы) *ж сокр* (= *перфораци́онная ле́нта*) punched tape.

пе́рхот|ь (-и) *ж собир* dandruff.

пе́рц|а *итп сущ см* **пе́рец**.

перча́т|ка (-ки; *gen pl* -ок) *ж* glove; (*боксёра*) (boxing) glove; **пе́рвая ~** (*СПОРТ*) champion boxer.

перч|и́ть (-у́, -и́шь; *perf* **наперчи́ть** *или* **поперчи́ть**) *сов перех* to pepper.

перш|и́ть (*3sg* -и́т) *несов безл* (*разг*): **у меня́ ~и́т в го́рле** I've got a frog in my throat.

пе́рья *итп сущ см* **перо́**.

пёс (пса) *м* dog.

пе́сен *сущ см* **пе́сня**.

пе́сенник (-а) *м* songbook; (*композитор*) songwriter.

пес|е́ц (-ца́) *м* arctic fox.

песка́ *итп сущ см* **песо́к**.

песка́р|ь (-я́) *м* gudgeon.

песк|и́ (-о́в) *мн* sands *мн*.

песн|ь (-и; *gen pl* -ей) *ж* (*в поэме*) canto.

пе́с|ня (-ни; *gen pl* -ен) *ж* song; **ста́рая ~** (*разг*) the same old story.

пес|о́к (-ка́; *part gen* -ку́) *м* sand; **са́харный ~** granulated sugar; *см также* **пески́**.

песо́чниц|а (-ы) *ж* sandpit (*BRIT*), sandbox (*US*).

песо́чный *прил* (*цвет*) sandy; (*тесто, печенье*) short; **песо́чные часы́** hourglass.

пессими́ст (-а) *м* pessimist.

пессимисти́чный (-ен, -на, -но) *прил* pessimistic.

пестици́д (-а) *м* pesticide.

пе́ст|овать (-ую; *perf* **вы́пестовать**) *несов перех* (*перен*) to nurture.

пестр|е́ть (*3sg* -ет, *3pl* -ют) *несов перех* (*виднеться*) to be colourful (*BRIT*) *или* colorful (*US*); (*3pl* -я́т; *мелькать*) to make a colo(u)rful display; **в саду́/на лугу́ ~ю́т цветы́** the garden/meadow is bright with flowers.

пестр|и́ть (*3sg* -и́т, *3pl* -я́т) *несов неперех*: **~ +instr** to be full of.

пёстр|ый (-, -а́, -о) *прил* (*ткань, ковёр*) multi-coloured (*BRIT*), multi-colored (*US*); (*перен: разнородный*) mixed.

песца́ *итп сущ см* **песе́ц**.

песча́ник (-а) *м* sandstone.

песча́н|ый *прил* (*берег, дно реки*) sandy; **песча́ная бу́ря** sandstorm.

пе́тель *сущ см* **пе́тля**.

Петербу́рг *сущ =* **Санкт-Петербу́рг**.

пети́ци|я (-и) *ж* petition.

петли́ц|а (-ы) *ж* (*петля*) buttonhole; (*нашивка*) tab (*on uniform*).

пе́т|ля (-ли; *gen pl* -ель) *ж* loop; (*в вязании*) stitch; (*двери, крышки*) hinge; (*на одежде: для пуговицы*) buttonhole; (: *для крючка*) eye.

петля́|ть (-ю) *несов неперех* to meander.

петру́ш|ка (-и) *ж* parsley.

пету́нь|я (-и) *ж* petunia.

пету́х (-а́) *м* cock, rooster (*US*).

петуши́ный *прил* (*пение*) cocks'; **~ бой** cockfight; **~ го́лос** a squeaky voice.

пе|ть (пою́, поёшь; *pt* -л, -ла, -ло, *imper* по́й(те), *perf* **спеть**) *несов перех* to sing.

пехо́т|а (-ы) *ж* infantry.

пехо́т|инец (-ца) *м* infantryman (*мн* infantrymen).

пехо́тный *прил* infantry *опред*.

печа́лен *прил см* **печа́льный**.

печа́л|иться (-юсь, -ишься; *perf* **опеча́литься**) *несов возв* to be sad.

печа́л|ь (-и) *ж* (*грусть*) sadness, sorrow; **не́ было ~и!** (*разг*) what a nuisance!

печа́льно *нареч* (*петь, выглядеть*) sadly ◆ **как сказ** it's sad; **~, что мы не встре́тились** it's sad that we didn't meet; **~ изве́стный** notorious.

печа́льн|ый (-ен, -ьна, -ьно) *прил* sad; (*ошибка, судьба, память*) unhappy; **~ьная изве́стность** *или* **сла́ва** ill repute.

печа́та|ть (-ю; *perf* **напеча́тать**) *несов перех* (*также ФОТО*) to print; (*публиковать*) to publish; (*на пишущей машинке*) to type

▶ **печа́таться** (*perf* **напеча́таться**) *несов возв* to have one's work published.

печа́тающий (-ая, -ее, -ие) *прил*: **~ая голо́вка** (*КОМП*) printhead; **~ее колесо́** (*КОМП*) printwheel.

печа́т|ка (-ки; *gen pl* -ок) *ж* signet.

печа́тник (-а) *м* (*работник*) printer.

печа́тн|ый *прил* (*станок*) printing *опред*; (*цех*) print *опред*; (*интервью итп*) published; **писа́ть (написа́ть** *perf*) **~ыми бу́квами** to print; **печа́тные бу́квы** block letters; **печа́тный лист** (*единица измерения*) printer's sheet.

печа́ток *сущ см* **печа́тка**.

печа́т|ь (-и) *ж* stamp, seal; (*на дверях, на сейфе*) seal; (*издательское дело*) printing; (*след: страданий*) mark ◆ *собир* (*пресса*) press; **выходи́ть (вы́йти** *perf*) **из ~и** to come out, be published.

пе́чек *сущ см* **пе́чка**.

печён|ка (-ки; *gen pl* -ок) *ж* liver; **в ~х сиде́ть** (*impf*) **у кого́-н** (*разг*) to get on sb's nerves.

печёный *прил* baked.

пе́чен|ь (-и) *ж* (*АНАТ*) liver.

пе́чень|е (-я) *ср* biscuit (*BRIT*), cookie (*US*).

пе́ч|ка (-ки; *gen pl* -ек) *ж* stove.

печ|ь (-чи; *loc sg* -чи́, *gen pl* -е́й) *ж* stove; (*ТЕХ*) furnace; (: *обжиговая*) kiln; ◆ (-у́, -чёшь *итп*, -у́т; *pt* пёк, -кла́, -кло́, *perf* **испе́чь**) *несов перех* to bake; **микроволно́вая ~** microwave oven

▶ **пе́чься** (*perf* **испе́чься**) *несов возв* to bake; (*заботиться*): **пе́чься о +prp** to look after (*BRIT*), take care of (*US*).

пе́шек *сущ см* **пе́шка**.

пешехо́д (-а) *м* pedestrian.

пешехо́дный *прил* pedestrian *опред*; (*совершаемый пешком*) on foot; **пешехо́дный мост** footbridge.

пе́ш|ий (-ая, -ее, -ие) *прил* (*солдат*) foot *опред*; (*движение*) pedestrian *опред*; (*совершаемый пешком*) on foot; **~им хо́дом** on foot.

пе́ш|ка (-ки; *gen pl* -ек) *ж* (*также перен*) pawn.

пешко́м *нареч* on foot.

пеще́р|а (-ы) ж cave.
пеще́рный прил (живопись) cave опред; **пеще́рный челове́к** caveman (мн cavemen).
ПЗУ ср сокр (= постоя́нное запомина́ющее устро́йство) ROM (= read-only memory).
пиал|а́ (-ы́) ж handleless cup used in Central Asia.
пиани́но ср нескл (upright) piano.
пиани́ст (-а) м pianist.
пиани́ст|ка (-ки; gen pl -ок) ж см **пиани́ст**.
пивн|а́я (-о́й; decl like adj) ж ≈ bar, ≈ pub (BRIT).
пивно́й прил (бар, бочка) beer опред; (дрожжи) brewer's.
пи́в|о (-а) ср beer.
пи́галиц|а (-ы) ж (перен: пренебр) pipsqueak.
пигме́|й (-я) м pygmy.
пигме́нт (-а) м pigment.
пигмента́ци|я (-и) ж pigmentation.
пиджа́к (-а́) м jacket.
пижа́м|а (-ы) ж pyjamas мн.
пи́жм|а (-ы) ж (трава) feverfew; (дерево) wild rowan.
пижо́н (-а) м (разг: пренебр) pose(u)r.
пик (-а) м (также перен) peak ♦ прил неизм (часы, период, время) peak опред; **часы́ ~** (в работе транспорта) rush hour; (электростанции, телефона итп) peak period.
пи́к|а (-и) ж (рыцаря) lance; (солдата) pike; **в ~у кому́-н** to get at sb.
пика́нтный (-ен, -на, -но) прил (вкус) piquant; (случай, слухи) spicy; (женщина, внешность) alluring.
пике́т (-а) м picket.
пикети́р|овать (-ую) несов перех to picket.
пи́к|и (-) мн (в картах) spades мн.
пики́р|овать (-ую) (не)сов неперех (АВИА) to dive.
пикиро́вщик (-а) м (АВИА) dive-bomber.
пикни́к (-а́) м picnic.
пи́кн|уть (-у, -ешь) сов неперех (разг: животное) to let out a squeak; (: птица) to let out a squawk; **он при ней не сме́л и ~** he wouldn't dare speak out in her presence.
пи́ков|ый прил (наивысший) peak опред; (в картах) of spades; **~ое положе́ние** (разг) mess.
пи́ксел|ь (-я) м (КОМП) pixel.
пил итп несов см **пить**.
пил|а́ (-ы́; nom pl -ы) ж saw.
пилигри́м (-а) м pilgrim.
пили́к|ать (-ю) несов неперех (разг): **~ на** +prp (на скри́пке) to scrape away on.
пил|и́ть (-ю́, -ишь) несов перех to saw; (перен: разг) to nag.
пи́л|ка (-ки; gen pl -ок) ж nail file.
пиломатериа́л|ы (-ов) мн sawn timber ед.
пило́т (-а) м pilot; (СПОРТ) driver.
пилоти́р|овать (-ую) несов перех to pilot.

пило́т|ка (-ки; gen pl -ок) ж cloth cap worn as part of uniform.
пилю́л|я (-и) ж pill; **проглоти́ть** (perf) **~ю** (перен) to swallow a bitter pill.
пиля́стр|а (-ы) ж pilaster.
пина́|ть (-ю) несов перех to kick.
пингви́н (-а) м penguin.
пинг-по́нг (-а) м table tennis, ping-pong.
пине́т|ка (-ки; gen pl -ок) ж (обычно мн) bootee.
пин|о́к (-ка́) м kick.
пинце́т (-а) м (МЕД) tweezers мн; (ТЕХ) pincers мн.
пио́н (-а) м peony.
пионе́р (-а) м pioneer; (в СССР) member of Communist Youth organisation.
пипе́т|ка (-ки; gen pl -ок) ж pipette.
пир (-а; loc sg -у́, nom pl -ы́) м feast.
пирами́д|а (-ы) ж pyramid.
пира́т (-а) м pirate.
пира́тский (-ая, -ое, -ие) прил pirate опред.
Пирене́|и (-ев) мн Pyrenees.
пир|ова́ть (-у́ю) несов неперех to feast.
пиро́г (-а́) м pie.
пирожка́ итп сущ см **пирожо́к**.
пирожко́в|ая (-ой; decl like adj) ж (тип закусочной) snack-bar.
пиро́жн|ое (-ого; decl like adj) ср cake, sweet pastry.
пирож|о́к (-ка́) м (с мя́сом) pasty, pie; (с варе́ньем) turnover, tart.
пирс (-а) м pier.
пиру́эт (-а) м pirouette.
пи́ршеств|о (-а) ср feast.
писа́к|а (-и) м/ж (разг: пренебр) scribbler.
писа́ни|е (-я) ср (действие) writing; **Свяще́нное П~** Holy Scripture.
писани́н|а (-ы) ж (разг: пренебр) scribblings мн.
пи́сан|ый прил (разг): **она́ ~ая краса́вица** she is a picture of beauty ♦ (-ого; decl like adj) м: **говори́ть как по ~ому** to speak fluently.
пи́сар|ь (-я) м clerk.
писа́тел|ь (-я) м writer.
писа́тельниц|а (-ы) ж см **писа́тель**.
пи|са́ть (-шу́, -шешь; perf написа́ть) несов перех to write; (картину, пейзаж) to paint ♦ неперех (no perf; ребёнок, ученик) to be able to write; (ручка) to write; **он написа́л, как дое́хал/где устро́ился** he wrote to say he had arrived safely/where he was staying; **~ши пропа́ло** (разг) it is as good as lost
▶ **пи́саться** несов возв (слово) to be spelt или spelled; **как пи́шется э́то сло́во?** how do you spell this word?; **мне сего́дня не пи́шется** I don't feel like writing today.
пи́сем сущ см **письмо́**.
пис|е́ц (-ца́) м (ист) scribe.
писк (-а) м (ребёнка) squeak; (птицы) cheep.
пискли́вый прил (голос) squeaky.
пискля́вый прил = **пискли́вый**.

The spelling rules for Russian are shown on page xvii.

пи́скн|уть (**-у, -ешь**) *сов неперех* (*ребёнок,*
животное) to give a squeak; (*птица*) to give a
cheep.

пистоле́т (**-а**) *м* pistol.

писто́н (**-а**) *м* (*в патроне*) percussion cap.

писца́ *итп сущ см* **писе́ц**.

писчебума́жный *прил*: ~ **магази́н** stationer's.

пи́сч|ий (**-ая, -ее, -ие**) *прил* writing *опред*.

пи́сьменно *нареч* in writing.

пи́сьменность (**-и**) *ж* written language;
(*памятники*) literary texts *мн*.

пи́сьменн|ый *прил* (*просьба, экзамен*) written;
(*стол, прибор*) writing; **в ~ой фо́рме** in
writing.

письм|о́ (**-ьма́**; *nom pl* **-ьма, *gen pl* -ем**) *ср* letter;
(*no pl*; *иероглифическое, алфавитное*) script;
(*искусство: манера*) style.

пита́ни|е (**-я**) *ср* (*больного, ребёнка*) feeding;
(*ТЕХ*) supply; (*вегетарианское, плохое*) diet;
обще́ственное ~ public catering.

пита́тел|ьный *прил* (*соли, вещества*)
nutritious; (*крем, лосьон итп*) nourishing;
(*клапан, станция, насос*) supply *опред*; (**-ен,**
-ьна, -ьно; *каша, бульон*) filling; **пита́тельная**
среда́ (*БИО: перен*) breeding ground.

пита́|ть (**-ю**) *несов перех* (*кормить*) to feed;
(*снабжать*) to supply; (*перен: испытывать*) to
feel

▸ **пита́ться** *несов возв*: ~**ся** +*instr* (*человек,*
растение) to live on; (*животное*) to feed on;
(*ТЕХ*) to run on, use.

пито́м|ец (**-ца**) *м* (*воспитанник*) pupil.

пито́мник (**-а**) *м* (*БОТ*) nursery.

пито́мца *итп сущ см* **пито́мец**.

пито́н (**-а**) *м* python.

пи|ть (**пью, пьёшь**; *pt* **-л, -ла́, -ло,** *imper* **пе́й(те),**
perf **вы́пить**) *несов перех* to drink ♦ *неперех*: ~
за кого́-н/что-н to drink to sb/sth; **как ~ дать**
(*разг*) for sure.

питьев|о́й *прил*: ~**а́я вода́** drinking water.

пиха́|ть (**-ю**) *несов перех* (*разг: толкать*) to
shove; (*разг: засовывать*) to cram

▸ **пиха́ться** *несов возв* to push and shove (each
other).

пихн|у́ть (**-у́, -ёшь**) *сов перех* to give a shove;
(*сунуть*) to push.

пи́хт|а (**-ы**) *ж* fir (tree).

пи́цц|а (**-ы**) *ж* pizza.

пиццери́|я (**-и**) *ж* pizzeria.

пи́чка|ть (**-ю**; *perf* **напи́чкать**) *несов перех*
(*разг*): ~ **кого́-н чем-н** (*конфетами итп*) to
stuff sb with sth; (*лекарствами*) to pour sth
down sb's neck.

пишу́(сь) *итп несов см* **писа́ть(ся)**.

пи́шущ|ий (**-ая, -ее, -ие**) *прил*: ~**ая маши́нка**
typewriter.

пи́щ|а (**-и**) *ж* food; ~ **для размышле́ний** или **ума́**
food for thought; ~ **для воображе́ния** fuel to
the imagination.

пища́|ть (**-у́, -и́шь**) *несов неперех* (*птицы*) to
cheep; (*животные*) to squeak; (*ребёнок*) to cry.

пищебло́к (**-а**) *м* kitchen (*for catering*).

пищваре́ни|е (**-я**) *ср* digestion.

пищево́й *прил* food *опред*; (*соль*) edible;
пищева́я со́да baking soda.

пия́в|ка (**-ки**; *gen pl* **-ок**) *ж* leech.

ПК *м сокр* (= **персона́льный компью́тер**) PC (=
personal computer).

пл. *сокр* (= **пло́щадь**) Sq. (= *Square*).

плав (**-а**) *м*: **на ~у́** afloat.

пла́вани|е (**-я**) *ср* swimming; (*на судне*) sailing;
(*рейс*) voyage; **занима́ться** (*impf*) ~**м** to train as
a swimmer; **пла́вание бассе́йн** swimming pool.

пла́вательный *прил* swimming *опред*.

пла́ва|ть (**-ю**) *несов неперех* (*человек,*
животное) to swim; (*корабль*) to sail; (*лист,*
облако) to float; (*перен: на экзамене итп*) to be
out of one's depth; (*служить на судне*): ~ +*instr*
to work (at sea) as.

пла́вен *прил см* **пла́вный**.

пла́в|ить (**-лю, -ишь**; *perf* **распла́вить**) *несов*
перех to smelt

▸ **пла́виться** (*perf* **распла́виться**) *несов возв* to
smelt; (*стекло, пластмасса*) to melt.

пла́в|ка (**-ки**; *gen pl* **-ок**) *ж* (*действие*) smelting;
(*продукт*) smelt.

пла́в|ки (**-ок**) *мн* swimming trunks *мн*.

плавле́ни|е (**-я**) *ср*: **температу́ра** или **то́чка ~я**
melting point.

пла́вленый *прил*: ~ **сыр** processed cheese.

пла́влю(сь) *несов см* **пла́вить(ся)**.

плавни́к (**-а́**) *м* (*у рыб*) fin; (*у водных*
животных) flipper.

пла́вн|ый (**-ен, -на, -но**) *прил* smooth.

пла́вок *сущ см* **пла́вка, пла́вки**.

плаву́ч|ий (**-ая, -ее, -ие**) *прил* floating;
плаву́чая ба́за (*в рыболовстве*) *floating unit*
for storing and processing fish.

плагиа́т (**-а**) *м* plagiarism.

плагиа́тор (**-а**) *м* plagiarist.

пла́зм|а (**-ы**) *ж* plasma.

плака́т (**-а**) *м* poster.

пла́ка|ть (**-чу, -чешь**) *несов неперех* to cry,
weep; ~ (*impf*) **от** +*gen* (*от боли итп*) to cry
from; (*от радости*) to cry with; (*от горя*) to
cry in; ~**кал мой выходно́й** (*разг*) so much for
my day off; ~**кали мои́ де́ньги** (*разг*) that's my
money up the spout; **па́лка по нему́ ~чет** (*разг*)
he's asking for a beating

▸ **пла́каться** *несов возв* (*разг*): ~**ся (на** +*acc*)
(*на судьбу, на участь*) to moan (about).

плакир|ова́ть (**-у́ю**) (*не*)*сов перех* (*ТЕХ*) to
plate.

пла́кс|а (**-ы**) *м/ж* crybaby.

плаку́ч|ий (**-ая, -ее, -ие**) *прил*: ~**ая и́ва** weeping
willow.

пла́мени *итп сущ см* **пла́мя**.

пла́менный *прил* (*цвета пламени*) flame-
coloured (*BRIT*), flame-colored (*US*); (*горячий*)
burning; (*перен: страстный*) ardent.

пла́м|я (**-ени**; *как* **вре́мя**; *см* **Table 4**) *ср* flame.

план (**-а**) *м* plan; (*чертёж*) plan, map; **кру́пный**

~ (КИНО, ФОТО) close-up; **пла́ны на бу́дущее**
future plans; **пере́дний** ~ foreground; **за́дний** ~
background; **на пе́рвом пла́не у неё учёба** her
priority is studying; **в теорети́ческом пла́не** in
theory; **отходи́ть (отойти́** *perf*) *или* **отступа́ть**
(**отступи́ть** *perf*) **на второ́й** ~ to become less
important.
планёр (-а) *м* glider.
планери́зм (-а) *м* gliding.
плане́т|а (-ы) *ж* planet.
планета́ри|й (-я) *м* planetarium.
плани́ровани|е (-я) *ср* planning.
плани́р|овать (-ую) *несов перех* to plan; (АВИА)
to glide; (*perf* **заплани́ровать**; **намерева́ться**)
to plan.
планиров|а́ть (-у́ю); *perf* **распланирова́ть**)
несов перех to lay out.
планиро́в|ка (-и) *ж* (*участка, кварти́ры*)
layout.
планиро́вщик (-а) *м* planner.
пла́н|ка (-ки; *gen pl* -ок) *ж* (*деревя́нная*) strip of
wood; (*металли́ческая*) strip of metal.
планкто́н (-а) *м* plankton.
планови́к (-а́) *м* planner.
пла́новый *прил* (*зада́ние, проду́кция*) planned;
(*отде́л, коми́ссия*) planning.
пла́нок *сущ см* **пла́нка**.
планоме́р|ный (-ен, -на, -но) *прил* systematic.
планта́ци|я (-и) *ж* plantation.
планше́т (-а) *м* mapcase.
пласт (-а́) *м* (*также перен*) stratum (*мн* strata).
пла́стик (-а) *м* = **пластма́сса**.
пла́стик|а (-и) *ж* (*скульпту́ра*) the plastic arts
мн; (*гармо́ния*) grace; (*бале́тная*) eurhythmics;
(МЕД) plastic surgery.
пластили́н (-а) *м* plasticine.
пласти́н|а (-ы) *ж* (ГЕО) plate.
пласти́н|ка (-ки; *gen pl* -ок) *ж* (*уменьш от*
пласти́на; (МУЗ) record; **долгоигра́ющая** ~
album, L.P. (= *long-playing record*).
пласти́чен *прил см* **пласти́чный**.
пласти́ческ|ий (-ая, -ое, -ие) *прил* plastic
опред; **пласти́ческая ма́сса** plastic;
пласти́ческая опера́ция (МЕД) plastic surgery.
пласти́чный (-ен, -на, -но) *прил* (*же́сты,
движе́ния*) graceful; (*материа́лы, вещества́*)
plastic *опред*.
пластма́сс|а (-ы) *ж сокр* (= **пласти́ческая
ма́сса**) plastic.
пласту́нск|ий (-ая, -ое, -ие) *прил*: **ползти́
по**-~ to crawl on one's belly.
пла́стыр|ь (-я) *м* (МЕД) plaster.
пла́т|а (-ы) *ж* (*за труд, за услу́ги*) pay, salary; (*за
кварти́ру*) payment; (*за прое́зд*) fee; (*перен:
награ́да, ка́ра*) reward; **за́работная** ~ wages
мн.
плата́н (-а) *м* plane (tree).
платёж (-ежа́) *м* payment; **нало́женным** ~**ежо́м**

cash on delivery.
платёжеспосо́бен *прил см*
платёжеспосо́бный.
платёжеспосо́бност|ь (-и) *ж* solvency.
платёжеспосо́б|ный (-ен, -на, -но) *прил*
(КОММ) solvent.
платёж|ный *прил* (КОММ): ~ **бланк** payslip; ~**ая
ве́домость** payroll; ~**ое поруче́ние** *или*
тре́бование payment order.
пла́тин|а (-ы) *ж* platinum.
пла|ти́ть (-чу́, -тишь; *perf* **заплати́ть** *или*
уплати́ть) *несов перех* to pay; (*перен*): ~
чем-н за что-н to repay sth with sth; ~
(**заплати́ть** *или* **уплати́ть** *perf*) **нали́чными/
нату́рой** to pay in cash/in kind.
▶ **плати́ться** (*perf* **поплати́ться**) *несов возв*:
~**ся чем-н за что-н** to pay for sth with sth.
платка́ *итп сущ см* **плато́к**.
пла́т|ный *прил* (*вход, стоя́нка*) chargeable;
(*шко́ла*) fee-paying; (*больни́ца*) private.
плато́ *ср нескл* plateau.
плат|о́к (-ка́) *м* (*головно́й*) headscarf (*мн*
headscarves); (*наплечны́й*) shawl; (*также*:
носово́й ~) handkerchief.
платфо́рм|а (-ы) *ж* platform; (*ма́ленькая
ста́нция*) halt; (*откры́тый ваго́н*) open goods
truck; (*основа́ние*) foundation.
пла́ть|е (-я; *gen pl* -ев) *ср* dress ◆ *собир* (*оде́жда*)
clothing, clothes *мн*.
плафо́н (-а) *м* decorated ceiling; (*абажу́р*) shade
(*for ceiling light*).
пла́х|а (-и; *ист*) (executioner's) block.
плац (-а; *loc sg* -у́) *м* (ВОЕН) parade ground.
плацда́рм (-а) *м* (ВОЕН) bridgehead.
плаце́нт|а (-ы) *ж* placenta.
плацка́р|тный *прил*: ~ **ваго́н** *railway car with
open berths instead of compartments*.
плач (-а) *м* crying.
плаче́в|ный (-ен, -на, -но) *прил* (*бе́дственный*)
lamentable; (*жа́лкий*) pitiful.
пла́чу(сь) *итп несов см* **пла́кать(ся)**.
плачу́(сь) *несов см* **плати́ть(ся)**.
плашмя́ *нареч* flat.
плащ (-а́) *м* cloak; (*пальто́*) raincoat.
плащани́ц|а (-ы) *ж* (РЕЛ) the shroud of Christ.
плащ-пала́т|ка (-ки; *gen pl* -ок) *ж* (ВОЕН)
waterproof cape.
плебе́|й (-я) *м* plebeian.
плебе́йск|ий (-ая, -ое, -ие) *прил* plebeian
опред.
пл|ева́ть (-юю́) *несов неперех* to spit; (*perf*
наплева́ть; *перен*): ~ **на** +*acc* (*разг: на
пра́вила, на мне́ние други́х*) to not give a damn
about; ~ (*impf*) **в потоло́к** (*разг*) to loaf (about)
▶ **плева́ться** *несов возв* to spit.
плев|о́к (-ка́) *м* spit, spittle.
плеври́т (-а) *м* pleurisy.
плёвый *прил*: (э́то) ~**ое де́ло** (*разг*) it's a piece

of cake.

плед (-а) *м* (tartan) rug.

плéйер (-а) *м* Walkman®.

плёл *итп несов см* **плестú**.

плéмени *итп сущ см* **плéмя**.

племеннóй *прил* (*язык, территория*) tribal; (*с.-х.: скот*) purebred; (*хозяйство, животноводство*) (pure-strain) stockbreeding *опред*; **племеннóй бык** pedigree bull; **племеннáя лóшадь** thoroughbred (horse).

плéм|я (-ени; *как* **врéмя**; *см* **Table 4**) *ср* (*также перен*) tribe; **молодóе ~** the younger generation.

племя́нник (-а) *м* nephew.

племя́нниц|а (-ы) *ж* niece.

плен (-а; *loc sg* -ý) *м* captivity; **брать (взять** *perf*) **когó-н в ~** to take sb prisoner; **попадáть (попáсть** *perf*) **в ~** to be taken prisoner.

пленáрный *прил* plenary.

пленúтел|ьный (-ен, -ьна, -ьно) *прил* captivating, charming.

пленúть (-ю́, -úшь; *impf* **пленя́ть**) *сов перех* (*очаровывать*) to captivate, charm.

плёнк|а (-и; *gen pl* -ок) *ж* (*также* ФОТО) film; (*кожица*) film, membrane; (*магнитофонная*) tape; **запúсывать (записáть** *perf*) **чтó-н на ~ку** to record sth (on tape).

плéнн|ая (-ой; *decl like adj*) *ж см* **плéнный**.

плéнник (-а) *м* (*пленный*) prisoner, captive.

плéнниц|а (-ы) *ж см* **плéнник**.

плéнн|ый *прил* captive *опред* ♦ (-ого; *decl like adj*) *м* prisoner, captive.

плёнок *сущ см* **плёнка**.

плéнум (-а) *м* plenum.

пленя́ть (-ю) *несов от* **пленúть**.

плéсен|ь (-и) *ж* mould (*BRIT*), mold (*US*).

плеск (-а) *м* splash.

пле|скáть (-щý, -щешь) *несов неперех* to splash; (*слегка*) to lap.

▶ **плескáться** *несов возв* to splash; (*волны: слегка*) to lap.

плéснев|еть (*3sg* -ет, *3pl* -ют, *perf* **заплéсневеть**) *несов неперех* to go mouldy (*BRIT*) *или* moldy (*US*).

пл|естú (-етý, -етёшь; *pt* -ёл, -елá, -елó, *perf* **сплестú**) *несов перех* (*сети*) to weave; (*венок, волосы*) to plait; (*глупости*) to spout; **~ (*impf*) интрúги** *или* **кóзни** to weave a web of intrigue; **~ (*impf*) небылúцы** (*разг*) to spin yarns

▶ **плестúсь** *несов возв* (*разг: человек: медленно идти*) to trudge, plod.

плетёный *прил* (*корзина, мебель*) wicker; (*сандалии*) woven.

плетéн|ь (-ня́) *м* wattle fence.

плéт|ка (-ки; *gen pl* -ок) *ж* whip.

плетня́ *итп сущ см* **плетéнь**.

плéток *сущ см* **плётка**.

плету́(сь) *итп несов см* **плестú(сь)**.

плéт|ь (-и; *gen pl* -éй) *ж* whip.

плéчик|и (-ов) *мн* (*вешалка*) coat hangers *мн*; (*подкладки*) shoulder pads *мн*.

плечúст|ый (-, -а, -о) *прил* broad-shouldered.

плеч|ó (-á; *nom pl* -и) *ср* shoulder; **~м к ~ý** shoulder to shoulder; **э́то мне не по ~ý** I am not up to it; **за ~áми у негó 5 лет учёбы** he has 5 years of study behind him *или* under his belt; **с чужóго ~á** (*одежда*) second-hand; **вы́нести** *perf* **чтó-н на свои́х ~áх** to carry sth on one's shoulders.

плешúв|ый (-, -а, -о) *прил* bald.

плеш|ь (-и) *ж* bald patch.

плéщет(ся) *итп несов см* **плескáть(ся)**.

плещу́сь *итп несов см* **плескáться**.

плея́д|а (-ы) *ж* (*учёных, музыкантов итп*) galaxy.

Плúмут (-а) *м* Plymouth.

плúнтус (-а) *м* skirting board (*BRIT*), baseboard (*US*).

плиссé *ср нескл* pleats *мн* ♦ *прил неизм*: **ю́бка/плáтье ~** pleated skirt/dress.

плит|á (-ы́; *nom pl* -ы) *ж* (*каменная*) slab; (*металлическая*) plate; (*печь*) cooker, stove.

плúт|ка (-ки; *gen pl* -ок) *ж* (*керамическая, кафельная*) tile; (*шоколада*) bar; (*электрическая*) hot plate; (*газовая*) camping stove.

плов (-а) *м* pilaff.

пловéц (-цá) *м* swimmer.

пловчú|ха (-и) *ж см* **пловéц**.

плод (-á) *м* (БОТ) fruit; (БИО) foetus (*BRIT*), fetus (*US*); **~ +gen** (*перен*) fruits of.

плод|úться (*3sg* -úтся, *3pl* -я́тся, *perf* **расплодúться**) *несов возв* (*также перен*) to multiply.

плодовúт|ый (-, -а, -о) *прил* fertile; (*перен*) prolific.

плодовóдств|о (-а) *ср* fruit-growing.

плодорóд|ный (-ен, -на, -но) *прил* fertile.

плодотвóр|ный (-ен, -на, -но) *прил* fruitful.

плóмб|а (-ы) *ж* (*в зубе*) filling; (*на дверях, на сейфе*) seal.

пломбúр (-а) *м rich creamy ice-cream*.

пломбир|овáть (-ую; *perf* **запломбировáть**) *несов перех* (*зуб*) to fill; (*perf* **опломбировáть**; *дверь, сейф*) to seal.

плóск|ий (-ая, -ое, -ие; -ок, -á, -ко) *прил* flat; (*перен: неоригинальный*) feeble.

плоскогу́бц|ы (-ев) *мн* pliers *мн*.

плóскост|ь (-и; *gen pl* -éй) *ж* (*также перен*) plane.

плóсок *прил см* **плóский**.

плот (-á; *loc sg* -ý) *м* raft.

плóт|ен *прил см* **плóтный**.

плотú|на (-ы) *ж* dam.

плóтник (-а) *м* carpenter.

плóтно *нареч* (*закрыть дверь*) tightly; (*пообедать*) well.

плóтност|ь (-и) *ж* density.

плóт|ный (-ен, -нá, -но) *прил* (*дым, туман*) dense, thick; (*население, толпа, лес*) dense; (*бумага, кожа*) thick; (*тело, человек*) thick-set; (*завтрак, обед*) substantial.

плотоя́д|ный (-ен, -на, -но) *прил* carnivorous; (*перен*) lustful.

пло́тск|ий (-ая, -ое, -ие) *прил* (*желания*) carnal.

пло́ттер (-а) *м* (*комп*) plotter.

плот|ь (-и) *ж* flesh; ~ **и кровь** flesh and blood; **а́нгел/дья́вол во ~й** angel/devil incarnate.

пло́хо *нареч* (*учиться, работать*) badly ♦ *как сказ* it's bad ♦ *ср нескл* (*ПРОСВЕЩ*) ≈ poor (*school mark*); **без друзе́й** ~ it's bad not to have friends; **мне** ~ I feel bad; **в го́роде** ~ **с хле́бом** there's a shortage of bread in the town; **у меня́** ~ **с деньга́ми** I am short of money.

плох|о́й (-а́я, -о́е, -и́е; -, -а́, -о) *прил* bad; **мать ста́ла** ~**а́** mother is in a bad way.

площа́д|ка (-ки; *gen pl* -ок) *ж* (*детская*) playground; (*спортивная*) ground; (*строительная*) site; (*часть вагона*) corridor; **ле́стничная** ~ landing; **поса́дочная** ~ landing pad.

пло́щад|ь (-и; *gen pl* -е́й) *ж* (*место*) square; (*пространство, также МАТ*) area; (*разг: также: жила́я* ~) living space.

пло́ще *сравн прил от* **пло́ский**.

плуг (-а; *nom pl* -и́) *м* plough (*BRIT*), plow (*US*).

плут (-а́) *м* (*мошенник*) cheat; (*хитрец*) rogue.

плута́|ть (-ю) *несов неперех* (*разг*) to wander.

плутова́|ть (-ю; *perf* **сплутова́ть**) *несов неперех* to cheat.

Плуто́н (-а) *м* Pluto.

плуто́ний (-я) *м* plutonium.

плы|ть (-ву́, -вёшь; *pt* -л, -ла́, -ло) *несов неперех* (*человек, животное*) to swim; (*судно*) to sail; (*лист, облако*) to float.

плюга́в|ый (-, -а, -о) *прил* (*разг: пренебр*) wimpish.

плю́н|уть (-у, -ешь) *сов неперех* to spit; ~ (*perf*) **на что-н** (*разг*) to stop bothering about sth; **плюнь!** (*разг*) forget it!; **э́то мне раз** ~ (*разг*) it's a doddle (for me).

плюрали́зм (-а) *м* pluralism.

плюралисти́ческ|ий (-ая, -ое, -ие) *прил* pluralist(ic).

плюс *м нескл, союз* plus ♦ *м* (*разг: преимущество*) plus (*мн* plusses); **два** ~ **два – четы́ре** two plus two is four; ~**-ми́нус 2см** plus or minus *или* give or take 2cm.

плю́хн|уться (-усь, -ешься; *impf* **плю́хаться**) *сов возв* (*человек*) to flop down.

плюш (-а) *м* plush.

плю́ш|ка (-ки; *gen pl* -ек) *ж* bun.

плющ (-а́) *м* ivy.

плю́щ|ить (-у, -ишь; *perf* **сплю́щить**) *несов перех* to flatten.

пляж (-а) *м* beach.

пля|са́ть (-шу́, -шешь; *perf* **спляса́ть**) *несов перех* to dance.

пля́с|ка (-ки; *gen pl* -ок) *ж* dance.

пляшу́ *итп несов см* **пляса́ть**.

пневмати́ческ|ий (-ая, -ое, -ие) *прил* pneumatic.

пневмони́|я (-и) *ж* pneumonia.

Пномпе́н|ь (-я) *м* Pnomh Penh.

пн|уть (-у, -ёшь) *сов перех* (*разг*) to boot.

пня *итп сущ см* **пень**.

ПО *ср сокр* = *произво́дственное объедине́ние*.

KEYWORD

по *предл* (+*dat*) **1** (*о месте действия, вдоль*) along; **де́вочка идёт по у́лице** the little girl is walking along the street; **по берега́м расту́т кусты́** bushes grow along the banks; **ло́дка плывёт по реке́** the boat is sailing on the river; **спуска́ться (спусти́ться** *perf*) **по ле́стнице** to go down the stairs

2 (*при глаголах движения*) round; **ходи́ть** (*impf*) **по ко́мнате/са́ду** to walk round the room/garden; **путеше́ствовать** (*impf*) **по стране́** to travel round the country; **плыть** (*impf*) **по тече́нию** to go downstream; (*перен*) to swim with the tide; **идти́** (*impf*) **по ве́тру** to sail with the wind

3 (*об объекте воздействия*) on; **уда́рить** (*impf*) **кого́-н по плечу́/лицу́** to hit on the shoulder/face; **уда́рить** (*impf*) **по врагу́/по контрабанди́стам** to deal a blow to the enemy/to the smugglers

4 (*в соответствии с*): **де́йствовать по зако́ну/пра́вилу** to act in accordance to the law/the rules; **по расписа́нию/пла́ну** according to schedule/plan; **он ушёл по со́бственному жела́нию** he left voluntarily; **получа́ть (получи́ть** *perf*) **де́ньги по счёту** to receive payment of a bill

5 (*об основании*): **суди́ть по вне́шности** to judge by appearances; **жени́ться** (*impf/perf*) **по любви́** to marry for love

6 (*вследствие*) due to; **отсу́тствовать** (*impf*) **по боле́зни** to be absent due to illness; **по невнима́тельности** due to carelessness; **по необходи́мости** out of necessity

7 (*посредством*): **говори́ть по телефо́ну** to speak on the phone; **отправля́ть (отпра́вить** *perf*) **что-н по по́чте** to send sth by post; **передава́ть (переда́ть** *perf*) **что-н по ра́дио/по телеви́дению** to broadcast sth on radio/television

8 (*с целью, для*): **рабо́та по повыше́нию эффекти́вности** work towards increased efficiency; **о́рганы по борьбе́ с престу́пностью** organizations in the fight against crime; **опера́ция по захва́ту моста́** an operation to seize the bridge; **я позва́л тебя́ по де́лу** I called on you on business

9 (*о какой-н характеристике объекта*) in; **по интере́сам/до́лжности** in interests/position; **по профе́ссии** by profession; **дед по ма́тери** maternal grandfather; **това́рищ по шко́ле**

---

school friend
10 (*о сфере де́ятельности*) in; **заня́тия по литерату́ре** studies in literature; **иссле́дование по хи́мии** research in chemistry
11 (*о ме́ре вре́мени*): **по вечера́м/утра́м** in the evenings/mornings; **по воскресе́ньям/пя́тницам** on Sundays/Fridays; **я рабо́таю по це́лым дням** I work all day long; **рабо́та рассчи́тана по мину́там** the work is planned by the minute
12 (*о едини́чности предме́тов*): **ма́ма дала́ всем по я́блоку** Mum gave them each an apple; **мы купи́ли по одно́й кни́ге** we bought a book each
♦ *предл* (+*acc*) **1** (*вплоть до*) up to; **стоя́ть** (*impf*) **по по́яс в воде́** to stand up to the waist in water; **по настоя́щее вре́мя** up to the present time; **с пе́рвой по пя́тую главу́** from the first to (*BRIT*) *или* through (*US*) the fifth chapter; **я за́нят по го́рло** (*разг: перен*) I am up to my eyes in work; **он по́ уши в неё влюблён** he is head over heels in love with her
2 (*при обозначе́нии цены́*): **по два/три рубля́ за шту́ку** two/three roubles each
3 (*при обозначе́нии коли́чества*): **по два/три челове́ка** in twos/threes
♦ *предл* (+*prp*; *по́сле*) on; **по оконча́нии рабо́ты** on finishing work; **по прие́зде** on arrival.

по- *пре́фикс* (*in verbs*; *о нача́ле де́йствия*) *indicating the beginning of an action eg.* побежа́ть; (*об ограни́ченном де́йствии*) *indicating limitation of an action eg.* поговори́ть; (*о преры́вистом де́йствии*) *indicating action carried out at intervals eg.* погля́дывать; (*о де́йствии, соверша́ем мно́гими*) *indicating action undertaken by many people eg.* повскака́ть; (*in adjectives and adverbs*; *о неинтенси́вном ка́честве*) *indicating non-intensive quality of sth eg.* помя́гче; (*подо́бно чем-н*) *indicating comparison with sth eg.* по-но́вому.
п/о *сокр* = **почто́вое отделе́ние**; **произво́дственное объедине́ние**.
по-англи́йски *нареч* in English; **как ~ э́то сло́во?** what is this word in English?
побагрове́ть (-ю) *сов от* багрове́ть.
поба́иваться (-юсь) *несов возв*: ~ +*gen* to be a bit frightened of.
поба́ливать (*3sg* -ет, *3pl* -ют) *несов неперех* (*разг: иногда́*) to ache now and again; (: *слегка́*) to hurt a bit.
побе́г (-а) *м* (*из тюрьмы́*) escape; (*БОТ*) shoot, sprout.
побегу́ *итп сов см* побежа́ть.
побегу́шки *мн* (*разг*): **быть на ~ах у кого́-н** to run errands for sb; (*перен*) to be at sb's beck and call.
побе́д|а (-ы) *ж* victory; **оде́рживать** (**одержа́ть** *perf*) **~у над кем-н/чем-н** to win a victory over

sb/sth.
победи́тел|ь (-я) *м* (*в войне́*) victor; (*в состяза́нии*) winner.
победи́тельниц|а (-ы) *ж см* победи́тель.
победи́ть (*2sg* -и́шь, *3sg* -и́т, *impf* побежда́ть) *сов перех* to defeat ♦ *неперех* to win.
побе́дный *прил* victorious, triumphant; (*марш, салю́т*) victory *опред*.
победоно́сный (-ен, -на, -но) *прил* (*а́рмия, ата́ка*) victorious; (*перен: вид, слова́*) triumphant.
побежа́ть (*как* бежа́ть; *см* Table 20) *сов неперех* (*челове́к, живо́тное*) to start running; (*дни, го́ды*) to start to fly by; (*ручьи́, слёзы*) to begin to flow.
побежда́ть (-ю) *несов от* победи́ть.
побежи́шь *итп сов см* побежа́ть.
побеле́ть (-ю) *сов от* беле́ть.
побели́ть (-ю́, -и́шь) *сов от* бели́ть.
побе́лк|а (-и) *ж* whitewash; (*де́йствие*) whitewashing.
поберёг(ся) *итп сов см* побере́чь(ся).
побережёт(сь) *итп сов см* побере́чь(ся).
побере́жь|е (-я) *ср* coast.
побере́|чь (-гу́, -жёшь *итп*, -гу́т; *pt* -ёг, -гла́, -гло́) *сов перех* (*де́ньги, вре́мя*) to save; (*здоро́вье, мать*) to take care of, look after
▸ **побере́чься** *сов возв* to take care of o.s.
побесе́довать (-ую) *сов неперех* to have a chat.
побеспоко́|ить (-ю, -ишь) *сов перех* to disturb, bother; **позво́льте Вас ~** may I trouble you?; ~ (*perf*) **кого́-н прие́здом** to inconvenience sb by one's arrival
▸ **побеспоко́иться** *сов возв* (*проя́вить забо́ту*) to concern o.s.
поб|и́ть (-ью́, -ьёшь) *сов от* бить ♦ *перех* (*повреди́ть*) to destroy; (*переби́ть*) to kill; (*разби́ть*) to break; (*impf* побива́ть, *СПОРТ*) to beat; **побива́ть** (~ *perf*) **реко́рд** to break a record.
поблагодар|и́ть (-ю́, -и́шь) *сов от* благодари́ть.
побла́ж|ка (-ки; *gen pl* -ек) *ж* (*разг*) indulgence.
побледне́ть (-ю) *сов от* бледне́ть.
поблёк|нуть (-ну, -нешь; *pt* -, -ла, -ло) *сов от* блёкнуть.
поблизости *нареч* nearby ♦ *предл*: ~ **от** +*gen* near (to), close to.
побо́|и (-ев) *мн* beating *ед*.
побо́рник (-а) *м* champion (*of cause*).
побо́рниц|а (-ы) *ж см* побо́рник.
побор|о́ть (-ю́, -орешь) *сов перех* (*также перен*) to overcome.
побо́р|ы (-ов) *мн* (*ИСТ*) taxes *мн*, levies *мн*.
побо́чный (-ен, -на, -но) *прил* (*проду́кт, реа́кция*) secondary; ~ **эффе́кт** side effect.
побо|я́ться (-ю́сь, -и́шься) *сов от* боя́ться ♦ *возв*: **побо́йся Бо́га!** (*разг*) have a heart!
побрати́м (-а) *м*: **города́-~ы** twin towns *или* cities.

побреду́ *итп сов см* **побрести́.**

побре́зга|ть (-ю) *сов от* **брезговать.**

побре́зг|овать (-ую) *сов от* **бре́зговать.**

побр|ести́ (-еду́, -едёшь; *pt* -ёл, -ела́, -ело́) *сов непepex* to trudge.

побри́ть(ся) (-е́ю(сь), -е́ешь(ся)) *сов от* **бри́ть(ся).**

поброса́|ть (-ю) *сов переx* (*вещи*) to throw about.

побряку́ш|ка (-ки; *gen pl* -ек) *ж* (*обычно мн*) trinket.

побуди́|ть (-ужу́, -у́дишь; *impf* **побужда́ть**) *сов переx*: ~ кого́-н к чему́-н/+*infin* to prompt sb (in)to sth/to do.

побу́ду *итп сов см* **побы́ть.**

побужда́|ть (-ю) *несов от* **побуди́ть.**

побужде́ни|е (-я) *ср* (*действие*) prompting; (*стремление*) motive.

побужу́ *сов см* **побуди́ть.**

побыва́|ть (-ю) *сов непepex*: ~ в Áфрике/у роди́телей to visit Africa/one's parents.

поб|ы́ть (*как* **быть**; *см* **Table 21**) *сов непepex* to stay.

побью́ *итп сов см* **побить.**

пова́|диться (-жусь, -дишься) *сов непepex*: ~ +*infin* to get into the way of doing.

пова́д|ка (-ки; *gen pl* -ок) *ж* (*разг*) way.

пова́жусь *сов см* **пова́диться.**

пова́лен *прил см* **пова́льный.**

пов|али́ть (-алю́, -а́лишь) *сов от* **вали́ть** ♦ *непepex* (*снег, град*) to begin to fall; (*толпа*) to come pouring in

▶ **повали́ться** *сов от* **вали́ться.**

пова́л|ьный (-ен, -ьна, -ьно) *прил* mass.

по́вар (-а; *nom pl* -á) *м* cook.

пова́ренн|ый *прил*: ~ая кни́га cookery (*BRIT*) *или* cook (*US*) book; ~ая соль table salt.

повари́х|а (-и) *ж см* **по́вар.**

пове́да|ть (-ю) *сов* (*не)переx*: ~ что-н *или* о чём-н кому́-н to tell sb sth.

поведе́ни|е (-я) *ср* behaviour (*BRIT*), behavior (*US*).

поведу́(сь) *итп сов см* **повести́(сь).**

повез|ти́ (-у́, -ёшь; *pt* -ёз, -езла́, -езло́) *сов от* **везти́** ♦ *переx* to take.

повели́тельн|ый (-ен, -ьна, -ьно) *прил* imperious; **повели́тельное наклоне́ние** (*линг*) imperative mood.

повенча́|ть (-ю) *сов от* **венча́ть.**

поверг|ну́ть (-у, -ешь; *impf* **поверга́ть**) *сов переx* (*перен: врага*) to conquer; **поверга́ть** (~ *perf*) **кого́-н в** +*acc* (*в отча́яние, в уны́ние итп*) to plunge sb into.

пове́ренн|ый (-ого; *decl like adj*) *м*: ~ в дела́х chargé d'affaires; **прися́жный** ~ (*ИСТ*) barrister (*in tsarist Russia*).

пове́р|ить (-ю, -ишь) *сов от* **ве́рить** ♦ (*impf* **поверя́ть**) *переx*: ~ что-н кому́-н to confide sth

to sb

▶ **пове́риться** *сов от* **ве́риться.**

пове́рк|а (-и) *ж* (*перекли́чка*) rollcall; **на ~у** in fact.

поверн|у́ть (-у́, -ёшь; *impf* **повора́чивать**) *сов* (*не)переx* to turn

▶ **поверну́ться** (*impf* **повора́чиваться**) *сов возе* to turn; **де́ло ~у́лось к лу́чшему/ ху́дшему** things took a turn for the better/worse; **у меня́ язы́к не ~ётся сказа́ть э́то** (*разг*) I wouldn't have the guts to say that; ~**ся не́где** there isn't even room to turn round.

пове́рх *предл* (+*gen*) over.

пове́рхностн|ый *прил* surface *опред*; (-ен, -на, -но; *перен*) superficial.

пове́рхност|ь (-и) *ж* surface; **лежа́ть** (*impf*) **на ~и** to be perfectly obvious.

пове́рь|е (-я; *gen pl* -ий) *ср* (popular) belief.

поверя́|ть (-ю) *несов от* **пове́рить.**

повесел|е́ть (-ю) *сов от* **веселе́ть.**

пове́|сить(ся) (-шу(сь), -сишь(ся)) *сов от* **ве́шать(ся).**

повествова́ни|е (-я) *ср* narrative.

повеств|ова́ть (-у́ю) *несов непepex*: ~ о +*prp* (*роман итп*) to tell (the story) of.

пов|ести́ (-еду́, -едёшь; *pt* -ёл, -ла́, -ло́) *сов переx* (*начать вести́: человека*) to take; (: *войска*) to lead; (*машину, поезд*) to drive; (*войну, сле́дствие итп*) to begin ♦ (*impf* **поводи́ть**) *непepex*: ~ +*instr* (*бровью*) to raise; (*плечом*) shrug; (*perf*) **себя́ наха́льно** to start to behave impudently; **он и бро́вью не ~ёл** (*разг*) he didn't bat an eyelid

▶ **повести́сь** *сов возе* (*войти́ в обыкнове́ние*) to become the custom; ~**сь** (*perf*) **с кем-н** to become friends with sb.

пове́ст|ка (-ки; *gen pl* -ок) *ж* summons (*мн* summonses); (*также:* ~ **дня**) agenda.

по́вест|ь (-и) *ж* story.

пове́три|е (-я) *ср* tendency.

пове́шени|е (-я) *ср* hanging; **сме́ртная казнь че́рез** ~ sentence of death by hanging.

пове́шу(сь) *сов см* **пове́сить(ся).**

пове́|ять (3*sg* -ет, 3*pl* -ют) *сов безл* (+*instr*): ~**яло прохла́дой/све́жестью** there was a breath of cool/fresh air; ~**яло свобо́дой/ сча́стьем** there was a feeling of freedom/ happiness in the air.

повздо́р|ить (-ю, -ишь) *сов от* **вздо́рить.**

повзросл|е́ть (-ю) *сов от* **взросле́ть.**

повида́|ть(ся) (-ю(сь)) *сов от* **вида́ть(ся).**

по-ви́димому *вводн сл* apparently.

пови́дл|о (-а) *ср* jam (*BRIT*), jelly (*US*).

пови́нн|ая (-ой; *decl like adj*) *ж* confession; **яви́ться** (*perf*) *или* **прийти́** (*perf*) **с ~ой** to give o.s. up.

пови́нност|ь (-и) *ж* duty; **во́инская** ~ conscription.

пови́н|ный (-ен, -на, -но) *прил* guilty.
повин|ова́ться (-у́юсь) *сов возв* (+*dat*) to obey.
повинове́ни|е (-я) *ср* obedience.
пови́с|нуть (-ну, -нешь; *pt* -, -ла, -ло, *impf* **повиса́ть**) *сов неперех* to hang; (*тучи*) to hang motionless; (*птица, вертолёт*) to hover.
повл|е́чь (-еку́, -ечёшь *итп*, -еку́т; *pt* -ёк, -екла́, -екло́) *сов от* **влечь**.
по́в|од (-ода; *loc sg* -оду́, *nom pl* -о́дья, *gen pl* -ьев) *м* (*лошади*) rein; (*nom pl* -оды; *причина*) reason ◆ *предл*: по ~у +*gen* regarding, concerning; **дава́ть** (**дать** *perf*) **кому́-н ~ для чего́-н** to give sb cause for sth; **идти́** (*impf*) *или* **быть** (*impf*) **на поводу́ у кого́-н** to be under sb's thumb.
пов|оди́ть (-ожу́, -о́дишь) *несов от* **повести́** ◆ *перех* (*водить недолго*) to walk.
повод|о́к (-ка́) *м* lead, leash.
пово́дья *итп сущ см* **по́вод**.
повожу́ *сов см* **поводи́ть**.
пово́з|ка (-ки; *gen pl* -ок) *ж* cart.
поволо́к|а (-и) *ж* shroud, haze.
повора́чива|ть (-ю) *несов от* **поверну́ть**
▶ **повора́чиваться** *несов от* **поверну́ться** ◆ *возв* (*разг: быстро действовать*) to get a move on.
поворо́т (-а) *м* (*действие*) turning; (*место*) bend, turn; (*перен*) turning point.
поворо́тлив|ый (-, -а, -о) *прил* (*человек*) agile, nimble.
поворо́тный *прил* (*тех*) revolving; **~ пункт** *или* **моме́нт** (*перен*) turning point; **~ день** crucial day; **поворо́тный круг** turntable.
повре|ди́ть (-жу́, -ди́шь) *сов от* **вреди́ть** ◆ (*impf* **поврежда́ть**) *перех* (*поранить*) to injure; (*поломать*) to damage.
поврежде́ни|е (-я) *ср* (*см глаг*) injury; damage.
повре́жу *сов см* **повреди́ть**.
повремен|и́ть (-ю́, -и́шь) *сов неперех*: **~ с чем-н** to delay sth a little; **~** (*perf*) **с отве́том** to wait a little before answering.
повре́менный *прил*: **повре́менная опла́та** payment by the hour.
повседне́вен *прил см* **повседне́вный**.
повседне́вность (-и) *ж* everyday routine.
повседне́в|ный (-ен, -на, -но) *прил* everyday; (*занятия, встречи*) daily.
повсеме́ст|ный (-ен, -на, -но) *прил* widespread.
повск|ака́ть (*3sg* -а́чет, *3pl* -а́чут) *сов неперех* (*разг*) to jump up.
повстреча́|ть (-ю) *сов перех* (*разг*) to bump into
▶ **повстреча́ться** *сов возв* (*разг*): **~ся с кем-н** to bump into sb.
повсю́ду *нареч* everywhere.
по-вся́кому *нареч* in different ways.
повто́рен *прил см* **повто́рный**.
повторе́ни|е (-я) *ср* repetition.
повтор|и́ть (-ю́, -и́шь; *impf* **повторя́ть**) *сов перех* to repeat

▶ **повтори́ться** (*impf* **повторя́ться**) *сов возв* (*ситуация*) to repeat itself; (*болезнь*) to recur.
повто́р|ный (-ен, -на, -но) *прил* repeated.
повторя́|ть(ся) (-ю(сь)) *несов от* **повтори́ть(ся)**.
повы́|сить (-шу, -сишь; *impf* **повыша́ть**) *сов перех* to increase; (*интерес*) to heighten; (*качество, культуру*) to improve; (*работника*) to promote; **повыша́ть** (**~** *perf*) **кого́-н в обще́ственном мне́нии** to raise sb in the opinion of the public; **повыша́ть** (**~** *perf*) **го́лос** to raise one's voice
▶ **повы́ситься** (*impf* **повыша́ться**) *сов возв* to increase; (*интерес*) to heighten; (*качество, культура*) to improve.
повы́шенный *прил* (*спрос*) increased; (*интерес, чувствительность*) heightened; (*качество*) improved; **повы́шенное давле́ние** high blood pressure.
повы́шу(сь) *сов см* **повы́сить(ся)**.
повя|за́ть (-жу́, -жешь; *impf* **повя́зывать**) *сов перех* to tie.
повя́з|ка (-ки; *gen pl* -ок) *ж* bandage; (*стерильная*) dressing; **ги́псовая ~** plaster.
повя́зыва|ть (-ю) *несов от* **повяза́ть**.
погада́|ть (-ю) *сов от* **гада́ть**.
пога́н|ить (-ю, -ишь; *perf* **опога́нить**) *несов перех* (*разг*) to mess up.
пога́н|ка (-ки; *gen pl* -ок) *ж* toadstool.
пога́ный *прил* (*разг: отвратительный*) lousy; **~ гриб** toadstool.
пога́с *итп сов см* **пога́снуть**.
пог|аси́ть (-ашу́, -а́сишь) *сов от* **гаси́ть** ◆ (*impf* **погаша́ть**) *перех* (*задолженность, вексель,*) to pay (off).
пога́с|нуть (-ну, -нешь; *pt* -, -ла, -ло) *сов от* **га́снуть**.
погаша́|ть (-ю) *несов от* **погаси́ть**.
погаше́ни|е (-я) *ср*: **срок ~я** (*комм*) maturity date.
погашу́ *сов см* **погаси́ть**.
поги́б *итп сов см* **поги́бнуть**.
погиба́|ть (-ю) *несов от* **поги́бнуть**.
поги́бель (-и) *ж*: **согну́ться в три ~и** (*разг*) to bend double.
поги́б|нуть (-ну, -нешь; *pt* -, -ла, -ло) *сов от* **ги́бнуть**.
поги́бш|ий (-его; *decl like adj*) *м* dead person; **~ие** the dead.
погла́|дить (-жу, -дишь) *сов от* **гла́дить**.
погл|оти́ть (-ощу́, -о́тишь; *impf* **поглоща́ть**) *сов перех* to absorb; (*средства, время*) to take up; (*: усилия*) to demand.
поглоще́ни|е (-я) *ср*: **попы́тка ~я** (*комм*) takeover bid.
поглощу́ *сов см* **поглоти́ть**.
поглупе́|ть (-ю) *сов от* **глупе́ть**.
погля|де́ть (-жу́, -ди́шь) *сов от* **гляде́ть**.
погля́дыва|ть (-ю) *несов неперех* (*разг*) to have *или* take a squint.
погляжу́ *сов см* **погляде́ть**.

пог|на́ть (-оню́, -о́нишь) *сов перех* (*стадо, лошадь*) to drive; (*машину, поезд*) to drive fast
▸ **погна́ться** *сов возв*: ~ся за кем-н/чем-н (*также перен*) to set off in pursuit of sb/sth.
погнуша́|ться (-юсь) *несов от* **гнуша́ться**.
погова́рива|ть (-ю) *несов неперех*: ~ о +*prp* to talk about; ~ют, что ... they say that ....
погово́р|ка (-ки; *gen pl* -ок) *ж* saying.
пого́д|а (-ы) *ж* weather; э́то не де́лает ~у it doesn't make a lot of difference.
пого|ди́ть (-жу́, -ди́шь) *сов неперех*: ~ с +*instr* (*разг: подождать*) to take one's time with; немно́го ~дя́ after a while; ~ди́! (*угроза*) just you wait!
пого́дный *прил* weather *опред*.
пого́ж|ий (-ая, -ее, -ие; -, -а, -е) *прил* fine.
погожу́ *сов см* **погоди́ть**.
пого́ло́вный *прил* (*всеобщий*) general.
поголо́вь|е (-я) *ср* (*скота, лошадей*) total number.
поголубе́|ть (-ю) *сов от* **голубе́ть**.
пого́н (-а) *м* (*обычно мн*) (shoulder) stripe.
пого́нщик (-а) *м* (cattle) driver.
погоню́(сь) *итп сов см* **погна́ть(ся)**.
пого́н|я (-и) *ж*: ~ за +*instr* (*также перен*) pursuit of ◆ *собир* (*преследователи*) pursuers *мн*; в ~е за +*instr* in pursuit of.
погоня́|ть (-ю) *несов перех* (*лошадь, скот*) to drive; (*перен: разг*): ~ кого́-н to hurry sb up.
погор|е́ть (-ю́, -и́шь; *impf* **погора́ть**) *сов неперех* to lose everything (*in a fire*); **погора́ть** (~ *perf*) на взя́тках/кра́же (*разг*) to be caught taking bribes/stealing.
погоряч|и́ться (-у́сь, -и́шься) *сов возв* to get worked up.
погранзаста́в|а (-ы) *ж сокр* (= *пограни́чная заста́ва*) frontier post.
пограни́чник (-а) *м* frontier *или* border guard.
пограни́чный *прил* (*город, район*) frontier *опред*, border *опред*; (*конфликт, знак*) border *опред*.
по́греб (-а; *nom pl* -а́) *м* cellar; ви́нный ~ wine cellar.
погреба́льный *прил* funeral *опред*.
погребе́ни|е (-я) *ср* (*похороны*) burial, interment; (*могила*) grave.
погрему́ш|ка (-ки; *gen pl* -ек) *ж* rattle.
погре́|ть (-ю; *impf* **погрева́ть**) *сов перех* to warm up
▸ **погре́ться** *сов возв* to warm up.
погреш|и́ть (-у́, -и́шь) *сов от* **греши́ть**.
погре́шность (-и) *ж* error, mistake.
погро|зи́ть (-жу́, -зи́шь) *сов от* **грози́ть**.
погро́м (-а) *м* pogrom; (*разг: беспорядок*) chaos.
погруб|е́ть (-ю) *сов от* **грубе́ть**.
погр|узи́ть (-ужу́, -у́зишь) *сов перех от* **грузи́ть** ◆ *перех*: (-ужу́, -узи́шь; *impf*

погружа́ть; ~ что-н в +*acc*) to immerse sth in
▸ **погру|зи́ться** *сов от* **грузи́ться** ◆ (*impf* **погружа́ться**) *возв* (*человек*) to immerse o.s.; (*предмет*) to sink; **погружа́ться** (~ся *perf*) в +*acc* (*в сон, в апатию*) to sink into; **погружа́ться** (~ся *perf*) в размышле́ния to be deep in thought.
погру́з|ка (-ки; *gen pl* -ок) *ж* loading.
погру́зочный *прил* (*машина*) loading *опред*; ~ые рабо́ты loading.
погры́з|ться (-у́сь, -ёшься) *несов от* **гры́зться**.
погря́зн|уть (-у, -ешь; *impf* **погряза́ть**) *сов неперех*: ~ в +*prp* (*в грязи*) to get stuck in; (*в долгах, во лжи*) to sink into; (*в разврате*) to wallow in.
погуб|и́ть (-ублю́, -у́бишь) *сов от* **губи́ть**.
погуля́|ть (-ю) *сов от* **гуля́ть**.
погусте́|ть (-ю) *сов от* **густе́ть**.

┌─────────┐
│ KEYWORD │
└─────────┘
под *предл* (+*acc*) **1** (*в направлении ниже*) under; я положи́л су́мку под стол I put the bag under the table; **идти́** (*impf*) **под го́ру** to go downhill
2 (*поддерживая снизу*) by; **брать (взять** *perf*) **кого́-н под руку** to take sb by the arm
3 (*указывает на положение, состояние*) under; **под контро́ль/наблюде́ние** under control/ observation; **отдава́ть (отда́ть** *perf*) **кого́-н под суд** to prosecute sb; **попада́ть (попа́сть** *perf*) **под дождь** to be caught in the rain
4 (*близко к*): **под у́тро/ве́чер** towards morning/ evening; **под пра́здники** coming up to the holidays; **под ста́рость** approaching old age
5 (*указывает на функцию*) as; **мы приспосо́били помеще́ние под магази́н** we fitted out the premises as a shop
6 (*в виде чего-н*): **ва́за под хруста́ль** an imitation crystal vase; **сте́ны под мра́мор** marble-effect walls
7 (*в обмен на*) on; **брать (взять** *perf*) **что-н под зало́г/че́стное сло́во** to take sth on security/ trust
8 (*в сопровождении*): **под роя́ль/скри́пку** to the piano/violin; **мне э́то не под си́лу** that is beyond my powers
◆ *предл* (+*instr*) **1** (*ниже чего-н: о расположении*) under; **чемода́н под столо́м** the suitcase is under the table
2 (*около*) near; **под Петербу́ргом** near St. Petersburg; **под бо́ком у кого́-н** very near to sb; **под но́сом у кого́-н** under sb's nose; **под руко́й** to hand, at hand
3 (*об условиях существования объекта*) under; **быть** (*impf*) **под наблюде́нием/аре́стом** to be under observation/arrest; **под назва́нием, под и́менем** under the name of
4 (*вследствие*) under; **под влия́нием/ тя́жестью чего-н** under the influence/weight of

sth; **понима́ть** *(impf)*/**подразумева́ть** *(impf)* **под чем-н** to understand/imply by sth.

под- *префикс (in verbs; о движении снизу вверх) indicating movement upwards eg.* **подбро́сить**; *(о действии, содержащемся внизу) indicating movement below sth eg.* **подби́ть**; *(приближение) indicating movement towards eg.* **подбежа́ть**; *(добавление) indicating addition to sth eg.* **подли́ть**; *(ослабленная степень действия) indicating non-intensive quality of sth eg.* **подкра́сить**; *(тайное действие) indicating undercover nature of sth eg.* **подслу́шать**; *(in adjectives; расположенный ниже какой-нибудь поверхности)* under-; *(находящийся в ведении) indicating supervision of sth eg.* **поднадзо́рный**; *(in nouns; часть чего-н)* sub-; *(ниже по званию) indicating lower position or rank eg.* **подмасте́рье**.

пода|ва́ть(ся) (-ю́(сь)) *несов от* **пода́ть(ся)**.
пода|ви́ть (-авлю́, -а́вишь; *impf* **подавля́ть)** *сов перех* to suppress; **подави́ть (~** *perf*) **кого́-н чем-н** to intimidate sb with sth
▸ **подави́ться** *сов от* **дави́ться**.
подавле́ни|е (-я) *ср (восстания)* suppression.
пода́вленност|ь (-и) *ж* depression.
пода́вленный *прил (настроение, состояние, человек)* depressed; *(смех, стон)* suppressed.
подавлю́(сь) *сов см* **подави́ть(ся)**.
подавля́|ть (-ю) *несов от* **подави́ть**.
подавля́|ющий (-ая, -ее, -ие) *прил* overwhelming.
пода́вно *нареч:* **он бога́т, а она́ и ~** *(разг)* he is rich and she is even more so; **е́сли я не могу́ э́то сде́лать, то ты и ~** *(разг)* if I can't do this, then you certainly can't.
пода́м(ся) *итп сов см* **пода́ть(ся)**.
пода|ри́ть (-арю́, -а́ришь) *сов от* **дари́ть**.
пода́р|ок (-ка) *м* gift, present.
пода́рочный *прил (магазин итп)* gift *опред*.
пода́ст(ся) *сов см* **пода́ть(ся)**.
пода́тлив|ый (-, -а, -о) *прил* pliable; *(тело)* supple.
по́дат|ь (-и) *ж (ИСТ)* tax.
пода́|ть (как дать; *см* **Table 14;** *impf* **подава́ть)** *сов перех* to give; *(еду)* to serve up; *(поезд, такси итп)* to bring; *(заявление, жалобу итп)* to submit; *(СПОРТ: в теннисе)* to serve; *(: в футболе)* to pass; **подава́ть (~** *perf*) **что-н кому́-н** to give sth to sb, give sb sth; *(еду)* to serve sb up with sth; **подава́ть (~** *perf*) **го́лос за** +*acc* to cast a vote for; **подава́ть (~** *perf*) **иде́ю** to put forward an idea; **подава́ть (~** *perf*) **ре́плику** to make a comment; **подава́ть (~** *perf*) **в отста́вку** to hand in *или* submit one's resignation; **подава́ть (~** *perf*) **на кого́-н в суд** to take sb to court; **подава́ть (~** *perf*) **кому́-н ру́ку** *(при встрече)* to give sb one's hand; *(в трудной ситуации)* to give sb a hand; **подава́ть (~** *perf*) **кому́-н пальто́** to help sb into

their coat
▸ **пода́ться** *(impf* **подава́ться)** *сов возв (сдвинуться)* to give way; *(разг: уехать)* to make tracks.
пода́ч|а (-и) *ж (действие: заявления, прошения)* submission; *(: обеда)* serving up; *(СПОРТ: в теннисе)* serve; *(: в футболе)* pass.
пода́ч|ка (-ки; *gen pl* **-ек)** *ж (собаке)* scraps *мн*; *(человеку)* hand-out.
пода́шь(ся) *сов см* **пода́ть(ся)**.
подая́ни|е (-я) *ср* alms *мн*.
подба́в|ить (-лю, -ишь; *impf* **подбавля́ть)** *сов перех* to add.
подба́дрива|ть (-ю) *несов от* **подбодри́ть**.
подбежа́ть (как бежа́ть; *см* **Table 20;** *impf* **подбега́ть)** *сов неперех* to run up.
подберёзовик (-а) *м (БОТ)* shaggy boletus.
подберу́(сь) *итп сов см* **подобра́ть(ся)**.
подбива́|ть (-ю) *несов от* **подби́ть**.
подбира́|ть(ся) (-ю(сь)) *несов от* **подобра́ть(ся)**.
подби́ть (-обью́, -обьёшь; *impf* **подбива́ть)** *сов перех (птицу, самолёт)* to shoot down; *(глаз, крыло)* to injure; **подбива́ть (~** *perf*) **каблуки́ на** +*prp* to reheel.
подбодр|и́ть (-ю́, -и́шь; *impf* **подба́дривать)** *сов перех* to cheer up.
подбо́р (-а) *м* selection; *(собрание)* collection; **как на ~** *all alike and all the very best*.
подбо́рк|а (-и) *ж (журнальная)* collection of articles on one general theme.
подборо́д|ок (-ка) *м* chin.
подбро́|сить (-шу, -сишь; *impf* **подбра́сывать)** *сов перех (мяч, шар, камень итп)* to toss; *(+acc или +gen; добавить)* to put; *(тайно подложить: анонимку)* to leave; *(: ворованный товар, наркотик)* to plant; *(разг: подвезти)* to give a lift.
подва́л (-а) *м* cellar; *(для жилья)* basement.
подва́льный *прил (помещение)* basement *опред*; **подва́льный эта́ж** basement.
подведу́ *итп сов см* **подвести́**.
подведе́ни|е (-я) *ср (линии электропередачи)* connecting; **подведе́ние ито́гов** summing-up.
подве|зти́ (-зу́, -зёшь; *pt* **-ёз, -езла́, -езло́,** *impf* **подвози́ть)** *сов перех (машину, товар)* to take up; *(человека)* to give a lift.
подве́рг|нуть (-ну, -нешь; *pt* **-, -ла, -ло,** *impf* **подверга́ть)** *сов перех:* **~ кого́-н/что-н чему́-н** to subject sb/sth to sth; **подверга́ть (~** *perf*) **кого́-н ри́ску/опа́сности** to put sb at risk/in danger
▸ **подве́ргнуться** *(impf* **подверга́ться)** *сов возв:* **~ся** +*dat* to be subjected to.
подве́рженный (-, -а, -о) *прил:* **~** +*dat (дурному влиянию)* subject to; *(простуде)* susceptible to.
подверн|у́ть (-у́, -ёшь; *impf* **подвора́чивать)** *сов перех (сделать короче)* to turn up; **подвора́чивать (~** *perf*) **но́гу** to turn *или* twist one's ankle

▶ **подверну́ться** (*impf* **подвора́чиваться**) *сов возв* (*разг: попасться*) to turn up; **мне ~у́лась по́д руку интере́сная кни́га** I came across an interesting book; **у меня́ нога́ ~у́лась** I've twisted my ankle.

подве́|сить (**-шу, -сишь**; *impf* **подве́шивать**) *сов перех* to hang up.

подве́с|ка (**-ки**; *gen pl* **-ок**) *ж* pendant.

подвесно́й *прил* (*в висячем положении*) hanging *опред*; **подвесно́й мост** suspension bridge.

подве́сок *сущ см* **подве́ска**.

подве|сти́ (**-еду́, -еде́шь**; *pt* **-ёл, -ела́, -ело́**, *impf* **подводи́ть**) *сов перех*: **~ к** +*dat* (*человека*) to bring up to; (*машину*) to drive up to; (*поезд*) to bring into; (*корабль*) to sail up to; (*электричество*) to bring to; (*доро́гу*) to link to; (*разочаровать*) to let down; **подводи́ть** (**~** *perf*) **глаза́/гу́бы** to put eyeliner/lipstick on; **подводи́ть** (**~** *perf*) **ито́ги** to sum up.

подве́шива|ть (**-ю**) *несов от* **подве́сить**.

подве́шу *сов см* **подве́сить**.

по́двиг (**-а**) *м* exploit.

подвига́|ть(ся) (**-ю(сь)**) *несов от* **подви́нуть(ся)**.

подви́жен *прил см* **подви́жный**.

подви́жник (**-а**) *м* devotee.

подвижно́й *прил*: **~ соста́в** (*на желе́зной доро́ге*) rolling stock.

подви́ж|ный (**-ен, -на, -но**) *прил* (*человек, живо́тное*) agile; (*no short form*; *войска́, конта́кт*) mobile.

подви́|нуть (**-у, -ешь**; *impf* **подвига́ть**) *сов перех* (*передви́нуть: человека, предмет*) to move; (*перен: работу, дело*) to push ahead with.

▶ **подви́|нуться** (*impf* **подвига́ться**) *сов возв* (*человек*) to move.

подвла́ст|ный (**-ен, -на, -но**) *прил*: **~** +*dat* (*зако́ну*) subject to; (*президенту*) under the control of.

подво́д|а (**-ы**) *ж* cart.

подво|ди́ть (**-ожу́, -о́дишь**) *несов от* **подвести́**.

подво́дник (**-а**) *м* (*моряк*) submariner; (*водола́з*) diver.

подво́дный *прил* (*расте́ние, рабо́ты*) underwater *опред*; **подво́дная ло́дка** submarine; **подво́дное тече́ние** undercurrent.

подвожу́ *сов см* **подводи́ть**.

подво|зи́ть (**-ожу́, -о́зишь**) *несов от* **подвезти́**.

подвора́чива|ть (**-ю**) *несов от* **подверну́ть**.

подворо́т|ня (**-ни**; *gen pl* **-ен**) *ж* passage(way).

подво́х (**-а**) *м* (*разг: лову́шка*) catch.

подвя|за́ть (**-жу́, -жешь**; *impf* **подвя́зывать**) *сов перех* to tie.

подгиба́|ть(ся) (**-ю(сь)**) *несов от* **подогну́ть(ся)**.

подгля|де́ть (**-жу́, -ди́шь**; *impf* **подгля́дывать**)

сов перех to peep through.

подговор|и́ть (**-ю́, -и́шь**; *impf* **подгова́ривать**) *сов перех*: **~ кого́-н на что-н**/+*infin* to put sb up to sth/to doing.

подгоню́ *итп сов см* **подогна́ть**.

подгоня́|ть (**-ю**) *несов от* **подогна́ть**.

подгор|е́ть (*3sg* **-и́т**, *3pl* **-я́т**, *impf* **подгора́ть**) *сов непepex* (*мясо, пирог*) to burn slightly.

подгота́влива|ть(ся) (**-ю(сь)**) *несов от* **подгото́вить(ся)**.

подготови́тельный *прил* (*предвари́тельный*) preparatory; **подготови́тельный класс** (*в нача́льной шко́ле*) reception.

подгото́в|ить (**-лю, -ишь**; *impf* **подгота́вливать**) *сов перех* to prepare.

▶ **подгото́в|иться** (*impf* **подгота́вливаться**) *сов возв* to prepare (o.s.).

подгото́в|ка (**-и**) *ж* (*к экза́мену, к отъе́зду*) preparation; (*запас зна́ний, уме́ний*) training.

подгото́влю(сь) *сов см* **подгото́вить(ся)**.

подгу́зник (**-а**) *м* nappy (*BRIT*), diaper (*US*).

подда|ва́ться (**-ю́сь**) *несов от* **подда́ться** ♦ *возв*: **не ~ сравне́нию/описа́нию** to be beyond comparison/words.

поддади́мся *итп сов см* **подда́ться**.

подда́кива|ть (**-ю**) *несов непepex*: **~** +*dat* (*разг*) to agree with.

подда́мся *сов см* **подда́ться**.

по́дданн|ая (**-ой**; *decl like adj*) *ж см* **по́дданный**.

по́дданн|ый (**-ого**; *decl like adj*) *м* subject, citizen.

по́дданств|о (**-а**) *ср* nationality, citizenship.

подда́ться (*как* **дать**; *см* **Table 14**; *impf* **поддава́ться**) *сов возв* (*дверь итп*) to give way; **поддава́ться** (**~** *perf*) +*dat* (*па́нике*) to give way to; (*влия́нию, собла́зну*) to give in to; **поддава́ться** (**~** *perf*) +*dat или* **на** +*acc* (*на про́сьбы*) to give in to.

поддева́|ть (**-ю**) *несов от* **подде́ть**.

подде́ла|ть (**-ю**; *impf* **подде́лывать**) *сов перех* to forge.

▶ **подде́ла|ться** (*impf* **подде́лываться**) *сов возв*: **~ся под** +*acc* to imitate.

подде́л|ка (**-ки**; *gen pl* **-ок**) *ж* forgery.

подде́лыва|ть(ся) (**-ю(сь)**) *несов от* **подде́лать(ся)**.

подде́льный *прил* (*докуме́нт*) forged; (*ра́дость, гостеприи́мство*) feigned.

подде́ну *итп сов см* **подде́ть**.

поддер|жа́ть (**-жу́, -жишь**; *impf* **подде́рживать**) *сов перех* to support; (*па́дающего*) to hold on to; (*выступле́ние, предложе́ние итп*) to second; (*бесе́ду*) to keep up.

подде́ржива|ть (**-ю**) *несов от* **поддержа́ть** ♦ *перех* to support; (*перепи́ску*) to keep up; (*поря́док, отноше́ния*) to maintain.

подде́ржк|а (**-и**) *ж* support.

подде́|ть (-ну, -нешь; *impf* **поддева́ть**) *сов перех* (*приподнять*) to prise (*BRIT*) *или* prize (*US*) off; (*перен: разг*) to gibe at; **поддева́ть** (~ *perf*) **сви́тер под ку́ртку** to put on a sweater under(neath) one's jacket; **поддева́ть** (~ *perf*) **крючко́м** to hook.

поддо́н (-а) *м* (*для грузов*) pallet; (*для жидкости*) tray.

поддува́л|о (-а) *ср* damper.

подева́|ть(ся) (-ю(сь)) *сов от* **дева́ть(ся)**.

поде́йств|овать (-ую) *сов от* **де́йствовать**.

поде́ла|ть (-ю) *сов перех* (*разг*) to do; ~**ешь, ничего́ не** ~**ешь, ничего́ нельзя́** ~ (*разг*) it can't be helped.

поде|ли́ть(ся) (-елю́(сь), -е́лишь(ся)) *сов от* **дели́ть(ся)**.

поде́л|ка (-ки; *gen pl* -ок) *ж any kind of handmade craft.*

подело́м *нареч*: ~ **ему́** it serves him right.

подёргива|ться (-юсь) *несов от* **подёрнуться ♦** *возв* (*лицо*) to twitch.

поде́ржанный *прил* (*одежда, мебель итп*) second-hand.

подёрн|уться (*3sg* -ется, *3pl* -утся, *impf* **подёргиваться**) *сов возв*: ~ +*instr* (*покрыться*) to be covered with; **у него́ во́лосы** ~**улись седино́й** he had a lot of grey hair.

подеру́сь *итп сов см* **подра́ться**.

подешеве́|ть (-ю) *сов от* **дешеве́ть**.

поджа́рист|ый (-, -а, -о) *прил* (*мясо*) well-done; (*картошка, пирожок*) crisp.

поджа́р|ый (-, -а, -о) *прил* lean.

поджа́|ть (-ожму́, -ожмёшь; *impf* **поджима́ть**) *сов перех* (*губы*) to purse; (*живот*) to pull in; **поджима́ть** (~ *perf*) **но́ги под себя́** to tuck one's legs under o.s.; **поджима́ть** (~ *perf*) **коле́ни** to pull one's knees up.

поджелу́дочн|ый *прил*: ~**ая железа́** pancreas.

поджё|чь (-жгу́, -жжёшь *итп*, -жгу́т; *impf* **поджига́ть**) *сов перех* to set fire to.

поджига́тел|ь (-я) *м* arsonist.

поджига́|ть (-ю) *несов от* **подже́чь**.

поджида́|ть (-ю) *несов перех* to wait for.

поджима́|ть (-ю) *несов от* **поджа́ть ♦** *перех* (*разг*): **нас**~**ют сро́ки** we are working to a tight deadline.

поджо́г (-а) *м* arson.

подзаголо́в|ок (-ка) *м* subheading.

подзаты́льник (-а) *м* (*разг*) clip round the ear.

подзащи́тн|ая (-ой; *decl like adj*) *ж* (*ЮР*) *см* **подзащи́тный**.

подзащи́тн|ый (-ого; *decl like adj*) *м* (*ЮР*) client.

подземе́л|ье (-ья; *gen pl* -ий) *ср* (*комната*) vault; (*проход*) underground passage; (*ряд помещений*) catacombs *мн*.

подзе́мный *прил* underground.

подзову́ *итп сов см* **подозва́ть**.

подзо́рн|ый *прил*: ~**ая труба́** telescope.

подзыва́|ть (-ю) *несов от* **подозва́ть**.

подй *сов* (*разг*) go **♦** *вводн сл* (*наверное*) probably.

подира́|ть (*3sg* -ет) *несов безл*: **у меня́ моро́з по ко́же** ~**ет от э́того** (*разг*) it makes my skin crawl *или* my flesh creep.

подка́лыва|ть (-ю) *несов от* **подколо́ть**.

подка́пыва|ться (-юсь) *несов от* **подкопа́ться**.

подкарау́л|ить (-ю, -ишь; *impf* **подкарау́ливать**) *сов перех* (*разг*) to lie in wait for.

подка́рмлива|ть (-ю) *несов от* **подкорми́ть**.

подкати́ть (-ачу́, -а́тишь; *impf* **подка́тывать**) *сов перех* (*что-н круглое*) to roll; (*что-н на колёсах*) to wheel **♦** *неперех* (*машина, экипаж*) to race up.

подкача́|ть (-ю) *сов (не)перех* (*разг*) to fail.

подкачу́ *сов см* **подкати́ть**.

подка́шива|ть(ся) (-ю(сь)) *несов от* **подкоси́ть(ся)**.

подки́дыва|ть (-ю) *несов от* **подки́нуть**.

подки́дыш (-а) *м* abandoned baby.

подки́н|уть (-у, -ешь; *impf* **подки́дывать**) *сов перех* (*кинуть вверх*) to toss; (+*acc или* +*gen*; *добавить*) to put; (*тайно подложить*: *анонимку*) to leave; (: *ворованный товар, наркотик*) to plant; **подки́дывать** (~ *perf*) **кому́-н де́нег** (*разг*) to give sb a sub; **подки́дывать** (~ *perf*) **кого́-н** (*разг*) to give sb a lift.

подкла́д|ка (-ки; *gen pl* -ок) *ж* lining.

подкла́дыва|ть (-ю) *несов от* **подложи́ть**.

подкле́|ить (-ю, -ишь; *impf* **подкле́ивать**) *сов перех* to stick together.

подключ|и́ть (-у́, -и́шь; *impf* **подключа́ть**) *сов перех* (*телефон*) to connect; (*лампу*) to plug in; (*специалистов*) to involve; **подключа́ть** (~ *perf*) **к систе́ме/центра́льной се́ти** (*КОМП*) to network, hook up to the main network

▶ **подключи́ться** (*impf* **подключа́ться**) *сов возв* to get involved.

подко́в|а (-ы) *ж* (*лошадь итп*) shoe.

подкова́ть (-ую́) *сов от* **кова́ть ♦** (*impf* **подко́вывать**) *перех* (*лошади итп*) to shoe.

подкол|о́ть (-олю́, -о́лешь; *impf* **подка́лывать**) *сов перех* (*скрепить*) to pin up; (*разг: уязвить*) to taunt; **подка́лывать** (~ *perf*) **докуме́нт к де́лу** to file a document.

подко́п (-а) *м* (*ход*) secret underground passage.

подкопа́|ться (-юсь; *impf* **подка́пываться**) *сов возв*: ~ **под** +*acc* (*под здание*) to tunnel under; (*разг: под начальника итп*) to undermine.

подкорм|и́ть (-ормлю́, -о́рмишь; *impf* **подка́рмливать**) *сов перех* (*животных*) to fatten up; (*ребёнка, больного*) to feed up.

подкос|и́ть (-ошу́, -о́сишь; *impf* **подка́шивать**) *сов перех* (*подлеж: удар, пуля*) to fell; (*несчастье*) to devastate; (*усталость*) to overcome

▶ **подкоси́ться** (*impf* **подка́шиваться**) *сов возв*: **у него́ но́ги/коле́ни** ~**оси́лись** his legs/ knees gave way.

подкра́|сться (-ду́сь, -дёшься; *impf*

подкрáдываться) *сов возв* to sneak *или* steal up.

подкреп|и́ть (-лю́, -и́шь; *impf* **подкрепля́ть**) *сов перех* (*стену, крышу*) to support; (*мысли, утверждение*) to support, back up

▸ **подкрепи́ться** (*impf* **подкрепля́ться**) *несов возв* to fortify o.s.

подкрепле́ни|е (-я) *ср* (*ВОЕН*) reinforcement.

подкреплю́(сь) *сов см* **подкрепи́ть(ся)**.

подкрепля́|ть(ся) (-ю(сь)) *несов от* **подкрепи́ть(ся)**.

пóдкуп (-а) *м* bribery.

подк|упи́ть (-уплю́, -у́пишь; *impf* **подкупа́ть**) *сов перех* to bribe; (*перен: добротой*) to win over.

подлá|мываться (*3sg* -ется, *3pl* -ются) *несов от* **подломи́ться**.

пóдле *нареч* (*рядом*) nearby ♦ *предл* (+*gen*) beside, next to.

подлежа́ть (*3sg* -и́т, *3pl* -áт) *несов неперех*: ~ +*dat* (*проверке, обложению налогом*) to be subject to; **пригово́р не** ~**и́т обжа́лованию** (*ЮР*) the sentence is not open to appeal; **э́то не** ~**и́т сомне́нию** there can be no doubt about that.

подлежа́щее (-его; *decl like adj*) *ср* (*ЛИНГ*) subject.

подле|те́ть (-чу́, -ти́шь; *impf* **подлета́ть**) *сов неперех* (*самолёт*) to fly in; (*птица*) to fly up; (*разг: человек*) to race up.

подле́ц (-á) *м* scoundrel.

подл|ечи́ть (-ечу́, -е́чишь; *impf* **подле́чивать**) *сов перех* to treat

▸ **подлечи́ться** (*impf* **подле́чиваться**) *сов возв* to undergo a short course of treatment.

подлечу́ *сов см* **подлете́ть**.

подлива́|ть (-ю) *несов от* **подли́ть**.

подли́в|ка (-ки; *gen pl* -ок) *ж* (*КУЛИН*) sauce.

подли́з|а (-ы) *ж* crawler.

подли́зыва|ться (-юсь; *perf* **подлиза́ться**) *несов возв*: ~ **к** +*dat* (*разг*) to crawl to.

пóдлинен *прил см* **пóдлинный**.

пóдлинник (-а) *м* original.

пóдлин|ный (-ен, -на, -но) *прил* original; (*документ*) authentic; (*no short form; герой, друг*) true.

под|ли́ть (-олью́, -ольёшь; *pt* -ли́л, -лила́, -ли́ло, *impf* **подлива́ть**) *сов перех* to add; **подлива́ть** (~ *perf*) **вина́ в стака́н** to top up a glass with wine; **подлива́ть** (~ *perf*) **мáсла в огóнь** to add fuel to the fire *или* flames.

пóдло *нареч* (*поступить*) meanly ♦ *как сказ* it's mean.

подлóг (-а) *м* forgery.

подлóжен *прил см* **подлóжный**.

подл|ожи́ть (-ожу́, -óжишь; *impf* **подкла́дывать**) *сов перех* (*анонимку*) to leave; (*ворованный товар*) to plant; (+*acc или* +*gen*;

добавить) to put; (*дров, сахара*) to add; **подкла́дывать** (~ *perf*) **что-н под что-н** to put sth under sth.

подлóж|ный (-ен, -на, -но) *прил* forged.

подлокóтник (-а) *м* arm(rest).

подл|оми́ться (*3sg* -óмится, *3pl* -óмятся, *impf* **подла́мываться**) *сов возв*: ~ **под тя́жестью чего-н** to give way under the weight of sth.

пóдлост|ь (-и) *ж* (*качество*) baseness; **какáя** ~! what a base thing to do!

пóдл|ый (-, -á, -о) *прил* base.

подмастéр|ье (-я) *м* apprentice.

подмáчива|ть (-ю) *несов от* **подмочи́ть**.

подм|ени́ть (-еню́, -éнишь, *impf* **подмéнивать**) *сов перех* (*заменить*) to substitute; **подмéнивать** (~ *perf*) **когó-н** (*разг*) to stand in for sb.

подм|ести́ (-ету́, -етёшь; *pt* -ёл, -ела́, -елó) *сов от* **мести́** ♦ (*impf* **подметáть**) *перех* (*пол*) to sweep; (*мусор*) to sweep up.

подмé|тить (-чу, -тишь; *impf* **подмечáть**) *сов перех* to notice.

подмёт|ка (-и) *ж* (*подошва*) sole; **он в** ~**и ей не годи́тся** (*разг*) he's not worth her little finger.

подмету́ *итп сов см* **подмести́**.

подмечá|ть (-ю) *несов от* **подмéтить**.

подмéчу *сов см* **подмéтить**.

подмигн|у́ть (-у́, -ёшь; *impf* **подми́гивать**) *сов неперех*: ~ **кому́-н** to wink at sb.

подмина́|ть (-ю) *несов от* **подмя́ть**.

подмóг|а (-и) *ж* (*разг*) help.

подмóстк|и (-ов) *мн* (*ТЕАТР*) stage *ед*.

подм|очи́ть (-очу́, -óчишь; *impf* **подмáчивать**) *сов перех* to dampen, moisten; (*разг: репутацию*) to blacken.

подмóю *итп сов см* **подмы́ть**.

подмыва́|ть (-ю) *несов от* **подмы́ть** ♦ *безл* (*разг*): **егó** ~**ло** +*infin* ... he felt an urge to ....

подм|ы́ть (-óю, -óешь; *impf* **подмыва́ть**) *сов перех* (*ребёнка, больного*) to wash; (*берег, мост*) to undermine.

подмы́ш|ка (-ки; *gen pl* -ек) *ж* armpit.

подм|я́ть (-омну́, -омнёшь; *impf* **подмина́ть**) *сов перех* to crush.

подневóль|ный (-ен, -ьна, -ьно) *прил* (*человек*) subordinate; (*труд*) forced.

поднес|ти́ (-у́, -ёшь; *impf* **подноси́ть**) *сов перех*: ~ **к** +*dat* to bring up to; (*подарить*): ~ **что-н кому́-н** to present sth to sb.

поднима́|ть(ся) (-ю(сь)) *несов от* **подня́ть(ся)**.

подниму́(сь) *итп сов см* **подня́ть(ся)**.

поднов|и́ть (-лю́, -и́шь; *impf* **подновля́ть**) *сов перех* (*здание*) to refurbish; (*краску*) to touch up.

подногóтн|ая (-ой; *decl like adj*) *ж*: **(вся)** ~ the true nature.

поднóжек *сущ см* **поднóжка**.

поднóжи|е (-я) *ср* (*горы, памятника*) foot.

поднóж|ка (-ки; *gen pl* -ек) ж (*трамвая, автобуса итп*) step; **дать** (*perf*) *или* **постáвить** (*perf*) ~**ку кому́-н** to trip sb up.

поднóжн|ый *прил*: **быть на** ~**ом корму́** (*с.-х.*) to be out at pasture.

поднóс (-а) *м* tray.

поднос|и́ть (-ошу́, -óсишь) *несов от* **поднести́**.

подн|я́ть (-иму́, -и́мешь; *impf* **поднимáть**) *сов перех* to raise; (*что-н лёгкое*) to pick up; (*что-н тяжёлое*) to lift (up); (*флаг*) to hoist; (*спящего человека*) to rouse; (*пани́ку, восстание*) to start; (*экономику, дисциплину*) to improve; (*архивные материалы, документацию итп*) to unearth; **поднимáть** (~ *perf*) **крик** *или* **шум** to make a fuss; **поднимáть** (~ *perf*) **чьё-н настроéние** *или* **чей-н дух** to raise sb's spirits; **поднимáть** (~ *perf*) **когó-н нá смех** to make a laughing stock of sb

▸ **подня́ться** (*impf* **поднимáться**) *сов возв* to rise; (*на другой этаж, на сцену*) to go up; (*с постели, со стула*) to get up; (*пани́ка, метéль, дра́ка*) to break out; **поднимáться** (~**ся** *perf*) **нá гóру** to climb a hill; ~**я́лся крик** there was an uproar; ~**я́лся вéтер** the wind got up.

подо *предл см* **под**.

подоба́|ть (*3sg* -ет, *3pl* -ют) *несов неперех*: ~ +*dat* to befit; **Вам не** ~**ет отка́зываться** it does not befit you to refuse.

подоба́ющий (-ая, -ее, -ие) *прил* appropriate.

подóбен *прил см* **подóбный**.

подóбно *предл*: ~ +*dat* like, similar to ♦ *союз*: ~ **тому́ как** in the same way as, just as.

подóбн|ый (-ен, -на, -но) *прил*: ~ +*dat* (*сходный с*) like, similar to; ~**ные лю́ди – рéдкость** there are very few people like this *или* of this type; **и тому́** ~**ное** et cetera, and so on; **ничегó** ~**ного** (*разг*) nothing of the sort.

подобостра́стн|ый (-ен, -на, -но) *прил* obsequious, servile.

подо|бра́ть (-беру́, -берёшь; *impf* **подбира́ть**) *сов перех* to pick up; (*приподнять вверх*) to gather (up); (*выбрать подходящее*) to select, pick

▸ **подобра́ться** (*impf* **подбира́ться**) *сов возв* (*коллектив*) to get together; (*библиотека, коллекция*) to be built up; (*подкрасться*) to steal up.

подобрé|ть (-ю) *сов от* **добрéть**.

подобру́-поздорóву *нареч* (*разг*): **убира́йся** ~**!** get out while the going's good!

подоби́|ть *итп сов см* **подби́ть**.

подо|гна́ть (-гоню́, -гóнишь; *impf* **подгоня́ть**) *сов перех*: ~ **к** +*dat* (*стадо, машину*) to drive up to; (*лодку*) to take in to; **подгоня́ть** (~ *perf*) **под** +*acc* to fit.

подогн|у́ть (-у́, -ёшь; *impf* **подгиба́ть**) *сов перех* (*рукава, штани́ну*) to turn up

▸ **подогну́ться** (*impf* **подгиба́ться**) *сов возв* to curl under; **у негó нóги/колéни** ~**у́лись** his legs/knees gave way.

подогрé|ть (-ю; *impf* **подогрева́ть**) *сов перех* to warm up; (*перен: любопытство*) to heighten.

пододви́н|уть (-у, -ешь; *impf* **пододвига́ть**) *сов перех* to move closer.

пододея́льник (-а) *м* ≈ duvet cover.

подожда́ть (-у́, -ёшь; *pt* -а́л, -ала́, -а́ло) *сов перех* to wait for; ~ (*perf*) **с чем-н** to put sth off; ~ (*perf*) +*infin* to put off doing; ~**йте!** wait a minute!; ~**йте, мóжет всё не так плóхо** wait a bit, maybe it won't be all that bad; ~**йте, я ведь знал Ва́шего отца́** wait a minute, I think I knew your father.

подожгу́ *итп сов см* **поджéчь**.

подожму́ *итп сов см* **поджа́ть**.

подо|зва́ть (-зову́, -зовёшь; *pt* -озва́л, -озвала́, -озва́ло, *impf* **подзыва́ть**) *сов перех* to call over.

подозрева́|ть (-ю) *несов перех* to suspect; ~ (*impf*) **когó-н в чём-н** to suspect sb of sth; ~ (*impf*) (**о чём-н**) to have an idea (about sth).

подозрéни|е (-я) *ср* suspicion; ~ **на** +*acc* (*предположение*) suspicion of; **быть** (*impf*) **под** ~**м** *или* **на** ~**и** to be under suspicion; **он был задéржан/арестóван по** ~**ю в уби́йстве** he was held/arrested on suspicion of murder.

подозри́тель|ный (-ен, -ьна, -ьно) *прил* suspicious.

подо|йти́ (-ю́, -ишь) *сов от* **дойти́**.

подой|ти́ (*как* **идти́**; *см* **Table 18**; *impf* **подходи́ть**) *сов неперех*: ~ **к** +*dat* (*также перен*) to approach; (*соответствовать*): ~**ти́ к** +*dat* (*юбка*) to go (well) with; **подходи́ть** (~ *perf*) **на дóлжность** to be suited to a position; **э́то мне подхóдит** this suits me; **подходи́ть** (~ *perf*) **к концу́** to come to an end.

подокóнник (-а) *м* windowsill.

подóл (-а) *м* hem.

подóлгу *нареч* for a long time.

подолью́ *итп сов см* **подли́ть**.

подомну́ *итп сов см* **подмя́ть**.

подóн|ок (-ка) *м* scum.

подопéчн|ый (-ого; *decl like adj*) *м* ward ♦ *прил*: ~ **ребёнок** ward; **подопéчная террито́рия** (*под опéкой ООН*) trust territory, trusteeship.

подоплё|ка (-и) *ж* underlying reason.

подопру́ *итп сов см* **подперéть**.

подóпытн|ый *прил*: ~**ое живóтное** animal used in experiments; ~ **крóлик** (*перен*) guinea pig.

подорв|а́ть (-у́, -ёшь; *pt* -а́л, -ала́, -а́ло, *impf* **подрыва́ть**) *сов перех* to blow up; (*перен: авторитет, доверие*) to undermine; (: *здорóвье*) to destroy

▸ **подорва́ться** (*impf* **подрыва́ться**) *сов возв* to be blown up; (*перен: авторитет*) to be undermined; (: *здорóвье*) to be destroyed.

подорожа́|ть (-ю) *сов от* **дорожа́ть**.

подорóжник (-а) *м* plantain.

подо|сла́ть (-шлю́, -шлёшь; *impf* **подсыла́ть**) *сов перех* to send (*secretly*).

подоспе́|ть (-ю; *impf* **подоспева́ть**) *сов неперех* to arrive in time.

подотру́ *итп сов см* **подтере́ть**.

подотчёт|ный (-ен, -на, -но) *прил* (*организация, работник итп*) accountable; **счёт ~ных сумм** expense account; **подотчётные де́ньги** expenses.

подо́хн|уть (-у, -ешь) *сов от* **до́хнуть**.

подохо́дный *прил*: ~ **нало́г** income tax.

подо́шв|а (-ы) *ж* (*обуви*) sole.

подошёл *итп сов см* **подойти́**.

подошлю́ *итп сов см* **подосла́ть**.

подошью́ *итп сов см* **подши́ть**.

подпа́|сть (-ду́, -дёшь) *сов неперех*: ~ **под** +*acc* to fall under.

подпева́|ть (-ю; *perf* **подпе́ть**) *несов неперех* (+*dat*) to join in with; (*перен: разг: пренебр*) to echo.

подпере́ть (-опру́, -опрёшь; *pt* -пёр, -пёрла, -пёрло, *impf* **подпира́ть**) *сов перех*: ~ **что-н чем-н** to prop up; **подпира́ть** (~ *perf*) **щёку кула́ком** to rest one's head in one's hands.

подпе́ть (-ою́, -оёшь) *сов от* **подпева́ть**.

подпира́|ть (-ю) *несов от* **подпере́ть**.

подписа́ни|е (-я) *ср* signing.

подп|иса́ть (-ишу́, -и́шешь; *impf* **подпи́сывать**) *сов перех* to sign

▸ **подписа́ться** (*impf* **подпи́сываться**) *сов возв*: ~**ся под** +*instr* to sign; **подпи́сываться** (~**ся** *perf*) **на** +*acc* (*на газету, на журнал*) to subscribe to.

подпи́с|ка (-ки; *gen pl* -ок) *ж* subscription; (*о невыезде, о неразглашении*) signed statement.

подписно́й *прил* subscription *опред*; ~ **акционе́рный капита́л** (*КОММ*) subscribed capital; **подписно́й лист** list of subscribers.

подпи́сок *сущ см* **подпи́ска**.

подпи́счик (-а) *м* subscriber.

подпи́сыва|ть(ся) (-ю(сь)) *несов от* **подписа́ть(ся)**.

по́дпис|ь (-и) *ж* (*фамилия*) signature; (*под картиной*) title, caption; (*под стихами*) title.

подпишу́(сь) *итп сов см* **подписа́ть(ся)**.

подплы́|ть (-ву́, -вёшь; *pt* -л, -ла́, -ло, *impf* **подплыва́ть**) *сов неперех* (*лодка* итп) to sail (up); (*пловец, рыба*) to swim (up).

подполко́вник (-а) *м* lieutenant colonel.

подпо́ль|е (-я) *ср* (*подвал*) cellar; (*конспирация*) underground activities *мн*; **уходи́ть** (**уйти́** *perf*) **в** ~ to go underground.

подпо́льный *прил* underground *опред*.

подпо́р|ка (-ки; *gen pl* -ок) *ж* prop, support.

подпою́ *итп сов см* **подпе́ть**.

подпоя́|сать (-шу, -шешь; *impf* **подпоя́сывать**) *сов перех* to belt.

подпра́в|ить (-лю, -ишь; *impf* **подправля́ть**) *сов перех* to make minor corrections to.

подпрогра́мм|а (-ы) *ж* (*КОМП*) subroutine.

подпру́г|а (-и) *ж* girth.

подпры́гн|уть (-у, -ешь; *impf* **подпры́гивать**) *сов неперех* to jump.

подпуска́|ть (-ю) *несов от* **подпусти́ть** ♦ *перех*: ~ **к** +*dat* to allow access to.

подп|усти́ть (-ущу́, -у́стишь; *impf* **подпуска́ть**) *сов перех* (*человека, зверя*) to allow to approach.

подрабо́та|ть (-ю; *impf* **подраба́тывать**) *сов перех* (*статью*) to polish up ♦ (*не*)*перех* (+*acc или* +*gen*) to earn extra.

подра́внива|ть (-ю) *несов от* **подровня́ть**.

подра́гива|ть (-ю) *сов неперех* to tremble; (*ресницы*) to flutter.

подража́ни|е (-я) *ср* imitation.

подража́|ть (-ю) *несов неперех* (+*dat*) to imitate.

подразделе́ни|е (-я) *ср* (*воинское*) subunit; (*производственное*) subdivision.

подраздел|и́ть (-ю́, -и́шь; *impf* **подразделя́ть**) *сов перех* to subdivide.

подразделя́|ться (*3sg* -ется, *3pl* -ются) *несов возв* to be subdivided.

подразумева́|ть (-ю) *несов перех* to mean

▸ **подразумева́ться** *несов возв* to be implied.

подра́мник (-а) *м* stretcher.

подр|асти́ (-асту́, -астёшь; *pt* -о́с, -осла́, -осло́, *impf* **подраста́ть**) *сов неперех* to grow (a little).

подр|а́ться (-еру́сь, -ерёшься) *сов от* **дра́ться**.

подре́|зать (-жу, -жешь; *impf* **подреза́ть**) *сов перех* (*платье* итп) to shorten; (*волосы*) to cut; ~ (*perf*) **кры́лья кому́-н** (*перен*) to clip sb's wings.

подро́бен *прил см* **подро́бный**.

подро́бност|ь (-и) *ж* detail; **вдава́ться** (*impf*) **в** ~**и** to go into detail.

подро́б|ный (-ен, -на, -но) *прил* detailed.

подровня́|ть (-ю; *impf* **подра́внивать**) *сов перех* to trim.

подро́с *итп сов см* **подрасти́**.

подро́стка *сущ см* **подро́сток**.

подростко́вый *прил* (*одежда* итп) teenage *опред*; (*проблемы*) adolescent *опред*; **подростко́вый во́зраст** teens *мн*.

подро́ст|ок (-ка) *м* teenager, adolescent.

подру́г|а (-и) *ж* (girl)friend; **подру́га жи́зни** wife.

по-друго́му *нареч* (*иначе*) differently.

подруж|и́ть (-ужу́, -у́жишь) *сов от* **дружи́ть**

▸ **подружи́ться** *сов от* **дружи́ться** ♦ *возв*: ~**ся с** +*instr* to make friends with; **они́ бы́стро ~ужи́лись** they quickly became friends.

подрул|и́ть (-ю́, -и́шь; *impf* **подру́ливать**) *сов неперех* (*самолёт*) to taxi; (*автомобиль*) to drive (up).

подрумя́н|иться (-юсь, -ишься) *сов от* **румя́ниться** ♦ (*impf* **подрумя́ниваться**) *возв* (*женщина*) to put on blusher; (*пирожки,* *бу́лочки*) to brown.

подру́чн|ый *прил*: ~ **материа́л/инструме́нт** the material/instrument to hand ◆ (**-ого**; *decl like adj*) *м* assistant.

подрыва́|ть(ся) (**-ю(сь)**) *несов от* **подорва́ть(ся)**.

подрывно́й *прил* subversive.

подря́д *нареч* in succession ◆ (**-а**) *м* (*рабо́чий догово́р*) contract; **рабо́тали 5 дней** ~ they worked 5 days in a row *или* in succession; **все/всё** ~ everyone/everything without exception.

подря́дный *прил* contract *опред*.

подря́дчик (**-а**) *м* contractor.

подряхле́|ть (**-ю**) *сов от* **дряхле́ть**.

подса|ди́ть (**-ажу́, -а́дишь**; *impf* **подса́живать**) *сов перех* (*на коня́*) to help to mount; (*на высо́кий стул*) to help up; (*посади́ть ря́дом*) to place nearby.

подса́жива|ться (**-юсь**) *несов от* **подсе́сть**.

подсажу́ *сов см* **подсади́ть**.

подсве́чник (**-а**) *м* candlestick.

подсе́к *итп сов см* **подсе́чь**.

подсека́|ть (**-ю**) *несов от* **подсе́чь**.

подсеку́ *итп сов см* **подсе́чь**.

подсе́|сть (**-я́ду, -я́дешь**; *impf* **подса́живаться**) *сов неперех*: ~ **к** +*dat* to sit down beside.

подсе́|чь (**-еку́, -ечёшь** *итп*, **-еку́т**; *pt* **-ёк, -екла́, -екло́**, *impf* **подсека́ть**) *сов перех* to cut down; (*перен: по́длеж: несча́стье, боле́знь*) to lay low.

подсини́|ть (**-ю́, -и́шь**) *сов от* **сини́ть**.

подск|аза́ть (**-ажу́, -а́жешь**; *impf* **подска́зывать**) *сов перех* (*перен: иде́ю, реше́ние*) to suggest; (*разг: а́дрес, телефо́н*) to tell; **подска́зывать** (~ *perf*) **что-н кому́-н** to prompt sb with sth; **не ~а́жите, где у́лица Пу́шкина?** can you please tell me where Pushkin Street is?

подска́з|ка (**-ки**; *gen pl* **-ок**) *ж* prompt; **де́йствовать** (*impf*) **по чье́й-н ~ке** (*перен*) to do as sb says.

подска́зыва|ть (**-ю**) *несов от* **подсказа́ть**.

подск|очи́ть (**-очу́, -о́чишь**; *impf* **подска́кивать**) *сов неперех* (*та́кже перен*) to jump; (*подбежа́ть*) to run up; **подска́кивать** (~ *perf*) **от испу́га/неожи́данности** to start (in fright/surprise).

подсла|сти́ть (**-щу́, -сти́шь**; *impf* **подсла́щивать**) *сов перех* to sweeten.

подсле́дственн|ая (**-ой**; *decl like adj*) *ж см* **подсле́дственный**.

подсле́дственн|ый (**-ого**; *decl like adj*) *м* the accused, the defendant; **~ые** the accused.

подслу́ша|ть (**-ю**; *impf* **подслу́шивать**) *сов перех* to eavesdrop on.

подсма́трива|ть (**-ю**) *несов от* **подсмотре́ть**.

подсме́ива|ться (**-юсь**) *сов возв*: ~ **над** +*instr* to poke gentle fun at.

подсм|отре́ть (**-отрю́, -о́тришь**; *impf* **подсма́тривать**) *сов перех* (*уви́деть*) to spy

on; ~ (*perf*), **что** ... to notice that ...; **я ~отре́л, как он брал конфе́ты** I saw him take the sweets.

подсне́жник (**-а**) *м* snowdrop.

подсо́бный *прил* (*помеще́ние, хозя́йство*) subsidiary; **подсо́бный рабо́чий** auxiliary.

подсо́выва|ть (**-ю**) *несов от* **подсу́нуть**.

подсозна́ни|е (**-я**) *ср* the subconscious.

подсозна́тел|ьный (**-ен, -ьна, -ьно**) *прил* subconscious.

подсо́лнечник (**-а**) *м* sunflower.

подсо́лнечн|ый *прил*: **~ое ма́сло** sunflower oil.

подсо́лнух (**-а**) *м* (*разг*) sunflower.

подсо́х|нуть (**-ну, -нешь**; *pt* **-, -ла, -ло**, *impf* **подсыха́ть**) *сов неперех* to dry out a little.

подспо́рь|е (**-я**) *ср* help.

подспу́дный (**-ен, -на, -но**) *прил* hidden.

подста́в|ить (**-лю, -ишь**; *impf* **подставля́ть**) *сов перех*: ~ **под** +*acc* to put under; **подставля́ть** (~ *perf*) **кого́-н под уда́р** (*перен*) to lay sb open to attack.

подста́в|ка (**-ки**; *gen pl* **-ок**) *ж* stand.

подста́влю *сов см* **подста́вить**.

подставля́|ть (**-ю**) *несов от* **подста́вить**.

подставно́й *прил* (*ло́жный*) false.

подста́вок *сущ см* **подста́вка**.

подстака́нник (**-а**) *м* glassholder.

подста́нци|я (**-и**) *ж* substation.

подстегн|у́ть (**-у́, -ёшь**; *impf* **подстёгивать**) *сов перех* to urge on; (*перен: разг*): ~ **кого́-н** to get sb moving.

подстел|и́ть (**-ю́, -ешь**; *impf* **подстила́ть**) *сов перех* (*плед, простыню́*) to spread out.

подстерега́|ть (**-ю**) *несов от* **подстере́чь** ◆ *перех* (*ожида́ть*) to await.

подстере́|чь (**-гу́, -жёшь** *итп*, **-гу́т**; *impf* **подстерега́ть**) *сов перех* to lie in wait for.

подстила́|ть (**-ю**) *несов от* **подстели́ть**.

подсти́л|ка (**-ки**; *gen pl* **-ок**) *ж* covering.

подстра́ива|ть (**-ю**) *несов от* **подстро́ить**.

подстрах|ова́ть (**-у́ю**; *impf* **подстрахо́вывать**) *сов перех* (*гимна́ста*) to be on hand for; (*в риско́ванном де́ле*) to insure.

подстрека́тель (**-я**) *м* instigator.

подстрека́|ть (**-ю**) *несов перех*: ~ **кого́-н к** +*dat* to drive sb to.

подстрел|и́ть (**-ю́, -ешь**; *impf* **подстре́ливать**) *сов перех* to wing.

подстри́|чь (**-гу́, -жёшь** *итп*, **-гу́т**; *pt* **-г, -ла, -ло**, *impf* **подстрига́ть**) *сов перех* to trim; (*для уко́рачивания*) to cut

▶ **подстри́чься** (*impf* **подстрига́ться**) *сов возв* to have one's hair cut.

подстро́|ить (**-ю, -ишь**; *impf* **подстра́ивать**) *сов перех* to fix.

подстро́чн|ый *прил*: **~ое примеча́ние** footnote; **~ перево́д** word-for-word translation.

по́дступ (**-а**) *м* (*обы́чно мн*) approach.

подступ|и́ть (**-уплю́, -у́пишь**; *impf* **подступа́ть**) *сов неперех* (*слёзы*) to well up; (*рыда́ния*) to

rise; **подступа́ть** (~ _perf_) **к** +_dat_ to approach
▸ **подступи́ться** (_impf_ **подступа́ться**) _сов возв_: ~**ся к** +_dat_ to approach.
подсу́ден _прил см_ **подсу́дный**.
подсуди́м|ая (-**ой**; _decl like adj_) _ж см_ **подсуди́мый**.
подсуди́м|ый (-**ого**; _decl like adj_) _м_ (_ЮР_) the accused, the defendant; ~**ые** the accused.
подсу́д|ный (-**ен**, -**на**, -**но**) _прил_ (_ЮР_) sub judice; ~**ное де́ло** (_подлежащий суду_) case due to come before court; (_преступление_) crime.
подсу́н|уть (-**у**, -**ешь**; _impf_ **подсо́вывать**) _сов перех_ to shove; (_разг: что-н ненужное, плохое_) to get rid of.
подсуш|и́ть (-**у́**, -**у́шишь**; _impf_ **подсу́шивать**) _сов перех_ to dry slightly.
подсчёт (-**а**) _м_ counting; (_обычно мн: итог_) calculation.
подсчита́|ть (-**ю**; _impf_ **подсчи́тывать**) _сов перех_ to count (up).
подсыла́|ть (-**ю**) _несов см_ **подосла́ть**.
подсыха́|ть (-**ю**) _несов от_ **подсо́хнуть**.
подся́ду _итп сов см_ **подсе́сть**.
подта́лкива|ть (-**ю**) _несов от_ **подтолкну́ть**.
подтас|ова́ть (-**у́ю**; _impf_ **подтасо́вывать**) _сов перех_ to juggle (with).
подта́чива|ть (-**ю**) _несов от_ **подточи́ть**.
подтверд|и́ть (-**жу́**, -**ди́шь**; _impf_ **подтвержда́ть**) _сов перех_ to confirm; (_фактами, цифрами_) to back up
▸ **подтверди́ться** (_impf_ **подтвержда́ться**) _сов возв_ to be confirmed.
подтвержде́ни|е (-**я**) _ср_ confirmation.
подтвержу́(сь) _сов см_ **подтверди́ть(ся)**.
подтёк (-**а**) _м_ bruise.
подте́кст (-**а**) _м_ hidden meaning.
подт|ере́ть (-**отру́**, -**отрёшь**; _impf_ **подтира́ть**) _сов перех_ to mop up.
подтолкн|у́ть (-**у́**, -**ёшь**; _impf_ **подта́лкивать**) _сов перех_ to nudge; (_перен_) to urge on.
подт|очи́ть (-**очу́**, -**о́чишь**; _impf_ **подта́чивать**) _сов перех_ to sharpen (a little); (_перен: силы_) to weaken; (: _здоровье_) to destroy.
подтя́гива|ть(ся) (-**ю(сь)**) _несов от_ **подтяну́ть(ся)**.
подтя́ж|ка (-**ки**; _gen pl_ -**ек**) _ж_ (_обычно мн_) braces _мн_ (_BRIT_), suspenders _мн_ (_US_).
подтя́нут|ый (-, -**а**, -**о**) _прил_ smart.
подтя|ну́ть (-**ну́**, -**нешь**; _impf_ **подтя́гивать**) _сов перех_ (_тяжёлый предмет_) to haul up; (_гайку, болт_) to tighten; (_войска_) to bring up
▸ **подтяну́ться** (_impf_ **подтя́гиваться**) _сов возв_ (_на брусьях, на перекладине_) to pull o.s. up; (_войска_) to move up; (_перен_) to get one's act together.
поду́ма|ть (-**ю**) _сов от_ **ду́мать** ♦ _неперех_: ~ (_о_ +_prp_) to think (about); ~ (_perf_) **над** +_instr или_ **о** +_prp_ to think about; ~, **что...** to think that ...; **он**

и не ~**л извини́ться** he didn't even think of apologizing _или_ to apologize; ~**ешь**! **купи́л но́вую маши́ну** so what if he's bought a new car!; ~ **то́лько**! (_разг_) just think!; **кто бы мог** ~**!** who would have thought it!; **и не** ~**ю**! (_разг_) I won't hear of it!
▸ **поду́маться** _сов от_ **ду́маться**.
поду́мыва|ть (-**ю**) _несов неперех_ (_разг_): ~ **о** +_prp_/+_infin_ to think about/of doing.
подурне́|ть (-**ю**) _сов от_ **дурне́ть**.
поду́|ть (-**ю**) _сов неперех_ to blow; (_ветер_) to begin to blow.
подуч|и́ть (-**у́**, -**у́чишь**; _impf_ **поду́чивать**) _сов перех_ (_разг: выучить_) to learn; (_научить_) to teach.
поду́шек _сущ см_ **поду́шка**.
подуш|и́ть (-**у́**, -**у́шишь**) _сов перех_ to spray lightly with perfume.
поду́ш|ка (-**ки**; _gen pl_ -**ек**) _ж_ (_для сидения_) cushion; (_под голову_) pillow.
поду́шный _прил_: ~ **нало́г** poll tax.
подхали́м (-**а**) _м_ toady.
подхали́м|ка (-**ки**; _gen pl_ -**ок**) _ж см_ **подхали́м**.
подхва́т (-**а**) _м_: **быть на** ~**е** (_разг_) to be at hand.
подхв|ати́ть (-**ачу́**, -**а́тишь**; _impf_ **подхва́тывать**) _сов перех_ (_падающее_) to catch; (_подлеж: течение, толпа_) to carry away; (_слова, идею, болезнь_) to pick up; (_песню, мелодию_) to join in.
подхлестн|у́ть (-**у́**, -**ёшь**; _impf_ **подхлёстывать**) _сов перех_ to whip on.
подхо́д (-**а**) _м_ approach; **экза́мены на** ~**е** the exams are approaching.
подх|оди́ть (-**ожу́**, -**о́дишь**) _несов от_ **подойти́**.
подходя́щ|ий (-**ая**, -**ее**, -**ие**) _прил_ (_дом_) suitable; (_момент, слова_) appropriate.
подхожу́ _несов см_ **подходи́ть**.
подцеп|и́ть (-**лю́**, -**ишь**) _сов перех_ to attach; (_разг: болезнь, девушку, жениха_) to pick up.
подча́с _нареч_ at times.
подчеркн|у́ть (-**у́**, -**ёшь**; _impf_ **подчёркивать**) _сов перех_ (_в тексте_) to underline; (_в речи_) to emphasize.
подчине́ни|е (-**я**) _ср_ obedience.
подчинённый _прил_ subordinate _опред_ ♦ (-**ого**; _decl like adj_) _м_ subordinate.
подчин|и́ть (-**ю́**, -**и́шь**; _impf_ **подчиня́ть**) _сов перех_ (_народ, страну_) to subjugate; **подчиня́ть** (~ _perf_) **что-н кому́-н** to place sth under the control of sb
▸ **подчини́ться** (_impf_ **подчиня́ться**) _сов возв_ (+_dat_) to obey.
подчи́|стить (-**щу**, -**стишь**; _impf_ **подчища́ть**) _сов перех_ (_пол итп_) to clean; (_написанное_) to erase.
подше́й(те) _сов см_ **подши́ть**.
подше́фный _прил_: ~ **де́тский дом** children's

home under patronage.

подшивáть (-ю) *несов от* **подшúть**.

подшúв|ка (-ки; *gen pl* -ок) *ж* (*газет, документов*) bundle.

подшúпник (-а) *м* (*ТЕХ*) bearing.

подшúть (-ошью, -ошьёшь; *imper* -шéй(те), *impf* **подшивáть**) *сов перех* (*рукав*) to hem; (*подол*) to take up; (*документ*) to file; (*пачку газет*) to bundle up.

подшут|úть (-учý, -ýтишь; *impf* **подшýчивать**) *сов неперех*: ~ **над** +*instr* to make fun of.

подъ- *префф см* **под-**.

подъéду *итп сов см* **подъéхать**.

подъéзд (-а) *м* (*к городу, к дому*) approach; (*в здании*) entrance.

подъезжáй(те) *сов см* **подъéхать**.

подъезжáть (-ю) *несов см* **подъéхать**.

подъём (-а) *м* (*груза*) lifting; (*флага*) raising; (*на гору*) ascent; (*промышленный, культурный итп*) revival; (*в речи, в действиях*) enthusiasm; (*сигнал: к пробуждению*) reveille.

подъёмник (-а) *м* lift (*BRIT*), elevator (*US*).

подъёмн|ые (-ых; *decl like adj*) *мн* (*также:* ~ **дéньги**) relocation costs *мн*.

подъёмный *прил* lifting *опред*; **подъёмный кран** crane.

подъéхать (*как* **éхать**; *см* **Table 19**; *impf* **подъезжáть**) *сов неперех* (*на автомобиле*) to drive up; (*на коне*) to ride up; (*разг*) to call in.

подыгрáть (-ю; *impf* **подыгрывать**) *сов неперех* (+*dat; разг*) to accompany.

поды|скáть (-щý, -щешь; *impf* **подыскивать**) *сов перех* to find.

подытóж|ить (-у, -ишь) *сов перех* (*расходы, доходы*) to add up; (*сделанное, сказанное*) to sum up.

подыхáть (-ю) *несов неперех* (*животные*) to be dying; (*разг*): ~ **от** +*gen* (*от голода, от скуки итп*) to be dying of.

подышáть (-ышý, -ышешь) *сов неперех* to breathe.

подыщý *итп сов см* **подыскáть**.

поедá|ть (-ю) *несов см* **поéсть**.

поéдешь *итп сов см* **поéхать**.

поедúм *итп сов см* **поéсть**.

поедúн|ок (-ка) *м* duel.

поедúте *сов см* **поéсть**.

поéду *итп сов см* **поéхать**.

поедя́т *сов см* **поéсть**.

поёж|иться (-усь, -ишься; *impf* **поёживаться**) *сов возв* to shiver slightly.

пóезд (-а; *nom pl* -á) *м* train; **скóрый** ~ express train; ~ **дáльнего слéдования** long-distance train; **éхать** (*impf*) ~**ом** *или* **на** ~**е** to travel by train; **éхать** (*impf*) **в** ~**е метрó** to travel by tube (*BRIT*) *или* subway (*US*).

поéзд|ка (-ки; *gen pl* -ок) *ж* trip.

поезжáй(те) *сов см* **поéхать**.

поéсть (*как* **есть**; *см* **Table 15**) *сов от* **есть** ♦ (*impf* **поедáть**) *перех*: ~ **чегó-н** to eat a little bit of sth; (*съесть всё*) to eat up; (*подлеж: моль*) to

eat away.

поéхать (*как* **éхать**; *см* **Table 19**) *сов неперех* (*автомобиль, поезд итп*) to set off.

поéшь *сов см* **поéсть**.

пожáдничать (-ю) *сов от* **жáдничать**.

пожалé|ть (-ю) *сов от* **жалéть**.

пожáл|овать (-ую) *сов от* **жáловать** ♦ *неперех*: ~ **к** +*dat* (*посетить*) to visit; **добрó** ~ welcome.

пожáлуй *вводн сл* (*возможно*) perhaps; (*выражает предпочтение*) likely; **он**, ~, **не придёт** he may not come; **я**, ~, **пойдý** I am likely to go.

пожáлуйста *част* please; (*в ответ на благодарность*) don't mention it, you're welcome; ~, **помогúте мне** please help me; **скажúте** ~! you don't say!; **закóнчил шкóлу и,** ~, **женúлся** he left school and then, would you believe it, he got married.

пожáр (-а) *м* fire; (+*gen*; *перен: войны, революции*) the inferno.

пожáрище (-а) *ср* site of fire.

пожáрник (-а) *м* (*разг*) fireman (*мн* firemen).

пожáрн|ый (-ого; *decl like adj*) *м* fireman (*мн* firemen) ♦ *прил*: ~**ая комáнда** fire brigade (*BRIT*) *или* department (*US*); ~**ая машúна** fire engine; **на всякий** ~ (**слýчай**) (*разг*) in case of emergency.

пожáти|е (-я) *ср*: ~ (**рукú**) handshake.

пож|áть (-мý, -мёшь; *impf* **пожимáть**) *сов перех* to squeeze; **он** ~**áл мне рýку** he shook my hand; **пожимáть** (~ *perf*) **плечáми** to shrug one's shoulders.

пожелáни|е (-я) *ср* wish; **примúте мой наилýчшие** ~**я** pass on my best wishes.

пожелá|ть (-ю) *сов от* **желáть**.

пожелтé|ть (-ю) *сов от* **желтéть**.

пож|енúть (-еню́, -éнишь) *сов от* **женúть** ♦ *перех* (*разг*) to marry

► **поженúться** *сов от* **женúться** ♦ *возв* to marry, get married.

пожéртвовани|е (-я) *ср* donation.

пожéртв|овать (-ую) *несов от* **жéртвовать**.

поживá|ть (-ю) *несов неперех* (*разг*): **как ты** ~**ешь?** how are you?

пожив|úться (-лю́сь, -úшься) *сов возв* (+*instr*; *разг*) to live off.

поживý *итп сов см* **пожúть**.

пожúзненный *прил* lifelong, life *опред*; **пожúзненное заключéние** life imprisonment.

пожилóй *прил* elderly.

пожимá|ть (-ю) *несов от* **пожáть**.

пожирá|ть (-ю) *несов неперех* ♦ *перех* (*книги*) to devour; **любопытство/честолюбие** ~**ло егó** he was devoured by curiosity/ambition; ~ (*impf*) **когó-н глазáми** to devour sb with one's eyes.

пожúтк|и (-ов) *мн* (*разг*) belongings *мн*.

пожúть (-ивý, -ивёшь; *pt* -úл, -илá, -úло) *сов неперех* (*пробыть где-нибудь*) to stay for a while; ~**ивём – увúдим** we shall see.

пожму́ *итп сов см* **пожа́ть.**

пожр|а́ть (**-у́, -ёшь;** *impf* **пожира́ть**) *сов перех* (*подлеж: животное*) to devour; (*no impf*; *разг: подлеж: человек*) to gobble up.

по́з|а (**-ы**) *ж* posture; (*перен: поведение*) pose.

позабо́|титься (**-чусь, -тишься**) *сов от* **забо́титься.**

позави́довать (**-ую**) *сов от* **зави́довать.**

поза́втрака|ть (**-ю**) *несов от* **за́втракать.**

позавчера́ *нареч* the day before yesterday.

позади́ *нареч* (*сзади*) behind; (*в прошлом*) in the past ◆ *предл* (*+gen*) behind.

позаи́мств|овать (**-ую**) *сов от* **заи́мствовать.**

позапро́шл|ый *прил* before last; **~ая неде́ля** the week before last.

позаре́з *нареч* (*разг*) terribly.

поз|ва́ть (**-ову́, -овёшь**) *сов от* **звать.**

позволе́ни|е (**-я**) *ср* permission; **с Ва́шего ~я** with your permission.

позво́л|ить (**-ю, -ишь;** *impf* **позволя́ть**) *сов неперех* (*погода, обстоятельства*) to permit ◆ *перех*: **~ что-н кому́-н** to allow sb sth; **позволя́ть** (**~** *perf*) **кому́-н** *+infin* to allow sb to do; **~ьте!** excuse me!; **~ьте мне предста́вить моего́ колле́гу** allow me to introduce my colleague; **~ьте пройти́** excuse me please; **позволя́ть** (*impf*) **себе́ что-н** to afford sth.

позвон|и́ть (**-ю́, -и́шь**) *сов от* **звони́ть.**

позвон|о́к (**-ка́**) *м* vertebra (*мн* vertebrae).

позвоно́чник (**-а**) *м* spine, spinal column.

поздне́е *сравн нареч от* **по́здно** ◆ *нареч* later ◆ *предл* (*+gen*) after; (**не**) **~** *+gen* (no) later than.

по́здн|ий (**-яя, -ее, -ие**) *прил* late; **са́мое ~ее** (*раза*) at the latest.

по́здно *нареч* late ◆ *как сказ* it's late.

поздоро́ва|ться (**-юсь**) *сов от* **здоро́ваться.**

поздоро́в|иться (*3sg* **-ится**) *сов возв*: **ему́ не ~ится** (*раза*) he's in trouble.

поздрави́тельный *прил* greetings *опред.*

поздра́в|ить (**-лю, -ишь;** *impf* **поздравля́ть**) *сов перех*: **~ кого́-н с** *+instr* to congratulate sb on; **поздравля́ть** (**~** *perf*) **кого́-н с днём рожде́ния** to wish sb a happy birthday.

поздравле́ни|е (**-я**) *ср* congratulation; (*с днём рождения*) greeting.

поздра́влю *сов см* **поздра́вить.**

поздравля́|ть (**-ю**) *несов от* **поздра́вить.**

позелене́|ть (**-ю**) *сов от* **зелене́ть.**

по́зже *нареч* = **позднее.**

пози́р|овать (**-ую**) *сов неперех* (*+dat*) to pose for.

позити́в (**-а**) *м* (*ФОТО*) positive.

позити́вный (**-ен, -на, -но**) *прил* positive.

пози́ци|я (**-и**) *ж* position; (*контракта, проекта*) item.

познава́тельный (**-ен, -ьна, -ьно**) *прил* educational.

позна|ва́ть (**-ю́**) *несов от* **позна́ть**

▶ **познава́ться** *несов возв* to become known.

познако́м|ить(ся) (**-лю(сь), -ишь(ся)**) *сов от* **знако́мить(ся).**

позна́ни|е (**-я**) *ср* familiarization; (*приобретение знаний*) cognition; *см также* **позна́ния.**

позна́ни|я (**-й**) *мн* knowledge *ед.*

позна́|ть (**-ю;** *impf* **познава́ть**) *сов перех* (*любовь, бедность итп*) to experience.

позову́ *итп сов см* **позва́ть.**

позоло́т|а (**-ы**) *ж* gilding, gilt.

позоло|ти́ть (**-чу́, -ти́шь**) *сов от* **золоти́ть.**

позо́р (**-а**) *м* disgrace; **выставля́ть** (**вы́ставить** *perf*) **кого́-н на ~** to bring disgrace on sb.

позо́рен *прил см* **позо́рный.**

позо́р|ить (**-ю, -ишь;** *perf* **опозо́рить**) *несов перех* to disgrace

▶ **позо́риться** (*perf* **опозо́риться**) *несов возв* to disgrace o.s.

позо́рный (**-ен, -на, -но**) *прил* disgraceful.

позывн|ы́е (**-ы́х;** *decl like adj*) *мн* call sign *ед.*

поимённый *прил*: **~ спи́сок** list of names.

по́йм|ка (**-ки;** *gen pl* **-ок**) *ж* capture.

по-ино́му *нареч* differently.

поинтерес|ова́ться (**-у́юсь**) *сов возв* (*+instr*) to take an interest in.

по́иск (**-а**) *м* (*научный, творческий итп*) quest; (*КОМП*) search; **"~ и заме́на"** "search and replace"; *см также* **по́иски.**

поиска́ть (**-ищу́, -и́щешь**) *сов перех* to have a look for.

по́иск|и (**-ов**) *мн*: **~** (*+gen*) search *ед* (for); **в ~ах** *+gen* in search of.

по́йстине *нареч* truly.

по|и́ть (**-ю́, -ишь;** *imper* **пои́(те),** *perf* **напои́ть**) *несов перех*: **~ кого́-н чем-н** to give sb sth to drink; **его́ напои́ли во́дкой** he was plied with vodka.

поищу́ *итп сов см* **поиска́ть.**

пойду́ *итп сов см* **пойти́.**

по́йм|а (**-ы**) *ж* flood plain.

пойма́|ть (**-ю**) *сов перех* to catch.

пойму́ *итп сов см* **поня́ть.**

по́йнтер (**-а**) *м* pointer (*dog*).

пой(те) *несов см* **петь.**

пойти́ (*как* **идти́;** *см* **Table 18**) *сов неперех* to set off; (*по пути реформ*) to start off; (*о механизмах, к цели*) to start working; (*дождь, снег*) to begin to fall; (*дым, пар*) to begin to rise; (*кровь*) to start flowing; (*фильм итп*) to start showing; (*подойти*): **~** *+dat или* **к** *+dat* (*шляпа, поведение*) to suit; **~** (*perf*) **в кого́-н** (*в мать, в деда итп*) to look like sb; **е́сли на то пошло́** if it comes to that; **так не пойдёт** that won't work.

KEYWORD

пока́ *нареч* **1** (*некоторое время*) for a while; **я пока́ подожду́** I'll wait for a while **2** (*тем временем*) in the meantime; **я ушёл, а**

она́ пока́ остава́лась в до́ме I left, and in the meantime she stayed at home
♦ *союз* **1** (*в то время как*) while; **пока́ он чита́л, я вы́шел на балко́н** while he was reading, I went out onto the balcony
2 (*до того времени как*) **пока́ не** until; **ребёнок бу́дет крича́ть, пока́ не полу́чит конфе́ту** the child will go on shouting until he gets a sweet; **пока́!** so long!; **пока́ что** for the moment.

покажу́(сь) *итп сов см* **показа́ть(ся)**.
пока́з (**-а**) *м* (*фильма*) showing; (*опыта*) demonstration; (*изменений, тенденций итп*) portrayal, depiction.
показа́ни|**е** (**-я**) *ср* (*ЮР: обычно мн*) evidence *ед*; (*на счётчике итп*) reading.
показа́телен *прил см* **показа́тельный**.
показа́тел|**ь** (**-я**) *м* indicator; (*МАТ, ЭКОН*) index (*мн* indices).
показа́тел|**ьный** (**-ен, -ьна, -ьно**) *прил* (*явление, пример итп*) revealing; (*no short form*): **~ное выступле́ние гимна́стов** gymnastics display; **~ о́пыт** demonstration (*of an experiment*).
пока|**за́ть** (**-жу́, -жешь**; *impf* **пока́зывать**) *сов перех* to show; (*подлеж: часы, счётчик итп*) to say; (*на суде*) to testify; **пока́зывать** (**~** *perf*) **что-н/кого́-н кому́-н** to show sth/sb to sb; **пока́зывать** (**~** *perf*) **на что-н/кого́-н** to point to sth/sb; **пока́зывать** (**~** *perf*) **приме́р** to set an example; **пока́зывать** (**~** *perf*) **себя́** to prove o.s.; **он ~за́л себя́ не в лу́чшем све́те** he didn't show himself in a very good light; **я тебе́ ~жу́!** (*разг*) I'll show you!
▶ **пока**|**за́ться** *сов от* **каза́ться** ♦ (*impf* **пока́зываться**) *возв* to appear; **~ся** (*perf*) **врачу́** to see a doctor.
показно́й *прил* (*энтузиазм, радость итп*) affected; (*роскошь*) ostentatious.
пока́зыва|**ть(ся)** (**-ю(сь)**) *несов от* **показа́ть(ся)**.
пока́ка|**ть** (**-ю**) *сов от* **ка́кать**.
покале́ч|**ить** (**-у, -ишь**) *сов от* **кале́чить**.
пока́лыва|**ть** (*3sg* **-ет**) *несов неперех*: **у меня́ ~ет се́рдце/желу́док** I keep getting stabbing pains in my chest/stomach.
пока́мест *нареч* (*разг*) in the meantime ♦ *союз* (*разг*) while.
покапри́знича|**ть** (**-ю**) *сов от* **капри́зничать**.
покара́|**ть** (**-ю**) *сов от* **кара́ть**.
поката́|**ть** (**-ю**) *сов перех*: **~ кого́-н на маши́не** to take sb for a drive; (*perf*) **ребёнка на саня́х** to take a child sledging
▶ **поката́ться** *сов возв* to go for a ride.
пока|**ти́ть** (**-ачу́, -а́тишь**) *сов перех* (*что-н круглое*) to roll; (*что-н на колёсах*) to wheel ♦ *неперех* (*машина*) to shoot off
▶ **покати́ться** *сов возв* to start rolling, start to roll; **~ся** (*perf*) **со́ смеху** (*разг*) to burst out laughing.

пока́тыва|**ться** (**-юсь**) *несов возв*: **~ со́ смеху** (*разг*) to roll about with laughter *или* laughing.
пока́тый (**-, -а, -о**) *прил* sloping.
покача́|**ть** (**-ю**) *сов перех* to rock; **~** (*perf*) **голово́й** to shake one's head
▶ **покача́ться** *сов возв* (*на качелях*) to swing.
пока́чива|**ться** (**-юсь**) *несов возв* to rock.
покачу́(сь) *сов см* **покати́ть(ся)**.
пока́яни|**е** (**-я**) *ср* repentance.
пока́|**яться** (**-юсь**) *несов от* **ка́яться**.
по́кер (**-а**) *м* poker (*CARDS*).
поки́н|**уть** (**-у, -ешь**; *impf* **покида́ть**) *сов перех* to abandon.
поклада́|**ть** (**-ю**) *несов перех*: **не ~я рук** tirelessly.
покла́дист|**ый** (**-, -а, -о**) *прил* flexible.
покло́н (**-а**) *м* (*жест*) bow; (*приветствие*) greeting; **посыла́ть** (**посла́ть** *perf*) *или* **передава́ть** (**переда́ть** *perf*) **кому́-н ~** to send sb one's regards.
покл|**они́ться** (**-оню́сь, -о́нишься**) *сов от* **кла́няться** ♦ (*impf* **поклоня́ться**) *возв*: **~** (**+dat**) (*святым местам*) to pay homage (at).
покло́нник (**-а**) *м* admirer.
поклоня́|**ться** (**-юсь**) *несов от* **поклони́ться** ♦ *возв* (**+dat**) to worship.
покля́|**сться** (**-ну́сь, -нёшься**) *сов от* **кля́сться**.
поко́|**иться** (**-юсь, -ишься**) *несов возв* (*быть похороненным*) to be at rest; (*основываться*): **~ на +prp** to rest on.
поко́|**й** (**-я**) *м* peace; **оставля́ть** (**оста́вить** *perf*) **кого́-н в ~е** to leave sb in peace; **он не даёт мне ~я** he doesn't give me any peace.
поко́йн|**ая** (**-ой**; *decl like adj*) *ж см* **поко́йный**.
поко́йник (**-а**) *м* the deceased.
поко́йни|**ца** (**-ы**) *ж см* **поко́йник**.
поко́йн|**ый** *прил* the late ♦ (**-ого**; *decl like adj*) *м* the deceased.
поколеба́|**ть** (**-ю**) *сов от* **колеба́ть**
▶ **поколеба́ться** *сов от* **колеба́ться** ♦ *возв* to waver.
поколе́ни|**е** (**-я**) *ср* generation.
поко́нч|**ить** (**-у, -ишь**) *сов неперех*: **~ с +instr** (*с делами, с ремонтом итп*) to be finished with; (*с бедностью, с проблемой*) to put an end to; **~** (*perf*) **с собо́й** to kill o.s., commit suicide.
покорёж|**ить** (**-у, -ишь**) *несов от* **корёжить**.
поко́рен *прил см* **поко́рный**.
покори́тел|**ь** (**-я**) *м* conqueror.
покор|**и́ть** (**-ю́, -и́шь**; *impf* **покоря́ть**) *сов перех* (*страну, народ*) to conquer; (*подлеж: женщина, стихи*) to conquer the heart of; **~** (*perf*) **чьё-н се́рдце** to win sb's heart
▶ **покори́ться** (*impf* **покоря́ться**) *сов возв*: **~ся** (**+dat**) to submit (to).
пок|**орми́ть** (**-ормлю́, -о́рмишь**) *сов от* **корми́ть**.
поко́рн|**ый** (**-ен, -на, -но**) *прил* submissive.
покоро́б|**ить(ся)** (**-лю(сь), -ишь(ся)**) *сов от* **коро́бить(ся)**.

покоря́|ть(ся) (-ю(сь)) несов от покори́ть(ся).

поко́с (-а) м (трав) mowing; (время покоса) haymaking.

поко|си́ть(ся) (-шу́(сь), -си́шь(ся)) сов от коси́ть(ся).

покра́|сить(ся) (-шу(сь), -сишь(ся)) сов от кра́сить(ся).

покрасне́|ть (-ю) сов от красне́ть.

покрас|ова́ться (-у́юсь) сов от красова́ться.

покра́шу(сь) сов см покра́сить(ся).

покриви́ть(ся) (-лю́(сь), -и́шь(ся)) несов от криви́ть(ся).

покри́кива|ть (-ю) несов неперех (разг): ~ (на +acc) to yell (at).

покро́в (-а) м (верхний слой) layer; (РЕЛ) shroud; сне́жный ~ a blanket of snow; под ~ом но́чи under cover of darkness.

покрови́тел|ь (-я) м protector.

покрови́тельниц|а (-ы) ж см покрови́тель.

покрови́тельствен|ный (-ен, -на, -но) прил patronizing.

покрови́тельств|о (-а) ср protection.

покро́|й (-я) ср cut (of clothing).

покро́ю(сь) итп сов см покры́ть(ся).

покрупне́|ть (-ю) сов от крупне́ть.

покрыва́л|о (-а) ср bedspread.

покрыва́|ть(ся) (-ю(сь)) несов от покры́ть(ся).

покры́ти|е (-я) ср covering; ~ дивиде́нда (КОММ) dividend cover.

покр|ы́ть (-о́ю, -о́ешь) сов от крыть ♦ (impf покрыва́ть) перех (звуки, шум) to cover up; (расходы, убытки, расстояние) to cover; покрыва́ть (~ perf) (что-н/кого-н чем-н) to cover (sth/sb with sth)

► покры́ться (impf покрыва́ться) сов возв (+instr; одеялом) to cover o.s. with; (румянцем, снегом итп) to be covered in.

покры́ш|ка (-ки; gen pl -ек) ж (АВТ) tyre (BRIT), tire (US).

покупа́тел|ь (-я) м (в магазине) customer; (товара, дома итп) buyer, purchaser.

покупа́тельниц|а (-ы) ж см покупа́тель.

покупа́тельн|ый прил: ~ая спосо́бность purchasing power.

покупа́тельск|ий (-ая, -ое, -ие) прил (спрос, интересы) consumer опред.

покупа́|ть (-ю) несов от купи́ть.

поку́п|ка (-ки; gen pl -ок) ж purchase; де́лать (сде́лать perf) ~ки to go shopping.

покупно́й прил (торг) bought.

поку́почн|ый прил: ~ая цена́ purchase price.

покуша́|ть (-ю) сов от ку́шать ♦ (не)перех: ~ чего-н to have sth to eat.

покуша́|ться (-юсь) несов возв: ~ на +acc to attempt to take.

покуше́ни|е (-я) ср: ~ (на +acc) (на свободу, на права) infringement (of); (на жизнь) attempt

(on); соверша́ть (соверши́ть perf) ~ на кого́-н to make an attempt on sb's life.

пол (-а; loc sg -у́, nom pl -ы́) м floor; (nom pl -ы, gen pl -о́в, dat pl -а́м) sex, gender.

пол|а́ (-ы́; nom pl -ы) ж (обычно мн: пальто, пиджака итп) side; продава́ть (прода́ть perf) из-под ~ы́ to sell under the counter.

полага́|ть (-ю) несов неперех (думать) to suppose; на́до ~ supposedly; ~ (impf) нача́ло чему́-н to make a start on sth; ~ (impf) коне́ц чему́-н to put an end to sth.

полага́|ться (-юсь) несов от положи́ться ♦ возв (быть должным) to be expected; ~ется приходи́ть во́ время one is expected to be punctual.

пола́|дить (-жу, -дишь) сов от ла́дить.

пола́ком|иться (-люсь, -ишься) сов от ла́комиться.

полбеды́ ж нескл: э́то ещё ~ (разг) it could be worse.

пол|ве́ка (-уве́ка) м half a century.

пол|го́да (-уго́да) м half a year.

по́лдень (полу́дня или по́лдня) м midday, noon; 2 часа́ по́сле полу́дня 2 p.m.

по́лдник (-а) м (afternoon) tea.

по́лдня сущ см по́лдень.

полдоро́г|и (-) ж: на ~е halfway; остана́вливаться (останови́ться perf) на ~е (также перен) to stop halfway.

по́л|е (-я; nom pl -я́, gen pl -е́й) ср field; ~ де́ятельности sphere of activity; ~ зре́ния field of vision; см также поля́.

полево́дств|о (-а) ср crop cultivation.

полево́й прил field опред; ~ы́е рабо́ты work in the fields; полево́й госпита́ль field hospital.

полёг итп сов см поле́чь.

полеж|а́ть (-у́, -и́шь) сов неперех (человек) to have a lie down; (книга на полке, продукты в ящике итп) to lie.

полеза́й(те) сов см лезть.

поле́з|ный (-ен, -на, -но) прил useful; (пища) healthy; чем могу́ быть ~ен? how can I be of help?; ~ная нагру́зка (КОММ) payload; поле́зные ископа́емые minerals; поле́зная жила́я пло́щадь living space.

поле́з|ть (-у, -ешь) сов неперех (начать лезть) to start climbing, start to climb; (в драку, в спор) to get involved.

поле́мик|а (-и) ж polemic.

полеми́ческ|ий (-ая, -ое, -ие) прил polemical.

поле|ни́ться (-ню́сь, -нишься) сов от лени́ться.

поле́н|о (-а; nom pl -ья, gen pl -ьев) ср log.

полёт (-а) м flight; ~ фанта́зии или мы́сли flight of fancy.

поле|те́ть (-чу́, -ти́шь) сов от лете́ть ♦ неперех (птица, самолёт) to fly off; (годы, дни) to start to fly by; (слухи, новости) to start to fly.

поле́чь (-я́гу, -я́жешь *итп*, -я́гут; *pt* -ёг, -егла́, -егло́) *сов неперех* (*травы*) to be flattened; (*перен: погибнуть*) to fall, perish.

по́лзать (-ю) *несов неперех* to crawl; ~ (*impf*) **в нога́х у кого́-н** to come crawling to sb.

ползко́м *нареч*: **продвига́ться** ~ to crawl along on one's stomach.

полз|ти́ (-у́, -ёшь; *pt* -, -ла́, -ло́) *несов неперех* to crawl; (*разг: медленно двигаться*) to crawl (along).

ползунк|и́ (-о́в) *мн* (*одежда*) rompers *мн*.

ползу́ч|ий (-ая, -ее, -ие) *прил* (*животные*) crawling *опред*; (*растения*) creeping *опред*.

полива́ть (-ю) *несов от* **поли́ть**.

поливитами́н|ы (-ов) *мн* multivitamins *мн*.

полига́ми|я (-и) *ж* polygamy.

полиго́н (-а) *м* (*для учений*) shooting range; (*для испытания оружия*) test(ing) site.

полиграфи́ст (-а) *м* printer.

полигра́фи|я (-и) *ж* printing.

поликли́ник|а (-и) *ж* clinic.

полиня́ть (*3sg* -ет, *3pl* -ют) *сов от* **линя́ть**.

полиомиели́т (-а) *м* polio(myelitis).

полир|ова́ть (-у́ю; *perf* **отполирова́ть**) *несов перех* to polish.

по́лис (-а) *м*: **страхово́й** ~ insurance policy.

полисеми́|я (-и) *ж* polysemy.

политбюро́ *ср нескл* the Politburo.

полите́хникум (-а) *м* technical college.

политехни́ческ|ий (-ая, -ое, -ие) *прил*: ~ **институ́т** polytechnic.

поли́тик (-а) *м* politician.

поли́тик|а (-и) *ж* (*курс*) policy; (*события, наука*) politics.

политика́н (-а) *м* (*пренебр*) politico.

полити́ческ|ий (-ая, -ое, -ие) *прил* political; **полити́ческая эконо́мия** political economy; **полити́ческий обозрева́тель** political observer.

полито́лог (-а) *м* political scientist.

пол|и́ть (-ью, -ьешь; *pt* -и́л, -ила́, -и́ло, *impf* **полива́ть**) *сов неперех* (*дождь*) to start pouring, start to pour ♦ *перех*: ~ **что-н чем-н** to pour sth on sth; **полива́ть** (~ *perf*) **цветы́** to water the flowers

▶ **поли́ться** *сов возв* to pour out.

политэконо́ми|я (-и) *ж сокр* (= полити́ческая эконо́мия) Pol. Econ. (= *political economy*).

полице́йск|ий (-ая, -ое, -ие) *прил* police *опред* ♦ (-ого; *decl like adj*) *м* policeman (*мн* policemen); **полице́йский уча́сток** police station.

поли́ци|я (-и) *ж* the police; **вызыва́ть** (**вы́звать** (*perf*)) ~**ю** to call the police.

поли́чн|ое (-ого; *decl like adj*) *ср*: **пойма́ть кого́-н с** ~**ым** to catch sb at the scene of a crime; (*перен*) to catch sb red-handed *или* in the act.

полиэтиле́н (-а) *м* polythene.

полиэтиле́новый *прил* polythene *опред*.

полк (-а́; *loc sg* -у́) *м* regiment.

по́л|ка (-ки; *gen pl* -ок) *ж* shelf; (*в поезде: для багажа*) luggage rack; (: *для лежания*) berth.

полко́вник (-а) *м* colonel.

полково́д|ец (-ца) *м* commander.

пол-ли́тра (**полули́тра**) *м* half a litre (*BRIT*) *или* liter (*US*).

полне́ть (-ю; *perf* **пополне́ть**) *несов неперех* to put on weight.

по́лно *как сказ* that's enough; ~ **серди́ться/ расстра́иваться** stop getting so angry/upset.

полно́ *как сказ* (+*gen*; *разг*): **в до́ме** ~ **книг** the house is stacked full of books; **наро́ду** ~ there are a lot of people.

полнове́с|ный (-ен, -на, -но) *прил* (*аргумент, статья*) weighty; (*описание*) full-bodied.

полновла́ст|ный (-ен, -на, -но) *прил* fully empowered.

полново́д|ный (-ен, -на, -но) *прил* deep.

полнокро́в|ный (-ен, -на, -но) *прил* (*жизнь*) full-blooded.

полнолу́ни|е (-я) *ср* full moon.

полнометра́жный *прил*: ~ **фильм** full-length film.

полномо́чный *прил см* **полномо́чный**.

полномо́чи|е (-я) *ср* authority; (*обычно мн: право*) power; **облека́ть** (**обле́чь** (*perf*)) **кого́-н** ~**ями** +*infin* to authorize sb to do; **слага́ть** (**сложи́ть** (*perf*)) **с себя́** ~**я** to relinquish one's authority; **э́то не вхо́дит в мои́** ~**я** it is not within my jurisdiction.

полномо́ч|ный (-ен, -на, -но) *прил* fully authorized.

полноправ|ный (-ен, -на, -но) *прил* (*гражданин*) fully-fledged; (*наследник*) rightful; **он** ~ **владе́лец** he has full ownership rights.

по́лностью *нареч* fully, completely.

полнот|а́ (-ы́) *ж* (*целостность*) completeness; (*тучность*) stoutness; **облада́ть** (*impf*) **всей** ~**ой вла́сти/прав** to enjoy full power/rights; **опи́сывать** (**описа́ть** *perf*) **что-н во всей** ~**е́** to describe sth in its entirety; **от** ~**ы́ чувств** *или* **души́** overcome by emotion.

полноце́н|ный (-ен, -на, -но) *прил* (*отдых, пища*) proper; (*работа, исследование*) valuable; (*деньги, валюта*) valued.

по́л|ночь (-уночи) *ж* midnight.

по́л|ный (-он, -на́, -но́ *или* -но) *прил* full; (*no short form*; *победа, власть, счастье итп*) complete, total (*толстый*) stout; ~ +*gen* *или* +*instr* full of; (*тревоги, любви итп*) filled with; **ведро́,** ~**ное воды́** a bucket, full of water; **ко́мната была́ полна́ людьми́** the room was full of people; **она́ была́ полна́ трево́ги** she was filled with anxiety; ~**ным хо́дом** at full speed; **в** ~**ную си́лу** at full strength; **полны́м-полно́** (+*gen*) (*разг*) loads and loads (of); **по́лное собра́ние сочине́ний** complete works.

по́ло *ср нескл*: (**во́дное**) ~ (water) polo.

полови́к (-а́) *м* mat.

полови́н|а (-ы) *ж* half; **на** ~**е доро́ги** halfway; **сейча́с** ~ **пе́рвого/второ́го** it's (now) half past twelve/one; **приходи́те в ~е двена́дцатого** come at half past eleven; **встре́ча назна́чена на ~у деся́того** the meeting has been set for half past nine.

полови́нчат|ый (-, -а, -о) *прил* (*меры, реше́ние*) half-baked.

поло́вник (-а) *м* ladle.

полово́дь|е (-я) *ср* high water.

полово́й *прил* (*тряпка, мастика*) floor *опред*; (*БИО*) sexual; **полова́я жизнь** sex life; **полова́я зре́лость** puberty; **полово́й о́рган** reproductive organ; **половы́е о́рганы** genitals.

поло́г|ий (-ая, -ое, -ие; -, -а, -о) *прил* (*склон*) gentle; (*гора, бе́рег*) gently sloping.

положе́ни|е (-я) *ср* situation; (*географи́ческое*) location, position; (*те́ла, головы итп*) position; (*социа́льное, семе́йное итп*) status; (*пра́вила*) regulations *мн*; (*обы́чно мн: те́зис*) point; **быть** (*impf*) **на высоте́ ~я** to be on top of the situation; **входи́ть** (**войти́** *perf*) **в чьё-н ~** to put o.s. in sb's position; **выходи́ть** (**вы́йти** *perf*) **из тру́дного/неприя́тного ~я** to get o.s. out of a difficult/unpleasant situation; **она́ в ~и** (*разг*) she's expecting; **положе́ние дел** the state of affairs.

поло́женный *прил* fixed.

положи́тел|ьный (-ен, -ьна, -ьно) *прил* positive.

пол|ожи́ть (-ожу́, -о́жишь) *сов от* **класть ♦** (*не*)*перех*: **~о́жим, ты прав/э́то так** let us assume that you're right/this is the case; **~ожа́ ру́ку на́ се́рдце** (*перен*) with hand on heart

▶ **положи́ться** (*impf* **полага́ться**) *сов возв*: **~ся на** +*acc* to count on.

по́л|оз (-оза; *nom pl* -о́зья) *м* (*обы́чно мн*) runner (*on sledge*).

поло́к *сущ см* **по́лка, по́лька**.

полома́|ть(ся) (-ю(сь)) *сов от* **лома́ть(ся)**.

поло́м|ка (-ки; *gen pl* -ок) *ж* (*де́йствие*) breakdown; (*повреждённое ме́сто*) damage.

по́лон *прил см* **по́лный**.

полос|а́ (-ы́; *nom pl* **по́лосы**, *gen pl* **поло́с**, *dat pl* **по́лосам**) *ж* (*тка́ни, мета́лла итп*) strip; (*на тка́ни, на рису́нке итп*) stripe; (*тума́на, ле́са итп*) belt; (*неуда́ч, плохо́й пого́ды*) spell; (*в газе́те*) column.

полоса́тый (-, -а, -о) *прил* striped, stripy.

поло́с|ка (-ки; *gen pl* -ок) *ж* (*тка́ни, бума́ги, мета́лла*) (thin) strip; (*на оде́жде, на тка́ни*) (thin) stripe; **в ~ку** striped.

пол|оска́ть (-ощу́, -о́щешь; *perf* **прополоска́ть**) *несов перех* (*бельё, посу́ду*) to rinse; (*рот*) to rinse out; **~** (**прополоска́ть** *perf*) **го́рло** to gargle.

поло́сок *сущ см* **поло́ска**.

по́лост|ь (-и; *gen pl* -е́й) *ж* (*АНАТ*) cavity.

полоте́н *сущ см* **полотно́**.

полоте́н|це (-ца; *gen pl* -ец) *ср* towel.

поло́тнищ|е (-а) *ср*: **~ фла́га** flag.

пол|отно́ (-отна́; *nom pl* -о́тна, *gen pl* -о́тен) *ср* (*ткань*) sheet; (*карти́на*) canvas; **бле́дный как ~** white as a sheet.

пол|о́ть (-ю́, -ешь; *perf* **прополо́ть**) *несов перех* to weed.

полоу́мный *прил* (*разг: иде́я, речь*) crackpot *опред*.

полощу́ *итп несов см* **полоска́ть**.

полпре́д (-а) *м* (= **полномо́чный представи́тель**) plenipotentiary.

полпути́ *м нескл* half (*of journey*); **на ~** halfway; (*перен: останови́ться, бро́сить де́ло итп*) halfway through; **верну́ться** (*perf*) **с ~ to** turn back halfway.

полсло́ва (- *или* **полусло́ва**) *ср* half of the word; **мо́жно Вас на ~?** could I have a quick word?; **прерыва́ть** (**прерва́ть** *perf*) **кого́-н на пол(у)сло́ве** to cut sb short; **понима́ть** (**поня́ть** *perf*) **с пол(у)сло́ва** to understand in an instant.

полти́нник (-а) *м* (*су́мма*) 50 kopecks; (*моне́та*) 50-kopeck piece.

пол|тора́ (-у́тора; *f* **полторы́**) *м/ср чис* one and a half; **ей ~ го́да** she is one and a half; **ей о́коло ~у́тора лет** she is about one and a half; **кни́га сто́ит ~ рубля́/полторы́ ма́рки** the book costs one and a half roubles/one and a half marks.

пол|тора́ста (-у́тораста) *чис* one hundred and fifty.

полуботи́н|ок (-ка) *м* (*обы́чно мн*) man's desert boot.

полуве́ка *сущ см* **полве́ка**.

полуго́да *сущ см* **полго́да**.

полуго́ди|е (-я) *ср* (*ПРОСВЕЩ*) semester; (*ЭКОН*) half (*of the year*).

полугоди́чный *прил* six-month.

полугодово́й *прил* six-monthly, half-yearly.

полу́дня *сущ см* **по́лдень**.

полузащи́т|а (-ы) *ж* midfield.

полузащи́т|ник (-а) *м* midfielder.

полукру́г (-а) *м* semicircle.

полукру́глый *прил* semicircular.

полуме́р|а (-ы) *ж* half-measure (*fig*).

полуме́сяц (-а) *м* half-moon.

полумра́к (-а) *м* semidarkness.

полу́ночи *сущ см* **по́лночь**.

полуо́стров (-а) *м* peninsular.

полупальто́ *ср нескл* jacket, short coat.

полупроводни́к (-а́) *м* (*ЭЛЕК*) semiconductor.

полусапо́ж|ек (-ка; *gen pl* -ек) *м* (*обы́чно мн*) half-boot.

полусло́ва *сущ см* **полсло́ва**.

полуто́н (-а) *м* (*МУЗ*) semitone, half step (*US*).

полу́тора *чис см* **полтора́**.

полуфабрика́т (-а) *м* (*КУЛИН*) *any products such as frozen foods and cake mixes which require partial preparation*; (*ТЕХ*) semifinished article.

полуфина́л (-а) *м* semifinal.
получа́са *сущ см* **полчаса́**.
получа́тель (-я) *м* recipient.
получа́|ть(ся) (-ю(сь)) *несов от* **получи́ть(ся)**.
полу́чек *сущ см* **полу́чка**.
получе́ни|е (-я) *ср* receipt; (*урожая*, *результата*) obtaining.
пол|учи́ть (-учу́, -у́чишь; *impf* **получа́ть**) *сов перех* to receive, get; (*урожай*, *результат*, *насморк*, *удово́лствие*) to get; (*изве́стность*, *распростране́ние*, *примене́ние итп*) to gain ♦ *неперех* (*разг: быть нака́занным*) to get it in the neck
▸ **получи́ться** (*impf* **получа́ться**) *сов возв* to turn out; (*удаться*) to work; (*фотогра́фия*) to come out; **из него́** ~**у́чится хоро́ший учи́тель** he'll make a good teacher; **пиро́г хорошо́** ~**учи́лся** the pie turned out well; **у меня́ э́то не** ~**уча́ется** I can't do it; **из э́того ничего́ не** ~**у́чится** it won't come to anything.
полу́ч|ка (-ки; *gen pl* -ек) *ж* (*разг*) pay.
полуша́ри|е (-я) *ср* hemisphere.
полушу́б|ок (-ка) *м* (*из овчины*) sheepskin jacket; (*из меха*) short fur coat.
полцены́ *ж нескл* (*разг*): **за** ~ for next to nothing.
полчаса́ (-уча́са) *м* half an hour; **ка́ждые** ~ every half hour; **прошло́** *или* **прошли́** ~ half an hour went by.
по́лчищ|е (-а) *ср* (*обычно мн: враго́в*) horde; (: *насеко́мых, крыс*) swarm.
по́л|ый (-, -а, -о) *прил* hollow.
полы́н|ь (-и) *ж* wormwood.
полысе́|ть (-ю) *сов от* **лысе́ть**.
полыха́|ть (-ю) *несов неперех* to blaze.
по́льз|а (-ы) *ж* benefit; **в** ~**у** +*gen* in favour (*BRIT*) *или* favor (*US*) of; **идти́** (**пойти́** *perf*) **на** ~**у кому́-н** to be of benefit to sb.
по́льзовани|е (-я) *ср*: ~ (+*instr*) use (of).
по́льзовател|ь (-я) *м* (*также КОМП*) user.
по́льз|оваться (-уюсь; *perf* **воспо́льзоваться**) *несов возв* (+*instr*) to use; (*no perf*; *авторите́том, успе́хом итп*) to enjoy.
по́ль|ка (-ьки; *gen pl* -ек) *ж см* **поля́к**; (*танец*) polka.
по́льск|ий (-ая, -ое, -ие) *прил* Polish; ~ **язы́к** Polish.
польсти́ть (-щу́, -сти́шь) *сов от* **льстить**.
По́льш|а (-и) *ж* Poland.
польщё́н|ный (-, -а́, -о́) *прил*: ~ (+*instr*) flattered (by).
польщу́ *сов см* **польсти́ть**.
полью́(сь) *итп сов см* **поли́ть(ся)**.
полюб|и́ть (-лю́, -и́шь) *сов перех* (*челове́ка*) to come to love; ~ (*perf*) **что-н**/+*infin* to develop a love for sth/doing.
полюб|ова́ться (-у́юсь) *сов от* **любова́ться** ♦ *возв* (*разг*): ~**у́йтесь на его́/э́то!** take a look at him/that!
по́люс (-а; *nom pl* -а́) *м* (*ГЕО, ЭЛЕК*) pole.
пол|я́ (-е́й) *мн* (*шля́пы*) brim *ед*; (*на страни́це*)

margin *ед*.
поля́гу *итп сов см* **поле́чь**.
поля́к (-а) *м* Pole.
поля́н|а (-ы) *ж* glade.
поля́рный *прил* (*ГЕО*) polar *опред*; (*интере́сы*, *точки зре́ния итп*) diametrically opposed; **поля́рная звезда́** the Pole Star; **поля́рная ночь** Arctic night; **поля́рный день** Arctic day.
пома́д|а (-ы) *ж* (*также: губна́я* ~) lipstick.
пома́|зать (-жу, -жешь) *сов от* **ма́зать**.
помале́ньку *нареч* (*разг*) bit by bit; **живём** ~ we're getting by.
пома́лкива|ть (-ю) *несов неперех* (*разг*) to keep quiet.
пом|ани́ть (-аню́, -а́нишь) *сов от* **мани́ть**.
пома́р|ка (-ки; *gen pl* -ок) *ж* crossing out (*мн* crossings out).
пома́сл|ить (-ю, -ишь) *сов от* **ма́слить**.
пом|аха́ть (-ашу́, -а́шешь) *сов неперех* (+*instr*) to wave.
помедл|ить (-ю, -ишь) *сов неперех*: ~ **с** +*instr*/ +*infin* to linger over sth/over doing.
помелю́ *итп сов см* **помоло́ть**.
поменя́|ть(ся) (-ю(сь)) *сов от* **меня́ть(ся)**.
помере́щ|иться (*3sg* -ится, *3pl* -атся) *сов от* **мере́щиться**.
поме́р|ить(ся) (-ю(сь), -ишь(ся)) *сов от* **ме́рить(ся)**.
поме́ркн|уть (-у, -ешь) *сов от* **ме́ркнуть**.
помертве́|ть (-ю) *сов от* **мертве́ть**.
пом|ести́ть (-ещу́, -ести́шь; *impf* **помеща́ть**) *сов перех* to put; (*поста́вить*) to place, put; (*посели́ть*) to put up; (*устро́ить*) to settle
▸ **помести́ться** (*impf* **помеща́ться**) *сов возв* (*умести́ться*) to fit.
поме́сть|е (-ья; *gen pl* -ий) *ср* estate.
помё́т (-а) *м* dung.
поме́т|а (-ы) *ж* (*в словаре*) explanatory note.
поме́|тить (-чу, -тишь) *сов от* **ме́тить** ♦ (*impf* **помеча́ть**) *перех* to note.
поме́т|ка (-ки; *gen pl* -ок) *ж* note.
помех|а (-и) *ж* hindrance; (*связь: обычно мн*) interference *ед*.
помеча́|ть (-ю) *несов от* **поме́тить**.
помечу́ *сов см* **поме́тить**.
поме́шан|ный (-, -а, -о) *прил* mad; (*разг*): ~ **на** +*prp* (*перен*) crazy about.
помеша́тельств|о (-а) *ср* madness.
помеша́|ть (-ю) *сов от* **меша́ть**.
▸ **помеша́ться** *сов возв* to go mad; (*разг*): ~**ся на** +*prp* to be crazy about.
помеща́|ть (-ю) *несов от* **помести́ть**.
▸ **помеща́ться** *несов от* **помести́ться** ♦ *возв* (*находи́ться*) to be situated.
помеще́ни|е (-я) *ср* room; (*под офис*) premises *мн*; **жило́е** ~ living space.
поме́щик (-а) *м* landowner.
поме́щиц|а (-ы) *ж см* **поме́щик**.
помещу́(сь) *сов см* **помести́ть(ся)**.
помидо́р (-а) *м* tomato (*мн* tomatoes).
поми́ловани|е (-я) *ср* (*престу́пника*) pardon.

помúл|овать (-ую) *сов от* мúловать ♦
~**уйте**! (*разг*) you can't be serious!

помúмо *предл* (+*gen*) besides; (*без участия*)
bypassing; ~ **дéнег нам нужнá машúна** besides
money we need a car; ~ **тогó/всегó прóчего**
apart from that/everything else.

помúн (-а) *м*: **этого и в** ~**е нет** it's nowhere to
be found; **егó у нас и в** ~**е нé было** we haven't
seen hide nor hair of him; **лёгок на** ~**е** (*разг*)
speak of the devil.

поминáльный *прил* (*РЕЛ*) funeral *опред*.

помина|ть (-ю) *несов от* помянýть ♦ *неперех*:
~**й как звáли** (*разг*) just like that.

помúн|ки (-ок) *мн* wake *ед*; **справля|ть**
(**спрáвить** *perf*) ~ **по комý-н** to give a wake for
sb.

поминýт|ный (-ен, -на, -но) *прил* at intervals of
one minute; (*очень частый*) constant; (*оплата*)
by the minute.

помир|úть(ся) (-ю́(сь), -úшь(ся)) *сов от*
мирúть(ся).

пóмн|ить (-ю, -ишь) *несов* (*не*)*перех*: ~ (**о** +*prp*/
про +*acc*) to remember; **я** ~**ю о Вáшу прóсьбу**
или **о Вáшей прóсьбе** I remember your request;
я ~**ю, что Вы просúли об этом** I remember
that you asked about that

▶ **пóмниться** *несов возв* to be remembered; **мне**
~**ится нáша встрéча** I remember our meeting;
~**ится, мы об этом говорúли** I remember that
we spoke about that.

помножá|ть (-ю) *несов перех* = мнóжить.

помнóж|ить (-у, -ишь) *сов от* мнóжить.

помнý(сь) *итп сов см* помя́ть(ся).

помóг *итп сов см* помóчь.

помогá|ть (-ю) *несов от* помóчь.

помогý *итп сов см* помóчь.

помóек *сущ см* помóйка.

по-мóему *нареч* my way ♦ *вводн сл* in my
opinion.

помóжешь *итп сов см* помóчь.

помó|и (-ев) *мн* dishwater; (*отходы*) slops *мн*.

помóй|ка (-йки; *gen pl* -ек) *ж* (*помойная яма*)
cesspit; (*для мусора*) rubbish (*BRIT*) *или* garbage
(*US*) heap.

помóл (-а) *м*: **мукá/кóфе мéлкого/крýпного**
~**а** fine-/coarse-ground flour/coffee.

помóлв|ить (-лю, -ишь) *сов перех*: **онú** ~**лены**
they are engaged; **онá** ~**лена с ним** she is
engaged to him.

помол|úться (-юсь, -ишься) *сов от*
молúться.

помолодé|ть (-ю) *сов от* молодéть.

помол|óть (-ю, -ешь) *несов от* молóть.

помолчá|ть (-ý, -úшь) *сов неперех* to pause.

помор|úть (-ю́, -úшь) *сов от* морúть.

помóр|щиться (-усь, -ишься) *сов возв* to
screw up one's face.

помóст (-а) *м* (*для обозрения*) platform; (*для

выступлений) rostrum; (*для казни*) scaffold.

помотá|ть (-ю) *сов от* мотáть.

помоч|úться (-очýсь, -óчишься) *сов от*
мочúться.

помóчь (-огý, -óжешь *итп*, -óгут; *pt* -óг, -оглá,
-огло́, *impf* помогáть) *сов неперех* (+*dat*) to
help; (*в работе*) to help, assist; (*другой
стране*) to aid.

помóщник (-а) *м* helper; (*должностное лицо*)
assistant; ~ **капитáна** mate.

пóмощь (-и) *ж* help, assistance; **с** ~**ю, при
пóмощи** with; **звать (позвáть** *perf*) **на** ~ to call
for help; **окáзывать (оказáть** *perf*) **комý-н** ~ to
help *или* assist sb; **просúть (попросúть** *perf*) **о**
~**и** to ask for help.

помóю(сь) *итп сов см* помы́ть(ся).

помпóн (-а) *м* pompom.

помрачнé|ть (-ю) *сов от* мрачнéть.

помут|úть(ся) (*3sg* -úт(ся), *3pl* -я́т(ся)) *сов от*
мутúть(ся).

помутнé|ть (-ю) *сов от* мутнéть.

помýч|ить (-у, -ишь) *несов перех* to torment

▶ **помýчиться** *сов возв* to suffer.

пóмысел (-ла) *м* intention.

помы́сл|ить (-ю, -ишь; *impf* помышля́ть) *сов
неперех*: ~ **о чём-н** to have sth in mind.

помы́|ть(ся) (-ю(сь), -ешь(ся)) *сов от*
мы́ть(ся).

помышля́|ть (-ю) *несов от* помы́слить.

помя|нýть (-нý, -нешь; *impf* поминáть) *сов
перех* (*упомянуть*) to mention; (*устроить
поминки*) to give a wake for; ~**нúте моё слóво**
mark my words.

помя́т|ый (-, -а, -о) *прил* (*разг: одежда,
внешность*) rumpled; (*бок машины*) dented.

помя́|ть(ся) (-нý(сь), -нёшь(ся)) *сов от*
мя́ть(ся).

понадé|яться (-юсь) *сов от* надéяться.

понадóб|иться (-люсь, -ишься) *сов возв* to
need, require.

понаслы́шке *нареч*: **знать** ~ **о ком-н/чём-н** to
hear a rumour (*BRIT*) *или* rumor (*US*) about sb/
sth.

по-настоя́щему *нареч* properly.

поначáлу *нареч* (*разг*) at first.

по-нáшему *нареч* our way ♦ *вводн сл* in our
opinion.

поневóле *нареч* against one's will.

понедéльник (-а) *м* Monday; *см также*
вто́рник.

понемнóгу *нареч* a little; (*постепенно*) little by
little; **как поживáете?** – ~ how's life? – not too
bad.

пон|естú (-есý, -есёшь; *pt* -ёс, -еслá, -еслó) *сов
от* нестú ♦ *перех* (*начать нести*) to take

▶ **понестúсь** *сов возв* (*человек*) to tear off;
(*лошадь*) to charge off; (*машина*) to speed off.

по́ни *м нескл* pony.

понижа́|ть(ся) (-ю(сь)) *несов от* **пони́зить(ся)**.

пониже́ни|е (-я) *ср* reduction; (*в должности*) demotion.

пони́|зить (-жу, -зишь; *impf* **понижа́ть**) *сов перех* to reduce; (*в должности*) to demote; (*голос*) to lower

▸ **пони́зиться** (*impf* **понижа́ться**) *сов возв* to be reduced.

по́низу *нареч* (*близко к земле*) low.

пони́к|нуть (-у, -ешь) *сов от* **ни́кнуть**.

понима́ни|е (-я) *ср* (*способность ума*) understanding; (*толкование*) interpretation; **относи́ться** (**отнести́сь** *perf*) **к чему́-н с ~м** to be understanding about sth; **то вы́ше моего́ ~я** this is beyond me.

понима́|ть (-ю) *несов от* **поня́ть** ♦ *перех* to understand ♦ *неперех*: **~ в** +*prp* to know about; **~ете** you see; **вот э́то ~ю!** (*разг*) that's great!

пономар́|ь (-я́) *м* (*РЕЛ*) ≈ acolyte.

поно́с (-а) *м* diarrhoea (*BRIT*), diarrhea (*US*).

поно|си́ть (-шу́, -о́сишь) *сов перех* to carry for a while; (*одежду*) to wear ♦ *несов перех* (*ругать*) to curse.

поно́шен|ный (-, -на, -но) *прил* (*одежда*) worn.

поношу́ (*не*)*сов см* **поноси́ть**.

понра́в|иться (-люсь, -ишься) *сов от* **нра́виться**.

понто́н (-а) *м* pontoon bridge.

понука́|ть (-ю) *несов перех* (*также перен*) to urge on.

пону́р|ить (-ю, -ишь) *сов перех*: **~ го́лову** to hang one's head.

пону́рый *прил* downcast.

по́нчик (-а) *м* doughnut (*BRIT*), donut (*US*).

поны́не *нареч* to this day.

поню́ха|ть (-ю) *сов от* **ню́хать**.

поня́тен *прил см* **поня́тный**.

поня́ти|е (-я) *ср* (*времени, пространства итп*) conception; (*о политике, о литературе*) idea; **~я не име́ю** (*разг*) I've no idea.

поня́тлив|ый (-, -а, -о) *прил* quick.

поня́тно *нареч* intelligibly ♦ *как сказ*: **мне ~** I understand; **~!** I see!

поня́т|ный (-ен, -на, -но) *прил* intelligible; (*ясный*) clear; (*оправданный*) understandable.

понят|о́й (-о́го; *decl like adj*) *м* (*ЮР*) witness (*during official search*).

по|ня́ть (-йму́, -ймёшь; *pt* -нял, -няла́, -няло, *impf* **понима́ть**) *сов перех* to understand; **дава́ть** (**дать** *perf*) **~ кому́-н** to give sb to understand.

пообе́да|ть (-ю) *сов от* **обе́дать**.

пообеща́|ть (-ю) *сов от* **обеща́ть**.

пода́ль *нареч* a little way away ♦ *предл*: **~ от** +*gen* a little way from.

поодино́чке *нареч* one at a time.

поочерёдный *прил* (*дежурство, обслуживание*) alternating.

поощре́ни|е (-я) *ср* (*действие*) encouragement; (*то, чем поощряют*) incentive.

поощри́тельн|ый *прил*: **~ая пла́та** (*КОММ*) incentive bonus.

поощр|и́ть (-ю́, -и́шь; *impf* **поощря́ть**) *сов перех* to encourage.

поп (-а́) *м* (*разг*) priest.

по́п|а (-ы) *ж* (*разг*) bottom, bum.

попада́ни|е (-я) *ср* hit.

попада́|ть(ся) (-ю(сь)) *несов от* **попа́сть(ся)**.

попаду́(сь) *итп сов см* **попа́сть(ся)**.

попа́рно *нареч* in pairs.

попа́|сть (-ду́, -дёшь; *impf* **попада́ть**) *сов неперех*: **~ в** +*acc* (*в цель*) to hit; (*в ворота*) to end up in; (*в чужой город*) to find o.s. in; (*в беду*) to land in; **мы́ло ~ло в глаза́** the soap got in my eyes; **он ~л мячо́м в корзи́ну** he put the ball in the basket; **~** (*perf*) **университе́т/на ку́рсы** to get into university/onto a course; **попада́ть** (**~** *perf*) **в ава́рию** to have an accident; **~** (*perf*) **в плен** to be taken prisoner; **попада́ть** (**~** *perf*) **под дождь** to be caught in the rain; **ему́ ~ло** (*разг*) he got a hiding; (**Вы**) **не туда́ ~ли** you've got the wrong number; **где ~ло** (*разг*) anywhere; **как ~ло** (*разг*) anyhow; **что ~ло** (*разг*) anything

▸ **попа́сться** (*impf* **попада́ться**) *сов возв* (*быть по́йманным*) to be caught; **~ся** (*perf*) **на взя́тках/воровстве́** to be caught taking bribes/stealing; **мне ~лась интере́сная кни́га** I came across an interesting book; **попада́ться** (**~ся** *perf*) **кому́-н на глаза́** to catch sb's eye.

попе́й(те) *сов см* **попи́ть**.

попере́к *нареч* crossways ♦ *предл* (+*gen*) across.

попереме́нно *нареч* in turns.

попере́чный *прил* horizontal.

поперхн|у́ться (-у́сь, -ёшься) *сов возв* to choke.

поперч|и́ть (-у́, -и́шь) *сов от* **перчи́ть**.

попече́ни|е (-я) *ср* (*о детях*) care; (*о делах, о доме*) charge; **оставля́ть** (**оста́вить** *perf*) **кого́-н/что-н на чьё-н ~** to leave sb/sth in sb's care.

попечи́тел|ь (-я) *м* guardian; (*КОММ*) trustee.

попира́|ть (-ю) *несов от* **попра́ть**.

попи|са́ть (-шу́, -шешь) *сов* (*не*)*перех* to write; **ничего́ не ~шешь** (*разг*) there's nothing you can do.

поп|и́ть (-ью́, -ьёшь; *pt* -и́л, -ила́, -и́ло, *imper* -е́й(те)) *сов перех* to have a drink of.

попишу́ *итп сов см* **описа́ть**.

по́пкорн (-а) *м* popcorn.

поплав|о́к (-ка́) *м* (*на удочке*) float.

попл|ати́ться (-ачу́сь, -а́тишься) *сов от* **плати́ться**.

попли́н (-а) *м* poplin.

попл|ы́ть (-ву́, -вёшь; *pt* -л, -ла́, -ло) *сов неперех* (*человек, животное*) to start swimming; (*судно*) to set sail.

попола́м *нареч* in half; **~ с** +*instr* mixed with.

пополне́ни|е (-я) *ср* (*запасов*) replenishment; (*коллекции*) expansion; (*то, чем пополняется*) reinforcement.

пополне́ть (-ю) *сов от* **полне́ть.**

попо́лн|ить (-ю, -ишь; *impf* **пополня́ть**) *сов перех*: ~ **что-н** +*instr* (*запасы*) to replenish sth with; (*коллекцию*) to expand sth with; (*коллектив*) to reinforce sth with; (*образование*) to supplement sth with

▶ **попо́лниться** (*impf* **пополня́ться**) *сов возв* (*запасы*) to be replenished; (*коллекция*) to be expanded.

поправи́м|ый (-, -а, -о) *прил* (*дело, ошибка*) rectifiable.

попра́в|ить (-лю, -ишь; *impf* **поправля́ть**) *сов перех* to correct; (*галстук, платье итп*) to straighten; (*причёску*) to tidy; (*здоровье, дела*) to improve

▶ **попра́виться** (*impf* **поправля́ться**) *сов возв* to improve; (*пополне́ть*) to put on weight.

попра́в|ка (-ки; *gen pl* -ок) *ж* (*в решение, в закон*) amendment; **вноси́ть** (**внести́** *perf*) ~**ку в зако́н** to make an amendment to a law; **де́ло идёт на** ~**ку** things are looking up.

попра́влю(сь) *сов см* **попра́вить(ся).**

поправля́|ть(ся) (-ю(сь)) *несов от* **попра́вить(ся).**

попра́вок *сущ см* **попра́вка.**

попра́|ть (*pt* -л, -ла, -ло, *impf* **попира́ть**) *сов перех* (*права*) to disregard; (*гордость*) to offend; (*закон*) to flout.

по-пре́жнему *нареч* as before.

попрека́|ть (-ю) *несов перех* to reproach.

попрекн|у́ть (-у́, -ёшь) *сов перех* to reproach.

привё́тствовать (-ую) *сов от* **приве́тствовать.**

по́прищ|е (-а) *ср* (*науки итп*) field.

попро́б|овать (-ую) *сов от* **про́бовать** ♦ *неперех*: ~**уйте!** (*разг*) just you try!

попро|си́ть(ся) (-ошу́(сь), -о́сишь(ся)) *сов от* **проси́ть(ся).**

по́просту *част* simply; **он** ~ **уста́л** he's just *или* simply tired.

попро́шу(сь) *сов см* **попроси́ть(ся).**

попроща́|ться (-юсь) *сов возв*: ~ **с** +*instr* to say goodbye to.

попуга́|й (-я) *м* parrot.

популя́рен *прил см* **популя́рный.**

популяризи́р|овать (-ую) (*не*)*сов перех* to popularize.

популяриз|ова́ть (-у́ю) (*не*)*сов* = **популяризи́ровать.**

популя́рност|ь (-и) *ж* popularity.

популя́рн|ый (-ен, -на, -но) *прил* popular; (*изложение*) accessible.

популя́ци|я (-и) *ж* population (*of plants or animals*).

попурри́ *ср нескл* (*муз*) medley.

попусти́тельств|овать (-ую) *несов неперех* (+*dat*) to tolerate.

по́пусту *нареч* (*разг*) in vain.

попу́тн|ый *прил* (*замечание, исправление*) accompanying; (*машина*) passing; (*ветер*) favourable (*BRIT*), favorable (*US*); (: *МОР*) fair.

попу́тчик (-а) *м* travelling (*BRIT*) *или* traveling (*US*) companion.

попыта́|ть (-ю) *сов перех*: ~ **сча́стья** to try one's luck

▶ **попыта́ться** *сов от* **пыта́ться.**

попы́т|ка (-ки; *gen pl* -ок) *ж* attempt; ~ **к бе́гству** attempted escape; **со второ́й/с тре́тьей** ~**ки** on *или* at the second/third attempt.

попью́ *итп сов см* **попи́ть.**

попя́|титься (-чусь, -тишься) *сов возв* to take a few steps backward.

попя́тн|ый *прил*: **идти́** *или* **пойти́ на** ~ *или* **на** ~**ую** to go back on one's word.

попя́чусь *сов см* **попя́титься.**

по́р|а (-ы) *ж* pore.

пор|а́ (-ы́; *acc sg* -у, *dat sg* -е́, *nom pl* -ы) *ж* time ♦ **как сказ** it's time; **до каки́х** ~**р?** until when?; **до** ~**ры́ до вре́мени** for the time being; **до сих пор** (*раньше*) up till now; (*всё ещё*) still; **до тех пор** until then; **до тех пор, пока́** until; **на пе́рвых** ~**х** at first; **с каки́х пор?** since when?; (**мне**) ~ it's time (for me) to go; (**мне**) ~ **спать/рабо́тать** it's time (for me) to go to bed/ to work.

порабо|ти́ть (-щу́, -ти́шь; *impf* **порабоща́ть**) *сов перех* to enslave.

порабоще́ни|е (-я) *ср* enslavement.

порабощу́ *сов см* **порабо́тить.**

поравня́|ться (-юсь) *сов возв*: ~ **с** +*instr* (*человек*) to draw level with; (*машина*) to come alongside.

пора́д|овать(ся) (-ую(сь)) *сов от* **ра́довать(ся).**

поража́|ть(ся) (-ю(сь)) *несов от* **порази́ть(ся).**

пораже́ни|е (-я) *ср* (*цели*) hitting; (*МЕД*: *лёгких*) damage; (*в войне, в состязании итп*) defeat; **наноси́ть** (**нанести́** *perf*) **кому́-н** ~ to defeat sb; **терпе́ть** (**потерпе́ть** *perf*) ~ to be defeated.

поражу́(сь) *сов см* **порази́ть(ся).**

порази́тельн|ый (-ен, -ьна, -ьно) *прил* (*красота, талант*) striking; (*жестокость*) astonishing.

пора|зи́ть (-жу́, -зи́шь; *impf* **поража́ть**) *сов перех* (*цель*) to hit; (*подлеж: болезнь*) to affect; (*изумить*) to astonish

▶ **порази́ться** (*impf* **поража́ться**) *сов возв* to be astonished.

пора́н|ить (-ю, -ишь) *сов перех* to hurt.

пор|асти́ (*3sg* -асте́т, *3pl* -асту́т, *pt* -о́с, -осла́, -осло́, *impf* **пораста́ть**) *сов неперех*: ~ +*instr* to become overgrown with.

порв|а́ть (-у́, -ёшь) *сов от* **рвать** ♦ *перех* to tear ♦ (*impf* **порыва́ть**) *неперех*: ~ **с** +*instr* (*с женой, с друзьями*) to break up with; **порыва́ть** (~ *perf*) **что-н с кем-н** to break off sth with sb

▶ **порва́ться** *сов от* **рва́ться** ♦ *возв* (*нить*) to break; (*платье*) to tear.

пореде́ть (*3sg* -ет, *3pl* -ют) *несов от* **реде́ть**.

поре́жу(сь) *итп сов см* **поре́зать(ся)**.

поре́з (-а) *м* cut.

поре́|зать (-жу, -жешь) *сов перех* to cut

▶ **поре́заться** *сов возв* to cut o.s.

поре́|й (-я) *м* leek.

порекомендова́ть (-у́ю) *сов от* **рекомендова́ть**.

по́ристый (-, -а, -о) *прил* porous.

порица́ни|е (-я) *ср* reprimand.

порица́ть (-ю) *несов перех* to reprimand.

порнографи́ческ|ий (-ая, -ое, -ие) *прил* pornographic.

порногра́фи|я (-и) *ж* pornography.

по́ровну *нареч* equally.

поро́г (-а) *м* (*также перен*) threshold; (*на реке*) rapids *мн*; **переступа́ть** (**переступи́ть** *perf*) ~ to cross the threshold; **я его́ на** ~ **не пущу́** he won't darken my door again.

поро́д|а (-ы) *ж* (*животных*) breed; (*древесная*) species; (*горная*) rock; (*перен: людей*) type.

поро́дистый (-, -а, -о) *прил* pedigree *опред*; (*лицо*) aristocratic.

поро|ди́ть (-жу́, -ди́шь; *impf* **порожда́ть**) *сов перех* (*стать причиной*) to give rise to.

породни́ться (-ю́сь, -и́шься) *сов от* **родни́ться**.

порожда́|ть (-ю) *несов от* **породи́ть**.

поро́жн|ий (-яя, -ее, -ие) *прил* empty; **перелива́ть** (*impf*) **из пусто́го в** ~**ее** to rabbit on.

порожня́к (-а́) *м* empty vehicle.

порожняко́м *нареч* without a load.

порожу́ *итп сов см* **породи́ть**.

по́рознь *нареч* apart.

порозове́|ть (-ю) *сов от* **розове́ть**.

поро́й *нареч* from time to time.

поро́к (-а) *м* vice; **поро́к се́рдца** heart disease.

пороло́н (-а) *м* foam rubber.

поро́с *итп сов см* **порасти́**.

поросёнок (-ёнка; *nom pl* -я́та, *gen pl* -я́т) *м* piglet.

по́росл|ь (-и) *ж* (*побеги*) shoots *мн*; (*перен*) generation.

порося́та *итп сущ см* **поросёнок**.

пор|о́ть (-ю́, -ешь; *perf* **распоро́ть**) *несов перех* (*швы*) to unpick; (*perf* **вы́пороть**; *бить*) to belt; ~ (**напоро́ть** *perf*) **чушь** *или* **ерунду́** *или* **чепуху́** to talk nonsense; ~ (*impf*) **горя́чку** (*разг*) to get a move on.

по́рох (-а; *part gen* -у) *м* gunpowder.

поро́чен *прил см* **поро́чный**.

поро́ч|ить (-у, -ишь; *perf* **опоро́чить**) *несов перех* to bring shame on; (*чернить: человека*) to defame; (: *работу*) to bring into disrepute.

поро́ч|ный (-ен, -на, -но) *прил* (*безнравственный*) depraved; (*неправильный*) flawed.

порош|о́к (-ка́) *м* powder.

поро́ю *нареч* = **поро́й**.

порт (-а; *loc sg* -у́, *nom pl* -ы, *gen pl* -о́в) *м* port; **возду́шный** ~ airport.

порта́л (-а) *м* (*АРХИТ*) portal.

портати́вный *прил* portable.

портве́йн (-а) *м* port (*wine*).

по́р|тить (-чу, -тишь; *perf* **испо́ртить**) *несов перех* (*механизм, здоровье, карьеру*) to damage; (*настроение, праздник, ребёнка*) to spoil; ~ (*impf*) **себе́ не́рвы** to worry

▶ **по́ртиться** (*perf* **испо́ртиться**) *сов возв* (*механизм*) to be damaged; (*здоровье, погода*) to deteriorate; (*настроение*) to be spoiled; (*молоко*) to go off; (*мясо, овощи*) to go bad.

портни́х|а (-и) *ж* dressmaker.

портн|о́й (-о́го; *decl like adj*) *м* tailor.

порто́вый *прил* port *опред*.

портре́т (-а) *м* portrait.

портсига́р (-а) *м* cigarette case.

Портсму́т (-а) *м* Portsmouth.

Португа́ли|я (-и) *ж* Portugal.

португа́льск|ий (-ая, -ое, -ие) *прил* Portuguese; ~ **язы́к** Portuguese.

портфе́л|ь (-я) *м* briefcase; (*ПОЛИТ, КОММ*) portfolio; ~ **це́нных бума́г** (*КОММ*) investment portfolio.

портье́ *м нескл* (*в гостинице*) porter.

портье́р|а (-ы) *ж* curtain.

портя́нк|а (-ки; *gen pl* -ок) *ж* (*обычно мн*) puttee.

поруга́ни|е (-я) *ср* desecration.

поруга́|ть (-ю) *сов перех* (*разг*) to scold

▶ **поруга́ться** *сов от* **руга́ться** ♦ *возв* (*разг*): ~**ся** (**с** +*instr*) to fall out (with).

пору́к|а (-и) *ж*: **брать кого́-н на** ~**и** to take sb on probation; (*ЮР*) to stand bail for sb; **кругова́я** ~ mutual dependence; (*у преступников*) mutual cover-up; **отпуска́ть** (**отпусти́ть** *perf*) **кого́-н на** ~**и** to release sb on bail.

по-ру́сски *нареч* (*разговаривать, написать*) in Russian; **говори́ть** (*impf*)/**понима́ть** (*impf*) ~ to speak/understand Russian; **как** ~ „**book**"**?** what is the Russian for "book"?

поруча́|ть (-ю) *несов от* **поручи́ть**.

поруче́ни|е (-я) *ср* (*задание*) errand; (: *важное*) mission; **по** ~**ю** +*gen* on behalf of.

по́руч|ень (-ня) *м* handrail.

пору́чик (-а) *м* (*ИСТ*) first lieutenant.

поручи́тел|ь (-я) *м* (*КОММ*) guarantor.

поручи́тельств|о (-а) *ср* guarantee.

пор|учи́ть (-учу́, -у́чишь; *impf* **поруча́ть**) *сов неперех*: ~ **кому́-н что́-н** to entrust sb with sth; **поруча́ть** (~ *perf*) **кому́-н** +*infin* to instruct sb to do; **поруча́ть** (~ *perf*) **кому́-н кого́-н/что́-н** (*отдать на попечение*) to leave sb/sth in sb's care.

пор|учи́ться (-учу́сь, -у́чишься) *сов от* **руча́ться**.

по́ручня *итп сущ см* **по́ручень**.

порха́|ть (-ю) *несов неперех* (*бабочка*) to flutter about; (*птица*) to flit about.

по́рци|я (-и) *ж* portion; **принеси́те нам две** ~**и**

жа́реной говя́дины bring us two steaks.
по́рч|а (-и) ж damage.
по́рчу(сь) сов см **по́ртить(ся)**.
по́рш|ень (-ня) м (в двигателе) piston; (в насосе) plunger.
поры́в (-а) м (ветра) gust; (негодования, восторга итп) surge.
порыва́|ть (-ю) несов от **порва́ть**
▸ **порыва́ться** несов возв: **~ся** +infin (стремиться) to strive to do.
поры́вист|ый (-, -а, -о) прил (ветер) gusty; (движения) jerky; (характер, человек) impetuous.
поря́дка итп сущ см **поря́док**.
поря́дков|ый прил (номер) ordinal;
поря́дковое числи́тельное ordinal number.
поря́дком нареч (разг) pretty; **я ~ уста́л** I'm pretty tired.
поря́д|ок (-ка) м order; (правила) procedure; **в ~ке** +gen (в качестве) as; **~ка** +gen about; **в рабо́чем ~ке** in the course of the proceedings; **э́то в ~ке веще́й** (это нормально) that's nothing out of the ordinary; **в ~ке** in order; **всё в ~ке** everything's OK; **поря́док дня** agenda; **поря́док слов** (линг) word order.
поря́дочно нареч decently; (устал) pretty; (хорошо) quite well.
поря́доч|ный (-ен, -на, -но) прил (честный) decent; (значительный) fair.
пос. сокр = **посёлок**.
поса|ди́ть (-жу́, -́дишь) сов от **сажа́ть**.
поса́д|ка (-ки; gen pl -ок) ж (овощей, деревьев) planting; (пассажиров) boarding; (самолёта итп) landing; **произво́дится ~ на самолёт ...** the flight ... is boarding.
поса́дочн|ый прил (трап, талон) boarding опред; (площадка, огни) landing опред.
посажу́ сов см **посади́ть**.
посва́та|ть(ся) (-ю(сь)) сов от **сва́таться**.
посве́ж|еть (-ю) сов от **свеже́ть**.
посве|ти́ть (-чу́, -тишь) сов от **свети́ть**.
посветле́|ть (-ю) сов от **светле́ть**.
посвечу́ сов см **посвети́ть**.
по-сво́ему нареч his итп way.
посвя|ти́ть (-щу́, -ти́шь; impf **посвяща́ть** сов перех: **~ что-н** +dat to devote sth to; (книгу, стихи) to dedicate sth to; **посвяща́ть** (**~ perf**) **кого́-н в** +acc (в тайну) to let sb into.
посвяща́|ть (-ю) несов от **посвяти́ть**.
посвяще́ни|е (-я) ср (в книге) dedication.
посвящу́ сов см **посвяти́ть**.
посе́в (-а) м sowing; см также **посе́вы**.
посевн|о́й прил: **~ы́е рабо́ты** sowing; **посевны́е пло́щади** (с.-х.) area sown with crops.
посе́в|ы (-ов) мн crops мн.
поседе́|ть (-ю) сов от **седе́ть**.
поселе́н|ец (-ца) м settler; (высланный)

deportee.
поселе́ни|е (-я) ср (селение) settlement; (как наказание) deportation.
поселе́нца итп сущ см **поселе́нец**.
посе|ли́ть(ся) (-елю́(сь), -́елишь(ся)) сов от **сели́ть(ся)**.
посёл|ок (-ка) м village; **да́чный ~** village made up of dachas.
поселя́|ть(ся) (-ю(сь)) несов = **посели́ть(ся)**.
посеребр|и́ть (-ю́, -и́шь) сов от **серебри́ть**.
посереди́не нареч in the middle ♦ предл (+gen) in the middle of.
посере́|ть (-ю) сов от **сере́ть**.
посети́тель (-я) м visitor.
посети́тельниц|а (-ы) ж см **посети́тель**.
посе|ти́ть (-щу́, -ти́шь; impf **посеща́ть** сов перех to visit.
посе́т|овать (-ую) сов от **се́товать**.
посеща́емость (-и) ж attendance.
посеща́|ть (-ю) несов от **посети́ть**.
посеще́ни|е (-я) ср visit.
посещу́ сов см **посети́ть**.
посе́|ять (-ю) сов от **се́ять** ♦ перех (разг: потерять) to lose.
посиде́|ть (-жу́, -ди́шь) сов неперех to sit for a while.
посил|ьный (-ен, -ьна, -ьно) прил feasible.
посине́|ть (-ю) сов от **сине́ть**.
посин|и́ть (-ю́, -и́шь) сов от **сини́ть**.
поска|ка́ть (-чу́, -чешь) сов от **скака́ть**.
посканда́л|ить (-ю, -ишь) сов от **сканда́лить**.
поска́чу итп сов см **поскака́ть**.
поскользн|у́ться (-у́сь, -ёшься) сов возв to slip.
поско́льку союз as.
поскуп|и́ться (-лю́сь, -и́шься) сов от **скупи́ться**.
посла́ итп сущ см **посо́л**.
послабле́ни|е (-я) ср leniency.
посла́н|ец (-ца) м envoy.
посла́ни|е (-я) ср (официальное) dispatch; (дружеское, любовное) message.
посла́нник (-а) м (дипломатический) diplomat.
посла́нца итп сущ см **посла́нец**.
по|сла́ть (-шлю́, -шлёшь; impf **посыла́ть** сов перех to send; **посыла́ть** (**~ perf**) **кого́-н к чёрту** (разг) to tell sb to go to hell.
по́сле нареч (потом) afterwards ♦ предл (+gen) after ♦ союз: **~ того́ как** after.
послевое́нный прил postwar.
после́д (-а) м placenta.
после́дн|ее (-его; decl like adj) ср the last; **до ~его** to the utmost.
после́дн|ий (-яя, -ее, -ие) прил last; (новости, мода) latest; (разг); **~ негодя́й** utter rascal; **за или в ~ее вре́мя** recently; **руга́ться** (impf) **~ими слова́ми** to use foul language.
после́дователь (-я) м follower.

после́довательность (-и) *ж* sequence;
(*поли́тики*) consistency.

после́довательный *прил* (*эта́пы, движе́ния*)
consecutive; (*вы́вод, ход мы́сли*) consistent.

после́довать (-ую) *сов от* сле́довать.

после́дствие (-я) *ср* consequence.

после́дующий (-ая, -ее, -ие) *прил* subsequent.

послеза́втра *нареч* the day after tomorrow.

послеродово́й *прил* postnatal.

послесло́вие (-я) *ср* (*в кни́ге*) epilogue.

посло́вица (-ы) *ж* proverb, saying; **войти́** (*perf*)
в ~у to become proverbial.

послужи́ть (-ужу́, -у́жишь) *сов от* служи́ть.

послужно́й *прил*: ~ спи́сок (*вое́нного*) service
record; (*рабо́тника*) work record.

послуша́ние (-я) *ср* (*поко́рность*) obedience.

послу́шать (-ю) *сов от* слу́шать ♦ *перех*: ~
что-н to listen to sth for a while; ~йте! listen!

▶ **послу́шаться** *сов от* слу́шаться.

послу́шен *прил см* послу́шный.

послу́шник (-а) *м* (*РЕЛ*) novice.

послу́шница (-ы) *ж см* послу́шник.

послу́шный (-ен, -на, -но) *прил* (*ребёнок,
учени́к*) obedient; (*механи́зм*) user-friendly.

послы́шаться (*3sg* -ется, *3pl* -атся) *сов от*
слы́шаться.

послюня́вить (-лю, -ишь) *сов от* слюня́вить.

посма́тривать (-ю) *несов неперех* to glance
occasionally.

посме́иваться (-юсь) *несов возв* (*смея́ться*)
to chuckle; ~ (*impf*) (**над** +*instr*) (*насмеха́ться*)
to laugh at.

посме́нный *прил* shift *опред*.

посме́ртный *прил* posthumous.

посме́ть (-ю) *сов от* сметь.

посме́шище (-а) *ср* laughing stock;
выставля́ть (*impf*) **кого́-н на** ~ to make a
laughing stock of sb.

посмея́ться (-ю́сь, -ёшься) *сов от* смея́ться.

посмотре́ть (-отрю́, -о́тришь) *сов от*
смотре́ть ♦ *неперех*: ~о́трим (*разг*) we'll see;
там ~о́трим (*разг*) we'll see later

▶ **посмотре́ться** *сов от* смотре́ться.

посо́бие (-я) *ср* (*по́мощь*) benefit; (*ПРОСВЕЩ*:
уче́бное) handout; (: *нагля́дное*) visual aids *мн*;
посо́бие по безрабо́тице unemployment
benefit; **посо́бие по инвали́дности** disability
living allowance.

посо́бник (-а) *м* accomplice.

посове́товать(ся) (-ую(сь)) *сов от*
сове́товать(ся).

посоде́йствовать (-ую) *сов от*
соде́йствовать.

посо́л (-ла́) *м* ambassador; (-о́ла; *засо́л*) salting.

посоли́ть (-олю́, -о́лишь) *сов от* соли́ть.

посо́льство (-а) *ср* embassy.

поспе́ть (-ю) *сов от* спеть ♦ (*impf* поспева́ть)
неперех (*успе́ть*) to make it.

поспе́шен *прил см* поспе́шный.

поспеши́ть (-у́, -и́шь) *сов от* спеши́ть.

поспе́шный (-ен, -на, -но) *прил* rushed.

поспо́рить (-ю, -ишь) *сов от* спо́рить ♦
неперех to argue.

поспосо́бствовать (-ую) *сов от*
спосо́бствовать.

посрами́ть (-лю́, -и́шь; *impf* посрамля́ть) *сов*
перех to disgrace.

посреди́ *нареч* in the middle ♦ *предл* (+*gen*) in
the middle of; ~ **толпы́** in the midst of the
crowd.

посреди́не *нареч* in the middle ♦ *предл* (+*gen*)
in the middle of.

посре́дник (-а) *м* intermediary; (*при
конфли́кте*) mediator; **торго́вый** ~ middleman
(*мн* middlemen).

посре́днический (-ая, -ое, -ие) *прил* (*КОММ*)
intermediary *опред*.

посре́дничество (-а) *ср* mediation.

посре́дственно *нареч* (*учи́ться, писа́ть,
сочиня́ть*) averagely ♦ *ср нескл* (*ПРОСВЕЩ*) ≈
satisfactory (*school mark*).

посре́дственный (-, -на, -но) *прил* mediocre.

посре́дство (-а) *ср*: **при** ~**е** или **че́рез** ~ +*gen*
by means of.

посре́дством *предл* (+*gen*) by means of.

поссо́рить(ся) (-ю(сь), -ишь(ся)) *сов от*
ссо́рить(ся).

пост (-а́; *loc sg* -у́) *м* (*лю́ди*) guard; (*ме́сто*)
lookout post; (*до́лжность*) position, post; (*РЕЛ*)
fast; ~ **автоинспе́кции** (traffic) police
checkpoint.

поста́вить (-лю, -ишь) *сов от* ста́вить ♦ (*impf*
поставля́ть) *перех* (*това́р*) to supply.

поста́вка (-ки; *gen pl* -ок) *ж* (*снабже́ние*) supply.

поставлю́ *сов см* поста́вить.

поставля́ть (-ю) *несов от* поста́вить.

поста́вок *сущ см* поста́вка.

поставщи́к (-а́) *м* supplier; **судово́й** ~ ship
chandler.

постаме́нт (-а) *м* pedestal.

постанови́ть (-овлю́, -о́вишь; *impf*
постановля́ть) *сов неперех*: ~ +*infin* to resolve
to do.

постано́вка (-ки; *gen pl* -ок) *ж* (*па́мятника*)
erection; (*уче́бного проце́сса*) organization;
(*ТЕА́ТР*) production; **у неё хоро́шая** ~ **головы́**
she holds her head well; ~ **вопро́са/пробле́мы**
the formulation of the question/problem.

постановле́ние (-я) *ср* (*реше́ние*) resolution;
(*распоряже́ние*) decree.

постановлю́ *сов см* постанови́ть.

постановля́ть (-ю) *несов от* постанови́ть.

постано́вок *сущ см* постано́вка.

постано́вщик (-а) *м* producer.

постара́ться (-юсь) *сов от* стара́ться.

постаре́ть (-ю) *сов от* старе́ть.

постели́ть(ся) (-елю́(сь), -е́лишь(ся)) *сов от*
стели́ть(ся).

посте́ль (-и) *ж* bed.

посте́льный *прил*: ~**ое бельё** bedclothes *мн*;
он на ~**ом режи́ме** he is confined to bed.

постелю́ *итп сов см* постла́ть.

постепéнно *нареч* gradually.
постепéн|ный (-ен, -на, -но) *прил* gradual.
постесня́ться (-юсь) *сов от* **стесня́ться**.
постиг *итп сов см* **пости́чь**.
постига́|ть (-ю) *несов от* **пости́чь**.
пости́гну *итп сов см* **пости́чь**.
пости́г|нуть (-ну, -нешь; *pt* -, -ла, -ло) *сов* = **пости́чь**.
постила́|ть (-ю) *несов* = **стели́ть**.
постира́|ть (-ю) *сов от* **стира́ть**.
по|сти́ться (-щу́сь, -сти́шься) *несов возв* (*РЕЛ*) to fast.
пости́|чь (-гну, -гнешь; *pt* -г, -гла, -гло, *impf* **постига́ть**) *сов перех* (*смысл, значение*) to grasp; (*подлеж: несчастье*) to befall; **я не могу́ ~, как он мог э́то сде́лать** I can't comprehend how he could do something like that; **его́ ~гло разочарова́ние** he was disappointed.
пост|ла́ть (-елю́, -е́лешь) *сов от* **стлать**.
пóстный *прил* (*суп, обед*) vegetarian; (*мясо*) lean; (*разг: хмурый*) cheesed off; **пóстное мáсло** vegetable oil.
постов|óй *прил* (*служба, будка*) sentry *опред* ♦ (-óго; *decl like adj*) *м* militiaman on duty.
постóльку *союз*: ~ ... **поскóльку** in so far as ....
постор|они́ться (-оню́сь, -о́нишься) *сов от* **сторони́ться**.
посторóнн|ий (-яя, -ее, -ие) *прил* (*чужой*) strange; (*помощь, влияние*) outside; (*вопрос*) irrelevant ♦ (-его; *decl like adj*) *м* stranger, outsider; **~им вход воспрещён** authorized entry only.
постоя́н|ный (-ен, -на, -но) *прил* (*работа, адрес*) permanent; (*шум, разговоры*) constant; (*вкус, взгляды*) consistent; **постоя́нная áрмия** regular army; **постоя́нный ток** direct current.
посто|я́ть (-ю́, -и́шь) *сов от* **стоя́ть** ♦ *неперех* (*стоять недолго*) to stand for a while; **постóйте!** (*подождите*) hang on!; **он за ценóй не ~и́т** (*разг*) money is no object to him.
пострада́|ть (-ю) *сов от* **страда́ть**.
постри́г(ся) *итп сов см* **постри́чь(ся)**.
постригу́(сь) *итп сов см* **постри́чь(ся)**.
постриже́ни|е (-я) *ср* (*мужчины*) taking the habit; (*женщины*) taking the veil.
постри́|чь (-гу́, -жёшь *итп*, -гу́т; *pt* -г, -гла, -гло) *сов перех*: ~ **когó-н** to cut sb's hair; ~ (*perf*) **когó-н в монасты́рь** to initiate sb into a monastery
▶ **постри́чься** *сов возв* to have a haircut; **~ся** (*perf*) **в монасты́рь** to be initiated into a monastery.
пострóек *сущ см* **пострóйка**.
построéни|е (-я) *ср* (*предложения, фразы*) construction.
пострó|ить(ся) (-ю(сь), -ишь(ся)) *сов от* **стрóить(ся)**.
пострóй|ка (-ки; *gen pl* -ек) *ж* construction.

поступáтельн|ый *прил* (*движение*) forward *опред*; **~ое развѝтие** progress.
пост|упи́ть (-уплю́, -у́пишь; *impf* **поступáть**) *сов неперех* (*благорóдно, разýмно*) to act; (*товар, известия*) to come in; (*жалоба: в суд*) to be received; **поступáть** (~ *perf*) **в** +*acc* (*в университéт*) to enter; **поступáть** (~ *perf*) **на** +*acc* (*на рабóту, на кýрсы*) to start
▶ **поступи́ться** (*impf* **поступáться**) *сов возв*: **~ся** +*instr* to give up.
поступка *сущ см* **постýпок**.
поступлéни|е (-я) *ср* (*действие: в университéт*) entrance; (: *на рабóту*) starting; (: *жáлобы: в суд*) receipt; (*то, что поступи́ло: бюджéтное*) revenue; (: *в библиотéке*) acquisition.
поступлю́(сь) *сов см* **поступи́ть(ся)**.
постýп|ок (-ка) *м* (*благорóдный, пóдлый*) deed.
постýп|ь (-и) *ж* (*похóдка*) gait.
постучá|ть(ся) (-ý(сь), -и́шь(ся)) *сов от* **стучáть(ся)**.
посты́ден *прил см* **посты́дный**.
постыди́|ться (-жу́сь, -ди́шься) *сов от* **стыди́ться**.
посты́д|ный (-ен, -на, -но) *прил* shameful.
постыжу́сь *сов см* **постыди́ться**.
посýд|а (-ы) *ж собир* crockery; **кýхонная ~** kitchenware; **стекля́нная ~** glassware; **мы́ть (помы́ть** *perf*) **~у** to wash *или* (*BRIT*) the dishes.
посуди́|ть (-жу́, -дишь) *сов*: **~ди́те сáми** judge for yourself.
посул|и́ть (-ю́, -и́шь) *сов от* **сули́ть**.
посчастли́в|иться (*3sg* -ится) *сов безл*: **мне ~илось** +*infin* ... I was lucky enough to ....
посчитá|ть(ся) (-ю(сь), -ю(сь)) *сов от* **считáть(ся)**.
посылá|ть (-ю) *несов от* **послáть**.
посы́л|ка (-ки; *gen pl* -ок) *ж* (*действие: книг, дéнег*) sending; (*отправлéние*) parcel; (*основáние*) premise.
посы́льн|ый (-ого; *decl like adj*) *м* messenger.
посы́п|ать (-лю, -лешь) *сов перех* to sprinkle.
посягáтельств|о (-а) *ср*: ~ **на что-н** infringement on *или* of sth; ~ **на чью-н жизнь** an attempt on sb's life.
посяг|нýть (-ý, -ёшь; *impf* **посягáть**) *сов неперех*: ~ **на** +*acc* to infringe; **посягáть (~** *perf*) **на чью-н жизнь** to make an attempt on sb's life.
пот (-а; *part gen* -у, *loc sg* -ý, *nom pl* -ы́) *м* sweat; **в пóте лицá** hard; **пóтом и крóвью добывáть (добы́ть** *perf*) **что-н** to sweat blood to get sth; **рабóтать (** *impf*) **в пóте лицá** to sweat blood.
потайнóй *прил* secret *опред*.
потакá|ть (-ю) *несов неперех*: ~ +*dat* (*агрéссии*) to turn a blind eye to; (*агрéссору*) to ignore.
потаскýх|а (-и) *ж* (*разг: пренебр*) hussy.
потасóв|ка (-ки; *gen pl* -ок) *ж* (*разг*) punch-up.

по-тво́ему *нареч* your way ♦ *вводн сл* in your opinion.

потво́рств|овать (-ую) *несов неперех*: ~ +*dat* (*агрессии*) to turn a blind eye to; (*агрессору*) to ignore.

потёк *итп сов см* **поте́чь.**

потеку́т *сов см* **поте́чь.**

потём|ки (-ок) *мн* darkness *ед.*

потемне́|ть (-ю) *сов от* **темне́ть.**

потёмок *сущ см* **потёмки.**

потенциа́л (-а) *м* potential.

потенциа́л|ьный (-ен, -ьна, -ьно) *прил* potential.

потепле́ни|е (-я) *ср* warmer spell.

потепле́|ть (*3sg* -ет, *3pl* -ют) *сов от* **тепле́ть.**

пот|ере́ть (-ру́, -рёшь; *pt* -ёр, -ёрла, -ёрло) *сов перех* (*уши*) to rub; (*морковь*) to grate.

▶ **потере́ться** *сов от* **тере́ться.**

потерпе́вш|ая (-ей; *decl like adj*) *ж см* **потерпе́вший.**

потерпе́вш|ий (-его; *decl like adj*) *м* (*ЮР*) victim ♦ *прил*: (-ая, -ее, -ие) ~ая сторона́ injured party.

пот|ерпе́ть (-ерплю́, -е́рпишь) *сов от* **терпе́ть.**

потёртый *прил* (*одежда*) worn.

поте́р|я (-и) *ж* loss; **нести́ (понести́** *perf*) ~и (*в войне́*) to suffer losses.

поте́рянно *нареч* (*смотреть*) lost.

поте́рян|ный (-, -на, -но) *прил* (*растерянный: вид ити*) lost.

потеря́|ть(ся) (-ю(сь)) *сов от* **теря́ть(ся).**

потесни́|ть (-ю, -и́шь) *сов от* **тесни́ть** ♦ *перех*: ~ кого́-н to make sb squeeze up.

▶ **потесни́ться** *сов возв* to squeeze up.

поте́|ть (-ю) (*impf* **вспоте́ть**) *несов неперех* to sweat.

пот|е́чь (*3sg* -ечёт, *3pl* -еку́т, *pt* -ёк, -екла́, -екло́) *сов неперех* (*вода*) to start flowing; (*дни, жизнь*) to begin.

поте́ш|ить(ся) (-у(сь)) *сов от* **те́шить(ся).**

потихо́ньку *нареч* (*разг: медленно*) at a snail's pace; (: *тайно*) on the sly.

потни́ц|а (-ы) *ж* (*МЕД*) heat rash.

по́тный *прил* sweaty.

потого́нн|ый *прил* (*перен*): ~ая систе́ма slave labour (*BRIT*) *или* labor (*US*).

пото́к (-а) *м* (*также ПРОСВЕЩ*) stream; **положи́тельный/отрица́тельный** ~ **нали́чности** (*КОММ*) positive/negative cash flow.

потол|о́к (-ка́) *м* (*также перен*) ceiling; **брать** (**взять** *perf*) **что-н с** ~**ка́** (*разг*) to pluck sth out of thin air.

потолсте́|ть (-ю) *сов от* **толсте́ть.**

пото́м *нареч* (*после: пойдем, закончим итп*) later ♦ *союз* (*после*) then; (*разг: кроме того*) anyhow; **на** ~ (*разг*) for later.

пото́м|ки (-ов) *мн* descendants *мн.*

пото́мственный *прил* (*имение, деньги*) inherited; **он** – ~ **музыка́нт** he is descended from a family of musicians.

пото́мств|о (-а) *ср собир* descendants *мн*; (*дети*) offspring *мн.*

потому́ *нареч*: ~ (**и**) that's why; **я не приду́,** ~ **что уста́л** I'm not coming because I'm tired; **потому́ что** because.

пот|ону́ть (-ону́, -о́нешь) *сов от* **тону́ть.**

пото́п (-а) *м* flood.

пот|опи́ть (-оплю́, -о́пишь) *сов от* **топи́ть.**

потоп|та́ть (-чу́, -чешь) *сов от* **топта́ть.**

потора́плива|ть (-ю) *несов перех*: ~ кого́-н to hurry sb up.

▶ **потора́пливаться** *несов возв* to hurry.

потороп|и́ть(ся) (-лю́(сь), -и́шь(ся)) *сов от* **торопи́ть(ся).**

пото́чный *прил* (*производство*) mass *опред*; **пото́чная ли́ния** production line.

потрав|и́ть (-лю́, -ишь) *сов от* **трави́ть.**

потра́|тить(ся) (-чу(сь), -тишь(ся)) *сов от* **тра́тить(ся).**

потреби́тел|ь (-я) *м* consumer.

потреби́тельск|ий (-ая, -ое, -ие) *прил* (*спрос, товар*) consumer *опред*; **потреби́тельская коопера́ция** cooperative (society).

потреб|и́ть (-лю́, -и́шь) *сов от* **потребля́ть.**

потребле́ни|е (-я) *ср* (*действие*) consumption; **това́ры широ́кого** ~**я** consumer goods.

потреблю́ *сов см* **потреби́ть.**

потребля́|ть (-ю; *perf* **потреби́ть**) *несов перех* to consume.

потре́бность (-и) *ж* (*надобность*) requirement, demand; (*желание*) need.

потре́б|овать(ся) (-ую(сь)) *сов от* **тре́бовать(ся).**

Потребсою́з (-а) *м сокр* = **Сою́з потреби́тельских коопера́ций.**

потрево́ж|ить(ся) (-у(сь), -ишь(ся)) *сов от* **трево́жить(ся).**

потрёпан|ный (-, -на, -но) *прил* (*книга, одежда*) tattered, tatty; (*вид, лицо*) worn.

потреп|а́ть(ся) (-лю́(сь), -лешь(ся)) *сов от* **трепа́ть(ся).**

потре́ска|ться (*3sg* -ется, *3pl* -ются) *сов от* **тре́скаться.**

потроха́ (-о́в) *мн* (*птицы*) giblets *мн.*

потрош|и́ть (-у́, -и́шь; *perf* **вы́потрошить**) *несов перех* (*курицу, рыбу*) to gut.

потру́(сь) *итп сов см* **потере́ть(ся).**

потруд|и́ться (-жу́сь, -дишься) *сов возв* to work; ~ (*perf*) +*infin* to take the trouble to do; ~**ди́тесь переда́ть э́то письмо́** if you could be so kind as to pass on this letter.

потряса́|ть (-ю) *несов от* **потрясти́.**

потряса́ющ|ий (-ая, -ее, -ие) *прил* (*музыка, стихи*) fantastic; (*красота*) stunning.

потрясе́ни|е (-я) *ср* breakdown.

потряс|ти́ (-у́, -ёшь; *pt* -, -ла́, -ло́) *сов перех* to shake; (*impf* **потряса́ть**; *взволновать*) to stun ♦ *неперех*: ~ +*instr* to shake.

поту́г|а (-и) *ж* (*обычно мн*) contraction; (*перен: пренебр: усилия*) pathetic attempt.

поту́п|ить (-лю, -ишь; *impf* **потупля́ть**) *сов*

перех (*голову, глаза*) to lower
▶ поту́питься *сов возв* to lower one's eyes.
потускне́|ть (-ю) *сов от* тускне́ть.
потусторо́нн|ий (-яя, -ее, -ие) *прил* (*РЕЛ*) on
the other side.
поту́хн|уть (*3sg* -ет, *3pl* -ут, *impf* потуха́ть) *сов
неперех* (*лампа, свет*) to go out; (*жизнь,
веселье*) to end.
поту́ш|и́ть (-у́шу, -у́шишь) *сов от* туши́ть.
потя́га́|ться (-юсь) *сов от* тяга́ться.
потя́гива|ть (-ю) *несов перех* (*верёвку*) to pull;
(*вино, чай*) to sip
▶ потя́гиваться *несов от* потяну́ться.
потяжеле́|ть (-ю) *сов от* тяжеле́ть.
потя́н|уть (-я́ну́, -я́нешь) *сов от* тяну́ть
▶ потяну́ться *сов возв* to start to drag; (*impf*
потя́гиваться; *в постели, в кресле*) to stretch
out.
поу́жина|ть (-ю) *сов от* у́жинать.
поумне́|ть (-ю) *сов от* умне́ть.
поуча́|ть (-ю) *несов перех* to teach.
поуче́ни|е (-я) *ср* preaching.
поучи́|тельный (-ен, -ьна, -ьно) *прил* (*пример,
история*) instructive; (*тон, голос*) didactic; **его́
приме́р был для нас ~ен** we learnt from his
example.
поха́б|ный (-ен, -на, -но) *прил* (*непристойный*)
dirty.
поха́жива|ть (-ю) *несов неперех* (*в парке итп*)
to stroll.
похвал|а́ (-ы́) *ж* praise; **отзыва́ться
(отозва́ться** *perf*) **с ~о́й о ком-н** to praise sb.
похва́лен *прил см* похва́льный.
похва́л|и́ть(ся) (-алю́(сь), -а́лишь(ся)) *сов от*
хвали́ть(ся).
похва́л|ьный (-ен, -ьна, -ьно) *прил*
praiseworthy; (*отзыв*) complimentary; **~ьное
сло́во** word of praise; **похва́льная гра́мота**
certificate of merit.
похва́ста|ть(ся) (-ю(сь)) *сов от* хва́стать(ся).
похити́тел|ь (-я) *м* (*см глаг*) thief; abductor;
kidnapper.
похити́тельниц|а (-ы) *ж см* похити́тель.
похи́|тить (-щу, -тишь; *impf* похища́ть) *сов
перех* (*предмет*) to steal; (*человека*) to abduct;
(: *для выкупа*) to kidnap.
похище́ни|е (-я) *ср* (*см глаг*) theft; abduction;
kidnap(ping).
похи́щу *сов см* похи́тить.
похло́па|ть (-ю) *сов перех* to pat ◆ *неперех*
(*человек: в ладоши*) to clap; (*птица*) to flap.
похлоп|ота́ть (-очу́, -о́чешь) *сов от*
хлопота́ть.
похме́ль|е (-я) *ср* hangover.
похо́д (-а) *м* (*военный*) campaign;
(*туристический*) hike (*walking and camping
expedition*).
похода́тайств|овать (-ую) *сов от*
ходатайствовать.

пох|оди́ть (-ожу́, -о́дишь) *несов неперех*: ~ **на
кого-н/что-н** to resemble sb/sth ◆ *сов неперех*
to walk.
похо́дк|а (-и) *ж* gait.
похожде́ни|е (-я) *ср* (*обычно мн*) adventure.
похо́ж|ий (-ая, -ее, -ие) *прил*: ~ (**на** +*acc или с*
+*instr*) similar (to); **он похо́ж на бра́та, они́ с
бра́том ~и** he looks like his brother; **они́ ~и**
they look alike; **~е на то, что ...** it looks as if ...;
э́то на него́ не ~е it's not like him.
похожу́ (*не*)*сов см* походи́ть.
похолода́ни|е (-я) *ср* cold spell.
похолода́|ть (*3sg* -ет) *сов от* холода́ть.
похолоде́|ть (-ю) *сов от* холоде́ть.
похор|они́ть (-оню́, -о́нишь) *сов от* хорони́ть.
похоро́нный *прил* funeral *опред*; **похоро́нное
бюро́** undertaker's.
по́хор|оны (-о́н; *dat pl* -она́м) *мн* funeral *ед*.
похороше́|ть (-ю) *сов от* хороше́ть.
по́хот|ь (-и) *ж* lust.
похуде́|ть (-ю) *сов от* худе́ть.
поцара́па|ть (-ю) *сов от* цара́пать.
поцел|ова́ть(ся) (-у́ю(сь)) *сов от*
целова́ть(ся).
поцелу́|й (-я) *м* kiss.
поцеремо́н|иться (-юсь) *сов от*
церемо́ниться.
почасови́к (-а́) *м* part-time worker (*paid by the
hour*).
почасов|о́й *прил* (*оплата*) hourly; **~а́я рабо́та**
hourly-paid work.
поча́т|ок (-ка) *м* (*кукурузы*) cob.
по́чв|а (-ы) *ж* soil; (*перен*) basis; **на ~е** +*gen*
owing to; **он потеря́л ~у под нога́ми** he lost
his confidence.
по́чек *сущ см* по́чка.
почём *нареч* (*разг*) how much; ~ **я́блоки?** how
much are the apples?
почему́ *нареч* why; (**и**) **вот** ~ and that is why.
почему́-либо *нареч* for some reason.
почему́-нибудь *нареч* = почему́-либо.
почему́-то *нареч* for some reason.
по́черк (-а) *м* handwriting; (*перен: художника,
грабителя*) hallmark.
почерне́|ть (-ю) *сов от* черне́ть.
почерпн|у́ть (-у́, -ёшь) *сов перех* (*сведения*) to
obtain; (*идею*) to draw.
почерстве́|ть (-ю) *сов от* черстве́ть.
поче|са́ть(ся) (-шу́(сь), -шешь(ся)) *сов от*
чеса́ть(ся).
по́чест|ь (-и) *ж* (*обычно мн*) homage *ед*;
воздава́ть (возда́ть *perf*) **~и кому́-н** to pay
homage to sb.
поч|е́сть (-ту́, -тёшь; *pt* -ёл, -ла́, -ло́, *impf*
почита́ть) *сов неперех*: ~ **за долг/честь** +*infin*
to consider it one's duty/an honour (*BRIT*) *или*
honor (*US*) to do.

почёт (-а) *м* honour (*BRIT*), honor (*US*).
почётный *прил* (*гость*) honoured (*BRIT*),
honored (*US*); (*член академии*) honorary;
(*обязанность*) honourable (*BRIT*), honorable
(*US*); **почётный карау́л** guard of honour (*BRIT*)
или honor (*US*).
по́чечный *прил* kidney *опред*, renal; (*камни*)
kidney *опред*.
почешу́(сь) *итп сов см* **почеса́ть(ся)**.
почи́н (-а) *м* initiative.
почини́ть (-иню́, -и́нишь) *сов от* **чини́ть**.
почи́н|ка (-ки; *gen pl* -ок) *ж* (*обуви, телевизора*)
repair.
почи́стить (-щу, -стишь) *сов от* **чи́стить**.
почита́тель (-я) *м* admirer.
почита́тельниц|а (-ы) *ж см* **почита́тель**.
почита́ть (-ю) *несов от* **поче́сть** ♦ *перех*
(*поклоняться*) to admire ♦ *сов перех* to read.
почи́щу *сов см* **почи́стить**.
по́ч|ка (-ки; *gen pl* -ек) *ж* (*БОТ*) bud; (*АНАТ*)
kidney; **~ки** (*КУЛИН*) kidneys.
по́чт|а (-ы) *ж* (*учреждение*) post office;
(*корреспонденция*) mail, post; **отправля́ть**
(**отпра́вить** *perf*) **что-н ~ой** *или* **по ~е** to send
sth by post.
почтальо́н (-а) *м* postman (*BRIT*) (*мн* postmen),
mailman (*US*) (*мн* mailmen).
почта́мт (-а) *м* main post office.
почте́ни|е (-я) *ср* esteem.
почте́нный *прил* venerable; **~ые го́ды**
advanced years.
почти́ *нареч* almost, nearly; **~ что** (*разг*) almost.
почти́тельный (-ен, -ьна, -ьно) *прил*
respectful; **на ~ном расстоя́нии** at a
respectful distance.
почти́ть (*как* чтить; *см* Table 17) (-у́, -и́шь) *сов*
перех (*память*) to pay homage to; **~** *(perf)*
кого́-н свои́м прису́тствием to honour (*BRIT*)
или honor (*US*) sb with one's presence.
почто́вый *прил* (*служба, связь*) postal; (*марка*)
postage *опред*; **почто́вая откры́тка** postcard;
почто́вая бума́га writing paper; **почто́вый**
и́ндекс postcode (*BRIT*), zip code (*US*);
почто́вый перево́д (*деньги*) postal order;
почто́вый я́щик postbox.
почту́ *итп сов см* **поче́сть**.
почу́вств|овать (-ую) *сов от* **чу́вствовать**.
почу́диться (*3sg* -ится, *3pl* -ятся) *сов от*
чу́диться.
почу́ять (-ю) *сов от* **чу́ять**.
пошатну́ть (-у́, -ёшь) *сов перех* (*веру*) to shake;
(*здоровье*) to affect
▸ **пошатну́ться** *сов возв* to sway;
(*авторитет*) to be undermined; (*здоровье*) to
suffer.
пошатыва|ться (-юсь) *несов возв* (*человек*) to
sway slightly.
пошеве́лива|ться (-юсь) *несов возв* to stir;
(*разг: поторапливаться*) to get a move on.
пошевел|и́ть(ся) (-ю́(сь), -и́шь(ся)) *сов от*
шевели́ть(ся).

пошевельн|у́ться (-у́сь, -ёшься) *сов возв* to
stir.
пошёл *сов см* **пойти́**.
пошелохн|у́ться (-у́сь, -ёшься) *сов* =
шелохну́ться.
поши́б (-а) *м* (*разг: пренебр*): **они́ лю́ди одного́**
~а they are cut from the same cloth; **ни́зкий** *или*
невысо́кий ~ second-rate.
поши́в (-а) *м* (*действие*) sewing;
индивидуа́льный ~ tailoring.
пошла́ *итп сов см* **пойти́**.
по́шлин|а (-ы) *ж* duty; **суде́бная ~** legal costs
или expenses; **облага́ть** (**обложи́ть** *perf*) **что-н**
~ой to impose a duty on sth.
по́шлинный *прил* customs *опред*.
пошло́ *сов см* **пойти́**.
по́шлост|ь (-и) *ж* vulgarity; **говори́ть** (*impf*) **~и**
to make trite and vulgar comments.
по́шл|ый (-, -а́, -о) *прил* (*человек, посту́пок*)
vulgar; (*анекдот*) corny; (*карти́нка*) kitsch;
(*речи*) trite and vulgar.
пошлю́ *итп сов см* **посла́ть**.
пошля́к (-а́) *м* (*разг*) vulgar person.
пошут|и́ть (-чу́, -у́тишь) *сов от* **шути́ть**.
поща́д|а (-ы) *ж* mercy.
пощад|и́ть (-жу́, -ди́шь) *сов от* **щади́ть**.
пощек|ота́ть (-очу́, -о́чешь) *сов от* **щекота́ть**.
пощёчин|а (-ы) *ж* slap in the face.
пощу́па|ть (-ю) *сов от* **щу́пать**.
пощу́сь *несов см* **пости́ться**.
поэ́зи|я (-и) *ж* (*также перен*) poetry.
поэ́м|а (-ы) *ж* poem.
поэ́т (-а) *м* poet.
поэте́сс|а (-ы) *ж см* **поэ́т**.
поэтизи́р|овать (-ую; *perf* **опоэтизи́ровать**)
несов перех to wax poetic about.
поэти́ческ|ий (-ая, -ое, -ие) *прил* poetic.
поэ́тому *нареч* therefore.
пою́ *итп несов см* **петь, пойть**.
появ|и́ться (-явлю́сь, -я́вишься) *impf*
появля́ться) *сов возв* to appear; **у него́**
~яви́лись иде́и/сомне́ния he has had an idea/
begun to have doubts; **появля́ться** (**~** *perf*) **на**
свет to come into the world.
появле́ни|е (-я) *ср* appearance.
появлю́сь *сов см* **появи́ться**.
появля́|ться (-юсь) *несов от* **появи́ться**.
по́яс (-а; *nom pl* -а́) *м* (*ремень*) belt; (*та́лия*)
waist; (*ГЕО*) zone; **спаса́тельный ~** life belt;
тари́фный ~ (*ЭКОН*) tariff zone.
поясне́ни|е (-я) *ср* explanation.
поясн|и́ть (-ю́, -и́шь; *impf* **поясня́ть**) *сов перех*
to explain.
поясни́ц|а (-ы) *ж* small of the back.
поясня́|ть (-ю) *несов от* **поясни́ть**.
ППГ *м сокр* (= полево́й подвижно́й го́спиталь)
field hospital; ≈ MASH (*US*) (= *mobile army*
surgical hospital).
пр. *сокр* = прое́зд, проспе́кт, про́чее, про́чие.
прааба́б|ка (-ки; *gen pl* -ок) *ж* great-grandmother.
прааба́буш|ка (-ки; *gen pl* -ек) *ж* = **прааба́бка**.

прав‌а́ (-) _мн (также: водительские_ ~) driving licence (_BRIT_), driver's license (_US_); **прав‌а́ челове́ка** human rights.

пра́вд‌а (-ы) _ж_ truth ◆ _нареч_ really ◆ _вводн сл_ true; **он ~ измени́лся** he really has changed; **он, ~, сам созна́лся** true, he did confess; **ты винова́т в э́том – ~** you are to blame, it's true; **~у или по ~е говоря́** или **сказа́ть** to tell the truth; **он уже́ уе́хал, не ~ ли?** he's already gone, hasn't he?; **хоро́шая пого́да, не ~ ли?** the weather's good, isn't it?

правди́в‌ый (-, -а, -о) _прил_ truthful.

правдоподо́бн‌ый (-ен, -на, -но) _прил_ plausible.

пра́ведн‌о _прил см_ **пра́ведный.**

пра́ведник (-а) _ж (РЕЛ)_ righteous man (_мн_ men).

пра́вед‌ный (-ен, -на, -но) _прил (человек)_ righteous; (_суд_) just.

пра́вилен _прил см_ **пра́вильный.**

пра́вил‌о (-а) _ср_ rule; **э́то не в мои́х ~ах** that's not my way; **как ~** as a rule; **по всем ~ам** by the rules; **пра́вила доро́жного движе́ния** rules of the road, ≈ Highway Code.

пра́вильно _нареч_ correctly ◆ _как сказ_ that's correct.

пра́вил‌ьный (-ен, -ьна, -ьно) _прил (написание, произношение итп)_ correct; (_вывод, ответ_) right; (_совет, суждение_) sound.

прави́тел‌ь (-я) _м_ ruler.

прави́тельственный _прил_ government _опред._

прави́тельств‌о (-а) _ср_ government.

пра́в‌ить (-лю, -ишь) _несов перех (исправлять)_ to correct ◆ _неперех:_ ~ +_instr (страной)_ to rule, govern; (_машиной_) to drive.

пра́вк‌а (-ки; _gen pl_ -ок) _ж_ proofreading.

правле́ни‌е (-я) _ср_ government; (_орган_) board.

пра́влю _несов см_ **пра́вить.**

пра́внук (-а) _м_ great-grandson.

пра́в‌о (-а; _nom pl_ -а́) _ср (нормы, наука)_ law; (_свобода_) right ◆ _вводн сл (разг)_ really; **име́ть** (_impf_) ~ **на что-н/**+_infin_ to have the right или be entitled to sth/to do; **быть** (_impf_) **в ~е** +_infin_ to be entitled или have the right to do; **на права́х** +_gen_ as; **по ~у** (_законно_) by rights; (_с полным основанием_) rightly; **на ра́вных права́х с** +_instr_ on equal terms with; _см также_ **права́.**

правове́д (-а) _м_ jurisprudent.

правове́дени‌е (-я) _ср_ jurisprudence.

правове́р‌ный (-ен, -на, -но) _прил_ orthodox.

правово́й _прил (нормы)_ legal; **правово́е госуда́рство** lawful state.

правозащи́тник (-а) _м_ human rights activist.

правозащи́тниц‌а (-ы) _ж см_ **правозащи́тник.**

пра́вок _сущ см_ **пра́вка.**

правоме́р‌ный (-ен, -на, -но) _прил (вопрос)_ valid; (_сомнения_) justifiable; (_действие, поступок_) lawful.

правомо́ч‌ный (-ен, -на, -но) _прил (орган)_ competent; (_лицо_) authorized.

правонаруше́ни‌е (-я) _ср_ offence.

правонаруши́тел‌ь (-я) _м_ offender.

правописа́ни‌е (-я) _ср_ spelling.

правопоря́д‌ок (-ка) _м_ law and order.

правосла́ви‌е (-я) _ср_ orthodoxy.

правосла́вн‌ая (-ой; _decl like adj_) _ж см_ **правосла́вный.**

правосла́вн‌ый _прил (церковь, обряд)_ orthodox ◆ (_decl like adj_) _м member of the Orthodox Church._

правоспосо́б‌ный (-ен, -на, -но) _прил (ЮР)_ capable.

правосу́ди‌е (-я) _ср_ justice.

правот‌а́ (-ы́) _ж_ correctness; **я не сомнева́юсь в Ва́шей ~е́** I don't doubt that you are right.

пра́в‌ый _прил_ right; (_ПОЛИТ_) right-wing; (-, -а́, -о; _справедливый_) just; (_невиновный_) innocent; (_no full form_) **он прав** he is right; ~ **суд** fair trial.

пра́вящий (-ая, -ее, -ие) _прил_ ruling _опред._

Пра́г‌а (-и) _ж_ Prague.

прагмати́зм (-а) _м_ pragmatism.

прагма́тик (-а) _м_ pragmatist.

пра́дед (-а) _м_ great-grandfather.

праде́душ‌ка (-ки; _gen pl_ -ек) _м_ = **пра́дед.**

пра́зден _прил см_ **пра́здный.**

пра́зднеств‌о (-а) _ср_ festival.

пра́здник (-а) _м (по случаю какого-н события)_ public holiday; (_религиозный_) festival; (_нерабочий день_) holiday; (_радость, торжество_) celebration; **с ~ом!** best wishes!

пра́зднич‌ный (-ен, -на, -но) _прил (салют, обед)_ celebratory; (_одежда, настроение_) festive; ~ **день, пра́здничная да́та** holiday.

пра́здновать (-ую) _несов перех_ to celebrate.

пра́здн‌ый (-ен, -на, -но) _прил_ idle; ~**ная жизнь** life of idleness.

пра́ктик (-а) _м (о каком-н специалисте)_ expert; (_практичный человек_) practical person (_мн_ people); **он хоро́ший ~, но плохо́й теоре́тик** he's technically very good, but not so good at the theory.

пра́ктик‌а (-и) _ж_ practice; (_часть учёбы_) practical experience или work; **на ~е** in practice.

практика́нт (-а) _м_ trainee (_on a placement_).

практика́нт‌ка (-ки; _gen pl_ -ок) _ж см_ **практика́нт.**

практикова́ть (-ую) _несов перех_ to practise (_BRIT_), practice (_US_)

▸ **практикова́ться** _несов возв (методы, приёмы)_ to be used; (_обучаться_): ~**ся в чём-н** to practise sth.

практи́чен _прил см_ **практи́чный.**

практи́чески _нареч (на практике)_ in practice; (_по сути дела_) practically.

практи́ч‌еский (-ая, -ое, -ие) _прил_ practical.

практи́ч‌ный (-ен, -на, -но) _прил_ practical.

пра́порщик (-а) _м (ВОЕН)_ ≈ warrant officer.

прах (-а) *м* (*умершего*) ashes *мн*; **пойти́** (*perf*) **пра́хом** (*усилия, работа*) to be wasted.

пра́чек *сущ см* **пра́чка**.

пра́чечн|ая (-ой; *decl like adj*) *ж* laundry.

пра́ч|ка (-ки; *gen pl* -ек) *ж* laundress.

преа́мбул|а (-ы) *ж* preamble.

пребыва́ни|е (-я) *ср* (*в каком-н месте*) stay; ~ **у вла́сти** term of office.

пребыва́|ть (-ю) *несов неперех* (*находиться*) to be.

превали́р|овать (-ую) *несов неперех*: ~ (**над** +*instr*) to prevail (over).

превенти́вный *прил* preventive; ~ **уда́р** pre-emptive strike.

превзойти́ (*как* **идти́**; *см* **Table 18**; *impf* **превосходи́ть**) *сов перех* (*соперника, врага*) to beat; (*прежние результаты, ожидания*) to surpass; (*доходы, скорость*) to exceed; ~ (*perf*) **самого́ себя́** to surpass o.s.

превозм|о́чь (-огу́, -о́жешь *итп*, -о́гут; *pt* -о́г, -огла́, -огло́, *impf* **превозмога́ть**) *сов перех* to overcome.

превозн|ести́ (-есу́, -есёшь; *pt* -ёс, -есла́, -есло́) *сов перех* to extol.

превосхо́ден *прил см* **превосхо́дный**.

превосходи́ть (-жу́, -дишь) *несов от* **превзойти́**.

превосхо́дно *нареч* excellently ◆ *как сказ* it's excellent.

превосхо́дный (-ен, -на, -но) *прил* superb; **превосхо́дная сте́пень** superlative degree.

превосхо́дств|о (-а) *ср* superiority.

превосхожу́ *несов см* **превосходи́ть**.

превра́тен *прил см* **превра́тный**.

превра|ти́ть (-щу́, -ти́шь; *impf* **превраща́ть**) *сов перех*: ~ **что-н в** +*acc* to turn sth into; **превраща́ть** (~ *perf*) **кого́-н в** +*acc* to turn *или* transform sb into

▸ **преврати́ться** (*impf* **превраща́ться**) *сов возв* to turn.

превра́тный (-ен, -на, -но) *прил* wrong.

превраща́|ть(ся) (-ю(сь)) *несов от* **преврати́ть(ся)**.

превраще́ни|е (-я) *ср* transformation.

превращу́(сь) *сов см* **преврати́ть(ся)**.

превы́|сить (-шу́, -сишь; *impf* **превыша́ть**) *сов перех* to exceed; (*рекорд*) to break.

прегра́д|а (-ы) *ж* barrier.

прегра|ди́ть (-жу́, -ди́шь; *impf* **прегражда́ть**) *сов перех*: ~ **кому́-н доро́гу/вход** to block *или* bar sb's way/entrance.

преда|ва́ть(ся) (-ю́(сь)) *несов от* **преда́ть(ся)**.

преда́м(ся) *итп сов см* **преда́ть(ся)**.

преда́ни|е (-я) *ср* legend.

пре́дан|ный (-, -на, -но) *прил* devoted; **он пре́дан де́лу/жене́** he is devoted to the cause/ his wife.

преда́ст(ся) *сов см* **преда́ть(ся)**.

преда́тел|ь (-я) *м* traitor.

преда́тельниц|а (-ы) *ж см* **преда́тель**.

преда́тельск|ий (-ая, -ое, -ие) *прил* treacherous.

преда́тельств|о (-а) *ср* treachery.

преда́|ть (*как* **дать**; *см* **Table 14**; *impf* **предава́ть**) *сов перех* to betray; **предава́ть** (~ *perf*) **что-н гла́сности** to make sth public; **предава́ть** (~ *perf*) **кого́-н су́ду** to prosecute sb; **предава́ть** (~ *perf*) **забве́нию** to consign to oblivion

▸ **преда́ться** (*impf* **предава́ться**) *сов возв*: ~**ся** +*dat* (*мечтам итп*) to give o.s. up to.

предвари́тел|ьный (-ен, -ьна, -ьно) *прил* preliminary; (*продажа билетов*) advance *опред*; ~ **счёт-факту́ра** (*КОММ*) pro-forma invoice; **предвари́тельное заключе́ние** (*ЮР*) remand.

предвар|и́ть (-ю́, -и́шь; *impf* **предваря́ть**) *сов перех* (*события*) to anticipate.

предве́сти|е (-я) *ср* indication.

предвеща́|ть (-ю) *несов перех* (*будущее, успех*) to foretell; (*изменения, кризис*) to portend; (*плохую погоду*) to herald.

предвзя́|тый (-, -а, -о) *прил* prejudiced.

предви́дени|е (-я) *ср* foresight; (*предположение*) prediction.

предви́|деть (-жу, -дишь) *сов перех* to foresee, predict

▸ **предви́деться** *сов неперех* to be expected.

предвкуша́|ть (-ю) *несов перех* to look forward to, anticipate.

предвкуше́ни|е (-я) *ср* anticipation.

предводи́тел|ь (-я) *м* leader.

предвосхи́|тить (-щу́, -ти́шь; *impf* **предвосхища́ть**) *сов перех* to anticipate.

предвы́борн|ый *прил* (*собрание*) pre-election *опред*; ~**ая кампа́ния** election campaign.

предго́рн|ый *прил*: ~ **райо́н** foothills *мн*.

преддве́ри|е (-я) *ср*: **в ~и чего́-н** on the threshold of sth.

преде́л (-а) *м* (*обычно мн: города, страны*) boundary; (*перен: приличия*) bound; (: *терпения*) limit; (*изнеможения*) peak; (*совершенства, подлости*) height; (*мечтаний, желаний*) pinnacle; **на ~е** at breaking point; **дойти́** (*perf*) **до ~а** to reach the limit; **в ~ах** +*gen* (*закона, года*) within; (*приличия*) within the bounds of; **за ~ами** +*gen* (*страны, города*) outside.

преде́л|ьный (-ен, -ьна, -ьно) *прил* maximum; (*восторг, важность*) utmost; **преде́льный срок** deadline.

предзнаменова́ни|е (-я) *ср* omen.

предика́т (-а) *м* (*линг*) predicate.

предисло́ви|е (-я) *ср* foreword, preface.

пре́дка *сущ см* **пре́док**.

пре́дк|и (-ов) *мн* ancestors *мн*.

предлага́|ть (-ю) *несов от* **предложи́ть**.

предло́г (-а) *м* pretext; (*линг*) preposition; **под ~ом** +*gen* on the pretext of; **под ~ом того́ что, под тем ~ом что** on the pretext that.

предложе́ни|е (-я) *ср* (*конкретное, умное*) proposal, suggestion; (*замужества*) proposal;

(*КОММ*) offer; (*ЭКОН*) supply; (*ЛИНГ*) sentence; **де́лать (сде́лать** *perf*) ~ **кому́-н** (*де́вушке*) to propose to sb; (*КОММ*) to make sb an offer; **вноси́ть (внести́** *perf*) ~ (*на собра́нии, на съе́зде*) to propose a motion.

предл|ожи́ть (-ожу́, -о́жишь; *impf* **предлага́ть**) *сов перех* to offer; (*план, кандидату́ру*) to propose ♦ *неперех* to suggest, propose; (*попроси́ть*) to ask, invite; (*потре́бовать*) to ask; **предлага́ть** (~ *perf*) **что-н кому́-н** to offer sth to sb, offer sb sth; **он ~ожи́л нам пойти́ туда́** he suggested that we went there.

предло́жный *прил* (*ЛИНГ*) prepositional; **предло́жный паде́ж** prepositional case.

предме́сть|е (-я) *ср* suburb.

предме́т (-а) *м* object; (*обсужде́ния, изуче́ния*) subject; **на** ~ +*gen* concerning; **предме́ты дома́шнего обихо́да** household goods; **предме́ты пе́рвой необходи́мости** necessities.

предназнача́|ть (-ю) *несов от* **предназна́чить**
▸ **предназнача́ться** *несов возв* (+*dat*) to be destined for.

предназначе́ни|е (-я) *ср* role.

предназна́ч|ить (-у, -ишь; *impf* **предназнача́ть**) *сов перех*: ~ **что-н/кого́-н** +*dat* to intend sth/sb for.

преднаме́рен|ный (-, -на, -но) *прил* (*преступле́ние*) premeditated; (*обма́н итп*) deliberate.

пре́д|ок (-ка) *м* ancestor; *см та́кже* **пре́дки**.

предопредел|и́ть (-ю́, -и́шь; *impf* **предопределя́ть**) *сов перех* (*определи́ть*) to predetermine; (*обусло́вить*) to bring about.

предоста́в|ить (-лю, -ишь) *сов перех*: ~ **что-н кому́-н** to give sb sth ♦ *неперех*: ~ **кому́-н** +*infin* (*выбира́ть, реша́ть*) to let sb do; **предоставля́ть** (~ *perf*) **кого́-н самому́ себе́** to leave sb to his own devices; **предоставля́ть** (~ *perf*) **кому́-н сло́во** to call upon sb to speak.

предостерёг *итп сов см* **предостере́чь**.

предостерега́|ть (-ю) *несов от* **предостере́чь**.

предостерегу́ *итп сов см* **предостере́чь**.

предостереже́ни|е (-я) *ср* warning.

предостер|е́чь (-егу́, -ежёшь *итп*, -егу́т; *pt* -ёг, -егла́, -егло́, *impf* **предостерега́ть**) *сов перех*: ~ **кого́-н** (**от** +*gen*) to warn sb (about).

предосторо́жность (-и) *ж* caution; **ме́ры ~и** precautionary measures, precautions.

предосуди́тел|ьный (-ен, -ьна, -ьно) *прил* reprehensible.

предотвра|ти́ть (-щу́, -ти́шь; *impf* **предотвраща́ть**) *сов перех* (*войну́, кри́зис*) to avert; (*боле́знь, ава́рии*) to prevent.

предотвраще́ни|е (-я) *ср* (*см глаг*) averting; prevention.

предотвращу́ *сов см* **предотврати́ть**.

предохрани́тел|ь (-я) *м* safety device; (*электри́ческий*) fuse (*BRIT*), fuze (*US*); (*ружёйный*) safety catch; (*замка́*) snib.

предохрани́тельный *прил* (*ТЕХ*) safety *опред*.

предохран|и́ть (-ю́, -и́шь; *impf* **предохраня́ть**) *сов перех* to protect.

предписа́ни|е (-я) *ср* (*распоряже́ние*) instruction; (*: президе́нта, поли́ции*) order; (*: врача́*) prescription.

предпи|са́ть (-шу́, -́шешь; *impf* **предпи́сывать**) *сов перех*: ~ **что-н кому́-н** (*назна́чить*) to prescribe sth for sb ♦ *неперех*: ~ **кому́-н** +*infin* to order sb to do.

предполага́|ть (-ю) *несов от* **предположи́ть** ♦ *перех* to demand ♦ *неперех*: ~ +*infin* (*намерева́ться*) to intend to do
▸ **предполага́ться** *несов неперех* (*намеча́ться*) to be planned.

предположе́ни|е (-я) *ср* (*дога́дка*) supposition; (*наме́рение*) intention.

предположи́тел|ьный (-ен, -ьна, -ьно) *прил* (*результа́т, вопро́с*) hypothetical; (*срок, дохо́д*) anticipated.

предпол|ожи́ть (-ожу́, -о́жишь; *impf* **предполага́ть**) *сов перех* (*допусти́ть возмо́жность*) to allow for; ~**о́жим** (*возмо́жно*) suppose; ~**о́жим, он опозда́ет** suppose he is late.

предпо|сла́ть (-шлю́, -шлёшь; *impf* **предпосыла́ть**) *сов перех*: ~ **что-н чему́-н** to preface sth with sth.

предпосле́дн|ий (-яя, -ее, -ие) *прил* (*но́мер журна́ла*) penultimate; (*в о́череди*) last but one.

предпосыла́|ть (-ю) *несов от* **предпосла́ть**.

предпосы́л|ка (-ки; *gen pl* -ок) *ж* (*усло́вие*) precondition, prerequisite; (*исхо́дное положе́ние*) premise.

предпоч|е́сть (-ту́, -тёшь; *pt* -ёл, -ла́, -ло́, *impf* **предпочита́ть**) *сов перех*: ~ **что-н/кого́-н** +*dat* to prefer sth/sb to ♦ *неперех*: ~ +*infin* to prefer to do.

предпочте́ни|е (-я) *ср* preference; **ока́зывать (оказа́ть** *perf*) *или* **отдава́ть (отда́ть** *perf*) **кому́-н/чему́-н** ~ to show a preference for sb/sth.

предпочти́тел|ьный (-ен, -ьна, -ьно) *прил* preferable.

предпочту́ *итп сов см* **предпоче́сть**.

предпошлю́ *итп сов см* **предпосла́ть**.

предприи́мчив|ый (-, -а, -о) *прил* enterprising.

предприму́ *итп сов см* **предприня́ть**.

предпринима́тел|ь (-я) *м* entrepreneur, businessman; (*мн* businessmen)

предпринима́тельск|ий (-ая, -ое, -ие) *прил* enterprise *опред*, business *опред*.

предпринима́тельств|о (-а) *ср* enterprise.

предпр|иня́ть (-иму́, -и́мешь; *pt* -и́нял, -иняла́,-и́няло, *impf* **предпринима́ть**) *сов перех* to undertake; (*атаку, наступление итп*) to launch; (*меры*) to take.

предприя́ти|е (**-я**) *ср* enterprise, business.

предрасположе́ни|е (**-я**) *ср* predisposition.

предрасполо́женност|ь (**-и**) *ж* = **предрасположе́ние**.

предрассу́д|ок (**-ка**) *м* prejudice.

предрека́|ть (**-ю**) *несов перех* (*успех*) to foretell; (*плохую погоду*) to herald.

предреш|и́ть (**-у́, -и́шь**; *impf* **предреша́ть**) *сов перех* to predetermine.

председа́тел|ь (**-я**) *м* chairman (*мн* chairmen).

председа́тельств|о (**-а**) *ср* chairmanship; **под ~м** +*gen* under the chairmanship of.

председа́тельств|овать (**-ую**) *несов неперех* (*на заседании*) to be in the chair; (*работать председателем*) to be chairman; ~ (*impf*) **на собра́нии** to chair a meeting.

предскажу́ *итп сов см* **предсказа́ть**.

предсказа́ни|е (**-я**) *ср* (*действие*) predicting; (*то, что предсказано*) prediction.

предск|аза́ть (**-ажу́, -а́жешь**; *impf* **предска́зывать**) *сов перех* to predict; (*чью-н судьбу*) to foretell.

предсме́ртный *прил* (*агония*) death *опред*; (*вздох*) dying; (*воля*) last.

предста|ва́ть (**-ю́**) *несов от* **предста́ть**.

представи́тел|ь (**-я**) *м* representative; (*разряда животных итп*) specimen.

представи́тельниц|а (**-ы**) *ж* representative.

представи́тельный *прил* representative; (*видный*) imposing.

представи́тельств|о (**-а**) *ср* (*учреждение*) representatives *мн*; (*наличие представителей*) representation; **торго́вое** ~ trade mission; **дипломати́ческое** ~ diplomatic corps.

предста́в|ить (**-лю, -ишь**; *impf* **представля́ть**) *сов перех* to present; **представля́ть** (~ *perf*) **кого́-н кому́-н** (*познакомить*) to introduce sb to sb; **представля́ть** (**представить** *perf*) **кого́-н к** +*dat* (*к награде, к премии итп*) to recommend sb for, put sb forward for; **представля́ть** (~ *perf*) **интере́с** to be of interest; **представля́ть** (~ *perf*) **себе́** to imagine; **~ьте** (**себе́**)! (just) imagine!

▶ **предста́виться** (*impf* **представля́ться**) *несов возв* (*при знакомстве*) to introduce o.s.; (*появиться: возможность*) to present itself; **представля́ться** (**~ся** *perf*) **кому́-н** (*вид*) to appear before sb; (*интересная картина*) to meet sb's eyes; **ему́** ~**лась бу́дущая встре́ча** he pictured the future meeting; **ей** ~**лась возмо́жность пое́хать в Ло́ндон** an opportunity arose for her to go to London; **представля́ться** (**~ся** *perf*) **больны́м/спя́щим** to pretend to be ill/asleep.

представле́ни|е (**-я**) *ср* presentation; (*документу*) statement; (*ТЕАТР*) performance; (*знание*) idea; (*ПСИХОЛ*) representation; **не име́ть** (*impf*) (**никако́го**) ~**я о** +*prp* to have no idea about.

предста́влю(сь) *сов см* **предста́вить(ся)**.

представля́|ть (**-ю**) *несов от* **предста́вить** ◆ *перех* (*действовать от имени*) to represent; ~ (*impf*) **собо́й** *или* **из себя́** (*являться*) to be; ~ (*impf*) **себе́ что-н** (*понимать*) to understand sth; (*осознавать*) to appreciate sth; **он ничего́ из себя́ не** ~**ет** he doesn't amount to much

▶ **представля́ться** *несов от* **предста́виться** ◆ *возв*: **мне** ~**ется, (что) он прав** I think he's right; ~**ется, что ...** it appears that ....

предста́|ть (**-ну, -нешь**; *impf* **представа́ть**) *сов неперех*: ~ **пе́ред** +*instr* (*появиться*) to appear before; (*проявиться: человек*) to show o.s.; (*: характер*) to show itself.

предсто|я́ть (*3sg* **-и́т**, *3pl* **-я́т**) *несов неперех* to lie ahead; **нам** ~**и́т мно́го рабо́ты** there is a lot of work ahead of us.

предстоя́щий (**-ая, -ее, -ие**) *прил* (*сезон*) coming; (*трудности*) impending; (*работа, встреча*) forthcoming.

предубежде́ни|е (**-я**) *ср* prejudice.

предугада́|ть (**-ю**; *impf* **предуга́дывать**) *сов перех* to anticipate.

предупреди́тельный (**-ен, -ьна, -ьно**) *прил* (*предохраняющий*) preventive; (*любезный*) solicitous, attentive.

предупре|ди́ть (**-жу́, -ди́шь**; *impf* **предупрежда́ть**) *сов перех* (*учесть*) to warn; (*предотвратить*) to prevent; (*опередить*) to anticipate; **предупрежда́ть** (~ *perf*) **кого́-н о** +*prp* to warn sb about.

предупрежде́ни|е (**-я**) *ср* warning; (*аварии, заболевания*) prevention; (*извещение*) notice.

предупрежу́ *сов см* **предупреди́ть**.

предусм|отре́ть (**-отрю́, -о́тришь**; *impf* **предусма́тривать**) *сов перех* (*учесть*) to foresee; (*принять меры*) to make provision for; (*подлеж: программа, закон*) to provide for.

предусмотри́тельный (**-ен, -ьна, -ьно**) *прил* prudent.

предчу́встви|е (**-я**) *ср* premonition.

предчу́вств|овать (**-ую**) *несов перех* to have a premonition of.

предше́ственник (**-а**) *м* predecessor.

предше́ствующ|ий (**-ая, -ее, -ие**) *прил* previous; (*событие*) foregoing.

предъяви́тел|ь (**-я**) *м* bearer.

предъяви́тельниц|а (**-ы**) *ж см* **предъяви́тель**.

предъ|яви́ть (**-явлю́, -я́вишь**; *impf* **предъявля́ть**) *сов перех* (*паспорт, билет итп*) to show; (*доказательства*) to produce; (*требования, претензии*) to make; (*иск*) to bring; **предъявля́ть** (~ *perf*) **права́ на что-н** to lay claim to sth.

предъявле́ни|е (**-я**) *ср* (*паспорта, билета итп*) showing; (*претензий*) making; (*иска*) bringing; **по** ~ (*комм*) at sight.

предъявлю́ *сов см* **предъяви́ть**.

предъявля́|ть (**-ю**) *несов от* **предъяви́ть**.

предыду́щий (**-ая, -ее, -ие**) *прил* previous.

предысто́ри|я (-и) *ж* background.
прее́мник (-а) *м* successor.
прее́мниц|а (-ы) *ж см* **прее́мник**.
прее́мственност|ь (-и) *ж* (*власти, тради́ций*) continuity.
прее́мственный *прил* successive.
пре́жде *нареч* (*в прошлом*) formerly; (*снача́ла*) first ♦ *предл* (+*gen*) before; ~ **всего́** first of all; ~ **чем** before; ~ **она́ никогда́ об э́том не ду́мала** she never used to think about it.
преждевре́мен|ный (-ен, -на, -но) *прил* premature.
пре́жн|ий (-яя, -ее, -ие) *прил* former.
презента́ци|я (-и) *ж* presentation.
презервати́в (-а) *м* condom.
президе́нт (-а) *м* president.
прези́диум (-а) *м* presidium.
презира́|ть (-ю) *несов перех* to hold in contempt.
презре́ни|е (-я) *ср* (*ко лжи, к преда́телю*) contempt; (*к опа́сности*) disregard; (*к бога́тству итп*) scorn.
презри́тел|ьный (-ен, -ьна, -ьно) *прил* contemptuous.
преиму́щественно *нареч* chiefly.
преиму́ществ|о (-а) *ср* advantage; (*ЮР*) privilege; **по** ~**у** (*гла́вным о́бразом*) chiefly; **име́ть** (*impf*) ~ **пе́ред** +*instr* to have an advantage over.
преиспо́лн|иться (-юсь; *impf* **преисполня́ться**) *сов возв*: ~ +*instr* to be filled with.
прейскура́нт (-а) *м* price list.
преклоне́ни|е (-я) *ср*: ~ (**пе́ред** +*instr*) admiration (for).
прекло́нный *прил*: ~ **во́зраст** old age.
преклоня́|ться (-юсь) *несов возв*: ~ **пе́ред** +*instr* to admire.
прекра́сен *прил см* **прекра́сный**.
прекра́сн|ое (-ого; *decl like adj*) *ср* beauty.
прекра́с|ный (-ен, -на, -но) *прил* (*краси́вый*: *же́нщина, приро́да*) beautiful; (: *го́род, вид, день*) fine, beautiful; (*отли́чный*) excellent; **в оди́н** ~ **день** (*одна́жды*) one fine day.
прекра|ти́ть (-щу́, -ти́шь; *impf* **прекраща́ть**) *сов перех* to stop; (*пода́чу эне́ргии*) to cut off ♦ *неперех*: ~ +*infin* to stop doing; **прекраща́ть** (~ *perf*) **отноше́ния с кем-н** to break off relations with sb
▶ **прекрати́ться** (*impf* **прекраща́ться**) *сов возв* (*дождь, заня́тия*) to stop; (*отноше́ния, знако́мство*) to end.
прекраще́ни|е (-я) *ср* (*рабо́ты*) stopping; (*поста́вок*) cutting off; (*отноше́ний*) breaking off.
прекращу́(сь) *сов см* **прекрати́ть(ся)**.
преле́ст|ный (-ен, -на, -но) *прил* charming.
пре́лест|ь (-и) *ж* charm; **кака́я** ~**!** how charming!
прел|оми́ться (*3sg* -о́мится, *3pl* -о́мятся, *impf* **преломля́ться**) *сов возв* (*ФИЗ*) to be refracted; (*перен*) to take on a different cast.
пре́лый *прил* rotten.
прель|сти́ть (-щу́, -сти́шь; *impf* **прельща́ть**) *сов перех* to attract; (*увле́чь*): ~ **кого́-н чем-н** to entice sb with sth
▶ **прельсти́ться** (*impf* **прельща́ться**) *сов возв*: ~**ся** +*instr* (*возмо́жностями*) to be attracted by; (*бога́тством*) to be enticed by.
прелю́ди|я (-и) *ж* prelude.
премиа́льн|ые (-ых; *decl like adj*) *мн* bonus *ед*.
премиа́льный *прил* bonus *опред; см также* **премиа́льные**.
премир|ова́ть (-у́ю) (*не*)*сов перех* (*рабо́тника*) to give a bonus to; (*победи́теля*) to award a prize to.
пре́ми|я (-и) *ж* (*рабо́тнику*) bonus; (*победи́телю*) prize; (*КОММ*) premium.
прему́дрост|ь (-и) *ж* (*разг*: *обычно мн*) ins *мн* and outs *мн*.
премье́р (-а) *м* (*также*: ~-**мини́стр**) prime minister, premier.
премье́р|а (-ы) *ж* première.
премье́р-мини́стр (-а) *м* prime minister, premier.
пренебрёг *итп сов см* **пренебре́чь**.
пренебрега́|ть (-ю) *несов от* **пренебре́чь**.
пренебрегу́ *итп сов см* **пренебре́чь**.
пренебреже́ни|е (-я) *ср* (*зако́нами итп*) disregard; (: *обя́занностями*) neglect; (*высокоме́рие*) contempt.
пренебрежёшь *итп сов см* **пренебре́чь**.
пренебрежи́тел|ьный (-ен, -ьна, -ьно) *прил* contemptuous.
пренебре|чь (-гу́, -жёшь итп, -гу́т; *pt* -ёг, -егла́, -его́, *impf* **пренебрега́ть**) *сов неперех*: ~ +*instr* (*опа́сностью, после́дствиями*) to disregard; (*мо́дной оде́ждой, пра́вилами*) to scorn; (*сове́том, про́сьбой*) to ignore.
пре́ни|я (-й) *мн* debate *ед*.
преоблада́|ть (*3sg* -ет, *3pl* -ют) *несов неперех*: ~ (**над** +*instr*) to predominate (over).
преобра|зи́ть (-жу́, -зи́шь; *impf* **преображáть**) *сов перех* to transform
▶ **преобрази́ться** (*impf* **преобража́ться**) *сов возв* to be transformed.
преобразова́ни|е (-я) *ср* (*о́бщества, жи́зни*) transformation; (*то́ка, эне́ргии*) conversion; (*революцио́нное, социа́льное*) reform.
преобразова́тел|ь (-я) *м* (*то́ка, радиосигна́лов*) transformer; (*о́бщества*) reformer.
преобраз|ова́ть (-у́ю; *impf* **преобразо́вывать**) *сов перех* to reorganize; **преобразо́вывать** (~ *perf*) **что-н в** +*acc* (*преврати́ть*) to convert sth into.

преодоле́|ть (-ю; *impf* **преодолева́ть**) *сов перех* to overcome; (*преграду*) to break down; (*трудный переход итп*) to get through.

препара́т (-а) *м* (*МЕД, ХИМ*) preparation.

препина́ни|е (-я) *ср*: **зна́ки ~я** punctuation marks *мн*.

препира́|ться (-юсь) *несов возв*: **~ (с** +*instr*) to squabble *или* bicker (with).

преподава́ни|е (-я) *ср* teaching.

преподава́тел|ь (-я) *м* (*школы, курсов*) teacher; (*вуза*) lecturer.

преподава́тельниц|а (-ы) *ж см* **преподава́тель**.

препода|ва́ть (-ю́, -ёшь) *несов перех* to teach.

препода́ть (*как* **дать**; *см* **Table 14**) *сов перех* to teach; **~** (*perf*) **кому́-н уро́к терпе́ния** to teach sb patience.

препод|нести́ (-есу́, -есёшь; *pt* -ёс, -есла́, -есло́, *impf* **преподноси́ть**) *сов перех*: **~ что-н кому́-н** to present sb with sth; (*новость, сюрприз*) to give sb sth.

преподо́би|е (-я) *ср* (*РЕЛ*): **Ва́ше/Его́ ~** Your/His Eminence.

преподо́бный *прил* (*РЕЛ*) venerable.

препя́тстви|е (-я) *ср* obstacle.

препя́тств|овать (-ую; *perf* **воспрепя́тствовать**) *несов неперех* (+*dat*) to impede.

прерв|а́ть (-у́, -ёшь; *impf* **прерыва́ть**) *сов перех* (*разговор, работу итп*) to cut short; (*отношения, знакомство*) to break off; (*говорящего*) to interrupt; (*КОМП*) to abort

▶ **прерва́ться** (*impf* **прерыва́ться**) *сов возв* (*разговор, игра*) to be cut short; (*отношения, знакомство*) to be broken off.

пререка́|ться (-юсь) *несов возв* to squabble *или* bicker.

прерогати́в|а (-ы) *ж* prerogative.

прерыва́|ть(ся) (-ю(сь)) *несов от* **прерва́ть(ся)**.

прерыви́стый (-, -а, -о) *прил* (*звонок*) intermittent; (*линия*) broken.

пресёк *итп сов см* **пресе́чь**.

пресека́|ть (-ю) *несов от* **пресе́чь**.

пресеку́ *итп сов см* **пресе́чь**.

пре́сен *прил см* **пре́сный**.

пресече́ни|е (-я) *ср* suppression; **ме́ра ~я** (*ЮР*) injunction.

пресе́|чь (-ку́, -чёшь *итп*, -ку́т; *pt* -ёк, -екла́, -екло́, *impf* **пресека́ть**) *сов перех* to suppress.

пресле́довани|е (-я) *ср* pursuit; (*инакомыслия*) persecution.

пресле́д|овать (-ую) *несов перех* to pursue; (*перен: женщину*) to chase; (*подлеж: мысли, чувства*) to haunt; (*правозащитника*) to persecute.

пресловутый *прил* notorious.

пресмыка́|ться (-юсь) *несов возв* (*пренебр*): **~ пе́ред** +*instr* (*унижаться*) to crawl to.

пресмыка́ющееся (-егося; *nom pl* -иеся) *ср* reptile.

пресново́дный *прил* freshwater.

пре́с|ный (-ен, -на, -но) *прил* (*вода*) fresh; (*пища*) bland; (*перен: шутка*) feeble; (: *история, разговоры итп*) tedious.

пресс (-а) *м* (*ТЕХ*) press.

пре́сс|а (-ы) *ж собир* the press; **общенациона́льная ~** national press.

пресс-конфере́нци|я (-и) *ж* press conference.

пресс|ова́ть (-у́ю; *perf* **спрессова́ть**) *несов перех* (*детали*) to press; (*порошок, газ*) to compress.

пресс-центр (-а) *м* press office.

престаре́л|ый *прил* aged; **дом (для) ~ых** old people's home.

прести́ж (-а) *м* prestige.

прести́жный (-ен, -на, -но) *прил* prestigious.

престо́л (-а) *м* (*трон*) throne; **вступа́ть (вступи́ть** *perf*) *или* **восходи́ть (взойти́** *perf*) **на ~** to ascend the throne; **сверга́ть (све́ргнуть** *perf*) **кого́-н с ~а** to dethrone sb.

престу́пен *прил см* **престу́пный**.

преступ|и́ть (-уплю́, -у́пишь; *impf* **преступа́ть**) *сов перех* to breach.

преступле́ни|е (-я) *ср* crime.

преступлю́ *сов см* **преступи́ть**.

престу́пник (-а) *м* criminal.

престу́пниц|а (-ы) *ж см* **престу́пник**.

престу́пност|ь (-и) *ж* criminal nature; (*количество*) crime; **организо́ванная ~** organized crime.

престу́пный (-ен, -на, -но) *прил* criminal.

пресы́|титься (-щусь, -тишься; *impf* **пресыща́ться**) *сов возв* (+*instr*) to satiate o.s. with.

претвор|и́ть (-ю́, -и́шь; *impf* **претворя́ть**) *сов перех*: **~ что-н в жизнь** *или* **в де́ло** *или* **в действи́тельность** (*планы, замыслы*) to put sth into practice; (*мечту*) to realize sth.

претенде́нт (-а) *м* (*на престол*) claimant; (*на должность*) candidate; (*на руку женщины*) suitor; (*СПОРТ*) contender; (*ШАХМАТЫ*) challenger.

претенд|ова́ть (-у́ю) *несов неперех*: **~ на** +*acc* (*стремиться*) to aspire to; (*заявлять права*) to lay claim to.

прете́нзи|я (-и) *ж* (*обычно мн: на наследство, на престол*) claim *ед*; (: *на ум, на красоту итп*) pretension; (*жалоба*) complaint; **быть** (*impf*) **в ~и на** +*acc* to bear a grudge against.

претенцио́з|ный (-ен, -на, -но) *прил* pretentious.

прет|ерпе́ть (-ерплю́, , -е́рпишь; *impf* **претерпева́ть**) *сов перех* (*изменения*) to undergo; (*невзгоды*) to suffer.

прет|и́ть (*3sg* -и́т, *3pl* -я́т) *несов безл* (+*dat*): **ему́ ~и́т жа́дность** greed disgusts *или* sickens him.

преткнове́ни|е (-я) *ср*: **ка́мень ~я** stumbling block.

Прето́ри|я (-и) *ж* Pretoria.

пре|ть (-ю; *perf* **сопре́ть**) *несов неперех* (*листья*) to rot; (*пища*) to stew.

преувеличе́ни|е (-я) *ср* exaggeration.
преувели́ч|ить (-у, -ишь; *impf*
преувели́чивать) *сов перех* to exaggerate.
преуме́ньш|ить (-у, -ишь; *impf*
преуменьша́ть) *сов перех* (*недооценивать*) to
underestimate; (*показать в меньших размерах*)
to understate.
преуспева́|ть (-ю) *несов от* **преуспе́ть** ♦
неперех (*бизнесмен, писатель*) to be
successful.
преуспе́|ть (-ю; *impf* **преуспева́ть)** *сов неперех*
to be successful.
префе́кт (-а) *м administrative area of Moscow.*
преходя́щ|ий (-ая, -ее, -ие; -, -а, -е, -и) *прил*
(*временный*) transient.
прецеде́нт (-а) *м* precedent.

KEYWORD

при *предл* (+*prp*) **1** (*возле*) by, near; **при**
доро́ге/до́ме by *или* near the road/house;
сраже́ние при Ватерло́о the battle of Waterloo
2 (*указывает на прикреплённость*) at; **при**
институ́те есть столо́вая there is a canteen at
the institute; **я бу́ду при гостя́х** I will be with
the guests
3 (*в присутствии*) in front of; **при мне он не**
хо́чет говори́ть he doesn't want to speak in
front of me; **при свиде́телях** in front of *или* in
the presence of witnesses; **он всегда́ чита́ет**
при све́те ла́мпы he always reads by the light
of a lamp
4 (*о времени*) under; **при коммуни́стах/**
Консерва́торах under the communists/
Conservatives; **при короле́ве Викто́рии** in the
time of Queen Victoria
5 (*о наличии чего-н у кого-н*) on; **он всегда́ при**
деньга́х he always has money on him; **я**
оста́влю э́то при себе́ I'll keep it on me; **при**
жела́нии мо́жно всё измени́ть if you wish
everything can be changed; **при слу́чае**
переда́й ему́ приве́т if the occasion arises; **он**
при́ смерти he is close to death; **я здесь ни при**
чём it has nothing to do with me.

при- *префикс* (*in verbs*; *о доведении движения до*
конечной цели) indicating achievement of final
goal *eg.* прибежа́ть; (*добавление*) indicating
addition *eg.* пристро́ить; (*скрепление*)
indicating fastening onto sth *eg.* привинти́ть;
(*сближение*) indicating approach of sth *eg.*
придви́нуться; (*о слабой мере действия*)
indicating slight action *eg.* приоткры́ть; (*о*
сопутствующем действии) indicating
accompanying action *eg.* припева́ть; (*in nouns*
and adjectives; *примыкающий*) indicating
adjoining position *eg.* примо́рский.

приба́в|ить (-лю, -ишь; *impf* **прибавля́ть)** *сов*
перех to add; (*увеличить*) to increase;
прибавля́ть (~ *perf*) **в ве́се** to put on weight

приба́виться (*impf* **прибавля́ться**) *сов возв*
(*проблемы, работа итп*) to mount up ♦ *безл*
(*воды в реке*) to rise; (*народу в толпе*) to grow.
прибавле́ни|е (-я) *ср* addition; (*к зарплате*,
воды в реке) rise; **~ семе́йства** new addition to
the family.
приба́влю(сь) *сов см* **приба́вить(ся)**.
прибавля́|ть (-ю) *несов от* **приба́вить**.
прибау́т|ка (-ки; *gen pl* **-ок)** *ж* catch phrase.
прибега́|ть (-ю) *несов от* **прибе́гнуть**,
прибежа́ть.
прибе́гн|уть (-у, -ешь; *impf* **прибега́ть)** *сов*
неперех: **~ к** +*dat* to resort to.
прибегу́ *итп сов см* **прибежа́ть**.
прибедня́|ться (-юсь) *несов возв* (*разг*) to
pretend to be poor; (*преуменьшать свои*
возможности) to show false modesty.
прибежа́ть (*как* **бежа́ть;** *см* **Table 20**) *сов*
неперех to come running.
прибе́жищ|е (-а) *ср* refuge; **находи́ть (найти́**
perf) **~ в** +*prp* to find refuge in.
прибе́й(те) *сов см* **приби́ть**.
приберу́ *итп сов см* **прибра́ть**.
прибива́|ть(ся) (-ю(сь)) *несов от*
приби́ть(ся).
прибира́|ть (-ю) *несов от* **прибра́ть**.
приб|и́ть (-ью, -ьёшь; *imper* **-е́й(те),** *impf*
прибива́ть) *сов перех* (*прикрепить гвоздями*)
to nail; (*подлеж: вода, волна итп*) to wash up
приби́ться (*impf* **прибива́ться**) *сов возв*
(*лодка к берегу*) to be washed up.
приближа́|ть(ся) (-ю(сь)) *несов от*
прибли́зить(ся).
приближе́ни|е (-я) *ср* (*дня, события*) approach.
прибли́жу(сь) *сов см* **прибли́зить(ся)**.
приблизи́тел|ьный (-ен, -ьна, -ьно) *прил*
approximate.
прибли́|зить (-жу, -зишь; *impf* **приближа́ть)**
сов перех (*придвинуть*) to move nearer;
(*ускорить*) to bring nearer.
прибли́зиться (*impf* **приближа́ться**) *сов*
возв (*человек к окну, машина к дому*) to
approach; (*развязка, победа итп*) to draw near.
прибо́|й (-я) *м* breakers *мн*.
прибо́р (-а) *м* (*измерительный*) device;
(*оптический*) instrument; (*нагревательный*)
appliance; (*бритвенный, чернильный*) set.
прибра́|ть (-еру́, -ерёшь; *impf* **прибира́ть)** *сов*
перех to clear up; **прибира́ть (~** *perf*) **что-н к**
рука́м to lay one's hands on sth; **прибира́ть (~**
perf) **кого́-н к рука́м** to take sb in hand.
прибре́жный *прил* (*у берега моря*) coastal; (*у*
берега реки) riverside *опред*.
прибу́ду *итп сов см* **прибы́ть**.
прибыва́|ть (-ю) *несов от* **прибы́ть**.
прибы́лен *итп сов см* **прибы́льный**.
при́был|ь (-и) *ж* profit; **нереализо́ванная ~**
(*КОММ*) paper profit.

при́быль|ный (-ен, -ьна, -ьно) *прил* profitable.
прибы́ти|е (-я) *ср* arrival.
прибы́|ть (*как* **быть**; *см* **Table 21**; *impf*
　прибыва́ть) *сов неперех* to arrive; (*вода в*
　реке) to rise.
прибью́(сь) *итп сов см* **прибй́ть(ся)**.
прива́л (-а) *м* (*в пути*) stop; (*место остановки*)
　stopping place.
привали́ть (-алю́, -а́лишь; *impf* **прива́ливать**)
　сов перех (*придвинуть что-н тяжёлое*) to
　heave ◆ *неперех* (*перен: разг*) to turn up.
приватиза́ци|я (-и) *ж* (*экон*) privatization.
приватизи́р|овать (-ую) (*не*)*сов перех* to
　privatize.
приведе́ни|е (-я) *ср* (*чего-н в порядок*)
　bringing; (*примеров*) introduction; ~ **к прися́ге**
　swearing in; ~ **пригово́ра в исполне́ние** (*ЮР*)
　carrying out of a sentence; ~ **в движе́ние**
　setting in motion.
приведу́ *итп сов см* **привести́**.
приве|зти́ (-зу́, -зёшь; *pt* -зё, -зла́, -зло́,
　impf **привози́ть**) *сов перех* to bring.
привере́дливый (-, -а, -о) *прил* fussy.
приве́ржен|ец (-ца) *м* (*идеи, традиции*)
　adherent.
приве́ржен|ный (-, -а, -о) *прил*: ~ (**к** +*dat*)
　dedicated (to).
приве́рженца *итп сущ см* **приве́рженец**.
приве|сти́ (-еду́, -едёшь; *pt* -ёл, -ела́, -ело́, *impf*
　приводи́ть) *сов перех* (*ребёнка: домой*) to
　bring; (*подлеж: дорога: к дому*) to take;
　(*пример*) to give; (*чьи-н слова*) to quote; ~ (*perf*)
　в у́жас to horrify; ~ (*perf*) **в отча́яние** to bring to
　the point of despair; ~ (*perf*) **в восто́рг** to
　delight; ~ (*perf*) **в изумле́ние** to astonish; ~
　(*perf*) **в исполне́ние** to put into effect; ~ (*perf*) **в**
　гото́вность to make ready; ~ (*perf*) **в поря́док**
　to put in order; ~ (*perf*) **в движе́ние** to set in
　motion.
приве́т (-а) *м* greetings *мн*, regards *мн*; (*разг:*
　при встрече) hi; (: *при расставании*) bye;
　посыла́ть (**посла́ть** *perf*) *или* **передава́ть**
　(**переда́ть** *perf*) **кому́-н** ~ to send one's regards
　to sb; ~**! рад тебя́ ви́деть** hi! it's nice to see
　you.
приве́тлив|ый (-, -а, -о) *прил* friendly.
приве́тстви|е (-я) *ср* (*при встрече*) greeting;
　(*съезду, делегации*) welcome.
приве́тств|овать (-ую; *perf*
　поприве́тствовать) *несов перех* (*также*
　перен) to welcome.
привива́|ть(ся) (-ю(сь)) *несов от*
　приви́ть(ся).
приви́в|ка (-ки; *gen pl* -ок) *ж* (*МЕД*) vaccination.
привиде́ни|е (-я) *ср* ghost.
приви́|деться (*3sg* -ится, *3pl* -ятся, *impf*
　ви́деться) *сов безл* (+*dat*) to appear to; **мне**
　~**елся стра́шный сон** I had a terrifying dream.
привилегиро́ванный *прил* privileged.
привиле́ги|я (-и) *ж* privilege.
привинти́|ть (-чу́, -ти́шь; *impf* **приви́нчивать**)

сов перех to screw on.
приви́|ть (-ью, -ьёшь; *impf* **привива́ть**) *сов*
　перех (*растение*) to graft; (*МЕД*): ~ **кому́-н**
　что-н to inoculate *или* vaccinate sb against sth;
　(*перен*) to cultivate sth in sb
▶ **приви́ться** (*impf* **привива́ться**) *сов возв*
　(*прививка, черенок*) to take; (*новшество*) to
　catch on.
при́вкус (-а) *м* flavour (*BRIT*), flavor (*US*).
привлёк *итп сов см* **привле́чь**.
привлека́тел|ьный (-ен, -ьна, -ьно) *прил*
　attractive.
привлека́|ть (-ю) *несов от* **привле́чь**.
привлеку́ *итп сов см* **привле́чь**.
привлече́ни|е (-я) *ср* (*покупателей, внимания*)
　attraction; (*ресурсов*) use; ~ **к суду́** taking to
　court; ~ **к отве́тственности** calling to account.
привл|е́чь (-еку́, -ечёшь *итп*, -еку́т; *pt* -ёк,
　-екла́, -екло́, *impf* **привлека́ть**) *сов перех* to
　attract; **привлека́ть** (~ *perf*) **кого́-н к** +*dat* (*к*
　работе, к участию) to coax sb into; (*к суду*) to
　take sb to; **привлека́ть** (~ *perf*) **кого́-н к**
　разгово́ру to draw sb into a conversation;
　привлека́ть (~ *perf*) **кого́-н к отве́тственности**
　to call sb to account.
привн|ести́ (-есу́, -есёшь; *pt* -ёс, -есла́, -есло́,
　impf **привноси́ть**) *сов перех*: ~ **что-н в** +*acc* to
　inject sth into.
привн|оси́ть (-ошу́, -о́сишь) *несов от*
　привнести́.
при́вод (-а) *м* (*электрический*) drive; (*ручной*)
　gear.
приво́д (-а) *м* (*ЮР*) arrest.
прив|оди́ть (-ожу́, -о́дишь) *несов от*
　привести́.
привожу́ *несов см* **привози́ть**.
приво́з (-а) *м* (*товаров, сырья*) supply.
прив|ози́ть (-ожу́, -о́зишь) *несов от* **привезти́**.
привозно́й *прил* imported.
приво́л|ье *итп сов см* **приво́льный**.
приво́л|ье (-я) *ср* (*степное, полевое*) expanse.
приво́льный (-ен, -ьна, -ьно) *прил* (*луга, поля*
　итп) expansive; (*жизнь*) free and easy.
привра́тник (-а) *м* doorman (*мн* doormen).
привста|ва́ть (-ю́) *несов от* **привста́ть**.
привста́|ть (-ну, -нешь; *impf* **привстава́ть**) *сов*
　неперех to half rise.
привы́к|нуть (-ну, -нешь; *pt* -, -ла, -ло, *impf*
　привыка́ть) *сов неперех*: ~ +*infin* (*гулять,*
　тратить деньги) to get into the habit of doing;
　привыка́ть (~ *perf*) **к** +*dat* (*к новым друзьям, к*
　школе) to get used to; **он** ~, **что́бы ему́ все**
　помога́ли he is used to everyone helping him.
привы́чек *сущ см* **привы́чка**.
привы́чен *прил см* **привы́чный**.
привы́ч|ка (-ки; *gen pl* -ек) *ж* habit; **по** ~**ке** out of
　habit.
привы́чный (-ен, -на, -но) *прил* (*работа,*
　звуки) familiar.
привью́(сь) *итп сов см* **приви́ть(ся)**.
привяжу́(сь) *итп сов см* **привяза́ть(ся)**.

привя́занност|ь (-и) *ж* attachment.
прив|яза́ть (-яжу́, -я́жешь; *impf* **привя́зывать**) *сов перех*: ~ что-н/кого-н к +*dat* to tie sth/sb to; **привя́зывать** (~ *perf*) **к себе́** +*acc* (*вызвать любовь*) to endear o.s. to
▸ **привяза́ться** (*impf* **привя́зываться**) *сов возв*: ~**ся к** +*dat* (*ремнём к сиде́нью*) to fasten o.s. to; (*полюби́ть*) to become attached to; (*разг*: *надоеда́ть*) to pester.
при́вяз|ь (-и) *ж* tie.
пригиба́|ть(ся) (-ю(сь)) *несов от* **пригну́ть(ся)**.
пригла́|дить (-жу, -дишь; *impf* **пригла́живать**) *сов перех* (*скла́дки на пла́тье*) to smooth out; (*во́лосы*) to smooth back.
пригласи́тельный *прил*: ~ **биле́т** invitation.
пригла|си́ть (-шу́, -си́шь; *impf* **приглаша́ть**) *сов перех* to invite; (*врача́*) to call; **приглаша́ть** (~ *perf*) **кого́-н в го́сти** to invite sb; **приглаша́ть** (~ *perf*) **кого́-н на та́нец** to ask sb to dance.
приглаше́ни|е (-я) *ср* invitation; (*комп*) prompt.
приглашу́ *сов см* **пригласи́ть**.
приглуш|и́ть (-у́, -и́шь; *impf* **приглуша́ть**) *сов перех* (*зву́ки*) to deaden; (*ра́дио*) to turn down; (*кра́ски*) to tone down; (*тона́*) to soften; (*перен*: *боль, тоску́*) to lessen.
пригля|де́ть (-жу́, -ди́шь; *impf* **пригля́дывать**) *сов непере*: ~ **за** +*instr* to look after ◆ *перех* to search out, find
▸ **пригляде́ться** (*impf* **пригля́дываться**) *сов возв*: ~**ся (к** +*dat*) (*к карти́не, к незнако́мцу*) to look closely (at).
пригл|яну́ться (-яну́сь, -я́нешься) *сов возв*: ~ **кому́-н** to attract sb.
приг|на́ть (-оню́, -о́нишь; *impf* **пригоня́ть**) *сов перех* to drive; (*костю́м*) to adjust, alter.
пригну́ть (-у́, -ёшь; *impf* **пригиба́ть**) *сов перех* (*ве́тку, кусты́*) to bend
▸ **пригну́ться** (*impf* **пригиба́ться**) *сов возв* (*нагну́ться*: *челове́к*) to bend down; (*ве́тки, кусты́*) to bend.
пригова́рива|ть (-ю) *несов от* **приговори́ть** ◆ *непере* (*сопровожда́ть слова́ми*) to talk at the same time (*as doing sth*).
пригово́р (-а) *м* (*ЮР*) sentence; (*перен*) condemnation; **выноси́ть** (**вы́нести** *perf*) ~ to pass sentence.
приговор|и́ть (-ю́, -и́шь; *impf* **пригова́ривать**) *сов перех*: ~ **кого́-н к** +*dat* to sentence sb to.
приго́ден *прил см* **приго́дный**.
приго|ди́ться (-жу́сь, -ди́шься; *impf* **пригожда́ться**) *сов возв* (+*dat*) to be useful to.
приго́д|ный (-ен, -на, -но) *прил* suitable.
пригожда́|ться (-юсь) *несов от* **пригоди́ться**.
пригожу́сь *сов см* **пригоди́ться**.
пригоню́ *итп сов см* **пригна́ть**.
пригоня́|ть (-ю) *несов от* **пригна́ть**.

пригора́|ть (*3sg* -ет, *3pl* -ют) *несов от* **пригоре́ть**.
пригоре́лый *прил* burnt.
пригор|е́ть (*3sg* -и́т, *3pl* -я́т, *impf* **пригора́ть**) *сов непере* to burn.
приго́рка *сущ см* **приго́рок**.
при́город (-а) *м* suburb.
при́городный *прил* (*посёлок, жи́тель*) suburban; (*по́езд, авто́бус*) local.
приго́р|ок (-ка) *м* hillock.
при́горш|ня (-ни; *gen pl* -ен) *ж* handful.
пригото́в|ить (-лю, -ишь) *сов от* **гото́вить** ◆ (*impf* **приготавливать** или **приготовля́ть**) *перех* to prepare; (*посте́ль*) to make; (*ва́нну*) to run
▸ **пригото́виться** *сов от* **гото́виться** ◆ *возв*: ~**ся (к** +*dat*) (*к путеше́ствию*) to get ready (for); (*к уро́ку*) to prepare (o.s.) (for).
приготовле́ни|е (-я) *ср* preparation.
пригото́влю(сь) *сов см* **пригото́вить(ся)**.
приготовля́|ть (-ю) *несов от* **пригото́вить**.
пригрева́|ть (-ю) *несов от* **пригре́ть**.
пригре́|зиться (-жусь, -зишься) *сов от* **гре́зиться**.
пригре́|ть (-ю; *impf* **пригрева́ть**) *сов перех* (*подлеж*: *со́лнце*: *зе́млю*) to warm; (*перен*: *сироту́*) to take in.
пригро|зи́ть(ся) (-жу́(сь), -зи́шь(ся)) *сов от* **грози́ть(ся)**.
пригу́б|ить (-лю, -ишь; *impf* **пригу́бливать**) *сов перех* to take a sip of.
придава́|ть (-ю, -ёшь) *несов от* **прида́ть**.
придав|и́ть (-авлю́, -а́вишь; *impf* **прида́вливать**) *сов перех* to press, to squash.
прида́м *итп сов см* **прида́ть**.
прида́н|ое (-ого; *decl like adj*) *ср* (*неве́сты*) dowry; (*новорождённого*) layette.
прида́ст *сов см* **прида́ть**.
прида́т|ок (-ка) *м* (*также перен*) appendage.
прида́точный *прил*: **прида́точное предложе́ние** (*линг*) subordinate clause.
прида́ть (*как* **дать**; *см* **Table 14**; *impf* **придава́ть**) *сов перех*: ~ **чего́-н кому́-н** (*уве́ренности*) to instil sth in sb; **придава́ть** (~ *perf*) **что-н чему́-н** (*вид, фо́рму*) to give sth to sth; (*ва́жность*) to attach sth to sth; **придава́ть** (~ *perf*) **бо́дрости кому́-н** to hearten sb; **придава́ть** (~ *perf*) **сил кому́-н** to strengthen sb.
прида́ч|а (-и) *ж*: **в** ~**у** in addition.
прида́шь *сов см* **прида́ть**.
придви́|нуть (-у, -ешь; *impf* **придвига́ть**) *сов перех*: ~ (**к** +*dat*) to move over или up (to).
придво́рн|ый *прил* court *опред* ◆ (-ого; *decl like adj*) *м* courtier.
приде́ла|ть (-ю; *impf* **приде́лывать**) *сов перех*: ~ **что-н к** +*dat* to attach или fix sth to.
придерж|а́ть (-ержу́, -е́ржишь; *impf* **приде́рживать**) *сов перех* (*дверь*) to hold

(steady); (*лошадь*) to restrain.

придёрживаꞁться (-юсь) *несов возв* (+*gen*; *каких-н взглядов*) to hold; (*за перила*): ~ **за** +*acc* to hold onto.

придерýсь *итп сов см* **придрáться**.

придирáться (-ю) *несов от* **придрáться**.

придúрꞁка (-ки; *gen pl* -ок) *ж* quibble.

придúрчивꞁый (-, -а, -о) *прил* (*человек*) fussy; (*замечание, взгляд*) critical.

придрáться (-ерýсь, -ерёшься; *impf* **придирáться**) *сов возв*: ~ **к** +*dat* to find fault with.

придý(сь) *итп сов см* **прийтú(сь)**.

придýмаꞁть (-ю; *impf* **придýмывать**) *сов перех* (*отговорку, причину*) to think of *или* up; (*новый прибор*) to devise; (*песню, стихотворение*) to make up; **он ~л, как спастú положéние** he thought of how to save the situation.

придýриваꞁться (-юсь) *несов возв* (*разг*) to pretend to be ignorant.

придýсь *итп сов см* **прийтúсь**.

придыхáниꞁе (-я) *ср* (*линг*) aspiration.

приедáꞁться (-юсь) *несов от* **приéсться**.

приедúмся *итп сов см* **приéсться**.

приéду *итп сов см* **приéхать**.

приедятся *итп сов см* **приéсться**.

приéзд (-а) *м* arrival.

приезжáꞁть (-ю) *несов от* **приéхать**.

приéзжꞁий (-ая, -ее, -ие) *прил* visiting.

приéмся *сов см* **приéсться**.

приём (-а) *м* reception; (*у врача*) surgery (*BRIT*), office (*US*); (*борьбы, гимнастический*) technique; (*наказания, воздействия*) means; **за одúн ~** in one go; **в два/в три ~а** in two/three attempts; **устрáивать (устрóить** *perf*) **~** to organize a reception; **запúсываться (записáться** *perf*) **на ~ к** +*dat* to make an appointment to see.

приёмꞁка (-и) *ж* (*товаров*) receipt.

приёмнꞁая (-ой; *decl like adj*) *ж* (*также:* ~ **кóмната**) reception.

приёмник (-а) *м* (*радиоприёмник*) radio; (*связь*) receiver.

приёмный *прил* (*часы*) reception *опред*; (*день*) visiting *опред*; (*экзамены*) entrance *опред*; (*комиссия*) selection *опред*; (*родители, дети*) adoptive; **приёмный покóй** *room where newly-arrived patients register and are given inital checkup before going to the ward*.

приꞁéсться (*как* **есть;** *см* **Table 15;** *impf* **приедáться**) *сов возв*: ~ **комý-н** (*разг*) to bore sb stiff.

приꞁéхать (*как* **éхать;** *см* **Table 19;** *impf* **приезжáть**) *сов неперех* to arrive *или* come (*by transport*).

приéшься *сов см* **приéсться**.

прижáꞁть (-мý, -мёшь; *impf* **прижимáть**) *сов перех* (*разг: притеснить*) to put the screws on; **прижимáть** (~ *perf*) **что-н/кого-н к** +*dat* to press sth/sb to *или* against

▸ **прижáться** (*impf* **прижимáться**) *сов возв*:

~**ся к** +*dat* to press o.s. against; (*ребёнок к грýди*) to snuggle up to.

прижꞁéчь (-гý, -жёшь *итп*, -гýт; *impf* **прижигáть**) *сов перех* to cauterize.

приживáꞁться (-юсь) *несов от* **прижúться**.

приживýсь *итп сов см* **прижúться**.

прижигáꞁть (-ю) *несов от* **прижéчь**.

прижúзненнꞁый *прил*: ~**ая слáва** fame during one's lifetime; **он вúдел мнóго** ~**ых издáний свойх поэм** many books of his poems were published during his lifetime.

прижимáꞁть(ся) (-ю(сь)) *несов от* **прижáть(ся)**.

прижúмистꞁый (-, -а, -о) *прил* (*разг*) tightfisted.

прижꞁúться (-вýсь, -вёшься; *pt* -лся, -лáсь, -лось, *impf* **приживáться**) *сов возв* (*человек*) to settle in, get o.s. settled; (*животные*) to adapt, become acclimatized (*BRIT*) *или* acclimated (*US*); (*растения*) to take rest.

прижмý(сь) *сов см* **прижáть(ся)**.

приз (-а; *nom pl* -**ы́**) *м* prize.

призадýмаꞁться (-юсь; *impf* **призадýмываться**) *сов возв*: ~ **над** +*instr или* **о** +*prp* to reflect upon.

призвáниꞁе (-я) *ср* (*к искусству, к наýке итп*) vocation; (*предназначение*) calling; ~ **теáтра – воспúтывать** the purpose of the theatre is to educate.

призꞁвáть (-овý, -овёшь; *pt* -вáл, -валá, -вáло, *impf* **призывáть**) *сов перех* (*на борьбý, к защúте страны*) to call, summon; **призывáть** (~ *perf*) **к мúру/разоружéнию** to call for peace/disarmament; **призывáть** (~ *perf*) **когó-н к спокóйствию/повиновéнию** to appeal to sb to be calm/obedient; **призывáть** (~ *perf*) **когó-н к порядку** to call sb to order; **призывáть** (~ *perf*) **в áрмию** to call up (to join the army).

призéмистꞁый (-, -а, -о) *прил* (*человек*) squat.

приземлꞁúть (-ю́, -úшь; *impf* **приземлять**) *сов перех* to land

▸ **приземлúться** (*impf* **приземляться**) *сов возв* to land.

призёр (-а) *м* prizewinner.

прúзмꞁа (-ы) *ж* prism; **сквозь** *или* **чéрез** ~**у** +*gen* (*перен*) in the light of.

признаꞁвáть(ся) (-ю́(сь), -ёшь(ся)) *несов от* **признáть(ся)**.

прúзнак (-а) *м* (*кризиса, успéха*) sign; (*отравления*) symptom; **без** ~**ов жúзни** not showing any sign of life.

признáниꞁе (-я) *ср* (*госудáрства, писáтеля*) recognition; (*своегó бессúлия, чьúх-н достижéний*) acknowledgment, recognition; (*в любвú*) declaration; (*в преступлéнии*) confession.

прúзнаннꞁый (-, -а, -о) *прил* recognized.

признáтелен *прил см* **признáтельный**.

признáтельностꞁь (-и) *ж* gratitude.

признáтельнꞁый (-ен, -ьна, -ьно) *прил* grateful.

признáꞁть (-ю; *impf* **признавáть**) *сов перех*

(*правительство, чьи-н права*) to recognize; (*положительно оценить: книгу, фильм*) to acclaim; (*счесть*): ~ что-н/кого-н +*instr* to recognize sth/sb as

▶ **призна́|ться** (*impf* **признава́ться**) *сов возв*: ~**ся кому́-н в чём-н** (*в преступлении*) to confess sth to sb; **признава́ться** (~**ся** *perf*) **кому́-н в любви́** to make a declaration of love to sb; ~**ся** *или* **признаю́сь, я Вас не понима́ю** I have to admit that I don't understand you.

призово́й *прил* (*деньги*) prize *опред*; ~**я́я меда́ль** prizewinner's medal; ~**о́е ме́сто** medal position.

призову́ *итп сов см* **призва́ть**.

призо́р (-а) *м*: **без ~а** (*разг*) unattended.

при́зрак (-а) *м* ghost.

при́зрач|ный (-ен, -на, -но) *прил* (*успех, надежды*) illusory; (*опасность*) imagined.

призы́в (-а) *м* (*к восстанию, к защите*) call; (: *в армию*) conscription; (*лозунг*) slogan ◆ *собир* call-up.

призыва́|ть (-ю) *несов от* **призва́ть**.

призывни́|к (-á) *м* conscript.

призывно́й *прил* (*возраст*) call-up *опред*; (*пункт*) recruiting *опред*.

призы́вный *прил* summoning *опред*.

при́иск (-а) *м* mine.

прийти́ (*как* **идти́**; *см* **Table 18**; *impf* **приходи́ть**) *сов неперех* (*идя, достичь*) to come (*on foot*); (*письмо, телеграмма*) to arrive; (*весна, час свободы*) to come; (*достигнуть*): ~ **к** +*dat* (*к власти, к выводу*) to come to; (*к демократии*) to achieve; **приходи́ть** (~ *perf*) **в у́жас/недоуме́ние** to be horrified/bewildered; **приходи́ть** (~ *perf*) **в восто́рг** to go into raptures; **приходи́ть** (~ *perf*) **в него́дность** to become worthless; **приходи́ть** (~ *perf*) **в упа́док** to go into decline; **приходи́ть** (~ *perf*) **в запу́щенность** to fall into neglect; **приходи́ть** (~ *perf*) **кому́-н в го́лову** *или* **на ум** to occur to sb; **приходи́ть** (~ *perf*) **в себя́** (*после обморока*) to come to *или* round; (*успокоиться*) to come to one's senses

▶ **прийти́сь** (*impf* **приходи́ться**) *сов возв*: ~**сь на** +*acc* to fall on; (*попасть*): ~**сь по** +*dat* to land on; (*подойти*): ~**сь по** +*dat*/**к** +*dat* (*одежда, ключ*) to fit; (*вещь: по вкусу*) to suit ◆ *безл* (+*infin*): *уступить*, **пойти на уступки итп**) to have to do; (**нам**) **придётся согласи́ться** we'll have to agree; **нам пришло́сь тяжело́** we had a hard time; **как придётся** anyhow; **где придётся** anywhere; **что придётся** anything.

прикажу́ *итп сов см* **приказа́ть**.

прика́з (-а) *м* order; **отдава́ть** (**отда́ть** *perf*) ~ to give an order.

приказа́ни|е (-я) *ср* = **прика́з**.

приказа́|ть (-ажу́, -а́жешь; *impf* **прика́зывать**) *сов неперех*: ~ **кому́-н** +*infin* to order sb to do;

как ~а́жете as you like.

приказно́й *прил* (*тон, жест*) commanding; **в приказно́м поря́дке** in the form of an order.

прика́зчик (-а) *м* (*в магазине*) sales assistant (*BRIT*) *или* clerk (*US*); (*в помещичьем хозяйстве*) *manager of estate or farm*.

прика́зыва|ть (-ю) *несов от* **приказа́ть**.

прика́лыва|ть (-ю) *несов от* **приколо́ть**.

прика́нчива|ть (-ю) *несов от* **прикончить**.

прикарма́н|ить (-ю, -ишь; *impf* **прикарма́нивать**) *сов перех* (*разг*) to pocket.

прика́рмлива|ть (-ю) *несов перех* (*младенца*) to supplement the diet of.

прикаса́ни|е (-я) *ср* (*рук*) touch.

прикаса́|ться (-юсь) *несов от* **прикосну́ться**.

прика|ти́ть (-ачу́, -а́тишь; *impf* **прика́тывать**) *сов перех* to roll up ◆ *неперех* (*разг: приехать*) to show up.

прики́н|уть (-у, -ешь; *impf* **прики́дывать**) *сов неперех* (*разг: посчитать*) to work out (roughly)

▶ **прики́нуться** (*impf* **прики́дываться**) *сов возв* (+*instr*, *разг*) to pretend to be.

прикла́д (-а) *м* (*ружья, автомата*) butt (*of gun etc*).

прикладно́й *прил* applied; **прикладна́я програ́мма** (*КОМП*) application program; **прикладно́е иску́сство** applied art.

прикла́дыва|ть(ся) (-ю(сь)) *несов от* **приложи́ть(ся)**.

прикле́|ить (-ю, -ишь; *impf* **прикле́ивать**) *сов перех* to glue, stick

▶ **прикле́иться** (*impf* **прикле́иваться**) *сов возв* to stick.

приключа́|ться (*3sg* -ется, *3pl* -ются) *несов от* **приключи́ться**.

приключе́ни|е (-я) *ср* adventure.

приключе́нчес|кий (-ая, -ое, -ие) *прил* adventure *опред*.

приключ|и́ться (*3sg* -и́тся, *3pl* -а́тся, *impf* **приключа́ться**) *сов возв* (*разг: произойти*) to happen.

прико́выва|ть (-ю; *impf* **прико́вывать**) *сов перех* (*перен: внимание, взгляд*) to fix; **прико́вывать** (~ *perf*) **кого́-н к** +*dat* to chain sb to; (*перен*) to confine sb to.

прико́л (-а) *м*: **стоя́ть на ~е** to be moored.

прико|ло́ть (-олю́, -о́лешь; *impf* **прика́лывать**) *сов перех* to fasten, fix.

прикомандир|ова́ть (-у́ю; *impf* **прикомандиро́вывать**) *сов перех* to second.

прико́нч|ить (-у, -ишь; *impf* **прика́нчивать**) *сов перех* (*умертвить*) to finish off.

прикорн|у́ть (-у́, -ёшь) *сов неперех* (*разг*) to curl up.

прикосну́ться (-у́сь, -ёшься; *impf* **прикаса́ться**) *сов возв*: ~ **к** +*dat* to touch lightly.

прикреп|и́ть (-лю́, -и́шь; *impf* **прикрепля́ть**) *сов перех*: ~ **что-н к** +*dat* (*деталь, бант*) to fix sth to; **прикрепля́ть** (~ *perf*) **кого-н/что-н к** +*dat* (*советника к предприятию, институт к заводу*) to attach sb/sth to.

прикри́к|нуть (-у, -ешь; *impf* **прикри́кивать**) *сов неперех*: ~ **на** +*acc* to shout *или* yell at.

прикро́ю(сь) *итп сов см* **прикры́ть(ся)**.

прикрыва́|ть(ся) (-ю) *несов от* **прикры́ть(ся)**.

прикры́ти|е (-я) *ср* (*махинаций*) cover-up; (*тыла, ВОЕН*) cover; **под** ~**м** +*gen* under the guise of.

прикр|ы́ть (-о́ю, -о́ешь; *impf* **прикрыва́ть**) *сов перех* to cover; (*закрыть*) to close (over); (*разг: ликвидировать*) to wind up; (*скрывать*) to cover up

▶ **прикры́ться** (*impf* **прикрыва́ться**) *сов возв* (+*instr*; *одеялом, плащом*) to cover o.s. with; (*отговорками, риторикой*) to hide behind; (*разг: ликвидироваться*) to close down.

прикур|и́ть (-урю́, -у́ришь; *impf* **прику́ривать**) *сов неперех* to get a light (*from lit cigarette*).

прикус|и́ть (-ушу́, -у́сишь; *impf* **прику́сывать**) *сов перех* (*губу, язык*) to bite.

прила́в|ок (-ка) *м* (*в магазине*) counter; (*на рынке*) stall.

прилага́тельн|ое (-ого; *decl like adj*) *ср* (*ЛИНГ: также: и́мя* ~) adjective.

прилага́|ть (-ю) *несов от* **приложи́ть**.

прила́|дить (-жу, -дишь; *impf* **прила́живать**) *сов перех*: ~ **что-н к** +*dat* to fit sth on to.

приласка́|ть(ся) (-ю(сь)) *сов от* **ласка́ть(ся)**.

прилёг *итп сов см* **приле́чь**.

прилега́|ть (*3sg* -ет, *3pl* -ют) *несов неперех*: ~ **к** +*dat* (*касаться*) to fit tightly; (*находиться рядом*) to adjoin.

прилежа́ни|е (-я) *ср* diligence.

приле́ж|ный (-ен, -на, -но) *прил* diligent.

прилеп|и́ть (-еплю́, -е́пишь; *impf* **прилепля́ть**) *сов перех* to stick.

приле|те́ть (-чу́, -ти́шь; *impf* **прилета́ть**) *сов неперех* to arrive (*by air*), fly in.

приле́|чь (-я́гу, -я́жешь *итп*, -я́гут; *pt* -ёг, -егла́, -егло́) *сов неперех* to lie down for a while.

прили́в (-а) *м* (*в море, в океане*) tide; (*денег, туристов*) flood; (*негодования, энергии*) surge.

прилива́|ть (-ю) *несов от* **прили́ть**.

прилижу́ *итп сов см* **прилиза́ть**.

прили́занный *прил* (*разг: волосы*) slicked-down; (*вид*) fastidious; (*человек*) pernickety (*BRIT*), persnickety (*US*).

прилиз|а́ть (-ижу́, -и́жешь; *impf* **прили́зывать**) *сов перех* (*разг: волосы*) to slick down.

прили́п|нуть (-ну, -нешь; *pt* -, -ла, -ло, *impf* **прилипа́ть** *или* **ли́пнуть**) *сов неперех*: ~ **к** +*dat* to stick to; (*разг: к девушке, к незнакомцу*) to cling to.

прил|и́ть (*3sg* -ьёт, *3pl* -ью́т, *pt* -и́л, -ила́, -и́ло, *impf* **прилива́ть**) *сов неперех* (*вода в море*) to flow; (*кровь*) to rush.

прили́чен *прил см* **прили́чный**.

прили́чи|е (-я) *ср* decency; (*обычно мн*) manners *мн*.

прили́ч|ный (-ен, -на, -но) *прил* (*пристойный: человек*) decent; (: *манеры*) proper; (*достаточно хороший, большой*) fair, decent.

приложе́ни|е (-я) *ср* (*силы, энергии*) application; (*к журналу*) supplement; (*к документации*) addendum (*мн* addenda).

прил|ожи́ть (-ожу́, -о́жишь; *impf* **прилага́ть**) *сов перех* (*присоединить*) to affix; (*силу, знания итп*) to apply; (*impf* **прикла́дывать**): ~ **что-н к** +*dat* (*руку ко лбу*) to put sth to; (*трубку к уху*) to hold sth to; **прилага́ть** (~ *perf*) **ру́ку к** +*dat* to put one's hand to; **ума́ не** ~**ожу́** (*разг*) I don't have a clue

▶ **приложи́ться** (*impf* **прикла́дываться**) *сов возв*: ~**ся у́хом/губа́ми к** +*dat* to press one's ear/lips against; **остально́е** ~**о́жится** the rest is a matter of course.

прильёт *итп сов см* **прили́ть**.

прильн|у́ть (-у́, -ёшь) *сов от* **льнуть** ◆ *неперех* (*приникнуть*): ~ **к** +*dat* (*к чьей-н груди*) to cling to; (*к двери, к окну*) to press o.s. against.

приля́гу *итп сов см* **приле́чь**.

при́м|а (-ы) *ж* (*МУЗ: ведущий голос*) lead; (*разг: о балерине*) prima ballerina.

при́м|а-балери́н|а (-ы, -ы) *ж* prima ballerina.

прим|ани́ть (-аню́, -а́нишь) *сов перех* (*разг*) to lure.

прима́н|ка (-ки; *gen pl* -ок) *ж* bait.

примелька́|ться (-юсь) *сов возв* to become familiar.

примене́ни|е (-я) *ср* (*оружия*) use; (*машин, лекарств*) application; (*мер, метода*) adoption; **в** ~ **и к** +*dat* in application to.

примени́м|ый (-, -а, -о) *прил* applicable.

примени́тельно *предл*: ~ **к** +*dat* in conformity with.

прим|ени́ть (-еню́, -е́нишь; *impf* **применя́ть**) *сов перех* (*меры*) to implement; (*силу*) to use; **применя́ть** (~ *perf*) **что-н** (**к** +*dat*) (*метод, теорию*) to apply sth (to); **применя́ть** (~ *perf*) **са́нкции к** +*dat* to impose sanctions on.

применя́|ться (*3sg* -ется, *3pl* -ются) *несов неперех* (*использоваться*) to be used.

приме́р (-а) *м* example; **к** ~**у** for example; **не в** ~ +*dat* unlike; **по** ~**у** +*gen* (*сходно с*) after the example of; **ста́вить** (**поста́вить** *perf*) **кого́-н/что-н в** ~ to hold sb/sth up as an example; **брать** (**взять** *perf*) ~ **с** +*gen* to follow the example of.

приме́рен *прил см* **приме́рный**.

примёрз|нуть (-ну, -нешь; *pt* -, -ла, -ло, *impf* **примерза́ть**) *сов неперех*: ~ (**к** +*dat*) to freeze (to).

приме́р|ить (-ю, -ишь; *impf* **примеря́ть**) *сов перех* to try on.

приме́р|ка (-ки; *gen pl* -ок) *ж* trying on.

приме́рно *нареч* (*образцово*) in an exemplary fashion; (*приблизительно*) approximately.

примéр|ный (-ен, -на, -но) *прил* (*образцовый*)
exemplary; (*приблизительный*) approximate.
примéрок *сущ см* **примéрка**.
примеря|ть (-ю) *несов от* **примéрить**.
при́месь (-и) *ж* dash.
примéт|а (-ы) *ж* (*признак*) sign; (*суеверная*)
omen; **онá у негó на** ~е he has his eye on her.
примета|ть (-ю; *impf* **примётывать**) *сов перех*
to stitch on, tack on (*BRIT*).
примéтен *прил см* **примéтный**.
примé|тить (-чу, -тишь; *impf* **примечáть**) *сов
перех* (*разг*) to notice.
примéт|ный (-ен, -на, -но) *прил* (*заметный:
человек*) conspicuous; (: *событие*) prominent.
примётыва|ть (-ю) *несов от* **приметáть**.
примечáни|е (-я) *ср* note, comment.
примечá|тельный (-ен, -ьна, -ьно) *прил*
(*событие, внешность*) remarkable;
(*изменение*) notable.
примечá|ть (-ю) *несов от* **примéтить**.
примечý *сов см* **примéтить**.
примеша|ть (-ю; *impf* **примéшивать**) *сов перех*
(*перен*) to bring; **примéшивать** (~ *perf*) (**в** +*acc*)
to add (to), mix in(to).
примина|ть (-ю) *несов от* **примя́ть**.
примирéни|е (-я) *ср* reconciliation.
примир|и́ть (-ю́, -и́шь; *impf* **примиря́ть** *или*
мири́ть) *сов перех*: ~ **когó-н с кем-н** to
reconcile sb with sb; **примиря́ть** (~ *perf*) **когó-н
с чем-н** to help sb come to terms with sth
▶ **примири́ться** (*impf* **примиря́ться**) *сов возв*:
~**ся с** +*instr* (*с врагом, с мужем*) to be
reconciled with; (*с действительностью*) to
reconcile o.s. to.
примити́в|ный (-ен, -на, -но) *прил* primitive.
примкн|у́ть (-у́, -ёшь; *impf* **примыкáть**) *сов
неперех*: ~ **к** +*dat* (*к партии*) to join; (*к
большинству*) to side with.
примнý *итп сов см* **примя́ть**.
примóлкн|уть (-у, -ешь) *сов неперех* (*разг*:
умолкнуть) to shush.
примóрск|ий (-ая, -ое, -ие) *прил* seaside *опред*.
примóрь|е (-я) *ср* seaside.
примо|сти́ться (-щу́сь, -сти́шься) *сов возв*
(*разг*) to perch o.s.
примóч|ка (-ки; *gen pl* -ек) *ж* (*процедура*)
bathing; (*лекарство*) lotion.
примощу́сь *сов см* **примости́ться**.
прим|у́(сь) *итп сов см* **приня́ть(ся)**.
при́мул|а (-ы) *ж* (*БОТ*) primrose.
при́мус (-а) *м* Primus (stove) ®.
примч|áться (-у́сь, -и́шься) *несов возв* to come
tearing up.
примыка|ть (-ю) *несов от* **примкну́ть** ◆
неперех (*прилегать*): ~ **к** +*dat* to adjoin.
прим|я́ть (-ну́, -нёшь; *impf* **примина́ть**) *сов
перех* (*траву*) to trample on.
принадлеж|а́ть (-у́, -и́шь) *несов неперех*: ~

+*dat* to belong to; (*заслуга*) to go to; (*роль*) to be
played by; ~ (*impf*) **к** +*dat* (*входить в состав*) to
belong to, be a member of.
принадлéжность (-и) *ж* characteristic;
(*обычно мн*: *охотничьи, рыболовные*) tackle;
(*письменные*) accessories *мн*; (*вхождение в
состав*): ~ **к** +*dat* membership of.
приневóл|ить (-ю, -ишь) *сов от* **невóлить**.
прин|ести́ (-есу́, -есёшь; *pt* -ёс, -еслá, -еслó,
impf **приноси́ть**) *сов перех* (*стул, ребёнка,
удачу итп*) to bring; (*подлеж: животные*) to
bear; (: *растения*) to yield; (*доход, прибыль
итп*) to bring in; (*извинения, благодарность
итп*) to express; (*присягу*) to take; **приноси́ть** (~
perf) **пóльзу** to be of use; **приноси́ть** (~ *perf*)
вред to harm; **приноси́ть** (~ *perf*) **что-н в
жéртву** to sacrifice sth.
прини|зи́ть (-жу, -зишь; *impf* **принижáть**) *сов
перех* (*унизить*) to humiliate; (*умалить*) to
belittle.
прини́к|нуть (-ну, -нешь; *pt* -, -ла, -ло, *impf*
приникáть) *сов неперех*: ~ **к** +*dat* (*к земле*) to
press o.s. to; (*к подушке итп*) to nestle up
against; (*к другу*) to snuggle up to; (*к двери, к
окну*) to press o.s. against.
принима|ть(ся) (-ю(сь)) *несов от*
приня́ть(ся).
принорóв|иться (-лю́сь, -и́шься; *impf*
принорáвливаться) *сов возв*: ~ **к** +*dat* (*к
обстоятельствам*) to adapt to; (*к машине*) to
get used to; (+*infin*) to get used to doing.
прино|си́ть (-ошу́, -óсишь) *несов от*
принести́.
при́нтер (-а) *м* (*КОМП*) printer.
принуди́тельный (-ен, -ьна, -ьно) *прил*
(*труд, лечение итп*) forced; (*меры*)
compulsory.
прину́|дить (-жу, -дишь; *impf* **принуждáть**) *сов
перех*: ~ **когó-н/что-н к** +*dat/*+*infin* to force
sb/sth into/to do.
принуждéни|е (-я) *ср* compulsion; **по** ~**ю** under
compulsion.
принуждённый (-ён, -на, -но) *прил* forced.
прину́жу *сов см* **прину́дить**.
принц (-а) *м* prince.
принцéсс|а (-ы) *ж* princess.
при́нцип (-а) *м* principle; **в** ~**е** (*в основном*) in
principle; **из** ~**а** on principle; **по** ~**у** +*gen* on the
principle of.
принципиáльный (-ен, -ьна, -ьно) *прил*
(*человек, политика*) of principle; (*согласие,
договорённость*) in principle.
при́нятый (-, -а, -о) *прил* accepted.
при|ня́ть (-му́, -мешь; *pt* -ня́л, -нялá, -ня́ло, *impf*
принимáть) *сов перех* to take; (*подарок,
критику, условия*) to accept; (*какóй-н пост*) to
take up; (*гостéй, делегáцию, телегрáмму*) to
receive; (*закон, резолю́цию, попрáвку*) to pass;

(*отноше́ние, вид*) to take on; (*христиа́нство итп*) to adopt; **принима́ть** (~ *perf*) **в/на** +*acc* (*в университе́т, на рабо́ту*) to accept; **принима́ть** (~ *perf*) **что-н/кого́-н за** +*acc* to mistake sth/sb for; (*счесть*) to take sth/sb as; **принима́ть** (~ *perf*) **ро́ды** to deliver a baby

▶ **приня́ться** (*impf* **принима́ться**) *сов возв* (*расте́ние*) to take root; (+*infin*; *приступи́ть*) to get down to doing; **принима́ться** (~*ся perf*) **за** +*acc* (*приступи́ть*) to get down to; (*за лентя́ев, за престу́пников*) to take in hand; (*за десе́рт, за вино́*) to start *или* get started on.

приободр|и́ть (-ю́, -и́шь; *impf* **приободря́ть**) *сов перех* to cheer up

▶ **приободри́ться** (*impf* **приободря́ться**) *несов возв* to cheer up.

приобр|ести́ (-ету́, -ете́шь; *pt* -ёл, -ела́, -ело́, *impf* **приобрета́ть**) *сов перех* to acquire; (*друзе́й, враго́в*) to make; (*о́пыт*) to gain.

приобрете́ни|е (-я) *ср* acquisition; (*комм*) procurement.

приобрету́ *итп сов см* **приобрести́**.

приобщ|и́ть (-у́, -и́шь; *impf* **приобща́ть**) *сов перех* (*приложи́ть*) to attach; (*познако́мить*): ~ **кого́-н/что-н к** +*dat* to introduce sb/sth to; **приобща́ть** (~ *perf*) **к де́лу** to file

▶ **приобщ|и́ться** (*impf* **приобща́ться**) *сов возв*: ~ **к** +*dat* to become involved in.

приоде́|ть (-ну, -нешь) *сов перех* (*разг*) to dress up.

приорите́т (-а) *м* priority.

приорите́т|ный (-ен, -на, -но) *прил* main.

приостан|ови́ть (-овлю́, -о́вишь; *impf* **приостана́вливать**) *сов перех* to suspend.

приоткр|ы́ть (-о́ю, -о́ешь; *impf* **приоткрыва́ть**) *сов перех* (*дверь*) to open slightly; (*глаза́*) to half open.

припада́|ть (-ю) *несов от* **припа́сть**.

припа́д|ок (-ка) *м* (*серде́чный*) attack; (*гне́ва*) fit; (*весе́лья*) outburst; **истери́ческий** ~ fit of hysterics.

припаду́ *итп сов см* **припа́сть**.

припа́ива|ть (-ю) *несов от* **припая́ть**.

припа́р|ка (-ки; *gen pl* -ок) *ж* (*мед*) poultice.

прип|асти́ (-асу́, -асёшь; *pt* -а́с, -асла́, -асло́, *impf* **припаса́ть**) *сов перех* (*еду́*) to store up; (*де́ньги*) to save up.

припа́|сть (-ду́, -дёшь; *impf* **припада́ть**) *сов неперех*: ~ **к** +*dat* to throw o.s. at.

припасу́ *итп сов см* **припасти́**.

припа́с|ы (-ов) *мн* (*еды́, де́нежные*) supplies; (*воен*: *боевы́е, руже́йные*) ammunition.

припая́|ть (-ю; *impf* **припа́ивать**) *сов перех* (*приде́лать пая́нием*) to solder on.

припе́в (-а) *м* (*пе́сни*) chorus, refrain.

припева́|ючи *нареч* (*разг*): **жить** ~ to live the life of Riley.

припека́|ть (*3sg* -ет) *несов неперех* (*со́лнце*) to be burning hot.

прип|ере́ть (-ру́, -рёшь; *pt* -ёр, -ёрла, -ёрло, *impf* **припира́ть**) *сов перех* (*разг*): ~ **к** +*dat*

(*прижа́ть*) to shove against; **припира́ть** (~ *perf*) **к сте́нке** (*перен*: *разг*) to put in a tight spot.

припи|са́ть (-шу́, -шешь; *impf* **припи́сывать**) *сов перех* (*написа́ть в дополне́ние*) to add; (*прикрепи́ть*): ~ **кого́-н/что-н к** +*dat* to attach sb/sth to; (*счесть сле́дствием*): ~ **что-н чему́-н** to put sth down to sth; (*счесть принадлежа́щим*): ~ **что-н кому́-н** to attribute sth to sb.

припи́с|ка (-ки; *gen pl* -ок) *ж* (*в письме́*) postscript; (: *в докуме́нте*) addition; (*обы́чно мн*: *ло́жные да́нные*: *в отчёте, в докла́де*) tampering with facts and figures.

припи́сыва|ть (-ю) *несов от* **приписа́ть**.

припишу́ *итп сов см* **приписа́ть**.

припл|ести́ (-ету́, -ете́шь; *pt* -ёл, -ела́, -ело́, *impf* **приплета́ть**) *сов перех* (*вплета́я, присоедини́ть*) to plait in; (*перен*: *разг*: *и́мя*) to drag in; (: *собы́тие, факт*) to drag up

▶ **приплести́сь** *сов возв* (*разг*) to drag o.s. along.

приплю́снут|ый (-, -а, -о) *прил* (*нос*) flat.

приплю́сыва|ть (-ю) *несов неперех* to skip.

приподнима́|ть(ся) (-ю(сь)) *несов от* **приподня́ть(ся)**.

приподниму́(сь) *итп сов см* **приподня́ть(ся)**.

припо́днят|ый (-, -а, -о) *прил* (*оживлённый*) cheerful; (*торже́ственный*) elevated.

приподн|я́ть (-иму́, -и́мешь; *impf* **приподнима́ть**) *сов перех* (*чемода́н*) to lift slightly; (*за́навес*) to raise slightly

▶ **приподня́ться** (*impf* **приподнима́ться**) *сов возв* to raise o.s. a little.

припо́мн|ить (-ю, -ишь; *impf* **припомина́ть**) *сов перех* to remember; **примина́ть** (~ *perf*) **что-н кому́-н** to make sb remember sth.

припра́в|а (-ы) *ж* seasoning.

припру́ *итп сов см* **припере́ть**.

припря́|тать (-чу, -чешь; *impf* **припря́тывать**) *сов перех* (*разг*) to stash (away).

припугн|у́ть (-у́, -ёшь; *impf* **припу́гивать**) *сов перех* (*разг*) to put the wind up.

при́пуск (-а) *м* allowance.

припу|сти́ть (-щу́, -у́стишь; *impf* **припуска́ть**) *сов неперех* (*разг*: *побежа́ть*) to speed up.

припу́хлый *прил* slightly swollen.

припущу́ *сов см* **припусти́ть**.

прира́внива|ть (-ю; *impf* **прира́внивать**) *сов перех*: ~ **кого́-н/что-н к** +*dat* to equate sb/sth with.

прир|асти́ (-асту́, -асте́шь; *pt* -о́с, -осла́, -осло́, *impf* **прираста́ть**) *сов неперех* (*приживи́ться*) to take; (*увели́читься*) to increase; (*перен*): ~ **к** +*dat* to become rooted to.

приро́д|а (-ы) *ж* nature; (*места́ вне го́рода*) countryside; **от** ~**ы**, **по** ~**е** by nature; **живу́ю** ~ natural world.

приро́дный *прил* natural; (*врождённый*) innate; **приро́дные бога́тства** natural resources; **приро́дный газ** natural gas.

природове́дени|е (-я) *ср* natural history.

природоохра́н|а (-ы) ж nature conservation.
прирождённый *прил* (*чувство, грация*) inborn; (*учитель, художник*) born.
приро́с *итп сов см* **прирасти́**.
приро́ст (-а) *м* (*населения*) growth; (*доходов, урожая*) increase.
приручи́|ть (-у́, -и́шь; *impf* **прируча́ть**) *сов перех* (*животное*) to tame; (*перен: человека*) to bring to heel.
приса́жива|ться (-юсь) *несов от* **присе́сть**.
приса́сыва|ться (-юсь) *несов от* **присоса́ться**.
присво́|ить (-ю, -ишь; *impf* **присва́ивать**) *сов перех* to appropriate; (*дать*): ~ **что-н кому́-н** to confer sth on sb.
приседа́ни|е (-я) *ср* squatting (*physical exercise*).
приседа́|ть (-ю) *несов от* **присе́сть**.
присе́ст (-а) *м* (*разг*): **в** *или* **за оди́н** ~ at one sitting *или* a single sitting.
присе́|сть (-я́ду, -я́дешь; *impf* **приседа́ть**) *сов неперех* to squat; (*impf* **приса́живаться**) to sit down (*for a short while*).
приск|ака́ть (-ачу́, -а́чешь; *impf* **приска́кивать**) *сов неперех* (*лошадь, всадник*) to gallop up, come galloping up; (*разг: быстро прийти/приехать*) to come tearing up.
приско́рбен *прил см* **приско́рбный**.
приско́рби|е (-я) *ср*: **к мо́ему глубо́кому** ~**ю** to my deepest regret; **с глубо́ким** ~**м** with deepest regret.
приско́рб|ный (-ен, -на, -но) *прил* regrettable.
при|сла́ть (-шлю́, -шлёшь; *impf* **присыла́ть**) *сов перех* to send.
прислон|и́ть (-ю́, -и́шь; *impf* **прислоня́ть**) *сов перех*: ~ **что-н к** +*dat* to lean sth against
▸ **прислони́ться** (*impf* **прислоня́ться**) *сов возв*: ~**ся к** + *dat* to lean against.
прислу́г|а (-и) *ж собир* servants *мн*.
прислу́жива|ть (-ю) *несов неперех* (+*dat*; *официант*) to wait on
▸ **прислу́живаться** *несов возв* to ingratiate o.s., grovel.
прислу́ша|ться (-юсь; *impf* **прислу́шиваться**) *сов возв*: ~ **к** +*dat* (*к звуку*) to listen to; (*к совету*) to take heed of.
присма́трива|ть (-ю) *несов от* **присмотре́ть**
♦ *перех* to look for
▸ **присма́триваться** *несов от* **присмотре́ться**.
присмире́|ть (-ю) *сов неперех* to quieten (*BRIT*) *или* quiet (*US*) down, calm down.
присмир|и́ть (-ю́, -и́шь; *impf* **присмиря́ть**) *сов перех* to quieten (*BRIT*), quiet (*US*).
присмо́тр (-а) *м* care.
присм|отре́ть (-отрю́, -о́тришь) *сов перех* (*разг*) to find ♦ (*impf* **присма́тривать**) *неперех*: ~ **за** +*instr* to look after

присмотре́ться (*impf* **присма́триваться**) *сов возв*: ~**ся (к** +*dat*) to take a good look (at).
присн|и́ться (*3sg* -и́тся, *3pl* -я́тся) *сов от* **сни́ться**.
присовокуп|и́ть (-лю́, -и́шь; *impf* **присовокупля́ть**) *сов перех* (*к делу*) to file; (*к сказанному*) to add.
присоедине́ни|е (-я) *ср* (*см глаг*) attachment; connection; annexation; (*к протесту итп*) joining; (*к чьему-н мнению*) supporting.
присоедин|и́ть (-ю́, -и́шь; *impf* **присоединя́ть**) *сов перех*: ~ **что-н к** +*dat* to attach sth to; (*провод*) to connect sth to; (*территорию*) to annex sth to
▸ **присоедини́ться** (*impf* **присоединя́ться**) *сов возв*: ~**ся к** +*dat* (*к экскурсии, к протесту итп*) to join; (*к чьему-н мнению*) to support.
присос|а́ться (-у́сь, -ёшься; *impf* **приса́сываться**) *сов возв* to attach itself by suction.
приспе́шник (-а) *м* (*пренебр*) accomplice.
приспосо́б|ить (-лю, -ишь; *impf* **приспоса́бливать** *или* **приспособля́ть**) *сов перех* to adapt
▸ **приспосо́биться** (*impf* **приспоса́бливаться** *или* **приспособля́ться**) *сов возв* (*к условиям, к климату*) to adapt (o.s.); (*делать что-н*) to get used to.
приспосо́блен *прил см* **приспосо́бленный**.
приспособле́ни|е (-я) *ср* (*к условиям итп*) adaptation; (*устройство, механизм итп*) appliance.
приспосо́блен|ный (-, -а, -о) *прил*: ~ **к** +*dat* (*пригодный*) fit for, well-suited to.
приспосо́блю(сь) *сов см* **приспосо́бить(ся)**.
приспособл|я́ть(ся) (-ю(сь)) *несов от* **приспосо́бить(ся)**.
приставáни|е (-я) *ср* pestering.
приста|ва́ть (-ю́, -ёшь) *несов от* **приста́ть**.
приста́в|ить (-лю, -ишь; *impf* **приставля́ть**) *сов перех*: ~ **что-н к** +*dat* to put sth against; (*пистолет: к груди*) to put sth to; **приставля́ть** (~ *perf*) **кого́-н к** +*dat* to assign sb to look after.
приста́в|ка (-ки; *gen pl* -ок) *ж* fitting; (*линг*) prefix.
приста́влю *сов см* **приста́вить**.
приставл|я́ть (-ю) *несов от* **приста́вить**.
приста́вок *сущ см* **приста́вка**.
при́сталь|ный (-ен, -ьна, -ьно) *прил* (*взгляд, внимание*) fixed; (*интерес, наблюдение*) determined, resolute.
приста́нищ|е (-а) *ср* refuge.
приста́ну *итп сов см* **приста́ть**.
при́стан|ь (-и) *ж* pier.
приста́|ть (-ну, -нешь; *impf* **пристава́ть**) *сов неперех*: ~ **к** +*dat* (*прилипнуть*) to stick to; (*присоединиться*) to join; (*разг: с вопросами*) to pester; (*причалить*) to put into; **ему́ не** ~**ло**

так поступа́ть (*разг*) he shouldn't behave like that.

пристегну́ть (-у́, -ёшь; *impf* **пристёгивать**) *сов перех* to fasten

▶ **пристегну́ться** (*impf* **пристёгиваться**) *сов возв* (*в самолёте, в автомобиле*) to fasten one's seat belt.

присто́йный (-ен, -йна, -йно) *прил* (*приличный*) decent.

пристра́ива|ть(ся) (-ю(сь)) *несов от* **пристро́ить(ся)**.

пристра́стен *прил см* **пристра́стный**.

пристра́сти|е (-я) *ср* (*склонность*) passion; (*предубеждение*) bias.

пристра|сти́ться (-щу́сь, -сти́шься) *сов возв*: ~ к +*dat* to develop a liking for.

пристра́ст|ный (-ен, -на, -но) *прил* bias(s)ed.

пристращу́сь *сов см* **пристрасти́ться**.

пристре|ли́ть (-елю́, -е́лишь; *impf* **пристре́ливать**) *сов перех* (*животное*) to put down; (*разг: человека*) to shoot.

пристро́|ить (-ю, -ишь; *impf* **пристра́ивать**) *сов перех* (*комнату*) to build onto; (*разг: устроить*) to fix up

▶ **пристро́иться** (*impf* **пристра́иваться**) *сов возв* (*на диване, в углу*) to settle o.s.; (*разг: на работу, на службу*) to get fixed up.

пристро́йк|а (-йки; *gen pl* -ек) *ж* extension.

при́ступ (-а) *м* (*атака*) attack; (*смеха, гнева*) fit; (*кашля*) bout; (*припадок*): серде́чный ~ heart attack; ~ удушья asthma attack.

приступ|и́ть (-уплю́, -у́пишь; *impf* **приступа́ть**) *сов неперех*: ~ к +*dat* (*начать*) to get down to.

пристыди́ть (-жу́, -ди́шь) *сов от* **стыди́ть**.

присуди́ть (-ужу́, -у́дишь; *impf* **присужда́ть**) *сов перех*: ~ что-н кому́-н (*приз, алименты итп*) to award sth to sb; (*учёную степень*) to confer sth on sb; (*приговорить*): ~ кого́-н к +*dat* to sentence sb to.

прису́тственный *прил* (*день, часы*) working опред.

прису́тстви|е (-я) *ср* presence; в ~и +*gen* in the presence of; ~ ду́ха presence of mind.

прису́тств|овать (-ую) *несов неперех* to be present.

прису́тствующ|ие (-их; *decl like adj*) *мн* those present.

прису́щ|ий (-ая, -ее, -ие; -, -а, -о) *прил*: ~ +*dat* characteristic of.

присыла́|ть (-ю) *несов от* **присла́ть**.

присы́лк|а (-ки; *gen pl* -ок) *ж* (*письма*) sending.

присы́пк|а (-ки; *gen pl* -ок) *ж* powder.

прися́г|а (-и) *ж* oath; под ~ой under oath.

присяга́|ть (-ю; *perf* **присягну́ть**) *несов неперех* (+*dat*) to swear an oath to.

прися́ду *итп сов см* **присе́сть**.

прися́жн|ый (-ого; *decl like adj*) *м* (*ЮР: также*: ~ заседа́тель) juror; суд ~ых jury.

притаи́ться (-ю́сь, -и́шься; *impf* **прита́иваться**) *сов возв* to hide.

прит|ащи́ть (-ащу́, -а́щишь; *impf* **прита́скивать**) *сов перех* (*что-н тяжёлое или громоздкое*) to drag; (*заставить пойти*) to drag along.

притво́рен *прил см* **притво́рный**.

притвор|и́ть (-орю́, -о́ришь; *impf* **притворя́ть**) *сов перех* to shut (*not fully*).

притвор|и́ться (-ю́сь, -и́шься; *impf* **притворя́ться**) *сов возв* (+*instr*) to pretend to be.

притво́р|ный (-ен, -на, -но) *прил* feigned.

притво́рств|о (-а) *ср* pretence.

притворю́(сь) *сов см* **притвори́ть(ся)**.

притворя́|ть(ся) (-ю(сь)) *несов от* **притвори́ть(ся)**.

притесне́ни|е (-я) *ср* (*людей*) oppression; (*обычно мн: гонения*) persecution.

притесни́тел|ь (-я) *м* oppressor.

притесн|и́ть (-ю́, -и́шь; *impf* **притесня́ть**) *сов перех* to oppress.

прити́х|нуть (-ну, -нешь; *pt* -, -ла, -ло, *impf* **притиха́ть**) *сов неперех* to grow quiet.

приткн|у́ть (-у́, -ёшь; *impf* **притыка́ть**) *сов перех* to stick.

прито́к (-а) *м* (*река*) tributary; ~ +*gen* (*сил, энергии, средств*) supply of; (*населения*) influx of.

прито́м *союз* and what's more.

прито́н (-а) *м* den.

при́тор|ный (-ен, -на, -но) *прил* (*вкус, торт итп*) sickly sweet; (*перен: улыбка, выражение лица*) unctuous.

притро́н|уться (-усь, -ешься; *impf* **притра́гиваться**) *сов возв*: ~ к +*dat* to touch.

прит|упи́ться (*3sg* -у́пится, *3pl* -у́пятся, *impf* **притупля́ться**) *сов возв* (*нож, бритва, топор*) to go blunt; (*перен: внимание итп*) to diminish; (: *чувства*) to fade; (: *слух*) to fail.

при́тч|а (-и) *ж* parable.

притыка́|ть (-ю) *несов от* **приткну́ть**.

притяга́тел|ьный (-ен, -ьна, -ьно) *прил* attractive.

притя́гива|ть (-ю) *несов от* **притяну́ть**.

притяжа́тельный *прил* (*линг*) possessive.

притяза́ни|е (-я) *ср*: ~ на +*acc* (*на наследство, на территорию*) claim to; (*на остроумие, на красоту итп*) pretensions *мн* of.

притя|ну́ть (-ну́, -я́нешь; *impf* **притя́гивать**) *сов перех* (*подтащить*) to drag up; (*привлечь*) to attract; **притя́гивать (~ *perf*) факт за́ уши** to come up with a far-fetched fact.

приукра́|сить (-шу, -сишь; *impf* **приукра́шивать**) *сов перех* (*события, чьи-н достоинства*) to exaggerate.

приумно́ж|ить (-у, -ишь; *impf* **приумножа́ть**) *сов перех* to increase.

приуны́ть (-о́ю, -о́ешь; *impf* **приуныва́ть**) *сов неперех* to get depressed.

приуро́ч|ить (-у, -ишь; *impf* **приуро́чивать**) *сов перех*: ~ что-н к +*dat* to time sth to coincide with.

приуса́дебный *прил*: ~ уча́сток allotment.

приу́чи́ть (-учу́, -у́чишь; *impf* приуча́ть) *сов перех*: ~ кого́-н к +*dat*/+*infin* to train sb for/to do

▶ **приучи́ться** (*impf* приуча́ться) *сов возв*: ~ся к +*dat*/+*infin* to train for/to do.

прифронтово́й *прил* front(line) *опред*.

прихвастн|у́ть (-у́, -ёшь) *сов неперех* (*разг*) to blow one's own trumpet a bit.

прихв|ати́ть (-ачу́, -а́тишь; *impf* прихва́тывать) *сов перех* (*разг*: схвати́ть) to grab; (: взять с собой) to take ◆ *безл* (о боли) to grip.

прихлеба́тел|ь (-я) *м* (*разг*: пренебр*) sponger.

прихло́пн|уть (-у, -ешь; *impf* прихло́пывать) *сов перех* (крышку) to slam shut; (*разг*: насекомое) to swat.

прихлы́н|уть (*3sg* -ет, *3pl* -ут) *сов перех* (волна, толпа) to surge; (*перен*: воспоминания) to come flooding back.

прихо́д (-а) *м* (поезда, гостя, весны) arrival; (*КОММ*) receipts *мн*; (*РЕЛ*) parish; ~ и расхо́д (*КОММ*) credit and debit.

прих|оди́ть (-ожу́, -о́дишь) *несов от* прийти́

▶ **приходи́ться** *несов от* прийти́сь ◆ *возв*: ~ся кому́-н дя́дей/ро́дственником to be sb's uncle/relative; раз на раз не ~о́дится no two times are ever the same.

прихо́дный *прил* (*КОММ*): ~ая кни́га receipt book.

прихо́д|овать (-ую; *perf* оприхо́довать) *несов перех* (*КОММ*: сумму) to enter (*in receipt book*).

прихо́дск|ий (-ая, -ое, ие) *прил* (*РЕЛ*) parish *опред*.

приходя́щ|ий (-ая, -ее, -ие) *прил* nonresident; (медсестра) visiting *опред*; ~ая ня́ня babysitter; ~ больно́й outpatient.

прихожа́н|ин (-ина; *nom pl* -е) *м* (*РЕЛ*) parishioner.

прихожа́н|ка (-ки; *gen pl* -ок) *ж* (*РЕЛ*) см прихожа́нин.

прихо́ж|ая (-ей; *decl like adj*) *ж* entrance hall.

прихожу́(сь) *несов см* приходи́ть(ся).

прихора́шива|ться (-юсь) *несов возв* (*разг*) to smarten o.s. up.

прихотли́в|ый (-, -а, -о) *прил* (человек) capricious, whimsical; (вкус) quirky; (узор) intricate.

при́хот|ь (-и) *ж* whim.

прихра́мыва|ть (-ю) *сов неперех* to limp slightly.

прице́л (-а) *м* (ружья́, пушки) sight(s); (прицеливание) aiming; брать (взять *perf*) кого́-н/что-н на ~ to aim at sb/sth; (*перен*) to keep a close watch on sb/sth.

прице́л|иться (-юсь, -ишься; *impf* прице́ливаться) *сов возв* to take aim.

прицен|и́ться (-ю́сь, -е́нишься; *impf* прице́ниваться) *сов возв*: ~ к +*dat* to enquire about the price of.

прице́п (-а) *м* trailer.

прицеп|и́ть (-еплю́, -е́пишь; *impf* прицепля́ть) *сов перех* (вагон) to couple

▶ **прицепи́ться** (*impf* прицепля́ться) *сов возв* (перен: разг: пристать) to be a pain in the neck; **прицепля́ться** (~ся *perf*) к +*dat* to stick to; (перен: разг: к человеку) to nag; (: к слова́м) to find fault with.

прича́л (-а) *м* mooring; (пассажирский) quay; (грузовой, ремонтный) dock.

прича́л|ить (-ю, -ишь; *impf* прича́ливать) *сов (не)перех* to moor.

прича́стен *прил см* прича́стный.

прича́сти|е (-я) *ср* (*ЛИНГ*) participle; (*РЕЛ*) communion.

прича|сти́ть (-щу́, -сти́шь; *impf* причаща́ть) *перех* (*РЕЛ*) to give communion to

▶ **причасти́ться** (*impf* причаща́ться) *сов возв* (*РЕЛ*) to receive communion.

прича́стный *прил* (*ЛИНГ*) participial; (-ен, -на, -но; связанный): ~ к +*dat* connected with.

причаща́|ть(ся) (-ю(сь)) *несов от* причасти́ть(ся).

причаще́ни|е (-я) *ср* (*РЕЛ*) Eucharist.

причащу́(сь) *сов см* причасти́ть(ся).

причём *союз* moreover.

причес|а́ть (-ешу́, -е́шешь; *impf* причёсывать) *сов перех* (во́лосы) to comb, brush; **причёсывать** (~ *perf*) кого́-н to comb *или* brush sb's hair; **причёсывать** (~ *perf*) го́лову to do one's hair

▶ **причеса́ться** (*impf* причёсываться) *сов возв* to comb *или* brush one's hair.

причёс|ка (-ки; *gen pl* -ок) *ж* hairstyle.

причёсыва|ть(ся) (-ь(сь)) *несов от* причеса́ть(ся).

причешу́(сь) *итп сов см* причеса́ть(ся).

причи́н|а (-ы) *ж* cause, reason; по ~е +*gen* on account of.

причин|и́ть (-ю́, -и́шь; *impf* причиня́ть) *сов перех* to cause.

причи́сл|ить (-ю, -ишь; *impf* причисля́ть) *сов перех*: ~ кого́-н/что-н к +*dat* (отнести́ к) to number sb/sth among.

причита́ни|е (-я) *ср* lamentation; (похоро́нные) keening; сва́дебные ~я *old Russian wedding ritual where women wail and lament the bride*.

причита́|ть (-ю) *несов неперех* (на похоро́нах) to wail

▶ **причита́ться** *несов возв*: мне ~ется 10 рубле́й I am owed 10 roubles; с Вас ~ется 10 рубле́й you owe 10 roubles.

причу́д|а (-ы) *ж* whim.

причу́дливый (-, -а, -о) *прил* (узор) intricate.

пришварт|ова́ть (-ую) *сов от* швартова́ть.

пришёл|(те) *сов см* прийти́.

пришёл(ся) *сов см* прийти́(сь).

пришёл|ец (-ьца) *м* stranger.

пришéстви|е (-я) *ср* (*РЕЛ*) advent.
приши́бленный *прил* crestfallen.
приши́ть (-ью, -ьёшь; *imper* **-éй(те)**, *impf*
пришивáть) *сов перех* to sew on; (*перен: разг*):
~ **комý-н что-н** to pin sth on sb.
пришлá *итп сов см* **прийти́**.
при́шлый *прил* (*человек*) strange; (*кошка*)
stray.
пришлю́ *итп сов см* **присла́ть**.
пришпóр|ить (-ю, -ишь; *impf* **пришпóривать**)
сов перех to spur.
пришью́ *итп сов см* **приши́ть**.
прищем|и́ть (-лю́, -и́шь; *impf* **прищемля́ть**) *сов*
перех to catch.
прищéп|ка (-ки; *gen pl* **-ок**) *ж* clothes peg (*BRIT*),
clothespin (*US*).
прищýр|ить (-ю, -ишь; *impf* **прищýривать**) *сов*
перех (*глаза*) to screw up
▶ **прищýриться** (*impf* **прищýриваться**) *сов*
возв to screw up one's eyes.
прию́т (-а) *м* shelter; (*для сирот*) orphanage.
приюти́ть (-чý, -ти́шь) *сов перех* to shelter
▶ **приюти́ться** *сов возв* to take shelter.
прия́тел|ь (-я) *м* friend.
прия́тельниц|а (-ы) *ж см* **прия́тель**.
прия́тен *прил см* **прия́тный**.
прия́тно *нареч* (*удивлён, поражён*) pleasantly ◆
как сказ it is nice *или* pleasant; **мне** ~ **э́то**
слы́шать I'm glad to hear that; **óчень** ~ (*при*
знакомстве) pleased to meet you.
прия́т|ный (-ен, -на, -но) *прил* (*встреча,*
поездка) pleasant, enjoyable; (*разговор, вкус*)
pleasant; (*человек, лицо, улыбка*) nice, pleasant.
ПРО *ж сокр* (= *противоракéтная оборóна*)
antimissile defence (*BRIT*) *или* defense (*US*)
system.
про *предл* (+*acc*) about.
про- *префикс* (*in verbs*; *о действии,*
направленном сквозь что-н) *indicating action*
through sth eg. прострели́ть; (*о действии,*
распространяющемся на весь предмет)
indicating action involving whole object eg.
прогрéть; (*о движении мимо чего-н*) *indicating*
movement past sth eg. проéхать; (*об*
исчерпанности действия) *indicating*
completion of action eg. пронумеровáть; (*о*
звучании, осуществляемом в один приём)
indicating single occurence of sound eg.
протруби́ть; (*о длительном действии*)
indicating prolonged action eg. прорабóтать;
(*in nouns and adjectives*; *сторонник чего-н*) pro-.
проанали́зир|овать (-ую) *сов от*
анализи́ровать.
проанноти́р|овать (-ую) *сов от*
анноти́ровать.
прóб|а (-ы) *ж* (*испытание*) test; (*образец*)
sample; (*драгоценного металла*) standard (*of*
precious metals); (*клеймо*) hallmark.
пробéг (-а) *м* (*СПОРТ: автомобильный,*
марофонский) race; (: *лыжный*) run; (*АВТ*)
mileage.

пробéга|ть (-ю) *сов неперех* to run around.
пробе|жа́ть (*как* **бежа́ть**; *см* **Table 20**; *impf*
пробега́ть) *сов перех* (*бегло прочитать*) to
skim ◆ *неперех* (5 *километров*) to cover;
(*время, годы*) to pass; (*миновать бегом*): ~
ми́мо +*gen* to run past; (*появиться и*
исчезнуть): ~ **по** +*dat* (*шум, дрожь*) to run
through; (*по земле*) to run along; **пробега́ть** (~
perf) **чéрез** +*acc* to run through
▶ **пробежа́ться** *сов возв* to run.
пробéж|ка (-ки; *gen pl* **-ек**) *ж* run.
пробéл (-а) *м* (*также перен*) gap.
проберý(сь) *итп сов см* **пробра́ть(ся)**.
пробива́ть(ся) (-ю(сь)) *несов от*
проби́ть(ся).
пробивнóй *прил* (*сила снаряда*) penetrating;
(*перен: разг: человек*) pushy.
пробира́ть(ся) (-ю(сь)) *несов от*
пробра́ть(ся).
проби́р|ка (-ки; *gen pl* **-ок**) *ж* test-tube.
проб|и́ть (-ью́, -ьёшь) *сов от* **бить** ◆ (*impf*
пробива́ть) *перех* (*дыру, отверстие*) to
knock; (*крышу, стену*) to make a hole in; (*разг:*
с трудом добиться) to force through;
пробива́ть (~ *perf*) **себé дорóгу** (*перен*) to
carve one's way
▶ **проби́ться** (*impf* **пробива́ться**) *сов возв*
(*прорваться*) to fight one's way through;
(*растения, ростки*) to push through *или* up;
(*разг: прожить с трудом*) to struggle through.
прóб|ка (-ки; *gen pl* **-ок**) *ж* (*no pl*; *древесной коры*)
cork; (*для закупоривания*) cork, stopper;
(*перен: транспортная*) jam; (*ЭЛЕК*) fuse.
проблéм|а (-ы) *ж* problem.
проблема́тик|а (-и) *ж собир* problems *мн*.
проблемати́чен *прил см* **проблемати́чный**.
проблемати́ческ|ий (-ая, -ое, -ие) *прил*
problematic(al).
проблемати́|чный (-ен, -на, -но) *прил* =
проблемати́ческий.
прóблеск (-а) *м* (*блеск*) ray; (*таланта,*
понимания) hint; ~ **надéжды** ray of hope.
прóбный *прил* (*образец, экземпляр*) trial
опред; (*полёт*) test *опред*; ~ **ка́мень** (*перен*)
touchstone.
прóб|овать (-ую; *perf* **попрóбовать**) *несов*
перех (*мотор*) to test; (*пирог, вино*) to taste;
(+*infin*; *пытаться*) to try to do.
прободéни|е (-я) *ср* (*МЕД*) perforation.
пробóин|а (-ы) *ж* hole.
прóбок *сущ см* **прóбка**.
проболта́|ться (-юсь) *сов возв* (*разг:*
проговориться) to blab; (: *пробездельничать*)
to loaf about.
пробóр (-а) *м* parting (*of hair*).
пробра́ть (-ерý, -ерёшь; *impf* **пробира́ть**) *сов*
перех (*разг: страх*) to strike; (*дрожь*) to come
over; (*мороз*) to chill
▶ **пробра́ться** (*impf* **пробира́ться**) *сов возв* (*с*
трудом пройти) to fight one's way through;

(*тихо пройти*) to steal past *или* through.

пробу́дешь *итп сов см* **пробы́ть**.

проб|уди́ть (-ужу́, -у́дишь) *impf* **пробужда́ть** *или* **буди́ть**) *сов перех* (*массы, людей*) to rouse, stir; (*перен: желания, чувства*) to arouse

▶ **пробуди́ться** (*impf* **пробужда́ться**) *сов возв* (*проснуться*) to awake, wake up; (*перен: появиться*) to appear.

пробу́ду *итп сов см* **пробы́ть**.

пробу́дь(те) *сов см* **пробы́ть**.

пробужда́|ть(ся) (-ю(сь)) *несов от* **пробуди́ть(ся)**.

пробужде́ни|е (-я) *ср* (*ото сна*) waking up; (*сознания, чувств*) awakening.

пробужу́(сь) *сов см* **пробуди́ть(ся)**.

пробура́вить (-лю, -ишь) *сов от* **бура́вить**.

пробур|и́ть (-ю́, -и́шь) *сов от* **бури́ть**.

пробурча́|ть (-у́, -и́шь) *сов от* **бурча́ть**.

пробы́ть (*как* **быть**; *см* **Table 21**) *сов неперех* (*прожить*) to stay, remain; (*провести*) to go; **он пробы́л 10 лет учи́телем** he was a teacher for 10 years.

пробью́(сь) *итп сов см* **проби́ть(ся)**.

прова́л (-а) *м* (*в почве, в стене*) hole; (*перен: неудача*) flop; (: *памяти*) failure.

прова́л|ить (-аю́, -а́лишь) *impf* **прова́ливать**) *сов перех* (*крышу, пол*) to cause to collapse; (*разг: перен: дело, затею*) to make a mess of; (: *студента*) to fail

▶ **провали́ться** (*impf* **прова́ливаться**) *сов возв* (*упасть*) to fall; (*рухнуть*) to collapse; (*разг: перен: студент, попытка*) to fail; (: *исчезнуть*) to vanish; **как сквозь зе́млю ~али́лся** he disappeared into thin air.

прова́р|ить (-арю́, -а́ришь) *impf* **прова́ривать**) *сов перех* to boil (*for a long time*).

прове́да|ть (-ю) *impf* **прове́дывать**) *сов перех* (*навестить*) to call on; (*разг: узнать*) to find out.

проведе́ни|е (-я) *ср* (*урока*) taking; (*репетиции, конкурса*) holding; (*границы*) drawing; (*линии передачи*) installation; (*машины*) driving; (*судна*) piloting.

проведу́ *итп сов см* **провести́**.

прове́дыва|ть (-ю) *несов от* **прове́дать**.

провез|ти́ (-у́, -ёшь; *pt* -ёз, -езла́, -езло́, *impf* **провози́ть**) *сов перех* (*везя, доставить*): **~ по** +*dat*/**ми́мо** +*gen*/**че́рез** +*acc* to take along/ past/across; (*контрабанду, наркотики*) to smuggle.

провентили́р|овать (-ую) *сов от* **вентили́ровать**.

прове́р|ить (-ю, -ишь; *impf* **проверя́ть**) *сов перех* to check; (*выполнение правил*) to monitor; (*знание ученика, двигатель*) to test

▶ **прове́риться** (*impf* **проверя́ться**) *сов возв* (*у врача*) to get a check-up.

прове́р|ка (-ки; *gen pl* -ок) *ж* (*см глаг*) check;

monitoring; test.

провер|ну́ть (-у́, -ёшь; *impf* **провора́чивать**) *сов перех* (*кран, винт*) to crank; (*перен: разг: дело, обмен кварти́ры*) to rush through.

прове́рок *прил см* **прове́рка**.

проверя́ющий (-его; *decl like adj*) *м* examiner.

проверя́|ть(ся) (-ю(сь)) *несов от* **прове́рить(ся)**.

пров|ести́ (-еду́, -едёшь; *pt* -ёл, -ела́, -ело́, *impf* **проводи́ть**) *сов перех* (*черту, границу*) to draw; (*дорогу, ход итп*) to build; (*линию передачи*) to install; (*план, реформу*) to implement; (*урок, репетицию*) to hold; (*операцию*) to carry out; (*детство, день*) to spend; (*обмануть*) to trick; **проводи́ть** (**~** *perf*) **ми́мо** +*gen*/**че́рез** +*acc* (*людей, экскурсантов*) to take past/across; **проводи́ть** (**~** *perf*) **что-н в жизнь** to put sth into effect.

прове́тр|ить (-ю, -ишь; *impf* **прове́тривать**) *сов перех* to air

▶ **прове́триться** (*impf* **прове́триваться**) *сов возв* (*комната, одежда*) to have an airing; (*человек: на свежем воздухе*) to take a breath of fresh air; (*перен: разг*) to have a change of scene.

прове́|ять (-ю) *сов от* **ве́ять**.

прови́а́нт (-а) *м* provisions *мн*.

прови́дени|е (-я) *ср* foresight.

провиде́ни|е (-я) *ср* (*РЕЛ*) Providence.

провин|и́ться (-ю́сь, -и́шься) *сов возв*: **~** (**в** +*prp*) to be guilty (of).

прови́нност|ь (-и) *ж* fault.

провинциа́л (-а) *м* provincial.

провинциа́л|ка (-ки; *gen pl* -ок) *ж см* **провинциа́л**.

провинциа́льный *прил* provincial.

прови́нци|я (-и) *ж* province; (*отдалённая местность*) provinces *мн*.

про́вод (-а; *nom pl* -а́) *м* cable.

проводи́мост|ь (-и) *ж* conductivity.

пров|оди́ть (-ожу́, -о́дишь) *несов от* **провести́**
♦ (*impf* **провожа́ть**) *сов перех* to see off; (*сына: в армию*) to send off; **провожа́ть** (**~** *perf*) **глаза́ми/взгля́дом кого́-н** to follow sb with one's eyes/gaze.

прово́д|ка (-ки; *gen pl* -ок) *ж* (*ЭЛЕК*) wiring.

проводни́к (-а́) *м* (*в горах*) guide; (*в поезде*) steward (*BRIT*) *или* porter (*US*); (*ЭЛЕК*) conductor; (*перен: идей, политики итп*) vehicle.

проводни́ц|а (-ы) *ж* (*в поезде*) stewardess (*BRIT*) *или* porter (*US*).

прово́док *сущ см* **прово́дка**.

про́вод|ы (-ов) *мн* (*прощание*) send-off *ед*.

провожа́т|ый (-ого; *decl like adj*) *м* escort.

провожа́|ть (-ю) *несов от* **проводи́ть**.

провожу́ (*не*)*сов см* **проводи́ть**.

провожу́(сь) *несов см* **провози́ть(ся)**.

провóз (-а) *м* (*багажа*) transport; (*незаконный*) smuggling.

провозгла|сить (-шý, -сишь; *impf* **провозглашáть**) *сов перех* to proclaim; **провозглашáть** (~ *perf*) **когó-н/чтó-н** +*instr* to hail sb/sth as.

провозглашéни|е (-я) *ср* proclamation.

провозглашý *сов см* **провозгласить**.

пров|озить (-ожý, -óзишь) *несов от* **провезти**
▸ **провозиться** *сов возв* (*разг*) to muck around *или* about; ~**ся** (*perf*) **с кем-н/чем-н** to spend time with sb/on sth.

провокáтор (-а) *м* agent provocateur.

провокациóнный *прил* provocative.

провокáци|я (-и) *ж* provocation; **поддавáться** (**поддáться** *perf*) **на** ~**ю** to give in to provocation.

прóволок|а (-и) *ж* wire.

проволóч|ка (-ки; *gen pl* -ек) *ж* (*разг*) hold-up.

проворáчива|ть (-ю) *несов от* **провернýть**.

провóр|ный (-ен, -на, -но) *прил* agile.

провор|овáться (-ýюсь; *impf* **проворóвываться**) *сов возв* (*разг*) to be caught stealing.

провор|óнить (-ю, -ишь) *сов от* **ворóнить**.

проворч|áть (-ý, -ишь) *сов неперех* (*человек*) to grumble ◆ *перех* to mutter.

провоци́р|овать (-ую; *perf* **спровоци́ровать**) *несов перех* to provoke; ~ (**спровоци́ровать** *perf*) **когó-н/чтó-н на чтó-н** to provoke sb/sth into sth.

провя́л|ить (-ю, -ишь) *сов от* **вя́лить**.

прогадá|ть (-ю; *impf* **прогáдывать**) *сов неперех* (*разг*) to miscalculate.

прогиб (-а) *м* (*пола, балки*) sagging; (*место*) sag.

прогибá|ть(ся) (-ю(сь)) *несов от* **прогнýть(ся)**.

прогл|отить (-очý, -óтишь; *impf* **проглáтывать** *или* **глотáть**) *сов перех* (*также перен*) to swallow; (*перен: разг: книгу*) to devour; **язы́к** ~**óтишь, так вкýсно** (*разг*) it's so tasty it makes your mouth water.

прогля|дéть (-жý, -ди́шь) *сов перех* (*ошибку, изменения*) to overlook.

прогл|яну́ть (*3sg* -я́нет, *3pl* -я́нут) *сов перех* (*солнце*) to peek out; **на егó лицé** ~**яну́ла улы́бка** there was a hint of a smile on his face.

прог|нáть (-оню́, -óнишь; *pt* -нáл, -налá, -нáло, *impf* **прогоня́ть**) *сов перех* (*заставить двигаться*) to drive; (*заставить уйти*) to turn out; (*уволить*) to dismiss; (*избавиться*) to drive away.

прогнев|и́ть (-лю́, -и́шь) *сов от* **гневи́ть**.

прогни|ть (*3sg* -ёт, *3pl* -ю́т, *impf* **прогнивáть**) *сов неперех* to rot through.

прогнóз (-а) *м* forecast.

прогнози́р|овать (-ую) (*не*)*сов перех* to forecast.

прогн|у́ть (-ý, -ёшь; *impf* **прогибáть**) *сов перех*: ~ **чтó-н** to cause sth to sag

▸ **прогну́ться** (*impf* **прогибáться**) *сов возв* to sag.

проговор|и́ть (-ю́, -и́шь; *impf* **проговáривать**) *сов перех* (*произнести*) to utter ◆ *неперех* (*no impf*; *разговаривать*) to chat

▸ **проговори́ться** (*impf* **проговáриваться**) *сов возв* to let out a secret; ~**ся** (*perf*) **о чём-н** to reveal sth.

прогого|тáть (-чý, -чешь) *сов от* **гоготáть**.

проголос|овáть (-ýю) *сов от* **голосовáть**.

прогоню́ *итп сов см* **прогнáть**.

прогоня́|ть (-ю) *несов от* **прогнáть**.

прогор|éть (-ю́, -и́шь; *impf* **прогорáть**) *сов неперех* (*дрова*) to burn through; (*перен: разг: дело*) to go bust.

прогóрклый *прил* (*масло*) rancid.

прогóркн|уть (*3sg* -ет, *3pl* -ут) *сов от* **гóркнуть**.

прогрáмм|а (-ы) *ж* programme (*BRIT*), program (*US*); (*ПОЛИТ*) manifesto; (*также:* **вещáтельная** ~) channel; (*ПРОСВЕЩ*) curriculum; (*КОМП*) program.

программи́ровани|е (-я) *ср* (*КОМП*) programming.

программи́р|овать (-ую; *perf* **запрограмми́ровать**) *несов перех* (*КОМП*) to program.

программи́ст (-а) *м* (*КОМП*) programmer.

прогрáмм|ка (-ки; *gen pl* -ок) *ж* (*разг: в театре*) programme (*BRIT*), program (*US*).

прогрáммный *прил* programmed (*BRIT*), programed (*US*); (*экзамен, зачёт*) set; (*КОМП*) programming (*BRIT*), programming (*US*); **прогрáммное обеспéчение** (*КОМП*) software; **прогрáммное управлéние** (*КОМП*) programmed (*BRIT*) *или* programed (*US*) control.

прогревá|ть (-ю) *сов от* **прогрéть**.

прогрем|éть (-лю́, -и́шь) *сов от* **гремéть**.

прогрéсс (-а) *м* progress.

прогресси́вный *прил* (*писатель, идеи*) progressive.

прогресси́р|овать (-ую) *несов неперех* to progress.

прогрé|ть (-ю; *impf* **прогревáть**) *сов перех* to warm up

▸ **прогрéться** (*impf* **прогревáться**) *сов возв* to warm up.

прогромыхá|ть (-ю) *сов от* **громыхáть**.

прогрохо|тáть (-чý, -чешь) *сов от* **грохотáть**.

прогры́з|ть (-ý, -ёшь; *pt* -, -ла, -ло, *impf* **прогрызáть**) *сов перех* to gnaw through.

прогу|дéть (-жý, -ди́шь) *сов от* **гудéть**.

прогу́л (-а) *м* (*на работе*) absence; (*в школе*) truancy.

прогу́лива|ть (-ю) *несов от* **прогуля́ть** ◆ *перех* (*разг: собаку*) to take

▸ **прогу́ливаться** *несов от* **прогуля́ться**.

прогу́л|ка (-ки; *gen pl* -ок) *ж* walk; (*недалекая поездка*) trip.

прогу́льщик (-а) *м* (*работник*) absentee; (*ученик*) truant.

прогу́льщиц|а (-ы) *ж см* **прогу́льщик**.

прогуля́|ть (-ю; *impf* **прогу́ливать**) *сов перех* (*работу*) to be absent from; (*уроки*) to miss ◆ *неперех* (*no impf*) to walk
▸ **прогуля́ться** (*impf* **прогу́ливаться**) *сов возв* to go for a walk.
продава́|ть(ся) (-ю́(сь)) *несов от* **прода́ть(ся)**.
продав|е́ц (-ца́) *м* seller; (*в магазине*) (shop-)assistant.
прода|ви́ть (-авлю́, -а́вишь; *impf* **прода́вливать**) *сов перех* (*стекло*) to go through; **прода́вливать** (~ *perf*) **сиде́нье сту́ла** to make the seat of a chair sag.
продавца́ *итп сущ см* **продаве́ц**.
продавщи́ц|а (-ы) *ж см* **продаве́ц**.
продади́м(ся) *итп сов см* **прода́ть(ся)**.
прода́ж|а (-и) *ж* (*дома, товара*) sale; (*торговля*) trade; **быть** (*impf*) **в ~е, поступа́ть** (**поступи́ть** *perf*) **в ~у** to be on sale.
прода́ж|ный *прил* (*цена*) sale *опред*; (*вещь*) for sale; (-ен, -на, -но; *человек, пресса*) corrupt.
прода́лблива|ть (-ю) *несов от* **продолби́ть**.
прода́ть (*как* **дать**; *см* **Table 14**; *impf* **продава́ть**) *сов перех* to sell; (*перен: дру́га*) to betray
▸ **прода́ться** (*impf* **продава́ться**) *сов возв* (*врага́м*) to sell out.
продвига́|ть(ся) (-ю(сь)) *несов от* **продви́нуть(ся)**.
продвиже́ни|е (-я) *ср* (*по территории*) advance; (*по службе*) promotion.
продви́|нуть (-у, -ешь; *impf* **продвига́ть**) *сов перех* to move; (*перен: работник*) to promote
▸ **продви́нуться** (*impf* **продвига́ться**) *сов возв* to move; (*войска́*) to advance; (*перен: работник*) to be promoted; (: *работа, строи́тельство*) to progress.
продева́|ть (-ю) *несов от* **проде́ть**.
продезинфици́р|овать (-ую) *сов от* **дезинфици́ровать**.
продеклами́р|овать (-ую) *сов от* **деклами́ровать**.
проде́ла|ть (-ю; *impf* **проде́лывать**) *сов перех* (*отверстие*) to make; (*работу*) to do.
проде́л|ка (-ки; *gen pl* -ок) *ж* trick.
проде́лыва|ть (-ю) *несов от* **проде́лать**.
продемонстри́р|овать (-ую) *сов от* **демонстри́ровать**.
проде́ну *итп сов см* **проде́ть**.
проде|ржа́ть (-ержу́, -е́ржишь) *сов перех* (*держа́ть*) to hold; (: *библиоте́чную кни́гу, челове́ка*) to keep
▸ **продержа́ться** *сов возв* (*держа́ться*) to hold out.
продеру́сь *итп сов см* **продра́ться**.
проде́|ть (-ну, -нешь; *impf* **продева́ть**) *сов перех* to thread; **продева́ть** (~ *perf*) **ни́тку в иго́лку** to thread a needle.
продикт|ова́ть (-у́ю) *сов от* **диктова́ть**.

продира́|ться (-юсь) *несов от* **продра́ться**.
продлева́|ть (-ю) *несов от* **продли́ть**.
продле́ни|е (-я) *ср* (*см глаг*) extension; prolongation.
продлённый *прил*: ~ **день** (*ПРОСВЕЩ*) extended school day (*for children whose parents work late*)
продл|и́ть (-ю́, -и́шь; *impf* **продлева́ть**) *сов перех* (*командиро́вку, о́тпуск*) to extend; (*жизнь*) to prolong.
продл|и́ться (*3sg* -и́тся, *3pl* -я́тся) *сов от* **дли́ться**.
продма́г (-а) *м* (= **продово́льственный магази́н**) grocer's (shop) (*BRIT*), grocery (*US*).
продово́льственный *прил* food *опред*; **продово́льственный магази́н** grocer's (shop) (*BRIT*), grocery (*US*).
продово́льстви|е (-я) *ср* provisions *мн*.
продолб|и́ть (-лю́, -и́шь) *сов от* **долби́ть**.
продолгова́т|ый (-, -а, -о) *прил* elongated.
продолжа́тел|ь (-я) *м* successor.
продолжа́|ть (-ю; *perf* **продо́лжить**) *несов перех* to continue, carry on; (~ *perf*) +*impf infin* to continue *или* carry on doing
▸ **продолжа́ться** (*perf* **продо́лжиться**) *несов возв* to continue, carry on.
продолже́ни|е (-я) *ср* (*борьбы, лекции*) continuation; (*рома́на, расска́за*) sequel; **в ~** +*gen* for the duration of.
продолжи́телен *прил см* **продолжи́тельный**.
продолжи́тельност|ь (-и) *ж* duration; **сре́дняя ~** life expectancy; **продолжи́тельность жи́зни** lifespan.
продолжи́тель|ный (-ен, -ьна, -ьно) *прил* (*боле́знь, разгово́р*) prolonged; (*уро́к*) extended.
продо́лж|ить(ся) (-у(сь), -ишь(ся)) *сов от* **продолжа́ть(ся)**.
продо́льный *прил* longitudinal.
продра́|ться (-еру́сь, -ерёшься; *impf* **продира́ться**) *сов возв*: ~ **сквозь** +*acc* to fight one's way through.
продро́г|нуть (-у, -ешь) *сов неперех* to be frozen to the bone.
продува́|ть (-ю) *несов от* **проду́ть** ◆ *перех*: **сквозня́к ~л ко́мнату** the draught blew through the room.
проду́кт (-а) *м* product; *см также* **проду́кты**.
продукти́вен *прил см* **продукти́вный**.
продукти́вност|ь (-и) *ж* productivity; (*КОМП*) throughput.
продукти́в|ный (-ен, -на, -но) *прил* productive.
продукто́вый *прил* food *опред*.
проду́кт|ы (-ов) *мн* (*также*: ~ **пита́ния**) foodstuffs *мн*.
проду́кци|я (-и) *ж* produce.
проду́ман|ный (-, -на, -но) *прил* well thought-out.
проду́ма|ть (-ю; *impf* **проду́мывать**) *сов перех*

(*действия, выступление*) to think out; (*ответ*) to consider ♦ *неперех* to think.

проду́|ть (-ю, -ешь; *impf* **продува́ть**) *сов перех* (*трубу*) to blow through; (*разг: проиграть*) to lose ♦ *безл* (+*acc*): **меня́ ~ло** I've caught a chill.

продыря́в|ить (-лю, -ишь) *сов перех* to make a hole in.

продю́сер (-а) *м* producer.

проеда́|ть (-ю) *несов от* **прое́сть**.

прое́дешь *итп сов см* **прое́хать**.

прое́дим *итп сов см* **прое́сть**.

прое́ду(сь) *итп сов см* **прое́хать(ся)**.

проедя́т *сов см* **прое́сть**.

прое́зд (-а) *м* (*в транспорте*) journey; (*место*) passage.

проездно́й *прил* (*документ*) travel *опред*; **проездно́й биле́т** travel card.

прое́здом *нареч* en route.

проезжа́й(те) *сов см* **прое́хать**.

проезжа́|ть (-ю) *несов от* **прое́хать**.

прое́зж|ий (-ая, -ее, -ие) *прил* (*человек*) passing ♦ (**-его**; *decl like adj*) *м* traveller (*BRIT*), traveler (*US*); **~ая часть (у́лицы)** roadway.

прое́кт (-а) *м* (*дома, памятника итп*) design; (*закона, договора*) draft; (*замысел*) project.

проекти́р|овать (-ую; *perf* **спроекти́ровать**) *несов перех* (*дом*) to design; (*perf* **запроекти́ровать**; *наметить*) to plan.

проекти́ро|вщик (-а) *м* designer.

прое́ктор (-а) *м* (*ОПТИКА*) projector.

прое́кци|я (-и) *ж* (*также ГЕОМ*) projection.

проём (-а) *м* (*дверной, оконный*) aperture.

прое́сть (*как* **есть**; *см* **Table 15**; *impf* **проеда́ть**) *сов перех* to eat through; (*разг: деньги*) to blow on food.

прое́хать (*как* **е́хать**; *см* **Table 19**) *сов перех* (*миновать*) to pass; (*остановку, поворот итп*) to miss ♦ (*impf* **проезжа́ть**) *неперех*: **~ ми́мо** +*gen*/**по** +*dat*/**че́рез** +*acc итп* to drive past/along/across *итп*

▶ **прое́хаться** *сов возв* (*на велосипеде, на санках*) to go for a ride; (*на машине*) to go for a drive.

прое́шь *сов см* **прое́сть**.

прожа́р|ить (-ю, -ишь; *impf* **прожа́ривать**) *сов перех* to fry

▶ **прожа́риться** (*impf* **прожа́риваться**) *сов возв* to be well-fried.

прожгу́ *итп сов см* **проже́чь**.

прожда́|ть (-у́, -ёшь) *сов перех* to wait a long time for.

прожёг *итп сов см* **проже́чь**.

проже́ктор (-а) *м* floodlight.

прож|е́чь (-гу́, -жёшь *итп*, -гу́т; *pt* -ёг, -гла́, -гло́, *impf* **прожига́ть**) *сов перех* (*огнём, кислотой*) to burn a hole in.

прожива́ни|е (-я) *ср* (*в гостинице*) stay.

прожива́|ть (-ю) *несов от* **прожи́ть** ♦ *неперех* to live.

проживу́ *итп сов см* **прожи́ть**.

прожига́|ть (-ю) *несов от* **проже́чь** ♦ *перех*: **~**

жизнь (*перен*) to live life in the fast lane.

прожи́л|ка (-ки; *gen pl* -ок) *ж* vein; (*дерева*) grain.

прожи́ти|е (-я) *ср*: **на ~** to live on.

прожи́точный *прил*: **~ ми́нимум** minimum living wage.

прожи́|ть (-ву́, -вёшь) *сов неперех* (*пробыть живым*) to live; (*жить*) to spend ♦ *перех* (*деньги, состояние*) to squander.

прожо́рлив|ый (-, -а, -о) *прил* voracious.

про́з|а (-ы) *ж* prose; (*повседневность*) routine.

проза́ик (-а) *м* prosaist.

прозаи́ческ|ий (-ая, -ое, -ие) *прил* (*произведение*) prose *опред*; (*жизнь*) prosaic.

прозва́ни|е (-я) *ср* nickname.

проз|ва́ть (-ову́, -овёшь; *impf* **прозыва́ть**) *сов перех* to nickname.

прозвен|е́ть (*3sg* -и́т, *3pl* -я́т) *сов от* **звене́ть**.

про́зви|ще (-а) *ср* nickname.

прозвуч|а́ть (*3sg* -и́т, *3pl* -а́т) *сов неперех* (*стать слышным*) to resound; (*проявиться*) to come through.

прозева́|ть (-ю) *сов от* **зева́ть**.

прозимова́|ть (-у́ю) *сов от* **зимова́ть**.

прозову́ *итп сов см* **прозва́ть**.

прозонди́р|овать (-ую) *сов от* **зонди́ровать**.

прозорли́в|ый (-, -а, -о) *прил* (*человек, ум*) perceptive; (*политика*) farsighted.

прозра́ч|ный (-ен, -на, -но) *прил* (*стекло, намерение*) transparent; (*воздух, вода*) clear; (*ткань, одежда*) see-through.

прозре́|ть (-ю; *impf* **прозрева́ть**) *сов неперех* to gain one's sight; (*перен*) to see the light.

прозыва́|ть (-ю) *несов от* **прозва́ть**.

прозяба́|ть (-ю) *несов неперех* (*человек*) to vegetate.

проигнори́р|овать (-ую) *сов от* **игнори́ровать**.

проигра́|ть (-ю; *impf* **прои́грывать**) *сов перех* to lose; (*играть*) to play ♦ *неперех* (*no impf*; *играть*) to play.

прои́грыватель (-я) *м* record player.

прои́грыва|ть (-ю) *несов от* **проигра́ть**.

про́игрыш (-а) *м* loss.

произведе́ни|е (-я) *ср* (*литературы, искусства*) work; (*МАТ*) product.

произв|ести́ (-еду́, -едёшь; *pt* -ёл, -ела́, -ело́, *impf* **производи́ть**) *сов перех* (*обыск, операцию*) to carry out; (*впечатление, суматоху*) to create; **производи́ть** (**~** *perf*) **поса́дку** to land; **производи́ть** (**~** *perf*) **кого́-н в офице́ры/в генера́лы** to confer the rank of an officer/a general on sb.

производи́телен *прил см* **производи́тельный**.

производи́тел|ь (-я) *м* producer.

производи́тельность (-и) *ж* productivity.

производи́тельн|ый (-ен, -ьна, -ьно) *прил* (*продуктивный*) productive; **производи́тельные си́лы** (*ЭКОН*) labour (*BRIT*) *или* labor (*US*) force.

произв|одить (-ожу́, -о́дишь) *несов от*
произвести́ ♦ *перех* (*изготовлять*) to
produce.

произво́дный *прил* derivative *опред*;
произво́дное сло́во derivative.

произво́дственный *прил* (*процесс, план*)
production *опред*; ~ **спрос** (*комм*) derived
demand; ~ **несча́стный слу́чай** occupational
accident; **произво́дственные отноше́ния**
industrial relations.

произво́дств|о (-а) *ср* (*товаров*) production,
manufacture; (*отрасль*) industry; (*завод,
фабрика*) factory; (*опыта*) carrying out;
сельскохозя́йственное ~ agricultural yield;
(*отрасль*) agriculture; **промы́шленное** ~
industrial output; (*отрасль*) industry.

произвожу́ *несов см* **производи́ть**.

произво́л (-а) *м* (*самовластие*) arbitrary rule;
оставля́ть (**оста́вить** *perf*) *или* **броса́ть**
(**бро́сить** *perf*) **кого́-н на** ~ **судьбы́** to leave sb
in the hands of fate.

произво́л|ьный (-ен, -ьна, -ьно) *прил*
(*свободный*) free; (*no short form*; СПОРТ)
freestyle *опред*; (*неосновательный*) arbitrary.

произн|ести́ (-есу́, -есёшь; *pt* -ёс, -есла́, -есло́,
impf **произноси́ть**) *сов перех* (*выговорить*) to
pronounce; (*сказать*) to say; **произноси́ть** (~
perf) **речь/тост** to make a speech/toast.

произн|оси́ть (-ошу́, -о́сишь) *несов от*
произнести́.

произноше́ни|е (-я) *ср* pronunciation.

произношу́ *несов см* **произноси́ть**.

произойти́ (*как* **идти́**; *см* **Table 18**; *impf*
происходи́ть) *сов неперех* (*случиться*) to
occur; **происходи́ть** (~ *perf*) **от** +*gen* to come
from.

проиллюстри́р|овать (-ую) *сов от*
иллюстри́ровать.

проинспекти́р|овать (-ую) *сов от*
инспекти́ровать.

проинструкти́р|овать (-ую) *сов от*
инструкти́ровать.

проинтервью́и́р|овать (-ую) *сов от*
интервью́и́ровать.

проинформи́р|овать (-ую) *сов от*
информи́ровать.

про́иск|и (-ов) *мн* machinations *мн*.

проистека́|ть (*3sg* -ет, *3pl* -ют) *несов неперех*:
~ **из/от** +*gen* to result from.

происх|оди́ть (-ожу́, -о́дишь) *несов от*
произойти́ ♦ *неперех*: ~ **от/из** +*gen* to come
from.

происхожде́ни|е (-я) *ср* origin; **по** ~**ю** by birth.

происхожу́ *несов см* **происходи́ть**.

происше́стви|е (-я) *ср* event; **доро́жное** ~ road
accident.

пройдёшь(ся) *итп сов см* **пройти́(сь)**.

пройдо́х|а (-и) *м/ж* (*разг*) cad.

пройду́(сь) *итп сов см* **пройти́(сь)**.

пройму́ *итп сов см* **проня́ть**.

пройти́ (*как* **идти́**; *см* **Table 18**; *impf*
проходи́ть) *сов неперех* to pass; (*расстояние*)
to cover; (*слух, весть итп*) to spread; (*дорога,
канал итп*) to stretch; (*дождь, снег*) to fall;
(*состояться: операция, переговоры итп*) to
go ♦ *перех* (*завершить: практику, службу
итп*) to complete; (*изучить: тему итп*) to do;
проходи́ть (~ *perf*) **в** +*acc* (*в институте итп*)
to get into

▶ **пройти́сь** (*impf* **проха́живаться**) *сов возв* (*по
комнате*) to pace; (*по парку*) to stroll; ~**сь** (*perf*)
на чей-н счёт *или* **по чьему́-н а́дресу** (*разг*) to
give sb a bad write-up.

прок (-а; *gen part* -у) *м* (*разг*) use.

прока́з|а (-ы) *ж* mischief; (*мед*) leprosy.

прока́зник (-а) *м* mischief-maker.

прока́знича|ть (-ю; *perf* **напрока́зничать**)
несов неперех to get up to mischief.

прока́лыва|ть (-ю) *несов от* **проколо́ть**.

прока́пчива|ть (-ю) *несов от* **прокопти́ть**.

прока́пыва|ть (-ю) *несов от* **прокопа́ть**.

прока́т (-а) *м* (*телевизора, палатки итп*) hire;
(*металл*) rolled iron; **брать** (**взять** *perf*) **что-н
на** ~ to hire sth; **выпуска́ть** (**вы́пустить** *perf*)
фильм в ~ to release a film.

прок|ати́ть (-ачу́, -а́тишь; *impf* **прока́тывать**)
сов перех (*разг: раскритиковать*) to pick holes
in ♦ *неперех* (*разг*) to whizz past; **прока́тывать**
(~ *perf*) **кого́-н** (*на машине итп*) to take sb for a
ride

▶ **прокати́ться** (*impf* **прока́тываться**) *сов возв*
(*также перен: гром*) to roll; (*на машине*) to go
for a spin; (*перен: выстрел*) to ring out.

прока́тк|а (-и) *ж* (ТЕХ) rolling.

прока́тный *прил* (*производство, цех*) rolling;
(*пункт, плата*) hire.

прока́тчик (-а) *м* (*в цеху*) worker (*in steel
rolling mill*).

прока́тыва|ть(ся) (-ю(сь)) *несов от*
прокати́ть(ся).

прокачу́(сь) *сов см* **прокати́ть(ся)**.

прокипя́|ти́ть (-чу́, -ти́шь) *сов перех* to boil.

проки́с|нуть (*3sg* -нет, *3pl* -нут, *pt* -, -ла, -ло) *сов
от* **ки́снуть** ♦ (*impf* **прокиса́ть**) *неперех* to go
off.

прокла́д|ка (-ки; *gen pl* -ок) *ж* (*действие: труб*)
laying out; (: *линий передачи*) laying;
(*защитная*) padding.

прокла́дыва|ть (-ю) *несов от* **проложи́ть**.

проклина́|ть (-ю) *несов от* **прокля́сть** ♦ *перех*
to curse.

прокл|я́сть (-яну́, -янёшь; *pt* -ял, -яла́, -яло,
impf **проклина́ть**) *сов перех* to curse.

прокля́ти|е (-я) *ср* curse.

прокля́тый *прил* damned; **рабо́тать** (*impf*) **как
про́клятый** (*разг*) to work like a dog.

прокóл (-а) *м* (*действие: шины*) puncturing; (*: нарыва*) lancing; (*: ушей*) piercing; (*отверстие: в шине*) puncture; (*в ушах*) hole; (*разг: неудача*) flop.

прокол|óть (-олю́, -óлешь; *impf* **прокáлывать**) *сов перех* (*шину*) to puncture; (*уши*) to pierce; (*нарыв*) to lance.

прокомменти́р|овать (-ую) *сов от* **комменти́ровать**.

прокомпости́р|овать (-ую) *сов от* **компости́ровать**.

проконсульти́р|овать(ся) (-ую(сь)) *сов от* **консульти́ровать(ся)**.

прокопá|ть (-ю; *impf* **прокáпывать**) *сов перех* (*канаву, ход*) to dig out.

прокоп|ти́ть (-чу́, -ти́шь) *сов от* **копти́ть** ♦ (*impf* **прокáпчивать**) *перех* (*копотью*) to cover with soot; (*дымом*) to fill with smoke.

прокóрм (-а) *м* feeding.

прок|орми́ть(ся) (-ормлю́(сь), -óрмишь(ся)) *сов от* **корми́ть(ся)**.

прокорректи́р|овать (-ую) *сов от* **корректи́ровать**.

прокрá|сться (-ду́сь, -дёшься; *impf* **прокрáдываться**) *сов возв*: ~ **в** +*acc*/**ми́мо** +*gen*/**чéрез** +*acc* *итп* to creep (*BRIT*) *или* sneak (*US*) in(to)/past/through *итп*.

прокрич|áть (-у́, -и́шь) *сов перех* (*выкрикнуть*) to shout out ♦ *непер* (*ребёнок*) to cry.

прокру|ти́ть (-учу́, -у́тишь; *impf* **прокру́чивать**) *сов перех* (*провернуть*) to turn; (*мясо*) to mince; (*КОМП*) to scroll; (*разг: фильм*) to roll; (*: пластинку, видеоплёнку*) to play.

прокру́чивани|е (-я) *ср* (*см глаг*) turning; mincing; rolling; playing.

прокру́чива|ть (-ю) *несов от* **прокрути́ть**.

прокручу́ *сов см* **прокрути́ть**.

прокуратýр|а (-ы) *ж* (*ЮР*) public prosecution office ♦ *собир* procurators *мн*.

прокур|и́ть (-ю́, -у́ришь; *impf* **проку́ривать**) *сов перех* to fill with smoke.

прокурóр (-а) *м* (*района, города*) procurator; (*на суде*) counsel for the prosecution; **Генерáльный** ~ (*ЮР*) general procurator, attorney general (*US*).

прокурóрск|ий (-ая, -ое, -ие) *прил*: ~ **надзóр** (*ЮР*) procurator's powers *мн*.

прокус|и́ть (-ушу́, -у́сишь; *impf* **проку́сывать**) *сов перех* to bite through.

пролагá|ть (-ю) *несов от* **проложи́ть**.

пролáмыва|ть (-ю) *несов от* **проломи́ть**.

пролá|ять (-ю) *сов от* **лáять**.

пролегá|ть (*3sg* -ет, *3pl* -ют) *несов от* **пролéчь**.

пролеж|áть (-у́, -и́шь) *сов непер* to lie.

пролéз|ть (-у, -ешь; *impf* **пролезáть**) *сов непер* to get through; (*перен: разг: руководство*) to worm one's way in.

пролёт (-а) *м* span; ~ **лéстницы** a flight of stairs.

пролетариáт (-а) *м* proletariat.

пролетáрск|ий (-ая, -ое, -ие) *прил* proletarian.

проле|тéть (-чу́, -ти́шь; *impf* **пролетáть**) *сов непер* to fly; (*человек, поезд*) to fly past; (*лето, отпуск*) to fly by.

прол|éчь (*3sg* -я́жет, *3pl* -я́гут, *impf* **пролегáть**) *сов непер* (*дорога, тропинка*) to stretch.

проли́в (-а) *м* strait(s) (*мн*).

пролива́|ть(ся) (-ю(сь)) *несов от* **проли́ть(ся)**.

проливнóй *прил*: ~ **дождь** pouring rain.

проль|и́ть (-ью́, -ьёшь; *pt* -и́л, -илá, -и́ло, *impf* **пролива́ть**) *сов перех* to spill; **пролива́ть** (~ *perf*) **чью-н кровь** to spill sb's blood

▶ **проли́ться** (*impf* **пролива́ться**) *сов возв* to spill.

пролоѓ (-а) *м* prologue (*BRIT*), prolog (*US*).

прол|ожи́ть (-ожу́, -óжишь; *impf* **проклáдывать**) *сов перех* (*протянуть*) to lay; **проклáдывать** (~ *perf*) **что-н чем-н** to interlay sth with sth; ~ (*perf*) **дорóгу** *или* **путь кому-н/чему-н** to pave the way for sb/sth.

пролóм (-а) *м* (*льда*) cracking; (*место*) crack.

пролома́|ть (-ю; *impf* **пролáмывать**) *сов перех* to break through.

прол|оми́ть (-омлю́, -óмишь; *impf* **пролáмывать**) *сов перех* (*лёд*) to break; (*череп*) to fracture; **пролáмывать** (~ *perf*) **дыру́ в чём-н** to make a hole in sth.

пролью́(сь) *итп сов см* **проли́ть(ся)**.

проля́жет *итп сов см* **пролéчь**.

пром|áзать (-жу, -жешь) *сов от* **мáзать**.

промарширова́|ть (-ю́) *сов непер* to march past.

промáсл|ить (-ю, -ишь; *impf* **промáсливать**) *сов перех* (*растительным маслом*) to oil; (*сливочным маслом*) to grease.

промáтыва|ть (-ю) *несов от* **промота́ть**.

прóмах (-а) *м* miss; (*перен*) blunder; **дава́ть** (**дать** *perf*) ~ to miss the target; (*перен*) to make a blunder.

промахн|у́ться (-у́сь, -ёшься; *impf* **промáхиватся**) *сов возв* to miss; (*перен: разг*) to blunder.

промáчива|ть (-ю) *несов от* **промочи́ть**.

промáшк|а (-ки; *gen pl* -ек) *ж* stroke of bad luck; (*упущение*) blunder.

промедлéни|е (-я) *ср* delay.

промéдл|ить (-ю, -ишь) *сов непер*: ~ **с** +*instr* to delay.

промежу́т|ок (-ка) *м* (*пространство*) gap; (*перерыв*) break.

промежу́точный *прил* (*участок, период*) intervening; (*стадия, положение*) intermediate.

промелькн|у́ть (-у́, -ёшь) *сов непер* to flash past; ~ (*perf*) **в** +*prp* (*в голове, в памяти*) to flash through.

променя́|ть (-ю; *impf* **промéнивать**) *сов перех*: ~ **когó-н/что-н на** +*acc* to prefer sb/sth to.

промёрз|нуть (-у, -ешь; *impf* **промерзáть**) *сов непер* (*комната, дом*) to be chilled through; (*человек*) to freeze.

промет|áть (-ю) *сов от* **метáть**.

промо́зглый *прил* cold and wet.

промока́тельный *прил*: **~ая бума́га** blotting paper.

промока́|ть (-ю) *несов от* **промо́кнуть ♦** *неперех* to let water through.

промока́ш|ка (-ки; *gen pl* -ек) *ж* (*разг*) blotting paper.

промо́кн|уть (-у, -ешь; *impf* **промока́ть**) *сов неперех* (*одежда, ноги*) to get soaked.

промокн|у́ть (-у́, -ёшь; *impf* **промока́ть**) *сов перех* to blot.

промо́лв|ить (-лю, -ишь) *сов перех* to utter.

промолч|а́ть (-у́, -и́шь) *сов неперех* to say nothing.

промота́|ть (-ю; *impf* **прома́тывать**) *сов перех* (*разг*) to blow.

пром|очи́ть (-очу́, -о́чишь; *impf* **прома́чивать**) *сов перех* to get wet.

промо́ю *итп сов см* **промы́ть**.

промтова́рный *прил*: **~ магази́н** *shop selling manufactured goods*.

промтова́р|ы (-ов) *мн* (= **промы́шленные това́ры**) manufactured goods *мн*.

промурлы́ка|ть (-ю) *сов от* **мурлы́кать**.

промч|а́ться (-у́сь, -и́шься) *сов возв* (*год, лето, жизнь*) to fly by; **~** (*perf*) **ми́мо** +*gen*/ **че́рез** +*acc* (*поезд, человек*) to fly past/through.

промыва́ни|е (-я) *ср* (*желудка*) pumping; (*гла́за, раны*) bathing.

промыва́|ть (-ю) *несов от* **промы́ть**.

про́мыс|ел (-ла) *м* (*ремесло*) trade; **охо́тничий ~** hunting; **пушно́й ~** trapping; **ры́бный ~** fishing; *см также* **про́мыслы**.

промысло́вый *прил* trading; (*рыба, зверь*) marketable.

про́мысл|ы (-ов) *мн* (*нефтяные*) fields *мн*; (*горные, соляные*) mines *мн*.

пром|ы́ть (-о́ю, -о́ешь; *impf* **промыва́ть**) *сов перех* (*желудок*) to pump; (*рану, глаз*) to bathe; (*золотой песок*) to pan out.

промыч|а́ть (-у́, -и́шь) *сов от* **мыча́ть**.

промы́шленник (-а) *м* industrialist.

промы́шленност|ь (-и) *ж* industry; **лёгкая/тяжёлая ~** light/heavy industry.

промы́шленный *прил* industrial.

промышля́|ть (-ю) *несов неперех*: **~ охо́той** to hunt; **~** (*impf*) **ры́бой** to fish; **~** (*impf*) **перево́дами** (*разг*) to earn a living from translation.

промя́мл|ить (-ю, -ишь) *сов от* **мя́млить**.

промя́ука|ть (-ю) *сов от* **мяу́кать**.

пронаблюда́|ть (-ю) *сов от* **наблюда́ть**.

прон|ести́ (-есу́, -есёшь; *pt* -ёс, -есла́, -есло́, *impf* **проноси́ть**) *сов перех* to carry; (*тайком*) to sneak in; (*сохранить*) to preserve **♦** *безл* (*перен*) to blow over

▶ **пронести́сь** (*impf* **проноси́ться**) *сов возв* (*машина, пуля, бегун*) to shoot by; (*лето, годы*)

итп) to fly by; (*буря, тайфун итп*) to whirl past.

пронжу́ *сов см* **пронзи́ть**.

пронза́|ть (-ю) *несов от* **пронзи́ть**.

пронзи́тельный (-ен, -ьна, -ьно) *прил* piercing; (*свет, цвет*) glaring.

прон|зи́ть (-жу́, -зи́шь; *impf* **пронза́ть**) *сов перех* (*также перен*) to pierce.

прон|иза́ть (-ижу́, -и́жешь; *impf* **прони́зывать**) *сов перех* to penetrate (into).

прони́к(ся) *итп сов см* **прони́кнуть(ся)**.

проника́|ть(ся) (-ю(сь)) *несов от* **прони́кнуть(ся)**.

проникнове́нный (-ен, -на, -но) *прил* (*слова*) heartfelt; (*голос*) emotional.

прони́кнут|ый (-, -а, -о) *прил* (+*instr*) full of.

прони́к|нуть (-ну, -нешь; *pt* -, -ла, -ло, *impf* **проника́ть**) *сов перех*: **~ в** +*acc* to penetrate (into); (*залечь*) to break into; (*распространиться*) to spread into; (*понять*) to understand

▶ **прони́кнуться** (*impf* **проника́ться**) *сов возв* (+*instr*) to be filled with.

пронима́|ть (-ю) *несов от* **проня́ть**.

проница́тельный (-ен, -ьна, -ьно) *прил* (*человек, ум*) shrewd; (*взгляд*) penetrating.

проница́|ть (-ю) *несов неперех*: **~ в** +*acc* (*свет*) to penetrate (into).

прон|оси́ть(ся) (-ошу́(сь), -о́сишь(ся)) *несов от* **пронести́(сь)**.

пронумер|ова́ть (-у́ю) *сов от* **нумерова́ть**.

проны́р|а (-ы) *ж* (*разг*) dodgy character.

проны́рливый (-, -а, -о) *прил* (*разг*) dodgy.

прон|я́ть (-йму́, -ймёшь; *impf* **пронима́ть**) *сов перех* (*разг: подлеж: холод*) to seize; (: *музыка*) to move.

проо́браз (-а) *м* (*образец*) model; (*прототип*) prototype.

прооперир|ова́ть (-ую) *сов от* **опери́ровать**.

пропага́нд|а (-ы) *ж* propaganda; (*спорта*) promotion.

пропаганди́р|овать (-ую) *несов перех* (*политическое учение*) to spread propaganda about; (*знаний, спорт*) to promote.

пропаганди́ст (-а) *м* propagandist.

пропаганди́стск|ий (-ая, -ое, -ие) *прил* (*шумиха, кампания*) propagandist *опред*.

пропада́|ть (-ю) *несов от* **пропа́сть ♦** *неперех* (*разг*) to stay for a long time; **он вечера́ми ~ет на рабо́те** he spends all his evenings at work.

про́падом *нареч*: **пропади́ ~** (*разг*) to hell with it.

пропаду́ *итп сов см* **пропа́сть**.

пропа́ж|а (-и) *ж* (*денег, документов*) loss; (*то, что пропало*) lost object.

пропа́лыва|ть (-ю) *несов от* **прополо́ть**.

про́пас|ть (-и) *ж* precipice; (*перен: во взглядах*) abyss; (*no pl*; *разг*) masses *мн*.

проп|а́сть (-аду́, -адёшь; *impf* **пропада́ть**) *сов неперех* to disappear; (*деньги, письмо*) to go missing; (*аппетит, голос, слух*) to go; (*усилия, билет в театр*) to be wasted; (*погибнуть*) to die; **пропада́ть** (~ *perf*) **бе́з вести** (*человек*) to go missing.

проп|аха́ть (-ашу́, -а́шешь; *impf* **пропа́хивать**) *сов перех* to plough (*BRIT*), plow (*US*).

пропа́х|нуть (-ну, -нешь; *pt* -, -ла, -ло) *сов неперех* (+*instr*) to become filled with the smell of.

пропашу́ *итп сов см* **пропаха́ть**.

пропа́щ|ий (-ая, -ее, -ие) *прил* (*разг: безнадёжный*) hopeless; (*долго не приходивший*) long-lost; **э́ти де́ньги – ~ие** (*разг*) that money is lost for good.

пропе́й(те) *сов см* **пропи́ть**.

пропё́к(ся) *итп сов см* **пропе́чь(ся)**.

пропека́|ть(ся) (-ю(сь)) *несов от* **пропе́чь(ся)**.

пропеку́(сь) *сов см* **пропе́чь(ся)**.

пропе́ллер (-а) *м* (*АВИА*) propeller.

проп|е́ть (-ою́, -оёшь) *сов от* **петь** ♦ *перех* (*петь*) to sing.

проп|е́чь (-еку́, -ечёшь *итп*, -еку́т; *pt* -ёк, -екла́, -екло́, *impf* **пропека́ть**) *сов перех* to bake

▶ **пропе́чься** (*impf* **пропека́ться**) *сов возв* to be well-baked.

пропива́|ть (-ю) *несов от* **пропи́ть**.

проп|или́ть (-илю́, -и́лишь; *impf* **пропи́ливать**) *сов перех* to saw through.

проп|иса́ть (-ишу́, -и́шешь; *impf* **пропи́сывать**) *сов перех* (*человека*) to register; (*лекарство*) to prescribe; (*статью, письмо*) to write

▶ **прописа́ться** *сов возв* to register.

пропи́с|ка (-ки; *gen pl* -ок) *ж* (*в городе, в доме*) registration.

прописн|о́й *прил* (*общеизвестный*) commonplace; **~а́я и́стина** truism; **прописна́я бу́ква** capital letter.

пропи́сыва|ть (-ю) *несов от* **прописа́ть**.

про́пис|ь (-и) *ж* (*ПРОСВЕЩ*) writing samples *мн*.

про́писью *нареч* in full; **писа́ть (написа́ть** *perf***) су́мму ~** to write out a sum *или* amount in words.

пропита́ни|е (-я) *ср* food.

пропита́|ть (-ю; *impf* **пропи́тывать**) *сов перех* (*смочить*) to soak; (*насытить: бумагу*) to saturate; (*: комнату, воздух*) to fill

▶ **пропита́ться** (*impf* **пропи́тываться**) *сов возв*: **~ся чем-н** (*водой*) to be soaked in sth; (*запахом: воздух*) to be filled with sth; (*: одежда*) to be saturated with sth.

пропи́т|ка (-ки; *gen pl* -ок) *ж* (*ткани, дерева*) soaking; (*водонепроницаемая*) impregnation; (*ромовая*) flavouring.

пропи́тыва|ть(ся) (-ю(сь)) *несов от* **пропита́ть(ся)**.

проп|и́ть (-ью́, -ьёшь; *pt* -и́л, -ила́, -и́ло, *imper* **пропе́й(те)**, *impf* **пропива́ть**) *сов перех* (*деньги, состояние*) to squander on drink; (*талант, карьеру*) to ruin (*through drinking*); (*no impf, пить*) to drink.

пропихн|у́ть (-у́, -ёшь) *сов перех* (*разг: в дверь итп*) to shove; (*: в университет итп*) to push.

пропишу́(сь) *итп сов см* **прописа́ть(ся)**.

проплава́|ть (-ю) *сов неперех* (*человек*) to swim; (*судно*) to sail.

пропла́|кать (-чу, -чешь) *сов неперех* to cry; ~ (*perf*) **все глаза́** to cry one's eyes out.

проплута́|ть (-ю) *сов неперех* to wander.

проплы́|ть (-ву́, -вёшь; *impf* **проплыва́ть**) *сов неперех* (*человек*) to swim; (*: миновать*) to swim past; (*судно*) to sail; (*: миновать*) to sail past; (*перен: птица, облака*) to sail by *или* past; (*: воспоминания, мысли итп*) to flash past.

пропове́дник (-а) *м* (*РЕЛ*) preacher; (*перен: убеждений, теории*) advocate.

пропове́дниц|а (-ы) *ж см* **пропове́дник**.

пропове́д|овать (-ую) *несов перех* (*РЕЛ*) to preach; (*идею*) to advocate.

про́повед|ь (-и) *ж* (*РЕЛ*) preaching; (*идей*) endorsement; (*речь*) sermon.

пропо́йц|а (-ы) *м* (*разг*) soak.

прополаскива|ть (-ю) *несов от* **прополоска́ть**.

прополз|ти́ (-у́, -ёшь; *pt* -, -ла́, -ло́) *сов неперех*: ~ **по** +*dat*/**в** +*acc итп* (*насекомое, человек*) to crawl along/in(to) *итп*; (*змея*) to slither along/in(to) *итп*.

пропо́лис (-а) *м* propolis.

пропо́л|ка (-ки; *gen pl* -ок) *ж* weeding.

прополоска́|ть (-ю; *impf* **прополаскивать** *или* **полоска́ть**) *сов перех* to rinse (out); **прополаскивать** *или* **полоска́ть** (~ *perf*) **го́рло** to gargle.

проп|оло́ть (-олю́, -о́лешь; *impf* **пропа́лывать** *или* **поло́ть**) *сов перех* (*грядку итп*) to weed.

пропорциона́лен *прил см* **пропорциона́льный**.

пропорциона́льность (-и) *ж* proportion.

пропорциона́л|ьный (-ен, -ьна, -ьно) *прил* (*фигура, тело*) well-proportioned; (*развитие, распределение*) proportional; **пропорциона́льное представи́тельство** proportional representation.

пропо́рци|я (-и) *ж* proportion.

пропот|е́ть (-ю; *impf* **пропотева́ть**) *сов неперех* to sweat profusely; (*пропитаться потом*) to be soaked with sweat.

пропою́ *итп сов см* **пропе́ть**.

про́пуск (-а) *м* (*действие: в зал, через границу итп*) admission; (*: в школе*) non-attendance; (*в тексте, в изложении*) gap; (*неявка: на работу, в школу*) absence; (*nom pl* -а́; *документ*) pass.

пропуска́|ть (-ю) *несов от* **пропусти́ть** ♦ *перех* (*чернила, свет итп*) to let through; (*воду, холод*) to let in.

проп|усти́ть (-ущу́, -у́стишь; *impf* **пропуска́ть**) *сов перех* to miss; (*дать дорогу, обслужить*) to admit; (*разрешить*) to allow; (*заставить пройти*) to put through; (*выпустить*) to miss out; **пропуска́ть** (~ *perf*) **кого́-н че́рез грани́цу** to let sb across the border; **пропуска́ть** (~ *perf*)

кого́-н вперёд to let sb go ahead.
пропылесо́с|ить (-ю, -ишь) *сов от*
пылесо́сить.
пропыл|и́ться (-ю́сь, -и́шься) *сов возв* to be
full of dust.
пропью́ *итп сов см* **пропи́ть.**
прора́б (-а) *м* (= *производи́тель рабо́т*)
foreman (*мн* foremen).
прорабо́та|ть (-ю; *impf* **прораба́тывать**) *сов*
неперех to work ♦ *перех* (*уче́бник, статью́,*
уро́к) to study in detail; (*разг: критикова́ть*) to
rip into.
прор|асти́ (*3sg* -асте́т, *3pl* -асту́т, *pt* -о́с, -осла́,
-осло́, *impf* **прораста́ть**) *сов непepex* (*семена́*)
to germinate; (*трава́*) to sprout.
про́рв|а (-ы) *ж* (*разг: о́чень мно́го*) heaps *мн*,
masses *мн*; (: *о челове́ке*) pig.
прорв|а́ть (-у́, -ёшь; *pt* -а́л, -ала́, -а́ло, *impf*
прорыва́ть) *сов перех* (*оде́жду, су́мку*) to tear;
(*плоти́ну*) to burst; (*оборо́ну, фронт*) to break
through ♦ *безл* (+*acc*; *перен*) to explode;
наконе́ц его́ ~а́ло (*перен*) he finally exploded
▸ **прорва́ться** (*impf* **прорыва́ться**) *сов возв*
(*карма́н, су́мка*) to tear; (*плоти́на, ша́рик*) to
burst; (*гнев, раздраже́ние*) to erupt; (*го́ре*) to
break out; **прорыва́ться** (~**ся** *perf*) **в** +*acc* to
burst in(to).
прореаги́р|овать (-ую) *сов от* **реаги́ровать.**
проре|ди́ть (-жу́, -ди́шь; *impf* **проре́живать**)
сов (*гря́дки, всхо́ды*) to thin out.
проре́|зать (-жу, -жешь) *сов от* **ре́зать** ♦ (*impf*
проре́зывать) *перех* to cut through; (*ре́зать:*
мя́со, ры́бу итп) to cut; (: *о́вощи, фру́кты итп*)
to chop
▸ **проре́заться** *сов от* **ре́заться** ♦ (*impf*
проре́зываться) *возв* (*появи́ться: зу́бы*) to
come through; (: *ли́стья*) to come out.
прорези́н|ить (-ю, -ишь; *impf* **прорези́нивать**)
сов перех to cover with rubber.
прорезн|о́й *прил:* ~ **карма́н** slit pocket; ~**а́я**
пе́тля buttonhole.
проре́зыва|ть(ся) (-ю(сь)) *несов от*
проре́зать(ся).
про́рез|ь (-и) *ж* (*на тка́ни*) slit; (*на прице́ле*
ору́дия) aperture.
проре́ктор (-а) *м* vice-principal.
прорепети́р|овать (-ую) *сов от*
репети́ровать.
прорефери́р|овать (-ую) *сов от*
рефери́ровать.
проре́х|а (-и) *ж* (*дыра́*) tear; (*разг: недоста́ток*)
shortcoming.
прорецензи́р|овать (-ую) *сов от*
рецензи́ровать.
проржа́ве|ть (*3sg* -ет, *3pl* -ют) *сов непepex* to
rust through.
прорица́ни|е (-я) *ср* prophecy.
прорица́тел|ь (-я) *м* prophet.

прорица́тельниц|а (-ы) *ж см* **прорица́тель.**
прорица́|ть (-ю) *несов перех* to prophesy.
проро́к (-а) *м* (*РЕЛ, перен*) prophet.
прор|они́ть (-оню́, -о́нишь) *сов перех*
(*сказа́ть*) to utter.
проро́с *итп сов см* **прорасти́.**
проро́ческ|ий (-ая, -ое, -ие) *прил* (*сон, слова́,*
дар) prophetic.
проро́честв|о (-а) *ср* prophecy.
проро́ч|ить (-у, -ишь; *perf* **напроро́чить**) *несов*
перех to predict.
проро́ю *итп сов см* **проры́ть.**
прор|уби́ть (-ублю́, -у́бишь; *impf* **проруба́ть**)
сов перех (*сте́ну, лёд, го́ру*) to make a hole in;
проруба́ть (~ *perf*) **про́секу в лесу́** to make a
clearing in a forest.
про́руб|ь (-и) *ж* ice-hole.
проры́в (-а) *м* (*фро́нта*) break-through;
(*плоти́ны*) bursting; (*про́рванное ме́сто*)
breach.
прорыва́|ть(ся) (-ю(сь)) *несов от*
прорва́ть(ся).
прор|ы́ть (-о́ю, -о́ешь; *impf* **прорыва́ть**) *сов*
перех (*прокопа́ть*) to dig.
прос|ади́ть (-ажу́, -а́дишь; *impf* **проса́живать**)
сов перех (*разг: истра́тить*) to blow.
проса́чива|ться (*3sg* -ется, *3pl* -ются) *несов*
от **просочи́ться.**
просверл|и́ть (-ю́, -и́шь; *impf* **просверливать**
или **сверли́ть**) *сов перех* to bore, drill.
просве́т (-а) *м* (*в ту́чах, в облака́х*) break; (*в*
забо́ре, в заве́се) crack; (*перен: в тяжёлой*
ситуа́ции) light at the end of the tunnel.
просвети́тел|ь (-я) *м person who enlightens*
others about progressive ideas.
просвети́тельниц|а (-ы) *ж см* **просвети́тель.**
просве|ти́тельный *прил* enlightening.
просве|ти́ть (-щу́, -ти́шь; *impf* **просвеща́ть**)
сов перех to enlighten; (-чу́, -ти́шь; *impf*
просве́чивать; *лёгкие*) to x-ray
▸ **просве|ти́ться** ♦ (-щу́сь, -ти́шься; *impf*
просвеща́ться) *сов возв* to enlighten o.s.
просветле́ни|е (-я) *ср* (*я́сность*) lucidity.
просветлённый *прил* lucid.
просветле́|ть (-ю) *сов от* **светле́ть.**
просве́чива|ть (-ю) *несов от* **просвети́ть** ♦
непepex (*со́лнце*) to shine through; (*не́бо*) to be
visible through; (*ткань*) to let light through.
просвечу́ *сов см* **просвети́ть.**
просвеща́|ть(ся) (-ю(сь)) *несов от*
просвети́ть(ся).
просвеще́ни|е (-я) *ср* education;
Министе́рство ~**я** ≈ Department of Education.
просвещённый *прил* (-, -на, -но) *прил* educated.
просвещу́(сь) *сов см* **просвети́ть(ся).**
просви́р|а (-ы) *ж* (*РЕЛ*) communion bread, Host.
просвисте́|ть (-щу́, -сти́шь) *сов от* **свисте́ть** ♦

(*impf* **просви́стывать**) *перех* (*мотив, песню*) to whistle (through) ♦ *неперех* (*пуля, снаряд*) to whistle past.

про́седь (-и) *ж* grey (*BRIT*) или gray (*US*) streak.

просе́ивани|е (-я) *ср* (*муки, песка*) sifting.

просе́ива|ть (-ю) *несов от* **просе́ять**.

про́сек|а (-и) *ж* (*в лесу*) clearing.

просёл|ок (-ка) *м* dirt-track.

просёлочн|ый *прил*: ~**ая доро́га** dirt-track.

просе́|ять (-ю; *impf* **просе́ивать**) *сов перех* (*муку, песок*) to sift.

просигнализи́р|овать (-ую) *сов от* **сигнализи́ровать**.

просигна́л|ить (-ю, -ишь) *сов от* **сигна́лить**.

просиде́ть (-жу́, -ди́шь; *impf* **проси́живать**) *сов неперех* (*сидеть*) to sit; (*пробыть*) to stay.

про|си́ть (-шу́, -сишь; *perf* **попроси́ть**) *несов перех* to ask; (*приглашать*) to invite; ~**шу́ Вас!** if you please!; ~ (**попроси́ть** *perf*) **кого́-н о чём-н**/+*infin* to ask sb for sth/to do; ~ (**попроси́ть** *perf*) **кого́-н за кого́-н** to ask sb a favour (*BRIT*) или favor (*US*) on behalf of sb

▶ **проси́ться** (*perf* **попроси́ться**) *несов возв* (*просить разрешения*) to ask permission; **сло́во так и** ~**ся** (*impf*) **языка́** to have a word on the tip of one's tongue; **её лицо́ про́сится на карти́ну** her face was crying out to be painted.

просия́|ть (-ю) *сов неперех* (*солнце*) to begin to shine; (*радуга*) to appear; (*перен: человек*) to beam; (: *лицо*) to light up.

проск|ака́ть (-ачу́, -а́чешь) *сов неперех* (*человек*) to hop; ~ (*perf*) **че́рез/сквозь** +*acc* (*лошадь*) to gallop across/through; (*олень, заяц*) to bound across или by/through.

проска́кива|ть (-ю) *несов от* **проскочи́ть**.

проска́льзыва|ть (-ю) *несов от* **проскользну́ть**.

проскачу́ *итп сов см* **проскака́ть**.

просквоз|и́ть (*3sg* -и́т, *3pl* -я́т) *сов безл* (+*acc*): **меня́** ~**и́ло** I caught a chill.

проскло́ня́|ть (-ю) *сов от* **склоня́ть**.

проскользн|у́ть (-у́, -ёшь; *impf* **проска́льзывать**) *сов неперех* (*монета*) to slide in; (*человек*) to slip in; (*перен: сомнение, страх*) to creep in.

проск|очи́ть (-очу́, -о́чишь; *impf* **проска́кивать**) *сов неперех* (*проскользнуть*) to slide in; (*пройти, проехать*): ~ **в** +*acc*/**ми́мо** +*gen итп* to race in(to)/past *итп*; (*проникнуть*): ~ **в/че́рез** +*acc* to break in(to)/through.

проску́ча|ть (-ю) *сов неперех* to be bored.

просла́б|ить (*3sg* -ит, *3pl* -ят) *сов от* **сла́бить**.

просла́в|ить (-лю, -ишь; *impf* **прославля́ть**) *сов перех* (*сделать известным*) to make famous; (*impf* **прославля́ть** или **сла́вить**; *восхвалить*) to glorify

▶ **просла́виться** (*impf* **прославля́ться**) *сов возв* (*актёр, писатель*) to become famous; (*перен: разг: преступник*) to become notorious.

просла́вленный *прил* renowned.

просла́влю(сь) *сов см* **просла́вить(ся)**.

прославля́ть(ся) (-ю(сь)) *несов от* **просла́вить(ся)**.

проследи́ть (-жу́, -ди́шь; *impf* **просле́живать**) *сов перех* (*следить глазами*) to follow; (*исследовать*) to trace ♦ *неперех*: ~ **за** +*instr* to follow; (*за выполнением приказа, за чьим-н поведением*) to monitor.

просле́д|овать (-ую) *сов неперех*: ~ (**ми́мо** +*gen*/**сквозь** +*acc*) to pass slowly (by/through).

просле́жива|ть (-ю) *несов от* **проследи́ть**.

прослежу́ *сов см* **проследи́ть**.

просле|зи́ться (-жу́сь, -зи́шься) *сов возв* to cry.

просло́йка (-йки; *gen pl* -ек) *ж* (*слой*) layer; (*в горной породе*) stratum (*мн* strata).

прослу|жи́ть (-ужу́, -у́жишь) *сов неперех* to serve; (*туфли, пальто итп*) to last.

прослу́ша|ть (-ю; *impf* **прослу́шивать**) *сов перех* to listen to; (*курс, лекции*) to attend; (*ответ, объяснение итп*) to miss; (*no impf*; *радио, музыку*) to listen to.

прослу́шива|ть (-ю) *несов от* **прослу́шать** ♦ *перех*: **их кварти́ру** ~**ют** their flat (*BRIT*) или apartment (*US*) is bugged.

просл|ы́ть (-ыву́, -ывёшь) *сов неперех* (+*instr*) to acquire a reputation as.

прослы́ша|ть (-у, -ишь) *сов неперех* (*разг*): ~ **о** +*prp* to hear about.

просма́лива|ть (-ю) *несов от* **просмоли́ть**.

просма́трива|ть (-ю) *несов от* **просмотре́ть**.

▶ **просма́триваться** *несов возв* to be visible.

просмол|и́ть (-ю́, -и́шь; *impf* **просма́ливать**) *сов перех* to coat with tar.

просмо́тр (-а) *м* (*фильма, спектакля*) viewing; (*документов*) inspection; (*ошибка*) blunder.

просм|отре́ть (-отрю́, -о́тришь; *impf* **просма́тривать**) *сов перех* (*ознакомиться: читая*) to look through; (: *смотря*) to view; (*пропустить*) to overlook.

просн|у́ться (-у́сь, -ёшься; *impf* **просыпа́ться**) *сов возв* to wake up; (*перен: любовь, страх итп*) to be awakened.

про́с|о (-а) *ср* millet.

просо́выва|ть(ся) (-ю(сь)) *несов от* **просу́нуть(ся)**.

просо́ди|я (-и) *ж* prosody.

просол|и́ть (-олю́, -о́лишь; *impf* **проса́ливать**) *сов перех* to salt.

просо́х|нуть (-ну, -нешь; *pt* -, -ла, -ло, *impf* **просыха́ть**) *сов неперех* to dry out.

проса́чива|ться (*3sg* -ится, *3pl* -а́тся, *impf* **проса́чиваться**) *сов возв* (*также перен*) to filter through.

просп|а́ть (-лю́, -и́шь; *pt* -а́л, -ала́, -а́ло) *сов неперех* (*спать*) to sleep; (*impf* **просыпа́ть**; *встать поздно*) to oversleep ♦ *перех* (*разг: остановку*) to sleep through.

проспе́кт (-а) *м* avenue; (*план*) draft; (*издание*) brochure.

проспли́ю *сов см* **проспа́ть**.

проспо́р|ить (-ю, -ишь; *impf* **проспо́ривать**) *сов перех* to lose in a bet ♦ *неперех* (*no impf*; *спорить*) to argue.

проспряга́|ть (-ю) *сов от* **спряга́ть**.

просро́чек *сущ см* **просро́чка**.

просро́ч|ить (-у, -ишь; *impf* **просро́чивать**) *сов перех* (*платёж*) to be late with; (*паспорт, билет*) to let expire.

просро́ч|ка (-ки; *gen pl* -ек) *ж* (*платежа*) expiry of time limit; (*паспорта, билета*) expiry.

проста́в|ить (-лю, -ишь; *impf* **проставля́ть**) *сов перех* to fill in.

проста́ива|ть (-ю) *несов от* **простоя́ть**.

проста́к (-а́) *м* simpleton.

простега́|ть (-ю) *сов от* **стега́ть**.

просте́н|ок (-ка) *м section of wall between windows or doors.*

простере́ть(ся) (*pt* -ёр(ся), -ёрла(сь), -ёрло(сь)) *сов от* **простира́ть(ся)**.

просте́цк|ий (-ая, -ое, -ие) *прил* (*разг*) informal.

простира́|ть (-ю; *perf* **простере́ть**) *несов перех* (*планы, замыслы*) to raise; (*протягивать*): ~ **ру́ки** to hold out one's hands ♦ (*impf* **прости́рывать**) *сов перех* (*стирать тщательно*) to wash thoroughly ♦ *неперех* (*стирать*) to wash

▶ **простира́ться** (*perf* **простере́ться**) *несов возв* to extend.

простирн|у́ть (-у́, -ёшь) *сов перех* (*разг*): ~ **что-н** to give sth a quick wash.

прости́рыва|ть (-ю) *несов от* **простира́ть**.

прости́тел|ьный (-ен, -ьна, -ьно) *прил* excusable, forgivable.

проститу́т|ка (-ки; *gen pl* -ок) *ж* prostitute.

проститу́ци|я (-и) *ж* prostitution.

прости́ть (**прощу́**, **прости́шь**; *impf* **проща́ть**) *сов перех* (*врага, ошибку итп*) to forgive; **проща́ть** (~ *perf*) **что-н кому́-н** to excuse *или* forgive sb (for) sth; **проща́ть** (~ *perf*) **долг кому́-н** to cancel sb's debt; **прости́те меня́, я был о́чень груб** forgive me, I was very rude; **прости́те, как пройти́ на ста́нцию?** excuse me, how do I get to the station?; **нет (уж) прости́те, я не согла́сен** I'm sorry, but I cannot agree

▶ **прости́ться** (*impf* **проща́ться**) *сов возв*: ~**ся с** +*instr* to say goodbye to; (*покинуть*) to leave.

про́сто *нареч* (*делать*) easily; (*интерпретировать*) simply ♦ *част* just; **я зашёл** ~ **повида́ться** I just popped in to see you; **всё э́то** ~ **недоразуме́ние** all this is simply a misunderstanding; ~ **(так)** for no particular reason; ~-**на́просто** (*разг*) just.

простова́тый (-, -а, -о) *прил* simple-minded.

простоволо́сый *прил* (*разг*) bareheaded.

простоду́шен *прил см* **простоду́шный**.

простоду́ши|е (-я) *ср* ingenuousness.

простоду́ш|ный (-ен, -на, -но) *прил* ingenuous.

прост|о́й (-, -а́, -о) *прил* simple;

(*незамысловатый, грубый*) plain; (*не трудный*) easy, simple; (*прямой и нецеремонный*) unaffected; (*no short form*; *обыкновенный*) ordinary ♦ (-о́я) *м* downtime, idle time; (*рабочих*) stoppage; **маши́на на** ~**о́е** the machine is standing idle; **пла́та за** ~ **су́дна** demurrage; ~**им гла́зом** with the naked eye; **про́ще** ~**о́го** (*разг*) as easy as pie; **просто́е письмо́** ordinary letter; **просто́й каранда́ш** lead pencil; **просты́е чулки́** cotton stockings.

простоква́ш|а (-и) *ж* soured milk (*type of yoghurt*).

простонаро́дный *прил* of the common people.

простон|а́ть (-ону́, -о́нешь) *сов* (*не*)*перех* to groan.

просто́р (-а) *м* expanse; (*свобода*) scope.

просто́рен *прил см* **просто́рный**.

просторе́чи|е (-я) *ср* common speech; **э́то** ~ it's a colloquial expression.

просторе́чный *прил* common.

просто́р|ный (-ен, -на, -но) *прил* roomy.

простосерде́ч|ный (-ен, -на, -но) *прил* open-hearted.

простот|а́ (-ы́) *ж* simplicity; (*задачи*) easiness, simplicity; (*одежды, рисунка*) plainness; (*характера*) unaffectedness; **по** ~**е́ душе́вной** *или* **серде́чной** in all innocence.

простофи́л|я (-и) *м/ж* dimwit.

просто|я́ть (-ю́, -и́шь; *impf* **проста́ивать**) *сов неперех* to stand; (*бездействуя*) to stand idle; (*no impf*; *просуществовать*) to stand.

простра́н|ный (-ен, -на, -но) *прил* (*подробный*) verbose.

простра́нственный *прил* spatial.

простра́нств|о (-а) *ср* (*также* АСТРОНОМИЯ) space; (*территория*) expanse.

простре́л (-а) *м* backache.

простре́лива|ть (-ю) *несов от* **прострели́ть** ♦ *перех* (*обстреливать*) to cover (*with artillery fire*).

прострел|и́ть (-елю́, -е́лишь; *impf* **простре́ливать**) *сов перех* to shoot through.

простро́ч|ить (-очу́, -о́чишь) *сов от* **строчи́ть**.

просту́д|а (-ы) *ж* (МЕД) cold.

простуд|и́ть (-ужу́, -у́дишь; *impf* **простужа́ть**) *сов перех*: ~ **кого́-н** to give a cold to sb; **простужа́ть** (~ *perf*) **у́ши/го́рло** to get a cold in one's ears/throat

▶ **простуди́ться** (*impf* **простужа́ться**) *сов возв* to catch a cold.

просту́дный *прил* cold-related.

простужа́|ть(ся) (-ю(сь)) *несов от* **простуди́ть(ся)**.

просту́жен|ный (-, -а, -о) *прил*: **ребёнок просту́жен** the child has got a cold; **у Вас** ~ **го́лос** you sound as if you've got a cold.

простужу́(сь) *сов см* **простуди́ть(ся)**.

прост|упи́ть (*3sg* -у́пит, *3pl* -у́пят, *impf*

проступа́ть) *сов неперех* (*пот, пятна*) to come through; (*очертания*) to appear.

просту́п|ок (-ка) *м* misconduct; (*ЮР*) misdemeanour (*BRIT*), misdemeanor (*US*).

простыва́|ть (-ю) *несов от* **просты́ть**.

просты́|ну *итп сов см* **просты́ть**.

простыня́ (-и́; *nom pl* **про́стыни**, *gen pl* **просты́нь**, *dat pl* -**я́м**) *ж* sheet.

просты́|ть (-ну, -нешь; *impf* простыва́ть) *сов неперех* (*разг*) to catch a cold; **его́ и след** ~**л** (*разг*) he disappeared without a trace.

просу́н|уть (-у, -ешь; *impf* просо́вывать) *сов перех*: ~ **сквозь/в** +*acc итп* to push through/in *to итп*

▸ **просу́нуться** (*impf* просо́вываться) *сов возв* (*разг*): **в дверь/в окно́** ~**улась голова́** a head came round the door/appeared at the window.

просу́ши|ть (-ушу́, -у́шишь; *impf* просу́шивать) *сов перех* to dry.

просуществ|ова́ть (-у́ю) *сов неперех* to exist.

просфор|а́ (-ы́) *ж* (*РЕЛ*) communion bread, Host.

просчёт (-а) *м* (*счёт*) counting; (*ошибка: в подсчёте*) error; (: *в действиях*) miscalculation.

просчита́|ть (-ю; *impf* просчи́тывать) *сов перех* (*считать*) to count; (*ошибиться*) to miscount

▸ **просчита́ться** (*impf* просчи́тываться) *сов возв* (*при счёте*) to miscount; (*в планах, в предположениях*) to miscalculate; **мы** ~**лись на сто рубле́й** we are out by one hundred roubles.

просы́п|ать (-лю, -лешь; *impf* просыпа́ть) *сов перех* to spill.

▸ **просы́паться** (*impf* просыпа́ться) *сов возв* to spill.

просыпа́|ть (-ю) *несов от* **проспа́ть**, **просы́пать**.

▸ **просыпа́ться** *несов от* **проснуться**, **просы́паться**.

просы́плю(сь) *итп сов см* **просы́пать(ся)**.

просыха́|ть (-ю) *сов от* **просо́хнуть**.

про́сьб|а (-ы) *ж* request; **выполня́ть** (**вы́полнить** *perf*) ~**у** to fulfil a request; **обраща́ться** (**обрати́ться** *perf*) **к кому́-н с** ~**ой** to make a request to sb.

прота́лин|а (-ы) *ж* bare patch (*where snow has melted*).

прота́лкива|ть(ся) (-ю(сь)) *несов от* **протолкну́ть(ся)**.

прота́плива|ть (-ю) *несов от* **протопи́ть**.

прота́птыва|ть (-ю) *несов от* **протопта́ть**.

протара́н|ить (-ю, -ишь) *сов от* **тара́нить**.

протаска́|ть (-ю) *сов перех* (*разг: сумку*) to carry round; (: *платье*) to wear.

прота́скива|ть (-ю) *несов от* **протащи́ть**.

прота́чива|ть (-ю) *несов от* **проточи́ть**.

прот|ащи́ть (-ащу́, -а́щишь; *impf* прота́скивать) *сов перех* (*разг: перен: силой устроить*) to wangle; (: *критиковать*) to pan; **прота́скивать** (~ *perf*) **что-н по** +*dat*/**сквозь** +*acc* to drag sth along/through.

протеже́ *м/ж нескл* protégé(e).

проте́з (-а) *м* artificial *или* prosthetic limb; **зубно́й** ~ denture.

проте́ин (-а) *м* protein.

протеи́новый *прил* protein *опред*.

протёк *итп сов см* **проте́чь**.

протека́ни|е (-я) *ср* (*болезни, явлений*) progression; (*в крыше*) leakage.

протека́|ть (*3sg* -ет, *3pl* -ют) *несов от* **проте́чь** ◆ *неперех* (*вода*) to flow, run; (*болезнь, явление*) to progress.

протеку́т *итп сов см* **проте́чь**.

протекциони́зм (-а) *м* (*ЭКОН*) protectionism.

проте́кци|я (-и) *ж* patronage; **ока́зывать** (**оказа́ть** *perf*) ~**ю кому́-н** to use one's influence on behalf of sb.

протелеграфи́р|овать (-ую) *сов от* **телеграфи́ровать**.

прот|ере́ть (-ру́, -рёшь; *pt* -ёр, -ёрла, -ёрло, *impf* протира́ть) *сов перех* (*сделать дыру*) to wear a hole in; (*очистить*) to wipe; **протира́ть** (~ *perf*) **что-н че́рез си́то** to rub sth through a sieve; (~ *perf*) **глаза́** to rub one's eyes

▸ **протере́ться** (*impf* протира́ться) *сов возв* (*одежда итп*) to wear through.

протёртый *прил* mashed.

проте́ст (-а) *м* protest; (*ЮР*) objection.

протеста́нт (-а) *м* Protestant.

протеста́нтск|ий (-ая, -ое, -ие) *прил* Protestant *опред*.

протест|ова́ть (-у́ю) *несов неперех*: ~ (**про́тив** +*gen*) to protest (against) ◆ (*perf* **опротестова́ть**) *перех* (*вексель, решение суда*) to object to.

протесту́ющ|ий (-его; *decl like adj*) *м* (*обычно мн*) protestor.

проте́чек *сущ см* **проте́чка**.

протечёт *итп сов см* **проте́чь**.

проте́ч|ка (-ки; *gen pl* -ек) *ж* leak.

прот|е́чь (*3sg* -ечёт, *3pl* -еку́т, *pt* -ёк, -екла́, -екло́, *impf* протека́ть) *сов неперех* (*вода*) to seep; (*крыша*) to leak; (*время, юность итп*) to pass by.

про́тив *предл* (+*gen*) against; (*прямо перед*) opposite ◆ *как сказ*: **я** ~ **да́нного предложе́ния** I am against the motion; **кто** ~? who is against?; ~ **до́ма магази́н** opposite the house (there) is a shop; ~ **и́мени/наименова́ния** against a name/designation; ~ **ве́тра/тече́ния/со́лнца** against the wind/current/sun; ~ **пра́вил/во́ли роди́телей** against the rules/one's parents wishes; ~ **ожида́ния** contrary to expectation; ~ **конкуре́нтов/врага́** against the competition/enemy; **лека́рство** ~ **ка́шля/головно́й бо́ли** medicine for a cough/headache.

проти́вен *прил см* **проти́вный**.

про́тив|ень (-ня) *м* baking tray.

проти́в|иться (-люсь, -ишься; *perf* воспроти́виться) *несов возв* (+*dat*) to oppose.

проти́вник (-а) *м* opponent ◆ *собир* (*ВОЕН*) the enemy.

проти́вниц|а (-ы) ж opponent.
проти́вно нареч offensively ◆ как сказ безл it's disgusting; **мне ~ ви́деть э́то** it disgusts me to see this.
проти́вн|ое (-ого; decl like adj) ср the opposite.
проти́в|ный прил (точка зрения, мнение) opposite опред, contrary опред; (**-ен, -на, -но**; человек, работа) disgusting, revolting; **~** +dat (закону, разуму) contrary to; **в ~ном слу́чае** otherwise; **проти́вная сторона́** the opposing side.
про́тивня итп сущ см **про́тивень**.
противоа́том|ный прил (защита) antinuclear; **~ое укры́тие** nuclear shelter.
противобо́рств|о (-а) ср struggle.
противобо́рств|овать (-ую) несов неперех (+dat) to fight.
противове́с (-а) м (ТЕХ, перен) counterbalance; **в ~ обще́ственному мне́нию** contrary to public opinion.
противовозду́шный прил anti-aircraft.
противога́з (-а) м gas mask.
противоде́йстви|е (-я) ср opposition; **встреча́ть (встре́тить** perf**) ~ чему́-н** to meet with opposition over sth.
противоде́йств|овать (-ую) несов неперех (+dat) to oppose.
противоесте́ствен|ный (**-, -на, -но**) прил unnatural.
противозако́н|ный (**-ен, -на, -но**) прил unlawful.
противозача́точный прил contraceptive опред; **противозача́точное сре́дство** contraceptive.
противопожа́рный прил (меры) fire-prevention; (техника) fire-fighting.
противопоказа́ни|е (-я) ср contraindication.
противопока́зан|ный (**-, -а, -о**) прил: **ему́ ~о есть жи́рное** he's been advised not to eat fatty things.
противополо́жен прил см **противополо́жный**.
противополо́жност|ь (-и) ж (мнений, политики) contrast; (противоположное явление) opposite; **в ~** +dat in contrast to.
противополо́ж|ный (**-ен, -на, -но**) прил (берег, сторона итп) opposite; (мнение, политика итп) opposing.
противопоста́в|ить (**-лю, -ишь**; impf **противопоставля́ть**) сов перех: **~ кого́-н/что́-н** +dat to contrast sb/sth with; (направить против) to oppose sb/sth with.
противопоставле́ни|е (-я) ср (мнений, взглядов) contrasting; (силы) opposing.
противопоста́влю сов см **противопоста́вить**.
противопоставля́|ть (-ю) несов от **противопоста́вить**.

противоречи́вост|ь (-и) ж paradox.
противоречи́в|ый (**-, -а, -о**) прил paradoxical.
противоре́чи|е (-я) ср contradiction; (классовое, политические) conflict; (возражение): **~** (+dat) (закону, старшим) defiance (of); **быть** (impf) **в ~и с** +instr to be in conflict with.
противоре́ч|ить (**-у, -ишь**) несов неперех: **~** +dat (человеку) to contradict; (логике, закону итп) to defy; **их показа́ния ~ат друг дру́гу** their evidence is contradictory.
противосто|я́ть (**-ю́, -и́шь**) несов неперех: **~** +dat (ветру, буре) to withstand; (уговорам, давлению) to resist; **~** (impf) **друг дру́гу** to confront each other.
противоя́ди|е (-я) ср (также перен) antidote.
протира́|ть(ся) (**-ю(сь)**) несов от **протере́ть(ся)**.
проти|сну́ть (**-у, -ешь**; impf **проти́скивать**) сов перех to squeeze through
▸ **проти́снуться** (impf **проти́скиваться**) сов возв: **~ся в** +acc/**сквозь** +acc to squeeze in(to)/through; **~ся** (impf) **вперёд** to push forward.
проткн|у́ть (**-у́, -ёшь**; impf **протыка́ть**) сов перех to pierce.
протодья́кон (-а) м archdeacon.
протоиере́|й (-я) м high priest.
прото́к (-а) м (рукав реки) tributary; (соединяющая река) channel; (МЕД) duct.
протоко́л (-а) м (собрания) minutes мн; (допроса) transcript; (соглашения) protocol; **Дипломати́ческий ~** Diplomatic Protocol; **вести́** (impf) **~ собра́ния** to take the minutes of a meeting; **составля́ть (соста́вить** perf**) ~ о́быска** to record the details of a search; **журна́л ~ов** minute book.
протоколи́р|овать (-ую; perf **запротоколи́ровать**) несов перех (собрание, заседание) to minute; (осмотр, обыск) to record.
протоко́льный прил (стиль) condensed; **протоко́льная за́пись** record of proceedings; **~ журна́л** minutes book.
протолкн|у́ть (**-у́, -ёшь**; impf **прота́лкивать**) сов перех (также перен) to push through
▸ **протолкну́ться** (impf **прота́лкиваться**) сов возв to push one's way through.
прот|опи́ть (**-оплю́, -о́пишь**; impf **прота́пливать**) сов перех (комнату, дом) to warm through; (печь) to stoke up.
прот|опта́ть (**-опчу́, -о́пчешь**; impf **прота́птывать**) сов перех (тропинку, дорожку) to beat.
проторг|ова́ть (**-у́ю**; impf **проторго́вывать**) сов перех (потерять) to make a loss of; (no impf; торговать: товары) to sell; (жизнь) to fritter away.
проторён|ный прил (дорога, путь) well-

trodden.

проторить (-ю, -ишь; *impf* **проторять**) *сов перех* to beat.

прототип (-а) *м person upon which a character of a novel, play etc is based.*

проточить (-очу, -очишь; *impf* **протачивать**) *сов перех* (*прогрызть отверстие*) to nibble through; (*ТЕХ*) to bore.

проточный *прил* (*вода*) running; **~ое озеро** *lake with rivers flowing out of it;* **~ая труба** pipe.

протралить (-ю, -ишь) *сов от* **траить**.

протрезветь (-ю) *сов неперех* = **протрезвиться**.

протрезвить (-лю, -ишь; *impf* **протрезвлять**) *сов перех:* **~ кого-н** to sober sb up

▶ **протрезвиться** (*impf* **протрезвляться**) *сов возв* to sober up.

протру(сь) *итп сов см* **протереть(ся)**.

протрубить (-лю, -ишь) *сов от* **трубить**.

протухнуть (*3sg* -ет, *3pl* -ут, *impf* **протухать** *или* **тухнуть**) *сов неперех* to go bad *или* off.

протыкать (-ю) *несов от* **проткнуть**.

протягивать(ся) (-ю(сь)) *несов от* **протянуть(ся)**.

протяжен *прил см* **протяжный**.

протяжение (-я) *ср:* **на ~и двух недель/месяцев** over a period of; **на всём ~и пути** the whole way; **на ~и всего нашего визита** for the whole duration of our visit.

протяжённость (-и) *ж* length.

протяжённый (-, -на, -но) *прил* prolonged.

протяжный (-ен, -на, -но) *прил* (*песня, крик итп*) long drawn-out.

протянуть (-яну, -янешь; *impf* **протягивать**) *сов перех* (*верёвку*) to stretch; (*линию передачи*) to extend; (*руки, ноги*) to stretch (out); (*предмет*) to hold out; (*слово, ответ итп*) to say slowly; (*разг: критиковать*) to pan ◆ *неперех* (*разг: прожить*) to last; **~** (*perf*) **ноги** (*разг*) to turn up one's toes; **протягивать** (**~** *perf*) **руку помощи** to lend a (helping) hand

▶ **протянуться** (*impf* **протягиваться**) *сов возв* (*дорога*) to stretch; (*линия передачи*) to extend; (*рука*) to stretch out.

проулок (-ка) *м* (*разг*) lane.

проучить (-учу, -учишь; *impf* **проучивать**) *сов перех* (*разг: наказать*) to teach a lesson; (*no impf; учить*) to study

▶ **проучиться** *сов возв* to study.

проф. *сокр* (= **профессор**) Prof. (= *Professor*).

профан (-а) *м* ignoramus.

профанация (-и) *ж* (*непочтительное отношение*) profanity; (*обман*) sham.

профашист (-а) *м* fascist sympathizer.

профашистский (-ая, -ое, -ие) *прил* fascist *опред*.

профбюро *ср нескл сокр* (= **профсоюзное бюро**) trade-union office.

профессионал (-а) *м* professional.

профессионализм (-а) *м* professionalism.

профессиональный *прил* professional *опред*; (*болезнь, привычка, обучение*) occupational; **профессиональный союз** trade (*BRIT*) *или* labor (*US*) union.

профессия (-и) *ж* profession; **по ~и он инженер** he is an engineer by profession; **получать** (**получить** *perf*) *или* **приобретать** (**приобрести** *perf*) **~ю** to get professional qualifications.

профессор (-а; *nom pl* -á) *м* professor.

профессура (-ы) *ж* professorship ◆ *собир* professors *мн*.

профилактика (-и) *ж* prevention.

профилактический (-ая, -ое, -ие) *прил* (*меры*) prevent(at)ive; (*прививка*) prophylactic *опред*; **~ое средство** prophylactic.

профиль (-я) *м* profile; (*предмета, дороги*) cross section; (*учебного заведения*) type; (*работника*) field.

профильтровать (-ую) *сов от* **фильтровать**.

профком (-а) *м сокр* (= **профсоюзный комитет**) trade-union committee.

профорг (-а) *м сокр* (= **профсоюзный организатор**) trade-union boss.

проформа (-ы) *ж* formality.

профсоюз (-а) *м сокр* (= **профессиональный союз**) trade (*BRIT*) *или* labor (*US*) union.

профсоюзный *прил* trade-union.

прохаживаться (-юсь) *несов от* **пройтись**.

прохватить (*3sg* -атит, *3pl* -атят, *impf* **прохватывать**) *сов перех* (*подлеж: холод, мороз итп*) to chill to the bone.

прохвост (-а) *м* (*разг*) crook.

прохлада (-ы) *ж* cool.

прохладительный *прил:* **~ напиток** cool soft drink.

прохладно *нареч* (*встретить*) coolly ◆ *как сказ* it's cool.

прохладный *прил* (*также перен*) cool.

прохладца (-ы) *ж:* **с ~ей** coolly.

прохлаждаться (-юсь) *несов возв* (*разг: бездельничать*) to doss about.

прохлопать (-ю; *impf* **прохлопывать**) *сов перех* (*разг*) to miss.

проход (-а) *м* passage; **задний ~** (*АНАТ*) back passage, anus; **~а нет от кого-н/чего-н** you can't get away from sb/sth; **не давать** (*impf*) **~а кому-н** to pester sb.

проходимец (-ца) *м* swindler.

проходимость (-и) *ж* (*местности*) passability; (*АВТ*) off-road capability; (*МЕД*) permeability.

проходимца *итп сущ см* **проходимец**.

проходимый (-, -а, -о) *прил* passable.

проходить (-ожу, -одишь) *несов от* **пройти** ◆ *сов неперех* (*ходить*) to walk.

проходка (-ки; *gen pl* -ок) *ж* sinking of shafts.

проходная (-ой; *decl like adj*) *ж* checkpoint (*at entrance to factory etc*).

проходной *прил:* **~ая комната** hall;

.**проходно́й балл** pass mark.
прохо́док *сущ см* **прохо́дка**.
прохо́дчик (-а) *м person who sinks shafts*.
прохо́жая (-ей; *decl like adj*) *ж см* **прохо́жий**.
прохожде́ни|**е** (-я) *ср* (*по доро́ге*) passage; (*испыта́ний*) passing; (*слу́жбы*) term.
прохо́жий (-его; *decl like adj*) *м* passer-by.
прохожу́ (*не*)*сов см* **проходи́ть**.
прохуд|**и́ться** (*3sg* -**и́тся**, *3pl* -**я́тся**) *сов непе́рех* (*раза*) to wear thin.
процвета́|**ть** (-ю) *несов непе́рех* (*фирма, бизнесме́н*) to prosper; (*теа́тр, нау́ка*) to flourish; (*разг: челове́к, семья́*) to thrive.
процеди́ть (-ежу́, -е́дишь; *impf* **проце́живать**) *сов пе́рех* (*бульо́н, сок*) to strain; (*no impf*; *произнести́*) : ~ (**сквозь зу́бы**) to say through one's teeth.
процеду́р|**а** (-ы) *ж* procedure; (*МЕД: обы́чно мн*) course of treatment.
процеду́рн|**ый** *прил* procedural; (*МЕД*): ~**ая сестра́** nurse; ~ **кабине́т** treatment room.
проце́жива|**ть** (-ю) *несов от* **процеди́ть**.
процежу́ *сов см* **процеди́ть**.
проце́нт (-а) *м* percentage; **в разме́ре 5** ~**ов годовы́х** at a yearly rate of 5 percent; **на все сто** ~**ов** (*доверя́ть, подде́рживать*) one hundred percent; *см та́кже* **проце́нты**.
проце́нтный *прил* (*вы́раженный в проце́нтах*) percentage *опред*; **проце́нтная ста́вка** interest rate.
проце́нт|**ы** (-ов) *мн* (*КОММ*) interest *ед*; (: *вознагражде́ние*) commission; **просты́е/ сло́жные/наро́сшие** ~ simple/compound/ accrued interest.
проце́сс (-а) *м* process; (*ЮР: поря́док разбира́тельства*) proceedings *мн*; (: *та́кже*: **суде́бный** ~) trial; **воспали́тельный** ~ inflammation; **в** ~**е** +*gen* in the course of; **возбужда́ть** (**возбуди́ть** *perf*) ~ to institute proceedings.
проце́сси|**я** (-и) *ж* procession.
проце́ссор (-а) *м* word processor.
процессуа́льный *прил* (*ЮР*) procedural; **процессуа́льный ко́декс** procedural code.
процити́р|**овать** (-ую) *сов от* **цити́ровать**.
прочёл *сов см* **проче́сть**.
про́чен *прил см* **про́чный**.
про́черк (-а) *м* line.
проч|**ерти́ть** (-ерчу́, -е́ртишь; *impf* **проче́рчивать**) *сов пе́рех*: ~ **ли́нию** to draw a line.
проч|**еса́ть** (-ешу́, -е́шешь; *impf* **прочёсывать**) *сов пе́рех* (*та́кже пере́н*) to comb.
проч|**е́сть** (-ту́, -тёшь; *pt* -**ёл**, -**ла́**, -**ло́**) *сов от* **чита́ть**.
прочёсыва|**ть** (-ю) *несов от* **прочеса́ть**.
прочешу́ *итп сов см* **прочеса́ть**.
про́чий (-ая, -ее, -ие) *прил* other; **поми́мо всего́** ~**его** on top of everything else; **и про́чее** and so on.

прочи́|**стить** (-щу, -стишь; *impf* **прочища́ть**) *сов пе́рех* to clean out; (*нос*) to clear.
прочита́|**ть** (-ю) *сов от* **чита́ть**.
про́ч|**ить** (-у, -ишь) *несов пе́рех*: ~ **что-н кому́-н** to predict sth for sb; **его́ роди́тели** ~**или его́ во врачи́** his parents intended him to be a doctor.
прочища́|**ть** (-ю) *несов от* **прочи́стить**.
прочи́щу *сов см* **прочи́стить**.
прочла́ *итп сов см* **проче́сть**.
про́чно *нареч* (*закрепи́ть*) firmly; (*зау́чить*) well.
про́чность (-и) *ж* (*материа́ла итп*) durability; (*отноше́ний, семьи́*) stability; **запа́с** ~**и** reliability.
про́чн|**ый** (-ен, -на́, -но) *прил* (*материа́л итп*) durable; (*постро́йка*) solid, stable; (*зна́ния*) sound; (*отноше́ние, семья́*) stable; (*мир, сча́стье*) lasting.
прочте́ни|**е** (-я) *ср* reading.
прочту́ *итп сов см* **проче́сть**.
прочу́вствованный *прил* heartfelt.
прочу́вств|**овать** (-ую) *сов пе́рех* to feel deeply; ~ (*perf*) **роль** to get inside a role.
прочь *нареч* (*в сто́рону*) away; **ру́ки** ~! hands off!; ~ **с доро́ги**! get out of the way!; **он не** ~ **вы́пить** he won't say no to a drink.
прошвырн|**у́ться** (-у́сь, -ёшься) *сов возв* (*разг*) to stretch one's legs.
проше́дший (-ая, -ее, -ие) *прил* (*про́шлый*) past; **проше́дшее вре́мя** past tense.
прошёл(ся) *сов см* **пройти́(сь)**.
проше́ни|**е** (-я) *ср* plea; (*пи́сьменное хода́тайство*) petition; **подава́ть** (**пода́ть** *perf*) ~ **в** +*acc* to present a petition to.
прош|**епта́ть** (-епчу́, -е́пчешь) *сов пе́рех* to whisper.
проше́стви|**е** (-я) *ср*: **по** ~**и го́да/ме́сяца** after a year's/month's lapse.
прошиб|**и́ть** (-у́, -ёшь; *pt* -, -**ла́**, -**ло́**, *impf* **прошиба́ть**) *сов пе́рех* (*разг: дверь, окно́ итп*) to smash through; **пот прошиб его́** he broke out in a sweat; **дрожь** ~**и́ла её** a shiver went down her spine.
прош|**и́ть** (-ью, -ьёшь; *imper* -**е́й(те)**, *impf* **прошива́ть**) *сов пе́рех* (*пришить*) to sew a seam on; (*пере́н: пу́лями сте́ны*) to pepper.
прошла́ *итп сов см* **пройти́**.
прошлого́дн|**ий** (-яя, -ее, -ие) *прил* last year's; ~**ие собы́тия** the events of last year.
про́шло|**е** (-го; *decl like adj*) *ср* the past; **отходи́ть** (**отойти́** *perf*) **в** ~ to become a thing of the past.
про́шл|**ый** *прил* last; (*пре́жний*) past; **в** ~ **раз** last time; **на** ~**ой неде́ле** last week; **в** ~**ом году́/ме́сяце** last year/month; **де́ло** ~**ое** it's in

the past.

прошмыгну́ть (-у́, -ёшь; *impf* **прошмы́гивать**) *сов неперех*: ~ **ми́мо** +*gen*/**сквозь** +*acc итп* (*разг*) to dart past/through *итп*.

проштампова́ть (-у́ю) *сов от* **штампова́ть**.

проштра́ф|**иться** (-люсь, -ишься) *сов возв* (*разг*) to lapse.

проштуди́р|**овать** (-ую) *сов от* **штуди́ровать**.

прошу́(сь) *несов см* **проси́ть(ся)**.

прошью́ *итп сов см* **проши́ть**.

проща́йте *част* goodbye, farewell.

проща́льный *прил* parting *опред*; (*вечер, визит*) farewell *опред*.

проща́ни|**е** (-я) *ср* (*действие*) parting; **на** ~ on parting; **они́ ему́ подари́ли на** ~ they gave him a leaving present.

проща́|**ть(ся)** (-ю(сь)) *несов от* **прости́ть(ся)**.

про́ще *сравн нареч от* **про́сто** ♦ *сравн прил от* **просто́й**.

проще́ни|**е** (-я) *ср* (*ребёнка, друга итп*) forgiveness; (*преступника*) pardon; **проси́ть** (**попроси́ть** *perf*) ~**я** to say sorry; **прошу́** ~**я!** (I'm) sorry!

прощу́(сь) *сов см* **прости́ть(ся)**.

прощу́па|**ть** (-ю; *impf* **прощу́пывать**) *сов перех* to feel for; (*перен*) to check out; **прощу́пывать** (~ *perf*) **по́чву** to explain how the land lies.

проэкзамен|**ова́ть** (-у́ю) *сов от* **экзаменова́ть**.

прояви́тел|**ь** (-я) *м* (*ФОТО*) developer.

про|**яви́ть** (-явлю́, -я́вишь; *impf* **проявля́ть**) *сов перех* to display; (*ФОТО*) to develop; **проявля́ть** (~ *perf*) **себя́ пло́хо/хорошо́** to show o.s. in a bad/good light

▶ **прояви́ться** (*impf* **проявля́ться**) *сов возв* (*талант, потенциал итп*) to reveal itself; (*решительность, смелость итп*) to show itself; (*ФОТО*) to be developed.

проявле́ни|**е** (-я) *ср* display; (*обычно мн: жизни*) manifestation.

проявлю́(сь) *сов см* **прояви́ть(ся)**.

проявля́|**ть(ся)** (-ю(сь)) *несов от* **прояви́ть(ся)**.

проясне́ни|**е** (-я) *ср* (*погоды*) brightening *или* clearing up; (*ситуации*) clarification; **у меня́ наступи́ла** ~ **созна́ния** *или* **ума́** my mind cleared.

проясн|**и́ть** (-ю́, -и́шь; *impf* **проясня́ть**) *сов перех* (*обстановку*) to clarify; (*мысли*) to sort out; **проясня́ть** (~ *perf*) **чьё-н созна́ние** to bring sb round

▶ **проясни́ться** (*impf* **проясня́ться**) *сов возв* (*погода, небо*) to brighten *или* clear up; (*обстановка*) to be clarified; (*мысли*) to be sorted out; **у него́** ~**и́лось созна́ние** his mind cleared.

пру(сь) *итп несов см* **пере́ть(ся)**.

пруд (-а́; *loc sg* -у́) *м* (*естественный*) pool, pond; (*искусственный*) pond.

пр|**уди́ть** (-ужу́, -у́дишь; *perf* **запруди́ть**) *несов перех* to dam; **де́нег у него́ хоть** ~**уд пруди́**

(*разг*) he is rolling in cash.

пружи́н|**а** (-ы) *ж* (*ТЕХ*) spring; (*перен: движущая сила*) mainspring.

пружи́нист|**ый** (-, -а, -о) *прил* springy; **у него́** ~ **шаг** he has a spring in his step.

пружу́ *сов см* **пруди́ть**.

прут (-а́; *nom pl* -ья) *м* (*БОТ*) twig; (*ТЕХ*) rod.

прыга́лк|**а** (-ки; *gen pl* -ок) *ж* skipping-rope (*BRIT*), skip rope (*US*).

пры́га|**ть** (-ю) *несов неперех* to jump; (*мяч*) to bounce.

пры́гн|**уть** (-у, -ешь) *сов неперех* to jump; (*мяч*) to bounce.

прыгу́н (-а́) *м* (*СПОРТ*) jumper; ~ **в длину́** long jumper; ~ **в высоту́** high jumper.

прыгу́нь|**я** (-и; *gen pl* -ий) *ж см* **прыгу́н**.

прыж|**о́к** (-ка́) *м* (*через лужу, с парашютом*) jump; (*в воду*) dive; ~**ки́ в высоту́/длину́** high/long jump; ~**ки́ с шесто́м** pole vault; **опо́рный** ~ (*СПОРТ*) vault.

пры́сн|**уть** (-у, -ешь; *impf* **пры́скать**) *сов неперех* (*кровь*) to spurt; (+*instr*: *водой*) to sprinkle with; (*духами*) to spray with; **пры́скать** (~ *perf*) **со́ смеху** (*разг*) to go into a fit of giggles.

пры́т|**кий** (-кая, -кое, -кие; -ок, -ка́, -ко) *прил* (*разг: подвижный*) bouncy.

прыт|**ь** (-и) *ж* (*разг: быстрота*) bounce; **во всю** ~ (*разг*) at full tilt.

прыщ (-а́) *м* spot.

прыща́в|**ый** (-, -а, -о) *прил* spotty.

пряди́льный *прил* spinning *опред*.

пряди́льщик (-а) *м* spinner.

пряди́льщиц|**а** (-ы) *ж см* **пряди́льщик**.

пряду́ *итп несов см* **прясть**.

прядь (-и) *ж* lock (*of hair*).

пря́ж|**а** (-и) *ж* yarn.

пря́жк|**а** (-ки; *gen pl* -ек) *ж* (*на ремне*) buckle; (*на юбке*) clasp.

пря́лк|**а** (-ки; *gen pl* -ок) *ж* spinning wheel.

пряма́|**я** (-я́я; *decl like adj*) *ж* straight line; **по** ~**о́й** in a straight line.

прямико́м *нареч*: **он прошёл** ~ **че́рез сад** (*разг*) he went straight across the garden.

пря́мо *нареч* (*в прямом направлении*) straight ahead; (*ровно*) upright; (*непосредственно*) straight; (*откровенно*) directly ♦ *част* (*действительно*) really; **приступа́ть** (**приступи́ть** *perf*) ~ **к де́лу** to get straight down to business; **у меня́** ~ **сил нет!** I really haven't (got) the strength!; **помоги́те ему́ – (ну)** ~**!** (*разг*) help him? no way!

прямоду́ш|**ный** (-ен, -на, -но) *прил* (*человек*) forthright; (*ответ*) candid.

прям|**о́й** (-, -а́, -о) *прил* straight; (*путь, слова, человек*) direct; (*ответ, политика*) open; (*вызов, обман*) obvious; (*улики*) solid; (*no short form*; *сообщение, рейс, обязанность итп*) direct; (*выгода, смысл, польза итп*) real; (*значение слова*) literal; ~**ые изде́ржки** direct cost; **пряма́я кишка́** rectum; **пряма́я**

трансля́ция live broadcast; **прямо́е
дополне́ние** direct object; **прямо́е попада́ние**
direct hit; **прямо́й до́ступ** (КОМП) direct access;
прямо́й репорта́ж live coverage; **прямо́й у́гол**
right angle; **прямы́е вы́боры/нало́ги** direct
elections/taxes.

прямолине́йный (-ен, -йна, -йно) прил
(движение) along a straight line; (перен) blunt.

пря́мо-таки нареч (разг) really.

прямоуго́льник (-а) м rectangle.

прямоуго́льный прил rectangular.

пря́ник (-а) м ≈ gingerbread.

пря́ность (-и) ж spice.

пря́ный (-, -а, -о) прил spicy.

прясть (-ду́, -дёшь; perf **спрясть**) несов перех
to spin.

пря́тать (-чу, -чешь; perf **спря́тать**) несов
перех to hide; **он ~тал глаза́ от меня́** he didn't
look me straight in the eye

▶ **пря́таться** (perf **спря́таться**) несов возв to
hide; (человек: от холода, ветра) to shelter;
(солнце) to hide; **~ся** (**спря́таться** perf) **за
чужу́ю спи́ну** to redirect responsibility.

пря́тки (-ок; dat pl -кам) мн hide-and-seek ед;
игра́ть (impf) **в ~ с кем-н** to play hide-and-seek
with sb; (перен) to avoid sb.

пря́чу(сь) итп несов см **пря́тать(ся)**.

пса итп сущ см **пёс**.

псало́м (-ма́) м psalm.

псало́мщик (-а) м sexton.

псалты́рь (-и) ж Psalter.

пса́рня (-и) ж kennels мн (for hunting dogs).

псевдони́м (-а) м pseudonym.

псих (-а) м (разг) psycho.

психиа́тр (-а) м psychiatrist.

психиатри́ческий (-ая, -ое, -ие) прил
psychiatric.

психиатри́я (-и) ж psychiatry.

пси́хика (-и) ж psyche.

психи́ческий (-ая, -ое, -ие) прил (заболевание,
отклонение итп) mental.

психоана́лиз (-а) м psychoanalysis.

психова́ть (-у́ю) несов неперех (разг) to freak
out.

психо́з (-а) м (МЕД) psychosis; (странность в
психике) neurosis.

психо́лог (-а) м psychologist.

психологи́ческий (-ая, -ое, -ие) прил
psychological.

психоло́гия (-и) ж psychology.

психопа́т (-а) м psychopath.

психопа́тия (-и) ж psychopathy.

психотерапе́вт (-а) м psychotherapist.

психотерапи́я (-и) ж psychotherapy.

ПСС м сокр = по́лное собра́ние сочине́ний.

пта́ха (-и) ж (разг) bird.

пта́шка (-ки; gen pl -ек) ж bird.

птене́ц (-ца́) м chick.

пти́ца (-ы) ж bird ♦ собир: (дома́шняя) ~
poultry; **ва́жная ~** (разг) big shot.

птицево́д (-а) м poulterer, poultry farmer.

птицево́дство (-а) ср poultry farming.

птицево́дческий (-ая, -ое, -ие) прил: **~ая
фе́рма** poultry farm.

птицефа́брика (-и) ж poultry farm.

пти́чек сущ см **пти́чка**.

пти́чий (-ья, -ье, -ьи) прил (корм, клетка) bird
опред; **вид с высоты́ ~ьего полёта** bird's eye
view; **я сам здесь на ~ьих права́х** I don't have
any rights here myself; **пти́чий база́р** bird
colony.

пти́чка (-ки; gen pl -ек) ж уменьш от **пти́ца**;
(разг: в тексте) tick (BRIT), check (US).

пти́чник (-а) м ≈ hen house.

ПТУ ср сокр (= профессиона́льно-техни́ческое
учи́лище) ≈ tech (= technical college).

пуа́нт (-а) м (БАЛЕТ) ballet shoe.

пу́блика (-и) ж собир audience; **широ́кая ~** the
public; **игра́ть** (impf) **на ~у** to show off; **на ~у** in
company.

публика́ция (-и) ж publication.

публикова́ть (-у́ю; perf **опубликова́ть**) несов
перех to publish.

публици́ст (-а) м writer of sociopolitical
literature.

публици́стика (-и) ж собир sociopolitical
journalism.

публицисти́ческий (-ая, -ое, -ие) прил
sociopolitical.

публи́чный (-ен, -на, -но) прил public;
публи́чный дом brothel; **публи́чные торги́,
публи́чная прода́жа** (public) auction, public
sale.

пу́гало (-а) ср scarecrow; (перен: некраси́вый
челове́к) fright.

пуга́ть (-ю; perf **испуга́ть** или **напуга́ть**) несов
перех to frighten, scare

▶ **пуга́ться** (perf **испуга́ться** или **напуга́ться**)
несов возв to be frightened или scared.

пугли́вый (-, -а, -о) прил timid.

пу́говица (-ы) ж button; **застёгивать
(застегну́ть** perf) **~у** to fasten a button.

пуд (-а; nom pl -ы́) м pood (Russian measure of
weight equivalent to 16 kilogrammes).

пу́дель (-я) м poodle.

пу́динг (-а) м ≈ pudding.

пудо́вый прил: **~ая ги́ря** a pood weight.

пу́дра (-ы) ж powder; **са́харная ~** icing sugar.

пу́дреница (-ы) ж powder compact.

пу́дрить (-ю, -ишь; perf **напу́дрить**) несов
перех to powder; **~** (impf) **мозги́ кому́-н** (разг)
to pull the wool over sb's eyes

▶ **пу́дриться** (perf **напу́дриться**) несов возв to
powder one's face.

пуза́тый (-, -а, -о) прил (разг: челове́к) tubby;
(перен: ча́йник, комо́д) rounded.

пу́з|о (-а) *ср (разг: живот)* belly; *(брюхо)* paunch.

пузыр|ёк (-ька́) *м (уменьш)* от **пузы́рь**; *(для лекарства, чернил)* vial.

пузыри́ться (3sg -и́тся, 3pl -я́тся) *несов возв (жидкость)* to bubble; *(краска)* to blister; *(разг: одежда)* to blow up.

пузы́р|ь (-я́) *м (мыльный)* bubble; *(на коже)* blister; *(с водой)* water bottle; **жёлчный ~** gall bladder; **мочево́й ~** (urinary) bladder.

пузырька́ *итп сущ см* **пузырёк**.

пук (-а́) *м* bundle.

пу́ка|ть (-ю; perf пу́кнуть) *несов неперех* to fart.

пулево́й *прил* bullet *опред*.

пулемёт (-а) *м* machine gun.

пулемётчик (-а) *м* machine gunner.

пуленепробива́емый *прил* bullet-proof.

пуло́вер (-а) *м* pullover.

пульвериза́тор (-а) *м* atomizer.

пульс (-а) *м (МЕД, перен)* pulse.

пульси́р|овать (3sg -ует, 3pl -уют) *несов неперех (артерии)* to pulsate; *(кровь)* to pulse; *(нарыв)* to throb.

пульт (-а) *м* panel; *(музыканта)* stand; **пульт управле́ния** control panel.

пу́л|я (-и) *ж* bullet; **~ей вы́лететь** *(perf)* *(перен: разг)* to shoot out (from).

пу́м|а (-ы) *ж* puma.

пункт (-а) *м* point; *(документа)* clause; *(медицинский)* centre *(BRIT)*, center *(US)*; *(наблюдательный, командный)* post; **населённый ~** inhabited area.

пункти́р (-а) *м* dotted line.

пунктуа́л|ьный (-ен, -ьна, -ьно) *прил (человек)* punctual.

пунктуа́ци|я (-и) *ж* punctuation.

пу́нкци|я (-и) *ж (МЕД)* lumber puncture.

пунцо́вый *прил* scarlet *опред*.

пунш (-а) *м (кулин)* punch.

пуп (-а́) *м (разг)* belly button; **~ земли́** *(разг)* the bee's knees.

пупка́ *сущ см* **пупо́к**.

пупови́н|а (-ы) *ж* umbilical cord.

пуп|о́к (-ка́) *м (АНАТ)* navel.

пупы́рыш|ек (-ка) *м (разг: на коже)* pimple.

пург|а́ (-и́) *ж* snowstorm.

пурге́н (-а) *м* phenol phthalene *(used as laxative)*.

пурита́н|ин (-ина, nom pl -е, gen pl -) *м* puritan.

пурита́н|ка (-ки; gen pl -ок) *ж см* **пурита́нин**.

пурита́нский (-ая, -ое, -ие) *прил* puritanical.

пурпу́р (-а) *м* wine, Burgundy.

пурпу́рный *прил* wine *опред*, Burgundy *опред*.

пуск (-а) *м (завода итп)* starting up; **~ в эксплуата́цию** commission.

пуска́й *част, союз (разг) =* **пусть**.

пуска́ть(ся) (-ю(сь)) *несов от* **пусти́ть(ся)**.

пусково́й *прил (период)* initial *опред*; *(механизм, установка)* starting *опред*; *(платформа)* launching *опред*.

пусте́ть (3sg -ет, 3pl -ют, perf опусте́ть) *несов*

неперех to become empty.

пу|сти́ть (-щу́, -стишь; impf пуска́ть) *сов перех (руку, человека)* to let go of; *(лошадь, санки итп)* to send off; *(завод, станок, электростанцию)* to start; *(в вагон, в зал)* to let in; *(пар, дым)* to give off; *(камень, снаряд)* to throw; *(сплетни)* to spread; *(корни)* to put out; **пуска́ть (~ perf) что-н на** +*acc*/**под** +*acc* *(использовать)* to use sth as/for; **пуска́ть (~ perf) кого́-н куда́-нибудь** to let sb go somewhere; **пуска́ть (~ perf) това́р в прода́жу** to put goods onto the market; **пуска́ть (~ perf) пузыри́** to blow bubbles; **пуска́ть (~ perf) слньй** to dribble; **пуска́ть (~ perf) во́ду/газ** to turn on the water/gas

▶ **пусти́ться (impf пуска́ться)** *сов возв:* **~ся в** +*acc (в объяснение)* to go into; **пуска́ться (~ся perf) в подро́бности** to go into detail; **пуска́ться (~ся perf) в пляс** *или* **пляса́ть** to start dancing; **пуска́ться (~ся perf) в путь** to set off.

пу́сто *нареч* empty ♦ *как сказ (ничего нет)* there's nothing there; *(никого нет)* there's no-one there; **в го́роде/холоди́льнике ~** the town/fridge is empty.

пуст|ова́ть (3sg -у́ет, 3pl -у́ют) *несов неперех* to be empty.

пуст|о́й (-, -а́, -о, -ы́) *прил* empty; *(взгляд)* vacant; *(предлог, причина, затея)* trifling; **он – ~о́е ме́сто** he's a real nobody; **с ~ыми рука́ми** empty-handed.

пустосло́ви|е (-я) *ср* idle talk.

пуст|ота́ (-оты́; nom pl -о́ты) *ж* emptiness; *(полое место)* cavity.

пу́стош|ь (-и) *ж* wasteland.

пусты́н|ный *прил* desert *опред*; *(-ен, -на, -но; безлюдный)* deserted.

пусты́н|я (-и; gen pl -ь) *ж* desert; *(безлюдное место)* wilderness.

пусты́рник (-а) *м* motherwort.

пусты́р|ь (-я́) *м* wasteland.

пусты́ш|ка (-ки; gen pl -ек) *ж (разг: соска)* dummy *(BRIT)*, pacifier *(US)*; *(перен: о человеке)* airhead.

KEYWORD

пусть *част (+3sg/pl)* **1** *(выражает приказ, угрозу):* **пусть он придёт у́тром** let him come in the morning; **пусть она́ то́лько попро́бует отказа́ться** let her just try to refuse **2** *(выражает согласие):* **пусть бу́дет так** so be it; **пусть бу́дет по-тво́ему** have it your way **3** *(всё равно)* OK, all right; **она́ вини́т меня́, пусть!** OK *или* all right, so she blames me! ♦ *союз (допустим)* even if; **пусть он плохо́й дире́ктор, зато́ хоро́ший челове́к** even if he is a bad director, he is a good person; **на́до оправда́ть все, пусть да́же небольши́е, затра́ты** all expenses, even small ones, must be justified.

пустя́к (-а́) *м* trifle; *(неценный предмет)* trinket

◆ *как сказ*: э́то ~ it's nothing; **говори́ть** *(impf)* **пустяки́** to talk nonsense; **Вы огорчены́? – пустяки́!** are you upset? – it's nothing!
пустяко́вый *прил (разг: повод, жалоба)* trivial; **э́то пустяко́вая рабо́та** it's a piece of cake.
пустя́чный *прил* = **пустяко́вый**.
пута́н|а (-ы) *ж prostitute working for hard currency.*
пу́таниц|а (-ы) *ж (в мыслях, в делах)* muddle; *(дорог, дверей)* maze.
пу́тан|ый *прил (объяснение, рассказ)* muddled.
пу́та|ть (-ю; *perf* **запу́тать** *или* **спу́тать)** *несов перех (нитки, волосы)* to tangle (up); *(разг: сбить с толку;* (*perf* **спу́тать** *или* **перепу́тать;** *бумаги, факты итп)* to mix up; *(perf* **впу́тать;** *разг)*: ~ **кого́-н в** +*acc* to get sb mixed up in; **я его́ с кем-то ~ю** I'm confusing him with somebody else; **он всегда́ ~л на́ши имена́** he always got our names mixed up
▶ **пу́таться** *(perf* **запу́таться** *или* **спу́таться)** *несов возв* to get tangled (up); *(в рассказе, в объяснении)* to get mixed up; *(perf* **спу́таться;** *общаться)*: ~**ся с** +*instr (с мошенниками, с хулиганами итп)* to get mixed up with.
путёв|ка (-ки; *gen pl* **-ок)** *ж* holiday voucher *(given by employer)*; *(водителя)* manifest *(of cargo drivers).*
путеводи́тел|ь (-я) *м* guidebook.
путево́дн|ый *прил (перен: идея, теория)* guiding; ~**ая нить** guiding light.
путево́й *прил (пост, сигнал)* railway *опред*; *(записки, дневник)* travel *опред*; **путево́й лист** *(водителя)* = **путёвка**.
путёвок *сущ см* **путёвка**.
путёвый *прил (разг)* = **пу́тный**.
путе́й *сущ см* **пути́**.
путём *сущ см* **путь** ◆ *предл* (+*gen*) by means of.
путеше́ственник (-а) *м* traveller *(BRIT)*, traveler *(US)*.
путеше́стви|е (-я) *ср* journey, trip; *(морской)* voyage.
путеше́ств|овать (-ую) *несов неперех* to travel.
пут|и́ *сущ см* **путь** ◆ **(-е́й)** *мн:* **дыха́тельные ~** respiratory tract.
пу́тник (-а) *м* traveller *(BRIT)*, traveler *(US)*.
пу́тный *прил (человек)* decent; *(план, предложение)* practical.
путч (-а) *м (полит)* putsch.
пу́т|ы (-) *мн (также перен)* fetters *мн*.
путь (-й; *см* **Table 3)** *м (также перен)* way; *(платформа)* platform; *(рельсы)* track; *(путешествие)* journey; **запасно́й ~** siding; **во́дные ~й** waterways; **возду́шные ~й** air lanes; **нам с Ва́ми не по ~й** we're not going the same way; *(перен)* we don't see eye to eye; **счастли́вого ~й!** have a good trip!; **быть** *(impf)*

на ~й к +*dat* to be on the road *или* way to; **провожа́ть (проводи́ть** *perf)* **кого́-н в после́дний ~** to lay sb to rest; **пути́ сообще́ния** transport network *ед*; *см также* **пути́**.
пуф (-а) *м* pouffe.
пух (-а; *loc sg* **-у́)** *м (у животных)* fluff; *(у птиц, у человека)* down; **в ~ и прах** *(разг)* totally and utterly; **ни пу́ха ни пера́!** good luck!
пух *итп несов см* **пу́хнуть**.
пу́хл|ый (-, -а́, -о) *прил (щёки, человек)* chubby; *(губы)* full; *(портфель, папка)* bulging.
пу́х|нуть (-ну, -нешь; *pt* **-, -ла, -ло,** *perf* **вспу́хнуть** *или* **опу́хнуть)** *несов неперех* to swell (up); **у меня́ голова́ ~нет** *(разг)* my head's buzzing.
пухо́в|ый *прил (подушка)* feather *опред*; *(платок)* angora *опред*; ~**ая ку́ртка** padded jacket.
пучегла́зый *прил (разг)* goggle-eyed, pop-eyed.
пучи́н|а (-ы) *ж* the deep.
пу́ч|ить (-у, -ишь; *perf* **вы́пучить)** *несов перех*: ~ **глаза́** to goggle; **он вы́пучил глаза́** his eyes popped out of his head; **меня́ ~ит** I have flatulence
▶ **пу́читься** *(perf* **вспу́читься)** *несов возв* to swell (up).
пуч|о́к (-ка́) *м* bunch; *(света)* beam.
пу́шек *сущ см* **пу́шка**.
пуши́н|ка (-ки; *gen pl* **-ок)** *ж* piece of fluff; *(снега)* flake.
пуши́ст|ый (-, -а, -о) *прил (мех, ковёр итп)* fluffy; *(волосы)* fuzzy; *(ткань)* fleecy; *(кот)* furry; *(цыплёнок)* downy.
пу́ш|ка (-ки; *gen pl* **-ек)** *ж (на танке)* artillery gun; *(ист)* cannon.
пушни́н|а (-ы) *ж собир* furs *мн*.
пушно́й *прил* furry; ~ **това́р** furs *мн*.
пуш|о́к (-ка́) *м уменьш от* **пух**; *(над губой)* fluff.
пу́щ|а (-и) *ж* dense forest.
пу́щий (-ая, -ее, -ие) *прил*: **для ~ей ва́жности** *(разг)* for more impact.
пущу́(сь) *сов см* **пусти́ть(ся)**.
пфе́нниг (-а) *м* pfennig.
Пхенья́н (-а) *м* Pyongyang.
пчел|а́ (-ы́; *nom pl* **пчёлы)** *м* bee.
пчели́ный *прил (мёд)* bee's; ~ **воск** beeswax; ~ **рой** swarm of bees.
пчелово́д (-а) *м* bee-keeper.
пчелово́дств|о (-а) *ср* bee-keeping.
пшени́ц|а (-ы) *ж* wheat.
пшени́чный *прил* wheat *опред*.
пшён|ка (-ки) *ж (разг)* millet porridge.
пшённ|ый *прил*: ~**ая ка́ша** millet porridge.
пшен|о́ (-а́) *ср* millet.
пы́ж|иться (-усь, -ишься; *perf* **напы́житься)** *несов возв (разг: напрягаться)* to puff and pant; *(держаться важно)* to puff up.

пыл (-а; *loc sg* -ý) *м* (*перен*) ardour (*BRIT*), ardor (*US*); **в ~ý спо́ра/сраже́ния** in the heat of the argument/battle.

пыла́|ть (-ю) *несов неперех* (*костёр*) to blaze; (*перен: лицо*) to burn; (*+instr; перен: любовью, гне́вом итп*) to burn with.

пы́лен *прил см* **пы́льный**.

пылесо́с (-а) *м* vacuum cleaner, hoover®.

пылесо́с|ить (-ю, -ишь; *perf* **пропылесо́сить**) *сов перех* to vacuum, hoover®.

пыли́н|ка (-ки; *gen pl* -ок) *ж* speck of dust.

пыли́|ть (-ю, -ишь; *perf* **напыли́ть**) *несов неперех* to raise dust

▸ **пыли́ться** (*perf* **запыли́ться**) *несов возв* to get dusty.

пы́л|кий (-кая, -кое, -кие; -ок, -ка́, -ко) *прил* passionate.

пыль (-и; *loc sg* -и́) *ж* dust; **вытира́ть (вы́тереть** *perf*) ~ to dust; **пуска́ть (пусти́ть** *perf*) ~ **в глаза́ кому́-н** to give sb the wrong idea.

пы́льный (-ен, -ьна, -ьно) *прил* dusty.

пыльца́ (-ы́) *ж* pollen.

пырну́|ть (-ý, -ёшь) *сов перех* (*разг*) to stab; ~ (*perf*) **ножо́м** to knife.

пыта́|ть (-ю) *несов перех* to torture; ~ (*impf*) **кого́-н о чём-н** to grill sb about sth

▸ **пыта́ться** (*perf* **попыта́ться**) *несов возв:* ~**ся** +*infin* to try to do.

пы́т|ка (-ки; *gen pl* -ок) *ж* torment.

пытли́вый (-, -а, -о) *прил* inquisitive.

пы́ток *сущ см* **пы́тка**.

пы́хать (-шу, -шешь) *несов неперех:* ~ +*instr* to give off; ~ (*impf*) **зло́бой/за́вистью** to burn with anger/envy; **она́ ~шет здоро́вьем** she's bursting with health.

пых|те́ть (-чý, -ти́шь) *несов неперех* (*тяжело дыша́ть*) to pant; (*самова́р*) to steam; (*парово́з*) to chug; ~ (*impf*) **над чем-н** (*разг*) to sweat over sth.

пы́шек *сущ см* **пы́шка**.

пы́шен *прил см* **пы́шный**.

пы́ш|ка (-ки; *gen pl* -ек) *ж* doughnut (*BRIT*), donut (*US*).

пышноволо́сый (-, -а, -о) *прил* fuzzy-haired.

пышногру́дый (-, -а, -о) *прил* busty.

пы́шност|ь (-и) *ж* (*волос*) luxuriance; (*хвоста́ итп*) bushiness; (*обстано́вки, приёма итп*) splendour (*BRIT*), splendor (*US*); **придава́ть (прида́ть** *perf*) ~ **волоса́м** to give body to one's hair.

пы́шный (-ен, -на́, -но) *прил* (*во́лосы, хвост, усы́ итп*) bushy; (*по́лный*) voluptuous; (*роско́шный*) splendid.

пышу́ *итп несов см* **пы́хать**.

пьедеста́л (-а) *м* (*основа́ние*) pedestal; (*для победи́телей*) winners' rostrum.

пье́с|а (-ы) *ж* (*ЛИТЕРАТУРА*) play; (*МУЗ*) piece.

пью *итп несов см* **пить**.

пью́щий (-его; *decl like adj*) *м* heavy drinker.

пьяне́|ть (-ю; *perf* **опьяне́ть**) *несов неперех* to get drunk; (*перен*) to become intoxicated.

пьян|и́ть (-ю́, -и́шь; *perf* **опьяни́ть**) *несов перех* to get drunk; (*перен: подлеж: во́здух, сча́стье итп*) to intoxicate.

пья́ниц|а (-ы) *м/ж* drunkard.

пья́н|ка (-ки; *gen pl* -ок) *ж* (*разг*) booze-up.

пья́нств|о (-а) *ср* heavy drinking; **борьба́ с ~м** anti-drinking campaign.

пья́нств|овать (-ую) *несов неперех* to drink heavily.

пьянчу́г|а (-и) *м/ж* (*разг*) (old) soak.

пья́ный (-, -á, -о) *прил* (*челове́к*) drunk; (*кри́ки, пе́сни итп*) drunken ♦ (-ого; *decl like adj*) *м* drunk; **под ~ую ру́ку** (*разг*) in a drunken rage.

пэр (-а) *м* peer.

пюпи́тр (-а) *м* lectern.

пюре́ *ср нескл* (*фрукто́вое*) purée; **карто́фельное** ~ mashed potato.

п/я *сокр* (= **почто́вый я́щик**) POB (= *Post Office Box*).

пяд|ь (-и) *ж* (*ме́ра*) span; (*небольшо́е простра́нство*) stretch; **семи́ пя́дей во́ лбу** extraordinarily intelligent.

пя́лец *сущ см* **пя́льцы**.

пя́л|иться (-юсь, -ишься) *несов возв* (*разг*) to gawk.

пя́ль|цы (-ец; *dat pl* -ьцам) *мн* tambour *ед*.

пят|а́ (-ы́) *ж:* **до пят** (*о́чень дли́нный*) to the ground; **с головы́ до пят** from head to toe; **ходи́ть** (*impf*) или **гна́ться** (*impf*) **за кем-н по ~м** to follow hot on sb's heels.

пята́к (-á) *м* (*разг*) five-kopeck piece.

пятачо́к (-ка́) *м* five-kopeck piece; (*небольша́я площа́дка*) spot; (*небольшо́е простра́нство*) stretch; (*сви́ный*) snout.

пя́т|ая (-ой; *decl like adj*) *ж:* **одна́** ~ one fifth.

пя́тен *сущ см* **пятно́**.

пятёр|ка (-ки; *gen pl* -ок) *ж* (*ци́фра, ка́рта*) five; (*разг: де́нежный знак*) fiver; (*ПРОСВЕЩ*) ≈ A (*school mark*); (*гру́ппа из пяти́*) group of five; (*разг: авто́бус, трамва́й итп*) (number) five (*bus, tram etc*).

пятерн|я́ (-и́) *ж* (*разг*) paw.

пя́тер|о (-ы́х; *как* **че́тверо**; *см* **Table 36b**) *чис* five; *см также* **дво́е**.

пятёрок *сущ см* **пятёрка**.

пяти́ *чис см* **пять**.

пятибо́р|ье (-я) *ср* pentathlon.

пятидеся́ти *чис см* **пятьдеся́т**.

пятидесятиле́ти|е (-я) *ср* fifty years *мн*; (*годовщи́на*) fiftieth anniversary.

пятидесятиле́тн|ий (-яя, -ее, -ие) *прил* (*пери́од*) fifty-year; (*челове́к*) fifty-year-old.

пятидеся́тый (-ая, -ое, -ые) *чис* fiftieth; **чита́ю ~ую страни́цу** I am on page fifty; **я живу́ в ~ой кварти́ре** I live in flat fifty; **я прие́хал в Петербу́рг в ~ом году́** I came to Petersburg in nineteen fifty; **~ые го́ды** the Fifties; **в ~ых года́х** in the Fifties.

пятидне́в|ка (-ки; *gen pl* -ок) *ж* (*разг*) five-day week.

пятидне́вный *прил* five-day.

пятикла́ссник (-а) *м pupil in fifth year at school (usually eleven years old)*.

пятикла́ссниц|а (-ы) *ж см* **пятикла́ссник**.

пятикопе́ечный *прил* five-kopeck.

пятикра́тн|ый *прил*: ~ **чемпио́н** five-times champion; **в ~ом разме́ре** fivefold.

пятиле́ти|е (-я) *ср (срок)* five years; *(юбилей)* fifth anniversary.

пятиле́т|ка (-ки; *gen pl* -ок) *ж (ИСТ, ЭКОН)* five-year plan.

пятиле́тн|ий (-яя, -ее, -ие) *прил (промежуток)* five-year; *(ребёнок)* five-year-old.

пятиле́ток *сущ см* **пятиле́тка**.

пятиме́сячный *прил* five-month; *(ребёнок)* five-month-old.

пятимину́т|ка (-ки; *gen pl* -ок) *ж (разг)* short meeting *(at work)*.

пятинеде́льный *прил* five-week; *(ребёнок)* five-week-old.

пятисо́т *чис см* **пятьсо́т**.

пятисотле́ти|е (-я) *ср (срок)* five hundred years; *(годовщина)* quincentenary.

пятисотле́тн|ий (-яя, -ее, -ие) *прил (период)* five-hundred-year; *(дерево)* five hundred-year-old.

пятисо́т|ый (-ая, -ое, -ые) *чис* five-hundredth.

пя́|титься (-чусь, -тишься; *perf* **попя́титься**) *несов возв* to move backwards; **он попя́тился от меня́** he backed away from me.

пятиуго́льник (-а) *м* pentagon.

пятичасово́й *прил (рабочий день)* five-hour; *(поезд)* five o'clock.

пятиэта́ж|ка (-ки; *gen pl* -ек) *м (разг)* five-storey block of flats *(ВRIT)*, five-story apartment block *(US)*.

пятиэта́жный *прил* five-storey.

пя́т|ка (-ки; *gen pl* -ок) *ж* heel; **наступа́ть** *(impf)* **кому́-н на ~ки** *(перен)* to tread on sb's toes.

пятна́дцатый (-ая, -ое, -ые) *чис* fifteenth; *см также* **пя́тый**.

пятна́дцат|ь (-и; *как* **пять**; *см* **Table 27**) *чис* fifteen; *см также* **пять**.

пятна́|ть (-ю; *perf* **запятна́ть**) *несов перех* to tarnish.

пятни́ст|ый (-, -а, -о) *прил* spotted.

пя́тниц|а (-ы) *ж* Friday; **в ~у** on Friday; **по ~м** on Fridays; **в сле́дующую/про́шлую ~у** next/

last Friday; **сего́дная ~, деся́тое ма́я** today is Friday (the) tenth (of) May.

пятн|о́ (-а́; *nom pl* **пя́тна**, *gen pl* -ен) *ср (также перен)* stain; *(выделяющееся по цвету)* spot.

пя́ток *сущ см* **пя́тка**.

пят|о́к (-ка) *м (разг)* five *(when buying eggs etc)*.

пя́т|ый (-ая, -ое, -ые) *чис* fifth; **сего́дня ~ое ию́ля** today is the fifth of July *или* July the fifth; **прие́ду ~ого ию́ля** I will arrive on the fifth of July; **встре́ча отло́жена до ~ого ию́ля** the meeting was postponed until the fifth of July; **сего́дня у́же ~ое (число́)** today is already the fifth; **сейча́с де́сять мину́т ~ого** it is ten minutes past five; **я прие́хал в Петербу́рг в ты́сяча девятьсо́т пятьдеся́т ~ом году́** I came to Petersburg in nineteen fifty five; **ле́кция бу́дет в ~ой аудито́рии** the lecture will take place in room five; **я зако́нчил ~ым** I finished fifth; **я был ~ым ребёнком в семье́** I was child number five in the family; **~ое – деся́тое** *(разг)* this and that; **переска́кивать** *(impf)* **с ~ого на деся́тое** *(разг)* to skip from one subject to another.

пят|ь (-и́; *см* **Table 27**) *чис* five; *(ПРОСВЕЩ)* ≈ А *(school mark)*; **ей ~ лет** she is five years old; **они́ живу́т в до́ме но́мер ~** they live at number five; **о́коло ~и́** about five; **кни́га сто́ит ~ рубле́й** the book costs five roubles; **~ с полови́ной часо́в** five and a half hours; **сейча́с ~ часо́в** it is five o'clock; **я́блоки продаю́тся по ~ штук** the apples are sold in fives; **дели́ть (раздели́ть** *perf)* **что-н на ~** to divide sth into five.

пятьдеся́т (-и́десяти; *см* **Table 29**) *чис* fifty; **здесь о́коло ~и́десяти челове́к** there are about fifty people here; **на сле́дующей неде́ле ему́ испо́лнится ~ (лет)** he will be fifty next week; **ему́ о́коло ~и́десят (лет)** he is about fifty (years old); **маши́на е́дет со ско́ростью ~ киломе́тров в час** the car is going at fifty miles per hour.

пять|со́т (-исо́т; *см* **Table 34**) *чис* five hundred; *см также* **сто**.

пя́тью *нареч* five times; **~ два – де́сять** five times two is ten.

пятью́ *чис см* **пять**.

пя́чусь *несов см* **пя́титься**.

~ Р, р ~

Р, р *сущ нескл (буква)* the 17th letter of the Russian alphabet.

р. *сокр* (= **река́**) R., r. (= *river*); (= *роди́лся*) b. (= *born*); (= **рубль**) R., r. (= *rouble*).

раб (-á) *м (также перен)* slave; ~ **любви́/мо́ды** *итп* a slave to love/fashion *итп*.

раба́ (-ы́; *no pl*) *ж см* **раб**.

рабовладе́лец (-ьца) *м* slave owner.

рабовладе́льческий (-ая, -ое, -ие) *прил* slave-owning.

раболе́п|ный (-ен, -на, -но) *прил* servile.

раболе́пств|овать (-ую) *несов неперех*: ~ (**пе́ред** +*instr*) to crawl (to).

рабо́т|а (-ы) *ж (труд, произведение)* work; *(источник заработка)* work, job; *(функционирование)* working; **поступа́ть** (**поступи́ть** *perf*) **на** ~**у** to start a job; **постоя́нная/вре́менная/случа́йная** ~ permanent/temporary/casual work *или* employment; **сде́льная** ~ piecework; **сме́нная** ~ shiftwork.

рабо́та|ть (-ю) *несов неперех* to work; *(магазин, библиотека итп)* to be open; ~ *(impf)* **на кого́-н/что-н** to work for sb/sth; ~ *(impf)* **над чем-н** to work on sth; **кем Вы** ~**ете?** what do you do for a living?; **я** ~**ю инжене́ром** I'm an engineer

▸ **рабо́таться** *несов возв* (+*dat*): **сего́дня мне не** ~**ется** I can't get down to work today; **в библиоте́ке хорошо́** ~**ется** the library is a good place to work.

рабо́тник (-а) *м* worker; *(учреждения)* employee; **руководя́щие** ~**и** management; **нау́чный** ~ researcher.

рабо́тниц|а (-ы) *ж* (female) worker.

работода́тел|ь (-я) *м* employer.

работоспосо́бност|ь (-и) *ж (человека)* ability to work hard; *(машины)* efficiency.

работоспосо́бный *прил (человек)* able to work hard; *(население)* working *опред*.

работя́г|а (-и) *м/ж (разг)* workhorse *(fig)*.

работя́щий (-ая, -ее, -ие) *прил (разг)* hard-working.

рабо́чая (-ей; *decl like adj*) *ж см* **рабо́чий**.

рабо́чий (-ая, -ее, -ие) *прил (движение, посёлок, столовая)* worker's *опред*; *(человек, одежда, часть механизма, чертёж)* working *опред* ◆ (-его; *decl like adj*) *м* worker; **в** ~**ее вре́мя** during working hours; **у нас нехва́тка**

~**их рук** we are undermanned; **в** ~**ем поря́дке** in working order; **рабо́чая ло́шадь** workhorse; **рабо́чая си́ла** workforce; **рабо́чая ста́нция** *(КОМП)* work station; **рабо́чее ме́сто** *(помещение)* workplace; *(пост)* position; **рабо́чие ру́ки** workers; **рабо́чий визи́т** working visit; **рабо́чий день** working day *(BRIT)*, workday *(US)*; **рабо́чий класс** the working class.

ра́бский (-ая, -ое, -ие) *прил (существование, условия)* slave-like; *(послушание, подражание)* slavish; ~ **труд** slave labour *(BRIT)* *или* labor *(US)*.

ра́бств|о (-а) *ср* slavery.

рабфа́к (-а) *м (ист* = **рабо́чий факульте́т)** ≈ working man's college.

рабы́н|я (-и) *ж* slave.

равви́н (-а) *м* rabbi.

ра́вен *прил см* **ра́вный**.

ра́венств|о (-а) *ср* equality; *(чисел)* equal value; **знак** ~**а** *(МАТ)* equals sign; **ста́вить** (**поста́вить** *perf)* **знак** ~**а ме́жду чем-н и чем-н** to equate sth with sth.

равни́н|а (-ы) *ж* plain.

равно́ *нареч* equally ◆ *союз*: ~ **(как) и** as well as ◆ *как сказ*: **э́то всё** ~ it doesn't make any difference; **мне всё** ~ it's all the same to me; **я всё** ~ **приду́** I'll come just the same; **два плюс пять** ~ **семи́** two plus five equals seven.

равнове́си|е (-я) *ср (также перен)* equilibrium; **теря́ть** (**потеря́ть** *perf)* ~ to lose one's balance; ~ **сил** balance of power.

равноде́нстви|е (-я) *ср* equinox.

равноду́шен *прил см* **равноду́шный**.

равноду́ши|е (-я) *ср*: ~ **(к** +*dat)* indifference (to).

равноду́шно *нареч* indifferently.

равноду́ш|ный (-ен, -на, -но) *прил*: ~ **(к** +*dat)* indifferent (to).

равноме́р|ный (-ен, -на, -но) *прил* even.

равнопра́вен *прил см* **равнопра́вный**.

равнопра́ви|е (-я) *ср* equal rights *мн*.

равнопра́в|ный (-ен, -на, -но) *прил* equal.

равноси́л|ьный (-ен, -ьна, -ьно) *прил*: ~ +*dat* equivalent *или* equal to.

равноце́н|ный (-ен, -на, -но) *прил* of equal value *или* worth.

ра́в|ный (-ен, -на́, -но) *прил* equal; ~**ным о́бразом** equally; **на** ~**ных** *(разг)* on an equal footing.

равня́|ть (-ю; *perf* **сравня́ть**) *несов перех*: ~ (**с** +*instr*) (*делать равным*) to make equal (with); (*одинаково оценивать*): ~ **кого́-н/что-н с** +*instr* to treat sb/sth the same as

▸ **равня́ться** (*perf* **сравня́ться**) *несов возв*: ~**ся по** +*dat* to draw level with; (*считать себя равным*): ~**ся с** +*instr* to compare o.s. with; (*быть равносильным*): ~**ся** +*dat* to be equal to; (*следовать примеру*): ~**ся на** +*acc* to emulate; **два плюс два** ~**ется четырём** two plus two equals four.

рагу́ *ср нескл* ragout.

рад (-а, -о, -ы) *как сказ*: ~ (+*dat*) glad (of); ~ +*infin* glad *или* pleased to do; ~ **познако́миться с Ва́ми** pleased to meet you; **я** ~ **за него́** I'm pleased *или* happy for him; **я всегда́** ~ **помо́чь** I'm always glad to be of help; **я уже́ и не ра́да, что согласи́лась** I'm already regretting that I agreed.

ра́ди *предл*: ~ (+*gen*) for the sake of; **чего́** ~? (*разг*) what for?; **шу́тки** ~ (*разг*) for a joke; ~ **Бо́га!** (*разг*) for God's sake!

радиа́льный *прил* radial.

радиа́тор (-а) *м* radiator.

радиа́ция (-и) *ж* radiation.

ра́ди|й (-я) *м* radium.

радика́л (-а) *м* (*ПОЛИТ, МАТ*) radical.

радика́л|ьный (-ен, -ьна, -ьно) *прил* radical.

радикули́т (-а) *м* lower back pain.

ра́дио *ср нескл* radio; **по** ~ on the radio; **слу́шать** (*impf*) ~ to listen to the radio.

радиоакти́вност|ь (-и) *ж* radioactivity.

радиоакти́вный *прил* radioactive.

радиовеща́ни|е (-я) *ср* (radio) broadcasting.

радиолока́тор (-а) *м* radar (*device*).

радиолока́ци|я (-и) *ж* radar (*system*).

радиолюби́тел|ь (-я) *м* radio ham.

радиопереда́ч|а (-и) *ж* radio programme (*BRIT*) *или* program (*US*).

радиоприёмник (-а) *м* radio (set).

радиосвя́з|ь (-и) *ж* radiocommunication.

радиослу́шател|ь (-я) *м* (radio) listener.

радиослу́шательниц|а (-ы) *ж см* **радиослу́шатель**.

радиоста́нци|я (-и) *ж* radio station.

радиотелефо́н (-а) *м* radiotelephone.

радиоте́хник|а (-и) *ж* radio engineering.

радиоу́зел (-ла́) *м* public-address facilities *мн*.

радиоэлектро́ник|а (-и) *ж* radio electronics.

ради́ст (-а) *м* radio operator.

ради́ст|ка (-ки; *gen pl* -ок) *ж см* **ради́ст**.

ра́ди|ус (-а) *м* radius; (*перен: влияния, действия*) range.

ра́д|овать (-ую; *perf* **обра́довать**) *несов перех*: ~ **кого́-н** to make sb happy, please sb; ~ (*impf*) **глаз/слух** to be a joy to behold/hear

▸ **ра́доваться** *несов возв* (*перен: душа,* сердце) to rejoice; (*perf* **обра́доваться**; +*dat*; *солнцу, успехам*) to take pleasure in; **я обра́довалась ему́** *или* **встре́че с ним** I was overjoyed to see him.

ра́достен *прил см* **ра́достный**.

ра́достно *нареч* joyfully; **они́ меня́** ~ **встре́тили** they gave me a very warm welcome.

ра́дост|ный (-ен, -на, -но) *прил* joyful; (*день, новость*) joyous.

ра́дост|ь (-ти) *ж* joy; **от** ~**ти** (*плакать, смеяться*) with joy; **пры́гать** (*impf*) **от** ~**ти** to jump for joy; **с** ~**ю** gladly; **на** ~**тях я его́ прости́л** (*разг*) I was so happy, I forgave him.

ра́дуг|а (-и) *ж* rainbow.

ра́дуж|ный (-ен, -на, -но) *прил* (*перен: настроение, надежды*) bright; ~**ные цвета́** rainbow colours; **ра́дужная оболо́чка** (*АНАТ*) iris.

раду́шен *прил см* **раду́шный**.

раду́ши|е (-я) *ср* warmth.

раду́ш|ный (-ен, -на, -но) *прил* warm.

раз (-а; *nom pl* -**ы́**, *gen pl* -**) *м* time ◆ *нескл* (*один*) one ◆ *нареч* (*раз: однажды*) once ◆ *союз* (*разг: если*) if; **в два/три/четы́ре ра́за бо́льше/ме́ньше** two/three/four times bigger/smaller; **в пять/шесть/семь** *итп* ~ **бо́льше/ме́ньше** five/six/seven *итп* times bigger/smaller; **не** ~ more than once; ~ **в пе́рвый** ~ (*впервые*) for the first time; (*в первом случае*) on the first occasion; **в тот/про́шлый/сле́дующий** ~ that/last/next time; **на э́тот** ~ this time; **ещё** ~ (once) again; **и навсегда́** once and for all; **ни ра́зу** not once; (**оди́н**) ~ **в день** once a day; **вот тебе́ и** ~! (*раза*) that's a turn up for the books!; **в са́мый** ~ (*разг: о размере*) just right; (: *о времени*) at just the right time; ~... **то** ... (*разг*) if ... then ...; ~ **на** ~ **не прихо́дится** you can't win all the time; ~ **пришёл – сади́сь** now that you're here, have a seat.

раз- *префикс* (*in verbs*; *о разделении на части*) *indicating division into parts eg.* **развяза́ть**; (*о распределении по местам, по поверхности*) *indicating positioning of sth somewhere eg.* **разложи́ть**; (*об интенсивном действии*) *indicating intensive action eg.* **разбушева́ться**; (*о направлении движения в разные стороны*) *indicating movement in different directions eg.* **разбежа́ться**; (*о прекращении действия*) *indicating cessation of action eg.* **разлюби́ть**; (*in adjectives*; *раза: о высшей степени качества*) *indicating a great degree of a certain quality eg.* **развесёлый**.

разба́в|ить (-лю, -ишь; *impf* **разбавля́ть**) *сов перех* to dilute.

разбаза́р|ить (-ю, -ишь; *impf* **разбаза́ривать**) *сов перех* to squander.

разба́лива|ться (-юсь) *несов от* **разболе́ться**.

разба́лтыва|ть(ся) (-ю(сь)) *несов от* **разболта́ть(ся)**.

разбе́г (-а) *м* (*машины*) acceleration; (*атлета*) run-up; **прыжо́к с ~а** *или* **~у** running jump.

разбежа́ться (*как* **бежа́ть**; *см* Table 20; *impf* **разбега́ться**) *сов возв* to run off, scatter; (*перед прыжком*) to take a run-up; (*перен: мысли*) to wander; **у меня́ глаза́ разбега́ются** (*разг*) I'm spoilt for choice.

разбе́й(те) *сов см* **разби́ть**.

разберу́(сь) *сов см* **разобра́ть(ся)**.

разбива́|ть(ся) (-ю(сь)) *несов от* **разби́ть(ся)**.

разби́в|ка (-ки; *gen pl* -ок) *ж* (*данных, людей*) arranging; (*сада, парка*) layout.

разбира́тельств|о (-а) *ср* (*ЮР*) examination.

разбира́|ть (-ю) *несов от* **разобра́ть ◆** *перех* (*разг: сотрудника, нарушителя итп*) to take to task

▶ **разбира́ться** *несов от* **разобра́ться ◆** *возв* (*разг: понимать*): **~ся в** +*prp* to understand.

разбитно́й *прил* carefree.

разб|и́ть (-обью́, -обьёшь; *imper* -е́й(те), *impf* **разбива́ть**) *сов перех* (*стекло, тарелку, го́лову*) to break; (*машину*) to smash up; (*врага́, а́рмию*) to crush; (*на уча́стки, на ча́сти*) to break up; (*алле́ю, клу́мбу*) to lay; (*сча́стье, мечты́*) to ruin; **разбива́ть** (**~** *perf*) **ла́герь** to set up camp

▶ **разби́ться** (*impf* **разбива́ться**) *сов возв* to break, smash; (*при паде́нии, в ава́рии*) to be badly hurt; (*на гру́ппы, на уча́стки*) to break up.

разбогате́|ть (-ю) *сов от* **богате́ть**.

разбо́|й (-я) *м* robbery.

разбо́йник (-а) *м* robber; (*разг: шалу́н*) troublemaker.

разбо́йниц|а (-ы) *ж см* **разбо́йник**.

разбо́йнича|ть (-ю) *несов неперех* to thieve; (*разг: шали́ть*) to get up to mischief.

разбо́йн|ый *прил*: **~ое нападе́ние** (*ЮР*) armed assault.

разболе́|ться (-юсь; *impf* **разба́ливаться**) *сов возв* (*разг: челове́к*) to be taken ill; (: *рука́, живо́т итп*) to hurt badly; **у меня́ голова́ ~лась** I've got a splitting headache.

разбо́лтан|ный (-, -на, -но) *прил* (*разг*) slack; **~ная похо́дка** swagger.

разболта́|ть (-ю; *impf* **разба́лтывать**) *сов перех* (*порошо́к, смесь итп*) to mix in; (*замо́к, га́йку*) to weaken; (*разг: секре́т, но́вость*) to blab; **~** (*perf*) **дисципли́ну** (*разг*) to let discipline slip; **~** (*perf*) **ребёнка** (*разг*) to lose control over a child

▶ **разболта́ться** (*impf* **разба́лтываться**) *сов возв* (*порошо́к, мука́*) to mix in; (*дверь, запо́р*) to come loose; (*дисципли́на, поведе́ние*) to slacken off; (*no impf*; *болта́ть*) to babble on.

разбомб|и́ть (-лю́, -и́шь) *сов перех* to bomb.

разбо́р (-а) *м* (*статьи́, вопро́са итп*) analysis; (*ЮР*) examination; (*линг*) parsing; **без ~а** without exception.

разбо́рный *прил* collapsible.

разбо́рчивост|ь (-и) *ж* (*требовательность*)

discernment; (*почерка*) legibility.

разбо́рчив|ый (-, -а, -о) *прил* (*челове́к, вкус*) discerning; (*почерк*) legible.

разбра́сыва|ть (-ю) *несов от* **разброса́ть**

▶ **разбра́сываться** *несов возв* (*разг*) to try to do too much (at once); (+*instr*; *друзья́ми, покло́нниками итп*) to underrate.

разбр|ести́сь (-еду́сь, -едёшься; *pt* -ёлся, -ела́сь, -ело́сь, *impf* **разбреда́ться**) *сов возв* to wander off (*in different directions*).

разброса́|ть (-ю; *impf* **разбра́сывать**) *сов перех* to scatter.

разбу|ди́ть (-ужу́, -у́дишь) *сов от* **буди́ть**.

разбу́х|нуть (-ну, -нешь; *pt* -, -ла, -ло, *impf* **разбуха́ть**) *сов неперех* to swell; (*папка, чемода́н итп*) to bulge; (*лицо́, рука́ итп*) to swell up.

разбуше|ва́ться (-у́юсь) *сов возв* (*мо́ре*) to rage; (*разг*) to rant.

разва́л (-а) *м* (*в кварти́ре, в дела́х*) chaos; (*эконо́мики*) ruin; (*систе́мы*) break-up; **у нас до́ма по́лный ~** our home is in a state of chaos.

разва́лива|ть(ся) (-ю(сь)) *несов от* **развали́ть(ся)**.

разва́лин|а (-ы) *ж* (*обычно мн*) ruins *мн*; (*перен: челове́к*) wreck.

разв|али́ть (-алю́, -а́лишь; *impf* **разва́ливать**) *сов перех* (*сте́ну, дом*) to knock down; (*де́ло, хозя́йство*) to ruin

▶ **развали́ться** (*impf* **разва́ливаться**) *сов возв* to collapse; **он ~али́лся в кре́сле** he sat slumped in the armchair.

разв|ари́ться (*3sg* -а́рится, *3pl* -а́рятся, *impf* **разва́риваться**) *сов возв* to be overcooked; **бы́стро ~а́риваться** (*impf*) to cook quickly.

ра́зве *част* really; **~ он согласи́лся/не знал?** did he really agree/not know?; **~ то́лько** *или* **что** except that.

развева́|ться (*3sg* -ется, *3pl* -ются) *несов возв* (*фла́га*) to flutter; (*во́лосы*) to flow.

разве́да|ть (-ю; *impf* **разве́дывать**) *сов перех* (*ГЕО*) to prospect; (*ВОЕН*) to reconnoitre (*BRIT*), reconnoiter (*US*); **~** (*perf*)(**о** +*prp*) to find out (about).

разведе́ни|е (-я) *ср* (*живо́тных*) breeding; (*расте́ний*) cultivation; (*костра́*) building; (*кле́я, кра́ски*) dilution; **~ пчёл** beekeeping.

разведён|ный (-, -а́, -ы́) *прил* (*в разводе*) divorced; (*no short form*; *раство́р, во́дка*) diluted.

разве́д|ка (-ки; *gen pl* -ок) *ж* (*ГЕО*) prospecting; (*ПОЛИТ*) intelligence; (*ВОЕН*) reconnaissance.

разведу́(сь) *итп сов см* **развести́(сь)**.

разве́дчик (-а) *м* (*ГЕО*) prospector; (*полит*) intelligence agent; (*ВОЕН*) scout; (*самолёт*) reconnaissance plane.

разве́дчиц|а (-ы) *ж* (*ВОЕН*) scout.

разве́дыва|ть (-ю) *несов от* **разве́дать**.

разв|езти́ (-езу́, -езёшь; *pt* -ёз, -езла́, -езло́, *impf* **развози́ть**) *сов перех* to deliver **◆** *безл*: **меня́ ~езло́ от жары́/во́дки** the heat/vodka knocked me out; **доро́гу ~езло́** the road has become impassable.

разве́ива|**ть(ся)** (-ю(сь)) *несов от*
разве́ять(ся).
разве́й(те) *сов см* **разви́ть**.
развенча́|**ть** (-ю; *impf* **разве́нчивать**) *сов перех*
to discredit.
развёрну́т|**ый** (-, -а, -о) *прил* detailed;
(*строи́тельство*) extensive.
разверну́ть (-у́, -ёшь; *impf* **развёртывать** *или*
развора́чивать) *сов перех* (*бума́гу, ка́рту*) to
unfold; (*ковёр*) to unroll; (*па́рус, флаг*) to
unfurl; (*прое́кт, торго́влю итп*) to launch;
(*вы́ставку, ла́герь*) to set up; (*свои́ си́лы,
тала́нт*) to develop fully; (*кора́бль, маши́ну,
самолёт*) to turn around; (*батальо́н, полк итп*)
to deploy; **~** (*perf*) **пле́чи** to pull one's shoulders
back
▶ **разверну́ться** (*impf* **развёртываться** *или*
развора́чиваться) *сов возв* (*борьба́, кампа́ния,
рабо́та*) to get under way; (*тала́нт, челове́к*)
to develop fully; (*автомоби́ль, су́дно*) to turn
around; (*батальо́н*) to be deployed; (*вид,
зре́лище*) to open up.
развесел|**и́ть** (-ю́, -и́шь) *сов от* **весели́ть**.
разве́сист|**ый** (-, -а, -о) *прил* spreading *опред*.
разве́|**сить** (-шу, -сишь; *impf* **разве́шивать**) *сов
перех* (*ве́тви*) to spread; (*карти́ны, ве́щи*) to
hang; (*бельё*) to hang up *или* out; **~** (*perf*) **у́ши**
(*разг*) to listen wide-eyed.
развесно́й *прил* sold by weight.
разве|**сти́** (-еду́, -еде́шь; *pt* -ёл, -ела́, -ело́, *impf*
разводи́ть) *сов перех* to take; (*разъедини́ть*)
to divorce; (*порошо́к*) to dissolve; (*сок, кра́ску*) to
dilute; (*живо́тных*) to breed; (*цветы́, сад*) to
grow; (*мост*) to raise; **разводи́ть** (**~** *perf*) **дете́й
по дома́м** to take the children home; **разводи́ть**
(**~** *perf*) **ого́нь** to get a fire going; **разводи́ть** (**~**
perf) **рука́ми** ≈ to shrug one's shoulders;
разводи́ть (**~** *perf*) **пусту́ю болтовню́** (*разг*) to
talk hot air
▶ **развести́сь** (*impf* **разводи́ться**) *сов возв*
(*живо́тные*) to breed; **разводи́ться** (**~сь** *perf*)
(**с** +*instr*) to divorce, get divorced (from).
разветв|**и́ть** (-лю́, -и́шь; *impf* **разветвля́ть**) *сов
перех* to expand
▶ **разветви́ться** (*impf* **разветвля́ться**) *сов возв*
(*де́рево, река́, доро́га*) to branch; (*компа́ния,
учрежде́ние*) to branch out.
разветвле́ни|**е** (-я) *ср* (*де́йствие: доро́г, кро́ны
дере́вьев*) branching; (: *компа́нии*) expansion;
(*ме́сто: желе́зной доро́ги, кана́ла*) fork.
разветвлённый (-ён, -ена́, -ено́) *прил*
extensive.
разветвлю́(сь) *сов см* **разветви́ть(ся)**.
разветвля́|**ть(ся)** (-ю(сь)) *несов от*
разветви́ть(ся).
разве́ша|**ть** (-ю; *impf* **разве́шивать**) *сов перех*
(*карти́ны, фотогра́фии*) to hang; (*бельё*) to
hang up *или* out.

разве́шива|**ть** (-ю) *несов от* **разве́сить**,
разве́шать.
разве́шу *сов см* **разве́сить**.
разве́|**ять** (-ю; *impf* **разве́ивать**) *сов перех*
(*облака́, тума́н*) to disperse; (*подозре́ния,
сомне́ния, грусть*) to dispel; **разве́ивать** (**~**
perf) **миф** to shatter a myth
▶ **разве́яться** (*impf* **разве́иваться**) *сов возв*
(*облака́*) to disperse; (*тума́н*) to lift; (*тоска́,
сомне́ния, мра́чные мы́сли*) to be dispelled;
(*челове́к*) to relax.
развива́|**ть(ся)** (-ю(сь)) *несов от* **разви́ть(ся)**.
развива́ющ|**ийся** (-аяся, -оеся, -иеся) *прил*:
~аяся страна́ developing country.
разви́л|**ка** (-ки; *gen pl* -ок) *ж* fork (*in road*).
разви́ти|**е** (-я) *ср* development; **высо́кое/
ни́зкое ~** a high/low level of development.
ра́зви́т|**ой** (-, -а, -о) *прил* developed; (*духо́вно
зре́лый*) mature.
разв|**и́ть** (-овью́, -овьёшь; *pt* -и́л, -ила́,
-и́ло, *imper* -ве́й(те), *impf* **развива́ть**) *сов
перех* to develop; (*наступле́ние,
де́ятельность*) to step up; (*верёвку, плётку*) to
unwind; (*во́лосы*) to straighten; **развива́ть** (**~**
perf) **ско́рость** to gather speed; **развива́ть** (**~**
perf) **ребёнка** to help a child to develop
▶ **разви́ться** (*impf* **развива́ться**) *сов возв* to
develop; (*ско́рость*) to build up; (*верёвка, коса́,
плётка*) to come unwound; (*во́лосы*) to become
straighter.
развлёк(ся) итп *сов см* **развле́чь(ся)**.
развлека́тел|**ьный** (-ен, -ьна, -ьно) *прил*
entertaining.
развлека́|**ть(ся)** (-ю(сь)) *несов от*
развле́чь(ся).
развлеку́(сь) итп *сов см* **развле́чь(ся)**.
развлече́ни|**е** (-я) *ср* (*госте́й, пу́блики*)
entertaining; (*спекта́кль итп*) entertainment.
развл|**е́чь** (-еку́, -ечёшь итп, -еку́т; *pt* -ёк,
-екла́, -екло́, *impf* **развлека́ть**) *сов перех* to
entertain
▶ **развле́чься** (*impf* **развлека́ться**) *сов возв* to
have fun.
разво́д (-а) *м* (*расторже́ние бра́ка*) divorce;
(*моста́*) opening; **они́ в ~е** they are divorced;
подава́ть (**пода́ть** *perf*) **на ~** to apply for a
divorce.
разв|**оди́ть(ся)** (-ожу́(сь), -о́дишь(ся)) *несов
от* **развести́(сь)**.
разводно́й *прил*: **~ ключ** monkey wrench;
разводно́й мост drawbridge.
разво́д|**ы** (-ов) *мн* (*узо́р*) design *ед*; (*подтёки,
пя́тна*) stains *мн*.
развожу́(сь) *несов см* **разводи́ть(ся)**.
разв|**ози́ть** (-ожу́, -о́зишь) *несов от* **развезти́**.
разволно́|**вать** (-у́ю) *сов перех* to alarm
▶ **разволнова́ться** *сов возв* to be alarmed.
развора́чива|**ть(ся)** (-ю(сь)) *несов от*

разверну́ть(ся).

разворо́|ва́ть (-у́ю; *impf* **разворо́вывать**) *сов перех* to loot.

разворо́т (-а) *м* (*машины*) U-turn; (*в книге*) double page.

разворо́|ти́ть (-чу́, -тишь) *сов перех* (*дорогу*) to dig up.

развра́т (-а) *м* promiscuity; (*духовный*) depravity.

развра́тен *прил см* **развра́тный**.

развра|ти́ть (-щу́, -ти́шь; *impf* **развраща́ть**) *сов перех* to pervert; (*деньгами*) to corrupt.

► **разврати́ться** (*impf* **развраща́ться**) *сов возв* (*см перех*) to become promiscuous; to become corrupted.

развра́тник (-а) *м* promiscuous man (*мн* men).

развра́тниц|а (-ы) *ж* promiscuous woman (*мн* women).

развра́тнича|ть (-ю) *несов неперех* to lead a life of promiscuity.

развра́т|ный (-ен, -на, -но) *прил* promiscuous.

развраща́|ть(ся) (-ю(сь)) *несов от* **разврати́ть(ся)**.

развращу́(сь) *несов см* **разврати́ть(ся)**.

разв|яза́ть (-яжу́, -я́жешь; *impf* **развя́зывать**) *сов перех* (*узел, шнурки, мешок*) to untie; (*перен: инициативу*) to unshackle; (: *войну, реакцию*) to unleash; **развя́зывать** (~ *perf*) кому́-н ру́ки (*перен*) to free sb's hands; **развя́зывать** (~ *perf*) кому́-н язы́к to loosen sb's tongue

► **развяза́ться** (*impf* **развя́зываться**) *сов возв* (*шнурки, бант итп*) to come untied; ~**ся с** +*instr* (*разг: с людьми, с экзаменами*) to be through with; (: *с долгами*) to get rid of.

развя́з|ка (-ки; *gen pl* -ок) *ж* (*конец*) ending; (*авт*) junction.

развя́з|ный (-ен, -на, -но) *прил* overly familiar.

развя́зок *сущ см* **развя́зка**.

развя́зыва|ть(ся) (-ю(сь)) *несов от* **развяза́ть(ся)**.

разгада́|ть (-ю; *impf* **разга́дывать**) *сов перех* (*кроссворд, загадку*) to solve; (*замыслы, тайну*) to guess; (*сны*) to decipher; (*человека*) to fathom out.

разга́д|ка (-ки; *gen pl* -ок) *ж* (*снов, мыслей*) deciphering; (*тайны*) key; (*феномена*) explanation; (*решение загадки*) solution.

разга́дыва|ть (-ю) *несов от* **разгада́ть**.

разга́р (-а) *м*: **в** ~**е** +*gen* (*сезона*) at the height of; (*боя*) in the heart of; **кани́кулы в (по́лном)** ~**е** the holidays are in full swing.

разгиба́|ть(ся) (-ю(сь)) *несов от* **разогну́ть(ся)**.

разгильдя́|й (-я) *м* (*разг*) layabout.

разгла́|дить (-жу, -дишь; *impf* **разгла́живать**) *сов перех* to smooth out.

разгла|си́ть (-шу́, -си́шь; *impf* **разглаша́ть**) *сов перех* to divulge, disclose.

разгля|де́ть (-жу́, -ди́шь; *impf* **разгля́дывать**) *сов перех* (*рассмотреть*) to scrutinize; (*no impf*;

понять) to discern.

разгне́ван|ный (-, -а, -о) *прил*: ~ (+*instr*) angry (with).

разгова́рива|ть (-ю) *несов неперех*: ~ (**с** +*instr*) to talk (to); **она́ бо́льше со мной не** ~**ет** she doesn't talk to me any more.

разгово́р (-а) *м* conversation; **э́то друго́й** ~! (*раз*) that's another matter! **без** ~**ов** without a word; *см также* **разгово́ры**.

разгово́рник (-а) *м* phrase book.

разгово́рный *прил* colloquial.

разгово́рчив|ый (-, -а, -о) *прил* talkative.

разгово́р|ы (-ов) *мн* (*толки*) gossip *ед*.

разго́н (-а) *м* (*демонстрации*) breaking up; (*самолёта, автомобиля*) acceleration; **устра́ивать** (**устро́ить** *perf*) **кому́-н** ~ (*разг*) to give sb a roasting.

разгоня́|ть(ся) (-ю(сь)) *несов от* **разогна́ть(ся)**.

разгор|е́ться (*3sg* -и́тся, *3sg* -я́тся, *impf* **разгора́ться**) *сов возв* (*костёр, спор*) to flare up; (*закат*) to be ablaze; (*щёки, уши*) to burn; (*перен: страсти, любопытство*) to become inflamed.

разгорячён|ный (-, -а́, -о́) *прил*: ~ (+*instr*) (*человек*) inflamed (by); (-, на́, -но́; *лицо*) excited.

разгорячи́|ться (-у́сь, -и́шься) *сов от* **горячи́ться** ♦ *возв* (*от волнения, от работы*) to get het up; (*от бега*) to be hot.

разграни́ч|ить (-у, -ишь; *impf* **разграни́чивать**) *сов перех* (*район, земли*) to demarcate; (*обязанности, понятия*) to delimit.

разграф|и́ть (-лю́, -и́шь) *сов от* **графи́ть**.

разгр|ести́ (-ебу́, -ебёшь; *pt* -ёб, -ебла́, -ебло́, *impf* **разгреба́ть**) *сов перех* to sweep aside.

разгро́м (-а) *м* (*разг: беспорядок*) mayhem, havoc; (*статьи*) savaging.

разгром|и́ть (-лю́, -и́шь) *сов перех* (*врага, сопротивление*) to crush; (*город, страну*) to destroy; (*политику, статью, соперника*) to savage.

разгро́мный *прил* (*речь, критика*) savage.

разгру|зи́ть (-жу́, -у́зишь; *impf* **разгружа́ть**) *сов перех* to unload; (*программу*) to ease; **разгружа́ть** (~ *perf*) **кого́-н** to lighten sb's load.

разгру́з|ка (-ки; *gen pl* -ок) *ж* (*вагонов, баржи*) unloading; (*перен: человека*) unburdening; (: *программы, плана*) easing up.

разгру́зоч|ный *прил*: ~**ые рабо́ты** unloading; **разгру́зочный день** *day during dieting programme on which diet is relaxed*.

разгры́з|ть (-у, -ёшь) *сов от* **грызть** ♦ *impf* **разгрыза́ть**) *сов перех* (*редиску, кость*) to gnaw at; (*орех*) to crack open.

разгу́л (-а) *м* revelry; (+*gen*; *реакции, национализма итп*) outburst of.

разгу́лива|ть (-ю) *несов неперех* to have a wander

► **разгу́ливаться** *несов от* **разгуля́ться**.

разгуля́|ться (-юсь; *impf* **разгу́ливаться**) *сов*

возв (*дать себе волю*) to let o.s. go; (*перен:
ветер, море*) to get up; (: *погода, день*) to clear
up.

разда|ва́ть(ся) (**-ю́(сь), -ёшь(ся)**) *несов от*
разда́ть(ся).

раздав|и́ть (**-авлю́, -а́вишь**) *сов от* **дави́ть** ♦
(*impf* **разда́вливать**) *перех* to squash.

разда́м(ся) *итп сов см* **разда́ть(ся)**.

разда́точный *прил*: ~ **пункт** distribution centre
(*BRIT*) *или* center (*US*).

разда́ть (*как* **дать**; *см* **Table 14**; *impf*
раздава́ть) *сов перех* to give out, distribute

▸ **разда́ться** (*impf* **раздава́ться**) *сов возв*
(*голос, шум итп*) to be heard; (*толпа*) to make
way; (*обувь, сапоги*) to stretch; **раздава́ться**
(**~ся** *perf*) **в бёдрах** (*разг*) to put weight on
around the hips.

разда́ч|а (**-и**) *ж* distribution.

разда́шь(ся) *сов см* **разда́ть(ся)**.

раздва́ива|ться (**-юсь**) *несов от*
раздво́иться.

раздвига́|ть(ся) (**-ю**) *несов от*
раздви́нуть(ся).

раздвижно́й *прил*: ~ **за́навес** curtain (*THEAT*);
~ **стол** extending table.

раздви́н|уть (**-у, -ешь**; *impf* **раздвига́ть**) *сов
перех* to move apart; (*шторы*) to open; (*толпу*)
to part; (*перен: рамки наблюдения,
исследования*) to broaden

▸ **раздви́нуться** (*impf* **раздвига́ться**) *сов возв*
(*шторы*) to open; (*толпа*) to part; (*перен: мир,
возможности*) to open up.

раздво́ени|е (**-я**) *ср*: ~ **ли́чности** split
personality.

раздво́иться (**-ю́сь, -и́шься**; *impf*
раздва́иваться) *сов возв* (*дорога, река*) to
divide into two; (*перен: мнение*) to be divided.

раздева́л|ка (**-ки**; *gen pl* **-ок**) *ж* changing room.

раздева́|ть(ся) (**-ю(сь)**) *несов от* **разде́ть(ся)**.

разде́л (**-а**) *м* (*действие: имущества*) division;
(*часть, область*) section.

разде́ла|ть (**-ю**; *impf* **разде́лывать**) *сов перех*
(*мясо, рыбу*) to dress; (*грядки*) to prepare;
(*мебель*): ~ **что-н под дуб/мра́мор** to give sth
an oak/a marble finish

▸ **разде́латься** (*impf* **разде́лываться**) *сов возв*
(*разг*): **~ся с** +*instr* (*с делами, с долгами*) to
settle; (*с соперником, с хулиганом*) to take care
of.

разделе́ни|е (**-я**) *ср* division; ~ **труда́** division
of labour (*BRIT*) *или* labor (*US*).

раздел|и́ть (**-елю́, -е́лишь**) *сов от* **дели́ть** ♦
(*impf* **разделя́ть**) *перех* (*мнение, взгляды,
энтузиазм*) to share

▸ **раздели́ться** *сов от* **дели́ться** ♦ (*impf*
разделя́ться) *возв* (*мнения, общество*) to
become divided.

разде́лыва|ть(ся) (**-ю(сь)**) *несов от*

разде́лать(ся).

разделя́|ть(ся) (**-ю(сь)**) *несов от*
раздели́ть(ся).

раздеру́ *итп сов см* **разодра́ть**.

разде́|ть (**-ну, -нешь**; *impf* **раздева́ть**) *сов перех*
to undress; (*разг: ограбить*): ~ **кого́-н** to strip
sb bare

▸ **разде́ться** (*impf* **раздева́ться**) *сов возв* to get
undressed.

раздира́|ть (**-ю**) *несов от* **разодра́ть** ♦ *перех*
(*душу, человека, общество*) to tear apart.

раздобре́|ть (**-ю**) *сов от* **добре́ть**.

раздобы́|ть (*как* **быть**; *см* **Table 21**; *impf*
раздобыва́ть) *сов перех* (*разг*) to get hold of,
lay one's hands on.

раздо́лен *прил см* **раздо́льный**.

раздо́ль|е (**-я**) *ср* expanse; (*перен*) freedom;
мне здесь ~ I feel free here.

раздо́л|ьный (**-ен, -ьна, -ьно**) *прил* vast;
(*перен*) free.

раздо́р (**-а**) *м* (*обычно мн*) strife *ед*.

раздоса́д|овать (**-ую**) *сов перех* to upset.

раздража́|ть(ся) (**-ю(сь)**) *несов от*
раздражи́ть(ся).

раздраже́ни|е (**-я**) *ср* irritation.

раздражённо *нареч* (*сказать*) irritably.

раздражённый (**-ён, -ена́, -ено́**) *прил*
(*человек, голос*) irritated; (**-ён, -енна́, -енно́**;
тон) irritable; **у меня́ не́рвы ~ены́ до
преде́ла** my nerves are on edge.

раздражи́тел|ьный (**-ен, -ьна, -ьно**) *прил*
irritable.

раздраж|и́ть (**-у́, -и́шь**; *impf* **раздража́ть**) *сов
перех* (*также МЕД*) to irritate; (*нервы*) to
agitate; (*аппетит*) to stimulate

▸ **раздражи́ться** (*impf* **раздража́ться**) *сов возв*
(*кожа, глаза*) to become irritated; (*человек*):
~ся (+*instr*) to be irritated (by).

раздроб|и́ть (**-лю́, -и́шь**) *сов от* **дроби́ть** ♦
(*impf* **раздробля́ть**) *перех* to shatter.

раздро́блен|ный (**-, -а, -о**) *прил* fragmented.

раздроблю́ *сов см* **раздроби́ть**.

раздробля́|ть (**-ю**) *несов от* **раздроби́ть**.

раздува́|ть(ся) (**-ю(сь)**) *несов от* **разду́ть(ся)**.

разду́ма|ть (**-ю**; *impf* **разду́мывать**) *сов
неперех*: ~ +*infin* (*пойти, жениться итп*) to
decide not to do, decide against doing.

разду́мыва|ть (**-ю**) *несов от* **разду́мать** ♦
неперех: ~ (**о** +*prp*) (*долго думать*) to
contemplate.

разду́м|ье (**-я**; *gen pl* **-ий**) *ср* contemplation;
(*обычно мн*) thought; **впада́ть** (**впасть** *perf*) **в** ~
to sink deep into thought; **по́сле до́лгих ~ий** on
или after lengthy consideration.

разду́|ть (**-ю**; *impf* **раздува́ть**) *сов перех*
(*огонь, костёр*) to fan; (*пузырь*) to blow; (*разг:
дело, скандал*) to blow up; (: *штаты*) to
overstaff; **раздува́ть** (**~** *perf*) **но́здри** to flare

one's nostrils; **у неё ~у́ло шёку/но́гу** her cheek/leg has swollen up

▶ **разду́ться** (*impf* **раздува́ться**) *сов возв* (*парус*) to swell; (*щека, губа, также перен*) to swell up; (*карманы, портфель*) to bulge.

разева́ть (-ю) *несов от* **рази́нуть**.

разжа́лоб|ить (-лю, -ишь) *сов перех*: ~ **кого́-н** to evoke sympathy in sb.

разжа́л|овать (-ую) *сов перех* to demote; ~ (*perf*) **кого́-н в рядовы́е** to reduce sb to the ranks.

разж|а́ть (-ожму́, -ожмёшь; *impf* **разжима́ть**) *сов перех* (*пальцы, губы*) to relax; (*пружину*) to uncoil.

▶ **разжа́ться** (*impf* **разжима́ться**) *сов возв* (*см перех*) to relax; to uncoil.

разж|ева́ть (-ую; *impf* **разжёвывать**) *сов перех* to chew; (*перен: разг: мысль*) to spell out in simple terms.

разж|е́чь (-огу́, -ожжёшь *итп* -огу́т; *pt* -жёг, -ожгла́, -ожгло́, *impf* **разжига́ть**) *сов перех* (*также перен*) to kindle; (*войну, ненависть*) to incite.

разживу́сь *итп сов см* **разжи́ться**.

разжига́ть (-ю) *несов от* **разже́чь**.

разжима́ть(ся) (-ю(сь)) *несов от* **разжа́ть(ся)**.

разжире́ть (-ю) *сов от* **жире́ть**.

разж|и́ться (-иву́сь, -ивёшься; *pt* -и́лся, -ила́сь, -ило́сь) *сов возв* (*разг: жить в доста́тке*) to do well for o.s.; ~ (*perf*) +*instr* (*деньга́ми*) to rake in.

раззадо́р|ить (-ю, -ишь; *impf* **раззадо́ривать**) *сов перех* to excite.

рази́н|уть (-у, -ешь; *impf* **разева́ть**) *сов перех* (*разг*): ~ **рот** to gape; **слу́шать** (*impf*) **~ув рот** to listen open-mouthed.

рази́н|я (-и) *м/ж* (*разг*) scatterbrain.

рази́тел|ьный (-ен, -ьна, -ьно) *прил* striking.

раз|и́ть (-жу́, -зи́шь) *сов перех* to strike; (*перен: пороки*) to strike out at ♦ *безл* (+*instr; разг*): **от неё ~зи́т духа́ми/чесноко́м** she reeks of perfume/garlic.

разлага́ть(ся) (-ю(сь)) *несов от* **разложи́ть(ся)**.

разла́д (-а) *м* (*в дела́х, в рабо́те*) disorder; (*с жено́й*) discord.

разла́мыва|ть (-ю) *несов от* **разлома́ть, разломи́ть**.

▶ **разла́мываться** *несов от* **разлома́ться, разломи́ться** ♦ *возв* (*разг*): **у меня́ ~ется спина́/голова́** my back/head is killing me.

разлёгся *итп сов см* **разле́чься**.

разле|те́ться (-чу́сь, -ти́шься; *impf* **разлета́ться**) *сов возв* (*птицы, перья*) to fly off (*in different directions*); (*перен: вы́росшие де́ти*) to fly the nest; (*разг: стекло́, ва́за итп*) to shatter; (*: но́вости*) to get around; (*: по́езд*) to speed up.

разл|е́чься (-я́гусь, -я́жешься *итп*, -я́гутся; *pt* -ёгся, -егла́сь, -егло́сь) *сов возв* (*разг*) to

stretch out.

разли́в (-а) *м* flooding; (*место, зали́тое водо́й*) flood plain; (*вина, воды*) bottling; (*металла*) casting.

разлива́|ть (-ю) *несов от* **разли́ть**

▶ **разлива́ться** *несов от* **разли́ться** ♦ *возв* (*соловьи́*) to sing; (*перен*): **~ся соловьём** to wax lyrical.

разливн|о́й *прил*: **~о́е пи́во** beer on tap.

разлин|ова́ть (-у́ю; *impf* **разлино́вывать**) *сов перех* to rule (*page*).

разл|и́ть (-олью́, -ольёшь; *pt* -ли́л, -лила́, -ли́ло, *impf* **разлива́ть**) *сов перех* to pour out; (*по буты́лкам*) to bottle; (*проли́ть*) to spill; **их водо́й не ~ольёшь** they are never apart

▶ **разли́ться** (*impf* **разлива́ться**) *сов возв* (*проли́ться*) to spill; (*река́*) to overflow; **румя́нец ~ли́лся по его́ щека́м** the colour flooded into his cheeks; **по её лицу́ улы́бка ~лила́сь** a smile spread across her face.

различа́|ть (-ю) *несов от* **различи́ть**

▶ **различа́ться** *несов возв*: **~ся по** +*dat* to differ in.

различён *прил см* **разли́чный**.

разли́чи|е (-я) *ср* difference; **без ~я** indiscriminately.

различ|и́ть (-у́, -и́шь; *impf* **различа́ть**) *сов перех* (*уви́деть, услы́шать*) to make out; (*отличи́ть*): ~ (**по** +*dat*) to distinguish (by); **я их не ~а́ю** I can't tell them apart.

различ|ный (-ен, -на, -но) *прил* different.

разложе́ни|е (-я) *ср* (*ХИМ, БИО*) decomposition; (*о́бщества, а́рмии итп*) disintegration; (*МАТ*) expansion (*of equation*).

разл|ожи́ть (-ожу́, -о́жишь; *impf* **раскла́дывать**) *сов перех* (*расположи́ть*) to place, arrange; (*еду́ по таре́лкам*) to dish out, serve; (*ка́рту, дива́н, стол*) to open out; (*impf* **разлага́ть**; *ХИМ, БИО*) to decompose; (*МАТ*) to expand; (*перен: а́рмию*) to demoralize; **раскла́дывать** (~ *perf*) **костёр** to build a fire

▶ **разложи́ться** (*impf* **раскла́дываться**) *сов возв* (*разг: размести́ть свои́ ве́щи*) to spread; (*impf* **разлага́ться**; *ХИМ, БИО*) to decompose; (*МАТ*) to expand; (*перен: а́рмия, о́бщество*) to fall apart.

разлома́|ть (-ю) *сов от* **лома́ть** ♦ (*impf* **разла́мывать**) *перех* to break up

▶ **разлома́ться** (*impf* **разла́мываться**) *сов возв* to break up; (*постро́йка*) to fall to pieces.

разл|оми́ть (-омлю́, -о́мишь; *impf* **разла́мывать**) *сов перех* (*на ча́сти: хлеб итп*) to break up

▶ **разломи́ться** (*impf* **разла́мываться**) *сов возв* to break up.

разлу́к|а (-и) *ж* separation; **жить** (*impf*) **в ~е с кем-н** to live apart from sb.

разлуч|и́ть (-у́, -и́шь; *impf* **разлуча́ть**) *сов перех*: ~ **кого́-н с** +*instr* to separate sb from

▶ **разлучи́ться** (*impf* **разлуча́ться**) *сов возв*: **~ся (с** +*instr*) to be separated (from).

разлюб|и́ть (-ю́блю́, -ю́бишь) *сов перех*: ~
+*infin* (*читать, гулять итп*) to lose one's
enthusiasm for doing; **он меня́ ~юби́л** he
doesn't love me any more.

разля́гусь *итп сов см* **разле́чься**.

разма́|зать (-жу, -жешь; *impf* **разма́зывать**) *сов*
перех to smear

▶ **разма́заться** (*impf* **разма́зываться**) *сов возв*
to be smeared.

размазн|я́ (-и́) *м/ж* ditherer.

разма́зыва|ть(ся) (-ю) *несов от*
разма́зать(ся).

разма́лыва|ть (-ю) *несов от* **размоло́ть**.

разма́рива|ть (*3sg* -ет, *3pl* -ют) *несов от*
размори́ть

▶ **разма́риваться** *несов от* **размори́ться**.

разма́тыва|ть (-ю) *несов от* **размота́ть**.

разма́х (-а) *м* (*рук, кры́льев*) span; (*маятника,*
ко́локола) swing; (*перен: де́ятельности*)
scope; (: *проекта*) scale; **уда́рить** (*perf*) **кого́-н**
с ~у to take a swing at sb; **он челове́к с ~ом** he
thinks on a large scale.

разма́хива|ть (-ю) *несов от* **размахну́ть** ◆
неперех: ~ +*instr* (*рука́ми, флажко́м*) to wave;
(*ша́шкой*) to brandish

▶ **разма́хиваться** *несов от* **размахну́ться**.

размахн|у́ть (-у́, -ёшь; *impf* **разма́хивать**) *сов*
перех (*руку, крыло́*) to spread ◆ *неперех*: ~
+*instr* (*кнуто́м, топоро́м*) to swing

▶ **размахну́ться** (*impf* **разма́хиваться**) *сов*
возв to swing one's arm back; (*перен: разг: со*
сва́дьбой, в дела́х итп) to go to town.

разма́шист|ый (-, -а, -о) *прил* sweeping.

размельч|и́ть (-у́, -и́шь) *сов от* **мельчи́ть**.

размелю́ *итп сов см* **размоло́ть**.

разме́н (-а) *м* (*де́нег, пле́нных*) exchange; ~
кварти́ры flat swap (*in which one large flat is*
exchanged for two smaller ones).

разме́нива|ть(ся) (-ю(сь)) *несов от*
разменя́ть(ся).

разме́нн|ый *прил*: ~ **автома́т** change machine;
~**ая моне́та** (small) change.

разменя́|ть (-ю; *impf* **разме́нивать**) *сов перех*
(*де́ньги*) to change; (*кварти́ру*) to exchange;
(*перен: тала́нт*) to waste; ~ (*perf*) **со́весть** to
sell out (*fig*)

▶ **разменя́ться** (*impf* **разме́ниваться**) *сов возв*
(*перен: разг: обменя́ть жилпло́щадь*) to do a
flat swap (*of one large flat for two smaller ones*);
разме́ниваться (*impf*) **по мелоча́м** *или*
пустяка́м (*разг*) to waste o.s.

разме́р (-а) *м* size; (*обы́чно мн:*
строи́тельства: масшта́бы) dimension;
(*линг*) metre (*BRIT*), meter (*US*); **како́й у тебя́**
~? what size do you take?

разме́рен|ный (-, -на, -но) *прил* (*звон, шаги́*)
measured; (*жизнь*) well-regulated.

разме|сти́ть (-щу́, -сти́шь; *impf* **размеща́ть**) *сов*
перех (*найти́ ме́сто для*) to place;
(*расположи́ть*) to arrange

▶ **размести́ться** (*impf* **размеща́ться**) *сов возв*
to accommodate o.s.; **го́сти ~сти́лись за**
столо́м the guests took their seats at the table.

разме|та́ть (-чу́, -чешь) *сов перех* (*листву́,*
пе́пел итп) to scatter; (*руки*) to fling open

▶ **размета́ться** *сов возв* (*во́лосы*) to fly
everywhere; (*челове́к: во сне*) to sprawl out.

разме́|тить (-чу, -тишь; *impf* **размеча́ть**) *сов*
перех to mark out.

размечта́|ться (-юсь) *сов возв* to start
dreaming.

размечу́ *сов см* **разме́тить**.

размечу́(сь) *итп сов см* **размета́ть(ся)**.

размеша́|ть (-ю; *impf* **разме́шивать**) *сов перех*
to stir.

размеща́|ть(ся) (-ю(сь)) *несов от*
размести́ть(ся).

размеще́ни|е (-я) *ср* (*веще́й*) placing;
(*расположе́ние*) arrangement; (*люде́й: по*
ко́мнатам) accommodation.

размещу́(сь) *сов см* **размести́ть(ся)**.

размина́|ть(ся) (-ю(сь)) *несов от* **размя́ть(ся)**.

размини́р|овать (-ую) (*не*)*сов перех*: ~ **по́ле**
to clear a field of mines.

разми́н|ка (-ки; *gen pl* -ок) *ж* (*ног, му́скулов*)
loosening up; (*спортсме́нов*) warm-up.

размин|у́ться (-у́сь, -ёшься) *сов возв* (*не*
встре́титься) to miss each other; (*дать*
пройти́) to pass; **мы с ним ~у́лись (на 5**
мину́т) we missed each other (by 5 minutes).

размножа́|ть (-ю) *несов от* **размно́жить**

▶ **размножа́ться** *несов от* **размно́житься** ◆
возв (*БИО*) to reproduce.

размноже́ни|е (-я) *ср* (*также БИО*)
reproduction.

размно́ж|ить (-у, -ишь; *impf* **размножа́ть**) *сов*
перех to make (multiple) copies of

▶ **размно́житься** (*perf* **размножа́ться**) *сов возв*
(*БИО*) to reproduce.

размо́ет *итп сов см* **размы́ть**.

размозж|и́ть (-у́, -и́шь) *сов перех* to smash.

размо́к|нуть (-ну, -нешь; *pt* -, -ла, -ло, *impf*
размока́ть) *сов неперех* (*хлеб, карто́н*) to go
soggy; (*по́чва*) to become sodden.

размо́лв|ка (-ки; *gen pl* -ок) *ж* squabble.

размол|о́ть (-елю́, -е́лешь; *impf* **разма́лывать**)
сов перех to grind.

размора́жива|ть(ся) (-ю(сь)) *несов от*
разморо́зить(ся).

размор|и́ть (*3sg* -и́т, *3pl* -я́т, *impf* **разма́ривать**)
сов перех (*сон, уста́лость*) to come over; **меня́**
~**и́ло от жары́/све́жего во́здуха** the heat/fresh
air has made me drowsy

▶ **размори́ться** (*impf* **разма́риваться**) *сов возв*
to become drowsy.

разморо́|зить (-жу, -зишь; *impf*

размора́живать) *сов перех* to defrost
▶ **разморо́зиться** (*impf* **размора́живаться**) *сов возв* to defrost.
размота́|ть (-ю; *impf* **разма́тывать**) *сов перех* to unwind.
размыва́|ть (*3sg* -**ет**, *3pl* -**ют**) *несов от* **размы́ть**.
размыка́|ть(ся) (-ю) *несов от* **разомкну́ть(ся)**.
размы́т|ый (-, -а, -о) *прил* blurred.
размы́|ть (*3sg* -**о́ет**, *3sg* -**о́ют**, *impf* **размыва́ть**) *сов перех* to wash away.
размышле́ни|е (-я) *ср* reflection.
размышля́|ть (-ю) *несов неперех*: ~ (o +*prp*) to think (about), reflect (on).
размягч|и́ть (-у́, -и́шь; *impf* **размягча́ть**) *сов перех* (*воск, кожу, душу*) to soften; (*перен: человека*) to soften up.
размя́к|нуть (-ну, -нешь; *pt* -, -ла, -ло, *impf* **размяка́ть**) *сов неперех* (*глина, земля*) to soften; (*перен: от спиртного, от духоты*) to (become) mellow; (: *от похвалы*) to soften up.
раз|мя́ть (-омну́, -омнёшь) *сов от* мять ◆ (*impf* **размина́ть**) *перех* to loosen up
▶ **размя́ться** (*impf* **размина́ться**) *сов возв* to warm up.
разнаря́д|ка (-ки; *gen pl* -ок) *м* directive.
разна́шива|ть(ся) (-ю) *несов от* **разноси́ть(ся)**.
разн|ести́ (-есу́, -есёшь; *pt* -ёс, -есла́, -есло́, *impf* **разноси́ть**) *сов перех* (*письма, посылки*) to deliver; (*еду*) to serve (up); (*тарелки, чашки*) to put out; (*тучи, обрывки бумаги*) to disperse; (*заразу, слухи*) to spread; (*разг: разбить*) to smash up; (: *раскритиковать*) to slam, pan ◆ *безл* (*разг: опухнуть*) to puff up; (: *пополнеть*) to get fat; **разноси́ть** (~ *perf*) **что-н в кло́чья** to smash sth to pieces
▶ **разнести́сь** (*impf* **разноси́ться**) *сов возв* (*весть, слух, запах*) to spread; (*звон, гудок, крик*) to resound.
разнима́|ть (-ю) *несов от* **разня́ть**.
разниму́ *итп сов см* **разня́ть**.
ра́зниц|а (-ы) *ж* difference; **кака́я** ~? what difference does it make?; ~ **в ве́се/в во́зрасте** weight/age difference; **без** ~**ы** (*разг*) it makes no difference.
разнобо́|й (-я) *м* (*в работе, в действиях*) lack of coordination; (*в правилах*) contradictions *мн*.
разнове́с (-а) *м* weights *мн* (*for set of scales*).
разнови́дност|ь (-и) *ж* (*био*) variety; (*людей*) type, kind.
разногла́си|е (-я) *ср* disagreement.
разнообра́жу *сов см* **разнообра́зить**.
разнообра́зен *прил см* **разнообра́зный**.
разнообра́зи|е (-я) *ср* variety; **для** ~**я** for a change.
разнообра́|зить (-жу, -зишь) *несов перех* to vary.
разнообра́з|ный (-ен, -на, -но) *прил* (*вкусы, звуки, мнения*) various; ~**ные лю́ди** different sorts of people; ~**ная пу́блика** a diverse

audience.
разнорабо́ч|ий (-его; *decl like adj*) *м* labourer (*BRIT*), laborer (*US*).
разноречи́в|ый (-, -а, -о) *прил* conflicting.
разноро́д|ный (-ен, -на, -но) *прил* (*состав*) heterogeneous; (*вещества, предметы*) of various sorts; (*впечатления*) varied.
разно́с (-а) *м* delivery; (*разг: выговор*) pounding.
разн|оси́ть (-ошу́, -о́сишь) *несов от* **разнести́** ◆ (*impf* **разна́шивать**) *сов перех* (*туфли, сапоги*) to break in
▶ **разноси́ться** *несов от* **разнести́сь** ◆ (*impf* **разна́шиваться**) *сов возв* to wear loose.
разносторо́н|ний (-няя, -нее, -нее; -ен, -ня, -не) *прил* (*деятельность*) wide-ranging; (*соглашение, договор*) multilateral; (*ум, личность*) multifaceted; **он** ~ **челове́к** he has a wide range of interests; ~**ее образова́ние** a broad education.
ра́зност|ь (-и) *ж* (*также мат*) difference.
разно́счик (-а) *м* (*товара*) delivery man (*мн* men); (*телеграмм*) bearer; (*инфекции*) carrier.
разноцве́т|ный *прил* multicoloured (*BRIT*), multicolored (*US*).
разночи́н|ец (-ца) *м* (*ист*) raznochinets (*educated person of nonaristocratic descent in 19th century Russia*).
разношёрстный *прил* (*перен*) motley.
разношу́(сь) (*не)сов см* **разноси́ть(ся)**.
разноязы́чный *прил* speaking different languages.
разну́здан|ный (-, -на, -но) *прил* (*человек, поведение*) unruly.
ра́зный *прил* different.
разн|я́ть (-иму́, -и́мешь; *pt* -я́л, -яла́, -яло́, *impf* **разнима́ть**) *сов перех* (*руки, зубы*) to unclench; (*драчунов, боксёров*) to separate, pull apart.
разоблач|и́ть (-у́, -и́шь; *impf* **разоблача́ть**) *сов перех* to expose.
раз|обра́ть (-беру́, -берёшь; *impf* **разбира́ть**) *сов перех* (*разг: раскупить, взять*) to snatch up; (*привести в порядок*) to sort out; (*подвергнуть анализу*) to analyse (*BRIT*), analyze (*US*); (*распознать: вкус, подпись итп*) to make out; **разбира́ть** (~ *perf*) (**на ча́сти**) (*часы, механизм итп*) to take apart; **его́** ~**ба́ет смех** (*разг*) he can hardly control his laughter
▶ **разобра́ться** (*impf* **разбира́ться**) *сов возв*: ~**ся в** +*prp* (*в вопросе, в деле*) to form an understanding of.
разобщён|ный (-, -на, -но) *прил* isolated.
ра́зовый *прил*: ~ **биле́т** single (*BRIT*) *или* one-way ticket.
разовью́(сь) *итп сов см* **разви́ть(ся)**.
раз|огна́ть (-гоню́, -го́нишь; *pt* -огна́л, -огнала́, -огна́ло, *impf* **разгоня́ть**) *сов перех* (*толпу, демонстрацию*) to break up; (*разг: организацию*) to purge; (: *бездельников, тунея́дцев*) to come down on; (*тучи, туман*) to

disperse; (*перен: сон, тоску, мысли*) to drive away; (*машину, самолёт*) to speed up
▸ **разогна́ться** (*impf* **разгоня́ться**) *сов возв* to build up speed.
разогн|у́ть (-у́, -ёшь; *impf* **разгиба́ть**) *сов перех* (*спину*) to straighten up; (*проволоку, скрепку*) to straighten out
▸ **разогну́ться** (*impf* **разгиба́ться**) *сов возв* to straighten up.
разогре́|ть (-ю; *impf* **разогрева́ть**) *сов перех* (*чайник, суп*) to heat
▸ **разогре́ться** (*impf* **разогрева́ться**) *сов возв* (*суп*) to heat up; (*человек, двигатель*) to warm up.
разоде́т|ый (-, -а, -о) *прил* overdressed.
разоде́|ться (-нусь, -нешься) *сов возв* (*разг*) to get dressed up.
раз|одра́ть (-деру́, -дерёшь; *impf* **раздира́ть**) *сов перех* to tear up.
разожгу́ *итп сов см* **разже́чь**.
разожму́(сь) *итп сов см* **разжа́ть(ся)**.
разозл|и́ть (-ю́, -и́шь) *сов от* **злить ♦** *перех* to anger
▸ **разозли́ться** *сов от* **зли́ться ♦** *возв* to get angry.
разойти́сь (*как* **идти́**; *см* **Table 18**; *impf* **расходи́ться**) *сов возв* (*гости*) to leave; (*облака, туман, толпа*) to disperse; (*запасы, деньги*) to run out; (*тираж*) to sell out; (*не встретиться*) to miss each other; (*дать дорогу*) to pass each other; (*супруги*) to split up; (*прекратить дружбу*) to part company; (*шов, крепления*) to come apart; (*перен: мнения, взгляды*) to diverge; (: *разг: дать волю себе*) to get going; **на э́той доро́ге не ~** the road is too narrow for passing.
разолью́(сь) *итп сов см* **разли́ть(ся)**.
ра́зом *нареч* (*разг: все вместе*) all at once; (: *в один приём*) all in one go.
разомкн|у́ть (-у́, -ёшь; *impf* **размыка́ть**) *сов перех* (*цепь, крепление*) to unfasten; (*пальцы*) to uncurl; **~** (*perf*) **ру́ки** to let go (of each other's hands)
▸ **разомкну́ться** (*impf* **размыка́ться**) *сов возв* (*цепь, крепление*) to come unfastened; (*пальцы*) to open.
разомну́(сь) *итп сов см* **размя́ть(ся)**.
разопью́ *итп сов см* **распи́ть**.
разорв|а́ть (-у́, -ёшь; *pt* -а́л, -ала́, -а́ло) *сов от* **рвать ♦** (*impf* **разрыва́ть**) *перех* (*письмо, бумагу*) to tear *или* rip up; (*конверт, обёртку*) to tear *или* rip open; (*одежду*) to tear, rip; (*перен: знакомство, связь*) to break off; (: *договор, контракт*) to break **♦** *безл* (*ногу, руку*) to be blown off; (*танк, стену*) to be blown up
▸ **разорва́ться** *сов от* **рва́ться ♦** (*impf* **разрыва́ться**) *возв* (*одежда*) to tear, rip; (*верёвка, цепь*) to break; (*связь, знакомство*)

to be severed; (*снаряд, ракета*) to explode.
разоре́ни|е (-я) *ср* (*см глаг*) plundering; impoverishment; ruin.
разори́тельный (-ен, -ьна, -ьно) *прил* ruinous.
разор|и́ть (-ю́, -и́шь; *impf* **разоря́ть**) *сов перех* (*деревню, гнездо*) to plunder; (*семью, население*) to impoverish; (: *компанию, страну*) to ruin
▸ **разори́ться** (*impf* **разоря́ться**) *сов возв* to go to rack and ruin; (*человек*) to become impoverished; (*разг*): **~ся на** +*acc* (*потратить деньги*) to splash out on.
разоружа́|ть(ся) (-ю(сь)) *несов от* **разоружи́ть(ся)**.
разоруже́ни|е (-я) *ср* (*противника, пленных*) disarming; (*политический процесс*) disarmament.
разоруж|и́ть (-у́, -и́шь; *impf* **разоружа́ть**) *сов перех* (*также перен*) to disarm
▸ **разоружи́ться** (*impf* **разоружа́ться**) *сов возв* to disarm.
разоря́|ть(ся) (-ю(сь)) *несов от* **разори́ть(ся)**.
разо|сла́ть (-шлю́, -шлёшь; *impf* **рассыла́ть**) *сов перех* to send out.
разостла́ть (**расстелю́, рассте́лишь**) *несов* = **расстели́ть**.
разотру́ *итп сов см* **растере́ть(ся)**.
разочарова́ни|е (-я) *ср* disappointment; (*потеря веры*): **~ в** +*prp* (*в друге, в идеалах*) disenchantment with.
разочаро́ван|ный (-, -на, -но) *прил* disappointed; (-, -а, -о): **~ в** +*prp* disenchanted with.
разочар|ова́ть (-у́ю; *impf* **разочаро́вывать**) *сов перех* to disappoint
▸ **разочарова́ться** (*impf* **разочаро́вывать**) *сов возв*: **~ся в** +*prp* to become disenchanted with.
разошёлся *итп сов см* **разойти́сь**.
разошлю́ *итп сов см* **разосла́ть**.
разошью́ *итп сов см* **расши́ть**.
разрабо́та|ть (-ю; *impf* **разраба́тывать**) *сов перех* (*план, технологию, теорию*) to develop; (*месторождение*) to exploit.
разрабо́т|ка (-ки) *ж* (*см глаг*) development; exploitation; (*gen pl* -ок; *обычно мн: научные*) groundwork *ед*; *см также* **разрабо́тки**.
разрабо́т|ки (-ок) *мн* (ГЕО): **га́зовые ~** gas fields *мн*; **нефтяны́е ~** oilfields *мн*; **методи́ческие ~** guidelines *мн*.
разра́вн|ивать (-ю) *несов от* **разровня́ть**.
разра|зи́ться (-жу́сь, -зи́шься; *impf* **разража́ться**) *сов возв* (*гроза, катастрофа*) to break out; **~** (*perf*) **аплодисме́нтами/сме́хом** to break into applause/laughter.
разр|асти́сь (*3sg* -асётётся, *3pl* -асту́тся, *pt* -о́сся, -осла́сь, -осло́сь, *impf* **разраста́ться**)

сов возв (*лес, растение*) to spread; (*город, движение*) to grow.

разреве́|ться (-у́сь, -ёшься) *сов возв* (*разг*) to start bawling.

разрежён|ный (-, -а́, -о́) *прил* rarified.

разре́жу *сов см* **разре́зать**.

разре́з (-а) *м* (*на юбке*) slit; (*ГЕОМ*) section; **в ~е** +*gen* in the context of; **~ глаз** the shape of one's eyes.

разре́|зать (-жу, -жешь) *сов от* **ре́зать**.

разреза́|ть (-ю) *несов перех* to cut up.

разрекла́ми́р|овать (-ую) *сов перех* to publicize.

разреша́|ть (-ю) *несов от* **разреши́ть**

▶ **разреша́ться** *несов от* **разреши́ться** ◆ *неперех* (*допускаться*) to be allowed *или* permitted; **здесь не ~ется кури́ть** smoking is not permitted here.

разреше́ни|е (-я) *ср* (*действие*) authorization; (*позволение, право*) permission, authorization; (*документ*) permit; (*решение*) resolution; **с Ва́шего ~я** with your permission.

разреш|и́ть (-у́, -и́шь; *impf* **разреша́ть**) *сов перех* (*задачу*) to resolve; (*позволить*): **~ кому́-н** +*infin* to allow *или* permit sb to do; **~и́те** +*infin* ... may I ...; **~?** may I come in?; **~и́те пройти́** let me through; **разреша́ть** (**~** *perf*) **фильм/кни́гу** to pass a film for screening/book for publication

▶ **разреши́ться** (*impf* **разреша́ться**) *сов возв* to be resolved.

разрис|ова́ть (-у́ю; *impf* **разрисо́вывать**) *сов перех* (*карандашом*) to draw all over; (*краской*) to paint all over.

разровня́|ть (-ю) *сов от* **ровня́ть** ◆ (*impf* **разра́внивать**) *перех* to level.

разро́знен|ный (-, -на, -но) *прил* (*действия, силы*) uncoordinated; (*коллекция, сервиз*) made up of odd parts; (*тома*) odd.

разро́сся *итп сов см* **разрасти́сь**.

разруб|и́ть (-лю́, -убишь; *impf* **разруба́ть**) *сов перех* to chop in two; **разруба́ть** (**~** *perf*) **на куски́** to chop up.

разрумя́н|ить(ся) (-ю(сь)) *сов от* **румя́нить(ся)**.

разру́х|а (-и) *ж* ruin; **в стране́ ~** the country is in ruins.

разруша́|ть(ся) (-ю(сь)) *несов от* **разру́шить(ся)**.

разруши́тель|ный (-ен, -ьна, -ьно) *прил* destructive.

разру́ш|ить (-у, -ишь; *impf* **разруша́ть**) *сов перех* to destroy; (*планы, жизнь*) to ruin

▶ **разру́шиться** (*impf* **разруша́ться**) *сов возв* (*см перех*) to be destroyed; to be ruined.

разры́в (-а) *м* (*дипломатических отношений, связей*) severance; (*провода, цепи*) breaking; (*разорванная часть*) tear; (*снаряда, гранаты*) explosion; (*несоответствие, промежуток времени*) gap; **с ~ом в 10 лет** with a gap of 10 years; **разры́в се́рдца** (*МЕД*) heart attack.

разрыва́|ть(ся) (-ю(сь)) *несов от* **разорва́ть(ся)**.

разрыхли́|ть (-ю́, -и́шь) *сов от* **рыхли́ть**.

разря́д (-а) *м* (*людей, растений*) class; (*спортивный*) grade; (*профессиональный*) status; (*ФИЗ*) discharge.

разря|ди́ть (-жу́, -ди́шь; *impf* **разряжа́ть**) *сов перех* (*ружьё, батарейку*) to discharge; **разряжа́ть** (**~** *perf*) **обстано́вку** to diffuse the situation

▶ **разряди́ться** (*impf* **разряжа́ться**) *сов возв* (*перен*) to become less tense.

разря́д|ка (-ки; *gen pl* -ок) *ж* release, outlet; (*в тексте*) spacing; **~ (междунаро́дной) напряжённости** détente.

разряжа́|ть(ся) (-ю(сь)) *несов от* **разряди́ть(ся)**.

разряжу́(сь) *сов см* **разряди́ть(ся)**.

разубе|ди́ть (-жу́, -ди́шь; *impf* **разубежда́ть**) *сов перех*: **~ кого́-н (в** +*prp*) to dissuade sb (from).

разува́|ть(ся) (-ю(сь)) *несов от* **разу́ть(ся)**.

разуве́р|иться (-юсь, -ишься; *impf* **разуверя́ться**) *сов возв*: **~ в** +*prp* to lose faith in.

разузна́|ть (-ю; *impf* **разузнава́ть**) *сов перех* (*разг*) to find out.

разукра́|сить (-шу, -сишь; *impf* **разукра́шивать**) *сов перех* to decorate.

ра́зум (-а) *м* reason.

разу́мен *прил см* **разу́мный**.

разуме́|ться (*3sg* -ется) *сов возв*: **под э́тим ~ется, что ...** by this is meant that ...; **само́ собо́й ~ется** that goes without saying; **он, ~ется, не знал об э́том** it goes without saying that he knew nothing about it.

разу́м|ный (-ен, -на, -но) *прил* intelligent; (*поступок, решение, довод*) reasonable.

разу́|тый (-, -а, -о) *прил* (*без обуви*) barefoot; (*разг: нуждающийся в обуви*) shoeless.

разу́|ть (-ю; *impf* **разува́ть**) *сов перех*: **~ кого́-н** to take sb's shoes off

▶ **разу́ться** (*impf* **разува́ться**) *сов возв* to take one's shoes off.

разучи́|ть (-учу́, -у́чишь; *impf* **разу́чивать**) *сов перех* to learn

▶ **разучи́ться** (*impf* **разу́чиваться**) *сов возв*: **~ся** +*infin* to forget how to do.

разъеда́|ть (*3sg* -ет, *3pl* -ют) *несов от* **разъе́сть** ◆ *перех* (*перен: душу*) to eat away at

▶ **разъеда́ться** *несов от* **разъе́сться**.

разъе́дешься *итп сов см* **разъе́хаться**.

разъеди́м(ся) *сов см* **разъе́сть(ся)**.

разъедин|и́ть (-ю́, -и́шь; *impf* **разъединя́ть**) *сов перех* (*провода, телефон*) to disconnect; (*друзей, любимых*) to separate.

разъеди́н(ся) *сов см* **разъе́сть(ся)**.

разъе́дусь *итп сов см* **разъе́хаться**.

разъедя́т(ся) *сов см* **разъе́сть(ся)**.

разъе́зд (-а) *м* (*гостей*) departure; (*для поездов*) siding (*BRIT*), sidetrack (*US*); *см также*

разъе́зды.

разъе́зд|ы (-ов) *мн* (*поездки*) travel *ед*; **он всё
вре́мя в ~ах** he does a lot of travelling.

разъезжа́|ть (-ю) *несов неперех* (*по делам, по
городам*) to travel around; (*кататься: на
тройке, на автомобиле*) to ride about; ~ (*impf*)
по гостя́м to go around visiting friends

▶ **разъезжа́ться** *несов от* **разъе́хаться.**

разъе́сть (*как* **есть;** *см* **Table 15;** *impf*
разъеда́ть) *сов перех* to corrode

▶ **разъе́сться** (*impf* **разъеда́ться**) *сов возв*
(*разг*) to get fat.

разъе́|хаться (*как* **е́хать;** *см* **Table 19;** *impf*
разъезжа́ться) *сов возв* to leave; (*разг: лыжи,
ноги на льду*) to slide apart; **она́ ~халась с
му́жем/ма́терью** she doesn't live with her
husband/mother any more; **мы с ни́ми ~хались
в темноте́** we missed each other in the darkness;
маши́ны не могли́ ~ the cars couldn't get past
each other.

разъе́шь(ся) *сов см* **разъе́сть(ся).**

разъярённый *прил* (*зверь, человек, лицо*)
furious; (*перен: река, стихия*) raging.

разъяр|и́ть (-ю́, -и́шь; *impf* **разъяря́ть**) *сов
перех* (*толпу, человека*) to infuriate, enrage;
(*зверя*) to provoke

▶ **разъяри́ться** (*impf* **разъяря́ться**) *сов возв* to
become infuriated.

разъясне́ни|е (-я) *ср* clarification.

разъясн|и́ть (-ю́, -и́шь; *impf* **разъясня́ть**) *сов
перех* to clarify

▶ **разъясни́ться** (*impf* **разъясня́ться**) *сов возв*
to be clarified.

разыгра́|ть (-ю; *impf* **разы́грывать**) *сов перех*
(*МУЗ, СПОРТ*) to play; (*сцену*) to act out; (*в
лотерею, по жребию*) to raffle; (*разг:
подшутить*) to play a joke *или* trick on

▶ **разыгра́ться** (*impf* **разы́грываться**) *сов возв*
(*увлечься игрой*) to get carried away with one's
game; (*начать лучше играть*) to get going;
(*перед концертом*) to warm up; (*перен: буря*)
to rage; (*: драма, сражение*) to unfold; **у меня́
~лась мигре́нь** I had a nasty migraine; **по́сле
прогу́лки у него́ ~лся аппети́т** the walk gave
him a big appetite.

разыска́|ть (-ищу́, -и́щешь; *impf* **разы́скивать**)
сов перех to find

▶ **разыска́ться** (*impf* **разы́скиваться**) *сов возв*
to turn up.

РАИС *ср сокр* (= *Российское аге́нтство
интеллектуа́льной со́бственности*) copyright
protection agency.

ра|й (-я; *loc sg* -ю́) *м* (*также перен*) paradise.

райко́м (-а) *м сокр* (*ИСТ:* = *райо́нный комите́т*)
district committee (*of Communist Party or
Komsomol*).

райо́н (-а) *м* region; (*ПОЛИТ*) district.

райо́нный *прил* district *опред*.

ра́йск|ий (-ая, -ое, -ие) *прил* (*также перен*)
heavenly.

райце́нтр (-а) *м сокр* (= *райо́нный центр*) main
town (*of district*).

рак (-а) *м* (*ЗООЛ: речной*) crayfish (*мн* crayfish);
(*: морской*) crab; (*МЕД*) cancer; (*созвездие*): **Р~**
Cancer.

раке́т|а (-ы) *ж* (*также КОСМОС*) rocket; (*ВОЕН*)
missile; (*судно*) hydrofoil.

раке́т|ка (-ки; *gen pl* -ок) *ж* (*СПОРТ*) racket;
пе́рвая ~ (*перен*) the top player.

раке́тный *прил* (*также КОСМОС*) rocket *опред*;
(*ВОЕН*) missile *опред*; **раке́тное ору́жие** (*ВОЕН*)
missiles *мн*.

раке́ток *сущ см* **раке́тка.**

ра́ковин|а (-ы) *ж* (*ЗООЛ*) shell; (*для умывания*)
sink; **ушна́я ~** aural cavity.

ра́ковый *прил* (*ЗООЛ, КУЛИН*) crab *опред*; (*МЕД*)
cancer *опред*; **ра́ковая о́пухоль** malignant
tumour.

ра́лли *ср нескл* (*СПОРТ*) rally.

ра́м|а (-ы) *ж* frame; (*АВТ*) chassis; **двойны́е ~ы**
double glazing.

рамаза́н (-а) *м* Ramadan.

ра́м|ка (-ки; *gen pl* -ок) *ж* (*для фотографии, для
картины*) frame; (*текста, рисунка*) border; *см
также* **ра́мки.**

ра́м|ки (-ок) *мн*: ~ +*gen* (*рассказа, разговора,
обязанностей*) framework *ед* of; (*закона,
устава*) limits *мн* of; **в ~ках** +*gen* (*закона,
приличия*) within the bounds of; (*дискуссии,
переговоров*) within the framework of; **за
~ками** +*gen* beyond the bounds of; **держа́ть**
(*impf*) **себя́ в ~ках** to control o.s.

ра́мп|а (-ы) *ж* (*ТЕАТР*): **огни́ ~ы** footlights *мн*.

РАН *м сокр* (= *Росси́йская акаде́мия нау́к*)
Russian Academy of Sciences.

ра́н|а (-ы) *ж* (*также перен*) wound.

Рангу́н (-а) *м* Rangoon.

ра́нен|ая (-ой; *decl like adj*) *ж см* **ра́неный.**

ране́ни|е (-я) *ср* injury.

ра́нен|ый *прил* injured; (*ВОЕН*) wounded ♦ (-ого;
decl like adj) *м* injured person (*мн* people); (*ВОЕН*)
wounded person (*мн* people).

ра́н|ец (-ца) *м* (*школьный*) satchel; (*солдатский,
походный*) backpack.

рани́м|ый (-, -а, -о) *прил* vulnerable.

ра́н|ить (-ю, -ишь) (*не*)*сов перех* (*также перен*)
to wound; ~ (*impf/perf*) **кого́-н в ру́ку/но́гу** to
wound sb in the arm/leg; ~ (*impf/perf*) **кому́-н
ду́шу** to wound sb (*fig*).

ра́нн|ий (-яя, -ее, -ие) *прил* early.

ра́но *нареч* early ♦ *как сказ* it's early; **ещё ~** (*о
раннем времени*) it's still early; ~ **де́лать** (*impf*)
вы́воды it's too early to draw conclusions; **он
жени́лся/у́мер ~** he married/died young; **~ и́ли
по́здно** sooner or later.

ра́нца *итп сущ см* **ра́нец.**

рань (-и) ж (разг) early morning.

ра́ньше сравн нареч от **ра́но** ♦ нареч (прежде) before; (сначала) earlier ♦ предл: ~ +gen before; ~ **он жил в го́роде** he used to live in the city; ~ **поду́май, пото́м отвеча́й** think before you answer; ~ **вре́мени** (радоваться итп) too soon; ~ **ве́чера мы не зако́нчим** we won't finish before the evening; **он зако́нчил ~ всех** he finished before everybody else.

папи́р|а (-ы) ж foil (for fencing).

ра́порт (-а) м report; **подава́ть** (**пода́ть** perf) ~ to submit a report.

рапорт|ова́ть (-у́ю; perf **отрапортова́ть**) (не)сов неперех: ~ (кому́-н о +prp) to report back (to sb on).

рас- префикс см **раз-**.

ра́с|а (-ы) ж race.

раси́зм (-а) м racism.

раси́ст (-а) м racist.

раси́ст|ка (-ки; gen pl -ок) ж см **раси́ст**.

раси́стск|ий (-ая, -ое, -ие) прил racist опред.

раска́ива|ться (-юсь) несов от **раска́яться**.

раскалённый прил burning hot.

раскал|и́ть (-ю́, -и́шь; impf **раскаля́ть**) сов перех to bring to a high temperature
▸ **раскали́ться** (impf **раскаля́ться**) сов возв to get very hot.

раска́лыва|ть (-ю) несов от **расколо́ть**
▸ **раска́лываться** несов от **расколо́ться** ♦ возв: **у меня́ ~ется голова́** I have a splitting headache.

раскаля́|ть(ся) (-ю(сь)) несов от **раскали́ть(ся)**.

раска́пыва|ть (-ю) несов от **раскопа́ть**.

раска́рмлива|ть (-ю) несов от **раскорми́ть**.

раска́т (-а) м (обычно мн: грома, смеха) peal.

раската́|ть (-ю; impf **раска́тывать**) сов перех (ковёр, рулон) to unroll; (тесто) to roll out; (дорогу, горку) to flatten (out); (брёвна, шары) to send rolling (in different directions).

раска́тист|ый (-, -а, -о) прил (гром, хохот) booming.

раска́тыва|ть (-ю) несов от **раската́ть**.

раскача́|ть (-ю; impf **раска́чивать**) сов перех to swing; (качели, ребёнка) to push
▸ **раскача́ться** (impf **раска́чиваться**) сов возв (лодка) to rock; (качели) to swing; (разг: медлить: человек) to dither.

раска́яни|е (-я) ср repentance.

раска́я|ться (-юсь; impf **раска́иваться**) сов возв: ~ (в +prp) to repent (of).

расквита́|ться (-юсь) сов возв (разг): ~ **с** +instr (с кредиторами) to settle up with; (перен: с врагом, с обидчиком) to settle a score with.

раскида́|ть (-ю; impf **раски́дывать**) сов перех to throw around, scatter; **жизнь ~ла их по всему́ све́ту** life has scattered them across the globe.

раски́дист|ый (-, -а, -о) прил (дерево) spreading.

раски́дыва|ть (-ю) несов от **раскида́ть,**
раски́нуть.

раски́н|уть (-у, -ешь; impf **раски́дывать**) сов перех (руки) to throw open; (ковёр, сети) to spread out; (лагерь) to set up; (палатку, шатёр) to pitch; ~ (perf) **что-н умо́м** или **мозга́ми** (разг) to think sth over
▸ **раски́нуться** (impf **раски́дываться**) сов возв to stretch out.

раскла́д|ка (-и) ж (действие) arranging; (соотношение: сил, средств) balance.

раскладно́й прил folding опред.

расклад|у́шка (-ки; gen pl -ек) ж (разг) camp bed (BRIT), cot (US).

раскла́дыва|ть(ся) (-ю(сь)) несов от **разложи́ть(ся)**.

раскла́ня|ться (-юсь; impf **раскла́ниваться**) сов возв (актёр, выступающий) to take a bow; (при встрече, при расставании) to bow.

раскле́|ить (-ю, -ишь; impf **раскле́ивать**) сов перех (конверт) to unglue; (плакаты, афиши, рекламы) to paste up
▸ **раскле́иться** (impf **раскле́иваться**) сов возв to come unstuck; (перен: разг: свадьба, дело) to fall through; **я совсе́м ~ился** (разг) I feel (like) a complete wreck.

раско́ван|ный (-, -на, -но) прил relaxed.

раско́л (-а) м (организации, движения) split; (РЕЛ) schism.

раскол|о́ть (-олю́, -о́лешь; impf **раска́лывать**) сов перех (дрова, страну, движение) to split; (лёд, орех) to crack
▸ **расколо́ться** (impf **раска́лываться**) сов возв (полено, орех) to split open; (перен: движение, организация) to be split.

раскопа́|ть (-ю; impf **раска́пывать**) сов перех (также перен) to dig up.

раско́п|ка (-ки; gen pl -ок) ж (действие) excavation; см также **раско́пки**.

раско́п|ки (-ок) мн (работы) excavations мн; (место) (archaeological) dig ед.

раскорм|и́ть (-ормлю́, -о́рмишь; impf **раска́рмливать**) сов перех to overfeed.

раско́сый прил (глаза) slanting.

раскоше́л|иться (-юсь, -ишься; impf **раскоше́ливаться**) сов возв (разг): ~ **(на** +acc) to fork out (for).

раскра́ива|ть (-ю) несов от **раскро́ить**.

раскра́|сить (-шу, -сишь; impf **раскра́шивать**) сов перех (рисунок, картинку) to colour (BRIT), color (US); (вазу, поделку) to paint.

раскра́с|ка (-и) ж (см глаг) colouring (BRIT), coloring (US); painting; (цветовая гамма) colours мн (BRIT), colors мн (US).

раскрасне́|ться (-юсь) сов возв to go red.

раскра́шива|ть (-ю) несов от **раскра́сить**.

раскра́шу сов см **раскра́сить**.

раскритик|ова́ть (-у́ю) сов перех to criticize severely.

раскро́|ить (-ю́, -и́шь; impf **раскра́ивать**) сов перех to cut.

раскру|ти́ть (-учу́, -у́тишь; impf **раскру́чивать**)

сов перех (что-н сплетённое) to untwist; *(что-н закрученное)* to unscrew; *(интригу, тайну)* to unravel.

раскр|ы́ть (-о́ю, -о́ешь; *impf* **раскрыва́ть**) *сов перех* to open; *(перен)* to discover; **раскрыва́ть** (~ *perf*) **свои́ ка́рты** *(перен)* to show one's hand
▸ **раскры́ться** (*impf* **раскрыва́ться**) *сов возв* to open; *(перен: характер, дарование)* to be revealed; **~ся** *(perf)* **пе́ред кем-н** to open up to sb.

раск|упи́ть (-уплю́, -у́пишь; *impf* **раскупа́ть**) *сов перех* to buy up.

раск|уси́ть (-ушу́, -у́сишь) *сов перех (разг: понять)* to suss out; *(impf* **раску́сывать**; *яблоко, конфету)* to bite into.

ра́совый *прил* racial.

распа́д (-а) *м* break-up, collapse; *(хим)* decomposition.

распада́|ться (*3sg* -ется, *3pl* -ются) *несов от* **распа́сться** ♦ *возв (состоять из частей)*: ~ **на** +*acc* to be divided into.

распадётся *итп сов см* **распа́сться**.

распа́рыва|ть (-ю; *perf* **распоро́ть**) *несов перех* = **поро́ть**.

распа́|сться (*3sg* -дётся, *3pl* -ду́ться, *impf* **распада́ться**) *сов возв* to break up; *(вещество, молекула)* to decompose; **распада́ться** (~ *perf*) **на ча́сти** to fall apart.

расп|аха́ть (-ашу́, -а́шешь; *impf* **распа́хивать**) *сов перех* to plough (*BRIT*) *или* plow (*US*) up.

распахн|у́ть (-у́, -ёшь; *impf* **распа́хивать**) *сов перех* to throw open; ~ *(perf)* **ду́шу** to bare one's soul
▸ **распахну́ться** (*impf* **распа́хиваться**) *сов возв (дверь, шуба)* to fly open; *(поля, равнина)* to open out.

распашо́н|ка (-ки; *gen pl* -ок) *ж cotton baby top without buttons*.

распашу́ *итп сов см* **распаха́ть**.

распева́|ть (-ю) *несов неперех (разг)* to sing loudly ♦ *перех (разг)*: ~ **пе́сню** to sing away.

распелена́|ть (-ю; *impf* **распелёнывать**) *сов перех* to unwrap.

распеча́та|ть (-ю; *impf* **распеча́тывать**) *сов перех (письмо, пакет)* to open; *(помещение)* to unseal; *(размножить)* to print off; *(КОМП)* to print out.

распеча́т|ка (-ки; *gen pl* -ок) *ж (доклада)* printout; *(КОМП)* hard copy.

распеча́тыва|ть (-ю) *несов от* **распеча́тать**.

распива́|ть (-ю) *несов от* **распи́ть**.

расп|или́ть (-илю́, -и́лишь; *impf* **распи́ливать**) *сов перех* to saw up.

распина́|ть (-ю) *несов от* **распя́ть**
▸ **распина́ться** *несов возв (разг)*: **~ся пе́ред** +*instr* to go out of one's way for.

расписа́ни|е (-я) *ср* timetable.

расп|иса́ть (-ишу́, -и́шешь; *impf* **распи́сывать**)

сов перех (дела, мероприятия, расходы итп) to arrange; *(день, месяц)* to fill up; *(стены, шкатулку, вазу)* to paint; *(перен: разг: будущее, приключения)* to paint a rosy picture of; *(разг: жениха и невесту)* to marry (*in registry office*)
▸ **расписа́ться** (*impf* **распи́сываться**) *сов возв (поставить подпись)* to sign one's name; *(перен)*: **~ся в** +*prp (в невежестве, в бессилии)* to acknowledge; *(разг)*: **~ся (с** +*instr) (зарегистрировать брак)* to get married (to) (*in registry office*); **распи́сываться** (**~ся** *perf*) **в получе́нии чего́-н** to sign for sth.

распи́с|ка (-ки; *gen pl* -ок) *ж (о получении денег)* receipt; *(гарантия)* warrant; **принима́ть** (**приня́ть** *perf*) **что-н под ~ку** to sign for sth.

расписно́й *прил* painted.

расписо́к *сущ см* **распи́ска**.

распи́сыва|ть(ся) (-ю(сь)) *несов от* **расписа́ть(ся)**.

расп|и́ть (**разопью́, разопьёшь**; *pt* -и́л, -ила́, -и́ло, *impf* **распива́ть**) *сов перех (разг)* to get through.

распиха́|ть (-ю; *impf* **распи́хивать**) *сов перех (разг: толпу, очередь)* to push through; *(: вещи, бумаги)*: ~ **по** +*dat* to stuff into.

распишу́(сь) *итп сов см* **расписа́ть(ся)**.

распла́в|ить (-лю, -ишь) *сов от* **пла́вить** ♦ (*impf* **расплавля́ть**) *перех* to melt
▸ **распла́виться** *сов от* **пла́виться** ♦ (*impf* **расплавля́ться**) *возв* to melt.

распла́|каться (-чусь, -чешься) *сов возв* to burst into tears.

распласта́|ть (-ю; *impf* **распла́стывать**) *сов перех (крылья, руки)* to spread
▸ **распласта́ться** (*impf* **распла́стываться**) *сов возв* to sprawl out.

распла́т|а (-ы) *ж* payment; *(перен)* retribution; **час ~ы** *(перен)* the day of reckoning.

распл|ати́ться (-ачу́сь, -а́тишься; *impf* **распла́чиваться**) *сов возв*: ~ **(с** +*instr) (с продавцом, с кредитором)* to pay; *(перен: с предателем, с негодяем)* to get even (with); **распла́чиваться** (**~** *perf*) **за оши́бку/преступле́ние** to pay for a mistake/crime.

распла́чусь *итп сов см* **распла́каться**.

расплёл(ся) *итп сов см* **расплести́(сь)**.

распле|ска́ть (-щу́, -ещешь; *impf* **расплёскивать**) *сов перех* to spill
▸ **расплеска́ться** (*impf* **расплёскиваться**) *сов возв* to spill.

распл|ести́ (-ету́, -етёшь; *pt* -ёл, -ела́, -ело́, *impf* **расплета́ть**) *сов перех (плётку)* to untwist; *(косу)* to unplait
▸ **расплести́сь** (*impf* **расплета́ться**) *сов возв* to come untwisted; *(коса)* to come out.

расплещу́(сь) *сов см* **расплеска́ть(ся)**.

расплод|и́ться (*3sg* -и́тся, *3pl* -я́тся) *сов от* **плоди́ться**.

расплыва́|ться (-юсь) *несов от* **распльы́ться**.

расплыву́сь *итп сов см* **распльы́ться**.

распльы́вчат|ый (-, -а, -о) *прил* (*рисунок, очертания*) blurred; (*перен: мысли, ответ, намёк*) vague.

распльы́|ться (-ву́сь, -вёшься; *pt* -лся, -ла́сь, -ло́сь, *impf* **расплыва́ться**) *сов возв* (*утки итп*) to swim off; (*чернила, краски*) to run; (*нефть, дым*) to diffuse; (*облака*) to disperse; (*перен: фигуры, силуэт*) to blur; (*разг: располнеть*) to spread; (: *широко улыбнуться*) to beam; **он ~лся** *или* **его́ лицо́ ~лось в улы́бке** a smile spread across his face.

расплю́щ|ить (-у, -ишь; *impf* **расплю́щивать**) *сов перех* to crush.

распну́ *итп сов см* **распя́ть**.

распого́д|иться (*3sg* -ится) *сов возв* to clear up (*weather*).

распозна́|ть (-ю; *impf* **разпознава́ть**) *сов перех* to identify.

располага́|ть (-ю) *несов от* **расположи́ть** ♦ *неперех*: ~ +*instr* (*данными, временем итп*) to have at one's disposal, have available; **Вы мо́жете мной** ~ I am entirely at your disposal

▸ **располага́|ться** *несов от* **расположи́ться** ♦ *возв* (*находиться*) to be situated *или* located.

располага́ющ|ий (-ая, -ее, -ие) *прил* welcoming.

располз|ти́сь (*3sg* -ётся, *3pl* -у́тся, *impf* **располза́ться**) *сов возв* to crawl off; (*туман, плющ*) to spread; (*пятно, строчки*) to smudge; (*разг: ткань, одежда*) to become threadbare.

расположе́ни|е (-я) *ср* (*действие: предметов*) arranging; (*место: отряда, лагеря*) location; (*комнат*) layout; (*мебели*) arrangement; (*симпатия*) disposition; ~ **ду́ха** mood; **я испы́тываю к нему́** ~ he is well-disposed towards me; **у меня́ нет сейча́с ~я е́хать туда́** I'm not in the mood for going there right now.

расположен|ный (-, -а, -о) *прил*: ~ **к** +*dat* (*к человеку*) well-disposed towards; (*к инфекции, к простуде*) susceptible to; ~ +*infin* (*читать, работать, играть*) in the mood for doing; **я не расположен э́то сейча́с обсужда́ть** I am not in the mood to discuss it right now.

распол|ожи́ть (-ожу́, -о́жишь; *impf* **располага́ть**) *сов перех* (*мебель, вещи итп*) to arrange; (*отряд*) to station; (*лагерь*) to set up; **располога́ть** (~ *perf*) **кого́-н к себе́** to win sb over

▸ **расположи́ться** (*impf* **располага́ться**) *сов возв* (*человек: в кресле, под деревом итп*) to settle down; (*отряд*) to position itself.

распор|о́ть (-орю́, -о́решь) *сов от* **поро́ть**.

распоряди́тел|ь (-я) *м* (*КОММ*) manager; (*церемониала, вечера*) organizer.

распоряди́тельный *прил* (*хозяйка, начальник*) efficient; **распоряди́тельный дире́ктор** managing director;

распоряди́тельный комите́т management committee.

распоря|ди́ться (-жу́сь, -ди́шься; *impf* **распоряжа́ться**) *сов возв* to give out instructions; (+*infin*; *сделать что-н*) to order to do; (+*instr*; *деньгами, ресурсами*) to manage; **он ~ди́лся, что́бы все яви́лись к шести́** he instructed everyone to be there by six (o'clock).

распоря́д|ок (-ка) *м* routine; **пра́вила вну́треннего ~ка** regulations *мн*.

распоряжа́|ться (-юсь) *несов от* **распоряди́ться** ♦ *возв*: ~ (+*instr*) to be in charge (of).

распоряже́ни|е (-я) *ср* (*управление*) management; (*приказ*) instructions *мн*; (*указ*) enactment; **ба́нковское** ~ banker's order; **в** ~ +*gen* at sb's/sth's disposal; **предоставля́ть** (**предоста́вить** *perf*) **что-н в чьё-н** ~ to place sth at sb's disposal; **я с Ва́шем ~и** I am at your disposal.

распоряжу́сь *сов см* **распоряди́ться**.

распоя́са|ться (-юсь; *impf* **распоя́сываться**) *сов возв* (*перен: разг*) to get cocky.

распра́в|а (-ы) *ж* reprisals *мн*.

распра́в|ить (-лю, -ишь; *impf* **расправля́ть**) *сов перех* (*складки, смятую бумагу*) to straighten out; (*грудь, плечи*) to straighten (up); (*крылья*) to spread

▸ **распра́виться** (*impf* **расправля́ться**) *сов возв* (*см перех*) to be straightened out; to straighten up; to spread; (*парус*) to unfurl; (*наказать*): ~**ся с** +*instr* (*с демонстра́нтами, с забасто́вщиками*) to take reprisals against; (*перен: разг*: *с дела́ми, с обе́дом итп*) to be finished with.

распределе́ни|е (-я) *ср* distribution; (*после института*) work placement.

распредел|и́ть (-ю́, -и́шь; *impf* **распределя́ть**) *сов перех* (*обязанности, доходы*) to distribute; (*книги по полкам*) to arrange; (*учеников по классам*) to divide up; (*разг*): ~ **кого́-н** (*выпускника*) to give sb a work placement

▸ **распредели́ться** (*impf* **распределя́ться**) *сов возв* (*разг: выпускники*) to get work placements; **распределя́ться** (~**ся** *perf*) (**по** +*dat*) (*по гру́ппам, по брига́дам*) to divide up (into).

распрода|ва́ть (-ю́, -ёшь) *несов от* **распрода́ть**.

распродади́м *итп сов см* **распрода́ть**.

распрода́ж|а (-и) *ж* sale.

распрода́ть (*как* дать; *см* **Table 14**; *impf* **распродава́ть**) *сов перех* (*вещи, имущество, това́р*) to sell off; (*биле́ты*) to sell out of.

распростёртый *прил* (*руки*) outstretched; (*тело*) prostrate; **встреча́ть** (**встре́тить** *perf*) **кого́-н с распростёртыми объя́тиями** to welcome sb with open arms.

распро|сти́ться (-щу́сь, -сти́шься) *сов возв*: ~ **с** +*instr* to say *или* bid farewell to.

распростране́ни|е (-я) *ср* (*информа́ции,*

опыта, знаний) dissemination; (*инфекции*)
spreading; (*ядерного оружия*) proliferation;
(*приказа, правила*) extension.
распространён|ный (**-**, **-на**, **-но**) *прил*
widespread.
распростран|и́ть (**-ю́**, **-и́шь**; *impf*
распространя́ть) *сов перех* (*информацию*,
знания) to disseminate; (*опыт*) to share;
(*сплетни, инфекцию*) to spread; (*правило*,
приказ) to apply; (*владения*) to widen;
(*газеты*) to distribute; (*запах*) to emit
▸ **распространи́ться** (*impf*
распространя́ться) *сов возв* to spread; (*разг:*
подробно говорить) to go into detail; **~ся** (*perf*)
на +*acc* to extend to; **э́тот прика́з ~я́ется на**
всех this order applies to everybody.
распроща́|ться (**-юсь**) *сов возв* =
распрости́ться.
распрощу́сь *сов см* **распрости́ться**.
ра́спр|я (**-и**; *gen pl* **-ей**) *ж* (*обычно мн*) feud.
распря́г *итп сов см* **распря́чь**.
распряга́|ть (**-ю**) *несов от* **распря́чь**.
распрягу́ *итп сов см* **распря́чь**.
распряжёшь *итп сов см* **распря́чь**.
распрям|и́ть (**-лю́**, **-и́шь**; *impf* **распрямля́ть**)
сов перех (*проволоку, крючок*) to straighten
(out); (*спину, грудь, плечи*) to straighten (up).
распря́|чь (**-гу́**, **-жёшь** *итп*, **-гу́т**; *pt* **-г**, **-гла́**, **-гло́**,
impf **распряга́ть**) *сов перех* to unharness.
распуга́|ть (**-ю**; *impf* **распу́гивать**) *сов перех* to
scare away *или* off.
расп|усти́ть (**-ущу́**, **-у́стишь**; *impf* **распуска́ть**)
сов перех (*армию*) to disband; (*студентов*,
школьников) to dismiss; (*шнурки, корсет*,
ремень) to loosen; (*волосы, косу*) to let down;
(*шов, вязанье*) to unpick; (*перен*): **~ кого́-н**
(*ребёнка итп*) to let sb run wild; **распуска́ть** (**~**
perf) **парла́мент** to dissolve parliament;
распуска́ть (**~** *perf*) **слу́хи** to spread rumours
▸ **распусти́ться** (*impf* **распуска́ться**) *сов возв*
(*цветы, почки*) to open out; (*шнуровка*,
завязки) to come undone; (*дети, люди*) to get
out of hand.
распу́та|ть (**-ю**; *impf* **распу́тывать**) *сов перех*
(*узел, нитки*) to untangle; (*перен: дело*,
преступление, загадку) to unravel; (*лошадь*) to
unfetter
▸ **распу́таться** (*impf* **распу́тываться**) *сов возв*
(*см перех*) to come untangled; to unravel itself.
распу́тиц|а (**-ы**) *ж period during autumn and*
spring when the roads become impassable.
распу́тник (**-а**) *м* libertine.
распу́тниц|а (**-ы**) *ж см* **распу́тник**.
распу́тный (**-ен**, **-на**, **-но**) *прил* depraved.
распу́тыва|ть(ся) (**-ю(сь)**) *несов от*
распу́тать(ся).
распу́ть|е (**-ья**; *nom pl* **-ий**) *ср* crossroads; **быть**
(*impf*) **на ~** (*перен*) to be at a crossroads.

распу́хн|уть (**-у**, **-ешь**; *impf* **распуха́ть**) *сов*
неперех (*лицо, нога итп*) to swell up;
(*бумажник, папка*) to bulge.
распу́щен|ный (**-**, **-на**, **-но**) *прил* unruly;
(*безнравственный*) dissolute.
распущу́(сь) *сов см* **распусти́ть(ся)**.
распыли́тел|ь (**-я**) *м* spray.
распыл|и́ть (**-ю́**, **-и́шь**; *impf* **распыля́ть**) *сов*
перех to spray.
распя́ти|е (**-я**) *ср* crucifixion.
расп|я́ть (**-ну́**, **-нёшь**; *impf* **распина́ть**) *сов перех*
to crucify.
расса́д|а (**-ы**) *ж собир* (*БОТ*) seedlings *мн*.
рассад|и́ть (**-ажу́**, **-а́дишь**; *impf* **расса́живать**)
сов перех (*гостей, публику*) to seat;
(*болтунов*) to seat apart; (*цветы*) to thin out.
расса́дник (**-а**) *м* (*перен*) hotbed.
расса́жива|ть (**-ю**) *несов от* **рассади́ть**
▸ **расса́живаться** *несов от* **рассе́сться**.
рассажу́ *сов см* **рассади́ть**.
расса́сыва|ться (*3sg* **-ется**, *3pl* **-ются**) *несов*
от **рассоса́ться**.
рассве|сти́ (*3sg* **-тёт**, *pt* **-ло́**, *impf* **рассвета́ть**)
сов безл: **~та́ет** dawn is breaking; **уже́ ~ло́** it's
already light.
рассве́т (**-а**) *м* daybreak.
рассвета́|ть (*3sg* **-ет**) *несов от* **рассвести́**.
рассветёт *сов см* **рассвести́**.
рассвирепе́|ть (**-ю**) *сов от* **свирепе́ть**.
рассёдла|ть (**-ю**; *impf* **рассёдлывать**) *сов*
перех to unsaddle.
рассе́ива|ть(ся) (**-ю(сь)**) *несов от*
рассе́ять(ся).
рассёк *итп сов см* **рассе́чь**.
рассека́|ть (**-ю**) *несов от* **рассе́чь**.
рассеку́ *итп сов см* **рассе́чь**.
рассе́лин|а (**-ы**) *ж* fissure.
рассел|и́ть (**-елю́**, **-е́лишь**; *impf* **расселя́ть**) *сов*
перех (*по комнатам, по квартирам*) to
accommodate, put up; **расселя́ть** (**~** *perf*)
коммуна́льную кварти́ру *to move the*
occupants of a communal flat into self-contained
accommodation.
рассе́лся *итп сов см* **рассе́сться**.
расселя́|ть (**-ю**) *несов от* **рассели́ть**.
рассе́рд|ить(ся) (**-ержу́(сь)**, **-е́рдишь(ся)**) *сов*
от **серди́ть(ся)**.
рассе́|сться (**-я́дусь**, **-я́дешься**; *pt* **-е́лся**,
-е́лась, **-е́лось**) *сов возв* (*по столам, в зале*) to
take one's seat; (*разг: развалиться: на диване*,
в кресле) to slump.
рассе́|чь (**-еку́**, **-ечёшь** *итп*, **-еку́т**; *pt* **-ёк**, **-екла́**,
-екло́, *impf* **рассека́ть**) *сов перех* (*тушу*,
канат) to cut in two; (*губу, лоб*) to cut;
рассека́ть (**~** *perf*) **во́лны** to cut through the
water.
рассе́ян|ный (**-**, **-на**, **-но**) *прил* (*человек*)
absent-minded; (*свет*) diffuse.

рассе́|ять (-ю; *impf* **рассе́ивать**) *сов перех* (*семена, людей*) to scatter; (*свет*) to diffuse; (*перен: сомнения, подозрения*) to dispel; (*горе, тоску*) to alleviate

▶ **рассе́яться** (*impf* **рассе́иваться**) *сов возв* (*люди, семена*) to be scattered; (*тучи, туман, дым*) to disperse; (*сомнения, печаль*) to be dispelled; (*развлечься*) to find a distraction.

расскажу́ *итп сов см* **рассказа́ть**.

расска́з (-а) *м* story; (*свидетеля*) account.

расск|аза́ть (-ажу́, -а́жешь; *impf* **расска́зывать**) *сов перех* to tell.

расска́зчик (-а) *м* storyteller; (*автор*) narrator.

расска́зчиц|а (-ы) *ж см* **расска́зчик**.

расска́зыва|ть (-ю) *несов от* **рассказа́ть**.

рассла́б|ить (-лю, -ишь; *impf* **расслабля́ть**) *сов перех* (*мышцы, ноги, руки*) to relax; (*ремень, галстук*) to loosen; (*подлеж: болезнь, работа*) to weaken

▶ **рассла́биться** (*impf* **расслабля́ться**) *сов возв* to relax.

рассла́блен|ный (-, -на, -но) *прил* relaxed.

рассла́блю(сь) *сов см* **рассла́бить(ся)**.

расслабля́|ть(ся) (-ю(сь)) *несов от* **рассла́бить(ся)**.

рассла́ива|ться (*3sg* -ется, *3pl* -ются) *несов от* **рассло́йться**.

рассле́дование (-я) *ср* investigation.

рассле́д|овать (-ую) (*не)сов перех* to investigate.

рассло|и́ться (*3sg* -и́тся, *3pl* -я́тся, *impf* **рассла́иваться**) *сов возв* (*горная порода, общество*) to stratify; (*пирог, фанера*) to split.

расслы́ш|ать (-у, -ишь) *сов перех* to hear; **извини́те, я не ~ал** I'm sorry, I didn't catch what you said.

рассма́трива|ть (-ю) *несов от* **рассмотре́ть** ♦ *перех:* **~ что-н как** to regard sth as.

рассмеш|и́ть (-у́, -и́шь) *сов от* **смеши́ть**.

рассме|я́ться (-ю́сь, -ёшься) *сов возв* to start laughing.

рассмотре́ни|е (-я) *ср* examination.

рассм|отре́ть (-отрю́, -о́тришь; *impf* **рассма́тривать**) *сов перех* to examine; (*различить: в темноте, вдали*) to discern.

рассс|ова́ть (-ую́; *impf* **рассо́вывать**) *сов перех* (*разг*): **~ что-н в** +*acc или* **по** +*dat* to stuff sth into.

рассо́л (-а; *part gen* -у) *м* brine.

рассо́льник (-а; *part gen* -у) *м* *soup made with meat and pickled cucumbers*.

рассос|а́ться (*3sg* -ётся, *3pl* -у́тся, *impf* **расса́сываться**) *сов возв* (*опухоль*) to go down; (*перен: очередь, пробка*) to ease off; (*: толпа*) to thin out.

расспра́шива|ть (-ю) *несов от* **расспроси́ть**.

расспро́с (-а) *м* (*действие: свидетелей*) questioning; (*обычно мн: вопросы*) question.

расспр|оси́ть (-ошу́, -о́сишь; *impf* **расспра́шивать**) *сов перех:* **~ (о** +*prp*) to question (about).

рассро́ч|ка (-ки; *gen pl* -ек) *ж* installment (*BRIT*), instalment (*US*); **в ~ку** (*купить, продать*) on hire purchase (*BRIT*), on the installment plan (*US*); **выпла́чивать** (**вы́платить** *perf*) **в ~ку** to pay in instal(l)ments.

расстава́ни|е (-я) *ср* parting.

расста|ва́ться (-ю́сь, -ёшься) *сов от* **расста́ться**.

расста́в|ить (-лю, -ишь; *impf* **расставля́ть**) *сов перех* (*книги, мебель итп*) to arrange; (*шахматы*) to set up *или* out; (*знаки препинания, ударения*) to add; (*ножки циркуля*) to open; (*пальцы*) to splay; (*разг: расширить: платье, воротник*) to let out; **расставля́ть (~** *perf*) **но́ги** to open one's legs.

расстано́в|ка (-ки; *gen pl* -ок) *ж* (*мебели, книг*) arrangement; **~ сил** distribution of power; **чита́ть** (*impf*)/**говори́ть** (*impf*) **с ~кой** to read/speak slowly and clearly.

расста́|ться (-нусь, -нешься; *impf* **расстава́ться**) *сов возв:* **~ с** +*instr* to part with; (*с любимым делом*) to abandon; (*перен: с мечтой, с детством*) to say goodbye to.

расстегн|у́ть (-у́, -ёшь; *impf* **расстёгивать**) *сов перех* to undo

▶ **расстегну́ться** (*impf* **расстёгиваться**) *сов возв* (*человек*) to unbutton o.s.; (*рубашка, молния, пуговица*) to come undone.

рассте|ли́ть (-елю́, -е́лешь; *impf* **расстила́ть**) *сов перех* to spread out.

расстила́|ться (*3sg* -ется, *3pl* -ются) *несов возв* (*равнина, степь*) to extend; (*туман*) to spread.

расстоя́ни|е (-я) *ср* distance; **держа́ть** (*impf*) **кого́-н на ~и** (*перен*) to keep sb at arm's length; **держа́ться** (*impf*) **на ~и** to keep one's distance.

расстра́ива|ть(ся) (-ю(сь)) *несов от* **расстро́ить(ся)**.

расстре́л (-а) *м:* **~** +*gen* shooting *или* firing at; (*казнь*) execution (*by firing squad*); **приговри́вать** (**приговори́ть** *perf*) **кого́-н к ~у** to sentence sb to be shot.

расстреля́|ть (-ю; *impf* **расстре́ливать**) *сов перех* (*демонстрацию*) to open fire on; (*казнить*) to shoot; (*патроны, снаряды*) to use up.

расстро́ен|ный (-, -а, -о) *прил* (*здоровье, нервы*) weak; (*человек, вид*) upset; (*рояль, скрипка*) out of tune.

расстро́|ить (-ю, -ишь; *impf* **расстра́ивать**) *сов перех* (*планы, дела, свадьбу*) to disrupt; (*нервы*) to unsettle; (*человека, желудок*) to upset; (*здоровье*) to compromise; (*ряды противника*) to throw into confusion *или* disarray; (*МУЗ*) to put out of tune

▶ **расстро́иться** (*impf* **расстра́иваться**) *сов возв* (*поездка, планы*) to fall through; (*дела, бизнес*) to fall apart; (*человек*) to get upset; (*колонна, ряды*) to fall into disarray; (*нервы*) to weaken; (*здоровье*) to become poorly; (*МУЗ*) to go out of tune.

расстро́йств|о (-а) *ср* (*в делах, в хозяйстве*)

disorder; (*в рядах противника*) confusion, disarray; (*огорчение*) upset; (*речи, нервной системы*) dysfunction; ~ желу́дка stomach upset; **приходи́ть (прийти́** *perf*) **в** ~ (*дела, хозяйство*) to be thrown into confusion; (*человек*) to become upset.

расступи́ться (*3sg* -у́пится, *impf* **расступа́ться**) *сов возв* (*толпа*) to make way; (*перен: тайга, волны, земля*) to part.

расстык|ова́ться (-у́юсь; *impf* **расстыко́вываться**) *сов возв* (*космос*) to undock.

расстыко́в|ка (-ки) *ж* undocking.

расстыко́выва|ться (-юсь) *несов от* **расстыкова́ться**.

рассуди́тель|ный (-ен, -ьна, -ьно) *прил* judicious.

рассу|ди́ть (-жу́, -у́дишь) *сов перех* (*спор*) to settle; (*людей*) to settle a dispute between ♦ *неперех*: **она́ ~уди́ла пра́вильно** she made the correct decision.

рассу́д|ок (-ка) *м* reason; **быть** (*impf*) **в своём** ~**ке** to be in possession of one's facilities.

рассужда́|ть (-ю) *несов неперех* to reason; ~ (*impf*) **о** +*prp* to debate.

рассужде́ни|е (-я) *ср* (*умозаключения*: *логическое итп*) judg(e)ment; ~**я** (*о политике, о морали итп*) reasoning *ед*; **без** ~**й** without arguing.

рассужу́ *сов см* **рассуди́ть**.

рассчита́|ть (-ю; *impf* **рассчи́тывать**) *сов перех* (*стоимость, траекторию, политику*) to calculate; (*работника*) to lay off; **словарь рассчи́тан на студе́нтов** the dictionary is designed for students

▶ **рассчита́ться** (*impf* **рассчи́тываться**) *сов возв* (*уволиться*) to hand in one's notice; (*воен: в строю*) to call out one's number; **рассчи́тываться** (~**ся** *perf*) (**с** +*instr*) (*с продавцом, в гостинице*) to settle up (with); (*перен: с врагом, с обидчиком*) to settle a score (with).

рассчи́тыва|ть (-ю) *несов от* **рассчита́ть** ♦ *неперех*: ~ **на** +*acc* (*надеяться: на удачу, на друга*) to count *или* rely on; ~ (*impf*) +*infin* to count on doing

▶ **рассчи́тываться** *несов от* **рассчита́ться**.

рассыла́|ть (-ю) *несов от* **разосла́ть**.

рассы́п|ать (-лю, -лешь; *impf* **рассыпа́ть**) *сов перех* to spill; (*распределить*): ~ **по** +*dat* to pour into

▶ **рассы́паться** (*impf* **рассыпа́ться**) *сов возв* (*сахар, песок, бусы*) to spill; (*стена, холм*) to crumble; (*волосы*) to fall loose; (*толпа, стая*) to scatter; **он** ~**ался в благода́рностях** he was effusive in his thanks.

рассыпно́й *прил* sold loose.

рассы́пчат|ый (-, -а, -о) *прил* (*каша, рис*) fluffy;

(*печенье, пирог*) crumbly.

расся́|дусь *итп сов см* **рассе́сться**.

раста́лкива|ть (-ю) *несов от* **растолка́ть**.

раста́плива|ть (-ю) *несов от* **растопи́ть**.

раста́птыва|ть (-ю) *несов от* **растопта́ть**.

растаска́|ть (-ю; *impf* **раста́скивать**) *сов перех* (*разг: по комнатам*) to drag; (: *разворовать*) to filch.

раст|ащи́ть (-ащу́, -а́щишь) *сов* = **растаска́ть** ♦ *перех* (*разг: драчунов, мальчишек*) to drag apart.

раста́|ять (-ю) *сов от* **та́ять**.

раство́р (-а) *м* (*хим*) solution; (*циркуля*) span, spread; (*строительный*) mortar; **цеме́нтный** ~ cement.

раствори́м|ый (-, -а, -о) *прил* soluble; **раствори́мый ко́фе** instant coffee.

раствори́тель (-я) *м* solvent.

раствор|и́ть (-ю́, -и́шь; *impf* **растворя́ть**) *сов перех* (*окно, дверь*) to open; (*порошок, сахар*) to dissolve

▶ **раствори́ться** (*impf* **растворя́ться**) *сов возв* (*см перех*) to open; to dissolve; (*перен*): ~ **в** +*prp* (*в темноте, в тумане*) to vanish into.

растека́|ться (*3sg* -ется, *3pl* -ются) *несов от* **расте́чься**.

растёкся *итп сов см* **расте́чься**.

растеку́тся *итп сов см* **расте́чься**.

расте́ни|е (-я) *ср* plant.

растеннево́дств|о (-а) *ср* horticulture.

раст|ере́ть (разотру́, разотрёшь; *pt* -ёр, -ёрла, -ёрло, *impf* **растира́ть**) *сов перех* (*рану, тело*) to massage; **растира́ть** (~ *perf*) (**в порошо́к**) to grind (into a powder); **растира́ть** (~ *perf*) **кре́мом/ма́зью** to rub cream/ointment into; **растира́ть** (~ *perf*) **но́гу** to get blisters

▶ **растере́ться** (*impf* **растира́ться**) *сов возв*: ~**ся** (+*instr*) (*полотенцем, мочалкой*) to rub sb down (with).

растерза́|ть (-ю) *сов от* **терза́ть**.

растёрянность (-и) *м* confusion; **она́ стоя́ла в** ~**и** she stood there looking confused.

расте́рянн|ый (-, -а, -о) *прил* confused.

растеря́|ться (-юсь) *сов возв* to go missing.

расте́|чься (*3sg* -чётся, *3pl* -ку́тся, *pt* -ёкся, -екла́сь, -екло́сь, *impf* **растека́ться**) *сов возв* (*ручьи, вода*) to spill; (*чернила, краска*) to run.

раст|и́ (-у́, -ёшь; *pt* рос, росла́, росло́, *perf* **вы́расти**) *несов неперех* to grow; (*проводить детство*) to grow up; **он вы́рос за грани́цей** he grew up abroad; ~ (**вы́расти** *perf*) **в чьих-н глаза́х** to grow in sb's estimation.

растира́ть(ся) (-ю(сь)) *несов от* **растере́ть(ся)**.

расти́тельность (-и) *ж собир* vegetation.

расти́тельн|ый *прил* (*бот*) plant *опред*: **расти́тельное ма́сло** vegetable oil; **расти́тельный мир** the plant kingdom;

расти́тельный покро́в vegetation.

ра|сти́ть (-щу́, -сти́шь; *perf* вы́растить) несов перех (детей) to raise; (цветы) to grow; (животных) to rear; (перен: кадры) to nurture; (: талант, дарование) to cultivate.

растолка́|ть (-ю; *impf* раста́лкивать) сов перех (толпу, людей) to push away; (разг: разбудить) to shake.

растолк|ова́ть (-у́ю; *impf* растолко́вывать) сов перех: ~ что-н (кому́-н) to clarify sth (for sb).

растоло́|чь (-ку́, -чёшь итп, -ку́т; *pt* -о́к, -кла́, -кло́) сов от толо́чь.

растолсте́|ть (-ю) сов неперех to put on weight.

растоп|и́ть (-оплю́, -о́пишь; *impf* раста́пливать) сов перех (печку) to light; (воск, жир, лёд) to melt

▶ растопи́ться сов от топи́ться

растопта́|ть (-опчу́, -о́пчешь; *impf* раста́птывать) сов перех (также перен) to trample on.

растопы́р|ить (-ю, -ишь; *impf* растопы́ривать) сов перех to spread.

расто́рг|нуть (-ну, -нешь, *pt* -, -ла, -ло, *impf* расторга́ть) сов перех to annul.

растормош|и́ть (-у́, -и́шь) сов перех (разг) to shake.

растаро́п|ный (-ен, -на, -но) прил quick, efficient.

расточи́тел|ьный (-ен, -ьна, -ьно) прил extravagant.

расточи́тельств|о (-а) ср extravagance.

растр|а́вить (-авлю́, -а́вишь; *impf* растравля́ть) сов перех (перен): ~ кому́-н ду́шу to torment sb.

растранжи́р|ить (-ю, -ишь) сов от транжи́рить.

растра́т|а (-ы) ж (времени, сил, денег) waste; (хищение) embezzlement; (растраченная сумма) loss.

растра́|тить (-чу, -тишь; *impf* растра́чивать) сов перех to waste; (расхитить) to embezzle.

растрево́ж|ить (-у, -ишь) сов перех to alarm; ~ (perf) кому́-н ду́шу to stir sb's emotions

▶ растрево́житься сов возв to become alarmed.

растрёпан|ный (-, -на, -но) прил (вид, внешность) bedraggled; (волосы) tousled; (тетрадь, книга) tatty; быть (*impf*) в ~ных чу́вствах (разг) to be all confused.

растреп|а́ть (-еплю́, -е́плешь) сов перех (волосы) to mess up; (тетрадь, книгу) to tatter; (разг: разболтать) to blab

▶ растрепа́ться сов возв (разг: волосы) to get messed up; (: тетрадь, книга) to become tattered.

растро́ган|ный (-, -на, -но) прил (человек) moved, touched; (голос) full of emotion.

растро́га|ть (-ю) сов перех: ~ кого́-н (+instr) (письмом, вниманием) to touch или move sb (by)

▶ растро́гаться сов возв to be touched или moved; ~ся (perf) до слёз to be moved to tears.

раструб|и́ть (-лю́, -и́шь) сов от труби́ть.

растя́гива|ть(ся) (-ю(сь)) несов от растяну́ть(ся).

растяже́ни|е (-я) ср (МЕД) strain.

растяжи́м|ый (-, -а, -о) прил: ~ое поня́тие a loose concept.

растя́нут|ый (-, -а, -о) прил lengthy.

растя|ну́ть (-ну́, -нешь; *impf* растя́гивать) сов перех to stretch; (скатерть) to spread out; (связки, сухожилие) to strain; (ногу, руку) to sprain; (доклад, рассказ) to drag out; (удовольствие) to prolong; (средства) to stretch out

▶ растяну́ться (*impf* растя́гиваться) сов возв to stretch; (человек, обоз) to stretch out; (связки, сухожилие) to be strained; (собрание, работа) to drag on.

растя́п|а (-ы) м/ж (разг) bungler.

расфас|ова́ть (-у́ю) сов от фасова́ть.

расформир|ова́ть (-у́ю; *impf* расформиро́вывать) сов перех to disband.

расха́жива|ть (-ю) несов неперех to saunter.

расхвал|и́ть (-алю́, -а́лишь; *impf* расхва́ливать) сов перех to enthuse about.

расхвата́|ть (-ю; *impf* расхва́тывать) сов перех (разг) to snatch up.

расхити́тел|ь (-я) м embezzler.

расхи́|тить (-щу, -тишь; *impf* расхища́ть) сов перех to embezzle.

расхище́ни|е (-я) ср embezzlement.

расхля́баннный (-, -на, -но) прил (жест, движение) irreverent; (человек, поведение) lax.

расхо́д (-а) м (энергии, воды) consumption; (обычно мн: затраты) expense; (: комм: в бухгалтерской книге) expenditure; ~ы произво́дства production costs; вводи́ть (ввести́ *perf*) кого́-н в ~ to leave sb out of pocket.

расход|и́ться (-ожу́сь, -о́дишься) несов от разойти́сь.

расхо́дный прил: ~ о́рдер (КОММ) expenses form.

расхо́д|овать (-ую; *perf* израсхо́довать) несов перех (деньги) to spend; (материалы, энергию) to expend; (потреблять: бензин) to consume.

расхожде́ни|е (-я) ср (между словом и делом) discrepancy; (во взглядах) divergence.

расхо́ж|ий (-ая, -ее, -ие) прил (мнение) widely accepted.

расхожу́сь несов см расходи́ться.

расхоте́ть (как хоте́ть; см Table 16) сов неперех: ~ +infin (спать, гуля́ть итп) to no longer want to do; я расхоте́л есть I don't feel hungry any more

▶ расхоте́ться сов безл: (мне) расхоте́лось спать I don't feel sleepy any more.

расхох|ота́ться (-очу́сь, -о́чешься) сов возв to burst out laughing.

расхочу́(сь) *итп сов см* **расхоте́ть(ся)**.
расцара́па|ть (-ю) *сов перех* to scratch.
расцв|ести́ (-ету́, -етёшь; *pt* -ёл, -ела́, -ело́, *impf* **расцвета́ть**) *сов неперех* (*также перен*) to blossom; (*от радости*) to light up.
расцве́т (-а) *м* (*перен: науки, таланта*) blossoming; **он в ~е сил** he is in the prime of life.
расцвета́|ть (-ю) *несов от* **расцвести́**.
расцве́т|ка (-ки; *gen pl* -ок) *ж* colour (*BRIT*) *или* color (*US*) scheme.
расцвету́ *итп сов см* **расцвести́**.
расцел|ова́ть (-у́ю) *сов перех* to kiss
▸ **расцелова́ться** *сов возв* to kiss each other.
расце́нива|ться (*3sg* -ется, *3pl* -ются) *несов возв*: ~ **как** to be regarded as.
расцен|и́ть (-ю́, -ишь; *impf* **расце́нивать**) *сов перех* to judge; **расце́нивать** (~ *perf*) **что-н как** to regard sth as.
расце́н|ка (-ки; *gen pl* -ок) *ж* (*оплата работы*) rate; (*цена*) tariff.
расцеп|и́ть (-лю́, -е́пишь; *impf* **расцепля́ть**) *сов перех* (*состав*) to uncouple; (*дерущихся, пальцы*) to pull apart.
расч|ерти́ть (-ерчу́, -е́ртишь; *impf* **расче́рчивать**) *сов перех* to rule, line.
расч|еса́ть (-ешу́, -е́шешь; *impf* **расчёсывать**) *сов перех* (*волосы, гриву*) to comb; (*шерсть, лён*) to card; (*руку, царапину*) to scratch; **расчёсывать** (~ *perf*) **кого-н** to comb sb's hair.
расчё́с|ка (-ки; *gen pl* -ок) *ж* comb.
расчёсыва|ть (-ю) *несов от* **расчеса́ть**.
расчёт (-а) *м* (*налога, стоимости итп*) calculation; (*оплата*) payment; (*предложение*) calculation; (*выгода*) advantage; (*бережливость*) economy; (*увольнение*) dismissal; (*ВОЕН, МОР*) crew; **из ~а** +*gen* on the basis of; **из ~а 5 проце́нтов годовы́х** at 5 percent per annum; **он ведёт дела́ с ~ом** he runs his business economically; **де́йствовать** (*impf*) **по ~у** to act in a calculated way; **исходи́ть** (*impf*) **из ~а, что** ... to act on the assumption that ...; **брать** (**взять** *perf*) **что-н в ~** to take sth into account; **по мои́м ~ам мы зако́нчим к ве́черу** by my reckoning we will finish by evening; **я с Ва́ми в ~е** we are all even; **брать** (**взять** *perf*) ~ to hand in one's notice.
расчётлив|ый (-, -а, -о) *прил* (*экономный*) thrifty; (*руководитель, игрок*) calculating; (*движения*) deliberate.
расчётный *прил* (*ТЕХ: скорость итп*) estimated; **расчётный день** payday; **расчётный счёт** debit account.
расчешу́ *итп сов см* **расчеса́ть**.
расчи́|стить (-щу, -стишь; *impf* **расчища́ть**) *сов перех* to clear
▸ **расчи́ститься** (*impf* **расчища́ться**) *сов возв* to clear.

расчлен|и́ть (-ю́, -и́шь) *сов от* **расчленя́ть, члени́ть**.
расчленя́|ть (-ю) *несов от* **расчлени́ть**.
расчу́вств|оваться (-уюсь) *сов возв* (*разг*) to be overcome with emotion.
расшата́|ть (-ю; *impf* **расша́тывать**) *сов перех* (*стол, стул*) to make wobbly; (*здоровье*) to damage; **он ~л себе́ не́рвы** he's become a nervous wreck
▸ **расшата́ться** (*impf* **расша́тываться**) *сов возв* (*забор, столб*) to become wobbly; (*перен: нервы*) to give out; (*здоровье*) to be damaged.
расшвыр|я́ть (-ю) *сов перех* (*разг*) to hurl around; (: *перен: деньги*) to fritter away.
расшевел|и́ть (-ю́, -и́шь) *сов перех* (*разг*): ~ **кого́-н** to give sb a shake; (*перен: слушателей*) to liven sb up
▸ **расшевели́ться** *сов возв* to stir; (*перен: начальство, игроки*) to get moving.
расшиб|и́ть (-у́, -ёшь; *impf* **расшиба́ть**) *сов перех* (*разг*) to smash
▸ **расшиби́ться** (*impf* **расшиба́ться**) *сов возв* (*о дверь, при падении*) to hurt o.s.; (*разг: для друга, для семьи*) to put o.s. out.
расшива́|ть (-ю) *несов от* **расши́ть**.
расшире́ни|е (-я) *ср* widening; (*связей, производства*) expansion; (*знаний*) broadening.
расши́рен|ный (-, -на, -но) *прил* (*проход*) widened; (*комитет, заседание*) expanded; (*зрачки, сосуды*) dilated.
расши́р|ить (-ю, -ишь; *impf* **расширя́ть**) *сов перех* to widen; (*производство*) to expand; **расширя́ть** (~ *perf*) **кругозо́р** to broaden one's horizons
▸ **расши́риться** (*impf* **расширя́ться**) *сов возв* to widen; (*завод, контакты, знания*) to expand; (*зрачки*) to dilate.
расши́тый *прил* embroidered.
ра|сши́ть (-зошью́, -зошьёшь; *impf* **расшива́ть**) *сов перех* (*вышить*) to embroider.
расшифр|ова́ть (-у́ю; *impf* **расшифро́вывать**) *сов перех* (*текст, шифровку*) to decode, decipher; (*перен: тайну, смысл слов*) to decipher.
расшнур|ова́ть (-у́ю; *impf* **расшнуро́вывать**) *сов перех* to unlace.
расшум|е́ться (-лю́сь, -и́шься) *сов возв* (*разг*) to make a racket; (: *начать спорить*) to kick up a fuss.
расщедр|иться (-юсь, -ишься; *impf* **расще́дриваться**) *сов возв* (*разг*) to become generous.
расще́лин|а (-ы) *ж* (*скалы, горы*) crevice; (*в дереве, в камне*) cleft.
расщеп|и́ть (-лю́, -и́шь; *impf* **расщепля́ть**) *сов перех* (*также физ*) to split; (*хим*) to decompose
▸ **расщепи́ться** (*impf* **расщепля́ться**) *сов возв*

to splinter; (*ФИЗ*) to split; (*ХИМ*) to decompose.

расщепле́ни|е (-я) *ср* splintering; (*ФИЗ*) fission; (*ХИМ*) decomposition.

расщеплю́(сь) *сов см* **расщепи́ть(ся).**

расщепля́|ть(ся) (-ю) *несов от* **расщепи́ть(ся).**

ратифика́ци|я (-и) *ж* ratification.

ратифици́р|овать (-ую) *(не)сов перех* to ratify.

ра́унд (-а) *м* (*СПОРТ*) round; (*ПОЛИТ*): ~ **перегово́ров** round of talks.

ра́фик (-а) *м* (*разг*) minibus.

рафина́д (-а) *м* sugar cubes *мн*.

рафини́рованный *прил* refined.

рахи́т (-а) *м* (*МЕД*) rickets.

рацио́н (-а) *м* ration.

рациона́лен *прил см* **рациона́льный.**

рационализа́тор (-а) *м* innovator.

рационализа́ци|я (-и) *ж* rationalization.

рационализи́р|овать (-ую) *(не)сов перех* to rationalize.

рационали́ст (-а) *м* rationalist.

рациона́л|ьный (-ен, -ьна, -ьно) *прил* (*поступок*) rational; (*использование ресурсов, организация*) effective; **~ьное пита́ние** well-balanced diet.

ра́ци|я (-и) *ж* walkie-talkie.

рацпредложе́ни|е (-я) *ср сокр* (= *рационализа́торское предложе́ние*) innovation proposal.

рачи́тельный (-ен, -ьна, -ьно) *прил* thrifty.

рван|у́ть (-у, -ёшь) *сов перех* to pull at; (*разг*) to explode ♦ *неперех* (*разг: лошадь, бегун*) to shoot off; ~ *(perf)* **кого́-н за пиджа́к/за́ руку** to tug at sb's jacket/arm; ~ *(perf)* **пе́сню** (*разг*) to break into song

▶ **рвану́ться** *сов возв* to tear off.

рва́ный *прил* torn; (*ботинки*) ripped; (*рана*) lacerated.

рв|а́ть (-у, -ёшь), *perf* **порва́ть** *или* **разорва́ть)** *несов перех* (*письмо, одежду, книгу*) to tear, rip; (*перен: отношения, дружбу*) to break off; (*perf* **вы́рвать**; *предмет из рук*) to snatch; (*no perf*; *подлеж: ветер: одежды, занавес*) to tear at; (*perf* **сорва́ть**; *цветы, траву*) to pick; (*ветки*) to break off ♦ (*perf* **вы́рвать**) *безл*: **его́** *итп* **~а́ло всю ночь** he was vomiting *или* being sick all night; ~ (**разорва́ть** *perf*) **что-н на ча́сти** to tear sb/sth to bits; **меня́ ~ут на ча́сти** (*перен*) I'm in demand from all sides; ~ (**порва́ть** *perf*) **с про́шлым** to break with the past; ~ (**вы́рвать** *perf*) **кому́-н зуб** (*разг*) to pull sb's tooth out; ~ (*impf*) **и мета́ть** (*impf*) (*разг*) to rant and rave

▶ **рва́ться** (*perf* **порва́ться** *или* **разорва́ться**) *несов возв* (*бумага, одежда*) to tear, rip; (*обувь*) to rip; (*перен: отношения, связи*) to be severed; (*perf* **разорва́ться**; *снаряд*) to explode; **~а́ться** (*impf*) **к приключе́ниям/вла́сти** to be hungry for adventure/power; **~а́ться** (*impf*) **в дра́ку** to be spoiling for a fight; **у меня́ се́рдце** *или* **душа́ ~ётся на ча́сти** my heart is being torn in two.

рвач (-а́) *м* (*разг: пренебр*) taker.

рве́ни|е (-я) *ср* (*в учёбе, в работе*) enthusiasm; (*патриотический, религиозный*) zeal; ~ +*infin* desire to do.

рво́т|а (-ы) *ж* vomiting.

рво́т|ный *прил*: **~ое (сре́дство)** emetic.

ре *ср нескл* (*МУЗ*) re.

реабилита́ци|я (-и) *ж* rehabilitation.

реабилити́р|овать (-ую) *(не)сов перех* to rehabilitate.

реаги́р|овать (-ую) *несов неперех*: ~ (**на** +*acc*) (*на свет, на раздражение*) to react (to); (*perf* **отреаги́ровать** *или* **прореаги́ровать**; *на критику, на слова*) to react *или* respond (to).

реакти́в (-а) *м* (*ХИМ*) reagent.

реакти́вный *прил* (*ХИМ*) reactive; (*ТЕХ*) jet-propelled; **реакти́вный дви́гатель** jet engine; **реакти́вный самолёт** jet (plane).

реа́ктор (-а) *м* reactor.

реакционе́р (-а) *м* reactionary.

реакцио́нный *прил* reactionary.

реа́кци|я (-и) *ж* reaction.

реа́лен *прил см* **реа́льный.**

реализа́ци|я (-и) *ж* (*см глаг*) implementation; realization.

реали́зм (-а) *м* realism.

реализ|ова́ть (-у́ю) *(не)сов перех* (*реформы, проект, предложение*) to implement; (*товар, ценные бумаги*) to realize.

реали́ст (-а) *м* realist.

реалисти́чен *прил см* **реалисти́чный.**

реалисти́ческ|ий (-ая, -ое, -ие) *прил* realistic; (*искусство*) realist *опред*.

реалисти́ч|ный (-ен, -на, -но) *прил* realistic.

реа́льност|ь (-и) *ж* reality; (*политики, плана, задачи*) practicability, feasibility; **~и на́шего вре́мени** modern-day realities.

реа́л|ьный (-ен, -ьна, -ьно) *прил* (*не воображаемый*) real; (*осуществимый, практический*) realistic; **в ~ьном вре́мени** (*КОМП*) real-time; **реа́льная за́работная пла́та** (*ЭКОН*) real wage.

реанима́ци|я (-и) *ж* resuscitation; **отделе́ние ~и** intensive care unit.

ребён|ок (-ка; *nom pl* **де́ти** *или* **ребя́та)** *м* child (*мн* children); (*грудной*) baby; **дом ~ка** children's home.

ребр|о́ (-а́; *nom pl* **рёбра,** *gen pl* **рёбер)** *ср* (*АНАТ*) rib; (*монеты, стола, кубика итп*) edge; **ста́вить (поста́вить** *perf*) **вопро́с ~м** to put a question bluntly.

ре́бус (-а) *м* rebus; (*перен*) riddle.

ребя́т|а (-) *мн от* **ребёнок**; (*разг: парни*) guys *мн*.

ребя́ческ|ий (-ая, -ое, -ие) *прил* (*душа, сознание*) child's *опред*; (*перен: поведение, суждение*) childish.

рёв (-а) *м* roar; (*разг: громкий плач*) howling.

ревальва́ци|я (-и) *ж* (*ЭКОН*) revaluation.

рева́нш (-а) *м* revenge; (*игра*) revenge match; **взять** (*perf*) ~ to take revenge.

реваншизм (-а) *м* revanchism.
ревень (-я) *м* rhubarb.
реветь (-у́, -ёшь) *несов неперех* to roar; (*разг: плакать*) to howl.
ревизио́нный *прил*: ~ая коми́ссия audit commission.
реви́зи|я (-и) *ж* (*комм*) audit; (*взглядов, учения*) revision.
ревиз|ова́ть (-у́ю) (*не*)*сов перех* (*предприятие*) to inspect; (*бухгалтерские книги*) to audit.
ревизо́р (-а) *м* (*комм*) auditor.
ревмати́зм (-а) *м* rheumatism.
ревмати́ческ|ий (-ая, -ое, -ие) *прил* rheumatoid.
ревмато́лог (-а) *м* rheumatologist.
ревни́в|ый (-, -а, -о) *прил* jealous.
ревн|ова́ть (-у́ю) *несов неперех*: ~ (кого́-н) to be jealous (of sb); **он ~у́ет меня́ к своему́ бра́ту** he is jealous of my relationship with his brother.
ре́вност|ный (-ен, -на, -но) *прил* ardent, zealous.
ре́вность (-и) *ж* jealousy.
револьве́р (-а) *м* revolver.
революционе́р (-а) *м* revolutionary.
революционе́р|ка (-ки; *gen pl* -ок) *ж см* **революционе́р**.
революцио́нный *прил* revolutionary.
револю́ци|я (-и) *ж* revolution.
ревю́ *ср нескл* revue.
рега́ли|я (-и) *ж* (*обычно мн*) regalia *ед*.
рега́т|а (-ы) *ж* regatta.
ре́гби *ср нескл* rugby.
регби́ст (-а) *м* rugby player.
регио́н (-а) *м* region.
региона́льный *прил* regional.
реги́стр (-а) *м* (*муз, комп, мор*) register; (*на пишущей машинке*): **ве́рхний/ни́жний** ~ upper/lower case.
регистра́тор (-а) *м* (*в поликлинике*) receptionist; (*в загсе*) registrar.
регистрату́р|а (-ы) *ж* (*в поликлинике*) reception; (*на предприятии*) records department.
регистра́ци|я (-и) *ж* registration.
регистри́р|овать (-ую) *perf* **регистри́ровать** *или* **зарегистри́ровать**) *несов перех* to register
► **регистри́роваться** (*не*)*сов возв* to register; (*оформлять брак*) to get married (*at a registry office*).
регла́мент (-а) *м* (*порядок заседаний*) order of business; (*время для выступления*) speaking time.
регла́н *прил неизм* raglan ♦ (-а) *м*: (**пальто́**-)/(**пла́тье**-)~ raglan coat/dress.
регули́р|овать (-ую) *несов перех* to regulate; (*perf* **урегули́ровать**; *отношения*) to

normalize; (*perf* **отрегули́ровать**; *мотор, громкость*) to adjust.
регулиро́вщик (-а) *м* traffic policeman (*мн* policemen).
регуля́рен *прил см* **регуля́рный**.
регуля́рно *нареч* regularly.
регуля́рность (-и) *ж* regularity.
регуля́р|ный (-ен, -на, -но) *прил* regular; **регуля́рные войска́** regular army *ед*.
редакти́р|овать (-ую; *perf* **отредакти́ровать**) *несов перех* to edit.
реда́ктор (-а) *м* (*также комп*) editor.
редакцио́нн|ый *прил* (*поправки*): ~ая колле́гия editorial board; **редакцио́нная статья́** editorial.
реда́кци|я (-и) *ж* (*действие: текста, статьи*) editing; (*вариант произведения*) edition; (*формулировка: статьи закона*) wording; (*учреждение*) editorial offices *мн*; (*на радио*) desk; (*на телевидении*) division; **под** ~**ей** +*gen* edited by.
реде́|ть (*3sg* -ет, *3pl* -ют, *perf* **пореде́ть**) *несов неперех* to thin out.
реди́с (-а) *м* radish.
реди́ск|а (-и) *ж* (*разг*) (red) radish ♦ *собир* radishes *мн*.
ре́д|кий (-кая, -кое, -кие; -ок, -ка́, -ко) *прил* rare; (*выстрелы, письма, гость*) occasional; (*волосы*) thin; (*зубы*) gappy; (*лес*) sparse; (*ткань, материал*) loose-weave.
ре́дко *нареч* rarely, seldom; (*расти*) sparsely.
редколле́ги|я (-и) *ж сокр* = **редакцио́нная колле́гия**.
ре́дкость (-и) *ж* rarity; **на** ~ unusually; **он на** ~ **до́брый челове́к** he is a person of uncommon kindness; **таки́е приме́ры не** ~ such examples are not uncommon.
ре́док *прил см* **ре́дкий**.
ре́дьк|а (-и) *ж* (white) radish ♦ *собир* radishes *мн*.
режи́м (-а) *ж* (*питания, также полит*) regime; (*больничный, тюремный итп*) routine; (*условия работы*) conditions *мн*; (*комп*) mode; ~ **безопа́сности** security system; **рабо́чий** ~ **дви́гателя** the operating conditions of the engine.
режиссёр (-а) *м* director (*of film, play etc*); **режиссёр-постано́вщик** (stage) director.
режиссу́р|а (-ы) *ж* (*профессия*) directing; (*фильма, спектакля*) direction.
ре́|зать (-жу, -жешь; *perf* **разре́зать**) *несов перех* (*хлеб*) to slice, cut up; (*металл, кожу*) to cut; (*разг: нарыв, живот*) to cut open; (*perf* **заре́зать**; *разг: гуся, свинью*) to slaughter; (*перен: разг: диссертацию*) to flunk; (*perf* **сре́зать**; *студента*) to fail; (*no perf; ложки, фигурки итп*) to carve; (*причинять боль: подлеж: воротник*) to dig into; (: *дым, ветер*)

to sting; (*наносить изображения*): ~ **по** +*dat*
(*по дереву, по камню*) to carve; (*по стеклу*) to
cut; (*по металлу*) to engrave; **резáть** (*impf*)
слух *или* **ýхо** to grate

▶ **рéзаться** (*perf* **прорéзаться**) *несов возв*
(*зубы, рога*) to come through; (*no perf*; *разг*):
~**ся в** +*acc* (*в карты итп*) to play.

резвúться (-**лю́сь, -úшься**) *несов возв* to
frolic, frisk about.

рéзво *нареч* (*бежать*) energetically.

рéзв|ый (-, -á, -о) *прил* (*ребёнок*) playful;
(*быстрый в беге: конь, заяц*) frisky.

резéрв (-а) *м* (*СПОРТ*) reserve team; (*обычно мн*:
материальные итп) reserve; **кáссовый** ~
(*КОММ*) cash reserves.

резéрвн|ый *прил* reserve *опред*; (*КОМП*) backup
опред; ~**ые войскá** (army) reserves;
резéрвная валю́та reserve currency;
резéрвный капитáл capital reserve;
резéрвный фонд reserve fund.

резервуáр (-а) *м* reservoir (*tank*).

рез|éц (-цá) *м* (*инструмент*) cutting tool; (*АНАТ*)
incisor.

резидéнт (-а) *м* spy.

резидéнци|я (-и) *ж* residence.

резúн|а (-ы) *ж* rubber; **тянýть** (*impf*) ~**у** (*разг*) to
drag things out.

резúн|ка (-ки; *gen pl* -ок) *ж* (*ластик*) rubber
(*BRIT*), eraser (*esp US*); (*тесёмка*) elastic;
(*жвачка*) chewing gum.

резúновый *прил* rubber *опред*.

резúнок *сущ см* **резúнка**.

рéз|кий (-кая, -кое, -кие; -ок, -кá, -ко) *прил*
sharp; (*свет, звук, голос*) harsh; (*запах*)
pungent; (*стиль, манера*) abrupt.

рéзко *нареч* sharply; (*встать, высказать*)
abruptly.

рéзкост|ь (-и) *ж* (*поведения, манеры*)
abruptness; (*ФОТО*) focus; **говорúть (сказáть**
perf) **комý-н** ~**и** to be rude to sb.

резнóй *прил* carved.

резн|я́ (-и́) *ж* slaughter.

рéзок *прил см* **рéзкий**.

резолю́ци|я (-и) *ж* (*съезда, заседания*)
resolution; (*распоряжение*) directive.

резонáнс (-а) *м* (*физ*) resonance; (*перен*)
response.

резóн|ный (-ен, -на, -но) *прил* reasonable.

результáт (-а) *м* result; **в** ~**е** as a result; (*в*
итоге) in the end.

результатúвн|ый (-ен, -на, -но) *прил* (*дело,*
встреча) productive; (*спортсмен*) successful.

рéзче *сравн прил от* **рéзкий** ◆ *сравн нареч от*
рéзко.

рéзус (-а) *м* (*также:* ~-**фáктор**) rhesus factor.

резцá *итп сущ см* **резéц**.

рез|ь (-и) *ж* sharp pain.

резьб|á (-ы́) *ж* carving; (*винта, шурупа*) thread;
~ **по дéреву/кáмню** carving in wood/stone.

резюмé *ср нескл* resume, summary.

резюмúр|овать (-ую) (*не*)*сов перех* to

summarize.

рейд (-а) *м* raid; (*МОР*) anchorage.

рé|йка (-йки; *gen pl* **ек**) *ж* batten;
(*измерительная*) measuring rod.

Рéйкьявик (-а) *м* Reykjavik.

Рейн (-а) *м* (the) Rhine.

рейнвéйн (-а) *м* hock (*wine*).

рейс (-а) *м* (*самолёта*) flight; (*автобуса*) run;
(*парахода*) sailing.

рéйсовый *прил* regular.

рéйтинг (-а) *м* popularity rating.

рейтýз|ы (-) *мн* thermal pants.

рек|á (-и́; *acc sg* -**у**, *dat sg* -**é**, *nom pl* -**и**) *ж* (*также*
перен) river.

рéквием (-а) *м* requiem.

реквизúр|овать (-ую) (*не*)*сов перех* to
requisition.

реквизúт (-а) *м* (*ТЕАТР, КИНО*) props *мн*;
(*обычно мн: в документе*) stipulation.

реклáм|а (-ы) *ж* (*действие: торговая*)
advertising; (*средство*) advert (*BRIT*),
advertisement; (*театральная*) publicity;
дéлать (сдéлать *perf*) **себé** ~**у** to draw attention
to o.s.

рекламúр|овать (-ую) (*не*)*сов перех* to
advertise.

реклáмный *прил* (*отдел, колонка*) advertising
опред; (*статья, фильм, справочник*) publicity
опред; **реклáмный рóлик** advertisement;
(*фильма*) trailer.

рекомендáтельн|ый *прил*: ~**ое письмó** letter
of recommendation.

рекомендáци|я (-и) *ж* recommendation.

рекоменд|овáть (-ýю; *perf* **рекомендовáть**
или **порекомендовáть**) *несов перех* to
recommend; ~ (**порекомендовáть** *perf*) **когó-н**
комý-н/на рабóту to recommend sb to sb/for a
job; ~ (**порекомендовáть** *perf*) **комý-н** +*infin* to
recommend sb to do.

реконструúр|овать (-ую) (*не*)*сов перех*
(*промышленность*) to rebuild; (*памятник,*
здание) to reconstruct.

реконструкци|я (-и) *ж* reconstruction.

рекóрд (-а) *м* record; **устанáвливать**
(**установúть** *perf*)/**побúть** (*perf*) ~ to set/break a
record.

рекóрдный *прил* record(-breaking) *опред*.

рекордсмéн (-а) *м* recordholder.

рекордсмéн|ка (-ки; *gen pl* -ок) *ж см*
рекордсмéн.

рéктор (-а) *м* ≈ principal.

ректорáт (-а) *м* principal's office.

религиóзный (-ен, -на, -но) *прил* religious.

релúги|я (-и) *ж* religion.

релúкви|я (-и) *ж* relic; (*семейная*) heirloom.

рельéф (-а) *м* (*ГЕО, ИСКУССТВО*) relief.

рельс (-а) *м* (*обычно мн*) rail; **на рéльсы** +*gen*
(*перен*) towards.

рéльсовый *прил*: ~ **путь** railway (*BRIT*) *или*
railroad (*US*) track.

ремáрк|а (-и) *ж* (*ТЕАТР*) stage directions *мн*;

(*замечание*) remark.

рем|**éнь** (-нá) *м* (*брюк, платья, также тех*) belt; (*сумки*) strap; **привязны́|е ~ни** seat belt; **приводно́й ~** drive-belt.

ремёсел *сущ см* ремесло́.

реме́сленник (-а) *м* artisan, craftsman (*мн* craftsmen).

реме́сленный *прил* (*труд, мастерская*) artisan's, craftsman's; (*изделие*) handcrafted; (*перен*: *не творческий*) mechanical.

ремесл|**о́** (-á; *nom pl* ремёсла, *gen pl* ремёсел) *ср* trade; (*перен*: *нетворческая работа*) hack work.

ремеш|**о́к** (-ка́) *м* strap.

ремня́ *итп сущ см* реме́нь.

ремо́нт (-а) *м* repair; (*здания*) refurbishment; (: *мелкий*) redecoration; **на ~е** under repair; **теку́щий ~** maintenance; **сдава́ть (сдать** *perf*) **что-н в ~** to put sth in for repair; **у нас до́ма сейча́с идёт ~** our house is being redecorated.

ремонти́р|**овать** (-ую; *perf* **ремонти́ровать** *или* **отремонти́ровать**) *несов перех* to repair; (*квартиру, здание*) to do up.

ремо́нтн|**ый** *прил*: **~ые рабо́ты** repairs *мн*; **~ая мастерска́я** repair workshop.

ре́нт|**а** (-ы) *ж* rent; **земе́льная ~** ground rent.

рента́бел|**ьный** (-ен, -ьна, -ьно) *прил* profitable.

рентге́н (-а) *м* (*мед*) X-ray; (*физ*) roentgen; **де́лать (сде́лать** *perf*) **кому́-н ~** to X-ray sb.

рентге́новск|**ий** (-ая, -ое, -ие) *прил*: **~ кабине́т/аппара́т** X-ray room/machine; **~ сни́мок** X-ray; **~ие лучи́** X-rays.

рентгено́лог (-а) *м* radiologist.

реорганиза́ци|**я** (-и) *ж* reorganization.

реорганиз|**ова́ть** (-у́ю) (*не*)*сов перех* to reorganize.

ре́п|**а** (-ы) *ж* (*no pl*) swede (*brit*), rutabaga (*us*).

репатриа́нт (-а) *м* repatriate.

репатриа́ци|**я** (-и) *ж* repatriation.

репатрии́р|**овать** (-ую) (*не*)*сов перех* to repatriate.

реп|**е́й** (-ья́) *м* (*разг*) = репе́йник.

репе́йник (-а) *м* (*бот*) burdock.

репертуа́р (-а) *м* repertoire.

репети́р|**овать** (-ую; *perf* **отрепети́ровать** *или* **прорепети́ровать**) *несов* (*не*)*перех* (*диалог, спектакль*) to rehearse.

репети́тор (-а) *м* (*преподаватель*) coach, private tutor.

репети́ци|**я** (-и) *ж* rehearsal.

ре́плик|**а** (-и) *ж* (*слушателей*) remark; (*театр*) line; (*юр*) objection.

репорта́ж (-а) *м* (*статья, передача*) report.

репортёр (-а) *м* reporter.

репре́сси|**я** (-и) *ж* (*обычно мн*) repression.

репроду́ктор (-а) *м* loudspeaker.

репроду́кци|**я** (-и) *ж* reproduction (*of painting*

etc).

репти́ли|**я** (-и) *ж* reptile.

репута́ци|**я** (-и) *ж* reputation.

ре́пчатый *прил*: **~ лук** onions *мн*.

репья́ *итп сущ см* репе́й.

респи́ц|**а** (-ы) *ж* (*обычно мн*) eyelash.

респекта́бел|**ьный** (-ен, -ьна, -ьно) *прил* respectable.

респонде́нт (-а) *м* respondent.

респу́блик|**а** (-и) *ж* republic.

республика́нск|**ий** (-ая, -ое, -ие) *прил* republican.

рессо́р|**а** (-ы) *ж* spring.

реставра́тор (-а) *м* restorer.

реставра́ци|**я** (-и) *ж* restoration.

реставри́р|**овать** (-ую; *perf* **реставри́ровать** *или* **отреставри́ровать**) *несов перех* to restore.

рестора́н (-а) *м* restaurant.

ресу́рс (-а) *м* (*обычно мн*) resource; **приро́дные ~ы** natural resources.

ре́тро *прил неизм* (*мода, мебель*) retro.

ретрогра́д (-а) *м* reactionary.

ретроспекти́в|**а** (-ы) *ж* retrospective.

рефера́т (-а) *м* synopsis (*мн* synopses).

рефере́ндум (-а) *м* referendum (*мн* referenda).

рефере́нт (-а) *м* (*директора, министра*) aide.

рефери́ *м нескл* referee.

рефери́р|**овать** (-ую; *perf* **рефери́ровать** *или* **прорефери́ровать**) (*не*)*сов перех* to summarize.

рефле́кс (-а) *м* reflex.

рефле́ктор (-а) *м* reflector.

рефо́рм|**а** (-ы) *ж* reform.

реформа́тор (-а) *м* reformer.

рефрижера́тор (-а) *м* (*судно*) refrigerator ship; (*грузовик*) refrigerated lorry (*brit*) *или* truck (*us*).

рехн|**у́ться** (-у́сь, -ёшься) *сов возв* (*разг*) to crack (up), flip; **~ (***perf***) на чём-н** to be nuts about sth.

рецензи́р|**овать** (-ую; *perf* **прорецензи́ровать**) *несов перех* to review.

реце́нзи|**я** (-и) *ж*: **~ (на** +*acc*) review (of).

реце́пт (-а) *м* (*мед*) prescription; (*кулин, перен*) recipe.

рециди́в (-а) *м* (*преступления*) repetition; (*болезни*) recurrence.

рецидиви́ст (-а) *м* recidivist, habitual offender.

речев|**о́й** *прил* speech *опред*; **~ дефе́кт** speech defect; **~ы́е на́выки** speaking skills.

ре́ч|**ка** (-ки; *gen pl* -ек) *ж* stream; (*разг*) river.

речни́к (-а) *м* river-transport worker.

речн|**о́й** *прил* river *опред*; **~а́я ры́ба** freshwater fish; **речно́й трамва́й** river bus.

реч|**ь** (-и) *ж* speech; (*стиль: разговорная итп*) language; (*русская, французская*) spoken language; **ру́сская ~** spoken Russian; **часть ре́чи** part of speech; **прямáя/ко́свенная ~**

direct/indirect speech; **у́стная/пи́сьменная ~** spoken/written language; **дар ре́чи** the gift of speech; **теря́ть (потеря́ть** *perf***) дар ре́чи** to be left speechless; **произноси́ть** (*impf*) **у́мные/пусты́е ре́чи** to make clever/empty pronouncements; **~ идёт о** +*prp* ... we are talking about ...; **о чём идёт ~?** what are you talking about?; **~ идёт о том, как/где/кто** *итп* ... the matter in question is how/where/who *итп* ...; **заводи́ть (завести́** *perf***) ~ о** +*prp* to raise the matter of; **об э́том не мо́жет быть и ре́чи** there can be absolutely no question of this; **об э́том ре́чи не́ было** nothing was said about this; **о чём ~!** (*разг*) sure!, of course!

реша́ть(ся) (-ю(сь)) *несов от* **реши́ть(ся)**.

реша́ющий (-ая, -ее, -ие) *прил* decisive; (*слово, матч*) deciding *опред*; **реша́ющий го́лос** casting vote.

реше́ни|е (-я) *ср* (*суда, собрания итп*) decision; (*ответ к задаче*) solution; (*действие: вопроса, дела*) solution, solving; (: *судьбы*) deciding.

решётк|а (-ки; *gen pl* -ок) *ж* (*садовая*) trellis; (*оконная*) grille; (*в камине*) grate; (*в духовке*) oven rack; **за ~кой** (*разг*) behind bars.

решет|о́ (-а́) *ср* sieve.

решёток *сущ см* **решётка**.

решётчат|ый *прил* lattice *опред*, trellis *опред*; **~ое окно́** lattice window.

реши́мость (-и) *ж* resolve.

реши́телен *прил см* **реши́тельный**.

реши́тельно *нареч* (*заявить, отказать*) resolutely; (*действовать*) with resolve, decisively; **я ~ не понима́ю, о чём Вы говори́те** I've got absolutely no idea what you are talking about.

реши́тельн|ый (-ен, -ьна, -ьно) *прил* (*человек, взгляд*) resolute; (*меры*) drastic; (*решающий*) decisive.

реши́|ть (-у́, -йшь; *impf* **реша́ть**) *сов перех* to decide; (*задачу, вопрос*) to solve; **реша́ть (~** *perf***) +*infin* to decide to do

▶ **реши́ться** (*impf* **реша́ться**) *сов возв* (*вопрос, судьба*) to be decided; **реша́ться (~ся** *perf***) на** +*acc*/+*infin* to make up one's mind on/to do.

ре́шк|а (-и) *ж* (*на монете*) tails *мн*; **орёл или ~?** heads or tails?

рез́экспорт (-а) *м* re-export.

рез́экспорти́р|овать (-ую) (*не*)*сов перех* re-export.

ре|я́ть (*3sg* -ет, *3sg* -ют) *сов неперех* (*птица*) to soar; (*флаг*) to fly.

ржа́ве|ть (*3sg* -ет, *3pl* -ют, *perf* **заржа́веть**) *несов неперех* to rust, go rusty.

ржа́вчин|а (-ы) *ж* rust.

ржа́в|ый *прил* rusty; (*вода*) brown; (*листва*) rust-coloured (*BRIT*) *или* -colored (*US*); **~ое пятно́** rust mark.

ржано́й *прил* rye *опред*.

рж|ать (-у, -ёшь) *несов неперех* to neigh; (*разг: смеяться*) to roar with laughter.

ржи *итп сущ см* **рожь**.

РЖУ *ср сокр* = **райо́нное жили́щное управле́ние**.

РИА *м сокр* (= **Росси́йское информацио́нное аге́нтство**) Russian News Agency.

Ривье́р|а (-ы) *ж* the Riviera.

Ри́г|а (-и) *ж* Riga.

ри́з|а (-ы) *ж* (*одежда*) vestments *мн*; (*на иконе*) overlay.

рикоше́т (-а) *м* ricochet, rebound; **отска́кивать (отскочи́ть** *perf***) ~ом** to ricochet, rebound.

Рим (-а) *м* Rome.

ри́мск|ий (-ая, -ое, -ие) *прил* Roman; **ри́мские ци́фры** Roman numerals.

ри́мско-католи́ческ|ий (-ая, -ое, -ие) *прил* Roman Catholic.

ринг (-а) *м* (boxing) ring.

ри́н|уться (-усь, -ешься) *сов возв* to charge; **~ (*perf*) в рабо́ту** to throw o.s. into one's work.

Рио-де-Жане́йро *м нескл* Rio de Janeiro.

рис. *сокр* (= **рису́нок**) diag. (= *diagram*).

рис (-а) *м* rice.

риск (-а) *м* (*no pl*) risk; **на свой страх и ~** at one's own risk.

рискн|у́ть (-у́, -ёшь) *сов от* **рискова́ть**.

риско́ван|ный (-, -на, -но) *прил* risky; (*перен: разговор, шутка*) risqué.

риск|ова́ть (-у́ю; *perf* **рискну́ть**) *несов неперех* to take risks; **~ (рискну́ть** *perf***) +*instr* (*жизнью, здоровьем*) to risk; **~ (*impf*) +*infin* to risk doing; **Вы (си́льно) ~уете** you are taking a (big) risk.

ри́слинг (-а) *м* Riesling.

рисова́ни|е (-я) *ср* (*карандашом*) drawing; (*красками*) painting.

рис|ова́ть (-у́ю; *perf* **нарисова́ть**) *несов перех* (*карандашом*) to draw; (*красками*) to paint; (*перен: описывать*) to depict, portray; (: *подлеж: воображение, сознание*) to evoke a picture of

▶ **рисова́ться** *несов возв* (*виднеться*) to be seen; (*перен: в воображении*) to be conjured up; (*манерничать*) to show off.

ри́совый *прил* rice *опред*.

рису́н|ок (-ка) *м* drawing; (*на ткани, на обоях*) pattern; (*картины*) sketch; **акваре́льный ~** watercolour (*BRIT*), watercolor (*US*).

ритм (-а) *м* (*сердца, стиха*) rhythm; (*перен: жизни, работы*) pace.

ритми́чен *прил см* **ритми́чный**.

ритми́ческ|ий (-ая, -ое, -ие) *прил* rhythmic(al); **ритми́ческая гимна́стика** aerobics.

ритми́чн|ый (-ен, -на, -но) *прил* (*музыка, стук*) rhythmic(al); (*работа, процесс*) smooth-running.

рито́рик|а (-и) *ж* rhetoric.

ритуа́л (-а) *м* ritual.

риф (-а) *м* reef.

рифлёный *прил* (*подошва*) grooved; **рифлёное желе́зо** corrugated iron.

ри́фм|а (-ы) *ж* rhyme.

рифм|ова́ть (-у́ю; *perf* **срифмова́ть**) *несов перех* (*строчки, слова*) to make rhyme

▶ **рифмова́ться** *несов возв* to rhyme.
РКП(б) *м сокр* (*ист*) = *Росси́йская Коммунисти́ческая па́ртия* (*большевико́в*).
р-н *сокр* = **райо́н**.
РНК *ж сокр* (= *рибонуклеи́новая кислота́*) RNA (= *ribonucleic acid*).
робе́|ть (-ю; *perf* **оробе́ть**) *несов непе́рех* to go shy.
ро́б|кий (-кая, -кое, -кие; -ок, -ка́, -ко) *прил* shy.
ро́бот (-а) *м* robot.
робототе́хник|а (-и) *ж* robotics.
р|ов (-ва; *loc sg* **-ву**) *м* ditch.
ро́вен *прил см* **ро́вный**.
рове́сник (-а) *м*: **он мой** ~ he is the same age as me.
рове́сниц|а (-ы) *ж*: **она́ моя́** ~ she is the same age as me.
ро́вно *нареч* (*писа́ть*) evenly; (*черти́ть*) straight; (*дыша́ть*) regularly; (*через год*) exactly; ~ **в два часа́** at two o'clock sharp; **я** ~ **ничего́ не по́нял** I didn't understand a thing.
ро́в|ный (-ен, -на́, -но) *прил* even; (*степь*) flat; (*пробор, ли́ния*) straight; (*дыха́ние, пульс*) regular; (*перен: хара́ктер, челове́к*) stable; ~ **счёт** round number; **~ным счётом ничего́** (*разг*) absolutely nothing.
ровня́|ть (-ю; *perf* **сровня́ть** *или* **вы́ровнять**) *несов перех* (*строй, шере́нгу*) to straighten (up); (*perf* **разровня́ть** *или* **сровня́ть**; *доро́жку, площа́дку*) to level; **сровня́ть** (*perf*) **с землёй** to raze to the ground.
рог (-а; *nom pl* **-а́**) *м* (*та́кже муз*) horn; (*полуме́сяца*) cusp; **оле́ний** ~ antler; ~ **изоби́лия** horn of plenty; **у чёрта на** ~**а́х** (*разг*) in the middle of nowhere; **взять** (*perf*) **быка́ за** ~**а́** (*разг*) to take the bull by the horns.
рога́лик (-а) *м crescent-shaped roll*.
рога́т|ка (-ки; *gen pl* **-ок**) *ж* (*для мета́ния ка́мешков*) catapult; (*на доро́ге*) roadblock; **ста́вить** (*impf*) ~**ки кому́-н** to create obstacles for sb.
рога́т|ый (-, -а, -о) *прил* horned; **кру́пный** ~ **муж** cattle.
рогови́ц|а (-ы) *ж* cornea.
роговой *прил* horn *опред*; **роговая оболо́чка** cornea.
рого́ж|а (-и) *ж* (*ткань*) sacking.
род (-а; *part sg* **-у**, *loc sg* **-у́**, *nom pl* **-ы́**) *м* clan; (*ряд поколе́ний*) family; (*происхожде́ние*) stock; (*расте́ний, живо́тных*) genus (*мн* genera); (*де́ятельности, войск*) type; (*линг*) gender; (*одно поколе́ние*) generation; **он ро́дом из По́льши** he comes from Poland; **он ро́дом из дворя́н** he is of noble stock; **своего́ ро́да** a kind of; **в не́котором ро́де** to some extent; **что-то в э́том** *или* **тако́м ро́де** something like that; **вся́кого** *или* **ра́зного ро́да** all kinds of; **вести́** *perf* **свой** ~ **от кого́-н** to be descended from sb;

то у нас в ~**у́** it runs in the family; **из** ~ **ро́да в** ~ from generation to generation; **ему́ два́дцать лет от** ~**у** (*разг*) he is twenty years old; **он от** ~**у ничего́ тако́го не слы́шал** he had never heard anything like this in his life.
род. *сокр* (= *роди́лся*) b. (= *born*).
роддо́м (-а) *м сокр* (= *роди́льный дом*) maternity hospital.
роди́льный *прил*: ~ **дом** maternity hospital.
роди́мый *прил* (*разг: край, земля́*) native; ~ **дом** family home; **роди́мое пятно́** birthmark.
ро́дин|а (-ы) *ж* (*отечество*) homeland; (*ме́сто рожде́ния, появле́ния*) birthplace.
ро́дин|ка (-ки; *gen pl* **-ок**) *ж* birthmark.
роди́тел|и (-ей) *мн* parents *мн*.
роди́тельный *прил*: ~ **паде́ж** genitive case.
роди́тельский (-ая, -ое, -ие) *прил* (*обя́занности, права́, дом*) parental; (*де́ньги*) parents'; **роди́тельское собра́ние** parents' meeting.
ро|ди́ть (-жу́, -ди́шь; *pt perf* **-ди́л**, **-дила́**, **-ди́ло**, *pt impf* **-ди́л**, **-ди́ла**, **-ди́ло**, *impf* **рожа́ть** *или* **рожда́ть**) *сов перех* to give birth to; (*подлеж: земля́, я́блоня*) to bear a crop of.
▶ **роди́ться** (*impf* **рожда́ться**) *сов возв* to be born ◆ (*perf* **уроди́ться**) *несов* (*пшени́ца, я́блоки*) to give a good yield; **у них** ~**дила́сь дочь** they had a daughter; ~**ся** (*perf*) **в руба́шке** (*разг*) to always land on one's feet.
родни́к (-а́) *м* spring (*water*).
родн|и́ть (*3sg* **-и́т**, *3pl* **-я́т**) *несов перех*: ~ **кого́-н** (**с** +*instr*) to bring sb closer (to)
▶ **родни́ться** ◆ (**-ю́сь**, **-и́шься**; *perf* **породни́ться**) *несов возв*: ~**ся** (**с** +*instr*) to become related (to).
родно́й *прил* (*брат, мать итп*) natural *опред*; (*город, страна́*) native; (*в обраще́нии*) dear; **родно́й язы́к** mother tongue; *см та́кже* **родны́е**.
родны́|е (-х; *decl like adj*) *мн* relations *мн*, relatives *мн*.
родн|я́ (-и́) *ж собир* (*ро́дственники*) relations *мн*, relatives *мн* ◆ (*разг: ро́дственник*) relative.
родови́т|ый (-, -а, -о) *прил* of noble birth.
родово́й *прил* (*ист: строй, быт*) tribal; (*поня́тие, при́знак*) generic; (*линг*) gender *опред*; (*име́ние*) family *опред*; (*мед: су́дороги, тра́вма*) birth *опред*.
родовспоможе́ни|е (-я) *ср* midwifery.
родонача́льник (-а) *м* (*семьи́, дина́стии*) forefather; (*перен: уче́ния*) founder; (*: тео́рии*) originator.
родосло́ви|е (-я) *ср* genealogy.
родосло́вн|ая (-ой; *decl like adj*) *ж* (*семьи́*) ancestry; (*соба́ки*) pedigree.
родосло́вный *прил*: ~**ое де́рево** family tree.
ро́дственник (-а) *м* relation, relative.
ро́дственниц|а (-ы) *ж см* **ро́дственник**.

ро́дствен|ный (-, -на, -но) *прил* family *опред*; (*языки, науки*) related; **ро́дственные свя́зи** family ties.

родств|о́ (-а́) *ср* relationship; (*душ, идей итп*) affinity.

ро́д|ы (-ов) *мн* labour *ед* (*BRIT*), labor *ед* (*US*); **умере́ть** (*perf*) **от ~ов** to die in childbirth; **принима́ть** (**приня́ть** *perf*) ~ to deliver a baby.

ро́ж|а (-и) *ж* (*разг: лицо*) face; (*неприятное лицо*) mug; (*МЕД*) erysipelas (*skin complaint*); **стро́ить** (*impf*) **~и** (*разг*) to make faces.

рожа́|ть (-ю) *несов от* **роди́ть**.

рожда́емост|ь (-и) *ж* birth rate.

рожда́|ть(ся) (-ю(сь)) *несов от* **роди́ть(ся)**.

рожде́ни|е (-я) *ср* birth; **день ~я** birthday.

рожде́ственск|ий (-ая, -ое, -ие) *прил* Christmas *опред*.

Рождеств|о́ (-а́) *ср* (*РЕЛ*) Nativity; (*праздник*) Christmas; **с ~м!** Happy *или* Merry Christmas!

роже́ниц|а (-ы) *ж* (*рожающая женщина*) woman in labour; (*только что родившая*) woman who has given birth.

рожка́ *итп сущ см* **рожо́к**.

рожна́ *итп сущ см* **рожо́н**.

рож|о́к (-ка́) *м* (*МУЗ*) horn; (*рогалик*) crescent-shaped roll; (*для надевания обуви*) shoehorn; (*макароны*) macaroni.

рож|о́н (-на́) *м* (*разг*): **лезть на ~** to ask for trouble; **какого ~на́ тебе́ на́до?** (*разг*) what the hell do you want?

рожу́(сь) (*не*)*сов от* **роди́ть(ся)**.

рожь (ржи) *ж* rye.

ро́з|а (-ы) *ж* (*растение*) rose(bush); (*цветок*) rose.

роза́ри|й (-я) *м* rose garden.

ро́з|га (-ги; *gen pl* -ог) *ж* birch (*for punishment*).

розе́т|ка (-ки; *gen pl* -ок) *ж* power point; (*блюдечко*) jam (*BRIT*) *или* jelly (*US*) dish; (*украшение*) rosette.

ро́зниц|а (-ы) *ж* retail goods *мн*; **продава́ть** (*impf*) **в ~у** to retail.

ро́зничный *прил* retail; (**рекомендо́ванная**) **ро́зничная цена́** (recommended) retail price.

розн|ь (-и) *ж*: **студе́нт студе́нту ~** there are students and students.

розове́|ть (-ю; *perf* **порозове́ть**) *несов неперех* to turn *или* go pink; **у него́ на лбу ~л шрам** he had a pink scar on his forehead.

ро́зовый *прил* rose *опред*; (*цвет*) pink; (*ребёнок, мечты*) rosy; **ви́деть** (*impf*) **кого́-н/что-н в ро́зовом све́те** to see sb/sth through rose-coloured spectacles (*BRIT*) *или* rose-colored glasses (*US*).

ро́зог *сущ см* **ро́зга**.

ро́зыгрыш (-а) *м* draw; (*шутка*) prank.

ро́зыск (-а) *м* search; **уголо́вный ~** Criminal Investigation Department (*BRIT*), Federal Bureau of Investigation (*US*).

ро|и́ться (*3sg* -и́тся, *3pl* -я́тся) *несов возв* to swarm; (*перен: мысли*) to flood.

ро|й (-я; *nom pl* -и́) *м* (*пчёл, комаров*) swarm;

(*снежинок, искр*) flurry; (*пыли*) cloud; (*перен: воспоминаний*) flood.

рок (-а) *м* (*злая судьба*) fate; (*рок-музыка*) rock ◆ *прил неизм* (*танец, стиль*) rock *опред*.

ро́кер (-а) *м* (*разг*) rocker.

рок-му́зык|а (-и) *ж* rock music.

рок-н-ро́лл (-а) *м* rock and roll.

роково́й *прил* fatal.

ро́кот (-а) *м* rumble.

рок|ота́ть (*3sg* -о́чет, *3pl* -о́чут) *несов неперех* to rumble.

рокфо́р (-а) *м* Roquefort.

ро́лик (-а) *м* (*вращающийся валик*) roller; (*на ножке*) caster; (*ЭЛЕК*) cleat; (*фотоплёнки, бумаги*) roll; (*обычно мн: разг: коньки на колесиках*) roller skate; ~ **новосте́й** newsreel; **рекла́мный ~** advertisement; (*фильма*) trailer; *см также* **ро́лики**.

ро́лик|и (-ов) *мн* roller skates *мн*.

ро́ликов|ый *прил* (*ТЕХ*) roller *опред*; **~ые конько́** roller skates.

рол|ь (-и; *gen pl* -е́й, *dat pl* -я́м) *ж* role; (*текст*) part; **в ро́ли** +*gen* as; **игра́ть** (*impf*) ~ to play a part; **входи́ть** (**войти́** *perf*) **в ~** to get into the part.

ром (-а) *м* rum.

рома́н (-а) *м* (*исторический, биографический*) novel; (*любовная связь*) affair.

романи́ст (-а) *м* (*писатель*) novelist; (*учёный*) Romance language philologist.

рома́нс (-а) *м* (*МУЗ*) romance.

рома́нск|ий (-ая, -ое, -ие) *прил* Romance *опред*; (*архитектура*) Romanesque.

романти́зм (-а) *м* (*художественное течение*) Romanticism; (*умонастроение*) romantic mood.

рома́нтик (-а) *м* (*мечтатель*) romantic; (*писатель, композитор итп*) romanticist.

рома́нтик|а (-и) *ж* romance.

рома́ш|ка (-ки; *gen pl* -ек) *ж* camomile.

ромб (-а) *м* rhombus.

ро́мов|ый *прил* rum *опред*; **ро́мовая ба́ба** rum baba.

ромште́кс (-а) *м* rump steak.

РОНО *м сокр* (= ра́йонный отде́л наро́дного образова́ния) ≈ district education department.

рон|я́ть (-ю; *perf* **урони́ть**) *несов перех* to drop; (*перен: честь, авторитет*) to lose; (*no perf*; *листву, перья*) to shed; ~ (*impf*) **слёзы** to shed tears; ~ (*impf*) **себя́ в чьих-н глаза́х** to lose face with sb; ~ (*impf*) **слова́** to make haughty remarks.

ро́пот (-а) *м* rumble.

рос *итп несов см* **расти́**.

рос|а́ (-ы́; *nom pl* -ы) *ж* dew.

роси́н|ка (-ки; *gen pl* -ок) *ж* dewdrop.

роско́ш|ный (-ен, -на, -но) *прил* (*наряд, дом*) luxurious; (*еда*) sumptuous; (*разг: волосы, растительность*) luxuriant; (: *день, погода*) splendid; **~ная жизнь** a life of luxury.

ро́скош|ь (-и) *ж* luxury; (*излишества*)

extravagance; (*прирóды*) luxuriance; **предмéты**
~и luxury items; **жить** (*impf*) **в ~и** to live in
luxury.
рóслый *прил* tall.
рóспис|ь (**-и**) *ж* (*дéйствие: собóра, кýпола*)
painting; (*узóр: на шкатýлке*) design; (: *на*
стенáх) mural; (*расхóдов, имýщества*) list;
(*пóдпись*) signature.
рóспуск (**-а**) *м* (*áрмии*) disbandment;
(*парлáмента*) dissolution.
росси́йск|ий (**-ая, -ое, -ие**) *прил* Russian;
Росси́йская Федерáция the Russian
Federation.
Росси́|я (**-и**) *ж* Russia.
россия́н|ин (**-ина**; *nom pl* **-е**, *gen pl* **-**) *м* Russian.
россия́н|ка (**-ки**; *gen pl* **-ок**) *ж см* **россия́нин**.
рóссказн|и (**-ей**) *мн* (*разг*) old wives' tale.
рóссып|и (**-ей**) *мн* (*алмáзов, золоты́е итп*)
deposit *ед*.
рóссып|ь (**-и**) *ж* (*грибóв*) scattering; *см тáкже*
рóссыпи.
рост (**-а**) *м* growth; (*перéн: мастерствá,*
производи́тельности) increase; (*размéр:*
человéка) height; (*nom pl* **-á**; *длинá: пальтó,*
плáтья) length; **вставáть** (**встать** *perf*) **во весь**
~ (*человéк*) to stand up straight; (*проблéма,*
задáча) to become fully apparent.
рóстбиф (**-а**) *м* roast beef.
росткá *итп сущ см* **ростóк**.
ростовщи́к (**-á**) *м* moneylender.
ростовщи́ц|а (**-ы**) *ж см* **ростовщи́к**.
ростóк (**-ká**) *м* (*БОТ*) shoot; (*перéн*): **~ки** +*gen*
(*демокрáтии, нóвого*) beginnings *мн* of.
рóсчерк (**-а**) *м* stroke; **решáть** (**реши́ть** *perf*)
что-н одни́м ~ом перá to decide sth with one
stroke of the pen.
рот (**ртá**; *loc sg* **ртý**) *м* mouth; **говори́ть** (*impf*) **не**
закрывáя ртá (*разг*) to talk nonstop; **смотрéть**
(*impf*) **в ~ комý-н** (*перéн*) to hang on sb's every
word; **онá в ~ не берёт ры́бы** (*разг*) she
doesn't touch fish.
рóт|а (**-ы**) *ж* (*ВОЕН*) company.
ротапри́нт (**-а**) *м* offset duplicator.
ротозé|й (**-я**) *м* (*разг: бездéльник*) loafer;
(*рази́ня*) scatterbrain.
рóтор (**-а**) *м* rotor.
Рóттердам (**-а**) *м* Rotterdam.
рóщ|а (**-и**) *ж* grove.
роя́л|ь (**-я**) *м* grand piano.
р-р *сокр* (= **раствóр**) sol. (= *solution*).
р/с *сокр* = **расчётный счёт**.
РСО *сокр* (= *ракéта срéдней дáльности*)
MRBM (= *medium-range ballistic missile*).
РСУ *ср сокр* = *ремóнтно-строи́тельное*
управлéние.
РСФСР *ж сокр* (*ист*: = *Росси́йская Совéтская*
Федерати́вная Социалисти́ческая
Респýблика) RSFSR (= *Russian Soviet Federal*

Socialist Republic).
рта *итп сущ см* **рот**.
рту́тный *прил* mercury *опред*; **~ стóлбик**
mercury column.
рту́т|ь (**-и**) *ж* mercury.
руб. *сокр* (= **рубль**) R., r., rouble.
руба́н|ок (**-ка**) *м* plane (*tool*).
руба́х|а (**-и**) *ж* (*разг*) shirt; **~-пáрень** (*разг*)
straightforward chap (*BRIT*) *или* guy (*US*).
руба́ш|ка (**-ки**; *gen pl* **-ек**) *ж* (*мужска́я*) shirt;
(*игра́льной ка́рты*) back; **ни́жняя ~** (*же́нская*)
slip; **ночна́я ~** nightshirt; **смири́тельная ~**
(*перéн*) straitjacket.
рубéж (**-á**) *м* (*госудáрства*) border; (: *вóдный,*
леснóй) boundary; (*ВОЕН*) line; **он живёт за**
рубежóм he lives abroad; **он уéхал за ~** he
went abroad; **на рубежé эпóх** between the two
eras.
руб|éц (**-цá**) *м* (*от ран, пóсле операции*) scar;
(*кули́н*) tripe.
руби́льник (**-а**) *м* knife switch.
руби́н (**-а**) *м* ruby.
руби́новый *прил* ruby *опред*.
руб|и́ть (**-лю́, -ишь**; *perf* **сруби́ть**) *сов перех*
(*дéрево*) to fell; (*вéтку*) to chop off; (*no perf;*
мя́со, капýсту) to chop (up); (*гóлову*) to hack
off; (*дáчу, избý*) to erect; **он ~и́т сплеча́**
(*перéн*) he doesn't mince his words.
рубк|а (**-и**) *ж* (*дéйствие: дерéвьев*) felling;
(*избы́*) erection; (*мя́са*) chopping; (*на суднé, на*
радиостáнции) cabin.
рублёвый *прил* (*монéта, банкнóта*) rouble
опред; (*печéнье, конфéты*) for one rouble;
(*разг: товáр, подáрок*) cheap.
ру́блен|ый *прил* (*мя́со, óвощи*) chopped;
(*амбáр, избá*) made from logs; **~ые котлéты**
rissoles.
рубл|ь (**-я́**) *м* rouble; **переводнóй ~** convertible
rouble.
рублю́ *сов см* **руби́ть**.
ру́брик|а (**-и**) *ж* (*раздéл*) column; (*заголóвок*)
heading.
рубца́ *итп сущ см* **рубéц**.
рубцева́ться (*3sg* **-у́ется**, *3pl* **-у́ются**, *perf*
зарубцева́ться) *несов возв* to form a scar.
ру́бчат|ый (**-, -а, -о**) *прил* ribbed.
ру́бчик (**-а**) *м* rib.
ру́ган|ь (**-и**) *ж* bad language.
руга́тельн|ый *прил*: **~ое слóво** swearword;
пьéса получи́ла мнóго ~ых óтзывов the play
got a lot of bad reviews.
руга́тельств|о (**-а**) *ср* swearword.
руга́ть (**-ю**; *perf* **вы́ругать** *или* **отруга́ть**) *несов*
перех (*мýжа, ученика́*) to scold; (*perf* **обруга́ть**;
пьéсу, статью́) to take to pieces.
► **руга́ться** *несов возв* (*брани́ться*): **~ся с** +*instr*
to scold; (*perf* **вы́ругаться**) to swear; (*perf*
поруга́ться): **~ся с** +*instr* (*с мýжем, с родны́ми*)

to fall out with.

ругну́ться (-у́сь, -ёшься) *сов возв* (*разг*) to swear (*once*).

руд|а́ (-ы́; *nom pl* -ы) *ж* ore.

рудни́к (-а́) *м* mine.

рудниќовый *прил* (*предприятие*) ore-mining.

рудни́чный *прил* = **рудниќовый**.

руж|ьё (-ья́; *nom pl* -ья, *gen pl* -ей) *м* rifle.

руи́н|а (-ы) *ж* (*обычно мн*) ruin.

рук|а́ (-и́; *acc sg* -у, *nom pl* -и, *gen pl* -, *dat pl* -а́м) *ж* hand; (*верхняя конечность*) arm; (*разг: в верхах, в руководстве*) contact; **из пе́рвых рук** first hand; **в э́том чу́вствуется ~ ма́стера** one can tell this is the work of clever hands; **у неё на ~х трое дете́й** she has three children on her hands; **под руко́й, под ~ми** to hand, handy; **она́ шла с ним по́д ~у** she walked arm in arm with him; **проси́ть** (*impf*) **чьей-н ~й** to ask for sb's hand (in marriage); **подня́ть** (*perf*) **ру́ку на кого́-н** to raise one's hand to sb; **его́/э́то с ~ми оторву́т** (*разг*) he/it will be snapped up; **у меня́ всё ру́ки не дохо́дят до э́того** I haven't got round to (doing) it; **отсю́да до го́рода ~о́й пода́ть** it's a stone's throw from here to the town; **у меня́ ру́ки че́шутся** +*infin* ... (*разг*) I'm itching to ...; **э́то ему́ на́ ~у** that's what suits him; **брать** (**взять** *perf*) **себя́ в ру́ки** to get a grip of o.s.; **ему́ всё схо́дит с рук** (*разг*) he gets away with everything; **э́то де́ло рук ма́фии** this is the work of the Mafia; **у него́ золоты́е ру́ки** he's very good with his hands; **де́ла иду́т из рук вон пло́хо** things have hit rock bottom; **прибира́ть** (**прибра́ть** *perf*) **что-н к ~м** to get one's hands on sth.

рука́в (-а́) *м* (*одежды*) sleeve; (*реки*) branch; (*пожарный, напорный*) hose; (*зерновой*) chute.

рукави́ц|а (-ы) *ж* (*обычно мн*) mitten.

руководи́тел|ь (-я) *м* leader; (*кафедры, предприятия*) head.

руководи́тельниц|а (-ы) *ж см* **руководи́тель**.

руков|оди́ть (-ожу́, -оди́шь) *несов неперех:* ~ +*instr* (*наступлением, действиями*) to lead; (*учреждением, цехом, лабораторией*) to be in charge of; (*страной*) to govern; (*аспирантами*) to supervise; **им ~оди́ла жа́дность** he was governed by greed.

руково́дств|о (-а) *ср* (*походом, мероприятием*) leadership; (*заводом, институтом*) management; (*лабораторией*) supervision; (*к действию, в поведении*) guidelines *мн*; (*по рукоделию, по фотографии*) handbook, manual; (*по эксплуатации, по уходу*) instructions *мн* ♦ *собир* (*партии, страны*) leadership (*leaders*); **под ~м** +*gen* under the leadership of.

руково́дств|оваться (-уюсь) *несов возв:* ~ +*instr* to follow; (*здравым смыслом*) to be guided by.

руководя́щ|ий (-ая, -ее, -ие) *прил* (*работник, кадры*) managerial; (*орган*) governing *опред*;

~**ие указа́ния** instructions.

руковожу́ *несов см* **руководи́ть**.

рукоде́ли|е (-я) *ср* needlework.

рукоде́льниц|а (-ы) *ж* needlewoman (*мн* needlewomen).

рукомо́йник (-а) *м* washstand.

рукопа́шный *прил:* **они́ пошли́ в ~ бой** they went off to fight with their bare hands.

рукопи́сный *прил* (*текст*) handwritten; (*отдел библиотеки*) manuscript *опред*.

ру́копис|ь (-и) *ж* manuscript.

рукопл|еска́ть (-ещу́, -е́щешь) *несов неперех:* ~ +*dat* to applaud.

рукопожа́ти|е (-я) *ср* handshake.

рукоприкла́дств|о (-а) *ср* beating.

рукоя́т|ка (-ки; *gen pl* -ок) *ж* (*кинжала, молотка*) handle; (*пульта управления*) crank.

рулев|о́й (-о́го; *decl like adj*) *м* (*МОР*) helmsman (*мн* helmsmen); (*перен: ведущий вперёд*) leader ♦ *прил:* ~**ое колесо́** steering wheel; ~**ое управле́ние** steering.

руле́т (-а) *м* (*картофельный*) croquette; (*с маком, с джемом*) ≈ swiss roll; (*копчёный без кости*) boned ham; **мясно́й** ~ meat loaf.

руле́т|ка (-ки; *gen pl* -ок) *ж* (*для измерения*) tape measure; (*в игорных домах*) roulette.

рул|и́ть (-ю́, -и́шь) *несов перех* to steer.

руло́н (-а) *м* roll.

рул|ь (-я́) *м* steering wheel; **стоя́ть** (*impf*) **у ~я́** (*перен*) to be at the helm.

румы́н (-а) *м* Romanian.

Румы́ни|я (-и) *ж* Romania.

румы́н|ка (-ки; *gen pl* -ок) *ж см* **румы́н**.

румы́нск|ий (-ая, -ое, -ие) *прил* Romanian; ~ **язы́к** Romanian.

румя́н|а (-) *мн* blusher *ед*.

румя́н|ец (-ца) *м* glow.

румя́н|ить (-ю, -ишь; *perf* **нарумя́нить**) *несов перех* (*щёки, лицо*) to put blusher on; (*perf* **разрумя́нить**): **моро́з ~ит лица́** the frost makes her face glow.

▶ **румя́ниться** (*perf* **разрумя́ниться**) *несов возв* to flush; (*perf* **нарумя́ниться**; *женщина*) to put on blusher; (*perf* **подрумя́ниться**; *пирог*) to brown.

румя́нца *итп сущ см* **румя́нец**.

румя́н|ый (-, -а, -о) *прил* rosy; (*пирог, корочка*) browned.

ру́пор (-а) *м* loudspeaker; ~ +*gen* (*о газете, о журнале*) mouthpiece of.

руса́л|ка (-ки; *gen pl* -ок) *ж* mermaid.

руса́лоч|ий (-ья, -ье, -ьи) *прил* mermaid's *опред*.

ру́сел *сущ см* **ру́сло**.

руси́ст (-а) *м* Russianist.

руси́стик|а (-и) *ж* Russian studies.

руси́ст|ка (-ки; *gen pl* -ок) *ж см* **руси́ст**.

русифика́ци|я (-и) *ж* Russification.

русифици́р|овать (-ую) (*не*)*сов перех* to Russify

▶ **русифици́роваться** (*не*)*сов возв* to be

Russified.

ру́сл|о (-ла; *gen pl* **-ел**) *ср* bed (*of river, stream etc*); (*перен*: *путь развития чего-н*) course; **жизнь вошла́ в обы́чное** ~ life has taken its usual course.

ру́сск|ая (-ой; *decl like adj*) *ж см* **ру́сский**.

ру́сск|ий (-ая, -ое, -ие) *прил* Russian ♦ (-ого; *decl like adj*) *м* Russian; ~ **язы́к** Russian.

ру́с|ый *прил* (*волосы, борода*) light brown; (*человек*) with light brown hair.

Рус|ь (-и́) *ж* Russia.

рути́н|а (-ы) *ж* rut (*fig*).

рути́нный *прил* stale.

ру́хлядь (-и) *ж собир* (*разг*) junk.

ру́хн|уть (-у, -ешь) *сов* (*дерево, человек итп*) to crash down; (*дом, мост*) to collapse; (*перен: счастье, надежда*) to be shattered.

руча́тельств|о (-а) *ср* guarantee.

руча́|ться (-юсь; *perf* **поручи́ться**) *несов возв*: ~ **за** +*acc* to guarantee; **я голово́й** ~**юсь, что мы успе́ем** (*разг*) I'll bet my life that we'll do it.

руч|е́й (-ья́) *м* stream; ~ **слёз** floods of tears.

ру́ч|ка (-ки; *gen pl* -ек) *ж уменьш от* **рука́**; (*двери, чемодана итп*) handle; (*кресла, дивана*) arm; (*для письма*) pen; **ша́риковая** ~ ballpoint (pen).

ручн|о́й *прил* hand *опред*; (*животное, человек*) tame; ~**а́я прода́жа** sale without a prescription; **ручна́я кладь, ручно́й бага́ж** hand luggage; **ручны́е часы́** (wrist)watch.

ручья́ *сущ см* **руче́й**.

ру́ш|ить (-у, -ишь; *perf* **обру́шить**) *несов перех* (*дома, деревья*) to pull down; (*no perf*; *разг*: *счастье, семью*) to wreck.

▶ **ру́шиться** *несов возв* (*дом, строение*) to collapse; (*перен: семья, планы*) to be wrecked.

РФ *ж сокр* (= **Росси́йская Федера́ция**) the Russian Federation.

рыб|а (-ы) *м* fish; **ни** ~ **ни мя́со** neither here nor there; **чу́вствовать** (*impf*) **себя́ как** ~ **в воде́** to feel at home; *см также* **Ры́бы**.

рыба́к (-а́) *м* fisherman (*мн* fishermen).

рыба́л|ка (-ки; *gen pl* -ок) *ж* fishing.

рыба́цкий (-ая, -ое, -ие) *прил* fishing *опред*.

рыба́чек *сущ см* **рыба́чка**.

рыба́чий (-ья, -ье, -ьи) *прил* = **рыба́цкий**.

рыба́ч|ить (-у, -ишь) *несов неперех* to fish.

рыба́ч|ка (-ки; *gen pl* -ек) *ж* fisherwoman (*мн* fisherwomen); (*разг*: *жена рыбака*) fisherman's wife (*мн* wives).

ры́б|ий (-ья, -ье, -ьи) *прил* (*чешуя, хвост, клей*) fish *опред*; (*плавник*) fish's; **ры́бий жир** cod-liver oil.

рыбнадзо́р (-а) *м* fishing patrol.

ры́бный *прил* (*магазин*) fish *опред*; (*промышленность, хозяйство*) fishing *опред*; (*река, озеро*) full of fish; **ры́бные консе́рвы** tinned (*BRIT*) *или* canned fish; ~ **день** *day when*

only fish is served in a canteen or restaurant.

рыболо́в (-а) *м* fisherman (*мн* fishermen), angler.

рыболо́вный *прил* fishing *опред*.

Ры́б|ы (-) *мн* (*созвездие*) Pisces.

рыв|о́к (-ка́) *м* (*человека, машины*) jerk; (*перен: в работе*) push; (: *бегуна*) dash.

рыга́|ть (-ю) *несов неперех* (*разг*) to belch, burp.

рыда́ни|е (-я) *ср* sobbing.

рыда́|ть (-ю) *несов неперех* to sob.

рыжеволо́с|ый (-, -а, -о) *прил* red-haired.

ры́ж|ий (-ая, -ее, -ие; -, -а́, -е) *прил* (*усы, волосы, животное*) red *опред*; (*человек*) red-haired.

рыка́|ть (-ю) *несов неперех* to roar.

ры́лец *сущ см* **ры́льце**.

ры́л|о (-а) *ср* (*свиное*) snout; (*разг: лицо*) mug.

ры́ль|це (-ьца; *gen pl* -ец) *ср* (*БОТ*) stigma (*мн* stigmata).

ры́н|ок (-ка) *м* market; ~ **труда́** labour (*BRIT*) *или* labor (*US*) market; ~**ки сбы́та** markets.

ры́ночный *прил* (*КОММ*) market *опред*; (*яйца, овощи*) from the market; **ры́ночная цена́** market price; **ры́ночная сто́имость** market value.

рыса́к (-а́) *м* trotter (*horse*).

рыс|и́й (-ья, -ье, -ьи) *прил* lynx *опред*.

ры́ск|ать (-щу, -щешь) *несов неперех* to roam, rove; ~ (*impf*) **глаза́ми** (*перен*) to let one's eyes roam.

рысца́ (-ы́) *ж* jog trot.

рыс|ь (-и) *ж* lynx; (*бег лошади*) trot.

ры́твин|а (-ы) *ж* pothole.

рыть (ро́ю, ро́ешь; *perf* **вы́рыть**) *несов перех* (*окопы, канал*) to dig; (*картошку итп*) to dig up

▶ **ры́ться** *несов возв* (*в земле, в песке*) to dig; (*в карманах, в шкафу*) to rummage; (*перен: в бумагах, в книгах*) to dig about; **ры́ться** (*impf*) **в па́мяти** to delve into one's memory.

рыхл|и́ть (-ю́, -и́шь; *perf* **взрыхли́ть** *или* **разрыхли́ть**) *несов перех* to loosen.

ры́хл|ый (-, -а, -о) *прил* (*снег, земля*) loose; (*кирпич, камень*) crumbly; (*перен: статья, план*) rough; (: *разг: тело, человек*) podgy (*BRIT*), pudgy (*US*).

ры́царск|ий (-ая, -ое, -ие) *прил* (*доспехи, честь долг*) knight's; (*турнир*) jousting *опред*; (*поступок, поведение*) chivalrous, knightly; **ры́царский рома́н** tale of chivalry.

ры́цар|ь (-я) *м* knight; **он настоя́щий** ~ he's very chivalrous.

рыча́г (-а́; *м* (*ТЕХ: управления, скорости*) lever; (*телефона*) cradle; (*перен: воздействия, реформ*) linchpin.

рыча́|ть (-у́, -и́шь) *несов неперех* to growl; (*разг*): ~ **на** +*acc* (*на подчинённых, на учеников итп*) to snarl at.

ры́щу *итп несов см* **ры́скать**.

рья́н|ый (-, -а, -о) *прил* zealous.

рэкет (-а) *м* racket.
рэкетир (-а) *м* racketeer.
рюкзак (-á) *м* rucksack.
рюм|ка (-ки; *gen pl* -ок) *ж* (*сосуд*) ≈ liqueur glass; (*водки, коньяка итп*) shot.
рюмочн|ая (-ой; *decl like adj*) *ж small bar selling alcohol and sandwiches.*
рюш|ка (-ки; *gen pl* -ек) *ж* frill.
ряби́н|а (-ы) *ж* (*дерево*) rowan, mountain ash ♦ *собир* (*ягоды*) rowan berry; (*разг: на коже*) pockmark; (*тёмное пятно*) speck.
ряби́новый *прил* (*куст*) rowan *опред*, mountain ash *опред*; (*настойка, варенье*) rowan-berry.
ряб|и́ть (*3sg* -и́т) *несов перех* (*воду*) to ripple; **у меня́** **~и́т в глаза́х** I'm seeing stars.
ряб|о́й (-, -á, -о) *прил* (*лицо, тело*) pockmarked; (*курица, скворец*) speckled; (*гладь озера*) rippling; **Ку́рочка-ря́ба** speckled hen (*in fairytales*).
ря́бчик (-а) *м* hazelhen.

ряб|ь (-и) *ж* (*на воде*) ripple; (*в глазах*) stars *мн*.
ря́вка|ть (-ю) *несов неперех* (*разг*): **~** (**на** +*acc*) to bark (at).
ряд (-а; *loc sg* -ý, *nom pl* -ы́) *м* row; (*бойцов*) line; (*явлений, событий*) sequence; (*обычно мн: торговые, овощной*) stalls *мн*; (*prp sg* -е): **~** +*gen* (*вопросов, причин*) a number of; **из ря́да вон выходя́щий** extraordinary; *см также* **ряды́**.
рядов|о́й *прил* (*случай, жизнь, работник итп*) ordinary; (*член партии, боец*) rank-and-file ♦ (-о́го; *decl like adj*) *м* (*ВОЕН*) private.
ря́дом *нареч* close (by), near(by); **они́ сиде́ли ~** they sat side by side; **~ с** +*instr* next to; **это совсе́м ~** it's really near.
ряд|ы́ (-о́в) *мн* (*состав: армии, партии*) ranks *мн*.
ря́женк|а (-и) *ж type of yoghurt.*
Ряза́н|ь (-и) *ж* Ryazan.
ряс|а (-ы) *ж* cassock.

~ C, c ~

C, c *сущ нескл (буква)* the 18th letter of the Russian alphabet.

с *сокр* (= *се́вер*) N (= *North*;) (= **секу́нда**) s (= *second*).

KEYWORD

с *предл* (+*gen*) **1** (*указывает на объект, от которого что-н отделяется*) off; **лист упа́л с де́рева** a leaf fell off the tree; **ма́льчик пры́гнул с кры́ши** the boy jumped off the roof; **письмо́ с ро́дины/Украи́ны** a letter from home/the Ukraine; **с ле́кции/рабо́ты/ свида́ния** from a lecture/work/a meeting
2 (*следуя чему-н*) from; **эски́з с нату́ры** a sketch from nature; **перево́д с ру́сского** a translation from Russian; **ко́пия с докуме́нта** a copy of a document
3 (*об источнике*) from; **де́ньги с зака́зчика** money from a customer; **с ребёнка спрос ма́ленький** one can't demand much from a child; **с меня́/него́ доста́точно** I've/he's had enough
4 (*начиная с*) since; **жду тебя́ с утра́** I've been waiting for you since morning; **с января́ по май** from January to May; **с утра́ до ве́чера** from morning till evening
5 (*на основании чего-н*) with; **зако́н введён с одобре́ния парла́мента** the law was brought in with the approval of parliament
6 (*по причине*): **с го́лоду/хо́лода/го́ря** of hunger/cold/grief; **с испу́га/доса́ды** with fright/ anger; **со зла** out of spite; **я уста́л с доро́ги** I was tired from the journey
♦ *предл* (+*acc; приблизительно*) about; **с киломе́тр/то́нну** about a kilometre (*BRIT*) *или* kilometer (*US*)/ton *или* tonne
♦ *предл* (+*instr*) **1** (*совместно*) with; **я иду́ гуля́ть с дру́гом** I am going for a walk with a friend; **он познако́мился с де́вушкой** he has met a girl; **мы с ним о́чень ра́зные** he and I are very different
2 (*о наличии чего-н в чём-н*): **пиро́г с мя́сом** a meat pie; **хлеб с ма́слом** bread and butter; **дикта́нт с оши́бками** a dictation containing mistakes; **челове́к с ю́мором** a man with a sense of humour (*BRIT*) *или* humor (*US*)
3 (*при указании на образ действия*) with; **слу́шать** (*impf*) **с удивле́нием** to listen with *или* in surprise; **ждать** (*impf*) **с нетерпе́нием** to wait impatiently *или* with impatience; **ждём с нетерпе́нием встре́чи с Ва́ми** we look forward to meeting you; **одева́ться** (*impf*) **со вку́сом** to dress with (good) taste; **он ел с жа́дностью** he ate greedily
4 (*при посредстве*): **с курье́ром** by courier; **я уе́хал с пе́рвым по́ездом** I left on the first train
5 (*при наступлении чего-н*): **с во́зрастом** with age; **мы вы́ехали с рассве́том** we left at dawn; **с отъе́здом госте́й нам ста́ло ску́чно** when the guests left we got bored
6 (*об объекте воздействия*) with; **поко́нчить** (*perf*) **с несправедли́востью** to do away with injustice; **поспеши́ть** (*perf*) **с вы́водами** to draw hasty conclusions; **случа́ться** (**случи́ться** *perf*) **с** +*instr* to happen to; **что с тобо́й?** what's the matter with you?

с. *сокр* = **село́**, (= **страни́ца**) p. (= *page*).
СА *ж сокр* (*ИСТ*) = **Сове́тская А́рмия**.
са́бля (**-ли**; *gen pl* **-ель**) *ж* sabre (*BRIT*), saber (*US*).
сабо́ *м/ср нескл* (*обычно мн*) clog.
сабота́ж (**-а**) *м* sabotage.
саботи́р|овать (**-ую**) (*не*)*сов перех* to sabotage.
са́ван (**-а**) *м* shroud.
сава́нн|а (**-ы**) *ж* savannah.
са́г|а (**-и**) *ж* saga.
сагити́р|овать (**-ую**) *сов от* **агити́ровать**.
са́го *ср нескл* sago.
сад (**-а**; *loc sg* **-у́**, *nom pl* **-ы́**) *м* garden; (*фрукто́вый*) orchard; (*также:* **де́тский ~**) nursery (school) (*BRIT*), kindergarten (*US*).
сади́зм (**-а**) *м* sadism.
са́дик (**-а**) *м уменьш от* **сад**; (*разг: детский сад*) nursery (*BRIT*), kindergarten (*US*).
сади́ст (**-а**) *м* sadist.
сади́ться (**-жу́сь, -ди́шься**) *несов от* **сесть**.
садо́вник (**-а**) *м* (professional) gardener.
садово́д (**-а**) *м* (*любитель*) gardener; (*специалист*) horticulturalist.
садово́дств|о (**-а**) *ср* (*хобби*) gardening; (*наука*) horticulture.

The spelling rules for Russian are shown on page xvii.

садо́в|ый *прил* garden *опред*; **голова́ твоя́ ~ая** (*раза*) you've got a head like a sieve.
са́ек *сущ см* **са́йка.**
са́ж|а (-и) *ж* soot.
сажа́ть (-ю; *perf* **посади́ть)** *несов перех* (*человека: на стол, в кресло*) to seat; (: в поезд, в автобус) to put; (*растения, дерево*) to plant; (*раза: заключить*) to lock up; (*самолёт*) to land; ~ **(посади́ть** *perf*) **кого́-н в по́езд/на самолёт** to put sb on a train/plane; ~ **(посади́ть** *perf*) **кого́-н за рабо́ту** to sit sb down to work; ~ **(посади́ть** *perf*) **кого́-н в тюрьму́/под аре́ст** to put sb in prison/under arrest.
са́жен|ец (-ца) *м* (*дерева*) sapling; (*растения*) seedling.
сажу́сь *несов см* **сади́ться.**
саза́н (-а) *м* carp.
са́йка (-йки; *gen pl* **-ек)** *ж* (bread) roll.
сакво́яж (-а) *м* travelling (*BRIT*) *или* traveling (*US*) bag.
сакрамента́л|ьный (-ен, -ьна, -ьно) *прил* (*РЕЛ*) sacramental; (*перен*) sacred.
саксофо́н (-а) *м* saxophone.
сала́з|ки (-ок) *мн* (*сани*) toboggan *ед*.
сала́к|а (-и) *ж* Baltic herring.
сала́т (-а) *м* (*БОТ*) lettuce; (*КУЛИН*) salad.
сала́тни|ца (-ы) *ж* salad bowl.
сала́тный *прил* salad *опред*; (*цвет*) pale green.
са́л|о (-а) *ср* (*животного*) fat; (*КУЛИН*) lard.
сало́н (-а) *м* salon; (*автобуса, самолёта итп*) passenger section; (*в гостинице*) lounge; (*на корабле*) saloon; **худо́жественный** ~ art salon.
салфе́т|ка (-ки; *gen pl* **-ок)** *ж* (*столовая*) napkin, serviette (*BRIT*); (*маленькая скатерть*) doily.
Сальвадо́р (-а) *м* El Salvador.
сальди́р|овать (-ую) *несов перех* (*КОММ*) to balance.
са́льдо *ср нескл* (*КОММ*) balance; ~ **с перено́са** balance brought forward.
са́льный *прил* greasy; (*шутка, слова*) dirty.
са́льто *ср нескл* somersault.
салю́т (-а) *м* salute.
салют|ова́ть (-у́ю) (*не)сов неперех* (+*dat*) to salute.
саля́ми *ж нескл* salami.
сам (-ого́; *f* **сама́,** *nt* **само́,** *pl* **са́ми)** *мест* (*я*) myself; (*ты*) yourself; (*он*) himself; (*как таковой*) itself; **он ~ предложи́л э́то** he himself suggested it; **я ~ могу́ прове́рить** I can check it myself; **ты (и) ~ зна́ешь** you know yourself; **~á его́ принципа́льность важна́** his integrity itself is important; ~ **по себе́** (*в отдельности*) per se, by itself; ~ **собо́й** (*непроизвольно*) of its own accord, by itself; **фа́кты говоря́т ~-и за себя́** the facts speak for themselves.
сам|а́ (-о́й) *мест* (*я*) myself; (*ты*) yourself; (*она*) herself; *см также* **сам.**
Сама́р|а (-ы) *ж* Samara.
самби́ст (-а) *м* sambo wrestler.
са́мбо *ср нескл* sambo (wrestling).

сам|е́ц (-ца́) *м* male (*ZOOL*).
са́м|и (-йх) *мест* (*мы*) ourselves; (*они*) themselves; *см также* **сам.**
са́м|ка (-ки; *gen pl* **-ок)** *ж* female (*ZOOL*).
сам|о́ (-ого́) *мест* itself; ~ **собо́й (разуме́ется)** it goes without saying; *см также* **сам.**
самоана́лиз (-а) *м* self-analysis.
самобичева́ни|е (-я) *ср* (*перен*) self-reproach.
самобы́тен *прил см* **самобы́тный.**
самобы́тность (-и) *ж* originality.
самобы́т|ный (-ен, -на, -но) *прил* original.
самова́р (-а) *м* samovar.
самовлюблённый *прил* (*человек*) vain.
самово́льно *прил см* **самово́льный.**
самово́ли|е (-я) *ср* wilfulness (*BRIT*), willfulness (*US*).
самово́л|ьный (-ен, -ьна, -ьно) *прил* (*человек*) self-willed; (*уход*) unauthorized.
самого́н (-а) *м* home-made vodka.
самоде́л|ка (-ки; *gen pl* **-ок)** *ж* (*разг*) home-made thing.
самоде́льный *прил* home-made.
самодержа́ви|е (-я) *ср* autocracy.
самодержа́вный *прил* autocratic.
самоде́ятельность (-и) *ж* initiative, self-motivation; (*также:* **худо́жественная ~**) amateur art and performance.
самоде́ятельный *прил* (*по личному почину*) self-motivated; (*не профессиональный*) amateur.
самодисципли́н|а (-ы) *ж* self-discipline.
самодовле́ющий (-ая, -ее, -ие) *прил* self-sufficient.
самодово́л|ьный (-ен, -ьна, -ьно) *прил* self-satisfied.
самоду́р (-а) *м* tyrant (*fig*).
самозабве́нен *прил см* **самозабве́нный.**
самозабве́ни|е (-я) *ср* selflessness.
самозабве́н|ный (-ен, -на, -но) *прил* selfless.
самозва́н|ец (-ца) *м* impostor.
самозва́н|ка (-ки; *gen pl* **-ок)** *ж см* **самозва́нец.**
самозва́нный *прил* self-appointed.
самозва́нок *сущ см* **самозва́нка.**
самозва́нца *итп сущ см* **самозва́нец.**
са́мок *сущ см* **са́мка.**
самока́т (-а) *м* scooter (*child's*).
самоконтро́л|ь (-я) *м* self-control.
самокри́тик|а (-и) *ж* self-criticism.
самокрити́ч|ный (-ен, -на, -но) *прил* self-critical.
самолёт (-а) *м* (aero)plane (*BRIT*), (air)plane (*US*).
самолётострое́ни|е (-я) *ср* aircraft manufacturing.
самолюби́в|ый (-, -а, -о) *прил* self-enamoured.
самолюби|е (-я) *ср* self-esteem.
самомне́ни|е (-я) *ср* self-importance.
самонадея́н|ный (-, -на, -но) *прил* self-important.
самооблада́ни|е (-я) *ср* self-possession.
самообма́н (-а) *м* self-deception.
самооборо́н|а (-ы) *ж* self-defence (*BRIT*), self-

defense (*US*).
самообразова́ни|е (-я) *ср* self-education.
самообслу́живани|е (-я) *ср* self-service.
самоокупа́емост|ь (-и) *ж* (*ЭКОН*) self-sufficiency.
самоопределе́ни|е (-я) *ср* self-determination.
самоопредел|и́ться (-ю́сь, -йшься; *impf* **самоопределя́ться**) *сов возв* (*человек*) to determine one's position; (*нация*) to make its position clear.
самоотве́ржен|ный (-, -на, -но) *прил* self-sacrificing.
самоотво́д (-а) *м* withdrawal.
самоотрече́ни|е (-я) *ср* self-denial.
самооце́н|ка (-ки; *gen pl* -ок) *ж* self-appraisal.
самоочеви́д|ный (-ен, -на, -но) *прил* self-evident.
самопа́л (-а) *м* (*разг: кустарная вещь*) cheap fake.
самопоже́ртвовани|е (-я) *ср* self-sacrifice.
самопрове́р|ка (-ки; *gen pl* -ок) *ж* (*КОМП*) self-test.
самопроизво́л|ьный (-ен, -ьна, -ьно) *прил* spontaneous.
самореклам|а (-ы) *ж* self-advertisement.
саморо́д|ок (-ка) *м* (*золотой*) nugget; (*перен: талант*) natural.
самосва́л (-а) *м* dump truck.
самосоверше́нствовани|е (-я) *ср* self-improvement.
самосозна́ни|е (-я) *ср* self-awareness.
самосохране́ни|е (-я) *ср* self-preservation.
самостоя́телен *прил см* **самостоя́тельный**.
самостоя́тельно *нареч* (*независимо*) independently; (*без помощи других*) on one's own.
самостоя́тель|ный (-ен, -ьна, -ьно) *прил* independent.
самосу́д (-а) *м* mob law.
самотёк (-а) *м* (*перен*) chaos; **пуска́ть** (**пусти́ть** *perf*) **де́ло на** ~ to let things slide.
самоуби́йств|о (-а) *ср* suicide; **поко́нчить** (*perf*) **жизнь** ~**м** to commit suicide.
самоуби́йц|а (-ы) *м/ж* suicide (victim).
самоуваже́ни|е (-я) *ср* self-respect.
самоуве́рен|ный (-, -на, -но) *прил* self-confident, self-assured.
самоуниже́ни|е (-я) *ср* self-abasement, self-degradation.
самоуничиже́ни|е (-я) *ср* self-humiliation.
самоуправле́ни|е (-я) *ср* self-administration.
самоупра́вств|о (-а) *ср* (*произвол*) arbitrariness.
самоуспокое́ни|е (-я) *ср* complacency.
самоустран|и́ться (-ю́сь, -йшься) *сов возв*: ~ **от** +*gen* to evade, dodge.
самоутвержде́ни|е (-я) *ср* self-assertion.
самоу́чек *сущ см* **самоу́чка**.

самоучи́тел|ь (-я) *м* teach-yourself book.
самоу́ч|ка (-ки; *gen pl* -ек) *м/ж*: **он/она́** ~ he/she is self-taught.
самофинанси́ровани|е (-я) *ср* self-financing.
самохо́дный *прил* self-propelled.
самоцве́т (-а) *м* gem.
самоцве́тный *прил*: ~ **ка́мень** gemstone.
самоце́л|ь (-и) *ж* an end in itself.
самочу́вstvи|е (-я) *ср*: **как Ва́ше** ~? how are you feeling?
самца́ *итп сущ см* **саме́ц**.
са́м|ый (-ая, -ое, -ые) *мест* (+*noun*) the very; (+*adj*; *вкусный, красивый итп*) the most; **на** ~ **верх** to the very top; **в** ~**ом низу́** at the very bottom; **в** ~**ом нача́ле/конце́** right at the beginning/end; ~ **большо́й/ма́ленький/лу́чший/ху́дший** the biggest/smallest/best/worst; **тот же** ~ the same; **э́то тот** ~ **челове́к, о кото́ром мы говори́ли** this is the (same) person that we were talking about; ~**ое вре́мя** *или* ~**ая пора́ уйти́/нача́ть** it is high time to go/start; **в** ~ **раз** (*разг: вовремя*) at just the right time; **э́ти ту́фли мне в** ~ **раз** (*разг*) these shoes are a perfect fit; ~**ая ма́лость** the tiniest little bit; **в** ~**ом де́ле** really; **на** ~**ом де́ле** in actual fact.
сан (-а) *м* (*звание*) rank; **духо́вный** ~ holy orders *мн*.
санато́ри|й (-я) *м* sanatorium (*BRIT*), sanitarium (*US*) (*мн* sanatoriums *или* sanatoria).
санда́ли|я (-и) *ж* (*обычно мн*) sandal.
са́н|и (-е́й) *мн* sledge *ед* (*BRIT*), sled *ед* (*US*); (*спортивные*) toboggan *ед*.
санита́р (-а) *м* (*МЕД*) orderly.
санитари́|я (-и) *ж* sanitation.
санита́р|ка (-ки; *gen pl* -ок) *ж* auxiliary.
санита́рный *прил* sanitary; **санита́рная те́хника** = **санте́хника**;; **санита́рное состоя́ние** sanitation; **санита́рный день** cleaning day; **санита́рный инспе́ктор** environmental health officer.
санита́рок *сущ см* **санита́рка**.
са́н|ки (-ок) *мн* sledge *ед* (*BRIT*), sled *ед* (*US*).
Санкт-Петербу́рг (-а) *м* St. Petersburg.
санкт-петербу́ргск|ий (-ая, -ое, -ие) *прил* St. Petersburg *опред*.
санкциони́ровани|е (-я) *ср* sanctioning.
санкциони́р|овать (-ую) (*не*)*сов перех* to sanction.
са́нкци|я (-и) *ж* (*разрешение*) sanction; (*мера*): **экономи́ческие/полити́ческие** ~**и** economic/political sanctions; ~ **на о́быск** search warrant; **с** ~**и** +*gen* with the sanction of; **дава́ть** (**дать** *perf*) ~**ю на** +*acc* to sanction.
са́нок *сущ см* **са́нки**.
са́ночник (-а) *м* (*СПОРТ*) tobogganist.
санте́хник (-а) *м сокр* (= *санита́рный те́хник*) plumber.
санте́хник|а (-и) *ж сокр* (= *санита́рная*

те́хника) collective term for plumbing equipment and bathroom accessories.

сантиме́тр (-а) *м* centimetre (*BRIT*), centimeter (*US*); (*линейка*) tape measure.

Сантья́го *м нескл* Santiago.

сану́з|ел (-ла́) *м сокр* (= *санита́рный у́зел*) bathroom facilities *мн*.

Сан-Франци́ско *м нескл* San Francisco.

санча́ст|ь (-и) *ж сокр* = *санита́рная часть*; (*ВОЕН*) medical unit.

сапёр (-а) *м* field engineer, sapper.

сапо́г (-á; *nom pl* -и́, *gen pl* -) *м* boot.

сапо́жник (-а) *м* shoemaker; (*разг: пренебр*) bungler.

сапфи́р (-а) *м* sapphire.

сапфи́ровый *прил* sapphire *опред*.

Сара́ев|о (-а) *ср* Sarajevo.

сара́|й (-я) *м* (*для дров, скотины*) shed; (*для сена*) barn.

саранч|á (-и́) *ж собир* locusts *мн*.

сарафа́н (-а) *м* (*платье*) pinafore (dress) (*BRIT*), jumper (*US*).

сарде́л|ька (-ьки; *gen pl* -ек) *ж* sausage.

сарди́н|а (-ы) *ж* sardine.

cáрж|а (-и) *ж* serge.

сарка́зм (-а) *м* sarcasm.

саркасти́ческ|ий (-ая, -ое, -ие) *прил* sarcastic.

саркофа́г (-а) *м* sarcophagus (*мн* sarcophaguses *или* sarcophagi).

сары́ч (-á) *м* buzzard.

сатан|á (-ы́) *м* Satan.

сателли́т (-а) *м* (*также ПОЛИТ*) satellite.

сати́н (-а) *м* sateen.

сати́новый *прил* sateen *опред*.

сати́р|а (-ы) *ж* satire.

сати́рик (-а) *м* satirist.

сатири́ческ|ий (-ая, -ое, -ие) *прил* satirical.

Сату́рн (-а) *м* Saturn.

сау́довск|ий (-ая, -ое, -ие) *прил*: **С~ая Ара́вия** Saudi Arabia.

cáyн|а (-ы) *ж* sauna.

Сахали́н (-а) *м* Sakhalin.

cáxap (-а; *part gen* -у) *м* sugar; **рабо́та у меня́ не ~** (*разг*) my work is no picnic; **хара́ктер у неё не ~** (*разг*) she's not all sweetness and light.

Caxáp|a (-ы) *ж* Sahara.

сахари́н (-а) *м* saccharin.

cáxaрниц|а (-ы) *ж* sugar bowl.

cáxaрный *прил* sugary; (*перен: белый*) white; (: *слащавый*) sugary; **cáxaрная ва́та** candy floss; **cáxaрная кость** marrowbone; **cáxaрная свёкла** sugar beet; **cáxaрный диабе́т** diabetes; **cáxaрный песо́к** granulated sugar; **cáxaрный тростни́к** sugar cane.

caxapóз|a (-ы) *ж* sucrose.

сачо́к (-ка́) *м* (*для ловли рыб*) landing net; (*для бабочек*) butterfly net.

СБ *ж сокр* (= *слу́жба бы́та*) service industries *мн*.

сб. *сокр* (= *сбо́рник*) coll. (= *collection*).

сба́в|ить (-лю, -ишь; *impf* **сбавля́ть**) *сов перех* to reduce.

сба́гр|ить (-ю, -ишь) *сов перех* (*разг*) to get rid *или* shot of.

сбаланси́рованный *прил* balanced.

сбаланси́р|овать (-ую) *сов от* **баланси́ровать**.

сба́лтыва|ть (-ю) *несов от* **сболта́ть**.

сбе́га|ть (-ю) *сов неперех* (*разг*): **~ в магази́н/за молоко́м** to run to the shop/for milk.

сбе|жа́ть (*как* **бежа́ть**; *см* **Table 20**; *impf* **сбега́ть**) *сов неперех* (*убежа́ть*) to run away; **сбега́ть** (**~** *perf*) **с** +*gen* (*с горы итп*) to run down; **сбега́ть** (**~** *perf*) **с ле́стницы** to run downstairs; **сбега́ть** (**~** *perf*) **из тюрьмы́** to escape from prison; **улы́бка ~жа́ла с его́ лица́** the smile vanished from his face

▶ **сбежа́ться** (*impf* **сбега́ться**) *сов возв* to come running.

сбе́й(те) *сов см* **сбить**.

сберёг *итп сов см* **сбере́чь**.

сберега́тельный *прил*: **~ банк** savings bank; **сберега́тельная ка́сса** = **сберка́сса**; **сберега́тельная кни́жка** = **сберкни́жка**.

сберега́|ть (-ю) *несов от* **сбере́чь**.

сберегу́ *итп сов см* **сбере́чь**.

сбереже́ни|е (-я) *ср* (*действие*) saving; **~я** savings *мн*.

сбер|е́чь (-егу́, -ежёшь *итп*, -егу́т; *pt* -ёг, -егла́, -егло́, *impf* **сберега́ть**) *сов перех* (*имущество*) to protect; (*здоровье, любовь, отношение*) to preserve; (*де́ньги*) to save (up).

сберка́сс|а (-ы) *ж сокр* (= *сберега́тельная ка́сса*) savings bank.

сберкни́ж|ка (-ки; *gen pl* -ек) *ж сокр* (= *сберега́тельная кни́жка*) savings book.

сбива́|ть(ся) (-ю(сь)) *несов от* **сбить(ся)**.

сби́вчив|ый (-, -а, -о) *прил* confused.

сбить (собью́, собьёшь; *imper* **сбе́й(те)**, *impf* **сбива́ть**) *сов перех* (*птицу, самолёт*) to shoot down; (*каблуки, туфли*) to wear down; (*цену, температуру*) to bring down; (*ящик из досок*) to knock together; (*сливки, яйца*) to beat; **сбива́ть** (**~** *perf*) **кого́-н с пути́** (*перен*) to lead sb astray; **сбива́ть** (**~** *perf*) **кого́-н с то́лку** to mislead sb

▶ **сби́ться** (*impf* **сбива́ться**) *сов возв* (*шапка, повязка итп*) to slip; (*каблуки, копыта*) to wear down; (*собра́ться вместе*) to flock together; (*сливки, крем, яйца*) to stiffen; **сбива́ться** (**сби́ться** *perf*) **с пути́** (*также перен*) to lose one's way; **сбива́ться** (**сби́ться** *perf*) **со счёта** to lose count; **сбива́ться** (**сби́ться** *perf*) **с ног** to be run off one's feet.

сближа́|ть(ся) (-ю(сь)) *несов от* **сбли́зить(ся)**.

сближе́ни|е (-я) *ср* (*между государствами*) rapprochement; (*между людьми*) closeness.

сбли́|зить (-жу, -зишь; *impf* **сближа́ть**) *сов перех* to bring closer together

▶ **сбли́зиться** (*impf* **сближа́ться**) *сов возв*: **~ся (друг с дру́гом)** to approach (one another); (*люди, государства*) to become closer.

СБО м сокр = спра́вочно-библиографи́ческий отде́л.

сбо́|й (-я) м (перебой) failure; (в работе людей) disruption.

сбо́ку нареч at the side ♦ предл: ~ от +gen at the side of, beside.

сболта́|ть (-ю; impf сба́лтывать) сов перех to shake (up).

сболтну́|ть (-у́, -ёшь) сов перех (разг): ~ ли́шнее/глу́пость to say too much/something stupid.

сбор (-а) м (урожая, данных) gathering; (налогов, взносов) collection; (валовой, годовой) yield; (плата: страховой, аукционный итп) fee; (выручка: от концерта, спектакля) takings мн, receipts мн; (собрание) assembly, gathering; (обычно мн: армейского запаса, спортсменов) training ед; ~ фру́ктов fruit-picking; тамо́женный/ге́рбовый ~ customs/stamp duty; ~ информа́ции (комп) data capture; порто́вые сбо́ры harbour dues; все в сбо́ре everyone is present; см также сбо́ры.

сбо́рищ|е (-а) ср (разг: пренебр) gang; (: собрание) mob.

сбо́р|ка (-ки; gen pl -ок) ж (изделия) assembly; (обычно мн: на юбке) gather.

сбо́рн|ая (-ой; decl like adj) ж (также: ~ кома́нда) national team.

сбо́рник (-а) м collection (of stories, articles).

сбо́рный прил: ~ пункт assembly point; сбо́рная ме́бель kit furniture; сбо́рная моде́ль model kit.

сбо́рок сущ см сбо́рка.

сбо́рочный прил assembly опред; ~ конве́йер assembly line.

сбо́рщик (-а) м (данных, урожая) gatherer; (машин) assembler; сбо́рщик нало́гов tax collector.

сбо́р|ы (-ов) мн (приготовления) preparations мн.

сбра́сыва|ть(ся) (-ю(сь)) несов от сбро́сить(ся).

сбр|ить (-е́ю, -е́ешь; impf сбрива́ть) сов перех to shave off.

сброд (-а) м (разг: пренебр) rabble.

сброс (-а) м (отходов) discharge; (воды) overflow.

сбро́|сить (-шу, -сишь; impf сбра́сывать) сов перех (бросить вниз) to throw down; (спустить) to let down; (свергнуть) to overthrow; (пальто итп) to throw off; (скорость, давление) to reduce; (карту) to throw away; (комп) to reset.

▶ **сбро́ситься** (impf сбра́сываться) сов возв (разг: сложиться) to chip in; сбра́сываться (~ся perf) с +gen to throw o.s. from.

сбру|я (-и) ж harness.

СБСЕ ср сокр (= Совеща́ние по безопа́сности и сотру́дничеству в Евро́пе) CSCE (= Conference on Security and Cooperation in Europe).

сбу́ду(сь) итп сов см сбы́ть(ся).

сбыва́|ть(ся) (-ю(сь)) несов от сбы́ть(ся).

сбыт (-а) м sale; ры́нок сбы́та market; отде́л сбы́та sales department.

сбытово́й прил retail опред.

сб|ыть (как быть; см **Table 21**; impf сбыва́ть) сов перех (товар) to sell; (разг: избавиться) to get rid of; ~ (perf) кого́-н/что-н с рук to get sb/sth off one's hands

▶ **сбы́ться** (impf сбыва́ться) сов возв (надежды, предсказания) to come true.

СВ сокр (= сре́дние во́лны) MW= medium wave ед ♦ прил (средневолново́й) MW (= medium-wave).

св. сокр (= свято́й) St (= Saint).

сва́деб сущ см сва́дьба.

сва́дебный прил: ~ пода́рок wedding present; сва́дебное пла́тье wedding dress.

сва́дьб|а (-ьбы; gen pl -еб) ж wedding; игра́ть (сыгра́ть perf) ~ьбу to celebrate a wedding.

свал|и́ть (-алю́, -а́лишь) сов от вали́ть ♦ (impf сва́ливать) перех to throw down; (разг: свергнуть) to topple; меня́ ~или́а уста́лость (разг) I feel whacked; её ~или́ грипп (разг) she's come down with the flu

▶ **свали́ться** сов от вали́ться ♦ (impf сва́ливаться) возв (разг: появиться) to turn up; (: заболеть и слечь) to collapse; вся рабо́та ~или́ась на него́ he was landed with all (of) the work.

сва́л|ка (-ки; gen pl -ок) ж (действие) dumping; (место) rubbish dump.

сваля́|ть (-ю) сов от валя́ть

▶ **сваля́ться** сов возв (волосы, шерсть) to become matted.

СВАПО ж сокр SWAPO (= South-West Africa People's Organization).

свар|и́ть (-арю́, -а́ришь) сов от вари́ть ♦ (impf сва́ривать) перех (шов) to weld

▶ **свари́ться** сов от вари́ться

сва́р|ка (-и) ж welding.

сварли́в|ый (-, -а, -о) прил quarrelsome.

сва́рочный прил welding опред.

сва́рщик (-а) м welder.

сва́стик|а (-и) ж swastika.

сват (-а) м (сватающий) matchmaker; (родственник) the father of one's son-in-law or daughter-in-law.

сва́та|ть (-ю; perf посва́тать или сосва́тать) несов перех: ~ кого́-н (за +acc) (предлагать в супруги) to try to marry sb off (to); (no perf; перен): ~ кого́-н (кому́-н) to fix sb up (with sb)

▶ **сва́таться** (perf посва́таться) несов возв: ~ся к +dat или за +acc to court.

сва́ть|**я** (-и) *ж mother of one's son-in-law or daughter-in-law.*

сва́х|**а** (-и) *ж matchmaker.*

сва́|**я** (-и) *ж (строит) pile.*

сведе́ни|**е** (-я) *ср (обычно мн: известия, данные) information ед;* **доводи́ть (довести́** *perf)* **что-н до ~я кого́-н** to bring sth to sb's attention; **принима́ть (приня́ть** *perf)* **что-н к ~ю** to take sth into consideration; **к Ва́шему ~ю** for your information; *см также* **све́дения.**

сведе́ни|**е** (-я) *ср (пятен, грязи) removal; (в таблицу, в график итп) arrangement;* **~ к** +*dat* reduction to.

сведе́ни|**я** (-й) *мн (знания) knowledge ед.*

сведу́(сь) *итп сов см* **свести́(сь).**

све́дущ|**ий** (-ая, -ее, -ие; -, -а, -е) *прил:* **~ (в** +*prp)* knowledgeable (about).

свежезаморо́женный *прил fresh-frozen.*

свежеиспечённый *прил freshly-baked.*

све́жест|**ь** (-и) *ж (продуктов итп) freshness; (воздуха, воды) cleanliness; (погоды) briskness;* **э́ти о́вощи не пе́рвой ~и** these vegetables aren't very fresh.

свеже́ть (-ю; *perf* **посвеже́ть)** *несов неперех (ветер) to turn brisk; (воздух) to clear; (человек) to look fresher.*

све́ж|**ий** (-ая, -ее, -ие; -, -а́, -о́, -и) *прил fresh; (воздух, вода) clean; (ветер) brisk; (журнал) recent;* **к ве́черу ста́ло свежо́** it grew chilly towards evening; **обду́мывать (обду́мать** *perf)* **что-н на ~ую го́лову** to come back to sth with a clear head.

све́зти (-зу́, -зёшь; *pt* -ёз, -езла́, -езло́, *impf* **свози́ть)** *сов перех:* **~ (с** +*gen)* (спустить) to drive down; *(собрать)* to bring; *(разг: отвезти: на дачу)* to take.

свёкл|**а** (-ы) *ж beetroot.*

свеко́льный *прил beetroot* **опред;** *(цвет)* beetroot(-coloured (*BRIT*) или colored (*US*)).

свёкор (-ра) *м father-in-law, husband's father.*

свекро́в|**ь** (-и) *ж mother-in-law, husband's mother.*

свёл(ся) *итп сов см* **свести́(сь).**

сверг|**ну́ть** (-у, -ешь; *impf* **сверга́ть)** *сов перех to overthrow.*

сверже́ни|**е** (-я) *ср overthrow.*

све́р|**ить** (-ю, -ишь; *impf* **сверя́ть)** *сов перех:* **~ (с** +*instr)* to check (against)

▶ **све́риться** (*impf* **сверя́ться)** *сов возв:* **~ся с** +*instr* to check in.

сверка́|**ть** (-ю) *несов неперех (звезда, глаза) to twinkle; (огни) to flicker;* **~** *(impf)* **умо́м/красото́й** to sparkle with intelligence/beauty.

сверк|**ну́ть** (-у́, -ёшь) *сов неперех to flash;* **у меня́ ~у́ла мысль** a thought flashed through my mind.

сверли́льн|**ый** *прил (тех):* **~ стано́к** drill; **~ая голо́вка** drillstock.

сверл|**и́ть** (-ю́, -и́шь; *perf* **просверли́ть)** *несов перех to drill, bore; (no perf; подлеж: сомнения*

итп) *to gnaw away at.*

сверл|**о́** (-ерла́; *nom pl* **свёрла)** *ср drill.*

сверн|**у́ть** (-у́, -ёшь; *impf* **свёртывать** или **свора́чивать)** *сов перех (скатать: карту, ковёр итп)* to roll up; (: *сигарету*) to roll; *(сократить)* to cut, reduce; *(временно прекратить)* to hold up ♦ (*impf* **свора́чивать)** *неперех (повернуть)* to turn; **~** *(perf)* **себе́ ше́ю** to break one's neck; **~** *(perf)* **кому́-н ше́ю** *(перен)* to wring sb's neck; **свора́чивать (~** *perf)* **напра́во/нале́во** to turn right/left

▶ **сверну́ться** (*impf* **свёртываться** или **свора́чиваться)** *сов возв (карта, ковёр итп)* to roll up; *(человек, животное)* to curl up; *(молоко)* to curdle; *(кровь)* to clot.

сверста́ть (-ю) *сов от* **верста́ть.**

све́рстник (-а) *м peer;* **мы с ней ~и** she and I are the same age.

све́рстниц|**а** (-ы) *ж см* **све́рстник.**

свёрт|**ок** (-ка) *м package.*

свёртыва|**ть(ся)** (-ю(сь)) *несов от* **сверну́ть(ся).**

сверх *предл* (+*gen;* нормы) over and above; **э́то ~ мои́х возмо́жностей** it is out of my reach; **~ ожида́ния** beyond all expectation; **~ обыкнове́ния** unusually; **~ того́** moreover; **~ всего́** on top of everything else.

сверхзвуково́й *прил supersonic.*

сверхпла́новый *прил over and above the plan.*

сверхпри́был|**ь** (-и) *ж surplus profit.*

сверхсро́чный *прил:* **~ая вое́нная слу́жба** extended military service.

све́рху *нареч (о направлении)* from the top; *(в верхней части)* on the surface; **прика́зы ~** orders from above; **смотре́ть** *(impf)* **~ вниз на кого́-н** to look down on sb.

сверхуро́чно *нареч:* **рабо́тать ~** to work overtime.

сверхуро́чн|**ые** (-ых; *decl like adj) мн (плата)* overtime pay *ед.*

сверхуро́чный *прил:* **~ая рабо́та** overtime; **рабо́тать** *(impf)* **в ~ые часы́** to work on after hours.

сверхчелове́ческ|**ий** (-ая, -ое, -ие) *прил superhuman.*

сверхъесте́ственный *прил (РЕЛ)* supernatural; *(перен: усилие, терпение итп)* superhuman.

сверч|**о́к** (-ка́) *м (зоол) cricket.*

сверша́|**ть(ся)** (-ю(сь)) *несов от* **сверши́ть(ся).**

сверше́ни|**е** (-я) *ср (надежд) fulfilment (BRIT), fulfillment (US); (дел, подвига итп) accomplishment; (кары) exacting.*

сверш|**и́ть** (-у́, -и́шь; *impf* **сверша́ть)** *сов перех to accomplish*

▶ **сверши́ться** (*impf* **сверша́ться)** *сов возв (событие) to take place; (надежды, замыслы) to be fulfilled.*

сверя́|**ть(ся)** (-ю(сь)) *несов от* **све́рить(ся).**

све́|**сить** (-шу, -сишь; *impf* **све́шивать)** *сов*

перех to lower

▶ **свéситься** (*impf* **свéшиваться**) *сов возв*: ~**ся из** +*gen*/**чéрез** +*acc* to hang from/over; (*вéтви, дерéвья*) to overhang.

свести́ (**-едý, -едёшь**; *pt* **-ёл, -елá, -елó**, *impf* **своди́ть**) *сов перех*: ~ **с** +*gen* to lead down; (*направить в другýю стóрону*) to lead off; (*пятнó, грязь*) to shift; (*познакóмить*) to introduce; (*собрáть*) to arrange; **своди́ть** (~ *perf*) **к ми́нимуму** to minimize; **своди́ть** (~ *perf*) **когó-н с умá** to drive sb mad; **у меня́ ~елó нóгу** I've got cramp in my leg; **своди́ть** (~ *perf*) **брóви** to knit one's brows; **своди́ть** (~ *perf*) **рýки** to clasp one's hands (together)

▶ **свести́сь** (*impf* **своди́ться**) *сов возв*: ~**сь к** +*dat* to be reduced to; **своди́ться** (~**сь** *perf*) **к нулю́** to come to nothing.

свет (**-а**; *loc sg* **-ý**) *м* light; (*Земля́*) the world; (*аристокрáтия*) (high) society; **при свéте лунь́/свечи́** by moonlight/candlelight; **в свéте** +*gen* (*нóвой поли́тики, послéдних собы́тий*) in the light of; **в мрáчном/оптимисти́ческом свéте** in a gloomy/optimistic light; **ни ~ ни заря́** at the crack of dawn; **чуть ~** at daybreak; **выводи́ть** (**вы́вести** *perf*) **в ~** (*кни́га*) to be published; **выпускáть** (**вы́пустить** *perf*) **в ~** (*кни́гу*) to publish; **включáть** (**включи́ть** *perf*)/ **выключáть** (**вы́ключить** *perf*) to switch *или* turn the light on/off; **проливáть** (**проли́ть** *perf*) ~ **на что-н** to shed *или* throw light on sth; **тот ~** (*РЕЛ*) the next world; **ни за что на свéте не сдéлал бы э́то** (*разг*) I wouldn't do it for the world; **ругáть** (*impf*) *или* **брани́ть** (*impf*) **когó-н на чём ~ стои́т** (*разг*) to give sb hell.

светáть (*3sg* **-ет**) *несов безл* to get *или* grow light; **лéтом рáно ~ет** it gets light early in summer.

свéтел *прил см* **свéтлый**.

свети́л|о (**-а**) *ср*: **небéсное ~** heavenly body; (*перен: наýки итп*) leading light.

свети́льник (**-а**) *м* lamp.

свети́ть (**-ечý, -éтишь**) *несов неперех* to shine; (*perf* **посвети́ть**): ~ **комý-н** (*фонарём итп*) to light the way for sb

▶ **свети́ться** *несов возв* (*также перен*) to shine; **её глазá ~éтились любóвью** her eyes shone with love; **он ~éтился от рáдости** he was radiant with joy.

светлé|ть (**-ю**; *perf* **посветлéть** *или* **просветлéть**) *несов неперех* (*также перен*) to lighten; (*ткань, вóлосы*) to go lighter; (*no perf*; *ви́днеться*) to show light; **за óкнами ~ет** it's getting light outside.

светлó *как сказ*: **на ýлице ~** it's light outside.

свéт|лый (**-ел, -лá, -ло**) *прил* bright; (*кóмната*) light, bright; (*вóлосы, глазá, крáски*) light; (*ум, мы́сли*) lucid; ~**ло-крáсный/-зелёный** light-red/-green; **у негó ~лая головá** he is very

bright.

световóй *прил* light *опред*; **световóй день** time of the day during which it's light.

светопреставлéни|е (**-я**) *ср* doomsday.

светофóр (**-а**) *м* traffic light.

светочувстви́тельный *прил* light-sensitive.

свéтск|ий (**-ая, -ое, -ие**) *прил* (*круг, манéры*) refined; (*не духóвный*) secular; ~**ое óбщество** high society; ~ **человéк** man of the world.

свеч|á (**-и́**; *nom pl* **-и**, *gen pl* **-éй**) *ж* candle; (*МЕД*) suppository; (*ТЕХ*) spark(ing) plug; (*СПОРТ*) lob.

свéч|ка (**-ки**; *gen pl* **-ек**) *ж* candle.

свечý(сь) *сов см* **свети́ть(ся)**.

свéша|ть (**-ю**) *сов от* **вéшать**.

свéшива|ть(ся) (**-ю(сь)**) *несов от* **свéсить(ся)**.

свéшу(сь) *сов см* **свéсить(ся)**.

свивá|ть (**-ю**; *perf* **свить**) *несов перех* to weave

▶ **свивá|ться** *несов от* **сви́ться**.

свидáни|е (**-я**) *ср* rendezvous; (*деловóе*) appointment; (*с заключённым, с больны́м*) visit; (*влюблённых*) date; **до ~я** goodbye; **до скóрого ~я** see you soon; **назначáть (назнáчить** *perf*) **комý-н ~** to arrange to meet sb; (*о влюблённых*) to make a date with sb.

свидéтел|ь (**-я**) *м* witness.

свидéтельниц|а (**-ы**) *ж см* **свидéтель**.

свидéтельск|ий (**-ая, -ое, -ие**) *прил* witness's.

свидéтельств|о (**-а**) *ср* evidence; (*докумéнт*) certificate; **свидéтельство о рождéнии/брáке** birth/marriage certificate.

свидéтельств|овать (**-ую**) *несов неперех*: ~ **о** +*prp* (*свидéтель*) to give evidence about; (*ци́фры, собы́тия*) to testify to ◆ (*perf* **засвидéтельствовать**) *перех* (*пóдпись*) to certify.

свинáрник (**-а**) *м* (*также перен*) pigsty.

свин|éц (**-цá**) *м* lead (*metal*).

свини́н|а (**-ы**) *ж* pork.

сви́нк|а (**-и**) *ж* (*МЕД*) mumps; **морскáя ~** guinea pig.

свиновóдств|о (**-а**) *ср* pig farming.

свинóй *прил* (*сáло, корм*) pig *опред*; (*из свини́ны*) pork *опред*; **свинáя кóжа** pigskin.

сви́нск|ий (**-ая, -ое, -ие**) *прил* (*разг*) filthy.

сви́нств|о (**-а**) *ср* (*разг*) filth.

свин|ти́ть (**-чý, -ти́шь**; *impf* **сви́нчивать**) *сов перех* (*соедини́ть*) to screw together.

свинцá *итп сущ см* **свинéц**.

свинцóвый *прил* lead *опред*; (*цвет*) leaden.

сви́нчива|ть (**-ю**) *несов от* **свинти́ть**.

свинчý *сов см* **свинти́ть**.

свин|ья́ (**-ьи́**; *nom pl* **-ьи**, *gen pl* **-éй**) *ж* pig; (*разг: пренебр*) pig, swine; **подложи́ть** *perf* ~**ью́ комý-н** (*разг*) to do the dirty on sb.

свирéл|ь (**-и**) *ж* (*МУЗ*) reed pipe.

свирепé|ть (**-ю**; *perf* **рассвирепéть**) *несов неперех* to turn savage.

свире́пств|овать (-ую) *несов неперех* to rage.
свире́п|ый (-, -а, -о) *прил* fierce, ferocious.
свиса́ть (*3sg* -ет, *3pl* -ют) *несов неперех* to hang.
свист (-а) *м* whistle; (*ветра*) whistling.
свисте́ть (-щу́, -сти́шь; *perf* **просвисте́ть**) *несов неперех* to whistle.
свистка́ *сущ см* **свисто́к**.
сви́стн|уть (-у, -ешь) *сов неперех* to give a whistle ♦ *перех* (*разг: украсть*) to nick (*BRIT*), pinch.
свисто́к (-ка́) *м* whistle.
сви́т|а (-ы) *ж* retinue.
сви́тер (-а) *м* sweater.
свить (совью́, совьёшь) *сов от* **вить**, **свива́ть**
▶ **сви́ться** (*impf* **свива́ться**) *сов возв* (*растения*) to intertwine.
свихн|у́ться (-у́сь, -ёшься) *сов возв* (*разг: помешаться*) to go round the bend *или* twist; ~ (*perf*) **на чём-н** (*на футболе, на кино*) to be mad *или* crazy about sth.
свищ (-а́) *м* (*МЕД*) fistula.
свищу́ *несов от* **свисте́ть**.
свобо́д|а (-ы) *ж* freedom; **лише́ние** ~ы imprisonment; **лиша́ть** (**лиши́ть** *perf*) **кого́-н** ~ы to imprison sb; **выпуска́ть** (**вы́пустить** *perf*) **кого́-н на** ~у to set sb free; **свобо́да ли́чности/печа́ти** freedom of the individual/ press; **свобо́да сло́ва** freedom of speech.
свобо́ден *прил см* **свобо́дный**.
свобо́дно *нареч* (*передвигаться*) freely; (*говорить*) fluently; (*облегать*) loosely ♦ *как сказ*: **мне здесь** ~ I feel free here; **в до́ме** ~ there's a lot of room in the house; **здесь** ~? is this place free?; **он** ~ **говори́т по-ру́сски** he speaks Russian fluently.
свобо́дн|ый (-ен, -на, -но) *прил* free; (*незанятый: место, номер*) vacant; (: *комната*) spare; (*одежда*) loose-fitting; (*помещение*) spacious; (*движение, речь*) fluent; (*дыхание*) unrestricted; ~ **от** +*gen* (*от недостатков итп*) free from *или* of; **вход** ~ free admission; **телефо́н** ~ the telephone is free; **Вы** ~ны, **мо́жете идти́** you are free to go; **у меня́ сейча́с нет** ~ных **де́нег** I don't have any money to spare; **свобо́дный перево́д** free translation; **свобо́дный стиль** (*в плавании*) free style; **свобо́дный уда́р** (*в футболе*) free kick.
свободолюби́в|ый (-, -а, -о) *прил* freedom-loving.
свободомы́сли|е (-я) *ср* free thinking.
свод (-а) *м* (*пятен, грязи*) removal; (*частей в целое, данных в таблицу*) arrangement; (*правил итп*) set; (*летописей*) collection; (*здания, тоннеля*) vaulting; ~ **пра́вил** (*профессиональный*) code of practice; **свод зако́нов** legal code.
свод|и́ть (-ожу́, -о́дишь) *несов от* **свести́** ♦ *сов перех* (*отвести*) to take
▶ **своди́ться** *несов от* **свести́сь**.

сво́д|ка (-ки; *gen pl* -ок) *ж*: ~ **пого́ды/новосте́й** weather/news summary; **операти́вная** ~ (*ВОЕН*) situation report.
сво́дный *прил* (*таблица, график*) summary *опред*; **сво́дный брат** stepbrother; **сво́дная сестра́** stepsister.
сво́док *прил см* **сво́дка**.
сво́дчатый *прил* vaulted.
своё (-его́) *мест см* **свой**.
своево́л|ьный (-ен, -ьна, -ьно) *прил* self-willed.
своевре́мен|ный (-ен, -на, -но) *прил* timely.
своём *итп мест см* **свой**, **своё**.
своенра́в|ный (-ен, -на, -но) *прил* wilful (*BRIT*), willful (*US*).
своеобра́зен *прил см* **своеобра́зный**.
своеобра́зи|е (-я) *ср* distinctiveness.
своеобра́з|ный (-ен, -на, -но) *прил* (*оригинальный*) original; (*no short form*; *своего́ рода*) peculiar.
свожу́(сь) (не)*сов см* **своди́ть(ся)**.
св|ози́ть (-ожу́, -о́зишь) *несов от* **свезти́** ♦ *сов перех* to take; **он** ~**ози́л нас в кино́** he took us to the cinema.

KEYWORD

свой (-его́; *f* **своя́**, *nt* **своё**, *pl* **свои́**; *как мой*; *см* **Table 8**) *мест* **1** (*я*) my; (*ты*) your; (*он*) his; (*она*) her; (*оно*) its; (*мы*) our; (*вы*) your; (*они*) their; **я люблю́ свою́ рабо́ту** I love my work; **мы собра́ли свои́ ве́щи** we collected our things; **де́лать** (**сде́лать** *perf*) **что-н свои́ми рука́ми** to make sth oneself; **жить** (*impf*) **свои́м трудо́м** to live by one's own hard work; **крича́ть** (*impf*) **не свои́м го́лосом** to shout wildly; **называ́ть** (*impf*) **ве́щи свои́ми имена́ми** to call a spade a spade
2 (*собственный*) one's own; **у неё свой компью́тер** she has her own computer; **у меня́ своя́ маши́на** I have my own car
3 (*своеобразный*) its; **э́тот план име́ет свои́ недоста́тки** this plan has its shortcomings
4 (*близкий*): **свой челове́к** one of us; **он сам не свой по́сле случи́вшегося** he is not himself after what happened.

сво́йск|ий (-ая, -ое, -ие) *прил* (*разг*) easy-going, laid-back.
сво́йствен|ный (-, -на, -но) *прил* (+*dat*) characteristic of; **ему́** ~**но серди́ться** he has a tendency to get angry.
сво́йств|о (-а) *ср* (*человека*) characteristic; (*предмета*) property.
сво́лочь (-и; *gen pl* -е́й) *ж* (*груб!*) bastard (*!*)
сво́р|а (-ы) *ж собир* (*волков*) pack; (*перен*: *хулиганов, мошенников*) pack, gang.
свора́чива|ть (-ю) *несов от* **сверну́ть**, **свороти́ть**
▶ **свора́чиваться** *несов от* **сверну́ться**.
сворот|и́ть (-очу́, -о́тишь; *impf* **свора́чивать**) *сов неперех* (*разг: сдвинуть*) to shift, budge; (: *свернуть*) to turn.
сво|я́ (-е́й) *мест см* **свой**.

свояк (-á) *м* brother-in-law (*wife's sister's husband*).

свояченица (-ы) *ж* sister-in-law (*wife's sister*).

СВЧ *сокр* (= сверхвысокая частота) SHF, shf (= *superhigh frequency*) ♦ *прил сокр* (*сверхвысокочастотный*) SHF, shf (= *superhigh frequency*).

свыкнуться (-усь, -ешься; *impf* **свыкаться**) *сов возв*: ~ с +*instr* to get *или* become used to.

свысока *нареч* condescendingly; **смотреть** (*impf*) **на кого-н** ~ to look down on sb.

свыше *предл*: ~ +*gen* (*выше*) beyond; (*больше*) over, more than; **это ~ моих сил** it's beyond me.

свяжу(сь) *итп сов см* **связать(ся)**.

связанный (-, -а, -о) *прил*: ~ (с +*instr*) connected (to *или* with); (*имеющий связи*): ~ с +*instr* (*с деловыми кругами, с художниками итп*) associated with; (-, -на, -но; *несвободный*: *движения, речь*) restricted; **это ~о со значительными расходами** it involves considerable expense; **он был несколько лет связан с этой фирмой** he was involved with the company for several years.

связать (-жу, -жешь) *сов от* **вязать** ♦ (*impf* **связывать**) *перех* (*веревку итп*) to tie; (*вещи, человека*) to tie up; (*перен: действия, инициативу*) to bind; (*установить сообщение, зависимость*): ~ **что-н** с +*instr* to connect *или* link sth to; **с чем Вы это связываете?** to what do you attribute this?; **я могу Вас с ним** ~ I can put you in touch with him; **он ~зал свою жизнь с наукой** he devoted his life to science; **он двух слов** ~ **не может** (*перен*) he can't string two words together; **связывать** (~ *perf*) **кого-н по рукам и ногам** (*перен*) to bind sb hand and foot

▶ **связаться** (*impf* **связываться**) *сов возв*: ~**ся с** +*instr* to contact; (*разг: с ворами итп*) to get mixed up with; (: *с невыгодным делом*) to get o.s. caught up in; **связываться** (~**ся** *perf*) **с кем-н по телефону** to get in touch with sb by phone.

связи (-ей) *мн* (*знакомства*) connections *мн*.

связист (-а) *м* (ВОЕН) signalman (*мн* signalmen).

связка (-ки; *gen pl* -ок) *ж* (*ключей*) bunch; (*бумаг, дров*) bundle; (АНАТ) ligament; (ЛИНГ) copula.

связной (-ого; *decl like adj*) *м* messenger.

связный *прил* coherent.

связок *сущ см* **связка**.

связующий (-ая, -ее, -ие) *прил* connecting *опред*.

связывание (-я) *ср* tying.

связывать(ся) (-ю(сь)) *несов от* **связать(ся)**.

связь (-и) *ж* (*экономическая, дружеская итп*) tie; (*причинная*) connection, link; (*телеграфная, почтовая итп*) communications *мн*; (*также*: **любовная** ~)

relationship; **в** ~**й с** +*instr* (*вследствие*) due to; (*по поводу*) in connection with; **в этой** ~**й** in this regard; **Министерство Связи** Ministry of Communications; *см также* **связи**.

святая (-ой; *decl like adj*) *ж см* **святой**.

святилище (-а) *ср* (РЕЛ) sanctuary.

святить (-щу, -тишь; *perf* **освятить**) *несов перех* (РЕЛ) to sanctify.

святки (-ок) *мн* ≈ Christmas(tide) *ед*.

святой *прил* holy; (-, -а, -о; *дело, обязанность, истина*) sacred ♦ (-ого; *decl like adj*) *м* (РЕЛ) saint; ~**ая святых** the holy of holies; ~ **отец** father (*used to address a priest*); **он/она** ~ **человек** he/she is a real saint.

святок *сущ см* **святки**.

святость (-и) *ж* holiness; (*дела, чувства*) sanctity.

святотатство (-а) *ср* sacrilege.

святыня (-и) *ж* (*место*) sacred place; (*предмет*) sacred object.

священник (-а) *м* priest.

священнодействие (-я) *ср* religious ceremony.

священнодействовать (-ую) *несов неперех* to conduct a religious ceremony.

священнослужитель (-я) *м* clergyman (*мн* clergymen).

священный *прил* holy, sacred; (*долг, обязанность*) sacred; **Священное писание** Holy Scripture.

священство (-а) *ср собир* the priesthood.

святящ *несов см* **святить**.

с.г. *сокр* = сего года.

сгиб (-а) *м* bend.

сгибать (-ю; *perf* **согнуть**) *несов перех* to bend

▶ **сгибаться** (*perf* **согнуться**) *несов возв* to bend down.

сгинуть (-у, -ешь) *сов неперех* (*разг*) to vanish.

сгладить (-жу, -дишь; *impf* **сглаживать**) *сов перех* to smooth out; (*перен: противоречия, остроту горя*) to smooth over; **сглаживать** (~ *perf*) **углы** (*перен*) to iron out difficulties

▶ **сгладиться** (*impf* **сглаживаться**) *сов возв* to be smoothed out.

сглазить (-жу, -зишь) *сов перех* (РЕЛ) to put the evil eye on; (*разг*) to jinx.

сглупить (-лю, -ишь) *сов от* **глупить**.

сгнивать (*3sg* -ет, *3pl* -ют) *несов неперех* to rot.

сгнить (-ю, -ёшь) *сов от* **гнить**.

сгноить (-ю, -ишь) *сов от* **гноить**.

сговариваться (-юсь) *несов от* **сговориться**.

сговор (-а) *м* agreement.

сговориться (-юсь, -ишься; *impf* **сговариваться**) *сов возв*: ~ **с** +*instr* (*о встрече, о сделке*) to come to an arrangement with; (*в дискуссии, в беседе*) to reach an agreement with.

сговóрчив|ый (-, -а, -о) *прил* cooperative.
сгоню *итп сов см* **согнáть**.
сгоня|ть (-ю) *несов от* **согнáть** ♦ *сов неперех* (*разг: сбегать*) to run ♦ *перех* (*послать*) to send.
сгорáни|е (-я) *ср* (*ТЕХ*) combustion.
сгорá|ть (-ю) *несов от* **сгорéть** ♦ *неперех*: ~ **от** **любопы́тства/нетерпéния** to be burning with curiosity/impatience.
сгóрб|ить(ся) (-лю(сь), -ишь(ся)) *сов от* **гóрбить(ся)**.
сгорé|ть (-ю, -йшь; *impf* **сгорáть** *или* **горéть**) *сов неперех* to burn; (*impf* **сгорáть**; *ЭЛЕК*) to fuse; (*на солнце*) to get burnt; (*перен: на работе*) to burn o.s. out.
сгорячá *нареч* in the heat of the moment.
сготóв|ить (-лю, -ишь) *сов от* **готóвить**.
сгре|сти́ (-бу́, -бёшь; *pt* -ёб, -еблá, -еблó, *impf* **сгребáть**) *сов перех* (*собрать*) to rake up; (*скинуть*): ~ **с** +*gen* to shovel off.
сгру|ди́ться (*3sg* -ится, *1pl* -и́мся) *сов неперех* (*разг*) to crowd together.
сгру|зи́ть (-ужу́, -у́зишь; *impf* **сгружáть**) *сов перех*: ~ (**с** +*gen*) to unload (from).
сгруппир|овáть(ся) (-у́ю(сь)) *сов от* **группировáть(ся)**.
сгуб|и́ть (-ублю́, -у́бишь) *сов от* **губи́ть**.
сгу|сти́ть (-щу́, -усти́шь; *impf* **сгущáть**) *сов перех* to thicken; **сгущáть** (~ *perf*) **крáски** (*перен*) to paint an exaggerated picture
▸ **сгусти́ться** (*impf* **сгущáться**) *сов возв* to thicken.
сгу́ст|ок (-ка) *м* blob.
сгущá|ть(ся) (-ю(сь)) *несов от* **сгусти́ть(ся)**.
сгущённ|ый *прил*: ~**ое молокó** condensed milk.
сгущу́(сь) *сов см* **сгусти́ть(ся)**.
с.-д. *сокр* = **социáл-демократи́ческий**.
сда|вáть (-ю́, -ёшь; *imper* **-вáй(те)**) *несов от* **сдать** ♦ *перех*: ~ **экзáмен** to sit an exam
▸ **сдавáться** *несов от* **сдáться** ♦ *возв* (*отдаваться внаём*) to be leased out ♦ *безл* (+*dat*; *разг*): ~**ётся мне, что ...** I reckon that ...; „~**ётся внаём"** "to let".
сдав|и́ть (-авлю́, -áвишь; *impf* **сдáвливать**) *сов перех* to squeeze.
сдáвленн|ый (-, -на, -но) *прил* (*голос, плач*) choked.
сдáвлива|ть (-ю) *несов от* **сдави́ть**.
сдавлю́ *сов см* **сдави́ть**.
сдáм(ся) *итп сов см* **сдáть(ся)**.
сдáтчик (-а) *м* supplier.
сдать (*как* **дать**; *см* **Table 14**; *impf* **сдавáть**) *сов перех* (*пальто, багаж, работу*) to hand in; (*сырьё, продукцию*) to supply; (*дежурство, рабочее место итп*) to hand over; (*дом, комнату итп*) to rent out; (*город, позицию итп*) to surrender; (*сдачу*) to give (back); (*no impf*; *экзамен, зачёт итп*) to pass; (*ослабеть*) to give out; **сдать** (*perf*) **делá** to step down; **сдавáть** (**сдать** *perf*) **орýжие** to lay down one's arms; **он сдал мне 5 рублéй** he gave me 5

roubles change
▸ **сдáться** (*impf* **сдавáться**) *сов возв* to give up; (*солдат, город*) to surrender; **сдавáться** (~**ся** *perf*) **на** +*acc* (*на уговоры итп*) to give in to; **на что мне сдали́сь эти дéньги?** (*разг*) what use is this money to me?; **сдавáться** (~**ся** *perf*) **в плен комý-н** to give o.s. up to sb.
сдá|ча (-и) *ж* (*сырья*) supply; (*экзамена*) passing; (*дежурства*) handing over; (*дома*) letting; (*города врагу*) surrender; (*излишек денег*) change; (*КАРТЫ*) deal; **давáть** (**дать** *perf*) **комý-н** ~**у** to give sb his *итп* change; **дать** (*perf*) **комý-н** ~**и** (*разг*) to match sb blow for blow; ~ **с 10 рублéй** change from 10 roubles.
сдáшь(ся) *сов см* **сдáть(ся)**.
сдвиг (-а) *м* (*в работе, в учёбе*) progress; (*в сознании*) change; (*у негó* ~ (*разг*) he's not all there.
сдви́н|уть (-у, -ешь; *impf* **сдвигáть**) *сов перех* (*переместить*) to move; (*сблизить*) to move together; (*заставить тронуться*) to shift
▸ **сдви́нуться** (*impf* **сдвигáться**) *сов возв*: ~**ся** (**с мéста**) to move; (*сместиться*) to shift.
сдéла|ть(ся) (-ю(сь)) *сов от* **дéлать(ся)**.
сдéл|ка (-ки; *gen pl* -ок) *ж* deal; **заключи́ть** (**заключи́ть** *perf*) ~**ку** (**с** +*instr*) to do a deal (with); **пойти́** (*perf*) **на** ~**ку с сóвестью** to do a deal with the devil.
сдéльн|ый *прил*: ~**ая рабóта** piecework.
сдéльщик (-а) *м* pieceworker.
сдéльщиц|а (-ы) *ж см* **сдéльщик**.
сдёргива|ть (-ю) *несов от* **сдёрнуть**.
сдéржанно *нареч* (*сказать, плакать итп*) with restraint; (*отнестись, принять*) with reserve.
сдéржанн|ый (-, -на, -но) *прил* (*человек*) reserved; (*чувства*) contained.
сдерж|áть (-ержý, -éржишь; *impf* **сдéрживать**) *сов перех* to contain, hold back; **сдéрживать** (~ *perf*) **себя́** to contain o.s.; **сдéрживать** (~ *perf*) **слóво/обещáние** to keep one's word/promise; **сдéрживать** (~ *perf*) **кля́тву** to honour an oath
▸ **сдержáться** (*impf* **сдéрживаться**) *сов возв* to restrain o.s.
сдёрн|уть (-у, -ешь; *impf* **сдёргивать**) *сов перех* to pull off.
сдерý *итп сов см* **содрáть**.
сдирá|ть (-ю; *perf* **содрáть**) *несов перех* (*кожуру, кору*) to peel off.
сдóб|а (-ы) *ж* (*добавки*) shortening ♦ *собир* (*булки*) buns *мн*.
сдóбный *прил* rich.
сдóхн|уть (-у, -ешь) *сов от* **дóхнуть**.
сдр|ужи́ть (-ужý, -у́жишь) *сов перех* to bring together
▸ **сдружи́ться** *сов возв* to become friends.
сдубли́р|овать (-ую) *сов от* **дубли́ровать**.
сдувá|ть (-ю) *несов см* **сдуть**.
сдýру *нареч* (*разг*) stupidly.
сдý|ть (-ю; *impf* **сдувáть**) *сов перех* to blow away; (*разг: списать*) to copy.
сдыхá|ть (-ю) *несов неперех* (*разг: человек*) to

snuff it.

сё (**сего́**) *мест* this; **то да ~** (*разг*) this and that; **ни то ни ~** (*разг*) neither one thing nor the other.

сеа́нс (**-а**) *м* (*кино*) show; (*психотерапии итп*) session.

СЕАТО *ср сокр* (= Организа́ция догово́ра Юго-Восто́чной А́зии) SEATO (= *Southeast Asia Treaty Organization*).

себе́ *мест см* **себя́** ♦ *част* (*разг*): **так ~** so-so; **ничего́ ~**! wow!; **иди́ ~, не вме́шивайся!** just stay out of it!

себесто́имост|**ь** (**-и**) *ж* cost price.

┌─────────────┐
│ **KEYWORD** │
└─────────────┘
себя́ *мест* (*я*) myself; (*ты*) yourself; (*он*) himself; (*она́*) herself; (*оно́*) itself; (*мы*) ourselves; (*вы*) yourselves; (*они́*) themselves; **он тре́бователен к себе́** he asks a lot of himself; **она́ вини́т себя́** she blames herself; **представля́ть (предста́вить** *perf*) **что-н себе́** to imagine sth; **испы́тывать (испыта́ть** *perf*) **что-н на себе́** (*лекарство*) to test sth on o.s.; (*трудности*) to experience sth; **к себе́** (*домой*) home; (*в свою комнату*) to one's room; **к себе́** (*на двери*) "pull"; **„от себя́**" (*на двери*) "push"; **по себе́** (*по своим вкусам*) to one's taste; **убира́ть (убра́ть** *perf*) **по́сле себя́** to tidy up after o.s.; **приходи́ть (прийти́** *perf*) **в себя́** to come to one's senses; **говори́ть** (*impf*)/**чита́ть** (*impf*) **про себя́** to talk/read to o.s.; **она́ себе́ на уме́** (*разг*) she is secretive; **он у себя́** (*в своём доме*) he is at home; (*в своём кабинете*) he is in the office.

себялюби́в|**ый** (**-, -а, -о**) *прил* egotistical.

себялюби|**е** (**-я**) *ср* self-love.

сев (**-а**) *м* sowing.

Севасто́пол|**ь** (**-я**) *м* Sevastopol.

се́вер (**-а**) *м* north; **С~** (*Арктика*) the Arctic North.

се́верн|**ый** *прил* north опред; (*ветер, направление*) northerly; (*климат, полушарие*) northern; **С~ Кавка́з** the Northern Caucasus; **С~ая Коре́я** North Korea; **С~ Ледови́тый океа́н** Arctic Ocean; **се́верное сия́ние** the northern lights *мн*; **Се́верный по́люс** the North Pole.

се́веро-восто́к (**-а**) *м* northeast.

се́веро-за́пад (**-а**) *м* northwest.

северя́н|**ин** (**-ина**; *nom pl* **-е**, *gen pl* **-**) *м* northerner.

северя́н|**ка** (**-ки**; *gen pl* **-ок**) *ж см* **северя́нин**.

севрю́г|**а** (**-и**) *ж* sturgeon.

сегме́нт (**-а**) *м* segment.

сего́ *мест см* **сей, сие́**.

сего́дня *нареч, сущ нескл* today; **у́тром/ днём/ве́чером** this morning/afternoon/ evening; **встре́ча назна́чена на ~** this meeting

has been set for today; **на ~ у нас ма́ло ресу́рсов** we currently have very few resources; **не ~-за́втра** any day now.

сего́дняшн|**ий** (**-яя, -ее, -ие**) *прил* today's; **~ день** today; **на ~ день** at present; **жить** (*impf*) **~им днём** to live for the present.

сегрега́ци|**я** (**-и**) *ж* segregation.

сёдел *сущ см* **седло́**.

седе́ть (**-ю**; *perf* **поседе́ть**) *несов неперех* to go grey (*BRIT*) *или* gray (*US*).

седина́ (**-ины́**; *nom pl* **-и́ны**) *ж* grey (*BRIT*) *или* gray (*US*) hair.

седла́ть (**-ю**; *perf* **оседла́ть**) *несов перех* to saddle.

седл|**о́** (**-а́**; *nom pl* **сёдла**, *gen pl* **сёдел**) *ср* saddle; **вы́шибить** (*perf*) *или* **вы́бить** (*perf*) **кого́-н из ~а́** (*перен*) to knock sb out of his *итп* stride.

седовла́с|**ый** (**-, -а, -о**) *прил* grey-haired (*BRIT*), gray-haired (*US*).

седоволо́с|**ый** (**-, -а, -о**) *прил* = **седовла́сый**.

седо́й (**-, -а́, -о**) *прил* (*волосы*) grey (*BRIT*), gray (*US*); (*человек*) grey-haired (*BRIT*), gray-haired (*US*); **~ая старина́** ancient times.

седо́к (**-а́**) *м* (*всадник*) rider; (*пассажир*) passenger.

седьм|**о́й** (**-а́я, -о́е, -ы́е**) *чис* seventh; **сейча́с ~ час** it's after six; **быть** (*impf*) **на ~о́м не́бе** to be in seventh heaven; *см также* **пя́тый**.

сезо́н (**-а**) *м* season; **~ дожде́й** the rainy season.

сезо́нник (**-а**) *м* seasonal worker.

сезо́нн|**ый** *прил* seasonal; **сезо́нный биле́т** season ticket.

сей (**сего́**; *см* **Table 12**) *мест* this; **сию́ мину́ту** *или* **секу́нду!** this minute!; **на ~ раз** on this occasion; **по ~ день** to this day; **5-го ма́я сего́ го́да** on the 5th (of) May this year; **от сих до сих** (*разг*) from here to here.

сейсми́ческ|**ий** (**-ая, -ое, -ие**) *прил* (*колебания, волны*) seismic; (*станция, прибор*) seismological.

сейсмо́лог (**-а**) *м* seismologist.

сейф (**-а**) *м* (*ящик*) safe; (*помещение*) vault.

сейча́с *нареч* (*теперь*) now; (*скоро*) just now; (*разг*: *недавно*) (only) just; **он ~ рабо́тает** he's working just now; **~ приду́** I'm just on my way; **~ же!** right now!

сёк *итп сов см* **сечь**.

СЕКА́М *м сокр* (= систе́ма цветно́го телеви́дения) SECAM (= *séquentiel couleur à mémoire*).

сека́тор (**-а**) *м* secateurs *мн*.

секре́т (**-а**) *м* secret; **по ~у** in secret; **под ~ом** confidentially; **держа́ть** (*impf*) **что-н в ~е** to keep sth a secret.

секретариа́т (**-а**) *м* secretariat.

секрета́рш|**а** (**-и**) *ж* (*разг*) secretary (*female*).

секрета́р|**ь** (**-я́**) *м* secretary; **генера́льный ~** secretary-general; **секрета́рь-машини́стка**

secretary.
секре́тен *прил см* **секре́тный**.
секрете́р (-а) *м* bureau (*BRIT*), secretaire.
секре́тнича|ть (-ю) *несов неперех*
(*скрытничать*) to be secretive;
(*разговаривать по секрету*) to talk secretively.
секре́т|ный (-ен, -на, -но) *прил* secret.
секс (-а) *м* sex.
сексопи́льность (-и) *ж* sex appeal.
сексопи́льный *прил* sexy.
сексуа́л|ьный *прил* sexual; (-ен, -ьна, -ьно;
эротичный) sexy; **сексуа́льная жизнь** sex life;
сексуа́льное образова́ние sex education.
се́кт|а (-ы) *ж* sect.
секта́нт (-а) *м* sect member.
секта́нт|ка (-ки; *gen pl* -ок) *ж см* **секта́нт**.
секта́нтск|ий (-ая, -ое, -ие) *прил* sectarian.
се́ктор (-а) *м* (*также* ЭКОН, ГЕОМ) sector;
(*здания*) section; (*учреждения*) department.
се́кторный *прил*: **се́кторная диагра́мма** pie
chart.
секу́ *итп сов см* **сечь**.
секу́нд|а (-ы) *ж* second; (**одну́**) ~**у!** just one *или*
a second!
секунда́нт (-а) *м* second (*of boxer, duellist*).
секу́ндн|ый *прил* (*пауза, заминка*) second's;
~**ая стре́лка** second hand (*on clock*).
секундоме́р (-а) *м* stopwatch.
секцио́нный *прил* divided into sections.
се́кци|я (-и) *ж* section.
сел *итп сов см* **сесть**.
селёд|ка (-ки; *gen pl* -ок) *ж* herring.
селезёнк|а (-и) *ж* spleen.
се́лез|ень (-ня) *м* drake.
селе́ктор (-а) *м* (*ТЕЛ*) intercom.
селекционе́р (-а) *м* breeder.
селе́кци|я (-и) *ж* (*БИО*) selective breeding.
селе́ни|е (-я) *ср* village.
сел|и́ть (-ю́, -ишь; *perf* **посели́ть**) *несов перех* (*в
местности*) to settle; (*в доме*) to house
▶ **сели́ться** (*perf* **посели́ться**) *несов возв* to
settle.
сел|о́ (-а́; *nom pl* сёла) *ср* (*селение*) village; (*по
pl*; *местность*) the country; **ни к** ~**у́ ни к
го́роду** (*разг*) inappropriately.
сел|ь (-я) *м* mountain torrent.
сельдере́|й (-я) *м* celery.
сельд|ь (-и; *gen pl* -е́й) *ж* herring.
сельпо́ *ср нескл* (= се́льское потреби́тельское
о́бщество) village shop.
се́льск|ий (-ая, -ое, -ие) *прил* (*см сущ*) village
опред; country *опред*, rural; **се́льское
хозя́йство** agriculture.
сельскохозя́йственный *прил* agricultural.
сельча́н|ин (-ина; *nom pl* -е, *gen pl* -) *м* villager.
сельча́н|ка (-ки; *gen pl* -ок) *ж см* **сельча́нин**.
сём *мест см* **сей**, **сиё**.
сема́нтик|а (-и) *ж* semantics.
семанти́ческ|ий (-ая, -ое, -ие) *прил* semantic.
семафо́р (-а) *м* semaphore.
сёмг|а (-и) *ж* salmon.
семе́йный *прил* family *опред*; ~ **челове́к**

family man.
семе́йственность (-и) *ж* nepotism.
семе́йств|о (-а) *ср* family.
се́мени *итп сущ см* **се́мя**.
семен|и́ть (-ю́, -и́шь) *несов неперех* to mince.
семенно́й *прил* (*для посева*) seed *опред*; (*БИО*)
sperm *опред*.
семёр|ка (-ки; *gen pl* -ок) *ж* (*цифра, карта*)
seven; (*группа из семи*) group of seven; (*разг*:
автобус, трамвай итп) (number) seven (*bus,
tram etc*).
се́мер|о (-ы́х; *как* че́тверо; *см* Table 36b) *чис*
seven; *см также* **дво́е**.
семёрок *сущ см* **семёрка**.
семе́стр (-а) *м* term (*BRIT*), semester (*US*).
се́мечк|и (-ек) *мн* (*подсолнечника*) sunflower
seeds *мн*.
се́мечк|о (-ка; *gen pl* -ек) *ср* seed; *см также*
се́мечки.
семи́ *чис см* **семь**.
семи́десяти *чис см* **се́мьдесят**.
семидесятиле́ти|е (-я) *ср* (*промежуток*)
seventy years; (*годовщина*) seventieth
anniversary.
семидесятиле́тн|ий (-яя, -ее, -ие) *прил*
seventy-year; (*человек*) seventy-year-old.
семидеся́т|ый (-ая, -ое, -ые) *чис* seventieth; *см
также* **пятидеся́тый**.
семидне́вный *прил* seven-day.
семикла́ссник (-а) *м pupil in seventh year at
school (usually 13 years old)*.
семикла́ссниц|а (-ы) *ж см* **семикла́ссник**.
семикра́тн|ый *прил*: ~ **чемпио́н** seven-times
champion; **в** ~**ом разме́ре** sevenfold.
семиле́ти|е (-я) *ср* (*срок*) seven years;
(*годовщина*) seventh anniversary.
семиле́тн|ий (-яя, -ее, -ие) *прил* seven-year;
(*ребёнок*) seven-year-old.
семиме́сячный *прил* seven-month; (*ребёнок*)
seven-month-old.
семина́р (-а) *м* seminar.
семинари́ст (-а) *м* seminarist.
семина́ри|я (-и) *ж* seminary.
семинеде́льный *прил* seven-week; (*ребёнок*)
seven-week-old.
семисо́т *чис см* **семьсо́т**.
семисотле́ти|е (-я) *ср* (*срок*) seven hundred
years *мн*; (*годовщина*) seven hundredth
anniversary.
семисотле́тн|ий (-яя, -ее, -ие) *прил* (*период*)
seven-hundred-year; (*дерево*) seven-hundred-
year-old.
семисо́т|ый (-ая, -ое, -ые) *чис* seven hundredth.
семиуго́льник (-а) *м* heptagon.
семичасово́й *прил* (*рабочий день*) seven-hour;
(*поезд*) seven o'clock.
семна́дцати *чис см* **семна́дцать**.
семна́дцат|ый (-ая, -ое, -ые) *чис* seventeenth;
см также **пя́тый**.
семна́дцат|ь (-и; *как* пять; *см* Table 27) *чис*
seventeen; *см также* **пять**.

сему́ *мест см* **сей, сие́**.

семь (-и́; *как* **пять**; *см* **Table 27**) *чис* seven; *см также* **пять**.

се́м|**ьдесят** (-идесяти; *как* **пятьдеся́т**; *см* **Table 29**) *чис* seventy; *см также* **пятьдеся́т**.

семь|**со́т** (-исо́т; *как* **пятьсо́т**; *см* **Table 34**) *чис* seven hundred; *см также* **сто**.

се́мью *нареч*: ~ **пять** *итп* seven times five *итп*.

семью *чис см* **семь**.

семь|**я́** (-и́; *nom pl* -и) *ж* family.

семьяни́н (-а) *м* family man.

се́м|**я** (-ени; *как* **вре́мя**; *см* **Table 4**) *ср* (*БОТ, также перен*) seed; (*no pl; БИО*) semen.

Се́н|**а** (-ы) *ж* Seine.

сена́т (-а) *м* senate.

сена́тор (-а) *м* senator.

Сенега́л (-а) *м* Senegal.

се́н|**и** (-ей) *мн* hall *ед*.

сенн|**о́й** *прил*: ~**а́я лихора́дка** hay fever.

се́н|**о** (-а) *м* hay.

сенова́л (-а) *м* hayloft.

сеноко́с (-а) *м* (*косьба*) haymaking; (*место*) hayfield.

сенсацио́нный *прил* sensational.

сенса́ци|**я** (-и) *ж* sensation.

сенте́нци|**я** (-и) *ж* maxim.

сентимента́л|**ьный** (-ен, -ьна, -ьно) *прил* sentimental.

сентя́брь (-я́) *м* September; *см также* **октя́брь**.

сентя́брьск|**ий** (-ая, -ое, -ие) *прил* September *опред*.

сень (-и; *prp sg* -и́) *ж* canopy; **под се́нью** +*gen* under the protection of.

сепарати́зм (-а) *м* separatism.

сепара́тный *прил* separate.

се́псис (-а) *м* septicaemia (*BRIT*), septicemia (*US*).

септи́ческ|**ий** (-ая, -ое, -ие) *прил* septic.

се́р|**а** (-ы) *ж* sulphur (*BRIT*), sulfur (*US*); (*в ушах*) earwax.

серб (-а) *м* Serb.

Се́рби|**я** (-и) *ж* Serbia.

се́рб|**ка** (-ки; *gen pl* -ок) *ж см* **серб**.

се́рбск|**ий** (-ая, -ое, -ие) *прил* Serbian.

серва́нт (-а) *м* buffet unit.

серви́з (-а) *м*: **столо́вый/ча́йный** ~ dinner/tea service.

сервиро́вать (-у́ю) (*не*)*сов перех*: ~ **стол** to set *или* lay the table.

се́рвис (-а) *м* service (*in shop, restaurant etc*).

серде́ц *итп сущ см* **се́рдце**.

серде́чен *прил см* **серде́чный**.

серде́чник (-а) *м* (*ТЕХ*) core; (*разг*): **он** ~ he's got a bad heart.

серде́чниц|**а** (-ы) *ж* (*разг*) *см* **серде́чник**.

серде́чный *прил* heart *опред*, cardiac; (*любовный*) loving; (*волнения, обида*) deep-felt; (-ен, -на, -но; *человек*) warm-hearted; (*приём, разговор*) cordial; ~**ная тоска́**

---

heartache; **серде́чная боле́знь** heart disease; **серде́чный при́ступ** acute angina.

серди́т|**ый** (-, -а, -о) *прил* angry.

серди́ть (-жу́, -дишь; *perf* **рассерди́ть**) *несов перех* to anger, make angry

▶ **серди́ться** (*perf* **рассерди́ться**) *несов возв*: ~**ся (на кого́-н/что-н)** to be angry (with sb/about sth).

сердобо́л|**ьный** (-ен, -ьна, -ьно) *прил* soft-hearted.

сердоли́к (-а) *м* carnelian.

се́рдц|**е** (-а; *nom pl* -а́, *gen pl* -е́ц, *dat pl* -а́м) *ср* (*также перен*) heart; **в сердца́х** in a fit of temper; **в глубине́** ~**а** in one's heart of hearts; **от всего́** ~**а** from the bottom of one's heart; **принима́ть** (**приня́ть** *perf*) **что-н бли́зко к** ~**цу** to take sth to heart; **он мне по́ сердцу** he's a man after my own heart; **у него́** ~ **не лежи́т к э́той рабо́те** his heart isn't in the work.

сердцебие́ни|**е** (-я) *ср* (*нормальное*) heartbeat; (*учащённое*) palpitations *мн*.

сердцеви́н|**а** (-ы) *ж* (*стебля, плода*) core; (*перен: событий*) heart.

серебри́ст|**ый** (-, -а, -о) *прил* silver(-coloured (*BRIT*) *или* -colored (*US*)); (*перен: голос, смех*) silvery.

серебри́ть (-ю́, -и́шь; *perf* **посеребри́ть**) *несов перех* (*покрыть серебром*) to silver-plate; (*перен*) to turn silver.

серебр|**о́** (-а́) *ср, собир* silver.

серебряни́к (-а) *м* silversmith.

сере́бряный *прил* silver; **сере́бряная сва́дьба** silver wedding (anniversary).

серёг *сущ см* **серьга́**.

середи́н|**а** (-ы) *ж* middle; **в** ~**е** +*gen* in the middle of.

середи́нный *прил* middle-of-the-road.

серёдка (-и) *ж* (*разг*) middle.

серёж|**ка** (-ки; *gen pl* -ек) *ж уменьш от* **серьга́**; (*БОТ*) catkin.

серена́д|**а** (-ы) *ж* serenade.

сере́ть (-ю; *perf* **посере́ть**) *несов неперех* to turn grey (*BRIT*) *или* gray (*US*); (*no perf; цветы*) to show grey.

сержа́нт (-а) *м* sergeant.

сержу́(сь) *несов см* **серди́ть(ся)**.

сери́йн|**ый** *прил*: ~**ое произво́дство** serial production; **сери́йный но́мер** serial number.

се́ри|**я** (-и) *ж* series *ед*; (*кинофильма*) part.

се́рн|**а** (-ы) *ж* chamois.

се́рн|**ый** *прил*: ~**ая кислота́** sulphuric (*BRIT*) *или* sulfuric (*US*) acid.

серп (-а́) *м* sickle; **лу́нный** ~ crescent moon.

серпанти́н (-а) *м* (*бумажная лента*) streamer; (*дорога*) sharply winding road (*in the mountains*).

сертифика́т (-а) *м* certificate; (*товара*) guarantee (certificate).

The spelling rules for Russian are shown on page xvii.

се́р|ый *прил* grey (*BRIT*), gray (*US*); (-, -á, -o; *перен: погода, жизнь*) grey, drab; (*разг: малообразованный*) dim; **се́рый хлеб** brown bread.

сер|ьга́ (-ьги́; *nom pl* -ьги, *gen pl* -ёг, *dat pl* -ьга́м) ж earring.

серьёзен *прил см* серьёзный.

серьёзно *нареч, вводн сл* seriously; ~, **ты согла́сен?** do you really agree?

серьёзност|ь (-и) ж seriousness.

серьёз|ный (-ен, -на, -но) *прил* serious.

се́сси|я (-и) ж (*суда, парламента*) session; (*также: экзаменацио́нная* ~) examinations *мн*.

сестр|а́ (-ы́; *nom pl* сёстры, *gen pl* сестёр) ж sister; (*также: медици́нская* ~) nurse.

сесть (ся́ду, ся́дешь; *pt* сел, се́ла, се́ло, *impf* сади́ться) *сов неперех* to sit down; (*птица, самолёт*) to land; (*солнце, луна*) to go down; (*одежда*) to shrink; (*батаре́йка, аккумуля́тор*) to run down; сади́ться (~ *perf*) **в по́езд/на самолёт** to get on a train/plane; сади́ться (~ *perf*) **за руль** to get behind the wheel; сади́ться (~ *perf*) **за рабо́ту** to sit down to work; сади́ться (~ *perf*) **в тюрьму́** to go to prison; сади́ться (~ *perf*) **под аре́ст** to be placed under arrest; сади́ться (~ *perf*) **за стол** to sit down at the table.

сет (-а) м (*ТЕННИС итп*) set.

се́т|ка (-ки; *gen pl* -ок) ж net; (*разг: сумка*) string bag; **тари́фная** ~ scale of charges.

се́тование (-я) *ср* (*обычно мн*) complaint.

се́т|овать (-ую; *perf* посе́товать) *несов неперех:* ~ **на** +*acc* to complain about.

се́ток *сущ см* се́тка.

сет|ь (-и; *prp sg* -й, *gen pl* -е́й) ж (*для ло́вли рыб итп*) net; (*система, также КОМП*) network; **расставля́ть (расста́вить** *perf***) кому́-н се́ти** to set a trap for sb.

Сеу́л (-а) м Seoul.

сече́ни|е (-я) *ср* (*поперечное, продольное итп*) section; **ке́сарево** ~ Caesarean (*BRIT*) *или* Cesarean (*US*) (section).

се́ч|ка (-и) ж (*крупа*) chaff.

сечь (секу́, сечёшь итп, секу́т; *pt* сёк, секла́, секло́) *несов перех* (*рубить*) to cut up; (*perf* **вы́сечь;** *розгами итп*) to lash, flog.

се́ялк|а (-ки; *gen pl* -ок) ж seed drill.

се́|ять (-ю; *perf* посе́ять) *несов перех (также перен*) to sow ♦ *неперех* (*no perf*): ~**ет дождь** it's drizzling; ~ (**посе́ять** *perf*) **зна́ния/зло** to sow the seeds of knowledge/evil.

СЖ м *сокр* (= *Сою́з журнали́стов*) ≈ NUJ (= National Union of Journalists).

сжа́л|иться (-юсь, ишься) *сов возв:* ~ (**над** +*instr*) to have *или* take pity (on).

сжа́ти|е (-я) *ср* (*воздуха, газа*) compression; (*в груди, в го́рле*) constriction; (*се́рдца*) contraction.

сжа́т|ый (-, -а, -о) *прил* (*воздух, газ*) compressed; (*кра́ткий*) condensed; **в** ~**ые сро́ки** in a short space of time.

сжать (сожну́, сожнёшь) *сов от* жать ♦ (**сожму́, сожмёшь,** *impf* сжима́ть) *перех* to squeeze; (*воздух, газ*) to compress; (*текст, статью́*) to condense; (*срок*) to reduce; сжима́ть (~ *perf*) **зу́бы** to grit one's teeth; сжима́ть (~ *perf*) **гу́бы** to purse one's lips

► сжа́ться (*impf* сжима́ться) *сов возв* (*пружина, гу́бка, воздух*) to contract; (*человек: от бо́ли, испу́га*) to tense up; (*перен: се́рдце*) to seize up.

сжечь (сожгу́, сожжёшь итп, сожгу́т; *pt* сжёг, сожгла́, сожгло́, *impf* сжига́ть *или* жечь) *сов перех* to burn; (*impf* сжига́ть; *перен: подлеж: страсть, жела́ние*) to consume; (: *со́лнце*) to scorch; **его́ сжига́ла за́висть** he was consumed with envy; ~ (*perf*) **свои́ корабли́** *или* **за собо́й мосты́** to burn one's boats *или* bridges.

сжива́|ть(ся) (-ю(сь)) *несов от* сжи́ть(ся).

сживу́(сь) итп *сов см* сжи́ть(ся).

сжига́|ть (-ю) *несов от* сжечь.

сжима́|ть(ся) (-ю(сь)) *несов от* сжать(ся).

сжи|ть (-ву́, -вёшь; *pt* -л, -ла́, -ло, *impf* сжива́ть) *сов перех:* ~ **кого́-н со све́та** *или* **све́ту** to drive sb to his итп grave.

сжи́|ться (-ву́сь, -вёшься; *pt* -лся, -ла́сь, -лось, *impf* сжива́ться) *сов возв:* ~ **с** +*instr* to become close to; (*привы́кнуть*) to grow used to; ~ (*perf*) **с ро́лью** to get inside a role.

сжу́льнича|ть (-ю) *сов от* жу́льничать.

сза́ди *нареч* (*подойти́*) from behind; (*находи́ться*) behind ♦ *предл* (+*gen*) behind.

сзыва́|ть (-ю) *несов от* созва́ть.

си *ср нескл* (*МУЗ*) te.

сиби́рск|ий (-ая, -ое, -ие) *прил* Siberian.

Сиби́р|ь (-и) ж Siberia.

сибиря́к (-а́) м Siberian.

сибиря́чк|а (-ки; *gen pl* -ек) ж см сибиря́к.

си́вый *прил* (*масть ло́шади*) grey (*BRIT*), gray (*US*).

сига́р|а (-ы) ж cigar.

сигаре́т|а (-ы) ж cigarette.

сигна́л (-а) м signal; (*АВТ*) horn.

сигнализа́тор (-а) м signalling device.

сигнализа́ци|я (-и) ж (*действие*) signalling; (*система*) signalling system; (*в кварти́ре*) burglar alarm; **пожа́рная/автомоби́льная** ~ fire/car alarm.

сигнализи́р|овать (-ую) *perf* сигнализи́ровать *или* просигнализи́ровать) *несов неперех:* ~ (**о** +*prp*) to signal.

сигна́л|ить (-ю, -ишь; *perf* просигна́лить) *несов неперех* (*флажка́ми, фара́ми*) to signal; (*АВТ*) to honk.

сигна́льный *прил* signal *опред*; **сигна́льный экземпля́р** proof copy; **сигна́льная бу́дка** signal box; **сигна́льные огни́** (*АВТ*) indicators.

СИД м *сокр* (= *светоизлуча́ющий дио́д*) LED (= light-emitting diode).

сиде́л|ка (-ки; *gen pl* -ок) ж (sick) nurse.

сиде́ни|е (-я) *ср* sitting.

сиде́нь|е (-я) *ср* seat.

сиде́ть (-жу́, -ди́шь) *несов неперех* to sit; (*не*

работать, отдыхать) to sit around; (*одежда*) to fit; ~ (*impf*) **до́ма** to stay at home; ~ (*impf*) **в тюрьме́** to be in prison; ~ (*impf*) **с ребёнком** to look after a child; ~ (*impf*) **без де́нег/де́ла** to have no money/nothing to do; **он ~де́л за кни́гой/рабо́той** he was sitting reading a book/ doing his work; ~ (*impf*) **на телефо́не** (*разг*) to spend ages on the phone

▸ **сиде́ться** *безл*: **ему́ не ~дится на ме́сте/до́ма** he can't keep still/bear sitting at home.

Сидне́й (-я) *м* Sydney.

си́дя *нареч*: **рабо́тать/есть** ~ to work/eat sitting down.

сидя́ч|ий (-ая, -ее, -ие) *прил* (*положение*) sitting *опред*; (*образ жизни*) sedentary; **сидя́чая забасто́вка** sit-down strike; **сидя́чие места́** (*разг*) seats *мн*.

сие́ *мест см* **сей**.

сижу́ *несов см* **сиде́ть**.

СИЗО *сокр* = **сле́дственный изоля́тор**.

си́з|ый (-, -а́, -о) *прил* blue-grey (*BRIT*), blue-gray (*US*).

сий *мест см* **сей**.

си́л|а (-ы) *ж* strength; (*тока, ветра, закона*) force; (*воли, слова*) power; (*обычно мн: душевные, творческие*) energy; **в ~у того́, что ...** owing to the fact that ...; **и́зо всей ~ы** *или* **всех сил** as hard as one can; **от ~ы** (*разг*) at (the) most; **э́то зада́ние ему́ по ~м** *или* **под си́лу** he is capable of (doing) this task; **я не в ~х э́то сде́лать** I'm not able to do that; **он всё де́лает че́рез ~у** it's an effort for him to do anything; **он ест че́рез ~у** he's forcing himself to eat; **вступа́ть (вступи́ть** *perf*) *или* **входи́ть (войти́** *perf*) **в ~у** to come into *или* take effect; **теря́ть (потеря́ть** *perf*) *или* **утра́чивать (утра́тить** *perf*) **~у** to cease to be effective; **всё остаётся в ~е** everything will stay as it is; **применя́ть (примени́ть** *perf*) **~у** to use force; *см также* **си́лы**.

сила́ч (-а́) *м* strong man (*мн* men).

силён *прил см* **си́льный**.

си́л|иться (-юсь, -ишься) *несов возв*: ~ +*infin* to make an effort to do.

силово́й *прил* power *опред*; **силова́я борьба́** wrestling; **силово́й приём** throw (*in martial arts*).

си́лой *нареч* by force.

си́лос (-а) *м* silage.

силуэ́т (-а) *м* (*контур*) silhouette; (*одежды*) outline.

си́л|ы (-) *мн* forces *мн*; ~**ами кого́-н** with the help of; **свои́ми ~ами** by o.s.; **производи́тельные ~** production force; **си́лы бы́строго реаги́рования** quick-deployment forces.

си́льно *нареч* strongly; (*ударить*) hard;

(*хотеть, понравиться итп*) very much.

сильноде́йствующ|ий (-ая, -ее, -ие) *прил* (*лекарство, яд*) powerful.

си́л|ьный (-ён, -ьна́, -ьно) *прил* strong; (*мороз*) hard; (*впечатление, желание*) powerful; (*шум*) loud; (*дождь*) heavy.

сим *мест см* **сей, сие́, сий**.

си́мвол (-а) *м* symbol; (*КОМП*) character.

символизи́р|овать (-ую) *несов перех* to symbolize.

символи́зм (-а) *м* (*ИСКУССТВО*) symbolism.

символ|ика (-и) *ж* (*символическое значение*) symbolism ♦ *собир* (*военная, морская итп*) symbols *мн*.

символи́ческий (-ая, -ое, -ие) *прил* symbolic.

си́ми *мест см* **сий**.

симметри́ческий (-ая, -ое, -ие) *прил* symmetrical.

симметри́чный *прил* = **симметри́ческий**.

симметри́|я (-и) *ж* symmetry.

симпатизи́р|овать (-ую) *несов неперех*: ~ **кому́-н** to like *или* be fond of sb.

симпати́чный (-ен, -на, -но) *прил* nice, pleasant.

симпа́ти|я (-и) *ж* liking, fondness.

симпо́зиум (-а) *м* symposium.

симпто́м (-а) *м* symptom.

симптомати́чный (-ен, -на, -но) *прил* symptomatic.

симули́р|овать (-ую) (*не)сов перех* (*нападение*) to simulate; (*болезнь*) to fake.

симфони́ческий (-ая, -ое, -ие) *прил* symphonic; **симфони́ческий орке́стр** symphony orchestra.

симфо́ни|я (-и) *ж* (*МУЗ*) symphony.

синаго́г|а (-и) *ж* synagogue.

Сингапу́р (-а) *м* Singapore.

синдика́т (-а) *м* (*ЭКОН*) syndicate.

синдро́м (-а) *м* (*МЕД*) syndrome.

синев|а́ (-ы́) *ж* (*синий цвет*) blue; (*моря, неба*) blueness.

сине́|ть (-ю; *perf* **посине́ть**) *несов неперех* to turn blue; (*no perf*; *виднеться*) to show blue.

си́н|ий (-яя, -ее, -ие) *прил* blue; **си́ний чуло́к** bluestocking.

син|и́ть (-ю́, -и́шь; *perf* **посини́ть**) *несов перех* (*красить*) to paint blue.

сини́ц|а (-ы) *ж* tit.

синкрети́зм (-а) *м* syncretism.

сино́д (-а) *м* synod.

сино́ним (-а) *м* synonym.

синоними́ческий (-ая, -ое, -ие) *прил* synonymous.

синоними́|я (-и) *ж* synonimity.

сино́птик (-а) *м* weather forecaster.

си́нтаксис (-а) *м* syntax.

синтакси́ческий (-ая, -ое, -ие) *прил* syntactic; ~**ая оши́бка** (*КОМП*) syntax error.

си́нтез (-а) *м* (*также хим*) synthesis (*мн* syntheses).

синтези́р|овать (-ую) (*не*)*сов перех* (*также хим*) to synthesize.

синтети́к|а (-и) *ж собир* (*материалы*) synthetic material; (*изделия*) synthetics *мн*.

синтети́ческ|ий (-ая, -ое, -ие) *прил* (*материал*) synthetic.

синхро́нн|ый *прил* (*движение*) synchronous; (*перевод*) simultaneous; **~ое пла́вание** synchronized swimming.

синь (-и) *ж* = **синева́**.

си́ньк|а (-и) *ж* blue.

синя́к (-á) *м* bruise.

сиони́зм (-а) *м* Zionism.

сиони́ст (-а) *м* Zionist.

сип|е́ть (-лю́, -и́шь) *несов неперех* to croak.

си́пл|ый (-, -á, -о) *прил* hoarse.

сиплю *несов см* **сипе́ть**.

сипн|у́ть (-у, -ешь; *perf* **оси́пнуть**) *несов неперех* to grow hoarse.

сире́н|а (-ы) *ж* (*гудок*) siren.

сире́невый *прил* lilac.

сире́нь (-и) *ж* (*кустарник*) lilac bush ♦ *собир* (*цветы*) lilac.

сири́ек *сущ см* **сири́йка**.

сири́|ец (-йца) *м* Syrian.

сири́йка (-йки; *gen pl* -ек) *ж см* **сири́ец**.

сири́йск|ий (-ая, -ое, -ие) *прил* Syrian.

сири́йца *итп сущ см* **сири́ец**.

Си́ри|я (-и) *ж* Syria.

сиро́п (-а) *м* syrup.

сирот|а́ (-оты́; *nom pl* -о́ты) *м/ж* orphan.

сироте́|ть (-ю; *perf* **осироте́ть**) *несов неперех* to be orphaned.

сиротли́в|ый (-, -а, -о) *прил* sad and lonely.

систе́м|а (-ы) *ж* system; (*конструкция*) make; **приводи́ть (привести́** *perf*) **в ~у** to put into order.

систематизи́р|овать (-ую) (*не*)*сов перех* to order.

системати́ческ|ий (-ая, -ое, -ие) *прил* following a defined system; (*регулярный*) regular.

системати́чный *прил* = **системати́ческий**.

систе́мн|ый *прил* relating to or based on a system; **систе́мный ана́лиз** systems analysis; **систе́мный диск** (*КОМП*) system disk.

си́т|ец (-ца) *м* cotton.

си́течк|о (-а; *gen pl* -ек) *ср уменьш от* **си́то**; (*для чая*) (tea) strainer.

си́т|о (-а) *ср* sieve.

ситро́ *ср нескл* soft drink.

ситуа́ци|я (-и) *ж* situation.

си́тца *итп сущ см* **си́тец**.

си́тцевый *прил* (*ткань*) cotton.

СИФ *м сокр* c.i.f. (= cost, insurance, freight).

си́филис (-а) *м* syphilis.

сифо́н (-а) *м* siphon.

сих *мест см* **сий**.

сицилиа́нск|ий (-ая, -ое, -ие) *прил* Sicilian.

Сици́ли|я (-и) *ж* Sicily.

сию́ *мест см* **сия́**.

сиюмину́т|ный (-ен, -на, -но) *прил* immediate.

сия́ *мест см* **сей**.

сия́ни|е (-я) *ср* (*солнца, луны, глаз*) shining; (*лица*) radiance; (*славы, успеха*) dazzle; **се́верное ~** the Northern lights *мн*.

сия́|ть (-ю) *несов неперех* (*солнце, звезда*) to shine; (*огонь*) to glow; **~** (*impf*) **от сча́стья** to beam with happiness; **ко́мната ~ла чистото́й** the room was spotlessly clean; **же́нщина ~ла красото́й** the woman was dazzlingly beautiful.

сия́ющий (-ая, -ее, -ие) *прил* (*глаза*) shining; (*лицо, улыбка*) beaming; (*человек*) radiant.

СК *м сокр* (= Сою́з компози́торов) ≈ MU (= Musicians' Union).

скажу́(сь) *итп сов см* **сказа́ть(ся)**.

сказа́ни|е (-я) *ср* legend.

ск|аза́ть (-ажу́, -а́жешь) *сов от* **говори́ть** ♦ *перех*; **~а́жем** (*разг*) let's say; **~а́жите!** (*разг*) I say!; **как ~** (*разг*) how shall I put it; **кста́ти ~** by the way; **не́чего ~** (*разг: действительно*) indeed; **~а́жите пожа́луйста** could you please tell me; **~а́жите пожа́луйста!** well I never!; **так ~** so to speak

▶ **сказа́ться** (*impf* **ска́зываться**) *сов возв* (*способности, опыт итп*) to show; (*отразиться*): **~ся на** +*prp* to take its toll on; **ска́зываться** (**~ся** *perf*) +*instr* (*родственником, журналистом*) to pose as; **ска́зываться** (**~ся** *perf*) **больны́м** to pretend to be ill (*BRIT*) *или* sick (*US*).

ска́зк|а (-ки; *gen pl* -ок) *ж* fairy tale *или* story.

ска́зочен *прил см* **ска́зочный**.

ска́зочник (-а) *м* story teller.

ска́зочниц|а (-ы) *ж см* **ска́зочник**.

ска́зочн|ый *прил* fairy-tale; (-ен, -на, -но; *перен: необычайный*) fantastic.

сказу́ем|ое (-ого; *decl like adj*) *ср* (*линг*) predicate.

ска́зыва|ться (-юсь) *несов от* **сказа́ться**.

скак *м*: **на (всём) ~у́** at top speed.

скака́лк|а (-ки; *gen pl* -ок) *ж* skipping rope.

ск|ака́ть (-ачу́, -а́чешь) *несов неперех* (*человек*) to skip; (*животное*) to hop; (*мяч*) to bounce; (*разг: температура, цены итп*) to rise and fall; (*лошадь, всадник*) to gallop.

скакн|у́ть (-у́, -ёшь) *сов неперех* to leap.

скаков|о́й *прил*: **~а́я ло́шадь** racehorse; **скаковы́е соревнова́ния** race meeting.

скаку́н (-á) *м* racehorse.

скал|а́ (-алы́; *nom pl* -а́лы) *ж* cliff.

скаламбу́р|ить (-ю, -ишь) *сов от* **каламбу́рить**.

скали́ст|ый *прил* rocky; **С~ые го́ры** the Rocky Mountains *или* Rockies.

ск|а́лить (-ю, -ишь; *perf* **оска́лить**) *несов перех*: **~ зу́бы** to bare one's teeth

▶ **ска́литься** (*perf* **оска́литься**) *несов возв* to bare one's teeth.

ска́лк|а (-ки; *gen pl* -ок) *ж* (*кулин*) rolling-pin.

скалола́з (-а) *м* rock-climber.

скалола́зани|е (-я) *ср* rock-climbing.
ска́лыва|ть (-ю) *несов от* сколо́ть.
скалькѝр|овать (-ую) *сов от* кальки́ровать.
ска́льпел|ь (-я) *м* scalpel.
скаме́йка (-йки; *gen pl* -ек) *ж* bench.
скам|ья́ (-ьи́; *gen pl* -е́й) *ж* (*для сидения*) bench; ~ **подсуди́мых** (*ЮР*) the dock; **сесть** (*perf*) **на** ~**ью́ подсуди́мых** to stand trial; **со шко́льной/студе́нческой** ~**ьи́** from one's school/student days.
сканда́л (-а) *м* (*политический*) scandal; (*ссора*) quarrel.
сканда́лен *прил см* сканда́льный.
скандализи́р|овать (-ую) (*не*)*сов перех* to scandalize.
скандали́ст (-а) *м* troublemaker.
скандали́ст|ка (-ки; *gen pl* -ок) *ж см* скандали́ст.
сканда́л|ить (-ю, -ишь; *perf* наскáнда́лить) *несов неперех* to quarrel.
сканда́л|ьный (-ен, -ьна, -ьно) *прил* (*история, поступок*) scandalous; (*no short form*; *человек*) quarrelsome.
скандѝр|овать (-ую) (*не*)*сов перех* (*подлеж: толпа итп*) to chant.
ска́нер (-а) *м* scanner.
ска́плива|ть(ся) (-ю(сь)) *несов от* скопи́ть(ся).
скарб (-а) *м собир* (*разг: вещи*) stuff.
ска́ред|ный (-ен, -на, -но) *прил* (*разг*) mingy.
скарлати́н|а (-ы) *ж* scarlet fever.
ска́рмлива|ть (-ю) *несов от* скорми́ть.
скат (-а) *м* slope; (*АВТ: колесо*) wheel; (*ось*) axle.
ската́|ть (-ю) *сов от* ката́ть ◆ (*impf* ска́тывать) *перех* to roll up.
ска́терт|ь (-и; *gen pl* -е́й) *ж* tablecloth; ~**ю доро́га** (*разг*) good riddance.
скати́|ть (-ачу́, -а́тишь; *impf* ска́тывать) *сов перех* to roll down
▶ **скати́|ться** (*impf* ска́тываться) *сов возв* (*слеза*) to roll down; (*перен*): ~**ся к** +*dat*/**на** +*acc* to slide towards/into; ~**ся** (*perf*) **на лы́жах/на саня́х** to ski/sledge down.
ска́тыва|ть (-ю) *несов от* ската́ть, скати́ть
▶ **ска́тываться** *несов от* скати́ться.
скафа́ндр (-а) *м* (*водолаза*) diving suit; (*космонавта*) spacesuit.
ска́чек *итп сущ см* ска́чки.
ска́чк|а (-и) *ж* galloping.
скачка́ *итп сущ см* скачо́к.
ска́чк|и (-ек) *мн* the races *мн*.
скачо́к (-ка́) *м* leap.
скачу́(сь) *сов см* скати́ть(ся).
скачу́ *итп несов см* скака́ть.
ска́шива|ть (-ю) *несов от* скоси́ть.
скв *ж сокр* (= свобо́дно конверти́руемая валю́та) convertible currency.
сква́жин|а (-ы) *ж* (*нефтяная, газовая*) well;

замо́чная ~ keyhole; **бурова́я** ~ borehole.
сквер (-а) *м small public garden*.
скве́р|ен *прил см* скве́рный.
сквернослов|ие (-я) *ср* foul language.
скверносло́в|ить (-лю, -ишь) *несов неперех* to use foul language.
скве́р|ный (-ен, -на́, -но) *прил* foul; (*история, поступок*) nasty.
сквита́|ться (-юсь) *сов возв*: ~ (**с** +*instr*) (*отомстить*) to get even (with); (*рассчитаться*) to pay in full.
сквоз|и́ть (*3sg* -и́т, *3pl* -я́т) *несов неперех* (*чувство*) to show ◆ *безл*: **здесь** ~**и́т** it's draughty here.
сквозн|о́й *прил* (*поезд*) through *опред*; **он получи́л** ~**у́ю ра́ну** the bullet has gone right through him; ~ **ве́тер** crosswinds *мн*.
сквозня́к (-а́) *м* (*в комнате*) draught (*BRIT*), draft (*US*).
сквозь *предл* (+*acc*) through; **я слы́шал что́-то** ~ **сон** I heard something in my sleep.
скворе́ц (-ца́) *м* starling.
скворе́чник (-а) *м* nesting box.
скворца́ *итп сущ см* скворе́ц.
скеле́т (-а) *м* (*также перен*) skeleton.
ске́псис (-а) *м* scepticism.
ске́птик (-а) *м* sceptic.
скептици́зм (-а) *м* scepticism.
скепти́ческ|ий (-ая, -ое, -ие) *прил* sceptical.
ски́дк|а (-ки; *gen pl* -ок) *ж* (*с цены*) discount, reduction; **де́лать** (**сде́лать** *perf*) ~**ку на что-н** to make an allowance for sth; **со** ~**кой на что-н** taking sth into account; **нало́говая** ~ tax allowance.
ски́н|уть (-у, -ешь; *impf* ски́дывать) *сов перех* (*сбросить*) to throw down; (: *одежду, одеяло*) to throw off; (*разг: с цены*) to knock off
▶ **ски́нуться** *сов возв* (*разг*) to have a whip-round.
ски́петр (-а) *м* sceptre (*BRIT*), scepter (*US*).
скирд|а́ (-ы́) *ж* stack.
ски́с|нуть (-ну, -нешь; *pt* -, -ла, -ло) *сов от* ки́снуть ◆ (*impf* скиса́ть) *неперех* to turn sour; (*перен: разг*) to lose interest.
скита́л|ец (-ьца) *м* wanderer.
скита́ни|е (-я) *ср* wandering.
скита́|ться (-юсь) *несов возв* to wander.
склад (-а) *м* (*помещение: товарный*) store; (*жизни*) way; (*оружия итп*) cache; ~ **ума́** mentality; ~ **боеприпа́сов** ammunition dump.
скла́ден *прил см* скла́дный.
склади́р|овать (-ую) (*не*)*сов перех* to store.
скла́д|ка (-ки; *gen pl* -ок) *ж* (*на одежде*) pleat; (*на лице*) furrow; (*на ткани*) crease; **ю́бка в** ~**ку** *или* **со** ~**ми** pleated skirt.
складно́й *прил* folding.
скла́д|ный (-ен, -на, -но) *прил* (*статный*) well-built; (*связный*) coherent.

скла́док *сущ см* **скла́дка.**

складско́й *прил* storage *опред.*

скла́дчин|а (-ы) *ж* (*сбор*) pool; **купи́ть** (*perf*) **что-н в ~у** to pool together to buy sth.

скла́дывани|е (-я) *ср* (*действие: предметов*) stacking; (*чисел*) addition.

скла́дыва|ть(ся) (-ю(сь)) *несов от* **сложи́ть(ся).**

скле́|ить (-ю, -ишь) *сов от* **кле́ить** ◆ (*impf* **скле́ивать**) *перех* to glue together.

склеп (-а) *м* crypt.

склепа́|ть (-ю) *сов от* **клепа́ть.**

склеро́з (-а) *м* (*сосудов, лёгких*) sclerosis; **~ мо́зга** senility.

склеро́зный *прил* sclerotic.

склеро́тик (-а) *м* sclerotic.

склероти́ческ|ий (-ая, -ое, -ие) *прил* = **склеро́зный.**

склóк|а (-и) *ж* squabble.

склон (-а) *м* slope; **на скло́не лет** *или* **жи́зни** *или* **дней** in one's later life.

скло́нен *прил см* **скло́нный.**

склоне́ни|е (-я) *ср* (*линг*) declension.

скл|они́ть (-оню́, -о́нишь; *impf* **склоня́ть**) *сов перех* (*опустить*) to lower; **склоня́ть** (**~** *perf*) **кого́-н к побе́гу/на преступле́ние** to talk sb into escaping/committing a crime; **я ~они́л её на свою́ сто́рону** I talked her over to my side

▸ **склони́ться** (*impf* **склоня́ться**) *сов возв* (*нагнуться*) to bend; (*перен*): **~ся к** +*dat* to come round to.

скло́нност|ь (-и) *ж*: **~ к** +*dat* (*к музыке, к математике*) aptitude for; (*к меланхолии, к полноте*) tendency to.

скло́н|ный (-ен, -на́, -но) *прил*: **~ к** +*dat* (*к простуде*) prone *или* susceptible to; **~** +*infin* (*согласиться, помириться*) inclined to do; **он ~ен к фи́зике** he has an aptitude for physics.

склоня́емый *прил* declinable.

склоня́|ть (-ю) *несов от* **склони́ть** ◆ (*perf* **просклоня́ть**) *перех* (*линг*) to decline; **~** (*impf*) **кого́-н** to talk about sb a lot

▸ **склоня́ться** *несов от* **склони́ться** ◆ *возв* (*линг*) to decline.

скло́чен *прил см* **скло́чный.**

скло́чник (-а) *м* (*разг*) quarrelsome man (*мн* men).

скло́чниц|а (-ы) *ж* (*разг*) quarrelsome woman (*мн* women).

скло́ч|ный (-ен, -на, -но) *прил* quarrelsome.

скля́н|ка (-ки; *gen pl* -ок) *ж* (*разг: сосуд*) bottle.

ск|оба́ (-обы́; *nom pl* -о́бы) *ж* (*для опоры, для держания*) clamp; (*для крепления*) staple.

скоб|ка (-ки; *gen pl* -ок) *ж уменьш от* **скоба́**; (*обычно мн: знак*) bracket, parentheses *мн*; **кру́глые/квадра́тные ~ки** round/square brackets; **брать** (**взять** *perf*) **сло́во в ~ки** to put a word in brackets *или* parentheses.

скобл|и́ть (-ю́, -и́шь) *несов перех* to scrape.

скобо́к *сущ см* **скобка.**

ско́ван|ный (-, -на, -но) *прил* (*человек, движения*) inhibited.

ск|ова́ть (-ую́) *сов от* **кова́ть** ◆ (*impf* **ско́вывать**) *перех* (*соединить*) to weld together; **страх ~ова́л его́** he was paralysed with fear; **лёд ~ова́л ре́ку** the river froze over.

сковорода́ (-ы́; *nom pl* **ско́вороды**) *ж* frying-pan (*BRIT*), skillet (*US*).

сковоро́д|ка (-ки; *gen pl* -ок) *ж* = **сковорода́.**

ско́выва|ть (-ю) *несов от* **скова́ть.**

скол|оти́ть (-очу́, -о́тишь; *impf* **скола́чивать**) *сов перех* to hammer together; (*разг: банду, капитал*) to get together.

скол|о́ть (-олю́, -о́лешь; *impf* **ска́лывать**) *сов перех* (*снять*) to chop off; (*соединить*) to pin together.

сколочу́ *сов см* **сколоти́ть.**

сколь *нареч* (*как*) how; (*возможно*) as much as; **~ ... столь (же)** ... as much ... as ....

скольз|и́ть (-жу́, -зи́шь) *несов неперех* to glide; (*теряя устойчивость*) to slide.

ско́льз|кий (-кая, -кое, -кие; -ок, -ка, -ко) *прил* slippery; (*ситуация, тема*) tricky; (*вопрос*) sensitive.

скользн|у́ть (-у́, -ёшь) *сов неперех* to glide; (*быстро пройти*) to slip.

ско́льзок *прил см* **ско́льзкий.**

скользя́щ|ий (-ая, -ее, -ие) *прил* (*шаг*) gliding; (*непостоянный*) flexible.

KEYWORD

ско́льк|о (-их) *местоименное нареч* **1** (+*gen*; *книг, часов, дней итп*) how many; (*сахара, сил, работы итп*) how much; **ско́лько люде́й пришло́?** how many people came?; **ско́лько де́нег тебе́ на́до?** how much money do you need?; **ско́лько э́то сто́ит?** how much is it?; **ско́лько тебе́ лет?** how old are you? **2** (*относительно*) as much; **бери́, ско́лько хо́чешь** take as much as you want; **ско́лько уго́дно** as much as you like

◆ *нареч* **1** (*насколько*) as far as; **ско́лько по́мню, он всегда́ был агресси́вный** as far as I remember, he was always aggressive **2** (*много*): **ско́лько люде́й!** what a lot of people!; **ско́лько вре́мени он отня́л у нас!** what a long time he has kept us!; **не сто́лько ... ско́лько** ... not so much ... as ....

скома́нд|овать (-ую) *сов от* **кома́ндовать.**

скомбини́р|овать (-ую) *сов от* **комбини́ровать.**

скомка|ть (-ю) *сов от* **ко́мкать.**

скоморо́х (-а) *м* (*комедиант*) mummer; (*перен*) buffoon.

скомпили́р|овать (-ую) *сов от* **компили́ровать.**

скомплект|ова́ть (-у́ю) *сов от* **комплектова́ть.**

скомпон|ова́ть (-у́ю) *сов от* **компонова́ть.**

скомпромети́р|овать (-ую) *сов от* **компромети́ровать.**

сконструи́р|овать (-ую) *сов от*

конструи́ровать.

сконфу́зить(ся) (-жу(сь), -зишь(ся)) *сов от* конфу́зить(ся).

сконцентри́р|овать(ся) (-ую(сь)) *сов от* концентри́ровать(ся).

сконча́ни|е (-я) *ср*: до ~я ве́ка to the end of time.

сконча́|ться (-юсь) *сов возв* to pass away.

скоордини́р|овать (-ую) *сов от* координи́ровать.

скопидо́м (-а) *м* miser.

скопи́р|овать (-ую) *сов от* копи́ровать.

скопи́|ть(ся) (-лю́(сь), -ишь(ся)) *сов от* копи́ть(ся).

ско́пищ|е (-а) *ср* horde.

скопле́ни|е (-я) *ср* (*людей, предметов*) mass.

скоплю́(сь) *сов см* скопи́ть(ся).

ско́пом *нареч* (*разг*) in a crowd.

ско́р|ая (-ой; *decl like adj*) *ж* (*разг: также:* ~ по́мощь) ambulance.

ско́рбен *прил см* ско́рбный.

скорбе́|ть (-лю́, -йшь) *несов неперех*: ~ о +*prp* to grieve for.

ско́рб|ный (-ен, -на, -но) *прил* sorrowful; **в** ~ную мину́ту at a time of sorrow.

скорб|ь (-и; *gen pl* -е́й) *ж* grief.

скоре́е *сравн прил от* ско́рый ♦ *сравн нареч от* ско́ро ♦ *част* rather; ~...чем или нежели (*в большей степени*) more likely ... than; (*лучше, охотнее*) rather ... than; ~ всего́ они́ до́ма it's most likely they'll be (at) home; ~ всего́ он сего́дня не придёт he is most unlikely to come today; ~ бы он верну́лся I wish he would come back soon.

скорлу́п|а́ (-у́пы; *nom pl* -у́пы) *ж* shell; **яи́чная** ~ eggshell; **оре́ховая** ~ nutshell.

скорми́|ть (-лю́, -ишь; *impf* ска́рмливать) *сов перех*: ~ что-н кому́-н to feed sth to sb.

скорня́ж|ный *прил*: ~ая мастерска́я furrier's workshop; ~ое де́ло furriery.

скорня́к (-а́) *м* furrier.

ско́ро *нареч* soon ♦ *как сказ* it's soon; ~ зима́ it will soon be winter; я ~ верну́сь I will be back soon.

сковаро́в|ка (-ки; *gen pl* -ок) *ж* pressure cooker.

скорогово́р|ка (-ки; *gen pl* -ок) *ж* tongue-twister; (*быстрая речь*) gabble.

скоро́м|ный *прил*: ~ая пи́ща *food forbidden on fasting days.*

скоропали́тель|ный (-ен, -ьна, -ьно) *прил* hasty.

скоропо́ртящийся (-аяся, -ееся, -иеся) *прил* (*кулин*) perishable.

скоропости́ж|ный (-ен, -на, -но) *прил*: ~ная смерть sudden death.

скороспе́лый *прил* (*БОТ*) early.

скоростно́й *прил* (*поезд*) high-speed; (*строительство*) speedy.

ско́рост|ь (-и; *gen pl* -е́й) *ж* speed; (*ФИЗ*) velocity; со ~ю 5 киломе́тров в час at (a speed of) 5 kilometres (*BRIT*) или kilometers (*US*) per hour; на (большо́й) ~и at (great) speed; ~ переда́чи (в бо́дах) (*КОМП*) baud rate.

скоросшива́тель (-я) *м* (loose-leaf) binder.

скорота́|ть (-ю) *сов от* корота́ть.

скороте́ч|ный (ен, -на, -но) *прил* short-lived.

скорпио́н (-а) *м* scorpion; (*созвездие*): С~ Scorpio.

скорректи́р|овать (-ую) *сов от* корректи́ровать.

ско́рч|ить(ся) (-у(сь), -ишь(ся)) *сов от* ко́рчить(ся).

ско́р|ый (-, -а́, -о) *прил* (*езда, движение*) fast; (*разлука, визит*) impending; до ~ого свида́ния see you soon; в ~ом вре́мени shortly; приго́товить (*perf*) что-н на ~ую ру́ку to rustle sth up; ско́рая по́мощь (*учреждение*) ambulance service; (*автомашина*) ambulance; ско́рый по́езд express (train).

скос (-а) *м* (*скошенная сторона*) slant; (*склон*) slope.

скос|и́ть (-ошу́, -о́сишь) *сов от* коси́ть ♦ (*impf* ска́шивать) *перех* (*траву*) to mow; (*пшеницу*) to reap; (*крышу*) to set on a slant; ска́шивать или коси́ть (~ *perf*) глаза́ to squint

► **скоси́ться** *сов от* коси́ться.

скот (-а́) *м собир* livestock; (*перен: разг*) animal; моло́чный/мясно́й ~ dairy/beef cattle.

скоти́н|а (-ы) *ж собир* livestock ♦ *ж* (*разг: человек*) swine.

ско́тник (-а) *м* herdsman (*мн* herdsmen).

ско́тниц|а (-ы) *ж* dairy maid.

ско́тный *прил*: ~ двор cattle-yard.

скотово́дств|о (-а) *ср* livestock farming.

ско́тск|ий (-ая, -ое, -ие) *прил* (*подлый*) beastly; (*грязный*) bestial.

скошу́ *сов см* скоси́ть.

скра́дыва|ть (*3sg* -ет, *3pl* -ют) *несов перех* (*звуки*) to keep out; (*полноту, морщины*) to conceal.

скра́|сить (-шу, -сишь; *impf* скра́шивать) *сов перех* to ease.

скреб (-) *итп несов см* скрести́(сь).

скреб|о́к (-ка́) *м* scraper.

скребу́(сь) *итп несов см* скрести́(сь).

скре́жет (-а) *м* (*металла*) grating; (*колёс*) screech.

скреже|та́ть (-щу́, -щешь) *несов неперех* (*что-н металлическое*) to grate; ~ (*impf*) зуба́ми to grate one's teeth.

скреп|и́ть (-лю́, -йшь; *impf* скрепля́ть) *сов перех* (*соединить*) to fasten together; (*перен: дружбу*) to strengthen; (*удостоверить*) to endorse; ~й се́рдце reluctantly.

скре́п|ка (-ки; *gen pl* -ок) *ж* paperclip.

скреплю́ *сов см* скрепи́ть.

скрепля́|ть (-ю) *несов от* **скрепи́ть**.

скре́пок *сущ см* **скрепка**.

скр|ести́ (-ебу́, -ебёшь; *pt* -ёб, -ебла́, -ебло́) *несов неперех* (*мышь, кошка*) to scratch ♦ *перех* (*сковоро́дку*) to scour; (*де́рево*) to sand; **~ебёт на душе́** *или* **на се́рдце** he *итп* has a nagging feeling inside

▶ **скрести́сь** *несов возв* (*мышь*) to scratch about; **соба́ка ~ебётся в дверь** the dog is scratching at the door.

скре|сти́ть (-щу́, -сти́шь; *impf* **скре́щивать**) *сов перех* to cross

▶ **скрести́ться** (*impf* **скре́щиваться**) *сов возв* to cross; (*перен: интере́сы, устремле́ния*) to clash.

скреще́ни|е (-я) *ср* crossing; (*интере́сов*) clash; **~ доро́г** crossroads.

скре́щивани|е (-я) *ср* cross-breeding.

скре́щива|ть(ся) (-ю(сь)) *несов от* **скрести́ть(ся)**.

скрещу́(сь) *сов см* **скрести́ть(ся)**.

скрив|и́ть(ся) (-лю́(сь), -и́шь(ся)) *сов от* **криви́ть(ся)**.

скрип (-а) *м* (*две́ри, по́ла*) creak; (*мета́лла*) grate; (*сне́га*) crunch; **со скри́пом** (*перен: разг*) with a struggle.

скрипа́ч (-а́) *м* violinist.

скрипа́чк|а (-ки; *gen pl* -ек) *ж см* **скрипа́ч**.

скрип|е́ть (-лю́, -и́шь) *несов неперех* to creak; (*перен: разг*) to struggle along.

скри́п|ка (-ки; *gen pl* -ок) *ж* violin; (*в наро́дной му́зыке*) fiddle; **пе́рвая ~** (*в орке́стре*) first violin; (*в де́ле*) first fiddle.

скриплю́ *несов см* **скрипе́ть**.

скри́пок *сущ см* **скрипка**.

скрипу́чий (-ая, -ее, -ие) *прил* (*дверь, пол*) creaky; (*го́лос*) croaky.

скро|́ить (-ю́, -и́шь) *сов от* **крои́ть**.

скро́мен *прил см* **скро́мный**.

скро́мник (-а) *м* (*разг*) modest lad (*BRIT*) *или* guy (*US*).

скро́мниц|а (-ы) *ж* (*разг*) modest girl.

скро́мност|ь (-и) *ж* modesty; (*оде́жды итп*) plainness.

скро́м|ный (-ен, -на́, -но) *прил* modest; (*слу́жащий, до́лжность*) humble.

скро́ю(сь) *итп сов см* **скры́ть(ся)**.

скрупулёз|ный (-ен, -на, -но) *прил* scrupulous.

скр|ути́ть (-учу́, -у́тишь) *сов* ♦ (*impf* **скру́чивать**) *перех* (*провода́, во́лосы*) to twist together; (*разг: аресто́ванного*) to tie up; (: *подлеж: боле́знь, го́ре*) to take a grip

▶ **скрути́ться** *сов возв* to twist together.

скрыва́|ть (-ю) *несов от* **скрыть**.

▶ **скрыва́ться** *несов от* **скры́ться** ♦ *возв* (*от поли́ции, от власте́й*) to hide; (*раздраже́ние в го́лосе*) to lurk; **~ся** (*impf*) **под чужи́м и́менем** to hide behind another name.

скры́т|ный (-ен, -на, -но) *прил* secretive; (*возмо́жности*) potent.

скры́тый *прил* (*смысл, возмо́жности итп*)

hidden; (*не́нависть, оппози́ция*) secret; **скры́тая ка́мера** *или* **съёмка** hidden camera.

скр|ыть (-о́ю, -о́ешь; *impf* **скрыва́ть**) *сов перех* to hide; (*фа́кты*) to conceal

▶ **скры́ться** (*impf* **скрыва́ться**) *сов возв* (*от дождя́, от пого́ни*) to take cover; (*со́лнце, луна́*) to disappear; **от него́ ничего́ не ~о́ется** nothing escapes him.

скрю́ч|ить (-у, -ишь) *сов от* **крю́чить** ♦ (*impf* **скрю́чивать**) *перех* to bend

▶ **скрю́читься** *сов от* **крю́читься** ♦ (*impf* **скрю́чиваться**) *возв* to be stooped.

скря́г|а (-и) *м/ж* (*разг*) skinflint.

скуде́н *прил см* **скудный**.

скуде́|ть (-ю; *perf* **оскуде́ть**) *несов неперех* to run thin.

ску́д|ный (-ен, -на́, -но) *прил* (*запа́сы, сре́дства*) meagre (*BRIT*), meager (*US*); (*язык, све́дения*) limited; (*расти́тельность*) sparse; **~ +instr** (*собы́тиями, витами́нами*) lacking in.

ску́к|а (-и) *ж* boredom; **там ужа́сная ~** it's dreadfully boring there.

скул|а́ (-ы́; *nom pl* -ы) *ж* (*обы́чно мн*) cheekbone.

скула́ст|ый (-, -а, -о) *прил*: **~ое лицо́** a face with prominent cheekbones.

скул|и́ть (-ю́, -и́шь) *несов неперех* to whine.

ску́льптор (-а) *м* sculptor.

скульпту́р|а (-ы) *ж* sculpture.

ску́мбри|я (-и) *ж* mackerel.

скупа́|ть (-ю) *несов от* **скупи́ть** ♦ *перех* (*для перепрода́жи*) to buy up; (*кра́деное*) to buy.

скуп|и́ть (-лю́, -у́пишь; *impf* **скупа́ть**) *сов перех* to buy up.

скуп|и́ться (-лю́сь, -и́шься; *perf* **поскупи́ться**) *несов возв*: **~ на +acc** to skimp on; **он не ~и́тся на обеща́ния/комплиме́нты** he's generous with his promises/compliments.

ску́п|ка (-и) *ж* (*де́йствие*) buying up; (*магази́н*) second-hand shop.

скуплю́ *сов см* **скупи́ть**.

скуп|о́й (-, -а́, -о) *прил* mean; (*свет*) dim; (*речь*) terse; (*расти́тельность*) sparse; **он скуп на де́ньги/похвалу́** he's sparing with money/praise.

ску́почный *прил*: **~ магази́н** second-hand shop; **~ пункт** collection point.

ску́пщик (-а) *м* buyer.

скуфья́ (-и́; *gen pl* -ей) *ж tall hat worn by Orthodox priests*.

скуча́|ть (-ю) *несов неперех* to be bored; (*тоскова́ть*): **~ по +dat** *или* **о +prp** to miss.

ску́чен *прил см* **ску́чный**.

ску́чно *нареч* (*жить, расска́зывать итп*) boringly ♦ *как сказ*: **здесь ~** it's boring here; **мы о́чень ~ живём** we lead a boring life; **как ~!** oh, how boring!; **на уро́ке бы́ло ~** the lesson was boring; **мне ~** I'm bored.

ску́ч|ный (-ен, -на́, -но) *прил* (*челове́к, жизнь итп*) boring, dreary; (*испы́тывающий ску́ку: челове́к, го́лос итп*) bored.

ску́ша|ть (-ю) *сов от* **ку́шать**.

слабе́|ть (-ю; *perf* **ослабе́ть**) *несов неперех* (*человек*) to grow weak; (*здоровье, интерес итп*) to weaken; (*мороз*) to ease off; (*ветер*) to drop; (*дисциплина*) to slacken.

слаби́тельн|ое (-ого; *decl like adj*) *ср* laxative.

слаби́тельный *прил* laxative.

сла́б|ить (*3sg* -ит) *несов перех:* ~ кого́-н to give sb diarrhoea (*BRIT*) *или* diarrhea (*US*); **его́** ~**ит** he has diarrhoea.

сла́б|нуть (-ну, -нешь; *perf* **осла́бнуть**) *несов* = **слабе́ть**.

сла́бо *нареч* (*вскри́кнуть*) weakly; (*нажать*) lightly; (*знать*) badly.

слабово́л|ьный (-ен, -ьна, -ьно) *прил* weak-willed.

сла́бост|ь (-и) *ж* weakness; (*го́лоса*) feebleness; (*дисциплины*) slackness; (*пристрастие*): ~ **к** +*dat* weakness for.

слабоу́мный *прил* feeble-minded.

слабохара́ктер|ный (-ен, -на, -но) *прил* weak.

сла́б|ый (-, -а́, -о) *прил* weak; (*ветер*) light; (*го́лос*) feeble; (*знания, доказательство итп*) poor; (*резинка, дисциплина итп*) slack; **сла́бая сторона́, сла́бое ме́сто** weak spot.

сла́в|а (-ы) *ж* (*героя*) glory; (*писателя, актёра итп*) fame; (*дурная, хорошая*) repute; (*разг: слухи*) rumour (*BRIT*), rumor (*US*); **во** ~**у** +*gen* to the greater glory of; **на** ~**у** splendidly; ~ **Бо́гу!** thank God!

сла́вен *прил см* **сла́вный**.

сла́ви|ровать (-ую) *сов от* **лави́ровать**.

сла́в|ить (-лю, -ишь) *несов от* **просла́вить** ♦ *перех* (*героев*) to glorify

▸ **сла́виться** *несов возв:* ~**ся** +*instr* to be renowned for.

сла́в|ный (-ен, -на́, -но) *прил* (*человек, отдых*) pleasant; (*подвиг, имя*) famous.

славосло́в|ить (-лю, -ишь) *несов перех* to extol.

славяни́н (-яни́на; *nom pl* -я́не, *gen pl* -я́н) *м* Slav.

славя́н|ка (-ки; *gen pl* -ок) *ж см* **славяни́н**.

славя́нск|ий (-ая, -ое, -ие) *прил* Slavonic.

слага́ем|ое (-ого; *decl like adj*) *ср* (*МАТ*) item; (*успеха*) component.

слага́|ть (-ю) *несов от* **сложи́ть**.

сла́д|ить (-жу, -дишь; *impf* **сла́живать**) *сов неперех:* ~ **с** +*instr* (*с маши́ной, с ло́шадью*) to handle; (*с ребёнком*) to cope with.

сла́д|кий (-кая, -кое, -кие; -ок, -ка́, -ко) *прил* sweet; (*жизнь*) pleasant.

сла́дко *нареч* (*пахнуть*) sweet; (*спать*) deeply; (*улыбаться*) sweetly; ♦ *как сказ безл:* **во рту** ~ I am left with a sweet taste in my mouth; **мне здесь не** ~ (*разг*) I can't stand it here.

сла́дк|ое (-ого; *decl like adj*) *ср* sweet things *мн*; (*разг: десерт*) afters (*BRIT*), dessert (*US*); **что**

сего́дня на ~**?** what's for afters today?

сладкое́ж|ка (-ки; *gen pl* -ек) *м/ж* (*разг*) = **сластёна**.

сла́док *прил см* **сла́дкий**.

сла́достен *прил см* **сла́достный**.

сла́дост|и (-ей) *мн* sweet things *мн*.

сла́достный (-ен, -на, -но) *прил* sweet.

сладостра́стный (-ен, -на, -но) *прил* sensual.

сла́дост|ь (-и) *ж* (*см прил*) sweetness; pleasantness; *см также* **сла́дости**.

сла́жен|ный (-, -на, -но) *прил* orderly.

сла́жива|ть (-ю) *несов от* **сла́дить**.

сла́жу *сов от* **сла́дить**.

сла́|зить (-жу, -зишь) *сов неперех* to climb.

слайд (-а) *м* (*ФОТО*) slide.

сла́лом (-а) *м* slalom; **гига́нтский** ~ giant slalom.

сламоми́ст (-а) *м* slalom skier.

сластён|а (-ы) *м/ж:* **он/она́** ~ he/she has a sweet tooth.

сла|сти́ть (-щу́, -сти́шь) *несов перех* to sweeten.

слать (шлю, шлёшь) *несов перех* to send.

сла́ща|вый (-, -а, -о) *прил* sugary.

сла́ще *сравн прил от* **сла́дкий** ♦ *сравн нареч от* **сла́дко**.

слащу́ *сов см* **сласти́ть**.

сле́ва *нареч* on the left.

слёг *итп сов см* **слечь**.

слегка́ *нареч* slightly.

след (-а; *nom pl* -ы́) *м* trace; (*колёс*) track; (*перен*) sign; (*ноги*) footprint; **пре́жней уста́лости и** ~**а́ нет** all traces of my earlier tiredness have gone; **напада́ть** (**напа́сть** *perf*) **на чей-н** ~ (*также перен*) to get on sb's trail.

сле|ди́ть (-жу́, -ди́шь) *несов неперех:* ~ **за** +*instr* to follow; (*заботиться*) to take care of; (*за шпионом*) to watch; (*perf* **наследи́ть**; *гря́зными нога́ми*) to leave a trail; ~ (*impf*) **за собо́й** to take care of o.s..

сле́дование (-я) *ср* (*мо́де, сове́там итп*) following; **по́езд/авто́бус да́льнего** ~**я** long-distance train/bus.

сле́дователь (-я) *м* detective.

сле́довательно *вводн сл* consequently ♦ *союз* therefore.

сле́д|овать (-ую; *perf* **после́довать**) *несов неперех* (*вывод, неприя́тность*) to follow ♦ *безл:* **Вам** ~**ует поду́мать** you should think about it; **его́** ~**ует за э́то наказа́ть** he should be punished for this; ~ (**после́довать** *perf*) **за кем-н/чем-н** to follow sb/sth; ~ (**после́довать** *perf*) **чему́-н** (*правилам, сове́там*) to follow sth; **как** ~**ует** properly.

сле́дом *нареч:* **ходи́ть** ~ **за кем-н** to follow sb ♦ *предл:* ~ **за** +*instr* following.

сле́дственный *прил* investigative, investigatory.

сле́дстви|е (-я) *ср* (*последствие*) consequence;

(ЮР: *после преступления*) investigation.

сле́дующий (-ая, -ее, -ие) *прил* next ♦ *мест* following; **на ~ день** the next day; **кто ~?** who is next?

слеже́ни|е (-я) *ср* observation.

сле́ж|ка (-ки; *gen pl* -ек) *ж* shadowing.

слежу́ *сов см* **следи́ть**.

слез *итп сов см* **слезть**.

слез|а́ (-езы́; *nom pl* -ёзы, *dat pl* -еза́м) *ж* tear; **доводи́ть (довести́** *perf*) **кого́-н до ~ёз** to reduce sb to tears; **мне оби́дно до ~ёз** I'm so hurt I could cry.

слеза́|ть (-ю) *несов от* **слезть**.

слез|и́ться (*3sg* -и́тся, *3pl* -я́тся) *несов возв* (*глаза*) to water.

слезли́в|ый (-, -а, -о) *прил* (*человек*) weepy; (*перен: тон, голос*) tearful.

слёзный *прил* lacrimal; (*жалобный*) pitiful.

слезоточи́в|ый *прил*: **~ газ** tear gas.

слез|ть (-у, -ешь; *pt* -, ла, -ло, *impf* **слеза́ть**) *сов неперех*: **~ (с** +*gen*) (*с дерева*) to climb down; (*с лошади, с велосипеда*) to climb off; (*разг: с автобуса, с поезда итп*) to get off; (: *очки, платок*) to slip off; (*кожа, краска*) to peel off.

сле́й(те) *сов см* **слить**.

сленг (-а) *м* slang.

слеп|е́нь (-ня́) *м* horsefly (*мн* horseflies), cleg.

слеп|и́ть (*3sg* -и́т, *3pl* -я́т) *сов перех*: **~ глаза́ кому́-н** to blind sb.

слеп|и́ть (-еплю́, -е́пишь) *сов от* **лепи́ть** ♦ (*impf* **слепля́ть**) *перех* to stick together

► **слепи́ться** (*impf* **слепля́ться**) *сов возв* to stick together.

сле́пка *итп сущ см* **сле́пок**.

слеплю́(сь) *сов см* **слепя́ть(ся)**.

слепля́|ть(ся) (-ю(сь)) *несов от* **слепи́ть(ся)**.

сле́пн|уть (-у, -ешь; *perf* **осле́пнуть**) *несов неперех* to go blind.

слепня́ *итп сущ см* **слепе́нь**.

слеп|о́й (-, -а́, -о) *прил* (*также перен*) blind ♦ (-о́го; *decl like adj*) *м* blind person (*мн* people); **слепа́я кишка́** appendix (*мн* appendices); **слепо́й ме́тод печа́тания** touch-typing.

слеп|о́к (-ка) *м* cast.

слепот|а́ (-ы́) *ж* (*также перен*) blindness.

слеса́рный *прил*: **~ая мастерска́я** metal workshop; **~ стано́к** lathe.

слеса́р|ь (-я; *nom pl* -я́, *gen pl* -е́й) *м* maintenance man (*мн* men).

слёт (-а) *м* (*пионеров*) rally.

слета́|ть (-ю) *несов от* **слете́ть** ♦ *неперех* (*на юг, на море*) to fly; (*разг: сбегать*) to nip

► **слета́ться** *несов от* **слете́ться**.

слет|е́ть (-чу́, -ти́шь; *impf* **слета́ть**) *сов неперех*: **~ (с** +*gen*) (*птица*) to fly down (from); (*разг: спесь*) to vanish (from); (: *шляпа, ребёнок*) to fall off; **вопро́с ~те́л с губ** *или* **с языка́** the question slipped out

► **слете́ться** (*impf* **слета́ться**) *сов возв* (*птицы*) to flock; (*мухи*) to swarm.

сле|чь (-я́гу, -я́жешь *итп* -я́гут; *pt* -ёг, -егла́,

-егло́) *сов неперех* to take to one's bed.

слив (-а) *м* (*действие*) discharge; (*устройство*) drain.

сли́в|а (-ы) *ж* (*дерево*) plum (tree); (*плод*) plum.

слива́|ть(ся) (-ю(сь)) *несов от* **слить(ся)**.

сли́в|ки (-ок) *мн* (*также перен*) cream *ед*.

сли́вовый *прил* plum *опред*.

сли́вок *сущ см* **сли́вки**.

сли́вочный *прил made with cream*; **сли́вочное ма́сло** butter.

сли|за́ть (-ижу́, -и́жешь; *impf* **сли́зывать**) *сов перех* (*языком*) to lick off.

сли́зистый *прил* mucous *опред*; **сли́зистая оболо́чка** mucous membrane.

сли́зыва|ть (-ю) *несов от* **слиза́ть**.

слиз|ь (-и) *ж* mucus; (*от сырости, от грязи*) slime.

слипа́|ться (*3sg* -ется, *3pl* -ются) *несов от* **сли́пнуться** ♦ *возв* (*перен*): **у меня́ глаза́ ~ются** I can't keep my eyes open.

сли́п|нуться (*3sg* -нется, *3pl* -нутся, *pt* -ся, -лась, -лось, *impf* **слипа́ться**) *сов возв* to stick together.

сли́тка *итп сущ см* **сли́ток**.

сли́тн|ый *прил* (*звучание*) unified; **~ое написа́ние** spelt as one word.

сли́т|ок (-ка) *м* (*металлический*) bar; (*золота, серебра*) ingot.

сли|ть (-солью́, -сольёшь; *pt* -л, -ла́, -ло, *imper* **сле́й(те)**, *impf* **слива́ть**) *сов перех* to pour; (*вылить*) to pour out; (*перен: соединить*) to merge

► **сли́ться** (*impf* **слива́ться**) *сов возв* (*реки*) to flow together; (*голоса, судьбы, компании*) to merge.

слич|и́ть (-у́, -и́шь; *impf* **слича́ть**) *сов перех*: **~ что-н с чем-н** to check sth against sth.

сли́шком *нареч* too; **э́то уже́ ~** (*разг*) that's just too much.

слов|а́ (-) *мн*: **~ пе́сни** lyrics *мн*.

слова́к (-а) *м* Slovak.

Слова́ки|я (-и) *ж* Slovakia.

слова́рный *прил* (*работа, статья*) dictionary *опред*, lexicographic(al); (*фонд, состав языка*) lexical; **слова́рный запа́с** vocabulary.

слова́р|ь (-я́) *м* (*книга*) dictionary; (*запас слов*) vocabulary.

слова́цк|ий (-ая, -ое, -ие) *прил* Slovak, Slovakian.

слова́ч|ка (-ки; *gen pl* -ек) *ж см* **слова́к**.

слове́н|ец (-ца) *м* Slovene.

Слове́ни|я (-и) *ж* Slovenia.

слове́н|ка (-ки; *gen pl* -ок) *ж см* **слове́нец**.

слове́нск|ий (-ая, -ое, -ие) *прил* Slovene, Slovenian.

слове́нца *итп сущ см* **слове́нец**.

слове́сность (-и) *ж* literature.

слове́сный *прил* oral; (*заявление, протест*) verbal; **слове́сный портре́т** description.

сло́вно *союз* (*как*) like; (*как будто*) as if.

сло́в|о (-а; *nom pl* -а́) *ср* word; **~ в ~** word for word; **он двух слов связáть не мóжет** (*разг*) he can't put string words together; **на словáх** (*передать, согласиться*) verbally; **онá сочýвствует тóлько на словáх** her sympathy is just empty words; **со слов свидéтелей/егó друзéй** according to witnesses/his friends; **просúть (попросúть** *perf*) **~я** (*на собрáнии*) to ask to speak; **предоставлять (предостáвить** *perf*) **комý-н ~** to allow sb to speak; **лаборатóрия оборýдована по послéднему ~у наýки** the laboratory is equipped with the latest technology; **к ~у пришлóсь** it sprang to mind; **(однúм) ~м** in a word; **слов нет, ты прав** what can I say, you're right; *см также* **словá**.

словоизменéни|е (-я) *ср* inflection.
слóвом *вводн сл* in a word.
словообразовáни|е (-я) *ср* word formation.
словоохóтлив|ый (-, -а, -о) *прил* loquacious.
словосочетáни|е (-я) *ср* word combination.
словоупотреблéни|е (-я) *ср* word usage.
словцó (-á) *ср* witticism; **для крáсного ~á** for effect.

слог (-а; *nom pl* **-и,** *gen pl* **-óв)** *м* syllable; (*стиль*) style.
слóек *сущ см* **слóйка**.
слоёный *прил*: **~ое тéсто** puff pastry.
слóжен *прил см* **слóжный**.
сложéни|е (-я) *ср* (*в математике*) addition; (*телосложéние*) build; (*полномóчий, обязанностей*) relinquishing; (*чисел*) adding.
сложён|ный (-, -á, -о) *прил*: **он хорошó сложён** he is well-built.
сл|ожúть (-ожý, -óжишь; *impf* **склáдывать)** *сов перех* (*вещи*) to put; (*книги*) to stack; (*чемодáн, сýмку итп*) to pack; (*бумáгу, рубáшку итп*) to fold (up); (*impf* **склáдывать** *или* **слагáть;** *числá*) to add (up); (*картúнку*) to make; (*пéсню, стихи*) to make up; **~** (*perf*) **гóлову/орýжие** to lay down one's life/weapons; **~ рýки** to fold one's arms; **слагáть (~** *perf*) **с себя полномóчия/отвéтственность** to relinquish one's authority/responsibility; **сидéть** (*impf*) **~ожá рýки** to sit back and do nothing
▶ **сложúться** (*impf* **склáдываться**) *сов возв* (*коллектúв*) to come together; (*ситуáция, обстоятельства*) to turn out; (*харáктер*) to form; (*собрáть деньги*) to have a collection; (*зонт, палáтка*) to fold up; (*впечатлéние*) to form; **у нас ~ожúлось хорóшее впечатлéние о нём** we formed a good impression of him.
слóжно *нареч* (*дéлать*) in a complicated way; (*сложúться*) in a difficult way ♦ *как сказ* it's difficult; **мне ~ понять егó** I find it difficult to understand him.
сложносокращённ|ый *прил*: **~ое слóво** compound.
сложност|ь (-и) *ж* (*многообрáзие*) complexity;

(*затéйливость*) intricacy; (*обычно мн*: *трýдность*) difficulty; **в óбщей ~и** all in all.
слóж|ный (-ен, -нá, -но) *прил* (*дéло, предложéние, человéк*) complex; (*узóр*) intricate; (*вопрóс, рабóта*) difficult.
слóйст|ый (-, -а, -о) *прил* stratified.
слой (-я; *nom pl* **-и)** *м* layer.
слóй|ка (-йки; *gen pl* **-ек)** *ж* sweet pastry.
слом (-а) *м*: **на ~** for demolition; **дом идёт на ~** this house is due for demolition.
сломá|ть (-ю) *сов от* **ломáть**
▶ **сломáться** *сов от* **ломáться** ♦ *возв* (*перен*: *рáзг: человéк*) to break.
слом|úть (-лю́, -ишь) *сов перех* (*сопротивлéние, вóлю итп*) to break; (*подлеж*: *болéзнь, устáлость*) to knock out; **~я́ гóлову** (*рáзг*) at breakneck speed
▶ **сломúться** *сов возв* (*перен*: *человéк*) to break.
слон (-á) *м* elephant; (*ШАХМАТЫ*) bishop.
слонёнок (-ёнка; *nom pl* **-я́та,** *gen pl* **-я́т)** *м* elephant calf (*мн* calves).
слонúх|а (-и) *ж* cow (*elephant*).
слонóв|ый *прил* elephant *опред*; **слонóвая кость** ivory.
слоня́та *итп сущ см* **слонёнок**.
слоня́|ться (-юсь) *несов возв* (*рáзг*) to loaf around.
слóпа|ть (-ю) *сов от* **лóпать**.
слуг|á (-й; *nom pl* **-и)** *ж* servant.
служáк|а (-и) *м* (*рáзг*) trouper.
служáнк|а (-ки; *gen pl* **-ок)** *ж* maid.
служащ|ий (-его; *decl like adj*) *м* white collar worker; **госудáрственный ~** civil servant; **контóрский ~** clerk.
служб|а (-ы) *ж* service; (*рабóта*) work; **срок ~ы** durability; **Слýжба бы́та** consumer services; **Слýжба зáнятости** ≈ Employment Service.
служéбн|ый *прил* (*делá, обязанности итп*) official; (*роль, помещéние итп*) auxiliary; **~ое положéние** rank; **служéбное слóво** connective word; **служéбная собáка** working dog.
служéни|е (-я) *ср* (*дéйствие*: *рóдине*) serving; (*РЕЛ*) service.
служúтел|ь (-я) *м* (*в музéе, в зоопáрке*) keeper; (*на автозапрáвке*) attendant; (*наýки, искýсства*) servant; **служúтель цéркви** clergyman (*мн* clergymen).
служúтельниц|а (-ы) *ж* keeper.
служ|úть (-ý, -ужúшь) *несов непéрех* (*в бáнке, в контóре итп*) to work; (*в áрмии*) to serve ♦ *перех* (*РЕЛ*) to hear ♦ *непéрех* (*собáка*) to beg; (*perf* **послужúть,** +*instr*: *функционúровать*) to serve as; **~** (*impf*) **рóдине/пáртии** to serve one's country/party; **чем могý ~?** what can I do for you?
слукáв|ить (-лю, -ишь) *сов от* **лукáвить**.
слух (-а) *м* hearing; (*музыкáльный*) ear;

(*известие*) rumour (*BRIT*), rumor (*US*); **на ~** by hearing; **игра́ть** (*impf*) **по слу́ху** to play by ear; **о нём ни слу́ху ни ду́ху** there's been no word of him; **по слу́хам** from what people are saying.

слуховой *прил* (*нерв, орган*) auditory; **слуховой аппара́т** hearing aid.

случа́ен *прил см* **случа́йный**.

слу́ча|й (**-я**) *м* occasion; (*подходящий момент*) chance, opportunity; (*случайность*) chance; **в ~е** *+gen* in the event of; **в ~е чего́** (*разг*) if there is anything; **во вся́ком ~е** in any case; **на ~** *+gen* in case of; **на вся́кий ~** just in case; **по ~ю** *+gen* (*годовщины*) on the occasion of; **при ~е** if the opportunity arises; **несча́стный ~** accident.

случа́йно *нареч* accidentally, by chance ◆ *вводн сл* by any chance; **Вы, ~, не зна́ете, где здесь банк?** you don't by any chance know where there is a bank?; **не ~** not by chance.

случа́йност|ь (**-и**) *ж* (*chance*); **по счастли́вой ~и** by sheer luck.

случа́йный (**-ен, -йна, -йно**) *прил* (*встреча*) accidental, chance *опред*; (*знакомство*) casual; (*комп*) random; **~ за́работок** casual earnings.

случа́|ть (**-ю**) *несов от* **случи́ть**

▶ **случа́ться** *несов от* **случи́ться** ◆ *возв*: **он, ~ется, прихо́дит серди́тый** occasionally he arrives in a temper.

случи́|ть (**-у́, -ишь**; *impf* **случа́ть**) *сов перех* to mate

▶ **случи́ться** (*impf* **случа́ться**) *сов возв* (*произойти*) to happen ◆ *безл*: **мне ~лось с ним познако́миться** I happened to become acquainted with him.

слу́шани|е (**-я**) *ср* (*ЮР*) hearing.

слу́шател|ь (**-я**) *ср* listener; (*ПРОСВЕЩ*) student.

слу́шательни|ца (**-ы**) *ж см* **слу́шатель**.

слу́ша|ть (**-ю**) *несов перех* (*музыку, речь*) to listen to; (*ЮР*) to hear; (*курс лекций*) to attend; (*perf* **послу́шать**; *совет*) to listen to; (*perf* **вы́слушать**; *сердце, лёгкие*) to listen to; **~йте!** (*разг*) listen!

▶ **слу́шаться** (*perf* **послу́шаться**) *несов возв*: **~ся** *+gen* to obey; (*совета*) to follow; **~юсь!** yes, sir!

слы|ть (**-ву́, -вёшь**; *pt* **-л, -ла́, -ло**) *несов непepex*: **~** *+instr или* **за** *+acc* to be reputed to be.

слы́хан|ный *прил*: **где э́то ~о?** (*разг*) whoever heard of such a thing?

слыха́|ть (*pt* **-л, -ла, -ло**) *несов перех* to hear; **мне ничего́ не ~** (*разг*) I can't hear a thing.

слы́ш|ать (**-у, -ишь**) *несов перех* to hear ◆ (*perf* **услы́шать**) *перех* to hear; **~** (*impf*) **о** *+prp* to hear about; **и ~ об э́том не хочу́** I won't hear of it; **он пло́хо ~ит** he's hard of hearing

▶ **слы́шаться** *несов возв* to be heard.

слы́шен *прил см* **слы́шный**.

слы́шимост|ь (**-и**) *ж* (*в зале*) acoustics *мн*; (*радио, телевизора*) audibility.

слы́шно *как сказ* it can be heard; **мне ничего́ не ~** I can't hear a thing; **о ней ничего́ не ~** there's

no news of her; **что у Вас ~?** how are things?

слы́шный (**-ен, -на́, -но**) *прил* (*звук, пение*) audible ◆ *как сказ* (*no full form*): **в его́ го́лосе слышна́ трево́га** anxiety can be heard in his voice.

слюд|а́ (**-ы́**) *ж* mica.

слюн|а́ (**-ы́**) *ж* saliva.

слю́н|ки (**-ок**) *мн*: **у меня́ ~ теку́т** my mouth's watering.

слюня́в|ить (**-лю, -ишь**) *несов перех* (*разг*) to lick.

сля́гу *итп сов см* **слечь**.

сля́кот|ь (**-и**) *ж* slush.

сля́па|ть (**-ю**) *сов от* **ля́пать**.

см *сокр* (**= сантиме́тр**) cm(**= *centimetre* (*BRIT*)** *или* *centimeter* (*US*)).

см. *сокр* (**= смотри́**) v. (**= *vide*,**) qv (**= *quod vide***).

с.м. *сокр* (**= сего́ ме́сяца**) inst. (**= *instant***).

сма́з|ать (**-жу, -жешь**; *impf* **сма́зывать**) *сов перех* (*маслом*) to lubricate; (*разг: испортить впечатление*) to slur; **сма́зывать** (**~** *perf*) **что-н ма́зью** to put ointment on sth.

сма́з|ка (**-и**) *ж* (*действие*) lubrication; (*вещество*) lubricant.

смазли́в|ый (**-, -а, -о**) *прил* (*разг*) pretty.

сма́зочный *прил* lubricating.

сма́зыва|ть (**-ю**) *несов от* **сма́зать**.

смак|ова́ть (**-у́ю**) *несов перех* (*еду*) to savour (*BRIT*), savor (*US*); (*перен: новость, книгу итп*) to relish.

смалоду́шнича|ть (**-ю**) *сов от* **малоду́шничать**.

сма́льт|а (**-ы**) *ж* smalto.

сманеври́р|овать (**-ую**) *сов от* **маневри́ровать**.

см|ани́ть (**-аню́, -а́нишь**; *impf* **сма́нивать**) *сов перех* (*переманить*) to lure, entice.

смастери́|ть (**-ю́, -ишь**) *сов от* **мастери́ть**.

сма́тыва|ть(ся) (**-ю(сь)**) *несов от* **смота́ть(ся)**.

сма́хива|ть (**-ю**) *несов от* **смахну́ть** ◆ *неперех* (*разг*): **~ на** *+acc* (*походить*) to look a bit like.

смахну́|ть (**-у́, -ёшь**) *сов перех* to brush off.

сма́чен *прил см* **сма́чный**.

сма́чива|ть (**-ю**) *несов от* **смочи́ть**.

сма́чный (**-ен, -на́, -но**) *прил* (*разг: вкусный*) scrumptious; (*перен: слово*) juicy.

сме́жен *прил см* **сме́жный**.

сме́жник (**-а**) *м* (*предприятие*) related company.

сме́жный (**-ен, -на, -но**) *прил* (*с общей границей*) adjoining, adjacent; (*производство, предприятие*) affiliated; (*наука*) related.

смека́лист|ый (**-, -а, -о**) *прил* astute.

смека́л|ка (**-и**) *ж* astuteness.

смека́|ть (**-ю**; *perf* **смекну́ть**) *несов перех* to catch onto.

смеле́|ть (**-ю**; *perf* **осмеле́ть**) *несов неперех* to grow bolder.

сме́ло *нареч* boldly; (*без колебаний*) confidently.

сме́лост|ь (-и) *ж* (*храбрость*) bravery; (*поступка, поведения*) boldness, audacity; **брать** (**взять** *perf*) **на себя́** ~ +*infin* to have the audacity to do.

сме́л|ый (-, -á, -о) *прил* (*человек, поступок*) brave; (*идея, проект*) ambitious; (*перен: нескрайный*) risqué.

смельча́к (-á) *м* brave person (*мн* people).

смелю́ *итп сов см* **смоло́ть.**

смéн|а (-ы) *ж* (*руководства*) change; (*караула, одежды*) changing; (*на производстве*) shift; (*молодое поколение*) successors *мн*; (*также:* ~ **белья́**) change of sheets (*BRIT*) *или* bed-linen (*US*); **приходи́ть** (**прийти́** *perf*) **на** ~**у кому́-н/ чему́-н** to succeed sb/sth.

см|ени́ть (-еню́, -éнишь; *impf* **сменя́ть**) *сов перех* to change; (*коллегу*) to relieve

▸ **смени́ться** (*impf* **сменя́ться**) *сов возв* (*руководство*) to change; (*радость, день*): ~**ся** +*instr* to give way to; **сменя́ться** (~**ся** *perf*) (**с** +*gen*) (*с дежурства, с вахты*) to go off duty (from).

смéнн|ый *прил* (*работа, задание*) shift *опред*; (*колесо*) spare; ~**ое бельё** a change of sheets (*BRIT*) *или* bed-linen (*US*); (*нижнее*) a change of underwear.

сменя́ть(ся) (-ю(сь)) *несов от* **смени́ть(ся).**

смёрзн|уться (*3sg* -ется, *3pl* -утся) *сов возв* to freeze together.

смéр|ить (-ю, -ишь) *сов от* **мéрить.**

смерка́|ться (*3sg* -ется, *perf* **смéркнуться**) *несов безл* to start to get dark.

смертéл|ьный (-ен, -ьна, -ьно) *прил* mortal; (*рана*) fatal; (*скука, усталость*) deadly; **смертéльный исхо́д** fatal ending; **смертéльный слу́чай** fatality.

смéртен *прил см* **смéртный.**

смéртник (-а) *м* (*приговорённый к казни*) prisoner on death row; (*террорист*) kamikaze.

смéртность (-и) *ж* death-rate, mortality.

смéрт|ный (-ен, -на, -но) *прил* mortal; (*разг: скука*) deadly; ~ **час** hour of death; ~ **бой** (*перен*) fight to the death; **просто́й** ~ ordinary mortal; **смéртный пригово́р** death sentence; **смéртная казнь** death penalty.

смертоно́сный *прил* lethal.

смерт|ь (-и) *ж* death; **быть** (*impf*) **при** ~**и** to be at death's door; **умира́ть** (**умерéть** *perf*) **свое́й смéртью** to die a natural death; **я до́** ~**и бою́сь** I'm scared to death.

смерч (-а) *м* tornado.

смеси́тел|ь (-я) *м* mixer.

сме|си́ть (-шу́, -сишь) *сов от* **меси́ть.**

сме|сти́ (-ту́, -тёшь; *pt* -ёл, -елá, -ело́, *impf* **смета́ть**) *сов перех* to sweep; (*подлеж: ураган, смерч*) to sweep away.

сме|сти́ть (-щу́, -сти́шь; *impf* **смеща́ть**) *сов перех* (*уволить*) to remove; (*сдвинуть*) to shift

▸ **смести́ться** (*impf* **смеща́ться**) *сов возв* to shift.

смес|ь (-и) *ж* mixture; **моло́чная** ~ powdered baby milk.

смéт|а (-ы) *ж* (*ЭКОН*) estimate.

сметáн|а (-ы) *ж* sour cream.

смета́|ть (-ю) *несов от* **смести́** ◆ *сов от* **метáть.**

сметли́в|ый (-, -а, -о) *прил* quick.

смéтный *прил* estimated; **смéтная сто́имость** estimated cost.

сме|ть (-ю; *perf* **посмéть**) *несов неперех*: ~ +*infin* to dare to do; **как Вы смéете!** how dare you!; **не смей!** don't you dare!

смету́ *итп сов см* **смести́.**

смех (-а; *part gen* -у) *м* laughter ◆ *как сказ* (*смешно*) it's ridiculous; **слу́шать э́то** – ~ it makes me laugh to hear it; **поднимáть** (**подня́ть** *perf*) **кого́-н нá** ~ to make a laughing stock of sb; **и** ~ **и грех** one can see the funny side of it.

смехотво́р|ный (-ен, -на, -но) *прил* (*смешной*) funny; (*жалкий*) ludicrous.

смéшанный *прил* mixed.

смешá|ть (-ю) *сов от* **мешáть** ◆ (*impf* **смéшивать**) *перех* (*спутать*) to mix up; ~ (*perf*) **чьи-н кáрты** to spoil sb's plans

▸ **смешáться** *сов от* **мешáться** ◆ *возв* (*смутиться*) to be taken aback; (*impf* **смéшиваться**; *слиться*) to mingle; (*краски, цвета*) to blend; (*чувства*) to become confused.

смешéни|е (-я) *ср* (*стилей, чувств*) mixture.

смéшивани|е (-я) *ср* mixing.

смéшива|ть(ся) (-ю(сь)) *несов от* **смешáть(ся).**

смеш|и́ть (-ý, -и́шь; *perf* **насмеши́ть** *или* **рассмеши́ть**) *несов перех*: ~ **кого́-н** to make sb laugh.

смешкá *итп сущ см* **смешо́к.**

смешли́в|ый (-, -а, -о) *прил* (*человек*) jolly; (*настроение*) giggly.

смешно́ *нареч* (*смотрéться*) funny ◆ *как сказ* it's funny; (*глупо*) it's ludicrous; **мне не** ~ I don't find it funny; ~ **надéяться** it's ludicrous to hope; ~ **сказáть, но ...** it sounds funny, but ...; **э́то про́сто** ~ that's just ridiculous.

смеш|но́й (-о́н, -нá, -но́) *прил* funny; (*требования, претензии итп*) ludicrous; **до** ~**но́го** to the point of absurdity; **дохо́дит до** ~**но́го** it's a real joke.

смешо́к (-кá) *м* giggle.

смешо́н *прил см* **смешно́й.**

смещá|ть(ся) (-ю(сь)) *несов от* **смести́ть(ся).**

смещéни|е (-я) *ср* (*руководства*) removal; (*понятий, критериев*) shift.

смещённый (-ён, -енá, -ено́) *прил* upset; (*понятия*) disturbed.

смещу́(сь) *сов см* **смести́ть(ся).**

смея́ться (-ю́сь) *несов возв* to laugh;

(*шутить*) to joke; (*perf* **посмея́ться**; **насмеха́ться**): ~ **над** +*instr* to laugh at.

сми́лостив|иться (-люсь, -ишься) *сов возв*: ~ (**над** +*instr*) to take pity (on).

смина́|ть (-ю) *несов от* **смять**.

сми́рен *прил см* **сми́рный**.

смире́ни|е (-я) *ср* (*покорность*) humility.

смире́н|ный (-, -на, -но) *прил* humble.

смири́тельн|ый *прил*: ~**ая руба́шка** strait-jacket.

смир|и́ть (-ю́, -и́шь; *impf* **смиря́ть**) *сов перех* to subdue.

▶ **смири́ться** (*impf* **смиря́ться**) *сов возв* (*покориться*) to submit; (*примириться*): ~**ся с** +*instr* to resign o.s. to.

сми́рно *нареч* (*сидеть, вести себя*) quietly; (*ВОЕН: команда*) attention; **стоя́ть** (*impf*) **по сто́йке «~»** to stand to attention.

сми́р|ный (-ен, -на́, -но) *прил* docile.

смиря́|ть(ся) (-ю(сь)) *несов от* **смири́ть(ся)**.

смог (-а) *м* smog.

смог *итп сов см* **смочь**.

смогу́ *итп сов см* **смочь**.

смодели́р|овать (-ую) *сов от* **модели́ровать**.

смо́жешь *итп сов см* **смочь**.

смол|а́ (-ы́; *nom pl* -ы) *ж* (*дерево*) resin; (*дёготь*) tar.

смоли́ст|ый (-, -а, -о) *прил* (*дерево*) resinous.

смо́лк|нуть (-ну, -нешь; *pt* -, -ла, -ло, *impf* **смолка́ть**) *сов неперех* (*голоса*) to fall silent; (*звуки*) to fade away.

смо́лоду *нареч* from one's youth.

смол|оти́ть (-очу́, -о́тишь) *сов от* **молоти́ть**.

смол|о́ть (-елю́, -е́лешь) *сов от* **моло́ть**.

смолочу́ *сов см* **смолоти́ть**.

смолч|а́ть (-у́, -и́шь) *сов неперех* to keep quiet.

смоль (-и) *ж*: **чёрный как** ~ jet-black.

смонти́р|овать (-ую) *сов от* **монти́ровать**.

сморка́|ть (-ю; *perf* **вы́сморкать**) *несов перех*: ~ **нос** to blow one's nose.

▶ **сморка́ться** (*perf* **вы́сморкаться**) *несов возв* to blow one's nose.

сморо́дин|а (-ы) *ж*: **кра́сная** ~ (*кустарник*) redcurrant bush; (*ягоды*) redcurrants *мн*; **чёрная** ~ (*кустарник*) blackcurrant bush; (*ягоды*) blackcurrants *мн*.

сморо́|зить (-жу, -зишь) *сов перех* to say.

смо́рщенный *прил* wrinkled.

смо́рщ|ить (-у, -ишь) *сов от* **мо́рщить**.

▶ **смо́рщиться** *сов от* **мо́рщиться** ◆ *возв* to become wrinkled.

смота́|ть (-ю; *impf* **сма́тывать**) *сов перех* to wind.

▶ **смота́ться** (*impf* **сма́тываться**) *сов возв* (*нитки*) to wind; (*разг: убежать*) to leg it; (: *быстро пойти*) to nip.

смотр (-а; *loc sg* -у́, *nom pl* -ы) *м* presentation; (*ВОЕН*) inspection.

см|отре́ть (-отрю́, -о́тришь; *perf* **посмотре́ть**) *несов неперех* to look ◆ *перех* (*фильм, игру*) to watch; (*газеты, почту*) to look through;

(*квартиру, картину*) to look at; (*музей, выставку*) to look round; (*пациента*) to examine; (*следить*): ~ **за** +*instr* to look after; ~ (*impf*) **в/на** +*acc* to look onto; ~ (**посмотре́ть** *perf*) **на** +*acc* (*относиться*) to look at; ~**отри́те, не упади́те** watch, don't fall; ~**отрю́, ты осво́ился здесь** (*разг*) I see you've settled down here; ~**отря́ по** +*dat* depending on; **Вы хоти́те пойти́ погуля́ть? – ~отря́ куда́** would you like to go for a walk? – it depends where to

▶ **смотре́ться** (*perf* **посмотре́ться**) *несов возв*: ~**ся в** +*acc* (*в зеркало, в воду*) to look at o.s. in; (*разг: хорошо выглядеть*) to look good; **э́та вы́ставка ~о́трится легко́** this exhibition is not too demanding.

смотри́тель (-я) *м* (*в музее*) attendant.

смотри́тельниц|а (-ы) *ж см* **смотри́тель**.

смотров|о́й *прил* (*площадка*) viewing *опред*; ~**а́я ба́шня** watch tower; ~**о́е отве́рстие** peephole; **смотрово́й кабине́т** medical examination room.

см|очи́ть (-очу́, -о́чишь; *impf* **сма́чивать**) *сов перех* to dampen.

смо|чь (-гу́, -жешь *итп*, -гут; *pt* -г, -гла́, -гло́) *сов от* **мочь**.

смоше́ннича|ть (-ю) *сов от* **моше́нничать**.

смо́ю(ся) *итп сов от* **смы́ть(ся)**.

смрад (-а) *м* (*вонь*) stench.

смра́д|ный (-ен, -на, -но) *прил* stinking.

сму́глый (-, -а́, -о) *прил* swarthy.

сму́т|а (-ы) *ж* (*социальная*) unrest; **у меня́ на душе́** ~ my soul is troubled.

сму́тен *прил см* **сму́тный**.

смут|и́ть (-щу́, -ти́шь; *impf* **смуща́ть**) *сов перех* to embarrass

▶ **смути́ться** (*impf* **смуща́ться**) *сов возв* to get embarrassed.

сму́т|ный (-ен, -на, -но) *прил* (*очертания, воспоминания*) vague; (*настроение, время итп*) troubled.

смуща́|ть(ся) (-ю(сь)) *несов от* **смути́ть(ся)**.

смуще́ни|е (-я) *ср* embarrassment.

смущённый *прил* embarrassed.

смущу́(сь) *сов см* **смути́ть(ся)**.

смыва́|ть(ся) (-ю(сь)) *несов от* **смы́ть(ся)**.

смыка́|ть(ся) (-ю(сь)) *несов от* **сомкну́ть(ся)**.

смысл (-а) *м* (*книги, статьи*) point; (*слов*) meaning; (*линг*) sense; **в смы́сле** +*gen* as regards; **здра́вый** ~ common sense; **прямо́й/перено́сный** ~ **сло́ва** the literal/figurative sense of a word; **како́й** ~ **на э́то соглаша́ться?** what is the point of agreeing to that?; **есть** ~ **е́хать сего́дня** it makes sense to go today.

смы́сл|ить (-ю, -ишь) *несов неперех* (*разг: разбираться*): ~ **в** +*prp* (*в технике*) to have a knack for.

см|ы́ть (-о́ю, -о́ешь; *impf* **смыва́ть**) *сов перех* to wash off; (*подлеж: волна, течение*) to wash away

▶ **смы́ться** (*impf* **смыва́ться**) *сов возв* to wash

off; (*разг: незаметно уйти*) to do a bunk.

смычо́к (-ка́) *м* (*МУЗ*) bow.

смышлён|**ый** (-, -а, -о) *прил* sharp.

смягча́|**ть(ся)** (-ю(сь)) *несов от* **смягчи́ть(ся)**.

смягча́ющ|**ий** (-ая, -ее, -ие) *прил*: ~**ие обстоя́тельства** (*ЮР*) extenuating circumstances *мн*.

смягче́ни|**е** (-я) *ср* (*действие*) softening; (: *наказания*) mitigation.

смягчи́ть (-у́, -и́шь; *impf* **смягча́ть**) *сов перех* (*кожу, ткань, удар*) to soften; (*боль*) to ease; (*наказание, приговор*) to mitigate; (*человека*) to appease

▶ **смягчи́ться** (*impf* **смягча́ться**) *сов возв* to soften.

смяте́ни|**е** (-я) *ср* turmoil.

смять (**сомну́, сомнёшь**) *сов от* **мять** ♦ (*impf* **смина́ть**) *перех* (*противника, оборону*) to crush

▶ **смя́ться** *сов от* **мя́ться**.

сна *итп* *сущ см* **сон**.

снаб|**ди́ть** (-жу́, -ди́шь; *impf* **снабжа́ть**) *сов перех*: ~ **кого́-н/что-н чем-н** to supply sb/sth with sth.

снабже́ни|**е** (-я) *ср* supply.

снабжу́ *сов см* **снабди́ть**.

сна́йпер (-а) *м* (*стрелок*) sniper.

снару́жи *нареч* (*покрасить, расположиться*) on the outside; (*закрыть*) from the outside.

снаря́д (-а) *м* (*ВОЕН*) shell; (*СПОРТ*) apparatus.

снаря|**ди́ть** (-жу́, -ди́шь; *impf* **снаряжа́ть**) *сов перех* to equip.

снаряже́ни|**е** (-я) *ср* (*действие*) equipping; (*лыжное, охотничье*) equipment; (*солдата*) kit.

снаряжу́ *сов см* **снаряди́ть**.

снасть (-и) *ж* (*МОР: обычно мн*) rigging *только ед*; (*рыболовная*) tackle.

снача́ла *нареч* at first; (*ещё раз*) all over again.

сна́шива|**ть** (-ю) *несов от* **сноси́ть**.

СНГ *м сокр* (= **Содру́жество Незави́симых Госуда́рств**) CIS (= *Commonwealth of Independent States*).

снег (-а; *part gen* -у, *loc sg* -у́, *nom pl* -á) *м* snow; **идёт** ~ it's snowing; **вы́пал** ~ it's been snowing; **как** ~ **на́ голову** like a bolt from the blue.

снеги́р|**ь** (-я́) *м* bullfinch.

снегови́к (-á) *м* snowman (*мн* snowmen).

снегоочисти́тел|**ь** (-я) *м* snowplough (*BRIT*), snowplow (*US*).

снегопа́д (-а) *м* snowfall.

снегоубо́рочн|**ый** *прил*: ~**ая маши́на** snowplough (*BRIT*), snowplow (*US*).

снегу́роч|**ка** (-ки; *gen pl* -ек) *ж* Snow Maiden.

снедь (-и) *ж собир* food.

снежи́н|**ка** (-ки; *gen pl* -ок) *ж* snowflake.

снежка́ *итп* *сущ см* **снежо́к**.

сне́жн|**ый** *прил* snow *опред*; ~**ая зима́** snowy winter; **сне́жная ба́ба** snowman (*мн* snowmen).

снеж|**о́к** (-ка́) *м* (*комок*) snowball; **игра́ть** (*impf*) **в** ~**ки́** to have a snowball fight.

сн|**ести́** (-есу́, -есёшь; *pt* -ёс, -есла́, -есло́) *сов от* **нести́** ♦ (*impf* **сноси́ть**) *перех* (*отнести*) to take; (*подлеж: буря*) to carry away; (*сверху вниз*) to take down; (*перен: вытерпеть*) to take; (*дом*) to demolish

▶ **снести́сь** *сов от* **нести́сь** ♦ *возв* (*связаться*): ~**сь с** +*instr* to contact.

снижа́|**ть(ся)** (-ю(сь)) *несов от* **сни́зить(ся)**.

сниже́ни|**е** (-я) *ср* (*цен итп*) lowering; (*самолёта*) descent; (*производительности итп*) reduction.

сни́|**зить** (-жу, -зишь; *impf* **снижа́ть**) *сов перех* (*цены, давление итп*) to lower; (*самолёт*) to descend; (*скорость*) to reduce

▶ **сни́зиться** (*impf* **снижа́ться**) *сов возв* (*цены, производительность итп*) to fall; (*самолёт*) to descend.

снизойти́ (*как* **идти́**; *см* **Table 18**; *impf* **снисходи́ть**) *сов неперех*: ~ **к кому́-н** *или* **до кого́-н** to condescend to sb; **он снизошёл к мое́й про́сьбе** *или* **до мое́й про́сьбы** he condescended to grant my request.

сни́зу *нареч* (*внизу*) at the bottom; (*по направлению вверх*) from the bottom; (*перен: со стороны народа*) from the masses; ~ **до́верху** from top to bottom.

сни́к|**нуть** (-ну, -нешь; *pt* -, -ла, -ло) *сов от* **ни́кнуть** ♦ *неперех* to flag.

снима́|**ть(ся)** (-ю(сь)) *несов от* **снять(ся)**.

сни́м|**ок** (-ка) *м* (*ФОТО*) snap(shot).

сниму́ *итп* *сов см* **снять(ся)**.

сни́с|**кать** (-щу́, -щешь) *сов перех* to win; **э́тот посту́пок** ~**ска́л ему́ большу́ю сла́ву** this deed won him great fame.

снисходи́тельн|**ый** (-ен, -ьна, -ьно) *прил* (*не строгий*) lenient; (*с оттенком высокомерия*) condescending.

снисхо́|**ди́ть** (-ожу́, -о́дишь) *несов от* **снизойти́**.

снисхожде́ни|**е** (-я) *ср* leniency.

снисхожу́ *несов см* **снисходи́ть**.

сни́ться (-юсь, -ишься; *perf* **присни́ться**) *несов безл*: **мне** ~**и́лся стра́шный сон** I was having a terrible dream; **мне** ~**и́лось, что я в гора́х** I dreamt I was in the mountains; **ты ча́сто** ~**и́шься мне** I often dream of you.

снищу́ *итп* *сов см* **сниска́ть**.

сноб (-а) *м* snob.

сноби́зм (-а) *м* snobbery.

сно́ва *нареч* again.

сн|**ова́ть** (-ую́) *несов неперех* (*люди*) to dash about; (*машины*) to zoom about.

сновиде́ни|**е** (-я) *ср* dream.

сногсшиба́тельн|**ый** (-ен, -ьна, -ьно) *прил*

(разг) stunning.

сноп (-а́) м (с.-х.) sheaf; (перен) shaft.

сноро́вк|а (-и) ж knack.

снос (-а) м demolition; **дом идёт на ~** the house is due for demolition; **э́тим боти́нкам сно́су нет** these boots are hard-wearing.

сно́сен прил см **сно́сный**.

сн|оси́ть (-ошу́, -о́сишь) несов от **снести́** ◆ (impf **сна́шивать**) сов перех (износить) to wear out.

сно́с|ка (-ки; gen pl -ок) ж footnote.

сно́сный (-ен, -на, -но) прил (разг) tolerable.

сно́сок сущ см **сно́ска**.

снотво́рн|ое (-ого; decl like adj) ср sleeping pill или tablet.

снотво́рн|ый прил: **~ое сре́дство** sedative.

снох|а́ (-и́) ж daughter-in-law (of husband's father).

сноше́ни|е (-я) ср relations мн; **входи́ть** (**войти́** perf) **в ~я с** +instr to enter into relations with.

сношу́ (не)сов см **сноси́ть**.

сня́ти|е (-я) ср removal.

сн|ять (-иму́, -и́мешь; impf **снима́ть**) сов перех to take down; (плод) to pick; (одежду) to take off; (запрет, ответственность) to remove; (копию) to make; (дом, комнату итп) to rent; (уволить) to dismiss; **снима́ть** (**~** perf) **фотогра́фию** to take a picture; **снима́ть** (**~** perf) **фильм** to shoot a film; **снима́ть** (**~** perf) **показа́ния** to take down evidence; **снима́ть** (**~** perf) **урожа́й** to gather the harvest

▶ **сня́ться** (impf **снима́ться**) сов возв (сфотографироваться) to have one's photograph taken; (покинуть: со стоянки) to move off; (актёр) to appear; (корабль): **~я́ться с я́коря** to up anchor.

со предл = **с**.

соа́втор (-а) м coauthor.

соа́вторств|о (-а) ср coauthorship; **в ~е с** +instr in coauthorship with.

соба́к|а (-и) ж dog; (разг) rat, dog; **он на э́том ~у съел** (разг) he knows it inside out; **вот где ~ зары́та!** so that's what it is!

собаково́д (-а) м dog-breeder.

собаково́дств|о (-а) ср dog-breeding.

соба́ч|ий (-ья, -ье, -ьи) прил (лай, нюх) dog's; **~ья жизнь** (разг) it's a dog's life; **на у́лице хо́лод ~** (разг) it's blooming cold outside.

соба́чник (-а) м (ловящий собак) dog-catcher; (разг: любитель собак) dog-lover.

собезья́нничalть (-ю) сов от **обезья́нничать**.

соберу́(сь) итп сов см **собра́ть(ся)**.

собе́с (-а) м сокр = **социа́льное обеспе́чение** social security; (учреждение) ≈ social security department.

собесе́дник (-а) м interlocutor; **мой ~ замолча́л** the person I was talking to fell silent.

собесе́дниц|а (-ы) ж см **собесе́дник**.

собесе́довани|е (-я) ср interview.

собира́ни|е (-я) ср (материала, данных итп) collection, gathering; (коллекционирование) collecting; (ягод, грибов) picking; **~ ма́рок** итп stamp итп collecting.

собира́телен прил см **собира́тельный**.

собира́тел|ь (-я) м collector.

собира́тельный (-ен, -ьна, -ьно) прил (также линг) collective.

собира́|ть (-ю) несов от **собра́ть**.

▶ **собира́ться** несов от **собра́ться** ◆ возв: **я ~юсь пойти́ туда́** I'm going to go there.

собко́р (-а) м сокр = **со́бственный корреспонде́нт: э́то сообще́ние от на́шего ~а в Москве́** this report is from our own correspondent in Moscow.

собла́зн (-а) м temptation; **устоя́ть** (perf) **пе́ред ~ом** или **про́тив ~а** to resist temptation; **вводи́ть** (**ввести́** perf) **кого́-н в ~** to tempt sb.

соблазни́телен прил см **соблазни́тельный**.

соблазни́тел|ь (-я) м seducer.

соблазни́тельный (-ен, -ьна, -ьно) прил tempting; (женщина) seductive.

соблазн|и́ть (-ю́, -и́шь; impf **соблазня́ть**) сов перех to seduce; (прельстить): **~ кого́-н чем-н** to tempt sb with sth

▶ **соблазни́ться** (impf **соблазня́ться**) сов возв: **~ся** +instr/+infin to be tempted by/to do.

соблюда́|ть (-ю) несов от **соблюсти́** ◆ перех (дисциплину, порядок) to maintain; **«~йте чистоту́»** "please keep this area tidy".

соблю|сти́ (-ду́, -дёшь) сов от **блюсти́** ◆ (impf **соблюда́ть**) перех (закон, правила) to observe.

соболе́зновани|е (-я) ср condolences мн; **выража́ть** (**вы́разить** perf) **кому́-н ~** to express one's condolences to sb.

соболе́зн|овать (-ую) несов неперех: **~ кому́-н** to condole with sb.

со́бол|ь (-оля; nom pl -оля́) м sable.

собо́р (-а) м cathedral; (съезд) council (of churches).

собо́рный прил (здание, колокол) cathedral опред; **~ое постановле́ние** decree of the church council.

собра́ни|е (-я) ср (партийное, профсоюзное) meeting; (представителей) assembly; (картин итп) collection; **собра́ние сочине́ний** collected works мн.

со́бран|ный (-, -на, -но) прил self-disciplined.

соб|ра́ть (-еру́, -ерёшь; pt -ра́л, -рала́, -ра́ло, impf **собира́ть**) сов перех to gather (together); (ягоды, грибы) to pick; (урожай) to gather; (станок, приёмник итп) to assemble; (марки, налоги, подписи) to collect; (перен: мужество) to muster up; (: силы) to summon; (пригото́-вить): **~ кого́-н в** +acc (в школу итп) to get sb ready for; **собира́ть** (**~** perf) **чемода́н/ве́щи** to pack one's suitcase/things

▶ **собра́ться** (impf **собира́ться**) сов возв (гости, делегаты) to assemble, gather; (в экспедицию, на урок итп) to get ready to go; (приготовиться): **~ся** +infin to get ready to do; **собира́ться** (**~ся** perf) **с** +instr (с силами, с мыслями) to gather; **собира́ться** (**~ся** perf) **с** ду́хом to pluck up the courage; **ты куда́ ~ра́лся?** where were you going?; **то́лько ~ра́лся лечь спать, как зазвони́л телефо́н** I was about to go to bed when the telephone rang.

со́бственник (-а) *м* (*владелец*) owner.

со́бственниц|а (-ы) *ж см* **со́бственник.**

со́бственническ|ий (-ая, -ое, -ие) *прил* proprietorial.

со́бственно *част* actually ♦ *вводн сл:* **~ (говоря́)** as a matter of fact.

собственнору́чный *прил* (*расписка*) own.

со́бственност|ь (-и) *ж* (*имущество*) property; (*владение*) ownership; **~ на** +*acc* right of ownership of; **быть** (*impf*) *или* **находи́ться** (*impf*) **в чьей-н ~и** to be in sb's possession; **приобрета́ть (приобрести́** *perf*) **в ~ что-н** to become the owner of sth.

со́бственн|ый *прил* (one's) own; **по ~ому жела́нию** of one's own volition; **и́мя ~ое** proper name; **чу́вство ~ого досто́инства** self-respect; **со́бственный корреспонде́нт** *см* **собко́р.**

собуты́льник (-а) *м* (*разг: пренебр*) drinking mate (BRIT) *или* buddy (US).

собы́ти|е (-я) *ср* event.

собью́(сь) *итп сов см* **сби́ть(ся).**

сов|а́ (-ы́; *nom pl* -ы) *ж* owl.

сова́ть (су́ю, суёшь; *perf* **су́нуть**) *несов перех* to put in; **~ (су́нуть** *perf*) **нос во что-н** to poke one's nose into sth

▸ **сова́ться** (*perf* **су́нуться**) *несов возв* (*разг: лезть*): **~ся вперёд** to push through; **~ся (су́нуться** *perf*) **не в своё де́ло** to poke one's nose into other people's business.

сов|ёнок (-ёнка; *nom pl* -я́та, *gen pl* -я́т) *м* owlet.

соверша́ть(ся) (-ю(сь)) *несов от* **соверши́ть(ся).**

соверше́нен *прил см* **соверше́нный.**

соверше́ни|е (-я) *ср* (*сделки*) conclusion; (*преступления*) committing.

соверше́нно *нареч* (*играть, исполнять*) perfectly; (*совсем*) absolutely, completely; **у меня́ ~ нет сил** I have absolutely no energy; **э́то ~ ве́рно** it's absolutely *или* completely true.

совершеннолети|е (-я) *ср:* **дости́гнуть ~я** to come of age.

совершенноле́тн|ий (-яя, -ее, -ие) *прил:* **стать ~им** to come of age.

соверше́нн|ый (-ен, -на, -но) *прил* (*безукоризненный*) perfect; (*абсолютный*) absolute, complete; **соверше́нный вид** perfective aspect.

соверше́нств|о (-а) *ср* perfection; **доводи́ть (довести́** *perf*) **что-н до ~а** to do sth to perfection; **в ~е владе́ть** (*impf*) **чем-н** to have a perfect command of sth.

соверше́нств|овать (-ую; *perf* **усоверше́нствовать**) *несов перех* to improve

▸ **соверше́нствоваться** (*perf* **усоверше́нствоваться**) *несов возв:* **~ся в** +*prp* to improve.

соверш|и́ть (-у́, -и́шь; *impf* **соверша́ть**) *сов перех* to make; (*сделку*) to conclude; (*преступление, проступок итп*) to commit; (*богослужение, обряд, подвиг*) to perform

▸ **соверши́ться** (*impf* **соверша́ться**) *сов возв* to take place.

со́вестлив|ый (-, -а, -о) *прил* conscientious.

со́вестно *как сказ:* **мне ~** +*infin* ... I am ashamed to do; **как ему́ не ~!** he ought to be ashamed of himself!

со́вест|ь (-и) *ж* conscience; **на ~** (*сделанный*) very well; **по ~и говоря́** to be honest; **поступа́ть (поступи́ть** *perf*) **по ~и** to behave as one's conscience dictates; **со споко́йной ~ю** with a clear conscience.

сове́т (-а) *м* advice *только ед*; (*семейный*) discussion; (*военный*) council; (*ист*) Soviet; **учёный ~** academic council; **С~ Безопа́сности ООН** United Nations Security Council; **дава́ть (дать** *perf*) **кому́-н ~** to give sb advice; **держа́ть** (*impf*) **~** to hold a council.

сове́тник (-а) *м* (*юстиции итп*) councillor; (*президента*) adviser.

сове́т|овать (-ую; *perf* **посове́товать**) *несов неперех:* **~ кому́-н** +*infin* to advise sb to do; **~** (*impf*) **кому́-н что-н** to recommend sth to sb

▸ **сове́товаться** (*perf* **посове́товаться**) *несов возв:* **~ся с кем-н** (*с другом*) to ask sb's advice; (*с врачом, с юристом*) to consult sb.

сове́тск|ий (-ая, -ое, -ие) *прил* Soviet.

сове́тчик (-а) *м* confidant(e); **в да́нном вопро́се я тебе́ не ~** I can't advise you on this subject.

совеща́ни|е (-я) *ср* (*собрание*) meeting; (*конференция*) conference.

совеща́тельный *прил* (*орган, голос*) consultative.

совеща́|ться (-юсь) *несов возв* to deliberate.

Совинформбюро́ *ср нескл сокр* (*ист*) = *Сове́тское информацио́нное бюро́.*

совка́ *итп сущ см* **сово́к.**

совко́в|ый *прил:* **~ая лопа́та** shovel.

совлада́|ть (-ю) *сов неперех:* **~ с** +*instr* to control; **~** (*perf*) **с собо́й** to control o.s.

совладе́л|ец (-ьца) *м* joint owner.

совладе́ни|е (-я) *ср* joint ownership.

совме́стен *прил см* **совме́стный.**

совмести́мост|ь (-и) *ж* compatibility.

совмести́м|ый (-, -а, -о) *прил* compatible.

совмести́тельств|о (-а) *ср:* **я рабо́таю по ~у секретарём** my second job is as a secretary.

совме|сти́ть (-щу́, -сти́шь; *impf* **совмеща́ть**) *сов перех* to combine; **он ~ща́л в себе́ учёного и администра́тора** he was both a scholar and an administrator.

совме́стно *нареч (работать, решать итп)*
jointly; ~ **с** +*instr* jointly with.

совме́ст|ный (**-ен, -на, -но**) *прил (общий)* joint;
совме́стное предприя́тие joint venture.

совмеща́|ть (**-ю**) *несов от* **совмести́ть ♦ перех**
(две должности) to combine.

совмеще́ни|е (**-я**) *ср* combining.

совмещу́ *сов см* **совмести́ть**.

сов|о́к (**-ка́**) *м (для мусора)* dustpan; *(для муки)*
scoop; *(строительный)* shovel.

совоку́пен *прил см* **совоку́пный**.

совоку́пност|ь (**-и**) *ж (факторов, причин)*
combination; **в ~и** in total.

совоку́п|ный (**-ен, -на, -но**) *прил (усилие)*
combined, joint.

совпада́|ть (*3sg* **-ет**, *3pl* **-ют**) *несов от*
совпа́сть.

совпаде́ни|е (**-я**) *ср (событий,
обстоятельств)* coincidence; *(данных, цифр)*
tallying; *(интересов, мнений)* meeting.

совпа́|сть (*3sg* **-дёт**, *3pl* **-ду́т**, *impf* **совпада́ть**)
сов неперех (события) to coincide; *(данные,
цифры итп)* to agree; *(интересы, мнения)* to
meet.

соврати́тел|ь (**-я**) *м* seducer.

совра|ти́ть (**-щу́, -ти́шь**; *impf* **совраща́ть**) *сов
перех (сбить с пути)* to lead astray; *(женщину)*
to seduce.

совр|а́ть (**-у́, -ёшь**) *сов от* **врать**.

совраща́|ть (**-ю**) *несов от* **соврати́ть**.

совращу́ *сов см* **соврати́ть**.

совреме́нен *прил см* **совреме́нный**.

совреме́нник (**-а**) *м* contemporary.

совреме́нниц|а (**-ы**) *ж см* **совреме́нник**.

совреме́нно *нареч (одеваться)* fashionably;
(звучать) modern.

совреме́нност|ь (**-и**) *ж (взглядов, идей)*
progressiveness; *(современная эпоха)* the
present day.

совреме́н|ный *прил* contemporary; (**-ен, -на,
-но**; *техника)* up-to-date; *(человек, идеи)*
modern.

совсе́м *нареч (новый, негодный итп)*
completely; *(молодой)* very; *(нисколько: не
пригодный, не нужный)* totally; **не ~** *(не
вполне)* not quite.

совхо́з (**-а**) *м сокр* (= *сове́тское хозя́йство*)
Sovkhoz *(state farm in the Soviet Union)*.

совью́(сь) *итп сов см* **свить(ся)**.

совя́та *итп сущ см* **совёнок**.

согла́сен *прил см* **согла́сный**.

согла́си|е (**-я**) *ср* consent; *(в семье)* harmony,
accord; **в ~и с** +*instr (с человеком)* in agreement
with; **с чьего́-н ~я** with sb's consent; **дава́ть
(дать** *perf*) **~ на что-н** to give one's consent to
sth; **приходи́ть** (**прийти́** *perf*) **к ~ю** to come to
an agreement; **жить** (*impf*) **в ~и** to live in
harmony.

согла|си́ться (**-шу́сь, -си́шься**; *impf*
соглаша́ться) *сов возв*: ~ **на что-н**/+*infin* to
agree to sth/to do; ~ (*perf*) **с** +*instr (с мнением, с*

высказыванием) to agree with; ~ (*perf*) **на чём-н**
(разг) to agree on sth.

согла́сно *нареч (жить, работать)* in harmony
♦ предл: ~ +*dat или* **с** +*instr* in accordance with.

согла́с|ный *прил*: ~ **звук** consonant **♦ (-ного;**
decl like adj) м consonant; (**-ен, -на, -но**; *дающий
согласие*): ~ **на** +*acc (на условия, на
ограничения)* agreeable to; **Вы ~ны (со мной)?**
do you agree (with me)?; **все ~ны?** are we all
agreed?; **я не ~ен** +*infin* ... I am not prepared to
....

согласова́ни|е (**-я**) *ср (действий, мер)*
coordinating; *(обсуждение: плана)*
coordination.

согласо́ван|ный (**-, -на, -но**) *прил (политика)*
concerted; *(стратегия)* agreed.

согласова́ть (**-ую**; *impf* **согласо́вывать**) *сов
перех (усилия, действия)* to coordinate;
(обговорить): ~ **что-н с** +*instr (план, цену)* to
agree sth with; ~ (*perf*) **что-н с чем-н** *(спрос с
предложением)* to make sth meet sth;
(прилагательное с существительным) to
make sth agree with sth

► **согласова́ться** *(не)сов возв*: **~ся с** +*instr* to
correspond with.

соглаша́ться (**-юсь**) *несов от* **согласи́ться**.

соглаше́ни|е (**-я**) *ср* agreement; **приходи́ть
(прийти́** *perf*) **к ~ю** to come to an agreement;
заключа́ть (заключи́ть *perf*) ~ to conclude an
agreement.

соглашу́сь *сов см* **согласи́ться**.

согн|а́ть (**сгоню́, сго́нишь**; *pt* **-а́л, -ала́, -а́ло**,
impf **сгоня́ть**) *сов перех (заставить
удалиться)* to drive away; *(собрать)* to round
up; **сгоня́ть** (~ *perf*) **улы́бку с лица́** to wipe a
smile off somebody's face.

согн|у́ть (**-у́, -ёшь**) *сов от* **гнуть, сгиба́ть**.

согр|ажда́нин (**-ажда́нина**; *nom pl* **-а́ждане**, *gen
pl* **-а́ждан**) *м* fellow citizen.

согрева́ни|е (**-я**) *ср (воды, пищи)* heating up;
(тела) warming up.

согре́|ть (**-ю**; *impf* **согрева́ть**) *сов перех (воду)*
to heat up; *(землю, ноги, руки)* to warm up;
(подлеж: мысль, ласка) to warm

► **согре́ться** (*impf* **согрева́ться**) *сов возв (вода)*
to heat up; *(человек, печка)* to warm up.

согреши́ть (**-у́, -и́шь**) *сов от* **греши́ть**.

со́д|а (**-ы**) *ж* soda; **питьева́я ~** bicarbonate of
soda.

соде́йстви|е (**-я**) *ср* assistance.

соде́йств|овать (**-ую**) *(не)сов неперех* (+*dat*) to
assist.

содержа́ни|е (**-я**) *ср (семьи, детей)* upkeep;
(магазина, фермы) keeping; *(книги, статьи)*
contents *мн*; *(человека: под арестом)* holding;
(сахара, витаминов) content; *(заработная
плата)* allowance; *(оглавление)* contents *мн*;
о́тпуск без ~я unpaid leave.

содержа́телен *прил см* **содержа́тельный**.

содержа́тел|ь (**-я**) *м (ресторана)* owner;
(магазина, пансиона) keeper.

содержа́тел|ьный (-ен, -ьна, -ьно) *прил* (*статья, доклад*) informative.

содержа́ть (-ержу́, -е́ржишь) *несов перех* (*детей, родителей, магазин*) to keep; (*ресторан*) to own; (*сахар, ошибки, информацию итп*) to contain; (*человека: под аре́стом*) to hold; ~ (*impf*) **что-н в чистоте́/в поря́дке** to keep sth clean/in order

▶ **содержа́ться** *несов возв* (*под аре́стом*) to be held; **в кни́ге ~е́ржится интере́сная информа́ция** the book contains interesting information; **~ся** (*impf*) **в чистоте́/в поря́дке** to be kept clean/in order.

содержи́м|ое (-ого; *decl like adj*) *ср* (*банки, сумки итп*) contents *мн*.

со́довый *прил* (*раствор*) soda *опред*.

содра́ть (сдеру́, сдерёшь; *pt* -а́л, -ала́, -а́ло, *impf* **сдира́ть**) *сов перех* (*слой, одежду*) to tear off; **сдира́ть** (~ *perf*) **ко́жу с чего́-н** to skin sth; ~ (*perf*) **что-н с кого́-н** (*разг: дорого взять*) to sting sb for sth.

содрога́ни|е (-я) *ср* (*стен, стёкол*) shaking; (*от боли, от ужаса*) shuddering.

содрога́|ться (-юсь; *perf* **содрогну́ться**) *несов возв* (*стены, земля*) to shake; (*от боли, от страха итп*) to shudder.

содру́жеств|о (-а) *ср* (*дружба*) cooperation; (*союз*) commonwealth; **Содру́жество Незави́симых Госуда́рств** the Commonwealth of Independent States.

со́евый *прил* soya *опред*.

соедине́ни|е (-я) *ср* (*сил*) joining; (*проводов*) connection; (*учёбы с работой*) combination; (*место соединения*) contact; (*ВОЕН*) formation.

соедини́тел|ь (-я) *м* (*ЭЛЕК*) adaptor.

соедини́тельный *прил* (*провод, труба*) connecting.

соедини́|ть (-ю́, -йшь; *impf* **соединя́ть**) *сов перех* (*силы, усилия, детали*) to join; (*людей*) to unite; (*провода, трубы, по телефону*) to connect; (*установить сообщение*) to link; (*сочетать*): ~ **что-н с** +*instr* to combine sth with; **в ней ~ены́ ум и красота́** she is both clever and beautiful

▶ **соедини́ться** (*impf* **соединя́ться**) *сов возв* (*люди, отряды*) to join together; **~ся** (*perf*) **с кем** to make contact with sb.

сожале́ни|е (-я) *ср* (*сострадание*) pity; ~ (**о** +*prp*) (*о прошлом, о потере*) regret (about); **к ~ю** unfortunately; **к мо́ему (вели́кому** *или* **глубо́кому) ~ю** to my (great *или* deep) regret.

сожале́|ть (-ю) *несов неперех*: ~ (**о** +*prp*) (*об ошибке, о поступке*) to regret.

сожгу́ *итп сов см* **сжечь**.

сожже́ни|е (-я) *ср* (*еретика*) burning.

сожи́тел|ь (-я) *м* cohabiter.

сожи́тельниц|а (-ы) *ж см* **сожи́тель**.

сожму́(сь) *итп сов см* **сжа́ть(ся)**.

сожну́ *итп сов см* **сжать**.

сожр|а́ть (-у́, -ёшь) *сов от* **жрать**.

созва́ниваться (-юсь) *несов см* **созвони́ться**.

соз|ва́ть (-ову́, -овёшь; *pt* -ва́л, -вала́, -ва́ло, *impf* **сзыва́ть**) *сов перех* (*пригласить*) to summon; (*impf* **созыва́ть**; *съезд, конференцию итп*) to convene.

созве́зди|е (-я) *ср* constellation.

созвони́ться (-ю́сь, -йшься; *impf* **созва́ниваться**) *сов возв*: ~ +*instr* to phone (*BRIT*) *или* call (*US*); (*договориться*): **нам на́до** ~ we should fix something over the phone.

созву́чен *прил см* **созву́чный**.

созву́чи|е (-я) *ср* (*МУЗ*) sonority.

созву́чный (-ен, -на, -но) *прил* harmonious; (*слова*) assonant; ~**но** +*dat* (*соответствующий*) in keeping with; ~**но с** +*instr* in keeping with.

созда|ва́ть(ся) (-ю́(сь), -ёшь(ся)) *несов от* **созда́ть(ся)**.

созда́м(ся) *итп сов см* **созда́ть(ся)**.

созда́ни|е (-я) *ср* creation; (*школы*) foundation; (*человек, животное*) creature.

созда́ст(ся) *сов см* **созда́ть(ся)**.

созда́тел|ь (-я) *м* creator; (*школы*) founder.

созда́тельниц|а (-ы) *ж см* **созда́тель**.

созда́ть (*как* **дать**; *см* **Table 14**; *impf* **создава́ть**) *сов перех* to create; (*школу*) to found

▶ **созда́ться** (*impf* **создава́ться**) *сов возв* (*обстановка*) to emerge; (*впечатление*) to be created.

созерца́ни|е (-я) *ср* (*рассматривание*) contemplation; (*душевное*) reflection.

созерца́|ть (-ю) *несов перех* (*рассматривать*) to contemplate.

созида́тел|ьный (-ен, -ьна, -ьно) *прил* creative.

созна|ва́ть (-ю́, -ёшь) *несов от* **созна́ть** ♦ *перех* to be aware of; ~ (*impf*), **что** ... to realize that ...

▶ **сознава́ться** *несов от* **созна́ться**.

созна́ни|е (-я) *ср* consciousness; (*вины, долга*) awareness; **приходи́ть (прийти́** *perf*) **в** ~ to come round; **теря́ть (потеря́ть** *perf*) ~ to lose consciousness; **он рабо́тал до поте́ри ~я** he worked himself senseless.

созна́телен *прил см* **созна́тельный**.

созна́тельность (-и) *ж* (*политическая, социальная*) awareness.

созна́тел|ьный (-ен, -ьна, -ьно) *прил* (*жизнь, возраст*) conscious; (*отношение, человек*) intelligent; (*обман, поступок*) deliberate, intentional.

созна́|ть (-ю; *impf* **сознава́ть**) *сов перех* (*вину, долг*) to realize

▶ **созна́ться** (*impf* **сознава́ться**) *сов возв*: ~**ся** (**в** +*prp*) (*в ошибке, в каком-н намерении*) to admit (to); *(преступник)* to confess (to); **на́до** ~**ся** admittedly.

созову́ *итп сов см* **созва́ть**.

созрева́ть (-ю) *несов неперех* = **зреть**.

созре́ть (-ю) *сов от* **зреть**.

созы́в (-а) *м (съезда, собрания)* calling.

созыва́ть (-ю) *несов от* **созва́ть**.

СОИ *ж сокр* (= *стратеги́ческая оборо́нная инициати́ва*) SDI (*US*) (= *Strategic Defense Initiative*).

соизмери́м|ый (-, -а, -о) *прил (величины)* proportional; *(поня́тия, це́нности)* comparable.

соизме́р|ить (-ю, -ишь; *impf* **соизмеря́ть**) *сов перех* to compare.

соиска́ни|е (-я) *ср*: **на** ~ **чего́-н** pursuing sth.

соиска́тел|ь (-я) *м (приза, награды)* competitor; *(учёной сте́пени)* candidate.

сойти́ (*как* **идти́**; *см* **Table 18**; *impf* **сходи́ть**) *сов неперех (с горы, с ле́стницы)* to go down; *(с доро́ги)* to leave; *(подле́ж: кра́ска, зага́р итп)* to come off; *(разг)*: ~ **с** +*instr (с по́езда, с авто́буса)* to get off; ~ *(perf)* **за** +*acc (за актёра, за богача́)* to pass as; **сходи́ть** (~ *perf*) **с ума́** to go mad; **фильм** ~**шёл с экра́на** the film is not shown anymore; **с ума́ сойдёшь** *или* ~ *(разг)* the mind boggles; **всё** ~**шло́ благополу́чно** everything's turned out well; ~**йдёт и так)** *(разг)* it will do (as it is); **ему́ всё схо́дит с рук** he gets away with everything

▸ **сойти́сь** (*impf* **сходи́ться**) *сов возв (встре́титься)* to meet; *(собра́ться)* to gather; *(ци́фры, показа́ния)* to tally; *(перен)*: ~**сь с** +*instr (подружи́ться)* to become friendly with; ~**шли́сь на том, что ...** it was agreed that ...; ~**сь** *(perf)* **во взгля́дах/во вку́сах** *(перен)* to have similar views/tastes; **сойти́сь** (~**сь** *perf*) **на цене́/усло́виях** to agree on a price/conditions; ~**сь** *(perf)* **хара́ктерами** to get on.

сок (-а; *part gen* -у, *loc sg* -у́) *м* juice; *(также:* **фрукто́вый** ~) (fruit) juice.

соковыжима́л|ка (-ки; *gen pl* -ок) *ж* juice extractor.

со́кол (-а) *м* falcon.

сокол|ёнок (-ёнка; *nom pl* -**я́та**, *gen pl* -**я́т**) *ж* falcon chick.

соколи́н|ый *прил (гнездо́)* falcon's *опред;* ~**ая охо́та** falconry.

соколя́та *итп сущ см* **соколёнок**.

сокра|ти́ть (-щу́, -ти́шь; *impf* **сокраща́ть**) *сов перех (путь, рабо́чий день, статью́)* to shorten; *(расхо́ды)* to cut down, reduce

▸ **сократи́ться** (*impf* **сокраща́ться**) *сов возв (расстоя́ние, сро́ки)* to be shortened; *(расхо́ды, снабже́ние)* to be reduced.

сокраще́ни|е (-я) *ср (см глаг)* shortening; cutting down, reduction; *(сокращённое назва́ние)* abbreviation; *(также:* ~ **шта́тов)** staff reduction; **попада́ть** (**попа́сть** *perf*) **под** ~ **(шта́тов)** to be made redundant.

сокращённый *прил (вариа́нт те́кста)* abridged; *(рабо́чий день)* shortened; *(сло́во)* abbreviated.

сокращу́(сь) *сов см* **сократи́ть(ся)**.

сокрове́нный (-ен, -на, -но) *прил (мы́сли итп)* innermost; *(смысл, мечта́)* intimate.

сокро́вищ|е (-а) *ср (обычно мн: также перен)* treasure.

сокро́вищница (-ы) *ж (ме́сто)* treasury; *(совоку́пность)*: ~ +*gen* wealth.

сокруша́ть (-ю) *несов от* **сокруши́ть**

▸ **сокруша́ться** *несов возв (огорча́ться)* to be distressed.

сокруше́ни|е (-я) *ср (проти́вника)* destruction; *(огорче́ние)* distress.

сокруши́тел|ьный (-ен, -ьна, -ьно) *прил* devastating.

сокруши́|ть (-у́, -и́шь; *impf* **сокруша́ть**) *сов перех (а́рмию)* to crush; *(режи́м)* to overthrow.

соку́рсник (-а) *м*: **он мой** ~ he is in my year.

соку́рсниц|а (-ы) *ж*: **она́ моя́** ~ she is in my year.

сол|га́ть (-гу́, -жёшь *итп*, -гу́т) *сов от* **лгать**.

солда́т (-а) *м* soldier.

солда́тик (-а) *м уменьш от* **солда́т**; *(игру́шка)* toy soldier.

солда́т|ка (-ки; *gen pl* -ок) *ж* soldier's wife *(мн* wives).

солда́тск|ий (-ая, -ое, -ие) *прил* soldier's.

солдафо́н (-а) *м (разг: пренебр)* squaddie.

соле́ни|е (-я) *ср (огурцо́в)* pickling; *(ры́бы)* salting.

солёно|е (-ого; *decl like adj*) *ср* salty food.

солёный *прил (ве́тер)* salty; *(о́вощи)* pickled in brine; *(вода́)* salt *опред;* *(ры́ба)* salted; (-**он**, -**она́**, -**оно́**; *пи́ща)* salty.

соле́нь|е (-я) *ср (обычно мн)* ≈ pickle.

солжёшь *итп сов см* **солга́ть**.

солида́рен *прил см* **солида́рный**.

солида́рност|ь (-и) *ж* solidarity.

солида́р|ный (-ен, -на, -но) *прил*: **я с ним** ~**ен** I am on his side.

соли́д|ный (-ен, -на, -но) *прил (постро́йка)* solid; *(зна́ния, рабо́та)* sound; *(фи́рма, специали́ст)* established; *(челове́к, мане́ры)* respectable; *(ме́бель, оде́жда)* quality; ~ **во́зраст** respectable age.

соли́р|овать (-ую) *несов* to play a solo part.

соли́ст (-а) *м* soloist.

соли́стк|а (-ки; *gen pl* -ок) *ж см* **соли́ст**.

сол|и́ть (-ю́, -и́шь; *perf* **посоли́ть**) *несов перех (суп, рагу́)* to salt; *(заса́ливать)* to preserve in brine.

со́лнечный *прил (эне́ргия, лучи́ итп)* solar; (-**ен**, -**на**; *день, пого́да)* sunny; **со́лнечное сплете́ние** solar plexus; **со́лнечный уда́р** sunstroke; **со́лнечные очки́** sunglasses.

со́лнц|е (-а) *ср* sun.

солнцезащи́т|ный *прил*: ~ **крем** suncream.

солнцепёк (-а) *м*: **на** ~**е** in a sunny spot.

солнцестоя́ни|е (-я) *ср* solstice.

со́ло *ср нескл, нареч* solo.

солов|е́й (-ья́) *м* nightingale.

соловé|ть (-ю; *perf* **осоловéть**) *несов неперех* (*разг*) to become dazed.
соловьи́ный *прил* nightingale *опред*.
соловья́ *итп сущ см* **соловéй**.
сóлод (-а) *м* malt.
солóм|а (-ы) *ж* straw.
солóменный *прил* (*шляпа*) straw *опред*; (*крыша*) thatched; (*цвет*) straw-coloured (*BRIT*), straw-colored (*US*).
соломи́н|а (-ы) *ж* straw.
солóмин|ка (-ки; *gen pl* **-ок**) *ж уменьш от* **соломи́на**; (*перен*): **хвата́ться за** ~**ку** to clutch at straws.
солóм|ка (-ки; *gen pl* **-ок**) *ж уменьш от* **солóма**; (*печенье*) *long thin biscuit or bread stick*.
сóлон *итп прил см* **солёный**.
солóн|ка (-ки; *gen pl* **-ок**) *ж* saltcellar.
солонча́к (-á) *м* saltmarsh.
сол|ь (-и) *ж* salt; (*gen pl* **-éй**; *хим*) salt; (*перен*): ~ +*gen* (*вопроса, рассказа*) point of ♦ *ср нескл* (*муз*) soh; **столóвая** ~ table salt.
сóльный *прил* solo *опред*.
солью́(сь) *сов см* **сли́ть(ся)**.
соля́н|ка (-ки; *gen pl* **-ок**) *ж spicy meat and vegetable soup*; (*рагу*) ragout.
соляно́й *прил* (*раствор*) saline; (*промысел, залежи*) salt *опред*.
соля́нок *сущ см* **соля́нка**.
сом (-á) *м* catfish.
Сома́ли *ср нескл* Somalia.
сомкн|у́ть (-у́, **-ёшь**; *impf* **смыка́ть**) *сов перех* to close; **я глаз не** ~**у́л всю ночь** I didn't sleep a wink all night
▸ **сомкну́ться** (*impf* **смыка́ться**) *сов возв* to close.
сомнева́|ться (-юсь) *несов возв*: ~ (**в** +*prp*) to doubt; ~**юсь, что э́то пра́вда** I doubt that is true; **не** ~**йся приду́** don't worry, I'll come.
сомнéни|е (-я) *ср* (*неуверенность*) doubt; **вне** *или* **без** (**вся́кого**) ~**я** without a doubt; **брать** (**взять** *perf*) **что-н под** ~ to doubt sth.
сомни́телен *прил см* **сомни́тельный**.
сомни́тельно *как сказ* it's doubtful; ~, **что́бы он согласи́лся** it's doubtful he'll agree; **он придёт?-** ~ he's coming? - it's unlikely *или* not likely.
сомни́тел|ьный (-ен, -ьна, -ьно) *прил* (*дело, личность*) shady; (*предложение, знакомство*) dubious; (*комплимент, речи*) ambiguous; (*победа*) questionable.
сомну́(сь) *итп сов см* **смя́ть(ся)**.
сон (**сна**) *м* sleep; (*сновидение*) dream; **ви́деть** (**уви́деть** *perf*) **что-н во сне** to have a dream about sth; **ви́деть** (*impf*) ~ to have a dream; **сквозь** ~ **слы́шать** (**услы́шать** *perf*) to hear in one's sleep; **со сна** half-awake.
сона́т|а (-ы) *ж* sonata.
сонéт (-а) *м* sonnet.

сонли́вый *прил* sleepy.
сóнн|ый *прил* (*заспанный*) sleepy, somnolent; (*вялый*) drowsy; ~**ые виде́ния** dreams.
сóн|я (-и) *ж* (*животное*) dormouse (*мн dormice*) ♦ *м/ж* (*разг*) sleepyhead.
соображá|ть (-ю) *несов от* **сообрази́ть** ♦ *неперех* (*разг*: **быть собрази́тельным**) to be quick; (*смыслить*): ~ **в** +*prp* to be good at; **я сего́дня пло́хо** ~**ю** I'm slow on the uptake today.
соображéни|е (-я) *ср* (*суждение*) reasoning; (*обычно мн*: *мотивы*) reason; **из фина́нсовых/педагоги́ческих** ~**й** for financial/educational reasons.
соображу́ *сов см* **сообрази́ть**.
сообрази́тел|ьный (-ен, -ьна, -ьно) *прил* bright.
сообра|зи́ть (-жу́, **-зи́шь**; *impf* **соображáть**) *сов неперех* to work out; **нам на́до** ~, **что де́лать да́льше** we've got to work out what to do next.
сообра́зно *предл*: ~ +*dat или* **с** +*instr* in accordance with.
сообра́зный *прил*: ~ **с** +*instr* in agreement with.
сообща́ *нареч* together.
сообща́|ть (-ю) *несов от* **сообщи́ть**
▸ **сообща́ться** *несов от* **сообщи́ться** ♦ *возв*: ~**ся с** +*instr* (*связываться*) to communicate with.
сообщéни|е (-я) *ср* (*действие*: *новостей, результатов*) reporting; (*по радио*) report; (*правительственное*) announcement; (*срочное*) communication; (*автобусное, почтовое*) communications *мн*; ~ **об оши́бке** (*комп*) error message.
сообщéств|о (-а) *ср* association; **в** ~**е с** +*instr* in association with; **мировóе** *или* **междунарóдное** ~ international community.
сообщ|и́ть (-у́, **-и́шь**; *impf* **сообща́ть**) *сов неперех*: ~ **кому́-н о** +*prp* to inform sb of ♦ *перех* (*новости, тайну*) to tell
▸ **сообщи́ться** (*impf* **сообща́ться**) *сов возв* (+*dat*) to be communicated.
сообщник (-а) *м* accomplice.
сообщни́ц|а (-ы) *ж см* **сообщник**.
соору|ди́ть (-жу́, **-ди́шь**; *impf* **сооружа́ть**) *сов перех* (*построить*) to erect; (*разг*: **смастери́ть**) to put together; (: *ужин, выпить*) to knock up.
сооружá|ть (-ю) *несов от* **сооруди́ть**.
сооружéни|е (-я) *ср* (*действие*: *здания*) erection; (*крупная постройка*) structure.
сооружу́ *сов см* **сооруди́ть**.
соотвéтственно *нареч* (*как следует*) accordingly ♦ *предл*: ~ +*dat* (*обстано́вке*) according to; ~ **с** +*instr* in accordance with.
соотвéтствен|ный (-, **-на, -но**) *прил* (*оплата*) appropriate; (*результаты*) fitting.
соотвéтстви|е (-я) *ср* (*интересов, стилей*

итп) conformity; **в ~и с** +*instr* in accordance with.

соотвéтств|овать (-**ую**) *несов неперех:* ~ +*dat* (*интерéсам, дóлжности итп*) to correspond with; (*трéбованиям*) to meet; **э́то не ~ует действи́тельности** it does not correspond with reality.

соотвéтствующий (-**ая, -ее, -ие**) *прил* appropriate; **~им óбразом** accordingly.

соотéчественник (-**а**) *м* compatriot.

соотéчественниц|а (-**ы**) *ж см* **соотéчественник**.

соотн|ести́ (-**есу́, -есёшь;** *pt* **-ёс, -есла́, -есло́,** *impf* **соотноси́ть**) *сов перех:* ~ **что-н с чем-н** to correlate sth with sth.

соотноси́тельный (-**ен, -ьна, -ьно**) *прил* correlating.

соотн|оси́ть (-**ошу́, -óсишь**) *несов от* **соотнести́**

▸ **соотноси́ться** *несов возв* to correlate.

соотношéни|е (-**я**) *ср* correlation.

соотношу́(сь) *несов см* **соотноси́ть(ся)**.

сóпел *сущ см* **сóпло**.

сопережива́|ть (-**ю**) *несов неперех* to empathize.

сопéрник (-**а**) *м* rival; (*в спóрте*) competitor.

сопéрниц|а (-**ы**) *ж см* **сопéрник**.

сопéрнича|ть (-**ю**) *несов неперех:* ~ **с кем-н в чём-н** to rival sb in sth.

сопéть (-**лю́, -и́шь**) *несов неперех* to snort.

сóп|ка (-**ки;** *gen pl* **-ок**) *ж* (*холм*) hill; (*вулкáн*) volcano.

сóпл|и (-**ей**) *мн* (*разг*) snot *ед*.

сопли́вый *прил* (*разг: ребёнок*) snotty; **он ещё ~ мальчи́шка!** (*разг*) he's still just a young whippersnapper!

сóп|ло (-**лá;** *nom pl* **-ла,** *gen pl* **-ел**) *ср* nozzle.

соплю́ *несов см* **сопéть**.

сóпок *сущ см* **сóпка**.

сопостави́м|ый (-, **-а, -о**) *прил* comparable.

сопостáв|ить (-**лю, -ишь;** *impf* **сопоставля́ть**) *сов перех:* ~ **что-н (с** +*instr*) to collate sth (with).

сопрáно *ср нескл* soprano.

сопредéльный (-**ен, -ьна, -ьно**) *прил* (*óбласть, странá итп*) neighbouring *опред* (*BRIT*), neighboring *опред* (*US*); (*наýка, поня́тие*) related.

сопрéть (*3sg* **-ет,** *3pl* **-ют**) *сов от* **преть**.

соприкаса́|ться (-**юсь;** *perf* **соприкосну́ться**) *несов возв* (*предмéты, учáстки*) to adjoin; (*интерéсы*) to cross over; ~ (**соприкосну́ться** *perf*) **с кем-н** to come into contact with sb.

сопроводи́тель (-**я**) *м* escort.

сопроводи́тельный *прил* (*докумéнт*) accompanying *опред*; **сопроводи́тельное письмó** covering letter.

сопрово|ди́ть (-**жу́, -ди́шь;** *impf* **сопровожда́ть**) *сов перех* to accompany; (*no impf:* **дополнить**): ~ **что-н чем-н** to attach sth to sth.

сопровожда́|ть (-**ю**) *несов от* **сопроводи́ть** ◆

перех (*расскáз, пéние*) to accompany

▸ **сопровожда́ться** *несов возв:* ~**ся** +*instr* to be accompanied by.

сопровождéни|е (-**я**) *ср* (*дéйствие*) escorting; (*аккомпанемéнт*) accompaniment; **в ~и** +*gen* accompanied by.

сопровожу́ *сов см* **сопроводи́ть**.

сопротивлéни|е (-**я**) *ср* resistance; (*ИСТ*) the Resistance; **окáзывать (оказáть** *perf*) ~ **кому́-н** to put up resistance to sb.

сопротивля́емост|ь (-**и**) *ж* resistance.

сопротивля́|ться (-**юсь**) *несов возв* (+*dat*) to resist.

сопру́ *итп сов см* **спереть**.

сопряжён|ный (-, **-á, -о**) *прил:* ~ **с** +*instr* (*с опáсностями итп*) involving.

сопу́тств|овать (*3sg* **-ует,** *3pl* **-уют**) *несов неперех* (+*dat*) to accompany.

сопью́сь *итп сов см* **спи́ться**.

сор (-**а;** *part gen* **-у**) *м* rubbish; **выноси́ть** (*impf*) ~ **из избы́** (*перен*) to wash one's dirty linen in public.

соразмéрен *прил см* **соразмéрный**.

соразмéр|ить (-**ю, -ишь;** *impf* **соразмеря́ть**) *сов перех:* ~ **что-н с чем-н** to measure sth against sth.

соразмéрный (-**ен, -на, -но**) *прил:* ~ +*dat* proportionate to; ~**но** +*dat или* **с** +*instr* according to.

соразмеря́|ть (-**ю**) *несов от* **соразмéрить**.

сорáтник (-**а**) *м* comrade in arms.

сорáтниц|а (-**ы**) *ж см* **сорáтник**.

сорван|éц (-**цá**) *м* (*разг*) scamp.

сорв|а́ть (-**у́, -ёшь;** *pt* **-áл, -алá, -áло,** *impf* **срыва́ть**) *сов перех* (*цветóк, я́блоко*) to pick; (*дверь, крышу, одéжду итп*) to tear off; (*лéкцию, переговóры*) to sabotage; (*плáны*) to frustrate; (*разг: аплодисмéнты*) to get; (: *перен*): ~ **что-н на ком-н** (*гнев, злóбу*) to take sth out on sb; ~ (*perf*) **гóлос** to lose one's voice

▸ **сорва́ться** (*impf* **срыва́ться**) *сов возв:* ~**ся с** +*instr* (*с петéль*) to come away from; (*с лéстницы*) to fall off; (*перен: потеря́ть самооблада́ние*) to lose one's temper; (*плáны*) to be frustrated; (*лéкция*) to have to be cancelled; ~**ся** (*perf*) **с мéста** to dash off; **у негó срыва́лся гóлос** his voice was faltering; **он как с цéпи ~áлся** (*пренебр*) he's gone completely berserk.

сорганиз|ова́ться (-**у́юсь**) *сов от* **организова́ться**.

соревнова́ни|е (-**я**) *ср* competition; **кома́ндные ~я** team event; **отбóрочные ~я** elimination contests.

соревн|ова́ться (-**у́юсь**) *несов возв* to compete.

сориенти́р|оваться (-**уюсь**) *сов от* **ориенти́роваться**.

сори́н|ка (-**ки;** *gen pl* **-ок**) *ж* speck.

сор|и́ть (-**ю́, -и́шь;** *perf* **насори́ть**) *несов неперех* to make a mess; ~ (*impf*) **деньга́ми** to throw

one's money about *или* around.
сóрн|ый *прил* refuse *опред*; ~**ая травá** weeds.
сорня́к (-á) *м* weed.
сóрок (-á; *см* **Table 28)** *чис* forty; **емý за** ~ he's
over forty; *см также* **пятьдеся́т.**
соро́к|а (-и) *ж* magpie; *(о болтливом человеке)*
chatterbox.
сорокалéти|е (-я) *ср (срок)* forty years;
(годовщина события) fortieth anniversary.
сорокалéтн|ий (-яя, -ее, -ие) *прил (период)*
forty-year; *(человек)* forty-year-old.
сороков|óй (-áя, -óе, -ы́е) *чис* fortieth; *см
также* **пятидеся́тый.**
сороконóж|ка (-ки; *gen pl* **-ек)** *ж* centipede.
соро́ч|ка (-ки; *gen pl* **-ек)** *ж (мужская)* shirt;
нóчная ~ nightgown; **ни́жняя** ~ undergarment.
сорт (-а; *nom pl* **-á)** *м (товара, продукта)* sort;
(пшеницы) grade; **пéрвый** ~ Grade 1; *(перен)*
first rate; **товáр пéрвого сóрта** a Grade 1
product.
сортамéнт (-а) *м* assortment.
сортировáльный *прил* sorting *опред*.
сортиров|áть (-ýю) *несов перех (также КОМП)*
to sort; *(по сортам, качеству)* to grade.
сортирóв|ка (-ки; *gen pl* **-ок)** *ж (см глаг)* sorting;
grading.
сóртный *прил* ≈ Grade A *или* 1 *опред*.
сортовóй *прил* = **сóртный.**
сос|áть (-ý, -ёшь) *несов перех* to suck;
(младенец, детёныш) to suckle; **у меня́** ~**ёт
под лóжечкой** *(разг)* I've got a sore stomach.
сосвáта|ть (-ю) *сов от* **свáтать.**
сосéд (-а; *nom pl* **-и,** *gen pl* **-éй)** *м* neighbour
(BRIT), neighbor *(US)*.
сосéдн|ий (-яя, -ее, -ие) *прил* neighbouring
(BRIT), neighboring *(US)*.
сосéдств|о (-а) *ср*: **жить по** ~**у** to live nearby; **в**
~**е с** *+instr* near.
сóсен *сущ см* **соснá.**
соси́с|ка (-ки; *gen pl* **-ок)** *ж* sausage.
сóс|ка (-ки; *gen pl* **-ок)** *ж (на бутылке)* teat;
(пустышка) dummy.
соскá *итп сущ см* **сосóк.**
соскáблива|ть (-ю) *несов от* **соскобли́ть.**
соскáкива|ть (-ю) *несов от* **соскочи́ть.**
соскáльзыва|ть (-ю) *несов от* **соскользну́ть.**
соскобл|и́ть (-ю́, -и́шь; *impf* **соскáбливать)** *сов
перех* to scrape off.
соскользн|у́ть (-ý, -ёшь; *impf* **соскáльзывать)**
сов неперех (с горы) to slide down; *(платок)* to
slip off.
соскоч|и́ть (-очý, -óчишь; *impf* **соскáкивать)**
сов неперех (с лошади, с поезда итп) to jump
off; *(с головы, с ноги)* to slip off.
соскреб|áть (-ю) *несов от* **соскрести́.**
соскр|ести́ (-ебý, -ебёшь; *pt* **-ёб, -еблá, -еблó,**
impf **соскребáть)** *сов перех* to scrape away *или*
off.

соску́ч|иться (-усь, -ишься) *сов возв (в чужом
городе)* to be homesick; *(затосковать)* ~ **по**
+*dat* to miss.
сослагáтельн|ый *прил*: ~**ое наклонéние**
subjunctive mood.
со|слáть (-шлю́, -шлёшь; *impf* **ссылáть)** *сов
перех* to exile
▶ **сослáться** *(impf* **ссылáться)** *сов возв*: ~**ся на**
+*acc* to refer to.
сóслепу *нареч (разг)* being unable to see
properly.
сосло́ви|е (-я) *ср* social class.
сосло́вный *прил* class *опред*.
сослужи́в|ец (-ца) *м* colleague.
сослужи́вица (-ы) *ж см* **сослужи́вец.**
сослужи́вца *итп сущ см* **сослужи́вец.**
сослуж|и́ть (-ужý, -ýжишь) *сов перех*: ~
слýжбу комý-н *(человек)* to do sb a good turn;
(вещь) to serve sb well.
сос|нá (-ны́; *nom pl* **-ны,** *gen pl* **-ен)** *ж* pine (tree);
заблуди́ть|ся *(perf)* **в трёх сóснах** *(перен: разг)*
to fail to solve a simple problem; **сиби́рская** ~
cedar.
сосно́вый *прил* pine *опред*.
сосн|у́ть (-ý, -ёшь) *сов неперех* to take a nap.
сóсок *сущ см* **сóска.**
сос|óк (-кá) *м* nipple.
сосредотáчива|ть(ся) (-ю(сь)) *несов от*
сосредотóчить(ся).
сосредотóчен|ный (-, -на, -но) *прил (атака,
взгляд)* concentrated; *(ученик, работник)*
attentive.
сосредотóч|ить (-у, -ишь; *impf*
сосредотáчивать) *сов перех (войска)* to
concentrate; *(мысли, внимание)* to concentrate,
focus
▶ **сосредотóчиться** *(impf* **сосредотáчиваться)** *сов возв (войска)* to be
concentrated; *(внимание)* to concentrate, focus.
состáв (-а) *м (товарный, пассажирский)* train;
(классовый) structure; ~ +*gen (комитета,
комиссии)* members мн of; *(вещества)*
composition *мн*; **руководя́щий** ~ management
(staff); **преподавáтельский** ~ teaching staff; **в**
~**е** +*gen* among(st); **входи́ть** *(impf)* **в** ~ +*gen* to
be a member of; **войти́** *(perf)* **в** ~ +*gen* to become
a member of; **грýппа вернýлась в пóлном** ~**е**
all members of the group returned; **в** ~
делагáции вошли́ ... the delegation was made
up of ...; **коми́ссия в** ~**е 10 человéк** a
commission consisting of 10 members; **состáв
преступлéния** *(ЮР)* constitution of a crime.
состави́тел|ь (-я) *м (словаря)* compiler;
(сборника) editor.
состáв|ить (-лю, -ишь; *impf* **составля́ть)** *сов
перех (фразу)* to make; *(словарь, список)* to
compile; *(план)* to draw up; *(коллекцию,
мнение, впечатление)* to form; *(какую-нибудь*

сумму) to constitute; (*ме́бель*) to put together; ~ (*perf*) **себе́ и́мя** to make a name for o.s.;
составля́ть (~ *perf*) **кому́-н компа́нию** to join sb; **составля́ть** (~ *perf*) **себе́ представле́ние о чём-н** to form an impression about sth; **э́то не** ~**ит большо́го труда́** it won't take a lot of effort
▸ **соста́виться** (*impf* **составля́ться**) *сов возв* (*колле́кция, хор, коллекти́в*) to be formed; (*мне́ние, впечатле́ние*) to form; **у нас** ~**илось благоприя́тное мне́ние о нём** we formed a good impression of him.
составле́ни|е (**-я**) *ср* (*словаря́*) compilation; (*пла́на*) drawing up; (*колле́кции*) forming; (*фра́зы*) making.
составлю́(сь) *сов см* **соста́вить(ся)**.
составля́|ть(ся) (**-ю(сь)**) *несов от* **соста́вить(ся)**.
составн|о́й *прил*: ~**а́я ме́бель** kit furniture; ~**а́я часть**, ~ **элеме́нт** component.
соста́р|ить (**-ю, -ишь**) *сов от* **ста́рить**
▸ **соста́риться** *сов возв* (*челове́к*) to grow old.
состоя́ни|е (**-я**) *ср* (*экономи́ческое, эмоциона́льное*) state; (*больно́го*) condition; (*со́бственность*) capital; **быть** (*impf*) **в** ~**и** +*infin* to be able to do.
состоя́тель|ный (**-ен, -ьна, -ьно**) *прил* (*иде́я, вы́вод итп*) sound; (*бога́тый*) well-off.
состо|я́ть (**-ю́, -и́шь**) *несов неперех*: ~ **из** +*gen* (*кни́га*) to consist of; (*кварти́ра*) to comprise; (*заключа́ться*): ~ **в** +*prp* to be; (*в па́ртии*) to be a member of; ~ (*impf*) +*instr* (*дире́ктором итп*) to be; **пробле́ма** ~**и́т в том, что ...** the problem is that ...
▸ **состоя́ться** *несов возв* (*собра́ние, конце́рт*) to take place; **как учёный, он не** ~**я́лся** he didn't make it as a scholar.
сострада́ни|е (**-я**) *ср* compassion.
состри́г *итп сов см* **состри́чь**.
сострига́|ть (**-ю**) *несов от* **состри́чь**.
состригу́ *итп сов см* **состри́чь**.
состр|и́ть (**-ю́, -и́шь**) *сов от* **остри́ть**.
состри́|чь (**-гу́, -жёшь** *итп*, **-гу́т**; *pt* **-г, -гла, -гло**, *impf* **сострига́ть**) *сов перех* (*во́лосы*) to cut off; (*шерсть*) to shear off.
состро́|ить (**-ю, -ишь**) *сов от* **стро́ить**.
состря́па|ть (**-ю**) *несов от* **стря́пать** ◆ *сов перех* (*перен*: *сде́лать пло́хо*) to concoct.
состык|ова́ть(ся) (**-у́ю(сь)**) *сов от* **стыкова́ть(ся)**.
состяза́ни|е (**-я**) *ср* contest.
состяза́|ться (**-юсь**) *несов возв* to compete; ~ (*impf*) **в бе́ге**, ~ (*impf*) **в пла́вании** to race; **они́** ~**лись в ще́дрости** they were competing to show who was the most generous.
сосу́д (**-а**) *м* vessel.
сосу́дистый *прил* vascular.
сосу́|лька (**-ьки**; *gen pl* **-ек**) *ж* icicle.
сосуществова́ни|е (**-я**) *ср* coexistence.
сосуществ|ова́ть (**-у́ю**) *несов неперех* to coexist.

сосчита́|ть (**-ю**) *сов от* **счита́ть**.
сот *чис см* **сто**.
сот|а́я (**-о́й**; *decl like adj*) *ж*: **одна́** ~ one hundredth.
сотворе́ни|е (**-я**) *ср*: ~ **ми́ра** Creation.
сотвор|и́ть (**-ю́, -и́шь**) *сов от* **твори́ть** ◆ *перех* to create.
со́тен *сущ см* **со́тня**.
со́т|ка (**-ки**; *gen pl* **-ок**) *ж* one tenth of a hectare.
сотка́|ть (**-у́, -ёшь**) *сов от* **ткать**.
со́тник (**-а**) *м* sotnik (*lieutenant of Cossack troops*).
со́т|ня (**-ни**; *gen pl* **-ен**) *ж* (*сто*) a hundred; (*де́ньги*) one hundred roubles; (*во́йска*) Cossack *squadron*; ~**ни люде́й/вопро́сов/пи́сем** hundreds of people/questions/letters.
со́ток *сущ см* **со́тка**.
сотру́(сь) *итп сов см* **стере́ть(ся)**.
сотру́дник (**-а**) *м* (*служа́щий*) employee; (*колле́га*) colleague; **нау́чный** ~ research worker.
сотру́дниц|а (**-ы**) *ж см* **сотру́дник**.
сотру́днича|ть (**-ю**) *несов неперех* (*в газе́те, в учрежде́нии*) to work; ~ (*impf*) **с** +*instr* (*с фи́рмой*) to work with; (*с секре́тными слу́жбами*) to collaborate with.
сотру́дничеств|о (**-а**) *ср* (*культу́рное, экономи́ческое*) cooperation; (*в газе́те, в журна́ле*) work.
сотряс|а́ть(ся) (**-а́ю(сь)**) *несов от* **сотрясти́(сь)**.
сотрясе́ни|е (**-я**) *ср* (*от взры́ва, от уда́ра*) shaking; (*та́кже*: ~ **мо́зга**) concussion.
сотряс|ти́ (**-у́, -ёшь**; *impf* **сотряса́ть**) *сов перех* (*сте́ны, зе́млю*) to shake
▸ **сотрясти́сь** (*impf* **сотряса́ться**) *сов возв* (*сте́ны, земля́*) to shake.
со́т|ы (**-ов**) *мн*: (*пчели́ные*) ~ honeycomb *ед*.
со́тый (**-ая, -ое, -ые**) *чис* hundredth.
со́ус (**-а**) *м* sauce.
со́усник (**-а**) *м* ≈ gravy boat.
соуча́сти|е (**-я**) *ср* complicity.
соуча́стник (**-а**) *м* accomplice.
соуча́стниц|а (**-ы**) *ж см* **соуча́стник**.
соф|а́ (**-ы́**; *nom pl* **-ы**) *ж* sofa.
Софи́|я (**-и**) *ж* Sofia.
сох|а́ (**-и́**; *nom pl* **-и**) *ж* wooden plough (*BRIT*) *или* plow (*US*).
со́х|нуть (**-ну, -нешь**; *pt* **-, -ла, -ло**, *perf* **вы́сохнуть**) *несов неперех* (*мо́крое бельё, ко́жа*) to dry; (*perf* **вы́сохнуть** *или* **засо́хнуть**; *расте́ния, де́рево*) to wither; (*от боле́зни, от пережива́ний*) to go thin; (*кра́ска, клей*) to dry; (*черни́ла*) to dry up.
сохран|и́ть (**-ю́, -и́шь**; *impf* **сохраня́ть**) *сов перех* to preserve; (*КОМП*) to save
▸ **сохрани́ться** (*impf* **сохраня́ться**) *сов возв* to survive, be preserved; **она́ хорошо́** ~**и́лась** (*ра́за*) she's well-preserved.
сохра́нность (**-и**) *ж* (*гру́за*) good condition; (*вкла́дов, докуме́нтов*) security; **в (по́лной)** ~**и**

(fully) intact.

сохраня́|ть(ся) (-ю(сь)) *несов от* **сохрани́ть(ся)**.

соцве́ти|е (-я) *ср* inflorescence.

социа́л-демокра́т (-а) *м* social democrat.

социа́л-демократи́ческ|ий (-ая, -ое, -ие) *прил* social democrat *опред*.

социали́зм (-а) *м* socialism.

социали́ст (-а) *м* socialist.

социалисти́ческ|ий (-ая, -ое, -ие) *прил* socialist.

социа́льный *прил* social; **социа́льная защищённость** social security.

социо́лог (-а) *м* sociologist.

социоло́ги|я (-и) *ж* sociology.

сочé́льник (-а) *м* (*рождественский*) Christmas Eve; (*крещенский*) Twelfth Night.

со́чен *прил см* **со́чный**.

сочета́ни|е (-я) *ср* (*учёбы и работы*) combining; (*единство: красок, звуков*) combination.

сочета́|ть (-ю) (*не*)*сов перех* to combine

▶ **сочета́|ться** (*не*)*сов возв* (*соединиться*) to combine; (*гармонировать*) to match, go with; **в ней ~ются ум и доброта́** she is both kind and intelligent.

сочинé́ни|е (-я) *ср* (*музыки*) composing; (*стихов*) writing; (*литературное*) work; (*музыкальное*) composition; (*ПРОСВЕЩ*) essay.

сочин|и́ть (-ю́, -и́шь; *impf* **сочиня́ть**) *сов перех* (*музыку*) to compose; (*стихи, песню*) to write; (*разг: письмо*) to concoct; (: *солгать*) to make up.

соч|и́ться (*3sg* -и́тся, *3pl* -а́тся) *несов возв* to ooze; ~ (*impf*) **чем-н** to ooze with sth.

со́ч|ный (-ен, -на́, -но) *прил* (*плод*) juicy; (*трава*) lush; (*краски*) vibrant; (*язык*) expressive.

сочту́ *итп сов см* **счесть**.

сочу́вствен|ный (-ен, -на, -но) *прил* sympathetic.

сочу́встви|е (-я) *ср* sympathy; **встреча́ть (встре́тить** *perf*) **что-н с ~м** to be sympathetic to sth.

сочу́вств|овать (-ую) *несов неперех*: ~ +*dat* to sympathize with.

сочу́вствующий (-его; *decl like adj*) *м* sympathizer.

сошёл(ся) *итп сов см* **сойти́(сь)**.

сошлю́(сь) *итп сов см* **сосла́ть(ся)**.

сошью́ *итп сов см* **сшить**.

сощу́р|ить(ся) (-ю(сь), -ишь(ся)) *сов от* **щу́рить(ся)**.

сою́з (-а) *м* alliance; (*республик, профессиональный*) union; (*линг*) conjunction.

сою́зник (-а) *м* ally.

сою́зническ|ий (-ая, -ое, -ие) *прил* ally's.

сою́зный *прил* (*государство, армия*) allied;

(*слово, связь*) conjunctive.

со́|я (-и) *ж собир* soya beans *мн*.

СП *м сокр* = **Сою́з писа́телей** ♦ *ср сокр* = **совме́стное предприя́тие**.

спаге́тти *мн нескл* spaghetti *ед*.

спад (-а) *м* (*температуры, давления*) drop; **экономи́ческий** ~ recession; **идти́ (пойти́** *perf*) **на** ~ (*температура, давление*) to go down; (*экономика, производство*) to go into recession.

спада́|ть (*3sg* -ет, *3pl* -ют) *несов от* **спасть** ♦ *неперех* (*волосы, складки*) to fall.

спадёт *итп сов см* **спасть**.

спа́ек *сущ см* **спа́йка**.

спазм (-а) *м* spasm.

спа́ива|ть (-ю) *несов от* **спои́ть, спая́ть**.

спа́йк|а (-йки; *gen pl* -ек) *ж* (*действие*) soldering; (*место*) join (*from soldering*).

спа́лен *прил см* **спа́льня**.

спал|и́ть (-ю́, -и́шь) *сов от* **пали́ть**.

спа́льник (-а) *м* (*разг*) sleeping bag.

спа́льный *прил* (*место*) sleeping *опред*; **спа́льный ваго́н** sleeping car; **спа́льный мешо́к** sleeping bag.

спа́льн|я (-ьни; *gen pl* -ен) *ж* (*комната*) bedroom; (*мебель*) bedroom suite.

спа́рж|а (-и) *ж* asparagus.

спар|и́ть (-ю, -ишь; *impf* **спа́ривать**) *сов перех* (*телефон*) to connect (*to a shared line*); (*вагоны, трубы*) to couple; (*собак, кошек*) to mate.

спа́рыва|ть (-ю) *несов от* **спороть**.

Спас (-а) *м* (*РЕЛ*) the Day of the Saviour (*in the Orthodox Church*); (: *икона*) the Saviour.

спас(ся) *итп сов см* **спасти́(сь)**.

спаса́ни|е (-я) *ср* rescue.

спаса́тель (-я) *м* rescuer; (*судно*) lifeboat.

спаса́тельный *прил* (*станция*) rescue *опред*; **спаса́тельная ло́дка** lifeboat; **спаса́тельный жиле́т** lifejacket; **спаса́тельный по́яс** lifebelt.

спаса́|ть(ся) (-ю(сь)) *несов от* **спасти́(сь)**.

спасéни|е (-я) *ср* rescue; (*РЕЛ*) Salvation.

спаси́бо *част*: ~ (**Вам**) thank you; **большо́е ~!** thank you very much!; ~ **за по́мощь/сове́т** thanks for the help/advice; ~, **что мили́ция во́время пришла́** (*разг*) thank God the police got here on time.

спаси́телен *прил см* **спаси́тельный**.

спаси́тел|ь (-я) *м* saviour; (*РЕЛ*) the Saviour.

спаси́тельниц|а (-ы) *ж* saviour.

спаси́тельный (-ен, -ьна, -ьно) *прил* lifesaving.

спас|ова́ть (-у́ю) *сов от* **пасова́ть**.

спас|ти́ (-у́, -ёшь; *pt* -, -ла́, -ло́, *impf* **спаса́ть**) *сов перех* (*также РЕЛ*) to save; **спаса́ть** (~ *perf*) **кому́-н жизнь** to save sb's life; ~ (*perf*) **положе́ние** to rescue the situation

▶ **спас|ти́сь** (*impf* **спаса́ться**) *сов возв*: ~**сь** (**от** +*gen*) to escape; (*РЕЛ*) to be saved (from).

спа|сть (*3sg* -дёт, *3pl* -дýт, *impf* спадáть) *сов неперех* (*вода*) to drop; (*упасть вниз*): ~ **с** +*gen* (*одежда, покрывало*) to fall off; **жарá к вéчеру спáла** the heat lessened towards evening.

сп|ать (-лю, -ишь; *pt* -ал, -алá, -áло) *несов неперех* to sleep; (*перен: разг: быть невнимательным*) to daydream; **ложйться** (**лечь** *perf*) ~ to go to bed; **порá** ~ it's time for bed; ~ (*impf*) **крéпким сном** to sleep like a log; **пóсле рабóты хорошó ~йтся** one sleeps well after working

▶ **спáться** *несов возв*: **мне не ~йтся** I can't (get to) sleep.

спáян|ный (-, -на, -но) *прил* (*перен: коллектив*) unified.

спая|ть (-ю; *impf* спáивать) *сов перех* (*трубы*) to weld; (*перен: сплотить*) to unite.

СПБ *сокр* (= *Санкт-Петербýрг*) St Petersburg.

СПб *сокр* = **СПБ**.

Спб *сокр* = **СПБ**.

спектáкл|ь (-я) *м* performance.

спектр (-а) *м* (*также перен*) spectrum.

спекулй|ровать (-ую) *несов неперех* (*дефицитом*) to profiteer; (*КОММ*): ~ +*instr* (*на бирже: цéнными бумáгами*) to speculate in; (*с дурными целями*): ~ **на** +*prp* (*на трýдностях, на слáбостях*) to exploit.

спекулянт (-а) *м* (*КОММ: биржевóй*) speculator; (*дефицитом*) profiteer.

спекулятйв|ный (-ен, -на, -но) *прил* speculative.

спекуляци|я (-и) *ж* (*КОММ*) speculation; (*дефицитом*) profiteering.

спекýтся *итп сов см* **спéчься**.

спелена́|ть (-ю) *сов от* пеленáть.

спéл|ый (-, -á, -о) *прил* ripe.

спервá *нареч* (*разг: вначáле*) (at) first.

спéреди *нареч* in front ◆ *предл* (+*gen*) in front of.

сп|ерéть (сопрý, сопрёшь; *pt* -ёр, -ёрла, -ёрло) *сов от* перéть.

спéрм|а (-ы) *ж* sperm.

спёртый (-, -а, -о) *прил* (*разг: воздух*) stuffy.

спесйв|ый (-, -а, -о) *прил* (*человек, тон*) haughty, arrogant.

спес|ь (-и) *ж* haughtiness, arrogance.

сп|еть (*3sg* -éет, *3pl* -éют, *perf* поспéть) *несов неперех* (*фрýкты, овощи*) to ripen; ◆ (-ою, -оёшь) *сов от* петь

▶ **спéться** *сов возв* (*хор, ансáмбль*) to achieve a good sound; (*разг: пренебр*): ~**éться с** +*instr* (*с ворáми, со спекулянтами*) to get in. with. in Petersburg.

спех (-а) *м*: **мне не к спéху** (*разг*) I'm in no hurry.

спец (-á) *м сокр* = **специалйст**.

спец (-а) *м* (*разг: мáстер, знаток*) buff.

специализáци|я (-и) *ж* (*произвóдства*) specialization; (*научная*) specialism.

специализйрованный *прил* specialized.

специализй|роваться (-уюсь) (*не*)*сов возв*: ~ **в** +*prp* *или* **по** +*dat* to specialize in.

специалйст (-а) *м*: ~ (**по** +*dat*) specialist (in).

специалйст|ка (-ки; *gen pl* -ок) *ж см* **специалйст**.

специáльно *нареч* specially; (*намéренно*) on purpose.

специáльност|ь (-и) *ж* (*профéссия*) profession; (*ПРОСВЕЩ*) main subject.

специáльный *прил* (*помещéние, одéжда итп*) special; (*образовáние*) specialist; ~ **тéрмин** technical term; **специáльный корреспондéнт** special correspondent.

специфик|а (-и) *ж* specific nature.

спецификáци|я (-и) *ж* specification.

специфицй|ровать (-ую) (*не*)*сов перех* to specify.

специфйчен *прил см* **специфйчный**.

специфйческ|ий (-ая, -ое, -ие) *прил* specific.

специфйч|ный (-ен, -на, -но) *прил* = **специфйческий**.

спéци|я (-и) *ж* spice.

спецкóр (-а) *м сокр* = **специáльный корреспондéнт**.

спецкýрс (-а) *м сокр* = **специáльный курс**; (*в вýзе*) course of lectures in a specialist field.

спецóвк|а (-и) *ж* (*разг*) workman's jacket.

спецодéжд|а (-ы) *ж сокр* (= *специáльная одéжда*) work clothes *мн*.

спé|чься (*3sg* -чётся, *3pl* -кýтся) *сов* = запéчься.

спéшен *прил см* **спéшный**.

спеш|йть (-ý, -йшь; *perf* поспешйть) *несов неперех* (*часы*) to be fast; (*прийтй закончить*): ~ +*infin*/**с** +*instr* to be in a hurry to do/with; ~ (*impf*) **на пóезд/в шкóлу** to rush for the train/to school; ~ **-ý** (*домóй/на рабóту*) I am in a hurry (to get home/to work); **поспешй!** hurry up; **он поспешйл с отвéтом** he gave a rash answer; **~ý сообщйть, что ...** I hasten to inform you that ...; **рабóтать** (*impf*) **не** ~**á** to work at a relaxed pace.

спéшк|а (-и) *ж* (*разг*) hurry, rush; **в ~е я забýл шáпку** in the rush I forgot my hat; **нет никакóй ~и** there's no hurry.

спéшно *нареч* (*уйтй, закончить*) hurriedly.

спéш|ный (-ен, -на, -но) *прил* (*дéло, задáние*) urgent.

спивá|ться (-юсь) *несов от* спйться.

СПИД (-а) *м сокр* (= *синдрóм приобретённого иммунодефицйта*) AIDS (= *acquired immune deficiency syndrome*)

спидóметр (-а) *м* speedometer.

спйкер (-а) *м* speaker.

спикй|ровать (-ую) *сов от* пикйровать.

спил|йть (-ю, -ишь; *impf* спйливать) *сов перех* to saw down.

спин|á (-ы́; *acc sg* -у, *dat sg* -é, *nom pl* -ы́) *ж* (*человéка, живóтного*) back; **за ~óй у негó богáтая жизнь** he has lead a full life.

спйн|ка (-ки; *gen pl* -ок) *ж уменьш от* спинá; (*дивáна, стýла итп*) back; (*кровáти*) bedstead.

спйннинг (-а) *м* spinner.

спиннóй *прил* (*позвонóк*) spinal; **спиннóй мозг**

spinal cord.

спи́нок *сущ см* **спи́нка**.

спира́л|ь (-и) *ж (линия)* spiral; *(также:* **внутрима́точная ~)** coil *(contraceptive)*.

спира́льный *прил* spiral.

спирт (-а; *loc sg* **-у)** *м (технический, медицинский)* spirit.

спиртн|о́е (-о́го; *decl like adj) ср* alcohol.

спиртно́й *прил (запах, раствор)* of alcohol; **спиртно́й напи́ток** alcoholic drink.

списа́ни|е (-я) *ср (КОММ)* writing off; *(МОР)* discharge.

сп|иса́ть (-ишу́, -и́шешь; *impf* **спи́сывать)** *сов перех* to copy; *(КОММ)* to write off; *(МОР)* to discharge; **спи́сывать (~** *perf)* **что-н с** +*gen* to copy sth from

▸ **списа́ться** *(impf* **спи́сываться)** *сов возв (моряк)* to leave ship; **спи́сываться (~ся** *perf)* **с** +*instr (со ста́рым дру́гом)* to write to.

спи́с|ок (-ка) *м (делега́тов, прису́тствующих)* list; *(докуме́нтов, рома́на)* manuscript copy; **кни́га разошла́сь в ~ках** the book was distributed in handwritten copies.

спи́сыва|ть(ся) (-ю(сь)) *несов от* **списа́ть(ся)**.

спи́ться (сопью́сь, сопьёшься; *impf* **спива́ться)** *сов возв* to take to drink.

спихн|у́ть (-у́, -ёшь; *impf* **спи́хивать)** *сов перех* to push aside *или* down; *(разг: конкуре́нта, нача́льника)* to oust; **спи́хивать (~** *perf)* **что-н на кого́-н** *(разг: плохо́й това́р, отве́тственность)* to push sth onto sb.

спи́ц|а (-ы) *ж (для вяза́ния)* knitting needle; *(колеса́)* spoke.

спи́чек *сущ см* **спи́чка**.

спи́чечн|ый *прил:* **~ая коро́бка** matchbox; **~ая голо́вка** matchhead.

спи́ч|ка (-ки; *gen pl* **-ек)** *ж* match; *(разг: худо́й челове́к)* beanpole.

спишу́(сь) *итп сов см* **списа́ть(ся)**.

сплав (-а) *м ((не)металли́ческий)* alloy; *(ле́са)* floating.

спла́в|ить (-лю, -ишь; *impf* **сплавля́ть)** *сов перех (мета́ллы)* to alloy; *(лес)* to float; *(перен: разг: изба́виться)* to get rid of.

сплани́р|овать (-ую) *сов от* **плани́ровать**.

сплани́р|овать (-ую) *сов от* **планирова́ть**.

спла́чива|ть(ся) (-ю(сь)) *несов от* **сплоти́ть(ся)**.

сплёвыва|ть (-ю) *несов от* **сплюну́ть**.

спл|ести́ (-ету́, -етёшь; *pt* **-ёл, -ела́, -ело́)** *сов от* **плести́** ◆ *(impf* **сплета́ть)** *перех (па́льцы, но́ги, ру́ки)* to intertwine

▸ **сплести́сь** *(impf* **сплета́ться)** *сов возв (во́доросли)* to be interwoven; *(ру́ки, тела́)* to be intertwined.

сплётен *сущ см* **сплётня**.

сплете́ни|е (-я) *ср (лент, верёвок)* interlacing;

(то, что сплетено́) tissue; *(перен: причи́н, обстоя́тельств)* combination.

спле́тник (-а) *м* gossip.

спле́тниц|а (-ы) *ж см* **спле́тник**.

спле́тнича|ть (-ю) *несов неперех* to gossip.

спле́т|ня (-ни; *gen pl* **-ен)** *ж* gossip; **распуска́ть** *(impf)* **~ни** to spread gossip; **пуска́ть (пусти́ть** *perf)* **~ню** to start gossip.

сплету́(сь) *итп сов см* **сплести́(сь)**.

сплеча́ *нареч (уда́рить)* straight from the shoulder; *(разз: реша́ть)* impulsively.

спло|ти́ть (-чу́, -ти́шь; *impf* **спла́чивать)** *сов перех* to unite

▸ **сплоти́ться** *(impf* **спла́чиваться)** *сов возв* to unite.

сплох|ова́ть (-у́ю) *сов неперех (разг)* to slip up.

сплочённый *прил* united.

сплочу́(сь) *сов см* **сплоти́ть(ся)**.

сплошно́й *прил (стена́, пото́к итп)* continuous; *(гра́мотность, пе́репись)* universal; *(разг: муче́ние, неуда́чи)* utter; *(: восто́рг, мара́зм)* complete and utter.

сплошь *нареч (по всей пове́рхности)* all over; *(без исключе́ния)* completely; **~ и ря́дом** *(разг)* more often than not.

сплут|ова́ть (-у́ю) *сов от* **плутова́ть**.

сплы́ть (3sg **-вёт, 3pl** **-ву́т,** *impf* **сплыва́ть)** *сов неперех (уплы́ть)* to be carried away; **был да ~л** *(разг)* it's gone forever

▸ **сплы́ться** *(impf* **сплыва́ться)** *сов возв (бу́квы, кра́ски итп)* to run together, merge.

сплю *несов см* **спать**.

сплю́н|уть (-у, -ешь; *impf* **сплёвывать)** *сов перех* to spit; *(шелуху́)* to spit out.

сплю́щ|ить (-у, -ишь) *сов от* **плю́щить** ◆ *(impf* **сплю́щивать)** *перех* to flatten

▸ **сплю́щиться** *(impf* **сплю́щиваться)** *сов возв* to become flattened.

спля|са́ть (-шу́, -шешь) *сов от* **пляса́ть**.

сподви́жник (-а) *м* loyal supporter.

сподо́б|иться (-люсь, -ишься) *сов возв:* **~** +*infin (разг)* to be honoured *(BRIT)* или honored *(US)* to do.

спозара́нку *нареч (разг)* very early *(in the morning)*.

спо|и́ть (-ю́, -и́шь; *imper* **-и́(те),** *impf* **спа́ивать)** *сов перех:* **~ кого́-н** to get sb drunk; *(приучи́ть пья́нствовать)* to make a drunkard of sb.

споко́ен *прил см* **споко́йный**.

споко́йно *нареч (жить, говори́ть)* quietly; *(спать)* peacefully ◆ *как сказ безл* it's quiet; **у меня́ на душе́ ~** I feel calm.

споко́йный (-ен, -йна, -йно) *прил (мо́ре)* calm; *(у́лица, жизнь)* quiet; *(челове́к, тон, бесе́да)* serene; *(хара́ктер)* placid; *(цвет)* gentle, restful; **~йная со́весть** clear conscience.

споко́йстви|е (-я) *ср (в го́роде, в лесу́)* calm, tranquillity; *(на душе́)* calm; **сохраня́ть** *(impf)* **~**

споласкива|ть (-ю) *несов от* **сполоснуть**.

сполз|ти (-у, -ёшь; *pt* -, -ла, -ло, *impf* **сползать**) *сов неперех* to climb down; (*шапка, платок, чулки*) to slip down; (*перен: к национализму*) to slide

▸ **сползтись** (*impf* **сползаться**) *сов возв* to congregate.

сполна *нареч* in full.

сполосн|уть (-у, -ёшь; *impf* **споласкивать**) *сов перех* to rinse.

спонсор (-а) *м* sponsor.

спонсорск|ий (-ая, -ое, -ие) *прил* sponsoring *опред*.

спор (-а) *м* debate; (*имущественный*) dispute; (*спортивный*) competition; **вести** (*impf*) ~ to have an argument; **спору нет** there is no doubt; **на** ~ (*разг*) as a bet.

спор|а (-ы) *ж* (*БОТ*) spore.

спорадическ|ий (-ая, -ое, -ие) *прил* sporadic.

спорен *прил см* **спорный**.

спор|ить (-ю, -ишь; *perf* **поспорить**) *несов неперех* (*вести спор*) to argue, debate; (*держать пари*) to bet; ~ (*impf*) **с кем-н о чём-н** *или* **за что-н** (*о наследстве*) to dispute sth with sb; ~**им, ты не посмеешь ему возразить** I bet you wouldn't dare to contradict him

▸ **спор|иться** *несов возв* (*работа, дело*) to go well.

спор|ный (-ен, -на, -но) *прил* (*дело*) disputed; (*победа, преимущество*) doubtful; ~ **вопрос** moot point.

спор|оть (-ю, -ешь; *impf* **спарывать**) *сов перех* to nip off.

спорт (-а) *м* sport.

спортзал (-а) *м* sports hall, gymnasium.

спортивный *прил* (*площадка, комментатор*) sports *опред*; (*фигура, человек*) sporty; **спортивный костюм** tracksuit.

спортлото *ср нескл* sports lottery.

спортсмен (-а) *м* sportsman (*мн* sportsmen).

спортсмен|ка (-ки; *gen pl* -ок) *ж* sportswoman (*мн* sportswomen).

спорттовар|ы (-ов) *мн* sports goods *мн*.

спорхн|уть (-у, -ёшь) *сов неперех* to flutter off.

спорщик (-а) *м* debater.

спорщи|ца (-ы) *ж см* **спорщик**.

спорый *прил* efficient.

способ (-а) *м* way.

способен *прил см* **способный**.

способност|ь (-и) *ж* ability; (*обычно мн: талант*) aptitude *ед*; **математические** ~**и** aptitude for mathematics; **пропускная** ~ (*дороги, метро*) capacity; **покупательная** ~ **населения** purchasing power (of the population).

способ|ный (-ен, -на, -но) *прил* capable; (*талантливый*) able; ~ +*infin* capable of doing; **он** ~**ен к математике** he has a gift for mathematics; **она** ~**на на всё** she is capable of anything.

способств|овать (-ую) *сов неперех*: ~ +*dat* (*успеху, развитию*) to promote.

спотыкн|уться (-усь, -ёшься; *impf* **спотыкаться**) *сов возв* (*при ходьбе, при беге*) to trip; (*при чтении*) to get stuck; (*перен: совершить проступок*) to slip up.

спохва|титься (-ачусь, -атишься; *impf* **спохватываться**) *сов возв* (*вспомнить*) to remember suddenly; (*понять ошибку*) to realize.

спою *итп несов см* **спеть**.

справа *нареч* to the right; ~ **от чего-н** to the right of sth.

справедливо *нареч* fairly, justly ♦ *как сказ*: **это** ~ that's fair *или* just.

справедливост|ь (-и) *ж* justice; **отдать** (*perf*) **кому-н** ~ (*оценить по заслугам*) to do justice to sb; ~**и ради** ... to be fair ....

справедлив|ый (-, -а, -о) *прил* just; (*утверждение*) correct; (*подозрение*) justified.

справ|ить (-лю, -ишь; *impf* **справлять**) *сов перех* (*разг: дни рождения*) to celebrate; (*шубу, туфли*) to get

▸ **справ|иться** (*impf* **справляться**) *сов возв*: ~**ся с** +*instr* (*с работой, с заданием*) to manage; (*с противником*) to deal with; (*с волнением, с детьми*) to cope with; (*узнавать*): ~**ся о** +*prp* to enquire *или* ask about.

справ|ка (-ки; *gen pl* -ок) *ж* (*сведения*) information; (*документ*) certificate; **обраща|ться** (**обратиться** *perf*) **за** ~**кой** to apply for information; **наводить** (**навести** *perf*) ~**ки** to make enquiries.

справлю(сь) *сов см* **справить(ся)**.

справля|ть(ся) (-ю(сь)) *несов от* **справить(ся)**.

справок *сущ см* **справка**.

справочник (-а) *м* (*телефонный*) directory; (*грамматический*) reference book.

справочный *прил* (*литература, пособие*) reference *опред*; **справочное бюро** information office *или* bureau.

спрашива|ть (-ю) *несов от* **спросить**.

▸ **спрашиваться** *несов от* **спроситься** ♦ *возв*: ~**ется, где ты был в это время** the question is, where were you at that time?

спрессов|ать (-ую) *сов от* **прессовать**.

спринт (-а) *м* sprint.

спринтер (-а) *м* sprinter.

спрова|дить (-жу, -дишь; *impf* **спроваживать**) *сов перех* (*разг*) to send off.

спровоцир|овать (-ую) *сов от* **провоцировать**.

спроектир|овать (-ую) *сов от* **проектировать**.

спрос (-а) *м*: ~ **на** +*acc* (*на товары, на специалистов*) demand for; (*требование*): ~ **с** +*gen* (*с родителей, с начальника*) demands *мн* on; **без спроса** *или* **спросу** without permission; **с тебя** ~ **особый** there are special demands on you; ~ **и предложе́ние** (*ЭКОН*) supply and demand.

спр|оси́ть (-**ошу́**, -**о́сишь**; *impf* **спра́шивать**) *сов перех* (*доро́гу, вре́мя*) to ask; (*сове́та, де́нег*) to ask for; (*взыска́ть*): ~ **что-н с** +*gen* to demand sth from; (*осве́домиться*): ~ **кого́-н о чём-н** to call sb to account for sth; **спра́шивать** (~ *perf*) **учени́ка** to question *или* test a pupil; **я** ~**оси́л, кото́рый час/когда́ по́езд** I asked what the time was/when the train would be

▶ **спроси́ться** (*impf* **спра́шиваться**) *сов возв*: ~**ся** +*gen* *или* **у** +*gen* (**у** *роди́телей, у учи́теля итп*) to ask permission of; **с нас** ~**о́сится за э́то** we will be answerable for that.

спросо́нок *нареч* (*разг*) half asleep.

спрошу́(сь) *сов см* **спроси́ть(ся)**.

спрут (-**а**) *м* octopus.

спры́г|нуть (-**ну**, -**нешь**; *impf* **спры́гивать**) *сов непере*х: ~ **с** +*gen* to jump off.

спряга́|ть (-**ю**; *perf* **проспряга́ть**) *несов перех* (*ЛИНГ*) to conjugate.

спряду́ *итп сов см* **спрясть**.

спряже́ни|е (-**я**) *ср* (*ЛИНГ*) conjugation.

спря́|сть (-**ду́**, -**дёшь**) *сов от* **прясть**.

спря́|тать(ся) (-**чу(сь)**, -**чешь(ся)**) *сов от* **пря́тать(ся)**.

спуг|ну́ть (-**ну́**, -**нёшь**; *impf* **спу́гивать**) *сов перех* to frighten off.

спуд (-**а**) *м*: **держа́ть что-н под спу́дом** (*иде́ю, план*) to keep sth back; **извлека́ть** (**извле́чь** *perf*) **что-н из-под спу́да** to bring sth into the light of day.

спуск (-**а**) *м* (*де́йствие: фла́га*) lowering; (: *корабля́*) launch; (: *воды́, га́за*) draining; (*ме́сто: к реке́, с горы́*) descent; (*оружия*) trigger; **нажима́ть** (**нажа́ть** *perf*) (**на**) ~ to pull the trigger; **я не дал ему́ спу́ску** (*разг*) I didn't let him off.

спуска́емый *прил*: ~ **аппара́т** (*КОСМОС*) landing gear.

спуска́|ть (-**ю**) *несов от* **спусти́ть** ◆ *перех*: **я не** ~**л глаз с неё** I didn't take my eyes off her

▶ **спуска́ться** *несов от* **спусти́ться** ◆ *возв* (*доро́га, бе́рег*) to descend, go down; (*во́лосы, фа́лды*) to hang down.

спусково́й *прил* (*трап*) exit *опред*; (*механи́зм*) trigger *опред*.

спу|сти́ть (-**щу́**, -**стишь**; *impf* **спуска́ть**) *сов перех* to lower; (*директи́ву, план*) to send out; (*соба́ку*) to let loose; (*газ, во́ду*) to drain; (*разг: зарпла́ту, насле́дство*) to squander; (*прости́ть*): ~ **что-н кому́-н** to let sb off with sth, forgive sb for sth; ~**стя́ рукава́** (*разг: небре́жно*) carelessly; **спуска́ть** (~ *perf*) **кора́бль** (**на́ воду**) to launch a ship; **спуска́ть** (~ *perf*) **куро́к** to pull the trigger; **спуска́ть** (~ *perf*) **кого́-н с ле́стницы** to kick sb downstairs; (*вы́гнать*) to kick sb out; **у мое́й маши́ны**

~**сти́ла ши́на** my car has a flat tyre (*BRIT*) *или* tire (*US*)

▶ **спусти́ться** (*impf* **спуска́ться**) *сов возв* to go down; (*чулки́, ю́бка итп*) to slip down; (*тума́н, мгла, ночь итп*) to descend.

спустя́ *нареч*: ~ **три дня/год** three days/a year later.

спу́танный *прил* (*во́лосы, верёвки*) tangled; (*речь*) muddled.

спу́та|ть(ся) (-**ю(сь)**) *сов от* **пу́тать(ся)**.

спу́тник (-**а**) *м* (*в пути́*) travelling (*BRIT*) *или* traveling (*US*) companion; (*городо́к*) satellite town; (*АСТРОНО́МИЯ*) satellite; (*КОСМОС: та́кже*: **иску́сственный** ~) sputnik, satellite; (*пе́рен*): ~ +*gen* (*бе́дности, прогре́сса итп*) concomitant of; ~ **жи́зни** (*муж*) life's companion.

спу́тниковый *прил* (*связь*) satellite *опред*; **спу́тниковое телеви́дение** satellite TV.

спу́тниц|а (-**ы**) *ж* (*в пути́*) travelling (*BRIT*) *или* traveling (*US*) companion; ~ **жи́зни** (*жена́*) life's companion.

спу́тыва|ть (-**ю**; *perf* **спу́тать**) *несов перех* = **пу́тать**.

спущу́(сь) *сов см* **спусти́ть(ся)**.

спя́|тить (-**чу**, -**тишь**) *сов непере*х (*разг*) to go daft.

спя́чк|а (-**и**) *ж* (*живо́тных*) hibernation; (*пе́рен*: *безде́ятельность*) lethargy.

спя́чу *сов см* **спя́тить**.

ср. *сокр* (= **сравни́**) ср. (= *compare*).

сраба́тыва|ть (3*sg* -**ет**, 3*pl* -**ют**) *несов перех от* **срабо́тать**.

срабо́танност|ь (-**и**) *ж* harmony.

срабо́та|ть (3*sg* -**ет**, 3*pl* -**ют**, *impf* **сраба́тывать**) *сов непере*х to operate.

сравне́ни|е (-**я**) *ср* comparison; **в** ~**и** *или* **по** ~**ю с** +*instr* compared with; **не мо́жет быть никако́го** ~**я с** +*instr* there can be no comparison with; **не подда́ться** (*perf*) **никако́му** ~**ю** to be unspeakable.

сра́внива|ть (-**ю**) *несов от* **сравни́ть**, **сравня́ть**.

сравни́м|ый (-, -**а**, -**о**) *прил* comparable.

сравни́телен *прил см* **сравни́тельный**.

сравни́тельно *нареч* comparatively; ~ **с** +*instr* compared to *или* with.

сравни́тельн|ый (-**ен**, -**ьна**, -**ьно**) *прил* comparative; **сравни́тельная сте́пень** (*ЛИНГ*) comparative degree.

сравн|и́ть (-**ю́**, -**и́шь**; *impf* **сра́внивать**) *сов перех*: ~ **что-н/кого́-н** (**с** +*instr*) to compare sb/sth (with); (*уподо́бить*): ~ **что-н/кого́-н с** +*instr* to compare sb/sth to

▶ **сравни́ться** *сов возв*: ~**ся с** +*instr* to compare with.

сравня́|ть (-**ю**; *impf* **сра́внивать**) *сов перех* (*расхо́д с дохо́дом*) to balance; **сра́внивать** (~ *perf*) **счёт** to equalize

▸ **сравня́ться** *сов возв*: ~**ся с** +*instr* to become the equal of.

сража́|ть(ся) (**-ю(сь)**) *несов от* **срази́ть(ся)**.

сраже́ни|е (**-я**) *ср* (*битва*) battle.

сра|зи́ть (**-жу́, -зи́шь**; *impf* **сража́ть**) *сов перех* (*пулей, ударом*) to slay; (*подлеж: горе, тяжёлая весть*) to crush

▸ **срази́ться** (*impf* **сража́ться**) *сов возв* to join battle.

сра́зу *нареч* (*немедленно*) straight away; (*в один приём*) (all) at once; (*рядом*) right.

срам (**-а**) *м* (*разг*) shame; ~ **ви́деть тако́е** it's a disgrace *или* shame.

срами́ть (**-лю́, -и́шь**; *perf* **осрами́ть**) *несов перех* (*позорить*) to shame; (*бранить*) to put to shame

▸ **срами́ться** (*perf* **осрами́ться**) *несов возв* to bring shame on o.s.

сраста́ни|е (**-я**) *ср* (*костей*) knitting.

срас|ти́сь (*3sg* **-тётся**, *3pl* **-ту́тся**, *impf* **сраста́ться**) *сов возв* (*кости*) to knit (together); (*стволы*) to grow together; (*перен: компании*) to merge.

сраще́ни|е (**-я**) *ср* (*костей*) knitting.

среаги́р|овать (**-ую**) *сов от* **реаги́ровать**.

сред|а́ (**-ы́**; *nom pl* **-ы**) *ж* medium; (*no pl*; *природная, социальная*) environment; (*артистическая, литературная*) milieu; (*acc sg* **-у**; *день недели*) Wednesday; *см также* **пя́тница**; **окружа́ющая** ~ environment; **охра́на окружа́ющей ~ы** conservation.

среди́ *предл* (+*gen*) in the middle of; (*в пределах*) in the middle of, amidst; (*в окружении*) amidst; (*в среде, в числе*) among.

средизе́мн|ый *прил*: **С~ое мо́ре** the Mediterranean (Sea).

среди́н|а (**-ы**) *ж* = **середи́на**.

среди́нный *прил* = **середи́нный**.

среднеазиа́тск|ий (**-ая, -ое, -ие**) *прил* Central Asian.

средневеко́вый *прил* medieval.

средневеко́вь|е (**-я**) *ср* the Middle Ages *мн*.

средневолново́й *прил* medium-wave.

среднегодово́й *прил* average annual.

среднеме́сячный *прил* average monthly.

среднесу́точный *прил* average daily.

сре́дн|ий (**-яя, -ее, -ие**) *прил* medium; (*комната, окно итп*) middle; (*посредственный*) average; **в ~ем** on average; **вы́ше/ни́же ~его** above/below average; **он ~их лет** he is middle-aged; **сре́днее образова́ние** secondary education; **сре́дние века́** the Middle Ages *мн*; **сре́дний па́лец** middle finger; **сре́дняя шко́ла** secondary school.

средото́чи|е (**-я**) *ср* focus, centre (*BRIT*), center (*US*).

сре́дств|а (**-**) *мн* means *мн*; (*деньги*) means *мн*, funds *мн*; **отпуска́ть** (**отпусти́ть** *perf*) *или* **выделя́ть** (**вы́делить** *perf*) ~ **на что-н** to allocate funds to sth; **остава́ться** (**оста́ться** *perf*) **без средств** to be without means;

сре́дства произво́дства (*ЭКОН*) means of production; **сре́дства существова́ния** livelihood.

сре́дств|о (**-а**) *ср* means *мн*; (*лекарство*) remedy, medicine; **добива́ться** (*impf*) **чего́-н все́ми ~ами** to use all means to get sth; **сре́дство передвиже́ния** means of conveyance; *см также* **сре́дства**.

сре́жу(сь) *итп сов см* **сре́зать(ся)**.

срез (**-а**) *м* (*место*) cut; (*тонкий слой*) section.

сре́|зать (**-жу, -жешь**; *impf* **среза́ть**) *сов перех* (*траву, цветок*) to cut; (*разг: дотации, кредиты*) to cut off; (: *студента*) to flunk

▸ **сре́заться** (*impf* **среза́ться**) *сов возв* (*разг: студент*) to flunk.

Сре́тени|е (**-я**) *ср* (*РЕЛ*) Candlemas, Feast of the Purification.

срис|ова́ть (**-у́ю**; *impf* **срисо́вывать**) *сов перех* to copy.

срифм|ова́ть (**-у́ю**) *сов от* **рифмова́ть**.

сровня́|ть (**-ю**) *сов от* **ровня́ть**.

сро́дни *предл* (+*dat*) akin to.

сро|дни́ть (**-ню́, -ни́шь**) *сов перех*: ~ **кого́-н с** +*instr* to bring sb close to

▸ **сродни́ться** *сов возв*: ~**ся с** +*instr* to become close to.

сродств|о́ (**-а́**) *ср* affinity.

сро́ду *нареч*: ~ **не ви́дел/не слы́шал ...** never in my life have I seen/heard ....

сро|́иться (*3sg* **-и́тся**, *3pl* **-я́тся**) *сов от* **рои́ться**.

срок (**-а**; *part gen* **-у**) *м* (*длительность*) time, period; (*дата*) date; (*разг: тюремный*) term; **в ~** (*во время*) in time; **после́дний** *или* **преде́льный** ~ deadline; **сро́ком на** +*acc* for a term of; **испыта́тельный** ~ trial period; ~ **произво́дства платежа́** due date; **срок го́дности** (*товара*) sell-by date; **срок де́йствия** period of validity.

сро́чен *прил см* **сро́чный**.

сро́чно *нареч* quickly, urgently.

сро́чност|ь (**-и**) *ж* urgency; **нет никако́й ~и** there's no hurry.

сро́ч|ный (**-ен, -на, -но**) *прил* (*дело, заказ*) urgent; (*ссуда, вклад*) fixed-term; **сро́чная телегра́мма** express telegram.

сро́ю *итп сов см* **срыть**.

сруб (**-а**) *м* (*место сруба*) cut; (*постройка*) log shell (*of building, well etc*).

сруба́|ть (**-ю**; *perf* **сруби́ть**) *несов перех* = **руби́ть**.

сруб|и́ть (**-лю́, -убишь**) *сов от* **руби́ть**.

срыв (**-а**) *м* (*плана итп*) disruption; (*с горы, с крыши итп*) fall; (*на экзамене итп*) failure; (*обрыв*) precipice.

срыва́ни|е (**-я**) *ср* picking.

срыва́|ть (**-ю**) *несов от* **сорва́ть, срыть**

▸ **срыва́ться** *несов от* **сорва́ться**.

срыва́ющийся (**-аяся, -ееся, -иеся**) *прил* (*голос*) breaking.

сро|ы́ть (**-ю́, -о́ешь**; *impf* **срыва́ть**) *сов перех* (*насыпь, холм*) to level.

СС *м сокр* SS.

сса́дин|а (-ы) *ж* scratch.

ссадн́ть (-аж́у, -дишь; *impf* сса́живать) *сов перех* (*со стула, с колен*) to help down; (*безбилетника*) to put off.

ссо́р|а (-ы) *ж* quarrel.

ссо́р|ить (-ю, -ишь; *perf* поссо́рить) *несов перех* (*друзей, родственников*) to cause to quarrel; ~ (поссо́рить *perf*) кого́-н с +*instr* to make sb quarrel with

▶ **ссо́риться** (*perf* поссо́риться) *несов возв* to quarrel.

СССР *м сокр* (*ист*: = *Союз Сове́тских Социалисти́ческих Респу́блик*) USSR (= *Union of Soviet Socialist Republics*).

ссу́д|а (-ы) *ж* loan; **брать (взять** *perf*) ~у to take out a loan; ~ **под проце́нты** interest-bearing loan; ~ **под зало́г** loan on collateral.

ссуд́ить (-жу́, -дишь; *impf* ссужа́ть) *сов перех* (*деньги*) to lend.

ссу́дный *прил* (*операция, ведомость*) loan *опред*; **ссу́дный банк** lending bank; **ссу́дный капита́л** (*КОММ*) loan capital.

ссужа́|ть (-ю) *несов от* **ссуди́ть**.

ссужу́ *сов см* **ссуди́ть**.

ссуту́л|ить(ся) (-ю(сь), -ишь(ся)) *сов от* **суту́лить(ся)**.

ссыла́|ть(ся) (-ю(сь)) *несов от* **сосла́ть(ся)** ◆ *возв*: ~я́сь на +*acc* with reference to.

ссы́л|ка (-ки; *gen pl* -ок) *ж* exile; (*на автора, на источник*) reference; (*цитата*) quotation.

ссы́льн|ая (-ой; *decl like adj*) *ж см* **ссы́льный**.

ссы́льн|ый (-ого; *decl like adj*) *м* exile.

ссы́п|ать (-лю, -лешь; *impf* ссыпа́ть) *сов перех* (*насыпать*) to pour.

ст. *сокр* (= **ста́нция**) sta. (= *station*); (= **ста́рший**) Sen. (= *senior*); = **ста́рый**.

ста *чис см* **сто**.

стаби́лен *прил см* **стаби́льный**.

стабилиза́тор (-а) *м* (*ТЕХ*) stabilizer.

стабилиза́ци|я (-и) *ж* stabilization.

стабилизи́р|овать (-ую) (*не*)*сов перех* to stabilize

▶ **стабилизи́роваться** (*не*)*сов возв* to stabilize.

стаби́л|ьный (-ен, -ьна, -ьно) *прил* stable; **стаби́льный уче́бник** standard textbook.

ста́в|ень (-ня) *м* (*обычно мн*) shutter.

ста́в|ить (-лю, -ишь; *perf* поста́вить) *несов перех* to put; (*назначать: министром, дежурным*) to appoint; (*памятник*) to erect; (*телефон*) to install; (*парус, сроки*) to set; (*пятно, оценку*) to make; (*точку, запятую итп*) to put in; (*оперу, фильм итп*) to stage; (*выдвигать: задачу, цель*) to present; (: *вопрос*) to raise; ~ (поста́вить *perf*) де́ньги на что-н to put money on sth; ~ (поста́вить

perf) **печа́ть на что-н** to stamp sth; ~ (поста́вить *perf*) **часы́** to set a clock; ~ (поста́вить *perf*) **диа́гноз** to make a diagnosis; ~ (поста́вить *perf*) **что-н на голосова́ние** to put sth to the vote; ~ (поста́вить *perf*) **что-н кому́-н в вину́** to lay the blame for sth on sb; ~ (поста́вить *perf*) **что-н кому́-н в заслу́гу** to put sth at sb's service; ~ (поста́вить *perf*) **что-н кому́-н в досто́инство** to give sb credit for sth; ~ (поста́вить *perf*) **себе́ за пра́вило** to make it a rule; ~ (поста́вить *perf*) **кого́-н в изве́стность** to fill sb in; ~ (поста́вить *perf*) **что-н под контро́ль** to bring sth under control; **его́ здесь ни во что не** ~**ят** he counts for nothing here.

ста́в|ка (-ки; *gen pl* -ок) *ж* (*также КОММ*) rate; (*ВОЕН*) headquarters *мн*; (*в азартных играх*) stake; (*перен*): ~ **на** +*acc* (*расчёт*) counting on; **проце́нтные** ~**ки** (*КОММ*) interest rates; **ба́зовая ссу́дная** ~ base rate; **минима́льная ссу́дная** ~ minimum lending rate; **учётная** ~ (*банка*) discount rate.

ста́вленник (-а) *м* protégé.

ста́вленниц|а (-ы) *ж* protégée.

ста́влю *сов см* **ста́вить**.

ста́вн|я *итп сущ см* **ста́вень**.

ста́вок *сущ см* **ста́вка**.

ставри́д|а (-ы) *ж* (*ЗООЛ*) horse mackerel, scad.

стагна́ци|я (-и) *ж* stagnation.

стадио́н (-а) *м* stadium (*мн* stadia).

ста́ди|я (-и) *ж* stage.

ста́дный *прил* (*животное*) herd *опред*; (*перен: чувство*) gregarious.

ста́д|о (-а; *nom pl* -á) *ср* (*коров*) herd; (*овец*) flock.

стаж (-а) *м* (*рабочий*) length of service; **испыта́тельный** ~ probation.

стажёр (-а) *м* probationer.

стажир|ова́ться (-у́юсь) *несов возв* to work on probation.

стажиро́в|ка (-ки; *gen pl* -ок) *ж* probationary period.

ста́ива|ть (-ю) *несов от* **ста́ять**.

ста́йер (-а) *м* long-distance runner.

ста́йер|ский (-ая, -ое, -ие) *прил*: ~**ая диста́нция** long distance.

стака́н (-а) *м* glass; **бума́жный** ~ paper cup.

стака́нчик (-а) *м* glass; **моро́женое в** ~**ах** ice cream in tubs.

стакка́то *нареч* staccato.

сталагми́т (-а) *м* stalagmite.

сталакти́т (-а) *м* stalactite.

сталева́р (-а) *м* steel founder.

сталелите́йный *прил* steel-founding.

сталеплави́льный *прил* steel-smelting.

сталепрока́тный *прил* steel-rolling.

стали́йн|ый *прил*: ~**ое вре́мя** (*КОММ*) lay days *мн*.

сталини́зм (-а) *м* Stalinism.

ста́лкива|ть(ся) (**-ю(сь)**) *несов от*
столкну́ть(ся).
сталь (**-и**) *ж* steel.
стально́й *прил* (*кабель, рельсы, решимость*)
steel *опред*; (*мускулы, нервы*) of steel; (*воля*)
iron *опред*; (*цвет: глаза*) steel-blue; (: *море*)
steel-grey (*BRIT*), steel-gray (*US*).
стам *итп чис см* **сто**.
Стамбу́л (**-а**) *м* Istanbul.
стаме́с|ка (**-ки**; *gen pl* **-ок**) *ж* chisel.
стан (**-а**) *м* (*человека*) torso; (*стоянка*) camp;
(*ТЕХ*) mill.
станда́рт (**-а**) *м* (*также перен*) standard; **по ~у**
(*изготовить*) in line with the standard; (*перен:
действовать*) conventionally.
станда́ртен *прил см* **станда́ртный**.
стандартиза́ци|я (**-и**) *ж* standardization;
(*личности, отношений*) stereotyping.
стандартизи́р|овать (**-ую**) (*не)сов перех* to
standardize.
станда́рт|ный (**-ен, -на, -но**) *прил* (*детали,
машина*) standard; (*вопросы, тема*) stock.
стани́н|а (**-ы**) *ж* (*ТЕХ*) bed.
стани́ц|а (**-ы**) *ж* stanitsa (*large Cossack village*).
станка́ *итп сущ см* **стано́к**.
станко́вый *прил* (*живопись*) easel *опред*.
станкострое́ни|е (**-я**) *ср* machine-tool
construction.
станкостро́ительный *прил* (*завод,
промышленность*) machine-tool.
стан|ови́ться (**-овлю́сь, -о́вишься**) *несов от*
стать.
становле́ни|е (**-я**) *ср* formation.
становлю́сь *несов см* **станови́ться**.
стан|о́к (**-ка́**) *м* (*слесарный итп*) machine (tool);
(*искусство*) frame; (*балетный*) barre;
тока́рный ~ lathe.
ста́ну(сь) *итп сов см* **стать(ся)**.
станцио́нный *прил* station *опред*.
ста́нци|я (**-и**) *ж* station; **запра́вочная ~** filling
station; **телефо́нная ~** telephone exchange.
ста́пел|ь (**-я**; *nom pl* **-я́**) *м* (*МОР*) building berth
(*BRIT*), slip (*US*).
ста́плива|ть (**-ю**) *несов от* **стопи́ть**.
ста́птыва|ть(ся) (**-ю(сь)**) *несов от*
стопта́ть(ся).
стара́ни|е (**-я**) *ср* effort; **при всём ~и не смогу́
тебе́ помо́чь** no matter how much I try, I can't
help you.
стара́телен *прил см* **стара́тельный**.
стара́тел|ь (**-я**) *м* (gold) prospector.
стара́тельност|ь (**-и**) *ж* (*см прил*) diligence;
painstakingness.
стара́тел|ьный (**-ен, -ьна, -ьно**) *прил*
(*работник, ученик*) diligent; (*работа,
подсчёт*) painstaking.
стара́|ться (**-юсь**; *perf* **постара́ться**) *несов
возв*: **~ +**infin to try to do.
старе́йш|ий (**-ая, -ее, -ие**) *превос прил от*
ста́рый.
старе́йшин|а (**-ы**) *ж* elder.

старе́ни|е (**-я**) *ср* ageing.
старе́|ть (**-ю**; *perf* **постаре́ть**) *несов неперех*
(*человек*) to grow old(er), age; (*perf* **устаре́ть**;
оборудование) to become out of date.
ста́р|ец (**-ца**) *м* elder; (*РЕЛ*) elderly monk.
стари́к (**-а́**) *м* old man (*мн* men); **старики́** old
people.
старико́вск|ий (**-ая, -ое, -ие**) *прил* (*привычки*)
old people's.
старин|а́ (**-ы́**) *ж* (*прошлое*) the olden days *мн* ♦ *м*
(*обращение*) old man *или* chap (*BRIT*).
стари́н|ка (**-и**) *ж*: **по ~е** in the old way.
стари́нный *прил* ancient; (*давний: друг*) old.
ста́р|ить (**-ю, -ишь**; *perf* **соста́рить**) *несов перех*
to age.
ста́рк|а (**-и**) *ж* (*сорт водки*) starka (*type of
vodka*).
старо́ *как сказ*: **э́то всё ~** it's all outdated; (*не
ново*) there's nothing new in it; **~ как мир** it's as
old as the hills.
старове́р (**-а**) *м* (*РЕЛ*) Old Believer.
старове́р|ка (**-ки**; *gen pl* **-ок**) *ж см* **старове́р**.
старожи́л (**-а**) *м* old resident.
старомо́д|ный (**-ен, -на, -но**) *прил* old-
fashioned.
старообря́д|ец (**-ца**) *м* (*РЕЛ*) Old Believer.
старообря́д|ка (**-ки**; *gen pl* **-ок**) *ж см*
старообря́дец.
старообря́дца *итп сущ см* **старообря́дец**.
старообря́дчеств|о (**-а**) *ср* Old Belief.
старославя́нск|ий (**-ая, -ое, -ие**) *прил*:
старословя́нский язы́к Old Church Slavonic.
ста́рост|а (**-ы**) *м* (*курса*) senior student; (*класса:
мальчик*) head boy; (: *девушка*) head girl;
(*клуба*) head, president; (*артели*) foreman (*мн*
foremen).
ста́рост|ь (**-и**) *ж* (*человека*) old age; **на ~и лет**
in one's old age.
старпо́м (**-а**) *м* = **ста́рший помо́щник**; (*МОР*)
first mate.
старт (**-а**) *м* (*СПОРТ*) start; (*ракеты*) takeoff
point; **дава́ть** (**дать** *perf*) **~** to start; **брать**
(**взять** *perf*) **~** (*перен*) to take off.
ста́ртер (**-а**) *м* (*АВТ*) starter.
старте́р (**-а**) *м* (*СПОРТ*) starter.
старт|ова́ть (**-у́ю**) (*не)сов неперех* (*спортсмен*)
to start; (*ракета*) to take off.
ста́ртовый *прил* starting *опред*.
стару́х|а (**-и**) *ж* old woman (*мн* women).
стару́шек *сущ см* **стару́шка**.
стару́шечий (**-ья, -ье, -ьи**) *прил* old woman's.
стару́ш|ка (**-ки**; *gen pl* **-ек**) *ж* = **стару́ха**.
ста́рца *итп сущ см* **ста́рец**.
ста́рческ|ий (**-ая, -ое, -ие**) *прил* old person's
или people's; **ста́рческий во́зраст** old age;
ста́рческий мара́зм (*МЕД*) senility.
ста́рше *сравн прил от* **ста́рый** ♦ *как сказ*: **я ~
сестры́ на́ год** I am a year older than my sister;
я ~ его́ по зва́нию I am senior to him.
старшекла́ссник (**-а**) *м* senior pupil.
старшекла́ссниц|а (**-ы**) *ж см*

старшекла́ссник.

старшеку́рсник (-а) *м* senior student.

старшеку́рсница (-ы) *ж см* **старшеку́рсник.**

ста́рш|ий (-ая, -ее, -ие) *прил* senior *опред*; (*сестра, брат*) elder *опред* ♦ (-**его**; *decl like adj*) *м* (*группы, отделения*) senior; ~**ие** (*взрослые люди*) grown-ups *мн*, adults *мн*.

старшин|а́ (-ы́; *nom pl* -**ы**) *м* (*ВОЕН*) sergeant major; (*милиции*) sergeant.

старшинств|о́ (-а́) *ср* seniority; **по** ~**у́** by seniority.

ста́р|ый (-, -а́, -о́, -ы) *прил* old; **и стар и млад** old and young; **ста́рый стиль** (*летосчисления*) Old Style.

старь|ё (-я́) *ср собир* old things *мн*.

старьёвщик (-а) *м* junk dealer.

ста́скива|ть (-ю) *несов от* **стащи́ть.**

стасова́|ть (-ую) *сов от* **тасова́ть.**

ста́тен *прил см* **ста́тный.**

ста́тик|а (-и) *ж* (*наука*) statics; (*неподвижность*) stasis.

стати́ст (-а) *м* (*ТЕАТР*) extra.

стати́стик (-а) *м* statistician.

стати́стик|а (-и) *ж* statistics.

статисти́ческ|ий (-ая, -ое, -ие) *прил* statistical; **Центра́льное** ~**ое управле́ние** *central statistics office.*

стати́чен *прил см* **стати́чный.**

стати́ческ|ий (-ая, -ое, -ие) *прил* static.

стати́чн|ый (-ен, -на, -но) *прил* static.

ста́т|ный (-ен, -на, -но) *прил* stately.

ста́тус (-а) *м* status.

ста́тус-кво *м нескл* status quo.

стату́т (-а) *м* (*правила*) statute.

статуэ́т|ка (-ки; *gen pl* -**ок**) *ж* statuette.

стату́|я (-и) *ж* statue.

ста|ть (-ти) *ж* (*осанка*) bearing; ♦ (-**ну**, -**нешь**; *impf* **станови́ться**) *сов неперех* to stand; (*к станку, за прилавок*) to take up position; (*no perf, часы, завод, движение*) to stop; (*начать*): ~ +*infin* to begin *или* start doing; (*обойтись*): ~ **в** +*acc* to cost ♦ *безл* (*наличествовать*): **нас ста́ло бо́льше/тро́е** there are more/three of us; **под** ~ **кому́-н/чему́-н** (*подобно*) to be like sb/sth; **с какой ста́ти?** (*разг*) why?; **станови́ться** (~ *perf*) +*instr* (*учителем*) to become; **его́ не ста́ло** he passed away; **не ста́ло де́нег/сил** I have no more money/energy; **с него́ ста́нет** (*разг*) that's all you can expect from him; **ста́ло быть** (*значит*) so; **во что бы то ни ста́ло** no matter what; **что с ним ста́ло?** what has become of him?; **станови́ться** (~ *perf*) **у вла́сти** to come to power; **станови́ться** (~ *perf*) **на путь чего́-н** to set out on the path of sth

▶ **ста́ться** *сов безл* (*случиться*) to happen; **мо́жет ста́ться** it is possible.

стать|я́ (-и́; *gen pl* -**е́й**) *ж* (*в газете, в сборнике*) article; (*в словаре*) entry; (*в законе, в договоре*)

paragraph, clause; (*экспорта, импорта*) type; (*КОММ: расхода, дохода*) item; **по всем** ~**м** (*разг*) in all respects.

стафилоко́кк (-а) *м* (*МЕД*) staphylococcus.

стациона́р (-а) *м* (*МЕД*) hospital.

ста́чек *сущ см* **ста́чка.**

ста́чечник (-а) *м* striker.

ста́чечниц|а (-ы) *ж см* **ста́чечник.**

ста́чива|ть (-ю) *несов от* **сточи́ть.**

ста́ч|ка (-ки; *gen pl* -**ек**) *ж* (*ЭКОН*) strike.

стащ|и́ть (-у́, -ишь) *сов от* **тащи́ть** ♦ (*impf* **ста́скивать**) *перех* (*что-н сверху*) to pull down; (*что-н в подвал*) to drag down; (*сапоги, чулки*) to pull off; (*no impf, разг: украсть*) to nick.

ста́|я (-и) *ж* (*птиц*) flock; (*волков*) pack; (*рыб*) shoal.

ста́|ять (*3sg* -**ет**, *3pl* -**ют**, *impf* **ста́ивать**) *сов неперех* to melt.

ствол (-а́) *м* (*дерева*) trunk; (*ружья, пушки*) barrel.

ство́р|ка (-ки; *gen pl* -**ок**) *ж* door; (*ставней*) shutter; (*зеркала*) leaf.

ство́рчатый *прил* (*окно, шкаф*) double (*opening in the middle*).

стёб|ель (-ля) *м* (*цветка*) stem.

стёган|ка (-ки; *gen pl* -**ок**) *ж* quilted jacket.

стёганый *прил* quilted; **стёганое одея́ло** quilt.

стега́|ть (-ю; *perf* **простега́ть**) *несов перех* (*одеяло*) to quilt; (*no perf, хлыстом*) to lash.

стегн|у́ть (-у́, -ёшь) *сов перех* to lash.

стёж|ка (-ки; *gen pl* -**ек**) *ж* stitch.

стеж|о́к (-ка́) *м* stitch.

стез|я́ (-и́) *ж* path (*fig*).

стёк(ся) *итп сов см* **стечь(ся).**

стека́|ть(ся) (*3sg* -**ет(ся)**, *3pl* -**ют(ся)**) *несов от* **сте́чь(ся).**

стеклене́|ть (*3sg* -**ет**, *3pl* -**ют**, *perf* **остеклене́ть**) *несов неперех* to become glassy.

стекл|и́ть (-ю́, -и́шь; *perf* **остекли́ть**) *несов перех* (*окно*) to glaze.

стекл|о́ (-а́; *nom pl* **стёкла**, *gen pl* **стёкол**) *ср* glass; (*также: око́нное* ~) (window) pane; (*для очков*) lenses *мн* ♦ *собир* glassware.

стёклышко (-ка; *gen pl* -**ек**) *ср уменьш от* **стекло́**; (*осколок*) piece of glass.

стекля́нный *прил* glass; (*перен: взгляд, глаза*) glassy.

стекля́рус (-а) *м собир* glass beads *мн*.

стекля́ш|ка (-ки; *gen pl* -**ек**) *ж* (*осколок*) piece of glass; (*пренебр: изделие*) bauble.

стеко́л *сущ см* **стекло́.**

стеко́льный *прил* (*завод*) glass.

стеко́льщик (-а) *м* glazier.

стеку́т(ся) *итп сов см* **сте́чь(ся).**

сте́лек *сущ см* **сте́лька.**

стел|и́ть (-ю́, -ишь; *perf* **постели́ть**) *несов перех* (*скатерть, подстилку*) to spread out; (*perf*

настели́ть; *пол, паркет*) to lay; ~ **(постели́ть** *perf*) **посте́ль** to make up a bed
▶ **стели́ться** *несов возв (туман)* to spread; *(perf* **постели́ться**; *разг: приготовить постель)* to get ready for bed.
стелла́ж (-а́) *м* shelf (*мн* shelves).
стел|ька (-ьки; *gen pl* -ек) *ж (в обуви)* insole.
стелю́(сь) *итп несов см* **стла́ть(ся).**
стемне́|ть (*3sg* -ет) *сов от* **темне́ть.**
стен|а́ (-ы́; *acc sg* -у, *dat sg* -е́, *nom pl* -ы, *dat pl* -а́м) *ж (также перен)* wall; **в** ~**х** +*gen (школы, учреждения)* within the confines of; **сиде́ть** *(impf)* **в четырёх** ~**х** to be cooped up indoors.
стена́ни|е (-я) *ср* groan.
стена́|ть (-ю) *несов неперех* to groan.
стенгазе́т|а (-ы) *ж (= стенна́я газе́та) newsletter displayed on wall in school or place of work.*
стенд (-а) *м (выставочный)* display stand; *(испытательный)* test-bed; *(для стрельбы)* rifle range.
сте́ндовый *прил:* ~ **докла́д** presentation; **сте́ндовая стрельба́** shooting *(SPORT).*
сте́н|ка (-ки; *gen pl* -ок) *ж уменьш от* **стена́**; *(комнаты, желудка, также* ФУТБОЛ) wall; *(разг: мебель)* wall unit; *(ящика)* side; **прижима́ть (прижа́ть** *perf*) **кого́-н к** ~**ке** *(разг)* to push sb to the wall.
стенно́й *прил* wall *опред*; **стенна́я ро́спись** mural.
стеногра́мм|а (-ы) *ж* shorthand record.
стенографи́р|овать (-ую; *perf* **сренографи́ровать** *или* **застенографи́ровать)** *несов перех* to take down in shorthand.
стенографи́ст (-а) *м* shorthand typist (*BRIT*), stenographer (*US*).
стенографи́ст|ка (-ки; *gen pl* -ок) *ж см* **стенографи́ст.**
стеногра́фи|я (-и) *ж* shorthand (*BRIT*), stenography (*US*).
сте́нок *сущ см* **сте́нка.**
стенокарди́|я (-и) *ж* angina.
сте́нопись (-и) *ж* mural painting.
сте́ньг|а (-и) *ж (МОР)* topmast.
степе́нный (-ен, -на, -но) *прил* sedate.
сте́пен|ь (-и; *gen pl* -е́й) *ж (также* ПРОСВЕЩ) degree; *(МАТ)* power; **в вы́сшей** ~**и** in the extreme; **до изве́стной** *или* **не́которой** ~**и** to some *или* a certain extent; **ожо́г пе́рвой** *итп* ~**и** first *итп* degree burn.
степно́й *прил* steppe *опред*.
степь (-и; *loc sg* -и́, *gen pl* -е́й) *ж* the steppe.
сте́рв|а (-ы) *ж (груб!)* bastard (*!*); (: *женщина*) bitch (*!*).
стервене́|ть (-ю; *perf* **остервене́ть)** *несов неперех (разг)* to get mad.
стервя́тник (-а) *м* carrion crow.
стерёг *итп несов см* **стере́чь.**
стерегу́ *итп несов см* **стере́чь.**
стереоза́пис|ь (-и) *ж* stereo recording.

стереозвуча́ни|е (-я) *ср* stereo (*sound*).
стереомагнитофо́н (-а) *м* stereo tape recorder.
стереопро́игрыватель (-я) *м* stereo record player.
стереосисте́м|а (-ы) *ж* stereo.
стереоти́п (-а) *м (ТИПОГ, перен)* stereotype.
стереоти́пный *прил* (-ен, -на, -но; *ответ, мышление итп)* stereotyped.
стере́ть (сотру́, сотрёшь; *pt* стёр, стёрла, стёрло, *impf* **стира́ть)** *сов перех (грязь, пыль, грим)* to wipe off; *(надпись, память, различия)* to erase; **стира́ть** (~ *perf)* **что-н/кого́-н в порошо́к** *(также перен)* to pulverize sth/sb; **стира́ть** (~ *perf)* **с лица́ земли́** to wipe off the face of the earth
▶ **стере́ться** *(impf* **стира́ться)** *сов возв (надпись, краска)* to be worn away; *(подошвы)* to wear down; *(перен: различия, границы)* to be erased; **стира́ться** (~**ся** *perf)* **в па́мяти** to become blurred.
стер|е́чь (-егу́, -ежёшь *итп*, -егу́т; *pt* -ёг, -егла́, -егло́) *несов перех* to watch over; *(подстерегать)* to lie in wait for.
сте́рж|ень (-ня) *м* rod; *(винта)* stem; *(ось)* pivot; *(шариковой ручки)* (ink) cartridge; *(перен: политики, романа)* backbone.
стержнево́й *прил (осевой)* pivoted; *(перен: вопрос, проблема)* crucial.
сте́ржня *итп сущ см* **сте́ржень.**
стери́лен *прил см* **стери́льный.**
стерилиза́тор (-а) *м* sterilizer.
стерилиза́ци|я (-и) *ж* sterilization.
стерилиз|ова́ть (-у́ю) *(не)сов перех* to sterilize.
стери́льный (-ен, -ьна, -ьно) *прил* sterile, sterilized.
сте́рлинг (-а) *м (ЭКОН)* sterling; **10 фу́нтов** ~**ов** 10 pounds sterling.
сте́рляд|ь (-и; *gen pl* -е́й) *ж* sterlet.
стерп|е́ть (-лю́, -ишь) *сов перех* to endure
▶ **стерпе́ться** *сов возв:* ~**ся с** +*instr* to learn to endure.
стёртый (-, -а, -о) *прил (надпись)* worn; *(монета)* effaced; *(перен: фразы)* hackneyed.
сте|са́ть (-шу́, -шешь; *impf* **стёсывать)** *сов перех (кору)* to strip off.
стесне́ни|е (-я) *ср* constraints *мн*; *(в груди)* constriction; *(смущение)* shyness.
стеснённый *прил (дыхание)* constricted; **в** ~**ых обстоя́тельствах** in financial straits.
стесни́телен *прил см* **стесни́тельный.**
стесни́тельност|ь (-и) *ж* shyness.
стесни́тельный (-ен, -ьна, -ьно) *прил* shy.
стесн|и́ть (-ю́, -и́шь) *сов от* **тесни́ть** ♦ *(impf* **стесня́ть)** *перех (хозяев)* to inconvenience; *(дыхание)* to constrict; **стесня́ть** (~ *perf)* **кого́-н в расхо́дах** to restrict sb's spending.
стесня́|ться (-юсь; *perf* **постесня́ться)** *несов возв:* ~ (+*gen) (женщин, незнакомых)* to be shy (of); (+*infin*; *сказать, просить итп)* to be too

shy to do; ~ *(impf)* **пéред кем-н** to feel shy in sb's presence; **онá не ~ется в срéдствах** she won't stop at anything; **он не ~ется в выражéниях** he doesn't mince his words.

стёсыва|ть (-ю) *несов от* **стеса́ть**.

стетоскóп (-а) *м* stethoscope.

стечéни|е (-я) *ср (нарóда)* gathering; *(случáйностей)* combination; ~ **обстоя́тельств** coincidence; **при большóм ~и нарóда** in front of a large number of people.

стечь *(3sg* **-ечёт,** *3pl* **-екýт,** *pt* **-ёк, -еклá, -еклó,** *impf* **стекáть)** *сов неперех:* ~ **(с** +*gen)* to run down (from)

▶ **сте́чься** *(impf* **стекáться)** *сов возв (ручьи́, рéки)* to flow; *(люди)* to congregate.

стешý *итп сов см* **стеса́ть**.

сти́лен *прил см* **сти́льный**.

стилизáци|я (-и) *ж (подражáние)* imitation; *(о произведéнии)* stylized work.

стилизóван|ный (-, -на, -но) *прил* stylized.

стилизова́ть (-ýю) *(не)сов перех* to stylize.

стилисти́ческ|ий (-ая, -ое, -ие) *прил (приём)* stylistic.

стил|ь (-я) *м* style; *(летосчислéния)* calendar; **он в своём сти́ле** he's being his usual self; **6 ию́ня по стáрому/нóвому сти́лю** 6th June Old Style/New Style.

сти́л|ьный (-ен, -ьна, -ьно) *прил* stylish; *(разг: причёска, одéжда)* snazzy.

стиля́г|а (-и) *м/ж (разг: пренебр)* fashion victim.

сти́мул (-а) *м* incentive, stimulus *(мн* stimuli).

стимули́рование (-я) *ср* stimulation; **материáльное** ~ financial incentive.

стимули́р|овать (-ую) *(не)сов перех* to stimulate; *(работу, прогрéсс)* to encourage; ~ *(impf/perf)* **рост экономики** to encourage economic growth.

стимуля́ци|я (-и) *ж* stimulation; *(рóдов)* induction.

стипендиáльный *прил:* ~ **фонд** scholarship fund; **стипендиáльная коми́ссия** grants committee.

стипéнди|я (-и) *ж (государственная)* grant; *(за особые достижéния)* scholarship.

стипль-чéз (-а) *м (СПОРТ)* steeplechase.

стирáльный *прил:* ~ **порошóк** washing powder; **стирáльная маши́на** washing machine.

стирáни|е (-я) *ср (нáдписи)* erasure; *(различий)* erosion.

сти́раный *прил* washed.

стирá|ть (-ю) *несов от* **стерéть** ◆ *(perf* **вы́стирать** *или* **постирáть)** *перех* to wash

▶ **стирáться** *несов от* **стерéться**.

сти́р|ка (-ки; *gen pl* **-ок)** *ж* washing; **отдавáть (отдáть** *perf)* **что-н в ~ку** to put sth in for a service wash.

сти́сн|уть (-у, -ешь; *impf* **сти́скивать)** *сов перех*

(в рукé, в зубáх) to clench; *(подлеж: толпá)* to squeeze; **сти́скивать (~** *perf)* **когó-н в объя́тиях** to clutch sb in one's arms; ~ *(perf)* **зýбы** *(перен)* to grit one's teeth.

стих (-á) *м* verse.

стиха́|ть (-ю) *несов от* **сти́хнуть**.

стих|и́ (-óв) *мн (поэзия)* poetry *ед;* **ромáн в ~áх** novel in verse.

стихи́|йный (-ен, -йна, -йно) *прил (сила)* elemental; *(развúтие, становлéние)* uncontrolled; *(протéст, демонстрáции)* spontaneous; **стихи́йное бéдствие** natural disaster.

стихи́|я (-и) *ж (вода́, огóнь итп)* element; *(ры́нка, инфля́ции)* natural force; **борóться** *(impf)* **со ~ей** to do battle with the elements; **быть** *(impf)* **в своéй ~и** to be in one's element; **би́знес** — **егó** ~ business is his forte.

сти́х|нуть (-ну, -нешь; *pt* **-, -ла, -ло,** *impf* **стиха́ть)** *сов неперех* to die down.

стихосложéни|е (-я) *ср* versification.

стихотворéни|е (-я) *ср* poem.

стихотвóрный *прил (произведéние)* poetic; *(парóдия)* in verse; **стихотвóрный размéр** metre *(in poetry)*.

стлать (стелю́, стéлешь; *perf* **постлáть)** *несов перех* = **стели́ть**

▶ **стла́ться** *несов возв* = **стели́ться**.

сто (ста; *см* **Table 30)** *чис* one hundred; *(разг: мнóго):* ~ +*gen* hundreds of; ~ **книг/столóв** a hundred books/tables; **óколо ста** about a hundred; ~ **пéрвый** hundred and first; **я увéрен на** ~ **процéнтов** I am one hundred percent sure; **мнóго сот** many hundreds; **нéсколько сот** several hundred.

стог (-а; *loc sg* **-ý,** *nom pl* **-á)** *м:* ~ **сéна** haystack.

стограммóвый *прил (ги́ря)* one-hundred-gram; ~ **стакáн** ≈ shot glass.

стóек *сущ см* **стóйка** ◆ *прил см* **стóйкий**.

стóимостный *прил (ЭКОН):* ~**ые показáтели/отношéния** cost indices/relations.

стóимост|ь (-и) *ж* cost; *(цéнность)* value; ~ **по торгóвым кни́гам** *(КОММ)* book value; ~ **и фрахт** cost and freight.

стó|ить (-ю, -ишь) *несов (не)перех* (+*acc или* +*gen; дéнег)* to cost; *(усúлий, труда́ итп)* to take ◆ *неперех:* ~ +*gen (внимáния, любви́)* to be worth ◆ *безл:* ~**ить** +*infin* to be worth doing; **кни́га** ~**ит 10 рублéй** the book costs 10 roubles; **дом** ~**ит большúе дéньги** *или* **больши́х дéнег** the house costs a lot of money; **на эту вы́ставку** ~**ит пойти́** it is worth going to see this exhibition; **мне ничегó не** ~**ит сдéлать это** it's no trouble for me to do it; **спаси́бо! – не** ~**ит** thank you! – don't mention it; **чегó** ~**ят твои́ обещáния!** what are your promises worth?; ~**ит** *(тóлько)* **захотéть/постарáться** *(об услóвии)* you only have to wish/try; ~**ит мне** *(тóлько)*

войти в дом, как сразу начинает звонить телефон the minute I come through the door the phone starts ringing.

стойчески *нареч* stoically.

стойческ|ий (-ая, -ое, -ие) *прил* stoical.

стой(те) *несов см* **стоять**.

стойбище (-а) *ср (кочевников)* nomad camp.

сто|йка (-йки; *gen pl* **-ек)** *ж (положение тела)* stance; *(собаки)* pose; *(подпорка)* prop; *(прилавок)* counter; *(воротник)* stand-up collar; **стоять** *(impf)* **по ~йке смирно/вольно** to stand to attention/at ease; **стойка на руках** handstand; **стойка на голове** headstand.

сто|йкий (-йкая, -йкое, -йкие; -ек, -йка, -йко) *прил (человек, характер)* steadfast, resilient; *(краска, материал)* durable, hard-wearing; *(запах)* stubborn.

стойко *нареч* steadfastly.

стойкост|ь (-и) *ж (см прил)* resilience; durability; stubborness.

стойл|о (-а) *ср* stall *(in a stable)*.

стоймя *нареч* upright.

стойче *сравн прил от* **стойкий ♦** *сравн нареч от* **стойко**.

сток (-а) *м (действие)* drainage; *(приспособление)* drain.

Стокгольм (-а) *м* Stockholm.

стократный *прил* hundredfold.

стол (-а) *м* table; *(письменный)* desk; *(еда)* food; **адресный ~** *residents' registration office*; **круглый ~** round table *(fig)*; **садиться (сесть** *perf)* **за ~** to sit down at the table; **за ~ом** at table; **убирать (убрать** *perf)* **со ~а** to clear the table; **вставать (встать** *perf)* **из-за ~а** to get up from the table; **стол находок** lost property (office); **стол переговоров** negotiating table.

столб (-а) *м (пограничный, указательный)* post; *(телеграфный)* pole; *(перен: пыли, дыма)* cloud.

столбене|ть (-ю; *perf* **остолбенеть)** *несов неперех* to be rooted to the spot.

столб|ец (-ца) *м* column *(on page)*.

столбик (-а) *м уменьш от* **столб**; *(бумаг)* ream; *(цифр)* column; **ртутный ~** mercury column; **~ом** in a column.

столбняк (-а) *м* tetanus.

столбовой *прил*: **~ дворянин** *(ИСТ) a member of the old Russian nobility*; **столбовая дорога** *(ИСТ)* highway.

столбца *итп сущ см* **столбец**.

столети|е (-я) *ср (срок)* century; *(годовщина)*: **~** *+gen* centenary of.

столетн|ий (-яя, -ее, -ие) *прил (период)* hundred-year; *(старик, дерево)* hundred-year-old.

столетник (-а) *м (БОТ)* aloe.

столечко *нареч (разг)* = **столько**.

столик (-а) *м уменьш от* **стол**; *(в ресторане, в кафе)* table; **туалетный ~** dressing table.

столиц|а (-ы) *ж* capital (city).

столичный *прил (газеты, жители, театры)* of the capital; **столичный город** capital city.

столкновени|е (-я) *ср* clash; *(машин, судов)* collision; **вооружённое ~** armed clash.

столкн|уть (-у, -ёшь; *impf* **сталкивать)** *сов перех*: **~ (с** *+gen)* to push off; *(сблизить толчком)* to push together; *(подлеж: случай, судьба)* to bring together; **~** *(perf)* **кого-н в воду** to push sb into the water

▶ **столкнуться** *(impf* **сталкиваться)** *сов возв (машины, поезда)* to collide; *(интересы, характеры)* to clash; *(встречаться)*: **~ся с** *+instr (встречаться)* to come into contact with; *(случайно)* to bump *или* run into; *(с трудностями, с непониманием)* to encounter; **я сталкивался с ним по работе** I have come into contact with him through work.

столк|оваться (-уюсь; *impf* **столковываться)** *сов возв*: **~ (с** *+instr)* to come to an agreement (with).

столов|ая (-ой; *decl like adj)* *ж (заведение)* canteen; *(комната)* dining room.

столов|ка (-ки; *gen pl* **-ок)** *ж (разг)* canteen.

столов|ый *прил (мебель, часы)* dining room **опред**; **столовая ложка** *(для супа)* tablespoon; **столовая соль** table salt; **столовое вино** table wine; **столовый сервиз** dinner service.

столп (-а) *м (обычно мн: перен)* pillar.

столп|иться (3sg **-ится, 3pl** **-ятся)** *сов возв* to crowd.

столпотворени|е (-я) *ср* chaos.

столь *нареч так*; **~ же ... сколько ...** as ... as ....

стольк|о *нареч (об исчисляемом количестве)* so many; *(о неисчисляемом количестве)* so much **♦ (-их)** *мест (см нареч)* this many; this much; **я не хочу давать ему ~ денег** I don't want to give him that much money; **она ~ пережила!** she has been through so much!; **где ты был ~ времени?** where have you been all this time?; **у меня ~ (же) денег/проблем, сколько (и) у тебя** I've got as much money/as many problems as you; **он не ~ глуп, сколько ленив** he is not so much stupid as lazy.

столько-то *нареч (об исчисляемом количестве)* X number of; *(об неисчисляемом количестве)* X amount of; **~ сделано, ~ осталось** this much has been done and this much is left.

столяр (-а) *м* joiner.

столярнича|ть (-ю) *несов неперех (разг)* to do carpentry.

столярн|ый *прил*: **~ая мастерская** joiner's; **столярное дело** joinery; **столярные инструменты** carpentry tools; **столярный клей** wood glue.

стоматит (-а) *м* mouth ulcer.

стоматолог (-а) *м* dental surgeon.

стоматологическ|ий (-ая, -ое, -ие) *прил* dental; **стоматологический кабинет/ поликлиника** dental surgery/hospital.

стоматологи|я (-и) *ж* dentistry.

стометров|ка (-ки; *gen pl* **-ок)** *ж (разг: СПОРТ)*

the hundred metres (*BRIT*) *или* meters (*US*).

стометро́вый *прил*: ~**ая диста́нция** one hundred metres (*BRIT*) *или* meters (*US*).

стон (-**а**) *м* (*см глаг*) groan; moan.

стон|а́ть (-**у́**, -**ешь**) *несов неперех* to groan; (*перен: жаловаться*) to moan.

стоп *межд* stop.

стоп|а́ (-**ы́**; *nom pl* -**ы**) *ж* (*в стихах*) foot; (*nom pl* -**ы́**; *АНАТ*) sole; **идти́ (пойти́** *perf*) **по чьим-н** ~**м** to follow in sb's footsteps.

стоп|и́ть (-**лю́**, -**ишь**; *impf* **ста́пливать**) *сов перех* (*дрова*) to burn up.

сто́п|ка (-**ки**; *gen pl* -**ок**) *ж* (*бумаг, писем*) pile; (*стаканчик*) glass (*for vodka etc*).

стоп-кра́н (-**а**) *м* emergency handle (*on train*).

стоплю́ *сов см* **стопи́ть**.

сто́пок *сущ см* **сто́пка**.

сто́пор (-**а**) *м* (*ТЕХ*) lock.

стопор|и́ть (-**ю**, -**ишь**; *perf* **застопо́рить**) *несов перех* (*машину*) to stop; (*дело, работу*) to hold up; (*фиксировать*) to lock.

стопроце́нтный *прил* one-hundred percent; (*разг: негодяй, лгун итп*) absolute.

стоп|та́ть (-**чу́**, -**чешь**; *impf* **ста́птывать**) *сов перех* to wear out.

▶ **стопта́ться** (*impf* **ста́птываться**) *сов возв* to wear out.

сторг|ова́ть(ся) (-**у́ю(сь)**) *сов от* **торгова́ть(ся)**.

сторице́й *нареч*: **возда́ть** ~ **кому́-н** to reward sb in full.

сто́рож (-**а**; *nom pl* -**а́**, *gen pl* -**е́й**) *м* watchman (*мн* watchmen).

сторожево́й *прил*: ~ **пост** lookout post; **сторожева́я вы́шка** watchtower; **сторожево́й ка́тер** patrol boat.

сторо́жек *сущ см* **сторо́жка**.

сторож|и́ть (-**у́**, -**и́шь**) *несов перех* (*дом, сад*) to guard; (*зверя, вора*) to lie in wait for.

сторо́ж|ка (-**ки**; *gen pl* -**ек**) *ж* hut.

стор|она́ (-**оны́**; *acc sg* -**ону**, *dat sg* -**оне́**, *nom pl* -**оны**, *gen pl* -**о́н**, *dat pl* -**она́м**) *ж* side; (*направление: левая, правая*) direction; (*страна*) land; **стоя́ть** (*impf*) **в** ~**оне́ от** +*gen* to stand apart from; **в** ~**оне́** a little way off; **держа́ться** (*impf*) **в** ~**оне́** to keep one's distance; **в сто́рону** +*gen* towards; **смотре́ть (посмотре́ть** *perf*) **в сто́рону** to look away; **на́** ~**ону** (*разг: продавать*) on the side; **подраба́тывать** (*impf*) **на** ~**оне́** (*разг*) to work on the side; **брать (взять** *perf*) **кого́-н со** ~**оны́** to bring sb in from outside (*fig*); **со** ~**оны́** +*gen* from; **со** ~**оны́ ма́тери/отца́** on one's mother's/father's side; **э́то о́чень любе́зно с Ва́шей** ~**оны́** that is very good of you; **с одно́й** ~**оны́** ... **с друго́й** ~**оны́** ... on the one hand ... on the other hand ...; **принима́ть (приня́ть** *perf*) **чью-н сто́рону** to take sb's side; **встава́ть**

(**встать** *perf*) **на чью-н сто́рону** to come out in sb's defence (*BRIT*) *или* defense (*US*); **быть** (*impf*) **на чьей-н** ~**оне́** to be on sb's side; **смотре́ть** (*impf*) **по** ~**м** to look around; (*отвлекаться*) to let one's attention wander.

сторо|ни́ться (-**ню́сь**, -**о́нишься**; *perf* **посторони́ться**) *несов возв* (*дать дорогу*) to make way; (*избегать*): ~ +*gen* to avoid.

сторо́нн|ий (-**яя**, -**ее**, -**ие**) *прил* outside *опред*.

сторо́нник (-**а**) *м* supporter, advocate.

сторо́нниц|а (-**ы**) *ж см* **сторо́нник**.

сторубле́вый *прил* (*ассигнация*) one-hundred-rouble; (*о стоимости*) worth one hundred roubles.

стоск|ова́ться (-**у́юсь**) *сов возв*: ~ **по** +*dat* to miss.

сточ|и́ть (-**у́**, -**ишь**; *impf* **ста́чивать**) *сов перех* to smooth down.

сто́чный *прил*: ~**ая кана́ва** gutter (*in street*); **сто́чная труба́** drainpipe; **сто́чные во́ды** effluent; **сто́чный жёлоб** gutter (*on roof*).

стошн|и́ть (-**и́т**) *сов от* **тошни́ть**.

стоя́ *нареч* standing up.

стоя́ни|е (-**я**) *ср* standing.

стоя́н|ка (-**ки**; *gen pl* -**ок**) *ж* (*поезда, судна*) stop; (*автомобилей*) car park (*BRIT*), parking lot (*US*); (*геологов, путешественников*) camp; (*первобытного человека*) site; **стоя́нка такси́** taxi rank.

сто|я́ть (-**ю́**, -**и́шь**; *imper* **сто́й(те)**) *несов неперех* to stand; (*находиться*) to be; (*полк*) to be stationed; (*бездействовать*) to stand idle; (*сохраняться: цветы*) to last; (: *продукты*) to keep; (*perf* **постоя́ть**; *защищать*): ~ **за** +*acc* (*за друга, за идею*) to stand up for; **пе́ред на́ми** ~**и́т тру́дная зада́ча/интере́сная пробле́ма** we are faced with a difficult task/interesting problem; **на бла́нке** ~**и́т по́дпись дире́ктора** the document bears the director's signature; **по́езд** ~**и́т здесь 15 мину́т** the train stops here for 15 minutes; **ча́йник** ~**и́т на плите́** the kettle is on the stove; **цветы́** ~**я́т в ва́зе** the flowers are in the vase; **посу́да** ~**и́т в шкафу́** the crockery is in the cupboard; ~**я́ла весна́/о́сень** it was spring/autumn (*BRIT*) *или* fall (*US*); **всё ле́то** ~**я́ла жара́** it was hot all through the summer; **в до́ме** ~**я́л шум/смех** the house was full of noise/laughter; ~ (*impf*) **у вла́сти** to be in power; ~ (*impf*) **на свои́х пози́циях** to stand one's ground; **он** ~**и́т на своём** he refuses to budge.

стоя́ч|ий (-**ая**, -**ее**, -**ие**) *прил* (*предложение*) standing *опред*; (*воротник*) stand-up; (*вода*) stagnant.

сто́ящ|ий (-**ая**, -**ее**, -**ие**) *прил* (*дело, предложение*) worthwhile; (*человек*) worthy; (*вещь*) useful.

стр. *сокр* (= **страни́ца**) pg. (= *page*).

страв|и́ть (-лю́, -ишь) *сов от* **трави́ть** ◆ (*impf* **стра́вливать**) *перех* to set on; **он их ~и́л** he set them on each other.

страда́ (-ы́) *ж* harvesting.

страда́л|ец (-ьца) *м* martyr.

страда́лиц|а (-ы) *ж см* **страда́лец**.

страда́льца *итп сущ см* **страда́лец**.

страда́льческ|ий (-ая, -ое, -ие) *прил* martyred.

страда́ни|е (-я) *ср* suffering.

страда́тельный *прил* (*линг*): **~ зало́г** passive voice.

страда́|ть (-ю) *несов неперех* to suffer; (*дисциплина, грамотность итп*) to be poor; (*сочувствовать*): **~ за** +*acc* to suffer for; (*потерпеть ущерб*): **~ от** +*gen* (*от засухи, от инфляции итп*) to suffer as a result of; (*perf* **пострада́ть**; *поплати́ться*) to suffer; **~** (*impf*) (**от** +*gen*) (*от боли, от голода*) to suffer; **~** (*impf*) +*instr* (*болезнью, самомнением*) to suffer from; **~** (*impf*) **от любви́** to be lovesick.

страж (-а) *м* guardian.

стра́ж|а (-и) *ж собир* guard; **быть** (*impf*) *или* **стоя́ть** (*impf*) **на ~е** +*gen* to guard; **под ~ей** in custody; **брать** (**взять** *perf*) **кого́-н под ~у** to take sb into custody.

стран|а́ (-ы́; *nom pl* -ы) *ж* county; **стра́ны све́та** cardinal points (*on compass*).

стра́нен *прил см* **стра́нный**.

страни́ц|а (-ы) *ж* (*также перен*) page; (*перен: истории, жизни*) chapter; **на ~х газе́т** in the papers.

стра́нник (-а) *м* wanderer; (*РЕЛ*) pilgrim.

стра́нниц|а (-ы) *ж см* **стра́нник**.

стра́нно *нареч* strangely ◆ *как сказ* that is strange *или* odd; **он ~ вы́глядит** he looks strange; **~, что её ещё нет** it is strange *или* odd that she isn't here yet; **мне ~, что ...** I find it strange that ....

стра́нност|ь (-и) *ж* strangeness; (*обычно мн: человека, поведения*) oddity.

стра́н|ный (-ен, -на́, -но) *прил* strange; **~ное де́ло** that's strange *или* odd.

странове́дени|е (-я) *ср* national studies *мн*.

стра́нстви|е (-я) *ср* wandering.

стра́нств|овать (-ую) *несов неперех* to wander.

Стра́сбург (-а) *м* Strasbourg.

стра́стен *прил см* **стра́стный**.

страстно́й *прил*: **~ая неде́ля** Holy Week.

стра́стност|ь (-и) *ж* passion.

стра́ст|ный (-ен, -на́, -но) *прил* passionate; (*коллекционер итп*) ardent.

страст|ь (-и) *ж* passion; (*разг: ужас*) horror; **стра́сти разгоре́лись** passions were running high; **~ к му́зыке/кни́гам** a passion for music/books.

страте́г (-а) *м* strategist.

стратеги́ческ|ий (-ая, -ое, -ие) *прил* strategic.

страте́ги|я (-и) *ж* strategy.

стратосфе́р|а (-ы) *ж* stratosphere.

стра́ус (-а) *м* ostrich.

стра́усовый *прил* ostrich *опред*.

страх (-а) *м* fear; (*разг: обычно мн: стра́шное собы́тие*) horror; **~ за дете́й/за бли́зких** fear for one's children/loved ones; **~ сме́рти/ разоблаче́ния** fear of death/exposure; **~ пе́ред неизве́стным** fear of the unknown; **со стра́ху** in fright; **нача́льник держа́л их в стра́хе** they lived in fear of their boss; **под стра́хом сме́рти** on pain of death; **на свой ~ (и риск)** at one's own risk.

страхова́ни|е (-я) *ср* insurance; **~ от** +*gen* insurance against; **госуда́рственное ~** national insurance (*BRIT*); **страхова́ние жи́зни** life insurance; **страхова́ние иму́щества** property insurance.

страхова́тел|ь (-я) *м person taking out insurance*.

страх|ова́ть (-у́ю) *несов перех* (*гимна́ста*) to stand by (*to prevent sb from falling*); (*perf* **застрахова́ть**): **~ (от** +*gen*) (*имущество, автомобиль*) to insure (against); (*от неожи́данностей*) to protect (against)

▶ **страхова́ться** (*perf* **застрахова́ться**) *несов возв*: **~ся (от** +*gen*) to insure o.s. (against); (*от неожи́данностей*) to protect o.s (from).

страхо́в|ка (-ки; *gen pl* -ок) *ж* insurance; **для ~ки** to be on the safe side.

страхово́й *прил* (*фирма, агент*) insurance *опред*; **~ бро́кер** insurance broker; **страхово́й взнос** *или* **страхова́я пре́мия** insurance premium; **страхово́й по́лис** insurance policy.

страхо́вок *сущ см* **страхо́вка**.

страхо́вщик (-а) *м* insurer.

стра́шен *прил см* **стра́шный**.

страши́л|а (-ы) *м/ж* = **страши́лище**.

страши́лищ|е (-а; *gen pl* -) *ср* (*разг*) fright.

страш|и́ть (-у́, -и́шь) *несов перех* to frighten, scare

▶ **страши́ться** *несов возв*: **~ся** +*gen* to be frightened *или* scared of.

стра́шно *нареч* (*крича́ть*) in a frightening way; (*разг: уста́лый, дово́льный*) terribly ◆ *как сказ* it's frightening; **мне ~** I'm frightened *или* scared; **~ поду́мать** it's frightening to think; **он ~ дово́лен собо́й** (*разг*) he's awfully *или* terribly pleased with himself; **она́ ~ уста́ла** (*разг*) she's awfully *или* terribly tired; **она́ ~ лю́бит болта́ть** (*разг*) she really likes to chat.

стра́ш|ный (-ен, -на́, -но) *прил* terrible, awful; (*фильм, сон, путь*) terrifying; **ничего́ ~ного** it doesn't matter.

стре́ж|ень (-ня) *м* deep part (*of river*).

стрек|оза́ (-озы́; *nom pl* -о́зы) *ж* dragonfly (*мн* dragonflies); (*ребёнок*) fidget.

стрек|ота́ть (-очу́, -о́чешь) *несов неперех* to chirp.

стрел|а́ (-ы́; *nom pl* -ы) *ж* (*для стрельбы́*) arrow; (*крана*) arm; (*поезд*) express (train).

стрел|е́ц (-ьца́) *м* Strelets (*regular soldier of special regiment in 16th-17th century*); (*созве́здие*): **С~** Sagittarius.

стре́л|ка (-ки; *gen pl* -ок) ж уменьш от стрела́; (часо́в) hand; (ко́мпаса, баро́метра) needle; (знак) arrow; (железнодоро́жная) switch; (ГЕО) spit; (лука́) shoot.

стрелка́ *итп сущ см* стрело́к.

стрелко́вый *прил*: ~ полк infantry regiment; стрелко́вый спорт shooting.

стре́лок *сущ см* стре́лка.

стрело́к (-ка́) м (ВОЕН) rifleman (мн riflemen); он хоро́ший ~ he is a good shot.

стре́лочник (-а) м signalman (мн signalmen).

стре́лочниц|а (-ы) ж см стре́лочник.

стрельб|а́ (-ы́) ж shooting, firing.

стре́льбищ|е (-а) ср shooting range.

стрельца́ *итп сущ см* стреле́ц.

стре́льчатый *прил* (о́кна, свод) arched.

стре́ляный *прил* (дичь) shot опред; ~ патро́н spent cartridge; ~ солда́т *soldier who has been under fire*; ~ воробе́й (разг) old hand.

стреля́|ть (-ю) *несов неперех*: ~ (в +acc) (в цель, во врага́) to shoot (at); (мото́р) to backfire ♦ *перех* (убива́ть: птиц) to shoot; (выпра́шивать) to cadge; ~ (*impf*) из ружья́/пу́шки to fire a rifle/canon; у меня́ ~ет в боку́ I have a shooting pain in my side

► стреля́ться *несов возв* (самоуби́йца) to shoot o.s.; (на дуэли): ~ся с +instr to fight a duel with.

стремгла́в *нареч* headlong.

стре́мени *итп сущ см* стре́мя.

стреми́тельно *нареч* (мча́ться) headlong; (меня́ться) rapidly.

стреми́тельность (-и) ж (движе́ний) swiftness; (измене́ний) rapidity.

стреми́тельный *прил* (движе́ние, бег, ата́ка) swift; (челове́к) energetic; (измене́ния) rapid.

стреми́|ться (-лю́сь, -и́шься) *несов возв*: ~ в +acc (в университе́т, на ро́дину) to want to go to; (добива́ться): ~ к +dat (к сла́ве, к добру́, к пра́вде) to strive for.

стремле́ни|е (-я) ср: ~ (к +dat) striving (for).

стремлю́сь *несов см* стреми́ться.

стремни́н|а (-ы) ж rapid (*in river*).

стре́м|я (-ени; *как* вре́мя; *см* Table 4) ср stirrup.

стремя́н|ка (-ки; *gen pl* -ок) ж step-ladder.

стрептоко́кк (-а) м streptococcus.

стресс (-а) м stress.

стре́ссовый *прил* (состоя́ние) stressed; (ситуа́ция, нагру́зки) stressful.

стри́г(ся) *итп несов см* стри́чь(ся).

стригу́(сь) *итп несов см* стри́чь(ся).

стриж (-а́) м swift.

стри́жка *сущ см* стри́жка.

стри́женый *прил* shorn; (трава́) cut; (ма́льчик) short-haired.

стри́ж|ка (-ки; *gen pl* -ек) ж (*см глаг*) cutting; shearing; mowing; pruning; (причёска) haircut.

стрипти́з (-а) м striptease.

стрихни́н (-а) м strychnine.

стри́|чь (-гу́, -жёшь *итп*, -гу́т; *pt* -г, -гла, -гло, *perf* постри́чь *или* остри́чь) *несов перех* (во́лосы, тра́ву) to cut; (овцу́) to shear; (газо́н) to mow; (кусты́) to prune; ~ (постри́чь *perf*) кого́-н to cut sb's hair; ~ (*impf*) всех под одну́ гребёнку to tar everyone with the same brush

► стри́чься (*perf* постри́чься *или* остри́чься) *несов возв* (остри́чь себе́ во́лосы) to cut one's hair; (в парикма́херской) to have one's hair cut; (*no perf*; носи́ть коро́ткую стри́жку) to wear one's hair short.

стро́ганый *прил* planed.

строга́|ть (-ю; *perf* вы́строгать) *несов перех* to plane.

строг|ий (-ая, -ое, -ие; -, -а́, -о) *прил* strict; (красота́, причёска, наказа́ние, вы́говор) severe; (ме́ры) harsh; (черты́ лица́) regular.

стро́го *нареч* (воспи́тывать) strictly; (наказа́ть, сказа́ть) severely; ~-на́строго (разг) very strictly; ~ говоря́ strictly speaking.

стро́гост|ь (-и) ж (*см прил*) strictness; severity; harshness; regularity; (обы́чно мн: стро́гие поря́дки) harsh regulation.

строево́й *прил* (ВОЕН: команди́р) line опред; строева́я подгото́вка drill; строева́я часть line unit; строево́й лес timber forest; строево́й шаг goose step.

стро́ек *сущ см* стро́йка.

стро́ен *прил см* стро́йный.

строе́ни|е (-я) ср (зда́ние) building; (организа́ции, вещества́) structure.

стро́же *сравн прил от* стро́гий ♦ *сравн нареч* от стро́го.

стро́итель (-я) м builder; (+gen; но́вого о́бщества) creator of.

строи́тельный *прил* building опред, construction опред; строи́тельный уча́сток building site; строи́тельные материа́лы building materials.

строи́тельств|о (-а) ср (зда́ний) building, construction; (но́вого о́бщества) building.

стро́|ить (-ю, -ишь; *perf* вы́строить *или* постро́ить) *несов перех* (дом, доро́гу, мост) to build, construct; (*perf* постро́ить; о́бщество, быт, семью́) to create; (фра́зу, мысль) to compose; (план, дога́дку) to make; (полк, отря́д) to draw up; ~ (постро́ить *perf*) рома́н на чём-н to base a novel on sth; ~ (постро́ить *perf*) (из себя́) дурака́ to make o.s. out to be a fool; ~ (состро́ить *perf*) гла́зки кому́-н to make eyes at sb; ~ (состро́ить *perf*) грима́сы *или* pull faces

► стро́иться (*perf* постро́иться) *несов возв* to build o.s. a house; (*perf* вы́строиться; солда́ты, пле́нные) to form up; (*no perf*): ~ся на +prp (сюже́т, рома́н) to be based on.

стро|й (-я) м (социа́льный) system; (языка́, предложе́ния) structure; (*loc sg* -ю́; ВОЕН:

шере́нга) line; (: *похо́дный, боево́й*) formation; (: *де́йствующие войска́*) ranks *мн*; **входи́ть (войти́** *perf*) **в ~** (*заво́д*) to come into operation; **вводи́ть (ввести́** *perf*) **что-н в ~** (*заво́д*) to put sth into operation; **выводи́ть (вы́вести** *perf*) **что-н из стро́я** (*танк, маши́ну*) to put sth out of commission; **выходи́ть (вы́йти** *perf*) **из стро́я** to fall out; (*перен*) to break down; **~ мышле́ния** way of thinking.

стро́йка (-йки; *gen pl* -ек) *ж* (*зда́ния*) building; (*ме́сто*) building *или* construction site.

стройматериа́л|ы (-ов) *мн сокр* (= **строи́тельные материа́лы**) building materials *мн*.

стро́йный (-ен, -йна́, -йно) *прил* (*фигу́ра*) shapely; (*челове́к*) well-built; (*ряд, шере́нга*) orderly; (*речь, фра́за*) well-constructed; (*пе́ние*) harmonious.

строк|а́ (-и́; *nom pl* -и, *dat pl* -а́м) *ж* (*в те́ксте*) line; **кра́сная ~** new paragraph; **чита́ть** (*impf*) **ме́жду строк** to read between the lines.

стро́н|уться (-усь, -ешься) *сов возв* to start moving.

строп (-а) *м* sling.

стропи́л|о (-а) *ср* beam, rafter.

стропти́в|ый (-, -а, -о) *прил* headstrong.

строф|а́ (-ы́; *nom pl* -ы, *dat pl* -а́м) *ж* stanza.

стро́чек *сущ см* **стро́чка**.

строч|и́ть (-у́, -ишь; *perf* **прострочи́ть**) *несов перех* (*рука́в, подо́л*) to stitch; (*perf* **настрочи́ть**; *сочине́ние, статью́*) to scribble; (*no perf; перен*: *из автома́та*) to fire away.

стро́ч|ка (-ки; *gen pl* -ек) *ж уменьш от* **строка́**; (*шов*) stitch.

строчн|о́й *прил*: **~а́я бу́ква** small *или* lower case letter.

струга́|ть (-ю; *perf* **вы́стругать**) *несов перех* = **строга́ть**.

стру́ж|ка (-ки; *gen pl* -ек) *ж* shaving (*of wood, metal etc*).

стру|и́ться (*3sg* -и́тся, *3pl* -я́тся) *несов возв* (*вода́, руче́й*) to stream; (*пот, дым*) to pour.

стру́|йка (-йки; *gen pl* -ек) *ж* trickle.

стру́йный *прил*: **~ при́нтер** inkjet printer.

структу́р|а (-ы) *ж* structure.

структурали́зм (-а) *м* structuralism.

структу́рный *прил* structural.

струн|а́ (-ы́; *nom pl* -ы) *ж* (*скри́пки, раке́тки*) string; (*перен*: *поэти́ческая*) streak.

стру́н|ка (-ки; *gen pl* -ок) *ж* string; **стать** (*perf*) *или* **вытя́гиваться (вы́тянуться** *perf*) **в ~ку** to stand to attention; **ходи́ть** (*impf*) **по ~ке у кого́-н** *или* **пе́ред кем-н** to be under sb's thumb.

стру́нный *прил* (*инструме́нт*) stringed; **стру́нный кварте́т** string quartet.

стру́нок *сущ см* **стру́нка**.

струп (-а; *nom pl* -ья, *gen pl* -ьев) *м* scab.

стру́|сить (-шу, -сишь) *сов от* **тру́сить**.

струхн|у́ть (-у́, -ёшь) *сов неперех* (*разг*) to get a fright.

стручк|а́ *итп сущ см* **стручо́к**.

стручко́вый *прил*: **~ пе́рец** chilli; **стручко́вая фасо́ль** runner beans *мн*; **стручко́вый горо́х** peas *мн* in the pod.

стручо́к (-ка́) *м* pod.

стру́шу *сов см* **стру́сить**.

стру|я́ (-и́; *nom pl* -и) *ж* (*воды́, во́здуха*) stream; (*перен*: *сатири́ческая, бо́драя*) streak; **попа́сть** (*perf*) **в ~ю** (*перен*) to fit in.

стря́па|ть (-ю; *perf* **состря́пать**) *несов перех* (*разг*: *еду́*) to cook; (: *расска́з, стихи́*) to cobble together.

стряпн|я́ (-и́) *ж* (*разг*) cooking; (*перен*) rubbish.

стряс|ти́ (-у́, -ёшь; *pt* -, -ла́, -ло́, *impf* **стряса́ть**) *сов перех* to shake off

▶ **стрясти́сь** *сов возв* (*разг*) to happen; **с ним ~ла́сь беда́** he's in trouble; **что там ~ло́сь?** what happened here?

стряхн|у́ть (-у́, -ёшь; *impf* **стря́хивать**) *сов перех* (*также перен*) to shake off.

ст.с *сокр* (= *ста́рого сти́ля*) OS (= *Old Style*).

ст.ст. *сокр* = **ст.с.**

студен|е́ть (*3sg* -ет, *3pl* -ют) *несов неперех* (*заливно́е*) to gel.

студени́ст|ый (-, -а, -о) *прил* gelatinous.

студе́нт (-а) *м* student.

студе́нт|ка (-ки; *gen pl* -ок) *ж см* **студе́нт**.

студе́нческ|ий (-ая, -ое, -ие) *прил* student *опред*; **студе́нческий биле́т** student card.

студе́нчеств|о (-а) *ср* student days *мн* ◆ *собир* (*студе́нты*) students *мн*.

студён|ый (-, -а, -о) *прил* icy cold.

сту́д|ень (-ня) *м* jellied meat.

студи́|ец (-йца) *м* student (*at art or drama school*).

студи́|йка (-йки; *gen pl* -ек) *ж см* **студи́ец**.

студи́йца *итп сущ см* **студи́ец**.

студ|и́ть (-жу́, -дишь; *perf* **остуди́ть**) *несов перех* to cool.

сту́ди|я (-и) *ж* studio; (*шко́ла*) school (*for actors, dancers, artists etc*); (*мастерска́я*) workshop.

сту́дня *итп сущ см* **сту́день**.

сту́ж|а (-и) *ж* severe cold.

стужу́ *несов см* **студи́ть**.

стук (-а) *м* (*в дверь*) knock; (*маши́н, па́дающего предме́та*) thud; (*се́рдца*) thump; **входи́ть (войти́** *perf*) **без сту́ка** to enter without knocking.

сту́ка|ть(ся) (-ю(сь)) *несов от* **сту́кнуть(ся)**.

стука́ч (-а́) *м* (*разг*: *пренебр*) grass (*informer*).

сту́к|нуть (-ну, -ешь) *сов* (*в дверь, в окно́*) to knock; (*по столу́*) to bang; (*impf* **сту́кать**; *разг*: *уда́рить*) to knock ◆ *безл* (*no impf*): **мне ~уло 60** I've hit 60

▶ **сту́кнуться** (*impf* **сту́каться**) *сов возв* to bang o.s.

стул (-а; *nom pl* -ья, *gen pl* -ьев) *м* chair; (*no pl*; *физиоло́гия*) stools *мн*.

сту́п|а (-ы) *ж* mortar.

ступа́|ть (-ю) *несов от* **ступи́ть** ◆ *неперех*

(*осторожно, медленно*) to tread; ~**йте!** off you go!

ступе́нек *сущ см* **ступе́нька**.

ступе́нчат|**ый** (-, -а, -о) *прил* (*спуск, водопад*) terraced; (*процесс*) in stages.

ступе́н|**ь** (-и) *ж* step; (*gen pl* -**е́й**, *dat pl* -**я́м**; *процесса*) stage; (*МУЗ*) degree.

ступе́н|**ька** (-ьки; *gen pl* -ек) *ж* step.

ступ|**и́ть** (-лю́, -ишь; *impf* **ступа́ть**) *сов неперех* to step, tread.

ступи́ц|**а** (-ы) *ж* (*ТЕХ*) hub.

сту́п|**ка** (-ки; *gen pl* -ок) *ж* mortar.

ступлю́ *сов см* **ступи́ть**.

ступн|**я́** (-и́) *ж* (*стопа*) foot (*мн* feet); (*подошва*) sole.

сту́пок *сущ см* **сту́пка**.

сту́пор (-а) *м* stupor.

стуч|**а́ть** (-у́, -и́шь; *perf* **постуча́ть**) *несов неперех* (*в дверь, в окно*) to knock; (*по столу, по доске*) to bang; (*колёса*) to rattle; (*сердце*) to thump; (*зубы*) to chatter; (*perf* **настуча́ть**; *разг: доносить*) to grass; (**у меня́**) ~**и́т в виска́х** my temples are throbbing; ~ (**постуча́ть** *perf*) **в окно́/в дверь** to bang on the window/door

▸ **стуч**|**а́ться** (*perf* **постуча́ться**) *несов возв*: ~**ся в** (+*acc*) to knock (at); ~**ся** (**постуча́ться** *perf*) **к кому́-н** to knock at sb's door.

стуш|**ева́ться** (-у́юсь; *impf* **тушева́ться**) *сов возв* to go shy.

стыд (-а́) *м* shame; **к** ~**у́ своему́** to one's shame; **сгора́ть** (**сгоре́ть** *perf*) **от** ~**а́** to burn with shame; **у тебя́ нет ни** ~**а́, ни со́вести** (*разг*) you've no shame.

стыд|**и́ть** (-жу́, -ди́шь; *perf* **пристыди́ть**) *несов перех* to (put to) shame

▸ **стыд**|**и́ться** (*perf* **постыди́ться**) *несов возв*: ~**ся** +*gen*/+*infin* to be ashamed of/to do; ~**ся** (**постыди́ться** *perf*) **кого́-н/чего́-н пе́ред кем-н** to be ashamed of sb/sth in front of sb.

стыдли́в|**ый** (-, -а, -о) *прил* bashful.

сты́дно *как сказ* it's a shame; **мне** ~ I am ashamed; **мне** ~ **друзе́й** *или* **пе́ред друзья́ми** I'm ashamed in front of my friends; **как тебе́ не** ~**!** you ought to be ashamed of yourself!

стыжу́(сь) *несов см* **стыди́ть(ся)**.

стык (-а) *м* (*труб, рельсов*) join; (*улиц*) junction; (*перен: двух наук, двух эпох*) meeting point.

стык|**ова́ть** (-у́ю; *perf* **состыкова́ть**) *несов перех* (*рельсы, трубы*) to join; (*космос*) to dock

▸ **стык**|**ова́ться** (*perf* **состыкова́ться**) *несов возв* (*космос*) to dock.

стыко́в|**ка** (-ки; *gen pl* -ок) *ж* docking.

сты́н|**уть** (-у, -ешь; *perf* **осты́нуть**) *несов неперех* = **стыть**.

сты|**ть** (-ну, -нешь; *perf* **осты́ть**) *несов неперех* to go cold; (*perf* **просты́ть**; *мёрзнуть*) to freeze; **кровь сты́нет** (**в жи́лах**) the blood runs cold.

сты́ч|**ка** (-ки; *gen pl* -ек) *ж* (*военная*) clash; (*разг: с начальником, с милицией*) run-in.

стюа́рд (-а) *м* steward.

стюарде́сс|**а** (-ы) *ж* air hostess.

стяг (-а; *nom pl* -и) *м* banner.

стя́гива|**ть(ся)** (-ю(сь)) *несов от* **стяну́ть(ся)**.

стяжа́тел|**ь** (-я) *м* taker.

стяжа́тельниц|**а** (-ы) *ж см* **стяжа́тель**.

стяжа́тельск|**ий** (-ая, -ое, -ие) *прил* grasping.

стян|**у́ть** (-у́, -ешь; *impf* **стя́гивать**) *сов перех* (*пояс, шнуровку*) to tighten; (*войска*) to round up; (*no impf*; *разг: украсть*) to nick, pinch; (*перевязать*) ~ **что-н чем-н** (*талию поясом*) to pull sth in with sth; (*чемодан ремнём*) to strap sth up with sth; (*обувь, перчатку*) to pull off

▸ **стян**|**у́ться** (*impf* **стя́гиваться**) *сов возв* (*узел*) to tighten; (*войска*) to gather; (*разг: поясом*) to pull o.s. in.

СУ *ср сокр* (= *статисти́ческое управле́ние*) *statistics office*.

субаре́нд|**а** (-ы) *ж* sub-lease, sub-let.

суббо́т|**а** (-ы) *ж* Saturday; *см также* **пя́тница**.

суббо́тн|**ий** (-яя, -ее, -ие) *прил* (*вечер, работа*) Saturday *опред*; (*события*) Saturday's.

сублима́ци|**я** (-и) *ж* sublimation.

субордина́ци|**я** (-и) *ж* subordination.

субподря́д (-а) *м* subcontract; **заключа́ть** (**заключи́ть** *perf*) ~ to subcontract.

субподря́дчик (-а) *м* subcontractor.

субсиди́р|**овать** (-ую) (*не*)*сов перех* to subsidize.

субси́ди|**я** (-и) *ж* subsidy; **инвестицио́нные** ~**и** (*КОММ*) investment grant *ед*.

субстантиви́рованн|**ый** *прил*: ~**ое прилага́тельное** substantivized adjective.

субста́нци|**я** (-и) *ж* substance.

субти́тр (-а) *м* subtitle.

субтро́пик|**и** (-ов) *мн* subtropics *мн*.

субъе́кт (-а) *м* (*индивид, также ЮР*) individual; (*разг: о мужчине*) character.

субъекти́вность (-и) *ж* subjectivity.

субъекти́вн|**ый** *прил* subjective.

сувени́р (-а) *м* souvenir.

сувере́нен *прил см* **сувере́нный**.

суверените́т (-а) *м* sovereignty.

сувере́нн|**ый** (-ен, -на, -но) *прил* sovereign.

сугли́н|**ок** (-ка) *м* loam.

сугро́б (-а) *м* snowdrift.

сугу́бо *нареч* highly.

сугу́б|**ый** *прил* particular.

суд (-а́) *м* court session; (*орган*) court; (*процесс*) trial; (*мнение*) judgement, verdict ♦ *собир* the judges *мн*; **отдава́ть** (**отда́ть** *perf*) **кого́-н под** ~ to prosecute sb; **подава́ть** (**пода́ть** *perf*) **на кого́-н в** ~ to take sb to court; **предава́ть** (**преда́ть** *perf*) **кого́-н** ~**у** (*преступника*) to prosecute sb; **попада́ть** (**попа́сть** *perf*) **под** ~ to be taken to court; **встать, ~ идёт!** please stand for the court!; **на нет и ~á нет** oh well, that's that then.

суда́ *итп сущ см* **су́дно.**

суда́к (-á) *м* pike-perch.

Суда́н (-а) *м* (the) Sudan.

суда́рын|я (-и; *gen pl* -ь) *ж* Madame.

су́дар|ь (-я) *м* Sir.

суде́б *сущ см* **судьба́.**

суде́бно-медици́нск|ий (-ая, -ое, -ие) *прил*: **суде́бно-медици́нская эксперти́за** forensics.

суде́бн|ый *прил* (*заседание, органы*) court *опред*; (*издержки, практика*) legal; **~ая оши́бка** miscarriage of justice; **~ое реше́ние** adjudication; **суде́бное де́ло** court case; **суде́бный исполни́тель** bailiff; **суде́бный пригово́р** sentence.

суде́йск|ий (-ая, -ое, -ие) *прил* (ЮР) judge's; **суде́йская колле́гия** (ЮР) the bench; (СПОРТ) panel of judges.

суде́йств|о (-а) *ср* refereeing.

су́ден *сущ см* **су́дно.**

суди́мость (-и) *ж* conviction.

суди́ть (-жу́, -дишь) *несов перех* (*преступника*) to try; (*матч*) to referee; (*укорять*) to judge ♦ *неперех* (*на матче*) to referee; (*на соревнованиях*) to judge; ~ (*impf*) **о ком-н/чём-н** to judge sb/sth; **су́дя по** +*dat* judging by

▸ **суди́ться** *несов возв*: **~ся с кем-н** to take sb to court.

су́дн|о (-на; *nom pl* -á, *gen pl* -óв) *ср* vessel; (*gen pl* -ен; МЕД) bedpan.

су́дный *прил*: ~ **день** Judgement Day.

судове́рф|ь (-и) *ж сокр* (= **судострои́тельная верфь**) shipyard.

судовладе́л|ец (-ьца) *м* shipowner.

судовожде́ни|е (-я) *ср* navigation.

судов|о́й *прил*: **~ая кома́нда** ship's crew; **судово́й журна́л** ship's log.

судопроизво́дств|о (-а) *ср* legal proceedings *мн*.

судоремо́нтн|ый *прил*: **~ые мастерски́е** shipyards *мн*.

су́дорог|а (-и) *ж* (*от боли*) spasm; (*от холода, от отвращения итп*) shudder.

су́дорож|ный (-ен, -на, -но) *прил* (*движения, плач*) convulsive; (*перен: приготовления*) feverish.

судостро́ени|е (-я) *ср* ship building.

судострои́тельный *прил* ship-building.

судохо́дный *прил* navigable; ~ **кана́л** shipping canal.

судохо́дств|о (-а) *ср* navigation.

судьб|а́ (-ьбы́; *nom pl* -ьбы, *gen pl* -е́б) *ж* fate; (*будущее*) destiny; ~ **э́той пье́сы о́чень интере́сна** this play has had a very interesting fate; **каки́ми ~ми!** fancy seeing you here!; **(нам) не ~ встре́титься** we are not fated to meet.

судья́ (-ьи́; *nom pl* -ьи, *gen pl* -е́й) *ж* judge; (СПОРТ) referee; **я тебе́ не ~** who am I to judge

you?

суеве́рен *прил см* **суеве́рный.**

суеве́ри|е (-я) *ср* superstition.

суеве́р|ный (-ен, -на, -но) *прил* superstitious.

сует|а́ (-ы́) *ж* (*житейская, мелочная*) futility; (*хлопоты*) hustle and bustle.

су́етен *прил см* **су́етный.**

суе|ти́ться (-чу́сь, -ти́шься) *несов возв* to fuss (about).

суетли́в|ый (-, -а, -о) *прил* fussy; (*жизнь, работа*) busy.

су́ет|ный (-ен, -на, -но) *прил* (*интересы, желания, жизнь итп*) futile; (*человек*) superficial; (*день, жизнь*) busy.

суечу́сь *несов см* **суети́ться.**

сужа́|ть (-ю) *несов от* **су́зить.**

сужде́ни|е (-я) *ср* (*мнение*) opinion; (*заключение*) judgement.

суждено́ *как сказ*: **(нам) не ~ бы́ло встре́титься** we weren't fated to meet.

су́жен|ая (-ой; *decl like adj*) *ж*: **его́ ~** his intended.

суже́ни|е (-я) *ср* (*см глаг*) narrowing; taking in.

су́жен|ый (-ого; *decl like adj*) *м*: **её ~** her intended.

сужу́(сь) *несов см* **суди́ть(ся).**

су́|зить (-жу, -зишь; *impf* **сужа́ть**) *сов перех* to narrow; (*платье*) to take in

▸ **су́зиться** *несов возв* to narrow.

су|к (-ка́; *loc sg* -ку́, *nom pl* -чья, *gen pl* -чьев) *м* (*дерева*) bough.

су́к|а (-и) *ж* bitch ♦ *м/ж* (*груб!: о женщине*) bitch (*!*); (: *о мужчине*) bastard (*!*); **~ин сын** son of a bitch (*!*).

сукн|о́ (-á; *nom pl* -на, *gen pl* -он) *ср* (*шерстяное*) felt; (*хлопчатобумажное*) coarse cloth; **класть (положи́ть** *perf*) **что-н под ~** (*перен*) to shelve sth.

суко́нный *прил* (*см сущ*) felt *опред*; coarse cloth *опред*.

сул|и́ть (-ю́, -и́шь; *perf* **посули́ть**) *несов перех*: ~ **что-н кому́-н** (*обещать*) to promise sb sth, promise sth to sb; (*предвещать*) to bode for.

султа́н (-а) *м* (*монарх*) sultan; (*украшение*) plume.

сульфа́т (-а) *м* sulphate.

сум|а́ (-ы́) *ж* (*старушечья*) (tote) bag; (*охотничья*) pouch; **ходи́ть** (*impf*) **с ~о́й** (*перен*) to go begging.

сумасбро́д (-а) *м* maverick.

сумасбро́ден *прил см* **сумасбро́дный.**

сумасбро́д|ка (-ки; *gen pl* -ок) *ж см* **сумасбро́д.**

сумасбро́д|ный (-ен, -на, -но) *прил* (*человек, поведение*) maverick; (*идея*) madcap.

сумасбро́док *сущ см* **сумасбро́дка.**

сумасбро́дств|о (-а) *ср* (*поведение*) maverick behaviour; (*поступок*) exploit.

сумасше́дш|ая (-ей; *decl like adj*) *ж* madwoman (*мн* madwomen).

сумасше́дш|ий (-ая, -ее, -ие) *прил* mad; (*разг: успех*) amazing; (: *скорость*) lunatic ♦ (-его; *decl like adj*) *м* madman (*мн* madmen); ~**ие**

де́ньги ridiculous amounts of money;
сумасше́дший дом asylum; (*разг*) madhouse.
сумасше́стви|**е** (**-я**) *ср* madness, lunacy; **до ~я**
like mad.
сумато́х|**а** (**-и**) *ж* chaos.
сумато́ш|**ный** (**-ен, -на, -но**) *прил* (*разг*)
chaotic.
сумбу́р (**-а**) *м* muddle.
сумбу́р|**ный** (**-ен, -на, -но**) *прил* muddled.
су́мерек *сущ см* **су́мерки**.
су́мереч|**ный** (**-ен, -на, -но**) *прил* twilight.
су́мер|**ки** (**-ек**) *мн* twilight *ед*, dusk *ед*.
суме́|**ть** (**-ю**) *сов неперех*: ~ +*infin* to manage to
do.
су́м|**ка** (**-ки**; *gen pl* **-ок**) *ж* bag; (*кенгуру*) pouch.
су́мм|**а** (**-ы**) *ж* sum.
сумма́р|**ный** (**-ен, -на, -но**) *прил* (*количество,
затраты*) total *опред*; (*оценка, обзор,
описание*) overall.
сумми́р|**овать** (**-ую**) (*не*)*сов перех* (*затраты
итп*) to add up; (*информацию, данные,
сказанное*) to summarize.
су́мок *сущ см* **су́мка**.
су́моч|**ка** (**-ки**; *gen pl* **-ек**) *ж уменьш от* **су́мка**;
(*дамская, вечерняя*) handbag.
су́мрак (**-а**) *м* gloom.
су́мрачен *прил см* **су́мрачный**.
су́мрачно *нареч* (*посмотреть*) gloomily;
(*выглядеть*) gloomy ◆ *как сказ* (*на улице, в
доме*) it's gloomy; **у меня́ на душе́ ~** I have a
heavy heart.
су́мрач|**ный** (**-ен, -на, -но**) *прил* (*также перен*)
gloomy.
су́мчатый *прил* (*зоол*) marsupial *опред*.
сумя́тиц|**а** (**-ы**) *ж* mishmash.
сунду́к (**-а́**) *м* trunk, chest.
су́н|**уть(ся)** (**-у(сь), -ешь(ся)**) *сов от*
сова́ть(ся).
суп (**-а**; *part gen* **-у**, *nom pl* **-ы́**) *м* soup.
суперма́ркет (**-а**) *м* supermarket.
супермэ́н (**-а**) *м* superman (*мн* supermen).
супермо́дный *прил* very trendy.
суперобло́ж|**ка** (**-ки**; *gen pl* **-ек**) *ж* dust jacket.
су́пниц|**а** (**-ы**) *ж* soup tureen.
супру́г (**-а**; *nom pl* **-и**) *м* spouse; **~и** husband and
wife.
супру́г|**а** (**-и**) *ж* spouse.
супру́жеск|**ий** (**-ая, -ое, -ие**) *прил* marital;
(*чета*) married.
супру́жеств|**о** (**-а**) *ср* matrimony.
сургу́ч (**-а́**) *м* sealing wax.
суро́вость (**-и**) *ж* (*см прил*) bleakness; severity;
hardship; harshness; sternness.
суро́в|**ый** (**-, -а, -о**) *прил* (*природа, зима*) bleak;
(*приговор*) severe; (*жизнь*) tough;
(*действительность*) harsh; (*человек, взгляд*)
stern; (*no short form*; *ткань, нити*) coarse.
суррога́т (**-а**) *м* (*также перен*) substitute.

суррога́тный *прил* substitute *опред*.
суса́льный *прил*: **~ое зо́лото** gold leaf.
су́слик (**-а**) *м* ground squirrel (*BRIT*), gopher (*US*).
суспе́нзи|**я** (**-и**) *ж* suspension.
суста́в (**-а**) *м* (*АНАТ*) joint.
суста́вный *прил*: **~ ревмати́зм** rheumatism of
the joints.
сутенёр (**-а**) *м* pimp.
су́т|**ки** (**-ок**) *мн* twenty four hours *мн*; **кру́глые ~**
day and night.
су́толок|**а** (**-и**) *ж* hurly-burly.
су́точн|**ые** (**-ых**; *decl like adj*) *мн* subsistence
allowance *ед*.
су́точный *прил* twenty-four-hour.
суту́л|**ить** (**-ю, -ишь**; *perf* **ссуту́лить**) *несов
перех* to hunch
▶ **суту́литься** (*perf* **ссуту́литься**) *несов возв* to
stoop.
суту́л|**ый** (**-, -а, -о**) *прил* stooped.
сут|**ь** (**-и**) *ж* essence; **~ де́ла** the crux of the
matter; **по су́ти (де́ла)** as a matter of fact ◆ *как
сказ*: **э́то не ~ ва́жно** it's not all that important;
таки́е слу́чаи ~ гро́зное предупрежде́ние
such incidents serve as a severe warning.
суфле́ *ср нескл* soufflé.
суфлёр (**-а**) *м* prompter.
суфлёрск|**ий** (**-ая, -ое, -ие**) *прил*: **~ая бу́дка**
prompt box.
су́ффикс (**-а**) *м* suffix.
суха́р|**ь** (**-я́**) *м* cracker; (*разг: о человеке*) cold
fish.
су́хо *нареч* drily ◆ *как сказ* (*о сухой погоде*) it is
dry; **на у́лице ~** it's dry outside.
сухове́|**й** (**-я**) *м* hot dry wind.
сухогру́з (**-а**) *м* dry-cargo ship.
сухожи́ли|**е** (**-я**) *ср* tendon.
сух|**о́й** (**-, -а́, -о**) *прил* dry; (*ветка, листья*) dried;
(*no short form*; *фрукты, овощи*) dried; **сухо́е
вино́** dry wine; **сухо́е молоко́** dried milk;
сухо́й зако́н dry law, prohibition; **сухо́й счёт**
(*СПОРТ*) lockout.
сухопа́р|**ый** (**-, -а, -о**) *прил* bony.
сухопу́тный *прил* land *опред*; **сухопу́тные
войска́** ground forces *мн*.
су́хость (**-и**) *ж* dryness.
сухофру́кт|**ы** (**-ов**) *мн* dried fruit *ед*.
сухоща́в|**ый** (**-, -а, -о**) *прил* lean.
сучо́к (**-ка́**) *м* twig.
су́чья *итп сущ см* **сук**.
су́ш|**а** (**-и**) *ж* (dry) land.
су́ше *сравн прил от* **сухо́й** ◆ *сравн нареч от*
су́хо.
су́шек *сущ см* **су́шка**.
сушёный *прил* dried.
суши́л|**ка** (**-ки**; *gen pl* **-ок**) *ж* (*помещение*) drying
room; (*приспособление*) dryer.
суш|**и́ть** (**-у́, -ишь**; *perf* **вы́сушить**) *несов перех*
(*бельё, одежду, сено*) to dry; (*perf* **вы́сушить**

или **засушúть**; *травы итп*) to dry
▶ **сушúться** (*perf* **вы́сушиться**) *несов возв* to dry; (*человек*) to dry off.
сýш|ка (-ки; *gen pl* -**ек**) *ж* (*действие*) drying; (*бублик*) *small dry biscuit in the shape of a doughnut.*
сушь (-и) *ж* dry spell.
суще́ственно *нареч* (*улучшить, изменить*) subsantially.
суще́ствен|ный (-, -на, -но) *прил* (*черта, качество*) essential; (*изменения*) substantial; (*замечания*) major; (*вопрос*) important.
существúтельн|ое (-ого; *decl like adj*) *ср* (*также:* **úмя** ~) noun.
существ|ó (-á) *ср* (*вопроса, дела итп*) essence; (*nom pl* -á; *животное*) creature; (*человек*) being; **по** ~**ý** (*говорить*) to the point; (*вводн сл*) essentially; **всем своúм** ~**м** with one's whole being.
существова́ни|е (-я) *ср* existence; **прекраща́ть** (**прекратúть** *perf*) ~ to cease to exist; **сре́дства к** ~**ю** livelihood; **отравля́ть** (**отпра́вить** *perf*) **комý-н** ~ to make sb's life a misery.
существ|ова́ть (-ýю) *несов неперех* to exist; ~ (*impf*) +*instr или* **на** +*acc* to make one's living from.
сýщ|ий (-ая, -ее, -ие) *прил* (*правда*) honest; (*мучение, пустяки*) utter; **она́** ~ **ребёнок** she is a real baby.
сýщность (-и) *ж* (*вопроса, проблемы*) essence; **в** ~**и** (**говоря́**) in essence, essentially.
Суэ́ц (-а) *м* Suez.
суэ́цк|ий (-ая, -ое, -ие) *прил*: **С~ кана́л** the Suez Canal.
СФ *м сокр* (= *Сове́т Федера́ции*) *upper chamber of the Russian parliament.*
сфабрик|ова́ть (-ýю) *сов от* **фабрикова́ть**.
сфальшú|вить (-лю, -ишь) *сов от* **фальшú́вить**.
сфантазú́р|овать (-ую) *сов от* **фантазú́ровать**.
сфе́р|а (-ы) *ж* sphere; (*производства, торговли, науки*) area; (*театральная, дипломатическая*) circles *мн*; **земна́я** ~ the globe; **вы́сшие** ~**ы** upper echelons; **в** ~**е** +*gen* in the field of; **сфе́ра обслýживания** *или* **услýг** service industry.
сферú́ческ|ий (-ая, -ое, -ие) *прил* spherical.
сфинкс (-а) *м* sphinx.
сформúр|ова́ть(ся) (-ýю(сь)) *сов от* **формирова́ть(ся)**.
сформулú́р|овать (-ую) *сов от* **формулú́ровать**.
сфотографú́р|овать(ся) (-ую(сь)) *сов от* **фотографú́ровать(ся)**.
схалтýр|ить (-ю, -ишь) *сов от* **халтýрить**.
схва|тúть (-чý, -тишь) *сов* (*impf* **схва́тывать**) *перех* (*скрепить*) to secure; (*разг: простуду*) to catch; (*мысль, смысл*) to grasp; **у меня́** ~**тúло живо́т** I've got stomach cramps
▶ **схватúться** *сов от* **хвата́ться** ◆ (*impf*

схва́тываться) *возв* (*борцы, оппоненты*) to lock together.
схва́т|ка (-ки; *gen pl* -**ок**) *ж* fight; *см также* **схва́тки**.
схва́т|ки (-ок) *мн* (*МЕД*) contractions *мн*.
схва́тыва|ть(ся) (-ю(сь)) *несов от* **схватú́ть(ся)**.
схвачý(сь) *сов см* **схватú́ть(ся)**.
схе́м|а (-ы) *ж* (*метро, улиц*) plan; (*ЭЛЕК: радио итп*) circuit board; (*статьи итп*) outline.
схематизú́р|овать (-ую) (*не*)*сов перех* to schematize.
схематú́зм (-а) *м* schematism.
схематú́чен *прил см* **схематú́чный**.
схематú́ческ|ий (-ая, -ое, -ие) *прил* (*ТЕХ*) diagrammatic; (*изложение*) sketchy.
схематú́ч|ный (-ен, -на, -но) *прил* (*изложение*) sketchy.
схú́м|а (-ы) *ж* schema (*strict vow taken by orthodox monks*).
схú́мник (-а) *м monk who has taken strict vows.*
схитрú́|ть (-ю, -ишь) *сов от* **хитрú́ть**.
схлестн|ýться (-ýсь, -ёшься) *impf* **схлёстываться** *сов возв* (*разг*) to lock together.
схлоп|ота́ть (-очý, -о́чешь) *сов перех* (*разг*): ~ **вы́говор** to get a telling off; **ты у меня́** ~**о́чешь!** you're asking for it!
схлы́н|уть (*3sg* -**ет**, *3pl* -**ут**) *сов неперех* (*вода*) to subside; (*толпа*) to thin out.
сход (-а) *м* (*с горы, с трапа*) descent.
схо́ден *прил см* **схо́дный**.
схо|дú́ть (-жý, -дишь) *сов от* **ходú́ть** ◆ *неперех* (*разг: в театр, на прогýлку*) to go ◆ *несов от* **сойтú́**
▶ **сходú́ться** *несов от* **сойтú́сь**.
схо́д|ка (-ки; *gen pl* -**ок**) *ж* assembly.
схо́дн|и (-ей) *мн* gangplank *ед*.
схо́д|ный (-ен, -на́, -но) *прил* similar.
схо́док *сущ см* **схо́дка**.
схо́дств|о (-а) *ср* similarity.
схо́ж|ий (-ая, -ее, -ие) *прил* (*разг*) = **схо́дный**.
схожý(сь) (*не*)*сов см* **сходú́ть(ся)**.
схола́стик|а (-и) *ж* (*философия*) scholasticism; (*отвлечённые знания*) speculation.
схоластú́ч|ный (-ен, -на, -но) *прил* scholastic.
схоронú́|ть (-ю́, -ишь) *сов от* **хоронú́ть**.
сца́па|ть (-ю) *сов от* **ца́пать**.
сце|дú́ть (-жý, -дишь; *impf* **сце́живать**) *сов перех* (*жидкость, сок*) to strain off; (*грудно́е молоко́*) to express.
сцементú́р|овать (-ую) *сов от* **цементú́ровать**.
сце́н|а (-ы) *ж* (*подмостки*) stage; (*эпизод: в пьесе, на улице*) scene; **сходú́ть** (**сойтú́** *perf*) **со** ~**ы** to leave the stage; (*политик*) to fade from the scene; **устра́ивать** (**устро́ить** *perf*) ~**у** to make a scene.
сцена́ри|й (-я) *м* (*фильма*) script; (*вечера, праздника*) programme.
сценарú́ст (-а) *м* scriptwriter.
сценú́чен *прил см* **сценú́чный**.

сцени́ческ|ий (-ая, -ое, -ие) *прил* stage *опред*; **~ое масте́рство́** acting skills; **~ о́браз** dramatic character; **сцени́ческое иску́сство** dramatic art.

сцени́ч|ный (-ен, -на, -но) *прил*: **~ная пье́са** play well-suited for the theatre (*BRIT*) *или* theater (*US*).

сце́н|ка (-ки; *gen pl* **-ок)** *ж уменьш от* **сце́на**; (*зарисовка*) sketch.

сцеп|и́ть (-лю́, -ишь; *impf* **сцепля́ть)** *сов перех* (*вагоны, прицепы*) to couple; (*пальцы, руки*) to clasp

▸ **сцепи́ться** (*impf* **сцепля́ться**) *сов возв* (*ветви*) to be caught together; (*разг: схватиться*): **~ся (с** +*instr*) (*дети, спорщики*) to get into a fight (with).

сцепле́ни|е (-я) *ср* (*вагонов*) coupling; (*ТЕХ: механизм*) clutch.

сцеплю́(сь) *сов см* **сцепи́ть(ся)**.

сцепля́|ть(ся) (-ю(сь)) *несов от* **сцепи́ть(ся)**.

счастли́в|ец (-ца) *м* lucky man (*мн* men).

счастли́виц|а (-ы) *ж* lucky woman (*мн* women).

сча́стливо *нареч* (*жить, рассмеяться*) happily; **~ отде́латься** (*perf*) to have a lucky escape; **сча́стливо!** all the best!; **счастли́во остава́ться!** take care!

счастли́вца *итп сущ см* **счастли́вец**.

счастли́вчик (-а) *м* (*разг*) lucky devil.

счастли́вый (-ив, -ива, -иво) *прил* (*человек, жизнь, лицо*) happy; (*делец, игрок, случай*) lucky; **у него́ ~ивая рука́** he's got a lucky touch; **~ивого пути́!** have a good journey!

сча́сть|е (-я) *ср* (*личное, семейное*) happiness; (*удача*) luck; **к ~ю** luckily, fortunately; **на на́ше ~** luckily for us; **како́е ~, что ты пришёл** how nice that you've come; **возьми́ э́то на ~** take that for good luck; **твоё ~, что ...** you're lucky that ....

счесть (сочту́, сочтёшь; *pt* **счёл, сочла́, сочло́)** *сов от* **счита́ть ♦** *неперех*: **пробле́м у меня́ не ~** I've got countless problems.

счёт (-а; *part gen* **-у,** *loc sg* **-у́,** *nom pl* **-á)** *м* (*действие*) counting; (*КОММ: в банке*) account; (: *накладная*) invoice; (*ресторанный, телефонный*) bill; (*no pl*; *СПОРТ*) score; **в ~** +*gen* in lieu of; **за ~** +*gen* (*фирмы*) at the expense of; (*эффективности, внедрений итп*) due to; **на ~ кого́-н** at sb's expense; **на э́тот ~** in this respect; **быть** (*impf*) **на хоро́шем/плохо́м счету́ у** +*gen* to be in the good/bad books with; **у неё ка́ждая копе́йка на счету́** she counts every penny; **э́то не в ~** that doesn't count; **по большо́му ~у** having set a high standard; **име́ть** (*impf*) **что-н на счету́** (*победы*) to have sth to one's name; **предъявля́ть (предъяви́ть** *perf*) **~ кому́-н** to invoice sb; **принима́ть (приня́ть** *perf*) **что-н на свой ~** to take sth personally; **он не зна́ет ~а деньга́м** he's rolling

in money; **лицево́й ~** (*КОММ*) personal account; **теку́щий ~** (*КОММ*) current (*BRIT*) *или* checking (*US*) account; **~ поступле́ний** (*КОММ*) revenue account; **ссу́дный ~** (*КОММ*) loan account; **~ ассигнова́ний** (*КОММ*) appropriation account; **счета́ кредиторов/дебиторов** (*КОММ*) account payable/receivable; **открыва́ть (откры́ть** *perf*) **~ в ба́нке** to open a bank account.

счётн|ый *прил*: **~ая коми́ссия** vote counting committee; **счётная маши́на** calculator.

счётчик (-а) *м* (*человек: голосов*) counter; (*электричества, в такси*) meter.

счёт|ы (-ов) *мн* (*приспособление*) abacus; (*деловые*) dealings *мн*; **поко́нчить** (*perf*) **все ~ с кем-н** (*расчитаться*) to pay off one's debts to sb; (*прекратить связи*) to break off ties with sb; **сбра́сывать (сбро́сить** *perf*) **кого́-н/что-н со счето́в** to dismiss sb/sth; **своди́ть (свести́** *perf*) **~ с кем-н** to settle a score with sb; **у него́ с ни́ми свои́ ~** he's got his own scores to settle with them.

счи́|стить (-щу, -стишь; *impf* **счища́ть)** *сов перех* to clean off.

счита́л|ка (-ки; *gen pl* **-ок)** *ж* counting rhyme.

счи́танн|ый *прил*: **~ые дни/мину́ты** only a few days/minutes; **~ое коли́чество** very few.

счита́|ть (-ю) *несов неперех* to count **♦** (*perf* **посчита́ть** *или* **сосчита́ть**) *перех* (*деньги итп*) to count; (*perf* **посчита́ть** *или* **счесть**): **~ что-н/кого́-н** +*instr* to regard sb/sth as; **~ (посчита́ть** *или* **счесть** *perf*) **что-н необходи́мым** to consider sth (to be) necessary; **~я** +*gen* (*принимая в расчёт*) considering; **не ~я** +*gen* excluding; **~я от** +*gen или* **с** +*gen* starting with; **~ (счесть** *perf*) **что-н/кого́-н за** +*acc* to regard sb/sth as; **я ~ю, что ...** I believe *или* think that ...

▸ **счита́ться** *несов возв*: **~ся** +*instr* to be considered to be; (*уважать*): **~ся с** +*instr* (*с родителями, с другом итп*) to be considerate to.

счи́тыва|ть (-ю; *perf* **счита́ть**) *несов перех* to read (*meter etc*).

счища́|ть (-ю) *несов от* **счи́стить**.

счи́щу *сов см* **счи́стить**.

США *мн сокр* (= *Соединённые Шта́ты Аме́рики*) USA (= *United States of America*).

сшиба́|ть (-у́, -ёшь; *pt* **-, -ла, -ло,** *impf* **сшиба́ть**) *сов перех* (*разг: подлеж: машина*) to hit

▸ **сшиби́ться** (*impf* **сшиба́ться**) *сов возв* (*разг*) to get into a fight.

сшива́|ть (-ю) *несов от* **сшить**.

сшить (сошью́, сошьёшь; *imper* **сшей(те))** *сов от* **шить ♦** (*impf* **сшива́ть**) *перех* (*соединить шитьём*) to sew together.

съеда́|ть (-ю) *несов от* **съесть**.

съеде́м(ся) *сов см* **съе́хать(ся)**.

съеде́ни|е (-я) *ср*: **отдава́ть кого́-н на ~**

кому́-н (*также перен*) to leave sb at the mercy of sb.

съе́дешь(ся) *итп сов см* **съе́хать(ся)**.

съеди́м *итп сов см* **съесть**.

съедо́бный (**-ен, -на, -но**) *прил* edible.

съе́ду(сь) *итп сов см* **съе́хать(ся)**.

съедя́т *сов см* **съесть**.

съёжиться (**-усь, -ишься**) *сов от* **ёжиться ◆** *возв* (*от холода, от страха*) to huddle; (*листья*) to shrivel up.

съезд (**-а**) *м* (*действие: гостей, делегатов*) gathering; (*к реке, в долину*) descent; (*партийный*) congress.

съе́здить (**-жу, -дишь**) *сов неперех* (*за покупками, к родителям*) to go; ~ (*perf*) +*dat* (*разг: ударить*) to whack.

съе́здовский (**-ая, -ое, -ие**) *прил* (*документы, решения*) congress *опред*.

съезжа́ть(ся) (**-ю(сь)**) *несов от* **съе́хать(ся)**.

съе́зжу *сов см* **съе́здить**.

съем *сов см* **съесть**.

съём|ка (**-ки**; *gen pl* **-ок**) *ж* (*копии*) making, taking; (*местности*) survey; (*обычно мн: фильма*) shooting; (*гипса*) removal.

съёмный *прил* detachable.

съёмок *сущ см* **съёмка**.

съёмочный *прил*: ~**ая площа́дка** film set; **съёмочная гру́ппа** film crew.

съёмщик (**-а**) *м* tennant.

съёмщиц|а (**-ы**) *ж см* **съёмщик**.

съестн|о́й *прил*: ~**ы́е припа́сы** food supplies *мн*.

съе|сть (*как* **есть**; *см* **Table 15**; *impf* **есть** *или* **съеда́ть**) *сов перех* (*хлеб, кашу*) to eat; (*подлеж: моль, ржавчина*) to eat away at; (: *тоска, ревность*) to gnaw at; (*impf* **съеда́ть**; *разг: деньги, зарплату*) to eat up.

съе́хать (*как* **е́хать**; *см* **Table 19**; *impf* **съезжа́ть**) *сов неперех*: ~ (**с** +*gen*) (*спуститься: с горки*) to go down; (*платок*) to slip; (*шапка*) to tilt; **съезжа́ть** (~ *perf*) (**с кварти́ры**) to move out (of one's flat); ~ (*perf*) **с ле́стницы** (*упасть*) to tumble down the stairs

▶ **съе́хаться** (*impf* **съезжа́ться**) *сов возв* (*гости, делегаты*) to gather.

съехи́дничать (**-ю**) *сов от* **ехи́дничать**.

съешь *сов см* **съесть**.

съязв|и́ть (**-лю, -и́шь**) *сов от* **язви́ть**.

сы́ворот|ка (**-ки**; *gen pl* **-ок**) *ж* (*молочная*) whey; (*мед*) serum.

сы́гранный *прил* well-coordinated.

сыгра́ть (**-ю**) *сов от* **игра́ть**

▶ **сыгра́ться** (*impf* **сы́грываться**) *сов возв* (*музыканты*) to play well together; (*спортсмены*) to play well as a team.

сы́змала *нареч* from an early age.

сы́знова *нареч* (*разг*) anew.

сымити́р|овать (**-ую**) *сов от* **имити́ровать**.

сымпровизи́р|овать (**-ую**) *сов от* **импровизи́ровать**.

сын (**-а**; *nom pl* **-овья́**, *gen pl* **-ове́й**, *dat pl* **-овья́м**)

м son; (*nom pl* **-ы́**, *gen pl* **-о́в**; *перен*): ~ +*gen* (*народа*) son of.

сынка́ *итп сущ см* **сыно́к**.

сыновья́ *итп сущ см* **сын**.

сыно́вний (**-яя, -ее, -ие**) *прил* (*любовь, долг*) son's.

сын|о́к (**-ка́**) *м уменьш от* **сын**; (*как обращение*) son.

сы́п|ать (**-лю, -лешь**; *imper* **сы́пь(те)**) *несов перех* to pour **◆** *неперех*: ~ +*instr* (*цитатами, остротами*) to pour forth with

▶ **сы́паться** *несов возв* (*мука, песок, яблоки итп*) to pour; (*вопросы, письма итп*) to pour forth; **на него́ посы́пались уда́ры со всех сторо́н** blows rained down on him from all sides.

сыпно́й *прил*: ~ **тиф** typhus.

сыпу́ч|ий (**-ая, -ее, -ие**) *прил* (*вещество*) friable; (*грунт*) shifting.

сып|ь (**-и**) *ж* rash.

сыр (**-а**; *part gen* **-у**, *nom pl* **-ы́**) *м* cheese; **как** ~ **в ма́сле ката́ться** (*impf*) to live the life of Riley.

сыре́|ть (*3sg* **-ет**, *3pl* **-ют**) *несов неперех* to get damp.

сыр|е́ц (**-ца́**) *м*: **хло́пок-**~ rough cotton; **шёлк-**~ raw silk.

сырка́ *итп сущ см* **сыро́к**.

сырко́вый *прил*: ~**ая ма́сса** cream cheese.

сы́рник (**-а**) *м small thick pancake made with cream cheese*.

сы́ро *как сказ*: **здесь** ~ it's damp here.

сыроёжк|а (**-и**) *ж* russula.

сыр|о́й (**-, -а́, -о**) *прил* (*бельё, земля, воздух*) damp; (*статья, стихи*) rough; (*no short form; мясо, овощи*) raw, uncooked; **сыра́я вода́** tap water.

сыр|о́к (**-ка́**) *м*: **творо́жный** ~ sweet curd cheese; **пла́вленный** ~ processed cheese.

сы́рост|ь (**-и**) *ж* dampness.

сырца́ *итп сущ см* **сыре́ц**.

сырь|ё (**-я́**) *ср собир* raw material.

сырьев|о́й *прил* (*ресурсы, база*) raw material *опред*.

сыск (**-а**) *м* criminal detection.

сы|ска́ть (**-щу́, -щешь**) *сов перех* (*разг: отыскать*) to find

▶ **сыска́ться** *сов возв* (*разг: обнаружиться*) to turn up.

сы́тный (**-ен, -на́, -но**) *прил* filling.

сы́т|ый (**-, -а́, -о**) *прил* (*не голодный*) full, satisfied; (*откормленный*) well-fed; (*no short form; перен: вид, улыбка*) contented; (: *мещанство*) smug; **спаси́бо, я сыт** thank you, I'm full; **я сыт по го́рло** (*перен*) I'm fed up.

сыч (**-а́**) *м* little owl; (*о человеке*) loner.

сы́щик (**-а**) *м* detective.

сыщу́(сь) *итп сов см* **сыска́ть(ся)**.

СЭВ (**-а**) *м сокр* (*ист*: = **Сове́т Экономи́ческой Взаимопо́мощи**) Comecon, CMEA (= *Council for Mutual Economic Assistance*).

СЭЗ ж сокр = свобо́дная экономи́ческая зо́на.

сэконо́м|ить (-лю, -ишь) сов от **эконо́мить**.

СЭС м сокр = Сове́тский Энциклопеди́ческий Слова́рь.

сюда́ нареч here; **(и) туда́ и ~** both here and there; **то туда́, то ~** sometimes here, sometimes there; **ни туда́ ни ~** neither here nor there; **туда́-~** (туда и обратно) backwards and forwards; (в разные стороны) everywhere; **иди́ ~!** come here!; **э́то ещё туда́-~** that's bearable.

сюже́т (-а) м plot.

сюже́тн|ый прил: **~ая ли́ния** storyline; **сюже́тное разви́тие** development of the plot.

сюи́т|а (-ы) ж (муз) suite.

сюрпри́з (-а) м surprise.

сюрреали́зм (-а) м surrealism.

сюрреали́ст (-а) м surrealist.

сюрту́к (-а́) м frock-coat.

сюсю́кани|е (-я) ср (см глаг) lisping; fussing.

сюсю́ка|ть (-ю) несов неперех (в речи) to lisp; (потворствовать): **~ с кем-н** to fuss over sb

▶ **сюсю́каться** несов возв: **~ся с кем-н** to fuss over sb.

ся́ду итп сов см **сесть**.

сяк нареч: **(и) так и ~** или **то так, то ~** (разг) hy hook or by crook; **э́то ещё так-~** (разг) it's so-so.

сяко́й прил: **ах ты тако́й-~** (разг) you little so-and-so.

сям нареч: **(и) там и ~** (разг) here and there; **то там, то ~** now here, now there.

~ *T, m* ~

T, т *сущ нескл* (*буква*) the 19th letter of the Russian alphabet.

т *сокр* (= **то́нна**) t (= *tonne*).

т. *сокр* = **това́рищ**; (= **том**) v., vol. (= *volume*); = **ты́сяча**.

та (**той**) *мест см* **тот**.

таба́к (**-á**; *part gen* **-ý**) *м* tobacco.

табака́ *нескл*: **цыплёнок** ~ char-grilled chicken.

табаке́р|ка (**-ки**; *gen pl* **-ок**) *ж* snuffbox.

табаково́д (**-а**) *м* tobacco grower.

табаково́дств|о (**-а**) *ср* tobacco-growing.

таба́чный *прил* tobacco *опред*.

та́бел|ь (**-я**) *м* (*ПРОСВЕЩ*) school report (*BRIT*), report card (*US, SCOTTISH*); (*на работе*) *board on which employees mark their time of arrival and departure*; (*график*) chart.

табле́т|ка (**-ки**; *gen pl* **-ок**) *ж* tablet.

табли́ц|а (**-ы**) *ж* table; (*СПОРТ*) (league) table; **табли́ца умноже́ния** multiplication table.

табли́ч|ка (**-ки**; *gen pl* **-ек**) *ж* (*с названием улицы*) street sign; (*экспоната*) plate; (*на двери*) nameplate.

табло́ *ср нескл* (*на вокзале, в аэропорту*) (information) board; (*на стадионе*) scoreboard.

та́бор (**-а**) *м* camp.

табу́ *ср нескл* taboo; **налага́ть** (**наложи́ть** *perf*) **на что-н** ~ to make a taboo of sth.

табу́н (**-á**) *м* herd.

табуре́т (**-а**) *м* = **табуре́тка**.

табуре́т|ка (**-ки**; *gen pl* **-ок**) *ж* stool.

тавтоло́ги|я (**-и**) *ж* tautology.

таджи́к (**-а**) *м* Tajik.

Таджикиста́н (**-а**) *м* Tajikistan.

таджи́кск|ий (**-ая, -ое, -ие**) *прил* Tajiki.

таджи́ч|ка (**-ки**; *gen pl* **-ек**) *ж см* **таджи́к**.

таёжный *прил* taiga *опред*.

таз (**-а**; *loc sg* **-ý**, *nom pl* **-ы́**) *м* (*сосуд*) basin; (*АНАТ*) pelvis.

тазобе́дренный *прил*: ~ **суста́в** hip joint.

та́зовый *прил* (*АНАТ*) pelvic.

Таила́нд (**-а**) *м* Thailand.

таила́нд|ец (**-ца**) *м* Thai.

таила́нд|ка (**-ки**; *gen pl* **-ок**) *ж см* **таила́ндец**.

таила́ндца *итп сущ см* **таила́ндец**.

таи́нственн|ый (**-, -на, -но**) *прил* mysterious; (*цель, намерение*) secret.

та́инств|о (**-а**) *ср* (*РЕЛ*) sacrament.

Таи́ти *м нескл* Tahiti.

таи́|ть (**-ю́, -ишь**) *несов перех* to conceal;

(*перен*): ~ **в себе́** (*возможности, угрозу итп*) to conceal; ~ (*impf*) **зло́бу на кого́-н** to harbour (*BRIT*) *или* harbor (*US*) malice towards sb; **что греха́** ~ (*разг*) there's no point in pretending otherwise

▶ **таи́ться** *несов возв* (*скрывать что-н*) to cover up; (*опасность, неожиданность*) to lurk; **в нём** ~**и́тся наде́жда/зло́ба** he harbo(u)rs a secret hope/feeling of malice.

таитя́нск|ий (**-ая, -ое, -ие**) *прил* Tahitian.

Тайва́н|ь (**-я**) *м* Taiwan.

тайг|á (**-и**) *ж* the taiga.

тайко́м *нареч* in secret, secretly.

тайм (**-а**) *м* (*СПОРТ*) period; **пе́рвый/второ́й** ~ (*ФУТБОЛ*) the first/second half.

тайм-а́ут (**-а**) *м* (*СПОРТ*) time-out.

та́йн|а (**-ы**) *ж* (*секрет*) secret; (*загадка*) mystery; **держа́ть** (*impf*) **что-н в** ~**е** to keep sth secret; **храни́ть** (*impf*) ~**у** to keep a secret.

тайни́к (**-á**) *м* hiding place.

та́йный *прил* secret.

тайфу́н (**-а**) *м* typhoon.

KEYWORD

так *нареч* **1** (*указательное: таким образом*) like this, this way; **де́лайте так** do it like this *или* this way; **пусть бу́дет так** so be it; **так не пойдёт** that won't do; **она́ всё де́лает не так** she does everything wrong

2 (*настолько*) so; **я так испуга́лся, что на́чал крича́ть** I was so frightened I started to shout; **всё случи́лось так неожи́данно!** it all happened so unexpectedly!

3 (*без последствий*) just like that; **так э́то не пройдёт** you won't get away with it

4 (*разг: без какого-н намерения*) for no (special) reason; **я сказа́л э́то про́сто так** I said it for no (special) reason; **почему́ ты пла́чешь? – да так** why are you crying? – for no reason

♦ *част* **1** (*разг: ничего*) nothing; **что с тобо́й? – так** what's wrong? – nothing

2 (*разг: усилительная*): **а она́ так жа́ловалась!** she didn't half complain!; **так я тебе́ и пове́рил!** I'm not falling for that!

3 (*разг: приблизительно*) about; **дня так че́рез два** in about two days

4 (*например*) for example; **поведе́ние у него́ плохо́е; так, вчера́ слома́л окно́** his behaviour is bad, for example, yesterday he broke a window

5 (*да*) OK; **так, всё хорошо́/пра́вильно** OK, that's fine/correct
♦ *союз* **1** (*в тако́м слу́чае*) then; **пло́хо себя́ чу́вствуешь, так иди́ спать** if you feel ill, (then) go and have a sleep; **е́хать, так е́хать** if we are going, (then) let's go
2 (*таки́м о́бразом*) so; **так ты пое́дешь?** so, you are going?
3 (*но*) but; **я пыта́лся его́ убеди́ть, так он не слу́шает** I tried to convince him but he wouldn't listen
4 (*в раздели́тельных вопро́сах*): **э́то поле́зная кни́га, не так ли?** it's a useful book, isn't it?; **он хоро́ший челове́к, не так ли?** he's a good person, isn't he?; **у них есть соба́ка, не так ли?** they have a dog, don't they?
5 (*во фра́зах*): **и так** (*и без того́ уже́*) anyway; **е́сли** *или* **раз так** in that case; **так и быть!** so be it!; **так и есть** (*разг*) sure enough; **так ему́!** serves him right!; **та́к себе** (*разг*) so-so; **так как** since; **так что** so; **так что́бы** so that.

такела́ж (-а) *м* rigging.
та́кже *союз, нареч* also; **я ~ подде́рживаю Ва́ше предложе́ние** I also *или* too am in favour (*BRIT*) *или* favor (*US*) of your suggestion; **мне нра́вится ~ и Ва́ше предложе́ние** I like your suggestion too *или* as well; **с Но́вым Го́дом! – и Вас ~** Happy New Year! – the same to you; **а ~** and also.
-таки *част* (*разг: всё же*) *emphatic particle*; **ты~ отказа́лся** so you decided to refuse then; **он~ пришёл** so he did come then; **она́ пря́мо~ исхо́дит от гне́ва** she is really furious; **опя́ть~** but having said that; **та́к~** (*разг*) so that's the way it is.
тако́в (-а́, -о́, -ы́) *как сказ* such; **~ тебе́ мой сове́т** that is my advice to you; **ситуа́ция такова́, что ...** the situation is such that ...; **и был ~** (*разг*) and we never saw him again.
таково́й *мест*: **как ~** as such.
тако́|е (-ого) *ср* (*о чём-н интере́сном, ва́жном итп*) something; **я ~ слы́шала!** I've heard something; **~ происхо́дит!** something is going on!; **что тут ~ого?** what is so special about that?
тако́|й *мест* such; **~и́е лю́ди встреча́ются ре́дко** you rarely meet such people; **до ~ сте́пени** to such an extent; **~а́я жара́!** such heat!; **кто ~?** who is it?; **он сего́дня како́й-то не ~** he is not quite himself today; **что ~о́е?** what is it?; **~то** (*о лице́*) so-and-so; (*о предме́те*) such-and-such.
тако́й-сяко́й *мест* (*разг*): **ах ты ~** you little so-and-so.
та́кс|а (-ы) *ж* (*зоол*) dachshund; (*комм*) (fixed) rate; **пла́та по ~е** fixed-rate payment.
такса́ци|я (-и) *ж* rating.
такси́ *ср нескл* taxi.
такси́р|овать (-ую) (*не)сов перех* (*услуги итп*)

to set a rate for.
такси́ст (-а) *м* taxi driver.
таксомото́р (-а) *м* taxicab.
таксопа́рк (-а) *м сокр* (= таксомото́рный парк) taxi depot.
таксофо́н (-а) *м* payphone.
такт (-а) *м* (*такти́чность*) tact; (*муз*) bar (*BRIT*), measure (*US*); (*ритм*) beat; **в ~ му́зыке** in time with the music.
та́ктик (-а) *м* tactician.
та́ктик|а (-и) *ж* tactic; (*воен*) tactics *мн*.
такти́чен *прил см* **такти́чный**.
такти́ческ|ий (-ая, -ое, -ие) *прил* tactical.
такти́ч|ный (-ен, -на, -но) *прил* tactful.
тала́нт (-а) *м* talent.
тала́нтлив|ый (-, -а, -о) *прил* talented.
талисма́н (-а) *м* charm, talisman.
та́ли|я (-и) *ж* waist; **пла́тье в ~ю** dress fitted at the waist.
Та́ллин (-а) *м* Tallin(n).
талму́д (-а) *м* the Talmud.
тало́н (-а) *м* ticket; (*на бензи́н, на проду́кты итп*) coupon.
та́лый *прил* (*снег, лёд*) melted.
тальк (-а) *м* talcum powder, talc.
там *нареч* there; **бу́ду ~ ско́ро** I'll be there soon; **~ посмо́трим** (*разг*) we'll see; **каки́е ~ сомне́ния** (*разг*) what's there to be unsure about?; **како́е ~!** (*разг*) not a chance!; **я ду́мал, что он догада́ется – куда́ уж ~!** (*разг*) I thought he'd guess, but not a bit of it!; **что ~ ни говори́, а мы оши́блись** whatever you say, we still made a mistake; **и ~ и сям** (*разг*) here, there and everywhere.
тамада́ (-ы́) *ж* (*мужчи́на*) toastmaster; (*же́нщина*) toastmistress.
та́мбур (-а) *м* section at door of train carriage.
тамбури́н (-а) *м* (*бараба́н*) tambourin (*small drum*); (*бу́бен*) tambourine.
тамо́жен *сущ см* **тамо́жня**.
тамо́женник (-а) *м* customs officer.
тамо́женный *прил* (*досмо́тр*) customs *опред*; **тамо́женная по́шлина** customs (duty).
тамо́жн|я (-ни; *gen pl* -ен) *ж* customs.
та́мпекс (-а) *м* Tampax ®.
тампо́н (-а) *м* tampon.
та́нгенс (-а) *м* (*мат*) tangent.
та́нго *ср нескл* tango.
та́н|ец (-ца) *м* dance; *см также* **та́нцы**.
танзани́йск|ий (-ая, -ое, -ие) *прил* Tanzanian.
Танзани́|я (-и) *ж* Tanzania.
тани́н (-а) *м* tannin.
танк (-а) *м* (*воен, тех*) tank.
та́нкер (-а) *м* tanker (*ship*).
танке́т|ка (-ки; *gen pl* -ок) *ж* (*обы́чно мн: о́бувь*) wedge heel.
танки́ст (-а) *м* tank crew member.

та́нца *итп сущ см* **та́нец.**

танцева́льный *прил* dance *опред*; **~ зал** dance hall.

танцева́ть (**-у́ю**) *несов (не)перех* to dance.

танцо́вщик (**-а**) *м* dancer.

танцо́вщиц|а (**-ы**) *ж см* **танцо́вщик.**

танцплоща́д|ка (**-ки**; *gen pl* **-ок**) *ж сокр* (= **танцева́льная площа́дка**) dance floor.

танцо́р (**-а**) *м* dancer.

та́нц|ы (**-ев**) *мн* (*вечер*) dance *ед*; **идти́ (пойти́** *perf*) **на ~** to go dancing.

та́поч|ка (**-ки**; *gen pl* **-ек**) *ж* (*обычно мн: дома́шняя*) slipper; (: *спорти́вная*) plimsoll (*BRIT*), sneaker (*US*).

та́р|а (**-ы**) *ж собир* containers *мн.*

тараба́н|ить (**-ю, -ишь**) *несов неперех* (*разг*) to rap.

тараба́рщин|а (**-ы**) *ж* (*разг*) gobbledegook.

тарака́н (**-а**) *м* cockroach.

тара́н (**-а**) *м* (*ВОЕН*) ram.

тара́н|ить (**-ю, -ишь**; *perf* **протара́нить**) *несов перех* to ram.

таранта́с (**-а**) *м* tarantass (*large springless carriage*).

тара́нтул (**-а**) *м* tarantula.

тарара́м (**-а**) *м* (*разг*) hullaballoo.

тарато́р|ить (**-ю, -ишь**) *несов неперех* (*разг*) to gabble on.

тарах|те́ть (**-чу́, -ти́шь**) *несов неперех* (*колёса, мотор*) to rattle; (*челове́к*) to rattle on.

тара́щ|ить (**-у, -ишь**; *perf* **вы́таращить**) *несов перех*: **~ глаза́ (на +***acc*) to stare (at)

▸ **тара́щиться** (*perf* **вы́таращиться**) *несов возв* (*разг*): **~ся (на +***acc*) to gawp *или* gawk (at).

таре́л|ка (**-ки**; *gen pl* **-ок**) *ж* plate; **глубо́кая ~** soup plate; **лета́ющая ~** flying saucer; **я здесь не в свое́й ~ке** (*разг*) I feel out of place here; *см также* **таре́лки.**

таре́л|ки (**-ок**) *мн* (*МУЗ*) cymbals *мн.*

тари́ф (**-а**) *м* tariff.

тарифика́ци|я (**-и**) *ж* tariffing.

тарифици́р|овать (**-ую**) (*не*)*сов перех* (*перево́зки, услу́ги*) to tariff; **~** (*impf/perf*) **окла́ды/нало́ги** to fix the salary/tax scale.

тари́фн|ый *прил*: **~ая табли́ца/се́тка** list/scale of charges.

таска́|ть (**-ю**) *несов перех* to lug; (*разг: ворова́ть*) to pinch; (: *одева́ть*) to wear; **~** (*impf*) **с собо́й** to carry around; **~** (*impf*) **кого́-н за́ во́лосы** to pull sb's hair

▸ **таска́ться** *несов возв* (*по магази́нам итп*) to traipse around; **~ся** (*impf*) **за кем-н** to trail around after sb.

Тасма́ни|я (**-и**) *ж* Tasmania.

тас|ова́ть (**-у́ю**; *perf* **стасова́ть**) *несов перех* to shuffle.

ТАСС *м сокр* (= **Телегра́фное аге́нтство Сове́тского Сою́за**) Tass (*main news agency of the Soviet Union*).

тата́рин (**-а**; *nom pl* **тата́ры**) *м* Tatar.

тата́р|ка (**-ки**; *gen pl* **-ок**) *ж см* **тата́рин.**

тата́р|ы *итп сущ см* **тата́рин.**

татуиро́в|ка (**-ки**; *gen pl* **-ок**) *ж* tattoo.

тахт|а́ (**-ы́**) *ж* divan (*BRIT*), ottoman (*US*).

та́ч|ка (**-ки**; *gen pl* **-ек**) *ж* wheelbarrow.

Ташке́нт (**-а**) *м* Tashkent.

тащ|и́ть (**-у́, -ишь**) *несов перех* (*тяну́ть*) to pull; (*волочи́ть, также перен*) to drag; (*нести́*) to haul; (*perf* **вы́тащить**; *перен: в теа́тр, на прогу́лку*) to drag out; (*perf* **стащи́ть**; *разг: красть*) to nick; **он та́щит всю рабо́ту на себе́** he is lumbered with (*BRIT*) *или* has got landed with all the work

▸ **тащи́ться** *несов возв* (*ме́дленно е́хать*) to trundle along; (*идти́ нео́хотно*) to drag o.s. along; (*волочи́ться: подо́л*) to drag; **не хо́чется ~ся в таку́ю даль** I don't feel like traipsing all that way.

та́|ять (**-ю**; *perf* **раста́ять**) *несов неперех* to melt; (*перен: си́лы, де́ньги*) to dwindle; (: *от любви́, от похвал́*) to melt; (: *от боле́зни*) to waste away; **~** (*impf*) **во рту** (*перен*) to melt in the mouth.

Тбили́си *м нескл* Tbilisi.

ТВ *м сокр* (= **телеви́дение**) TV (= *television*).

твар|ь (**-и**) *ж* creature; (*разг: пренебр*) swine.

тверде́|ть (*3sg* **-ет**, *3pl* **-ют**, *perf* **затверде́ть**) *несов неперех* (*также перен*) to harden.

тверд|и́ть (**-жу́, -ди́шь**; *perf* **затверди́ть**) *несов перех* (*стихотворе́ние, уро́к итп*) to learn by rote; **~** (*impf*) **о +***prp* (*говори́ть*) to go on about.

твёрдо *нареч* (*ве́рить, сказа́ть*) firmly; (*зау́чить, запо́мнить*) properly; **я ~ зна́ю, что ...** I know for sure that ....

твердоло́б|ый (**-, -а, -о**) *прил* hard-headed.

твёрдост|ь (**-и**) *ж* firmness; (*цен*) stability; (*во́ли, хара́ктера*) toughness.

твёрд|ый *прил* (*ФИЗ*) solid; (**-, -а́, -о**; *земля́, предме́т*) hard; (*реше́ние, сторо́нник, тон итп*) firm; (*це́ны, ста́вки*) stable; (*поря́док*) set; (*зна́ния*) solid; (*во́ля, хара́ктер*) tough; (*ЛИНГ: звук*) hard, nonpalatalized; **здесь нужна́ ~ая рука́** a firm hand is needed; **твёрдый знак** (*ЛИНГ*) hard sign.

тверды́н|я (**-и**) *ж* (*перен*) stronghold.

твёрже *сравн прил от* **твёрдый** ♦ *сравн нареч от* **твёрдо.**

твержу́ *несов см* **тверди́ть.**

твид (**-а**) *м* tweed.

твист (**-а**) *м* the twist.

тво|й (**-его́**; *f* **-я́**, *nt* **-ё**, *pl* **-и́**; *как* **мой**; *см* **Table 8**) *притяж мест* your; **вот ~ чай** here is your tea; **мой оте́ц врач – а ~?** my father is a doctor – what does yours do?; **э́то всё ~ё** this is all yours; **приве́т (всем) ~им** say hello to your folks; **по-~ему мне́нию** in your opinion; **как по-тво́ему?** what is your opinion?; **дава́й сде́лаем по-тво́ему** let's do it your way.

творе́ни|е (**-я**) *ср* creation.

твор|е́ц (**-ца́**) *м* creator; **Т~** (*РЕЛ*) the Creator.

твори́тельный *прил*: **~ паде́ж** (*ЛИНГ*) the instrumental (case).

твор|и́ть (-ю́, -и́шь) *несов неперех* to create ◆ (*perf* **сотвори́ть**) *перех* (*шедевр, симфонию итп*) to create; (*perf* **натвори́ть**; *разг*) to get up to; ~ (**сотвори́ть** *perf*) **чудеса́** to work miracles; ~ (**сотвори́ть** *perf*) **добро́** to do good; ~ (*impf*) **беззако́ния** to commit unjust acts

▸ **твори́ться** *несов возв*: **что тут ~и́тся?** what's going on here?; **с ним ~и́тся что́-то стра́нное** something strange has come over him.

творо́г (-а́; *part gen* -**у́**) *м* ≈ curd cheese.

творо́жник (-а) *м* curd pancake.

творо́жный *прил* curd-cheese.

творца́ *итп сущ см* **творе́ц**.

тво́рческ|ий (-ая, -ое, -ие) *прил* creative; **тво́рческий о́тпуск** sabbatical.

тво́рчеств|о (-а) *ср* creative work; (*писателя, композитора*) work; **худо́жественное** ~ artistic creativity; **наро́дное** ~ folk art.

тво|я́ (-**ей**) *притяж мест см* **твой**.

ТВЧ *сокр* (= *то́ки высо́кой частоты́*) high frequency currents *мн*.

т.д. *сокр* (= **так да́лее**) etc. (= *et cetera*).

те (**тех**) *мест см* **тот**.

т.е. *сокр* (= **то есть**) i.e. (= *id est*).

теа́тр (-а) *м* theatre (*BRIT*), theater (*US*); ~ **Го́голя/Шекспи́ра** Gogol's/Shakespeare's theatrical works; ~ **вое́нных де́йствий** the theatre of operations.

театра́л (-а) *м* theatregoer (*BRIT*), theatergoer (*US*).

театрализ|ова́ть (-**у́ю**) (*не*)*сов перех* to dramatize.

театра́л|ка (-ки; *gen pl* -**ок**) *ж см* **театра́л**.

театра́льный *прил* (*афиша, сезон*) theatre *опред* (*BRIT*), theater *опред* (*US*); (*деятельность, жест*) theatrical; **театра́льная ка́сса** theatre box office; **театра́льная сту́дия** theatre studio; **театра́льный зал** theatre; **театра́льный институ́т** drama school.

театрове́д (-а) *м* theatre (*BRIT*) *или* theater (*US*) specialist.

тебе́ *мест см* **ты** ◆ *как част* (*разг*): **здесь** ~ **и по́мощь и понима́ние** you can get help and understanding here; **я** ~ **поспо́рю!** don't you dare to argue!; **я** ~ **дам** *или* **покажу́!** I'll show you!

тебя́ *мест см* **ты**.

Тегера́н (-а) *м* Teheran.

теза́урус (-а) *м* thesaurus.

те́зис (-а) *м* (*идея*) thesis (*мн* theses); (: *в логике*) proposition; (*обычно мн: доклада, статьи*) abstract.

тёз|ка (-ки; *gen pl* -**ок**) *м/ж* namesake.

тёк *итп несов см* **течь**.

текст (-а) *м* text; (*песни*) words *мн*, lyrics *мн*.

тексти́л|ь (-я) *м собир* textiles *мн*.

тексти́льн|ый *прил*: ~**ые изде́лия** textiles; ~**ая промы́шленность** textile industry.

теку́т *итп несов см* **течь**.

теку́чест|ь (-и) *ж* fluidity; ~ **ка́дров** high staff turnover.

теку́ч|ий (-ая, -ее, -ие; -, -а, -е) *прил* fluid; ~**ие ка́дры** fluctuating workforce.

теку́чк|а (-и) *ж* (*разг*) daily routine.

теку́щ|ий (-ая, -ее, -ие) *прил* (*год*) current; (*повседневный: дела*) routine; ~**ие обяза́тельства** (*КОММ*) current liabilities *мн*; **теку́щие собы́тия** current affairs; **теку́щий ремо́нт** running repairs, maintenance; **теку́щий счёт** (*КОММ*) current (*BRIT*) *или* checking (*US*) account.

тел. *сокр* (= **телефо́н**) tel. (= *telephone*).

телевеща́ни|е (-я) *ср* television broadcasting.

телеви́дени|е (-я) *ср* television; **по** ~**ю** on television.

телевизио́нный *прил* television *опред*.

телеви́зор (-а) *м* television (set); **смотре́ть** (*impf*) ~ to watch television; **по** ~**у** on television.

теле́г|а (-и) *ж* cart.

телегра́мм|а (-ы) *ж* telegram.

телегра́ф (-а) *м* (*способ связи*) telegraph; (*учреждение*) telegraph office.

телеграфи́р|овать (-**ую**) (*не*)*сов перех* to wire.

телеграфи́ст (-а) *м* telegraphist.

телеграфи́ст|ка (-ки; *gen pl* -**ок**) *ж см* **телеграфи́ст**.

телегра́фный *прил* (*также перен*) telegraphic; **телегра́фное аге́нтство** news agency; **телегра́фный де́нежный перево́д** telegraphic transfer; **телегра́фный столб** telegraph pole.

теле́ж|ка (-ки; *gen pl* -**ек**) *ж уменьш от* **теле́га**; (*для багажа, в супермаркете*) trolley.

телезри́тел|ь (-я) *м* viewer.

телека́мер|а (-ы) *ж* television camera.

те́лекс (-а) *м* telex.

телёнок (-ёнка; *nom pl* -**я́та**, *gen pl* -**я́т**) *м* calf (*мн* calves).

телепа́ти|я (-и) *ж* telepathy.

телепереда́ч|а (-и) *ж* TV programme (*BRIT*) *или* program (*US*).

теле́сен *прил см* **теле́сный**.

телеско́п (-а) *м* telescope.

телескопи́ческ|ий (-ая, -ое, -ие) *прил* (*антенна, очки*) telescopic; (*наблюдения*) long-distance.

теле́сн|ый (-ен, -на, -но) *прил* bodily; ~**ного цве́та** flesh-coloured; **теле́сное наказа́ние** corporal punishment.

телеста́нци|я (-и) *ж* television station.

телесту́ди|я (-и) *ж* television studio.

телета́йп (-а) *м* teleprinter (*BRIT*), teletypewriter (*US*), Teletype ®.

телефо́н (-а) *м* telephone; (*разг: номер*) (phone) number.

телефони́ст (-а) *м* telephonist.

телефони́ст|ка (-ки; *gen pl* -**ок**) *ж см*

телефони́ст.

телефóнный *прил* telephone *опред*; **телефóнная стáнция** telephone exchange; **телефóнная кни́га** telephone book *или* directory.

теле́ц *сущ см* **тéльце.**

Теле́ц (-ьцá) *м* (*созвездие*) Taurus.

телеце́нтр (-а) *м* television centre (*BRIT*) *или* center (*US*).

тели́ться (*3sg* -ится, *3pl* -ятся, *perf* **отели́ться**) *несов возв* to calve.

тёл|ка (-ки; *gen pl* -ок) *ж* heifer.

тéл|о (-а; *nom pl* -á) *ср* body; **небéсные телá** heavenly bodies; **дрожáть** (*impf*) **всем ~м** to tremble all over; **держáть** (*impf*) **когó-н в чёрном ~е** to treat sb badly.

телогрéй|ка (-йки; *gen pl* -ек) *ж* body warmer.

телодвижéни|е (-я) *ср* movement.

тёлок *сущ см* **тёлка.**

телосложéни|е (-я) *ср* physique.

телохрани́тел|ь (-я) *м* bodyguard.

Тель-Ави́в (-а) *м* Tel Aviv.

тельня́ш|ка (-ки; *gen pl* -ек) *ж* sailor top.

Тельцá *итп сущ см* **Теле́ц.**

тéль|це (-ьца; *nom pl* -ьцá, *gen pl* -éц) *ср уменьш от* **тéло**; (*ребёнка*) body; (*обычно мн*: *кровяные*) corpuscle.

теля́т|а *итп сущ см* **телёнок.**

теля́тин|а (-ы) *ж* veal.

теля́тник (-а) *м* (*помещение*) calf shed.

теля́чий (-ья, -ье, -ьи) *прил*: **~ья кóжа** calfskin *опред*; (*кулин*) veal *опред*; **~ьи нéжности** (*разг*) lovey-dovey behaviour; **~ восторг** (*разг*) wide-eyed enthusiasm.

тем *мест см* **тот, то** ◆ *союз* (+*comparative*): **чем бóльше, ~ лýчше** the more the better; **~ бóлее!** all the more so!; **~ бóлее, что ...** especially as ...; **э́то трýдно, ~ бóлее для меня́** it's difficult, especially for me; **~ лýчше/хýже** that's even better/worse; **~ лýчше для меня́** all the better for me; **не хóчет слýшать? ~ хýже для негó** if he doesn't want to listen then it's his loss; **~ не мéнее** nevertheless; **~ сáмым** thus.

тéм|а (-ы) *ж* subject, topic; (*МУЗ, ЛИТЕРАТУРА*) theme.

темáтик|а (-и) *ж* theme.

темати́ческ|ий (-ая, -ое, -ие) *прил* (*выставка, показ фильмов итп*) theme-based.

тембр (-а) *м* timbre.

тёмен *прил см* **тёмный.**

тéмени *итп сущ см* **тéмя.**

Тéмз|а (-ы) *ж* the Thames.

тéми *мест см* **тот, то.**

темнé|ть (*3sg* -ет, *3pl* -ют, *perf* **потемнéть**) *несов непереx* (*небо, краска*) to darken ◆ (*perf* **стемнéть**) *безл* to get dark; (*no perf*; *виднеться*) to loom dark; **зимóй рáно ~ет** it get's dark early in winter.

темни́ть (-ю, -и́шь) *несов непереx* (*разг*) to confuse the issue.

темни́ц|а (-ы) *ж* dungeon.

темнó *как сказ*: **на ýлице/в кóмнате ~** it's dark outside/inside; **на душé у неё бы́ло ~** she felt gloomy.

темнот|á (-ы́) *ж* darkness; (*перен: невежество*) ignorance.

тём|ный (-ен, -нá, -нó) *прил* dark; (*смысл, теория*) obscure; (*прошлое, дела*) shady; (*невежественный: человек*) ignorant; **~ное пятнó** (*перен*) blemish; **~ные временá** dark times.

темп (-а) *м* speed; (*МУЗ*) tempo; **в тéмпе** (*разг*) quickly; **ускоря́ть (ускóрить** *perf*) **~ +***gen* to speed up.

тéмпер|а (-ы) *ж* tempera.

темперáмент (-а) *м* temperament, disposition; **он человéк с ~ом** he is a temperamental character.

темперáмент|ный (-ен, -на, -но) *прил* (*речь, исполнение, человек*) spirited.

температýр|а (-ы) *ж* temperature; **у меня́ ~** I've got a temperature; **ходи́ть** (*impf*) **с ~ой** (*разг*) to go about with a temperature.

температýр|ить (-ю, -ишь) *несов непереx* (*разг*) to be running a temperature.

тéм|я (-ени; *как* **врéмя**; *см* **Table 4**) *ср* crown (*of the head*).

тéнг|е (-а) *м* tenga (*currency unit of Kazakhstan*).

тенденцио́зность (-и) *ж* bias.

тенденцио́зный *прил* bias(s)ed.

тендéнци|я (-и) *ж*: **~ (к** +*dat*) tendency (towards); (*предвзятость*) bias.

теневóй *прил* shady; (*перен: стороны жизни*) shadowy; **теневáя экономи́ка** shadow economy; **теневóй кабинéт** (*ПОЛИТ*) shadow cabinet.

тенелюби́в|ый (-, -а, -о) *прил* (*БОТ*) shade-loving.

тéн|и (-éй) *мн* (*также*: **~ для век**) eye shadow *ед*.

тени́ст|ый (-, -а, -о) *прил* shady.

тéннис (-а) *м* tennis.

тенниси́ст (-а) *м* tennis player.

тенниси́ст|ка (-ки; *gen pl* -ок) *ж см* **тенниси́ст.**

тéннис|ка (-ки; *gen pl* -ок) *ж* polo shirt.

тéннис|ный *прил*: **~ая ракéтка** tennis racket; **тéннисный корт/мяч** tennis court/ball.

тéннисок *сущ см* **тéнниска.**

тéнор (-а; *nom pl* -á) *м* (*МУЗ*) tenor.

тент (-а) *м* awning.

тен|ь (-и; *prp sg* -и́, *gen pl* -éй) *ж* (*тенистое место*) shade; (*предмета, человека*) shadow; (+*gen*; *перен: волнения, печали итп*) flicker; **отбрáсывать (отбрóсить** *perf*) **~** to cast a shadow; **держáться** (*impf*) **в ~и́** (*перен*) to remain in the background; **бросáть (брóсить** *perf*) **~ на** +*acc* (*перен*) to cast a slur on; **без тéни сомнéния** without a shadow of a doubt; **нет ни тéни сомнéния, что ...** there is not the slightest doubt that ...; *см также* **тéни.**

теологи́ческ|ий (-ая, -ое, -ие) *прил* theological.

теолóги|я (-и) *ж* theology.

теоре́м|а (-ы) *ж* theorem.
теоре́тик (-а) *м* theoretician.
теорети́ческ|ий (-ая, -ое, -ие) *прил* theoretical.
тео́ри|я (-и) *ж* theory.
тёпел *прил см* **тёплый**.
тепе́решн|ий (-яя, -ее, -ие) *прил* (*разг*) present.
тепе́рь *нареч* (*сейчас*) now; (*в наше время*) nowadays ♦ *союз*: ~ **обсу́дим сле́дующий вопро́с** let us now move on to the next question.
тепле́|ть (*3sg* -ет, *3pl* -ют, *perf* **потепле́ть**) *несов неперех* to get warmer; (*отношения*) to become warmer.
те́пл|иться (*3sg* -ится, *3pl* -ятся) *несов возв* to flicker; **в нём ещё ~ится наде́жда** he still holds out a faint hope.
тепли́ц|а (-ы) *ж* hothouse.
тепли́чный *прил* (*растение*) hothouse *опред*; (*перен: условия*) sheltered.
тепл|о́ *нареч* warmly ♦ (-а́) *ср* (*также перен*) warmth ♦ *как сказ* it's warm; **на у́лице/в ко́мнате ~** it's warm outside/inside; **нас ~ встре́тили** we were given a warm welcome; **10 гра́дусов ~а́** 10 degrees (centigrade); **мне ~** I'm warm.
теплово́з (-а) *м* locomotive.
теплово́й *прил* (*лучи, энергия*) thermal; **теплово́й дви́гатель** heat engine; **теплово́й уда́р** (*МЕД*) heatstroke.
теплолюби́в|ый (-, -а, -о) *прил* (*БОТ*) heat-loving.
теплообме́н (-а) *м* (*ФИЗ*) heat exchange.
теплот|а́ (-ы́) *ж* heat; (*перен: чувств, отношений, красок*) warmth.
теплохо́д (-а) *м* motor ship *или* vessel.
теплоцентра́л|ь (-и) *ж* generator plant (*supplying central heating systems*).
тё́пл|ый (-ел, -ла́, -ло́) *прил* warm; **~лое месте́чко** (*разг*) cushy job; **сказа́ть** (*perf*) **кому́-н па́ру ~лых слов** (*разг*) to give sb a piece of one's mind.
терапе́вт (-а) *м* ≈ general practitioner.
терапи́|я (-и) *ж* (*МЕД: наука*) internal medicine; (*лечение*) therapy; **интенси́вная ~** intensive care.
тереб|и́ть (-лю́, -и́шь) *несов перех* (*волосы, бороду*) to twiddle; (*разг: надоедать*) to pester.
тере́ть (**тру, трёшь**; *pt* **тёр, тёрла, тёрло**) *несов перех* to rub; (*чистить*) to scrub; (*овощи*) to grate ♦ *неперех* (*обувь, воротник*) to rub
▶ **тере́ться** *несов возв* (*человек*): **~ся о** +*acc* to rub o.s. up against; (*перен: разг*): **~ся о́коло** *или* **во́зле** +*gen* to hang around.
терза́ни|е (-я) *ср* (*обычно мн: душевные*) torment.
терза́|ть (-ю; *perf* **растерза́ть**) *несов перех* (*добычу*) to savage; (*perf* **истерза́ть**; *перен: упрёками, ревностью*) to torment
▶ **терза́ться** *несов возв* (+*instr*; *сомнениями,*

раскаянием) to be racked by.
тёр|ка (-ки; *gen pl* -ок) *ж* grater.
те́рмин (-а) *м* term.
термина́л (-а) *м* terminal.
терминологи́ческ|ий (-ая, -ое, -ие) *прил*: **~ слова́рь** specialized dictionary.
терминоло́ги|я (-и) *ж* terminology.
терми́ческ|ий (-ая, -ое, -ие) *прил* thermal.
термо́метр (-а) *м* thermometer.
те́рмос (-а) *м* Thermos®.
термоста́т (-а) *м* thermostat.
термосто́йк|ий (-ая, -ое, -ие) *прил* heat-resistant.
термоя́дерный *прил* thermonuclear; **термоя́дерное ору́жие** thermonuclear weapon.
терни́ст|ый (-, -а, -о) *прил*: **~ путь** (*перен*) difficult path.
терно́вник (-а) *м* blackthorn.
тёрок *сущ см* **тёрка**.
терпели́в|ый (-, -а, -о) *прил* patient.
терпе́ни|е (-я) *ср* patience; **выводи́ть** (**вы́вести** *perf*) **кого́-н из ~я** to exhaust sb's patience; **~ у меня́ ло́пнуло** I lost my patience; **запаса́ться** (**запасти́сь** *perf*) **~м** to call on one's reserve of patience.
терп|е́ть (-лю́, -ишь) *несов перех* (*боль, холод итп*) to suffer, endure; (*perf* **потерпе́ть**; *неудачу*) to suffer; (*мириться: грубость, наглеца итп*) to tolerate; **~** (**потерпе́ть** *perf*) **неуда́чу/пораже́ние** to suffer failure/a defeat; **~** (**потерпе́ть** *perf*) **круше́ние** (*корабль*) to be wrecked; (*поезд*) to crash; **вре́мя не те́рпит** time waits for no man; **де́ло не те́рпит отлага́тельств** this matter won't wait; **~ не могу́ таки́х люде́й** (*разг*) I can't stand people like that; **~ не могу́ спо́рить** (*разг*) I hate arguing
▶ **терпе́ться** *несов безл*: (**мне**) **не те́рпится** +*infin* I can't wait to do.
терпи́мост|ь (-и) *ж*: **~ (к** +*dat*) tolerance (of).
терпи́м|ый (-, -а, -о) *прил* tolerable; (*человек, отношение*): **~ (к** +*dat*) tolerant (towards).
тё́рп|кий (-кая, -кое, -кие; -ок, -ка, -ко) *прил* tart.
терпло́|сь *несов см* **терпе́ть(ся)**.
тё́рпок *прил см* **тё́рпкий**.
терракота (-ы) *ж* terracotta.
терракотовый *прил* terracotta.
терра́с|а (-ы) *ж* (*также ГЕО*) terrace.
территориа́льный *прил* territorial.
террито́ри|я (-и) *ж* (*страны*) territory; (*школы, усадьбы*) grounds *мн*; **о́бщая ~ заво́да – 100 кв миль** the plant occupies an area of 100 sq miles.
терро́р (-а) *м* terror.
терроризи́р|овать (-ую) (*не*)*сов перех* to terrorize.
террори́зм (-а) *м* terrorism.
террори́ст (-а) *м* terrorist.
террористи́ческ|ий (-ая, -ое, -ие) *прил*

terrorist *опред*.

террори́ст|ка (**-ки**; *gen pl* **-ок**) *ж см* **террори́ст**.

тёртый *прил* (*сыр, овощи*) grated; **челове́к он ~** (*разг*) he's been around.

терье́р (**-а**) *м* terrier.

теря́|ть (**-ю**; *perf* **потеря́ть**) *несов перех* to lose; **~** (**потеря́ть** *perf*) **го́лову** to lose one's head; **~** (**потеря́ть** *perf*) **из ви́ду** (*перестать видеть*) to lose sight of; (*не иметь сведений о*) to lose touch with; **~** (**потеря́ть** *perf*) **по́чву под нога́ми** (*перен*) to lose one's way

▶ **теря́ться** (*perf* **потеря́ться**) *несов возв* to get lost; (*робеть*) to lose one's nerve; (*утрачиваться: память, уверенность*) to disappear; **~ся** (*impf*) **в дога́дках** to get caught up in conjecture.

тёс (**-а**) *м собир* planks *мн*.

тёсаный *прил* hewn.

теса́|ть (**-шу́, -шешь**) *несов перех* to hew (out).

тесём|ка (**-ки**; *gen pl* **-ок**) *ж* = **тесьма́**; (*завязка*) drawstring.

тесен *прил см* **те́сный**.

тесн|и́ть (**-ю́, -и́шь**; *perf* **потесни́ть**) *несов перех* (*друг друга в толпе*) to squeeze; (*кого-н к стене*) to press; (*противника*) to press back; (*perf* **стесни́ть**; *перен*): **~и́т в груди́** he *итп* has got a tight feeling in his chest

▶ **тесни́ться** *несов возв* (*люди: в толпе, в тесной комнате*) to be squashed together; (*мысли*) to crowd; **семья́ ~и́тся в одно́й ко́мнате** the whole family lives crammed together in one room; **в голове́ ~я́тся воспомина́ния** his *итп* mind is crowded with memories.

те́сно *нареч* (*стоять, расположить итп*) close together; (*сотрудничать*) closely ♦ *как сказ*: **в кварти́ре о́чень ~** the flat is very cramped; **мы с ним ~ знако́мы** he and I know each other very well.

теснот|а́ (**-ы́**) *ж* (*помещения*) cramped conditions *мн*; (*скопление людей*) crowd; (*в груди*) tightness; **в ~é, да не в оби́де** ≈ the more the merrier.

те́с|ный (**-ен, -на́, -но**) *прил* (*проход*) narrow; (*помещение*) cramped; (*одежда*) tight; (*дружба, ряды*) close; **мир ~ен** it's a small world.

тест (**-а**) *м* test.

те́ст|о (**-а**) *ср* (*дрожжевое*) dough; (*слоёное, песочное*) pastry (*BRIT*), paste (*US*); (*для блинов*) batter; (*для кекса*) mixture; (*бетонное*) mix.

тест|ь (**-я**) *м* father-in-law, wife's father.

тесьм|а́ (**-ы́**) *ж* tape; (*для украшения*) trimming.

те́терев (**-а**) *м* black grouse.

тете́р|я (**-и**) *ж* (*разг*) clot; **глуха́я ~** cloth-ears; **со́нная ~** sleepyhead.

тетив|а́ (**-ы́**) *ж* (*лука*) bowstring.

тёт|ка (**-ки**; *gen pl* **-ок**) *ж* auntie; (*разг: пренебр: женщина*) old dear.

тетра́д|ка (**-ки**; *gen pl* **-ок**) *ж* exercise book.

тетра́д|ь (**-и**) *ж* exercise book; **но́тная ~** manuscript book.

тёт|я (**-и**; *gen pl* **-ь**) *ж* aunt; (*разг: женщина*) lady.

тефте́л|и (**-ей**) *мн* meatballs *мн*.

тех *мест см* **те**.

Теха́с (**-а**) *м* Texas.

те́хник (**-а**) *м* technician.

те́хник|а (**-и**) *ж* technology; (*приёмы: музыкальная, плавания итп*) technique ♦ *собир* (*машины*) machinery; (*разг: муз*) hi-fi; **вычисли́тельная ~** (*КОМП*) computers *мн*; **те́хника безопа́сности** industrial safety.

те́хникум (**-а**) *м* technical college.

техни́чек *сущ см* **техни́чка**.

техни́чен *прил см* **техни́чный**.

техни́ческ|ий (**-ая, -ое, -ие**) *прил* technical; (*масло, волокно*) industrial; **техни́ческие нау́ки** engineering sciences; **техни́ческие сре́дства обуче́ния** educational technology; **техни́ческий осмо́тр** (*АВТ*) ≈ МОТ (*BRIT*) (*annual roadworthiness check*); **техни́ческий реда́ктор** copy editor; **техни́ческое обслу́живание** maintenance, servicing.

техни́ч|ка (**-ки**; *gen pl* **-ек**) *ж* (*автомобиль*) emergency vehicle; (*уборщица*) cleaner.

техни́ч|ный (**-ен, -на, -но**) *прил* (*спортсмен, музыкант*) technically good.

технокра́т (**-а**) *м* technocrat.

техно́лог (**-а**) *м* technologist; (*производственного процесса*) process engineer.

технологи́ческ|ий (**-ая, -ое, -ие**) *прил* technological; (*не строительный*) engineering *опред*; (*не вспомогательный*) basic, major; **технологи́ческий институ́т** institute of technology.

техноло́ги|я (**-и**) *ж* technology.

тече́ни|е (**-я**) *ср* (*воды, жизни*) flow; (*поток: морское, атмосферное*) current; (*в политике, в искусстве*) trend, current; **в ~** +*gen* during; **с ~м вре́мени** in the course of time; **по ~ю** with the current; **плыть** (*impf*) **по ~ю** (*перен*) to go with the flow; **про́тив ~я** against the current.

те́ч|ка (**-и**) *ж* (*ЗООЛ*) heat; **у на́шей соба́ки ~** our dog is on *или* in heat.

те́|чь (*3sg* **-чёт**, *3pl* **-ку́т**, *pt* **тёк, текла́, текло́**) *несов неперех* (*вода, кровь итп*) to flow; (*крыша, лодка итп*) to leak; (*перен: жизнь, время*) to go by ♦ (*-чи*) *ж* leak; **дава́ть** (**дать** *perf*) **~** to spring a leak.

те́ш|ить (**-у, -ишь**; *perf* **поте́шить**) *несов перех* to amuse; (*самолюбие*) to indulge

▶ **те́шиться** (*perf* **поте́шиться**) *несов возв*: **~ся** +*instr* (*игрушкой*) to amuse o.s. with; (*мыслью*) to console o.s. with; (*издеваться*): **~ся над** +*instr* to make fun of.

тёща (**-и**) *ж* mother-in-law, wife's mother.

тешу́ *итп несов см* **теса́ть**.

Тибе́т (**-а**) *м* Tibet.

тибе́тск|ий (**-ая, -ое, -ие**) *прил* Tibetan.

Тибр (**-а**) *м* Tiber (*river*).

Тигр (**-а**) *м* Tigris (*river*).

тигр (-а) м tiger.

тигрёнок (-ёнка; *nom pl* -**я́та**, *gen pl* -**я́т**) м tiger cub.

тигри́ц|**а** (-ы) ж tigress.

тигро́вый *прил* tiger опред; **тигро́вый глаз** (*камень*) tiger's-eye.

тигря́та *итп сущ см* **тигрёнок**.

тик (-а) м (*нервный*) tic; (*ткань*) ticking.

ти́кани|**е** (-я) *ср* ticking.

ти́ка|**ть** (*3sg* -ет, *3pl* -**ют**) *несов неперех* to tick.

ти́н|**а** (-ы) ж slime; (*перен: обывательщины итп*) mire.

тип (-а) м type; (*разг: о мужчине*) character; **ти́па** +*gen* (*разг*) sort of.

типа́ж (-á) м character type.

типи́чен *прил см* **типи́чный**.

типи́ческ|**ий** (-ая, -ое, -ие) *прил* typical.

типи́ч|**ный** (-ен, -на, -но) *прил*: ~ (**для** +*gen*) typical (of).

типово́й *прил* standard-type.

типогра́фи|**я** (-и) ж press, printing house.

типогра́фск|**ий** (-ая, -ое, -ие) *прил* typographical; **типогра́фская кра́ска** printing ink; **типогра́фский стано́к** printing press.

типу́н (-а) м: ~ **тебе́ на язы́к!** (*разг*) don't say that!

тир (-а) м shooting gallery.

тира́д|**а** (-ы) ж tirade.

тира́ж (-á) м (*газеты*) circulation; (*книги*) printing; (*лотереи, облигаций*) drawing; **кни́га вы́шла тиражо́м в ты́сячу экземпля́ров** one thousand copies of the book were printed; **выходи́ть** (**вы́йти** *perf*) **в** ~ (*заём, облигации*) to be issued; (*книга*) to be printed; (*перен*) to fade from the scene.

тира́н (-а) м tyrant.

Тира́н|**а** (-ы) ж Tirana.

тира́н|**ить** (-ю, -ишь) *несов перех* to tyrannize.

тирани́ческий (-ая, -ое, -ие) *прил* tyrannical.

тирани|**я** (-и) ж tyranny.

тире́ *ср нескл* dash.

тис (-а) м yew (tree).

ти́ска|**ть** (-ю) *несов перех* to squeeze.

тиск|**и́** (-о́в) *мн* (*ТЕХ*) vice *ед* (*BRIT*), vise *ед* (*US*); **в** ~**áх** +*gen* (*перен*) in the grip of.

тисне́ни|**е** (-я) *ср* (*по коже*) stamping.

тиснённый *прил* (*переплёт*) impressed.

тита́н (-а) м (*в мифологии*) titan; (*перен: науки, мысли итп*) giant; (*хим*) titanium; (*для нагрева воды*) boiler, urn.

титани́ческий (-ая, -ое, -ие) *прил* titanic.

титр (-а) м (*обычно мн*) credit (*of a film*).

ти́тул (-а) м (*также КОММ*) title; ~ **на иму́щество** (*ЮР*) title (*to property*).

ти́тульный *прил*: ~ **лист** title page.

тиф (-а) м typhus; **брюшно́й** ~ typhoid fever.

тифо́зн|**ый** *прил*: ~**ая лихора́дка** typhoid fever ♦ (-**ого**; *decl like adj*) typhus patient.

ти́х|**ий** (-ая, -ое, -ие; -, -á, -о) *прил* quiet;

(*течение, ход*) gentle; **Ти́хий океа́н** the Pacific (Ocean).

ти́х|**нуть** (*3sg* -нет, *3pl* -нут, *pt* -, -ла, -ло) *несов неперех* to go quiet.

ти́хо *нареч* (*говорить, жить итп*) quietly; (*идти*) slowly ♦ *как сказ*: **в до́ме** ~ the house is quiet; ~! (be) quiet!

тихо́н|**я** (-и) *м/ж* (*разг*) quiet operator.

ти́ше *сравн прил от* **ти́хий** ♦ *сравн нареч от* **ти́хо**: ~! quiet!, hush!

тишина́ (-ы́) ж quiet.

тиш|**ь** (-и) ж = **тишина́**.

т.к. *сокр* = **так как**.

тка́ный *прил* woven.

ткан|**ь** (-и) ж fabric, material; (*АНАТ*) tissue; (*перен: рассказа*) fabric.

тк|**ать** (-у, -ёшь; *perf* **сотка́ть**) *несов перех* to weave; (*паутину*) to spin.

тка́цк|**ий** (-ая, -ое, -ие) *прил*: ~**ое произво́дство** weaving; **тка́цкая фа́брика** mill (*for fabric production*); **тка́цкий стано́к** loom.

ткач (-á) м weaver.

ткачи́х|**а** (-и) ж см ткач.

ткну́ть(ся) (-у́(сь), -ёшь(ся)) *сов от* **ты́кать(ся)**.

тлен (-а) м decay.

тлетво́рный (-ен, -на, -но) *прил* pernicious.

тле|**ть** (*3sg* -ет, *3pl* -**ют**) *несов неперех* (*навоз, мусор*) to decay; (*дрова, угли*) to smoulder (*BRIT*), smolder (*US*); (*пламя*) to die out; (*перен: надежда*) to flicker.

▶ **тле́ться** *несов возв* (*костёр, угли*) to smo(u)lder; (*надежда*) to flicker.

тл|**я** (-и) ж aphid.

тмин (-а) м (*БОТ*) tumin.

т.н. *сокр* = **так называемый**.

ТНК ж *сокр* = **транснациона́льная корпора́ция**.

то *союз* (*условный*): **е́сли ... ~ ...** if ... then ...; (*разделительный*): ~ **...** ~ **...** sometimes ... sometimes ...; **е́сли его́ не бу́дет там,** ~ **я не, пойду́** if he isn't going to be there, (then) I'm not going; **и** ~ even; **он и** ~ **зна́ет об э́том** even he knows about it; ~ **есть** that is; ~ **и де́ло** time and again.

то (*того́*) *мест см* **тот**.

т.о. *сокр* = **таки́м о́бразом**.

-то *част* (*для выделения*): **письмо́-то ты получи́л?** did you (at least) receive the letter?; **где-то она́ сейча́с** if only I knew where she is now; **когда́-то мы встре́тимся?** when on earth shall we meet?; **э́тот-то всё съел** this one here has eaten everything.

тобо́й *мест см* **ты**.

тобо́ю *мест* = **тобо́й**.

тов. *сокр* = **това́рищ**.

това́р (-а; *part gen* -у) м product; (*ЭКОН*) commodity ♦ *собир* goods *мн*.

това́рищ (-а) м (*приятель*) friend; (*по партии*)

comrade; ~ **по шко́ле/рабо́те** school-/
workmate.
това́рищеск|ий (-**ая, -ое, -ие**) *прил* comradely;
това́рищеский матч (*СПОРТ*) friendly (match).
това́рищество (-**а**) *ср* camaraderie; (*КОММ*)
partnership.
това́рный *прил* (*производство*) goods *опред*;
(*рынок*) commodity *опред*; **това́рная би́ржа**
commodity exchange; **това́рный ваго́н** goods
wagon (*BRIT*), freight car (*US*); **това́рный знак**
trademark; **това́рный по́езд** goods (*BRIT*) *или*
freight (*US*) train; **това́рный склад** warehouse.
товарове́д (-**а**) *м* merchandiser.
товарообме́н (-**а**) *м* barter.
товарооборо́т (-**а**) *м* turnover.
товаропроизводи́тел|ь (-**я**) *м* (goods)
manufacturer.
тогда́ *нареч* then; ~ **как** (*хотя*) while; (*при*
противопоставлении) whereas; **не хо́чешь,** ~
не на́до if you don't want to, then don't.
тогда́шн|ий (-**яя, -ее, -ие**) *прил* (*разг*): **в** ~**ие**
времена́ in those days.
того́ *мест см* **тот, то.**
тожде́ственн|ый (-, -**на, -но**) *прил* identical.
то́ждеств|о (-**а**) *ср* (*также МАТ*) identity.
то́же *нареч* (*также*) too, as well, also ◆ *част* as
if; **я** ~ **пойду́** I'm going too *или* as well, I'm also
going; ~ **мне поэ́т нашёлся!** as if he's a poet!;
я ~ **люблю́ я́блоки** I too like apples; **я иду́**
купа́ться – я ~! I'm going swimming – me too!
той *мест см* **та.**
ток (-**а**) *м* (*ЭЛЕК*) current; (*для зерна*) threshing
floor.
тока́рный *прил*: ~ **стано́к** lathe.
то́кар|ь (-**я**; *nom pl* -**я́**) *м* turner.
То́кио *м нескл* Tokyo.
токсико́з (-**а**) *м* toxicosis; (*беременной*)
hyperemesis.
токси́чен *прил см* **токси́чный.**
токси́ческий (-**ая, -ое, -ие**) *прил* toxic.
токси́чный (-**ен, -на, -но**) *прил* = **токси́ческий.**
толк (-**а**; *part gen* -**у**) *м* (*в рассуждениях*) sense;
(*разг: польза*) use; **рассужда́ть** (*impf*) *или*
говори́ть (*impf*) **с то́лком** to talk sense; **от него́**
нет то́лку (*разг*) he's no use; **всё без** ~**у** it's all
for nothing; **взять** (*perf*) **что-н себе́ в** ~ (*разг*)
to get sth; **знать** (*impf*) *или* **понима́ть** (*impf*) ~ **в**
чём-н to have a good understanding of sth;
сбива́ть (**сбить** *perf*) **кого́-н с то́лку** to confuse
sb.
толка́тел|ь (-**я**) *м*: ~ **ядра́** shot-putter.
толка́|ть (-**ю**; *perf* **толкну́ть**) *несов перех* to
push; (*перен*): ~ **кого́-н на** +*acc* (*подлеж:*
голод) to force sb into; (: *человек*) to put sb up
to; ~ (*impf*) **по́ктем** to nudge; ~ (*impf*) **ядро́** to
put the shot; ~ (*impf*) **шта́нгу** to lift weights; ~
(**толкну́ть** *perf*) **речь** (*разг*) to have one's say
▶ **толка́ться** *несов возв* (*в толпе*) to push
(one's way); (*разг: без дела*) to hang about *или*
around; ~**ся** (**толкну́ться** *perf*) **в** +*acc* (*разг: в*
дверь) to push; (*перен: в учрежде́ния*) to

approach.
то́лк|и (-**ов**) *мн* (*разг*) gossip *ед.*
толкну́ть(ся) (-**у́(сь), -ёшь(ся)**) *сов от*
толка́ть(ся).
толкова́ни|е (-**я**) *ср* interpretation; (*слова*)
definition.
толк|ова́ть (-**у́ю**) *несов перех* (*явления,*
события итп) to interpret; (*разг*): ~ **что-н** +*dat*
to spell sth out to; ~ (*impf*) **с кем-н о чём-н**
(*разг*) to have a chat with sb about sth.
толко́в|ый (-, -**а, -о**) *прил* (*ученик, работник*)
intelligent; (*объясне́ние*) clear; **толко́вый**
слова́рь dictionary with definitions.
то́лком *нареч* (*разг*) properly; **я** ~ **ничего́ не**
узна́л I didn't manage to find anything out.
толкотн|я́ (-**и́**) *ж* (*разг: в толпе, в о́череди*)
crush.
толку́(сь) *итп несов см* **толо́чь(ся).**
толку́ч|ка (-**ки**; *gen pl* -**ек**) *ж* (*разг: рынок*) flea
market; (*место скопления людей*) crush.
толо́к(ся) *итп несов см* **толо́чь(ся).**
тол|о́чь (-**ку́, -чёшь** *итп*, -**ку́т**; *pt* -**о́к, -кла́, -кло́**,
perf **истоло́чь** *или* **растоло́чь**) *несов перех*
(*зерна, сухари*) to pound; ~ (*impf*) **во́ду в сту́пе**
(*разг*) to pound the air
▶ **толо́чься** *несов возв* (*разг*) to crowd about
или around.
толп|а́ (-**ы́**; *nom pl* -**ы**) *ж* (*народа*) crowd; (*перен:*
в противопоставление ли́чности) the crowd.
толп|и́ться (*3sg* -**и́тся**, *3pl* -**я́тся**) *несов возв* to
crowd around.
толсте́|ть (-**ю**; *perf* **потолсте́ть**) *несов непе́рех*
to get fatter.
толст|и́ть (*3sg* -**и́т**, *3pl* -**я́т**) *несов перех* (*разг*):
Вас ~**и́т э́то пла́тье** that dress makes you look
fat.
толстоко́ж|ий (-**ая, -ее, -ие**; -, -**а, -о**) *прил*
(*также перен*) thick-skinned.
толсту́х|а (-**и**) *ж* (*разг*) = **толсту́шка.**
толсту́ш|ка (-**ки**; *gen pl* -**ек**) *ж* (*разг*) fatty.
то́лст|ый (-, -**а́, -о**) *прил* thick; (*человек, ноги*
итп) fat; **то́лстая кишка́** large intestine.
толстя́к (-**а́**) *м* (*разг*) fatso.
толчёный *прил* crushed.
толче|я́ (-**и́**) *ж* (*разг*) crush.
толч|о́к (-**ка́**) *м* (*в спину, в грудь*) shove; (*при*
торможении, при встряхивании) jolt; (*при*
землетрясении) tremor; (*перен: к работе, к*
началу) push; (*СПОРТ: штанги*) thrust; (: *ядра*)
put; (*разг: рынок*) flea market.
то́лщ|а (-**и**) *ж* (*льда, облако́в*) mass.
то́лще *сравн прил от* **то́лстый.**
толщин|а́ (-**ы́**) *ж* (*тела, фигуры*) corpulence;
(*слоя, бревна́*) thickness.
тол|ь (-**я**) *м* roofing felt.

KEYWORD

то́лько *част* **1** only; **то́лько 5 книг** only 5
books; **он чита́ет то́лько газе́ты** he only reads
newspapers
2 (+*pron*/+*adv*; *усиливает вырази́тельность*):

зачём то́лько я согласи́лся! why on earth did I agree!; где то́лько он не побыва́л where has he NOT been!; попро́буй то́лько отказа́ться! just try to refuse!; поду́мать то́лько! imagine that!
♦ *союз* **1** (*сразу после*) as soon as; **то́лько напи́шешь, я прие́ду** as soon as you write, I'll come
2 (*однако, но*) only; **позвони́, то́лько разгова́ривай недо́лго** phone (*BRIT*) *или* call (*US*), only don't talk for long
♦ *нареч* **1** (*недавно*) (only) just; **ты давно́ здесь?- нет, то́лько вошла́** have you been here long? – no, I've (only) just come in
2 (*во фразах*): **то́лько лишь** (*разг*) only; **то́лько и всего́** (*разг*) that's all; **как** *или* **лишь** *или* **едва́ то́лько** (*сразу после того, как*) as soon as; **не то́лько ..., но и ...** not only ... but also ...; **то́лько бы** if only; **то́лько бы знать, где он!** if only I knew where he was!; **то́лько что** only just.

том *мест см* **тот, то.**
том (-а; *nom pl* **-а́**) *м* volume.
тома́т (-а) *м* (*помидор*) tomato (*мн* tomatoes); (*соус*) tomato purée.
тома́тный *прил*: ~ **сок/суп** tomato juice/soup.
то́мен *прил см* **то́мный.**
томи́тельный (-ен, -ьна, -ьно) *прил* tormenting.
том|и́ть (-лю́, -и́шь; *perf* **истоми́ть**) *несов перех* (*расспросами, ожиданием*) to torment
▸ **томи́ться** (*perf* **истоми́ться**) *несов возв* (*ожиданием, жаждой*) to be tormented.
томле́ни|е (-я) *ср* languor.
томлю́(сь) *несов см* **томи́ть(ся).**
то́м|ный (-ен, -на, -но) *прил* languid.
тому́ *мест см* **тот, то.**
тон (-а) *м* (*также муз, мед*) tone.
тона́льност|ь (-и) *ж* (*муз*) key; (*картины*) tones *мн*; (*перен: стихотворения*) tone.
тонзилли́т (-а) *м* tonsillitis.
тонизи́рующий (-ая, -ее, -ие) *прил* (*прогулка, напиток*) refreshing; ~**ее сре́дство** tonic.
то́н|кий (-кая, -кое, -кие; -ок, -ка́, -ко) *прил* thin; (*фигура, пальцы*) slender; (*черты лица, работа, ум*) fine; (*запах, вкус*) delicate; (*обращение, различия, намёк*) subtle; (*слух*) sharp; **то́нкая кишка́** small intestine.
то́нко *нареч* (*резать*) thinly; (*пахнуть*) delicately; (*намекать, чувствовать*) subtly; **она́ ~ чу́вствует му́зыку/поэ́зию** she has a fine appreciation of music/poetry.
тонкоко́ж|ий (-ая, -ее, -ие; -, -а, -о) *прил* thin-skinned.
то́нкост|ь (-и) *ж* (*см прил*) thinness; slenderness; fineness; delicacy; subtlety; sharpness; (*частность*) detail; **до ~ей** down to the last detail; **вдава́ться** (*impf*) **в ~и** to go into detail.

то́нн|а (-ы) *ж* tonne.
тонна́ж (-а) *м* (*судна*) tonnage; (*вагона*) capacity.
тоннél|ь (-я) *м* tunnel.
то́нок *прил см* **то́нкий.**
то́нус (-а) *м* (*сердца, тканей*) tone; **жи́зненный ~** vitality.
тон|у́ть (-у́, -ешь; *perf* **утону́ть** *или* **потону́ть**) *несов неперех* (*человек*) to drown; (*perf* **утону́ть**; *дерево, камень*) to sink; (*perf* **затону́ть**; *корабль*) to sink; (*увязать*): ~ **в** +*prp* (*в снегу, в грязи*) to get stuck in; (*перен: в делах*) to be up to one's eyes in; (*no perf*; *перен: в зелени*) to get lost; (*в шуме*) to drown.
то́ньше *сравн прил от* **то́нкий** ♦ *сравн нареч от* **то́нко.**
топа́з (-а) *м* topaz.
то́па|ть (-ю) *несов неперех* (*разг: идти*) to go; ~ (*impf*) **нога́ми** to stamp one's feet; ~**й отсю́да!** (*разг*) scram!
топ|и́ть (-лю́, -ишь) *несов перех* (*печь*) to stoke (up); (*дом*) to warm (up); (*плавить: масло, воск*) to melt; (*perf* **утопи́ть** *или* **потопи́ть**; *корабль*) to sink; (*человека*) to drown; (*perf* **потопи́ть**; *перен: дело*) to ruin; ~ (**потопи́ть** *perf*) **го́ре** to drown one's sorrows
▸ **топи́ться** *несов возв* (*печь*) to burn; (*помещение*) to be heated; (*perf* **растопи́ться**; *воск*) to melt; (*perf* **утопи́ться**; *лишить себя жизни*) to drown o.s.
то́пк|а (-и) *ж* (*действие: печи*) stoking; (*часть печи*) furnace.
то́п|кий (-кая, -кое, -кие; -ок, -ка́, -ко) *прил* (*дорога, почва*) muddy.
топлён|ый *прил* (*кулин: масло, жир*) melted; ~**ое молоко́** boiled milk.
то́пливо (-а) *ср* fuel; **жи́дкое/твёрдое ~** liquid/solid fuel.
топлю́(сь) *несов см* **топи́ть(ся).**
топогра́фи|я (-и) *ж* topography.
то́пок *прил см* **то́пкий.**
то́пол|ь (-я) *м* poplar.
топони́мик|а (-и) *ж* toponymy.
топо́р (-а́) *м* axe (*BRIT*), ax (*US*).
топо́рен *прил см* **топо́рный.**
топори́щ|е (-а) *ср* axe (*BRIT*) *или* ax (*US*) handle.
топо́р|ный (-ен, -на, -но) *прил* (*перен: работа, стиль*) crude.
топо́рщ|ить (-у, -ишь; *perf* **встопо́рщить**) *несов перех* (*разг: перья, шерсть*) to fluff up
▸ **топо́рщиться** (*perf* **встопо́рщиться**) *несов возв* (*разг: усы, хвост*) to bristle; (*платье, складки*) to puff up.
то́пот (-а) *м* clatter.
топ|та́ть (-чу́, -чешь; *perf* **потопта́ть**) *несов перех* (*траву*) to trample; (*пол*) to dirty
▸ **топта́ться** *несов возв* to shift from one foot to the other; ~**ся** (*impf*) **на ме́сте** (*перен*) to

go round in circles.
топ-топ *звукоподражание* pitter-patter.
топча́н (-а́) *м* trestle bed.
топчу́(сь) *итп несов см* **топта́ть(ся)**.
топ|ь (-и) *ж* marsh.
торг (-а) *м* trading.
торга́ш (-а́) *м* (*разг: пренебр*) money-grubber.
торг|й (-о́в) *мн* (аукцион) auction *ед*;
(*состязание*) tender *ед*.
торг|ова́ть (-у́ю) *несов неперех* (*перен:*
совестью, убеждениями) to forfeit; (*магазин*)
to trade; ~ (*impf*) +*instr* (*мясом, мебелью*) to
trade in; ~ (*impf*) **с** +*instr* to (do) trade with
▶ **торгова́ться** (*perf* **сторгова́ться**) *несов возв*
(*разг: спорить о цене*) to haggle; (*перен:*
спорить) to bicker.
торго́в|ец (-ца) *м* merchant; (*мелкий, уличный*)
trader.
торго́в|ка (-ки; *gen pl* -ок) *ж* (*уличная, базарная*)
trader.
торго́вл|я (-и) *ж* trade.
торго́вок *сущ см* **торго́вка**.
торго́вца *итп сущ см* **торго́вец**.
торго́вый *прил* (*договор, прибыль, барьеры*)
trade *опред*; (*судно, флот*) merchant *опред*;
торго́вая сеть retail network; **торго́вая то́чка**
retail outlet; **торго́вое представи́тельство**
trade mission; **торго́вый рабо́тник** retail
industry worker; **торго́вый центр** shopping
centre (*BRIT*), mall (*US*).
торгпре́д (-а) *м сокр* (= **торго́вый**
представи́тель) head of the trade mission.
торгпре́дств|о (-а) *ср сокр* (= **торго́вое**
представи́тельство) trade mission.
тореадо́р (-а) *м* toreador.
тор|е́ц (-ца́) *м* (*доски, книги*) butt; (*здания*) gable
end.
торже́ственен *прил см* **торже́ственный**.
торже́ственно *нареч* (*обещать*) solemnly;
(*праздновать*) fully.
торже́ственн|ый *прил* (*день, случай*) special;
(*собрание*) celebratory; (*-ен, -на, -но; вид,*
обстановка) festive; (*no short form; обещание,*
клятва) solemn.
торжеств|о́ (-а́) *ср* (*семейное, национальное*)
celebration; (*в голосе, в словах*) triumph; ~
+*gen* (*справедливости итп*) the triumph of.
торжеств|ова́ть (-у́ю; *perf* **восторжествова́ть**)
несов неперех ~ (**над** +*instr*) to triumph (over);
(*no perf; внутренно, скрыто*) to rejoice.
торма́ш|ки (-ек) *мн* (*разг*): **вверх** ~**ками** upside
down.
торможе́ни|е (-я) *ср* (*машины*) braking;
(*рефлексов*) inhibition.
торможу́(сь) *несов см* **тормози́ть(ся)**.
то́рмоз (-а; *nom pl* -а́) *м* brake; (*nom pl* -ы; *перен:*
в работе) hindrance, obstacle.
тормо|зи́ть (-жу́, -зи́шь; *perf* **затормози́ть**)
несов перех (*машину, поезд*) to slow down;
(*перен: движение, работу*) to hamper, impede
♦ *неперех* (*машина, поезд*) to brake

▶ **тормози́ться** (*perf* **затормози́ться**) *несов*
возв (*дело, работа итп*) to be hindered *или*
impeded.
тормозн|о́й *прил* (*механизм, педаль*) brake
опред; (*био: рефлекс*) inhibitory; ~**а́я**
жи́дкость brake fluid.
тормош|и́ть (-у́, -и́шь) *несов перех* to shake; ~
(*impf*) **кого́-н за рука́в** to tug at sb's sleeve; ~
(*impf*) **кого́-н** (*вопросами*) to pester sb.
тор|опи́ть (-оплю́, -о́пишь; *perf* **поторопи́ть**)
несов перех (*коня*) to urge on; (*ребёнка,*
события) to hurry; ~ (**поторопи́ть** *perf*) **кого́-н**
с чем-н to hurry sb with sth
▶ **торопи́ться** (*perf* **поторопи́ться**) *несов возв*
(*на поезд, в школу итп*) to hurry; (*с работой, с*
выполнением): ~**ся с** +*instr* to hurry with.
торопли́в|ый (-, -а, -о) *прил* (*человек*) hasty;
(*шаг*) hurried; (*суждение, вывод*) hasty, hurried.
тороплю́(сь) *несов см* **торопи́ть(ся)**.
торпе́д|а (-ы) *ж* torpedo (*мн* torpedoes).
торпеди́р|овать (-ую) (*не*)*сов перех* (*также*
перен) to torpedo.
торс (-а) *м* torso.
торт (-а) *м* cake.
торф (-а) *м* peat.
торца́ *итп сущ см* **торе́ц**.
торч|а́ть (-у́, -и́шь) *несов неперех* (*вверх*) to
stick up; (*в стороны*) to stick out; (*разг: на*
улице, в ресторане) to hang around.
торчко́м *нареч* (*разг*) on end.
торше́р (-а) *м* standard lamp.
тоск|а́ (-и́) *ж* (*на сердце, во взгляде*) melancholy;
(*скука*) boredom; ~ **по ро́дине** homesickness.
тоскли́в|ый (-, -а, -о) *прил* (*настроение,*
музыка итп) melancholy; (*погода, разговор*
итп) dreary.
тоск|ова́ть (-у́ю) *несов неперех* to pine away; ~
(*impf*) **по** +*dat или* +*prp* to miss.
тост (-а) *м* toast; ~ **за** +*acc* toast to.

KEYWORD

то|т (-го́; *f* **та**, *nt* **то**, *pl* **те**; *см* **Table 11**) *мест* **1**
that; **тот дом** that house; **та ру́чка** that pen; **те**
кни́ги those books; **по ту сто́рону** on that side
2 (*указывает на ранее упомянутое*) that; **в тот**
раз/день that time/day
3 (*разг: о прошлом*) last; (: *о будущем*) next; **я**
ви́дел его́ на той неде́ле I saw him last week;
уви́димся на той неде́ле we'll meet next week
4 (*в главных предложениях*): **э́то тот челове́к,**
кото́рый приходи́л вчера́ it's the man who
came yesterday; **мы обра́довались тому́, что**
он ушёл we were pleased that he had gone
5 (*о последнем из названных лиц*): **я**
посмотре́л на дру́га, тот стоя́л мо́лча I
looked at my friend, he stood silently
6 (*обычно с отрицанием*): **зашёл не в тот дом**
I called at the wrong house; **э́то всё не то** it's
not that
7 (*об одном из перечисляемых предметов*): **ни**
тот, ни друго́й neither one nor the other; **тем**
или ины́м спо́собом by some means or other;

тот же the same; **та же маши́на, что и в про́шлый раз** the same car as last time; **он сказа́л то же са́мое** he said the same thing **8** (во фразах): **до того́** so; **он до того́ испуга́лся, что не мог усну́ть** he was so frightened he couldn't sleep; **мне не до того́** I have no time for that; **не то что(бы) ... , а ...** not so much that ... but ...; **она́ не то что(бы) глупа́, а засте́нчива** she's not so much stupid, as just shy; **к тому́ же** moreover; **с тем, что́бы** in order to; **ни с того́ ни с сего́** (разг) out of the blue; **тому́ наза́д** ago; **и тому́ подо́бное** et cetera, and so on.

тота́лен прил см **тота́льный**.

тотализа́тор (-а) м totalizer.

тоталитари́зм (-а) м totalitarianism.

тоталита́рный прил totalitarian.

тота́л∥**ьный** (-ен, -ьна, -ьно) прил total.

то-то част (разг: вот именно) exactly, that's just it; (вот почему) that's why; (выражает удовлетворение): **~ же** pleased to hear it; **он не сдал экза́мен – ~ он тако́й гру́стный** he didn't pass the exam – that's why he's so sad; **~ он удиви́тся!** he WILL be surprised!

то́тчас нареч immediately.

то́чек сущ см **то́чка**.

то́чен прил см **то́чный**.

точёный прил (острый: нож) sharpened; (деталь, грань итп) turned; (перен: фигура) shapely; (: черты лица) fine.

то́чечн∥**ый** прил (линия) dotted; **~ масса́ж** shiatsu, acupressure; **~ая электросва́рка** spot-welding.

точи́л∥**ка** (-ки; gen pl -ок) ж pencil sharpener.

точ∥**и́ть** (-у́, -ишь; perf **наточи́ть**) несов перех (нож, каранда́ш) to sharpen; (perf **вы́точить**; деталь) to turn; (no perf; подлеж: червь, ржавчина) to eat away at; (перен: подлеж: болезнь, тоска итп) to drain.

то́ч∥**ка** (-ки; gen pl -ек) ж point; (пятнышко) dot; (линг) full stop (BRIT), period (esp US); (действие: детали, карандаша) sharpening; **~ зре́ния** point of view; **попа́сть (попа́сть** perf**) в (са́мую) ~ку** to hit the bull's-eye; **дойти́** (perf) **до ~ки** (разг) to reach one's limit; **то́чка с запято́й** semicolon.

точне́е вводн сл to be exact или precise; **приходи́ вече́ром, ~, в 5 часо́в** come in the evening, at 5 o'clock to be exact или precise.

то́чно нареч exactly; (объясни́ть) exactly, precisely; (подсчита́ть, перевести́) accurately ◆ част (разг: действи́тельно) precisely ◆ союз (как бу́дто) as if или though; **~ тако́й дом** exactly the same house; **он ~ так и сде́лал/ сказа́л** that's exactly what he did/said; **~, он уе́хал** that's right, he's gone; **так ~!** yes, sir!; **распла́кался, ~ ребёнок** he burst into

tears, just like a child; **он говори́л со мной, ~ я ребёнок** he talked to me as if или though I were a child.

то́чност∥**ь** (-и) ж (часов, попадания) accuracy; (работы) precision; **я подсчита́л затра́ты с ~ю до рубля́** I counted the expenditure right down to the last rouble; **в ~** (разг) exactly.

то́чный (-ен, -на́, -но) прил (часы, перевод, попадание) accurate; (описание, приказ) precise; (адрес, копия) exact; **то́чное вре́мя** exact time; **то́чные нау́ки** exact sciences.

точь-в-точь нареч (разг) just like.

тошн∥**и́ть** (3sg -и́т, perf **стошни́ть**) несов безл: **меня́ ~и́т** I feel sick; (перен) it makes me sick; **меня́ ~и́т от твоего́ лицеме́рия** your hypocrisy makes me sick.

то́шно как сказ (перен: разг) it's nauseating или sickening.

тошнот∥**а́** (-ы́) ж (чувство) nausea; **мне э́то до ~ы́ надое́ло** I'm sick to death of it.

тошнотво́р∥**ный** (-ен, -на, -но) прил (также перен) nauseating, sickening.

то́щий (-ая, -ее, -ие; -, -á, -е) прил (человек) gaunt; (кошелёк) empty; (почва) poor; (растительность) sparse.

т.п. сокр (= тому́ подо́бное) etc. (= et cetera).

ТПП м сокр (= Торго́во-промы́шленная пала́та) ≈ Chamber of Commerce.

тпру межд (лошадям) whoa.

т-р сокр = теа́тр.

трав∥**а́** (-ы́; nom pl -ы) ж grass; (лека́рственная) herb; (сорная) weed; **хоть ~ не расти́** (разг) he итп couldn't care less.

трави́н∥**ка** (-ки; gen pl -ок) ж blade of grass.

трав∥**и́ть** (-лю́, -ишь) несов перех (также перен) to poison; (perf **потрави́ть**; посевы) to damage; (perf **затрави́ть**; дичь) to hunt; (перен: разг: притеснять) to harass, hound; (perf **вы́травить**; узор) to etch

▸ **трави́ться** (perf **отрави́ться**) несов возв to poison o.s.

травле́ни∥**е** (-я) ср etching.

травлю́(сь) несов см **трави́ть(ся)**.

тра́вл∥**я** (-и) ж hunting; (демокра́тов, радика́лов) hounding.

тра́вм∥**а** (-ы) ж (физи́ческая) injury; (психи́ческая) trauma.

травмато́лог (-а) м specialist in traumatology.

травматологи́ческ∥**ий** (-ая, -ое, -ие) прил: **~ отде́л** casualty; **~ пункт** first-aid room.

травматоло́ги∥**я** (-и) ж traumatology.

травми́р∥**овать** (-ую) (не)сов перех (голову) to injure; (перен: грубостью) to traumatize.

травоя́дный (-ен, -на, -но) прил herbivorous.

травяни́ст∥**ый** прил herbaceous; (-, -а, -о; луг) grassy.

травяно́й прил (насто́йка) herbal; **~ покро́в** grass.

The spelling rules for Russian are shown on page xvii.

трагéди|я (-и) ж tragedy.

траги́зм (-а) м tragedy.

трагикомéди|я (-и) ж tragicomedy.

трагикоми́ческ|ий (-ая, -ое, -ие) *прил* tragicomic.

траги́чен *прил см* **траги́чный**.

траги́ческ|ий (-ая, -ое, -ие) *прил* tragic; ~ **актёр** (*траги́к*) tragedy actor.

траги́ч|ный (-ен, -на, -но) *прил* tragic.

традицио́н|ный (-ен, -на, -но) *прил* traditional.

тради́ци|я (-и) ж tradition; **входи́ть** (**войти́** *perf*) **в ~ю** to become a tradition.

траекто́ри|я (-и) ж trajectory.

тракт (-а) м (*ист*) highway; (*АНАТ*): **пищевари́тельный ~** alimentary canal.

тракта́т (-а) м treatise.

тракти́р (-а) м inn.

тракти́рщик (-а) м innkeeper.

тракти́рщиц|а (-ы) ж см **тракти́рщик**.

тракт|ова́ть (-у́ю) *несов перех* to interpret.

тракто́в|ка (-ки; *gen pl* -ок) ж interpretation.

тра́ктор (-а) м tractor.

тракторист (-а) м tractor driver.

тракторист|ка (-ки; *gen pl* -ок) ж см **тракторист**.

трал (-а) м (*сеть*) trawl; **ми́нный ~** minesweeping operation.

тра́л|ить (-ю, -ишь; *perf* **протра́лить**) *несов перех* to trawl; **~** (**протра́лить** *perf*) **ми́ны** to sweep for mines.

трамб|ова́ть (-у́ю; *perf* **утрамбова́ть**) *несов перех* to tamp.

трамва́|й (-я) м tram (*BRIT*), streetcar (*US*); **éздить/éхать** (*impf*) **на ~е** to go by tram.

трамва́йный *прил* tram *опред* (*BRIT*), streetcar *опред* (*US*); **~ые пути́** tramlines; **трамва́йный парк** tram *или* streetcar depot.

трампли́н (-а) м (*также перен*) springboard; **лы́жный ~** ski jump.

транжи́р (-а) м spendthrift.

транжи́р|ить (-ю, -ишь; *perf* **растранжи́рить**) *несов перех* (*разг: де́ньги*) to blow.

транжи́р|ка (-ки; *gen pl* -ок) ж см **транжи́р**.

транзи́стор (-а) м (*усилитель*) transistor; (*радиоприёмник*) transistor (radio).

транзи́т (-а) м transit; (*о грузе*) transit goods.

транзи́тный *прил* transit *опред*.

транквилиза́тор (-а) м tranquillizer (*BRIT*), tranquilizer (*US*).

транс (-а) м (*ПСИХОЛ*) trance; (*КОММ: документ*) transport document; **но́мер тра́нса** trans number.

трансконтинента́льный *прил* transcontinental.

транскри́пци|я (-и) ж transcription.

трансли́р|овать (-ую) (*не*)*сов перех* to broadcast.

трансля́тор (-а) м (*ТЕХ*) translator.

трансля́ци|я (-и) ж (*передачи*) transmission, broadcasting; (*передача*) broadcast; **пряма́я ~** live broadcast.

транспара́нт (-а) м banner.

транспланта́ци|я (-и) ж transplant.

тра́нспорт (-а) м transport.

транспортёр (-а) м (*конвейер*) conveyor belt; (*ВОЕН*) troop carrier.

транспорти́р|овать (-ую) (*не*)*сов перех* to transport.

транспортиро́в|ка (-и) ж transportation.

тра́нспортный *прил* transport *опред*.

транссексуа́л (-а) м transsexual.

трансформа́тор (-а) м transformer.

трансформа́ци|я (-и) ж transformation.

трансформи́р|овать (-ую) (*не*)*сов перех* to transform.

траншé|я (-и) ж trench.

трап (-а) м gangway; **подава́ть** (**пода́ть** *perf*) **~** to put down the gangway.

тра́пез|а (-ы) ж *communal meal in monastery*.

тра́пезн|ая (-ой; *decl like adj*) ж refectory.

трапéци|я (-и) ж (*ГЕОМ*) trapezium; (*цирковая, гимнастическая*) trapeze.

тра́сс|а (-ы) ж (*лыжная*) run; (*трубопровода, канала*) route; **автомоби́льная ~** motorway (*BRIT*), expressway (*US*); **возду́шная ~** airway.

трасса́т (-а) м (*КОММ*) drawee.

тра́т|а (-ы) ж spending; **пуста́я ~ вре́мени/ де́нег** a waste of time/money.

тра́|тить (-чу, -тишь; *perf* **истра́тить** *или* **потра́тить**) *несов перех* to spend

▶ **тра́|титься** (*perf* **истра́титься** *или* **потра́титься**) *несов возв*: **~ся на** +*acc* to spend a lot of money on.

тра́улер (-а) м trawler.

тра́ур (-а) м mourning; **~ по** +*prp* mourning for; **носи́ть** (*impf*) **~** to wear mourning.

тра́ур|ный *прил* (*процессия, платье*) mourning *опред*; (-ен, -на, -но; *перен: обстановка, тон*) mournful.

трафарéт (-а) м stencil; **мы́слить** (*impf*) **по ~у** (*перен*) to think in clichés.

трафарéт|ный (-ен, -на, -но) *прил* (*рисунок, черчение*) stencilled; (*перен: фразы*) trite.

трах *межд* bang; **а он ~ по столу́** and he banged against the table.

тра́ха|ть(ся) (-ю(сь)) *несов от* **тра́хнуть(ся)**.

трахé|я (-и) ж trachea.

тра́хн|уть (-у, -ешь; *impf* **тра́хать**) *сов непрех* (*раз: выстрел*) to ring out ♦ *перех* (*ударить*) to thump; (*переспать: женщину*) to lay

▶ **тра́хн|уться** (*impf* **тра́хаться**) *сов возв* (*раз: удариться*) to bang o.s.; (: *мужчина и женщина*) to have it off; **тра́хаться** (**~ся** *perf*) **голово́й о стéнку** to bang one's head against the wall.

тра́чу(сь) *несов см* **тра́тить(ся)**.

трéбовани|е (-я) ср (*объяснений, денег*) request; (*решительное, категорическое*) demand; (*устава, экзаменационные*) requirement; (*документ: на книгу*) order; **~я** (*моральные, эстетические*) needs мн.

трéбовательный (-ен, -ьна, -ьно) *прил* demanding; (*тон, голос*) peremptory.

трéб|овать (-ую; *perf* **потрéбовать**) *несов перех* (*квитанцию*) to ask for; (*в суд, к* начальнику) to summon; ~ (**потре́бовать** *perf*) **что-н/**+*infin* to demand sth/to do; ~ (**потре́бовать** *perf*) +*gen* (*сочувствия, правдивости*) to expect; (*помощи, переделки*) to need, require

▶ **тре́боваться** (*perf* **потре́боваться**) *несов возв* to be needed *или* required.

требух|а́ (**-и́**) *ж* entrails *мн.*

трево́г|а (**-и**) *ж* (*волнение*) anxiety; (*на улице, в доме*) alarm; **возду́шная** ~ air-raid warning; **поднима́ть** (**подня́ть** *perf*) *или* **бить** (*impf*) ~**у** (*перен*) to raise the alarm.

трево́жен *прил см* **трево́жный**.

трево́ж|ить (**-у, -ишь**; *perf* **встрево́жить**) *несов перех* (*родителей, правительство*) to alarm; (*perf* **потрево́жить**; *подлеж:* **шум, посетители**) to disturb; (*перен:* **рану**) to reopen

▶ **трево́житься** (*perf* **встрево́житься**) *несов возв* (*за детей*) to be concerned; (*perf* **потрево́житься**; *затруднять себя*) to trouble o.s.

трево́жно *нареч* (*посмотреть*) anxiously ◆ **как сказ: на се́рдце** ~ I feel anxious; **в го́роде** ~ there is a sense of alarm in the city.

трево́ж|ный (**-ен, -на, -но**) *прил* (*голос, взгляд*) anxious; (*сведения*) alarming; ~**ное вре́мя** time of unrest; **трево́жный сигна́л** alarm.

тре́звенник (**-а**) *м* teetotaller.

трезве́|ть (**-ю**; *perf* **отрезве́ть**) *несов неперех* to sober up.

трезво́н (**-а**) *м* (*колокольный*) peal; (*разг: толки*) gossip.

трезво́н|ить (**-ю, -ишь**) *несов неперех* (*колокола*) to peal; (*телефон, звонок*) to ring; (*разг: сплетничать*) to spread gossip.

тре́звост|ь (**-и**) *ж* (*неупотребление алкоголя*) sobriety; (*перен: взгляда, суждений*) soberness.

тре́зв|ый (**-, -а́, -о**) *прил* (*состояние, человек*) sober; (*перен: рассуждение, решение*) sensible.

трек (**-а**) *м* track.

трель (**-и**) *ж* warble.

трелья́ж (**-а**) *м* (*зеркало*) triple mirror.

трём *итп чис см* **три**.

трёмста́м *итп чис см* **три́ста**.

тренажёр (**-а**) *м equipment used for physical training.*

тре́нер (**-а**) *м* coach; **гла́вный** ~ manager (*of sports team*).

тре́ни|е (**-я**) *ср* friction; (*обычно мн: перен*) friction *ед.*

трениров|а́ть (**-у́ю**; *perf* **натренирова́ть**) *несов перех* to train; (*спортсменов*) to coach.

▶ **тренирова́ться** (*perf* **натренирова́ться**) *несов возв* (*спортсмен*) to train; (*ученик, работник*) to train o.s.

трениро́в|ка (**-ки**; *gen pl* **-ок**) *ж* (*памяти, лошади итп*) training; (*отдельное занятие*) training (session).

трениро́вочный *прил* training *опред*; **трениро́вочный костю́м** tracksuit.

трено́жник (**-а**) *м* tripod.

трёп (**-а**; *part gen* **-у**) *м* (*разг*) blethering, blathering.

трепана́ци|я (**-и**) *ж* (*мед*) trepanation.

трёпаный *прил* (*разг*) tattered.

трепа́|ть (**-лю́, -лешь**; *perf* **потрепа́ть**) *несов перех* (*подлеж:* **ветер**) to blow about; (*по плечу*) to pat; (*перен:* **корабль**) to toss; (*perf* **истрепа́ть** *или* **потрепа́ть**; *разг:* **обувь, книги**) to wear out; ~ (**потрепа́ть** *perf*) **кого́-н за во́лосы/за у́ши** to pull sb's hair/ears; ~ (**потрепа́ть** *perf*) **не́рвы кому́-н** to wear sb's nerves down; ~ (*impf*) **языко́м** (*разг цми*) to chatter

▶ **трепа́ться** *несов возв* (*no perf; флаги, волосы*) to be blown about; (*perf* **истрепа́ться** *или* **потрепа́ться**; *разг: одежда, обувь*) to wear out; (*perf* **потрепа́ться**; *разг: о пустяках*) to chatter.

трепа́ч (**-а́**) *м* (*разг*) chatterbox.

тре́пет (**-а**) *м* (*листьев*) quivering; (*волнение*) tremor; (*страх*) trepidation.

треп|ета́ть (**-ещу́, -е́щешь**) *несов неперех* (*листья, флаги*) to quiver; (*от ужаса*) to quake, tremble.

тре́петный (**-ен, -на, -но**) *прил* tremulous.

трепещу́ *итп несов см* **трепета́ть**.

треплю́(сь) *итп несов см* **трепа́ть(ся)**.

трепыха́|ться (**-юсь**) *несов возв* (*разг: животное, рыба*) to wriggle; (*флаг, парус*) to flutter; (*перен: волноваться*) to be in a flutter.

треск (**-а**) *м* (*ломающихся сучьев*) snapping; (*выстрелов*) crackling; **с тре́ском прова́ливаться** (**провали́ться** *perf*) (*разг: пьеса*) to be a flop; (*: студент*) to come a cropper.

треска́ (**-и́**) *ж* cod.

тре́ска|ться (*3sg* **-ется**, *3pl* **-ются**, *perf* **потре́скаться**) *несов возв* (*земля, стекло*) to crack.

трескотн|я́ (**-и́**) *ж* (*разг: кузнечиков*) chirp; (*перен: болтовня*) chitchat.

треску́чий (**-ая, -ее, -ие**; **-, -а, -е**) *прил* (*перен: речи, слова*) bombastic; ~ **моро́з** hard frost.

тре́сн|уть (*3sg* **-ет**, *3pl* **-ут**) *сов неперех* (*ветка*) to snap; (*стакан, кожа*) to crack; (*разг*): ~ **чем-н по чему́-н** (*кулаком: по столу*) to bang sth on sth ◆ *перех* (*разг*): ~ **кого́-н по** +*dat* (*по шее, по руке*) to thump sb on

▶ **тре́снуться** *сов возв* (*разг*): ~**ся чем-н о** +*acc* to bang sth on.

трест (**-а**) *м* (*экон*) trust.

тре́т|ий (**-ья, -ье, -ьи**) *чис* third; **фильм/врач** ~**ьего со́рта** a third-rate film/doctor; ~**ьего дня** the day before yesterday; **Т**~ **мир** the Third World; **тре́тий сорт** (*товара*) Grade 3 (*denoting product of inferior quality*); **тре́тье**

лицо́ (*ЛИНГ*) the third person; **тре́тья сторона́, тре́тьи ли́ца** third party; *см также* **пя́тый**.

трети́р|овать (**-ую**) *сов перех* to patronize.

трети́чный *прил* tertiary.

треть (**-и**; *nom pl* **-и**, *gen pl* **-е́й**) *ж* third.

тре́ть|е (**-его**; *decl like adj*) *ср* (*КУЛИН*) sweet (*ВПГ*), dessert.

третьекла́ссник (**-а**) *м* pupil in third year at school (*usually nine years old*).

третьекла́ссни|ца (**-ы**) *ж см* **третьекла́ссник**.

третьесо́рт|ный (**-ен, -на, -но**) *прил* third-rate.

тре́ть|я (**-ей**; *decl like adj*) *ж*: **одна́ ~** one third.

треуго́льник (**-а**) *м* triangle.

треуго́льный *прил* triangular.

треф|ы (**-**) *мн* (*КАРТЫ*) clubs *мн*.

трёх *чис см* **три**.

трёхгоди́чный *прил* three-year.

трёхгодова́лый *прил* three-year-old.

трёхдне́вный *прил* three-day.

трёхкра́т|ный *прил*: **~ чемпио́н** three-times champion; **в ~ом разме́ре** threefold.

трёхле́ти|е (**-я**) *ср* (*срок*) three years; (*годовщина*) third anniversary.

трёхле́т|ний (**-яя, -ее, -ие**) *прил* (*период*) three-year; (*ребёнок*) three-year-old.

трёхме́рный *прил* 3-D, three-dimensional.

трёхме́сячный *прил* three-month; (*ребёнок*) three-month-old.

трёхнеде́льный *прил* three-week; (*ребёнок*) three-week-old.

трёхсо́т *чис см* **три́ста**.

трёхсотле́ти|е (**-я**) *ср* (*срок*) three hundred years; (*годовщина*) tercentenary.

трёхсотле́т|ний (**-яя, -ее, -ие**) *прил* (*период*) three hundred-year; (*дерево*) three hundred-year-old.

трёхсо́т|ый (**-ая, -ое, -ые**) *чис* three hundredth.

трёхста́х *чис см* **три́ста**.

трёхсторо́н|ний (**-яя, -ее, -ие**) *прил* (*соглашение, союз*) trilateral.

трёхчасово́й *прил* (*операция*) three-hour; (*поезд*) three o'clock.

трёшк|а (**-ки**; *gen pl* **-ек**) *ж* (*разг*) three-rouble note.

трещ|а́ть (**-у́, -и́шь**) *несов неперех* (*лёд, доски итп*) to crack; (*кузнечики*) to chip; (*пулемёты*) to crackle; (*разг: тараторить*) to jabber (on); **у меня́ ~и́т голова́** I've got a splitting headache; **~** (*impf*) **по швам** (*также перен*) to be falling apart at the seams.

тре́щин|а (**-ы**) *ж* (*также перен*) crack; **дава́ть** (**дать** *perf*) **~у** to crack.

трещо́т|ка (**-ки**; *gen pl* **-ок**) *ж* rattle ◆ *м/ж* (*перен: болтун*) chatterbox.

три (**-ёх**; *см* **Table 24**) *чис* three ◆ *нескл* (*ПРОСВЕЩ*) ≈ C (*school mark*); **ей ~ го́да** she is three (years old); **они́ живу́т в до́ме но́мер ~** they live at number three; **о́коло ~ёх** about three; **кни́га сто́ит ~ рубля́** the book costs three roubles; **~ с полови́ной часа́** three and a half hours; **сейча́с ~ часа́** it is three o'clock; **я́блоки**

продаю́тся по **~ шту́ки** the apples are sold in threes; **дели́ть** (**раздели́ть** *perf*) **что-н на ~** to divide sth into three.

трибу́н|а (**-ы**) *ж* platform; (*стадиона*) stand.

трибуна́л (**-а**) *м* tribunal; **вое́нный ~** military court.

тривиа́л|ьный (**-ен, -ьна, -ьно**) *прил* trivial.

тригономе́три|я (**-и**) *ж* trigonometry.

три́девять: **за ~ земе́ль** (*ФОЛЬКЛОР*) in far off lands.

тридеся́т|ый *прил* (*ФОЛЬКЛОР*): **в ~ом госуда́рстве** in a far off country.

тридцати́ *чис см* **три́дцать**.

тридцатиле́ти|е (**-я**) *ср* (*срок*) thirty years; (*годовщина события*) thirtieth anniversary.

тридцатиле́т|ний (**-яя, -ее, -ие**) *прил* (*период*) thirty-year; (*человек*) thirty-year-old.

тридца́т|ый (**-ая, -ое, -ые**) *чис* thirtieth; *см также* **пятидеся́тый**.

три́дцат|ь (**-и**; *как пять*; *см* **Table 27**) *чис* thirty; *см также* **пятьдеся́т**.

три́жды *нареч* three times; **~ два — шесть** three times two is six; **он ~ прав** he's absolutely right.

трико́ *ср нескл* leotard.

трикота́ж (**-а**) *м* (*ткань*) knitted fabric ◆ *собир* (*одежда*) knitwear.

трикота́жный *прил* knitted; **~ магази́н** knitwear shop.

три́лер (**-а**) *м* thriller.

трили́стник (**-а**) *м* trefoil.

триллио́н (**-а**) *м* trillion.

трило́ги|я (**-и**) *ж* trilogy.

трина́дцати *чис см* **трина́дцать**.

трина́дцат|ый (**-ая, -ое, -ые**) *чис* thirteenth; *см также* **пя́тый**.

трина́дцат|ь (**-и**; *как пять*; *см* **Table 27**) *чис* thirteen; *см также* **пять**.

три́о *ср нескл* trio.

Три́поли *м нескл* Tripoli.

три́птих (**-а**) *м* triptych.

три́ста (**трёхсо́т**; *как сто*; *см* **Table 32**) *чис* three hundred; *см также* **сто**.

трито́н (**-а**) *м* newt.

триу́мф (**-а**) *м* triumph.

триумфа́льный *прил* triumphant; **триумфа́льная а́рка** triumphal arch.

тро́гател|ьный (**-ен, -ьна, -ьно**) *прил* touching.

тро́га|ть (**-ю**; *perf* **тро́нуть**) *несов перех* (*также перен*) to touch; (*разг: беспокоить: вопросами*) to pester; (*подлеж: рассказ, событие*) to move ◆ *неперех* (*лошадь, повозка*) to start moving; **улы́бка тро́нула её гу́бы** a smile flickered across her lips; **седина́ тро́нула его́ во́лосы** his hair was touched with grey

▶ **тро́гаться** (*perf* **тро́нуться**) *несов возв* (*поезд*) to move off; (*лёд*) to (begin to) break; **~ся** (**тро́нуться** *perf*) **в путь** to set off.

тро́|е (**-о́их**; *см* **Table 35а**) *чис* three; *см также* **дво́е**.

троебо́рь|е (**-я**) *ср* triathlon.

тро́ек *сущ см* **тро́йка**.

тро́ен *сущ см* **тро́йня.**

трои́х *чис см* **тро́е.**

тро́иц|а (-ы) *ж* (*также:* **свята́я** ~) the Holy Trinity; (*праздник: также:* **Т**~**ын день**) ≈ Trinity Sunday; (*разг: о друзьях*) threesome.

тро́йк|а (-йки; *gen pl* -ек) *ж* (*цифра, карта*) three; (*ПРОСВЕЩ*) ≈ C (*school mark*); (*лошадей*) troika; (*группа людей*) threesome; (*разг: автобус, трамвай итп*) (number) three (*bus, tram etc*); (*костюм*) three-piece suit.

тройни́к (-á) *м* (*ЭЛЕК*) (three-way) adaptor.

тройн|о́й *прил* triple; **в** ~**о́м разме́ре** triple the size; **тройно́й прыжо́к** (*СПОРТ*) triple jump.

тро́йн|я (-йни; *gen pl* -ен) *ж* triplets *мн*.

тро́йствен|ный (-ен, -на, -но) *прил* (*связь*) threefold; (*no short form*; *ПОЛИТ: союз, соглашение*) tripartite.

тройча́тк|а (-и) *ж* (*разг*) mild painkiller taken for headaches etc.

тролле́йбус (-а) *м* trolleybus.

тромб (-а) *м* blood clot.

тромбо́з (-а) *м* thrombosis.

тромбо́н (-а) *м* trombone.

трон (-а) *м* throne.

тро́нн|ый *прил*: ~ **зал** throne room; ~**ая речь** royal address.

► **тро́н|уть** (-у, -ешь) *сов от* **тро́гать**

► **тро́нуться** *сов от* **тро́гаться** ♦ *возв*: ~**ся** (**умо́м**) (*разг*) to be (a bit) touched.

троп|á (-ы́; *nom pl* -ы) *ж* pathway.

тро́пик (-а) *м*: **се́верный/ю́жный** ~ the tropic of Cancer/Capricorn; *см также* **тро́пики.**

тро́пик|и (-ов) the tropics *мн*.

тропи́н|ка (-ки; *gen pl* -ок) *ж* footpath.

тропи́ческий (-ая, -ое, -ие) *прил* tropical.

трос (-а) *м* cable.

трости́н|ка (-ки; *gen pl* -ок) *ж* (*камыша*) cane; (*травинка*) stem.

тростни́к (-á) *м* reed; **са́харный** ~ sugar cane.

трость (-и; *gen pl* -е́й) *ж* walking stick.

тротуа́р (-а) *м* pavement (*BRIT*), sidewalk (*US*).

трофе́й (-я) *м* trophy.

трою́родный *прил*: ~ **брат** second cousin (*male*); **трою́родная сестра́** second cousin (*female*).

тро́я|кий (-ая, -ое, -ие; -, -а, -о) *прил* triple.

тру(сь) *итп несов см* **тере́ть(ся).**

труб|á (-ы́; *nom pl* -ы) *ж* (*газовая, водосточная итп*) pipe; (*дымовая*) chimney; (*МУЗ*) trumpet; (*АНАТ*): **фалло́пиева** ~ Fallopian tube; **в** ~**у́ вылета́ть** (**вы́лететь** *perf*) (*разг*) to go to the wall.

труба́ч (-á) *м* trumpeter.

труби́ть (-лю́, -и́шь; *perf* **протруби́ть**) *несов неперех*: ~ **в** +*acc* (*МУЗ*) to blow; (*подлеж: труба*) to sound; (*перен: разг*): ~ **о** +*prp* to trumpet ♦ *перех* (*сбор, отбой*) to sound.

тру́б|ка (-ки; *gen pl* -ок) *ж* tube; (*курительная*)

pipe; (*телефона*) receiver; (*МЕД*) stethoscope; **брать** (**взять** *perf*) *или* **поднима́ть** (**подня́ть** *perf*) ~**ку** (*ТЕЛ*) to pick up the receiver; **свора́чивать** (**сверну́ть** *perf*) **что-н в** ~**ку** to roll sth into a tube.

трублю́ *несов см* **труби́ть.**

тру́бок *сущ см* **тру́бка.**

трубопрово́д (-а) *м* pipeline.

трубо́чек *сущ см* **тру́бочка.**

трубочи́ст (-а) *м* chimney sweep.

тру́боч|ка (-ки; *gen pl* -ек) *ж уменьш от* **тру́бка**; (*кулин*) cream horn.

труд (-á) *м* work; (*ЭКОН*) labour (*BRIT*), labor (*US*); (*ПРОСВЕЩ*) home economics and design; **бескоры́стный** ~ labo(u)r of love; **брать** (**взять** *perf*) **на себя́** ~ +*infin* to take the trouble to do; **без** ~**á** without any difficulty; **с** (**больши́м**) ~**о́м** with (great) difficulty.

тру́ден *прил см* **тру́дный.**

тру|ди́ться (-жу́сь, -дишься) *несов возв* to work hard; ~ (*impf*) **над** +*instr* to labour (*BRIT*) *или* labor (*US*) over; **не** ~**ди́тесь писа́ть мне** don't bother to write.

тру́дно *как сказ* it's hard *или* difficult; **у меня́** ~ **с деньга́ми** I've got money problems; **мне** ~ **поня́ть э́то/найти́ вре́мя** I find it hard to understand/to find the time; (**мне**) ~ **бе́гать/ стоя́ть** I have trouble running/standing up; ~ **сказа́ть** it's hard to say.

трудновоспиту́емый (-, -а, -о) *прил*: ~ **ребёнок** problem child (*мн* children).

труднодосту́п|ный (-ен, -на, -но) *прил* (*горы, место*) hard to get to.

труднопроходи́м|ый (-, -а, -о) *прил* (*дорога*) almost impassable.

тру́дность (-и) *ж* difficulty.

тру́дный (-ен, -на́, -но) *прил* difficult.

трудов|о́й *прил* working; ~**о́е законода́тельство** employment legislation; ~**ы́е дохо́ды** earned income; ~ **стаж** working life; ~**ая дисципли́на** discipline in the workplace; **трудова́я кни́жка** employment record book; **трудово́е соглаше́ние** contract (of employment).

трудоёмк|ий (-кая, -кое, -кие; -ок, -ка, -ко) *прил* labour-intensive (*BRIT*), labor-intensive (*US*).

трудолюби́в|ый (-, -а, -о) *прил* hard-working, industrious.

трудоспосо́бность (-и) *ж* fitness to work; **утра́та** ~**и** disablement.

трудоспосо́бный *прил* fit to work.

трудотерапи́|я (-и) *ж* occupational therapy.

трудоустро́|ить (-ю, -ишь; *impf* **трудоустра́ивать**) *сов перех* to find work for.

трудоустро́йств|о (-а) *ср* placement.

трудя́щийся (-аяся, -ееся, -иеся) *прил* working ♦ (-егося; *decl like adj*) *м* worker.

тру́женик (-а) *м* worker.

тру́женица (-ы) ж см **тру́женик.**

тружу́сь несов см **труди́ться.**

труп (-а) м corpse; **то́лько че́рез мой ~!** over my dead body!

тру́пп|а (-ы) ж (ТЕАТР) company.

трус (-а) м coward.

тру́сик|и (-ов) мн (женские, детские) knickers мн (BRIT), panties мн (US).

тру́|сить (-шу, -сишь; perf **стру́сить**) несов неперех to get scared; ~ (impf) **пе́ред кем-н** to cower before sb.

тру|си́ть (-шу́, -си́шь) несов неперех to trot along ♦ перех (содержимое мешка) to shake out; (плоды: с дерева) to shake.

трусли́в|ый (-, -а, -о) прил cowardly.

тру́сость (-и) ж cowardice.

трусц|а́ (-ы́) ж trot; **бег ~о́й** jogging; **бе́гать** (impf) **~о́й** to jog.

трус|ы́ (-о́в) мн (бельё: обычно мужские) underpants мн; (спортивные) shorts мн.

тру́т|ень (-ня) м (ЗООЛ) drone; (перен: человек) parasite.

трух|а́ (-и́) ж dust.

трухля́в|ый (-, -а, -о) прил crumbly.

тру́шу несов см **тру́сить.**

трушу́ несов см **труси́ть.**

трущо́б|а (-ы) ж (бедный район) slum; (лесная) jungle (fig).

трюк (-а) м trick; (акробатический) stunt.

трюка́ч (-а́) м (в цирке) acrobat; (мошенник) fraudster.

трюм (-а) м hold (of ship).

трюмо́ ср нескл dresser (piece of furniture).

трюфел|ь (-я; nom pl -я́) м (также конфета) truffle.

тряпи́чн|ый прил: ~**ая ку́кла** rag doll.

тря́п|ка (-ки; gen pl -ок) ж (половая, для пыли) cloth; (лоскут) rag; (перен: разг: о человеке) drip; ~**ки** (разг: пренебр) rags.

тряпь|ё (-я́) ср собир rags мн.

тряси́н|а (-ы) ж quagmire; (перен) mire.

тря́ский (-кая, -кое, -кие; -ок, -ка, -ко) прил (вагон, машина) rickety; (дорога) bumpy.

трясогу́з|ка (-ки; gen pl -ок) ж wagtail.

тря́сок прил см **тря́ский.**

тряс|ти́ (-у́, -ёшь) несов перех to shake; (perf **вы́трясти**; ковёр, мешок) to shake down; ~ (impf) +instr (головой, кулаком) to shake; (гривой) to toss; **в маши́не ~ёт** the car is jolting; **его́ ~ёт от стра́ха** he's shaking with fear

▶ **тряс|ти́сь** несов возв (машина) to jolt; (разг: в машине, в поезде итп) to rattle along; ~**сь** (impf) **пе́ред** +instr (перед начальством) to tremble before; ~**сь** (impf) **над** +instr (разг: над ребёнком, над деньгами) to fret over или about; ~**сь** (impf) **от сме́ха/стра́ха/хо́лода** to shake with laughter/fear/cold.

трясн|у́ть (-у́, -ёшь) сов перех to shake; ~ (perf) **старино́й** (разг) to turn the clock back.

т/с сокр (= теку́щий счёт) C/A (= current account).

т/сче́т сокр = **т/с.**

тт сокр = **тома́.**

т.т. сокр = **това́рищи.**

ТУ м сокр = самолёт констру́кции А.Н.Ту́полева.

Ту м сокр = **ТУ.**

туале́т (-а) м toilet; (гардероб) outfit.

туале́тн|ый прил: ~**ая бума́га** toilet paper; **туале́тное мы́ло** toilet soap; **туале́тные принадле́жности** toiletries; **туале́тный сто́лик** dressing table.

туберкулёз (-а) м ТВ, tubercolosis.

туберкулёзный прил ТВ, tubercolosis опред.

ту́го нареч tightly; (набить) tight ♦ как сказ (разг): **(у нас) ~ с деньга́ми** money is tight (for us); **(у нас) ~ со вре́менем** we're hard-pressed for time; **дела́ иду́т ~** (разг) things aren't going too well.

тугоду́м (-а) м dimwit.

туг|о́й (-, -а́, -о) прил (струна, пружина) taut; (узел, одежда) tight; (чемодан) tightly-packed; (кошелёк) bulging; **он туг на́ ухо** (разг) he's a bit hard of hearing.

туда́ нареч there; ~ **и обра́тно** there and back; **биле́т ~ и обра́тно** return (BRIT) или round-trip (US) ticket; **ни ~ ни сюда́!** (разг) it won't budge!; ~ **ему́ и доро́га** (разг) that's the best place for him; **он тако́й молодо́й, а ~ же, кома́ндует** (разг) he is so young, and look at him ordering everyone around.

туда́-сюда́ нареч all over the place; (раскачиваться) backwards and forwards ♦ как сказ (разг) it's so-so.

ту́же сравн прил от **туго́й** ♦ сравн нареч от **ту́го.**

туж|и́ть (-у́, -ишь) несов неперех: ~ (**о** +prp) to pine (for).

туз (-а́) м (финансовый, городской) bigwig.

тузе́м|ец (-ца) м native.

тузе́м|ка (-ки; gen pl -ок) ж см **тузе́мец.**

тузе́мный прил (население, обычай) native опред.

тузе́мок сущ см **тузе́мка.**

тузе́мца итп сущ см **тузе́мец.**

тук межд knock.

ту́ловище (-а) ср torso.

тулу́п (-а) м (овчинный) sheepskin coat.

тума́к (-а́) м (разг) thump, whack.

тума́н (-а; part gen -у) м mist; (перен: в голове) haze.

тума́нен прил см **тума́нный.**

тума́н|ить (3sg -ит, 3pl -ят perf **затума́нить**); несов перех (подлеж: дым, дождь) to obscure; **слёзы затума́нили ей глаза́** her eyes were misty with tears; **вино́ затума́нило мне го́лову** the wine has addled my brain

▶ **тума́н|иться** (perf **затума́ниться**) несов возв to become shrouded in mist; (перен: глаза) to mist over; (: лицо) to cloud.

тума́нность (-и) ж (АСТРОНОМИЯ) nebula; (перен: в мыслях, в изложении) cloudiness.

тума́н|ный (-ен, -на, -но) *прил* (*воздух, утро*) misty; (*перен: взгляд*) dull; (: *смысл, объясне́ние*) nebulous.

ту́мб|а (-ы) *ж* (*прича́льная, у́личная*) bollard; (*для цвето́в*) stand; (*для скульпту́ры, стола́*) pedestal; **афи́шная ~** cylindrical advertising hoarding.

ту́мблер (-а) *м* (*КОМП*) toggle switch.

ту́мбоч|ка (-ки; *gen pl* -ек) *ж уменьш от* **ту́мба**; (*ме́бель*) bedside cabinet.

ту́ндр|а (-ы) *ж* tundra.

ту́ндровый *прил* tundra *опред*.

туне́ц (-ца́) *м* tuna (fish).

туне́я́д|ец (-ца) *м* parasite (*fig*).

туне́я́дств|о (-а) *ср* parasitism.

туне́я́дца *итп сущ см* **туне́я́дец**.

Туни́с (-а) *м* (*го́род*) Tunis; (*страна́*) Tunisia.

туни́сский (-ая, -ое, -ие) *прил* Tunisian.

тунне́л|ь (-я) *м* = **тонне́ль**.

тунца́ *итп сущ см* **туне́ц**.

тупе́|ть (-ю) *несов неперех* (*боль*) to become less acute; (*perf* **отупе́ть**; *разг: челове́к*) to become stupid; (*чу́вства*) to dull.

тупи́к (-а́) *м* (*у́лица*) dead end, cul-de-sac; (*для поездо́в*) siding; (*перен: в перегово́рах итп*) deadlock; **ста́вить (поста́вить** *perf*) **кого́-н в ~** to stump sb; **стать** (*perf*) **в ~** to be stumped; **заходи́ть (зайти́** *perf*) **в ~** (*перегово́ры*) to reach a deadlock.

тупико́вый *прил* (*ситуа́ция*) dead-end; (*ста́нция*) at the end of the line.

туп|и́ть (-лю́, -ишь; *perf* **затупи́ть**) *несов перех* to blunt

▸ **тупи́ться** (*perf* **затупи́ться**) *несов возв* to become blunt.

тупи́ц|а (-ы) *м/ж* (*разг*) dunce.

тупл́ю́(сь) *несов см* **тупи́ть(ся)**.

туп|о́й (-, -а́, -о) *прил* (*нож, каранда́ш*) blunt; (*челове́к*) stupid; (*боль, ум*) dull; (*поко́рность, страх*) blind; **тупо́й у́гол** obtuse angle.

ту́пость (-и) *ж* (*челове́ка, поведе́ния*) stupidity; (*ума́*) dullness.

тур (-а) *м* (*ко́нкурса, перегово́ров, вы́боров*) round; (*в та́нце*) turn; (*ЗООЛ*) mountain goat.

тур|а́ (-ы́) *ж* (*разг: в ша́хматах*) castle.

турби́н|а (-ы) *ж* turbine.

туре́цкий (-ая, -ое, -ие) *прил* Turkish; **~ язы́к** Turkish.

тури́зм (-а) *м* tourism.

тури́ст (-а) *м* tourist; (*в похо́де*) hiker.

туристи́ческий (-ая, -ое, -ие) *прил* tourist *опред*.

тури́стский (-ая, -ое, -ие) *прил* tourist's; **~ маршру́т** trail; **~ое снаряже́ние** camping and walking equipment.

ту́рка *итп сущ см* **ту́рок**.

туркме́н (-а) *м* Turkmen.

Туркме́ни|я (-и) *ж* Turkmenia.

туркме́н|ка (-ки; *gen pl* -ок) *ж см* **туркме́н**.

туркме́нский (-ая, -ое, -ие) *прил* Turkmenian.

турне́ *ср нескл* (*ТЕА́ТР, СПОРТ*) tour.

турне́пс (-а) *м* turnip.

турни́к (-а́) *м* horizontal bar.

турнике́т (-а) *м* turnstile.

турни́р (-а) *м* tournament.

ту́р|ок (-ка) *м* Turk.

Ту́рци|я (-и) *ж* Turkey.

турча́н|ка (-ки; *gen pl* -ок) *ж см* **ту́рок**.

ту́скл|ый (-, -а́, -о) *прил* (*стекло́*) opaque; (*лак, кра́ска, позоло́та*) matt; (*свет, стиль, взгляд*) dull.

тускне́|ть (*3sg* -ет, *3pl* -ют, *perf* **потускне́ть**) *несов неперех* (*кра́ска, тала́нт*) to fade; (*серебро́, позоло́та, кра́ски*) to tarnish.

тут *нареч* here; **что ~ говори́ть!** (*разг*) what is there to say?; **я ~ ни при чём** it has nothing to do with me; **и всё ~** (*разг*) and that's that; **он уже́ ~ как ~** (*разг*) right at that moment he appeared; **не ~-то бы́ло** (*разг*) it wasn't to be.

ту́тов|ый *прил*: **~ое де́рево** mulberry tree; **ту́товый шелкопря́д** silkworm.

ту́фл|я (-ли; *nom pl* -ли, *gen pl* -ель) *ж* (*обычно мн*) shoe.

ту́хл|ый (-, -а́, -о) *прил* (*еда́*) rotten; (*за́пах*) putrid.

ту́х|нуть (*3sg* -нет, *3pl* -нут, *pt* -, -ла, -ло, *perf* **поту́хнуть**) *несов неперех* (*костёр, свет, свеча́*) to go out; (*perf* **проту́хнуть**; *мя́со, ры́ба*) to go off.

ту́ч|а (-и) *ж* rain cloud; (*перен: мух, стрел*) cloud; **он сего́дня, как ~** he's been in a black mood all day.

ту́ч|ный (-ен, -на́, -но) *прил* (*челове́к*) stout; (*по́чва*) fertile; (*трава́, луга́*) lush.

туш (-а) *м* (*МУЗ*) flourish.

ту́ш|а (-и) *ж* carcass; (*разг: о ту́чном челове́ке*) hulk.

тушева́|ть (-ю́ю; *perf* **затушева́ть**) *несов перех* (*рису́нок, фотогра́фию*) to shade in; (*перен: ра́зницу, противоре́чия*) to gloss over.

тушева́ться (-у́юсь) *несов от* **стушева́ться**.

тушён|ка (-ки; *gen pl* -ок) *ж* (*разг*) tinned (*BRIT*) *или* canned meat.

тушёный *прил* (*КУЛИН*) braised.

туш|и́ть (-у́, -ишь; *perf* **затуши́ть** *или* **потуши́ть**) *несов перех* (*свечу́, костёр, пожа́р*) to put out; (*perf* **потуши́ть**; *свет*) to put out; (*КУЛИН*) to braise.

тушка́нчик (-а) *м* jerboa.

туш|ь (-и) *ж* (*для рисова́ния*) Indian ink; (*для ресни́ц*) mascara.

ту́|я (-и) *ж* red cedar.

т/х *сокр* = **теплохо́д**.

тчк *сокр* = **то́чка**.

тща́тел|ьный (-ен, -ьна, -ьно) *прил* thorough.

тщеду́ш|ный (-ен, -на, -но) *прил* feeble.

тщесла́вен *прил см* **тщесла́вный**.

тщесла́ви|е (-я) *ср* vanity.

тщесла́в|ный (-ен, -на, -но) *прил* vain.

тще́тен *прил см* **тще́тный**.

тще́тность (-и) *ж* futility.

тще́т|ный (-ен, -на, -но) *прил* futile.

ты (тебя́; *см* **Table 5а**) *мест* you; (*разг: для усиления*): **ах ~, кака́я жа́лость!** oh, what a pity!; **быть** *(impf)* **с кем-н на ~** to be on familiar terms with sb; **вот тебе́ раз!** good grief!

ты́|кать (-чу, -чешь; *perf* ткнуть) *несов перех* (*разг: ударять*): **тыка́ть что-н/кого́-н чем-н** to poke sth/sb with sth; (: *вонзать*): **тыка́ть что-н в** +*acc* to stick sth into; (: *обращаться на „ты"*) to address somebody using the informal form of *"you"*; **~** *(impf)* **кого́-н но́сом во что-н** (*разг*) to rub sb's face in sth; **~** (ткнуть *perf*) **па́льцем на** +*acc* (*разг*) to point at

▸ **ты́|каться** (*perf* ткну́ться) *несов возв* (*разг: суетливо двигаться*) to rush about; **~ся** (ткну́ться *perf*) **в** +*acc* (*в стену, в дверь итп*) to bang into; (*соваться*) to nuzzle.

ты́кв|а (-ы) *ж* pumpkin.

тыл (-а; *loc sg* -ý, *nom pl* -ы́) *м* (ВОЕН: *сторона, территория*) the rear; (: *вся страна*) the home front; (: *воинские организации*) rear units.

тылово́й *прил* (ВОЕН) rear.

ты́льный *прил* back; **~ая часть руки́** the back of one's hand.

тыс. *сокр* = **ты́сяча**.

ты́сяч|а (-и; *см* **Table 35**) *ж чис* thousand.

тысячеле́ти|е (-я) *ср* millenium; (*годовщина*) thousandth anniversary.

тысячеле́тн|ий (-яя, -ее, -ие) *прил* (*период*) thousand-year; (*дерево*) thousand-year-old.

ты́сячи *чис см* **ты́сяча**.

ты́сячн|ая (-ой; *decl like adj*) *ж*: **одна́ ~** one thousandth.

ты́сячн|ый (-ая, -ое, -ие) *чис* thousandth; (*толпа, армия*) of many thousands.

ты́сячу *чис см* **ты́сяча**.

тычи́н|ка (-ки; *gen pl* -ок) *ж* stamen.

ты́чу(сь) *итп несов см* **ты́кать(ся)**.

тьм|а (-ы) *ж* (*мрак*) darkness, gloom; (*множество*) swarm.

тьфу *межд* yuk.

ТЭС *ж сокр* = **теплоэлектроста́нция**.

ТЭЦ *ж сокр* = **теплоэлектроцентра́ль**.

тюбете́|йка (-йки; *gen pl* -ек) *ж* skullcap (*worn in Central Asia*).

тю́бик (-а) *м* tube.

ТЮЗ (-а) *м сокр* (= **теа́тр ю́ного зри́теля**) youth theatre (BRIT) *или* theater (US).

тюз (-а) *м сокр* = **ТЮЗ**.

тюк (-а́) *м* bale.

тю́левый *прил* tulle.

тюле́нь (-я) *м* (ЗООЛ) seal.

тюль (-я) *м* tulle.

тюльпа́н (-а) *м* tulip.

тюрба́н (-а) *м* turban.

тюре́мный *прил* prison *опред*; **тюре́мное заключе́ние** imprisonment.

тюрьм|а́ (-ы́) *ж* prison; **сажа́ть** (**посади́ть** *perf*) **кого́-н в ~ý** to put sb in prison.

тюфя́к (-а́) *м* straw mattress; (*разг: о человеке*) wimp.

тя́вка|ть (-ю) *несов неперех* to yap.

тя́вкнуть (-у, -ешь) *сов неперех* to yap.

тя́г|а (-и) *ж* (*в печи*) draught (BRIT), draft (US); (*насоса, пылесоса*) suction; (ТЕХ) traction; (*реактивная*) thrust; **~ к** +*dat* (*перен*) attraction to; **на электри́ческой ~е** powered by electricity; **на ко́нной ~е** horse-drawn.

тяга́|ться (-юсь; *perf* потяга́ться) *несов возв* (*разг*): **~ с кем-н (в** +*prp*) to compete with sb (in); **~** (потяга́ться *perf*) **с кем-н умо́м** to pit one's wits against sb.

тяга́ч (-а́) *м* tractor.

тя́гостн|ый (-ен, -на, -но) *прил* burdensome; (*впечатления*) depressing.

тя́гост|ь (-и) *ж* (*ожидания, зависимости*) burden; (*обычно мн: войны, бедности*) hardship; (*на сердце, на душе*) heavy feeling; **быть** *(impf)* **в ~ кому́-н** to be a burden to sb.

тяготе́ни|е (-я) *ср* (ФИЗ) gravity; (*перен*): **~ к** +*dat* attraction to.

тяготе́|ть (-ю) *несов неперех*: **~ к** +*dat* (*к культуре, к прогрессу, к общению*) to gravitate *или* be drawn towards; (*к мнению*) to tend towards; (*перен*): **~ над** +*instr* (*обвинение, подозрение*) to hang over; (*чья-н власть, воля*) to oppress.

тяго|ти́ть (-щу́, -ти́шь) *несов перех* to weigh (heavy) on

▸ **тяготи́ться** *несов возв* (+*instr*) to be weighed down by.

тя́готы (-) *мн* hardships *мн*.

тягощу́(сь) *несов см* **тяготи́ть(ся)**.

тягу́ч|ий (-ая, -ее, -ие; -, -а, -е) *прил* (*клей, краска итп*) viscous; (*резинка, ткань*) stretchy; (*перен: речь, голос*) droning.

тя́жб|а (-ы) *ж* dispute.

тя́жек *прил см* **тя́жкий**.

тяжеле́|ть (-ю; *perf* отяжеле́ть *или* потяжеле́ть) *несов неперех* to get heavier; (*голова, ноги: от усталости*) to grow heavy.

тяжело́ *нареч* heavily; (*больной, раненый*) seriously ◆ *как сказ* (*нести*) it's heavy; (*понять, согласиться*) it's hard; **мне ~ здесь** I find it hard here; **больно́му ~** the patient is suffering.

тяжелоатле́т (-а) *м* weightlifter.

тяжелоатлети́ческ|ий (-ая, -ое, -ие) *прил*: **~е соревнова́ния** weightlifting competiton.

тяжелове́с (-а) *м* (СПОРТ) heavyweight.

тяжелове́с|ный *прил* (-ен, -на, -но; *перен: речь, шутка, стиль*) laboured (BRIT), labored (US); (*архитектура*) heavy; **~ по́езд** freight train.

тяжёл|ый (-ёл, -ела́, -ело́) *прил* heavy; (*трудный: труд, обязанность, дорога итп*) hard, tough; (*сон*) restless; (*запах*) thick;

(*воздух*) close; (*преступление, болезнь, рана*) serious; (*горестный: зрелище, день трудный*) grim; (*мрачный: мысли, настроение*) sombre (BRIT), somber (US); (*no short form*; *трудный*: *человек, характер*) difficult; **с ~ёлым се́рдцем** with a heavy heart; **тяжёлая атле́тика** weightlifting; **тяжёлая промы́шленность** heavy industry.

тя́жесть (-и) *ж* heaviness, weight; (*работы, задачи*) difficulty; (*болезни, раны, преступления*) seriousness, severity; (*обычно мн: тяжёлый предмет*) weight; **си́ла ~и** (*физ*) gravitational pull; **центр ~и** (*физ*) centre of gravity.

тя́ж|кий (-кая, -кое, -кие; -ек, -ка́, -ко) *прил* (*труд*) arduous; (*характер*) oppressive; (*зрелище*) grim; (*сомнения, подозрение, преступление*) grave.

тяну́ть (-у́, -ешь) *несов перех* (*канат, сеть итп*) to pull; (*вытягивать: шею, руку*) to stretch out; (*дело, разговор, заседание*) to drag out; (*напиток*) to sip (at); (*perf* **протяну́ть**; *трубопровод, кабель*) to lay; (*perf* **вы́тянуть**; *жребий, номер*) to draw ♦ *неперех*: ~ **с** +*instr* (*с ответом, с решением*) to delay; (*разг*): ~ **на** +*acc* (*на килограмм итп*) to weigh; ~ (**потяну́ть** *perf*) **кого́-н за́ руку** to pull at sb's arm; ~ (*impf*) **кого́-н в кино́** to tempt sb out to the cinema; **меня́ тя́нет в Петербу́рг** I want to go to Petersburg; **меня́ тя́нет ко сну** I'm feeling drowsy; **он не тя́нет на ли́дера** he is not leadership material

▶ **тяну́ться** *несов возв* to stretch; (*заседание, дни, зима итп*) to drag on; (*дым, запах*) to waft; ~**ся** (*impf*) **к** +*dat* to be attracted *или* drawn to; **он тя́нется к зна́ниям** he has a thirst for knowledge; ~**ся** (*impf*) **за кем-н** to try to keep up with sb.

тяну́ч|ка (-ки; *gen pl* -ек) *ж* toffee.

тя́п|ка (-ки; *gen pl* -ок) *ж* hoe.

тяп-ля́п *нареч* (*разг: пренебр*): **де́лать что-н** ~ to do sth in a slapdash way.

тя́пнуть (-у, -ешь) *сов неперех* (*разг: укусить*) to nip.

тя́пок *сущ см* **тя́пка**.

~ У, у ~

У, у *сущ нескл (буква)* the 20th letter of the Russian alphabet.

KEYWORD

у *предл* (+*gen*) **1** (*около*) by; **у окна́/стены́** by the window/wall; **у мо́ря/реки́** by the sea/river; **у вхо́да** at the entrance

2 (*обозначает орудие, место работы*) at; **сиде́ть** (*impf*) **у руля́** to sit at the helm; **стоя́ть** (*impf*) **у станка́** to stand at the workbench

3 (*обозначает обладателя чего-н*): **у меня́ есть дом/де́ти** I have a house/children; **у таки́х люде́й быва́ют интере́сные иде́и** people like that have interesting ideas; **голова́ у меня́ совсе́м разболе́лась** I have a terrible headache

4 (*обозначает объект, с которым соотносится действие*): **я живу́ у друзе́й** I live with friends; **я учи́лся у него́** I was taught by him

5 (*указывает на источник получения чего-н*) from; **я взял/попроси́л у дру́га де́нег** I got/asked for money from a friend; **мы получи́ли разреше́ние у нача́льства** we got permission from the authorities

♦ *межд* (*выражает угрозу*) hey; (*выражает испуг, восторг*) oh; **у, негодя́й!** hey, you rascal!; **у, как высоко́!** oh, how high it is!; **у, кака́я красота́!** oh, how beautiful!

УАЗ *м сокр* = Улья́новский автомоби́льный заво́д; (*автомобиль*) *vehicle produced at the Ul'ianovskiy car factory.*

уба́в|ить (-лю, -ишь; *impf* **убавля́ть**) *сов перех* (*цену, размеры*) to reduce; (*рукава*) to shorten

▶ **уба́виться** (*impf* **убавля́ться**) *сов возв* (*расходы*) to decrease; (*срок*) to be reduced; (*дни*) to get shorter.

убаю́ка|ть (-ю) *сов от* **баю́кать.**

убега́|ть (-ю) *несов от* **убежа́ть.**

убегу́ *итп сов см* **убежа́ть.**

убеди́тельный (-ен, -ьна, -ьно) *прил* (*пример, доказательство*) convincing; (*просьба*) urgent.

убеди́|ть (-шь, -т; *impf* **убежда́ть**) *сов перех:* ~ **кого́-н** +*infin* to persuade sb to do; **убежда́ть** (~ *perf*) **кого́-н в чём-н** to convince sb of sth

▶ **убеди́ться** (*impf* **убежда́ться**) *сов возв:* ~**ся в чём-н** to be convinced of sth.

убежа́|ть (*как* **бежа́ть;** *см* **Table 20;** *impf* **убега́ть**) *сов неперех* to run away; **молоко́** ~**ло**

(*разг*) the milk has boiled over.

убежда́|ть(ся) (-ю(сь)) *несов от* **убеди́ть(ся).**

убежде́ни|е (-я) *ср* (*внушение*) assurance; (*взгляд*) conviction; **поддава́ться (подда́ться** *perf*) ~**ям** to give in to persuasion.

убеждённост|ь (-и) *ж* (*уверенность*) assurance, conviction.

убеждённый (-ён, -ена́, -ено́) *прил:* ~ **в** +*prp* convinced of; (-ён, -ённа, -ённо; *тон*) assured; (*no short form;* **като́лик**) convinced.

убежи́шь *итп сов см* **убежа́ть.**

убе́жищ|е (-а) *ср* (*от дождя, от бомб*) shelter; **полити́ческое** ~ political asylum.

убелённый *прил:* ~ **седи́нами** silver-haired.

убере́|чь (-гу́, -жёшь *итп,* -гу́т; *pt* -ёг, -егла́, -егло́, *impf* **уберега́ть**) *сов перех* to protect

▶ **убере́чься** (*impf* **уберега́ться**) *сов возв* (*от опасности итп*) to protect o.s.; ~**ся** (*perf*) **от просту́ды** to avoid catching cold.

уберу́(сь) *итп сов см* **убра́ть(ся).**

убива́|ть (-ю) *несов от* **уби́ть**

▶ **убива́ться** *несов возв* (*разг: страдать*) to grieve; (: *на работе*) to break one's back.

уби́йственный *прил* (*оружие*) deadly; (*новость, результат*) devastating; (*разг: жара, климат*) unbearable.

уби́йств|о (-а) *ср* murder.

уби́йц|а (-ы) *м/ж* murderer.

убира́|ть(ся) (-ю(сь)) *несов от* **убра́ть(ся).**

уби́т|ая (-ой; *decl like adj*) *ж* dead woman (*мн* women).

уби́тый *прил* (*перен: лицо*) crushed ♦ (-ого; *decl like adj*) *м* dead man (*мн* men); **спит как** ~ he is sleeping like a log.

уби́|ть (-ью, -ьёшь; *impf* **убива́ть**) *сов перех* to kill; (*совершить преступление*) to murder; (*перен: надежды, инициативу*) to destroy; ~ (*perf*) **вре́мя** (*перен*) to kill time.

ублаж|и́ть (-у́, -и́шь; *impf* **ублажа́ть**) *сов перех* (*разг*) to please.

убо́г|ий (-ая, -ое, -ие) *прил* (*дом, человек*) wretched; (*перен: идеи, фильм*) mediocre.

убо́жеств|о (-а) *ср* (*мыслей, идей*) mediocrity; (*обстановки*) wretchedness.

убо́й (-я) *м* slaughter.

убо́р (-а) *м:* **головно́й** ~ hat.

убо́ристый (-, -а, -о) *прил* (*почерк, печать*) close, dense.

убо́рк|а (-и) *ж* (*помещения*) cleaning;

занимáться (заня́ться *perf*) ~ to do the cleaning; ~ **урожáя** harvest.

убóрн|ая (-ой; *decl like adj*) *ж* (*артистическая*) dressing-room; (*туалет*) toilet, lavatory.

убóрочный *прил* harvesting *опред*; ~**ая машúна** harvester.

убóрщик (-а) *м* cleaner.

убóрщиц|а (-ы) *ж см* **убóрщик**.

убр|áть (уберу́, уберёшь; *pt* -áл, -алá, -áло, *impf* **убирáть**) *сов перех* (*унести: вещи*) to take away, remove; (*поместить*) to put away; (*паруса, якорь*) to stow; (*шасси*) to retract, draw in; (*комнату*) to tidy; (*разг: параграф: из текста*) to remove; (*урожай*) to gather in; **убирáть** (~ *perf*) **со столá** to clear the table

▶ **убрáться** (*impf* **убирáться**) *сов возв* (*разг: удалиться*) to get out; (*сделать уборку*) to clear *или* tidy up; **убирáйся отсю́да!** get lost!

убýду *итп сов см* **убы́ть**.

убывá|ть (-ю) *несов от* **убы́ть**.

у́был|ь (-и) *ж* (*рабочей силы*) decrease; **идтú** (**пойтú** *perf*) **на** ~ (*дни*) to get shorter; (*болезнь, эпидемия*) to run its course.

убы́т|ок (-ка) *м* loss; **терпéть** (*impf*) *или* **нестú** (*impf*) ~**ки** to incur losses.

убы́точный (-ен, -на, -но) *прил* unprofitable.

убы́ть (*как* **быть**; *см* **Table 21**; *impf* **убывáть**) *сов неперех* to decrease; **егó от э́того не убýдет** he won't be any worse off for it.

убью́ *итп сов см* **убúть**.

уважáемый *прил* respected, esteemed; **У**~**ые дáмы и господá!** Ladies and Gentlemen!

уважá|ть (-ю) *несов перех* to respect.

уважéни|е (-я) *ср* respect.

уважúтельный (-ен, -ьна, -ьно) *прил* (*отношение*) respectful; (*довод, причина*) respectable.

увá|жить (-у, -ишь) *сов перех* (*угодить*) to humour (*BRIT*), humor (*US*); ~ (*perf*) **чью-н прóсьбу** to grant sb's request.

у́вал|ень (-ьня) *м* lumbering oaf.

ув|арúться (*3sg* -áрится, *3pl* -áрятся, *impf* **увáриваться**) *сов возв* (*сироп, щи*) to boil down, reduce.

УВД *ср сокр* (= Управлéние внýтренних дел) *administration of internal affairs within a town or region*.

уведóм|ить (-лю, -ишь; *impf* **уведомля́ть**) *сов перех* to inform.

уведомлéни|е (-я) *ср* (*документ*) notification.

увéдомлю *сов см* **увéдомить**.

уведомля́|ть (-ю) *несов от* **увéдомить**.

уведý *итп сов см* **увестú**.

увез|тú (-ý, -ёшь; *pt* увёз, увезлá, увезлó, *impf* **увозúть**) *сов перех* to take away.

увековéч|ить (-у, -ишь) *сов перех* (*героя*) to immortalize.

увеличéни|е (-я) *ср* increase.

увелúчива|ть(ся) (-ю(сь)) *несов от* **увелúчить(ся)**.

увеличúтельн|ый *прил*: ~**ое стеклó** magnifying glass.

увелú|чить (-у, -ишь; *impf* **увелúчивать**) *сов перех* to increase; (*фотографию*) to enlarge

▶ **увелúчиться** (*impf* **увелúчиваться**) *сов возв* to increase, be increased.

увенчá|ться (-юсь) *сов возв*: ~ **успéхом** to result in success.

увéренност|ь (-и) *ж* confidence; ~ **в себé** self-confidence; **поколебáть** (*perf*) **чью-н** ~ **в чём-н/в том, что ...** to shake sb's conviction in sth/that ...; **я был в пóлной** ~**и, что ...** I was absolutely sure that ....

увéренн|ый (-, -на, -но, -ы) *прил* (*шаг, ответ, голос*) confident; (*рука*) sure; ~ **в** +*prp* sure of; ~ **в себé** self-confident, sure of o.s.

увéр|ить (-ю, -ишь) *сов от* **уверя́ть**.

уверн|ýться (-ýсь, -ёшься; *impf* **увёртываться**) *сов возв* to swerve; **увёртываться** (~ *perf*) **от удáра** to dodge a blow; **увёртываться** (~ *perf*) **от пря́мого отвéта** to avoid giving a straight answer.

увéр|овать (-ую) *сов неперех*: ~ **в** +*acc* to (come to) believe in.

увёртлив|ый (-, -а, -о) *прил* (*подвижный*) nimble; (*перен: хитрый*) evasive.

увёртыва|ться (-юсь) *несов от* **увернýться**.

увертю́р|а (-ы) *ж* overture.

уверя́|ть (-ю; *perf* **увéрить**) *несов перех*: ~ **когó-н/что-н (в чём-н)** to assure sb/sth (of sth); ~**ю Вас, что я был прóтив э́того** I assure you that I was against it.

увеселúтельный *прил* (*зрелище*) entertaining; ~**ая прогýлка** jaunt.

увéсист|ый (-, -а, -о) *прил* heavy.

уве|стú (-дý, -дёшь; *pt* -ёл, -елá, -елó, *impf* **уводúть**) *сов перех* to lead off *или* away; (*разг: похитить*) to nick.

увéчь|е (-я) *ср* injury; **наносúть** (**нанестú** *perf*) **комý-н** ~ to maim sb; **получáть** (**получúть** *perf*) ~ to be maimed.

увéша|ть (-ю; *impf* **увéшивать**) *сов перех*: ~ **когó-н/что-н чем-н** to cover sb/sth with sth.

увещевá|ть (-ю) *несов перех* to exhort.

увивá|ться (-юсь) *несов возв* (*ухаживать*): ~ (**за кем-н**) (*за женщиной*) to hang around (sb).

увú|деть (-жу, -дишь) *сов от* **вúдеть** ♦ *перех* to catch sight of

▶ **увúдеться** *сов от* **вúдеться**.

увильн|ýть (-ý, -ёшь) *сов неперех*: ~ **от** +*gen* (*разг*) to dodge; (*от ответственности*) to get *или* wriggle out of.

увлажн|úть (-ю, -úшь; *impf* **увлажня́ть**) *сов перех* to moisten

▶ **увлажнúться** (*impf* **увлажня́ться**) *сов возв* to become moist.

увлёк(ся) *итп сов см* **увлечь(ся)**.
увлека́тельный *прил* (*захватывающий*)
absorbing; (**-ен, -ьна, -ьно**; *занимательный*)
entertaining.
увлека́ть(ся) (**-ю(сь)**) *несов от* **увлечь(ся)**.
увлека́ющийся (**-аяся, -ееся, -иеся**) *прил*
easily carried away.
увлеку́(сь) *итп сов см* **увлечь(ся)**.
увлече́ни|е (**-я**) *ср* (*влюблённость*) infatuation;
~ (+*instr*) (*работой, балетом*) enthusiasm
или passion (for).
увле́чь (**-еку́, -ечёшь** *итп,* **-еку́т**; *pt* **-ёк, -екла́,
-екло́,** *impf* **увлека́ть**) *сов перех* to lead away;
(*перен*) to captivate
▸ **увле́чься** (*impf* **увлека́ться**) *сов возв:* ~**ся**
+*instr* to get carried away with; (*влюбиться*) to
fall for; (*шахматами итп*) to become keen on.
уво|ди́ть (**-ожу́, -о́дишь**) *несов от* **увести́**.
уво|зи́ть (**-ожу́, -о́зишь**) *несов от* **увезти́**.
увола́кивать (**-ю**) *несов от* **уволо́чь**.
уво́л|ить (**-ю, -ишь;** *impf* **увольня́ть**) *сов перех*
(*с работы*) to dismiss, sack; **увольня́ть** (~ *perf*)
в запа́с to transfer to the reserve
▸ **уво́литься** (*impf* **увольня́ться**) *сов возв:* ~**ся**
с рабо́ты to leave one's job.
уволо́чь (**-ку́, -чёшь** *итп,* **-ку́т**; *pt* **-к, -кла́, -кло́,**
impf **увола́кивать**) *сов перех* to drag away *или*
off; (*разг: украсть*) to nick.
увольне́ни|е (**-я**) *ср* (*со службы*) dismissal;
(*ВОЕН*) leave.
увольни́тельн|ая (**-ой;** *decl like adj*) *ж* (*ВОЕН*)
leave-pass.
увольня́|ть(ся) (**-ю(сь)**) *несов от*
уво́лить(ся).
УВЧ *сокр* (= *ультравысо́кая частота́*) UHF (=
ultrahigh frequency) ♦ *прил сокр*
(*ультравысокочасто́тный*) UHF (= *ultrahigh-
frequency*).
увы́ *межд* alas.
увяда́ни|е (**-я**) *ср* (*цветов*) withering;
(*красоты*) fading.
увя́дш|ий (**-ая, -ее, -ие**) *прил* (*цветок*) withered;
(*красота*) faded.
увя|за́ть (**-жу́, -жешь;** *impf* **увя́зывать**) *сов
перех* (*вещи*) to tie up; (*перен: согласовать*) to
tie in
▸ **увяза́ться** *сов возв* (*разг*): ~**ся** (**за** +*instr*) to
tag along (behind).
увя́зн|уть (**-у, -ешь**) *сов от* **вя́знуть**.
увя́зыва|ть (**-ю**) *несов от* **увяза́ть**.
увя́н|уть (**-у, -ешь**) *сов от* **вя́нуть**.
угада́|ть (**-ю;** *impf* **уга́дывать**) *сов перех* to
guess.
Уга́нд|а (**-ы**) *ж* Uganda.
уга́р (**-а**) *м* (*воздух*) fume-filled air;
(*отравление*) carbon-monoxide poisoning;
пья́ный ~ drunken haze.
уга́рный *прил:* ~ **дым** poisonous smoke;
уга́рный газ carbon monoxide.
угаса́|ть (**-ю;** *perf* **уга́снуть**) *несов неперех*
(*костёр, закат*) to die down.

уга́сн|уть (**-у, -ешь**) *сов от* **га́снуть**.
угла́ *итп сущ см* **у́гол**.
углево́д (**-а**) *м* carbohydrate.
углеводоро́д (**-а**) *м* hydrocarbon.
углекислот|а́ (**-ы́**) *ж* carbon dioxide.
углеки́слый *прил:* ~ **газ** carbon dioxide.
углепромы́шленност|ь (**-и**) *ж* coal industry.
углеро́д (**-а**) *м* (*ХИМ*) carbon.
углова́тост|ь (**-и**) *ж* (*лица*) angularity;
(*человека, движений*) awkwardness.
углова́тый *прил* (*лицо*) angular; (*человек,
движения*) awkward.
углово́й *прил* corner *опред;* (*также:* ~ **уда́р:**
СПОРТ) corner.
углуб|и́ть (**-лю́, -и́шь;** *impf* **углубля́ть**) *сов перех*
to deepen
▸ **углуби́ться** (*impf* **углубля́ться**) *сов возв*
(*также перен*) to deepen; **углубля́ться** (~**ся**
perf) **в** +*acc* (*в книгу, в чтение*) to become
absorbed in; ~**ся** (*perf*) **в воспомина́ния/
мы́сли** to become lost in memories/thought;
~**ся** (*perf*) **в лес** to go deep into the forest.
углубле́ни|е (**-я**) *ср* (*кризиса*) deepening;
(*впадина*) depression.
углублённый (**-ён, -ена́, -ено́**) *прил* profound.
углублю́(сь) *сов см* **углуби́ть(ся)**.
углубля́|ть(ся) (**-ю(сь)**) *несов от*
углуби́ть(ся).
угля́ *итп сущ см* **у́голь**.
угля|де́ть (**-жу́, -ди́шь**) *сов перех* (*разг:
увидеть*) to spot.
угн|а́ть (**угоню́, уго́нишь;** *pt* **-а́л, -ала́, -а́ло,** *impf*
угоня́ть) *сов перех* to drive off; (*разг: украсть*)
to steal; (*самолёт*) to hijack
▸ **угна́ться** *сов возв:* ~**ся за** +*instr* (*также
перен*) to catch up with.
угнета́тел|ь (**-я**) *м* oppressor.
угнета́|ть (**-ю**) *несов перех* (*притеснять*) to
oppress; (*мяготить*) to depress.
угнете́ни|е (**-я**) *ср* (*народа*) oppression.
угнетённост|ь (**-и**) *ж* depression.
угнетённый *прил* (*народ*) oppressed; (*МЕД*)
depressed.
угова́рива|ть (**-ю**) *несов от* **уговори́ть** ♦
перех to try to persuade.
угово́р (**-а**) *м* (*обычно мн: наставление*)
persuasion; (*соглашение*) agreement,
arrangement; **поддава́ться** (**подда́ться** *perf*) **на**
~**ы** to give in to persuasion.
угово|ри́ть (**-ю́, -и́шь;** *impf* **угова́ривать**) *сов
перех* to persuade.
уго́д|а (**-ы**) *ж:* **в** ~**у кому́-н** to please sb.
уго́ден *прил см* **уго́дный**.
уго|ди́ть (**-жу́, -ди́шь;** *impf* **угожда́ть**) *сов
неперех:* ~ +*dat*/**на** +*acc* to please; (*попасть*) to
end up; ~ (*perf*) **под маши́ну** to get run over; ~
(*perf*) **ного́й в я́му** to put one's foot in a hole.
уго́длив|ый (**-, -а, -о**) *прил* obsequious.
уго́дник (**-а**) *м* (*РЕЛ*) saint; **да́мский** ~ ladies'
man.
уго́днича|ть (**-ю**) *несов неперех:* ~ (**пе́ред**

+*instr*) to fawn (on).

угóдно *част*: **что** ~ whatever you like ◆ *как сказ*: **что Вам** ~? what can I do for you?; **кто** ~ anyone; **когдá/какóй** ~ whenever/whichever you like; **скóлько** ~ any amount; **комý** ~ **начáть?** who would like to start?; **возьмúте всё, что Вам** ~ take whatever you like; **от них мóжно ожидáть чегó** ~ they might do anything.

угóд|ный (**-ен, -на, -но**) *прил* (+*dat*; *родúтелям, властя́м*) pleasing to.

угóд|ья (**-ий**) *мн*: **земéльные** ~ arable and pasture land; **лесны́е** ~ forestry; **вóдные** ~ fisheries and waterways.

угождá|ть (**-ю**) *несов от* **угодúть**.

угожý *сов см* **угодúть**.

ýг|ол (**-лá**; *loc sg* **-лý**) *м* (*ГЕОМ*) angle; (*столá, дóма, кóмнаты*) corner; **завора́чивать (заверну́ть** *perf*) **зá угол** to turn the corner; **за углóм** round the corner; **из-за углá** from around the corner; ~ **зрéния** perspective, standpoint; **он снимáет** ~ he's renting a tiny little place.

уголкá *сущ см* **уголóк**.

уголóвник (**-а**) *м* criminal.

уголóвный *прил* criminal *опред*; **уголóвный кóдекс** criminal code; **уголóвный престýпник** criminal; **уголóвный рóзыск** Criminal Investigation Department.

уголóвщин|а (**-ы**) *ж* (*разг*) crime.

уголóк (**-кá**) *м уменьш от* **ýгол**; (*мéсто*) corner; **тúхий** ~ secluded spot.

ýг|оль (**-ля**; *nom pl* **-ли**, *gen pl* **-лéй**) *м* coal.

ýгольник (**-а**) *м* (*чертёжный*) set square.

ýгольный *прил* coal.

угомон|úться (**-ю́сь, -úшься**) *сов возв* (*разг*) to quieten down.

угóн (**-а**) *м* (*самолёта*) hijacking; (*машúны, коня́*) theft.

угóнщик (**-а**) *м* (*самолёта*) hijacker.

угоню́(сь) *итп сов см* **угнáть(ся)**.

угоня́|ть (**-ю**) *несов от* **угнáть**.

угорáзд|ить (*3sg* **-ит**) *сов безл*: ~**ило тебя́ сказáть э́то!** what on earth made you say that?; **как э́то тебя́** ~**ило** how on earth did you manage that?

угорéлый *прил*: **бéгать как** ~ to run around like a mad thing.

угор|éть (**-ю́, -úшь**) *сов неперех* to get gas-poisoning.

ýг|орь (**-ря́**; *nom pl* **-рú**) *м* (*ЗООЛ*) eel; (*на лицé*) blackhead.

уго|стúть (**-щý, -стúшь**; *impf* **угощáть**) *сов перех*: ~ **когó-н чем-н** (*дóма*) to offer sb sth; (*в рестора́не*) to treat sb to sth.

угощá|ться (**-юсь**) *несов возв*: ~**йтесь!** help yourselves!

угощéни|е (**-я**) *ср* (*гостéй*) entertaining; (*вкýсное, изы́сканное*) food.

угощý *сов см* **угостúть**.

угрóб|ить (**-лю, -ишь**) *сов от* **грóбить**.

угрожá|ть (**-ю**) *несов неперех*: ~ **комý-н (чем-н)** to threaten sb (with sth); **емý** ~**ет банкрóтство** he is threatened with bankruptcy.

угрожá|ющий (**-ая, -ее, -ие**) *прил* threatening; (*вид*) menacing.

угрóз|а (**-ы**) *ж* (*обычно мн*) threat.

угрóха|ть (**-ю**) *сов перех* (*разг*: *дéньги*) to blow; (*продýкты*) to use (up).

угрызéни|е (**-я**) *ж*: ~**я сóвести** pangs *мн* of conscience.

угрю́м|ый (**-, -а, -о**) *прил* gloomy.

угря́ *итп сущ см* **ýгорь**.

удáбрива|ть (**-ю**) *несов от* **удóбрить**.

удáв (**-а**) *м* boa constrictor.

удавá|ться (*3sg* **-ётся**, *3pl* **-ю́тся**) *несов от* **удáться**.

удадúмся *итп сов см* **удáться**.

удал|éц (**-ьцá**) *м* (*разг*) hero.

удал|úть (**-ю́, -úшь**; *impf* **удаля́ть**) *сов перех* (*детéй, посторóнних*) to send away, remove; (*игрокá*: *с пóля*) to send off; (*пятнó, зано́зу, óрган*) to remove; (*зуб*) to extract; (*КОМП*) to delete

▸ **удалúться** (*impf* **удаля́ться**) *сов возв* to move away; (*перен*: *от тéмы*) to digress; (*в свою́ кóмнату*) to withdraw.

удалóй *прил* daring.

ýдал|ь (**-и**) *ж* daring.

удальцá *итп сущ см* **удалéц**.

удаля́|ть(ся) (**-ю(сь)**) *несов от* **удалúть(ся)**.

удáр (**-а**) *м* blow; (*ногóй*) kick; (*звук, инсýльт*) stroke; (*пýльса, сéрдца*) beat; ~ **грóма** clap of thunder; **быть** (*impf*) **в** ~**е** (*разг*) to be on the ball; **стáвить (постáвить** *perf*) **когó-н под** ~ to put sb in a vulnerable position; **наносúть (нанестú** *perf*) ~ **комý-н** to deal a blow to sb.

ударéни|е (**-я**) *ср* (*тáкже линг*) stress.

удáр|ить (**-ю, -ишь**; *impf* **ударя́ть**) *сов перех* to hit; (*подлеж*: *часы́*) to strike; (: *морóзы*) to set in; **ударя́ть** (~ *perf*) **когó-н по головé/спинé** to hit sb on the head/back; **ударя́ть** (~ *perf*) **в бараба́н** to beat a drum; ~ (*perf*) **по спекуля́нтам** to crack down on profiteers; **винó** ~**ило емý в гóлову** the wine has gone to his head; ~**ил гром** there was a clap of thunder; **он не** ~**ил лицóм в грязь** he didn't disgrace himself

▸ **удáриться** (*impf* **ударя́ться**) *сов возв* (*натолкнýться на что-н*): ~**ся о** +*acc* (*о дверь, о стéну итп*) against; ~**ся** (*perf*) **в пáнику** to fly into a panic; ~**ся** (*perf*) **в спорт/в наýку/в полúтику** to become obsessed with sport/science/politics; **он** ~**ился головóй о шкаф** he hit his head *или* against the cupboard.

удáрник (**-а**) *м* (*музыкáнт*) percussionist; (*ружья́, пистолéта*) striker, firing pin.

уда́рный *прил* (*инструмент*) percussion *опред*; (*войска, труд*) shock *опред*; (*слог*) stressed; **уда́рная волна́** shock wave.

ударя́|ть(ся) (-ю(сь)) *несов от* уда́рить(ся).

уда́|ться (*как* дать; *см* **Table 14**; *impf* удава́ться) *сов возв* (*получиться: опыт, испытание*) to be successful, work; (*пирог*) to turn out well; **нам удало́сь/не удало́сь поговори́ть/зако́нчить рабо́ту** we managed/didn't manage to talk to one another/finish the work.

уда́ч|а (-и) *ж* (good) luck; **нам вы́пала больша́я ~** we had a great stroke of luck; **жела́ю ~и!** good luck!

уда́чен *прил см* уда́чный.

уда́члив|ый (-, -а, -о) *прил* lucky.

уда́ч|ный (-ен, -на, -но) *прил* successful; (*хороший: выбор, выражение*) good.

удва́ива|ть(ся) (-ю(сь)) *несов от* удво́ить(ся).

удво́ени|е (-я) *ср* doubling.

удво́енный *прил* (*зарплата*) doubled; (*энергия, сила итп*) redoubled.

удво́|ить (-ю, -ишь; *impf* удва́ивать) *сов перех* to double; (*внимание, усилия*) to redouble

▶ удво́иться (*impf* удва́иваться) *сов возв* to double; (*усилия итп*) to be redoubled.

уде́л (-а) *м* (*судьба*) lot, fate.

удел|и́ть (-ю́, -и́шь; *impf* уделя́ть) *сов перех*: **~ что-н кому́-н/чему́-н** to devote sth to sb/sth.

уде́льный *прил*: **~ вес** (*физ*) specific gravity.

уделя́|ть (-ю) *несов от* удели́ть.

у́держ (-у) *м*: **без ~у** uncontrollably; **он не зна́ет ~у в тра́тах** he doesn't know when to stop spending.

уд|ержа́ть (-ержу́, -е́ржишь; *impf* уде́рживать) *сов перех* to restrain; (*часть зарплаты*) to deduct; (*первенство, позиции*): **~ (за собо́й)** to retain; **~** (*perf*) **что-н в рука́х** to hold onto sth, not let go of sth; **уде́рживать** (**~** *perf*) **кого́-н от пое́здки** to keep sb from going on a journey; **уде́рживать** (**~** *perf*) **кого́-н до́ма** to keep sb at home

▶ удержа́ться (*impf* уде́рживаться) *сов возв* (*остановить себя*) to stop *или* restrain o.s.; (*устоять: на краю обрыва*) to hang on; **~ся** (*perf*) **на нога́х** to stay on one's feet; **~ся** (*perf*) **на свои́х пози́циях** to hold one's ground; **~ся** (*perf*) **от сме́ха** to stop *или* keep o.s. from laughing; **~ся** (*perf*) **от слёз** to hold back the tears.

удеру́ *итп сов см* удра́ть.

удесятер|и́ть (-ю́, -и́шь) *сов перех* to increase tenfold; (*усилия*) to triple.

удешев|и́ть (-лю́, -и́шь; *impf* удешевля́ть) *сов перех* to make cheaper

▶ удешеви́ться (*impf* удешевля́ться) *сов возв* to get cheaper.

удешевле́ни|е (-я) *ср*: **~ цен** (**на** +*acc*) reduction in the price of.

удешевлю́(сь) *сов см* удешеви́ть(ся).

удешевля́|ть(ся) (-ю(сь)) *несов от* удешеви́ть(ся).

удиви́телен *прил см* удиви́тельный.

удиви́тельно *нареч* (*красивый, вкусный*) amazingly ♦ *как сказ* it's amazing; **мне ~, что ты э́того не понима́ешь** I'm amazed that you don't understand this; **~, как ты не простуди́лся** it's amazing that you didn't catch (a) cold; **и не ~** and no wonder.

удиви́тельный (-ен, -ьна, -ьно) *прил* amazing.

удив|и́ть (-лю́, -и́шь; *impf* удивля́ть) *сов перех* to surprise

▶ удиви́ться (*impf* удивля́ться) *сов возв*: **~ся** +*dat* (*известию, приезду итп*) to be surprised at *или* by; **я ~и́лся, что он не позвони́л** I was surprised that he didn't phone.

удивле́ни|е (-я) *ср* surprise; **к на́шему ~ю, она́ ушла́** to our surprise she left; **с ~м** with surprise; **от ~я** in surprise; **краси́вый/у́мный на ~** amazingly beautiful/clever.

удивлённый *прил* surprised.

удивлю́(сь) *сов см* удиви́ть(ся).

удивля́|ть(ся) (-ю(сь)) *несов от* удиви́ть(ся).

удила́ (уди́л) *мн* bit *ед* (*of bridle*).

уди́лищ|е (-а) *ср* (*часть удочки*) (fishing-)rod.

удира́|ть (-ю) *несов от* удра́ть.

уди́ть (ужу́, у́дишь) *несов неперех* to angle.

удлине́ни|е (-я) *ср* (*рукава*) lengthening; (*срока*) extension.

удлинённый *прил* (*пальто*) long; (*лицо*) elongated.

удлин|и́ть (-ю́, -и́шь; *impf* удлиня́ть) *сов перех* (*рукав, пальто*) to lengthen; (*рабочий день, срок*) to extend

▶ удлини́ться (*impf* удлиня́ться) *сов возв* to grow longer.

удо́бен *прил см* удо́бный.

удо́бно *нареч* (*усесться, лечь*) comfortably ♦ *как сказ*: **мне здесь ~** I'm comfortable here; **мне ~ прийти́ ве́чером** it's convenient for me to come in the evening.

удо́б|ный (-ен, -на, -но) *прил* (*мебель*) comfortable; (*время, формат, место*) convenient; **дожида́ться** (**дожда́ться** *perf*) **~ного слу́чая** to wait for the right opportunity.

удобре́ни|е (-я) *ср* (*действие*) fertilizing; (*минеральное, химическое*) fertilizer.

удобр|и́ть (-ю, -ишь; *impf* удобря́ть **или** уда́бривать) *сов перех* to fertilize.

удо́бств|о (-а) *ср* comfort; **кварти́ра со все́ми ~ами** a flat with all (modern) conveniences.

удовлетворе́ни|е (-я) *ср* satisfaction; (*требований*) fulfilment.

удовлетворённый *прил* satisfied.

удовлетвори́телен *прил см* удовлетвори́тельный.

удовлетвори́тельно *нареч* satisfactorily; (*ПРОСВЕЩ*) ≈ satisfactory (*school mark*).

удовлетвори́тел|ьный (-ен, -ьна, -ьно) *прил* satisfactory.

удовлетвор|и́ть (-ю́, -и́шь; *impf* удовлетворя́ть) *сов перех* to satisfy;

(*потребности, спрос, просьбу*) to meet;
(*жалобу*) to respond to; **удовлетворя́ть** (~ *perf*)
+*dat* (*требованиям, вкусам, правилам*) to
satisfy

▶ **удовлетвори́ться** (*impf* **удовлетворя́ться**)
сов возв: ~ся +*instr* to be satisfied with.

удово́льстви|**е** (-**я**) *ср* pleasure; **получа́ть**
(**получи́ть** *perf*) ~ **от чего́-н** to enjoy sth;
доставля́ть (**доста́вить** *perf*) ~ **кому́-н** to make
sb happy; **с** ~**м** with pleasure; **я бы с** ~**м пошёл
с Ва́ми** I would love to go with you.

удово́льств|**оваться** (-**уюсь**) *сов от*
дово́льствоваться.

удо́д (-**а**) *м* (*ЗООЛ*) hoopoe.

удо́й (-**я**) *м* yield (*of milk*).

удо́йлив|**ый** (-, -**а**, -**о**) *прил*: ~**ая коро́ва** good
milking cow.

удорожа́ни|**е** (-**я**) *ср*: ~ **проду́ктов пита́ния**
rise in food prices.

удоста́ива|**ть(ся)** (-**ю(сь)**) *несов от*
удосто́ить(ся).

удостовере́ни|**е** (-**я**) *ср* (*подписи*) verification;
(*документ*) identification (card);
удостовере́ние ли́чности identity card.

удостове́р|**ить** (-**ю**, -**ишь**; *impf* **удостоверя́ть**)
сов перех (*факт*) to verify

▶ **удостове́риться** (*impf* **удостоверя́ться**) *сов
возв*: ~**ся в** +*prp* (*в чьей-н невиновности, в
верности сообщения*) to assure o.s. of; **он
~и́лся, что она́ до́ма** he made sure that she was
at home.

удосто́|**ить** (-**ю**, -**ишь**; *impf* **удоста́ивать**) *сов
перех*: ~ **кого́-н чего́-н** to bestow sth on sb;
удоста́ивать (~ *perf*) **кого́-н свои́м визи́том** to
honour (*BRIT*) *или* honor (*US*) sb with a visit; ~
(*perf*) **кого́-н улы́бки** to bestow a smile on sb

▶ **удосто́иться** (*impf* **удоста́иваться**) *сов возв*:
~**ся** +*gen* (*награды*) to be honoured (*BRIT*) *или*
honored (*US*) with.

удосу́ж|**иться** (-**усь**, -**ишься**; *impf*
удосу́живаться) *сов возв*: ~ +*infin* to find time
to do.

у́дочек *сущ см* **у́дочка**.

удочере́ни|**е** (-**я**) *ср* adoption (*of daughter*).

удочер|**и́ть** (-**ю**, -**и́шь**; *impf* **удочеря́ть**) *сов
перех* to adopt (*daughter*).

у́доч|**ка** (-**ки**; *gen pl* -**ек**) *ж* (fishing-)rod; **он
попа́лся на** ~**ку** (*перен*) he fell for it;
заки́дывать (**заки́нуть** *perf*) ~**ку** (*рыболов*) to
cast; (*перен*) to put out feelers.

удр|**а́ть** (**удеру́, удерёшь**; *pt* -**а́л**, -**ала́**, -**а́ло**, *impf*
удира́ть) *сов неперех* (*разг*) to make off.

удруж|**и́ть** (-**у́, -и́шь**) *сов неперех*: ~ **кому́-н** to
do sb a favour (*BRIT*) *или* favor (*US*).

удручённый *прил* (*взгляд, лицо, вид*) dejected;
(-**ён, -ена́, -ено́**; *человек*) dejected, depressed.

уд|**уши́ть** (-**ушу́, -у́шишь**) *сов от* **души́ть** ♦
(*impf* **удуша́ть**) *перех* (*человека*) to strangle;

(*свободу*) to stifle.

уду́шлив|**ый** *прил* (*газ, вещество*) suffocating;
(*жара*) stifling.

уду́шь|**е** (-**я**) *ср* (*no pl*) suffocation.

ужу́ *несов см* **уди́ть**.

уе́дешь *итп сов см* **уе́хать**.

уедине́ни|**е** (-**я**) *ср* solitude.

уединён|**ный** (-, -**на**, -**но**) *прил* (*место, остров*)
solitary.

уедин|**и́ться** (-**ю́сь, -и́шься**; *impf* **уединя́ться**)
сов возв to go off, withdraw.

уе́ду *итп сов см* **уе́хать**.

уе́зд (-**а**) *м* (*ИСТ*) uezd (*administrative division in
pre-Revolutionary Russia*).

уезжа́й(те) *сов см* **уе́хать**.

уезжа́|**ть** (-**ю**) *несов от* **уе́хать**.

УЕФА́ *м сокр* (= Европе́йский сою́з футбо́льных
ассоциа́ций) UEFA (= *Union of European
Football Associations*).

уе́ха|**ть** (*как* **е́хать**; *см* **Table 19**; *impf* **уезжа́ть**)
сов неперех to leave, go away; **он ~л в
о́тпуск/в Москву́** he has gone on holiday/to
Moscow; **мы ско́ро уезжа́ем** we are leaving
soon.

уж (-**а́**) *м* (*ЗООЛ*) grass snake ♦ *нареч* (*уже*)
already ♦ *част* (*выражает усиление*): **здесь не
так** ~ **пло́хо** it's not as bad as all that here; **э́то
~ о́чень до́рого** it really is too expensive.

ужа́л|**ить** (-**ю**, -**ишь**) *сов от* **жа́лить**.

у́жас (-**а**) *м* horror; (*страх*) terror ♦ *как сказ*
(*разг*): (**э́то**) ~! it's awful *или* terrible! ♦ *нареч*:
он ~ **како́й бога́тый** (*разг*) he's incredibly rich;
~**ы войны́** horrors of war; **прийти́** (*perf*) **в** ~ **от
чего́-н** to be horrified by sth; **к моему́** ~**у** to my
horror; **он дрожа́л от** ~**а** he was shaking in
terror; ~ **как бы́стро вре́мя идёт** it's awful *или*
terrible how time flies; **ти́хий** ~! (*разг*) horror of
horrors!; **до** ~**а** (*разг*) terribly.

ужасн|**у́ть** (-**у́, -ёшь**; *impf* **ужаса́ть**) *сов перех* to
horrify

▶ **ужасну́ться** (*impf* **ужаса́ться**) *сов возв* to be
horrified.

ужаса́ющий (-**ая, -ее, -ие**) *прил* (*крик,
зрелище*) horrific; (*запах, холод*) terrible.

ужа́сен *прил см* **ужа́сный**.

ужа́сно *нареч* (*разг*: умный, красивый итп)
terribly ♦ *как сказ*: **здесь сейча́с** ~ it's terrible
here now; **он чу́вствует себя́** ~ he feels
terrible.

ужа́с|**ный** (-**ен, -на, -но**) *прил* terrible, horrible,
awful.

у́же *сравн прил от* **у́зкий**.

уже́ *нареч, част* already; **мы не ви́делись** ~ **3
го́да** it's now 3 years since we've seen each
other; **ты же** ~ **не ма́ленький** you're not a child
any more; ~ **по э́тому мо́жно суди́ть, что ...**
one can judge from this alone that ....

ужива́|**ться** (-**юсь**) *несов от* **ужи́ться**.

уживу́сь *итп сов см* **ужи́ться**.

ужи́вчив|ый (-, -а, -о) *прил* (*человек*) easy to get along with.

ужи́м|ка (-ки; *gen pl* -ок) *ж* (*обычно мн*) grimace.

у́жин (-а) *м* supper.

у́жина|ть (-ю; *perf* **поу́жинать**) *несов неперех* to have supper.

ужи́ться (-ву́сь, -вёшься; *pt* -лся, -ла́сь, -ло́сь, *impf* **ужива́ться**) *сов возв*: ~ **с кем-н** to get on with sb.

узако́ненный *прил* (*порядок, ритуал*) established.

узако́н|ить (-ю, -ишь; *impf* **узако́нивать**) *сов перех* (*отношения, порядок*) to legalize.

узбе́к (-а) *м* Uzbek.

Узбекиста́н (-а) *м* Uzbekistan.

узбе́кск|ий (-ая, -ое, -ие) *прил* Uzbek; ~ **язы́к** Uzbek.

узбе́ч|ка (-ки; *gen pl* -ек) *ж см* **узбе́к**.

узда́ (-ы́; *nom pl* -ы) *ж* bridle; **держа́ть** (*impf*) **кого́-н в** ~**е́** to keep sb in check.

узде́чк|а (-и) *ж* = **узда́**.

уздцы́: **под** ~ by the bridle.

у́з|ел (-ла́) *м* knot; (*мешок*) bundle; **телефо́нный** ~ telephone exchange; **железнодоро́жный** ~ railway junction; **санита́рный** ~ bathroom and toilet; **морско́й** ~ hitch; **не́рвный** ~ ganglion; ~ **противоре́чий** a mass of contradictions.

у́з|кий (-кая, -кое, -кие; -ок, -ка́, -ко) *прил* narrow; (*тесный*) tight; (*перен: человек, взгляд*) narrow-minded; ~ **кая специа́льность** narrow specialism; ~ **круг друзе́й** small circle of friends.

узкоколе́йн|ый *прил*: ~**ая желе́зная доро́га** narrow-gauge railway.

узколо́бый *прил* (*перен*) narrow-minded.

узла́ *итп сущ см* **у́зел**.

узлова́т|ый (-, -а, -о) *прил* knotty.

узлово́й *прил* (*перен: вопрос, задачи*) key; ~**а́я ста́нция** junction.

узна́|ть (-ю; *impf* **узнава́ть**) *сов перех* (*знакомого, свою вещь итп*) to recognize; (*новости*) to find out, learn; (*познать: нужду, любовь*) to know; **я** ~**л, что ты прие́хал** I heard that you had come; **он** ~**л о состоя́нии дел** he found out how things stood.

у́зник (-а) *м* captive.

у́зок *прил см* **у́зкий**.

узо́р (-а) *м* pattern.

узо́рный *прил* = **узо́рчатый**.

узо́рчатый *прил* patterned.

у́зост|ь (-и) *ж* (*улиц, взглядов*) narrowness; (*платья*) tightness; (*человека*) narrow-mindedness.

узурпа́тор (-а) *м* usurper.

узурпи́р|овать (-ую) (*не*)*сов перех* to usurp.

у́зы (-) *мн* (*перен*) bonds *мн*.

уйду́ *итп сов см* **уйти́**.

у́йм|а (-ы) *ж* (*разг*): ~ **де́нег/вре́мени** heaps *или* loads of money/time.

уйму(сь) *итп сов см* **уня́ть(ся)**.

уйти́ (*как* **идти́**; *см* **Table 18**; *impf* **уходи́ть**) *сов неперех* (*человек*) to go away, leave; (*пароход, поезд*) to go, leave; (*молодость*) to go; (*время, годы*) to pass; (*отдаться*): ~ **в** +*acc* (*в бизнес*) to go into; (*избежать*): ~ **от** +*gen* (*от опасности итп*) to get away from; (*потребоваться*): ~ **на** +*acc* (*деньги, время*) to be spent on; **уходи́ть** (~ *perf*) **из до́ма** to leave the house; **уходи́ть** (~ *perf*) **со слу́жбы/со сце́ны** to leave one's job/the stage; **уходи́ть** (~ *perf*) **от му́жа** to leave one's husband; **уходи́ть** (~ *perf*) **из жи́зни** to pass away; **уходи́ть** (~ *perf*) **на пе́нсию** to retire; **у нас ушло́ мно́го де́нег на поку́пки** we spent a lot of money on shopping.

укажу́ *итп сов см* **указа́ть**.

ука́з (-а) *м* (*президента*) decree; **он мне не** ~ (*разг*) I don't take orders from him.

указа́ни|е (-я) *ср* pointing out, indication; (*разъяснение*) instruction; (: *начальства*) directive; ~**я врача́** doctor's orders.

указа́тел|ь (-я) *м* (*дорожный*) sign; (*книга*) guide; (*список в книге*) index; (*прибор*) indicator.

указа́тельный *прил* (*жест*) pointing; **указа́тельное местоиме́ние** demonstrative pronoun; **указа́тельный па́лец** index finger.

ук|аза́ть (-ажу́, -а́жешь; *impf* **ука́зывать**) *сов перех* to point out; (*дорогу*) to show; (*свой адрес, интересы, срок*) to indicate; (*движением, жестом*): ~ **на** +*acc* (*на дверь, на карти́ну итп*) to point to; (*на ошибки, на недоста́тки*) to point out; ~ (*perf*) **кому́-н на дверь** (*перен*) to show sb the door.

ука́з|ка (-ки; *gen pl* -ок) *ж* pointer; **де́лать** (**сде́лать** *perf*) **что́-нибудь по чужо́й** ~**ке** to blindly follow somebody else's directions.

ука́зыва|ть (-ю) *несов от* **указа́ть** ◆ *неперех* (*свидетельствовать*): ~ **на** +*acc* (*факты, цифры*) to indicate, point to.

ука́лыва|ть (-ю) *несов от* **уколо́ть**.

ука|та́ть (-ю; *impf* **ука́тывать**) *сов перех* (*дорогу*) to roll, flatten.

ук|ати́ть (-ачу́, -а́тишь) *сов перех* (*мяч*) to roll away; (*тачку*) to wheel away ◆ *неперех* (*разг*) *уехать*) to go off.

ука́тыва|ть (-ю) *несов от* **уката́ть**.

укача́|ть (-ю; *impf* **ука́чивать**) *сов перех* (*усыпить: ребёнка*) to rock to sleep; (*довести до тошноты*): **его́** ~**ло (в маши́не/на парохо́де)** he got (car-/sea-)sick.

укачу́ *сов см* **укати́ть**.

укла́д (-а) *м* (*экон: капиталисти́ческий, феода́льный*) order; ~ **жи́зни** way of life.

укла́д|ка (-и) *ж* (*действие: дров, рельс*) laying; (*причёска*) set.

укла́дчик (-а) *м* (*путей, парке́та*) layer.

укла́дывани|е (-я) *ср* (*вещей, чемода́на*) packing; (*ребёнка*) putting to bed.

укла́дыва|ть (-ю) *несов от* **уложи́ть**

► **укла́дываться** *несов от* **уложи́ться**,

улéчься ♦ *возв*: э́то не ~ется в обы́чные ра́мки this is out of the ordinary; э́то не ~ется в головé *или* в созна́нии it's beyond me.

уклóн (-а) *м* (*также перен*) slant; **пóезд/дорóга идёт под** ~ the train/road is going downhill.

уклонéни|е (-я) *ср* (*дороги в сторону*) bending; (*от ответа, от обязанностей*) evasion.

укл|они́ться (-оню́сь, -óнишься; *impf* **уклоня́ться**) *сов возв* (*отстрани́ться: в сторону*) to swerve; (*отойти от главного*): ~ **от** +*gen* to dodge; (*от темы, от предмета*) to digress from; (*от поручения*) to evade; **уклоня́ться** (~ *perf*) **от отвéта** to avoid giving an answer.

уклóнчив|ый (-, -а, -о) *прил* (*ответ*) evasive.

уклоня́|ться (-юсь) *несов от* **уклони́ться**.

уключин|а (-ы) *ж* rowlock.

укóл (-а) *м* (*иголкой*) prick; (*перен: замечание*) dig; (*МЕД*) injection; **дéлать** (**сдéлать** *perf*) **комý-н** ~ to give sb an injection; ~ **самолю́бию** blow to one's ego.

ук|олóть (-олю́, -óлешь) *сов от* **колóть** ♦ (*impf* **ука́лывать**) *перех* (*иглой, шипом*) to prick; (*перен: самолю́бие*) to wound

▶ **уколóться** *сов от* **колóться**.

укомплектóванный *прил* complete.

укомплект|ова́ть (-у́ю) *сов от* **комплектова́ть**.

укóр (-а) *м* (*упрёк*) reproach; ~**ы сóвести** the pangs of conscience; **живóй** ~ living indictment of sb; **ста́вить** (**поста́вить** *perf*) **комý-н что-н в** ~ to reproach sb with sth.

укора́чива|ть(ся) (-ю(сь)) *несов от* **укороти́ть(ся)**.

укоренéни|е (-я) *ср* taking root, establishment.

укорен|и́ть (-ю́, -и́шь; *impf* **укореня́ть**) *сов перех* (*рассаду*) to allow to take root.

укорен|и́ться (*3sg* -и́тся, *3pl* -я́тся, *impf* **укореня́ться**) *сов возв* (*также перен*) to take root.

укори́зн|а (-ы) *ж* (*укор*) reproach.

укори́зненно *нареч* reproachfully.

укори́зненн|ый (-, -на, -но) *прил* reproachful.

укор|и́ть (-ю́, -и́шь; *impf* **укоря́ть**) *сов перех* to reproach.

укоро|ти́ть (-чý, -ти́шь; *impf* **укора́чивать**) *сов перех* (*платье, палку, путь*) to shorten; (*жизнь, сроки*) to reduce; ~ (*perf*) **рýки комý-н** (*перен*) to take sb down a peg

▶ **укороти́ться** (*impf* **укора́чиваться**) *сов возв* (*юбка итп*) to be shortened; (*сроки*) to be reduced.

укорóченный *прил* (*пальто, юбка*) short; (*рабочий день*) reduced.

укорочý(сь) *сов см* **укороти́ть(ся)**.

укоря́|ть (-ю) *несов от* **укори́ть**.

укоря́ющий (-ая, -ее, -ие) *прил* (*взгляд*) reproachful.

укра́дкой *нареч* secretly.

украдý *итп сов см* **укра́сть**.

Украи́н|а (-ы) *ж* (the) Ukraine.

украи́н|ец (-ца) *м* Ukrainian.

украи́н|ка (-ки; *gen pl* -ок) *ж см* **украи́нец**.

украи́нск|ий (-ая, -ое, -ие) *прил* Ukrainian; ~ **язы́к** Ukrainian.

украи́нца *итп сущ см* **украи́нец**.

укра́|сить (-шу, -сишь; *impf* **украша́ть**) *сов перех* (*комнату*) to decorate; (*ёлку*) to decorate (*BRIT*), trim (*US*); (*речь*) to embellish; (*существование, жизнь итп*) to brighten

▶ **украси́ться** (*impf* **украша́ться**) *сов возв*: ~**ся** +*instr* (*деревья, поля*) to be decorated with (*fig*); (*жизнь, существование*) to be brightened up by.

укра́сть (-дý, -дёшь) *сов от* **красть**.

украша́|ть (-ю) *несов от* **укра́сить** ♦ *перех*: **такóе поведéние тебя́ не** ~**ет** that kind of behaviour doesn't suit you

▶ **украша́ться** *несов от* **украси́ться**.

украшéни|е (-я) *ср* decoration; (*коллектива*) pride; (*коллекции*) jewel; (*также*: **ювели́рное** ~) jewellery (*BRIT*), jewelry (*US*).

укра́шу(сь) *сов см* **укра́сить(ся)**.

укреп|и́ть (-лю́, -и́шь; *impf* **укрепля́ть**) *сов перех* (*мир, семью, организм*) to strengthen; (*стену, строение*) to reinforce; (*город, перевал*) to fortify; **укрепля́ть** (~ *perf*) **здорóвье** to get fit(ter)

▶ **укрепи́ться** (*impf* **укрепля́ться**) *сов возв* (*нервы, организм*) to become stronger; (*хозяйство, авторитет*) to become established; (*здоровье*) to improve; (*дисциплина*) to be tightened up; ~ **в свои́х убеждéниях** to become surer of one's convictions; **за ним ~и́лась дурна́я репута́ция** he has earned a bad reputation.

укреплéни|е (-я) *ср* (*здоровья*) improving; (*авторитета*) reinforcement; (*ВОЕН: обычно мн*) fortification.

укреплю́(сь) *сов см* **укрепи́ть(ся)**.

укрепля́|ть(ся) (-ю(сь)) *несов от* **укрепи́ть(ся)**.

укрепля́ющий (-ая, -ее, -ие) *прил* fortifying.

укрóмный *прил* (*уголок*) secluded.

укрóп (-а) *м, собир* dill.

укрóпный *прил* dill; **укрóпная вода́** (*МЕД*) gripe water.

укроти́тел|ь (-я) *м* tamer; ~ **львов** lion-tamer.

укроти́тельниц|а (-ы) *ж см* **укроти́тель**.

укро|ти́ть (-щý, -ти́шь; *impf* **укроща́ть**) *сов перех* (*животного, гнев, страсти*) to tame; (*человека*) to bring to heel.

укрощéни|е (-я) *ср* (*действие*) taming.

укрощý *сов см* **укроти́ть**.

укрóю(сь) *итп сов см* **укры́ть(ся)**.

укрупнéни|е (-я) *ср* enlargement.

укрупн|и́ть (-ю́, -и́шь; *impf* **укрупня́ть**) *сов*

перех to enlarge
▶ **укрупни́ться** (*impf* **укрупня́ться**) *сов возв*
(*завод, производство*) to get larger; (*черты
лица*) to grow more pronounced.
укрыва́тельств|о (-а) *ср* (*преступника итп*)
harbouring.
укрыва́ть(ся) (-ю(сь)) *несов от* **укры́ть(ся)**.
укры́ти|е (-я) *ср* (*место: подземное, от бомб*)
shelter.
укры́|ть (-о́ю, -о́ешь; *impf* **укрыва́ть**) *сов перех*
(*закрыть: платком, снегом*) to cover;
(*спрятать: преступника*) to harbour;
(*: беженца*) to shelter
▶ **укры́ться** (*impf* **укрыва́ться**) *сов возв*
(*одеялом, платком*) to cover o.s.; (*от
обстрела, от дождя*) to take cover; (*от
погони*) to hide; **от моего́ взгля́да не ~́ылось,
что ...** it has not escaped my notice that ....
у́ксус (-а) *м* vinegar.
у́ксусный *прил* (*запах, эссенция*) vinegar
опред; **у́ксусная кислота́** acetic acid.
уку́с (-а) *м* bite.
укуси́ть (-ушу́, -у́сишь) *сов перех* to bite.
уку́та|ть (-ю; *impf* **уку́тывать**) *сов перех*
(*больного, шею итп*) to wrap up
▶ **уку́таться** (*impf* **уку́тываться**) *сов возв* to
wrap o.s. up.
укушу́ *сов см* **укуси́ть**.
ул. *сокр* (= *у́лица*) St (= *street*).
ула́влива|ть (-ю) *несов от* **улови́ть**.
ула́|дить (-жу, -дишь; *impf* **ула́живать**) *сов
перех* to settle
▶ **ула́диться** (*impf* **ула́живаться**) *сов возв* to
sort o.s. out.
ула́живани|е (-я) *ср* (*ссоры, конфликта*)
settling.
ула́жива|ть(ся) (-ю(сь)) *несов от*
ула́дить(ся).
ула́жу(сь) *сов см* **ула́дить(ся)**.
ула́мыва|ть (-ю) *несов от* **уломать**.
ула́н (-а) *м* (*ИСТ*) uhlan (*lancer*).
Ула́н-Ба́тор (-а) *м* Ulan Bator.
улёгся *итп сов см* **уле́чься**.
у́л|ей (-ья) *м* (bee-)hive.
улете́|ть (-чу́, -ти́шь; *impf* **улета́ть**) *сов неперех*
(*птица*) to fly away; (*самолёт*) to leave;
(*перен: стремительно уйти*) to fly off.
улету́чи|ться (-усь, -ишься; *impf*
улету́чиваться) *сов возв* (*также перен*) to
evaporate; (*перен: разг*) to vanish.
улечу́ *сов см* **улете́ть**.
уле́|чься (-гусь, -я́жешься итп, -я́гутся; *pt*
-ёгся, -егла́сь, -егло́сь, *impf* **укла́дываться**)
сов возв to lie down; (*по impf; пыль*) to settle;
(*перен: буря, страсти, гнев*) to subside.
ули́к|а (-и) *ж* (piece) of evidence (*мн* evidence);
ко́свенная/пряма́я ~ circumstantial/hard
evidence.
ули́т|ка (-ки; *gen pl* -ок) *ж* snail.

у́лиц|а (-ы) *ж* (*в городе, в селе*) street; (*перен:
некультурная среда*) the gutter; **на ~е** outside;
остава́ться (оста́ться *perf*) **на ~е** to be out on
the street; **выбра́сывать (вы́бросить** *perf*) **на
~у** (*выселить*) to throw sb out onto the streets.
уличи́ть (-у́, -и́шь; *impf* **улича́ть**) *сов перех*: ~
кого́-н в чём-н to face sb with sth.
у́личный *прил* street *опред*; **у́личное движе́ние**
traffic.
уло́в (-а) *м* catch (*of fish*).
улови́мый (-, -а, -о) *прил*: **едва́** *или* **чуть** *или*
е́ле ~ barely perceptible.
уло́в|ить (-овлю́, -о́вишь; *impf* **ула́вливать**)
сов перех (*звуки, шум, запах*) to catch, detect;
(*перен: мысль, связь*) to catch, grasp;
ула́вливать (~ *perf*) **(подходя́щий) моме́нт** to
find the right moment.
уло́в|ка (-ки; *gen pl* -ок) *ж* ruse.
уловлю́ *сов см* **улови́ть**.
уло́вок *сущ см* **уло́вка**.
уло́ж|ить (-о́жу, -о́жишь; *impf* **укла́дывать**) *сов
перех* (*ребёнка*) to put to bed; (*вещи, чемодан*)
to pack; (*волосы*) to set; (*шпалы, рельсы*) to
lay; (*бельё*) to fold away; (*по impf; разг*): ~
кого́-н на ме́сте to kill sb; **хозя́йка ~ожи́ла
нас в гости́ной** our hostess put us (up) in the
living room
▶ **уложи́ться** (*impf* **укла́дываться**) *сов возв*
(*сложить вещи*) to pack; **укла́дываться (~ся**
perf) **в сро́ки** to keep to the deadline; **~ся** (*perf*) **в
получаса́** to keep it down to half an hour.
уломá|ть (-ю; *impf* **улáмывать**) *сов перех*
(*разг*): ~ **кого́-н** to talk sb round; **улáмывать
(~** *perf*) **кого́-н** +*infin* to talk sb into doing.
у́ло́ч|ка (-ки; *gen pl* -ек) *ж* lane.
улучш|и́ть (-у́, -и́шь; *impf* **улучáть**) *сов перех*
(*момент, полчаса*) to find.
улучшá|ть (-ю) *несов от* **улу́чшить**.
улучше́ни|е (-я) *ср* improvement.
улу́чш|ить (-у, -ишь; *impf* **улучшáть**) *сов перех*
to improve.
улыбá|ться (-юсь; *perf* **улыбну́ться**) *несов
возв*: ~ +*dat* to smile at; (*перен: счастье,
жизнь*) to smile on; **мне не ~ется э́та
рабо́та/пое́здка** this work/trip doesn't appeal to
me.
улы́б|ка (-ки; *gen pl* -ок) *ж* smile.
улыбн|у́ться (-у́сь, -ёшься) *сов от*
улыбáться.
улы́бок *сущ см* **улы́бка**.
улы́бчив|ый (-, -а, -о) *прил* smiley.
ультимáтум (-а) *м* ultimatum; **предъявля́ть
(предъяви́ть** *perf*) **кому́-н ~** to give sb an
ultimatum.
ультразву́к (-а) *м* ultrasound.
ультразвуково́й *прил* ultrasonic.
ультрамари́н (-а) *м* ultramarine.
ультрафиоле́тов|ый *прил*: ~**ые лучи́**
ultraviolet rays *мн*.
у́лья *итп сущ см* **у́лей**.
улюлю́ка|ть (-ю) *несов неперех* to halloo;

(перен) to hoot (*in derision*).

уля́гусь итп сов см **уле́чься**.

ум (-á) м mind; **быть** (*impf*) **без ~á от
кого́-н/чего́-н** to be wild about sb/sth; **в ~é**
(*считать, держать*) in one's head; **в своём ~é**
in one's right mind; **бра́ться (взя́ться** *perf*) **за ~**
to see sense; **сходи́ть (сойти́** *perf*) **с ~á** to go
mad; **своди́ть (свести́** *perf*) **кого́-н с ~á** to drive
sb mad; (*перен: увлечь*) to drive sb wild;
приро́дный ~ native wit; **~á не приложу́,
куда́/ско́лько/кто** ... I can't think where/how
much/who ...; **с ~óм** (*рассуди́тельно*) sensibly;
приходи́ть (прийти́ *perf*) **на ~ кому́-н** to come
into sb's head.

умал|и́ть (-ю́, -и́шь; *impf* **умаля́ть**) *сов перех*
(*значение, роль*) to diminish, belittle.

умалишённый *прил* insane.

умаля́|ть (-ю) *несов от* **умали́ть**.

ума́|яться (-юсь) *сов от* **ма́яться**.

уме́л|ец (-ьца) м skilled artisan.

уме́ло *нареч* skilfully (*BRIT*), skillfully (*US*).

уме́л|ый (-, -а, -о) *прил* (*рука, ремесленник,
политик*) skilful (*BRIT*), skillful (*US*);
(*работник*) able.

уме́льца итп *сущ см* **уме́лец**.

умён *прил см* **у́мный**.

уме́ни|е (-я) *ср* ability, skill; **с ~м** (*делать
что-н*) with skill.

уменьша́|ть(ся) (-ю(сь)) *несов от*
уме́ньшить(ся).

уменьше́ни|е (-я) *ж* reduction.

уменьши́тельный *прил* (*суффикс*)
diminutive.

уме́ньш|ить (-у, -ишь; *impf* **уменьша́ть**) *сов
перех* to reduce; **~** (*perf*) **шаг** to slow down

▶ **уме́ньшиться** (*impf* **уменьша́ться**) *сов возв*
(*объём, опасность*) to diminish, decrease.

уме́ренност|ь (-и) *ж* moderateness; (*климата*)
temperate nature.

уме́рен|ный (-, -на, -но) *прил* (*аппетит,
скорость, политика*) moderate; (*no short form*;
климат, характер) temperate.

умере́|ть (-ру́, -рёшь; *pt* -ер, -ерла́, -ерло, *impf*
умира́ть) *сов неперех* to die; (*традиция*) to die
out; **хоть ~ри́, но сде́лай** (*разг*) I'll do it if it
kills me; **~** (*perf*) **от го́лода/ра́ка** to die of
hunger/cancer; **со́ сме́ху ~ мо́жно** (*разг*) I
could die laughing.

уме́р|ить (-ю, -ишь; *impf* **умеря́ть**) *сов перех*
(*требования, желания*) to moderate; (*гнев*) to
restrain.

умер|тви́ть (-щвлю́, -тви́шь; *impf*
умерщвля́ть) *сов перех* (*также перен*) to kill.

умерщвле́ни|е (-я) *ср* killing.

умерщвлю́ итп *сов см* **умертви́ть**.

умерщвля́|ть (-ю) *несов от* **умертви́ть**.

умеря́|ть (-ю) *несов от* **уме́рить**.

уме|сти́ть (-щу́, -сти́шь; *impf* **умеща́ть**) *сов
перех* to fit, find room for

▶ **умести́ться** (*impf* **умеща́ться**) *сов возв* to fit;
мы все уме́стимся в маши́ну there's room for
all of us in the car; **мои́ ве́щи не ~ща́ются в
чемода́н** my things won't fit in my suitcase.

уме́|ть (-ю) *несов неперех* can, to be able to;
(*иметь способность*) to know how to; **он ~ет
пла́вать/чита́ть** he can swim/read; **Мари́я ~ет
хорошо́ одева́ться** Maria knows how to dress
well.

умеща́|ть(ся) (-ю(сь)) *несов от* **умести́ть(ся)**.

умещу́(сь) *сов см* **умести́ть(ся)**.

уме́ючи *нареч* (*разг*): **э́то на́до де́лать ~** you
need to have the knack (to do this).

умиле́ни|е (-я) *ср* tenderness; **слёзы ~я** fond
tears.

умили́тел|ьный (-ен, -ьна, -ьно) *прил*
touching.

умил|и́ть (-ю́, -и́шь; *impf* **умиля́ть**) *сов перех* to
touch

▶ **умили́ться** (*impf* **умиля́ться**) *сов возв* to be
touched.

уми́льный *прил* (*нежный*) touching;
(*льстивый*) smarmy.

умиля́|ть(ся) (-ю(сь)) *несов от* **умили́ть(ся)**.

умина́|ть (-ю) *несов от* **умя́ть**.

умира́ни|е (-я) *ср* dying.

умира́|ть (-ю) *несов от* **умере́ть** ◆ *неперех*
(*перен*): **~ю, как хочу́ есть/спать** I'm dying
for something to eat/to go to sleep; **я ~ю от
ску́ки** I'm bored to death.

умиротворе́ни|е (-я) *ср* (*сердца, души*)
bringing of peace; (*агрессора*) appeasement.

умиротворённый *прил* serene, tranquil.

умиротвор|и́ть (-ю́, -и́шь; *impf* **умиротворя́ть**)
сов перех (*душу*) to bring peace to;
(*враждующих*) to pacify; (*агрессора*) to appease

▶ **умиротвори́ться** (*impf* **умиротворя́ться**)
сов возв (*враждующие, спорщики итп*) to be
pacified.

умне́|ть (-ю; *perf* **поумне́ть**) *несов неперех*
(*человек*) to grow wiser; (*ребёнок*) to become
more intelligent; **э́то помо́жет тебе́ поумне́ть**
(*перен*) that'll teach you a lesson.

у́мник (-а) м clever boy; (*пренебр: умничающий*)
clever dick, knowall.

у́мниц|а (-ы) *ж* clever girl ♦ *м/ж* (*разг*): **вот ~!**
good for you!, well done!; **он ~** he's a clever
one.

у́мнича|ть (-ю) *несов неперех* (*разг: пренебр*)
to show off how clever one is, be clever;
(*своевольничать*) to try to be clever.

у́мно *нареч* (*вести себя*) sensibly; (*говорить*)
intelligently.

умножа́|ть (-ю) *несов от* **умно́жить**.

умноже́ни|е (-я) *ср* (*см глаг*) multiplication;
increase; **табли́ца ~я** (*МАТ*) multiplication table.

умно́ж|ить (-у, -ишь; *impf* **мно́жить** *или* **умножа́ть**) *сов перех* (МАТ) to multiply; (*дохо́ды, о́пыт, сла́ву итп*) to increase; **умножа́ть** (~ *perf*) **пять на́ два** to multiply five by two

▶ **умно́житься** *сов от* **мно́житься**.

умну́ *итп сов см* **умя́ть**.

у́мн|ый (-ён, -на́, -но́ *или* -но) *прил* (*челове́к*) clever, intelligent; (*лицо́*) intelligent; (*соба́ка, маши́на, прибо́р*) clever; (*ре́чи, сове́т, поли́тика*) sensible.

умозаключе́ни|е (-я) *ср* (*вы́вод*) deduction.

умозри́тел|ьный (-ен, -ьна, -ьно) *прил* (*построе́ние, рассужде́ния*) speculative.

умол|и́ть (-ю́, -и́шь; *impf* **умоля́ть**) *сов перех:* ~ **кого́-н** (+*infin*) to prevail upon sb (to do) (*by pleading*).

у́молк *м:* **без** ~**у** incessantly.

умо́лкн|уть (-у, -ешь; *impf* **умолка́ть**) *сов непере́х* (*го́лос, скри́пка*) to fall silent; (*смех, звон*) to stop.

умолча́ни|е (-я) *ср* (*фа́ктов*) supression, hushing up.

умолч|а́ть (-у́, -и́шь; *impf* **ума́лчивать**) *сов непере́х:* ~ **о чём-н** (*о преступле́нии, о недоста́тках итп*) to keep quiet about sth.

умол|я́ть (-ю) *несов от* **умоли́ть** ♦ *перех* to implore.

умоля́ющий (-ая, -ее, -ие) *прил* (*взгляд, го́лос*) pleading.

умонастрое́ни|е (-я) *ср* frame of mind.

умопомеша́тельств|о (-а) *ср* insanity.

умопомраче́ни|е (-я) *ср* temporary loss of one's senses; **до** ~**я** (*уста́ть*) terribly; (*люби́ть, влюби́ться*) madly; **рабо́тать** (*impf*)/**танцева́ть** (*impf*) **до** ~**я** to work/dance until one is ready to drop.

умопомрачи́тел|ьный (-ен, -ьна, -ьно) *прил* (*разг: красота́, бога́тство*) staggering.

умо́ра *ж нескл:* **э́то про́сто** ~ (*разг*) it's hilarious.

умори́тел|ьный (-ен, -ьна, -ьно) *прил* (*разг*) hilarious.

умор|и́ть (-ю́, -и́шь) *сов от* **мори́ть**.

умота́|ть (-ю) *сов от* **мота́ть**.

умру́ *итп сов см* **умере́ть**.

умо́ю(сь) *сов см* **умы́ть(ся)**.

у́мственно *нареч:* ~ **отста́лый** mentally retarded.

у́мственный *прил* (*спосо́бности*) mental; ~ **труд** brainwork.

умудрённый (-ён, -ена́, -ено́) *прил:* ~ **о́пытом/года́ми** wise from experience/with age.

умудр|и́ться (-ю́сь, -и́шься; *impf* **умудря́ться**) *сов возв* (*разг*) to manage; **я** ~**и́лся простуди́ться/опозда́ть на по́езд** I managed to catch a cold/miss the train.

умч|а́ть (-у́, -и́шь) *сов перех* to whisk off *или* away

▶ **умча́ться** *сов возв* (*ко́ни, вса́дники, де́ти*) to

dash off; (*го́ды, де́тство*) to fly by.

умыва́льник (-а) *м* washstand.

умыва́льн|ый *прил:* ~**ые принадле́жности** washing things *мн*.

умыва́ни|е (-я) *ср* washing.

умыва́|ть(ся) (-ю(сь)) *несов от* **умы́ть(ся)**.

умы́кн|уть (-у́, -ёшь; *impf* **умыка́ть**) *сов перех* (*разг: укра́сть*) to nick; (*неве́сту*) to abduct (*as part of wedding ritual*).

у́мыс|ел (-ла) *м* intent; **де́лать** (**сде́лать** *perf*) **что-н без** ~**ла/с у́мыслом** to do sth without/with intent.

умы́|ть (умо́ю, умо́ешь; *impf* **умыва́ть**) *сов перех* to wash

▶ **умы́ться** (*impf* **умыва́ться**) *сов возв* to wash.

умы́шленно *нареч* deliberately, intentionally.

умы́шленност|ь (-и) *ж* (*посту́пка*) deliberateness; (*преступле́ния*) premeditated nature.

умы́шлен|ный (-, -на, -но) *прил* (*посту́пок*) deliberate, intentional; (*преступле́ние, уби́йство*) premeditated.

умя́|ть (-ну́, -нёшь; *impf* **умина́ть**) *сов перех* (*снег, зе́млю*) to flatten; (*разг: съесть мно́го*) to stuff down.

унаво́зить (-жу, -зишь) *сов от* **наво́зить**.

унасле́д|овать (-ую) *сов от* **насле́довать**.

ун|ести́ (-есу́, -есёшь; *pt* -ёс, -есла́, -есло́, *impf* **уноси́ть**) *сов перех* to take away; (*разг: укра́сть*) to carry off; (*подлеж: война́, эпиде́мия*) to claim; **ло́дку** ~**есло́ тече́нием** the boat drifted away; **бума́ги** ~**есло́ ве́тром** the papers blew away

▶ **унести́сь** (*impf* **уноси́ться**) *сов возв* (*ту́чи, ко́ни, по́езд*) to speed off; **его́ мы́сли** ~**если́сь в про́шлое** his thoughts flashed back to the past; **он** ~**ёсся в мир фанта́зий** he was carried into the world of fantasy.

универма́г (-а) *м* (= **универса́льный магази́н**) department store.

универса́л (-а) *м* all-rounder.

универса́льност|ь (-и) *ж* (*зна́ний*) breadth; (*средств*) universality.

универса́льн|ый *прил* (*пробле́ма*) universal; (*образова́ние*) all-round; (*челове́к*) versatile, multitalented; (*зна́ния*) encyclopaedic (*BRIT*), encyclopedic (*US*); (*маши́на, инструме́нт*) versatile, multipurpose; ~**ое сре́дство** cure-all; ~**ая вычисли́тельная маши́на** (*КОМП*) mainframe; ~ **си́мвол** (*КОМП*) wildcard; **универса́льный магази́н** department store.

универса́м (-а) *м* supermarket.

университе́т (-а) *м* university.

университе́тск|ий (-ая, -ое, -ие) *прил* university *опред*.

унижа́|ть(ся) (-ю(сь)) *несов от* **уни́зить(ся)**.

униже́ни|е (-я) *ср* humiliation; **идти́** (**пойти́** *perf*) **на** ~ to humble o.s.

уни́жен|ный (-, -на, -но) *прил* (*челове́к*) humbled; (*взгляд, про́сьба*) humble.

уни́жу(сь) *сов см* **уни́зить(ся)**.

ун|изáть (-ижý, -и́жешь; *impf* уни́зывать) *сов перех* to string; (*пояс: жемчугом*) to stud.

унизи́телен *прил см* унизи́тельный.

унизи́тельность (-и) *ж* humiliation.

унизи́тель|ный (-ен, -ьна, -ьно) *прил* humiliating, degrading.

уни́|зить (-жу, -зишь; *impf* унижáть) *сов перех* to humiliate; **унижáть** (~ *perf*) **себя́** to abase o.s.

▶ **уни́зиться** (*impf* унижáться) *сов возв*: ~ся (пéред +*instr*) to abase o.s. (before).

уни́зыва|ть (-ю) *несов от* унизáть.

уникá|льный (-ен, -ьна, -ьно) *прил* unique.

у́никум (-а) *м*: **он настоя́щий** ~ he's one of a kind.

унимá|ть(ся) (-ю(сь)) *несов от* уня́ть(ся).

унисóн (-а) *м* unison; **в** ~ (**с** +*instr*) (*также перен*) in unison (with).

унитáз (-а) *м* toilet.

унификáци|я (-и) *ж* standardization.

унифици́р|овать (-ую) (*не*)*сов перех* to standardize.

унифóрм|а (-ы) *ж* (*одежда*) uniform.

уничижá|ть (-ю) *несов перех* to disparage.

уничижи́тель|ный (-ен, -ьна, -ьно) *прил* disparaging.

уничтожá|ть (-ю) *несов от* уничтóжить.

уничтожá|ющий (-ая, -ее, -ие) *прил* (*огонь, удар, критика*) devastating; (*взгляд*) scathing, withering.

уничтó|жить (-у, -ишь; *impf* уничтожáть) *сов перех* to destroy; (*насекомых, вредителей*) to exterminate; (*память о чём-н, следы*) to wipe out; (*безработицу, преступность итп*) to do away with; (*перен: унизить*) to crush.

ун|оси́ть(ся) (-ошу́(сь), -óсишь(ся)) *несов от* унести́(сь).

у́нтер-офицéр (-а) *м* non-commissioned officer.

у́нци|я (-и) *ж* ounce.

унывá|ть (-ю) *несов неперех* (*человек*) to be downcast *или* despondent; (*впадать в уныние*) to lose heart.

уны́ло *нареч* despondently.

уны́лый *прил* (*человек*) despondent; (*мысли*) depressing; (*природа*) cheerless, dreary.

уны́ни|е (-я) *ср* despondency.

уня́ть (уйму́, уймёшь; *pt* -л, -лá, -ло, *impf* **унимáть**) *сов перех* (*ребёнка, хулигана*) to restrain; (*слёзы, волнение*) to suppress

▶ **уня́ться** (*impf* **унимáться**) *сов возв* (*ребёнок, шалун итп*) to calm down; (*буря, боль*) to die down.

упáвш|ий (-ая, -ее, -ие) *прил* (*голос*) fallen.

упáд (-у) *м*: **мы танцевáли до** ~**у** (*разг*) we danced till we were ready to drop; **я смея́лся до** ~**у** (*разг*) I laughed my head off.

упáд|ок (-ка) *м* decline; ~ **сил** exhaustion; ~ **дýха** despondency.

упáдочническ|ий (-ая, -ое, -ие) *прил* decadent.

упадý *итп сов см* упáсть.

упак|овáть (-у́ю) *сов от* паковáть.

упакóвк|а (-и) *ж* packing; (*паковочный материал*) packaging.

упакóвочный *прил* packaging *опред*.

упакóвыва|ть (-ю; *perf* упаковáть) *несов* = паковáть ◆ *перех* (*КОМП*) to pack.

упакóвщик (-а) *м* packer.

упакóвщиц|а (-ы) *ж см* упакóвщик.

упасти́ *сов перех*: **упаси́ Бог** *или* **Бóже** *или* **Гóсподи**! God forbid!

упáсть (-дý, -дёшь) *сов от* пáдать ◆ *неперех*: ~ **в нóги кому́-н** to go down on one's knees to sb.

упекá|ть (-ю) *несов от* упéчь.

упекý *итп сов см* упéчь.

уперé|ть (упру́, упрёшь; *pt* упёр, упёрла, упёрло, *impf* **упирáть**) *сов перех* (*разг: украсть*) to nick, pinch; **упирáть** (~ *perf*) **что-н в** +*acc* (*в стену итп*) to prop sth against

▶ **уперéться** (*impf* **упирáться**) *сов возв*: ~**ся чем-н в** +*acc* (*в землю*) to dig sth into; (*в плот*) to stick sth into; (*натолкнуться на преграду*): ~**ся в** +*acc* (*в ограду, в забор итп*) to come up against; (*перен: взглядом, глазами*) to stare; **упирáться** (~**ся** *perf*) (**на** +*prp*) (*перен: разг: настоять*) to dig one's heels in (on).

упé|чь (-ку́, -чёшь итп, -ку́т; *impf* упекáть) *сов перех* (*разг: в тюрьму*) to fling.

упивá|ться (-юсь) *несов от* упи́ться.

упирá|ть (-ю) *несов от* уперéть

▶ **упирáться** *несов от* уперéться ◆ *возв* (*иметь причиной*): ~**ся в** +*prp* to arise from.

упи́тан|ный (-, -на, -но) *прил* plump.

упи́ться (-ью́сь, -ьёшься; *impf* упивáться) *сов возв* (*разг: напиться допьяна*) to get very drunk; (*перен*): ~ +*instr* (*счастьем, свободой итп*) to be intoxicated by; (: *чьим-н несчастьем*) to revel in.

УПК *м сокр* (= Уголóвно-процессуáльный кóдекс) criminal code.

уплáт|а (-ы) *ж* payment.

упл|ати́ть (-ачу́, -áтишь) *сов от* плати́ть.

уплáчива|ть (-ю; *perf* уплати́ть) *несов перех* = плати́ть.

уплачý *сов см* уплати́ть.

упл|ести́ (-ету́, -етёшь) *сов от* уплетáть.

уплетá|ть (-ю) *несов перех* (*разг*) to tuck *или* get stuck into.

уплотнéни|е (-я) *ср* (*почвы, снега*) compression; (*под кожей*) lump (*ANAT*).

уплотн|и́ть (-ю́, -и́шь; *impf* уплотня́ть) *сов перех* (*также перен*) to compress

▶ **уплотни́ться** (*impf* уплотня́ться) *сов возв* (*песок, грунт*) to become firmer; (*рабочий день, график*) to become busier.

уплы́|ть (-ву́, -вёшь; *pt* -л, -лá, -ло, *impf*

уплыва́ть *сов неперех (человек, рыба итп)* to swim away *или* off; *(пароход)* to sail away *или* off; *(плавно уйти)* to float away *или* off; *(перен: пройти)* to pass; *(: разг: деньги, наследство итп)* to vanish.

упова́ни|е *(-я) ср* hope; **возлага́ть** *(impf)* ~**я на** +*acc* to set one's hopes on.

упова́|ть *(-ю) несов неперех:* ~ **на** +*acc* to count on.

уподо́б|ить *(-лю, -ишь; impf* **уподобля́ть)** *сов перех:* ~ **что-н/кого́-н** +*dat* to compare sth/sb to

▶ **уподо́биться** *(impf* **уподобля́ться)** *сов возв:* ~**ся** +*dat* to become like.

упое́ни|е *(-я) ср* elation; **с** ~**м** with relish.

упо|ённый *(-ён, -ена́, -ено́) прил:* ~ +*instr (успехом итп)* elated by; *(счастьем)* intoxicated with.

упои́тельный *(-ен, -ьна, -ьно) прил (воздух)* intoxicating; *(поцелуй)* rapturous.

упоко́й *(-я) м:* **моли́тва за** ~ **(души́) кого́-н** prayer for sb's eternal rest.

уполз|ти́ *(-у́, -ёшь; pt -, -ла́, -ло́) сов неперех (змея)* to slither away; *(червь)* to wriggle away; *(ребёнок)* to crawl away.

уполномо́ченн|ая *(-ой; decl like adj) ж см* **уполномо́ченный.**

уполномо́ченн|ый *(-ого; decl like adj) м* authorized person *(мн* people).

уполномо́ч|ить *(-у, -ишь; impf* **уполномо́чивать)** *сов перех:* ~ **кого́-н** +*infin* to authorize sb to do.

упомина́ни|е *(-я) ср (см глаг)* mention; reference.

упомина́|ть *(-ю) несов от* **упомяну́ть**

▶ **упомина́ться** *несов неперех (имя, событие)* to be mentioned.

упом|яну́ть *(-яну́, -я́нешь; impf* **упомина́ть)** *сов перех (назвать):* ~ **о** +*prp* to mention; *(коснуться)* to refer to.

упо́р *(-а) м (для ног, для рук)* rest; **в** ~ *(стрелять)* point-blank; *(смотреть)* intently; **де́лать (сде́лать** *perf)* ~ **на** +*prp* to put emphasis on.

упо́рно *нареч* persistently.

упо́р|ный *(-ен, -на, -но) прил* persistent; *(сопротивление)* unrelenting.

упо́рств|о *(-а) ср* persistence.

упо́рств|овать *(-ую) несов неперех* to persist *или* be persistent.

упорхн|у́ть *(-у́, -ёшь) сов неперех (также перен)* to flit away.

упоря́дочени|е *(-я) ср (корреспонденции, информации)* sorting; *(торговли, процедуры)* regulation.

упоря́доченный *прил* ordered.

упоря́доч|ить *(-у, -ишь; impf* **упоря́дочивать)** *сов перех* to put in order; *(цены, процедуру)* to regulate

▶ **упоря́дочиться** *(impf* **упоря́дочиваться)** *сов возв (дела)* to be put in order; *(процедура)* to be regulated.

употреби́телен *прил см* **употреби́тельный.**

употреби́тельност|ь *(-и) ж* frequency *(of use).*

употреби́тел|ьный *(-ен, -ьна, -ьно) прил* frequently used.

употреб|и́ть *(-лю́, -и́шь; impf* **употребля́ть)** *сов перех* to use; **употребля́ть (**~ *perf)* **что-н в пи́щу** to eat sth.

употребле́ни|е *(-я) ср (лекарства, наркотиков)* taking; *(алкоголя)* consumption; *(слова, термина)* usage; **находи́ться** *(impf)* ~**и** to be in use; **выходи́ть (вы́йти** *perf)* **из** ~**я** *(слово)* to go out of usage; **вводи́ть (ввести́** *perf)* **в** ~ *(слово)* to introduce; *(одежду, предмет быта)* to bring into use.

употреблю́ *сов см* **употреби́ть.**

употребля́|ть *(-ю) несов от* **употреби́ть**

▶ **употребля́ться** *несов возв* to be used.

упр. *сокр* (= **управле́ние**) admin (= *administration*).

упра́в|а *(-ы) ж (ист)* office; *(разг: мера пресечения):* **иска́ть** ~**у** to seek justice; **найти́** *(perf)* ~**у на кого́-н** to make sure that sb is punished; **на него́ нет** ~**ы** there's no control over him.

упра́в|иться *(-люсь, -ишься; impf* **управля́ться)** *сов возв:* ~ **с** +*instr (разг: с делами, с уборкой)* to manage; *(с шалуном, с плохим учеником)* to deal with.

управле́ни|е *(-я) ср (судном, самолётом)* navigation; *(делами, финансами)* administration; *(оркестром, хором)* conducting; *(учреждение)* office; *(система приборов)* controls *мн;* **симфо́ния испо́лнена под** ~**м а́втора** the symphony was conducted by the composer; **теря́ть (потеря́ть** *perf)* ~ to lose control.

управле́нческ|ий *(-ая, -ое, -ие) прил:* ~ **аппара́т** ruling body.

управлю́сь *сов см* **упра́виться.**

управля́ем|ый *(-, -а, -о) прил:* ~**ая раке́та** guided missile; ~ **(с по́мощью) меню́** *(КОМП)* menu-driven.

управля́|ть *(-ю) несов неперех:* ~ +*instr (автомобилем)* to drive; *(судном)* to navigate; *(конём)* to ride; *(государством)* to govern; *(учреждением, фирмой итп)* to manage; *(оркестром, хором)* to conduct

▶ **управля́ться** *несов от* **упра́виться.**

управля́ющ|ий *(-его; decl like adj) м (хозяйством)* manager; *(имением, поместьем)* bailiff.

упражне́ни|е *(-я) ср (мускулов, памяти)* exercising; *(грамматические, гимнастические)* exercise.

упражня́|ть *(-ю) несов перех* to exercise

▶ **упражня́ться** *несов возв* to practise.

упраздн|и́ть *(-ю́, -и́шь; impf* **упразня́ть)** *сов перех* to abolish.

упра́шива|ть *(-ю) несов от* **упроси́ть.**

упрёк *(-а) м* reproach; **броса́ть (бро́сить** *perf)* ~ **кому́-н** to reproach sb; **ста́вить (поста́вить**

perf) **что-н в** ~ **кому́-н** to hold sth against sb.

упрека́|ть (-ю; *perf* **упрекну́ть**) *несов перех*: ~ **кого́-н (в** +*prp*) to reproach sb (for).

упр|оси́ть (-ошу́, -о́сишь; *impf* **упра́шивать**) *сов перех*: ~ **кого́-н** +*infin* to persuade sb to do.

упр|ости́ть (-щу́, -сти́шь; *impf* **упроща́ть**) *сов перех* to simplify; (*сделать слишком простым*) to oversimplify

▸ **упрости́ться** (*impf* **упроща́ться**) *сов возв* to become simpler.

упро́чени|е (-я) *ср* consolidation.

упро́ч|ить (-у, -ишь; *impf* **упро́чивать**) *сов перех* to consolidate

▸ **упро́читься** (*impf* **упро́чиваться**) *сов возв* (*работник*) to establish o.s.; (*положение, позиции*) to be consolidated; (*перен*): **за ним** ~**илась репута́ция хоро́шего реда́ктора** his reputation as a good editor was established.

упрошу́ *сов см* **упроси́ть**.

упроща́|ть(ся) (-ю(сь)) *несов от* **упрости́ть(ся)**.

упроще́ни|е (-я) *ср* simplification.

упрощённый *прил* (*простой*) simplified; (*излишне простой*) oversimplified.

упрощу́(сь) *сов см* **упрости́ть(ся)**.

упру́(сь) *итп сов см* **упере́ть(ся)**.

упру́г|ий (-ая, -ое, -ие; -, -а, -о) *прил* (*пружина, тело*) elastic; (*походка, движения*) bouncy, springy.

упру́гост|ь (-и) *ж* (*пружины, мышц*) elasticity; (*походки*) springiness.

упря́ж|ка (-ки; *gen pl* -ек) *ж* team (*of horses, dogs etc*); (*упряжь*) harness.

у́пряж|ь (-и) *ж* (*no pl*) harness.

упря́м|ец (-ца) *м* stubborn person (*мн* people).

упря́м|иться (-люсь, -ишься) *несов возв* to be obstinate *или* stubborn.

упря́миц|а (-ы) *ж см* **упря́мец**.

упря́мо *нареч* (*сказать*) obstinately, stubbornly; (*искать*) persistently.

упря́мств|о (-а) *ср* obstinacy, stubbornness.

упря́мца *итп сущ см* **упря́мец**.

упря́м|ый (-, -а, -о) *прил* obstinate, stubborn; (*поиски, стремление*) persistent.

упря́|тать (-чу, -чешь) *сов перех* (*разг*) to put away.

упуска́|ть (-ю; *perf* **упусти́ть**) *несов перех* (*мяч*) to let go of; (*момент, случай*) to miss; ~ (**упусти́ть** *perf*) **из ви́ду** to overlook.

уп|усти́ть (-ущу́, -у́стишь) *сов от* **упуска́ть**.

упуще́ни|е (-я) *ср* omission.

упы́р|ь (-я) *м* vampire.

упью́сь *итп сов см* **упи́ться**.

ура́ *межд* hooray, hurrah; **на** ~ (*с энтузиа́змом*) enthusiastically; (*без подгото́вки*) just like that.

уравне́ни|е (-я) *ср* (*сил*) equalization; (*МАТ*) equation.

ура́внива|ть (-ю) *несов от* **уравня́ть**,

уровня́ть.

уравни́ловк|а (-и) *ж* (*разг: пренебр*) *equal rewarding regardless of contribution*.

уравнове́|сить (-шу, -сишь; *impf* **уравнове́шивать**) *сов перех* to balance

▸ **уравнове́ситься** (*impf* **уравнове́шиваться**) *сов возв* (*чаши весов*) to balance; (*силы*) to be counterbalanced.

уравнове́шенность (-и) *ж* composure.

уравнове́шен|ный (-, -на, -но) *прил* balanced, steady.

уравнове́шива|ть(ся) (-ю(сь)) *несов от* **уравнове́сить(ся)**.

уравновешу(сь) *сов см* **уравнове́сить(ся)**.

уравня́|ть (-ю; *impf* **ура́внивать**) *сов перех* (*размеры, доли итп*) to make equal; **ура́внивать** (~ *perf*) **кого́-н в права́х с кем-н** to give sb the same rights as sb.

урага́н (-а) *м* hurricane; (*перен: страстей*) storm.

урага́нный *прил*: ~ **ве́тер** gale.

Уралма́ш (-а) *м сокр* = **Ура́льский машиностроительный заво́д**.

ура́н (-а) *м* uranium; (*планета*): **У**~ Uranus.

ура́новый *прил* uranium.

ура-патрио́т (-а) *м* (*пренебр*) jingoist.

ура-патриоти́зм (-а) *м* jingoism.

урбаниза́ци|я (-и) *ж* urbanization.

урв|а́ть (-у́, -ёшь; *impf* **урыва́ть**) *сов перех* (*разг: материа́льные бла́га*) to grab; (: *время*) to snatch.

урегули́ровани|е (-я) *ср* settlement.

урегули́р|овать (-ую) *сов от* **регули́ровать** ♦ *перех* (*отноше́ния*) to put to rights; (*конфликт*) to settle.

уре́жу *итп сов см* **уре́зать**.

уре́занный *прил* (*демокра́тия, свобо́да*) limited.

уре́|зать (-жу, -жешь; *impf* **уреза́ть**) *сов перех* (*расхо́ды, шта́ты*) to cut down.

урезо́н|ить (-ю, -ишь; *impf* **урезо́нивать**) *сов перех*: ~ **кого́-н** (*разг*) to make sb see reason.

уреми́|я (-и) *ж* uraemia (*BRIT*), uremia (*US*).

уре́тр|а (-ы) *ж* urethra.

у́рн|а (-ы) *ж* (*погреба́льная*) urn; (*для му́сора, для оку́рков*) bin; **избира́тельная** ~ ballot box.

у́ров|ень (-ня) *м* level; (*те́хники*) standard; (*зарпла́ты, дохо́дов*) rate; **в** ~ **с** +*instr* on a level with; **на** ~**не земли́** at ground level; **встре́ча на вы́сшем** ~**не** summit meeting; **вы́ше/ни́же** ~**ня мо́ря** above/below sea level; **моя́ рабо́та была́ на** ~**не** my work was up to standard; **у́ровень жи́зни** living standard.

уровня́|ть (-ю; *impf* **ура́внивать**) *сов перех* (*доро́гу, зе́млю*) to level.

уро́д (-а) *м person with a deformity*; (*нра́вственный*) monster.

уро́дин|а (-ы) *м/ж* ugly person (*мн* people).

уро|ди́ться (-жу́сь, -ди́шься) *сов возв*
(*пшеница*) to give a good yield; ~ (*perf*) **в кого́-н**
(*в де́да, в отца́ итп*) to take after sb.

уро́д|ка (-ки; *gen pl* -ок) *ж см* **уро́д**.

уро́дливость (-и) *ж* (*см прил*) deformity;
distortion; ugliness.

уро́длив|ый (-, -а, -о) *прил* (*с уро́дством*)
deformed; (*представле́ние*) distorted;
(*безобра́зный*) ugly.

уро́д|овать (-ую; *perf* **изуро́довать**) *несов
перех* (*кале́чить*) to deform; (*де́лать
некраси́вым*) to make ugly; (*созна́ние*) to
distort; (*ду́шу, молодёжь*) to corrupt.

уро́дств|о (-а) *ср* (*физи́ческий недоста́ток*)
deformity; (*некраси́вая вне́шность*) ugliness.

урожа́|й (-я) *м* (*зерна́, карто́феля итп*) harvest;
(*большо́е коли́чество*) abundance; **снима́ть
(снять** *perf*) **или собира́ть (собра́ть** *perf*) ~ to
gather the harvest; **убира́ть (убра́ть** *perf*) ~ to
take in the harvest.

урожа́йность (-и) *ж* yield.

урожа́йный *прил* (*год*) productive.

урождённая *прил* née.

уроже́н|ец (-ца) *м* native.

урожу́сь *сов см* **уроди́ться**.

уро́к (-а) *м* lesson; (*зада́ние*) task; (*обы́чно мн*:
дома́шняя рабо́та) homework *ед*; **де́лать
(сде́лать** *perf*) ~и to do one's homework; **э́то
послу́жит тебе́ хоро́шим ~ом** let it be a (good)
lesson to you; **брать** (*impf*) ~**и чего́-н у кого́-н** to
take lessons in sth from sb; **дава́ть** (*impf*) ~ to
give a lesson; **дава́ть** (*impf*) ~**и где́-нибудь/
кому́-н** to teach somewhere/sb.

уро́лог (-а) *м* urologist.

урологи́ческ|ий (-ая, -ое, -ие) *прил* urological.

уроло́ги|я (-и) *ж* urology.

уро́н (-а) *м* (*поте́ри*) losses *мн*; **нести́ (понести́**
perf) ~ to suffer losses; **наноси́ть (нанести́** *perf*)
кому́-н ~ to inflict loss on sb.

ур|они́ть (-оню́, -о́нишь) *сов от* **роня́ть**.

уро́чищ|е (-а) *ср* natural boundary.

Уругва́|й (-я) *м* Uruguay.

уругва́йск|ий (-ая, -ое, -ие) *прил* Uruguayan.

урча́ни|е (-я) *ср* (*воды́*) gurgling; (*соба́ки*)
growling; (*ко́шки*) purring.

урч|а́ть (-у́, -и́шь) *несов неперех* (*вода́*) to
gurgle; (*тигр*) to growl; (*ко́шка*) to purr; **у меня́
~и́т в желу́дке** my tummy's rumbling.

урыва́|ть (-ю) *несов от* **урва́ть**.

уры́вками *нареч* at odd times.

урю́к (-а) *м собир* dried apricots *мн*.

ус (-а) *м* whisker; *см та́кже* **усы́**.

ус|ади́ть (-ажу́, -а́дишь; *impf* **уса́живать**) *сов
перех*: ~ **госте́й** to show the guests to their
seats; (*заста́вить де́лать*): ~ **кого́-н за
что-н**/+*infin* to sit sb down to sth/to do;
уса́живать (~ *perf*) **сад цвета́ми** to plant the
garden with lots of flowers.

уса́дьб|а (-ы) *ж* (*поме́щичья*) country estate;
(*крестья́нская*) farmstead.

уса́жива|ть (-ю) *несов от* **усади́ть**

▶ **уса́живаться** *несов от* **усе́сться**.

усажу́ *сов см* **усади́ть**.

уса́т|ый (-, -а, -о) *прил*: ~ **мужчи́на** man with a
moustache; ~ **кот** cat with whiskers.

усва́ива|ть (-ю) *несов от* **усво́ить**.

усвое́ни|е (-я) *ср* (*уро́ка, нау́ки*) mastering;
(*пи́щи*) assimilation.

усво́|ить (-ю, -ишь; *impf* **усва́ивать**) *сов перех*
(*привы́чку*) to acquire; (*уро́к*) to master; (*пи́щу,
лека́рство*) to assimilate.

усвоя́емость (-и) *ж* assimilability.

усе́к *итп сов см* **усе́чь**.

усека́|ть (-ю) *несов от* **усе́чь**.

усеку́ *итп сов см* **усе́чь**.

усе́рден *прил см* **усе́рдный**.

усе́рди|е (-я) *ср* diligence.

усе́рдн|ый (-ен, -на, -но) *прил* diligent.

усе́рдств|овать (-ую) *несов неперех* to make
an effort.

усе́|сться (-я́дусь, -я́дешься; *pt* -е́лся, -е́лась,
-е́лось, *impf* **уса́живаться**) *сов возв* to settle
down; (*заня́ться чем-н*): ~ **за** +*acc* (*за рабо́ту,
за письмо́*) to sit down to.

усе́|чь (-еку́, -ечёшь *итп*, -еку́т; *pt* -ёк, -екла́,
-екло́, *impf* **усека́ть**) *сов перех* (*укороти́ть*) to
truncate; (*разг: поня́ть*) to catch on to.

усе́я|ть (-ю) *сов перех* (*по́ле, не́бо*) to cover

▶ **усе́яться** *сов возв*: ~**ся** +*instr* to be dotted *или*
strewn with; (*цвета́ми*) to be full of.

усиде́|ть (-жу́, -ди́шь) *сов неперех* (*оста́ться
сиде́ть*) to stay sitting; (*не упа́сть*) to stay in
one's seat; (*не е́ле* ~**де́л на ме́сте** he could
hardly sit still; **он не мог** ~ **до́ма** he couldn't
just sit at home.

уси́дчивость (-и) *ж* assiduity.

уси́дчив|ый (-, -а, -о) *прил* assiduous.

усижу́ *сов см* **усиде́ть**.

у́сик|и (-ов; *nom sg* -) *мн* (*ма́ленькие усы́*) small
moustache *ед*; (*у расте́ний*) tendril *ед*; (*у
членистоно́гих*) feelers *мн*.

уси́ленн|ый *прил* (*охра́на*) reinforced;
(*про́сьбы, напомина́ния*) persistent; (*внима́ние*)
increased; ~**ое пита́ние** high calorie diet.

уси́лива|ть(ся) (-ю(сь)) *несов от* **уси́лить(ся)**.

уси́ли|е (-я) *ср* effort; (*физи́ческое*) exertion;
де́лать (сде́лать *perf*) ~ **над собо́й** to force o.s.

уси́литель (-я) *м* amplifier.

уси́лительный *прил* amplifying.

уси́л|ить (-ю, -ишь; *impf* **уси́ливать**) *сов перех*
to intensify; (*охра́ну*) to reinforce; (*внима́ние*) to
increase; (*звук*) to amplify

▶ **уси́литься** (*impf* **уси́ливаться**) *сов возв*
(*ве́тер*) to get stronger; (*сопротивле́ние*) to
intensify; (*волне́ние*) to increase.

уск|а́ть (-ачу́, -а́чешь) *сов неперех* (*ко́ни*) to
gallop away *или* off; (*перен: разг: челове́к*) to
whizz off.

ускользн|у́ть (-у́, -ёшь; *impf* **ускольза́ть**) *сов
неперех* (*ры́ба, змея́ итп*) to slip off; (*перен*): ~
из +*gen*/**от** +*gen* to slip out of/away from;
ускольза́ть (~ *perf*) **от чьего́-н внима́ния** to

escape sb's attention.

ускоре́ни|е (-я) *ср* acceleration; (*шага*) quickening.

уско́ренный *прил* (*шаг*) quickened; (*дыхание, пульс, темпы*) accelerated; ~ **курс** crash course.

ускори́тель (-я) *м* accelerator; **раке́тный** ~ rocket booster.

уско́р|ить (-ю, -ишь; *impf* **ускоря́ть**) *сов перех* (*шаги*) to quicken; (*ход механизма, прогресс*) to accelerate; (*выздоровление, отъезд*) to speed up

▶ **уско́риться** (*impf* **ускоря́ться**) *сов возв* (*ход поезда*) to accelerate; (*шаги*) to quicken; (*отъезд, решение вопроса*) to speed up.

усла́влива|ться (-юсь) *несов от* **усло́виться**.

усла́д|а (-ы) *ж* delight, joy.

услад|и́ть (-жу́, -ди́шь; *impf* **услажда́ть**) *сов перех* (*слух, зрение*) to delight

▶ **услади́ться** (*impf* **услажда́ться**) *сов возв*: ~**ся** +*instr* (*зрелищем, ароматом*) to delight in.

усла́ть (ушлю́, ушлёшь; *impf* **усыла́ть**) *сов перех* (*курьера, слуг*) to dispatch; (*на каторгу*) to send away.

уследи́ть (-жу́, -ди́шь) *сов неперех*: ~ **за** +*instr* (*за ребёнком*) to keep an eye on; (*за ходом разговора*) to follow.

усло́вный *прил см* **усло́вный**.

усло́ви|е (-я) *ср* condition; (*договора, платежа*) term; (*соглашение*) agreement; (*обычно мн: поступления в институт, приёма на работу*) requirement; **ста́вить** (**поста́вить** *perf*) **что-н** ~**м** to make sth a condition; **при** ~**и хоро́шей пого́ды** on the condition that the weather is good; **при** ~**и, что он согласи́тся** on the condition *или* provided that he agrees; *см также* **усло́вия**.

усло́в|иться (-люсь, -ишься; *impf* **усла́вливаться**) *сов возв*: ~ **о** +*prp* (*договориться*) to agree on.

усло́ви|я (-й) *мн* (*природные*) conditions *мн*; (*задачи, теоремы*) factors *мн*; (*пользования чем-н, какого-н режима*) terms *мн*; **жили́щные** ~ living conditions; ~ **труда́** working conditions; **в** ~**х** +*gen* in an atmosphere of; **по** ~**м догово́ра** on the terms of the agreement; **на льго́тных** ~**х** on special terms; **на сле́дующих** ~**х** on the following conditions; **для рабо́ты здесь – все** ~ (*разг*) everything you need for working here is laid on.

усло́вленный *прил* agreed.

усло́влюсь *сов см* **усло́виться**.

усло́вность (-и) *ж* conditional nature; (*обычай*) convention.

усло́в|ный (-ен, -на, -но) *прил* (*срок, согласие итп*) conditional; (*знак, сигнал*) code *опред*; (*линия*) imaginary; (*no short form: термин, линг*) conditional; **усло́вный рефле́кс** conditional reflex; **усло́вный срок** suspended sentence.

усложн|и́ть (-ю́, -и́шь; *impf* **усложня́ть**) *сов перех* to complicate

▶ **усложни́ться** (*impf* **усложня́ться**) *сов возв* to get more complicated.

услу́г|а (-и) *ж* (*одолжение*) favour (*BRIT*), favor (*US*); (*обычно мн: облуживание*) service; **коммуна́льные** ~**и** public utilities; **бюро́ (до́брых) услу́г** domestic services agency; **к Ва́шим** ~**м!** at your service!; **ока́зывать** (**оказа́ть** *perf*) **кому́-н** ~**у** to do sb a good turn.

услуже́ни|е (-я) *ср*: **быть в** ~**и** (**у** +*gen*) to be in service (with).

услу́ж|и́ть (-ужу́, -у́жишь) *сов перех*: ~ **кому́-н** to do sb a good turn.

услу́жлив|ый (-, -а, -о) *прил* obliging.

услы́ш|ать (-у, -ишь) *сов от* **слы́шать**.

усма́трива|ть (-ю) *несов от* **усмотре́ть**.

усмехн|у́ться (-у́сь, -ёшься; *impf* **усмеха́ться**) *сов возв* to smile slightly.

усме́шк|а (-и) *ж* slight smile; **зла́я** ~ sneer.

усмире́ни|е (-я) *ср* (*тигра*) taming; (*страстей, мятежа*) suppression.

усмир|и́ть (-ю́, -и́шь; *impf* **усмиря́ть**) *сов перех* (*льва*) to tame; (*детей*) to discipline; (*страсти, мятеж, восстание*) to suppress

▶ **усмири́ться** (*impf* **усмиря́ться**) *сов возв* (*лев*) to become tame; (*дети*) to calm down.

усмотре́ни|е (-я) *ср* discretion; **предоставля́ть** (**предоста́вить** *perf*) **на** ~ **нача́льства** to be left to the management's discretion; **де́йствовать** (*impf*) **по своему́** ~**ю** to use one's own discretion *или* judgement; **на Ва́ше** ~ at your discretion.

усм|отре́ть (-отрю́, -о́тришь; *impf* **усма́тривать**) *сов перех* (*разг*) to spot; (*счесть*): ~ **что-н в** +*prp* to see sth in ◆ *неперех* (*разг: уследить*): ~ **за** +*instr* to keep an eye on.

усна|сти́ть (-щу́, -сти́шь; *impf* **уснаща́ть**) *сов перех*: ~ **что-н чем-н** to pepper sth with sth.

усн|у́ть (-у́, -ёшь) *сов неперех* (*заснуть*) to fall asleep; **go to sleep**; ~ (*perf*) **наве́ки** *или* **ве́чным сном** to go to one's eternal rest.

усоверше́нствовани|е (-я) *ср* improvement, refinement.

усоверше́нств|овать(ся) (-ую(сь)) *сов от* **соверше́нствовать(ся)**.

усове́|стить (-щу, -стишь; *impf* **усове́щивать**) *сов перех*: ~ **кого́-н** to make sb (feel) ashamed.

усомн|и́ться (-ю́сь, -и́шься) *сов возв*: ~ **в** +*prp* to doubt.

усо́пш|ая (-ей; *decl like adj*) *ж см* **усо́пший**.

усо́пш|ий (-его; *decl like adj*) *м* deceased.

усо́хн|уть (-у, -ешь; *impf* **усыха́ть**) *сов неперех* (*также перен*) to shrivel (up); (*шерсть*) to shrink.

успева́емость (-и) *ж* performance (*in studies*).

успева́|ть (-ю) *несов от* **успе́ть** ◆ *неперех* to make progress (*in one's studies*).

успе́ется *сов безл* there's no hurry *или* rush.

Успéни|е (-я) *ср* the Assumption.

успé|ть (-ю; *impf* **успевáть**) *сов неперех* (*сдéлать что-н в срок*) to manage; (*прийти вовремя*) to be *или* make it in time; **я не ~л это сдéлать, как** ... I'd hardly done it when ...; **не ~л оглянýться, как он ужé ушёл** I hardly had time to blink before he'd already gone.

успéх (-а) *м* success; (*обычно мн: в спóрте, в учёбе*) achievement; **как Вáши ~и?** how are you doing?; **с ~ом** (*успéшно*) successfully; (*без затруднéний*) easily; **добивáться (добиться** *perf*) **~а** to achieve success; **с тем же ~ом** just as well.

успéшно *нареч* successfully.

успéш|ный (-ен, -на, -но) *прил* successful.

успокáива|ть(ся) (-ю(сь)) *несов от* **успокóить(ся)**.

успокоéни|е (-я) *ср* (*бóли, сóвести*) easing; (*плáчущего*) pacifying; **эти мысли принеслú ей ~** these thoughts brought her peace of mind.

успокóенность (-и) *ж* complacency.

успокоúтельн|ое (-ого; *decl like adj*) *ср* sedative.

успокоúтельный *прил* (*извéстие, отвéт*) calming, soothing; (*лекáрство*) sedative *опред*.

успокó|ить (-ю, -ишь; *impf* **успокáивать**) *сов перех* to calm (down); (*сóвесть*) to ease; (*боль*) to soothe

► **успокóиться** (*impf* **успокáиваться**) *сов возв* (*человéк*) to calm down; (*мóре*) to calm; (*боль, сóвесть, волнéния*) to be eased; (*вéтер*) to drop; **успокáиваться (~ся** *perf*) **на достúгнутом** to be content with one's achievements; **он не ~ился, покá не раскрыли всё дéло** he couldn't rest until they'd uncovered the whole business.

уст|á (-) *мн* lips *мн*; **в егó ~х это звучúт стрáнно** it sounds strange coming from him; **из уст в ~** by word of mouth; **из пéрвых уст** from the horse's mouth; **это у всех на ~х** it's on everyone's lips.

устáв (-а) *м* (*партийный*) rules *мн*; (*воинский*) regulations *мн*; (*корпорáции*) statute; **~ акционéрной компáнии** (*комм*) articles of association.

уставá|ть (-ю, -ёшь) *несов от* **устáть**.

устáв|ить (-лю, -ишь; *impf* **уставлять**) *сов перех* (*разместить*) to place, put; (*занять*): **~ что-н чем-н** (*стол*) to cover sth with; (*пóлку*) to fill sth with; (*разг: устремить*): **~ что-н в** +*acc* to fix sth on

► **устáвиться** (*impf* **уставляться**) *сов возв* (*разг*): **~ся на/в** +*acc* (*на собесéдника, в стéну*) to gaze at.

устáвный *прил* statutory; **устáвный капитáл** (*комм*) authorized capital.

устáло *нареч* wearily.

устáлость (-и) *ж* tiredness, fatigue.

устáлый *прил* tired, weary.

устáл|ь (-и) *ж*: **без** *или* **не знáя ~и** tirelessly, indefatigably.

устан|овúть (-овлю, -óвишь; *impf* **устанáвливать**) *сов перех* to establish; (*размéр оплáты, срóки*) to set; (*прибóр, машину*) to install; **устанáвливать (~** *perf*) **рекóрд** to set a record

► **установúться** (*impf* **устанáвливаться**) *сов возв* to be established; (*погóда*) to become settled; (*харáктер*) to be formed.

устанóвк|а (-и) *ж* installation; (*директúва*) directive; (*цель*) objective.

установлю́(сь) *сов см* **установúть(ся)**.

устáн|у *итп сов см* **устáть**.

устарé|ть (-ю) *сов от* **старéть** ♦ (*impf* **устаревáть**) *неперех* (*оборýдование*) to become obsolete.

уст|áть (-áну, -áнешь; *impf* **уставáть**) *сов неперех* to get tired.

устл|áть (-елю, -éлешь; *impf* **устилáть**) *сов перех*: **~ что-н (чем-н)** to cover sth (with sth).

устный *прил* (*экзáмен*) oral; (*обещáние, прикáз*) verbal; **устная речь** spoken language.

устó|й (-я) *м* (*опóра*) support; **~и** (*оснóвы*) foundations.

устóйчивость (-и) *ж* stability.

устóйчив|ый (-, -а, -о) *прил* (*тáкже перен*) stable; (*лéстница*) steady; **устóйчивое (слóво)сочетáние** set phrase.

уст|оя́ть (-ю́, -ойшь) *сов неперех* (*не упáсть*) to remain standing; (*в спóре, в борьбé итп*) to stand one's ground; (*не поддáться*) to resist; **~ (perf) на ногáх** to keep one's balance

► **устоя́ться** *сов возв* (*харáктер*) to be formed; (*жúдкость*) to settle; (*взгляды*) to become fixed.

устрáива|ть(ся) (-ю(сь)) *несов от* **устрóить(ся)**.

устран|úть (-ю́, -úшь; *impf* **устранять**) *сов перех* (*препятствие*) to remove; (*недостáтки, сопéрника*) to eliminate; (*рабóтника*) to dismiss

► **устранúться** (*impf* **устраняться**) *сов возв* to resign.

устрашá|ть(ся) (-ю(сь)) *несов от* **устрашúть(ся)**.

устрашáющий (-ая, -ее, -ие) *прил* frightening.

устраш|úть (-ý, -úшь; *impf* **устрашáть**) *сов перех* to frighten

► **устрашúться** (*impf* **устрашáться**) *сов возв*: **~ся** +*gen* to be frightened of.

устрем|úть (-лю́, -úшь; *impf* **устремлять**) *сов перех* (*удáр, глазá итп*) to direct; (*внимáние, помыслы*) to focus

► **устремúться** (*impf* **устремляться**) *сов возв*: **~ся на** +*acc* (*кóнница, толпá*) to charge at; (*перен: внимáние, мысли*) to be focused on; (*взгляд, глазá*) to be fixed on.

устремлéни|е (-я) *ср* aspiration.

устремлённость (-и) *ж* tendency.

устремлю́(сь) *сов см* **устремúть(ся)**.

устремля́|ть(ся) (-ю(сь)) *несов от* **устремúть(ся)**.

устриц|а (-ы) *ж* oyster.

устричный *прил* oyster.

устро́ен|ный (-, -а, -о) *прил* (*жизнь*) ordered; (*кварти́ра*) habitable.

устро́ител|ь (-я) *м* organizer.

устро́ить (-ю, -ишь; *impf* **устра́ивать**) *сов перех* (*жизнь, дела́*) to organize; (*спекта́кль, вы́ставку*) to arrange; (*подле́ж: предложе́ние, цена́*) to suit; **устра́ивать** (~ *perf*) **кого́-н на рабо́ту/кварти́ру** to help sb find work/a flat; **устра́ивать** (~ *perf*) **сканда́л** to make a scene; **э́то меня́ ~ит** that suits me

▸ **устро́иться** (*impf* **устра́иваться**) *сов возв* (*расположи́ться*) to settle down; (*прийти́ в поря́док*) to work out; **устра́иваться** (**~ся** *perf*) **на рабо́ту** to get a job; **он ~ился на заво́д** he got a job in a factory.

устро́йств|о (-а) *ср* (*де́йствие: вы́ставки*) organization; (: *на рабо́ту*) finding; (*дома, прибо́ра*) construction; (*госуда́рственное, обще́ственное*) structure; (*техни́ческое*) device, mechanism; **~ опти́ческого счи́тывания си́мволов** (*комп*) optical character reader.

усту́п (-а) *м* ledge.

уступ|и́ть (-лю́, -у́пишь; *impf* **уступа́ть**) *сов перех*; **~ что-н кому́-н** to give sth up for sb ♦ *непере́х*: **~ кому́-н/чему́-н** (*си́льному, си́ле, жела́нию итп*) to give in to sb/sth; **уступа́ть** (**~ *perf*) в** +*prp* (*в си́ле, в уме́*) to be inferior in; **уступа́ть** (**~ *perf*) доро́гу кому́-н** to make way for sb; **он ~упи́л мне кни́гу за 10 рубле́й** he let me have the book for 10 roubles.

усту́п|ка (-ки; *gen pl* **-ок**) *ж* (*компроми́сс*) compromise; (*си́ле, врагу́*) surrender; (*ски́дка*) discount; **пойти́** (*perf*) **на ~ку** to compromise.

уступлю́ *сов см* **уступи́ть**.

усту́пок *сущ см* **усту́пка**.

усту́пчив|ый (-, -а, -о) *прил* compliant.

усты|ди́ть (-жу́, -ди́шь) *сов перех* to shame

▸ **усты́ди́ться** *сов возв*: **~ся** +*gen* to be ashamed of.

у́сть|е (-я) *ср* (*реки́*) mouth; (*ша́хты*) entrance.

усугу́б|ить (-лю, -ишь; *impf* **усугубля́ть**) *сов перех* (*вину́, опа́сность*) to increase; (*боле́знь, положе́ние*) to aggravate

▸ **усугу́биться** (*impf* **усугубля́ться**) *сов возв* (*вина́*) to increase; (*страда́ния, боле́знь*) to be aggravated.

усу́шк|а (-и) *ж* (*зерна́*) loss of weight (*through drying*).

ус|ы́ (-о́в) *мн* (*у челове́ка*) moustache *ед*; (*у живо́тных*) whiskers *мн*; **он** (**и**) **в ус** (**себе́**) **не ду́ет** (*разг*) he's completely unruffled; **на ус мота́ть** (**намота́ть** *perf*) **что-н** (*разг*) to take good note of sth; **са́ми с ~а́ми** (*разг*) we weren't born yesterday.

усыла́|ть (-ю) *несов от* **усла́ть**.

усынов|и́ть (-лю́, -и́шь; *impf* **усыновля́ть**) *сов перех* to adopt (*son*).

усыновле́ни|е (-я) *ср* adoption (*son*).

усыновлю́ *сов см* **усынови́ть**.

усыновля́|ть (-ю) *несов от* **усынови́ть**.

усыпа́льниц|а (-ы) *ж* burial chamber.

усы́п|ать (-лю, -лешь; *impf* **усыпа́ть**) *сов перех*: **~ что-н чем-н** (*путь, доро́гу*) to scatter sth with sth.

усып|и́ть (-лю́, -и́шь; *impf* **усыпля́ть**) *сов перех* (*больно́го*) to anaesthetize (*BRIT*), anesthetize (*US*); (*ребёнка*) to lull to sleep; (*перен: внима́ние, бди́тельность*) to weaken; (*больну́ю соба́ку итп*) to put to sleep; **он ~и́л меня́ свои́ми ску́чными разгово́рами** his boring conversation sent me to sleep.

усы́плю *итп сов см* **усы́пать**.

усыплю́ *сов см* **усыпи́ть**.

усыпля́|ть (-ю) *несов от* **усыпи́ть**.

усыха́|ть (-ю) *несов от* **усо́хнуть**.

уся́дусь *итп сов см* **усе́сться**.

ута|и́ть (-ю́, -и́шь; *impf* **ута́ивать**) *сов перех* (*пра́вду*) to keep secret; (*де́ньги, докуме́нты*) to appropriate.

ута́йк|а (-и) *ж*: **без ~и** (*разг*) openly.

ута́птыва|ть (-ю) *несов от* **утопта́ть**.

ута|щи́ть (-щу́, -а́щешь; *impf* **ута́скивать**) *сов перех* (*унести́*) to drag away *или* off; (*разг: укра́сть*) to make off with.

у́твар|ь (-и) *ж собир* utensils *мн*.

утверди́тельный (-ен, -ьна, -ьно) *прил* (*также линг*) affirmative.

утверд|и́ть (-жу́, -ди́шь; *impf* **утвержда́ть**) *сов перех* (*прое́кт, гра́фик*) to approve; (*госпо́дство, демокра́тию итп*) to establish; **~** (*perf*) **кого́-н в подозре́ниях** to confirm sb's suspicions; **~** (*perf*) **кого́-н в до́лжности** to approve sb's appointment to office; **~** (*perf*) **кого́-н в мне́нии/наме́рении** to strengthen sb's conviction/intention

▸ **утверди́ться** (*impf* **утвержда́ться**) *сов возв* to be established; (*увери́ться*): **~ся в** +*prp* (*в наме́рении*) to become convinced of.

утвержда́|ть (-ю) *несов от* **утверди́ть** ♦ *перех* (*пра́вильность, достове́рность*) to maintain; **он ~л, что ничего́ не зна́ет** he maintained that he didn't know anything

▸ **утвержда́ться** *несов от* **утверди́ться**.

утвержде́ни|е (-я) *ср* (*см глаг*) approval; establishment; (*пра́вильное, интере́сное*) statement.

утвержу́(сь) *сов см* **утверди́ть(ся)**.

утёк *итп сов см* **уте́чь**.

утека́|ть (*3sg* -ет, *3pl* -ют) *несов от* **уте́чь**.

утеку́т *итп сов см* **уте́чь**.

утёнок (-ёнка; *nom pl* -я́та, *gen pl* -я́т) *м* duckling.

утеплённый *прил* (*гара́ж*) insulated; (*о́бувь*) lined.

утепл|и́ть (-ю́, -и́шь; *impf* **утепля́ть**) *сов перех* to insulate.

уте|ре́ть (-ру́, -решь; pt -ёр, -ёрла, -ёрло, impf
утира́ть) сов перех (пот) to wipe off; (слёзы)
to wipe away; (лицо, нос) to wipe; ~ (perf) **нос**
кому́-н (перен: разг) to show sb what's what
▶ **утере́ться** (impf **утира́ться**) сов возв to wipe
one's face; (нос) to wipe one's nose.
уте́р|я (-и) ж loss.
утеря́|ть (-ю) сов от **теря́ть**.
утёс (-а) м cliff.
уте́чк|а (-и) ж (также перен) leak; (кадров)
turnover; **уте́чка мозго́в** brain drain.
уте́чь (3sg -ечёт, 3pl -еку́т, pt -ёк, -екла́, -екло́,
impf **утека́ть**) сов неперех (вода, газ) to leak;
(годы) to go by, pass; (информация) to be
leaked.
утеша́|ть(ся) (-ю(сь)) несов от **уте́шить(ся)**.
утеше́ни|е (-я) ср (плачущего) comforting; (о
чём-н утешающем) consolation.
уте́ш|ить (-у, -ишь; impf **утеша́ть**) сов перех
(плачущего, несчастного) to comfort, console;
(подлеж: мысль, успехи детей) to comfort
▶ **уте́шиться** (impf **утеша́ться**) сов возв to cheer
up.
утилиза́ци|я (-и) ж recycling.
утилизи́р|овать (-ую) (не)сов перех to recycle.
утилита́р|ный (-ен, -на, -но) прил (взгляды)
utilitarian; (знания) practical.
ути́л|ь (-я) м собир recyclable waste.
ути́ный прил (гнездо) duck's; (яйцо, охота)
duck опред.
утира́|ть(ся) (-ю(сь)) несов от **утере́ть(ся)**.
ути́хн|уть (-у, -ешь; impf **утиха́ть**) сов неперех
(спор) to calm down; (гром, звон) to die away;
(ветер) to drop; (вьюга) to die down.
утихоми́р|ить (-ю, -ишь; impf **утихоми́ривать**)
сов перех to pacify
▶ **утихоми́риться** (impf **утихоми́риваться**)
сов возв to calm down.
у́тк|а (-ки; gen pl -ок) ж duck; (ложный слух)
canard; (сосуд) bedpan; **пуска́ть (пусти́ть** perf)
~**ку** to spread a false rumour (BRIT) или rumor
(US).
уткн|у́ть (-у́, -ёшь) сов перех (разг: подбородок)
to bury; ~ (perf) **нос в** +acc to bury one's nose in;
~ (perf) **глаза́ в зе́млю** to fix one's eyes on the
ground
▶ **уткну́ться** сов возв (разг): ~**ся в** +acc (в
книгу, в газету) to bury one's nose in; **она́**
~**у́лась голово́й в поду́шку** she buried her face
in the pillow.
утконо́с (-а) м duck-billed platypus (мн
platypus).
у́тлый прил (лодка) decrepit.
у́ток сущ см **у́тка**.
утол|и́ть (-ю́, -и́шь; impf **утоля́ть**) сов перех
(жажду) to quench; (голод, любопытство) to
satisfy; (боль) to ease.
утол|сти́ть (-щу́, -сти́шь; impf **утолща́ть**) сов
перех to thicken.
утолще́ни|е (-я) ср widening.
утолщу́ сов см **утолсти́ть**.

утоля́|ть (-ю) несов от **утоли́ть**.
утоми́тел|ьный (-ен, -ьна, -ьно) прил tedious,
tiresome; (ребёнок) tiring.
утом|и́ть (-лю́, -и́шь; impf **утомля́ть**) сов перех
to tire
▶ **утоми́ться** (impf **утомля́ться**) сов возв to get
tired.
утомле́ни|е (-я) ср tiredness, fatigue.
утомлю́(сь) сов см **утоми́ть(ся)**.
утомля́емость (-и) ж (также тех) fatigue.
утомля́|ть(ся) (-ю(сь)) несов от **утоми́ть(ся)**.
ут|ону́ть (-ону́, -о́нешь) сов от **тону́ть**.
утончённост|ь (-и) ж refinement.
утончён|ный (-, -на, -но) прил refined.
утонч|и́ть (-у́, -и́шь) сов перех (нитку) to make
thinner
▶ **утончи́ться** сов возв (вкусы, восприятие) to
become refined.
утоп|а́ть (-ю) несов неперех (тонуть) to drown;
(перен): ~ **в** +prp (в кружевах, в цветах) to be
smothered in; (в роскоши, в разврате) to
wallow in.
утопи́ст (-а) м utopian.
ут|опи́ть(ся) (-оплю́(сь), -о́пишь(ся)) сов от
топи́ть(ся).
утопи́чен прил см **утопи́чный**.
утопи́ческ|ий (-ая, -ое, -ие) прил utopian.
утопи́|чный (-ен, -на, -но) прил utopian.
уто́пи|я (-и) ж utopia.
уто́пленник (-а) м drowned man (мн men).
уто́пленниц|а (-ы) ж drowned woman (мн
women).
утоплю́(сь) сов см **утопи́ть(ся)**.
ут|опта́ть (-опчу́, -о́пчешь; impf **ута́птывать**)
сов перех to stamp down.
уточне́ни|е (-я) ср elaboration; **вноси́ть**
(**внести́** perf) ~**я в** +acc to elaborate on.
уточн|и́ть (-ю́, -и́шь; impf **уточня́ть**) сов перех
(пункт договора, выводы) to elaborate on;
(сведения, факты) to clarify.
утрамб|ова́ть (-у́ю) сов от **трамбова́ть**.
утра́т|а (-ы) ж loss; ~ **трудоспосо́бности**
disablement; **понести́** (perf) ~**у** to suffer a loss.
утра́|тить (-чу, -тишь; impf **утра́чивать**) сов
перех (потерять) to lose; ~ (perf) **си́лу**
(документ итп) to become invalid.
у́тренн|ий (-яя, -ее, -ие) прил morning опред;
(событие, известие) this morning's.
у́тренник (-а) м matinée; (с участием детей)
children's party.
утри́рованный прил exaggerated.
утри́р|овать (-ую) (не)сов перех to exaggerate.
у́тр|о (-а; nom pl -а, gen pl -, dat pl -ам) ср morning;
до утра́ till morning; **с утра́** since this morning;
дава́й встре́тимся с утра́ let's meet in the
morning; **с утра́ до ́ночи** from morn till night;
до́брое ~!, **с до́брым** ~**м!** good morning!; **на**
~ next morning; **по утра́м** in the mornings; **под**
~, **к утру́** in the early hours of the morning.
утро́б|а (-ы) ж (матери́нская) womb; (брюхо)
belly.

утро́бный *прил* (*био*) f(o)etal; (*истошный*) hollow.

утро́|ить (**-ю, -ишь**) *сов перех* to treble, triple
► **утро́иться** *сов возв* to treble, triple.

у́тром *нареч* in the morning; **ра́но** ~ early in the morning.

утру́(сь) *итп сов см* **утере́ть(ся)**.

утружда́|ть (**-ю**) *несов перех*: ~ **кого́-н чем-н** to trouble sb with sth; **не** ~**йте себя́** don't trouble yourself
► **утружда́ться** *несов возв* to trouble o.s.

утру́ск|а (**-и**) *ж* spillage.

утр|ясти́ (**-ясу́, -ясёшь**; *impf* **утряса́ть**) *сов перех* (*перен: разг: вопрос, проблему*) to settle; (*муку*) to shake down
► **устрясти́сь** *сов возв* (*разг*) to settle.

уты́|кать (**-чу, -чешь**; *impf* **утыка́ть**) *сов перех*: ~ **что-н чем-н** to stick sth into sth.

утю́г (**-а́**) *м* iron (*appliance*).

утю́ж|ить (**-у, -ишь**; *perf* **вы́утюжить** *или* **отутю́жить**) *несов перех* to iron.

утяжел|и́ть (**-ю́, -и́шь**; *impf* **утяжеля́ть**) *сов перех* to make heavier, increase the weight of.

утя́та *итп сущ см* **утёнок**.

утя́тин|а (**-ы**) *ж* (*мясо*) duck.

уф *межд*: ~! phew!

ух *межд*: ~! ooh!

ух|а́ (**-и́**) *ж* fish broth.

уха́б (**-а**) *м* pothole.

уха́бист|ый (**-, -а, -о**) *прил*: ~**ая доро́га** road full of potholes.

ухажёр (**-а**) *м* (*разг*) admirer.

уха́живани|е (**-я**) *ср* courting.

уха́жива|ть (**-ю**) *несов неперех*: ~ **за** +*instr* (*за больным, за ранеными*) to nurse; (*за цветами, за садом*) to tend; (*за женщиной*) to court.

у́хань|е (**-я**) *ср* (*no pl*) hooting.

у́ха|ть (**-ю**) *несов от* **у́хнуть**.

ухва́т (**-а**) *м* oven fork.

ухва|ти́ть (**-чу́, -́тишь**; *impf* **ухва́тывать**) *сов перех* (*человека: за руку, за рукав*) to get hold of; (*перен: идею, смысл*) to grasp
► **ухвати́ться** (*impf* **ухва́тываться**) *сов возв*: ~**ся за** +*acc* (*за перила, за руку*) to grab hold of; (*за дело, за мысль*) to latch onto; (*за предложение*) to jump at.

ухва́т|ки (**-ок**) *мн* manners *мн*.

ухва́тыва|ть(ся) (**-ю(сь)**) *несов от* **ухвати́ть(ся)**.

ухвачу́(сь) *сов см* **ухвати́ть(ся)**.

ухитр|и́ться (**-ю́сь, -и́шься**; *impf* **ухитря́ться**) *сов возв* to manage.
► **умудри́ться**.

ухищре́ни|е (**-я**) *ср* (*уловка*) trick; **прибега́ть** (**прибе́гнуть** *perf*) **к ра́зным** ~**ям** to resort to various tricks.

ухищрённый *прил* crafty.

ухищря́|ться (**-юсь**) *несов возв* to contrive.

ухло́па|ть (**-ю**; *impf* **ухло́пывать**) *сов перех* (*разг: истратить*) to blow.

ухмы́лк|а (**-и**) *ж* (*разг*) smirk.

ухмыля́|ться (**-юсь**; *perf* **ухмыльну́ться**) *несов возв* (*разг*) to smirk.

у́хн|уть (**-у, -ешь**; *impf* **у́хать**) *сов неперех* (*снаряд*) to thud; (*гром*) to rumble; (*филин, сова*) to hoot; (*разг: упасть*) to come a cropper
♦ *перех* (*разг: все де́ньги*) to blow; (: *камень*) to hurl; ~ (*perf*) **кула́ком по столу́** to bang one's fist down on the table.

у́х|о (**-а**; *nom pl* **у́ши**, *gen pl* **уше́й**) *ср* ear; (*у шапки*) flap; **говори́ть** (**сказа́ть** *perf*) **что-н кому́-н на́ ухо** to whisper sth in sb's ear; **не вида́ть тебе́ де́нег как свои́х уше́й** you've got no chance of getting the money; **слу́шать** (*impf*) **во все у́ши** to be all ears; **слы́шать** (**услы́шать** *perf*) **что-н кра́ем** ~**а** *или* **одни́м** ~**ом** to listen to sth with half an ear; **по́ уши влюби́ться** (*perf*) **в кого́-н** (*разг*) to fall head over heels in love with sb; **у́ши вя́нут от твои́х шу́ток** your jokes make me sick.

ухо́д (**-а**) *м* (*со службы, из семьи*) leaving; (*от погони, от реальности*) escape; (*в монасты́рь*) retreat; (*с собрания, со сцены*) exit; (*за больны́м, за ребёнком*) care; ~ **в отста́вку** resignation; ~ **на пе́нсию** retirement.

ухо|ди́ть (**-ожу́, -́одишь**) *несов от* **уйти́** ♦ *неперех* (*простираться*) to extend.

ухо́женный *прил* (*лицо, руки*) well-looked-after; (*сад*) well-kept; (*лошадь, человек*) well-groomed.

ухожу́ *несов см* **уходи́ть**.

ухудша́|ть(ся) (**-ю(сь)**) *несов от* **уху́дшить(ся)**.

ухудше́ни|е (**-я**) *ср* deterioration, worsening.

уху́дш|ить (**-у, -ишь**; *impf* **ухудша́ть**) *сов перех* to make worse
► **уху́дшиться** (*impf* **ухудша́ться**) *сов возв* to get worse, deteriorate.

уцеле́|ть (**-ю**) *сов неперех* to survive.

уценённый *прил* reduced.

уцен|и́ть (**-ю́, -́енишь**; *impf* **уце́нивать**) *сов перех* to reduce (the price of).

уце́н|ка (**-ки**; *gen pl* **-ок**) *ж* reduction.

уцеп|и́ть (**-лю́, -́епишь**) *сов перех* to hook
► **уцепи́ться** *сов возв* (*ухвати́ться*): ~**ся за** +*acc* (*за руку*) to get hold of; (*за предложение, за возможность*) to jump at.

уча́ств|овать (**-ую**) *сов неперех*: ~ **в** +*prp* (*в собрании, в спекта́кле*) to take part in; (*в предприятии, в прибыля́х*) to have a share in.

уча́сти|е (**-я**) *ср* (*в собрании, в спекта́кле итп*) participation; (*в предприятии, в прибыля́х*) share; (*родственное, дружеское*) concern; **принима́ть** (**приня́ть** *perf*) ~ **в** +*prp* to take part in; **принима́ть** (**приня́ть** *perf*) ~ **в ком-н** to show concern for sb.

уча|сти́ть (**-щу́, -сти́шь**; *impf* **учаща́ть**) *сов* *перех* (*шаг*) to quicken; (*контакты, встречи*) to make more frequent

▸ **участи́ться** (*impf* **учаща́ться**) *сов возв* (*пульс, дыхание*) to quicken; (*столкновения, контакты*) to become more frequent.

уча́стка *сущ см* **уча́сток**.

участко́в|**ый** *прил* local ♦ (**-ого**; *decl like adj*) *м* (*разг*) local policeman (*мн* policemen); (*также*: **~ врач**) local GP *или* doctor; (*также*: **~ инспе́ктор**) local policeman (*мн* policemen).

уча́стливо *нареч* sympathetically.

уча́стливый *прил* sympathetic.

уча́стник (**-а**) *м* (*кружка, экспедиции*) member; (*восстания, репетиции, переговоров*) participant; **~ соревнова́ния** competitor, contestant; **~ вы́ставки** exhibitor; **~ войны́** (war) veteran.

уча́стница (**-ы**) *ж см* **уча́стник**.

уча́ст|**ок** (**-ка**) *м* (*земли, кожи итп*) area; (*дороги, реки, фронта*) stretch; (*врачебный*) catchment area; (*приусадебный, земельный*) plot; (*строительный*) site; (*работы, деятельности*) field; **избира́тельный ~** polling station; **садо́вый ~** allotment.

у́част|**ь** (**-и**) *ж* lot; **его́ пости́гла стра́шная ~** fate dealt him a terrible blow.

уча́ща|ть(ся) (**-ю(сь)**) *несов от* **участи́ть(ся)**.

уча́щаяся (**-ейся**; *decl like adj*) *ж см* **уча́щийся**.

уча́щийся (**-егося**; *decl like adj*) *м* (*школы*) pupil; (*училища*) student.

учащу́(сь) *сов см* **участи́ть(ся)**.

учёб|**а** (**-ы**) *ж* studies *мн*.

уче́бник (**-а**) *м* textbook; **~ исто́рии** *или* **по исто́рии** history textbook.

уче́бный *прил* (*работа*) academic; (*процесс, фильм*) educational; (*стрельба*) practice; (*бой*) mock; (*мастерская, судно*) training *опред*; (*методы*) teaching *опред*; **уче́бная програ́мма** curriculum; **уче́бное заведе́ние** educational establishment; **уче́бный год** academic year; **уче́бный план** course outline; **уче́бный о́тпуск** block release.

учёл *итп сов см* **уче́сть**.

учёная (**-ой**; *decl like adj*) *ж см* **учёный**.

уче́ни|**е** (**-я**) *ср* (*в школе, в вузе*) study; (*теория*) teachings *мн; см также* **уче́ния**.

учени́к (**-á**) *м* (*школы*) pupil; (*училища*) student; (*мастера*) apprentice; (*последователь*) follower.

учени́ца (**-ы**) *ж см* **учени́к**.

учени́ческий (**-ая, -ое, -ие**) *прил* (*дневник, тетради*) school *опред*; (*перен: рассуждение, работа*) primitive.

учени́честв|**о** (**-а**) *ср* (*у мастера*) apprenticeship; **го́ды ~а** schooldays *мн*.

уче́ния (**-й**) *мн* exercises *мн*.

учёность (**-и**) *ж* learning.

учён|**ый** *прил* (*спор, круги*) academic; (*разг: опытом, каким-н событием*) educated; (*труды*) scholarly; (*кот, собака*) trained; (**-, -а, -о**; *человек*) learned, scholarly ♦ (**-ого**; *decl like*

adj) *м* (*научный работник*) academic, scholar; (: **в области точных и естественных наук**) scientist; **учёное зва́ние** academic title; **учёный сове́т** academic council.

уче́сть (**-ту́, -тёшь**; *pt* **-ёл, -лá, -ло́**, *impf* **учи́тывать**) *сов перех* (*обстоятельства, сложности*) to take into account; (*материал, имущество*) to make an inventory of; (*присутствующих*) to make a list of; **~ти́те, что ...** bear in mind that ...; **~** (*perf*) **ве́ксель** to discount a bill.

учёт (**-а**) *м* (*потребностей, обстоятельств*) consideration; (*товара*) stock-taking; (*военный, медицинский*) registration; (*векселей*) discount; (*затрат, поступлений*) record; **бухга́лтерский ~** (*учебный предмет*) accountancy; (*практическая деятельность*) bookkeeping; **брать** (**взять** *perf*) **на ~** to register; **вести** (*impf*) **~** to keep a record; **с ~ом всех обстоя́тельств** bearing in mind all the circumstances; **с ~ом сезо́нных колеба́ний** allowing for seasonal fluctuations.

учётн|**ый** *прил*: **~ая ка́рточка** registration form; **~ая кни́га** record book; **~ проце́нт** (*комм*) rate of discount; **~ дом** (*комм*) discount house.

учи́лище (**-а**) *ср* college; **профессиона́льно-техни́ческое ~** technical college.

учин|**и́ть** (**-ю́, -и́шь**; *impf* **учиня́ть**) *сов перех* (*драку*) to start; **учиня́ть** (**~** *perf*) **сканда́л** to make a scene.

учи́тель (**-я**; *nom pl* **-я́**) *м* (*школьный*) teacher; (*nom pl* **-и**; *мудрости*) master.

учи́тельница (**-ы**) *ж* teacher.

учи́тельск|**ая** (**-ой**; *decl like adj*) *ж* staffroom.

учи́тельств|**о** (**-а**) *ср* (*профессия*) teaching ♦ *собир* (*учителя*) teachers *мн*.

учи́тельств|**овать** (**-ую**) *несов неперех* to teach, work as a teacher.

учи́тыва|ть (**-ю**) *несов от* **уче́сть**.

уч|**и́ть** (**-у́, -ишь**; *perf* **вы́учить**) *несов перех* (*урок, роль*) to learn; (*perf* **вы́учить** *или* **научи́ть** *или* **обучи́ть**): **~ кого́-н чему́-н**/+*infin* to teach sb sth/to do; **исто́рия/э́та тео́рия у́чит, что ...** history/this theory teaches that ...

▸ **учи́ться** *несов возв* (*в школе, училище*) to study; (*perf* **вы́учиться** *или* **научи́ться**; *получить навыки*): **~ся чему́-н**/+*infin* to learn sth/to do.

учреди́тель (**-я**) *м* founder.

учреди́тельница (**-ы**) *ж см* **учреди́тель**.

учреди́тельный *прил*: **~ое собра́ние** inaugural meeting.

учре|**ди́ть** (**-жу́, -ди́шь**; *impf* **учрежда́ть**) *сов перех* (*фонд, банк*) to set up; (*контроль, порядок*) to introduce.

учрежде́ни|**е** (**-я**) *ср* (*фонда, организации итп*) setting up; (*контроля*) introduction; (*научное, исследовательское*) establishment; (*финансовое, общественное*) institution; (*страховое*) agency.

учрежу́ *сов см* **учреди́ть**.

учти́вост|ь (-и) *ж* courtesy.
учти́в|ый (-, -а, -о) *прил* courteous, civil.
учту́ *итп сов см* **уче́сть**.
учу́|ять (-ю, -ешь) *сов перех* (*разг: собака*) to sniff; (: *перен: человек*) to sense.
уша́н|ка (-ки; *gen pl* -ок) *ж cap with ear-flaps*.
уша́ст|ый (-, -а, -о) *прил*: ~ **ма́льчик** boy with big ears.
уша́т (-а) *м* tub.
у́шек *сущ см* **у́шко**.
ушёл *сов см* **уйти́**.
у́ши *итп сущ см* **у́хо**.
уши́б (-а) *м* bruise.
ушиб|и́ть (-у́, -ёшь; *pt* -, -ла, -ло, *impf* **ушиба́ть**) *сов перех* to bang
▶ **ушиби́ться** *сов возв* to bang o.s.
уш|и́ть (-ью́, -ьёшь; *impf* **ушива́ть**) *сов перех* (*сделать уже*) to take in; (*сделать короче*) to shorten, take up.
у́шк|о (-ка; *nom pl* -ки, *gen pl* -ек) *ср уменьш от* **у́хо**; (*медали*) eyelet; (*иголки*) eye.
ушла́ *итп сов см* **уйти́**.
у́шлый *прил* smart.
ушлю́ *итп сов см* **усла́ть**.
ушни́к (-а́) *м* (*разг*) ear specialist.
ушн|о́й *прил ear опред*; ~**а́я боль** earache; ~**а́я ра́ковина** (*АНАТ*) auricle.
ушью́ *итп сов см* **уши́ть**.
уще́л|ье (-ья; *gen pl* -ий) *ср* gorge, ravine.
ущем|и́ть (-лю́, -и́шь; *impf* **ущемля́ть**) *сов перех* (*права, возможности*) to limit; (*палец*) to trap; **ущемля́ть** (~ *perf*) **чьё-н самолю́бие** to hurt *или* wound sb's pride.
ущемле́ни|е (-я) *ср* (*прав, возможностей*) limitation; ~ **чьего́-н самолю́бия** wound to sb's pride.
ущемлённый *прил* (*самолюбие, гордость*) wounded; (*права*) limited.
ущемлю́ *сов см* **ущеми́ть**.
ущемля́|ть (-ю) *несов от* **ущеми́ть**.
уще́рб (-а) *м* (*материальный*) loss; (*здоровью*) detriment; **в** ~ +*dat* to the detriment of; **на** ~**е** on the wane; **наноси́ть (нанести́** *perf*) *или* **причиня́ть (причини́ть** *perf*) ~ **кому́-н/чему́-н** to inflict loss on sb/sth.
уще́рбен *прил см* **уще́рбный**.
уще́рбност|ь (-и) *ж* (*см прил*) waning; abnormality.
уще́рб|ный *прил* (*луна*) waning; (-ен, -на, -но; *характер, психика*) abnormal.
ущипн|у́ть (-у́, -ёшь) *сов перех* to nip, pinch.
Уэ́льс (-а) *м* Wales.
уэ́льск|ий (-ая, -ое, -ие) *прил* Welsh; ~ **язы́к** Welsh.
ую́т (-а) *м* comfort, cosiness.
ую́тен *прил см* **ую́тный**.
ую́тно *нареч* (*расположиться*) comfortably ♦ *как сказ*: **здесь** ~ it's cosy here; **мне здесь** ~ I feel comfortable here.
ую́т|ный (-ен, -на, -но) *прил* cosy.
уязви́мост|ь (-и) *ж* vulnerability.
уязви́м|ый (-, -а, -о) *прил* vulnerable; ~**ое ме́сто** weak spot.
уязв|и́ть (-лю́, -и́шь) *сов перех* to wound, hurt.
уясне́ни|е (-я) *ср* clarification.
уясн|и́ть (-ю́, -и́шь; *impf* **уясня́ть**) *сов перех* (*смысл, значение*) to comprehend; **уясня́ть** (~ *perf*) (**себе́**) to clarify for o.s.

~ Ф, ф ~

Ф, ф *сущ нескл* (*буква*) the 21st letter of the Russian alphabet.

фа *ср нескл* (*МУЗ*) fa.

фа́брик|а (-и) *ж* factory; (*ткацкая, бумажная*) mill.

фабрик|ова́ть (-у́ю; *perf* **сфабрикова́ть**) *несов перех* (*перен*) to fabricate.

фабри́чный *прил* factory *опред*; **фабри́чная ма́рка** trademark.

фа́бул|а (-ы) *ж* plot.

фавори́т (-а) *м* (*также СПОРТ*) the favourite (*BRIT*) *или* favorite (*US*).

фавори́т|ка (-ки; *gen pl* -ок) *ж см* **фавори́т**.

фаго́т (-а) *м* bassoon.

фа́з|а (-ы) *ж* phase; (*работы, строительства*) stage.

фаза́н (-а) *м* pheasant.

файл (-а) *м* (*КОМП*) file.

фак. *сокр* (= **факульте́т**) Fac. (= *Faculty*).

фа́кел (-а) *м* torch; (*дыма, выбросов*) column.

факс (-а) *м* fax; **посыла́ть** (**посла́ть** *perf*) ~ to send a fax.

факси́миле *ср нескл* facsimile.

факси́мильный *прил* facsimile *опред*.

факт (-а) *м* fact; **ста́вить** (**поста́вить** *perf*) **кого́-н пе́ред фа́ктом** to present sb with a fait accompli; **го́лые фа́кты** the bare facts; ~ **тот, что ...** (*разг*) the fact of the matter is that ....

факти́чески *нареч* actually, in fact.

факти́ческ|ий (-ая, -ое, -ие) *прил* (*материал, данные*) factual; (*руководитель, положение дел*) real, actual.

фа́ктор (-а) *м* factor.

факту́р|а (-ы) *ж* texture; (*КОММ*) invoice.

факультати́в (-а) *м* optional *или* elective course.

факультати́в|ный (-ен, -на, -но) *прил* optional, elective.

факульте́т (-а) *м* faculty.

фала́нг|а (-и) *ж* (*АНАТ, ВОЕН*) phalanx.

фа́лд|а (-ы) *ж* tail (*of coat*); (*складка*) crease.

фальсифика́тор (-а) *м* falsifier.

фальсифика́ци|я (-и) *ж* falsification.

фальсифици́р|овать (-ую) (*не*)*сов перех* to falsify.

фальста́рт (-а) *м* (*СПОРТ*) false start.

фальце́т (-а) *м* falsetto.

фальши́в|ить (-лю, -ишь; *perf* **сфальши́вить**) *несов неперех* (*петь*) to sing out of tune;

(*играть*) to play out of tune; (*лицемерить*) to pretend, put on an act.

фальши́в|ка (-ки; *gen pl* -ок) *ж* (*разг*) forgery.

фальши́влю *несов см* **фальши́вить**.

фальши́вок *сущ см* **фальши́вка**.

фальшивомоне́тчик (-а) *м* counterfeiter.

фальшивомоне́тчи|ца (-ы) *ж см* **фальшивомоне́тчик**.

фальши́в|ый *прил* (*документ, паспорт*) false, forged; (*монета, банкнот*) counterfeit; (*пение, инструмент*) out of tune; (*борода, улыбка, нота*) false; (-, -а, -о; *игра актёра*) unnatural, artificial; (*человек, поведение*) insincere.

фальш|ь (-и) *ж* insincerity.

фами́ли|я (-и) *ж* surname; (*королевская, старинная*) family; **де́вичья** ~ maiden name; **как Ва́ша** ~? what is your surname?; **моя́** ~ **Серо́в** my surname is Serov.

фами́льный *прил* family *опред*.

фамилья́рен *прил см* **фамилья́рный**.

фамилья́рнича|ть (-ю) *несов неперех*: ~ (**с** +*instr*) to be too familiar (with).

фамилья́р|ный (-ен, -на, -но) *прил* over(ly)-familiar.

фанати́зм (-а) *м* fanaticism.

фана́тик (-а) *м* (*также перен*) fanatic.

фанати́ч|ный (-ен, -на, -но) *прил* fanatical.

фане́р|а (-ы) *ж* (*для облицовки*) veneer; (*древесный материал*) plywood.

фане́рный *прил* plywood *опред*.

фант (-а) *м* forfeit.

фантазёр (-а) *м* dreamer.

фантазё́р|ка (-ки; *gen pl* -ок) *ж см* **фантазёр**.

фантази́р|овать (-ую) *несов неперех* (*мечтать*) to dream; (*выдумывать*) to make up stories.

фанта́зи|я (-и) *ж* (*художника, писателя*) imagination; (*мечта*) fantasy; (*выдумка*) fib; (*МУЗ*) fantasia.

фанта́ст (-а) *м* writer of fantasy; (*научный*) science-fiction writer.

фанта́стик|а (-и) *ж* (*сказок, преданий*) fantastic element ◆ *собир* (*ЛИТЕРАТУРА*) fantasy; **нау́чная** ~ science fiction; **э́то** ~! (*разг*) it's incredible!

фантасти́ческ|ий (-ая, -ое, -ие) *прил* fantastic; (*причудливый*) fantastical; (*проект*) fantastic, far-fetched.

фа́нтик (-а) *м* wrapper.

фанфа́р|а (-ы) *ж* (*инструмент*) bugle; (*обычно*

мн: *сигнал*) fanfare.

ФАО *сокр* FAO (= *Food and Agriculture Organization*).

фа́р|а (-ы) *ж* (*АВТ, АВИА*) light; **пере́дние** ~ы headlights, headlamps; **за́дние** ~ы rear lights (*BRIT*), taillamps *или* taillamps (*US*).

фарао́н (-а) *м* pharaoh.

фарва́тер (-а) *м* (*МОР*) fairway, channel.

Фаренге́йт (-а) *м* Fahrenheit; **70 гра́дусов по** ~**у** 70 degrees Fahrenheit.

фаре́рск|ий (-ая, -ое, -ие) *прил*: Ф~ие острова́ the Faroe Islands, the Faroes.

фаринги́т (-а) *м* pharyngitis.

фарисе́й (-я) *м* Pharisee.

фарисе́йств|о (-а) *ср* hypocrisy.

фармаколо́ги|я (-и) *ж* pharmacology.

фармаце́вт (-а) *м* chemist, pharmacist.

фарс (-а) *м* farce.

фа́ртук (-а) *м* apron.

фарфо́р (-а) *м*, *собир* porcelain, china.

фарфо́ровый *прил* porcelain, china.

фарцо́вщик (-а) *м* (*разг*) *illegal trader who sells imported goods to Russians.*

фарцо́вщиц|а (-ы) *ж см* **фарцо́вщик.**

фарш (-а) *м* stuffing, forcemeat; (*мясной*) mince, minced *или* ground (*US*) meat.

фарширо́ванный *прил* (*КУЛИН*) stuffed.

фарширова́ть (-у́ю; *perf* **зафарширова́ть**) *несов перех* to stuff.

ФАС *сокр* f.a.s. (= *free alongside ship*).

фас (-а) *м* (*ФОТО*) front.

фаса́д (-а) *м* (*лицевая сторона*) facade, front; **за́дний** ~ back; **боково́й** ~ side.

фас|ова́ть (-у́ю; *perf* **расфасова́ть**) *несов перех* to prepack.

фасо́вк|а (-и) *ж* packing.

фасо́вочн|ый *прил* (*цех, машина*) packing *опред*; ~ая бума́га wrapping paper.

фасо́л|ь (-и) *ж* (*растение*) bean plant ♦ *собир* (*БОТ*; *семена*) beans *мн*; **кра́сная** ~ kidney beans *мн.*

фасо́н (-а) *м* style.

фат|а́ (-ы́) *ж* veil.

фата́л|ьный (-ен, -ьна, -ьно) *прил* fatal, fateful.

фа́ун|а (-ы) *ж* fauna.

фаши́зм (-а) *м* fascism.

фаши́ст (-а) *м* fascist.

фаши́стск|ий (-ая, -ое, -ие) *прил* fascist.

фая́нс (-а) *м* (*материал*) faïence ♦ *собир* (*изделия*) faïence, glazed earthenware.

фая́нсовый *прил* (*посуда, изделия*) glazed earthenware *опред*.

ФБР *ср сокр* (= *Федера́льное бюро́ рассле́дований* (*США*)) FBI (= *Federal Bureau of Investigation*).

февра́л|ь (-я́) *м* February; *см также* **октя́брь.**

февра́льск|ий (-ая, -ое, -ие) *прил* February *опред*.

федера́льный *прил* federal; **Федера́льное бюро́ рассле́дований** Federal Bureau of Investigation; **Федера́льное собра́ние** (*ПОЛИТ*) the Federal Assembly (*upper house of the Russian Parliament*).

федерати́вный *прил* federal.

федера́ци|я (-и) *ж* federation; **Росси́йская Ф~** the Russian Federation; **Сове́т Ф~и** *upper chamber of the Russian parliament.*

фее́ри|я (-и) *ж* magic show.

фейерве́рк (-а) *м* firework.

фе́льдшер (-а) *м* medical assistant.

фельето́н (-а) *м* satirical article.

фемини́ст|ка (-ки; *gen pl* -ок) *ж* feminist.

фен (-а) *м* hairdryer.

фено́мен (-а) *м* phenomenon (*мн* phenomena).

феномена́л|ьный (-ен, -ьна, -ьно) *прил* phenomenal.

феода́л (-а) *м* feudal lord.

феодали́зм (-а) *м* feudalism.

феода́льный *прил* feudal.

ферз|ь (-я́) *м* (*ШАХМАТЫ*) queen.

фе́рм|а (-ы) *ж* farm.

ферме́нт (-а) *м* ferment, enzyme.

фе́рмер (-а) *м* farmer.

фе́рмерск|ий (-ая, -ое, -ие) *прил*: ~ое хозя́йство farm.

фестива́л|ь (-я) *м* festival.

фетр (-а) *м* felt.

фе́тровый *прил* felt.

фехтова́льщик (-а) *м* fencer.

фехтова́льщиц|а (-ы) *ж см* **фехтова́льщик.**

фехтова́ни|е (-я) *ср* (*СПОРТ*) fencing.

фешене́бел|ьный (-ен, -ьна, -ьно) *прил* fashionable.

фе́|я (-и) *ж* fairy.

фи *межд*: ~! ugh!

фиа́л|ка (-ки; *gen pl* -ок) *ж* violet.

фиа́ско *ср нескл* fiasco; **терпе́ть** (**потерпе́ть** *perf*) ~ to suffer an embarrassment.

фи́г|а (-и) *ж* (*БОТ*) fig; (*разг*) fig (*gesture of refusal*); **ни фига́ не полу́чишь** (**от них**) (*разг*) you won't get a thing out of them; **иди́ на́ фиг** (*разг*) get lost, clear off.

фи́говый *прил* fig *опред*.

фиго́вый *прил* (*разг*) lousy, rotten.

фигу́р|а (-ы) *ж* (*ГЕОМ, перен*) figure; (*ШАХМАТЫ*) (chess)piece; **фигу́ра вы́сшего пилота́жа** aerobatic figure.

фигура́л|ьный (-ен, -ьна, -ьно) *прил* figurative.

фигури́р|овать (-ую) *несов неперех* (*присутствовать*) to be present; (*имя, тема*) to figure; ~ (*impf*) **на суде́ в ка́честве свиде́теля** to appear as a witness.

фигури́ст (-а) *м* figure skater.

фигури́ст|ка (-ки; *gen pl* -ок) *ж см* **фигури́ст.**

фигу́р|ка (-ки; *gen pl* -ок) *ж* (*скульптура*) figurine, statuette; (*обычно мн*: *игральная*) piece.

фигу́рный *прил* (*резьба*) figured; (*СПОРТ*) figure *опред*; **фигу́рное ката́ние** figure skating; **фигу́рные ско́бки** curly *или* brace brackets.

фигу́рок *сущ см* **фигу́рка**.

Фи́джи *ср нескл* Fiji.

фи́зик (-а) *м* physicist.

фи́зик|а (-и) *ж* physics.

физио́лог (-а) *м* physiologist.

физиологи́ческ|ий (-ая, -ое, -ие) *прил* physiological.

физиоло́ги|я (-и) *ж* physiology.

физионо́ми|я (-и) *ж* (*разг*) face.

физиотерапе́вт (-а) *м* physiotherapist.

физиотерапевти́ческ|ий (-ая, -ое, -ие) *прил* physiotherapy *опред*.

физиотерапи́|я (-и) *ж* physiotherapy.

физи́ческ|ий (-ая, -ое, -ие) *прил* (*также СПОРТ, физ*) physical; (*труд*) manual; **физи́ческая культу́ра** physical education; **физи́ческие упражне́ния** physical exercise *ед*; **физи́ческое лицо́** (*ЮР*) individual; **физи́ческое наси́лие** physical violence.

физкульту́р|а (-ы) *ж сокр* (= **физи́ческая культу́ра**) PE (= *physical education*).

физма́т (-а) *м сокр* = **фи́зико-математи́ческий факульте́т**.

фикс *м*: **иде́я ~** idée fixe.

фикса́ж (-а) *м* (*ФОТО*) fixer.

фикса́ция (-и) *ж* (*ТЕХ*) clamping; (*ФОТО*) fixing.

фикси́р|овать (-ую; *perf* **зафикси́ровать**) *несов перех* (*события, факты, показания*) to record, chronicle; (*срок, дату, цены*) to fix, set; (*внимание, взгляд*) to fix; (*груз, тормоз*) to clamp, fix.

фикти́вн|ый (-ен, -на, -но) *прил* fictitious; **фикти́вный брак** (*ЮР*) marriage of convenience.

фи́кус (-а) *м* ficus; (*каучуконосный*) rubber plant.

фи́кци|я (-и) *ж* fiction.

филармо́ни|я (-и) *ж* (*зал*) concert hall; (*организация*) philharmonic society.

филатели́ст (-а) *м* philatelist.

филе́ *ср нескл* (*сорт мяса*) fillet.

филиа́л (-а) *м* branch.

филигра́нн|ый (-ен, -на, -но) *прил* (*изделия, орнамент*) filigree; (*перен: работа*) intricate.

фи́лин (-а) *м* eagle owl.

филиппи́н|ец (-ца) *м* Filipino.

филиппи́н|ка (-ки; *gen pl* -ок) *ж см* **филиппи́нец**.

филиппи́нск|ий (-ая, -ое, -ие) *прил* Filipino, Philippine.

филиппи́нца *итп сущ см* **филиппи́нец**.

Филиппи́н|ы (-) *мн* the Philippines *мн*.

фило́лог (-а) *м* philologist (*specialist in languages and literature*).

филологи́ческ|ий (-ая, -ое, -ие) *прил* philological; **филологи́ческий факульте́т** faculty of philology.

филоло́ги|я (-и) *ж* philology (*study of language*

and literature).

фило́н|ить (-ю, -ишь) *несов неперех* (*разг*) to skive.

фило́соф (-а) *м* philosopher.

филосо́фи|я (-и) *ж* philosophy.

филфа́к (-а) *м сокр* = **филологи́ческий факульте́т**.

фильм (-а) *м* film; **сего́дня идёт хоро́ший ~** there's a good film on today.

фильмоско́п (-а) *м* slide projector.

фильтр (-а) *м* filter.

фильтр|ова́ть (-у́ю; *perf* **профильтрова́ть**) *несов перех* to filter.

фин. *сокр* (= **фина́нсовый**) fin. (= *financial*).

фина́л (-а) *м* (*спектакля, концерта*) finale; (*СПОРТ*) final; **выходи́ть** (**вы́йти** *perf*) **в ~** to reach the final.

фина́льный *прил* (*также СПОРТ, КОММ*) final *опред*.

финанси́ровани|е (-я) *ср* financing.

финанси́р|овать (-ую) *несов перех* to finance.

финанси́ст (-а) *м* (*предприниматель*) financier; (*специалист*) *specialist in financial matters*.

фина́нсовый *прил* financial; (*год*) fiscal; (*отдел, инспектор, комиссия*) finance *опред*; **~ институ́т** institute of finance; **~ отчёт** financial statement.

фина́нс|ы (-ов) *мн* finances *мн*; (*деньги*) cash *ед*; **Министе́рство ~ов** ≈ the Treasury (*BRIT*), ≈ the Treasury Department *или* Department of the Treasury (*US*).

фи́ник (-а) *м* (*плод*) date; (*дерево*) date palm.

фини́фт|ь (-и) *ж, собир* decorated Russian enamel.

фи́ниш (-а) *м* (*СПОРТ*) finish; **приходи́ть** (**прийти́** *perf*) **к ~у** to reach the finish.

финиши́р|овать (-ую) (*не*)*сов неперех* to finish, come in.

фи́нишн|ый *прил* finishing *опред*; **выходи́ть** (**вы́йти** *perf*) **на ~ую прямую́** to reach the final straight; (*перен*) to be on the home straight; **~ая черта́/ле́нточка** finishing line/tape.

фи́н|ка (-ки; *gen pl* -ок) *ж см* **финн**; (*разг: нож*) Finnish knife.

Финля́нди|я (-и) *ж* Finland.

финн (-а) *ж* Finn.

фи́нн|ок (-ка) *ж см* **фи́нка**.

фи́нск|ий (-ая, -ое, -ие) *прил* Finnish; **~ язы́к** Finnish; **Фи́нский зали́в** Gulf of Finland.

финт (-а́) *м* (*СПОРТ*) feint; (*разг: уловка*) trick.

финт|и́ть (-чу́, -ти́шь) *несов неперех* (*разг*) to be tricky.

Ф.И.О. *сокр* (= **фами́лия, и́мя, о́тчество**) *surname, first name, patronymic*.

ф.и.о. *сокр* = **Ф.И.О.**.

фиоле́товый *прил* purple.

фи́рм|а (-ы) *ж* firm; (*разг: модная вещь*) quality; **секре́т ~ы** (*разг*) trade secret.

фи́рменный *прил* (*марка, ресторан*) firm's, company *опред*; (*магазин*) chain *опред*; (*разг:*

джинсы, юбка, костюм итп) quality *опред*
(*usually of imported brand names*);
фи́рменный знак brand name.
фиста́шк|а (**-и**) *ж* pistachio.
фити́л|ь (**-я́**) *м* wick; (*взрывных устройств*)
fuse.
ФИФА́ *ж сокр* (= *Междунаро́дная федера́ция*
футбо́ла) FIFA (= *Fédération Internationale*
de Football Association).
фи́ф|а (**-ы**) *ж* (*разг*) bimbo, dolly bird.
фи́шка (**-ки**; *gen pl* **-ек**) *ж* counter, chip.
флаг (**-а**) *м* flag.
фла́гман (**-а**) *м* (*командующий*) flag officer;
(*корабль*) flagship.
флагшто́к (**-а**) *м* flagpole.
флаж|о́к (**-ка́**) *ж* flag.
флако́н (**-а**) *м* bottle.
флама́нд|ец (**-ца**) *м* Fleming.
флама́нд|ка (**-ки**; *gen pl* **-ок**) *ж см* **флама́ндец**.
флама́ндск|ий (**-ая, -ое, -ие**) *прил* Flemish; ~
язы́к Flemish.
флама́ндца *итп сущ см* **флама́ндец**.
флами́нго *м нескл* flamingo.
фланг (**-а**) *м* flank.
Фла́ндри|я (**-и**) *ж* Flanders.
флане́левый *прил* flannel.
флане́л|ь (**-и**) *ж* flannel.
флегма́тик (**-а**) *м*: **он** ~ he is phlegmatic.
флегмати́ч|ный (**-ен, -на, -но**) *прил*
phlegmatic.
фле́йт|а (**-ы**) *ж* flute.
флейти́ст (**-а**) *м* flautist.
фле́кси|я (**-и**) *ж* inflection.
флекти́вный *прил* inflected.
фли́гел|ь (**-я**) *м* (*АРХИТ*) wing.
флирт (**-а**) *м* flirtation.
флирт|ова́ть (**-у́ю**) *несов неперех*: ~ (**с** +*instr*)
to flirt (with).
флокс (**-а**) *м* phlox.
флома́стер (**-а**) *м* felt-tip (pen).
флор|а (**-ы**) *ж* flora.
флоренти́йск|ий (**-ая, -ое, -ие**) *прил*
Florentine.
Флоре́нци|я (**-и**) *ж* Florence.
флот (**-а**) *м* (*ВОЕН*) navy; (*МОР*) fleet.
флоти́ли|я (**-и**) *ж* flotilla.
флю́гер (**-а**) *м* wind gauge; (*на башне*) weather
vane.
флюи́д|ы (**-ов**) *мн* (*разг*) vibes *мн*.
флюорогра́фи|я (**-и**) *ж* fluorography.
флюс (**-а**) *м* (dental) abscess, gumboil.
фля́г|а (**-и**) *ж* (*для воды, спирта*) flask; (*для*
молока, для сметаны) churn.
ФНО *м сокр* (= *Фронт национа́льного*
освобожде́ния) NLF (= *National Liberation*
Front).
ФОБ *сокр* (= *фра́нко-борт*) f.o.b. (= *free on*
board).
фойе́ *ср нескл* foyer.

фокстерье́р (**-а**) *м* fox terrier.
фокстро́т (**-а**) *м* foxtrot.
фо́кус (**-а**) *м* trick; (*ТЕХ, перен*) focus;
выки́дывать (вы́кинуть *perf*) ~ (*перен: разг*)
to start some nonsense.
фо́кусник (**-а**) *м* conjurer.
фолкле́ндск|ий (**-ая, -ое, -ие**) *прил*: Ф~ие
острова́ the Falkland Islands, the Falklands.
фольг|а́ (**-и́**) *ж* foil.
фолькло́р (**-а**) *м* folklore.
фолькло́рный *прил* (*фестиваль, ансамбль*)
folk *опред*.
фон (**-а**) *м* background; **на фо́не чего́-н** against a
background of sth; **на фо́не кого́-н** next to sb,
compared to sb.
фона́р|ь (**-я́**) *м* (*уличный*) lamp; (*карманный*)
torch; (*разг: синяк*) black eye, shiner; **ему́ всё**
до фонаря́ (*разг*) he doesn't give a toss about
anything.
фонд (**-а**) *м* (*организация*) fund, foundation;
(*денежные средства, запас*) fund; (*жилищный,*
семенной, земельный) resources *мн*; **фо́нды**
(*ценные бумаги*) stocks; **уставно́й** ~ (*КОММ*)
authorized capital.
фо́ндов|ый *прил*: ~**ая би́ржа** stock exchange.
фоне́тик|а (**-и**) *ж* phonetics.
фоногра́мм|а (**-ы**) *ж* recording; **петь (спеть**
perf) **под** ~**у** to mime to a recording.
фоноло́ги|я (**-и**) *ж* phonology.
фоноте́к|а (**-и**) *ж* record and tape collection.
фонта́н (**-а**) *м* fountain; (*нефти*) gusher.
фо́р|а (**-ы**) *ж*: **дать кому́-н** ~**у** (*разг*) to give sb a
start *или* an advantage; (*перен: разг*) to be miles
better than sb.
фо́рвард (**-а**) *м* forward.
форе́л|ь (**-и**) *ж* trout.
фо́рм|а (**-ы**) *ж* (*также линг*) form; (*одежда*)
uniform; (*ТЕХ*) mould; (*КУЛИН*) (cake) tin (*BRIT*)
или pan (*US*); **быть** (*impf*) **в** ~**е** to be in good
form; *см также* **фо́рмы**.
форма́лен *прил см* **форма́льный**.
формали́зм (**-а**) *м* (*в искусстве, в науке*)
formalism; ~ **в рабо́те** bureaucratic attitude to
work.
формали́ст (**-а**) *м* (*бюрократ*) bureaucrat.
формали́стик|а (**-и**) *ж* bureaucracy.
форма́льно *нареч* (*относиться*) formally; ~
он прав factually he's right.
форма́льность (**-и**) *ж* formality.
форма́льный (**-ен, -ьна, -ьно**) *прил*
(*отношение, подход*) bureaucratic; (*ответ*)
nominal; (*no short form; согласие, метод,*
логика) formal.
форма́т (**-а**) *м* format.
формати́р|овать (**-ую**) (*не)сов перех* (*КОМП*) to
format.
форма́ци|я (**-и**) *ж* (*общественная*) structure;
челове́к но́вой ~**и** forward-thinking person.

фо́рменн|ый прил (безобразие, негодяй) absolute; **~ бланк** official form; **фо́рменная оде́жда** uniform.

формирова́ни|е (-я) ср formation; **вое́нное ~** military unit.

формир|ова́ть (-у́ю; perf **сформирова́ть**) несов перех to form

▶ **формирова́ться** (perf **сформирова́ться**) несов возв to form.

фо́рмул|а (-ы) ж formula.

формули́р|овать (-у́ю; perf **сформули́ровать**) несов перех to formulate.

формулиро́в|ка (-ки; gen pl -ок) ж (мысли, предложения) formulation; (определение) definition.

формуля́р (-а) м library ticket или card.

фо́рм|ы (-) мн (раза) curves мн.

форпо́ст (-а) м (ВОЕН) outpost; (перен: демократии, науки) stronghold.

форс (-а) м (разг) swank.

форси́р|овать (-у́ю) (не)сов перех to force.

фор|си́ть (-шу́, -си́шь) несов неперех (разг) to show off.

форсу́н|ка (-ки; gen pl -ок) ж (двигателя) fuel injector.

форт (-а; loc sg -у́, nom pl -ы́) м fort.

фортепья́нный прил piano опред.

фортепья́но ср нескл piano.

фо́рточ|ка (-ки; gen pl -ек) ж hinged, upper pane for ventilation.

форту́н|а (-ы) ж fortune.

фо́рум (-а) м forum.

форшу́ несов см **форси́ть.**

фосфа́т (-а) м (обычно мн) phosphate.

фо́сфор (-а) м phosphorous.

фо́то ср нескл (разг) photo.

фотоаппара́т (-а) м camera.

фотоателье́ ср нескл photographic или photographer's studio.

фотобума́г|а (-и) ж photographic paper.

фотогени́ч|ный (-ен, -на, -но) прил photogenic.

фото́граф (-а) м photographer.

фотографи́р|овать (-ую; perf **сфотографи́ровать**) несов перех to photograph

▶ **фотографи́роваться** (perf **сфотографи́роваться**) несов возв to have one's photo(graph) taken.

фотогра́фи|я (-и) ж (занятие) photography; (снимок) photograph; (учреждение) photographer's studio.

фотока́рточ|ка (-ки; gen pl -ек) ж photo.

фотоси́нтез (-а) м photosynthesis.

фототелегра́мм|а (-ы) ж phototelegram.

фотоэлеме́нт (-а) м photocell.

фрагме́нт (-а) м (фильма, спектакля) excerpt; (древних сосудов итп) fragment.

фрагмента́р|ный (-ен, -на, -но) прил fragmentary.

фра́з|а (-ы) ж phrase.

фразеоло́ги|я (-и) ж (линг) phraseology;

(пустословие) rhetoric.

фрак (-а) м tail coat, tails мн.

фракцио́нный прил factional.

фра́кци|я (-и) ж faction.

франк (-а) м franc.

фра́нко прил неизм (КОММ): **~ вдоль бо́рта су́дна** free alongside ship; **~железнодоро́жный ваго́н** free on rail.

Фра́нкфурт (-а) м Frankfurt.

франт (-а) м dandy.

Фра́нци|я (-и) ж France.

францу́жен|ка (-ки; gen pl -ок) ж Frenchwoman (мн Frenchwomen).

францу́з (-а) м Frenchman (мн Frenchmen).

францу́зск|ий (-ая, -ое, -ие) прил French; **~ язы́к** French.

франши́з|а (-ы) ж (КОММ) franchise; **держа́тель/предостави́тель ~ы** franchisee/franchiser.

фрахт (-а) м freight; **~, упла́чиваемый по прибы́тие** (КОММ) freight inward; **~, упла́чиваемый в порту́ вы́грузки** (КОММ) freight forward.

фрахт|ова́ть (-у́ю; perf **зафрахтова́ть**) несов перех to charter.

ФРГ ж сокр (ИСТ: = Федерати́вная Респу́блика Герма́нии) FRG (= *Federal Republic of Germany*).

фрега́т (-а) м frigate.

фре́йлин|а (-ы) ж lady-in-waiting (мн ladies-in-waiting).

фре́с|ка (-ки; gen pl -ок) ж fresco.

фриво́лен прил см **фриво́льный.**

фриво́льность (-и) ж frivolity.

фриво́л|ьный (-ен, -ьна, -ьно) прил frivolous.

фриз (-а) м frieze.

фрикаде́л|ька (-ьки; gen pl -ек) ж meatball.

фронт (-а; nom pl -ы́) м front; **рабо́тать** (impf) **на два фро́нта** (перен) to do two things at the same time.

фронта́л|ьный (-ен, -ьна, -ьно) прил (ВОЕН) frontal; (перен) по́лный, general.

фронтиспи́с (-а) м frontispiece.

фронтови́к (-а́) м front line soldier; (ветеран) war veteran.

фронто́н (-а) м (АРХИТ) pediment.

фрукт (-а) м (БОТ) fruit; (раза: пренебр: человек) suspicious character.

фрукто́вый прил fruit опред.

фрукто́з|а (-ы) ж fructose.

ФСК ж сокр (= Федера́льная слу́жба контрразве́дки) *Russian counterespionage intelligence service.*

фтор (-а) м fluorin(e).

фу межд: **~! ugh!**

фу́г|а (-и) ж fugue.

фу́кси|я (-и) ж fuchsia.

фуже́р (-а) м wineglass; (для шампанского) flute.

фунда́мент (-а) м (СТРОИТ) foundation, base; (перен: семьи, науки) foundation, basis.

фундаментáл|ьный (-ен, -ьна, -ьно) *прил*
(*здание, мост*) sound, solid; (*перен: знания,
труд*) profound; ~**ьные наýки** basic science.
фундýк (-á) *м* (*кустарник*) hazel; (*плод*)
hazelnut.
функулёр (-а) *м* funicular railway.
функционáл|ьный (-ен, -ьна, -ьно) *прил*
functional; **функционáльная клáвиша** (*КОМП*)
function key.
функционéр (-а) *м* official, functionary.
функциони́р|овать (-ую) *несов неперех* to
function.
фу́нкци|я (-и) *ж* function; (*круг обязанностей*)
function, duties *мн*.
фунт (-а) *м* pound.
фура́ж (-á) *м* fodder.
фура́ж|ка (-ки; *gen pl* -ек) *ж* cap; (*ВОЕН*) forage
cap.
фургóн (-а) *м* (*АВТ*) van; (*конная повозка*)
(covered) wagon.
фу́ри|я (-и) *ж* (*разг*) virago.
фурóр (-а) *м* furore; **производи́ть (произвести́**

perf) ~ to create a furore.
фуру́нкул (-а) *м* boil.
фут (-а) *м* foot.
футбóл (-а) *м* football (*BRIT*), soccer;
америкáнский ~ (American) football.
футболи́ст (-а) *м* footballer (*BRIT*), soccer
player.
футбóл|ка (-ки; *gen pl* -ок) *ж* T-shirt, tee shirt.
футбóльный *прил* football *опред*, soccer
опред; **футбóльный мяч** football.
футля́р (-а) *м* case.
фуфá|йка (-йки; *gen pl* -ек) *ж* (*ватник*) padded
jacket; (*вязаная рубашка*) jersey.
фы́рка|ть (-ю) *несов неперех* (*животное*) to
snort; (*разг: смеяться*) to snort with laughter; (:
брюзжать) to complain.
фы́ркн|уть (-у, -ешь) *сов неперех* (*животное*)
to give a snort; (*разг: издать смешок*) to snort
with laughter.
фырчá|ть (-ý, -и́шь) *несов неперех* (*разг*) to
snort; (*брюзжать*) to whinge.
фью́черс|ы (-ов) *мн* (*КОММ*) futures *мн*.

~ X, x ~

X, x *сущ нескл (буква)* the 22nd letter of the Russian alphabet.

ха́ки *прил неизм, ср нескл* khaki.

хала́т (-а) *м (домашний)* dressing gown; **ба́нный** ~ bathrobe.

хала́тен *прил см* **хала́тный**.

хала́тность (-и) *ж* negligence.

хала́тный (-ен, -на, -но) *прил* negligent.

халва́ (-ы́) *ж* halva.

халту́ра (-ы) *ж (разг: плохая работа)* shoddy work; (: *работа на стороне)* moonlighting.

халту́рить (-ю, -ишь; *perf* **схалту́рить)** *несов неперех (разг)* to cut corners; (*no perf*; *разг*: *работать на стороне)* to moonlight.

хам (-а) *м (разг)* brute, lout.

хамелео́н (-а) *м (также перен)* chameleon.

хаме́ть (-ю; *perf* **охаме́ть)** *несов неперех* to become impudent.

хам|и́ть (-лю́, -и́шь; *perf* **нахами́ть)** *несов неперех:* ~ (+*dat*) *(разг)* to be cheeky (*BRIT*) или rude (*US*) (to).

ха́м|ка (-ки; *gen pl* -ок) *ж (разг)* hussy.

хамлю́ *сов см* **хами́ть**.

ха́мок *сущ см* **ха́мка**.

ха́мский (-ая, -ое, -ие) *прил (разг)* brutish, loutish.

ха́мство (-а) *ср* rudeness.

хан (-а) *м* khan.

хандра́ (-ы́) *ж* depression.

хандр|и́ть (-ю́, -и́шь) *несов неперех* to feel down.

ханж|а́ (-и́; *gen pl* -е́й) *м/ж* prude, prig.

ха́нжество (-а) *ср* prudishness, priggishness.

Хано́|й (-я) *м* Hanoi.

ха́ос (-а) *м* chaos.

хаоти́чен *прил см* **хаоти́чный**.

хаоти́ческий (-ая, -ое, -ие) *прил* chaotic.

хаоти́|чный (-ен, -на, -но) *прил* = **хаоти́ческий**.

ха́па|ть (-ю, -ешь) *несов перех (разг: хватать)* to grab at; (: *присваивать)* to swipe.

хара́ктер (-а) *м* nature; (*человека)* personality; **он челове́к с** ~**ом** he has a lot of character; **выде́рживать (вы́держать** *perf*) ~ to hold firm.

хара́ктерен *прил см* **характе́рный**.

характеризова́ть (-у́ю) *несов перех* to be typical of; (*perf* **охарактеризова́ть**; *персонаж, эпоху итп)* to characterize; **его́** ~**ует доброта́** he is a kind person

▶ **характеризова́ться** *несов возв* (+*instr*) to be characterized by.

характери́стик|а (-и) *ж (документ)* (character) reference; (*описание)* description.

характе́р|ный (-ен, -на, -но) *прил (внешность, поведение)* distinctive; (*свойственный*): ~ **(для** +*gen*) characteristic (of); (*no short form*; *обычаи, танцы итп)* typical; **для него́** ~ **перио́ды депре́ссии** he tends to go through bouts of depression.

ха́рка|ть (-ю) *несов неперех* (+*instr*; *кровью, слизью)* to cough up.

ха́рти|я (-и) *ж (документ)* charter.

харч (-а; *nom pl* -и́, *gen pl* -е́й) *м (обычно мн: разг)* grub *ед*, chow *ед*.

харчо́ *ср нескл* spicy Georgian meat and vegetable soup.

ха́р|я (-и) *ж (разг)* mug (*face*).

ха́т|а (-ы) *ж* cottage (*in Southern Russia and Ukraine*); **моя́** ~ **с кра́ю** *(разг)* it's nothing to do with me.

ха-ха́ *межд* ha-ha.

хачапу́ри *ср нескл* flat Georgian pie filled with cheese.

ха́я|ть (-ю) *несов перех (разг)* to slag off.

х/б *сокр* = **хлопчатобума́жный**.

хвал|а́ (-ы́) *ж* praise.

хвале́бный *прил* complimentary.

хвалёный *прил* celebrated.

хвал|и́ть (-ю́, -ишь; *perf* **похвали́ть)** *несов перех* to praise.

▶ **хвали́ться** (*perf* **похвали́ться)** *несов возв:* ~**ся** (+*instr*) *(разг)* to show off (about).

хваста́|ться (-юсь; *perf* **похва́статься)** *несов возв:* ~ (+*instr*) to boast (about).

хвастли́в|ый (-, -а, -о) *прил* boastful.

хвастовств|о́ (-а́) *ср* boasting.

хвасту́н (-а́) *м (разг)* show-off.

хвасту́н|ья (-ьи; *gen pl* -ий) *ж см* **хвасту́н**.

хвата́|ть (-ю; *perf* **схвати́ть)** *несов перех* to grab (hold of); (*преступника)* to arrest; (*разг: простуду, насморк)* to catch; (: *плохую отме́тку, оплеу́ху)* to get ♦ (*perf* **хвати́ть)** *безл* (+*gen*; *денег, времени итп)* to have enough; **мне** ~**ет де́нег на еду́** I've got enough to buy food; **его́ не хвати́ло на э́то** he wasn't up to it; **он** ~**л всё подря́д** *(разг)* he grabbed whatever he could; ~ (*impf*) **за́ душу** to tug at one's heartstrings; ~ **(схвати́ть** *perf*) **что-н на лету́** to grasp sth in an instant; **э́того ещё не** ~**ло!**

(*разг*) as if that wasn't enough!; **не ~ет то́лько, что́бы он отказа́лся** (*разг*) now all we need is for him to refuse

▶ **хвата́ться** (*perf* **схвати́ться**) *несов возв*: **~ся за** +*acc* (*за се́рдце*) to clutch at; (*за дверь, за ору́жие*) to grab; **~ся** (*impf*) **за всё сра́зу** (*разг*) to try to do everything at once; **~ся** (**схвати́ться** *perf*) **за соло́минку** to clutch at straws; **~ся** (**схвати́ться** *perf*) **за́ голову** (*перен*) to panic.

хва́ти́ть (**-чу́, -тишь**) *сов от* **хвата́ть** ♦ *перех* (*разг*): **~ по рю́мочке/ча́йку́** to have a quick drink/cuppa; (+*gen*; *беды, го́ря*) to suffer; (*разг: уда́рить*) to whack, thump ♦ *безл* (*разг*): **хва́тит!** that's enough!; **его́ ~ти́л парали́ч** he was paralysed; **её ~ти́л уда́р** she had a stroke; **он ~ти́л меня́ по голове́** he thumped me on the head; **он ~ти́л кулако́м по столу́** he banged on the table with his fist; **хва́тит спо́ров** *или* **спо́рить!** (*разг*) that's enough of this arguing!; **~** (*perf*) **че́рез край** to go too far; **с меня́ хва́тит!** I've had enough!

▶ **хвати́ться** *сов возв* (*разг*): **~ся чего́-н/кого́-н** to notice that sth/sb is gone.

хва́т|ка (**-ки**; *gen pl* **-ок**) *ж* grip; (*перен: ло́вкость*) skill; **делова́я ~** business acumen; **вцепля́ться** (**вцепи́ться** *perf*) **в что́-н/кого́-н мёртвой ~кой** (*также перен*) to cling onto sth/sb for dear life.

хвать *как сказ* (*разг*): **он меня́ ~ по голове́** he whacked me right in the head; **я поверну́лся, и ~ – нет кошелька́** I turned round and my purse (*BRIT*) *или* wallet (*US*) had vanished.

хвачу́(сь) *сов см* **хвати́ть(ся)**.

х-во *сокр* = **хозя́йство**.

хво́йный *прил* coniferous; **хво́йное де́рево** conifer.

хвора́|ть (**-ю**) *несов неперех* to feel poorly (*BRIT*), to feel sick (*US*).

хво́рост (**-а**; *part gen* **-у**) *м собир* firewood; (*кули́н*) *sugar-coated strips of dough fried in oil*.

хворости́н|а (**-ы**) *ж* switch.

хво́рый *прил* (*разг*) ill.

хвор|ь (**-и**) *ж* ailment.

хвост (**-а́**) *м* tail; (*по́езда*) tail end; (*перен: пы́ли, зева́к итп*) trail; (*разг: о́чередь*) queue (*BRIT*), line (*US*); (: *по матема́тике итп*) *an exam which has to be taken again*.

хво́стик (**-а**) *м* (*мы́ши, реди́ски*) tail; **ему́ 50 с ~ом** (*разг*) he's just over 50.

хвостов|о́й *прил* tail *опред*; **~а́я часть** (*самолёта, по́езда*) the tail end.

хвощ (**-а́**) *м* (*БОТ*) horsetail.

хво́|я (**-и**) *ж собир* needles *мн* (*of a conifer*).

ХДС *м сокр* (= **Христиа́нско-демократи́ческий сою́з**) CDU (= *Christian Democratic Union*).

хек (**-а**) *м* whiting.

хе́кер (**-а**) *м* (*КОМП*) hacker.

Хе́льсинки *м нескл* Helsinki.

хе́рес (**-а**; *part gen* **-у**) *м* sherry.

хи́жин|а (**-ы**) *ж* hut.

хи́л|ый (**-, -а́, -о**) *прил* (*мужчи́на, рука́*) puny; (*расте́ние, ребёнок*) sickly; (*дом, постро́йка*) rickety.

хи́мик (**-а**) *м* chemist.

химика́т (**-а**) *м* chemical.

химиотерапи́|я (**-и**) *ж* chemotherapy.

хими́ческ|ий (**-ая, -ое, -ие**) *прил* chemical *опред*; (*факульте́т, кабине́т*) chemistry *опред*; **хими́ческий каранда́ш** *graphite pencil which writes in purple when moistened*.

хи́ми|я (**-и**) *ж* chemistry; **бытова́я ~** household chemicals *мн*.

химчи́ст|ка (**-ки**; *gen pl* **-ок**) *ж сокр* = **хими́ческая чи́стка**; (*проце́сс*) dry-cleaning; (*пункт приёма*) dry-cleaner('s).

хини́н (**-а**) *м* quinine.

хи́ппи *м нескл* hippie.

хире́|ть (**-ю**; *perf* **захире́ть**) *несов неперех* (*челове́к*) to waste away; (*расте́ние*) to wither; (*перен: тво́рчество, тала́нт*) to dry up.

хирома́нти|я (**-и**) *ж* palmistry.

Хироси́м|а (**-ы**) *ж* Hiroshima.

хиру́рг (**-а**) *м* surgeon.

хирурги́ческ|ий (**-ая, -ое, -ие**) *прил* surgical; (*больно́й, кли́ника*) surgery *опред*.

хирурги́|я (**-и**) *ж* surgery.

хит (**-а**) *м* (*МУЗ*) hit.

хитёр *прил см* **хи́трый**.

хитре́ц (**-а́**) *м* cunning devil.

хитр|и́ть (**-ю́, -и́шь**; *perf* **схитри́ть**) *несов неперех* to act slyly.

хи́тро *нареч* cunningly; (*сде́ланный*) intricately.

хи́трост|ь (**-и**) *ж* slyness; (*уло́вка*) cunning.

хитроу́ми|е (**-я**) *ср* ingenuity.

хитроу́м|ный (**-ен, -на, -но**) *прил* ingenious.

хи́т|рый (**-ёр, -ра́, -ро**) *прил* sly, cunning; (*изобрета́тельный*) cunning; (*замыслова́тый*) intricate.

хихи́ка|ть (**-ю**) *несов неперех* (*разг*) to giggle; (: *смея́ться исподти́шка*) to snigger.

хи́щен *прил см* **хи́щный**.

хище́ни|е (**-я**) *ср* misappropriation.

хи́щник (**-а**) *м* (*также перен*) predator.

хи́щниц|а (**-ы**) *ж* (*перен*) predator.

хи́щническ|ий (**-ая, -ое, -ие**) *прил* (*поли́тика, инсти́нкт*) predatory; (*истребле́ние ле́са, охо́та*) ruthless; (*испо́льзование ресу́рсов*) rapacious.

хи́щ|ный (**-ен, -на, -но**) *прил* (*также перен*) predatory; (*де́лец, торга́ш*) cutthroat; **~ная пти́ца** bird of prey.

хладнокро́вен *прил см* **хладнокро́вный**.

хладнокро́ви|е (**-я**) *ср* composure.

хладнокро́в|ный (**-ен, -на, -но**) *прил* composed; (*уби́йство итп*) cold-blooded.

хлам (**-а**) *м собир* (*также перен*) junk.

хлеб (**-а**) *м* bread; (*зерно́*) grain; (*nom pl* **-ы́**) *формово́й, кру́глый*) loaf (*мн* loaves); (*nom pl* -а́; *ози́мые, ярово́е*) cereal; **зараба́тывать** (*impf*) **на ~** to earn a crust; **~ насу́щный** bread and butter (*fig*); **~-соль** bread and salt (*traditionally offered to guests as a symbol of hospitality*).

хлеба́|ть (-ю) *несов перех* (*разг*) to slurp.

хлеб|е́ц (-ца́) *м* loaf; **хрустя́щие ~цы́** ≈ crispbreads.

хле́бниц|а (-ы) *ж* bread basket; (*для хране́ния*) bread bin.

хлебн|у́ть (-у́, -ёшь) *сов перех* (*разг*: чай итп) to take a gulp of; **~** (*perf*) **го́ря** to see a lot of sorrow.

хле́бн|ый *прил* bread *опред*; (*злак, расте́ние*) corn *опред*; (*край, по́ле*) fertile; (*разг*: *месте́чко*) well-paid; **э́то год был ~** we had a good harvest this year; **~ые дро́жжи** baker's yeast.

хлебобу́лочн|ый *прил*: **~ые изде́лия** bread products *мн*.

хлебозаво́д (-а) *м* bakery.

хлеборе́з|ка (-ки; *gen pl* -ок) *ж* bread slicer.

хлеборо́б (-а) *м* harvester.

хлеборо́дный *прил* (*край, земля*) fertile; **э́то год был ~** we had a good harvest this year.

хлебосо́льный *прил* hospitable.

хлеб|ца́ *итп сущ см* **хлебе́ц**.

хлев (-а; *loc sg* -у́, *nom pl* -а́) *м* cowshed; (*перен*: *разг*) pigsty.

хлеста́|ть (-ещу́, -ещешь) *несов перех* (*ремнём, кнуто́м*) to whip; (*по лицу́, по щека́м*) to slap; (*разг*: *во́дку, пи́во*) to knock back ◆ *неперех* (*дождь*) to lash down; (*вода́, кровь*) to gush; (*пу́ли*) to rain down; **во́лны ~еста́ли о борт ло́дки** the waves lashed against the side of the boat.

хлёст|кий (-кая, -кое, -кие; -ок, -ка́, -ко) *прил* (*перен*) scathing.

хлестн|у́ть (-у́, -ёшь) *сов перех* to whip; (*по щеке́*) to slap.

хлёсток *прил см* **хлёсткий**.

хлещу́ *итп несов см* **хлеста́ть**.

хли́пк|ий (-ая, -ое, -ие) *прил* (*разг*: *здоро́вье*) poor; (: *челове́к, земля́*) weedy; (: *стол, строе́ние*) wobbly.

хлоп *как сказ* (*разг*): **он меня́ ~ по спине́** he whacked me right in the back; **он ~ на крова́ть** he flopped onto the bed.

хло́па|ть (-ю) *несов перех* (*ладо́нью*) to slap; (*кнуто́м*) to lash ◆ *неперех* (+*instr*; *две́рью, кры́шкой*) to slam; (+*dat*; *арти́сту, певцу́*) to clap; (*хлопу́шка, вы́стрел*) to go bang; **~** (*impf*) **уша́ми/глаза́ми** (*разг*) to look stupid/baffled.

хло́пка *сущ см* **хло́пок**.

хлопка́ *сущ см* **хлопо́к**.

хлопково́дство (-а) *ср* cotton growing.

хло́пковый *прил* cotton.

хло́пн|уть (-у, -ешь) *сов перех* (*по спине́*) to slap ◆ *неперех* (*в ладо́ни*) to clap; (*дверь*) to slam shut; (*хлопу́шка, вы́стрел*) to go bang; (+*instr*; *две́рью*) to slam; (*кнуто́м*) to crack.

хло́п|ок (-ка) *м* cotton.

хлоп|о́к (-ка́) *м* (*уда́р в ладо́ши*) clap; (*вы́стрела, кнута́*) crack; (*по спине́, по заты́лку*) slap.

хлопо|та́ть (-чу́, -чешь) *несов неперех* (*по дому, по хозя́йству*) to busy o.s.; (*добива́ться*): **~ о** +*prp* (*о разреше́нии, о посо́бии итп*) to be busy trying to get; **~** (*impf*) **о ком-н или за кого-н** to trouble o.s. on sb's behalf.

хлопотли́в|ый (-, -а, -о) *прил* (*челове́к*) busy; (*дело, обя́занности*) troublesome.

хло́потный *прил* (*разг*) troublesome.

хло́п|оты (-о́т; *dat pl* -о́там) *мн* (*по хозя́йству, по до́му итп*) things *мн* to do; (*о ком-н*) effort *ед*, trouble *ед*; **все мои́ ~ бы́ли напра́сны** all of my efforts were in vain; **хлопо́т по́лон рот** he *итп* has troubles galore.

хлопочу́ *итп несов см* **хлопота́ть**.

хлопу́ш|ка (-ки; *gen pl* -ек) *ж* (*для мух*) fly swatter; (*игру́шка*) (Christmas) cracker.

хлопча́тник (-а) *м* (*БОТ*: *расте́ние*) cotton.

хлопчатобума́жный *прил* cotton.

хло́пь|я (-ев) *мн* (*сне́га, мыла́*) flakes *мн*; (*ва́ты, овчи́ны*) clumps *мн*; **кукуру́зные ~** cornflakes.

хлор (-а) *м* chlorine.

хло́рк|а (-и) *ж* (*разг*) bleaching powder.

хло́рн|ый *прил*: **~ая и́звесть** bleaching powder; **хло́рная кислота́** hydrochloric acid.

хлын|у́ть (*3sg* -ет, *3pl* -ут) *сов неперех* to flood; (*перен*: *мы́сли, воспомина́ния*) to flood back.

хлыст (-а́) *м* whip.

хлыщ (-а́) *м* playboy.

хлю́па|ть (-ю) *несов неперех* (*разг*) to squelch; **~** (*impf*) **но́сом** to sniff.

хля́стик (-а) *м* half-belt.

хмеле́|ть (-ю) *несов неперех* to be drunk; **~** (*impf*) **от сча́стья/свобо́ды** to be drunk with happiness/freedom.

хмел|ь (-я) *м* (*БОТ*) hops *мн*; (*опьяне́ние*) drunkenness; **во ~ю́** drunk.

хмельно́й *прил* drunken; (*напи́ток*) alcoholic; (*во́здух, за́пах*) intoxicating.

хму́р|ить (-ю, -ишь; *perf* **нахму́рить**) *несов перех* (*лоб, бро́ви*) to furrow

▶ **хму́риться** *несов возв* to frown; (*небо*) to become overcast; (*пого́да, день*) to turn gloomy.

хму́ро *нареч* gloomily ◆ *как сказ*: **сего́дня на у́лице ~** it's very gloomy outside; **у него́ на душе́ ~** he's feeling very gloomy.

хму́рый *прил* gloomy.

хмы́ка|ть (-ю) *несов неперех* (*разг*) *to say "hmm" as a sign of surprise, annoyance etc*.

хмы́кн|уть (-у, -ешь) *сов неперех* *to say "hmm" as a sign of surprise, annoyance etc*.

хн|а (-ы) *ж* henna.

хны́ка|ть (-ю) *несов неперех* (*разг*: *пла́кать*) to whimper; (*перен*: *жа́ловаться*) to whine.

хо́бби *ср нескл* hobby.

хо́бот (-а) *м* (*слона́*) trunk.

хобот|о́к (-ка́) *м* (*насеко́мого*) proboscis.

ход (-а; *part gen* -у, *loc sg* -у́) *м* (*по́езда, маши́ны*, *руля, поршня*) movement; (*событий, дела итп*) course; (*часов, двигателя*) working; (*карты*) go; (*манёвр, также ШАХМАТЫ*) move; (*возможность*) chance; (*вход*) entrance; (*тоннель*) passage; **в хóде** +*gen* in the course of; ~ **мýслей** train of thought; **идтú (пойтú** *perf*) **в** ~ to come into use; **пускáть (пустúть** *perf*) **что-н в** ~ (*механизм*) to bring into use; (*слово, тип одежды*) to popularize; **быть** (*impf*) **в (большóм)** ~ý to be (very) popular; **на** ~ý (*есть, разговаривать*) on the move; (*делать замечания, шутить*) in passing; **с хóду** straight off; **он с хóду взбежáл на лéстницу** he ran straight upstairs; **до дóма три часá** ~ý it's three hours' walk to the house; **давáть (дать** *perf*) ~ **дéлу** to set things in motion; **давáть (дать** *perf*) ~ **нóвым лю́дям/мéтодам** to give new people/methods a chance; **давáть (дать** *perf*) **зáдний** (*АВТ*) to reverse; (*человеку*) to retreat; **знать** (*impf*) **все** ~**ы́ и вы́ходы** to know all the ins and outs; **дéло идёт свои́м хóдом** events are taking their natural course; **по хóду дéла** during the course of events; **чей** ~? (*в игре*) whose go is it?

ходáтайств|о (-а) *ср* petition; **подавáть (подáть** *perf*) ~ to submit a petition.

ходáтайств|овать (-ую) *perf* **походáтайствовать**) *несов неперех*: ~ **о чём-н/за когó-н** to petition for sth/on sb's behalf.

хóдик|и (-ов) *мн* wall clock *ед*.

ходúть (-жý, -дишь) *несов неперех* to walk; (*по магазинам, в гости, в кино итп*) to go (*on foot*); (*поезд, автобус итп*) to go; (*слухи, грипп*) to go round; (*часы*) to work; (+*instr; музом итп*) to play; (*конём, пешкой итп*) to move; (*носить*): ~ **в** +*prp* (*в пальто, в сапогах итп*) to wear; (*ухаживать*): ~ **за кем-н** to look after sb.

хóд|кий (-кая, -кое, -кие; -ок, -ká, -ко) *прил* (*разг: машина*) speedy; (: *товар*) popular.

ходовóй *прил* popular.

хóдок *прил см* **хóдкий**.

ходóк (-á) *м*: **он хорóший** ~ he's a good walker; **тудá я бóльше не** ~ (*разг*) I'm not going there again.

ходýл|я (-и; *gen pl* -ей) *ж* (*обычно мн*) stilt.

ходунóм *нареч*: **ходúть** ~ (*разг*) to shake.

ходьб|á (-ы́) *ж* walking; **полчасá** ~ы́ half an hour's walk.

ходя́ч|ий (-ая, -ее, -ие) *прил* trendy; (*избитый*) hackneyed; (*больной*) able to walk; **он** -~**ая добродéтель** he is a paragon of virtue.

хождéние (-я) *ср* walking; (*слухов*) circulation; **имéть** (*impf*) ~ (*валюта*) to be in circulation; (*выражение, товар*) to be popular.

хожý *несов см* **ходúть**.

хозрасчёт (-а) *м* (= хозяйственный расчёт) *system of management based on self-financing and self-governing principles.*

хозрасчётн|ый *прил*: ~**ое предприя́тие** self-financing, self-governing enterprise.

хозя́ева *итп сущ см* **хозя́ин**.

хозя́ек *сущ см* **хозя́йка**.

хозя́|ин (-ина; *nom pl* -ева, *gen pl* -ев) *м* (*владелец*) owner; (*сдающий жильё*) landlord; (*пользующийся наёмным трудом*) employer; (*принимающий гостей*) host; (*ведущий хозяйство*) manager; (*перен: положения, своей судьбы*) master.

хозя́|йка (-йки; *gen pl* -ек) *ж* (*владелица*) owner; (*сдающая жильё*) landlady; (*принимающая гостей*) hostess; (*разг: жена*) missus, old lady; **домáшняя** ~ housewife.

хозя́йнича|ть (-ю) *несов неперех* (*в доме, на кухне*) to be in charge; (*командовать*) to boss around.

хозя́йск|ий (-ая, -ое, -ие) *прил*: (**э́то) дéло** ~**ое** (*разг*) have it your own way.

хозя́йственник (-а) *м* manager.

хозя́йственный *прил* (*деятельность, управление*) economic *опред*; (*постройка, инвентарь*) domestic *опред*; (*человек*) thrifty; **хозя́йственные товáры** household goods; **хозя́йственный магази́н** hardware shop.

хозя́йств|о (-а) *ср* (*экон*) economy; (*производственная единица*) enterprise; (*оборудование*) equipment; (*предметы быта*) household goods *мн*; **городскóе/нарóдное** ~ urban/national economy; **домáшнее** ~ housekeeping; **вести́** (*impf*) ~ to run the house.

хозя́йств|овать (-ую) *несов неперех*: ~ **на предприя́тии/фи́рме** to manage an enterprise/firm; **он умéло** ~**ует** he is a good manager.

хоккеи́ст (-а) *м* hockey player.

хоккé|й (-я) *м* hockey; ~ **с ша́йбой/на травé** ice/field hockey.

хоккéйный *прил* hockey *опред*.

хóлдинг (-а) *м* (*КОММ*) holding.

хóлдингов|ый *прил*: ~**ая компáния** holding company.

хóленый *прил* (*человек, лошадь*) well-groomed; (*лицо, руки*) elegant.

холёный *прил* = **хóленый**.

холéр|а (-ы) *ж* (*МЕД*) cholera.

холестери́н (-а) *м* cholesterol.

холл (-а) *м* (*театра, гостиницы*) foyer, lobby; (*в квартире, в доме*) hall.

холм (-á) *м* hill.

хóлмик (-а) *м* hillock.

холми́ст|ый (-, -а, -о) *прил* hilly.

хóлод (-а; *nom pl* -á) *м* cold; (*осенний, зимний*) cold weather; (*перен: равнодушие*) coldness; (*озноб*) cold shiver.

холодá|ть (*3sg* -ет, *perf* **похолодáть**) *несов безл* to turn cold.

хóлоден *прил см* **холóдный**.

холодé|ть (-ю; *perf* **похолодéть**) *несов неперех*

(*руки, ноги*) to get cold; (*от страха, при смерти*) to go cold.

холод|е́ц (**-ца́**) *м* meat in aspic.

холоди́льник (**-а**) *м* (*домашний*) fridge, refrigerator; (*промышленный*) refrigerator; **двухка́мерный** ~ fridge-freezer.

хо́лодно *нареч* coldly ♦ *как сказ* it's cold; (+*dat*): **мне** *итп* ~ I'm *итп* cold; **на у́лице сего́дня** ~ it's cold outside today.

холо́|дный (**-оден, -одна́, -одно**) *прил* cold; **э́та ку́ртка** ~**о́дная** this jacket isn't very warm; **холо́дная война́** cold war; **холо́дное ору́жие** side arms *мн*.

холодца́ *итп сущ см* **холоде́ц**.

холост|о́й (**хо́лост**) *прил* (*мужчина*) unmarried, single; (*no short form*; *выстрел, патрон*) blank; **рабо́тать** (*impf*) **на** ~**о́м ходу́** (*АВТ, ТЕХ*) to idle, tick over; ~ **прого́н** dry run.

холостя́к (**-а́**) *м* bachelor.

холу́|й (**-я**) *м* sycophant.

холст (**-а́**) *м* canvas.

хому́т (**-а́**) *м* (*коня*) harness collar; (*ТЕХ*) clamp; (*перен*) bind; **пове́сить** (*perf*) *или* **наде́ть** (*perf*) **себе́** ~ **на ше́ю** to weigh o.s. down.

хомя́к (**-а́**) *м* hamster.

хор (**-а**) *м* choir; (*перен*) chorus.

хорва́т (**-а**) *м* Croatian.

Хорва́ти|я (**-и**) *ж* Croatia.

хорва́т|ка (**-ки**; *gen pl* **-ок**) *ж см* **хорва́т**.

хорва́тск|ий (**-ая, -ое, -ие**) *прил* Croatian.

хор|ёк (**-ька́**) *м* ferret.

хорео́граф (**-а**) *м* choreographer.

хореогра́фи|я (**-и**) *ж* choreography.

хори́ст (**-а**) *м* chorister.

хори́ст|ка (**-ки**; *gen pl* **-ок**) *ж см* **хори́ст**.

хорме́йстер (**-а**) *м* choirmaster.

хорово́д (**-а**) *м* round dance.

хорово́й *прил* choral.

хо́ром *нареч* in unison.

хоро́м|ы (**-**) *мн* mansion *ед*.

хор|они́ть (**-оню́, -о́нишь**; *perf* **похорони́ть**) *несов перех* to bury.

хорохо́р|иться (**-юсь, -ишься**) *несов возв* (*разг*) to brag.

хоро́шеньк|ий (**-ая, -ое, -ие**) *прил* (*симпатичный*) pretty; (*разг*: *плохой*) fine, nice.

хороше́нько *нареч* (*разг*) properly.

хороше́|ть (**-ю**; *perf* **похороше́ть**) *несов неперех* to become more attractive.

хоро́ш|ий (**-ая, -ее, -ие**; **-, -а́, -о́**) *прил* good; **он хоро́ш (собо́ю)** he's good-looking; **хоро́ш друг!** (*разг*) a fine friend!; **всего́** ~**его́!** all the best!

хорошо́ *нареч* well ♦ *как сказ* it's good; (+*dat*): **мне** ~ I feel good ♦ *част, вводн сл* okay, all right ♦ *ср нескл* (*ПРОСВЕЩ*) good (*school mark*); ~ **отдыха́ть (отдохну́ть** *perf*) to have a good rest; **на мо́ре** ~ it's nice by the sea; **мне здесь** ~ I like it here; ~, **я согла́сен** okay, I agree; **ну,** ~! (*разг*: *выражение угрозы*) right then!; ~ **бы пое́сть/поспа́ть** (*разг*) I wouldn't

mind a bite to eat/getting some sleep.

хо́р|ы (**-ов**) *мн* (*в церкви, в большом зале*) gallery *ед*.

хорька́ *итп сущ см* **хорёк**.

хот-до́г (**-а**) *м* hot dog.

хо|те́ть (*см* Table 16) *несов перех*: ~ +*infin* to want to do; **как** ~**ти́те** (*как вам угодно*) as you wish; (*а всё-таки*) no matter what you say; **хо́чешь не хо́чешь** whether you like it or not; ~ (*impf*) **есть/пить** to be hungry/thirsty

▶ **хоте́ться** *несов безл* (+*infin*): **мне** *итп* **хо́чется пла́кать/есть** I *итп* feel like crying/something to eat; **мне хо́чется ча́ю** I feel like some tea.

KEYWORD

хоть *союз* **1** (*несмотря на то, что*) (al)though; **хоть я и оби́жен, я помогу́ тебе́** although I am hurt, I will help you

2 (*до такой степени, что*) even if; **не соглаша́ется, хоть до утра́ проси́** he won't agree, even if you ask all night; **хоть умри́, а де́нег доста́нь** get hold of some money, even if it kills you; **хоть убе́й, не могу́ пойти́ на э́то** I couldn't do that to save my life; **хоть..., хоть** either ..., or; **езжа́й хоть сего́дня, хоть че́рез ме́сяц** go either today, or in a month's time

♦ *част* **1** (*служит для усиления*) at least; **подвези́ его́ хоть до ста́нции** take him to the station at least; **пойми́ хоть ты** you of all people should understand

2 (*разг*: *например*) for example; **взять хоть Мари́ю: она́ же всё вре́мя рабо́тает** take Maria for example, she works all the time

3 (*во фразах*): **хоть бы** at least; **хоть бы ты ему́ позвони́л!** you could at least phone him!; **хоть бы зако́нчить сего́дня!** if only we could get finished today!; **хоть кто** anyone; **хоть какой** any; **ему́ хоть бы что** it doesn't bother him; **хоть куда́!** (*разг*) excellent!; **хоть бы и так!** so what!

хотя́ *союз* although; ~ **и** even though; ~ **бы** at least; **он сра́зу всё по́нял,** ~ **и не знал подро́бностей** even without knowing the details, he was able to understand at once; **возьми́те** ~ **бы приме́р А́нглии** take England for example.

хотя́т(ся) *несов см* **хоте́ть(ся)**.

хохла́ *итп сущ см* **хохо́л**.

хохлом|а́ (**-ы́**) *ж* khokhloma (*traditional wooden articles decorated in red, gold and black*).

хо́хм|а (**-ы**) *ж* (*разг*) joke; (*что-н смешное*) laugh.

хох|о́л (**-ла́**) *м* (*клок волос*) tuft of hair; (*разг*: *пренебр*) Ukrainian.

хо́хот (**-а**) *м* guffaw; (*шакала*) laugh.

хох|ота́ть (**-очу́, -о́чешь**) *несов неперех* to laugh (loudly); (*филин, шакал*) to laugh; ~ (*impf*) **над** +*instr* to laugh at; **я** ~**о́тал до слёз** I laughed till the tears ran down my face.

хочу́(сь) *итп несов см* **хоте́ть(ся)**.

храбре́ц (-á) *м* brave person (*мн* people).
храби́ться (-ю́сь, -и́шься) *несов возв* (*разг*) to try to appear brave.
хра́бро *нареч* bravely.
хра́брост|**ь** (-и) *ж* bravery, courage.
хра́бр|**ый** (-, -á, -о) *прил* brave, courageous.
храм (-а) *м* (*РЕЛ*) temple.
хране́ни|**е** (-я) *ср* (*денег*) keeping; ~ ору́жия possession of firearms; ка́мера для ~я багажа́ left-luggage office (*BRIT*), checkroom (*US*); сдава́ть (сдать *perf*) ве́щи на ~ to put things in for safekeeping.
храни́лищ|**е** (-а) *ср* store.
храни́тел|**ь** (-я) *м* curator, keeper.
храни́ть (-ю́, -и́шь) *несов перех* to keep; (*границы, достоинство*) to protect; (*традиции*) to preserve; ~ (*impf*) что-н в та́йне to keep sth secret
▸ **храни́ться** *несов возв* to be kept.
храп (-а) *м* (*во сне*) snoring.
храп|**е́ть** (-лю́, -и́шь) *несов неперех* (*человек*) to snore; (*лошадь*) to snort.
хреб|**е́т** (-та́) *м* (*АНАТ*) spine; (*разг: спина*) back; (*ГЕО*) ridge.
хребто́вый *прил* (*позвонки*) spinal; (*перевал, гряда*) mountain *опред*.
хрен (-а) *м* (*БОТ, КУЛИН*) horseradish; (*груб!*) willy (*!*); ~ его́ зна́ет (*разг*) who the hell knows; ста́рый ~ (*разг*) old fool.
хрено́вый *прил* (*БОТ, КУЛИН*) horseradish *опред*; (*груб!*) crappy (*!*) (*BRIT*), lousy (*US*).
хрестомати́йный *прил* (*идея, образ*) basic.
хрестома́ти|**я** (-и) *ж* study aid, reader.
хризанте́м|**а** (-ы) *ж* chrysanthemum.
хрип (-а) *м* wheezing; предсме́ртный ~ dying gasp.
хрип|**е́ть** (-лю́, -и́шь) *несов неперех* (*лошадь, больной*) to wheeze; (*пластинка*) to crackle.
хрипл|**ый** (-, -á, -о) *прил* (*голос*) hoarse; (*гармонь, звук*) wheezing.
хриплю́ *несов см* **хрипе́ть**.
хри́пн|**уть** (-у, -ешь; *perf* охри́пнуть) *несов неперех* to become *или* grow hoarse.
хрипот|**á** (-ы́) *ж* hoarseness.
христиани́н (-ани́на; *nom pl* -а́не, *gen pl* -а́н) *м* Christian.
христиа́н|**ка** (-ки; *gen pl* -ок) *ж см* **христиани́н**.
христиа́нск|**ий** (-ая, -ое, -ие) *прил* Christian.
христиа́нств|**о** (-а) *ср* Christianity.
Христ|**о́с** (-á) *м* Christ; ~á ра́ди (*разг*) for Christ's sake.
хром (-а) *м* (*ХИМ*) chrome; (*краска*) chrome yellow; (*кожа*) box calf.
хрома́ть (-ю) *несов неперех* to limp; (*перен: разг: знания, дисциплина*) to be weak; моя́ матема́тика ~ет (*разг*) my maths is pretty shaky.
хро́мовый *прил* (*ХИМ*) chrome; (*кожа, сапоги*

итп) box-calf.
хром|**о́й** (-, -á, -о) *прил* lame; (*перен: разг: стол итп*) wobbly.
хромосо́м|**а** (-ы) *ж* chromosome.
хромот|**а́** (-ы́) *ж* limp.
хро́ник (-а) *м* (*разг*) bad case.
хро́ник|**а** (-и) *ж* chronicle; (*КИНО*) film chronicle.
хроника́льный *прил* chronicle *опред*.
хроникёр (-а) *м* (*журналист*) reporter.
хрони́ческ|**ий** (-ая, -ое, -ие) *прил* chronic.
хронологи́ческ|**ий** (-ая, -ое, -ие) *прил* chronological; в ~ой после́довательности in chronological order.
хроноло́ги|**я** (-и) *ж* chronology.
хронометра́ж (-а) *м* time-keeping.
хру́п|**кий** (-кая, -кое, -кие; -ок, -ка́, -ко) *прил* (*лёд, стекло итп*) fragile; (*печенье, кости*) brittle; (*перен: фигура, девушка*) delicate; (: *здоровье, организм*) frail.
хру́пкост|**ь** (-и) *ж* (*см прил*) fragility; brittleness; delicacy; frailty.
хру́пок *прил см* **хру́пкий**.
хруст (-а) *м* crunch.
хруста́лик (-а) *м* (*АНАТ*) lens.
хруста́л|**ь** (-я́) *м, собир* crystal; го́рный ~ rock crystal.
хруста́льный *прил* crystal *опред*; (*перен: лёд, звон*) crystal clear.
хру|**сте́ть** (-щу́, -сти́шь) *несов неперех* to crunch; (+*instr*; *редиской, сахаром итп*) to crunch.
хрустя́щ|**ий** (-ая, -ее, -ие) *прил* crunchy; (*скатерть, бельё*) crisp; хрустя́щий карто́фель potato crisps (*BRIT*) *или* chips (*US*) *мн*.
хрущу́ *несов см* **хрусте́ть**.
хрю́ка|**ть** (-ю) *несов неперех* to grunt.
хрящ (-á) *м* (*АНАТ*) cartilage.
ХСС *м сокр* (= Христиа́нско-социалисти́ческий сою́з) CSU (= *Christian Socialist Union*).
худе́ть (-ю) *несов неперех* to grow thin; (*быть на диете*) to slim.
худо́жественный *прил* artistic; (*школа, выставка*) art *опред*; худо́жественная литерату́ра fiction; худо́жественная самоде́ятельность *amateur art and performance*; худо́жественный сало́н (*выставка*) art exhibition; (*магазин*) ≈ craft shop; худо́жественный фильм feature film.
худо́жеств|**о** (-а) *ср*: акаде́мия худо́жеств art school.
худо́жник (-а) *м* artist.
худо́жниц|**а** (-ы) *ж см* **худо́жник**.
худ|**о́й** (-, -á, -о) *прил* thin; (*разг: плохой*) bad; (: *дырявый*) full of holes; на ~ коне́ц if the worst comes to the worst (*BRIT*), in the worst case scenario (*US*).
худоща́в|**ый** (-, -а, -о) *прил* thin.

ху́дш|ее (-его; *decl like adj*) *ср* the worst.
ху́дш|ий (-ая, -ее, -ие) *превос прил* the worst
   опред.
ху́же *сравн прил, нареч* worse.
ху|й (-я) *м* (*груб!*) cock (*!*), prick (*!*)
хулига́н (-а) *м* hooligan.
хулига́н|ить (-ю, -ишь; *perf* нахулига́нить)
   несов неперех to act like a hooligan.
хулига́н|ка (-ки; *gen pl* -ок) *ж см* хулига́н.
хулига́нск|ий (-ая, -ое, -ие) *прил*: ~ посту́пок
   act of hooliganism; ~ое поведе́ние
   hooliganism.
хулига́нств|о (-а) *ср* hooliganism.

хулиганьё (-я́) *ср собир* hooligans *мн*, yobs *мн*
   (*BRIT*).
хул|и́ть (-ю, -ишь) *несов перех* (*порочить*) to
   abuse.
ху́нт|а (-ы) *ж* (*полит*) junta.
хурм|а́ (-ы́) *ж* (*дерево*) persimmon tree; (*плод*)
   persimmon, sharon fruit.
ху́тор (-а) *м* (*ферма*) farmstead; (*селение*)
   village (*in Southern Russia and the Ukraine*).
хуторя́н|ин (-ина; *nom pl* -е, *gen pl* -) *м* (*владелец
   хутора*) farmer; (*житель хутора*) villager.
хуторя́н|ка (-ки; *gen pl* -ок) *ж см* хуторя́нин.

по ча́сти +*gen* when it comes to; **э́то не по мое́й ча́сти** this is not my department; **разрыва́ться** (*impf*) **на ча́сти** to have lots on the go at once; **её рвут на ча́сти** she is in constant demand; **часть ре́чи** part of speech; **часть све́та** continent.
ча́стью *нареч* partly.
час|ы́ (**-о́в**) *мн* (*карманные*) watch *ед*; (*стенные*) clock *ед*.
ча́хл|ый (**-**, **-а**, **-о**) *прил* (*цветок*) withered; (*человек*) sickly.
ча́х|нуть (**-ну**, **-нешь**; *pt* **-**, **-ла**, **-ло**, *perf* **зача́хнуть**) *несов неперех* (*растения*) to wither; (*человек, животное*) to fade away.
чахо́тк|а (**-и**) *ж* consumption.
ча́ш|а (**-и**) *ж* bowl; (*весов*) pan; **у них дом – по́лная** ~ they've got everything imaginable in their house; ~ **терпе́ния перепо́лнилась** this is the last straw.
ча́шек *сущ см* **ча́шка**.
ча́шечк|а (**-и**; *gen pl* **-ек**) *ж уменьш от* **ча́шка**; (*БОТ*) calyx; **коле́нная** ~ kneecap.
ча́шк|а (**-и**; *gen pl* **-ек**) *ж* cup; (*весов*) pan.
ча́щ|а (**-и**) *ж* (*лес*) thick forest.
ча́ще *сравн прил от* **ча́стый** ♦ *сравн нареч от* **ча́сто**.
ча́ян|е (**-я**) *ср* (*обычно мн*) aspiration.
ча́|ять (**-ю**) *несов перех*: **он в ней души́ не** ~**ет** he dotes on her.
чванли́в|ый (**-**, **-а**, **-о**) *прил* conceited.
чва́нств|о (**-а**) *ср* conceit.
чебуре́к (**-а**) *м* ≈ meat pasty.
чего́ *мест см* **что**.
чей (**чьего́**; *см* Table 7; *f* **чья**, *nt* **чьё**, *pl* **чьи**) *мест* whose; ~ **э́то ребёнок?** whose child is this?; ~ **бы то ни́ был** no matter whose it is.
чей-ли́бо (**чьего́-ли́бо**; *как* **чей**; *см* Table 7; *f* **чья-ли́бо**, *nt* **чьё-ли́бо**, *pl* **чьи-ли́бо**) *мест* = **чей-нибудь**.
чей-нибудь (**чьего́-нибудь**; *как* **чей**; *см* Table 7; *f* **чья-нибудь**, *nt* **чьё-нибудь**, *pl* **чьи-нибудь**) *мест* anyone's.
чей-то (**чьего́-то**; *как* **чей**; *см* Table 7; *f* **чья-то**, *nt* **чьё-то**, *pl* **чьи-то**) *мест* someone's, somebody's.
чек (**-а**) *м* (*банковский*) cheque (*BRIT*), check (*US*); (*товарный, кассовый*) receipt; **выбива́ть** (**вы́бить** *perf*) ~ to issue a receipt (*to be presented as proof of payment in Russian shops*).
Чека́ *ж сокр* (*ИСТ*: = *Чрезвыча́йная коми́ссия по борьбе́ с контрреволю́цией и сабота́жем*) Cheka (*state security police in Soviet Russia from 1918-1922*).
чека́н|ить (**-ю**, **-ишь**; *perf* **отчека́нить**) *несов перех* (*монеты*) to mint; (*узор*) to enchase; ~ (**отчека́нить** *perf*) **слова́** to enunciate one's words.
чека́нк|а (**-и**) *ж* (*монет*) minting; (*изделие*) enchased object.

чеки́ст (**-а**) *м* (*ИСТ*) Cheka officer.
че́ковый *прил* cheque *опред* (*BRIT*), check *опред* (*US*); **че́ковая кни́жка** cheque book.
чёл|ка (**-ки**; *gen pl* **-ок**) *ж* (*человека*) fringe (*BRIT*), bangs *мн* (*US*); (*лошади*) forelock.
челно́к (**-а́**) *м* (*лодка*) dugout; (*швейный*) shuttle.
челно́чный *прил* shuttle *опред*.
челове́к (**-а**; *nom pl* **лю́ди**, *gen pl* **люде́й**) *м* human (being); (*некто, личность*) person (*мн* people); **два/три/четы́ре** ~**а** two/three/four people; **пять/шесть** *итп* ~ five/six *итп* people; **будь** ~**ом, помоги́ нам!** (*разг*) be a sport and give us a hand!; **вот** ~! (*разг*) what a charcater!
челове́ко-д|ень (**-ня**; *gen pl* **-ней**) *м* man-day.
человеколю́би|е (**-я**) *ср* philanthropy.
человеконенави́стник (**-а**) *м* misanthrope.
человеконенави́стническ|ий (**-ая**, **-ое**, **-ие**) *прил* misanthropic.
челове́ко-час (**-а**) *м* man-hour.
челове́чен *прил см* **челове́чный**.
челове́ческ|ий (**-ая**, **-ое**, **-ие**) *прил* human *опред*; (*человечный*) humane; **по-~и** in a humane way.
челове́честв|о (**-а**) *ср* humanity, mankind.
челове́чный (**-ен**, **-на**, **-но**) *прил* humane.
чёлок *сущ см* **чёлка**.
че́люст|ь (**-и**) *ж* (*АНАТ*) jaw.
Челя́бинск (**-а**) *м* Chelyabinsk.
чем *мест см* **что** ♦ *союз* than; (*разг: вместо того чтобы*) instead of; **бо́льше**, ~ **де́сять челове́к** more than ten people; ~ **спо́рить, дава́й спро́сим кого́-нибудь** instead of arguing, let's ask someone; ~ **бо́льше/ра́ньше** *итп*, **тем лу́чше** the bigger/earlier *итп*, the better.
чемода́н (**-а**) *м* suitcase; **сиде́ть** (*impf*) **на** ~**ах** (*перен: разг*) to have one's bags packed.
чемпио́н (**-а**) *м* champion; ~ **по те́ннису** tennis champion.
чемпиона́т (**-а**) *м* championship; ~ **страны́ по хокке́ю** national hockey championships.
чемпио́н|ка (**-и**; *gen pl* **-ок**) *ж см* **чемпио́н**.
чему́ *мест см* **что**.
чепе́ *ср нескл* (*разг*) crisis.
чепух|а́ (**-и́**) *ж* (*разг*) rubbish (*BRIT*), garbage (*US*).
че́пчик (**-а**) *м* bonnet (*hat*).
че́рв|и (**-е́й**) *мн* (*КАРТЫ*) hearts *мн*.
черви́в|ый (**-**, **-а**, **-о**) *прил* maggoty.
черво́нец (**-ца**) *м* (*разг*: 10 *рублей*) ten roubles.
черво́нн|ый *прил* (*КАРТЫ*): ~**ая да́ма/деся́тка** the queen/ten of hearts.
черво́нца *итп сущ см* **черво́нец**.
черв|ь (**-я́**; *gen pl* **-е́й**) *м* worm; (*личинка*) maggot.
червя́к (**-а́**) *м* worm.
червя́чный *прил* (*ТЕХ*) worm *опред*.
черда́к (**-а́**) *м* attic, loft.
черда́чный *прил* attic *опред*.
черёд *м* (*разг*) turn; **всё идёт свои́м чередо́м**

everything is going as normal.

череда́ (-ы́) ж (людей) stream; (событий) sequence.

череду́|ова́ть (-у́ю) несов перех: ~ что-н с +instr to alternate sth with

▸ **чередова́ться** несов возв to alternate; ~**ся** (impf) с +instr to take turns with.

че́рез предл (+acc) **1** (поперёк) across, over; **мост че́рез кана́л/ре́ку** the bridge across или over the canal/river; **переходи́ть (перейти́** perf) **че́рез доро́гу** to cross the road
2 (сквозь) through; **он влез че́рез окно́** he climbed through the window; **че́рез лу́пу** through a magnifying glass
3 (поверх) over; **он переле́з че́рез забо́р** he climbed over the fence; **де́ти пры́гают че́рез верёвку** the children are jumping over a rope
4 (спустя) in; **че́рез час** in an hour('s time); **че́рез ме́сяц/год** in a month('s)/year('s) (time)
5 (минуя какое-н пространство): **че́рез три кварта́ла – ста́нция** the station is three blocks away
6 (при помощи) via; **он переда́л письмо́ че́рез знако́мого** he sent the letter via a friend
7 (при повторении действия) every; **принима́йте табле́тки че́рез ка́ждый час** take the tablets every hour.

черёмух|а (-и) ж bird cherry.
че́рен прил см **чёрный**.
черен|о́к (-ка́) м (рукоятка) handle; (БОТ) cutting.
че́реп (-а) м skull.
черепа́х|а (-и) ж tortoise; (морская) turtle.
черепа́ховый прил (суп) turtle; (гребень) tortoiseshell.
черепа́ш|ий (-ья, -ье, -ьи) прил tortoise's; (морской) turtle's; **идти́** (impf) ~**ьим ша́гом** to go at a snail's pace.
черепи́ц|а (-ы) ж tile ◆ собир tiles мн.
черепи́чный прил tiled.
черепка́ сущ см **черепо́к**.
черепно́й прил skull опред; **черепна́я коро́бка** cranium.
череп|о́к (-ка́) м pottery fragment.
чересчу́р нареч far too; **э́то уж** ~! that's just too much!
чере́ш|ня (-ни; gen pl -ен) ж (дерево) cherry (tree); (плод) cherry.
черка́|ть (-ю; perf **начерка́ть**) несов перех (разг) to draw lines on; (зачёркивать) to cross out.
черкн|у́ть (-у́, -ёшь) сов перех (разг: написать) to scribble.
черне́|ть (-ю; perf **почерне́ть**) несов неперех (становиться чёрным) to turn black; (no perf; виднеться) to show black.
черни́|ка (-и) ж (кустарник) bilberry (bush) ◆ собир bilberries мн.
черни́л|а (-) мн ink ед.
черни́льниц|а (-ы) ж inkwell.

черни́льный прил ink опред; **черни́льный каранда́ш** graphite pencil which writes in purple when moistened.
черн|и́ть (-ю́, -и́шь; perf **начерни́ть**) несов перех (брови) to tint; (perf **очерни́ть**; имя, репута́цию) to tarnish; (no perf; сталь, серебро) to tarnish.
чёрно-бе́лый прил black-and-white.
чернобу́рк|а (-и) ж (разг: мех) silver fox.
черно-бу́р|ый прил: ~**ая лиса́** silver fox.
черновик (-а́) м draft.
чернов|о́й прил draft опред; ~**а́я рабо́та** rough work.
черноволо́с|ый (-, -а, -о) прил black-haired.
черного́р|ец (-ца) м Montenegrin.
Черного́ри|я (-и) ж Montenegro.
черного́р|ка (-ки; gen pl -ок) ж см **черного́рец**.
черного́рск|ий (-ая, -ое, -ие) прил Montenegrin.
черного́рца итп сущ см **черного́рец**.
чернозём (-а) м black earth.
чернокож|ий (-ая, -ее, -ие) прил black (person)
◆ (-его; decl like adj) м black (person) (мн people).
чернорабо́ч|ий (-его; decl like adj) м unskilled worker.
черносли́в (-а) м собир prunes мн.
чернот|а́ (-ы́) ж blackness.
чё́рн|ый (-ен, -на́, -но́) прил black; (мрачный) gloomy; (no short form; преступный) wicked; (задний) back опред; **держа́ть** (impf) **кого́-н в** ~**ном те́ле** to treat sb badly; ~**ным по бе́лому** in black and white; ~**ная рабо́та** dirty work; **чё́рные мета́ллы** ferrous metals; **чё́рный ко́фе** black coffee; **чё́рный ры́нок** black market.
черпа́|ть (-ю) несов перех (жидкость) to ladle; (песок) to scoop (up); (перен: знания, силы) to derive.
черпн|у́ть (-у́, -ёшь) сов перех (жидкость) to ladle; (песок) to scoop (up).
черстве́|ть (-ю; perf **зачерстве́ть**) несов неперех (хлеб) to go stale; (perf **очерстве́ть**; человек, душа) to harden.
черств|ый (-, -а́, -о) прил (хлеб) stale; (человек, душа) hard.
чё́рт (-а; nom pl **че́рти**, gen pl **черте́й**) м (дьявол) devil; **у него́ де́нег до** ~**а** (разг) he's rolling in money; **иди́ к** ~**у!** (разг) go to hell!; **к** ~**у!** reply to a wish of good luck; **ни черта́** not a thing; ~ **меня́ дё́рнул** I don't know what got into me; **чем** ~ **не шу́тит** you never know; ~ **возьми́** или **побери́** или **подери́!** (разг) damn it!; ~ **его́ зна́ет!** (разг) God knows!; ~ **зна́ет что!** (разг) it's outrageous!; **он мо́жет** ~ **зна́ет что наде́лать** it's frightening to think what he might do; ~ **с ним!** (разг) to hell with him!; **он дал тебе́ де́нег?** – **а с два!** (разг) did he give you any money? – like hell he did!
черт|а́ (-ы́) ж (линия) line; (граница) limit; (признак) trait; **в о́бщих** ~**х** in general terms; см также **черты́**.

чертёж (-á) *м* draft.
чертёжник (-а) *м* draughtsman (*BRIT*) (*мн* draughtsmen), draftsman (*US*) (*мн* draftsmen).
чертёжный *прил* drawing *опред*.
чер|ти́ть (-чу́, -тишь; *perf* **начерти́ть**) *несов перех* (*линию*) to draw; (*план, графика*) to draw up.
чёртов (-а, -о, -ы) *прил* (*разг: холод, работа итп*) damn(ed); **чёртова дю́жина** baker's dozen.
черто́вски *нареч* (*разг*) dreadfully: **я ~ го́лоден** I'm ravenous.
черто́вск|ий (-ая, -ое, -ие) *прил* (*разг*) damn (ed).
чертополо́х (-а) *м* thistle.
чёрточ|ка (-ки; *gen pl* -ек) *ж уменьш от* **черта́**; (*дефис*) hyphen; **э́то сло́во пи́шется че́рез ~ку** this word is written with a hyphen.
черт|ы́ (-) *мн* (*также: ~ лица́*) features *мн*.
черче́ни|е (-я) *ср* (*действие*) drawing; (*ПРОСВЕЩ*) technical drawing.
черчу́ *несов см* **черти́ть**.
че|са́ть (-шу́, -шешь; *perf* **почеса́ть**) *несов перех* (*спину*) to scratch; (*no perf; разг: гребнем*) to comb; (: *щёткой*) to brush; **~** (*impf*) **язы́к** или **языко́м** to natter
▸ **чеса́ться** (*perf* **почеса́ться**) *несов возв* to scratch o.s.; (*no perf; зудеть*) to itch; **он и не че́шется** (*разг*) he doesn't lift a finger; **у меня́ ру́ки ~шу́тся** +*infin* (*разг*) I'm itching to do.
чесно́к (-á) *м* garlic.
чесо́тк|а (-и) *ж* (*МЕД*) scabies.
че́ствовани|е (-я) *ср* (*действие*) honouring (*BRIT*), honoring (*US*).
че́ств|овать (-ую) *несов перех* to honour (*BRIT*), honor (*US*).
че́стен *прил см* **че́стный**.
че́стно *нареч* honestly ♦ *как сказ*: **так бу́дет ~** that'll be fair.
че́стность (-и) *ж* honesty.
че́ст|ный (-ен, -нá, -но) *прил* honest; (*безупречный*) upright; **~ное и́мя** good name; **~ное сло́во** honest to God; **держа́ться** (*impf*) **на ~ном сло́ве** (*разг*) to hang by a thread.
честолю́б|ец (-ца) *м* ambitious person (*мн* people).
честолюби́в|ый (-, -а, -о) *прил* (*человек, план*) ambitious.
честолю́би|е (-я) *ср* ambition.
честолю́бца *итп сущ см* **честолю́бец**.
чест|ь (-и) *ж* honour (*BRIT*), honor (*US*); (*loc sg* -и́; *почёт*) glory; **в ~** +*gen* in hono(u)r of; **к че́сти кого́-н** to sb's credit; **де́лать** (*impf*) **~ кому́-н** to do sb credit; (*оказывать уважение*) to do sb an hono(u)r; **отдава́ть** (**отда́ть** *perf*) **кому́-н ~** to salute sb; **выходи́ть** (**вы́йти** *perf*) **с че́стью из чего́-н** to come out of sth with one's hono(u)r intact; **пора́ и ~ знать** (*разг*) it is time to wind

up.
чет|á (-ы́) *ж* couple; **он мне не ~** he is no match for me.
четве́рг (-á) *м* Thursday; *см также* **вто́рник**.
четвере́ньки (-ек) *мн*: **встава́ть** (**встать** *perf*) **на ~** to go down on all fours; **ходи́ть** (*impf*) **на ~ьках** to move on all fours.
четвёр|ка (-ки; *gen pl* -ок) *ж* (*цифра, карта*) four; (*ПРОСВЕЩ*) ≈ B (*school mark*); (*группа людей*) foursome; (*разг: автобус, трамвай итп*) (number) four (*bus, tram etc*).
четверн|я́ (-и́; *gen pl* -éй) *ж* quadruplets *мн*.
че́твер|о (*см* **Table 36а**: -ы́х) *чис* four; *см также* **дво́е**.
четвёрок *сущ см* **четвёрка**.
четверокла́ссник (-а) *м pupil in fourth year at school (usually ten years old)*.
четверокла́ссниц|а (-ы) *ж см* **четверокла́ссник**.
четвероно́г|ий (-ая, -ое, -ие) *прил* four-legged.
четверости́ши|е (-я) *ср* quatrain.
четвёрт|ая (-ой; *decl like adj*) *ж*: **одна́ ~** one quarter.
четверт|ова́ть (-у́ю) *несов перех* to quarter (*at execution*).
четвёрт|ый (-ая, -ое, -ые) *чис* fourth; **сейча́с ~ час** it's after three; *см также* **пя́тый**.
че́тверт|ь (-и) *ж* quarter; (*МУЗ*) crotchet (*BRIT*), quarter note (*US*); (*ПРОСВЕЩ*) term.
четвертьфина́л (-а) *м* (*СПОРТ*) quarter final.
четверы́м *итп чис см* **че́тверо**.
чёт|кий (-кая, -кое, -кие; -ок, -ка́, -ко) *прил* clear; (*движения, шаг*) precise.
чёткость (-и) *ж* (*см прил*) clarity; precision.
чётный *прил* (*число*) even.
чёток *сущ см* **чёткий**.
четы́р|е (-ёх; *instr sg* -ьмя́; *см* **Table 25**) *чис* (*цифра, число*) four; (*ПРОСВЕЩ*) ≈ B (*school mark*); **ей ~ го́да** she is four (years old); **они́ живу́т в до́ме но́мер ~** they live at number four; **о́коло четырёх** about four; **кни́га сто́ит ~ рубля́** the book costs four roubles; **~ с полови́ной часа́** four and a half hours; **сейча́с ~ часа́** it is four o'clock; **я́блоки продаю́тся по ~ шту́ки** the apples are sold in fours; **дели́ть** (**раздели́ть** *perf*) **что-н на ~** to divide sth into four.
четы́р|еста (-ёхсо́т; *см* **Table 33**) *чис* four hundred; *см также* **сто**.
четырёх *чис см* **четы́ре**.
четырёхдне́вный *прил* four-day.
четырёхкра́т|ный *прил*: **~ чемпио́н** four-times champion; **в ~ом разме́ре** fourfold.
четырёхле́ти|е (-я) *ср* (*срок*) four years; (*годовщина*) fourth anniversary.
четырёхле́т|ний (-яя, -ее, -ие) *прил* (*период*) four-year; (*ребёнок*) four-year-old.
четырёхме́сячный *прил* four-month;

(*ребёнок*) four-month-old.
четырёхнедéльный *прил* four-week; (*ребёнок*) four-week-old.
четырёхсóт *чис см* **четы́реста**.
четырёхсотлéти|е (**-я**) *ср* (*срок*) four hundred years; (*годовщина*) quartercentenary.
четырёхсотлéтн|ий (**-яя, -ее, -ие**) *прил* (*период*) four-hundred-year; (*дерево*) four-hundred-year-old.
четырёхсóт|ый (**-ая, -ое, -ые**) *чис* four-hundredth.
четырёхстá|х *чис см* **четы́реста**.
четырёхугóльник (**-а**) *м* quadrangle.
четырёхугóльный *прил* quadrangular.
четырёхчасовóй *прил* (*рабочий день*) four-hour; (*поезд*) four o'clock.
четы́рнадцат|ый (**-ая, -ое, -ые**) *чис* fourteenth; *см также* **пя́тый**.
четы́рнадцат|ь (**-и**; *как* **пять**; *см* **Table 27**) *чис* fourteen; *см также* **пять**.
четырьмя́ *чис см* **четы́ре**.
четырьмястáми *чис см* **четы́реста**.
чех (**-а**) *м* Czech.
чехард|á (**-ы́**) *ж* (*разг: игра*) leapfrog; (*перен: путаница*) muddle.
Чéхи|я (**-и**) *ж* the Czech Republic.
чех|óл (**-лá**) *м* (*для мебели*) cover; (*для гитары, для оружия*) case.
Чехословáки|я (**-и**) *ж* (*ист*) Czechoslovakia.
чечеви́ц|а (**-ы**) *ж* lentil ♦ *собир* lentils *мн*.
чечéн|ец (**-ца**) *м* Chechen.
Чечéни|я (**-и**) *ж* Chechenia.
чечéн|ка (**-ки**; *gen pl* **-ок**) *ж см* **чечéнец**.
чечéнца *итп сущ см* **чечéнец**.
чечётк|а (**-и**) *ж* tap dance.
чéш|ка (**-ки**; *gen pl* **-ек**) *ж см* **чех**.
чéшск|ий (**-ая, -ое, -ие**) *прил* Czech; ~ **язы́к** Czech.
чешу́(сь) *итп несов см* **чесáть(ся)**.
чешуйк|а (**-и**) *ж* scale.
чешу́йчатый *прил* scaly.
чешу|я́ (**-и́**) *ж собир* scales *мн*.
чи́бис (**-а**) *м* lapwing.
чиж (**-á**) *м* siskin.
чи́збургер (**-а**) *м* cheeseburger.
Чикáго *м нескл* Chicago.
Чи́ли *ср нескл* Chile.
чили́йск|ий (**-ая, -ое, -ие**) *прил* Chilean.
чин (**-а**; *nom pl* **-ы́**) *м* rank; **повышáть (повы́сить** *perf*) **когó-н в чи́не** to promote sb to a higher rank.
чин|и́ть (**-ю́, -ишь**; *perf* **почини́ть**) *несов перех* to mend, repair; (*perf* **очини́ть**; *карандаш*) to sharpen; (**-ю́, -и́шь**; *perf* **учини́ть**; *насилие, произвол*) to commit; (*no perf*; *препятствия*) to create.
чинóвник (**-а**) *м* (*служащий*) official; (*бюрократ*) bureaucrat.
чинóвнический (**-ая, -ое, -ие**) *прил* (*должность*) official; (*аппарат*) bureaucratic.
чи́пс|ы (**-ов**) *мн* crisps *мн*.
чири́ка|ть (**-ю**) *несов неперех* to twitter.

чи́рка|ть (**-ю**) *несов неперех*: ~ **спи́чкой** to strike a match.
чи́ркн|уть (**-у, -ешь**) *сов неперех* to strike.
чи́сел *сущ см* **числó**.
чи́сленность (**-и**) *ж* (*армии*) numbers *мн*; (*учащихся*) number; ~ **населéния** population.
чи́сленный *прил* (*количественный*) numerical; **чи́сленное превосхóдство** numerical advantage; **чи́сленный состáв** (*армии*) total numbers *мн*.
числи́тель (**-я**) *м* numerator.
числи́тельн|ое (**-ого**; *decl like adj*) *ср* numeral.
чи́сл|иться (**-юсь, -ишься**) *несов возв* (*в организации*) to be registered; ~ (*impf*) +*instr* (*больным, должником итп*) to be registered as; **он ~ится дирéктором фи́рмы** he's officially the director of the firm; **за ним ~ится долг** he owes some money; **в спи́ске егó фами́лия не ~ится** his family is not on the books.
чис|ло́ (**-лá**; *nom pl* **-ла**, *gen pl* **-ел**) *ср* number; (*день месяца*) date; **еди́нственное** ~ singular; **мнóжественное** ~ plural; **быть** (*impf*) **в ~лé** +*gen* to be among(st); **какóе сегóдня ~?** what is the date today?; **прие́ду в пéрвых чи́слах мáрта** I am coming at the beginning of March; **отмечáть (отмéтить** *perf*) **что-н зáдним ~м** to backdate sth; **узнавáть (узнáть** *perf*) **зáдним ~м** (*разг*) to find out later; **в том ~лé** including; **оши́бкам нет ~лá** there are countless mistakes.
числов|óй *прил*: ~**óе прогрáммное управлéние** (*комп*) numerically programmed (*BRIT*) *или* programed (*US*) control.
чисти́лище (**-а**) *ср* purgatory.
чи́|стить (**-щу, -стишь**; *perf* **вы́чистить** *или* **почи́стить**) *несов перех* to clean; (*зубы*) to brush, clean; (*perf* **почи́стить**; *яблоко, картошку*) to peel; (*рыбу*) to scale; (*perf* **очи́стить**; *дно реки*) to dredge; (*сад*) to clean up; (*perf* **обчи́стить**, *разг: кассу, человека*) to clean out.
чи́ст|ка (**-ки**; *gen pl* **-ок**) *ж* (*действие*) cleaning; (: *овощей*) peeling; (*в партии*) purge.
чи́сто *нареч* (*только*) purely; (*убранный, сделанный*) neatly ♦ *как сказ*: **в дóме** ~ the house is clean.
чистови́к (**-á**) *м* fair copy.
чистовóй *прил* fair.
чи́сток *сущ см* **чи́стка**.
чистокрóвный *прил* pure-breed; ~**ая лóшадь** thoroughbred.
чистоплóтен *прил см* **чистоплóтный**.
чистоплóтность (**-и**) *ж* cleanliness.
чистоплóтн|ый (**-ен, -на, -но**) *прил* clean; (*перен: порядочный*) decent.
чистопрóбный *прил* (*золото*) pure.
чистосердéчн|ый (**-ен, -на, -но**) *прил* sincere.
чистот|á (**-ы́**) *ж* (*воздуха, спирта, раствора*) purity; **у негó в дóме всегдá** ~ his house is always extremely clean.
чи́ст|ый (**-, -á, -о**) *прил* (*одежда, комната*) clean; (*любовь, сердце, человек*) pure and innocent;

(*сóвесть, нéбо, произношéние*) clear; (*зóлото, спирт*) pure; (*язык*) proper; (*no short form*; *прибыль, вес*) net; (*совпадéние, случáйность*) pure; **выводи́ть** (**вы́вести** *perf*) **когó-н на ~ую вóду** (*разоблачить*) to expose sb.

читáльный *прил*: ~ **зал** reading room.

читáтел|ь (-я) *м* reader.

читáтельниц|а (-ы) *ж см* **читáтель**.

читá|ть (-ю; *perf* **прочéсть** *или* **прочитáть**) *несов перех* to read; (*декламировать*) to recite; (*курс*) to teach; (*лéкцию*) to give.

чихá|ть (-ю; *perf* **чихнýть**) *несов неперех* to sneeze; (*разг: мотор*) to splutter: **емý ~ на прáвила/свои́х роди́телей** he doesn't give a damn about the rules/his parents.

чи́ще *сравн прил от* **чи́стый** ♦ *сравн нареч от* **чи́сто**.

чи́щу *несов см* **чи́стить**.

ЧК *ж сокр* = **Чекá**.

член (-а) *м* member; (*обычно мн: конéчности*) limb; **половóй ~** penis; **~ предложéния** part of a sentence.

член|и́ть (-ю́, -и́шь; *perf* **расчлени́ть**) *несов перех* to break up.

членкóр (-а) *м сокр* = **член-корреспондéнт**.

член-корреспондéнт (-а, -а) *м* (*звáние*) *academic title junior to academician*.

членоразде́л|ьный (-ен, -ьна, -ьно) *прил* intelligible.

чле́нск|ий (-ая, -ое, -ие) *прил* membership.

чле́нств|о (-а) *ср* membership.

ЧМ *сокр* (= *частóтная модуляция*) FM (= *frequency modulation*).

чóка|ться (-юсь; *perf* **чóкнуться**) *несов возв* to clink glasses (*during a toast*).

чóкнут|ый (-, -а, -о) *прил* (*разг: человéк*) barmy, crazy.

чóкн|уться (-усь, -ешься) *сов от* **чóкаться**.

чóпор|ный (-ен, -на, -но) *прил* prim.

ЧП *ср сокр* = **чрезвычáйное происшéствие**.

ЧПУ *ср сокр* = **числовóе прогрáммное управлéние**.

чрезвычá|ен *прил см* **чрезвычáйный**.

чрезвычáйно *нареч* extremely.

чрезвычáйн|ый (-ен, -йна, -йно) *прил* (*исключи́тельный*) extraordinary; (*no short form*; *экстрéнный*) emergency *опред*; **чрезвычáйный и полномóчный посóл** ambassador extraordinary and plenipotentiary; **чрезвычáйное положéние** state of emergency; **чрезвычáйное происшéствие** crisis.

чрезме́р|ный (-ен, -на, -но) *прил* excessive.

чтéни|е (-я) *ср* reading; *см также* **чтéния**.

чтéни|я (-й) *мн* course *ед* of lectures.

чтец (-á) *м* reader.

чт|ить (*см* **Table 17**) *несов перех* to honour (*BRIT*), honor (*US*).

KEYWORD

что (**чегó**; (*см* **Table 6**) *мест* **1** (*вопроси́тельное*) what; **что ты сказáл?** what did you say?; **что с тобóй?** what's the matter (with you)?; **что Вы говори́те?** you don't say!; **к чемý** *или* **на что тебé э́то?** what do you need it for?

2 (*относи́тельное*) which; **онá не поздорóвалась, что бы́ло мне неприя́тно** she did not say hello, which was unpleasant for me; **что ни говори́ ...** whatever you say ...

3 (*стóлько скóлько*): **онá закричáла что бы́ло сил** she shouted with her all might

4 (*котóрый*) that; **дéрево, что растёт у дóма** the tree that grows by the house

5 (*разг: что-нибудь*) anything; **éсли что случи́тся** if anything happens; should anything happen; **в слýчае чегó** if anything crops up; **чуть что – срáзу скажи́ мне** get in touch at the slightest thing

♦ *нареч* (*почемý*) why; **что ты грусти́шь?** why are you sad?; **мне не хóчется идти́ – что так?** I don't feel like going – why's that?

♦ *союз* **1** (*при сообщéнии, выскáзывании*): **я знáю, что нáдо дéлать** I know what must be done; **я знáю, что он приéдет** I know that he will come; **стрáнно то, что он молчи́т** it is strange that he remains silent; **что ни день, то нóвые проблéмы** there isn't a day without new problems

2 (*во фрáзах*): **а что?** (*разг*) why (do you ask)?; **к чемý** (*зачéм*) why; **нé за что!** not at all! (*BRIT*), you're welcome! (*US*); **не зá что!** (*разг*) no way!; **ни за что ни про что** (*разг*) for no (good) reason; **что ты!** (*при возражéнии*) what!; **я здесь ни при чём** it has nothing to do with me; **э́то тут ни при чём** that's beside the point; **чегó там!** forget it!; **что ж** (*да*) oh well; **что за чепухá?** what kind of nonsense is this!; **сáмый что ни на есть лýчший/óпытный** best/most experienced there is; **что к чемý** (*разг*) what's what; **поéхали, что ли?** (*разг*) shall we go or not?

чтоб *союз* = **чтóбы**.

KEYWORD

чтóбы *союз*: **чтóбы** +*infin* (*выражáет цель*) in order *или* so as to do; **я бýду рабóтать нóчью, чтóбы сдать сочинéние зáвтра** I will work at night in order *или* so as to hand in the composition tomorrow

♦ *союз* (+*pt*) **1** (*выражáет цель*) so that; **учи́тель говори́т мéдленно, чтóбы мы всё понимáли** the teacher speaks slowly so that we understand everything

2 (*выражáет желáтельность*): **я хочý, чтóбы онá пришлá** I want her to come

3 (*выражáет возмóжность*): **не мóжет быть,**

что́бы он так поступи́л it can't be possible that he should have acted like that
♦ *част 1 (выражает пожелание)*: что́бы она́ заболе́ла! I hope she gets ill!
2 (выражает требование): что́бы я его́ здесь бо́льше не ви́дел! I hope (that) I never see him here again!

что́-либо (чего́-либо; *как что; см* **Table 6**) *мест* = что́-нибудь.

что́-нибудь (чего́-нибудь; *как что; см* **Table 6**) *мест (в утвердительных предложениях)* something; *(в вопросительных предложениях)* anything; **скажи́** ~ say something; **есть** ~ **интере́сное?** is there anything interesting?

что́-то (чего́-то; *как что; см* **Table 6**) *мест* something; *(приблизительно)* something like ♦ *нареч (раз)*: почему́-то somehow; **он получи́л** ~ **о́коло ста пи́сем** he got something like a hundred letters; ~ **не по́мню тако́го** somehow I don't remember that.

чуб (-а) *м* forelock.

чува́ш (-а) *м* Chuvash.

чува́шек *сущ см* **чува́шка**.

Чува́ши|я (-и) *ж* Chuvashia.

чува́ш|ка (-ки; *gen pl* -ек) *ж см* **чува́ш**.

чу́вствен|ный (-, -на, -но) *прил (удовольствие, любовь итп)* sensual; *(no short form; восприятия)* sensory.

чувстви́телен *прил см* **чувстви́тельный**.

чувстви́тельност|ь (-и) *ж* sensitivity; *(стихов, музыки)* sentimentality.

чувстви́тель|ный (-ен, -ьна, -ьно) *прил* sensitive; *(стихи, музыка)* sentimental; *(удар)* heavy; *(оскорбление)* deep; *(потери)* considerable.

чу́вств|о (-а) *ср (эмоция, ощущение)* feeling; *(+gen; юмора, долга, ответственности)* sense of; **лиша́ться (лиши́ться** *perf*) **чувств** to faint, lose consciousness; **приводи́ть (привести́** *perf*) **кого́-н в** ~ to bring sb round.

чу́вств|овать (-ую; *perf* почу́вствовать) *несов перех* to feel; *(присутствие, опасность)* to sense; ~ *(impf)* **себя́ хорошо́/пло́хо/нело́вко** to feel good/bad/awkward

▶ чу́вствоваться *несов возв (жара, усталость)* to be felt; ~ **, что он волну́ется** you can tell he's worried.

чугу́н (-а́) *м* cast iron.

чугу́нный *прил* cast-iron.

чуда́к (-а́) *м* eccentric.

чу́ден *прил см* **чу́дный**.

чудён *прил см* **чудно́й**.

чудеса́ *итп сущ см* **чу́до**.

чуде́сен *прил см* **чуде́сный**.

чуде́сно *нареч* wonderfully ♦ *как сказ* it's wonderful.

чуде́с|ный (-ен, -на, -но) *прил (необычный)* miraculous; *(очень хороший)* marvellous (*BRIT*), marvelous (*US*), wonderful.

чуди́|ть (2sg -и́шь, 3sg -и́т) *несов неперех* to behave oddly.

чу́ди|ться (3sg -ится, 3pl -ятся, *perf* почу́диться) *несов возв (+dat)* to appear.

чу́дище (-а) *ср* monster.

чудн|о́й (-ён, -на́, -но́) *прил (разг)* odd.

чу́д|ный (-ен, -на, -но) *прил (великолепный)* marvellous (*BRIT*), marvelous (*US*).

чу́д|о (-а; *nom pl* -еса́) *ср* miracle.

чудо́вищ|е (-а) *ср* monster.

чудо́вищ|ный (-ен, -на, -но) *прил (преступление, факт)* monstrous; *(перен: ураган, мороз)* terrible.

чудоде́йствен|ный (-ен, -на, -но) *прил (средство)* miraculous.

чу́дом *нареч (спастись)* by a miracle.

чужа́к (-а́) *м* stranger.

чужби́н|а (-ы) *ж* foreign country.

чужда́|ться (-юсь) *несов возв*: ~ +*gen (также перен)* to shun.

чу́жд|ый (-, -а́, -о) *прил (взгляды, ценности)* alien; ~ +*gen* devoid of; **ему́ чужда́ за́висть** he is devoid of envy.

чужезе́м|ец (-ца) *м* stranger.

чужезе́мный *прил* from foreign parts.

чужезе́мца *итп сущ см* **чужезе́мец**.

чужеро́дный *прил (элемент)* alien.

чуж|о́й *прил (принадлежащий другому)* someone или somebody else's; *(речь, обычай)* foreign; *(человек)* strange ♦ (-о́го; *decl like adj*) *м* stranger; **под** ~**и́м и́менем** under an assumed name.

чу́кч|а (-и) *м/ж нескл* Chukchi.

чула́н (-а) *м* storeroom.

чул|о́к (-ка́; *gen pl* -о́к, *dat pl* -ка́м) *м (обычно мн)* stocking.

чум|а́ (-ы́) *ж* plague.

чума́з|ый (-, -а, -о) *прил (разг)* mucky.

чур *межд (разг)*: ~ **я пе́рвый**! mind out, I'm first!; ~ **меня́!** get away from me! *(to keep evil at bay)*

чурба́н (-а) *м (деревянный)* block; *(разг: пренебр: человек)* blockhead.

чу́т|кий (-кая, -кое, -кие; -ок, -ка́, -ко) *прил* sensitive; *(натура)* sympathetic; ~ **сон** light sleep.

чу́ткост|ь (-и) *ж (см прил)* sensitivity; sympathy.

чу́ток *прил см* **чу́ткий**.

чу́точк|а (-и) *ж (разг)*: ~**у** a bit; **ни** ~**и** not a bit.

чуть *нареч (разг: едва)* hardly; *(немного)* a little ♦ *союз (как только)* as soon as; ~ **(бы́ло) не** almost, nearly; ~ **ли не** almost certainly; ~ **что** *(разг)* at the slightest thing.

чуть|ё (-я́) *ср (у животных)* scent; *(у людей)* intuition.

чу́чел|о (-а) *ср (также перен)* scarecrow; ~ **живо́тного/пти́цы** stuffed animal/bird.

чуш|ь (-и) *ж (разг)* rubbish (*BRIT*), garbage (*US*).

чу́|ять (-ю) *несов перех (также перен)* to scent; **я ног под собо́й не** ~**ю** I'm walking on air; *(от усталости)* my legs are giving way beneath me.

чьё (чьего́) *мест см* **чей**.

чьи (чьих) *мест см* **чей**.

чья (чьей) *мест см* **чей**.

~ Ш, ш ~

Ш, ш *сущ нескл* (*буква*) the 25th letter of the Russian alphabet.
ш *сокр* (= **широта́**) w. (= *width*).
ш. *сокр* (= **шту́ка**) ea. (= *each*).
шаба́ш (-а) *м* Sabbath.
шаба́ш *част* (*кончено*) that's enough.
шабло́н (-а) *м* (*ТЕХ*) pattern, gauge; (*перен: в речи, в письме*) cliché.
шабло́н|ный *прил* (*об инструменте, о чертеже*) pattern *опред*; (-ен, -на, -но; *перен: фраза, ответ*) trite.
шаг (-а; *part gen* -у, *loc sg* -у́, *nom pl* -и́) *м* (*также перен*) step; **на ка́ждом ~у́** (*перен*) continually; **~ за ша́гом** step by step; **ша́гу не даю́т ступи́ть** (*перен*) one has no freedom of action; **прибавля́ть** (**приба́вить** *perf*) **ша́гу** to quicken one's pace; **предпринима́ть** (**предприня́ть** *perf*) **но́вые ~и́** to take a new initiative; **я услы́шал ~и́** I heard footsteps.
шага́ть (-ю) *несов неперех* to march; (*делать шаг*) to step; **~й отсю́да!** (*разг*) get lost!
шагну́ть (-у́, -ёшь) *сов неперех* to step, take a step; **~** (*perf*) **вперёд** (*также перен*) to take a step forward.
ша́гом *нареч* (*идти*) at a walk, at walking pace; **~ марш!** (*ВОЕН*) quick march!
ша́ек *сущ см* **ша́йка**.
ша́йб|а (-ы) *ж* (*ТЕХ: прокладка*) spacer; (: *болта*) washer; (*СПОРТ*) puck.
ша́йка (-йки; *gen pl* -ек) *ж* (*бандитская*) gang.
шака́л (-а) *м* jackal.
шала́нд|а (-ы) *ж* scow, barge.
шала́ш (-á) *м* hut (*made of branches*).
ша́левый *прил*: **~ плато́к** shawl; **ша́левый воротни́к** shawl collar.
шале́ть (-ю; *perf* **ошале́ть**) *несов неперех* (*разг*) to go crazy; **~** (**ошале́ть** *perf*) **от ра́дости** to go mad with joy.
шали́ть (-ю́, -и́шь) *несов неперех* (*дети*) to be mischevious; (*разг: мотор, сердце*) to play up.
шаловли́в|ый (-, -а, -о) *прил* (*ребёнок*) mischevious; (*тон, глаза*) playful.
шалопа́й (-я) *м* (*разг*) loafer, skiver.
ша́лост|ь (-и) *ж* (*проказа*) mischief.
шалу́н (-á) *м* mischevious boy.
шалу́нь|я (-ьи; *gen pl* -ий) *ж* mischevious girl.

шалфе́й (-я) *м* (*БОТ*) sage.
шаль (-и) *ж* shawl.
шально́й *прил* (*разг*) wild; (*пуля*) stray; (*деньги*) easy.
шаля́й-валя́й *нареч* (*разг: небрежно*) any(old) how.
шама́н (-а) *м* (*колдун*) shaman.
шама́н|ка (-ки; *gen pl* -ок) *ж см* **шама́н**.
ша́мка|ть (-ю) *несов неперех* to mumble.
шампа́нск|ое (-ого; *decl like adj*) *ср* champagne.
шампиньо́н (-а) *м* (*БОТ*) (field) mushroom.
шампу́нь (-я) *м* shampoo.
шампу́р (-а) *м* skewer.
шанс (-а) *м* chance; **~ на что-н** chance of sth.
шансоне́т|ка (-ки; *gen pl* -ок) *ж см* **шансонье́**.
шансонье́ *м нескл* singer.
шанта́ж (-á) *м* blackmail.
шантажи́р|овать (-ую) *несов перех* to blackmail.
шантажи́ст (-а) *м* blackmailer.
шантажи́ст|ка (-ки; *gen pl* -ок) *ж см* **шантажи́ст**.
шантрапа́ (-ы́) *м/ж собир* (*разг*) yobs *мн*.
Шанха́й (-я) *м* Shanghai.
ша́п|ка (-ки; *gen pl* -ок) *ж* hat; (*перен: снежная*) cap; (*заголовок*) headline; **по ~ке дава́ть** (**дать** *perf*) **+dat** (*перен: разг*) to punish; **по ~ке получа́ть** (**получи́ть** *perf*) (*разг*) to be punished; **на воре́ ~ гори́т** he's given the game away.
ша́почн|ый *прил* of a hat; **~ое знако́мство** nodding acquaintance; **приходи́ть** (**прийти́** *perf*) **к ~ому разбо́ру** (*перен*) to miss the bus.
шар (-а; *nom pl* -ы́) *м* (*ГЕОМ*) sphere; (*кегли, бильярдный итп*) ball; **возду́шный ~** balloon; **земно́й ~** the Earth; **в до́ме хоть ~о́м покати́** the house is completely empty.
шара́д|а (-ы) *ж* charade.
шара́хн|уть (-у, -ешь; *impf* **шара́хать**) *сов* (*не*)*перех* (*разг*): **~ +acc или +instr** (*ударять*) to thump
▸ **шара́хнуться** (*impf* **шара́хаться**) *сов возв* (*разг: отпрянуть*) to leap back; (: *удариться*): **~ся о +acc** to bang into.
шара́шкин *прил*: **~а конто́ра** dodgy enterprise; (*несолидное учреждение*) pathetic place.
шарж (-а) *м* caricature.
шаржи́р|овать (-ую) *несов перех* to caricature.

шáрик (-а) *м уменьш от* **шар**; (*АНАТ*): **кровянóй** ~ blood corpuscle.

шáриковый *прил* (*подшипник*) ball *опред*; ~**ая рýчка** ballpoint pen.

шарикоподшúпник (-а) *м* (*ТЕХ*) ball bearing.

шáр|ить (-ю, -ишь) *несов неперех* (*разг*) to grope; ~ (*impf*) **глазáми** to sweep; ~ (*impf*) **по** (**чужúм**) **кармáнам** (*разг*) to pick pockets.

шáркань|е (-я) *ср* shuffling.

шáрка|ть (-ю) *несов неперех* ~ +*instr* to shuffle.

шáркн|уть (-у, -ешь) *сов неперех* ~ **ногóй** to click one's heels.

шарлатáн (-а) *м* charlatan.

шарлатáн|ка (-ки; *gen pl* -ок) *ж см* **шарлатáн**.

шарлатáнств|о (-а) *ср* charlatanism.

шарлóт|ка (-ки; *gen pl* -ок) *ж* (*КУЛИН*) charlotte.

шарм (-а) *м* (*обаяние*) charm.

шармáн|ка (-ки; *gen pl* -ок) *ж* (*МУЗ*) barrel organ.

шарнúр (-а) *м* (*ТЕХ*) hinge; (*АВТ*) (suspension) joint.

шаровáр|ы (-) *мн* baggy trousers *мн*.

шаровúдный (-ен, -на, -но) *прил* spherical.

шаровóй *прил* (*ГЕОМ*) spherical; ~ **клáпан** ball valve; **шаровáя мóлния** (*ГЕО*) fireball, globe lightning.

шарообрáз|ный (-ен, -на, -но) *прил* = **шаровúдный**.

шарф (-а) *м* scarf.

шассú *ср нескл* (*самолёта*) landing gear; (*автомобиля*) chassis.

шáста|ть (-ю) *несов неперех* (*разг*) to mooch about.

шатáни|е (-я) *ср* (*хождение*) mooching about; (*раскачивание*) swaying; (*перен: идейные*) vacillation.

шатá|ть (-ю) *несов перех* (*раскачивать*) to rock; **меня́** ~**ет от устáлости** I am reeling with tiredness

▸ **шатáться** *несов возв* (*зуб*) to be loose *или* wobbly; (*столб*) to shake; (*от усталости*) to reel, stagger; (*разг: по городу, по улицам итп*) to mooch about.

шатéн (-а) *м* man with *auburn hair*.

шатёр (-рá) *м* tent.

шáт|кий (-кая, -кое, -кие; -ок, -ка, -ко) *прил* (*стул*) wobbly, rickety; (*перен: положение*) precarious; (: *доводы*) shaky.

шáткост|ь (-и) *ж* (*см прил*) wobbliness; precariousness; shakiness.

шатн|ýть (-ý, -ёшь) *сов перех* (*столб*) to shake

▸ **шатнýться** *сов возв* (*столб*) to be unsteady; (*от усталости*) to reel.

шáток *прил см* **шáткий**.

шатрá *итп сущ см* **шатёр**.

шатрóвый *прил* (*крыша, купол*) hipped; **шатрóвая архитектýра** hipped architecture.

шатýн (-á) *м* (*ТЕХ*) connecting rod.

шáфер (-а) *м* best man (*мн* men).

шафрáн (-а) *м* (*БОТ*) saffron.

шах (-а) *м* (*монарх*) shah; (*в шахматах*) check.

шахматúст (-а) *м* chess player.

шахматúст|ка (-ки; *gen pl* -ок) *ж см* **шахматúст**.

шáхматный *прил* (*кружок, чемпионат*) chess *опред*; (*порядок, рисунок*) staggered; **шáхматная доскá** chessboard.

шáхмат|ы (-) *мн* (*игра*) chess *ед*; (*фигуры*) chessmen *мн*.

шáхт|а (-ы) *ж* (*выработка*) mine, pit; (*предприятие*) mine; (*лифта*) shaft.

шахтёр (-а) *м* miner.

шáшек *сущ см* **шáшки**.

шашúст (-а) *м* draughts (*BRIT*) *или* checkers (*US*) player.

шашúст|ка (-ки; *gen pl* -ок) *ж см* **шашúст**.

шáшк|а (-и) *ж* (*игральная*) draught (*BRIT*), checker (*US*); (*взрывчатка*) blasting cartridge; (*оружие*) sabre (*BRIT*), saber (*US*); *см также* **шáшки**.

шáш|ки (-ек) *мн* (*игра*) draughts *мн* (*BRIT*), checkers *мн* (*US*).

шашлы́к (-á) *м* shashlik, kebab.

шашлы́чн|ая (-ой; *decl like adj*) *ж* kebab-house.

шáшн|и (-ей) *мн* (*разг*) affair *ед*.

шва *итп сущ см* **шов**.

швáбр|а (-ы) *ж* mop.

швáркн|уть (-у, -ешь; *impf* **швáркать**) *сов перех* (*разг*) to hurl.

швартóв (-а) *м* (*МОР*) mooring line; **отдавáть** (**отдáть** *perf*) ~**ы** to cast off.

швартовáть (-ýю; *perf* **пришвартовáть** *или* **ошвартовáть**) *несов перех* (*МОР*) to moor.

швед (-а) *м* Swede.

швéд|ка (-ки; *gen pl* -ок) *ж см* **швед**.

швéдск|ий (-ая, -ое, -ие) *прил* Swedish; ~ **язы́к** Swedish.

швéйный *прил* (*машина, нитки*) sewing *опред*; (*фабрика*) clothing *опред*.

швейцáр (-а) *м* doorman (*мн* doormen).

швейцáр|ец (-ца) *м* Swiss.

Швейцáри|я (-и) *ж* Switzerland.

швейцáр|ка (-ки; *gen pl* -ок) *ж см* **швейцáрец**.

швейцáрск|ий (-ая, -ое, -ие) *прил* Swiss.

швейцáрца *итп сущ см* **швейцáрец**.

Швéци|я (-и) *ж* Sweden.

шве|я́ (-и́) *ж* seamstress.

швырн|ýть (-ý, -ёшь) *сов (не)перех* ~ +*acc или* +*instr* to hurl.

швыря́|ть (-ю) *несов перех* to hurl, fling; ~ (*impf*) **дéньги** *или* **деньгáми** (*разг*) to throw one's money about

▸ **швыря́ться** *несов возв* (*разг*) to throw at each other; (*перен*): ~**ся** +*instr* (*людьми*) to treat lightly; ~**ся** (*impf*) **деньгáми** (*разг*) to throw one's money about.

шевел|и́ть (-ю́, -и́шь; *perf* **пошевели́ть**) *несов перех* (*сено*) to turn over; (*подлеж: ветер*) to stir ◆ *неперех*: ~ +*instr* (*пальцами, губами*) to move; ~ (**пошевели́ть** *perf*) **мозгáми** (*перен: разг*) to use one's head

▸ **шевели́ться** (*perf* **пошевели́ться**) *несов возв* to stir; ~**и́сь!** (*разг*) get a move on!

шевельн|ýть (-ý, -ёшь) *сов неперех*: ~ +*instr*

(пальцами, плечом) to move
▶ **шевельну́ться** *сов возв* to stir.
шевелю́р|а (**-ы**) *ж* (head of) hair.
шевро́н (**-а**) *м* (*нашивка*) chevron, long-service stripe.
шеде́вр (**-а**) *м* masterpiece.
ше́ек *сущ см* **ше́йка**.
шезло́нг (**-а**) *м* deckchair.
ше́|йка (**-йки**; *gen pl* **-ек**) *ж уменьш от* **ше́я**; (*рельса*) web; (*гильзы*) neck; **ше́йка ма́тки** (*АНАТ*) cervix.
ше́йный *прил* (*мышца*) neck *опред*; (*позвонок*) cervical; **~ плато́к** neckerchief.
шейх (**-а**) *м* sheikh.
шёл *несов см* **идти́**.
ше́лест (**-а**) *м* rustle.
шелесте́ть (**-и́шь**) *несов неперех* to rustle.
шёлк (**-а**; *nom pl* **-á**) *м* silk.
шелкови́ст|ый (**-**, **-а**, **-о**) *прил* (*гладкий*) silky.
шелкови́чный *прил*: **~ червь** silkworm.
шелково́дств|о (**-а**) *ср* sericulture, silkworm breeding.
шёлковый *прил* (*нить, одежда*) silk; (*перен: разг: человек*) meek.
шелкопря́д (**-а**) *м* silkworm.
шелкопряди́льный *прил* silk-spinning.
шелоткáц|кий (**-ая**, **-ое**, **-ие**) *прил* silk-weaving.
шелохну́ть (**-у́**, **-ёшь**) *сов перех* to stir, agitate
▶ **шелохну́ться** *сов возв* to stir, move.
шелух|á (**-и́**) *ж* (*картофельная*) skin, peel; (*гороховая*) pod; (*семечек*) chaff; (*перен*) dross.
шелуше́ни|е (**-я**) *ср* (*зерна*) shelling; (*кожи*) peeling.
шелуш|и́ть (**-у́**, **-и́шь**) *несов перех* to shell
▶ **шелуши́ться** *несов возв* to peel.
ше́льм|а (**-ы**) *м/ж* (*разг*) rascal.
шельф (**-а**) *м* (*ГЕО*) shelf.
шепеля́в|ить (**-лю**, **-ишь**) *несов неперех* to lisp.
шепеля́в|ый (**-**, **-а**, **-о**) *прил* (*человек, речь*) lisping.
шепну́ть (**-у́**, **-ёшь**) *сов перех* to whisper.
шёпот (**-а**) *м* whisper; (*перен: ручья, листьев*) murmuring.
шёпотом *нареч* (*сказать, подсказать*) in a whisper.
шепта́ни|е (**-я**) *ср* (*см глаг*) whispering; murmuring.
шепт|а́ть (**-чу́**, **-чешь**) *несов перех* to whisper ♦ *неперех* (*перен: ручей, листья*) to murmur
▶ **шепта́ться** *несов возв* to whisper to each other.
шербе́т (**-а**) *м* sherbet.
шере́нг|а (**-и**) *ж* (*солдат*) rank; (*машин*) line.
шери́ф (**-а**) *м* sheriff.
шерохова́тость (**-и**) *ж* (*см прил*) roughness; uneveness; (*шероховатое место*) rough area.

шерохова́т|ый (**-**, **-а**, **-о**) *прил* (*доска, кожа*) rough; (*перен: изложение*) uneven.
шерсти́н|ка (**-ки**; *gen pl* **-ок**) *ж* strand of wool.
шерстопряди́льный *прил* wool-spinning.
шерст|ь (**-и**) *ж* (*животного*) hair; (*пряжа, ткань*) wool.
шерстяно́й *прил* (*пряжа, ткань*) woollen (*BRIT*), woolen (*US*).
шерша́в|ый (**-**, **-а**, **-о**) *прил* (*руки, ткань*) rough.
шест (**-á**) *м* pole; **прыжо́к с ~о́м** pole vault.
шест|а́я (**-о́й**; *decl like adj*) *ж*: **одна́ ~** one sixth.
ше́стви|е (**-я**) *ср* procession.
ше́ств|овать (**-ую**) *несов неперех* to walk in procession.
шестерён|ка (**-ки**; *gen pl* **-ок**) *ж* (*ТЕХ*) gear (wheel).
шестёр|ка (**-и**) *ж* (*цифра, карта*) six; (*шлюпка*) six-oar boat; (*группа из шести*) group of six; (*разг: автобус, трамвай итп*) (number) six (*bus, tram etc*).
ше́стер|о (**-ы́х**; *см* **Table 36b**) *чис* six; *см также* **дво́е**.
шести́ *чис см* **шесть**.
шестидеся́т *чис см* **шестьдеся́т**.
шестидесятиле́ти|е (**-я**) *ср* (*срок*) sixty years *мн*; (*годовщина события*) sixtieth anniversary.
шестидесятиле́тн|ий (**-яя**, **-ее**, **-ие**) *прил* (*период*) sixty-year; (*юбилей*) sixtieth; (*человек*) sixty-year-old.
шестидеся́т|ый (**-ая**, **-ое**, **-ые**) *чис* sixtieth; *см также* **пятидеся́тый**.
шестидне́вный *прил* six-day.
шестикла́ссник (**-а**) *м pupil in sixth year at school (usually twelve years old)*.
шестикла́ссниц|а (**-ы**) *ж см* **шестикла́ссник**.
шестикра́т|ный *прил*: **~ чемпио́н** six-times champion; **в ~ом разме́ре** sixfold.
шестиле́ти|е (**-я**) *ср* (*срок*) six years; (*годовщина*) sixth anniversary.
шестиле́тн|ий (**-яя**, **-ее**, **-ие**) *прил* (*отсутствие*) six-year; (*ребёнок*) six-year-old.
шестиме́сячный *прил* six-month; (*ребёнок*) six-month-old.
шестинеде́льный *прил* six-week; (*ребёнок*) six-week-old.
шестисо́т *чис см* **шестьсо́т**.
шестисотле́ти|е (**-я**) *ср* (*срок*) six hundred years *мн*; (*годовщина*) six hundredth anniversary, sexcentenary.
шестисотле́тн|ий (**-яя**, **-ее**, **-ие**) *прил* (*период*) six hundred-year; (*дерево*) six hundred-year-old.
шестисо́т|ый (**-ая**, **-ое**, **-ые**) *чис* six-hundredth.
шестиуго́льник (**-а**) *м* hexagon.
шестичасово́й *прил* (*рабочий день*) six-hour; (*поезд*) six-o'clock.
шестна́дцати *чис см* **шестна́дцать**.
шестна́дцат|ый (**-ая**, **-ое**, **-ые**) *чис* sixteenth; *см*

также **пя́тый.**

шестнáдцат|ь (-и; *как* **пять**; *см* **Table 27)** *чис* sixteen; *см также* **пять.**

шест|óй (-áя, -óе, -ы́е) *чис* sixth; *см также* **пя́тый.**

шест|ь (-и́; *как* **пять**; *см* **Table 27)** *чис* six; *см также* **пять.**

шест|ьдеся́т (-и́десяти; *как* **пятьдеся́т**; *см* **Table 29)** *чис* sixty; *см также* **пятьдеся́т.**

шест|ьсóт (-исóт; *как* **пятьсóт**; *см* **Table 34)** *чис* six hundred; *см также* **сто.**

шéстью *нареч* six times.

шéстью *чис см* **шесть.**

шестьюстáми *чис см* **шестьсóт.**

шетлáндск|ий (-ая, -ое, -ие) *прил:* **Ш~ие островá** Shetland Islands.

шеф (-а) *м* (*полиции*) chief; (*разг: начальник*) boss; (*обычно мн: детского дома*) patron.

шéфск|ий (-ая, -ое, -ие) *прил* (*помощь*) patronal.

шéфств|о (-а) *ср:* ~ **над** +*instr* patronage of.

шéфств|овать (-ую) *несов неперех:* ~ **над** +*instr* to be patron of.

ше́|я (-и) *ж* (*АНАТ*) neck; **на свою** ~**ю** (*разг*) to our loss; **сидéть** (*impf*) *или* **висéть** (*impf*) **у когó-н на** ~**е** to live off sb; **гнать** (*impf*) **когó-н в** ~**ю** (*разг*) to throw sb out on his *итп* ear.

ши́бко *нареч* terribly.

ши́ворот (-а) *м* (*разг*): **за** ~ by the collar; ~**навы́ворот** back to front.

шизофрéник (-а) *м* schizophrenic.

шизофрени́|я (-и) *ж* schizophrenia.

шик (-а; *part gen* -у) *м* chic, stylishness.

шикáрен *прил см* **шикáрный.**

шикáрно *нареч* (*разг: жить*) in style; (*обставленный*) stylishly ♦ *как сказ:* **в гости́нице** ~ the hotel is stylish.

шикáр|ный (-ен, -на, -но) *прил* (*разг*) smart, stylish.

ши́ка|ть (-ю) *несов неперех* (*разг*): ~ **на когó-н** to hush sb.

ши́кн|уть (-у, -ешь) *сов неперех:* ~ **на когó-н** to hush sb.

шик|овáть (-у́ю) *несов неперех* (*разг*) to show off.

ши́ллинг (-а) *м* (*денежная единица*) shilling.

ши́л|о (-а; *nom pl* -ья, *gen pl* -ьев) *ср* awl.

шимпанзé *м нескл* chimpanzee.

шин|á (-ы́) *ж* (*АВТ*) tyre (*BRIT*), tire (*US*); (*МЕД*) splint.

шинéл|ь (-и) *ж* (*солдатская*) greatcoat, overcoat.

шинковáни|е (-я) *ср* shredding.

шинк|овáть (-у́ю; *perf* **нашинковáть**) *несов перех* (*овощи*) to shred.

шиньóн (-а) *м* chignon.

шип (-á) *м* (*растения*) thorn; (*соединительный*) tenon, tongue; (*на колесе*) stud; (*на ботинке*) spike.

шипéни|е (-я) *ср* hissing.

шип|éть (-лю́, -и́шь) *несов неперех* (*также*

разг) to hiss; (*шампанское, газировка*) to fizz.

шипóв|ки (-ок) *мн* (*СПОРТ*) spikes *мн.*

шипóвник (-а) *м* (*куст*) wild rose; (*плод*) (rose)hip; (*настой*) rosehip drink.

шипóвок *сущ см* **шипóвки.**

шипу́ч|ий (-ая, -ее, -ие; -, -а, -е) *прил* fizzy; (*вино*) sparkling.

шипя́щий (-ая, -ее, -ие) *прил* (*линг*) sibilant *опред.*

ши́ре *сравн прил от* **широ́кий** ♦ *сравн нареч от* **широкó.**

ширин|á (-ы́) *ж* width; **доро́жка метр** ~**óй** *или* **в** ~**ý** a path a metre (*BRIT*) *или* meter (*US*) wide.

ширин|ка (-ки; *gen pl* -ок) *ж* (*брюк*) fly.

шир|иться (3*sg* -ится, 3*pl* -ятся) *несов возв* (*дела*) to expand; (*движение*) to grow.

ши́рм|а (-ы) *ж* (*также перен*) screen.

широ́к|ий (-ая, -ое, -ие; -, -á, -ó) *прил* wide; (*степи, фронт, планы*) extensive; (*перен: общественность, публика*) general; (: *смысл, интерпретация*) broad; (: *масштабы*) large; (: *натура, жест*) generous; (: *образ жизни*) grand; **товáры** ~**ого потреблéния** (*ЭКОН*) consumer goods; **жить** (*impf*) **на** ~**ую нóгу** to live in grand style; **широ́кий экрáн** (*КИНО*) wide screen.

широкó *нареч* (*раскинуться*) widely; (*улыбаться, интерпретировать*) broadly; (*жить*) in grand style; ~ **раскрывáть** (**раскры́ть** *perf*) **глазá** to open one's eyes wide; (*перен*) to be amazed.

широковещáтел|ьный (-ен, -ьна, -ьно) *прил* broadcasting *опред;* **широковещáтельная сеть** (*КОМП*) broadcast network.

широкопле́ч|ий (-ая, -ее, -ие; -, -а, -е) *прил* (*человек*) broad-shouldered.

широкопóлый *прил* (*шляпа*) wide-brimmed; (*пальто*) with a full skirt.

широкоформáтный *прил* (*экран*) wide-format.

широкофюзеля́жный *прил* (*самолёт*) wide-bodied.

широкоэкрáнный *прил* (*фильм*) wide-screen.

широт|á (-оты́) *ж* breadth; (*nom pl* -óты; *ГЕО*) latitude.

ширпотрéб (-а) *м сокр* = **широ́кое потреблéние**; (*разг: о товарах*) consumer goods *мн*; (: *о плохом товаре*) low-quality goods *мн.*

шир|ь (-и) *ж* expanse; **развора́чиваться** (**разверну́ться** *perf*) **во всю** ~ (*перен*) to develop to one's full potential.

ши́то-кры́то *нареч* (*разг*): **всё** ~ it's all being kept under wraps.

ши́тый *прил* embroidered.

шить (**шью, шьёшь**; *perf* **сшить**) *несов перех* (*платье итп*) to sew ♦ *неперех:* ~ +*instr* (*шёлком итп*) to embroider.

шить|ё (-я́) *ср* (*см глаг*) sewing; embroidery.

ши́фер (-а) *м* (*натуральный*) slate; (*СТРОИТ*) corrugated asbestos board.

шифóн (-а) *м* chiffon.

шифоньéр (-а) *м* wardrobe.

шифр (**-а**) *м* (*для секретного письма*) code, cipher; (*книги, документа*) pressmark.

шифрова́льщик (**-а**) *м* cipher-clerk; (*расшифровывающий*) code cracker.

шифр|ова́ть (**-у́ю**; *perf* **зашифрова́ть**) *несов перех* (*донесение*) to encode, encipher.

шифро́в|ка (**-ки**; *gen pl* **-ок**) *ж* (*см глаг*) encoding, enciphering; (*сообщение*) coded message.

шиш (**-а́**) *м* (*разг: кукиш*) fig (*rude gesture*); **ни ~а́** (*разг*) damn all; **~ ты от меня полу́чишь** (*разг*) you'll get damn all from me; **на каки́е ~й?** (*разг*) who's paying?

ши́ш|ка (**-ки**; *gen pl* **-ек**) *ж* (*БОТ*) cone; (*на лбу*) bump, lump; (*разг: важный человек*) bigwig.

шишкова́т|ый (**-, -а, -о**) *прил* (*руки*) knobbly; (*лоб*) lumpy; (*доска*) rough.

шкал|а́ (**-ы́**; *nom pl* **-ы**) *ж* scale; (*приёмника*) dial.

шкату́л|ка (**-ки**; *gen pl* **-ок**) *ж* casket; **музыка́льная ~** musical box.

шкаф (**-а**; *loc sg* **-у́**, *nom pl* **-ы́**) *м* (*для одежды*) wardrobe; (*для посуды*) cupboard; (*ТЕХ: сушильный итп*) oven; **духово́й ~** airing cupboard; **кни́жный ~** bookcase.

шквал (**-а**) *м* (*ветер*) squall; **~ +gen** (*оваций, огня*) burst of.

шква́льный *прил* (*ветер*) squally; (*огонь*) heavy.

шкив (**-а**) *м* (*ТЕХ*) pulley.

шки́пер (**-а**) *м* (*МОР*) skipper.

шки́р|ка (**-и**) *ж*: **брать кого́-н за ~у** (*разг*) to take sb by the scruff of the neck; (*перен*) to twist sb's arm.

шко́л|а (**-ы**) *ж* school; (*милиции*) college, academy; (*выучка*) education, training; (*СПОРТ*) training; **вы́сшая ~** higher education; **нача́льная ~** primary (*BRIT*) *или* elementary (*US*) school; **сре́дняя ~** secondary (*BRIT*) *или* high (*US*) school.

шко́ла-интерна́т (**-ы, -а**) *м* boarding school.

шко́льник (**-а**) *м* schoolboy.

шко́льниц|а (**-ы**) *ж* schoolgirl.

шко́льный *прил* (*здание*) school *опред*; **шко́льные го́ды** schooldays; **шко́льный во́зраст** school age; **шко́льный уче́бник** school book; **шко́льный учи́тель** school teacher.

шку́р|а (**-ы**) *ж* (*животного*) fur; (*убитого животного*) skin; (: *обработанная*) hide ♦ *м/ж* (*разг: продажный человек*) self-seeker; **быть** (*impf*) **в чьей-н ~е** to be in sb's shoes (*fig*); **спаса́ть** (*impf*) **свою́ ~у** (*разг*) to save one's (own) skin; **на свое́й ~е узна́ть** (*perf*) (*разг*) to experience first-hand.

шку́р|ить (**-ю, -ишь**) *сов перех* (*шлифовать*) to sand(paper).

шку́р|ка (**-и**) *ж уменьш от* **шку́ра**; (*разг: плода*) rind, peel; (*абразив*) sandpaper.

шку́рник (**-а**) *м* (*разг: пренебр*) self-seeker.

шку́рный *прил* (*интересы*) selfish.

шла *несов см* **идти́**.

шлагба́ум (**-а**) *м* barrier.

шлак (**-а**) *м* (*ТЕХ*) slag.

шлакобето́нный *прил* (*панель, кирпич*) slag-concrete.

шланг (**-а**) *м* hose.

шлейф (**-а**) *м* (*платья*) train; (*дыма*) trail.

шлем (**-а**) *м* helmet.

шлёпан|ец (**-ца**) *ж* (*разг: обычно мн*) bedroom slipper.

шлёпа|ть (**-ю**) *несов перех* (*бить*) to slap ♦ *неперех*: **~ по** +*acc* (*по полу*) to shuffle; (*по воде*) to splash

▸ **шлёпаться** (*perf* **шлёпнуться**) *несов возв* (*разг*) to plop.

шли *несов см* **идти́**.

шлифова́льный *прил* (*ТЕХ*) grinding *опред*.

шлиф|ова́ть (**-у́ю**; *perf* **отшлифова́ть**) *несов перех* (*ТЕХ*) to grind; (*перен: стиль*) to polish.

шлифо́в|ка (**-и**) *ж* (*детали*) grinding.

шли́ц|а (**-ы**) *ж* (*ТЕХ*) spline; (*юбки*) slit.

шло *несов см* **идти́**.

шлю *итп несов см* **слать**.

шлюз (**-а**) *м* (*на канале*) lock; (*на реке*) sluice.

шлю́п|ка (**-ки**; *gen pl* **-ок**) *ж* (*МОР*) dinghy; **спаса́тельная ~** lifeboat.

шлю́х|а (**-и**) *ж* (*разг*) tart.

шля́гер (**-а**) *м* (*МУЗ*) hit.

шля́п|а (**-ы**) *ж* hat ♦ *м/ж* (*перен: разг: человек*) wimp; **де́ло в ~е** (*разг*) it's in the bag.

шля́п|ка (**-ки**; *gen pl* **-ок**) *ж* hat; (*гвоздя*) head; (*гриба*) cap.

шля́пник (**-а**) *м* (*мужской*) hatter; (*женский*) milliner.

шля́пный *прил* hat *опред*.

шля́пок *сущ см* **шля́пка**.

шля́|ться (**-юсь**) *несов возв* (*разг*) to mooch about.

шмель (**-я́**) *м* bumblebee.

шмо́т|ки (**-ок**) *мн* (*разг*) clobber *ед*.

шмы́га|ть (**-ю**) *несов неперех* (*разг: шнырять*) to rush; (*исчезнуть*) to slip, dart; **~** (*impf*) **но́сом** to sniff.

шмыгн|у́ть (**-у́, -ёшь**) *сов неперех* (*быстро пройти*) to dart, nip; (*исчезнуть*) to slip, dart.

шмя́кн|уть (**-у, -ешь**; *impf* **шмя́кать**) *сов перех* (*разг: бросить*) to thump down

▸ **шмя́кнуться** (*impf* **шмя́каться**) *сов возв* (*разг: упасть*) to topple over.

шни́цел|ь (**-я**) *м* (*КУЛИН*) schnitzel.

шнур (**-а́**) *м* (*верёвка*) cord; (*телефонный, лампы*) flex.

шнурка́ *итп сущ см* **шнуро́к**.

шнур|ова́ть (**-у́ю**; *perf* **зашнурова́ть**) *несов перех* (*ботинки*) to lace (up); (*perf* **прошнурова́ть**; *прошивать шнуром*) to tie, bind.

шнуро́вк|а (-и) ж (см глаг) lacing up; tying, binding; (на одежде, на обуви) lacing.

шнур|о́к (-ка́) м (ботинка) lace.

шныря́|ть (-ю) несов неперех (разг: в толпе, по улицам) to dash about; **он ~л глаза́ми** (перен: разг) his eyes darted about.

шов (шва) м (швейный) seam; (хирургический) stitch, suture; (намёточный, тамбурный итп) stitch; (кровельный) joint, seam; **сварно́й ~** joint weld, weld seam; **накла́дывать (наложи́ть** perf)/**снима́ть (снять** perf) **швы** (МЕД) to put in/take out stitches; **треща́ть** (impf) **по всем швам** (перен: разг) to fall apart at the seams; **ру́ки по швам** stand at attention.

шовини́зм (-а) м chauvinism.

шовини́ст (-а) м chauvinist.

шовинисти́ческ|ий (-ая, -ое, -ие) прил chauvinist.

шок (-а) м (МЕД, перен) shock.

шоки́р|овать (-ую) (не)сов перех to shock.

шо́ков|ый прил: **~ое состоя́ние** state of shock; **шо́ковая терапи́я** (МЕД, перен) shock therapy.

шокола́д (-а) м chocolate; (напиток) (hot) chocolate.

шокола́д|ка (-ки; gen pl -ок) ж (разг) bar of chocolate.

шокола́дн|ый прил (конфета) chocolate; (цвет) chocolate-brown; **~ая пли́тка** bar of chocolate.

шокола́док сущ см **шокола́дка**.

шо́мпол (-а) м (ВОЕН) cleaning rod.

шо́рох (-а) м rustle.

шо́рт|ы (-) мн shorts мн.

шоссе́ ср нескл highway.

шоссе́йн|ый прил: **~ая доро́га** highway.

шотла́нд|ец (-ца) м Scotsman (мн Scotsmen).

Шотла́нди|я (-и) ж Scotland.

шотла́нд|ка (-ки; gen pl -ок) ж Scotswoman (мн Scotswomen); (ткань) tartan (BRIT), plaid (US).

шотла́ндск|ий (-ая, -ое, -ие) прил Scottish, Scots.

шотла́ндца итп сущ см **шотла́ндец**.

шо́у ср нескл (также перен) show.

шофёр (-а) м driver.

шпа́г|а (-и) ж sword.

шпага́т (-а) м (бечёвка) string, twine; (СПОРТ) the splits.

шпажи́ст (-а) м (СПОРТ) fencer.

шпажи́ст|ка (-ки; gen pl -ок) ж см **шпажи́ст**.

шпакл|ева́ть (-юю; perf **зашпаклева́ть**) несов перех (трещины, дыры) to fill.

шпаклёвк|а (-и) ж (действие) filling; (замазка) filler.

шпа́л|а (-ы) ж sleeper (RAIL).

шпале́р|а (-ы) ж (обои) handpainted wallpaper; (для растений) trellis.

шпан|а́ (-ы́) ж собир (разг) rabble.

шпарга́л|ка (-ки; gen pl -ок) ж (разг: для экзаменов) crib.

шпа́р|ить (-ю, -ишь) несов неперех (разг) **~ на гита́ре** to play away on the guitar; **~** (impf)

по-англи́йски (разг) to speak fluent English; **~** (impf) **по у́лице** (разг) to rush along the street.

шпа́тел|ь (-я) м (для шпаклёвки, для краски) palette knife (мн knives); (МЕД) spatula.

шпиг|ова́ть (-у́ю; perf **нашпигова́ть**) несов перех (КУЛИН, перен) to lard.

шпик (-а; part gen -у) м (сало) lard; (разг: сыщик) detective.

шпи́лек сущ см **шпи́лька**.

шпил|ь (-я) м spire.

шпи́л|ька (-ьки; gen pl -ек) ж (для волос) hairpin; (для шляпы) hatpin; (каблук) stiletto (heel); (перен: разг: замечание) dig; **ту́фли на ~ьке** stilettos.

шпина́т (-а) м spinach.

шпингале́т (-а) м (на окне) catch; (разг: о мальчишке) little boy.

шпио́н (-а) м spy.

шпиона́ж (-а) м espionage.

шпио́н|ить (-ю, -ишь) несов неперех (разг) to spy; **~** (impf) **за** +instr (за врагом, за женой) to spy on.

Шпицбе́рген (-а) м Spitzbergen.

шпо́р|а (-ы) ж spur.

шприц (-а) м syringe.

шпро́т|ы (-ов) мн sprats мн.

шпу́ль|ка (-и) ж spool, bobbin.

шрам (-а) м (на теле) scar.

шрапне́л|ь (-и) ж (ВОЕН) shrapnel только ед.

Шри-Ла́нк|а (-и) ж Sri Lanka.

шрифт (-а; nom pl -ы́) м type, print; **жи́рный/ курси́вный ~** bold/italic type; **набо́рный ~** (ТИПОГ) printing type.

шт. сокр = **ш.**

штаб (-а; nom pl -ы́) м headquarters мн; (люди) staff.

шта́бел|ь (-я; nom pl -я́) м (дров) stack.

штаб-кварти́р|а (-ы) ж (ВОЕН) headquarters мн.

штабно́й прил (разведка, офицер) staff опред.

штаке́тник (-а) м (ограда) palings мн.

штамп (-а) м (печать) stamp; (перен: в речи) cliché; (ТЕХ) die, stamp.

штамп|ова́ть (-у́ю; perf **проштампова́ть**) несов перех (справки, документы) to stamp; (perf **отштампова́ть**; детали) to punch, press; (no perf; решения, ответы) to rubber-stamp.

штампо́вочный прил (ТЕХ) punching опред, pressing опред.

шта́нг|а (-и) ж (СПОРТ: в тяжёлой атлетике) weight; (: ворот) post.

штангенци́ркул|ь (-я) м (ТЕХ) sliding calipers мн, slide gauge.

штанги́ст (-а) м (СПОРТ) weightlifter.

штанда́рт (-а) м (ВОЕН) standard.

штани́н|а (-ы) ж (разг) trouser leg.

штан|ы́ (-о́в) мн trousers мн.

шта́пел|ь (-я) м (ткань) viscose manufactured to resemble cotton.

шта́пельный прил (ткань, платье) made with viscose manufactured to resemble cotton.

штат (-а) м (государства) state; (работники)

staff; (*положение*) staff regulations мн; **э́та до́лжность полага́ется по шта́ту** this job is stipulated by the regulations; **зачисля́ть (зачи́слить** *perf*) **кого́-н в ~** to take sb onto the staff.

штати́в (-а) *м* (*ФОТО*) tripod; (*микроско́па*) stand.

шта́тный *прил* (*сотру́дник*) permanent; **шта́тная до́лжность** (*АДМИН*) established post; **шта́тное расписа́ние** (*АДМИН*) staff register.

шта́тск|ий (-ая, -ое, -ие) *прил* (*оде́жда*) civilian *опред* ♦ (-**ого**; *decl like adj*) *м* civilian.

шта́тск|ое (-**ого**; *decl like adj*) *ср* civilian clothes *мн*, civies *мн* (*inf*).

ште́мпел|ь (-я) *м*: **почто́вый ~** postmark.

ште́псел|ь (-я) *м* (*ЭЛЕК*) plug.

ште́псельн|ый *прил*: **~ая розе́тка** electric socket.

штибле́т|ы (-) *мн* lace-up boots *мн*.

штилево́й *прил* (*пого́да*) calm.

штил|ь (-я) *м* (*МОР*) calm.

штифт (-а́) *м* (*ТЕХ*) pin.

што́л|ьня (-ьни; *gen pl* -**ен**) *ж* (*ГЕО*) gallery.

што́паный *прил* darned.

што́па|ть (-ю; *perf* **зашто́пать**) *несов перех* to darn.

што́пк|а (-и) *ж* (*де́йствие*) darning; (*ни́тки*) darning thread; (*разг*: зашто́панное ме́сто) darn.

што́пор (-а) *м* corkscrew.

што́р|а (-ы) *ж* drapery; (*поднима́ющаяся*) blind.

шторм (-а) *м* gale.

шторм|и́ть (*3sg* -**и́т**) *несов неперех* (*мо́ре*) to be rough; **сего́дня ~и́т** it is rough today.

шторм|о́вка (-ки; *gen pl* -**ок**) *ж* oilskin coat.

штормово́й *прил* (*пого́да*) stormy; (*ве́тер*) gale-force; **штормово́е предупрежде́ние** (*МОР*) gale warning.

шторм|о́вок *сущ см* **шторм|о́вка**.

штраф (-а) *м* (*де́нежный*) fine; (*СПОРТ*) punishment; **накла́дывать (наложи́ть** *perf*) **~ на** +*acc* to impose a fine on.

штрафни́к (-а́) *м* (*СПОРТ*) *player who has been sent off*; **скаме́йка штрафнико́в** penalty box (*in ice-hockey*).

штрафн|о́й *прил* penal ♦ (-**о́го**; *decl like adj*) *м* (*СПОРТ*: *та́кже*: **~ уда́р**) penalty (kick); **штрафно́е очко́** (*СПОРТ*) penalty point.

штраф|ова́ть (-у́ю; *perf* **оштрафова́ть**) *несов перех* to fine; (*СПОРТ*) to penalize.

штрейкбре́хер (-а) *м* strikebreaker, blackleg.

штрек (-а) *м* (*ГЕО*) drift.

штрих (-а́) *м* (*черта́*) stroke; (*ча́стность*) feature.

штрих|ова́ть (-у́ю; *perf* **заштрихова́ть**) *несов перех* (*рису́нок*) to shade.

штуди́р|овать (-ую; *perf* **проштуди́ровать**) *несов перех* to study.

шту́к|а (-и) *ж* (*отде́льный предме́т*) item; (*разг*: *тру́дная, заба́вная*) thing; (: *проде́лка*) trick; **вот так ~!** (*разг*) what do you know!

штукату́р (-а) *м* plasterer.

штукату́р|ить (-ю, -ишь; *perf* **отштукату́рить** *или* **оштукату́рить**) *несов перех* to plaster.

штукату́рк|а (-и) *ж* (*де́йствие*) plastering; (*раство́р*) plaster; (*на стене́*) plaster, stucco.

штукату́рный *прил* (*рабо́ты*) plaster *опред*.

штуко́вин|а (-ы) *ж* (*разг*) thing.

штурва́|л (-а) *м* (*су́дна, комба́йна*) wheel; (*самолёта*) controls *мн*.

штурва́льный *прил* steering *опред*.

штурм (-а) *м* (*ВОЕН*) storm; (*перен*: *го́рной верши́ны*) conquest; **брать (взять** *perf*) **что-н шту́рмом** to take sth by storm.

шту́рман (-а) *м* (*МОР, АВИА*) navigator.

шту́рманск|ий (-ая, -ое, -ие) *прил* navigator's.

штурм|ова́ть (-у́ю) *несов перех* (*ВОЕН*) to storm; (*перен*) to conquer.

шту́чный *прил* (*това́р, изде́лие*) sold by the piece; (*рабо́та, опла́та*) piece *опред*.

штык (-а́) *м* (*ВОЕН*) bayonet; **принима́ть (приня́ть** *perf*) *или* **встреча́ть (встре́тить** *perf*) **что-н/кого́-н в ~й** (*перен*) to give sth/sb a hostile reception; **как ~** (*разг*) on the dot.

штыково́й *прил* (*ата́ка*) bayonet *опред*; **штыкова́я лопа́та** sharp-bladed spade.

штыр|ь (-я́) *м* (*ТЕХ*) pin, pintle.

шу́б|а (-ы) *ж* (*мехова́я*) fur coat; (*разг*: *живо́тного*) coat; **селёдка под ~ой** (*КУЛИН*) herring served with an elaborate topping.

шу́лер (-а) *м* cardsharper.

шум (-а; *part gen* -**у**) *м* (*звук*) noise; (*перен*: *ажиота́ж*) stir, sensation; (*МЕД*) murmur; (*разг*: *ссо́ра*) row, racket; (*суета́*) bustle, fuss; **вызыва́ть (вы́звать** *perf*) *или* **наде́лать** (*perf*) to cause a sensation.

шу́мен *прил см* **шу́мный**.

шум|е́ть (-лю́, -и́шь) *несов неперех* to make a noise; (*разглаша́ть*) to create a scene; (*ссо́риться*) to kick up a row; **у меня́ ~и́т в голове́/в уша́х** I have a buzzing in my head/ears.

шуми́х|а (-и) *ж* (*разг*: *пренебр*: *то́лки*) sensation, stir; **поднима́ть (подня́ть** *perf*) **~у вокру́г чего́-н** to create a sensation around sth; **газе́тная ~** *sensation created by the press*.

шумли́вый (-, -а, -о) *прил* noisy.

шумлю́ *несов см* **шуме́ть**.

шу́мно *нареч* noisily ♦ *как сказ* it is noisy.

шу́мн|ый (-ен, -на́, -но) *прил* noisy; (*разгово́р, компа́ния*) loud; (*оживлённый*: *у́лица, за́лы итп*) bustling; (*перен*: *успе́х*) sensational.

шумо́в|ка (-ки; *gen pl* -**ок**) *ж* perforated spoon.

шумово́й *прил* (*оформле́ние*) sound *опред*.

шумо́вок *сущ см* **шумо́вка**.

шумо́к *м* (*разг*): **под ~** (*разг*) on the quiet.

шу́рин (-a) *м* brother-in-law, wife's brother.
шуру́п (-a) *м* (*ТЕХ*) screw.
шурш|а́ть (-у́, -и́шь) *несов неперех* to rustle.
шу́ры-му́ры *мн нескл* (*разг*) love affairs *мн*.
шу́стр|ый (-, -а́, -о) *прил* (*разг*) nimble.
шут (-а́) *м* (*придворный*) jester; (*разг: человек*) fool, clown; ~ **горо́ховый** (*разг*) buffoon; ~ **с ним** (*разг*) forget it.
шу|ти́ть (-чу́, -тишь; *perf* **пошути́ть**) *несов неперех* to joke; (*смеяться*): ~ **над** +*instr* to make fun of; (*no perf; пренебрегать*): ~ +*instr* (*здоровьем*) to disregard; ~ (*impf*) **с огнём** (*перен*) to play with fire; **чем чёрт не шу́тит!** (*разг*) anything might happen!
шу́т|ка (-ки; *gen pl* -ок) *ж* joke; **без ~ок** joking apart, seriously; **кро́ме ~ок, ты пра́вда согла́сен?** joking apart *или* seriously, do you really agree?; **не на ~ку** (*рассердился, испугался итп*) in earnest; **сказа́ть** (*perf*) **что-н в ~ку** to say sth as a joke; **~ки пло́хи с**

кем-н/чем-н sb/sth is not to be trifled with.
шутли́в|ый (-, -а, -о) *прил* (*человек, тон, замечание*) humourous (*BRIT*), humorous (*US*); (*настроение*) light-hearted.
шутни́к (-а́) *м* joker.
шутовск|о́й *прил*: ~**и́е вы́ходки** buffoonery; ~ **колпа́к** jester's cap.
шутовств|о́ (-а́) *ср* buffoonery.
шу́ток *сущ см* **шу́тка**.
шу́точ|ный (-ен, -на, -но) *прил* (*рассказ*) comic, funny; **э́то де́ло не ~ное** it's no laughing matter.
шутя́ *нареч* (*разг: без труда*) easily.
шучу́ *несов см* **шути́ть**.
шу́шер|а (-ы) *ж собир* (*разг*) riffraff.
шушу́ка|ться (-юсь) *несов возв*: ~ (**с** +*instr*) to whisper (to).
шху́н|а (-ы) *ж* (*МОР*) schooner.
ш-ш *межд* sh.
шью *итп несов см* **шить**.

~ Щ, щ ~

Щ, щ *сущ нескл* (*буква*) the 26th letter of the Russian alphabet.

щаве́л|ь (-**я́**) *м* sorrel.

ща|ди́ть (-**жу́**, -**ди́шь**; *perf* **пощади́ть**) *несов перех* to spare; **он на ~ди́щем режи́ме** (*МЕД*) he's not allowed to exert himself.

щам *итп сущ см* **щи**.

щебёнк|а (-**и**) *ж* = **ще́бень**.

ще́бень (-**ня**) *м* (*СТРОИТ*) ballast.

ще́бет (-**а**) *м* twitter.

щеб|ета́ть (-**ечу́**, -**е́чешь**) *несов неперех* (*также перен*) to twitter.

ще́бня *итп сущ см* **ще́бень**.

щег|о́л (-**ла́**) *м* goldfinch.

щеголева́т|ый (-, -**а**, -**о**) *прил* (*одежда*) fancy; (*мужчина*) stylish.

щёгол|ь (-**я**) *м* dandy.

щегольну́ть (-**у́**, -**ёшь**) *сов неперех*: ~ +*instr* to show off.

щегольско́й *прил* stylish.

щегольств|о́ (-**а́**) *ср* dandyism.

щеголя́ть (-**ю**) *несов неперех* to dress up; ~ (*impf*) +*instr* to show off; ~ (*impf*) **в** +*prp* to rig o.s. out in.

ще́дрост|ь (-**и**) *ж* generosity.

ще́др|ый (-, -**а́**, -**о**) *прил* generous; (*природа*) lush; (*климат*) fertile; ~ **на** +*acc* generous with.

щей *сущ см* **щи**.

щек|а́ (*щеки́*; *nom pl* **щёки**, *gen pl* **щёк**, *dat pl* **щека́м**) *ж* cheek; **за о́бе щеки́ есть** (*impf*) *или* **упи́сывать** (*impf*) (*разг*) to gobble one's food up *или* down.

щеко́лд|а (-**ы**) *ж* latch.

щек|ота́ть (-**очу́**, -**о́чешь**; *perf* **пощекота́ть**) *несов неперех* (*пятки итп*) to tickle; ~ (*impf*) **кому́-н не́рвы** to excite sb; **у меня́ ~о́чет в го́рле/носу́** I've got a tickle in my throat/nose.

щеко́тк|а (-**и**) *ж* tickling.

щекотли́в|ый (-, -**а**, -**о**) *прил* (*вопрос итп*) delicate.

щеко́тно *как сказ*: **мне** ~ it's tickling me; **здесь** ~ **ходи́ть босико́м** it's ticklish going barefoot here.

щекочу́ *итп несов см* **щекота́ть**.

щёлк|а (-**и**) *ж* small hole.

щёлка|ть (-**ю**) *несов перех* (*человека*) to flick; (*орехи, семечки*) to crack (open) ◆ *неперех*: ~ +*instr* (*языком*) to click; (*кнутом*) to crack.

щёлкн|уть (-**у**, -**ешь**) *сов неперех* to click; (*хлыстом*) to crack.

щелочно́й *прил* alkaline.

щёлоч|ь (-**и**) *ж* alkali.

щелч|о́к (-**ка́**) *м* flick; (*звук*) click; (*перен*: *оскорбление*) jibe.

щел|ь (-**и**; *loc sg* -**и́**, *gen pl* -**е́й**) *ж* (*отверстие*) crack; (*ТЕХ*) slit; **смотрова́я** ~ vision slit.

щем|и́ть (*3sg* -**и́т**, *3pl* -**я́т**) *несов перех* (*перен*: *тревожить*) to trouble ◆ *безл* (*ныть*): ~**и́т в боку́** his *итп* side is aching; ~**и́т в груди́** his *итп* heart is heavy.

щемя́щ|ий (-**ая**, -**ее**, -**ие**) *прил* aching.

щен|и́ться (*3sg* -**и́тся**, *3pl* -**я́тся**, *perf* **ощени́ться**) *несов возв* (*собака*) to have pups; (*волчица, лиса*) to have cubs.

щен|о́к (-**ка́**; *nom pl* -**я́та**, *gen pl* -**я́т**) *м* (*собаки*) pup; (*лисы, волчицы*) cub; (*перен*: *разг*) whippersnapper.

щепети́лен *прил см* **щепети́льный**.

щепети́льност|ь (-**и**) *ж* (*в отношениях, денежных делах*) scrupulousness.

щепети́льн|ый (-**ен**, -**ьна**, -**ьно**) *прил* scrupulous.

ще́п|ка (-**ки**; *gen pl* -**ок**) *ж* splinter; (*для растопки*): ~**ки** chippings *мн*; **худо́й как** ~ thin as a rake.

щепо́т|ка (-**ки**; *gen pl* -**ок**) *ж* (*соли, табака*) pinch.

щерба́т|ый (-, -**а**, -**о**) *прил* (*рот*) gap-toothed; (*лицо*) pock-marked.

щерби́н|а (-**ы**) *ж* (*на лице, на коже*) pock-mark; (*во рту*) gap (between teeth); (*на посуде*) chink.

щети́н|а (-**ы**) *ж* (*животных, щётки*) bristle; (*у мужчины*) stubble.

щети́нист|ый (-, -**а**, -**о**) *прил* (*жёсткий*) bristly; (*небритый*) stubbly.

щети́н|иться (*3sg* -**ится**, *3pl* -**ятся**, *perf* **ощети́ниться**) *несов возв* (*также перен*) to bristle.

щёт|ка (-**ки**; *gen pl* -**ок**) *ж* brush; **зубна́я** ~ toothbrush; ~ **для воло́с** hairbrush.

щи (*щей*; *dat pl* **щам**) *мн* cabbage soup *ед*; **ки́слые** ~ sour cabbage soup; **зелёные** ~ sorrel soup.

щи́колот|ка (-ки; *gen pl* -ок) ж ankle.

щип|а́ть (-лю́, -лешь) *несов перех* (защемлять до боли) to nip, pinch; (*no perf*; *подлеж*: мороз) to bite; (: *специя, кислое*) to sting; (*perf* ощипа́ть; *волосы, курицу*) to pluck

▸ щипа́ться *несов возв* (*разг*) to nip, pinch.

щипка́ *итп сущ см* щипо́к.

щипко́вый *прил* (*муз*): ~ инструме́нт plucked (*BRIT*) *или* picked (*US*) instrument.

щиплю́(сь) *итп несов см* щипа́ть(ся).

щип|ну́ть (-у́, -ёшь) *сов перех* to nip, pinch.

щип|о́к (-ка́) *м* nip, pinch.

щипц|ы́ (-о́в) *мн*: ками́нные ~ tongs *мн*; кузне́чные ~ pliers *мн*; хирурги́ческие ~ forceps *мн*; ~ для са́хара sugar-tongs *мн*.

щи́пчик|и (-ов) *мн уменьш от* щипцы́; (*для ногтей, бровей*) tweezers *мн*.

щит (-а́) *м* shield; (*фанерный, металлический итп*) barrier; (*рекламный, баскетбольный*) board; (*ТЕХ*) panel; ~ управле́ния control panel.

щитови́дн|ый *прил*: ~ая железа́ thyroid gland.

щу́к|а (-и) ж pike (*мн* pike).

щуп (-а) *м* (*ТЕХ*) probe.

щу́пальце (-ьца; *nom pl* -ьца, *gen pl* -ец) *ср* (*осьминога*) tentacle; (*насекомых*) feeler.

щу́па|ть (-ю; *perf* пощу́пать) *несов перех* (*опухоль, пульс*) to feel for; (*карманы*) to grope in.

щу́пл|ый (-, -а́, -о) *прил* (*разг*) puny.

щу́р|ить (-ю, -ишь; *perf* сощу́рить) *несов перех*: ~ глаза́ to screw up one's eyes

▸ щу́риться (*perf* сощу́риться) *несов возв* (*от солнца*) to squint.

щу́ч|ий (-ья, -ье, -ьи) *прил*: по ~ьему веле́нью (as if) by magic.

~ Э, э ~

Э, э *сущ нескл* (*буква*) the 30th letter of the Russian alphabet.

э *межд* (*выражает недоумение*) er ...; um ...; (*выражает решимость*) oh; **э, нет, я не пойду!** oh, no, I'm not going!

эбони́т (-а) *м* vulcanite, ebonite.

эвакуацио́нный *прил* (*пункт*) evacuation *опред*; (*госпиталь*) evacuee *опред*.

эвакуа́ци|я (-и) *ж* evacuation.

эваку́и́р|овать (-ую) (*не*)*сов перех* to evacuate

▸ **эваку́и́роваться** (*не*)*сов возв* to be evacuated.

Эвере́ст (-а) *м* Mount Everest.

эвкали́пт (-а) *м* eucalyptus.

эвкали́птов|ый *прил*: **~ое ма́сло** eucalyptus oil.

ЭВМ *ж сокр* (= **электро́нная вычисли́тельная маши́на**) computer.

эволюциони́р|овать (-ую) (*не*)*сов неперех* to evolve.

эволюцио́нный *прил* evolutionary.

эволю́ци|я (-и) *ж* evolution.

эвфеми́зм (-а) *м* euphemism.

эвфемисти́ческий (-ая, -ое, -ие) *прил* euphemistic.

эги́д|а (-ы) *ж*: **под ~ой** +*gen* under the aegis of.

эгои́зм (-а) *м* egoism.

эгои́ст (-а) *м* egoist.

эгоисти́чен *прил см* **эгоисти́чный**.

эгоисти́ческий (-ая, -ое, -ие) *прил* egotistic(al).

эгоисти́ч|ный (-ен, -на, -но) *прил* = **эгоисти́ческий**.

эгои́ст|ка (-ки; *gen pl* -ок) *ж см* **эгои́ст**.

эгоцентри́ст (-а) *м*: **он настоя́щий ~** he is very egocentric.

эдельве́йс (-а) *м* edelweiss.

Эдинбу́рг (-а) *м* Edinburgh.

эй *межд* (*разг*) hey; **~, кто идёт?** hey, who's there?

Эй-би-си *м сокр* (= **Америка́нская радиовеща́тельная компа́ния**) ABC (= *American Broadcasting Company*).

Эквадо́р (-а) *м* Ecuador.

эквадо́рский (-ая, -ое, -ие) *прил* Ecuadorian.

эква́тор (-а) *м* equator.

экваториа́льный *прил* equatorial.

эквивале́нт (-а) *м* equivalent.

эквивале́нт|ный (-ен, -на, -но) *прил* equivalent.

эквилибри́стик|а (-и) *ж* tightrope walking.

ЭКГ *ж сокр* (= **электрокардиогра́мма**) ECG (= *electrocardiogram*).

экзальта́ци|я (-и) *ж* exhilaration.

экзальти́рован|ный (-, -на, -но) *прил* exhilarated.

экза́мен (-а) *м*: **~** (**по** +*dat*) (*по истории, по языку*) exam(ination) (in); (*для получения звания, должности*): **~ на перево́дчика** translator's test; (*перен*): **~** (**на** +*acc*) test (of); **выпускны́е ~ы** Finals *мн*; **сдава́ть** (*impf*) **~** to sit (*BRIT*) *или* take an exam(ination); **сдать** (*perf*) *или* **выде́рживать** (**вы́держать** *perf*) **~** to pass an exam(ination); **прова́ливать** (**провали́ть** *perf*) **~** to fail an exam(ination); **принима́ть** (**приня́ть** *perf*) **~** to hold an exam(ination).

экзамена́тор (-а) *м* examiner.

экзаменацио́нный *прил* (*комиссия, сессия*) examination *опред*; **экзаменацио́нный биле́т** exam(ination) paper.

экзамен|ова́ть (-у́ю) *perf* **проэкзаменова́ть**) *несов перех* to examine.

экзе́м|а (-ы) *ж* eczema.

экземпля́р (-а) *м* (*рукописи, документа*) copy; (*животного, растения*) specimen; **в двух/трёх ~ах** in duplicate/triplicate.

экзистенциали́зм (-а) *м* existentialism.

экзо́тик|а (-и) *ж* exotica *мн*.

экзоти́чен *прил см* **экзоти́чный**.

экзоти́ческий (-ая, -ое, -ие) *прил* (*растение, страна*) exotic.

экзоти́ч|ный (-ен, -на, -но) *прил* (*наряд, декорации*) exotic.

э́к|ий (-ая, -ое, -ие; -а, -о, -и) *мест*: **~ая незада́ча!** what a nuisance!; **~ ты стра́нный** what a strange one you are!

экипа́ж (-а) *м* (*коляска*) carriage; (*команда*) crew.

экипир|ова́ть (-у́ю) (*не*)*сов перех* (*бойцов, экспедицию*) to equip.

экипиро́вк|а (-и) *ж* (*действие*) equipping; (*снаряжение*) equipment.

The spelling rules for Russian are shown on page xvii.

экологи́ческ|ий (-ая, -ое, -ие) *прил* ecological.
эколо́ги|я (-и) *ж* ecology.
эконо́мен *прил см* **эконо́мный**.
эконо́мик|а (-и) *ж* (*страны, региона*) economy;
(*наука*) economics.
эконо́ми́ст (-а) *м* economist.
эконо́м|ить (-лю, -ишь; *perf* **сэконо́мить**) *несов
перех* (*энергию, деньги*) to save;
(*выгадывать*): ~ **на** +*prp* to economize *или*
save on.
экономи́чен *прил см* **экономи́чный**.
экономи́ческ|ий (-ая, -ое, -ие) *прил* economic.
экономи́ч|ный (-ен, -на, -но) *прил* economical.
эконо́ми|я (-и) *ж* (*в работе, в использовании
чего-н*) economy; (*выгода*): ~ **в** +*prp* (*в
топливе, в ресурсах*) economizing in;
соблюда́ть (*impf*) ~**ю** to economize;
полити́ческая ~ political economy.
эконо́м|ка (-ки; *gen pl* -ок) *ж* housekeeper.
эконо́млю *несов см* **эконо́мить**.
эконо́м|ный (-ен, -на, -но) *прил* (*хозяин*) thrifty;
(*метод*) economical.
эконо́мок *сущ см* **эконо́мка**.
экосисте́м|а (-ы) *ж* ecosystem.
экра́н (-а) *м* screen.
экраниза́ци|я (-и) *ж* screen adaptation.
экранизи́р|овать (-ую) (*не*)*сов перех* to screen.
экра́нн|ый *прил*: ~**ая па́мять** (*КОМП*) screen
memory; ~**ое реда́кти́рование** (*КОМП*) screen
editing.
экс- *префикс* ex-; ~**чемпио́н** ex-champion.
экскава́тор (-а) *м* excavator, digger.
экскава́торщик (-а) *м* excavator operator.
эксклюзи́вный *прил* exclusive.
э́кскурс (-а) *м* excursus, digression.
экскурса́нт (-а) *м* tour group member.
экскурсио́нный *прил* excursion *опред*.
экску́рси|я (-и) *ж* (*посещение*) excursion;
(*группа*) party.
экскурсово́д (-а) *м* guide.
экспанси́в|ный (-ен, -на, -но) *прил*
enthusiastic.
экспа́нси|я (-и) *ж* (*полит*) expansion.
экспеди́тор (-а) *м* shipping agent.
экспеди́ци|я (-и) *ж* (*научная, студенческая*)
field work; (*группа людей*) expedition;
(*газетная*) dispatch.
экспериме́нт (-а) *м* experiment.
эксперимента́льный *прил* experimental.
эксперименти́р|овать (-ую) *несов неперех*: ~
(**над** *или* **с** +*instr*) to experiment (on *или* with).
экспе́рт (-а) *м* expert.
эксперти́з|а (-ы) *ж* (*медицинская*) medical
assessment; (*судебная*) legal evaluation.
экспе́ртный *прил* expert *опред*.
эксплуата́тор (-а) *м* exploiter.
эксплуата́ци|я (-и) *ж* (*человека, ресурсов*)
exploitation; (*машин, месторождений*)
utilization; **сдава́ть** (**сдать** *perf*) **что-н в** ~**ю** to
put sth into commission.
эксплуати́р|овать (-ую) *несов перех* to
exploit; (*машины, дороги*) to use.

экспози́ци|я (-и) *ж* (*музейная*) exhibition;
(*фото*) exposure.
экспона́т (-а) *м* exhibit.
экспони́р|овать (-ую) (*не*)*сов перех* to exhibit.
э́кспорт (-а) *м* export; **на** ~ for export.
экспортёр (-а) *м* exporter.
экспорти́р|овать (-ую) *несов перех* to export.
э́кспортный *прил* (*товар*) exported; (*правила*)
export *опред*.
экспре́сс (-а) *м* (*транспорт*) express.
экспресси́в|ный (-ен, -на, -но) *прил*
expressive.
экспре́сси|я (-и) *ж* expression.
экспро́мт (-а) *м* impromptu.
экспро́мтом *нареч* spontaneously.
экста́з (-а) *м* ecstasy.
экстенси́в|ный (-ен, -на, -но) *прил* extensive.
экстравага́нт|ный (-ен, -на, -но) *прил*
extravagant.
экстра́кт (-а) *м* extract.
экстраордина́р|ный (-ен, -на, -но) *прил*
extraordinary.
экстрасе́нс (-а) *м* psychic.
экстрема́л|ьный (-ен, -ьна, -ьно) *прил*
extreme.
экстреми́зм (-а) *м* extremism.
экстреми́ст (-а) *м* extremist.
экстреми́стск|ий (-ая, -ое, -ие) *прил* extremist.
э́кстрен|ный (-ен, -на, -но) *прил* (*отъезд,
вызов*) urgent; (*расходы, заседание*) emergency
опред.
эксце́нтрик (-а) *м* eccentric.
эксцентри́чен *прил см* **эксцентри́чный**.
эксцентри́ческ|ий (-ая, -ое, -ие) *прил*
eccentric.
эксцентри́ч|ный (-ен, -на, -но) *прил* eccentric.
эксце́сс (-а) *м* excess.
ЭКЮ *сокр* ECU (= *European Currency Unit*).
эла́стик (-а) *м* stretchy material.
эласти́ч|ный (-ен, -на, -но) *прил* (*материал*)
stretchy; (*походка*) springy.
элева́тор (-а) *м* (*С.-Х.*) grain store *или* elevator
(*US*); (*ТЕХ*) elevator.
элега́нт|ный (-ен, -на, -но) *прил* elegant.
эле́ги|я (-и) *ж* elegy.
электриз|ова́ть (-у́ю; *perf* **наэлектризова́ть**)
несов перех (*физ*) to electrify; (*перен*:
человека, атмосферу) to stir up.
эле́ктрик (-а) *м* electrician.
электрифика́ци|я (-и) *ж* electrification.
электрифици́р|овать (-ую) (*не*)*сов перех* to
connect an electricity supply to.
электри́чек *сущ см* **электри́чка**.
электри́ческ|ий (-ая, -ое, -ие) *прил* electric.
электри́честв|о (-а) *ср* (*энергия*) electricity;
(*освещение*) light; **зажига́ть** (**заже́чь** *perf*) ~ to
turn on the light.
электри́ч|ка (-ки; *gen pl* -ек) *ж* electric train.
электробытов|о́й *прил*: ~**ы́е прибо́ры**
electrical appliances.
электрово́з (-а) *м* electric locomotive.
эле́ктрогита́р|а (-ы) *ж* electric guitar.

электро́д (-а) *м* electrode.

электрокардиогра́мм|а (-ы) *ж* electrocardiogram.

электромонтёр (-а) *м* electrician.

электромото́р (-а) *м* electric motor.

электро́н (-а) *м* electron.

электро́ник|а (-и) *ж* electronics *мн.*

электро́нн|ый *прил*: ~ **микроско́п** electron microscope; **~ая доска́ объявле́ний** (*КОМП*) bulletin board; **~ая по́чта** (*КОМП*) electronic mail; **~ая табли́ца** (*КОМП*) spreadsheet; **электро́нная вычисли́тельная маши́на** computer.

электропереда́ч|а (-и) *ж* power transmission; **ли́ния ~и** power line.

электропо́езд (-а) *м* electric train.

электроприбо́р (-а) *м* electrical device.

электропрово́дк|а (-и) *ж* (electrical) wiring.

электропрово́дность (-и) *ж* conductivity.

электросва́рк|а (-и) *ж* (electric) welding.

электроста́нци|я (-и) *ж* (electric) power station.

электроте́хник (-а) *м* electrical engineer.

электроте́хник|а (-и) *ж* electrical engineering.

электроэне́рги|я (-и) *ж* electric power.

элеме́нт (-а) *м* (*также хим. ЭЛЕК*) element; **престу́пные ~ы** criminal element; **прогресси́вные ~ы о́бщества** progressive elements in society.

элемента́р|ный *прил* (*также физ*) elementary; (-**ен, -на, -но**; *правила. условия*) basic.

эликси́р (-а) *м* elixir.

эли́т|а (-ы) *ж собир* elite.

элита́рный *прил* elite.

э́ллипс (-а) *м* ellipse.

эл|ь (-я) *м* ale.

Э́льб|а (-ы) *ж* (*о́стров*) Elba; (*река́*) Elbe.

Эльза́с (-а) *м* Alsace.

эльза́сск|ий (-**ая, -ое, -ие**) *прил* Alsatian.

эльф (-а) *м* elf.

эма́левый *прил* enamel.

эмалиро́ванный *прил* enamelled.

эмали́р|ова́ть (-**у́ю**) *несов перех* to enamel.

эма́л|ь (-и) *ж* enamel.

эмансипа́ци|я (-и) *ж* emancipation.

эмансипи́рованный *прил* emancipated.

эмба́рго *ср нескл* embargo; **налага́ть** (**наложи́ть** *perf*) ~ **на** +*acc* to place an embargo on.

эмбле́м|а (-ы) *ж* emblem.

эмбриоло́ги|я (-и) *ж* embryology.

эмбрио́н (-а) *м* embryo.

эмигра́нт (-а) *м* emigrant.

эмигра́нтск|ий (-**ая, -ое, -ие**) *прил* (*поселе́ние*) emigrant *опред*; (*литерату́ра*) emigré *опред*.

эмиграцио́нный *прил* emigration *опред*.

эмигра́ци|я (-и) *ж* emigration ◆ *собир* emigrants *мн.*

эмигри́р|овать (-**ую**) (*не*)*сов неперех* to emigrate.

эмоциона́льный (-**ен, -ьна, -ьно**) *прил* emotional.

эмо́ци|я (-и) *ж* emotion.

эму́льси|я (-и) *ж* emulsion.

эмфати́ческ|ий (-**ая, -ое, -ие**) *прил* emphatic.

эндокри́нн|ый *прил* (*ФИЗИОЛОГИЯ*) endocrine; **~ые же́лезы** endocrine glands.

эндокриноло́ги|я (-и) *ж* endocrinology.

энерге́тик|а (-и) *ж* (*отдел физики*) energetics; (*промышленность*) power industry; (*наука*) power engineering.

энергети́ческ|ий (-**ая, -ое, -ие**) *прил* (*проблемы, ресурсы*) energy *опред*; **энергети́ческий кри́зис** energy crisis.

энерги́ч|ный (-**ен, -на, -но**) *прил* (*человек, движе́ния*) energetic; (*меры*) effective.

эне́рги|я (-и) *ж* energy.

энергонезави́сим|ый *прил*: **~ая па́мять** (*КОМП*) nonvolatile memory.

э́нн|ый *прил*: **~ое число́/коли́чество вре́мени** X number/amount of time; **в ~ раз** yet again; **в ~ой сте́пени** to the nth degree.

энтузиа́зм (-а) *м* enthusiasm.

энтузиа́ст (-а) *м* enthusiast.

энциклопеди́ческ|ий (-**ая, -ое, -ие**) *прил* (*ум*) encyclopaedic (*BRIT*), encyclopedic (*US*); **энциклопеди́ческий слова́рь** encyclopaedia (*BRIT*), encyclopedia (*US*).

энциклопе́ди|я (-и) *ж* encyclopaedia (*BRIT*), encyclopedia (*US*).

эпигра́мм|а (-ы) *ж* epigram.

эпи́граф (-а) *м* epigraph.

эпиде́ми|я (-и) *ж* epidemic.

эпизо́д (-а) *м* episode.

эпизоди́ческ|ий (-**ая, -ое, -ие**) *прил* (*случай, факт*) random.

эпизоди́чный *прил* = **эпизоди́ческий**.

эпиле́пси|я (-и) *ж* epilepsy.

эпиле́птик (-а) *м* epileptic.

эпило́г (-а) *м* epilogue (*BRIT*), epilog (*US*).

эпистоля́рный *прил* epistolary.

эпи́тет (-а) *м* epithet.

эпице́нтр (-а) *м* epicentre (*BRIT*), epicenter (*US*).

эпи́ческ|ий (-**ая, -ое, -ие**) *прил* epic.

эполе́т|а (-ы) *ж* (*обычно мн*) epaulette.

эпопе́|я (-и) *ж* epic.

э́пос (-а) *м* epic literature.

эпо́х|а (-и) *ж* epoch.

эпоха́льный (-**ен, -на, -но**) *прил* epoch-making.

э́р|а (-ы) *ж* era; **1-ый век на́шей ~ы/до на́шей ~ы** the first century AD/BC.

эре́кци|я (-и) *ж* (*АНАТ*) erection.

эрза́ц (-а) *м* substitute.

Эритре́|я (-и) *ж* Eritrea.

эритроци́т (-а) *м* erythrocyte, red blood cell.

эро́зи|я (-и) *ж* erosion.

эро́тик|а (-и) *ж* erotica *мн.*

эроти́ческ|ий (-ая, -ое, -ие) *прил* erotic.
Эр-Рия́д (-а) *м* Riyadh.
эруди́рован|ный (-, -на, -но) *прил* erudite.
эруди́т (-а) *м*: **он настоя́щий** ~ he knows an enormous amount.
эруди́ци|я (-и) *ж* erudition.
эска́др|а (-ы) *ж* squadron (*navy*).
эскадри́ль|я (-и) *ж* squadron (*air force*).
эскадро́н (-а) *м* squadron (*army*).
эскала́тор (-а) *м* escalator.
эскала́ци|я (-и) *ж* escalation.
эскало́п (-а) *м* escalope.
эски́з (-а) *м* (*к картине*) sketch; (*к проекту*) draft.
эскимо́ *ср нескл* choc-ice, Eskimo (*US*).
эскимо́с (-а) *м* Eskimo.
эскимо́с|ка (-ки; *gen pl* -ок) *ж см* **эскимо́с**.
эско́рт (-а) *м* escort.
эсми́н|ец (-ца) *м* (= эска́дренный миноно́сец) destroyer.
эссе́ *ср нескл* essay.
эссе́нци|я (-и) *ж* essence.
эстака́д|а (-ы) *ж* (*на автомагистрали*) flyover (*BRIT*), overpass; (*на железной дороге*) viaduct; (*на пристани*) pier.
эста́мп (-а) *м* (*ИСКУССТВО*) print.
эстафе́т|а (-ы) *ж* (*СПОРТ*) relay (race); (: *палочка*) baton.
эсте́тик|а (-и) *ж* aesthetics.
эстети́чен *прил см* **эстети́чный**.
эстети́ческ|ий (-ая, -ое, -ие) *прил* aesthetic.
эстети́ч|ный (-ен, -на, -но) *прил* aesthetic.
эсто́н|ец (-ца) *м* Estonian.
Эсто́ни|я (-и) *ж* Estonia.
эсто́н|ка (-ки; *gen pl* -ок) *ж см* **эсто́нец**.
эсто́нск|ий (-ая, -ое, -ие) *прил* Estonian; ~ **язы́к** Estonian.
эсто́нца *итп сущ см* **эсто́нец**.
эстра́д|а (-ы) *ж* (*для оркестра*) platform; (*вид искусства*) variety.
эстра́дный *прил*: ~ **конце́рт** variety show; ~ **арти́ст** variety performer.
э́т|а (-ой) *мест см* **э́тот**.
эта́ж (-а́) *м* floor, storey (*BRIT*), story (*US*); **пе́рвый/второ́й/тре́тий** ~ ground/first/second floor (*BRIT*), first/second/third floor (*US*).
этаже́р|ка (-ки; *gen pl* -ок) *ж* (stack of) shelves.
э́так *нареч* (*разг*: таким образом) in such a way
   ♦ *вводн сл* (*приблизительно*): ~ **25 лет** 25 years or so; ~ **у нас ничего́ не полу́чится** we won't get anywhere this way; **и так и** ~ (*разг*) this way and that (way).
э́так|ий (-ая, -ое, -ие) *мест* (*разг*) such.
этало́н (-а) *м* (*веса, меры*) standard; (*перен*: *красоты, благородства итп*) model; **брать (взять** *perf*) **что-н за** ~ to use sth as a standard.
эта́п (-а) *м* (*развития, работы*) stage; (*гонки*) lap; **ссы́лный** ~ stopping point (*for deported convicts*); **отправля́ть** (*impf*) ~**ом** *или* **по** ~**у** to deport (*under convoy*).
эта́пн|ый *прил* (*работа, произведение*)

prominent; ~**ое собы́тие** an event of great significance.
э́ти (-их) *мест см* **э́тот**.
э́тик|а (-и) *ж* ethics.
этике́т (-а) *м* etiquette.
этике́т|ка (-ки; *gen pl* -ок) *ж* label.
эти́л (-а) *м* ethyl.
эти́ловый *прил* ethyl *опред*.
э́тим *мест см* **э́тот**, **э́то**, **э́ти**.
э́тими *мест см* **э́ти**.
этимоло́ги|я (-и) *ж* etymology.
эти́ч|ный (-ен, -на, -но) *прил* ethical.
этни́ческ|ий (-ая, -ое, -ие) *прил* ethnic.
этнографи́ческ|ий (-ая, -ое, -ие) *прил* ethnographic.
этногра́фи|я (-и) *ж* ethnography.

KEYWORD

э́т|о (-ого; *см* **Table 10**) *мест* **1** (*указательное*) this; **на́до успе́ть к ве́черу; э́то бу́дет тру́дно** we need to finish by this evening, this will be difficult; **он на всё соглаша́ется; э́то о́чень стра́нно** he is agreeing to everything, this is most strange
2 (*связка в сказуемом*): **любо́вь – э́то проще́ние** love is forgiveness
3 (*как подлежащее*): **с кем ты разгова́ривал? – э́то была́ моя́ сестра́** who were you talking to? – that was my sister; **как э́то произошло́?** how did it happen?
4 (*для усиления*): **э́то он во всём винова́т** he is the one who is to blame for everything; **э́то они́ нас подвели́** they are the ones who let us down
   ♦ *част* **1** (*служит для усиления*): **кто э́то звони́л?** who was it who phoned (*BRIT*) *или* called (*US*)?; **о чём э́то ты так беспоко́ишься?** what is it that you are so worried about?
2 (*указательная*): **э́то ты так крича́л?** was it you who called out?

KEYWORD

э́т|от (-ого; *f* **э́та**, *nt* **э́то**, *pl* **э́ти**; *см* **Table 10**) *мест* **1** (*указательное*: *о близком предмете*) this; (: *о близких предметах*) these; **э́тот дом** this house; **э́ти кни́ги** these boots
2 (*о данном времени*) this; **э́тот год осо́бенно тру́дный** this year is particularly hard; **в э́ти дни я при́нял реше́ние** in the last few days I have come to a decision; **э́тот са́мый** that very
3 (*о чём только что упомянутом*) this; **он ложи́лся в 10 часо́в ве́чера; э́та привы́чка меня́ всегда́ удивля́ла** he used to go to bed at 10 pm, this habit always amazed me
   ♦ *ср* (*как сущ*: *об одном предмете*) this one; (: *о многих предметах*) these ones; **дай мне вот э́ти** give me these ones; **э́тот не всё спосо́бен** this one is capable of anything; **при э́том** in addition.

этю́д (-а) *м* (*ИСКУССТВО*) sketch; (*ЛИТЕРАТУРА*) study; (*МУЗ*) étude; (*шахматный*) problem.
эфеме́р|ный (-ен, -на, -но) *прил* ephemeral.
эфе́с (-а) *м* (*шпаги, сабли*) hilt.

эфиóп (-а) *м* Ethiopian.
Эфиóпи|я (-и) *ж* Ethiopia.
эфиóп|ка (-ки; *gen pl* -ок) *ж см* эфиóп.
эфиóпск|ий (-ая, -ое, -ие) *прил* Ethiopian.
эфи́р (-а) *м* (*хим*) ether; (*воздушное
пространство*) air; **выходи́ть** (**вы́йти** *perf*) **в** ~
to go on the air; **прямóй** ~ live broadcast.
эфи́рн|ый *прил*: ~ое ма́сло essential oil; ~ое
вре́мя airtime.
эффéкт (-а) *м* effect; (*обычно мн: шумовы́е,
свéтовые*) effects *мн*; **экономи́ческий** ~
economic result; **производи́ть** (**произвести́**
perf) ~ **на** +*acc* to have an effect on; **дава́ть**
(**дать** *perf*) **жела́емый** ~ to have the desired
effect.
эффéктен *прил см* эффéктный.
эффекти́вен *прил см* эффекти́вный.
эффекти́вность (-и) *ж* effectiveness.
эффекти́в|ный (-ен, -на, -но) *прил* effective.
эффéкт|ный (-ен, -на, -но) *прил* (*одéжда*)
striking; (*речь*) impressive.
эх *межд* (*разг*) oh; ~ **ты, лентя́й**! oh, you're
such a lazybones!
э́х|о (-а) *ср* echo (*мн* echoes).
эшафóт (-а) *м* scaffold; **всходи́ть** (**взойти́** *perf*)
на ~ to mount the scaffold.
эшелóн (-а) *м* echelon; (*поезд*) special train; ~ы
вла́сти echelons of power.

~ Ю, ю ~

Ю, ю *сущ нескл* (*буква*) the 31st letter of the Russian alphabet.

ю. *сокр* (= **юг**) S (= *South*); (= **южный**) S (= *South*).

юа́нь (**-я**) *м* yuan (*мн* yuan).

ЮАР *ж сокр* (= Южно-Африка́нская Респу́блика) RSA (= *Republic of South Africa*).

юбиле́й (**-я**) *м* (*годовщина*) anniversary; (*празднование*) jubilee.

юбиле́йный *прил* (*торжество*) anniversary *опред*; (*монета, значок итп*) jubilee *опред*.

юбиля́р (**-а**) *м*: учёный-/заво́д-~ scientist/ factory whose anniversary is being celebrated.

ю́б|ка (**-ки**; *gen pl* **-ок**) *ж* skirt; **держа́ться** (*impf*) **за чью-н ~ку** (*разг*) to be tied to sb's apron strings.

ювели́р (**-а**) *м* jeweller (*BRIT*), jeweler (*US*).

ювели́рный *прил* jewellery *опред* (*BRIT*), jewelery *опред* (*US*); (*перен: работа, точность*) painstaking; **~ые изде́лия** jewel(l)ery; **~ магази́н** jeweller's (*BRIT*) *или* jeweler's (*US*) (shop).

юг (**-а**) *м* south; **на ю́ге страны́** in the south of the country; **к ю́гу от го́рода** to the south of the town.

ю́го-восто́к (**-а**) *м* south-east.

ю́го-за́пад (**-а**) *м* south-west.

Югосла́вия (**-и**) *ж* (*ИСТ*) Yugoslavia.

южа́н|ин (**-ина**; *nom pl* **-е**, *gen pl* **-**) *м* southerner.

южа́н|ка (**-ки**; *gen pl* **-ок**) *ж см* южа́нин.

ю́жный *прил* southern; **Ю́жная Коре́я** South Korea; **Ю́жный по́люс** the South Pole.

юла́ (**-ы́**) *ж* (*игрушка*) (spinning) top ◆ *м/ж* (*перен: разг*) fidget.

юли́ть (**-ю́, -и́шь**) *несов неперех* (*разг: суетиться*) to fidget; (: *хитрить*) to be shifty; **~** (*impf*) **пе́ред** +*instr* (*заискивать*) to play up to.

ю́мор (**-а**) *м* humour (*BRIT*), humor (*US*).

юморе́с|ка (**-ки**; *gen pl* **-ок**) *ж* (*МУЗ*) humoresque; (*ЛИТЕРАТУРА*) short comedy.

юмори́ст (**-а**) *м* (*автор*) humorist; (*шутливый человек*) comedian.

юмори́стик|а (**-и**) *ж* (*ЛИТЕРАТУРА*) humour (*BRIT*), humor (*US*).

юмористи́ческий (**-ая, -ое, -ие**) *прил* humorous; **~ журна́л** satirical magazine.

юмори́ст|ка (**-ки**; *gen pl* **-ок**) *ж* comedienne.

ю́нг|а (**-и**) *м* cabin boy; (*младший матрос*) trainee sailor.

ЮНЕСКО *ср сокр* UNESCO (= *United Nations*

Educational Scientific and Cultural Organization).

юне́ц (**-ца́**) *м* (*разг: юноша*) youth.

юнио́р (**-а**) *м* junior.

ЮНИСЕ́Ф *м сокр* UNICEF (= *United Nations (International) Children's (Emergency) Fund*).

ю́нкер (**-а**; *nom pl* **-á**) *м* (*ИСТ*) cadet.

ю́нкерский (**-ая, -ое, -ие**) *прил* cadet *опред*; **~ое учи́лище** military school.

ю́ность (**-и**) *ж* youth ◆ *собир* (*юношество*) young people *мн*; **в ~и он был любозна́телен** in his youth he was greedy for knowledge.

ю́нош|а (**-и**; *nom pl* **-и**, *gen pl* **-ей**) *м* young man (*мн* men).

ю́ношеск|ий (**-ая, -ое, -ие**) *прил* youthful; (*журнал*) young person's; (*организация, клуб*) youth; **~ие го́ды** youth.

ю́ношеств|о (**-а**) *ср собир* young people *мн*; (*юность*) youth.

юнца́ *итп сущ см* юне́ц.

ю́ный (**-, -á, -о**) *прил* (*молодой*) young; (*силы, задор*) youthful; **теа́тр ~ого зри́теля** children's theatre (*BRIT*) *или* theater (*US*).

ЮПИ *м сокр* UPI (= *United Press International*).

юпи́тер (**-а**) *м* (*прибор*) floodlight; **Ю~** Jupiter.

юриди́чески *нареч*: **~ обяза́тельный** legally binding.

юриди́ческий (**-ая, -ое, -ие**) *прил* (*сила*) juridical; (*образование*) legal; **~ факульте́т** law faculty; **юриди́ческая консульта́ция** ≈ legal advice office; **юриди́ческое лицо́** body corporate.

юрисди́кци|я (**-и**) *ж* (*ЮР*) jurisdiction; **подлежа́ть** (*impf*) **чьей-н ~и** to come under sb's jurisdiction.

юриско́нсульт (**-а**) *м* legal adviser.

юриспруде́нци|я (**-и**) *ж* (*правоведение*) jurisprudence; (*практика юриста*) law.

юри́ст (**-а**) *м* lawyer.

ю́рк|ий (**-ая, -ое, -ие**; **-ок, -ка́, -ко**) *прил* nimble.

юркн|у́ть (**-у, -ешь**) *сов неперех* to scurry away.

юро́див|ый *прил* (*разг*) crazy ◆ (**-ого**; *decl like adj*) *м* (*РЕЛ*) holy fool.

юро́дствовать (**-ую**) *несов неперех* (*перен*) to behave like a lunatic.

юро́к *прил см* ю́ркий.

ю́рский (**-ая, -ое, -ие**) *прил* (*ГЕО*) Jurassic.

ю́рт|а (**-ы**) *ж* yurt (*skin tent used by nomads in*

Central Asia and Siberia).
ЮСИА м сокр USIA (= *United States Information Agency).*
юсти́ци|я (-и) ж (*правовые учреждения*) the judiciary; **Министе́рство** ~и the Ministry of

Justice.
ю|ти́ться (-чу́сь, -ти́шься) несов неперех (*располагаться*) to huddle together; (*иметь приют*) to live in cramped conditions.

~ Я, я ~

Я, я *сущ нескл* (*буква*) the 32nd letter of the Russian alphabet.

я (*меня*; *см* **Table 5a**) *мест* I ♦ *сущ нескл* (*личность*) the self, the ego; ~ **тебя** *или* **тебе́!** (*раза: угроза*) I'll teach you!; **не** ~ **бу́ду, е́сли не** ... (*разг*) I'll be damned if I don't ...; **второ́е "я"** alter ego.

я́беда (-ы) *м/ж* sneak.

я́бедник (-а) *м* = **я́беда.**

я́бедничать (-ю; *perf* **наябедничать**) *несов неперех*: ~ **на** +*acc* (*разг*) to tell tales about.

я́блоко (-а; *nom pl* -и) *ср* apple; **глазно́е** ~ eyeball; **в** ~**ах** (*о масти лошадей*) dappled; ~**у не́где упа́сть** (*перен*) there's not enough room to swing a cat.

я́блоневый *прил* (*цвет*) apple-green; ~**ая ве́тка** branch of an apple tree.

я́блоня (-и) *ж* apple tree.

я́блочко (-а) *ср уменьш от* **я́блоко**; (*на мишени*) bull's-eye.

я́блочный *прил* apple *опред*.

я́вен *прил см* **я́вный.**

яви́ться (-лю́сь, -ишься; *impf* **явля́ться**) *сов возв* (*в суд*) to appear; (*на службу*) to report; (*домой, в гости*) to arrive; (*мысль, образ*) to arise; **явля́ться** (~ *perf*) +*instr* (*причиной, следствием*) to turn out to be.

я́вка (-ки; *gen pl* -ок) *ж* (*действие: в суд, на допрос*) appearance; (: *на интервью итп*) attendance; (*место: конспираторов*) secret meeting place.

явле́ние (-я) *ср* phenomenon (*мн* phenomena); (*событие*) occurrence; (*ТЕАТР*) scene; (*РЕЛ*) manifestation.

явлю́сь *сов см* **яви́ться.**

явля́ться (-юсь) *несов от* **яви́ться** ♦ *возв*: ~ +*instr* to be.

я́вно *нареч* (*очевидно*) obviously.

я́вный (-ен, -на, -но) *прил* (*вражда, благосклонность*) overt; (*ложь, лесть итп*) obvious.

я́вок *сущ см* **я́вка.**

я́вочный *прил*; ~**ая кварти́ра** secret meeting place; ~ **пункт** (*ВОЕН*) reporting point; ~**ым поря́дком** without permission; **я́вочный лист** attendance sheet.

я́вственный (-, -на, -но) *прил* (*звук*) distinct; (*сознание, понимание итп*) clear.

я́вствовать (*3sg* -ует) *несов неперех* to be

obvious; **из показа́ний** ~**ует, что он невино́вен** from the evidence it is obvious that he is innocent.

явь (-и) *ж* reality.

яга́ (-и́) *ж* Baba-Yaga (*witch in Russian folk tales*).

я́гель (-я) *м* Iceland moss.

ягнёнок (-ёнка; *nom pl* -я́та, *gen pl* -я́т) *м* lamb.

ягни́ться (*3sg* -и́тся, *3pl* -я́тся, *perf* **оягни́ться**) *несов возв* to lamb.

ягня́та *итп сущ см* **ягнёнок.**

я́года (-ы) *ж* berry; **одного́ по́ля** ~ kindred spirit.

ягоди́ца (-ы) *ж* buttock.

я́годник (-а) *м* (*место*) berry patch; (*кустарник*) berry bush; (*разг: сборщик*) berry picker.

я́годный *прил* berry *опред.*

ягуа́р (-а) *м* jaguar.

яд (-а; *part sing* -у) *м* poison.

я́дер *сущ см* **ядро́.**

я́дерный *прил* nuclear.

я́дерщик (-а) *м* (*разг*) nuclear physicist.

ядови́тый (-, -а, -о) *прил* poisonous; (*перен: человек, слова*) venomous.

ядохимика́т (-а) *м* (*обычно мн*) chemical (*used as weedkiller or pesticide*).

ядрёный (-, -а, -о) *прил* (*яблоко*) juicy; (*перен: воздух*) fresh; (: *мороз*) hard.

ядро́ (-ра́; *nom pl* -ра, *gen pl* -ер) *ср* nucleus; (*ореха*) kernel; (*Земли, древесины*) core; (*ВОЕН*) projectile; (*СПОРТ*) shot; **толка́ние** ~**ра́** (*СПОРТ*) shot put.

яз. *сокр* (= **язы́к**) lang. (= *language*).

я́зва (-ы) *ж* (*МЕД*) ulcer; (*перен: общества*) evil ♦ *м/ж* (*перен: разг*) sarcastic person (*мн* people); **я́зва желу́дка** stomach ulcer.

я́звенный *прил*: ~**ая боле́знь** stomach ulcer.

язви́тельный (-ен, -ьна, -ьно) *прил* scathing.

язви́ть (-лю́, -и́шь; *perf* **съязви́ть**) *несов неперех* (+*dat*) to speak sharply to; ~ (**съязви́ть** *perf*) **на чей-н счёт** to be scathing at sb's expense.

язы́к (-а́) *м* tongue; (*русский, разговорный итп*) language; (*ВОЕН: разг*) *prisoner captured for information*; **держа́ть** (*impf*) ~ **за зуба́ми** (*разг*) to hold one's tongue; **вопро́с (был) у него́ на** ~**е** (*разг*) the question was on the tip of his tongue; **прикуси́ть** (*perf*) ~ (*разг*) to bite one's tongue; **тяну́ть** *(perf)* **кого́-н за** ~ *(разг)* to make sb talk; ~ **не повернётся сказа́ть/попроси́ть** *(разг)* I could not bring myself to say/ask; **владе́ть** *(impf)* **языко́м** to speak a language; **находи́ть (найти́** *perf)* **о́бщий** ~ to find a common language; ~ **программи́рования высо́кого/ни́зкого у́ровня** *(КОМП)* high-level/ low-level language; ~ **ассе́мблера** *(КОМП)* assembly language.

языка́ст|ый (-, -а, -о) *прил (человек)* sharp-tongued.

языкове́д (-а) *м* linguist.

языкове́ди|е (-я) *ср* linguistics.

языков|о́й *прил (факультет, система)* language *опред;* ~**о́е прави́ло** rule of a language.

языкозна́ни|е (-я) *ср* linguistics.

язы́ческ|ий (-ая, -ое, -ие) *прил* pagan *опред.*

язы́честв|о (-а) *ср* paganism.

язычка́ *итп сущ см* **язычо́к.**

язы́чник (-а) *м* pagan.

язы́чниц|а (-ы) *ж см* **язы́чник.**

язычо́к (-ка́) *м уменьш от* **язы́к;** *(АНАТ)* uvula; *(ботинка)* tongue; *(замка)* catch.

яйц *сущ см* **яйцо́.**

яи́чк|о (-ка; *gen pl* -ек) *ср уменьш от* **яйцо́;** *(АНАТ)* testicle.

яи́чник (-а) *м* ovary.

яи́чниц|а (-ы) *ж* fried eggs *мн.*

яи́чн|ый *прил:* ~ **бело́к** egg white; ~**ая скорлупа́** eggshell.

яйцеви́д|ный (-ен, -на, -но) *прил* egg-shaped.

яйцево́д (-а) *м* oviduct.

яйцекле́т|ка (-ки; *gen pl* -ок) *ж* ovule.

яйцо́ (**яйца́;** *nom pl* **яйца,** *gen pl* **яйц,** *dat pl* **я́йцам)** *ср* egg; *(АНАТ)* ovum; ~ **всмя́тку/ вкруту́ю** soft-boiled/hard-boiled egg.

ЯК (-а) *м сокр = самолёт констру́кции А.С. Я́ковлева.*

Як (-а) *м сокр =* **ЯК.**

як (-а) *м* yak.

я́кобы *союз (будто бы)* that ♦ *част* supposedly; **он утвержда́ет,** ~ **ничего́ не зна́ет** he claims that he doesn't know anything; **он предлага́ет** ~ **вы́годную сде́лку** he is supposedly proposing a good deal.

я́корный *прил* anchor *опред.*

я́кор|ь (-я; *nom pl* -**я́)** *м (МОР)* anchor; **броса́ть (бро́сить** *perf)* ~ to cast anchor; **стоя́ть** *(impf)* **на** ~**е** to ride at anchor; **снима́ться (сня́ться** *perf)* **с** ~**я** to weigh anchor.

яку́т (-а) *м* Yakut.

Яку́ти|я (-и) *ж* Yakutia.

яку́т|ка (-ки; *gen pl* -ок) *ж см* **яку́т.**

якша́|ться (-юсь) *несов возв:* ~ **с** +*instr* to consort with.

Ялт|а (-ы) *ж* Yalta.

я́м|а (-ы) *ж (в земле)* pit; *(разг: впадина)* hollow;

ры́ть *(impf)* ~**у кому́-н** to lay a trap for sb; **возду́шная** ~ air pocket; **оркестро́вая** ~ orchestra pit.

Яма́йк|а (-и) *ж* Jamaica.

яма́йск|ий (-ая, -ое, -ие) *прил* Jamaican.

я́мочк|а (-ки; *gen pl* -ек) *ж* dimple.

ямщи́к (-а́) *м* coachman *(мн* coachmen).

январ|ь (-я́) *м* January; *см также* **октя́брь.**

янта́рный *прил* amber *опред.*

янта́р|ь (-я́) *м* amber.

япо́н|ец (-ца) *м* Japanese.

Япони|я (-и) *ж* Japan.

япо́н|ка (-ки; *gen pl* -ок) *ж см* **япо́нец.**

япо́нск|ий (-ая, -ое, -ие) *прил* Japanese; ~ **язы́к** Japanese.

япо́нца *итп сущ см* **япо́нец.**

ярд (-а) *м* yard.

я́рк|ий (-кая, -кое, -кие; -ок, -ка́, -ко) *прил* bright; *(перен: человек, речь)* brilliant; *(: тала́нт)* outstanding.

я́ркост|ь (-и) *ж (цвета, краски)* brightness; *(человека, речи)* brilliance.

ярлы́к (-а́) *м* label; **ему́ накле́или** ~ **реакционе́ра** he was labelled as a reactionary.

я́рмар|ка (-ки; *gen pl* -ок) *ж* fair; **междунаро́дная** ~ international trade fair.

ярм|о́ (-а́) *ср (также перен)* yoke.

яров|о́й *прил (злаки)* spring *опред;* ~**о́е по́ле** field sown with spring crops.

я́рок *прил см* **я́ркий.**

я́рост|ный (-ен, -на, -но) *прил (взгляд, слова)* furious; *(перен: атака, критика)* fierce.

я́рост|ь (-и) *ж* fury; **приходи́ть (прийти́** *perf)* **в** ~ to fly into a rage.

я́рус (-а) *м (в зри́тельном за́ле)* circle; *(ряд)* tier; *(ГЕО)* layer.

я́рый *прил (преданный)* ardent.

я́сен *прил см* **я́сный.**

я́сен|ь (-я) *м* ash (tree).

я́сл|и (-ей) *мн (для скота)* trough *ед; (также:* **де́тские** ~**)** crèche, day nursery *(BRIT).*

ясне́|ть *(3sg* -ет, *3pl* -ют) *несов неперех* to clear, become clear.

я́сно *нареч* clearly ♦ *как сказ (о погоде)* it's fine; *(понятно)* it's clear; **я** ~ **выража́юсь?** do I make myself clear?; **на у́лице сего́дня** ~ it's fine outside today; **тепе́рь мне всё** ~ it's all clear to me now; ~, **что он недово́лен** it's clear that he's not happy; **с ним всё** ~ nothing more needs to be said about him.

яснови́дени|е (-я) *ср* clairvoyance.

яснови́д|ец (-ца) *м* clairvoyant.

яснови́дящ|ий (-ая, -ее, -ие) *прил (человек)* clairvoyant *опред* ♦ (-**его**; *decl like adj) м* clairvoyant.

я́сност|ь (-и) *ж* clarity; **вноси́ть (внести́** *perf)* ~ **в что-н** to clarify sth.

я́сн|ый (-ен, -на́, -но) *прил* clear.

я́стреб (-а) м (ЗООЛ) hawk.
ястреби́н|ый прил (клюв) hawk's; ~**ая охо́та**
falconry; ~ **нос** (перен) hooked nose.
я́хонт (-а) м (рубин) ruby; (сапфир) sapphire.
я́хт|а (-ы) ж yacht.
яхт-клу́б (-а) м yacht club.
яхтсме́н (-а) м yachtsman (мн yachtsmen).
яче́|йка (-йки; gen pl -ек) ж (сотовая,
партийная) cell; (профсоюзная) branch; (для
почты) pigeonhole; **яче́йка па́мяти** (КОМП)
memory cell.
ячме́нный прил barley опред.
ячме́н|ь (-я́) м (С.-Х.) barley; (МЕД) sty(e).

я́чневый прил crushed-barley.
я́шм|а (-ы) ж jasper.
я́щериц|а (-ы) ж lizard.
я́щик (-а) м (вместилище: большой) chest;
(: маленький) box; (в письменном столе итп)
drawer; (также: мусо́рный ~) dustbin (BRIT),
garbage can (US); **почто́вый ~** (домашний)
letter box (BRIT), mailbox (US); (уличный: как
адрес) post office box; (разг: об учреждении)
secret plant, institution etc; (: ТЕЛ) the box;
откла́дывать (**отложи́ть** perf) **что-н в до́лгий
~** (перен) to shelve sth.
я́щур (-а) м (болезнь) foot-and-mouth disease.

GUIDE TO RUSSIAN GRAMMAR

It is not the purpose of this grammar section to attempt to give an exhaustive treatment of Russian grammar. Instead it is intended to outline the basic grammatical principles and to draw the user's attention to the most commonly encountered irregular forms.

NOUNS

1 Gender

A Russian noun has either masculine, feminine or neuter gender. In most cases it is grammatically determinable by its ending:

дом *m*
картина *f*
кресло *nt*

Gender of nouns is significant since, for example, it determines the ending of a qualifying adjective:

большой дом
большая картина
большое кресло

1.1 Masculine noun categories

I) All nouns ending in a hard consonant eg. кот, собор, адрес or in -й eg. крематорий, музей.
II) Some nouns ending in -а/-я which are natural masculine nouns eg.мужчина, дядя and masculine first names eg. Саша.
III) Numerous nouns ending in a soft sign, including:
    i) natural masculines eg. парень, король.
    ii) months of the year eg. июль.

1.2 Feminine noun categories

I) The majority of nouns ending in -а/-я, eg. дорога, комната, тётя.
II) The majority of nouns ending in a soft sign, including:
    i) natural feminines eg. мать
    ii) all nouns ending in -жь,-чь,-шь,-щь,-знь,-мь,-пь,-фь.
    iii) most nouns ending in -сть,-бь,-вь,-дь,-зь,-сь,-ть.

1.3 Neuter noun categories

a) Almost all nouns ending in -о eg. окно
b) Almost all nouns ending in -е eg. солнце
c) Nouns ending in -ё eg. копьё.
d) Nouns ending in -мя eg. время, племя.
e) Most indeclinable loan words eg. виски, радио (a notable exception being кофе, which is masculine).

2 Declension

There are three declension patterns for nouns. The first covers most masculine and neuter nouns, the second most feminine nouns and the third is specific to feminine nouns ending in a soft sign. For the first declension pattern hard-ending masculine and neuter nouns (eg. мост, óзеро) have the genitive singular ending -a, whereas soft-ending masculine and neuter nouns (eg. кремато́рий, гость, го́ре) have the genitive ending -я. Similarly, the second declension pattern has a split between hard-ending feminine nouns (eg. ла́мпа), which have the genitive singular ending -ы, and soft-ending feminine nouns (eg. ба́шня), which have the genitive ending -и. All nouns in the third declension pattern, as they are soft-ending, have the genitive ending -и.

The genitive singular declension generally sets the pattern for the other oblique cases of a noun, ie. whether these will be hard- or soft-ending. The general pattern followed in all three declensions is illustrated by the following table, using specific noun examples:

[NB. The table does not, of course, cover all the variations in declension or stress that exist]

Nom	Acc	*Singular* Gen	Dat	Instr	Prp	Nom	Acc	*Plural* Gen	Dat	Instr	Prp
Masculine											
заво́д	~	~а	~у	~ом	~е	~ы	~ы	~ов	~ам	~ами	~ах
музе́й	~й	~я	~ю	~ем	~е	~и	~и	~ев	~ям	~ями	~ях
гость	~я	~я	~ю	~ем	~е	~и	~éй	~éй	~я́м	~я́ми	~я́х
писа́тель	~я	~я	~ю	~ем	~е	~и	~ей	~ей	~ям	~ями	~ях
дви́гатель	~ь	~я	~ю	~ем	~е	~и	~и	~ей	~ям	~ями	~ях
Neuter											
ме́сто	~о	~а	~у	~ом	~е	~á	~á	~	~áм	~áми	~áх
по́ле	~е	~я	~ю	~ем	~е	~я́	~я́	~éй	~я́м	~я́ми	~я́х
зда́ние	~е	~я	~ю	~ем	~и	~я	~я	~й	~ям	~ями	~ях
Feminine											
ла́мпа	~у	~ы	~е	~ой	~е	~ы	~ы	~	~ам	~ами	~ах
ба́шня	~ню	~ни	~не	~ней	~не	~ни	~ни	~ен	~ням	~нями	~нях
по́весть	~ь	~и	~и	~ью	~и	~и	~и	~ей	~ям	~ями	~ях
ста́нция	~ю	~и	~и	~ей	~и	~и	~и	~й	~ям	~ями	~ях

One particularly important rule to bear in mind is that the accusative case of animate masculine singular nouns and of all animate plural nouns is identical with the genitive.

3 Stress patterns

Stress varies a great deal from one Russian noun to the next, and even oblique cases of a particular noun frequently differ from each other in this respect.

Nouns ending in unstressed -а/-я and in -ия/-ие do not undergo any stress changes.

Fixed stem-stress is found in first declension masculine nouns such as стул, музе́й, локомоти́в, in nouns with medial stress, in nouns of three or more syllables, and in nouns with unstressed prefixes or suffixes.

Fixed end-stress is found in many hard-ending and soft-ending first declension masculine nouns such as стол, дождь, слова́рь, as well as in almost all nouns with the stressed suffixes -а́к/-я́к,-а́ч, -е́ж, -ёж,-и́к,-и́ч,-у́н,-у́х.

A shift of stress from the stem in the singular to the end in the plural is found in first declension masculine nouns such as мост and сад, as well as in many nouns with nominative plural endings -ья́,-а́/-я́. A similar stress shift occurs in neuter nouns such as де́ло and ме́сто. The reverse happens (ie. a shift of stress from the end in the singular to the stem in the plural) in other neuter nouns eg. письмо́, вино́, окно́. This is also true for many second declension feminine nouns eg. война́, игра́, страна́ and others which undergo a vowel mutation in the stress change eg. жена́ » жёны, сестра́ » сёстры.

Irregularity of stress pattern is greatest in end-stressed second declension feminine nouns, where the following patterns are possible: the accusative singular and nominative/ accusative plural have stem stress eg. рука́, нога́, сторона́, or only the nominative/ accusative plural have stem stress eg. губа́, волна́. Alternatively, stem stress may be confined to: the singular accusative and all plural forms, as in the case of вода́, цена́, стена́; all plural forms with the exception of the genitive and animate accusative, as in the case of семья́, судья́; the accusative singular and all plural forms excepting the genitive, as in the case of земля́.

2 ADJECTIVES

Russian adjectives generally have a long (attributive) form eg. ве́жливый, ве́жливая, ве́жливое, ве́жливые and a short (predicative) form eg. ве́жлив, ве́жлива, ве́жливо, ве́жливы.

1 Long form

Russian long adjectives are mostly used attributively and the majority have hard endings, the first vowel of the ending being -ы,-а or -о. The declension of such adjectives is seen as the regular one for the purposes of this dictionary. Thus, adjectives such as ста́рый decline as follows:

	m	*f*	*nt*	*pl*
Nom	ста́р|ый	ста́р|ая	ста́р|ое	ста́р|ые
Acc	~ый/~ого	~ую	~ое	~ые/~ых
Gen	~ого	~ой	~ого	~ых
Dat	~ому	~ой	~ому	~ым
Instr	~ым	~ой	~ым	~ыми
Prp	о ~ом	о ~ой	о ~ом	о ~ых

(NB. The alternative forms of the accusative are animate and identical with the genitive. The feminine instrumental ending -ою also exists)

End-stressed adjectives with hard endings, eg. живо́й, decline similarly, with the only difference being the masculine nominative singular and inanimate accusative singular, where the ending -о́й replaces -ый. Alternative endings are determined by Russian spelling rules, according to which и replaces ы after г,к,х,ж,ч,ш,щ, and е replaces an unstressed о after ж,ч,ш,щ and ц. Thus, a stem-stressed adjective such as гла́дкий declines as follows:

	m	f	nt	pl
Nom	гла́дк|ий	гла́дк|ая	гла́дк|ое	гла́дк|ие
Acc	~ий/~ого	~ую	~ое	~ие/~их
Gen	~ого	~ой	~ого	~их
Dat	~ому	~ой	~ому	~им
Instr	~им	~ой	~им	~ими
Prp	о ~ом	о ~ой	о ~ом	о ~их

(NB. The alternative forms of the accusative are animate and identical with the genitive. The feminine instrumental ending -ою also exists)

End-stressed adjectives such as большо́й decline similarly, with only the masculine nominative and inanimate accusative singular differing in that they have the ending -о́й instead of -ий. In stem-stressed adjectives such as хоро́ший, however, the declensions are as follows:

	m	f	nt	pl
Nom	хоро́ш|ий	хоро́ш|ая	хоро́ш|ее	хоро́ш|ие
Acc	~ий/~его	~ую	~ее	~ие/~их
Gen	~его	~ей	~его	~их
Dat	~ему	~ей	~ему	~им
Instr	~им	~ей	~им	~ими
Prp	о ~ем	о ~ей	о ~ем	о ~их

(NB. The alternative forms of the accusative are animate and identical with the genitive. The feminine instrumental ending -ею also exists)

Soft-ending adjectives, ie. those ending in -ний, decline differently again. Thus, adjectives such as о́сенний or сосе́дний decline as follows:

	m	f	nt	pl
Nom	о́сенн|ий	о́сенн|яя	о́сенн|ее	о́сенн|ие
Acc	~ий/~его	~юю	~ее	~ие/~их
Gen	~его	~ей	~его	~их
Dat	~ему	~ей	~ему	~им
Instr	~им	~ей	~им	~ими
Prp	о ~ем	о ~ей	о ~ем	о ~их

(NB. The alternative forms of the accusative are animate and, therefore, identical with the genitive. The feminine instrumental ending -ею also exists)

1.1 Possessive adjectives

These follow one of two declension patterns. Possessive adjectives like соба́чий and де́вичий decline as follows:

	m	f	nt	pl
Nom	соба́ч|ий	соба́ч|яя	соба́ч|ье	соба́ч|ьи
Acc	~ий/~ьего	~ью	~ье	~ьи/~ьих
Gen	~ьего	~ьей	~ьего	~ьих
Dat	~ьему	~ьей	~ьему	~ьим
Instr	~ьим	~ьей	~ьим	~ьими
Prp	о ~ьем	о ~ьей	о ~ьем	о ~ьих

(NB. The alternative forms of the accusative are animate and identical with the genitive. The feminine instrumental ending -ьею also exists. The ordinal numeral трéтий declines according to the above table)

In addition, there are those possessive adjectives formed by adding the suffixes -ин,-нин or -ов to the stems of nouns. This form is mainly used with reference to particular family members, eg. мáмин, мýжнин, дéдов, but can also be derived from the familiar forms of first names, eg. Лéнин, Сáшин. These decline as follows:

	m	*f*	*nt*	*pl*
Nom	Сáшин	Сáшин|а	Сáшин|о	Сáшин|ы
Acc	~/~ого	~у	~о	~ы/~ых
Gen	~ого	~ой	~ого	~ых
Dat	~у	~ой	~у	~ым
Instr	~ым	~ой	~ым	~ыми
Prp	о ~ом	о ~ой	о ~ом	о ~ых

(NB. The alternative forms of the accusative are animate and identical with the genitive. The feminine instrumental ending -ою also exists)

Note that the animate accusative/genitive rule which affects nouns also applies to long adjectives.

1.2 Usage

Long adjectives are typically used attributively, for example:

на ýлице стоúт **бéлая** машúна "a white car is parked on the street"

or showing the use of the accusative case:

он вóдит **бéлую** машúну "he drives a white car"

Long adjectives may be used predicatively when they denote characteristics inherent to the nouns they refer to.

эта ýлица – **длúнная** "this street is long"
этот груз – **тяжёлый** "this load is heavy"

2 Short adjectives

Short adjectives can be derived from most long adjectives. They are formed by replacing the long-form endings with contracted ones eg. вéжливый. This declines as follows:

	Long Form	*Short Form*
m	вéжлив|ый	вéжлив
f	~ая	~а
nt	~ое	~о
pl	~ые	~ы

The masculine short form of many adjectives requires a buffer vowel (е,о or ё) to be inserted between the last two consonants or to replace a soft sign. Thus, вáжный has masculine short form вáжен, вúдный has вúден, лёгкий лёгок, ýмный умён etc. Masculine short forms of adjectives ending in -енный (ie. unstressed) generally have -ен endings, whereas those in -éнный (ie. stressed) are replaced by the short form -éнен.

Short-form adjectives have either fixed stem stress, eg. вéжлив, вéжлива, вéжливо, вéжливы, end stress in feminine, neuter and plural, eg. хорóш, хорошá, хорошó, хоро́ши, end stress in the feminine, eg. жив, жива́, жи́во, жи́вы, or end stress in the feminine and plural, eg. ви́ден, видна́, ви́дно, видны́.

2.1 Usage

In contrast to the predicative use of long adjectives, the short form on the whole is used when talking about a temporary state. For example, он **плох** "he is poorly" contrasts with он – плохо́й "he is bad".

3 VERBS

1 Conjugation

Russian verbs can be divided into two groups, according to their endings when conjugated. The two groups are often referred to as "first-conjugation" and "second-conjugation" verbs, and the following examples – one from either group – show the pattern of endings encountered in the present-tense conjugations of verbs from each group:

	1st Conjugation	*2nd Conjugation*
	рабо́тать	говори́ть
я	рабо́таю	говорю́
ты	рабо́таешь	говори́шь
он/она́	рабо́тает	говори́т
мы	рабо́таем	говори́м
вы	рабо́таете	говори́те
они́	рабо́тают	говоря́т

1.1 First-conjugation verbs

These include verbs with infinitive endings in -ать (eg. рабо́тать: see above), in -ять (eg. стреля́ть: стреля́ю,стреля́ешь etc), in -овать/-евать (eg. интересова́ть: интерес-у́ю,интересу́ешь etc), in -уть (eg. махну́ть: махну́,махнёшь etc), in -авать (eg. узнава́ть: узнаю́,узнаёшь etc), in -ыть (eg. мыть: мо́ю,мо́ешь etc), and in -зть,-оть,-сть and -ти, as well as monosyllabic verbs in -ить (eg. шить: шью,шьёшь etc). Note how under stress e is replaced by ё.

Many first-conjugation verbs – generally those with end-stressed infinitives – undergo consonant mutation in conjugation, which is frequently accompanied by a stress shift from the end to the stem after the first person singular; this is the general pattern for stress changes within the conjugation of first-conjugation verbs. For example:

	писа́ть	иска́ть
я	пишу́	ищу́
ты	пи́шешь	и́щешь
он/она́	пи́шет	и́щет
мы	пи́шем	и́щем
вы	пи́шете	и́щете
они́	пи́шут	и́щут

Stress change does not occur in first-conjugation verbs where the stress falls on the stem of the infinitive, eg. пла́кать: пла́чу, пла́чешь etc, and дви́гать: дви́жу,дви́жешь etc.

1.2 Second-conjugation verbs

These include most verbs with infinitive endings in -ить (the main exception being the monosyllabic ones), many verbs in -еть, some in -ать and two in -ять (боя́ться and стоя́ть).

Note that у replaces ю and а replaces я after ж,ч,ш, or щ. Thus, смотре́ть conjugates: смотрю́,смо́тришь,...смо́трят, whereas слы́шать conjugates: слы́шу,слы́шишь,...слы́шат.

As with first-conjugation verbs, stress change in second-conjugation verbs that are end-stressed in the infinitive is often accompanied by a consonant change in conjunction, eg. плати́ть: плачу́,пла́тишь,...пла́тят and суди́ть: сужу́,су́дишь,...су́дят. However, this mutation applies consistently only to the first person singular of second-conjugation verbs in -ить and -еть. Furthermore, the addition of л in the first person singular of verbs with the stem ending in п, б, в, ф and м is a salient feature of the second conjugation, eg. люби́ть: люблю́,лю́бишь,...лю́бят and корми́ть: кормлю́, ко́рмишь,...ко́рмят. In fact, a consonant change of one form or other, in the first person singular, is found in all second conjugation verbs in -ить whose stems end in -б,-в,-д,-з,-с,-т and -ф, and those in -еть and -ить whose stems end in -м,-п, and -ст.

2 Past Tense

The past tense for most Russian verbs, including all those with infinitive endings in -сть and -ть, is formed by replacing the infinitive ending by -л,-ла,-ло,-ли, giving the masculine, feminine, neuter and plural forms respectively.

For example:

infinitive	*past tense*
молча́ть	он молча́л
	она́ молча́ла
	оно́ молча́ло
	они́ молча́ли
укра́сть	он укра́л
	она́ укра́ла
	оно́ укра́ло
	они́ укра́ли
звони́ть	он звони́л
	она́ звони́ла
	оно́ звони́ло
	они́ звони́ли

The singular past tense always reflects the gender of the subject, so that even after the personal pronouns я and ты the gender is always marked, eg. я сказа́л (masculine subject)
я сказа́ла (feminine subject)

Verbs with infinitives ending in -ереть,-зть,-чь, and many in -ти have no -л on the masculine past tense, eg. умере́ть (у́мер,умерла́), лезть (лез,ле́зла), мочь (мог,могла́), нести́ (нёс,несла́). This is also the case with some verbs in -нуть, привы́кнуть (привы́к, привы́кла).

The verb быть, while not used in the present tense, is encountered frequently in the past tense:

был, была́, бы́ло, бы́ли

Note the stress changes when used in the negative, ie. preceded by не:

не́ был, не была́, не́ было, не́ были

3 Imperative Mood

The imperative mood has two forms – the familiar and the formal - which are used in accordance with the mode of address (ie. the familiar ты or the formal Вы) appropriate in any given situation. The formal imperative is obtained by simply adding -те to the end of the familiar form. The familiar imperative is formed by replacing the third person plural ending of a verb by -й where it is directly preceded by a vowel, eg.:

де́лать (*infin*) » де́лают (*3rd person pl*) » де́лай(те) (*imperative*)

similarly:

чита́ть » чита́ют » чита́й(те)

Alternatively, -и(те) replaces the third person plural ending where this is directly preceded by a consonant and the verb has mobile or end stress in conjunction, eg.:

подчеркну́ть » подчеркну́т » подчеркни́(те)
держа́ть » де́ржат » держи́(те)

The imperative ending -ь(те) replaces the third person plural ending where this is directly preceded by no more than one consonant and the verb has fixed stem stress in conjugation, eg.:

поста́вить » поста́вят » поста́вь(те)
оде́ть » оде́нут » оде́нь(те)

Note: stress in imperative forms is identical to that of the first person singular.

– дава́|ть and its compounds have imperative -й(те).

– пить has imperative пей(те) (compare петь which has imperative по́й(те)). бить, вить, лить and шить also form the imperative like пить.

– the imperative of быть is бу́дь(те).

4 Aspect

The majority of Russian verbs have two verb aspects, the **imperfective** for conveying the **frequency** of an action or describing a **process**, and the **perfective** for emphasis on a **single action** or a **result**. It follows that the perfective can only be used in the past and future, while the imperfective can also be used in the present tense.

Aspectual pairs can be differentiated either by the presence of a prefix in the perfective aspect, eg. сде́лать (cf imperfective де́лать), by the presence of a suffix in the imperfective aspect, eg. пока́зывать (cf perfective показа́ть), or by a change in conjugation, eg. perfective ко́нчить (2nd conjugation) and its imperfective counterpart конча́ть (1st conjugation).

It should be noted, though, that some aspectual pairs do not follow this pattern, for instance those that derive from different roots, eg. говори́ть (*impf*)/сказа́ть (*perf*), брать (*impf*)/взять (*perf*). Then there are a minority of verbs which exist in one aspect only, eg. сто́ить (*impf*), while some verbs incorporate the two aspects in one form, eg. иссле́довать (*impf/perf*).

Aspect also has a bearing on the use of the imperative mood, where, generally speaking, the perfective aspect is used in positive commands (ie. telling someone to do something), while the imperfective is used in negative commands (ie. telling someone not to do something), in other words where the imperative form is preceded by "не".

~ A, a ~

A, a [eɪ] *n* (*letter*) 1-ая бу́ква англи́йского алфави́та; (*SCOL: mark*) ≈ отли́чно; ~ **road** (*BRIT: AUT*) шоссе́ *nt ind* (пе́рвой катего́рии); ~ **shares** (*BRIT: STOCK EXCHANGE*) а́кции *fpl* с ограни́ченным пра́вом го́лоса; **from** ~ **to Z** от "а" до "я".

A [eɪ] *n* (*MUS*) ля *nt ind*.

KEYWORD
---

a [eɪ] (*before vowel or silent h* **an**) *indef art*: **1**: **a book** кни́га; **an apple** я́блоко; **she's a student** она́ студе́нтка
2 (*instead of the number "one"*): **a week ago** неде́лю наза́д; **a hundred/thousand** *etc* **pounds** сто/ты́сяча *etc* фу́нтов
3 (*in expressing time*) в +*acc*; **3 a day/week** 3 в день/неде́лю; **10 km an hour** 10 км в час
4 (*in expressing prices*): **30p a kilo** 30 пе́нсов килогра́мм; **£5 a person** с ка́ждого 5 фу́нтов.

a. *abbr* = **acre**.

AA *n abbr* (*BRIT*: = *Automobile Association*) Автомоби́льная ассоциа́ция; (*US*: = *Associate in/of Arts*) член ассоциа́ции рабо́тников иску́сства; (= *Alcoholics Anonymous*) о́бщество анони́много излече́ния от алкоголи́зма; (= *anti-aircraft*) противовозду́шный.

AAA *n abbr* (= *American Automobile Association*) Америка́нская автомоби́льная ассоциа́ция; (*BRIT*: = *Amateur Athletics Association*) Люби́тельская ассоциа́ция лёгкой атле́тики.

A & R *n abbr* (*MUS*: = *artists and repertoire*) исполни́тели и репертуа́р.

AAUP *n abbr* = *American Association of University Professors*.

AB *abbr* (*BRIT*) = **able-bodied seaman**; (*CANADA*) = *Alberta*.

abaci ['æbəsaɪ] *npl of* **abacus**.

aback [ə'bæk] *adv*: **I was taken** ~ я был поражён.

abacus ['æbəkəs] (*pl* **abaci**) *n* счёты *pl*.

abandon [ə'bændən] *vt* (*person*) покида́ть (поки́нуть *perf*); (*car*) броса́ть (бро́сить* *perf*); (*search, research*) прекраща́ть (прекрати́ть* *perf*); (*idea, hope*) отка́зываться (отказа́ться*

perf) от +*gen* ♦ *n* (*wild behaviour*): **with** ~ самозабве́нно; **to** ~ **ship** покида́ть (поки́нуть *perf*) кора́бль.

abandoned [ə'bændənd] *adj* поки́нутый; (*unrestrained*) безу́держный.

abase [ə'beɪs] *vt*: **to** ~ **o.s. (before)** унижа́ться (уни́зиться* *perf*) (пе́ред +*instr*).

abashed [ə'bæʃt] *adj* смущённый* (смущён).

abate [ə'beɪt] *vi* (*storm*) утиха́ть (ути́хнуть* *perf*); (*anger, terror*) ослабева́ть (ослабе́ть *perf*).

abatement [ə'beɪtmənt] *n*: **noise** ~ сниже́ние у́ровня шу́ма.

abattoir ['æbətwɑ:'] *n* (*BRIT*) скотобо́йня.

abbey ['æbɪ] *n* абба́тство.

abbot ['æbət] *n* абба́т.

abbreviate [ə'bri:vɪeɪt] *vt* (*essay, word*) сокраща́ть (сократи́ть* *perf*).

abbreviation [əbri:vɪ'eɪʃən] *n* сокраще́ние.

ABC *n abbr* = *American Broadcasting Company*.

abdicate ['æbdɪkeɪt] *vt* (*responsibility, right*) слага́ть (сложи́ть *perf*) с себя́ ♦ *vi* (*monarch*) отрека́ться (отре́чься* *perf*) от престо́ла.

abdication [æbdɪ'keɪʃən] *n* (*see vb*) скла́дывание; отрече́ние престо́ла.

abdomen ['æbdəmɛn] *n* брюшна́я по́лость *f*, живо́т.

abdominal [æb'dɔmɪnl] *adj* брюшно́й; ~ **pain** бо́ли *fpl* в брюшно́й по́лости *or* в животе́.

abduct [æb'dʌkt] *vt* похища́ть (похи́тить* *perf*).

abduction [æb'dʌkʃən] *n* похище́ние.

Aberdeen [æbə'di:n] *n* Аберди́н.

Aberdonian [æbə'dəunɪən] *adj* аберди́нский ♦ *n* аберди́нец(-нка).

aberration [æbə'reɪʃən] *n* аберра́ция, отклоне́ние (от но́рмы); **in a moment of mental** ~ в мину́ту помраче́ния рассу́дка.

abet [ə'bɛt] *vt see* **aid**.

abeyance [ə'beɪəns] *n*: **in** ~ приостано́вленный (приостано́влен).

abhor [əb'hɔ:'] *vt* испы́тывать (*impf*) отвраще́ние к +*dat*.

abhorrent [əb'hɔrənt] *adj* отврати́тельный* (отврати́телен).

abide [ə'baɪd] *vt*: **I can't** ~ **it/him** я э́того/его́ не выношу́

---

* marks translations which have irregular inflections. The Russian-English side of the dictionary gives inflectional information.

▶ **abide by** *vt fus* (*law, decision*) соблюда́ть (соблюсти́* *perf*).

abiding [ə'baɪdɪŋ] *adj* неослабева́ющий.

ability [ə'bɪlɪtɪ] *n* (*capacity*) спосо́бность *f*; (*talent, skill*) спосо́бности *fpl*; **to the best of my ~** в ме́ру мои́х спосо́бностей.

abject ['æbdʒɛkt] *adj* (*poverty, coward*) жа́лкий*; (*apology*) уни́женный*.

ablaze [ə'bleɪz] *adj* (*building etc*) в огне́; **the city was ~ with light** го́род был зали́т огня́ми.

able ['eɪbl] *adj* (*capable*) спосо́бный* (спосо́бен); (*skilled*) уме́лый (уме́л); **he is/ was ~ to ...** он спосо́бен/был спосо́бен +*infin* ....

able-bodied ['eɪbl'bɔdɪd] *adj* (*person*) кре́пкий*; **~ seaman** (*BRIT*) матро́с пе́рвого кла́сса.

ablutions [ə'bluːʃənz] *npl* омове́ние *ntsg*.

ably ['eɪblɪ] *adv* (*skilfully*) уме́ло.

ABM *n abbr* (= *anti-ballistic missile*) ≈ ЗУРС= зени́тный управля́емый реакти́вный снаря́д.

abnormal [æb'nɔːml] *adj* ненорма́льный* (ненорма́лен).

abnormality [æbnɔː'mælɪtɪ] *n* ненорма́льность *f*, анома́лия.

aboard [ə'bɔːd] *prep* (*position: NAUT, AVIAT*) на борту́ +*gen*; (: *train, bus*) в +*prp*; (*motion: NAUT, AVIAT*) на борт +*gen*; (: *train, bus*) в +*acc* ◆ *adv*: **to climb ~** (*ship*) сади́ться (сесть* *perf*) на кора́бль; (*train*) сади́ться (сесть* *perf*) в по́езд.

abode [ə'bəud] *n* (*LAW*): **of no fixed ~** без постоя́нного местожи́тельства.

abolish [ə'bɔlɪʃ] *vt* отменя́ть (отмени́ть* *perf*).

abolition [æbə'lɪʃən] *n* отме́на.

abominable [ə'bɔminəbl] *adj* отврати́тельный* (отврати́телен).

abominably [ə'bɔminəblɪ] *adv* отврати́тельно.

aborigine [æbə'rɪdʒɪnɪ] *n* абориге́н(ка).

abort [ə'bɔːt] *vt* (*plan, activity*) прекраща́ть (прекрати́ть* *perf*); (*COMPUT*) прерыва́ть (прерва́ть* *perf*); (*MED*): **to ~ a baby** де́лать (сде́лать *perf*) або́рт.

abortion [ə'bɔːʃən] *n* (*MED*) або́рт; **to have an ~** де́лать (сде́лать *perf*) або́рт.

abortionist [ə'bɔːʃənɪst] *n* челове́к, де́лающий подпо́льные або́рты.

abortive [ə'bɔːtɪv] *adj* неуда́чный* (неуда́чен).

abound [ə'baund] *vi* быть* (*impf*) в изоби́лии; **to ~ in** *or* **with** изоби́ловать (*impf*) +*instr*.

┌─────────────────┐
│ **KEYWORD** │
└─────────────────┘

about [ə'baut] *adv* **1** (*approximately: referring to time, price etc*) приблизи́тельно +*acc*, приме́рно +*acc*, о́коло +*gen*; **it will take me about 3 hours** э́то займёт у меня́ приме́рно *or* приблизи́тельно 3 часа́; **at about 2 (o'clock)** приблизи́тельно *or* приме́рно в 2 (часа́), часа́ в 2, о́коло двух (часо́в); **I've just about finished** я почти́ зако́нчил

2 (*approximately: referring to height, size etc*) приме́рно +*nom*, приблизи́тельно +*nom*; **the room is about 10 metres wide** ко́мната

приме́рно *or* приблизи́тельно 10 ме́тров в ширину́; **she is about your height/age** она́ приме́рно *or* приблизи́тельно Ва́шего ро́ста/во́зраста

3 (*referring to place*) повсю́ду; **to leave things lying about** разбра́сывать (разброса́ть *perf*) ве́щи повсю́ду; **to run/walk etc about** бе́гать (*impf*)/ходи́ть* (*impf*) *etc*

4: **to be about to do** собира́ться (собра́ться* *perf*) +*infin*; **he was about to go to bed** он собра́лся спать

◆ *prep* **1** (*relating to*) о(б) +*prp*; **a book about London** кни́га о Ло́ндоне; **what is it about?** о чём э́то?; **we talked about it** мы говори́ли *or* разгова́ривали об э́том; **what *or* how about doing this?** как насчёт того́, что́бы +*infin*?

2 (*referring to place*) по +*dat*; **to walk about the town** ходи́ть* (*impf*) по го́роду; **her clothes were scattered about the room** её оде́жда была́ разбро́сана по ко́мнате.

about-face [ə'baut'feɪs] *n* (*MIL*) поворо́т круго́м; (*fig*) поворо́т на 180 гра́дусов.

about-turn [ə'baut'tə:n] *n* = **about-face**.

above [ə'bʌv] *adv* (*higher up*) наверху́; (*greater, more*) вы́ше, свы́ше ◆ *prep* (*higher than*) над +*instr*; (: *in rank etc*) вы́ше +*gen*; (: *in number*) свы́ше +*gen*, бо́лее +*gen*; **from ~** све́рху; **costing ~ £10** сто́ящий свы́ше £10; **~ the knees** вы́ше коле́н; **mentioned ~** вышеупомя́нутый; **he's not ~ a bit of blackmail** он не погнуша́ется шантажо́м; **~ suspicion/criticism** вне подозре́ния/кри́тики; **~ all** пре́жде всего́.

above board *adj* че́стный* (че́стен), откры́тый (откры́т).

abrasion [ə'breɪʒən] *n* тре́ние; (*on skin*) сса́дина.

abrasive [ə'breɪzɪv] *adj* (*substance*) абрази́вный; (*manner*) жёсткий* (жёсток).

abreast [ə'brɛst] *adv* (*people, vehicles*) в ряд; **three ~** по́ трое в ряд; **to keep ~ of** (*fig*) быть* (*impf*) в ку́рсе +*gen*.

abridge [ə'brɪdʒ] *vt* (*novel, play*) сокраща́ть (сократи́ть* *perf*).

abroad [ə'brɔːd] *adv* (*to be*) за грани́цей *or* рубежо́м; (*to go*) за грани́цу *or* рубе́ж; (*from abroad*) из-за грани́цы *or* рубежа́; **there is a rumour ~ that ...** (*fig*) хо́дит слух, что ....

abrupt [ə'brʌpt] *adj* (*action, ending etc*) внеза́пный* (внеза́пен); (*person, manner*) ре́зкий* (ре́зок).

abruptly [ə'brʌptlɪ] *adv* (*leave, end*) внеза́пно; (*speak*) ре́зко.

abscess ['æbsɪs] *n* абсце́сс.

abscond [əb'skɔnd] *vi* (*thief*): **to ~ with** скры́ться* (*perf*) с +*instr*; (*prisoner*): **to ~ (from)** сбега́ть (сбежа́ть* *perf*) (из +*gen*).

abseil ['æbseɪl] *vi* спуска́ться (спусти́ться* *perf*) при по́мощи кана́та.

absence ['æbsəns] *n* (*of person, thing*)

отсу́тствие; **in the ~ of** (*person*) в отсу́тствие +*gen*; (*thing*) при отсу́тствии +*gen*; **~ without leave** (*MIL*) самово́льная отлу́чка.
absent [*adj* 'æbsənt, *vb* æb'sɛnt] *adj* отсу́тствующий* ◆ *vt*: **to ~ o.s.** отлуча́ться (отлучи́ться *perf*).
absentee [æbsən'tiː] *n* отсу́тствующий*(-ая) *m(f) adj*.
absenteeism [æbsən'tiːɪzəm] *n* прогу́лы *mpl*.
absent-minded ['æbsənt'maɪndɪd] *adj* рассе́янный* (рассе́ян).
absent-mindedly ['æbsənt'maɪndɪdlɪ] *adv* рассе́янно.
absent-mindedness ['æbsənt'maɪndɪdnɪs] *n* рассе́янность *f*.
absolute ['æbsəluːt] *adj* абсолю́тный*.
absolutely [æbsə'luːtlɪ] *adv* (*totally*) абсолю́тно, соверше́нно; (*certainly*) безусло́вно.
absolute monopoly *n* абсолю́тная монопо́лия.
absolution [æbsə'luːʃən] *n* (*REL*) отпуще́ние грехо́в.
absolve [əb'zɔlv] *vt*: **to ~ sb (from sth)** отпуска́ть (отпусти́ть* *perf*) кому́-н (что-н).
absorb [əb'zɔːb] *vt* (*liquid, information*) впи́тывать (впита́ть *perf*); (*light, business*) поглоща́ть (поглоти́ть* *perf*); (*changes, effects*) воспринима́ть (восприня́ть* *perf*); **he is ~ed in a book** он поглощён кни́гой.
absorbent [əb'zɔːbənt] *adj* гигроскопи́чный.
absorbent cotton *n* (*US*) гигроскопи́ческая ва́та.
absorbing [əb'zɔːbɪŋ] *adj* (*book, film etc*) увлека́тельный* (увлека́телен).
absorption [əb'sɔːpʃən] *n* (*see adj*) впи́тывание; поглоще́ние; восприя́тие; (*interest*) увлечённость *f*.
abstain [əb'steɪn] *vi*: **to ~ (from)** возде́рживаться (воздержа́ться* *perf*) (от +*gen*).
abstemious [əb'stiːmɪəs] *adj* (*person*) возде́ржанный* (возде́ржан).
abstention [əb'stɛnʃən] *n* (*refusal to vote*) неуча́стие в голосова́нии.
abstinence ['æbstɪnəns] *n* воздержа́ние.
abstract [*adj, n* 'æbstrækt, *vb* æb'strækt] *adj* абстра́ктный*; (*idea, quality*) отвлечённый ◆ *n* (*summary*) анноти́ция ◆ *vt* (*dissertation*) рефера́т ◆ *vt* (*remove*) извлека́ть (извле́чь* *perf*); (*summarize*) анноти́ровать (проанноти́ровать *perf*).
abstruse [æb'struːs] *adj* замыслова́тый.
absurd [əb'sɔːd] *adj* абсу́рдный* (абсу́рден), неле́пый (неле́п).
absurdity [əb'sɔːdɪtɪ] *n* абсу́рдность *f*, неле́пость *f*.
ABTA ['æbtə] *n abbr* = Association of British Travel Agents.

Abu Dhabi ['æbu'dɑːbɪ] *n* Абу-Да́би.
abundance [ə'bʌndəns] *n* изоби́лие; **in ~** в изоби́лии.
abundant [ə'bʌndənt] *adj* изоби́льный* (изоби́лен).
abundantly [ə'bʌndəntlɪ] *adv* в изоби́лии; **~ clear/obvious** соверше́нно я́сно/очеви́дно.
abuse [*n* ə'bjuːs, *vb* ə'bjuːz] *n* (*insults*) брань *f*; (*ill-treatment*) жесто́кое обраще́ние; (*misuse: of power, drugs etc*) злоупотребле́ние ◆ *vt* (*insult*) оскорбля́ть (оскорби́ть* *perf*); (*ill-treat*) жесто́ко обраща́ться (*impf*) с +*instr*; (*misuse*) злоупотребля́ть (злоупотреби́ть* *perf*) +*instr*; **this system is open to ~** э́той систе́мой легко́ злоупотребля́ть.
abuser [ə'bjuːzə'] *n*: **drug ~** наркома́н; **child ~** челове́к, подверга́ющий дете́й физи́ческому и́ли сексуа́льному наси́лию.
abusive [ə'bjuːsɪv] *adj* (*person*) гру́бый (груб); **~ language** брань *f*.
abysmal [ə'bɪzməl] *adj* (*performance, failure*) плаче́вный* (плаче́вен); (*ignorance etc*) вопию́щий* (вопию́щ).
abysmally [ə'bɪzməlɪ] *adv* (*see adj*) плаче́вно, вопию́ще.
abyss [ə'bɪs] *n* про́пасть *f*.
AC *abbr* = **alternating current**; (*US*: = **athletic club**) легкоатлети́ческий клуб.
a/c *abbr* (*COMM*) = **account**; (= **account current**) теку́щий* счёт*.
academic [ækə'dɛmɪk] *adj* (*system, standards*) академи́ческий*; (*qualifications*) учёный; (*work, books*) нау́чный*; (*person, child*) интеллектуа́льный*; (*pej: issue*) академи́чный (академи́чен) ◆ *n* учёный(-ая) *m(f) adj*.
academic year *n* (*in school*) уче́бный год*; (*in higher education*) академи́ческий* год*.
academy [ə'kædəmɪ] *n* (*learned body*) акаде́мия; (*school*) учи́лище; (: *in Scotland*) сре́дняя шко́ла; **~ of music** консервато́рия; **military/naval ~** вое́нная/вое́нно-морска́я акаде́мия.
ACAS ['eɪkæs] *n abbr* (*BRIT*: = Advisory, Conciliation and Arbitration Service) слу́жба юриди́ческих консульта́ций и арбитра́жа.
accede [æk'siːd] *vi*: **to ~ to** (*request*) удовлетворя́ть (удовлетвори́ть *perf*); (*opinion, contention*) соглаша́ться (согласи́ться* *perf*) с +*instr*.
accelerate [æk'sɛləreɪt] *vt* (*process*) ускоря́ть (уско́рить *perf*) ◆ *vi* (*AUT*) разгоня́ться (разогна́ться *perf*).
acceleration [æksɛlə'reɪʃən] *n* (*see vb*) ускоре́ние; разго́н.
accelerator [æk'sɛləreɪtə'] *n* акселера́тор.
accent ['æksɛnt] *n* акце́нт; (*stress mark*) знак

---

* marks translations which have irregular inflections. The Russian-English side of the dictionary gives inflectional information.

ударе́ния; **to speak with an Irish ~** говори́ть *(impf)* с ирла́ндским акце́нтом; **to have a strong ~** име́ть *(impf)* си́льный акце́нт.
accented [æk'sɛntɪd] *adj* с акце́нтом; **heavily ~** с си́льным акце́нтом.
accentuate [æk'sɛntjueɪt] *vt (syllable)* акценти́ровать *(impf/perf)*, проставля́ть (проста́вить *perf)* ударе́ние на +*acc*; *(need, difference)* подчёркивать (подчеркну́ть *perf)*.
accept [ək'sɛpt] *vt (gift, proposal etc)* принима́ть (приня́ть* *perf)*; *(fact, situation, risk)* мири́ться (примири́ться *perf)* с +*instr*; *(responsibility, blame)* принима́ть (приня́ть* *perf)* на себя́.
acceptable [ək'sɛptəbl] *adj* прие́млемый (прие́млем).
acceptance [ək'sɛptəns] *n (of gift, offer etc)* приня́тие; *(of fact, situation)* прия́тие; **to meet with general ~** находи́ть* (найти́* *perf)* всео́бщее одобре́ние.
access ['æksɛs] *n* до́ступ ◆ *vt (COMPUT)* испо́льзовать *(impf/perf)* до́ступ к +*dat*; (: *data)* обраща́ться (обрати́ться* *perf)* к +*dat*; **to have ~ to** *(child)* име́ть *(impf)* возмо́жность обще́ния с +*instr*; **the burglars gained ~ through a window** взло́мщики прони́кли че́рез окно́.
accessible [æk'sɛsəbl] *adj* досту́пный* (досту́пен).
accession [æk'sɛʃən] *n* прихо́д к вла́сти; *(of king)* вступле́ние на престо́л; *(to library)* поступле́ние.
accessory [æk'sɛsərɪ] *n (COMM, TECH, AUT)* принадле́жность *f*; *(LAW):* **~ to** соуча́стник(-ица) +*gen*; **accessories** *npl (DRESS)* аксессуа́ры *mpl*; **toilet accessories** *(BRIT)* туале́тные принадле́жности *fpl*.
access road *n* подъездно́й путь* *m*.
access time *n (COMPUT)* вре́мя* *nt* до́ступа.
accident ['æksɪdənt] *n (chance event)* случа́йность *f*; *(mishap, disaster)* несча́стный слу́чай, ава́рия; **to meet with** *or* **to have an ~** попада́ть (попа́сть *perf)* в ава́рию *or* катастро́фу; **he had an ~** с ним произошёл несча́стный слу́чай; **by ~** *(unintentionally)* неча́янно; *(by chance)* случа́йно.
accidental [æksɪ'dɛntl] *adj* случа́йный* (случа́ен).
accidentally [æksɪ'dɛntəlɪ] *adv* случа́йно, неча́янно.
accident insurance *n* страхова́ние от несча́стных слу́чаев.
accident-prone ['æksɪdənt'prəun] *adj* невезу́чий; **he is ~** его́ пресле́дуют несча́стья.
acclaim [ə'kleɪm] *n* призна́ние ◆ *vt:* **he was ~ed for his achievements** он получи́л призна́ние за свои́ достиже́ния.
acclamation [æklə'meɪʃən] *n (approval)* бу́рное *or* шу́мное одобре́ние; *(applause)* бу́рные аплодисме́нты *mpl*.

acclimate [ə'klaɪmət] *vt (US)* = **acclimatize**.
acclimatize [ə'klaɪmətaɪz] *(US* **acclimate**) *vt:* **to become ~d (to)** *(surroundings)* акклиматизи́роваться *(impf/perf)* (в +*prp)*, осва́иваться (осво́иться *perf)* (в +*prp)*; *(heat, cold)* привыка́ть (привы́кнуть* *perf)* (к +*dat)*.
accolade ['ækəleɪd] *n* по́честь *f*.
accommodate [ə'kɔmədeɪt] *vt (subj: person)* предоставля́ть (предоста́вить* *perf)* жильё +*dat*; (: *car, hotel etc)* вмеща́ть (вмести́ть* *perf)*; *(oblige, help)* ока́зывать (оказа́ть* *perf)* услу́гу +*dat*; **to ~ one's plans to** приспоса́бливать (приспосо́бить* *perf)* свои́ пла́ны к +*dat*.
accommodating [ə'kɔmədeɪtɪŋ] *adj* услу́жливый (услу́жлив).
accommodation [əkɔmə'deɪʃən] *n (to live in)* жильё; *(to work in)* помеще́ние; **~s** *npl (US: lodgings)* жильё *ntsg*; **"accommodation to let"** *(living)* "сдаётся жильё"; *(office)* "сдаётся помеще́ние"; **they have ~ for 500** они́ мо́гут размести́ть 500 челове́к; **the hall has seating ~ for 600** *(BRIT)* зал расчи́тан на 600 мест; **do you have any ~?** *(for yourself)* Вам есть где жить?; *(for me)* Вы предоставля́ете жильё?
accompaniment [ə'kʌmpənɪmənt] *n* сопровожде́ние; *(MUS)* аккомпанеме́нт.
accompanist [ə'kʌmpənɪst] *n* аккомпаниа́тор.
accompany [ə'kʌmpənɪ] *vt (escort, go along with)* сопровожда́ть (сопроводи́ть* *perf)*; *(MUS)* аккомпани́ровать *(impf)* +*dat*.
accomplice [ə'kʌmplɪs] *n* соуча́стник(-ица), соо́бщник(-ица).
accomplish [ə'kʌmplɪʃ] *vt (task)* заверша́ть (заверши́ть *perf)*; *(goal)* достига́ть (дости́гнуть* *or* дости́чь* *perf)* +*gen*.
accomplished [ə'kʌmplɪʃt] *adj (person)* тала́нтливый (тала́нтлив); *(performance)* соверше́нный* (соверше́нен).
accomplishment [ə'kʌmplɪʃmənt] *n (completion, bringing about)* заверше́ние; *(achievement)* достиже́ние; *(skill: usu pl)* уме́ние.
accord [ə'kɔːd] *n* соглаше́ние ◆ *vt* ока́зывать (оказа́ть* *perf)*; **of his own ~** по со́бственному жела́нию; **of its own ~** сам по себе́; **with one ~** единоду́шно; *(movement)* как по кома́нде; **he and I are in ~ on this issue** мы с ним в согла́сии на э́тот счёт *or* по э́тому по́воду.
accordance [ə'kɔːdəns] *n:* **in ~ with** в согла́сии *or* соотве́тствии с +*instr*.
according [ə'kɔːdɪŋ] *prep:* **~ to** согла́сно +*dat*; **~ to plan** по пла́ну.
accordingly [ə'kɔːdɪŋlɪ] *adv (appropriately)* соотве́тствующим о́бразом; *(as a result)* соотве́тственно.
accordion [ə'kɔːdɪən] *n* аккордео́н.
accost [ə'kɔst] *vt* пристава́ть* (приста́ть* *perf)* к +*dat*.
account [ə'kaunt] *n (bill)* счёт*; *(monthly*

account) ежемéсячныи счёт; (*in bank*) (расчётный) счёт; (*report*) отчёт; ~**s** *npl* (*COMM*) счетá* *mpl*; (*books*) бухгáлтерские кни́ги *fpl*; **"account payee only"** (*BRIT*) "подлежи́т упла́те тóлько на счёт получáтеля"; **to keep an ~ of** вести́* (*impf*) счёт* +*gen or* +*dat*; **to bring sb to ~ for sth** призывáть (призвáть* *perf*) когó-н к отвéту за что-н; **by all ~s** по всем свéдениям; **of no ~** не вáжно; **on ~** в креди́т; **to pay £5 on ~** плати́ть* (заплати́ть* *perf*) £5 в задáток; **to buy sth on ~** покупáть (купи́ть* *perf*) что-н в крéдит; **on no ~** ни в кóем слýчае; **on ~ of** по причи́не +*gen*; **to take into ~, take ~ of** принимáть (приня́ть* *perf*) в расчёт

▸ **account for** *vt fus* (*money spent, expenses*) отчи́тываться (отчитáться *perf*) за +*acc*; (*absence, failure*) объясня́ть (объясни́ть *perf*); (*represent*) составля́ть (состáвить* *perf*); **all the children were ~ed for** все дéти бы́ли на мéсте; **four people are still not ~ed for** не досчитáлись четырёх.

accountability [əˈkauntəˈbɪlɪtɪ] *n* отчётность *f*.

accountable [əˈkauntəbl] *adj* подотчётный* (подотчётен); **to be ~ to sb for sth** отвечáть (*impf*) за что-н пéред кем-н.

accountancy [əˈkauntənsɪ] *n* бухгалтéрия.

accountant [əˈkauntənt] *n* бухгáлтер.

account executive *n* делопроизводи́тель *m*.

accounting [əˈkauntɪŋ] *n* бухгáлтерское дéло*.

accounting period *n* отчётный перйод.

account number *n* (*at bank etc*) нóмер* счёта.

account payable *n* счёт кредитóров (*в балáнсе*).

account receivable *n* счёт дебитóров (*в балáнсе*).

accredited [əˈkrɛdɪtɪd] *adj* (*agent etc*) аккредитóванный.

accretion [əˈkriːʃən] *n* (*process*) нарастáние; (*layer*) нарóст.

accrue [əˈkruː] *vi* (*mount up*) нарастáть (нарасти́* *perf*); **to ~ to** доставáться* (достáться* *perf*) +*dat*.

accrued charges *npl* нарóсшие процéнты *mpl*.

accrued interest *n* нарóсшие процéнты *mpl*.

accumulate [əˈkjuːmjuleɪt] *vt* накáпливать (накопи́ть* *perf*) ♦ *vi* накáпливаться (накопи́ться* *perf*).

accumulation [əkjuːmjuˈleɪʃən] *n* накоплéние.

accuracy [ˈækjurəsɪ] *n* тóчность *f*.

accurate [ˈækjurɪt] *adj* тóчный* (тóчен); (*person, device*) аккурáтный* (аккурáтен); (*shot*) мéткий*.

accurately [ˈækjurɪtlɪ] *adv* тóчно; (*shoot*) мéтко.

accusation [ækjuˈzeɪʃən] *n* обвинéние.

accusative [əˈkjuːzətɪv] *n* (*LING*) вини́тельный падéж*.

accuse [əˈkjuːz] *vt*: **to ~ sb (of sth)** обвиня́ть (обвини́ть *perf*) когó-н (в чём-н).

accused [əˈkjuːzd] *n* (*LAW*): **the ~** обвиня́емый(-ая) *m(f) adj*.

accuser [əˈkjuːzə] *n* обвини́тель *m*.

accusing [əˈkjuːzɪŋ] *adj* обвиня́ющий.

accustom [əˈkʌstəm] *vt* приучáть (приучи́ть* *perf*); **to ~ o.s. to sth** приучáться (приучи́ться* *perf*) or привыкáть (привы́кнуть* *perf*) к чемý-н.

accustomed [əˈkʌstəmd] *adj* (*usual*) привы́чный*; **I'm ~ to working late/to the heat** я привы́к рабóтать пóздно/к жарý.

AC/DC *abbr* (= *alternating current/direct current*) перемéнный ток/постоя́нный ток.

ACE [eɪs] *n abbr* = *American Council on Education*.

ace [eɪs] *n* (*CARDS*) туз; (*TENNIS*) вы́игрыш с подáчи.

acerbic [əˈsɜːbɪk] *adj* (*remark*) éдкий* (éдок).

acetate [ˈæsɪteɪt] *n* ацетáт.

ache [eɪk] *n* боль *f* ♦ *vi* (*be painful*) болéть (*impf*); (*yearn*): **to ~ to do** томи́ться* (*impf*) желáнием +*infin*; **I've got stomach ~** or **a stomach ~** у меня́ боли́т живóт; **I'm aching all over** у меня́ всё тéло нóет; **my head ~s** у меня́ боли́т голова́.

achieve [əˈtʃiːv] *vt* (*aim, result*) достигáть (дости́гнуть *or* дости́чь* *perf*) +*gen*; (*success, victory*) добивáться (доби́ться* *perf*) +*gen*.

achievement [əˈtʃiːvmənt] *n* достижéние.

Achilles heel [əˈkɪliːz-] *n* Ахиллéсова пятá.

acid [ˈæsɪd] *adj* (*CHEM: soil etc*) кислóтный*; (*taste*) ки́слый* ♦ *n* (*CHEM*) кислотá*; (*inf: DRUGS*) ЛСД (*наркóтик*).

acid house *n* áсид хáус (*стиль поп-мýзыки*).

acidic [əˈsɪdɪk] *adj* ки́слый* (кисл).

acidity [əˈsɪdɪtɪ] *n* кислóтность *f*.

acid rain *n* кислóтный* дождь* *m*.

acid test *n* прóбный кáмень* *m*.

acknowledge [əkˈnɒlɪdʒ] *vt* (*letter etc: also: ~ receipt of*) подтверждáть (подтверди́ть* *perf*) получéние +*gen*; (*fact, situation*) признавáть* (признáть *perf*).

acknowledgement [əkˈnɒlɪdʒmənt] *n* (*of letter etc*) подтверждéние получéния; ~**s** *npl* (*in book*) выражéние *ntsg* благодáрности (*в предислóвии кни́ги*).

ACLU *n abbr* = *American Civil Liberties Union*.

acme [ˈækmɪ] *n* верх*, верши́на.

acne [ˈæknɪ] *n* угри́* *mpl*, прыщи́ *mpl*.

acorn [ˈeɪkɔːn] *n* жёлудь *m*.

acoustic [əˈkuːstɪk] *adj* (*guitar etc*) акусти́ческий*.

acoustic coupler *n* (*COMPUT*) акусти́ческий* соедини́тель *m*.

acoustics [əˈkuːstɪks] *n* (*science*) акýстика ♦ *npl* (*of hall, room*) акýстика *fsg*.

---

* marks translations which have irregular inflections. The Russian-English side of the dictionary gives inflectional information.

acquaint [əˈkweɪnt] *vt*: **to ~ sb with sth** (*inform*) ознако́мить* (*perf*) кого́-н с чем-н; **I am/was ~ed with** (*person, fact*) я знако́м/был знако́м с +*instr*.

acquaintance [əˈkweɪntəns] *n* (*person*) знако́мый(-ая) *m(f) adj*; (*with person, subject*) знако́мство; **to make sb's ~** познако́миться* (*perf*) с кем-н.

acquiesce [ækwɪˈɛs] *vi*: **to ~ to** соглаша́ться (согласи́ться* *perf*) на +*acc*.

acquire [əˈkwaɪəʳ] *vt* приобрета́ть (приобрести́* *perf*).

acquired [əˈkwaɪəd] *adj* приобретённый; **it's an ~ taste** к э́тому на́до привы́кнуть.

acquisition [ækwɪˈzɪʃən] *n* приобрете́ние.

acquisitive [əˈkwɪzɪtɪv] *adj* (*greedy*) приобрета́тельский.

acquit [əˈkwɪt] *vt* (*LAW*) опра́вдывать (оправда́ть *perf*); **to ~ o.s. well** хорошо́ проявля́ть (прояви́ть* *perf*) себя́.

acquittal [əˈkwɪtl] *n* оправда́ние.

acre [ˈeɪkəʳ] *n* акр.

acreage [ˈeɪkərɪdʒ] *n* пло́щадь* *f* в а́крах.

acrid [ˈækrɪd] *adj* е́дкий* (е́док).

acrimonious [ækrɪˈməunɪəs] *adj* язви́тельный* (язви́телен).

acrimony [ˈækrɪmənɪ] *n* язви́тельность *f*.

acrobat [ˈækrəbæt] *n* акроба́т.

acrobatic [ækrəˈbætɪk] *adj* (*movement, display*) акробати́ческий; (*person*) ги́бкий* (ги́бок) и ло́вкий* (ло́вок).

acrobatics [ækrəˈbætɪks] *npl* акроба́тика *fsg*.

acronym [ˈækrənɪm] *n* бу́квенная аббревиату́ра.

Acropolis [əˈkrɔpəlɪs] *n*: **the ~** (*GEO*) Акро́поль *m*.

across [əˈkrɔs] *prep* (*from one side to the other of*) че́рез +*acc*; (*on the other side of*) на друго́й стороне́ +*gen*; (*crosswise over*) поперёк +*gen* ♦ *adv* на ту́ *or* другу́ю сто́рону; (*measurement: width*) ширино́й; **to walk ~ the road** переходи́ть* (перейти́* *perf*) доро́гу; **to take sb ~ the road** переводи́ть* (перевести́* *perf*) кого́-н че́рез доро́гу; **a road ~ the wood** доро́га че́рез лес; **the lake is 12 km ~** ширина́ о́зера – 12 км; **~ from** напро́тив +*gen*; **to get sth ~ (to sb)** втолко́вывать (втолкова́ть *perf*) что-н (кому́-н).

acrylic [əˈkrɪlɪk] *adj* акри́ловый ♦ *n* акри́л; **~s** *npl* (*ART*) акри́ловые кра́ски *fpl*.

ACT *n abbr* = **American College Test**.

act [ækt] *n* (*action, also LAW*) акт; (*deed*) посту́пок*; (*of play*) де́йствие, акт; (*in music-hall etc*) но́мер* ♦ *vi* (*do sth, take action*) де́йствовать* (*impf*); (*behave*) вести́* (*impf*) себя́; (*have effect*) де́йствовать (поде́йствовать *perf*); (*THEAT*) игра́ть (сыгра́ть *perf*); (*pretend*) разы́грывать (разыгра́ть *perf*) ♦ *vt* (*part*) игра́ть (сыгра́ть *perf*); **it's only an ~** э́то всего́ лишь игра́; **~ of God** (*LAW*) стихи́йное бе́дствие; **in the ~ of** в проце́ссе +*gen*; **to catch sb in the ~** пойма́ть (*perf*) кого́-н на ме́сте преступле́ния; **to ~ as** де́йствовать* (*impf*) в ка́честве +*gen*; **it ~s as a deterrent** э́то де́йствует в ка́честве сде́рживающей си́лы; **~ing in my capacity as chairman, I** ... выступа́я в ка́честве преседа́теля, я ...; **to ~ the fool** (*BRIT*) валя́ть (сваля́ть *perf*) дурака́

▸ **act on** *vt*: **to ~ on sth** де́йствовать (поде́йствовать *perf*) на что-н

▸ **act out** *vt* (*event*) разы́грывать (разыгра́ть *perf*); (*fantasies*) выплёскивать (вы́плеснуть *perf*).

acting [ˈæktɪŋ] *adj*: **~ manager/director** исполня́ющий обя́занности управля́ющего/дире́ктора ♦ *n* (*activity, profession*) актёрская профе́ссия.

action [ˈækʃən] *n* (*deed*) де́йствие; (*motion*) движе́ние; (*MIL*) вое́нные де́йствия *ntpl*; (*LAW*) иск; **to bring an ~ against sb** (*LAW*) предъявля́ть (предъяви́ть* *perf*) иск кому́-н; **he was killed in ~** (*MIL*) он был уби́т в бою́; **she/the machine was out of ~ for a week** она́/маши́на вы́шла из стро́я на неде́лю; **to take ~** принима́ть (приня́ть* *perf*) ме́ры; **to put a plan into ~** реализо́вывать (реализова́ть *perf*) план.

action replay *n* (*TV*) повторе́ние ка́дра (*ча́сто заме́дленное*).

activate [ˈæktɪveɪt] *vt* (*mechanism*) приводи́ть* (привести́* *perf*) в де́йствие; (*CHEM*) активи́ровать (*impf/perf*); (*PHYS*) де́лать (сде́лать *perf*) радиоакти́вным.

active [ˈæktɪv] *adj* (*person, life*) акти́вный* (акти́вен); (*volcano*) де́йствующий*; **to play an ~ part in** игра́ть (сыгра́ть *perf*) акти́вную роль в +*prp*.

active duty *n* (*US: MIL*) де́йствующая а́рмия.

actively [ˈæktɪvlɪ] *adv* (*participate*) акти́вно; (*discourage, dislike*) си́льно.

active partner *n* (*COMM*) гла́вный партнёр с ограни́ченной (иму́щественной) отве́тственностью.

active service *n* (*BRIT: MIL*) де́йствующая а́рмия.

active suspension *n* автомати́ческая систе́ма амортиза́ции го́ночного автомоби́ля, реаги́рующая на ка́чество пове́рхности.

activist [ˈæktɪvɪst] *n* активи́ст(ка).

activity [ækˈtɪvɪtɪ] *n* (*being active*) акти́вность *f*; (*action*) де́ятельность *f*; (*pastime, pursuit*) заня́тие.

actor [ˈæktəʳ] *n* актёр.

actress [ˈæktrɪs] *n* актри́са.

actual [ˈæktjuəl] *adj* (*real*) действи́тельный* (действи́телен); (*emphatic use*): **the ~ work hasn't begun yet** сама́ рабо́та ещё не начала́сь.

actually [ˈæktjuəlɪ] *adv* (*really*) действи́тельно; (*in fact*) факти́чески, на са́мом де́ле; (*even*) да́же.

actuary ['æktjuərɪ] *n* (*COMM*) актуа́рий.

actuate ['æktjueɪt] *vt* приводи́ть* (привести́* *perf*) в де́йствие.

acuity [ə'kju:ɪtɪ] *n* острота́.

acumen ['ækjumən] *n* сообрази́тельность *f*; **business** ~ делова́я хва́тка*.

acupuncture ['ækjupʌŋktʃə'] *n* иглоука́лывание, акупункту́ра.

acute [ə'kju:t] *adj* (*illness, mind, angle*) о́стрый* (остр); (*anxiety*) си́льный*; (*person, observer*) проница́тельный* (проница́телен); (*LING*): ~ **accent** аку́т.

AD *adv abbr* (= *Anno Domini*) н.э.= *на́шей э́ры* ♦ *n abbr* (*US*: *MIL*) = **active duty**.

ad [æd] *n abbr* (*inf*) = **advertisement**.

adage ['ædɪdʒ] *n* погово́рка*.

adamant ['ædəmənt] *adj* непрекло́нный* (непрекло́нен).

Adam's apple ['ædəmz-] *n* ада́мово я́блоко*, кады́к*.

adapt [ə'dæpt] *vt* (*alter, change*) приспоса́бливать {or) приспособля́ть (приспосо́бить* *perf*) ♦ *vi*: **to** ~ (**to**) приспоса́бливаться *or* приспособля́ться (приспосо́биться* *perf*) *or* адапти́роваться (*impf/perf*) (к +*dat*).

adaptability [ədæptə'bɪlɪtɪ] *n* приспособ-ля́емость *f*.

adaptable [ə'dæptəbl] *adj* (*device*) приспособля́емый; (*person*) легко́ приспоса́бливающийся.

adaptation [ædæp'teɪʃən] *n* (*of story, novel etc*) переложе́ние; (*of machine, equipment etc*) приспособле́ние.

adapter [ə'dæptə'] *n* (*ELEC*) ада́птер, переходни́к.

adaptor [ə'dæptə'] *n* = **adapter**.

ADC *n abbr* (*MIL*) = **aide-de-camp**; (*US*: = *Aid to Dependent Children*) по́мощь нужда́ющимся де́тям.

add [æd] *vt* (*to a collection etc*) прибавля́ть (приба́вить* *perf*); (*comment etc*) добавля́ть (доба́вить* *perf*); (*figures: also*: ~ **up**) скла́дывать (сложи́ть* *perf*), сумми́ровать (*impf/perf*) ♦ *vi*: **to** ~ **to** (*increase*) увели́чивать (увели́чить *perf*)

► **add on** *vt*: ~ **on** (**to**) прибавля́ть (приба́вить* *perf*) (к +*dat*)

► **add up** *vt* скла́дываться (сложи́ться *perf*) в +*acc* ♦ *vi* (*fig*): **it doesn't** ~ **up** концы́ не схо́дятся; **it doesn't** ~ **up to much** (*fig*) э́то не впечатля́ет.

addenda [ə'dɛndə] *npl of* **addendum**.

addendum [ə'dɛndəm] (*pl* **addenda**) *n* приложе́ние.

adder ['ædə'] *n* гадю́ка.

addict ['ædɪkt] *n* (*also*: **drug** ~) наркома́н;

(*enthusiast*) фана́тик.

addicted [ə'dɪktɪd] *adj*: **to be** ~ **to** (*drugs, drink etc*) пристрасти́ться* (*perf*) к +*dat*; (*fig*): **he's** ~ **to football/golf** он зая́длый люби́тель футбо́ла/го́льфа.

addiction [ə'dɪkʃən] *n* пристра́стие; **drug** ~ наркома́ния.

addictive [ə'dɪktɪv] *adj* (*drug*) вызыва́ющий* привыка́ние; (*activity*) захва́тывающий*.

adding machine ['ædɪŋ-] *n* счётная маши́на.

Addis Ababa ['ædɪs'æbəbə] *n* (*GEO*) Адди́с-Абе́ба *f*.

addition [ə'dɪʃən] *n* (*MATH*) сложе́ние; (*thing added*) добавле́ние; (*to collection*) пополне́ние; **in** ~ вдоба́вок; **in** ~ **to** в дополне́ние к +*dat*.

additional [ə'dɪʃənl] *adj* дополни́тельный*.

additive ['ædɪtɪv] *n* доба́вка*.

addled ['ædld] *adj* (*BRIT*: *egg*) ту́хлый*; **his brain is** ~ он сбит с то́лку.

address [ə'drɛs] *n* а́дрес*; (*speech*) речь* *f* ♦ *vt* (*letter, parcel*) адресова́ть (*impf/perf*); (*person, problem*) обраща́ться (обрати́ться* *perf*) к +*dat*; **form of** ~ фо́рма обраще́ния; **absolute/ relative** ~ (*COMPUT*) абсолю́тный/ относи́тельный а́дрес; **to** ~ **o.s. to** обраща́ться (обрати́ться* *perf*) к +*dat*.

address book *n* записна́я кни́жка.

addressee [ædrɛ'si:] *n* адреса́т.

Aden ['eɪdən] *n*: **Gulf of** ~ А́денский зали́в.

adenoids ['ædɪnɔɪdz] *npl* адено́иды *mpl*.

adept ['ædɛpt] *adj*: ~ **at** иску́сный* (иску́сен) +*prp*.

adequacy ['ædɪkwəsɪ] *n* (*in quantity*) доста́точность *f*; (*in quality*) адеква́тность *f*.

adequate ['ædɪkwɪt] *adj* (*sufficient*) доста́точный (доста́точен); (*satisfactory*) удовлетвори́тельный (удовлетвори́телен), адеква́тный* (адеква́тен).

adequately ['ædɪkwɪtlɪ] *adv* адеква́тно.

adhere [əd'hɪə'] *vi*: **to** ~ **to** прилипа́ть (прили́пнуть* *perf*) к +*dat*; (*fig*) приде́рживаться (*impf*) +*gen*.

adhesion [əd'hi:ʒən] *n* прилипа́ние; (*fig*) приве́рженность *f*.

adhesive [əd'hi:zɪv] *adj* кле́йкий* ♦ *n* клей*.

adhesive tape *n* (*BRIT*) кле́йкая ле́нта; (*US*: *MED*) лейкопла́стырь *m*.

ad hoc [æd'hɔk] *adj* (*decision*) момента́льный; (*committee*) со́зданный на ме́сте ♦ *adv* (*decide, appoint*) тут же.

ad infinitum ['ædɪnfɪ'naɪtəm] *adv* до бесконе́чности.

adjacent [ə'dʒeɪsənt] *adj*: ~ (**to**) сме́жный* (сме́жен) (с +*instr*).

adjective ['ædʒɛktɪv] *n* прилага́тельное *nt adj*.

adjoining [ə'dʒɔɪnɪŋ] *adj* (*room*) сме́жный.

adjourn [ə'dʒə:n] *vt* откла́дывать (отложи́ть*

---

* marks translations which have irregular inflections. The Russian-English side of the dictionary gives inflectional information.

perf) ◆ *vi*: **the meeting ~ed** собрáние бы́ло отло́жено; **to ~ a meeting till the following week** отложи́ть* *(perf)* заседáние до слéдующей недéли; **they ~ed to the restaurant** (*BRIT: inf*) они перебрáлись в ресторáн.

adjournment [ə'dʒə:nmənt] *n* (*period*) перерыв.

Adjt. *abbr* (*MIL*) = **adjutant.**

adjudicate [ə'dʒu:dɪkeɪt] *vt* (*claim*) рассмáтривать (рассмотрéть* *perf*); (*competition*) суди́ть* (*impf*) ◆ *vi* суди́ть* (*impf*).

adjudication [ədʒu:dɪ'keɪʃən] *n* (*LAW*) решéние судá.

adjudicator [ə'dju:dɪkeɪtə'] *n* судья́* *m/f.*

adjust [ə'dʒʌst] *vt* (*plans, views*) приспосáбливать (приспособить *perf*); (*clothing*) поправля́ть (попрáвить* *perf*); (*mechanism*) регули́ровать (отрегули́ровать *perf*) ◆ *vi*: **to ~ (to)** приспосáбливаться (приспособиться* *perf*) (к +*dat*).

adjustable [ə'dʒʌstəbl] *adj* регули́руемый.

adjuster [ə'dʒʌstə'] *n see* **loss.**

adjustment [ə'dʒʌstmənt] *n* (*to surroundings*) адаптáция; (*of prices, wages*) регули́рование; **to make ~s to** вноси́ть* (внести́* *perf*) изменéния в +*acc*.

adjutant ['ædʒətənt] *n* адъютáнт.

ad-lib [æd'lɪb] *vti* импровизи́ровать (симпровизи́ровать *perf*) ◆ *adv*: **ad lib** (*speak*) экспро́мтом.

adman ['ædmæn] *irreg n* (*inf*) реклами́ст.

admin ['ædmɪn] *n abbr* (*inf*) = **administration.**

administer [əd'mɪnɪstə'] *vt* (*country, department*) управля́ть (*impf*) +*instr*, руководи́ть* (*impf*) +*instr*; (*justice*) отправля́ть (*impf*); (*test*) проводи́ть* (провести́* *perf*); (*drug*) вводи́ть* (ввести́* *perf*).

administration [ədmɪnɪs'treɪʃən] *n* (*management*) администрáция; **the A~** (*US*) прави́тельство; **the Clinton A~** администрáция Кли́нтона.

administrative [əd'mɪnɪstrətɪv] *adj* админи-страти́вный.

administrator [əd'mɪnɪstreɪtə'] *n* админи-стрáтор.

admirable ['ædmərəbl] *adj* (*quality*) восхити́тельный* (восхити́телен); (*action*) замечáтельный* (замечáтелен).

admiral ['ædmərəl] *n* адмирáл.

Admiralty ['ædmərəltɪ] *n* (*BRIT*): **the ~** (*also*: **the ~ Board**) ≈ адмиралтéйство (*воéнно-морскоé вéдомство*).

admiration [ædmə'reɪʃən] *n* восхищéние; **I have great ~ for her** онá вызывáет у меня большóе восхищéние.

admire [əd'maɪə'] *vt* (*respect, appreciate*) восхищáться (восхити́ться *perf*) +*instr*; (*gaze at*) любовáться (*impf*) +*instr*.

admirer [əd'maɪərə'] *n* покло́нник(-ица).

admiring [əd'maɪərɪŋ] *adj* восхищённый (восхищён), восто́рженный* (восто́ржен).

admissible [əd'mɪsəbl] *adj* приéмлемый (приéмлем), допусти́мый (допусти́м); **it is ~ evidence** э́то мо́жет быть* при́нято в кáчестве доказáтельства.

admission [əd'mɪʃən] *n* (*admittance*) до́пуск; (*entry fee*) входнáя плáта; (*confession*) признáние; **to gain ~ to** (*official permission*) получáть (получи́ть* *perf*) до́пуск в/на +*acc*; **"admission free", "free ~"** "вход свобо́дный"; **by his own ~** по его́ со́бственному признáнию.

admit [əd'mɪt] *vt* (*confess, accept*) признавáть* (признáть* *perf*); (*permit to enter*) впускáть (впусти́ть* *perf*); (*to club, organization*) принимáть (приня́ть* *perf*); (*to hospital*) госпитализи́ровать (*impf/perf*); **"children not ~ted"** "дéтям вход воспрещён"; **this ticket ~s two** э́тот билéт нá два лицá

▶ **admit of** *vt fus* (*allow*) допускáть (*impf*)

▶ **admit to** *vt fus* (*murder etc*) сознавáться* (сознáться *perf*) в +*instr*.

admittance [əd'mɪtəns] *n* до́пуск; **no ~** вход воспрещён.

admittedly [əd'mɪtɪdlɪ] *adv*: **~ it is not easy** признáться, э́то не легко́.

admonish [əd'mɔnɪʃ] *vt* дéлать (сдéлать *perf*) внушéние +*dat*; (*LAW*) дéлать (сдéлать *perf*) предупреждéние +*dat*.

ad nauseam [æd'nɔ:sɪæm] *adv* бесконéчно.

ado [ə'du:] *n*: **without (any) more ~** без дальнéйших церемо́ний.

adolescence [ædəu'lɛsns] *n* подростко́вый во́зраст.

adolescent [ædəu'lɛsnt] *adj* подростко́вый ◆ *n* подро́сток*.

adopt [ə'dɔpt] *vt* (*son*) усыновля́ть (усынови́ть* *perf*); (*daughter*) удочеря́ть (удочери́ть *perf*); (*policy*) придéрживаться (*impf*) +*gen*; **to ~ sb as a candidate** выдвигáть (вы́двинуть *perf*) кого́-н в кандидáты.

adopted [ə'dɔptɪd] *adj* (*child*) приёмный.

adoption [ə'dɔpʃən] *n* (*see vb*) усыновлéние; удочерéние; приня́тие.

adoptive [ə'dɔptɪv] *adj* (*parent*) приёмный.

adorable [ə'dɔ:rəbl] *adj* прелéстный* (прелéстен).

adoration [ædə'reɪʃən] *n* (*of person*) обожáние.

adore [ə'dɔ:'] *vt* обожáть (*impf*).

adoring [ə'dɔ:rɪŋ] *adj* обожáющий.

adoringly [ə'dɔ:rɪŋlɪ] *adv* с обожáнием.

adorn [ə'dɔ:n] *vt* украшáть (укрáсить* *perf*).

adornment [ə'dɔ:nmənt] *n* украшéние.

ADP *n abbr* = **automatic data processing.**

adrenalin [ə'drɛnəlɪn] *n* адреналин; **to get the ~ going** давáть* (дать* *perf*) заря́д энéргии.

Adriatic [eɪdrɪ'ætɪk] *n*: **the ~** Адриáтика.

adrift [ə'drɪft] *adv* (*NAUT*): **to be ~** дрейфовáть (*impf*); (*fig*) плыть* (*impf*) по течéнию; **to go ~**

(*plans etc*) расстра́иваться (расстро́иться *perf*); **to come** ~ (*boat*) лечь* (*perf*) в дрейф; (*fastening*) расслабля́ться (рассла́биться *perf*).

adroit [ə'drɔɪt] *adj* ло́вкий* (ло́вок).

adroitly [ə'drɔɪtlɪ] *adv* ло́вко.

ADT *abbr* (*US*) = Atlantic Daylight Time.

adulation [ædju'leɪʃən] *n* обожа́ние.

adult ['ædʌlt] *n* взро́слый(-ая) *m adj* ♦ *adj* (*grown-up*) взро́слый; (*for adults*) для взро́слых.

adult education *n* образова́ние для взро́слых.

adulterate [ə'dʌltəreɪt] *vt* (*food, drink*: *with additives*) по́ртить* (испо́ртить* *perf*) (доба́вками); (: *with water*) разбавля́ть (разба́вить* *perf*).

adulterer [ə'dʌltərə'] *n* неве́рный муж.

adulteress [ə'dʌltərɪs] *n* неве́рная жена́.

adultery [ə'dʌltərɪ] *n* супру́жеская неве́рность *f*.

adulthood ['ædʌlthud] *n* зре́лый во́зраст.

advance [əd'vɑːns] *n* (*progress*) успе́х; (*MIL*) наступле́ние; (*movement*) продвиже́ние; (*money*) ава́нс ♦ *adj* (*booking*) предвари́тельный ♦ *vt* (*theory, idea*) выдвига́ть (вы́двинуть *perf*) ♦ *vi* (*move forward*: *also fig*) продвига́ться (продви́нуться *perf*) вперёд; (*MIL*) наступа́ть (*impf*); **in** ~ предвари́тельно, зара́нее; **to make ~s (to sb)** заи́грывать (*impf*) (с кем-н); **to give sb** ~ **notice** *or* ~ **warning (of sth)** предупрежда́ть (предупреди́ть* *perf*) кого́-н зара́нее (о чём-н); **to** ~ **sb money** плати́ть* (заплати́ть* *perf*) кому́-н ава́нсом; **we** ~**d 20 km** мы продви́нулись на 20 киломе́тров.

advanced [əd'vɑːnst] *adj* (*studies, course*) для продви́нутого у́ровня; (*child, country*) разви́той* (ра́звит); (*ideas, views*) прогресси́вный* (прогресси́вен); ~ **maths** вы́сшая матема́тика; **a man of** ~ **years** *or* ~ **in years** челове́к прекло́нного во́зраста.

advancement [əd'vɑːnsmənt] *n* (*of science*) прогре́сс; (*in job, rank*) продвиже́ние (по слу́жбе).

advancing [əd'vɑːnsɪŋ] *adj* надвига́ющийся.

advantage [əd'vɑːntɪdʒ] *n* преиму́щество; (*TENNIS*) "бо́льше"; **to take** ~ **of** (*person*) испо́льзовать (*perf*); (*sb's hospitality*) злоупотребля́ть (злоупотреби́ть* *perf*) +*instr*; (*opportunity*) воспо́льзоваться (*perf*) +*instr*; **to our/his** ~ в на́ших/его́ интере́сах; **to turn sth to one's** ~ обраща́ть (обрати́ть* *perf*) что-н в свою́ по́льзу.

advantageous [ædvən'teɪdʒəs] *adj* (*position, situation*) вы́годный* (вы́годен); **it's** ~ **to us** нам э́то вы́годно.

advent ['ædvənt] *n* появле́ние; (*REL*): **A**~ *ме́сяц*

до Рождества́.

Advent calendar *n* календа́рь с две́рцами на ка́ждый день ме́сяца до Рождества́.

adventure [əd'vɛntʃə'] *n* (*exciting event*) приключе́ние; **to look for** ~ иска́ть* (*impf*) приключе́ний.

adventure playground *n* де́тская игрова́я площа́дка.

adventurous [əd'vɛntʃərəs] *adj* (*action*) риско́ванный (риско́ван); (*person*) сме́лый (смел); **an** ~ **life** жизнь по́лная приключе́ний.

adverb ['ædvəːb] *n* наре́чие.

adversarial [ædvə'sɛərɪəl] *adj* противо-бо́рствующий.

adversary ['ædvəsərɪ] *n* проти́вник(-ница).

adverse ['ædvəːs] *adj* неблагоприя́тный; **in** ~ **circumstances** при неблагоприя́тных обстоя́тельствах.

adversity [əd'vəːsɪtɪ] *n* бе́дствие, несча́стие.

advert ['ædvəːt] *n abbr* (*BRIT*) = advertisement.

advertise ['ædvətaɪz] *vti* реклами́ровать (*impf*); **to** ~ **on television/in a newspaper** дава́ть* (дать* *perf*) рекла́му по телеви́дению/в газе́ту; **to** ~ **a job** объявля́ть (объяви́ть* *perf*) ко́нкурс на ме́сто; **to** ~ **for staff/accommodation** дава́ть* (дать* *perf*) объявле́ние, что тре́буется рабо́тники/жильё.

advertisement [əd'vəːtɪsmənt] *n* рекла́ма; (*in classified ads*) объявле́ние.

advertiser ['ædvətaɪzə'] *n* (*professional*) реклами́ст(ка); (*in newspaper, on television etc*) рекламода́тель *m*.

advertising ['ædvətaɪzɪŋ] *n* рекла́ма.

advertising agency *n* рекла́мное аге́нтство.

advertising campaign *n* рекла́мная кампа́ния.

advice [əd'vaɪs] *n* сове́т; (*notification*) уведомле́ние, извеще́ние; **a piece of** ~ сове́т; **to ask sb for** ~ (*friend*) (посове́товаться *perf*) с кем-н; (*professional*) обраща́ться (обрати́ться* *perf*) (за сове́том) к кому́-н; **to take legal** ~ обраща́ться (обрати́ться* *perf*) (за сове́том) к юри́сту.

advice note *n* (*BRIT*) извеще́ние.

advisable [əd'vaɪzəbl] *adj* целесообра́зный* (целесообра́зен).

advise [əd'vaɪz] *vt* сове́товать (посове́товать *perf*) +*dat*; (*professionally*) консульти́ровать (проконсульти́ровать *perf*) +*gen*; (*inform*): **to** ~ **sb of sth** извеща́ть (извести́ть* *perf*) кого́-н о чём-н; **to** ~ (**sb**) **against doing** отсове́товать (*perf*) (кому́-н) +*impf infin*; **you would be well-/ill-**~**d to go** Вам бы сле́довало пойти́/не сле́довало ходи́ть ....

advisedly [əd'vaɪzɪdlɪ] *adv* наме́ренно.

adviser [əd'vaɪzə'] *n* сове́тник, консульта́нт;

---

* marks translations which have irregular inflections. The Russian-English side of the dictionary gives inflectional information.

legal ~ юрисконсульт.
advisor [əd'vaɪzəʳ] *n* = **adviser**.
advisory [əd'vaɪzərɪ] *adj* (*body, role*)
консультати́вный; **in an ~ capacity** в
ка́честве сове́тника *or* консульта́нта.
advocate [*vb* 'ædvəkeɪt, *n* 'ædvəkɪt] *vt*
выступа́ть (*impf*) за +*acc* ♦ *n* (*LAW*) защи́тник,
адвока́т; (*supporter*): ~ **of** сторо́нник(-ица)
+*gen*.
advt. *abbr* = **advertisement**.
AEA *n abbr* (*BRIT*: = *Atomic Energy Authority*)
Управле́ние а́томной эне́ргии.
AEC *n abbr* (*US*: = *Atomic Energy Commission*)
Коми́ссия по а́томной эне́ргии.
AEEU *n abbr* (*BRIT*) = *Amalgamated Engineering
and Electrical Union.*
Aegean [iː'dʒiːən] *n*: **the** ~ Эге́йское Мо́ре.
aegis ['iːdʒɪs] *n*: **under the** ~ **of** под
эги́дой +*gen*.
aeon ['iːən] *n*: **for** ~**s** це́лую ве́чность.
aerial ['ɛərɪəl] *n* анте́нна ♦ *adj* возду́шный*; ~
photography аэрофотосъёмка.
aerobatics ['ɛərəʊ'bætɪks] *npl* вы́сший*
пилота́ж *msg*.
aerobics [ɛə'rəʊbɪks] *n* аэро́бика.
aerodrome ['ɛərədrəʊm] *n* (*BRIT*) аэродро́м.
aerodynamic ['ɛərəʊdaɪ'næmɪk] *adj*
аэродинами́ческий*.
aeronautics [ɛərə'nɔːtɪks] *n* аэрона́втика.
aeroplane ['ɛərəpleɪn] *n* (*BRIT*) самолёт.
aerosol ['ɛərəsɔl] *n* аэрозо́ль *m*.
aerospace industry ['ɛərəʊspeɪs-] *n*
аэро-косми́ческая промы́шленность *f*.
aesthetic [iːs'θɛtɪk] *adj* эстети́ческий*.
aesthetically [iːs'θɛtɪklɪ] *adv* эстети́чески.
afar [ə'fɑː'] *adv*: **from** ~ издалека́.
AFB *n abbr* (*US*) = *Air Force Base.*
AFDC *n abbr* (*US*) = *Aid to Families with
Dependent Children.*
affable ['æfəbl] *adj* (*person*) добродуш́ный*
(добродуш́ен); (*behaviour*)
доброжела́тельный* (доброжела́телен).
affair [ə'fɛəʳ] *n* (*matter*) де́ло*; (*also:* **love** ~)
рома́н; ~**s** *npl* (*business*) дела́* *ntpl*.
affect [ə'fɛkt] *vt* (*influence*) де́йствовать
(поде́йствовать *perf*) на +*acc*, влия́ть
(повлия́ть *perf*) на +*acc*; (*afflict*) поража́ть
(порази́ть* *perf*); (*move deeply*) тро́гать
(тро́нуть *perf*); (*feign*) каса́ться (косну́ться
perf); **to** ~ **an American accent** говори́ть (*impf*)
с де́ланным америка́нским акце́нтом.
affectation [æfɛk'teɪʃən] *n* (*in manner, speech*)
наи́гранность *f*.
affected [ə'fɛktɪd] *adj* (*person*) претенцио́зный*
(претенцио́зен); (*manner*) де́ланный.
affection [ə'fɛkʃən] *n* привя́занность *f*.
affectionate [ə'fɛkʃənɪt] *adj* не́жный*.
affectionately [ə'fɛkʃənɪtlɪ] *adv* не́жно.
affidavit [æfɪ'deɪvɪt] *n* (*LAW*) пи́сьменное
свиде́тельство, афида́вит.
affiliated [ə'fɪlieɪtɪd] *adj* (*company*) доче́рний*;

to be ~ **to** (*body*) явля́ться (*impf*) филиа́лом
+*gen*.
affinity [ə'fɪnɪtɪ] *n*: **to have an** ~ **with** (*bond*)
ощуща́ть (ощути́ть* *perf*) бли́зость с +*instr*;
(*resemblance*) обнару́живать (обнару́жить
perf) родство́ с +*instr*.
affirm [ə'fəːm] *vt* утвержда́ть (утверди́ть* *perf*).
affirmation [æfə'meɪʃən] *n* (*of facts*)
подтвержде́ние; (*of ideas*) утвержде́ние.
affirmative [ə'fəːmətɪv] *adj* утверди́тельный*
♦ *n*: **in the** ~ утверди́тельно.
affix [ə'fɪks] *vt* прикрепля́ть (прикрепи́ть* *perf*).
afflict [ə'flɪkt] *vt* постига́ть (пости́чь* *perf*); **to
be** ~**ed by** (*illness*) страда́ть (*impf*) от +*gen*.
affliction [ə'flɪkʃən] *n* несча́стье.
affluence ['æfluəns] *n* благосостоя́ние.
affluent ['æfluənt] *adj* благополу́чный*
(благополу́чен); **the** ~ **society** о́бщество
благосостоя́ния.
afford [ə'fɔːd] *vt* позво́лить (*perf*) себе́;
(*provide*) предоставля́ть (предоста́вить*
perf); **I can't** ~ **it** мне э́то не по карма́ну; **can
we** ~ **a car?** мы мо́жем себе́ позво́лить
купи́ть маши́ну?; **I can't** ~ **the time** мне
вре́мя не позволя́ет.
affordable [ə'fɔːdəbl] *adj* досту́пный по цене́.
affray [ə'freɪ] *n* (*BRIT*: *LAW*) дра́ка в
обще́ственном ме́сте.
affront [ə'frʌnt] *n* оскорбле́ние.
affronted [ə'frʌntɪd] *adj* оскорблённый
(оскорблён).
Afghan ['æfgæn] *adj* афга́нский ♦ *n*
афга́нец*(-нка).
Afghanistan [æf'gænɪstæn] *n* Афганиста́н.
afield [ə'fiːld] *adv*: **far** ~ вдалеке́, вдали́; **from
far** ~ издалека́.
AFL-CIO *n abbr* = *American Federation of Labor
and Congress of Industrial Organizations.*
afloat [ə'fləʊt] *adv* (*floating*) на плаву́; **to stay** ~
(*fig*) держа́ться (*impf*) на пове́рхности; **to
keep a business** ~ не дава́ть* (дать* *perf*)
потону́ть предприя́тию.
afoot [ə'fʊt] *adv*: **there is something** ~ что́-то
затева́ется.
aforementioned [ə'fɔːmɛnʃənd] *adj*
вышеупомя́нутый.
aforesaid [ə'fɔːsɛd] *adj* вышеупомя́нутый.
afraid [ə'freɪd] *adj* (*frightened*) испу́ганный
(испу́ган); **to be** ~ **of sth/sb/of doing** боя́ться*
(*impf*) чего́-н/кого́-н/+*infin*; **to be** ~ **to** боя́ться
(побоя́ться *perf*) +*infin*; **I am** ~ **that** (*apology*)
бою́сь, что; **I am** ~ **that I'll be late** бою́сь, что
я опозда́ю; **I am** ~ **so/not** бою́сь, что да/нет.
afresh [ə'frɛʃ] *adv* за́ново.
Africa ['æfrɪkə] *n* А́фрика.
African ['æfrɪkən] *adj* африка́нский* ♦ *n*
африка́нец*(-нка).
Afrikaans [æfrɪ'kɑːns] *n* (*язы́к*) африка́анс.
Afrikaner [æfrɪ'kɑːnəʳ] *n* африка́нер (*урожёнец
Южной Африки голландского
происхождёния*).

Afro-American [ˈæfrəʊəˈmɛrɪkən] *adj* афро-американский*.

Afro-Caribbean [ˈæfrəkærɪˈbiːən] *adj* афро-карибский.

AFT *n abbr* (*US*) = *American Federation of Teachers*.

after [ˈɑːftəʳ] *prep* (*time*) после +*gen*, спустя +*acc*; (*place, order*) за +*instr*; (*style, technique*) в стиле +*gen* ♦ *adv* потом, после ♦ *conj* после того как; ~ **dinner** после обеда; **the day** ~ **tomorrow** послезавтра; ~ **three years they divorced** спустя три года они развелись; **what/who are you** ~? что/кто Вам нужно/нужен?; **the police are** ~ **him** его разыскивает полиция; **to name sb** ~ **sb** называть (назвать* *perf*) кого-н в честь кого-н; **it's twenty** ~ **eight** (*US*) сейчас двадцать минут девятого; **to ask** ~ **sb** справляться (справиться* *perf*) о ком-н; ~ **all** в конце концов; ~ **you!** после Вас!; ~ **he left** после того, как он ушёл; ~ **having done this** сделав это.

afterbirth [ˈɑːftəbəːθ] *n* послед.

aftercare [ˈɑːftəkɛəʳ] *n* (*BRIT: MED*) уход за выздоравливающим.

after-effects [ˈɑːftərɪfɛkts] *npl* последствия *ntpl*.

afterlife [ˈɑːftəlaɪf] *n* загробная жизнь *f*.

aftermath [ˈɑːftəmɑːθ] *n* последствия *ntpl*; **in the** ~ **of** после +*gen*.

afternoon [ˈɑːftəˈnuːn] *n* вторая половина дня; **in the** ~ днём; **good** ~! (*goodbye*) до свидания!; (*hello*) добрый день!

afters [ˈɑːftəz] *n* (*inf: dessert*): **for** ~ на третье *or* десерт.

after-sales service [ɑːftəˈseɪlz-] *n* (*BRIT*) гарантированное техобслуживание.

after-shave (lotion) [ˈɑːftəʃeɪv-] *n* одеколон после бритья.

aftershock [ˈɑːftəʃɔk] *n* толчок* (*после основного землетрясения*).

aftertaste [ˈɑːftəteɪst] *n* привкус.

afterthought [ˈɑːftəθɔːt] *n*: **as an** ~ машинально.

afterward [ˈɑːftəwəd] *adv* (*US*) = **afterwards**.

afterwards [ˈɑːftəwədz] (*US* **afterward**) *adv* позже, потом.

again [əˈgɛn] *adv* (*once more*) ещё раз, снова; (*repeatedly*) опять; **I won't see him/go there** ~ я больше не увижу его/пойду туда; **to do sth** ~ делать (сделать *perf*) что-н ещё раз *or* снова; **to begin** ~ начать* (*perf*) сначала; **to see** ~ смотреть* (посмотреть* *perf*) *or* видеть* (увидеть* *perf*) ещё раз; **he opened the door** ~ он опять *or* снова открыл дверь; ~ **and** ~ снова и снова; **now and** ~ время от времени.

against [əˈgɛnst] *prep* (*lean*) к +*dat*; (*hit, rub*) о +*acc*; (*standing*) у +*gen*; (*in opposition to*)

против +*gen*; (*at odds with*) вопреки +*dat*; (*compared to*) по сравнению с +*instr*; ~ **a blue background** на синем фоне; (**as**) ~ в сравнении с +*instr*.

age [eɪdʒ] *n* (*of person*) возраст; (*period in history*) век* ♦ *vi* (*person*) стареть (постареть *perf*) ♦ *vt* (*subj: hairstyle, dress*) старить (*impf*); **what** ~ **is he?** сколько ему лет?; **he is 20 years of** ~ ему двадцать лет; **under** ~ несовершеннолетний*; **to come of** ~ достигать (достичь* *perf*) совершеннолетия; **it's been** ~**s since I saw you** я не видел Вас целую вечность.

aged[1] [ˈeɪdʒd] *adj*: **a boy** ~ **ten** мальчик десяти лет.

aged[2] [ˈeɪdʒɪd] *npl*: **the** ~ престарелые *pl adj*.

age group *n* возрастная группа; **the forty to fifty** ~ ~ люди возрастом от сорока до пятидесяти лет.

ageing [ˈeɪdʒɪŋ] *adj* стареющий ♦ *n* старение.

ageless [ˈeɪdʒlɪs] *adj* (*building, ritual*) вечный* (вечен).

age limit *n* возрастной предел.

agency [ˈeɪdʒənsɪ] *n* (*COMM*) агентство, бюро *nt ind*; (*government body*) управление; **through** *or* **by the** ~ **of** при посредстве +*gen*.

agenda [əˈdʒɛndə] *n* (*of meeting*) повестка* (дня); **on the** ~ на повестке (дня).

agent [ˈeɪdʒənt] *n* (*representative, spy*) агент; (*COMM*) посредник; (*CHEM*) реактив; (*fig*) фактор.

aggravate [ˈægrəveɪt] *vt* (*situation*) усугублять (усугубить* *perf*); (*person*) раздражать (раздражить *perf*).

aggravating [ˈægrəveɪtɪŋ] *adj*: **his behaviour is** ~ его поведение раздражает меня.

aggravation [ægrəˈveɪʃən] *n* (*see vt*) усугубление; раздражение.

aggregate [ˈægrɪgɪt] *n* (*total*) совокупность *f* ♦ *vt* группировать (сгруппировать *perf*) в +*acc*.

aggression [əˈgrɛʃən] *n* агрессия.

aggressive [əˈgrɛsɪv] *adj* (*belligerent*) агрессивный* (агрессивен); (*assertive*) напористый (напорист).

aggressiveness [əˈgrɛsɪvnɪs] *n* агрессивность *f*.

aggressor [əˈgrɛsəʳ] *n* агрессор.

aggrieved [əˈgriːvd] *adj* огорчённый* (огорчён).

aggro [ˈægrəu] *n* (*inf: aggressive behaviour*) напряжёнка; (*difficulties*) возня.

aghast [əˈgɑːst] *adj*: **to be** ~ **at** быть* (*impf*) в ужасе от +*gen*.

agile [ˈædʒaɪl] *adj* (*person*) проворный* (проворен); (*mind*) живой*.

agility [əˈdʒɪlɪtɪ] *n* подвижность *f*; **mental** ~ живость *f* ума.

agitate [ˈædʒɪteɪt] *vt* (*person*) возбуждать

---

* marks translations which have irregular inflections. The Russian-English side of the dictionary gives inflectional information.

(возбуди́ть* *perf*); (*liquid*) взба́лтывать (взболта́ть *perf*) ◆ *vi*: **to ~ for/against** агити́ровать (сагити́ровать *perf*) за +*acc*/ про́тив +*gen.*

agitated ['ædʒɪteɪtɪd] *adj* возбуждённый* (возбуждён), взволно́ванный (взволно́ван).

agitator ['ædʒɪteɪtə^r] *n* агита́тор.

AGM *n abbr* (= *annual general meeting*) ежего́дное о́бщее собра́ние.

agnostic [æg'nɒstɪk] *n* агно́стик.

ago [ə'gəʊ] *adv*: **two days ~** два дня наза́д; **not long ~** неда́вно; **as long ~ as 1960** ещё в 1960 году́; **how long ~?** как давно́?

agog [ə'gɒg] *adj* (*excited*) взволно́ванный (взволно́ван); **to be (all) ~** (*with anticipation*) сгора́ть (*impf*) от нетерпе́ния.

agonize ['ægənaɪz] *vi*: **he ~d over the problem** он му́чился над пробле́мой.

agonizing ['ægənaɪzɪŋ] *adj* мучи́тельный* (мучи́телен).

agony ['ægənɪ] *n* (*pain*) мучи́тельная боль *f*; (*torment*) му́ка, муче́ние; **to be in ~** му́читься (*impf*) от бо́ли.

agony aunt *n* психо́лог *"по́чты дове́рия"*, отвеча́ющий на вопро́сы чита́телей.

agony column *n* ру́брика *"по́чта дове́рия"*.

agree [ə'gri:] *vt* согласо́вывать (согласова́ть *perf*) ◆ *vi*: **to ~ with** (*have same opinion*) соглаша́ться (согласи́ться *perf*) с +*instr*; (*correspond*) согласова́ться (*impf/perf*) с +*instr*; **to ~ that** согласи́ться* (*perf*), что; **it was ~d that ...** бы́ло решено́, что ...; **the price is still to be ~d** це́ну всё ещё на́до согласова́ть; **I ~ (with you)** я согла́сен (с Ва́ми); **to ~ (with)** (*LING*) согласо́вывать (согласова́ть* *perf*) (с +*instr*); **garlic doesn't ~ with me** я не переношу́ чеснока́; **to ~ on sth** догова́риваться (договори́ться *perf*) о чём-н; **they ~d on this** они́ сошли́сь на э́том; **they ~d on going/on a price** они́ договори́лись пойти́/о цене́; **to ~ to sth/to do** соглаша́ться (согласи́ться* *perf*) на что-н/+*infin*.

agreeable [ə'grɪəbl] *adj* (*pleasant*) прия́тный* (прия́тен); (*willing*) согла́сен; **are you ~ to this?** Вы согла́сны на э́то?

agreed [ə'gri:d] *adj* усло́вленный (усло́влен).

agreement [ə'gri:mənt] *n* (*consent*) согла́сие; (*arrangement*) соглаше́ние, догово́р; **in ~ with** в согла́сии с +*instr*; **we are in complete ~** ме́жду на́ми по́лное согла́сие; **by mutual ~** по взаи́мному соглаше́нию.

agricultural [ægrɪ'kʌltʃərəl] *adj* се́льско-хозя́йственный; **~ land** земе́льные уго́дья *ntpl*.

agriculture ['ægrɪkʌltʃə^r] *n* се́льское хозя́йство.

aground [ə'graʊnd] *adv*: **to run ~** сади́ться* (сесть* *perf*) на мель.

ahead [ə'hɛd] *adv* вперед́и́; (*direction*) вперёд; **~ of** (*more advanced than*) вперед́и́ +*gen*;

(*earlier than*) ра́ньше +*gen*; **~ of time** *or* **schedule** досро́чно; **go right** *or* **straight ~** иди́те вперёд *or* пря́мо; **go ~!** (*permission*) дава́йте!; **they were (right) ~ of us** они́ бы́ли (пря́мо) пе́ред на́ми.

AI *n abbr* (= *Amnesty International*) Междунаро́дная амни́стия; (*COMPUT*) = **artificial intelligence.**

AIB *n abbr* (*BRIT*) = *Accident Investigation Bureau.*

AID *n abbr* = *artificial insemination by donor* иску́сственное оплодотворе́ние се́менем до́нора; (*US*) = *Agency for International Development.*

aid [eɪd] *n* (*assistance*) по́мощь *f*; (*device*) приспособле́ние ◆ *vt* помога́ть (помо́чь* *perf*) +*dat*; **with the ~ of** при по́мощи +*gen*; **in ~ of** в по́мощь +*dat*; **to ~ and abet** (*LAW*) подстрека́ть (*impf*); *see also* **hearing.**

aide [eɪd] *n* помо́щник.

aide-de-camp ['eɪddə'kɒŋ] *n* адъюта́нт.

AIDS [eɪdz] *n abbr* (= *acquired immune deficiency syndrome*) СПИД= *синдро́м приобретённого иммунодефици́та.*

AIH *n abbr* (= *artificial insemination by husband*) иску́сственное оплодотворе́ние се́менем му́жа.

ailing ['eɪlɪŋ] *adj* больно́й* (бо́лен); **an ~ economy** эконо́мика прише́дшая в упа́док.

ailment ['eɪlmənt] *n* неду́г.

aim [eɪm] *n* (*objective*) цель *f* ◆ *vi* (*also*: **take ~**) це́литься (наце́литься *perf*) ◆ *vt*: **to ~ (at)** (*gun, camera*) наводи́ть* (навести́* *perf*) (на +*acc*); (*missile, blow*) це́лить (*impf*) *or* наце́ливать (наце́лить *perf*) (на +*acc*); (*remark*) направля́ть (напра́вить* *perf*) (на +*acc*); **to ~ at** це́литься (*impf*) в +*acc*, прице́ливаться (прице́литься *perf*) в +*acc*; (*fig*) стреми́ться* (*impf*) к +*dat*; **to ~ to do** ста́вить (поста́вить* *perf*) свое́й це́лью +*infin*; **he has a good ~** он ме́ткий стрело́к.

aimless ['eɪmlɪs] *adj* бесце́льный* (бесце́лен).

aimlessly ['eɪmlɪslɪ] *adv* бесце́льно.

ain't [eɪnt] (*inf*) **= am not, aren't, isn't**; *see* be.

air [ɛə^r] *n* во́здух; (*tune*) моти́в; (*appearance*) вид ◆ *vt* (*room, bedclothes*) прове́тривать (прове́трить *perf*); (*views*) обнаро́довать (*perf*) ◆ *cpd* (*currents, attack etc*) возду́шный; **to throw sth into the ~** подбра́сывать (подбро́сить* *perf*) что-н в во́здух; **by ~** самолётом; **everything's still very much in the ~** всё до сих пор виси́т в во́здухе; **on the ~** в эфи́ре; **to go on the ~** выходи́ть* (вы́йти* *perf*) в эфи́р.

airbag ['ɛəbæg] *n воздушная подушка, надувающаяся автоматически между рулём и шофёром, в случае аварии.*

air base *n* авиаба́за.

airbed ['ɛəbɛd] *n* (*BRIT*) надувно́й матра́с.

airborne ['ɛəbɔ:n] *adj* возду́шный (возду́шен); (*troops*) возду́шно-деса́нтный; (*particles*) летучий*; **as soon as the plane was**

~ как то́лько самолёт подня́лся в во́здух.
air cargo *n* возду́шный груз.
air-conditioned ['ɛəkən'dɪʃənd] *adj* конициони́рованный.
air conditioning *n* кондициони́рование.
air-cooled ['ɛəku:ld] *adj* охлажда́емый во́здухом.
aircraft ['ɛəkrɑ:ft] *n inv* самолёт.
aircraft carrier *n* авиано́сец*.
air cushion *n* возду́шная поду́шка*.
airfield ['ɛəfi:ld] *n* аэродро́м.
Air Force *n* Вое́нно-Возду́шные Си́лы *fpl*.
air freight *n* авиагру́з.
air freshener *n* освежи́тель *m* во́здуха.
air gun *n* духово́е ружьё*.
air hostess *n* (*BRIT*) бортпроводни́ца, стюарде́сса.
airily ['ɛərɪlɪ] *adv* с лёгкостью, небре́жно.
airing ['ɛərɪŋ] *n*: **to give an** ~ **to** (*ideas, views etc*) обнаро́довать (*perf*).
air letter *n* (*BRIT*) письмо́* а́виа.
airlift ['ɛəlɪft] *n* возду́шная перебро́ска ♦ *vt* перебра́сывать (перебро́сить* *perf*) по во́здуху.
airline ['ɛəlaɪn] *n* авиакомпа́ния.
airliner ['ɛəlaɪnə'] *n* пассажи́рский* (авиа)ла́йнер.
airlock ['ɛəlɔk] *n* возду́шная про́бка.
air mail *n*: **by** ~ ~ авиапо́чтой.
air mattress *n* надувно́й матра́с.
airplane ['ɛəpleɪn] *n* (*US*) самолёт.
air pocket *n* возду́шная я́ма.
airport ['ɛəpɔ:t] *n* аэропо́рт.
air raid *n* возду́шный налёт.
air rifle *n* пневмати́ческая винто́вка.
airsick ['ɛəsɪk] *adj*: **to be** ~ страда́ть (*impf*) возду́шной боле́знью.
airspace ['ɛəspeɪs] *n* возду́шное простра́нство.
airspeed ['ɛəspi:d] *n* возду́шная ско́рость *f*, ско́рость *f* в во́здухе.
airstrip ['ɛəstrɪp] *n* взлётно-поса́дочная полоса́*.
air terminal *n* аэровокза́л.
airtight ['ɛətaɪt] *adj* гермети́ческий.
air time *n* вре́мя* *nt* в эфи́ре.
air-traffic control ['ɛətræfɪk-] *n* возду́шно-диспе́тчерская слу́жба.
air-traffic controller *n* возду́шный диспе́тчер.
airway ['ɛəweɪ] *n* возду́шная тра́сса.
air waybill *n* тра́нспортная накладна́я для авиагру́за.
airy ['ɛərɪ] *adj* (*room*) просто́рный* (просто́рен); (*manner*) беспе́чный* (беспе́чен).
aisle [aɪl] *n* прохо́д.
ajar [ə'dʒɑ:'] *adj* приоткры́тый (приоткры́т).
AK *abbr* (*US*: *POST*) = *Alaska*.
aka *abbr* (= *also known as*) изве́стный та́кже

под и́менем.
akin [ə'kɪn] *adj*: ~ **to** сродни́ +*dat*.
AL (*US*: *POST*) *abbr* = *Alabama*.
ALA *n abbr* = *American Library Association*.
alabaster ['æləbɑ:stə'] *n* алеба́стр.
à la carte [ɑ:lɑ:'kɑ:t] *adv*: **dinner** ~ ~ ~ обе́д с зака́зом блюд по меню́.
alacrity [ə'lækrɪtɪ] *n* гото́вность *f*; **with** ~ с гото́вностью.
alarm [ə'lɑ:m] *n* (*anxiety*) трево́га; (*device*) сигнализа́ция ♦ *vt* (*person*) трево́жить (встрево́жить *perf*); (*car, house*) устана́вливать (установи́ть* *perf*) сигнализа́цию в +*prp*.
alarm call *n*: **I would like an** ~ ~ **for 6 a.m.** позвони́те, пожа́луйста, в 6 часо́в и разбуди́те меня́.
alarm clock *n* буди́льник.
alarmed [ə'lɑ:md] *adj* встрево́женный* (встрево́жен); **his car is** ~ у него́ в маши́не сигнализа́ция.
alarming [ə'lɑ:mɪŋ] *adj* трево́жный* (трево́жен).
alarmist [ə'lɑ:mɪst] *n* паникёр(ша).
alas [ə'læs] *excl* увы́.
Alaska [ə'læskə] *n* Аля́ска.
Albania [æl'beɪnɪə] *n* Алба́ния.
Albanian [æl'beɪnɪən] *adj* алба́нский* ♦ *n* алба́нец*(-нка); (*LING*) алба́нский* язы́к*.
albatross ['ælbətrɔs] *n* (*ZOOL*) альбатро́с.
albeit [ɔ:l'bi:ɪt] *conj* хотя́ и.
album ['ælbəm] *n* альбо́м.
albumen ['ælbjumɪn] *n* бело́к*.
alchemy ['ælkɪmɪ] *n* алхи́мия.
alcohol ['ælkəhɔl] *n* алкого́ль *m*.
alcohol-free ['ælkəhɔl'fri:] *adj* безалкого́льный.
alcoholic [ælkə'hɔlɪk] *adj* алкого́льный ♦ *n* алкого́лик(-и́чка).
alcoholism ['ælkəhɔlɪzəm] *n* алкоголи́зм.
alcove ['ælkəuv] *n* алько́в.
Ald. *abbr* = *alderman*.
alderman ['ɔ:ldəmən] *irreg n* глава́ муниципалите́та.
ale [eɪl] *n* пи́во (пригото́вленное без хме́ля).
alert [ə'lɜ:t] *adj* (*attentive*) внима́тельный* (внима́телен); (*to danger*) бди́тельный* (бди́телен) ♦ *n* (*alarm*) трево́га ♦ *vt* (*police etc*) предупрежда́ть (предупреди́ть* *perf*); **to be on the** ~ (*also MIL*) быть* (*impf*) начеку́; **to** ~ **sb to sth** предупрежда́ть (предупреди́ть* *perf*) кого́-н о чём-н; **to** ~ **sb to the dangers of sth** предостерега́ть (предостере́чь* *perf*) кого́-н от опа́сности чего́-н.
Aleutian Islands [ə'lu:ʃən-] *npl* Алеу́тские острова́ *mpl*.
Alexandria [ælɪg'zɑ:ndrɪə] *n* Александри́я.
alfresco [æl'frɛskəu] *adj, adv* под откры́тым

---

* marks translations which have irregular inflections. The Russian-English side of the dictionary gives inflectional information.

не́бом.

algebra [ˈældʒɪbrə] *n* а́лгебра.

Algeria [ælˈdʒɪərɪə] *n* Алжи́р.

Algerian [ælˈdʒɪərɪən] *adj* алжи́рский* ♦ *n* алжи́рец*(-рка).

Algiers [ælˈdʒɪəz] *n* Алжи́р (*го́род*).

algorithm [ˈælgərɪðəm] *n* алгори́тм.

alias [ˈeɪlɪəs] *n* (*of criminal*) вы́мышленное и́мя* *nt*; (*of writer*) псевдони́м ♦ *adv*: ~ **John Green** он же Джон Грин.

alibi [ˈælɪbaɪ] *n* а́либи *nt ind*.

alien [ˈeɪlɪən] *n* (*foreigner*) иностра́нец*(-нка); (*extraterrestrial*) инопланетя́нин*(-я́нка) ♦ *adj*: ~ **(to)** чу́ждый* (чужд) (+*dat*); **pity was ~ to his nature** чу́вство жа́лости ему́ бы́ло чу́ждо.

alienate [ˈeɪlɪəneɪt] *vt* (*person*) отчужда́ть (*impf*), отта́лкивать (оттолкну́ть *perf*).

alienation [eɪlɪəˈneɪʃən] *n* отчужде́ние.

alight [əˈlaɪt] *adj*: **to be ~** горе́ть (*impf*); (*eyes, face*) сия́ть (*impf*) ♦ *adv*: **to set ~** поджига́ть (подже́чь* *perf*) ♦ *vi*: **to ~ on** опуска́ться (опусти́ться* *perf*) на +*acc*; **to ~ from** (*boat*) сходи́ть* (сойти́* *perf*) с +*gen*; (*bus, train*) выходи́ть* (вы́йти* *perf*) из +*gen*.

align [əˈlaɪn] *vt* (*objects*) выра́внивать (вы́ровнять *perf*); **to ~ o.s. with** присоединя́ться (присоедини́ться *perf*) к +*dat*.

alignment [əˈlaɪnmənt] *n* сою́з; (*POL*) алья́нс; **out of ~** неро́вно.

alike [əˈlaɪk] *adj* одина́ковый (одина́ков) ♦ *adv* одина́ково; **they look ~** они́ похо́жи друг на дру́га; **winter and summer ~** и зимо́й и ле́том.

alimony [ˈælɪmənɪ] *n* алиме́нты* *pl*.

alive [əˈlaɪv] *adj* жив; (*place*) оживлённый*; (*active: person*) живо́й*; **~ with** по́лон +*gen*; **to be ~ to sth** осознава́ть (осозна́ть *perf*) что-н.

alkali [ˈælkəlaɪ] *n* щёлочь* *f*.

alkaline [ˈælkəlaɪn] *adj* щелочно́й.

KEYWORD

---

all [ɔːl] *adj* весь* (*f* вся, *nt* всё, *pl* все); **all day** весь день* *m*; **all night** всю ночь* *f*; **all men are equal** все лю́ди равны́; **all five stayed** все пя́теро оста́лись; **all the books** все кни́ги; **all the time** всё вре́мя; **all his life** всю свою́ жизнь

♦ *pron* **1** всё; **I ate it all, I ate all of it** я всё съел; **all of us stayed** мы все оста́лись; **we all sat down** мы все се́ли; **is that all?** э́то всё?; (*in shop*) всё?

2 (*in phrases*): **above all** пре́жде всего́; **after all** в конце́ концо́в; **all in all** в це́лом *or* о́бщем; **not at all** (*in answer to question*) совсе́м нет, ничу́ть нет; (*in answer to thanks*) не́ за что; **I'm not at all tired** я совсе́м не уста́л

♦ *adv* совсе́м; **I am all alone** совсе́м оди́н; **I did it all by myself** я всё сде́лал сам; **it's not as hard as all that** э́то совсе́м не так уж тру́дно; **all the more/the better** тем бо́лее/лу́чше; **I**

have all but finished я почти́ что зако́нчил; **the score is two all** счёт-два два.

allay [əˈleɪ] *vt* (*fears etc*) разве́ивать (разве́ять *perf*).

all clear *n* отбо́й.

allegation [ælɪˈgeɪʃən] *n* обвине́ние; **according to his ~s** согла́сно его́ утвержде́ниям.

allege [əˈlɛdʒ] *vt* (*claim*) утвержда́ть (*impf*); **he is ~d to have said that ...** утвержда́ют, что он сказа́л что ....

alleged [əˈlɛdʒd] *adj* подозрева́емый.

allegedly [əˈlɛdʒɪdlɪ] *adv* я́кобы.

allegiance [əˈliːdʒəns] *n* (*to people*) ве́рность *f*; (*to ideas*) приве́рженность *f*.

allegory [ˈælɪgərɪ] *n* аллего́рия.

all-embracing [ˈɔːlɪmˈbreɪsɪŋ] *adj* всеобъе́млющий* (всеобъе́млющ).

allergic [əˈlɜːdʒɪk] *adj* аллерги́ческий*; **he is ~ to** у него́ аллерги́я на +*acc*; (*fig*) он не выно́сит.

allergy [ˈælədʒɪ] *n* (*MED*) аллерги́я.

alleviate [əˈliːvɪeɪt] *vt* облегча́ть (облегчи́ть *perf*).

alley [ˈælɪ] *n* (*street*) переу́лок*.

alleyway [ˈælɪweɪ] *n* проу́лок*.

alliance [əˈlaɪəns] *n* сою́з; (*POL*) алья́нс.

allied [ˈælaɪd] *adj* (*POL, MIL*) сою́зный; (*industries*) сме́жный*.

alligator [ˈælɪgeɪtə] *n* аллига́тор.

all-important [ˈɔːlɪmˈpɔːtnt] *adj* суще́ственный.

all-in [ˈɔːlɪn] *adj* (*BRIT: cost*) о́бщий*; **it cost me £100 ~** в о́бщей сло́жности мне э́то сто́ило £100.

all-in wrestling *n* во́льная борьба́.

alliteration [əlɪtəˈreɪʃən] *n* аллитера́ция.

all-night [ˈɔːlˈnaɪt] *adj* (*café, cinema*) ночно́й.

allocate [ˈæləkeɪt] *vt* (*money, time, room*) выделя́ть (вы́делить *perf*); (*tasks*) поруча́ть (поручи́ть* *perf*).

allocation [æləuˈkeɪʃən] *n* (*of responsibilty*) распределе́ние; (*of resources*) выделе́ние; (*of money*) ассигнова́ние.

allot [əˈlɔt] *vt*: **to ~ (to)** отводи́ть* (отвести́* *perf*) (+*dat*); **in the ~ed time** в отведённое вре́мя.

allotment [əˈlɔtmənt] *n* (*share*) до́ля*; (*garden*) (земе́льный) уча́сток*.

all-out [ˈɔːlaut] *adj* (*effort*) максима́льный; (*attack*) масси́рованный; (*strike*) всео́бщий* ♦ *adv* по́лностью; **to go all out (for)** по́лностью выкла́дываться (вы́ложиться *perf*) (для +*gen*).

allow [əˈlau] *vt* (*permit*) разреша́ть (разреши́ть *perf*); (*: claim, goal*) признава́ть* (призна́ть *perf*) действи́тельным; (*set aside: sum*) выделя́ть (вы́делить *perf*); (*concede*): **to ~ that** допуска́ть (допусти́ть* *perf*), что; **to ~ sb to do** разреша́ть (разреши́ть *perf*) *or* позволя́ть (позво́лить *perf*) кому́-н +*infin*; **he was ~ed to ...** ему́ бы́ло разрешено́ +*infin* ...; **smoking is not ~ed** кури́ть воспреща́ется *or* запреща́ется; **we must ~ 3 days for the journey** мы должны́ оста́вить три дня на доро́гу

▶ **allow for** *vt fus* учи́тывать (уче́сть* *perf*), принима́ть (приня́ть* *perf*) в расчёт.

allowance [ə'lauəns] *n* (*company expenses*) де́ньги* *pl* на расхо́ды; (*pocket money*) карма́нные де́ньги; (*welfare payment*) посо́бие; (*tax allowance*) нало́говая ски́дка*; **to make ~s for sb/sth** де́лать (сде́лать *perf*) ски́дку для кого́-н/на что-н.

alloy ['ælɔɪ] *n* сплав.

all right *adv* хорошо́, норма́льно; (*as answer: in agreement*) хорошо́, ла́дно ♦ *adj* неплохо́й*, норма́льный; **is everything ~~?** всё норма́льно *or* в поря́дке?; **are you ~~?** как Вы (себя́ чу́вствуете)?; **do you like him? – he's ~~** он Вам нра́вится? – ничего́.

all-rounder [ɔ:l'raundə*] *n* универса́л.

allspice ['ɔ:lspaɪs] *n* души́стый пе́рец*.

all-time ['ɔ:l'taɪm] *adj* (*record*) непревзойдённый; **inflation is at an ~ low** инфля́ция на небыва́ло ни́зком у́ровне.

allude [ə'lu:d] *vi*: **to ~ to** намека́ть (намекну́ть *perf*) на +*acc*.

alluring [ə'ljuərɪŋ] *adj* соблазни́тельный* (соблазни́телен).

allusion [ə'lu:ʒən] *n*: **~ (to)** намёк (на +*acc*); (*LITERATURE*) аллю́зия (на +*acc*).

alluvium [ə'lu:vɪəm] *n* аллю́вий.

ally [*n* 'ælaɪ, *vb* ə'laɪ] *n* сою́зник ♦ *vt*: **to ~ o.s. with** объединя́ться (объедини́ться *perf*) с +*instr*.

Alma-Ata [ælmə:ə'ta:] *n* А́лма-Ата́ *f ind*.

almighty [ɔ:l'maɪtɪ] *adj* (*omnipotent*) всемогу́щий* (всемогу́щ); (*tremendous*) колосса́льный.

almond ['ɑ:mənd] *n* минда́ль* *m*.

almost [ɔ:lməust] *adv* почти́; (*all but*) чуть *or* едва́ не; **he ~ fell** он чуть не упа́л.

alms [ɑ:mz] *npl* ми́лостыня *fsg*, подая́ние *ntsg*.

aloft [ə'lɔft] *adv* (*hold, carry*) над голово́й.

alone [ə'ləun] *adj, adv* оди́н (одна́); **to leave sb/sth ~** оставля́ть (оста́вить* *perf*) кого́-н/что-н в поко́е; **let ~ ...** не говоря́ уже́ о +*prp* ....

along [ə'lɔŋ] *prep* (*motion*) по +*dat*, вдоль +*gen*; (*position*) вдоль +*gen* ♦ *adv*: **is he coming (with us)?** он идёт с на́ми?; **he was limping ~** он шёл хрома́я; **~ with** вме́сте с +*instr*; **all ~** с са́мого нача́ла.

alongside [ə'lɔŋ'saɪd] *prep* (*position*) ря́дом с +*instr*, вдоль +*gen*; (*motion*) к +*dat* ♦ *adv* ря́дом; **we brought our boat ~** мы прича́лили ло́дку.

aloof [ə'lu:f] *adj* отрешённый (отрешён) ♦ *adv*: **to stand ~** держа́ться (*impf*) в стороне́.

aloofness [ə'lu:fnɪs] *n* отрешённость *f*.

aloud [ə'laud] *adv* (*read, speak*) вслух.

alphabet ['ælfəbɛt] *n* алфави́т.

alphabetical [ælfə'bɛtɪkl] *adj* алфави́тный; **in ~ order** в алфави́тном поря́дке.

alphanumeric ['ælfənju:'mɛrɪk] *adj* алфави́тно-цифрово́й.

alpine ['ælpaɪn] *adj* высокого́рный, альпи́йский*.

Alps [ælps] *npl*: **the ~** А́льпы* *pl*.

already [ɔ:l'rɛdɪ] *adv* уже́.

alright ['ɔ:l'raɪt] *adv* (*BRIT*) = **all right**.

Alsace ['ælsæs] *n* Эльза́с.

Alsatian [æl'seɪʃən] *n* (*BRIT: dog*) неме́цкая овча́рка*; (*person*) эльза́сец(-ска).

also ['ɔ:lsəu] *adv* (*referring to subject*) та́кже, то́же; (*referring to object*) та́кже; (*moreover*) кро́ме того́, к тому́ же; **he ~ likes apples** он та́кже *or* то́же лю́бит я́блоки; **he likes apples ~** он лю́бит та́кже я́блоки.

altar ['ɔltə*] *n* алта́рь* *m*.

alter ['ɔltə*] *vt* изменя́ть (измени́ть* *perf*) ♦ *vi* изменя́ться (измени́ться* *perf*).

alteration [ɔltə'reɪʃən] *n* измене́ние; **~s** *npl* (*SEWING*) переде́лки *fpl*; **to make ~s to a building** перестра́ивать (перестро́ить *perf*) зда́ние.

altercation [ɔltə'keɪʃən] *n* препира́тельство.

alternate [*adj* ɔl'tə:nɪt, *vb* 'ɔltə:neɪt] *adj* череду́ющийся; (*US: alternative*) альтернати́вный ♦ *vi*: **to ~ (with)** чередова́ться (*impf*) (с +*instr*); **on ~ days** че́рез день.

alternately [ɔl'tə:nɪtlɪ] *adv* попереме́нно.

alternating current ['ɔltə:neɪtɪŋ-] *n* переме́нный ток*.

alternative [ɔl'tə:nətɪv] *adj* альтернати́вный ♦ *n* альтернати́ва.

alternatively [ɔl'tə:nətɪvlɪ] *adv*: **~ one could ...** кро́ме того́ мо́жно ....

alternative medicine *n* альтернати́вная *or* нетрадицио́нная медици́на.

alternator ['ɔltə:neɪtə*] *n* (*AUT*) генера́тор переме́нного то́ка.

although [ɔ:l'ðəu] *conj* хотя́.

altitude ['æltɪtju:d] *n* (*of plane*) высота́*; (*of place*) высота́ над у́ровнем мо́ря.

alto ['æltəu] *n* (*female*) контра́льто *nt ind*; (*male*) альт*.

altogether [ɔ:ltə'gɛðə*] *adv* (*completely*) соверше́нно; (*in all*) в о́бщем, в о́бщей сло́жности; **how much is that ~?** ско́лько бу́дет в о́бщей сло́жности?

altruism ['æltruɪzəm] *n* альтруи́зм.

altruistic [æltru'ɪstɪk] *adj* (*action*) альтруисти́ческий; (*person*) альтруисти́чный (альтруисти́чен).

aluminium [ælju'mɪnɪəm] *n* (*BRIT*) алюми́ний.

---

* marks translations which have irregular inflections. The Russian-English side of the dictionary gives inflectional information.

aluminum [ə'lu:mɪnəm] *n* (*US*) = **aluminium.**
always ['ɔ:lweɪz] *adv* всегда́.
Alzheimer's disease ['æltshaɪməz-] *n* боле́знь
f Алцхе́ймера.
AM *abbr* (= *amplitude modulation*)
амплиту́дная модуля́ция.
am [æm] *vb see* **be.**
a.m. *adv abbr* (= *ante meridiem*) до полу́дня.
AMA *n abbr* = *American Medical Association.*
amalgam [ə'mælgəm] *n* амальга́ма.
amalgamate [ə'mælgəmeɪt] *vi* слива́ться
(сли́ться *perf*) ♦ *vt* слива́ть (слить *perf*).
amalgamation [əmælgə'meɪʃən] *n* (*of
companies*) слия́ние.
amass [ə'mæs] *vt* нака́пливать (накопи́ть*
perf).
amateur ['æmətə] *n* люби́тель *m*; ~ **sport/
dramatics** люби́тельский* спорт/теа́тр; ~
photographer фото́граф-люби́тель *m*.
amateurish ['æmətərɪʃ] *adj* (*work, efforts*)
непрофессиона́льный (непрофессиона́лен).
amaze [ə'meɪz] *vt* поража́ть (порази́ть* *perf*),
изумля́ть (изуми́ть* *perf*); **I was ~d (at)** я был
поражён (+*instr*).
amazement [ə'meɪzmənt] *n* изумле́ние.
amazing [ə'meɪzɪŋ] *adj* (*surprising*)
порази́тельный* (порази́телен); (*fantastic*)
изуми́тельный* (изуми́телен),
замеча́тельный* (замеча́телен).
amazingly [ə'meɪzɪŋlɪ] *adv* порази́тельно.
Amazon ['æməzən] *n* (*river*) Амазо́нка;
(*woman*) амазо́нка*; **the ~ basin** бассе́йн
реки́ Амазо́нки; **the ~ jungle** джу́нгли *pl*
Амазо́нки.
Amazonian [æmə'zəʊnɪən] *adj* (*GEO*)
амазо́нский.
ambassador [æm'bæsədə] *n* посо́л*.
amber ['æmbə] *n* янта́рь* *m*; **the lights were at
~** на светофо́ре был жёлтый свет.
ambidextrous [æmbɪ'dekstrəs] *adj* одина́ково
владе́ющий пра́вой и ле́вой руко́й.
ambience ['æmbɪəns] *n* атмосфе́ра.
ambiguity [æmbɪ'gjuɪtɪ] *n* двусмы́сленность *f*,
нея́сность *f*.
ambiguous [æm'bɪgjuəs] *adj* двусмы́сленный,
нея́сный*.
ambition [æm'bɪʃən] *n* (*quality: positive*)
честолю́бие; (: *negative*) амби́ция; (*aim*)
цель *f*; **to achieve one's ~** достига́ть
(дости́чь* *perf*) свое́й це́ли.
ambitious [æm'bɪʃəs] *adj* честолюби́вый
(честолюби́в); амбицио́зный*
(амбицио́зен).
ambivalence [æm'bɪvələns] *n* (*indecision*)
дво́йственное отноше́ние; (*ambiguity*)
несоотве́тствия *ntpl*.
ambivalent [æm'bɪvələnt] *adj* (*attitude*)
дво́йственный (дво́йствен); (*person*)
противоречи́вый (противоречи́в).
amble ['æmbl] *vi* прогу́ливаться (прогуля́ться
perf).

ambulance ['æmbjuləns] *n* ско́рая по́мощь *f*.
ambulanceman ['æmbjulənsmən] *irreg n*
фе́льдшер ско́рой по́мощи.
ambush ['æmbuʃ] *n* заса́да ♦ *vt* устра́ивать
(устро́ить* *perf*) заса́ду +*dat*.
ameba [ə'mi:bə] *n* (*US*) = **amoeba.**
ameliorate [ə'mi:lɪəreɪt] *vt* (*situation*) улучша́ть
(улу́чшить *perf*).
amen ['ɑ:'mɛn] *excl* ами́нь.
amenable [ə'mi:nəbl] *adj*: ~ **to** пода́тливый
(пода́тлив) на +*acc*; **he's ~ to advice** он
прислу́шивается к сове́там; ~ **to the law**
отве́тственный (отве́тствен) пе́ред
зако́ном.
amend [ə'mɛnd] *vt* пересма́тривать
(пересмотре́ть *perf*); (*habits*) исправля́ть
(испра́вить* *perf*) ♦ *vi* исправля́ться
(испра́виться* *perf*) ♦ *n*: **to make ~s**
загла́живать (загла́дить* *perf*) вину́.
amendment [ə'mɛndmənt] *n* попра́вка*.
amenities [ə'mi:nɪtɪz] *npl* удо́бства *ntpl*.
amenity [ə'mi:nɪtɪ] *n* удо́бство.
America [ə'mɛrɪkə] *n* Аме́рика.
American [ə'mɛrɪkən] *adj* америка́нский* ♦ *n*
америка́нец*(-нка).
americanize [ə'mɛrɪkənaɪz] *vt*
американизи́ровать (*impf/perf*).
amethyst ['æmɪθɪst] *n* амети́ст.
Amex ['æmɛks] *n abbr* = *American Stock
Exchange.*
amiable ['eɪmɪəbl] *adj* дружелю́бный*
(дружелю́бен).
amiably ['eɪmɪəblɪ] *adv* дружелю́бно.
amicable ['æmɪkəbl] *adj* (*relationship*)
дру́жеский*; (*divorce*) ми́рный* (ми́рен).
amicably ['æmɪkəblɪ] *adv* по-дру́жески, ми́рно.
amid(st) [ə'mɪd(st)] *prep* посреди́ +*gen*.
amiss [ə'mɪs] *adj, adv*: **to take sth ~** оши́бочно
истолко́вывать (истолкова́ть* *perf*) что-н;
there's something ~ что́-то нела́дно.
ammeter ['æmɪtə] *n* ампермéтр.
ammo ['æməu] *n abbr* (*inf*) = **ammunition.**
ammonia [ə'məunɪə] *n* (*gas*) аммиа́к; (*liquid*)
нашаты́рный спирт*.
ammunition [æmju'nɪʃən] *n* (*MIL*) боеприпа́сы
pl; (*for gun*) патро́ны *mpl*; (*fig*) ору́жие.
ammunition dump *n* склад боеприпа́сов.
amnesia [æm'ni:zɪə] *n* амнези́я, утра́та
па́мяти.
amnesty ['æmnɪstɪ] *n* амни́стия; **to grant an ~
to** объявля́ть (объяви́ть* *perf*) амни́стию
+*dat*.
amoeba [ə'mi:bə] *n* (*US* **ameba**) *n* амёба.
amok [ə'mɔk] *adv*: **to run ~** (*people*)
беснова́ться (*impf*); (*animals*) беси́ться*
(взбеси́ться *perf*).
among(st) [ə'mʌŋ(st)] *prep* среди́ +*gen*;
(*between*) ме́жду +*instr*.
amoral [æ'mɔrəl] *adj* безнра́вственный
(безнра́вствен), амора́льный* (амора́лен).
amorous ['æmərəs] *adj* любо́вный.

amorphous [ə'mɔːfəs] *adj* амо́рфный* (амо́рфен).

amortization [əmɔːtaɪ'zeɪʃən] *n* (*COMM*) амортиза́ция.

amount [ə'maunt] *n* коли́чество; (*sum of money*) су́мма ♦ *vi*: **to ~ to** (*total*) составля́ть (соста́вить* *perf*); **this ~s to a refusal** э́то равноси́льно отка́зу; **the total ~** (*of money*) о́бщая су́мма.

amp(ère) ['æmp(ɛəʳ)] *n* ампе́р*; **a 13 amp plug** ви́лка в 13 ампе́р.

ampersand ['æmpəsænd] *n* знак "&" (*обозначающий "и"*).

amphetamine [æm'fɛtəmiːn] *n* амфетами́н.

amphibian [æm'fɪbɪən] *n* амфи́бия, земново́дное живо́тное *nt adj*.

amphibious [æm'fɪbɪəs] *adj* (*animal*) земново́дный; (*vehicle*) амфиби́йный; **~ tank** танк-амфи́бия.

amphitheatre ['æmfɪθɪətəʳ] (*US* **amphitheater**) *n* амфитеа́тр.

ample ['æmpl] *adj* (*large*) большо́й; (*abundant*) оби́льный* (оби́лен); (*enough*) доста́точный (доста́точен); **to have ~ time/room** име́ть (*impf*) доста́точно вре́мени/ме́ста; **this is ~** э́того вполне́ доста́точно.

amplifier ['æmplɪfaɪəʳ] *n* усили́тель *m*.

amplify ['æmplɪfaɪ] *vt* усиливать (уси́лить *perf*).

amply ['æmplɪ] *adv* вполне́.

ampoule ['æmpuːl] (*US* **ampule**) *n* а́мпула.

amputate ['æmpjuteɪt] *vt* ампути́ровать (*impf/perf*).

amputation [æmpju'teɪʃən] *n* ампута́ция.

amputee [æmpju'tiː] *n* инвали́д.

Amsterdam ['æmstədæm] *n* Амстерда́м.

amt *abbr* (= **amount**) кол-во= *количество*.

amuck [ə'mʌk] *adv* = **amok**.

amuse [ə'mjuːz] *vt* развлека́ть (развле́чь* *perf*); **to ~ o.s. with sth** заня́ться (*perf*) *or* развлека́ться (развле́чься* *perf*) чем-н; **he was ~d at this** его́ э́то позаба́вило; **he was not ~d** ему́ бы́ло не до сме́ха.

amusement [ə'mjuːzmənt] *n* (*mirth*) удово́льствие; (*pastime*) развлече́ние; **much to my ~** к моему́ осо́бенному удово́льствию.

amusement arcade *n* павильо́н с развлека́тельными аппара́тами.

amusement park *n* луна́-парк.

amusing [ə'mjuːzɪŋ] *adj* заба́вный* (заба́вен), занима́тельный* (занима́телен).

an [æn] *indef art see* **a**.

ANA *n abbr* = *American Newspaper Association*; *American Nurses Association*.

anachronism [ə'nækrənɪzəm] *n* анахрони́зм.

anaemia [ə'niːmɪə] (*US* **anemia**) *n* анеми́я, малокро́вие.

anaemic [ə'niːmɪk] (*US* **anemic**) *adj* (*MED*, *fig*) анеми́чный* (анеми́чен).

anaesthetic [ænɪs'θɛtɪk] (*US* **anesthetic**) *n* нарко́з; **under the ~** под нарко́зом; **local/general ~** ме́стный/о́бщий* нарко́з.

anaesthetist [æ'niːsθɪtɪst] (*US* **anesthetist**) *n* анестезио́лог.

anagram ['ænəgræm] *n* анагра́мма.

anal ['eɪnl] *adj* ана́льный, заднепрохо́дный.

analgesic [ænæl'dʒiːsɪk] *adj* обезбо́ливающий* ♦ *n* обезбо́ливающее сре́дство.

analog ['ænəlɔg] *adj* = **analogue**.

analogous [ə'næləgəs] *adj* аналоги́чный* (аналоги́чен).

analogue ['ænəlɔg] *adj* (*computer*) ана́логовый.

analogy [ə'nælədʒɪ] *n* анало́гия; **to draw an ~ between** проводи́ть* (провести́* *perf*) анало́гию ме́жду +*instr*; **by ~** по анало́гии.

analyse ['ænəlaɪz] (*US* **analyze**) *vt* анализи́ровать (проанализи́ровать *perf*); (*PSYCH*): **to ~ sb** подверга́ть (подве́ргнуть* *perf*) кого́-н психоана́лизу.

analyses [ə'næləsiːz] *npl of* **analysis**.

analysis [ə'næləsɪs] (*pl* **analyses**) *n* ана́лиз; (*PSYCH*) психоана́лиз; **in the last ~** в коне́чном ито́ге.

analyst ['ænəlɪst] *n* (*political*) коммента́тор; (*financial, economic*) экспе́рт; (*US*: *psychiatrist*) психиа́тр.

analytic(al) [ænə'lɪtɪk(l)] *adj* аналити́ческий.

analyze ['ænəlaɪz] *vt* (*US*) = **analyse**.

anarchic [æ'naːkɪk] *adj* анархи́ческий.

anarchist ['ænəkɪst] *adj* анархи́ческий ♦ *n* анархи́ст.

anarchy ['ænəkɪ] *n* ана́рхия.

anathema [ə'næθɪmə] *n*: **that is ~ to him** для него́ э́то ана́фема.

anatomical [ænə'tɔmɪkl] *adj* анатоми́ческий.

anatomy [ə'nætəmɪ] *n* анато́мия; (*body*) органи́зм.

ANC *n abbr* (= *African National Congress*) АНК = *Африка́нский* *национа́льный конгре́сс*.

ancestor ['ænsɪstəʳ] *n* пре́док*.

ancestral [æn'sɛstrəl] *adj* родово́й; **~ home** родово́е поме́стье.

ancestry ['ænsɪstrɪ] *n* происхожде́ние.

anchor ['æŋkəʳ] *n* я́корь* *m* ♦ *vi* (*also*: **to drop ~**) броса́ть (бро́сить* *perf*) я́корь; **to weigh ~** поднима́ть (подня́ть* *perf*) я́корь.

anchorage ['æŋkərɪdʒ] *n* я́корная стоя́нка*.

anchor man *n* веду́щий* *m adj* (програ́ммы).

anchovy ['æntʃəvɪ] *n* анчо́ус.

ancient ['eɪnʃənt] *adj* (*civilization, person*) дре́вний*; (*monument*) стари́нный.

ancient monument *n* па́мятник старины́.

ancillary [æn'sɪlərɪ] *adj* подсо́бный.

---

* marks translations which have irregular inflections. The Russian-English side of the dictionary gives inflectional information.

and [ænd] *conj* и; (*with pronouns*) с +*instr*;
you ~ I мы с Вáми; **my father ~ I** мы с отцóм;
bread ~ butter хлеб с мáслом; **~ so on** и так
дáлее; **try ~ come** постарáйтесь прийти; **he
talked ~ talked** он всё говорил и говорил.

Andes ['ændi:z] *npl*: **the ~** Áнды* *pl*.

Andorra [æn'dɔ:rə] *n* Андóрра.

anecdote ['ænɪkdəut] *n* забáвная истóрия.

anemia *etc n* (*US*) = **anaemia** *etc*.

anemone [ə'nɛmənɪ] *n* вéтреница, анемóна.

anesthetic *etc* (*US*) = **anaesthetic** *etc*.

anew [ə'nju:] *adv* зáново.

angel ['eɪndʒəl] *n* áнгел.

angel dust *n* один из галлюцинатóрных
лекáрственных препарáтов.

angelic [æn'dʒɛlɪk] *adj* áнгельский*.

anger ['æŋgə] *n* гнев, возмущéние ♦ *vt*
сердить* (рассердить* *perf*), возмущáть
(возмутить* *perf*).

angina [æn'dʒaɪnə] *n* груднáя жáба.

angle ['æŋgl] *n* (*corner*) ýгол*; (*viewpoint*): **from
their ~** с их тóчки зрéния ♦ *vi*: **to ~ for**
(*invitation*) напрáшиваться (напроситься*
perf) на +*acc* ♦ *vt*: **the idea is/was ~d towards** *or*
to идéя расчи́тана/былá расчи́тана на +*acc*.

angler ['æŋglə] *n* рыболóв.

Anglican ['æŋglɪkən] *adj* англикáнский* ♦ *n*
англикáнин(-áнка).

anglicize ['æŋglɪsaɪz] *vt* англизи́ровать (*impf*).

angling ['æŋglɪŋ] *n* рыбная лóвля.

Anglo- ['æŋgləu] *prefix* áнгло-.

Anglo-Saxon ['æŋgləu'sæksən] *adj* англо-
саксóнский; (*LING*) древнеанглийский ♦ *n*
англосáкс; (*LING*) древнеанглийский язы́к*.

Angola [æŋ'gəulə] *n* Ангóла.

Angolan [æŋ'gəulən] *adj* ангóльский* ♦ *n*
ангóлец*(-лка*).

angrily ['æŋgrɪlɪ] *adv* серди́то, гнéвно.

angry ['æŋgrɪ] *adj* серди́тый (серди́т),
гнéвный* (гнéвен); (*wound*) воспалённый
(воспалён); **to be ~ with sb/at sth** серди́ться*
(*impf*) *or* зли́ться (*impf*) на когó-н/что-н; **to get
~** серди́ться* (рассерди́ться* *perf*), зли́ться
(разозли́ться *perf*); **he gets ~ easily** егó легкó
рассерди́ть; **to make sb ~** серди́ть*
(рассерди́ть* *perf*) *or* злить (разозли́ть *perf*)
когó-н.

anguish ['æŋgwɪʃ] *n* мýка.

anguished ['æŋgwɪʃt] *adj* страдáльческий*.

angular ['æŋgjulə] *adj* (*person, features*)
угловáтый (угловáт).

animal ['ænɪməl] *n* живóтное *nt adj*; (*wild
animal*) зверь* *m*; (*pej: person*) зверь,
живóтное ♦ *adj* живóтный.

animal rights [-raɪts] *npl* правá *ntpl* живóтных;
the ~ ~ movement движéние за правá
живóтных.

animate [*vb* 'ænɪmeɪt, *adj* 'ænɪmɪt] *vt* оживлять
(оживить* *perf*) ♦ *adj* живóй* (жив); (*LING*)
одушевлённый.

animated ['ænɪmeɪtɪd] *adj* оживлённый*

(оживлён), живóй* (жив); (*film*)
мультипликациóнный.

animation [ænɪ'meɪʃən] *n* (*CINEMA*)
мультипликáция; (*enthusiasm*) оживлéние.

animosity [ænɪ'mɔsɪtɪ] *n* враждéбность *f*.

aniseed ['ænɪsi:d] *n* анис ♦ *adj* анисовый.

Ankara ['æŋkərə] *n* Анкарá.

ankle ['æŋkl] *n* лодыжка*.

ankle sock *n* носóк*.

annex ['ænɛks] *n* (*also:* **~e**: *BRIT*) пристрóйка;
(: *separate building*) отдéльный кóрпус ♦ *vt*
аннекси́ровать (*impf/perf*).

annexation [ænɛk'seɪʃən] *n* аннéксия.

annihilate [ə'naɪəleɪt] *vt* уничтожáть
(уничтóжить *perf*).

annihilation [ənaɪə'leɪʃən] *n* уничтожéние.

anniversary [ænɪ'və:sərɪ] *n* годовщи́на.

Anno Domini ['ænəu'dɔmɪnaɪ] *adv* нáшей эры.

annotate ['ænəuteɪt] *vt* аннотировать
(проаннотировать *perf*).

announce [ə'nauns] *vt* (*decision, engagement*)
объявлять (объяви́ть* *perf*) (о +*prp*); (*birth,
death etc*) извещáть (известить* *perf*) о +*prp*;
he ~d that he wasn't going он заяви́л, что не
пойдёт.

announcement [ə'naunsmənt] *n* объявлéние;
(*in newspaper etc*) сообщéние; (*in letter etc*)
извещéние; **I'd like to make an ~** я бы хотéл
сдéлать заявлéние.

announcer [ə'naunsə] *n* (*RADIO, TV*) ди́ктор.

annoy [ə'nɔɪ] *vt* раздражáть (раздражи́ть
perf); **I am ~ed with him** он меня раздражáет;
don't get ~ed! не раздражáйтесь *or*
серди́тесь!

annoyance [ə'nɔɪəns] *n* (*feeling*) раздражéние,
досáда.

annoyed [ə'nɔɪd] *adj* раздражённый*
(раздражён).

annoying [ə'nɔɪɪŋ] *adj* (*noise*) раздражáющий*;
(*mistake, event*) досáдный* (досáден); **he is ~**
он меня раздражáет.

annual ['ænjuəl] *adj* (*meeting*) ежегóдный;
(*income*) годовóй ♦ *n* (*BOT*) однолéтнее
растéние; (*book*) ежегóдник.

annual general meeting *n* (*BRIT*) ежегóдное
óбщее собрáние.

annually ['ænjuəlɪ] *adv* ежегóдно.

annual report *n* годовóй отчёт.

annuity [ə'nju:ɪtɪ] *n* рéнта; **life ~** пожизненная
рéнта.

annul [ə'nʌl] *vt* (*contract*) аннули́ровать (*impf/
perf*); (*marriage*) расторгáть (растóргнуть*
perf); (*law*) отменять (отмени́ть* *perf*).

annulment [ə'nʌlmənt] *n* (*see vt*)
аннули́рование; расторжéние; отмéна.

annum ['ænəm] *n see* **per**.

Annunciation [ənʌnsɪ'eɪʃən] *n* Благовéщение.

anode ['ænəud] *n* анóд.

anodyne ['ænədaɪn] *n* успокáивающее
срéдство ♦ *adj* нейтрáльный* (нейтрáлен).

anoint [ə'nɔɪnt] *vt* помáзывать (помáзать*

perf).

anomalous [ə'nɔmələs] *adj* аномáльный* (аномáлен).

anomaly [ə'nɔməlɪ] *n* аномáлия.

anon. [ə'nɔn] *abbr* = **anonymous**.

anonymity [ænə'nɪmɪtɪ] *n* анонѝмность *f*.

anonymous [ə'nɔnɪməs] *adj* анонѝмный* (анонѝмен); (*place*) безлѝкий* (безлѝк); **to remain ~** сохранять (сохранѝть *perf*) анонѝмность.

anorak ['ænəræk] *n* кýртка* с капюшóном.

anorexia [ænə'rɛksɪə] *n* анорéксия.

anorexic [ænə'rɛksɪk] *adj*: **she is ~** онá страдáет анорексѝей.

another [ə'nʌðəʳ] *pron* другóй ♦ *adj*: **~ book** (*additional*) ещё однá кнѝга; (*different*) другáя кнѝга; **I waited ~ week** я ждал ещё однý недéлю; **~ drink?** Вам ещё налѝть?; **in ~ 5 years** ещё чéрез 5 лет; *see also* **one**.

ANSI *n abbr* (= *American National Standards Institute*) Институт америкáнскиих национáльных стандáртов.

answer ['ɑ:nsəʳ] *n* отвéт; (*to problem*) решéние ♦ *vi* отвечáть (отвéтить* *perf*) ♦ *vt* (*letter, question*) отвечáть (отвéтить* *perf*) на +*acc*; (*person*) отвечáть (отвéтить* *perf*) +*dat*; **in ~ to your letter** в отвéт на Вáше письмó; **to ~ the phone** подходѝть* (подойтѝ* *perf*) к телефóну; **to ~ the bell** *or* **the door** открывáть (открыть* *perf*) дверь; **our prayers were ~ed** нáши молѝтвы бы́ли услышаны

▸ **answer back** *vi* огрызáться (*impf*)

▸ **answer for** *vt fus* отвечáть (отвéтить* *perf*) за +*acc*

▸ **answer to** *vt fus* (*description*) соответствовать (*impf*) +*dat*.

answerable ['ɑ:nsərəbl] *adj*: **~ to sb for sth** отвéтственный пéред кем-н за что-н; **I am ~ to no-one** я не отвечáю ни пéред кем.

answering machine ['ɑ:nsərɪŋ-] *n* автоотвéтчик.

ant [ænt] *n* муравéй*.

ANTA *n abbr* = *American National Theater and Academy*.

antagonism [æn'tægənɪzəm] *n* антагонѝзм.

antagonist [æn'tægənɪst] *n* протѝвник.

antagonistic [æntægə'nɪstɪk] *adj* (*feelings*) враждéбный* (враждéбен); **he is ~ to the government** он враждéбен по отношéнию к правѝтельству.

antagonize [æn'tægənaɪz] *vt*: **to ~ sb** вызывáть (вызвать* *perf*) чьё-н враждéбное отношéние.

Antarctic [ænt'ɑ:ktɪk] *n*: **the ~** Антáрктика.

Antarctica [ænt'ɑ:ktɪkə] *n* Антарктѝда.

Antarctic Circle *n*: **the ~ ~** Южный полярный круг.

Antarctic Ocean *n*: **the ~ ~** Антарктѝческий*

океáн.

ante ['æntɪ] *n*: **to up the ~** повышáть (повысить* *perf*) стáвку.

ante... ['æntɪ] *prefix* до..., пред....

anteater ['ænti:təʳ] *n* муравьéд.

antecedent [æntɪ'si:dənt] *n* предшéственник; (*ancestor*) прéдок*.

antechamber ['æntɪtʃeɪmbəʳ] *n* перéдняя *f adj*, прихóжая *f adj*.

antelope ['æntɪləup] *n* антилóпа.

antenatal ['æntɪ'neɪtl] *adj* дородовóй.

antenatal clinic *n* ≈ жéнская консультáция.

antenna [æn'tɛnə] (*pl* **~e**) *n* ýсик; (*RADIO, TV*) антéнна.

antennae [æn'tɛni:] *npl of* **antenna**.

anteroom ['æntɪrum] *n* приёмная *f adj*.

anthem ['ænθəm] *n*: **national ~** госудáрственный гѝмн.

ant hill *n* муравéйник.

anthology [æn'θɔlədʒɪ] *n* антолóгия.

anthropologist [ænθrə'pɔlədʒɪst] *n* антропóлог.

anthropology [ænθrə'pɔlədʒɪ] *n* антропологѝя.

anti... ['æntɪ] *prefix* áнти..., прóтиво....

anti-aircraft ['æntɪ'ɛəkrɑ:ft] *adj* (*missile*) противовоздýшный.

anti-aircraft defence *n* противовоздýшная оборóна.

antiballistic ['æntɪbə'lɪstɪk] *adj* (*missile*) антибаллистѝческий.

antibiotic ['æntɪbaɪ'ɔtɪk] *n* (*MED*) антибиóтик.

antibody ['æntɪbɔdɪ] *n* антитéло*.

anticipate [æn'tɪsɪpeɪt] *vt* (*expect*) ожидáть (*impf*) +*gen*; (*foresee*) предвѝдеть* (*impf/perf*); (*look forward to*) предвкушáть (*impf*); (*forestall*) предвосхищáть (предвосхѝтить* *perf*); **this is worse than I ~d** это хýже, чем я ожидáл; **as ~d** как предполагáлось.

anticipation [æntɪsɪ'peɪʃən] *n* (*expectation*) ожидáние; (*eagerness*) предвкушéние; **thanking you in ~** зарáнее благодарю́ Вас.

anticlimax [æntɪ'klaɪmæks] *n* разочарованѝе.

anticlockwise ['æntɪ'klɔkwaɪz] *adv* (*BRIT*) прóтив часовóй стрéлки.

antics ['æntɪks] *npl* (*of animal, child*) шáлости *fpl*; (*of clown*) продéлки *pl*; (*of politicians etc*) выходки *pl*.

anticyclone ['æntɪ'saɪkləun] *n* антициклóн.

antidote ['æntɪdəut] *n* (*also fig*) противоя́дие.

antifreeze ['æntɪfri:z] *n* антифрѝз.

antihistamine ['æntɪ'hɪstəmɪn] *n* антигистамѝн.

Antilles [æn'tɪli:z] *npl*: **the ~** Антѝльские островá *mpl*.

antipathy [æn'tɪpəθɪ] *n* антипáтия.

antiperspirant ['æntɪ'pə:spɪrənt] *n* дезодорáнт.

Antipodean [æntɪpə'di:ən] *adj* антипóдный

(*обычно о жителях Австра́лии и Но́вой Зела́ндии*).

Antipodes [æn'tɪpədi:z] *npl*: **the ~** Австра́лия и Но́вая Зела́ндия.

antiquarian [æntɪ'kwɛərɪən] *n* антиква́р ◆ *adj*: **~ bookshop** букинисти́ческий* магази́н.

antiquated ['æntɪkweɪtɪd] *adj* устаре́лый.

antique [æn'ti:k] *n* предме́т старины́ ◆ *adj* (*furniture etc*) антиква́рный*; (*pre-medieval*) анти́чный.

antique dealer *n* антиква́р.

antique shop *n* антиква́рный магази́н.

antiquity [æn'tɪkwɪtɪ] *n* анти́чность *f.*

anti-Semitic ['æntɪsɪ'mɪtɪk] *adj* анти-семи́тский*.

anti-Semitism ['æntɪ'sɛmɪtɪzəm] *n* анти-семити́зм.

antiseptic [æntɪ'sɛptɪk] *n* антисе́птик ◆ *adj* антисепти́ческий*.

antisocial ['æntɪ'səuʃəl] *adj* (*behaviour*) антиобще́ственный; (*person*) необщи́тельный* (необщи́телен).

antitank ['æntɪ'tæŋk] *adj* противота́нковый.

antitheses [æn'tɪθɪsi:z] *npl of* **antithesis**.

antithesis [æn'tɪθɪsɪs] (*pl* **antitheses**) *n* антите́за.

antitrust ['æntɪ'trʌst] *adj*: **~ legislation** антимонопо́льное законода́тельство.

antlers ['æntləz] *npl* (оле́ньи) рога́* *mpl.*

Antwerp ['æntwɜ:p] *n* Антве́рпен.

anus ['eɪnəs] *n* за́дний* прохо́д.

anvil ['ænvɪl] *n* накова́льня*.

anxiety [æŋ'zaɪətɪ] *n* (*also MED*) трево́га; **~ to do** стремле́ние +*infin.*

anxious ['æŋkʃəs] *adj* (*person*) беспоко́йный* (беспоко́ен); (*expression*) озабо́ченный* (озабо́чен); (*worrying*) трево́жный* (трево́жен); (*keen*): **she is ~ to do** она́ о́чень хо́чет +*infin*; **to be ~ about** беспоко́иться (*impf*) о +*prp*; **I'm very ~ about you** я о́чень беспоко́юсь за Вас.

anxiously ['æŋkʃəslɪ] *adv* беспоко́йно, трево́жно.

KEYWORD

any ['ɛnɪ] *adj* **1** (*in questions etc*): **have you any butter/children?** у Вас есть ма́сло/де́ти?; **do you have any questions/doubts?** у Вас есть каки́е-нибу́дь вопро́сы/сомне́ния?; **if there are any tickets left** е́сли ещё оста́лись биле́ты

2 (*with negative*): **I haven't any bread/books** у меня́ нет хле́ба/книг; **I didn't buy/read any newspapers** я не купи́л/не чита́л газе́ты

3 (*no matter which*) любо́й; **any colour will do** любо́й цвет пойдёт; **choose any book you like** выбира́йте любу́ю кни́гу, кака́я Вам понра́вится

4 (*in phrases*): **in any case** в любо́м слу́чае; **any day now** сейча́с в любо́й день; **at any moment** в любо́й моме́нт; **at any rate** во вся́ком слу́чае; (*anyhow*) так и́ли ина́че; **any time** (*at any moment*) в любо́й моме́нт;

(*whenever*) в любо́е вре́мя; (*in answer to thanks*) не́ за что; **I need some black leather boots – have you any?** мне нужны́ чёрные ко́жаные сапоги́ – у Вас таки́е есть?; **I have run out of sugar, you don't have any?** у меня́ ко́нчился са́хар, у Вас не найдётся немно́го?

◆ *pron* **1** (*in questions etc*): **I need some money, have you got any?** мне нужны́ де́ньги, у Вас они́ есть?; **can any of you sing?** кто́-нибудь из Вас уме́ет петь?

2 (*with negative*) ни оди́н (*f* одна́, *nt* одно́, *pl* одни́); **I haven't any (of those)** у меня́ таки́х нет

3 (*no matter which one(s)*) любо́й; **take any you like** возьми́те то, что Вам нра́вится

◆ *adv* **1** (*in questions etc*): **do you want any more soup/sandwiches?** хоти́те ещё су́па/бутербро́ды?; **are you feeling any better?** Вам хоть ско́лько-нибудь лу́чше?

2 (*with negative*): **I can't hear him any more** я бо́льше его́ не слы́шу; **don't wait any longer** не жди́те бо́льше; **he isn't any better** ему́ ниско́лько *or* ничу́ть не лу́чше.

anybody ['ɛnɪbɒdɪ] *pron* = **anyone**.

anyhow ['ɛnɪhau] *adv* (*at any rate*) так и́ли ина́че; (*haphazardly*): **the work is done ~** рабо́та сде́лана ко́е-как *or* как попа́ло; **I shall go ~** я так и́ли ина́че пойду́; **she leaves things just ~** она́ разбра́сывает ве́щи как попа́ло.

anyone ['ɛnɪwʌn] *pron* (*in questions etc*) кто́-нибудь; (*with negative*) никто́; (*no matter who*) кто уго́дно, любо́й, вся́кий*; **can you see ~?** Вы ви́дите кого́-нибудь?; **I can't see ~** я никого́ не ви́жу; **~ could do it** кто уго́дно *or* любо́й *or* вся́кий* мо́жет э́то сде́лать; **you can invite ~** Вы мо́жете пригласи́ть кого́ уго́дно.

anyplace ['ɛnɪpleɪs] *adv* (*US*) = **anywhere**.

KEYWORD

anything ['ɛnɪθɪŋ] *pron* **1** (*in questions etc*) что́-нибудь; **can you see anything?** Вы ви́дите что́-нибудь?

2 (*with negative*) ничего́; **I can't see anything** я ничего́ не ви́жу

3 (*no matter what*) (всё,) что уго́дно; **anything (at all) will do** всё, (что уго́дно) подойдёт; **he'll eat anything** он ест всё, что ему́ ни дай.

anyway ['ɛnɪweɪ] *adv* (*at any rate*) всё равно́; (*besides*) всё равно́, в любо́м слу́чае; **I will be there ~** я всё равно́ там бу́ду; **~, I couldn't stay even if I wanted to** всё равно́ *or* в любо́м слу́чае, я не мог бы оста́ться, да́же е́сли бы я захоте́л; **why are you phoning, ~?** а что Вы звони́те?

KEYWORD

anywhere ['ɛnɪwɛə'] *adv* **1** (*in questions etc*: *position*) где́-нибудь; (: *motion*) куда́-

нибудь; **can you see him anywhere?** Вы его
где-нибудь ви́дите?; **did you walk anywhere
yesterday?** Вы вчера́ куда́-нибудь ходи́ли?
2 (*with negative: position*) нигде́; (: *motion*)
никуда́; **I can't see him anywhere** я нигде́ его́
не ви́жу; **I'm not walking anywhere today**
сего́дня я никуда́ не иду́
3 (*no matter where: position*) где уго́дно; (:
motion) куда́ уго́дно; **anywhere in the world**
где уго́дно в ми́ре; **put the books down
anywhere** положи́те кни́ги куда́ уго́дно.

Anzac ['ænzæk] *n abbr* = Australia-New Zealand
  Army Corps.
apace [ə'peɪs] *adv* стреми́тельно.
apart [ə'pɑːt] *adv* (*position*) в стороне́; (*motion*)
в сто́рону; (*separately*) разде́льно, врозь;
they are ten miles/a long way ~ они́
нахо́дятся на расстоя́нии де́сяти миль/на
большо́м расстоя́нии друг от дру́га; **they
are living** ~ они́ живу́т врозь; **they jumped** ~
они́ отпры́гнули в сто́роны; **with one's legs**
~ с расста́вленными нога́ми; **to take** ~
разбира́ть (разобра́ть* *perf*) (на ча́сти); ~
from кро́ме +*gen*.
apartheid [ə'pɑːteɪt] *n* апартеи́д.
apartment [ə'pɑːtmənt] *n* (*US*) кварти́ра;
(*room*) ко́мната.
apartment building *n* (*US*) многокварти́рный
дом*.
apathetic [æpə'θɛtɪk] *adj* апати́чный*
(апати́чен).
apathy ['æpəθɪ] *n* апа́тия.
APB *n abbr* (*US*: = *all points bulletin*) ≈ сигна́л
всем поста́м.
ape [eɪp] *n* (*ZOOL*) человекообра́зная обезья́на
♦ *vt* копи́ровать (скопи́ровать *perf*).
Apennines ['æpənaɪnz] *npl*: **the** ~ Апенни́ны *pl*.
aperitif [ə'pɛrɪtiːf] *n* аперити́в.
aperture ['æpətʃjuəʳ] *n* отве́рстие; (*PHOT*)
диафра́гма.
apex ['eɪpɛks] *n* (*also fig*) верши́на.
aphid ['æfɪd] *n* тля*.
aphorism ['æfərɪzəm] *n* афори́зм.
aphrodisiac [æfrəu'dɪzɪæk] *n* сре́дство,
возбужда́ющее полово́е влече́ние ♦ *adj*
возбужда́ющий* полово́е влече́ние.
API *n abbr* = *American Press Institute*.
apiece [ə'piːs] *adv* (*each person*) на ка́ждого;
(*each thing*) за шту́ку.
aplomb [ə'plɔm] *n* апло́мб.
APO *n abbr* (*US*) = *Army Post Office*.
apocalypse [ə'pɔkəlɪps] *n* (*end of world*) коне́ц*
све́та; (*destruction*) катастро́фа.
apolitical [eɪpə'lɪtɪkl] *adj* аполити́чный*
(аполити́чен).
apologetic [əpɔlə'dʒɛtɪk] *adj* (*tone*)
извиня́ющийся*; (*person, expression*)
винова́тый; **an** ~ **letter** письмо́* с

извине́ниями; **he's very** ~ **about** ... он
прино́сит свои́ извине́ния за +*acc* ....
apologize [ə'pɔlədʒaɪz] *vi*: **to** ~ **(for sth to sb)**
извиня́ться (извини́ться *perf*) (за что-н
пе́ред кем-н).
apology [ə'pɔlədʒɪ] *n* извине́ние; **to send one's
apologies** извиня́ться (извини́ться* *perf*) за
своё отсу́тствие; **please accept my apologies**
пожа́луйста, прими́те мои́ извине́ния.
apoplectic [æpə'plɛktɪk] *adj* (*MED*)
апоплекси́ческий; (*fig*): ~ **with rage**
разъярённый (разъярён).
apoplexy ['æpəplɛksɪ] *n* апопле́ксия.
apostle [ə'pɔsl] *n* апо́стол.
apostrophe [ə'pɔstrəfɪ] *n* апостро́ф.
apotheosis [əpɔθɪ'əusɪs] *n* (*deification*)
обожествле́ние; (*fig*) апофео́з.
appal [ə'pɔːl] *vt* ужаса́ть (ужасну́ть *perf*); **to be
~led by** ужаса́ться (ужасну́ться *perf*) +*dat*.
Appalachian Mountains [æpə'leɪʃən-] *npl*: **the**
~ ~ Аппала́чи *pl*.
appalling [ə'pɔːlɪŋ] *adj* (*awful*) ужа́сный*
(ужа́сен); (*shocking*) ужаса́ющий*; **she's an** ~
cook она́ ужа́сно гото́вит.
apparatus [æpə'reɪtəs] *n* аппарату́ра; (*in
gymnasium*) (гимнасти́ческий) снаря́д; (*of
organization*) аппара́т.
apparel [ə'pærl] *n* (*esp US*) одея́ние.
apparent [ə'pærənt] *adj* (*seeming*) ви́димый;
(*obvious*) очеви́дный* (очеви́ден); **it is** ~ **that**
... очеви́дно, что ....
apparently [ə'pærəntlɪ] *adv* по всей
ви́димости.
apparition [æpə'rɪʃən] *n* виде́ние, при́зрак.
appeal [ə'piːl] *vi* (*LAW*) аппели́ровать (*impf/perf*),
подава́ть* (пода́ть* *perf*) апелля́цию ♦ *n*
(*attraction*) привлека́тельность *f*; (*plea*)
призы́в; (*LAW*) апелля́ция, обжа́лование; **to**
~ **(to sb) for** (*help, funds*) призыва́ть
(обрати́ться* *perf*) (к кому́-н) за +*instr*; (*calm,
order*) призыва́ть (призва́ть* *perf*) (кого́-н) к
+*dat*; **to** ~ **to** (*be attractive to*) привлека́ть
(привле́чь* *perf*), нра́виться (понра́виться
perf) +*dat*; **to** ~ **to sb for mercy** взыва́ть
(воззва́ть* *perf*) к кому́-н о милосе́рдии; **the
idea doesn't** ~ **to me** э́та иде́я не привлека́ет
меня́; **right of** ~ пра́во на апелля́цию *or* на
обжа́лование; **on** ~ (*LAW*) на апелля́ции.
appealing [ə'piːlɪŋ] *adj* (*attractive*)
привлека́тельный* (привлека́телен);
(*touching*) тро́гательный* (тро́гателен);
(*pleading*) умоля́ющий*.
appear [ə'pɪəʳ] *vi* (*come into view, develop*)
появля́ться (появи́ться* *perf*); (*seem*)
каза́ться* (показа́ться* *perf*); (*be published*)
выходи́ть* (вы́йти* *perf*); **to** ~ **in court**
представа́ть* (предста́ть* *perf*) пе́ред судо́м;
to ~ **on TV** выступа́ть (вы́ступить* *perf*) на

---

* marks translations which have irregular inflections. The Russian-English side of the dictionary gives inflectional information.

телеви́дении; **to ~ in "Hamlet"** игра́ть (сыгра́ть *perf*) в "Га́млете"; **it would ~ that ...** похо́же (на то), что ....

appearance [ə'pıərəns] *n* (*arrival*) появле́ние; (*look, aspect*) вне́шность *f*; (*in public, on TV*) выступле́ние; **to put in** *or* **make an ~** появля́ться (появи́ться* *perf*); **cast in** *or* **by order of ~** (*THEAT*) соста́в исполни́телей в поря́дке появле́ния; **to keep up ~s** соблюда́ть (соблюсти́* *perf*) прили́чия; **to** *or* **by all ~s** су́дя по всему́.

appease [ə'piːz] *vt* (*person, country*) умиротворя́ть (умиротвори́ть *perf*).

appeasement [ə'piːzmənt] *n* (*POL*) умиротворе́ние.

append [ə'pɛnd] *vt* (*COMPUT*) добавля́ть (доба́вить* *perf*) (в коне́ц), присоединя́ть (присоедини́ть *perf*).

appendage [ə'pɛndıdʒ] *n* прида́ток*.

appendices [ə'pɛndısiːz] *npl of* **appendix**.

appendicitis [əpɛndı'saıtıs] *n* аппендици́т.

appendix [ə'pɛndıks] (*pl* **appendices**) *n* приложе́ние; (*ANAT*) аппе́ндикс; **he had his ~ out** ему́ вы́резали аппендици́т.

appetite ['æpıtaıt] *n* аппети́т; (*fig*) страсть* *f*; **that walk has given me an ~** по́сле прогу́лки у меня́ разыгра́лся.

appetizer ['æpıtaızə'] *n* (*food*) заку́ска*; (*drink*) аперити́в.

appetizing ['æpıtaızıŋ] *adj* (*smell*) аппети́тный.

applaud [ə'plɔːd] *vi* (*clap*) аплоди́ровать (*impf*), рукоплеска́ть* (*impf*) ◆ *vt* аплоди́ровать (*impf*) +*dat*, рукоплеска́ть* (*impf*) +*dat*; (*praise*) одобря́ть (одо́брить *perf*).

applause [ə'plɔːz] *n* (*clapping*) аплодисме́нты *pl*.

apple ['æpl] *n* я́блоко*; **he's the ~ of her eye** она́ в нём души́ не ча́ет.

apple tree *n* я́блоня.

apple turnover *n* *сло́ённый пирожо́к с я́блоком.*

appliance [ə'plaıəns] *n* (*electrical, domestic*) прибо́р.

applicable [ə'plıkəbl] *adj*: **~ (to)** примени́мый (примени́м) (к +*dat*); **the law is ~ from January** зако́н вступа́ет в си́лу с января́.

applicant ['æplıkənt] *n* (*for job, scholarship*) кандида́т; (*for college*) абитурие́нт.

application [æplı'keıʃən] *n* (*for a job, a grant etc*) заявле́ние; (*hard work*) стара́ние; (*of cream, paint*) нанесе́ние; **on ~** (*of rule, knowledge*) по зая́вке; (*of methods*) примене́ние.

application form *n* заявле́ние-анке́та.

application program *n* (*COMPUT*) прикладна́я програ́мма.

applications package *n* (*COMPUT*) паке́т прикладны́х програ́мм.

applied [ə'plaıd] *adj* (*science, art*) прикладно́й.

apply [ə'plaı] *vt* (*paint, makeup*) наноси́ть* (нанести́* *perf*); (*bandage*) накла́дывать (наложи́ть *perf*); (*theory, law*) применя́ть

(примени́ть* *perf*) ◆ *vi*: **to ~ to** (*be applicable*) применя́ться (*impf*) к +*dat*; (*ask*) обраща́ться (обрати́ться* *perf*) (с про́сьбой) к +*dat*; **to ~ the brakes** нажима́ть (нажа́ть* *perf*) на тормоза́; **to ~ o.s. to** сосредота́чиваться (сосредото́читься *perf*) на +*prp*; **to ~ for a grant/job** подава́ть* (пода́ть* *perf*) заявле́ние на стипе́ндию/о приёме на рабо́ту.

appoint [ə'pɔınt] *vt* назнача́ть (назна́чить *perf*).

appointed [ə'pɔıntıd] *adj*: **at the ~ time** в назна́ченное вре́мя*.

appointee [əpɔın'tiː] *n* получи́вший(-ая) *m(f)* *adj* назначе́ние.

appointment [ə'pɔıntmənt] *n* (*of person*) назначе́ние; (*post*) до́лжность* *f*; (*arranged meeting*) приём; **to make an ~ (with sb)** назнача́ть (назна́чить *perf*) (кому́-н) встре́чу *or* свида́ние; **I have an ~ with the director/the doctor** я запи́сан на приём к мини́стру/к врачу́; **to make an ~ with the hairdresser/doctor** записа́ться* (*perf*) в парихма́херскую/на приём к врачу́; **by ~** по за́писи.

apportion [ə'pɔːʃən] *vt* распределя́ть (распредели́ть *perf*); **to ~ sth to sb** наделя́ть (надели́ть *perf*) кого́-н чем-н; **to ~ blame to sb** возлага́ть (возложи́ть *perf*) вину́ на кого́-н.

apposition [æpə'zıʃən] *n* приложе́ние.

appraisal [ə'preızl] *n* оце́нка*.

appraise [ə'preız] *vt* оце́нивать (оцени́ть* *perf*).

appreciable [ə'priːʃəbl] *adj* значи́тельный.

appreciably [ə'priːʃəblı] *adv* заме́тно, ощути́мо.

appreciate [ə'priːʃıeıt] *vt* (*value*) цени́ть* (*impf*); (*understand*) понима́ть (поня́ть* *perf*) ◆ *vi* (*COMM*) повыша́ться (повы́ситься* *perf*) в цене́; **I ~ your help** я благода́рен Вам за по́мощь; **he ~s good cooking/opera** он цени́тель хоро́шей ку́хни/о́перы.

appreciation [əpriːʃı'eıʃən] *n* (*understanding*) понима́ние; (*gratitude*) призна́тельность *f*; (*COMM*) повыше́ние сто́имости.

appreciative [ə'priːʃıətıv] *adj* (*person, audience*) призна́тельный* (призна́телен); (*comment*) одобри́тельный* (одобри́телен).

apprehend [æprı'hɛnd] *vt* (*arrest*) заде́рживать (задержа́ть* *perf*); (*understand*) понима́ть (поня́ть* *perf*).

apprehension [æprı'hɛnʃən] *n* опасе́ние; (*of criminal*) задержа́ние.

apprehensive [æprı'hɛnsıv] *adj* (*glance etc*) опа́сливый; **to be ~ about sth** опаса́ться (*impf*) за что-н.

apprentice [ə'prɛntıs] *n* подмасте́рье*, учени́к* ◆ *vt*: **to be ~d to sb** быть (*impf*) в уче́нии у кого́-н.

apprenticeship [ə'prɛntısʃıp] *n* (*also fig*) учени́чество; **to serve one's ~** проходи́ть* (пройти́* *perf*) обуче́ние.

appro. ['æprəu] *abbr* (*BRIT: inf: COMM:*) = *approval*): **on ~** на про́бу.

approach [ə'prəutʃ] *vi* приближа́ться
(прибли́зиться* *perf*) ◆ *vt* (*ask, apply to*)
обраща́ться (обрати́ться* *perf*) к +*dat*; (*come
to*) приближа́ться (прибли́зиться* *perf*) к
+*dat*; (*consider*) подходи́ть* (подойти́* *perf*) к
+*dat* ◆ *n* (*advance: also fig*) приближе́ние;
(*access: on foot*) подхо́д; (: *by transport*)
подъе́зд; (*to problem, situation*) подхо́д; **to ~
sb about sth** обраща́ться (обрати́ться* *perf*) к
кому́-н с предложе́нием о чём-н.
approachable [ə'prəutʃəbl] *adj* (*person, place*)
досту́пный* (досту́пен).
approach road *n* подъездно́й путь* *m*.
approbation [æprə'beɪʃən] *n* одобре́ние.
appropriate [*adj* ə'prəuprɪɪt, *vb* ə'prəuprɪeɪt] *adj*
(*behaviour*) подоба́ющий*; (*remarks*)
уме́стный; (*tools*) подходя́щий* ◆ *vt*
присва́ивать (присво́ить *perf*); **it would not
be ~ for me to comment** бы́ло бы неуме́стно
с мое́й стороны́ комменти́ровать; **it is not ~
for you to behave like that** Вам не подоба́ет
вести́ себя́ так.
appropriately [ə'prəuprɪɪtlɪ] *adv* подоба́ющим
or соотве́тствующим о́бразом.
appropriation [əprəuprɪ'eɪʃən] *n* присвое́ние.
appropriation account *n* счёт ассигнова́ний.
approval [ə'pru:vəl] *n* одобре́ние; (*permission*)
согла́сие; **to meet with sb's ~** получа́ть
(получи́ть* *perf*) чьё-н одобре́ние; **on ~**
(*COMM*) на про́бу.
approve [ə'pru:v] *vt* (*motion, decision*)
одобря́ть (одо́брить *perf*); (*publication,
product*) утвержда́ть (утверди́ть* *perf*)
▸ **approve of** *vt fus* одобря́ть (одо́брить *perf*).
approved school [ə'pru:vd-] *n* (*BRIT: formerly*)
исправи́тельная шко́ла.
approvingly [ə'pru:vɪŋlɪ] *adv* одобри́тельно.
approx. *abbr* = **approximately**.
approximate [*adj* ə'prɔksɪmɪt, *vb* ə'prɔksɪmeɪt]
adj приблизи́тельный* (приблизи́телен) ◆ *vi*:
to ~ to приближа́ться (прибли́зиться* *perf*) к
+*dat*.
approximately [ə'prɔksɪmɪtlɪ] *adv* приблиз-
и́тельно.
approximation [ə'prɔksɪ'meɪʃən] *n* прибли-
же́ние.
APR *n abbr* (= *annual percentage rate*) годова́я
проце́нтная ста́вка.
Apr. *abbr* = **April**.
apricot ['eɪprɪkɔt] *n* абрико́с.
April ['eɪprəl] *n* апре́ль *m*; ~ **fool!** пе́рвое
Апре́ля – никому́ не ве́рю!; *see also* **July**.
April Fool's Day *n* день *m* дурако́в.
apron ['eɪprən] *n* пере́дник, фа́ртук; (*AVIAT*)
площа́дка пе́ред анга́ром.
apse [æps] *n* апси́да.
APT *n abbr* (*BRIT*: = *advanced passenger train*)
пассажи́рский* суперэкспре́сс.

apt [æpt] *adj* (*suitable: comment, description etc*)
уда́чный* (уда́чен), уме́стный (уме́стен); ~
to do скло́нный +*infin*.
Apt. *abbr* (= **apartment**) кв.= *кварти́ра*.
aptitude ['æptɪtju:d] *n* скло́нность *f*.
aptitude test *n* тест на выявле́ние
скло́нностей.
aptly ['æptlɪ] *adv* уме́стно; (*accurately*) то́чно.
aqualung ['ækwəlʌŋ] *n* аквала́нг.
aquarium [ə'kwɛərɪəm] *n* аква́риум.
Aquarius [ə'kwɛərɪəs] *n* Водоле́й; **he is ~** он –
Водоле́й.
aquatic [ə'kwætɪk] *adj* во́дный.
aqueduct ['ækwɪdʌkt] *n* акведу́к.
AR *abbr* (*US: POST*) = *Arkansas*.
ARA *n abbr* (*BRIT*) = *Associate of the Royal
Academy*.
Arab ['ærəb] *adj* ара́бский* ◆ *n* ара́б(ка).
Arabia [ə'reɪbɪə] *n* Ара́вия.
Arabian [ə'reɪbɪən] *adj* ара́бский*.
Arabian Desert *n*: **the ~ ~** Арави́йская
пусты́ня.
Arabian Sea *n*: **the ~ ~** Арави́йское мо́ре*.
Arabic ['ærəbɪk] *adj* ара́бский* ◆ *n* ара́бский*
язы́к*.
arable ['ærəbl] *adj* (*land*) па́хотный; (*farm*)
полево́дческий.
Aral Sea ['ærəl-] *n* Ара́льское мо́ре.
ARAM *n abbr* (*BRIT*) = *Associate of the Royal
Academy of Music*.
arbiter ['ɑ:bɪtə] *n* арби́тр (*в спо́ре*).
arbitrary ['ɑ:bɪtrərɪ] *adj* произво́льный*
(произво́лен).
arbitrate ['ɑ:bɪtreɪt] *vi* выноси́ть* (вы́нести*
perf) трете́йское реше́ние.
arbitration [ɑ:bɪ'treɪʃən] *n* (*of quarrel*)
трете́йский суд*; (*INDUSTRY*) арбитра́ж; **the
dispute went to ~** спо́р пе́редан в арбитра́ж.
arbitrator ['ɑ:bɪtreɪtə] *n* трете́йский судья́*,
арби́тр.
ARC *n abbr* = *American Red Cross*.
arc [ɑ:k] *n* (*also MATH*) дуга́*.
arcade [ɑ:'keɪd] *n* (*round a square*) арка́да;
(*shopping mall*) пасса́ж.
arch [ɑ:tʃ] *n* а́рка*, свод; (*of foot*) свод ◆ *vt*
(*back*) выгиба́ть (вы́гнуть *perf*) ◆ *adj* (*playful*)
игри́вый; (*knowing*) многозначи́тельный ◆
prefix а́рхи-.
archaeological [ɑ:kɪə'lɔdʒɪkl] (*US
archeological*) *adj* археологи́ческий*.
archaeologist [ɑ:kɪ'ɔlədʒɪst] (*US archeologist*) *n*
архео́лог.
archaeology [ɑ:kɪ'ɔlədʒɪ] (*US archeology*) *n*
археоло́гия.
archaic [ɑ:'keɪɪk] *adj* архаи́ческий.
Archangel ['ɑ:keɪndʒəl] *n* Арха́нгельск.
archangel ['ɑ:keɪndʒəl] *n* арха́нгел.
archbishop [ɑ:tʃ'bɪʃəp] *n* архиепи́скоп.

---

* marks translations which have irregular inflections. The Russian-English side of the dictionary gives inflectional information.

arch-enemy [ˈɑːtʃˈɛnəmɪ] *n* заклятый враг*.
archeology *etc* [ɑːkɪˈɔlədʒɪ] (*US*) = **archaeology** *etc*.
archery [ˈɑːtʃərɪ] *n* стрельба* из лука.
archetypal [ˈɑːkɪtaɪpəl] *adj* типичный*.
archetype [ˈɑːkɪtaɪp] *n* образец.
archipelago [ɑːkɪˈpɛlɪɡəu] *n* архипелаг.
architect [ˈɑːkɪtɛkt] *n* (*of building*) архитектор.
architectural [ɑːkɪˈtɛktʃərəl] *adj* архитектурный.
architecture [ˈɑːkɪtɛktʃə*] *n* архитектура.
archive [ˈɑːkaɪvz] *n* архив.
archive file *n* (*COMPUT*) архивный файл.
archives [ˈɑːkaɪvz] *npl* архив *msg*.
archivist [ˈɑːkɪvɪst] *n* архивариус.
archway [ˈɑːtʃweɪ] *n* арочный проход.
ARCM *n abbr* (*BRIT*) = *Associate of the Royal College of Music.*
Arctic [ˈɑːktɪk] *adj* арктический* ♦ *n*: **the ~** Арктика.
Arctic Circle *n*: **the ~~** Северный Полярный круг.
Arctic Ocean *n*: **the ~~** Северный Ледовитый океан.
ARD *n abbr* (*US: MED*: = *acute respiratory disease*) ОРЗ= *острое респираторное заболевание*.
ardent [ˈɑːdənt] *adj* пылкий* (пылок).
ardour [ˈɑːdə*] (*US* **ardor**) *n* пыл*.
arduous [ˈɑːdjuəs] *adj* тяжёлый* (тяжёл).
are [ɑː*] *vb see* **be**.
area [ˈɛərɪə] *n* (*of country, knowledge*) область *f*; (*part: of place*) участок*; (: *of room*) часть *f*; (*GEOM etc*) площадь* *f*; **in the London ~** в районе Лондона.
area code *n* код зоны.
arena [əˈriːnə] *n* (*also fig*) арена.
aren't [ɑːnt] = **are not;** *see* **be**.
Argentina [ɑːdʒənˈtiːnə] *n* Аргентина.
Argentinian [ɑːdʒənˈtɪnɪən] *adj* аргентинский* ♦ *n* аргентинец*(-нка*).
arguable [ˈɑːɡjuəbl] *adj* спорный* (спорен); **it is ~ whether this is necessary** нужно ли это – вопрос спорный; **it is ~ that ...** можно утверждать, что ....
arguably [ˈɑːɡjuəblɪ] *adv* возможно; **he is ~ the best in his profession** можно утверждать, что он лучший специалист в своей области.
argue [ˈɑːɡjuː] *vi* (*quarrel*) ссориться (поссориться *perf*); (*reason*) доказывать (доказать* *perf*) ♦ *vt* обсуждать (обсудить* *perf*); **to ~ that ...** доказывать (доказать* *perf*), что ...; **to ~ about sth** спорить (поспорить *perf*) о чём-н; **to ~ for/against sth** приводить* (привести* *perf*) доводы в пользу/против чего-н.
argument [ˈɑːɡjumənt] *n* (*quarrel*) ссора; (*reasons*) аргумент, довод; (*debate*) обсуждение, спор*; **~ for/against** аргумент *or* довод в пользу/против +*gen*.
argumentative [ɑːɡjuˈmɛntətɪv] *adj* (*person*) конфликтный*; (*voice*) вызывающий*.

aria [ˈɑːrɪə] *n* ария.
ARIBA *n abbr* (*BRIT*) = *Associate of the Royal Institue of British Architects.*
arid [ˈærɪd] *adj* безводный* (безводен); (*fig*) сухой.
aridity [əˈrɪdɪtɪ] *n* сухость *f*.
Aries [ˈɛərɪz] *n* Овен*; **he is ~** он – Овен.
arise [əˈraɪz] (*pt* **arose**, *pp* **arisen**) *vi* (*occur*) возникать (возникнуть* *perf*); **to ~ from** возникать (возникнуть* *perf*) вследствие +*gen*; **should the need ~** если возникнет необходимость.
arisen [əˈrɪzn] *pp of* **arise**.
aristocracy [ærɪsˈtɔkrəsɪ] *n* аристократия.
aristocrat [ˈærɪstəkræt] *n* аристократ(ка*).
aristocratic [ærɪstəˈkrætɪk] *adj* (*family*) аристократический*; (*features*) аристократичный.
arithmetic [əˈrɪθmətɪk] *n* (*MATH*) арифметика; (*calculation*) подсчёт.
arithmetical [ærɪθˈmɛtɪkl] *adj* арифметический*.
ark [ɑːk] *n*: **Noah's A~** Ноев ковчег.
arm [ɑːm] *n* рука*; (*of chair*) ручка*; (*of clothing*) рукав*; (*of organization*) подразделение ♦ *vt* вооружать (вооружить* *perf*); **~s** *npl* (*MIL*) вооружение *ntsg*; (*HERALDRY*) герб; **~ in ~** под руку.
armaments [ˈɑːməmənts] *npl* вооружение *sg*.
armband [ˈɑːmbænd] *n* нарукавная повязка.
armchair [ˈɑːmtʃɛə*] *n* кресло*.
armed [ɑːmd] *adj* вооружённый (вооружён); **the ~ forces** вооружённые силы.
armed robbery *n* вооружённый грабёж*.
Armenia [ɑːˈmiːnɪə] *n* Армения.
Armenian [ɑːˈmiːnɪən] *adj* армянский* ♦ *n* армянин(-нка); (*LING*) армянский* язык*.
armful [ˈɑːmful] *n* охапка.
armistice [ˈɑːmɪstɪs] *n* перемирие.
armor *etc* (*US*) = **armour** *etc*.
armour [ˈɑːmə*] (*US* **armor**) *n* (*also:* **suit of ~**) доспехи *mpl*; (*also:* **~-plating**) броня; (*tanks*) бронесилы *fpl*.
armoured car [ˈɑːməd-] *n* бронемашина.
armoury [ˈɑːmərɪ] *n* (*also fig*) арсенал.
armpit [ˈɑːmpɪt] *n* подмышка*.
armrest [ˈɑːmrɛst] *n* подлокотник.
arms control [ɑːmz-] *n* контроль *m* вооружений.
arms race *n*: **the ~~** гонка вооружений.
army [ˈɑːmɪ] *n* (*also fig*) армия.
aroma [əˈrəumə] *n* аромат.
aromatherapy [ərəuməˈθɛrəpɪ] *n* аромотерапия.
aromatic [ærəˈmætɪk] *adj* ароматный* (ароматен).
arose [əˈrəuz] *pt of* **arise**.
around [əˈraund] *adv* вокруг ♦ *prep* (*encircling*) вокруг +*gen*; (*near, about*) около +*gen*; **is he ~?** он здесь?; **~ £5/3 o'clock** около £5/3 часов*; **~ here** здесь поблизости.

arousal [ə'rauzəl] *n* возбужде́ние.
arouse [ə'rauz] *vt* (*sleeping person*) буди́ть*
(разбуди́ть* *perf*); (*interest, passions*)
возбужда́ть (возбуди́ть* *perf*).
arpeggio [ɑː'pɛdʒɪəu] *n* арпе́джио *nt ind*.
arrange [ə'reɪndʒ] *vt* (*organize*) устра́ивать
(устро́ить *perf*); (*put in order*) расставля́ть
(расста́вить *perf*); (*MUS*) аранжи́ровать (*impf/
perf*) ♦ *vi*: **we have ~d for a car to pick you up**
мы договори́лись, что́бы маши́на зае́хала
за Ва́ми; **it was ~d that ...** бы́ло усло́влено,
что ...; **to ~ to do** усла́вливаться
(усло́виться* *perf*) +*infin*, догова́риваться
(договори́ться *perf*) +*infin*.
arrangement [ə'reɪndʒmənt] *n* (*agreement*)
договорённость *f*; (*MUS*) аранжиро́вка*;
(*order, layout*) расположе́ние; **~s** *npl*
(*preparations, plans*) приготовле́ния *ntpl*; **to
come to an ~ with sb** приходи́ть* (прийти́*
perf) к соглаше́нию с кем-н; **home deliveries
by ~** доста́вка на́ дом по договорённости;
I'll make ~s for you to be met я договорю́сь,
что́бы Вас встре́тили.
arrant ['ærənt] *adj* отъя́вленный.
array [ə'reɪ] *n* (*MATH, COMPUT*) масси́в; **~ of**
ма́сса +*gen*, мно́жество +*gen*.
arrears [ə'rɪəz] *npl* задо́лженность *fsg*; **to be in
~ with one's rent** име́ть (*impf*)
задо́лженность по квартпла́те.
arrest [ə'rɛst] *vt* (*criminal*) аресто́вывать
(арестова́ть *perf*); (*sb's attention*)
прико́вывать (прикова́ть *perf*) ♦ *n* аре́ст,
задержа́ние; **under ~** под аре́стом.
arresting [ə'rɛstɪŋ] *adj* порази́тельный.
arrival [ə'raɪvl] *n* прибы́тие; (*COMM*) приво́з;
new ~ (*person*) новичо́к*; (*baby*)
новорождённый(-ая) *m(f) adj*.
arrive [ə'raɪv] *vi* (*traveller*) прибыва́ть
(прибы́ть* *perf*); (*letter, news*) приходи́ть*
(прийти́* *perf*); (*baby*) рожда́ться (роди́ться*
perf)
▶ **arrive at** *vt fus* (*fig*) приходи́ть* (прийти́* *perf*)
к +*dat*.
arrogance ['ærəgəns] *n* высокоме́рие.
arrogant ['ærəgənt] *adj* высокоме́рный*
(высокоме́рен).
arrow ['ærəu] *n* (*weapon*) стрела́*; (*sign*)
стре́лка*.
arse [ɑːs] *n* (*BRIT* *inf!*) жо́па (*!*)
arsenal ['ɑːsɪnl] *n* арсена́л.
arsenic ['ɑːsnɪk] *n* мышья́к*.
arson ['ɑːsn] *n* поджо́г.
art [ɑːt] *n* (*also fig*) иску́сство; (*also:* **Fine A~**)
изобрази́тельное иску́сство; **A~s** *npl*
гуманита́рные нау́ки *fpl*; **work of ~**
произведе́ние иску́сства.
artefact ['ɑːtɪfækt] *n* худо́жественное изде́лие,
поде́лка.

arterial [ɑː'tɪərɪəl] *adj* (*ANAT*) артериа́льный; **~
road** магистра́ль *f*.
artery ['ɑːtərɪ] *n* (*also fig*) арте́рия.
artful ['ɑːtful] *adj* ло́вкий*.
art gallery *n* (*national*) карти́нная галере́я;
(*private*) галере́я.
arthritic [ɑː'θrɪtɪk] *adj* артрити́ческий*.
arthritis [ɑː'θraɪtɪs] *n* артри́т.
artichoke ['ɑːtɪtʃəuk] *n* (*also:* **globe ~**)
артишо́к; (*also:* **Jerusalem ~**) земляна́я
гру́ша.
article ['ɑːtɪkl] *n* (*object, item*) предме́т; (*LING*)
арти́кль *m*; (*in newspaper*) статья́*; (*in
document*) пункт; **~s** *npl* (*BRIT: LAW*) курс
профессиона́льной подгото́вки адвока́тов; **~
of clothing** предме́т оде́жды.
articles of association *npl* (*COMM*) уста́в
акционе́рной компа́нии.
articulate [*adj* ɑː'tɪkjulɪt, *vb* ɑː'tɪkjuleɪt] *adj*
(*speech, writing*) вразуми́тельный*
(вразуми́телен) ♦ *vt* (*fears, ideas*) выража́ть
(вы́разить* *perf*) ♦ *vi*: **to ~ well/badly** чётко/
нечётко выгова́ривать (вы́говорить *perf*);
she is very ~ она́ чётко *or* я́сно выража́ет
свои́ мы́сли.
articulated lorry *n* (*BRIT*) грузови́к* с
прице́пом.
artifice ['ɑːtɪfɪs] *n* (*trick*) приём; (*skill*)
иску́сность *f*.
artificial [ɑːtɪ'fɪʃəl] *adj* иску́сственный*;
(*affected*) неесте́ственный* (неесте́вен).
artificial insemination [-ɪnsɛmɪ'neɪʃən] *n*
иску́сственное оплодотворе́ние.
artificial intelligence *n* иску́сственный
интелле́кт.
artificial respiration *n* иску́сственное
дыха́ние.
artillery [ɑː'tɪlərɪ] *n* (*MIL: corps*) артилле́рия.
artisan ['ɑːtɪzæn] *n* реме́сленник(-ица).
artist ['ɑːtɪst] *n* худо́жник(-ица); (*performer*)
арти́ст(ка).
artistic [ɑː'tɪstɪk] *adj* худо́жественный; **an ~
person** худо́жественная ли́чность *f*.
artistry ['ɑːtɪstrɪ] *n* мастерство́.
artless ['ɑːtlɪs] *adj* безыску́сный (безыску́сен).
art school *n* худо́жественное учи́лище.
artwork ['ɑːtwɔːk] *n* оформле́ние.
ARV *n abbr* (*BIBLE*: = *American Revised Version*)
америка́нский вариа́нт Би́блии.
AS *n abbr* (*US*: = *Associate in/of Science*) член
ассоциа́ции нау́чных рабо́тников ♦ *abbr*
(*POST*) = *American Samoa*.

KEYWORD

as [æz] *conj* **1** (*referring to time*) когда́; **as the
years went by** с года́ми; **he came in as I was
leaving** он вошёл, когда́ я уходи́л; **as from
tomorrow** с за́втрашнего дня
2 (*in comparisons*): **as big as** тако́й же

---

* marks translations which have irregular inflections. The Russian-English side of the dictionary gives inflectional information.

большóй, как; **twice as big as** в два рáза
бóльше, чем; **as white as snow** бéлый как
снег; **as much money/many books as** стóлько
же дéнег/книг, скóлько; **as soon as** как
тóлько; **as soon as possible** как мóжно
скорéе
3 (*since, because*) поскóльку, так как
4 (*referring to manner, way*) как; **do as you
wish** дéлайте как хотúте; **as she said** как онá
сказáла
5 (*concerning*) **as for** *or* **to** что касáется +*gen*;
6: **as if** *or* **though** так, как бýдто бы; **he looked
as if he had been ill** он вúглядел так, как
бýдто бы он был бóлен
♦ *prep* (*in the capacity of*): **he works as a driver/
waiter** он рабóтает шофёром/официáнтом;
as chairman of the company, he … как главá
компáнии, он …; *see also* **long, same, such,
well**.

ASA *n abbr* (= *American Standards Association*)
Америкáнская ассоциáция стандáртов.
a.s.a.p. *adv abbr* (= *as soon as possible*) как
мóжно скорéе.
asbestos [æz'bɛstəs] *n* асбéст.
ascend [ə'sɛnd] *vt* (*hill*) всходúть* (взойтú* *perf*)
на +*acc*; (*stairs*) всходúть* (взойтú* *perf*) по
+*dat*; (*throne*) взойтú* (*perf*) на +*acc*.
ascendancy [ə'sɛndənsɪ] *n* госпóдство; ~ **over
sb** госпóдство над кем-н.
ascendant [ə'sɛndənt] *n*: **to be in the ~**
госпóдствовать (*impf*).
ascension [ə'sɛnʃən] *n*: **the A~** (*REL*)
Вознесéние.
Ascension Island *n* Óстров Вознесéния.
ascent [ə'sɛnt] *n* (*slope*) подъём; (*climb*)
восхождéние.
ascertain [æsə'teɪn] *vt* устанáвливать
(установúть* *perf*).
ascetic [ə'sɛtɪk] *adj* аскетúческий*.
asceticism [ə'sɛtɪsɪzəm] *n* аскетúзм.
ASCII ['æski:] *n abbr* (*COMPUT*. = *American
Standard Code for Information Interchange*)
*америкáнский стандáртный код для обмéна
информáцией*.
ascribe [ə'skraɪb] *vt*: **to ~ sth to** припúсывать
(приписáть* *perf*) что-н +*dat*.
ASCU *n abbr* (*US*) = *Association of State Colleges
and Universities*.
ASEAN ['æsɪæn] *n abbr* (= *Association of South-
East Asian Nations*) АСЕАН.
ASH [æʃ] *n abbr* (*BRIT*) = *Action on Smoking and
Health*) Óбщество борьбý с курéнием.
ash [æʃ] *n* (*of fire*) золá, пéпел*; (*of cigarette*)
пéпел; (*wood, tree*) ясень *m*.
ashamed [ə'ʃeɪmd] *adj*: **to be ~ (of)** стыдúться
(*impf*) (+*gen*); **I'm ~ of …** мне стúдно +*gen* …;
I'm ~ of myself for having done that мне
стúдно, что я сдéлал это.
ashen ['æʃən] *adj* (*face*) мёртвенно-блéдный*.
Ashkhabad [aʃxa'bat] *n* Ашхабáд.

ashore [ə'ʃɔ:'] *adv* (*be*) на берегý; (*swim, go*) на
бéрег.
ashtray ['æʃtreɪ] *n* пéпельница.
Ash Wednesday *n* пéрвый день* *m* Велúкого
Постá.
Asia ['eɪʃə] *n* Áзия.
Asia Minor *n* Мáлая Áзия.
Asian ['eɪʃən] *adj* азиáтский* ♦ *n* азиáт(ка*).
Asiatic [eɪsɪ'ætɪk] *adj* азиáтский*.
aside [ə'saɪd] *adv* в стóрону ♦ *n* рéплика ♦ *prep*:
~ **from** помúмо +*gen*; **to brush objections ~**
отметáть (отместú* *perf*) возражéния в
стóрону.
ask [ɑ:sk] *vt* (*inquire*) спрáшивать (спросúть*
perf); (*invite*) звать* (позвáть* *perf*); **to ~ sb for
sth/sb to do** просúть* (попросúть* *perf*) что-н
у когó-н/когó-н +*infin*; **to ~ sb the time**
спрáшивать (спросúть* *perf*) когó-н,
котóрый час; **to ~ sb about sth** спрáшивать
(спросúть* *perf*) когó-н о чём-н; **to ~ about
the price** спрáшивать (спросúть* *perf*) о ценé;
to ~ (sb) a question задавáть* (задáть* *perf*)
(комý-н) вопрóс; **to ~ sb out to dinner**
приглашáть (пригласúть* *perf*) когó-н в
ресторáн
▸ **ask after** *vt fus* (*person*) справляться
(спрáвиться* *perf*) о +*prp*
▸ **ask for** *vt fus* (*request*) просúть* (попросúть*
perf); (*look for: trouble*) напрáшиваться
(напросúться* *perf*) на +*acc*; **he's just ~ing for
trouble** *or* **for it** он прóсто напрáшивается на
неприятности.
askance [ə'skɑ:ns] *adv*: **to look ~ at sb/sth**
смотрéть* (посмотрéть* *perf*) на когó-н/
что-н кóсо.
askew [ə'skju:] *adv* (*clothes*) крúво, кóсо.
asking price ['ɑ:skɪŋ-] *n*: **the ~ ~**
запрáшиваемая ценá*.
asleep [ə'sli:p] *adj* спящий; **to be ~** спать*
(*impf*); **to fall ~** засыпáть (заснýть *perf*).
ASLEF ['æzlɛf] *n abbr* (*BRIT*) = *Associated Society
of Locomotive Engineers and Firemen*.
asp [æsp] *n* áспид.
asparagus [əs'pærəgəs] *n* спáржа.
asparagus tips *npl* спáржевые головки* *fpl*.
ASPCA *n abbr* (= *American Society for the
Prevention of Cruelty to Animals*)
Америкáнское óбщество защúты
живóтных.
aspect ['æspɛkt] *n* (*element*) аспéкт, сторонá*;
(*quality, air*) вид*; **a room with a southern ~**
кóмната с вúдом на юг.
aspersions [əs'pə:ʃənz] *npl*: **to cast ~ on**
(*integrity, ability*) стáвить* (постáвить* *perf*)
под сомнéние; (*person*) очернять (очернúть*
perf).
asphalt ['æsfælt] *n* асфáльт.
asphyxiate [æs'fɪksɪeɪt] *vt* душúть* (задушúть*
perf).
asphyxiation [æsfɪksɪ'eɪʃən] *n* удýшье.
aspirate [*vt* 'æspəreɪt, *adj* 'æspərɪt] *vt*

произноси́ть* (произнести́* *perf*) с
придыха́нием ◆ *adj* придыха́тельный.
aspirations [æspə'reɪʃənz] *npl*
устремле́ния *ntpl*.
aspire [əs'paɪəʳ] *vi*: **to ~ to** стреми́ться* (*impf*) к
+*dat*.
aspirin ['æsprɪn] *n* аспири́н.
aspiring [əs'paɪərɪŋ] *adj* начина́ющий*.
ass [æs] *n* (*also fig*) осёл*; (*US*: *infl*) жо́па (*!*)
assail [ə'seɪl] *vt* (*person*) напада́ть (напа́сть*
perf) на +*acc*; (*fig*): **he was ~ed by doubts** его́
одоле́ли сомне́ния.
assailant [ə'seɪlənt] *n*: **his/her ~** напа́вший(-ая)
m(f) adj на него́/неё.
assassin [ə'sæsɪn] *n* полити́ческий* уби́йца *m/f*.
assassinate [ə'sæsɪneɪt] *vt* соверша́ть
(соверши́ть *perf*) покуше́ние на +*acc*.
assassination [əsæsɪ'neɪʃən] *n* полити́ческое
уби́йство.
assault [ə'sɔ:lt] *n* нападе́ние; (*MIL*, *fig*) ата́ка ◆
vt напада́ть (напа́сть* *perf*) на +*acc*; (*MIL*)
атакова́ть (*impf/perf*); (*sexually*) наси́ловать
(изнаси́ловать *perf*); **~ and battery** (*LAW*)
оскорбле́ние де́йствием.
assemble [ə'sɛmbl] *vt* собира́ть (собра́ть* *perf*)
◆ *vi* собира́ться (собра́ться* *perf*).
assembly [ə'sɛmblɪ] *n* (*meeting*) собра́ние;
(*institution*) ассамбле́я, законода́тельное
собра́ние; (*construction*) сбо́рка; **General A~
of the UN** Генера́льная Ассамбле́я ООН.
assembly language *n* (*COMPUT*) язы́к*
ассе́мблера.
assembly line *n* сбо́рочный конве́йер.
assent [ə'sɛnt] *n* согла́сие ◆ *vi*: **to ~ (to)**
соглаша́ться (согласи́ться* *perf*) (на +*acc*).
assert [ə'sə:t] *vt* (*opinion, authority*)
утвержда́ть (утверди́ть* *perf*); (*rights,
innocence*) отста́ивать (отстоя́ть *perf*); **to ~
o.s.** самоутвержда́ться (самоутверди́ться*
perf).
assertion [ə'sə:ʃən] *n* (*claim*) утвержде́ние.
assertive [ə'sə:tɪv] *adj* самоуве́ренный
(самоуве́рен).
assess [ə'sɛs] *vt* оце́нивать (оцени́ть* *perf*); **to
~ for tax** оцени́ть (*perf*) сто́имость для це́лей
налогообложе́ния.
assessment [ə'sɛsmənt] *n*: **~ (of)** оце́нка*
(+*gen*); **tax ~** оце́нка сто́имости для це́лей
налогообложе́ния.
assessor [ə'sɛsəʳ] *n* (*LAW*) экспе́рт-
(-консульта́нт).
asset ['æsɛt] *n* (*useful quality*) досто́инство; **~s**
npl (*property, funds*) акти́вы *mpl*; (*COMM*)
акти́в *msg* бала́нса; **he's an ~ to the company**
он представля́ет собо́й большу́ю це́нность
для компа́нии.
asset-stripping ['æsɛt'strɪpɪŋ] *n* (*COMM*)
распрода́жа непри́быльных акти́вов (*при*

поглаще́ние одно́й компа́нии друго́й).
assiduous [ə'sɪdjuəs] *adj* (*care, work*)
усе́рдный* (усе́рден).
assign [ə'saɪn] *vt* (*task*) поруча́ть (поручи́ть*
perf), предпи́сывать (предписа́ть* *perf*);
(*significance*) придава́ть* (прида́ть* *perf*);
(*resources, role*) предназнача́ть
(предназна́чить *perf*); **to ~ a date for a
meeting** назнача́ть (назна́чить *perf*) да́ту
заседа́ния.
assignment [ə'saɪnmənt] *n* (*task*) предписа́ние;
(*SCOL*) зада́ние.
assimilate [ə'sɪmɪleɪt] *vt* (*ideas*) усва́ивать
(усво́ить *perf*); (*immigrants*): **to be ~d**
ассимили́роваться (*impf/perf*).
assimilation [əsɪmɪ'leɪʃən] *n* усвое́ние; (*of
immigrants etc*) ассимиля́ция.
assist [ə'sɪst] *vt* помога́ть (помо́чь* *perf*) +*dat*;
(*financially*) соде́йствовать (*impf/perf*) +*dat*.
assistance [ə'sɪstəns] *n* по́мощь *f*; (*financial*)
соде́йствие.
assistant [ə'sɪstənt] *n* помо́щник(-ица); (*in
office etc*) ассисте́нт(ка); (*BRIT: also: **shop ~**)
продаве́ц*(-вщи́ца); **laboratory ~**
лабора́нт(ка).
assistant manager *n* замести́тель *m*
заве́дующего.
assizes [ə'saɪzɪz] *npl* (*BRIT: LAW*) выездна́я
се́ссия суда́ прися́жных.
associate [*n, adj* ə'səʊʃɪɪt, *vb* ə'səʊʃɪeɪt] *n*
(*colleague*) колле́га *m/f* ◆ *adj* (*member,
director, professor*) ассоции́рованный ◆ *vt*
(*mentally*) ассоции́ровать (*impf/perf*); **to ~
with sb** обща́ться (*impf*) с кем-н.
associated company [ə'səʊʃɪeɪtɪd-] *n* доче́рнее
предприя́тие.
association [əsəʊsɪ'eɪʃən] *n* (*group, PSYCH*)
ассоциа́ция; (*involvement*) связь* *f*; **in ~ with**
в сотру́дничестве с +*instr*.
association football *n* футбо́л.
assorted [ə'sɔ:tɪd] *adj* разнообра́зный*; **hats in
~ sizes** шля́пы ра́зных разме́ров.
assortment [ə'sɔ:tmənt] *n* (*of clothes, colours*)
ассортиме́нт; (*of books, people*) подбо́р.
Asst. *abbr* (= **assistant**) ассисте́нт.
assuage [ə'sweɪdʒ] *vt* (*grief, pain*) смягча́ть
(смягчи́ть *perf*); (*thirst, hunger*) утоля́ть
(утоли́ть *perf*).
assume [ə'sju:m] *vt* (*suppose*) предполага́ть
(предположи́ть* *perf*), допуска́ть
(допусти́ть* *perf*); (*responsibilities*) брать*
(взять* *perf*) на себя́; (*command, appearance,
air*) принима́ть (приня́ть* *perf*); (*power*)
брать* (взять* *perf*).
assumed name [ə'sju:md-] *n* вы́мышленное
и́мя* *nt*.
assumption [ə'sʌmpʃən] *n* (*supposition*)
предположе́ние; (*of control, responsibility*)

---

* marks translations which have irregular inflections. The Russian-English side of the dictionary gives inflectional information.

приня́тие на себя́; ~ **of power** при́ход к
вла́сти; **on the ~ that** ... предполага́я, что ....
assurance [ə'ʃuərəns] *n* (*promise*) завере́ние;
(*confidence*) уве́ренность *f*; (*insurance*)
страхова́ние; **I can give you no ~s** я не могу́
дать Вам никаки́х гара́нтий.
assure [ə'ʃuə'] *vt* (*reassure*) уверя́ть (уве́рить
perf), заверя́ть (заве́рить *perf*); (*guarantee*)
обеспе́чивать (обеспе́чить *perf*).
assured [ə'ʃuəd] *adj* (*voice*) уве́ренный*
(уве́рен); (*sucess*) несомне́нный*
(несомне́нен).
AST *abbr* (*US*) = *Atlantic Standard Time.*
asterisk ['æstərɪsk] *n* звёздочка* (знак "*").
astern [ə'stɜːn] *adv* (*NAUT*: *on ship*: *position*) на
корме́; (: *motion*) на корму́; (*behind ship*) за
кормо́й; **to move ~** идти́* (*impf*) за́дним
хо́дом.
asteroid ['æstərɔɪd] *n* астеро́ид.
asthma ['æsmə] *n* а́стма.
asthmatic [æs'mætɪk] *adj* (*breathing*)
астмати́ческий* ♦ *n* астма́тик; **~ attack**
при́ступ а́стмы.
astigmatism [ə'stɪgmətɪzəm] *n* астигмати́зм.
astir [ə'stɜː'] *adv* на нога́х.
astonish [ə'stɒnɪʃ] *vt* изумля́ть (изуми́ть* *perf*),
поража́ть (порази́ть* *perf*).
astonishing [ə'stɒnɪʃɪŋ] *adj* порази́тельный*
(порази́телен); **I find it ~ that** ... меня́
поража́ет, что ....
astonishingly [ə'stɒnɪʃɪŋlɪ] *adv* порази́тельно;
the play, ~, was successful порази́тельным
о́бразом пье́са была́ уда́чной.
astonishment [ə'stɒnɪʃmənt] *n* удивле́ние,
изумле́ние; **to my ~** к моему́ изумле́нию.
astound [ə'staund] *vt* поража́ть (порази́ть*
perf), изумля́ть (изуми́ть* *perf*).
astounded [ə'staundɪd] *adj* поражённый
(поражён), изумлённый (изумлён).
astounding [ə'staundɪŋ] *adj* порази́тельный*
(порази́телен), изуми́тельный*
(изуми́телен).
astray [ə'streɪ] *adv*: **to go ~** (*letter*) затеря́ться
(*perf*); (*fig*) сбива́ться (сби́ться* *perf*) с пути́;
to lead ~ (*fig*) сбива́ть (сбить* *perf*) с пути́; **to
go ~ in one's calculations** сбива́ться
(сби́ться* *perf*) со счёта.
astride [ə'straɪd] *prep* верхо́м на +*prp* ♦ *adv*
верхо́м.
astringent [əs'trɪndʒənt] *adj* вя́жущий* ♦ *n*
вя́жущее вещество́.
astrologer [əs'trɒlədʒə'] *n* астро́лог.
astrology [əs'trɒlədʒɪ] *n* астроло́гия.
astronaut ['æstrənɔːt] *n* астрона́вт,
космона́вт.
astronomer [əs'trɒnəmə'] *n* астроно́м.
astronomical [æstrə'nɒmɪkl] *adj* (*also fig*)
астрономи́ческий*.
astronomy [əs'trɒnəmɪ] *n* астроно́мия.
astrophysics ['æstrəu'fɪzɪks] *n* астрофи́зика.
astute [əs'tjuːt] *adj* (*person*) проница́тельный*

(проница́телен); (*decision*) дальнови́дный*
(дальнови́ден).
asunder [ə'sʌndə'] *adv*: **to tear ~** разрыва́ть
(разорва́ть* *perf*) на куски́.
ASV *n abbr* (*BIBLE*: = *American Standard Version*)
америка́нский* станда́ртный вариа́нт
Би́блии.
asylum [ə'saɪləm] *n* (*refuge*) убе́жище; (*mental
hospital*) сумасше́дший дом*; **to seek
political ~** иска́ть* (*perf*) полити́ческого
убе́жища.
asymmetrical [eɪsɪ'mɛtrɪkl] *adj*
ассиметри́чный* (ассиметри́чен).

─────────────────────────
KEYWORD
─────────────────────────

at [æt] *prep* **1** (*referring to position*) в/на +*prp*; **at
the top** наверху́; **at home** до́ма; **at school** в
шко́ле; **at the theatre** в теа́тре; **at the baker's**
в бу́лочной; **at a concert** на конце́рте; **at the
station** на ста́нции; **they are sitting at the
table** они́ сидя́т за столо́м; **at my friend's
(house)** у моего́ дру́га; **at the doctor's** у врача́
2 (*referring to direction*) в/на +*acc*; **to look at
sb/sth** смотре́ть (посмотре́ть *perf*) на
кого́-н/что-н; **to throw sth at sb** (*several
objects*) броса́ться (*impf*) чем-н в кого́-н; (*one
object*) броса́ть (бро́сить* *perf*) что-н в
кого́-н
3 (*referring to time*): **at four o'clock** в четы́ре
часа́; **at half past two** в полови́не тре́тьего; **at
a quarter to two** без че́тверти два; **at a
quarter past two** в че́тверть тре́тьего; **at
dawn** на заре́; **at night** но́чью; **at Christmas**
на Рождество́; **at lunch** за обе́дом; **at times**
времена́ми
4 (*referring to rates*): **at £1 a kilo** по фу́нту за
килогра́мм; **two at a time** по два за раз; **at
fifty km/h** со ско́ростью пятьдеся́т км/ч; **at
full speed** на по́лной ско́рости
5 (*referring to manner*): **at a stroke** одни́м
ма́хом; **at peace** в ми́ре
6 (*referring to activity*): **to be at home/work**
быть (*impf*) до́ма/на рабо́те; **to play at
cowboys** игра́ть (*impf*) в ковбо́и; **to be good at
doing sth** хорошо́ уме́ть (*impf*) что-н де́лать
(*impf*)
7 (*referring to cause*): **shocked/surprised/
annoyed at sth** шоки́рован/удивлён*/
раздражён* чем-н; **I am surprised at you** Вы
меня́ удивля́ете; **I stayed at his suggestion** я
оста́лся по его́ предложе́нию.

─────────────────────────

ate [eɪt] *pt of* **eat.**
atheism ['eɪθɪɪzəm] *n* атеи́зм.
atheist ['eɪθɪɪst] *n* атеи́ст(ка*).
Athenian [ə'θiːnɪən] *adj* афи́нский ♦ *n*
афиня́нин(-нка).
Athens ['æθɪnz] *n* Афи́ны* *pl.*
athlete ['æθliːt] *n* спортсме́н(ка*).
athletic [æθ'lɛtɪk] *adj* спорти́вный; (*physique*)
атлети́ческий*.
athletics [æθ'lɛtɪks] *n* лёгкая атле́тика.

Atlantic [ət'læntɪk] *adj* атланти́ческий* ◆ *n*: **the ~ (Ocean)** Атланти́ческий* Океа́н.
atlas ['ætləs] *n* а́тлас.
Atlas Mountains *npl*: **the ~~** Атла́сские Го́ры* *fpl*.
ATM *abbr* (= *Automated Telling Machine*) ба́нковский* автома́т.
atmosphere ['ætməsfɪəʳ] *n* атмосфе́ра; (*air*) во́здух.
atmospheric [ætməs'fɛrɪk] *adj* атмосфе́рный.
atmospherics [ætməs'fɛrɪks] *npl* (*RADIO*) атмосфе́рные поме́хи *fpl*.
atoll ['ætɔl] *n* ато́лл.
atom ['ætəm] *n* а́том.
atomic [ə'tɔmɪk] *adj* а́томный.
atom(ic) bomb *n* а́томная бо́мба.
atomizer ['ætəmaɪzəʳ] *n* (*for perfume*) пульвериза́тор.
atone [ə'təun] *vi*: **to ~ for** искупа́ть (искупи́ть* *perf*).
atonement [ə'təunmənt] *n* искупле́ние.
ATP *n abbr* = *Association of Tennis Professionals*.
atrocious [ə'trəuʃəs] *adj* ужа́сный* (ужа́сен).
atrocity [ə'trɔsɪtɪ] *n* (*act*) зве́рство.
atrophy ['ætrəfɪ] *n* атрофи́я ◆ *vt* атрофи́ровать (*impf/perf*) ◆ *vi* атрофи́роваться (*impf/perf*).
attach [ə'tætʃ] *vt* прикрепля́ть (прикрепи́ть* *perf*); (*document, letter*) прилага́ть (приложи́ть* *perf*); **he is/was ~ed to** (*fond of*) он привя́зан/был привя́зан к +*dat*; (*connected with*) он свя́зан/был свя́зан с +*instr*; **to ~ importance to** придава́ть (прида́ть* *perf*) значе́ние +*dat*; **the ~ed letter** прилага́емое письмо́.
attaché [ə'tæʃeɪ] *n* атташе́ *m ind*.
attaché case *n* диплома́т (*портфе́ль*).
attachment [ə'tætʃmənt] *n* (*fastening*) крепле́ние; (*device*) приспособле́ние, наса́дка; (*love*): **~ (to sb)** привя́занность *f* (к кому́-н).
attack [ə'tæk] *vt* (*MIL, fig*) атакова́ть (*impf/perf*); (*assault*) напада́ть (напа́сть* *perf*) на +*acc*; (*tackle: problem*) бра́ться* (взя́ться* *perf*) энерги́чно за +*acc* ◆ *n* (*criticism, MIL*) ата́ка; (*assault*) нападе́ние; (*of illness*) при́ступ*; **heart ~** серде́чный при́ступ.
attacker [ə'tækəʳ] *n*: **his/her ~** напа́вший(-ая) *m(f) adj* на него́/неё.
attain [ə'teɪn] *vt* (*happiness, success*) достига́ть (дости́гнуть* *or* дости́чь* *perf*) +*gen*; добива́ться (доби́ться* *perf*) +*gen*; (*knowledge*) приобрета́ть (приобрести́* *perf*).
attainments [ə'teɪnmənts] *npl* достиже́ния *ntpl*.
attempt [ə'tɛmpt] *n* (*try*) попы́тка* ◆ *vt* (*try*) пыта́ться (попыта́ться* *perf*) +*infin*; **to make an ~ on sb's life** соверша́ть (соверши́ть *perf*) покуше́ние на чью-н жизнь; **he made no ~ to help** он соверше́нно не пыта́лся помо́чь.
attempted [ə'tɛmptɪd] *adj*: **~ murder**

покуше́ние на жизнь; **~ suicide** попы́тка* самоуби́йства; **~ burglary** попы́тка* ограбле́ния.
attend [ə'tɛnd] *vt* (*school, church, lectures*) посеща́ть (*impf*); (*patient*) уха́живать (*impf*) за +*instr*; (*course*) слу́шать (прослу́шать *perf*); (*meeting, talk*) прису́тствовать (*impf*) на +*prp*
▶ **attend to** *vt fus* (*needs, patient*) занима́ться (заня́ться* *perf*) +*instr*; (*customer*) обслу́живать (обслужи́ть *perf*).
attendance [ə'tɛndəns] *n* прису́тствие; (*in school*) посеща́емость *f*; (*SPORT: gate*) коли́чество боле́льщиков на ма́тче.
attendant [ə'tɛndənt] *n* сопровожда́ющий(-ая) *m(f) adj*; (*in garage etc*) служи́тель(ница) *m(f)* ◆ *adj* (*dangers, risks*) сопу́тствующий.
attention [ə'tɛnʃən] *n* (*concentration*) внима́ние; (*care*) ухо́д ◆ *excl* (*MIL*) сми́рно; **~s** *npl* (*acts of courtesy*) зна́ки *mpl* внима́ния; **for the ~ of ...** (*ADMIN*) к све́дению +*gen*; **it has come to my ~ that ...** мне ста́ло изве́стно, что ...; **to stand to/at ~** (*MIL*) стоя́ть (*impf*) по сто́йке "сми́рно".
attentive [ə'tɛntɪv] *adj* (*audience*) внима́тельный* (внима́телен); (*polite*) предупреди́тельный* (предупреди́телен); (*kind*) забо́тливый (забо́тлив).
attentively [ə'tɛntɪvlɪ] *adv* внима́тельно, забо́тливо.
attenuate [ə'tɛnjueɪt] *vt* ослабля́ть (осла́бить* *perf*) ◆ *vi* ослабля́ться (осла́биться* *perf*).
attest [ə'tɛst] *vi*: **to ~ to** (*demonstrate*) свиде́тельствовать (*impf*) о +*prp*; (*LAW*) свиде́тельствовать (засвиде́тельствовать *perf*).
attic ['ætɪk] *n* (*living space*) манса́рда; (*storage space*) черда́к*.
attire [ə'taɪəʳ] *n* одея́ние.
attitude ['ætɪtjuːd] *n* (*view, behaviour*): **~ (to or towards)** отноше́ние (к +*dat*); (*posture*) по́за.
attorney [ə'təːnɪ] *n* (*US: lawyer*) юри́ст; (*having proxy*) пове́ренный(-ая) *m(f) adj*; **power of ~** дове́ренность *f*.
Attorney General *n* (*BRIT*) мини́стр юсти́ции; (*US*) Генера́льный прокуро́р.
attract [ə'trækt] *vt* привлека́ть (привле́чь* *perf*).
attraction [ə'trækʃən] *n* (*charm, appeal*) привлека́тельность *f*; (*usu pl: amusements*) аттракцио́ны *mpl*; (*PHYS*) притяже́ние; (*fig: towards sb, sth*) влече́ние.
attractive [ə'træktɪv] *adj* привлека́тельный* (привлека́телен).
attribute [*n* 'ætrɪbjuːt, *vb* ə'trɪbjuːt] *n* при́знак, атрибу́т ◆ *vt*: **to ~ sth to** (*cause*) относи́ть* (отнести́* *perf*) что-н за счёт +*gen*; (*painting, quality*) припи́сывать (приписа́ть* *perf*) что-н +*dat*.
attribution [ætrɪ'bjuːʃən] *n* припи́сывание.

---

* marks translations which have irregular inflections. The Russian-English side of the dictionary gives inflectional information.

attrition [ə'trɪʃən] *n*: **war of** ~ война* на
изнуре́ние.
Atty. Gen. *abbr* = **Attorney General**.
ATV *n abbr* (= *all terrain vehicle*) вездехо́д.
atypical [ei'tɪpɪkl] *adj* нетипи́чный
(нетипи́чен).
aubergine ['əubəʒi:n] *n* (*vegetable*) баклажа́н;
(*colour*) тёмно-лило́вый.
auburn ['ɔ:bən] *adj* (*hair*) тёмно-ры́жий*.
auction ['ɔ:kʃən] *n* (also: **sale by** ~) аукцио́н ◆ *vt*
продава́ть (прода́ть* *perf*) с аукцио́на.
auctioneer [ɔ:kʃə'nɪə'] *n* аукциони́ст.
auction room *n* аукцио́нный зал.
audacious [ɔ:'deiʃəs] *adj* (*behaviour*) де́рзкий*
(де́рзок).
audacity [ɔ:'dæsɪtɪ] *n* де́рзость *f*.
audible ['ɔ:dɪbl] *adj* слы́шный* (слы́шен).
audience ['ɔ:dɪəns] *n* аудито́рия, пу́блика;
(*with queen etc*) аудиенция.
audio typist ['ɔ:dɪəu-] *n* фономашини́стка.
audiovisual ['ɔ:dɪəu'vɪzjuəl] *adj* (*materials,
equipment*) а́удио-визуа́льный*.
audiovisual aids ['ɔ:dɪəu'vɪzjuəl-] *npl*
техни́ческие сре́дства *ntpl* обуче́ния.
audit ['ɔ:dɪt] *vt* (*COMM*) проводи́ть* (провести́*
perf) реви́зию +*gen* ◆ *n* реви́зия, ауди́т.
audition [ɔ:'dɪʃən] *n* (*CINEMA, THEAT etc*)
прослу́шивание ◆ *vi*: **to** ~ **(for)** проходи́ть*
(пройти́* *perf*) прослу́шивание (на +*acc*).
auditor ['ɔ:dɪtə'] *n* реви́зия, ауди́тор.
auditorium [ɔ:dɪ'tɔ:rɪəm] *n* зал.
Aug. *abbr* = **August**.
augment [ɔ:g'mɛnt] *vt* (*income etc*)
увели́чивать (увели́чить *perf*).
augur ['ɔ:gə'] *vi*: **it** ~**s well** э́то хоро́шее
предзнаменова́ние.
August ['ɔ:gəst] *n* а́вгуст; *see also* **July**.
august [ɔ:'gʌst] *adj* (*figure, building*)
вели́чественный.
aunt [ɑ:nt] *n* тётя*.
auntie ['ɑ:ntɪ] *n dimin of* **aunt**.
aunty ['ɑ:ntɪ] *n dimin of* **aunt**.
au pair ['əu'pɛə'] *n* (*also*: ~ ~ **girl**) *молода́я
ня́ня-иностра́нка, живу́щая в семье́.*
aura ['ɔ:rə] *n* (*fig: air*) орео́л.
auspices ['ɔ:spɪsɪz] *npl*: **under the** ~ **of** под
эги́дой +*gen*.
auspicious [ɔ:s'pɪʃəs] *adj* благоприя́тный.
austere [ɔs'tɪə'] *adj* (*room etc*) стро́гий*;
(*person, manner*) суро́вый (суро́в).
austerity [ɔs'tɛrɪtɪ] *n* (*simplicity*) стро́гость *f*;
(*ECON: hardship*) лишения *ntpl*.
Australasia [ɔ:strə'leɪzɪə] *n* Австра́лия и
Но́вая Зела́ндия.
Australasian [ɔ:strə'leɪzɪən] *adj* австра́ло-
азиа́тский*.
Australia [ɔs'treɪlɪə] *n* Австра́лия.
Australian [ɔs'treɪlɪən] *adj* австрали́йский* ◆ *n*
австрали́ец*(-и́йка).
Austria ['ɔstrɪə] *n* А́встрия.
Austrian ['ɔstrɪən] *adj* австри́йский* ◆ *n*

австри́ец*(-и́йка).
AUT *n abbr* (*BRIT*) = **Association of University
Teachers**.
authentic [ɔ:'θɛntɪk] *adj* по́длинный*.
authenticate [ɔ:'θɛntɪkeɪt] *vt* удостоверя́ть
(удостове́рить *perf*) по́длинность +*gen*.
authenticity [ɔ:θɛn'tɪsɪtɪ] *n* по́длинность *f*.
author ['ɔ:θə'] *n* (*of text, plan*) а́втор;
(*profession*) писа́тель*(ница).
authoritarian [ɔ:θɔrɪ'tɛərɪən] *adj* (*attitudes,
conduct*) авторита́рный*.
authoritative [ɔ:'θɔrɪtətɪv] *adj* авторите́тный*
(авторите́тен).
authority [ɔ:'θɔrɪtɪ] *n* (*power*) власть *f*;
(*government body*) управле́ние; (*expert*)
авторите́т; (*official permission*) полномо́чие;
the authorities *npl* (*ruling body*) вла́сти *fpl*; **to
have the** ~ **to do** име́ть (*impf*) полномо́чия
+*infin*.
authorization [ɔ:θəraɪ'zeɪʃən] *n*: ~ **(for)**
са́нкция (на +*acc*).
authorize ['ɔ:θəraɪz] *vt* санкциони́ровать (*impf/
perf*); **to** ~ **sb to do** уполномо́чивать
(уполномо́чить *perf*) кого́-н +*infin*.
authorized capital ['ɔ:θəraɪzd-] *n* (*COMM*)
уста́вный капита́л.
authorship ['ɔ:θəʃɪp] *n* а́вторство.
autistic [ɔ:'tɪstɪk] *adj* (*person*) страда́ющий
аути́змом.
auto ['ɔ:təu] *n* (*US: inf*) авто́ *nt ind*.
autobiographical ['ɔ:təbaɪə'græfɪkl] *adj*
автобиографи́ческий.
autobiography [ɔ:təbaɪ'ɔgrəfɪ] *n*
автобиогра́фия.
autocracy [ɔ:'tɔkrəsɪ] *n* автокра́тия.
autocratic [ɔ:tə'krætɪk] *adj* автократи́ческий.
Autocue® ['ɔ:təukju:] *n* телесуфлёр.
autograph ['ɔ:təgrɑ:f] *n* авто́граф ◆ *vt*
надпи́сывать (надписа́ть* *perf*).
auto-immune [ɔ:təu'mju:n] *adj*
аутоимму́нный.
automat ['ɔ:təmæt] *n* (*vending machine*)
автома́т; (*US: place*) кафе́-автома́т.
automata [ɔ:'tɔmətə] *npl of* **automaton**.
automate ['ɔ:təmeɪt] *vt* автоматизи́ровать
(*impf/perf*).
automated ['ɔ:təmeɪtɪd] *adj* автоматиз-
и́рованный.
automatic [ɔ:tə'mætɪk] *adj* автомати́ческий* ◆
n (*US: gun*) (самозаря́дный) пистоле́т; (*car*)
автомоби́ль *m* с автомати́ческим
переключе́нием скоросте́й; (*washing
machine*) стира́льная маши́на-автома́т.
automatically [ɔ:tə'mætɪklɪ] *adv*
автомати́чески.
automatic data processing *n*
автомати́ческая обрабо́тка да́нных.
automation [ɔ:tə'meɪʃən] *n* автоматиза́ция.
automaton [ɔ:'tɔmətən] (*pl* **automata**) *n*
автома́т.
automobile ['ɔ:təməbi:l] *n* (*US*) автомоби́ль *m*.

autonomous [ɔː'tɒnəməs] *adj* (*region*)
автоно́мный* (автоно́мен); (*person,
organization*) самостоя́тельный*
(самостоя́телен).
autonomy [ɔː'tɒnəmɪ] *n* (*of organization, country
etc*) автоно́мия, самостоя́тельность *f*.
autopsy ['ɔːtɒpsɪ] *n* вскры́тие (*трупа*).
autumn ['ɔːtəm] *n* о́сень *f*; **in** ~ о́сенью.
autumnal [ɔː'tʌmnəl] *adj* осе́нний*.
auxiliary [ɔːg'zɪlɪərɪ] *adj* вспомога́тельный ♦ *n*
помо́щник.
AV *n abbr* (*BIBLE*: = *Authorized Version*) перево́д
Би́блии, при́нятый в англика́нской це́ркви ♦
abbr = **audiovisual**.
Av. *abbr* = **avenue**.
avail [ə'veɪl] *vt*: **to** ~ **o.s. of** воспо́льзоваться
(*perf*) +*instr* ♦ *n*: **to no** ~ напра́сно.
availability [əveɪlə'bɪlɪtɪ] *n* (*supply*) нали́чие.
available [ə'veɪləbl] *adj* (*article, service*)
име́ющийся в нали́чии, досту́пный*
(досту́пен); (*person, time*) свобо́дный*
(свобо́ден); **every** ~ **means** все досту́пные
сре́дства; **is the manager** ~? заве́дующий *m*
adj свобо́ден?; **to make sth** ~ **to sb**
предоставля́ть (предоста́вить* *perf*) что-н
кому́-н.
avalanche ['ævəlɑːnʃ] *n* (*also fig*) лави́на.
avant-garde ['ævɒŋˈgɑːd] *adj*
авангарди́стский*.
avarice ['ævərɪs] *n* а́лчность *f*.
avaricious [ævə'rɪʃəs] *adj* а́лчный* (а́лчен).
avdp. *abbr* (= *avoirdupois*) *систе́ма едини́ц
ве́са, испо́льзуемая в англоязы́чных
стра́нах*.
Ave. *abbr* = **avenue**.
avenge [ə'vɛndʒ] *vt* мстить* (отомсти́ть* *perf*)
за +*acc*.
avenue ['ævənjuː] *n* (*street*) у́лица; (*drive*)
алле́я; (*means, solution*) путь* *m*.
average ['ævərɪdʒ] *n* сре́днее *nt adj* ♦ *adj*
сре́дний* ♦ *vt* достига́ть (дости́чь* *perf*) в
сре́днем +*gen*, составля́ть (соста́вить* *perf*) в
сре́днем; **on** ~ в сре́днем; **above/below (the)**
~ вы́ше/ни́же сре́днего у́ровня.
▶ **average out** *vi*: **to** ~ **out at** равня́ться (*impf*) в
сре́днем +*dat*.
averse [ə'vəːs] *adj*: **to be** ~ **to sth/doing** быть*
(*impf*) про́тив чего́-н/того́, что́бы +*infin*; **I
wouldn't be** ~ **to a drink** я непро́чь что́-
нибудь вы́пить.
aversion [ə'vəːʃən] *n* неприя́знь *f*; **to have an** ~
to sb/sth испы́тывать (*impf*) неприя́знь к
кому́-н/чему́-н.
avert [ə'vəːt] *vt* (*accident, war*) предотвраща́ть
(предотврати́ть* *perf*); (*blow, eyes*)
отводи́ть* (отвести́* *perf*).
aviary ['eɪvɪərɪ] *n* пти́чий* вольёр.
aviation [eɪvɪ'eɪʃən] *n* авиа́ция.

avid ['ævɪd] *adj* (*supporter, viewer*) стра́стный.
avidly ['ævɪdlɪ] *adv* стра́стно.
avocado [ævə'kɑːdəu] *n* (*also:* ~ **pear**: *BRIT*)
авока́до *nt ind*.
avoid [ə'vɔɪd] *vt* избега́ть* (избежа́ть* *perf*).
avoidable [ə'vɔɪdəbl] *adj* (*death, accident*)
предотврати́мый.
avoidance [ə'vɔɪdəns] *n*: ~ (**of**) (*of tax, issue*)
уклоне́ние (от +*gen*).
avowed [ə'vaud] *adj* откры́тый.
AVP *n abbr* (*US*: = *assistant vice-president*)
помо́щник ви́це-президе́нта.
avuncular [ə'vʌŋkjuləʳ] *adj* (*expression, tone*)
оте́ческий*; (*person*) забо́тливый.
AWACS ['eɪwæks] *n abbr* (= *airborne warning
and control system*) АВАКС (*авиацио́нная
систе́ма да́льнего радиолокацио́нного
обнаруже́ния и управле́ния*).
await [ə'weɪt] *vt* ожида́ть (*impf*) +*gen*; ~**ing
delivery** (*COMM*) отпра́вка предстои́т; **long**
~**ed** долгожда́нный.
awake [ə'weɪk] (*pt* **awoke**, *pp* **awoken** *or*
awaked) *vt* буди́ть* (разбуди́ть* *perf*) ♦ *vi*
просыпа́ться (просну́ться *perf*) ♦ *adj*: **he is** ~
он просну́лся; **to be** ~ **to** (*dangers,
possibilities*) сознава́ть* (*impf*); **he was still** ~
он ещё не спал.
awakening [ə'weɪknɪŋ] *n* (*also fig*)
пробужде́ние.
award [ə'wɔːd] *n* награ́да; (*LAW*) возмеще́ние
♦ *vt* награжда́ть (награди́ть* *perf*); (*LAW*)
присужда́ть (присуди́ть* *perf*).
aware [ə'wɛəʳ] *adj*: **to be** ~ (**of**) (*realize*)
сознава́ть* (*impf*) (+*acc*); **to become** ~ **of/that**
осознава́ть* (осозна́ть *perf*) +*acc*/, что;
politically/socially ~ полити́чески/социа́льно
созна́тельный; **I am fully** ~ **that** я по́лностью
сознаю́, что.
awareness [ə'wɛənɪs] *n* осозна́ние; **to develop
people's** ~ **of** развива́ть (разви́ть* *perf*)
обще́ственное осозна́ние +*gen*.
awash [ə'wɔʃ] *adj* зато́пленный; (*fig*): ~ **with**
наводнённый (наводнён) +*instr*.
away [ə'weɪ] *adv* (*movement*) в сто́рону;
(*position*) в стороне́, пода́ль; (*far away*)
далеко́; (*in time*): **the holidays are two weeks**
~ до кани́кул (оста́лось) две неде́ли; ~ **from**
(*movement*) от +*gen*; (*position*) пода́ль от
+*gen*; **two kilometres** ~ **from the town** в двух
киломе́трах от го́рода; **two hours** ~ **by car** в
двух часа́х езды́ на маши́не; **he's** ~ **for a
week** он в отъе́зде на неде́лю; **he's** ~ **in Milan**
он в отъе́зде в Мила́н; **to take** ~ (**from**)
(*remove*) забира́ть (забра́ть* *perf*) (у +*gen*);
(*subtract*) отнима́ть (отня́ть* *perf*) (от +*gen*);
he is working ~ он продолжа́ет рабо́тать; **to
fade** ~ (*colour*) выцвета́ть (вы́цвести* *perf*);
(*enthusiasm, light*) угаса́ть (уга́снуть *perf*).

away game *n* (*SPORT*) игра́ на вы́езде.
awe [ɔ:] *n* благогове́ние.
awe-inspiring [ˈɔːɪnspaɪərɪŋ] *adj* (*person, thing*) внуша́ющий благогове́ние.
awesome [ˈɔːsəm] *adj* = awe-inspiring.
awestruck [ˈɔːstrʌk] *adj* охва́ченный (охва́чен) благогове́нием.
awful [ˈɔːfəl] *adj* ужа́сный* (ужа́сен); **an ~ lot (of)** ужа́сно мно́го (+*gen*).
awfully [ˈɔːfəlɪ] *adv* ужа́сно.
awhile [əˈwaɪl] *adv* недо́лго, како́е-то вре́мя; **wait ~** подожди́те немно́го.
awkward [ˈɔːkwəd] *adj* (*clumsy*) неуклю́жий* (неуклю́ж); (*inconvenient*) неудо́бный* (неудо́бен); (*embarrassing*) нело́вкий*.
awkwardness [ˈɔːkwədnɪs] *n* (*see adj*) неуклю́жесть *f*; неудо́бство; нело́вкость *f*.
awl [ɔ:l] *n* ши́ло*.
awning [ˈɔːnɪŋ] *n* (*of tent*) навес; (*of shop, hotel*) тент.
awoke [əˈwəuk] *pt of* awake.
awoken [əˈwəukən] *pp of* awake.
AWOL [ˈeɪwɔl] *abbr* (*MIL*: = *absent without leave*) (находя́щийся) в самово́льной отлу́чке.
awry [əˈraɪ] *adv* (*crooked*) кри́во, ко́со; **to go ~** (*plan*) спу́тываться (спу́таться *perf*).
axe [æks] (*US* **ax**) *n* топо́р* ◆ *vt* (*employee*) увольня́ть (уво́лить *perf*); (*project etc*)

уре́зывать (уре́зать* *perf*); (*jobs*) сокраща́ть (сократи́ть* *perf*); **to have an ~ to grind** (*fig*) име́ть (*impf*) коры́стные побужде́ния.
axes[1] [ˈæksɪz] *npl of* ax(e).
axes[2] [ˈæksi:z] *npl of* axis.
axiom [ˈæksɪəm] *n* аксио́ма.
axiomatic [æksɪəuˈmætɪk] *adj* аксиомати́чный (аксиомати́чен).
axis [ˈæksɪs] (*pl* **axes**) *n* ось* *f*.
axle [ˈæksl] *n* (*also:* ~**tree**: *AUT*) ось* *f*.
aye [aɪ] *excl* да; **the ~s** *npl* голосу́ющие "за".
AYH *n abbr* = *American Youth Hostels*.
AZ *abbr* (*US*: *POST*) = *Arizona*.
azalea [əˈzeɪlɪə] *n* аза́лия.
Azerbaijan [[ae]zəbaɪˈdʒɑːn] *n* Азербайджа́н.
Azerbaijani [[ae]zəbaɪˈdʒɑːnɪ] *n* (*person*) азербайджа́нец*(-а́нка*); (*LING*) азербайджа́нский* язы́к* ◆ *adj* азербайджа́нский*.
Azores [əˈzɔːz] *npl*: **the ~** Азо́рские острова́ *mpl*.
Azov [ˈɑːzɔv] *n*: **Sea of ~** Азо́вское мо́ре.
AZT *n abbr* (= *azidothymidine*) аздотимиди́н.
Aztec [ˈæztɛk] *n* ацте́к ◆ *adj*: ~ **civilization/art** цивилиза́ция/исску́ство ацте́ков.
azure [ˈeɪʒə] *adj* лазу́рный.

~ B, b ~

B, b [bi:] *n* (*letter*) 2-áя бу́ква англи́йского алфави́та; (*SCOL: mark*) ≈ хорошо́; ~ **road** (*BRIT: AUT*) шоссе́ *nt ind* (второ́й катего́рии).
B [bi:] *n* (*MUS*) си *nt ind*.
b. *abbr* (= **born**) род.= *роди́лся*.
BA *n abbr* (= *Bachelor of Arts*) бакала́вр гуманита́рных нау́к; (= *British Academy*) Брита́нская акаде́мия (*гуманита́рных нау́к*).
babble ['bæbl] *vi* лепета́ть* (залепета́ть* *perf*) ♦ *n*: **a ~ of voices** го́мон голосо́в.
babe [beɪb] *n* (*inf*) де́тка*, кро́шка*.
baboon [bə'bu:n] *n* бабуи́н.
baby ['beɪbɪ] *n* ребёнок*; (*US: inf*) де́тка*.
baby carriage *n* (*US*) коля́ска*.
baby grand *n* (*also:* ~ ~ **piano**) кабине́тный роя́ль *m*.
babyhood ['beɪbɪhud] *n* младе́нчество.
babyish ['beɪbɪʃ] *adj* де́тский*.
baby-minder ['beɪbɪˌmaɪndə'] *n* (*BRIT*) ня́ня* (*присма́тривающая за детьми́ у себя́ до́ма*).
baby-sit ['beɪbɪsɪt] *vi* смотре́ть (*impf*) за детьми́.
baby-sitter ['beɪbɪsɪtə'] *n* приходя́щая ня́ня*.
bachelor ['bætʃələ'] *n* холостя́к*; **B~ of Arts/ Science** ≈ бакала́вр гуманита́рных/ есте́ственных нау́к; **B~ of Arts/Science degree** ≈ сте́пень *f* бакала́вра гуманита́рных/есте́ственных нау́к.
bachelorhood ['bætʃələhud] *n* холостя́цкая жизнь *f*.
bachelor party *n* (*US*) мальчи́шник.

<hr>

KEYWORD

back [bæk] *n* **1** (*of person, animal*) спина́; **the back of the hand** ты́льная сторона́ ладо́ни; **he has his back to the wall** (*fig*) он прижа́т к сте́нке
2 (*of house, car etc*) за́дняя часть *f*; (*of chair*) спи́нка*; (*of page*) обра́тная сторона́, оборо́т; (*back cover: of book*) оборо́т; **back to front** за́дом наперёд; **to break the back of a job** (*BRIT*) выполня́ть (вы́полнить *perf*) гла́вную часть рабо́ты; **at the back** (*of crowd*) в за́дних ряда́х; (*of book*) в конце́
3 (*FOOTBALL*) защи́тник
♦ *vt* **1** (*candidate: also:* **back up**)

подде́рживать (поддержа́ть *perf*)
2 (*financially: person*) финанси́ровать (*impf*), ока́зывать (оказа́ть *perf*) фина́нсовую подде́ржку; (: *horse*) ста́вить* (поста́вить* *perf*) на +*acc*
3 (*car*): **he backed the car into the garage** он дал за́дний ход и поста́вил маши́ну в гара́ж
♦ *vi* (*car etc: also:* **back up**) дава́ть* (дать* *perf*) за́дний* ход
♦ *adv* **1** (*not forward*) обра́тно, наза́д; **he ran back** он побежа́л обра́тно *or* наза́д
2 (*returned*): **he's back** он верну́лся; **when will you be back?** когда́ Вы вернётесь?
3 (*restitution*): **to throw the ball back** кида́ть (ки́нуть *perf*) мяч обра́тно; **can I have the pen back?** верни́те мне ру́чку, пожа́луйста
4 (*again*): **to call back** (*TEL*) перезва́нивать (перезвони́ть *perf*); (*visit again*) заходи́ть (зайти́ *perf*) ещё раз
♦ *cpd* **1** (*payment*) за́дним число́м
2 (*AUT: seat, wheels*) за́дний*; (*room, garden*) вну́тренний*; **to take a back seat** (*fig*) станови́ться* (стать* *perf*) пасси́вным наблюда́телем
▶ **back down** *vi* отступа́ть (отступи́ть* *perf*)
▶ **back on to** *vt fus*: **the house backs on to a park** дом выхо́дит за́дним фаса́дом в парк
▶ **back out** *vi* (*of promise*) отступа́ться (отступи́ться* *perf*)
▶ **back up** *vt* (*person, theory etc*) подде́рживать (поддержа́ть* *perf*); (*COMPUT*) резерви́ровать (*impf/perf*).

<hr>

backache ['bækeɪk] *n* постре́л, боль *f* в поясни́це.
backbencher ['bæk'bɛntʃə'] *n* (*BRIT*) "заднескаме́ечник".
backbiting ['bækbaɪtɪŋ] *n* злосло́вие.
backbone ['bækbəun] *n* позвоно́чник; **he's the ~ of the organization** на нём де́ржится вся организа́ция.
backchat ['bæktʃæt] *n* (*BRIT: inf*) препира́тельство.
backcloth ['bækklɔθ] *n* (*BRIT: THEAT*) за́дник.
backcomb ['bækkəum] *vt* (*BRIT*) начёсывать (начеса́ть* *perf*).

backdate [bæk'deɪt] *vt* (*pay rise*) проводи́ть*
(провести́* *perf*) за́дним число́м; (*letter*)
помеча́ть (поме́тить* *perf*) за́дним число́м;
~d pay rise (of 20%) повыше́ние зарпла́ты
за́дним число́м (на 20%).
backdrop ['bækdrɒp] *n* = **backcloth**.
backer ['bækə'] *n* (*COMM*) финанси́рующая
сторона́*.
backfire [bæk'faɪə'] *vi* (*AUT*) дава́ть* (дать* *perf*)
обра́тную вспы́шку; **his plan ~d** его́ план
оберну́лся про́тив него́.
backgammon ['bækgæmən] *n* триктра́к.
background ['bækgraund] *n* (*of picture*)
за́дний* план; (*of events*) предысто́рия;
(*COMPUT*) фон; (*experience*) о́пыт ♦ *cpd* (*noise,
music*) посторо́нний*; **he's from a working
class ~** он из рабо́чей семьи́; **against a ~ of ...**
на фо́не +*gen* ...; ~ **reading (on)**
дополни́тельное чте́ние (по +*dat*).
backhand ['bækhænd] *n* (*TENNIS*) уда́р сле́ва.
backhanded ['bæk'hændɪd] *adj* (*fig*)
двусмы́сленный (двусмы́слен).
backhander ['bæk'hændə'] *n* (*BRIT: inf*) взя́тка*.
backing ['bækɪŋ] *n* (*support*) подде́ржка*;
(*COMM*) финанси́рование; (*MUS*)
сопровожде́ние.
back issue *n* ста́рый но́мер*.
backlash ['bæklæʃ] *n* (*fig*) обра́тная реа́кция.
backlog ['bæklɒg] *n*: ~ **of work** невы́полненная
рабо́та.
back number *n* = **back issue**.
backpack ['bækpæk] *n* рюкза́к*.
backpacker ['bækpækə'] *n* молодо́й челове́к,
путеше́ствующий с рюкза́ком.
back pay *n* пла́та за́дним число́м.
backpedal ['bækpɛdl] *vi* (*fig*) идти́* (пойти́*
perf) на попя́тный.
backseat driver ['bæksiːt-] *n* пассажи́р,
даю́щий сове́ты шофёру.
backside ['bæksaɪd] *n* (*inf*) зад*.
backslash ['bækslæʃ] *n* коса́я черта́ вле́во.
backslide ['bækslaɪd] *vi* принима́ться
(приня́ться *perf*) за ста́рое.
backspace ['bækspeɪs] *vi* реверси́ровать (*impf/
perf*).
backstage [bæk'steɪdʒ] *adv* за кули́сами.
backstreet ['bækstriːt] *n* окра́ина ♦ *cpd*: ~
abortionist челове́к, *де́лающий подпо́льные
або́рты.*
backstroke ['bækstrəuk] *n* пла́вание на спине́;
to do the ~ пла́вать (*impf*) на спине́.
backtrack ['bæktræk] *vi* (*fig*) идти́* (пойти́* *perf*)
на попя́тный.
backup ['bækʌp] *adj* (*train, plane*)
дополни́тельный*; (*COMPUT*) резе́рвный ♦ *n*
(*support*) подде́ржка*; (*also:* ~ **disk**)
дублика́т (ги́бкого ди́ска).
backward ['bækwəd] *adj* (*movement*)
обра́тный; (*person, country*) отста́лый.
backwards ['bækwədz] *adv* наза́д; (*in reverse
order*) наоборо́т; (*fall*) на́взничь; **to know sth**

~ *or* (*US*) ~ **and forwards** знать (*impf*) что-н
вдоль и поперёк; **to walk ~** пя́титься*
(попя́титься* *perf*).
backwater ['bækwɔːtə'] *n* (*fig*) боло́то.
backyard [bæk'jɑːd] *n* (*of house*) за́дний*
двор*.
bacon ['beɪkən] *n* беко́н.
bacteria [bæk'tɪərɪə] *npl* бакте́рии *fpl*.
bacteriology [bæktɪərɪ'ɒlədʒɪ] *n*
бактериоло́гия.
bad [bæd] *adj* плохо́й*; (*mistake*) серьёзный;
(*injury, crash*) тяжёлый (тяжёл); (*food*)
ту́хлый*; **his ~ leg** его́ больна́я нога́; **to go ~**
(*food*) ту́хнуть (проту́хнуть *perf*), по́ртиться*
(испо́ртиться* *perf*); (*milk*) скиса́ть (ски́снуть
perf); **she's having a ~ time of it** у неё тяжёлый
пери́од; **I feel ~ about it** я чу́вствую себя́
винова́тым; **in ~ faith** нейскренне.
bad debt *n* спи́санный долг (по
несостоя́тельности должника́).
baddy ['bædɪ] *n* (*inf*) плохо́й* *m adj* (*в кни́ге,
фи́льме*).
bade [bæd] *pt of* **bid**.
badge [bædʒ] *n* значо́к*; (*of policeman*) бля́ха;
(*sew-on*) наши́вка; (*fig*) си́мвол.
badger ['bædʒə'] *n* барсу́к ♦ *vt* пристава́ть*
(приста́ть* *perf*) к +*dat*.
badly ['bædlɪ] *adv* пло́хо; ~ **wounded** тяжело́
ра́неный; **he needs it** ~ он си́льно в э́том
нужда́ется; **to be ~ off (for money)** нужда́ться
(*impf*) (в деньга́х).
bad-mannered ['bæd'mænəd] *adj*
невоспи́танный.
badminton ['bædmɪntən] *n* бадминто́н.
bad-tempered ['bæd'tɛmpəd] *adj* (*by nature*)
вспы́льчивый (вспы́льчив); (*on
one occasion*) раздражённый (раздражён).
baffle ['bæfl] *vt* озада́чивать (озада́чить *perf*).
baffling ['bæflɪŋ] *adj*: **I find his behaviour** ~ его́
поведе́ние меня́ озада́чивает.
bag [bæg] *n* су́мка; (*paper, plastic*) паке́т;
(*handbag*) су́мочка*; (*satchel*) ра́нец*; (*case*)
портфе́ль *m*; (*of hunter*) ягдта́ш; (*pej:
woman*) карга́*; ~**s of** (*inf*) у́йма +*gen*; **to pack
one's ~s** собира́ть (собра́ть* *perf*) чемода́ны;
~**s under the eyes** мешки́ под глаза́ми.
bagful ['bægful] *n* (*of flour etc*) (по́лный)
паке́т; (*of shopping*) (по́лная) су́мка*.
baggage ['bægɪdʒ] *n* (*US*) бага́ж*.
baggage car *n* (*US*) бага́жный ваго́н.
baggage claim *n* (*US*) вы́дача багажа́.
baggy ['bægɪ] *adj* мешкова́тый.
Baghdad [bæg'dæd] *n* Багда́д.
bag lady *n* (*esp US*) бездо́мная ни́щая *f adj*.
bagpipes ['bægpaɪps] *npl* волы́нка* *fsg*.
bag-snatcher ['bægsnætʃə'] *n* (*BRIT*) вор*,
выхва́тывающий су́мки.
Bahamas [bə'hɑːməz] *npl*: **the** ~ Бага́мские
острова́ *mpl*.
Bahrain [bɑː'reɪn] *n* Бахре́йн.

Baikal [baɪˈkɑ:l] *n*: **Lake ~** Байка́л.
bail [beɪl] *n* (*payment*) зало́г ♦ *vt* (*also:* **to grant ~ to**) выпуска́ть (вы́пустить* *perf*) под зало́г; **he was released on ~** он был вы́пущен на пору́ки
▶ **bail out** *vt* (*LAW*) плати́ть* (заплати́ть* *perf*) зало́говую су́мму за +*acc*; (*boat*) выче́рпывать (вы́черпать *perf*) во́ду из +*gen*; (*firm, friend*) выруча́ть (вы́ручить *perf*) ♦ *vi* выбра́сываться (вы́броситься* *perf*) с парашю́том.
bailiff [ˈbeɪlɪf] *n* (*LAW*: *BRIT*) суде́бный исполни́тель *m*; (: *US*) помо́щник шери́фа; (*BRIT*: *of estate*) управля́ющий(-ая) *m(f)* *adj* име́нием.
bait [beɪt] *n* (*for fish*) нажи́вка*; (*for animal, criminal*) прима́нка* ♦ *vt* (*hook, trap*) наживля́ть (наживи́ть* *perf*); (*person*) дразни́ть* (*impf*).
baize [beɪz] *n* (зелёное) сукно́.
bake [beɪk] *vt* печь* (испе́чь* *perf*); (*clay etc*) обжига́ть (обже́чь* *perf*) ♦ *vi* (*bread etc*) пе́чься* (испе́чься* *perf*); (*make cakes etc*) печь* (испе́чь* *perf*) пироги́.
baked beans [beɪkt-] *npl* консерви́рованная фасо́ль *fsg*.
baker [ˈbeɪkə] *n* пе́карь* *m*; (*also:* **the ~'s**) бу́лочная *f adj*.
baker's dozen *n* чёртова дю́жина.
bakery [ˈbeɪkərɪ] *n* (*factory*) пека́рня; (*shop*) бу́лочная *f adj*.
baking [ˈbeɪkɪŋ] *n* вы́печка ♦ *adj* (*inf*): **it's ~ hot today** сего́дня печёт; **she does her ~ once a week** она́ печёт раз в неде́лю.
baking powder *n* разрыхли́тель *m*.
baking tin *n* (*for cake, meat*) фо́рма.
baking tray *n* про́тивень* *m*.
Baku [baˈku] *n* Баку́ *m ind*.
balaclava [bæləˈklɑ:və] *n* (*also:* **~ helmet**) вя́заный шлем.
balance [ˈbæləns] *n* (*equilibrium*) равнове́сие; (*COMM*: *in account*) бала́нс; (: *remainder*) оста́ток*; (*scales*) весы́ *pl* ♦ *vt* (*budget, account*) баланси́ровать (сбаланси́ровать *perf*); (*make equal*) уравнове́шивать (уравнове́сить* *perf*); **on ~** по зре́лом размышле́нии; **~ of trade/payments** торго́вый/платёжный бала́нс; **~ carried forward** бала́нс к перено́су; **~ brought forward** бала́нс с перено́са; **to ~ the books** баланси́ровать (сбаланси́ровать *perf*) кни́ги; **to ~ the pros and cons** взве́шивать (взве́сить* *perf*) все за и про́тив.
balanced [ˈbælənst] *adj* (*report*) взве́шенный (взве́шен); (*diet*) сбаланси́рованный (сбаланси́рован); (*personality*) уравнове́шенный.
balance sheet *n* сво́дный бала́нс.

balcony [ˈbælkənɪ] *n* балко́н.
bald [bɔ:ld] *adj* (*head*) лы́сый*; (*tyre*) стёртый; (*statement*) прямо́й*.
baldness [ˈbɔ:ldnɪs] *n* лы́сина.
bale [beɪl] *n* (*of hay etc*) тюк*; (*of papers etc*) ки́па
▶ **bale out** *vti see* **bail out**.
Balearic Islands [bælɪˈærɪk-] *npl*: **the ~ ~** Бале́рские острова́ *mpl*.
baleful [ˈbeɪlful] *adj* (*glance*) злове́щий* (злове́щ).
balk [bɔ:k] *vi*: **he ~ed at the idea** ему́ прети́ла э́та иде́я; (*subj: horse*): **to ~ (at)** заарта́читься (*perf*) (пе́ред +*instr*).
Balkan [ˈbɔ:lkən] *adj* балка́нский; **the ~s** *npl* Балка́ны *pl*.
ball [bɔ:l] *n* (*for football*) мяч*; (*for tennis, golf*) мя́чик; (*of wool, string*) клубо́к*; (*dance*) бал*; **to set the ~ rolling** (*fig*) пуска́ть (пусти́ть* *perf*) де́ло в ход; **to play ~ (with sb)** (*fig*) подъи́грывать (подыгра́ть *perf*) (кому́-н); **to be on the ~** (*fig*) быть* (*impf*) на коне́; **the ~ is in their court** (*fig*) о́чередь за ни́ми.
ballad [ˈbæləd] *n* балла́да.
ballast [ˈbæləst] *n* балла́ст.
ball bearing *n* ша́рик подши́пника.
ballcock [ˈbɔ:lkɔk] *n* шарово́й кла́пан.
ballerina [bæləˈri:nə] *n* балери́на.
ballet [ˈbæleɪ] *n* бале́т.
ballet dancer *n* арти́ст(ка) бале́та.
ballistic [bəˈlɪstɪk] *adj* баллисти́ческий*.
ballistic missile *n* баллисти́ческий* снаря́д.
ballistics [bəˈlɪstɪks] *n* балли́стика.
balloon [bəˈlu:n] *n* возду́шный шар; (*also:* **hot air ~**) аэроста́т; (*in comic strip*) ко́нтур, в кото́рый впи́сываются ре́плики геро́ев ко́миксов.
balloonist [bəˈlu:nɪst] *n* воздухопла́ватель *m*.
ballot [ˈbælət] *n* голосова́ние, баллотиро́вка*.
ballot box *n* избира́тельная у́рна.
ballot paper *n* избира́тельный бюллете́нь *m*.
ballpark [ˈbɔ:lpɑ:k] *n* (*US*) бейсбо́льное по́ле.
ballpark figure *n* (*inf*) приблизи́тельный подсчёт.
ballpoint (pen) [ˈbɔ:lpɔɪnt(-)] *n* ша́риковая ру́чка*.
ballroom [ˈbɔ:lrum] *n* ба́льный зал.
balls [bɔ:lz] *npl* (*inf!*) я́йца* *ntpl* (*!*); (: *nonsense*) фигня́ *fsg* (*!*)
balm [bɑ:m] *n* бальза́м.
balmy [ˈbɑ:mɪ] *adj* (*breeze*) ласка́ющий (ласка́ющ); (*day*) прия́тный* (прия́тен); (*BRIT*: *inf*) = **barmy**.
BALPA [ˈbælpə] *n abbr = British Airline Pilots' Association*.
balsam [ˈbɔ:lsəm] *n* бальза́м.
balsa (wood) [ˈbɔ:lsə-] *n* ба́льзовое де́рево*.

Baltic [bɔːltɪk] *n*: **the ~** Балти́йское Мо́ре ♦ *adj*: **the ~ States** прибалти́йские госуда́рства *ntpl*.

balustrade [bæləs'treɪd] *n* балюстра́да.

bamboo [bæm'buː] *n* бамбу́к.

bamboozle [bæm'buːzl] *vt* (*inf*) одура́чивать (одура́чить *perf*).

ban [bæn] *vt* (*prohibit*) запреща́ть (запрети́ть* *perf*); (*suspend, exclude*) отстраня́ть (отстрани́ть *perf*) ♦ *n* (*prohibition*) запре́т; (*suspension*): **~ from** отстране́ние от +*gen*; **he was ~ned from driving** (*BRIT*) у него́ отобра́ли води́тельские права́.

banal [bə'nɑːl] *adj* (*remark, idea etc*) бана́льный* (бана́лен).

banana [bə'nɑːnə] *n* бана́н.

band [bænd] *n* (*group: of people, rock musicians*) гру́ппа; (: *of jazz, military musicians*) орке́стр; (*strip: of light, colour*) полоса́*; (: *of cloth*) ле́нта; (*range*) диапазо́н

▶ **band together** *vi* объединя́ться (объедини́ться *perf*).

bandage ['bændɪdʒ] *n* повя́зка* ♦ *vt* (*wound, leg*) бинтова́ть (забинтова́ть *perf*); (*person*) перевя́зывать (перевяза́ть* *perf*).

bandaid® ['bændeɪd] *n* (*US*) пла́стырь *m*.

bandit ['bændɪt] *n* банди́т.

bandstand ['bændstænd] *n* эстра́да.

bandwagon ['bændwægən] *n*: **to jump on the ~** примкну́ть (*perf*) к си́льной стороне́ *or* мо́дному тече́нию.

bandy ['bændɪ] *vt* (*jokes, ideas*) перебра́сываться (перебро́ситься* *perf*) +*instr*

▶ **bandy about** *vt* бесконе́чно упомина́ть (*impf*).

bandy-legged ['bændɪ'lɛgɪd] *adj* (*person*) кривоно́гий*.

bane [beɪn] *n*: **it/he is the ~ of my life** э́то/он несча́стье мое́й жи́зни.

bang [bæŋ] *n* стук; (*explosion*) вы́стрел; (*blow*) уда́р ♦ *excl* бах ♦ *vt* (*door*) хло́пать (хло́пнуть *perf*) +*instr*; (*one's head etc*) ударя́ть (уда́рить *perf*) ♦ *vi* (*door*) захло́пываться (захло́пнуться *perf*); (*fireworks*) хлопа́ть (*impf*) ♦ *adv*: **~ on time** (*BRIT*: *inf*) как ра́з во вре́мя; **to ~ at the door** колоти́ть* (*impf*) в дверь; **to ~ into sth** ста́лкиваться (столкну́ться *perf*) с чем-н.

banger ['bæŋə'] *n* (*BRIT*: *inf*: *also*: **old ~**) драндуле́т; (: *sausage*) сарде́лька*; (: *firework*) хлопу́шка.

Bangkok [bæŋ'kɔk] *n* Бангко́к.

Bangladesh [bæŋglə'dɛʃ] *n* Бангладе́ш.

Bangladeshi [bæŋglə'dɛʃɪ] *n* (*person*) бангладе́шец*(-е́шка*) ♦ *adj* бангладе́шский.

bangle ['bæŋgl] *n* брасле́т.

bangs [bæŋz] *npl* (*US*) чёлка* *fsg*.

banish ['bænɪʃ] *vt* высыла́ть (вы́слать* *perf*).

banister ['bænɪstə'] *n* (*usu pl*) пери́ла *pl*.

banjo ['bændʒəu] (*pl* **~es** *or* **~s**) *n* ба́нджо *nt ind*.

bank [bæŋk] *n* банк; (*of river, lake*) бе́рег*; (*of earth*) на́сыпь *f*; (*of switches*) пане́ль *f* ♦ *vi* (*AVIAT*) крени́ться (накрени́ться *perf*); (*COMM*): **they ~ with Pitt's** они́ де́ржат де́ньги в ба́нке Питт

▶ **bank on** *vt fus* полага́ться (положи́ться* *perf*) на +*acc*.

bank account *n* ба́нковский* счёт.

bank balance *n* коли́чество де́нег на ба́нковском счету́.

bank card *n* ба́нковская ка́рточка*.

bank charges *npl* (*BRIT*) *пла́та, взима́емая ба́нком за услу́ги*.

bank draft *n* ба́нковская тра́тта.

banker ['bæŋkə'] *n* банки́р.

banker's card *n* (*BRIT*) = **bank card**.

banker's order *n* (*BRIT*) ба́нковское поруче́ние.

Bank Giro *n* жи́ро *nt ind* банк.

bank holiday *n* (*BRIT*) нерабо́чий* день *m* (*обы́чно понеде́льник*).

banking ['bæŋkɪŋ] *n* ба́нковское де́ло*.

banking hours *npl* часы́ *mpl* рабо́ты ба́нка.

bank loan *n* ба́нковский заём*.

bank manager *n* управля́ющий(-ая) *m(f) adj* ба́нком.

banknote ['bæŋknəut] *n* банкно́т.

bank rate *n* учётная ста́вка* ба́нка.

bankroll ['bæŋkrəul] *vt* обеспе́чивать (обеспе́чить *perf*) деньга́ми ♦ *n* (*esp US*) фина́нсовые ресу́рсы *pl*.

bankrupt ['bæŋkrʌpt] *adj* обанкро́тившийся ♦ *n* банкро́т; **to go ~** обанкро́титься* (*perf*); **I am ~** я – банкро́т.

bankruptcy ['bæŋkrʌptsɪ] *n* (*COMM, fig*) банкро́тство, несостоя́тельность *f*.

bank statement *n* вы́писка* с ба́нковского счёта.

banner ['bænə'] *n* транспара́нт.

banner headline *n* (газе́тная) ша́пка*.

bannister ['bænɪstə'] *n* = **banister**.

banns [bænz] *npl* *оглаше́ние в це́ркви имён вступа́ющих в брак*.

banquet ['bæŋkwɪt] *n* банке́т.

bantamweight ['bæntəmweɪt] *n* (*BOXING*) боксёр лёгкого ве́са.

banter ['bæntə'] *n* подшу́чивание.

BAOR *n abbr* = **British Army of the Rhine**.

baptism ['bæptɪzəm] *n* креще́ние.

Baptist ['bæptɪst] *n* бапти́ст(ка).

baptize [bæp'taɪz] *vt* крести́ть* (окрести́ть* *perf*).

bar [bɑː'] *n* (*in pub*) бар; (*counter*) сто́йка; (*rod*) прут; (*cake: of soap*) брусо́к*; (: *of chocolate*) пли́тка*; (*obstacle*) прегра́да; (*prohibition*) запре́т; (*MUS*) такт ♦ *vt* (*door, way*) загора́живать (загороди́ть* *perf*); (*road*) прегражда́ть (прегради́ть *perf*); (*person*) не допуска́ть (допусти́ть* *perf*); (*activity*) запреща́ть (запрети́ть* *perf*); **~s** *npl* (*on window etc*) решётка *fsg*; **behind ~s** за решёткой; **the B~** адвокату́ра; **~ none** без

исключе́ния.
Barbados [bɑ:ˈbeɪdɔs] n Барба́дос.
barbaric [bɑːˈbærɪk] adj ва́рварский*.
barbarous [ˈbɑːbərəs] adj ва́рварский*.
barbecue [ˈbɑːbɪkjuː] n барбекю́ nt ind.
barbed wire [ˈbɑːbd-] n колю́чая про́волока.
barber [ˈbɑːbəˀ] n парикма́хер.
barbiturate [bɑːˈbɪtjʊrɪt] n барбитура́т.
Barcelona [bɑːsəˈləʊnə] n Барсело́на.
bar chart n гисторгра́мма.
bar code n штрихово́й код.
bare [bɛəˀ] adj (body) го́лый*, обнажённый
(обнажён); (trees) оголённый (оголён) ♦ vt
(one's body) обнажа́ть (обнажи́ть perf);
(teeth) ска́лить (оска́лить perf); **in** or **with ~
feet** босико́м; **the ~ essentials** предме́ты mpl
пе́рвой необходи́мости; **~ minimum** то́лько
ми́нимум; **to ~ one's soul** раскрыва́ть
(раскры́ть* perf) свою́ ду́шу.
bareback [ˈbɛəbæk] adv без седла́.
barefaced [ˈbɛəfeɪst] adj бессты́дный*.
barefoot [ˈbɛəfʊt] adj босо́й* (бос) ♦ adv
босико́м.
bareheaded [bɛəˈhɛdɪd] adj, adv с непокры́той
голово́й.
barely [ˈbɛəlɪ] adv едва́.
Barents Sea [ˈbærənts-] n: **the ~ ~** Ба́ренцево
мо́ре.
bargain [ˈbɑːgɪn] n сде́лка*; (good buy)
вы́годная поку́пка* ♦ vi: **to ~ (with sb)**
торгова́ться (сторгова́ться perf) (с кем-н);
into the ~ в прида́чу
▸ **bargain for** vt fus: **he got more than he ~ed for**
он получи́л бо́льше, чем ожида́л.
bargaining [ˈbɑːgənɪŋ] n торг.
bargaining position n пози́ция, с кото́рой
предъявля́ются тре́бования и усло́вия
сде́лки и́ли догово́ра.
barge [bɑːdʒ] n ба́ржа
▸ **barge in** vi (enter) вва́ливаться (ввали́ться*
perf); (interrupt) влеза́ть (влезть* perf)
▸ **barge into** vt fus (person) ната́лкиваться
(натолкну́ться perf) на +acc.
bargepole [ˈbɑːdʒpəʊl] n: **I wouldn't touch him
with a ~** я к э́тому на пу́шечный вы́стрел не
подойду́.
baritone [ˈbærɪtəʊn] n барито́н.
barium meal [ˈbɛərɪəm-] n ба́риевая
миксту́ра.
bark [bɑːk] n (of tree) кора́; (of dog) лай ♦ vi
(dog) ла́ять (impf); **she's ~ing up the wrong
tree** она́ обраща́ется не по а́дресу.
barley [ˈbɑːlɪ] n ячме́нь* m.
barley sugar n ≈ ледене́ц*.
barmaid [ˈbɑːmeɪd] n буфе́тчица.
barman [ˈbɑːmən] irreg n ба́рмен.
barmy [ˈbɑːmɪ] adj (BRIT: inf: person) чо́кнутый;
(: idea) неле́пый.

barn [bɑːn] n амба́р.
barn owl n сипу́ха.
barnacle [ˈbɑːnəkl] n моллю́ск.
barometer [bəˈrɔmɪtəˀ] n баро́метр.
baron [ˈbærən] n баро́н; (of press, industry)
магна́т.
baroness [ˈbærənɪs] n бароне́сса.
baronet [ˈbærənɪt] n бароне́т.
barracking [ˈbærəkɪŋ] n вы́крики mpl,
неодобри́тельные во́згласы mpl.
barracks [ˈbærəks] npl (MIL) каза́рма fsg.
barrage [ˈbærɑːʒ] n (MIL) загради́тельный
ого́нь m; (dam) да́мба; (fig) лави́на.
barrel [ˈbærəl] n (of wine, beer) бо́чка*; (of oil)
барре́ль m; (of gun) ствол*.
barrel organ n шарма́нка*.
barren [ˈbærən] adj (land) беспло́дный*
(беспло́ден).
barricade [bærɪˈkeɪd] n баррика́да ♦ vt
баррикади́ровать (забаррикади́ровать
perf); **to ~ o.s. in** баррикади́роваться
(забаррикади́роваться perf).
barrier [ˈbærɪəˀ] n (at entrance) барье́р; (at
frontier) шлагба́ум; (BRIT: also: **crash ~**)
предохрани́тельный барье́р на шоссе́ и
доро́гах; (fig: to progress etc) препя́тствие;
(: to communication) поме́ха.
barrier cream n (BRIT) защи́тный крем.
barring [ˈbɑːrɪŋ] prep за исключе́нием +gen.
barrister [ˈbærɪstəˀ] n (BRIT) адвока́т.
barrow [ˈbærəʊ] n (also: **wheelbarrow**) та́чка*;
(cart) двухколёсная теле́жка*.
bar stool n высо́кое сиде́нье во́зле сто́йки
ба́ра.
Bart. abbr (BRIT: = baronet) бароне́т.
bartender [ˈbɑːtɛndəˀ] n (US) ба́рмен.
barter [ˈbɑːtəˀ] vi производи́ть* (произвести́*
perf) ба́ртерный обме́н ♦ n ба́ртер.
base [beɪs] n основа́ние; (of monument etc)
постаме́нт; (of make up) осно́ва; (MIL) ба́за;
(for organization) местонахожде́ние ♦ adj
ни́зкий* (ни́зок) ♦ vt: **to ~ sth on** (opinion,
belief) осно́вывать (impf) что-н на +prp; **to be
~d at** бази́роваться (impf) в/на +prp; **the film
is ~d on the book** фильм осно́ван на кни́ге;
I'm ~d in London for now сейча́с я бази́руюсь
в Ло́ндоне (inf); **a Paris-~d firm** фи́рма
бази́рующаяся в Пари́же; **computer-~d
teaching** обуче́ние при по́мощи
компью́теров.
baseball [ˈbeɪsbɔːl] n бейсбо́л.
baseboard [ˈbeɪsbɔːd] n (US) пли́нтус.
base camp n ба́зовый ла́герь* m.
Basel [ˈbɑːl] n = **Basle**.
baseline [ˈbeɪslaɪn] n (SPORT) ли́ния пода́чи;
(starting point) исхо́дная черта́.
basement [ˈbeɪsmənt] n подва́л.
base rate n тари́фная ста́вка.

---

* marks translations which have irregular inflections. The Russian-English side of the dictionary gives inflectional information.

bases[1] ['beɪsɪz] *npl of* **base**.
bases[2] ['beɪsi:z] *npl of* **basis**.
bash [bæʃ] (*inf*) *vt* колоти́ть* (поколоти́ть*
perf) ♦ *n*: **I'll have a ~ (at it)** (*BRIT*) я попыта́юсь
▸ **bash up** *vt* (*car*) разбива́ть (разби́ть* *perf*);
(*BRIT: person*) избива́ть (изби́ть* *perf*).
bashful ['bæʃful] *adj* засте́нчивый (засте́нчив).
bashing ['bæʃɪŋ] *n* (*inf*): **union-~** я́ростные
напа́дки на профсою́зы.
BASIC ['beɪsɪk] *n* (*COMPUT*) Бэ́йсик.
basic ['beɪsɪk] *adj* (*fundamental*)
фундамента́льный; (*elementary*)
нача́льный; (*primitive*) элемента́рный
(элемента́рен).
basically ['beɪsɪklɪ] *adv* по существу́; (*on the
whole*) в основно́м.
basic rate *n* ба́зисная ста́вка.
basics ['beɪsɪks] *npl*: **the ~** осно́вы *fpl*.
basil ['bæzl] *n* базили́к.
basin ['beɪsn] *n* (*also*: **washbasin**) ра́ковина;
(*BRIT: for food*) ми́ска*; (*GEO*) бассе́йн.
basis ['beɪsɪs] (*pl* **bases**) *n* основа́ние; **on a part-
time ~** на непо́лной ста́вке; **on a trial ~** на
испыта́тельный срок; **on the ~ of what
you've said** на осно́ве ска́занного Ва́ми.
bask [bɑ:sk] *vi*: **to ~ in the sun** гре́ться (*impf*) на
со́лнце.
basket ['bɑ:skɪt] *n* корзи́на.
basketball ['bɑ:skɪtbɔ:l] *n* баскетбо́л.
basketball player *n* баскетболи́ст(ка).
Basle [bɑ:l] *n* Ба́зель *m*.
Basque [bæsk] *adj* ба́скский ♦ *n* баск.
bass [beɪs] *n* бас* ♦ *adj* бассо́вый.
bass clef *n* басо́вый ключ*.
bassoon [bə'su:n] *n* фаго́т.
bastard ['bɑ:stəd] *n* внебра́чный ребёнок*;
(*inf!*) ублю́док* (*!*)
baste [beɪst] *vt* (*CULIN*) полива́ть (поли́ть* *perf*)
жи́ром и со́ком; (*SEWING*) смётывать
(смета́ть* *perf*).
bastion ['bæstɪən] *n* (*fig*) опло́т.
bat [bæt] *n* (*ZOOL*) лету́чая мышь *f*; (*SPORT*)
бита́; (*BRIT: TABLE TENNIS*) раке́тка* ♦ *vt*: **he
didn't ~ an eyelid** он и гла́зом не моргну́л;
off one's own ~ по со́бственному почи́ну.
batch [bætʃ] *n* (*of bread*) вы́печка*; (*of papers
etc*) па́чка*; (*of applicants, goods*) па́ртия.
batch processing *n* (*COMPUT*) паке́тная
обрабо́тка (*да́нных*).
bated ['beɪtɪd] *adj*: **with ~ breath** затаи́в
дыха́ние.
bath [bɑ:θ] *n* ва́нна ♦ *vt* купа́ть (вы́купать
perf); **to have a ~** принима́ть (приня́ть* *perf*)
ва́нну; *see also* **baths**.
bathe [beɪð] *vi* (*swim*) купа́ться (*impf*); (*US: have
a bath*) принима́ть (приня́ть* *perf*) ва́нну ♦ *vt*
(*wound*) промыва́ть (промы́ть* *perf*).
bather ['beɪðə'] *n* купа́льщик(-ица).
bathing ['beɪðɪŋ] *n* купа́ние.
bathing cap *n* купа́льная ша́почка*.
bathing costume (*US* **bathing suit**) *n*

купа́льный костю́м.
bath mat *n* ко́врик для ва́нной.
bathrobe ['bɑ:θrəub] *n* купа́льный хала́т.
bathroom ['bɑ:θrum] *n* ва́нная *f adj*.
baths [bɑ:ðz] *npl* (*also*: **swimming ~**)
пла́вательный бассе́йн *msg*.
bath towel *n* ба́нное полоте́нце.
bathtub ['bɑ:θtʌb] *n* ва́нна.
batman ['bætmən] *irreg n* (*BRIT*) денщи́к.
baton ['bætən] *n* (*MUS*) дирижёрская па́лочка*;
(*ATHLETICS*) эстафе́тная па́лочка*; (*POLICE*)
дуби́нка*.
battalion [bə'tælɪən] *n* батальо́н.
batten ['bætn] *n* (*CARPENTRY*) ре́йка; (*NAUT*) ре́я
▸ **batten down** *vt* (*NAUT*): **to ~ down the
hatches** задра́ивать (задра́ить *perf*) лю́ки.
batter ['bætə'] *vt* (*child, wife*) бить (изби́ть*
perf); (*subj: wind, rain*) бить* (поби́ть* *perf*) ♦ *n*
(*CULIN*) жи́дкое те́сто.
battered ['bætəd] *adj* (*hat*) потрёпанный
(потрёпан); (*pan*) покорёженный (покорё-
жен); **~ wife** подверга́емая побо́ям жена́*.
battering ram ['bætərɪŋ-] *n* тара́н.
battery ['bætərɪ] *n* (*of torch etc*) батаре́йка*;
(*AUT*) аккумуля́тор; (*of tests, reporters*) ряд*.
battery charger *n* заря́дное устро́йство
(батаре́и).
battery farm *n* птицефа́брика.
battery hens *npl* инкуба́торные ку́ры *mpl*.
battle ['bætl] *n* би́тва, бой* ♦ *vi* боро́ться*
(*impf*), сража́ться (*impf*); **that's half the ~** э́то
уже́ пол де́ла; **it's a** *or* **we're fighting a losing ~**
(*fig*) э́то безнадёжная борьба́, мы ведём
безнадёжную борьбу́.
battle dress *n* похо́дная фо́рма.
battlefield ['bætlfi:ld] *n* по́ле* би́твы *or* бо́я.
battlements ['bætlmənts] *npl* сте́ны* *fpl* с
бойни́цами.
battleship ['bætlʃɪp] *n* вое́нный кора́бль* *m*.
batty ['bætɪ] *adj* (*inf*) чо́кнутый (чо́кнут).
bauble ['bɔ:bl] *n* безделу́шка*.
baud [bɔ:d] *n* (*COMPUT*) бод.
baud rate *n* (*COMPUT*) ско́рость *f* переда́чи (в
бо́дах).
baulk [bɔ:lk] *vi* = **balk**.
bauxite ['bɔ:ksaɪt] *n* бокси́т.
Bavaria [bə'vɛərɪə] *n* Бава́рия.
Bavarian [bə'vɛərɪən] *adj* бава́рский* ♦ *n*
бава́рец(-рка).
bawdy ['bɔ:dɪ] *adj* (*joke, song*) скабрёзный*
(скабрёзен).
bawl [bɔ:l] *vi* ора́ть* (заора́ть* *perf*).
bay [beɪ] *n* зали́в; (*smaller*) бу́хта; (*horse*)
гнеда́я ло́шадь *f*; **parking ~** (*BRIT*) ме́сто*
парко́вки; **loading ~** погру́зочная
площа́дка*; **to hold sb at ~** держа́ть (*impf*)
кого́-на расстоя́нии.
bay leaf *n* лавро́вый лист*.
bayonet ['beɪənɪt] *n* штык*.
bay tree *n* ла́вровое де́рево*.
bay window *n* э́ркер*.

bazaar [bə'zɑːʳ] *n* (*market*) база́р, ры́нок*; (*fete*) благотвори́тельный база́р.

bazooka [bə'zuːkə] *n* базу́ка, гранатомёт.

BB *n abbr* (*BRIT*: = *Boys' Brigade*) ≈ отря́д бойска́утов.

B & B *n abbr* = **bed and breakfast**.

b & b *n abbr* = **B & B**.

BBC *n abbr* (= *British Broadcasting Corporation*) Би-Би-Си *nt ind*.

BC *adv abbr* (= *before Christ*) до рождества́ Христо́ва ♦ *abbr* (*CANADA*) = **British Columbia**.

BCG *n abbr* (= *Bacillus Calmette-Guérin*) БЦЖ.

BD *n abbr* (= *Bachelor of Divinity*) бакала́вр богосло́вия.

B/D *abbr* = **bank draft**.

BDS *n abbr* (= *Bachelor of Dental Surgery*) бакала́вр стоматоло́гии.

KEYWORD
---

be [biː] (*pt* **was**, **were**, *pp* **been**) *aux vb* **1** (*with present participle: forming continuous tenses*): **what are you doing?** что Вы де́лаете?; **it is raining** идёт дождь; **they're working tomorrow** они́ рабо́тают за́втра; **the house is being built** дом стро́ится/стро́ят; **I've been waiting for you for ages** я жду Вас уже́ це́лую ве́чность

2 (*with pp: forming passives*): **he was killed** он был уби́т; **the box had been opened** я́щик открыва́ли; **the thief was nowhere to be seen** во́ра нигде́ не́ было ви́дно

3 (*in tag questions*) пра́вда, да; **she's back again, is she?** она́ верну́лась, да?; **she is pretty, isn't she?** она́ хоро́шенькая, пра́вда?

4 (*to +infin*): **the house is to be sold** дом бу́дет про́дан; **you're to be congratulated for all your work** Вы бу́дете отме́чены за всю ва́шу рабо́ту; **he's not to open it** он не до́лжен открыва́ть это

♦ *vb* **1** (+ *complement: in present tense*): **he is English** он англича́нин; (*in past/future tense*) быть (*impf*) +*instr or* +nom; **he was a doctor** он был врачо́м; **she is going to be very tall** она́ бу́дет о́чень высо́кая *or* высо́кой; **he is going to be an actor** он бу́дет актёром; **I'm tired** я уста́л; **I was hot/cold** мне бы́ло жа́рко/хо́лодно; **two and two are four** два́жды два — четы́ре; **she's tall/pretty** она́ высо́кая/симпати́чная; **be careful!** бу́дьте осторо́жны!; **be quiet!** ти́ше!

2 (*of health*): **how are you feeling?** как Вы себя́ чу́вствуете?; **he's very ill** он о́чень бо́лен; **I'm better now** мне сейча́с лу́чше

3 (*of age*): **how old are you?** ско́лько Вам лет?; **I'm sixteen (years old)** мне шестна́дцать (лет); **I was only 5 (years old) then** мне тогда́ бы́ло всего́ 5 (лет)

4 (*cost*): **how much is/was the wine?** ско́лько сто́ит/сто́ило вино́?; **that'll be £5.75, please** с Вас £5.75, пожа́луйста

♦ *vi* **1** (*exist*) быть (*impf*); **there are people who...** есть лю́ди, кото́рые...; **there is one drug that...** есть одно́ лека́рство, кото́рое...; **is there a God?** Бог есть на све́те?

2 (*occur*) быва́ть (*impf*); **there are frequent accidents on this road** на э́той доро́ге ча́сто быва́ют ава́рии; **be that as it may** как бы ни́ было; **so be it** так и бы́ть, быть по сему́

3 (*referring to place*): **I won't be here tomorrow** меня́ здесь за́втра не бу́дет; **Edinburgh is in Scotland** Эдинбу́рг нахо́дится в Шотла́ндии; **the book is on the table** кни́га на столе́; **there are pictures on the wall** на стене́ карти́ны; **there is someone in the house** в до́ме кто-то есть; **we've been here for ages** мы здесь уже́ о́чень давно́

4 (*referring to movement*) быть (*impf*); **where have you been?** где Вы бы́ли?; **I've been to the post office** я был на по́чте

♦ *impers vb* **1** (*referring to time*): **it's five o'clock (now)** сейча́с пять часо́в; **it's the 28th of April (today)** сего́дня 28-ое апре́ля

2 (*referring to distance, weather: in present tense*): **it's 10 km to the village** до дере́вни 10 км; (: *in past/future tense*) быть (*impf*); **it's too hot/cold (today)** сего́дня сли́шком жа́рко/хо́лодно; **it was very windy yesterday** вчера́ бы́ло о́чень ве́тренно; **it will be sunny tomorrow** за́втра бу́дет со́лнечно

3 (*emphatic*): **it's (only) me/the postman** э́то я/почтальо́н; **it was Maria who paid the bill** счёт оплати́ла Мари́я.

B/E *abbr* = **bill of exchange**.

beach [biːtʃ] *n* (*stony*) бе́рег* мо́ря; (*sandy*) пляж ♦ *vt* (*boat*) выта́скивать (вы́тащить *perf*) на бе́рег.

beach buggy *n* пля́жный вездехо́д.

beachcomber ['biːtʃkəuməʳ] *n* бич*.

beachwear ['biːtʃwɛəʳ] *n* пля́жная оде́жда.

beacon ['biːkən] *n* (*lighthouse*) мая́к*; (*marker*) сигна́льный ого́нь* *m*; (*also:* **radio** ~) радиомая́к*.

bead [biːd] *n* бу́сина; (*of sweat*) ка́пля*; ~**s** *npl* (*necklace*) бу́сы *pl*.

beady ['biːdɪ] *adj*: ~ **eyes** глаза́-бу́синки *mpl*.

beagle ['biːgl] *n* го́нчая *f adj* (соба́ка).

beak [biːk] *n* клюв.

beaker ['biːkəʳ] *n* (*cup*) пласстма́ссовый стака́н.

beam [biːm] *n* (*ARCHIT*) ба́лка*; (*of light*) луч*; (*RADIO*) радиосигна́л ♦ *vi* (*smile*) сия́ть (*impf*) ♦ *vt* (*signal*) передава́ть* (переда́ть* *perf*); **to drive on full or main** *or* (*US*) **high** ~ е́хать* (*impf*) с включёнными да́льними фа́рами.

beaming ['biːmɪŋ] *adj* сия́ющий*.

---

* marks translations which have irregular inflections. The Russian-English side of the dictionary gives inflectional information.

bean [bi:n] *n* боб*; **French ~** фасо́ль *f no pl*; **runner ~** фасо́ль о́гненная; **coffee ~** кофе́йное зерно́.
beanpole ['bi:npəul] *n* (*inf*) каланча́* (*высо́кий челове́к*).
beansprouts ['bi:nsprauts] *npl* побе́ги *mpl* бобо́в.
bear [bɛəʳ] (*pt* bore, *pp* borne) *n* медве́дь(-дица) *m(f)*; (*STOCK EXCHANGE*) "медве́дь" (*спекуля́нт, игра́ющий на пониже́ние ку́рса*) ♦ *vt* (*responsibility, cost*) нести́* (понести́* *perf*); (*weight*) нести́* (*impf*); (*examination, scrutiny*) выде́рживать (вы́держать* *perf*); (*situation, person*) выноси́ть* (вы́нести* *perf*); (*traces, signs*) нести́* (*impf*) на себе́; (*children*) рожда́ть (роди́ть* *perf*); (*fruit*) приноси́ть* (принести́* *perf*); (*COMM:*) **to ~ interest** приноси́ть* (принести́* *perf*) проце́нты ♦ *vi*: **to ~ right/left** (*AUT*) держа́ться (*impf*) пра́вого/ле́вого поворо́та; **to ~ the responsibility of** нести́* (понести́* *perf*) отве́тственность за +*acc*; **to ~ comparison with** выде́рживать (вы́держать* *perf*) сравне́ние с +*instr*; **I can't ~ him** я его́ не выношу́; **the road ~s to the right/left** доро́га идёт впра́во/вле́во; **to bring pressure to ~ on sb** ока́зывать (оказа́ть* *perf*) давле́ние на кого́-н
▶ **bear out** *vt* подде́рживать (поддержа́ть *perf*)
▶ **bear up** *vi* держа́ться (*impf*); **he bore up well** он держа́лся молодцо́м
▶ **bear with** *vt fus* терпе́ть (*impf*) с +*instr*; **~ with me a minute** потерпи́те мину́ту.
bearable ['bɛərəbl] *adj* терпи́мый (терпи́м).
beard [bɪəd] *n* борода́*.
bearded ['bɪədɪd] *adj* борода́тый.
bearer ['bɛərəʳ] *n* (*of letter*) пода́тель(ница) *m(f)*; (*of news*) ве́стник; (*of cheque, passport etc*) владе́лец*, предъяви́тель *m*; (*of title*) носи́тель(ница) *m(f)*.
bearing ['bɛərɪŋ] *n* (*manner*) мане́ра держа́ть себя́; (*connection*) отноше́ние; (*TECH*) подши́пник; **~s** *npl* (*also:* **ball ~s**) ша́рики *mpl* подши́пника; **to take a ~** ориенти́роваться (*impf/perf*); **to get one's ~s** ориенти́роваться (сориенти́роваться *perf*).
beast [bi:st] *n* (*also inf*) зверь* *m*.
beastly ['bi:stlɪ] *adj* ужа́сный (ужа́сен), жу́ткий* (жу́ток).
beat [bi:t] (*pt* beat, *pp* beaten) *n* (*of heart*) бие́ние; (*MUS: rhythm*) ритм; (: *in bar*) такт; (*POLICE*) уча́сток* ♦ *vt* (*wife, child*) бить* (поби́ть* *perf*); (*eggs etc*) взбива́ть (взби́ть* *perf*); (*opponent, record*) побива́ть (поби́ть* *perf*); (*drum*) бить* (*impf*) в +*acc* ♦ *vi* (*heart*) би́ться* (*impf*); (*rain, wind*) стуча́ть (*impf*); **to ~ time** отбива́ть (*impf*) такт; **~ it!** (*inf*) кати́сь!; **that ~s everything** э́то превосхо́дит всё; **to ~ about the bush** ходи́ть* (*impf*) вокру́г да о́коло; **off the ~en track** по непроторённому пути́

▶ **beat down** *vt* (*door*) выла́мывать (вы́ломать *perf*); (*price*) сбива́ть (сбить* *perf*); (*seller*) добива́ться (доби́ться* *perf*) ски́дки у +*gen* ♦ *vi* (*rain*) хлеста́ть* (*impf*); (*sun*) пали́ть (*impf*)
▶ **beat off** *vt* отбива́ть (отби́ть* *perf*)
▶ **beat up** *vt* (*person*) избива́ть (изби́ть* *perf*); (*eggs etc*) взбива́ть (взби́ть* *perf*).
beaten ['bi:tn] *pp of* beat.
beater ['bi:təʳ] *n* ве́нчик.
beating ['bi:tɪŋ] *n* (*thrashing*) по́рка*; **to take a ~** (*fig*) терпе́ть* (потерпе́ть* *perf*) пораже́ние.
beat-up ['bi:t'ʌp] *adj* (*inf*) раздо́лбанный (раздо́лбан).
beautician [bju:'tɪʃən] *n* космети́чка*.
beautiful ['bju:tɪful] *adj* (*woman, place*) краси́вый (краси́в); (*day, experience*) прекра́сный* (прекра́сен).
beautifully ['bju:tɪflɪ] *adv* (*play, sing etc*) краси́во, прекра́сно; (*quiet, empty etc*) замеча́тельно.
beautify ['bju:tɪfaɪ] *vt* украша́ть (укра́сить* *perf*).
beauty ['bju:tɪ] *n* красота́*; (*woman*) краса́вица; **the ~ of it is that ...** (*fig*) пре́лесть *f* э́того в том, что ....
beauty contest *n* ко́нкурс красоты́.
beauty queen *n* короле́ва красоты́.
beauty salon *n* сало́н красоты́.
beauty sleep *n* сон до полу́ночи, по пове́рию де́лающий челове́ка молоды́м и здоро́вым.
beauty spot *n* (*BRIT: TOURISM*) живопи́сная ме́стность *f*.
beaver ['bi:vəʳ] *n* (*ZOOL*) бобр*.
becalmed [bɪ'kɑ:md] *adj* заштиле́вший.
became [bɪ'keɪm] *pt of* become.
because [bɪ'kɔz] *conj* потому́ что; (*since, as*) так как; **~ of** (*illness etc*) из-за +*gen*.
beck [bɛk] *n*: **to be at sb's ~ and call** быть* (*impf*) у кого́-н на побегу́шках.
beckon ['bɛkən] *vt* (*also:* **~ to**) мани́ть* (помани́ть* *perf*) ♦ *vi* (*fame, glory*) мани́ть* (*impf*).
become [bɪ'kʌm] (*irreg: like* come) *vi* станови́ться* (стать* *perf*) +*instr*; **to ~ fat** толсте́ть (потолсте́ть *perf*); **to ~ thin** худе́ть (похуде́ть *perf*); **to ~ angry** серди́ться* (рассерди́ться* *perf*); **it became known that** ста́ло изве́стно, что; **what has ~ of him?** что с ним ста́лось?
becoming [bɪ'kʌmɪŋ] *adj* (*behaviour*) прили́чествующий; (*clothes*): **your dress is ~** э́то пла́тье Вам к лицу́.
BECTU *n abbr* (*BRIT*) = Broadcasting Entertainment Cinematographic and Theatre Union.
BEd *n abbr* (= Bachelor of Education) бакала́вр педаго́гики.
bed [bɛd] *n* крова́ть *f*; (*of coal, clay*) пласт*; (*of river, sea*) дно*; (*of flowers*) клу́мба; **to go to ~** ложи́ться (лечь* *perf*) спать

▶ **bed down** *vi* располага́ться (расположи́ться* *perf*) на ночле́г.

bed and breakfast *n* ма́ленькая ча́стная гости́ница с за́втраком; (*terms*) ночле́г и за́втрак.

bedbug ['bɛdbʌg] *n* клоп*.

bedclothes ['bɛdkləuðz] *npl* посте́льное бельё *ntsg*.

bedding ['bɛdɪŋ] *n* посте́льные принадле́жности *fpl*.

bedevil [bɪ'dɛvl] *vt* (*person*) опу́тывать (опу́тать *perf*); (*plans*) спу́тывать (спу́тать *perf*); **to be ~led by** вя́знуть (увя́знуть *perf*) в +*prp*.

bedfellow ['bɛdfɛləu] *n*: **they are strange ~s** (*fig*) они́ стра́нная па́ра.

bedlam ['bɛdləm] *n* бедла́м.

bedpan ['bɛdpæn] *n* (покладно́е) су́дно*.

bedpost ['bɛdpəust] *n* сто́лбик крова́тного по́лоса.

bedraggled [bɪ'drægld] *adj* (*person, clothes*) потрёпанный (потрёпан); (*hair*) всклоко́ченный (всклоко́чен).

bedridden ['bɛdrɪdn] *adj* прико́ванный (прико́ван) к посте́ли.

bedrock ['bɛdrɔk] *n* (*fig*) краеуго́льный ка́мень *m*; (*GEO*) материко́вая поро́да.

bedroom ['bɛdrum] *n* спа́льня*.

Beds *abbr* (*BRIT: POST*) = *Bedfordshire*.

bed settee *n* дива́н-крова́ть *f*.

bedside ['bɛdsaɪd] *n*: **at sb's ~** у посте́ли кого́-н ◆ *cpd* (*lamp, cabinet*) прикрыва́тный.

bedsit(ter) ['bɛdsɪt(ə⁰)] *n* (*BRIT*) ко́мната, соединя́ющая в себе́ спа́льню, гости́ную и иногда́ ку́хню.

bedspread ['bɛdsprɛd] *n* покрыва́ло.

bedtime ['bɛdtaɪm] *n* вре́мя* *nt* ложи́ться спа́ть; **it's ~** пора́ (ложи́ться) спа́ть.

bee [bi:] *n* пчела́*; **to have a ~ in one's bonnet about sth** помеша́ться (*impf*) на чём-н.

beech [bi:tʃ] *n* бук*.

beef [bi:f] *n* говя́дина; **roast ~** ро́стбиф

▶ **beef up** *vt* (*inf: support*) придава́ть (прида́ть* *perf*) си́лы +*dat*; (: *essay*) напо́лнить (*perf*) +*instr*.

beefburger ['bi:fbə:gə⁰] *n* говя́жья котле́та, га́мбургер.

Beefeater ['bi:fi:tə⁰] *n* лейб-гварде́ец охра́ны Та́уэра в Ло́ндоне.

beehive ['bi:haɪv] *n* у́лей*.

beekeeping ['bi:ki:pɪŋ] *n* пчелово́дство.

beeline ['bi:laɪn] *n*: **to make a ~ for** мча́ться (помча́ться *perf*) пря́мо в +*acc*.

been [bi:n] *pp of* **be**.

beep [bi:p] *n* гудо́к* ◆ *vi* сигна́лить (просигна́лить *perf*).

beer [bɪə⁰] *n* пи́во.

beer belly *n* (*inf*) брю́хо.

beer can *n* ба́нка из-под пи́ва.

beet [bi:t] *n* (*vegetable*) кормова́я свёкла; (*US: also: red ~*) свёкла.

beetle ['bi:tl] *n* жук*.

beetroot ['bi:tru:t] *n* (*BRIT*) свёкла *no pl*.

befall [bɪ'fɔ:l] (*irreg: like* **fall**) *vt* выпада́ть (вы́пасть* *perf*) +*dat*.

befit [bɪ'fɪt] *vt* прили́чествовать (*impf*) +*dat*.

before [bɪ'fɔ:⁰] *prep* пе́ред +*instr*, до +*gen* ◆ *conj* до того́ *or* пе́ред тем, как ◆ *adv* (*time*) ра́ньше, пре́жде; (*space*) впереди́; **the day ~ yesterday** позавчера́; **do this ~ you forget** сде́лайте э́то пока́ Вы не забы́ли; **~ going** пе́ред ухо́дом; **~ she goes** до того́ *or* пе́ред тем, как она́ уйдёт; **the week ~** неде́лю наза́д, на про́шлой неде́ле; **I've never seen it ~** я никогда́ э́того ра́ньше не ви́дел.

beforehand [bɪ'fɔ:hænd] *adv* зара́нее.

befriend [bɪ'frɛnd] *vt* подружи́ться (*perf*) с +*instr*.

befuddled [bɪ'fʌdld] *adj* одурма́ненный (одурма́нен).

beg [bɛg] *vi* ни́щенствовать (*impf*) ◆ *vt* (*also: ~ for: food, money*) проси́ть* (*impf*); (: *forgiveness, mercy etc*) умоля́ть (умоли́ть *perf*) о +*prp*; **to ~ sb to do** умоля́ть (умоли́ть *perf*) кого́-н +*infin*; **I ~ your pardon** (*apologizing*) прошу́ проще́ния; (*not hearing*) прости́те, не расслы́шал; **to ~ the question** счита́ть (счесть* *perf*) спо́рный вопро́с решённым; **to ~ a favour of sb** проси́ть* (попроси́ть* *perf*) об одолже́нии у кого́-н.

began [bɪ'gæn] *pt of* **begin**.

beggar ['bɛgə⁰] *n* ни́щий*(-ая) *m(f) adj*.

begin [bɪ'gɪn] (*pt* **began**, *pp* **begun**) *vt* начина́ть (нача́ть* *perf*) ◆ *vi* начина́ться (нача́ться* *perf*); **to ~ doing** *or* **to do** начина́ть (нача́ть* *perf*) +*impf infin*; **~ning (from) Monday** начина́я с понеде́льника; **I can't ~ to thank you** не зна́ю, как Вас благодари́ть; **we'll have soup to ~ with** мы начнём с су́па; **to ~ with, I'd like to know ...** для нача́ла, я бы хоте́л знать ....

beginner [bɪ'gɪnə⁰] *n* начина́ющий*(-ая) *m(f) adj*.

beginning [bɪ'gɪnɪŋ] *n* нача́ло; **right from the ~** с са́мого нача́ла.

begrudge [bɪ'grʌdʒ] *vt*: **he ~s me my success** он зави́дует моему́ успе́ху.

beguile [bɪ'gaɪl] *vt* соблазня́ть (соблазни́ть *perf*).

beguiling [bɪ'gaɪlɪŋ] *adj* соблазни́тельный, зама́нчивый.

begun [bɪ'gʌn] *pp of* **begin**.

behalf [bɪ'hɑ:f] *n*: **on** *or* (*US*) **in ~ of** от и́мени +*gen*; (*for benefit of*) ра́ди +*gen*, в интере́сах +*gen*; **on my/his ~** от моего́/его́ и́мени.

behave [bɪ'heɪv] *vi* вести́* (*impf*) себя́; (*well: also: ~ o.s.*) вести́* (*impf*) себя́ хорошо́.

---

* marks translations which have irregular inflections. The Russian-English side of the dictionary gives inflectional information.

behaviour [bɪ'heɪvjəʳ] (*US* **behavior**) *n* поведéние.

behead [bɪ'hɛd] *vt* обезглáвливать (обезглáвить* *perf*).

beheld [bɪ'hɛld] *pt, pp of* **behold**.

behind [bɪ'haɪnd] *prep* (*at the back of*) за +*instr*, позадú +*gen*; (*supporting*) за +*instr*; (*lower in rank etc*) нúже +*gen* ◆ *adv* сзáди, позадú ◆ *n* (*buttocks*) зад*; ~ **the scenes** за кулúсами; **we're ~ them in technology** мы отстáли от них в технолóгии; **to be ~ schedule** отставáть* (отстáть* *perf*) от грáфика; **to leave sth ~** (*forget*) оставлять (остáвить* *perf*) что-н.

behold [bɪ'həuld] (*irreg: like* **hold**) *vt* узрéть (*perf*).

beige [beɪʒ] *adj* бéжевый.

Beijing ['beɪ'dʒɪŋ] *n* Пекúн.

being ['bi:ɪŋ] *n* (*creature*) существó*; (*existence*) существовáние; **to come into ~** возникáть (вознúкнуть* *perf*).

Beirut [beɪ'ru:t] *n* Бейрýт.

Belarus [bɛlə'rus] *n* Беларýсь *f*.

belated [bɪ'leɪtɪd] *adj* запоздáлый.

belch [bɛltʃ] *vi* отрыгивать (отрыгнýть *perf*) ◆ *vt* (*also:* ~ **out**) извергáть (извéргнуть* *perf*).

beleaguered [bɪ'li:gɪd] *adj* (*also fig*) осаждённый (осаждён); (*army*) окружённый*.

Belfast ['bɛlfɑ:st] *n* Бéлфаст.

belfry ['bɛlfrɪ] *n* колокóльня*.

Belgian ['bɛldʒən] *adj* бельгúйский* ◆ *n* бельгúец*(-ийка).

Belgium ['bɛldʒəm] *n* Бéльгия.

Belgrade [bɛl'greɪd] *n* Белгрáд.

belie [bɪ'laɪ] *vt* (*give false impression of*) давáть* (дать* *perf*) невéрное представлéние о +*prp*; (*disprove*) опровергáть (опровéргнуть *perf*).

belief [bɪ'li:f] *n* (*conviction*) убеждéние; (*trust, faith*) вéра; **it's beyond ~** это невероятно; **in the ~ that** полагáя, что.

believable [bɪ'li:vəbl] *adj* правдоподóбный* (правдоподóбен).

believe [bɪ'li:v] *vt* вéрить (повéрить *perf*) +*dat or* в(о) +*acc* ◆ *vi* вéрить (*impf*); **to ~ in** вéрить (повéрить *perf*) в +*acc*; **I don't ~ in corporal punishment** я не вéрю в телéсные наказáния; **he is ~d to be abroad** полагáют, что он за гранúцей.

believer [bɪ'li:vəʳ] *n* сторóнник(-ица); (*REL*) вéрующий*(-ая) *m(f) adj*; **she's a great ~ in healthy eating** она – сторóнница здорóвого питáния.

belittle [bɪ'lɪtl] *vt* преуменьшáть (преумéньшить *perf*), уничижáть (*impf*).

Belize [bɛ'li:z] *n* Белúз.

bell [bɛl] *n* кóлокол*; (*small*) колокóльчик; (*on door*) звонóк*; **that rings a ~** я чтó-то припоминáю.

bell-bottoms ['bɛlbɒtəmz] *npl* брюки клёш *pl*.

bellboy ['bɛlbɔɪ] *n* (*BRIT*) коридóрный *m adj*.

bellhop ['bɛlhɒp] *n* (*US*) = **bellboy**.

belligerence [bɪ'lɪdʒərəns] *n* воúнственность *f*.

belligerent [bɪ'lɪdʒərənt] *adj* (*person, attitude*) воúнственный (воúнственен).

bellow ['bɛləu] *vi* ревéть* (*impf*) ◆ *vt* (*orders*) проревéть* (*perf*).

bellows ['bɛləuz] *npl* (*for fire*) мехú *mpl*.

bell push *n* (*BRIT*) звонóк*.

belly ['bɛlɪ] *n* брюхо.

bellyache ['bɛlɪeɪk] (*inf*) *n* боли *fpl* в животé ◆ *vi* ныть* (*impf*).

bellybutton ['bɛlɪbʌtn] *n* пупóк*.

bellyful ['bɛlɪful] *n*: **I've had a ~ of it** я сыт по гóрло этим.

belong [bɪ'lɒŋ] *vi*: **to ~ to** принадлежáть (*impf*) +*dat*; (*club etc*) состоять (*impf*) в +*prp*; **this book ~s here** мéсто этой кнúги здесь.

belongings [bɪ'lɒŋɪŋz] *npl* вéщи *fpl*; **personal ~** лúчные принадлéжности *fpl*.

Belorussia [bɛlɛu'rʌʃə] *n* Белорýссия.

Belorussian [bɛlɛu'rʌʃən] *n* (*person*) белорýс(ка*); (*LING*) белорýсский* язык* ◆ *adj* белорýсский*.

beloved [bɪ'lʌvɪd] *adj* любúмый ◆ *n* возлюбленный(-ая) *m(f) adj*.

below [bɪ'ləu] *prep* (*position*) под(о) +*instr*; (*motion*) под(о) +*acc*; (*less than*) нúже +*gen* ◆ *adv* (*position*) внизý; (*motion*) вниз; **temperatures ~ normal** температýры нúже нормáльных; **see ~** смотрúте нúже.

belt [bɛlt] *n* (*leather etc*) ремéнь* *m*; (*cloth*) пóяс*; (*of land*) пóяс*, зóна; (*TECH*) приводнóй ремéнь* ◆ *vt* (*thrash*) порóть* (выпороть *perf*) ◆ *vi* (*BRIT: inf*): **to ~ along** *or* **down the road** жáрить (*impf*) по дорóге; **industrial ~** индустриáльная зóна

▶ **belt out** *vt* горлáнить (*impf*)

▶ **belt up** *vi* (*inf: BRIT*) заткнýться (*perf*); (: *AUT*) застёгиваться (застегнýться *perf*).

beltway ['bɛltweɪ] *n* (*US: AUT*) кольцевáя дорóга; (*motorway*) кольцевáя скоростнáя автомагистрáль *f*.

bemoan [bɪ'məun] *vt* оплáкивать (оплáкать* *perf*).

bemused [bɪ'mju:zd] *adj* озадáченный.

bench [bɛntʃ] *n* скамья*; (*in workshop*) верстáк*; (*in laboratory*) лаборатóрный стол*; (*BRIT: POL*) местá пáртий в Парлáменте; **the B~** (*LAW*) судéйская коллéгия.

benchmark ['bɛntʃmɑ:k] *n* критéрий.

bend [bɛnd] (*pt, pp* **bent**) *vt* (*pipe, leg etc*) гнуть (согнýть *perf*), сгибáть (*impf*) ◆ *vi* (*person*) гнýться (согнýться *perf*) ◆ *n* (*BRIT: in road*) поворóт; (*in pipe*) изгúб; (*in river*) излýчина; **~s** *npl* (*MED*): **the ~s** кессóнная болéзнь *fsg*

▶ **bend down** *vi* наклонúться (наклонúться *perf*), нагибáться (нагнýться *perf*)

▶ **bend over** *vt fus* (*book, child*) склоняться (склонúться* *perf*) над +*instr*; (*fence*) перегибáться (перегнýться *perf*) чéрез +*acc*.

beneath [bɪ'ni:θ] *prep* (*position*) под +*instr*; (*motion*) под(о) +*acc*; (*unworthy of*) ни́же +*gen* ◆ *adv* внизу́.

benefactor ['bɛnɪfæktə'] *n* (*to person*) благоде́тель *m*; (*to institution*) благотвори́тель *m*.

benefactress ['bɛnɪfæktrɪs] *n* благоде́тельница; благотвори́тельница.

beneficial [bɛnɪ'fɪʃəl] *adj*: ~ (**to**) благотво́рный* (благотво́рен) (для +*gen*).

beneficiary [bɛnɪ'fɪʃərɪ] *n* (*LAW*) бенефициа́рий.

benefit ['bɛnɪfɪt] *n* (*advantage*) вы́года; (*money*) посо́бие; (*also:* ~ **concert**) благотвори́тельный конце́рт; (*also:* ~ **match**) благотвори́тельный матч ◆ *vt* приноси́ть* (принести́* *perf*) по́льзу +*dat* ◆ *vi*: **he'll** ~ **from it** он полу́чит от э́того вы́году.

Benelux ['bɛnɪlʌks] *n* Бенилю́кс.

benevolent [bɪ'nɛvələnt] *adj* (*person*) доброжела́тельный* (доброжела́телен); (*organization*) благотвори́тельный* (благотвори́телен).

BEng *n abbr* (= *Bachelor of Engineering*) ≈ бакала́вр инжене́рного де́ла.

Bengal [bɛn'gɔ:l] *n*: **Bay of** ~ Бенга́льский зали́в.

Bengali [bɛn'gɔ:lɪ] *n* (*person*) бенга́лец*(-а́лка*); (*LING*) бенга́льский язы́к* ◆ *adj* бенга́льский.

benign [bɪ'naɪn] *adj* добросерде́чный* (добросерде́чен); (*MED*) доброка́чественный.

bent [bɛnt] *pt, pp of* **bend** ◆ *adj* (*wire, pipe*) по́гнутый; (*inf: dishonest*) жуликова́тый (жуликова́т); (: *pej: homosexual*): **he is** ~ он голубо́й ◆ *n*: **a** ~ **for** скло́нность *f* к +*dat*; **he is** ~ **on doing** он реши́тельно настро́ен +*infin*.

bequeath [bɪ'kwi:ð] *vt* завеща́ть (*impf/perf*).

bequest [bɪ'kwɛst] *n* насле́дство.

bereaved [bɪ'ri:vd] *adj* поне́сший тяжёлую утра́ту ◆ *n*: **the** ~ друзья́ *mpl* и ро́дственники *mpl* поко́йного.

bereavement [bɪ'ri:vmənt] *n* тяжёлая утра́та.

bereft [bɪ'rɛft] *adj*: ~ **of** лишённый (лишён) +*gen*.

beret ['bɛreɪ] *n* бере́т.

Bering Sea ['beɪrɪŋ-] *n*: **the** ~ ~ Бе́рингово мо́ре.

berk [bə:k] *n* (*inf: pej*) крети́н, деби́л.

Berks *abbr* (*BRIT: POST*) = **Berkshire**.

Berlin [bə:'lɪn] *n* Берли́н; **East/West** ~ (*formerly*) Восто́чный/За́падный Берли́н.

Bermuda [bə:'mju:də] *n* Берму́дские острова́ *mpl*.

Bermuda shorts *npl* берму́ды *pl*.

Bern [bə:n] *n* Берн.

berry ['bɛrɪ] *n* я́года.

berserk [bə'sə:k] *adj*: **to go** ~ разъяря́ться (разъяри́ться *perf*).

berth [bə:θ] *n* (*bed: in caravan*) ко́йка*; (: *on ship*) каю́та; (: *on train*) по́лка*; (*mooring*) прича́л ◆ *vi* прича́ливать (прича́лить *perf*); **to give sb/sth a wide** ~ обходи́ть* (обойти́* *perf*) кого́-н/что-н за версту́*.

beseech [bɪ'si:tʃ] (*pt, pp* **besought**) *vt* моли́ть* (*impf*).

beset [bɪ'sɛt] (*pt, pp* **beset**) *vt*: **we have been** ~ **with problems** нас одолева́ми пробле́мы.

beside [bɪ'saɪd] *prep* ря́дом с +*instr*, о́коло +*gen*, у +*gen*; (*compared with*) ря́дом с +*instr*; **to be** ~ **o.s. (with)** быть* (*impf*) вне себя́ (от +*gen*); **that's** ~ **the point** э́то к де́лу не отно́сится.

besides [bɪ'saɪdz] *adv* кро́ме того́ ◆ *prep* кро́ме +*gen*, помимо +*gen*.

besiege [bɪ'si:dʒ] *vt* (*also fig*) осажда́ть (осади́ть* *perf*).

besmirch [bɪ'smə:tʃ] *vt* очерня́ть (очерни́ть *perf*).

besotted [bɪ'sɔtɪd] *adj* (*BRIT*): ~ **with** опьянённый (опьянён) +*instr*.

besought [bɪ'sɔ:t] *pt, pp of* **beseech**.

bespectacled [bɪ'spɛktɪkld] *adj* в очка́х.

bespoke [bɪ'spəuk] *adj* (*BRIT*) поши́тый (поши́т); ~ **tailor** портно́й, рабо́тающий на зака́з.

best [bɛst] *adj* лу́чший* ◆ *adv* лу́чше всего́; **the** ~ **thing to do is …** лу́чше всего́ +*infin* …; **the** ~ **part of** (*quantity*) больша́я часть +*gen*; **at** ~ в лу́чшем слу́чае; **to make the** ~ **of sth** испо́льзовать (*impf*) что-н наилу́чшим о́бразом; **to do one's** ~ де́лать (сде́лать *perf*) всё возмо́жное; **to the** ~ **of my knowledge** наско́лько мне изве́стно; **to the** ~ **of my ability** в ме́ру мои́х спосо́бностей; **he's not exactly patient at the** ~ **of times** он не отлича́ется осо́бым терпе́нием.

bestial ['bɛstɪəl] *adj* ско́тский*.

best man *n* ша́фер*.

bestow [bɪ'stəu] *vt*: **to** ~ **sth on sb** (*title*) дарова́ть (*impf/perf*) что-н кому́-н; (*affection*) ода́ривать (одари́ть *perf*) кого́-н чем-н.

bestseller ['bɛst'sɛlə'] *n* бестсе́ллер.

bet [bɛt] (*pt, pp* **bet** *or* **betted**) *n* (*wager*) пари́ *nt ind*; (*in gambling*) ста́вка ◆ *vi* (*wager*) держа́ть (*impf*) пари́; (*expect, guess*) би́ться* (*impf*) об закла́д ◆ *vt*: **to** ~ **sb sth** би́ться* (поби́ться* *perf*) об закла́д с кем-н о чём-н, спо́рить (поспо́рить *perf*) с кем-н на что-н; **it's a safe** ~ (*fig*) э́то ве́рное де́ло; **to** ~ **money on sth** ста́вить* (поста́вить* *perf*) де́ньги на что-н.

Bethlehem ['bɛθlɪhɛm] *n* Вифлее́м.

betray [bɪ'treɪ] *vt* (*friends*) предава́ть* (преда́ть* *perf*); (*trust*) обма́нывать (обману́ть* *perf*); (*emotion*) выдава́ть* (вы́дать* *perf*).

---

betrayal [bɪˈtreɪəl] *n* преда́тельство.
better [ˈbɛtəʳ] *adj* лу́чший* ◆ *adv* лу́чше ◆ *vt* (*score*) улучша́ть (улу́чшить *perf*) ◆ *n*: **to get the ~ of** бра́ть* (взять* *perf*) верх над +*instr*; **I feel ~** я чу́вствую себя́ лу́чше; **to get ~** (*MED*) поправля́ться (попра́виться* *perf*); **that's ~!** вот та́к(-то) лу́чше!; **I had ~ go** мне лу́чше уйти́; **he thought ~ of it** он переду́мал; **a change for the ~** измене́ние к лу́чшему.
better off *adj* (*wealthier*) бо́лее состоя́тельный* (состоя́телен); (*more comfortable etc*) лу́чше; (*fig*): **you'd be ~ ~ this way** так Вам бу́дет лу́чше.
betting [ˈbɛtɪŋ] *n* пари́ *nt ind*.
betting shop *n* (*BRIT*) ме́сто, где де́лают ста́вки.
between [bɪˈtwiːn] *prep* ме́жду +*instr* ◆ *adv*: **in ~** ме́жду тем; **the road ~ here and London** доро́га отсю́да до Ло́ндона; **we only had £5 ~ us** у нас на двои́х бы́ло всего́ £5.
bevel [ˈbɛvəl] *n* (*also:* **~ edge**) скос.
bevelled [ˈbɛvəld] *adj*: **a ~ edge** ско́шенный край*.
beverage [ˈbɛvərɪdʒ] *n* напи́ток*.
bevy [ˈbɛvɪ] *n*: **a ~ of** (*people*) гру́ппа +*gen*; (*things*) ряд +*gen*.
bewail [bɪˈweɪl] *vt* скорбе́ть (*impf*) о +*prp*.
beware [bɪˈwɛəʳ] *vi*: **to ~ (of)** остерега́ться (остере́чься* *perf*) (+*gen*); **"beware of the dog"** "осторо́жно, (зла́я) соба́ка".
bewildered [bɪˈwɪldəd] *adj* изумлённый (изумлён).
bewildering [bɪˈwɪldrɪŋ] *adj* изуми́тельный* (изуми́телен).
bewitching [bɪˈwɪtʃɪŋ] *adj* (*smile, person*) чару́ющий.
beyond [bɪˈjɔnd] *prep* (*position*) за +*instr*; (*motion*) за +*acc*; (*understanding*) вы́ше +*gen*; (*expectations*) сверх +*gen*; (*age*) бо́льше +*gen*; (*date*) по́сле +*gen* ◆ *adv* (*position*) вдали́; (*motion*) вда́ль; **~ doubt** вне сомне́ния; **it's ~ repair** э́то невозмо́жно почини́ть; **it's ~ me** э́то вы́ше моего́ понима́ния.
b/f *abbr* (*COMM*: = **brought forward**) перенесённый на сле́дующую страни́цу.
BFPO *n abbr* = **British Forces Post Office**.
bhp *n abbr* (*AUT*: = **brake horsepower**) эффекти́вная мо́щность дви́гателя вну́треннего сгора́ния в лошади́ных си́лах.
bi... [baɪ] *prefix* би..., дву(х)....
biannual [baɪˈænjuəl] *adj* выходя́щий два ра́за в год.
bias [ˈbaɪəs] *n* (*against*) предубежде́ние; (*towards*) пристра́стие.
bias(s)ed [ˈbaɪəst] *adj* (*jury*) пристра́стный* (пристра́стен); (*judgement*) предвзя́тый (предвзя́т); **he is/was ~ against** он предубеждён/был предубеждён про́тив +*gen*.
bib [bɪb] *n* (*child's*) нагру́дник.
Bible [ˈbaɪbl] *n* Би́блия.

biblical [ˈbɪblɪkl] *adj* библе́йский*.
bibliography [bɪblɪˈɔɡrəfɪ] *n* библиогра́фия.
bicarbonate of soda [baɪˈkɑːbənɪt-] *n* питьева́я *or* пищева́я со́да.
bicentenary [baɪsɛnˈtiːnərɪ] *n* двухсотле́тие.
bicentennial [baɪsɛnˈtɛnɪəl] *n* (*US*) = **bicentenary**.
biceps [ˈbaɪsɛps] *n* би́цепс.
bicker [ˈbɪkəʳ] *vi* препира́ться (*impf*).
bickering [ˈbɪkərɪŋ] *n* препира́тельство.
bicycle [ˈbaɪsɪkl] *n* велосипе́д.
bicycle path *n* велосипе́дная доро́жка.
bicycle pump *n* велосипе́дный насо́с.
bicycle track *n* велотре́к.
bid [bɪd] (*pt* **bade** *or* **bid**, *pp* **bid(den)**) *n* (*at auction*) предложе́ние цены́; (*in tender*) зая́вка*; (*attempt*) попы́тка* ◆ *vt* (*offer*) предлага́ть (предложи́ть* *perf*) ◆ *vi*: **to ~ for** (*at auction*) предлага́ть (предложи́ть* *perf*) це́ну за +*acc*; (*CARDS*) объявля́ть (объяви́ть* *perf*) (*масть или коли́чество взя́ток*); **to ~ sb good day** здоро́ваться (поздоро́ваться *perf*) с кем-н.
bidden [ˈbɪdn] *pp of* **bid**.
bidder [ˈbɪdəʳ] *n*: **the highest ~** лицо́, предлага́ющее наивы́сшую це́ну.
bidding [ˈbɪdɪŋ] *n* (*at auction*) предложе́ние цены́, торги́ *pl*; (*command*): **to do sb's ~** исполня́ть (испо́лнить *perf*) чьй-н приказа́ния.
bide [baɪd] *vt*: **to ~ one's time** дожида́ться (дожда́ться *perf*) своего́ ча́са.
bidet [ˈbiːdeɪ] *n* биде́ *nt ind*.
bidirectional [ˈbaɪdɪˈrɛkʃənl] *adj* (*COMPUT*: *printing*) двунапра́вленный; (: *drive*) реверси́вный.
biennial [baɪˈɛnɪəl] *adj* происходя́щий раз в два го́да ◆ *n* двухле́тник.
bier [bɪəʳ] *n* катафа́лк.
bifocals [baɪˈfəuklz] *npl* бифока́льные очки́ *pl*.
big [bɪɡ] *adj* большо́й; (*important*) ва́жный* (ва́жен); (*bulky*) кру́пный*; (*older: brother, sister*) ста́рший*; **to do things in a ~ way** де́лать (сде́лать *perf*) что-н с широ́ким разма́хом.
bigamist [ˈbɪɡəmɪst] *n* (*man*) двоеже́нец*.
bigamous [ˈbɪɡəməs] *adj* бига́мный.
bigamy [ˈbɪɡəmɪ] *n* бига́мия.
big dipper [-ˈdɪpəʳ] *n* аттракцио́н "америка́нские го́ры".
big end *n* больша́я голо́вка (шатуна́).
biggish [ˈbɪɡɪʃ] *adj* дово́льно большо́й *or* кру́пный.
bigheaded [ˈbɪɡˈhɛdɪd] *adj* зано́счивый (зано́счив).
big-hearted [ˈbɪɡˈhɑːtɪd] *adj* великоду́шный* (великоду́шен).
bigot [ˈbɪɡət] *n* фана́тик.
bigoted [ˈbɪɡətɪd] *adj* фанати́чный* (фанати́чен).
bigotry [ˈbɪɡətrɪ] *n* фанати́зм.

big toe *n* большо́й па́лец* ноги́.
big top *n* ку́пол* ци́рка.
big wheel *n* колесо́* обозре́ния.
bigwig ['bɪgwɪg] *n* (*inf*) (ва́жная) ши́шка*.
bike [baɪk] *n* (*bicycle*) ве́лик; (*motorcycle*) мотоци́кл.
bikini [bɪ'kiːnɪ] *n* бики́ни *nt ind.*
bilateral [baɪ'lætərl] *adj* двусторо́нний*.
bile [baɪl] *n* жёлчь *f*; (*fig*) жёлчность *f*.
bilingual [baɪ'lɪŋgwəl] *adj* двуязы́чный*.
bilious ['bɪlɪəs] *adj* (*also fig*) тошнотво́рный (тошнотво́рен).
bill [bɪl] *n* (*invoice*) счёт*; (*POL*) законопрое́кт; (*US: banknote*) банкно́та; (*beak*) клюв ♦ *vt* (*item*) реклами́ровать (*impf*/*perf*); (*customer*) присыла́ть (присла́ть* *perf*) счёт +*dat*; "*post no ~s*" "помеща́ть афи́ши воспреща́ется"; **to fit** *or* **fill the ~** (*fig*) отвеча́ть (*impf*) всем тре́бованиям; **on the ~** (*THEAT*) в афи́шах *or* програ́мме; **~ of exchange** ве́ксель* *m*; **~ of fare** меню́ *nt ind*; **~ of lading** коносаме́нт, (тра́нспортная) накладна́я *f adj*; **~ of sale** ку́пчая *f adj.*
billboard ['bɪlbɔːd] *n* доска́ объявле́ний.
billet ['bɪlɪt] *n* (*MIL*) кварти́ры *fpl* ♦ *vt* расквартиро́вывать (расквартирова́ть* *perf*).
billfold ['bɪlfəʊld] *n* (*US*) бума́жник.
billiards ['bɪljədz] *n* билья́рд.
billion ['bɪljən] *n* (*BRIT*) биллио́н; (*US*) миллиа́рд.
billow ['bɪləʊ] *n* (*of smoke, steam*) клуб ♦ *vi* (*smoke*) клуби́ться (*impf*); (*sail*) надува́ться (наду́ться* *perf*).
billy goat ['bɪlɪ-] *n* козёл*.
bimbo ['bɪmbəʊ] *n* (*inf*) ку́кла (*хоро́шенькая, но не у́мная же́нщина*).
bin [bɪn] *n* (*BRIT: also: rubbish ~*) му́сорное ведро́*; (*container*) я́щик.
binary ['baɪnərɪ] *adj* (*MATH, COMPUT*) дво́ичный, бина́рный.
bind [baɪnd] (*pt, pp* **bound**) *vt* (*tie*) привя́зывать (привяза́ть* *perf*); (*tie together: hands and feet*) свя́зывать (связа́ть* *perf*); (*oblige*) обя́зывать (обяза́ть* *perf*); (*book*) переплета́ть (переплести́* *perf*) ♦ *n* (*inf*) обу́за
▶ **bind over** *vt* (*LAW*) обя́зывать (обяза́ть* *perf*)
▶ **bind up** *vt* (*wound*) перевя́зывать (перевяза́ть* *perf*); **he is/was bound up in** (*work etc*) он вовлечён/был вовлечён в +*acc*; **he is/was bound up with** (*person*) он свя́зан/ был свя́зан с +*instr.*
binder ['baɪndə'] *n* (*file*) скоросшива́тель *m.*
binding ['baɪndɪŋ] *adj* обя́зывающий ♦ *n* (*of book*) переплёт.
binge [bɪndʒ] *n* (*inf*): **to go on a ~** (*drink a lot*) пья́нствовать (*impf*).
bingo ['bɪŋgəʊ] *n* лото́ *nt ind.*
bin-liner ['bɪnlaɪnə'] *n* мешо́к* для му́сора.

binoculars [bɪ'nɔkjuləz] *npl* бино́кль *msg.*
bio... [baɪəʊ] *prefix* био...; **~chemistry** биохи́мия.
biodegradable ['baɪəʊdɪ'greɪdəbl] *adj* биологи́чески разложи́мый (разложи́м).
biodiversity ['baɪəʊdaɪ'vəːsɪtɪ] *n* биолог- и́ческое разнообра́зие.
biographer [baɪ'ɔgrəfə'] *n* био́граф.
biographic(al) [baɪə'græfɪk(l)] *adj* биографи́ческий.
biography [baɪ'ɔgrəfɪ] *n* биогра́фия.
biological [baɪə'lɔdʒɪkl] *adj* (*science*) биологи́ческий*; (*warfare*) бактериолог- и́ческий*; (*washing powder*) содержа́щий* биопрепара́ты.
biological clock *n* биологи́ческие часы́ *pl*; **to upset sb's ~ ~** наруша́ть (нару́шить *perf*) чей-н ре́жим.
biologist [baɪ'ɔlədʒɪst] *n* био́лог.
biology [baɪ'ɔlədʒɪ] *n* биоло́гия.
biophysics ['baɪəʊ'fɪzɪks] *n* биофи́зика.
biopic ['baɪəʊpɪk] *n* (*inf*) биографи́ческий фильм.
biopsy ['baɪɔpsɪ] *n* биопси́я.
biosphere ['baɪəsfɪə'] *n* биосфе́ра.
biotechnology ['baɪəʊtɛk'nɔlədʒɪ] *n* биотехноло́гия.
biped ['baɪpɛd] *n* двуно́гое *nt adj.*
birch [bəːtʃ] *n* берёза.
bird [bəːd] *n* пти́ца; (*BRIT: inf: girl*) деви́ца.
bird of prey *n* хи́щная пти́ца.
bird's-eye view ['bəːdzaɪ-] *n* (*aerial view*) вид* с высоты́ пти́чьего полёта; (*overview*) о́бщая карти́на.
bird-watcher ['bəːdwɔtʃə'] *n* орнито́лог- люби́тель *m.*
Birmingham ['bəːmɪŋəm] *n* Бирмингем.
Biro® ['baɪərəʊ] *n* ша́риковая ру́чка*.
birth [bəːθ] *n* рожде́ние; **to give ~ to** рожа́ть (роди́ть* *perf*).
birth certificate *n* свиде́тельство о рожде́нии.
birth control *n* (*policy*) контро́ль *m* рожда́емости; (*methods*) противо- зача́точные ме́ры *fpl.*
birthday ['bəːθdeɪ] *n* день* *m* рожде́ния ♦ *cpd* ко дню рожде́ния; *see also* **happy**.
birthmark ['bəːθmɑːk] *n* (*large*) роди́мое пятно́*; (*small*) роди́нка*.
birthplace ['bəːθpleɪs] *n* (*also fig*) ро́дина.
birth rate *n* рожда́емость *f.*
Biscay ['bɪskeɪ] *n*: **the Bay of ~** Биска́йский зали́в.
biscuit ['bɪskɪt] *n* (*BRIT*) пече́нье; (*US*) ≈ кекс.
bisect [baɪ'sɛkt] *vt* (*MATH*) дели́ть* (раздели́ть* *perf*).
bisexual ['baɪ'sɛksjuəl] *adj* бисексуа́льный* (бисексуа́лен).
bishop ['bɪʃəp] *n* (*REL*) епи́скоп; (*CHESS*) слон*.

---

* marks translations which have irregular inflections. The Russian-English side of the dictionary gives inflectional information.

bistro ['bi:strəu] *n* бистро́ *nt ind.*

bit [bɪt] *pt of* **bite** ◆ *n* (*piece*) кусо́к*, кусо́чек*; (*of tool*) сверло́*; (*COMPUT*) бит; (*of horse*) удила́* *pl*; (*US: coin*) (ме́лкая) моне́та; **a ~ of** немно́го +*gen*; **a ~ dangerous** слегка́ опа́сный; **~ by ~** ма́ло-пома́лу; **to come to ~s** разла́мываться (разлома́ться* *perf*); **bring all your ~s and pieces** принесёте все Ва́ши пожи́тки; **to do one's ~** вноси́ть* (внести́* *perf*) свой вклад.

bitch [bɪtʃ] *n* (*also inf!*) су́ка (*also !*)

bitching ['bɪtʃɪŋ] *n* хула́.

bite [baɪt] (*pt* **bit**, *pp* **bitten**) *vt* куса́ть (укуси́ть* *perf*) ◆ *vi* куса́ться (*impf*) ◆ *n* (*insect bite*) уку́с; **to ~ one's nails** куса́ть (*impf*) но́гти; **let's have a ~ (to eat)** (*inf*) дава́йте переку́сим; **he had a ~ of cake** он откуси́л кусо́к пирога́.

biting ['baɪtɪŋ] *adj* (*wind*) прони́зывающий; (*wit*) язви́тельный* (язви́телен).

bit part *n* проходна́я роль* *f*.

bitten ['bɪtn] *pp of* **bite**.

bitter ['bɪtə'] *adj* го́рький*; (*wind*) прони́зывающий; (*struggle*) ожесточённый ◆ *n* (*BRIT*) пи́во с горькова́тым при́вкусом; **to the ~ end** до са́мого конца́.

bitterly ['bɪtəlɪ] *adv* го́рько; (*oppose, criticize*) ожесточённо; (*jealous*) ужа́сно; **it's ~ cold today** сего́дня прони́зывающий хо́лод.

bitterness ['bɪtənɪs] *n* (*anger*) го́речь *f*, ожесточённость *f*; (*taste*) го́речь.

bittersweet ['bɪtəswi:t] *adj* горькова́то-сла́дкий*.

bitty ['bɪtɪ] *adj* (*BRIT: inf*) неро́вный* (неро́вен).

bitumen ['bɪtjumɪn] *n* биту́м.

bivouac ['bɪvuæk] *n* бива́к.

bizarre [bɪ'zɑ:'] *adj* стра́нный, причу́дливый.

bk *abbr* = **bank**, **book**.

BL *n abbr* (= *Bachelor of Law*) ≈ бакала́вр правове́дения; (= *Bachelor of Letters*) ≈ бакала́вр литературове́дения; (*US*: = *Bachelor of Literature*) ≈ бакала́вр литературове́дения.

bl *abbr* (= *bill of lading*) ≈ тра́нспортная накладна́я *f adj.*

blab [blæb] *vi* (*inf*) проба́лтываться (проболта́ться *perf*).

black [blæk] *adj* чёрный*; (*tea, coffee*) без молока́; (*person*) черноко́жий* ◆ *n* (*colour*) чёрный цвет, чёрное *nt adj*; (*person*): **B~** негр(итя́нка) ◆ *vt* (*BRIT: INDUSTRY*) бойкоти́ровать (*impf/perf*); **to give sb a ~ eye** подбива́ть (подби́ть* *perf*) кому́-н глаз; **~ and blue** в синяка́х; **there it is in ~ and white** (*fig*) вот оно́, чёрным по бе́лому напи́санно; **to be in the ~** име́ть (*impf*) де́ньги в ба́нке

▶ **black out** *vi* па́дать (упа́сть* *perf*) в о́бморок.

black belt *n* (*JUDO*) чёрный по́яс*; (*US: area*) *ю́жные райо́ны США, в кото́рых преоблада́ет негритя́нское населе́ние.*

blackberry ['blækbərɪ] *n* ежеви́ка *no pl.*

blackbird ['blækbə:d] *n* (чёрный) дрозд*.

blackboard ['blækbɔ:d] *n* кла́ссная доска́*.

black box *n* (*AVIAT*) чёрный я́щик.

black coffee *n* чёрный ко́фе *m ind.*

Black Country *n* (*BRIT*): **the ~~** *индустриа́льные райо́ны Се́веро-За́падной А́нглии.*

blackcurrant ['blæk'kʌrənt] *n* чёрная сморо́дина.

black economy *n*: **the ~~** теневая эконо́мика.

blacken ['blækn] *vt* (*fig*) черни́ть (очерни́ть *perf*).

black eye *n* синя́к* *or* фона́рь* *m* под гла́зом.

Black Forest *n*: **the ~~** Шварцва́льд.

blackhead ['blækhɛd] *n* у́горь* *m.*

black hole *n* чёрная дыра́*.

black ice *n* гололе́дица.

blackjack ['blækdʒæk] *n* (*CARDS*) блэкдже́к; (*US: truncheon*) дуби́нка.

blackleg ['blæklɛg] *n* (*BRIT: INDUSTRY*) штрейкбре́хер.

blacklist ['blæklɪst] *n* чёрный спи́сок* ◆ *vt* (*person*) заноси́ть* (занести́* *perf*) в чёрный спи́сок.

blackmail ['blækmeɪl] *n* шанта́ж ◆ *vt* шантажи́ровать (*impf*).

blackmailer ['blækmeɪlə'] *n* шантажи́ст.

black market *n* чёрный ры́нок*.

blackout ['blækaut] *n* (*in wartime*) затемне́ние; (*ELEC*) обесто́чка*; (*TV, RADIO*) приостановле́ние переда́ч; (*MED*) о́бморок.

black pepper *n* чёрный пе́рец*.

Black Sea *n*: **the ~~** Чёрное мо́ре.

black sheep *n* (*fig*) парши́вая овца́.

blacksmith ['blæksmɪθ] *n* кузне́ц*.

black spot *n* (*AUT*) гу́блое ме́сто*; (*ECON*) мёртвая зо́на.

bladder ['blædə'] *n* (*ANAT*) мочево́й пузы́рь* *m.*

blade [bleɪd] *n* ле́звие; (*of oar, propeller*) ло́пасть* *f*, **a ~ of grass** трави́нка*.

blame [bleɪm] *n* вина́* ◆ *vt*: **to ~ sb for sth** вини́ть (*impf*) кого́-н в чём-н; **he is/was to ~ (for sth)** он винова́т *or* вино́вен/был винова́т *or* вино́вен (в чём-н); **who's to ~?** кого́ сле́дует в э́том вини́ть?; **I'm not to ~** э́то не моя́ вина́.

blameless ['bleɪmlɪs] *adj* (*person*) невино́вый, безупре́гный.

blanch [blɑ:ntʃ] *vi* беле́ть (побеле́ть *perf*) ◆ *vt* (*CULIN*) обва́ривать (обвари́ть* *perf*) кипятко́м.

blancmange [blə'mɔnʒ] *n* бланманже́ *nt ind.*

bland [blænd] *adj* (*taste, food*) пре́сный (пре́сен).

blank [blæŋk] *adj* (*paper*) чи́стый* (чист); (*look*) безуча́стный* (безуча́стен) ◆ *n* (*of memory*) пробе́л; (*on form*) про́пуск; (*for gun*) холосто́й патро́н; **we drew a ~** (*fig*) мы оста́лись ни с чем.

blank cheque *n* незапо́лненный чек; **to give sb a ~~** (*fig*) предоставля́ть (предоста́вить*

perf) кому́-н карт-бланш.
blanket ['blæŋkɪt] *n* одея́ло; (*of snow*) покро́в; (*of fog*) пелена́ ♦ *adj* всеобъе́млющий*.
blanket cover *n* (*INSURANCE*) бла́нковый *or* блок по́лис.
blare [blɛəˈ] *vi* реве́ть (*impf*)
▶ **blare out** *vi* прореве́ть (*perf*).
blarney ['blɑːnɪ] *n* лесть *f*.
blasé ['blɑːzeɪ] *adj* пресы́щенный.
blaspheme [blæsˈfiːm] *vi* богоху́льствовать (*impf*), святота́тствовать (*impf*).
blasphemous ['blæsfɪməs] *adj* (*words*) богоху́льный; **a ~ person** богоху́льник.
blasphemy ['blæsfɪmɪ] *n* богоху́льство, святота́тство.
blast [blɑːst] *n* (*of wind*) поры́в; (*of air, steam*) волна́*; (*of whistle*) пронзи́тельный свист; (*explosion*) взрыв ♦ *vt* (*blow up*) взрыва́ть (взорва́ть* *perf*) ♦ *excl* (*BRIT: inf*) пропади́ (всё) про́падом; **at full ~** (*play music etc*) на по́лную мо́щность
▶ **blast off** *vi* взлета́ть (взлете́ть* *perf*), взмыва́ть (взмыть* *perf*).
blast furnace *n* до́менная печь* *f*.
blast-off ['blɑːstɔf] *n* старт.
blatant ['bleɪtənt] *adj* я́вный (я́вен), неприкры́тый.
blatantly ['bleɪtəntlɪ] *adv* я́вно, неприкры́то; **it's ~ obvious** э́то я́сно как день.
blaze [bleɪz] *n* (*fire*) пла́мя* *nt*; (*of colour*) полыха́ние; (*of glory*) сия́ние ♦ *vi* (*fire*) пыла́ть (*impf*); (*guns*) пали́ть (*impf*); (*fig: eyes*) сверка́ть (*impf*) ♦ *vt*: **to ~ a trail** пролага́ть (проложи́ть* *perf*) путь; **in a ~ of publicity** в газе́тной шуми́хе.
blazer ['bleɪzəˈ] *n* фо́рменная ку́ртка.
bleach [bliːtʃ] *n* (*also*: **household ~**) отбе́ливатель *m* ♦ *vt* (*fabric*) отбе́ливать (отбели́ть* *perf*); (*hair*) обесцве́чивать (обесцве́тить* *perf*).
bleached [bliːtʃt] *adj* (*hair*) обесцве́ченный (обесцве́чен).
bleachers ['bliːtʃəz] *npl* (*US: SPORT*) откры́тая трибу́на *fsg*.
bleak [bliːk] *adj* (*weather, expression*) уны́лый (уны́л); (*prospect*) безра́достный* (безра́достен).
bleary-eyed ['blɪərɪ'aɪd] *adj* с воспалёнными глаза́ми.
bleat [bliːt] *vi* (*animal*) бле́ять (забле́ять *perf*) ♦ *n* (*of animal*) бле́яние.
bled [blɛd] *pt, pp of* **bleed**.
bleed [bliːd] (*pt, pp* **bled**) *vi* кровото́чить (*impf*); (*colour*) течь* (поте́чь* *perf*) ♦ *vt* (*brakes, radiator*) опорожня́ть (опорожни́ть* *perf*); **my nose is ~ing** у меня́ идёт кровь из но́са.
bleep [bliːp] *n* сигна́л; (*TEL*) гудо́к* ♦ *vi* сигна́лить (просигна́лить *perf*) ♦ *vt* (*doctor*)

вызыва́ть (вы́звать* *perf*).
bleeper ['bliːpəˈ] *n* переносна́я ра́ция.
blemish ['blɛmɪʃ] *n* пятно́*.
blend [blɛnd] *n* (*of tea, whisky*) буке́т ♦ *vt* (*CULIN*) сме́шивать (смеша́ть *perf*); (*colours, styles etc*) сочета́ть (*impf*) ♦ *vi* (*also*: **~ in**) сочета́ться (*impf*), слива́ться (сли́ться* *perf*).
blender ['blɛndəˈ] *n* смеси́тель *m*, ми́ксер.
bless [blɛs] (*pt, pp* **blessed** *or* **blest**) *vt* (*REL*) благословля́ть (благослови́ть* *perf*); **he is ~ed with** Бог награди́л его́ +*instr*; **~ you!** бу́дьте здоро́вы!
blessed ['blɛsɪd] *adj* блаже́нный; **it rains every ~ day** (*inf*) дождь идёт ка́ждый Бо́жий день.
blessing ['blɛsɪŋ] *n* благослове́ние; (*godsend*) благода́ть *f*; **to count one's ~s** не гневи́ть* (*impf*) Бо́га, не ропта́ть* (*impf*) по́пусту на судьбу́; **it was a ~ in disguise** ≈ не́ бы́ло бы сча́стья, да несча́стье помогло́.
blest [blɛst] *pt, pp of* **bless**.
blew [bluː] *pt of* **blow**.
blight [blaɪt] *vt* губи́ть* (погуби́ть* *perf*) ♦ *n* (*of plants*) головня́*.
blimey ['blaɪmɪ] *excl* (*BRIT: inf*) чтоб мне провали́ться.
blind [blaɪnd] *adj* слепо́й* ♦ *n* што́ра; (*also*: **Venetian ~**) жалюзи́ *pl ind* ♦ *vt* ослепля́ть (ослепи́ть* *perf*); **the ~** *npl* (*blind people*) слепы́е *pl adj*; **to be ~ (to)** (*fig*) не ви́деть* (*impf*) (+*acc*); **to turn a ~ eye (on** *or* **to)** закрыва́ть (закры́ть* *perf*) глаза́ (на +*acc*).
blind alley *n* (*fig*) тупи́к.
blind corner *n* (*BRIT*) непросма́тривающийся поворо́т.
blind date *n* свида́ние с незнако́мцем.
blinders ['blaɪndəz] *npl* (*US*) = **blinkers**.
blindfold ['blaɪndfəuld] *n* повя́зка ♦ *adv* вслепу́ю ♦ *vt* завя́зывать (завяза́ть* *perf*) глаза́ +*dat*.
blinding ['blaɪndɪŋ] *adj* ослепля́ющий (ослепля́юш), слепя́щий; (*fig*) ослепи́тельный (ослепи́телен).
blindly ['blaɪndlɪ] *adv* (*without seeing*) вслепу́ю; (*without thinking*) сле́по.
blindness ['blaɪndnɪs] *n* слепота́; (*fig*) ослепле́ние.
blind spot *n* (*AUT*) опа́сное ме́сто*; (*fig*) сла́бое ме́сто*.
blink [blɪŋk] *vi* (*person, animal*) морга́ть (*impf*); (*light*) мига́ть (*impf*) ♦ *n*: **the TV's on the ~** (*inf*) телеви́зор барахли́т.
blinkers ['blɪŋkəz] *npl* шо́ры *fpl*.
blinking ['blɪŋkɪŋ] *adj* (*BRIT: inf*): **this ~ weather** прокля́тая пого́да.
blip [blɪp] *n* вспы́шка* (*на экра́не*); (*scientific*) отражённый и́мпульс.
bliss [blɪs] *n* блаже́нство.
blissful ['blɪsful] *adj* блаже́нный (блаже́н);

---

* marks translations which have irregular inflections. The Russian-English side of the dictionary gives inflectional information.

(*event*) счастли́вый (сча́стлив); **in ~ ignorance** в счастли́вом неве́дении.

blissfully ['blɪsfəlɪ] *adv* бла́женно; **~ happy** бесконе́чно счастли́вый; **~ unaware of ...** в счастли́вом неве́дении о +*prp* ....

blister ['blɪstə'] *n* (*on skin*) волды́рь* *m*; (*in paint, rubber*) пузы́рь* *m* ♦ *vi* (*paint*) пузыри́ться (*impf*).

blithely ['blaɪðlɪ] *adv* беспе́чно.

blithering ['blɪðərɪŋ] *adj* (*inf*): **this ~ idiot** э́тот зако́нченный дура́к.

BLit(t) *n abbr* = *Bachelor of Literature, Bachelor of Letters.*

blitz [blɪts] *n* (*MIL*) бомбёжка*; **to have a ~ on sth** (*fig*) нава́ливаться (навали́ться* *perf*) на что-н.

blizzard ['blɪzəd] *n* вью́га.

BLM *n abbr* (*US*) = *Bureau of Land Management.*

bloated ['bləʊtɪd] *adj* (*face, stomach*) взду́тый (взду́т); **I feel ~** я ве́сь разду́лся.

blob [blɔb] *n* (*of glue, paint*) сгу́сток*; (*indistinct shape*) сму́тное очерта́ние.

bloc [blɔk] *n* блок; **the Eastern ~** (*formerly*) стра́ны Восто́чного бло́ка.

block [blɔk] *n* (*of buildings*) кварта́л; (*of stone etc*) плита́*; (*in pipe etc*) про́бка; (*toy*) ку́бик ♦ *vt* (*entrance, road*) загора́живать (загороди́ть* *perf*); (*progress*) препя́тствовать (*impf*); (*COMPUT*) блоки́ровать (*impf*/*perf*); **~ of flats** (*BRIT*) многокварти́рный дом*; **three ~s from here** че́рез три у́лицы; **mental ~** прова́л па́мяти; **~ and tackle** лебёдка*; **to ~ sb's way** прегражда́ть (прегради́ть* *perf*) кому́-н доро́гу

► **block up** *vt* затыка́ть (заткну́ть *perf*) ♦ *vi* засоря́ться (засори́ться *perf*); **my nose is ~ed up** у меня́ нос заложи́ло.

blockade [blɔ'keɪd] *n* блока́да ♦ *vt* блоки́ровать (заблоки́ровать *perf*).

blockage ['blɔkɪdʒ] *n* блоки́рование.

block booking *n* группова́я бронь *f*.

blockbuster ['blɔkbʌstə'] *n* боеви́к*.

block capitals *npl* печа́тные бу́квы *fpl*.

blockhead ['blɔkhɛd] *n* (*inf*) болва́н.

block letters *npl* печа́тные бу́квы *fpl*.

block release *n* (*BRIT*) уче́бный о́тпуск.

block vote *n* (*BRIT*) представи́тельное голосова́ние.

bloke [bləʊk] *n* (*BRIT: inf*) па́рень* *m*.

blond(e) [blɔnd] *adj* белоку́рый (белоку́р) ♦ *n*: **blonde** (*woman*) блонди́нка*.

blood [blʌd] *n* кровь* *f*; **new ~** (*fig*) све́жие си́лы *fpl*.

blood bank *n* храни́лище кро́ви.

bloodbath ['blʌdbɑːθ] *n* бо́йня.

blood count *n* о́бщий ана́лиз кро́ви.

bloodcurdling ['blʌdkɜːdlɪŋ] *adj* леденя́щий* кровь.

blood donor *n* до́нор.

blood group *n* гру́ппа кро́ви.

bloodhound ['blʌdhaund] *n* ище́йка*.

bloodless ['blʌdlɪs] *adj* бескро́вный* (бескро́вен).

bloodletting ['blʌdlɛtɪŋ] *n* кровопуска́ние; (*fig*) кровопроли́тие.

blood poisoning *n* зараже́ние кро́ви.

blood pressure *n* кровяно́е давле́ние; **he has high/low ~ ~** у него́ высо́кое/ни́зкое давле́ние.

bloodshed ['blʌdʃɛd] *n* кровопроли́тие.

bloodshot ['blʌdʃɔt] *adj* (*eyes*) нали́тый кро́вью.

blood sport *n* охо́та (*как вид спо́рта*).

bloodstained ['blʌdsteɪnd] *adj* запя́тнанный кро́вью.

bloodstream ['blʌdstriːm] *n* кровообраще́ние.

blood test *n* ана́лиз кро́ви.

bloodthirsty ['blʌdθɜːstɪ] *adj* кровожа́дный (кровожа́ден).

blood transfusion *n* перелива́ние кро́ви.

blood type *n* гру́ппа кро́ви.

blood vessel *n* кровено́сный сосу́д.

bloody ['blʌdɪ] *adj* (*battle*) крова́вый; (*nose*) окрова́вленный (окрова́влен); (*BRIT: inf*!): **this ~ weather** э́та прокля́тая пого́да (!); **~ strong/good** (*inf*!) ужа́сно си́льный/ хоро́ший*.

bloody-minded ['blʌdɪ'maɪndɪd] *adj* (*BRIT: inf*) по́длый (подл).

bloom [bluːm] *n* (*BOT*) цвето́к ♦ *vi* (*BOT*) цвести́ (*impf*); (*talent, person*) расцвета́ть (расцвести́* *perf*); **to be in ~** быть* (*impf*) в цвету́, цвести́* (*impf*).

blooming ['bluːmɪŋ] *adj* (*BRIT: inf*): **this ~ weather** э́та чёртова пого́да.

blossom ['blɔsəm] *n* цвет ♦ *vi* цвести́* (*impf*); (*fig*): **to ~ into** расцвести́* (*perf*) в +*acc*.

blot [blɔt] *n* (*on text*) кля́кса; (*on name etc*) пятно́* ♦ *vt* (*with ink etc*) ста́вить* (поста́вить* *perf*) кля́ксу на +*acc*; **to be a ~ on the landscape** по́ртить* (*impf*) вид; **to ~ one's copy book** (*fig*) мара́ть (замара́ть *perf*) свою́ репута́цию

► **blot out** *vt* (*view*) заслоня́ть (заслони́ть *perf*); (*memory*) уничтожа́ть (уничто́жить *perf*).

blotchy ['blɔtʃɪ] *adj* (*complexion*) пятни́стый (пятни́ст).

blotter ['blɔtə'] *n* бюва́р.

blotting paper ['blɔtɪŋ-] *n* промока́тельная бума́га.

blotto ['blɔtəu] *adj* (*inf*) пья́ный (пьян) в сте́льку.

blouse [blauz] *n* блу́за, блу́зка*.

blow [bləu] (*pt* **blew**, *pp* **blown**) *n* (*also fig*) уда́р ♦ *vi* (*wind, person*) дуть (поду́ть *perf*); (*fuse*) перегора́ть (перегоре́ть *perf*) ♦ *vt* (*subj: wind*) гнать* (*impf*); (*instrument*) дуть (*impf*) в +*acc*; **to ~ one's nose** сморка́ться (вы́сморкаться *perf*); **to ~ a whistle** свисте́ть (просвисте́ть *perf*) в свисто́к; **to come to ~s** доходи́ть* (дойти́* *perf*) до дра́ки

▶ **blow away** *vt* сдува́ть (сдуть *perf*) ◆ *vi* уноси́ться* (унести́сь* *perf*)

▶ **blow down** *vt* вали́ть* (повали́ть* *perf*)

▶ **blow off** *vt* сдува́ть (сдуть *perf*) ◆ *vi* слета́ть (слете́ть* *perf*); (*NAUT*): **the ship was ~n off course** кора́бль снесло́ с ку́рса

▶ **blow out** *vi* га́снуть* (пога́снуть *perf*)

▶ **blow over** *vi* (*storm, crisis*) проходи́ть* (пройти́* *perf*)

▶ **blow up** *vi* (*storm, crisis*) разража́ться (разрази́ться* *perf*) ◆ *vt* (*bridge*) взрыва́ть (взорва́ть* *perf*); (*tyre*) надува́ть (наду́ть *perf*); (*PHOT*) увели́чивать (увели́чить *perf*).

blow-dry ['bləʊdraɪ] *n* укла́дка воло́с фе́ном ◆ *vt* укла́дывать (уложи́ть* *perf*) во́лосы фе́ном.

blowlamp ['bləʊlæmp] *n* (*BRIT*) пая́льная ла́мпа.

blown [bləʊn] *pp of* **blow**.

blow-out ['bləʊaʊt] *n* (*of tyre*) разры́в; (*of oil well*) проры́в; (*inf*: *big meal*) кутёж*.

blowtorch ['bləʊtɔ:tʃ] *n* = **blowlamp**.

blow-up ['bləʊʌp] *n* увели́ченный сни́мок*.

blowzy ['blaʊzɪ] *adj* (*BRIT*) обрю́згший.

BLS *n abbr* (*US*) = **Bureau of Labor Statistics**.

blubber ['blʌbə'] *n* вы́топленный жир ◆ *vi* (*pej*) реве́ть* (зареве́ть* *perf*).

bludgeon ['blʌdʒən] *vt* бить* (изби́ть* *perf*) дуби́нкой; (*fig*): **to ~ sb into doing** заставля́ть (заста́вить* *perf*) кого́-н из-под па́лки +*impf infin*.

blue [blu:] *adj* (*colour: light*) голубо́й; (: *dark*) си́ний*; (*depressed*) гру́стный, пода́вленный; **~s** *npl* (*MUS*): **the ~s** блю́з *msg*; **~ film** поха́бный фильм; (**only**) **once in a ~ moon** раз в сто лет; **out of the ~** (*fig*) как с не́ба свали́ться.

blue baby *n* сини́юшный младе́нец*.

bluebell ['blu:bɛl] *n* колоко́льчик.

bluebottle ['blu:bɔtl] *n* наво́зная му́ха.

blue cheese *n* сыр* ти́па рокфо́р.

blue-chip ['blu:tʃɪp] *adj*: **~ investment** надёжное капиталовложе́ние.

blue-collar worker ['blu:kɔlə'-] *n* рабо́чий*(-ая) *m(f) adj*.

blue jeans *npl* джи́нсы *pl*.

blueprint ['blu:prɪnt] *n* (*fig*): **a ~** (**for**) прое́кт (+*gen*).

bluff [blʌf] *vi* (*pretend, threaten*) блефова́ть (*impf*) ◆ *n* блеф; (*GEO*) утёс*; **to call sb's ~** заставля́ть (заста́вить* *perf*) кого́-н раскры́ть ка́рты.

blunder ['blʌndə'] *n* про́мах ◆ *vi* (*make mistake*) допуска́ть (допусти́ть* *perf*) про́мах; **to ~ into sb/sth** натыка́ться (наткну́ться *perf*) на кого́-н/что-н.

blunt [blʌnt] *adj* тупо́й* (туп); (*person*) прямолине́йный* (прямолине́ен); (*talk*)

открове́нный* (открове́нен) ◆ *vt* (*chisel etc*) затупля́ть (затупи́ть* *perf*); (*feelings*) тупи́ть (притупи́ть* *perf*); **~ instrument** (*LAW*) тупо́е ору́дие.

bluntly ['blʌntlɪ] *adv* пря́мо.

bluntness ['blʌntnɪs] *n* (*of person*) прямолине́йность *f*.

blur [blə:'] *n* сму́тное очерта́ние; (*memory*) сму́тное воспомина́ние ◆ *vt* (*vision*) затума́нивать (затума́нить *perf*); (*distinction*) стере́ть* (стира́ть *perf*).

blurb [blə:b] *n* (*about book etc*) рекла́ма.

blurred [blə:d] *adj* стёртый.

blurt out [blə:t-] *vt* выпа́ливать (вы́палить *perf*).

blush [blʌʃ] *vi* красне́ть (покрасне́ть *perf*) ◆ *n* румя́нец*.

blusher ['blʌʃə'] *n* румя́на *pl*.

bluster ['blʌstə'] *n* взрыв гне́ва ◆ *vi* разбушева́ться* (*perf*).

blustering ['blʌstərɪŋ] *adj* (*person*) бу́йный* (бу́ен); (*tone etc*) громогла́сный* (громогла́сен).

blustery ['blʌstərɪ] *adj* ве́треный.

Blvd *abbr* = **boulevard**.

BM *n abbr* = **British Museum**; (= *Bachelor of Medicine*) ≈ бакала́вр медици́ны.

BMA *n abbr* = **British Medical Association**.

BMJ *n abbr* = **British Medical Journal**.

BMus *n abbr* (= *Bachelor of Music*) ≈ бакала́вр музыкове́дения.

BMX *n abbr* (= *bicycle motorcross*) велосипе́дные го́нки *pl*; **~ bike** *ма́рка велосипе́да*.

BNP *n abbr* (= *British National Party*) Брита́нская национа́льная па́ртия.

BO *n abbr* (*inf*: = *body odour*): **he has ~** от него́ па́хнет по́том; (*US*) = **box office**.

boar [bɔ:'] *n* бо́ров; (*wild pig*) каба́н*.

board [bɔ:d] *n* доска́*; (*cardboard*) карто́н; (*committee*) комите́т; (*in firm*) правле́ние ◆ *vt* (*ship*) сади́ться* (сесть* *perf*) на +*acc*; (*train*) сади́ться* (сесть* *perf*) в/на +*acc*; **on ~** (*NAUT, AVIAT*) на борту́; **full ~** (*BRIT*) по́лный пансио́н; **half ~** (*BRIT*) пансио́н с за́втраком и у́жином; **~ and lodging** прожива́ние и пита́ние; **the plan went by the ~** (*fig*) план был вы́брошенным за́ борт; **above ~** (*fig*) зако́нным о́бразом; **across the ~** (*fig*) по всем катего́риям

▶ **board up** *vt* забива́ть (заби́ть* *perf*), закола́чивать (заколоти́ть* *perf*).

boarder ['bɔ:də'] *n* (*SCOL*) учени́к*(-и́ца) шко́лы-интерна́та.

board game *n* насто́льная игра́*.

boarding card ['bɔ:dɪŋ-] *n* (*AVIAT, NAUT*) = **boarding pass**.

boarding house *n* пансио́н.

---

* marks translations which have irregular inflections. The Russian-English side of the dictionary gives inflectional information.

boarding party *n* спецгру́ппа тамо́женников и́ли полице́йских, проводя́щая инспе́кцию судо́в, подозрева́емых в прово́зе контраба́нды и нарко́тиков.
boarding pass *n* поса́дочный тало́н.
boarding school *n* шко́ла-интерна́т.
board meeting *n* совеща́ние правле́ния.
board room *n* зал заседа́ний.
boardwalk ['bɔ:dwɔ:k] *n* (*US*) доща́тый насти́л.
boast [bəust] *vt* горди́ться (*impf*) +*instr* ◆ *vi*: **to ~ (about** *or* **of)** хва́статься (похва́статься *perf*) (+*instr*).
boastful ['bəustful] *adj* хвастли́вый (хвастли́в).
boastfulness ['bəustfulnɪs] *n* хвасто́вство.
boat [bəut] *n* (*small*) ло́дка*; (*large*) кора́бль* *m*; **to go by ~** плы́ть* (поплы́ть* *perf*); **to be in the same ~** (*fig*) быть (*impf*) това́рищами по несча́стью.
boater ['bəutə'] *n* соло́менная шля́па.
boating ['bəutɪŋ] *n* ката́ние на ло́дке.
boatswain ['bəusn] *n* бо́цман.
bob [bɔb] *vi* (*boat: also:* **~ up and down**) пока́чиваться (*impf*) ◆ *n* (*BRIT: inf*) = **shilling**
▸ **bob up** *vi* выска́кивать (вы́скочить *perf*).
bobbin ['bɔbɪn] *n* шпу́лька.
bobby ['bɔbɪ] *n* (*BRIT: inf*) мент.
bobsleigh ['bɔbsleɪ] *n* бо́бслей.
bode [bəud] *vi*: **to ~ well/ill** предвеща́ть (*impf*) *or* сули́ть (*impf*) хоро́шее/недо́брое.
bodice ['bɔdɪs] *n* корса́ж.
bodily ['bɔdɪlɪ] *adj* физи́ческий* ◆ *adv* целико́м.
body ['bɔdɪ] *n* те́ло*; (*torso*) ту́ловище; (*of speech, document*) основна́я часть* *f*; (*of car*) ко́рпус; (*of plane*) фюзеля́ж; (*fig: group*) гру́ппа; (: *organization*) о́рган, организа́ция; (*of information*) ма́сса; (*of wine*) консисте́нция; (*also:* **~stocking**) сви́тер-гольф (*по ти́пу закры́того купа́льника*), трико́ *nt ind*; **ruling ~** о́рган правле́ния; **in a ~** в по́лном соста́ве.
body blow *n* сокруши́тельный уда́р.
body-building ['bɔdɪ'bɪldɪŋ] *n* бо́ди-би́лдинг, атлети́зм.
body-double ['bɔdɪdʌbl] *n* актёр, снима́ющийся в обнажённом ви́де вме́сто веду́щего актёра.
bodyguard ['bɔdɪgɑ:d] *n* телохрани́тель *m*.
body language *n* язы́к* жестов.
body repairs *npl* ремо́нт ко́рпуса.
body search *n* ли́чный досмо́тр.
bodywork ['bɔdɪwɔ:k] *n* ко́рпус.
boffin ['bɔfɪn] *n* (*BRIT: inf*) спец.
bog [bɔg] *n* (*GEO*) боло́то, трясина ◆ *vt*: **to get ~ged down in** (*fig*) вя́знуть (увя́знуть *perf*) в +*prp*.
bogey ['bəugɪ] *n* (*worry*) пу́гало; (*also:* **~man**) бу́ка *m/f*.
boggle ['bɔgl] *vi*: **the mind ~s** уму́ непостижи́мо.

bogie ['bəugɪ] *n* (*RAIL*) двухо́сная теле́жка*.
Bogotá [bɔgə'tɑ:] *n* Богота́.
bogus ['bəugəs] *adj* (*claim*) фикти́вный* (фикти́вен); (*person*) сомни́тельный (сомни́телен).
Bohemia [bəu'hi:mɪə] *n* Боге́мия.
Bohemian [bəu'hi:mɪən] *adj* (*GEO*) боге́мский ◆ *n* боге́мец(ка); (*non-conformist: also:* **b~**) представи́тель(ница) *m(f)* боге́мы.
boil [bɔɪl] *vt* (*water*) кипяти́ть* (вскипяти́ть* *perf*); (*eggs, potatoes etc*) вари́ть (свари́ть *perf*), отва́ривать (отвари́ть *perf*) ◆ *vi* (*also fig*) кипе́ть* (вскипе́ть* *perf*) ◆ *n* фуру́нкул; **to come to the** (*BRIT*) **or a** (*US*) **~** вскипе́ть* (*perf*)
▸ **boil down to** *vt fus* (*fig*) своди́ться (свести́сь* *perf*) к +*dat*
▸ **boil over** *vi* (*milk*) убега́ть (убежа́ть* *perf*); (*potatoes*) выкипа́ть (вы́кипать *impf*).
boiled egg [bɔɪld-] *n* варёное яйцо́*.
boiled potatoes *npl* варёная карто́шка *fsg*.
boiler ['bɔɪlə'] *n* (*device*) парово́й котёл*, бо́йлер.
boiler suit *n* (*BRIT*) комбинезо́н.
boiling ['bɔɪlɪŋ] *adj*: **I'm ~ (hot)** (*inf*) я запа́рился; **it's ~!** (*of weather*) жара́!, жари́ща!
boiling point *n* (*of liquid*) то́чка кипе́ния.
boisterous ['bɔɪstərəs] *adj* развито́й.
bold [bəuld] *adj* (*brave*) сме́лый* (смел); (*pej: cheeky*) на́глый (нагл); (*pattern, colours*) бро́ский* (бро́сок).
boldly ['bəuldlɪ] *adv* (*bravely*) сме́ло; (*impudently*) на́гло.
boldness ['bəuldnɪs] *n* (*see adv*) сме́лость *f*; на́глость *f*.
bold type *n* жи́рный шрифт.
Bolivia [bə'lɪvɪə] *n* Боли́вия.
Bolivian [bə'lɪvɪən] *adj* боливи́йский ◆ *n* боливи́ец(-и́йка).
bollard ['bɔləd] *n* (*BRIT: AUT*) ту́мба, (: *NAUT*) швартова́я ту́мба.
bolshy ['bɔlʃɪ] *adj* (*BRIT: inf*) агресси́вный* (агресси́вен), вои́нственный.
bolster ['bəulstə'] *n* ва́лик
▸ **bolster up** *vt* подкрепля́ть (подкрепи́ть* *perf*).
bolt [bəult] *n* (*lock*) засо́в; (*with nut*) болт* ◆ *vt* (*lock*) запира́ть (запере́ть* *perf*) на засо́в; (*also:* **~ together**) скрепля́ть (скрепи́ть* *perf*) болта́ми; (*devour*) загла́тывать (заглотну́ть* *perf*) ◆ *vi* (*run away*) понести́сь* (*perf*) ◆ *adv*: **~ upright** вытяну́вшись в стру́нку; **a ~ of lightning** разря́д мо́лнии; **a ~ from the blue** (*fig*) гром среди́ я́сного не́ба.
bomb [bɔm] *n* бо́мба ◆ *vt* бомби́ть* (*impf*).
bombard [bɔm'bɑ:d] *vt* (*MIL, fig*) бомбардирова́ть (*impf*).
bombardment [bɔm'bɑ:dmənt] *n* бомбардиро́вка.
bombastic [bɔm'bæstɪk] *adj* претенцио́зный* (претенцио́зен).

bomb disposal *n*: ~ ~ **unit** отря́д сапёров; ~ ~ **expert** сапёр.
bomber ['bɔmə'] *n* (*AVIAT*) бомбардиро́вщик; (*person*) террори́ст.
bombing ['bɔmɪŋ] *n* бомбардиро́вка, бомбёжка.
bombshell ['bɔmʃɛl] *n* (*fig*): **my sacking was a real** ~ изве́стие о моём увольне́нии произвело́ эффе́кт разорва́вшейся бо́мбы.
bomb site *n* разбомблённый уча́сток*.
bona fide ['bəunə'faɪdɪ] *adj* (*traveller etc*) по́длинный*; (*offer*) настоя́щий*.
bonanza [bə'nænzə] *n* золото́е дно.
bond [bɔnd] *n* у́зы *pl*; (*binding promise*) обяза́тельство; (*FINANCE*) облига́ция; (*COMM*): **goods in** ~ това́ры, неопла́ченные по́шлиной.
bondage ['bɔndɪdʒ] *n* (*slavery*) нево́ля.
bonded goods ['bɔndɪd-] *npl* храня́щиеся това́ры *mpl* на тамо́женных скла́дах.
bonded warehouse *n* тамо́женный склад (*для товаров неопла́ченных по́шлиной*).
bone [bəun] *n* кость* *f* ♦ *vt* отделя́ть (отдели́ть* *perf*) от косте́й; **I've got a** ~ **to pick with you** у меня́ к тебе́ прете́нзия.
bone china *n* костяно́й фарфо́р.
bone-dry ['bəun'draɪ] *adj* соверше́нно сухо́й*.
bone idle *adj* пра́здный* (пра́зден); **he is** ~ ~ он безде́льник.
bone marrow *n* ко́стный мозг.
boner ['bəunə'] *n* (*US*) про́мах*.
bonfire ['bɔnfaɪə'] *n* костёр*.
bonk [bɔŋk] (*inf*) *vt* тра́хать (тра́хнуть *perf*) ♦ *vi* тра́хаться (тра́хнуться *perf*).
bonkers ['bɔŋkəz] *adj* (*inf*) чо́кнутый (чо́кнут).
Bonn [bɔn] *n* Бонн.
bonnet ['bɔnɪt] *n* (*hat*) ка́пор; (*BRIT*: *of car*) капо́т.
bonny ['bɔnɪ] *adj* (*esp SCOTTISH*) краси́вый (краси́в).
bonus ['bəunəs] *n* (*payment*) пре́мия; (*on wages*) премиа́льные *pl adj*; (*fig*) дополни́тельное преиму́щество.
bony ['bəunɪ] *adj* (*person, fingers*) костля́вый (костля́в); (*meat, fish*) кости́стый.
boo [buː] *excl* фу ♦ *vt* освистывать (освиста́ть* *perf*).
boob [buːb] *n* (*inf*: *breast*) грудь *f*; (*BRIT*: *mistake*) глу́пость *f*.
booby prize ['buːbɪ-] *n* приз* проигра́вшему игроку́.
booby trap *n* (*MIL*) ми́на-лову́шка*; (*fig*) лову́шка*.
booby-trapped ['buːbɪtræpt] *adj*: **a** ~ **car** маши́на с подло́женной ми́ной.
book [buk] *n* кни́га; (*of stamps, tickets*) кни́жечка* ♦ *vt* (*ticket, table*) зака́зывать (заказа́ть* *perf*); (*seat, room*) брони́ровать

(заброни́ровать *perf*); (*subj*: *policeman, referee*) штрафова́ть (оштрафова́ть *perf*); ~**s** *npl* (*COMM*: *accounts*) бухга́лтерские кни́ги *fpl*; **to keep the** ~**s** вести́* (*impf*) бухга́лтерские кни́ги; **by the** ~ согла́сно инстру́кции; **to throw the** ~ **at sb** обвиня́ть (обвини́ть *perf*) кого́-н во всех сме́ртных греха́х
▸ **book in** *vi* (*BRIT*: *at hotel*) регистри́роваться (зарегистри́роваться *perf*)
▸ **book up** *vt*: **all seats are** ~**ed up** все биле́ты про́даны; **the hotel is** ~**ed up** в гости́нице нет мест; **I'm** ~**ed up that week** у меня́ э́та неде́ля по́лностью за́нята.
bookable ['bukəbl] *adj*: **all seats are** ~ все биле́ты по предвари́тельным зака́зам.
bookcase ['bukkeɪs] *n* кни́жный шкаф*.
book end *n* книгодержа́тель *m*.
booking ['bukɪŋ] *n* (*BRIT*) зака́з.
booking office *n* (*BRIT*) биле́тная ка́сса.
book-keeping ['buk'kiːpɪŋ] *n* бухгалте́рия, счетово́дство.
booklet ['buklɪt] *n* брошю́ра.
bookmaker ['bukmeɪkə'] *n* букме́кер.
bookseller ['buksɛlə'] *n* книготорго́вец*.
bookshelf ['bukʃɛlf] *n* кни́жная по́лка.
bookshop ['bukʃɔp] *n* кни́жный магази́н.
bookstall ['bukstɔːl] *n* кни́жный кио́ск.
book store *n* = **bookshop**.
book token *n* пода́рочный тало́н на поку́пку *книги*.
book value *n* сто́имость *f* по торго́вым кни́гам.
bookworm ['bukwɔːm] *n* кни́жный червь *m*.
boom [buːm] *n* (*noise*) ро́кот; (*growth: in population etc*) бы́стрый рост; (*ECON*) бум ♦ *vi* (*guns, thunder*) грохота́ть* (прогрохота́ть* *perf*); (*voice*) рокота́ть* (пророкота́ть* *perf*); (*business*) процвета́ть (*impf*).
boomerang ['buːməræŋ] *n* бумера́нг ♦ *vi*: **to** ~ **on sb** верну́ться (*perf*) к кому́-н бумера́нгом.
boom town *n* го́род, процвета́ющий во вре́мя экономи́ческого подъёма.
boon [buːn] *n* бла́го.
boorish ['buərɪʃ] *adj* неотёсанный (неотёсан).
boost [buːst] *n* (*to confidence etc*) толчо́к*, сти́мул ♦ *vt* стимули́ровать (*impf*), дава́ть (дать* *perf*) толчо́к +*dat*; **to give a** ~ **to sb's spirits** *or* **to sb** окрыля́ть (окрыли́ть *perf*) кого́-н.
booster ['buːstə'] *n* (*MED*) повто́рная приви́вка*; (*TV, ELEC*) усили́тель *m*; (*also:* ~ **rocket**) раке́та-носи́тель *m*.
booster cushion *n* сиде́нье для дете́й в маши́не.
boot [buːt] *n* (*for winter*) сапо́г*; (*for football*) бу́тса; (*for walking*) боти́нок*; (*BRIT*: *of car*) бага́жник ♦ *vt* (*COMPUT*) загружа́ть (загрузи́ть* *perf*); ... **to** ~ (*in addition*) ... в

---

* marks translations which have irregular inflections. The Russian-English side of the dictionary gives inflectional information.

придачу; **to give sb the ~** (inf) вытурить (perf) кого-н.

booth [buːð] n (at fair) ларёк*; (TEL, for voting) будка*.

bootleg ['buːtlɛg] adj контрабандный.

bootlegger ['buːtlɛgə] n контрабандист.

booty ['buːtɪ] n трофеи mpl.

booze [buːz] (inf) n выпивка ♦ vi выпивать (impf).

boozer ['buːzə] n (BRIT: inf: pub) пивнушка*; **he's a real ~** (inf) он настоящий* пьянчуга.

border ['bɔːdə] n (of a country) граница; (for flowers) бордюр; (on cloth etc) кайма* ♦ vt (road, river etc) окаймлять (окаймить* perf); (another country: also: ~ on) граничить (impf) с +instr; **B~s** n: **the B~s** район на границе между Англией и Шотландией

▸ **border on** vt fus (fig) граничить (impf) с +instr.

borderline ['bɔːdəlaɪn] n: **on the ~** на грани.

borderline case n промежуточный случай.

bore [bɔː] pt of **bear** ♦ vt (hole) сверлить (просверлить perf); (well, tunnel) бурить (пробурить perf); (person) наскучить (perf) +dat ♦ n (person) зануда m/f; (of gun) канал ствола, калибр; **to be ~d** скучать (impf); **he's ~d to tears** or **~d to death** or **~d stiff** ему смертельно скучно.

boredom ['bɔːdəm] n (condition) скука; (boring quality) занудство.

boring ['bɔːrɪŋ] adj скучный*.

born [bɔːn] adj рождённый; **to be ~** рождаться (родиться* perf); **I was ~ in 1960** я родился в 1960 году; **~ blind** слепорождённый; **a ~ comedian** прирождённый комик.

born-again [bɔːnə'gɛn] adj: **~ Christian** новообращённый(-ая) христианин*(-анка).

borne [bɔːn] pp of **bear**.

Borneo ['bɔːnɪəʊ] n Борнео m ind.

borough ['bʌrə] n административный округ*.

borrow ['bɔrəʊ] vt: **to ~ sth from sb** занимать (занять* perf) что-н у кого-н; **to ~ books from the library** брать* (взять* perf) книги в библиотеке; **may I ~ your car?** можно взять на время вашу машину?

borrower ['bɔrəʊə] n заёмщик.

borrowing ['bɔrəʊɪŋ] n (word, custom) заимствование; (of money) заём*.

borstal ['bɔːstl] n (BRIT) исправительная колония для несовершеннолетних преступников.

Bosnia ['bɔznɪə] n Босния; **~-Herzogovina** Босния-Герцеговина.

Bosnian ['bɔznɪən] n житель(ница) m(f) Боснии.

bosom ['buzəm] n грудь* f; (fig: of family) лоно.

bosom friend n закадычный друг*.

Bosphorus ['bɔsfərəs] n: **the ~** Босфор.

boss [bɔs] n (employer) хозяин*(-яйка*), босс; (leader) лидер, вожак ♦ vt (also: ~ **around**, ~ **about**) распоряжаться (impf), командовать (impf) +instr; **stop ~ing everyone about!**

перестань всеми командовать!

bossy ['bɔsɪ] adj властный (властен).

bosun ['bəʊsn] n боцман.

botanical [bə'tænɪkl] adj ботанический.

botanist ['bɔtənɪst] n ботаник.

botany ['bɔtənɪ] n ботаника.

botch [bɔtʃ] vt (also: ~ **up**) состряпать (perf).

both [bəʊθ] adj, pron оба* (f обе*) ♦ adv: **~ A and B** и А, и Б; **~ (of them)** оба (они); **~ of us went, we ~ went** мы оба пошли; **they sell ~ meat and poultry** они торгуют и мясо и птицей.

bother ['bɔðə] vt (worry) беспокоить (обеспокоить perf); (disturb) беспокоить (побеспокоить perf) ♦ vi (also: ~ **o.s.**) беспокоиться (impf) ♦ n (trouble) беспокойство; (nuisance) хлопоты* pl ♦ excl: **~! чёрт возьми!; to ~ doing** брать* (взять* perf) на себя труд +infin; **I'm sorry to ~ you** извините за беспокойство; **please don't ~** пожалуйста, не беспокойтесь; **don't ~!** не надо!; **it is a ~ to have to do** это так хлопотно +infin; **it's no ~** это меня не затруднит; **I can't be ~ed** мне лень.

Botswana [bɔt'swaːnə] n Ботсвана.

bottle ['bɔtl] n бутылка*; (for baby) рожок*; (BRIT: inf: courage) смелость f ♦ vt (beer, wine) разливать (разлить* perf) по бутылкам; (fruit) консервировать (законсервировать perf); **~ of wine/milk** бутылка* вина/молока; **wine/milk ~** бутылка* из-под вина/молока

▸ **bottle up** vt скрывать (скрыть* perf).

bottle bank n мусорный ящик для стеклянной тары.

bottle-fed ['bɔtlfɛd] adj: **~ baby** искусственник.

bottleneck ['bɔtlnɛk] n (AUT) узкий* езд; (fig) затор.

bottle-opener ['bɔtləʊpnə] n штопор.

bottom ['bɔtəm] n (of container, sea etc) дно*; (ANAT) зад*; (of page, list) низ*; (of class) неуспевающий*(-ая) m(f) adj; (of mountain etc) подножие ♦ adj (lowest) нижний*; (last) последний*; **at the ~ of** на дне +gen; **to get to the ~ of sth** (fig) добираться (добраться* perf) до сути чего-н.

bottomless ['bɔtəmlɪs] adj (funds, store) бездонный* (бездонен).

bottom line n суть f дела.

botulism ['bɔtjulɪzəm] n ботулизм.

bough [bau] n сук*.

bought [bɔːt] pt, pp of **buy**.

boulder ['bəʊldə] n валун*.

boulevard ['buːləvaːd] n бульвар.

bounce [bauns] vi (ball) отскакивать (отскочить perf); (cheque) вернуться (perf) (о чеке, ввиду отсутствия денег на счету) ♦ vt (ball) ударять (ударить perf); (signal) отражать (отразить perf) ♦ n (of ball) отскок; **he's got plenty of ~** (fig) он очень живой.

bouncer ['baunsə'] *n* (*inf*) вышибала *m*.
bouncy castle ['baunsɪ-] *n надувная конструкция в форме замка, на которой могут прыгать дети*.
bound [baund] *pt, pp of* **bind** ◆ *n* (*leap*) прыжок*, скачок* ◆ *vi* (*leap*) прыгать (прыгнуть *perf*) ◆ *vt* (*border*) служить (*impf*) границей +*gen* ◆ *adj*: **he is ~ by law to ...** его обязывает закон +*infin*...; **~s** *npl* (*limits*) пределы *mpl*; **he is/was ~ to do** он обязан/был обязан +*infin*; **he's ~ to come** он обязательно *or* непременно придёт; **~ for** направляющийся* в/на +*acc*; **this area is out of ~s** (*fig: place*) это место является запретным.
boundary ['baundrɪ] *n* граница.
boundless ['baundlɪs] *adj* безграничный* (безграничен).
bountiful ['bauntɪful] *adj* (*person*) щедрый* (щедр); (*supply*) обильный* (обилен).
bounty ['bauntɪ] *n* (*generosity*) щедрость *f*; (*reward*) вознаграждение.
bounty hunter *n* охотник за наградой.
bouquet ['bukeɪ] *n* букет.
bourbon ['buəbən] *n* (*US: also:* **~ whiskey**) кукурузное виски *nt ind*, бурбон.
bourgeois ['buəʒwɑ:] *adj* буржуазный* ◆ *n* буржуа *m ind*.
bout [baut] *n* (*of illness*) приступ; (*of activity*) всплеск; (*BOXING etc*) схватка*.
boutique [bu:'ti:k] *n* лавка*.
bow¹ [bəu] *n* (*knot*) бант; (*weapon*) лук; (*MUS*) смычок.
bow² [bau] *n* (*of the head, body*) поклон; (*NAUT: also:* **~s**) нос ◆ *vi* (*with head, body*) кланяться (поклониться* *perf*); (*yield*): **to ~ to** *or* **before** поддаваться* (поддаться* *perf*) +*dat or* на +*acc*; **to ~ to the inevitable** покоряться (покориться *perf*) неизбежному.
bowels ['bauəlz] *npl* кишечник *msg*; (*of the earth etc*) недра *pl*.
bowl [bəul] *n* миска*, чаша; (*for washing*) таз*; (*ball*) шар*; (*of pipe*) головка*; (*US: stadium*) арена ◆ *vi* подавать* (подать* *perf*) мяч
▸ **bowl over** *vt* (*fig*) сбивать (сбить* *perf*).
bow-legged ['bəu'lɛgɪd] *adj* кривоногий*.
bowler ['bəulə'] *n* боулер, подающий мяч; (*BRIT: also:* **~ hat**) котелок*.
bowling ['bəulɪŋ] *n* (*game*) кегельбан.
bowling alley *n* кегельбан.
bowling green *n* площадка* для игры в шары.
bowls [bəulz] *n* игра* в шары.
bow tie [bəu-] *n* бабочка*.
box [bɔks] *n* ящик, коробка*; (*also:* **cardboard ~**) картонная коробка*; (*THEAT*) ложа; (*BRIT: AUT*) разграничительная линия; (*ADMIN: on form*) графа* ◆ *vt* (*put in a box*) упаковывать (упаковать* *perf*) в коробку; (*SPORT*) ударять

(ударить *perf*) ◆ *vi* (*SPORT*) боксировать (*impf*); **what's on the ~?** (*inf: TV*) что сегодня по ящику?; **to ~ sb's ears** надирать (надрать* *perf*) кому-н уши
▸ **box in** *vt* окружать (окружить *perf*)
▸ **box off** *vt* отгораживать (отгородить* *perf*).
boxer ['bɔksə'] *n* боксёр.
box file *n* ящик для хранения документов.
boxing ['bɔksɪŋ] *n* бокс.
Boxing Day *n* (*BRIT*) *день после Рождества*.
boxing gloves *npl* боксёрские перчатки* *fpl*.
boxing ring *n* ринг.
box number *n* номер* абонентского ящика.
box office *n* театральная касса.
boxroom ['bɔksrum] *n* чулан.
boy [bɔɪ] *n* мальчик; (*son*) сынок*.
boycott ['bɔɪkɔt] *n* бойкот ◆ *vt* бойкотировать (*impf/perf*).
boyfriend ['bɔɪfrɛnd] *n* друг*.
boyish ['bɔɪʃ] *adj* мальчишеский*.
boy scout *n* бойскаут.
Bp *abbr* = **bishop**.
BR *abbr* = **British Rail**.
bra [brɑ:] *n* лифчик.
brace [breɪs] *n* (*on leg*) шина; (*on teeth*) пластинки *pl*; (*tool*) коловорот; (*also:* **~ bracket**) скобка* ◆ *vt* (*knees, shoulders*) напрягать (напрячь* *perf*); **~s** *npl* (*BRIT: for trousers*) подтяжки* *pl*; **to ~ o.s.** (*for shock*) собираться (собраться* *perf*) с духом.
bracelet ['breɪslɪt] *n* браслет.
bracing ['breɪsɪŋ] *adj* бодрящий.
bracken ['brækən] *n* орляк.
bracket ['brækɪt] *n* (*TECH*) кронштейн; (*group, range*) категория; (*also:* **brace ~**) скобка*; (*also:* **round ~**) круглая скобка*; (*also:* **square ~**) квадратная скобка* ◆ *vt* (*fig: also:* **~ together**) группировать (сгруппировать* *perf*); (*word, phrase*) заключать (заключить *perf*) в скобки; **income ~** уровень *m* дохода; **in ~s** в скобках.
brackish ['brækɪʃ] *adj* солоноватый (солноват*).
brag [bræg] *vi* хвастаться (похвастаться *perf*).
braid [breɪd] *n* (*for clothes etc*) тесьма; (*of hair*) коса*.
Braille [breɪl] *n* шрифт Брайля.
brain [breɪn] *n* (*ANAT, fig*) мозг*; **~s** *npl* (*CULIN*) мозги *mpl*; (*intelligence*) мозги *mpl*, сообразительность *f*; **he's got ~s** он парень с головой.
brainchild ['breɪntʃaɪld] *n* детище.
braindead ['breɪndɛd] *adj*: **the patient was ~** у пациента наступила биологическая смерть.
brain drain *n*: **the ~ ~** утечка мозгов.
brainless ['breɪnlɪs] *adj* безмозглый.
brainstorm ['breɪnstɔ:m] *n* (*fig*) умопомрачение; (*US: brainwave*) озарение.

---

* marks translations which have irregular inflections. The Russian-English side of the dictionary gives inflectional information.

brainwash ['breɪnwɔʃ] *vt* промыва́ть (промы́ть* *perf*) мозги́ +*dat*.

brainwave ['breɪnweɪv] *n* озаре́ние; **he had a ~** на него́ нашло́ озаре́ние.

brainy ['breɪnɪ] *adj* мозгови́тый.

braise [breɪz] *vt* туши́ть* (потуши́ть* *perf*).

brake [breɪk] *n* (*also fig*) то́рмоз* ♦ *vi* тормози́ть* (затормози́ть* *perf*).

brake fluid *n* тормозна́я жи́дкость *f*.

brake light *n* тормозно́й сигна́л.

brake pedal *n* педа́ль *f* то́рмоза, то́рмоза* *mpl*.

bramble ['bræmbl] *n* ежеви́ка.

bran [bræn] *n* о́труби *pl*.

branch [brɑːntʃ] *n* (*of tree*) ве́тка*, ветвь* *f*; (*fig: of family, organization*) ветвь*; (*COMM: of bank, company etc*) филиа́л ♦ *vi* разветвля́ться (разветви́ться* *perf*)
▸ **branch out** *vi* (*fig*) разветвля́ться (разветви́ться *perf*).

branch line *n* (железнодоро́жная) ве́тка*.

branch manager *n* дире́ктор* филиа́ла.

brand [brænd] *n* (*also:* ~ **name**) фи́рменная ма́рка*; (*fig: type*) сорт ♦ *vt* (*cattle*) клейми́ть* (заклейми́ть* *perf*); (*fig: pej*): **to ~ sb a communist** *etc* клейми́ть* (заклейми́ть* *perf*) кого́-н коммуни́стом *etc*.

brandish ['brændɪʃ] *vt* разма́хивать (*impf*) +*instr*; (*weapon*) потряса́ть (*impf*) +*instr*.

brand name *n* фи́рменная ма́рка.

brand-new ['brænd'njuː] *adj* соверше́нно но́вый*.

brandy ['brændɪ] *n* бре́нди *nt ind*, конья́к*.

brash [bræʃ] *adj* наха́льный* (наха́лен).

Brasilia [brə'zɪlɪə] *n* Брази́лия.

brass [brɑːs] *n* (*metal*) лату́нь *f*; **the ~** (*MUS*) духовы́е инструме́нты *mpl*.

brass band *n* духово́й орке́стр.

brassiere ['bræsɪəʳ] *n* бюстга́льтер.

brass tacks *npl*: **to get down to ~ ~** доходи́ть* (дойти́* *perf*) до су́ти.

brassy ['brɑːsɪ] *adj* (*colour*) ме́дный; (*sound*) ре́зкий*; (*behaviour*) вызыва́ющий*.

brat [bræt] *n* (*pej*) отро́дье*.

Bratislava [brætɪ'slɑːvə] *n* Братисла́ва.

bravado [brə'vɑːdəu] *n* брава́да.

brave [breɪv] *adj* сме́лый (смел), хра́брый (храбр) ♦ *n* инде́йский во́ин ♦ *vt* сме́ло *or* хра́бро встреча́ть (встре́тить* *perf*).

bravely ['breɪvlɪ] *adv* сме́ло, хра́бро.

bravery ['breɪvərɪ] *n* сме́лость *f*, хра́брость *f*.

bravo [brɑː'vəu] *excl* бра́во.

brawl [brɔːl] *n* дра́ка ♦ *vi* дра́ться* (подра́ться* *perf*).

brawn [brɔːn] *n* (*strength*) му́скулы *mpl*; (*meat*) зельц, сту́день *m*.

brawny ['brɔːnɪ] *adj* мускули́стый (мускули́ст).

bray [breɪ] *vi* (*donkey*) реве́ть* (*impf*) ♦ *n* рёв осла́.

brazen ['breɪzn] *adj* (*woman*) бессты́жий

(бессты́ж); (*lie, accusation*) на́глый (нагл) ♦ *vt*: **to ~ it out** выкру́чиваться (вы́крутиться* *perf*).

brazier ['breɪzɪəʳ] *n* жаро́вня*.

Brazil [brə'zɪl] *n* Брази́лия.

Brazilian [brə'zɪljən] *adj* брази́льский* ♦ *n* брази́лец*(-лья́нка*).

Brazil nut *n* америка́нский* оре́х.

breach [briːtʃ] *vt* (*defence, wall*) пробива́ть (проби́ть* *perf*) брешь в +*acc* ♦ *n* (*gap*) брешь *f*; (*estrangement*) разры́в; **~ of contract** наруше́ние догово́ра; **~ of the peace** наруше́ние обще́ственного поря́дка; **~ of trust** злоупотребле́ние дове́рием.

bread [brɛd] *n* хлеб; (*inf: money*) ба́бки *fpl*; **to earn one's daily ~** зараба́тывать (зарабо́тать *perf*) на хлеб *or* на жизнь; **to know which side one's ~ is buttered (on)** знать (*impf*) свою́ вы́году.

bread and butter *n* хлеб с ма́слом; (*fig*) хлеб насу́щный, жи́зненная осно́ва.

breadbin ['brɛdbɪn] *n* (*BRIT*) хле́бница.

breadboard ['brɛdbɔːd] *n* хле́бная доска́*; (*COMPUT*) маке́т, маке́тная пла́та.

breadbox ['brɛdbɔks] *n* (*US*) хле́бница.

breadcrumbs ['brɛdkrʌmz] *npl* кро́шки* *fpl*; (*CULIN*) паниро́вочные сухари́ *mpl*.

breadline ['brɛdlaɪn] *n*: **on the ~** за черто́й бе́дности.

breadth [brɛtθ] *n* (*of cloth etc*) ширина́; (*fig: of knowledge, subject*) широта́.

breadwinner ['brɛdwɪnəʳ] *n* корми́лец*(-лица).

break [breɪk] (*pt* **broke**, *pp* **broken**) *vt* (*cup, glass*) разбива́ть (разби́ть* *perf*); (*leg, arm*) лома́ть (слома́ть *perf*); (*promise, law*) наруша́ть (нару́шить *perf*); (*record*) побива́ть (поби́ть* *perf*) ♦ *vi* (*crockery*) разбива́ться (разби́ться *perf*); (*storm*) разрази́ться (*perf*); (*weather*) по́ртиться (испо́ртиться *perf*); (*dawn*) бре́зжить (забре́зжить *perf*); (*story, news*) сообща́ть (сообщи́ть *perf*) ♦ *n* (*gap*) пробе́л; (*fracture*) перело́м; (*rest*) переды́шка*; (*interval*) переры́в; (*playtime*) переме́на; (*chance*) шанс; (*holiday*) о́тпуск*, о́тдых; **to ~ the news to sb** сообща́ть (сообщи́ть *perf*) кому́-н но́вость; **to ~ even** (*COMM*) зако́нчиться (*perf*) без убы́тка; **to ~ with sb** порыва́ть (порва́ть* *perf*) с кем-н; **to ~ free** *or* **loose** вы́рваться* (*perf*) на свобо́ду; **to take a ~** (*few minutes*) де́лать (сде́лать *perf*) небольшо́й переры́в; (*holiday*) брать* (взять* *perf*) о́тпуск; **without a ~** без переры́ва; **a lucky ~** счастли́вый слу́чай
▸ **break down** *vt* (*figures etc*) разбива́ть (разби́ть* *perf*) по статья́м; (*door etc*) взла́мывать (взлома́ть *perf*) ♦ *vi* (*machine, car*) лома́ться (слома́ться *perf*); (*resistance*) быть* (*impf*) сло́мленным(-ой); (*person*) сломи́ться (*perf*); (*talks*) срыва́ться (сорва́ться* *perf*)
▸ **break in** *vt* (*horse*) обу́здывать (обузда́ть

perf) ◆ *vi (burglar)* взла́мывать (взлома́ть *perf);* (*interrupt*) вме́шиваться (вмеша́ться *perf)*
▶ **break into** *vt fus (house)* вла́мываться (вломи́ться* *perf)* в +*acc*
▶ **break off** *vi (branch)* отла́мываться (отломи́ться* *perf);* (*speaker*) прерыва́ться (прерва́ться* *perf)* ◆ *vt (talks)* прерыва́ть (прерва́ть* *perf);* (*engagement*) расторга́ть (расто́ргнуть *perf)*
▶ **break open** *vt* взла́мывать (взлома́ть *perf)*
▶ **break out** *vi (begin)* разража́ться (разрази́ться* *perf);* (*escape*) сбега́ть (сбежа́ть* *perf);* **to ~ out in spots/a rash** покрыва́ться (покры́ться* *perf)* прыща́ми/ сы́пью
▶ **break through** *vt fus* прорыва́ться (прорва́ться* *perf)* сквозь +*acc* ◆ *vi:* **the sun broke through** со́лнце проби́лось сквозь ту́чи
▶ **break up** *vi (ship)* разбива́ться (разби́ться* *perf);* (*crowd, meeting*) расходи́ться* (разойти́сь* *perf);* (*marriage, partnership*) распада́ться (распа́сться *perf);* (*SCOL*) закрыва́ться (закры́ться* *perf)* на кани́кулы ◆ *vt (rocks etc)* разла́мывать (разломи́ть* *perf);* (*journey*) прерыва́ть (прерва́ть* *perf);* (*fight etc*) прекраща́ть (прекрати́ть* *perf);* (*meeting*) распуска́ть (распусти́ть* *perf);* (*marriage*) разбива́ть (разби́ть* *perf)*
breakable ['breɪkəbl] *adj* хру́пкий* (хру́пок), ло́мкий* (ло́мок) ◆ *n:* ~s хру́пкие предме́ты *mpl.*
breakage ['breɪkɪdʒ] *n (act of breaking)* поло́мка*; (*object*) бой; **to pay for** ~s плати́ть* (заплати́ть* *perf)* за бой.
breakaway ['breɪkəweɪ] *adj (group etc)* отдели́вшийся, отколо́вшийся.
break-dancing ['breɪkdɑ:nsɪŋ] *n* брейк.
breakdown ['breɪkdaun] *n (AUT)* небольша́я ава́рия; (*in communications*) наруше́ние; (*of marriage*) распа́д; (*of statistics*) разби́вка*; (*also:* **nervous** ~) не́рвный срыв.
breakdown service *n (BRIT)* авари́йная слу́жба.
breakdown van *n (BRIT)* фурго́н авари́йной слу́жбы.
breaker ['breɪkə'] *n* вал*.
breakeven ['breɪk'i:vn] *cpd:* ~ **chart** гра́фик рента́бельности; ~ **point** то́чка* без- убы́точности.
breakfast ['brɛkfəst] *n* за́втрак ◆ *vi* за́втракать (поза́втракать *perf)*.
breakfast cereal *n* крупа́ для за́втраков.
break-in ['breɪkɪn] *n* взлом.
breaking and entering ['breɪkɪŋən'ɛntrɪŋ] *n (LAW)* вторже́ние с взло́мом.
breaking point *n* преде́л.

breakthrough ['breɪkθru:] *n (fig: in technology)* перело́мное откры́тие.
break-up ['breɪkʌp] *n (of partnership, marriage)* распа́д.
break-up value *n (COMM)* ликвидацио́нная сто́имость *f.*
breakwater ['breɪkwɔ:tə'] *n* волноре́з, мол*.
breast [brɛst] *n* грудь* *f;* (*of meat*) груди́нка; (*of poultry*) бе́лое мя́со.
breast-feed ['brɛstfi:d] *(irreg: like* **feed**) *vt* корми́ть* (покорми́ть* *perf)* гру́дью ◆ *vi* корми́ть *(impf)* (гру́дью).
breast pocket *n (of jacket etc)* нагру́дный карма́н.
breast-stroke ['brɛststrəuk] *n* брасс.
breath [brɛθ] *n* вдох; (*breathing*) дыха́ние; **to go out for a ~ of air** выходи́ть* (вы́йти* *perf)* подыша́ть *or* на све́жий во́здух; **to be out of** ~ запыха́ться (запыха́ться *perf);* **to get one's ~ back** отдыша́ться *(perf).*
breathalyse ['brɛθəlaɪz] *vt* проверя́ть (прове́рить *perf)* дыха́ние на алкого́ль.
Breathalyser® ['brɛθəlaɪzə'] *n* спирто́метр.
breathe [bri:ð] *vt* вдыха́ть (вдохну́ть *perf)* ◆ *vi* дыша́ть* *(impf);* **I won't ~ a word about it** я сло́вом не обмо́лвлюсь об э́том
▶ **breathe in** *vt* вдыха́ть (вдохну́ть *perf)* ◆ *vi* де́лать (сде́лать *perf)* вдох
▶ **breathe out** *vt* выдыха́ть (вы́дохнуть *perf)* ◆ *vi* де́лать (сде́лать *perf)* вы́дох.
breather ['bri:ðə'] *n* переды́шка*.
breathing ['bri:ðɪŋ] *n* дыха́ние.
breathing space *n (fig)* переды́шка*.
breathless ['brɛθlɪs] *adj (from exertion)* запы́хавшийся; (*after illness*) безды́ханный; **he was ~ with excitement** у него́ перехвати́ло дыха́ние от волне́ния.
breathtaking ['brɛθteɪkɪŋ] *adj* захва́тывающий* дух.
breath test *n* дыха́тельная про́ба.
bred [brɛd] *pt, pp of* **breed**.
-bred [brɛd] *suffix:* **well/ill-**~ хорошо́/пло́хо воспи́танный* (воспи́тан).
breed [bri:d] *(pt, pp* **bred**) *vt (animals, plants)* разводи́ть* (развести́* *perf);* (*fig: give rise to*) порожда́ть (породи́ть* *perf)* ◆ *vi* размножа́ться *(impf)* ◆ *n (ZOOL)* поро́да; (*type, class*) сорт*, род*.
breeder ['bri:də'] *n (person)* селекционе́р; (*PHYS: also:* ~ **reactor**) реа́ктор- размножи́тель *m;* **cattle** ~ скотово́д.
breeding ['bri:dɪŋ] *n* воспита́ние.
breeding ground *n* ме́сто* размноже́ния; (*fig*) расса́дник.
breeze [bri:z] *n* бриз.
breezeblock ['bri:zblɔk] *n (BRIT)* шлако- бето́нный кирпи́ч.
breezy ['bri:zɪ] *adj (manner, tone)* оживлённый

(оживлён); (*weather*) прохла́дный* (прохла́ден).
Bremen ['breɪmən] *n* Бре́мен.
Breton ['brɛtən] *adj* брето́нский ♦ *n* брето́нец*(-нка*).
brevity ['brɛvɪtɪ] *n* кра́ткость *f*.
brew [bruː] *vt* (*tea*) зава́ривать (завари́ть* *perf*); (*beer*) вари́ть* (свари́ть* *perf*) ♦ *vi* (*tea*) зава́риваться (завари́ться* *perf*); (*beer*) броди́ть* (вы́бродить* *perf*); (*storm*) надвига́ться (надви́нуться *perf*); (*fig: trouble*) назрева́ть (назре́ть *perf*).
brewer ['bruːə'] *n* пивова́р.
brewery ['bruːərɪ] *n* пивова́ренный заво́д.
briar ['braɪə'] *n* (*thorny bush*) колю́чий* куста́рник; (*wild rose*) шипо́вник.
bribe [braɪb] *n* взя́тка*, по́дкуп ♦ *vt* (*person*) подкупа́ть (подкупи́ть* *perf*), дава́ть* (дать* *perf*) взя́тку; **to ~ sb to do** подкупа́ть (подкупи́ть* *perf*) кого́-н +*infin*.
bribery ['braɪbərɪ] *n* по́дкуп.
bric-a-brac ['brɪkəbræk] *n* безделу́шки* *fpl*.
brick [brɪk] *n* кирпи́ч*; (*of ice cream*) брике́т.
bricklayer ['brɪkleɪə'] *n* ка́менщик.
brickwork ['brɪkwəːk] *n* (кирпи́чная) кла́дка.
bridal ['braɪdl] *adj* подвене́чный, сва́дебный.
bride [braɪd] *n* неве́ста.
bridegroom ['braɪdgruːm] *n* жени́х*.
bridesmaid ['braɪdzmeɪd] *n* подру́жка* неве́сты.
bridge [brɪdʒ] *n* (*TECH, ARCHIT, DENTISTRY*) мост*; (*NAUT*) капита́нский* мо́стик; (*CARDS*) бридж; (*of nose*) перено́сица ♦ *vt* (*fig: gap, gulf*) преодолева́ть (преодоле́ть *perf*); **to ~ a river** стро́ить (постро́ить *perf*) мост че́рез ре́ку.
bridging loan ['brɪdʒɪŋ-] *n* (*BRIT: COMM*) промежу́точный заём.
bridle ['braɪdl] *n* узде́чка*, узда́ ♦ *vt* (*horse*) взну́здывать (взнузда́ть *perf*) ♦ *vi*: **to ~ at** взвива́ться (взви́ться* *perf*) на дыбы́, возмуща́ться (возмути́ться* *perf*).
bridle path *n* верхова́я тропа́*.
brief [briːf] *adj* (*period of time*) коро́ткий* (ко́роток); (*description*) кра́ткий* (кра́ток) ♦ *n* (*LAW*) изложе́ние де́ла; (*task*) зада́ние ♦ *vt* (*inform*) знако́мить* (ознако́мить* *perf*) с +*instr*; (*MIL etc*): **to ~ sb (about)** инструкти́ровать (проинструкти́ровать *perf*) кого́-н (о +*prp*); **~s** *npl* (*for men*) трусы́ *pl*; (*for women*) тру́сики *pl*; **in ~** ... вкра́тце ....
briefcase ['briːfkeɪs] *n* портфе́ль *m*.
briefing ['briːfɪŋ] *n* инструкта́ж; (*PRESS*) бри́финг.
briefly ['briːflɪ] *adv* (*glance, smile*) бе́гло; (*visit*) на коро́ткое вре́мя; (*explain*) вкра́тце; **to glimpse ~** бро́сать (бро́сить* *perf*) бе́глый взгляд.
Brig. *abbr* = **brigadier**.
brigade [brɪˈɡeɪd] *n* (*MIL*) брига́да.
brigadier [brɪɡəˈdɪə'] *n* бригади́р.

bright [braɪt] *adj* (*light, colour*) я́ркий* (я́рок); (*room, future*) све́тлый* (све́тел); (*clever: person, idea*) блестя́щий*; (*lively: person*) живо́й*, весёлый*; **to look on the ~ side** ви́деть* (*impf*) све́тлую сто́рону.
brighten ['braɪtn] *vt* (*also: ~ up: room, event*) оживля́ть (оживи́ть* *perf*); (: *person*) ра́довать (обра́довать *perf*) ♦ *vi* (*weather*) проясня́ться (проясни́ться* *perf*); (*person*) оживля́ться (оживи́ться* *perf*); (*face*) светле́ть (просветле́ть *perf*); (*prospects*) улучша́ться (улу́чшиться *perf*).
brightly ['braɪtlɪ] *adv* (*shine*) я́рко; (*smile, talk*) ра́достно.
brill [brɪl] (*inf*) *adj* здо́рово.
brilliance ['brɪljəns] *n* блеск, я́ркость *f*; (*fig: of person*) гениа́льность *f*.
brilliant ['brɪljənt] *adj* блестя́щий* (блестя́щ); (*sunshine, light*) я́ркий* (я́рок); (*inf: holiday etc*) великоле́пный* (великоле́пен).
brilliantly ['brɪljəntlɪ] *adv* (*see adj*) блестя́ще; я́рко.
brim [brɪm] *n* (*of cup*) край; (*of hat*) поля́ *ntpl*.
brimful ['brɪmˈful] *adj*: **~ (of)** по́лный (по́лон) до краёв (+*gen*); (*fig*) перепо́лненный (перепо́лнен) (+*instr*).
brine [braɪn] *n* (*CULIN*) рассо́л.
bring [brɪŋ] (*pt, pp* **brought**) *vt* (*thing*) приноси́ть* (принести́* *perf*); (*person: on foot*) приводи́ть* (привести́* *perf*); (: *by transport*) привози́ть* (привезти́* *perf*); (*fig: satisfaction, trouble*) доставля́ть (доста́вить* *perf*); **to ~ sth to an end** поко́нчить (*perf*) с чем-н; **I can't ~ myself to tell him** я не могу́ заста́вить себя́ сообщи́ть ему́
▸ **bring about** *vt* (*cause: unintentionally*) вызыва́ть (вы́звать* *perf*), порожда́ть (породи́ть *perf*); (: *intentionally*) осуществля́ть (осуществи́ть* *perf*)
▸ **bring back** *vt* (*restore*) возрожда́ть (возроди́ть* *perf*); (*return*) возвраща́ть (возврати́ть* *perf*), верну́ть (*perf*)
▸ **bring down** *vt* (*government*) сверга́ть (све́ргнуть* *perf*); (*plane*) сбива́ть (сбить* *perf*); (*price*) снижа́ть (сни́зить* *perf*)
▸ **bring forward** *vt* (*meeting*) переноси́ть* (перенести́* *perf*) на бо́лее ра́нний срок; (*proposal*) выдвига́ть (вы́двинуть *perf*); (*BOOKKEEPING*) переноси́ть* (перенести́* *perf*) на сле́дующую страни́цу
▸ **bring in** *vt* (*money*) приноси́ть* (принести́* *perf*); (*person, legislation*) вводи́ть* (ввести́* *perf*); (*verdict*) выноси́ть* (вы́нести* *perf*)
▸ **bring off** *vt* (*task, plan*) исполня́ть (испо́лнить* *perf*); (*deal*) заключа́ть (заключи́ть *perf*)
▸ **bring out** *vt* вынима́ть (вы́нуть *perf*); (*meaning*) выявля́ть (вы́явить* *perf*); (*publish*) выпуска́ть (вы́пустить* *perf*)
▸ **bring round** *vt* (*MED*) приводи́ть* (привести́* *perf*) в чу́вство

▶ **bring up** *vt* (*carry up*) приноси́ть* (принести́* *perf*) наве́рх; (*educate*) воспи́тывать (воспита́ть *perf*); (*question*) поднима́ть (подня́ть* *perf*); (*vomit*): **he brought up his food** его́ стошни́ло.

bring and buy sale *n* благотвори́тельная перепрода́жа веще́й ме́жду её организа́торами.

brink [brɪŋk] *n* (*of disaster, war etc*) грань *f*; **on the ~ of doing** чуть не +*infin*; **she was on the ~ of tears** она́ е́ле сде́рживала слёзы.

brisk [brɪsk] *adj* (*tone*) отры́вистый (отры́вист); (*person, trade*) оживлённый* (оживлён); **business is ~** дела́ иду́т по́лном хо́дом.

bristle ['brɪsl] *n* щети́на ◆ *vi* (*in anger*) щети́ниться (ощети́ниться *perf*); **bristling with** по́лный (по́лон) +*instr or* +*gen*.

bristly ['brɪslɪ] *adj* щети́нистый; **your chin's all ~** у тебя́ подборо́док щети́нистый.

Brit [brɪt] *n abbr* (*inf*: = *British person*) брита́нец*(-нка*).

Britain ['brɪtən] *n* (*also*: **Great ~**) Брита́ния; **in ~** в Брита́нии.

British ['brɪtɪʃ] *adj* брита́нский*; **the ~** *npl* брита́нцы* *mpl*.

British Isles *npl*: **the ~ ~** Брита́нские острова́* *mpl*.

British Rail *n* Брита́нская желе́зная доро́га.

British Summer Time *n* Брита́нское ле́тнее вре́мя* *nt*.

Briton ['brɪtən] *n* брита́нец*(-нка*).

Brittany ['brɪtənɪ] *n* Брета́нь *f*.

brittle ['brɪtl] *adj* хру́пкий* (хру́пок), ло́мкий* (ло́мок).

Bro. *abbr* (*REL*) = **brother**.

broach [brəutʃ] *vt* (*subject*) поднима́ть (подня́ть *perf*) вопро́с о +*prp*.

broad [brɔːd] *adj* (*wide*) широ́кий* (широ́к); (*general*) о́бщий*; (*strong*) си́льный* ◆ *n* (*US*: *inf*) ба́ба; **in ~ daylight** средь бе́ла дня; **~ hint** прозра́чный намёк.

broad bean *n* фасо́ль *f no pl*.

broadcast ['brɔːdkɑːst] (*pt, pp* **broadcast**) *n* (*RADIO*) (ра́дио)переда́ча; (*TV*) (теле)-переда́ча ◆ *vt* (*RADIO*) передава́ть* (переда́ть* *perf*) по ра́дио, трансли́ровать (*impf*); (*TV*) передава́ть* (переда́ть* *perf*) по телеви́дению, трансли́ровать (*impf*) ◆ *vi* трансли́роваться (*impf*).

broadcaster ['brɔːdkɑːstə'] *n* (*RADIO*) ра́дио-журнали́ст; (*TV*) теле-журнали́ст.

broadcasting ['brɔːdkɑːstɪŋ] *n* (*RADIO*) радиовеща́ние; (*TV*) телевеща́ние.

broadcasting station *n* (*RADIO*) радиоста́нция; (*TV*) телеста́нция.

broaden ['brɔːdn] *vt* расширя́ть (расши́рить *perf*) ◆ *vi* расширя́ться (расши́риться *perf*); **to ~ one's horizons** расширя́ть (расши́рить *perf*) свой кругозо́р.

broadly ['brɔːdlɪ] *adv* вообще́.

broad-minded ['brɔːd'maɪndɪd] *adj* с широ́кими взгля́дами.

broadsheet ['brɔːdʃiːt] *n* (*advertisement*) рекла́мный плака́т *or* рекла́мная афи́ша; (*newspaper*) газе́та, отпеча́танная на одно́м развёрнутом листе́ бума́ги.

broccoli ['brɔkəlɪ] *n* бро́кколи *nt ind*.

brochure ['brəuʃjuə'] *n* брошю́ра.

brogue [brəug] *n* (*accent*) провинциа́льный акце́нт (осо́бенно ирла́ндский *или* шотла́ндский); (*shoe*) башма́к.

broil [brɔɪl] *vt* жа́рить (зажа́рить *perf*).

broiler ['brɔɪlə'] *n* бро́йлер.

broke [brəuk] *pt of* **break** ◆ *adj* (*inf*) прогоре́вший; **to go ~** прогора́ть (прогоре́ть *perf*).

broken ['brəukn] *pp of* **break** ◆ *adj* (*window, cup etc*) разби́тый (разби́т); (*machine*) сло́манный (сло́ман); (*promise, vow*) нару́шенный (нару́шен); **a ~ leg** сло́манная нога́*; **a ~ marriage** распа́вшийся брак; **a ~ home** неблагополу́чная семья́; **in ~ English/Russian** на ло́маном англи́йском/ру́сском.

broken-down ['brəukn'daun] *adj* (*car*) сло́манный (сло́ман); (*house*) полу-разру́шенный.

broken-hearted ['brəukn'hɑːtɪd] *adj* уби́тый го́рем, с разби́тым се́рдцем.

broker ['brəukə'] *n* (*COMM*: *in shares*) бро́кер; (: *in insurance*) страхово́й аге́нт.

brokerage ['brəukrɪdʒ] *n* (*COMM*: *commission*) брокера́ж; (: *business*) бро́керское аге́нтство.

brolly ['brɔlɪ] *n* (*BRIT*: *inf*) зонт.

bronchitis [brɔŋ'kaɪtɪs] *n* бронхи́т.

bronze [brɔnz] *n* (*metal*) бро́нза; (*sculpture*) бро́нзовая скульпту́ра.

bronzed [brɔnzd] *adj* (*person, body*) загоре́лый, бро́нзовый.

brooch [brəutʃ] *n* брошь *f*.

brood [bruːd] *n* вы́водок* ◆ *vi* (*hen*) сиде́ть* (*impf*) на я́йцах; (*person*) размышля́ть (*impf*)

▶ **brood on** *or* **over** *vt fus* грусти́ть* (*impf*) *or* размышля́ть (*impf*) о +*prp*.

broody ['bruːdɪ] *adj* (*thoughtful, moody*) угрю́мый (угрю́м); **~ hen** насе́дка*.

brook [bruk] *n* ручей*.

broom [brum] *n* метла́*; (*BOT*) раки́тник.

broomstick ['brumstɪk] *n* (*broom handle*) ру́чка метлы́.

Bros. *abbr* (*COMM*: = *brothers*) бра́тья* *mpl*.

broth [brɔθ] *n* похлёбка*.

brothel ['brɔθl] *n* публи́чный дом*, борде́ль *m*.

brother ['brʌðə'] *n* (*also REL*) брат*; (*in association*) собра́т*.

---

* marks translations which have irregular inflections. The Russian-English side of the dictionary gives inflectional information.

brotherhood ['brʌðəhud] *n* бра́тство.
brother-in-law ['brʌðərɪn'lɔ:] *n* (*sister's husband*) зять* *m*; (*wife's brother*) шу́рин*; (*husband's brother*) де́верь* *m*.
brotherly ['brʌðəlɪ] *adj* бра́тский*.
brought [brɔ:t] *pt, pp of* **bring**.
brought forward *adj* перенесённый на сле́дующую страни́цу.
brow [brau] *n* (*forehead*) лоб*, чело́*; (*also:* **eyebrow**) бровь *f*; (*of hill*) гре́бень *m*.
browbeat ['braubi:t] *vt*: **to ~ sb (into doing)** запу́гивать (запуга́ть *perf*) кого́-н (для того́, что́бы +*infin*).
brown [braun] *adj* кори́чневый; (*hair*) кашта́новый; (*eyes*) ка́рий*; (*tanned*) загоре́лый ♦ *n* (*colour*) кори́чневый цвет ♦ *vt* (*CULIN*) подрумя́нивать (подрумя́нить *perf*); **to go ~** (*person*) загора́ть (загоре́ть *perf*); (*leaves*) желте́ть (пожелте́ть *perf*).
brown bread *n* чёрный хлеб.
Brownie ['braunɪ] *n* (*also:* **~ Guide**) *мла́дшая де́вочка-ска́ут*.
brownie ['braunɪ] *n* (*US: cake*) *шокола́дное пиро́жное с оре́хами.*
brown paper *n* обёрточная бума́га.
brown rice *n* неочи́щенный рис.
brown sugar *n* неочи́щенный са́хар.
browse [brauz] *vi* (*in shop*) рассма́тривать (*impf*), разгля́дывать (*impf*); (*animal*) пита́ться (*impf*) пожо́жным ко́рмом ♦ *n*: **to have a ~ (around)** рассма́тривать (*impf*) *or* разгля́дывать (*impf*); **to ~ through a book** проли́стывать (пролиста́ть *perf*) кни́гу.
bruise [bru:z] *n* (*on face etc*) синя́к*; (*on fruit*) вмя́тина ♦ *vt* ушиба́ть (ушиби́ть* *perf*); (*fruit*) помя́ть* (*perf*) ♦ *vi* (*fruit*) помя́ться* (*perf*).
bruising ['bru:zɪŋ] *n* синяки́* *mpl*.
Brum [brʌm] *n abbr* (*BRIT: inf*) = **Birmingham**.
Brummie ['brʌmɪ] *n* (*inf*) бирмингéмец(-емка).
brunch [brʌntʃ] *n* по́здний* за́втрак.
brunette [bru:'nɛt] *n* брюне́тка*.
brunt [brʌnt] *n*: **to bear the ~ of** принима́ть (приня́ть* *perf*) на себя́ основно́й уда́р +*gen*.
brush [brʌʃ] *n* (*for cleaning*) щётка*; (*for painting*) кисть* *f*; (*for shaving*) помазо́к*; (*quarrel*) столкнове́ние ♦ *vt* (*sweep*) подмета́ть (подмести́* *perf*); (*groom*) чи́стить* (почи́стить* *perf*) щёткой; (*also:* **~ against**) слегка́ задева́ть (заде́ть* *perf*); **to have a ~ with sb** (*verbally*) вздо́рить (повздо́рить *perf*) с ке́м-н; (*physically*) дра́ться* (подра́ться* *perf*) с ке́м-н; **to have a ~ with the police** име́ть (*impf*) столкнове́ние с поли́цией
► **brush aside** *vt* (*criticism, emotion*) отмета́ть (отмести́ *perf*)
► **brush past** *vt* проноси́ться* (пронести́сь* *perf*) ми́мо +*gen*
► **brush up** *vt* (*subject, language*) шлифова́ть (отшлифова́ть *perf*); (*knowledge*) освежа́ть (освежи́ть *perf*).

brushed [brʌʃt] *adj* (*steel, chrome etc*) ма́товый; (*nylon, denim etc*) ворси́стый.
brush-off ['brʌʃɔf] *n* (*inf*): **to give sb the ~** отбрива́ть (отбри́ть* *perf*) кого́-н.
brushwood ['brʌʃwud] *n* хво́рост.
brusque [bru:sk] *adj* бесцеремо́нный*.
Brussels ['brʌslz] *n* Брюссéль *m*.
Brussels sprout *n* брюссéльская капу́ста.
brutal ['bru:tl] *adj* (*person*) жесто́кий*; (*actions*) зве́рский*; (*honesty, frankness*) жёсткий*.
brutality [bru:'tælɪtɪ] *n* (*see adj*) жесто́кость *f*; зве́рство.
brutalize ['bru:təlaɪz] *vt* ожесточа́ть (ожесточи́ть *perf*).
brute [bru:t] *n* зверь* *m* ♦ *adj*: **by ~ force** гру́бой си́лой.
brutish ['bru:tɪʃ] *adj* зве́рский*, ско́тский*.
BS *n abbr* (*US*: = *Bachelor of Science*) ≈ бакала́вр есте́ственных нау́к.
bs *abbr* = **bill of sale**.
BSA *n abbr* (= *Boy Scouts of America*) Сою́з америка́нских бойска́утов.
BSE *n abbr* (= *bovine spongiform encephalopathy*) энцефалопа́тия кру́пного рога́того скота́.
BSc *abbr* (= *Bachelor of Science*) ≈ бакала́вр есте́ственных нау́к.
BSI *n abbr* (= *British Standards Institution*) Брита́нский* институ́т станда́ртов.
BST *abbr* = *British Summer Time*.
Bt. *abbr* (*BRIT*) = **Bart**.
btu *n abbr* (= *British thermal unit*) брита́нская теплова́я едини́ца.
bubble ['bʌbl] *n* пузы́рь* *m* ♦ *vi* (*liquid*) пе́ниться (вспе́ниться *perf*); (*fig*): **to ~ with laughter** залива́ться (*impf*) смéхом.
bubble bath *n* пéнистая ва́нна.
bubble gum *n* жева́тельная рези́нка (*образу́ющая пузыри́*).
bubblejet printer ['bʌbldʒɛt-] *n тип компью́терного при́нтера.*
bubble pack *n* бли́стерная упако́вка*.
bubbly ['bʌblɪ] *adj* (*inf: girl*) живо́й; (*mineral water*) шипу́чий*, газиро́ванный ♦ *n* (*inf*) шипу́чка*.
Bucharest [bu:kə'rɛst] *n* Бухарéст.
buck [bʌk] *n* (*rabbit*) кро́лик; (*deer*) самéц оле́ня; (*US: inf*) бакс ♦ *vi* (*horse*) брыка́ться (*impf*); **to pass the ~ (to sb)** перекла́дывать (переложи́ть *perf*) отвéтственность (на кого́-н)
► **buck up** *vi* (*cheer up*) встряхну́ться (*perf*); (*hurry up*) пошевéливаться (*impf*) ♦ *vt*: **to ~ one's ideas up** исправля́рься (испра́виться* *perf*).
bucket ['bʌkɪt] *n* ведро́* ♦ *vi* (*BRIT: inf*): **the rain is ~ing (down)** дождь льёт как из ведра́.
buckle ['bʌkl] *n* пря́жка ♦ *vt* (*shoe, belt*) застёгивать (застегну́ть *perf*); (*wheel*) деформи́ровать (*impf/perf*) ♦ *vi* (*wheel*) деформи́роваться (*impf/perf*); (*bridge,*

support) прогибáться (прогнýться *perf*);
(*knees, legs*) подгибáться (подогнýться *perf*)
▶ **buckle down** *vi*: **to ~ down (to sth)** засéсть*
(*perf*) (за что-н).
Bucks [bʌks] *abbr* (*BRIT: POST*) = Buckingham-
shire.
bud [bʌd] *n* (*of tree*) пóчка*; (*of flower*) бутóн ◆
vi (*flower*) распускáться (распустúться* *perf*);
the trees are ~ding на дерéвьях
распускáются пóчки; **to nip in the ~**
пресекáть (пресéчь* *perf*) в кóрне.
Budapest [bjuːdəˈpɛst] *n* Будапéшт.
Buddha [ˈbudə] *n* Бýдда *m*.
Buddhism [ˈbudɪzəm] *n* буддúзм.
Buddhist [ˈbudɪst] *adj* буддúйский ◆ *n*
буддúст.
budding [ˈbʌdɪŋ] *adj* подаю́щий надéжды.
buddy [ˈbʌdɪ] *n* (*US*) прия́тель *m*.
budge [bʌdʒ] *vt* (*object*) сдвигáть (сдвúнуть
perf) (с мéста); (*fig: person*) заставля́ть
(застáвить* *perf*) уступúть* ◆ *vi* сдвúнуться
(*perf*) (с мéста).
budgerigar [ˈbʌdʒərɪɡɑːˈ] *n* волнúстый
попугáйчик.
budget [ˈbʌdʒɪt] *n* бюджéт ◆ *vi*: **to ~ for sth**
ассигновáть (*impf/perf*) *or* откла́дывать
(отложúть *perf*) дéньги на что-н; **I'm on a
tight ~** у меня́ тýго с финáнсами; **she works
out her ~ every month** онá рассчúтывает
свой бюджéт кáждый мéсяц.
budgie [ˈbʌdʒɪ] *n* = budgerigar.
Buenos Aires [ˈbwemɔsˈaɪrɪz] *n* Буэ́нос-Áйрес.
buff [bʌf] *adj* корúчневый ◆ *n* (*inf: enthusiast*)
знатóк*.
buffalo [ˈbʌfələu] (*pl* ~ *or* ~es) *n* (*BRIT*) бýйвол;
(*US: bison*) бизóн.
buffer [ˈbʌfəˈ] *n* бýфер*.
buffering [ˈbʌfərɪŋ] *n* (*COMPUT*) буферизáция,
использовáние бýфера.
buffer state *n* бýферное госудáрство.
buffer zone *n* бýферная зóна.
buffet[1] [ˈbufeɪ] *n* (*BRIT: in station*) буфéт; (*food*)
швéдский* стол*.
buffet[2] [ˈbʌfɪt] *vt* (*subj: wind, sea*) трепáть*
(*perf*), швыря́ть (*impf*).
buffet car *n* (*BRIT: RAIL*) вагóн-ресторáн.
buffet lunch *n* швéдский* стол*.
buffoon [bəˈfuːn] *n* фигля́р.
bug [bʌɡ] *n* (*esp US: insect*) насекóмое *nt adj*;
(*COMPUT: of program*) ошúбка*; (*fig: germ*)
вúрус, зарáза; (*hidden microphone*)
микрофóн, подслýшивающее устрóйство ◆
vt (*inf: annoy*) раздражáть (раздражúть *perf*);
(: *bother*) надоедáть (надоéсть* *perf*) +*dat*;
(*room etc*) прослýшивать (*impf*); **I've got the
travel ~** (*fig*) я помéшан на путешéствиях.
bugbear [ˈbʌɡbeə] *n* проблéма.
bugger [ˈbʌɡəˈ] (*infl*) *n* свóлочь *m/f* (*!*) ◆ *vb*: ~

off! катúсь отсю́да! (*!*); **~ (it)!** твою́ мать! (*!*)
buggy [ˈbʌɡɪ] *n* (*also: baby ~*) складнáя
дéтская коля́ска*.
bugle [ˈbjuːɡl] *n* горн.
build [bɪld] (*pt, pp* **built**) *n* (*of person*)
телосложéние ◆ *vt* стрóить (пострóить *perf*)
▶ **build on** *vt fus* (*fig*) пóльзоваться
(воспóльзоваться *perf*) +*instr*
▶ **build up** *vt* (*forces, production*) нарáщивать
(*impf*); (*morale*) укрепля́ть (укрепúть* *perf*);
(*stocks*) накáпливать (накопúть* *perf*);
(*business*) создавáть* (создáть* *perf*); **don't ~
your hopes up too soon** не рáдуйтесь рáньше
врéмени.
builder [ˈbɪldəˈ] *n* строúтель *m*.
building [ˈbɪldɪŋ] *n* (*industry, construction*)
строúтельство; (*structure*) строéние; (:
residential, offices) здáние.
building contractor *n* строúтельный
подря́дчик.
building industry *n* строúтельная
промы́шленность *f*.
building site *n* строúтельный учáсток*.
building society *n* (*BRIT*) ≈ "строúтельное
óбщество".
building trade *n* = building industry.
build-up [ˈbɪldʌp] *n* (*of gas etc*) скоплéние;
(*publicity*): **to give sb/sth a good ~**
обеспéчивать (обеспéчить *perf*) комý-н/
чемý-н хорóшую реклáму.
built [bɪlt] *pt, pp of* build ◆ *adj*: ~**-in** встрóенный;
well-~ person хорóшо сложённый* человéк.
built-in obsolescence [ˈbɪltɪn-] *n*
запланúрованное устаревáние.
built-up area [ˈbɪltʌp-] *n* застрóенный райóн.
bulb [bʌlb] *n* (*BOT*) лýковица; (*ELEC*) лáмпа,
лáмпочка*.
bulbous [ˈbʌlbəs] *adj* пузáтый (пузáт); (*nose*)
тóлстый (толст).
Bulgaria [bʌlˈɡɛərɪə] *n* Болгáрия.
Bulgarian [bʌlˈɡɛərɪən] *adj* болгáрский* ◆ *n*
болгáрин*(-рка*); (*LING*) болгáрский язы́к*.
bulge [bʌldʒ] *n* (*bump*) вы́пуклость *f*; (*in birth
rate*) врéменное увеличéние ◆ *vi* (*stomach*)
выпя́чиваться (вы́пятиться* *perf*); (*pocket,
file*) трещáть (*impf*) по швам; **her purse is
bulging with money** её кошелёк набúт
дéньгами.
bulimia [bəˈlɪmɪə] *n* булимúя.
bulimic [bəˈliːmɪk] *adj*: **she is ~** онá страдáет
булимúей.
bulk [bʌlk] *n* громáда; **in ~** óптом; **the ~ of**
бóльшая часть +*gen*.
bulk buying [-ˈbaɪŋ] *n* оптóвая закýпка*.
bulk carrier *n* грузовóе сýдно, грузовóй
корáбль *m*.
bulkhead [ˈbʌlkhɛd] *n* перегорóдка.
bulky [ˈbʌlkɪ] *adj* громóздкий (громóздок).

---

* marks translations which have irregular inflections. The Russian-English side of the dictionary gives inflectional information.

bull [bul] n (ZOOL) бык*; (male: whale) самéц* китá; (: elephant) слон; (STOCK EXCHANGE) спекуля́нт, игра́ющий* на повыше́ние на би́рже; (REL) бу́лла.

bulldog ['buldɔg] n бульдо́г.

bulldoze ['buldəuz] vt (flatten) расчища́ть (расчи́стить* perf) бульдо́зером; (knock down) лома́ть (слома́ть perf) бульдо́зером; **I was ~d into it** (fig: inf) меня́ заста́вили сде́лать э́то.

bulldozer ['buldəuzə'] n бульдо́зер.

bullet ['bulɪt] n пу́ля.

bulletin ['bulɪtɪn] n: **news ~** сво́дка* новосте́й; (journal) бюллете́нь m.

bulletin board n (COMPUT) электро́нная доска́ объявле́ний.

bulletproof ['bulɪtpru:f] adj пулене-проби́ваемый.

bullfight ['bulfaɪt] n бой* быко́в.

bullfighter ['bulfaɪtə'] n тореадо́р.

bullfighting ['bulfaɪtɪŋ] n бой быко́в.

bullion ['buljən] n сли́ток*.

bullock ['bulək] n вол*.

bullring ['bulrɪŋ] n аре́на (на кото́рой происхо́дит бой быко́в).

bull's-eye ['bulzaɪ] n (on a target) я́блоко* мише́ни.

bullshit ['bulʃɪt] (infl) n бред (соба́чий) (!) ◆ vt нести́* (impf) бред (!)

bully ['bulɪ] n задира m/f ◆ vt трави́ть* (затрави́ть* perf); (frighten) запу́гивать (запуга́ть perf).

bullying ['bulɪŋ] n тра́вля, запу́гивание.

bum [bʌm] n (inf: backside) за́дница; (esp US: tramp) бродя́га m/f; (: good-for-nothing) безде́льник

▶ **bum around** vi (inf) шата́ться (impf).

bumblebee ['bʌmblbi:] n шмель* m.

bumf [bʌmf] n (inf) бума́жки* fpl.

bump [bʌmp] n (minor accident) столкнове́ние; (jolt) толчо́к; (swelling) ши́шка; (on road) уха́б ◆ vt (strike) ударя́ть (уда́рить perf); (dent) помя́ть* (perf); **he ~ed his head on the door** он уда́рился or сту́кнулся голово́й о дверь

▶ **bump along** vi трясти́сь* (impf) по +dat

▶ **bump into** vt fus ната́лкиваться (натолкну́ться perf) на +acc.

bumper ['bʌmpə'] n (AUT) ба́мпер ◆ adj: **~ crop** or **harvest** небыва́лый урожа́й.

bumper cars npl (US) аттракцио́нный электромоби́ль m.

bumper sticker n накле́йка на ба́мпер.

bumph [bʌmf] n = **bumf**.

bumptious ['bʌmpʃəs] adj самоуве́ренный (самоуве́рен).

bumpy ['bʌmpɪ] adj уха́бистый; **it was a ~ flight** нас всю доро́гу трясло́.

bun [bʌn] n (CULIN) сдо́бная бу́лка*; (of hair) у́зел*.

bunch [bʌntʃ] n (of flowers) буке́т; (of keys) свя́зка*; (of bananas) гроздь f; (of people) компа́ния; **~es** npl (in hair) хво́стики mpl; **~ of grapes** гроздь or кисть* f виногра́да.

bundle ['bʌndl] n (of clothes) у́зел*; (of sticks) вяза́нка*; (of papers) па́чка* ◆ vt (also: **~ up**) свя́зывать (связа́ть* perf) в у́зел; (put): **to ~ sth/sb into** зата́лкивать (затолкну́ть perf) что-н/кого́-н в +acc

▶ **bundle off** vt отсыла́ть (отосла́ть* perf)

▶ **bundle out** vt бы́стро уходи́ть* (уйти́* perf).

bun fight n (BRIT: inf: official function) банке́т; (: tea party) чаепи́тие.

bung [bʌŋ] n про́бка* ◆ vt (BRIT: throw) запи́хивать (запиха́ть perf); (also: **~ up**: pipe, hole) затыка́ть (заткну́ть perf); **my nose is ~ed up** у меня́ зало́жен нос.

bungalow ['bʌŋgələu] n бунга́ло nt ind.

bungee jumping ['bʌndʒi:'dʒʌmpɪŋ] n прыжки́ с высоты́ вниз голово́й, в кото́рых челове́к привя́зан за но́ги к эласти́чному кана́ту.

bungle ['bʌŋgl] vt зава́ливать (завали́ть perf).

bunion ['bʌnjən] n нато́птыш.

bunk [bʌŋk] n (bed) ко́йка.

bunk beds npl двухъя́русная крова́ть fsg.

bunker ['bʌŋkə'] n бу́нкер*; (GOLF) я́ма с песко́м (на по́ле для го́льфа).

bunny ['bʌnɪ] n (also: **~ rabbit**) за́йчик.

bunny girl n (BRIT) официа́нтка ночно́го клу́ба, в облега́ющем костю́ме с кро́личьим хвосто́м и уша́ми.

bunny hill n (US: SKIING) лягуша́тник.

bunting ['bʌntɪŋ] n флажки́ mpl.

buoy [bɔɪ] n буй*, ба́кен

▶ **buoy up** vt (fig) подба́дривать (подбодри́ть perf).

buoyancy ['bɔɪənsɪ] n плаву́честь f.

buoyant ['bɔɪənt] adj (ship) плаву́чий*; (economy, market) оживлённый* (оживлён); (prices, currency) твёрдый*; (fig: person) жизнера́достный* (жизнера́достен).

burden ['bə:dn] n (responsibility) бре́мя* nt; (load) но́ша ◆ vt (trouble): **to ~ sb with** обременя́ть (обремени́ть perf) кого́-н +instr; **to be a ~ to sb** быть* (impf) в тя́гость кому́-н.

bureau ['bjuərəu] (pl **~x**) n (BRIT) бюро́ nt ind; (US) комо́д.

bureaucracy [bjuə'rɔkrəsɪ] n (POL, COMM) бюрокра́тия; (system) бюрократи́зм.

bureaucrat ['bjuərəkræt] n бюрокра́т.

bureaucratic [bjuərə'krætɪk] adj бюрократи́ческий*.

bureaux ['bjuərəuz] npl of **bureau**.

burgeon ['bə:dʒən] vi (fig) расцвета́ть (расцвести́* perf).

burger ['bə:gə'] n бу́ргер.

burglar ['bə:glə'] n взло́мщик.

burglar alarm n сигнализа́ция.

burglarize ['bə:gləraɪz] vt (US) соверша́ть (соверши́ть perf) кра́жу со взло́мом.

burglary ['bə:glərɪ] n (crime) кра́жа со взло́мом; (act) взлом.

burgle ['bə:gl] *vt* совершáть (соверши́ть *perf*) крáжу со взлóмом.
Burgundy ['bə:gəndɪ] *n* (*GEO*) Бургýндия.
burial ['bɛrɪəl] *n* погребéние, пóхороны *pl*.
burial ground *n* мéсто* погребéния.
burlesque [bə:'lɛsk] *n* парóдия.
burly ['bə:lɪ] *adj* дю́жий.
Burma ['bə:mə] *n* Би́рма.
Burmese [bə:'mi:z] *adj* бирмáнский ◆ *n inv* бирмáнец*(-нка*); (*LING*) бирмáнский язы́к*.
burn [bə:n] (*pt, pp* **burned** *or* **burnt**) *vt* жечь* (сжечь* *perf*), сжигáть (сжечь* *perf*); (*arson*) поджигáть (поджéчь* *perf*) ◆ *vi* (*house, wood*) горéть (сгорéть *perf*), сгорáть (сгорéть *perf*); (*cakes*) подгорáть (подгорéть *perf*) ◆ *n* ожóг; **the cigarette ~t a hole in her dress** сигарéта прожглá ды́рку в её на плáтье; **she always ~s the meat** у неё всегдá подгорáет мя́со; **I've ~t myself!** я обжёгся!
▶ **burn down** *vt* сжигáть (сжечь* *perf*) дотлá
▶ **burn out** *vt*: **to ~ o.s. out** вымáтываться (вы́мотаться *perf*); **the fire ~t itself out** огóнь догорéл.
burner ['bə:nəʳ] *n* горéлка*.
burning ['bə:nɪŋ] *adj* (*building, forest*) горя́щий; (*sand, desert*) раскалённый; (*issue, ambition*) жгýчий*.
burnish ['bə:nɪʃ] *vt* полировáть (отполировáть *perf*).
burnt [bə:nt] *pt, pp of* **burn**.
burnt sugar *n* (*BRIT*) жжёный сáхар.
burp [bə:p] *n* отры́жка* ◆ *vt*: **to ~ a baby** вызвáть (вы́звать* *perf*) отры́жку у ребёнка ◆ *vi* отры́гивать (отрыгнýть *perf*).
burrow ['bʌrəu] *n* норá* ◆ *vi* (*dig*) рыть* (вы́рыть* *perf*) норý; (*rummage*) ры́ться* (*impf*).
bursar ['bə:səʳ] *n* казначéй.
bursary ['bə:sərɪ] *n* (*BRIT*) стипéндия.
burst [bə:st] (*pt, pp* **burst**) *vt* (*bag etc*) разрывáть (разорвáть* *perf*) ◆ *vi* (*pipe*) прорывáться (прорвáться* *perf*); (*tyre, balloon*) лóпаться (лóпнуть *perf*) ◆ *n* (*of gunfire*) залп; (*of shelling*) разры́в; (*also:* **~ pipe**) проры́в; **the river has ~ its banks** рекá вы́шла из берегóв; **to ~ into flames** вспы́хивать (вспы́хнуть *perf*); **to ~ into tears** расплáкаться* (*perf*); **to ~ out laughing** расхохотáться* (*perf*); **to ~ into a room** врывáться (ворвáться* *perf*) в кóмнату; **~ blood vessel** разóрванный кровенóсного сосýда; **the room is/was ~ing with people** кóмната наби́та/былá наби́та до откáза людьми́; **to be ~ing with** (*pride, anger*) раздувáться (раздýться *perf*) от +*gen*; **a ~ of energy/enthusiasm** прили́в энéргии/энтузиáзма; **~ of laughter/applause** взрыв смéха/рукоплескáний; **~ of machine gun fire** пулемётная óчередь *f*

▶ **burst into** *vt fus* (*room*) врывáться (ворвáться* *perf*)
▶ **burst open** *vi* (*door etc*) распáхиваться (распахнýться *perf*).
bury ['bɛrɪ] *vt* (*object*) зарывáть (зары́ть* *perf*), закáпывать (закопáть *perf*); (*person*) хорони́ть* (похорони́ть* *perf*); **many people were buried in the rubble** мнóго людéй бы́ли зары́ты под облóмками; **to ~ one's face in one's hands** пря́тать* (спря́тать* *perf*) лицó в ладóни; **to ~ one's head in the sand** (*fig*) зарывáть (зары́ть* *perf*) гóлову в песóк; **to ~ the hatchet** (*fig*) забывáть (забы́ть* *perf*) раздóры, мири́ться (помири́ться *perf*).
bus [bʌs] *n* автóбус; (*double decker*) (двухэтáжный) автóбус.
bus boy *n* (*US*) *помóщник официáнта, убирáющий гря́зную посýду со столá*.
bush [buʃ] *n* куст*; (*scrubland*) *прострáнства, покры́тые кустáрниками (в Австрáлии и m.n.)*; **to beat about the ~** ходи́ть* (*impf*) вокрýг да óколо.
bushed [buʃt] *adj* (*inf*) вы́мотанный (вы́мотан).
bushel ['buʃl] *n* бýшель *m*.
bush fire *n* леснóй пожáр.
bushy ['buʃɪ] *adj* (*tail*) пуши́стый (пуши́ст); (*hair, eyebrows*) густóй* (густ); (*plant*) кусти́стый.
busily ['bɪzɪlɪ] *adv* (*actively*) делови́то, энерги́чно; **to be ~ doing sth** энерги́чно занимáться (*impf*) чем-н.
business ['bɪznɪs] *n* (*matter*) дéло*; (*trading*) би́знес; (*firm*) предприя́тие, фи́рма; (*occupation*) заня́тие; **to be away on ~** быть (*impf*) в командирóвке; **I'm here on ~** я здесь по дéлу; **he's in the insurance/transport ~** он рабóтает в страховóм/трáнспортном би́знесе; **to do ~ with sb** имéть (*impf*) делá с кем-н; **it's my ~ to ...** это моя́ обя́занность +*infin* ...; **it's none of my ~** это не моё дéло; **he means ~** он серьёзно настрóен.
business address *n* áдрес* фи́рмы.
business card *n* визи́тная кáрточка*.
businesslike ['bɪznɪslaɪk] *adj* делови́тый (делови́т).
businessman ['bɪznɪsmən] *irreg n* бизнесмéн.
business trip *n* командирóвка*.
businesswoman ['bɪznɪswumən] *irreg n* жéнщина-бизнесмéн, деловáя жéнщина.
busker ['bʌskəʳ] *n* (*BRIT*) *ýличный музыкáнт*.
bus lane *n* (*BRIT*) *часть дорóги, отведённая для движéния автóбусов*.
bus shelter *n* автóбусная останóвка (*с навéсом*).
bus station *n* абтóбусная стáнция, автовокзáл.
bus-stop ['bʌsstɔp] *n* автóбусная останóвка*.

---

* marks translations which have irregular inflections. The Russian-English side of the dictionary gives inflectional information.

bust [bʌst] *n* (ANAT) бюст, грудь* *f*; (*measurement*) объём груди́; (*sculpture*) бюст ◆ *adj* (*inf: broken*) сло́манный (сло́ман) ◆ *vt* (*inf: arrest*) накрыва́ть (накры́ть* *perf*); **to go ~** (*company etc*) прогора́ть (прогоре́ть *perf*), вылета́ть (вы́лететь* *perf*) в трубу́.

bustle ['bʌsl] *n* (*activity*) сумато́ха, суета́ ◆ *vi* (*person*) суети́ться* (*impf*).

bustling ['bʌslɪŋ] *adj* (*place*) оживлённый, шу́мный*.

bust-up ['bʌstʌp] *n* (BRIT: *inf*) сканда́л, ссо́ра.

BUSWE *n abbr* (BRIT) = British Union of Social Work Employees.

busty ['bʌstɪ] *adj* (*inf*) груда́стый (груда́ст).

busy ['bɪzɪ] *adj* (*person*) занято́й; (*street*) оживлённый (оживлён), шу́мный* (шу́мен); (TEL): **the line is ~** ли́ния занята́ ◆ *vt*: **to ~ o.s. with** занима́ть (заня́ть* *perf*) себя́ +*instr*, занима́ться (заня́ться* *perf*) +*instr*; **he's a ~ man** (*normally*) он занято́й челове́к; **he's ~** (*temporarily*) он за́нят; **it's usually a very ~ shop** в э́том магази́не обы́чно мно́го наро́ду.

busybody ['bɪzɪbɔdɪ] *n*: **he is a ~** он суёт нос в чужи́е дела́.

busy signal *n* (US: TEL) коро́ткие гудки́ *mpl*.

KEYWORD

but [bʌt] *conj* **1** (*yet*) но; (: *in contrast*) а; **he's not very bright, but he's hard-working** он не о́чень умён, но усе́рден; **I'm tired but Paul isn't** я уста́л, а Па́вел не уста́л

2 (*however*) но; **I'd love to come, but I'm busy** я бы с удово́льствием пришёл, но я за́нят

3 (*showing disagreement, surprise etc*) но; **but that's fantastic!** но э́то же потряса́юще!

◆ *prep* (*apart from, except*): **no-one but him can do it** никто́, кро́ме него́, не мо́жет э́то сде́лать; **nothing but trouble/bad luck** сплошны́е неприя́тности/неуда́чи; **but for you/your help** е́сли бы не Вы/ва́ша по́мощь; **I'll do anything but that** я сде́лаю всё, что уго́дно, но то́лько не э́то

◆ *adv* (*just, only*): **she's but a child** она́ всего́ лишь ребёнок; **had I but known** е́сли бы то́лько я знал; **I can but try** ну я, коне́чно, могу́ попро́бовать; **the work is all but finished** рабо́та почти́ зако́нчена.

butane ['bju:teɪn] *n* (*also: ~ gas*) бута́н.

butch [butʃ] *adj* (*pej: woman*) мужеподо́бный* (мужеподо́бен); **he's very ~** он (настоя́щий) мужи́к.

butcher ['butʃə'] *n* мясни́к*; (*pej: murderer*) пала́ч* ◆ *vt* (*cattle*) бить* (заби́ть* *perf*), ре́зать* (заре́зать* *perf*); (*prisoners*) выреза́ть* (вы́резать* *perf*).

butcher's (shop) ['butʃəz-] *n* мясно́й магази́н.

butler ['bʌtlə'] *n* дворе́цкий *m adj*.

butt [bʌt] *n* (*large barrel*) бо́чка*; (*thick end*) утолщённый коне́ц*; (*of rifle*) прикла́д; (*of pistol*) рукоя́тка; (*of cigarette*) оку́рок*; (BRIT: *of teasing*) посме́шище; (: *of criticism*) предме́т; (US: *inf!*) за́дница (*!*) ◆ *vt* (*subj: goat*) бода́ть (*impf*)

▶ **butt in** *vi* встрева́ть (встрять* *perf*) в +*acc*.

butter ['bʌtə'] *n* (сли́вочное) ма́сло* ◆ *vt* (*bread*) нама́зывать (нама́зать* *perf*) (сли́вочным) ма́слом.

buttercup ['bʌtəkʌp'] *n* лю́тик.

butter dish *n* маслёнка*.

butterfingers ['bʌtəfɪŋɡəz] *n* (*inf*) растя́па *m/f*.

butterfly ['bʌtəflaɪ] *n* ба́бочка*; (*also: ~ stroke*) баттерфля́й.

buttocks ['bʌtəks] *npl* я́годицы *fpl*.

button ['bʌtn] *n* (*on clothes*) пу́говица; (*on machine*) кно́пка*; (US: *badge*) значо́к* ◆ *vt* (*also: ~ up*) застёгивать (застегну́ть* *perf*).

buttonhole ['bʌtnhəul] *n* петля́*, петли́ца ◆ *vt*: **to ~ sb** приста(ва́ть (приста́ть* *perf*) к кому́-н с разгово́рами.

buttress ['bʌtrɪs] *n* контрфо́рс.

buxom ['bʌksəm] *adj* (*woman*) полногру́дый (полнлгру́д).

buy [baɪ] (*pt, pp* bought) *vt* покупа́ть (купи́ть* *perf*); (COMM) приобрета́ть (приобрести́* *perf*) ◆ *n* поку́пка*; **to ~ sb sth/sth from sb** покупа́ть (купи́ть* *perf*) кому́-н что-н/что-н у кого́-н; **to ~ sb a drink** покупа́ть (купи́ть* *perf*) кому́-н вы́пить что́-нибудь; **that was a good/bad ~** э́то была́ уда́чная/неуда́чная поку́пка

▶ **buy back** *vt* выкупа́ть (вы́купить* *perf*)

▶ **buy in** *vt* (BRIT) закупа́ть (закупи́ть* *perf*)

▶ **buy into** *vt fus* (BRIT) покупа́ть (купи́ть* *perf*) часть +*gen*, входи́ть* (войти́* *perf*) в до́лю с +*instr*

▶ **buy off** *vt* подкупа́ть (подкупи́ть* *perf*)

▶ **buy out** *vt* выкупа́ть (вы́купить* *perf*)

▶ **buy up** *vt* скупа́ть (скупи́ть* *perf*).

buyer ['baɪə'] *n* покупа́тель(ница) *m(f)*; (COMM) заку́пщик(-ица).

buyer's market ['baɪəz-] *n* ры́нок, вы́годный для покупа́теля.

buy-out ['baɪaut] *n*: **management ~** вы́куп ча́стной фи́рмы у её владе́льца чле́нами администра́ции, рабо́тающими на фи́рме.

buzz [bʌz] *n* жужжа́ние ◆ *vi* (*insect, saw*) жужжа́ть* (прожужжа́ть* *perf*); (*inf: place*) гуде́ть* (*impf*) ◆ *vt* (*call on intercom*) звони́ть (позвони́ть *perf*) по вну́треннему телефо́ну; (*with buzzer*) звони́ть (позвони́ть *perf*); (AVIAT) соверша́ть (соверши́ть *perf*) бре́ющий полёт над +*instr*; **to give sb a ~** (*inf: TEL*) звя́кнуть (*perf*) кому́-н; **my head is ~ing** меня́ голова́ гуди́т

▶ **buzz off** *vi* (*inf*) отва́ливать (отвали́ть* *perf*).

buzzard ['bʌzəd] *n* каню́к*, сары́ч*.

buzzer ['bʌzə'] *n* зу́ммер, звоно́к.

buzz word *n* (*inf*) мо́дное слове́чко*.

KEYWORD

by [baɪ] *prep* **1** (*referring to cause, agent*): **he was killed by lightning** он был уби́т мо́лнией; **a**

painting by Van Gogh карти́на Ван Го́га; **it's
by Shakespeare** э́то Шекспи́р
2 (*referring to manner, means*): **by bus/train** на
авто́бусе/по́езде, авто́бусом/по́ездом; **by
car** на маши́не; **by phone** по телефо́ну; **to pay
by cheque** плати́ть* (заплати́ть* *perf*) че́ком;
by moonlight при све́те луны́; **by candlelight**
при свеча́х; **by working constantly, he...**
благодаря́ тому́, что он рабо́тал без
остано́вки, он...
3 (*via, through*) че́рез +*acc*; **by land/sea** по
су́ше/мо́рю; **by the back door** че́рез за́днюю
дверь
4 (*close to*) о́коло +*gen*, у +*gen*; **the house is by
the river** дом* нахо́дится о́коло *or* у реки́; **a
holiday by the sea** о́тпуск на мо́ре
5 (*past*) ми́мо +*gen*; **she rushed by me** она́
пронесла́сь ми́мо меня́
6 (*not later than*) к +*dat*; **by four o'clock** к
четырём часа́м; **by the time I got here it was
too late** к тому́ вре́мени, когда́ я добра́лся
сюда́, бы́ло сли́шком по́здно
7 (*during*): **by day** днём; **by night** но́чью
8 (*amount*): **to sell by the kilo/metre**
продава́ть* (*impf*) в килогра́ммах/ме́трах;
she is paid by the hour у неё почасова́я
опла́та
9 (*MATH, measure*) на +*acc*; **to divide/multiply
by three** дели́ть* (раздели́ть* *perf*)/умножа́ть
(умно́жить *perf*) на три; **a room three metres
by four** ко́мната разме́ром три ме́тра на
четы́ре
10 (*according to*) по +*dat*; **to play by the rules**
игра́ть (*impf*) по пра́вилам; **it's all right by me**
я не возража́ю; **by law** по зако́нам
11: **(all) by oneself** (*alone*) (соверше́нно) оди́н
(*f* одна́, *nt* одно́, *pl* одни́); (*unaided*) сам (*f*
сама́, *nt* само́, *pl* сами́); **I did it all by myself** я
сде́лал всё сам; **he was standing by himself in
the corner** он стоя́л в углу́ оди́н/сам по себе́
12: **by the way** кста́ти, ме́жду про́чим; **this
wasn't my idea by the way** кста́ти *or* ме́жду
про́чим, э́то была́ не моя́ иде́я
♦ *adv* **1** *see* **go, pass** *etc*
2: **by and by** вско́ре; **by and large** в це́лом.

bye(-bye) ['baɪ('baɪ)] *excl* пока́, всего́.
by(e)-law ['baɪlɔ:] *n* постановле́ние ме́стной
вла́сти.
by-election ['baɪlɛkʃən] *n* (*BRIT*)
дополни́тельные вы́боры *mpl*.
Byelorussia [bjɛləu'rʌʃə] *n* Белору́ссия.
bygone ['baɪɡɔn] *adj* мину́вший* ♦ *n*: **let ~s be
~s** что бы́ло, то прошло́.
bypass ['baɪpɑ:s] *n* (*AUT*) объе́зд; (*MED*)
обходно́е шунти́рование (*обы́чно в
кардиохирурги́и*) ♦ *vt* (*town*) объезжа́ть
(объе́хать* *perf*); (*fig*) обходи́ть* (обойти́*
perf).
by-product ['baɪprɔdʌkt] *n* (*of industrial
process*) побо́чный проду́кт; (*of situation*)
побо́чный результа́т.
byre ['baɪə'] *n* (*BRIT*) коро́вник.
bystander ['baɪstændə'] *n* свиде́тель(ница) *m(f)*,
прохо́жий(-ая) *m(f) adj*.
byte [baɪt] *n* (*COMPUT*) байт.
byway ['baɪweɪ] *n* (*in country*) просёлочная
доро́га; (*in city*) у́лочка.
byword ['baɪwə:d] *n*: **to be a ~ for** быть* (*impf*)
олицетворе́нием *or* си́мволом +*gen*.
by-your-leave ['baɪjɔ:'li:v] *n*: **without so much
as a ~** без вся́кого разреше́ния.

---

* marks translations which have irregular inflections. The Russian-English side of the dictionary gives inflectional information.

~ C, c ~

C, c [siː] n (letter) 3-ья бу́ква англи́йского алфави́та; (SCOL: mark) ≈ удовлетвори́тельный.
C [siː] n (MUS) до nt ind.
C. abbr = **Celsius, centigrade.**
c abbr (= **century**) в. = век; (= circa) о́коло +gen; (US etc: = cents) це́нты mpl.
CA n abbr (BRIT) = **chartered accountant** ♦ abbr = **Central America**; (US: POST) = California.
ca. abbr (= circa) о́коло +gen.
c/a abbr (COMM) = **capital account, credit account, current account.**
CAA n abbr (BRIT: = Civil Aviation Authority) Управле́ние гражда́нской авиа́ции; (US) = Civil Aeronautics Authority.
CAB n abbr (BRIT: = Citizens' Advice Bureau) бюро́, даю́щее беспла́тные сове́ты по широ́кому спе́ктру пробле́м.
cab [kæb] n такси́ nt ind; (of truck etc) каби́на; (horse-drawn) экипа́ж, кэб.
cabaret ['kæbəreɪ] n кабаре́ nt ind.
cabbage ['kæbɪdʒ] n капу́ста.
cabbie ['kæbɪ] n такси́ст.
cab driver n шофёр такси́.
cabin ['kæbɪn] n (on ship) каю́та; (on plane) каби́на; (house) хи́жина.
cabin cruiser n пассажи́рский* ка́тер*.
cabinet ['kæbɪnɪt] n шкаф*; (also: display ~) го́рка; (POL) кабине́т (мини́стров).
cabinet-maker ['kæbɪnɪt'meɪkə'] n красно-дере́вщик.
cabinet minister n член кабине́та мини́стров.
cable ['keɪbl] n (strong rope) кана́т; (metal) трос; (ELEC, TEL, TV) ка́бель m; (also: ~gram) каблогра́мма, телегра́мма ♦ vt (message) телеграфи́ровать (impf/perf); (money) посыла́ть (посла́ть* perf) телегра́фом.
cable car n кана́тная доро́га.
cable railway n фуникулёр.
cable television n ка́бельное телеви́дение.
cache [kæʃ] n та́йный склад; **a ~ of food** запа́с продово́льствия.
cackle ['kækl] vi (person) хихи́кать (impf); (hen) куда́хтать* (impf).
cacti ['kæktaɪ] npl of **cactus.**
cactus ['kæktəs] (pl **cacti**) n ка́ктус.
CAD n abbr (= computer-aided design) автоматизи́рованное проекти́рование.

caddie ['kædɪ] n (GOLF) подру́чный m adj игрока́ в гольф.
caddy ['kædɪ] n = **caddie.**
cadence ['keɪdəns] n (of voice) интона́ция.
cadet [kə'dɛt] n курса́нт; **police ~** курса́нт полице́йской шко́лы.
cadge [kædʒ] vt (inf): **to ~ (from** or **off)** выкля́нчивать (вы́клянчить perf) (у +gen).
cadger ['kædʒə'] n (BRIT: inf) попроша́йка m/f.
cadre ['kædrɪ] n ка́дры mpl.
Caesarean [siː'zɛərɪən] n (also: ~ **section**) ке́сарево сече́ние.
CAF abbr (BRIT: = cost and freight) КАФ (сто́имость и фрахт).
café ['kæfeɪ] n кафе́ nt ind.
cafeteria [kæfɪ'tɪərɪə] n кафете́рий.
caffein(e) ['kæfiːn] n кофеи́н.
cage [keɪdʒ] n (of animal) кле́тка; (of lift) каби́на ♦ vt сажа́ть (посади́ть* perf) в кле́тку.
cagey ['keɪdʒɪ] adj (inf: person) скры́тный* (скры́тен); (: answer) укло́нчивый (укло́нчив).
cagoule [kə'guːl] n дождеви́к.
cahoots [kə'huːts] npl: **to be in ~ with sb** быть* (impf) в сго́воре с кем-н.
CAI n abbr (= computer-aided instruction) автоматизи́рованное обуче́ние.
Cairo ['kaɪərəu] n Каи́р.
cajole [kə'dʒəul] vt: **to ~ sb** склоня́ть (склони́ть perf) ле́стью кого́-н.
cake [keɪk] n (large) торт; (small) пиро́жное nt adj; (of soap) брусо́к*; **it's a piece of ~** (inf) э́то пустяко́вое де́ло*; **his books sell like hot ~s** его́ кни́ги иду́т на расхва́т.
caked [keɪkt] adj: ~ **with** облеплённый +instr.
cake shop n бу́лочная-конди́терская f adj.
calamine lotion ['kæləmaɪn-] n калами́нный лосьо́н.
calamitous [kə'læmɪtəs] adj бе́дственный.
calamity [kə'læmɪtɪ] n бе́дствие.
calcium ['kælsɪəm] n ка́льций.
calculate ['kælkjuleɪt] vt (work out: numbers, cost) подсчи́тывать (подсчита́ть perf); (: distance) вычисля́ть (вы́числить perf); (estimate) рассчи́тывать (рассчита́ть perf)
▸ **calculate on** vt fus: **to ~ on sth** рассчи́тывать (impf) на что-н.
calculated ['kælkjuleɪtɪd] adj наме́ренный (наме́рен); **a ~ risk** созна́тельный риск.

calculating [ˈkælkjuleɪtɪŋ] *adj* расчётливый (расчётлив).

calculation [kælkjuˈleɪʃən] *n* (*see vb*) подсчёт; вычисле́ние; расчёт.

calculator [ˈkælkjuleɪtəʳ] *n* калькуля́тор.

calculus [ˈkælkjuləs] *n* исчисле́ние; **integral/ differential ~** интегра́льное/ дифференциа́льное исчисле́ние.

Calcutta [kælˈkʌtə] *n* Кальку́тта.

calendar [ˈkæləndəʳ] *n* календа́рь* *m* ◆ *cpd*: **~ month/year** календа́рный ме́сяц*/год*.

calf [kɑːf] (*pl* **calves**) *n* (*of cow*) телёнок*; (*of elephant, seal*) детёныш; (*also:* **~skin**) теля́чья ко́жа; (*ANAT*) икра́*.

caliber [ˈkælɪbəʳ] (*US*) *n* = **calibre**.

calibrate [ˈkælɪbreɪt] *vt* калиброва́ть (*impf*).

calibre [ˈkælɪbəʳ] (*US* **caliber**) *n* (*of gun, person*) кали́бр.

calico [ˈkælɪkəu] *n* (*BRIT*) митка́ль* *m*; (*US*) си́тец*.

California [kælɪˈfɔːnɪə] *n* Калифо́рния.

calipers [ˈkælɪpəz] (*US*) *npl* = **callipers**.

call [kɔːl] *vt* (*name, label*) называ́ть (назва́ть* *perf*); (*TEL*) звони́ть (позвони́ть *perf*) +*dat*; (*summon*) вызыва́ть (вы́звать* *perf*); (*arrange*) созыва́ть (созва́ть* *perf*); (*announce*) объявля́ть (объяви́ть* *perf*) ◆ *vi* (*shout*) крича́ть (кри́кнуть *perf*); (*telephone*) звони́ть (позвони́ть *perf*); (*visit: also:* **~ in**, **~ round**) заходи́ть* (зайти́* *perf*) ◆ *n* (*shout, cry*) крик; (*TEL*) звоно́к*; (*visit*) посеще́ние; (*demand*) призы́в; (*summons: for flight*) объявле́ние; (*fig: lure*) зов*; **she is ~ed Suzanne** её зову́т Сюза́нна; **the mountain is ~ed Ben Nevis** гора́ называ́ется Бен Не́вис; **to ~ sb as a witness** призыва́ть (призва́ть* *perf*) кого́-н в свиде́тели; **who is ~ing?** (*TEL*) кто звони́т?; **London ~ing** (*RADIO*) говори́т Ло́ндон; **please give me a ~ at 7** позвони́те мне, пожа́луйста, в 7 часо́в; **to make a ~** звони́ть (позвони́ть *perf*); **to pay a ~ on sb** навеща́ть (навести́ть* *perf*) кого́-н; **there's not much ~ for these items** нет большо́го спро́са; **to be on ~** (*nurse, doctor*) дежу́рить (*impf*); (*army, fire brigade*) быть* (*impf*) нагото́ве

▶ **call at** *vt fus* (*subj: ship*) заходи́ть* (зайти́* *perf*) в +*prp*; (: *train*) остана́вливаться (останови́ться* *perf*) в +*prp*

▶ **call back** *vi* (*return*) заходи́ть* (зайти́* *perf*) опя́ть; (*TEL*) перезва́нивать (перезвони́ть *perf*) ◆ *vt* (*TEL*) перезва́нивать (перезвони́ть *perf*) +*dat*

▶ **call for** *vt fus* (*demand*) призыва́ть (призва́ть* *perf*) к +*dat*; (*fetch*) заходи́ть (зайти́* *perf*) за +*instr*

▶ **call in** *vt* (*doctor*) вызыва́ть (вы́звать* *perf*) ◆ *vi* (*visit*) заходи́ть* (зайти́* *perf*); **to ~ sth in**

(*books, stock*) отзыва́ть (отозва́ть* *perf*)

▶ **call off** *vt* отменя́ть (отмени́ть* *perf*); **the strike was ~ed off** забасто́вка была́ отменена́

▶ **call on** *vt fus* (*visit*) заходи́ть* (зайти́* *perf*) к +*dat*; (*appeal to*) призыва́ть (призва́ть* *perf*) к +*dat*; (*request*): **to ~ on sb to do** призыва́ть (призва́ть* *perf*) кого́-н +*infin*

▶ **call out** *vi* крича́ть (кри́кнуть *perf*) ◆ *vt* (*doctor, police*) вызыва́ть (вы́звать* *perf*)

▶ **call up** *vt* (*MIL*) призыва́ть (призва́ть* *perf*) (в а́рмию); (*TEL*) звони́ть (позвони́ть *perf*) +*dat*.

Callanetics® [kæləˈnɛtɪks] *n* каллане́тика (*вид оздорови́тельной гимна́стики*).

call box *n* (*BRIT*) телефо́нная бу́дка.

caller [ˈkɔːləʳ] *n* (*visitor*) посети́тель(ница) *m(f)*; (*TEL*) звоня́щий(-ая) *m(f) adj*; **hold the line, ~!** не кла́дите тру́бку!

call girl *n* проститу́тка* (*кото́рую вызыва́ют по телефо́ну*).

call-in [ˈkɔːlɪn] *n* (*US*) програ́мма, приглаша́ющая звонки́ (*от телезри́телей и́ли радиослу́шателей*).

calling [ˈkɔːlɪŋ] *n* призва́ние.

calling card *n* (*US*) визи́тная ка́рточка*.

callipers [ˈkælɪpəz] (*US* **calipers**) *npl* (*MATH*) штангенци́ркуль *msg*.

callous [ˈkæləs] *adj* (*heartless*) безду́шный (безду́шен).

callousness [ˈkæləsnɪs] *n* безду́шие.

callow [ˈkæləu] *adj*: **~ youth** птене́ц*.

calm [kɑːm] *adj* споко́йный (споко́ен); (*place*) ти́хий*; (*weather*) безве́тренный ◆ *n* тишина́, поко́й; (*at sea*) штиль *m* ◆ *vt* успока́ивать (успоко́ить* *perf*)

▶ **calm down** *vt* (*person, animal*) успока́ивать (успоко́ить *perf*) ◆ *vi* (*person*) успока́иваться (успоко́иться *perf*).

calmly [ˈkɑːmlɪ] *adv* споко́йно.

calmness [ˈkɑːmnɪs] *n* споко́йствие.

Calor gas® [ˈkæləʳ-] *n* фи́рменная ма́рка балло́ного га́за.

calorie [ˈkælərɪ] *n* кало́рия; **low-~ product** низкокалори́йный проду́кт.

calve [kɑːv] *vi* (*cow*) тели́ться (отели́ться* *perf*); (*elephant, seal*) рожда́ть (роди́ть* *perf*) детёныша.

calves [kɑːvz] *npl of* **calf**.

CAM *n abbr* (= *computer-aided manufacturing*) автоматизи́рованное произво́дство.

camber [ˈkæmbəʳ] *n* попере́чный укло́н.

Cambodia [kæmˈbəudɪə] *n* Камбо́джа.

Cambodian [kæmˈbəudɪən] *adj* камбоджи́йский* ◆ *n* камбоджи́ец(-и́йка).

Cambridge [ˈkeɪmbrɪdʒ] *n* Ке́мбридж.

Cambs *abbr* (*BRIT: POST*) = *Cambridgeshire*.

camcorder [ˈkæmkɔːdəʳ] *n* видеока́мера.

came [keɪm] *pt of* **come**.

---

* marks translations which have irregular inflections. The Russian-English side of the dictionary gives inflectional information.

camel ['kæməl] *n* верблю́д.
cameo ['kæmɪəu] *n* (*jewellery*) каме́я; (*THEAT, LITERATURE*) миниатю́ра.
camera ['kæmərə] *n* (*PHOT*) фотоаппара́т; (*also:* cine ~, **movie** ~) кинока́мера; (*TV*) телека́мера; **35 mm** ~ кинока́мера для 35-мм плёнки; **in** ~ (*LAW*) при закры́тых дверя́х.
cameraman ['kæmərəmæn] *irreg n* (*CINEMA*) (кино)опера́тор; (*TV*) (теле)опера́тор.
Cameroon [kæmə'ru:n] *n* Камеру́н.
Cameroun [kæmə'ru:n] *n* = **Cameroon**.
camomile ['kæməumaɪl] *n* рома́шка; ~ **tea** рома́шковый чай*.
camouflage ['kæməfla:ʒ] *n* (*MIL*) камуфля́ж, маскиро́вка; (*ZOOL*) защи́тная окра́ска ◆ *vt* (*also MIL*) маскирова́ть (замаскирова́ть *perf*).
camp [kæmp] *n* ла́герь* *m*; (*MIL*) вое́нный городо́к* ◆ *vi* (*set up camp*) разбива́ть (разби́ть* *perf*) ла́герь; (*go camping*) жить* (*impf*) в пала́тках ◆ *adj* (*effeminate*) женоподо́бный.
campaign [kæm'peɪn] *n* кампа́ния ◆ *vi*: **to** ~ (**for/against**) вести́* (*impf*) кампа́нию (за +*acc*/ про́тив +*gen*).
campaigner [kæm'peɪnə'] *n*: ~ (**for/against**) боре́ц* (за +*acc*/про́тив +*gen*).
camp bed *n* (*BRIT*) раскладу́шка*.
camper ['kæmpə'] *n* (*person*) тури́ст(ка) (*живу́щий* в пала́тке*); (*vehicle*) фурго́н (*обору́дованный для похо́дной жи́зни*).
camping ['kæmpɪŋ] *n* ке́мпинг; **to go** ~ отправля́ться (отпра́виться* *perf*) в похо́д.
camping site *n* = **camp site**.
camp site *n* ке́мпинг.
campus ['kæmpəs] *n* университе́тский* *or* студе́нческий* городо́к*.
camshaft ['kæmʃɑ:ft] *n* кулачко́вый вал*.
can¹ [kæn] *n* (*for foodstuffs*) консе́рвная ба́нка; (*for oil, beer*) ба́нка ◆ *vt* консерви́ровать (законсерви́ровать *perf*); **a** ~ **of beer** ба́нка пи́ва; **he had to carry the** ~ (*BRIT: inf*) ему́ пришло́сь за всё отдува́ться.

KEYWORD

can² (*negative* **cannot, can't**, *conditional, pt* **could**)
aux vb **1** (*be able to*) мочь* (смочь* *perf*); **you can do it (if you try)** Вы смо́жете э́то сде́лать(, е́сли Вы постара́етесь); **I'll help you all I can** я помогу́ Вам всем, чем могу́; **I can't go on any longer** я бо́льше не могу́; **I can't see/hear you** я не ви́жу/слы́шу Вас; **she couldn't sleep that night** в ту ночь она́ не могла́ усну́ть
2 (*know how to*) уме́ть (*impf*); **I can swim** я уме́ю пла́вать; **can you speak Russian?** Вы говори́те *or* уме́ете говори́ть по-ру́сски?
3 (*may*) мо́жно; **can I use your phone?** мо́жно от Вас позвони́ть?; **could I have a word with you?** мо́жно с Ва́ми поговори́ть?; **you can smoke if you like** Вы мо́жете кури́ть, е́сли хоти́те; **can I help you with that?** могу́ я Вам

в э́том помо́чь?
4 (*expressing disbelief, puzzlement*): **it can't be true!** не мо́жет быть!; **what CAN he want?** что ему́ ну́жно?
5 (*expressing possibility, suggestion etc*): **he could be in the library** он мо́жет быть в библиоте́ке, возмо́жно, он в библиоте́ке; **she could have been delayed** возмо́жно, её что́-то задержа́ло.

Canada ['kænədə] *n* Кана́да.
Canadian [kə'neɪdɪən] *adj* кана́дский* ◆ *n* кана́дец*(-дка*).
canal [kə'næl] *n* кана́л.
Canaries [kə'nɛərɪz] *npl* = **Canary Islands**.
canary [kə'nɛərɪ] *n* канаре́йка*.
Canary Islands *npl*: **the** ~ ~ Кана́рские острова́ *mpl*.
Canberra ['kænbərə] *n* Канбе́рра.
cancel ['kænsəl] *vt* отменя́ть (отмени́ть* *perf*); (*contract, cheque, visa*) аннули́ровать (*impf/ perf*); (*words, figures*) вычёркивать (вы́черкнуть *perf*); (*stamp*) погаша́ть (погаси́ть* *perf*)
▶ **cancel out** *vt* нейтрализова́ть (*impf/perf*); **they** ~ **each other out** они нейтрализу́ют друг дру́га.
cancellation [kænsə'leɪʃən] *n* отме́на, аннули́рование.
cancer ['kænsə'] *n* (*MED*) рак; (*fig*) бич; **C**~ (*ASTROLOGY*) Рак; **he is C**~ он – Рак.
cancerous ['kænsrəs] *adj* ра́ковый.
cancer patient *n* ра́ковый(-ая) больно́й(-а́я) *m(f) adj*.
cancer research *n* онкологи́ческие иссле́дования *ntpl*.
C and F *abbr* (*BRIT: COMM*) = **CAF**.
candid ['kændɪd] *adj* и́скренний* (и́скренен), чистосерде́чный* (чистосерде́чен).
candidacy ['kændɪdəsɪ] *n* кандидату́ра.
candidate ['kændɪdeɪt] *n* (*for job*) претенде́нт; (*in exam*) экзамену́емый(-ая) *m(f) adj*; (*POL*) кандида́т.
candidature ['kændɪdətʃə'] (*BRIT*) *n* = **candidacy**.
candied ['kændɪd] *adj*: ~ **fruit** цука́ты *mpl*; ~ **apple** (*US*) я́блочный цука́т.
candle ['kændl] *n* свеча́*; (*smaller*) све́чка*.
candleholder ['kændlhəuldə'] *n* = **candlestick**.
candlelight ['kændllaɪt] *n*: **by** ~ при свеча́х.
candlestick ['kændlstɪk] *n* подсве́чник.
candour ['kændə'] (*US* **candor**) *n* и́скренность *f*.
candy ['kændɪ] *n* (*also*: **sugar**-~) караме́ль *f*, ледене́ц*; (*US*) конфе́та.
candyfloss ['kændɪflɒs] *n* (*BRIT*) са́харная ва́та.
candy store *n* (*US*) конди́терская *f adj*.
cane [keɪn] *n* (*BOT*) тростни́к*; (*stick*) ро́зга*; (*for walking*) трость* *f* ◆ *vt* (*BRIT*) нака́зывать (наказа́ть* *perf*) ро́згами.
canine ['keɪnaɪn] *adj* соба́чий*.
canister ['kænɪstə'] *n* (*for tea etc*) жестяна́я ба́нка*; (*pressurized container*) балло́н; (*of chemicals etc*) кани́стра.

cannabis ['kænəbɪs] *n* гашиш; (*also:* ~ **plant**) конопля.

canned [kænd] *adj* (*fruit, vegetables etc*) консервированный; (*inf: music*) в записи; (*BRIT: inf: drink*) баночный; (: *drunk*) наклюкавшийся.

cannibal ['kænɪbəl] *n* (*animal*) каннибал; (*person*) каннибал, людоед.

cannibalism ['kænɪbəlɪzəm] *n* каннибализм, людоедство.

cannon ['kænən] (*pl* ~ *or* ~**s**) *n* (*gun*) пушка*.

cannonball ['kænənbɔ:l] *n* пушечное ядро*.

cannon fodder *n* пушечное мясо.

cannot ['kænɔt] = **can not**; *see* **can**[2].

canny ['kænɪ] *adj* смекалистый (смекалист).

canoe [kə'nu:] *n* (*boat*) челнок*; (*for competition*) каноэ *nt ind*.

canoeing [kə'nu:ɪŋ] *n* гребля на каноэ.

canon ['kænən] *n* (*clergyman*) каноник; (*rule*) канон; (*standard*) критерий.

canonize ['kænənaɪz] *vt* канонизировать (*impf/perf*).

can-opener ['kænəupnəʳ] *n* консервный нож* *or* ключ*.

canopy ['kænəpɪ] *n* (*above bed etc*) балдахин, полог; (*of leaves etc*) свод.

cant [kænt] *n* ханжество.

can't [kænt] = **can not**; *see* **can**[2].

Cantab. *abbr* (*BRIT: in degree titles*) = *Cantabrigiensis*.

cantankerous [kæn'tæŋkərəs] *adj* сварливый (сварлив), придирчивый (придирчив).

canteen [kæn'ti:n] *n* столовая *f adj*; (*mobile*) походная кухня*; (*BRIT*): ~ **of cutlery** *походный ящик со столовыми принадлежностями*.

canter ['kæntəʳ] *vi* ездить*/ехать* (*impf*) лёгким галопом ♦ *n* лёгкий* галоп.

cantilever ['kæntɪli:vəʳ] *n* консоль *f*, кронштейн; ~ **bridge** консольный мост*.

canvas ['kænvəs] *n* (*fabric, also ART*) холст*; (*for tents*) брезент; (*NAUT*) парусина ♦ *adj* (*shoes, bag*) парусиновый; **under** ~ (*camping*) в палатках.

canvass ['kænvəs] *vi*: **to** ~ **for** агитировать (*impf/perf*) за +*acc* ♦ *vt* (*opinions*) собирать (*impf*).

canvasser ['kænvəsəʳ] *n* агитатор.

canvassing ['kænvəsɪŋ] *n* предвыборная агитация.

canyon ['kænjən] *n* каньон.

CAP *n abbr* (= *Common Agricultural Policy*) общая сельскохозяйственная политика (*в странах Общего рынка*).

cap [kæp] *n* (*hat*) кепка*; (*of uniform*) фуражка*; (*of pen*) колпачок*; (*of bottle*) крышка*; (*also:* **Dutch** ~: *contraceptive*) колпачок*; (*for toy gun*) пистон; (*FOOTBALL*) футбольный игрок,

который получает кепку как знак отличия ♦ *vt* (*outdo*) превосходить* (превзойти* *perf*); (*SPORT*): **he was ~ped ten times** он играл в сборной команде страны десять раз; **swimming** ~ купальная шапочка; **to be ~ped with** увенчаться (увенчаться *perf*) +*instr*; **and to** ~ **it all, he ...** в довершение ко всему, он ....

capability [keɪpə'bɪlɪtɪ] *n* (*competence*) способность *f*; (*MIL*) потенциал.

capable ['keɪpəbl] *adj* (*person*) способный* (способен); ~ **of sth/doing** (*person, object*) способен к чему-н/+*infin*.

capacious [kə'peɪʃəs] *adj* вместительный* (вместителен).

capacity [kə'pæsɪtɪ] *n* (*of container*) ёмкость *f*; (*of ship, theatre etc*) вместительность *f*; (*of lift*) подъёмная способность *f*; (*of person: capability*) способность; (: *role*) роль* *f*; (*of factory*) производственная мощность *f*; **filled to** ~ заполнен до предела; **in his** ~ **as** в роли +*gen*; **in an advisory** ~ в роли советника; **this work is beyond my** ~ эта работа вне моей компетенции; **to work at full** ~ работать (*impf*) на полную мощность.

cape [keɪp] *n* (*GEO*) мыс*; (*cloak*) плащ.

Cape of Good Hope *n*: **the** ~ ~ ~ ~ Мыс Доброй Надежды.

caper ['keɪpəʳ] *n* (*CULIN: usu pl*) каперсы *mpl*; (*prank*) розыгрыш.

Cape Town *n* Кейптаун.

capita ['kæpɪtə] *see* **per capita**.

capital ['kæpɪtl] *n* (*also:* ~ **city**) столица; (*money*) капитал; (*also:* ~ **letter**) заглавная буква.

capital account *n* баланс движения капитала.

capital allowance *n* налоговая скидка, связанная с инвестициями в основной капитал.

capital assets *npl* основной капитал *msg*, основные фонды *mpl*.

capital employed *n* применяемый капитал.

capital expenditure *n* капиталовложение.

capital gains tax *n* налог на реализованный прирост капитала.

capital goods *npl* капитальные товары *mpl*, средства *ntpl* производства.

capital-intensive ['kæpɪtlɪn'tɛnsɪv] *adj* капиталоёмкий.

capital investment *n* капиталовложение.

capitalism ['kæpɪtəlɪzəm] *n* капитализм.

capitalist ['kæpɪtəlɪst] *adj* капиталистический* ♦ *n* капиталист.

capitalize ['kæpɪtəlaɪz] *vt* (*COMM*) капитализировать (*impf/perf*) ♦ *vi*: **to** ~ **on** извлекать (извлечь* *perf*) выгоду из +*gen*.

capital punishment *n* смертная казнь *f*.

---

capital transfer tax *n* (*BRIT*) нало́г на перево́д капита́ла.
Capitol ['kæpɪtl] *n*: **the ~** Капито́лий.
capitulate [kə'pɪtjuleɪt] *vi*: **to ~ (to)** капитули́ровать (*impf*/*perf*) (пе́ред +*instr*).
capitulation [kəpɪtju'leɪʃən] *n* капитуля́ция.
capricious [kə'prɪʃəs] *adj* (*person*) капри́зный* (капри́зен), прихотли́вый (прихотли́в).
Capricorn ['kæprɪkɔːn] *n* (*ASTROLOGY*) Козеро́г; **he is ~** он – Козеро́г.
caps [kæps] *abbr* = **capital letters**.
capsize [kæp'saɪz] *vt* опроки́дывать (опроки́нуть *perf*) ◆ *vi* опроки́дываться (опроки́нуться *perf*).
capstan ['kæpstən] *n* (*NAUT*) кабеста́н.
capsule ['kæpsjuːl] *n* ка́псула.
Capt. *abbr* (*MIL*) = **captain**.
captain ['kæptɪn] *n* (*of ship, plane*) команди́р; (*of team, army*) капита́н ◆ *vt* (*ship*) кома́ндовать (*impf*); (*team*) явля́ться (*impf*) капита́ном +*gen*.
caption ['kæpʃən] *n* по́дпись *f*.
captivate ['kæptɪveɪt] *vt* пленя́ть (плени́ть *perf*).
captive ['kæptɪv] *adj* пле́нный ◆ *n* пле́нник(-ица).
captivity [kæp'tɪvɪtɪ] *n* плен*; **in ~** (*animal*) в нево́ле; (*person*) в плену́.
captor ['kæptəʳ] *n* (*unlawful*) похити́тель(ница) *m(f)*; (*lawful*) взя́вший(-ая) *m(f)* adj в плен; **his ~s** взя́вшие его́ в плен.
capture ['kæptʃəʳ] *vt* (*animal*) лови́ть* (пойма́ть *perf*); (*person, city, also COMM*) захва́тывать (захвати́ть* *perf*); (*attention*) прико́вывать (прикова́ть *perf*) ◆ *n* (*of person, town etc*) захва́т; (*of animal*) пой́мка*; (*COMPUT*): **data ~** сбор информа́ции; **to ~ the screen** (*COMPUT*) хвата́ть (хвати́ть* *perf*) *or* фикси́ровать (зафикси́ровать *perf*) изображе́ние с экра́н.
car [kɑːʳ] *n* автомоби́ль *m*, маши́на; (*RAIL*) ваго́н; **by ~** на автомоби́ле *or* маши́не; **dining ~** (*BRIT*) ваго́н-рестора́н.
Caracas [kə'rækəs] *n* Карака́с.
carafe [kə'ræf] *n* графи́н.
caramel ['kærəməl] *n* (*sweet*) караме́ль *f*; (*burnt sugar*) жжёный са́хар*.
carat ['kærət] *n* (*of diamond, gold*) кара́т; **24 ~ gold** чи́стое зо́лото.
caravan ['kærəvæn] *n* (*BRIT*) жило́й-автоприце́п; (*in desert*) карава́н.
caravan site *n* (*BRIT*) *площа́дка для стоя́нки жилы́х-автоприце́пов.*
caraway ['kærəweɪ] *n*: **~ seeds** тмин *msg*.
carbohydrate [kɑːbəu'haɪdreɪt] *n* углево́д.
carbolic acid [kɑː'bɔlɪk-] *n* карбо́ловая кислота́.
car bomb *n* бо́мба, подло́женная в *or* под маши́ну.
carbon ['kɑːbən] *n* углеро́д.
carbonated ['kɑːbəneɪtɪd] *adj* газиро́ванный.

carbon copy *n* ко́пия (*сде́ланная под копи́рку*).
carbon dioxide *n* двуо́кись *f* углеро́да.
carbon monoxide [mɔ'nɔksaɪd] *n* моноксѝд углеро́да.
carbon paper *n* копирова́льная бума́га, копи́рка.
carbon ribbon *n* ле́нта (*для пи́шущей маши́нки или при́нтера*).
car boot sale *n* барахо́лка, на кото́рой това́р разло́жен на капо́тах маши́н.
carburettor [kɑːbju'rɛtəʳ] (*US* **carburetor**) *n* карбюра́тор.
carcass ['kɑːkəs] *n* ту́ша.
carcinogenic [kɑːsɪnə'dʒɛnɪk] *adj* канцероге́нный.
card [kɑːd] *n* (*material*) карто́н; (*also*: **record ~**) ка́рточка*; (*also*: **membership ~**) чле́нский* биле́т; (*also*: **playing ~**) (игра́льная) ка́рта; (*also*: **greetings ~**) откры́тка; (*also*: **visiting ~**, **business ~**) визи́тная ка́рточка*; **to play ~s** игра́ть (*impf*) в ка́рты.
cardamom ['kɑːdəməm] *n* кардамо́н.
cardboard ['kɑːdbɔːd] *n* карто́н.
cardboard box *n* карто́нная коро́бка*.
cardboard city (*inf*) *n* райо́н го́рода, за́нятый бездо́мными, живу́щими в карто́нных я́щиках.*
card-carrying ['kɑːd'kærɪŋ] *adj*: **~ member** *полнопра́вный член полити́ческой организа́ции.*
card game *n* игра́* в ка́рты.
cardiac ['kɑːdɪæk] *adj* серде́чный; (*unit*) кардиологи́ческий*.
Cardiff ['kɑːdɪf] *n* Ка́рдифф.
cardigan ['kɑːdɪɡən] *n* жаке́т (*вя́заный*).
cardinal ['kɑːdɪnl] *adj* (*also*: **~ number**) коли́чественное числи́тельное *nt adj*; (*sin*) сме́ртный; (*principle, importance*) кардина́льный ◆ *n* кардина́л.
card index *n* картоте́ка.
cardsharp ['kɑːdʃɑːp] *n* шу́лер*.
card vote *n* (*BRIT*) манда́тное голосова́ние.
CARE [kɛəʳ] *n abbr* = *Cooperative for American Relief Everywhere.*
care [kɛəʳ] *n* (*worry*) забо́та; (*of the ill*) ухо́д; (*attention*) внима́ние ◆ *vi*: **to ~ about** (*person, animal*) забо́титься* (позабо́титься* *perf*) о +*prp*; **in sb's ~** на чьём-н попече́нии; **the child has been taken into ~** ребёнок был взят в де́тский дом; **"handle with ~"** "не кантова́ть"; **to take ~ (to do)** позабо́титься (*perf*) (+*infin*); **to take ~ of** (*patient, child etc*) забо́титься* (позабо́титься* *perf*) о +*prp*; (*problem, situation*) занима́ться (заня́ться* *perf*) +*instr*; **~ of** для переда́чи +*dat*; **he ~s about environmental issues** его́ волну́ют пробле́мы защи́ты окружа́ющей среды́; **would you ~ to/for ...?** не хоти́те ли +*infin*/+*acc*; **I wouldn't ~ to repeat the experience** мне бы не хоте́лось испыта́ть э́то сно́ва; **I**

don't ~ мне всё равно; **I couldn't ~ less** мне наплева́ть
► **care for** *vt fus* (*look after*) забо́титься* (позабо́титься* *perf*) о +*prp*; (*like*): **he ~s for her** он неравноду́шен к ней.
career [kə'rɪə*] *n* карье́ра ♦ *vi* мча́ться* (помча́ться* *perf*); **my school ~** (*life*) мои́ шко́льные го́ды.
career girl *n* = **career woman**.
careers officer [kə'rɪəz-] *n* консульта́нт по профессиона́льной ориента́ции.
career woman *irreg n* делова́я же́нщина.
carefree ['kɛəfri:] *adj* беззабо́тный* (беззабо́тен).
careful ['kɛəful] *adj* (*cautious*) осторо́жный* (осторо́жен); (*thorough*) тща́тельный* (тща́телен); **(be) ~!** осторо́жно!, береги́сь!; **he is/was ~ with his money** он эконо́мен/был эконо́мен.
carefully ['kɛəfəlɪ] *adv* (*see adj*) осторо́жно; тща́тельно.
careless ['kɛəlɪs] *adj* (*negligent*) невнима́тельный* (невнима́телен); (*casual: remark*) небре́жный* (небре́жен); (*untroubled*) беззабо́тный* (беззабо́тен).
carelessly ['kɛəlɪslɪ] *adv* (*see adj*) невнима́тельно; небре́жно; беззабо́тно.
carelessness ['kɛəlɪsnɪs] *n* (*negligence*) невнима́тельность *f*; (*casualness*) небре́жность *f*; (*lack of concern*) беззабо́тность *f*.
carer ['kɛərə*] *n* челове́к, уха́живающий за больны́ми, престаре́лыми и т.п.
caress [kə'rɛs] *n* ла́ска* ♦ *vt* ласка́ть (*impf*).
caretaker ['kɛəteɪkə*] *n* (*of building*) завхо́з.
caretaker government *n* (*BRIT*) вре́менное прави́тельство.
car ferry *n* автомоби́льный паро́м.
cargo ['ka:gəu] (*pl* **~es**) *n* груз.
cargo boat *n* грузово́е су́дно*.
cargo plane *n* грузово́й самолёт.
car hire *n* (*BRIT*) прока́т автомоби́лей.
Caribbean [kærɪ'bi:ən] *adj* кари́бский ♦ *n*: **the ~ (Sea)** Кари́бское мо́ре*.
caricature ['kærɪkətjuə*] *n* карикату́ра; **~ of the truth** карикату́ра на пра́вду.
caring ['kɛərɪŋ] *adj* забо́тливый (забо́тлив).
carjack ['ka:dʒæk] *n* домкра́т.
carnage ['ka:nɪdʒ] *n* резня́.
carnal ['ka:nl] *adj* пло́тский*.
carnation [ka:'neɪʃən] *n* гвозди́ка.
carnival ['ka:nɪvl] *n* карнава́л; (*US: funfair*) аттракцио́нный городо́к*.
carnivorous [ka:'nɪvərəs] *adj* (*animal*) плотоя́дный*; (*plant*) насекомоя́дный.
carol ['kærəl] *n* (*also*: **Christmas ~**) Рожде́ственский* гимн.
carouse [kə'rauz] *vi* бра́жничать (*impf*).

carousel [kærə'sɛl] *n* (*US*) карусе́ль *f*.
carp [ka:p] *n* карп
► **carp at** *vt fus* придира́ться (придра́ться* *perf*) к +*dat*.
car park *n* (*BRIT*) автостоя́нка*.
Carpathian Mountains [ka:'peɪθɪən-] *npl* Карпа́ты *pl*.
carpenter ['ka:pɪntə*] *n* пло́тник.
carpentry ['ka:pɪntrɪ] *n* пло́тницкое де́ло.
carpet ['ka:pɪt] *n* (*also fig*) ковёр*; (*of snow*) покро́в ♦ *vt* (*room*) устила́ть (устла́ть* *perf*) ковра́ми; **fitted ~** (*BRIT*) ковро́вое покры́тие.
carpet bombing *n* ковро́вый налёт.
carpet slippers *npl* шлёпанцы *mpl*.
carpet sweeper [-'swi:pə*] *n* щётка для ковра́.
car phone *n* ра́дио-телефо́н (*в маши́не*).
carport ['ka:pɔ:t] *n* навес для маши́ны.
car rental *n* прока́т автомоби́лей.
carriage ['kærɪdʒ] *n* (*BRIT: RAIL*) (пассажи́рский*) ваго́н; (*horse-drawn*) экипа́ж; (*of goods*) перево́зка; (*of typewriter*) каре́тка*; (*transport costs*) сто́имость *f* перево́зки; **~ forward** сто́имость перево́зки подлежи́т опла́те получа́телем; **~ free** перево́зка осуществля́ется беспла́тно; **~ inwards** су́мма, опла́чиваемая покупа́телем за доста́вку полу́ченного гру́за; **~ outwards** су́мма, предста́вленная продавцо́м к опла́те на покры́тие расхо́дов по доста́вке; **~ paid** за перево́зку упла́чено.
carriage return *n* перево́д каре́тки.
carriageway ['kærɪdʒweɪ] *n* (*BRIT*) прое́зжая часть* *f* доро́ги.
carrier ['kærɪə*] *n* (*transporter*) транспорти́ровщик; (*MED*) носи́тель *m*.
carrier bag *n* (*BRIT*) паке́тик (*для поку́пок*).
carrier pigeon *n* почто́вый го́лубь* *m*.
carrion ['kærɪən] *n* па́даль *f*.
carrot ['kærət] *n* морко́вь *f*; (*fig*): **~ and stick policy** поли́тика кнута́ и пря́ника.
carry ['kærɪ] *vt* (*take*) носи́ть*/нести́* (*impf*); (*transport*) вози́ть*/везти́* (*impf*); (*a motion, bill*) проводи́ть* (провести́* *perf*); (*involve*) влечь* (повле́чь* *perf*); (*MED*) переноси́ть* (*impf*); (*have: picture, slogan*) содержа́ть* (*impf*) ♦ *vi* (*sound*) передава́ться* (*impf*); **he carries the virus** он носи́тель ви́руса; **this loan carries 10% interest per annum** э́тот заём предоставля́ется под 10% годовы́х; **to get carried away (by)** (*fig*) увлека́ться (увле́чься* *perf*) (+*instr*)
► **carry forward** *vt* (*also COMM*) переноси́ть* (перенести́* *perf*) на другу́ю страни́цу
► **carry on** *vi* продолжа́ться (продо́лжиться *perf*); (*inf: make a fuss*) заводи́ться* (завести́сь* *perf*) ♦ *vt* продолжа́ть (продо́лжить *perf*); **to ~ on with sth/doing** продолжа́ть (продо́лжить *perf*) что-н/+*impf*

---

* marks translations which have irregular inflections. The Russian-English side of the dictionary gives inflectional information.

infin

▶ **carry out** *vt* (*orders*) выполня́ть (вы́полнить *perf*), исполня́ть (испо́лнить *perf*); (*investigation*) проводи́ть* (провести́* *perf*); (*threat*) осу⁻ ъществля́ть (осуществи́ть* *perf*).

carrycot ['kærɪkɔt] *n* (*BRIT*) переносна́я колыбе́ль *f*.

carry-on ['kærɪˈɔn] *n* (*inf*: *fuss*) сумато́ха, суета́; (: *annoying behaviour*) капри́зы *mpl*; **I've had enough of your ~**! надое́ли мне твои́ капри́зы!; **what a ~**! кака́я сумато́ха *or* суета́!

cart [kɑːt] *n* теле́га, пово́зка; (*handcart*) теле́жка* ◆ *vt* (*inf*: *people, objects*) таска́ть/ тащи́ть* (*impf*).

carte blanche ['kɑːt'blɔnʃ] *n*: **to give sb ~ ~** предоставля́ть (предоста́вить* *perf*) кому́-н по́лную свобо́ду де́йствий.

cartel [kɑːˈtɛl] *n* карте́ль *m*.

cartilage ['kɑːtɪlɪdʒ] *n* хрящ*.

cartographer [kɑːˈtɔɡrəfəʳ] *n* карто́граф.

cartography [kɑːˈtɔɡrəfɪ] *n* картогра́фия.

carton ['kɑːtən] *n* (*large box*) карто́нная коро́бка*; (*container*) паке́т.

cartoon [kɑːˈtuːn] *n* (*drawing*) карикату́ра; (*BRIT*: *comic strip*) ко́микс; (*TV*) мультфи́льм= *мультипликацио́нный фильм*.

cartoonist [kɑːˈtuːnɪst] *n* карикатури́ст(ка).

cartridge ['kɑːtrɪdʒ] *n* (*for gun*) ги́льза; (*for camera*) кассе́та с фотоплёнкой; (*music tape*) кассе́та; (*of record-player*) голо́вка*; (*of pen*) (черни́льный) балло́нчик; (*of printer*) ка́ртридж.

cartwheel ['kɑːtwiːl] *n* колесо́* теле́ги; **to turn a ~** де́лать (сде́лать *perf*) колесо́.

carve [kɑːv] *vt* (*meat*) нареза́ть (наре́зать* *perf*); (*initials, design*) выреза́ть (вы́резать* *perf*); (*wood, stone*) выреза́ть (*impf*).

▶ **carve up** *vt* (*land, property*) раздробля́ть (раздроби́ть* *perf*); (*meat*) разреза́ть (разре́зать* *perf*).

carving ['kɑːvɪŋ] *n* (*object*) резно́е изде́лие; (*design*) резьба́; (*art*) иску́сство резьбы́.

carving knife *n* разде́лочный нож*.

car wash *n* мо́йка автомоби́лей.

Casablanca [kæsəˈblæŋkə] *n* Касабла́нка.

cascade [kæsˈkeɪd] *n* (*waterfall*) каска́д ◆ *vi* (*water*) низверга́ться (*impf*); (*hair*) ниспада́ть (*impf*).

case [keɪs] *n* (*instance, problem*) слу́чай; (*MED*: *patient*) больно́й(-а́я) *m(f) adj*; (*LAW*) (суде́бное) де́ло*; (*criminal investigation*) рассле́дование; (*for spectacles etc*) футля́р; (*BRIT*: *also*: **suitcase**) чемода́н; (*of wine etc*) я́щик (*содержа́щий* 12 буты́лок); (*TYP*): **lower/upper ~** ни́жный/ве́рхний* реги́стр; **to have a good ~** име́ть (*impf*) убеди́тельные до́воды; **there's a strong ~ for reform** есть все основа́ния для проведе́ния рефо́рмы; **in ~** (**of**) (*fire, emergency*) в слу́чае (+*gen*); **in ~ he**

comes в слу́чае, е́сли он придёт; **in any ~** во вся́ком слу́чае; **just in ~** на вся́кий* слу́чай.

case history *n* (*MED*) исто́рия боле́зни.

case study *n* изуче́ние конкре́тного слу́чая.

cash [kæʃ] *n* нали́чные *pl adj* (де́ньги) ◆ *vt*: **to ~ a cheque** обме́нивать (обменя́ть *perf*) чек на де́ньги; **to pay (in) ~** плати́ть* (заплати́ть* *perf*) нали́чными; **~ on delivery** нало́женный платёж; **~ with order** опла́та при соверше́нии зака́за.

▶ **cash in** *vt* получа́ть (получи́ть* *perf*) де́ньги по +*dat*

▶ **cash in on** *vt fus* испо́льзовать (*impf*) в свои́х интере́сах.

cash account *n* нали́чный счёт*.

cash-and-carry [kæʃənˈkærɪ] *n* мелкоопто́вый магази́н.

cash-book ['kæʃbuk] *n* ка́ссовая кни́га.

cash box *n* коро́бка для хране́ния ка́ссы.

cash card *n* (*BRIT*) ка́рточка для получе́ния нали́чных из автома́та.

cash cow *n* (*enterprise*) хле́бное де́ло*; (*product*) золото́е де́ло.

cash crop *n* това́рная культу́ра.

cash desk *n* (*BRIT*) ка́сса.

cash discount *n* ски́дка с цены́ това́ра в слу́чае упла́ты нали́чными.

cash dispenser *n* (*BRIT*) автома́т для вы́дачи нали́чных с ба́нковского счёта.

cashew [kæˈʃuː] *n* (*also*: **~ nut**) оре́х ке́шью *m ind*.

cash flow *n* движе́ние де́нежной нали́чности.

cashier [kæˈʃɪəʳ] *n* касси́р.

cashmere ['kæʃmɪəʳ] *n* (*wool, jersey*) кашеми́р.

cash point *n* автома́т для вы́дачи нали́чных с ба́нковского счёта.

cash price *n* цена́ това́ра при прода́же за нали́чные.

cash register *n* ка́ссовый аппара́т.

cash reserves *npl* ка́ссовый резе́рв *msg*.

cash sale *n* прода́жа за нали́чные *pl adj*.

casing ['keɪsɪŋ] *n* оболо́чка*, футля́р.

casino [kəˈsiːnəu] *n* казино́ *nt ind*.

cask [kɑːsk] *n* бочо́нок*.

casket ['kɑːskɪt] *n* шкату́лка; (*US*: *coffin*) гроб*.

Caspian Sea ['kæspɪən-] *n* (*GEO*): **the ~ ~** Каспи́йское мо́ре*.

casserole ['kæsərəul] *n* рагу́ *nt ind*; (*also*: **~ dish**) ла́тка*.

cassette [kæˈsɛt] *n* кассе́та.

cassette deck *n* кассе́тный магнитофо́н (*стациона́рный*).

cassette player *n* кассе́тный пле́йер.

cassette recorder *n* кассе́тный магнитофо́н (*портати́вный*).

cast [kɑːst] (*pt, pp* **cast**) *vt* (*light, shadow, glance*) броса́ть (бро́сить* *perf*); (*net, fishing line*) забра́сывать (забро́сить* *perf*); (*doubts*) се́ять (посе́ять *perf*); (*spell*) околдо́вывать (околдова́ть *perf*); (*skin*) сбра́сывать (сбро́сить* *perf*); (*statue*) отлива́ть (отли́ть*

perf) ♦ *vi (FISHING)* забра́сывать (забро́сить*
perf) се́ти ♦ *n (THEAT)* соста́в (исполни́телей);
(mould) фо́рма *(для отли́вки)*; *(also: plaster
~)* ги́псовый слепо́к*; **to ~ one's vote (for sb)**
отдава́ть* (отда́ть* *perf)* свой го́лос (за
кого́-н); **to ~ sb as Hamlet** *(THEAT)* назнача́ть
(назна́чить *perf)* кого́-н на роль Га́млета;
the ~ was full of celebrities в спекта́кле
игра́ло мно́го знамени́тостей
▶ **cast aside** *vt* отверга́ть (отве́ргнуть *perf)*
▶ **cast off** *vi (NAUT)* отча́ливать (отча́лить
perf); *(KNITTING)* сбра́сывать (сбро́сить* *perf)*
пе́тлю ♦ *vt (KNITTING)* сбра́сывать (сбро́сить*
perf) (*пе́тлю*)
▶ **cast on** *vi (KNITTING)* набира́ть (набра́ть*
perf) пе́тли ♦ *vt* набира́ть (набра́ть* *perf)*
(*пе́тли*).
castaway ['kɑ:stəweɪ] *n попа́вший по́сле
кораблекруше́ния на необита́емый о́стров.*
caste [kɑ:st] *n* ка́ста; **the ~ system** ка́стовая
систе́ма.
caster sugar ['kɑ:stə-] *n (BRIT)* са́харная пу́дра.
casting vote ['kɑ:stɪŋ-] *n (BRIT)* реша́ющий*
го́лос *(при ра́вном числе́ голосо́в "за" и
"про́тив")*.
cast iron *n* чугу́н* ♦ *adj:* ~~ *(fig)* желе́зный.
castle ['kɑ:sl] *n* за́мок*; *(fortified)* кре́пость *f*;
(CHESS) ладья́*, тура́.
cast-offs ['kɑ:stɔfs] *npl* обно́ски *mpl.*
castor ['kɑ:stə'] *n (wheel)* ро́лик.
castor oil *n* касто́ровое ма́сло.
castrate [kæs'treɪt] *vt* кастри́ровать *(impf/perf).*
casual ['kæʒjul] *adj (meeting)* случа́йный*
(случа́ен); *(attitude)* небре́жный* (небре́жен);
(clothes) повседне́вный; **to do ~ work** де́лать
(impf) случа́йную рабо́ту; **~ wear**
повседне́вная оде́жда.
casual labour *n* вре́менные рабо́тники *mpl.*
casually ['kæʒjulɪ] *adv (behave)* небре́жно;
(dress) повседне́вно; *(by chance)* случа́йно;
he was ~ dressed он был оде́т в повсе-
дне́вную оде́жду.
casualty ['kæʒjultɪ] *n (sb injured)*
пострада́вший(-ая) *m(f) adj; (sb killed, victim)*
же́ртва; *(MED: department)* травмотоло́гия;
heavy casualties тяжёлые поте́ри *fpl.*
casualty ward *n (BRIT)* травмотологи́ческое
отделе́ние.
cat [kæt] *n (pet)* ко́шка*; *(tomcat)* кот; **big ~s**
коша́чьи *pl adj.*
catacombs ['kætəku:mz] *npl* катако́мбы *fpl.*
catalogue ['kætəlɔg] *(US catalog) n* катало́г; *(of
events, faults)* пе́речень *m* ♦ *vt (books,
collection)* каталогизи́ровать *(impf/perf);
(events)* перечисля́ть (перечи́слить *perf).*
catalyst ['kætəlɪst] *n (CHEM, fig)* катализа́тор.
catalytic converter [kætə'lɪtɪk kən'vɜ:tə'] *n
(AUT)* каталити́ческий нейтрализа́тор.

catapult ['kætəpʌlt] *n (BRIT)* рога́тка*; *(MIL)*
катапу́льта ♦ *vi* катапульти́роваться *(impf/
perf)* ♦ *vt* катапульти́ровать *(impf/perf).*
cataract ['kætərækt] *n* катара́кта.
catarrh [kə'tɑ:'] *n* ката́р.
catastrophe [kə'tæstrəfɪ] *n* катастро́фа.
catastrophic [kætə'strɔfɪk] *adj*
катастрофи́ческий*.
catcall ['kætkɔ:l] *n* осви́стывание.
catch [kætʃ] *(pt, pp* **caught**) *vt* лови́ть* (пойма́ть
perf); *(bus etc)* сади́ться (сесть* *perf)* на +*acc*;
(breath) зата́ивать (затаи́ть *perf)*; *(attention)*
привлека́ть (привле́чь* *perf)*; *(hit)* ударя́ть
(уда́рить *perf)*; *(hear)* ула́вливать (улови́ть*
perf); *(illness)* подхва́тывать (подхвати́ть*
perf); *(person)* застава́ть* (заста́ть* *perf)* ♦ *vi
(become trapped)* застрева́ть (застря́ть *perf)*
♦ *n (of fish)* уло́в; *(criminal caught)*
заде́ржанный(-ая) *m(f) adj; (of ball)* захва́т;
(hidden problem) подво́х; *(of lock)* защёлка;
(game) пятна́шки *pl;* **to ~ sb's attention** *or* **eye**
привлека́ть (привле́чь* *perf)* чьё-н внима́ние;
to ~ sight of уви́деть* (*perf)*; **to ~ fire**
загоре́ться *(perf)*
▶ **catch on** *vi (grow popular)* прижива́ться
(прижи́ться* *perf)*; *(understand):* **to ~ on (to
sth)** понима́ть (поня́ть* *perf)* (что-н)
▶ **catch out** *vt (BRIT: fig)* лови́ть* (пойма́ть *perf)*
▶ **catch up** *vi (fig)* нагоня́ть (нагна́ть* *perf)* ♦ *vt
(also: ~ up with)* догоня́ть (догна́ть* *perf).*
catching ['kætʃɪŋ] *adj (fig)* зарази́тельный*;
(MED) зара́зный*.
catchment area ['kætʃmənt-] *n (BRIT: of school
etc)* микрорайо́н; *(GEO)* бассе́йн.
catch phrase *n* мо́дное выраже́ние.
catch-22 ['kætʃtwɛntɪ'tu:] *n:* **it's a ~ situation**
э́то безвы́ходная ситуа́ция.
catchy ['kætʃɪ] *adj* легко́ запомина́ющийся.
catechism ['kætɪkɪzəm] *n* катехи́зис.
categoric(al) [kætɪ'gɔrɪk(l)] *adj*
категори́ческий*.
categorize ['kætɪgəraɪz] *vt (classify)*
классифици́ровать *(impf/perf).*
category ['kætɪgərɪ] *n* катего́рия.
cater ['keɪtə'] *vi (provide food):* **to ~ (for)**
организо́вывать (организова́ть *perf)*
пита́ние *(для +gen)*
▶ **cater for** *vt fus (BRIT: needs, tastes)*
удовлетворя́ть (удовлетвори́ть *perf)*;
(: readers, consumers) обслу́живать
(обслужи́ть* *perf).*
caterer ['keɪtərə'] *n* организа́тор пита́ния.
catering ['keɪtərɪŋ] *n (trade, business)*
обще́ственное пита́ние.
caterpillar ['kætəpɪlə'] *n* гу́сеница ♦ *cpd
(vehicle)* гу́сеничный.
caterpillar track *n* гу́сеница *(TEX)*
cat flap *n* коша́чий* лаз* *(в двери́)*, коша́чья

---

* marks translations which have irregular inflections. The Russian-English side of the dictionary gives inflectional information.

две́рца.
cathedral [kə'θi:drəl] *n* собо́р.
cathode ['kæθəud] *n* като́д.
cathode-ray tube [kæθəud'reɪ-] *n* электроннолучева́я тру́бка*.
Catholic ['kæθəlɪk] *adj* католи́ческий* ♦ *n* като́лик(-и́чка).
catholic *adj* (*tastes, interests*) разносторо́нний*.
CAT scanner *n abbr* (MED: = *computerized axial tomography scanner*) аксиа́льный компью́терный томо́граф.
Catseye® ['kæts'aɪ] *n* (BRIT: AUT) "коша́чий глаз" (*вмонти́рованный в доро́гу отража́тель све́та фар*).
catsup ['kætsəp] *n* (US) ке́тчуп.
cattle ['kætl] *npl* скот* *msg*.
catty ['kætɪ] *adj* ехи́дный*.
catwalk ['kætwɔ:k] *n* (*at fashion show*) помо́ст *or* эстра́да (*для демонстра́ции моде́лей оде́жды*).
Caucasian [kɔ:'keɪzɪən] *adj* кавка́зский ♦ *n* кавка́зец*(-зка).
Caucasus ['kɔ:kəsəs] *n* Кавка́з.
caucus ['kɔ:kəs] *n* (POL: *group*) влия́тельная группиро́вка внутри́ па́ртии; (: US) предвы́борный ми́тинг сторо́нников па́ртии.
caught [kɔ:t] *pt, pp of* **catch**.
cauliflower ['kɔlɪflauə] *n* цветна́я капу́ста.
cause [kɔ:z] *n* (*reason*) причи́на; (*aim*) де́ло* ♦ *vt* явля́ться (яви́ться* *perf*) причи́ной +*gen*; **there is no ~ for concern** нет причи́н для беспоко́йства; **to ~ sb trouble/harm** причиня́ть (причини́ть *perf*) кому́-н неприя́тности/вред; **to ~ sb to do** (*force*) заставля́ть (заста́вить* *perf*) кого́-н +*infin*.
causeway ['kɔ:zweɪ] *n* доро́га (*проло́женная че́рез то́пкое ме́сто*).
caustic ['kɔ:stɪk] *adj* каусти́ческий*; (*fig*) е́дкий*.
cauterize ['kɔ:təraɪz] *vt* прижига́ть (прижечь* *perf*).
caution ['kɔ:ʃən] *n* осторо́жность *f*; (*warning*) предупрежде́ние, предостереже́ние ♦ *vt* предупрежда́ть (предупреди́ть *perf*).
cautious ['kɔ:ʃəs] *adj* осторо́жный* (осторо́жен).
cautiously ['kɔ:ʃəslɪ] *adv* осторо́жно.
cautiousness ['kɔ:ʃəsnɪs] *n* осторо́жность *f*.
cavalier [kævə'lɪə] *adj* надме́нный*, пренебрежи́тельный.
cavalry ['kævəlrɪ] *n* кавале́рия; (*mechanized*) мотопехо́та.
cave [keɪv] *n* пеще́ра ♦ *vi*: **to go caving** занима́ться (*impf*) спелеоло́гией
▶ **cave in** *vi* (*roof etc*) обва́ливаться (обвали́ться *perf*); (*inf: give in*) сдава́ться (сда́ться* *perf*).
caveman ['keɪvmæn] *irreg n* пеще́рный челове́к*.
cavern ['kævən] *n* пеще́ра.

caviar(e) ['kævɪɑ:'] *n* икра́*.
cavity ['kævɪtɪ] *n* по́лость* *f*; (*in tooth*) дупло́*.
cavity wall insulation *n* двойна́я стена́ с изоля́цией.
cavort [kə'vɔ:t] *vi* скака́ть* (*impf*).
cayenne [keɪ'ɛn] *n* (*also:* ~ **pepper**) кра́сный стручко́вый пе́рец.
CB *n abbr* (= *Citizens' Band (Radio)*) диапазо́н часто́т люби́тельской радиосвя́зи; (BRIT: = *Companion of (the Order of) the Bath*) кавале́р о́рдена Ба́ни.
CBC *n abbr* = *Canadian Broadcasting Corporation*.
CBE *n abbr* (BRIT: = *Companion of (the Order of) the British Empire*) кавале́р о́рдена Брита́нской Импе́рии.
CBI *n abbr* (= *Confederation of British Industries*) Конфедера́ция брита́нской промы́шленности.
CBS *n abbr* (US) = *Columbia Broadcasting System*.
CC *abbr* (BRIT: = *county council*) ≈ сове́т гра́фства.
cc *abbr* (= *cubic centimetre*) куби́ческий* сантиме́тр; = **carbon copy**.
CCA *n abbr* (US: = *Circuit Court of Appeals*) Окружно́й апелляцио́нный суд.
CCU *n abbr* (US: = *coronary care unit*) отделе́ние интенси́вной терапи́и для больны́х с о́строй серде́чной недоста́точностью.
CD *n abbr* (= *Corps Diplomatique*) ≈ дипко́рпус= *дипломати́ческий ко́рпус* ♦ *abbr* (MIL: BRIT: = *Civil Defence (Corps)*) гражда́нская оборо́на; (: US: = *Civil Defense*) гражда́нская оборо́на; = **compact disc**; ~ **player** про́игрыватель *m* для компа́кт-ди́сков.
CDC *n abbr* (US) = *Center for Disease Control*.
CD-I *n abbr* (= *compact disc interactive*) компа́ктный диск-интеракти́вный (*устро́йство, позволя́ющее передава́ть содержа́ние компа́ктного ди́ска на телеэкра́н*).
Cdr. *abbr* (MIL) = **commander**.
CD-ROM *abbr* (= *compact disc read-only memory*) па́мять, счи́тывающая информа́цию с компа́кт-ди́ска.
CDT *abbr* (US) = *Central Daylight Time*.
cease [si:s] *vt* прекраща́ть (прекрати́ть* *perf*) ♦ *vi* прекраща́ться (прекрати́ться* *perf*).
cease-fire ['si:sfaɪə'] *n* прекраще́ние огня́.
ceaseless ['si:slɪs] *adj* непреры́вный*.
CED *n abbr* (US) = *Committee for Economic Development*.
cedar ['si:də'] *n* кедр.
cede [si:d] *vt* уступа́ть (уступи́ть* *perf*).
cedilla [sɪ'dɪlə] *n* седи́ль *m* (*орфографи́ческий знак*).
CEEB *n abbr* (US) = *College Entry Examination Board*.
Ceefax ['si:fæks] *n информацио́нная слу́жба*

БиБиСи, *осуществляемая путём вывода на*
экран телевизора информации,
классифицированной по различным
направлениям.
ceilidh ['keɪlɪ] *n вечер с народной музыкой и*
танцами в Шотландии или Ирландии.
ceiling ['si:lɪŋ] *n* (*also fig*) потолок*.
celebrate ['sɛlɪbreɪt] *vt* праздновать
(отпраздновать *perf*) ♦ *vi* веселиться
(повеселиться *perf*); **to ~ mass** отправлять
(*impf*) церковную службу.
celebrated ['sɛlɪbreɪtɪd] *adj* знаменитый
(знаменит).
celebration [sɛlɪ'breɪʃən] *n* (*event*) праздник;
(*of anniversary etc*) празднование.
celebrity [sɪ'lɛbrɪtɪ] *n* знаменитость *f*.
celeriac [sə'lɛrɪæk] *n* корнеплод сельдерея.
celery ['sɛlərɪ] *n* сельдерей.
celestial [sɪ'lɛstɪəl] *adj* небесный.
celibacy ['sɛlɪbəsɪ] *n* сексуальное
воздержание; (*unmarried state*) безбрачие.
cell [sɛl] *n* (*in prison*) камера; (*in monastery*)
келья*; (*of revolutionaries etc*) ячейка*; (*BIO*)
клетка*; (*ELEC*) элемент.
cellar ['sɛlə˞] *n* подвал; (*also:* **wine ~**) винный
погреб*.
cellist ['tʃɛlɪst] *n* виолончелист(ка).
cello ['tʃɛləu] *n* виолончель *f*.
cellophane ['sɛləfeɪn] *n* целлофан.
cellphone ['sɛlfəun] *n* портативный телефон.
cellular ['sɛljulə˞] *adj* (*BIO*) клеточный; (*fabrics*)
сетчатый.
celluloid ['sɛljulɔɪd] *n* целлулоид.
cellulose ['sɛljuləus] *n* клетчатка, целлюлоза.
Celsius ['sɛlsɪəs] *adj:* **30 degrees ~** 30 градусов
по Цельсию.
Celt [kɛlt] *n* кельт.
Celtic ['kɛltɪk] *adj* кельтский* ♦ *n* (*LING*)
кельтский* язык*.
cement [sə'mɛnt] *n* цемент; (*glue*) клей* ♦ *vt*
(*also fig*) цементировать (*impf/perf*); (*stick,*
glue): **to ~ to** приклеивать (приклеить *perf*)
or прикреплять (прикрепить* *perf*) к +*dat*.
cement mixer *n* бетономешалка*.
cemetery ['sɛmɪtrɪ] *n* кладбище.
cenotaph ['sɛnəta:f] *n памятник погибшим*
солдатам.
censor ['sɛnsə˞] *n* цензор ♦ *vt* подвергать
(подвергнуть* *perf*) цензуре.
censorship ['sɛnsəʃɪp] *n* цензура.
censure ['sɛnʃə˞] *vt* осуждать (осудить* *perf*),
порицать (*impf*) ♦ *n* осуждение, порицание.
census ['sɛnsəs] *n* (*of population*) перепись *f*.
cent [sɛnt] *n* (*US etc: coin*) цент; *see also* **per**.
centenary [sɛn'ti:nərɪ] *n* столетие.
centennial [sɛn'tɛnɪəl] *n* (*US*) столетие.
center *etc n* (*US*) = **centre** *etc*.
centigrade ['sɛntɪgreɪd] *adj:* **30 degrees ~** 30

градусов по Цельсию.
centilitre ['sɛntɪli:tə˞] (*US* **centiliter**) *n*
центилитр.
centimetre ['sɛntɪmi:tə˞] (*US* **centimeter**) *n*
сантиметр.
centipede ['sɛntɪpi:d] *n* многоножка*.
central ['sɛntrəl] *adj* центральный*; **this flat is**
very ~ эта квартира расположена близко к
центру города.
Central African Republic *n* Центрально-
Африканская республика.
Central America *n* Центральная Америка.
central heating *n* центральное отопление.
centralize ['sɛntrəlaɪz] *vt* централизовать (*impf/*
perf).
central processing unit *n* центральный
процессор.
central reservation *n* (*BRIT: AUT*)
разделительная полоса.
centre ['sɛntə˞] (*US* **center**) *n* центр ♦ *vt* (*PHOT,*
TYP) центрировать (*impf/perf*); (*SPORT: ball*)
подавать* (подать* *perf*) в центр;
(*concentrate on*): **to ~ (on)**
сосредоточивать (сосредоточиться *perf*)
(на +*prp*); **to ~ sth on** сосредоточивать
(сосредоточить *perf*) что-н на +*acc*.
centrefold ['sɛntəfəuld] (*US* **centerfold**) *n*
центральная вкладка*.
centre forward *n* (*SPORT*) центральный
нападающий* *m adj*, центр-форвард.
centre half *n* (*SPORT*) центральный
полузащитник.
centrepiece ['sɛntəpi:s] (*US* **centerpiece**) *n*
декоративный предмет, выставленный
посередине стола, полки итд; (*fig*) главное
украшение.
centre spread *n* (*BRIT: PRESS*) разворот.
centre-stage [sɛntə'steɪdʒ] *n* центр сцены.
centrifugal [sɛn'trɪfjugl] *adj* (*PHYS*)
центробежный.
centrifuge ['sɛntrɪfju:ʒ] *n* центрифуга.
century ['sɛntjurɪ] *n* век*; (*CRICKET*) сто очков;
twentieth ~ двадцатый век; **in the twentieth**
~ в двадцатом веке.
CEO *n abbr* (*US:* = *chief executive officer*)
главный администратор.
ceramic [sɪ'ræmɪk] *adj* керамический*.
ceramics [sɪ'ræmɪks] *npl* керамика *fsg*.
cereal ['si:rɪəl] *n* (*plant, crop*): **~s** зерновые *pl*
adj; (*also:* **breakfast ~**) хлопья *pl* к завтраку.
cerebral ['sɛrɪbrəl] *adj* (*MED*) мозговой,
церебральный*; (*intellectual*)
умозрительный* (умозрителен); **~ palsy**
церебральный паралич.
ceremonial [sɛrɪ'məunɪəl] *n* церемониал ♦ *adj*
обрядовой.
ceremony ['sɛrɪmənɪ] *n* церемония;
(*behaviour*) церемонии *fpl*; **with ~** со всеми

формáльностями; **to stand on ~** настáивать (настоя́ть* *perf*) на соблюдéнии формáльностей.
cert [sə:t] *n* (*BRIT*: *inf*): **it's a dead ~** э́то дéло вéрное.
certain ['sə:tən] *adj* (*sure*): **I'm ~ (that)** я увéрен (что); (*particular*): **~ days** определённые дни; (*some*): **a ~ pleasure** нéкоторое удовóльствие; **it's ~ (that)** несомнéнно (что); **in ~ circumstances** при определённых обстоя́тельствах; **a ~ Mr Smith** нéкий Ми́стер Смит; **to make ~ of/that** удостоверя́ться (удостовéриться *perf*) в +*prp*/что; **for ~** навернякá.
certainly ['sə:tənlɪ] *adv* (*undoubtedly*) несомнéнно; (*of course*) конéчно.
certainty ['sə:təntɪ] *n* (*assurance*) увéренность *f*; (*inevitability*) несомнéнность *f*.
certificate [sə'tɪfɪkɪt] *n* (*doctor's etc*) спрáвка; (*diploma*) диплóм; **birth ~** свидéтельство рождéнии; **marriage ~** свидéтельство о заключéнии брáка.
certified letter ['sə:tɪfaɪd-] *n* (*US*) гаранти́рованное письмó.
certified mail *n* (*US*) гаранти́рованная пóчта.
certified public accountant *n* (*US*) бухгáлтер вы́сшей квалификáции.
certify ['sə:tɪfaɪ] *vt* (*fact*) удостоверя́ть (удостовéрить *perf*); (*after studies*) выдавáть* (вы́дать* *perf*) диплóм +*dat*; (*also:* **~ insane**) признавáть* (признáть* *perf*) душевнобольны́м(-ой); **he is a certified lawyer** он дипломи́рованный юри́ст.
cervical ['sə:vɪkl] *adj*: **~ cancer** рак шéйки мáтки; **~ smear** мазóк* с шéйки мáтки.
cervix ['sə:vɪks] *n* шéйка мáтки.
Cesarean [si:'zɛərɪən] *adj*, *n* (*US*) = **Caesarean**.
cessation [sə'seɪʃən] *n* прекращéние.
cesspit ['sɛspɪt] *n* выгребнáя я́ма.
CET *abbr* (= *Central European Time*) центральноевропéйское врéмя* *nt*.
Ceylon [sɪ'lɔn] *n* Цейлóн.
cf. *abbr* = **compare**.
c/f *abbr* (*COMM*: = *carried forward*) перенесенó на слéдующую страни́цу.
CFC *n abbr* (= *chlorofluorocarbon*) хлор-фтороуглерóд.
CG *n abbr* (*US*) = **coastguard**.
cg *abbr* (= *centigram*) сантигрáмм.
CH *n abbr* (*BRIT*: = *Companion of Honour*) кавалéр óрдена.
ch. *abbr* (= *chapter*) гл.= *главá*.
c.h. *abbr* (*BRIT*) = **central heating**.
Chad [tʃæd] *n* Чад.
chafe [tʃeɪf] *vt* (*rub*) натирáть (натерéть *perf*) ♦ *vi* (*fig*): **to ~ at/under** раздражáться (*impf*) из-за +*gen*.
chaffinch ['tʃæfɪntʃ] *n* зя́блик.
chagrin ['ʃægrɪn] *n* (*annoyance*) досáда; (*disappointment*) огорчéние.
chain [tʃeɪn] *n* (*also fig*) цепь* *f*; (*decorative, on*

bicycle) цепóчка*; (*of shops, hotels*) сеть* *f*; (*of events, ideas*) верени́ца ♦ *vt* (*also:* **~ up**: *person*) прикóвывать (прикóвáть* *perf*); (*dog*) сажáть (посади́ть* *perf*) на цепь; **a ~ of mountains** гóрная цепь.
chain reaction *n* цепнáя реáкция.
chain-smoke ['tʃeɪnsməuk] *vi* кури́ть* (*impf*) одну́ сигарéту за другóй.
chain store *n* филиáл (*магази́на*).
chair [tʃɛəʳ] *n* стул*; (*also:* **armchair**) крéсло*; (*of university*) кáфедра; (*of meeting: also:* **~person**) председáтель *m* ♦ *vt* председáтельствовать (*impf*) на +*prp*; **the ~** (*US: also:* **the electric ~**) электри́ческий* стул*; **to take the ~** председáтельствовать (*impf*).
chair lift *n* канáтный подъёмник.
chairman ['tʃɛəmən] *irreg n* председáтель *m*; (*BRIT: of company*) президéнт.
chairperson ['tʃɛəpə:sn] *n* председáтель *m*.
chairwoman ['tʃɛəwumən] *irreg n* председáтель *m*.
chalet ['ʃæleɪ] *n* ≈ коттéдж.
chalice ['tʃælɪs] *n* (*REL*) поти́р.
chalk [tʃɔ:k] *n* мёл*
▸ **chalk up** *vt* (*fig: success etc*) заноси́ть* (занести́* *perf*) в спи́сок свои́х достижéний.
challenge ['tʃælɪndʒ] *n* вы́зов; (*challenging task*) испытáние ♦ *vt* (*rival: also SPORT*) бросáть (брóсить* *perf*) вы́зов +*dat*; (*authority, right etc*) оспáривать (оспóрить *perf*); **to ~ sb to sth** вызывáть (вы́звать* *perf*) когó-н на что-н.
challenger ['tʃælɪndʒəʳ] *n* (*in sport*) претендéнт(ка).
challenging ['tʃælɪndʒɪŋ] *adj* (*task*) трýдный* (трýден); (*tone, look*) вызывáющий*; **this work is very ~** э́та рабóта трéбует большóй отдáчи.
chamber ['tʃeɪmbəʳ] *n* (*room*) кáмера; (*POL*) палáта; (*BRIT: LAW: usu pl*) адвокáтская контóра; **~ of commerce** Торгóвая Палáта.
chambermaid ['tʃeɪmbəmeɪd] *n* гóрничная *f adj*.
chamber music *n* кáмерная мýзыка.
chamber pot *n* ночнóй горшóк*.
chameleon [kə'mi:lɪən] *n* хамелеóн.
chamois ['ʃæmwɑ:] *n* (*ZOOL*) сéрна; (*also:* **~ leather**) зáмша.
champagne [ʃæm'peɪn] *n* шампáнское *nt adj*.
champers ['ʃæmpəz] *n* (*inf*) шампáнское *nt adj*.
champion ['tʃæmpɪən] *n* (*SPORT*) чемпиóн; (*of cause*) побóрник(-ица); (*of person*) защи́тник(-ица) ♦ *vt* защищáть (защити́ть* *perf*).
championship ['tʃæmpɪənʃɪp] *n* (*contest*) чемпионáт; (*title*) звáние чемпиóна.
chance [tʃɑ:ns] *n* (*hope, possibility*) шанс; (*opportunity*) возмóжность *f*; (*risk*) риск ♦ *vt* (*risk*) рисковáть (*impf*) +*instr* ♦ *adj* случáйный; **the ~s are that ...** все шáнсы за то, что ...;

there is little ~ of his coming маловероя́тно,
что он придёт; **to take a ~** рискну́ть *(perf)*; **by
~** случа́йно; **to leave to ~** оставля́ть
(оста́вить* *perf*) на во́лю слу́чая; **it's the ~ of
a lifetime** така́я возмо́жность
предоставля́ется раз в жи́зни; **to ~ it**
рискну́ть *(perf)*; **to ~ to overhear/see** *(happen)*
случа́йно подслу́шать *(perf)/уви́деть (perf)*
► **chance (up)on** *vt fus* случа́йно наткну́ться
(perf) на +*acc*.
chancel ['tʃɑːnsəl] *n* алта́рная часть *f*.
chancellor ['tʃɑːnsələ'] *n* (POL) ка́нцлер; (BRIT:
of university) почётный ре́ктор
(*номина́льный пост*).
Chancellor of the Exchequer *n* (BRIT) ка́нцлер
казначе́йства (*мини́стр фина́нсов*).
chancy ['tʃɑːnsɪ] *adj* риско́ванный (риско́ван).
chandelier [ʃændə'lɪə'] *n* лю́стра.
change ['tʃeɪndʒ] *vt* меня́ть (поменя́ть *perf*);
(*wheel, bulb etc*) заменя́ть (замени́ть* *perf*);
(*job, address*) сменя́ть (смени́ть* *perf*);
(*money: to different currency*) обме́нивать
(обменя́ть *perf*); (: *for smaller notes or coins*)
разме́нивать (разменя́ть *perf*) ♦ *vi* (*alter*)
меня́ться (*impf*), изменя́ться (измени́ться*
perf); (*one's clothes*) переодева́ться
(переоде́ться* *perf*); (*change trains, buses*)
де́лать (сде́лать *perf*) переса́дку ♦ *n*
(*alteration*) измене́ние; (*difference*) переме́на;
(*replacement*) сме́на; (*coins: also:* **small** *or*
loose ~) ме́лочь *f*; (*money returned*) сда́ча; **to
~ sth into** превраща́ть (преврати́ть* *perf*)
кого́-н в +*acc*; **to ~ one's mind** переду́мывать
(переду́мать *perf*); **to ~ gear** (AUT)
переключа́ть (переключи́ть *perf*) ско́рость;
to ~ a baby's nappy перепелёнывать
(перепелена́ть *perf*) ребёнка; **to ~ into** (*be
transformed*) превраща́ться (преврати́ться*
perf) в +*acc*; **a ~ of clothes** сме́на оде́жды; **to
give sb** *or* **of ten pounds** дава́ть* (дать*
perf) кому́-н сда́чу с десяти́ фу́нтов; **keep the
~** сда́чи не на́до; **for a ~** для разнообра́зия.
changeable ['tʃeɪndʒəbl] *adj* (*weather, mood*)
изме́нчивый (изме́нчив); (*person*)
непостоя́нный* (непостоя́нен).
change machine *n* разме́нный автома́т.
changeover ['tʃeɪndʒəʊvə'] *n*: ~ (**to**) (*to new
system*) перехо́д (к +*dat*).
changing ['tʃeɪndʒɪŋ] *adj* (*world*)
изменя́ющийся; (*colours*) меня́ющийся.
changing room *n* (BRIT: *in shop*) приме́рочная
f adj; (: SPORT) раздева́лка*.
channel ['tʃænl] *n* кана́л; (*for shipping*) тра́сса;
(*groove*) жёлоб ♦ *vt*: **to ~ into** (*money,
interest*) направля́ть (напра́вить* *perf*) на
+*acc*; **through the usual ~s** че́рез обы́чные
кана́лы; **~s of communication** кана́лы свя́зи;
green/red ~ зелёный/кра́сный кана́л (*при*

тамо́женном контро́ле); **the (English) C~**
Ла-Ма́нш; **the C~ Islands** Норма́ндские
острова́ *mpl*.
Channel Tunnel *n* тунне́ль *m* под
Ла-Ма́ншем.
chant ['tʃɑːnt] *n* (*of crowd, fans etc*)
сканди́рование; (REL: *song*) пе́ние ♦ *vti*
(*shout*) сканди́ровать (*impf*); **the
demonstrators ~ed their disapproval**
демонстра́нты хо́ром выража́ли
неодобре́ние.
chaos ['keɪɔs] *n* хао́с.
chaos theory *n*: **the ~ ~** тео́рия хао́са.
chaotic [keɪ'ɔtɪk] *adj* (*mess, situation*)
хаоти́чный* (хаоти́чен).
chap ['tʃæp] *n* (BRIT: *inf*) па́рень* *m*; (*term of
address*): **old ~** старина́ *m*, стари́к.
chapel ['tʃæpl] *n* (*in church*) приде́л; (*in
hospital, prison, school etc*) це́рковь* *f*; (BRIT:
also: **non-conformist ~**) протеста́нтская
нон-конформи́стская це́рковь*; (: *of trade
union*) *отделе́ние профсою́за рабо́тников
изда́тельства.*
chaperone ['ʃæpərəʊn] *n* (*for woman*)
компаньо́нка ♦ *vt* сопровожда́ть
(сопроводи́ть* *perf*).
chaplain ['tʃæplɪn] *n* капелла́н.
chapped ['tʃæpt] *adj* (*skin, lips etc*)
потре́скавшийся.
chapter ['tʃæptə'] *n* (*of book*) глава́*; (*of life,
history*) страни́ца; **a ~ of accidents** череда́
неуда́ч.
char ['tʃɑː'] *vt* (*burn*) обу́гливать (обу́глить
perf) ♦ *vi* (BRIT) рабо́тать (*impf*) убо́рщицей ♦ *n*
(BRIT) = **charlady**.
character ['kærɪktə'] *n* (*personality*) ли́чность *f*;
(*nature, strength of character*) хара́ктер; (*in
novel, film*) персона́ж; (*eccentric*) оригина́л;
(*letter, symbol*) знак; (: COMPUT) си́мвол; **a
person of good ~** поря́дочный челове́к.
character code *n* (COMPUT) код си́мвола.
characteristic ['kærɪktə'rɪstɪk] *n* характе́рная
черта́ ♦ *adj*: ~ (**of**) характе́рный*
(характе́рен +*gen*); **it is ~ of him** э́то
характе́рно для него́.
characterize ['kærɪktəraɪz] *vt* (*typify*)
характеризова́ть (*impf/perf*); (*describe*): **to ~
(as)** характеризова́ть (*impf/perf*) (как); **to be
~d by** характеризова́ться (*impf*) +*instr*.
charade [ʃə'rɑːd] *n* шара́да; (*fig*) коме́дия.
charcoal ['tʃɑːkəʊl] *n* (*fuel*) древе́сный у́голь*
m; (*for drawing*) у́голь.
charge ['tʃɑːdʒ] *n* (*fee*) пла́та; (LAW: *accusation*)
обвине́ние; (*responsibility*) отве́тственность
f; (*of gun, battery*) заря́д; (MIL: *attack*) ата́ка ♦
vi (*also* MIL) атакова́ть (*impf/perf*); (*rush*)
кида́ться (ки́нуться *perf*), броса́ться
(бро́ситься *perf*) ♦ *vt* (*battery, gun*) заряжа́ть

---

* marks translations which have irregular inflections. The Russian-English side of the dictionary gives inflectional information.

(заряди́ть* perf); (LAW: accuse): **to ~ sb with** обвиня́ть (обвини́ть perf) кого́-н в +prp; (entrust) поруча́ть (поручи́ть* perf) кому́-н +acc; **~s** npl (bank charges) де́нежный сбор msg; (telephone charges) телефо́нный тари́ф msg; **labour ~s** сто́имость fsg рабо́чей си́лы; **to reverse the ~s** (TEL) звони́ть (impf) по колле́кту; **is there a ~?** за э́то ну́жно плати́ть?; **at no extra ~** без дополни́тельной опла́ты; **free of ~** беспла́тно; **to take ~ of** (child) брать* (взять* perf) на попече́ние; (company) брать* (взять* perf) на себя́ руково́дство +instr; **to be in ~ of** отвеча́ть (impf) за +acc; **who's in ~ here?** кто здесь гла́вный?; **to ~** (sb) (for) (demand fee) проси́ть* (попроси́ть* perf) (у кого́-н) пла́ту (за +acc); **they ~d us £10 for the meal** с нас взя́ли £10 за еду́; **how much do you ~ for?** ско́лько Вы про́сите за +acc?; **to ~ an expense (up) to sb's account** переводи́ть* (перевести́* perf) расхо́ды на чей-н счёт.

charge account n креди́т по откры́тому счёту.

charge card n креди́тная ка́рточка* (определённого магази́на).

chargé d'affaires ['ʃɑ:ʒeɪ dæ'fɛə] n пове́ренный* m adj в дела́х.

charge hand n (BRIT) ма́стер* (на произво́дстве).

charger ['tʃɑ:dʒə'] n (also: battery ~) заря́дное устро́йство; (warhorse) боево́й конь m.

chariot ['tʃærɪət] n колесни́ца.

charisma [kæ'rɪsmə] n обая́ние.

charitable ['tʃærɪtəbl] adj (organization) благотвори́тельный; (person) милосе́рдный* (милосе́рден).

charity ['tʃærɪtɪ] n (organization) благотвори́тельная организа́ция; (kindness) милосе́рдие; (money, gifts) ми́лостыня.

charlady ['tʃɑ:leɪdɪ] n (BRIT) убо́рщица.

charlatan ['ʃɑ:lətən] n шарлата́н.

charm [tʃɑ:m] n (attractiveness) обая́ние, очарова́ние; (spell) заклина́ние; (talisman) амуле́т; (on bracelet etc) брело́к ♦ vt (please, delight) очаро́вывать (очарова́ть perf).

charm bracelet n брасле́т с брелка́ми.

charming ['tʃɑ:mɪŋ] adj очарова́тельный* (очарова́телен).

chart [tʃɑ:t] n (graph, diagram) гра́фик; (NAUT) навигацио́нная ка́рта; (ASTRONOMY) ка́рта звёздного не́ба; (weather chart) синопти́ческая ка́рта ♦ vt (put on map) наноси́ть* (нанести́* perf) на ка́рту; (keep track of) фикси́ровать (impf); **~s** npl (hit parade) хит-пара́д msg; **to be in the ~s** (record) быть в спи́ске наибо́лее популя́рных ди́сков.

charter ['tʃɑ:tə'] vt (plane, ship etc) фрахтова́ть (зафрахтова́ть perf) ♦ n (of company) уста́в; (document, constitution) ха́ртия; **on ~** (plane,

train etc) по ча́ртеру.

chartered accountant ['tʃɑ:təd-] n (BRIT) бухга́лтер вы́сшей квалифика́ции.

charter flight n ча́ртерный рейс.

charwoman ['tʃɑ:wumən] irreg n = charlady.

chary ['tʃɛərɪ] adj: **to be ~ of** остерега́ться (impf) +gen.

chase [tʃeɪs] vt (pursue: also fig) гна́ться*/ гоня́ться (impf) за +instr ♦ n пого́ня; **to ~ away** or **off** прогоня́ть (прогна́ть* perf)
  ▸ **chase down** vt (US) = chase up
  ▸ **chase up** vt (BRIT: information) разы́скивать (разыска́ть* perf); (: person: remind) напомина́ть (напо́мнить perf) +dat.

chasm ['kæzəm] n (GEO) уще́лье; (between people) про́пасть* f.

chassis ['ʃæsɪ] n шасси́ nt ind.

chaste [tʃeɪst] adj (person, relationship etc) целому́дренный*.

chastened ['tʃeɪsnd] adj присты́женный (присты́жен).

chastening ['tʃeɪsnɪŋ] adj (sobering) отрезвля́ющий.

chastise [tʃæs'taɪz] vt отчи́тывать (отчита́ть perf).

chastity ['tʃæstɪtɪ] n целому́дрие.

chat [tʃæt] vi болта́ть (поболта́ть perf) ♦ n бесе́да; **idle ~** болтовня́
  ▸ **chat up** vt (BRIT: inf) заи́грывать (impf) с +instr.

chatline ['tʃætlaɪm] n телефо́нная слу́жба, предоставля́ющая собесе́дника.

chat show n (BRIT) ≈ шо́у с уча́стием знамени́тостей.

chattel ['tʃætl] n see goods.

chatter ['tʃætə'] vi (person, monkey, parrot) треща́ть (impf); (magpie) стрекота́ть* (impf); (teeth) стуча́ть (impf) ♦ n (of people) болтовня́; (of birds, animals) трескотня́; **my teeth are ~ing** я стучу́ зуба́ми.

chatterbox ['tʃætəbɔks] n (inf) трещо́тка.

chattering classes ['tʃætərɪŋ 'klɑ:sɪz] npl: **the ~** ~ псевдоинтеллиге́нция, лю́бящая обсужда́ть совреме́нные полити́ческие и обще́ственные пробле́мы.

chatty ['tʃætɪ] adj (letter) живо́й; (person) говорли́вый (говорли́в).

chauffeur ['ʃəufə'] n (персона́льный) шофёр.

chauvinism ['ʃəuvɪnɪzəm] n (also: male ~) мужско́й шовини́зм; (nationalism) шовини́зм.

chauvinist ['ʃəuvɪnɪst] n (also: male ~) шовини́ст.

chauvinistic [ʃəuvɪ'nɪstɪk] adj (ideas, views) шовинисти́ческий*.

ChE abbr = chemical engineer.

cheap [tʃi:p] adj (also fig) дешёвый*; (reduced) со ски́дкой ♦ adv: **to buy/sell sth ~** дёшево покупа́ть (купи́ть* perf)/продава́ть* (прода́ть* perf) что-н.

cheapen ['tʃi:pn] vt (person) унижа́ть

(уни́зить* *perf*).
cheaper ['tʃiːpəʳ] *adj* деше́вле.
cheaply ['tʃiːplɪ] *adv* дёшево.
cheap money *n*: ~ ~ **policy** ситуа́ция, когда́ вла́сти стремя́тся стимули́ровать экономи́ческий рост с по́мощью ни́зких ста́вок.
cheat [tʃiːt] *vi* (*at cards*) жу́льничать (*impf*); (*in exam*) спи́сывать (списа́ть* *perf*) ◆ *n* (*person*) жу́лик ◆ *vt*: **to ~ sb (out of £10)** наду́ть (*perf*) кого́-н (на £10); **to ~ on sb** (*inf*: *husband, wife etc*) изменя́ть (измени́ть* *perf*) кому́-н.
cheating ['tʃiːtɪŋ] *n* жу́льничество, надува́тельство.
check [tʃɛk] *vt* проверя́ть (прове́рить *perf*); (*halt*) приостана́вливать (приостанови́ть* *perf*); (*restrain*) сде́рживать (сдержа́ть* *perf*); (*US: items on list*) отмеча́ть (отме́тить* *perf*) ◆ *vi* проверя́ть (прове́рить *perf*) ◆ *n* (*inspection*) прове́рка*; (*US: bill*) счёт*; (: *COMM*) = **cheque**; (*pattern*: *usu pl*) кле́тка* ◆ *adj* (*cloth, skirt*) кле́тчатый; **to ~ with sb** посове́товаться (*perf*) с кем-н; **to keep a ~ on sb/sth** контроли́ровать (*impf*) кого́-н/что-н; **to act as a ~ on** (*curb*) явля́ться (яви́ться* *perf*) ме́рой контро́ля +*gen*
▶ **check in** *vi* (*at hotel, airport*) регистри́роваться (зарегистри́роваться *perf*) ◆ *vt* (*luggage*) сдава́ть* (сдать* *perf*)
▶ **check off** *vt* (*items on list etc*) отмеча́ть (отме́тить* *perf*)
▶ **check out** *vi* (*of hotel*) выпи́сываться (вы́писаться* *perf*); (*investigate*: *story*) проверя́ть (прове́рить *perf*); (: *building*) прочёсывать (прочеса́ть *perf*)
▶ **check up** *vi*: **to ~ up on sb/sth** наводи́ть (навести́* *perf*) спра́вки о ком-н/чём-н.
checkered ['tʃɛkəd] *adj* (*US*) = **chequered**.
checkers ['tʃɛkəz] *npl* (*US: draughts*) ша́шки *pl*.
check guarantee card *n* (*US*) = **cheque card**.
check-in (desk) ['tʃɛkɪn-] *n* (*at airport*) сто́йка регистра́ции.
checking account ['tʃɛkɪŋ-] *n* (*US: current account*) теку́щий* счёт*.
check list *n* контро́льный спи́сок*.
checkmate ['tʃɛkmeɪt] *n* (*CHESS*) мат.
checkout ['tʃɛkaut] *n* (*in shop*) контро́ль *m*, ка́сса.
checkpoint ['tʃɛkpɔɪnt] *n* (*on border*) контро́льно-пропускно́й пункт.
checkroom ['tʃɛkrum] *n* (*US*) ка́мера хране́ния.
checkup ['tʃɛkʌp] *n* (*MED*) осмо́тр.
cheek [tʃiːk] *n* (*ANAT*) щека́*; (*impudence*) на́глость *f*; (*nerve*) де́рзость *f*.
cheekbone ['tʃiːkbəun] *n* скула́*.
cheeky ['tʃiːkɪ] *adj* наха́льный* (наха́лен), на́глый (нагл).

cheep [tʃiːp] *vi* пища́ть* (*impf*) ◆ *n* писк.
cheer [tʃɪəʳ] *vt* (*encourage*) приве́тствовать (поприве́тствовать *perf*); (*gladden*) ободря́ть (обо́дрить *perf*) ◆ *vi* одобри́тельно восклица́ть (*impf*); ~**s** *npl* (*of crowd: of welcome*) приве́тственные во́згласы *mpl*; (: *of approval*) одобри́тельные во́згласы *mpl*; ~**s!** (*toast*) (за) Ва́ше здоро́вье!
▶ **cheer on** *vt* ободри́ть (ободря́ть *perf*)
▶ **cheer up** *vi* развеселя́ться (*perf*), повеселе́ть (*perf*) ◆ *vt* (*person*) развесели́ть (*perf*); ~ **up!** не грусти́(те)!
cheerful ['tʃɪəful] *adj* весёлый* (ве́сел).
cheerfulness ['tʃɪəfulnɪs] *n* весёлость *f*.
cheerio [tʃɪəɪ'əu] *excl* (*BRIT*) пока́.
cheerleader ['tʃɪəliːdəʳ] *n* заводи́ла (де́вушка, подстрека́ющая боле́льщиков в спорти́вных состяза́ниях).
cheerless ['tʃɪəlɪs] *adj* уны́лый* (уны́л).
cheese [tʃiːz] *n* сыр*.
cheeseboard ['tʃiːzbɔːd] *n* доска́* для сы́ра; (*with cheese on it*) доска́* с сы́ром.
cheeseburger ['tʃiːzbəːgəʳ] *n* чи́збургер.
cheesecake ['tʃiːzkeɪk] *n* ≈ творо́жный кекс.
cheetah ['tʃiːtə] *n* гепа́рд.
chef [ʃɛf] *n* шеф-по́вар*.
chemical ['kɛmɪkl] *adj* хими́ческий* ◆ *n* химика́т; (*in laboratory*) реакти́в.
chemical engineering *n* хими́ческая техноло́гия.
chemist ['kɛmɪst] *n* (*BRIT*: *pharmacist*) фармаце́вт; (*scientist*) хи́мик.
chemistry ['kɛmɪstrɪ] *n* хи́мия.
chemist's (shop) ['kɛmɪsts-] *n* (*BRIT*) апте́ка.
chemotherapy [kiːməu'θɛrəpɪ] *n* химотерапи́я.
cheque [tʃɛk] *n* (*BRIT*) чек; **to pay by ~** плати́ть* (заплати́ть* *perf*) че́ком.
chequebook ['tʃɛkbuk] *n* (*BRIT*) че́ковая кни́жка.
cheque card *n* (*BRIT*) ка́рточка, подтвержда́ющая платёжеспосо́бность владе́льца.
chequered ['tʃɛkəd] (*US* **checkered**) *adj* (*fig*: *career*) пёстрый.
cherish ['tʃɛrɪʃ] *vt* леле́ять (взлеле́ять *perf*).
cheroot [ʃə'ruːt] *n* сига́р (с уплощёнными конца́ми).
cherry ['tʃɛrɪ] *n* (*fruit, tree*) чере́шня*; (: *sour variety*) ви́шня.
chervil ['tʃəːvɪl] *n* купы́рь *m*.
Ches *abbr* (*BRIT*: *POST*) = **Cheshire**.
chess [tʃɛs] *n* ша́хматы *pl*.
chessboard ['tʃɛsbɔːd] *n* ша́хматная доска́*.
chessman ['tʃɛsmən] *irreg n* ша́хматная фигу́ра.
chess player *n* шахмати́ст.
chest [tʃɛst] *n* (*ANAT*) грудь* *f*; (*box*) сунду́к*;

I'm glad I got it off my ~ (*inf*) я рад, что облегчи́л ду́шу.
chest measurement *n* окру́жность *f* груди́.
chestnut ['tʃɛsnʌt] *n* кашта́н ♦ *adj* (*hair*) кашта́новый; (*horse*) гнедо́й.
chest of drawers *n* комо́д.
chesty ['tʃæstɪ] *adj* грудно́й.
chew [tʃu:] *vt* (*food*) жева́ть (*impf*); (*nails*) грызть* (*impf*); (*a hole*) прогрыза́ть (прогры́зть* *perf*).
chewing gum ['tʃu:ɪŋ-] *n* жева́тельная рези́нка.
chic [ʃi:k] *adj* шика́рный*, элега́нтный* (элега́нтен).
Chicago [ʃɪ'ka:geu] *n* Чика́го *m ind*.
chick [tʃɪk] *n* (*of hen*) цыплёнок; (*of wild bird*) птене́ц*; (*inf: girl*) пта́шка.
chicken ['tʃɪkɪn] *n* (*bird, meat*) ку́рица; (*inf: coward*) труси́шка *m/f*.
▶ **chicken out** *vi* (*inf*) тру́сить (стру́сить* *perf*);
he ~ed out of going он стру́сил и не пошёл.
chicken feed *n* (*fig*) прощи́ *mpl*.
chickenpox ['tʃɪkɪnpɔks] *n* ветря́нка.
chickpeas ['tʃɪkpi:z] *npl* туре́цкий горо́х* *msg*.
chicory ['tʃɪkərɪ] *n* цико́рий.
chide [tʃaɪd] *vt* (*person*): **to ~ sb (for)** брани́ть (вы́бранить *perf*) кого́-н (за +*acc*).
chief [tʃi:f] *n* (*of tribe*) вождь* *m*; (*of organization, department*) нача́льник ♦ *adj* гла́вный, основно́й.
chief constable *n* (*BRIT*) нача́льник поли́ции.
chief executive (*US* **chief executive officer**) *n* гла́вный исполни́тельный дире́ктор.
chiefly ['tʃi:flɪ] *adv* гла́вным о́бразом.
Chief of Staff *n* (*MIL*) нача́льник шта́ба.
chiffon ['ʃɪfɔn] *n* шифо́н.
chilblain ['tʃɪlbleɪn] *n* обморо́женное ме́сто* (*на па́льцах*).
child [tʃaɪld] (*pl* **~ren**) *n* ребёнок*; (*fig*): **~ (of)** дитя́ (+*gen*); **do you have any ~ren?** у Вас есть де́ти?
child benefit *n* (*BRIT*) *де́нежное посо́бие на ребёнка.*
childbirth ['tʃaɪldbə:θ] *n* ро́ды *pl*.
childhood ['tʃaɪldhud] *n* де́тство.
childish ['tʃaɪldɪʃ] *adj* (*games, attitude*) ребя́ческий*; (*person*) ребя́чливый (ребя́лчив).
childless ['tʃaɪldlɪs] *adj* безде́тный* (безде́тен).
childlike ['tʃaɪldlaɪk] *adj* (*smile, figure*) де́тский*.
child minder *n* (*BRIT*) ня́ня.
child prodigy *n* вундерки́нд.
children ['tʃɪldrən] *npl of* **child**.
children's home ['tʃɪldrənz-] *n* де́тский* дом*.
child's play ['tʃaɪldz-] *n*: **it was ~ ~** (*fig*) э́то бы́ло пустяко́вое де́ло.
Chile ['tʃɪlɪ] *n* Чи́ли *nt ind*.
Chilean ['tʃɪlɪən] *adj* чили́йский* ♦ *n* чили́ец(-и́йка).
chili ['tʃɪlɪ] *n* (*US*) = **chilli**.

chill [tʃɪl] *n* (*coldness*) прохла́да; (*MED*) просту́да ♦ *adj* холо́дный* ♦ *vt* (*food, drinks*) охлажда́ть (охлади́ть* *perf*); **to catch a ~** простужа́ться (простуди́ться* *perf*); **his words sent a ~ down my spine** от его́ слов у меня́ пробежа́л холодо́к по спине́; **a ~ reminder** (*fig*) злове́щее предзнаменова́ние; **I'm ~ed to the bone** я промёрз до косте́й; **"serve ~ed"** "подава́ть в охлаждённом ви́де"
▶ **chill out** *vi* (*inf*) кайфова́ть (*impf*).
chilli ['tʃɪlɪ] (*US* **chili**) *n* (*CULIN*) кра́сный стручко́вый пе́рец*.
chilling ['tʃɪlɪŋ] *adj* (*wind*) прохла́дный* (прохла́ден), холо́дный* (хо́лоден); (*tale*) ужаса́ющий*.
chilly ['tʃɪlɪ] *adj* (*weather*) холо́дный, промо́зглый; (*response, person*) холо́дный* (хо́лоден); **to feel ~** зя́бнуть* (*impf*).
chime [tʃaɪm] *n* (*of bell*) звон; (*of clock*) бой* ♦ *vi* (*bell*) звони́ть (*impf*); (*clock*) бить* (про́бить* *perf*).
chimney ['tʃɪmnɪ] *n* (*дымова́я*) труба́.
chimney sweep *n* трубочи́ст.
chimpanzee [tʃɪmpæn'zi:] *n* шимпанзе́ *m ind*.
chin [tʃɪn] *n* подборо́док*.
China ['tʃaɪnə] *n* Кита́й.
china ['tʃaɪnə] *n* фарфо́р.
Chinese [tʃaɪ'ni:z] *adj* кита́йский* ♦ *n inv* (*person*) кита́ец(-а́янка); (*LING*) кита́йский* язы́к*.
chink [tʃɪŋk] *n* (*crack*) щель* *f*; (*clink*) звя́канье.
chintz [tʃɪnts] *n* набивно́й си́тец.
chinwag ['tʃɪnwæg] *n* (*inf*) дру́жеская болтовня́; **we had a good ~** мы хорошо́ поболта́ли.
chip [tʃɪp] *n* (*of wood*) ще́пка*; (*of glass, stone*) оско́лок*; (*in glass, cup etc*) щерби́нка; (*in gambling*) фи́шка*; (*COMPUT: also:* **microchip**) микросхе́ма ♦ *vt* (*cup, plate*) обива́ть (оби́ть* *perf*); **~s** *npl* (*BRIT: CULIN*) карто́фель *msg*-фри; (*US: also:* **potato ~s**) чи́псы *mpl*; **when the ~s are down** (*fig*) когда́ уда́ча отвернётся
▶ **chip in** *vi* (*inf: contribute*) сбра́сываться (сбро́ситься* *perf*); (: *interrupt*) встрева́ть (встрять* *perf*).
chipboard ['tʃɪpbɔ:d] *n* древесно-стру́жечная плита́.
chipmunk ['tʃɪpmʌŋk] *n* бурунду́к.
chippings ['tʃɪpɪŋz] *npl*: **loose ~** ще́пки* *fpl*.
chiropodist [kɪ'rɔpədɪst] *n* (*BRIT*) мозо́льный опера́тор *m/f*.
chiropody [kɪ'rɔpədɪ] *n* (*BRIT*) *ухо́д за нога́ми.*
chirp [tʃə:p] *vi* (*bird*) чири́кать (*impf*); (*cricket, grasshopper*) стрекота́ть* (*impf*).
chirpy ['tʃə:pɪ] *adj* (*inf*) жизнера́достный* (жизнера́достен).
chisel ['tʃɪzl] *n* (*for wood*) долото́; (*for stone*) зуби́ло; (*of sculptor*) резе́ц*.
chit [tʃɪt] *n* (*note*) запи́ска*; (*receipt*) распи́ска.
chitchat ['tʃɪtʃæt] *n* болтовня́.

chivalrous ['ʃɪvəlrəs] *adj* гала́нтный*
(гала́нтен).
chivalry ['ʃɪvəlrɪ] *n* гала́нтность *f.*
chives [tʃaɪvz] *npl* лук-ре́занец *msg.*
chloride ['klɔːraɪd] *n* хлори́д.
chlorinate ['klɔrɪneɪt] *vt* хлори́ровать *(impf).*
chlorine ['klɔːriːn] *n* хлор.
chock [tʃɔk] *n* (*AUT, AVIAT*) тормозна́я
коло́дка*.
chock-a-block ['tʃɔkə'blɔk] *adj* битко́м
наби́тый (наби́т).
chock-full [tʃɔk'ful] *adj* = chock-a-block.
chocolate ['tʃɔklɪt] *n* шокола́д; (*sweet*)
шокола́дная конфе́та ♦ *cpd* шокола́дный.
choice [tʃɔɪs] *n* (*selection*) вы́бор ♦ *adj* (*cut of
meat, fruit etc*) отбо́рный; **this is a possible ~**
э́то возмо́жный вариа́нт; **by** *or* **from ~**
доброво́льно; **a wide ~** большо́й вы́бор; **to
have first ~** выбира́ть (вы́брать* *perf*)
пе́рвым; **I have no ~, but/but to** у меня́ нет
друго́го вы́хода кро́ме +*gen*/кро́ме как
+*infin.*
choir ['kwaɪə'] *n* хор*; (*area of church*) хо́ры *pl.*
choirboy ['kwaɪəbɔɪ] *n* пе́вчий *m adj.*
choke [tʃəuk] *vi* (*on food, drink*) дави́ться*
(подави́ться* *perf*); (*with smoke, anger*)
задыха́ться (задохну́ться *perf*) ♦ *vt* (*strangle*)
души́ть* (задуши́ть* *or* удуши́ть* *perf*) ♦ *n*
(*AUT*) возду́шная засло́нка; **~d (with)**
(*blocked*) засорённый (засорён) (+*instr*).
cholera ['kɔlərə] *n* холе́ра.
cholesterol [kə'lɛstərɔl] *n* холестери́н; **high/
low ~** высо́ким/ни́зким содержа́нием
холестери́на.
choose [tʃuːz] (*pt* chose, *pp* chosen) *vt*
выбира́ть (вы́брать *perf*); (*elect*) избира́ть
(избра́ть* *perf*) ♦ *vi*: **to ~ between/from**
выбира́ть (вы́брать* *perf*) ме́жду +*instr*/из
+*gen*; **to ~ to do** реша́ть (реши́ть *perf*) +*infin.*
choosy ['tʃuːzɪ] *adj* привере́дливый
(привере́длив); **he is ~ about his food** он
привере́длив в еде́.
chop [tʃɔp] *vt* (*wood*) руби́ть* (наруби́ть* *perf*);
(*also:* **~ up**: *vegetables, meat*) ре́зать*
(наре́зать* *or* поре́зать* *perf*) ♦ *n* (*CULIN*) ≈
отбивна́я (котле́та); **~s** *npl* (*inf: jaws*): **to lick
one's ~s** обли́зываться (облиза́ться* *perf*);
he got the ~ (*BRIT: inf*) его́ вы́гнали с рабо́ты
▶ **chop down** *vt* (*tree*) руби́ть* (сруби́ть* *perf*).
chopper ['tʃɔpə'] *n* (*helicopter*) вертолёт.
choppy ['tʃɔpɪ] *adj* (*sea*) неспоко́йный*
(неспоко́ен).
chopsticks ['tʃɔpstɪks] *npl* па́лочки* *fpl* для
еды́.
choral ['kɔːrəl] *adj* хорово́й; (*in church*)
хора́льный.
chord [kɔːd] *n* (*MUS*) акко́рд; (*MATH*) хо́рда.
chore [tʃɔː'] *n* (*domestic task*) рабо́та по до́му;

(*routine task*) повседне́вная обя́занность *f*;
household ~s дома́шние хло́поты.
choreographer [kɔrɪ'ɔgrəfə'] *n* хорео́граф; (*of
ballet*) балетме́йстер*.
choreography [kɔrɪ'ɔgrafɪ] *n* хореогра́фия.
chorister ['kɔrɪstə'] *n* пе́вчий *m adj*, хори́ст.
chortle ['tʃɔːtl] *vi* хохота́ть* *(impf).*
chorus ['kɔːrəs] *n* (*choir, song, also fig*) хор*;
(*church song*) хора́л; (*refrain*) припе́в; **in ~**
хо́ром.
chose [tʃəuz] *pt of* choose.
chosen ['tʃəuzn] *pp of* choose.
chow [tʃau] *n* (*dog*) ча́у-ча́у *m/f ind.*
chowder ['tʃaudə'] *n* ≈ похлёбка.
Christ [kraɪst] *n* Христо́с.
christen ['krɪsn] *vt* крести́ть* (окрести́ть* *perf*);
(*with nickname*) окрести́ть* (*perf*) +*instr.*
christening ['krɪsnɪŋ] *n* креще́ние.
Christian ['krɪstɪən] *adj* христиа́нский* ♦ *n*
христиани́н*(-а́нка).
Christianity [krɪstɪ'ænɪtɪ] *n* христиа́нство.
Christian name *n* и́мя* *nt.*
Christmas ['krɪsməs] *n* Рождество́; **Happy** *or*
Merry ~! Счастли́вого Рождества́!
Christmas card *n* рожде́ственская откры́тка*.
Christmas Day *n* день *m* Рождества́.
Christmas Eve *n* соче́льник.
Christmas Island *n* о́стров* Рождества́.
Christmas tree *n* рожде́ственская ёлка*.
chrome [krəum] *n* = chromium.
chromium ['krəumɪəm] *n* хром; (*also:* **~
plating**) хроми́рование.
chromosome ['krəuməsəum] *n* хромосо́ма.
chronic ['krɔnɪk] *adj* хрони́ческий*.
chronicle ['krɔnɪkl] *n* (*of events*) хро́ника.
chronological [krɔnə'lɔdʒɪkl] *adj* (*order*)
хронологи́ческий*.
chrysanthemum [krɪ'sænθəməm] *n*
хризанте́ма.
chubby ['tʃʌbɪ] *adj* пу́хлый*.
chuck [tʃʌk] (*inf*) *vt* швыря́ть (швырну́ть *perf*);
(*BRIT: also:* **~ up, ~ in**: *job, girlfriend*) броса́ть
(бро́сить* *perf*)
▶ **chuck out** *vt* (*person, rubbish*) вышвы́ривать
(вы́швырнуть *perf*).
chuckle ['tʃʌkl] *vi* посме́иваться *(impf)*; **"Yes",
he ~d** Да, – сказа́л он, посме́иваясь.
chuffed [tʃʌft] *adj* (*inf*) дово́льный (дово́лен).
chug [tʃʌg] *vi* пыхте́ть* *(impf)*; (*also:* **~ along**)
пыхте́ть* (пропыхте́ть* *perf*).
chum [tʃʌm] *n* (*inf: friend*) закады́чный друг*.
chump [tʃʌmp] *n* (*inf*) болва́н.
chunk [tʃʌŋk] *n* (*of meat*) кусо́к*; (*of bread*)
ло́моть* *m.*
chunky ['tʃʌŋkɪ] *adj* (*furniture etc*) громо́здкий*
(громо́здок); (*person*) корена́стый
(корена́ст); (*knitwear*) то́лстый.
church [tʃəːtʃ] *n* це́рковь* *f*; **the C~ of England**

---

* marks translations which have irregular inflections. The Russian-English side of the dictionary gives inflectional information.

Англика́нская Це́рковь*.
churchyard ['tʃə:tʃjɑ:d] *n* пого́ст.
churlish ['tʃə:lɪʃ] *adj* гру́бый (груб).
churn [tʃə:n] *n* (*machine*) маслобо́йка; (*also:* milk ~) бидо́н
▶ **churn out** *vt* производи́ть* (произвести́* *perf*) в бо́льшом коли́честве.
chute [ʃu:t] *n* (*also:* rubbish ~) мусоропрово́д; (*for parcels etc*) жёлоб*; (*BRIT:* slide) го́рка*.
chutney ['tʃʌtnɪ] *n* ча́тни *nt ind* (*инди́йская припра́ва*).
CIA *n abbr* (*US:* = Central Intelligence Agency) ЦРУ.
cicada [sɪ'kɑ:də] *n* цика́да.
CID *n abbr* (*BRIT:* = Criminal Investigation Department*) Уголо́вный ро́зыск.
cider ['saɪdə˚] *n* сидр.
c.i.f. *abbr* (*COMM:* = cost, insurance and freight) СИФ (*сто́имость, страхова́ние, фрахт*).
cigar [sɪ'gɑ:˚] *n* сига́ра.
cigarette [sɪgə'rɛt] *n* сигаре́та.
cigarette case *n* портсига́р.
cigarette end *n* оку́рок*.
cigarette holder *n* мундшту́к*.
C-in-C *abbr* (*MIL:* = commander in chief) главнокома́ндующий*.
cinch [sɪntʃ] *n* (*inf*): **it's a** ~ э́то пустя́к.
Cinderella [sɪndə'rɛlə] *n* Зо́лушка.
cinders ['sɪndəz] *npl* зола́ *fsg*.
cine camera ['sɪnɪ-] *n* (*BRIT*) кинока́мера.
cine film *n* (*BRIT*) киноплёнка*.
cinema ['sɪnəmə] *n* кинотеа́тр; (*film-making*) кинематогра́фия.
cine projector *n* (*BRIT*) кинопрое́ктор.
cinnamon ['sɪnəmən] *n* кори́ца.
cipher ['saɪfə˚] *n* шифр; (*fig*) пе́шка*; **a letter in** ~ зашифро́ванное письмо́.
circa ['sə:kə] *prep* о́коло +*gen*.
circle ['sə:kl] *n* круг*; (*THEAT*) балко́н; (*of trees*) кольцо́ ♦ *vi* (*bird, plane*) кружи́ть* (*impf*) ♦ *vt* (*move round*) дви́гаться* (*impf*) вокру́г +*gen*; (*surround*) окружа́ть (окружи́ть *perf*); **to form a** ~ встава́ть* (встать* *perf*) в круг.
circuit ['sə:kɪt] *n* (*ELEC*) цепь *f*; (*tour*) турне́ *nt ind*; (*track*) трек; (*lap*) заéзд.
circuit board *n* монта́жная пла́та.
circuitous [sə:'kjuɪtəs] *adj* око́льный.
circular ['sə:kjulə˚] *adj* (*plate, pond etc*) кру́глый*; (*route*) окружно́й; (*argument*) несконча́емый ♦ *n* (*letter*) циркуля́р; (*advertisement*) проспе́кт.
circulate ['sə:kjuleɪt] *vi* (*blood, traffic*) циркули́ровать (*impf*); (*news, rumour etc*) передава́ться* (переда́ться* *perf*) ♦ *vt* передава́ть* (переда́ть* *perf*); **to** ~ **amongst the guests** переходи́ть (*impf*) от одного́ го́стя к друго́му.
circulating capital [sə:kju'leɪtɪŋ-] *n* оборо́тный капита́л.
circulation [sə:kju'leɪʃən] *n* (*of newspaper*) тира́ж*; (*MED*) кровообраще́ние; (*of money*)

обраще́ние; (*of air, traffic*) циркуля́ция.
circumcise ['sə:kəmsaɪz] *vt* обреза́ть (обре́зать* *perf*) (*РЕЛ*).
circumference [sə'kʌmfərəns] *n* окру́жность *f*.
circumflex ['sə:kəmflɛks] *n* (*also:* ~ accent) циркумфле́кс.
circumscribe ['sə:kəmskraɪb] *vt* (*GEOM*) впи́сывать (вписа́ть* *perf*) в окру́жность; (*fig*) ограни́чивать (ограни́чить *perf*).
circumspect ['sə:kəmspɛkt] *adj* осмотри́тельный* (осмотри́телен).
circumstances ['sə:kəmstənsɪz] *npl* обстоя́тельства *ntpl*; **in** *or* **under the** ~ в да́нных обстоя́тельствах; **under no** ~ ни в ко́ем слу́чае.
circumstantial [sə:kəm'stænʃl] *adj* обстоя́тельный* (обстоя́телен); ~ **evidence** ко́свенные ули́ки *fpl*.
circumvent [sə:kəm'vɛnt] *vt* обходи́ть* (обойти́* *perf*).
circus ['sə:kəs] *n* цирк; (*also:* C~: *in place names*) ≈ пло́щадь *f*.
cirrhosis [sɪ'rəʊsɪs] *n* цирро́з.
CIS *n abbr* (= Commonwealth of Independent States) СНГ = *Содру́жество Незави́симых Госуда́рств*.
cissy ['sɪsɪ] *n* (*boy*) девчо́нка*; (*girl*) не́женка*.
cistern ['sɪstən] *n* (*water tank*) цисте́рна; (*of toilet*) бак.
citation [saɪ'teɪʃən] *n* (*from book etc*) цита́та; (*for bravery etc*) благода́рность *f*; (*US: LAW*) пове́стка (*в суд*).
cite [saɪt] *vt* (*quote*) цити́ровать (процити́ровать *perf*); (*LAW*) вызыва́ть (вы́звать* *perf*) в суд.
citizen ['sɪtɪzn] *n* (*of a country*) граждани́н*(-а́нка); (*of town*) жи́тель(ница) *m(f)*.
Citizens' Advice Bureau ['sɪtɪznz-] *n* бюро́, *даю́щее беспла́тные сове́ты по широ́кому кру́гу вопро́сов*.
citizenship ['sɪtɪznʃɪp] *n* (*of a country*) гражда́нство.
citric acid ['sɪtrɪk-] *n* лимо́нная кислота́*.
citrus fruit ['sɪtrəs-] *n* ци́трус.
city ['sɪtɪ] *n* го́род*; **the C~** Си́ти *nt ind*.
city centre *n* центр (го́рода).
City Hall *n* ра́туша.
civic ['sɪvɪk] *adj* муниципа́льный; (*duties, pride*) гражда́нский*.
civic centre *n* (*BRIT*) ≈ Дом* Культу́ры.
civil ['sɪvɪl] *adj* гражда́нский*; (*authorities*) госуда́рственный*; (*polite*) учти́в).
Civil Aviation Authority *n* (*BRIT*) Управле́ние гражда́нской авиа́ции.
civil defence *n* гражда́нская оборо́на.
civil disobedience *n* гражда́нское неповинове́ние.
civil engineer *n* инжене́р-строи́тель *m*.
civil engineering *n* гражда́нское строи́тельство.

civilian [sɪ'vɪlɪən] *adj* (*life*) общественный ♦ *n* мирный(-ая) житель(ница) *m(f)*; ~ **casualties** жертвы среди мирного населения.
civilization [sɪvɪlaɪ'zeɪʃən] *n* цивилизация.
civilized ['sɪvɪlaɪzd] *adj* (*society*) цивилизованный; (*person*) культурный; (*place*) комфортабельный.
civil law *n* Гражданское право.
civil liberties *npl* гражданские свободы *fpl*.
civil rights *npl* гражданские права *ntpl*.
civil servant *n* государственный служащий* *m adj*.
Civil Service *n* государственная служба.
civil war *n* гражданская война*.
civvies ['sɪvɪz] *npl* (*inf*) цивильная одежда *fsg*.
cl *abbr* = **centilitre**.
clad [klæd] *adj*: ~ **(in)** облачённый (облачён) (в +*acc*).
claim [kleɪm] *vt* (*responsibility, credit*) приписывать (приписать* *perf*) себе; (*rights, inheritance*) претендовать (*impf*) *or* притязать (*impf*) на +*acc*; (*compensation, damages*) требовать (потребовать *perf*) ♦ *vi* (*for insurance*) делать (сделать *perf*) страховую заявку ♦ *n* (*assertion*) утверждение; (*for compensation, pension*) требование; (*right*) право; (*to inheritance, land*) претензия, притязание; (*for expenses*) заявка; **to ~ (that)** *or* **to be** (*assert*) утверждать (*impf*), что; **(insurance)** ~ страховая заявка; **to put in a ~ for** (*expenses*) подавать* (подать* *perf*) заявку на +*acc*.
claimant ['kleɪmənt] *n* (*LAW*) претендент; (*ADMIN*) податель(ница) *m(f)* заявления.
claim form *n* бланк заявления.
clairvoyant [klɛə'vɔɪənt] *n* ясновидец*(-дица).
clam [klæm] *n* двухстворчатый моллюск
▶ **clam up** *vi* (*inf*) уходить* (уйти* *perf*) в себя.
clamber ['klæmbə'] *vi* карабкаться (вскарабкаться *perf*).
clammy ['klæmɪ] *adj* (*hands*) липкий*; (*weather*) душный*.
clamour ['klæmə'] (*US* **clamor**) *n* (*noise*) гул; (*protest*) ропот ♦ *vi*: **to ~ for** шумно требовать (*impf*) +*gen*.
clamp [klæmp] *n* зажим ♦ *vt* зажимать (зажать* *perf*)
▶ **clamp down on** *vt fus* повести* (*perf*) наступление против +*gen*.
clampdown ['klæmpdaun] *n*: ~ **(on)** строгие меры *fpl* (против +*gen*); **there was a ~ on drug dealing in the area** в районе прикрыли торговлю наркотиками.
clan [klæn] *n* клан.
clandestine [klæn'dɛstɪn] *adj* подпольный.
clang [klæŋ] *vi* (*bell*) звенеть (*impf*); (*metal object*) лязгать (*impf*) ♦ *n* (*see vi*) звон; лязг.
clanger ['klæŋə'] *n* (*inf*) ляпсус.

clansman ['klænzmən] *irreg n* член клана.
clap [klæp] *vi* хлопать (*impf*) ♦ *vt*: **to ~ one's hands** хлопать (*impf*) в ладоши; **a ~ of thunder** удар грома.
clapping ['klæpɪŋ] *n* хлопки *mpl*, аплодисменты *fpl*.
claptrap ['klæptræp] *n* (*inf*) белиберда.
claret ['klærət] *n* бордо *nt ind*.
clarification [klærɪfɪ'keɪʃən] *n* (*fig*) разъяснение.
clarify ['klærɪfaɪ] *vt* (*fig*) разъяснять (разъяснить *perf*).
clarinet [klærɪ'nɛt] *n* кларнет.
clarity ['klærɪtɪ] *n* (*of explanation, thought*) ясность *f*.
clash [klæʃ] *n* столкновение; (*of events etc*) совпадение; (*of metal objects*) звяканье ♦ *vi* (*gangs*) иметь (*impf*) столкновение; (*political opponents*) вступать (вступить* *perf*) в столкновение; (*beliefs*) сталкиваться (столкнуться *perf*); (*colours*) не совмещаться (*impf*); (*events etc*) совпадать (совпасть* *perf*) (по времени); (*metal objects*) звякать (*impf*).
clasp [klɑːsp] *n* (*hold*) хватка*; (*of necklace, bag*) застёжка* ♦ *vt* сжимать (сжать* *perf*).
class [klɑːs] *n* (*in school, society*) класс; (*lesson*) урок; (*of goods: type*) разряд; (: *quality*) сорт ♦ *adj* классовый ♦ *vt* классифицировать (*impf/ perf*).
class-conscious ['klɑːs'kɔnʃəs] *adj* (*person*) осознающий классовое разделение.
class-consciousness ['klɑːs'kɔnʃəsnɪs] *n* классовое сознание.
classic ['klæsɪk] *adj* классический* ♦ *n* (*film, novel etc*) классическое произведение; (*author*) классик; **C~s** *npl* (*SCOL*) классическая филология *fsg*.
classical ['klæsɪkl] *adj* классический*.
classification [klæsɪfɪ'keɪʃən] *n* классификация; (*category*) разряд.
classified ['klæsɪfaɪd] *adj* засекреченный.
classified advertisement *n* объявления под рубрикой.
classify ['klæsɪfaɪ] *vt* классифицировать (*impf/ perf*).
classless ['klɑːslɪs] *adj* бесклассовый.
classmate ['klɑːsmeɪt] *n* одноклассник(-ица).
classroom ['klɑːsrum] *n* класс.
classy ['klɑːsɪ] *adj* (*inf: car, flat*) классный.
clatter ['klætə'] *n* (*of dishes etc*) звяканье; (*of hooves*) цоканье ♦ *vi* (*see n*) звякать (*impf*); цокать (*impf*).
clause [klɔːz] *n* (*LAW*) пункт; (*LING*): **principal/ subordinate** ~ главное/придаточное предложение.
claustrophobia [klɔːstrə'fəubɪə] *n* клаустрофобия.
claustrophobic [klɔːstrə'fəubɪk] *adj*: **she is** ~

она́ страда́ет клаустрофо́бией, у неё
клаустрофо́бия.
claw [klɔ:] *n* (*of animal, bird*) ко́готь* *m*;
(*of lobster*) клешня́*
▶ **claw at** *vt fus* цепля́ться (*impf*) за +*acc.*
clay [kleɪ] *n* гли́на.
clean [kli:n] *adj* (*person*) чи́стый*; (*fight*) че́стный*;
(*reputation*) незапя́тнанный (незапя́тан);
(*joke*) прили́чный* (прили́чен); (*edge,
fracture*) ро́вный* (ро́вен) ♦ *vt* (*hands, face*)
мыть (вы́мыть* *perf*); (*car, cooker*) чи́стить*
(почи́стить* *perf*) ♦ *adv*: **he ~ forgot** он
на́чисто забы́л; **~ driving licence** *or* (*US*)
record чи́стые води́тельские права́ *ntpl*; **to ~
one's teeth** (*BRIT*) чи́стить* (почи́стить *perf*)
зу́бы; **the thief got ~ away** во́ра и след
просты́л; **to come ~** (*inf*) выкла́дывать
(вы́ложить *perf*) всё начисту́ю
▶ **clean off** *vt* (*wash*) смыва́ть (смыть* *perf*);
(*brush, dust etc*) счища́ть (счи́стить* *perf*)
▶ **clean out** *vt* (*cupboard etc*) вычища́ть
(вы́чистить* *perf*); (*inf: person*) обчища́ть
(обчи́стить* *perf*)
▶ **clean up** *vt* (*room*) убира́ть (убра́ть* *perf*);
(*child*) мыть* (помы́ть* *perf*); (*fig*) проводи́ть*
(провести́* *perf*) чи́стку в +*prp* ♦ *vi* убира́ться
(убра́ться* *perf*); (*fig*) загреба́ть (загрести́*
perf) больши́е де́ньги; **to ~ up after sb/sth**
убира́ть (убра́ть* *perf*) за кем-н/чем-н.
clean-cut [ˈkli:nˈkʌt] *adj* (*person*) опря́тный*
(опря́тен); (*situation*) я́сный* (я́сен).
cleaner [ˈkli:nə'] *n* (*person*) убо́рщик(-ица);
(*substance*) мо́ющее сре́дство.
cleaner's [ˈkli:nəz] *n* (*also:* **dry ~**) химчи́стка*.
cleaning [ˈkli:nɪŋ] *n* убо́рка*.
cleaning lady *n* убо́рщица.
cleanliness [ˈklɛnlɪnɪs] *n* чистопло́тность *f.*
cleanly [ˈkli:nlɪ] *adv* чи́сто.
cleanse [klɛnz] *vt* (*purify*) очища́ть (очи́стить*
perf); (*face*) мыть* (вы́мыть* *perf*); (*cut*)
промыва́ть (промы́ть* *perf*).
cleanser [ˈklɛnzə'] *n* (*for face*) очища́ющий
лосьо́н.
clean-shaven [ˈkli:nˈʃeɪvn] *adj* чи́сто
вы́бритый.
cleansing department [ˈklɛnzɪŋ-] *n* (*BRIT*)
санита́рное управле́ние.
clean sweep *n*: **to make a ~ ~** (*in tournaments*)
забира́ть (забра́ть* *perf*) все призы́.
cleanup [ˈkli:nʌp] *n* (*of house, room*) убо́рка*;
(*of river, air*) очи́стка.
clear [klɪə'] *adj* я́сный* (я́сен); (*report,
argument*) я́сный* (я́сен), поня́тный*;
(*footprint*) чёткий*; (*writing*) разбо́рчивый
(разбо́рчив); (*majority*) подавля́ющий*;
(*glass, water*) прозра́чный* (прозра́чен);
(*road*) свобо́дный* (свобо́ден); (*conscience,
profit*) чи́стый* ♦ *vt* (*space, room*)
освобожда́ть (освободи́ть* *perf*); (*ground*)
расчища́ть (расчи́стить* *perf*); (*weeds, slums*)
убира́ть (убра́ть* *perf*); (*suspect*)

опра́вдывать (оправда́ть *perf*); (*fence etc*)
брать* (взять* *perf*); (*goods*) распродава́ть*
(распрода́ть* *perf*) ♦ *vi* (*sky*) проясня́ться
(проясни́ться *perf*); (*fog, smoke*)
рассе́иваться (рассе́яться *perf*); (*room etc*)
обезлю́деть (*perf*) ♦ *adv*: **~ of** (*trouble, ground*)
пода́льше от +*gen* ♦ *n*: **he is/was in the ~** (*out
of debt*) он свобо́ден/был свобо́ден от
долго́в; **to be in the ~** (*free of suspicion*)
быть* (*impf*) вне подозре́ния; (*out of danger*)
быть* (*impf*) вне опа́сности; **have I made
myself ~?** я я́сно вы́разился?; **to make it ~ to
sb that ...** дава́ть* (дать* *perf*) кому́-н поня́ть,
что ...; **I have a ~ day tomorrow** (*BRIT*) у меня́
за́втра свобо́дный день; **to ~ the table**
убира́ть (убра́ть* *perf*) со стола́; **to ~ one's
throat** прочища́ть (прочи́стить* *perf*) го́рло;
to ~ a cheque выпла́чивать (вы́платить* *perf*)
де́ньги по че́ку; **to ~ a profit** получа́ть
(получи́ть* *perf*) чи́стую при́быль; **to keep ~
of sb/sth** держа́ться* (*impf*) пода́льше от
кого́-н/чего́-н
▶ **clear off** *vi* (*inf: leave*) убира́ться (убра́ться*
perf)
▶ **clear up** *vt* (*room*) убира́ть (убра́ть* *perf*);
(*mystery, problem*) разреша́ть (разреши́ть
perf) ♦ *vi* убира́ться (убра́ться* *perf*); (*illness*)
проходи́ть* (пройти́* *perf*); (*weather*)
проясня́ться (проясни́ться *perf*).
clearance [ˈklɪərəns] *n* (*removal*) расчи́стка*;
(*permission*) разреше́ние; (*above vehicle*)
габари́тная высота́*.
clearance sale *n* распрода́жа.
clear-cut [ˈklɪə'ˈkʌt] *adj* (*decision, issue*) я́сный*
(я́сен); (*division*) чёткий*.
clearing [ˈklɪərɪŋ] *n* поля́на; (*BRIT: COMM*)
кли́ринг.
clearing bank *n* (*BRIT*) кли́ринговый банк.
clearing house *n* кли́ринговая пала́та.
clearly [ˈklɪəlɪ] *adv* (*distinctly*) я́сно, отчётливо;
(*obviously*) я́вно, очеви́дно; (*coherently*)
я́сно, поня́тно.
clearway [ˈklɪəweɪ] *n* (*BRIT*) *автодоро́га, где
остано́вка тра́нспорта запрещена́*.
cleavage [ˈkli:vɪdʒ] *n* я́мка*.
cleaver [ˈkli:və'] *n* (*for meat*) топо́рик.
clef [klɛf] *n* (*MUS*) ключ*.
cleft [klɛft] *n* рассе́лина.
cleft palate *n* за́ячья губа́.
clemency [ˈklɛmənsɪ] *n* милосе́рдие.
clement [ˈklɛmənt] *adj* мя́гкий*.
clench [klɛntʃ] *vt* сжима́ть (сжать* *perf*).
clergy [ˈklə:dʒɪ] *n* духове́нство.
clergyman [ˈklə:dʒɪmən] *irreg n* свяще́нник,
священнослужи́тель *m.*
clerical [ˈklɛrɪkl] *adj* (*job, error*) канцеля́рский*;
(*skills*) секрета́рский*; (*REL*) церко́вный.
clerk [klɑ:k, (*US*) klə:rk] *n* (*BRIT: office worker*)
клерк, делопроизводи́тель*(ница) *m(f)*; (*US:
sales person*) продаве́ц*(-вщи́ца).
Clerk of Court *n* секрета́рь* *m* суда́.

clever [ˈklɛvəʳ] *adj* (*intelligent*) у́мный* (умён); (*deft, crafty*) ло́вкий* (ло́вок).

cleverly [ˈklɛvəlɪ] *adv* ло́вко.

clew [kluː] *n* (*US*) = **clue**.

cliché [ˈkliːʃeɪ] *n* клише́ *nt ind*, штамп.

click [klɪk] *vt* (*tongue, heels*) щёлкать (щёлкнуть *perf*) +*instr* ♦ *vi* (*device, switch etc*) щёлкать (щёлкнуть *perf*).

client [ˈklaɪənt] *n* клие́нт.

clientele [kliːɑ̃ːnˈtɛl] *n* клиенту́ра.

cliff [klɪf] *n* скала́*, утёс.

cliffhanger [ˈklɪfhæŋəʳ] *n* (*TV, also fig*) напряжённый моме́нт.

climactic [klaɪˈmæktɪk] *adj* кульминацио́нный.

climate [ˈklaɪmɪt] *n* (*weather, fig*) кли́мат; ~ **of opinion** состоя́ние обще́ственного мне́ния.

climax [ˈklaɪmæks] *n* кульмина́ция; (*during sex*) орга́зм.

climb [klaɪm] *vi* (*sun*) поднима́ться (подня́ться* *perf*); (*plant*) ви́ться (*impf*); (*plane*) набира́ть (набра́ть* *perf*) высоту́; (*prices, shares*) поднима́ться (подня́ться* *perf*) ♦ *vt* (*stairs, ladder*) взбира́ться (взобра́ться* *perf*) по +*prp*; (*tree, hill*) взбира́ться (взобра́ться* *perf*) *or* поднима́ться (подня́ться* *perf*) на +*acc* ♦ *n* подъём; **to ~ over a wall** перелеза́ть (перелезть* *perf*) че́рез сте́ну

► **climb down** *vi* (*BRIT: fig*) уступа́ть (уступи́ть *perf*).

climb-down [ˈklaɪmdaun] *n* (*BRIT*) усту́пка*.

climber [ˈklaɪməʳ] *n* (*mountaineer*) альпини́ст(ка*); (*plant*) вью́щееся расте́ние.

climbing [ˈklaɪmɪŋ] *n* альпини́зм.

clinch [klɪntʃ] *vt* (*deal*) заключа́ть (заключи́ть *perf*); (*argument*) разреша́ть (разреши́ть *perf*).

clincher [ˈklɪntʃəʳ] *n* реша́ющий* до́вод.

cling [klɪŋ] (*pt, pp* **clung**) *vi* (*clothes, dress*) облега́ть (*impf*); **to ~ to** (*mother, support*) вцепля́ться (вцепи́ться* *perf*) в +*acc*; (*idea, belief*) цепля́ться (*impf*) за +*acc*.

clingfilm [ˈklɪŋfɪlm] *n* обёрточная плёнка для проду́ктов.

clinic [ˈklɪnɪk] *n* (*medical centre*) кли́ника; (*session*) консульта́ция.

clinical [ˈklɪnɪkl] *adj* (*MED*) клини́ческий*; (*fig: attitude*) бесстра́стный (бесстра́стен); (: *room*) стери́льный.

clink [klɪŋk] *vi* звене́ть (*impf*) ♦ *vt* (*glasses*) чо́каться (чо́кнуться *perf*) +*instr*.

clip [klɪp] *n* (*also:* **paper ~**) скре́пка*; (*BRIT: also:* **bulldog ~**) зажи́м; (*for hair*) зако́лка*; (*TV, CINEMA*) клип ♦ *vt* (*fasten*) прикрепля́ть (прикрепи́ть* *perf*); (*also:* ~ **together**: *papers*) скрепля́ть (скрепи́ть* *perf*); (*cut*) подстрига́ть (подстри́чь* *perf*).

clippers [ˈklɪpəz] *npl* (*for gardening*) сека́тор *msg*; (*also:* **nail ~**) щи́пчики *pl*.

clipping [ˈklɪpɪŋ] *n* (*PRESS*) вы́резка*.

clique [kliːk] *n* кли́ка.

clitoris [ˈklɪtərɪs] *n* кли́тор.

cloak [kləuk] *n* (*cape*) плащ* ♦ *vt* (*fig: in mist*) оку́тывать (оку́тать *perf*) +*instr*; ~**ed in** оку́танный (оку́тан) +*instr*.

cloakroom [ˈkləukrum] *n* (*for coats*) гардеро́б; (*BRIT: toilet*) убо́рная *f adj*.

clobber [ˈklɔbəʳ] *(inf) n* мона́тки *pl* ♦ *vt* (*hit*) колошма́тить (исколошма́тить *perf*); (*defeat*) отколошма́тить* (*perf*).

clock [klɔk] *n* часы́ *pl*; (*of taxi*) счётчик; **to sleep/work round the ~** спать* (*impf*)/ рабо́тать (*impf*) кру́глые су́тки; **this car has 30,000 miles on the ~** (*BRIT*) э́та маши́на нае́здила 30,000 миль; **to work against the ~** рабо́тать (*impf*) наперегонки́ со вре́менем

► **clock in** *vi* (*BRIT: for work*) отмеча́ться (отме́титься* *perf*) (приходя́ на рабо́ту)

► **clock off** *vi* (*BRIT: from work*) отмеча́ться (отме́титься* *perf*) (уходя́ с рабо́ты)

► **clock on** *vi* (*BRIT*) = **clock in**

► **clock out** *vi* (*BRIT*) = **clock off**

► **clock up** *vt* (*debts*) нака́пливать (накопи́ть* *perf*); (*miles*) накру́чивать (накрути́ть* *perf*); (*hours*) набира́ть (набра́ть* *perf*).

clockwise [ˈklɔkwaɪz] *adv* по часово́й стре́лке.

clockwork [ˈklɔkwəːk] *n* заво́д ♦ *adj* (*toy*) заводно́й.

clog [klɔg] *n* сабо́* *nt ind* ♦ *vt* (*drain*) засоря́ть (засори́ть *perf*) ♦ *vi* (*also:* ~ **up**: *sink*) засоря́ться (засори́ться *perf*); **my nose is ~ged (up)** у меня́ зало́жен нос.

cloister [ˈklɔɪstəʳ] *n* кры́тая галере́я.

clone [kləun] *n* (*BIO*) клон.

close[1] [kləus] *adj* (*near*) бли́зкий* (бли́зок); (*writing*) убо́рстый (убо́рист); (*contact, ties*) те́сный* (те́сен); (*watch, attention*) при́стальный* (при́стален); (*weather, room*) ду́шный* (ду́шен) ♦ *adv* бли́зко; **to ~** (*near*) бли́зкий (бли́зок) к +*dat*; ~ **to** *or* **on** (*almost*) бли́зко к +*dat*; ~ **by** *or* **at hand** ря́дом; **how ~ is Edinburgh to Glasgow?** как бли́зко от Эдинбу́рга нахо́дится Гла́зго?; **a ~ friend** бли́зкий* друг*; **a ~ contest** борьба́ на ра́вных; **I had a ~ shave** (*fig*) я был на волосо́к от э́того; **to keep a ~ eye on sb/sth** внима́тельно следи́ть (*impf*) за +*instr*; **at ~ quarters** на бли́зком расстоя́нии

close[2] [kləuz] *vt* (*shut*) закрыва́ть (закры́ть* *perf*); (*finalize*) заключа́ть (заключи́ть *perf*); (*end*) заверша́ть (заверши́ть *perf*) ♦ *vi* (*shut*) закрыва́ться (закры́ться* *perf*); (*end*) заверша́ться(заверши́ться *perf*) ♦ *n* коне́ц*; **to bring sth to a ~** заверша́ть (заверши́ть *perf*) что-н

► **close down** *vt* закрыва́ть (закры́ть* *perf*) ♦ *vi* закрыва́ться (закры́ться* *perf*)

---

* marks translations which have irregular inflections. The Russian-English side of the dictionary gives inflectional information.

▸ **close in** vi (*night, fog*) опуска́ться
(опусти́ться* *perf*); (*hunters*): **to ~ in (on sb/
sth)** окружа́ть (окружи́ть *perf*) (кого́-н/
что-н); **the days are closing in** дни стано́вятся
коро́че

▸ **close off** vt (*area*) огора́живать (огороди́ть*
perf); (*road*) блоки́ровать (*impf/perf*).

closed [kləuzd] *adj* закры́тый (закры́т).

closed-circuit ['kləuzd'sə:kɪt] *adj*: **~ television**
за́мкнутая телевизио́нная систе́ма.

closed shop n (*union*) *предприя́тие, на
кото́ром рабо́тают то́лько чле́ны
определённого профсою́за*.

close-knit ['kləus'nɪt] *adj* сплочённый
(сплочён).

closely ['kləuslɪ] *adv* (*watch, examine*)
при́стально; (*connected, related*) те́сно; **he ~
resembles his father** он о́чень похо́ж на отца́;
we are ~ related мы бли́зкие ро́дственники;
a ~ guarded secret тща́тельно оберега́емый
секре́т.

close season ['kləus-] n закры́тый сезо́н.

closet ['klɔzɪt] n (*cupboard*) шкаф*; (*room*)
чула́н.

close-up ['kləusʌp] n (*PHOT*) кру́пный план.

closing ['kləuzɪŋ] *adj* (*stages, remarks*)
заключи́тельный.

closing price n (*COMM*) после́дняя цена́ *or*
ста́вка*.

closing time n вре́мя* nt закры́тия (*бáра*).

closure ['kləuʒə'] n (*of factory*) закры́тие; (*of
road*) блоки́рование.

clot [klɔt] n (*of blood etc*) сгу́сток*; (*inf*) балда́
m/f ◆ vi (*blood*) свора́чиваться (сверну́ться
perf).

cloth [klɔθ] n (*material*) ткань f; (*for cleaning
etc*) тря́пка*; (*BRIT: also:* **teacloth**) ку́хонное
полоте́нце*; (*also:* **tablecloth**) ска́терть* f.

clothe [kləuð] vt одева́ть (оде́ть* *perf*).

clothes [kləuðz] npl оде́жда fsg; **to put one's ~
on** одева́ться (оде́ться* *perf*); **to take one's ~
off** раздева́ться (разде́ться* *perf*); **to change
one's ~** переодева́ться (переоде́ться* *perf*).

clothes brush n оде́жная щётка*.

clothesline ['kləuðzlaɪn] n бельева́я верёвка*.

clothes peg (*US* **clothes pin**) n прище́пка*.

clothing ['kləuðɪŋ] n = **clothes**.

clotted cream ['klɔtɪd-] n (*BRIT*) густы́е сли́вки
pl.

cloud [klaud] n о́блако* ◆ vt (*liquid*) мути́ть*
(замути́ть* *perf*); **every ~ has a silver lining** нет
ху́да без добра́; **to ~ the issue** запу́тывать
(запу́тать *perf*) де́ло

▸ **cloud over** vi (*sky*) покрыва́ться
(покры́ться* *perf*) облака́ми; (*face*)
тума́ниться (затума́ниться *perf*).

cloudburst ['klaudbə:st] n ли́вень* m.

cloud-cuckoo-land [klaud'kuku:lænd] n (*BRIT*):
he is living in ~ он живёт в безо́блачном
ца́рстве.

cloudy ['klaudɪ] *adj* (*sky*) о́блачный* (о́блачен);

(*liquid*) му́тный* (му́тен).

clout [klaut] vt (*inf*) долбану́ть (*perf*) ◆ n (*fig*)
влия́ние.

clove [kləuv] n гвозди́ка; **~ of garlic** до́лька
чеснока́.

clover ['kləuvə'] n кле́вер.

cloverleaf ['kləuvəli:f] n лист* кле́вера; (*AUT*)
кле́верный лист* (*о констру́кции
пересече́ния автомоби́льных доро́г*).

clown [klaun] n кло́ун ◆ vi (*also: ~* **about,** ~
around) пая́сничать (*impf*).

cloying ['klɔɪŋ] *adj* (*taste, smell*) при́торный*
(при́торен).

club [klʌb] n (*society, place*) клуб; (*weapon*)
дуби́нка; (*implement: also:* **golf ~**) клю́шка*
◆ vt (*hit*) избива́ть (изби́ть* *perf*) ◆ vi: **to ~
together** скла́дываться (сложи́ться* *perf*); **~s**
npl (*CARDS*) тре́фы fpl; **king of ~s** трефо́вый
коро́ль m.

club car n (*US: RAIL*) ваго́н-рестора́н.

club class n осо́бый класс (*в самолётах*).

clubhouse ['klʌbhaus] n спорти́вный клуб
(*зда́ние*).

club soda n со́довая вода́.

cluck [klʌk] vi (*hen*) куда́хтать (*impf*).

clue [klu:] n ключ*; (*for police*) ули́ка; **I haven't
a ~** я поня́тия не име́ю.

clued-up ['klu:dʌp] (*US* **clued in**) *adj* (*inf*): **to be
~** быть* (*impf*) в ку́рсе (дел).

clueless ['klu:lɪs] *adj* без поня́тия.

clump [klʌmp] n (*of trees, plants*) за́росли fpl;
(*of buildings*) скопле́ние.

clumsy ['klʌmzɪ] *adj* (*person, movement*)
неуклю́жий* (неуклю́ж); (*object*) неудо́бный
(неудо́бен).

clung [klʌŋ] pt, pp of **cling**.

cluster ['klʌstə'] n (*of people, stars*) скопле́ние;
(*of flowers*) пучо́к* ◆ vi (*people*) сгруди́ться
(*perf*); (*things*) ска́пливаться (скопи́ться*
perf).

clutch [klʌtʃ] n (*grip*) хва́тка; (*AUT*) сцепле́ние
◆ vt сжима́ть (сжать* *perf*) ◆ vi: **to ~ at**
цепля́ться (*impf*) за +acc; **he has me in his ~es**
я у него́ в рука́х.

clutter ['klʌtə'] vt (*also: ~* **up**: *room, table*)
захламля́ть (захлами́ть* *perf*) ◆ n хлам.

CM *abbr* (*US: POST*) = **North Mariana Islands**.

cm *abbr* (= **centimetre**) см= *сантиме́тр*.

CNAA n *abbr* (*BRIT*) = **Council for National
Academic Awards**.

CND n *abbr* = **Campaign for Nuclear
Disarmament**.

CO n *abbr* = **commanding officer**; (*BRIT*: =
Commonwealth Office) *отде́л по дела́м на́ций
брита́нского Содру́жества* ◆ *abbr* (*US: POST*)
= **Colorado**.

Co. *abbr* = **company, county**.

c/o *abbr* (= **care of**) для переда́чи +dat.

coach [kəutʃ] n (*bus*) авто́бус; (*horse-drawn*)
каре́та; (*of train*) ваго́н; (*SPORT*) тре́нер;
(*SCOL*) репети́тор ◆ vt (*SPORT*) тренирова́ть

(натренировáть *perf*); (*SCOL*): **to ~ sb for sth** готóвить* (подготóвить* *perf*) когó-н к чему́-н.
coach trip *n* автóбусная экскýрсия.
coagulate [kəu'ægjuleɪt] *vi* (*blood*) св오рáчиваться (сверну́ться *perf*); (*paint*) сгущáться (сгусти́ться* *perf*).
coal [kəul] *n* ýголь* *m*.
coalface ['kəulfeɪs] *n* забóй.
coalfield ['kəulfi:ld] *n* каменноýгольный бассéйн.
coalition [kəuə'lɪʃən] *n* (*also POL*) коали́ция.
coalman ['kəulmən] *irreg n* ýгольщик.
coalmine ['kəulmaɪn] *n* ýгольная шáхта.
coal miner *n* шахтёр.
coal mining *n* добы́ча угля́.
coarse [kɔ:s] *adj* грýбый*; (*hair*) жёсткий*; (*salt, sand etc*) крýпный*.
coast [kəust] *n* бéрег*; (*area*) побережье ◆ *vi* (*car etc*) кати́ться* (покати́ться* *perf*) по инéрции.
coastal ['kəustl] *adj* прибрéжный; (*services*) береговóй.
coaster ['kəustə'] *n* (*NAUT*) кабота́жное сýдно*; (*for glass*) подстáвка* для стакáна.
coastguard ['kəustgɑ:d] *n* (*officer*) офицéр береговóй слýжбы; **the ~** (*service*) береговáя слýжба.
coastline ['kəustlaɪn] *n* береговáя ли́ния.
coat [kəut] *n* пальтó *nt ind*; (*on animal: fur*) мех*; (: *wool*) шерсть*; (*of paint*) слой* ◆ *vt* покрывáть (покры́ть* *perf*).
coat hanger *n* вéшалка*.
coating ['kəutɪŋ] *n* слой.
coat of arms *n* герб*.
coauthor ['kəu'ɔ:θə'] *n* соáвтор.
coax [kəuks] *vt* угова́ривать (уговори́ть *perf*) лáской.
cob [kɔb] *n see* **corn.**
cobbler ['kɔblə'] *n* сапóжник.
cobbles ['kɔblz] *npl* булы́жники *mpl*.
cobblestones ['kɔblstəunz] *npl =* **cobbles.**
COBOL ['kəubɔl] *n* Кóбол.
cobra ['kəubrə] *n* кóбра.
cobweb ['kɔbwɛb] *n* паути́на.
cocaine [kə'keɪn] *n* кокаи́н.
cock [kɔk] *n* (*rooster*) петýх*; (*male bird*) самéц* ◆ *vt* (*gun*) взводи́ть* (взвести́* *perf*); **to ~ one's ears** (*fig*) навостри́ть (*perf*) ýши.
cock-a-hoop [kɔkə'hu:p] *adj*: **to be ~** балдéть (*impf*).
cockerel ['kɔkərl] *n* петýх*.
cockeyed ['kɔkaɪd] *adj* (*fig*) дурáцкий*.
cockle ['kɔkl] *n* моллю́ск.
cockney ['kɔknɪ] *n* (*person*) кóкни *m/f ind* (*урожéнец райóна Ист-Энд в Лóндоне*); (*LING*) кóкни *m ind* (*диалéкт урожéнцев Ист-Энда*).

cockpit ['kɔkpɪt] *n* каби́на.
cockroach ['kɔkrəutʃ] *n* таракáн.
cocktail ['kɔkteɪl] *n* (*drink*) коктéйль *m*; (*with fruit, prawns etc*) салáт, закýска.
cocktail cabinet *n* бар (*в сервáнте*).
cocktail party *n* приём.
cocktail shaker [-'ʃeɪkə'] *n* ми́ксер.
cockup ['kɔkʌp] *n* (*inf!*) лáжа (*!*)
cocky ['kɔkɪ] *adj* дéрзкий* (дéрзок), зади́ристый (зади́рист).
cocoa ['kəukəu] *n* какáо *nt ind*.
coconut ['kəukənʌt] *n* (*fruit*) кокóсовый орéх; (*flesh*) кокóс.
cocoon [kə'ku:n] *n* (*of butterfly*) кóкон; (*fig*) оболóчка.
COD *abbr* (= *cash on delivery*) налóженный платёж; (*US*: = *collect on delivery*) налóженный платёж *pl*.
cod [kɔd] *n* трескá *f no pl*.
code [kəud] *n* (*of behaviour*) кóдекс; (*cipher, TEL*) код; **post ~** почтóвый и́ндекс; **~ of practice** свод прáвил (*профессионáльной дéятельности*).
codeine ['kəudi:n] *n* кодеи́н.
codger ['kɔdʒə'] *n* чудáк*.
codicil ['kɔdɪsɪl] *n* (*LAW*) дополни́тельный парáграф завещáния.
codify ['kəudɪfaɪ] *vt* кодифици́ровать (*impf/perf*).
cod-liver oil ['kɔdlɪvə-] *n* ры́бий* жир.
co-driver ['kəu'draɪvə'] *n* (*in race*) штýрман; (*of lorry*) смéнный води́тель.
co-ed ['kəu'ɛd] *adj abbr* (*SCOL*) = **coeducational** ◆ *n abbr* (*US*: *female student*) студéнтка (*в учéбных заведéниях смéшанного ти́па*); (*BRIT*: *school*) смéшанная шкóла.
coeducational ['kəuɛdju'keɪʃənl] *adj* (*school*) смéшанный.
coerce [kəu'ə:s] *vt* принуждáть (прину́дить* *perf*).
coercion [kəu'ə:ʃən] *n* принуждéние.
coexistence ['kəuɪg'zɪstəns] *n* сосуществовáние.
C. of C. *n abbr* (= *chamber of commerce*) Торгóвая палáта.
C of E *abbr* = **Church of England.**
coffee ['kɔfɪ] *n* кóфе *m ind*; **black ~** чёрный кóфе; **white ~** кóфе с молокóм; **~ with cream** кóфе со сли́вками.
coffee bar *n* (*BRIT*) кофéйная *f adj*.
coffee beans *npl* кофéйные зёрна *ntpl*.
coffee break *n* переры́в на кóфе.
coffee cake *n* (*US*) торт к кóфе.
coffee cup *n* кофéйная чáшка*.
coffeepot ['kɔfɪpɔt] *n* кофéйник.
coffee table *n* кофéйный стóлик.
coffin ['kɔfɪn] *n* гроб*.
C of I *abbr* = *Church of Ireland.*
C of S *abbr* = *Church of Scotland.*

---

* marks translations which have irregular inflections. The Russian-English side of the dictionary gives inflectional information.

cog [kɔg] n (wheel) зу́бчатое колесо́*; (tooth) зубе́ц*.

cogent ['kəudʒənt] adj внуши́тельный* (внуши́телен).

cognac ['kɔnjæk] n конья́к*.

cogwheel ['kɔgwi:l] n зу́бчатое колесо́*.

cohabit [kəu'hæbɪt] vi: **to ~ (with sb)** сожи́тельствовать (impf) (с кем-н).

coherent [kəu'hɪərənt] adj свя́зный; **she was very ~** её речь была́ о́чень свя́зной.

cohesion [kəu'hi:ʒən] n це́льность f.

cohesive [kə'hi:sɪv] adj (fig) це́льный* (це́лен).

COI n abbr (BRIT: = Central Office of Information) Центра́льное управле́ние информа́ции.

coil [kɔɪl] n (of rope, wire) мото́к*; (one loop) вито́к*; (of smoke) кольцо́*; (AUT) кату́шка*; (contraceptive) спира́ль f ♦ vt (rope) сма́тывать (смота́ть perf).

coin [kɔɪn] n моне́та ♦ vt (phrase) приду́мывать (приду́мать perf).

coinage ['kɔɪnɪdʒ] n (money) де́нежные зна́ки mpl; (system) де́нежная систе́ма; (LING) неологи́зм.

coin box n (BRIT) телефо́н-автома́т.

coincide [kəuɪn'saɪd] vi совпада́ть (совпа́сть* perf).

coincidence [kəu'ɪnsɪdəns] n совпаде́ние.

coin-operated ['kɔɪn'ɔpəreɪtɪd] adj: **~ machine** автома́т.

Coke® [kəuk] n (drink) ко́ка-ко́ла; **I would like a ~, please** да́йте пожа́луйста ко́ка-ко́лу.

coke [kəuk] n (coal) кокс.

Col. abbr = colonel.

COLA n abbr (US: = cost-of-living adjustment) индекса́ция за́работной пла́ты.

colander ['kɔləndəʳ] n (CULIN) дуршла́г.

cold [kəuld] adj холо́дный* ♦ n хо́лод; (MED) просту́да; **it's ~** хо́лодно; **I am** or **feel ~** мне хо́лодно; **the wall is ~** э́та стена́ холо́дная; **to catch ~** or **a ~** простужа́ться (простуди́ться* perf); **in ~ blood** хладнокро́вно; **to have ~ feet** (fig) тру́сить* (стру́сить* perf); **I gave her the ~ shoulder** я был неприве́тлив с ней.

cold-blooded ['kəuld'blʌdɪd] adj (ZOOL) холоднокро́вный (холоднокро́вен); (callous) хладнокро́вный* (хладнокро́вен).

cold cream n ко́льд крем.

coldly ['kəuldlɪ] adv хо́лодно.

cold-shoulder [kəuld'ʃəuldəʳ] vt относи́ться* (отнести́сь* perf) неприве́тливо к +dat.

cold sore n лихора́дка* (на губе́ и́ли носу́).

cold sweat n холо́дный пот.

cold turkey n (inf): **he is going through ~ ~** у него́ ло́мка.

cold war n: **the ~ ~** холо́дная война́.

coleslaw ['kəulslɔ:] n капу́стный сала́д с майоне́зом.

colic ['kɔlɪk] n ко́лики pl.

colicky ['kɔlɪkɪ] adj страда́ющий ко́ликами.

collaborate [kə'læbəreɪt] vi сотру́дничать

(impf).

collaboration [kəlæbə'reɪʃən] n сотру́дничество.

collaborator [kə'læbəreɪtəʳ] n (on book etc) соа́втор; (with enemy) коллаборациони́ст.

collage [kɔ'lɑ:ʒ] n (ART) колла́ж.

collagen ['kɔlədʒən] n коллаге́н.

collapse [kə'læps] vi (building, system, plans) ру́шиться (ру́хнуть perf); (table etc) скла́дываться (сложи́ться perf); (company) разоря́ться (разори́ться perf); (government) разва́ливаться (развали́ться perf); (resistance) сломи́ться (perf); (MED: person) свали́ться (perf) ♦ n (of building) обва́л; (of system, plans) круше́ние; (of company) разоре́ние; (of government) паде́ние; (MED) упа́док сил, колла́пс; **a ~d lung** колла́пс лёгкого.

collapsible [kə'læpsəbl] adj складно́й.

collar ['kɔləʳ] n (of shirt etc) воротни́к*; (of dog etc) оше́йник; (TECH) ше́йка* ♦ vt (inf: physically) схва́тывать (схвати́ть* perf); (to speak to) заде́рживать (задержа́ть* perf).

collarbone ['kɔləbəun] n ключи́ца.

collate [kɔ'leɪt] vt сопоставля́ть (сопоста́вить* perf).

collateral [kə'lætərl] n (COMM) обеспече́ние креди́та.

collateral damage n сопу́тствующее разруше́ние.

collation [kə'leɪʃən] n сопоставле́ние, сличе́ние; **a cold ~** холо́дный буфе́т.

colleague ['kɔli:g] n колле́га m/f.

collect [kə'lɛkt] vt (gather) собира́ть (собра́ть* perf); (stamps etc) коллекциони́ровать (impf); (BRIT: on foot) заходи́ть* (зайти́* perf) за +instr; (: by vehicle) заезжа́ть* (зае́хать* perf) за +instr; (debts etc) взы́скивать (взыска́ть* perf); (mail) забира́ть (забра́ть* perf) ♦ vi (crowd) собира́ться (собра́ться* perf); **to call ~** (US) звони́ть (impf) по колле́кту; **to ~ one's thoughts** собира́ться (собра́ться perf) с мы́слями; **~ on delivery** (US) нало́женный платёж.

collected [kə'lɛktɪd] adj: **~ works** собра́ние сочине́ний.

collection [kə'lɛkʃən] n (of stamps etc) колле́кция; (of poems etc) сбо́рник; (for charity, also REL) поже́ртвования ntpl; (of mail) вы́емка*.

collective [kə'lɛktɪv] adj коллекти́вный ♦ n коллекти́в.

collective bargaining n перегово́ры ме́жду предпринима́телем и профсою́зами об опла́те труда́ рабо́чих.

collector [kə'lɛktəʳ] n (of stamps etc) коллекционе́р; (of taxes etc) сбо́рщик(-ица); (of cash) инкасса́тор; **~'s item** or **piece** вещь, представля́ющая интере́с для коллекционе́ра.

college ['kɔlɪdʒ] n (of university) колле́дж; (of

technology etc) институ́т; **to go to** ~
поступа́ть (поступи́ть* perf) в институ́т; ~ **of
education** уче́бное заведе́ние.
collide [kə'laɪd] vi (cars, people) ста́лкиваться
(столкну́ться perf); **to** ~ **with sth**
ната́лкиваться (натолкну́ться perf) на что-н.
collie ['kɔlɪ] n ко́лли m ind.
colliery ['kɔlɪərɪ] n (BRIT) у́гольная ша́хта.
collision [kə'lɪʒən] n (of vehicles)
столкнове́ние; **to be on a** ~ **course**
находи́ться* (impf) на пути́, веду́щем к
столкнове́нию; (fig) вставать* (встать* perf)
на путь конфронта́ции.
collision damage waiver n страхо́вка,
освобожда́ющая от вы́платы компенса́ции
за поврежде́ние взя́той на прока́т маши́ны.
colloquial [kə'ləukwɪəl] adj разгово́рный.
collusion [kə'luːʒən] n (collaboration) сго́вор; **in**
~ **with** в сго́воре с +instr.
Cologne [kə'ləun] n Кёльн.
cologne [kə'ləun] n (also: **eau de** ~) одеколо́н.
Colombia [kə'lɔmbɪə] n Колу́мбия.
Colombian [kə'lɔmbɪən] adj колумби́йский* ◆
n колумби́ец(-и́йка).
colon ['kəulən] n (LING) двоето́чие; (ANAT)
пряма́я кишка́.
colonel ['kəːnl] n полко́вник.
colonial [kə'ləunɪəl] adj колониа́льный.
colonize ['kɔlənaɪz] vt (country etc)
колонизи́ровать (impf/perf).
colony ['kɔlənɪ] n (of people, animals) коло́ния.
color etc (US) = **colour** etc.
Colorado beetle [kɔlə'rɑːdəu-] n колора́дский
жук*.
colossal [kə'lɔsl] adj колосса́льный*
(колосса́лен).
colour ['kʌləʳ] (US color) n цвет*; (of spectacle
etc) кра́сочность f ◆ vt (paint) раскра́шивать
(раскра́сить* perf); (dye) кра́сить*
(покра́сить* perf); (fig: judgement etc)
окра́шивать (окра́сить* perf) ◆ vi (blush)
красне́ть (покрасне́ть perf) ◆ cpd цветно́й; ~**s**
npl (of club etc) эмбле́ма fsg; (MIL) флаг msg;
skin ~ цвет ко́жи; **in** ~ в цве́те; **with flying** ~**s**
с триу́мфом.
▶ **colour in** vt раскра́шивать (раскра́сить*
perf).
colour bar n ра́ссовый барье́р.
colour-blind ['kʌləblaɪnd] adj: **he is** ~ он
дальто́ник.
coloured ['kʌləd] adj цветно́й.
colour film n цветна́я плёнка.
colourful ['kʌləful] adj (cloth) цвети́стый
(цвети́ст); (story) кра́сочный* (кра́сочен);
(personality) я́ркий*.
colouring ['kʌlərɪŋ] n (complexion) цвет лица́;
(in food) краси́тель m.
colour scheme n цветова́я га́мма.

colour supplement n (BRIT: PRESS)
иллюстри́рованное приложе́ние.
colour television n цветно́й телеви́зор.
colt [kəult] n жеребёнок*.
column ['kɔləm] n (of people, also ARCHIT)
коло́нна; (of smoke) столб*; (PRESS)
ру́брика; **the editorial** ~ реда́кторская
статья́*.
columnist ['kɔləmnɪst] n (PRESS) обозрева́тель
m.
coma ['kəumə] n (MED): **to be in a** ~
находи́ться* (impf) в ко́ме.
comb [kəum] n (for hair) расчёска; (:
ornamental) гре́бень* m ◆ vt (hair)
расчёсывать (расчеса́ть* perf); (area)
прочёсывать (прочеса́ть* perf).
combat [n 'kɔmbæt, vt kɔm'bæt] n (fighting)
бой*; (battle) би́тва ◆ vt боро́ться* (impf)
про́тив +gen.
combination [kɔmbɪ'neɪʃən] n (mixture)
сочета́ние, комбина́ция; (code) код.
combination lock n замо́к* с ши́фром.
combine [vb kəm'baɪn, n 'kɔmbaɪn] vt
комбини́ровать (скомбини́ровать perf) ◆ vi
(groups) объединя́ться (объедини́ться perf);
(CHEM) вступа́ть (вступи́ть* perf) в
соедине́ние ◆ n (ECON) объедине́ние; (also: ~
harvester) комба́йн; **to** ~ **sth with sth**
(qualities) сочета́ть perf что-н с чем-н;
(activities) совмеща́ть (совмести́ть* perf)
что-н с чем-н; **a** ~**d effort** совме́стное
уси́лие.
combo ['kɔmbəu] n (JAZZ) ко́мбо.
combustible [kəm'bʌstɪbl] adj горю́чий*.
combustion [kəm'bʌstʃən] n (act) сгора́ние;
(process) горе́ние.

┌─────────────┐
│ **KEYWORD** │
└─────────────┘

come [kʌm] (pt **came**, pp **come**) vi **1** (move
towards: on foot) подходи́ть* (подойти́* perf);
(: by transport) подъезжа́ть (подъе́хать* perf);
they came to a river (on foot) они́ подошли́ к
реке́; (by transport) они́ подъе́хали к реке́; **he
came running up to us** он подбежа́л к нам; **to
come running** подбега́ть (подбежа́ть* perf)
2 (arrive: on foot) приходи́ть* (прийти́* perf);
(: by transport) приезжа́ть (прие́хать* perf); **to
come home** (on foot) приходи́ть* (прийти́*
perf) домо́й; (by transport) приезжа́ть
(прие́хать* perf) домо́й; **he came running to
tell us** он прибежа́л, сказа́ть нам; **are you
coming to my party?** Вы придёте ко мне на
вечери́нку?; **I've only come for an hour** я
зашёл то́лько на час
3 (reach: power, decision, conclusion): **to come
to** приходи́ть* (прийти́* perf) к +dat; **the bill
came to £40** счёт был £40; **her hair came to
her waist** у неё бы́ли во́лосы до по́яса
4 (occur): **an idea came to me** мне в го́лову

пришла́ иде́я
5 (*be, become*): **to come into being** возника́ть
(возни́кнуть *perf*); **to come loose** отходи́ть*
(отойти́* *perf*); **I've come to like him** он стал
мне нра́виться
► **come about** *vi*: **how did it come about?**
каки́м о́бразом э́то получи́лось?; **it came**
about through... э́то получи́лось из-за +*gen*
► **come across** *vt fus* ната́лкиваться
(натолкну́ться *perf*) на +*acc*
  ♦ *vi*: **to come across well/badly** производи́ть*
(произвести́* *perf*) хоро́шее/плохо́е
впечатле́ние
► **come along** *vi* (*pupil, work*) продвига́ться
(продви́нуться *perf*); **come along!** идёмте!,
пошли́!
► **come apart** *vi* (*break*) лома́ться (слома́ться
perf); (*can be dismantled*) разбира́ться (*impf*);
(*tear*) рва́ться* (разорва́ться* *perf*)
► **come away** *vi* (*leave*) уходи́ть* (уйти́* *perf*);
(*to become detached*) отходи́ть* (отойти́*
perf)
► **come back** *vi* (*return*) возвраща́ться
(верну́ться *perf*); (*inf*): **can I come back to you**
on that one? я ещё верну́сь к Вам с э́тим,
ла́дно?
► **come by** *vt fus* (*acquire*) достава́ть* (доста́ть*
perf)
► **come down** *vi* (*price*) понижа́ться
(пони́зиться* *perf*); **the tree came down in the**
storm де́рево снесло́ бу́рей; **the building will**
have to come down soon зда́ние должны́
ско́ро снести́
► **come forward** *vi* (*volunteer*) вызыва́ться
(вы́зваться* *perf*)
► **come from** *vt fus* (*place, source etc*): **she**
comes from India она́ из Инди́и
► **come in** *vi* (*person*) входи́ть* (войти́* *perf*);
(*on deal etc*): **to come in on** вступа́ть
(вступи́ть* *perf*) в +*acc*; **where does he come**
in? в чём его́ роль?
► **come in for** *vt fus* подверга́ться
(подве́ргнуться* *perf*) +*dat*
► **come into** *vt fus* (*fashion*) входи́ть* (войти́*
perf) в +*acc*; (*be involved in*) игра́ть (*impf*) роль
в +*prp*; **to come into money** получа́ть
(получи́ть* *perf*) су́мму де́нег
► **come off** *vi* (*button*) отрыва́ться
(оторва́ться* *perf*); (*handle*) отла́мываться
(отлома́ться* *perf*); (*can be taken off*)
снима́ться (*impf*); (*attempt*) удава́ться*
(уда́ться* *perf*)
► **come on** *vi* (*pupil*) де́лать (сде́лать *perf*)
успе́хи; (*work etc*) продвига́ться (*impf*); (*lights*
etc) включа́ться (включи́ться* *perf*); **come**
on! (ну,) дава́йте!
► **come out** *vi* (*fact*) станови́ться (стать* *perf*)
изве́стным(-ой); (*book, sun*) выходи́ть*
(вы́йти* *perf*); (*stain*) сходи́ть* (сойти́* *perf*);
(*person*) выходи́ть* (вы́йти* *perf*); (*workers*):
to come out on strike выходи́ть* (вы́йти* *perf*)

на забасто́вку
► **come over** *vt fus*: **I don't know what's come**
over him! я не зна́ю, что с ним тако́е!
► **come round** *vi* (*MED*) очну́ться (*perf*),
приходи́ть* (прийти́* *perf*) в себя́
► **come through** *vt fus* (*survive*) пережи́ть*
(*perf*); (: *operation*) переноси́ть* (перенести́*
perf)
  ♦ *vi*: **his visa came through yesterday** его́ ви́за
пришла́ вчера́
► **come to** *vi* (*MED*) очну́ться (*perf*), приходи́ть*
(прийти́* *perf*) в себя́
  ♦ *vt fus*: **how much does it come to?** ско́лько
э́то всё бу́дет?
► **come under** *vt fus*: **to come under (the**
heading) идти́* (*impf*) под заголо́вком; **to**
come under criticism from ... подверга́ться
(подве́ргнуться *perf*) кри́тике со стороны́
+*gen* ...; **he has come under pressure from his**
boss его́ нача́льник ока́зывал на него́
давле́ние
► **come up** *vi* (*sun*) всходи́ть* (взойти́* *perf*);
(*approach: event*) приближа́ться (*impf*); (*arise*:
questions) встава́ть (встать* *perf*); (*to be*
mentioned) быть (*impf*) затро́нутым; **I can't**
come with you, something important has
come up я не смогу́ пойти́ с тобо́й, у меня́
возни́кло ва́жное де́ло
► **come up against** *vt fus* ната́лкиваться
(натолкну́ться *perf*) на +*acc*
► **come up to** *vt fus*: **the film didn't come up to**
our expectations фильм не оправда́л на́ши
ожида́ния
► **come up with** *vt fus* (*idea, solution*)
приду́мывать (приду́мать *perf*); (*money*)
найти́* (*perf*)
► **come upon** *vt fus* ната́лкиваться
(натолкну́ться *perf*) на +*acc*.

comeback ['kʌmbæk] *n* (*reaction*)
язви́тельный отве́т; (*response*) возраже́ние;
to make a ~ (*of actor etc*) обрета́ть (обрести́*
perf) но́вую популя́рность.
Comecon ['kɔmɪkɔn] *n abbr* (= *Council for*
Mutual Economic Aid) ≈ СЭВ= *Сове́т*
Экономи́ческой Взаимопо́мощи.
comedian [kə'miːdiən] *n* ко́мик.
comedienne [kəmiːdɪ'ɛn] *n* коми́ческая
актри́са.
comedown ['kʌmdaun] *n* (*inf: humiliation*)
униже́ние; (: *demotion*) пониже́ние.
comedy ['kɔmɪdɪ] *n* (*play, film*) коме́дия;
(*humour*) коми́зм.
comet ['kɔmɪt] *n* коме́та.
comeuppance [kʌm'ʌpəns] *n*: **to get one's ~**
получа́ть (получи́ть* *perf*) по заслу́гам.
comfort ['kʌmfət] *n* (*well-being*) комфо́рт;
(*solace*) утеше́ние; (*relief*) облегче́ние ♦ *vt*
утеша́ть (уте́шить *perf*); **~s** *npl* (*luxuries*)
удо́бства *ntpl*.
comfortable ['kʌmfətəbl] *adj* (*furniture, room*)

удо́бный* (удо́бен), комфорта́бельный*
(комфорта́белен); (*walk etc*) лёгкий*;
(*majority*) прили́чный* (прили́чен); **to be ~**
(*person: physically*) чу́вствовать (*impf*) себя́
удо́бно; (: *financially*) жить (*impf*) в доста́тке;
(*patient*) чу́вствовать (*impf*) себя́ норма́льно;
I don't feel very ~ about it я чу́вствую себя́
нело́вко в да́нном слу́чае; **make yourself ~**
располага́йтесь поудо́бнее.
comfortably ['kʌmfətəblɪ] *adv* удо́бно.
comforter ['kʌmfətəʳ] *n* (*US*) со́ска-пусты́шка*.
comfort station *n* (*US*) обще́ственный туале́т.
comic ['kɔmɪk] *adj* коми́ческий*, смешно́й ♦ *n*
(*comedian*) ко́мик; (*BRIT: magazine*) ко́микс.
comical ['kɔmɪkl] *adj* смешно́й* (смешо́н),
коми́чный* (коми́чен).
comic strip *n* ко́микс (*се́рия рису́нков*).
coming ['kʌmɪŋ] *n* прибы́тие ♦ *adj*
(*approaching*) приближа́ющийся; (*next*)
сле́дующий*; (*future*) бу́дущий*; **in the ~**
weeks в тече́ние сле́дующих неде́ль.
coming(s) and going(s) *n(pl)* прихо́д *msg* и
ухо́д *msg.*
Comintern ['kɔmɪntəːn] *n* (*POL*) Коминте́рн.
comma ['kɔmə] *n* (*LING*) запята́я *f adj.*
command [kə'mɑːnd] *n* (*order*) кома́нда;
(*control*) контро́ль *m*; (*MIL*) кома́ндование;
(*mastery*) владе́ние; (*COMPUT*) кома́нда,
директи́ва ♦ *vt* (*troops*) кома́ндовать (*impf*)
+*instr*; (*be able to get*) располага́ть (*impf*)
+*instr*; (*deserve*) заслу́живать (*impf*) +*gen*; **to**
be in ~ of (*situation*) владе́ть (овладе́ть *perf*)
+*instr*; **to take ~ of** (*MIL*) принима́ть (приня́ть*
perf) кома́ндование +*instr*; **to have at one's ~**
(*resources etc*) име́ть (*impf*) в своём
распоряже́нии; **he has a good ~ of English** он
хорошо́ владе́ет англи́йским языко́м; **to ~**
sb to do прика́зывать (приказа́ть* *perf*)
кому́-н +*infin.*
commandant ['kɔməndænt] *n* коменда́нт.
command economy *n* кома́ндная
эконо́мика.
commandeer [kɔmən'dɪəʳ] *vt* (*requisition*)
реквизи́ровать (*impf/perf*); (*fig*) присва́ивать
(присво́ить *perf*).
commander [kə'mɑːndəʳ] *n* (*MIL: of troops*)
кома́ндующий *m adj*; (: *of batallion*)
команди́р.
commander in chief *n* главнокома́ндующий
m adj.
commanding [kə'mɑːndɪŋ] *adj* (*appearance*)
внуши́тельный*; (*voice etc*) вла́стный*;
(*situation*) госпо́дствующий*.
commanding officer *n* команди́р.
commandment [kə'mɑːndmənt] *n* за́поведь *f.*
command module *n* (*SPACE*) кома́ндный
отсе́к корабля́.
commando [kə'mɑːndəu] *n* (*group*) деса́нтные

войска́ *ntpl*; (*soldier*) деса́нтник.
commemorate [kə'mɛməreɪt] *vt* (*with statue*
etc) увекове́чивать (увекове́чить *perf*); (*with*
celebration etc) отмеча́ть (отме́тить* *perf*).
commemoration [kəmɛmə'reɪʃən] *n*
ознаменова́ние.
commemorative [kə'mɛmərətɪv] *adj* (*stamp*)
юбиле́йный; (*plaque*) мемориа́льный.
commence [kə'mɛns] *vt* приступа́ть
(приступи́ть* *perf*) к +*dat* ♦ *vi* начина́ться
(нача́ться* *perf*).
commend [kə'mɛnd] *vt* хвали́ть* (похвали́ть*
perf); (*recommend*): **to ~ sth to sb**
рекомендова́ть (порекомендова́ть *perf*)
что-н кому́-н.
commendable [kə'mɛndəbl] *adj* похва́льный*
(похва́лен).
commendation [kɔmɛn'deɪʃən] *n*
благода́рность *f.*
commensurate [kə'mɛnʃərɪt] *adj*: **~ with**
соразме́рный* (соразме́рен) +*dat or c* +*instr.*
comment ['kɔmɛnt] *n* (*remark*) замеча́ние; (*on*
situation) коммента́рий ♦ *vi*: **to ~ (on)**
комменти́ровать (прокомменти́ровать *perf*)
(+*acc*); **to ~ that** поясня́ть (поясни́ть *perf*),
что; *"no ~"* "возде́рживаюсь от
коммента́риев".
commentary ['kɔməntərɪ] *n* репорта́ж; (*book,*
article) коммента́рий.
commentator ['kɔmənteɪtəʳ] *n* (*TV, RADIO*)
коммента́тор; (**sports**) ~ спорти́вный
коммента́тор.
commerce ['kɔməːs] *n* комме́рция.
commercial [kə'məːʃəl] *adj* (*organization*)
комме́рческий*; (*success, failure*)
фина́нсовый ♦ *n* (*TV, RADIO*) рекла́ма.
commercial bank *n* комме́рческий* банк.
commercial break *n* рекла́мная па́уза.
commercial college *n* институ́т комме́рции.
commercialism [kə'məːʃəlɪzəm] *n*
меркантили́зм.
commercialized [kə'məːʃəlaɪzd] *adj* (*pej*)
поста́вленный на комме́рческую осно́ву.
commercial radio *n* комме́рческое ра́дио.
commercial television *n* комме́рческое
телеви́дение.
commercial traveller *n* коммивояжёр.
commercial vehicle *n* комме́рческий
тра́нспорт.
commiserate [kə'mɪzəreɪt] *vi*: **to ~ with**
сочу́вствовать (посочу́вствовать *perf*) +*dat.*
commission [kə'mɪʃən] *n* (*order for work*)
зака́з; (*COMM*) комиссио́нные *pl adj*,
комиссио́нное вознагражде́ние; (*committee*)
коми́ссия; (*MIL*) офице́рский* чин ♦ *vt* (*order*)
зака́зывать (заказа́ть* *perf*); (*MIL*)
присва́ивать (присво́ить *perf*) офице́рский
чин +*dat*; **out of ~** (*NAUT*) не приго́дный

---

* marks translations which have irregular inflections. The Russian-English side of the dictionary gives inflectional information.

(приго́ден) к пла́ванию; (*machine*)
неиспра́вный* (неиспра́вен); **I get 10% ~** я
получа́ю 10% комиссио́ных; **~ of inquiry**
сле́дственная коми́ссия; **to ~ sb to do**
поруча́ть (поручи́ть* *perf*) кому́-н +*infin*; **to ~**
sth from sb зака́зывать (заказа́ть* *perf*) что-н
кому́-н.
commissionaire [kəmɪʃə'nɛəʳ] *n* (*BRIT*)
швейца́р.
commissioner [kə'mɪʃənəʳ] *n*: (**police**) ~
полице́йский* комисса́р.
commit [kə'mɪt] *vt* (*crime*) соверша́ть
(соверши́ть *perf*); (*money*) выделя́ть
(вы́делить *perf*); (*entrust*) вверя́ть (вве́рить
perf); **to ~ o.s.** принима́ть (приня́ть* *perf*) на
себя́ обяза́тельства; **to ~ suicide** соверша́ть
(соверши́ть *perf*) самоуби́йство; **to ~ to**
writing запи́сывать (записа́ть* *perf*); **to ~ to**
memory запомина́ть (запо́мнить *perf*); **to ~**
sb for trial отдава́ть* (отда́ть* *perf*) кого́-н
под суд.
commitment [kə'mɪtmənt] *n* (*belief*)
пре́данность *f*; (*obligation*) обяза́тельство.
committed [kə'mɪtɪd] *adj* (*supporter*)
приве́рженный (приве́ржен).
committee [kə'mɪtɪ] *n* комите́т; **to be on a ~**
входи́ть* (*impf*) в соста́в комите́та.
committee meeting *n* заседа́ние комите́та.
commodity [kə'mɔdɪtɪ] *n* (*saleable item*) това́р;
(*food*) проду́кт.
commodity exchange *n* това́рная би́ржа.
common ['kɔmən] *adj* (*shared*) о́бщий*; (*usual*,
ordinary) обы́чный; (*vulgar*) вульга́рный*
(вульга́рен) ◆ *n* обще́ственный луг*; **the C~s**
npl (*also*: **the House of C~s**: *BRIT*) Пала́та *fsg*
О́бщин; **to have sth in ~ (with sb)** име́ть (*impf*)
что-н о́бщее (с кем-н); **in ~ use** в широ́ком
употребле́нии; **it's ~ knowledge that**
общеизве́стно, что; **to** *or* **for the ~ good** для
всео́бщего бла́га.
common cold *n* обыкнове́нная просту́да.
common denominator *n* (*MATH*) о́бщий*
знамена́тель *m*; (*characteristic*) о́бщая черта́;
(*attitude*) о́бщее* мне́ние.
commoner ['kɔmənəʳ] *n* простолюди́н.
common ground *n* (*fig*) то́чки *fpl*
соприкоснове́ния.
common land *n* обще́ственная земля́*.
common law *n* обы́чное пра́во.
common-law ['kɔmənlɔ:] *adj* гражда́нский*.
commonly ['kɔmənlɪ] *adv* обы́чно.
Common Market *n*: **the ~ ~** О́бщий* ры́нок*.
commonplace ['kɔmənpleɪs] *adj* обы́чный,
обы́денный.
common room *n* ко́мната о́тдыха (*для*
студе́нтов, учителе́й и т.д.).
common sense *n* здра́вый смысл.
Commonwealth ['kɔmənwɛlθ] *n* (*BRIT*): **the ~**
Содру́жество.
commotion [kə'məuʃən] *n* сумато́ха.
communal ['kɔmju:nl] *adj* (*shared*) о́бщий*;

(*life*) обще́ственный; **a ~ flat** коммуна́льная
кварти́ра.
commune [*n* 'kɔmju:n, *vi* kə'mju:n] *n* комму́на
◆ *vi*: **to ~ with** обща́ться (*impf*) с +*instr*.
communicate [kə'mju:nɪkeɪt] *vt* передава́ть*
(переда́ть* *perf*) ◆ *vi*: **to ~ (with)** обща́ться
(*impf*) (с +*instr*); **to ~ (by letter)** обраща́ться
(обрати́ться* *perf*) пи́сьменно.
communication [kəmju:nɪ'keɪʃən] *n* (*process*)
коммуника́ция; (*letter etc*) сообще́ние.
communication cord *n* (*BRIT*) авари́йный
сигна́л "стоп".
communications network [kəmju:nɪ'keɪʃənz-]
n систе́ма коммуника́ций.
communications satellite *n* спу́тник свя́зи.
communicative [kə'mju:nɪkətɪv] *adj* (*person*)
общи́тельный* (общи́телен).
communion [kə'mju:nɪən] *n* (*also*: **Holy C~**)
Свято́е Прича́стие.
communiqué [kə'mju:nɪkeɪ] *n* коммюнике́ *nt*
ind.
communism ['kɔmjunɪzəm] *n* коммуни́зм.
communist ['kɔmjunɪst] *adj* коммунист-
и́ческий* ◆ *n* коммуни́ст(ка).
community [kə'mju:nɪtɪ] *n* (*public*)
обще́ственность *f*; (*within larger group*)
о́бщина; **the business ~** делов́ые круги́ *mpl*.
community centre *n* ≈ обще́ственный центр.
community charge *n* (*BRIT*: *formerly*)
поду́шный нало́г.
community chest *n* (*US*) объединённый
благотвори́тельный фонд.
community health centre *n* райо́нная
поликли́ника.
community home *n* (*BRIT*: *for children*)
де́тский* дом.
community service *n* трудова́я пови́нность *f*
(*как фо́рма наказа́ния*).
community spirit *n* чу́вство о́бщности *or*
това́рищества.
commutation ticket [kɔmju'teɪʃən-] *n* (*US*)
сезо́нный биле́т.
commute [kə'mju:t] *vi* (*to work*) *е́здить на*
рабо́ту из при́города в го́род ◆ *vt* (*LAW*)
смягча́ть (смягчи́ть *perf*) наказа́ние.
commuter [kə'mju:təʳ] *n* челове́к, кото́рый
е́здит на рабо́ту из при́города в го́род; **~**
train при́городный по́езд.
compact [*adj* kəm'pækt, *n* 'kɔmpækt] *adj*
компа́ктный* (компа́ктен) ◆ *n* (*also*: **powder**
~) пу́дреница.
compact disc *n* компа́кт-диск.
compact-disc player [kɔmpækt'dɪsk-] *n*
прои́грыватель *m* для компа́кт-ди́сков.
companion [kəm'pænjən] *n* спу́тник(-ица).
companionship [kəm'pænjənʃɪp] *n* обще́ние.
companionway [kəm'pænjənweɪ] *n* (*NAUT*)
трап.
company ['kʌmpənɪ] *n* (*COMM*) компа́ния;
(*THEAT*) тру́ппа; (*MIL*) ро́та; (*companionship*)
компа́ния, о́бщество; **he's good ~** его́

óбщество приятно; **we have ~** у нас гости; **to keep sb ~** составлять (составить* *perf*) кому-н компанию; **to part ~ with** расходиться* (разойтись* *perf*) с +*instr*; **Smith and C~** Смит и Компания.

company car *n* служебная машина.

company director *n* директор* компании.

company secretary *n* (*BRIT*) секретарь* *m(f)* фирмы.

comparable [ˈkɔmpərəbl] *adj* (*size*) сравнимый (сравним); (*style*) сопоставимый (сопоставим); (*car, property etc*) подобный* (подобен).

comparative [kəmˈpærətɪv] *adj* (*also LING*) сравнительный; (*relative*) относительный (относителен).

comparatively [kəmˈpærətɪvlɪ] *adv* (*relatively*) относительно.

compare [kəmˈpɛəʳ] *vt*: **to ~ sb/sth with** *or* **to** (*liken*) сравнивать (сравнить *perf*) кого-н/что-н с +*instr*; (*set side by side*) сопоставлять (сопоставить* *perf*) кого-н/что-н с +*instr* ◆ *vi*: **to ~ (with)** соотноситься (*impf*) (с +*instr*); **how do the prices ~?** как соотносятся цены?; **~d with** *or* **to** по сравнению *or* в сравнении с +*instr*.

comparison [kəmˈpærɪsn] *n* (*see vt*) сравнение; сопоставление; **in ~ (with)** по сравнению *or* в сравнении (с +*instr*).

compartment [kəmˈpɑːtmənt] *n* (*RAIL*) купе *nt ind*; (*section*) отделение.

compass [ˈkʌmpəs] *n* (*instrument*) компас; (*fig*) диапазон; **~es** *npl* (*also:* **pair of ~es**) циркуль *msg*; **beyond the ~ of** за пределами +*gen*; **within the ~ of** в пределах +*gen*.

compassion [kəmˈpæʃən] *n* сострадание.

compassionate [kəmˈpæʃənɪt] *adj* сострадательный* (сострадателен); **on ~ grounds** по состоянию здоровья; **~ leave** отпуск по семейным обстоятельствам.

compatibility [kəmpætɪˈbɪlɪtɪ] *n* совместимость *f*.

compatible [kəmˈpætɪbl] *adj* (*also COMPUT*) совместимый (совместим).

compel [kəmˈpɛl] *vt* вынуждать (вынудить* *perf*).

compelling [kəmˈpɛlɪŋ] *adj* (*fig: argument*) убедительный* (убедителен); (: *reason*) настоятельный.

compendium [kəmˈpɛndɪəm] *n* (*summary*) резюме *nt ind*.

compensate [ˈkɔmpənseɪt] *vt*: **to ~ sb for sth** компенсировать (*impf/perf*) кому-н что-н ◆ *vi*: **to ~ for** (*loss, distress etc*) компенсировать (*impf/perf*).

compensation [kɔmpənˈseɪʃən] *n* компенсация; (*money*) денежная компенсация.

compère [ˈkɔmpɛəʳ] *n* (*TV, RADIO*) ведущий*(-ая) *m(f)* *adj*.

compete [kəmˈpiːt] *vi* (*in contest etc*) соревноваться (*impf*); **to ~ (with)** (*companies*) конкурировать (*impf*) (с +*instr*); (*rivals*) соперничать (*impf*) (с +*instr*); **to ~ (with one another)** соперничать (*impf*) друг с другом.

competence [ˈkɔmpɪtəns] *n* компетенция.

competent [ˈkɔmpɪtənt] *adj* (*person*) компетентный* (компетентен); (*piece of work*) искусный.

competing [kəmˈpiːtɪŋ] *adj* (*firms*) конкурирующий; (*claims, explanations*) разноречивый (разноречив).

competition [kɔmpɪˈtɪʃən] *n* (*contest*) соревнование; (*between firms*) конкуренция; (*between rivals*) соперничество; **to be in ~ with** конкурировать (*impf*) с +*instr*.

competitive [kəmˈpɛtɪtɪv] *adj* (*industry*) основанный на конкуренции; (*person*) честолюбивый (честолюбив); (*price etc*) конкурентоспособный* (конкурентоспособен); (*sport*) состязательный.

competitive examination *n* конкурс.

competitor [kəmˈpɛtɪtəʳ] *n* (*rival*) соперник, конкурент; (*in musical competition*) конкурсант; (*participant*) участник(-ица) соревнования.

compile [kəmˈpaɪl] *vt* составлять (составить* *perf*).

complacency [kəmˈpleɪsnsɪ] *n* безмятежность *f*.

complacent [kəmˈpleɪsnt] *adj* безмятежный (безмятежен).

complain [kəmˈpleɪn] *vi*: **to ~ (about)** жаловаться (пожаловаться *perf*) (на +*acc*); **to ~ of a pain** жаловаться (пожаловаться *perf*) на боль.

complaint [kəmˈpleɪnt] *n* жалоба; **to make a ~ against** подавать* (подать* *perf*) жалобу на +*acc*.

complement [*n* ˈkɔmplɪmənt, *vb* ˈkɔmplɪmɛnt] *n* (*supplement*) дополнение; (*ship's crew*) экипаж ◆ *vt* (*enhance*) дополнять (*impf*); **to have a full ~ of** иметь (*impf*) полный комплект +*gen*.

complementary [kɔmplɪˈmɛntərɪ] *adj*: **they are ~ (to one another)** они дополняют друг друга.

complete [kəmˈpliːt] *adj* полный*; (*finished*) завершённый (завершён) ◆ *vt* (*building, task*) завершать (завершить* *perf*); (*set etc*) комплектовать (укомплектовать* *perf*); (*a form*) заполнять (заполнить* *perf*); **it's a ~ disaster** это полный провал.

completely [kəmˈpliːtlɪ] *adv* полностью,

совершённо.

completion [kəmˈpliːʃən] n (of building) завершёние; (of contract) совершёние; **to be nearing** ~ бли́зиться (impf) к завершёнию; **on** ~ по завершёнии.

complex [ˈkɔmplɛks] adj сло́жный*, ко́мплексный ◆ n (also PSYCH) ко́мплекс.

complexion [kəmˈplɛkʃən] n (of face) цвет* лица́; (nature) хара́ктер.

complexity [kəmˈplɛksɪtɪ] n сло́жность f.

compliance [kəmˈplaɪəns] n (submission) послуша́ние; (agreement) согла́сие; ~ **with** слёдование +dat; **in** ~ **with** в соотвётствии с +instr.

compliant [kəmˈplaɪənt] adj послу́шный* (послу́шен).

complicate [ˈkɔmplɪkeɪt] vt усложня́ть (усложни́ть perf).

complicated [ˈkɔmplɪkeɪtɪd] adj сло́жный* (сло́жен).

complication [kɔmplɪˈkeɪʃən] n (also MED) осложнёние.

complicity [kəmˈplɪsɪtɪ] n соуча́стие.

compliment [n ˈkɔmplɪmənt, vb ˈkɔmplɪmɛnt] n комплимёнт, хвала́ ◆ vt хвали́ть (похвали́ть perf); ~**s** npl (regards) приве́ты mpl; **to** ~ **sb, pay sb a** ~ де́лать (сде́лать perf) кому́-н комплимёнт; **to** ~ **sb (on sth** or **on doing)** поздравля́ть (поздра́вить* perf) кого́-н (с чем-н).

complimentary [kɔmplɪˈmɛntərɪ] adj (remark) лёстный* (лёстен); (ticket etc) да́рственный.

compliments slip n фи́рменный бланк для неофициа́льных запи́сок.

comply [kəmˈplaɪ] vi: **to** ~ **(with)** подчиня́ться (подчини́ться perf) (+dat).

component [kəmˈpəunənt] adj составно́й ◆ n компонёнт.

compose [kəmˈpəuz] vt (write) сочиня́ть (сочини́ть perf); (form) **to be** ~**d of** состоя́ть (impf) из +gen; **to** ~ **o.s.** успока́иваться (успоко́иться perf).

composed [kəmˈpəuzd] adj споко́йный* (споко́ен).

composer [kəmˈpəuzə'] n компози́тор.

composite [ˈkɔmpəzɪt] adj составно́й; (BOT) сложноцвётный; (MATH) сло́жный.

composition [kɔmpəˈzɪʃən] n (structure) соста́в; (essay) сочинёние; (MUS) компози́ция.

compositor [kəmˈpɔzɪtə'] n набо́рщик.

compos mentis [ˈkɔmpɔs ˈmɛntɪs] adj вменя́емый (вменя́ем).

compost [ˈkɔmpɔst] n компо́ст; (also: **potting** ~) удо́бренная земля́.

composure [kəmˈpəuʒə'] n самооблада́ние.

compound [n, adj ˈkɔmpaund, vt kəmˈpaund] n (CHEM) соединёние; (enclosure) укреплённый ко́мплекс; (LING) сло́жное сло́во* ◆ adj сло́жный ◆ vt (problem etc) осложня́ть (осложни́ть perf).

compound fracture n откры́тый перело́м.

compound interest n сло́жные процёнты pl.

comprehend [kɔmprɪˈhɛnd] vt постига́ть (пости́гнуть or пости́чь* perf).

comprehension [kɔmprɪˈhɛnʃən] n понима́ние.

comprehensive [kɔmprɪˈhɛnsɪv] adj исчёрпывающий* (исчёрпывающ) ◆ n = **comprehensive school**; ~ **insurance** всеобъёмлющее страхова́ние.

comprehensive school n (BRIT) срёдняя шко́ла.

compress [vt kəmˈprɛs, n ˈkɔmprɛs] vt (air) сжима́ть (сжать* perf); (cotton, paper) прессова́ть (спрессова́ть perf); (text etc) сокраща́ть (сократи́ть* perf) ◆ n компрёсс.

compressed air [kəmˈprɛst-] n сжа́тый во́здух.

compression [kəmˈprɛʃən] n (of air) сжа́тие; (of text) сокращёние.

comprise [kəmˈpraɪz] vt (also: **be** ~**d of**) включа́ть (impf) в себя́, состоя́ть (impf) из +gen; (constitute) составля́ть (соста́вить* perf).

compromise [ˈkɔmprəmaɪz] n компроми́сс ◆ vt компромети́ровать (скомпромети́ровать perf) ◆ vi (make concessions) идти́* (пойти́* perf) на компроми́сс ◆ cpd компроми́ссный.

compulsion [kəmˈpʌlʃən] n (desire) влечёние; (force) принуждёние; **under** ~ по принуждёнию.

compulsive [kəmˈpʌlsɪv] adj (gambler etc) безрассу́дный; (behaviour) маниака́льный; (reading etc) захва́тывающий* (захва́тывающ); **he's a** ~ **liar** он неисправи́мый лгун.

compulsory [kəmˈpʌlsərɪ] adj (attendance) обяза́тельный* (обяза́телен); (redundancy) принуди́тельный* (принуди́телен).

compulsory purchase n обяза́тельная поку́пка*.

compunction [kəmˈpʌŋkʃən] n раска́яние; **to have no** ~ **about doing** де́лать (сде́лать perf) что-н без вся́кого сожалёния.

computer [kəmˈpjuːtə'] n компью́тер ◆ cpd компью́терный; **the process is done by** ~ процёсс выполня́ется при по́мощи компью́тера.

computer game n компью́терная игра́*.

computerization [kəmpjuːtəraɪˈzeɪʃən] n компьютериза́ция.

computerize [kəmˈpjuːtəraɪz] vt компьютеризова́ть (impf/perf); **to** ~ **information** обраба́тывать (обрабо́тать perf) информа́цию на компью́тере.

computer literate adj: **to be** ~ ~ уме́ть (impf) по́льзоваться компью́тером.

computer peripheral n перифери́йное устро́йство (компью́тера).

computer programmer n программи́ст.

computer programming n программи́рование.

computer science n электро́нно-вычисли́тельная нау́ка.

computer scientist *n* специали́ст в о́бласти ЭВМ.

computing [kəmˈpjuːtɪŋ] *n* (*activity*) рабо́та на компью́тере; (*science*) электро́нно-вычисли́тельная нау́ка; **I've never done any ~** я никогда́ не рабо́тал на компью́тере.

comrade [ˈkɔmrɪd] *n* (*POL, MIL*) сора́тник; (*friend*) това́рищ.

comradeship [ˈkɔmrɪdʃɪp] *n* това́рищество.

Comsat® [ˈkɔmsæt] *n abbr* = **communications satellite**.

con [kɔn] *vt* надува́ть (наду́ть *perf*) ◆ *n* (*trick*) обма́н; **to ~ sb into doing** обма́ном заставля́ть (заста́вить* *perf*) кого́-н +*infin*.

concave [ˈkɔnkeɪv] *adj* (*mirror etc*) во́гнутый; (*cheeks*) впа́лый.

conceal [kənˈsiːl] *vt* (*hide*) укрыва́ть (укры́ть* *perf*); (*keep back*) скрыва́ть (скрыть* *perf*).

concede [kənˈsiːd] *vt* признава́ть* (призна́ть *perf*) ◆ *vi* (*admit error*) признава́ться (призна́ться *perf*); (*admit defeat*) сдава́ться* (сда́ться* *perf*).

conceit [kənˈsiːt] *n* высокоме́рие.

conceited [kənˈsiːtɪd] *adj* высокоме́рный.

conceivable [kənˈsiːvəbl] *adj* мы́слимый (мы́слим); **it is ~ that ...** вполне́ допусти́мо, что ....

conceivably [kənˈsiːvəblɪ] *adv*: **he may ~ be right** возмо́жно, что он прав.

conceive [kənˈsiːv] *vt* (*child*) зача́ть* (*perf*); (*idea*) заду́мывать (заду́мать *perf*) ◆ *vi* (*BIO*) забере́менеть (*perf*); **to ~ of sth** представля́ть (предста́вить* *perf*) что-н.

concentrate [ˈkɔnsəntreɪt] *vi* сосредо-то́чиваться (сосредото́читься *perf*), концентри́роваться (сконцентри́роваться *perf*) ◆ *vt*: **to ~ (on)** (*energies etc*) сосредото́чивать (сосредото́чить *perf*) *or* концентри́ровать (скноцентри́ровать *perf*) (на +*prp*).

concentration [kɔnsənˈtreɪʃən] *n* сосредото́чение, концентра́ция; (*attention*) сосредото́ченность *f*; (*CHEM*) концентра́ция.

concentration camp *n* концентрацио́нный ла́герь* *m*.

concentric [kɔnˈsɛntrɪk] *adj* концентри́ческий*.

concept [ˈkɔnsɛpt] *n* поня́тие.

conception [kənˈsɛpʃən] *n* (*idea*) конце́пция; (*BIO*) зача́тие.

concern [kənˈsəːn] *n* (*affair*) де́ло*; (*worry*) озабо́ченность *f*; (*COMM*) предприя́тие ◆ *vt* (*worry*) беспоко́ить (*impf*); (*involve*) вовлека́ть (вовле́чь* *perf*); (*relate to*) каса́ться (*impf*) +*gen*; **to be ~ed (about)** беспоко́иться (*impf*) (о +*prp*); **"to whom it may ~"** "надлежа́щему лицу́"; **as far as I am ~ed** что каса́ется меня́; **the department ~ed** (*relevant*)

отде́л, о кото́ром идёт речь; (*involved*) отде́л, кото́рый э́тим занима́ется.

concerning [kənˈsəːnɪŋ] *prep* относи́тельно +*gen*.

concert [ˈkɔnsət] *n* конце́рт; **to be in ~** (*MUS*) дава́ть* (*impf*) конце́рт; **in ~ with** (*activities etc*) совме́стно *or* во взаимоде́йствии с +*instr*.

concerted [kənˈsəːtɪd] *adj* совме́стный.

concert hall *n* конце́ртный зал.

concertina [kɔnsəˈtiːnə] *n* гармо́ника ◆ *vi* (*fig*) скла́дываться (сложи́ться* *perf*) гармо́никой.

concerto [kənˈtʃəːtəu] *n* (*MUS*) конце́рт; **piano/violin ~** конце́рт для фортепья́но/скри́пки с орке́стром.

concession [kənˈsɛʃən] *n* (*compromise*) усту́пка*; (*right*) конце́ссия; (*for pensioners, the unemployed*) льго́та; **tax ~** нало́говая ски́дка*.

concessionaire [kənsɛʃəˈnɛəʳ] *n* концессионе́р.

concessionary [kənˈsɛʃənrɪ] *adj* льго́тный.

conciliation [kənsɪlɪˈeɪʃən] *n* примире́ние.

conciliatory [kənˈsɪlɪətrɪ] *adj* примири́тельный* (примири́телен).

concise [kənˈsaɪs] *adj* кра́ткий*.

conclave [ˈkɔnkleɪv] *n* та́йное совеща́ние; (*REL*) конкла́в.

conclude [kənˈkluːd] *vt* (*speech, chapter*) зака́нчивать (зако́нчить *perf*); (*treaty, deal etc*) заключа́ть (заключи́ть* *perf*); (*decide*) приходи́ть* (прийти́* *perf*) к заключе́нию *or* вы́воду ◆ *vi* (*speaker*) заключа́ть (заключи́ть *perf*) речь; (*events*): **to ~ (with)** заверша́ться (заверши́ться *perf*) (+*instr*); **"that," he ~d, "is why we did it"** "вот почему́, – заключи́л он, – мы сде́лали э́то"; **I ~ that ...** я прихожу́ к заключе́нию, что ....

concluding [kənˈkluːdɪŋ] *adj* заключи́тельный.

conclusion [kənˈkluːʒən] *n* заключе́ние; (*of speech*) оконча́ние; (*of events*) заверше́ние; **to come to the ~ that** приходи́ть* (прийти́* *perf*) к заключе́нию, что ....

conclusive [kənˈkluːsɪv] *adj* (*evidence*) неопровержи́мый (неопровержи́м); (*defeat*) оконча́тельный* (оконча́телен).

concoct [kənˈkɔkt] *vt* (*excuse*) приду́мывать (приду́мать *perf*); (*meal*) гото́вить* (пригото́вить* *perf*).

concoction [kənˈkɔkʃən] *n* смесь *f*.

concord [ˈkɔnkɔːd] *n* (*harmony*) согла́сие; (*treaty*) соглаше́ние.

concourse [ˈkɔnkɔːs] *n* (*hall*) вестибю́ль *m*; (*crowd*) стече́ние.

concrete [ˈkɔnkriːt] *n* бето́н ◆ *adj* бето́нный; (*fig*) конкре́тный* (конкре́тен).

concrete mixer *n* бетономеша́лка.

concur [kənˈkəːʳ] *vi* (*events*) совпада́ть

---

* marks translations which have irregular inflections. The Russian-English side of the dictionary gives inflectional information.

(совпа́сть* *perf*); **to ~ (with)** соглаша́ться (согласи́ться* *perf*) (с +*instr*).
concurrently [kən'kʌrntlɪ] *adv* одновреме́нно.
concussion [kən'kʌʃən] *n* сотрясе́ние мо́зга.
condemn [kən'dɛm] *vt* осужда́ть (осуди́ть* *perf*); (*building*) бракова́ть (забракова́ть *perf*).
condemnation [kɔndɛm'neɪʃən] *n* (*criticism*) осужде́ние.
condensation [kɔndɛn'seɪʃən] *n* конденса́ция.
condense [kən'dɛns] *vi* конденси́роваться (*impf*/*perf*) ♦ *vt* сжима́ть (сжать* *perf*).
condensed milk [kən'dɛnst-] *n* сгущённое молоко́.
condescend [kɔndɪ'sɛnd] *vi* вести́ (*impf*) себя́ снисходи́тельно; **to ~ to do** соизволя́ть (соизво́лить *perf*) +*infin*.
condescending [kɔndɪ'sɛndɪŋ] *adj* снисходи́тельный* (снисходи́телен).
condition [kən'dɪʃən] *n* (*also MED*) состоя́ние; (*requirement*) усло́вие ♦ *vt* (*person*) формирова́ть (сформирова́ть *perf*); (*hair, skin*) обраба́тывать (обрабо́тать *perf*); **~s** *npl* (*circumstances*) обстоя́тельства *ntpl*; **in good/ poor ~** в хоро́шем/плохо́м состоя́нии; **a heart ~** боле́знь *f* се́рдца; **weather ~s** пого́дные усло́вия; **~s of sale** усло́вия прода́жи; **on ~ that** при усло́вии, что.
conditional [kən'dɪʃənl] *adj* усло́вный; **to be ~ upon** зави́сеть* (*impf*/*perf*) от +*gen*.
conditioner [kən'dɪʃənə'] *n* (*for hair*) бальза́м; (*for fabrics*) смягча́ющий* раство́р.
condo ['kɔndəu] *n abbr* (*US: inf*) = **condominium**.
condolences [kən'dəulənsɪz] *npl* соболе́знования *ntpl*.
condom ['kɔndəm] *n* презервати́в.
condominium [kɔndə'mɪnɪəm] *n* (*US: building*) *кооперати́вный многокварти́рный дом*; (: *rooms*) кооперати́вная кварти́ра.
condone [kən'dəun] *vt* мири́ться (примири́ться *perf*) с +*instr*.
conducive [kən'dju:sɪv] *adj*: **~ to** спосо́бствующий +*dat*.
conduct [*n* 'kɔndʌkt, *vt* kən'dʌkt] *n* (*of person*) поведе́ние ♦ *vt* (*survey etc*) проводи́ть* (провести́* *perf*); (*MUS*) дирижи́ровать (*impf*); (*PHYS*) проводи́ть* (*impf*); **to ~ o.s.** (*behave*) вести́* (повести́* *perf*) себя́.
conducted tour [kən'dʌktɪd-] *n* (*of museum etc*) экску́рсия с ги́дом.
conductor [kən'dʌktə'] *n* (*MUS*) дирижёр; (*US: RAIL*) контролёр; (*PHYS*) проводни́к*; (*on bus*) конду́ктор.
conductress [kən'dʌktrɪs] *n* конду́ктор.
conduit ['kɔndjuɪt] *n* (*ELEC*) труба́ для электропрово́дки; (*TECH*) трубопрово́д.
cone [kəun] *n* (*shape*) ко́нус; (*on road*) *конусообра́зное доро́жное загражде́ние*; (*BOT*) ши́шка*; (*CULIN*) ва́фельная тру́бочка* (*для моро́женого*).

confectioner [kən'fɛkʃənə'] *n* конди́тер.
confectioner's (shop) [kən'fɛkʃənəz-] *n* конди́терская *f adj*.
confectionery [kən'fɛkʃənrɪ] *n* конди́терские изде́лия *ntpl*.
confederate [kən'fɛdrɪt] *adj* конфедерати́вный ♦ *n* (*pej*) соо́бщник; (*US*) конфедера́т.
confederation [kənfɛdə'reɪʃən] *n* конфедера́ция.
confer [kən'fə:'] *vi* совеща́ться (*impf*) ♦ *vt*: **to ~ sth (on sb)** (*honour*) ока́зывать (оказа́ть* *perf*) что-н (кому́-н); (*degree*) присужда́ть (присуди́ть* *perf*) что-н (кому́-н); (*advantage*) дава́ть* (дать* *perf*) что-н (кому́-н); **to ~ (with sb about sth)** совеща́ться (*impf*) (с кем-н о чём-н).
conference ['kɔnfərəns] *n* конфере́нция; **to be in ~** быть* (*impf*) на совеща́нии.
conference room *n* зал заседа́ний, конфере́нцзал.
confess [kən'fɛs] *vt* (*guilt, ignorance*) признава́ть* (призна́ть* *perf*); (*sin*) испове́доваться (испове́даться *perf*) в +*prp*; (*crime*) сознава́ться* (созна́ться* *perf*) в +*prp* ♦ *vi* (*admit to crime*) признава́ться* (призна́ться* *perf*); **to ~ to sth** сознава́ться* (созна́ться* *perf*) в чём-н; **I must ~ that I didn't enjoy it at all** до́лжен призна́ться, мне э́то соверше́нно не понра́вилось.
confession [kən'fɛʃən] *n* призна́ние; (*REL*) и́споведь *f*; **to make a ~** де́лать (сде́лать *perf*) призна́ние.
confessor [kən'fɛsə'] *n* испове́дник.
confetti [kən'fɛtɪ] *n* конфетти́ *nt ind*.
confide [kən'faɪd] *vi*: **to ~ in** доверя́ться (дове́риться *perf*) +*dat*.
confidence ['kɔnfɪdns] *n* (*faith*) уве́ренность *f*; (*self-assurance*) уве́ренность в себе́; (*secret*) секре́т; **I have ~ in him** я уве́рен в нём; **she has (every) ~ that** она́ по́лностью уве́рена в том, что; **motion of no ~** выраже́ние недове́рия; **in ~** конфиденциа́льно; **to tell sb sth in strict ~** рассказа́ть* (*perf*) кому́-н что-н стро́го конфиденциа́льно.
confidence trick *n* моше́нничество.
confident ['kɔnfɪdənt] *adj* (*positive*) уве́ренный (уве́рен); (*self-assured*) уве́ренный (уве́рен) в себе́.
confidential [kɔnfɪ'dɛnʃəl] *adj* (*report etc*) конфиденциа́льный (конфиденциа́лен); (*tone*) довери́тельный (довери́телен); (*secretary*) по́льзующийся дове́рием.
confidentiality [kɔnfɪdɛnʃɪ'ælɪtɪ] *n* конфиденциа́льность *f*.
configuration [kənfɪgju'reɪʃən] *n* (*also COMPUT*) конфигура́ция.
confine [kən'faɪm] *vt* (*lock up*) запира́ть (запере́ть* *perf*); (*limit*): **to ~ (to)** ограни́чивать (ограни́чить *perf*) (+*instr*); **to ~ o.s. to sth** ограни́чиваться (ограни́читься *perf*) чем-н.

confined [kənˈfaɪnd] *adj* закры́тый.
confinement [kənˈfaɪnmənt] *n* (тюре́мное)
заключе́ние; (*MED*) ро́ды *pl*.
confines [ˈkɒnfaɪnz] *npl* (*also fig*) преде́лы *mpl*.
confirm [kənˈfɜːm] *vt* подтвержда́ть
(подтверди́ть* *perf*); **to be ~ed** (*REL*) получа́ть
(получи́ть* *perf*) конфирма́цию.
confirmation [kɒnfəˈmeɪʃən] *n*
подтвержде́ние; (*REL*) конфирма́ция.
confirmed [kənˈfɜːmd] *adj* убеждённый.
confiscate [ˈkɒnfɪskeɪt] *vt* конфиско́вывать
(конфискова́ть* *perf*).
confiscation [kɒnfɪsˈkeɪʃən] *n* конфиска́ция.
conflagration [kɒnfləˈɡreɪʃən] *n* пожа́рище.
conflict [*n* ˈkɒnflɪkt, *vi* kənˈflɪkt] *n* конфли́кт; (*of
interests*) столкнове́ние ♦ *vi* противоре́чить
(*impf*) друг дру́гу; **to ~ with sth**
противоре́чить (*impf*) чему́-н.
conflicting [kənˈflɪktɪŋ] *adj* (*reports*)
противоречи́вый (противоречи́в); (*interests*)
противополо́жный* (противополо́жен).
conform [kənˈfɔːm] *vi*: **to ~ (to)** подчиня́ться
(подчини́ться *perf*) (+*dat*).
conformist [kənˈfɔːmɪst] *n* конформи́ст.
confound [kənˈfaʊnd] *vt* (*confuse*) озада́чивать
(озада́чить *perf*); (*amaze*) поража́ть
(порази́ть* *perf*).
confounded [kənˈfaʊndɪd] *adj* (*nuisance*)
прокля́тый; (*idiot*) зако́нченный.
confront [kənˈfrʌnt] *vt* (*problems*)
ста́лкиваться (столкну́ться *perf*) с +*instr*;
(*enemy*) противостоя́ть (*impf*) +*dat*.
confrontation [kɒnfrənˈteɪʃən] *n*
конфронта́ция.
confuse [kənˈfjuːz] *vt* (*perplex, complicate*)
запу́тывать (запу́тать *perf*); (*mix up: two
things, people etc*) пу́тать (спу́тать *perf*).
confused [kənˈfjuːzd] *adj* (*person*)
озада́ченный (озада́чен); (*situation*)
запу́танный (запу́тан); **to get ~**
запу́тываться (запу́таться *perf*).
confusing [kənˈfjuːzɪŋ] *adj* запу́танный.
confusion [kənˈfjuːʒən] *n* (*mix-up*) пу́таница;
(*perplexity*) замеша́тельство; (*disorder*)
беспоря́док.
congeal [kənˈdʒiːl] *vi* (*blood*) запека́ться
(запе́чься* *perf*); (*sauce, fat*) застыва́ть
(засты́ть* *perf*).
congenial [kənˈdʒiːnɪəl] *adj* (*atmosphere*)
благоприя́тный* (благоприя́тен); (*person*)
ро́дственный (*place, job etc*) подходя́щий*.
congenital [kənˈdʒɛnɪtl] *adj* (*MED*)
врождённый.
conger eel [ˈkɒŋɡər-] *n* морско́й у́горь* *m*.
congested [kənˈdʒɛstɪd] *adj* (*road*)
перегру́женный (перегру́жен); (*area*)
перенаселённый (перенаселён); (*MED*)
засто́йный.

congestion [kənˈdʒɛstʃən] *n* (*of road*)
перегру́женность *f*; (*of area*)
перенаселённость *f*; (*MED*) засто́й.
conglomerate [kənˈɡlɒmərɪt] *n* (*COMM*)
конгломера́т.
conglomeration [kənɡlɒməˈreɪʃən] *n*
конгломера́ция.
Congo [ˈkɒŋɡəʊ] *n* Ко́нго *ind*.
congratulate [kənˈɡrætjʊleɪt] *vt*: **to ~ sb (on)**
поздравля́ть (поздра́вить* *perf*) кого́-н (с
+*instr*).
congratulations [kənɡrætjʊˈleɪʃənz] *npl*
поздравле́ния *ntpl*; **~ (on)** (*from one person*)
поздравля́ю (с +*instr*); (*from several people*)
поздравля́ем (с +*instr*).
congregate [ˈkɒŋɡrɪɡeɪt] *vi* собира́ться
(собра́ться* *perf*).
congregation [kɒŋɡrɪˈɡeɪʃən] *n* прихожа́не*
mpl.
congress [ˈkɒŋɡrɛs] *n* (*conference*) конгре́сс;
(*US*): **C~** конгре́сс США.
congressman [ˈkɒŋɡrɛsmən] *irreg n* (*US*)
конгрессме́н.
congresswoman [ˈkɒŋɡrɛswʊmən] *irreg n* (*US*)
конгрессме́н.
conical [ˈkɒnɪkl] *adj* кони́ческий*.
conifer [ˈkɒnɪfə] *n* хво́йное де́рево*.
coniferous [kəˈnɪfərəs] *adj* хво́йный.
conjecture [kənˈdʒɛktʃər] *n* предположе́ние ♦ *vi*
предполага́ть (предположи́ть *perf*).
conjugal [ˈkɒndʒʊɡl] *adj* супру́жеский*.
conjugate [ˈkɒndʒʊɡeɪt] *vt* (*LING*) спряга́ть
(проспряга́ть *perf*).
conjugation [kɒndʒəˈɡeɪʃən] *n* (*LING*)
спряже́ние.
conjunction [kənˈdʒʌŋkʃən] *n* (*LING*) сою́з; **in ~
with** совме́стно с +*instr*.
conjunctivitis [kəndʒʌŋktɪˈvaɪtɪs] *n* (*MED*)
коньюнктиви́т.
conjure [ˈkʌndʒə] *vt* (*fig*) создава́ть* (созда́ть*
perf) из ничего́ ♦ *vi* (*magician*) пока́зывать
(показа́ть* *perf*) фо́кусы
▸ **conjure up** *vt* (*ghost*) вызыва́ть* (вы́звать*
perf); (*memories*) пробужда́ть (пробуди́ть*
perf).
conjurer [ˈkʌndʒərə] *n* фо́кусник.
conjuring trick [ˈkʌndʒərɪŋ-] *n* фо́кус.
conker [ˈkɒŋkə] *n* (*BRIT*) ко́нский* кашта́н.
conk out [kɒŋk-] *vi* (*inf*) сдыха́ть (сдо́хнуть
perf).
con man *irreg n* моше́нник.
connect [kəˈnɛkt] *vt* (*ELEC*) подсоединя́ть
(подсоедини́ть *perf*); (*TEL: subscriber*)
подключа́ть (подключи́ть *perf*); (*fig:
associate*) свя́зывать (связа́ть* *perf*) ♦ *vi*: **to ~
with** согласо́вываться (согласова́ться *perf*)
по расписа́нию с +*instr*; **to ~ sb/sth (to)** (*also
TEL*) соединя́ть (соедини́ть *perf*) кого́-н/что-н

---

* marks translations which have irregular inflections. The Russian-English side of the dictionary gives inflectional information.

(c +*instr*); **he is/was ~ed with** он свя́зан/был свя́зан с +*instr*; **I am trying to ~ you** (*TEL*) я пыта́юсь нала́дить связь.

connection [kə'nɛkʃən] *n* (*also fig, ELEC*) связь* *f*; (*train etc*) переса́дка*; (*TEL: caller*) соедине́ние; (: *subscriber*) подключе́ние; **in ~ with** в связи́ с +*instr*; **what is the ~ between them?** кака́я связь ме́жду ни́ми?; **business ~s** деловы́е свя́зи; **to miss one's ~** опа́здывать (опозда́ть *perf*) на переса́дку; **to get one's ~** де́лать (сде́лать *perf*) переса́дку.

connexion [kə'nɛkʃən] *n* (*BRIT*) = **connection.**

conning tower ['kɔnɪŋ-] *n* (*NAUT*) ру́бка*.

connive [kə'naɪv] *vi*: **to ~ at** потво́рствовать (*impf*) +*dat*.

connoisseur [kɔnɪ'sə:ʳ] *n* знато́к*.

connotation [kɔnə'teɪʃən] *n* коннота́ция.

connubial [kə'nju:bɪəl] *adj* бра́чный.

conquer ['kɔŋkə'] *vt* (*MIL*) завоёвывать (завоева́ть* *perf*); (*overcome*) поборо́ть* (*perf*).

conqueror ['kɔŋkərə'] *n* завоева́тель *m*.

conquest ['kɔŋkwɛst] *n* (*MIL*) завоева́ние; (*prize*) побе́да; (*of space*) покоре́ние.

cons [kɔnz] *npl see* **convenience, pro.**

conscience ['kɔnʃəns] *n* со́весть *f*; **he has a guilty/clear ~** у него́ со́весть нечиста́/чиста́; **in all ~** по со́вести.

conscientious [kɔnʃɪ'ɛnʃəs] *adj* добро-со́вестный* (добро-со́вестно).

conscientious objector *n* отка́зывающийся *от призы́ва в а́рмию по убежде́нию.*

conscious ['kɔnʃəs] *adj* (*deliberate*) созна́тельный (созна́телен); (*aware*): **to be ~ of sth/that** сознава́ть* (*impf*) что-н/, что; (*awake*): **the patient was ~** пацие́нт находи́лся в созна́нии; **to become ~ of sth/ that** осознава́ть (осозна́ть *perf*) что-н/, что.

consciousness ['kɔnʃəsnɪs] *n* (*also MED*) созна́ние; (*of society etc*) самосозна́ние; **to lose ~** теря́ть (потеря́ть *perf*) созна́ние; **to regain ~** приходи́ть* (прийти́* *perf*) в созна́ние.

conscript ['kɔnskrɪpt] *n* призывни́к*, новобра́нец*.

conscription [kən'skrɪpʃən] *n* во́инская пови́нность *f*.

consecrate ['kɔnsɪkreɪt] *vt* (*building etc*) освяща́ть (освяти́ть* *perf*).

consecutive [kən'sɛkjutɪv] *adj*: **on three ~ occasions** в трёх слу́чаях подря́д; **on three ~ days** три дня подря́д.

consensus [kən'sɛnsəs] *n* (*medical, scientific*) еди́ное мне́ние; **~ (of opinion)** консе́нсус.

consent [kən'sɛnt] *n* согла́сие ♦ *vi*: **to ~ to** соглаша́ться (согласи́ться* *perf*) на +*acc*; **age of ~** совершенноле́тие; **by common ~** с о́бщего согла́сия.

consenting [kən'sɛntɪŋ] *adj*: **~ adult** совершенноле́тний*(-яя) *m(f) adj*.

consequence ['kɔnsɪkwəns] *n* (*result*)

сле́дствие; (*significance*): **of ~** значи́тельный (значи́телен); **it's of little ~** э́то не име́ет большо́го значе́ния; **in ~** (*consequently*) всле́дствие.

consequently ['kɔnsɪkwəntlɪ] *adv* сле́довательно.

conservation [kɔnsə'veɪʃən] *n* (*preservation*) сохране́ние; (*also: nature ~*) охра́на приро́ды, природоохра́на; **energy ~** эконо́мия эне́ргии.

conservationist [kɔnsə'veɪʃnɪst] *n* челове́к, *вступа́ющий за природоохра́ну.*

conservative [kən'sə:vətɪv] *adj* (*person*) консервати́вный*; (*estimate*) скро́мный*; (*BRIT*): **C~** консервати́вный ♦ *n* (*BRIT*): **C~** консерва́тор.

conservatory [kən'sə:vətrɪ] *n* застеклённая вера́нда; (*MUS*) консервато́рия.

conserve [kən'sə:v] *vt* (*preserve*) сохраня́ть (сохрани́ть *perf*); (*energy*) рациона́льно испо́льзовать (*impf*) ♦ *n* варе́нье*.

consider [kən'sɪdə'] *vt* (*believe*) счита́ть (посчита́ть *perf*); (*study*) рассма́тривать (рассмотре́ть* *perf*); (*take into account*) учи́тывать (уче́сть* *perf*); (*regard*): **to ~ that ...** полага́ть (*impf*), что ...; **to ~ sth** поду́мывать (*impf*) о чём-н; **they ~ themselves to be superior** они́ счита́ют себя́ вы́ше; **she ~ed it a disaster** она́ счита́ла, что э́то катастро́фа; **~ yourself lucky** счита́йте, что Вам повезло́; **all things ~ed** приня́в всё во внима́ние.

considerable [kən'sɪdərəbl] *adj* значи́тельный* (значи́телен).

considerably [kən'sɪdərəblɪ] *adv* (*improve, deteriorate etc*) значи́тельно; (*bigger, smaller etc*) гора́здо.

considerate [kən'sɪdərɪt] *adj* (*person*) забо́тливый (забо́тлив); (*action*) внима́тельный (внима́телен).

consideration [kənsɪdə'reɪʃən] *n* (*deliberation*) рассмотре́ние, обду́мывание; (*factor*) соображе́ние; (*thoughtfulness*) внима́ние; (*reward*) вознагражде́ние; **out of ~ for** из уваже́ния к +*dat*; **to take sth into ~** принима́ть (приня́ть *perf*) что-н во внима́ние; **under ~** на рассмотре́нии; **my first ~ is my family** я пре́жде всего́ забо́чусь о свое́й семье́.

considered [kən'sɪdəd] *adj* (*approach, answer*) обду́манный; **it is my ~ opinion that ...** у меня́ сложи́лось мне́ние, что ...

considering [kən'sɪdərɪŋ] *prep* учи́тывая +*acc*; **~ (that)** учи́тывая (, что).

consign [kən'saɪn] *vt* (*send: goods*) отправля́ть (отпра́вить* *perf*); **to ~ to** (*thing: to place*) забра́сывать (забро́сить* *perf*) в +*acc*; (*person: to sb's care*) поруча́ть (поручи́ть *perf*) +*dat*; (: *to poverty*) обрека́ть (обре́чь* *perf*) на +*acc*.

consignee [kɔnsaɪ'ni:] *n* грузополуча́тель *m*.

consignment [kən'saɪnmənt] *n* (*COMM*) па́ртия.

consignment note *n* (*COMM*) тра́нспортная накладна́я *f adj.*

consignor [kən'saɪnəʳ] *n* грузоотправи́тель *m.*

consist [kən'sɪst] *vi*: **to ~ of** состоя́ть (*impf*) из +*gen.*

consistency [kən'sɪstənsɪ] *n* (*of actions etc*) после́довательность *f*; (*of yoghurt etc*) консисте́нция.

consistent [kən'sɪstənt] *adj* (*person, argument*) после́довательный* (после́дователен); **~ with** соотве́тствующий* +*dat.*

consolation [kɔnsə'leɪʃən] *n* утеше́ние.

console [*vt* kən'səul, *n* 'kɔnsəul] *vt* утеша́ть (уте́шить *perf*) ♦ *n* (*panel*) пане́ль *f.*

consolidate [kən'sɔlɪdeɪt] *vt* (*position, power*) укрепля́ть (укрепи́ть* *perf*).

consolidated balance sheet [kən'sɔlɪdeɪtɪd-] *n* сво́дный бала́нсовый отчёт.

consols ['kɔnsɔlz] *npl* (*BRIT*) консо́ли *fpl* (*прави́тельственные облига́ции*).

consommé [kən'sɔmeɪ] *n* прозра́чный бульо́н*.

consonant ['kɔnsənənt] *n* согла́сный *m adj.*

consort [*n* 'kɔnsɔ:t, *vb* kən'sɔ:t] *n* супру́г(а) ♦ *vi*: **to ~ with sb** свя́зываться (связа́ться* *perf*) с кем-н; **prince ~** принц-консо́рт, супру́г ца́рствующей короле́вы.

consortium [kən'sɔ:tɪəm] *n* консо́рциум.

conspicuous [kən'spɪkjuəs] *adj* (*person, feature*) заме́тный* (заме́тен); **to make o.s. ~** обраща́ть (обрати́ть* *perf*) на себя́ внима́ние.

conspiracy [kən'spɪrəsɪ] *n* за́говор.

conspiratorial [kən'spɪrə'tɔ:rɪəl] *adj* загово́рщический.

conspire [kən'spaɪəʳ] *vi* (*people*) устра́ивать (устро́ить *perf*) за́говор; **circumstances ~d against us** обстоя́тельства скла́дывались про́тив нас.

constable ['kʌnstəbl] (*BRIT*) *n* полице́йский *m adj*; **chief ~** нача́льник поли́ции.

constabulary [kən'stæbjulərɪ] *n* (*BRIT*) поли́ция.

constant ['kɔnstənt] *adj* (*continuous*) постоя́нный*; (*fixed*) неизме́нный*.

constantly ['kɔnstəntlɪ] *adv* (*continually*) постоя́нно.

constellation [kɔnstə'leɪʃən] *n* (*ASTRONOMY*) созве́здие.

consternation [kɔnstə'neɪʃən] *n* смяте́ние.

constipated ['kɔnstɪpeɪtɪd] *adj*: **he/she is ~** у него́/неё запо́р.

constipation [kɔnstɪ'peɪʃən] *n* запо́р.

constituency [kən'stɪtjuənsɪ] *n* (*area*) избира́тельный о́круг*; (*electors*) избира́тели *mpl* о́круга.

constituency party *n* ме́стная парти́йная организа́ция.

constituent [kən'stɪtjuənt] *n* (*POL*)

избира́тель(ница) *m(f)*; (*component*) компоне́нт.

constitute ['kɔnstɪtju:t] *vt* (*represent*) явля́ться (яви́ться* *perf*) +*instr*; (*make up*) составля́ть (соста́вить* *perf*).

constitution [kɔnstɪ'tju:ʃən] *n* (*of country*) конститу́ция; (*of organization*) уста́в; (*health*) органи́зм; (*of committee etc*) строе́ние.

constitutional [kɔnstɪ'tju:ʃənl] *adj* конституцио́нный*; **~ monarchy** конституцио́нная мона́рхия.

constrain [kən'streɪn] *vt* (*force*) вынужда́ть (вы́нудить* *perf*); (*limit*) сде́рживать (сдержа́ть *perf*).

constrained [kən'streɪnd] *adj* принуждённый*.

constraint [kən'streɪnt] *n* (*restriction*) ограниче́ние; (*compulsion*) принужде́ние; (*embarrassment*) стесне́ние.

constrict [kən'strɪkt] *vt* (*squeeze*) сжима́ть (сжать* *perf*); (*limit*) стесня́ть (стесни́ть *perf*).

constriction [kən'strɪkʃən] *n* (*in throat*) стесне́ние; (*restriction*) ограниче́ние.

construct [kən'strʌkt] *vt* (*build*) сооружа́ть (сооруди́ть* *perf*); (*formulate*) стро́ить (постро́ить *perf*).

construction [kən'strʌkʃən] *n* (*of building etc*) сооруже́ние; (*structure*) констру́кция; (*fig: interpretation*) истолкова́ние; **the building is under ~** зда́ние стро́ится.

construction industry *n* строи́тельная промы́шленность *f.*

constructive [kən'strʌktɪv] *adj* конструкти́вный* (конструкти́вен).

construe [kən'stru:] *vt* истолко́вывать (истолкова́ть *perf*).

consul ['kɔnsl] *n* ко́нсул.

consulate ['kɔnsjulɪt] *n* ко́нсульство.

consult [kən'sʌlt] *vt* (*friend*) сове́товаться (посове́товаться *perf*) с +*instr*; (*book, map etc*) справля́ться (спра́виться* *perf*) с +*instr*; **to ~ sb (about sth)** (*doctor etc*) консульти́роваться (проконсульти́роваться *perf*) с кем-н (о чём-н).

consultancy [kən'sʌltənsɪ] *n* (*company*) консульти́рующая фи́рма; (*MED*) до́лжность *f* врача́-консульта́нта.

consultant [kən'sʌltənt] *n* (*MED*) врач-консульта́нт; (*other specialist*) консульта́нт ♦ *cpd*: **~ engineer/paediatrician** инжене́р-/педиа́тр-консульта́нт; **legal ~** юриско́нсульт; **management ~** консульта́нт по ме́неджменту.

consultation [kɔnsəl'teɪʃən] *n* (*MED*) консульта́ция; (*discussion*) совеща́ние; (*LAW*) юриди́ческая консульта́ция; **in ~ with** с по́мощью +*gen.*

consultative [kən'sʌltətɪv] *adj* консультати́вный.

---

* marks translations which have irregular inflections. The Russian-English side of the dictionary gives inflectional information.

consulting room [kən'sʌltɪŋ-] *n* (*BRIT*) враче́бный кабине́т.

consume [kən'sju:m] *vt* (*food, drink*) потребля́ть (потреби́ть* *perf*); (*fuel, energy etc*) расхо́довать (израсхо́довать *perf*); (*subj: emotion, fire etc*) охва́тывать (охвати́ть* *perf*).

consumer [kən'sju:mə*r*] *n* (*COMM, also of gas etc*) потреби́тель *m*.

consumer credit *n* потреби́тельский* креди́т.

consumer durables *npl* потреби́тельские това́ры *mpl* дли́тельного по́льзования.

consumer goods *npl* потреби́тельские това́ры *mpl*.

consumerism [kən'sju:mərɪzəm] *n* защи́та прав потреби́телей.

consumer society *n* о́бщество потребле́ния.

consummate ['kɔnsʌmeɪt] *vt* (*marriage, ambition etc*) осуществля́ть (осуществи́ть* *perf*).

consumption [kən'sʌmpʃən] *n* потребле́ние; (*amount consumed*) расхо́д; (*MED*) туберкулёз лёгких; **not fit for human ~** не го́ден к потребле́нию.

cont. *abbr* (= *continued*): **~ on** продолже́ние на +*prp*.

contact ['kɔntækt] *n* (*communication*) конта́кт; (*touch*) соприкоснове́ние; (*person*) делово́й(-а́я) знако́мый(-ая) *m(f) adj* ♦ *vt* свя́зываться (связа́ться* *perf*) с +*instr*; **to lose/be in ~ with sb/sth** теря́ть (потеря́ть *perf*)/подде́рживать (*impf*) конта́кт с кем-н/ чем-н; **business ~s** деловы́е свя́зи.

contact lenses *npl* конта́ктные ли́нзы *fpl*.

contagious [kən'teɪdʒəs] *adj* (*disease*) зара́зный* (зара́зен); (*fig*) зарази́тельный* (зарази́телен).

contain [kən'teɪn] *vt* (*hold*) вмеща́ть (вмести́ть* *perf*); (*include*) содержа́ть* (*impf*); (*curb*) сде́рживать (сдержа́ть* *perf*); **to ~ o.s.** сде́рживаться (сдержа́ться* *perf*).

container [kən'teɪnə*r*] *n* (*also COMM*) конте́йнер ♦ *cpd* (*ship, lorry etc*) конте́йнерный.

containerization [kəntenməraɪ'zeɪʃən] *n* упако́вка* гру́зов в конте́йнеры.

containerize [kən'teɪnəraɪz] *vt* осуществля́ть (осуществи́ть* *perf*) конте́йнерные перево́зки.

contaminate [kən'tæmɪneɪt] *vt* загрязня́ть (загрязни́ть *perf*).

contamination [kəntæmɪ'neɪʃən] *n* загрязне́ние.

cont'd *abbr* (= *continued*): **~ on** продолже́ние на +*prp*; **to be ~** продолже́ние сле́дует.

contemplate ['kɔntəmpleɪt] *vt* (*consider*) размышля́ть (*impf*) о +*prp*; (*look at*) созерца́ть (*impf*).

contemplation [kɔntəm'pleɪʃən] *n* (*see vb*) разымшле́ние; созерца́ние.

contemporary [kən'tɛmpərərɪ] *adj* (*present-day*) совреме́нный*; (*belonging to same time*) относя́щийся к тому́ вре́мени ♦ *n* совреме́нник(-ица); **Samuel Pepys and his contemporaries** Самю́ель Пипс и его́ совреме́нники.

contempt [kən'tɛmpt] *n* презре́ние; **~ of court** оскорбле́ние суда́; **to have/ hold sb/sth in ~** презира́ть (*impf*) кого́-н/ что-н.

contemptible [kən'tɛmptəbl] *adj* (*conduct*) презре́нный.

contemptuous [kən'tɛmptjuəs] *adj* презри́тельный* (презри́телен).

contend [kən'tɛnd] *vt*: **to ~ that** утвержда́ть (*impf*), что ♦ *vi* (*struggle*): **to ~ with** (*problem etc*) боро́ться* (*impf*) с +*instr*; (*compete*): **to ~ for** (*power etc*) боро́ться* (*impf*) за +*acc*; **to have to ~ with** ста́лкиваться (столкну́ться *perf*) с +*instr*; **he has a lot to ~ with** ему́ прихо́дится справля́ться со мно́гим.

contender [kən'tɛndə*r*] *n* претенде́нт(ка).

content [*n* 'kɔntɛnt, *adj, vt* kən'tɛnt] *n* содержа́ние ♦ *adj* дово́льный* (дово́лен) ♦ *vt* (*satisfy*) удовлетворя́ть (удовлетвори́ть* *perf*); **~s** *npl* (*of bottle etc*) содержи́мое *ntsg adj*; (*of book*) содержа́ние *ntsg*; (**table of**) **~s** оглавле́ние; **she is ~ with her life** она́ дово́льна жи́знью; **to ~ o.s. with sth** дово́льствоваться (*impf*) чем-н.

contented [kən'tɛntɪd] *adj* дово́льный* (дово́лен).

contentedly [kən'tɛntɪdlɪ] *adv* дово́льно, удовлетворённо.

contention [kən'tɛnʃən] *n* (*assertion*) утвержде́ние; (*argument*) разногла́сие; **bone of ~** я́блоко* раздо́ра.

contentious [kən'tɛnʃəs] *adj* спо́рный* (спо́рен).

contentment [kən'tɛntmənt] *n* удовлетво- рённость *f*.

contest [*n* 'kɔntɛst, *vt* kən'tɛst] *n* (*competition: sport*) соревнова́ние; (: *beauty*) ко́нкурс; (*for power etc*) борьба́* ♦ *vt* (*statement, decision, LAW*) оспа́ривать (оспо́рить *perf*); (*compete for*) боро́ться* (*impf*) за +*acc*; (*election, competition*) боро́ться* (*impf*) на +*prp*.

contestant [kən'tɛstənt] *n* (*in competition*) уча́стник(-ница); (*in fight*) проти́вник(-ница).

context ['kɔntɛkst] *n* конте́кст; **in ~** в конте́ксте; **out of ~** вне конте́кста.

continent ['kɔntɪnənt] *n* контине́нт, матери́к; **the C~** (*BRIT*) Евро́па (*кро́ме брита́нских острово́в*); **on the C~** в Евро́пе (*кро́ме брита́нских острово́в*).

continental [kɔntɪ'nɛntl] *adj* (*BRIT*) европе́йский* ♦ *n* европе́ец(-е́йка).

continental breakfast *n* европе́йский* за́втрак (*лёгкий за́втрак из ко́фе и бу́лочки*).

continental quilt *n* (*BRIT*) стёганое одея́ло.

contingency [kən'tɪndʒənsɪ] *n* возмо́жность *f*.

contingency plan *n* план де́йствий на слу́чай

непредвиденных обстоятельств.
contingent [kən'tɪndʒənt] *n* (*also* MIL)
контингéнт ♦ *adj*: **to be ~ upon** зави́сеть*
(*impf*) от +*gen*.
continual [kən'tɪnjuəl] *adj* непреры́вный*.
continually [kən'tɪnjuəlɪ] *adv* непреры́вно,
постоя́нно.
continuation [kəntɪnju'eɪʃən] *n* продолже́ние.
continue [kən'tɪnju:] *vi* (*carry on*)
продолжа́ться (*impf*); (*after interruption: talk*)
продолжа́ться (продо́лжиться *perf*);
(: *person*) продложа́ть (продо́лжить *perf*) ♦ *vt*
продолжа́ть (продо́лжить *perf*); **to ~ to do**
продолжа́ть (продо́лжить *perf*) +*impf infin*; **to
be ~d** продолже́ние сле́дует; **~d on page 10**
продолже́ние на страни́це 10.
continuing education [kən'tɪnjuɪŋ-] *n* ку́рсы
mpl вече́рнего обуче́ния.
continuity [kəntɪ'nju:ɪtɪ] *n* (*in management*)
прее́мственность *f*; (*TV, CINEMA*)
непреры́вность *f* (*телевизио́нных програ́мм
и фи́льмов*); ~ **announcer** ди́ктор,
заполня́ющий пробе́лы; ~ **department** отде́л,
обеспе́чивающий непреры́вность
телевизио́нных програ́мм.
continuous [kən'tɪnjuəs] *adj* (*process, growth
etc*) непреры́вный*; (*line*) сплошно́й; (*LING*)
дли́тельный*; ~ **performance** (*CINEMA*) пока́з
кинофи́льма без переры́ва ме́жду сеа́нсами.
continuously [kən'tɪnjuəslɪ] *adv* (*repeatedly*)
неоднокра́тно, постоя́нно; (*uninterruptedly*)
непреры́вно.
continuous stationery *n* (*COMPUT*) руло́нная
бума́га (*для печа́тающего устро́йства*).
contort [kən'tɔ:t] *vt* (*body*) искривля́ть
(искриви́ть* *perf*); (*face*) криви́ть* (скриви́ть*
perf).
contortion [kən'tɔ:ʃən] *n* искривле́ние.
contortionist [kən'tɔ:ʃənɪst] *n*
пласти́ческий*(-ая) акроба́т(ка).
contour ['kɔntuə^r] *n* (*also:* ~ **line**) ко́нтурная
ли́ния; (*outline: usu pl*) ко́нтур.
contraband ['kɔntrəbænd] *n* контраба́нда ♦ *adj*
контраба́ндный.
contraception [kɔntrə'sɛpʃən] *n* пред-
упрежде́ние бере́менности.
contraceptive [kɔntrə'sɛptɪv] *adj* противо-
зача́точный ♦ *n* противозача́точное
сре́дство, контрацепти́в.
contract [*n, cpd* 'kɔntrækt, *vb* kən'trækt] *n* (*LAW,
COMM*) догово́р, контра́кт ♦ *vi* (*become
smaller*) сжима́ться (сжа́ться* *perf*) ♦ *vt*
(*illness*) заболева́ть (заболе́ть *perf*) +*instr* ♦
cpd (*price, date*) догово́рный; ~ **of
employment** служе́бный контра́кт; ~ **of
service** догово́р ме́жду компа́нией и
руководя́щим сотру́дником; **to ~ to do**
(*COMM*) обя́зывать (обяза́ть *perf*) +*infin*; ~

work рабо́та по контра́кту
► **contract in** *vi* (*BRIT*) официа́льно заявля́ть
(заяви́ть* *perf*) о жела́нии уча́ствовать в +*prp*.
► **contract out** *vi* (*BRIT*) официа́льно
отка́зываться (отказа́ться* *perf*) от уча́стия
в +*prp*.
contraction [kən'trækʃən] *n* (*of metal*) сжа́тие;
(*LING*) сокраще́ние; (*MED*) родова́я поту́га.
contractor [kən'træktə^r] *n* подря́дчик.
contractual [kən'træktʃuəl] *adj* (*agreement etc*)
догово́рный.
contradict [kɔntrə'dɪkt] *vt* (*person*) возража́ть
(возрази́ть* *perf*) +*dat*; (*statement*) возража́ть
(возрази́ть* *perf*) на +*acc*; (*be contrary to*)
противоре́чить (*impf*) +*dat*.
contradiction [kɔntrə'dɪkʃən] *n* противоре́чие;
to be in ~ with находи́ться* (*impf*) в
противоре́чии с +*instr*; **a ~ in terms**
логи́ческое противоре́чие.
contradictory [kɔntrə'dɪktərɪ] *adj*
противоречи́вый (противоречи́в).
contralto [kən'træltəu] *n* (*MUS*) контра́льто *nt
ind*.
contraption [kən'træpʃən] *n* дура́цкая вещь *f*.
contrary[1] ['kɔntrərɪ] *adj* (*opposite, different*)
противополо́жный*; (*unfavourable*)
неблагоприя́тный ♦ *n* противополо́жность
f; ~ **to what we thought** в противо-
поло́жность тому́, что мы ду́мали; **on the ~**
напро́тив, наоборо́т; **unless you hear to the
~** е́сли не бу́дет други́х инстру́кций.
contrary[2] [kən'trɛərɪ] *adj* своенра́вный*.
contrast [*n* 'kɔntrɑːst, *vt* kən'trɑːst] *n* (*difference*)
контра́ст ♦ *vt* сопоставля́ть (сопоста́вить*
perf); **in ~ to** *or* **with** по контра́сту с +*instr*.
contrasting [kən'trɑːstɪŋ] *adj* (*colours*)
контрасти́рующий; (*attitudes, views*)
противополо́жный.
contravene [kɔntrə'viːn] *vt* преступа́ть
(преступи́ть* *perf*).
contravention [kɔntrə'vɛnʃən] *n*: **in ~ of** в
наруше́ние +*gen*.
contribute [kən'trɪbjuːt] *vi* (*give*) де́лать
(сде́лать *perf*) вклад ♦ *vt* (*money, an article*)
вноси́ть* (внести́* *perf*); **to ~ to** (*to charity*)
же́ртвовать (поже́ртвовать *perf*) на +*acc or
для* +*gen*; (*to newspaper*) писа́ть* (написа́ть*
perf) для +*gen*; (*to discussion*) уча́ствовать
(*impf*) в +*prp*; (*to problem*) усугубля́ть
(усугуби́ть* *perf*).
contribution [kɔntrɪ'bjuːʃən] *n* (*donation*)
поже́ртвование; (*BRIT: for social security*)
взнос; (*to debate, campaign*) вклад; (*to
journal*) публика́ция.
contributor [kən'trɪbjutə^r] *n* (*to appeal*)
же́ртвователь *m*; (*to newspaper*) а́втор.
contributory [kən'trɪbjutərɪ] *adj*
спосо́бствующий; **it was a ~ factor in ...** э́то

---

* marks translations which have irregular inflections. The Russian-English side of the dictionary gives inflectional information.

яви́лось одни́м из спосо́бствующих
фа́кторов в ....

contributory pension scheme n (BRIT)
пенсио́нный догово́р, по кото́рому рабо́тник
принима́ет части́чное уча́стие в
формирова́нии свое́й бу́дущей пе́нсии.

contrite ['kɔntraɪt] adj (person) винова́тый; **she
looked ~** у неё был винова́тый вид.

contrivance [kən'traɪvəns] n (scheme) уло́вка;
(device) приспособле́ние.

contrive [kən'traɪv] vt (meeting) затева́ть
(зате́ять perf) ♦ vi: **to ~ to do** ухитря́ться
(ухитри́ться perf) +infin.

control [kən'trəul] vt контроли́ровать (impf) ♦ n
(of country, organization) контро́ль m; (of
oneself) самооблада́ние; (also: ~ **group**)
контро́льная гру́ппа; ~**s** npl (of vehicle)
рычаги́ mpl управле́ния; (on radio etc) ру́чки
fpl настро́йки; **to ~ o.s.** сохраня́ть
(сохрани́ть perf) самооблада́ние; **to take ~ of**
брать* (взять* perf) в свои́ ру́ки управле́ние
+instr; (COMM) брать* (взять* perf) под
контро́ль +acc; **to be in ~ of** контроли́ровать
(impf); **under ~** споко́йный; **everything is
under ~** всё под контро́лем; **out of ~**
неуправля́емый; **the car went out of ~**
маши́на потеря́ла управле́ние;
circumstances beyond our ~ не зави́сящие от
нас обстоя́тельства; **governmental ~s**
госуда́рственный контро́ль msg.

control key n управля́ющая кла́виша,
кла́виша управле́ния.

controller [kən'trəulə'] n (head) руководи́тель
m.

controlling interest [kən'trəulɪŋ-] n (COMM)
контро́льный паке́т а́кций.

control panel n пульт управле́ния.

control point n контро́льный пункт.

control room n (NAUT, MIL) пункт управле́ния;
(RADIO, TV) аппара́тная f adj.

control tower n контро́льно-диспе́тчерский*
пункт.

control unit n (COMPUT) блок управле́ния.

controversial [kɔntrə'və:ʃl] adj (topic etc)
спо́рный* (спо́рен); (person, writer)
неоднозна́чный* (неоднозна́чен).

controversy ['kɔntrəvə:sɪ] n диску́ссия, спор.

conurbation [kɔnə'beɪʃən] n агломера́ция.

convalesce [kɔnvə'lɛs] vi выздора́вливать
(вы́здороветь perf).

convalescence [kɔnvə'lɛsns] n вы-
здоровле́ние.

convalescent [kɔnvə'lɛsnt] n вы-
здора́вливающий*(-ая)m(f) adj ♦ adj: ~ **home**
санато́рий; ~ **leave** о́тпуск* по
выздоровле́нию.

convector [kən'vɛktə'] n (also: ~ **heater**)
конве́ктор.

convene [kən'viːn] vt (meeting) созыва́ть
(созва́ть* perf) ♦ vi (parliament etc)
собира́ться (собра́ться* perf).

convener [kən'viːnə'] n (ADMIN) челове́к,
отве́тственный за подгото́вку и созы́в
собра́ния, заседа́ния итп.

convenience [kən'viːnɪəns] n удо́бство; **at your
~** когда́ or как Вам бу́дет удо́бно; **at your
earliest ~** при пе́рвой возмо́жности; **a flat
with all modern ~s** or (BRIT) **all mod cons**
кварти́ра со все́ми удо́бствами.

convenience foods npl пищевы́е
полуфабрика́ты.

convenient [kən'viːnɪənt] adj удо́бный*
(удо́бен); **if it is ~ to you** е́сли Вам удо́бно.

conveniently [kən'viːnɪəntlɪ] adv (happen) как
раз; (situated) удо́бно.

convenor [kən'viːnə'] n = **convener**.

convent ['kɔnvənt] n (REL) (же́нский*)
монасты́рь* m.

convention [kən'vɛnʃən] n (custom)
усло́вность f; (conference) конфере́нция;
(agreement) конве́нция; (in art, literature)
приём.

conventional [kən'vɛnʃənl] adj обы́чный.

convent school n монасты́рская шко́ла.

converge [kən'vəːdʒ] vi (roads) сходи́ться*
(сойти́сь* perf); (people) съезжа́ться
(съе́хаться* perf); (ideas) совпада́ть
(совпа́сть* perf).

conversant [kən'vəːsnt] adj: **he is/was ~ with**
он све́дущ/был све́дущ в +prp.

conversation [kɔnvə'seɪʃən] n бесе́да,
разгово́р; **to have a ~ with sb** разгова́ривать
(impf) or бесе́довать (perf) с кем-н.

conversational [kɔnvə'seɪʃənl] adj
разгово́рный; (COMPUT) диало́говый.

conversationalist [kɔnvə'seɪʃnəlɪst] n: **a good ~**
интере́сный(-ая) собесе́дник(-ница).

converse [n 'kɔnvəːs, vb kən'vəːs] n (of
statement) противополо́жность f ♦ vi: **to ~
(with sb) (about sth)** бесе́довать
(побесе́довать perf) (с кем-н) (о чём-н).

conversely [kɔn'vəːslɪ] adv наоборо́т.

conversion [kən'vəːʃən] n (of weights) перево́д;
(of substances) превраще́ние; (of currency,
REL) обраще́ние; (BRIT: of house)
перестро́йка; (RUGBY) оди́н из приёмов
получе́ния очко́в.

conversion table n табли́ца преобразова́ния.

convert [vt kən'vəːt, n 'kɔnvəːt] vt (person: REL,
POL) обраща́ть (обрати́ть* perf); (building,
vehicle) преобразо́вывать (преобразова́ть
perf); (COMM) переводи́ть* (перевести́* perf) ♦
n (REL, POL) новообращённый(-ая)m(f) adj; **to
~ sth into** превраща́ть (преврати́ть* perf)
что-н в +acc.

convertible [kən'vəːtəbl] adj (currency)
конверти́руемый ♦ n автомоби́ль m с
отки́дным ве́рхом; ~ **loan stock** (COMM)
конверта́бельные а́кции.

convex ['kɔnvɛks] adj вы́пуклый.

convey [kən'veɪ] vt (information, idea, thanks)
передава́ть* (переда́ть* perf); (cargo, person)

перевози́ть* (перевезти́* *perf*).

conveyance [kən'veɪəns] *n* (*of goods*) перево́зка*; (*vehicle*) тра́нспортное сре́дство.

conveyancing [kən'veɪənsɪŋ] *n* (*LAW*) составле́ние нотариа́льного а́кта о переда́че прав на недви́жимость.

conveyor belt [kən'veɪəʳ-] *n* конве́йер.

convict [*vt* kən'vɪkt, *n* 'kɔnvɪkt] *vt* осужда́ть (осуди́ть* *perf*) ◆ *n* ка́торжник.

conviction [kən'vɪkʃən] *n* (*belief*) убежде́ние; (*certainty*) убеждённость *f*; (*LAW: decision*) осужде́ние; (*previous*) суди́мость *f*.

convince [kən'vɪns] *vt* (*assure*) уверя́ть (уве́рить *perf*); (*persuade*) убежда́ть (убеди́ть* *perf*); **to ~ sb (of sth/that)** убежда́ть (убеди́ть* *perf*) кого́-н (в чём-н/, что).

convinced [kən'vɪnst] *adj*: ~ **of/that** убеждённый в +*prp*/, что.

convincing [kən'vɪnsɪŋ] *adj* убеди́тельный* (убеди́телен).

convincingly [kən'vɪnsɪŋlɪ] *adv* убеди́тельно.

convivial [kən'vɪvɪəl] *adj* (*atmosphere*) дру́жеский*; (*person*) дружелю́бный* (дружелю́бен).

convoluted ['kɔnvəluːtɪd] *adj* замыслова́тый (замvillслова́т).

convoy ['kɔnvɔɪ] *n* (*of trucks*) коло́нна; (*of ships*) конво́й.

convulse [kən'vʌls] *vt*: **to be ~d with laughter/ pain** содрога́ться (*impf*) от сме́ха/бо́ли.

convulsion [kən'vʌlʃən] *n* су́дорога, конву́льсия.

coo [kuː] *vi* (*dove, person*) воркова́ть (*impf*).

cook [kuk] *vt* (*food*) гото́вить* (пригото́вить* *perf*) ◆ *vi* (*person*) гото́вить* (*impf*); (*food*) гото́виться* (*impf*) ◆ *n* по́вар*

► **cook up** *vt* (*inf*) стря́пать (состря́пать *perf*).

cookbook ['kukbuk] *n* пова́ренная *or* кулина́рная кни́га.

cook-chill ['kuktʃɪl] *adj*: ~ **food** заморо́женные полуфабрика́ты *mpl*.

cooker ['kukəʳ] *n* (*stove*) плита́*.

cookery ['kukərɪ] *n* кулинари́я.

cookery book *n* (*BRIT*) = **cookbook**.

cookie ['kukɪ] *n* (*US*) пече́нье*.

cooking ['kukɪŋ] *n* гото́вка ◆ *cpd* (*apples, chocolate*) испо́льзуемый в кулинари́и; **her ~ is very good** она́ хорошо́ гото́вит; **Italian ~** италья́нская ку́хня; ~ **utensils** ку́хонные принадле́жности.

cookout ['kukaut] *n* (*US*) приготовле́ние пи́щи на откры́том во́здухе.

cool [kuːl] *adj* (*temperature, drink etc*) прохла́дный*; (*dress, clothes*) лёгкий* (лёгок); (*person: calm, unemotional*) невозмути́мый (невозмути́м); (: *unfriendly*) холо́дный* (хо́лоден) ◆ *vt* (*tea, room*) охлажда́ть (охлади́ть* *perf*) ◆ *vi* (*water, air*) остыва́ть (осты́ть* *perf*); **it's ~** прохла́дно; **to keep sth ~** *or* **in a ~ place** держа́ть* (*impf*) что-н в прохла́дном ме́сте; **to keep one's ~** сохраня́ть (сохрани́ть *perf*) хладнокро́вие; **to lose one's ~** теря́ть (потеря́ть *perf*) самооблада́ние

► **cool down** *vi* остыва́ть (осты́ть* *perf*); (*situation*) нормализова́ться (*impf/perf*).

coolant ['kuːlənt] *n* хладаге́нт.

cool box (*US* **cooler**) *n* холоди́льный я́щик.

cooler ['kuːləʳ] *n* (*US*) = **cool box**.

cooling ['kuːlɪŋ] *n* охлажде́ние ◆ *adj* прохлади́тельный, освежа́ющий (освежа́ющ).

cooling tower *n* гради́рня*.

coolly ['kuːlɪ] *adv* (*calmly*) невозмути́мо; (*coldly*) хо́лодно.

coolness ['kuːlnɪs] *n* (*see adj*) прохла́да; лёгкость *f*; невозмути́мость *f*; хо́лодность *f*.

coop [kuːp] *n* кле́тка* ◆ *vt*: **to ~ up** (*fig*) запира́ть (запере́ть* *perf*).

co-op ['kəuɔp] *n abbr* (= *cooperative (society)*) кооперати́вное о́бщество.

cooperate [kəu'ɔpəreɪt] *vi* (*collaborate*) сотру́дничать (*impf*); (*assist*) соде́йствовать (*impf*); **to ~ with sb** сотру́дничать (*impf*) с кем-н.

cooperation [kəuɔpə'reɪʃən] *n* (*see vb*) коопера́ция, сотру́дничество; соде́йствие.

cooperative [kəu'ɔpərətɪv] *adj* кооперати́вный ◆ *n* кооперати́в; **he is very ~** он всегда́ гото́в оказа́ть по́мощь.

coopt [kəu'ɔpt] *vt*: **to ~ sb onto a committee** коопти́ровать (*impf/perf*) кого́-н в чле́ны комите́та.

coordinate [*vt* kəu'ɔːdɪneɪt, *n* kəu'ɔːdɪnət] *vt* (*activity, attack*) согласовыва́ть (согласова́ть *perf*); (*movements*) координи́ровать (*impf/perf*) ◆ *n* (*MATH*) координа́та; ~**s** *npl* (*clothes*) предме́ты оде́жды, составля́ющие оди́н анса́мбль.

coordination [kəuɔːdɪ'neɪʃən] *n* координа́ция.

co-ownership ['kəu'əunəʃɪp] *n* совме́стное владе́ние.

cop [kɔp] *n* (*inf*) мент.

cope [kəup] *vi*: **to ~ with** справля́ться (спра́виться* *perf*) с +*instr*.

Copenhagen ['kəupn'heɪɡən] *n* Копенга́ген.

copier ['kɔpɪəʳ] *n* (*also*: **photocopier**) (фото)копирова́льная маши́на.

co-pilot ['kəu'paɪlət] *n* второ́й пило́т.

copious ['kəupɪəs] *adj* оби́льный* (оби́лен).

copper ['kɔpəʳ] *n* (*metal*) медь *f*; (*BRIT: inf*) лега́вый *m adj*; ~**s** *npl* (*small change*) медяки́* *mpl*.

coppice ['kɔpɪs] *n* ро́щица.

copse [kɔps] *n* = **coppice**.

---

* marks translations which have irregular inflections. The Russian-English side of the dictionary gives inflectional information.

copulate ['kɔpjuleɪt] *vi* совокупля́ться (совокупи́ться* *perf*).

copy ['kɔpɪ] *n* (*duplicate*) ко́пия; (*of book etc*) экземпля́р; (*material: for printing*) пи́сьменный экземпля́р, ру́копись *f* ♦ *vt* (*person, idea, text*) копи́ровать (скопи́ровать *perf*); **to make good ~** (*PRESS*) составля́ть (соста́вить* *perf*) хоро́ший материа́л (для печа́ти)

► **copy out** (*text*) копи́ровать (скопи́ровать *perf*)

► **copy down** (*text*) копи́ровать (скопи́ровать *perf*).

copycat ['kɔpɪkæt] *n* (*inf*) обезья́на *m/f*.

copyright ['kɔpɪraɪt] *n* а́вторское пра́во*; **~ reserved** а́вторское пра́во сохранено́.

copy typist *n* машини́стка*.

copywriter ['kɔpɪraɪtə'] *n* реклами́ст.

coral ['kɔrəl] *n* кора́лл.

coral reef *n* кора́лловый риф.

Coral Sea *n*: **the ~ ~** Кора́лловое мо́ре*.

cord [kɔ:d] *n* (*string*) верёвка*; (*ELEC*) шнур*; (*fabric*) вельве́т; **~s** *npl* (*trousers*) вельве́товые брю́ки *pl*.

cordial ['kɔ:dɪəl] *adj* (*friendly*) серде́чный* ♦ *n* (*BRIT*) фрукто́вый напи́ток*.

cordless ['kɔ:dlɪs] *adj* переносно́й.

cordon ['kɔ:dn] *n* кордо́н, оцепле́ние

► **cordon off** *vt* оцепля́ть (оцепи́ть* *perf*).

cordon bleu [kɔ:dɔn 'blə:] *adj* (*cookery, cook*) вы́сшего кла́сса (*о кулина́рном иску́сстве*).

corduroy ['kɔ:dərɔɪ] *n* вельве́т*.

CORE [kɔ:'] *n* *abbr* (*US*) = *Congress of Racial Equality*.

core [kɔ:'] *n* (*of fruit, organization*) сердцеви́на; (*of earth*) ядро́*; (*of nuclear reactor*) серде́чник; (*of problem*) суть *f* ♦ *vt* выреза́ть (вы́резать* *perf*) сердцеви́ну +*gen*; **rotten to the ~** (*fig*) прогни́вший до основа́ния.

Corfu [kɔ:'fu:] *n* Ко́рфу *m ind*.

coriander [kɔrɪ'ændə'] *n* (*spice*) ки́нза, кориа́ндр.

cork [kɔ:k] *n* про́бка*.

corkage ['kɔ:kɪdʒ] *n* дополни́тельная опла́та в рестора́не за отку́поривание и пода́чу принесённого с собо́й вина́.

corked [kɔ:kt] (*US* **corky**) *adj* пропа́хший про́бкой.

corkscrew ['kɔ:kskru:] *n* што́пор.

corky ['kɔ:kɪ] *adj* (*US*) = **corked**.

cormorant ['kɔ:mərnt] *n* бакла́н.

Corn *abbr* (*BRIT*: *POST*) = **Cornwall**.

corn [kɔ:n] *n* (*BRIT*) зерно́*; (*US*: *maize*) кукуру́за; (*on foot*) мозо́ль *f*; **~ on the cob** поча́тки* кукуру́зы.

cornea ['kɔ:nɪə] *n* рогова́я оболо́чка*.

corned beef ['kɔ:nd-] *n* консерви́рованная говя́дина.

corner ['kɔ:nə'] *n* у́гол*; (*SPORT*: *also*: ~ **kick**) углово́й *m adj* (уда́р) ♦ *vt* (*trap*) загоня́ть (загна́ть* *perf*) в у́гол; (*COMM*: *market*)

приобрета́ть (приобрести́* *perf*) контро́ль над +*instr* ♦ *vi* (*in car*) де́лать (сде́лать *perf*) поворо́т; **to cut ~s** (*fig*) среза́ть (*impf*) углы́.

corner flag *n* углово́й флажо́к*.

corner kick *n* углово́й уда́р.

cornerstone ['kɔ:nəstəun] *n* (*fig*) крае-уго́льный ка́мень* *m*.

cornet ['kɔ:nɪt] *n* (*MUS*) корне́т; (*BRIT*: *of ice-cream*) моро́женое в ва́фельной тру́бочке.

cornflakes ['kɔ:nfleɪks] *npl* кукуру́зные хло́пья* *pl*.

cornflour ['kɔ:nflauə'] *n* (*BRIT*) кукуру́зная мука́.

cornice ['kɔ:nɪs] *n* карни́з.

Cornish ['kɔ:nɪʃ] *adj* корнуэ́льский.

corn oil *n* кукуру́зное ма́сло*.

cornstarch ['kɔ:nstɑ:tʃ] *n* (*US*) = **cornflour**.

cornucopia [kɔ:nju'kəupɪə] *n* рог* изоби́лия.

Cornwall ['kɔ:nwəl] *n* Ко́рнуолл.

corny ['kɔ:nɪ] *adj* (*inf*) пло́ский* (пло́сок).

corollary [kə'rɔlərɪ] *n* сле́дствие.

coronary ['kɔrənərɪ] *n* (*also*: ~ **thrombosis**) корона́рный тромбо́з.

coronation [kɔrə'neɪʃən] *n* корона́ция.

coroner ['kɔrənə'] *n* (*LAW*) ко́ронер (*судья́, рассле́дующий причи́ны сме́рти, происше́дшей при подозри́тельных обстоя́тельствах*).

coronet ['kɔrənɪt] *n* диаде́ма.

Corp. *abbr* = **corporation**; (*MIL*) = **corporal**.

corporal ['kɔ:pərl] *n* капра́л ♦ *adj*: ~ **punishment** теле́сное наказа́ние.

corporate ['kɔ:pərɪt] *adj* (*COMM*) корпорацио́нный; (*ownership, effort*) о́бщий*; (*identity*) корпорати́вный.

corporate hospitality *n* спецобслу́живание и привиле́гии, ока́зываемые корпора́цией осо́бо ва́жным и́ли це́нным клие́нтам.

corporation [kɔ:pə'reɪʃən] *n* (*COMM*) корпора́ция; (*of town*) муниципалите́т.

corporation tax *n* корпорацио́нный нало́г.

corps [kɔ:'] (*pl* ~) *n* (*also MIL*) ко́рпус*; **the press ~** корреспонде́нтский ко́рпус.

corpse [kɔ:ps] *n* труп.

corpuscle ['kɔ:pʌsl] *n* (*BIO*) те́льце* (*кровяны́е*).

corral [kə'rɑ:l] *n* заго́н.

correct [kə'rɛkt] *adj* (*accurate*) пра́вильный* (пра́вилен); (*proper*) соотве́тствующий* ♦ *vt* (*mistake, fault*) исправля́ть (испра́вить* *perf*); (*exam*) проверя́ть (прове́рить *perf*); **you are ~** Вы пра́вы.

correction [kə'rɛkʃən] *n* (*act of correcting*) исправле́ние; (*mistake corrected*) попра́вка*; (*of proofs*) корректу́ра.

correctly [kə'rɛktlɪ] *adv* пра́вильно.

correlate ['kɔrɪleɪt] *vt* соотноси́ть* (соотнести́* *perf*) ♦ *vi*: **to ~ with** соотноси́ться* (*impf*) *or* коррели́ровать (*impf*) с +*instr*.

correlation [kɔrɪ'leɪʃən] *n* соотноше́ние, корреля́ция.

correspond [kɔrɪs'pɔnd] *vi*: **to ~ (with)** (*write*)

перепи́сываться (*impf*) (c +*instr*); (*tally*) согласо́вываться (*impf*) (c +*instr*); (*equate*): **to ~ (to)** соотве́тствовать (*impf*) (+*dat*).

correspondence [kɔrɪs'pɔndəns] *n* (*letters*) корреспонде́нция, перепи́ска; (*relationship*) соотноше́ние.

correspondence course *n* зао́чный курс.

correspondent [kɔrɪs'pɔndənt] *n* (*PRESS*) корреспонде́нт(ка).

corresponding [kɔrɪs'pɔndɪŋ] *adj* соотве́тствующий*.

corridor ['kɔrɪdɔ:ʳ] *n* (*in building etc*) коридо́р; (*in train*) прохо́д.

corroborate [kə'rɔbəreɪt] *vt* подтвержда́ть (подтверди́ть* *perf*).

corrode [kə'rəud] *vt* (*metal*) разъеда́ть (разъе́сть* *perf*) ♦ *vi* (*metal*) ржаве́ть (заржаве́ть *perf*).

corrosion [kə'rəuʒən] *n* (*damage*) ржа́вчина; (*process*) корро́зия.

corrosive [kə'rəuzɪv] *adj* коррози́йный.

corrugated ['kɔrəgeɪtɪd] *adj* рифлёный.

corrugated iron *n* рифлёное желе́зо.

corrupt [kə'rʌpt] *adj* (*person*) прода́жный* (прода́жен), коррумпи́рованный; (*COMPUT*) испо́рченный, искажённый ♦ *vt* развраща́ть (разврати́ть* *perf*); (*COMPUT*) искажа́ть (искази́ть* *perf*); **~ practices** бесче́стные приёмы.

corruption [kə'rʌpʃən] *n* (*see adj*) корру́пция, прода́жность *f*; искаже́ние.

corset ['kɔ:sɪt] *n* (*also MED*) корсе́т.

Corsica ['kɔ:sɪkə] *n* Ко́рсика.

Corsican ['kɔ:sɪkən] *adj* корсика́нский ♦ *n* корсика́нец*(-нка*).

cortège [kɔ:'teɪʒ] *n* (*also:* **funeral ~**) проце́ссия.

cortisone ['kɔ:tɪzəun] *n* кортизо́н.

coruscating ['kɔrəskeɪtɪŋ] *adj* сверка́ющий.

c.o.s. *abbr* (= *cash on shipment*) *опла́та нали́чными при отпра́вке*.

cosh [kɔʃ] *n* (*BRIT*) дуби́нка*.

cosignatory ['kəu'sɪgnətərɪ] *n* одна́ из сторо́н, подпи́сывающих докуме́нт.

cosiness ['kəuzɪnɪs] *n* ую́т.

cos lettuce ['kɔs-] *n* лату́к (*сала́т*).

cosmetic [kɔz'mɛtɪk] *n* (*usu pl*) косме́тика ♦ *adj* (*fig*) космети́ческий*; **~ surgery** космети́ческая хирурги́я.

cosmic ['kɔzmɪk] *adj* косми́ческий*.

cosmonaut ['kɔzmənɔ:t] *n* космона́вт.

cosmopolitan [kɔzmə'pɔlɪtn] *adj* (*place*) космополити́ческий.

cosmos ['kɔzmɔs] *n*: **the ~** ко́смос.

cosset ['kɔsɪt] *vt* балова́ть (избалова́ть* *perf*).

cost [kɔst] (*pt, pp* **cost**) *n* сто́имость *f*; (*fig*) цена́* ♦ *vt* (*be priced at*) сто́ить (*impf*); (*pt, pp* **costed**) *find out cost of*) оце́нивать (оцени́ть* *perf*) сто́имость +*gen*; **~s** *npl* (*COMM*) расхо́ды *mpl*;

(*LAW*) суде́бные изде́ржки* *fpl*; **how much does it ~?** ско́лько э́то сто́ит?; **it ~s £5/too much** э́то сто́ит £5/сли́шком до́рого; **what will it ~ to have it repaired?** ско́лько бу́дет сто́ить ремо́нт?; **to ~ sb time/effort** сто́ить (*impf*) кому́-н вре́мени/уси́лий; **it ~ him his life/job** э́то сто́ило ему́ жи́зни/рабо́ты; **the ~ of living** сто́имость жи́зни; **to sell/buy at ~** продава́ть* (прода́ть* *perf*)/покупа́ть (купи́ть* *perf*) по себесто́имости; **at all ~s** любо́й цено́й.

cost accountant *n* бухга́лтер (*веду́щий учёт затра́т*).

co-star ['kəustɑ:ʳ] *n* партнёр (*гла́вной ро́ли*).

Costa Rica ['kɔstə'ri:kə] *n* Ко́ста-Ри́ка.

cost-benefit analysis ['kɔstbɛnɪfɪt-] *n* ана́лиз изде́ржек и при́были.

cost centre *n* счёт, фикси́рующий *произво́дственные изде́ржки*.

cost control *n* контро́ль *m* за у́ровнем изде́ржек.

cost-effective ['kɔstɪ'fɛktɪv] *adj* вы́годный* (вы́годен); (*COMM*) рента́бельный.

cost-effectiveness ['kɔstɪ'fɛktɪvnɪs] *n* (*see adj*) вы́годность *f*; рента́бельность *f*.

costing ['kɔstɪŋ] *n* (*COMM*) оце́нка сто́имости.

costly ['kɔstlɪ] *adj* (*expensive*) дорого́й* (до́рог); (*in time, effort*) дорогосто́ящий*.

cost of living *n* сто́имость *f* жи́зни.

cost price *n* (*BRIT*) себесто́имость *f*; **to sell/buy at ~ ~** продава́ть* (прода́ть* *perf*)/покупа́ть (купи́ть* *perf*) по себесто́имости.

costume ['kɔstju:m] *n* костю́м; (*BRIT: also:* **swimming ~**) купа́льник, купа́льный костю́м.

costume jewellery *n* бижуте́рия.

cosy ['kəuzɪ] (*US* **cozy**) *adj* (*room, atmosphere*) ую́тный* (ую́тен); (*bed*) удо́бный* (удо́бен); (*scarf, gloves*) тёплый*; (*person*) забо́тливый; (*chat, evening*) прия́тный* (прия́тен).

cot [kɔt] *n* (*BRIT: for baby*) де́тская крова́тка*; (*US: camp bed*) ко́йка*.

cot death *n* внеза́пная сме́рть здоро́вого грудно́го ребёнка во сне.

Cotswolds ['kɔtswəuldz] *npl*: **the ~** Ко́тсвольд *msg*.

cottage ['kɔtɪdʒ] *n* котте́дж.

cottage cheese *n* творо́г.

cottage industry *n* надо́мный труд*.

cottage pie *n* запека́нка из мя́са и карто́феля.

cotton ['kɔtn] *n* (*fabric*) хлопо́к*, хлопчатобума́жная ткань *f*; (*plant*) хло́пчатник; (*thread*) (шве́йная) ни́тка*; **~ dress** *etc* хлопчатобума́жное пла́тье* *etc*.

► **cotton on** *vi* (*inf*): **he has ~ed on to the fact that ...** до него́ дошло́, что ....

---

* marks translations which have irregular inflections. The Russian-English side of the dictionary gives inflectional information.

cotton candy n (US) са́харная ва́та.
cotton wool n (BRIT) ва́та.
couch [kautʃ] n тахта́, дива́н; (for patients) кушётка* ♦ vt излага́ть (изложи́ть* perf).
couchette [kuːˈʃɛt] n спа́льное ме́сто*, по́лка*.
couch potato n лежебо́ка m/f.
cough [kɔf] vi (person) ка́шлять (impf); (engine) тараха́ть (impf) ♦ n ка́шель f.
cough drop n табле́тка* от ка́шля.
cough mixture n миксту́ра от ка́шля.
cough syrup n = cough mixture.
could [kud] pt of can².
couldn't [ˈkudnt] = could not; see can².
council [ˈkaunsl] n сове́т; city or town ~ городско́й сове́т, муниципалите́т; C~ of Europe Сове́т Европе́йского Соо́бщества.
council estate n (BRIT) жило́й, принадлежа́щий масси́в муниципалите́ту.
council house n (BRIT) дом, принадлежа́щий муниципалите́ту.
council housing n (BRIT) жильё, принадлежа́щее муниципалите́ту и сдава́емое в аре́нду.
councillor [ˈkaunslə'] n ≈ член муниципалите́та.
council tax n муниципа́льный нало́г.
counsel [ˈkaunsl] n (advice) сове́т; (lawyer) адвока́т, юрисконсу́льт ♦ vt: to ~ sth/sb to do сове́товать (посове́товать perf) что-н/ кому́-н +infin; ~ for the defence защи́тник; ~ for the prosecution обвини́тель m.
counsellor [ˈkaunslə'] n (advisor) сове́тник; (US: lawyer) адвока́т.
count [kaunt] vt (add up) счита́ть (посчита́ть perf); (include) счита́ть (impf) ♦ vi пересчи́тывать (пересчита́ть perf); (qualify) счита́ться (impf); (matter) име́ть (impf) значе́ние ♦ n (of things, people) подсчёт; (level) у́ровень* m; (nobleman) граф; to ~ (up) to 10 счита́ть (посчита́ть perf) до 10; not ~ing the children не счита́я дете́й; 10 ~ing him 10, счита́я его́; to ~ the cost of оце́нивать (оцени́ть perf) сто́имость +gen; it ~s for very little э́то име́ет о́чень ма́ленькое значе́ние; ~ yourself lucky счита́йте, что Вам повезло́; to keep/lose ~ of sth вести́* (impf)/ теря́ть (потеря́ть perf) счёт чего́-н
  ▶ **count on** vt fus рассчи́тывать (impf) на +acc; to ~ on doing рассчи́тывать (impf) +infin
  ▶ **count up** vt подсчи́тывать (подсчита́ть perf).
countdown [ˈkauntdaun] n счёт в обра́тном направле́нии.
countenance [ˈkauntɪnəns] n лицо́* ♦ vt одобря́ть (одо́брить perf).
counter [ˈkauntə'] n (in shop, café) прила́вок*; (in bank, post office) сто́йка*; (in game) фи́шка*; (TECH) счётчик ♦ vt (oppose) опроверга́ть (опрове́ргнуть perf); (blow) отража́ть (отрази́ть perf) ♦ adv: to ~ противове́с +dat; to buy under the ~ (fig) покупа́ть (купи́ть* perf) из-под прила́вка; to

~ sth with sth противостоя́ть (impf/perf) чему́-н чем-н.
counteract [ˈkauntər'ækt] vt (effect etc) противоде́йствовать (impf) +dat; (poison etc) нейтрализова́ть (impf/perf), обезвре́живать (обезвре́дить* perf).
counterattack [ˈkauntərə'tæk] n контрата́ка ♦ vi контратакова́ть (impf/perf).
counterbalance [ˈkauntə'bæləns] vt уравнове́шивать (уравнове́сить* perf).
counterclockwise [ˈkauntə'klɔkwaiz] adv про́тив часово́й стре́лки.
counterespionage [ˈkauntər'ɛspiənɑ:ʒ] n контрразве́дка*.
counterfeit [ˈkauntəfit] n подде́лка* ♦ vt подде́лывать (подде́лать perf) ♦ adj (coin) фальши́вый.
counterfoil [ˈkauntəfɔil] n (of cheque, money order) корешо́к*.
counterintelligence [ˈkauntərɪn'tɛlidʒəns] n контрразве́дка*.
countermand [ˈkauntəmɑ:nd] vt (order) отменя́ть (отмени́ть* perf).
countermeasure [ˈkauntəmɛʒə'] n контрме́ра.
counteroffensive [ˈkauntərə'fɛnsiv] n контрнаступле́ние.
counterpane [ˈkauntəpein] n покрыва́ло.
counterpart [ˈkauntəpɑ:t] n (of person) колле́га m/f; (of document etc) ко́пия.
counterproductive [ˈkauntəprə'dʌktiv] adj непродукти́вный (непродукти́вен).
counterproposal [ˈkauntəprə'pəuzl] n встре́чное предложе́ние.
countersign [ˈkauntəsain] vt заверя́ть (заве́рить*, perf), засвиде́тельствовать (perf).
countersink [ˈkauntəsiŋk] vt зенкова́ть (impf).
countess [ˈkauntis] n графи́ня.
countless [ˈkauntlis] adj несчётный*, бесчи́сленный.
countrified [ˈkʌntrifaid] adj дереве́нский*.
country [ˈkʌntri] n (state, nation) страна́*; (native land) ро́дина; (rural area) дере́вня*; (region) райо́н; in the ~ за́ городом; mountainous ~ гори́стая ме́стность f.
country and western (music) n ка́нтри n ind.
country dancing n (BRIT) наро́дные та́нцы mpl.
country house n за́городный дом*, ≈ да́ча.
countryman [ˈkʌntrimən] irreg n (compatriot) земля́к*, соотече́ственник; (country dweller) дереве́нский* or се́льский* жи́тель m.
countryside [ˈkʌntrisaid] n се́льская ме́стность f.
countrywide [ˈkʌntri'waid] adj обще-национа́льный ♦ adv по всей стране́.
county [ˈkaunti] n гра́фство*.
county council n ≈ областно́й сове́т, сове́т гра́фства.
county town n (BRIT) гла́вный го́род* гра́фства.
coup [kuː] (pl ~s) n (also: ~ d'état)

госуда́рственный переворо́т; (*fig*)
переворо́т.
coupé [kuː'peɪ] *n* (*AUT*) закры́тый автомоби́ль
с двумя́ дверя́ми и накло́нным ку́зовом.
couple ['kʌpl] *n* (*married couple*) супру́ги *pl*; (*of
people, things*) па́ра ♦ *vt* (*ideas, names*)
свя́зывать (связа́ть* *perf*); (*machinery*)
сцепля́ть (сцепи́ть* *perf*); **a ~ of** (*two, a few*)
па́ра +*gen*.
couplet ['kʌplɪt] *n* двусти́шие.
coupling ['kʌplɪŋ] *n* (*RAIL*) сцепле́ние.
coupon ['kuːpɔn] *n* (*voucher*) купо́н;
(*detachable form*) тало́н; (*COMM*) отрывно́й
бланк.
courage ['kʌrɪdʒ] *n* сме́лость *f*, хра́брость *f*,
му́жество.
courageous [kə'reɪdʒəs] *adj* сме́лый* (смел),
хра́брый (храбр), му́жественный
(му́жественен).
courgette [kuə'ʒet] *n* (*BRIT*) молодо́й кабачо́к*.
courier ['kurɪəʳ] *n* (*messenger*) курье́р; (*for
tourists*) руководи́тель *m* гру́ппы.
course [kɔːs] *n* (*SCOL, MED, NAUT*) курс; (*of
events, time etc*) ход; (*of argument, action*)
направле́ние; (*of river*) тече́ние; (*part of
meal*): **first/next/last ~** пе́рвое/второ́е/
сла́дкое блю́до; **~ of lectures/treatment** курс
ле́кций/лече́ния; **in the ~ of the next few days**
в тече́ние сле́дующих не́скольких дней; **in
due ~** в своё вре́мя; **~** (*of action*) ли́ния
поведе́ния; **the best ~ would be ...** лу́чшим
вы́ходом бы́ло бы ...; **we have no other ~ but
to ...** у нас нет друго́го вы́хода, кро́ме как ...;
of ~ (*naturally*) коне́чно; (*certainly*)
безусло́вно; **of ~!** коне́чно!; **(no) of ~ not!**
(нет,) коне́чно, нет!; **golf ~** по́ле для игры́ в
гольф.
court [kɔːt] *n* (*LAW*) суд*; (*SPORT*) корт; (*royal*)
двор* ♦ *vt* (*woman*) уха́живать (*impf*) за +*instr*;
(*fig: favour*) добива́ться (доби́ться* *perf*)
+*gen*; (: *death, disaster*) заи́грывать (*impf*) с
+*instr*; **to settle out of ~** приходи́ть* (прийти́*
perf) к соглаше́нию без суде́бного
разбира́тельства; **to take sb to ~** подава́ть*
(пода́ть* *perf*) на кого́-н в суд.
courteous ['kəːtɪəs] *adj* ве́жливый (ве́жлив).
courtesan [kɔːtɪ'zæn] *n* куртиза́нка*.
courtesy ['kəːtəsɪ] *n* ве́жливость *f*; **(by) ~ of**
благодаря́ любе́зности +*gen*.
courtesy light *n* ла́мпочка в сало́не
автомоби́ля.
courthouse ['kɔːthaus] *n* (*US*) зда́ние суда́.
courtier ['kɔːtɪəʳ] *n* придво́рный *m adj*.
court martial (*pl* **~s**) *n* вое́нный трибуна́л.
court of appeal (*pl* **~s ~ ~**) *n* апелляцио́нный
суд*.
court of inquiry (*pl* **~s ~ ~**) *n* сле́дственная
коми́ссия.

courtroom ['kɔːtrum] *n* зал суда́.
court shoe *n* ло́дочки *pl*.
courtyard ['kɔːtjɑːd] *n* вну́тренний* двор*.
cousin ['kʌzn] *n* (*relative: male*) неродно́й
брат*; (: *female*) неродна́я сестра́*; **first ~**
(*male*) двою́родный брат*; (*female*)
двою́родная сестра́*.
cove [kəuv] *n* (*bay*) бу́хточка*.
covenant ['kʌvənənt] *n* (*promise*)
обяза́тельство ♦ *vt*: **to ~ £200 per year to
charity** обя́зываться (обяза́ться* *perf*)
перечисля́ть £200 в год в благо-
твори́тельный фонд.
Coventry ['kɔvəntrɪ] *n*: **send sb to ~** (*fig*)
бойкоти́ровать (*impf/perf*) кого́-н.
cover ['kʌvəʳ] *vt* (*protect, hide*) закрыва́ть
(закры́ть* *perf*), укрыва́ть (укры́ть* *perf*);
(*distance*) покрыва́ть (покры́ть* *perf*); (*MIL*)
прикрыва́ть (прикры́ть* *perf*); (*INSURANCE*)
предусма́тривать (предусмотре́ть* *perf*);
(*topic*) рассма́тривать (рассмотре́ть* *perf*);
(*include*) охва́тывать (охвати́ть* *perf*);
(*PRESS*) освеща́ть (освети́ть* *perf*) ♦ *n* (*for
furniture, machinery etc*) чехо́л*; (*of book,
magazine*) обло́жка*; (*shelter*) укры́тие;
(*INSURANCE*) покры́тие; (*MIL*) прикры́тие;
(*fig*) прикры́тие; **~s** *npl* (*bedclothes*)
посте́льные принадле́жности *fpl*; **he was ~ed
in** *or* **with** (*mud*) он был весь в +*prp*; **to take ~**
укрыва́ться (укры́ться* *perf*); **under ~** в
укры́тии; **under ~ of darkness** под покро́вом
темноты́; **under separate ~** (*COMM*) в
отде́льном паке́те; **£10 will ~ my expenses**
£10 покро́ют мои́ расхо́ды
▶ **cover up** *vt* (*protect, hide*) закрыва́ть
(закры́ть* *perf*); (*fig: facts, feelings*) скрыва́ть
(скрыть* *perf*) ♦ *vi* (*fig*): **to ~ up for sb**
покрыва́ть (покры́ть* *perf*) кого́-н.
coverage ['kʌvərɪdʒ] *n* (*TV, PRESS*) освеще́ние;
television ~ of the conference освеще́ние
конфере́нции по телеви́дению; **to give full ~
to** дава́ть* (дать* *perf*) по́лное освеще́ние
+*gen*.
coveralls ['kʌvərɔːlz] *npl* (*US*) рабо́чий*
комбинезо́н *msg*.
cover charge *n* (*in restaurant*) наце́нка.
covering ['kʌvərɪŋ] *n* (*layer*) пласт*; (*of snow,
dust etc*) слой*; (*on floor*) насти́л.
covering letter (*US* **cover letter**) *n*
сопроводи́тельное письмо́*.
cover note *n* докуме́нт, удостоверя́ющий
факт страхова́ния.
cover price *n* цена́, ука́занная на обло́жке.
covert ['kʌvət] *adj* (*threat*) скры́тый; (*attack*)
неожи́данный*; **she gave me a ~ glance** она́
укра́дкой на меня́ посмотре́ла.
cover-up ['kʌvərʌp] *n* ши́рма, прикры́тие.
covet ['kʌvɪt] *vt* жа́ждать (*impf*) +*gen*.

---

* marks translations which have irregular inflections. The Russian-English side of the dictionary gives inflectional information.

cow [kau] *n* (*also inf!*) коро́ва (*also !*) ◆ *vt* запу́гивать (запуга́ть *perf*).

coward ['kauəd] *n* трус(и́ха).

cowardice ['kauədɪs] *n* тру́сость *f*.

cowardly ['kauədlɪ] *adj* трусли́вый (трусли́в).

cowboy ['kaubɔɪ] *n* (*in US*) ковбо́й; (*pej: tradesman*) шаба́шник.

cow elephant *n* слони́ха.

cower ['kauə[r]] *vi* съёживаться (съёжиться *perf*).

cow shed *n* коро́вник.

cowslip ['kauslɪp] *n* первоцве́т (настоя́щий* *or* весе́нний*).

cox [kɔks] *n abbr* = **coxswain**.

coxswain ['kɔksn] *n* (*ROWING*) старшина́ (байда́рки).

coy [kɔɪ] *adj* (*shy*) засте́нчивый (засте́нчив).

coyote [kɔɪ'əutɪ] *n* койо́т.

cozy ['kəuzɪ] *adj* (*US*) = **cosy**.

CP *n abbr* = **Communist Party**.

cp. *abbr* (= **compare**) ср.= *сравни́*.

c/p *abbr* (*BRIT*: = **carriage paid**) с опла́ченной доста́вкой.

CPA *n abbr* (*US*) = **certified public accountant**.

CPI *n abbr* (= **Consumer Price Index**) и́ндекс потреби́тельских цен.

Cpl. *abbr* (*MIL*) = **corporal**.

CP/M *n abbr* (= **Central Program for Microprocessors**) CPM (*операцио́нная систе́ма для микроЭВМ*).

c.p.s. *abbr* (*COMPUT, TYP*: = **characters per second**) зна́ков в секу́нду.

CPSA *n abbr* (*BRIT*) = **Civil and Public Services Association**.

CPU *n abbr* (*COMPUT*) (= **central processing unit**) ЦП = *центра́льный проце́ссор*.

cr. *abbr* = **credit**, **creditor**.

crab [kræb] *n* краб.

crab apple *n* ди́кое я́блоко*.

crack [kræk] *n* (*noise*) треск; (*gap*) щель* *f*; (*in bone, dish, wall*) тре́щина; (*joke*) хо́хма; (*DRUGS*) крэк (*фо́рма кокаи́на*) ◆ *vt* (*whip, twig*) щёлкать (щёлкнуть *perf*) +*instr*; (*bone, dish etc*) раска́лывать (расколо́ть* *perf*); (*nut*) коло́ть* (расколо́ть* *perf*); (*problem*) реша́ть (реши́ть *perf*); (*code*) разга́дывать (разгада́ть *perf*); (*joke*) отпуска́ть (отпусти́ть* *perf*) ◆ *adj* первокла́ссный*; **at the ~ of dawn** на заре́; **to have a ~ (at sth)** (*inf*) пыта́ть (попыта́ть *perf*) свои́ си́лы (в чём-н); **to get ~ing** (*inf*) пошеве́ливаться (*impf*)

▶ **crack down on** *vt fus* расправля́ться (распра́виться* *perf*) с +*instr*

▶ **crack up** *vi* (*with laughter*) пры́скать (при́снуть *perf*) со́ смеху; **she ~ed up** (*under strain*) у неё был не́рвный срыв.

crackdown ['krækdaun] *n*: **~ (on)** распра́ва (с +*instr*).

cracked [krækt] *adj* (*inf*) сло́манный (сло́ман).

cracker ['krækə[r]] *n* (*biscuit*) кре́кер; (*Christmas cracker*) хлопу́шка*; (*firework*) шути́ха; **a ~ of**

a goal (*BRIT*: *inf*) сногсшиба́тельный гол; **she's a ~** (*BRIT*: *inf*) она́ сногсшиба́тельная же́нщина; **he's ~s** (*BRIT*: *inf*) он спя́тил.

crackle ['krækl] *vi* потре́скивать (*impf*).

crackling ['kræklɪŋ] *n* треск; (*of pork*) шква́рки *fpl*.

crackpot ['krækpɔt] *n* (*inf*) полоу́мный(-ая) *m(f)* *adj* ◆ *adj* полоу́мный.

cradle ['kreidl] *n* (*for baby*) колыбе́ль *f* ◆ *vt* прижима́ть (*impf*) к груди́.

craft [krɑ:ft] *n* (*skill*) мастерство́; (*trade*) ремесло́*; (*boat: pl inv*) кора́бль* *f*.

craftsman ['krɑ:ftsmən] *irreg n* (*artisan*) реме́сленник.

craftsmanship ['krɑ:ftsmənʃɪp] *n* (*quality*) вы́делка; (*skill*) мастерство́.

crafty ['krɑ:ftɪ] *adj* лука́вый (лука́в).

crag [kræg] *n* утёс.

craggy ['krægɪ] *adj* (*mountain, cliff*) отве́сный*; (*face*) с ре́зкими черта́ми.

cram [kræm] *vi* (*for exams*) зубри́ть (вы́зубрить *perf*) ◆ *vt* (*fill*): **to ~ sth with** набива́ть (наби́ть* *perf*) что-н +*instr*; (*put*): **to ~ sth into** вти́скивать (вти́снуть *perf*) что-н в +*acc*.

cramming ['kræmɪŋ] *n* зубрёжка.

cramp [kræmp] *n* су́дорога ◆ *vt* стесня́ть (стесни́ть *perf*).

cramped [kræmpt] *adj* (*accommodation*) те́сный (те́сен).

crampon ['kræmpən] *n* (*CLIMBING*) клещи́ *pl*.

cranberry ['krænbərɪ] *n* клю́ква.

crane [kreɪn] *n* (*machine*) (подъёмный) кран; (*bird*) жура́вль* *m* ◆ *vt*: **to ~ one's neck** вытя́гивать (вы́тянуть *perf*) ше́ю ◆ *vi*: **to ~ forward** высо́вываться (вы́сунуться *perf*).

crania ['kreɪnɪə] *npl of* **cranium**.

cranium ['kreɪnɪəm] (*pl* **crania**) *n* че́реп*.

crank [kræŋk] *n* (*person*) чуда́к*; (*handle*) заводна́я рукоя́тка.

crankshaft ['kræŋkʃɑ:ft] *n* коле́нчатый вал*.

cranky ['kræŋkɪ] *adj* чудакова́тый (чудакова́т).

cranny ['krænɪ] *n see* **nook**.

crap [kræp] (*inf!*) *n* дерьмо́ (*!*) ◆ *vi* срать* (*impf*) (*!*); **to have a ~** поcра́ть* (*perf*) (*!*).

crappy ['kræpɪ] *adj* (*inf!*) дерьмо́вый (*!*).

crash [kræʃ] *n* (*noise*) грохо́т; (*of car*) ава́рия; (*of plane, train*) круше́ние; (*COMM*) крах ◆ *vt* (*car, plane*) разбива́ть (разби́ть* *perf*) ◆ *vi* (*car, plane*) разбива́ться (разби́ться* *perf*); (*two cars*) ста́лкиваться (столкну́ться *perf*); (*COMM*) потерпе́ть* (*perf*) крах; **to ~ into** вреза́ться (вре́заться* *perf*) в +*acc*; **he ~ed the car into a wall** он вре́зался на маши́не в сте́ну.

crash barrier *n* (*BRIT*) предохрани́тельный барье́р (на доро́ге).

crash course *n* нтенси́вный курс.

crash helmet *n* защи́тный шлем.

crash landing *n* вы́нужденная поса́дка*.

crass [kræs] *adj* тупóй (туп).
crate [kreɪt] *n* (*box*) деревя́нный я́щик;
(*for bottles*) упакóвочный я́щик (*для
буты́лок*); (*inf: car*) драндулéт.
crater [ˈkreɪtəʳ] *n* (*of volcano*) крáтер; (*of bomb
blast*) ворóнка*.
cravat [krəˈvæt] *n* шéйный платóк*.
crave [kreɪv] *vti*: **to ~ sth** *or* **for sth** жáждать
(*impf*) чегó-н.
craven [ˈkreɪvən] *adj* трусли́вый (трусли́в).
craving [ˈkreɪvɪŋ] *n*: **~ (for)** жáжда (+*gen*).
crawl [krɔ:l] *vi* пóлзать/ползти́* (*impf*); (*inf:
grovel*) пресмыкáться (*impf*) ◆ *n* (*SWIMMING*)
кроль *f*; **to ~ to sb** (*inf*) пресмыкáться (*impf*)
пéред кем-н; **I was driving along at a ~** моя́
маши́на éле ползлá.
crayfish [ˈkreɪfɪʃ] *n inv* (*freshwater*) речнóй рак;
(*saltwater*) лангýст.
crayon [ˈkreɪən] *n* цветнóй мелóк*.
craze [kreɪz] *n* повáльное увлечéние.
crazed [kreɪzd] *adj*; (*look, person*) безýмный*;
(*pottery etc*) потрéскавшийся.
crazy [ˈkreɪzɪ] *adj* сумасшéдший*; (*inf*): **he's ~
about skiing** (*inf*) он помéшан на лы́жах; **to
go ~** помешáться (*perf*).
crazy paving *n* (*BRIT*) насти́л из кáменных
плит разли́чной фóрмы.
creak [kri:k] *vi* скрипéть* (*impf*).
cream [kri:m] *n* (*of milk*) сли́вки* *pl*; (*made
artificially*) иску́сственные сли́вки*;
(*cosmetic*) крем ◆ *adj* (*colour*) крéмовый;
whipped ~ взби́тые сли́вки*; **soured ~**
сметáна; **the ~ of society** сли́вки* óбщества
▶ **cream off** *vt* (*fig: best talents*) отбирáть
(отобрáть* *perf*); (*part of profits*) снимáть
(*impf*) пéнки.
cream cake *n* пиро́жное *nt adj* с крéмом.
cream cheese *n* сли́вочный сыр*.
creamery [ˈkri:mərɪ] *n* (*shop*) молóчный
магази́н; (*factory*) маслобóйный завóд.
creamy [ˈkri:mɪ] *adj* (*colour*) крéмовый; (*taste*)
сли́вочный.
crease [kri:s] *n* (*fold*) склáдка*; (: *in trousers*)
стрéлка*; (*wrinkle: in dress, on brow*)
морщи́на ◆ *vt* мять* (помя́ть* *perf*) ◆ *vi*
мя́ться* (помя́ться* *perf*).
crease-resistant [ˈkri:srɪzɪstənt] *adj*
немнýщийся*.
create [kri:ˈeɪt] *vt* (*cause to happen, exist*)
твори́ть (сотвори́ть *perf*), порождáть
(породи́ть* *perf*); (*produce: impression*)
создавáть* (создáть* *perf*).
creation [kri:ˈeɪʃən] *n* создáние; (*REL*)
сотворéние.
creative [kri:ˈeɪtɪv] *adj* (*artistic*) твóрческий*;
(*inventive*) изобретáтельный*
(изобретáтелен).
creativity [kri:eɪˈtɪvɪtɪ] *n* твóрчество.

creator [kri:ˈeɪtəʳ] *n* создáтель *m*.
creature [ˈkri:tʃəʳ] *n* (*animal*) существó;
(*person*) создáние.
creature comforts [- ˈkʌmfəts] *npl* удóбства
ntpl.
crèche [krɛʃ] *n* (дéтские) я́сли *pl*.
credence [ˈkri:dns] *n*: **to lend** *or* **give ~ to**
придавáть* (придáть* *perf*) правдо-
подóбность +*dat*.
credentials [krɪˈdɛnʃlz] *npl* (*references*)
квалификáция *fsg*, достижéния *ntpl*; (*identity
papers*) рекомендáция, рекомендáтельное
письмó.
credibility [krɛdɪˈbɪlɪtɪ] *n* (*of fact*)
правдоподóбность *f*; (*of person*) авторитéт.
credible [ˈkrɛdɪbl] *adj* (*thing*) вероя́тный*
(вероя́тен), правдоподóбный*
(правдоподóбен); (*person*) авторитéтный*
(авторитéтен).
credit [ˈkrɛdɪt] *n* (*COMM*) креди́т; (*recognition*)
дóлжное *nt adj*; (*SCOL*) курс, необходи́мый
для получéния дипло́ма ◆ *adj* (*COMM*)
прихóдный ◆ *vt* (*COMM*) кредитовáть (*impf/
perf*); (*believe: also*: **give ~ to**) вéрить
(повéрить *perf*) +*dat*; **~s** *npl* (*CINEMA, TV*)
(вступи́тельные) ти́тры *mpl*; **he is/was in ~**
он платёжеспосóбен/был платёжеспосóбен;
on ~ в креди́т; **to sb's ~** к чьéй-н чéсти; **to
take the ~ for** припи́сывать (приписáть* *perf*)
себé +*acc*; **it does him ~** э́то дéлает ему́
честь; **he's a ~ to his family** он дéлает честь
своéй семьé; **to ~ sb with sth** (*fig*)
припи́сывать (приписáть* *perf*) кому́-н
что-н; **to ~ £5 to sb** вноси́ть* (внести́* *perf*) £5
на чей-н счёт.
creditable [ˈkrɛdɪtəbl] *adj* (*behaviour*)
достóйный; (*mark*) похвáльный* (похвáлен).
credit account *n* креди́тный счёт (*в
отдéльном магази́не*).
credit agency *n* (*BRIT*) креди́тно-
информацио́нное бюрó.
credit balance *n* креди́тный остáток* на
счёте.
credit bureau *n* (*US*) = **credit agency**.
credit card *n* креди́тная кáрточка*.
credit control *n* (*ECON*) креди́тный контрóль
m.
credit facilities *npl* креди́тный лими́т
(*креди́тной кáрточки заёмщика*).
credit limit *n* креди́тный лими́т (*в
применéнию к индивидуáльному заёмщику
и́ли определя́емый креди́тной ли́нией бáнка*).
credit note *n* (*BRIT*) докумéнт, позволя́ющий
купи́ть товáр взамéн неиспрáвного.
creditor [ˈkrɛdɪtəʳ] *n* кредитóр.
credit transfer *n* креди́тный перевóд, жи́ро.
creditworthy [ˈkrɛdɪtˌwə:ðɪ] *adj*
кредитоспосóбный*.

---

* marks translations which have irregular inflections. The Russian-English side of the dictionary gives inflectional information.

credulity [krɪ'dju:lɪtɪ] *n* дове́рчивость *f*.
creed [kri:d] *n* (*REL*) вероуче́ние.
creek [kri:k] *n* у́зкий* зали́в; (*US*)руче́й*; **to be up the ~** (*inf*) вли́пнуть (*perf*) в исто́рию.
creel [kri:l] *n* (*also:* **lobster ~**) *кле́тка для ло́вли лангу́стов*.
creep [kri:p] (*pt, pp* **crept**) *vi* (*person, animal*) кра́сться* (*impf*); (*plant*) ви́ться* (*impf*) ♦ *n* (*inf*) подхали́м(ка); **it gives me the ~s** от э́того у меня́ моро́з по ко́же подира́ет; **to ~ up on sb** подкра́дываться (подкра́сться* *perf*) к кому́-н.
creeper ['kri:pə'] *n* ползу́чее расте́ние.
creepers ['kri:pəz] *npl* (*US*) ползунки́ *pl*.
creepy ['kri:pɪ] *adj* жу́ткий*.
creepy-crawly ['kri:pɪ'krɔ:lɪ] *n* (*inf*) бука́шка*.
cremate [krɪ'meɪt] *vt* крема́ровать (*impf/perf*).
cremation [krɪ'meɪʃən] *n* крема́ция.
crematoria [krɛmə'tɔ:rɪə] *npl of* **crematorium**.
crematorium [krɛmə'tɔ:rɪəm] (*pl* **crematoria**) *n* кремато́рий.
creosote ['krɪəsəut] *n* креозо́т.
crêpe [kreɪp] *n* (*fabric*) креп; (*rubber*) *сорт каучу́ка*.
crêpe bandage *n* (*BRIT*) эласти́чная повя́зка*.
crêpe paper *n* крепи́рованная бума́га.
crêpe sole *n* каучу́ковая подо́шва.
crept [krɛpt] *pt, pp of* **creep**.
crescendo [krɪ'ʃɛndəu] *n* (*MUS*) креще́ндо *nt ind*; **the noise reached a ~** шум нараста́л креще́ндо.
crescent ['krɛsnt] *n* (*shape*) полуме́сяц; (*street*) серпообра́зная у́лица.
cress [krɛs] *n* кресс-сала́т.
crest [krɛst] *n* (*of hill*) гре́бень* *m*; (*of bird*) хохоло́к*, гребешо́к; (*coat of arms*) герб.
crestfallen ['krɛstfɔ:lən] *adj* удручённый* (удручён); **he looked ~** у него́ был удручённый вид.
Crete [kri:t] *n* Крит.
crevasse [krɪ'væs] *n* рассе́лина *or* расще́лина (*в леднике́*).
crevice ['krɛvɪs] *n* щель *f*.
crew [kru:] *n* (*NAUT, AVIAT*) экипа́ж; (*TV, CINEMA*) съёмочная гру́ппа; (*gang*) компа́ния.
crew cut *n* ёжик; **to have a ~~** стри́чься (подстри́чься* *perf*) под ёжик.
crew neck *n* вы́рез под го́рло.
crib [krɪb] *n* (*cot*) де́тская крова́тка*; (*REL*) я́сли *pl* ♦ *vt* (*inf*) сдува́ть (сдуть* *perf*).
cribbage ['krɪbɪdʒ] *n* кри́ббидж.
crick [krɪk] *n* (*in back*) боле́зненный спазм; **~ in the neck** вы́вих шейно́го позвонка́.
cricket ['krɪkɪt] *n* (*game*) кри́кет; (*insect*) сверчо́к*.
cricketer ['krɪkɪtə'] *n* игро́к* в кри́кет.
crime [kraɪm] *n* (*also fig*) преступле́ние; (*illegal activity*) престу́пность *f*; **petty ~** ме́лкое хулига́нство.
Crimea [kraɪ'mɪə] *n*: **the ~** Крым.
crime wave *n* волна́* престу́пности.
criminal ['krɪmɪnl] *n* престу́пник*(-ица) ♦ *adj*

(*illegal*) кримина́льный, уголо́вный; (*morally wrong*) престу́пный*; **~ law** уголо́вное пра́во; **C~ Investigation Department** Уголо́вный ро́зыск.
criminal code *n* уголо́вный ко́декс.
crimp [krɪmp] *vt* (*fabric*) гофри́рова́ть (*impf/ perf*); (*pastry*) защи́пывать (защипну́ть *perf*); (*hair*) завива́ть (зави́ть* *perf*).
crimson ['krɪmzn] *adj* мали́новый, тёмно-кра́сный*.
cringe [krɪndʒ] *vi* съёживаться (съёжиться *perf*).
crinkle ['krɪŋkl] *vt* мять* (измя́ть* *perf*).
cripple ['krɪpl] *n* кале́ка *m/f* ♦ *vt* (*person*) кале́чить (искале́чить *perf*); (*ship, plane*) повреждать* (повреди́ть* *perf*); (*production, exports*) наноси́ть* (нанести́* *perf*) вред +*dat*; **~d with rheumatism** искале́ченный ревмати́змом.
crippling ['krɪplɪŋ] *adj* (*disease*) веду́щий* к инвали́дности; (*taxation, debts*) разори́тельный (разори́телен).
crises ['kraɪsi:z] *npl of* **crisis**.
crisis ['kraɪsɪs] (*pl* **crises**) *n* кри́зис.
crisp [krɪsp] *adj* (*vegetables*) хрустя́щий*; (*weather*) све́жий* (свеж); (*reply*) чёткий* (чёток).
crisps [krɪsps] *npl* (*BRIT*) чи́псы *pl*.
crisscross ['krɪskrɔs] *adj* перекрёстный ♦ *vt* пересека́ть (пересе́чь* *perf*).
criteria [kraɪ'tɪərɪə] *npl of* **criterion**.
criterion [kraɪ'tɪərɪən] (*pl* **criteria**) *n* крите́рий.
critic ['krɪtɪk] *n* кри́тик.
critical ['krɪtɪkl] *adj* (*time, situation, analysis*) крити́ческий*; (*person, opinion*) крити́чный* (крити́чен); **he is ~** (*MED*) он в крити́ческом состоя́нии; **she is ~ of him/the system** она́ крити́чна по отноше́нию к нему́/систе́ме.
critically ['krɪtɪklɪ] *adv* (*speak, look*) крити́чески; (*ill*) опа́сно; (*examine*) крити́чно.
criticism ['krɪtɪsɪzəm] *n* кри́тика; (*of book, play*) крити́ческий* разбо́р.
criticize ['krɪtɪsaɪz] *vt* (*find fault with*) критикова́ть (*impf*).
critique [krɪ'ti:k] *n* крити́ческий* ана́лиз.
croak [krəuk] *vi* (*frog*) ква́кать (*impf*); (*bird*) ка́ркать (*impf*); (*person*) хрипе́ть (*impf*) ♦ *n* (*see vi*) ква́канье; ка́рканье; хрип.
Croatia [krəu'eɪʃə] *n* Хорва́тия.
Croatian [krəu'eɪʃən] *n* (*person*) хорва́т(ка*) ♦ *adj* хорва́тский*.
crochet ['krəuʃeɪ] *n* вяза́ние крючко́м.
crock [krɔk] *n* гли́няный кувши́н; (*inf: also:* **old ~**) разва́лина.
crockery ['krɔkərɪ] *n* гли́няная *or* фая́нсовая посу́да.
crocodile ['krɔkədaɪl] *n* крокоди́л.
crocus ['krəukəs] *n* шафра́н.
croft [krɔft] *n* (*BRIT: small farm*) ху́тор*.
crofter ['krɔftə'] *n* (*BRIT*) хуторя́нин(-нка*).

crone [krəun] *n* карга́.

crony ['krəunɪ] *n* (*inf*) закады́чный друг*.

crook [kruk] *n* (*criminal*) жу́лик; (*of shepherd*) по́сох; **the ~ of the arm** вну́тренний* сгиб ло́ктя.

crooked ['krukɪd] *adj* криво́й* (крив); (*dishonest*) нече́стный*.

crop [krɔp] *n* (*produce grown*) (сельскохозя́йственная) культу́ра; (*amount produced: cereals etc*) урожа́й; (: *honey, herbs*) сбор; (*also:* **riding ~**) плеть *f*; (*of bird*) зоб* ♦ *vt* (*hair*) ко́ротко подстрига́ть (подстри́чь* *perf*); (*subj: animal*) щипа́ть* (*impf*)

▶ **crop up** *vi* неожи́данно возника́ть (возни́кнуть* *perf*).

crop circle *n* таи́нственные круги́ из сло́манных коло́сьев, *появля́ющиеся на засе́янных зерновы́ми поля́х.*

cropper ['krɔpə'] *n* (*inf*): **to come a ~** (*fail*) сади́ться* (сесть *perf*) в лу́жу *or* в кало́шу; (*fall*) шлёпаться (шлёпнуться *perf*).

crop spraying [-'spreɪŋ] *n* опры́скивание посе́вов.

croquet ['krəukeɪ] *n* (*BRIT*) кроке́т.

croquette [krə'kɛt] *n* (*CULIN*) кроке́ты *pl*.

cross [krɔs] *n* (*shape, also REL*) крест; (*mark*) кре́стик; (*BIO*) по́месь *f*; (*BOT*) гибри́д ♦ *vt* (*street, room etc*) пересека́ть (пересе́чь* *perf*), переходи́ть* (перейти́* *perf*); (*cheque*) кросси́ровать (*impf/perf*); (*BIO, BOT, also arms etc*) скре́щивать (скрести́ть* *perf*); (*thwart: person, plan*) препя́тствовать* (*impf*) +*dat* ♦ *adj* серди́тый ♦ *vi*: **the boat ~es from ... to ...** кора́бль плывёт из +*gen*... в +*acc*...; **to ~ o.s.** крести́ться* (перекрести́ться* *perf*); **we have a ~ed line** (*BRIT: TEL*) кто́-то подсоедини́лся к на́шей ли́нии; **they've got their lines or wires ~ed** (*fig*) они́ совсе́м запу́тались; **the thought did not ~ my mind** э́та мысль не приходи́ла мне в го́лову; **to be/get ~ with sb (about sth)** серди́ться (*impf*)/рассерди́ться* *perf* на кого́-н (из-за чего́-н)

▶ **cross out** *vt* вычёркивать (вы́черкнуть *perf*).

crossbar ['krɔsbɑ:'] *n* (*FOOTBALL*) перекла́дина; (*on bicycle*) попере́чная пла́нка.

crossbow ['krɔsbəu] *n* самостре́л, арбале́т.

crossbreed ['krɔsbri:d] *n* по́месь *f*.

cross-Channel ferry ['krɔs'tʃænl-] *n* паро́м, че́рез Ла-Ма́нш.

crosscheck ['krɔstʃɛk] *n* перепрове́рка ♦ *vt* перепроверя́ть (перепрове́рить *perf*).

cross-country (race) ['krɔs'kʌntrɪ-] *n* бег по пересечённой ме́стности.

cross-dressing [krɔs'drɛsɪŋ] *n* переодева́ние в *оде́жду противополо́жного по́ла.*

cross-examination ['krɔsɪgzæmɪ'neɪʃən] *n* перекре́стный допро́с.

cross-examine ['krɔsɪg'zæmɪn] *vt* (*LAW*) подверга́ть (подве́ргнуть* *perf*) перекрёстному допро́су.

cross-eyed ['krɔsaɪd] *adj* косогла́зый.

crossfire ['krɔsfaɪə'] *n* перекрёстный ого́нь* *m*; **to get caught in the ~** (*MIL*) оказа́ться (*perf*) под перекрёстным огнём; (*fig*) оказа́ться (*perf*) ме́жду двух огне́й.

crossing ['krɔsɪŋ] *n* (*sea passage*) перепра́ва; (*also:* **pedestrian ~**) перехо́д.

crossing guard *n* (*US*) *регулиро́вщик и́ли регулиро́вщица движе́ния, кото́рый обеспе́чивает безопа́сный перехо́д у́лицы шко́льниками.*

cross-purposes ['krɔs'pə:pəsɪz] *npl*: **to be at ~ with sb** не находи́ть* (*impf*) о́бщего языка́ с кем-н; **we're (talking) at ~** мы говори́м о ра́зных веща́х.

cross-question ['krɔs'kwɛstʃən] *vt* подверга́ть (подве́ргнуть *perf*) перекрёстному допро́су.

cross-reference ['krɔs'rɛfrəns] *n* перекрёстная ссы́лка*.

crossroads ['krɔsrəudz] *n* перекрёсток*.

cross section *n* (*of population*) про́филь *m*; (*of object*) попере́чное сече́ние; (*BIO*) попере́чный разре́з *or* срез.

crosswalk ['krɔswɔ:k] *n* (*US*) перехо́д.

crosswind ['krɔswɪnd] *n* боково́й ве́тер*.

crosswise ['krɔswaɪz] *adv* крест-на́крест.

crossword ['krɔswə:d] *n* кроссво́рд.

crotch [krɔtʃ] *n* (*ANAT*) проме́жность *f*; **the trousers are tight in the ~** брю́ки жмут в шагу́.

crotchet ['krɔtʃɪt] *n* четвертна́я но́та.

crotchety ['krɔtʃɪtɪ] *adj* раздражи́тельный* (раздражи́телен), брюзгли́вый (брюзгли́в).

crouch [krautʃ] *vi* (*person, animal*) приседа́ть (присе́сть* *perf*).

croup [kru:p] *n* круп.

croupier ['kru:pɪə'] *n* крупье́ *m ind*.

crouton ['kru:tɔn] *n* грено́к*.

crow [krəu] *n* (*bird*) воро́на; (*of cock*) кукаре́канье ♦ *vi* (*cock*) кукаре́кать (*impf*); (*fig: boast*): **to ~ about** хва́статься (*impf*) +*instr*.

crowbar ['krəubɑ:'] *n* лом*.

crowd [kraud] *n* толпа́*; (*clique*) компа́ния ♦ *vt* (*fill*) заполня́ть (запо́лнить *perf*); (*cram*): **to ~ sb/sth into sth** набива́ть (наби́ть* *perf*) что-н кем-н/чем-н ♦ *vi* (*gather*): **to ~ round** толпи́ться (*impf*); (*cram*): **to ~ into sth** набива́ться (наби́ться* *perf*) в что-н; **~s of people** то́лпы люде́й.

crowded ['kraudɪd] *adj* (*overpopulated*) перенаселённый (перенаселён); (*full*): **the room was ~** ко́мната была́ запо́лнена наро́дом; **~ with** по́лный* +*gen*, напо́лненный +*instr*.

---

crowd scene n массо́вка*, ма́ссовая сце́на.

crown [kraun] n (of monarch) коро́на; (of head) маку́шка; (of hill) верши́на; (of tooth) коро́нка*; (of hat) тулья́* ♦ vt (monarch) коронова́ть (impf/perf); (tooth) ста́вить* (поста́вить* perf) коро́нку на +acc; (fig) венча́ть (увенча́ть perf); **the C~** (monarchy) коро́на; **and to ~ it all ...** (fig) и в доверше́ние всего́ ....

crown court n (BRIT) коро́нный суд (в отли́чие от магистрату́р с постоя́нными судья́ми и прися́жными заседа́телями).

crowning ['kraunıŋ] adj блиста́тельный*.

crown jewels npl короле́вские рега́лии fpl.

crown prince n кронпри́нц.

crow's-feet ['krəuzfi:t] npl гуси́ные ла́пки* fpl, морщи́нки fpl (в уголка́х глаз).

crow's-nest ['krəuznɛst] n (NAUT) воро́нье гнездо́.

crucial ['kru:ʃl] adj (event, moment) реша́ющий*; (work) ва́жный* (ва́жен); **~ to** ва́жный (ва́жен) для +gen.

crucifix ['kru:sıfıks] n распя́тие.

crucifixion [kru:sı'fıkʃən] n распя́тие на кресте́.

crucify ['kru:sıfaı] vt (also fig) распина́ть (распя́ть* perf).

crude [kru:d] adj (materials) сыро́й*; (fig: basic) примити́вный* (примити́вен); (: vulgar) гру́бый* (груб).

crude (oil) n сыра́я нефть f.

cruel ['kruəl] adj жесто́кий* (жесто́к).

cruelty ['kruəltı] n жесто́кость f.

cruet ['kru:ıt] n судо́к*.

cruise [kru:z] n (on ship) круи́з ♦ vi (ship, aircraft) крейси́ровать (impf).

cruise missile n управля́емый снаря́д с я́дерной боеголо́вкой.

cruiser ['kru:zəʳ] n (motorboat) ка́тер*; (warship) кре́йсер*.

cruising speed ['kru:zıŋ-] n сре́дняя (экономи́ческая) ско́рость f.

crumb [krʌm] n (of bread, cake) кро́шка*; (fig: of information) обры́вок; (: of sympathy, hope) крупи́ца.

crumble ['krʌmbl] vt (bread, biscuit etc) кроши́ть* (раскроши́ть* perf) ♦ vi осыпа́ться (осыпа́ться* perf); (fig) ру́шиться (impf), ру́хнуть (perf).

crumbly ['krʌmblı] adj рассы́пчатый.

crummy ['krʌmı] adj (inf) задри́панный.

crumpet ['krʌmpıt] n ≈ блин.

crumple ['krʌmpl] vt мять* (измя́ть* perf).

crunch [krʌntʃ] vt (food etc) грызть* (сгрызть* perf); (stones, glass etc) скрипе́ть* (impf), хрусте́ть* (impf) ♦ n (fig): **the ~** крити́ческий* or реша́ющий* моме́нт; **if it comes to the ~** е́сли насту́пит крити́ческий моме́нт; **when the ~ comes** когда́ насту́пит крити́ческий моме́нт.

crunchy ['krʌntʃı] adj хрустя́щий*.

crusade [kru:'seıd] n (campaign) кресто́вый похо́д ♦ vi (fig): **to ~ for/against** боро́ться* (impf) за +acc/про́тив +gen.

crusader [kru:'seıdəʳ] n крестоно́сец*; (fig): **~ (for)** боре́ц* (за +acc).

crush [krʌʃ] vt (squash) выжима́ть (вы́жать* perf); (: grapes) дави́ть* (impf); (crumple) мять* (смять* perf); (grind: garlic, ice) размельча́ть (размельчи́ть* perf); (defeat) сокруша́ть (сокруши́ть perf); (devastate) уничтожа́ть (уничто́жить perf) ♦ n (crowd) да́вка; (infatuation): **to have a ~ on sb** сходи́ть* (сойти́* perf) с ума́ по кому́-н; (drink): **lemon ~** лимо́нный напи́ток*.

crush barrier n (BRIT) огражде́ние (сде́рживающее толпу́).

crushing ['krʌʃıŋ] adj сокруши́тельный*.

crust [krʌst] n ко́рка*; (of earth) кора́.

crustacean [krʌs'teıʃən] n ракообра́зное nt adj (живо́тное).

crusty ['krʌstı] adj хрустя́щий*; (fig) раздражи́тельный* (раздражи́телен); (bread) ко́рочкой; (old gentleman) жёлчный.

crutch [krʌtʃ] n (MED) косты́ль* m; (support, TECH) опо́ра; (ANAT, in garment) see **crotch**.

crux [krʌks] n суть f.

cry [kraı] vi (weep) пла́кать* (impf); (also: **~ out**) крича́ть* (impf) ♦ n крик; **what are you ~ing about?** почему́ Вы пла́чете?; **he began to ~** он заплакал or на́чал пла́кать; **to ~ for help** звать* (позва́ть* perf) на по́мощь; **she cried out suddenly in pain** она́ вскри́кнула от бо́ли; **she had a good ~** она́ вы́плакалась; **it's a far ~ from ...** (fig) э́то си́льно отлича́ется от +gen

▸ **cry off** vi (inf) отка́зываться (отказа́ться* perf).

crying ['kraıŋ] adj (fig: need) о́стрый*; **it's a ~ shame** э́то весьма́ приско́рбно.

crypt [krıpt] n склеп.

cryptic ['krıptık] adj (remark) зага́дочный* (зага́дочен); (clue) зашифро́ванный.

crystal ['krıstl] n го́рный хруста́ль* m; (glass) хруста́ль*; (CHEM) криста́лл.

crystal clear adj (water, air) криста́льно чи́стый*; (sound, idea) соверше́нно я́сный.

crystallize ['krıstəlaız] vt (opinion etc) формирова́ть (сформирова́ть perf) ♦ vi (sugar etc) кристаллизова́ться (impf/perf); **~d fruits** (BRIT) заса́харенные фру́кты.

CSA n abbr = Confederate States of America.

CSC n abbr (= Civil Service Commission) Коми́ссия гражда́нской слу́жбы.

CSE n abbr (BRIT: formerly: = Certificate of Secondary Education) аттеста́т о сре́днем образова́нии.

CS gas n (BRIT) слезоточи́вый газ*.

CST abbr (US) = Central Standard Time.

CT abbr (US: POST) = Connecticut.

ct abbr = carat.

CTC n abbr (BRIT: = city technology college)

тéхникум.

cu. *abbr* (= **cubic**) куб.= *кубический*.

cub [kʌb] *n* детёныш; (*also:* ~ **scout**) член *младшего отряда бойскаутов*.

Cuba [ˈkjuːbə] *n* Кýба.

Cuban [ˈkjuːbən] *adj* кубинский* ♦ *n* кубинец*(-нка*).

cubbyhole [ˈkʌbɪhəul] *n* закутóк*.

cube [kjuːb] *n* (*also MATH*) куб* ♦ *vt* возводить* (возвести* *perf*) в куб; **the ~ of 4 is 64** 4 в кýбе равняется 64.

cube root *n* кубический* кóрень* *m*.

cubic [ˈkjuːbɪk] *adj* кубический*; ~ **metre** *etc* кубический* метр *etc*.

cubic capacity *n* кубический* объём.

cubicle [ˈkjuːbɪkl] *n* (*at pool*) кабинка*; (*in hospital*) бокс.

cuckoo [ˈkuku:] *n* кукýшка*.

cuckoo clock *n* часы *pl* с кукýшкой.

cucumber [ˈkjuːkʌmbəʳ] *n* огурéц*.

cud [kʌd] *n*: **to chew the ~** жевáть* (*impf*) жвáчку.

cuddle [ˈkʌdl] *vt* обнимáть (обнять* *perf*) ♦ *vi* обнимáться (обняться* *perf*) ♦ *n* лáска.

cuddly [ˈkʌdlɪ] *adj* миленький*.

cudgel [ˈkʌdʒl] *n* дубина ♦ *vt*: **to ~ one's brains about sth** ломáть (*impf*) гóлову над чем-н.

cue [kjuː] *n* (*SNOOKER etc*) кий*; (*THEAT etc*) рéплика.

cuff [kʌf] *n* (*of sleeve*) манжéта; (*US: of trousers*) отворóт; (*blow*) шлепóк* ♦ *vt* (*hit*) шлёпать (шлёпнуть *perf*); **off the ~** экспрóмтом.

cuff links *npl* зáпонки* *fpl*.

cu. in. *abbr* (= *cubic inches*) кубические дюймы.

cuisine [kwɪˈziːn] *n* кýхня* (*кýшанья*).

cul-de-sac [ˈkʌldəsæk] *n* (*road*) тупик*.

culinary [ˈkʌlɪnərɪ] *adj* кулинáрный.

cull [kʌl] *vt* (*story, idea*) отбирáть (отобрáть* *perf*); (*animals*) отбракóвывать (отбраковáть *perf*) ♦ *n* отбракóвка*.

culminate [ˈkʌlmɪneɪt] *vi*: **to ~ in** завершáться (завершиться* *perf*) +*instr*.

culmination [kʌlmɪˈneɪʃən] *n* кульминáция.

culottes [kjuːˈlɔts] *npl* юбка-брюки *pl*.

culpable [ˈkʌlpəbl] *adj*: ~ (**of**) винóвный (винóвен +*prp*).

culprit [ˈkʌlprɪt] *n* (*of crime*) винóвник(-ница).

cult [kʌlt] *n* (*also REL*) культ.

cult figure *n* кумир.

cultivate [ˈkʌltɪveɪt] *vt* (*crop, feeling*) культивировать (*impf*); (*land*) возделывать (*impf*); (*person*) обхáживать (*impf*).

cultivation [kʌltɪˈveɪʃən] *n* (*AGR*) культивáция.

cultural [ˈkʌltʃərəl] *adj* культýрный*.

culture [ˈkʌltʃəʳ] *n* (*also BIO*) культýра.

cultured [ˈkʌltʃəd] *adj* (*individual*) культýрный; (*pearl*) культивированный.

cumbersome [ˈkʌmbəsəm] *adj* (*object, process*)

громóздкий* (громóздок).

cumin [ˈkʌmɪn] *n* (*spice*) тмин*.

cumulative [ˈkjuːmjulətɪv] *adj* (*effect, result*) суммáрный; (*process*) нарастáющий.

cunning [ˈkʌnɪŋ] *n* хитрость *f* ♦ *adj* (*crafty*) хитрый* (хитёр).

cunt [kʌnt] *n* (*infl*) пизда́ (*!*)

cup [kʌp] *n* чáшка*; (*as prize*) кýбок*; (*of bra*) чáшечка*; **a ~ of tea** чáшка* чáя.

cupboard [ˈkʌbəd] *n* шкаф*; (*built-in*) стеннóй шкаф*.

cup final *n* (*BRIT: SPORT*) финáл рóзыгрыша кýбка.

cupful [ˈkʌpful] *n* пóлная чáшка*.

cupid [ˈkjuːpɪd] *n* (*figurine*) пýтти *pl ind*; **C~** Купидóн, Амýр.

cupidity [kjuːˈpɪdɪtɪ] *n* áлчность *f*.

cupola [ˈkjuːpələ] *n* кýпол*.

cuppa [ˈkʌpə] (*inf*) *n* чáшка чáя.

cup tie *n* (*BRIT: SPORT*) кýбковый матч.

curable [ˈkjuərəbl] *adj* излечимый (излечим).

curate [ˈkjuərɪt] *n* викáрий.

curator [kjuəˈreɪtə] *n* (*in museum*) хранитель *m*.

curb [kəːb] *vt* (*powers, expenditure*) обуздывать (обуздáть *perf*); (*person*) сдéрживать (сдержáть* *perf*); *n* ограничéние; (*US*) бордюр (*тротуáра*).

curd cheese [kəːd-] *n* творóг*.

curdle [ˈkəːdl] *vi* (*milk*) свёртываться (свернýться *perf*).

curds [kəːdz] *npl* простоквáша *fsg*.

cure [kjuəʳ] *vt* (*illness, patient*) вылéчивать (вылечить *perf*); (*CULIN*) обрабáтывать (обрабóтать *perf*); (*problem*) устранять (устранить *perf*) ♦ *n* (*MED*) лекáрство; (*solution*) срéдство; **to be ~d of sth** вылечиться (*perf*) *or* излечиться* (*perf*) от чегó-н.

cure-all [ˈkjuərɔːl] *n* (*also fig*) панацéя.

curfew [ˈkəːfjuː] *n* комендáнтский* час*.

curio [ˈkjuərɪəu] *n* рéдкая антиквáрная вéщь* *f*.

curiosity [kjuərɪˈɔsɪtɪ] *n* (*see adj*) любознáтельность *f*; любопытство.

curious [ˈkjuərɪəs] *adj* (*interested*) любознáтельный* (любознáтелен); (*nosy, strange*) любопытный* (любопытен); **I'm ~ about him** он меня интересýет.

curiously [ˈkjuərɪəslɪ] *adv* стрáнно; (*inquisitively*) с любопытством; ~ **enough, ...** как ни стрáнно, ...

curl [kəːl] *n* (*of hair*) лóкон, завитóк; (*of smoke etc*) кольцó* ♦ *vt* (*hair: loosely*) завивáть (завить* *perf*); (*: tightly*) закрýчивать (закрутить* *perf*) ♦ *vi* (*hair*) виться* (*impf*); (*smoke*) клубиться (*impf*)

▶ **curl up** *vi* свóрачиваться (свернýться *perf*); **to ~ up into a ball** свóрачиваться (свернýться *perf*) клубкóм.

---

* marks translations which have irregular inflections. The Russian-English side of the dictionary gives inflectional information.

curler ['kə:lə^r] *n* бигуди́ *ntpl ind*; (*SPORT*) игро́к в кэ́рлинг.

curlew ['kə:lu:] *n* большо́й кроншне́п.

curling ['kə:lɪŋ] *n* (*SPORT*) кэ́рлинг (*шотла́ндская игра́ на льду, в кото́рой игро́ки сбива́ют цель при по́мощи специа́льных камне́й*).

curling tongs (*US* **curling irons**) *npl* щипцы́ *pl* для зави́вки.

curly ['kə:lɪ] *adj* вью́щийся; (*tightly curled*) кудря́вый.

currant ['kʌrnt] *n* (*dried grape*) изю́минка; (*bush, fruit*) сморо́динка; ~**s** (*dried grapes*) изю́м *msg*; (*fruit*) сморо́дина *fsg*.

currency ['kʌrnsɪ] *n* (*system*) де́ньги *pl* в обраще́нии; (*money*) валю́та; **to gain** ~ (*fig*) получа́ть (получи́ть *perf*) распростране́ние.

current ['kʌrnt] *n* (*of air, water*) струя́*, пото́к; (*ELEC*) ток*; (*of opinion*) направле́ние ◆ *adj* (*present*) теку́щий*, совреме́нный; (*accepted*) общепри́нятый; **direct/alternating** ~ постоя́нный/переме́нный ток*; **the** ~ **issue of a magazine** теку́щий* но́мер* журна́ла; **this word is in** ~ **use** э́то сло́во явля́ется общепри́нятым.

current account *n* (*BRIT*) теку́щий* счёт*.

current affairs *npl* теку́щие собы́тия *ntpl*.

current assets *npl* теку́щие оборо́тные акти́вы *mpl*.

current liabilities *npl* теку́щие обяза́тельства *ntpl*.

currently ['kʌrntlɪ] *adv* в да́нный *or* настоя́щий моме́нт.

curricula [kə'rɪkjulə] *npl of* **curriculum**.

curriculum [kə'rɪkjuləm] (*pl* ~**s** *or* **curricula**) *n* (*SCOL*) уче́бный план.

curriculum vitae [-'vi:taɪ] *n* автобиогра́фия (*обы́чно пи́шущаяся при поступле́нии на учёбу и́ли рабо́ту* *).

curry ['kʌrɪ] *n* блю́до, с кэ́рри ◆ *vt*: **to** ~ **favour with** заи́скивать (*impf*) пе́ред +*instr*.

curry powder *n* порошо́к* кэ́рри *nt ind*.

curse [kə:s] *vi* (*swear*) руга́ться (*impf*) ◆ *vt* проклина́ть (прокля́сть* *perf*) ◆ *n* (*spell, problem*) прокля́тие; (*swearword*) руга́тельство.

cursor ['kə:sə^r] *n* ку́рсор.

cursory ['kə:sərɪ] *adj* (*glance, examination*) бе́глый.

curt [kə:t] *adj* ре́зкий*.

curtail [kə:'teɪl] *vt* (*freedom, rights*) ограни́чивать (ограни́чить *perf*); (*expenses, visit*) сокраща́ть (сократи́ть* *perf*).

curtain ['kə:tn] *n* (*light*) занаве́ска*; (*heavy, also* THEAT) за́навес*; **to draw the** ~**s** (*together*) задёргивать (задёрнуть *perf*) занаве́ски; (*apart*) отдёргивать (отдёрнуть *perf*) занаве́ски.

curtain call *n* (*THEAT*) покло́ны *mpl*; **they took four** ~~**s** их вызыва́ли четы́ре ра́за.

curts(e)y ['kə:tsɪ] *vi* де́лать (сде́лать *perf*)

реверá́нс, приседа́ть (присе́сть* *perf*) в реверá́нсе ◆ *n* реверá́нс.

curvature ['kə:vətʃə^r] *n* (*of the earth*) кривизна́; (*of spine*) искривле́ние.

curve [kə:v] *n* изги́б ◆ *vi* изгиба́ться (изогну́ться *perf*) ◆ *vt* сгиба́ть (согну́ть *perf*), изгиба́ть (изогну́ть *perf*).

curved [kə:vd] *adj* изо́гнутый, со́гнутый.

cushion ['kuʃən] *n* поду́шка* ◆ *vt* (*collision, effect*) смягча́ть (смягчи́ть *perf*); (*seat*) подкла́дывать (подложи́ть *perf*) поду́шку.

cushy ['kuʃɪ] *adj* (*inf*): **a** ~ **job** тёпленькое месте́чко*; **to have a** ~ **time** бить* (*impf*) баклу́ши.

cussed ['kʌsɪd] *adj* упря́мый (упря́м).

custard ['kʌstəd] *n* заварно́й крем.

custard powder *n* (*BRIT*) заварно́й крем (порошо́к).

custodial [kʌs'təudɪəl] *adj*: ~ **care** опеку́нство; **he was given a** ~ **sentence** он был приговорён к тюре́мному заключе́нию.

custodian [kʌs'təudɪən] *n* попечи́тель *m*.

custody ['kʌstədɪ] *n* (*of child*) опе́ка; (*for offenders*) содержа́ние под стра́жей, заключе́ние; **to take into** ~ (*suspect*) брать* (взять* *perf*) под стра́жу, аресто́вывать (арестова́ть *perf*); **he was remanded in** ~ он был оста́влен под стра́жей; **in the** ~ **of** под опе́кой +*gen*; **the mother has** ~ **of the children** де́ти нахо́дятся под опе́кой ма́тери.

custom ['kʌstəm] *n* (*traditional*) тради́ция; (*convention*) обы́чай; (*habit*) привы́чка*; **we get a lot of** ~ **from the locals** бо́льшая часть на́ших покупа́телей *or* на́шей клиенту́ры – ме́стные жи́тели.

customary ['kʌstəmərɪ] *adj* обы́чный*, традицио́нный; **it is** ~ **to** при́нято +*infin*.

custom-built ['kʌstəm'bɪlt] *adj* изгото́вленный на зака́з.

customer ['kʌstəmə^r] *n* (*of shop*) покупа́тель*(ница) *m(f)*; (*of small business*) клие́нт; (*of large company*) зака́зчик; **he's an awkward** ~ (*inf*) он тру́дный тип.

customer profile *n* про́филь *m* покупа́теля.

customized ['kʌstəmaɪzd] *adj* изгото́вленный на зака́з.

custom-made ['kʌstəm'meɪd] *adj* изгото́вленный на зака́з.

customs ['kʌstəmz] *npl* тамо́жня *fsg*; **to go through (the)** ~ проходи́ть* (пройти́* *perf*) тамо́женный досмо́тр.

Customs and Excise *n* (*BRIT*) тамо́женно-акци́зное управле́ние.

customs officer *n* тамо́женник.

cut [kʌt] (*pt, pp* **cut**) *vt* (*bread, meat*) ре́зать* (разре́зать* *perf*); (*hand, knee*) ре́зать* (поре́зать* *perf*); (*grass, hair*) стричь* (постри́чь* *perf*); (*text, spending, supply*) уреза́ть (уре́зать* *perf*); (*prices*) снижа́ть (сни́зить* *perf*); (*cloth*) крои́ть (раскрои́ть *perf*); (*inf: lecture, appointment*) прогу́ливать

(прогуля́ть *perf*) ♦ *vi* (*knife, scissors*) ре́зать*
(*impf*); (*lines*) пересека́ться (пересе́чься* *perf*)
♦ *n* (*in skin*) поре́з; (*in salary, spending etc*)
сниже́ние; (*of meat*) кусо́к*; (*of garment*)
покро́й; (*of jewel*) отде́лка*; **she is ~ting a
tooth** у неё прореза́ется зуб; **to ~ one's finger**
ре́зать (поре́зать* *perf*) па́лец*; **to get one's
hair ~** стри́чься* (подстри́чься* *perf*); **to ~ sth
short** прерыва́ть (прерва́ть* *perf*) что-н; **to ~
sb short** обрыва́ть (оборва́ть* *perf*) кого́-н; **to
~ sb dead** соверше́нно игнори́ровать (*impf/
perf*) кого́-н; **cold ~s** (*US*) холо́дные мясны́е
заку́ски*; **we had a power ~** у нас
отключи́лось электри́чество

▶ **cut back** *vt* (*plants*) подреза́ть (подре́зать*
perf); (*production, expenditure*) сокраща́ть
(сократи́ть* *perf*)

▶ **cut down** *vt* (*tree*) сруба́ть (сруби́ть* *perf*);
(*consumption*) сокраща́ть (сократи́ть* *perf*);
to ~ sb down to size (*fig*) поста́вить* (*perf*)
кого́-н на ме́сто

▶ **cut down on** *vt fus*: **to ~ down on smoking/
drinking** ме́ньше кури́ть (*impf*)/пить (*impf*)

▶ **cut in** *vi* (*AUT*) пересека́ть (пересе́чь* *perf*)
путь*; (*interrupt*): **to ~ in on** вме́шиваться
(вмеша́ться *perf*) (в +*acc*)

▶ **cut off** *vt* (*also fig*) отреза́ть (отре́зать* *perf*);
(*water, electricity*) отключа́ть (отключи́ть
perf); (*food*) прекраща́ть (прекрати́ть* *perf*)
снабже́ние +*gen*; (*TEL*) разъединя́ть
(разъедини́ть *perf*); **we've been ~ off** (*TEL*) нас
разъедини́ли

▶ **cut out** *vt* (*remove*) выреза́ть (вы́резать*
perf); (*stop*) прекраща́ть (прекрати́ть* *perf*)

▶ **cut up** *vt* разреза́ть (разре́зать* *perf*); **it really
~ me up** (*inf*) э́то о́чень подкоси́ло меня́; **she
still feels ~ up about her sister's death** (*inf*)
она́ всё ещё не опра́вилась по́сле сме́рти
свое́й сестры́.

cut-and-dried [ˈkʌtənˈdraɪd] *adj* (*answer,
solution*) гото́вый.

cut-and-dry [ˈkʌtənˈdraɪ] *adj* = **cut-and-dried**.

cutaway [ˈkʌtəweɪ] *n* (*coat*) визи́тка*; (*of
machine, engine etc*): **a ~ model** моде́ль *f* в
разре́зе; (*CINEMA, TV*) вста́вка*.

cutback [ˈkʌtbæk] *n* сокраще́ние.

cute [kjuːt] *adj* (*sweet*) ми́лый (мил),
преле́стный (преле́стен); (*clever*) у́мный
(умён).

cut glass *n* гранёное стекло́*.

cuticle [ˈkjuːtɪkl] *n* (*of nail*) ко́жица; **~ remover**
*жи́дкость и́ли крем размягча́ющий и
уничтожа́ющий ко́жицу вокру́г ногтево́й
лу́нки.*

cutlery [ˈkʌtləɪ] *n* столо́вый прибо́р.

cutlet [ˈkʌtlɪt] *n* котле́та.

cutoff [ˈkʌtɔf] *n* (*also:* **~ point**) преде́л ♦ *cpd*: **~
date** преде́льный срок.

cutoff switch *n* автомати́ческий*
выключа́тель *m*.

cutout [ˈkʌtaut] *n* (*switch*) автомати́ческий*
выключа́тель *m*; (*shape*) вы́резанная
фигу́ра; (*paper figure*) апплика́ция.

cut-price [ˈkʌtˈpraɪs] (*US* **cut-rate**) *adj* по
сни́женной цене́.

cut-rate [ˈkʌtˈreɪt] *adj* (*US*) = **cut-price**.

cutthroat [ˈkʌtθrəut] *n* головоре́з* ♦ *adj* (*fig*)
беспоща́дный; **~ competition** жёсткая
конкуре́нция.

cutting [ˈkʌtɪŋ] *adj* (*edge*) о́стрый*; (*remark etc*)
язви́тельный*; (*: RAIL*) вы́емка*; (*from plant*) черено́к*.

cutting edge *n* остриё.

cuttlefish [ˈkʌtlfɪʃ] *n* карака́тица.

CV *n abbr* = **curriculum vitae**.

C & W *n abbr* = **country and western (music)**.

c.w.o. *abbr* (*COMM:* = *cash with order*) вы́дача
това́ра по нали́чному расчёту.

cwt. *abbr* = **hundredweight**.

cyanide [ˈsaɪənaɪd] *n* циан, циа́нистый ка́лий.

cybernetics [saɪbəˈnɛtɪks] *n* киберне́тика.

cyclamen [ˈsɪkləmən] *n* (*BOT*) цикламе́н.

cycle [ˈsaɪkl] *n* (*bicycle*) велосипе́д; (*series, also
TECH*) цикл ♦ *vi* е́здить* (*impf*) на велосипе́де.

cycle race *n* велого́нка*.

cycle rack *n* металли́ческая ра́ма для
стоя́нки велосипе́дов.

cycling [ˈsaɪklɪŋ] *n* езда́ на велосипе́де; (*in
competition*) велоспо́рт; **to go on a ~ holiday**
(*BRIT*) е́хать (пое́хать* *perf*) в о́тпуск на
велосипе́де.

cyclist [ˈsaɪklɪst] *n* велосипеди́ст.

cyclone [ˈsaɪkləun] *n* цикло́н.

cygnet [ˈsɪgnɪt] *n* (*ZOOL*) лебедёнок*.

cylinder [ˈsɪlɪndə] *n* (*also TECH*) цили́ндр; (*of
gas*) балло́н; **a five ~ engine**
пятицилиндро́вый дви́гатель *m*.

cylinder head *n* кры́шка* цили́ндра.

cylinder-head gasket [ˈsɪlɪndəhɛd-] *n*
прокла́дка* кры́шки цили́ндра.

cymbals [ˈsɪmblz] *npl* (*MUS*) таре́лки* *fpl*.

cynic [ˈsɪnɪk] *n* ци́ник.

cynical [ˈsɪnɪkl] *adj* цини́чный (цини́чен).

cynicism [ˈsɪnɪsɪzəm] *n* цини́зм.

CYO *n abbr* (*US*) = *Catholic Youth Organization*.

cypress [ˈsaɪprɪs] *n* (*tree*) кипари́с.

Cypriot [ˈsɪprɪət] *adj* ки́прский ♦ *n*
киприо́т(ка*).

Cyprus [ˈsaɪprəs] *n* Кипр.

cyst [sɪst] *n* киста́.

cystitis [sɪsˈtaɪtɪs] *n* цисти́т.

CZ *n abbr* (*US*) = *Canal Zone*.

czar [zɑː] *n* царь *m*.

Czech [tʃɛk] *adj* че́шский ♦ *n* чех (че́шка*);
(*LING*) че́шский* язы́к*.

Czech Republic *n* Че́шская Респу́блика.

---

* marks translations which have irregular inflections. The Russian-English side of the dictionary gives inflectional information.

~ D, d ~

D, d [di:] n (letter) 4-ая буква английского алфавита; (SCOL) ≈ неудовлетворительный.
D [di:] n (MUS) ре.
D abbr (US: POL) = **democrat(ic)**.
d abbr (BRIT: formerly) = **penny**.
d. abbr = **died**.
DA n abbr (US) = **district attorney**.
dab [dæb] vt (eyes, wound) промокнуть* (perf); (paint, cream) наносить* (нанести* perf) ◆ n мазок*; **she's a ~ hand at sth/doing** она дока в чём-н/+infin
▶ **dab at** vt fus промокнуть (perf).
dabble ['dæbl] vi: **to ~ in** (politics, antiques etc) баловаться (impf) +instr.
dachshund ['dækshund] n такса.
dad [dæd] n (inf) папа m, папочка* m.
daddy ['dædɪ] n (inf) = **dad**.
daddy-longlegs [dædɪ'lɒŋlɛgz] n (inf) долгоножка*.
daffodil ['dæfədɪl] n нарцисс.
daft [dɑ:ft] adj (ideas) дурацкий*; (person) чокнутый, ненормальный; **to be ~ about sb/sth** рехнуться (perf) на ком-н/чём-н.
dagger ['dægə*] n кинжал; **to be at ~s drawn with sb** быть* (impf) на ножах с кем-н; **to look ~s at sb** пронзать (пронзить* perf) кого-н злобным взглядом.
dahlia ['deɪljə] n георгин.
daily ['deɪlɪ] adj (dose) суточный; (routine) повседневный; (wages) дневной ◆ n (also: ~ paper) ежедневная газета; (BRIT: also: ~ help) приходящая домработница ◆ adv ежедневно; **twice ~** два раза or дважды в день.
dainty ['deɪntɪ] adj изящный* (изящен).
dairy ['dɛərɪ] n (BRIT: shop) молочный магазин; (company) ≈ молочная фирма; (on farm: for making butter) маслодельня*; (: for making cheese) сыроварня* ◆ cpd молочный.
dairy farm n молочная ферма.
dairy products npl молочные продукты mpl.
dairy store n (US) молочный магазин.
dais ['deɪs] n помост.
daisy ['deɪzɪ] n маргаритка*.
daisywheel ['deɪzɪwi:l] n лепестковый шрифтоноситель m.
daisywheel printer n (COMPUT) лепестковый принтер.
Dakar ['dækə*] n Дакар.

dale [deɪl] n (BRIT) долина.
dally ['dælɪ] vi болтаться (impf) без дела; **to ~ with** (idea, plan) носиться* (impf) с +instr.
dalmatian [dæl'meɪʃən] n далматский дог.
dam [dæm] n (on river) дамба; (reservoir) водохранилище ◆ vt перекрывать (перекрыть* perf) дамбой.
damage ['dæmɪdʒ] n (harm) ущерб; (dents etc) повреждение; (fig) вред* ◆ vt (object) повреждать (повредить perf); (reputation, economy) вредить (повредить perf) +dat; **~s** npl (LAW) компенсация fsg; **~ to property** имущественный ущерб; **to pay £5,000 in ~s** выплачивать (выплатить* perf) компенсацию в размере £5.000.
damaging ['dæmɪdʒɪŋ] adj: **~ (to)** вредный* (для +gen).
Damascus [də'mɑ:skəs] n Дамаск.
dame [deɪm] n (US: inf) баба; (THEAT) комическая старуха; (title): **D~** Леди f ind.
damn [dæm] vt (condemn) осуждать (осудить* perf); (curse at) проклинать (проклясть* perf) ◆ adj (inf: also: ~ed) проклятый ◆ n (inf): **I don't give a ~** мне плевать; **~ (it)!** чёрт возьми or побери!; **~ good** (inf) чертовски хороший.
damnable ['dæmnəbl] adj отвратный* (отвратен).
damnation [dæm'neɪʃən] n, excl (REL: also inf) проклятие.
damning ['dæmɪŋ] adj изобличительный.
damp [dæmp] adj (building, wall) сырой*; (cloth) влажный* ◆ n сырость f ◆ vt (also: ~en: cloth etc) смачивать (смочить* perf); (: enthusiasm etc) охлаждать (охладить* perf).
dampcourse ['dæmpkɔ:s] n гидроизоляция.
damper ['dæmpə*] n (MUS) демпфер; (of fire) заслонка*; **to put a ~ on** (fig: atmosphere) портить* (испортить* perf); (enthusiasm) охлаждать (охладить* perf).
dampness ['dæmpnɪs] n сырость f.
damson ['dæmzən] n (fruit) тернослива.
dance [dɑ:ns] n танец*; (social event) танцы* mpl ◆ vi танцевать (impf); **to ~ about** скакать* (impf).
dance hall n танцевальный зал.
dancer ['dɑ:nsə*] n (for pleasure) танцор(ка*); (professional) танцовщик(-ица).

dancing ['dɑːnsɪŋ] *n* та́нец.
D and C *n abbr* (*MED*: = *dilation and curettage*)
расшире́ние ше́йки ма́тки и
выска́бливание.
dandelion ['dændɪlaɪən] *n* одува́нчик.
dandruff ['dændrəf] *n* пе́рхоть *f*.
dandy ['dændɪ] *n* де́нди *m ind*, щёголь *m* ♦ *adj*
(*US*: *inf*) кла́ссный.
Dane [deɪn] *n* датча́нин*(-а́нка*).
danger ['deɪndʒə'] *n* опа́сность *f*; **there is a** ~
of ... есть *or* существу́ет опа́сность +*gen* ...;
"danger!" "опа́сно!"; **in/out of** ~ в/вне
опа́сности; **he is in** ~ **of losing his job** ему́
рози́т поте́ря рабо́ты.
danger list *n*: **on the** ~~ (*MED*) в спи́ске *or*
числе́ осо́бо тяжёлых больны́х.
dangerous ['deɪndʒrəs] *adj* опа́сный* (опа́сен).
dangerously ['deɪndʒrəslɪ] *adv* с ри́ском; ~
close (to) в опа́сной бли́зости (к +*dat*); **he is** ~
ill он опа́сно бо́лен.
danger zone *n* опа́сная зо́на.
dangle ['dæŋgl] *vt* болта́ть (*impf*) +*instr* ♦ *vi*
болта́ться (*impf*).
Danish ['deɪnɪʃ] *adj* да́тский* ♦ *n* (*LING*)
да́тский* язы́к*; **the** ~ *npl* датча́не.
Danish pastry *n* пиро́жное *nt adj* по-да́тски (*с*
откры́той начи́нкой из фру́ктов и́ли
оре́хов).
dank [dæŋk] *adj* сыро́й*.
Danube ['dænjuːb] *n*: **the** ~ Дуна́й.
dapper ['dæpə'] *adj* щеголева́тый (щеголева́т).
Dardanelles [dɑːdə'nɛlz] *npl*: **the** ~
Дарданéллы *pl*.
dare [dɛə'] *vt*: **to** ~ **sb to do** вызыва́ть
(вы́звать* *perf*) кого́-н +*infin* ♦ *vi*: **to** ~ **(to) do**
сметь (посме́ть *perf*) +*infin*; **I** ~**n't tell him**
(*BRIT*) я не могу́ осме́литься сказа́ть ему́;
how ~ **you say that!** как Вы сме́ете так
говори́ть!; **I** ~ **say** сме́ю заме́тить.
daredevil ['dɛədɛvl] *n* сорвиголова́* *m*/*f*.
Dar es Salaam ['dɑːrɛssə'lɑːm] *n* Да́р-
эс-Сала́м.
daring ['dɛərɪŋ] *adj* (*audacious*) де́рзкий*
(де́рзок); (*bold*) сме́лый* (смел) ♦ *n* де́рзость
f.
dark [dɑːk] *adj* тёмный* (тёмен); (*complexion*)
сму́глый*; (*fig*: *deed*) чёрный ♦ *n*: **in the** ~ в
темноте́; ~ **blue** *etc* тёмно-си́ний* *etc*; **it is**
getting ~ темне́ет; **it is** ~ темно́; ~ **chocolate**
чёрный шокола́д*; **to be in the** ~ **about** (*fig*)
быть* (*impf*) в неве́дении относи́тельно +*gen*;
after ~ по́сле наступле́ния темноты́.
Dark Ages *npl*: **the** ~~ ра́ннее средневеко́вье
ntsg.
darken [dɑːkn] *vt* затемня́ть (затемни́ть *perf*) ♦
vi (*sky, room*) темне́ть (потемне́ть *perf*).
dark glasses *npl* тёмные очки́ *pl*.
dark horse *n* тёмная лоша́дка*.

darkly ['dɑːklɪ] *adv* мра́чно.
darkness ['dɑːknɪs] *n* темнота́.
darkroom ['dɑːkrum] *n* тёмная ко́мната,
прояви́тельная лаборато́рия.
darling ['dɑːlɪŋ] *adj* (*child, spouse*) люби́мый ♦
n дорого́й(-а́я) *m(f) adj*; (*favourite*): **he is the** ~
of он люби́мец +*gen*; **she is a** ~ она́ пре́лесть.
darn [dɑːn] *vt* што́пать (зашто́пать *perf*).
dart [dɑːt] *n* (*in game*) стре́лка* (*для игры́ в*
дартс); (*in sewing*) вы́тачка* ♦ *vi*: **to (make a)**
~ **towards** броса́ться (бро́ситься* *perf*)
навстре́чу +*dat*; **to** ~ **along** промча́ться (*perf*);
to ~ **away** умча́ться (*perf*).
dartboard ['dɑːtbɔːd] *n* мише́нь *f* в да́рте.
darts [dɑːts] *n* дартс.
dash [dæʃ] *n* (*drop*) ка́пелька*; (*pinch*)
щепо́тка*; (*sign*) тире́ *nt ind*; (*rush*) рыво́к* ♦ *vt*
(*throw*) швыря́ть (швырну́ть *perf*); (*shatter*:
hopes) разруша́ть (разру́шить *perf*),
разбива́ть (разби́ть* *perf*) ♦ *vi*: **to** ~ **towards**
рва́ться (*perf*) к +*dat*; **we'll have to make a** ~
for the house мы должны́ бежа́ть к до́му
▶ **dash away** *vi* умча́ться (*perf*)
▶ **dash off** *vi* = **dash away**.
dashboard ['dæʃbɔːd] *n* (*AUT*) прибо́рная
пане́ль *f*.
dashing ['dæʃɪŋ] *adj* шика́рный* (шика́рен).
dastardly ['dæstədlɪ] *adj* по́длый*, ме́рзкий*.
DAT *n abbr* (= *digital audio tape*)
дискретизи́рованная аудиокассе́та.
data ['deɪtə] *npl* да́нные *pl adj*.
database ['deɪtəbeɪs] *n* ба́за да́нных.
data capture *n* сбор да́нных.
data processing *n* обрабо́тка да́нных.
data transmission *n* переда́ча да́нных.
date [deɪt] *n* (*day*) число́*, да́та; (*with friend*)
свида́ние; (*fruit*) фи́ник ♦ *vt* дати́ровать (*impf*
perf); (*person*) встреча́ться (*impf*) с +*instr*;
what's the ~ **today?** како́е сего́дня число́?; ~
of birth да́та рожде́ния; **the closing** ~ **for**
applications is ... срок пода́чи заявле́ний
истека́ет +*gen* ...; **to** ~ на сего́дняшний день;
out of ~ (*old-fashioned*) устаре́лый
(устаре́л); (*expired*) просро́ченный
(просро́чен); **up to** ~ совреме́нный; **to bring**
up to ~ (*method*) обновля́ть (обнови́ть* *perf*);
(*correspondence, information*) пополня́ть
(попо́лнить *perf*); (*person*) вводи́ть* (ввести́*
perf) в курс де́ла; **letter** ~**d 5th July** *or* (*US*) **July**
5th письмо́, дати́рованное 5-ым ию́ля.
dated ['deɪtɪd] *adj* устаре́лый.
dateline ['deɪtlaɪn] *n* указа́ние ме́ста и да́ты
(*опи́сываемого собы́тия*).
date rape *n* изнаси́лование во вре́мя свида́ния.
date stamp *n* календа́рный штёмпель* *m*.
dative ['deɪtɪv] *n* (*also*: ~ **case**) да́тельный
паде́ж*.
daub [dɔːb] *vt* разма́зывать (разма́зать* *perf*);

---

* marks translations which have irregular inflections. The Russian-English side of the dictionary gives inflectional information.

(*wall, face*): **to ~ with** ма́зать* (нама́зать* *perf*) +*instr*.

daughter ['dɔ:tə^r] *n* дочь* *f*.

daughter-in-law ['dɔ:tərɪnlɔ:] *n* неве́стка*, сноха́*.

daunt [dɔ:nt] *vt* страши́ть (*impf*).

daunting ['dɔ:ntɪŋ] *adj* устраша́ющий*.

dauntless ['dɔ:ntlɪs] *adj* бесстра́шный* (бесстра́шен).

dawdle ['dɔ:dl] *vi* копа́ться (*impf*), вози́ться* (*impf*); **to ~ over one's work** вози́ться* (*impf*) с рабо́той.

dawn [dɔ:n] *n* (*of day*) рассве́т; (*of period, situation*) заря́ ♦ *vi* рассвета́ть (рассвести́* *perf*), света́ть (*impf*); (*fig*): **it ~ed on him that …** его́ осени́ло, что …; **from ~ to dusk** с рассве́та до зака́та, от зари́ до зари́.

dawn chorus *n* пе́ние птиц на рассве́те.

day [deɪ] *n* (*period*) су́тки *pl*, день* *m*; (*daylight*) день*; (*working day*) рабо́чий* день*; (*heyday*) вре́мя *nt*; **the ~ before** накану́не; **the ~ after** на сле́дующий* день; **the ~ after tomorrow** послеза́втра; **the ~ before yesterday** позавчера́; **the following ~** на сле́дующий* день; **the ~ that …** в тот день, когда́ …; **~ by ~** ка́ждый день; **~ after ~** изо дня в день; **by ~** днём; **he is paid by the ~** ему́ пла́тят подённо; **I have a ~ off tomorrow** за́втра у меня́ отгу́л; **to work an 8 hour ~** рабо́тать (*impf*) 8 часо́в в день; **these ~s, in the present ~** в на́ши дни, в настоя́щее вре́мя.

daybook ['deɪbuk] *n* (*BRIT: ADMIN*) журна́л.

dayboy ['deɪbɔɪ] *n* приходя́щий учени́к* (*в интерна́те*).

daybreak ['deɪbreɪk] *n* рассве́т.

day-care centre ['deɪkɛə-] *n* (*BRIT*) дневно́й це́нтр по ухо́ду за больны́ми и престаре́лыми.

daydream ['deɪdri:m] *vi* предава́ться (*impf*) мечта́ниям, гре́зить* (*impf*) ♦ *n* мечта́ние, грёза.

daygirl ['deɪɡə:l] *n* приходя́щая учени́ца (*в интерна́те*).

daylight ['deɪlaɪt] *n* дневно́й свет*.

daylight robbery *n* грабёж средь бе́ла дня.

Daylight Saving Time *n* (*US*) ле́тнее вре́мя* *nt*.

day release *n*: **to be on ~ ~** находи́ться на дневны́х ку́рсах по повыше́нию квалифика́ции.

day return *n* (*BRIT*) обра́тный биле́т (*действи́тельный в тече́ние одного́ дня*).

day shift *n* дневна́я сме́на.

daytime ['deɪtaɪm] *n* день* *m*.

day-to-day ['deɪtə'deɪ] *adj* (*life, organization*) повседне́вный*, ежедне́вный; **on a ~ basis** ежедне́вно.

day trip *n* однодне́вная экску́рсия.

day-tripper ['deɪ'trɪpə^r] *n* челове́к на однодне́вной экску́рсии.

daze [deɪz] *vt* (*stun*) ошеломля́ть (ошеломи́ть*

perf); (*subj: drug*) тума́нить (затума́нить *perf*) созна́ние +*gen*; (: *blow*) ошеломля́ть (ошеломи́ть *perf*) ♦ *n*: **in a ~** как в тума́не.

dazed [deɪzd] *adj* ошеломлённый.

dazzle ['dæzl] *vt* (*bewitch*) завора́живать (заворожи́ть *perf*); (*blind*) ослепля́ть (ослепи́ть* *perf*).

dazzling ['dæzlɪŋ] *adj* (*also fig*) ослепи́тельный* (ослепи́телен).

DC *abbr* = **direct current**; (*US: POST*) = **District of Columbia**.

DD *n abbr* (= *Doctor of Divinity*) ≈ до́ктор богосло́вия.

dd. *abbr* (*COMM*) = **delivered**.

D/D *abbr* = **direct debit**.

D-day ['di:deɪ] *n* пе́рвый день генера́льного сраже́ния.

DDS *n abbr* (*US:* = *Doctor of Dental Surgery*) до́ктор стоматоло́гии.

DDT *n abbr* (= *dichlorodiphenyltrichloroethane*) ДДТ= *дихлордифени́л трихлорэта́н*.

DE *abbr* (*US: POST*) = **Delaware**.

DEA *n abbr* (*US:* = *Drug Enforcement Administration*) Управле́ние по соблюде́нию зако́нов о нарко́тиках.

deacon ['di:kən] *n* дья́кон*.

dead [dɛd] *adj* (*person, place, flowers*) мёртвый* (мёртв); (*silence*) мёртвый*; (*arm, leg*) онеме́лый; (*centre*) са́мый ♦ *adv* (*completely*) внеза́пно; (*inf: directly*) пря́мо ♦ *npl*: **the ~** мёртвые *pl adj*; (*in an accident, war*) поги́бшие *pl adj*; **the battery is ~** батаре́йка се́ла; **the telephone is ~** телефо́н отключи́лся; **to shoot sb ~** застрели́ть* (*perf*) кого́-н; **~ on time** то́чно во́-время; **to stop ~** (*person*) остана́вливаться (останови́ться* *perf*) как вко́панный; **~ tired** смерте́льно уста́лый* (уста́л); **the line has gone ~** телефо́н замолча́л.

dead-beat ['dɛdbi:t] *adj* смерте́льно уста́вший, соверше́нно вы́мотанный (вы́мотан).

deaden [dɛdn] *vt* (*pain, sound*) заглуша́ть (заглуши́ть *perf*).

dead end *n* тупи́к*.

dead-end ['dɛdɛnd] *adj*: **a ~ job** бес-перспекти́вная рабо́та.

dead heat *n*: **to finish in a ~ ~** приходи́ть* (прийти́* *perf*) к фи́нишу одновреме́нно.

dead-letter office [dɛd'lɛtə-] *n* отде́л невостре́бованной или недоста́вленной корреспонде́нции.

deadline ['dɛdlaɪn] *n* после́дний* *or* преде́льный срок; **to work to a ~** рабо́тать (*impf*) в ра́мках ограни́ченного сро́ка.

deadlock ['dɛdlɔk] *n* тупи́к; **the meeting ended in ~** собра́ние зашло́ в тупи́к.

dead loss *n* (*inf*): **she is a ~ ~** она́ никчёмна.

deadly ['dɛdlɪ] *adj* (*poison, weapon*) смертоно́сный* (смертоно́сен); (*insult*) смерте́льный* (смерте́лен); (*accuracy*)

ги́бельный ♦ *adv* (*dull*) смерте́льно.
deadpan ['dɛdpæn] *adj* невозмути́мый
(невозмути́м).
Dead Sea *n*: the ~~ Мёртвое мо́ре.
dead season *n* мёртвый сезо́н.
deaf [dɛf] *adj* (*totally*) глухо́й* (глух); (*partially*)
тугоу́хий (тугоу́х); **to turn a ~ ear to sth**
игнори́ровать (*impf*) что-н.
deaf aid *n* (*BRIT*) слухово́й аппара́т.
deaf-and-dumb ['dɛfən'dʌm] *adj* глухонемо́й;
~ **alphabet** алфави́т для глухонемы́х.
deafen [dɛfn] *vt* оглуша́ть (оглуши́ть *perf*).
deafening ['dɛfnɪŋ] *adj* оглуши́тельный*
(оглуши́телен).
deaf-mute ['dɛfmju:t] *n* глухонемо́й(-а́я) *m(f)*
adj.
deafness ['dɛfnɪs] *n* глухота́.
deal [di:l] (*pt, pp* **dealt**) *n* (*agreement*) сде́лка* ♦
vt (*blow*) наноси́ть* (нанести́* *perf*); (*cards*)
сдава́ть* (сдать* *perf*); **to strike a ~ with sb**
заключа́ть (заключи́ть *perf*) сде́лку с кем-н;
it's a ~! (*inf*) по рука́м!; **he got a fair/bad ~**
from them с ним обошли́сь че́стно/
нече́стно; **a good ~ (of)** мно́го (+*gen*); **a great**
~ **(of)** о́чень мно́го (+*gen*)
▶ **deal in** *vt fus* (*COMM*) торгова́ть (*impf*) +*instr*;
(*drugs*) занима́ться (*impf*) прода́жей +*gen*
▶ **deal with** *vt fus* (*person, company*) име́ть
(*impf*) де́ло с +*instr*; (*problem*) реша́ть
(реши́ть *perf*); (*subject*) занима́ться
(заня́ться* *perf*) +*instr*.
dealer ['di:ləʳ] *n* (*COMM*) торго́вец*; (*also*: **art** ~)
ди́лер; (*CARDS*) сдаю́щий(-ая) *m(f) adj* ка́рты,
банкомёт; **drug** ~ торго́вец* нарко́тиками.
dealership ['di:ləʃɪp] *n* (*COMM*) аге́нтство (*по*
прода́же проду́кции определённой фи́рмы).
dealings ['di:lɪŋz] *npl* (*transactions*) опера́ции
fpl; (*in business*) дела́ *ntpl*.
dealt [dɛlt] *pt, pp of* **deal**.
dean [di:n] *n* (*REL*) настоя́тель *m*; (*SCOL*) дека́н.
dear [dɪəʳ] *adj* (*person*) дорого́й*, ми́лый*;
(*expensive*) дорого́й* ♦ *n*: (**my**) ~ (*to man,*
boy) дорого́й (мой); (*to woman, girl*)
дорога́я (моя́) ♦ *excl*: ~ **me!** о, Го́споди!; **D~**
Sir уважа́емый господи́н; **D~ Madam**
уважа́емая госпожа́; **D~ Mr Smith** дорого́й
or уважа́емый ми́стер Смит; **D~ Mrs Smith**
дорога́я *or* уважа́емая ми́ссис Смит.
dearly ['dɪəlɪ] *adv* (*love*) о́чень; (*pay*) до́рого.
dear money *n* (*COMM*) "дороги́е" де́ньги *pl*.
dearth [də:θ] *n*: **a ~ of** нехва́тка +*gen*,
недоста́ток* +*gen*.
death [dɛθ] *n* смерть* *f*.
deathbed ['dɛθbɛd] *n*: **to be on one's ~** быть*
(*impf*) на сме́ртном одре́.
death certificate *n* свиде́тельство о сме́рти.
deathly ['dɛθlɪ] *adj* (*colour*) смерте́льный*;
(*silence*) мёртвый ♦ *adv* смерте́льно.

death penalty *n* сме́ртная казнь *f*.
death rate *n* сме́ртность *f*.
death row [-rəu] *n* часть тюрьмы́, где
располо́жены ка́меры приговорённых к
сме́ртной ка́зни; **prisoners on ~ ~**
заключённые *pl adj*, ожида́ющие сме́ртной
ка́зни.
death sentence *n* сме́ртный пригово́р.
death toll *n* число́* поги́бших.
deathtrap ['dɛθtræp] *n* ги́блое ме́сто*.
deb [dɛb] *n abbr* (*inf*) = **debutante**.
debacle [deɪ'bɑ:kl] *n* (*defeat*) разгро́м; (*failure*)
фиа́ско *nt ind*.
debar [dɪ'bɑ:ʳ] *vt*: **to ~ sb from doing** лиша́ть
(лиши́ть *perf*) кого́-н возмо́жности +*infin*; **to**
~ **sb from a club** изгоня́ть (изгна́ть* *perf*)
кого́-н из клу́ба.
debase [dɪ'beɪs] *vt* (*value, quality*) снижа́ть
(сни́зить* *perf*); (*person*) унижа́ть (уни́зить*
perf); **to ~ o.s.** унижа́ться (уни́зиться* *perf*).
debatable [dɪ'beɪtəbl] *adj* спо́рный*; **it is ~**
whether he can come смо́жет ли он прийти́ –
вопро́с спо́рный.
debate [dɪ'beɪt] *n* деба́ты *pl* ♦ *vt* (*topic*)
обсужда́ть (обсуди́ть* *perf*); (*course of action*)
обду́мывать (обду́мать *perf*); **he ~d whether**
to stay он размышля́л, сле́дует ли оста́ться.
debauchery [dɪ'bɔ:tʃərɪ] *n* (*drunkenness etc*)
распу́щенность *f*.
debenture [dɪ'bɛntʃəʳ] *n* (*bond*) це́нная бума́га*;
~ **capital** ссу́да, обеспе́ченная
фикси́рованными и́ли други́ми акти́вами
компа́нии.
debilitate [dɪ'bɪlɪteɪt] *vt* истоща́ть (истощи́ть*
perf).
debilitating [dɪ'bɪlɪteɪtɪŋ] *adj* изнури́тельный*
(изнури́телен).
debit ['dɛbɪt] *n* де́бет ♦ *vt*: **to ~ a sum to sb** *or* **to**
sb's account дебетова́ть (*impf/perf*) су́мму с
кого́-н *or* с чьего́-н счёта; *see also* **direct debit**.
debit balance *n* дебето́вый оста́ток*.
debit note *n* дебето́вое авви́зо.
debonaire [dɛbə'nɛəʳ] *adj* гала́нтный.
debrief [di:'bri:f] *vt* опра́шивать (опроси́ть*
perf).
debriefing [di:'bri:fɪŋ] *n* расспро́с.
debris ['dɛbri:] *n* (*rubble*) обло́мки *mpl*,
разва́лины *fpl*.
debt [dɛt] *n* (*sum*) долг*; (*state of owing money*)
задо́лженность *f*; **to be in ~** быть* (*impf*) в
долгу́; **bad ~** безнадёжный долг*.
debt collector *n* челове́к, взы́скивающий
долги́.
debtor ['dɛtəʳ] *n* должни́к*.
debug ['di:'bʌg] *vt* отла́живать (отла́дить*
perf).
debunk [di:'bʌŋk] *vt* (*claim*) опроверга́ть
(опрове́ргнуть *perf*); (*person, institution*,

---

myth) разве́нчивать (развенча́ть *perf*).

début [ˈdeɪbjuː] *n* дебю́т.

debutante [ˈdɛbjutænt] *n де́вушка, выходя́щая в (вы́сший) свет.*

Dec. *abbr* = **December**.

decade [ˈdɛkeɪd] *n* десятиле́тие.

decadence [ˈdɛkədəns] *n* упа́док*.

decadent [ˈdɛkədənt] *adj* (*sentiments*) упа́дочнический*; (*class*) упа́дочный.

de-caff [ˈdiːkæf] (*inf*) *adj* без кофеи́на ♦ *n* ко́фе без кофеи́на.

decaffeinated [dɪˈkæfɪneɪtɪd] *adj* без кофеи́на.

decamp [dɪˈkæmp] *vi* (*inf*) удира́ть (удра́ть* *perf*).

decant [dɪˈkænt] *vt* перелива́ть (перели́ть* *perf*).

decanter [dɪˈkæntə'] *n* графи́н.

decarbonize [diːˈkɑːbənaɪz] *vt* очища́ть (очи́стить* *perf*) от нага́ра.

decathlon [dɪˈkæθlɒn] *n* десятибо́рье.

decay [dɪˈkeɪ] *n* разруше́ние; (*of society*) разложе́ние ♦ *vi* (*body, leaves, society etc*) разлага́ться (разложи́ться* *perf*); (*teeth*) разруша́ться (разру́шиться *perf*).

decease [dɪˈsiːs] *n* (*LAW*): **upon your ~** по Ва́шей кончи́не.

deceased [dɪˈsiːst] *n*: **the ~** поко́йный(-ая) *m(f) adj*.

deceit [dɪˈsiːt] *n* обма́н.

deceitful [dɪˈsiːtful] *adj* лжи́вый (лжив).

deceive [dɪˈsiːv] *vt* обма́нывать (обману́ть* *perf*); **to ~ o.s.** обма́нываться (обману́ться* *perf*).

decelerate [diːˈsɛləreɪt] *vi* замедля́ть (заме́длить *perf*) ско́рость.

December [dɪˈsɛmbə'] *n* дека́брь* *m*; *see also* **July**.

decency [ˈdiːsənsɪ] *n* (*propriety*) благопристо́йность *f*; (*kindness*) поря́дочность *f*.

decent [ˈdiːsənt] *adj* (*wages, meal, sleep*) прили́чный* (прили́чен); (*interval, behaviour, person*) поря́дочный* (поря́дочен); **we expect you to do the ~ thing** мы ожида́ем, что Вы посту́пите поря́дочно; **they were very ~ about it** они́ отреаги́ровали на э́то о́чень благоро́дно; **it was very ~ of him** э́то бы́ло о́чень поря́дочно с его́ стороны́; **are you ~?** Вы прили́чно оде́ты?

decently [ˈdiːsəntlɪ] *adv* (*respectably*) прили́чно; (*kindly*) поря́дочно.

decentralization [ˈdiːsɛntrəlaɪˈzeɪʃən] *n* децентрализа́ция.

decentralize [diːˈsɛntrəlaɪz] *vt* децентрализ- ова́ть (*impf/perf*).

deception [dɪˈsɛpʃən] *n* обма́н.

deceptive [dɪˈsɛptɪv] *adj* обма́нчивый* (обма́нчив).

decibel [ˈdɛsɪbɛl] *n* дециба́л.

decide [dɪˈsaɪd] *vt* (*person: persuade*) убежда́ть (убеди́ть *perf*); (*settle*) реша́ть (реши́ть *perf*)

♦ *vi*: **to ~ to do/that** реша́ть (реши́ть *perf*) +*infin*/, что; **to ~ on sth** остана́вливаться (останови́ться* *perf*) на что-н; **to ~ on doing/ against doing** реша́ть (реши́ть *perf*) +*infin*/не +*infin*.

decided [dɪˈsaɪdɪd] *adj* (*character*) реши́тельный* (реши́телен); (*views, opinions*) определённый; (*dangers, improvement*) несомне́нный* (несомне́нен).

decidedly [dɪˈsaɪdɪdlɪ] *adv* (*distinctly*) несомне́нно; (*emphatically*) реши́тельно.

deciding [dɪˈsaɪdɪŋ] *adj* реша́ющий*.

deciduous [dɪˈsɪdjuəs] *adj* листопа́дный.

decimal [ˈdɛsɪməl] *adj* десяти́чный ♦ *n* десяти́чная дробь *f*; **to three ~ places** с то́чностью до тре́тьего зна́ка.

decimalize [ˈdɛsɪməlaɪz] *vt* (*BRIT*) переводи́ть* (перевести́* *perf*) в метри́ческую систе́му мер.

decimal point *n* то́чка* *or* запята́я *f adj* (*отделя́ющая це́лое от дро́би*).

decimate [ˈdɛsɪmeɪt] *vt* истребля́ть (истреби́ть* *perf*).

decipher [dɪˈsaɪfə'] *vt* (*message etc: enigmatic*) расшифро́вывать (расшифрова́ть *perf*); (: *illegible*) разбира́ть (разобра́ть* *perf*).

decision [dɪˈsɪʒən] *n* реше́ние; (*decisiveness*) реши́мость *f*; **to make a ~** принима́ть (приня́ть* *perf*) реше́ние.

decisive [dɪˈsaɪsɪv] *adj* реши́тельный* (реши́телен).

deck [dɛk] *n* (*NAUT*) па́луба; (*of cards*) коло́да; (*also*: **record ~**) прои́грыватель *m*; (*of bus*): **top ~** ве́рхний* эта́ж*; **to go up on ~** поднима́ться (подня́ться* *perf*) на па́лубу; **below ~** под па́лубой; **cassette ~** кассе́тная де́ка.

deck chair *n* шезло́нг.

deck hand *n* матро́с.

declaration [dɛkləˈreɪʃən] *n* (*statement*) деклара́ция; (*public announcement*) заявле́ние.

declare [dɪˈklɛə'] *vt* (*state*) объявля́ть (объяви́ть* *perf*); (*for tax*) деклари́ровать (*impf/perf*).

declassify [diːˈklæsɪfaɪ] *vt* рассекре́чивать (рассекре́тить* *perf*).

decline [dɪˈklaɪn] *n* (*drop*) паде́ние; (*lessening*) уменьше́ние; (*decay*) упа́док* ♦ *vt* (*invitation*) отклоня́ть (отклони́ть* *perf*) ♦ *vi* (*strength*) па́дать (*impf*); (*business*) приходи́ть* (прийти́* *perf*) в упа́док; **~ in living standards** сниже́ние у́ровня жи́зни; **to be in** *or* **on the ~** быть* (*impf*) в упа́дке.

declutch [ˈdiːˈklʌtʃ] *vi* выключа́ть (вы́ключить *perf*) сцепле́ние.

decode [ˈdiːˈkəʊd] *vt* (*message*) декоди́ровать (*impf/perf*), расшифро́вывать (расшифрова́ть *perf*).

decoder [diːˈkəʊdə'] *n* (*person*) челове́к, *обраща́ющийся к словарю́ с це́лью поня́ть* смысл слóва в инострáнном языкé; (*machine*) декóдер.

decompose [di:kəm'pəuz] *vi* разлагáться (разложи́ться* *perf*).

decomposition [di:kɔmpə'zıʃən] *n* разложéние.

decompression [di:kəm'prɛʃən] *n* декомпрéссия.

decompression chamber *n* декомпрессиóнная кáмера.

decongestant [di:kən'dʒɛstənt] *n* сосудосужáющее срéдство.

decontaminate [di:kən'tæmıneıt] *vt* обеззарáживать (обеззарáзить* *perf*).

decontrol [di:kən'trəul] *vt* освобождáть (освободи́ть* *perf*) от (госудáрственного) контрóля.

décor ['deıkɔː'] *n* отдéлка*; (*THEAT*) декорáция.

decorate ['dɛkəreıt] *vt* (*room etc*) отдéлывать (отдéлать *perf*); (*adorn*): **to ~ (with)** украшáть (украсить* *perf*) +*instr*.

decoration [dɛkə'reıʃən] *n* (*on tree, dress etc*) украшéние; (*of room*) отдéлка*; (*medal*) нагрáда.

decorative ['dɛkərətıv] *adj* декорати́вный*.

decorator ['dɛkəreıtə'] *n* обóйщик; **painter and ~** маля́р и обóйщик.

decorum [dı'kɔːrəm] *n* благопристóйность *f*, декóрум.

decoy ['di:kɔı] *n* примáнка*.

decrease ['di:kri:s] *vt* уменьшáть (умéньшить *perf*) ♦ *vi* уменьшáться (умéньшиться *perf*) ♦ *n*: **~ (in)** уменьшéние (+*gen*); **to be on the ~** идти́* (пойти́* *perf*) на у́быль.

decreasing [di:'kri:sıŋ] *adj* уменьшáющийся.

decree [dı'kri:] *n* (*ADMIN, LAW*) постановлéние; (*POL, REL*) укáз ♦ *vt*: **to ~ (that)** (*ADMIN, LAW*) постановля́ть (постанови́ть* *perf*)(, что).

decree absolute *n* окончáтельное решéние о развóде.

decree nisi [-'naısaı] *n* усло́вно-оконча́тельное *реше́ние суда́ о разво́де*.

decrepit [dı'krɛpıt] *adj* дря́хлый* (дряхл).

decry [dı'kraı] *vt* порицáть (*impf*).

dedicate ['dɛdıkeıt] *vt*: **to ~ to** посвящáть (посвяти́ть* *perf*) +*dat*.

dedicated ['dɛdıkeıtıd] *adj* (*person*) прéданный* (прéдан); (*COMPUT*) вы́деленный, назнáченный; **~ word processor** специализи́рованный процéссор для обрабóтки тéкстов.

dedication [dɛdı'keıʃən] *n* (*devotion*) прéданность *f*; (*in book etc*) посвящéние.

deduce [dı'dju:s] *vt*: **to ~ that** заключáть (заключи́ть *perf*), что.

deduct [dı'dʌkt] *vt* вычитáть (вы́честь* *perf*); **to ~ sth (from)** (*from wage etc*) вычитáть (вы́честь* *perf*) что-н (из +*gen*).

deduction [dı'dʌkʃən] *n* (*conclusion*) умозаключéние; (*subtraction*) вычитáние; (*amount*) вы́чет.

deed [di:d] *n* (*feat*) дея́ние, посту́пок*; (*LAW*) акт; **~ of covenant** акт о передáче.

deem [di:m] *vt* (*formal*) полагáть (*impf*); **to ~ it wise to do** полагáть (*impf*) целесообрáзным +*infin*.

deep [di:p] *adj* глубóкий* (глубóк); (*voice*) ни́зкий* (ни́зок) ♦ *adv*: **the spectators stood 20 ~** зри́тели стоя́ли в 20 рядóв; **the lake is 4 metres ~** глубинá óзера – 4 мéтра; **knee-~ in water** по колéно в водé; **he took a ~ breath** он сдéлал глубóкий вздóх; **~ blue** тёмно-си́ний*.

deepen [di:pn] *vt* (*hole etc*) углубля́ть (углуби́ть* *perf*) ♦ *vi* (*crisis, mystery*) углубля́ться (углуби́ться* *perf*).

deepfreeze ['di:p'fri:z] *n* морози́льная кáмера.

deep-fry ['di:p'fraı] *vt* жáрить (зажáрить *perf*) во фритю́ре.

deeply ['di:plı] *adv* глубокó.

deep-rooted ['di:p'ru:tıd] *adj* (*prejudice*) глубокó укорени́вшийся; (*affection*) глубóкий* (глубóк); (*habit*) закоренéлый (закоренéл).

deep-sea ['di:p'si:] *cpd* (*fishing*) глубоковóдный*; **~ diver** водолáз.

deep-seated ['di:p'si:tıd] *adj* укорени́вшийся.

deep-set ['di:psɛt] *adj* глубокó посáженный (посáжен).

deer [dıə'] *n inv* олéнь *m*; (*red*) **~** благорóдный олéнь; (*roe*) **~** косу́ля; (*fallow*) **~** лань *f*.

deerskin ['dıəskın] *n* зáмша.

deerstalker ['dıəstɔːkə'] *n* (*hat*) охóтничья *во́йлочная шля́па*.

deface [dı'feıs] *vt* обезобрáживать (обезобрáзить* *perf*).

defamation [dɛfə'meıʃən] *n* клеветá, диффамáция.

defamatory [dı'fæmətrı] *adj* клеветни́ческий*.

default [dı'fɔːlt] *n* (*COMPUT: also: ~* value) значéние по умолчáнию ♦ *vi*: **to ~ on a debt** не выплáчивать (вы́платить* *perf*) долг; **by ~** (*win*) за нея́вкой проти́вника.

defaulter [dı'fɔːltə'] *n* неплатéльщик.

default option *n* (*COMPUT*) парáметр *or* вариáнт, выбирáемый по умолчáнию.

defeat [dı'fi:t] *n* поражéние ♦ *vt* наноси́ть* (нанести́* *perf*) поражéние +*dat*.

defeatism [dı'fi:tızəm] *n* поражéнчество.

defeatist [dı'fi:tıst] *adj* поражéнческий ♦ *n* поражéнец*.

defecate ['dɛfəkeıt] *vi* испражня́ться (испражни́ться *perf*).

defect ['di:fɛkt] *n* (*of product*) дефéкт; (*of plan, society*) недостáток* ♦ *vi*: **to ~ to the enemy**

перебега́ть (перебежа́ть* *perf*) на сто́рону врага́; **physical/mental** ~ физи́ческий*/ у́мственный недоста́ток*.

defective [dɪ'fɛktɪv] *adj* (*goods*) дефе́ктный (дефе́ктен).

defector [dɪ'fɛktə'] *n* перебе́жчик(-ица).

defence [dɪ'fɛns] (*US* **defense**) *n* (*protection, justification*) защи́та; (*MIL*) оборо́на; **in** ~ **of** в защи́ту +*gen*; **witness for the** ~ свиде́тель *m* защи́ты; **the Ministry of D**~ Министе́рство оборо́ны; **the Department of Defense** (*US*) Департа́мент по оборо́не.

defenceless [dɪ'fɛnslɪs] *adj* беззащи́тный* (беззащи́тен).

defend [dɪ'fɛnd] *vt* (*also SPORT*) защища́ть (защити́ть* *perf*); (*LAW*) защища́ть (*impf*).

defendant [dɪ'fɛndənt] *n* (*in criminal case*) подсуди́мый(-ая) *m(f) adj*, обвиня́емый(-ая) *m(f) adj*; (*in civil case*) отве́тчик(-ица).

defender [dɪ'fɛndə'] *n* (*also fig*) защи́тник(-ица); (*SPORT*) защи́тник.

defending champion [dɪ'fɛndɪŋ-] *n* чемпио́н, защища́ющий своё зва́ние.

defending counsel *n* адвока́т подсуди́мого.

defensive [dɪ'fɛnsɪv] *adj* (*weapons, measures*) оборони́тельный; (*behaviour, manner*) вызыва́ющий* ♦ *n*: **he was on the** ~ он был гото́в к оборо́не.

defer [dɪ'fə:'] *vt* отсро́чивать (отсро́чить *perf*).

deference ['dɛfərəns] *n* почте́ние; **out of** *or* **in** ~ **to** из почте́ния к +*dat*.

deferential [dɛfə'rɛnʃəl] *adj* почти́тельный* (почти́телен).

deferred creditor [dɪ'fə:d-] *n* кредито́р, получи́вший отсро́чку.

defiance [dɪ'faɪəns] *n* вы́зов; **in** ~ **of** вопреки́ +*dat*.

defiant [dɪ'faɪənt] *adj* (*person, reply*) де́рзкий* (де́рзок); (*tone*) вызыва́ющий*.

defiantly [dɪ'faɪəntlɪ] *adv* де́рзко, вызыва́юще.

deficiency [dɪ'fɪʃənsɪ] *n* (*lack*) нехва́тка*; (*inadequacy*) недоста́ток*; (*COMM*) дефици́т.

deficiency disease *n* авитамино́з.

deficient [dɪ'fɪʃənt] *adj* (*inadequate*) несоверше́нный* (несоверше́нен); (*lacking*): **to be** ~ **in** испы́тывать (*impf*) недоста́ток в +*prp*.

deficit ['dɛfɪsɪt] *n* (*COMM*) дефици́т.

defile [dɪ'faɪl] *vt* оскверня́ть (оскверни́ть *perf*) ♦ *n* ущелье*.

define [dɪ'faɪn] *vt* (*limits etc*) определя́ть (определи́ть *perf*); (*word etc*) дава́ть* (дать* *perf*) определе́ние +*dat*.

definite ['dɛfɪnɪt] *adj* определённый* (определён); **he was** ~ **about it** его́ мне́ние на э́тот счёт бы́ло определённым.

definite article *n* определённый арти́кль *m*.

definitely ['dɛfɪnɪtlɪ] *adv* (*positively*) определённо; (*certainly*) несомне́нно.

definition [dɛfɪ'nɪʃən] *n* (*of word*) определе́ние;

(*of photograph etc*) чёткость *f*.

definitive [dɪ'fɪnɪtɪv] *adj* оконча́тельный* (оконча́телен).

deflate [di:'fleɪt] *vt* (*tyre, balloon*) спуска́ть (спусти́ть* *perf*); (*person*) сбива́ть (сбить* *perf*) спесь с +*gen*; (*ECON*): **to** ~ **the money supply** осуществля́ть (осуществи́ть* *perf*) дефля́цию.

deflation [di:'fleɪʃən] *n* (*ECON*) дефля́ция.

deflationary [di:'fleɪʃənrɪ] *adj* дефляцио́нный.

deflect [dɪ'flɛkt] *vt* (*criticism, shot*) отклоня́ть (отклони́ть* *perf*); (*attention*) отвлека́ть (отвле́чь* *perf*).

defog ['di:'fɔg] *vt* (*US*) устраня́ть (устрани́ть *perf*) запотева́ние стекла́.

defogger ['di:'fɔgə'] *n* (*US: AUT*) устро́йство, устраня́ющее запотева́ние стекла́.

deform [dɪ'fɔ:m] *vt* (*damage*) деформи́ровать (*impf/perf*); (*distort*) искажа́ть (искази́ть* *perf*).

deformed [dɪ'fɔ:md] *adj* (*see vt*) деформи́рованный (деформи́рован); искажённый (искажён).

deformity [dɪ'fɔ:mɪtɪ] *n* (*distorted part*) физи́ческий* недоста́ток; (*condition*) деформа́ция.

defraud [dɪ'frɔ:d] *vt*: **to** ~ **sb of sth** обма́ном лиша́ть (лиши́ть *perf*) кого́-н чего́-н.

defray [dɪ'freɪ] *vt*: **to** ~ **sb's expenses** возмеща́ть (возмести́ть* *perf*) чьи-н расхо́ды.

defrost [di:'frɔst] *vt* (*fridge, food*) размора́живать (разморо́зить* *perf*); (*windscreen*) очища́ть (очи́стить* *perf*) ото льда́.

defroster [di:'frɔstə'] *n* (*US: demister*) дефро́стер.

deft [dɛft] *adj* ло́вкий* (ло́вок).

defunct [dɪ'fʌŋkt] *adj* безде́йственный (безде́йствен).

defuse [di:'fju:z] *vt* (*also fig*) разряжа́ть (разряди́ть* *perf*).

defy [dɪ'faɪ] *vt* (*resist*) оспа́ривать (оспо́рить *perf*); (*fig: description, explanation*) не поддава́ться* (*impf*) +*dat*; (*challenge*): **to** ~ **sb to do** призыва́ть (призва́ть* *perf*) кого́-н +*infin*.

degenerate [*vb* dɪ'dʒɛnəreɪt, *adj* dɪ'dʒɛnərɪt] *vi* ухудша́ться (уху́дшиться *perf*) ♦ *adj* растле́нный (растле́н).

degradation [dɛgrə'deɪʃən] *n* деграда́ция.

degrade [dɪ'greɪd] *vt* (*debase: person*) унижа́ть (уни́зить* *perf*); (*worsen*) ухудша́ть (уху́дшить *perf*).

degrading [dɪ'greɪdɪŋ] *adj* унизи́тельный* (унизи́телен).

degree [dɪ'gri:] *n* (*extent*) сте́пень *f*; (*unit of measurement*) гра́дус; (*SCOL*) (учёная) сте́пень*; **10** ~**s below (zero)** 10 гра́дусов ни́же нуля́; **a considerable** ~ **of risk** значи́тельная сте́пень* ри́ска; **by** ~**s** постепе́нно; **to some** ~, **to a certain** ~

до не́которой сте́пени.

dehydrated [di:haɪˈdreɪtɪd] *adj* (*MED*) обезво́женный (обезво́жен); (*milk, eggs*) порошко́вый.

dehydration [di:haɪˈdreɪʃən] *n* обезво́живание, дегидрата́ция.

de-ice [ˈdi:ˈaɪs] *vt* удаля́ть (удали́ть *perf*) лёд.

de-icer [ˈdi:ˈaɪsə] *n* антиобледени́тель *m*.

deign [deɪn] *vi*: **to ~ to do** соизволя́ть (соизво́лить *perf*) +*infin*.

deity [ˈdi:ɪtɪ] *n* божество́*.

déjà vu [deɪʒɑːˈvuː] *n* чу́вство узнава́ния в незнако́мом ме́сте; **I had a sense of ~ ~** у меня́ бы́ло тако́е чу́вство, бу́дто я здесь уже́ был.

dejected [dɪˈdʒɛktɪd] *adj* уны́лый.

dejection [dɪˈdʒɛkʃən] *n* уны́ние.

del. *abbr* = **delete**.

delay [dɪˈleɪ] *vt* (*decision, ceremony etc*) откла́дывать (отложи́ть* *perf*); (*person, plane etc*) заде́рживать (задержа́ть* *perf*) ♦ *vi* ме́длить (*impf*) ♦ *n* заде́ржка; **to be ~ed** заде́рживаться (*impf*); **without ~** без отлага́тельств.

delayed-action [dɪˈleɪdˈækʃən] *adj*: **~ device** приспособле́ние с регули́руемой заде́ржкой де́йствия.

delectable [dɪˈlɛktəbl] *adj* (*person*) притяга́тельный* (притяга́телен); (*food*) ла́комый (ла́ком).

delegate [*n* ˈdɛlɪgɪt, *vt* ˈdɛlɪgeɪt] *n* делега́т ♦ *vt* (*person*) делеги́ровать (*impf/perf*); (*task*) поруча́ть (поручи́ть *perf*); **to ~ sth to sb/sb to do** поруча́ть (поручи́ть *perf*) что-н кому́-н/ кому́-н +*infin*.

delegation [dɛlɪˈgeɪʃən] *n* (*group*) делега́ция; (*by manager, leader*) переда́ча.

delete [dɪˈliːt] *vt* вычёркивать (вы́черкнуть *perf*); (*COMPUT*) удаля́ть (удали́ть *perf*).

Delhi [ˈdɛlɪ] *n* Де́ли *m ind*.

deli [ˈdɛlɪ] (*inf*) *n* магази́н "деликате́сы".

deliberate [*adj* dɪˈlɪbərɪt, *vi* dɪˈlɪbəreɪt] *adj* (*intentional*) наме́ренный* (наме́рен); (*slow*) неторопли́вый (неторопли́в) ♦ *vi* обду́мывать (обду́мать *perf*).

deliberately [dɪˈlɪbərɪtlɪ] *adv* (*see adj*) наме́ренно, наро́чно; неторопли́во.

deliberation [dɪlɪbəˈreɪʃən] *n* (*consideration*) размышле́ние; (*usu pl*: *discussion*) обсужде́ние.

delicacy [ˈdɛlɪkəsɪ] *n* то́нкость *f*; (*food*) деликате́с.

delicate [ˈdɛlɪkɪt] *adj* то́нкий* (то́нок); (*colour*) не́жный (не́жен); (*approach, problem*) делика́тный* (делика́тен); (*health*) хру́пкий* (хру́пок).

delicately [ˈdɛlɪkɪtlɪ] *adv* то́нко.

delicatessen [dɛlɪkəˈtɛsn] *n* магази́н деликате́сов.

delicious [dɪˈlɪʃəs] *adj* (*food*) о́чень вку́сный* (вку́сен); (*smell, feeling, person*) восхити́тельный* (восхити́телен).

delight [dɪˈlaɪt] *n* (*feeling*) восто́рг; (*person, experience etc*) пре́лесть *f* ♦ *vt* ра́довать (пора́довать *perf*); **to take (a) ~ in** находи́ть* (найти́* *perf*) удово́льствие в +*prp*; **her son was her ~** она́ души́ не ча́яла в своём сы́не; **she was a ~ to interview** брать (*impf*) у неё интервью́ было и́стинным удово́льствием; **the ~s of country life** пре́лести дереве́нской жи́зни.

delighted [dɪˈlaɪtɪd] *adj*: **(to be) ~ (at** *or* **with)** (быть (*impf*)) в восто́рге (от +*gen*); **he was ~ to see her** он был рад ви́деть её; **I'd be ~ to help** я с ра́достью помогу́; **I am ~ to meet you** о́чень прия́тно познако́миться.

delightful [dɪˈlaɪtful] *adj* восхити́тельный* (восхити́телен).

delimit [di:ˈlɪmɪt] *vt* определя́ть (определи́ть *perf*) грани́цы +*gen*.

delineate [dɪˈlɪnɪeɪt] *vt* оче́рчивать (очерти́ть* *perf*).

delinquency [dɪˈlɪŋkwənsɪ] *n* правонаруше́ние.

delinquent [dɪˈlɪŋkwənt] *adj* престу́пный ♦ *n* несовершенноле́тний(-яя) правонаруши́тель(ница) *m(f)*.

delirious [dɪˈlɪrɪəs] *adj*: **to be ~** (*with fever*) быть* (*impf*) в бреду́; (*with excitement*) быть* (*impf*) в забытье́.

delirium [dɪˈlɪrɪəm] *n* (*MED*) бред*.

deliver [dɪˈlɪvə] *vt* (*goods*) доставля́ть (доста́вить* *perf*); (*letter*) вруча́ть (вручи́ть *perf*); (*message*) передава́ть* (переда́ть* *perf*); (*speech*) произноси́ть* (произнести́* *perf*); (*blow*) наноси́ть* (нанести́* *perf*); (*baby*) принима́ть (приня́ть* *perf*); (*warning, ultimatum*) предъявля́ть (предъяви́ть* *perf*); (*person*): **to ~ (from)** избавля́ть (изба́вить* *perf*) (от +*gen*); **to ~ the goods** (*fig*) выполня́ть (вы́полнить *perf*) обе́щанное.

deliverance [dɪˈlɪvrəns] *n* избавле́ние.

delivery [dɪˈlɪvrɪ] *n* (*of goods*) доста́вка*; (*of speaker*) стиль *m* изложе́ния; (*MED*) ро́ды *pl*; **to take ~ of** получа́ть (получи́ть* *perf*).

delivery note *n* тра́нспортная накладна́я *f adj*.

delivery van (*US* **delivery truck**) *n* автофурго́н для доста́вки това́ров.

delouse [ˈdiːˈlaus] *vt* избавля́ть (изба́вить* *perf*) от вшей.

delta [ˈdɛltə] *n* (*GEO*) де́льта.

delude [dɪˈluːd] *vt* вводи́ть* (ввести́* *perf*) в заблужде́ние; **to ~ o.s.** заблужда́ться (*impf*).

deluge [ˈdɛljuːdʒ] *n* ли́вень *m*; (*fig*) лави́на.

delusion [dɪˈluːʒən] *n* заблужде́ние; **he has ~s of grandeur** у него́ ма́ния вели́чия.

---

* marks translations which have irregular inflections. The Russian-English side of the dictionary gives inflectional information.

de luxe [də'lʌks] *adj* роско́шный* (роско́шен);
a ~ ~ **car/hotel** маши́на/гости́ница люкс.
delve [dɛlv] *vi*: **to ~ into** (*subject*) углубля́ться
(углуби́ться* *perf*) в +*acc*; (*handbag etc*)
ры́ться* (*impf*) в +*acc*.
Dem. *abbr* (*US*: *POL*) = **democrat(ic)**.
demagogue ['dɛməɡɔɡ] *n* демаго́г.
demand [dɪ'mɑːnd] *vt* тре́бовать
(потре́бовать *perf*) +*gen* ♦ *n* (*request, claim*)
тре́бование; (*ECON*): ~ **(for)** спрос (на +*acc*);
to ~ sth (from *or* **sb)** тре́бовать
(потре́бовать *perf*) чего́-н (от кого́-н); **to be
in ~** (*commodity*) по́льзоваться (*impf*)
спро́сом; **specialists are in great ~** на
специали́стов большо́й спрос; **on ~**
(*available, payable*) по тре́бованию.
demand draft *n* (*COMM*) *ве́сель, опла́чиваемый
при предъявле́нии.*
demanding [dɪ'mɑːndɪŋ] *adj* (*boss, parents*)
тре́бовательный* (тре́бователен); (*child*)
тру́дный; (*work: involving responsibility*)
отве́тственный*; (: *requiring effort*) тяжёлый.
demarcation [diːmɑː'keɪʃən] *n* разграниче́ние.
demarcation dispute *n* (*INDUSTRY*)
разногла́сие по по́воду разделе́ния.
demean [dɪ'miːn] *vt*: **to ~ o.s.** унижа́ться
(уни́зиться *perf*).
demeanour [dɪ'miːnə'] (*US* **demeanor**) *n*
мане́ра поведе́ния.
demented [dɪ'mɛntɪd] *adj* (*person*)
поме́шанный* (поме́шан).
demilitarized zone [diː'mɪlɪtəraɪzd-] *n* (*MIL*)
демилитаризо́ванная зо́на.
demise [dɪ'maɪz] *n* упа́док; (*death*) кончи́на.
demist [diː'mɪst] *vt* (*BRIT*: *AUT*): **to ~ the
windscreen** *суши́ть обогрева́телем
запоте́вшее лобово́е стекло́.*
demister [diː'mɪstə'] *n* (*BRIT*: *AUT*) *обогрева́тель
для су́шки запоте́вших стёкол.*
demiveg ['dɛmɪvɛdʒ] *n* полу-
вегетариа́нец*(-нка*).
demo ['dɛməu] *n abbr* (*inf*) = **demonstration**.
demob [diː'mɔb] *vt* (*MIL*: *inf*) демобилизова́ть
(*impf/perf*).
demobilize [diː'məubɪlaɪz] *vt* (*MIL*)
демобилизова́ть (*impf/perf*).
democracy [dɪ'mɔkrəsɪ] *n* (*system*)
демокра́тия; (*country*) демократи́ческая
страна́*.
democrat ['dɛməkræt] *n* демокра́т; **D~** (*US*)
член па́ртии демокра́тов.
democratic [dɛmə'krætɪk] *adj*
демократи́ческий*; **D~ Party** (*US*) па́ртия
демокра́тов.
demography [dɪ'mɔɡrəfɪ] *n* демогра́фия.
demolish [dɪ'mɔlɪʃ] *vt* (*building*) сноси́ть*
(снести́* *perf*); (*argument*) разгроми́ть* (*perf*).
demolition [dɛmə'lɪʃən] *n* (*of building*) снос; (*of
argument*) разгро́м.
demon ['diːmən] *n* де́мон ♦ *adj* (*skilled*)
гениа́льный* (гениа́лен).

demonstrate ['dɛmənstreɪt] *vt*
демонстри́ровать (продемонстри́ровать
perf) ♦ *vi* (*POL*): **to ~ (for/against)**
демонстри́ровать (*impf*) (за +*acc*/про́тив
+*gen*).
demonstration [dɛmən'streɪʃən] *n*
демонстра́ция; **to hold a ~** (*POL*) проводи́ть*
(провести́* *perf*) демонстра́цию.
demonstrative [dɪ'mɔnstrətɪv] *adj* (*LING*)
указа́тельный; **she's very ~** она́ откры́то
выража́ет свои́ чу́вства.
demonstrator ['dɛmənstreɪtə'] *n* (*POL*)
демонстра́нт; (*sales person*) демонстра́тор.
demoralize [dɪ'mɔrəlaɪz] *vt* деморализова́ть
(*impf/perf*).
demote [dɪ'məut] *vt* понижа́ть (пони́зить* *perf*)
в до́лжности.
demotion [dɪ'məuʃən] *n* пониже́ние в
до́лжности.
demur [dɪ'məːˈ] *vi* (*formal*) возража́ть
(возрази́ть* *perf*) ♦ *n*: **without ~** без
возраже́ний; **they ~red at his suggestion** они́
возрази́ли на его́ предложе́ние.
demure [dɪ'mjuə'] *adj* (*smile, person*) чи́нный;
(*dress*) скро́мный* (скро́мен).
demurrage [dɪ'mʌrɪdʒ] *n* (*COMM*) *пла́та за
просто́й су́дна.*
den [dɛn] *n* (*of animal, person*) ло́гово; (*of
thieves*) прито́н.
denationalization [diː'næʃnəlaɪ'zeɪʃən] *n*
денационализа́ция.
denationalize [diː'næʃnəlaɪz] *vt*
денационализи́ровать (*impf/perf*).
denatured alcohol [diː'neɪtʃəd-] *n* (*US*)
денатура́т.
denial [dɪ'naɪəl] *n* отрица́ние; (*refusal*) отка́з.
denier ['dɛnɪə'] *n* (*of tights, stockings*) денье́ *nt
ind*.
denigrate ['dɛnɪɡreɪt] *vt* принижа́ть
(прини́зить* *perf*).
denim ['dɛnɪm] *n* джинсо́вая ткань *f*; **~s** *npl*
(*jeans*) джи́нсы *pl*.
denim jacket *n* джинсо́вая ку́ртка*.
denizen ['dɛnɪzn] *n* (*inhabitant*)
обита́тель(ница) *m(f)*.
Denmark ['dɛnmɑːk] *n* Да́ния.
denomination [dɪnɔmɪ'neɪʃən] *n* (*of money*)
досто́инство; (*REL*) испове́дание.
denominator [dɪ'nɔmɪneɪtə'] *n* (*MATH*)
знамена́тель *m*.
denote [dɪ'nəut] *vt* (*indicate*) ука́зывать
(указа́ть* *perf*) на +*acc*; (*represent*)
обознача́ть (обозна́чить *perf*).
denounce [dɪ'nauns] *vt* (*condemn*) осужда́ть
(осуди́ть* *perf*); (*give information against*)
доноси́ть* (донести́* *perf*) на +*acc*.
dense [dɛns] *adj* (*crowd*) пло́тный*; (*smoke,
foliage etc*) густо́й* (густ); (*inf*: *person*)
тупо́й* (туп).
densely ['dɛnslɪ] *adv*: **~ populated** гу́сто
населённый; **~ wooded** покры́тый (покры́т)

густы́м ле́сом.

density ['dɛnsɪtɪ] n (of population: also PHYS)
пло́тность f; **single/double-~ disk** (COMPUT)
диск с одина́рной/двойно́й пло́тностью.

dent [dɛnt] n (in metal) вмя́тина ♦ vt (also: **make
a ~ in**: car etc) оставля́ть (оста́вить* perf)
вмя́тину в +acc; (ego) уда́рить (perf) по +dat.

dental ['dɛntl] adj зубно́й.

dental floss [-flɔs] n нить для чи́стки
межзу́бных промежу́тков.

dental surgeon n зубно́й врач*, стомато́лог.

dentifrice ['dɛntɪfrɪs] n (MED: paste) зубна́я
па́ста; (: powder) зубно́й порошо́к*.

dentist ['dɛntɪst] n зубно́й врач*, стомато́лог;
(also: ~'s surgery) зубоврачéбный кабине́т,
стоматологи́ческий* кабине́т.

dentistry ['dɛntɪstrɪ] n стоматоло́гия.

dentures ['dɛntʃəz] npl зубно́й проте́з sg.

denuded [di:'nju:dɪd] adj оголённый* (оголён);
~ **of** (fig) лишённый (лишён) +gen.

denunciation [dɪnʌnsɪ'eɪʃən] n (accusation)
обличе́ние; (condemnation) осужде́ние.

deny [dɪ'naɪ] vt (refute) отрица́ть (impf);
(allegation) отверга́ть (отве́ргнуть perf);
(disown) отрека́ться (отре́чься* perf) от +gen;
(refuse): **to ~ sb sth** отка́зывать (отказа́ть*
perf) кому́-н в чём-н; **he denies having said it**
он отрица́ет, что он э́то сказа́л.

deodorant [di:'əudərənt] n дезодора́нт.

depart [dɪ'pɑːt] vi (person) отбыва́ть (отбы́ть*
perf); (bus, train) отправля́ться
(отпра́виться* perf); (plane) улета́ть
(улете́ть* perf); **to ~ from** (fig) отклоня́ться
(отклони́ться* perf) от +gen.

departed [dɪ'pɑːtɪd] adj поко́йный ♦ n
поко́йный(-ая) m(f) adj, у́мерший*(-ая) m(f)
adj.

department [dɪ'pɑːtmənt] n (in shop) отде́л; (in
university, school) отделе́ние*; (POL)
ве́домство, департа́мент; **D~ of Trade and
Industry** Министе́рство торго́вли и
промы́шленности; **that's not my ~** (fig) я не
специали́ст в э́том де́ле; **D~ of State** (US)
Госуда́рственный департа́мент.

departmental [di:pɑːt'mɛntl] adj (COMM,
ADMIN): ~ **meeting/activities** собра́ние/
де́ятельность f отде́ла; ~ **manager**
заве́дующий*(-ая) m(f) adj отде́лом.

department store n универса́льный магази́н.

departure [dɪ'pɑːtʃəʳ] n (of visitor etc) отъе́зд;
(of employee) ухо́д; (of bus, train)
отправле́ние; (of plane) отлёт; (fig): ~ **from**
отклоне́ние от +gen; **a new ~** но́вое
направле́ние.

departure lounge n (at airport) зал отлёта.

depend [dɪ'pɛnd] vi: **to ~ on** зави́сеть* (impf) от
+gen; (trust) полага́ться (положи́ться* perf)
на +acc; **it ~s** смотря́ по обстоя́тельствам,

как полу́чится; ~**ing on the outcome** ... в
зави́симости от исхо́да ....

dependable [dɪ'pɛndəbl] adj надёжный*
(надёжен).

dependant [dɪ'pɛndənt] n иждиве́нец(-нка).

dependence [dɪ'pɛndəns] n зави́симость f.

dependent [dɪ'pɛndənt] adj: ~ **(on)** зави́симый
(зави́сим) (от +gen) ♦ n = **dependant**.

depict [dɪ'pɪkt] vt изобража́ть (изобрази́ть*
perf).

depilatory [dɪ'pɪlətrɪ] n (also: ~ **cream**) крем
для удале́ния воло́с.

depleted [dɪ'pliːtɪd] adj истощённый*
(истощён).

deplorable [dɪ'plɔːrəbl] adj (conditions)
плаче́вный* (плаче́вен); (behaviour)
возмути́тельный* (возмути́телен).

deplore [dɪ'plɔː] vt (condemn) негодова́ть
(impf) по по́воду +gen.

deploy [dɪ'plɔɪ] vt (troops) дислоци́ровать
(impf/perf).

depopulate [di:'pɔpjuleɪt] vt обезлю́дить (perf).

depopulation ['di:pɔpju'leɪʃən] n
опустоше́ние.

deport [dɪ'pɔːt] vt депорти́ровать (impf/perf),
высыла́ть (вы́слать* perf).

deportation [di:pɔː'teɪʃən] n депорта́ция,
вы́сылка*.

deportation order n (LAW) прика́з о
депорта́ции.

deportee [di:pɔː'tiː] n депорти́рованный(-ая)
m(f) adj.

deportment [dɪ'pɔːtmənt] n оса́нка.

depose [dɪ'pəuz] vt (remove) смеща́ть
(смести́ть* perf); (overthrow) низлага́ть
(низложи́ть perf).

deposit [dɪ'pɔzɪt] n (in account) депози́т,
вклад; (down payment) пе́рвый взнос,
зада́ток*; (: when hiring, renting) зало́г; (on
bottle etc) сто́имость f посу́ды; (CHEM)
оса́док*; (of ore, oil) за́лежь f ♦ vt (money)
помеща́ть (помести́ть* perf); (subj: river:
sand, silt etc) намыва́ть (намы́ть* perf); (case,
bag) сдава́ть* (сдать* perf); **to put down a ~ of
£50** дава́ть* (дать* perf) зада́ток £50.

deposit account n депози́тный счёт*.

depositor [dɪ'pɔzɪtəʳ] n вкла́дчик* m/f.

depository [dɪ'pɔzɪtərɪ] n (person) дове́ренное
лицо́*; (place) храни́лище.

depot ['dɛpəu] n (storehouse) склад; (for buses)
парк; (for trains) депо́ nt ind; (US: station)
ста́нция.

depraved [dɪ'preɪvd] adj развращённый
(развращён).

depravity [dɪ'prævɪtɪ] n развращённость f.

deprecate ['dɛprɪkeɪt] vt порица́ть (impf).

deprecating ['dɛprɪkeɪtɪŋ] adj
неодобри́тельный* (неодобри́телен).

---

* marks translations which have irregular inflections. The Russian-English side of the dictionary gives inflectional information.

depreciate [dɪ'priːʃieɪt] *vi* обесце́ниваться (обесце́ниться *perf*).
depreciation [dɪpriːʃɪ'eɪʃən] *n* обесце́нивание.
depress [dɪ'prɛs] *vt* (*PSYCH*) подавля́ть (*impf*), угнета́ть (*impf*); (*prices, profits*) снижа́ть (сни́зить* *perf*); (*lever, pedal*) нажима́ть (нажа́ть* *perf*) на +*acc*.
depressant [dɪ'prɛsnt] *n* (*MED*) депресса́нт, успокои́тельное сре́дство.
depressed [dɪ'prɛst] *adj* (*person*) пода́вленный* (пода́влен), угнетённый* (угнетён); (*prices*) сни́женный; (*industry*): **to be ~** находи́ться* (*impf*) в состоя́нии спа́да; **to get ~** впада́ть (впасть* *perf*) в депре́ссию; **~ area** райо́н, находя́щийся в состоя́нии экономи́ческого упа́дка.
depressing [dɪ'prɛsɪŋ] *adj* (*time*) тяжёлый; (*news, outlook*) удруча́ющий.
depression [dɪ'prɛʃən] *n* (*PSYCH, ECON*) депре́ссия; (*METEOROLOGY*) о́бласть *f* ни́зкого давле́ния; (*hollow*) углубле́ние; (: *in landscape*) впа́дина.
deprivation [dɛprɪ'veɪʃən] *n* (*poverty*) нужда́; (*depriving*) лише́ние.
deprive [dɪ'praɪv] *vt*: **to ~ sb of** лиша́ть (лиши́ть* *perf*) кого́-н +*gen*.
deprived [dɪ'praɪvd] *adj* (*area, family*) бе́дный* (бе́ден); **~ child** ребёнок из бе́дной семьи́.
dept. *abbr* = **department**.
depth [dɛpθ] *n* глубина́*; **in the ~s of despair/a crisis** в глубо́ком отча́янии/кри́зисе; **the ~s of winter** глубо́кой зимо́й; **at a ~ of three metres** на глубине́ трёх ме́тров; **to be out of one's ~** (*in water*) не достава́ть* (*impf*) до дна; **I'm out of my ~ with this job** мне э́та рабо́та не по плечу́; **to study sth in ~** изуча́ть (изучи́ть* *perf*) что-н углублённо.
depth charge *n* глуби́нная бо́мба.
deputation [dɛpju'teɪʃən] *n* депута́ция.
deputize ['dɛpjutaɪz] *vi*: **to ~ for sb** замеща́ть (*impf*) кого́-н.
deputy ['dɛpjutɪ] *n* замести́тель *m*; (*POL*) депута́т; (*US: also:* **~ sheriff**) исполня́ющий обя́занности шери́фа ♦ *cpd*: **~ leader/ chairman** замести́тель ли́дера/ председа́теля; **~ head** (*BRIT: SCOL*) замести́тель дире́ктора.
derail [dɪ'reɪl] *vt*: **to be ~ed** сходи́ть* (сойти́* *perf*) с ре́льсов.
derailment [dɪ'reɪlmənt] *n*: **the cause of the ~ is unknown** причи́на, по кото́рой по́езд сошёл с ре́льсов неизве́стна.
deranged [dɪ'reɪndʒd] *adj* (*person*) психи́чески больно́й; **he is ~** он психи́чески бо́лен.
derby ['dəːrbɪ] *n* (*US: bowler hat*) котело́к.
Derbys *abbr* (*BRIT: POST*) = **Derbyshire**.
deregulate [dɪ'rɛgjuleɪt] *vt* (*INDUSTRY*) ослабля́ть (осла́бить* *perf*) госуда́рственный контро́ль.
deregulation [dɪ'rɛgju'leɪʃən] *n* ослабле́ние госуда́рственного контро́ля.

derelict ['dɛrɪlɪkt] *adj* забро́шенный* (забро́шен).
deride [dɪ'raɪd] *vt* насмеха́ться (*impf*) над +*instr*.
derision [dɪ'rɪʒən] *n* презре́ние.
derisive [dɪ'raɪsɪv] *adj* презри́тельный* (презри́телен).
derisory [dɪ'raɪsərɪ] *adj* (*ridiculous*) смехотво́рный* (смехотво́рен); (*derisive*) презри́тельный* (презри́телен).
derivation [dɛrɪ'veɪʃən] *n* происхожде́ние.
derivative [dɪ'rɪvətɪv] *n* (*CHEM*) дерива́т; (*LING*) произво́дное сло́во, дерива́т ♦ *adj* (*word, form*) произво́дный; (*not original*) неоригина́льный* (неоригина́лен).
derive [dɪ'raɪv] *vt* (*get*): **to ~ (from)** (*pleasure*) получа́ть (получи́ть* *perf*) (от +*gen*); (*benefit*) извлека́ть (извле́чь* *perf*) (из +*gen*) ♦ *vi* (*originate in*): **to ~ from** происходи́ть* (*impf*) от +*gen*.
derived demand [dɪ'raɪvd-] *n* ко́свенный *or* произво́дственный спрос.
dermatitis [dəːmə'taɪtɪs] *n* дермати́т.
dermatology [dəːmə'tɔlədʒɪ] *n* дерматоло́гия.
derogatory [dɪ'rɔgətərɪ] *adj* пренебрежи́тельный* (пренебрежи́телен).
derrick ['dɛrɪk] *n* (*on ship*) де́ррик; (*on well*) бурова́я вы́шка*.
derv [dəːv] *n* (*BRIT: AUT*) ди́зельное то́пливо.
DES *n abbr* (*BRIT: formerly:* = *Department of Education and Science*) Министе́рство просвеще́ния и нау́ки.
desalination [diːsælɪ'neɪʃən] *n* опресне́ние.
descend [dɪ'sɛnd] *vt* (*stairs*) спуска́ться (спусти́ться* *perf*) по +*dat*; (*hill*) спуска́ться (спусти́ться* *perf*) с +*gen* ♦ *vi* (*go down*) спуска́ться (спусти́ться* *perf*); **to ~ from** (*family, person*) происходи́ть* (*impf*) из +*gen*; **to ~ to** (*lying, begging etc*) опуска́ться (опусти́ться* *perf*) до +*gen*; **in ~ing order of importance** в нисходя́щем поря́дке
▶ **descend on** *vt fus* (*subj: enemy, misfortune*) обру́шиваться (обру́шиться *perf*); (: *gloom, darkness*) опуска́ться (опусти́ться* *perf*); (: *silence*) воцаря́ться (воцари́ться *perf*); **visitors ~ed (up)on us** к нам нагря́нули го́сти.
descendant [dɪ'sɛndənt] *n* пото́мок*.
descent [dɪ'sɛnt] *n* (*stairs*): **to be ~** спуск; (*AVIAT*) сниже́ние; (*origin*) происхожде́ние.
describe [dɪs'kraɪb] *vt* опи́сывать (описа́ть* *perf*).
description [dɪs'krɪpʃən] *n* описа́ние; (*sort*) род*; **of every ~** всевозмо́жного ро́да.
descriptive [dɪs'krɪptɪv] *adj* (*writing, passage*) описа́тельный.
desecrate ['dɛsɪkreɪt] *vt* оскверня́ть (оскверни́ть *perf*).
desegregate [diː'sɛgrɪgeɪt] *vt*: **to ~ a society/ school** ликвиди́ровать (*impf/perf*) сегрега́цию в о́бществе/шко́ле.
desert [*n* 'dɛzət, *vb* dɪ'zəːt] *n* (*also fig*) пусты́ня ♦

vt покида́ть (поки́нуть *perf*) ♦ *vi* (*MIL*) дезерти́ровать (*impf/perf*); *see also* **deserts**.
deserter [dɪ'zɜːtəʳ] *n* (*MIL*) дезерти́р.
desertion [dɪ'zɜːʃən] *n* (*MIL*) дезерти́рство; (*LAW*) оставле́ние.
desert island *n* необита́емый о́стров*.
deserts [dɪ'zɜːts] *npl*: **to get one's just ~** получа́ть (получи́ть* *perf*) по заслу́гам.
deserve [dɪ'zɜːv] *vt* заслу́живать (заслужи́ть* *perf*).
deservedly [dɪ'zɜːvɪdlɪ] *adv* заслу́женно.
deserving [dɪ'zɜːvɪŋ] *adj* досто́йный*.
desiccated ['dɛsɪkeɪtɪd] *adj* (*coconut*) сушёный.
design [dɪ'zaɪn] *n* диза́йн; (*process: of dress*) модели́рование; (*sketch: of building*) прое́кт; (*type: of appliance etc*) моде́ль *f*; (*pattern*) рису́нок*; (*intention*) за́мысел* ♦ *vt* (*house, kitchen*) проекти́ровать (спроекти́ровать *perf*); (*product, test*) разраба́тывать (разрабо́тать *perf*); **to have ~s on** име́ть (*impf*) ви́ды на +*acc*; **by ~** с у́мыслом.
designate [*vt* 'dɛzɪgneɪt, *adj* 'dɛzɪgnɪt] *vt* (*nominate*) назнача́ть (назна́чить *perf*); (*indicate*) обознача́ть (обозна́чить *perf*) ♦ *adj*: **minister ~** назна́ченный мини́стр (*до вступле́ния в до́лжность*).
designation [dɛzɪg'neɪʃən] *n* (*description, name*) обозначе́ние.
designer [dɪ'zaɪnəʳ] *n* (*ART*) диза́йнер; (*of program*) разрабо́тчик; (*of building*) проектиро́вщик; (*of machine*) констру́ктор; (*also: fashion ~*) модельер ♦ *adj* (*clothes*) моде́льный; **~ label** фи́рменный знак (моде́льера).
desirability [dɪzaɪərə'bɪlɪtɪ] *n*: **the ~ of** жела́тельность *f* +*gen*.
desirable [dɪ'zaɪərəbl] *adj* (*proper*) жела́тельный* (жела́телен); (*attractive*) привлека́тельный* (привлека́телен); **it is ~ that** жела́тельно, чтобы.
desire [dɪ'zaɪəʳ] *n* жела́ние ♦ *vt* (*want*) жела́ть (*impf*); **to ~ to do/that** жела́ть (*impf*) +*infin*/, чтобы.
desirous [dɪ'zaɪərəs] *adj*: **to be ~ of doing** жела́ть (*impf*) +*infin*.
desist [dɪ'zɪst] *vi*: **to ~ (from)** возде́рживаться (воздержа́ться *perf*) (от +*gen*).
desk [dɛsk] *n* (*in office, study*) (пи́сьменный) стол*; (*for pupil*) па́рта; (*in hotel, at airport*) сто́йка*; (*BRIT: also: cash-~*) ка́сса.
desk job *n* канцеля́рская рабо́та.
desktop ['dɛsktɔp] *adj* насто́льный.
desktop publishing *n* (*COMPUT*) насто́льное изда́тельство, насто́льная типогра́фия.
desolate ['dɛsəlɪt] *adj* (*place*) забро́шенный*; (*person*) поки́нутый.
desolation [dɛsə'leɪʃən] *n* (*action*) опустоше́ние; (*quality*) опустошённость *f*.

despair [dɪs'pɛəʳ] *n* отча́яние ♦ *vi*: **to ~ of sth/ doing** отча́иваться (отча́яться *perf*) в +*prp*/ +*infin*; **to be in ~** быть* (*impf*) в отча́янии.
despatch [dɪs'pætʃ] *n, vt* = **dispatch**.
desperate ['dɛspərɪt] *adj* (*action, situation*) отча́янный* (отча́ян); (*criminal*) отъя́вленный; (*person*): **he/she is ~** он/она́ в отча́янии; **to be ~ to do** жа́ждать (*impf*) +*infin*; **to be ~ for money** стра́шно нужда́ться (*impf*) в деньга́х.
desperately ['dɛspərɪtlɪ] *adv* отча́янно; (*very*) чрезвыча́йно.
desperation [dɛspə'reɪʃən] *n* отча́яние; **in (sheer) ~** в (по́лном) отча́янии.
despicable [dɪs'pɪkəbl] *adj* презре́нный* (презре́нен).
despise [dɪs'paɪz] *vt* презира́ть (*impf*).
despite [dɪs'paɪt] *prep* несмотря́ на +*acc*.
despondent [dɪs'pɔndənt] *adj* уны́лый (уны́л).
despot ['dɛspɔt] *n* де́спот.
dessert [dɪ'zɜːt] *n* десе́рт.
dessertspoon [dɪ'zɜːtspuːn] *n* десе́ртная ло́жка*.
destabilize [diː'steɪbɪlaɪz] *vt* (*also fig*) дестабилизи́ровать (*impf/perf*).
destination [dɛstɪ'neɪʃən] *n* (*of traveller*) цель *f*; (*of mail*) ме́сто* назначе́ния.
destined ['dɛstɪnd] *adj*: **he/she is ~ to do** ему́/ей суждено́ +*infin*; **to be ~ for** предназнача́ться (*impf*) для +*gen*.
destiny ['dɛstɪnɪ] *n* судьба́*.
destitute ['dɛstɪtjuːt] *adj* (*person*) обездо́ленный (обездо́лен).
destroy [dɪs'trɔɪ] *vt* (*also fig*) уничтожа́ть (уничто́жить *perf*), разруша́ть (разру́шить *perf*); (*kill: pet*) усыпля́ть (усыпи́ть* *perf*); (: *farm animal*) забива́ть (заби́ть* *perf*).
destroyer [dɪs'trɔɪəʳ] *n* (*NAUT*) миноно́сец*.
destruction [dɪs'trʌkʃən] *n* уничтоже́ние, разруше́ние; (*fig: of reputation etc*) ги́бель *f*.
destructive [dɪs'trʌktɪv] *adj* (*capacity, force*) разруши́тельный; (*criticism*) деструкти́вный; (*emotion*) губи́тельный* (губи́телен); (*child*): **he's very ~** он всё лома́ет.
desultory ['dɛsəltərɪ] *adj* (*attempt*) сла́бый (слаб); (*reading, work*) беспоря́дочный (беспоря́дочен).
detach [dɪ'tætʃ] *vt* снима́ть (снять* *perf*); (*unstick*) отделя́ть (отдели́ть *perf*).
detachable [dɪ'tætʃəbl] *adj* съёмный.
detached [dɪ'tætʃt] *adj* (*objective*) беспристра́стный* (беспристра́стен); **~ house** особня́к*.
detachment [dɪ'tætʃmənt] *n* (*aloofness*) отдалённость *f*; (*MIL*) отря́д.
detail ['diːteɪl] *n* дета́ль *f*, подро́бность *f* ♦ *vt* (*list*) перечисля́ть (перечи́слить *perf*); **in ~**

подро́бно, в дета́лях; **to go into ~s**
вдава́ться* *(impf)* в дета́ли *or* подро́бности.
detailed ['di:teɪld] *adj* дета́льный* (дета́лен),
подро́бный* (подро́бен).
detain [dɪ'teɪn] *vt (delay, confine)* заде́рживать
(задержа́ть* *perf)*; **to ~ in hospital** оставля́ть
(оста́вить* *perf)* в больни́це.
detainee [di:teɪ'ni:] *n (POL)* у́зник(-ица).
detect [dɪ'tɛkt] *vt (sense)* чу́вствовать
(почу́вствовать *perf)*; *(discover)*
обнару́живать (обнару́жить *perf)*.
detection [dɪ'tɛkʃən] *n (discovery)*
обнаруже́ние; **crime ~** уголо́вный ро́зыск;
the criminal escaped ~ престу́пник не
обнару́жен; **the mistake escaped ~** оши́бка
оста́лась незаме́ченной.
detective [dɪ'tɛktɪv] *n (POLICE)* сы́щик,
детекти́в.
detective story *n* детекти́в.
detector [dɪ'tɛktə'] *n (TECH)* дете́ктор.
détente [deɪ'tɑ:nt] *n (POL)* разря́дка.
detention [dɪ'tɛnʃən] *n (arrest)* задержа́ние;
(imprisonment) содержа́ние под стра́жей;
(SCOL): **to give sb ~** оставля́ть (оста́вить*
perf) кого́-н по́сле уро́ков.
deter [dɪ'tə:'] *vt* уде́рживать (удержа́ть *perf)*.
detergent [dɪ'tə:dʒənt] *n* мо́ющее сре́дство.
deteriorate [dɪ'tɪərɪəreɪt] *vi* ухудша́ться
(уху́дшиться *perf)*.
deterioration [dɪtɪərɪə'reɪʃən] *n* ухудше́ние.
determination [dɪtə:mɪ'neɪʃən] *n (resolve)*
реши́мость *f, (establishment)* установле́ние.
determine [dɪ'tə:mɪn] *vt (find out)*
устана́вливать (установи́ть* *perf)*; *(establish,
dictate)* определя́ть (определи́ть *perf)*; **to ~
that** *(establish)* устана́вливать (установи́ть*
perf), что; **to ~ to do** *(decide)* реша́ть (реши́ть
perf) +*infin*.
determined [dɪ'tə:mɪnd] *adj (person, effort)*
реши́тельный* (реши́телен); *(quantity)*
определённый*; **~ to do** по́лный (по́лон*)
реши́мости +*infin*.
deterrence [dɪ'tɛrəns] *n* сде́рживание.
deterrent [dɪ'tɛrənt] *n* сре́дство сде́рживания,
сде́рживающее сре́дство; **nuclear ~**
сре́дство я́дерного сде́рживания; **to act as a
~** явля́ться (яви́ться* *perf)* сре́дством
сде́рживания.
detest [dɪ'tɛst] *vt* ненави́деть* *(impf)*.
detestable [dɪ'tɛstəbl] *adj* отврати́тельный*
(отврати́телен).
detonate ['dɛtəneɪt] *vi* взрыва́ться
(взорва́ться* *perf)* ◆ *vt* взрыва́ть (взорва́ть*
perf).
detonator ['dɛtəneɪtə'] *n* детона́тор.
detour ['di:tuə'] *n (in vehicle, also US)* объе́зд;
(on foot) обхо́д; **to make a ~** *(in vehicle)*
пое́хать* *(perf)* в объе́зд; *(on foot)* пойти́*
(perf) в обхо́д.
detract [dɪ'trækt] *vi*: **to ~ from** умаля́ть
(умали́ть *perf)*.

detractor [dɪ'træktə'] *n* недоброжела́тель *m*.
detriment ['dɛtrɪmənt] *n*: **to the ~ of** в уще́рб
+*dat*; **without ~ to** без уще́рба для +*gen*.
detrimental [dɛtrɪ'mɛntl] *adj*: **~ to** вре́дный*
(вре́ден) для +*gen*.
deuce [dju:s] *n (TENNIS)* „ро́вно“.
devaluation [dɪvælju'eɪʃən] *n (ECON)*
девальва́ция.
devalue ['di:'vælju:] *vt (currency)*
обесце́нивать (обесце́нить *perf)*; *(person,
work)* недооце́нивать (недооцени́ть *perf)*.
devastate ['dɛvəsteɪt] *vt* опустоша́ть
(опустоши́ть *perf)*; *(fig)*: **she is ~d by** она́
потрясена́ +*instr*.
devastating ['dɛvəsteɪtɪŋ] *adj (weapon, storm)*
разруши́тельный* (разруши́телен); *(news,
effect)* ошеломля́ющий*.
devastation [dɛvəs'teɪʃən] *n* разруше́ние,
опустоше́ние.
develop [dɪ'vɛləp] *vt (idea, industry)* развива́ть
(разви́ть* *perf)*; *(plan, resource)*
разраба́тывать (разрабо́тать *perf)*; *(land)*
застра́ивать (застро́ить *perf)*; *(PHOT)*
проявля́ть (прояви́ть* *perf)*; *(disease)*
заболева́ть (заболе́ть *perf)* +*instr* ◆ *vi (evolve,
advance)* развива́ться (разви́ться* *perf)*;
(appear) проявля́ться (прояви́ться* *perf)*; **the
machine ~ed a fault** в маши́не возни́кли
непола́дки; **to ~ a taste for sth**
пристрасти́ться* *(perf)* к чему́-н; **to ~ into**
превраща́ться (преврати́ться* *perf)* в +*acc*.
developer [dɪ'vɛləpə'] *n (also: property ~*:
company) строи́тельная фи́рма; (: *person)*
разрабо́тчик.
developing country [dɪ'vɛləpɪŋ-] *n*
развива́ющаяся страна́*.
development [dɪ'vɛləpmənt] *n* разви́тие; *(of
resources)* разрабо́тка; *(of land)* застро́йка;
housing ~ жили́щный ко́мплекс.
development area *n террито́рия, на
разви́тие кото́рой напра́влены
дополни́тельные прави́тельственные
сре́дства.*
deviant ['di:vɪənt] *adj* отклоня́ющийся от
но́рмы.
deviate ['di:vɪeɪt] *vi*: **to ~ (from)** отклоня́ться
(отклони́ться *perf)* (от +*gen*).
deviation [di:vɪ'eɪʃən] *n*: **~ (from)** отклоне́ние
(от +*gen*).
device [dɪ'vaɪs] *n* устро́йство, прибо́р; *(ploy,
stratagem)* сре́дство; **explosive ~** взры́вчатое
устро́йство.
devil ['dɛvl] *n* дья́вол, чёрт*; **go on, be a ~!**
дава́й, позво́ль себе́!; **talk of the ~!** лёгок* на
поми́не!
devilish ['dɛvlɪʃ] *adj* дья́вольский*.
devil's advocate [dɛvlz-] *n* провока́тор.
devious ['di:vɪəs] *adj* лука́вый (лука́в); *(route,
path)* изви́листый (изви́лист).
devise [dɪ'vaɪz] *vt* разраба́тывать
(разрабо́тать *perf)*.

devoid [dɪ'vɔɪd] *adj*: ~ **of** лишённый (лишён) +*gen.*

devolution [di:və'lu:ʃən] *n* (*POL*) переда́ча вла́сти (*ме́стным о́рганам*).

devolve [dɪ'vɔlv] *vt* (*power, duty etc*) передава́ть* (переда́ть* *perf*) ♦ *vi*: **to** ~ **(up)on** переходи́ть* (перейти́* *perf*) к +*dat.*

devote [dɪ'vəut] *vt*: **to** ~ **sth to** посвяща́ть (посвяти́ть* *perf*) что-н +*dat.*

devoted [dɪ'vəutɪd] *adj* (*admirer, partner*) пре́данный* (пре́дан); (*service, friendship*) ве́рный; **he is** ~ **to her** он пре́дан ей; **his book is** ~ **to the history of Scotland** его́ кни́га посвящена́ исто́рии Шотла́ндии.

devotee [dɛvəu'ti:] *n* (*fan*) приве́рженец*; (*REL*) правове́рный(-ая) *m(f) adj.*

devotion [dɪ'vəuʃən] *n* пре́данность *f*; (*REL*) поклоне́ние.

devour [dɪ'vauəʳ] *vt* (*also fig*) пожира́ть (пожра́ть* *perf*).

devout [dɪ'vaut] *adj* (*REL*) благочести́вый (благочести́в).

dew [dju:] *n* роса́*.

dexterity [dɛks'tɛrɪtɪ] *n* (*manual*) ло́вкость *f*; (*mental*) сообрази́тельность *f.*

dext(e)rous ['dɛkstrəs] *adj* (*see n*) ло́вкий* (ло́вок); сообрази́тельный* (сообрози́телен).

dg *abbr* (= *decigram*) децигра́мм.

DH *n abbr* (*BRIT*: = *Department of Health*) Министе́рство здравоохране́ния.

Dhaka ['dækə] *n* Да́ка.

DHSS *n abbr* (*BRIT*: formerly: = *Department of Health and Social Security*) Министе́рство здравоохране́ния и социа́льного обеспе́чения.

diabetes [daɪə'bi:ti:z] *n* диабе́т.

diabetic [daɪə'bɛtɪk] *n* диабе́тик ♦ *adj* диабети́ческий.

diabolical [daɪə'bɔlɪkl] *adj* дья́вольский*; (*inf*: *dreadful*) жу́ткий*.

diaeresis [daɪ'ɛrɪsɪs] *n* диере́за.

diagnose [daɪəg'nəuz] *vt* (*illness*) диагности́ровать (*impf/perf*); (*problem*) определя́ть (определи́ть *perf*).

diagnoses [daɪəg'nəusi:z] *npl of* diagnosis.

diagnosis [daɪəg'nəusɪs] (*pl* diagnoses) *n* диа́гноз.

diagonal [daɪ'ægənl] *adj* диагона́льный ♦ *n* (*MATH*) диагона́ль *f.*

diagram ['daɪəgræm] *n* схе́ма.

dial ['daɪəl] *n* (*of clock*) цифербла́т; (*of indicator*) шкала́; (*of phone*) диск; (*of radio*) регуля́тор настро́йки ♦ *vt* (*number*) набира́ть (набра́ть* *perf*); **to** ~ **a wrong number** не туда́ попада́ть (попа́сть* *perf*); **can I** ~ **London direct?** могу́ я набра́ть в Ло́ндон по автома́ту?

dial. *abbr* = dialect.

dial code *n* (*US*) = dialling code.

dialect ['daɪəlɛkt] *n* диале́кт.

dialling code ['daɪəlɪŋ-] (*US* dial code) *n* код; **the** ~ ~ **for London** код Ло́ндона.

dialling tone (*US* dial tone) *n* непреры́вный гудо́к*.

dialogue ['daɪəlɔg] (*US* dialog) *n* диало́г.

dial tone *n* (*US*) = dialling tone.

dialysis [daɪ'ælɪsɪs] *n* (*MED*) диа́лиз.

diameter [daɪ'æmɪtəʳ] *n* диа́метр.

diametrically [daɪə'mɛtrɪklɪ] *adv*: ~ **opposed (to)** диаметра́льно противополо́жный* (противополо́жен) (+*dat*).

diamond ['daɪəmənd] *n* алма́з; (*cut diamond*) бриллиа́нт; (*shape*) ромб; ~**s** *npl* (*CARDS*) бу́бны* *fpl.*

diamond ring *n* бриллиа́нтовое кольцо́*.

diaper ['daɪəpəʳ] *n* (*US*) подгу́зник.

diaphragm ['daɪəfræm] *n* диафра́гма.

diarrhoea [daɪə'ri:ə] (*US* diarrhea) *n* поно́с.

diary ['daɪərɪ] *n* (*journal*) дневни́к*; (*engagements book*) записна́я кни́жка*; **to keep a** ~ вести́* (*impf*) дневни́к.

diatribe ['daɪətraɪb] *n* ре́зкая кри́тика.

dice [daɪs] *npl of* die; (*in game*) ку́бик; (*game*) ко́сти* *fpl* ♦ *vt* (*CULIN*) ре́зать (наре́зать* *perf*) ку́биками.

dicey ['daɪsɪ] *adj* (*inf*): **it's a bit** ~ э́то немно́го риско́ванно.

dichotomy [daɪ'kɔtəmɪ] *n* дихотоми́я.

dickhead ['dɪkhɛd] *n* (*inf*) пень* *m.*

Dictaphone® ['dɪktəfəun] *n* диктофо́н.

dictate [dɪk'teɪt] *vt* диктова́ть (продиктова́ть *perf*) ♦ *vi*: **to** ~ **to** диктова́ть (продиктова́ть *perf*) +*dat*; **the** ~**s of** веле́ние +*gen*; **I won't be** ~**d to by him** я не позволю́, что́бы он мне диктова́л.

dictation [dɪk'teɪʃən] *n* (*of letter*) дикто́вка*; (*SCOL*) дикта́нт; **at** ~ **speed** со ско́ростью дикто́вки.

dictator [dɪk'teɪtəʳ] *n* дикта́тор.

dictatorship [dɪk'teɪtəʃɪp] *n* диктату́ра.

diction ['dɪkʃən] *n* ди́кция.

dictionary ['dɪkʃənrɪ] *n* слова́рь* *m.*

did [dɪd] *pt of* do.

didactic [daɪ'dæktɪk] *adj* дидакти́ческий*, поучи́тельный* (поучи́телен).

diddle ['dɪdl] *vt* (*inf*) надува́ть (наду́ть* *perf*).

didn't ['dɪdnt] = did not.

die [daɪ] *n* (*pl* dice; *in game*) игра́льная кость* *f*; (*pl* ~**s**; *TECH*) ма́трица, штамп ♦ *vi* (*person, emotion*) умира́ть (умере́ть* *perf*); (*smile, light*) угаса́ть (уга́снуть* *perf*); **to** ~ **of** *or* **from** умира́ть (умере́ть* *perf*) от +*gen*; **to be dying** умира́ть (*impf*); **to be dying for sth/to do** до́ смерти хоте́ть* (*impf*) чего́-н/+*infin*

▶ **die away** *vi* (*sound*) замира́ть (замере́ть*

---

* marks translations which have irregular inflections. The Russian-English side of the dictionary gives inflectional information.

perf); (*light*) угасáть (угáснуть* *perf*)
► **die down** *vi* (*wind, noise*) утихáть
(утихнуть* *perf*); (*fire*) потухáть (потухнуть*
perf); (*excitement*) улéчься* (*perf*)
► **die out** *vi* (*custom*) умирáть (умерéть* *perf*);
(*species*) вымирáть (вымереть* *perf*).
diehard ['daɪhɑ:d] *n* ретрогрáд ♦ *adj*
непреклóнный.
diesel ['di:zl] *n* дизель* *m*; (*also:* ~ **oil**)
дизельное тóпливо.
diesel engine *n* дизельный мотóр.
diet ['daɪət] *n* диéта ♦ *vi* (*also:* **be on a** ~) быть*
(*impf*) на диéте; **to live on a** ~ **of** питáться
(*impf*) одним(-óй) +*instr*.
dietician [daɪə'tɪʃən] *n* диетóлог.
differ ['dɪfə'] *vi*: **to** ~ (**from**) отличáться (*impf*)
(от +*gen*); (*disagree*): **to** ~ **about** расходиться*
(разойтись* *perf*) в вопрóсе +*gen*; **we agreed
to** ~ кáждый из нас остáлся при своём
мнéнии.
difference ['dɪfrəns] *n* (*dissimilarity*) разлúчие;
(: *in size, age*) рáзница; (*disagreement*)
разноглáсие; **it makes no** ~ **to me** мне всё
равнó; **a** ~ **of opinion** расхождéние во
мнéниях; **to settle one's** ~**s** улáживать
(улáдить* *perf*) разноглáсия.
different ['dɪfrənt] *adj* (*other*) другóй, инóй;
(*various*) разлúчный, рáзный; **to be** ~ **from**
отличáться (*impf*) от +*gen*.
differential [dɪfə'rɛnʃəl] *n* (MATH)
дифференциáл; (BRIT: *in wages*) рáзница в
тарúфах.
differentiate [dɪfə'rɛnʃɪeɪt] *vi*: **to** ~ (**between**)
проводить* (провести* *perf*) разлúчие
(мéжду +*instr*) ♦ *vt*: **to** ~ **from** отличáть
(отличúть* *perf*) от +*gen*.
differently ['dɪfrəntlɪ] *adv* (*otherwise*) инáче,
по-другóму; (*in different ways*) по-рáзному.
difficult ['dɪfɪkəlt] *adj* трýдный* (трýден);
(*person*) тяжёлый; ~ **to understand/see**
трýдно понять/видеть.
difficulty ['dɪfɪkəltɪ] *n* трýдность *f*,
затруднéние; **to have difficulties** испытывать
(испытáть* *perf*) трýдности; **to be in
difficulties** находиться* (*impf*) в трýдном
положéнии.
diffidence ['dɪfɪdəns] *n* застéнчивость *f*.
diffident ['dɪfɪdənt] *adj* застéнчивый
(застéнчив).
diffuse [*vt* dɪ'fju:z, *adj* dɪ'fju:s] *vt* (*information*)
распространять (распространить* *perf*) ♦ *adj*
(*idea, sense*) расплывчатый (расплывчат);
(*light*) рассéянный*.
dig [dɪg] (*pt, pp* **dug**) *vt* (*hole*) копáть (выкопать
perf), рыть* (вырыть* *perf*); (*garden*)
вскáпывать (вскопáть* *perf*) ♦ *n* (*prod*)
толчóк*; (*archaeological excavation*)
раскóпки* *fpl*; (*remark*): **to have a** ~ **at sb**
подкáлывать (подколóть *perf*) кого-н; **to** ~
one's nails/claws into sth впивáться
(впиться* *perf*) ногтями/когтями во что-н

► **dig in** *vi* (*inf*: *eat*): **to** ~ **in** (**to**) налегáть
(налéчь* *perf*) (на +*acc*) ♦ *vt*: **to** ~ **in** (**to**)
(*compost*) вкáпывать (вкопáть* *perf*) (в +*acc*);
(*knife*) вонзáть (вонзить* *perf*) (в +*acc*); **to** ~ **in
one's heels** (*fig*) упирáться (уперéться* *perf*)
► **dig into** *vt fus* (*snow, soil*) зарывáть (зарыть*
perf), закáпывать (закопáть* *perf*); **to** ~ **into
one's savings** начáть (*perf*) трáтить
сбережéния; **to** ~ **into one's pockets** (**for sth**)
запускáть (запустить* *perf*) рукý в кармáн
(за чем-н)
► **dig out** *vt* (*from snow, earth*) откáпывать
(откопáть *perf*)
► **dig up** *vt* (*plant*) выкáпывать (выкопать
perf); (*information*) раскáпывать (раскопáть
perf).
digest [*vt* daɪ'dʒɛst, *n* 'daɪdʒɛst] *vt* (*food*)
перевáривать (переварить* *perf*); (*facts*)
усвáивать (усвóить *perf*) ♦ *n* (*book*) сбóрник
(*адаптированных произведéний*).
digestible [dɪ'dʒɛstəbl] *adj* удобоваримый
(удобоварим).
digestion [dɪ'dʒɛstʃən] *n* пищеварéние.
digestive [dɪ'dʒɛstɪv] *adj* пищеварительный ♦
n (*also:* ~ **biscuit**) *печéнье из муки грýбого
помóла*.
digit ['dɪdʒɪt] *n* (*number*) цифра; (*finger*)
пáлец*.
digital ['dɪdʒɪtl] *adj*: ~ **watch** электрóнные
часы *mpl*; ~ **recording** электрóнная зáпись.
digital compact cassette *n*
дисскретизированная компáктная кассéта.
digital computer *n* электрóнно-
вычислительная машина.
dignified ['dɪgnɪfaɪd] *adj* пóлный* (пóлон)
достóинства.
dignitary ['dɪgnɪtərɪ] *n* высокопостáвленное
лицó*.
dignity ['dɪgnɪtɪ] *n* достóинство.
digress [daɪ'grɛs] *vi*: **to** ~ (**from**) отступáть
(отступить* *perf*) (от +*gen*).
digression [daɪ'grɛʃən] *n* отступлéние.
digs [dɪgz] *npl* (BRIT: *inf*) жилище.
dike [daɪk] *n* = **dyke**.
dilapidated [dɪ'læpɪdeɪtɪd] *adj* вéтхий*.
dilate [daɪ'leɪt] *vi* расширяться (расшириться
perf) ♦ *vt* расширять (расширить *perf*).
dilatory ['dɪlətərɪ] *adj* (*influence*)
замедляющий; (*person*) медлительный*
(медлителен).
dilemma [daɪ'lɛmə] *n* дилéмма; **to be in a** ~
стоять (*impf*) пéред дилéммой.
diligence ['dɪlɪdʒəns] *n* усéрдие, прилежáние.
diligent ['dɪlɪdʒənt] *adj* (*worker*) усéрдный*
(усéрден), прилéжный* (прилéжен); (*work*)
тщáтельный* (тщáтелен).
dill [dɪl] *n* укрóп*; (*seed*) укрóпное сéмя*.
dilly-dally ['dɪlɪ'dælɪ] *vi* мéшкать (*impf*).
dilute [daɪ'lu:t] *vt* (*liquid*) разбавлять
(разбáвить* *perf*); (*belief, principle*)
ослаблять (ослáбить* *perf*) ♦ *adj*

разба́вленный (разба́влен).
dim [dɪm] adj (outline, feeling, memory)
сму́тный* (сму́тен); (light) ту́склый* (тускл);
(room) пло́хо освещённый (освещён);
(eyesight) сла́бый* (слаб); (future, prospects)
мра́чный* (мра́чен); (inf: person) тупо́й*
(туп) ♦ vt (also US: light) пригаша́ть
(пригаси́ть* perf); **to take a ~ view of sth**
неодобри́тельно смотре́ть* (impf) на что-н.
dime [daɪm] n (US) десятице́нтовая моне́та.
dimension [daɪˈmɛnʃən] n (measurement)
измере́ние; (also pl: scale, size) разме́ры mpl;
(aspect) аспе́кт.
diminish [dɪˈmɪnɪʃ] vi уменьша́ться
(уме́ньшиться perf) ♦ vt (belittle) принижа́ть
(прини́зить* perf).
diminished [dɪˈmɪnɪʃt] adj: **~ responsibility**
(LAW) ограни́ченная отве́тственность f.
diminutive [dɪˈmɪnjutɪv] adj кро́шечный ♦ n
(LING) уменьши́тельно-ласка́тельное сло́во.
dimly [ˈdɪmlɪ] adv (glow, illuminate) ту́скло;
(see, remember) сму́тно.
dimmer [ˈdɪməʳ] n (also: ~ **switch**) регуля́тор
освещённости.
dimmers [ˈdɪməz] npl (US: dipped headlights)
бли́жний* свет msg фар; (parking lights)
стоя́ночный свет msg.
dimple [ˈdɪmpl] n я́мочка*.
dim-witted [ˈdɪmˈwɪtɪd] adj (inf) тупоу́мный*
(тупоу́мен).
din [dɪn] n гро́хот ♦ vt (inf): **to ~ sth into sb**
вда́лбивать (вдолби́ть* perf) что-н в кого́-н.
dine [daɪn] vi обе́дать (пообе́дать perf).
diner [ˈdaɪnəʳ] n (person) обе́дающий(-ая) m(f)
adj; (US) дешёвый ресторанчик.
dinghy [ˈdɪŋgɪ] n (also: **sailing ~**) шлю́пка*;
(also: **rubber ~**) надувна́я ло́дка.
dingy [ˈdɪndʒɪ] adj (streets, room) мра́чный*
(мра́чен); (clothes, curtains etc)
замы́зганный.
dining car [ˈdaɪnɪŋ-] n (BRIT) ваго́н-рестора́н.
dining room n столо́вая f adj.
dinner [ˈdɪnəʳ] n (evening meal) у́жин; (lunch,
banquet) обе́д.
dinner jacket n смо́кинг.
dinner party n зва́ный обе́д.
dinner service n столо́вый серви́з.
dinner time n (midday) обе́денное вре́мя* nt;
(evening) вре́мя* у́жина.
dinosaur [ˈdaɪnəsɔːʳ] n диноза́вр.
dint [dɪnt] n: **by ~ of** посре́дством +gen.
diocese [ˈdaɪəsɪs] n епа́рхия.
dioxide [daɪˈɔksaɪd] n двуо́кись f.
dip [dɪp] n (slope) укло́н; (depression) впа́дина;
(CULIN) со́ус*; (AGR: for sheep)
дезинфици́рующий раство́р ♦ vt (immerse)
погружа́ть (погрузи́ть* perf), окуна́ть
(окуну́ть perf); (: in liquid) обма́кивать

(обмакну́ть perf); (BRIT: AUT: lights)
пригаша́ть (пригаси́ть* perf) ♦ vi (ground,
road) идти́* (пойти́* perf) под уклон; **to go for
a ~ in the sea** окуна́ться (окуну́ться perf) в
мо́ре.
Dip. abbr (BRIT) = **diploma**.
diphtheria [dɪfˈθɪərɪə] n дифтери́т.
diphthong [ˈdɪfθɔŋ] n дифто́нг.
diploma [dɪˈpləumə] n дипло́м.
diplomacy [dɪˈpləuməsɪ] n диплома́тия.
diplomat [ˈdɪpləmæt] n диплома́т.
diplomatic [dɪpləˈmætɪk] adj (POL)
дипломати́ческий*; (tactful)
дипломати́чный* (дипломати́чен); **to break
off ~ relations (with)** (POL) разрыва́ть
(разорва́ть* perf) дипломати́ческие
отноше́ния (с +instr).
diplomatic corps n дипломати́ческий*
ко́рпус*.
diplomatic immunity n дипломати́ческая
неприкоснове́нность f.
dip stick n (BRIT: AUT) щуп для измере́ния
у́ровня ма́сла.
dip switch n (BRIT: AUT) переключа́тель m
све́та фар.
dire [daɪəʳ] adj (consequences) злове́щий*;
(poverty, situation) жу́ткий*.
direct [daɪˈrɛkt] adj прямо́й ♦ adv пря́мо ♦ vt
(company, project etc) руководи́ть* (impf)
+instr; (play, film, programme) ста́вить*
(поста́вить* perf); (letter): **to ~ to** направля́ть
(напра́вить* perf) +dat; (attention, remark): **to
~ (towards** or **at)** направля́ть (напра́вить*
perf) (на +acc); (order): **to ~ sb to do** веле́ть
(impf) кому́-н +infin; **can you ~ me to ...?** Вы не
ука́жите где находи́ться ...?
direct access n (COMPUT) прямо́й до́ступ.
direct cost n (COMM) прямы́е затра́ты fpl.
direct current n постоя́нный ток.
direct debit n (BRIT: COMM) прямо́е
дебетова́ние.
direct dialling n автомати́ческая телефо́нная
связь f.
direct hit n (MIL) прямо́е попада́ние.
direction [dɪˈrɛkʃən] n (way) направле́ние; (TV,
CINEMA) постано́вка; **~s** npl (instructions)
указа́ния ntpl; **to have a good sense of ~**
хорошо́ ориенти́роваться (impf/perf); **~s for
use** инстру́кция (по эксплуата́ции); **to ask for
~s (to)** спра́шивать (спроси́ть* perf) доро́гу
(к +dat); **in the ~ of** в направле́нии +gen.
directional [dɪˈrɛkʃənl] adj (TECH)
напра́вленный.
directive [dɪˈrɛktɪv] n (POL, ADMIN) директи́ва,
постановле́ние; **a government ~**
прави́тельственное постановле́ние.
direct labour n (BRIT) постоя́нная рабо́чая
си́ла.

---

* marks translations which have irregular inflections. The Russian-English side of the dictionary gives inflectional information.

directly [dɪ'rɛktlɪ] *adv* пря́мо; (*at once*) сейча́с же; (*as soon as*) как то́лько.

direct mail *n* прода́жа това́ров по по́чте.

direct-mail shot [dɪ'rɛkt'meɪl-] *n* (*BRIT*) почто́вая рекла́ма.

directness [daɪ'rɛktnɪs] *n* прямота́.

director [dɪ'rɛktə'] *n* (*COMM*) дире́ктор*; (*of project*) руководи́тель(ница) *m(f)*; (*TV, RADIO, CINEMA*) режиссёр.

Director of Public Prosecutions *n* (*BRIT*) Гла́вный прокуро́р.

directory [dɪ'rɛktərɪ] *n* (*also COMPUT*) спра́вочник; (*also: street ~*) указа́тель *m*.

directory enquiries (*US* **directory assistance**) *n* (телефо́нная) спра́вочная *f adj.*

dirt [də:t] *n* грязь* *f*; **to treat sb like ~** ни во что́ не ста́вить (*impf*) кого́-н.

dirt-cheap ['də:t'tʃi:p] *adv* по дешёвке.

dirt road *n* грунтова́я доро́га.

dirty ['də:tɪ] *adj* гря́зный* ♦ *vt* па́чкать (испа́чкать *perf*).

dirty trick *n* зла́я шу́тка*.

disability [dɪsə'bɪlɪt] *n* (*physical*) инвали́дность *f no pl*; (*mental*) у́мственная неполноце́нность *f*; **physical disabilities** физи́ческие недоста́тки.

disability allowance *n* посо́бие по инвали́дности.

disable [dɪs'eɪbl] *vt* (*subj: illness, accident*) кале́чить (искале́чить *perf*); (*tank, gun*) выводи́ть* (вы́вести* *perf*) из стро́я.

disabled [dɪs'eɪbld] *adj* (*mentally*) у́мственно неполноце́нный; (*physically*): **~ person** инвали́д ♦ *npl*: **the ~** инвали́ды *mpl*.

disabuse [dɪsə'bju:z] *vt*: **to ~ sb (of)** разуверя́ть (разуве́рить *perf*) кого́-н (в +*prp*).

disadvantage [dɪsəd'va:ntɪdʒ] *n* недоста́ток*; **to be at a ~** быть* (*impf*) в невы́годном положе́нии.

disadvantaged [dɪsəd'va:ntɪdʒd] *adj* (*person, region*) обездо́ленный* (обездо́лен).

disadvantageous [dɪsædvə:n'teɪdʒəs] *adj* невы́годный* (невы́годен).

disaffected [dɪsə'fɛktɪd] *adj* разочаров-а́вшийся.

disaffection [dɪsə'fɛkʃən] *n*: **~ (with)** поте́ря дове́рия (к +*dat*).

disagree [dɪsə'gri:] *vi* (*differ*) расходи́ться* (разойти́сь* *perf*); (*be against, think otherwise*): **to ~ (with)** не соглаша́ться (согласи́ться* *perf*) (с +*instr*); **I ~ with you** я с Ва́ми не согла́сен; **we ~ on many things** мы во мно́гом расхо́димся; **garlic ~s with me** я пло́хо переношу́ чесно́к.

disagreeable [dɪsə'gri:əbl] *adj* неприя́тный* (неприя́тен).

disagreement [dɪsə'gri:mənt] *n* (*lack of consensus, argument*) разногла́сие; (*opposition*): **~ with sb/sth** несогла́сие с кем-н/чем-н; **to have a ~ with sb** име́ть (*impf*) разногла́сие с кем-н.

disallow ['dɪsə'lau] *vt* (*appeal*) отклоня́ть (отклони́ть *perf*); (*goal*) не засчи́тывать (засчита́ть *perf*).

disappear [dɪsə'pɪə'] *vi* исчеза́ть (исче́знуть* *perf*).

disappearance [dɪsə'pɪərəns] *n* исчезнове́ние.

disappoint [dɪsə'pɔɪnt] *vt* разочаро́вывать (разочарова́ть *perf*).

disappointed [dɪsə'pɔɪntɪd] *adj* разочаро́ванный* (разочаро́ван).

disappointing [dɪsə'pɔɪntɪŋ] *adj*: **the film is rather ~** э́тот фильм разочаро́вывает; **the election results were ~ for the Democrats** демокра́ты бы́ли разочаро́ваны результа́тами вы́боров.

disappointment [dɪsə'pɔɪntmənt] *n* разочарова́ние.

disapproval [dɪsə'pru:vəl] *n* неодобре́ние.

disapprove [dɪsə'pru:v] *vi*: **to ~ (of)** не одобря́ть (*impf*) (+*acc*).

disapproving [dɪsə'pru:vɪŋ] *adj* неодобри́тельный* (неодобри́телен).

disarm [dɪs'ɑ:m] *vt* (*MIL*) разоружа́ть (разоружи́ть *perf*); (*fig*) обезору́живать (обезору́жить *perf*) ♦ *vi* разоружа́ться (разоружи́ться *perf*).

disarmament [dɪs'ɑ:məmənt] *n* разоруже́ние.

disarming [dɪs'ɑ:mɪŋ] *adj* обезору́живающий.

disarray [dɪsə'reɪ] *n*: **in ~** (*army, organization, thoughts*) в смяте́нии; (*hair, clothes*) в беспоря́дке; **to throw into ~** приводи́ть* (привести́* *perf*) в смяте́ние.

disaster [dɪ'zɑ:stə'] *n* (*natural*) бе́дствие; (*man-made, also fig*) катастро́фа.

disaster area *n* (*also fig*) зо́на бе́дствия.

disastrous [dɪ'zɑ:strəs] *adj* губи́тельный* (губи́телен).

disband [dɪs'bænd] *vt* распуска́ть (распусти́ть* *perf*) ♦ *vi* расформиро́вываться (расформирова́ться *perf*).

disbelief ['dɪsbə'li:f] *n* неве́рие; **in ~** с неве́рием.

disbelieve ['dɪsbə'li:v] *vt* (*person*) не ве́рить (*impf*) +*dat*; (*story*) не ве́рить (*impf*) +*dat or* в +*acc*; **I don't ~ you** я не могу́ сказа́ть, что не ве́рю Вам.

disc [dɪsk] *n* (*ANAT*) межпозвоно́чный хрящ*; (*record*) диск; (*COMPUT*) = **disk**.

disc. *abbr* (*COMM*) = **discount**.

discard [dɪs'kɑ:d] *vt* (*old things*) выбра́сывать (вы́бросить* *perf*); (*idea, plan*) отбра́сывать (отбро́сить* *perf*).

disc brake *n* ди́сковый то́рмоз*.

discern [dɪ'sə:n] *vt* (*see*) различа́ть (различи́ть *perf*); (*identify*) определя́ть (определи́ть *perf*).

discernible [dɪ'sə:nəbl] *adj* различи́мый.

discerning [dɪ'sə:nɪŋ] *adj* разбо́рчивый (разбо́рчив); **he has ~ tastes** он то́нкий* цени́тель.

discharge [*vt* dɪs'tʃɑ:dʒ, *n* 'dɪstʃɑ:dʒ] *vt* (*duties*) выполня́ть (вы́полнить *perf*); (*debt*)

распла́чиваться (расплати́ться* *perf*) с +*instr*;
(*waste*) выбра́сывать (вы́бросить* *perf*);
(*ELEC*) разряжа́ть (разряди́ть* *perf*); (*pus etc*)
выделя́ть (*impf*); (*patient*) выпи́сывать
(вы́писать* *perf*); (*employee*) увольня́ть
(уво́лить *perf*); (*soldier*) демобилизова́ть
(*impf/perf*); (*defendant*) опра́вдывать
(оправда́ть *perf*) ♦ *n* (*CHEM, MED*) выделе́ние;
(*ELEC*) разря́д; (*of patient*) вы́писка; (*of
employee*) увольне́ние; (*of soldier*)
демобилиза́ция; (*of defendant*) оправда́ние;
to ~ a gun разряжа́ть (разряди́ть* *perf*)
ружьё.
discharged bankrupt [dɪs'tʃɑːdʒd-] *n лицо́,
восстано́вленное в права́х по́сле
банкро́тства*.
disciple [dɪ'saɪpl] *n* (*REL*) апо́стол; (*fig*)
учени́к*(-и́ца).
disciplinary ['dɪsɪplmərɪ] *adj* (*code, measures*)
дисциплина́рный; **~ problems** пробле́мы с
дисципли́ной; **to take ~ action against sb**
принима́ть (приня́ть* *perf*) дисциплина́рные
ме́ры к кому́-н.
discipline ['dɪsɪplɪn] *n* дисципли́на ♦ *vt* (*train*)
дисциплини́ровать (*impf/perf*); (*punish*)
налага́ть (наложи́ть* *perf*) дисциплина́рное
взыска́ние на +*acc*; **to ~ o.s. to do** приуча́ться
(приучи́ться* *perf*) +*impf infin*.
disc jockey *n* диск-жоке́й.
disclaim [dɪs'kleɪm] *vt* отрица́ть (*impf*).
disclaimer [dɪs'kleɪmə^r] *n* отка́з от
отве́тственности; **to issue a ~** обнаро́довать
(*perf*) отка́з *or* отрече́ние от отве́тств-
енности.
disclose [dɪs'kləuz] *vt* раскрыва́ть (раскры́ть*
perf).
disclosure [dɪs'kləuʒə^r] *n* раскры́тие.
disco ['dɪskəu] *n abbr* = **discotheque**.
discolour [dɪs'kʌlə^r] (*US* **discolor**) *vt*
обесцве́чивать (обесцве́тить* *perf*) ♦ *vi*
обесцве́чиваться (обесцве́титься* *perf*).
discolouration [dɪskʌlə'reɪʃən] (*US*
discoloration) *n* обесцве́чивание.
discoloured [dɪs'kʌləd] (*US* **discolored**) *adj*
вы́цветший.
discomfort [dɪs'kʌmfət] *n* (*unease*) нело́вкость
f; (*pain etc*) недомога́ние.
disconcert [dɪskən'sə:t] *vt* смуща́ть (смути́ть*
perf).
disconcerting [dɪskən'sə:tɪŋ] *adj*
вызыва́ющий* чу́вство нело́вкости.
disconnect [dɪskə'nɛkt] *vt* (*pipe, telephone*)
разъединя́ть (разъедини́ть *perf*); (*ELEC,
RADIO*) отключа́ть (отключи́ть *perf*).
disconnected [dɪskə'nɛktɪd] *adj* (*speech,
thoughts*) бессвя́зный* (бессвя́зен).
disconsolate [dɪs'kɔnsəlɪt] *adj* неуте́шный*
(неуте́шен), безуте́шный* (безуте́шен).

discontent [dɪskən'tɛnt] *n* недово́льство.
discontented [dɪskən'tɛntɪd] *adj*: **~ (with)**
недово́льный* (недово́лен) (+*instr*).
discontinue [dɪskən'tɪnjuː] *vt* прекраща́ть
(прекрати́ть* *perf*); **"discontinued"** (*COMM*)
"сня́то с произво́дства".
discord ['dɪskɔːd] *n* разла́д; (*MUS*) диссона́нс.
discordant [dɪs'kɔːdənt] *adj* (*fig: note*)
несогласу́ющийся; (*MUS*) диссон-
и́рующий.
discotheque ['dɪskəutɛk] *n* дискоте́ка.
discount [*n* 'dɪskaunt, *vt* dɪs'kaunt] *n* ски́дка* ♦ *vt*
(*COMM*) снижа́ть (сни́зить* *perf*) це́ну на +*acc*;
(*idea, fact*) не принима́ть (приня́ть* *perf*) в
расчёт; **to give sb a ~ on sth** де́лать (сде́лать
perf) кому́-н ски́дку на что-н; **~ for cash**
ски́дка* при усло́вии опла́ты нали́чными; **at
a ~** со ски́дкой.
discount house *n* (*esp BRIT: FINANCE*) учётный
дом*; (*esp US: also:* **discount store**) *магази́н,
торгу́ющий по сни́женным це́нам*.
discount rate *n* сни́женная цена́.
discourage [dɪs'kʌrɪdʒ] *vt* (*dishearten*)
отбива́ть (отби́ть* *perf*) жела́ние у +*gen*;
(*advise against*): **to ~ sb from doing**
отгова́ривать (отговори́ть *perf*) кого́-н
+*infin*.
discouragement [dɪs'kʌrɪdʒmənt] *n* (*feeling*)
разочарова́ние; **to act as a ~ to sb** отбива́ть
(отби́ть* *perf*) охо́ту у кого́-н *or* +*infin or* к
+*dat*.
discouraging [dɪs'kʌrɪdʒɪŋ] *adj* рас-
хола́живающий.
discourteous [dɪs'kə:tɪəs] *adj* нелюбе́зный*
(нелюбе́зен).
discover [dɪs'kʌvə^r] *vt* обнару́живать
(обнару́жить *perf*).
discovery [dɪs'kʌvərɪ] *n* (*of object etc*)
откры́тие; (*thing found*) нахо́дка.
discredit [dɪs'krɛdɪt] *vt* дискредити́ровать
(*impf/perf*) ♦ *n*: **it is to his ~ that he ...** его́
дискредити́рует то, что он ....
discreet [dɪs'kriːt] *adj* (*tactful*) такти́чный*
(такти́чен); (*careful*) осмотри́тельный*
(осмотри́телен); (*barely noticeable*)
незаме́тный* (незаме́тен).
discreetly [dɪs'kriːtlɪ] *adv* (*see adj*) такти́чно;
осмотри́тельно; незаме́тно.
discrepancy [dɪs'krɛpənsɪ] *n* расхожде́ние.
discretion [dɪs'krɛʃən] *n* (*tact*) такти́чность *f*; **at
the ~ of** на усмотре́ние +*gen*; **use your (own)
~** поступа́йте, по своему́ усмотре́нию.
discretionary [dɪs'krɛʃənrɪ] *adj* (*powers etc*)
дискрецио́нный.
discriminate [dɪs'krɪmɪneɪt] *vi*: **to ~ between**
различа́ть (различи́ть* *perf*); **to ~ against**
дискримини́ровать (*impf/perf*).
discriminating [dɪs'krɪmɪneɪtɪŋ] *adj* (*discerning*)

---

* marks translations which have irregular inflections. The Russian-English side of the dictionary gives inflectional information.

разбо́рчивый (разбо́рчив); (*tax etc*) дифференциа́льный.

discrimination [dɪskrɪmɪ'neɪʃən] *n* (*bias*) дискримина́ция; (*discernment*) разбо́рчивость *f*; **racial** ~ ра́совая дискримина́ция; **sexual** ~ дискримина́ция по полово́му при́знаку.

discus ['dɪskəs] *n* (*object*) диск; (*event*) мета́ние ди́ска.

discuss [dɪs'kʌs] *vt* обсужда́ть (обсуди́ть* *perf*).

discussion [dɪs'kʌʃən] *n* (*talk*) обсужде́ние; (*debate*) диску́ссия; **the matter is under** ~ э́тот вопро́с обсужда́ется.

disdain [dɪs'deɪn] *n* презре́ние ◆ *vt* презира́ть (*impf*) ◆ *vi*: **to** ~ **to do** счита́ть (посчита́ть *perf*) ни́же своего́ досто́инства +*infin*.

disease [dɪ'ziːz] *n* боле́знь *f*.

diseased [dɪ'ziːzd] *adj* (*also fig*) больно́й* (бо́лен).

disembark [dɪsɪm'bɑːk] *vt* (*goods*) выгружа́ть (вы́грузить* *perf*); (*passengers*) выса́живать (вы́садить* *perf*) ◆ *vi* выса́живаться (вы́садиться* *perf*).

disembarkation [dɪsɛmbɑː'keɪʃən] *n* (*see vt*) вы́грузка*; вы́садка*.

disembodied ['dɪsɪm'bɔdɪd] *adj* (*limb, head*) отчленённый; (*voice*) бестеле́сный.

disembowel ['dɪsɪm'bauəl] *vt* потроши́ть (вы́потрошить *perf*).

disenchanted ['dɪsɪn'tʃɑːntɪd] *adj*: ~ (**with**) разочаро́ванный* (разочаро́ван) (+*instr*).

disenfranchise ['dɪsɪn'fræntʃaɪz] *vt* (*POL*) лиша́ть (лиши́ть *perf*) избира́тельных прав; (*COMM*) лиша́ть (лиши́ть *perf*) франши́зы.

disengage [dɪsɪn'geɪdʒ] *vt* (*TECH*) расцепля́ть (расцепи́ть* *perf*); (*AUT*): **to** ~ **the clutch** выключа́ть (вы́ключить *perf*) сцепле́ние.

disengagement [dɪsɪn'geɪdʒmənt] *n* освобожде́ние; **military** ~ вы́вод вооружённых сил.

disentangle [dɪsɪn'tæŋgl] *vt* (*from wreckage*) высвобожда́ть (вы́свободить* *perf*); (*wool, wire*) распу́тывать (распу́тать *perf*); **to** ~ **o.s. (from)** выпу́тываться (вы́путаться *perf*) (из +*gen*).

disfavour [dɪs'feɪvəʳ] (*US* **disfavor**) *n* неми́лость *f*.

disfigure [dɪs'fɪgəʳ] *vt* уро́довать (изуро́довать *perf*).

disgorge [dɪs'gɔːdʒ] *vt* (*subj: river*) выбра́сывать (вы́бросить* *perf*); (: *building, vehicle*) изверга́ть (изве́ргнуть* *perf*).

disgrace [dɪs'greɪs] *n* позо́р ◆ *vt* позо́рить (опозо́рить *perf*).

disgraceful [dɪs'greɪsful] *adj* позо́рный* (позо́рен).

disgruntled [dɪs'grʌntld] *adj* недово́льный* (недово́лен).

disguise [dɪs'gaɪz] *n* (*make-up, costume*) маскиро́вка*; (*art*) гримиро́вка, маскиро́вка

◆ *vt* (*object*) маскирова́ть (замаскирова́ть *perf*); (*feelings*) скрыва́ть (скрыть* *perf*); (*person*): **to** ~ (**as**) (*dress up*) переодева́ть (переоде́ть* *perf*) (+*instr*); (*make up*) гримирова́ть (загримирова́ть *perf*) (+*instr*); **in** ~ (*person*) переоде́тый; **to** ~ **o.s. as** переодева́ться (переоде́ться* *perf*) +*instr*; **there's no disguising the fact that ...** нельзя́ скрыть того́, что ....

disgust [dɪs'gʌst] *n* отвраще́ние ◆ *vt* внуша́ть (внуши́ть *perf*) отвраще́ние +*dat*; **she walked off in** ~ она́ с возмуще́нием ушла́.

disgusting [dɪs'gʌstɪŋ] *adj* отврати́тельный* (отврати́телен).

dish [dɪʃ] *n* (*plate, food*) блю́до; (*also:* **satellite** ~) параболи́ческая анте́нна; **to do** *or* **wash the** ~**es** мыть* (вы́мыть* *perf*) посу́ду

▶ **dish out** *vt* (*money, advice etc*) раздава́ть* (разда́ть* *perf*); (*food*) раскла́дывать (разложи́ть* *perf*) (по таре́лкам)

▶ **dish up** *vt* (*food*) подава́ть* (пода́ть* *perf*) к столу́; (*inf: facts*) преподноси́ть* (преподнести́* *perf*).

dishcloth ['dɪʃklɔθ] *n* тря́пка* для мытья́ посу́ды.

dishearten [dɪs'hɑːtn] *vt* приводи́ть* (привести́* *perf*) в уны́ние.

dishevelled [dɪ'ʃɛvəld] (*US* **disheveled**) *adj* растрёпанный* (растрёпан).

dishonest [dɪs'ɔnɪst] *adj* нече́стный* (нече́стен).

dishonesty [dɪs'ɔnɪstɪ] *n* нече́стность *f*.

dishonour [dɪs'ɔnəʳ] (*US* **dishonor**) *n* бесче́стье.

dishonourable [dɪs'ɔnərəbl] *adj* бесче́стный* (бесче́стен).

dish soap *n* (*US*) хозя́йственное мы́ло*.

dishtowel ['dɪʃtauəl] *n* (*esp US*) ку́хонное *or* посу́дное полоте́нце*.

dishwasher ['dɪʃwɔʃəʳ] *n* (*machine*) посудомо́ечная маши́на.

dishy [dɪʃɪ] *adj* (*inf*): ~ **bloke** клёвый па́рень *m*.

disillusion [dɪsɪ'luːʒən] *vt* разочаро́вывать (разочарова́ть *perf*) ◆ *n* разочарова́ние; **to become** ~**ed (with)** разочаро́вываться (разочарова́ться *perf*) (в +*prp*).

disillusionment [dɪsɪ'luːʒənmənt] *n* разочарова́ние.

disincentive [dɪsɪn'sɛntɪv] *n* сде́рживающее обстоя́тельство; **to be a** ~ **to sb** явля́ться (*impf*) сде́рживающим обстоя́тельством для кого́-н.

disinclined [dɪsɪn'klaɪnd] *adj*: **I am** ~ **to do it** мне не хо́чется э́то де́лать.

disinfect [dɪsɪn'fɛkt] *vt* дезинфици́ровать (*impf/perf*).

disinfectant [dɪsɪn'fɛktənt] *n* дезинфици́рующее сре́дство.

disinflation [dɪsɪn'fleɪʃən] *n* (*ECON*) дез-инфля́ция.

disinformation [dɪsɪnfə'meɪʃən] *n* дезинформа́ция.

disingenuous [dısın'dʒɛnjuəs] *adj* нейскренный* (нейскренен).

disinherit [dısın'hɛrıt] *vt*: **to ~ sb** лишáть (лишить* *perf*) когó-н наслéдства.

disintegrate [dıs'ıntıgreıt] *vi* (*break up*) распадáться (распáсться* *perf*) на чáсти; (*decay*) разлагáться (разложиться* *perf*).

disinterested [dıs'ıntrəstıd] *adj* (*impartial*) бескорыстный* (бескорыстен).

disjointed [dıs'dʒɔıntıd] *adj* бессвязный* (бессвязен).

disk [dısk] *n* (*COMPUT*) диск; **single-/double-sided ~** односторо́нний/двусторо́нний диск.

disk drive *n* дисковóд.

diskette [dıs'kɛt] *n* (*US*) = **disk**.

disk operating system *n* дисковая операцио́нная систéма.

dislike [dıs'laık] *n* (*feeling*) неприязнь *f*; (*usu pl*: *object of dislike*) нелюбимая вещь *f* ♦ *vt* не любить* (*impf*) +*gen*; **to take a ~ to sb/sth** невзлюбить* (*perf*) когó-н/что-н; **I ~ the idea** мне не нрáвится идéя; **he ~s cooking** он не любит гото́вить.

dislocate ['dısləkeıt] *vt* вывихнуть (*perf*); **he has ~d his shoulder** он вывихнул плечó.

dislodge [dıs'lɔdʒ] *vt* смещáть (сместить* *perf*).

disloyal [dıs'lɔıəl] *adj*: **~ (to)** невéрный* (невéрен) (+*dat*).

dismal ['dızml] *adj* унылый (уныл), мрáчный* (мрáчен); **a ~ failure** ужáсная неудáча.

dismantle [dıs'mæntl] *vt* разбирáть (разобрáть* *perf*).

dismast [dıs'mɑ:st] *vt* (*NAUT*) снимáть (снять* *perf*) мáчты.

dismay [dıs'meı] *n* смятéние ♦ *vt* приводить* (привести* *perf*) в смятéние; **much to my ~** к моему́ смятéнию; **he gasped in ~** он áхнул в смятéнии.

dismiss [dıs'mıs] *vt* (*worker*) увольнять (уво́лить *perf*); (*pupils, soldiers*) распускáть (распустить* *perf*); (*LAW*: *case*) прекращáть (прекратить* *perf*); (*possibility, idea*) отбрáсывать (отбро́сить* *perf*).

dismissal [dıs'mısl] *n* (*sacking*) увольнéние.

dismount [dıs'maunt] *vi* (*from horse*) спéшиваться (спéшиться *perf*); (*from bicycle*) слезáть (слезть *perf*).

disobedience [dısə'bi:dıəns] *n* непослушáние.

disobedient [dısə'bi:dıənt] *adj* непослу́шный* (непослу́шен).

disobey [dısə'beı] *vt* не слу́шаться (послу́шаться *perf*) +*gen*.

disorder [dıs'ɔ:də*] *n* беспоря́док*; (*MED*) расстро́йство; **civil ~** социáльные беспоря́дки.

disorderly [dıs'ɔ:dəlı] *adj* (*room etc*) беспоря́дочный; (*meeting*)

неорганизо́ванный* (неорганизо́ван); (*behaviour*) бесчинствующий.

disorderly conduct *n* нарушéние обще́ственного поря́дка.

disorganize [dıs'ɔ:gənaız] *vt* дезорганизовáть (*impf/perf*).

disorganized [dıs'ɔ:gənaızd] *adj* неорганизо́ванный.

disorientated [dıs'ɔ:rıenteıtıd] *adj* лишённый (лишён) чу́вства ориентáции.

disown [dıs'əun] *vt* (*action*) отказываться (отказáться* *perf*) от +*gen*; (*person*) отрекáться (отрéчься* *perf*) от +*gen*.

disparaging [dıs'pærıdʒıŋ] *adj* пренебрежительный* (пренебрежителен); **to be ~ about sb/sth** относить* (отнести́сь* *perf*) пренебрежительно к кому́-н/чему́-н.

disparate ['dıspərıt] *adj* несравнимый.

disparity [dıs'pærıtı] *n* нерáвенство.

dispassionate [dıs'pæʃənət] *adj* бесстрáстный* (бесстрáстен).

dispatch [dıs'pætʃ] *vt* (*send*) отправлять (отпрáвить* *perf*); (*deal with*) разде́лываться (разде́латься *perf*) с +*instr*; (*kill*) поконьчи́ть (*perf*) с +*instr* ♦ *n* (*sending*) отпрáвка; (*PRESS*) сообщéние; (*MIL*) донесéние.

dispatch department *n* отдéл отпрáвки.

dispatch rider *n* (*MIL*) мотоцикли́ст свя́зи.

dispel [dıs'pɛl] *vt* рассéивать (рассéять *perf*).

dispensary [dıs'pɛnsərı] *n* аптéка.

dispensation [dıspən'seıʃən] *n* (*of justice, treatment*) осуществлéние; (*permission*): (*special*) **~** особо́е разрешéние.

dispense [dıs'pɛns] *vt* (*medicines*) приготовля́ть (приготовить* *perf*) и отпускáть (отпусти́ть* *perf*); (*charity, advice*) раздавáть (раздáть* *perf*); **to ~ justice** отправлять (*impf*) правосу́дие

▸ **dispense with** *vt fus* (*do without*) обходиться* (обойти́сь* *perf*) без +*gen*; (*make unnecessary*) освобождáть (освободи́ть* *perf*) от необходи́мости +*gen*.

dispenser [dıs'pɛnsə*] *n* (*machine*) торго́вый автомáт.

dispensing chemist [dıs'pɛnsıŋ-] *n* (*BRIT*: *shop*) аптéка.

dispersal [dıs'pə:sl] *n* рассéивание.

disperse [dıs'pə:s] *vt* (*objects*) рассéивать (рассéять *perf*); (*crowd*) разгоня́ть (разогнáть* *perf*); (*knowledge*) распространя́ть (распространи́ть *perf*) ♦ *vi* (*crowd, clouds*) рассéиваться (рассéяться *perf*).

dispirited [dıs'pırıtıd] *adj* удручённый* (удручён).

displace [dıs'pleıs] *vt* замещáть (замести́ть* *perf*).

displaced person [dıs'pleıst-] *n* перемещённое лицó*.

---

* marks translations which have irregular inflections. The Russian-English side of the dictionary gives inflectional information.

displacement [dɪsˈpleɪsmənt] n замещéние; (PHYS) вытеснéние.

display [dɪsˈpleɪ] n демонстрáция; (exhibition) вы́ставка*; (pej: bad manners) выставлéние напокáз; (COMPUT, TECH) дисплéй ♦ vt (emotion, quality) выкáзывать (вы́казать* perf); (goods, exhibits) выставля́ть (вы́ставить* perf) (напокáз); (results, departure times) покáзывать (показáть* perf); **on ~** (exhibits) на вы́ставке; (goods in window) на витри́не.

display advertising n витри́нно-вы́ставочная реклáма.

displease [dɪsˈpliːz] vt раздражáть (раздражи́ть perf).

displeased [dɪsˈpliːzd] adj: **~ with** раздражённый* (раздражён) +gen.

displeasure [dɪsˈplɛʒəʳ] n неудовóльствие.

disposable [dɪsˈpəuzəbl] adj (lighter, bottle) однорáзового употреблéния; (syringe) однорáзовый; **~ income** дохóд, котóрым населéние располагáет пóсле уплáты налóгов.

disposable nappy n (BRIT) однорáзовая пелёнка*.

disposal [dɪsˈpəuzl] n (of goods for sale) реализáция; (of property etc: by selling) распродáжа; (: by giving away) удалéние; (of rubbish) удалéние; **to have sth at one's ~** располагáть (impf) чем-н; **to put sth at sb's ~** предоставля́ть (предостáвить* perf) что-н в чьё-н распоряжéние.

dispose [dɪsˈpəuz] vi: **~ of** (body, unwanted goods) избавля́ться (избáвиться* perf) от +gen; (problem, task) управля́ться (упрáвиться* perf) с +instr; (COMM: stock) реализóвывать (реализовáть perf).

disposed [dɪsˈpəuzd] adj: **I am ~ to do** я настрóен +infin; **to be well ~ towards sb** хорошó относи́ться* (impf) к комý-н.

disposition [dɪspəˈzɪʃən] n (nature) нрав; (inclination) склóнность f.

dispossess [ˈdɪspəˈzɛs] vt: **to ~ sb (of)** лишáть (лиши́ть perf) когó-н (+gen).

disproportion [dɪsprəˈpɔːʃən] n диспропóрция.

disproportionate [dɪsprəˈpɔːʃənət] adj (excessive) неопрáвданно большóй; **our income is ~ to our expenditure** нáши дохóды не соизмери́мы с нáшими расхóдами.

disprove [dɪsˈpruːv] vt опровергáть (опровéргнуть* perf).

dispute [dɪsˈpjuːt] n (domestic) ссóра; (POL, MIL, INDUSTRY) спор; (LAW) тя́жба ♦ vt оспáривать (оспóрить perf); **to be in** or **under ~** (matter) опротестóвываться (impf); (territory) оспáриваться (impf).

disqualification [dɪskwɔlɪfɪˈkeɪʃən] n: **~ from sth** лишéние прáва на учáстие в чём-н; **~ from driving** (BRIT) лишéние води́тельских прав.

disqualify [dɪsˈkwɔlɪfaɪ] vt (SPORT)

дисквалифици́ровать (impf/perf); **to ~ sb for sth/from doing** (status, situation) лишáть (лиши́ть perf) когó-н прáва на учáстие в чём-н/+infin; (authority) лишáть (лиши́ть perf) +gen; **to ~ sb from driving** (BRIT) лишáть (лиши́ть perf) когó-н води́тельских прав.

disquiet [dɪsˈkwaɪət] n беспокóйство.

disquieting [dɪsˈkwaɪətɪŋ] adj тревóжный* (тревóжен).

disregard [dɪsrɪˈgɑːd] vt пренебрегáть (пренебрéчь* perf) ♦ n: **~ (for)** пренебрежéние (к +dat).

disrepair [ˈdɪsrɪˈpɛəʳ] n: **to fall into ~** приходи́ть* (прийти́* perf) в негóдность.

disreputable [dɪsˈrɛpjutəbl] adj (person, behaviour) недостóйный.

disrepute [ˈdɪsrɪˈpjuːt] n дурнáя слáва; **to fall into ~** приобретáть (приобрести́* perf) дурнýю слáву; **to bring sb/sth into ~** навлекáть (навлéчь* perf) на когó-н/что-н дурнýю слáву.

disrespectful [dɪsrɪˈspɛktful] adj непочти́тельный* (непочти́телен).

disrupt [dɪsˈrʌpt] vt нарушáть (нарýшить perf).

disruption [dɪsˈrʌpʃən] n (interruption) нарушéние; (disturbance) социáльные беспоря́дки mpl.

disruptive [dɪsˈrʌptɪv] adj (influence) подрывнóй; (action) разруши́тельный.

dissatisfaction [dɪssætɪsˈfækʃən] n недовóльство, неудовлетворённость f.

dissatisfied [dɪsˈsætɪsfaɪd] adj: **~ (with)** недовóльный* (недовóлен) (+instr).

dissect [dɪˈsɛkt] vt (ANAT) вскрывáть (вскрыть* perf); (theory, article) анализи́ровать (проанализи́ровать perf).

disseminate [dɪˈsɛmɪneɪt] vt распространя́ть (распространи́ть perf).

dissent [dɪˈsɛnt] n инакомы́слие; **~ from the party line** отхóд от парти́йной ли́нии.

dissenter [dɪˈsɛntəʳ] n (REL, POL) инакомы́слящий*(-ая) m(f) adj.

dissertation [dɪsəˈteɪʃən] n диссертáция.

disservice [dɪsˈsəːvɪs] n: **to do sb a ~** окáзывать (оказáть* perf) комý-н плохýю услýгу.

dissident [ˈdɪsɪdnt] adj (faction, voice) диссидéнтский ♦ n (POL, REL) диссидéнт.

dissimilar [dɪˈsɪmɪləʳ] adj: **~ (to)** несхóдный (с +instr); **this is not ~ to ...** э́то схóдно с +instr ....

dissipate [ˈdɪsɪpeɪt] vt (heat, clouds) рассéивать (рассéять perf); (money, effort) растрáчивать (растрáтить* perf).

dissipated [ˈdɪsɪpeɪtɪd] adj (debauched) распýщенный* (распýщен).

dissociate [dɪˈsəuʃɪeɪt] vt: **to ~ from** отделя́ть (отдели́ть* perf) от +gen; **to ~ o.s. from** отмежёвываться (отмежевáться perf) от +gen.

dissolute [ˈdɪsəluːt] adj разврáтный* (разврáтен).

dissolution [dɪsəˈluːʃən] n (of parliament,

organization) ро́спуск; (of marriage)
расторже́ние.
dissolve [dɪ'zɒlv] vt (substance) растворя́ть
(раствори́ть perf); (organization, parliament)
распуска́ть (распусти́ть* perf); (marriage)
расторга́ть (расто́ргнуть* perf) ♦ vi
растворя́ться (раствори́ться perf); **to ~ in(to)
tears** залива́ться (зали́ться* perf) слеза́ми.
dissuade [dɪ'sweɪd] vt: **to ~ sb (from sth)**
отгова́ривать (отговори́ть perf) кого́-н (от
чего́-н).
distaff ['dɪstɑːf] n: **on the ~ side** по же́нской
ли́нии.
distance ['dɪstns] n (in space) расстоя́ние; (in
sport) диста́нция; (in time) отдалённость f;
(reserve) сде́ржанность f ♦ vt: **to ~ o.s. (from)**
отдаля́ться (отдали́ться perf) (от +gen); **in
the ~** вдалеке́, вдали́; **from a ~** издалека́,
и́здали; **what's the ~ to London?** каково́
расстоя́ние до Ло́ндона; **into the ~** вдаль;
it's within walking ~ туда́ мо́жно дойти́
пешко́м; **the town is some ~ from the sea**
го́род нахо́диться в не́котором отдале́нии
от мо́ря; **at a ~ of two metres** на расстоя́нии
двух ме́тров; **keep your ~!** соблюда́йте
диста́нцию!; **to keep sb at a ~** держа́ть (impf)
кого́-н на расстоя́нии.
distant ['dɪstnt] adj (place, time) далёкий*;
(relative) да́льний*; (manner) сде́ржанный*;
in the ~ past/future в далёком про́шлом/-
бу́дущем.
distaste [dɪs'teɪst] n неприя́знь f.
distasteful [dɪs'teɪstful] adj неприя́тный*
(неприя́тен).
Dist. Atty. abbr (US) = **district attorney.**
distemper [dɪs'tɛmpəʳ] n (paint) те́мпера;
(disease: of dogs) (соба́чья) чума́.
distend [dɪs'tɛnd] vt расширя́ть (расши́рить
perf), раздува́ть (разду́ть perf) ♦ vi
раздува́ться (разду́ться perf).
distended [dɪs'tɛndɪd] adj (stomach) взду́тый.
distil [dɪs'tɪl] (US **distill**) vt (water)
дистилли́ровать (impf/perf); (whisky)
перегоня́ть (перегна́ть* perf); (information
etc) извлека́ть (извле́чь* perf).
distillery [dɪs'tɪlərɪ] n спи́рто-во́дочный заво́д.
distinct [dɪs'tɪŋkt] adj (clear) отчётливый
(отчётлив); (unmistakable) определённый;
(different): **~ (from)** отли́чный* (отли́чен) (от
+gen); **as ~ from** в отли́чие от +gen.
distinction [dɪs'tɪŋkʃən] n (difference) отли́чие;
(honour) честь f; (in exam) ≈ "отли́чно"; **to
draw a ~ between** проводи́ть* (провести́*
perf) разли́чие ме́жду +instr; **to pass an exam
with ~** сдава́ть* (сдать* perf) экза́мен на
отли́чно; **he is a writer of ~** он выдаю́щийся
писа́тель.
distinctive [dɪs'tɪŋktɪv] adj (voice, walk etc)

своеобра́зный* (своеобра́зен),
характе́рный* (характе́рен); (feature)
отличи́тельный.
distinctly [dɪs'tɪŋktlɪ] adv (remember, specify)
отчётливо; (unhappy, better) определённо.
distinguish [dɪs'tɪŋgwɪʃ] vt различа́ть
(различи́ть perf); **to ~ (between)** проводи́ть*
(провести́* perf) разли́чие (ме́жду +instr); **to ~
o.s.** отлича́ться (отличи́ться perf).
distinguished [dɪs'tɪŋgwɪʃt] adj (eminent)
выдаю́щийся*; (in appearance)
благоро́дный* (благоро́ден).
distinguishing [dɪs'tɪŋgwɪʃɪŋ] adj (feature)
отличи́тельный.
distort [dɪs'tɔːt] vt искажа́ть (искази́ть* perf).
distortion [dɪs'tɔːʃən] n искаже́ние.
distract [dɪs'trækt] vt отвлека́ть (отвле́чь* perf).
distracted [dɪs'træktɪd] adj (dreaming)
невнима́тельный* (невнима́телен); (look)
отсу́тствующий*; (anxious) встрево́женный*
(встрево́жен).
distraction [dɪs'trækʃən] n (inattention)
отвлече́ние; (confusion) пу́таница;
(amusement) развлече́ние; **to drive sb to ~**
доводи́ть* (довести́* perf) кого́-н до
безу́мия.
distraught [dɪs'trɔːt] adj: **~ (with)** (pain, worry)
обезу́мевший (от +gen).
distress [dɪs'trɛs] n (extreme worry, hardship)
отча́яние; (through pain) страда́ние ♦ vt
огорча́ть (огорчи́ть perf); **the ship is in ~**
кора́бль те́рпит бе́дствие; **he is in ~** он в
бе́дственном положе́нии; **~ed area** (BRIT)
райо́н бе́дствия.
distressing [dɪs'trɛsɪŋ] adj огорчи́тельный*
(огорчи́телен).
distress signal n сигна́л бе́дствия.
distribute [dɪs'trɪbjuːt] vt (leaflets, prizes etc)
раздава́ть* (разда́ть* perf); (profits, weight)
распределя́ть (распредели́ть* perf).
distribution [dɪstrɪ'bjuːʃən] n (of goods)
распростране́ние; (of profits, weight)
распределе́ние.
distribution cost n изде́ржки fpl обраще́ния.
distributor [dɪs'trɪbjuːtəʳ] n (COMM)
дисстрибью́тер; (AUT, TECH) распредели́тель
m зажига́ния.
district ['dɪstrɪkt] n райо́н.
district attorney n (US) ≈ окружно́й
прокуро́р.
district council n (BRIT) райо́нный сове́т.
district nurse n (BRIT) участко́вая медсестра́*.
distrust [dɪs'trʌst] n недове́рие ♦ vt не
доверя́ть (impf) +dat.
distrustful [dɪs'trʌstful] adj: **~ (of)**
недове́рчивый (недове́рчив) (к +dat).
disturb [dɪs'təːb] vt (person) беспоко́ить
(побеспоко́ить perf); (interrupt: thoughts,

---

* marks translations which have irregular inflections. The Russian-English side of the dictionary gives inflectional information.

peace etc) меша́ть (помеша́ть *perf)* +*dat;*
(*disorganize*) наруша́ть (нару́шить *perf);*
sorry to ~ you извини́те за беспоко́йство.
disturbance [dɪs'tə:bəns] *n* расстро́йство;
(*political etc*) волне́ния *ntpl;* (*violent event*)
беспоря́дки *mpl;* (*of mind*) расстро́йство; (*by
drunks etc*) наруше́ние (обще́ственного)
поря́дка; **to cause a ~** (*in street etc*) вызыва́ть
(вы́звать* *perf*) беспоря́дки; **~ of the peace**
наруше́ние обще́ственного поря́дка.
disturbed [dɪs'tə:bd] *adj* (*person: upset*)
расстро́енный* (расстро́ен); (*childhood*)
неспоко́йный; **mentally ~** душевнобольно́й;
emotionaly ~ психи́чески неуравно-
ве́шенный.
disturbing [dɪs'tə:bɪŋ] *adj* трево́жный*
(трево́жен).
disuse [dɪs'ju:s] *n:* **to fall into ~** выходи́ть*
(вы́йти* *perf*) из употребле́ния.
disused [dɪs'ju:zd] *adj* забро́шенный*
(забро́шен).
ditch [dɪtʃ] *n* ров, кана́ва; (*for irrigation*) кана́л
◆ *vt* (*inf: person, car*) броса́ть (бро́сить* *perf*);
(: *plan*) забра́сывать (забро́сить* *perf*).
dither ['dɪðəʳ] *vi* колеба́ться* (*impf*).
ditto ['dɪtəu] *adv* так же.
divan [dɪ'væn] *n* (*also:~ bed*) тахта́.
dive [daɪv] *n* (*from board*) пыжо́к* (*в во́ду*);
(*underwater*) ныря́ние; (*of submarine*)
погруже́ние; (*pej: place*) забега́ловка ◆ *vi*
ныря́ть (*impf*); (*submarine*) погружа́ться
(погрузи́ться* *perf*); **to ~ into** (*bag, drawer etc*)
запуска́ть (запусти́ть* *perf*) ру́ку в +*acc;*
(*shop, car etc*) ныря́ть (нырну́ть* *perf*) в +*acc.*
diver ['daɪvəʳ] *n* водола́з.
diverge [daɪ'və:dʒ] *vi* расходи́ться (разойти́сь*
perf).
divergent [daɪ'və:dʒənt] *adj* расходя́щийся*.
diverse [daɪ'və:s] *adj* разнообра́зный*
(разнообра́зен).
diversification [daɪvə:sɪfɪ'keɪʃən] *n*
диверсифика́ция.
diversify [daɪ'və:sɪfaɪ] *vi* разнообра́зить* (*impf*);
(*COMM*) расширя́ть (расши́рить *perf*) вы́бор.
diversion [daɪ'və:ʃən] *n* (*BRIT: AUT*) объе́зд; (*of
attention, funds*) отвлече́ние.
diversionary [daɪ'və:ʃənrɪ] *adj* диверсио́нный*.
diversity [daɪ'və:sɪtɪ] *n* разнообра́зие,
многообра́зие.
divert [daɪ'və:t] *vt* (*funds, attention*) отвлека́ть
(отвле́чь* *perf*); (*traffic*) отводи́ть* (отвести́*
perf).
divest [daɪ'vest] *vt:* **to ~ sb of** лиша́ть (лиши́ть
perf) кого́-н +*gen.*
divide [dɪ'vaɪd] *vt* (*separate*) разделя́ть
(раздели́ть* *perf*); (*MATH*) дели́ть*
(раздели́ть* *perf*); (*share out*) дели́ть*
(подели́ть* *perf*) ◆ *vi* (*cells etc*) дели́ться*
(раздели́ться* *perf*); (*road*) разделя́ться
(раздели́ться* *perf*); (*people, groups*)
дели́ться* *or* разделя́ться (раздели́ться* *perf*)

◆ *n* расхожде́ние; **to ~ (between** *or* **among)**
дели́ть* (подели́ть* *perf*) (ме́жду +*instr*); **40
~d by 5** 40 раздели́ть на 5
▶ **divide out** *vt:* **to ~ out (between** *or* **among)**
разделя́ть (раздели́ть* *perf*) (ме́жду +*instr*).
divided [dɪ'vaɪdɪd] *adj* (*fig: country, couple*)
разделённый* (разделён); **opinions were ~**
мне́ния раздели́лись.
divided highway *n* (*US*) шоссе́ *nt ind.*
dividend ['dɪvɪdɛnd] *n* (*COMM*) дивиде́нд; (*fig*):
to pay ~s окупа́ться (окупи́ться *perf*).
dividend cover *n* (*COMM*) покры́тие
дивиде́нда.
dividers [dɪ'vaɪdəz] *npl* (*MATH, TECH*)
раздели́тельный ци́ркуль *msg.*
divine [dɪ'vaɪn] *adj* (*also fig*) боже́ственный ◆ *vt*
(*future, truth*) уга́дывать (угада́ть *perf*);
(*water, metal*) иска́ть* (*impf*).
diving ['daɪvɪŋ] *n* ныря́ние; (*SPORT*) прыжки́
mpl в во́ду.
diving board *n* вы́шка* (*для прыжко́в в во́ду*).
diving suit *n* гидрокостю́м.
divinity [dɪ'vɪnɪtɪ] *n* (*holiness*) боже́ственность
f; (*god*) божество́*; (*SCOL*) богосло́вие.
divisible [dɪ'vɪzəbl] *adj* (*MATH*): **~ (by)** дели́мый
(на +*acc*); **to be ~ into** подразделя́ться (*impf*)
на +*acc.*
division [dɪ'vɪʒən] *n* (*also MATH*) деле́ние;
(*sharing out*) разделе́ние; (*disagreement*)
разногла́сие; (*BRIT: POL*) парла́ментское
голосова́ние, соверша́емое в ра́зных
ко́мнатах; (*COMM*) подразделе́ние,
отделе́ние; (*MIL*) диви́зия; (*SPORT*) ли́га; **~ of
labour** разделе́ние труда́.
divisive [dɪ'vaɪsɪv] *adj* (*tactics, system etc*)
вызыва́ющий* разногла́сия.
divorce [dɪ'vɔ:s] *n* разво́д ◆ *vt* (*spouse*)
разводи́ться* (развести́сь* *perf*) с +*instr;*
(*dissociate*) отделя́ть (отдели́ть* *perf*).
divorced [dɪ'vɔ:st] *adj* разведённый*
(разведён).
divorcee [dɪvɔ:'si:] *n* разведённый(-ая) *m(f) adj.*
divot ['dɪvət] *n* вы́рванный кусо́к* дёрна.
divulge [daɪ'vʌldʒ] *vt* разглаша́ть
(разгласи́ть* *perf*).
DIY *n abbr* (*BRIT*) = **do-it-yourself.**
dizziness ['dɪzɪnɪs] *n* головокруже́ние.
dizzy ['dɪzɪ] *adj* (*height*) головокружи́тельный;
~ turn *or* **spell** при́ступ головкруже́ния; **I feel
~** у меня́ кру́жится голова́; **to make sb ~**
приводи́ть* (привести́* *perf*) кого́-н в
смяте́ние.
DJ *n abbr* = **disc jockey.**
d.j. *n abbr* = **dinner jacket.**
Djakarta [dʒə'kɑ:tə] *n* Джака́рта.
DJIA *n abbr* (*US*: = *Dow-Jones Industrial
Average*) и́ндекс Доу Джо́нса.
dl *abbr* (= *decilitre*) дециди́тр.
DLit(t) *n abbr* (= *Doctor of Literature, Doctor of
Letters*) до́ктор филоло́гии.
DLO *n abbr* (= *dead-letter office*) Отде́л

недоста́вленной корреспонде́нции.

dm *abbr* (= *decimetre*) дм= *дециме́тр*.

DMus *n abbr* (= *Doctor of Music*) до́ктор музыкове́дения.

DMZ *n abbr* (= *demilitarized zone*) демилитаризо́ванная зо́на.

DNA *n abbr* (= *deoxyribonucleic acid*) ДНК= *дезоксирибонуклеи́новая кислота́*.

Dnieper [ˈdniːpəˀ] *n*: **the ~** Днепр.

KEYWORD

do [duː] (*pt* **did**, *pp* **done**) *aux vb* **1** (*in negative constructions and questions*); **I don't understand** я не понима́ю; **she doesn't want it** она́ не хо́чет э́то; **didn't you know?** ра́зве Вы не зна́ли?; **what do you think?** что Вы ду́маете?

2 (*for emphasis*) да; **she does look rather pale** да, она́ вы́глядит о́чень бле́дной; **oh do shut up!** ну, замолчи́те же!

3 (*in polite expressions*) пожа́луйста; **do sit down/help yourself** пожа́луйста, сади́тесь/-угоща́йтесь; **do take care!** пожа́луйста, береги́те себя́!

4 (*used to avoid repeating vb*): **she swims better than I do** она́ пла́вает лу́чше меня́ *or* чем я; **do you read/buy newspapers? – yes, I do/no, I don't** Вы чита́ете/покупа́ете газе́ты? – да, (чита́ю/покупа́ю)/нет, (не чита́ю/-покупа́ю); **she lives in Glasgow – so do I** она́ живёт в Гла́зго – а, я то́же; **he didn't like it and neither did we** ни ему́, ни нам, э́то не понра́вилось; **who made this mess? – I did** кто здесь насори́л? – я; **he asked me to help him and I did** он попроси́л меня́ помо́чь ему́, что я и сде́лал

5 (*in question tags*) ве́рно, ведь; **you like him, don't you?** он Вам нра́вится, ве́рно?, он ведь Вам нра́вится; **I don't know him, do I?** я ведь его́ не зна́ю

♦ *vt* **1** де́лать (сде́лать *perf*); **what are you doing tonight?** что Вы де́лаете сего́дня ве́чером?; **I've got nothing to do** мне не́чего де́лать; **what can I do for you?** чем я могу́ Вам помо́чь?; **we're doing "Othello" at school** (*studying*) мы прохо́дим "Оте́лло" в шко́ле; (*performing*) мы ста́вим "Оте́лло" в шко́ле; **to do one's teeth** чи́стить* (почи́стить* *perf*) зу́бы; **to do one's hair** причёсываться (причеса́ться *perf*); **to do the washing-up** мыть (помы́ть *perf*) посу́ду

2 (*AUT etc*): **the car was doing 100 (km/h)** маши́на шла со ско́ростью 100 км/ч; **we've done 200 km already** мы уже́ прое́хали 200 км; **he can do 100 mph in that car** на э́той маши́не он мо́жет е́хать со ско́ростью 100 миль в час

♦ *vi* **1** (*act, behave*) де́лать (сде́лать *perf*); **do**

as I do де́лайте, как я; **you did well to react so quickly** Вы молоде́ц, что так бы́стро среаги́ровали

2 (*get on, fare*): **he's doing well/badly at school** он хорошо́/пло́хо у́чится; **the firm is doing well** дела́ в фи́рме иду́т успе́шно; **how do you do?** о́чень прия́тно

3 (*be suitable*) подходи́ть (подойти́ *perf*); **will it do?** э́то подойдёт?

4 (*be sufficient*) хвата́ть (хвати́ть *perf*) +*gen*; **will ten pounds do?** десяти́ фу́нтов хва́тит?; **that'll do** ла́дно, хорошо́; **that'll do!** (*in annoyance*) дово́льно!, хва́тит!; **to make do (with)** обходи́ться (обойти́сь *perf*) (+*instr*)

♦ *n* (*inf*): **we're having a bit of a do on Saturday** у нас бу́дет вечери́нка в суббо́ту; **it was a formal do** э́то был официа́льный приём

▸ **do away with** *vt fus* (*kill*) прико́нчить (*perf*); (*abolish*) поко́нчить (*perf*) с +*instr*

▸ **do for** *vt fus* (*BRIT: inf*) убира́ть (*impf*) у +*gen*

▸ **do up** *vt* (*laces*) завя́зывать (завяза́ть* *perf*); (*dress, buttons*) застёгивать (застегну́ть *perf*); (*room, house*) ремонти́ровать* (отремонти́ровать* *perf*)

▸ **do with** *vt fus*: **I could do with a drink** я бы вы́пил чего́-нибудь; **I could do with some help** по́мощь мне бы не помеша́ла; **what has it got to do with you?** како́е э́то к Вам име́ет отноше́ние?; **I won't have anything to do with it** я не жела́ю име́ть к э́тому никако́го отноше́ния; **it has to do with money** э́то относи́тельно де́нег

▸ **do without** *vt fus* обходи́ться* (обойти́сь* *perf*) без +*gen*; **if you're late for tea then you'll do without** е́сли Вы опозда́ете, то оста́нетесь без ча́я.

---

do. *abbr* = **ditto**.

DOA *abbr* (= *dead on arrival*): **he was ~** по прибы́тии в больни́цу он был мёртв.

d.o.b. *abbr* = **date of birth**.

doc [dɔk] *n* (*inf*) до́ктор.

docile [ˈdəʊsaɪl] *adj* кро́ткий* (кро́ток).

dock [dɔk] *n* (*NAUT*) док; (*LAW*) скамья́ подсуди́мых; (*BOT*) щаве́ль* *m* ♦ *vi* (*NAUT*) прича́ливать (прича́лить *perf*); (*SPACE*) стыкова́ться (состыкова́ться *perf*) ♦ *vt*: **they ~ed a third of his wages** они́ удержа́ли треть его́ зарпла́ты; **~s** *npl* (*NAUT*) док, верфь *f*.

dock dues [-djuːz] *npl* (*COMM*) пла́та за по́льзование до́ком.

docker [ˈdɔkəˀ] *n* до́кер.

docket [ˈdɔkɪt] *n* (*ADMIN, COMM: certificate*) квита́нция; (*on parcel*) о́пись *f*.

dockyard [ˈdɔkjɑːd] *n* док, верфь *f*.

doctor [ˈdɔktəˀ] *n* (*MED*) врач*; (*SCOL*) до́ктор* ♦ *vt*: **I ~ed his coffee with arsenic** я подмеша́л в его́ ко́фе мышья́к; **~'s office** (*US*) враче́бный

---

* marks translations which have irregular inflections. The Russian-English side of the dictionary gives inflectional information.

кабинéт.
doctorate ['dɔktərɪt] *n* (*thesis*) дóкторская
рабóта; (*degree*) дóкторская стéпень* *f.*
Doctor of Philosophy *n* (*degree, person*)
дóктор филосóфии *or* филосóфских наýк.
doctrine ['dɔktrɪn] *n* доктрúна.
docudrama ['dɔkjudrɑːmə] *n* фильм úли
прогрáмма, в оснóву котóрых вошлú
реáльные собы́тия.
document [*n* 'dɔkjumənt, *vb* 'dɔkjumɛnt] *n*
докумéнт ◆ *vt* документúровать (*impf/perf*).
documentary [dɔkju'mɛntərɪ] *adj*
документáльный ◆ *n* (*TV, CINEMA*)
документáльный фúльм.
documentation [dɔkjumən'teɪʃən] *n* (*also*
COMPUT) документáция.
DOD *n abbr* (*US:* = *Department of Defense*)
Департáмент оборóны.
doddering ['dɔdərɪŋ] *adj* дря́хлый* (дряхл).
doddery ['dɔdərɪ] *adj* = **doddering**.
doddle ['dɔdl] *n* (*inf*) пустя́к, пáра пустякóв.
Dodecanese [dəudɪkə'niːz] *n:* the ~ (**Islands**)
Докеданéзские островá* *mpl.*
dodge [dɔdʒ] *n* (*trick*) увéртка*, улóвка ◆ *vt*
увéртываться (увернýться *perf*) от +*gen* ◆ *vi*
увéртываться (увернýться *perf*); (*SPORT*)
дéлать (сдéлать *perf*) обмáнное движéние;
to ~ out of the way отскáкивать (отскочúть*
perf) в сторонý; **to ~ through the traffic**
лавúровать (*impf*) в потóке машúн.
dodgems ['dɔdʒəmz] *npl* (*BRIT*)
аттракциóнный электромобúль *msg.*
dodgy ['dɔdʒɪ] *adj* (*inf: plan*) рискóванный*
(рискóван); (: *person*): ~ **character**
подозрúтельный тип.
DOE *n abbr* (*BRIT:* = *Department of the*
Environment) Департáмент охрáны
окружáющей среды́; (*US:* = *Department of*
Energy) Департáмент энергéтики.
doe [dəu] *n* (*deer*) сáмка* олéня; (*rabbit*) сáмка*
крóлика.
does [dʌz] *vb see* **do**.
doesn't ['dʌznt] = **does not**.
dog [dɔg] *n* собáка ◆ *vt* преслéдовать (*impf*); **to**
go to the ~s (*fig*) приходúть* (прийтú* *perf*) в
упáдок.
dog biscuits *npl* галéты *fpl* для собáк.
dog collar *n* ошéйник; (*REL*) высóкий жёсткий
воротнúк у свящéнников.
dog-eared ['dɔgɪəd] *adj* потрёпанный*
(потрёпан).
dog food *n* корм* для собáк.
dogged ['dɔgɪd] *adj* упóрный.
doggy bag ['dɔgɪ-] *n* пакéт, в котóром
посетúтели ресторáна мóгут унестú
объéдки.
dogma ['dɔgmə] *n* дóгма.
dogmatic [dɔg'mætɪk] *adj* догматúческий*.
do-gooder [duː'gudəʳ] *n* (*pej*) благо-
дéтель(ница) *m(f).*
dogsbody ['dɔgzbɔdɪ] *n* (*BRIT: inf*) ишáк*.

doily ['dɔɪlɪ] *n* ажýрная *or* кружевнáя
салфéточка.
doing ['duɪŋ] *n:* **this is your** ~ э́то твоúх рук
дéло.
doings ['duɪŋz] *npl* (*activities*) дéйствия *ntpl.*
do-it-yourself ['duːɪtjɔː'sɛlf] *n* сдéлай сам.
doldrums ['dɔldrəmz] *npl:* **to be in the** ~
(*person*) хандрúть (*impf*); (*business*)
находúться (*impf*) в упáдке.
dole [dəul] *n* (*BRIT*) посóбие по безрабóтице; **to**
be on the ~ получáть (*impf*) посóбие по
безрабóтице
► **dole out** *vt* (*food, money*) раздавáть*
(раздáть* *perf*).
doleful ['dəulful] *adj* скóрбный* (скóрбен).
doll [dɔl] *n* (*also US: inf*) кýкла*.
dolled up *adj* (*inf*) разря́женный (разря́жен).
dollar ['dɔləʳ] *n* дóллар.
dollar area *n* дóлларовая зóна.
dollop ['dɔləp] *n:* **a** ~ (**of**) лóжка (+*gen*).
dolly ['dɔlɪ] *n* кýкла.
Dolomites ['dɔləmaɪts] *npl:* **the** ~
Доломúтовые Áльпы *fpl.*
dolphin ['dɔlfɪn] *n* дельфúн.
domain [də'meɪn] *n* (*sphere*) сфéра; (*empire*)
владéние.
dome [dəum] *n* кýпол*.
domestic [də'mɛstɪk] *adj* домáшний*; (*trade,*
politics) внýтренний*; (*happiness*) семéйный.
domesticated [də'mɛstɪkeɪtɪd] *adj* (*animal*)
одомáшенный*; (*person*) домовúтый
(домовúт); **he's very** ~ он óчень домовúтый.
domesticity [dəumɛs'tɪsɪtɪ] *n* домáшняя жизнь
f.
domestic servant *n* прислýга.
domicile ['dɔmɪsaɪl] *n* (*LAW, ADMIN*) мéсто*
жúтельства.
dominant ['dɔmɪnənt] *adj* (*share, role*)
преобладáющий, доминúрующий; (*partner*)
влáстный* (влáстен).
dominate ['dɔmɪneɪt] *vt* доминúровать (*impf*)
над +*instr.*
domination [dɔmɪ'neɪʃən] *n* преобладáние,
доминúрование.
domineering [dɔmɪ'nɪərɪŋ] *adj* влáстный*
(влáстен).
Dominican Republic [də'mɪnɪkən-] *n:* **the** ~ ~
Доминикáнская Респýблика.
dominion [də'mɪnɪən] *n* (*territory*) доминиóн;
(*authority*): **to have** ~ **over** влады́чествовать
(*impf*) над +*instr.*
domino ['dɔmɪnəu] (*pl* ~**es**) *n* доминó *nt ind.*
domino effect *n* цепнáя реáкция.
dominoes ['dɔmɪnəuz] *n* (*game*) доминó *nt ind.*
don [dɔn] *n* (*BRIT: SCOL*) преподавáтель(ница)
m(f) ◆ *vt* (*clothing*) надевáть (надéть* *perf*).
donate [də'neɪt] *vt:* **to** ~ (**to**) жéртовать
(пожéртвовать *perf*) (+*dat or* на +*acc*).
donation [də'neɪʃən] *n* пожéртвование.
done [dʌn] *pp of* **do**.
donkey ['dɔŋkɪ] *n* осёл*.

donkey-work [ˈdɒŋkɪwəːk] *n* (*BRIT: inf*) ишáчья рабóта.
donor [ˈdəʊnəʳ] *n* (*MED: of blood, heart etc*) дóнор; (*to charity*) жéртвователь(ница) *m(f)*.
donor card *n* дóнорская кáрточка.
don't [dəʊnt] = **do not**.
donut [ˈdəʊnʌt] *n* (*US*) = **doughnut**.
doodle [ˈduːdl] *vi* чúркать (*impf*) ♦ *n* карáкули* *fpl*.
doom [duːm] *n* рок ♦ *vt*: **the plan was ~ed to failure** план был обечён на провáл.
doomsday [ˈduːmzdeɪ] *n* стрáшный суд*.
door [dɔːʳ] *n* дверь* *f*; **to go from ~ to ~** ходúть* (*impf*) от дóма к дóму.
doorbell [ˈdɔːbɛl] *n* (двернóй) звонóк*.
door handle *n* двернáя рýчка*; (*of car*) рýчка* двéри.
doorman [ˈdɔːmən] *irreg n* (*in hotel*) швейцáр; (*in block of flats*) приврáтник.
doormat [ˈdɔːmæt] *n* (*mat*) половúк*; (*inf: person*) трáпка* *m/f*.
doorpost [ˈdɔːpəʊst] *n* дpepнóй косáк*.
doorstep [ˈdɔːstɛp] *n* порóг; **on the ~** на порóге.
door-to-door [ˈdɔːtəˈdɔːʳ] *adj*: **~ salesman** агéнт, сбывáющий товáры и различные виды услýг непосрéдственно в домáх потребúтелей; **~ selling** продáжа вразнóс.
doorway [ˈdɔːweɪ] *n* двернóй проём; **in the ~** в дверáх.
dope [dəʊp] *n* (*inf: drug*) наркóтик; (: *in sport*) дóпинг; (: *person*) придýрок*; (: *information*) секрéтная информáция ♦ *vt* (*horse, person*) водúть* (вестú* *perf*) наркóтик +*dat*.
dopey [ˈdəʊpɪ] *adj* (*inf: groggy*) одурмáненный; (: *stupid*) одурéлый.
dormant [ˈdɔːmənt] *adj* (*plant*) покóящийся; (*volcano*) спящий; (*idea, report etc*): **to lie ~** бездéйствовать (*impf*).
dormer [ˈdɔːməʳ] *n* (*also: ~* **window**) мансáрдное окнó*.
dormice [ˈdɔːmaɪs] *npl of* **dormouse**.
dormitory [ˈdɔːmɪtrɪ] *n* (*room*) óбщая спáльня*; (*US: building*) общежúтие.
dormouse [ˈdɔːmaʊs] (*pl* **dormice**) *n* (*ZOOL*) сóня.
Dors *abbr* (*BRIT: POST*) = **Dorset**.
DOS [dɒs] *n abbr* (*COMPUT: = disk operating system*) ДОС = *дúсковая операцибнная систéма*.
dosage [ˈdəʊsɪdʒ] *n* дóза.
dose [dəʊs] *n* дóза; (*BRIT: bout*) прúступ ♦ *vt*: **~ o.s. with** принимáть (принять* *perf*); **I had a ~ of flu last week** на прóшлой недéле у меня был грипп.
dosh [dɒʃ] *n* (*inf*) бáбки *pl*.
dosser [ˈdɒsəʳ] (*inf*) *n* (*tramp*) бомж; (*layabout*) разгильдяй.

doss house [ˈdɒs-] *n* (*BRIT: inf*) ночлéжка*.
dossier [ˈdɒsɪeɪ] *n* досьé *nt ind*.
DOT *n abbr* (*US: = Department of Transportation*) департáмент путéй сообщéния.
dot [dɒt] *n* тóчка*; (*speck*) пятнышко* ♦ *vt*: **~ted with** усéянный (усéян) +*instr*; **on the ~** минýта в минýту.
dote [dəʊt]: **to ~ on** *vt fus* душú не чáять (*impf*) в +*prp*.
dot-matrix printer [dɒtˈmeɪtrɪks-] *n* (*COMPUT*) мáтричный прúнтер.
dotted line [ˈdɒtɪd-] *n* пунктúрная лúния; **to sign on the ~ ~** (*fig*) окончáтельно соглашáться (согласúться *perf*).
dotty [ˈdɒtɪ] *adj* (*inf*) трóнутый.
double [ˈdʌbl] *adj* двойнóй ♦ *adv*: **to cost ~** стóить (*impf*) вдвóе дорóже ♦ *n* двойнúк* ♦ *vt* удвáивать (удвóить *perf*); (*fold in two*) склáдывать (сложúть* *perf*) вдвóе ♦ *vi* (*increase*) удвáиваться (удвóиться *perf*); **to ~ as** (*person*) совмещáть (*impf*) обязанности +*gen*; (*object*) служúть* (*impf*) одноврéменно +*instr*; **he ~s as a servant in this play** он тáкже исполнáет роль слугú в этом спектáкле; **on the ~**, (*BRIT*) **at the ~** бегóм; **~ five two six (5526)** (*BRIT: TEL*) пятьдесят пять двáдцать шесть; **it's spelt with a ~ "l"** пúшется с двумя „л"

▶ **double back** *vi* развóрáчиваться (развернýться *perf*) и идтú* (пойтú* *perf*) назáд
▶ **double up** *vi* (*bend over*) скóрчиваться (скóрчиться *perf*); (*share room*) делúть (*impf*).
double bass *n* контрабáс.
double bed *n* двуспáльная кровáть *f*.
double bend *n* (*BRIT*) извúлистая дорóга.
double blind *n* сравнúтельный эксперимéнт, в котóром лúчность учáстников неизвéстна ни эксперимéнтатором ни эксперимéнтúруемым.
double-breasted [ˈdʌblˈbrɛstɪd] *adj* двубóртный.
double-check [ˈdʌblˈtʃɛk] *vti* перепроверáть (перепровéрить *perf*).
double cream (*BRIT*) *n* густы́е слúвки* *pl*.
doublecross [ˈdʌblˈkrɒs] *vt* надувáть (надýть *perf*).
doubledecker [ˈdʌblˈdɛkəʳ] *n* (*also:* **double-decker bus**) двухэтáжный автóбус.
double exposure *n* (*PHOT*) двойнáя экспозúция.
double glazing [-ˈgleɪzɪŋ] *n* (*BRIT*) двойны́е рáмы *fpl*.
double indemnity *n* (*US*) вы́плата страховóй сýммы в двойнóм размéре.
double-page spread [ˈdʌblpeɪdʒ-] *n* двойнóй разворóт (*газéты, журнáла*).
double parking *n* парковка вторы́м рядом.

---

double room n (*in hotel*) двухме́стный но́мер*; (*in house*) ко́мната на двои́х.
doubles ['dʌblz] n (*TENNIS*) па́ры fpl.
double time n двойна́я опла́та.
double whammy [-'wæmɪ] n двойно́й уда́р.
doubly ['dʌblɪ] adv вдвойне́.
doubt [daut] n сомне́ние ◆ vt сомнева́ться (*impf*); (*mistrust*) сомнева́ться (*impf*) в +prp, недоверя́ть (*impf*) +dat; **without (a)** ~ без сомне́ния; **I** ~ **it (very much)** я (о́чень) сомнева́юсь; **I** ~ **if** or **whether she'll come** я сомнева́юсь, что она́ придёт; **I don't** ~ **that** ... я не сомнева́юсь, что ....
doubtful ['dautful] adj сомни́тельный; **to be** ~ **about sth** сомнева́ться (*impf*) насчёт чего-н; **I'm a bit** ~ я неско́лько сомнева́юсь; **it's** ~ **whether** ... сомни́тельно, что ....
doubtless ['dautlɪs] adv несомне́нно.
dough [dəu] n те́сто; (*inf: money*) ба́бки* fpl.
doughnut ['dəunʌt] (*US* **donut**) n по́нчик.
dour [duə'] adj суро́вый* (суро́в).
douse [dauz] vt: **to** ~ **(with)** облива́ть (обли́ть* perf) (+instr) ◆ vt (*extinguish*) туши́ть (потуши́ть perf), гаси́ть (погаси́ть perf).
dove [dʌv] n го́лубь m.
Dover ['dəuvə'] n Дувр; **Straits of** ~ Па-де--Кале́ m ind.
dovetail ['dʌvteɪl] vi (*fig*) совпада́ть (совпа́сть* perf); (*schedules*) дополня́ть (допо́лнить perf) друг дру́га ◆ n (*TECH*): ~ **joint** ла́сточкин хвост*.
dowager ['dauədʒə'] n престаре́лая све́тская да́ма; **the** ~ **duchess** вдо́вствующая герцоги́ня.
dowdy ['daudɪ] adj неказ́и́стый* (неказ́и́ст).
Dow-Jones average ['dau'dʒəunz-] n (*US*) и́ндекс веду́щих монопо́лий До́у Джо́нса.
down [daun] n пух*; (*hill*) холм* ◆ adv (*motion*) вниз; (*position*) внизу́ ◆ prep (*towards lower level*) (вниз) с +gen or по +dat; (*movement along*) (вдоль) по +dat ◆ vt (*inf: drink*) прогла́тывать (проглоти́ть* perf); ~ **there** вон там; ~ **here** вот здесь; **the price of meat is** ~ цена́ на мя́со упа́ла; **I've got it** ~ **somewhere** у меня́ где́-то это запи́сано; **to pay £2** ~ плати́ть* (заплати́ть* perf) пе́рвый взнос £2; **England is two goals** ~ А́нглия прои́грывает на два очка́; **to** ~ **tools** (*BRIT*) прекраща́ть (прекрати́т perf) рабо́тать; ~ **with the government!** доло́й прави́тельство!
down-and-out ['daunəndaut] n бездо́мный(-ая) m(f) adj.
down-at-heel ['daunət'hiːl] adj (*shoes etc*) сто́птанный (сто́птан); (*appearance, person*) потрёпанный* (потрёпан).
downbeat ['daunbiːt] n (*MUS*) си́льная до́ля ◆ adj небре́жный* (небре́жен).
downcast ['daunkɑːst] adj (*person*) пода́вленный* (пода́влен); (*eyes*) опу́щенный (опу́щен).
downer ['daunə'] n (*inf: drug*) успокои́тельное

nt adj; **to be on a** ~ (*depressed*) быть* (*impf*) в депре́ссии.
downfall ['daunfɔːl] n паде́ние; (*from drinking, gambling etc*) ги́бель f.
downgrade ['daungreɪd] vt: **he was** ~**d** его́ пони́зили.
downhearted ['daun'hɑːtɪd] adj упа́вший* ду́хом.
downhill ['daun'hɪl] n (*also:* ~ **race**: *SKIING*) скоростно́й спуск ◆ adv (*face, look*) вниз; **to go** ~ (*person*) идти́* (пойти́* perf) под го́ру; (*road*) идти́* (пойти́* perf) под укло́н; (*car*) е́хать* (пое́хать* perf) под го́ру; (*fig: person*) кати́ться (покати́ться perf) по накло́нной пло́скости; (: *business*) идти́* (пойти́* perf) под го́ру or под укло́н.
Downing Street ['daunɪŋ-] n (*BRIT: POL*) Да́унинг Стрит.
download ['daunləud] vt (*COMPUT*) загружа́ть (загрузи́ть* perf) (*в па́мять*).
down-market ['daun'mɑːkɪt] adj (*product*) дешёвый.
down payment n пе́рвый взнос.
downplay ['daunpleɪ] vt (*US*) преуменьша́ть (преуме́ньшить perf).
downpour ['daunpɔː'] n ли́вень* m.
downright ['daunraɪt] adj я́вный; (*refusal*) по́лный ◆ adv соверше́нно.
Downs [daunz] npl (*BRIT: GEO*): **the** ~ Да́унз (*известко́вые холмы́ на ю́ге А́нглии*).
Down's syndrome [daunz-] n синдро́м Да́уна.
downstairs ['daun'stɛəz] adv (*position*) внизу́; (*motion*) вниз.
downstream ['daunstriːm] adv вниз по тече́нию.
downtime ['dauntaɪm] n просто́й.
down-to-earth ['dauntuː'əːθ] adj (*person*) просто́й; (*solution*) практи́чный* (практи́чен).
downtown ['daun'taun] adv (*position*) в це́нтре; (*motion*) в центр ◆ adj (*US*): ~ **Chicago** центр Чика́го.
downtrodden ['dauntrɔdn] adj (*person*) заби́тый (заби́т).
down under adv (*BRIT: inf: Australia etc*) друго́й коне́ц све́та (*Австра́лия и Но́вая Зела́ндия*); **he lives** ~ ~ он живёт на друго́м конце́ све́та.
downward ['daunwəd] adj напра́вленный вниз ◆ adv вниз; **a** ~ **trend** понижа́тельная тенде́нция.
downwards ['daunwədz] adv = **downward**.
dowry ['daurɪ] n прида́ное nt adj.
doz. abbr = **dozen**.
doze [dəuz] vi дрема́ть* (*impf*)
▶ **doze off** vi задрема́ть* (*perf*).
dozen ['dʌzn] n дю́жина; **a** ~ **books** дю́жина книг; **80 pence a** ~ 80 пе́нсов за дю́жину; ~**s of** деся́тки +gen.
DPh n abbr (= *Doctor of Philosophy*) до́ктор

философии.
DPhil *n abbr* (= *Doctor of Philosophy*) до́ктор
философии.
DPP *n abbr* (*BRIT*: = *Director of Public
Prosecutions*) Генера́льный прокуро́р.
DPT *n abbr* (= *diphtheria, pertussis, tetanus*)
коклю́шно-дифтери́йно-столбня́чная
вакци́на.
DPW *n abbr* (*US*: = *Department of Public Works*)
Департа́мент обще́ственного
строи́тельства.
Dr *abbr* = **doctor**.
Dr. *abbr* (*in street names*) = **Drive**.
dr *abbr* (*COMM*) = **debtor**.
drab [dræb] *adj* (*weather, building, clothes*)
се́рый (сер), уны́лый (уны́л).
draft [drɑ:ft] *n* (*first version*) чернови́к*,
набро́сок*; (*POL*: *of bill*) прое́кт; (*COMM*)
тра́тта; (*US*: *MIL*) призы́в ♦ *vt* (*plan*)
составля́ть (соста́вить* *perf*); (*write roughly*)
писа́ть* (написа́ть* *perf*) на́черно; *see also*
draught.
draftsman ['drɑ:ftsmən] *irreg n* (*US*) =
draughtsman.
draftsmanship ['drɑ:ftsmənʃɪp] *n* (*US*) =
draughtsmanship.
drag [dræg] *vt* тащи́ть* (*impf*); (*lake, pond*)
прочёсывать (прочеса́ть* *perf*) ♦ *vi* (*time, a
concert etc*) тяну́ться* (*impf*) ♦ *n* (*inf*: *person*)
обу́за; (: *task*) бре́мя* *nt*; (*NAUT, AVIAT*)
лобово́е сопротивле́ние; **in** ~ в костю́ме
же́нщины (*о мужчи́не*)
▸ **drag away** *vt*: **to** ~ **sb away (from)**
отта́скивать (оттащи́ть* *perf*) кого́-н (от
+*gen*)
▸ **drag on** *vi* тяну́ться* (*impf*).
dragnet ['drægnɛt] *n* не́вод*, бре́день* *m*; (*fig*)
обла́ва.
dragon ['drægn] *n* драко́н.
dragonfly ['drægənflaɪ] *n* стрекоза́*.
dragoon [drə'gu:n] *n* драгу́н* ♦ *vt*: **to** ~ **sb into
sth** (*BRIT*) втя́гивать (втяну́ть* *perf*) кого́-н во
что-н.
drain [dreɪn] *n* (*in street*) водосто́к, водоотво́д;
(*on resources, manpower*) уте́чка*; (*on health,
energy*) расхо́д ♦ *vt* (*land, glass etc*) осуша́ть
(осуши́ть* *perf*); (*vegetables*) слива́ть (слить*
perf) ♦ *vi* (*liquid*) стека́ть (стечь* *perf*); **I feel**
~**ed** я истощён; **I feel** ~**ed of emotion** у меня́
истощи́лись эмо́ции.
drainage ['dreɪnɪdʒ] *n* (*system*) канализа́ция;
(*process*) дрена́ж, осуше́ние.
drainboard ['dreɪnbɔ:d] *n* (*US*) = **draining board**.
draining board ['dreɪnɪŋ-] (*US* **drainboard**) *n*
су́шка*.
drainpipe ['dreɪnpaɪp] *n* водосто́чная труба́*.
drake [dreɪk] *n* се́лезень* *m*.
dram [dræm] *n* (*SCOTTISH*: *drink*) глото́к* (*о

спиртно́м*).
drama ['drɑ:mə] *n* (*also fig*) дра́ма.
dramatic [drə'mætɪk] *adj* драмати́ческий*;
(*increase etc*) ре́зкий*; (*change*)
рази́тельный.
dramatically [drə'mætɪklɪ] *adv* драмати́чески;
(*increase, change*) ре́зко.
dramatist ['dræmətɪst] *n* драмату́рг.
dramatize ['dræmətaɪz] *vt* (*exaggerate*)
драматизи́ровать (*impf*/*perf*); (*adapt*: *for TV,
cinema*) инсцени́ровать (*impf*/*perf*).
drank [dræŋk] *pt of* **drink**.
drape [dreɪp] *vt* драпирова́ть (задрапирова́ть
perf).
drapes [dreɪps] *npl* (*US*: *curtains*) занаве́ски* *fpl*.
drastic ['dræstɪk] *adj* (*measure*) реши́тельный*
(реши́телен); (*change*) коренно́й.
drastically ['dræstɪklɪ] *adv* (*change*) коренны́м
о́бразом; (*reduce*) ре́зко.
draught [drɑ:ft] (*US* **draft**) *n* (*of air*) сквозня́к*;
(*NAUT*) оса́дка*; (*of chimney*) тя́га; **on** ~ (*beer*)
из бо́чки.
draught beer *n* бо́чковое пи́во.
draughtboard ['drɑ:ftbɔ:d] *n* (*BRIT*) ша́шечная
доска́*.
draughts [drɑ:fts] *n* (*BRIT*) ша́шки* *pl*.
draughtsman ['drɑ:ftsmən] *irreg* (*US*
draftsman) *n* чертёжник(-ица).
draughtsmanship ['drɑ:ftsmənʃɪp] (*US*
draftsmanship) *n* черче́ние; (*art*) иску́сство
черче́ния.
draw [drɔ:] (*pt* **drew**, *pp* **drawn**) *vt* (*ART*)
рисова́ть (*impf*); (*TECH*) черти́ть* (*impf*); (*pull*:
cart) тащи́ть* (*impf*); (: *curtains*) заё́ргивать
(задё́рнуть* *perf*); (*gun, tooth*) вырыва́ть
(вы́рвать* *perf*); (*attention*) привлека́ть
(привле́чь* *perf*); (*crowd*) собира́ть (собра́ть*
perf); (*money*) снима́ть (снять* *perf*); (*wages*)
получа́ть (получи́ть* *perf*) ♦ *vi* (*SPORT*) игра́ть
(сыгра́ть* *perf*) в ничью́ ♦ *n* (*SPORT*) ничья́*;
(*lottery*) лотере́я; (: *of teams*) жеребьёвка*; **to**
~ **near** приближа́ться (прибли́зиться* *perf*);
to ~ **to a close** подходи́ть* (подойти́* *perf*) к
концу́; **to** ~ **a conclusion** де́лать (сде́лать
perf) вы́вод; **to** ~ **a comparison between**
проводи́ть* (провести́* *perf*) сравне́ние
ме́жду +*instr*
▸ **draw back** *vi*: **to** ~ **back (from)** отпря́нуть
(*perf*) (от +*gen*)
▸ **draw in** *vi* (*BRIT*: *car*) остана́вливаться
(останови́ться* *perf*); (: *train*) подъезжа́ть
(подъе́хать* *perf*); (*nights*) станови́ться*
(стать* *perf*) длинне́е
▸ **draw on** *vt* испо́льзовать (*impf*/*perf*)
▸ **draw out** *vi* (*lengthen*) растя́гивать
(растяну́ть* *perf*) ♦ *vt* (*money*) снима́ть
(снять* *perf*)
▸ **draw up** *vi* (*train, bus etc*) подъезжа́ть

---

* marks translations which have irregular inflections. The Russian-English side of the dictionary gives inflectional information.

(подъе́хать* *perf*) ◆ *vt* (*chair etc*) придвига́ть (придви́нуть* *perf*); (*document*) составля́ть (соста́вить* *perf*).

drawback ['drɔːbæk] *n* недоста́ток*.

drawbridge ['drɔːbrɪdʒ] *n* подъёмный *or* разводно́й мост*.

drawee [drɔːˈiː] *n* трасса́т.

drawer [drɔː] *n* я́щик.

drawing ['drɔːɪŋ] *n* (*picture*) рису́нок*; (*act*) рисова́ние.

drawing board *n* чертёжная доска́*; **to go back to the ~ ~** (*fig*) всё начина́ть (нача́ть* *perf*) снача́ла.

drawing pin *n* (*BRIT*) (канцеля́рская) кно́пка*.

drawing room *n* гости́ная *f adj*.

drawl [drɔːl] *n* протя́жное произноше́ние ◆ *vi* протя́гивать (протяну́ть* *perf*).

drawn [drɔːn] *pp of* **draw** ◆ *adj* изму́ченный* (изму́чен).

drawstring ['drɔːstrɪŋ] *n* шнур* (*кото́рый проде́рнут во что́-нибудь*).

dread [drɛd] *n* у́жас ◆ *vt* боя́ться (*impf*) +*gen*.

dreadful ['drɛdful] *adj* ужа́сный*; **I feel ~!** я ужа́сно себя́ чу́вствую!

dream [driːm] (*pt, pp* **dreamed** *or* **dreamt**) *n* сон*; (*ambition*) мечта́ ◆ *vt*: **I must have ~t it** мне, наве́рное, э́то присни́лось ◆ *vi* ви́деть (*impf*) сон*; (*wish*) мечта́ть (*impf*); **I had a ~ about you** ты мне присни́лся; **sweet ~s!** прия́тных сновиде́ний!

▶ **dream up** *vt* выду́мывать (вы́думать *perf*).

dreamer ['driːmə] *n* (*fig*) мечта́тель*(ница) *m(f)*.

dreamt [drɛmt] *pt, pp of* **dream**.

dream world *n*: **to live in a ~ ~** жить* (*impf*) в приду́манном ми́ре.

dreamy ['driːmɪ] *adj* (*expression, person*) мечта́тельный* (мечта́телен); (*music*) убаю́кивающий.

dreary ['drɪərɪ] *adj* тоскли́вый (тоскли́в).

dredge [drɛdʒ] *vt* драги́ровать (*impf*/*perf*)

▶ **dredge up** *vt* драги́ровать (*impf*/*perf*); (*fig: facts*) выта́скивать (вы́тащить *perf*).

dredger ['drɛdʒə] *n* (*ship*) землечерпа́лка, дра́га; (*BRIT: also*: **sugar ~**) сосу́д с ма́ленькими ды́рочками в кры́шке для са́хара.

dregs [drɛgz] *npl* муть* *fsg*; **~ of society** отбро́сы о́бщества.

drench [drɛntʃ] *vt*: **to be ~ed** мо́кнуть (промо́кнуть* *perf*); **~ed to the skin** насквозь промо́кший.

Dresden ['drɛzdən] *n* Дре́зден.

dress [drɛs] *n* (*frock*) пла́тье*; (*no pl: clothing*) оде́жда ◆ *vt* одева́ть (оде́ть* *perf*); (*wound*) перевя́зывать (перевяза́ть* *perf*) ◆ *vi* одева́ться (оде́ться* *perf*); **she ~es very well** она́ о́чень хорошо́ одева́ется; **to ~ a shop window** оформля́ть (офо́рмить* *perf*) витри́ну; **to get ~ed** одева́ться (оде́ться* *perf*)

▶ **dress up** *vi* наряжа́ться (наряди́ться* *perf*).

dress circle *n* (*BRIT*) бельэта́ж.

dress designer *n* модельёр.

dresser ['drɛsə] *n* (*BRIT*) ку́хонный шкаф*; (*US*: *chest of drawers*) туале́тный сто́лик; (*also*: **window ~**) оформи́тель(ница) *m(f)* витри́н.

dressing ['drɛsɪŋ] *n* (*MED*) повя́зка*; (: *process*) перевя́зка*; (*CULIN*) запра́вка*.

dressing gown *n* (*BRIT*) хала́т.

dressing room *n* (*THEAT*) артисти́ческая убо́рная *f adj*; (*SPORT*) раздева́лка*.

dressing table *n* туале́тный сто́лик.

dressmaker ['drɛsmeɪkə] *n* портни́ха.

dressmaking ['drɛsmeɪkɪŋ] *n* поши́в же́нского пла́тья.

dress rehearsal *n* генера́льная репети́ция.

dressy ['drɛsɪ] *adj* (*inf*) наря́дный* (наря́ден).

drew [druː] *pt of* **draw**.

dribble ['drɪbl] *vi* (*liquid*) ка́пать* (*impf*); (*baby*) пуска́ть (пусти́ть* *perf*) слю́ни; (*SPORT*) вести́* (*impf*) мяч ◆ *vt* (*ball*) вести́* (*impf*).

dried [draɪd] *adj* (*fruit*) сушёный*; (*milk*) сухо́й.

drier ['draɪə] *n* = **dryer**.

drift [drɪft] *n* (*of current etc*) ско́рость *f*; (*of snow*) зано́с, сугро́б; (*meaning*) смысл ◆ *vi* (*boat*) дрейфова́ть (*impf*); **sand/snow had ~ed over the road** доро́гу занесло́ песко́м/сне́гом; **to let things ~** пуска́ть (пусти́ть* *perf*) всё на самотёк; **to ~ apart** расходи́ться* (разойти́сь* *perf*); **I get** *or* **catch your ~** я понима́ю куда́ Вы кло́ните.

drifter ['drɪftə] *n* (*person*) бродя́га *m/f*.

driftwood ['drɪftwud] *n* плавни́к.

drill [drɪl] *n* (*drill bit*) сверло́*; (*machine*) дрель *f*; (: *for mining etc*) бура́в*; (*MIL*) уче́ние ◆ *vt* (*hole*) сверли́ть (просверли́ть* *perf*); (*troops*) муштрова́ть (вы́муштровать *perf*); (*pupils*) ната́скивать (натаска́ть *perf*) ◆ *vi* (*for oil*) бури́ть (*impf*).

drilling ['drɪlɪŋ] *n* (*for oil*) буре́ние.

drilling rig *n* бурова́я устано́вка*.

drily ['draɪlɪ] *adv* = **dryly**.

drink [drɪŋk] (*pt* **drank**, *pp* **drunk**) *n* напи́ток*; (*alcoholic drink*) (спиртно́й) напи́ток*; (*sip*) глото́к* ◆ *vt* пить* (вы́пить* *perf*) ◆ *vi* пить* (*impf*); **to have a ~** попи́ть* (*perf*); (*alcohol*) вы́пить* (*perf*); **a ~ of water** глото́к* воды́; (*glassful*) стака́н воды́; **would you like something to ~?** хоти́те чего́-нибудь вы́пить?; **we had ~s before lunch** мы вы́пили пе́ред обе́дом

▶ **drink in** *vt* упива́ться (*impf*) +*instr*.

drinkable ['drɪŋkəbl] *adj* (*water*) питьево́й; (*palatable: wine etc*) неплохо́й (непло́х), прия́тный* (прия́тен).

drink-driving ['drɪŋk'draɪvɪŋ] *n* вожде́ние в нетре́звом состоя́нии ◆ *cpd*: **they are running a ~ campaign** они́ веду́т кампа́нию про́тив води́телей, садя́щихся за руль в нетре́звом состоя́нии.

drinker ['drɪŋkə] *n* (*of alcohol*) пью́щий*(-ая)

m(f) adj.

drinking ['drɪŋkɪŋ] *n* питьё*; **there was a lot of ~ at the party** на вечери́нке мно́го пи́ли.

drinking fountain *n* питьево́й фонта́нчик.

drinking water *n* питьева́я вода́*.

drip [drɪp] *n* ка́панье; (*one drip*) ка́пля*; (*MED*) ка́пельница ♦ *vi* (*water, rain*) ка́пать* (*impf*); **the tap is ~ping** кран течёт; **the washing is ~ping** с белья́ ка́пает.

drip-dry ['drɪp'draɪ] *adj:* ~ **material** ткань, кото́рой даю́т стечь по́сле сти́рки и кото́рую не гла́дят.

drip-feed ['drɪpfiːd] *vt* (*MED*) влива́ть (влить* *perf*) че́рез ка́пельницу ♦ *n:* **to be on a ~** быть* (*impf*) на ка́пельнице.

dripping ['drɪpɪŋ] *n* (*CULIN*) (то́плёный) жир ♦ *adj* (*very wet*) мо́крый (мокр); **I'm ~** с меня́ течёт; ~ **wet** соверше́нно мо́крый (мокр).

drive [draɪv] (*pt* **drove**, *pp* **driven**) *n* (*journey*) пое́здка*; (*also:* ~**way**) подъе́зд; (*energy*) напо́ристость *f*; (*campaign*) кампа́ния; (*FOOTBALL*) уда́р; (*TENNIS*) дра́йв; (*COMPUT: also:* **disk** ~) дисково́д; (*in street names*): **Rose D~** Ро́уз Драйв ♦ *vt* (*vehicle*) води́ть*/вести́* (*impf*); (*TECH: machine, motor, wheel*) приводи́ть* (привести́* *perf*) в движе́ние; (*animal*) гнать* (*impf*); (*ball*) ударя́ть (уда́рить *perf*) (пло́ско); (*nail, stake etc*): **to ~ sth into sth** вбива́ть (вбить* *perf*) что-н в что-н ♦ *vi* (*AUT: at controls*) води́ть* (вести́* *perf*) (маши́ну); (*travel*) е́здить*/е́хать* (*impf*); **to go for a ~** пое́хать (*perf*) поката́ться; **the town is three hours' ~ from London** го́род в трёх часа́х езды́ от Ло́ндона; **left-/right-hand ~** (*AUT*) пра́во-/левосторо́нее управле́ние; **front-/rear-wheel ~** (*AUT*) приво́д на пере́дние/за́дние колёса; **economy ~** борьба́ за эконо́мию; **he ~s a taxi** он во́дит такси́; **to ~ at 50 km an hour** е́здить*/е́хать* (*impf*) со ско́ростью 50 км в час; **to ~ sb home/to the airport** отвози́ть* (отвезти́* *perf*) кого́-н домо́й/в аэропо́рт; **to ~ sb mad** своди́ть* (свести́* *perf*) кого́-н с ума́; **to ~ sb to sth** доводи́ть* (довести́* *perf*) кого́-н до чего́-н; **what are you driving at?** куда́ Вы кло́ните?

▸ **drive off** *vt* (*repel*) отбра́сывать (отбро́сить* *perf*)

▸ **drive out** *vt* (*force to leave*) вытесня́ть (вы́теснить *perf*); (*person, animal, evil*) выгоня́ть (вы́гнать* *perf*).

drive-by shooting ['draɪvbaɪ-] *n* стрельба́ из дви́жущегося автомоби́ля.

drive-in ['draɪvɪn] *n* (*esp US: restaurant*) кафе́, где мо́жно купи́ть еду́ не выходя́ из маши́ны.

drivel ['drɪvl] *n* (*inf*) чушь *f*.

driven ['drɪvn] *pp of* **drive**.

driver ['draɪvə^r] *n* води́тель *m*; (*of train*)

машини́ст.

driver's license ['draɪvəz-] *n* (*US*) води́тельские права́ *nt pl*.

driveway ['draɪvweɪ] *n* подъе́зд.

driving ['draɪvɪŋ] *n* вожде́ние ♦ *adj:* ~ **rain** проливно́й дождь* *m*; ~ **snow** мете́ль *f*.

driving belt *n* приводно́й реме́нь* *m*.

driving force *n* дви́жущая си́ла.

driving instructor *n* инстру́ктор* по вожде́нию.

driving lesson *n* уро́к по вожде́нию.

driving licence *n* (*BRIT*) води́тельские права́ *ntpl*.

driving mirror *n* зе́ркало за́днего ви́да.

driving school *n* автошко́ла.

driving test *n* экза́мен по вожде́нию.

drizzle ['drɪzl] *n* моро́ся́щий дождь* *m* ♦ *vi* мороси́ть (*impf*).

droll [drəul] *adj* заба́вный.

dromedary ['drɒmədərɪ] *n* одного́рбый верблю́д.

drone [drəun] *n* (*noise*) гуде́ние; (*male bee*) тру́тень* *m* ♦ *vi* (*bee*) жужжа́ть (*impf*); (*engine etc*) гуде́ть (*impf*); (*also:* ~ **on**) бубни́ть (*impf*).

drool [druːl] *vi:* **he is ~ing** у него́ теку́т слю́ни; **to ~ over sth/sb** (*inf*) роня́ть (*impf*) слю́ни по по́воду чего́-н/кого́-н.

droop [druːp] *vi* (*flower, head*) поника́ть (пони́кнуть *perf*); (*shoulders*) ссуту́литься (*perf*).

drop [drɒp] *n* (*of water*) ка́пля*; (*reduction*) паде́ние; (*fall: distance*) расстоя́ние (све́рху вниз); (*also:* **parachute** ~) сбра́сывание на парашю́те (*продово́льствия, боеприпа́сов*) ♦ *vt* (*allow to fall: object*) роня́ть (урони́ть* *perf*); (*eyes*) опуска́ть (опусти́ть* *perf*); (*voice, price*) понижа́ть (пони́зить* *perf*); (*set down from car*) выса́живать (вы́садить* *perf*); (*exclude*) исключа́ть (исключи́ть *perf*) ♦ *vi* па́дать (упа́сть* *perf*); (*wind*) стиха́ть (сти́хнуть* *perf*); ~**s** *npl* (*MED*) ка́пли *fpl*; **cough ~s** леденцы́ от ка́шля; **there is a 30 ft ~ from the window to the ground** высота́ от окна́ до земли́ 30 фу́тов; **there's been a ~ of 10% in profits** при́быль упа́ла на 10%; **to ~ anchor** броса́ть (бро́сить* *perf*) я́корь; **to ~ sb a line** черкну́ть* (*perf*) кому́-н не́сколько стро́чек

▸ **drop in** *vi* (*inf*): **to ~ in on sb** загля́дывать (загляну́ть* *perf*) к кому́-н

▸ **drop off** *vi* (*go to sleep*) засыпа́ть (засну́ть *perf*) ♦ *vt* (*passenger*) выса́живать (вы́садить* *perf*)

▸ **drop out** *vi* (*of game, agreement*) выходи́ть* (вы́йти* *perf*); **to ~ out of college** броса́ть (бро́сить* *perf*) ко́лледж.

droplet ['drɒplɪt] *n* ка́пелька*.

drop-out ['drɒpaut] *n* (*from society*)

---

* marks translations which have irregular inflections. The Russian-English side of the dictionary gives inflectional information.

отщепе́нец*(-нка*); (*SCOL*) недоу́чка* *m/f*.
dropper ['drɔpə'] *n* пипе́тка*.
droppings ['drɔpɪŋz] *npl* помёт *msg*.
dross [drɔs] *n* шлак; (*rubbish*) му́сор.
drought [draut] *n* за́суха.
drove [drəuv] *pt of* **drive** ♦ *n*: ~**s of people** то́лпы
fpl люде́й.
drown [draun] *vt* топи́ть* (утопи́ть* *perf*); (*also*:
~ **out**: *sound, voice*) заглуша́ть (заглуши́ть
perf) ♦ *vi* тону́ть* (утону́ть* *perf*).
drowse [drauz] *vi* дрема́ть* (*impf*).
drowsy ['drauzɪ] *adj* со́нный.
drudge [drʌdʒ] *n* (*person*) рабо́тяга *m/f*.
drudgery ['drʌdʒəɪ] *n* тяжёлая, ну́дная
рабо́та; **housework is sheer** ~ рабо́та по
до́му – тяжёлый труд.
drug [drʌg] *n* (*MED*) лека́рство; (*narcotic*)
нарко́тик ♦ *vt* (*person, animal*) вводи́ть*
(ввести́* *perf*) нарко́тик +*dat*; **to be on** ~**s**
быть* (*impf*) на нарко́тиках; **hard/soft** ~**s**
си́льные/сла́бые нарко́тики.
drug addict *n* наркома́н.
druggist ['drʌgɪst] *n* (*US*) апте́карь *m*.
drug peddler *n* торго́вец* нарко́тиками.
drugstore ['drʌgstɔ:'] *n* (*US*) апте́ка (*иногда с
небольши́м кафе́*).
drum [drʌm] *n* бараба́н; (*for oil*) бо́чка* ♦ *vi*
бараба́нить (*impf*); ~**s** *npl* (*kit*) уда́рные
инструме́нты *mpl*
▶ **drum up** *vt* (*support*) призыва́ть (призва́ть*
perf).
drummer ['drʌmə'] *n* (*with military band*)
бараба́нщик; (*in rock group*) уда́рник.
drum roll *n* бараба́нный бой*.
drumstick ['drʌmstɪk] *n* бараба́нная па́лочка*;
(*of chicken*) но́жка*.
drunk [drʌŋk] *pp of* **drink** ♦ *adj* пья́ный* ♦ *n*
пья́ный*(-ая) *m(f) adj*; (*also*: ~**ard**) пья́ница
m/f; **to get** ~ напива́ться (напи́ться* *perf*); ~
driving вожде́ние в нетре́звом состоя́нии.
drunken ['drʌŋkən] *adj* пья́ный* (пьян); ~
driving вожде́ние в нетре́звом состоя́нии.
drunkenness ['drʌŋkənnɪs] *n* пья́нство.
dry [draɪ] *adj* (*also fig*) сухо́й* (сух); (*lake,
riverbed*) вы́сохший; (*humour*) сде́ржанный*
(сде́ржан); (*lecture, subject*) скучны́й*
(ску́чен) ♦ *vt* (*clothes, ground*) суши́ть*
(вы́сушить *perf*); (*surface*) вытира́ть
(вы́тереть* *perf*) ♦ *vi* (*paint, washing*) со́хнуть
(вы́сохнуть *perf*); **on** ~ **land** на су́ше; **to** ~
one's hands/eyes вытира́ть (вы́тереть* *perf*)
ру́ки/глаза́; **to** ~ **one's hair** (*with towel*)
вытира́ть (вы́тереть* *perf*) во́лосы; (*with
hairdryer*) суши́ть* (вы́сушить *perf*) во́лосы;
to ~ **the dishes** вытира́ть (вы́тереть* *perf*)
посу́ду
▶ **dry up** *vi* (*river, well*) высыха́ть (вы́сохнуть*
perf); (*resources, speaker*) иссяка́ть
(исся́кнуть* *perf*).
dry clean *vt* чи́стить* (почи́стить* *perf*) (*в
химичи́стке*).

dry cleaner *n* рабо́тник химчи́стки.
dry-cleaner's ['draɪ'kli:nəz] *n* химчи́стка*.
dry-cleaning ['draɪ'kli:nɪŋ] *n* хими́ческая
чи́стка.
dry dock *n* (*NAUT*) сухо́й док.
dryer ['draɪə'] *n* (*for clothes*) суши́лка*.
dry goods *npl* (*US*) галантере́я *fsg* и тка́ни *fpl*.
dry ice *n* сухо́й* лёд*.
dryly ['draɪlɪ] *adv* ирони́чно.
dryness ['draɪnɪs] *n* су́хость *f*.
dry rot *n* суха́я гниль *f* (*боле́знь древеси́ны*).
dry run *n* (*fig: inf*) холосто́й прого́н.
dry ski slope *n* склон с иску́сственным
покры́тием.
DSc *n abbr* (= *Doctor of Science*) до́ктор
естествозна́ния.
DSS *n abbr* (*BRIT*: = *Department of Social
Security*) Министе́рство социа́льного
обеспе́чения.
DST *abbr* (*US*: = *Daylight Saving Time*) ле́тнее
вре́мя* *nt*.
DT *n abbr* (*COMPUT*: = *data transmission*)
переда́ча да́нных.
DTI *n abbr* (*BRIT*: = *Department of Trade and
Industry*) Министе́рство промы́шленности
и торго́вли.
DTP *n abbr* = **desktop publishing**.
DT's *npl abbr* (*inf*: = *delirium tremens*) бе́лая
горя́чка; **to have the** ~ страда́ть (*impf*) бе́лой
горя́чкой.
dual ['djuəl] *adj* двойно́й; (*function, number*)
дво́йственный.
dual carriageway *n* (*BRIT*) шоссе́ *nt ind*.
dual nationality *n* двойно́е гражда́нство.
dual-purpose ['djuəl'pə:pəs] *adj* двойно́го
назначе́ния.
dubbed [dʌbd] *adj* (*CINEMA*) дубли́рованный
(дубли́рован); (*nicknamed*) про́званный
(про́зван).
dubious ['dju:bɪəs] *adj* сомни́тельный; **I'm very
~ about it** у меня́ серьёзные сомне́ния на
э́тот счёт.
Dublin ['dʌblɪn] *n* Ду́блин.
Dubliner ['dʌblɪnə'] *n* ду́блинец*(-нка*).
duchess ['dʌtʃɪs] *n* герцоги́ня*.
duck [dʌk] *n* у́тка* ♦ *vi* (*also*: ~ **down**)
пригиба́ться (пригну́ться *perf*) ♦ *vt* (*blow*)
увёртываться (уверну́ться *perf*) от +*gen*;
(*responsibility etc*) ува́ливать (увильну́ть
perf) от +*gen*.
duckling ['dʌklɪŋ] *n* утёнок*.
duct [dʌkt] *n* (*ELEC*) ка́бельный кана́л; (*TECH*)
трубопрово́д; (*ANAT*) прото́к, кана́л.
dud [dʌd] *adj* (*object, tool*) бесполе́зный*
(бесполе́зен); (*grenade*) неразорва́вшийся*;
(*BRIT*: *cheque*) недействи́тельный ♦ *n* (*note,
coin*) подде́лка*.
due [dju:] *adj* (*expected*) предполага́емый;
(*attention, consideration, owed*):
I am ~ £20 мне должны́ *or* прилага́ются £20
♦ *n*: **to give sb his** (*or* **her**) ~ отдава́ть*

(отда́ть* *perf*) кому́-н до́лжное ◆ *adv*: ~ **north** пря́мо на се́вер; ~**s** *npl* (*for club, union*) взно́сы *mpl*; (*in harbour*) порто́вые сбо́ры *mpl*; **in** ~ **course** в своё вре́мя; ~ **to** из-за +*gen*; **he is** ~ **to go** он до́лжен идти́; **the rent is** ~ **on the 30th** за кварти́ру должно́ быть* запла́чено 30-ого числа́; **the train is** ~ **at 8** по́езд до́лжен прийти́ в 8 часо́в; **she is** ~ **back tomorrow** она́ должна́ верну́ться за́втра; **I am** ~ **6 days' leave** мне причита́ется 6 свобо́дных дней.

due date *n* срок произво́дства платежа́.

duel ['djuəl] *n* дуэ́ль *f*; (*fig*) поеди́нок.

duet [dju:'ɛt] *n* дуэ́т.

duff [dʌf] *adj* (*BRIT: inf*) дрянно́й*
▶ **duff up** *vt* (*inf*) колошма́тить* (исколошма́тить* *perf*).

duffel bag ['dʌfl-] *n* су́мка-мешо́к*.

duffel coat *n* шерстяно́е пальто́ с капюшо́ном.

duffer ['dʌfə'] *n* (*inf*) тупи́ца *m/f*.

dug [dʌg] *pt, pp of* **dig**.

dugout ['dʌgaut] *n* (*canoe*) челно́к; (*shelter*) земля́нка.

duke [dju:k] *n* ге́рцог.

dull [dʌl] *adj* (*light, colour*) ту́склый* (тускл); (*weather, day*) се́рый* (сер); (*sound*) глухо́й* (глух); (*pain, wit*) тупо́й* (туп); (*event*) ску́чный* (ску́чен) ◆ *vt* притупля́ть (притупи́ть* *perf*).

duly ['dju:lɪ] *adv* (*properly*) до́лжным о́бразом; (*on time*) своевре́менно.

dumb [dʌm] *adj* (*mute*) немо́й*; (*inf: pej: stupid: person*) тупо́й*; (: *idea*) дура́цкий*; **to be struck** ~ онеме́ть (*perf*).

dumbbell ['dʌmbɛl] *n* (*SPORT*) ганте́ль *f*.

dumbfounded [dʌm'faundɪd] *adj* ошеломлённый (ошеломлён).

dummy ['dʌmɪ] *n* (*tailor's model*) манеке́н; (*TECH*) маке́т; (*COMM*) моде́ль *f*; (*SPORT*) обма́нный приём; (*BRIT: for baby*) со́ска*, пусты́шка* ◆ *adj* (*bullet*) холосто́й*; (*firm*) фикти́вный.

dummy run *n* испыта́тельный прого́н.

dump [dʌmp] *n* (*also: rubbish* ~) сва́лка*; (*inf: pej: place*) дыра́*; (*MIL*) полево́й склад ◆ *vt* (*put down*) сва́ливать (свали́ть* *perf*), выбра́сывать (вы́бросить* *perf*); (*car*) броса́ть (бро́сить* *perf*); (*COMPUT: data*) выгружа́ть (вы́грузить* *perf*), сбра́сывать (сбро́сить* *perf*); **to be down in the** ~**s** (*inf*) хандри́ть (*impf*); "**no** ~**ing**" "сва́лка му́сора запрещена́".

dumpling ['dʌmplɪŋ] *n* (*CULIN*) клёцка*.

dumpy ['dʌmpɪ] *adj* кря́жистый* (кря́жист).

dunce [dʌns] *n* тупи́ца *m/f*.

Dundee [dʌn'di:] *n* Данди́ *m ind*.

Dundonian [dʌn'dəʊnɪən] *adj* го́рода Данди́ ◆

n жи́тель(ница) *m(f)* го́рода Данди́.

dune [dju:n] *n* дю́на.

dung [dʌŋ] *n* наво́з*.

dungarees [dʌŋgə'ri:z] *npl* комбинезо́н *msg*.

dungeon ['dʌndʒən] *n* темни́ца.

dunk [dʌŋk] *vt* мака́ть (макну́ть *perf*).

Dunkirk [dʌn'kə:k] *n* Данке́рк.

duo ['dju:əu] *n* дуэ́т.

duodenal [dju:əu'di:nl] *adj* дуодена́льный; ~ **ulcer** я́зва двенадцатипе́рстной кишки́.

duodenum [dju:əu'di:nəm] *n* двенадцатипе́рстная кишка́.

dupe [dju:p] *n* проста́к*, простофи́ля* *m/f* ◆ *vt* надува́ть (наду́ть* *perf*).

duplex ['dju:plɛks] *n* (*US: also:* ~ **house**) одна́ из часте́й двухкварти́рного до́ма; (*also:* ~ **apartment**) двухэта́жная кварти́ра.

duplicate [*n, adj* 'dju:plɪkət, *vt* 'dju:plɪkeɪt] *n* (*of document, key etc*) дублика́т, ко́пия ◆ *adj* (*key, copy etc*) запасно́й ◆ *vt* копи́ровать (скопи́ровать *perf*); (*repeat*) дубли́ровать (продубли́ровать *perf*); **in** ~ в двойно́м экземпля́ре.

duplicating machine ['dju:plɪkeɪtɪŋ-] *n* копирова́льная маши́на.

duplicator ['dju:plɪkeɪtə'] *n* копирова́льная маши́на.

duplicity [dju:'plɪsɪtɪ] *n* двули́чие.

Dur *abbr* (*BRIT: POST*) = **Durham**.

durability [djuərə'bɪlɪtɪ] *n* про́чность *f*.

durable ['djuərəbl] *adj* про́чный.

duration [djuə'reɪʃən] *n* продолжи́тельность *f*.

duress [djuə'rɛs] *n*: **under** ~ под давле́нием.

Durex® ['djuərɛks] *n* (*BRIT*) ма́рка презервати́в.

during ['djuərɪŋ] *prep* (*in the course of*) во вре́мя +*gen*, в тече́ние +*gen*; (*from beginning to end*) в тече́ние +*gen*.

Dushanbe [du:'ʃɑ:nbɪ] *n* Душанбе́ *m ind*.

dusk [dʌsk] *n* су́мерки *pl*.

dusky ['dʌskɪ] *adj* (*light*) су́меречный*; (*room*) тёмный.

dust [dʌst] *n* пыль* *f* ◆ *vt* вытира́ть (вы́тереть* *perf*) пыль с +*gen*; (*cake etc*): **to** ~ **with** посыпа́ть (посы́пать* *perf*) +*instr*
▶ **dust off** *vt* (*also fig*) стря́хивать (стряхну́ть *perf*) пыль с +*gen*.

dustbin ['dʌstbɪn] *n* (*BRIT*) му́сорное ведро́*.

dustbin liner *n* целофа́новая прокла́дка для му́сорного ведра́.

duster ['dʌstə'] *n* (*cloth*) тря́пка* для пы́ли.

dust jacket *n* суперобло́жка*.

dustman ['dʌstmən] *irreg n* (*BRIT*) му́сорщик.

dustpan ['dʌstpæn] *n* сово́к* для му́сора.

dusty ['dʌstɪ] *adj* пы́льный*.

Dutch [dʌtʃ] *adj* голла́ндский* ◆ *n* (*LING*) голла́ндский* язы́к*; **the** ~ *npl* (*people*) голла́ндцы* *mpl*; **they decided to go** ~ (*inf*) они́ реши́ли, что ка́ждый пла́тит за себя́.

---

* marks translations which have irregular inflections. The Russian-English side of the dictionary gives inflectional information.

Dutch auction *n* "голла́ндский* аукцио́н" (*аукцио́н со сниже́нием цен, пока́ не найдётся покупа́тель*).
Dutchman ['dʌtʃmən] *irreg n* голла́ндец*.
Dutchwoman ['dʌtʃwumən] *irreg n* голла́ндка*.
dutiable ['djuːtɪəbl] *adj* (*COMM: goods*) облага́емый по́шлиной.
dutiful ['djuːtɪful] *adj* (*son, daughter*) послу́шный* (послу́шен); (*husband, wife*) поко́рный* (поко́рен); (*employee*) исполни́тельный* (исполни́телен).
duty ['djuːtɪ] *n* (*responsibility*) обя́занность *f*; (*obligation*) долг; (*tax*) по́шлина; **duties** *npl* (*functions*) обя́занности *fpl*; **to make it one's ~ to do** счита́ть (посчита́ть *perf*) свои́м до́лгом +*infin*; **to pay ~ on sth** плати́ть* (заплати́ть* *perf*) по́шлину за что-н; **on ~** на дежу́рстве; **off ~** вне слу́жбы.
duty-free ['djuːtɪ'friː] *adj* беспо́шлинный; **~ shop** магази́н това́ров не облага́емых по́шлиной.
duty officer *n* (*MIL*) дежу́рный офице́р.
duvet ['duːveɪ] *n* (*BRIT*) пухо́вое одея́ло.
DV *abbr* (= *Deo volente*) Бог даст.
DVLA *n abbr* (*BRIT*) = *Driver and Vehicle Licensing Authority*.
DVLC *n abbr* (*BRIT*) = *Driver and Vehicle Licensing Centre*.
DVM *n abbr* (*US*: = *Doctor of Veterinary Medicine*) до́ктор ветерина́рных нау́к.
dwarf [dwɔːf] (*pl* **dwarves**) *n* ка́рлик ♦ *vt* де́лать (сде́лать *perf*) кро́хотным.
dwarves [dwɔːvz] *npl of* **dwarf**.
dwell [dwɛl] (*pt, pp* **dwelt**) *vi* прожива́ть (прожи́ть* *perf*)
▸ **dwell on** *vt fus* заде́рживаться (задержа́ться* *perf*) на +*prp*.
dweller ['dwɛləʳ] *n* жи́тель(ница) *m(f)*, обита́тель(ница) *m(f)*; **city ~** городско́й(-а́я) жи́тель(ница).
dwelling ['dwɛlɪŋ] *n* (*house*) жили́ще.
dwelt [dwɛlt] *pt, pp of* **dwell**.
dwindle ['dwɪndl] *vi* (*interest, attendance*) сокраща́ться (сократи́ться* *perf*).
dwindling ['dwɪndlɪŋ] *adj* (*strength, interest*) убыва́ющий; (*resources, supplies*) сокраща́ющийся.
dye [daɪ] *n* (*for hair, cloth*) краси́тель *m*, кра́ска* ♦ *vt* кра́сить* (покра́сить* *perf*).
dyestuffs ['daɪstʌfs] *npl* краси́тели *mpl*.
dying ['daɪɪŋ] *adj* умира́ющий; (*moments, words*) предсме́ртный.
dyke [daɪk] *n* (*BRIT: wall*) да́мба; (*channel*) кана́ва; (*causeway*) на́сыпь *f*.
dynamic [daɪ'næmɪk] *adj* (*leader, force*) динами́чный.
dynamics [daɪ'næmɪks] *n or npl* (*TECH*) дина́мика *fsg*.
dynamite ['daɪnəmaɪt] *n* динами́т ♦ *vt* взрыва́ть (взорва́ть* *perf*) динами́том.
dynamo ['daɪnəməu] *n* (*ELEC*) дина́мо-маши́на.
dynasty ['dɪnəstɪ] *n* дина́стия.
dysentery ['dɪsntrɪ] *n* дизентери́я.
dyslexia [dɪs'lɛksɪə] *n* дисле́ксия.
dyslexic [dɪs'lɛksɪk] *adj* дислекти́ческий ♦ *n* дисле́ктик.
dyspepsia [dɪs'pɛpsɪə] *n* диспепси́я.

~ E, e ~

E, e [iː] n (letter) 5-ая бу́ква англи́йского алфави́та; (SCOL: mark) ≈ о́чень пло́хо.

E [iː] n (MUS) ми nt ind.

E abbr (= east) В= восто́к ◆ n abbr (= Ecstacy) "Экста́з" (нарко́тик).

E111 n abbr (also: form ~) спра́вка, обеспе́чивающая медици́нскую по́мощь за преде́лами Великобрита́нии.

ea. abbr = each.

E.A. n abbr (US) = educational age.

each [iːtʃ] adj ка́ждый ◆ pron (each one) ка́ждый; ~ **other** друг дру́га; **they hate ~ other** они́ ненави́дят друг дру́га; **they don't talk to ~ other** они́ не разгова́ривают друг с дру́гом; **they think about ~ other** они́ ду́мают друг о дру́ге; **they are jealous of ~ other** они́ зави́дуют друг дру́гу; ~ **day** ка́ждый де́нь; **they have two books ~** у ка́ждого из них по две кни́ги; **they cost £5 ~** они́ сто́ят £5 шту́ка or за шту́ку; ~ **of us** ка́ждый из нас.

eager ['iːgəʳ] adj (keen) нетерпели́во ожида́ющий; **to be ~ for** жа́ждать (impf) +gen; **he is ~ to ...** он по́лон жела́ния +infin ....

eagerly ['iːgəlɪ] adv с воодушевле́нием; (awaited) с нетерпе́нием.

eagle ['iːgl] n орёл*.

ear [ɪəʳ] n (ANAT) у́хо*; (of corn) ко́лос*; **up to one's ~s in debt/work/paint** по́ уши в долгу́/в рабо́те/в кра́ске; **to give sb a thick ~** дать* (perf) кому́-н в у́хо; **we'll play it by ~** (fig) мы посмо́трим по ситуа́ции.

earache ['ɪəreɪk] n боль f в у́хе; **I have ~** у меня́ боли́т у́хо.

eardrum ['ɪədrʌm] n бараба́нная перепо́нка*.

earful ['ɪəful] n (inf): **to give sb an ~** устра́ивать (устро́ить perf) разно́с кому́-н.

earl [əːl] n (BRIT) граф.

earlier ['əːlɪəʳ] adj бо́лее ра́нний* ◆ adv ра́ньше; **I can't come any ~** я не могу́ прийти́ ра́ньше.

early ['əːlɪ] adv ра́но ◆ adj ра́нний*; (death, departure) преждевре́менный; (quick: reply) незамедли́тельный; (Christians, settlers) пе́рвый; ~ **in the morning** ра́но у́тром; **to have an ~ night** ра́но ложи́ться (лечь* perf) спать; **in the ~ spring**, ~ **in the spring** ра́нней весно́й; **in the ~ 19th century**, ~ **in the 19th century** в нача́ле 19-го ве́ка; **you need to take the ~ train** Вам на́до е́хать* ра́нним по́ездом; **you're ~!** Вы пришли́ ра́но!; **she's in her ~ forties** ей немно́го за со́рок; **at your earliest convenience** в ближа́йшее удо́бное для Вас вре́мя.

early retirement n: **to take ~ ~** ра́но уходи́ть* (уйти́* perf) на пе́нсию.

early warning system n (MIL) систе́ма ра́ннего предупрежде́ния.

earmark ['ɪəmɑːk] vt: **to ~ for** (funds) предназнача́ть (предназна́чить perf) для +gen.

earn [əːn] vt (salary) зараба́тывать (зарабо́тать perf); (interest) приноси́ть* (принести́* perf); (praise) заслу́живать (заслужи́ть* perf); **to ~ one's living** зараба́тывать (impf) на жизнь; **this ~ed him much praise, he ~ed much praise for this** э́то принесло́ ему́ мно́го похва́л, он заслужи́л мно́го похва́л за э́то; **he's ~ed his rest/reward** он заслужи́л свой о́тдых/свою́ награ́ду.

earned income [əːnd-] n (COMM) трудово́й дохо́д.

earnest ['əːnɪst] adj (person, manner) серьёзный* (серьёзен); (wish, desire) и́скренний* ◆ n (also: ~ **money**) зада́ток*; **in ~** всерьёз; **work on the tunnel soon began in ~** рабо́та по прокла́дке тунне́ля вско́ре начала́сь всерьёз; **is he in ~ about these proposals?** всерьёз ли он говори́т об э́тих предложе́ниях?

earnings ['əːnɪŋz] npl (personal) за́работок* msg; (of company etc) при́быль fsg.

ear nose and throat specialist n (MED) отоларинго́лог, врач* у́хо-го́рло-но́с.

earphones ['ɪəfəunz] npl нау́шники mpl.

earplugs ['ɪəplʌgz] npl заты́чки fpl для уше́й.

earring ['ɪərɪŋ] n серьга́*.

earshot ['ɪəʃɔt] n: **within/out of ~** в преде́лах/вне преде́лов слы́шимости.

earth [əːθ] n земля́*; (BRIT: ELEC) заземле́ние; (of fox) нора́* ◆ vt (BRIT: ELEC) заземля́ть (заземли́ть perf); **E~** (planet) Земля́*.

---

* marks translations which have irregular inflections. The Russian-English side of the dictionary gives inflectional information.

earthenware ['ə:θnwɛə'] *n* кера́мика, гонча́рные изде́лия *pl* ♦ *adj* гли́няный.

earthly ['ə:θlı] *adj* земно́й; ~ **paradise** земно́й рай*; **there is no ~ reason to think** ... нет ни мале́йшей причи́ны ду́мать ....

earthquake ['ə:θkweık] *n* землетрясе́ние.

earthshattering ['ə:θʃætərıŋ] *adj* (*surprising*) потряса́ющий* (потряса́ющ).

earth tremor *n* подзе́мный толчо́к*.

earthworks ['ə:θwə:ks] *npl* земляны́е рабо́ты *fpl*.

earthworm ['ə:θwə:m] *n* земляно́й червь* *m*.

earthy ['ə:θı] *adj* (*humour*) грубова́тый (грубова́т).

earwig ['ıəwıg] *n* ухове́ртка*.

ease [i:z] *n* лёгкость *f*; (*comfort*) поко́й* ♦ *vt* (*pain*) облегча́ть (облегчи́ть *perf*); (*problem*) уменьша́ть (уме́ньшить *perf*; (*tension*) ослабля́ть (осла́бить* *perf*); (*loosen: grip, belt*) отпуска́ть (отпусти́ть* *perf*) ♦ *vi* (*situation*) упроща́ться (упрости́ться* *perf*); (*pain, grief, grip*) слабе́ть (ослабе́ть *perf*); (*rain, snow*) станови́ться* (стать* *perf*) ти́ше; **to ~ sth into sth** вставля́ть (вста́вить* *perf*) что-н в что-н; **to ~ sth out of sth** выдвига́ть (вы́двинуть *perf*) что-н из чего́-н; **to ~ o.s. into** опуска́ться (опусти́ться *perf*) в +*acc*; **at ~!** (*MIL*) во́льно!; **with ~** с лёгкостью; **life of ~** жизнь в поко́е и дово́льстве

▶ **ease off** *vi* станови́ться* (стать* *perf*) ти́ше; (*slow down*) замедля́ться (заме́длиться *perf*)

▶ **ease up** *vi* = **ease off**.

easel ['i:zl] *n* мольбе́рт.

easily ['i:zılı] *adv* легко́; (*in a relaxed manner*) непринуждённо; (*without doubt*) несомне́нно.

easiness ['i:zınıs] *n* лёгкость *f*; (*of manner*) непринуждённость *f*.

east [i:st] *n* восто́к ♦ *adj* восто́чный ♦ *adv* на восто́к; **the E~** Восто́к.

Easter ['i:stə'] *n* па́сха ♦ *adj* пасха́льный.

Easter egg *n* (*painted*) пасха́льное яйцо́*; (*chocolate*) шокола́дное пасха́льное яйцо́*.

Easter Island *n* о́стров Па́схи.

easterly ['i:stəlı] *adj* восто́чный.

Easter Monday *n* ≈ све́тлый понеде́льник.

eastern ['i:stən] *adj* восто́чный; (*POL*) восто́чно-европе́йский; **E~ Europe** Восто́чная Евро́па; **the E~ bloc** (*formerly*) Восто́чно-Европе́йский* блок.

Easter Sunday *n* ≈ све́тлое *or* христо́во воскресе́нье.

East Germany *n* (*formerly*) Восто́чная Герма́ния.

eastward(s) ['i:stwəd(z)] *adv* на восто́к.

easy ['i:zı] *adj* лёгкий*; (*manner*) непринуждённый* ♦ *adv*: **to take it** *or* **things ~** не напряга́ться (*impf*); (*not worry*) не волнова́ться (*impf*); **payment on ~ terms** (*COMM*) платёж* на лёгких усло́виях; **that's easier said than done** ле́гче сказа́ть, чем

сде́лать; **I'm ~** (*inf*) мне всё равно́.

easy chair *n* удо́бное кре́сло*.

easy-going ['i:zı'gəuıŋ] *adj* с лёгким хара́ктером.

easy touch *n* (*inf*): **she is an ~ ~** её легко́ убеди́ть.

eat [i:t] (*pt* **ate**, *pp* **eaten**) *vt* есть* (съесть* *perf*) ♦ *vi* есть* (*impf*)

▶ **eat away** *vt* (*rock, metal*) разъеда́ть (разъе́сть* *perf*); (*savings*) съеда́ть (съесть* *perf*)

▶ **eat away at** *vt fus* = **eat away**

▶ **eat into** *vt fus* = **eat away**

▶ **eat out** *vi* (*in restaurant*) есть* (*impf*) в рестора́не

▶ **eat up** *vt* (*food*) доеда́ть (дое́сть* *perf*); **it ~s up electricity** э́то потребля́ет мно́го электроэне́ргии.

eatable ['i:təbl] *adj* съедо́бный*.

eaten ['i:tn] *pp of* **eat**.

eau de Cologne ['əudəkə'ləun] *n* одеколо́н*.

eaves [i:vz] *npl* (*of house*) карни́з *msg*.

eavesdrop ['i:vzdrɔp] *vi*: **to ~ (on)** подслу́шивать (подслу́шать *perf*).

ebb [ɛb] *n* отли́в ♦ *vi* (*tide, sea*) отлива́ть (*impf*); (*fig: also*: ~ **away**) угаса́ть (уга́снуть *perf*); **the ~ and flow** отли́в и прили́в; **to be at a low ~** (*fig*) находи́ться* (*impf*) в состоя́нии упа́дка.

ebb tide *n* отли́в.

ebony ['ɛbənı] *n* эбе́новое *or* чёрное де́рево.

ebullient [ı'bʌlıənt] *adj* по́лный* (по́лон) энтузиа́зма.

EC *n abbr* (= *European Community*) ЕС = *Европе́йское соо́бщество*.

eccentric [ık'sɛntrık] *adj* (*choice, views*) эксцентри́чный* ♦ *n* эксцентри́чный челове́к.

ecclesiastic(al) [ıkli:zı'æstık(l)] *adj* духо́вный.

ECG *n abbr* = **electrocardiogram**.

echo ['ɛkəu] (*pl* ~**es**) *n* э́хо *no pl* ♦ *vt* (*repeat*) вто́рить (*impf*) ♦ *vi* (*sound*) отдава́ться* (*impf*) э́хом; (*place*) воспроизводи́ть* (воспроизвести́* *perf*).

éclair ['eıklɛə'] *n* экле́р.

eclipse [ı'klıps] *n* затме́ние ♦ *vt* (*also fig*) затмева́ть (затми́ть* *perf*).

ECM *n abbr* (*US*: = *European Common Market*) О́бщий* ры́нок*.

eco- ['i:kəu] *prefix* э́ко-.

eco-friendly ['i:kəu'frɛndlı] *adj* экологи́чески безопа́сный* (безопа́сен).

ecological [i:kə'lɔdʒıkəl] *adj* экологи́ческий*.

ecologist [ı'kɔlədʒıst] *n* эко́лог.

ecology [ı'kɔlədʒı] *n* (*SCOL*) эколо́гия; (*environment*) окружа́ющая среда́.

economic [i:kə'nɔmık] *adj* экономи́ческий*; (*profitable*) рента́бельный* (рента́белен).

economical [i:kə'nɔmık] *adj* (*cheap to run*) экономи́чный* (экономи́чен); (*thrifty*) эконо́мный*.

economically [i:kə'nɔmıklı] *adv* эконо́мно;

(*regarding economics*) экономи́чески.
economics [i:kə'nɔmɪks] *n* экономика ◆ *npl* (*of project, situation*) экономи́ческий* расчёт *msg*.
economic warfare *n* экономи́ческая война́.
economist [ɪ'kɔnəmɪst] *n* экономи́ст.
economize [ɪ'kɔnəmaɪz] *vi* эконо́мить* (сэконо́мить* *perf*).
economy [ɪ'kɔnəmɪ] *n* экономика, хозя́йство; (*financial prudence*) эконо́мия; **economies of scale** (*COMM*) экономи́чность за счёт кру́пных объёмов опера́ций.
economy class *n* (*AVIAT*) наибо́лее дешёвые посадо́чные места́.
economy size *n* (*COMM*) больша́я упако́вка како́го-либо това́ра, сто́ящая деше́вле, чем ма́ленькая.
ecosystem ['i:kəusɪstəm] *n* экосисте́ма.
ECSC *n abbr* (= *European Coal & Steel Community*) европе́йское соо́бщество производи́телей угля́ и ста́ли.
ecstasy ['ɛkstəsɪ] *n* экста́з; **to go into ecstasies over** впада́ть (впасть* *perf*) в экста́з от +*gen*; **in ecstacy** в экста́зе.
ecstatic [ɛks'tætɪk] *adj* восто́рженный*.
ECT *n abbr* = **electroconvulsive therapy**.
ECU *n abbr* (= *European Currency Unit*) экю́ *ind*.
Ecuador ['ɛkwədɔ:ʳ] *n* Эквадо́р.
ecumenical [i:kju'mɛnɪkl] *adj* вселе́нский.
eczema ['ɛksɪmə] *n* экзе́ма.
eddy ['ɛdɪ] *n* (*of water*) водоворо́т; (*of air*) вихрь *m*.
edge [ɛdʒ] *n* край*; (*of knife etc*) остриё* ◆ *vt* (*trim*) окаймля́ть (окайми́ть* *perf*) ◆ *vi*: **to ~ forward** ме́дленно продвига́ться (продви́нуться *perf*); **on ~** (*fig*) = **edgy**; **to have the ~ on** име́ть (*impf*) преиму́щество пе́ред +*instr*; **to ~ past** проти́снуться (*perf*); **~ away from** отходи́ть* (отойти́* *perf*) бочко́м от +*gen*; **to ~ up** (*COMM*) незначи́тельно изменя́ться.
edgeways ['ɛdʒweɪz] *adv*: **he couldn't get a word in ~** он не мог слове́чка вверну́ть *or* сло́ва вста́вить.
edging ['ɛdʒɪŋ] *n* кайма́*.
edgy ['ɛdʒɪ] *adj* (*nervous, agitated*) раздражённый*.
edible ['ɛdɪbl] *adj* съедо́бный* (съедо́бен).
edict ['i:dɪkt] *n* ука́з.
edifice ['ɛdɪfɪs] *n* вели́чественное зда́ние.
edifying ['ɛdɪfaɪŋ] *adj* поучи́тельный* (поучи́телен).
Edinburgh ['ɛdɪnbərə] *n* Эдинбург.
edit ['ɛdɪt] *vt* (*text, newspaper, COMPUT*) редакти́ровать (отредакти́ровать *perf*); (*book*) гото́вить* (подгото́вить* *perf*) к печа́ти; (*film, broadcast*) монти́ровать (смонти́ровать *perf*).

edition [ɪ'dɪʃən] *n* (*of book*) изда́ние; (*of newspaper, TV programme*) вы́пуск.
editor ['ɛdɪtəʳ] *n* реда́ктор*; **foreign/political ~** (*PRESS*) реда́ктор* отде́ла зарубе́жных новосте́й/поли́тики.
editorial [ɛdɪ'tɔ:rɪəl] *adj* редакцио́нный ◆ *n* передови́ца, передова́я статья́*.
EDP *n abbr* (*COMPUT*) = **electronic data processing**.
EDT *abbr* (*US*) = *Eastern Daylight Time*.
educate ['ɛdjukeɪt] *vt* (*teach*) дава́ть* (дать* *perf*) образова́ние +*dat*; (*instruct*) просвеща́ть (просвети́ть* *perf*); **to be ~d at ...** получа́ть (получи́ть *perf*) образова́ние в +*prp*.
educated guess ['ɛdjukeɪtɪd-] *n* дога́дка располага́ющего предвари́тельной информа́цией.
education [ɛdju'keɪʃən] *n* (*schooling*) образова́ние; (*teaching*) обуче́ние; (*knowledge*) образо́ванность *f*; **primary or** (*US*) **elementary/secondary ~** нача́льное/сре́днее образова́ние.
educational [ɛdju'keɪʃənl] *adj* (*institution*) уче́бный; (*staff*) преподава́тельский; (*policy, practice*) уче́бный, воспита́тельный*; (*toy*) обуча́ющий; **~ system** систе́ма образова́ния; **~ technology** техни́ческие сре́дства обуче́ния.
Edwardian [ɛd'wɔ:dɪən] *adj* эпо́хи англи́йского короля́ Эдуа́рда VII.
EE *abbr* = **electrical engineer**.
EEC *n abbr* (= *European Economic Community*) ЕЭС= *Европе́йское экономи́ческое соо́бщество*.
EEG *n abbr* = **electroencephalogram**.
eel [i:l] *n* у́горь* *m*.
EENT *n abbr* (*US*: *MED*: = *eye, ear, nose and throat*) ≈ у́хо-го́рло-нос.
EEOC *n abbr* (*US*: = *Equal Employment Opportunity Commission*) коми́ссия ра́вных возмо́жностей при на́йме на рабо́ту.
eerie ['ɪərɪ] *adj* жу́ткий*.
EET *abbr* (= *Eastern European Time*) восточноевропе́йское вре́мя* *nt*.
efface [ɪ'feɪs] *vt* (*erase*) стира́ть (стере́ть* *perf*); **to ~ o.s.** держа́ться* (*impf*) в тени́.
effect [ɪ'fɛkt] *n* (*result*) эффе́кт, после́дствие; (*impression*) впечатле́ние, эффе́кт ◆ *vt* (*carry out*) производи́ть (произвести́* *perf*); **~s** *npl* (*property*) иму́щество *ntsg*; (*THEAT, CINEMA*) эффе́кты *mpl*; **to take ~** (*drug*) де́йствовать (поде́йствовать *perf*); (*law*) вступа́ть (вступи́ть* *perf*) в си́лу; **to put into ~** осуществля́ть (осуществи́ть* *perf*); **to have an ~ on sb/sth** де́йствовать (поде́йствовать *perf*) на кого́-н/что-н; **in ~** в су́щности; **his letter is to the ~ that ...** суть его́ письма́ заключа́ется в том, что ....

---

* marks translations which have irregular inflections. The Russian-English side of the dictionary gives inflectional information.

effective [ɪ'fɛktɪv] *adj* (*successful*) эффекти́вный* (эффекти́вен); (*actual*) действи́тельный*; **to become ~** (*LAW*) входи́ть* (войти́* *perf*) в си́лу; **~ date** да́та вступле́ния в си́лу.

effectively [ɪ'fɛktɪvlɪ] *adv* (*successfully*) эффекти́вно; (*in reality*) факти́чески.

effectiveness [ɪ'fɛktɪvnɪs] *n* (*success*) эффекти́вность *f*.

effeminate [ɪ'fɛmɪnɪt] *adj* женоподо́бный* (женоподо́бен).

effervescent [ɛfə'vɛsnt] *adj* (*drink*) шипу́чий*.

efficacy ['ɛfɪkəsɪ] *n* эффекти́вность *f*.

efficiency [ɪ'fɪʃənsɪ] *n* (*see adj*) эффекти́вность *f*; делови́тость *f*.

efficiency apartment *n* (*US*) кварти́ра, соединя́ющая в себе́ спа́льную, гости́ную и иногда́ ку́хню.

efficient [ɪ'fɪʃənt] *adj* (*organization, method, machine*) эффекти́вный* (эффекти́вен); (*person*) делови́тый.

efficiently [ɪ'fɪʃəntlɪ] *adv* эффекти́вно.

effigy ['ɛfɪdʒɪ] *n* (*dummy*) чу́чело; (*image*) изображе́ние.

effluent ['ɛfluənt] *n* сток, жи́дкие отхо́ды *mpl*.

effort ['ɛfət] *n* (*attempt*) попы́тка*; (*exertion, concerted attempt*) уси́лие; **to make an ~ to do** прикла́дывать (приложи́ть *perf*) уси́лия, чтобы +*infin*.

effortless ['ɛfətlɪs] *adj* (*achievement*) не тре́бующий уси́лий; (*style*) лёгкий*.

effrontery [ɪ'frʌntərɪ] *n* наха́льство, на́глость *f*; **to have the ~ to do** име́ть (*impf*) наха́льство *or* на́глость, чтобы +*infin*.

effusive [ɪ'fjuːsɪv] *adj* экспанси́вный*.

EFL *n abbr* (*SCOL*) = *English as a Foreign Language.*

EFTA ['ɛftə] *n abbr* (= *European Free Trade Association*) ЕАСТ= *Европе́йская ассоциа́ция свобо́дной торго́вли.*

e.g. *adv abbr* (*for example*: = *exempli gratia*) наприме́р.

egalitarian [ɪgælɪ'tɛərɪən] *adj* эгалита́рный ♦ *n* (*person*) побо́рник(-ица) равнопра́вия.

egg [ɛg] *n* яйцо́; **hard-boiled/soft-boiled ~** яйцо́ вкруту́ю/всмя́тку

▸ **egg on** *vt* (*encourage*) подстрека́ть (подстрекну́ть *perf*).

egg cup *n* рю́мка* для яйца́.

eggplant ['ɛgplɑːnt] *n* (*esp US*) баклажа́н*.

eggshell ['ɛgʃɛl] *n* яи́чная скорлупа́* ♦ *adj* (*paint*) ма́товый.

egg timer *n* та́ймер.

egg white *n* яи́чный бело́к*.

egg yolk *n* яи́чный желто́к*.

ego ['iːgəu] *n* (*self-esteem*) самолю́бие.

egoism ['ɛgəuɪzəm] *n* эгои́зм.

egoist ['ɛgəuɪst] *n* эгои́ст(ка*).

egotism ['ɛgəutɪzəm] *n* эготи́зм.

egotist ['ɛgəutɪst] *n* эготи́ст(ка*).

ego trip *n* (*pej*) самоублаже́ние.

Egypt ['iːdʒɪpt] *n* Еги́пет*.

Egyptian [ɪ'dʒɪpʃən] *adj* еги́петский* ♦ *n* египтя́нин*(-я́нка*).

eiderdown ['aɪdədaun] *n* (*quilt*) ва́тное одея́ло.

eight [eɪt] *n* во́семь*; *see also* **five.**

eighteen [eɪ'tiːn] *n* восемна́дцать*; *see also* **five.**

eighteenth [eɪ'tiːnθ] *adj* восемна́дцатый; *see also* **fifth.**

eighth [eɪtθ] *adj* восьмо́й ♦ *n* (*fraction*) восьма́я *f adj*; *see also* **fifth.**

eightieth ['eɪtɪəθ] *adj* восьмидеся́тый; *see also* **fifth.**

eighty ['eɪtɪ] *n* во́семьдесят*; *see also* **fifty.**

Eire ['ɛərə] *n* Э́йре *nt ind*.

EIS *n abbr* = *Educational Institute of Scotland.*

either ['aɪðə'] *adj* (*one or other*) любо́й (из двух); (*both, each*) ка́ждый ♦ *adv* та́кже ♦ *pron*: **~** (**of them**) любо́й (из них) ♦ *conj*: **~ yes or no** ли́бо "да", ли́бо "нет"; **on ~ side** на обе́их сторона́х; **I don't smoke – I don't ~** я не курю́ – я то́же; **I don't like ~** мне не нра́вится ни то, ни друго́е; **there was no sound from ~ of the flats** не́ бы́ло зву́ка ни из одно́й из кварти́р; **I haven't seen ~** я не ви́дел ни того́, ни друго́го.

ejaculation [ɪdʒækju'leɪʃən] *n* (*PHYSIOL*) эякуля́ция.

eject [ɪ'dʒɛkt] *vt* выбра́сывать (вы́бросить* *perf*); (*tenant*) выселя́ть (вы́селить *perf*); (*gatecrasher*) выгоня́ть (вы́гнать* *perf*) ♦ *vi* (*pilot*) катапульти́роваться (*impf/perf*).

ejector seat [ɪ'dʒɛktə-] *n* (*AVIAT*) катапульти́руемое кре́сло*.

Ekaterinburg [jɪkətɪrin'burk] *n* Екатеринбу́рг.

eke [iːk] *vt*: **to ~ out** (*income*) растя́гивать (растяну́ть *perf*); **to ~ out a living from** существова́ть (*impf*) за счёт +*gen*.

EKG *n abbr* (*US*) = **electrocardiogram.**

el [ɛl] *n abbr* (*US*: *inf*: = *elevated railroad*) надзе́мная желе́зная доро́га.

elaborate [*adj* ɪ'læbərɪt, *vb* ɪ'læbəreɪt] *adj* сло́жный* ♦ *vt* (*expand*) развива́ть (разви́ть* *perf*); (*refine*) тща́тельно разраба́тывать (разрабо́тать *perf*) ♦ *vi*: **to ~ on** (*idea, plan etc*) рассма́тривать (рассмотре́ть* *perf*) в дета́лях.

elapse [ɪ'læps] *vi* (*time*) проходи́ть* (пройти́* *perf*).

elastic [ɪ'læstɪk] *n* (*material*) рези́нка ♦ *adj* (*stretchy*) эласти́чный* (эласти́чен); (*adaptable*) ги́бкий* (ги́бок).

elastic band *n* (*BRIT*) рези́нка*.

elasticity [ɪlæs'tɪsɪtɪ] *n* эласти́чность *f*.

elated [ɪ'leɪtɪd] *adj*: **to be ~** быть* (*impf*) в припо́днятом настрое́нии.

elation [ɪ'leɪʃən] *n* припо́днятое настрое́ние.

elbow ['ɛlbəu] *n* ло́коть *m* ♦ *vt*: **to ~ one's way through the crowd** прота́лкиваться (*impf*) в толпе́.

elbow grease *n*: **a lot of ~ ~ is required** придётся хороше́нько потруди́ться.

elbowroom [ˈɛlbəʊrum] *n* просто́р.
elder [ˈɛldəʳ] *adj* (*brother, sister etc*) ста́рший* ♦ *n* (*tree*) бузина́; (*older person*): ~**s** ста́ршие *pl adj*.
elderly [ˈɛldəlɪ] *adj* пожило́й; **the** ~ *npl* ста́рые лю́ди *pl*, престаре́лые *pl adj*.
elder statesman *irreg n* заслу́женный полити́ческий* де́ятель *m*.
eldest [ˈɛldɪst] *adj* (*child*) (са́мый) ста́рший* ♦ *n* ста́рший*(-ая) *m(f) adj*.
elect [ɪˈlɛkt] *vt* избира́ть (избра́ть* *perf*) ♦ *adj*: **the president** ~ и́збранный президе́нт; **to** ~ **to do** (*choose*) предпочита́ть (предпоче́сть* *perf*) +*infin*.
election [ɪˈlɛkʃən] *n* (*voting*) вы́боры *pl*; (*installation*) избра́ние; **to hold an** ~ проводи́ть* (провести́* *perf*) вы́боры.
election campaign *n* избира́тельная кампа́ния.
electioneering [ɪlɛkʃəˈnɪərɪŋ] *n* агита́ция.
elector [ɪˈlɛktəʳ] *n* избира́тель(ница) *m(f)*.
electoral [ɪˈlɛktərəl] *adj* избира́тельный.
electoral college *n* колле́гия вы́борщиков.
electorate [ɪˈlɛktərɪt] *n*: **the** ~ избира́тели *mpl*.
electric [ɪˈlɛktrɪk] *adj* электри́ческий*.
electrical [ɪˈlɛktrɪkl] *adj* электри́ческий*; ~ **failure** отключе́ние то́ка.
electrical engineer *n* инжене́р-эле́ктрик.
electric blanket *n* одея́ло-гре́лка*.
electric chair *n* (*US*) электри́ческий* стул*.
electric cooker *n* электри́ческая плита́*.
electric current *n* электри́ческий* ток.
electric fire *n* (*BRIT*) электри́ческий* ками́н.
electrician [ɪlɛkˈtrɪʃən] *n* электромонтёр, эле́ктрик.
electricity [ɪlɛkˈtrɪsɪtɪ] *n* электри́чество ♦ *cpd* электри́ческий*; **to switch on/off the** ~ подключа́ть (подключи́ть* *perf*)/отключа́ть (отключи́ть* *perf*) электри́чество; ~ **bill** счёт* за электри́чество.
electricity board *n* (*BRIT*) управле́ние электрифика́ции.
electric light *n* электри́ческий* свет.
electric shock *n* уда́р то́ком.
electrify [ɪˈlɛktrɪfaɪ] *vt* (*fence, rail network*) электрифици́ровать (*impf/perf*); (*thrill*) электрифизова́ть (наэлектризова́ть* *perf*).
electro... [ɪˈlɛktrəʊ] *prefix* эле́ктро....
electrocardiogram [ɪˈlɛktrəˈkɑːdɪəɡræm] *n* электрокардиогра́мма.
electroconvulsive therapy [ɪˈlɛktrəkənˈvʌlsɪv-] *n* электрото́ковая терапи́я.
electrocute [ɪˈlɛktrəkjuːt] *vt* (*person: kill*) убива́ть (уби́ть* *perf*) электри́ческим то́ком; (: *injure*) ударя́ть (уда́рить *perf*) электри́ческим то́ком.
electrode [ɪˈlɛktrəʊd] *n* электро́д.

electroencephalogram [ɪˈlɛktrəʊɛnˈsɛfələɡræm] *n* электро-энцефалогра́мма.
electrolysis [ɪlɛkˈtrɔlɪsɪs] *n* электро́лиз.
electromagnetic [ɪˈlɛktrəmæɡˈnɛtɪk] *adj* электромагни́тный.
electron [ɪˈlɛktrɔn] *n* электро́н.
electronic [ɪlɛkˈtrɔnɪk] *adj* электро́нный.
electronic data processing *n* электро́нная обрабо́тка информа́ции.
electronic mail *n* (*COMPUT*) электро́нная по́чта.
electronics [ɪlɛkˈtrɔnɪks] *n* электро́ника.
electron microscope *n* электро́нный микроско́п.
electroplated [ɪˈlɛktrəˈpleɪtɪd] *adj* покры́тый мета́ллом с по́мощью электро́лиза.
electrotherapy [ɪˈlɛktrəˈθɛrəpɪ] *n* электро-терапи́я.
elegance [ˈɛlɪɡəns] *n* элега́нтность *f*.
elegant [ˈɛlɪɡənt] *adj* элега́нтный* (элега́нтен).
element [ˈɛlɪmənt] *n* (*also CHEM*) элеме́нт; (*of heater, kettle etc*) электронагрева́тельный элеме́нт; **the** ~**s** *npl* стихи́я *fsg*; **you are in your** ~ Вы в свое́й стихи́и.
elementary [ɛlɪˈmɛntərɪ] *adj* элемента́рный* (элемента́рен); (*school, education*) нача́льный.
elephant [ˈɛlɪfənt] *n* слон*(и́ха).
elevate [ˈɛlɪveɪt] *vt* (*in rank*) повыша́ть (повы́сить* *perf*); (*in importance*) возводи́ть (возвести́* *perf*); (*physically*) поднима́ть (подня́ть* *perf*).
elevated railroad [ˈɛlɪveɪtɪd-] *n* (*US*) надзе́мная желе́зная доро́га.
elevation [ɛlɪˈveɪʃən] *n* (*see vb*) повыше́ние; возведе́ние; подня́тие; (*height*) высота́*; (*ARCHIT*) фаса́д.
elevator [ˈɛlɪveɪtəʳ] *n* (*US*) лифт; (*in warehouse etc*) грузоподъёмник.
eleven [ɪˈlɛvn] *n* оди́ннадцать*; *see also* **five**.
elevenses [ɪˈlɛvnzɪz] *npl* (*BRIT*) лёгкий за́втрак о́коло оди́ннадцати часо́в утра́.
eleventh [ɪˈlɛvnθ] *adj* оди́ннадцатый; **at the** ~ **hour** в после́днюю мину́ту; *see also* **fifth**.
elf [ɛlf] (*pl* **elves**) *n* эльф.
elicit [ɪˈlɪsɪt] *vt*: **to** ~ (**from**) (*information*) извлека́ть (извле́чь* *perf*) (из +*gen*); (*response, reaction*) вызыва́ть (вы́звать* *perf*) (от +*gen*); **to** ~ **a reply** добива́ться (доби́ться* *perf*) отве́та; **to** ~ **applause from the audience** вызыва́ть (вы́звать* *perf*) аплодисме́нты ауди́тории.
eligible [ˈɛlɪdʒəbl] *adj* (*for marriage*) подходя́щий*; **to be** ~ **for sth** (*qualified, suitable*) быть* (*impf*) подходя́щей кандидату́рой для чего́-н; **to be** ~ **for a pension** име́ть (*impf*) пра́во на пе́нсию.

---

eliminate [ɪ'lɪmɪneɪt] *vt* ликвиди́ровать *(impf/ perf)*, исключа́ть (исключи́ть *perf*); *(candidate, team, contestant)* отсе́ивать (отсе́ять *perf*); **they were ~d in the first round** они́ бы́ли отсе́яны на пе́рвом ту́ре.

elimination [ɪlɪmɪ'neɪʃən] *n* ликвида́ция, исключе́ние; *(of team, candidate)* устране́ние; **by process of ~** путём исключе́ния *or* ликвида́ции.

élite [eɪ'liːt] *n* эли́та.

élitist [eɪ'liːtɪst] *adj (pej)* элита́рный.

elixir [ɪ'lɪksə'] *n* эликси́р.

Elizabethan [ɪlɪzə'biːθən] *adj (house, music, period)* эпо́хи короле́вы Елизаве́ты.

ellipse [ɪ'lɪps] *n (MATH)* э́ллипс.

elliptical [ɪ'lɪptɪkl] *adj (MATH)* эллипти́ческий.

elm [ɛlm] *n* вяз.

elocution [ɛlə'kjuːʃən] *n* ора́торское иску́сство.

elongated ['iːlɒŋɡeɪtɪd] *adj* удлинённый* (удлинён).

elope [ɪ'ləʊp] *vi:* **to ~ (with)** та́йно сбежа́ть* *(impf)* (с +*instr*).

elopement [ɪ'ləʊpmənt] *n* та́йное бе́гство.

eloquence ['ɛləkwəns] *n (see adj)* красноре́чие; я́ркость *f*.

eloquent ['ɛləkwənt] *adj (description, person)* красноречи́вый; *(speech)* я́ркий*.

El Salvador [ɛl'sælvədɔː'] *n* Сальвадо́р.

else [ɛls] *adv (other)* ещё; **nothing ~** бо́льше ничего́; **somewhere ~** *(be)* где́-нибудь ещё; *(go)* куда́-нибудь ещё; *(come from)* отку́да-то ещё; **everywhere ~** ве́зде; **where ~?** *(position)* где ещё?; *(motion)* куда́ ещё?; **is there anything ~ I can do to help?** я могу́ че́м-нибудь ещё помо́чь?; **there was little ~ to do** ма́ло, что мо́жно бы́ло де́лать; **everyone ~** все остальны́е; **nobody ~ spoke** бо́льше никто́ не выступа́л; **or ~ ...** не то (бу́дет ху́же) ....

elsewhere [ɛls'wɛə'] *adv (be)* где́-нибудь ещё *(в друго́м ме́сте)*; *(go)* куда́-нибудь ещё *(в друго́е ме́сто)*.

ELT *n abbr (SCOL)* = **English Language Teaching**.

elucidate [ɪ'luːsɪdeɪt] *vt* разъясня́ть (разъясни́ть *perf*).

elude [ɪ'luːd] *vt (captor, capture)* ускольза́ть (ускользну́ть *perf*) от +*gen*; *(subj: fact, idea):* **to ~ sb** не приходи́ть *(impf)* кому́-н на ум.

elusive [ɪ'luːsɪv] *adj (person, animal)* неулови́мый; *(quality)* не поддаю́щийся описа́нию; **he's very ~** он о́чень за́мкнутый.

elves [ɛlvz] *npl of* **elf**.

emaciated [ɪ'meɪsɪeɪtɪd] *adj (person, animal)* истощённый*.

E-mail *n abbr (= electronic mail)* электро́нная по́чта.

emanate ['ɛməneɪt] *vi:* **to ~ from** исходи́ть *(impf)* от +*gen*.

emancipate [ɪ'mænsɪpeɪt] *vt* освобожда́ть (освободи́ть* *perf*), эмансипи́ровать *(impf/*

perf).

emancipation [ɪmænsɪ'peɪʃən] *n* освобожде́ние, эмансипа́ция.

emasculate [ɪ'mæskjuleɪt] *vt (weaken)* ослабля́ть (осла́бить* *perf*).

embalm [ɪm'bɑːm] *vt* бальзами́ровать (забальзами́ровать *perf*).

embankment [ɪm'bæŋkmənt] *n (of road, railway)* на́сыпь *f*; *(of river)* на́бережная *f adj*.

embargo [ɪm'bɑːɡəʊ] *(pl ~es)* *n* эмба́рго *nt ind* ◆ *vt* запреща́ть (запрети́ть* *perf*); **to put** *or* **impose** *or* **place an ~ on sth** накла́дывать (наложи́ть* *perf*) эмба́рго на что-н; **to lift an ~ from** снима́ть (снять* *perf*) эмба́рго с +*gen*.

embark [ɪm'bɑːk] *vi:* **to ~ (on)** *(ship)* грузи́ться* (погрузи́ться* *perf*) (на +*acc*); **to ~ on** *(journey)* отправля́ться (отпра́виться* *perf*) в +*acc*; *(task, course of action)* принима́ть (предприня́ть* *perf*).

embarkation [ɛmbɑː'keɪʃən] *n (of people)* поса́дка; *(of cargo)* погру́зка.

embarkation card *n* поса́дочный тало́н.

embarrass [ɪm'bærəs] *vt* смуща́ть (смути́ть* *perf*); *(politician, government)* затрудня́ть (затрудни́ть *perf*).

embarrassed [ɪm'bærəst] *adj (laugh, silence)* смущённый*; **to be ~** смуща́ться (смути́ться* *perf*).

embarrassing [ɪm'bærəsɪŋ] *adj* вызыва́ющий* смуще́ние, щекотли́вый.

embarrassment [ɪm'bærəsmənt] *n (feeling)* смуще́ние; *(problem)* стыд*.

embassy ['ɛmbəsɪ] *n* посо́льство; **the French E~** Францу́зское посо́льство, посо́льство Фра́нции.

embedded [ɪm'bɛdɪd] *adj (object)* заде́ланный; *(attitude, belief)* устоя́вшийся.

embellish [ɪm'bɛlɪʃ] *vt (story)* приукра́шивать (приукра́сить* *perf*); *(place, dress):* **~ed with** укра́шенный +*instr*.

embers ['ɛmbəz] *npl* тле́ющие уголь́ки *mpl*.

embezzle [ɪm'bɛzl] *vt* присва́ивать (присво́ить* *perf*).

embezzlement [ɪm'bɛzlmənt] *n* растра́та.

embezzler [ɪm'bɛzlə'] *n* растра́тчик(-ица).

embitter [ɪm'bɪtə'] *vt (fig)* озлобля́ть (озло́бить* *perf*).

embittered [ɪm'bɪtəd] *adj (person)* озло́бленный*.

emblem ['ɛmbləm] *n* эмбле́ма.

embodiment [ɪm'bɒdɪmənt] *n:* **she is the ~ of** она́ — воплоще́ние +*gen*.

embody [ɪm'bɒdɪ] *vt (incarnate)* воплоща́ть (воплоти́ть* *perf*); *(include, contain)* содержа́ть *(impf)* (в себе́).

embolden [ɪm'bəʊldn] *vt* ободря́ть (ободри́ть *perf*).

embolism ['ɛmbəlɪzəm] *n* эмболи́я.

embossed [ɪm'bɒst] *adj (design, word)* рельéфный*; **~ with his initials** с рельéфными инициа́лами.

embrace [ɪm'breɪs] *vt* обнима́ть (обня́ть* *perf*);
(*include*) охва́тывать (охвати́ть* *perf*) ◆ *vi*
обнима́ться (*impf*) ◆ *n* объя́тие.
embroider [ɪm'brɔɪdə'] *vt* (*cloth*) вышива́ть
(вы́шить* *perf*); (*fig: story*) приукра́шивать
(приукра́сить* *perf*).
embroidery [ɪm'brɔɪdərɪ] *n* (*stitching*)
вы́шивка; (*activity*) вышива́ние.
embroil [ɪm'brɔɪl] *vt:* **to become ~ed (in sth)**
ока́зываться (оказа́ться* *perf*)
вовлечённым(-ой) (во что-н).
embryo ['ɛmbrɪəu] *n* (*BIO*) эмбрио́н; (*fig*)
заро́дыш.
emend [ɪ'mɛnd] *vt* (*text*) исправля́ть
(испра́вить* *perf*).
emerald ['ɛmərəld] *n* изумру́д.
emerge [ɪ'mə:dʒ] *vi* (*fact*) всплыва́ть (всплыть*
perf); (*new industry, society*) появля́ться
(появи́ться* *perf*); **to ~ from** (*from room,
imprisonment*) выходи́ть (вы́йти* *perf*) из
+*gen*; (*from sleep*) пробужда́ться
(пробуди́ться* *perf*) от +*gen*; **it ~s that** (*BRIT*)
вы́яснилось, что.
emergence [ɪ'mə:dʒəns] *n* (*of new idea etc*)
появле́ние.
emergency [ɪ'mə:dʒənsɪ] *n* (*crisis*) кра́йняя
необходи́мость *f* ◆ *cpd:* **~ repair** сро́чный
ремо́нт; **in an ~** в слу́чае опа́сности; **state of
~** чрезвыча́йное положе́ние; **~ talks**
экстренные переговоры.
emergency cord *n* (*US*) ≈ стоп-кра́н.
emergency exit *n* запа́сный вы́ход.
emergency landing *n* (*AVIAT*) вы́нужденная
поса́дка.
emergency lane *n* (*US: AUT*) авари́йная
полоса́*.
emergency road service *n* (*US*) авари́йная
доро́жная слу́жба.
emergency services *npl:* **the ~ ~** авари́йная
слу́жба *fsg*.
emergency stop *n* (*BRIT: AUT*) внеза́пная
остано́вка (*в крити́ческой ситуа́ции*).
emergent [ɪ'mə:dʒənt] *adj* (*nation, group*)
получи́вший незави́симость,
образова́вшийся; **an ~ industrial class**
зая́вивший о себе́ промы́шленный класс.
emeritus [ɪ'mɛrɪtəs] *adj:* **professor ~**
заслуженный профе́ссор в отста́вке.
emery board ['ɛmərɪ-] *n* па́лочка для ногте́й
(*покрытая кору́ндом*).
emery paper *n* нажда́чная бума́га.
emetic [ɪ'mɛtɪk] *n* (*MED*) рво́тное *nt adj*.
emigrant ['ɛmɪgrənt] *n* эмигра́нт(ка*).
emigrate ['ɛmɪgreɪt] *vi* эмигри́ровать (*impf/
perf*).
emigration [ɛmɪ'greɪʃən] *n* эмигра́ция.
émigré ['ɛmɪgreɪ] *n* полити́ческий*
эмигра́нт(ка).

eminence ['ɛmɪnəns] *n* (*importance*)
знамени́тость *f*.
eminent ['ɛmɪnənt] *adj* (*scientist, writer*)
знамени́тый (знамени́т).
eminently ['ɛmɪnəntlɪ] *adv* (*practical etc*)
весьма́.
emirate ['ɛmɪrɪt] *n* эмира́т.
emission [ɪ'mɪʃən] *n* (*of gas, heat*) выделе́ние
no pl; (*of light, radiation*) излуче́ние.
emit [ɪ'mɪt] *vt* (*smoke, smell*) испуска́ть
(испусти́ть* *perf*); (*sound*) издава́ть* (изда́ть*
perf); (*light, heat*) излуча́ть (*impf*).
emolument [ɪ'mɔljumənt] *n* (*usu pl*) дохо́д;
(*fee*) вознагражде́ние; (*salary*) жа́лованье*.
emotion [ɪ'məuʃən] *n* чу́вство; (*as opposed to
reason*) эмо́ция.
emotional [ɪ'məuʃənl] *adj* эмоциона́льный*
(эмоциона́лен); (*issue*) волну́ющий.
emotionally [ɪ'məuʃnəlɪ] *adv* (*behave, speak*)
эмоциона́льно; **~ disturbed** эмоциона́льно
неуравнове́шенный*.
emotive [ɪ'məutɪv] *adj* (*subject, language*)
вызыва́ющий эмо́ции, эмоциона́льно
волну́ющий; **~ power** эмоциона́льная си́ла.
empathy ['ɛmpəθɪ] *n* сочу́вствие; **to feel ~ with
sb** сочу́вствовать (*impf*) кому́-н.
emperor ['ɛmpərə'] *n* импера́тор.
emphases ['ɛmfəsi:z] *npl of* **emphasis**.
emphasis ['ɛmfəsɪs] (*pl* **emphases**) *n* значе́ние;
(*in speaking*) ударе́ние, акце́нт; **to lay** *or* **place
~ on sth** (*fig*) подчёркивать (подчеркну́ть
perf) что-н; **the ~ is on reading** наибо́льшее
значе́ние придаётся чте́нию.
emphasize ['ɛmfəsaɪz] *vt* подчёркивать
(почеркну́ть* *perf*); **I must ~ that ...** я до́лжен
подчеркну́ть, что ....
emphatic [ɛm'fætɪk] *adj* (*statement, denial*)
убеди́тельный* (убеди́телен); (*person,
manner*) насто́йчиво убежа́ющий; **to be ~
about sth** насто́йчиво убежда́ть (*impf*) в
чём-н.
emphatically [ɛm'fætɪklɪ] *adv* насто́йчиво;
(*certainly*) убеди́тельно.
emphysema [ɛmfɪ'si:mə] *n* эмфизе́ма.
empire ['ɛmpaɪə'] *n* (*also fig*) импе́рия.
empirical [ɛm'pɪrɪkl] *adj* (*knowledge, study*)
эмпири́ческий.
employ [ɪm'plɔɪ] *vt* (*workforce, person*)
нанима́ть (наня́ть* *perf*), трудоустра́ивать
(трудоустро́ить* *perf*), дава́ть* (дать* *perf*)
рабо́ту +*dat*; (*tool, weapon*) применя́ть
(примени́ть* *perf*); **he's ~ed in a bank** он
рабо́тает в ба́нке.
employee [ɪmplɔɪ'i:] *n* рабо́тник.
employer [ɪm'plɔɪə'] *n* работода́тель *m*.
employment [ɪm'plɔɪmənt] *n* рабо́та; **to find ~**
трудоустра́иваться (трудоустро́иться *perf*);
without ~ без рабо́ты; **place of ~** ме́сто

---

* marks translations which have irregular inflections. The Russian-English side of the dictionary gives inflectional information.

рабо́ты.

employment agency n бюро́ nt ind по трудоустро́йству.

employment exchange n (*BRIT: formerly*) би́ржа труда́.

empower [ɪm'pauə'] vt: **to ~ sb to do** уполномо́чивать (уполномо́чить *perf*) кого́-н +*infin*.

empress ['ɛmprɪs] n императри́ца.

empties ['ɛmptɪz] npl (*bottles*) та́ра fsg.

emptiness ['ɛmptɪnɪs] n пустота́.

empty ['ɛmptɪ] adj (*also fig*) пусто́й* ◆ vt (*container*) опорожня́ть (опорожни́ть *perf*); (*place, house etc*) опустоша́ть (опустоши́ть *perf*) ◆ vi (*house, container*) пусте́ть (опусте́ть *perf*); (*liquid*) вытека́ть (вы́течь* *perf*); **on an ~ stomach** на пусто́й желу́док; **to ~ into** (*river*) впада́ть (*impf*) в +*acc*.

empty-handed ['ɛmptɪ'hændɪd] adj с пусты́ми рука́ми; **he returned ~** он верну́лся с пусты́ми рука́ми.

empty-headed ['ɛmptɪ'hɛdɪd] adj (*person*) пустоголо́вый.

EMS n abbr (= *European Monetary System*) ЕВС= *Европе́йская валю́тная систе́ма*.

EMT n abbr = *emergency medical technician*.

EMU n abbr = *economic and monetary union*.

emu ['iːmjuː] n стра́ус эму m ind.

emulate ['ɛmjuleɪt] vt (*hero, idol*) подража́ть (*impf*) +*dat*.

emulsion [ɪ'mʌlʃən] n (*liquid*) эму́льсия; (*also: ~ paint*) эму́льсия, эмульсио́нная кра́ска*.

enable [ɪ'neɪbl] vt (*make possible*) спосо́бствовать (*impf*) +*dat*; **to ~ sb to do** (*permit, allow*) дава́ть* (дать* *perf*) возмо́жность кому́-н +*infin*.

enact [ɪ'nækt] vt (*law*) вводи́ть* (ввести́* *perf*); (*play*) ста́вить* (поста́вить* *perf*); (*role*) игра́ть (сыгра́ть *perf*).

enamel [ɪ'næməl] n эма́ль f; (*also: ~ paint*) эма́ль, эма́левая кра́ска*.

enamoured [ɪ'næməd] (*US* **enamored**) adj: **to be ~ of** (*pastime, idea, belief*) пита́ть (*impf*) сла́бость к +*dat*.

encampment [ɪn'kæmpmənt] n ла́герная стоя́нка.

encased [ɪn'keɪst] adj: **~ in** (*in plaster, armour*) зако́ванный в +*acc*; (*in shell*) заключённый в +*acc*.

encash [ɪn'kæʃ] vt инкасси́ровать *perf*.

enchant [ɪn'tʃɑːnt] vt (*delight*) очаро́вывать (очарова́ть *perf*).

enchanted [ɪn'tʃɑːntɪd] adj (*under a spell*) заколдо́ванный, зачаро́ванный.

enchanting [ɪn'tʃɑːntɪŋ] adj обворожи́тельный* (обворожи́телен).

encircle [ɪn'səːkl] vt (*place, prisoner*) окружа́ть (окружи́ть *perf*).

encl. abbr (*on letters etc: = enclosed, enclosure*) приложе́ние.

enclave ['ɛnkleɪv] n: **an ~ of** анкла́в +*gen*,

о́стров +*gen*.

enclose [ɪn'kləuz] vt (*land, space*) огора́живать (огороди́ть* *perf*); (*object*) заключа́ть (заключи́ть *perf*); (*letter etc*): **to ~ (with)** прилага́ть (приложи́ть *perf*) (к +*dat*); **please find ~d a cheque for £100** здесь прилага́ется чек на £100.

enclosure [ɪn'kləuʒə'] n (*area of land*) огоро́женное ме́сто*; (*in letter etc*) приложе́ние.

encoder [ɪn'kəudə'] n (*COMPUT*) коди́рующее устро́йство, ко́дер.

encompass [ɪn'kʌmpəs] vt (*include*) охва́тывать (охвати́ть* *perf*).

encore [ɔŋ'kɔː'] excl бис ◆ n: **as an ~** на "бис".

encounter [ɪn'kauntə'] n встре́ча; (*problem*) столкнове́ние ◆ vt (*person*) встре́титься (*perf*) с +*instr*; (*new experience, problem*) ста́лкиваться (столкну́ться *perf*) с +*instr*.

encourage [ɪn'kʌrɪdʒ] vt поощря́ть (поощри́ть *perf*); (*growth*) спосо́бствовать (*impf*) +*dat*; **to ~ sb to do** убежда́ть (*impf*) кого́-н +*infin*.

encouragement [ɪn'kʌrɪdʒmənt] n (*see vt*) поощре́ние; подде́ржка.

encouraging [ɪn'kʌrɪdʒɪŋ] adj (*situation, meeting, news*) обнадёживающий.

encroach [ɪn'krəutʃ] vi: **to ~ (up)on** (*rights, property, time*) покуша́ться (покуси́ться* *perf*) or посяга́ть (посягну́ть *perf*) на +*acc*.

encrusted [ɪn'krʌstɪd] adj: **~ with** покры́тый +*instr*.

encumber [ɪn'kʌmbə'] vt: **~ed with** (*suitcase, baggage etc*) загромождённый (загромождён) +*instr*; (*debts*) обременённый (обременён) +*instr*.

encyclop(a)edia [ɛnsaɪkləu'piːdɪə] n энциклопе́дия.

end [ɛnd] n коне́ц*; (*of town*) часть f; (*aim*) цель f ◆ vt (*also:* **bring to an ~**, **put an ~ to**) зака́нчивать (зако́нчить *perf*), прекраща́ть (прекрати́ть* *perf*) ◆ vi (*situation, activity, period etc*) конча́ться (ко́нчиться *perf*); **from ~ to ~** с нача́ла до конца́; **to come to an ~** подходи́ть* (подойти́* *perf*) к концу́, конча́ться (ко́нчиться *perf*); **to be at an ~** зака́нчиваться (зако́нчиться *perf*); **in the ~** в конце́ концо́в; **on ~** (*hair*) стоя́ть (стать* *perf*) ды́бом; **for hours on ~** часа́ми; **for 5 hours on ~** 5 часо́в подря́д; **at the ~ of the street** в конце́ у́лицы; **at the ~ of the day** (*BRIT: fig*) в конце́ концо́в; **to this ~**, **with this ~ in view** с э́той це́лью.

► **end up** vi: **to ~ up in** (*place*) конча́ть (ко́нчить *perf*) в +*prp*; **we ~ed up taking a taxi** мы ко́нчили тем, что взя́ли такси́.

endanger [ɪn'deɪndʒə'] vt подверга́ть (подве́ргнуть* *perf*) опа́сности; **an ~ed species** вымира́ющий вид.

endear [ɪn'dɪə'] vt: **to ~ o.s. to sb** внуша́ть (внуши́ть *perf*) кому́-н симпа́тию к себе́.

endearing [ɪn'dɪərɪŋ] adj (*personality, conduct*)

покоря́ющий.

endearment [ɪnˈdɪəmənt] *n*: **to whisper ~s** шепта́ть *(impf)* ла́сковые слова́; **term of ~** ла́сковое обраще́ние.

endeavour [ɪnˈdɛvəʳ] *n* (*attempt*) попы́тка*; (*effort*) стара́ние ♦ *vi*: **to ~ to do** (*attempt*) стара́ться (постара́ться *perf*) +*infin*; (*strive*) стреми́ться* (*impf*) +*infin*.

endemic [ɛnˈdɛmɪk] *adj* эндеми́ческий.

ending [ˈɛndɪŋ] *n* (*of book, play etc*) коне́ц*; (*LING*) оконча́ние.

endive [ˈɛndaɪv] *n* (*curly*) энди́вый сала́т; (*chicory*) цико́рный сала́т.

endless [ˈɛndlɪs] *adj* бесконе́чный* (бесконе́чен); (*forest, beach*) бескра́йний; (*patience, resources*) беспреде́льный* (беспреде́лен); (*possibilities*) неограни́ченный* (неограни́чен).

endorse [ɪnˈdɔːs] *vt* (*cheque, document*) распи́сываться (расписа́ться* *perf*) на +*prp*; (*approve: proposal, candidate*) подде́рживать (поддержа́ть* *perf*).

endorsee [ɪndɔːˈsiː] *n* индосса́т.

endorsement [ɪnˈdɔːsmənt] *n* (*approval*) индоссаме́нт; (*BRIT: on driving licence*) отме́тка*.

endorser [ɪnˈdɔːsəʳ] *n* индосса́нт.

endow [ɪnˈdau] *vt* (*provide with money*) обеспе́чивать (обеспе́чить *perf*); **~ed with** (*talent, quality*) наделён (наделён) +*instr*.

endowment [ɪnˈdaumənt] *n* (*money*) поже́ртвование (*для обеспече́ния ежего́дным дохо́дом*); (*quality*) спосо́бности *fpl*.

endowment mortgage *n* ипоте́чная ссу́да сочета́нии со страхова́нием жи́зни.

endowment policy *n* по́лис включа́ющий страхова́ние жи́зни.

end product *n* (*INDUSTRY*) коне́чный проду́кт; (*fig*) результа́т.

end result *n* коне́чный результа́т.

endurable [ɪnˈdjuərəbl] *adj* терпи́мый.

endurance [ɪnˈdjuərəns] *n* выно́сливость *f*.

endurance test *n* испыта́ние на про́чность.

endure [ɪnˈdjuəʳ] *vt* (*bear*) переноси́ть* (перенести́* *perf*) ♦ *vi* (*last*) выде́рживать (вы́держать *perf*) (*испыта́ние вре́менем*).

enduring [ɪnˈdjuərɪŋ] *adj* (*lasting*) про́чный* (про́чен).

end user *n* (*COMPUT*) коне́чный по́льзователь *m*.

enema [ˈɛnɪmə] *n* (*MED*) кли́зма.

enemy [ˈɛnəmɪ] *adj* (*forces, strategy*) неприя́тельский, вра́жеский ♦ *n* враг*; (*opponent*) проти́вник; (*MIL*) враг*, неприя́тель *m*; **to make an ~ of sb** нажива́ть (нажи́ть* *perf*) врага́ в ком-н.

energetic [ɛnəˈdʒɛtɪk] *adj* энерги́чный*

(энерги́чен).

energy [ˈɛnədʒɪ] *n* эне́ргия; **Department of E~** Управле́ние энергоснабже́нием.

energy crisis *n* энергети́ческий* кри́зис.

energy-saving [ˈɛnədʒɪˈseɪvɪŋ] *adj* (*device*) сокраща́ющий расхо́д эне́ргии; **~ policy** поли́тика эконо́мии эне́ргии.

enervating [ˈɛnəveɪtɪŋ] *adj* обесси́ливающий, отнима́ющий си́лы.

enforce [ɪnˈfɔːs] *vt* (*law*) следи́ть* (*impf*) за соблюде́нием +*gen*.

enforced [ɪnˈfɔːst] *adj* (*inactivity, unemployment*) вы́нужденный.

enfranchise [ɪnˈfræntʃaɪz] *vt* предоставля́ть (предоста́вить* *perf*) избира́тельные права́ +*dat*.

engage [ɪnˈgeɪdʒ] *vt* (*attention, interest*) привлека́ть (привле́чь* *perf*); (*employ*) нанима́ть (наня́ть* *perf*); (*AUT: clutch*) зацепля́ть (зацепи́ть* *perf*); (*MIL: enemy*) вступа́ть (вступи́ть* *perf*) в бой с +*instr* ♦ *vi* (*TECH*) входи́ть* (войти́* *perf*) в зацепле́ние; **to ~ in** занима́ться (заня́ться* *perf*) +*instr*; **to ~ sb in conversation** вовлека́ть (вовле́чь* *perf*) кого́-н в разгово́р.

engaged [ɪnˈgeɪdʒd] *adj* обручённый (обручён); (*BRIT: busy*) за́нят; **~ to** обручён с +*instr*; **to get ~** обручи́ться (*perf*); **he is ~ in research** он занима́ется иссле́дованием.

engaged tone *n* (*BRIT: TEL*) гудки́ *pl* "за́нято".

engagement [ɪnˈgeɪdʒmənt] *n* (*appointment*) договорённость *f*; (*hiring*) контра́кт; (*to marry*) обруче́ние; (*MIL*) бой*; **I have a previous ~** у меня́ уже́ есть договорённость.

engagement ring *n* обруча́льное кольцо́*.

engaging [ɪnˈgeɪdʒɪŋ] *adj* привлека́тельный* (привлека́телен).

engender [ɪnˈdʒɛndəʳ] *vt* порожда́ть (породи́ть* *perf*).

engine [ˈɛndʒɪn] *n* (*AUT*) дви́гатель *m*, мото́р; (*RAIL*) локомоти́в.

engine driver *n* (*BRIT*) маши́ни́ст.

engineer [ɛndʒɪˈnɪəʳ] *n* (*designer*) инжене́р; (*for repairs, also NAUT*) меха́ник; (*US: RAIL*) маши́ни́ст; **civil ~** инжене́р-строи́тель *m*; **mechanical ~** инжене́р-меха́ник.

engineering [ɛndʒɪˈnɪərɪŋ] *n* (*science*) инжене́рное де́ло; (*design*) техни́ческий дизайн; (*construction: of roads, ships*) строи́тельство; (*of cars, machines*) произво́дство ♦ *cpd*: **~ works** *or* **factory** машинострои́тельный заво́д.

engine failure *n* отка́з дви́гателя.

engine trouble *n* неиспра́вность *f* дви́гателя.

England [ˈɪŋglənd] *n* А́нглия.

English [ˈɪŋglɪʃ] *adj* англи́йский* ♦ *n* (*LING*) англи́йский язы́к; **the ~** *npl* (*people*) англича́не *mpl*; **an ~ speaker**

англоговоря́щий(-ая) *m(f) adj.*
English Channel *n*: **the ~ ~** Ла-Ма́нш.
Englishman ['ɪŋglɪʃmən] *irreg n* англича́нин*.
English-speaking ['ɪŋglɪʃ'spi:kɪŋ] *adj*
англоговоря́щий.
Englishwoman ['ɪŋglɪʃwumən] *irreg n*
англича́нка*.
engrave [ɪn'greɪv] *vt* гравирова́ть
(вы́гравировать *perf*).
engraving [ɪn'greɪvɪŋ] *n* гравю́ра.
engrossed [ɪn'grəust] *adj*: **~ in** поглощённый
(поглощён) +*instr*.
engulf [ɪn'gʌlf] *vt* (*subj: water*) поглоща́ть
(поглоти́ть* *perf*); (: *panic, fear, fire*)
охва́тывать (охвати́ть* *perf*).
enhance [ɪn'hɑ:ns] *vt* (*enjoyment*) увели́чивать
(увели́чить *perf*); (*beauty, reputation*)
улучша́ть (улу́чшить *perf*).
enigma [ɪ'nɪgmə] *n* зага́дка.
enigmatic [ɛnɪg'mætɪk] *adj* зага́дочный*
(зага́дочен).
enjoy [ɪn'dʒɔɪ] *vt* люби́ть (*impf*); (*have benefit
of*) облада́ть (*impf*) +*instr*; **to ~ o.s.** хорошо́
проводи́ть* (провести́* *perf*) вре́мя; **I ~**
dancing я люблю́ танцева́ть.
enjoyable [ɪn'dʒɔɪəbl] *adj* прия́тный*
(прия́тен).
enjoyment [ɪn'dʒɔɪmənt] *n* (*feeling of pleasure*)
удово́льствие.
enlarge [ɪn'lɑ:dʒ] *vt* увели́чивать (увели́чить
perf) ♦ *vi*: **to ~ on** распространя́ться (*impf*) о
+*prp*.
enlarged [ɪn'lɑ:dʒd] *adj* (*edition*)
допо́лненный; (*MED, PHOT*) увели́ченный
(увели́чен).
enlargement [ɪn'lɑ:dʒmənt] *n* (*PHOT*)
увеличе́ние.
enlighten [ɪn'laɪtn] *vt* просвеща́ть
(просвети́ть* *perf*).
enlightened [ɪn'laɪtnd] *adj* просвещённый.
enlightening [ɪn'laɪtnɪŋ] *adj* просвеща́ющий.
enlightenment [ɪn'laɪtnmənt] *n*: **the E~**
Просвеще́ние.
enlist [ɪn'lɪst] *vt* (*person*) вербова́ть
(завербова́ть *perf*); (*support*) заруча́ться
(заручи́ться *perf*) +*instr* ♦ *vi*: **to ~ in** (*army,
navy etc*) идти́* (пойти́* *perf*) в +*acc*; **~ed man**
(*US: MIL*) военнослу́жащий* *m adj* (*рядово́го
и́ли сержа́нтского соста́ва*).
enliven [ɪn'laɪvn] *vt* (*events*) оживля́ть
(оживи́ть* *perf*); (*people*) подбодря́ть
(подбодри́ть *perf*).
enmity ['ɛnmɪtɪ] *n* вражде́бность *f*.
ennoble [ɪ'nəubl] *vt* возводи́ть* (возвести́* *perf*)
в ти́тул; (*fig*) облагора́живать
(облагоро́дить* *perf*).
enormity [ɪ'nɔ:mɪtɪ] *n* (*of problem, danger*)
величина́.
enormous [ɪ'nɔ:məs] *adj* грома́дный*
(грома́ден).
enormously [ɪ'nɔ:məslɪ] *adv* чрезвыча́йно.

enough [ɪ'nʌf] *adj* (*time, books, people etc*)
доста́точно +*gen* ♦ *pron* доста́точно ♦ *adv*: **big
~** доста́точно большо́й; **I've had ~!** с меня́
хва́тит!; **have you got ~ work to do?** у Вас
доста́точно рабо́ты?; **have you had ~ to eat?**
Вы нае́лись?; **that's ~, thanks** доста́точно,
спаси́бо; **I've had ~ of him** он мне надое́л; **he
has not worked ~** он недоста́точно рабо́тал;
will five pounds be ~? пяти́ фу́нтов бу́дет
доста́точно?; **I do not have ~ money to buy it**
у меня́ не хвата́ет де́нег, что́бы купи́ть э́то;
it's hot ~ as it is и та́к дово́льно жа́рко; **he
was kind ~ to lend me the money** он был
насто́лько добр, что́бы одолжи́ть мне
де́ньги; **~!** дово́льно!; **strangely** *or* **oddly ~ ...**
как э́то ни стра́нно ....
enquire [ɪn'kwaɪə'] *vti* = **inquire**.
enrage [ɪn'reɪdʒ] *vt* беси́ть* (взбеси́ть* *perf*).
enrich [ɪn'rɪtʃ] *vt* обогаща́ть (обогати́ть *perf*).
enrol [ɪn'rəul] (*US* **enroll**) *vt* (*subj: administrator*)
зачисля́ть (зачи́слить *perf*); (: *parents etc*)
запи́сывать (записа́ть* *perf*) ♦ *vi* (*see vt*)
зачисля́ться (зачи́слиться *perf*);
запи́сываться (записа́ться* *perf*).
enrolment [ɪn'rəulmənt] (*US* **enrollment**) *n*
(*registration*) зачисле́ние; (*for course, club*)
за́пись *f*.
en route [ɔn'ru:t] *adv* по пути́; **~ ~ for** *or* **to/
from** по пути́ в +*acc*/из +*gen*.
ensconce [ɪn'skɔns] *vt*: **to ~ o.s. in**
устра́иваться (устро́иться *perf*) в +*prp*.
ensemble [ɔn'sɔmbl] *n* анса́мбль *m*.
enshrine [ɪn'ʃraɪn] *vt* (*belief, right*) храни́ть
(*impf*); **to be ~d in** сохраня́ться (сохрани́ться
perf) в +*prp*.
ensue [ɪn'sju:] *vi* сле́довать (после́довать *perf*);
a terrible argument ~d (за э́тим)
после́довала ужа́сная ссо́ра.
ensuing [ɪn'sju:ɪŋ] *adj* после́дующий*.
ensure [ɪn'ʃuə'] *vt* обеспе́чивать (обеспе́чить
perf); **to ~ that** обеспе́чивать (обеспе́чить
perf), что.
ENT *n abbr* (*MED*: = *Ear, Nose and Throat*)
у́хо-го́рло-нос.
entail [ɪn'teɪl] *vt* влечь* (повле́чь* *perf*) за
собо́й.
entangled [ɪn'tæŋgld] *adj*: **to become ~ (in)** (*in
net, rope etc*) запу́тываться (запу́таться *perf*)
(в +*prp*).
enter ['ɛntə'] *vt* (*room, building*) входи́ть*
(войти́* *perf*) в +*acc*; (*university, college*)
поступа́ть (поступи́ть* *perf*); (*club,
profession, contest*) вступа́ть (вступи́ть* *perf*)
в +*acc*; (*in book*) запи́сывать (записа́ть* *perf*);
(*COMPUT*) вводи́ть* (ввести́* *perf*) ♦ *vi*
входи́ть* (войти́* *perf*); **I ~ed my son in the
marathon** я по́дал зая́вку на включе́ние
моего́ сы́на в марафо́н
► **enter for** *vt fus* (*competition, examination*)
подава́ть* (пода́ть* *perf*) зая́вку на уча́стие в
+*prp*

▶ **enter into** *vt fus* (*discussion, correspondence, agreement*) вступа́ть (вступи́ть* *perf*) в +*acc*
▶ **enter (up)on** *vt fus* (*career, policy*) начина́ть (нача́ть* *perf*).
enteritis [ɛntəˈraɪtɪs] *n* энтери́т.
enterprise [ˈɛntəpraɪz] *n* (*company, undertaking*) предприя́тие; (*initiative*) предприи́мчивость *f*; **free/private ~** свобо́дное/ча́стное предпринима́тельство.
enterprising [ˈɛntəpraɪzɪŋ] *adj* (*person*) предприи́мчивый (предприи́мчив); (*scheme*) предпринима́тельский*.
entertain [ɛntəˈteɪn] *vt* (*amuse*) развлека́ть (развле́чь* *perf*); (*play host to*) принима́ть (приня́ть* *perf*); (*idea*) разду́мывать (*impf*) над +*instr*.
entertainer [ɛntəˈteɪnəʳ] *n* веду́щий*(-ая) *m(f) adj* развлека́тельной програ́ммы.
entertaining [ɛntəˈteɪnɪŋ] *adj* занима́тельный* (занима́телен), развлека́тельный ♦ *n*: **we do a lot of ~** мы ча́сто приглаша́ем к себе́ госте́й.
entertainment [ɛntəˈteɪnmənt] *n* (*amusement*) развлече́ние; (*show*) представле́ние.
entertainment allowance *n* сре́дства на представи́тельские расхо́ды.
enthral [ɪnˈθrɔːl] (*US* **enthrall**) *vt* приводи́ть* (привести́* *perf*) в восто́рг.
enthralled [ɪnˈθrɔːld] *adj* увлечённый (увлечён); **he was ~ by** *or* **with the book** он был увлечён кни́гой.
enthralling [ɪnˈθrɔːlɪŋ] *adj* увлека́тельный* (увлека́телен).
enthuse [ɪnˈθuːz] *vi*: **to ~ about** *or* **over** приходи́ть* (прийти́* *perf*) в восто́рг от +*gen*.
enthusiasm [ɪnˈθuːzɪæzəm] *n* энтузиа́зм.
enthusiast [ɪnˈθuːzɪæst] *n* энтузиа́ст; **a jazz** *etc* **~** энтузиа́ст джа́за *etc*.
enthusiastic [ɪnθuːzɪˈæstɪk] *adj* по́лный* (по́лон) энтузиа́зма; (*response, reception*) восто́рженный; **he is ~ about** он по́лон энтузиа́зма по по́воду +*gen*.
entice [ɪnˈtaɪs] *vt* (*lure*) зама́нивать (замани́ть* *perf*); (*tempt*) соблазня́ть (соблазни́ть *perf*).
enticing [ɪnˈtaɪsɪŋ] *adj* (*offer, food*) соблазни́тельный.
entire [ɪnˈtaɪəʳ] *adj* весь*.
entirely [ɪnˈtaɪəlɪ] *adv* по́лностью; (*for emphasis*) соберше́нно; **~ different** соверше́нно разли́чный.
entirety [ɪnˈtaɪərətɪ] *n*: **in its ~** весь целико́м.
entitle [ɪnˈtaɪtl] *vt*: **to ~ sb to sth/to do** дава́ть* (дать* *perf*) пра́во кому́-н на что-н/+*infin*.
entitled [ɪnˈtaɪtld] *adj* (*book, film etc*) озагла́вленный; **to be ~ to sth/to do** име́ть (*impf*) пра́во на что-н/на то, что́бы +*infin*.
entity [ˈɛntɪtɪ] *n* (еди́ная) су́щность *f*; **a separate ~** (*person*) отде́льная ли́чность.

entourage [ɔntuˈrɑːʒ] *n* антура́ж, окруже́ние.
entrails [ˈɛntreɪlz] *npl* вну́тренности *fpl*.
entrance [*n* ˈɛntrns, *vt* ɪnˈtrɑːns] *n* (*way in*) вход; (*arrival*) вступле́ние, появле́ние; (*THEAT*) вы́ход (на сце́ну) ♦ *vt* (*enchant*) очаро́вывать (очарова́ть *perf*); **to gain ~ to** (*university*) поступа́ть (поступи́ть* *perf*) в +*acc*; (*profession*) получа́ть (получи́ть *perf*) до́ступ к +*dat*; **to make an ~** вступа́ть (вступи́ть* *perf*).
entrance examination *n* вступи́тельный экза́мен.
entrance fee *n* (*for museum etc*) входна́я пла́та.
entrance ramp *n* (*US*: *AUT*) въезд на автостра́ду.
entrancing [ɪnˈtrɑːnsɪŋ] *adj* восхити́тельный* (восхити́телен).
entrant [ˈɛntrnt] *n* уча́стник(-ица).
entreat [ɛnˈtriːt] *vt* (*implore*): **to ~ sb to do** умоля́ть (умоли́ть *perf*) кого́-н +*infin*.
entreaty [ɛnˈtriːtɪ] *n* мольба́.
entrée [ˈɔntreɪ] *n* (*CULIN*: *main course*) гла́вное блю́до.
entrenched [ɛnˈtrɛntʃt] *adj* (*ideas etc*) укорени́вшийся.
entrepreneur [ˈɔntrəprəˈnəːʳ] *n* предпринима́тель(ница) *m(f)*.
entrepreneurial [ˈɔntrəprəˈnəːrɪəl] *adj* предпринима́тельский*.
entrust [ɪnˈtrʌst] *vt* (*possessions, task*): **to ~ sth to sb** доверя́ть (дове́рить *perf*) что-н кому́-н; **to ~ sb with sth** (*task*) возлага́ть (возложи́ть* *perf*) на кого́-н что-н.
entry [ˈɛntrɪ] *n* (*way in*) вход; (*in register, account book*) за́пись *f*; (*in reference book*) статья́*; (*in competition: participants*) число́ уча́стников; (*arrival: in country*) въезд; (: *in room*) вход; **"no ~"** (*to room, building*) "нет вхо́да"; (*AUT*) "нет въе́зда"; **single/double ~ book-keeping** (*COMM*) проста́я/двойна́я бухгалте́рия.
entry form *n* зая́вка* на уча́стие.
entry phone *n* (*BRIT*) входно́е переговоро́ное устро́йство.
entwine [ɪnˈtwaɪn] *vt*: **to ~ (with)** переплета́ть (переплести́* *perf*) (с +*instr*).
enumerate [ɪˈnjuːməreɪt] *vt* перечисля́ть (перечи́слить *perf*).
enunciate [ɪˈnʌnsɪeɪt] *vt* (*word*) произноси́ть* (произнести́* *perf*); (*principle, plan etc*) излага́ть (изложи́ть* *perf*).
envelop [ɪnˈvɛləp] *vt* (*cover, enclose*) облега́ть (обле́чь* *perf*).
envelope [ˈɛnvələup] *n* конве́рт.
enviable [ˈɛnvɪəbl] *adj* зави́дный* (зави́ден).
envious [ˈɛnvɪəs] *adj* зави́стливый (зави́стлив); **to be ~ of sth/sb** зави́довать

---

* marks translations which have irregular inflections. The Russian-English side of the dictionary gives inflectional information.

(*impf*) чему́-н/кому́-н.

environment [ɪn'vaɪərnmənt] *n* среда́; **the ~** окружа́ющая среда́; **Department of the E~** (*BRIT*) отде́л охра́ны окружа́ющей среды́.

environmental [ɪnvaɪərn'mɛntl] *adj* свя́занный с окружа́ющей средо́й, экологи́ческий*; **children respond to ~ stimuli** де́ти реаги́руют на сти́мулы предлага́емые средо́й; **~ studies** эколо́гия.

environmentalist [ɪnvaɪərn'mɛntlɪst] *n* сторо́нник(-ица) защи́ты окружа́ющей среды́.

environmentally [ɪnvaɪərn'mɛntlɪ] *adv* экологи́чески.

Environmental Protection Agency *n* (*US*) *аге́нтство по охране́ окружа́ющей среды́.*

envisage [ɪn'vɪzɪdʒ] *vt* (*foresee*) предви́деть* (*impf*); **I ~ that** ... я предви́жу, что ....

envision [ɪn'vɪʒən] *vt* (*US*) = **envisage**.

envoy ['ɛnvɔɪ] *n* посла́нник.

envy ['ɛnvɪ] *n* за́висть *f* ◆ *vt* зави́довать (позави́довать *perf*) +*dat*; **to ~ sb sth** зави́довать (позави́довать *perf*) кому́-н из-за чего́-н.

enzyme ['ɛnzaɪm] *n* (*BIO, MED*) энзи́м.

EPA *n abbr* (*US*: = *Environmental Protection Agency*) *аге́нтство по охра́не окружа́ющей среды́.*

ephemeral [ɪ'fɛmərl] *adj* эфеме́рный* (эфеме́рен).

epic ['ɛpɪk] *n* эпопе́я; (*poem*) эпи́ческая поэ́ма ◆ *adj* (*journey*) эпоха́льный* (эпоха́лен).

epicentre ['ɛpɪsɛntə'] (*US* **epicenter**) *n* эпице́нтр.

epidemic [ɛpɪ'dɛmɪk] *n* эпиде́мия.

epigram ['ɛpɪɡræm] *n* эпигра́мма.

epilepsy ['ɛpɪlɛpsɪ] *n* эпиле́псия.

epileptic [ɛpɪ'lɛptɪk] *adj* эпилепти́ческий ◆ *n* эпиле́птик.

epilogue ['ɛpɪlɔɡ] *n* эпило́г.

Epiphany [ɪ'pɪfənɪ] *n* Богоявле́ние, Креще́ние.

episcopal [ɪ'pɪskəpl] *adj* (*REL*) епи́скопский; **the E~ Church** Епископа́льная Це́рковь*.

episode ['ɛpɪsəud] *n* эпизо́д.

epistle [ɪ'pɪsl] *n* посла́ние.

epitaph ['ɛpɪtɑ:f] *n* эпита́фия.

epithet ['ɛpɪθɛt] *n* эпи́тет.

epitome [ɪ'pɪtəmɪ] *n* воплоще́ние.

epitomize [ɪ'pɪtəmaɪz] *vt* воплоща́ть (воплоти́ть* *perf*).

epoch ['ɪ:pɔk] *n* эпо́ха.

epoch-making ['ɪ:pɔkmeɪkɪŋ] *adj* эпоха́льный* (эпоха́лен).

eponymous [ɪ'pɔnɪməs] *adj:* **~ hero** геро́й, и́менем кото́рого на́звано произведе́ние.

EPOS *n abbr* (= *electronic point of sale*) *электро́нное счи́тывание информа́ции с това́рных этике́ток.*

equable ['ɛkwəbl] *adj* ро́вный* (ро́вен).

equal ['ɪ:kwl] *adj* ра́вный* (ра́вен); (*intensity, quality*) одина́ковый ◆ *n* ра́вный(-ая) *m(f) adj*

◆ *vt* (*number*) равня́ться (*impf*) +*dat*; (*quality*) не уступа́ть (уступи́ть* *perf*) +*dat or* по +*dat*; **they are roughly ~ in size** они́ приме́рно равны́ по разме́ру; **the number of exports should be ~ to imports** коли́чество э́кспорта должно́ быть* равно́ коли́честву и́мпорта; **he is ~ to** (*task*) он мо́жет спра́виться с +*instr*.

Equal Employment Opportunity Commission *n* (*US*) = **Equal Opportunities Commission**.

equality [i:'kwɔlɪtɪ] *n* ра́венство, равнопра́вие; **~ of opportunity** ра́венство возмо́жностей.

equalize ['ɪ:kwəlaɪz] *vt* ура́внивать (уравня́ть* *perf*) ◆ *vi* (*SPORT*) сра́внивать (сравня́ть *perf*) счёт.

equally ['ɪ:kwəlɪ] *adv* (*share etc*) равно́; (*good, bad*) одина́ково; **they are ~ clever** они́ в ра́вной сте́пени умны́.

Equal Opportunities Commission (*US* **Equal Employment Opportunity Commission**) *n* коми́ссия ра́вных возмо́жностей при на́йме на рабо́ту.

equal(s) sign *n* знак ра́венства.

equanimity [ɛkwə'nɪmɪtɪ] *n* (*calm*) хладнокро́вие; **with ~** хладнокро́вно.

equate [ɪ'kweɪt] *vt:* **to ~ sth with sth, ~ sth to sth** прира́внивать (приравня́ть *perf*) что-н к чему́-н.

equation [ɪ'kweɪʃən] *n* (*MATH*) уравне́ние.

equator [ɪ'kweɪtə'] *n* эква́тор.

equatorial [ɛkwə'tɔ:rɪəl] *adj* экваториа́льный.

Equatorial Guinea *n* Экваториа́льная Гвине́я.

equestrian [ɪ'kwɛstrɪən] *adj* ко́нный ◆ *n* вса́дник(-ица).

equilibrium [i:kwɪ'lɪbrɪəm] *n* равнове́сие.

equinox ['i:kwɪnɔks] *n* равноде́нствие; **the spring/autumn ~** весе́ннее/осе́ннее равноде́нствие.

equip [ɪ'kwɪp] *vt:* **to ~ (with)** (*person, army*) снаряжа́ть (снаряди́ть* *perf*) (+*instr*); (*room, car etc*) обору́довать (*impf*/*perf*) (+*instr*); **to ~ sb for** (*prepare*) гото́вить* (подгото́вить* *perf*) кого́-н к +*dat*.

equipment [ɪ'kwɪpmənt] *n* обору́дование.

equitable ['ɛkwɪtəbl] *adj* справедли́вый (справедли́в).

equities ['ɛkwɪtɪz] *npl* (*BRIT*) обыкнове́нные а́кции *fpl*.

equity ['ɛkwɪtɪ] *n* справедли́вость *f*.

equity capital *n* капита́л в фо́рме а́кций.

equivalent [ɪ'kwɪvələnt] *n* эквивале́нт ◆ *adj:* **~ (to)** эквивале́нтный* (эквивале́нтен) (+*dat*); **it is ~ to** э́то эквивале́нтно +*dat*.

equivocal [ɪ'kwɪvəkl] *adj* (*ambiguous*) двусмы́сленный* (двусмы́слен); (*open to suspicion*) сомни́тельный* (сомни́телен).

equivocate [ɪ'kwɪvəkeɪt] *vi* говори́ть (*impf*) двусмы́сленно.

equivocation [ɪkwɪvə'keɪʃən] *n* укло́нчивость *f*.

ER *abbr* (*BRIT*) = *Elizabeth Regina*.
ERA *n abbr* (*US*: *POL*: = *Equal Rights Amendment*) попра́вка о ра́вных права́х (*к конститу́ции США*).
era ['ɪərə] *n* э́ра.
eradicate [ɪ'rædɪkeɪt] *vt* искореня́ть (искорени́ть *perf*).
erase [ɪ'reɪz] *vt* стира́ть (стере́ть* *perf*).
eraser [ɪ'reɪzə^r] *n* рези́нка*, ла́стик для стира́ния.
erect [ɪ'rɛkt] *adj* (*posture*) прямо́й* (прям), вертика́льный* (вертика́лен); (*tail, ears*) по́днятый (по́днят) ♦ *vt* (*build*) возводи́ть* (возвести́* *perf*); (*assemble*) ста́вить* (поста́вить* *perf*).
erection [ɪ'rɛkʃən] *n* возведе́ние; (*of tent, machinery*) устано́вка*; (*PHYSIOL*) эре́кция.
ergonomics [ə:gə'nɔmɪks] *n* эргоно́мика.
ERISA *n abbr* (*US*) = *Employee Retirement Income Security Act*.
ERM *n abbr* (= *Exchange Rate Mechanism*) МВК= *механи́зм валю́тных ку́рсов*.
ermine ['ə:mɪn] *n* горноста́й.
ERNIE ['ə:nɪ] *n abbr* (*BRIT*: = *Electronic Random Number Indicator Equipment*) ЭВМ, *определя́ющая вы́игрышные номера́ госуда́рственного вы́игрышного за́йма*.
erode [ɪ'rəud] *vt* (*soil, rock: subj: wind*) выве́тривать (вы́ветрить *perf*); (: *water*) размыва́ть (размы́ть* *perf*); (*metal*) разъеда́ть (разъе́сть* *perf*); (*confidence, power*) подрыва́ть (подорва́ть* *perf*).
erogenous [ɪ'rɔdʒənəs] *adj* эроге́нный.
erosion [ɪ'rəuʒən] *n* эро́зия.
erotic [ɪ'rɔtɪk] *adj* эроти́ческий*.
eroticism [ɪ'rɔtɪsɪzəm] *n* эроти́зм.
err [ə:^r] *vi* допуска́ть (допусти́ть* *perf*) оши́бку; **to ~ on the side of** ... сли́шком склоня́ться (*impf*) к +*dat* ....
errand ['ɛrənd] *n* поруче́ние; **to run ~s** выполня́ть (*impf*) поруче́ния; **~ of mercy** пое́здка* с до́брой ми́ссией.
erratic [ɪ'rætɪk] *adj* (*attempts*) беспоря́дочный* (беспоря́дочен); (*behaviour*) сумасбро́дный* (сумасбро́ден).
erroneous [ɪ'rəunɪəs] *adj* оши́бочный* (оши́бочен).
error ['ɛrə^r] *n* оши́бка*; **typing ~** опеча́тка*; **spelling ~** орфографи́ческая оши́бка*; **in ~** по оши́бке; **~s and omissions excepted** не счита́я оши́бки и про́пуски.
error message *n* (*COMPUT*) сообще́ние об оши́бке.
erstwhile ['ə:stwaɪl] *adj* бы́вший*.
erudite ['ɛrjudaɪt] *adj* (*person*) эруди́рованный* (эруди́рован).
erupt [ɪ'rʌpt] *vi* (*war, crisis*) разража́ться (разрази́ться* *perf*); **the volcano ~ed**

произошло́ изверже́ние вулка́на.
eruption [ɪ'rʌpʃən] *n* (*of volcano*) изверже́ние; (*of fighting*) взры́в.
ESA *n abbr* (= *European Space Agency*) ЕКА= *Европе́йское косми́ческое аге́нтство*.
escalate ['ɛskəleɪt] *vi* обостря́ться (обостри́ться *perf*).
escalation [ɛskə'leɪʃən] *n* обостре́ние, эскала́ция.
escalation clause *n оговóрка о скользя́щих це́нах и́ли скользя́щей зарпла́те*.
escalator ['ɛskəleɪtə^r] *n* эскала́тор.
escapade [ɛskə'peɪd] *n* (*adventure*) эскапа́да, авантю́ра.
escape [ɪs'keɪp] *n* (*from prison*) побе́г; (*from person*) избега́ние; (*TECH*) вы́ход; (*of gas*) выделе́ние, вы́пуск ♦ *vi* (*get away*) убега́ть (убежа́ть* *perf*); (*from jail*) бежа́ть* (*impf/perf*); (*leak*) утека́ть (уте́чь* *perf*), дава́ть* (дать* *perf*) уте́чку ♦ *vt* (*avoid: consequences etc*) избега́ть (избежа́ть* *perf*) +*gen*; (*elude*): **his name ~s me** его́ и́мя вы́пало у меня́ из па́мяти; **to ~ from** (*place*) сбега́ть (сбежа́ть* *perf*) *or* убега́ть (убежа́ть* *perf*) из/от +*gen*; (*person*) сбега́ть (сбежа́ть* *perf*) *or* убега́ть (убежа́ть* *perf*) от +*gen*; **he ~d with minor injuries** он спа́сся отде́лавшись небольши́ми поврежде́ниями; **to ~ to** (*another place*) сбега́ть (сбежа́ть* *perf*) *or* убега́ть (убежа́ть* *perf*) в/на +*prp*; **to ~ to safety** скрыва́ться (скры́ться* *perf*) в безопа́сном ме́сте; **to ~ notice** ускольза́ть (ускользну́ть *perf*) незаме́ченным.
escape artist *n* трюка́ч.
escape clause *n пункт договóра, избавля́ющий сто́рону от отве́тственности*.
escapee [ɪskeɪ'pi:] *n* сбежа́вший(-ая) *m(f) adj*.
escape hatch *n* авари́йный люк.
escape key *n* (*COMPUT*) кла́виша вы́хода.
escape route *n* (*from fire*) запасно́й (пожа́рный) вы́ход; (*of prisoners etc*) маршру́т побе́га.
escapism [ɪs'keɪpɪzəm] *n* бе́гство от действи́тельности, эскапи́зм.
escapist [ɪs'keɪpɪst] *adj* (*literature*) уводя́щий от о́стрых пробле́м жи́зни, эскапи́стский.
escapologist [ɛskə'pɔlədʒɪst] *n* (*BRIT*) = **escape artist**.
escarpment [ɪs'kɑ:pmənt] *n* отко́с.
eschew [ɪs'tʃu:] *vt* (*company, violence*) сторони́ться (*impf*) +*gen*.
escort [*n* 'ɛskɔ:t, *vt* ɪs'kɔ:t] *n* (*companion: male*) сопровожда́ющий *m adj*; (: *female*) сопровожда́ющая *f adj*; (*MIL, POLICE*) конво́й ♦ *vt* сопровожда́ть (*impf*); **his/her ~** его́/её сопровожда́ющий(-ая).
escort agency *n* бюро́ *nt ind* по на́йму

сопровождающих.

Eskimo [ˈɛskɪməu] *n* эскимос(ка*).

ESL *n abbr* (*SCOL*) = *English as a Second Language*.

esophagus [iːˈsɒfəgəs] *n* (*US*) = **oesophagus**.

esoteric [ɛsəˈtɛrɪk] *adj* эзотерический.

ESP *n abbr* = **extrasensory perception**; (*SCOL*) = *English for Special Purposes*.

esp. *abbr* = **especially**.

especially [ɪsˈpɛʃlɪ] *adv* особенно.

espionage [ˈɛspɪɒnɑːʒ] *n* шпионаж.

esplanade [ɛspləˈneɪd] *n* эспланада.

espouse [ɪsˈpauz] *vt* (*policy, idea*) (целиком) отдаваться* (отдаться* *perf*) +*dat*, поддерживать (*impf*).

Esq. *abbr* = **Esquire**.

Esquire [ɪsˈkwaɪəʳ] *n*: **J. Brown,** ~ Дж. Браун, эсквайр.

essay [ˈɛseɪ] *n* (*SCOL*) сочинение; (*LITERATURE*) очерк.

essence [ˈɛsns] *n* сущность *f*; (*CULIN*) эссенция; **in** ~ в сущности; **speed is of the** ~ всё дело в скорости.

essential [ɪˈsɛnʃl] *adj* (*vital*) существенно необходимый* (необходим); (*basic*) основной ♦ *n* (*see adj*) существенно необходимая вещь *f*; основное *nt adj*; **it is** ~ **that** существенно важно, чтобы.

essentially [ɪˈsɛnʃəlɪ] *adv* в сущности.

EST *abbr* (*US*) = *Eastern Standard Time*.

est. *abbr* = *established*; *estimate(d)*.

establish [ɪsˈtæblɪʃ] *vt* (*organization*) учреждать (учредить* *perf*); (*facts, contact*) устанавливать (установить* *perf*); (*reputation*) утверждать (утвердить* *perf*) за собой.

established [ɪsˈtæblɪʃt] *adj* (*business*) упрочненный; (*custom, practice*) признанный.

establishment [ɪsˈtæblɪʃmənt] *n* (*see vb*) учреждение; установление; утверждение; (*shop etc*) заведение; **the E**~ истеблишмент.

estate [ɪsˈteɪt] *n* (*land*) поместье*; (*BRIT: also*: **housing** ~) жилой комплекс; (*LAW*) состояние.

estate agency *n* (*BRIT*) агенство по продаже недвижимости.

estate agent *n* (*BRIT*) агент по продаже недвижимости.

estate car *n* (*BRIT*) автомобиль *m*-пикап.

esteem [ɪsˈtiːm] *n*: **to hold sb in high** ~ относиться* (отнестись* *perf*) к кому-н с большим почтением.

esthetic [ɪsˈθɛtɪk] *adj* (*US*) = **aesthetic**.

estimate [*vb* ˈɛstɪmeɪt, *n* ˈɛstɪmət] *vt* (*reckon, calculate*) предварительно подсчитывать (подсчитать* *perf*); (: *chances*) оценивать (оценить* *perf*) ♦ *n* (*calculation*) подсчёт; (*assessment*) оценка*; (*builder's etc*) смета ♦ *vi* (*BRIT: COMM*): **to** ~ **for** составлять (составить* *perf*) смету +*gen*; **I** ~ **that** я полагаю, что; **to give sb an** ~ давать* (дать*

perf) кому-н оценку; **at a rough** ~ по грубым подсчётам.

estimation [ɛstɪˈmeɪʃən] *n* (*opinion*) оценка*; (*calculation*) подсчёт; **in my** ~ по моим подсчётам.

estimator [ˈɛstɪmeɪtəʳ] *n* оценщик.

Estonia [ɛsˈtəunɪə] *n* Эстония.

Estonian [ɛsˈtəunɪən] *n* (*person*) эстонец*-(-онка*); (*LING*) эстонский* язык* ♦ *adj* эстонский*.

estranged [ɪsˈtreɪndʒd] *adj* (*from spouse, family*) отчуждённый* (отчуждён); **his** ~ **wife** ушедшая от него жена; **he is** ~ **from his wife** он разошёлся с женой.

estrangement [ɪsˈtreɪndʒmənt] *n* отчуждение.

estrogen [ˈiːstrəudʒən] *n* (*US*) = **oestrogen**.

estuary [ˈɛstjuərɪ] *n* устье*.

ET *n abbr* (*BRIT*: = *Employment Training*) профессиональная подготовка ♦ *abbr* (*US*) = *Eastern Time*.

ETA *n abbr* (= *estimated time of arrival*) ожидаемое время* *nt* прибытия.

et al. *abbr* (*and others*: = *et alii*) и другие.

etc. *abbr* (= *et cetera*) и т.д.= *и так далее*.

etch [ɛtʃ] *vt* (*surface*) гравировать (выгравировать *perf*); (*design*): **to** ~ (**on**) травить* (вытравить* *perf*) (на +*prp*); **it will be** ~**ed on my memory** это запечатлеется в моей памяти.

etching [ˈɛtʃɪŋ] *n* (*craft*) гравировка*; (*product*) гравюра, офорт.

ETD *n abbr* (= *estimated time of departure*) ожидаемое время* *nt* отправления.

eternal [ɪˈtəːnl] *adj* вечный* (вечен).

eternity [ɪˈtəːnɪtɪ] *n* вечность *f*.

ether [ˈiːθəʳ] *n* эфир*.

ethereal [ɪˈθɪərɪəl] *adj* (*delicate*) эфирный.

ethical [ˈɛθɪkl] *adj* (*relating to ethics*) этический; (*morally right*) этичный* (этичен).

ethics [ˈɛθɪks] *n*, *npl* этика *fsg*.

Ethiopia [iːθɪˈəupɪə] *n* Эфиопия.

Ethiopian [iːθɪˈəupɪən] *adj* эфиопский* ♦ *n* эфиоп(а).

ethnic [ˈɛθnɪk] *adj* этнический*.

ethnic cleansing *n* этническая чистка*.

ethnology [ɛθˈnɒlədʒɪ] *n* этнология.

ethos [ˈiːθɒs] *n* этос.

etiquette [ˈɛtɪkɛt] *n* этикет.

ETV *n abbr* (*US*) = *Educational Television*.

etymology [ɛtɪˈmɒlədʒɪ] *n* этимология.

eucalyptus [juːkəˈlɪptəs] *n* эвкалипт.

Eucharist [ˈjuːkərɪst] *n* (*REL*): **the** ~ евхаристия, причастие.

eulogy [ˈjuːlədʒɪ] *n* восхваление.

euphemism [ˈjuːfəmɪzəm] *n* эвфемизм.

euphemistic [juːfəˈmɪstɪk] *adj* эвфемистический*.

euphoria [juːˈfɔːrɪə] *n* эйфория.

Eurasia [juəˈreɪʒə] *n* Евразия.

Eurasian [juəˈreɪʒən] *adj* евразийский* ♦ *n* евразиец* (-ийка*).

Euratom [juə'rætəm] *n abbr* (= *European Atomic Energy Community*) Европейский* комитет по атомной энергии.
Euro- ['juərəu] *prefix* евро-.
eurocheque ['juərəut∫ɛk] *n* еврочек.
Eurocrat ['juərəukræt] *n служащий в организации Европейского Сообщества.*
Eurodollar ['juərəudɔləˈ] *n* евродоллар.
Europe ['juərəp] *n* Европа.
European [juərə'pi:ən] *adj* европейский* ◆ *n* европеец(-ейка).
European Community *n*: the~~ Европейское Сообщество.
European Court of Justice *n*: the ~~~~ Европейский* Суд*.
European Economic Community *n*: the ~~ ~ Европейское Экономическое Сообщество.
Euro-sceptic ['juərəuskɛptɪk] *n* евроскептик (*человек, относящийся с недоверием к идее Европейского Союза*).
euthanasia [ju:θə'neɪzɪə] *n* эйтаназия (*безнадёжно больных*).
evacuate [ɪ'vækjueɪt] *vt* (*people*) эвакуировать (*impf/perf*); (*place*) очищать (очистить* *perf*).
evacuation [ɪvækju'eɪ∫ən] *n* (*see vb*) эвакуация; очистка*.
evacuee [ɪvækju'i:] *n* эвакуированный(-ая) *m(f) adj.*
evade [ɪ'veɪd] *vt* (*duties, question*) уклоняться (уклониться* *perf*) от +*gen*; (*person*) избегать (*impf*) +*gen*.
evaluate [ɪ'væljueɪt] *vt* оценивать (оценить* *perf*).
evangelical [i:væn'dʒɛlɪkl] *adj* евангелический*.
evangelist [ɪ'vændʒəlɪst] *n* евангелист.
evangelize [ɪ'vændʒəlaɪz] *vi* проповедовать (*impf*) евангелизм.
evaporate [ɪ'væpəreɪt] *vi* испаряться (испариться* *perf*); (*feeling, attitude*) пропадать (пропасть* *perf*).
evaporated milk [ɪ'væpəreɪtɪd-] *n* сгущённое молоко (*без сахара*).
evaporation [ɪvæpə'reɪ∫ən] *n* испарение.
evasion [ɪ'veɪʒən] *n* (*of responsibility, tax etc*) уклонение.
evasive [ɪ'veɪsɪv] *adj* (*reply, action*) уклончивый (уклончив).
eve [i:v] *n*: **on the ~ of** накануне +*gen*; **Christmas E~** канун Рождество; **New Year's E~** канун Нового года.
even ['i:vn] *adj* (*level, smooth*) ровный* (ровен); (*equal*) равный* (равен); (*number*) чётный ◆ *adv* даже; **~ if** даже если; **~ though** хотя и; **~ more** ещё больше; **he loves her ~ more** он любит её ещё больше; **the work is going ~ better/faster** работа идёт ещё

лучше/быстрее; **~ so** всё же; **not ~** даже не; **~ he was there** даже он там был; **~ on Sundays** даже по воскресеньям; **I am ~ more likely to leave now** теперь даже ещё более вероятно, что я уеду; **to break ~** работать на уровне самоокупаемости (*но без дохода*); **to get ~ with sb** (*inf*) расквитаться (*perf*) с кем-н
► **even out** *vt* выравнивать (выравнять *perf*) ◆ *vi* выравниваться (выравняться *perf*).
even-handed ['i:vnhændɪd] *adj* беспристрастный (беспристрастен).
evening ['i:vnɪŋ] *n* вечер*; **in the ~** вечером; **this ~** сегодня вечером; **tomorrow/yesterday ~** завтра/вчера вечером.
evening class *n* вечерние курсы *mpl*.
evening dress *n* (*no pl: formal clothes*) вечерний туалет; (*gown*) вечернее платье*.
evenly ['i:vnlɪ] *adv* (*distribute*) равномерно; (*divide, breathe*) ровно.
evensong ['i:vnsɔŋ] *n* вечерня*.
event [ɪ'vɛnt] *n* (*occurrence*) событие; (*SPORT: competition*) соревнование, вид; **in the normal course of ~s** при нормальном течении событий; **in the ~ of** в случае +*gen*; **in the ~** в конечном счёте; **at all ~s** (*BRIT*), **in any ~** во всяком *or* любом случае.
eventful [ɪ'vɛntful] *adj* насыщенный* (насыщен) событиями.
eventing [ɪ'vɛntɪŋ] *n* (*HORSE-RIDING*) участие в ряде состязаний по верховой езде.
eventual [ɪ'vɛnt∫uəl] *adj* (*outcome, goal*) конечный.
eventuality [ɪvɛnt∫u'ælɪtɪ] *n* (*possibility*) возможность *f*.
eventually [ɪ'vɛnt∫uəlɪ] *adv* в конце концов.
ever ['ɛvəˈ] *adv* (*always*) всегда; (*at any time*) когда-либо, когда-нибудь; **why ~ not?** почему же нет?; **the best ~** самый лучший*; **have you ~ been to Russia?** Вы когда-либо *or* когда-нибудь были в России?; **for ~** навсегда; **hardly ~** почти никогда; **I hardly ~ read** я почти никогда не читаю; **better than ~** лучше чем бы то ни было *or* чем когда-либо; **~ since** с тех пор, как; **~ since that day** с того дня; **~ so pretty** ужасно симпатичная; **thank you ~ so much** я Вам так благодарен; **yours ~** (*BRIT: in letters*) преданный Вам.
Everest ['ɛvərɪst] *n* (*also*: **Mount ~**) Эверест.
evergreen ['ɛvəgri:n] *n* вечнозелёный.
everlasting [ɛvə'lɑ:stɪŋ] *adj* (*love, life etc*) вечный* (вечен).

KEYWORD
---

every ['ɛvrɪ] *adj* **1** (*each*) каждый; **every child will receive a present** каждый ребёнок получит подарок; **every one of them** каждый из них; **every shop in the town was closed** все

магази́ны в го́роде бы́ли закры́ты
2 (*all possible*): **I gave you every assistance** я
помо́г Вам, всем чем то́лько мо́жно; **I tried
every option** я испро́бовал все пути́; **I have
every confidence in him** я в нём соверше́нно
уве́рен; **we wish you every success** мы
жела́ем Вам вся́ческого успе́ха; **he's every
bit as clever/stupid as his brother** он столь же
умён/глуп, как и его́ брат
3 (*showing recurrence*) ка́ждый; **every week**
ка́ждую неде́лю; **every other car** ка́ждая
втора́я маши́на; **she visits me every third/
other day** она прихо́дит ко мне ка́ждые два
дня/че́рез день; **every now and then** вре́мя*
от вре́мени.

everybody ['ɛvrɪbɔdɪ] *pron* (*each*) ка́ждый; (*all*)
все *pl*; ~ **knows about it** об э́том ка́ждый
зна́ет; ~ **else** все остальны́е.
everyday ['ɛvrɪdeɪ] *adj* (*daily*) ежедне́вный;
(*common*) повседне́вный*.
everyone ['ɛvrɪwʌn] *pron* = **everybody**.
everything ['ɛvrɪθɪŋ] *pron* всё; ~ **is ready** всё
гото́во; **he did** ~ **possible** он сде́лал всё
возмо́жное; **you think of** ~ Вы ду́маете обо
всём; **I don't agree with** ~ **he says** я не
согла́сен со всем, что он говори́т.
everywhere ['ɛvrɪwɛə'] *adv* везде́, повсю́ду; ~
you go you meet … куда́ ни пойдёшь, везде́ *or*
повсю́ду встреча́ешь ….
evict [ɪ'vɪkt] *vt* выселя́ть (вы́селить *perf*).
eviction [ɪ'vɪkʃən] *n* выселе́ние.
eviction notice *n* предупрежде́ние о
выселе́нии.
eviction order *n* прика́з о выселе́нии.
evidence ['ɛvɪdns] *n* (*proof*) доказа́тельство;
(*testimony*) показа́ние; (*indication*) при́знаки
mpl; **to give** ~ дава́ть* (дать* *perf*)
(свиде́тельские) показа́ния; **to show** ~ **of**
проявля́ть (проя́вить* *perf*) при́знаки +*gen*; **in**
~ (*obvious*) заме́тен.
evident ['ɛvɪdnt] *adj* заме́тный* (заме́тен).
evidently ['ɛvɪdntlɪ] *adv* очеви́дно.
evil ['iːvl] *adj* (*person, spirit*) злой* (зол);
(*system, influence*) дурно́й* ♦ *n* зло.
evocative [ɪ'vɔkətɪv] *adj* (*description, music*)
навева́ющий чу́вства и воспомина́ния.
evoke [ɪ'vəuk] *vt* вызыва́ть (вы́звать* *perf*).
evolution [iːvə'luːʃən] *n* эволю́ция.
evolve [ɪ'vɔlv] *vt* развива́ть (разви́ть* *perf*) ♦ *vi*
(*animal, plant*) эволюциони́ровать (*impf/perf*);
(*plan, idea*) развива́ться (разви́ться* *perf*).
ewe [juː] *n* овца́*.
ewer ['juːə'] *n* кувши́н*.
ex- [ɛks] *prefix* (*former*) экс-, бы́вший*; (*out of*):
the price ex works цена́ с предприя́тия.
exacerbate [ɛks'æsəbeɪt] *vt* (*situation, pain*)
обостря́ть (обостри́ть *perf*).
exact [ɪg'zækt] *adj* то́чный* (то́чен) ♦ *vt*: **to** ~
sth from (*obedience*) тре́бовать
(потре́бовать *perf*) чего́-н от +*gen*; (*payment*)
взы́скивать (взыска́ть* *perf*) что-н с +*gen*.

exacting [ɪg'zæktɪŋ] *adj* (*task*) тру́дный*;
(*person*) взыска́тельный* (взыска́телен).
exactly [ɪg'zæktlɪ] *adv* то́чно; ~! вот и́менно!
exaggerate [ɪg'zædʒəreɪt] *vti* преувели́чивать
(преувели́чить *perf*).
exaggerated [ɪg'zædʒəreɪtɪd] *adj* пре-
увели́ченный (преувели́чен).
exaggeration [ɪgzædʒə'reɪʃən] *n* пре-
увеличе́ние.
exalt [ɪg'zɔːlt] *vt* превозноси́ть* (превознести́*
perf).
exalted [ɪg'zɔːltɪd] *adj* (*prominent*) высо́кий*
(высо́к); (*elated*) восто́рженный*
(восто́ржен).
exam [ɪg'zæm] *n abbr* = **examination**.
examination [ɪgzæmɪ'neɪʃən] *n* (*inspection*)
изуче́ние; (*plan*) рассмотре́ние; (*SCOL*)
экза́мен; (*LAW*) допро́с; (*MED*) осмо́тр; **to
take** *or* (*BRIT*) **sit an** ~ сдава́ть* (сдать* *perf*)
экза́мен; **the matter is under** ~ де́ло
нахо́дится на рассмотре́нии.
examine [ɪg'zæmɪn] *vt* (*scrutinize*) смотре́ть
(посмотре́ть *perf*) на +*acc*; (*inspect*)
осма́тривать (осмотре́ть *perf*); (*plan*)
рассма́тривать (рассмотре́ть *perf*); (*SCOL*)
экзаменова́ть (проэкзаменова́ть *perf*); (*LAW*)
допра́шивать (допроси́ть* *perf*); (*MED*)
осма́тривать (осмотре́ть* *perf*).
examiner [ɪg'zæmɪnə'] *n* (*SCOL*) экзамена́тор.
example [ɪg'zɑːmpl] *n* приме́р; **for** ~
наприме́р; **to set a good/bad** ~ подава́ть*
(пода́ть* *perf*) хоро́ший*/плохо́й приме́р.
exasperate [ɪg'zɑːspəreɪt] *vt* изма́тывать
(измота́ть *perf*); ~**d by** *or* **with** измо́танный
+*instr*.
exasperating [ɪg'zɑːspəreɪtɪŋ] *adj* раз-
дража́ющий.
exasperation [ɪgzɑːspə'reɪʃən] *n* раздраже́ние;
in ~ в раздраже́нии.
excavate ['ɛkskəveɪt] *vt* (*site*) раска́пывать
(раскопа́ть *perf*); (*hole*) выка́пывать
(вы́копать *perf*) ♦ *vi* производи́ть*
(произвести́* *perf*) раско́пки.
excavation [ɛkskə'veɪʃən] *n* (*activity*)
раска́пывание; (*archeological dig*): ~**s**
раско́пки *fpl*.
excavator ['ɛkskəveɪtə'] *n* экскава́тор.
exceed [ɪk'siːd] *vt* превыша́ть (превы́сить*
perf); (*hopes*) превосходи́ть* (превзойти́*
perf).
exceedingly [ɪk'siːdɪŋlɪ] *adv* чрезвыча́йно.
excel [ɪk'sɛl] *vt* превосходи́ть* (превзойти́*
perf) ♦ *vi*: **to** ~ (**in** *or* **at**) отлича́ться
(отличи́ться *perf*) (в +*prp*); **to** ~ **o.s.** (*BRIT*)
превосходи́ть* (превзойти́* *perf*) самого́
себя́.
excellence ['ɛksələns] *n* (*in sport, business*)
мастерство́*; (*superiority*) превосхо́дство.
Excellency ['ɛksələnsɪ] *n*: **His** ~ его́
Превосходи́тельство.
excellent ['ɛksələnt] *adj* отли́чный* (отли́чен),

превосхо́дный* (превосхо́ден) ◆ *excl*: ~!
отли́чно!, превосхо́дно!

except [ɪkˈsɛpt] *prep* (*also:* ~ **for**) кро́ме +*gen* ◆
vt: **to** ~ **sb** (**from**) исключа́ть (исключи́ть *perf*)
кого́-н (из +*gen*); ~ **if/when** кро́ме *or* за
исключе́нием тех слу́чаев е́сли/когда́; ~ **that**
кро́ме того́, что.

excepting [ɪkˈsɛptɪŋ] *prep* за исключе́нием
+*gen*.

exception [ɪkˈsɛpʃən] *n* исключе́ние; **to take** ~
to обижа́ться (оби́деться* *perf*) на +*acc*; **with
the** ~ **of** за исключе́нием +*gen*.

exceptional [ɪkˈsɛpʃənl] *adj* исключи́тельный*
(исключи́телен).

excerpt [ˈɛksəːpt] *n* отры́вок*.

excess [ɪkˈsɛs] *n* избы́ток*; (*INSURANCE*)
превыше́ние; ~**es** *npl* (*of cruelty etc*) эксце́ссы
mpl, кра́йности *fpl*; **an** ~ **of £15, a £15** ~
изли́шек* в £15; **in** ~ **of** сверх +*gen*, свы́ше
+*gen*; **to drink to** ~ пить (*impf*) сверх ме́ры.

excess baggage *n* изли́шек* багажа́.

excess fare *n* (*BRIT*) допла́та (*за биле́т*).

excessive [ɪkˈsɛsɪv] *adj* чрезме́рный*
(чрезме́рен).

excess supply *n* избы́точное предложе́ние.

exchange [ɪksˈtʃeɪndʒ] *n* (*conversation*) обме́н
мне́ниями; (*argument*) перепа́лка*; (*also:*
telephone ~) коммута́тор ◆ *vt*: **to** ~ (**for**)
(*goods etc*) обме́нивать (обменя́ть *perf*) (на
+*acc*); ~ (**of**) обме́н (+*instr*); **in** ~ **for** в обме́н
на +*acc*; **foreign** ~ валю́тная би́ржа.

exchange control *n* валю́тный контро́ль *m*.

exchange market *n* валю́тный ры́нок*.

exchange rate *n* валю́тный *or* обме́нный
курс.

Exchequer [ɪksˈtʃɛkəʳ] *n* (*BRIT*): **the** ~
казначе́йство.

excisable [ɪkˈsaɪzəbl] *adj* (*goods*) облага́емый
акци́зным сбо́ром.

excise [*n* ˈɛksaɪz, *vt* ɛkˈsaɪz] *n* акци́з, акци́зный
сбор ◆ *vt* (*remove*) выреза́ть (вы́резать* *perf*).

excise duties *npl* акци́зный сбор *msg*.

excitable [ɪkˈsaɪtəbl] *adj* (легко́) возбуди́мый.

excite [ɪkˈsaɪt] *vt* возбужда́ть (возбуди́ть* *perf*);
(*stimulate*) заинтересо́вать (заинтересова́ть
perf); **to get** ~**d** волнова́ться (взволнова́ться
perf).

excitement [ɪkˈsaɪtmənt] *n* (*agitation*)
возбужде́ние; (*exhilaration*) оживле́ние.

exciting [ɪkˈsaɪtɪŋ] *adj* восхити́тельный.

excl. *abbr* = **excluding**, **exclusive (of)**.

exclaim [ɪksˈkleɪm] *vi* восклица́ть
(воскли́кнуть *perf*).

exclamation [ɛkskləˈmeɪʃən] *n* восклица́ние.

exclamation mark *n* восклица́тельный знак.

exclude [ɪksˈkluːd] *vt* исключа́ть (исключи́ть
perf).

excluding [ɪksˈkluːdɪŋ] *prep* исключа́я +*acc*.

exclusion [ɪksˈkluːʒən] *n* исключе́ние; **to the** ~
of исключа́я +*acc*.

exclusion clause *n* статья́* об исключе́ниях.

exclusion zone *n* запре́тная зо́на.

exclusive [ɪksˈkluːsɪv] *adj* (*select*)
недосту́пный* (недосту́пен), для
и́збранных; (*use*) исключи́тельный*
(исключи́телен); (*interview*) уника́льный*
(уника́лен); (*PRESS*) эксклюзи́вный
материа́л (*напеча́танный то́лько в одно́й
газе́те*) ◆ *adv*: ~ **of** (*COMM*) не счита́я +*gen*;
mutually ~ взаимоисключа́ющие; ~ **of
postage** без сто́имости почто́вых расхо́дов; ~
from the 1st to the 15th March ~ с 1-ого до
15-ого ма́рта, включи́тельно; ~ **of tax** не
счита́я нало́га.

exclusively [ɪksˈkluːsɪvlɪ] *adv* исключи́тельно.

exclusive rights *npl* исключи́тельные права́
ntpl.

excommunicate [ɛkskəˈmjuːnɪkeɪt] *vt*
отлуча́ть (отлучи́ть *perf*) от це́ркви.

excrement [ˈɛkskrəmənt] *n* экскреме́нты *mpl*.

excruciating [ɪksˈkruːʃieɪtɪŋ] *adj* мучи́тельный*
(мучи́телен).

excursion [ɪksˈkəːʃən] *n* экску́рсия.

excursion ticket *n* дешёвый биле́т на
коро́ткую экску́рсию.

excusable [ɪksˈkjuːzəbl] *adj* прости́тельный*
(прости́телен).

excuse [*n* ɪksˈkjuːs, *vt* ɪksˈkjuːz] *n* оправда́ние ◆
vt (*justify*) опра́вдывать (оправда́ть *perf*);
(*forgive*) проща́ть (прости́ть* *perf*); **to make
~s for sb** находи́ть* (найти́* *perf*) оправда́ние
кому́-н; **that's no** ~! э́то не причи́на!; ~ **sb
from sth/doing** освобожда́ть (освободи́ть*
perf) кого́-н от чего́-н/от того́, что́бы +*infin*;
~ **me!** (*attracting attention*) извини́те!,
прости́те!; (*as apology*) извини́те *or*
прости́те (меня́)!; **if you will** ~ **me, I have to** ...
Вы прости́те, мне на́до ...; **to** ~ **o.s. for sth/
for having done sth** извиня́ться (извини́ться
perf) за что-н/за то, что сде́лал что-н.

ex-directory [ˈɛksdɪˈrɛktərɪ] *adj* (*BRIT: number*)
не включённый (включён) в телефо́нный
спра́вочник; **she's** ~ её но́мер не включён в
телефо́нный спра́вочник.

execrable [ˈɛksɪkrəbl] *adj* отврати́тельный*
(отврати́телен).

execute [ˈɛksɪkjuːt] *vt* (*kill*) казни́ть (*impf/perf*);
(*carry out, perform*) выполня́ть (вы́полнить
perf).

execution [ɛksɪˈkjuːʃən] *n* (*see vb*) казнь *f*;
выполне́ние.

executioner [ɛksɪˈkjuːʃnəʳ] *n* пала́ч*.

executive [ɪgˈzɛkjutɪv] *n* (*person*)
руководи́тель *m*; (*committee*)
исполни́тельный о́рган ◆ *adj* (*board, role*)
руководя́щий*; (*secretary*) отве́тственный;

(*car, plane, chair, toys*) для руководя́щих рабо́тников.
executive director *n* дире́ктор*-распоряди́тель *m*.
executor [ɪɡ'zɛkjutə'] *n* (*LAW*) исполни́тель *m*.
exemplary [ɪɡ'zɛmplərɪ] *adj* приме́рный* (приме́рен).
exemplify [ɪɡ'zɛmplɪfaɪ] *vt* (*typify*) служи́ть* (послужи́ть *perf*) приме́ром +*gen*; (*illustrate*) поясня́ть (поясни́ть *perf*) приме́ром.
exempt [ɪɡ'zɛmpt] *adj*: ~ **from** освобожд-ённый (освобождён) от +*gen* ♦ *vt*: **to ~ sb from** освобожда́ть (освободи́ть* *perf*) кого́-н от +*gen*.
exemption [ɪɡ'zɛmpʃən] *n* освобожде́ние.
exercise ['ɛksəsaɪz] *n* (*no pl*) гимна́стика; (*keep-fit*) заря́дка*; (*SCOL*, *MUS*) упражне́ние; (*of authority etc*) проявле́ние ♦ *vt* (*patience, authority*) проявля́ть (прояви́ть* *perf*); (*right*) осуществля́ть (осуществи́ть* *perf*); (*dog*) выгу́ливать (*impf*); (*mind*) занима́ть (*impf*) ♦ *vi* (*also*: **to take ~**) упражня́ться (*impf*); **military ~s** вое́нные уче́ния; **you need more ~** Вам на́до бо́льше дви́гаться.
exercise bike *n* велосипе́д-тренажёр.
exercise book *n* тетра́дь *f*.
exert [ɪɡ'zə:t] *vt* (*influence, pressure*) ока́зывать (оказа́ть* *perf*); (*authority*) применя́ть (примени́ть* *perf*); **to ~ o.s.** напряга́ться (напря́чься* *perf*).
exertion [ɪɡ'zə:ʃən] *n* (*effort*) уси́лие; (*strain*) напряже́ние.
ex gratia ['ɛks'ɡreɪʃə] *adj*: ~~ **payment** де́нежное вознагражде́ние.
exhale [ɛks'heɪl] *vti* выдыха́ть (вы́дохнуть *perf*).
exhaust [ɪɡ'zɔ:st] *n* (*also*: ~ **pipe**) выхлопна́я труба́; (*fumes*) выхлопны́е га́зы *mpl* ♦ *vt* (*person*) изнуря́ть (изнури́ть *perf*); (*money, resources etc*) истоща́ть (истощи́ть *perf*); (*topic*) исче́рпывать (исче́рпать *perf*); **to ~ o.s.** доводи́ть* (довести́* *perf*) себя́ до изможже́ния *or* изнуре́ния.
exhausted [ɪɡ'zɔ:stɪd] *adj* (*person*) изнурённый* (изнурён), изнеможённый* (изнеможён).
exhausting [ɪɡ'zɔ:stɪŋ] *adj* изнури́тельный* (изнури́телен).
exhaustion [ɪɡ'zɔ:stʃən] *n* (*tiredness*) изможже́ние; **nervous ~** не́рвное истоще́ние.
exhaustive [ɪɡ'zɔ:stɪv] *adj* исче́рпывающий*.
exhibit [ɪɡ'zɪbɪt] *n* экспона́т; (*LAW*) веще́ственное доказа́тельство ♦ *vt* (*paintings*) экспони́ровать (*impf/perf*); (*quality, emotion*) проявля́ть (прояви́ть* *perf*).
exhibition [ɛksɪ'bɪʃən] *n* (*of paintings etc*) вы́ставка*; (*of ability, emotion*) проявле́ние; **to make an ~ of o.s.** выставля́ть (вы́ставить* *perf*) себя́ на посме́шище.
exhibitionist [ɛksɪ'bɪʃənɪst] *n* эксгибициони́ст;

(*show-off*): **he's a real ~** он всё де́лает напока́з.
exhibitor [ɪɡ'zɪbɪtə'] *n* экспоне́нт.
exhilarating [ɪɡ'zɪləreɪtɪŋ] *adj* волну́ющий.
exhilaration [ɪɡzɪlə'reɪʃən] *n* взволно́ванность *f*.
exhort [ɪɡ'zɔ:t] *vt*: **to ~ sb to do** увещева́ть (*impf*) кого́-н +*infin*.
exile ['ɛksaɪl] *n* (*banishment*) ссы́лка*, изгна́ние; (*person*) ссы́льный(-ая) *m(f) adj*, изгна́нник ♦ *vt* ссыла́ть (сосла́ть* *perf*); (*abroad*) высыла́ть (вы́слать* *perf*); **in ~** в ссы́лке *or* изгна́нии.
exist [ɪɡ'zɪst] *vi* существова́ть (*impf*).
existence [ɪɡ'zɪstəns] *n* существова́ние; **to be in ~** существова́ть (*impf*).
existentialism [ɛɡzɪs'tɛnʃlɪzəm] *n* экзистенциали́зм.
existing [ɪɡ'zɪstɪŋ] *adj* существу́ющий.
exit ['ɛksɪt] *n* (*way out*) вы́ход; (*on motorway*) вы́езд; (*departure*) ухо́д ♦ *vi* (*THEAT*) уходи́ть* (уйти́* *perf*); (*COMPUT*) выходи́ть* (вы́йти* *perf*); (*leave*): **to ~ from** (*room*) выходи́ть* (вы́йти* *perf*) из +*gen*; (*motorway*) съезжа́ть (съе́хать* *perf*) с +*gen*.
exit poll *n* предвари́тельный подсчёт голосо́в.
exit ramp *n* (*US*: *AUT*) съезд с автостра́ды.
exit visa *n* выездна́я ви́за.
exodus ['ɛksədəs] *n* ма́ссовое бе́гство; **the ~ to the cities** ма́ссовое переселе́ние в города́.
ex officio ['ɛksə'fɪʃɪəu] *adv* по до́лжности.
exonerate [ɪɡ'zɔnəreɪt] *vt*: **to ~ sb from guilt/ responsibility** снима́ть (снять* *perf*) с кого́-н обвине́ние/отве́тственность.
exorbitant [ɪɡ'zɔ:bɪtnt] *adj* непоме́рный* (непоме́рен).
exorcize ['ɛksɔ:saɪz] *vt* (*person, place*) изгоня́ть (изгна́ть* *perf*) дья́вола из +*gen*; (*spirit*) изгоня́ть (изгна́ть* *perf*).
exotic [ɪɡ'zɔtɪk] *adj* экзоти́ческий*.
expand [ɪks'pænd] *vt* (*area, business, influence*) расширя́ть (расши́рить *perf*); (*numbers*) увели́чивать (увели́чить *perf*) ♦ *vi* (*gas, metal, business*) расширя́ться (расши́риться *perf*); (*population*) увели́чиваться (увели́читься *perf*); **to ~ on** (*story, idea etc*) подро́бно разъясня́ть (разъясни́ть *perf*).
expanse [ɪks'pæns] *n*: **an ~ of sea/sky** морско́й/ небе́сный просто́р.
expansion [ɪks'pænʃən] *n* расшире́ние; (*of population*) увеличе́ние; (*of economy*) рост.
expansionism [ɪks'pænʃənɪzəm] *n* (*ECON*) экспансиони́зм.
expansionist [ɪks'pænʃənɪst] *adj* (*policy*) экспансиони́стский.
expatriate [ɛks'pætrɪət] *n* эмигра́нт(ка*).
expect [ɪks'pɛkt] *vt* (*anticipate, hope for, await*) ожида́ть (*impf*); (*baby*) ждать* (*impf*); (*suppose*) полага́ть (*impf*) ♦ *vi*: **to be ~ing** (*be pregnant*) ждать* (*impf*) ребёнка; **he ~s me to**

finish by Tuesday он ожида́ет, что я зако́нчу ко вто́рнику; **to ~ to do** рассчи́тывать *(impf)* +*infin*; **as ~ed** как и ожида́лось; **I ~ so** я полага́ю.

expectancy [ɪks'pɛktənsɪ] *n* предвкуше́ние; **life ~** сре́дняя продолжи́тельность *f* жи́зни.

expectant [ɪks'pɛktənt] *adj (silence, crowd)* выжида́ющий.

expectantly [ɪks'pɛktəntlɪ] *adv* с наде́ждой.

expectant mother *n* бере́менная же́нщина.

expectation [ɛkspɛk'teɪʃən] *n (hope)* ожида́ние; **in ~ of** в ожида́нии +*gen*; **contrary to** *or* **against all ~(s)** вопреки́ всем ожида́ниям; **to come** *or* **live up to sb's ~s** опра́вдывать (оправда́ть *perf*) чьи-н ожида́ния.

expedience [ɪks'pi:dɪəns] *n* = **expediency**.

expediency [ɪks'pi:dɪənsɪ] *n* вы́года; **for the sake of ~** ра́ди вы́годы.

expedient [ɪks'pi:dɪənt] *adj* целесообра́зный* (целесообра́зен). ♦ *n* уло́вка.

expedite ['ɛkspədaɪt] *vt* ускоря́ть (уско́рить *perf*).

expedition [ɛkspə'dɪʃən] *n* экспеди́ция; *(for shopping etc)* похо́д.

expeditionary force [ɛkspə'dɪʃənrɪ-] *n* экспедицио́нные войска́* *pl*.

expeditious [ɛkspə'dɪʃəs] *adj* эффекти́вный* (эффекти́вен).

expel [ɪks'pɛl] *vt (person: from school, organization)* исключа́ть (исключи́ть *perf*); (: *from place)* изгоня́ть (изгна́ть* *perf*); *(substance: from body etc)* выводи́ть* (вы́вести* *perf*).

expend [ɪks'pɛnd] *vt* расхо́довать (израсхо́довать *perf*), тра́тить* (затра́тить* *perf*).

expendable [ɪks'pɛndəbl] *adj (resources)* подлежа́щий списа́нию; **he is entirely ~** его́ мо́жно сбро́сить со счётов.

expenditure [ɪks'pɛndɪtʃə'] *n (money spent)* затра́ты *fpl*; *(of money)* расхо́дование; *(of energy, time)* затра́та.

expense [ɪks'pɛns] *n (cost)* сто́имость *f*; **~s** *npl (travelling expenses etc)* расхо́ды *mpl*; *(expenditure)* затра́ты *fpl*; **at the ~ of** за счёт +*gen*; **to go to the ~ of doing** тра́титься* (потра́титься* *perf*) +*infin*; **at great/little ~** с больши́ми/небольши́ми затра́тами.

expense account *n* счёт подотчётных сумм.

expensive [ɪks'pɛnsɪv] *adj* дорого́й* (до́рог); **to be ~** до́рого сто́ить *(impf)*; **to have ~ tastes** име́ть *(impf)* вкус к дороги́м веща́м.

experience [ɪks'pɪərɪəns] *n (in job, of situation)* о́пыт; *(event, activity)* слу́чай; (: *difficult, painful)* испыта́ние; *(of emotion)* пережива́ние ♦ *vt* испы́тывать (испыта́ть *perf*), пережива́ть (пережи́ть* *perf*); **to know**

by *or* **from ~** знать *(impf)* по о́пыту; **to learn by ~** учи́ться *(impf)* на о́пыте.

experienced [ɪks'pɪərɪənst] *adj* о́пытный* (о́пытен).

experiment [ɪks'pɛrɪmənt] *n* экспериме́нт, о́пыт ♦ *vi*: **to ~ (with/on)** эксперименти́ровать *(impf)* (с +*instr*/на +*prp*); **to carry out** *or* **perform an ~** проводи́ть* (провести́* *perf*) экспериме́нт; **as an ~** в ка́честве экспериме́нта; **to ~ with a new vaccine** проводи́ть* (провести́* *perf*) о́пыты с но́вой вакци́ной.

experimental [ɪksperɪ'mɛntl] *adj (methods, ideas)* эксперимента́льный; *(tests)* про́бный; **at the ~ stage** на ста́дии экспериме́нта.

expert ['ɛkspə:t] *n* экспе́рт, специали́ст ♦ *adj (person)* уме́лый; **~ opinion/advice** мне́ние/ сове́т экспе́рта *or* специали́ста; **~ on** *or* **on sth** специали́ст по чему́-н; **she is ~ at resolving disputes** она́ прекра́сно уме́ет разреша́ть спо́ры; **~ witness** *(LAW)* суде́бный экспе́рт.

expertise [ɛkspə:'ti:z] *n* зна́ния *or* о́пыт.

expire [ɪks'paɪə'] *vi* истека́ть (исте́чь* *perf*); **my passport ~s in January** срок де́йствия моего́ па́спорта истека́ет в январе́.

expiry [ɪks'paɪərɪ] *n* истече́ние сро́ка.

expiry date *n* да́та истече́ния сро́ка.

explain [ɪks'pleɪn] *vt* объясня́ть (объясни́ть *perf*)

▶ **explain away** *vt (mistake, situation)* находи́ть* (найти́* *perf*) оправда́ние +*gen*.

explanation [ɛksplə'neɪʃən] *n* объясне́ние; **to find an ~ for sth** находи́ть* (найти́* *perf*) объясне́ние чему́-н.

explanatory [ɪks'plænətrɪ] *adj (comment etc)* объясни́тельный; **~ notes** примеча́ния *ntpl*.

expletive [ɛks'pli:tɪv] *n* бра́нное сло́во*, руга́тельство.

explicable [ɪks'plɪkəbl] *adj* объясни́мый; **for no ~ reason** по необъясни́мой причи́не.

explicit [ɪks'plɪsɪt] *adj* я́вный* (я́вен); *(sex, violence)* открове́нный.

explode [ɪks'pləud] *vi (bomb, person)* взрыва́ться (взорва́ться* *perf*); *(population)* ре́зко возраста́ть (возрасти́* *perf*) ♦ *vt (bomb)* взрыва́ть (взорва́ть* *perf*); *(myth, theory)* опроверга́ть* (опрове́ргнуть* *perf*); **to ~ with laughter** разража́ться (разрази́ться* *perf*) сме́хом.

exploit [*vt* ɪks'plɔɪt, *n* 'ɛksplɔɪt] *vt (resources, also pej: person, idea)* эксплуати́ровать *(impf)*; *(opportunity)* испо́льзовать *(impf/perf)* ♦ *n* по́двиг.

exploitation [ɛksplɔɪ'teɪʃən] *n (see vb)* эксплуата́ция; испо́льзование.

exploration [ɛksplə'reɪʃən] *n (of place)* иссле́дование; *(of idea)* изуче́ние.

exploratory [ɪks'plɔrətrɪ] *adj (expedition)*

---

* marks translations which have irregular inflections. The Russian-English side of the dictionary gives inflectional information.

исследовательский*; (*talks, operation*) предварительный.

explore [ɪks'plɔ:ʳ] *vt* (*place*) исследовать (*impf/ perf*); (*with hands etc*) ощупывать (ощупать *perf*); (*idea, suggestion*) изучать (изучить* *perf*).

explorer [ɪks'plɔ:rəʳ] *n* исследователь(ница) *m(f)*.

explosion [ɪks'pləuʒən] *n* взрыв; **population** ~ демографический* взрыв.

explosive [ɪks'pləusɪv] *adj* (*device, effect*) взрывной; (*situation*) взрывоопасный* (взрывоопасен) ◆ *n* (*substance*) взрывчатое вещество*; (*device*) взрывное устройство; **he has an ~ temper** он очень вспыльчивый.

exponent [ɪks'pəunənt] *n* (*of idea, theory*) сторонник(-ица); (*of skill, activity*) мастер; (*MATH*) показатель *m* степени.

exponential [ɛkspəu'nɛnʃl] *adj* (*growth*) стремительный* (стремителен); (*MATH*) экспоненциальный ◆ *n* (*MATH*) экспонента.

export [*n, cpd* 'ɛkspɔ:t, *vt* ɛks'pɔ:t] *n* (*process*) экспорт, вывоз; (*product*) предмет экспорта ◆ *vt* экспортировать (*impf/perf*), вывозить* (вывезти* *perf*) ◆ *cpd* (*duty, licence*) экспортный.

exportation [ɛkspɔ:'teɪʃən] *n* экспортирование.

exporter [ɛks'pɔ:təʳ] *n* экспортёр.

expose [ɪks'pəuz] *vt* (*object*) обнажать (обнажить *perf*); (*truth, plot*) раскрывать (раскрыть* *perf*); (*person*) разоблачать (разоблачить *perf*); (*PHOT*) экспонировать (*impf/perf*); **to ~ sb to sth** подвергать (подвергнуть* *perf*) кого-н чему-н; **to ~ o.s.** (*LAW*) демонстрировать (*impf*) половые органы.

exposé [ɛks'pəuzeɪ] *n* разоблачение.

exposed [ɪks'pəuzd] *adj* (*wire*) оголённый; (*place*): ~ **(to)** открытый (открыт) (+*dat*).

exposition [ɛkspə'zɪʃən] *n* (*explanation*) изложение; (*exhibition*) экспозиция.

exposure [ɪks'pəuʒəʳ] *n* (*of culprit*) разоблачение; (*PHOT*) экспозиция, выдержка; (: *shot*) кадр; ~ **to radiation** пребывание под воздействием радиации; **to suffer/die from** ~ (*MED*) страдать (пострадать *perf*)/умирать (умереть* *perf*) от переохлаждения.

exposure meter *n* (*PHOT*) экспонометр.

expound [ɪks'paund] *vt* излагать (изложить* *perf*).

express [ɪks'prɛs] *adj* (*clear*) чёткий*; (*BRIT: service*) срочный ◆ *n* (*train, coach etc*) экспресс ◆ *adv* (*send*) экспрессом ◆ *vt* выражать (выразить* *perf*); **to ~ o.s.** выражать (выразить* *perf*) себя.

expression [ɪks'prɛʃən] *n* выражение; (*expressiveness*) выразительность *f*.

expressionism [ɪks'prɛʃənɪzəm] *n* экспрессионизм.

expressive [ɪks'prɛsɪv] *adj* выразительный* (выразителен).

expressly [ɪks'prɛslɪ] *adv* (*clearly*) определённо; (*intentionally*) специально.

expressway [ɪks'prɛsweɪ] *n* (*esp US*) скоростная автострада.

expropriate [ɛks'prəuprɪeɪt] *vt* (*money, property*) экспроприировать (*impf/perf*).

expulsion [ɪks'pʌlʃən] *n* (*from school*) исключение; (*from country*) изгнание; (*of substance*) вывод.

expurgate ['ɛkspə:geɪt] *vt*: **to ~ a text** вычёркивать (вычеркнуть *perf*) нежелательные места из текста; **the ~d version** вариант с купюрами.

exquisite [ɛks'kwɪzɪt] *adj* (*face, lace, taste, workmanship*) изысканный* (изыскан); (*pain, pleasure*) острый.

exquisitely [ɛks'kwɪzɪtlɪ] *adv* (*dressed, polite, carved*) изысканно; (*sensitive*) обострённо.

ex-serviceman ['ɛks'sə:vɪsmən] *irreg n* бывший* военнослужащий* *m adj*.

ext. *abbr* (*TEL*) = **extension**.

extemporize [ɪks'tɛmpəraɪz] *vi* импровизировать (*impf*).

extend [ɪks'tɛnd] *vt* (*visit, deadline*) продлевать (продлить *perf*); (*building*) расширять (расширить *perf*); (*arm, hand*) протягивать (протянуть* *perf*); (*offer*) оказывать (оказать* *perf*); (*credit, help*) предоставлять (предоставить* *perf*) ◆ *vi* (*land, road*) простираться (*impf*); (*period*) продолжаться (продолжиться *perf*); **to ~ an invitation to sb** приглашать (пригласить* *perf*) кого-н.

extension [ɪks'tɛnʃən] *n* (*of time*) продление; (*of campaign, rights*) расширение; (*of building*) пристройка*; (*of road*) продолжение; (*ELEC*) удлинитель *m*; (*TEL: in house*) параллельный телефон; (: *in office*) добавочный телефон; ~ **3718** (*TEL*) добавочный (номер) 3718.

extension cable *n* удлинитель *m*.

extension lead *n* = **extension cable**.

extensive [ɪks'tɛnsɪv] *adj* обширный* (обширен); ~ **damage** значительный ущерб.

extensively [ɪks'tɛnsɪvlɪ] *adv*: **he has travelled** ~ он много путешествовал.

extent [ɪks'tɛnt] *n* (*size: of area etc*) протяжённость *f*; (: *of problem etc*) масштаб; (*degree: of damage, loss*) размер; **to some** ~ до некоторой степени; **to a large** ~ в значительной степени; **to go to the ~ of ...** доходить* (дойти* *perf*) до того, что ...; **to such an ~ that ...** до такой степени, что ...; **to what ~?** до какой степени?

extenuating [ɪks'tɛnjueɪtɪŋ] *adj*: ~ **circumstances** смягчающие обстоятельства *ntpl*.

exterior [ɛks'tɪərɪəʳ] *adj* (*drain, light, paint*) наружный; (*world*) внешний* ◆ *n* (*outside*) внешняя сторона*; (*appearance*) внешность *f*.

exterminate [ɪks'tə:mɪneɪt] *vt* истреблять
(истребить* *perf*).
extermination [ɪkstə:mɪ'neɪʃən] *n*
истребление.
external [ɛks'tə:nl] *adj* внешний*; **the ~s** *npl*
внешняя сторона* *sg*; **"for ~ use only"** "для
наружного употребления"; ~ **affairs** (*POL*)
внешняя политика*; ~ **evidence**
свидетельство со стороны.
externally [ɛks'tə:nəlɪ] *adv* внешне.
extinct [ɪks'tɪŋkt] *adj* (*animal*) вымерший;
(*plant*) исчезнувший; (*volcano*) потухший; **to**
become ~ вымирать (вымереть* *perf*).
extinction [ɪks'tɪŋkʃən] *n* (*see adj*) вымирание;
исчезновение.
extinguish [ɪks'tɪŋgwɪʃ] *vt* (*fire*) тушить*
(потушить* *perf*); (*light*) гасить* (погасить*
perf); (*memory, hope*) уничтожать
(уничтожить *perf*).
extinguisher [ɪks'tɪŋgwɪʃəʳ] *n* (*also:* **fire ~**)
огнетушитель *m*.
extol [ɪks'təul] (*US* **extoll**) *vt* превозносить*
(превознести* *perf*).
extort [ɪks'tɔ:t] *vt*: **to ~ sth (from)** вымогать
(*impf*) что-н (у +*gen*).
extortion [ɪks'tɔ:ʃən] *n* вымогательство.
extortionate [ɪks'tɔ:ʃnɪt] *adj* (*price*) граб-
ительский*; (*demands*) вымогательский.
extra ['ɛkstrə] *adj* (*additional*)
дополнительный; (*spare*) лишний ◆ *adv* (*in*
addition) дополнительно; (*especially*)
особенно ◆ *n* (*luxury*) излишество;
(*surcharge*) доплата; (*CINEMA*) статист(ка*);
wine will cost ~ за вино нужно будет
заплатить отдельно; **the room charge does**
not include ~s цена номера не включает
плату за дополнительные услуги и
удобства.
extra... ['ɛkstrə] *prefix* экстра..., особо...,
сверх....
extract [*vt* ɪks'trækt, *n* 'ɛkstrækt] *vt* (*tooth*)
удалять (удалить *perf*); (*mineral*) добывать
(добыть* *perf*); (*money, promise*) вытягивать
(вытянуть *perf*) ◆ *n* (*from novel, recording*)
отрывок*; (*CULIN*) экстракт; **to ~ sth (from)**
извлекать (извлечь* *perf*) что-н (из +*gen*).
extraction [ɪks'trækʃən] *n* (*of object*)
извлечение; (*of tooth*) удаление; (*of minerals*
etc) добыча; (*descent*): **of Scottish ~**
шотландец(-дка) по происхождению.
extractor fan [ɪks'træktə-] *n* вытяжное
устройство, вентилятор.
extracurricular ['ɛkstrəkə'rɪkjuləʳ] *adj*
внеклассный, внеучебный.
extradite ['ɛkstrədaɪt] *vt*: **to ~ sb to/from**
выдавать (выдать* *perf*) кого-н +*dat*/из +*gen*.
extradition [ɛkstrə'dɪʃən] *n* выдача
(*преступника*) ◆ *cpd*: ~ **order/treaty** просьба/

соглашение о выдаче.
extramarital ['ɛkstrə'mærɪtl] *adj* внебрачный.
extramural ['ɛkstrə'mjuərl] *adj* заочный.
extraneous [ɛks'treɪnɪəs] *adj* посторонний*.
extraordinary [ɪks'trɔ:dnrɪ] *adj* незаурядный*
(незауряден), необычайный* (необычаен);
(*meeting*) чрезвычайный; **the ~ thing is that**
... самое удивительное в том, что ....
extraordinary general meeting *n*
чрезвычайное общее собрание.
extrapolation [ɛkstræpə'leɪʃən] *n*
экстраполяция.
extrasensory perception ['ɛkstrə'sɛnsərɪ-] *n*
сверхчувственное *or* экстрасенсорное
восприятие.
extra time *n* дополнительное время* *rt*.
extravagance [ɪks'trævəgəns] *n* (*of behaviour*)
экстравагантность *f*; (*with money*)
расточительство.
extravagant [ɪks'trævəgənt] *adj* (*lavish*)
экстравагантный* (экстравагантен);
(*wasteful: person*) расточительный*
(расточителен); (*: machine*) неэкономный*
(неэкономен); (*wild: ideas, claims*)
сумасбродный* (сумасброден).
extreme [ɪks'tri:m] *adj* крайний*; (*heat, cold*)
сильнейший ◆ *n* (*of behaviour*) крайность *f*;
the ~ right/left (*POL*) крайне правые *pl adj*/
левые *pl adj*; **~s of temperature** перепады
температуры.
extremely [ɪks'tri:mlɪ] *adv* крайне.
extremist [ɪks'tri:mɪst] *n* экстремист(ка*) ◆ *adj*
экстремистский.
extremities [ɪks'trɛmɪtɪz] *npl* (*ANAT*)
конечности *fpl*.
extremity [ɪks'trɛmɪtɪ] *n* конечность *f*; (*of*
situation) крайность *f*.
extricate ['ɛkstrɪkeɪt] *vt*: **to ~ sb/sth (from)**
высвобождать (высвободить* *perf*) кого-н/
что-н (из +*gen*); **to ~ o.s. (from)**
выпутываться (выпутаться *perf*) (из +*gen*).
extrovert ['ɛkstrəvə:t] *n* экстроверт.
exuberance [ɪg'zju:bərns] *n* экспансивность *f*.
exuberant [ɪg'zju:bərnt] *adj* (*person, behaviour*)
экспансивный* (экспансивен); (*imagination*)
буйный* (буен).
exude [ɪg'zju:d] *vt* (*confidence, enthusiasm*)
источать (*impf*); (*liquid*) выделять (выделить
perf); (*smell*) издавать* (*impf*).
exult [ɪg'zʌlt] *vi* (*rejoice*): **to ~ (in)** ликовать*
(*impf*) (по поводу +*gen*).
exultant [ɪg'zʌltənt] *adj* ликующий,
торжествующий; **to be ~** ликовать (*impf*),
торжествовать (*impf*).
exultation [ɛgzʌl'teɪʃən] *n* экзальтация,
ликование.
eye [aɪ] *n* (*ANAT*) глаз*; (*of needle*) ушко* ◆ *vt*
разглядывать (разглядеть* *perf*); **to keep an**

---

* marks translations which have irregular inflections. The Russian-English side of the dictionary gives inflectional information.

~ on (*person, object*) присма́тривать (присмотре́ть* *perf*) за +*instr*; (*time*) следи́ть* (*impf*) за +*instr*; **in the public ~** на виду́, в це́нтре внима́ния; **to have an ~ for sth** знать (*impf*) толк в чём-н; **with an ~ to doing** (*BRIT*) с расчётом +*infin*; **as far as the ~ can see** насколько мо́жно охвати́ть взгля́дом; **there's more to this than meets the ~** э́то не так про́сто, как ка́жется на пе́рвый взгляд.
eyeball ['aɪbɔːl] *n* глазно́е я́блоко*.
eyebath ['aɪbɑːθ] *n* (*BRIT*) глазна́я ва́нночка*.
eyebrow ['aɪbrau] *n* бровь* *f*.
eyebrow pencil *n* каранда́ш* для брове́й.
eye-catching ['aɪkætʃɪŋ] *adj* броса́ющийся в глаза́.
eyecup ['aɪkʌp] *n* (*US*) = **eyebath**.
eye drops *npl* глазны́е ка́пли *fpl*.
eyeful ['aɪful] *n*: **an ~ of sand/dust** по́лные глаза́ песка́*/пы́ли; **to get an ~ of sb/sth** (*inf*) разгляде́ть* (*perf*) кого́-н/что-н.
eyeglass ['aɪglɑːs] *n* моно́кль *m*.
eyelash ['aɪlæʃ] *n* ресни́ца.
eyelet ['aɪlɪt] *n* фесто́н.

eye level *n*: **at ~** на у́ровне глаз.
eyelevel ['aɪlɛvl] *adj* (*grill*) располо́женный на у́ровне глаз.
eyelid ['aɪlɪd] *n* ве́ко*.
eyeliner ['aɪlaɪnə*r*] *n* каранда́ш* для глаз.
eye-opener ['aɪəupnə*r*] *n* открове́ние.
eye shadow *n* те́ни* *fpl* (для век).
eyesight ['aɪsaɪt] *n* зре́ние.
eyesore ['aɪsɔː*r*] *n*: **that building is a real ~** э́то зда́ние как бельмо́ на глазу́.
eyestrain ['aɪstreɪn] *n* чрезме́рное напряже́ние глаз.
eyeteeth ['aɪtiːθ] *npl of* **eyetooth**.
eyetooth ['aɪtuːθ] (*pl* **eyeteeth**) *n* глазно́й зуб; **to give one's eyeteeth for sth/to do** же́ртвовать (поже́ртвовать *perf*) всем за что-н/за то, что́бы +*infin*.
eyewash ['aɪwɔʃ] *n* примо́чка* для глаз; (*fig: inf*) очковтира́тельство.
eyewitness ['aɪwɪtnɪs] *n* очеви́дец* ♦ *cpd*: **an ~ account** свиде́тельство очеви́дца.
eyrie ['ɪərɪ] *n* (*nest*) орли́ное гнездо́*.

~ F, f ~

F, f [ɛf] n (letter) 6-ая бу́ква англи́йского алфави́та.

F [ɛf] n (MUS) фа.

F abbr = **Fahrenheit**.

FA n abbr (BRIT. = Football Association) Футбо́льная ассоциа́ция.

FAA n abbr (US: = Federal Aviation Administration) Федера́льное управле́ние авиа́цией.

fable ['feɪbl] n ба́сня*.

fabric ['fæbrɪk] n (cloth) ткань f; (of society) структу́ра; (of building) констру́кция.

fabricate ['fæbrɪkeɪt] vt (make up) фабрикова́ть (сфабрикова́ть perf); (make) производи́ть* (произвести́* perf).

fabrication [fæbrɪ'keɪʃən] n (lie) фабрика́ция; (making) произво́дство.

fabric ribbon n (for typewriter) печа́тная ле́нта.

fabulous ['fæbjuləs] adj (extraordinary) невероя́тный* (невероя́тен); (mythical) ска́зочный*; (inf: super) ска́зочный* (ска́зочен).

façade [fə'sɑːd] n фаса́д; (fig: pretence) ви́димость f; **a ~ of gaiety/indifference** фаса́д весе́лья/равноду́шия.

face [feɪs] n (of person, organization) лицо́*; (grimace) грима́са; (of clock) цифербла́т; (of mountain, cliff) склон; (of building) фаса́д; (surface: of cube etc) сторона́* ♦ vt (fact) признава́ть* (призна́ть* perf); **the house is facing the sea** дом обращён к мо́рю; **he was facing the door** он был обращён лицо́м к две́ри; **we are facing difficulties** нам предстоя́т тру́дности; **~ down** лицо́м вниз; **to lose/save** теря́ть (потеря́ть perf)/спаса́ть (спасти́ perf) репута́цию; **to make** or **pull a ~** де́лать (сде́лать perf) грима́су; **in the ~ of** (difficulties etc) несмотря́ на +acc; **on the ~ of it** на пе́рвый взгляд; **~ to ~ (with)** (with person, problem) лицо́м к лицу́ (с +instr); **to ~ the fact that ...** признава́ть* (призна́ть* perf) тот факт, что ...

▶ **face up to** vt fus (obligations, responsibility) признава́ть* (призна́ть* perf); (difficulties) справля́ться (спра́виться* perf) с +instr.

face cloth n (BRIT) махро́вая салфе́тка (для обтира́ния лица́).

face cream n крем* для лица́.

faceless ['feɪslɪs] adj безли́кий*.

face-lift ['feɪslɪft] n подтя́жка* ко́жи на лице́; (of building etc) облицо́вка*.

face powder n пу́дра для лица́.

face-saving ['feɪs'seɪvɪŋ] adj для спасе́ния репута́ции.

facet ['fæsɪt] n (also fig) грань f.

facetious [fə'siːʃəs] adj остроу́мный*.

face to face adv лицо́м к лицу́.

face value n номина́льная сто́имость f; **to take sth at ~ ~** (fig) принима́ть (приня́ть* perf) что-н за чи́стую моне́ту.

facia ['feɪʃə] n = **fascia**.

facial ['feɪʃl] n космети́ческая обрабо́тка лица́ ♦ adj: **~ expression** выраже́ние лица́; **~ hair** во́лосы, расту́щие на лице́.

facile ['fæsaɪl] adj пове́рхностный*.

facilitate [fə'sɪlɪteɪt] vt спосо́бствовать (impf/ perf) +dat.

facilities npl (buildings) помеще́ние ntsg; (equipment) обору́дование ntsg; **credit ~** креди́тный лими́т (креди́тной ка́рточки заёмщика); **cooking ~** усло́вия ntpl для приготовле́ния пи́щи.

facility [fə'sɪlɪtɪ] n (feature) приспособле́ние; (service) услу́га; (aptitude): **to have a ~ for** име́ть (impf) спосо́бности к +dat.

facing ['feɪsɪŋ] prep (opposite) напро́тив +gen ♦ n (SEWING) отде́лка*.

facsimile [fæk'sɪmɪlɪ] n факси́миле nt ind; (machine, document) факс.

fact [fækt] n факт; **in ~** факти́чески; **to know for a ~ that ...** знать (impf) наверняка́, что ...; **the ~ (of the matter) is that ...** де́ло в том, что ...; **the ~s of life** (sex) полова́я сторона́ жи́зни, (fig) реа́льности fpl жи́зни.

fact-finding ['fæktfaɪndɪŋ] adj для рассле́дования фа́ктов.

faction ['fækʃən] n (group) фра́кция.

factor ['fæktə] n фа́ктор; (COMM) комиссионе́р; (: agent) аге́нт; **safety ~** фа́ктор безопа́сности; **human ~** челове́ческий* фа́ктор.

---

* marks translations which have irregular inflections. The Russian-English side of the dictionary gives inflectional information.

factory ['fæktərɪ] *n* (*for textiles etc*) фа́брика; (*for machinery etc*) заво́д.
factory farming *n* (*BRIT*) веде́ние животново́дства промы́шленными ме́тодами.
factory floor *n* (*fig: workers*) рабо́чие *pl adj* у станка́.
factory ship *n* плаву́чая фа́брика.
factual ['fæktjuəl] *adj* факти́ческий*.
faculty ['fækəltɪ] *n* спосо́бность *f*; (*of university*) факульте́т; (*US: teaching staff*) профе́ссорско-преподава́тельский соста́в.
fad [fæd] *n* причу́да.
fade [feɪd] *vi* (*colour*) выцвета́ть (вы́цвести* *perf*); (*light*) угаса́ть (уга́снуть* *perf*); (*sound*) замира́ть (замере́ть* *perf*); (*flower*) вя́нуть* (завя́нуть* *perf*); (*hope, smile*) угаса́ть (уга́снуть* *perf*); (*memory*) сгла́живаться (сгла́диться* *perf*)
▶ **fade in** *vt*: to ~ the picture/sound in постепе́нно увели́чивать (*impf*) чёткость изображе́ния/си́лу зву́ка
▶ **fade out** *vt*: to ~ the picture/sound out постепе́нно уменьша́ть (*impf*) чёткость изображе́ния/си́лу зву́ка.
faeces ['fi:si:z] (*US* feces) *npl* фека́лии *fpl*.
fag [fæg] (*inf*) *n* (*BRIT: cigarette*) сигаре́та; (*US: pej: homosexual*) го́мик; (*BRIT: chore*): what a ~! ну и работёнка!
Fahrenheit ['færənhaɪt] *n* Фаренге́йт.
fail [feɪl] *vt* (*exam, candidate*) прова́ливать (провали́ть* *perf*); (*subj: person, memory*) изменя́ть (измени́ть *perf*), подводи́ть (подвести́ *perf*); (: *courage*) покида́ть (покину́ть *perf*) ♦ *vi* (*candidate, attempt*) прова́ливаться (провали́ться* *perf*); (*brakes*) отка́зывать (отказа́ть* *perf*); my eyesight/ health is ~ing у меня́ слабе́ет зре́ние/ здоро́вье; to ~ to do не смочь* (*perf*) +*infin*; without ~ обяза́тельно; the light is ~ing смерка́ется.
failing ['feɪlɪŋ] *n* недоста́ток* ♦ *prep* за неиме́нием +*gen*; ~ that за неиме́нем э́того.
fail-safe ['feɪlseɪf] *adj* (*device*) предохрани́тельный.
failure ['feɪljə'] *n* неуда́ча; (*mechanical*) поврежде́ние; (*of crops*) неурожа́й; (*in exam*) прова́л; (*person*) неуда́чник(-ица); his ~ to complete the work то, что он не смог вы́полнить рабо́ту; the evening was a complete ~ ве́чер был по́лным прова́лом.
faint [feɪnt] *adj* сла́бый* (слаб); (*recollection*) сму́тный* (сму́тен); (*mark*) едва́ заме́тный* (заме́тен); (*breeze, trace*) лёгкий* ♦ *n* (*MED*) о́бморок ♦ *vi* (*MED*) па́дать (упа́сть* *perf*) в о́бморок; to feel ~ чу́вствовать (почу́вствовать *perf*) сла́бость.
faintest ['feɪntɪst] *adj* мале́йший*; I haven't the ~ idea я не име́ю ни мале́йшего поня́тия.
faint-hearted ['feɪnt'hɑ:tɪd] *adj* малоду́шный* (малоду́шен).

faintly ['feɪntlɪ] *adv* (*a bit*) сла́бо; (*hardly*) едва́.
fair [fɛə'] *adj* (*person, decision*) справедли́вый (справедли́в); (*size, number*) значи́тельный (*chance, guess*) хоро́ший*; (*skin, hair*) све́тлый* (све́тел); (*weather*) хоро́ший*, я́сный* ♦ *n* (*also:* trade ~) я́рмарка*; (*BRIT: also:* funfair) аттракцио́ны *mpl* ♦ *adv*: to play ~ вести́* (*impf*) дела́ разу́мно *or* че́стно; it's not ~! э́то нече́стно!; a ~ amount of money значи́тельная су́мма де́нег; a ~ amount of success значи́тельный успе́х; I had a pretty ~ idea у меня́ была́ дово́льно хоро́шая иде́я; ~ wear and tear обосно́ванный изно́с.
fair copy *n* чистово́й экземпля́р.
fair game *n*: he is ~ он зако́нная добы́ча.
fairground ['fɛəgraʊnd] *n* лу́на-парк.
fair-haired [fɛə'hɛəd] *adj* светловоло́сый (светово́лос).
fairly ['fɛəlɪ] *adv* (*justly*) справедли́во; (*quite*) дово́льно; I'm ~ sure я почти́ уве́рен.
fairness ['fɛənɪs] *n* (*justice*) справедли́вость *f*; in all ~ со всей справедли́востью.
fair play *n* че́стная игра́.
fairway ['fɛəweɪ] *n* (*GOLF*): the ~ *трави́нистая доро́жка ме́жду лу́нками в го́льфе.*
fairy ['fɛərɪ] *n* фе́я.
fairy godmother *n* до́брая волше́бница.
fairy lights *npl* (*BRIT*) электри́ческая гирля́нда *fsg*.
fairy tale *n* ска́зка*.
faith [feɪθ] *n* (*also* REL) ве́ра; to have ~ in sb/sth ве́рить (*impf*) в кого́-н/что-н.
faithful ['feɪθful] *adj*: ~ (to) ве́рный* (ве́рен) (+*dat*).
faithfully ['feɪθfəlɪ] *adv* ве́рно.
faith healer *n* зна́харь(-рка*) *m(f)*.
fake [feɪk] *n* (*painting, document*) подде́лка*; (*person*) притво́рщик(-ица) ♦ *adj* фальши́вый, подде́льный ♦ *vt* (*painting, document*) подде́лывать (подде́лать *perf*); (*illness, emotion*) симули́ровать (*impf*); his illness is a ~ его́ боле́знь – симуля́ция.
falcon ['fɔ:lkən] *n* со́кол.
Falkland Islands ['fɔ:lklənd-] *npl*: the ~~ Фолкле́ндские острова́* *mpl*.
fall [fɔ:l] (*pt* fell, *pp* fallen) *n* паде́ние; (*US: autumn*) о́сень *f* ♦ *vi* па́дать (упа́сть* *perf*); (*government, country*) пасть* (*perf*); (*rain, snow*) па́дать (вы́пасть* *perf*); (*silence, hush, night*) наступа́ть (наступи́ть* *perf*); (*sadness*) охва́тывать (охвати́ть *perf*); ~s *npl* (*waterfall*) водопа́д; a ~ of snow снегопа́д; a ~ of earth обва́л; to ~ flat (*plan*) не удава́ться (уда́ться* *perf*); (*joke*) не име́ть (*impf*) успе́ха; to ~ flat (on one's face) па́дать (упа́сть* *perf*) ничко́м; to ~ in love (with sb/sth) влюбля́ться (влюби́ться* *perf*) (в кого́-н/во что-н); to ~ short of (sb's expectations) неопра́вдывать (неоправда́ть *perf*) (чьих-н ожида́ний); a lot of rain/snow fell yesterday вчера́ вы́пало мно́го сне́га/дождя́; darkness/

night fell наступи́ла темнота/ночь
▸ **fall apart** *vi* разва́ливаться (развали́ться*
perf); (*inf: emotionally*) расклеиваться
(расклеиться *perf*)
▸ **fall back** *vt fus* (*MIL*) отступа́ть (отступи́ть*
perf)
▸ **fall back on** *vt fus* прибега́ть (прибе́гнуть*
perf) к +*dat*; **to have sth to ~ back on** (*money,
job etc*) име́ть (*impf*) что-н в запа́се
▸ **fall behind** *vi* отстава́ть (отста́ть* *perf*); **to ~
behind with the payments** просро́чивать
(просро́чить *perf*) платежи́
▸ **fall down** *vi* (*person*) па́дать (упа́сть* *perf*);
(*building*) ру́шиться (ру́хнуть *perf*)
▸ **fall for** *vt fus* (*trick etc*) попада́ться
(попа́сться* *perf*) на у́дочку; (*story*) ве́рить
(пове́рить *perf*) +*dat*; (*person*) влюбля́ться
(влюби́ться* *perf*) в +*acc*
▸ **fall in** *vi* (*roof*) обва́ливаться (обвали́ться*
perf); (*MIL*) стро́иться (постро́иться *perf*)
▸ **fall in with** *vt fus* (*sb's plans etc*) соглаша́ться
(согласи́ться* *perf*) с +*instr*
▸ **fall off** *vi* па́дать (упа́сть* *perf*)
▸ **fall out** *vi* (*hair, teeth*) выпада́ть (вы́пасть*
perf); (*friends etc*): **to ~ out with sb** ссо́риться
(поссо́риться *perf*) с кем-н
▸ **fall over** *vi* упа́сть* (*perf*) ♦ *vt*: **to ~ over o.s. to
do** лезть* (вы́лезть* *perf*) из ко́жи вон, что́бы
+*infin*
▸ **fall through** *vi* (*plan*) прова́ливаться
(провали́ться* *perf*).
fallacy ['fæləsɪ] *n* (*misconception*)
заблужде́ние.
fall-back ['fɔːlbæk] *adj*: **~ position** пози́ция для
отступле́ния.
fallen ['fɔːlən] *pp of* **fall**.
fallible ['fæləbl] *adj* спосо́бный* (спосо́бен)
ошиба́ться (ошиби́ться *perf*).
falling ['fɔːlɪŋ] *adj*: **~ market** (*COMM*)
понижа́тельная ры́ночная коньюнкту́ра.
falling off *n* сниже́ние.
falling out *n* размо́лвка.
Fallopian tube [fə'ləʊpɪən-] *n* фалло́пиевы
тру́бы *fpl*.
fallout ['fɔːlaʊt] *n* радиоакти́вные оса́дки *pl*.
fallout shelter *n* убе́жище от радиоакти́вных
оса́дков.
fallow ['fæləʊ] *adj* (*land, field*) парово́й.
false [fɔːls] *adj* (*untrue, wrong*) ло́жный*
(ло́жен); (*insincere, artificial*) фальши́вый
(фальши́в); **~ imprisonment** незако́нное
лише́ние свобо́ды.
false alarm *n* ло́жная трево́га.
falsehood ['fɔːlshʊd] *n* ложь* *f*.
falsely ['fɔːlslɪ] *adv* (*accuse*) ло́жно.
false pretences *npl*: **under ~ ~** под ло́жным
предло́гом.
false teeth *npl* (*BRIT*) иску́сственные зу́бы* *mpl*.

falsify ['fɔːlsɪfaɪ] *vt* фальсифици́ровать (*impf/
perf*), подде́лывать (подде́лать *perf*).
falter ['fɔːltə'] *vi* (*engine*) ка́шлять (*impf*);
(*person: hesitate*) замя́ться* (*perf*); (: *in
speech*) запина́ться (запну́ться *perf*); (: *while
moving*) спотыка́ться (споткну́ться *perf*).
fame [feɪm] *n* сла́ва.
familiar [fə'mɪlɪə'] *adj* (*well-known*) знако́мый
(знако́м); (*intimate*) дру́жеский*; **he is/was ~
with** (*subject*) он знако́м/был знако́м с +*instr*;
to make o.s. ~ with sth знако́миться*
(ознако́миться* *perf*) с чем-н; **to be on ~
terms with sb** быть* (*impf*) в прия́тельских *or*
дру́жеских отноше́ниях с кем-н.
familiarity [fəmɪlɪ'ærɪtɪ] *n* (*knowledge*) зна́ние;
(*informality*) фамилья́рность *f*.
familiarize [fə'mɪlɪəraɪz] *vt*: **to ~ o.s. with sth**
ознакомля́ться (ознако́миться* *perf*) с
чем-н.
family ['fæmɪlɪ] *n* семья́*; (*children*) де́ти* *pl*.
family business *n* семе́йный би́знес.
family credit *n* де́нежное посо́бие,
*выпла́чиваемое госуда́рством се́мьям с
ни́зким у́ровнем дохо́дов*.
family doctor *n* семе́йный врач*.
family life *n* семе́йная жизнь *f*.
family man *n* семьяни́н*, семе́йный челове́к*.
family planning *n* контро́ль *m* рожда́емости;
~ ~ clinic ≈ же́нская консульта́ция.
family tree *n* родосло́вное де́рево*.
famine ['fæmɪn] *n* го́лод*.
famished ['fæmɪʃt] (*inf*) *adj* голо́дный; **I'm ~** я
умира́ю с го́лоду.
famous ['feɪməs] *adj* знамени́тый (знамени́т).
famously ['feɪməslɪ] *adv* (*get on*) великоле́пно.
fan [fæn] *n* (*folding*) ве́ер*; (*ELEC*) вентиля́тор;
(*of famous person*) покло́нник(-ица); (*of
sports team*) боле́льщик(-ица) ♦ *vt* (*face*)
обма́хивать (обмахну́ть *perf*); (*fire, quarrel*)
раздува́ть (разду́ть *perf*)
▸ **fan out** *vi* (*people*) развёртываться
(разверну́ться *perf*) ве́ером; (*roads*)
расходи́ться* (разойти́сь* *perf*) ве́ером.
fanatic [fə'nætɪk] *n* (*extremist*) фана́тик.
fanatical [fə'nætɪkl] *adj* (*support, dedication*)
фанати́чный* (фанати́чен).
fan belt *n* (*AUT*) вентиля́торный реме́нь* *m*.
fanciful ['fænsɪful] *adj* причу́дливый
(причу́длив).
fan club *n* клуб покло́нников.
fancy ['fænsɪ] *n* (*whim*) при́хоть *f*; (*imagination*)
воображе́ние; (*fantasy*) фанта́зия ♦ *adj*
изы́сканный ♦ *vt* (*feel like, want*) хоте́ть*
(захоте́ть* *perf*); (*imagine*) вообража́ть
(вообрази́ть* *perf*); (*think*) ду́мать (*impf*); **to
take a ~ to** увлека́ться (увле́чься* *perf*) +*instr*;
when the ~ takes him когда́ ему́ взду́мается;
the idea took *or* **caught my ~** иде́я пришла́сь

---

* marks translations which have irregular inflections. The Russian-English side of the dictionary gives inflectional information.

мне по вку́су; **to ~ that** ду́мать *(impf)*, что; **he fancies her** *(inf)* она́ ему́ нра́вится; **~ that!** предста́вьте себе́.

fancy dress *n* маскара́дный костю́м.

fancy-dress ball ['fænsɪdrɛs-] *n* костюм-и́рованный бал*.

fancy goods *npl* украше́ния *ntpl (обы́чно для до́ма)*.

fanfare ['fænfɛə'] *n* фанфа́ра.

fanfold paper ['fænfəuld-] *n* перфори́рованная *or* фальцо́ванная бума́га.

fang [fæŋ] *n* клык*; *(of snake)* ядови́тый зуб*.

fan heater *n (BRIT)* электрообогрева́тель *m (нагнета́ющий тёплый во́здух при по́мощи вентиля́тора)*.

fanlight ['fænlaɪt] *n* веерообра́зное окно́ над две́рью.

fanny ['fænɪ] *n (inf)* за́дница.

fantasize ['fæntəsaɪz] *vi* фантази́ровать *(impf)*.

fantastic [fæn'tæstɪk] *adj* фантасти́ческий*; **that's ~!** э́то фанта́стика!

fantasy ['fæntəsɪ] *n* фанта́зия.

fanzine ['fænziːn] *n* журна́л и́ли газе́та, самоде́ятельно издава́емый покло́нниками попгру́ппы, телепрогра́ммы, спо́рта *итп*.

FAO *n abbr (= Food and Agriculture Organization)* ФАО *(продово́льственная и сельскохозя́йственная организа́ция ООН)*.

f.a.q. *abbr (= free alongside quay)* фра́нко на́бережная.

far [fɑː'] *adj (distant)* да́льний* ◆ *adv (a long way)* далеко́; *(much)* гора́здо; **at the ~ end** в да́льнем конце́; **at the ~ side** на друго́й стороне́; **the ~ left/right** *(POL)* кра́йне ле́вый/пра́вый; **~ away, ~ off** далеко́; **~ better** гора́здо лу́чше; **he was ~ from poor** он был далеко́ *or* отню́дь не бе́дным; **by ~** намно́го; **is it ~ to London?** далеко́ ли до Ло́ндона?; **it's not ~ from here** э́то недалеко́ отсю́да; **go as ~ as the post office** дойди́те до по́чты; **as ~ back as the 13th century** ещё в 13-ом ве́ке; **as ~ as I know** наско́лько мне изве́стно; **as ~ as possible** наско́лько возмо́жно; **how ~?** *(distance)* как далеко́?; *(to what extent)* наско́лько?; **how ~ have you got with your work?** наско́лько Вы продви́нулись в свое́й рабо́те?

faraway ['fɑːrəweɪ] *adj (place)* да́льний*, далёкий*; *(look)* отсу́тствующий*.

farce [fɑːs] *n (also fig)* фарс.

farcical ['fɑːsɪkl] *adj (fig)* неле́пый.

fare [fɛə'] *n (on trains, buses)* пла́та за прое́зд; *(in taxi)* сто́имость *f* прое́зда; *(: passenger)* пассажи́р; *(food)* еда́ ◆ *vi*: **how did you ~?** как успе́хи?; **half/full ~** полсто́имости/по́лная сто́имость; **bus/train ~** пла́та за прое́зд в авто́бусе/на по́езде; **they ~ better than we do under the present system** с ни́ми обраща́ются лу́чше, чем с на́ми при ны́нешней систе́ме; **they ~d well/badly in the recent elections** им повезло́/не повезло́ на

неда́вних вы́борах.

Far East *n*: **the ~~** Да́льний* Восто́к.

farewell [fɛə'wɛl] *excl* проща́йте ◆ *n* проща́ние ◆ *cpd (party etc)* проща́льный.

far-fetched ['fɑː'fɛtʃt] *adj* неправдоподо́бный, невероя́тный.

farm [fɑːm] *n* фе́рма ◆ *vt (land)* обраба́тывать (обрабо́тать *perf*)

▶ **farm out** *vt* отдава́ть* (отда́ть* *perf)*.

farmer ['fɑːmə'] *n* фе́рмер.

farm hand *n* рабо́тник(-ица) фе́рмы.

farmhouse ['fɑːmhaʊs] *n* фе́рмерский дом*.

farming ['fɑːmɪŋ] *n (agriculture)* се́льское хозя́йство; *(of crops)* выра́щивание; *(of animals)* разведе́ние; **sheep ~** разведе́ние ове́ц, овцево́дство; **intensive ~** интенси́вно веде́ние се́льского хозя́йства.

farm labourer *n* рабо́тник на фе́рме.

farmland ['fɑːmlænd] *n* сельско-хозя́йственные уго́дья* *ntpl*.

farm produce *n* проду́кты *mpl* се́льского хозя́йства.

farm worker *n* = **farm hand**.

farmyard ['fɑːmjɑːd] *n* фе́рмерский двор*.

Faroe Islands ['fɛərəu-] *npl*: **the ~~** Фаре́рские острова́* *mpl*.

Faroes ['fɛərəuz] *npl* = **Faroe Islands**.

far-reaching ['fɑː'riːtʃɪŋ] *adj (reform)* далеко́ иду́щий; *(effect)* глубо́кий*.

far-sighted ['fɑː'saɪtɪd] *adj (US)* дальнозо́ркий* (дальнозо́рок); *(fig)* дальнови́дный* (дальнови́ден); **he is ~** *(US)* у него́ дальнозо́ркость.

fart [fɑːt] *(inf!)* *vi* перде́ть* (пёрнуть *perf*) *(!)* ◆ *n* перде́ние *(!)*.

farther ['fɑːðə'] *adv* да́льше ◆ *adj* бо́лее да́льний*, далёкий*.

farthest ['fɑːðɪst] *superl of* **far**.

f.a.s. *abbr (BRIT: = free alongside ship)* ФАС *(свобо́дно вдоль бо́рта су́дна)*.

fascia ['feɪʃə] *n (AUT)* пане́ль *f*.

fascinate ['fæsɪneɪt] *vt* захва́тывать (захвати́ть* *perf)*; *(subj: person)* очаро́вывать (очарова́ть *perf*).

fascinating ['fæsɪneɪtɪŋ] *adj (story)* захва́тывающий*; *(person)* очарова́тельный* (очарова́телен).

fascination [fæsɪ'neɪʃən] *n* очарова́ние.

fascism ['fæʃɪzəm] *n (POL)* фаши́зм.

fascist ['fæʃɪst] *adj* фаши́стский* ◆ *n* фаши́ст(ка).

fashion ['fæʃən] *n (trend)* мо́да; *(fashion industry)* инду́стрия мо́ды ◆ *vt (make)* мастери́ть (смастери́ть *perf*); **in/out of ~** в/не в мо́де; **in an animated ~** оживлённо; **in a friendly ~** по-дру́жески; **he did it after a ~** он сде́лал э́то кое-ка́к; **in the Greek ~** в гре́ческом сти́ле.

fashionable ['fæʃnəbl] *adj* мо́дный* (мо́ден).

fashion designer *n* модельѐр.

fashion show *n* пока́з *or* демонстра́ция мод.

fast [fɑːst] *adv* (*quickly*) бы́стро; (*firmly: stick*) про́чно; (: *hold*) кре́пко ♦ *n* (REL) пост* ♦ *vi* (REL) пости́ться* (*impf*) ♦ *adj* бы́стрый* (быстр); (*progress*) стреми́тельный*; (*car*) скоростно́й; (*dye, colour*) про́чный; (*clock*): **to be** ~ спеши́ть (*impf*); **he is** ~ **asleep** он кре́пко спит; **as** ~ **as possible** как мо́жно быстре́е; **to make a boat** ~ (BRIT) кре́пко привяза́ть* (*perf*) ло́дку; **my watch is 5 minutes** ~ мои́ часы́ спеша́т на 5 мину́т.

fasten ['fɑːsn] *vt* закрепля́ть (закрепи́ть* *perf*); (*door*) запира́ть (запере́ть* *perf*); (*shoe*) завя́зывать (завяза́ть* *perf*); (*coat, dress*) застёгивать (застегну́ть* *perf*); (*seat belt*) пристёгивать (пристегну́ть* *perf*) ♦ *vi* (*coat, belt*) застёгиваться (застегну́ться* *perf*); (*door*) запира́ться (запере́ться* *perf*)

▶ **fasten (up)on** *vt fus* (*idea etc*) сосредото́чиваться (сосредото́читься *perf*) на +*acc*.

fastener ['fɑːsnə^r] *n* (*for clothing*) застёжка*.

fastening ['fɑːsnɪŋ] *n* = **fastener**.

fast food *n* быстроприготавливаемая еда́ ♦ *cpd*: ~~ **restaurant** рестора́н быстро-приго́товливаем еды́.

fastidious [fæs'tɪdɪəs] *adj* (*fussy*) скрупулёзный* (скрупулёзен).

fast lane *n* (BRIT: AUT): **the** ~~ скоростно́й ряд*.

fat [fæt] *adj* то́лстый* (толст); (*inf: profit*) соли́дный* ♦ *n* жир*; **that's a** ~ **lot of use to us** (*inf*) нам э́то нигде́ не на́до; **to live off the** ~ **of the land** как сыр в ма́сле ката́ться (*impf*).

fatal ['feɪtl] *adj* (*mistake*) фата́льный* (фата́лен), роково́й; (*injury, illness*) смерте́льный* (смерте́лен).

fatalistic [feɪtə'lɪstɪk] *adj* (*attitude*) фаталисти́ческий.

fatality [fə'tælɪtɪ] *n* (*death*) смерте́льный слу́чай.

fatally ['feɪtəlɪ] *adv* (*injured*) смерте́льно; (*flawed*) фата́льно, роковы́м о́бразом.

fate [feɪt] *n* судьба́*, рок; **to meet one's** ~ находи́ть* (найти́* *perf*) свой коне́ц.

fated ['feɪtɪd] *adj* обречённый* (обречён); **it seemed** ~ каза́лось, э́то бы́ло суждено́му случи́тся.

fateful ['feɪtful] *adj* роково́й.

fat-free ['fæt'friː] *adj* обезжи́ренный.

father ['fɑːðə^r] *n* оте́ц*.

Father Christmas *n* ≈ Дед Моро́з.

fatherhood ['fɑːðəhud] *n* отцо́вство.

father-in-law ['fɑːðərənlɔː] *n* (*wife's father*) свёкор*; (*husband's father*) тесть *m*.

fatherland ['fɑːðəlænd] *n* оте́чество.

fatherly ['fɑːðəlɪ] *adj* оте́ческий*.

fathom ['fæðəm] *n* (NAUT) фа́том, морска́я са́жень *f* ♦ *vt* (*understand: also:* ~ **out**)

постига́ть (пости́чь* *perf*).

fatigue [fə'tiːg] *n* утомле́ние; ~**s** *npl* (MIL) солда́тская рабо́чая оде́жда *fsg*; **metal** ~ уста́лость *f* мета́лла.

fatness ['fætnɪs] *n* (*of person*) полнота́; (*of wallet*) толщина́.

fatten ['fætn] *vt* (*animal*) отка́рмливать (откорми́ть* *perf*) ♦ *vi* жире́ть (разжире́ть *perf*); **chocolate is** ~**ing** от шокола́да толсте́ют.

fatty ['fætɪ] *adj* (*food*) жи́рный* ♦ *n* (*inf*) толстя́к*.

fatuous ['fætjuəs] *adj* бессмы́сленный*.

faucet ['fɔːsɪt] *n* (US) (водопрово́дный) кран.

fault [fɔːlt] *n* (*blame*) вина́*; (*defect: in person*) недоста́ток*; (: *in machine*) дефе́кт; (GEO) разло́м; (TENNIS) оши́бка* при пода́че ♦ *vt* (*criticise*) придира́ться (*impf*) к +*dat*; **it's my** ~ э́то моя́ вина́; **to find** ~ **with** придира́ться (придра́ться* *perf*) к +*dat*; **I am at** ~ я винова́т; **if my memory is not at** ~ е́сли мне не изменя́ет па́мять; **generous to a** ~ чрезме́рно ще́дрый*.

faultless ['fɔːltlɪs] *adj* безупре́чный* (безупре́чен).

faulty ['fɔːltɪ] *adj* (*goods*) испо́рченный*; (*machine*) повреждённый.

fauna ['fɔːnə] *n* фа́уна.

faux pas ['fəu'pɑː] *n inv* неве́рный шаг*.

favour ['feɪvə^r] (US **favor**) *n* (*approval*) расположе́ние; (*help*) одолже́ние ♦ *vt* (*prefer: solution*) ока́зывать (оказа́ть* *perf*) предпочте́ние +*dat*; (: *pupil etc*) выделя́ть (вы́делить *perf*); (*assist*) благоприя́тствовать (*impf*) +*dat*; **to ask a** ~ **of sb** проси́ть (попроси́ть* *perf*) кого́-н об одолже́нии; **to do sb a** ~ ока́зывать (оказа́ть* *perf*) кому́-н услу́гу; **in** ~ **of** в по́льзу +*gen*; **to be in** ~ **of sth/doing** быть* (*impf*) за что-н/за то, что́бы +*infin*; **to find** ~ **with sb** (*subj: person*) завоёвывать (завоева́ть* *perf*) расположе́ние кого́-н; (: *suggestion*) находи́ть* (найти́* *perf*) подде́ржку у кого́-н.

favourable ['feɪvrəbl] (US **favorable**) *adj* благоприя́тный* (благоприя́тен).

favourably ['feɪvrəblɪ] (US **favorably**) *adv* (*react*) положи́тельно, благоприя́тно; **to compare** ~ **with** выи́грывать (*impf*) в сравне́нии с +*instr*.

favourite ['feɪvrɪt] (US **favorite**) *adj* люби́мый* ♦ *n* (*of teacher, parent*) люби́мец*; (SPORT) фавори́т*.

favouritism ['feɪvrɪtɪzəm] (US **favoritism**) *n* фавори́тизм.

fawn [fɔːn] *n* молодо́й оле́нь *m* ♦ *adj* (*also:* ~**-coloured**) желтова́то-кори́чневый ♦ *vi*: **to** ~ **(up)on** заи́скивать (*impf*) пе́ред +*instr*.

fax [fæks] *n* факс ♦ *vt* (*letter, document*)

посыла́ть (посла́ть* *perf*) фа́ксом.

FBI *n abbr* (*US*: = Federal Bureau of Investigation) ФБР= *Федера́льное бюро́ рассле́дований.*

FCC *n abbr* (*US*: = Federal Communications Commission) Федера́льная коми́ссия свя́зи.

FCO *n abbr* (*BRIT*: = Foreign and Commonwealth Office) *Министе́рство иностра́нных дел и сноше́ний со стра́нами Брита́нского содру́жества.*

FD *n abbr* (*US*) = **fire department**.

FDA *n abbr* (*US*: = Food and Drug Administration) *управле́ние по контро́лю за проду́ктами и медикаме́нтами.*

FE *abbr* (= Further Education) ≈ профессиона́льно-техни́ческое образова́ние.

fear [fɪəʳ] *n* страх; (*less strong*) боя́знь *f*; (*worry*) опасе́ние ♦ *vt* боя́ться (*impf*) +*gen* ♦ *vi* боя́ться (*impf*); **to ~ for** боя́ться (*impf*) за +*acc*; **to ~ that** боя́ться (*impf*), что; **~ of heights** боя́знь высоты́; **for ~ of missing my flight** (*in case*) боя́сь опозда́ть на самолёт.

fearful ['fɪəful] *adj* (*person*) боязли́вый (боязли́в); (*sight*) ужаса́ющий*; (*risk, noise*) стра́шный* (стра́шен); **to be ~ of** страши́ться (*impf*) +*gen*.

fearfully ['fɪəfəlɪ] *adv* (*timidly*) боязли́во; (*inf*: *very*) ужа́сно.

fearless ['fɪəlɪs] *adj* бесстра́шный* (бесстра́шен).

fearsome ['fɪəsəm] *adj* (*opponent*) внуша́ющий страх; (*sight*) устраша́ющий.

feasibility [fiːzə'bɪlɪtɪ] *n* (*of plan*) осуществи́мость *f*.

feasibility study *n* те́хнико-экономи́ческое обоснова́ние.

feasible ['fiːzəbl] *adj* осуществи́мый (осуществи́м).

feast [fiːst] *n* (*banquet*) пир*; (*REL*: *also*: ~ **day**) пра́здник ♦ *vi* пирова́ть (*impf*); **to ~ on** ла́комиться* (*impf*) +*instr*; **to ~ one's eyes on sth** любова́ться (*impf*) чем-н.

feat [fiːt] *n* по́двиг.

feather ['fɛðəʳ] *n* перо́* ♦ *cpd* перьево́й ♦ *vt*: **to ~ one's nest** набива́ть (наби́ть* *perf*) себе́ карма́н; ~ **bed** пери́на.

featherweight ['fɛðəweɪt] *n* (*BOXING*) боксёр полулёгкого ве́са.

feature ['fiːtʃəʳ] *n* черта́, осо́бенность *f*; (*of landscape*) осо́бенность; (*PRESS*) о́черк; (*TV, RADIO*) переда́ча ♦ *vt*: **the film ~s 2 famous actors** в фи́льме снима́ются 2 изве́стные актёра; ~**s** *npl* (*of face*) черты́ *fpl*; **a film featuring ...** фильм с уча́стием ...; **his article ~d in all the newspapers** его́ статья́ фигури́ровала во всех газе́тах; **a special ~ on sth/sb** специа́льная переда́ча о чём-н/ком-н.

feature film *n* худо́жественный фильм.

featureless ['fiːtʃəlɪs] *adj* невырази́тельный* (невырази́телен).

Feb. *abbr* = **February**.

February ['fɛbruərɪ] *n* февра́ль *m*; *see also* **July**.

feces ['fiːsiːz] *npl* (*US*) = **faeces**.

feckless ['fɛklɪs] *adj* безотве́тственный.

Fed *abbr* (*US*) = **federal, federation**.

fed [fɛd] *pt, pp of* **feed**.

Fed. *n abbr* (*US*: *inf*: = Federal Reserve Board) *сове́т, управля́ющий федера́льной резе́рвной систе́мой.*

federal ['fɛdərəl] *adj* федера́льный.

Federal Republic of Germany *n* Федерати́вная Респу́блика Герма́нии.

Federal Reserve Board *n* (*US*) Федера́льное резе́рвное правле́ние.

Federal Trade Commission *n* (*US*) Федера́льная торго́вая коми́ссия.

federation [fɛdə'reɪʃən] *n* федера́ция.

fed up *adj*: **he is ~ ~** ему́ надое́ло.

fee [fiː] *n* пла́та; (*of doctor, lawyer*) пла́та, гонора́р; **school ~s** пла́та за обуче́ние; **entrance ~** входна́я пла́та; **membership ~** чле́нский* взнос; **for a small ~** за небольшо́е вознагражде́ние.

feeble ['fiːbl] *adj* хи́лый (хил); (*joke*) сла́бый.

feeble-minded ['fiːbl'maɪndɪd] *adj* слабоу́мный.

feed [fiːd] (*pt, pp* **fed**) *n* (*feeding*) кормле́ние; (*fodder*) корм*; (*on printer*) загру́зка* ♦ *vt* корми́ть* (накорми́ть* *perf*); **to ~ sth into sth** (*data, information*) загружа́ть (загрузи́ть* *perf*) что-н во что-н; (*material*) подава́ть* (пода́ть* *perf*) что-н во что-н

▶ **feed back** *vt* (*results*) подава́ть* (пода́ть* *perf*) обра́тно

▶ **feed on** *vt fus* пита́ться (*impf*) +*instr*.

feedback ['fiːdbæk] *n* (*response*) обра́тная связь *f*; (*from person*) о́тзыв.

feeding bottle ['fiːdɪŋ-] *n* (*BRIT*) буты́лочка* (*для кормле́ния младе́нца*).

feel [fiːl] (*pt, pp* **felt**) *n* ощуще́ние ♦ *vt* (*touch*) тро́гать (потро́гать *perf*); (*experience*) чу́вствовать (*impf*); (*think, believe*): **to ~ (that)** счита́ть (*impf*) (, что); **to get the ~ of sth** осва́иваться (осво́иться *perf*) с чем-н; **I ~ that you ought to do it** я счита́ю, что Вы должны́ э́то сде́лать; **he ~s hungry** он го́лоден; **she ~s cold** ей хо́лодно; **to ~ lonely/better** чу́вствовать (*impf*) себя́ одино́ким/лу́чше; **I don't ~ well** я пло́хо себя́ чу́вствую; **he ~s sorry for me** ему́ меня́ жа́лко *or* жаль; **the material ~s soft/like velvet** э́тот материа́л на о́щупь мя́гкий/как ба́рхат; **it ~s colder here** здесь холодне́е; **I ~ like ...** (*want*) мне хо́чется ...; **I'm still ~ing my way** я всё ещё осва́иваюсь *or* присма́триваюсь ...

▶ **feel about** *vi*: **to ~ about for sth** иска́ть (*impf*) что-н на о́щупь; **to ~ about** *or* **around in one's pocket for** ша́рить (поша́рить *perf*) в карма́не в по́исках +*gen*

▶ **feel around** *vi* = **feel about**.

feeler ['fiːləʳ] *n* (*of insect*) у́сик, щу́пальце*;

to put out a ~ *or* ~**s** (*fig*) зондировать
(прозондировать *perf*) по́чву.
feeling ['fi:lɪŋ] *n* (*emotion, impression*)
чу́вство; (*physical sensation*) ощуще́ние; ~**s**
ran high стра́сти разгоре́лись; **what are your**
~**s about the matter?** како́во Ва́ше
отноше́ние к э́тому вопро́су?; **I have a** ~ **that**
... у меня́ тако́е ощуще́ние, что ...; **my** ~ **is**
that ... по-мо́ему мне́нию ...; **to hurt sb's** ~**s**
задева́ть (заде́ть* *perf*) чьи-н чу́вства.
fee-paying ['fi:peɪŋ] *adj*: ~ **school** пла́тная
шко́ла; ~ **student** студе́нт, пла́тящий за
обуче́ния.
feet [fi:t] *npl of* **foot**.
feign [feɪn] *vt* (*injury, interest*) симули́ровать
(*impf/perf*).
feigned [feɪnd] *adj* притво́рный* (притво́рен).
feint [feɪnt] *n* (*of paper*) линёвка; **a pad of**
narrow ~ блокно́т в у́зкую лине́йку.
felicitous [fɪ'lɪsɪtəs] *adj* уда́чный* (уда́чен).
feline ['fi:laɪn] *adj* коша́чий*.
fell [fɛl] *pt of* **fall** ♦ *vt* вали́ть (свали́ть *perf*) ♦ *n*
(*BRIT*) гора́, холм и́ли боло́та в назва́ниях ♦
adj: **in one** ~ **swoop** одни́м ма́хом; **the** ~**s** *npl*
(*moorland*) боло́тистая ме́стность *fsg*.
fellow ['fɛləu] *n* (*man*) па́рень *m*; (*comrade*)
това́рищ; (*of learned society*)
действи́тельный член; (*of university*) член
сове́та ♦ *cpd*: **their** ~ **prisoners/students** их
сока́мерники/соку́рсники; **his** ~ **workers** его́
това́рищи по рабо́те.
fellow citizens *npl* согра́ждане* *mpl*.
fellow countryman *irreg n* соotéчественник.
fellow men *npl* бли́жние *pl adj*.
fellowship ['fɛləuʃɪp] *n* (*comradeship*)
содру́жество; (*society*) чле́нство; (*SCOL*)
стипе́ндия аспира́нта (*зва́ние чле́на сове́та*
колле́джа и́ли нау́чного о́бщества).
fell-walking ['fɛlwɔːkɪŋ] *n* (*BRIT*) восхожде́ние по
гора́м, боло́тистой ме́стности итп.
felon ['fɛlən] *n* (*LAW*) уголо́вный престу́пник.
felony ['fɛlənɪ] *n* (*LAW*) уголо́вное
преступле́ние.
felt [fɛlt] *pt, pp of* **feel** ♦ *n* (*fabric*) фетр.
felt-tip pen ['fɛltɪp-] *n* флома́стер.
female ['fi:meɪl] *n* (*also pej*) са́мка ♦ *adj* (*sex,*
character, profession) же́нский*; (*child*)
же́нского по́ла; (*ELEC*) охва́тывающий; ~
suffrage избира́тельное пра́во для же́нщин;
male and ~ **students** студе́нты и студе́нтки.
female impersonator *n* (*THEAT*) актёр,
игра́ющий же́нщин.
Femidom® ['fɛmɪdəm] *n* фемидо́м (*же́нский*
презервати́в).
feminine ['fɛmɪnɪn] *adj* (*clothes, behaviour*)
же́нственный* (же́нственен); (*LING*)
же́нского ро́да ♦ *n* (*LING*) же́нский* род.
femininity [fɛmɪ'nɪnɪtɪ] *n* же́нственность *f*.

feminism ['fɛmɪnɪzəm] *n* фемини́зм.
feminist ['fɛmɪnɪst] *n* фемини́ст(ка).
fen [fɛn] *n* (*BRIT*) *n* (*marsh*) боло́та; **the F**~**s**
ни́зкая боло́тистая ме́стность в
Ке́ймбредшире и Ли́нкольншире.
fence [fɛns] *n* (*barrier*) забо́р, и́згородь *f*;
(*SPORT*) препя́тствие ♦ *vt* (*also*: ~ **in**)
огора́живать (огороди́ть* *perf*) ♦ *vi* (*SPORT*)
фехтова́ть (*impf*); **to sit on the** ~ (*fig*)
занима́ть (*impf*) выжида́тельную пози́цию в
спо́ре.
fencing ['fɛnsɪŋ] *n* (*SPORT*) фехтова́ние.
fend [fɛnd] *vi*: **to** ~ **for o.s.** забо́титься*
(позабо́титься* *perf*) о себе́
▶ **fend off** *vt* отража́ть (отрази́ть* *perf*).
fender ['fɛndə] *n* (*of fireplace*) ками́нная
решётка*; (*on boat*) кра́нец*; (*US: of car*)
крыло́*.
fennel ['fɛnl] *n* фе́нхель *m* обыкнове́нный,
сла́дкий* укро́п*.
ferment [*n* 'fə:mɛnt, *vi* fə'mɛnt] *n* (*unrest*)
броже́ние ♦ *vi* броди́ть* (*impf*).
fermentation [fə:mɛn'teɪʃən] *n* броже́ние.
fern [fə:n] *n* па́поротник.
ferocious [fə'rəuʃəs] *adj* (*animal*) свире́пый
(свире́п); (*behaviour*) ди́кий* (дик);
(*competition, opposition, criticism*) жесто́кий*
(жесто́к); (*heat*) ужа́сный* (ужа́сен).
ferocity [fə'rɔsɪtɪ] *n* жесто́кость *f*; (*of*
opposition) я́рость *f*; **the** ~ **of the sun**
невыноси́мое пе́кло.
ferret ['fɛrɪt] *n* хорёк*
▶ **ferret about** *vi* ша́рить (*impf*)
▶ **ferret around** *vi* = **ferret about**
▶ **ferret out** *vt* выве́дывать (вы́ведать *perf*).
ferry ['fɛrɪ] *n* (*also*: ~**boat**) паро́м ♦ *vt*
перевози́ть* (перевезти́* *perf*); **to** ~ **sth/sb**
across *or* **over** переправля́ть (перепра́вить
perf) что-н/кого́-н.
ferryman ['fɛrɪmən] *irreg n* паро́мщик.
fertile ['fə:taɪl] *adj* (*land, soil*) плодоро́дный*
(плодоро́ден); (*imagination*) бога́тый
(бога́т); (*woman*) спосо́бный к зача́тию; ~
period плодотво́рный пери́од.
fertility [fə'tɪlɪtɪ] *n* (*see adj*) плодоро́дие;
бога́тство; спосо́бность *f* к зача́тию.
fertility drug *n* препара́т от беспло́дия.
fertilization [fə:tɪlaɪ'zeɪʃən] *n* (*of egg*)
оплодотворе́ние.
fertilize ['fə:tɪlaɪz] *vt* (*land*) удобря́ть
(удо́брить *perf*); (*egg*) оплодотворя́ть
(оплодотвори́ть *perf*); (*plant*) опыля́ть
(опыли́ть *perf*).
fertilizer ['fə:tɪlaɪzə] *n* удобре́ние.
fervent ['fə:vənt] *adj* (*admirer, belief*) пы́лкий*.
fervour ['fə:və] (*US* **fervor**) *n* пыл*.
fester ['fɛstə] *vi* (*wound*) гнои́ться
(загнои́ться *perf*); (*insult, row*) разраста́ться

(разрости́сь* *perf*).

festival ['fɛstɪvəl] *n* (*REL*) пра́здник; (*ART, MUS*) фестива́ль *m*.

festive ['fɛstɪv] *adj* (*mood, atmosphere*) пра́здничный* (пра́здничен); **the ~ season** (*BRIT*) свя́тки* *pl*.

festivities [fɛs'tɪvɪtɪz] *npl* пра́зднества *ntpl*.

festoon [fɛs'tu:n] *vt*: **to ~ with** украша́ть (укра́сить* *perf*) +*instr*.

fetch [fɛtʃ] *vt* (*object*) приноси́ть* (принести́* *perf*); (*person*) приводи́ть* (привести́* *perf*); (*by transport*) привози́ть* (привезти́* *perf*); **would you ~ me a jug of water please?** принеси́те мне, пожа́луйста, кувши́н воды́; **how much did the book ~?** ско́лько Вы вы́ручили за кни́гу?; **his pictures ~ very high prices** его́ карти́ны продаю́тся по высо́ким це́нам

▸ **fetch up** *vi* (*BRIT*) оказа́ться* (*perf*).

fetching ['fɛtʃɪŋ] *adj* преле́стный* (преле́стен).

fête [feɪt] *n* благотвори́тельный пра́здник-база́р.

fetid ['fɛtɪd] *adj* воню́чий*.

fetish ['fɛtɪʃ] *n* (*also fig*) фети́ш*.

fetter ['fɛtə] *vt* (*person*) зако́вывать (закова́ть *perf*); (*horse*) спу́тывать (спу́тать *perf*); (*fig*) ско́вывать (скова́ть *perf*).

fetters ['fɛtəz] *npl* (*also fig*) око́вы *pl*.

fettle ['fɛtl] *n* (*BRIT*): **in fine ~** (*person*) в прекра́сной фо́рме.

fetus ['fi:təs] *n* (*US*) = **foetus**.

feud [fju:d] *n* вражда́ ◆ *vi* враждова́ть (*impf*); **a family ~** фами́льная вражда́ (*ме́жду двумя́ се́мьями*).

feudal ['fju:dl] *adj* феода́льный.

feudalism ['fju:dlɪzəm] *n* феодали́зм.

fever ['fi:və] *n* (*temperature*) жар; (*disease*) лихора́дка*; **he has a ~** у него́ жар.

feverish ['fi:vərɪʃ] *adj* (*also fig*) лихора́дочный* (лихора́дочен); (*person: with excitement*) возбуждённый* (возбуждён); **he is ~** у него́ жар, его́ лихора́дит.

few [fju:] *adj* (*not many*) немно́гие; (*several*): **a ~** (*number*) не́сколько +*gen*; (*some*) не́которые *pl adj* ◆ *pron*: **(a) ~** немно́гие *pl adj*; **a ~ more** ещё не́сколько; **for a ~ days** на не́сколько дней; **with a ~ of them** с не́которыми из них; **they were ~** их бы́ло ма́ло *or* немно́го; **~ succeed** немно́гим удаётся; **very ~ survive** о́чень немно́гие выжива́ют; **I know a ~** я зна́ю не́скольких; **a good ~** дово́льно мно́гие; **quite a ~** дово́льно мно́го; **in the next ~ days** в ближа́йшие не́сколько дней; **in the past ~ days** за после́дние не́сколько дней; **every ~ days/months** че́рез ка́ждые не́сколько дней/ме́сяцев.

fewer ['fju:ə'] *adj* ме́ньше +*gen*; **they are ~** их ме́ньше; **there are ~ buses on Sundays** по воскресе́ньям хо́дит ме́ньше авто́бусов.

fewest ['fju:ɪst] *adj* ме́ньше всего́ +*gen*.

FFA *n abbr* = *Future Farmers of America*.

FH *n abbr* (*BRIT*) = **fire hydrant**.

FHA *n abbr* (*US*) = *Federal Housing Administration*.

fiancé [fɪ'ɑ̃:ŋseɪ] *n* жени́х*.

fiancée [fɪ'ɑ̃:ŋseɪ] *n* неве́ста.

fiasco [fɪ'æskəu] *n* фиа́ско *nt ind*.

fib [fɪb] *n* враньё *nt no pl*; **to tell ~s** привира́ть (привра́ть* *perf*); **a few small ~s don't hurt** немно́жко привра́ть (*perf*) не побреди́т.

fibre ['faɪbə] (*US* **fiber**) *n* волокно́*; (*dietary*) клетча́тка.

fibreboard ['faɪbəbɔ:d] (*US* **fiberboard**) *n* фи́бровый карто́н*.

fibreglass ['faɪbəglɑ:s] (*US* **fiberglass**) *n* стекловолокно́.

fibrositis [faɪbrə'saɪtɪs] *n* фибро́з.

FICA *n abbr* (*US*) = *Federal Insurance Contributions Act*.

fickle ['fɪkl] *adj* непостоя́нный* (непостоя́нен).

fiction ['fɪkʃən] *n* (*LITERATURE*) худо́жественная литерату́ра; (*invention*) вы́мысел*; (*lie*) вы́думка*.

fictional ['fɪkʃənl] *adj* (*character, event*) вы́мышленный (вы́мылен); (*relating to fiction*) беллетристи́ческий.

fictionalize ['fɪkʃnəlaɪz] *vt* беллетризи́ровать (*impf/perf*).

fictitious [fɪk'tɪʃəs] *adj* (*false, invented*) фикти́вный* (фикти́вен); (*character, event*) вы́мышленный* (вы́мышлен).

fiddle ['fɪdl] *n* (*MUS*) скри́пка*; (*swindle*) обма́н ◆ *vt* (*BRIT: accounts*) подде́лывать (подде́лать *perf*); **tax ~** махина́ции с нало́гами; **to work a ~** моше́нничать (смоше́нничать *perf*)

▸ **fiddle with** *vt fus* верте́ть* (*impf*) в рука́х.

fiddler ['fɪdlə] *n* скрипа́ч*(ка*).

fiddly ['fɪdlɪ] *adj* (*task*) трудновыполни́мый; (*object*) неудо́бный в обраще́нии.

fidelity [fɪ'dɛlɪtɪ] *n* ве́рность *f*; (*accuracy*) то́чность *f*.

fidget ['fɪdʒɪt] *vi* ёрзать (*impf*).

fidgety ['fɪdʒɪtɪ] *adj* беспоко́йный* (беспоко́ен).

fiduciary [fɪ'dju:ʃɪərɪ] *n* (*LAW*) дове́ренное лицо́*.

field [fi:ld] *n* (*also ELEC, COMPUT*) по́ле; (*SPORT*) по́ле, площа́дка*; (*fig: area of interest*) о́бласть* *f* ◆ *cpd* (*study, trip, scientist etc*) полево́й; **the ~** (*competitors, entrants*) уча́стники *mpl* состяза́ния; **they lead the ~** (*COMM*) они́ веду́щие в свое́й о́бласти.

field day *n*: **to have a ~ ~** (*fig*) пра́здновать (*impf*), торжествова́ть (*impf*).

field glasses *npl* полево́й бино́кль *msg*.

field hospital *n* полево́й го́спиталь *m*.

field marshal *n* фельдма́ршал.

field work *n* полевы́е иссле́дования *ntpl*; (*GEO*) рабо́та в по́ле.

fiend [fi:nd] *n* злоде́й.

fiendish ['fi:ndɪʃ] *adj* дья́вольский*.

fierce ~ fill

fierce [fɪəs] *adj* (*animal, person, look*) свире́пый; (*fighting*) я́ростный; (*loyalty*) горя́чий* (горя́ч); (*enemy, cold, hatred*) лю́тый* (лют); (*wind, heat, storm*) стра́шный* (стра́шен).

fiery [ˈfaɪərɪ] *adj* (*burning*) жгу́чий*; (*sunset*) о́гненный; (*taste*) обжига́ющий; (*temperament*) горя́чий* (горя́ч); ~ **red** о́гненно-кра́сный.

FIFA [ˈfiːfə] *n abbr* (= *Fédération Internationale de Football Association*) ФИ́ФА.

fifteen [fɪfˈtiːn] *n* пятна́дцать*; *see also* **five**.

fifteenth [fɪfˈtiːnθ] *adj* пятна́дцатый; *see also* **fifth**.

fifth [fɪfθ] *adj* пя́тый ◆ *n* (*fraction*) пя́тая *f adj*; (*AUT: also:* ~ **gear**) пя́тая ско́рость *f*; **he came** ~ **in the competition** он за́нял пя́тое ме́сто в соревнова́нии; ~ **form** (*BRIT: SCOL*) пя́тый класс; **I was (the)** ~ **to arrive** я пришёл пя́тым; **Henry the F**~ Ге́нрих Пя́тый; **the** ~ **of July, July the** ~ пя́тое ию́ля; **I wrote to him on the** ~ я написа́л ему́ пя́того числа́.

fifth column *n* пя́тая коло́нна (*преда́тели внутри́ страны́ и́ли организа́ции*).

fiftieth [ˈfɪftɪθ] *adj* пятидеся́тый; *see also* **fifth**.

fifty [ˈfɪftɪ] *n* пятьдеся́т*; **there are about** ~ **people here** здесь о́коло пяти́десяти челове́к; **he'll be** ~ **(years old) next week** на сле́дующей неде́ле ему́ бу́дет пятьдеся́т (лет); **he's about** ~ ему́ о́коло пяти́десяти; **the Fifties (1950s)** пятидеся́тые го́ды; **he is in his fifties** ему́ за пятьдеся́т лет; **the temperature was in the fifties** температу́ра была́ вы́ше пяти́десяти гра́дусов; **to do** ~ **(miles per hour)** (*AUT*) е́хать (*impf*) со ско́ростью пятьдеся́т миль в час.

fifty-fifty [ˈfɪftɪˈfɪftɪ] *adj* (*deal, split*) ра́вный* ◆ *adv* попола́м, по́ровну; **to share** ~ **with sb** дели́ть* (раздели́ть* *perf*) попола́м с кем-н; **to have a** ~ **chance (of success)** име́ть (*impf*) ра́вные ша́нсы (на успе́х).

fig [fɪg] *n* инжи́р*.

fight [faɪt] (*pt, pp* **fought**) *n* дра́ка; (*MIL*) бой*; (*campaign, struggle*) борьба́ ◆ *vt* (*person*) дра́ться* (подра́ться* *perf*) с +*instr*; (*MIL*) воева́ть* (*impf*) с +*instr*; (*illness, problem, emotion*) боро́ться* (*impf*) с +*instr*; (*election*) уча́ствовать (*impf*) в предвы́борной борьбе́; (*LAW: case*) защища́ть* (*impf*) ◆ *vi* (*people*) дра́ться* (*impf*); (*MIL*) воева́ть* (*impf*); **to put up a** ~ упо́рно сопротивля́ться (*impf*); **to** ~ **one's way through a crowd/the undergrowth** прокла́дывать (*impf*) себе́ доро́гу че́рез толпу́/за́росли; **to** ~ **with sb** дра́ться* (*impf*) с кем-н; **to** ~ **(for/against)** боро́ться* (*impf*) (за +*acc*/про́тив +*gen*)

▸ **fight back** *vi* защища́ться (защити́ться *perf*); (*SPORT, after illness*) верну́ть (*perf*) себе́ спорти́вную фо́рму ◆ *vt fus* (*tears, fear etc*)

сде́рживать (сдержа́ть* *perf*)

▸ **fight down** *vt* (*urge, emotion*) подавля́ть (подави́ть* *perf*)

▸ **fight off** *vt* (*attacker*) отбива́ть (отби́ть* *perf*); (*sleep*) отгоня́ть (отогна́ть* *perf*)

▸ **fight out** *vt*: **to** ~ **it out** отста́ивать (отстоя́ть *perf*) что́-нибудь в борьбе́.

fighter [ˈfaɪtə] *n* (*also fig*) боре́ц*; (*MIL: soldier*) бое́ц*; (: *plane*) истреби́тель *m*.

fighter pilot *n* лётчик-истреби́тель *m*.

fighting [ˈfaɪtɪŋ] *n* (*battle*) бой*; (*brawl*) дра́ка.

figment [ˈfɪgmənt] *n*: **a** ~ **of the imagination** плод* воображе́ния.

figurative [ˈfɪgjurətɪv] *adj* (*style*) о́бразный*; (*sense*) перено́сный.

figure [ˈfɪgə] *n* (*shape, body, also GEOM*) фигу́ра; (*number*) ци́фра; (*personality*) ли́чность *f* ◆ *vt* (*esp US: think*) счита́ть (*impf*) ◆ *vi* (*appear*) фигури́ровать (*impf*); **to put a** ~ **on** назнача́ть (назна́чить *perf*) це́ну +*gen or* на +*acc*; **public** ~ изве́стная ли́чность

▸ **figure out** *vt* понима́ть (поня́ть* *perf*); (*cost*) подсчи́тывать (подсчита́ть *perf*).

figurehead [ˈfɪgəhɛd] *n* (*NAUT*) фигу́ра на носу́ корабля́; (*pej: leader*) номина́льная глава́ *m*.

figure of speech *n* фигу́ра ре́чи.

figure skating *n* фигу́рное ката́ние.

Fiji (Islands) [ˈfiːdʒi:-] *n(pl)* Фи́джи *ntpl ind*.

filament [ˈfɪləmənt] *n* (*ELEC, TECH*) нить *f* нака́ла; (*BIO*) тычи́ночная нить.

filch [fɪltʃ] *vt* (*inf*) стяну́ть (*perf*).

file [faɪl] *n* (*dossier*) де́ло*; (*in cabinet*) картоте́ка; (*folder*) скоросшива́тель *m*; (: *for loose leaf*) па́пка*; (*COMPUT*) файл; (*row*) коло́нна; (*tool*) напи́льник ◆ *vt* (*papers, document*) подшива́ть (подши́ть* *perf*); (*in card index*) вноси́ть* (внести́* *perf*); (*LAW: claim*) подава́ть* (пода́ть* *perf*); (*wood, fingernails*) шлифова́ть (отшлифова́ть *perf*) ◆ *vi*: **to** ~ **in/out/past** входи́ть* (войти́* *perf*)/выходи́ть* (вы́йти* *perf*)/проходи́ть* (пройти́* *perf*) коло́нной; **in single** ~ в коло́нну по одному́; **to** ~ **a suit against sb** подава́ть* (пода́ть* *perf*) в суд на кого́-н; **to** ~ **for divorce** подава́ть* (пода́ть* *perf*) на разво́д.

filename [ˈfaɪlneɪm] *n* (*COMPUT*) и́мя* *nt* фа́йла.

filibuster [ˈfɪlɪbʌstə] *n* (*esp US: POL*) *n* (*also:* ~**er**) обструкциони́ст ◆ *vi* тормози́ть (*impf*) пня́тие зако́на путём обстру́кции.

filing [ˈfaɪlɪŋ] *n* (*of papers, letters etc*) системати́зация.

filing cabinet *n* картоте́чный шкаф*, шкаф* с картоте́кой.

filing clerk *n* делопроизводи́тель *m*.

Filipino [fɪlɪˈpiːnəu] *n* филиппи́нец*(-нка*); (*LING*) филиппи́нксий* язы́к*.

fill [fɪl] *vi* (*room, hall*) наполня́ться

---

* marks translations which have irregular inflections. The Russian-English side of the dictionary gives inflectional information.

(напо́лниться *perf*) ♦ *vt* (*tooth*) пломбирова́ть (запломбирова́ть *perf*); (*vacancy*) заполня́ть (запо́лнить *perf*); (*need*) удовлетворя́ть (удовлетвори́ть *perf*) ♦ *n*: **to eat one's ~** наеда́ться (нае́сться* *perf*); **to ~ (with)** (*container*) наполня́ть (напо́лнить *perf*) (+*instr*); (*space, area*) заполня́ть (запо́лнить *perf*) (+*instr*)

▶ **fill in** *vt* (*cavity, form*) заполня́ть (запо́лнить *perf*); (*time*) корота́ть (*impf*) ♦ *vi*: **to ~ in for sb** замеща́ть (*impf*) кого́-н вре́менно; **to ~ sb in** (*inf*) вводи́ть* (ввести́* *perf*) кого́-н в курс де́ла

▶ **fill out** *vt* (*form, receipt*) заполня́ть (запо́лнить *perf*)

▶ **fill up** *vt* (*container*) наполня́ть (напо́лнить *perf*); (*space*) заполня́ть (запо́лнить *perf*) ♦ *vi* (*AUT*) заправля́ться (запра́виться* *perf*); **~ it up, please** (*AUT*) запра́вьте мне маши́ну, пожа́луйста.

fillet ['fɪlɪt] *n* филе́ *nt ind* ♦ *vt* отделя́ть (отдели́ть *perf*) от косте́й.

fillet steak *n* вы́резка.

filling ['fɪlɪŋ] *n* (*for tooth*) пло́мба; (*of pie*) начи́нка; (*of layer cake*) просло́йка.

filling station *n* запра́вочная ста́нция.

fillip ['fɪlɪp] *n* (*fig*) толчо́к.

filly ['fɪlɪ] *n* молода́я кобы́ла.

film [fɪlm] *n* (*CINEMA*) фи́льм; (*PHOT, COMM*) плёнка*; (*of powder, liquid etc*) то́нкий* слой ♦ *vti* снима́ть (снять *perf*)

film star *n* кинозвезда́* *m/f*.

film strip *n* диафи́льм.

film studio *n* киносту́дия.

Filofax® ['faɪleufæks] *n* записна́я кни́жка или дневни́к.

filter ['fɪltə*] *n* фильтр ♦ *vt* (*liquid*) фильтрова́ть (профильтрова́ть *perf*)

▶ **filter in** *vi* (*news*) проса́чиваться (просочи́ться *perf*)

▶ **filter through** *vi* = **filter in.**

filter coffee *n* ко́фе то́нкого помо́ла для кофева́рок с фи́льтром.

filter lane *n* (*BRIT: AUT*) полоса́, по кото́рой Вы должны́ е́хать, чтобы поверну́ть по указа́нию стре́лки светофо́ра.

filter tip *n* фильтр (*сигаре́ты*).

filter-tipped ['fɪltə'tɪpt] *adj* с фи́льтром.

filth [fɪlθ] *n* грязь *f*; (*fig: on TV etc*) непристо́йность *f*.

filthy ['fɪlθɪ] *adj* гря́зный* (гря́зен); (*fig*) ме́рзкий* (ме́рзок).

fin [fɪn] *n* (*of fish*) плавни́к*; (*TECH: of rocket*) стабилиза́тор.

final ['faɪnl] *adj* (*last*) после́дний*; (*SPORT*) фина́льный; (*ultimate*) заключи́тельный; (*definitive*) оконча́тельный* ♦ *n* (*SPORT*) фина́л; **~s** *npl* (*SCOL*) выпускны́е экза́мены *mpl*.

final demand *n* (*for bill etc*) оконча́тельное тре́бование.

final dividend *n* оконча́тельный дивиде́нд.

finale [fɪ'nɑ:lɪ] *n* фина́л.

finalist ['faɪnlɪst] *n* финали́ст.

finality [faɪ'nælɪtɪ] *n* оконча́тельность *f*; **to speak with an air of ~** говори́ть (*impf*) то́ном, не допуска́ющим возраже́ния.

finalize ['faɪnəlaɪz] *vt* (*arrangements, plans*) оконча́тельно уточня́ть (уточни́ть *perf*).

finally ['faɪnlɪ] *adv* (*eventually*) в конце́ концо́в; (*lastly*) наконе́ц; (*irrevocably*) оконча́тельно.

finance [faɪ'næns] *n* фина́нсы *pl* ♦ *vt* (*back, fund*) финанси́ровать (*impf/perf*); **~s** *npl* (*personal finances*) фина́нсы *pl*.

financial [faɪ'nænʃəl] *adj* (*difficulties, venture*) фина́нсовый; **~ statement** фина́нсовый отчёт.

financially [faɪ'nænʃəlɪ] *adv* в фина́нсовом отноше́нии.

financial management *n* фина́нсовое руково́дство.

financial year *n* фина́нсовый год*.

financier [faɪ'nænsɪə*] *n* финанси́ст.

find [faɪnd] (*pt, pp* **found**) *vt* находи́ть* (найти́* *perf*); (*discover*) обнару́живать (обнару́жить *perf*) ♦ *n* нахо́дка*; **to ~ sb at home** застава́ть* (заста́ть* *perf*) кого́-н до́ма; **to ~ sb guilty** (*LAW*) признава́ть* (призна́ть* *perf*) кого́-н вино́вным(-ой)

▶ **find out** *vt* (*fact, truth*) узнава́ть* (узна́ть* *perf*); (*person*) разоблача́ть (разоблачи́ть *perf*) ♦ *vi*: **to ~ out about** узнава́ть* (узна́ть* *perf*) о +*prp*.

findings ['faɪndɪŋz] *npl* (*LAW*) заключе́ние *ntsg*; (*in research*) результа́ты *mpl*.

fine [faɪn] *adj* (*quality, performance etc*) прекра́сный* (прекра́сен); (*hair, features*) то́нкий*; (*sand, powder, detail*) ме́лкий*; (*adjustment*) то́чный* (то́чен) ♦ *adv* (*well*) прекра́сно; (*small*) ме́лко ♦ *n* штраф ♦ *vt* штрафова́ть (оштрафова́ть *perf*); **he's ~** (*not ill*) он чу́вствует себя́ хорошо́; (*without problems*) у него́ всё в поря́дке; **the weather is ~** пого́да хоро́шая; **to cut it ~** (*of time*) оставля́ть (оста́вить* *perf*) сли́шком ма́ло вре́мени; **you're doing ~** у Вас всё в поря́дке.

fine arts *npl* изя́щные иску́сства *nt pl*.

finely ['faɪnlɪ] *adv* (*splendidly*) превосхо́дно; (*chop*) ме́лко; (*adjust: instrument*) то́нко.

fine print *n* напи́санное *or* напеча́танное ме́лким шри́фтом.

finery ['faɪnərɪ] *n* (*dress*) наря́д; (*jewellery*) украше́ния *ntpl*.

finesse [fɪ'nɛs] *n* то́нкость *f*, изя́щество.

fine-tooth comb ['faɪntu:θ-] *n*: **to go through sth with a ~ ~** (*fig*) скрупулёзно изуча́ть (изучи́ть* *perf*) что-н.

finger ['fɪŋgə*] *n* па́лец ♦ *vt* тро́гать (потро́гать *perf*); **little ~** мизи́нец*; **index ~** указа́тельный па́лец*.

fingernail ['fɪŋgəneɪl] *n* но́готь* *m*.

fingerprint ['fɪŋgəprɪnt] n отпеча́ток* па́льца ◆ vt (person) брать* (взять* perf) отпеча́тки па́льцев у +gen.

fingerstall ['fɪŋgəstɔ:l] n па́льчник.

fingertip ['fɪŋgətɪp] n ко́нчик па́льца; **to have sth at one's ~s** (at one's disposal) име́ть (impf) что-н под руко́й; (know well) знать* (impf) что-н как свои пять па́льцев.

finicky ['fɪnɪkɪ] adj привере́дливый (привере́длив).

finish ['fɪnɪʃ] n коне́ц*; (SPORT) фи́ниш; (polish etc) отде́лка* ◆ vt зака́нчивать (зако́нчить perf), конча́ть (ко́нчить perf) ◆ vi зака́нчиваться (зако́нчиться perf); (person) зака́нчивать (зако́нчить perf); **have you ~ed?** Вы уже́ зако́нчили?; **to ~ doing** конча́ть (ко́нчить perf) +infin; **he ~ed third** (in race etc) он зако́нчил тре́тьим; **to ~ with sth** поко́нчить (perf) с чем-н; **she's ~ed with him** у неё с ним всё ко́нчено

▶ **finish off** vt (complete) зака́нчивать (зако́нчить perf); (kill) прика́нчивать (прико́нчить perf)

▶ **finish up** vt (food) доеда́ть (дое́сть* perf); (drink) допива́ть (допи́ть* perf) ◆ vi (end up) конча́ть (ко́нчить perf).

finished ['fɪnɪʃt] adj (product) отде́ланный (отде́лан); (performance) отто́ченный (отто́чен); (inf: tired) изм́отанный (изм́отан).

finishing line ['fɪnɪʃɪŋ-] n (SPORT) фи́нишная черта́.

finishing school n ча́стный же́нский пансио́н.

finishing touches npl после́дние штрихи́* mpl.

finite ['faɪnaɪt] adj (time, space) ограни́ченный (ограни́чен), коне́чный* (коне́чен); (verb) ли́чный.

Finland ['fɪnlənd] n Финля́ндия; **Gulf of ~** Фи́нский зали́в.

Finn [fɪn] n финн (фи́нка).

Finnish ['fɪnɪʃ] adj фи́нский* ◆ n фи́нский* язы́к*.

fiord [fjɔ:d] n = **fjord**.

fir [fə:ʳ] n ель f.

fire ['faɪəʳ] n (flames) пла́мя* nt; (in hearth) ого́нь* m; (accidental fire) пожа́р; (bonfire) костёр* ◆ vt (shoot: gun, arrow etc) вы́стрелить (perf) из +gen; (stimulate: imagination etc) разжига́ть (разже́чь* perf); (inf: dismiss) увольня́ть (уво́лить perf) ◆ vi (shoot) вы́стрелить (perf); **the house is on ~** дом* гори́т; **to set ~ to sth, set sth on ~** поджига́ть (подже́чь* perf) что-н; **the house is insured against ~** дом* застрахо́ван на слу́чай пожа́ра; **electric ~** электро-обогрева́тель m; **to come under ~ (from)** (fig) ока́зываться (оказа́ться* perf) под обстре́лом (со стороны́ +gen); **to be under ~**

быть* (impf) под обстре́лом; **to ~ a gun** стреля́ть (вы́стрелить perf) из пу́шки.

fire alarm n пожа́рная сигнализа́ция.

firearm ['faɪərɑ:m] n огнестре́льное ору́жие nt no pl.

fire brigade n пожа́рная кома́нда.

fire chief n нача́льник пожа́рной кома́нды.

fire department n (US) = **fire brigade**.

fire door n пожа́рная дверь* f.

fire drill n пожа́рное уче́ние.

fire engine n пожа́рная маши́на.

fire escape n пожа́рная ле́стница.

fire-extinguisher ['faɪərɪk'stɪŋgwɪʃəʳ] n огнетуши́тель m.

fireguard ['faɪəgɑ:d] n (BRIT) ками́нная решётка*.

fire hazard n: **that's a ~ ~** э́то огнеопа́сно.

fire hydrant n пожа́рный насо́с.

fire insurance n страхова́ние на слу́чай пожа́ра.

fireman ['faɪəmən] irreg n пожа́рный m adj, пожа́рник.

fireplace ['faɪəpleɪs] n ками́н.

fireplug ['faɪəplʌg] n (US) = **fire hydrant**.

fire practice n = **fire drill**.

fireproof ['faɪəpru:f] adj (objects) несгора́емый; (materials) огнеупо́рный*.

fire regulations npl пра́вила ntpl пожа́рной безопа́сности.

fire screen n (decorative) ками́нный экра́н; (for protection) противопожа́рное загражде́ние.

fireside ['faɪəsaɪd] n: **by the ~** (indoors) у ками́на.

fire station n пожа́рное депо́ nt ind.

firewood ['faɪəwud] n дрова́ pl.

fireworks ['faɪəwə:ks] npl фейерве́рк msg; (display) фейерве́рк msg, салю́т msg.

firing line ['faɪərɪŋ-] n ли́ния огня́; **to be in the ~ ~** (fig) находи́ться* (impf) на ли́нии огня́.

firing squad n взвод, наря́женный для расстре́ла.

firm [fə:m] adj (ground, decision, faith) твёрдый* (твёрд); (mattress) жёсткий*; (grasp, body, muscles) кре́пкий* (кре́пок); (offer) оконча́тельный* (оконча́телен) ◆ n фи́рма; **to be a ~ believer in sth** твёрдо ве́рить (impf) во что-н.

firmly ['fə:mlɪ] adv (believe, stand) твёрдо; (grasp, shake hands) кре́пко.

firmness ['fə:mnɪs] n (of ground, decision, faith) твёрдость f; (of mattress) жёсткость f; (of grip, hold) кре́пость f.

first [fə:st] adj пе́рвый ◆ adv (before all others) пе́рвый; (before other things) снача́ла; (when listing reasons etc) во-пе́рвых; (for the first time) впервы́е ◆ n (person: in race) пе́рвый(-ая) m(f) adj; (AUT: also: ~ gear)

пе́рвая ско́рость *f*; (*BRIT: SCOL: degree*) дипло́м пе́рвой сте́пени; **the ~ of January** пе́рвое января́; **at ~** снача́ла; **~ of all** пре́жде всего́; **in the ~ instance** в пе́рвую о́чередь; **I'll do it ~ thing (tomorrow)** я сде́лаю э́то за́втра в пе́рвую о́чередь; **from the very ~** с са́мого нача́ла; *see also* **fifth.**

first aid *n* пе́рвая по́мощь *f*.

first-aid kit [fəːstˈeɪd-] *n* паке́т пе́рвой по́мощи.

first-class [ˈfəːstˈklɑːs] *adj* пе́рвого кла́сса; (*excellent*) первокла́ссный* ♦ *adv* пе́рвым кла́ссом.

first-hand [ˈfəːstˈhænd] *adj* (*experience, knowledge*) ли́чный; **a ~ account** расска́з очеви́дца.

first lady *n* (*US*) пе́рвая ле́ди *f ind*; **the ~ ~ of jazz** короле́ва джа́за.

firstly [ˈfəːstlɪ] *adv* во-пе́рвых.

first name *n* и́мя* *nt*.

first night *n* (*THEAT*) премье́ра.

first-rate [ˈfəːstˈreɪt] *adj* первокла́ссный*; (*liar*) отме́нный.

first-time buyer [ˈfəːsttaɪm-] *n* челове́к, впервы́е покупа́ющий дом и́ли кварти́ру.

fir tree *n* ель *f*.

FIS *n abbr* (*BRIT*: = *Family Income Supplement*) дополне́ние к семе́йному дохо́ду (*посо́бие для малоиму́щих*).

fiscal [ˈfɪskl] *adj* фиска́льный; **~ year** фиска́льный *or* фина́нсовый год.

fish [fɪʃ] *n inv* ры́ба ♦ *vt* (*river, area*) лови́ть* (*impf*) ры́бу в +*prp* ♦ *vi* (*commercially*) занима́ться (*impf*) рыболо́вством; (*as sport, hobby*) занима́ться (*impf*) ры́бной ло́влей; **to go ~ing** ходи́ть*/идти́* (пойти́* *perf*) на рыба́лку

▸ **fish out** *vt* (*from water*) выу́живать (вы́удить* *perf*); (*from box etc*) выта́скивать (вы́тащить *perf*).

fishbone [ˈfɪʃbəʊn] *n* ры́бья кость* *f*.

fish cake *n* ры́бная котле́та.

fisherman [ˈfɪʃəmən] *irreg n* рыба́к*.

fishery [ˈfɪʃərɪ] *n* (*fishing ground*) ры́бные места́ *ntpl*; (*fish farm*) рыбово́дческое хозя́йство.

fish factory *n* (*BRIT*) рыбозаво́д.

fish farm *n* рыбово́дческая фе́рма.

fish fingers *npl* (*BRIT*) ры́бные па́лочки* *fpl*.

fish hook *n* рыболо́вный крючо́к*.

fishing boat [ˈfɪʃɪŋ-] *n* рыболо́вное су́дно*.

fishing line *n* (*on rod*) ле́са*.

fishing net *n* рыболо́вная сеть *f*.

fishing rod *n* у́дочка*.

fishing tackle *n* рыболо́вная снасть *f*.

fish market *n* ры́бный ры́нок*.

fishmonger [ˈfɪʃmʌŋɡə*] *n* (*esp BRIT*) торго́вец* ры́бой.

fishmonger's (shop) [ˈfɪʃmʌŋɡəz-] *n* (*esp BRIT*) ры́бный магази́н.

fish slice *n* (*BRIT*) лопа́точка для

переора́чивания ры́бы на сковороде́.

fish sticks *npl* (*US*) = **fish fingers.**

fishy [ˈfɪʃɪ] *adj* (*inf: tale, story etc*) сомни́тельный.

fission [ˈfɪʃən] *n* расщепле́ние; **atomic** *or* **nuclear ~** а́томное *or* я́дерное расщепле́ние.

fissure [ˈfɪʃə*] *n* (*in rock*) расще́лина; (*in ground*) щель* *f*, тре́щина.

fist [fɪst] *n* кула́к*.

fistfight [ˈfɪstfaɪt] *n* дра́ка, кула́чный бой*.

fit [fɪt] *adj* (*suitable*) приго́дный* (приго́ден); (*healthy*) в хоро́шей фо́рме ♦ *vt* (*be the right size for*) быть* (*impf*) впо́ру +*dat*, подходи́ть* (подойти́* *perf*) по разме́ру +*dat*; (*adjust to the right size*) подгоня́ть (подогна́ть* *perf*); (: *clothes*) примеря́ть (приме́рить *perf*); (*match: facts, description*) соотве́тствовать (*impf*) +*dat*; (*put in: kitchen etc*) устана́вливать (установи́ть* *perf*); (*equip*) обору́довать (*impf*); (*suit: person*) подходи́ть (подойти́* *perf*) +*dat* ♦ *vi* (*clothes*) подходи́ть* (подойти́* *perf*) по разме́ру, быть* (*impf*) впо́ру; (*parts*) подходи́ть* (подойти́* *perf*) ♦ *n* (*MED*) припа́док*; (*of coughing, giggles*) при́ступ; **~ to do** (*ready*) гото́вый (гото́в) +*infin*; **~ to keep** приго́дный (приго́ден) для хране́ния; **~ for** (*suitable for*) приго́дный (приго́ден) для +*gen*; **to keep ~** сохраня́ть (*impf*) фо́рму; **~ for work** го́дный (го́ден) к рабо́те; **she's not ~ to be a teacher** рабо́та учи́теля ей не подхо́дит; **do as you think** *or* **see ~** де́лайте так, как Вы счита́ете ну́жным; **the suit ~s her** костю́м сиди́т на ней хорошо́; **to ~ into** входи́ть* (войти́* *perf*) в +*acc*; **a ~ of anger** при́ступ гне́ва; **a ~ of pride** поры́в го́рдости; **he had a ~** (*MED*) у него́ был припа́док; **he nearly had a ~ when he learned about it** (*fig: inf*) его́ чуть уда́р не хвати́л когда́ он об э́том узна́л; **this dress is a good ~** э́то пла́тье хорошо́ сиди́т; **by ~s and starts** урывка́ми

▸ **fit in** *vi* (*person, object*) впи́сываться (вписа́ться* *perf*) ♦ *vt* (*fig: appointment, visitor*) находи́ть* (найти́* *perf*) вре́мя для +*gen*; **to ~ in with sb's plans** совпада́ть (совпа́сть* *perf*) с чьи́ми-н пла́нами.

fitful [ˈfɪtful] *adj* (*sleep*) преры́вистый (преры́вист).

fitment [ˈfɪtmənt] *n* (*in room, cabin*) предме́т обстано́вки, обору́дование.

fitness [ˈfɪtnɪs] *n* (*MED*) состоя́ние здоро́вья.

fitted carpet [ˈfɪtɪd-] *n* ковро́вое покры́тие.

fitted cupboards *npl* встро́енные шкафы́ *mpl*.

fitted kitchen *n* (*BRIT*) по́лностью обору́дованная ку́хня.

fitter [ˈfɪtə*] *n* (*of machinery*) меха́ник; (*of equipment*) устано́вщик.

fitting [ˈfɪtɪŋ] *adj* (*thanks*) надлежа́щий* ♦ *n* (*of dress*) приме́рка*; (*of piece of equipment*) устано́вка; **~s** *npl* (*in building*) обстано́вка *fsg*.

fitting room *n* (*in shop*) приме́рочная *f adj*.

five [faɪv] *n* пять*; **she is ~ (years) old** ей пять лет; **they live at number 5/at 5 Green Street** они живут в доме номер 5/в доме номер 5 по Зелёной улице; **there are ~ of us** нас пятеро; **all ~ of them came** все пятеро пришли; **about ~** около пяти; **the book costs ~ pounds** книга стоит пять фунтов; **~ and a half/quarter** пять с половиной/и одна четверть; **it's ~ (o'clock)** сейчас пять часов; **to divide sth into ~** делить (разделить *perf*) что-н на пять; **they are sold in ~s** они продаются по пять.

five-day week ['faɪvdeɪ-] *n* пятиднéвная рабочая неделя.

fiver ['faɪvəʳ] *n* (*inf: money: BRIT*) пять фунтов; (*: US*) пять долларов.

fix [fɪks] *vt* (*sort out, arrange: amount*) устанавливать (установить* *perf*); (*: date*) назначать (назначить *perf*); (*mend*) налаживать (наладить* *perf*); (*inf: meal, drink*) организовать (*impf/perf*); (*: game etc*) подстраивать (подстроить *perf*) ♦ *n* (*inf*): **to be in a ~** быть* (*impf*) в трудном положении; **to ~ sth to** (*attach*) прикреплять (прикрепить *perf*) что-н к +*dat*; **to ~ one's eyes on** останавливать (остановить* *perf*) глаза на +*prp*; **to ~ one's attention on** сосредотачивать (сосредоточить *perf*) внимание на +*prp*; **the fight was a ~** (*inf*) исход поединка был предрешён

▸ **fix up** *vt* (*meeting*) устраивать (устроить *perf*); **to ~ sb up with sth** устраивать (устроить *perf*) кому-н что-н.

fixation [fɪk'seɪʃən] *n* помешательство; (*fig*): **she has a ~ about cleanliness** чистота – её пунктик.

fixative ['fɪksətɪv] *n* фиксатив.

fixed [fɪkst] *adj* (*price*) твёрдый*; (*amount*) установленный; (*ideas*) навязчивый; (*smile*) застывший*; **there's a ~ charge** существует установленная плата; **how are you ~ for money?** как у тебя с деньгами?

fixed assets *npl* недвижимое имущество *ntsg*.

fixed charge *n* (*COMM*) постоянные издержки* *pl*.

fixed-price contract [['fɪkstpraɪs-]] *n* контракт с фиксированной ценой.

fixture ['fɪkstʃəʳ] *n* (*fitting*) оборудование; (*SPORT*) назначенный матч.

fizz [fɪz] *vi* (*drink*) шипеть (*impf*).

fizzle out ['fɪzl-] *vi* (*event*) оканчиваться (окончиться *perf*) неудачей; (*interest*) угасать (угаснуть* *perf*); (*plan*) проваливаться (провалиться *perf*).

fizzy ['fɪzɪ] *adj* (*drink*) шипучий*, газированный.

fjord [fjɔːd] *n* фьорд, фиорд.

FL *abbr* (*US: POST*) = **Florida**.

flabbergasted ['flæbəgɑːstɪd] *adj* изумлённый (изумлён).

flabby ['flæbɪ] *adj* дряблый*.

flag [flæg] *n* флаг; (*for signalling*) флажок*; (*also: ~stone*) каменная плита* ♦ *vi* (*person*) выдыхаться (выдохнуться *perf*); (*spirits*) пропадать* (пропасть* *perf*); **~ of convenience** "удобный" флаг (*плавание под которым является особенно выгодным*); **to ~ down** (*taxi, car etc*) останавливать (остановить* *perf*).

flagging ['flægɪŋ] *adj*: **~ spirits** упадок духа.

flagon ['flægən] *n* бутыль *f*; (*for cider, wine*) кувшин.

flagpole ['flægpəʊl] *n* флагшток.

flagrant ['fleɪgrənt] *adj* (*injustice*) вопиющий*.

flagship ['flægʃɪp] *n* (*also fig*) флагман.

flagstone ['flægstəʊn] *n* каменная плита.

flag stop *n* (*US: for bus*) остановка* по требованию.

flair [flɛəʳ] *n* (*style*) стиль *m*; (*talent*): **a ~ for** склонность *f* к +*dat*; **political ~** политический* талант.

flak [flæk] *n* (*MIL*) зенитная артиллерия; (*inf: criticism*) нахлобучка*.

flake [fleɪk] *n* (*of snow, soap powder, cereal*) хлопья* *pl*; (*of rust, paint*) слой ♦ *vi* (*also: ~ off: enamel*) лупиться (облупиться *perf*); (*: paint*) трескаться (потрескаться *perf*); (*skin*) шелушиться (*impf*)

▸ **flake out** *vi* (*inf: person*) отключаться (отключиться *perf*).

flaky ['fleɪkɪ] *adj* (*paintwork*) облупленный; (*skin*) шелушащийся.

flaky pastry *n* слоёное тесто.

flamboyant [flæm'bɔɪənt] *adj* (*dress, design*) броский* (бросок); (*person*) колоритный* (колоритен).

flame [fleɪm] *n* (*of fire*) пламя* *nt*; **to burst into ~s** вспыхнуть (*perf*); **to be in ~s** пылать (*impf*); **an old ~** (*inf*) старая страсть.

flaming ['fleɪmɪŋ] *adj* (*inf*) дьявольский*.

flamingo [fləˈmɪŋgəʊ] *n* фламинго *m ind*.

flammable ['flæməbl] *adj* легко воспламеняющийся.

flan [flæn] *n* (*BRIT*) открытый круглый пирог*.

Flanders ['flɑːndəz] *n* Фландрия.

flange [flændʒ] *n* кромка.

flank [flæŋk] *n* (*of animal*) бок*; (*of army*) фланг ♦ *vt* окаймлять (*impf*); **~ed by** между +*instr*.

flannel ['flænl] *n* (*fabric*) фланель *f*; (*BRIT: also: face ~*) махровая салфетка для лица; **~s** *npl* (*trousers*) фланелевые брюки; **to give sb some ~** (*BRIT: inf*) морочить (*impf*) кому-н голову.

flannelette [flænə'lɛt] *n* байка.

flap [flæp] *n* (*of envelope*) отворот; (*of pocket*) клапан; (*of jacket*) пола* ♦ *vt* (*arms*) махать*

---

* marks translations which have irregular inflections. The Russian-English side of the dictionary gives inflectional information.

(*impf*) +*instr*; (*wings*) хло́пать (*impf*) +*instr* ♦ *vi*
(*sail, flag*) колыха́ться* (*impf*); (*inf: also:* be in a
~) волнова́ться (*impf*).

flapjack ['flæpdʒæk] *n* (*US: pancake*) ола́дья*;
(*BRIT: biscuit*) овся́ное пече́нье*.

flare [flɛəʳ] *n* (*signal*) сигна́льная раке́та; (*in
skirt etc*) клёш

▶ **flare up** *vi* (*fire*) вспы́хивать (вспы́хнуть *perf*)
я́рким пла́менем; (*fig: person, fighting,
trouble*) вспы́хивать (вспы́хнуть *perf*).

flared ['flɛəd] *adj*: ~ **trousers** брю́ки-клёш; ~
skirt ю́бка-клёш.

flash [flæʃ] *n* (*of light, also PHOT*) вспы́шка*;
(*also:* **news** ~) "мо́лния"; (*US: torch*) фона́рик
♦ *vt* (*light*) (внеза́пно) освеща́ть (освети́ть*
perf); (*send: news, message*) посыла́ть
(посла́ть* *perf*) мо́лнией; (*look*) мета́ть*
(метну́ть *perf*) ♦ *vi* (*lightning, light, eyes*)
сверка́ть (сверкну́ть *perf*); (*light on
ambulance etc*) мига́ть (*impf*); **in a** ~
мгнове́нно; **quick as a** ~ с быстрото́й
мо́лнии; ~ **of inspiration** поры́в
вдохнове́ния; **to** ~ **one's headlights**
сигна́лить (просигна́лить *perf*); **to** ~ **a smile
at sb** улыба́ться (улыбну́ться *perf*)
мимохо́дом кому́-н; **the thought** ~**ed
through his mind** у него́ промелькну́ла
мысль; **to** ~ **by** *or* **past** (*person*) мча́ться
(промча́ться *perf*) ми́мо +*gen*.

flashback ['flæʃbæk] *n* (*CINEMA*)
ретроспекти́вный кадр.

flashbulb ['flæʃbʌlb] *n* фотовспы́шка*,
ла́мпа-вспы́шка*.

flash card *n* (*SCOL*) ка́рточка *со сло́вом и́ли
бу́квой, испо́льзуемая при обуче́нии чте́нию*.

flashcube ['flæʃkjuːb] *n* фотовспы́шка.

flasher ['flæʃəʳ] *n* (*AUT*) поворо́та; (*inf: man*)
эксгибициони́ст.

flashlight ['flæʃlaɪt] *n* фона́рь* *m*, прожéктор.

flash point *n* (*fig*): **to be at** ~ ~ находи́ться*
(*impf*) на гра́ни взры́ва.

flashy ['flæʃɪ] *adj* (*pej*) крича́щий*.

flask [flɑːsk] *n* (*bottle*) фля́жка*; (*CHEM*) ко́лба;
(*also:* **vacuum** ~) те́рмос.

flat [flæt] *adj* (*surface*) пло́ский*; (*tyre*)
спу́щенный; (*battery*) се́вший; (*beer*)
вы́дохшийся; (*refusal, denial*)
категори́ческий*; (*MUS: note*) бемо́льный*;
(*voice*) однотóнный; (*rate, fee*) еди́ный
(еди́н) ♦ *n* (*BRIT: apartment*) кварти́ра; (*AUT:
also:* ~ **tyre**) спу́щенная ши́на; (*MUS*) бемо́ль
m; **to work** ~ **out** выкла́дываться (*impf*)
по́лностью, рабо́тать (*impf*) на изно́с; ~ **rate
of pay** еди́ная ста́вка.

flat-footed ['flæt'futɪd] *adj*: **he is** ~ у него́
плоскостóпие.

flatly ['flætlɪ] *adv* (*deny*) на́чисто; (*refuse*)
наотре́з.

flatmate ['flætmeɪt] *n* (*BRIT*) сосе́д*(ка*) по
кварти́ре.

flatness ['flætnɪs] *n* (*of land*) ро́вность *f*.

flat-screen ['flætskriːn] *adj* с пло́ским
экра́ном; ~ **TV set** телеви́зор с пло́ским
экра́ном.

flatten ['flætn] *vt* (*also:* ~ **out**) выра́внивать
(вы́ровнять *perf*); (*building*) сноси́ть*
(снести́* *perf*); (*crop*) побива́ть (поби́ть* *perf*);
(*city*) сравня́ть (*perf*) с землёй; (*fig: inf:
person*) разбива́ть (разби́ть* *perf*) в пух и
прах; **to** ~ **o.s. against a wall/door** *etc* пло́тно
прижима́ться (прижа́ться* *perf*) к стене́/двéри
etc.

flatter ['flætəʳ] *vt* льсти́ть* (польсти́ть* *perf*).

flatterer ['flætərəʳ] *n* льстéц*.

flattering ['flætərɪŋ] *adj* (*comment*) лéстный*
(лéстен); (*clothes*): **that dress is very** ~ э́то
пла́тье скрыва́ет все недоста́тки.

flattery ['flætərɪ] *n* лесть *f*.

flatulence ['flætjuləns] *n* (*MED*) метеори́зм.

flaunt [flɔːnt] *vt* щеголя́ть (*impf*).

flavour ['fleɪvəʳ] (*US* **flavor**) *vt* (*soups etc*)
приправля́ть (припра́вить* *perf*) ♦ *n* (*of food,
drink*) вкус; (*of ice-cream etc*) сорт*; (*fig*):
music with an African ~ му́зыка с
африка́нскими моти́вами *or* в африка́нском
сти́ле; **strawberry-**~**ed** с клубни́чным
при́вкусом; **to give** *or* **add** ~ **to** придава́ть*
(прида́ть* *perf*) вкус +*dat*.

flavouring ['fleɪvərɪŋ] *n* аромати́ческое
вещество́.

flaw [flɔː] *n* (*in argument, character*)
недоста́ток*, изъя́н; (*in cloth, glass*) дефéкт.

flawless ['flɔːlɪs] *adj* безупрéчный*.

flax [flæks] *n* лён*.

flaxen ['flæksən] *adj* (*hair*) льняно́й.

flea [fliː] *n* блоха́*.

flea market *n* барахо́лка*.

fleck [flɛk] *n* (*mark*) кра́пинка* ♦ *vt*: **to** ~ **(with)**
забры́згивать (*perf*) (+*instr*); **brown** ~**ed with
white** кори́чневый в бéлую кра́пинку.

fled [flɛd] *pt, pp of* **flee**.

fledg(e)ling ['flɛdʒlɪŋ] *n* (опери́вшийся)
птенéц*.

flee [fliː] (*pt, pp* **fled**) *vt* (*danger, famine*) бежа́ть*
(*impf*) от +*gen*; (*country*) бежа́ть* (*impf/perf*) из
+*gen* ♦ *vi* (*refugees, escapees*) спаса́ться (*impf*)
бéгством.

fleece [fliːs] *n* (*sheep's coat*) руно́*; (*sheep's
wool*) овéчья шерсть *f* ♦ *vt* (*inf: cheat*)
обира́ть (обобра́ть* *perf*).

fleecy ['fliːsɪ] *adj* пуши́стый.

fleet [fliːt] *n* (*of ships*) флот*; (*of lorries, cars*)
парк.

fleeting ['fliːtɪŋ] *adj* мимолётный*.

Flemish ['flɛmɪʃ] *adj* флама́ндский* ♦ *n* (*LING*)
флама́ндский язы́к*; **the** ~ *npl* (*GEO*)
Флама́ндцы* *mpl*.

flesh [flɛʃ] *n* (*ANAT*) плоть *f*; (*skin*) тéло; (*of
fruit*) мя́коть *f*

▶ **flesh out** *vt* излага́ть (изложи́ть* *perf*) во
всех дета́лях.

flesh wound [-wuːnd] *n* повéрхностная ра́на.

flew [flu:] *pt of* **fly**.
flex [flɛks] *n* гибкий* шнур* ♦ *vt* (*leg, muscles*) разминать (размять* *perf*).
flexibility [flɛksɪ'bɪlɪtɪ] *n* гибкость *f*.
flexible ['flɛksəbl] *adj* гибкий*.
flexitime ['flɛksɪtaɪm] *n* гибкий* график (*рабочего дня*).
flick [flɪk] *n* щелчок* ♦ *vt* (*with finger*) смахивать (смахнуть* *perf*); (*ash*) стряхивать (стряхнуть* *perf*); (*towel, whip*) хлестнуть (*perf*) +*instr*; (*switch*) щёлкнуть (*perf*) +*instr*; ~**s** *npl* (*inf*) кинóшка *fsg*
▶ **flick through** *vt fus* просматривать (просмотреть* *perf*).
flicker ['flɪkəʳ] *vi* (*light, flame*) мерцать (*impf*); (*eyelids*) трепетать (*impf*) ♦ *n* (*of light*) мерцáние; (*of pain, fear*) вспышка*; (*of suspicion, doubt*) тень *f*; (*of interest, hope*) проблеск; (*of eyelid*) трепетáние.
flick knife *n* (*BRIT*) кнóпочный нож.
flier ['flaɪəʳ] *n* (*pilot*) лётчик.
flight [flaɪt] *n* полёт; (*escape*) бегство; (*of steps*) пролёт (*лестницы*); **to take** ~ обращáться (обратиться* *perf*) в бегство; **to put to** ~ обращáть (обратить* *perf*) в бегство.
flight attendant *n* (*US*) стюáрд(éсса).
flight crew *n* экипáж самолёта.
flight deck *n* (*AVIAT*) кабина экипáжа; (*NAUT*) взлётно-посáдочная полосá на пáлубе.
flight path *n* (*of plane*) курс полёта; (*of rocket*) траектóрия полёта.
flight recorder *n* "чёрный ящик".
flimsy ['flɪmzɪ] *adj* (*shoes, clothes*) лёгкий*; (*building, structure*) непрóчный*; (*excuse, evidence*) слáбый*.
flinch [flɪntʃ] *vi* (*in pain, shock*) вздрáгивать (вздрóгнуть* *perf*); **to** ~ **from** (*unpleasant duty*) уклоняться (уклониться* *perf*) от +*gen*.
fling [flɪŋ] (*pt, pp* flung) *vt* (*throw*) швырять (швырнуть* *perf*) ♦ *n* (*love affair*) ромáн; **to** ~ **one's arms around sb's neck** обнимáть (обнять* *perf*) когó-н за шéю; **to** ~ **o.s.** (*move quickly*) кидáться (кинуться* *perf*), бросáться (брóситься* *perf*).
flint [flɪnt] *n* кремéнь* *m*.
flip [flɪp] *vt* (*switch*) щёлкать (щёлкнуть *perf*) +*instr*; (*coin*) подбрáсывать (подбрóсить* *perf*) щелчкóм; (*US: pancake*) подбрáсывать (подбрóсить* *perf*) ♦ *vi*: **to** ~ **for sth** (*US*) бросáть (брóсить* *perf*) монéту
▶ **flip through** *vt fus* просмáтривать (просмотрéть *perf*).
flippant ['flɪpənt] *adj* несерьёзный*.
flipper ['flɪpəʳ] *n* (*of seal etc*) плавник*; (*for swimming*) ласт*.
flip side *n* оборóт.
flirt [flɜ:t] *vi* (*with person*) флиртовáть (*impf*),

заигрывать (*impf*); (*with idea*) заигрывать (*impf*) ♦ *n* кокéтка*, любитель(ница) *m(f)* пофлиртовáть.
flirtation [flɜ:'teɪʃən] *n* флирт.
flit [flɪt] *vi* (*birds*) перелетáть (перелетéть* *perf*); (*butterfly*) порхáть (*impf*); (*expression, smile*) мелькáть (*impf*).
float [fləut] *n* (*for fishing*) поплавóк*; (*for swimming*) пеноплáстовая доскá для обучáющихся плáвать; (*lorry*) укрáшенная платфóрма на колёсах в прáздничной процéссии; (*money*) размéнные дéньги *pl* ♦ *vi* (*object: on water*) плáвать (*impf*), держáться (*impf*) на повéрхности; (*swimmer*) плыть* (*impf*); (*sound, smell, cloud*) плыть* (*impf*); (*paper*) летáть (*impf*); (*COMM: currency*) свобóдно колебáться* (*impf*) ♦ *vt* (*idea, plan*) пускáть (пустить* *perf*) в ход; **to** ~ **currency** вводить* (ввести* *perf*) плáвающий валютный курс; **to** ~ **a company** выпускáть (выпустить* *perf*) áкции компáнии чéрез биржу
▶ **float around** *vi* (*idea, rumour*) носиться* (*impf*) в вóздухе; (*person, object*) плáвать (*impf*).
flock [flɒk] *n* (*of sheep*) стáдо; (*of birds*) стáя; (*REL*) пáства ♦ *vi*: **to** ~ **to** (*place, event*) стекáться (стéчься *perf*) в +*prp*.
floe [fləu] *n* (*also*: **ice** ~) плавýчая льдина.
flog [flɒg] *vt* (*whip*) сечь* (высечь* *perf*); (*inf: sell*) сплавлять (сплавить* *perf*).
flood [flʌd] *n* (*of water*) наводнéние; (*of letters, imports etc*) потóк ♦ *vt* (*subj: water*) зáливать (залить* *perf*); (: *people*) наводнять (наводнить* *perf*); (*AUT: carburettor*) наполнять (напóлнить *perf*) ♦ *vi* (*place*) наполняться (напóлниться *perf*) водóй; (*people, goods*): **to** ~ **into** хлынуть (*perf*) в/на +*acc*; **the river is in** ~ рекá вышла из берегóв; **to** ~ **the market with** (*COMM*) наводнять (наводнить* *perf*) рынок +*instr*.
flooding ['flʌdɪŋ] *n* наводнéние.
floodlight ['flʌdlaɪt] *n* прожéктор* ♦ *vt* освещáть (осветить* *perf*) прожéктором.
floodlit ['flʌdlɪt] *pt, pp of* **floodlight** ♦ *adj* освещённый прожéктором.
flood tide *n* прилив.
flood water *n* (*разлившаяся*) водá* (*во врéмя наводнéния*).
floor [flɔ:ʳ] *n* (*of room*) пол*; (*storey*) этáж*; (*of sea, valley*) днó* ♦ *vt* (*subj: blow*) валить* (повалить* *perf*) нá пол, сбивáть (сбить* *perf*) с ног; (: *question, remark*) сражáть (сразить* *perf*); **on the** ~ на полý; **ground** *or* (*US*) **first** ~ пéрвый этáж*; **first** *or* (*US*) **second** ~ вторóй этáж*; **top** ~ послéдний этáж*; **to take the** ~ (*fig*) брать* (взять* *perf*) слóво; **to have the** ~ (*speaker*) получáть (получить *perf*) слóво.

---

* marks translations which have irregular inflections. The Russian-English side of the dictionary gives inflectional information.

floorboard ['flɔ:bɔ:d] *n* половѝца.
flooring ['flɔ:rɪŋ] *n* (*floor*) пол*; (*material to make floor*) настѝл; (*covering*) настѝлка полѐв.
floor lamp *n* (*US*) торшѐр.
floor show *n* (*in nightclub*) развлекѐтельная прогрѐмма.
floorwalker ['flɔ:wɔ:kə'] *n* (*esp US*) дежѐрный администрѐтор магазѝна.
floozy ['flu:zɪ] *n* (*inf*) шлю̀ха.
flop [flɔp] *n* (*failure*) провѐл ♦ *vi* (*fail*) провѐливаться (провалѝться* *perf*); (*fall: into chair, onto floor etc*) шлёпаться (шлёпнуться* *perf*).
floppy ['flɔpɪ] *adj* свисѐющий, отвѝслый ♦ *n* (*also:~disk*) гѝбкий* диск, дискѐта, флѐппи-диск; ~ **hat** шлѐпа с отвѝслыми полѐми.
flora ['flɔ:rə] *n* флѐра.
floral ['flɔ:rl] *adj* (*pattern*) цветѝстый.
Florence ['flɔrəns] *n* Флорѐнция.
Florentine ['flɔrəntaɪn] *adj* флорентѝйский*.
florid ['flɔrɪd] *adj* (*style*) цветѝстый; (*complexion*) крѐсный*.
florist ['flɔrɪst] *n* торгѐвец* цветѐми; (*female*) цветѐчница.
florist's (shop) ['flɔrɪsts-] *n* цветѐчный магазѝн.
flotation [fləu'teɪʃən] *n* (*of shares*) свобѐдная продѐжа; (*of company*) распродѐжа ѐкций компѐнии.
flotsam ['flɔtsəm] *n* (*also:~ and jetsam: rubbish*) мѐсор; (*: people*) бродѐги *pl*.
flounce [flauns] *n* (*frill*) обѐрка*
▶ **flounce out** *vi*: **she ~d out of the room** онѐ брѐсилась вон из кѐмнаты.
flounder ['flaundə'] *vi* (*in water*) барѐхтаться (*impf*); (*fig*) спотыкѐться (*impf*), пѐтаться (*impf*) ♦ *n* (*ZOOL*) кѐмбала.
flour ['flauə'] *n* мукѐ.
flourish ['flʌrɪʃ] *vi* (*business*) процветѐть (*impf*); (*plant*) пѝшно растѝ* (*impf*) ♦ *vt* (*document, handkerchief*) размѐхивать (*impf*) +*instr* ♦ *n* (*in writing*) завитѐшка; (*bold gesture*): **with a ~** демонстратѝвно.
flourishing ['flʌrɪʃɪŋ] *adj* (*company, trade*) процветѐющий.
flout [flaut] *vt* (*law, rules*) пренебрегѐть (пренебрѐчь* *perf*).
flow [fləu] *n* (*of blood, river*) течѐние; (*ELEC*) потѐк; (*of traffic, orders, information*) потѐк; (*of tide*) прилѝв ♦ *vi* течь* (*impf*); (*clothes, hair*) ниспадѐть (*impf*), пѐдать (*impf*).
flow chart *n* блок-схѐма.
flow diagram *n* = **flow chart**.
flower ['flauə'] *n* цветѐк* ♦ *vi* (*plant, tree*) цвестѝ* (*impf*); **~s** цветѝ; **in ~** в цветѐ.
flowerbed ['flauəbed] *n* клѐмба.
flowerpot ['flauəpɔt] *n* цветѐчный горшѐк*.
flowery ['flauərɪ] *adj* (*perfume*) цветѐчный; (*pattern, speech*) цветѝстый.

flown [fləun] *pp of* **fly**.
flu [flu:] *n* (*MED*) грипп*.
fluctuate ['flʌktjueɪt] *vi* (*price, rate, temperature*) колебѐться* (*impf*); (*opinions, attitudes*) менѝться (*impf*).
fluctuation [flʌktju'eɪʃən] *n*: ~ (**in**) колебѐние (в +*prp*).
flue [flu:] *n* дымохѐд.
fluency ['flu:ənsɪ] *n* бѐглость *f*; **his ~ in Russian** егѐ бѐглость в рѐсском языкѐ.
fluent ['flu:ənt] *adj* (*linguist*) бѐгло говорѝщий; (*speech, writing etc*) бѐглый, плѐвный*; **he's a ~ speaker** он ѐчень красноречѝв; **he's a ~ reader** он бѝстро читѐет; **he speaks ~ Russian, he's ~ in Russian** он свобѐдно *or* бѐгло говорѝт по-рѐсски.
fluently ['flu:əntlɪ] *adv* (*speak*) бѐгло; (*read, write*) свобѐдно.
fluff [flʌf] *n* (*on jacket, carpet*) ворс; (*fur, down*) пух* ♦ *vt* (*inf: do badly: lines*) спѐтывать (спѐтать *perf*); (*: exam*) завѐливать (завалѝть* *perf*); (*also:~ out: hair*) взбивѐть (взбѝть* *perf*); (*: feathers*) распушѐть (распушѝть *perf*).
fluffy ['flʌfɪ] *adj* пушѝстый; ~ **toy** мѝгкая игрѐшка*.
fluid ['flu:ɪd] *adj* (*movement*) текѐчий*; (*situation, arrangement*) переменчѝвый (переменчѝв); (*opinion*) неустѐйчивый (неустѐйчив) ♦ *n* жѝдкость *f*.
fluid ounce *n* (*BRIT*: = 0.028*l*; 0.05 *pints*) жѝдкая ѐнция.
fluke [flu:k] *n* (*inf*) везѐние.
flummox ['flʌməks] *vt* сбивѐть (сбѝть* *perf*) с тѐлку.
flung [flʌŋ] *pt, pp of* **fling**.
flunky ['flʌŋkɪ] *n* лакѐй.
fluorescent [fluə'resnt] *adj* (*dial, light*) флюоресцѝрующий; (*paint*) флюоресцѐнтный.
fluoride ['fluəraɪd] *n* фторѝд.
fluorine ['fluəri:n] *n* фтор.
flurry ['flʌrɪ] *n* (*of wind*) порѝв; **snow ~** снѐжный вихрь *m*; **a ~ of activity** бѐрная дѐятельность *f*; **a ~ of excitement** бѐрное возбуждѐние.
flush [flʌʃ] *n* (*on face*) румѝнец*; (*fig: of youth, beauty etc*) расцвѐт ♦ *vt* (*drains, pipe*) промывѐть (промѝть* *perf*) ♦ *vi* (*become red: face*) зардѐться (*perf*) ♦ *adj*: ~ **with** (*level*) на однѐм ѐровне с +*instr*; ~ **against** вплоть до +*gen*; **in the first ~ of youth/freedom** в упоѐнии мѐлодостью/свобѐдой; **hot ~es** (*BRIT: MED*) прилѝвы крѐви; **to ~ the toilet** спускѐть (спустѝть* *perf*) вѐду в туалѐте
▶ **flush out** *vt* (*game, birds*) вспѐгивать (вспугнѐть* *perf*); (*criminal*) спѐгивать (спугнѐть* *perf*).
flushed ['flʌʃt] *adj* раскраснѐвшийся.
fluster ['flʌstə'] *vt* (*person*) смущѐть (смутѝть* *perf*) ♦ *n*: **in a ~** в смущѐнии.
flustered ['flʌstəd] *adj* смущённый* (смущён).

flute [flu:t] *n* флéйта.
fluted ['flu:tɪd] *adj* рифлёный, гофрирóванный.
flutter ['flʌtə'] *n* (*of wings*) взмах; (*of panic, excitement*) трéпет ♦ *vi* (*bird*) взмáхивать (*impf*) крыльями; (*person*) метáться* (*impf*).
flux [flʌks] *n*: **in a state of** ~ в состоя́нии непрерывного изменéния.
fly [flaɪ] (*pt* **flew**, *pp* **flown**) *n* (*insect*) мýха; (*on trousers*: *also*: **flies**) ширúнка ♦ *vt* (*plane*) водúть/вестú* (*impf*); (*passengers, cargo*) перевозúть* (перевезтú* *perf*); (*distances*) пролетáть (пролетéть *perf*), преодолевáть (преодолéть *perf*); (*kite*) запускáть (запустúть* *perf*) ♦ *vi* (*also fig*) летáть/летéть (*impf*); (*escape*) спасáться (спастúсь* *perf*) бéгством, сбегáть (сбежáть *perf*); (*flag*) развевáться (*impf*); **to** ~ **open** распáхиваться (распахнýться *perf*); **to** ~ **off the handle** (*inf*) срывáться (сорвáться *perf*); **pieces of metal went** ~**ing everywhere** оскóлки метáлла полетéли во все стóроны; **she came** ~**ing into the room** онá влетéла в комнáту; **her glasses flew off** у неё слетéли очкú
▶ **fly away** *vi* улетáть (улетéть *perf*)
▶ **fly in** *vi* (*plane, person*) прилетáть (прилетéть* *perf*)
▶ **fly off** *vi* = **fly away**
▶ **fly out** *vi* (*person, plane*) вылетáть (вылететь* *perf*).
fly-fishing ['flaɪfɪʃɪŋ] *n* ужéние на блеснý.
flying ['flaɪɪŋ] *n* (*activity*) лётное дéло; (*action*) полёт ♦ *adj*: **a** ~ **visit** крáткий* визúт; **he doesn't like** ~ он не лю́бит летáть самолётом; **with** ~ **colours** блестя́ще.
flying buttress *n* áрочный контрфóрс.
flying picket *n группа профсою́зных агитáторов, объезжáющая фáбрики с цéлью убедúть рабóчих принять учáстие в забастóвке.*
flying saucer *n* летáющая тарéлка*.
flying squad *n* полицéйский спецотря́д (*для быстрого налёта*).
flying start *n*: **to get off to a** ~ ~ начинáть (начáть* *perf*) óчень успéшно.
flyleaf ['flaɪli:f] *n* фóрзац.
flyover ['flaɪəuvə'] *n* (*BRIT: overpass*) эстакáда.
fly-past ['flaɪpɑ:st] *n* воздýшный парáд.
fly sheet *n* (*for tent*) навéс.
flyweight ['flaɪweɪt] *n* боксёр лёгкой весовóй категóрии.
flywheel ['flaɪwi:l] *n* маховóе колесó*.
FM *abbr* (*BRIT: MIL*) = **field marshal**; (*RADIO*: = *frequency modulation*) ЧМ= *частóтная модуля́ция.*
FMB *n abbr* (*US*) = *Federal Maritime Board.*
FMCS *n abbr* (*US*) = *Federal Mediation and Conciliation Services*) *слýжба посрéдничества мéжду предпринимáтелями и рабóчими.*
FO *n abbr* (*BRIT*) = **Foreign Office.**
foal [fəul] *n* жеребёнок*.
foam [fəum] *n* пéна; (*also*: ~ **rubber**) пенорезúна ♦ *vi* пéниться (*impf*).
fob [fɔb] *n* (*also*: **watch** ~) цепóчка* для кармáнных часóв ♦ *vt*: **to** ~ **sb off (with sth)** всýчивать (всучúть* *perf*) *or* подсóвывать (подсýнуть *perf*) комý-н что-н.
f.o.b. *abbr* (*COMM*: = *free on board*) ФОБ= *фрáнко-бóрт.*
foc *abbr* (*COMM: BRIT*: = *free of charge*) беcплáтно.
focal point ['fəukl-] *n* средотóчие; (*PHOT*) фокáльная тóчка.
focus ['fəukəs] (*pl* ~**es**) *n* (*PHOT*) фóкус; (*of attention, interest, argument*) центр ♦ *vt* (*camera*) настрáивать* (настрóить* *perf*); (*light rays*) фокусúровать (сфокусúровать *perf*) ♦ *vi*: **to** ~ **(on)** (*PHOT*) настрáиваться (настрóиться *perf*) (на +*acc*); (*fig*): **to** ~ **on** сосредотáчиваться (сосредотóчиться *perf*) на +*prp*; **in** ~ в фóкусе; **out of** ~ не в фóкусе.
fodder ['fɔdə'] *n* корм*.
FOE *n abbr* (= *Friends of the Earth*) ОДЗ= *Óбщество "Друзья́ Землú"*; (*US*: = *Fraternal Order of Eagles*) Брáтский óрден орлóв.
foe [fəu] *n* нéдруг.
foetus ['fi:təs] (*US* **fetus**) *n* плод, зарóдыш.
fog [fɔg] *n* тумáн.
fogbound ['fɔgbaund] *adj* закры́тый *или* задержáнный из-за тумáна.
foggy ['fɔgɪ] *adj* тумáнный* (тумáнен); **it's** ~ стоúт тумáн.
fog lamp (*US* **fog light**) *n* (*AUT*) фáра для тумáна.
foible ['fɔɪbl] *n* причýда.
foil [fɔɪl] *vt* (*plan*) расстрáивать (рассстрóить* *perf*); (*attempt, attack*) срывáть (сорвáть* *perf*) ♦ *n* (*metal*) фольгá; (*FENCING*) рапúра; **to act as a** ~ **to** (*fig*) служúть* (*impf*) контрáстом +*dat*.
foist [fɔɪst] *vt*: **to** ~ **sth on sb** навя́зывать (навязáть* *perf*) что-н комý-н.
fold [fəuld] *n* (*crease*) склáдка*; (: *in paper*) сгиб; (*AGR*) загóн; (*fig*) лóно ♦ *vt* (*clothes, paper*) склáдывать (сложúть* *perf*); (*arms*) скрéщивать (скрестúть* *perf*) ♦ *vi* (*business*) свóрачиваться (свернýться *perf*)
▶ **fold up** *vi* склáдываться (сложúться* *perf*); (*business*) свóрачиваться (свернýться *perf*) ♦ *vt* (*object*) склáдывать (сложúть* *perf*).
folder ['fəuldə'] *n* (*for papers*) пáпка*, скоросшивáтель *m*; (: *binder*) пáпка* (*с металлúческим зажúмом*); (*brochure*) брошю́ра.
folding ['fəuldɪŋ] *adj* (*chair, bed*) складнóй.

---

foliage ['fəʊlɪdʒ] *n* листва́.
folk [fəʊk] *npl* лю́ди *pl*, наро́д* *msg* ♦ *cpd* (*art, music*) наро́дный; ~**s** *npl* (*inf: relatives*) бли́зкие *pl adj*.
folklore ['fəʊklɔ:'] *n* фолькло́р.
folk music *n* наро́дная му́зыка.
folk song *n* наро́дная пе́сня*.
follow ['fɒləʊ] *vt* (*leader, person*) сле́довать (после́довать *perf*) за +*instr*; (*example, advice*) сле́довать (после́довать *perf*) +*dat*; (*event, story*) следи́ть* (*impf*) за +*instr*; (*route, path*) держа́ться* (*impf*) +*gen*; (*with eyes*) провожа́ть (проводи́ть* *perf*) взгля́дом ♦ *vi* сле́довать (после́довать *perf*); **to ~ in sb's footsteps** идти́* (пойти́* *perf*) по чьи́м-н стопа́м; **I don't quite ~ you** я не совсе́м Вас понима́ю; **to ~ sb's advice** сле́довать (после́довать *perf*) чьему́-н сове́ту; **I left the room, and he ~ed** я вы́шел из ко́мнаты и он после́довал за мно́й; **it ~s that he ...** отсю́да сле́дует, что он ...; **to ~ suit** (*fig*) сле́довать (после́довать *perf*) приме́ру
► **follow on** *vi* (*continue*): **to ~ on from** сле́довать (после́довать *perf*) за +*instr*
► **follow out** *vt* (*idea, plan*) приводи́ть* (привести́* *perf*) в исполне́ние
► **follow through** *vt* = **follow out**
► **follow up** *vt* (*letter, offer*) рассма́тривать (рассмотре́ть* *perf*); (*case*) рассле́довать (*impf*).
follower ['fɒləʊə'] *n* (*of person*) после́дователь(ница) *m(f)*; (*of belief*) сторо́нник(-ица).
following ['fɒləʊɪŋ] *adj* сле́дующий* ♦ *n* (*followers*) сторо́нники *mpl*; **a large ~** мно́го сторо́нников.
follow-up ['fɒləʊʌp] *n* продолже́ние ♦ *adj* (*treatment, survey*) после́дующий*.
folly ['fɒlɪ] *n* (*foolishness*) глу́пость *f*; (*building*) декорати́вное па́рковое сооруже́ние.
fond [fɒnd] *adj* (*smile, look, parents*) ла́сковый* (ла́сков); (*memory*) прия́тный* (прия́тен); (*hopes, dreams*) тще́тный* (тще́тен); **to be ~ of** люби́ть* (*impf*); **she's ~ of swimming** она́ лю́бит пла́вать.
fondle ['fɒndl] *vt* ласка́ть (*impf*).
fondly ['fɒndlɪ] *adv* (*lovingly*) ла́сково; (*naïvely*) наи́вно; **he ~ believed that ...** он наи́вно ве́рил, что ....
fondness ['fɒndnɪs] *n* любо́вь* *f*; **a special ~ for** осо́бенная любо́вь к +*dat*.
font [fɒnt] *n* (*in church*) купе́ль *f*; (*TYP*) компле́кт (шри́фта).
food [fu:d] *n* еда́, пи́ща.
food chain *n* пищево́й симбио́з.
food mixer *n* ми́ксер.
food poisoning *n* пищево́е отравле́ние.
food processor *n* ку́хонный комба́йн.
food stamp *n* продукто́вый тало́н.
foodstuffs ['fu:dstʌfs] *npl* проду́кты *mpl* пита́ния.

fool [fu:l] *n* (*male*) дура́к*; (*female*) ду́ра; (*CULIN*) сла́дкое блю́до из сли́вок и фру́ктов ♦ *vt* (*deceive*) обма́нывать (обману́ть* *perf*), одура́чивать (одура́чить *perf*) ♦ *vi* (*be silly*) дура́читься (*impf*); **to make a ~ of sb** (*ridicule*) выставля́ть (вы́ставить* *perf*) кого́-н на посме́шище; (*trick*) одура́чивать (одура́чить *perf*) кого́-н; **to make a ~ of o.s.** ста́вить* (поста́вить* *perf*) себя́ в глу́пое положе́ние; **you can't ~ me** меня́ не проведёте
► **fool about** *vi* (*pej: waste time*) валя́ть (*impf*) дурака́; (*behave foolishly*) дура́читься *perf*
► **fool around** *vi* = **fool about**.
foolhardy ['fu:lhɑ:dɪ] *adj* безрассу́дный* (безрассу́ден).
foolish ['fu:lɪʃ] *adj* (*stupid*) глу́пый* (глуп); (*rash*) опроме́тчивый (опроме́тчив).
foolishly ['fu:lɪʃlɪ] *adv* (*see adj*) глу́по; опроме́тчиво.
foolishness ['fu:lɪʃnɪs] *n* дура́чество.
foolproof ['fu:lpru:f] *adj* (*plan*) надёжный* (надёжен).
foolscap ['fu:lskæp] *n* бума́га форма́та: 34 см x 43 см.
foot [fut] (*pl* **feet**) *n* (*of person*) нога́*, ступня́; (*of animal*) нога́*; (*of bed*) коне́ц*; (*of cliff*) подно́жие; (*measure*) фут; (*of page, stairs etc*) низ ♦ *vt*: **to ~ the bill** плати́ть* (*perf*); **on ~** пешко́м; **at the ~ of the page/stairs** внизу́ страни́цы/ле́стницы; **to find one's feet** (*fig*) встава́ть* (встать* *perf*) на́ ноги; **to put one's ~ down** (*AUT*) нажима́ть (нажа́ть* *perf*) на педа́ль; (*assert authority*) занима́ть (заня́ть* *perf*) твёрдую пози́цию.
footage ['fʊtɪdʒ] *n* (*CINEMA: material*) ка́дры *mpl*; (: *length*) ≈ метра́ж.
foot-and-mouth [fʊtən'maʊθ] *n* (*also: ~ disease*) я́щур.
football ['fʊtbɔ:l] *n* (*ball*) футбо́льный мяч*; (*sport: BRIT*) футбо́л; (: *US*) америка́нский футбо́л.
footballer ['fʊtbɔ:lə'] *n* (*BRIT*) футболи́ст.
football ground *n* футбо́льное по́ле.
football match *n* (*BRIT*) футбо́льный матч.
football player *n* футболи́ст.
foot brake *n* ножно́й то́рмоз*.
footbridge ['fʊtbrɪdʒ] *n* пешехо́дный мост*.
foothills ['fʊthɪlz] *npl* предго́рья* *ntpl*.
foothold ['fʊthəʊld] *n* опо́ра; (*fig*): **to get a ~** укрепля́ться (укрепи́ться* *perf*), утвержда́ться* (*perf*).
footing ['fʊtɪŋ] *n* (*fig: basis, relationship*) осно́ва; **to be on a friendly ~** быть* (*impf*) на дру́жеской ноге́; **to lose one's ~** (*fall*) теря́ть (потеря́ть *perf*) опо́ру; **on an equal ~** на ра́вных (основа́ниях).
footlights ['fʊtlaɪts] *npl* огни́ *mpl* ра́мпы.
footman ['fʊtmən] *irreg n* лаке́й.
footnote ['fʊtnəʊt] *n* сно́ска*.
footpath ['fʊtpɑ:θ] *n* тропи́нка*, доро́жка*; (*in street*) тротуа́р.

footprint ['futprɪnt] *n* след*, опеча́ток ноги́.
footrest ['futrest] *n* скаме́ечка* для ног.
footsie ['futsɪ] *n*: **to play ~ with sb** толка́ть
(толкну́ть *perf*) но́жкой кого́-н.
footsore ['futsɔː] *adj*: **I am ~** у меня́ боля́т
но́ги.
footstep ['futstεp] *n* (*sound*) шаг*; (*footprint*)
след*; (*fig*): **to follow in sb's ~s** идти́* (пойти́*
perf) по чьим-н стопа́м.
footwear ['futwεə] *n* о́бувь *f*.
footwork ['futwə:k] *n* фигу́ры *fpl* (*движе́ния
ног в та́нце*).

KEYWORD

for [fɔː] *prep* **1** (*indicating destination, intention*):
the train for London/Paris по́езд в Ло́ндон/
Пари́ж; **he left for Rome/work** он уе́хал в
Рим/на рабо́ту; **when does the train for
Moscow leave?** когда́ отправля́ется по́езд на
Москву́?; **he went for the paper/the doctor** он
пошёл за газе́той/врачо́м; **is this for me?** э́то
мне *or* для меня́?; **there's a letter for you** Вам
письмо́; **it's time for lunch/bed** пора́ обе́дать
(*impf*)/спать (*impf*)
2 (*indicating purpose*) для +*gen*; **what's it for?**
для чего́ э́то?; **give it to me – what for?** да́йте
э́то мне – заче́м?; **to pray for forgiveness**
моли́ть* (*impf*) о проще́нии; **to pray for peace**
моли́ться* (*impf*) о ми́ре
3 (*on behalf of, representing*): **to speak for sb**
говори́ть (*impf*) от лица́ кого́-н; **MP for
Brighton** член *m* парла́мента
представля́ющий Бра́йтон; **he works for the
government** он на госуда́рственной слу́жбе;
he works for a local firm он рабо́тает в
ме́стной фи́рме; **I'll ask him for you** я спрошу́
его́ от ва́шего и́мени; **to do sth for sb** (*on
behalf of*) де́лать (сде́лать *perf*) что-н за
кого́-н
4 (*because of*) из-за +*gen*; **for lack of funds**
из-за отсу́тствия средств; **for this reason** по
э́той причи́не; **for some reason, for whatever
reason** почему́-то; **for fear of being criticized**
боя́сь кри́тики; **to be famous for sth** быть
(*impf*) изве́стным чем-н
5 (*with regard to*): **it's cold for July** для ию́ля
сейча́с хо́лодно; **he's tall for fourteen/for his
age** для четы́рнадцати лет/для своего́
во́зраста он высо́кий; **a gift for languages**
спосо́бности к языка́м; **for everyone who
voted yes, 50 voted no** на ка́ждый го́лос „за",
прихо́дится 50 голосо́в „про́тив"
6 (*in exchange for, in favour of*): **I sold it
for £5** я про́дал э́то за £5; **I'm all for it** я
целико́м и по́лностью за э́то
7 (*referring to distance*): **there are roadworks
for five miles** доро́жные рабо́ты на
протяже́нии пяти́ миль; **to stretch for miles**
простира́ться (*impf*) на мно́го миль; **we**

walked for miles/for ten miles мы прошли́
мно́го миль/де́сять миль
8 (*referring to time*) на +*acc*; (: *in past*): **he was
away for 2 years** он был в отъе́зде 2 го́да; **she
will be away for a month** она́ уезжа́ет на
ме́сяц; **can you do it for tomorrow?** Вы
мо́жете сде́лать э́то на за́втра; **it hasn't
rained for 3 weeks** уже́ 3 неде́ли не́ было
дождя́; **for hours** часа́ми
9 (*with infinite clause*): **it is not for me to decide**
не мне реша́ть; **there is still time for you to do
it** у Вас ещё есть вре́мя сде́лать э́то; **for this
to be possible** ... что́бы э́то осуществи́ть ...
10 (*in spite of*) несмотря́ на +*acc*; **for all his
complaints** несмотря́ на все его́ жа́лобы
11 (*in phrases*): **for the first/last time** в
пе́рвый/после́дний раз; **for the time being**
пока́
♦ *conj* (*rather formal*) и́бо.

f.o.r. *abbr* (*COMM*: = *free on rail*) фра́нко-ваго́н.
forage ['fɔrɪdʒ] *n* корм ♦ *vi*: **to ~ for sth**
ры́скать* (*impf*) по́исках чего́-н.
forage cap *n* фура́жка, пило́тка.
foray ['fɔreɪ] *n* (*raid*) набе́г.
forbad(e) [fə'bæd] *pt of* **forbid**.
forbearing [fɔː'bεərɪŋ] *adj* сде́ржанный.
forbid [fə'bɪd] (*pt* **forbad(e)**, *pp* **forbidden**) *vt*
запреща́ть (запрети́ть* *perf*); **to ~ sb to do**
запреща́ть (запрети́ть* *perf*) +*infin*.
forbidden [fə'bɪdn] *pp of* **forbid** ♦ *adj* (*entry,
activity*) запрещённый* (запрещён); (*place*)
запре́тный; **it's ~ to** ... запрещено́ +*infin* ....
forbidding [fə'bɪdɪŋ] *adj* (*look etc*)
неприя́зненный; (*prospect*) мучи́тельный*
(мучи́телен).
force [fɔːs] *n* (*also PHYS*) си́ла; (*influence*)
возде́йствие ♦ *vt* (*compel*) заставля́ть
(заста́вить* *perf*), принужда́ть (принуди́ть*
perf); (*push*) толка́ть (толкну́ть *perf*); (*break
open*) взла́мывать (взлома́ть *perf*); **the F~s**
npl (*BRIT: MIL*) вооружённые си́лы *fpl*; **in ~** в
большо́м числе́; **to come into ~** вступа́ть
(вступи́ть* *perf*) в си́лу; **to join ~s**
объединя́ть (объедини́ть *perf*) уси́лия; **it's a
~ five wind** си́ла ве́тра – пять ба́ллов; **the
sales ~** (*COMM*) торго́вые аге́нты; **to ~ o.s. to
do** заставля́ть (заста́вить* *perf*) себя́ +*infin*; **to
~ sb to do** заставля́ть (заста́вить* *perf*) *or*
вынужда́ть (вы́нудить* *perf*) кого́-н +*infin*
► **force back** *vt* (*enemy*) отража́ть (отрази́ть*
perf); (*crowd, tears*) сде́рживать (сдержа́ть*
perf)
► **force down** *vt* (*food*) есть* (съесть* *perf*) с
трудо́м.
forced [fɔːst] *adj* (*landing*) вы́нужденный;
(*smile*) натя́нутый (натя́нут); **~ labour**
принуди́тельный труд.

---

* marks translations which have irregular inflections. The Russian-English side of the dictionary gives inflectional information.

force-feed [ˈfɔːsfiːd] *vt* насильно кормить*
(*impf*).
forceful [ˈfɔːsful] *adj* сильный* (силён).
forceps [ˈfɔːsɛps] *npl* щипцы *pl*.
forcible [ˈfɔːsəbl] *adj* (*action*) насильственный;
(*reminder, lesson*) убедительный.
forcibly [ˈfɔːsəblɪ] *adv* (*remove*) насильно;
(*express*) с силой.
ford [fɔːd] *n* (*in river*) брод* ♦ *vt* переходить*
(перейти* *perf*) вброд.
fore [fɔːʳ] *n*: **to come to the ~** выдвигаться
(выдвинуться *perf*).
forearm [ˈfɔːrɑːm] *n* предплечье*.
forebear [ˈfɔːbɛəʳ] *n* предок*.
foreboding [fɔːˈbəudɪŋ] *n* предчувствие.
forecast [ˈfɔːkɑːst] (*irreg: like* **cast**) *n* прогноз ♦
vt (*predict*) предсказывать (предсказать*
perf).
foreclose [fɔːˈkləuz] *vt* (*LAW: also:* ~ **on**)
лишать (лишить *perf*) прв собственности.
foreclosure [fɔːˈkləuʒəʳ] *n* (*COMM*) лишение
прав собственности.
forecourt [ˈfɔːkɔːt] *n* (*of garage*) передняя
площадка.
forefathers [ˈfɔːfɑːðəz] *npl* предки* *mpl*.
forefinger [ˈfɔːfɪŋgəʳ] *n* указательный палец*.
forefront [ˈfɔːfrʌnt] *n*: **in** *or* **at the ~ of** (*industry,
movement*) в авангарде +*gen*.
forego [fɔːˈgəu] (*irreg: like* **go**) *vt* поступаться
(поступиться *perf*) +*instr*.
foregoing [ˈfɔːgəuɪŋ] *adj* предшествующий* ♦
n: **the ~** вышеупомянутое *nt adj*.
foregone [ˈfɔːgɔn] *adj*: **it's a ~ conclusion** это
предрешённый исход.
foreground [ˈfɔːgraund] *n* (*also COMPUT*)
передний* план.
forehand [ˈfɔːhænd] *n* (*TENNIS*) удар справа.
forehead [ˈfɔrɪd] *n* лоб*.
foreign [ˈfɔrɪn] *adj* (*person, language*)
иностранный; (*country*) зарубежный; (*trade*)
внешний*; (*object*) посторонний*.
foreign body *n* инородное тело.
foreign currency *n* иностранная валюта.
foreigner [ˈfɔrɪnəʳ] *n* иностранец*(-нка*).
foreign exchange *n* (*system*) обмен валюты;
(*money*) валюта.
foreign-exchange market [fɔrɪnɪksˈtʃeɪndʒ-] *n*
валютный рынок*.
foreign-exchange rate *n* валютный курс.
foreign investment *n* иностранные
капиталовложения *ntpl*.
foreign minister *n* министр иностранных
дел.
Foreign Office *n* (*BRIT*) министерство
иностранных дел.
Foreign Secretary *n* (*BRIT*) министр
иностранных дел.
foreleg [ˈfɔːlɛg] *n* (*of animal*) передняя нога*.
foreman [ˈfɔːmən] *irreg n* (*in factory, on building
site etc*) мастер*; (*of jury*) старшина *m*
присяжных.

foremost [ˈfɔːməust] *adj* (*most important*)
наиболее важный* ♦ *adv*: **first and ~** в
первую очередь, прежде всего.
forename [ˈfɔːneɪm] *n* имя* *nt*.
forensic [fəˈrɛnsɪk] *adj* (*medicine, test*)
судебный*; **~ expert** специалист по
судебной медицине.
foreplay [ˈfɔːpleɪ] *n* возбуждающие ласки *fpl*.
forerunner [ˈfɔːrʌnəʳ] *n*
предшественник(-ница).
foresee [fɔːˈsiː] (*irreg: like* **see**) *vt* предвидеть*
(*impf/perf*).
foreseeable [fɔːˈsiːəbl] *adj* предвидимый; **in
the ~ future** в обозримом будущем.
foreseen [fɔːˈsiːn] *pp of* **foresee**.
foreshadow [fɔːˈʃædəu] *vt* (*event*)
предзнаменовать (*impf*).
foreshore [ˈfɔːˈʃɔːʳ] *n* береговая полоса,
затопляемая приливом.
foreshortened [fɔːˈʃɔːtnd] *adj* (*figure, scene*) в
ракурсе.
foresight [ˈfɔːsaɪt] *n* предусмотрительность *f*.
foreskin [ˈfɔːskɪn] *n* крайняя плоть *f*.
forest [ˈfɔrɪst] *n* лес*.
forestall [fɔːˈstɔːl] *vt* (*person*) при-
останавливать (приостановить* *perf*);
(*discussion*) опережать (опередить* *perf*).
forestry [ˈfɔrɪstrɪ] *n* лесоводство, лесничество.
foretaste [ˈfɔːteɪst] *n*: **a ~ of** представление о
+*prp*.
foretell [fɔːˈtɛl] (*irreg: like* **tell**) *vt* предсказывать
(предсказать* *perf*).
forethought [ˈfɔːθɔːt] *n* предусмотрительность *f*.
foretold [fɔːˈtəuld] *pt, pp of* **foretell**.
forever [fəˈrɛvəʳ] *adv* (*for good*) навсегда;
(*endlessly*) вечно; **that time has gone ~** то
время ушло навсегда; **it will last ~** это будет
длиться вечно; **you're ~ finding difficulties** Вы
вечно находите трудности.
forewarn [fɔːˈwɔːn] *vt* предупреждать
(предупредить* *perf*).
foreword [ˈfɔːwəːd] *n* (*in book*) предисловие.
forfeit [ˈfɔːfɪt] *n* (*penalty*) штраф ♦ *vt* (*right,
friendship etc*) терять (потерять *perf*); (*one's
happiness, health*) поплатиться* (*perf*) +*instr*.
forgave [fəˈgeɪv] *pt of* **forgive**.
forge [fɔːdʒ] *n* кузница ♦ *vt* (*signature, money*)
подделывать (подделать *perf*); (*metal*)
ковать (*impf*); **to ~ documents/a will**
подделывать (подделать *perf*) документы/
завещание
▶ **forge ahead** *vi* (*country, person*) вырываться
(вырваться* *perf*) вперёд.
forger [ˈfɔːdʒəʳ] *n* (*of documents, paintings*)
подделыватель *m*; (*of money*)
фальшивомонетчик.
forgery [ˈfɔːdʒərɪ] *n* подделка*.
forget [fəˈgɛt] (*pt* **forgot**, *pp* **forgotten**) *vt*
забывать (забыть* *perf*); (*appointment*)
забывать (забыть* *perf*) о +*prp* ♦ *vi* забывать

(забы́ть* *perf*); **to ~ o.s.** забы́ться* (*perf*).
forgetful [fə'gɛtful] *adj* (*person*) забы́вчивый
(забы́вчив); **~ of** забы́в о +*prp*.
forgetfulness [fə'gɛtfulnɪs] *n* забы́вчивость *f*;
(*oblivion*) забве́ние.
forget-me-not [fə'gɛtmɪnɔt] *n* незабу́дка*.
forgive [fə'gɪv] (*pt* **forgave**, *pp* **forgiven**) *vt*
(*pardon*) проща́ть (прости́ть* *perf*) +*dat or*
+*gen*; **to ~ sb for sth** (*excuse*) проща́ть
(прости́ть* *perf*) кому́-н *or* кого́-н за что-н; **I
forgave him for doing it** я прости́л ему́ *or* его́
за то, что он э́то сде́лал; **~ my ignorance, but
... прости́те моё неве́жество, но ...; they
could be ~n for thinking that ...** из мо́жно
прости́ть за то, что они́ ду́мают, что ....
forgiven [fə'gɪvn] *pp of* **forgive**.
forgiveness [fə'gɪvnɪs] *n* проще́ние.
forgiving [fə'gɪvɪŋ] *adj* великоду́шный*
(великоду́шен).
forgo [fɔː'gəu] *vt* = **forego**.
forgot [fə'gɔt] *pt of* **forget**.
forgotten [fə'gɔtn] *pp of* **forget**.
fork [fɔːk] *n* ви́лка*; (*for gardening*) ви́лы *pl*; (*in
road*) разви́лка*; (*in railway*) стык; (*in river,
tree*) разветвле́ние ◆ *vi* (*road*) разветвля́ться
(*impf*)
▶ **fork out** (*inf*) ◆ *vt* выкла́дывать (вы́ложить*
perf) ◆ *vi* раскоше́ливаться (раскоше́литься
perf).
forked [fɔːkt] *adj* (*lightning*) зигзагообра́зный.
fork-lift truck ['fɔːklɪft-] *n* грузоподъёмник.
forlorn [fə'lɔːn] *adj* (*person*) несча́стный;
(*place*) поки́нутый; (*hope, attempt*) сла́бый.
form [fɔːm] *n* (*type*) вид; (*shape*) фо́рма; (*SCOL*)
класс; (*questionnaire*) анке́та ◆ *vt* (*make*)
образо́вывать (образова́ть *perf*); (*set up:
organization, group*) формирова́ть
(сформирова́ть *perf*); (*idea, habit*)
выраба́тывать (вы́работать *perf*); **in the ~ of**
в фо́рме +*gen*; **to be in good ~** (*SPORT, fig*)
быть* (*impf*) в хоро́шей фо́рме; **in top ~** в
лу́чшей фо́рме; **on ~** в фо́рме; **to ~ part of
sth** явля́ться (яви́ться* *perf*) ча́стью чего́-н; **I
~ed a good impression of her** у меня́
созда́лось хоро́шее впечатле́ние о ней.
formal ['fɔːməl] *adj* форма́льный; (*statement*)
форма́льный* (форма́лен); (*person,
behaviour*) церемо́нный* (церемо́нен);
(*occasion, dinner*) официа́льный*
(официа́лен); (*garden*) англи́йский*; **~
clothes** официа́льная фо́рма оде́жды; **~
dress** (*evening dress*) вече́рняя оде́жда.
formalities [fɔː'mælɪtɪz] *npl* форма́льности *fpl*.
formality [fɔː'mælɪtɪ] *n* форма́льность *f*; (*of
person, behaviour*) церемо́нность *f*; (*of
occasion*) официа́льность *f*.
formalize ['fɔːməlaɪz] *vt* (*plan, arrangement*)
оформля́ть (офо́рмить* *perf*).

formally ['fɔːməlɪ] *adv* форма́льно; (*behave*)
церемо́нно; **to be ~ invited** получа́ть
(получи́ть* *perf*) официа́льное приглаше́ние.
format ['fɔːmæt] *n* (*form, style*) форма́т ◆ *vt*
(*COMPUT: disk*) формати́ровать (*impf/perf*).
formation [fɔː'meɪʃən] *n* формирова́ние; (*of
rocks*) форма́ция; (*of clouds*) скопле́ние.
formative ['fɔːmətɪv] *adj*: **in his ~ years** в го́ды
формирова́ния его́ хара́ктера.
former ['fɔːmə'] *adj* (*one-time*) бы́вший*;
(*earlier*) пре́жний*; **the ~ ... the latter ...**
пе́рвый ... после́дний*; **the ~ president**
бы́вший* президе́нт.
formerly ['fɔːməlɪ] *adv* ра́ньше, до э́того.
form feed *n* (*on printer*) пода́ча страни́ц.
Formica® [fɔː'maɪkə] *n* форма́йка
(*огнеупо́рная пластма́сса*).
formidable ['fɔːmɪdəbl] *adj* (*task*) чрезвыча́йно
тру́дный* (тру́ден); (*opponent*) гро́зный*
(гро́зен).
formula ['fɔːmjulə] (*pl* **~e** *or* **~s**) *n* (*MATH, CHEM*)
фо́рмула; (*plan*) схе́ма; **F~ One** (*AUT*)
обозначе́ние го́ночной маши́ны.
formulae ['fɔːmjuliː] *npl of* **formula**.
formulate ['fɔːmjuleɪt] *vt* (*plan, strategy*)
выраба́тывать (вы́работать *perf*); (*opinion,
thought*) формули́ровать (сформули́ровать
perf).
fornicate ['fɔːnɪkeɪt] *vi* прелюбоде́йствовать
(*impf*).
forsake [fə'seɪk] (*pt* **forsook**, *pp* **forsaken**) *vt*
(*abandon*) покида́ть (поки́нуть *perf*).
forsaken [fə'seɪkən] *pp of* **forsake**.
forsook [fə'suk] *pt of* **forsake**.
fort [fɔːt] *n* кре́пость *f*, форт*; **to hold the ~** (*fig*)
стоя́ть (*impf*) на стра́же.
forte ['fɔːtɪ] *n* (*strength*) си́льная сторона́.
forth [fɔːθ] *adv* (*out*): **to go ~** идти́* (*impf*)
вперёд; **to send ~** посла́ть* (*perf*); **to go back
and ~** ходи́ть* (*impf*) взад и вперёд; **to bring ~**
вынима́ть (вы́нуть *perf*); **and so ~** и так
да́лее.
forthcoming [fɔːθ'kʌmɪŋ] *adj* предстоя́щий;
(*person*) общи́тельный; **to be ~** (*help,
evidence*) ожида́ться (*impf*), появля́ться
(*impf*).
forthright ['fɔːθraɪt] *adj* (*condemnation,
opposition*) прямо́й.
forthwith ['fɔːθ'wɪθ] *adv* то́тчас.
fortieth ['fɔːtɪɪθ] *adj* сороково́й*; *see also* **fifth**.
fortification [fɔːtɪfɪ'keɪʃən] *n* (*MIL*) укрепле́ние.
fortified wine ['fɔːtɪfaɪd-] *n* креплёное вино́*.
fortify ['fɔːtɪfaɪ] *vt* (*city*) укрепля́ть (укрепи́ть*
perf); (*person*) придава́ть* (прида́ть* *perf*)
си́лы +*dat*.
fortitude ['fɔːtɪtjuːd] *n* сто́йкость *f*.
fortnight ['fɔːtnaɪt] (*BRIT*) *n* две неде́ли; **it's a ~**

---

since ... прошло две недели с тех пор, как ....

fortnightly ['fɔːtnaɪtlɪ] adv раз в две недели ♦ adj: ~ **magazine** журнал, выходящий раз в две недели.

FORTRAN ['fɔːtræn] n ФОРТРА́Н.

fortress ['fɔːtrɪs] n крепость f. `

fortuitous [fɔːˈtjuːɪtəs] adj случайный* (случаен).

fortunate ['fɔːtʃənɪt] adj (person) счастливый (счастлив); (event) счастливый; **he is/was** ~ ему везёт/повезло; **he is** ~ **to have** ... ему хорошо, что у него есть ...; **it is** ~ **that** ... удачно, что ....

fortunately ['fɔːtʃənɪtlɪ] adv к счастью.

fortune ['fɔːtʃən] n (wealth) состояние; (also: **good** ~) счастье, удача; **bad** or **ill** ~ несчастье, неудача; **to make a** ~ наживать (нажить* perf) себе состояние; **to tell sb's** ~ гадать (impf) кому-н, предсказывать (предсказать* perf) чью-н судьбу.

fortune-teller ['fɔːtʃəntɛlə'] n гадалка, предсказатель(ница) m(f).

forty ['fɔːtɪ] n сорок*; see also **fifty**.

forum ['fɔːrəm] n форум.

forward ['fɔːwəd] adv вперёд ♦ n (SPORT) нападающий*(-ая) m(f) adj ♦ vt (letter, parcel) пересылать (переслать* perf); (career) продвигать (продвинуть perf) ♦ adj (position) передний*; (not shy) дерзкий (дерзок); (COMM: delivery, sales) заблаговременный; **to move** ~ (progress) продвигаться (продвинуться perf); "**please** ~" „перешлите адресату"; ~ **movement** движение вперёд; ~ **planning** предварительное планирование.

forward contract n форвардный or срочный контракт.

forward rate n форвардный or срочный валютный курс, по которому заключается срочная валютная сделка.

forwards ['fɔːwədz] adv вперёд.

fossil ['fɒsl] n окаменелость f, ископаемое nt adj.

fossil fuel n топливо (образовавшееся из окаменелых останков растений и животных).

foster ['fɒstə'] vt (child) брать* (взять* perf) на воспитание; (activity) поощрять (impf); (hope) питать (impf); **to** ~ **an idea** вынашивать (impf) мысль.

foster child n ребёнок*.

foster mother n приёмная мать* f.

fought [fɔːt] pt, pp of **fight**.

foul [faul] adj отвратительный* (отвратителен); (language) непристойный* (непристоен); (temper) гневливый (гневлив) ♦ n (SPORT) нарушение ♦ vt загадить* (загадить* perf); (SPORT) нарушать (нарушить perf) правила против +gen; (entangle: anchor, propeller) опутывать (опутать perf).

foul play n (LAW) преступные действия ntpl; ~

~ **is not suspected** нет подозрения о преступных действиях.

found [faund] pt, pp of **find** ♦ vt (establish) основывать (основать perf).

foundation [faunˈdeɪʃən] n (act) основание; (base) основа; (fig) основа, устои mpl; (organization) общество, фонд; (also: ~ **cream**) крем под макияж; ~**s** npl (of building) фундамент msg; **the rumours are without** ~ слухи не имеют оснований; **to lay the** ~**s** (fig) закладывать (заложить* perf) основы.

foundation stone n краеугольный камень* m.

founder ['faundə'] n (of firm, college) основатель(ница) m(f) ♦ vi (ship) идти* (пойти* perf) ко дну.

founder member n член-учредитель(ница) m(f).

founding fathers ['faundɪŋ-] npl (esp US) основоположники mpl.

foundry ['faundrɪ] n литейная f adj, литейный цех.

fount [faunt] n источник; (TYP) комплект шрифта.

fountain ['fauntɪn] n фонтан.

fountain pen n чернильная ручка*.

four [fɔː'] n четыре*; **on all** ~**s** на четвереньках; see also **five**.

four-letter word ['fɔːlɛtə-] n ≈ мат.

four-poster ['fɔːˈpəustə'] n (also: ~ **bed**) кровать f с пологом.

foursome ['fɔːsəm] n четвёрка*.

fourteen ['fɔːˈtiːn] n четырнадцать*; see also **five**.

fourteenth ['fɔːˈtiːnθ] adj четырнадцатый*; see also **fifth**.

fourth ['fɔːθ] adj четвёртый ♦ n (AUT: also: ~ **gear**) четвёртая скорость f; see also **fifth**.

four-wheel drive ['fɔːwiːl-] n (AUT): **with** ~ ~ с приводом на четыре колеса.

fowl [faul] n птица; (wild) дичь f.

fox [fɒks] n лиса* ♦ vt озадачивать (озадачить perf).

foxglove ['fɒksglʌv] n (BOT) наперстянка*.

fox-hunting ['fɒkshʌntɪŋ] n охота на лис.

foxtrot ['fɒkstrɒt] n (dance) фокстрот.

foxy ['fɒksɪ] adj: ~ **lady** шикарная женщина.

foyer ['fɔɪeɪ] n фойе nt ind.

FPA n abbr (BRIT: = Family Planning Association) организация, обеспечивающая консультации по планированию дето-рождения.

Fr. abbr (REL) = **father, friar**.

fr. abbr = **franc**.

fracas ['frækɑː] n скандал.

fraction ['frækʃən] n (portion) небольшая часть f; (MATH) дробь f; **a** ~ **of a second** доля секунды.

fractionally ['frækʃnəlɪ] adv: ~ **smaller** etc незначительно меньше etc.

fractious ['frækʃəs] adj капризный* (капризен); **she was** ~ она капризничала.

fracture ['fræktʃə'] *n* (*of bone*) перело́м ◆ *vt* (*bone*) лома́ть (слома́ть *perf*).
fragile ['frædʒaɪl] *adj* хру́пкий* (хру́пок).
fragment ['frægmənt] *n* фрагме́нт; (*of stone, glass*) оско́лок*, обло́мок*.
fragmentary ['frægməntərɪ] *adj* (*evidence, knowledge*) отры́вочный* (отры́вочен).
fragrance ['freɪgrəns] *n* благоуха́ние.
fragrant ['freɪgrənt] *adj* души́стый (души́ст).
frail [freɪl] *adj* (*person*) сла́бый* (слаб); (*structure*) хру́пкий* (хру́пок), непро́чный* (непро́чен).
frame [freɪm] *n* (*of building, structure*) карка́с; (*of car, human, animal*) о́стов; (*of picture, door, window*) ра́ма; (*of spectacles: also:* ~**s**) опра́ва ◆ *vt* обрамля́ть (обра́мить* *perf*); (*reply, law, theory*) формули́ровать (сформули́ровать *perf*); ~ **of mind** настрое́ние; **to** ~ **sb** (*inf*) подста́вить* (*perf*) кого́-н.
framework ['freɪmwə:k] *n* (*structure*) карка́с; (*fig*) ра́мки *fpl*.
France [frɑ:ns] *n* Фра́нция.
franchise ['fræntʃaɪz] *n* (*POL*) пра́во го́лоса; (*COMM*) франши́за.
franchisee [fræntʃaɪ'zi:] *n* держа́тель *m* франши́зы.
franchiser ['fræntʃaɪzə'] *n* предостави́тель *m* франши́зы.
frank [fræŋk] *adj* (*discussion, person*) открове́нный* (открове́нен); (*look*) откры́тый ◆ *vt* (*letter*) франки́ровать (зафранки́ровать *perf*).
Frankfurt ['fræŋkfə:t] *n* Фра́нкфурт.
frankfurter ['fræŋkfə:tə'] *n* соси́ска*.
franking machine ['fræŋkɪŋ-] *n* франкирова́льная маши́на.
frankly ['fræŋklɪ] *adv* открове́нно.
frankness ['fræŋknɪs] *n* открове́нность *f*.
frantic ['fræntɪk] *adj* (*distraught*) обезу́мевший; (*hectic*) сумато́шный*; (*desperate: need, desire*) безу́мный*; (: *cry*) нейсто́вый; **we were** ~ **with worry** мы обезу́мели от волне́ния.
frantically ['fræntɪklɪ] *adv* отча́янно.
fraternal [frə'tə:nl] *adj* бра́тский*.
fraternity [frə'tə:nɪtɪ] *n* (*feeling*) бра́тство; (*club*) содру́жество.
fraternize ['frætənaɪz] *vi* обща́ться (*impf*).
fraud [frɔ:d] *n* (*crime*) моше́нничество; (*person*) моше́нник.
fraudulent ['frɔ:djulənt] *adj* (*scheme, claim*) моше́ннический*.
fraught [frɔ:t] *adj* (*person*) не́рвный* (не́рвен); (*situation*): ~ **with** (*danger, problems*) чрева́тый (чрева́т) +*instr*.
fray [freɪ] *vi* обтрёпываться (обтрепа́ться *perf*) ◆ *n* (*battle, fight*): **the** ~ бой, дра́ка; **tempers**

were ~**ed** все бы́ли на гра́ни от издёрганных не́рвов; **her nerves were** ~**ed** у неё бы́ли истрёпаны не́рвы; **to return to the** ~ сно́ва ри́нуться (*perf*) в бой *or* дра́ку.
FRB *n abbr* (*US*: = *Federal Reserve Board*) федера́льное резе́рвное правле́ние.
FRCM *n abbr* (*BRIT*) = *Fellow of the Royal College of Music*.
FRCO *n abbr* (*BRIT*) = *Fellow of the Royal College of Organists*.
FRCP *n abbr* (*BRIT*) = *Fellow of the Royal College of Physicians*.
FRCS *n abbr* (*BRIT*) = *Fellow of the Royal College of Surgeons*.
freak [fri:k] *n* (*event, accident*) стра́нный; (*person: in appearance*) уро́дец*(-дица), вы́родок* *m/f*; (: *in attitude, behaviour*): **he is a** ~ он со стра́нностями; (*pej: fanatic*): **she's an aerobics** ~ она́ помеша́лась на аэро́бике
▶ **freak out** *vi* (*inf: on drugs*) входи́ть* (войти́* *perf*) в раж.
freakish ['fri:kɪʃ] *adj* стра́нный.
freckle ['frɛkl] *n* весну́шка*.
freckled ['frɛkld] *adj* весну́шчатый.
free [fri:] *adj* свобо́дный* (свобо́ден); (*costing nothing*) беспла́тный* (беспла́тен) ◆ *vt* (*prisoner etc*) освобожда́ть (освободи́ть* *perf*), выпуска́ть (вы́пустить* *perf*) (на свобо́ду); (*jammed object*) высвобожда́ть (вы́свободить* *perf*), выта́скивать (вы́тащить *perf*); **to give sb a** ~ **hand** предоставля́ть (предоста́вить* *perf*) кому́-н свобо́ду де́йствовать по-сво́ему; ~ **and easy** непринуждённый; **admission** ~ свобо́дный вход; ~ (**of charge**), **for** ~ беспла́тно; ~ **alongside ship** фра́нко вдоль бо́рта су́дна; ~ **of tax** освобождённый от упла́ты нало́гов; ~ **on rail** фра́нко – железнодоро́жный ваго́н.
free agent *n*: **he's a** ~ ~ он сам себе́ хозя́ин.
freebie ['fri:bɪ] *n* (*inf: gift*) пода́рок*.
freedom ['fri:dəm] *n* свобо́да.
freedom fighter *n* боре́ц* за свобо́ду.
freedom of association *n* свобо́да объедине́ния *or* ассоциа́ции.
free enterprise *n* свобо́дное предпринима́тельство.
Freefone® ['fri:fəun] *n система, позволяющая звонить бесплатно в определённые организации.*
free-for-all ['fri:fərɔ:l] *n* (*fight*) всео́бщая дра́ка.
free gift *n* пода́рок*.
freehold ['fri:həuld] *n* (*of property*) по́лное пра́во на владе́ние.
free kick *n* (*FOOTBALL*) свобо́дный уда́р.
freelance ['fri:lɑ:ns] *adj* внешта́тный, рабо́тающий по догово́рам.
freelance work *n* рабо́та по контра́кту *or*

---

* marks translations which have irregular inflections. The Russian-English side of the dictionary gives inflectional information.

freeloader ['fri:ləudə^r] *n* (*pej*) дармоéд(ка*).
freely ['fri:lɪ] *adv* (*without restriction*) свобóдно; (*liberally*) обúльно; **drugs are ~ available in the city** наркóтики мóжно легкó достáть в гóроде.
free-market economy ['fri:'mɑ:kɪt-] *n* рýночная эконóмика.
Freemason ['fri:meɪsn] *n* масóн.
Freemasonry ['fri:meɪsnrɪ] *n* масóнство.
Freepost® ['fri:pəust] *n* (*BRIT*) бесплáтная пóчта.
free-range ['fri:'reɪndʒ] *adj*: ~ **eggs** я́йца от кур свобóдно-выгульного содержáния.
free sample *n* бесплáтный образéц*.
freesia ['fri:zɪə] *n* фрéзия.
free speech *n* свобóда слóва.
freestyle ['fri:staɪl] *n* (*in swimming*) кроль *m*.
free trade *n* неограниченная беспóшлинная торгóвля.
freeway ['fri:weɪ] *n* (*US: AUT*) скоростнáя автострáда.
freewheel [fri:'wi:l] *vi* (*on bicycle*) катúться* (покатúться* *perf*); (*in car*) идтú* (пойтú* *perf*) свобóдным хóдом.
free will *n* свобóда вóли; **of one's own** ~~ по дóброй вóле.
freeze [fri:z] (*pt* **froze**, *pp* **frozen**) *vi* (*weather*) холодáть (похолодáть *perf*); (*liquid, pipe, person*) замерзáть (замёрзнуть* *perf*); (*person: stop moving*) застывáть (засты́ть* *perf*) ♦ *vt* заморáживать (заморóзить* *perf*) ♦ *n* (*weather*) зáморозки *pl*; (*on arms, wages*) заморáживание; **it's freezing** óчень хóлодно.
▸ **freeze over** *vi* замерзáть (замёрзнуть* *perf*).
▸ **freeze up** *vi* замерзáть (замёрзнуть* *perf*).
freeze-dried ['fri:zdraɪd] *adj* обрабóтанный мéтодом заморáживания-высушивания.
freeze-dry ['fri:zdraɪ] *vt* бы́стро заморáживать и затéм высушивать в вáкуме.
freezer ['fri:zə^r] *n* морозúльник.
freezing ['fri:zɪŋ] *adj*: ~ (**cold**) ледянóй ♦ *n*: **3 degrees below** ~ мúнус 3 грáдуса, 3 грáдуса морóза; **I'm** ~ я замёрз.
freezing point *n* температýра замерзáния.
freight [freɪt] *n* фрахт; ~ **forward** фрахт уплáчиваемый в портý вы́грузки; ~ **inward** фрахт уплáчиваемый по прибы́тию.
freight car *n* (*US*) товáрный вагóн.
freighter ['freɪtə^r] *n* (*NAUT*) грузовóе сýдно*; (*AVIAT*) грузовóй самолёт.
freight forwarder [-'fɔ:wədə^r] *n* экспедúтор.
freight train *n* (*US*) товáрный пóезд*.
French [frɛntʃ] *adj* францýзский* ♦ *n* (*LING*) францýзский* язы́к*; **the** ~ *npl* (*people*) францýзы *mpl*.
French bean *n* (*BRIT*) стручкóвая фасóль *f*.
French Canadian *n* франкоязы́чный(-ая) канáдец*(-дка).
French-Canadian [frɛntʃkə'neɪdjən] *adj* франко-канáдский*.
French dressing *n* сóус для салáта из растúтельного мáсла и ýксуса.
French fried potatoes *npl* чúпсы *mpl*.
French fries [-fraɪz] *npl* (*US*) = French fried potatoes.
French Guiana [-gaɪ'ænə] *n* Францýзская Гвиáна.
Frenchman ['frɛntʃmən] *irreg n* францýз.
French Riviera *n*: **the** ~~ Францýзская Ривьéра.
French stick *n* длúнный фанзýский батóн.
French window *n* авуствóрчатое окнó до пóла.
Frenchwoman ['frɛntʃwumən] *irreg n* францýженка*.
frenetic [frə'nɛtɪk] *adj* лихорáдочный* (лихорáдочен).
frenzied ['frɛnzɪd] *adj* (*person*) бéшеный, взбешённый; (*behaviour*) нейстовый.
frenzy ['frɛnzɪ] *n* (*of violence*) бéшенство, нейстовство; ~ **of joy** безýмная рáдость; ~ **of excitement** безýмное возбуждéние; **to drive sb into a** ~ довестú* (*perf*) когó-н до бéшенства, привестú* (*perf*) когó-н в бéшенство; **to be in a** ~ быть* (*impf*) в бéшенстве.
frequency ['fri:kwənsɪ] *n* (*also RADIO*) частотá*.
frequency modulation *n* частóтная модуля́ция.
frequent [*adj* 'fri:kwənt, *vt* frɪ'kwɛnt] *adj* чáстый ♦ *vt* (*pub, restaurant*) посещáть (посетúть* *perf*).
frequently ['fri:kwəntlɪ] *adv* (*often*) чáсто.
fresco ['frɛskəu] *n* фрéска*.
fresh [frɛʃ] *adj* свéжий* (свеж); (*instructions, approach*) нóвый* (нов); (*cheeky: person*) нахáльный* (нахáлен), фамилья́рный* (фамилья́рен); **to make a ~ start** начáть* *perf* зáново; ~ **in one's mind** свежó в пáмяти.
freshen ['frɛʃən] *vi* (*wind, air*) свежéть (*impf*).
▸ **freshen up** *vi* (*person*) освежáться (освежúться* *perf*).
freshener ['frɛʃnə^r] *n*: **skin** ~ лосьóн для освежéния кóжи; **air** ~ освежúтель *m* вóздуха.
fresher ['frɛʃə^r] *n* (*BRIT: inf*) первокýрсник*.
freshly ['frɛʃlɪ] *adv*: ~ **made** свéжеприготóвленный; ~ **painted** свéжепокрáшенный.
freshman ['frɛʃmən] *irreg n* (*US*) = fresher.
freshness ['frɛʃnɪs] *n* свéжесть *f*.
freshwater ['frɛʃwɔ:tə^r] *adj* (*lake*) прéсный; (*fish*) пресновóдный.
fret [frɛt] *vi* волновáться (*impf*).
fretful ['frɛtful] *adj* (*child*) беспокóйный*.
Freudian ['frɔɪdɪən] *adj* фрейдúстский; ~ **slip** оговóрка по Фрéйду.
FRG *n abbr* (= *Federal Republic of Germany*) ФРГ = *Федератúвная Респýблика Гермáнии*.

Fri. *abbr* = **Friday**.
friar ['fraɪə'] *n* монáх.
friction ['frɪkʃən] *n* трéние; (*fig*) трéния *ntpl*.
friction feed *n* (*on printer*) подáча бумáги с
помóщью вáлика.
Friday ['fraɪdɪ] *n* пятница; *see also* **Tuesday**.
fridge [frɪdʒ] *n* (*BRIT*) холодильник.
fridge-freezer ['frɪdʒ'friːzə'] *n* холодильник с
большóй морозильной кáмерой.
fried [fraɪd] *pt, pp of* **fry** ♦ *adj* жáреный.
friend [frɛnd] *n* (*male*) друг*; (*female*) подрýга;
to make ~s with подружиться (*perf*) с +*instr*.
friendliness ['frɛndlɪnɪs] *n* дружелюбие.
friendly ['frɛndlɪ] *adj* (*person, smile etc*)
дружелюбный* (дружелюбен);
(*government, country*) дрýжественный*
(дрýжествен); (*place, restaurant*) приятный*
(приятен); (*game, match*) товáрищеский* ♦ *n*
(*also: ~* **match**) товáрищеская встрéча; **to be**
~ with дружить* (*impf*) с +*instr*; **to be ~ to sb**
относиться* (отнестись* *perf*) к комý-н
дружелюбно.
friendly fire *n* огóнь* *m* со своих позиций.
friendly society *n* óбщество *or* кáсса
взаимопóмощи.
friendship ['frɛndʃɪp] *n* дрýжба.
frieze [friːz] *n* фриз, бордюр.
frigate ['frɪgɪt] *n* фрегáт.
fright [fraɪt] *n* испýг; **to take ~** испугáться
(*perf*); **she looks a ~** онá выглядит как
пýгало.
frighten ['fraɪtn] *vt* пугáть (испугáть *or*
напугáть *perf*)
▶ **frighten away** *vt* (*birds, children etc*)
спýгивать (спугнýть *perf*)
▶ **frighten off** *vt* = **frighten away**.
frightened ['fraɪtnd] *adj* (*afraid*) испýганный*
(испýган); **I am ~** я боюсь; **to be ~ (of)**
боя́ться (*impf*) (+*gen*); **he is ~ by change** егó
пугáют изменéние.
frightening ['fraɪtnɪŋ] *adj* (*experience, prospect*)
стрáшный*.
frightful ['fraɪtful] *adj* (*dreadful*) кошмáрный*
(кошмáрен), ужáсный* (ужáсен).
frightfully ['fraɪtfəlɪ] *adv* ужáсно; **I'm ~ sorry**
мне ужáсно стыдно.
frigid ['frɪdʒɪd] *adj* (*woman*) фригидный.
frigidity [frɪ'dʒɪdɪtɪ] *n* фригидность *f*.
frill [frɪl] *n* (*of dress, shirt*) обóрка*; **without ~s**
(*fig*) без прикрáс.
frilly ['frɪlɪ] *adj* с обóрками.
fringe [frɪndʒ] *n* (*BRIT: of hair*) чёлка*; (*on shawl,
lampshade etc*) бахромá; (*of forest etc*) край*,
окрáина; (*fig: of activity, organization etc*)
перефéрия.
fringe benefits *npl* дополнительные льгóты
fpl.
fringe theatre *n* экспериментáльный теáтр.

Frisbee® ['frɪzbɪ] *n* тарéлки *fpl* (*летáющий
диск*).
frisk [frɪsk] *vt* (*search*) обыскивать (обыскáть*
perf) ♦ *vi* (*animal*) резвиться (порезвиться
perf).
frisky ['frɪskɪ] *adj* игривый (игрив).
fritter ['frɪtə'] *n* (*CULIN*) лóмтик чегó-нибудь,
обжáренный в кипящем мáсле
▶ **fritter away** *vt* (*money*) растрáчивать
(растрáтить* *perf*) по мелочáм; (*time*)
пóпусту терять (потерять *perf*).
frivolity [frɪ'vɔlɪtɪ] *n* легкомыслие.
frivolous ['frɪvələs] *adj* (*conduct, person*)
легкомысленный* (легкомыслен); (*object,
activity*) пустячный.
frizzy ['frɪzɪ] *adj* (*hair*) курчáвый, мéлко-
вьющийся.
fro [frəu] *adv*: **to and ~** тудá-сюдá.
frock [frɔk] *n* плáтье*.
frog [frɔg] *n* лягýшка*; **to have a ~ in one's
throat** хрипéть* (*impf*).
frogman ['frɔgmən] *irreg n* водолáз,
ныряльщик.
frogmarch ['frɔgmaːtʃ] *vt* (*BRIT*): **to ~ sb in/out**
втáскивать (втащить* *perf*)/вытáскивать
(вытащить *perf*) когó-н за рýки лицóм вниз.
frolic ['frɔlɪk] *vi* (*animals, children*) веселиться
(*impf*) ♦ *n* весéлье*.

KEYWORD
---

from [frɔm] *prep* **1** (*indicating starting place,
origin etc*): **where do you come from?** откýда
Вы?; **from London to Glasgow** из Лóндона в
Глáзго; **a letter from my sister** письмó от
моéй сестры; **a quotation from Dickens**
цитáта из Диккенса; **to drink from the bottle**
пить* (*impf*) из бутылки
2 (*indicating movement: from inside*) из +*gen*;
(: *away from*) от +*gen*; (: *off*) с(о) +*gen*; (: *from
behind*) из-за +*gen*; **she ran from the house**
онá выбежала из дóма; **the car drove away
from the house** машина отъéхала от дóма;
he took the magazine from the table он взял
журнáл со столá; **they got up from the table**
они встáли из-за столá
3 (*indicating time*) с +*gen*; **from two o'clock to**
or **until** *or* **till three** с двух часóв до трёх
(часóв); **from January (to August)** с января
(по áвгуст)
4 (*indicating distance: position*) от +*gen*; (:
motion) до +*gen*; **the hotel is 1 km from the
beach** гостиница нахóдится в киломéтре от
пляжа; **we're still a long way from home** нам
ещё далекó до дóма
5 (*indicating price, number etc: range*) от +*gen*;
(: *change*) с +*gen*; **prices range from £10 to £50**
цéны от £10 до £50; **the interest rate was
increased from nine per cent to ten per cent**
процéнты на вклáды повысили с девяти до

---
* marks translations which have irregular inflections. The Russian-English side of the dictionary gives inflectional information.

десяти (проце́нтов)

6 (*indicating difference*) от +*gen*; **to be different from sb/sth** отлича́ться (*impf*) от кого́-н/чего́-н

7 (*because of, on the basis of*): **from what he says** из того́, что он говори́л; **from what I understand** наско́лько я зна́ю; **to act from conviction** де́йствовать* (*impf*) по убежде́нию; **he is weak from hunger** он слаб от го́лода.

frond [frɔnd] *n* ветвь *f*; **palm ~** лист* па́льмы.

front [frʌnt] *n* (*of house, also fig*) фаса́д; (*of dress*) перёд; (*of train, car*) пере́дняя часть *f*; (*promenade: also:* **sea ~**) на́бережная *f adj*; (*MIL, METEOROLOGY*) фронт ◆ *adj* пере́дний ◆ *vi:* **to ~ onto sth** выходи́ть* (*impf*) фаса́дом на что-н; **in ~** вперёд; **in ~ of** перёд +*instr*; **on the political ~** на полити́ческом фро́нте.

frontage ['frʌntɪdʒ] *n* фаса́д.

frontal ['frʌntl] *adj* (*attack*) лобово́й, фронта́льный; **~ view** вид спе́реди.

front bench *n* (*POL: BRIT*) мини́стры пра́вящей па́ртии и руководи́тели па́ртии оппози́ции.

front desk *n* (*US: in hotel*) сто́йка администра́тора; (*: in doctor's surgery*) регистрату́ра.

front door *n* входна́я дверь* *f*.

frontier ['frʌntɪə] *n* грани́ца.

frontispiece ['frʌntɪspi:s] *n* фронтиспи́с.

front page *n* пе́рвая страни́ца (*газеты*).

front room *n* гости́ная *f adj*.

frontrunner ['frʌntrʌnə] *n* (*fig*) претенде́нт.

front-wheel drive ['frʌntwi:l-] *n* (*AUT*) пере́дний* при́вод.

frost [frɔst] *n* моро́з; (*also:* **hoarfrost**) и́ней.

frostbite ['frɔstbaɪt] *n* обмороже́ние.

frosted ['frɔstɪd] *adj* (*glass*) ма́товый; (*esp US: cake*) глазиро́ванный.

frosting ['frɔstɪŋ] *n* (*esp US: on cake*) глазу́рь *f*.

frosty ['frɔstɪ] *adj* (*weather, night*) моро́зный* (моро́зен); (*welcome, look*) ледяно́й; (*window*) покры́тый (покры́т) и́неем, замёрзший.

froth ['frɔθ] *n* (*on liquid*) пе́на.

frothy ['frɔθɪ] *adj* (*liquid*) пе́нистый.

frown [fraun] *n* нахму́ренный взгляд ◆ *vi* хму́риться (нахму́риться *perf*).

▶ **frown on** *vt fus* (*fig*) смотре́ть* (*impf*) с неодобре́нием на +*acc*.

froze [frəuz] *pt of* **freeze**.

frozen ['frəuzn] *pp of* **freeze** ◆ *adj* (*food*) моро́женый; (*COMM: assets*) заморо́женный.

FRS *n abbr* (*BRIT*) = Fellow of the Royal Society; (*US:* = Federal Reserve System) Федера́льная резе́рвная систе́ма.

frugal ['fru:gl] *adj* (*person*) бережли́вый (бережли́в); (*meal*) ску́дный* (ску́ден).

fruit [fru:t] *n inv* (*AGR*) фрукт; (*BOT*) плод; (*fig: results*) плоды́ *mpl*.

fruiterer ['fru:tərə] *n* торго́вец* фру́ктами.

fruit fly *n* фрукто́вая му́шка*.

fruitful ['fru:tful] *adj* плодотво́рный* (плодотво́рен).

fruition [fru:'ɪʃən] *n:* **to come to ~** осуществля́ться (осуществи́ться *perf*), реализо́вываться (реализова́ться *perf*).

fruit juice *n* фрукто́вый сок.

fruitless ['fru:tlɪs] *adj* (*fig*) беспло́дный* (беспло́ден).

fruit machine *n* (*BRIT*) игра́льный автома́т.

fruit salad *n* фрукто́вый сала́т.

fruity ['fru:tɪ] *adj* фрукто́вый; (*voice, laugh*) зы́чный* (зы́чен).

frump [frʌmp] *n* (*woman*) замухры́шка.

frustrate [frʌs'treɪt] *vt* (*person*) расстра́ивать (расстро́ить *perf*); (*plan, attempt*) срыва́ть (сорва́ть *perf*).

frustrated [frʌs'treɪtɪd] *adj* (*person*) неудовлетворённый (неудовлетворён); (*plan, attempt*) со́рванный (со́рван); **~ artist/poet** неуда́вшийся худо́жник/поэ́т.

frustrating [frʌs'treɪtɪŋ] *adj* (*day*) неуда́чный* (неуда́чен); **I find this job very ~** я о́чень неудовлетворён э́той рабо́той.

frustration [frʌs'treɪʃən] *n* (*irritation*) доса́да; (*thwarting*) круше́ние.

fry [fraɪ] (*pt, pp* **fried**) *vt* жа́рить (пожа́рить *or* поджа́рить *perf*); *see also* **small**.

frying pan ['fraɪŋ-] (*US* **fry-pan**) *n* сковорода́*.

fry-pan ['fraɪpæn] *n* (*US*) = **frying pan**.

FT *n abbr* (*BRIT*) = Financial Times; **the ~ index** фо́ндовый и́ндекс „Фа́йнэншл Таймс".

ft. *abbr* = **feet**, **foot**.

FTC *n abbr* (*US:* = Federal Trade Commission) Федера́льная торго́вая коми́ссия.

FTSE 100 Index *n* (*COMM*) показа́тель состоя́ния фо́ндовой би́ржи, публику́емый в газе́те „Фина́ншэл Таймс".

fuchsia ['fju:ʃə] *n* фу́ксия.

fuck [fʌk] (*inf!*) *vti* тра́хать (*impf*) (*!*); **~ off!** иди́ на́ фиг! (*!*)

fuddled ['fʌdld] *adj* одурма́ненный.

fuddy-duddy ['fʌdɪdʌdɪ] *n* (*pej*) ста́рый зану́да *m*.

fudge [fʌdʒ] *n* ≈ сли́вочная пома́дка ◆ *vt* (*issue, problem*) уклоня́ться (уклони́ться *perf*) от +*gen*.

fuel ['fjuəl] *n* (*for heating*) то́пливо; (*for plane, car*) горю́чее *nt adj* ◆ *vt* (*furnace etc*) топи́ть* (*impf*); (*aircraft, ship*) заправля́ть (запра́вить* *perf*).

fuel oil *n* мазу́т.

fuel pump *n* то́пливный насо́с.

fuel tank *n* то́пливный бак; (*in car*) бензоба́к.

fug [fʌg] *n* (*BRIT*) духота́.

fugitive ['fju:dʒɪtɪv] *n* бегле́ц*(-ля́нка*).

fulfil [ful'fɪl] (*US* **fulfill**) *vt* (*function*) исполня́ть (испо́лнить *perf*); (*ambition*) реализо́вывать (реализова́ть *perf*).

fulfilled [ful'fɪld] *adj* (*person*) состоя́вшийся; (*life*) напо́лненный.

fulfilment [ful'fɪlmənt] (*US* **fulfillment**) *n* (*of* *promise, desire*) исполне́ние; (*satisfaction*) удовлетворе́ние; (*of ambitions*) реализа́ция.

full [ful] *adj* по́лный* (по́лон); (*skirt*) широ́кий*; (*life*) напо́лненный; (*maximum*): **at ~ volume/power** на по́лную гро́мкость/мо́щность ♦ *adv*: **to know ~ well that** прекра́сно знать (*impf*), что; **I'm ~ (up)** я сыт; **he is ~ of enthusiasm/hope** он по́лон энтузиа́зма/наде́жды; **~ details** все дета́ли; **~ marks** отли́чные оце́нки; **at ~ speed** на по́лной ско́рости; **a ~ two hours** це́лых два часа́; **in ~** по́лностью.

fullback ['fulbæk] *n* (*SPORT*) защи́тник.

full-blooded ['ful'blʌdɪd] *adj* энерги́чный*.

full board *n*: **hotel with ~ ~** гости́ница с трёхра́зовым пита́нием.

full-cream ['ful'kriːm] *adj*: **~ milk** (*BRIT*) несня́тое молоко́.

full employment *n* по́лная за́нятость *f*.

full-grown ['ful'grəun] *adj* (*animal, person*) взро́слый; (*plant*) вы́росший.

full-length ['ful'leŋθ] *adj* (*film, novel*) полнометра́жный; (*coat*) дли́нный; (*portrait*) во весь рост.

full moon *n* по́лная луна́*.

fullness ['fulnɪs] *n*: **in the ~ of time** по проше́ствии вре́мени.

full-page ['fulpeɪdʒ] *adj* (*advertisement, picture*) на всю страни́цу.

full-scale ['fulskeɪl] *adj* (*model*) в натура́льную величину́; (*attack, war, search*) широко-масшта́бный.

full-sized ['ful'saɪzd] *adj* (*portrait*) в по́лную величину́.

full stop *n* (*BRIT*) то́чка*.

full-time ['ful'taɪm] *adj, adv* (*study*) на дне́вном отделе́нии; (*work*) на по́лной ста́вке, на по́лную ста́вку.

fully ['fulɪ] *adv* (*completely*) по́лностью, вполне́; (*at least*): **~ as big as** по кра́йней ме́ре тако́й же величины́, как.

fully fledged [-'fledʒd] *adj* (*teacher, barrister*) вполне́ сложи́вшийся; (*citizen, member*) полнопра́вный*; (*bird*) опери́вшийся.

fully-paid share ['fulɪpeɪd-] *n* по́лностью опла́ченная а́кция.

fulsome ['fulsəm] *adj* (*praise*) чрезме́рный.

fumble ['fʌmbl] *vi*: **to ~ with** (*catch, key*) вози́ться (*impf*) с *+instr* ♦ *vt*: **to ~ the ball** неуклю́же стара́ться (*impf*) пойма́ть (*perf*) мяч; **to ~ in** (*pocket*) ры́ться (*impf*) в *+prp*; **she ~d for the switch in the dark** она́ ша́рила в темноте́ в по́исках выключа́теля.

fume [fjuːm] *vi* дыми́ть (*impf*); **he was fuming** он был разъярён.

fumes [fjuːmz] *npl* пары́ *mpl*, испаре́ния *ntpl*.

fumigate ['fjuːmɪgeɪt] *vt* оку́ривать (окури́ть* *perf*).

fun [fʌn] *n*: **what ~!** как ве́село!; **to have ~** весели́ться (повесели́ться *perf*); **he's good ~ (to be with)** с ним ве́село; **for ~** для заба́вы; **it's not much ~** э́то дово́льно ску́чно; **to make ~ of** подшу́чивать (подшути́ть *perf*) над *+instr*; **to poke ~ at** насмеха́ться (*impf*) над *+instr*.

function ['fʌŋkʃən] *n* (*also MATH*) фу́нкция; (*product*) произво́дная *f adj*; (*social occasion*) приём ♦ *vi* (*operate*) функциони́ровать (*impf*); **to ~ as** выполня́ть (вы́полнить *perf*) *or* исполня́ть (испо́лнить *perf*) фу́нкции *+gen*.

functional ['fʌŋkʃənl] *adj* (*operational*) де́йствующий*; (*practical*) функциона́льный.

function key *n* (*COMPUT*) функциона́льная кла́виша.

fund [fʌnd] *n* (*of money*) фонд; (*of knowledge etc*) запа́с; **~s** *npl* (*money*) (де́нежные) сре́дства *ntpl*, фо́нды *mpl*.

fundamental [fʌndə'mɛntl] *adj* фундамента́льный*.

fundamentalism [fʌndə'mɛntəlɪzəm] *n* фундаментали́зм.

fundamentalist [fʌndə'mɛntəlɪst] *n* фундаментали́ст.

fundamentally [fʌndə'mɛntəlɪ] *adv* в свое́й осно́ве; **they are ~ different** они́ коре́нным о́бразом различа́ются.

fundamentals [fʌndə'mɛntlz] *npl* осно́вы *fpl*.

funding ['fʌndɪŋ] *n* финанси́рование.

fund raising [-reɪzɪŋ] *n* сбор средств.

funeral ['fjuːnərəl] *n* по́хороны* *pl*.

funeral director *n* распоряди́тель *m* на похорона́х.

funeral parlour *n* похоро́нное бюро́ *nt ind*.

funeral service *n* панихи́да.

funereal [fju:'nɪərɪəl] *adj* тра́урный.

funfair ['fʌnfɛər] *n* (*BRIT*) я́рмарка*.

fungi ['fʌŋgaɪ] *npl of* **fungus**.

fungus ['fʌŋgəs] (*pl* **fungi**) *n* (*plant*) гриб*; (*mould*) пле́сень *f*.

funicular [fju:'nɪkjuləʳ] *n* (*also: ~ railway*) фуникулёр.

funky ['fʌŋkɪ] *adj* о му́зыке с си́льным синкопи́рованным ри́тмом; (*inf*) клёвый.

funnel ['fʌnl] *n* (*for pouring*) воро́нка*; (*of ship*) труба́*.

funnily ['fʌnɪlɪ] *adv* (*strangely*) стра́нно; **~ enough** как ни стра́нно.

funny ['fʌnɪ] *adj* (*comical*) смешно́й* (смешо́н); (*amusing*) заба́вный* (заба́вен); (*strange*) стра́нный* (стра́нен), чудно́й.

funny bone *n* (*inf*) локтева́я кость *f*.

fun run *n* благотвори́тельный пробе́г.

fur [fəːʳ] *n* мех*; (*BRIT: in kettle*) на́кипь *f*.

fur coat *n* мехова́я шу́ба.

furious ['fjuərɪəs] *adj* (*person*) взбешённый (взбешён); (*exchange, argument*) бу́рный*

---

* marks translations which have irregular inflections. The Russian-English side of the dictionary gives inflectional information.

(бу́рен); (*effort, speed*) нейстовый; **I am ~ with her** я о́чень серди́т на неё.
furiously [ˈfjuərɪəslɪ] *adv* нейстово.
furl [fəːl] *vt* свёртывать (сверну́ть *perf*).
furlong [ˈfəːlɔŋ] *n 201.2 метр в ко́нных ска́чках*.
furlough [ˈfəːləu] *n* (*MIL*) увольне́ние.
furnace [ˈfəːnɪs] *n* печь* *f.*
furnish [ˈfəːnɪʃ] *vt* (*room, building*) обставля́ть (обста́вить* *perf*); (*supply*): **to ~ sb with sth** предоставля́ть (предоста́вить* *perf*) что-н кому́-н; **~ed flat** or (*US*) **apartment** мебели́рованная кварти́ра.
furnishings [ˈfəːnɪʃɪŋz] *npl* обстано́вка *fsg.*
furniture [ˈfəːnɪtʃə*] *n* ме́бель *f;* **piece of ~** предме́т ме́бели.
furniture polish *n* сре́дство для полиро́вки ме́бели.
furore [fjuəˈrɔːrɪ] *n* (*protests*) негодова́ние.
furrier [ˈfʌrɪə*] *n* (*fur seller*) меховщи́к*; (*artisan*) скорня́к*.
furrow [ˈfʌrəu] *n* борозда́* *vt:* **to ~ one's brow** хму́рить (нахму́рить *perf*) бро́ви.
furry [ˈfəːrɪ] *adj* пуши́стый (пуши́ст).
further [ˈfəːðə*] *adj* (*additional*) дополни́тельный *adv* (*farther*) да́льше; (*moreover*) бо́лее того́ *vt* (*career, project*) соде́йствовать (*impf/perf*) +*dat;* **until ~ notice** впредь до дальне́йшего уведомле́ния; **how much ~ is it to the station?** ско́лько ещё до вокза́ла?; **~ to your letter of ...** (*formal*) ссыла́ясь на Ва́ше письмо́ от +*gen* ...; **to ~ one's interests** пресле́довать (*impf*) свои́ интере́сы.
further education *n* (*BRIT*) дальне́йшее обуче́ние (*не включа́я вы́сшее образова́ние*).
furthermore [fəːðəˈmɔː*] *adv* (*moreover*) бо́лее того́.
furthermost [ˈfəːðəməust] *adj* са́мый да́льний*.
furthest [ˈfəːðɪst] *superl of* **far.**
furtive [ˈfəːtɪv] *adj:* **~ glance/movement** взгляд/ движе́ние укра́дкой.
furtively [ˈfəːtɪvlɪ] *adv* укра́дкой.
fury [ˈfjuərɪ] *n* (*anger, rage*) я́рость *f,* бе́шенство; **to be in a ~** быть* (*impf*) в бе́шенстве or в я́рости.
fuse [fjuːz] (*US* **fuze**) *n* (*ELEC*) предохрани́тель *m;* (*for bomb*) фити́ль* *m* *vt* (*metal*) пла́вить* (распла́вить* *perf*); (*ideas, systems*) слива́ть (слить* *perf*) *vi* (*see vt*) пла́виться

(распла́виться *perf*); слива́ться (сли́ться *perf*); **a ~ has blown** предохрани́тель перегоре́л; **to ~ the lights** (*BRIT*) вызыва́ть (вы́звать* *perf*) коро́ткое замыка́ние.
fuse box *n* блок предохрани́телей.
fuselage [ˈfjuːzəlɑːʒ] *n* фюзеля́ж.
fuse wire *n* пла́вкая про́волока (*для предохрани́телей*).
fusillade [fjuːzɪˈleɪd] *n* залп.
fusion [ˈfjuːʒən] *n* (*of ideas, qualities*) слия́ние; (*also:* **nuclear ~**) я́дерный си́нтез.
fuss [fʌs] *n* (*excitement*) сумато́ха; (*anxiety*) суета́; (*trouble*) шум *vi* суети́ться* (*impf*) *vt* надоеда́ть (*impf*) +*dat;* **to make** or **kick up a ~** поднима́ть (подня́ть* *perf*) шум; **to make a ~ of sb** носи́ться* (*impf*) с кем-н
  ► **fuss over** *vt fus* (*person*) трясти́сь* (*impf*) над +*instr.*
fusspot [ˈfʌspɔt] *n* (*inf*) хлопоту́н(ья).
fussy [ˈfʌsɪ] *adj* (*nervous*) суетли́вый; (*choosy*) ме́лочный* (ме́лочен), су́етный; (*clothes, room*) вы́чурный*; **I'm not ~** мне всё равно́.
fusty [ˈfʌstɪ] *adj* (*pej: archaic*) старомо́дный* (старомо́ден); (*musty*) за́тхлый.
futile [ˈfjuːtaɪl] *adj* (*attempt*) тще́тный* (тще́тен); (*comment, existence*) беспло́дный* (беспло́ден).
futility [fjuːˈtɪlɪtɪ] *n* (*see adj*) тще́тность *f,* беспло́дность *f.*
futon [ˈfuːtɔn] *n* фу́тон (*япо́нский матра́с*).
future [ˈfjuːtʃə*] *adj* бу́дущий* *n* бу́дущее *nt adj;* (*LING: also:* **~ tense**) бу́дущее вре́мя* *nt;* **~s** *npl* (*COMM*) фью́черсы *pl,* фью́черский това́р *msg* (*о согласо́ванной дато́й прода́жи*); **in (the) ~** в бу́дущем; **be more careful in ~** в бу́дущем бу́дьте осторо́жнее; **in the near/immediate ~** в недалёком/ ближа́йшем бу́дущем.
futuristic [fjuːtʃəˈrɪstɪk] *adj* футуристи́ческий.
fuze [fjuːz] (*US*) = **fuse.**
fuzz [fʌz] *n* (*inf: police*): **the ~** менты́ *mpl.*
fuzzy [ˈfʌzɪ] *adj* (*thoughts, also PHOT*) расплы́вчатый (расплы́вчат); (*hair*) кудря́вый (кудря́в).
fwd. *abbr* = **forward.**
f-word [ˈefwəːd] *n:* **the ~** ≈ сло́во на́ три бу́квы.
fwy *abbr* (*US*) = **freeway.**
FY *abbr* = **fiscal year.**
FYI *abbr* (= *for your information*) к Ва́шему све́дению.

~ G, g ~

G, g [dʒi:] *n* (*letter*) 7-áя бýква англи́йского алфави́та.

G [dʒi:] *n* (*MUS*) соль *nt ind*.

G *n abbr* (*BRIT: SCOL*) = *good*; (*US: CINEMA*: = *general* (*audience*)) фильм, приго́дный для пока́за всем возрастны́м гру́ппам; (*PHYS*): **G-force** си́ла тя́жести.

g. *abbr* (= **gram**) г= *грамм*; (*PHYS*) = **gravity.**

G7 *n abbr* (*POL*: = *Group of Seven*) „больша́я семёрка".

GA *n abbr* (*US: POST*) = *Georgia.*

gab [gæb] *n* (*inf*): **he has the gift of the ~** у него́ хорошо́ подве́шен язы́к.

gabble ['gæbl] *vi* тарато́рить (протарато́рить (*perf*)).

gaberdine [gæbə'di:n] *n* сукно́*, габарди́н.

gable ['geɪbl] *n* фронто́н.

Gabon [gə'bɒn] *n* Габо́н.

gad about [gæd-] *vi* (*inf*) болта́ться (*impf*) без де́ла.

gadget ['gædʒɪt] *n* приспособле́ние.

gadgetry ['gædʒɪtrɪ] *n* приспособле́ния *ntpl*.

Gaelic ['geɪlɪk] *adj* гэ́льский ♦ *n* (*LING*) гэ́льский язы́к* (*язы́к ке́льтского происхожде́ния*).

gaff [gæf] *n* (*NAUT*) га́фель *m*; (*inf: nonsense*): **he made a real ~** он тако́е ля́пнул.

gaffe [gæf] *n* опло́шность *f*.

gaffer ['gæfə'] (*inf*) *n* (*supervisor*) ста́рший *m adj*; (*fellow*) стари́к*.

gag [gæg] *n* (*on mouth*) кляп; (*joke*) хо́хма ♦ *vt* вставля́ть (вста́вить* *perf*) кляп +*dat*, завя́зывать (завяза́ть* *perf*) рот +*dat*; (*fig*) затыка́ть (заткну́ть *perf*) рот +*dat* ♦ *vi*: **the smell made him ~** у него́ го́рло перехвати́ло от за́паха.

gaga ['gɑːgɑː] *adj*: **he is ~** у него́ не все до́ма.

gage [geɪdʒ] *n, vt* (*US*) = **gauge.**

gaiety ['geɪɪtɪ] *n* весе́лье.

gaily ['geɪlɪ] *adv* ве́село; (*coloured*) я́рко.

gain [geɪn] *n* (*increase*) увеличе́ние; (*profit*) при́быль *f* ♦ *vt* (*confidence, experience*) приобрета́ть (приобрести́* *perf*); (*speed*) набира́ть (набра́ть* *perf*) ♦ *vi* (*clock, watch*) спеши́ть (*impf*); (*benefit*): **to ~ from sth** извлека́ть (извле́чь* *perf*) по́льзу из чего́-н; **to do sth for ~** де́лать (сде́лать *perf*) что-н

ра́ди вы́годы; **what will you ~ by that?** чего́ Вы э́тим добьётесь?; **to ~ ground** получа́ть (получи́ть *perf*) большо́е распростране́ние; **to ~ 3 pounds (in weight)** попра́виться (*perf*) на 3 фу́нта; **to ~ on sb** догоня́ть (догна́ть* *perf*) кого́-н.

gainful ['geɪnful] *adj* (*employment*) вы́годный* (вы́годен).

gainfully ['geɪnfəlɪ-] *adv*: **~ employed** по опла́чиваемой рабо́те.

gainsay [geɪn'seɪ] (*irreg: like* **say**) *vt* отрица́ть (*impf*).

gait [geɪt] *n* по́ступь *f*; **to walk with a slow/ confident ~** идти́* (*impf*) ме́дленной/ уве́ренной по́ступью.

gala ['gɑːlə] *n* (*festival*) пра́зднество; **swimming ~** пра́здник на воде́.

Galapagos Islands [gə'læpəgəs-] *npl*: **the ~ ~** Галапаго́сские острова́* *mpl*.

galaxy ['gæləksɪ] *n* гала́ктика.

gale [geɪl] *n* (*wind*) си́льный ве́тер*; **~ force ten** поры́вы ве́тра в де́сять ба́ллов.

gall [gɔːl] *n* (*ANAT*) жёлчь *f*; (*fig: impudence*) на́глость *f* ♦ *vt* раздража́ть (*impf*).

gall. *abbr* = **gallon.**

gallant ['gælənt] *adj* (*brave*) до́блестный*; (*chivalrous*) гала́нтный*.

gallantry ['gæləntrɪ] *n* (*see adj*) до́блесть *f*; гала́нтность *f*.

gall bladder *n* жёлчный пузы́рь* *m*.

galleon ['gælɪən] *n* галео́н.

gallery ['gælərɪ] *n* (*also*: **art ~**) галере́я; (*in hall, church, theatre*) балко́н.

galley ['gælɪ] *n* (*ship's kitchen*) ка́мбуз; (*ship*) гале́ра; (*PUBLISHING: also*: **~ proof**) гра́нка*.

Gallic ['gælɪk] *adj* га́лльский.

galling ['gɔːlɪŋ] *adj* раздража́ющий.

gallon ['gælən] *n* галло́н (*4,5 ли́тра*).

gallop ['gæləp] *n* гало́п ♦ *vi* (*horse*) скака́ть* (*impf*) (гало́пом), галопи́ровать (*impf*); (*person*) носи́ться*/нести́сь* (*impf*); **~ing inflation** галопи́рующая инфля́ция.

gallows ['gæləuz] *n* ви́селица.

gallstone ['gɔːlstəun] *n* жёлчный ка́мень* *m*.

Gallup Poll ['gæləp-] *n* оди́н из ви́дов опро́сов обще́ственного мне́ния.

---

* marks translations which have irregular inflections. The Russian-English side of the dictionary gives inflectional information.

galore [gə'lɔː'] *adv* в изоби́лии.
galvanize ['gælvənaɪz] *vt* (*person*) возбужда́ть (возбуди́ть* *perf*); (*support*) обеспе́чивать (обеспе́чить *perf*); **to ~ sb into action** побужда́ть (побуди́ть* *perf*) кого́-н к де́йствию.
Gambia ['gæmbɪə] *n* Га́мбия.
gambit ['gæmbɪt] *n* (*fig*): (**opening**) ~ пе́рвый ход.
gamble ['gæmbl] *n* риск, риско́ванное предприя́тие ♦ *vt* (*money*) ста́вить* (поста́вить* *perf*) ♦ *vi* (*take a risk*) рискова́ть (рискну́ть *perf*); (*bet*) игра́ть (*impf*) в аза́ртные и́гры; **to ~ on the Stock Exchange** игра́ть (*impf*) на би́рже; **to ~ on sth** (*also fig*) де́лать (сде́лать *perf*) ста́вку на что-н.
gambler ['gæmblə'] *n* игро́к*.
gambling ['gæmblɪŋ] *n* аза́ртные и́гры *fpl*.
gambol ['gæmbl] *vi* резви́ться* (*impf*).
game [geɪm] *n* игра́*; (*match*) матч; (*esp TENNIS*) гейм; (*also*: **board** ~) насто́льная игра́; (*CULIN, HUNTING*) дичь *f* ♦ *adj* (*willing*): ~ (**for**) гото́вый (гото́в) (на +*acc*); ~**s** *npl* (*SCOL*) спорти́вные и́гры *fpl*; **a ~ of football/tennis** футбо́льный/те́ннисный матч; **a ~ of chess** ша́хматная па́ртия; **big ~** (*lions, tigers etc*) кру́пный зверь.
game bird *n* перна́тая дичь *f*.
gamekeeper ['geɪmkiːpə'] *n* е́герь *m*.
gamely ['geɪmlɪ] *adv* хра́бро.
game reserve *n* охо́тничий* запове́дник.
games console ['geɪmz-] *n* пане́ль управле́ния компью́терными и́грами.
gamesmanship ['geɪmzmənʃɪp] *n* трюка́чество.
gaming ['geɪmɪŋ] *n* аза́ртные и́гры *fpl*.
gammon ['gæmən] *n* (*bacon*) о́корок*; (*ham*) ветчина́.
gamut ['gæmət] *n* (*range*) га́мма; **to run the ~ of emotions** пережива́ть (пережи́ть* *perf*) це́лую га́мму эмо́ций.
gander ['gændə'] *n* гусь* *m*.
gang [gæŋ] *n* ба́нда; (*of friends*) компа́ния; (*of workmen*) кома́нда
▸ **gang up** *vi*: **to ~ up on sb** ополча́ться (ополчи́ться *perf*) на *or* про́тив кого́-н.
Ganges ['gændʒiːz] *n*: **the ~** Ганг.
gangland ['gæŋlænd] *adj* (*boss, killers*) мафио́зный.
gangling ['gæŋglɪŋ] *adj* долговя́зый (долговя́з).
gangly ['gæŋglɪ] (*inf*) *adj* = **gangling**.
gangplank ['gæŋplæŋk] *n* трап.
gangrene ['gæŋgriːn] *n* гангре́на.
gangster ['gæŋstə'] *n* га́нгстер.
gangway ['gæŋweɪ] *n* (*from ship*) трап; (*BRIT: in cinema, bus etc*) прохо́д.
gantry ['gæntrɪ] *n* (*for crane*) порта́л; (*for railway signal*) сигна́льный мо́стик; (*for rocket*) раке́тная устано́вка.
GAO *n abbr* (*US*: = *General Accounting Office*) Центра́льное фина́нсово-контро́льное управле́ние.
gaol *etc* [dʒeɪl] (*BRIT*) = **jail** *etc*.
gap [gæp] *n* (*space*) промежу́ток*; (: *between teeth*) щерби́на; (: *in time*) интерва́л; (: *in market, records etc*) пробе́л; (*difference*) расхожде́ния *ntpl*; **generation ~** разногла́сия ме́жду поколе́ниями.
gape [geɪp] *vi* (*person*) рази́нуть (*perf*) рот от удивле́ния; (*hole*) зия́ть (*perf*); распа́хиваться (распахну́ться *perf*).
gaping ['geɪpɪŋ] *adj* (*hole*) зия́ющий; (*shirt*) распа́хнутый (распа́хнут).
garage ['gærɑːʒ] *n* гара́ж*; (*petrol station*) запра́вочная ста́нция, бензоколо́нка*.
garb [gɑːb] *n* оде́жда.
garbage ['gɑːbɪdʒ] *n* (*US: rubbish*) му́сор*; (*inf: nonsense*) ерунда́; (*fig: film, book*) дрянь *f*.
garbage can *n* (*US*) помо́йный я́щик.
garbage collector *n* (*US*) му́сорщик.
garbage disposal (unit) *n* (*US*) мусоропрово́д.
garbage truck *n* (*US*) мусороубо́рочная маши́на.
garbled ['gɑːbld] *adj* (*account, message*) запу́танный* (запу́тан).
garden ['gɑːdn] *n* сад* ♦ *vi* занима́ться (заня́ться* *perf*) садово́дством; ~**s** *npl* (*park*) парк *msg*; (*in street names*): **Rose G~s** Роуз Га́рденз; **she was busy ~ing** она́ рабо́тала в саду́.
garden centre *n* магази́н садо́вых принадле́жностей.
garden city *n* го́род*-сад*, зелёный го́род*.
gardener ['gɑːdnə'] *n* садово́д; (*employee*) садо́вник(-ица).
gardening ['gɑːdnɪŋ] *n* садово́дство.
gargle ['gɑːgl] *vi* полоска́ть* (прополоска́ть* *perf*) го́рло ♦ *n* полоска́ние.
gargoyle ['gɑːgɔɪl] *n* (*ARCHIT*) гарго́йл.
garish ['gɛərɪʃ] *adj* (*light*) ре́жущий глаз; (*dress, colour*) крича́щий.
garland ['gɑːlənd] *n* гирля́нда.
garlic ['gɑːlɪk] *n* чесно́к*.
garment ['gɑːmənt] *n* (*dress etc*) предме́т оде́жды.
garner ['gɑːnə'] *vt* добыва́ть (добы́ть* *perf*).
garnish ['gɑːnɪʃ] *vt* украша́ть (укра́сить* *perf*).
garret ['gærɪt] *n* камо́рка*.
garrison ['gærɪsn] *n* гарнизо́н.
garrulous ['gærjuləs] *adj* болтли́вый, говорли́вый.
garter ['gɑːtə'] *n* подвя́зка*.
garter belt *n* (*US*) по́яс* (*с подвя́зками*).
gas [gæs] *n* газ*; (*US: gasoline*) бензи́н*; (*as anaesthetic*) ингаляцио́нный анесте́тик ♦ *vt* (*kill*) удуша́ть (удуши́ть *perf*); (*MIL*) отравля́ть (отрави́ть* *perf*) га́зом.
gas cooker *n* (*BRIT*) га́зовая плита́*.
gas cylinder *n* га́зовый балло́н.
gaseous ['gæsɪəs] *adj* газообра́зный.

gas fire n (BRIT) га́зовый ками́н.
gas-fired ['gæsfaɪəd] adj га́зовый, рабо́тающий на га́зе.
gash [gæʃ] n (wound) глубо́кая ра́на; (cut, slash) глубо́кий* поре́з ♦ vt (person) наноси́ть* (нанести́* perf) глубо́кую ра́ну +dat; (object) распа́рывать (распоро́ть perf); наноси́ть* (нанести́* perf) глубо́кий поре́з +dat.
gasket ['gæskɪt] n (AUT) прокла́дка*.
gas mask n противога́з.
gas meter n га́зовый счётчик.
gasoline ['gæsəli:n] n (US) бензи́н*.
gasp [gɑ:sp] n (breath) вдох ♦ vi (pant) тяжело́ дыша́ть* (impf); (in surprise) издава́ть* (изда́ть* perf) вздох; **I am ~ing for a smoke** я умира́ю от жела́ния кури́ть
▶ **gasp out** vt выпа́ливать (вы́палить perf).
gas ring n камфо́рка*.
gas station n (US) запра́вочная ста́нция, бензоколо́нка*.
gas stove n (cooker) га́зовая плита́*.
gassy ['gæsɪ] adj (beer etc) газиро́ванный* (газиро́ван).
gas tank n бензоба́к.
gastric ['gæstrɪk] adj желу́дочный.
gastric ulcer n я́зва желу́дка.
gastroenteritis ['gæætrəuɛntə'raɪtɪs] n гастроэнтери́т.
gastronomy [gæs'trɔnəmɪ] n кулина́рное иску́сство.
gasworks ['gæswɔ:ks] n га́зовый заво́д.
gate [geɪt] n (single) кали́тка*; (double) воро́та mpl; (at airport) вы́ход; (of lock, level crossing etc) шлагба́ум.
gateau ['gætəu] (pl ~x) n торт.
gateaux ['gætəuz] npl of **gateau**.
gate-crash ['geɪtkræʃ] vt (BRIT): **to ~ a party** приходи́ть* (прийти́* perf) на вечери́нку без приглаше́ния.
gate-crasher ['geɪtkræʃəʳ] n (to party) незва́нный гость m.
gatehouse ['geɪthaus] n сторо́жка* у воро́т.
gateway ['geɪtweɪ] n (also fig) воро́та mpl.
gather ['gæðəʳ] vt собира́ть (собра́ть* perf); (understand) полага́ть (impf); (SEWING) собира́ть (собра́ть* perf) в скла́дки ♦ vi собира́ться (собра́ться* perf); (clouds) ска́пливаться (скопи́ться* perf); (dust) собира́ться (собра́ться* perf), оседа́ть (осе́сть* perf); **to ~ from sb** выясня́ть (вы́яснить perf) у кого́-н; **I ~ that** ... я полага́ю, что ...; **as far as I can ~** наско́лько я понима́ю; **to ~ speed** набира́ть (набра́ть* perf) ско́рость.
gathering ['gæðərɪŋ] n собра́ние.
GATT [gæt] n abbr (= General Agreement on Tariffs and Trade) ГАТТ (*Генера́льное*

соглаше́ние по тари́фам и торго́вле).
gauche [gəuʃ] adj нело́вкий*.
gaudy ['gɔ:dɪ] adj пёстрый*.
gauge [geɪdʒ] n (instrument) измери́тельный прибо́р; (RAIL) ширина́ колей ♦ vt (amount, quantity) измеря́ть (изме́рить perf); (fig: feelings, character etc) оце́нивать (оцени́ть* perf), получа́ть (получи́ть* perf) представле́ние о +prp; **petrol ~, fuel ~,** (US) **gas ~** указа́тель m у́ровня бензи́на; **to ~ the right moment** выбира́ть (вы́брать* perf) подходя́щий моме́нт.
Gaul [gɔ:l] n (country) Га́ллия; (person) галл.
gaunt [gɔ:nt] adj (haggard) измождённый* (измождён); (bare, stark) угрю́мый* (угрю́м).
gauntlet ['gɔ:ntlɪt] n перча́тка*; (fig): **to run the ~** подверга́ться (подве́ргнуться perf) напа́дкам; **to throw down the ~** броса́ть (бро́сить* perf) перча́тку.
gauze [gɔ:z] n (fabric) ма́рля.
gave [geɪv] pt of **give**.
gavel ['gævl] n молото́к (*председа́теля собра́ния, судьи́ или аукциони́ста*).
gawk [gɔ:k] vi (inf): **to ~ at** тара́щить (вы́таращить perf) глаза́ на +acc.
gawky ['gɔ:kɪ] adj неотёсанный* (неотёсан).
gawp [gɔ:p] vi: **to ~ at** тара́щить (вы́таращить perf) глаза́ на +acc.
gay [geɪ] adj (cheerful) весёлый* (ве́сел); (homosexual): **he is ~** он голубо́й or гомосексуали́ст; **~ bar** бар гомосексуали́стов or голубы́х.
gaze [geɪz] n (look, stare) (при́стальный) взгляд ♦ vi: **to ~ at sth** гляде́ть* (impf) на что-н.
gazelle [gə'zɛl] n газе́ль f.
gazette [gə'zɛt] n (newspaper) газе́та; (official publication) ве́домость f.
gazetteer [gæzə'tɪəʳ] n географи́ческий спра́вочник.
gazumping [gə'zʌmpɪŋ] n (BRIT: pej) увеличе́ние цены́ до́ма в после́дний моме́нт.
gazundering [gə'zʌndərɪŋ] n (BRIT: pej) пониже́ние предло́женную це́ну на поку́пку до́ма до подписа́ния контра́кта.
GB abbr = **Great Britain**.
GBH n abbr (BRIT: LAW: = grievous bodily harm) тяжёлые теле́сные поврежде́ния ntpl.
GC n abbr (BRIT: = George Cross) ≈ Гео́ргиевский крест.
GCE n abbr (BRIT: = General Certificate of Education) ≈ аттеста́т о сре́днем образова́нии.
GCHQ n abbr (BRIT: = Government Communications Headquarters) Гла́вный штаб служб прави́тельственной свя́зи.
GCSE n abbr (BRIT: = General Certificate of

---

* marks translations which have irregular inflections. The Russian-English side of the dictionary gives inflectional information.

Secondary Education) ≈ аттеста́т о сре́днем образова́нии.

Gdansk [gdænsk] *n* Гда́ньск.

Gdns. *abbr* (*in street names*) = **Gardens.**

GDP *n abbr* (= **gross domestic product**) ВВП= *валово́й вну́тренний проду́кт.*

GDR *n abbr* (*formerly:* = *German Democratic Republic*) ГДР= Герма́нская Демократи́ческая Респу́блика.

gear [gɪə'] *n* (*equipment, belongings etc*) принадле́жности *fpl*; (*for hunting*) снаряже́ние; (*for fishing*) сна́сти *fpl*; (*TECH*) зубча́тое колесо́; (*AUT*) ско́рость *f* ♦ *vt* (*fig*): **to ~ sth to** приспоса́бливать (приспосо́бить* *perf*) что-н к +*dat*; **top** *or* (*US*) **high/low/bottom ~** вы́сшая/ни́зкая/са́мая ма́лая переда́ча *or* ско́рость; **in ~** на переда́че *or* ско́рости, включённый (включён); **out of ~** не на переда́че *or* ско́рости, невключённый (невключён); **our service is ~ed to meet the needs of the disabled** на́ши услу́ги напра́влены на удовлетворе́ние потре́бностей инвали́дов

▶ **gear up** *vi*: **to ~ up (to do)** гото́виться* (пригото́виться* *or* подгото́виться* *perf*) (+*infin*) ♦ *vt*: **to ~ o.s. up (to do)** гото́вить* (пригото́вить* *or* подгото́вить* *perf*) себя́ (+*infin*).

gearbox ['gɪəbɔks] *n* коро́бка* переда́ч *or* скоросте́й.

gear lever (*US* **gear shift**) *n* переключа́тель *m* скоросте́й.

GED *n abbr* (*US*: *SCOL*) = *general educational development.*

geek [gi:k] *n* (*inf*) приду́рок*.

geese [gi:s] *npl of* **goose.**

geezer ['gi:zə'] *n* (*inf*) чува́к.

Geiger counter ['gaɪgə-] *n* счётчик Ге́йгера (*для измере́ния радиоакти́вности*).

gel [dʒɛl] *n* (*also CHEM*) гель *m.*

gelatin(e) ['dʒɛləti:n] *n* желати́н*.

gelignite ['dʒɛlɪgnaɪt] *n* гелигни́т.

gem [dʒɛm] *n* (*stone*) драгоце́нный ка́мень *m*, самоцве́т; (*fig*) сокро́вище.

Gemini ['dʒɛmɪnaɪ] *n* Близнецы́ *mpl*; **he is ~** он – Близне́ц.

gen [dʒɛn] *n* (*BRIT*: *inf*): **to give sb the ~ on sth** опи́сывать (описа́ть* *perf*) кому́-н что-н в о́бщих черта́х.

Gen. *abbr* (*MIL*) = **general.**

gen. *abbr* = **general, generally.**

gender ['dʒɛndə'] *n* (*sex*) пол; (*LING*) род.

gene [dʒi:n] *n* ген.

genealogy [dʒi:nɪ'ælədʒɪ] *n* генеало́гия.

general ['dʒɛnərl] *n* (*MIL*) генера́л ♦ *adj* о́бщий*; (*widespread*: *movement, interest*) всео́бщий*; **in ~** в о́бщем; **the ~ public** широ́кая пу́блика; **~ audit** (*COMM*) аудито́рская прове́рка.

general anaesthetic *n* о́бщий* нарко́з.

general delivery *n* (*US*) по́чта „до

востре́бования“.

general election *n* всео́бщие вы́боры *mpl.*

generalization ['dʒɛnrəlaɪ'zeɪʃən] *n* обобще́ние.

generalize ['dʒɛnrəlaɪz] *vi* обобща́ть (обобщи́ть *perf*).

generally ['dʒɛnrəlɪ] *adv* вообще́; (+*vb*) обы́чно; **it is ~ accepted that ...** обы́чно счита́ется, что ...; **to become ~ available** станови́ться* (стать* *perf*) общедосту́пным(-ой).

general manager *n* гла́вный управля́ющий* *m adj.*

general practitioner *n* врач-терапе́вт.

general strike *n* всео́бщая забасто́вка*.

generate ['dʒɛnəreɪt] *vt* (*power, electricity*) производи́ть* (произвести́* *perf*); (*excitement, interest*) вызыва́ть (вы́звать* *perf*); (*jobs*) создава́ть* (созда́ть* *perf*).

generation [dʒɛnə'reɪʃən] *n* поколе́ние; (*of electricity etc*) генери́рование; **for ~s** из поколе́ния в поколе́ние.

generator ['dʒɛnəreɪtə'] *n* генера́тор.

generic [dʒɪ'nɛrɪk] *adj* о́бщий*.

generosity [dʒɛnə'rɔsɪtɪ] *n* ще́дрость *f*; (*of spirit*) великоду́шие.

generous ['dʒɛnərəs] *adj* (*person: lavish*) ще́дрый (щедр); (: *unselfish*) великоду́шный* (великоду́шен); (*amount of money*) изря́дный.

genesis ['dʒɛnɪsɪs] *n* ге́незис, исто́ки *mpl*; **the ~ of an idea** восникнове́ние иде́и.

genetic [dʒɪ'nɛtɪk] *adj* генети́ческий*.

genetic engineering *n* генети́ческая инжене́рия.

genetic fingerprinting [-'fɪŋgəprɪntɪŋ] *n* установле́ние ли́чности челове́ка по его́ генети́ческим осо́бенностям (*по ДНК*).

genetics [dʒɪ'nɛtɪks] *n* гене́тика.

Geneva [dʒɪ'ni:və] *n* Жене́ва.

genial ['dʒi:nɪəl] *adj* (*smile, expression etc*) приве́тливый; (*host*) раду́шный*; (*climate*) мя́гкий*.

genitals ['dʒɛnɪtlz] *npl* половы́е о́рганы *mpl.*

genitive ['dʒɛnɪtɪv] *n* (*LING*) роди́тельный паде́ж*.

genius ['dʒi:nɪəs] *n* (*skill*) тала́нт; (*person*) ге́ний.

Genoa ['dʒɛnəuə] *n* Ге́нуя.

genocide ['dʒɛnəusaɪd] *n* геноци́д.

Genoese [dʒɛnəu'i:z] *adj* генуэ́зский ♦ *n inv* генуэ́зец*(-зка*).

gent [dʒɛnt] *n abbr* (*BRIT*: *inf*) = **gentleman.**

genteel [dʒɛn'ti:l] *adj* (*family*) благоро́дный*, благоро́дного происхожде́ния; (*person*) све́тский*.

gentle ['dʒɛntl] *adj* не́жный* (не́жен); (*movement, breeze, landscape, nature*) мя́гкий* (мя́гок); **a ~ hint** то́нкий* намёк.

gentleman ['dʒɛntlmən] *irreg n* (*man*) джентльме́н; (*referring to social position*)

дворянин*; ~'s agreement джентльме́нское
соглаше́ние.

gentlemanly ['dʒɛntlmənlɪ] *adj*
джентльме́нский.

gentleness ['dʒɛntlnɪs] *n (see adj)* не́жность *f*;
мя́гкость *f*.

gently ['dʒɛntlɪ] *adv (smile, treat)* не́жно; *(curve,
slope, move)* мя́гко; *(speak)* ла́сково.

gentry ['dʒɛntrɪ] *n inv:* **the ~** дворя́нство.

gents [dʒɛnts] *n:* **the ~** мужска́я убо́рная *f adj.*

genuine ['dʒɛnjuɪn] *adj (person, feeling)*
и́скренний*; *(painting etc)* по́длинный*.

genuinely ['dʒɛnjuɪnlɪ] *adv (sincerely)*
и́скренне; *(truly)* по-настоя́щему.

geographer [dʒɪˈɒɡrəfəʳ] *n* геогра́ф.

geographic(al) [dʒɪəˈɡræfɪk(l)] *adj*
географи́ческий.

geography [dʒɪˈɒɡrəfɪ] *n* геогра́фия.

geological [dʒɪəˈlɒdʒɪkl] *adj* геологи́ческий.

geologist [dʒɪˈɒlədʒɪst] *n* гео́лог.

geology [dʒɪˈɒlədʒɪ] *n* геоло́гия.

geometric(al) [dʒɪəˈmɛtrɪk(l)] *adj*
геометри́ческий.

geometry [dʒɪˈɒmətrɪ] *n* геоме́трия.

Geordie ['dʒɔːdɪ] *n (GEO: inf) уроже́нец го́рода
Нью́касл в А́нглии.*

Georgia ['dʒɔːdʒə] *n* Гру́зия.

Georgian ['dʒɔːdʒən] *adj* грузи́нский* ♦ *n*
грузи́н(ка*); *(LING)* грузи́нский* язы́к*.

geranium [dʒɪˈreɪnɪəm] *n* гера́нь *f*.

geriatric [dʒɛrɪˈætrɪk] *adj* гериатри́ческий ♦ *n*
дря́хлый стари́к.

germ [dʒɜːm] *n (MED)* микро́б; *(BOT, fig)*
заче́ток; **the ~ of an idea** заче́ток иде́и.

German ['dʒɜːmən] *adj* неме́цкий* ♦ *n*
неме́ц*(-мка*); *(LING)* неме́цкий* язы́к*.

German Democratic Republic *n (formerly)*
Герма́нская Демократи́ческая Респу́блика.

germane [dʒɜːˈmeɪn] *adj:* ~ **to** релева́нтный
+*dat.*

German measles *n (BRIT)* красну́ха.

Germany ['dʒɜːmənɪ] *n* Герма́ния.

germinate ['dʒɜːmɪneɪt] *vi (BOT)* прораста́ть
(прорасти́* *perf*); *(fig)* дава́ть* (дать* *perf*)
ростки́.

germination [dʒɜːmɪˈneɪʃən] *n (BOT)*
прораста́ние.

germ warfare *n* бактериологи́ческая война́.

gerrymandering ['dʒɛrɪmændərɪŋ] *n измене́ние
грани́ц избира́тельных округо́в с це́лью дать
преиму́щество определённой полити́ческой
па́ртии.*

gestation [dʒɛsˈteɪʃən] *n* созрева́ние плода́.

gesticulate [dʒɛsˈtɪkjuleɪt] *vi* жестикули́ровать
(impf).

gesture ['dʒɛstjəʳ] *n (movement, token)* жест; **as
a ~ of friendship** в знак дру́жбы.

KEYWORD

get [gɛt] *(pt, pp* **got**; *US) (pp* **gotten**) *vi* **1** *(become,
be):* **it's getting late** стано́вится* *(impf)*
по́здно; **to get old** старе́ть (постаре́ть *perf*);
to get tired устава́ть* (уста́ть* *perf*); **to get
cold** мёрзнуть (замёрзнуть *perf*); **to get
annoyed easily** ча́сто раздража́ться *(impf)*; **he
was getting bored** ему́ ста́ло ску́чно; **he gets
drunk quickly** он бы́стро пьяне́ет; **he gets
drunk every weekend** он напива́ется ка́ждый
выходно́й; **he got killed** его́ уби́ли; **when do I
get paid?** когда́ мне запла́тят?

2 *(go):* **to get to/from** добира́ться
(добра́ться* *perf*) до +*gen*/от +*gen*; **to get
home** приходи́ть* (прийти́* *perf*) домо́й; **how
did you get here/there?** как Вы сюда́/туда́
добрали́сь?

3 *(begin):* **to get to know sb** *(become
acquainted)* познако́миться* *(perf)* с кем-н; **to
get to know sb well** бли́зко познако́миться*
(perf) с кем-н; **I'm getting to like him** он
начина́ет мне нра́виться; **let's get started**
дава́йте начнём

♦ *modal aux vb:* **you've got to do it** Вы должны́
э́то сде́лать *(perf)*

♦ *vt:* **1: to get sth done** сде́лать *(perf)* что-н; **to
get the washing done** постира́ть *(perf)*; **to get
the dishes done** помы́ть* *(perf) or* вы́мыть
(perf) в посу́ду; **to get the car started** *or* **to start**
завести́* *(perf)* маши́ну; **to get sb to do**
заставля́ть (заста́вить* *perf*) кого́-н +*infin*; **to
get sb ready** собра́ть* *(perf)* кого́-н; **to get sth
ready** пригото́вить* *(perf)* что-н; **to get sb
drunk** напои́ть* *(perf)* кого́-н; **she got me into
trouble** я влип с ней в неприя́тности

2 *(obtain: permission, results)* получа́ть
(получи́ть* *perf*); *(: money)* достава́ть*
(доста́ть* *perf*); *(: find: job, flat)* находи́ть*
(найти́* *perf*); *(person: call)* звать* (позва́ть*
perf); *(: pick up)* забира́ть (забра́ть* *perf*); *(call
out: doctor, plumber etc)* вызыва́ть (вы́звать*
perf); *(object: carry)* приноси́ть* (принести́*
perf); *(: buy)* покупа́ть (купи́ть* *perf*); **I'll get
the car** я схожу́ за маши́ной; **can I get you
something to drink?** что Вам мо́жно
предложи́ть *(perf)*

3 *(receive)* получа́ть (получи́ть* *perf*); **to get a
reputation for sth** зарабо́тать *(perf)* дурну́ю
репута́цию +*instr*; **what did you get for your
birthday?** что Вам подари́ли на день
рожде́ния?

4 *(grab)* хвата́ть (схвати́ть* *perf*); *(hit):* **the
bullet got him in the leg** пу́ля попа́ла ему́ в
но́гу; **I'll get you there somehow** я Вас
ка́к-нибудь туда́ доста́влю; **do you think
we'll get the piano through the door?** как Вы
ду́маете, пиани́но пройдёт че́рез дверь?; **we
must get him to hospital** мы должны́ отвезти́

---

* marks translations which have irregular inflections. The Russian-English side of the dictionary gives inflectional information.

его в больни́цу; **I'll get the book to you tomorrow** за́втра кни́га бу́дет у Вас
5 (*catch, take*): **we got a taxi** мы взя́ли такси́; **did she get her plane?** она́ успе́ла на самолёт?; **what train are you getting?** каки́м по́ездом Вы е́дете?; **where do I get the train?** где мне сади́ться на по́езд?
6 (*understand*) понима́ть (поня́ть* *perf*); (*hear*) рассл́ышать (*perf*); **(do you) get it?** (*inf*) сечёшь?; **I've got it!** тепе́рь поня́тно!; **I'm sorry, I didn't get your name** прости́те, я не расслы́шал Ва́ше и́мя
7 (*have, possess*): **how many children have you got?** ско́лько у Вас дете́й?; **I've got very little time** у меня́ о́чень ма́ло вре́мени
▶ **get about** *vi* (*after illness*) ходи́ть* (*impf*); (*news*) распространя́ться (распространи́ться* *perf*); **I don't get about much now** (*go to places*) тепе́рь я ма́ло где быва́ю
▶ **get across** *vt* (*subj: speaker*) объясня́ть (объясни́ть* *perf*); **it's important to get this message across to them** ва́жно, что́бы они́ э́то по́няли
▶ **get along** *vi* (*agree*) ла́дить* (*impf*) с +*instr*; (*manage*) = **get by**; **I'd better be getting along** мне пора́
▶ **get around** *vt* = **get round**
▶ **get at** *vt fus* (*criticize*) придира́ться (придра́ться* *perf*) к +*dat*; (*reach*) дотя́гиваться (дотяну́ться* *perf*) до +*gen*; **what are you getting at?** ну что Вы хоти́те сказа́ть?
▶ **get away** *vi* (*leave*) уйти́* (*perf*); (*on holiday*) уе́хать* (*perf*); (*escape*) уйти́* (*perf*)
▶ **get away with** *vt fus*: **he always gets away with it** ему́ всё схо́дит с рук; **he'll never get away with it!** э́то ему́ да́ром не пройдёт!
▶ **get back** *vi* (*return*) возвраща́ться (верну́ться* *perf*)
◆ *vt* (*book, car*) получи́ть* (*perf*) обра́тно *or* наза́д; **get back!** отойди́те!
▶ **get back at** *vt fus* (*inf*): **I'll get back at you (for that)** ты у меня́ (за э́то) полу́чишь
▶ **to get back to** *vt fus* (*return to*) возвраща́ться (верну́ться* *perf*) к +*dat*; (*contact again*) связа́ться* (*perf*) с +*instr*; **to get back to sleep** сно́ва засыпа́ть (засну́ть* *perf*)
▶ **get by** *vi* (*pass: on foot*) проходи́ть* (пройти́* *perf*); (*manage*): **to get by without** обходи́ться* (обойти́сь* *perf*) без +*gen*; **I can/will get by** (*with little food, money*) мне хвата́ет/хва́тит; **I can get by in Dutch** я могу́ объясни́ться по-голла́ндски
▶ **get down** *vi*: **to get down from** слеза́ть (слезть* *perf*) с +*gen*
◆ *vt* (*depress*) де́йствовать* (*impf*) угнета́юще; (*write*) запи́сывать (записа́ть* *perf*); (*swallow*) впи́хивать (впихну́ть* *perf*) в себя́; **to get down on your hands and knees** встава́ть (встать* *perf*) на четвере́ньки
▶ **get down to** *vt fus* (*work, business*) сади́ться*

(засе́сть* *perf*) *or* бра́ться* (взя́ться* *perf*) за +*acc*)
▶ **get in** *vi* (*train*) прибыва́ть (прибы́ть* *perf*), приходи́ть* (прийти́* *perf*); (*arrive home: on foot*) приходи́ть* (прийти́* *perf*); (*by transport*) приезжа́ть (прие́хать* *perf*); (*be elected*): **he got in by ten votes** его́ избра́ли большинство́м в де́сять голосо́в; **as soon as the bus pulled up we all got in** как то́лько авто́бус подошёл, мы се́ли в него́; **we queued for a long time for the concert but couldn't get in** мы до́лго стоя́ли в о́череди, но так и не попа́ли на конце́рт
◆ *vt* (*harvest*) собира́ть (собра́ть* *perf*); (*coal, supplies*) заготавливать (загото́вить* *perf*); (*shopping*) закупа́ть (закупи́ть* *perf*); (*into conversation*) вставля́ть (вста́вить* *perf*)
▶ **get into** *vt fus* (*building*) входи́ть* (войти́* *perf*) в +*acc*; (*subj: train*) прибыва́ть (прибы́ть* *perf*) в/на +*acc*; (*vehicle*) сади́ться* (сесть* *perf*) в +*acc*; (*clothes*) влеза́ть (влезть* *perf*) в +*acc*; (*fight, argument*) вступа́ть (вступи́ть* *perf*) в +*acc*; (*university, college*) поступа́ть (поступи́ть* *perf*) в +*acc*; **to get into bed** ложи́ться (лечь* *perf*) в посте́ль; **I can't get into this skirt** э́та ю́бка не налеза́ет на меня́; **she has got into the habit of going for a walk before breakfast** у неё вошло́ в привы́чку выходи́ть гуля́ть до за́втрака
▶ **get off** *vi* (*escape*): **to get off lightly/with sth** отде́лываться (отде́латься* *perf*) легко́/чем-н
◆ *vt* (*clothes*) снима́ть (снять* *perf*); (*stain*) выводи́ть* (вы́вести* *perf*); (*letter etc*) отправля́ть (отпра́вить* *perf*); (*day, time*): **we got 2 days/2 weeks off last month** у нас бы́ло два выходны́х дня/две свобо́дных неде́ли в про́шлом ме́сяце
◆ *vt fus* (*train, bus*) сходи́ть* (сойти́* *perf*) с +*gen*; (*horse, bicycle*) слеза́ть (слезть* *perf*) с +*gen*; **to get off and walk** (*bicycle*) слеза́ть (слезть* *perf*) и идти́* (пойти́* *perf*) пешко́м; **you should get off at the next station** Вам на́до сойти́ (*perf*) на сле́дующей ста́нции; **to get off to a good/poor start** (*fig*) с бле́ском/пло́хо начина́ть (нача́ть* *perf*); **I'd better be getting off** (*departing*) мне пора́
▶ **get on** *vi* (*age*) старе́ть (*impf*); (*progress*): **how are you getting on?** у тебя́ подвига́ется де́ло?; **to get on (with)** (*agree*) ла́дить* (*impf*) (с +*instr*); (*manage*) справля́ться (спра́виться* *perf*) (с +*instr*)
◆ *vt fus* (*train, bus*) сади́ться* (сесть* *perf*) в +*acc*; (*horse, bicycle*) сади́ться* (сесть* *perf*) на +*acc*; **time is getting on** вре́мя идёт
▶ **get on to** *vt fus* (*BRIT: from one subject to another*) переходи́ть* (перейти́* *perf*) +*instr*; (*person*) свя́зываться (связа́ться* *perf*) с +*instr*; **how did we get on to this?** как мы к э́тому пришли́
▶ **get out** *vi* (*leave: building, vehicle*) выходи́ть* (вы́йти* *perf*); (*by transport*) выезжа́ть

(вы́ехать* perf); (: city) уезжа́ть (уе́хать* perf); (socialize) выбира́ться (вы́браться* perf) из до́ма

♦ vt (stain) выводи́ть* (вы́вести* perf); (object) доставá́ть (доста́ть* perf); (report) публикова́ть* (опубликова́ть* perf); **get out!** убира́йся!; **the news got out that...** ста́ло изве́стно, что...; **the news got out in the end** но́вости разошли́сь в конце́ концо́в

▶ **get out of** vt fus (duty etc) отде́лываться (отде́латься perf) от +gen

♦ vt (pleasure, satisfaction) получа́ть (получи́ть* perf) от +gen; (money): **to get out (of)** (from bank) бра́ть (взять* perf) (в +prp); (from account) снима́ть (снять* perf) с +gen; **I couldn't get a word out of him** я не мог и сло́ва доби́ться от него́

▶ **get over** vt fus (illness) поправля́ться (попра́виться* perf)

♦ vt: **to get sth over with** зако́нчить (perf) что-н; **to get the message over that...** объясни́ть (perf), что...; **let's get it over with!** дава́йте поко́нчим с э́тим де́лом!

▶ **get round** vt fus (law, rule) обходи́ть* (обойти́* perf); (fig: person) добива́ться (доби́ться* perf) своего́ от +gen

▶ **get round to** vt fus: **to get round to doing** собира́ться (собра́ться* perf) +infin; **I'll get around to it some day** когда́-н я доберу́сь до э́того

▶ **get through** vi (TEL) дозвони́ться (perf)

♦ vt fus (work, book) зака́нчивать (зако́нчить perf)

▶ **get through to** vt fus (TEL) дозвони́ться (perf) до +gen

▶ **get together** vi (several people) собира́ться (собра́ться* perf); (two people) встреча́ться (встре́титься* perf)

♦ vt (people) собира́ть (собра́ть perf); (project, plan etc) составля́ть (соста́вить* perf)

▶ **get up** vi встава́ть* (встать* perf)

♦ vt (person) поднима́ть (подня́ть* perf); **I can't get up any enthusiasm for it** у меня́ не возника́ет энтузиа́зма на э́тот счёт

▶ **get up to** vt fus (BRIT: prank etc) занима́ться (заня́ться* perf) +instr; **they're always getting up to mischief** они́ всегда́ прока́зничают.

getaway ['gɛtəweɪ] n: **to make a** or **one's** ~ бежа́ть* (impf).

getaway car n маши́на, испо́льзованная при побе́ге.

get-together ['gɛtəgɛðə'] n (meeting) неофициа́льное собра́ние; (party) вечери́нка*.

get-up ['gɛtʌp] n (inf) наря́д.

get-well card [gɛt'wɛl-] n откры́тка* с

пожела́ниями выздоровле́ния.

geyser ['giːzə'] n ге́йзер; (BRIT: water heater) га́зовая коло́нка*.

Ghana ['gɑːnə] n Га́на.

Ghanaian [gɑː'neɪən] adj га́нский ♦ n жи́тель(ница) m(f) Га́ны.

ghastly ['gɑːstlɪ] adj (horrible: person, situation) ужа́сный* (ужа́сен), отврати́тельный* (отврати́телен); (: building, appearance, behaviour) безобра́зный* (безобра́зен); (pale: complexion) ме́ртвенно-бле́дный* (ме́ртвенно-бле́ден); (ill): **you look** ~! Вы ужа́сно вы́глядите!

gherkin ['gɜːkɪn] n ме́лкий огуре́ц для маринова́ния.

ghetto ['gɛtəʊ] n ге́тто nt ind.

ghetto blaster [-'blɑːstə'] n переносно́й радиомагнитофо́н.

ghost [gəʊst] n (spirit) привиде́ние, при́зрак ♦ vt явля́ться (яви́ться* perf) та́йным а́втором +gen; **to give up the** ~ (fig) приказа́ть* (perf) до́лго жить.

ghost town n забро́шенный го́род.

ghostwriter ['gəʊstraɪtə'] n та́йный а́втор, писа́тель-неви́димка m.

ghoul [guːl] n (ghost) вурдала́к.

ghoulish ['guːlɪʃ] adj (tastes etc) ме́рзкий* (ме́рзок).

GHQ n abbr (MIL) = general headquarters.

GI n abbr (US: inf) = government issue.

giant ['dʒaɪənt] n (in myths, stories) велика́н; (fig: large company etc) гига́нт ♦ adj огро́мный.

giant killers npl кома́нда без и́мени, оде́рживающий побе́ды над кома́ндами мирово́го кла́сса.

gibber ['dʒɪbə'] vi говори́ть (проговори́ть perf) невня́тно.

gibberish ['dʒɪbərɪʃ] n тараба́рщина.

gibe [dʒaɪb] n насме́шка* ♦ vi: **to** ~ **at** смея́ться (impf) or издева́ться (impf) над +instr.

giblets ['dʒɪblɪts] npl (of chicken etc) потроха́* mpl.

Gibraltar [dʒɪ'brɔːltə'] n Гибралта́р.

giddiness ['gɪdɪnɪs] n головокруже́ние.

giddy ['gɪdɪ] adj (height) голово-кружи́тельный* (головокружи́телен); (dizzy): **I feel** ~ у меня́ кру́житься голова́; ~ **with success** опьянённый (опьянён) успе́хом.

gift [gɪft] n (present) пода́рок*; (donation) дар*; (COMM: also: **free** ~) беспла́тный пода́рок*; (ability) дар*, тала́нт; **to have a** ~ **for sth** облада́ть (impf) тала́нтом чего́-н.

gifted ['gɪftɪd] adj одарённый*.

gift token n пода́рочный купо́н.

gift voucher n = **gift token**.

gig [gɪg] n (inf: concert) конце́рт (рок- и́ли

---

* marks translations which have irregular inflections. The Russian-English side of the dictionary gives inflectional information.

поп-гру́ппы).

gigabyte ['dʒɪgəbaɪt] *n единúца измере́ния мóщности па́мяти компью́тера.*

gigantic [dʒaɪ'gæntɪk] *adj* гига́нтский*.

giggle ['gɪgl] *vi* хихúкать (*impf*) ♦ *n*: **it was just a ~!** э́то был про́сто смех!; **to do sth for a ~** де́лать (сде́лать *perf*) что-н для сме́ха.

GIGO ['gaɪgəu] *abbr* (*COMPUT: inf:* = *garbage in, garbage out*) МЗМП= *мяки́ну зало́жишь – мяки́ну полу́чишь.*

gild [gɪld] *vt* золотúть* (позолотúть* *perf*).

gill [dʒɪl] *n ме́ра жúдкости.*

gills [gɪlz] *npl* (*of fish*) жа́бры *fpl.*

gilt [gɪlt] *adj* позоло́ченный ♦ *n* позоло́та; **~s** *npl* (*COMM*) = **gilt-edged securities.**

gilt-edged ['gɪltɛdʒd] *adj*: **~ securities** золотобре́зные це́нные бума́ги *fpl* (*о надёжных áкциях*).

gimlet ['gɪmlɪt] *n* бура́вчик.

gimmick ['gɪmɪk] *n* (*sales*) уло́вка; (*electoral*) трюк.

gin [dʒɪn] *n* джин (*можжеве́ловая во́дка*).

ginger ['dʒɪndʒə'] *n* (*spice*) имбúрь* *m* ♦ *adj* (*in colour*) ры́жий*.

ginger ale *n* имбúрный эль.

ginger beer *n* имбúрное пúво.

gingerbread ['dʒɪndʒəbrɛd] *n* (*cake*) ≈ коврúжка, имбúрный пиро́г*; (*biscuit*) ≈ пря́ник, имбúрное пече́нье*.

ginger group *n* (*BRIT*) гру́ппа чле́нов организа́ции, наста́ивающая на бо́лее реши́тельных де́йствиях.

ginger-haired ['dʒɪndʒə'hɛəd] *adj* рыжеволóсый.

gingerly ['dʒɪndʒəlɪ] *adv* опа́сливо.

gingham ['gɪŋəm] *n* хлопчатобума́жная ткань в кле́тку.

ginseng ['dʒɪnsɛŋ] *n* жень-ше́нь *m.*

gipsy ['dʒɪpsɪ] *n* цыга́н*(ка*).

gipsy caravan *n* цыга́нская кибúтка.

giraffe [dʒɪ'rɑ:f] *n* жира́ф.

girder ['gə:də'] *n* металлúческая ба́лка*.

girdle ['gə:dl] *n* (*corset*) корсе́т ♦ *vt* (*encircle*) опоя́сывать (опоя́сать* *perf*).

girl [gə:l] *n* (*child*) де́вочка*; (*young unmarried woman*) де́вушка*; (*daughter*) до́чка*; **this is my little ~** э́то моя́ до́чка; **an English ~** англича́нка*.

girlfriend ['gə:lfrɛnd] *n* (*of girl*) подру́га; (*of boy*) де́вушка*, подру́га.

Girl Guide *n* де́вочка*-ска́ут *f.*

girlish ['gə:lɪʃ] *adj* деви́чий*.

Girl Scout *n* (*US*) = **Girl Guide.**

Giro ['dʒaɪrəu] *n*: **the National ~** (*BRIT*) спо́соб перево́да де́нег че́рез банк úли по по́чте.

giro ['dʒaɪrəu] *n* (*bank giro*) перево́д де́нег че́рез банк; (*post office giro*) перево́д де́нег че́рез по́чту; (*BRIT: welfare cheque*) чек, по кото́рому получа́ют посо́бия по безрабо́тице.

girth [gə:θ] *n* (*circumference*) окру́жность *f*; (*of*

horse) подпру́га.

gist [dʒɪst] *n* (*of speech, programme*) суть *f.*

give [gɪv] (*pt* **gave**, *pt* **given**) *vt* **1** (*hand over*): **to give sb sth** *or* **sth to sb** дава́ть* (дать* *perf*) кому́-н что-н; **they gave her a book for her birthday** они́ подарúли ей кнúгу на день рожде́ния

2 (*used with noun to replace a verb*): **to give a sigh** вздохну́ть (*perf*); **to give her a push** толкну́ть (*perf*); **to give a shrug** передёрнуть (*perf*) плеча́ми; **to give a speech** выступа́ть (вы́ступить* *perf*) с ре́чью; **to give a lecture** чита́ть (прочита́ть *perf*) ле́кцию; **to give three cheers** трúжды крича́ть (прокрича́ть *perf*) „ура́"

3 (*tell, deliver: news*) сообща́ть (сообщúть *perf*); (*advice*) дава́ть* (дать* *perf*); **could you give him a message for me please? tell him that...** переда́йте ему́, пожа́луйста, от меня́, что...; **I've got a message to give you from your brother** я тебе́ до́лжен что-то переда́ть от твоего́ бра́та; **let me give you some advice** разрешú мне дать Вам сове́т; **he gave me his new address over the phone** он дал мне свой но́вый а́дрес по телефо́ну;

4: **to give sb sth** (*clothing, food, right*) дава́ть* (дать* *perf*) кому́-н что-н; (*title*) присва́ивать (присво́ить *perf*) кому́-н что-н; (*honour, responsibility*) возлага́ть (возложúть* *perf*) на кого́-н что-н; **to give sb a surprise** удивúть* (*perf*) кого́-н; **that's given me an idea** э́то навело́ меня́ на мысль

5 (*dedicate: one's life*) отдава́ть* (отда́ть* *perf*); (*allow: time, attention*) уделя́ть (уделúть *perf*); **you'll need to give me more time** Вы должны́ дать мне бо́льше вре́мени; **she gave it all her attention** она́ отнесла́сь к э́тому с большúм внима́нием

6 (*organize*): **to give a party** устра́ивать (устро́ить *perf*) ве́чер, приглаша́ть (приласúть* *perf*) госте́й; **to give a dinner** *etc* дава́ть* (дать* *perf*) обе́д

♦ *vi* **1** (*stretch: fabric*) растя́гиваться (растяну́ться* *perf*)

2 (*break, collapse*) = **give way**

► **give away** *vt* (*money, object*) отдава́ть* (отда́ть* *perf*); (*betray: secret, information*) выдава́ть* (вы́дать* *perf*); (*: person*) выдава́ть* (вы́дать* *perf*); (*bride*) отдава́ть* (*impf*) за́муж

► **give back** *vt* отдава́ть* (отда́ть* *perf*) обра́тно

► **give in** *vi* (*yield*) сдава́ться* (сда́ться* *perf*) ♦ *vt* (*essay etc*) сдава́ть* (сдать* *perf*)

► **give off** *vt fus* (*smoke*) дымúть* (*impf*); **the radiator/coal fire gives off a lot of heat** от батаре́и/ками́на идёт тепло́

► **give out** *vt* (*distribute*) раздава́ть* (разда́ть* *perf*); (*make known*) объявля́ть (объявúть*

perf)
♦ *vi* (*be exhausted*) конча́ться (ко́нчиться *perf*); (*fail*) лома́ться (слома́ться *perf*)
▶ **give up** *vi* (*stop trying*) сдава́ться* (сда́ться* *perf*)
♦ *vt* (*job, boyfriend, habit*) броса́ть (бро́сить* *perf*); (*idea, hope*) оставля́ть (оста́вить* *perf*); **to give up smoking** броса́ть (бро́сить* *perf*) кури́ть; **to give o.s. up** сдава́ться* (сда́ться* *perf*)
▶ **give way** *vi* (*rope, ladder etc*) не вы́-де́рживать (вы́держать *perf*); (*wall, roof*) обва́ливаться (обвали́ться* *perf*); (*chair, floor*) прола́мываться (проломи́ться* *perf*); (*BRIT: AUT*) уступа́ть (уступи́ть* *perf*) доро́гу; **his legs gave way beneath him** его́ но́ги подогну́лись; **to give way (to)** (*to demands*) уступа́ть (уступи́ть* *perf*) +*dat*.

give-and-take ['gɪvənd'teɪk] *n* ги́бкость *f*, свобо́да.
giveaway ['gɪvəweɪ] (*inf*) *n*: **her expression was a ~** выраже́ние (её) лица́ вы́дало её ♦ *adj*: **~ prices** даровы́е це́ны; **the exam was a ~!** экза́мен был сундо́вый!
given ['gɪvn] *pp of* **give** ♦ *adj* да́нный ♦ *conj*: **~ the circumstances** ... с учётом обстоя́тельств ..., учи́тывая обстоя́тельства ...; **~ that** учи́тывая, что.
glacial ['gleɪsɪəl] *adj* (*also fig*) ледяно́й.
glacier ['glæsɪə'] *n* ледни́к*.
glad [glæd] *adj*: **I am ~** я рад; **I was ~ of his help** я был рад его́ по́мощи.
gladden ['glædn] *vt* (*heart*) ра́довать (пора́довать *perf*); (*person*) обра́довать *(perf)*; **it ~ed his heart to see her well again** у него́ пора́довалось се́рдце, когда́ он уви́дел, что ей ста́ло лу́чше.
glade [gleɪd] *n* поля́на.
gladioli [glædɪ'əʊlaɪ] *npl* гладио́лусы *mpl*.
gladly ['glædlɪ] *adv* (*willingly*) с ра́достью.
glamorous ['glæmərəs] *adj* очарова́тельный* (очаро́вателен).
glamour ['glæmə'] *n* очарова́ние.
glance [glɑːns] *n* (*look*) взгляд ♦ *vi*: **to ~ at** взгля́дывать (взгляну́ть* *perf*) на +*acc*
▶ **glance off** *vt fus* отска́кивать (отскочи́ть* *perf*) от +*gen*.
glancing ['glɑːnsɪŋ] *adj* (*blow*) боково́й.
gland [glænd] *n* железа́*.
glandular ['glændjulə'] *adj*: **~ fever** (*BRIT*) (инфекцио́нный) мононуклео́з.
glare [glɛə'] *n* (*angry*) свире́пый взгляд; (*hostile*) враждо́бный взгляд; (*of light*) ослепи́тельное сия́ние ♦ *vi* (*light*) ослепи́тельно сия́ть (*impf*); **she lives in the full ~ of publicity** все подро́бности её жи́зни стано́вятся достоя́нием пре́ссы; **to ~ at**

свире́по *or* при́стально смотре́ть* (посмотре́ть* *perf*) на +*acc*.
glaring ['glɛərɪŋ] *adj* (*mistake*) я́вный, очеви́дный.
Glasgow ['glɑːzgəu] *n* Гла́зго *m ind*.
glasnost ['glæznɒst] *n* гла́сность *f*.
glass [glɑːs] *n* (*substance*) стекло́; (*container, contents*) стака́н; **~es** *npl* (*spectacles*) очки́ *ntpl*.
glass-blowing ['glɑːsbləuɪŋ] *n* стеклоду́вное де́ло.
glass fibre *n* стекловолокно́.
glasshouse ['glɑːshaus] *n* тепли́ца, парни́к.
glassware ['glɑːswɛə'] *n* стекля́нная посу́да.
glassy ['glɑːsɪ] *adj* (*eyes, stare*) безжи́зненный* (безжи́зен).
Glaswegian [glæs'wiːdʒən] *adj* гла́зговский ♦ *n* жи́тель(ница) *m(f)* Гла́зго.
glaze [gleɪz] *vt* (*window*) застекля́ть (застекли́ть *perf*); (*pottery*) покрыва́ть (покры́ть* *perf*) глазу́рью ♦ *n* (*on pottery*) глазу́рь *f*.
glazed [gleɪzd] *adj* (*eyes*) му́тный*, ту́склый*; (*pottery*) покры́тый глазу́рью.
glazier ['gleɪzɪə'] *n* стеко́льщик.
gleam [gliːm] *vi* сия́ть (засия́ть *perf*) ♦ *n*: **a ~ of hope** луч* наде́жды.
gleaming ['gliːmɪŋ] *adj* сия́ющий*.
glean [gliːn] *vt* (*information*) добыва́ть (добы́ть* *perf*), собира́ть (собра́ть* *perf*).
glee [gliː] *n* (*joy*) ликова́ние.
gleeful ['gliːful] *adj* лику́ющий.
glen [glɛn] *n* (*SCOTTISH, IRISH*) доли́на реки́.
glib [glɪb] *adj* (*person*) болтли́вый (болтли́в); (*promise, response*) бо́йкий* (бо́ек).
glibly ['glɪblɪ] *adv* (*talk, answer*) бо́йко.
glide [glaɪd] *vi* скользи́ть* (*impf*); (*AVIAT*) плани́ровать (*impf*); (*bird*) пари́ть (*impf*) ♦ *n* скольже́ние.
glider ['glaɪdə'] *n* (*AVIAT*) планёр.
gliding ['glaɪdɪŋ] *n* (*AVIAT*) плани́рование.
glimmer ['glɪmə'] *n* (*of light*) мерца́ние; (*of interest, hope*) про́блеск ♦ *vi* (*light*) мерца́ть (*impf*).
glimpse [glɪmps] *n* мимолётное впечатле́ние ♦ *vt* ви́деть* (уви́деть* *perf*) ме́льком; **to catch a ~ of** уви́деть* (*perf*) ме́льком.
glint [glɪnt] *vi* блесте́ть* (блесну́ть *perf*), сверка́ть (сверкну́ть *perf*) ♦ *n* (*of metal, light*) блеск, сверка́ние; (*in eyes*) блеск.
glisten ['glɪsn] *vi* (*with sweat, rain etc*) блесте́ть* (*impf*).
glitter ['glɪtə'] *vi* сверка́ть (сверкну́ть *perf*) ♦ *n* сверка́ние.
glittering ['glɪtərɪŋ] *adj* (*eyes, career*) блестя́щий*; (*stars*) сия́ющий*; (*diamonds*) сверка́ющий.
glitz [glɪts] *n* (*inf*) блеск.

---

* marks translations which have irregular inflections. The Russian-English side of the dictionary gives inflectional information.

gloat [gləut] *vi*: **to ~ (over)** злора́дствовать (*impf*) (над +*instr*).

global ['gləubl] *adj* (*interest, attention*) всео́бщий*; (*overall: picture*) о́бщий*.

global warming [-'wɔ:mɪŋ] *n* всеми́рное *or* глоба́льное потепле́ние.

globe [gləub] *n* (*world*) земно́й шар*; (*model of world*) гло́бус; (*shape*) шар*.

globetrotter ['gləubtrɒtə'] *n* путеше́ственник(-ица).

globule ['glɒbju:l] *n* ка́пля*.

gloom [glu:m] *n* (*dark*) мрак; (*sadness*) уны́ние.

gloomily ['glu:mɪlɪ] *adv* уны́ло.

gloomy ['glu:mɪ] *adj* мра́чный.

glorification [glɔ:rɪfɪ'keɪʃən] *n* прославле́ние; **the ~ of war** прославле́ние войны́.

glorified ['glɔ:rɪfaɪd] *adj*: **she is merely a ~ secretary** она́ по су́ти де́ла про́сто секрета́рша.

glorify ['glɔ:rɪfaɪ] *vt* (*praise*) прославля́ть (просла́вить* *perf*).

glorious ['glɔ:rɪəs] *adj* (*sunshine, flowers, weather*) великоле́пный* (великоле́пен); (*victory*) сла́вный; (*future*) прекра́сный* (прекра́сен).

glory ['glɔ:rɪ] *n* (*prestige*) сла́ва; (*splendour*) великоле́пие ♦ *vi*: **to ~ in** упива́ться (*impf*) +*instr*.

glory hole *n* (*inf*) кладо́вка.

Glos *abbr* (*BRIT: POST*) = **Gloucestershire**.

gloss [glɒs] *n* блеск; (*also: ~ paint*) лак*
▶ **gloss over** *vt fus* (*error, problem*) зама́зывать (зама́зать* *perf*).

glossary ['glɒsərɪ] *n* глосса́рий.

glossy ['glɒsɪ] *adj* (*photograph, magazine*) гля́нцевый; (*hair*) блестя́щий* ♦ *n* (*also: ~ magazine*) журна́л в гля́нцевой обло́жке.

glove [glʌv] *n* перча́тка*.

glove compartment *n* (*AUT*) перча́точный я́щик, бардачо́к* (*разг*).

glow [gləu] *vi* (*embers, stars*) свети́ться (*impf*); (*face, eyes*) горе́ть (*impf*) ♦ *n* (*of eyes, stars*) свет; (*of face*) румя́нец*.

glower ['glauə'] *vi*: **to ~ at sb** смотре́ть* (посмотре́ть* *perf*) с негодова́нием на кого́-н.

glowing ['gləuɪŋ] *adj* (*fire*) я́рко светя́щийся; (*complexion*) румя́ный; (*fig: report etc*) блестя́щий*.

glow-worm ['gləuwə:m] *n* светлячо́к*.

glucose ['glu:kəus] *n* глюко́за.

glue [glu:] *n* клей* ♦ *vt*: **to ~ sth onto sth** прикле́ивать (прикле́ить *perf*) что-н на что-н.

glue-sniffing ['glu:snɪfɪŋ] *n* токсикома́ния.

glum [glʌm] *adj* мра́чный*.

glut [glʌt] *n* переизбы́ток* ♦ *vt*: **to be ~ted (with)** (*market, economy etc*) быть* (*impf*) зава́ленным(-ой) (+*instr*).

glutinous ['glu:tɪnəs] *adj* кле́йкий*.

glutton ['glʌtn] *n* обжо́ра *m/f*; **he is a ~ for work** он охо́ч до рабо́ты; **he is ~ for punishment** он жа́ден до рабо́ты.

gluttonous ['glʌtənəs] *adj* (*person, habits*) ненасы́тный* (ненасы́тен).

gluttony ['glʌtənɪ] *n* ненасы́тность *f*.

glycerin(e) ['glɪsəri:n] *n* глицери́н*.

gm *abbr* (= **gram**) г= *грамм*.

GMAT *n abbr* (*US*) = **Graduate Management Admissions Test**.

GMB *n abbr* (*BRIT*) = **General Municipal and Boilermakers (Union)**.

GMT *abbr* (= **Greenwich Mean Time**) сре́днее вре́мя* *nt* по Гри́нвичу.

gnarled [nɑ:ld] *adj* (*tree*) сучкова́тый (сучкова́т); (*hand*) скрю́ченный (скрю́чен).

gnash [næʃ] *vt*: **to ~ one's teeth** скрежета́ть* (*impf*) зуба́ми.

gnat [næt] *n* мо́шка*.

gnaw [nɔ:] *vt* грызть* (*impf*) ♦ *vi* (*doubts, suspicions*): **to ~ at** терза́ть (*impf*).

gnome [nəum] *n* гном.

GNP *n abbr* (= **gross national product**) ВНП= *валово́й национа́льный проду́кт*.

KEYWORD

go [gəu] (*pt* **went**, *pp* **gone**, *pl* **goes**) *vi* **1** (*move: on foot*) ходи́ть*/идти́* (пойти́* *perf*); (*travel: by transport*) е́здить*/е́хать (пое́хать* *perf*); **she went into the kitchen** она́ пошла́ на ку́хню; **he often goes to China** он ча́сто е́здит в Кита́й; **they are going to the theatre tonight** сего́дня ве́чером они́ иду́т в теа́тр

2 (*depart: on foot*) уходи́ть* (уйти́* *perf*); (: *by plane*) улета́ть (улете́ть* *perf*); (: *by train, car*) уезжа́ть (уе́хать* *perf*); **the plane goes at 6am** самолёт улета́ет в 6 часо́в утра́; **the train/ bus goes at 6pm** по́езд/авто́бус ухо́дит в 6 часо́в; **now I must go** тепе́рь я до́лжен идти́

3 (*attend*): **to go to** ходи́ть* (*impf*) в/на +*acc*; **she went to university in Aberdeen** она́ учи́лась в Абери́нском университе́те; **she doesn't go to lectures** она́ не хо́дит на ле́кции

4 (*take part in an activity*) ходи́ть*/идти́* (пойти́* *perf*)

5 (*work*): **is your watch going** ва́ши часы́ иду́т?; **the clock stopped going** часы́ останови́лись; **the bell went just then** зазвони́л звоно́к; **the tape recorder was still going** магнитофо́н не был вы́ключен

6 (*become*): **to go pale** бледне́ть (побледне́ть *perf*); **to go mouldy** пле́сневеть (запле́сневеть *perf*)

7 (*be sold*): **the books went for £10** кни́ги бы́ли про́даны за £10

8 (*fit, suit*): **to go with** подходи́ть* (подойти́* *perf*) к +*dat*

9 (*be about to, intend to*) собира́ться (собра́ться* *perf*) +*infin*

10 (*time: slowly*) тяну́ться (*impf*); (*quickly*) проходи́ть* (пройти́* *perf*)

11 (*event, activity*) проходи́ть* (пройти́* *perf*);

how did it go? ну как всё прошло?
12 (*be given*): **the job is to go to someone else** работу должны отдать кому-то другому; **the proceeds will go to charity** прибыль пойдёт на благотворительные цели
13 (*break etc*): **the fuse went** предохранитель *m* перегорел; **the leg of the chair went** ножка стула сломалась
14 (*be placed*): **the milk goes in the fridge** молоко нужно поставить в холодильник; **where does this cup go?** куда поставить эту чашку?; **the suitcase goes on top of the wardrobe** чемодан обычно лежит на шкафу
◆ *n* **1** (*try*): **to have a go (at sth/at doing sth)** пробовать* (попробовать* *perf*) (что-н/+*perf infin*)
2 (*turn*): **whose go is it?** (*in board games*) чей ход?; (*in sports*) чья (сейчас) очередь?
3 (*move*): **to be on the go** быть (*impf*) на ногах
▶ **go about** *vi* (*also:* **go around:** *rumour*) ходить* (*impf*)
◆ *vt fus:* **to go about one's business** заниматься (заняться* *perf*) своими делами; **how do I go about (doing) this?** как мне это сделать?
▶ **go after** *vt fus* (*person*) бежать (побежать* *perf*) (вдогонку) за +*instr*; **to go after a job** стремиться* (*impf*) получить работу
▶ **go against** *vt fus* (*subj: decision, verdict*): **to go against sb** быть (*impf*) не в чью-н пользу
▶ **go ahead** *vi* (*proceed*) продвигаться (продвинуться *perf*); (*event*): **to go ahead with** (*project*) приступить* (*perf*) к +*dat*; **may I begin? – yes, go ahead!** можно начать? – да, пожалуйста!
▶ **go along** *vi* идти (пойти* *perf*); **I went along with him/his decision** (*agree with*) я не стал противиться ему/его решению; **to go along with sb** (*accompany*) идти* (пойти* *perf*) с кем-н
▶ **go away** *vi* (*leave: on foot*) уходить* (уйти* *perf*); (*: by transport*) уезжать* (уехать* *perf*); **go away and think about it for a while** пойди и подумай немножко на этот счёт
▶ **go back** *vi* (*return*) возвращаться (вернуться* *perf*); (*go again: on foot*) идти* (пойти* *perf*) ещё раз *or* опять; (*: by transport*) ехать* (поехать* *perf*) ещё раз *or* опять; **we went back into the house** мы пошли обратно в дом; **I am never going back to her house again** я никогда больше не пойду к ней; **to go back to** (*date from*) относиться (*impf*) к +*dat*
▶ **go back on** *vt fus* (*promise, word*) не сдерживать (сдержать* *perf*) +*gen*
▶ **go by** *vi* (*years, time*) проходить (пройти* *perf*)
◆ *vt fus* (*book, rule*) делать (сделать *perf*) всё по +*dat*; **as time goes by** ... время идёт, и ...

▶ **go down** *vi* (*descend*) спускаться (спуститься* *perf*); (*ship*) тонуть* (затонуть* *perf*); (*sun*) заходить* (зайти* *perf*); (*prices, temperature*) падать (упасть* *perf*); (*swelling*) спадать (спасть* *perf*)
◆ *vt fus* (*stairs, ladder*) спускаться (спуститься* *perf*) с +*gen*; **that should go down well with him** это ему должно понравится; **he went to London/to see his sister** он поехал в Лондон/в гости к своей сестре
▶ **go for** *vt fus* (*fetch: paper, doctor*) идти* (пойти* *perf*) за +*instr*; (*choose, like*) любить* (*impf*); (*attack*) набрасываться (наброситься* *perf*) на +*acc*; **that goes for me too** и я тоже
▶ **go in** *vi* (*enter*) входить* (войти* *perf*); **it's time to go in** пора идти внутрь
▶ **go in for** *vt fus* принимать (принять* *perf*) участие в +*prp*; (*take up*) заняться* (*perf*) +*instr*
▶ **go into** *vt fus* (*enter*) входить* (войти* *perf*) в +*acc*; (*investigate*) рассматривать (рассмотреть* *perf*); (*take up*) заняться* (*perf*) +*instr*; **to go into detail** вдаваться* (*impf*) в подробности
▶ **go off** *vi* (*leave: on foot*) уходить* (уйти* *perf*); (*: by transport*) уезжать* (уехать* *perf*); (*food*) портиться* (испортиться* *perf*); (*bomb*) взрываться (взорваться* *perf*); (*gun*) выстрелить (*perf*); (*alarm*) звонить (зазвонить* *perf*); (*event*) проходить* (пройти* *perf*); (*lights*) выключаться (выключиться *perf*)
◆ *vt fus* разлюбить* (*perf*); **to go off to sleep** засыпать (заснуть *perf*)
▶ **go on** *vi*: **to go on (doing)** (*continue*) продолжать (*impf*) (+*infin*); (*happen*): **discussion, argument** идти* (*impf*); **life goes on** жизнь продолжается; **what's going on here?** что здесь происходит?; **we don't have enough evidence/information to go on** у нас нет достаточных доказательств/ информации
▶ **go on at** *vt fus* приставать* (*impf*) к +*dat*
▶ **go on with** *vt fus* продолжать (продолжить* *perf*)
▶ **go out** *vi* (*fire, light*) гаснуть* (погаснуть* *perf*); (*leave*): **to go out of** выходить* (выйти* *perf*) из +*gen*; **are you going out tonight?** (*for entertainment*) Вы сегодня вечером куда-нибудь идёте?
▶ **go over** *vi* идти* (пойти* *perf*)
◆ *vt fus* (*check*) просматривать (просмотреть* *perf*); **to go over sth in one's mind** повторять (повторить *perf*) что-н в уме
▶ **go round** *vi* (*circulate*) ходить* (*impf*); (*revolve*) вращаться (*impf*); (*suffice*) хватать (хватить *perf*) на всех; (*visit*): **to go round (to sb's)** заходить* (зайти* *perf*) (к кому-н);

---

* marks translations which have irregular inflections. The Russian-English side of the dictionary gives inflectional information.

(*make a detour*): **to go round (by)** (*on foot*)
идти* (пойти* *perf*) кругóм (чéрез +*acc*); (*by
transport*) éхать (поéхать *perf*) кругóм (чéрез
+*acc*)
▶ **go through** *vt fus* (*town etc*: *on foot*)
проходи́ть* (пройти́* *perf*) чéрез +*acc*; (: *by
transport*) проезжáть (проéхать* *perf*) чéрез
+*acc*; (*files, papers*) просмáтривать
(просмотрéть* *perf*); (*aloud: list*) читáть
(прочитáть* *perf*); (*practice*) проделывать
(проделать *perf*)
▶ **go through with** *vt fus* (*plan, crime*)
осуществля́ть (осуществи́ть* *perf*); **I couldn't
go through with it** я не мог осуществи́ть это
▶ **go under** *vi* (*also fig*) идти́* (пойти́* *perf*) под
вóду
▶ **go up** *vi* (*ascend*) поднимáться (подня́ться*
perf); (*price, level*) расти́* (вы́расти* *perf*);
(*buildings*) вырастáть (вы́расти* *perf*); **to go
up in flames** загорáться (*impf*)
▶ **go with** *vt fus* (*match*) походи́ть* (подойти́*
perf) к +*dat*
▶ **go without** *vt fus* (*treats*) остава́ться*
(остáться* *perf*) без +*gen*; **I can go without food
for 24 hours** я могу́ су́тки не есть.

goad [gəud] *vt* (*person*) подстрекáть (*impf*)
▶ **goad on** *vt* (*person*) подгоня́ть (*impf*).
go-ahead ['gəuəhɛd] *adj* предприи́мчивый
(предприи́чив) ♦ *n* (*for project*) добрó; **to give
sb the ~** давáть* (дать* *perf*) кому́-н добрó.
goal [gəul] *n* (*SPORT*) гол; (: *goal posts*) ворóта
mpl; (*aim*) цель *f*; **to score a ~** забивáть
(забить* *perf*) гол.
goal difference *n* рáзница мячéй.
goalie ['gəulɪ] *n* (*inf*) вратáрь* *m*, голки́пер.
goalkeeper ['gəulki:pəˀ] *n* вратáрь* *m*,
голки́пер.
goal post *n* боковáя штáнга, стóйка* ворóт.
goat [gəut] *n* (*billy*) козёл*; (*nanny*) козá.
gobble ['gɔbl] *vt* (*also:* ~ **down,** ~ **up**) лóпать
(слóпать *perf*), жрать* (сожрáть* *perf*).
go-between ['gəubɪtwi:n] *n* посрéдник(-ица).
Gobi Desert ['gəubɪ-] *n*: **the** ~ ~ пусты́ня
Гóби.
goblet ['gɔblɪt] *n* кýбок*.
goblin ['gɔblɪn] *n* гóблин.
gobsmacked ['gɔbsmækt] *adj*: **I was** ~ (*inf*) я
совершéнно обалдéл.
go-cart ['gəuka:t] *n* карт.
God [gɔd] *n* Бог ♦ *excl* Гóсподи!, о Бóже!
god [gɔd] *n* (*MYTHOLOGY, fig*) божествó*, бог*.
god-awful [gɔd'ɔ:fəl] *adj* (*inf!*) жýткий*,
кошмáрный*.
godchild ['gɔdtʃaɪld] *n* крéстник(-ица).
goddam ['gɔdæm] *adj* (*inf!*) прокля́тый (*!*)
goddamned ['gɔdæmd] *adj* (*inf!*) прокля́тый
(*!*)
goddaughter ['gɔdɔ:təˀ] *n* крéстница.
goddess ['gɔdɪs] *n* боги́ня.
godfather ['gɔdfɑ:ðəˀ] *n* крéстный отéц*.
God-fearing ['gɔdfɪərɪŋ] *adj* богобоя́зненный.

godforsaken ['gɔdfəseɪkən] *adj* забы́тый
Бóгом, забрóшенный*.
godmother ['gɔdmʌðəˀ] *n* крёстная мать* *f*.
godparent ['gɔdpɛərənt] *n* крёстный(-ая) *m(f)*
adj.
godsend ['gɔdsɛnd] *n* благодáть *f*.
godson ['gɔdsʌn] *n* крéстник.
goes [gəuz] *vb see* **go**.
gofer ['gəufəˀ] *n* (*inf*) мáльчик на побегýшках.
go-getter ['gəugɛtəˀ] *n* предприи́мчивый
человéк*.
goggle ['gɔgl] *vi* (*inf*): **to** ~ **at** тарáщиться
(вытарáщиться *perf*) на +*acc*.
goggles ['gɔglz] *npl* защи́тные очки́ *ntpl*.
going ['gəuɪŋ] *n* (*conditions*): **the** ~
обстоя́тельства *ntpl* ♦ *adj*: **the** ~ **rate**
существу́ющие расцéнки *fpl*; **this book is
heavy** ~ эта кни́га тру́дно читáется; **it was
hard** ~ поначáлу приходи́лось тру́дно; **a** ~
concern дéйствующее предприя́тие.
going-over [gəuɪŋ'əuvəˀ] *n* (*inf: examination*)
осмóтр; (*physical attack*) трёпка.
goings-on ['gəuɪŋz'ɔn] *npl* (*inf*) делá *ntpl*.
go-kart ['gəuka:t] *n* = **go-cart**.
gold [gəuld] *n* зóлото; (*SPORT: also:* ~ **medal**)
зóлото, золотáя медáль *f* ♦ *adj* золотóй; ~
reserves золотóй запáс.
golden ['gəuldən] *adj* (*made of gold*) золотóй;
(*gold in colour*) золоти́стый; (*opportunity,
future*) прекрáсный*.
golden age *n* золотóй век*.
golden handshake *n* (*BRIT*) *дéнежное
вознаграждéние при ухóде на пéнсию.*
golden rule *n* золотóе прáвило.
goldfish ['gəuldfɪʃ] *n* золотáя ры́бка*.
gold leaf *n* сусáльное зóлото.
gold medal *n* (*SPORT*) золотáя медáль *f*.
gold mine *n* золотóй при́иск *or* рудни́к*; (*fig*)
золотóе дно*.
gold-plated ['gəuld'pleɪtɪd] *adj* позолóченный.
goldsmith ['gəuldsmɪθ] *n* золоты́х дел
мáстер*.
gold standard *n* золотóй стандáрт.
golf [gɔlf] *n* гольф.
golf ball *n* мяч для игры́ в гольф; (*on
typewriter*) *металли́ческий шар с бу́квами в
электри́ческой печáтной маши́нке.*
golf club *n* (*organization*) клуб люби́телей
игры́ в гольф; (*stick*) клю́шка* для игры́ в
гольф.
golf course *n* пóле для игры́ в гольф.
golfer ['gɔlfəˀ] *n* игрóк* в гольф.
golfing ['gɔlfɪŋ] *adj* для игры́ в гольф.
gondola ['gɔndələ] *n* гондóла.
gondolier [gɔndə'lɪəˀ] *n* гондольéр.
gone [gɔn] *pp of* **go** ♦ *adj* уéхавший, ушéдший.
goner ['gɔnəˀ] *n* (*inf*) *n*: **I was a** ~ со мной бы́ло
всё покóнчено.
gong [gɔŋ] *n* гонг.
good [gud] *adj* хорóший*; (*pleasant*)
прия́тный*; (*kind*) дóбрый*; (*morally correct*)
прáвильный* ♦ *n* (*virtue*) добрó; (*benefit*)

по́льза; ~s *npl* (*COMM*) това́ры *mpl*; ~!
хорошо́!; **to be ~ at** име́ть (*impf*)
спосо́бности к +*dat*; **to be ~ for** (*useful*) быть*
(*impf*) поле́зным(-ой) для +*dat*; **it's ~ for you**
э́то Вам поле́зно (для здоро́вья); **it's a ~
thing you were there** хорошо́, что Вы бы́ли
там; **she is ~ with children** она́ уме́ет
обраща́ться с детьми́; **she is ~ with her
hands** у неё золоты́е ру́ки; **to feel ~**
чу́вствовать (*impf*) себя́ хорошо́; **it's ~ to see
you** о́чень прия́тно Вас ви́деть; **would you be
~ enough to ...?** не бу́дьте ли Вы так добры́
+*perf infin* ...?; **that's very ~ of you** э́то о́чень
ми́ло с Ва́шей стороны́; **is this any ~?** (*will it
do?*) э́то пойдёт?; (*what's it like?*)
понра́вилось ли э́то Вам?; **a ~ deal (of)**
большо́е коли́чество (+*gen*); **a ~ many** мно́го
+*gen*; **to take a ~ look** смотре́ть*
(посмотре́ть* *perf*) хороше́нько; **a ~ while
ago** о́чень давно́; **to make ~** (*damage*)
ремонти́ровать (отремонти́ровать *perf*);
(*loss*) восполня́ть (восполни́ть *perf*); **~
afternoon/evening!** до́брый день/ве́чер!; **~
morning!** до́брое у́тро!; **~ night!** (*on leaving*)
до свида́ния!; (*on going to bed*) споко́йной *or*
до́брой но́чи!; **he's up to no ~** он заду́мал
что́-то (плохо́е); **for the common ~** для
о́бщего бла́га; **it's no ~ complaining** что
то́лку жа́ловаться; **for ~** навсегда́; **~s and
chattels** ли́чные ве́щи*.

goodbye [gud'baɪ] *excl* до свида́ния; **to say ~
(to)** проща́ться (попроща́ться *perf*) (с +*instr*).

good-for-nothing ['gudfənʌθɪŋ] *adj*
никуды́шний.

Good Friday *n* Страстна́я пя́тница.

good-humoured ['gud'hju:məd] (*US* **good-
humored**) *adj* (*person*) добродушный*;
(*remark, joke*) до́брый*.

good-looking ['gud'lukɪŋ] *adj* краси́вый.

good-natured ['gud'neɪtʃəd] *adj* (*person*)
добродушный; (*pet*) послушный;
(*discussion*) споко́йный*.

goodness ['gudnɪs] *n* доброта́; **for ~ sake!**
ра́ди Бо́га!; **~ gracious!** Го́споди!

goods train *n* (*BRIT*) това́рный по́езд*.

goodwill [gud'wɪl] *n* (*of person*)
доброжела́тельность *f*; (*COMM*) прести́ж
фи́рмы.

goody-goody ['gudɪgudɪ] *n* (*pej*) па́инька* *m/f*.

gooey ['gu:ɪ] (*inf*) *adj* ли́пкий* (ли́пок).

goose [gu:s] (*pl* **geese**) *n* (*male*) гусь* *m*;
(*female*) гусы́ня.

gooseberry ['guzbərɪ] *n* крыжо́вник *no pl*; **he is
playing ~** (*BRIT*) он тре́тий ли́шний.

goose flesh *n* = **goose pimples**.

goose pimples *npl* гуси́ная ко́жа *fsg*.

goose step *n* (*MIL*) гуси́ный шаг.

GOP *n abbr* (*US*: *POL*: *inf*: = *Grand Old Party*)

неофициа́льное назва́ние Республика́нской
па́ртии США.

gopher ['gəufə'] *n* го́фер (колумби́йский
су́слик).

gore [gɔ:'] *vt* бода́ть (забода́ть *perf*) ♦ *n*
(запёкшаяся) кровь *f*.

gorge [gɔ:dʒ] *n* тесни́на, (у́зкое) уще́лье* ♦ *vt*:
to ~ o.s. (on) наеда́ться (нае́сться* *perf*)
(+*gen*).

gorgeous ['gɔ:dʒəs] *adj* великоле́пный,
прекра́сный.

gorilla [gə'rɪlə] *n* гори́лла.

gormless ['gɔ:mlɪs] *adj* (*BRIT*: *inf*) тупо́й*.

gorse [gɔ:s] *n* (*BOT*) утёсник.

gory ['gɔ:rɪ] *adj* (*details*) крова́вый; (*situation*)
кровопроли́тный*.

go-slow ['gəu'sləu] *n* (*BRIT*) сниже́ние те́мпа
рабо́ты (как вид забасто́вки).

gospel ['gɔspl] *n* (*REL*) ева́нгелие; (*doctrine*)
про́поведь *f*.

gossamer ['gɔsəmə'] *n* (*cobweb*) паути́нка;
(*light fabric*) газ.

gossip ['gɔsɪp] *n* (*rumours*) спле́тня*; (*chat*)
разгово́ры *mpl*; (*person*) спле́тник(-ица) ♦ *vi*
болта́ть (поболта́ть *perf*); **a piece of ~**
спле́тня*, слух.

gossip column *n* коло́нка* све́тской хро́ники.

got [gɔt] *pt*, *pp of* **get**.

Gothic ['gɔθɪk] *adj* готи́ческий*.

gotten ['gɔtn] *pp* (*US*) *of* **get**.

gouge [gaudʒ] *vt* (*also*: **~ out**: *hole etc*)
выда́лбливать (вы́долбить* *perf*); (: *initials*)
выреза́ть (вы́резать* *perf*); **to ~ sb's eyes out**
выка́лывать (вы́колоть *perf*) кому́-н глаза́.

gourd [guəd] *n* ты́ква.

gourmet ['guəmeɪ] *n* гурма́н.

gout [gaut] *n* (*MED*) пода́гра.

govern ['gʌvən] *vt* (*country, also LING*)
управля́ть (*impf*) +*instr*; (*event, conduct*)
руководи́ть* (*impf*) +*instr*.

governess ['gʌvənɪs] *n* гуверна́нтка*.

governing ['gʌvənɪŋ] *adj* (*POL*) пра́вящий*,
руководя́щий*.

governing body *n* (*of party*) руководя́щий*
о́рган; (*of university*) о́рган управле́ния.

government ['gʌvnmənt] *n* (*act of governing*)
управле́ние; (*governing body*)
прави́тельство ♦ *cpd* прави́тельственный;
local ~ ме́стное самоуправле́ние.

governmental [gʌvn'mɛntl] *adj*
прави́тельственный.

government housing *n* (*US*) жили́щный
ко́мплекс, постро́енный на госуда́рственные
сре́дства.

government stock *n* прави́тльственные
облига́ции и це́нные бума́ги.

governor ['gʌvənə'] *n* (*of state, colony*)
губерна́тор; (*of bank, school, hospital*)

---

* marks translations which have irregular inflections. The Russian-English side of the dictionary gives inflectional information.

дире́ктор*; (*BRIT: of prison*) нача́льник.
Govt *abbr* = **government**.
gown [gaun] *n* (*dress*) пла́тье*; (*of teacher: BRIT: of judge*) ма́нтия.
GP *n abbr* = **general practitioner**.
GPO *n abbr* (*BRIT: formerly*) = *General Post Office*; (*US*) *Government Printing Office*.
gr. *abbr* (*COMM*) = **gross**.
grab [græb] *vt* (*seize, also fig*) хвата́ть (схвати́ть* *perf*); (*food*) перехва́тывать (перехвати́ть* *perf*); (*sleep*) урыва́ть (урва́ть* *perf*) ♦ *vi*: **to ~ at** хвата́ться (ухвати́ться* *perf*) за +*acc*.
grace [greɪs] *n* гра́ция; (*REL*) моли́тва (*пе́ред едо́й*) ♦ *vt* (*honour*) удоста́ивать (удосто́ить *perf*); (*adorn*) украша́ть (укра́сить* *perf*); **5 days' ~** 5 дней отсро́чки; **with (a) good ~** любе́зно, с досто́инством; **with (a) bad ~** нелюбе́зно, бех досто́инства; **his sense of humour is his saving ~** его́ спаса́ет чу́вство ю́мора; **to say ~** моли́ться* (помоли́ться* *perf*) пе́ред едо́й.
graceful ['greɪsful] *adj* (*animal, person*) грацио́зный*; (*style, shape*) изя́щный*; (*refusal, behaviour*) досто́йный*.
gracious ['greɪʃəs] *adj* (*person, smile*) любе́зный*; (*house*) прекра́сный*; (*living*) краси́вый ♦ *excl*: (*good*) **~!** Бо́же мо́й!
gradation [grə'deɪʃən] *n* града́ция.
grade [greɪd] *n* (*COMM: quality*) сорт*; (*in hierarchy*) ра́нг; (*SCOL: mark*) оце́нка*; (*US: school year*) класс; (: *gradient*) укло́н ♦ *vt* (*rank, class*) распределя́ть (распредели́ть *perf*); (*products*) сортирова́ть (рассортирова́ть *perf*); **to make the ~** (*fig*) добива́ться (доби́ться* *perf*) своего́ *or* успе́ха.
grade crossing *n* (*US*) железнодоро́жный перее́зд.
grade school *n* (*US*) нача́льная шко́ла.
gradient ['greɪdɪənt] *n* (*of hill*) укло́н; (*GEOM*) градие́нт.
gradual ['grædjuəl] *adj* постепе́нный*.
gradually ['grædjuəlɪ] *adv* постепе́нно.
graduate [*n* 'grædjuɪt, *vi* 'grædjueɪt] *n* выпускни́к*(-и́ца) ♦ *vi*: **to ~ from** зака́нчивать (зако́нчить *perf*); **I ~d last year** я зако́нчил университе́т в про́шлом году́.
graduated pension ['grædjueɪtɪd-] *n* пе́нсия, увели́чивающаяся в зави́симости от ста́жа рабо́ты.
graduation [grædju'eɪʃən] *n* (*ceremony: at university*) церемо́ния вруче́ния дипло́ма; (: *US*) ≈ церемо́ния вруче́ния аттеста́та.
graffiti [grə'fi:tɪ] *n, npl* графи́ти *nt ind*.
graft [grɑ:ft] *n* (*AGR*) приви́вка*; (*MED*) переса́дка* (*ко́жи и́ли ко́стной тка́ни*); (*BRIT: inf: hard work*) тяжёлая рабо́та; (*bribery*) взя́точничество ♦ *vi*: **to ~** (**onto**) (*AGR, also fig*) привива́ть (приви́ть* *perf*) (к +*dat*); (*MED*) переса́живать (пересади́ть* *perf*)

(на +*acc*).
grain [greɪn] *n* (*seed*) зерно́*; (*no pl: cereals*) хле́бные зла́ки *mpl*; (*US: corn*) зерно́; (*of sand*) песчи́нка*; (*of salt*) крупи́ца; (*of wood*) воло́кно*; **however much it goes against the ~, I ...** (*fig*) как бы э́то ни противоре́чило мои́м при́нципам, я ....
gram [græm] *n* гра́мм.
grammar ['græmə*] *n* грамма́тика; (*book*) уче́бник грамма́тики.
grammar school *n* (*BRIT*) сре́дняя шко́ла (*для одарённых дете́й*).
grammatical [grə'mætɪkl] *adj* граммати́ческий*.
gramme [græm] *n* = **gram**.
gramophone ['græməfəun] *n* (*BRIT*) граммофо́н.
granary ['grænərɪ] *n* амба́р; (*larger*) зернохрани́лище.
Granary bread *or* **loaf®** *n* хлеб и́ли буха́нка из муки́ кру́пного помо́ла с це́лыми зёрнами внутри́.
grand [grænd] (*pl ~*) *adj* грандио́зный*; (*gesture*) вели́чественный*; (*inf: wonderful*) великоле́пный*, восхити́тельный* ♦ *n* (*inf*) ты́сяча.
grandchild ['græntʃaɪld] (*pl ~ren*) *n* внук(-у́чка*).
grandchildren ['græntʃɪldrən] *npl of* **grandchild**.
granddad ['grændæd] *n* (*inf*) де́душка* *m*.
granddaughter ['grændɔ:tə*] *n* вну́чка*.
grandeur ['grændjə*] *n* великоле́пие.
grandfather ['grændfɑ:ðə*] *n* де́душка* *m*.
grandiose ['grændɪəus] *adj* грандио́зный*.
grand jury *n* (*US*) прися́жные, реша́ющие вопро́с о преда́нии суду́.
grandma ['grænmɑ:] *n* (*inf*) ба́бушка*.
grandmother ['grænmʌðə*] *n* ба́бушка*.
grandpa ['grænpɑ:] *n* (*inf*) = **granddad**.
grandparents ['grændpɛərənts] *npl* де́душка* *m* и ба́бушка*.
grand piano *n* роя́ль *m*.
Grand Prix ['grɑ:'pri:] *n* гран-при́ *m ind*.
grandson ['grænsʌn] *n* внук.
grandstand ['grændstænd] *n* (*SPORT*) центра́льная трибу́на.
grand total *n* о́бщая су́мма.
granite ['grænɪt] *n* грани́т.
granny ['grænɪ] *n* (*inf*) ба́бушка*.
grant [grɑ:nt] *vt* (*money, visa*) выдава́ть (вы́дать* *perf*); (*pension*) назнача́ть (назна́чить *perf*); (*request*) удовлетворя́ть (удовлетвори́ть *perf*); (*admit*) признава́ть (призна́ть* *perf*) ♦ *n* (*SCOL*) стипе́ндия; (*ADMIN*) субси́дия; **to take sb/sth for ~ed** принима́ть (приня́ть* *perf*) кого́-н/что́-н как до́лжное; **to ~ that** признава́ть (призна́ть* *perf*), что.
granulated sugar ['grænjuleɪtɪd-] *n* са́харный песо́к*.
granule ['grænju:l] *n* (*of coffee*) гра́нула; (*of*

salt) крупи́ца.
grape [greɪp] *n* виногра́д* *no pl*; **a bunch of** ~s кисть* *f or* гроздь* *f* виногра́да.
grapefruit ['greɪpfruːt] (*pl* ~ *or* ~**s**) *n* грейпфру́т.
grapevine ['greɪpvaɪn] *n* виногра́дная лоза́*; **I heard on the** ~ **that** ... я слы́шал, что ..., говоря́т, что ....
graph [grɑːf] *n* (*diagram*) гра́фик.
graphic ['græfɪk] *adj* (*account, description*) я́ркий*; (*design*) изобрази́тельный; ~ **art** гра́фика; *see also* **graphics**.
graphic designer *n* худо́жник-офор́митель *m*.
graphic equalizer *n* графи́ческий* выра́вниватель *m*.
graphics ['græfɪks] *n* гра́фика ◆ *npl* рису́нки *mpl*.
graphite ['græfaɪt] *n* графи́т.
graph paper *n* миллиметро́вка.
grapple ['græpl] *vi*: **to** ~ **with sb** схва́тываться (схвати́ться* *perf*) с кем-н; **to** ~ **with a problem** би́ться* (*impf*) над пробле́мой.
grasp [grɑːsp] *vt* (*also fig*) схва́тывать (схвати́ть* *perf*) ◆ *n* (*grip*) хва́тка; (*understanding*) понима́ние; **the vase slipped from my** ~ ва́за выскользнула из мои́х рук; **success was now within his** ~ успе́х был тепе́рь в его́ рука́х; **to have a good** ~ **of sth** (*fig*) хорошо́ разбира́ться (*impf*) в чём-н
▸ **grasp at** *vt fus* (*rope etc*) хвата́ться (ухвати́ться* *perf*) за +*acc*; (*fig: opportunity*) цепля́ться (уцепи́ться* *perf*) за +*acc*.
grasping ['grɑːspɪŋ] *adj* (*greedy*) жа́дный*.
grass [grɑːs] *n* трава́*; (*lawn*) газо́н; (*BRIT: inf: informer*) стука́ч*; (: *ex-terrorist*) доно́счик.
grasshopper ['grɑːshɔpə'] *n* кузне́чик.
grass-roots ['grɑːsruːts] *adj* (*support*) низово́й; (*member*) рядово́й.
grass snake *n* уж*.
grassy ['grɑːsɪ] *adj* (*bank, slope*) травяни́стый.
grate [greɪt] *n* ками́нная решётка* ◆ *vt* (*CULIN*) тере́ть* (натере́ть* *perf*) ◆ *vi* (*metal, chalk*): **to** ~ (**on**) скрипе́ть* (*impf*) (по +*dat*).
grateful ['greɪtful] *adj* (*person*) благода́рный* (благода́рен); ~ **thanks** и́скренняя благода́рность.
gratefully ['greɪtfəlɪ] *adv* благода́рно.
grater ['greɪtə'] *n* тёрка*.
gratification [grætɪfɪ'keɪʃən] *n* удовлетворе́ние.
gratify ['grætɪfaɪ] *vt* (*person*) ра́довать (пора́довать *perf*); (*whim, desire*) удовлетворя́ть (удовлетвори́ть *perf*).
gratifying ['grætɪfaɪɪŋ] *adj* (*pleasing*) прия́тный* (прия́тен).
grating ['greɪtɪŋ] *n* решётка* ◆ *adj* (*noise*) ре́зкий*.
gratitude ['grætɪtjuːd] *n* благода́рность *f*.

gratuitous [grə'tjuːɪtəs] *adj* (*violence, cruelty*) бессмы́сленный* (бессмы́слен).
gratuity [grə'tjuːɪtɪ] *n* (*tip*) чаевы́е *pl adj*.
grave [greɪv] *n* моги́ла ◆ *adj* серьёзный* (серьёзен); (*mistake*) роково́й.
grave digger *n* моги́льщик.
gravel ['grævl] *n* гра́вий.
gravely ['greɪvlɪ] *adv* серьёзно; ~ **ill** тяжело́ больно́й* (бо́лен).
gravestone ['greɪvstəun] *n* надгро́бие.
graveyard ['greɪvjɑːd] *n* кла́дбище.
gravitas ['grævɪtæs] *n* многозначи́тельность *f*.
gravitate ['grævɪteɪt] *vi*: **to** ~ **towards** стреми́ться* (*impf*) *or* тяну́ться* (*impf*) к +*dat*.
gravity ['grævɪtɪ] *n* (*PHYS*) си́ла тя́жести; (*seriousness*) серьёзность *f*.
gravy ['greɪvɪ] *n* (*meat juices*) подли́вка; (*sauce*) со́ус*.
gravy boat *n* со́усник.
gravy train *n* (*inf*): **to ride the** ~ ~ име́ть (*impf*) лёгкий за́работок.
gray [greɪ] *adj* (*US*) = **grey**.
graze [greɪz] *vi* пасти́сь* (*impf*) ◆ *vt* (*touch lightly*) задева́ть (заде́ть* *perf*); (*scrape*) цара́пать (оцара́пать *perf*) ◆ *n* цара́пина.
grazing ['greɪzɪŋ] *n* (*pasture*) па́стбище.
grease [griːs] *n* (*lubricant*) сма́зка*; (*fat*) жир* ◆ *vt* сма́зывать (сма́зать* *perf*); **to** ~ **sb's palm** (*fig*) дава́ть* (дать* *perf*) кому́-н взя́тку.
grease gun *n* сма́зочный шприц.
greasepaint ['griːspeɪnt] *n* (театра́льный) грим.
greaseproof paper ['griːspruːf-] *n* (*BRIT*) жиронепроница́емая бума́га.
greasy ['griːsɪ] *adj* жи́рный*; (*clothes*) заса́ленный* (заса́лен); (*BRIT: road, surface*) ско́льзкий*.
great [greɪt] *adj* (*large*) большо́й*; (*heat, pain*) си́льный*; (*city*) знамени́тый*; (*man*) вели́кий*, знамени́тый*; (*inf: terrific*) замеча́тельный*; **they're** ~ **friends** они́ больши́е друзья́*; **we had a** ~ **time** мы замеча́тельно провели́ вре́мя; **it was** ~! э́то бы́ло замеча́тельно *or* здо́рово!; **the** ~ **thing is that** ... са́мое гла́вное то, что ....
Great Barrier Reef *n*: **the** ~ ~ ~ Большо́й Барье́рный риф.
Great Britain *n* Великобрита́ния.
greater ['greɪtə'] *adj*: ~ **Calcutta** больша́я Калькýтта; **G**~ **Manchester** большо́й Манче́стер.
great-grandchild [greɪt'græntʃaɪld] (*pl* ~**ren**) *n* пра́внук*(-учка*).
great-grandchildren [greɪt'græntʃɪldrən] *npl of* **great-grandchild**.
great-grandfather [greɪt'grænfɑːðə'] *n* праде́душка *m*.
great-grandmother [greɪt'grænmʌðə'] *n*

---

* marks translations which have irregular inflections. The Russian-English side of the dictionary gives inflectional information.

прабáбушка*.
Great Lakes *npl*: **the ~ ~** Большие Озёра *ntpl*.
greatly ['greItlI] *adv* óчень; (*influenced*) в
значительной стéпени.
greatness ['greItnIs] *n* (*importance*) велúчие.
Grecian ['gri:ʃən] *adj* грéческий*.
Greece [gri:s] *n* Грéция.
greed [gri:d] *n* (*greediness*) жáдность *f*; (*for
power, wealth*) жáжда.
greedily ['gri:dIlI] *adv* жáдно.
greedy ['gri:dI] *adj* жáдный* (жáден).
Greek [gri:k] *adj* грéческий ♦ *n* (*person*) грек
(гречáнка*); (*LING*) грéческий* язык*; **ancient/
modern ~** древнегрéческий*/совремéнный
грéческий* язык*.
green [gri:n] *adj* зелёный ♦ *n* (*colour*) зелёный
цвет; (*stretch of grass*) лужáйка*; (*on golf
course*) площáдка вокрýг лýнки, покрытая
травóй; (*also*: **village ~**) газóн в цéнтре
дерéвни; **~s** *npl* (*vegetables*) óвощи *mpl*; (*POL*)
:**the G~s** зелёные *pl adj*; **the G~ Party** пáртия
зелёных; **he has ~ fingers** *or* (*US*) **a ~ thumb**
(*fig*) что он ни посáдит, всё у негó растёт; **to
give sb the ~ light** давáть* (дать* *perf*) комý-н
зелёную улицу.
green belt *n* (*round town*) зелёная зóна,
зелёный пояс*.
green card *n* (*BRIT*: *AUT*) зелёная кáрточка
(*для страхóвки автомобиля за рубежóм*);
(*US*: *ADMIN*) зелёная кáрточка (*необходимый
для трудоустрóйства*).
greenery ['gri:nərI] *n* зéлень *f*.
greenfly ['gri:nflaI] *n* (*BRIT*) тля.
greengage ['gri:ngeIdʒ] *n* слúва-венчéрка.
greengrocer ['gri:ngrəusə'] *n* (*BRIT*) зеленщик*
(*продавéц овощéй и фрýктов*).
greenhouse ['gri:nhaus] *n* теплúца.
greenhouse effect *n*: **the ~ ~** парникóвый
эффéкт.
greenhouse gas *n* одúн из гáзов,
вызывáющий теплúчный эффéкт.
greenish ['gri:nIʃ] *adj* зеленовáтый.
Greenland ['gri:nlənd] *n* Гренлáндия.
Greenlander ['gri:nləndə'] *n* жúтель(ница) *m(f)*
Гренлáндии.
green pepper *n* зелёный пéрец*.
greet [gri:t] *vt* (*person*) привéтствовать*
(попривéтствовать *perf*), здорóваться
(поздорóваться *perf*); (*receive*: *news*)
встречáть (встрéтить* *perf*).
greeting ['gri:tIŋ] *n* (*welcome*) привéтствие;
Christmas/birthday ~s поздравляю с
Рождествóм/с днём рождéния; **Season's ~s**
поздравлéния с Рождествóм и Нóвым
гóдом.
greeting(s) card *n* поздравúтельная
открытка*.
gregarious [grə'gɛərIəs] *adj* общúтельный*
(общúтелен).
Grenada [grə'neIdə] *n* Гренáда.
grenade [grə'neId] *n* (*also*: **hand ~**) гранáта.

grew [gru:] *pt of* **grow**.
grey [greI] (*US* **gray**) *adj* сéрый* (сер); (*hair*)
седóй; (*dismal*) мрáчный* (мрáчен); **to go ~**
седéть (поседéть *perf*).
grey-haired [greI'hɛəd] *adj* седóй*.
greyhound ['greIhaund] *n* борзáя *f adj*.
grid [grId] *n* (*pattern*) сéтка*, сеть *f*; (*grating*)
решётка*; (*ELEC*) энергосистéма; (*US*: *AUT*)
решётка радиáтора.
griddle [grIdl] *n* (*on cooker*) плóский
металлúческий диск, испóльзуемый как
сковородá.
gridiron ['grIdaIən] *n* решётка грúля.
gridlock ['grIdlɒk] *n* (*US*: *of traffic etc*) затóр.
grief [gri:f] *n* гóре; **to come to ~** (*plan*)
рýшиться (рýхнуть *perf*); (*person*) терпéть*
(потерпéть* *perf*) неудáчу; **good ~!** Бóже
мой!
grievance ['gri:vəns] *n* (*complaint*) жáлоба.
grieve [gri:v] *vi* горевáть* (*impf*) ♦ *vt* огорчáть
(огорчúть *perf*); **to ~ for** горевáть (*impf*) о
+*prp*.
grievous ['gri:vəs] *adj* (*mistake, injury*)
серьёзный*; (*shock*) сúльный.
grievous bodily harm *n* (*LAW*) тяжёлые
телéсные повреждéния *ntpl*.
grill [grIl] *n* (*on cooker*) гриль *m*; (*grilled food*:
also: **mixed ~**) жáренные на грúле продýкты
mpl; (*restaurant*) = **grillroom** ♦ *vt* (*BRIT*) жáрить
(пожáрить *perf*) (на грúле); (*inf*: *question*)
допрáшивать (допросúть* *perf*) с
пристрáстием.
grille [grIl] *n* решётка*; (*AUT*) *решётка
радиáтора*.
grillroom ['grIlrum] *n* ≈ гриль-бар.
grim [grIm] *adj* (*place, person*) мрáчный*
(мрáчен); (*situation*) тяжёлый* (тяжёл).
grimace [grI'meIs] *n* гримáса ♦ *vi*
гримáсничать (*impf*).
grime [graIm] *n* (*from soot, smoke*) кóпоть *f*;
(*from mud*) грязь *f*.
grimy ['graImI] *adj* (*dirty*) грязный* (грязен).
grin [grIn] *n* ухмылка* ♦ *vi*: **to ~** (**at**) (широкó)
улыбáться (улыбнýться *perf*) (+*dat*).
grind [graInd] (*pt, pp* **ground**) *vt* (*coffee, pepper
etc*) молóть (смолóть* *perf*); (*US*: *meat*)
пропускáть (пропустúть* *perf*) чéрез
мясорýбку; (*make sharp*: *knife etc*) точúть*
(наточúть* *perf*); (*polish*: *gem, lens*)
шлифовáть (отшлифовáть *perf*) ♦ *vi* (*car
gears*) скрежетáть* (*impf*) ♦ *vt* (*work*)
изнурúтельная рабóта; **to ~ one's teeth**
скрежетáть* (*impf*) зубáми; **to ~ one's heel
into the ground** вдáвливать (вдавúть* *perf*)
каблýк в зéмлю; **to ~ to a halt** (*vehicle*)
останáвливаться (остановúться* *perf*) с
лязгом; (*fig*) застóпориться (*perf*); **the daily ~**
(*inf*) рутúна бýдней.
grinder ['graIndə'] *n* (*for coffee*) кофемóлка*;
(*for waste disposal etc*) дробúлка*.
grindstone ['graIndstəun] *n*: **to keep one's nose**

to the ~ рабо́тать *(impf)* без переды́шки.

grip [grɪp] *n* (*of person*) хва́тка; (: *control, grasp*) схва́тывание; (*of tyre*) сцепле́ние; (*handle*) ру́чка*; (*holdall*) доро́жная су́мка* ♦ *vt* (*object*) схва́тывать (схвати́ть* *perf*); (*audience, attention*) захва́тывать (захвати́ть* *perf*); **to come to** ~**s with** (*problem, difficulty*) бра́ться* (взя́ться* *perf*) за реше́ние +*gen*; **to** ~ **the road** (*car*) име́ть *(impf)* хоро́шее сцепле́ние с доро́гой; **to lose one's** ~ (*tyres*) стира́ться (стере́ться* *perf*); (*shoes*) изна́шиваться (износи́ться* *perf*); (*fig*) теря́ть (потеря́ть *perf*) хва́тку.

gripe [graɪp] *n* (*inf: complaint*) жа́лоба ♦ *vi* (*inf*) ворча́ть *(impf)*; **the** ~**s** (*MED*) ко́лики *pl*.

gripping ['grɪpɪŋ] *adj* захва́тывающий*.

grisly ['grɪzlɪ] *adj* ужа́сный*.

grist [grɪst] *n* (*fig*): **it's all** ~ **to the mill** э́то принесёт по́льзу.

gristle ['grɪsl] *n* (*on meat*) хрящ*.

grit [grɪt] *n* (*sand*) песо́к*; (*stone*) гра́вий; (*determination, courage*) вы́держка ♦ *vt* (*road*) посыпа́ть (посы́пать* *perf*) гра́вием; ~**s** *npl* (*US*) дроблёная кукуру́за *fsg*; **to** ~ **one's teeth** сти́скивать (сти́снуть *perf*) зу́бы; **I've got a piece of** ~ **in my eye** мне в глаз попа́ла сори́нка.

grizzle ['grɪzl] *vi* (*BRIT*) хны́кать* *(impf)*.

grizzly ['grɪzlɪ] *n* (*also*: ~ **bear**) гри́зли *m ind*.

groan [grəʊn] *n* (*of person*) стон ♦ *vi* (*person: in pain*) стона́ть* *(impf)*; (: *in disapproval*) тяжело́ вздыха́ть (вздохну́ть *perf*); (*tree, floorboard*) скрипе́ть *(impf)*.

grocer ['grəʊsə^r] *n* бакале́йщик.

groceries ['grəʊsərɪz] *npl* бакале́я *fsg*.

grocer's (shop) *n* бакале́йный магази́н.

grog [grɔg] *n* (*drink*) грог*.

groggy ['grɔgɪ] *adj*: **I feel** ~ у меня́ подка́шиваются но́ги.

groin [grɔɪn] *n* пах*.

groom [gru:m] *n* (*for horse*) ко́нюх; (*also*: **bridegroom**) жени́х* ♦ *vt* (*horse*) уха́живать *(impf)* за +*instr*; (*fig*): **to** ~ **sb for** (*job*) гото́вить* (пригото́вить* *perf*) кого́-н к +*dat*; **well-**~**ed** (*person*) ухо́женный* (ухо́жен).

groove [gru:v] *n* желобо́к*; (*habit*) рути́на.

grope [grəʊp] *vi*: **to** ~ **for** иска́ть *(impf)* о́щупью; (*fig*) нащу́пывать *(impf)*; **to** ~ **one's way to** дви́гаться *(impf)* о́щупью к +*dat*.

gross [grəʊs] *adj* (*vulgar*) вульга́рный*; (*flagrant: neglect, injustice*) вопию́щий*; (*COMM: income*) валово́й ♦ *n inv* (*twelve dozen*) гросс (*12 дю́жин*) ♦ *vt* (*COMM*): **to** ~ **£500,000** получа́ть (получи́ть* *perf*) о́бщую при́быль в £500.000; ~ **weight** вес бру́тто.

gross domestic product *n* валово́й вну́тренний* проду́кт.

grossly ['grəʊslɪ] *adv* (*greatly*) чрезме́рно.

gross national product *n* валово́й национа́льный проду́кт.

gross profit *n* валова́я при́быль *f*.

gross sales *npl* валово́й объём *msg* прода́жи.

grotesque [grə'tɛsk] *adj* гроте́скный*.

grotto ['grɔtəʊ] *n* грот.

grotty ['grɔtɪ] *adj* (*inf: dreadful*) парши́вый (парши́в).

grouch [graʊtʃ] (*inf*) *vi* брюзжа́ть *(impf)* ♦ *n* (*person*) брюзга́ *m/f*.

ground [graʊnd] *pt, pp of* **grind** ♦ *n* (*earth, land*) земля́*; (*floor*) пол; (*SPORT*) по́ле; (*US: also*: ~ **wire**) заземле́ние; (*reason: usu pl*) основа́ние ♦ *vt* (*US: ELEC*) заземля́ть (заземли́ть *perf*) ♦ *adj* (*coffee etc*) мо́лотый ♦ *vi* (*ship*) сади́ться* (сесть* *perf*) на мель; ~**s** *npl* (*of coffee*) гу́ща *fsg*; **school** ~**s** пришко́льный уча́сток*; **sports** ~ спорти́вная площа́дка*; **on the** ~ на земле́; **to the** ~ (*burnt*) дотла́; **below** ~ под землёй; **to gain** ~ продвига́ться (продви́нуться *perf*) вперёд; **to lose** ~ отступа́ть (отступи́ть* *perf*); **common** ~ вопро́с, в кото́ром спо́рящие сто́роны схо́дятся; **on the** ~**s that** на том основа́нии, что; **the plane was** ~**ed by the fog** самолёт не мог подня́ться в во́здух из-за тума́на.

ground cloth *n* (*US*) = **groundsheet**.

ground control *n* (*AVIAT, SPACE*) слу́жбы *fpl* назе́много контро́ля *or* управле́ния.

ground floor *n* пе́рвый эта́ж*.

grounding ['graʊndɪŋ] *n* (*in education*) подгото́вка.

groundless ['graʊndlɪs] *adj* беспо́чвенный*, необосно́ванный*.

groundnut ['graʊndnʌt] *n* земляно́й оре́х.

ground rent *n* (*BRIT*) земе́льная ре́нта.

ground rule *n* основно́е пра́вило.

groundsheet ['graʊndʃi:t] *n* (*BRIT*) водонепроница́емая ткань *f* (*испо́льзуемая в похо́дах для подкла́дки под спа́льные мешки́*).

groundskeeper ['graʊndzki:pə^r] *n* (*US*) = **groundsman**.

groundsman ['graʊndzmən] *irreg n* (*SPORT*) слу́жащий стадио́на и́ли па́рка поддержива́ющий поря́док.

ground staff *n* (*AVIAT*) назе́мный персона́л.

ground swell *n*: ~ ~ **of opinion (against)** нараста́ющее чу́вство проте́ста (про́тив +*gen*).

ground-to-air ['graʊntu'ɛə^r] *adj* противовозду́шный*.

ground-to-ground ['graʊntə'graʊnd] *adj*: ~ **missile** управля́емая раке́та кла́сса „земля́-земля́".

groundwork ['graʊndwə:k] *n* (*preparation*) фунда́мент, осно́ва.

group [gru:p] *n* гру́ппа ♦ *vt* (*also*: ~ **together**:

---

people, things etc) группирова́ть (сгруппирова́ть *perf*) ◆ *vi* (*also:* ~ **together**) группирова́ться (сгруппирова́ться *perf*).

groupie [ˈgruːpɪ] *n* деви́ца из антура́жа (*поп-гру́ппы, певца́ итп*).

group therapy *n* группова́я терапи́я.

grouse [graus] *n inv* (*bird*) (шотла́ндская) куропа́тка* ◆ *vi* (*complain*) ворча́ть (*impf*).

grove [grəuv] *n* ро́ща.

grovel [ˈgrɔvl] *vi* (*crawl*) по́лзать (*impf*); (*fig*): **to** ~ **(before)** заи́скивать (*impf*) (пе́ред +*instr*).

grow [grəu] (*pt* **grew**, *pp* **grown**) *vi* расти́* (вы́расти* *perf*); (*increase*) увели́чиваться (увели́читься *perf*); (*become*): **to** ~ **rich/weak** станови́ться* (стать* *perf*) бога́тым(-ой)/ сла́бым(-ой) ◆ *vt* (*roses, vegetables*) выра́щивать (вы́растить* *perf*); (*beard, hair*) отра́щивать (отрасти́ть* *perf*); **to** ~ **(out of** *or* **from)** (*city, society*) выраста́ть (вы́расти* *perf*) (из +*gen*); (*idea, plan*) возника́ть (возни́кнуть *perf*) (из +*gen*); **to** ~ **tired of waiting** устава́ть* (уста́ть* *perf*) от ожида́ния

▶ **grow apart** *vi* (*fig*) отдаля́ться (отдали́ться *perf*) друг от дру́га

▶ **grow away from** *vt fus* (*fig*) отдаля́ться (отдали́ться *perf*) от +*gen*

▶ **grow on** *vt fus*: **that painting is ~ing on me** э́та карти́на нра́вится мне всё бо́льше

▶ **grow out of** *vt fus* (*clothes*) выраста́ть (вы́расти* *perf*) из +*gen*; (*habit*) перераста́ть (перерасти́* *perf*); **he'll** ~ **out of it** он перераста́ть э́то

▶ **grow up** *vi* (*child*) расти́* (вы́расти* *perf*), взросле́ть (повзросле́ть *perf*); (*develop: idea, friendship*) возника́ть (возни́кнуть *perf*).

grower [ˈgrəuəʳ] *n* (*BOT*) садово́д; **lily/rose** ~ садово́д, разводя́щий ли́лии/ро́зы.

growing [ˈgrəuɪŋ] *adj* (*increasing*) расту́щий; ~ **pains** (*MED*) невралги́ческие или ревмати́ческие бо́ли в де́тском во́зрасте; (*fig*) боле́знь *f* ро́ста.

growl [graul] *vi* (*dog*) рыча́ть (зарыча́ть *perf*); (*person*) рыча́ть (прорыча́ть *perf*).

grown [grəun] *pp of* **grow**.

grown-up [grəunˈʌp] *n* (*adult*) взро́слый(-ая) *m(f) adj* ◆ *adj* (*son, daughter*) взро́слый.

growth [grəuθ] *n* (*development*) рост; (*increase*) приро́ст; (*of weeds*) за́росли *fpl*; (*of beard*) щети́на; (*MED*) о́пухоль *f*.

growth rate *n* темп ро́ста.

grub [grʌb] *n* (*larva*) личи́нка*; (*inf: food*) жратва́ ◆ *vi*: **to** ~ **about** *or* **around (for)** ры́ться* (*impf*) (в по́исках +*gen*).

grubby [ˈgrʌbɪ] *adj* (*also fig*) гря́зный* (гря́зен).

grudge [grʌdʒ] *n* (*grievance*) недово́льство ◆ *vt*: **to** ~ **sb sth** жале́ть (пожале́ть *perf*) что-н для кого́-н; **to bear sb a** ~ быть* (*impf*) на кого́-н в оби́де.

grudging [ˈgrʌdʒɪŋ] *adj* (*respect, silence*) вы́нужденный; (*praise*) скупо́й.

grudgingly [ˈgrʌdʒɪŋlɪ] *adv* неохо́тно.

gruelling [ˈgruəlɪŋ] (*US* **grueling**) *adj* изнури́тельный* (изнури́телен), тяжёлый* (тяжёл).

gruesome [ˈgruːsəm] *adj* (*tale, scene*) жу́ткий*.

gruff [grʌf] *adj* (*voice*) хри́плый* (хрипл); (*manner*) ре́зкий* (ре́зок).

grumble [ˈgrʌmbl] *vi* ворча́ть (*impf*).

grumpy [ˈgrʌmpɪ] *adj* сварли́вый (сварли́в).

grunge [grʌndʒ] *n* стиль *m* грю́ндж.

grunt [grʌnt] *vi* (*pig*) хрю́кать (хрю́кнуть *perf*); (*person*) бурча́ть (бу́ркнуть *perf*) ◆ *n* (*see vb*) хрю́канье; бурча́ние.

G-string [ˈdʒiːstrɪŋ] *n* (*garment*) тип откры́тых пла́вок.

GSUSA *n abbr* (= *Girl Scouts of the United States of America*) организа́ция де́вочек-ска́утов США.

GT *abbr* (*AUT*. = *gran turismo*) дорого́й двухме́стный закры́тый автомоби́ль.

GU *abbr* (*US*: *POST*) = Guam.

guarantee [gærənˈtiː] *n* (*assurance*) поручи́тельство; (*COMM*: *warranty*) гара́нтия ◆ *vt* гаранти́ровать (*impf/perf*); **he can't** ~ **(that) he'll come** он не мо́жет поручи́ться за то, что он придёт.

guarantor [gærənˈtɔː] *n* (*COMM*) поручи́тель (ница) *m(f)*.

guard [gɑːd] *n* (*one person*) часово́й, охра́нник; (*squad*) охра́на; (*MIL*) карау́л; (*BOXING, FENCING*) оборони́тельная сто́йка; (*BRIT: RAIL*) проводни́к*(-и́ца); (*on machine*) предохрани́тельное устро́йство; (*also:* **fireguard**) предохрани́тельная решётка* (*пе́ред ками́ном*) ◆ *vt* (*prisoner*) охраня́ть (*impf*); (*secret*) храни́ть (сохрани́ть *perf*); (*place, person*): **to** ~ **(against)** охраня́ть (*impf*) (от +*gen*); **to be on one's** ~ быть* (*impf*) насторо́же *or* начеку́

▶ **guard against** *vt fus* (*prevent: disease, damage etc*) предохраня́ть (*impf*) от +*gen*.

guard dog *n* сторожева́я соба́ка.

guarded [ˈgɑːdɪd] *adj* (*statement, reply*) осторо́жный* (осторо́жен).

guardian [ˈgɑːdɪən] *n* (*LAW: of minor*) опеку́н*; (*defender*) защи́тник(-ица).

guardrail [ˈgɑːdreɪl] *n* пери́ла *pl*.

guard's van *n* (*BRIT: RAIL*) бага́жный ваго́н.

Guatemala [gwɑːtɪˈmɑːlə] *n* Гватема́ла.

Guatemalan [gwɑːtɪˈmɑːlən] *adj* гватема́льский.

Guernsey [ˈgəːnzɪ] *n* Ге́рнси.

guerrilla [gəˈrɪlə] *n* партиза́н*(ка*).

guerrilla warfare *n* партиза́нская война́*.

guess [gɛs] *vt* (*estimate: number etc*) счита́ть (подсчита́ть *perf*) приблизи́тельно; (*: distance*) рассчи́тывать (рассчита́ть *perf*) приблизи́тельно; (*correct answer*) уга́дывать (угада́ть *perf*) ◆ *vi* дога́дываться (*impf*) ◆ *n* (*attempt at correct answer*) дога́дка; **to take** *or* **have a** ~ отга́дывать (отгада́ть *perf*); **my** ~ **is that ...** мне сдаётся, что ...; **I** ~ ...

(US) мне ка́жется ...; **I ~ you're right** Вы,
наве́рное, пра́вы; **to keep sb ~ing** держа́ть*
(impf) кого́-н в неве́дении.
guesstimate ['gɛstɪmɪt] n (inf) прики́дка.
guesswork ['gɛswɜ:k] n (speculation) дога́дки*
fpl, предположе́ния ntpl; **I got the answer by ~**
я угада́л отве́т.
guest [gɛst] n (visitor) гость*(я) m(f); (in hotel)
постоя́лец*, прожива́ющий(-ая) m(f) adj; **be
my ~** (inf) пожа́луйста.
guesthouse ['gɛsthaus] n пансио́н.
guest room n ко́мната для госте́й.
guff [gʌf] n (inf) трёп.
guffaw [gʌ'fɔ:] vi гогота́ть* (impf) ♦ n го́гот.
guidance ['gaɪdəns] n (advice) сове́т; **under the
~ of** с по́мощью +gen, под руково́дством
+gen; **vocational ~** сове́т по профориен-
та́ции; **marriage ~** сове́т по вопро́сам семьи́
и бра́ка.
guide [gaɪd] n (in museum, on tour) гид,
экскурсово́д; (mountain guide) проводни́к*;
(also: ~**book**) путеводи́тель m; (handbook)
руково́дство; (BRIT: also: **Girl G~**) де́вочка*-
ска́ут f ♦ vt (show around) води́ть* (impf),
вести́* (провести́* perf); (direct) направля́ть
(напра́вить* perf); **to be ~d by sb/sth** (fig)
руково́дствоваться (impf) чьим-н сове́том/
чем-ч.
guidebook ['gaɪdbuk] n путеводи́тель m.
guided missile n управля́емая раке́та.
guide dog n соба́ка-поводы́рь* f.
guidelines ['gaɪdlaɪnz] npl директи́ва fsg.
guild [gɪld] n ассоциа́ция; (HISTORY) ги́льдия.
guildhall ['gɪldhɔ:l] n (BRIT: in London): **the G~**
Ги́льдхолл (зда́ние ра́туши ло́ндонского
Си́ти).
guile [gaɪl] n хи́трость f.
guileless ['gaɪllɪs] adj бесхи́тростный*.
guillotine ['gɪləti:n] n гильоти́на; (for paper)
реза́льная маши́на.
guilt [gɪlt] n (remorse) вина́; (culpability)
вино́вность f.
guilty ['gɪltɪ] adj (person, expression) вино-
ва́тый; (of crime) вино́вный*; (secret)
позо́рный*; **to plead ~/not guilty**
признава́ть* (призна́ть* perf) себя́
вино́вным(-ой)/невино́вным(-ой); **to feel ~
about sth** чу́вствовать (impf) себя́
винова́тым(-ой) в чём-н.
Guinea ['gɪnɪ] n: **Republic of ~** Гвине́я.
guinea ['gɪnɪ] n (BRIT) гине́я.
guinea pig n (animal) морска́я сви́нка*; (fig)
„подо́пытный кро́лик".
guise [gaɪz] n: **in** or **under the ~ of** под ви́дом
+gen.
guitar [gɪ'tɑ:'] n гита́ра.
guitarist [gɪ'tɑ:rɪst] n гитари́ст(ка).
gulch [gʌltʃ] n (US) (у́зкое) уще́лье*.

gulf [gʌlf] n (GEO) зали́в; (also fig) про́пасть f;
the (Persian) G~ Перси́дский* зали́в.
Gulf States npl: **the ~ ~** стра́ны fpl
Перси́дского зали́ва.
Gulf Stream n: **the ~ ~** Гольфстри́м.
gull [gʌl] n ча́йка*.
gullet ['gʌlɪt] n пищево́д.
gullibility [gʌlɪ'bɪlɪtɪ] n легкове́рие.
gullible ['gʌlɪbl] adj (naive, trusting)
легкове́рный (легкове́рен).
gully ['gʌlɪ] n (ravine) глубо́кий* овра́г.
gulp [gʌlp] vi (swallow: from nerves,
excitement) сгла́тывать (сглотну́ть perf)
не́рвно ♦ vi (also: ~ **down**: food, drink)
прогла́тывать (проглоти́ть* perf) ♦ n: **to
drink at one ~** вы́пить* (perf) за́лпом.
gum [gʌm] n (ANAT) десна́*; (glue) клей*;
(sweet: also: ~**drop**) желе́йный мармела́д
(конфе́та); (also: **chewing~**) жева́тельная
рези́нка*, жва́чка* (разг) ♦ vt (stick): **to ~
(together)** скле́ивать (скле́ить perf)
▸ **gum up** vt: **to ~ up the works** (inf)
засто́порить (perf) рабо́ту.
gumboots ['gʌmbu:ts] npl (BRIT) рези́новые
сапоги́* mpl.
gumption ['gʌmpʃən] n (sense, wit)
сообрази́тельность f, нахо́дчивость f.
gumtree ['gʌmtri:] n: **to be up a ~** (fig: inf)
попада́ть (попа́сть* perf) в просо́к.
gun [gʌn] n (revolver, pistol) пистоле́т; (rifle,
airgun) ружьё*; (cannon) пу́шка* ♦ vt (also: ~
down) расстре́ливать (расстреля́ть perf),
застрели́ть* (perf); **to stick to one's ~s** (fig) не
скла́дывать (сложи́ть* perf) ору́жия.
gunboat ['gʌnbəut] n канонёрская ло́дка*.
gun dog n охо́тничья соба́ка.
gunfire ['gʌnfaɪə'] n оруди́йный ого́нь* m.
gung ho [gʌŋ həu] adj (inf) безрассу́дный*,
фанати́чный.
gunk [gʌŋk] n (inf) га́дость f.
gunman ['gʌnmən] irreg n вооружённый
банди́т.
gunner ['gʌnə'] n (MIL) артиллери́ст.
gunpoint ['gʌnpɔɪnt] n: **at ~** под ду́лом
пистоле́та, под прице́лом.
gunpowder ['gʌnpaudə'] n по́рох*.
gunrunner ['gʌnrʌnə'] n контрабанди́ст,
торгу́ющий ору́жием.
gunrunning ['gʌnrʌnɪŋ] n контрба́нда
ору́жием.
gunshot ['gʌnʃɔt] n вы́стрел.
gunsmith ['gʌnsmɪθ] n оруже́йный ма́стер*.
gurgle ['gə:gl] vi (baby) гу́кать (impf); (water)
журча́ть (impf).
guru ['guru:] n (REL) гуру́ m ind; (fig) духо́вный
наста́вник.
gush [gʌʃ] vi хлы́нуть (perf); (enthuse)
захлёбываться (захлебну́ться perf) от

---

* marks translations which have irregular inflections. The Russian-English side of the dictionary gives inflectional information.

восто́рга ♦ *n* (*of water etc*) пото́к.
gushing ['gʌʃɪŋ] *adj* (*female*) восто́рженный*
(восто́ржен); (*admiration, reverence*)
неуёмный* (неуёмен).
gusset ['gʌsɪt] *n* клин*.
gust [gʌst] *n* (*of wind*) поры́в.
gusto ['gʌstəu] *n*: **with ~** (*eat*) с удово́льст-
вием; (*work*) с жа́ром.
gusty ['gʌstɪ] *adj* (*wind*) поры́вистый
(поры́вист); (*day*) ве́треный (ве́трен).
gut [gʌt] *n* кишка́*; (*MUS, SPORT*) струна́* (*из
кишо́к живо́тных*) ♦ *vt* (*poultry, fish*)
потроши́ть (вы́потрошить *perf*); (*building*)
удаля́ть все вну́тренние ча́сти до́ма; **~s** *npl*
(*ANAT*) кишки́* *fpl*, вну́тренности *fpl*; (*inf:
courage*) му́жество *ntsg*; **the house was ~ted
by fire** дом сгоре́л по́лностью; **to hate sb's
~s** (*inf*) не принима́ть (приня́ть* *perf*) кого́-н
на́ дух, смерте́льно ненави́деть* (*impf*)
кого́-н.
gut reaction *n* инстинкти́вная реа́кция.
gutsy ['gʌtsɪ] (*inf*) *adj* напо́ристый.
gutted ['gʌtɪd] (*inf*) *adj*: **I was ~** (*very
disappointed*) я был соверше́нно уби́т.
gutter ['gʌtə'] *n* (*in street*) сто́чная кана́ва; (*of
roof*) водосто́чный жёлоб*.
gutter press (*inf: pej*) *n* бульва́рная пре́сса.
guttural ['gʌtərl] *adj* горта́нный.

guy [gaɪ] *n* (*inf: man*) па́рень* *m*; (*also: ~rope*)
шнуры́ *mpl* для натя́гивания пала́тки; (*effigy
of Guy Fawkes*) изображе́ние Га́я Фо́кса,
сжига́емое 5 ноября́.
Guyana [gaɪ'ænə] *n* Гайа́на.
guzzle ['gʌzl] *vt* (*drink*) пить* (вы́пить* *perf*) с
жа́дностью; (*food*) есть* (съесть* *perf*) с
жа́дностью.
gym [dʒɪm] *n* (*also: ~nasium*) гимнасти́ческий
зал; (*also: ~nastics*) гимна́стика.
gymkhana [dʒɪm'kɑːnə] *n* конноспорти́вные
состяза́ния *ntpl*.
gymnasium [dʒɪm'neɪzɪəm] *n* гимнасти́ческий
зал.
gymnast ['dʒɪmnæst] *n* гимна́ст(ка*).
gymnastics [dʒɪm'næstɪks] *n* гимна́стика.
gym shoes *npl* спорти́вные та́почки* *fpl*.
gymslip ['dʒɪmslɪp] *n* (*BRIT: tunic*) шко́льное
пла́тье без рукаво́в.
gynaecologist [gaɪnɪ'kɔlədʒɪst] (*US
gynecologist*) *n* гинеко́лог.
gynaecology [gaɪnə'kɔlədʒɪ] (*US gynecology*) *n*
гинеколо́гия.
gypsy ['dʒɪpsɪ] *n* = **gipsy**.
gyrate [dʒaɪ'reɪt] *vi* (*revolve*) враща́ться (*impf*)
по кру́гу.
gyroscope ['dʒaɪərəskəup] *n* гироско́п.

~ H, h ~

H, h [eɪtʃ] *n* (*letter*) 8-áя бýква английского алфавита.

habeas corpus [ˈheɪbɪəsˈkɔːpəs] *n* (*LAW*) Хáбеас Кóрпус (*закóн о неприкосновéнности лúчности*).

haberdashery [hæbəˈdæʃərɪ] *n* (*BRIT*) галантерéйные товáры *mpl*.

habit [ˈhæbɪt] *n* (*custom*) привы́чка*; (*addiction*) пристрáстие; (*REL: costume*) облачéние; **to get out of the ~ of doing** отвыкáть (отвы́кнуть* *perf*) +*infin*; **to get into the ~ of doing** привыкáть (привы́кнуть *perf*) +*infin*; **to be in the ~ of doing** имéть (*impf*) обыкновéние +*infin*.

habitable [ˈhæbɪtəbl] *adj* (*house etc*) пригóдный* для жилья́.

habitat [ˈhæbɪtæt] *n* (*BOT, ZOOL*) естéственная средá* обитáния.

habitation [hæbɪˈteɪʃən] *n* (*house etc*) жилúще; **fit for human ~** пригóдный* для жилья́.

habitual [həˈbɪtjuəl] *adj* (*action*) привы́чный* (привы́чен); (*drinker*) запóйный; (*liar*) отъя́вленный.

habitually [həˈbɪtjuəlɪ] *adv* (*late, untidy*) обы́чно.

hack [hæk] *vt* (*cut, slice*) отрубáть (отрубúть *perf*) ♦ *n* (*pej: writer*) писáка* *m/f*; (*horse*) лóшадь, сдавáемая напрокáт для верховóй езды́ ♦ *vi*: **to ~ into** (*COMPUT*) нелегáльно входúть* (войтú* *perf*) в +*acc*.

hacker [ˈhækə] *n* (*COMPUT*) хéкер.

hackles [ˈhæklz] *npl*: **to make sb's ~ rise** (*fig*) приводúть* (привестú *perf*) в состоя́ние раздражéния.

hackney cab [ˈhæknɪ-] *n* наёмный экипáж.

hackneyed [ˈhæknɪd] *adj* избúтый.

hacksaw [ˈhæksɔː] *n* ножóвка.

had [hæd] *pt, pp of* **have**.

haddock [ˈhædək] (*pl ~ or ~s*) *n* трескá; **smoked ~** копчёная трескá.

hadn't [ˈhædnt] = **had not**.

haematology [hiːməˈtɔlədʒɪ] (*US* **hematology**) *n* гематолóгия.

haemoglobin [hiːməˈɡləubɪn] (*US* **hemoglobin**) *n* гемоглобúн.

haemophilia [hiːməˈfɪlɪə] (*US* **hemophilia**) *n* гемофилúя.

haemorrhage [ˈhɛmərɪdʒ] (*US* **hemorrage**) *n* кровотечéние; **brain ~** кровоизлия́ние (в мозг).

haemorrhoids [ˈhɛmərɔɪdz] (*US* **hemorroids**) *npl* геморрóй *msg*.

hag [hæɡ] *n* (*woman*) каргá; (*witch*) вéдьма.

haggard [ˈhæɡəd] *adj* (*face, look*) изможлённый*.

haggis [ˈhæɡɪs] *n* (*SCOTTISH*) хáггис (*шотлáндское блю́до из барáньей или теля́чьей требухú с овся́ной крупóй и спéциями*).

haggle [ˈhæɡl] *vi* (*bargain*) торговáться (сторговáться *perf*); **to ~ over** спóрить (*impf*) о +*prp*.

haggling [ˈhæɡlɪŋ] *n* торгóвля.

Hague [heɪɡ] *n*: **The ~** (*GEO*) Гаáга.

hail [heɪl] *n* (*also fig*) град ♦ *vt* (*call*) окликáть (окликнуть *perf*); (*flag down*) подзывáть (подозвáть* *perf*); (*acclaim*) превозносúть* (превознестú* *perf*) ♦ *vi*: **it's ~ing** идёт град; **he ~s from Scotland** он рóдом из Шотлáндии.

hailstone [ˈheɪlstəun] *n* грáдина.

hailstorm [ˈheɪlstɔːm] *n* грозá* с грáдом.

hair [hɛəʳ] *n* вóлосы* *pl*; (*of animal*) шерсть *f*; (*single hair*) вóлос*; **to do one's ~** причёсываться (причесáться* *perf*); **to miss by a ~'s breadth** (*fig*) чуть-чуть промахнýться (*perf*).

hairbrush [ˈhɛəbrʌʃ] *n* щётка* для волóс.

haircut [ˈhɛəkʌt] *n* стрúжка*.

hairdo [ˈhɛəduː] *n* причёска*.

hairdresser [ˈhɛədrɛsəʳ] *n* парикмáхер.

hairdresser's [ˈhɛədrɛsəz] *n* парикмáхерская *f adj*.

hair dryer *n* фен.

-haired [hɛəd] *suffix*: **fair/long-~** светло-/длинноволóсый.

hairgrip [ˈhɛəɡrɪp] *n* невидúмка.

hairline [ˈhɛəlaɪn] *n* лúния волóс.

hairline fracture *n* трéщина.

hairnet [ˈhɛənɛt] *n* сéтка* для волóс.

hair oil *n* мáсло* для волóс.

hairpiece [ˈhɛəpiːs] *n* накладны́е вóлосы* *mpl*.

---

hairpin ['hɛəpɪn] *n* шпи́лька*.
hairpin bend (*US* **hairpin curve**) *n* круто́й поворо́т.
hair-raising ['hɛəreɪzɪŋ] *adj* (*experience, tale*) жу́ткий*.
hair remover *n* (*cream*) крем для удале́ния воло́с.
hair slide *n* зако́лка* для воло́с.
hair spray *n* лак для воло́с.
hairstyle ['hɛəstaɪl] *n* причёска*.
hairy ['hɛərɪ] *adj* (*person*) волоса́тый; (*animal*) мохна́тый (мохна́т); (*inf: situation*) риско́ванный*.
Haiti ['heɪtɪ] *n* Гаи́ти *m ind*.
hake [heɪk] (*pl ~ or ~s*) *n* серебри́стый хек.
halcyon ['hælsɪən] *adj*: ~ **days** безмяте́жные дни.
hale [heɪl] *adj*: ~ **and hearty** здоро́вый* (здоро́в) и бо́дрый* (бодр).
half [hɑːf] (*pl* **halves**) *n* полови́на; (*also*: ~ **pint**: *of beer etc*) полпи́нты *f*; (*RAIL, bus*) биле́т за полцены́ ♦ *adv* (*empty, closed, open, asleep*) наполови́ну; **first/second** ~ (*SPORT*) пе́рвый/ второ́й тайм; **one and a** ~ (*with m nouns*) полтора́ +*gen sg*; (*with f nouns*) полторы́ +*gen sg*; **three and a** ~ три с полови́ной; ~**-an-hour** полчаса́* *m*; ~ **a dozen (of)** полдю́жины* *f* (+*gen*); ~ **a pound (of)** полфу́нта *m* (+*gen*); **a week and a** ~ полторы́* *f* неде́ли; ~ (**of**) полови́на (+*gen*); ~ **the amount of** полови́на +*gen*; **to cut sth in** ~ разреза́ть* (разре́зать* *perf*) что-н попола́м; ~ **past three** полови́на четвёртого; **to go halves (with sb)** дели́ть* (подели́ть* *perf*) попола́м (с кем-н); **she never does things by halves** она́ никогда́ не остана́вливается на полпути́; **he's too clever by** ~ он чересчу́р уж у́мный; ~ **empty/closed** наполови́ну пусто́й*/закры́тый; **a** ~ **bottle (of)** полбуты́лки (+*gen*).
half-baked ['hɑːf'beɪkt] *adj* (*idea, scheme*) непроду́манный.
half board *n* пансио́н с за́втраком и у́жином.
half-breed ['hɑːfbriːd] *n* = **half-caste**.
half-brother ['hɑːfbrʌðəʳ] *n* (*with same mother*) единоутро́бный брат*; (*with same father*) единокро́вный брат*.
half-caste ['hɑːfkɑːst] *n* челове́к сме́шанной ра́сы.
half-day [hɑːf'deɪ] *n* коро́ткий* день* *m*.
half-hearted ['hɑːf'hɑːtɪd] *adj* лени́вый.
half-hour [hɑːf'auəʳ] *n* полчаса́* *m*.
half-life ['hɑːflaɪf] *n* (*TECH*) пери́од полураспа́да.
half-mast ['hɑːf'mɑːst] *adv*: **at** ~ (*flag*) приспу́щенный (приспу́щен).
halfpenny ['heɪpnɪ] *n* (*BRIT*) полпе́нса* *m*.
half-price ['hɑːf'praɪs] *adj, adv* за полцены́.
half-sister ['hɑːfsɪstəʳ] *n* (*with same mother*) единоутро́бная сестра́*; (*with same father*) единокро́вная сестра́*.
half term *n* (*BRIT*: *SCOL*) кани́кулы в середи́не

шко́льного триме́стра.
half-timbered [hɑːf'tɪmbəd] *adj* деревя́нно-кирпи́чный.
half-time [hɑːf'taɪm] *n* (*SPORT*) переры́в ме́жду та́ймами.
halfway ['hɑːf'weɪ] *adv* на полпути́; **I am prepared to meet you** ~ (*fig*) я гото́в пойти́ Вам навстре́чу.
halfway house *n* дом* на полпути́; (*fig*) середи́на.
halfwit ['hɑːfwɪt] *n* придуро́к*, полоу́мный(-ая) *m(f) adj*.
half-yearly [hɑːf'jɪəlɪ] *adv* раз в полго́да ♦ *adj* полугодово́й.
halibut ['hælɪbət] *n inv* па́лтус.
halitosis [hælɪ'təusɪs] *n* дурно́й за́пах изо рта́.
hall [hɔːl] *n* (*entrance way*) прихо́жая *f adj*; (*corridor*) коридо́р; (*mansion*) уса́дьба; (*for concerts, meetings etc*) зал; **to live in** ~**s** (*BRIT*: *students*) жить* (*impf*) в общежи́тии.
hallmark ['hɔːlmɑːk] *n* про́ба; (*fig*) отличи́тельная черта́*.
hallo ['hæ'ləu] *excl* = **hello**.
hall of residence (*pl* ~**s** ~ ~) *n* (*BRIT*) общежи́тие.
hallowed ['hæləud] *adj* (*REL*) свято́й*; (*fig*: *respected, revered*) почита́емый.
Hallowe'en ['hæləu'iːn] *n* кану́н Дня всех святы́х.
hallucination [həluːsɪ'neɪʃən] *n* галлюцина́ция.
hallucinogenic [həluːsɪnəu'dʒɛnɪk] *adj* галлюцинато́рный.
hallway ['hɔːlweɪ] *n* (*entrance hall*) прихо́жая *f adj*.
halo ['heɪləu] *n* (*REL*) нимб; (*circle of light*) орео́л.
halt [hɔːlt] *n* остано́вка* ♦ *vt* остана́вливать (останови́ть* *perf*) ♦ *vi* остана́вливаться (останови́ться* *perf*); **to call a** ~ **to sth** (*fig*) дава́ть* (дать* *perf*) отбо́й чему́-н.
halter ['hɔːltəʳ] *n* (*for horse*) по́вод*.
halterneck ['hɔːltənɛk] *adj*: ~ **dress** пла́тье с откры́той спино́й и завя́зками вокру́г ше́и.
halve [hɑːv] *vt* (*reduce*) сокраща́ть (сократи́ть* *perf*) наполови́ну; (*divide*) дели́ть* (раздели́ть* *perf*) попола́м.
halves [hɑːvz] *pl of* **half**.
ham [hæm] *n* ветчина́*; (*inf: also*: **radio** ~) радиолюби́тель *m*; (: *actor*) безда́рный(-ая) актёр(-три́са) ♦ *vt*: **to** ~ **it up** переи́грывать (переигра́ть* *perf*).
Hamburg ['hæmbəːg] *n* Га́мбург.
hamburger ['hæmbəːgəʳ] *n* га́мбургер.
ham-fisted ['hæm'fɪstɪd] *adj* нело́вкий*.
ham-handed ['hæm'hændɪd] *adj* = **ham-fisted**.
hamlet ['hæmlɪt] *n* дереву́шка*.
hammer ['hæməʳ] *n* молото́к*, мо́лот ♦ *vi* (*on door etc*) колоти́ть* (*impf*) ♦ *vt* (*criticize severely*) критикова́ть (раскритикова́ть* *perf*); (*nail*): **to** ~ **in** забива́ть (заби́ть* *perf*), вбива́ть (вбить* *perf*); (*fig: force*): **to** ~ **sth into**

sb вда́лбливать (вдолби́ть* perf) что-н кому́-н
▸ **hammer out** vt (metal) распплю́щивать (распплю́щить perf); (fig: solution, agreement) выраба́тывать (вы́работать perf).
hammock ['hæmək] n (on ship) ко́йка*; (in garden) гама́к*.
hamper ['hæmpə'] vt меша́ть (помеша́ть perf) +dat ♦ n (basket) больша́я корзи́на с кры́шкой.
hamster ['hæmstə'] n хомя́к*.
hamstring ['hæmstrɪŋ] n (ANAT) подколе́нное сухожи́лие ♦ vt (restrict) ограни́чивать (ограни́чить perf).
hand [hænd] n (ANAT) рука́*, кисть* f руки́; (of clock) стре́лка*; (handwriting) по́черк; (worker) рабо́чий* m adj; (of cards) ка́рты fpl (находя́щиеся на рука́х у игрока́); (measurement: of horse) ладо́нь f (ме́ра при измере́нии ро́ста ло́шади) ♦ vt (pass) передава́ть* (переда́ть* perf); (give) вруча́ть (вручи́ть perf); **to give** or **lend sb a ~** помога́ть (помо́чь* perf) кому́-н; **at ~** под руко́й; **by ~** вручну́ю; **in ~** (time) в распоряже́нии; (situation) под контро́лем; **the job in ~** теку́щее де́ло; **on ~** (person, services etc) в распоряже́нии; **to get out of ~** (child) отбива́ться (отби́ться* perf) от рук; (situation) выходи́ть* (вы́йти* perf) из-под контро́ля; **to dismiss out of ~** отве́ргнуть (perf) сра́зу; **I have the information to ~** распола́гаю информа́цией; **on the one ~ ...**, **on the other ~ ...** с одно́й стороны́ ..., с друго́й стороны́; **to force sb's ~** заставля́ть (заста́вить* perf) кого́-н раскры́ть свои́ ка́рты; **he has a free ~** у него́ развя́заны ру́ки; **to change ~s** (be sold etc) переходи́ть* (перейти́* perf) из рук в ру́ки; **to have in one's ~** (fig) держа́ть* (impf) под контро́лем; **~s off!** ру́ки прочь!
▸ **hand down** vt (knowledge, possessions) передава́ть* (переда́ть* perf); (LAW: judgement, sentence) выноси́ть* (вы́нести* perf)
▸ **hand in** vt (essay, work) сдава́ть* (сдать* perf)
▸ **hand out** vt раздава́ть* (разда́ть* perf)
▸ **hand over** vt передава́ть* (переда́ть* perf)
▸ **hand round** vt (BRIT) раздава́ть* (разда́ть* perf); (subj: hostess) разноси́ть* (разнести́* perf).
handbag ['hændbæg] n (да́мская) су́мочка*.
hand baggage n ручно́й бага́ж*.
handball ['hændbɔ:l] n гандбо́л.
hand basin n таз*.
handbook ['hændbuk] n руково́дство.
handbrake ['hændbreɪk] n ручно́й то́рмоз*.
h & c abbr (BRIT) = hot and cold (water).
hand cream n крем для рук.

handcuff ['hændkʌf] vt надева́ть (наде́ть* perf) нару́чники +dat or на +acc.
handcuffs ['hændkʌfs] npl нару́чники mpl.
handful ['hændful] n горсть* f; (fig: of people) го́рстка*.
hand-held ['hænd'hɛld] adj ручно́й.
handicap ['hændɪkæp] n (disability) физи́ческая неполноце́нность f; (disadvantage) препя́тствие; (SPORT) гандика́п ♦ vt препя́тствовать (воспрепя́тствовать perf) +dat; **mentally/physically ~ped** у́мственно/физи́чески неполноце́нный.
handicraft ['hændɪkrɑ:ft] n рукоде́лие; (objects) изде́лие ручно́й рабо́ты.
handiwork ['hændɪwəːk] n ручны́е изде́лия ntpl; **this looks like his ~** (pej) похо́же, что э́то его́ рук де́ло.
handkerchief ['hæŋkətʃɪf] n носово́й плато́к*.
handle ['hændl] n ру́чка*; (CB RADIO: name) про́звище ♦ vt (touch) держа́ть* (impf) в рука́х; (deal with) справля́ться (спра́виться* perf) с +instr; (treat: people) обраща́ться (impf) с +instr; **to fly off the ~** (inf) срыва́ться (сорва́ться* perf); **to get a ~ on a problem** (inf) бра́ться* (взя́ться* perf) за реше́ние пробле́мы; **"handle with care"** „обраща́ться осторо́жно".
handlebar(s) ['hændlbɑ:(z)] n(pl) руль* msg (велосипе́да и́ли мотоци́кла).
handling ['hændlɪŋ] n: **~ of** (of situation, problem etc) подхо́д к +dat; (luggage) обраще́ние +gen; (LAW) веде́ние +gen.
handling charges npl (COMM) пла́та fsg за услу́ги.
hand luggage n ручно́й бага́ж*.
handmade ['hænd'meɪd] adj ручно́й рабо́ты; **it's ~** э́то – ручна́я рабо́та.
hand-out ['hændaut] n (money, clothing, food) благотвори́тельная по́мощь f; (publicity leaflet) рекла́мный листо́к*; (summary: of lecture) проспе́кт.
hand-picked ['hænd'pɪkt] adj (produce) со́бранный вручну́ю; (staff etc) специа́льно подо́бранный.
handrail ['hændreɪl] n пери́ла pl.
handset ['hændsɛt] n телефо́нная тру́бка*.
handshake ['hændʃeɪk] n рукопожа́тие.
handsome ['hænsəm] adj (man) краси́вый (краси́в); (woman) интере́сный* (интере́сен); (building) внуши́тельный*; (gift) ще́дрый (щедр); (fig: profit, return) внуши́тельный* (внуши́телен).
hands-on ['hændz'ɔn] adj практи́ческий*.
handstand ['hændstænd] n: **to do a ~** де́лать (сде́лать perf) сто́йку на рука́х.
hand-to-mouth ['hændtə'mauθ] adj: **they live a ~ existence** они́ живу́т впро́голодь.
handwriting ['hændraɪtɪŋ] n по́черк.

---

handwritten ['hændrɪtn] *adj* напи́санный от руки́.

handy ['hændɪ] *adj* (*useful*) удо́бный*; (*skilful*) ло́вкий*; (*close at hand*) побли́зости; **to come in** ~ пригожда́ться* (пригоди́ться* *perf*).

handyman ['hændɪmæn] *irreg n* (*at home*) ма́стер* на все ру́ки; (*in hotel etc*) подру́чный *m adj*.

hang [hæŋ] (*pt, pp* **hung**) *vt* ве́шать (пове́сить* *perf*); (*pt, pp* **hanged**; *execute*) ве́шать (пове́сить* *perf*) ♦ *vi* висе́ть* (*impf*) ♦ *n*: **to get the** ~ **of sth** (*inf*) разбира́ться (разобра́ться* *perf*) в чём-н; **to** ~ **one's head** ве́шать (пове́сить* *perf*) го́лову

▸ **hang about** *vi* слоня́ться (*impf*)

▸ **hang around** *vi* = **hang about**

▸ **hang back** *vi* (*hesitate*): **to** ~ **back (from doing)** быть* (*impf*) в нереши́тельности (+*infin*)

▸ **hang on** *vi* (*wait*) подожда́ть* (*impf*) ♦ *vt fus* (*depend on*) зави́сеть (*impf*) от +*gen*; **to** ~ **on to** (*keep hold of*) цепля́ться (*impf*) за +*acc*; (*keep*) держа́ть (*impf*) у себя́

▸ **hang out** *vt* (*washing*) выве́шивать (вы́весить* *perf*) ♦ *vi* высо́вываться (вы́сунуться *perf*); **this is where the students always** ~ **out** (*inf*) студе́нты всегда́ там окола́чиваются

▸ **hang together** *vi* (*argument*) быть* (*impf*) убеди́тельным(-ой)

▸ **hang up** *vi* (*TEL*) ве́шать (пове́сить* *perf*) тру́бку ♦ *vt* веша́ть (пове́сить* *perf*).

hangar ['hæŋə] *n* анга́р.

hangdog ['hæŋdɔg] *adj* (*look, expression*) винова́тый.

hanger ['hæŋə] *n* (*for clothes*) ве́шалка*.

hanger-on [hæŋər'ɔn] *n* прихлеба́тель(ница) *m(f)*.

hang-glider ['hæŋglaɪdə] *n* (*craft*) дельтапла́н; (*pilot*) дельтапланери́ст.

hang-gliding ['hæŋglaɪdɪŋ] *n* дельта-планери́зм.

hanging ['hæŋɪŋ] *n* (*execution*) пове́шение; (*for wall*) портье́ра.

hangman ['hæŋmən] *irreg n* пала́ч*.

hangover ['hæŋəʊvə] *n* (*after drinking*) похме́лье; (*from past*) пережи́ток*.

hang-up ['hæŋʌp] *n* (*inhibition*) ко́мплекс.

hank [hæŋk] *n* мото́к*.

hanker ['hæŋkə] *vi*: **to** ~ **after** (*desire, long for*) мечта́ть (*impf*) о +*prp*.

hankering ['hæŋkərɪŋ] *n*: **I have a** ~ **for a beer** мне бы сейча́с пивка́.

hankie ['hæŋkɪ] *n abbr* = **handkerchief**.

hanky ['hæŋkɪ] *n abbr* = **handkerchief**.

Hanoi [hæ'nɔɪ] *n* Хано́й.

Hants *abbr* (*BRIT: POST*) = **Hampshire**.

haphazard [hæp'hæzəd] *adj* бессисте́мный*.

hapless ['hæplɪs] *adj* несча́стный*.

happen ['hæpən] *vi* случа́ться (случи́ться *perf*), происходи́ть* (произойти́* *perf*); (*chance*): **I**

~**ed to meet him in the park** я случа́йно встре́тил его́ в па́рке; **as it** ~**s** кста́ти; **what's** ~**ing?** что происхо́дит?; **she** ~**ed to be free** она́ оказа́лась свобо́дной; **if anything** ~**ed to him** е́сли с ним что-н случи́тся

▸ **happen (up)on** *vt fus* натыка́ться (наткну́ться *perf*) на +*acc*.

happening ['hæpnɪŋ] *n* слу́чай.

happily ['hæpɪlɪ] *adv* (*luckily*) к сча́стью; (*cheerfully*) ра́достно.

happiness ['hæpɪnɪs] *n* сча́стье.

happy ['hæpɪ] *adj* (*pleased*) счастли́вый (счастли́в); (*cheerful*) весёлый* (ве́сел); (*apt*) уда́чный* (уда́чен); **I am** ~ **(with it)** (*content*) я дово́лен (э́тим); **he is always** ~ **to help** (*willing*) он всегда́ с удово́льствием помога́ет; ~ **birthday!** с днём рожде́ния!

happy-go-lucky ['hæpɪgəʊ'lʌkɪ] *adj* беспе́чный* (беспе́чен).

happy hour *n вре́мя, в тече́ние кото́рого спиртны́е напи́тки в ба́рах продаю́тся по сни́женным це́нам.*

harangue [hə'ræŋ] *vt* (*audience, class*) увещева́ть (*impf*).

harass ['hærəs] *vt* изводи́ть* (извести́* *perf*).

harassed ['hærəst] *adj* (*person*) изнурённый* (изнурён).

harassment ['hærəsmənt] *n* пресле́дование; **sexual** ~ *злоупотребле́ние служе́бным положе́нием по отноше́нию к сотру́днику противополо́жного по́ла.*

harbour ['hɑ:bə] (*US* **harbor**) *n* га́вань *f* ♦ *vt* (*hope, fear etc*) зата́ивать (затаи́ть *perf*); (*criminal, fugitive*) укрыва́ть (укры́ть* *perf*); **to** ~ **a grudge against sb** держа́ть* (*impf*) зло на кого́-н.

harbour dues *npl* порто́вые сбо́ры *mpl*.

harbour master *n* нача́льник по́рта.

hard [hɑ:d] *adj* (*surface, object*) твёрдый (твёрд); (*question, problem*) тру́дный* (тру́ден); (*work, life*) тяжёлый (тяжёл); (*person*) суро́вый (суро́в); (*facts, evidence*) неопроверж́имый (неопроверж́им); (*drink*) кре́пкий*; (*drugs*) си́льный ♦ *adv*: **to work** ~ мно́го и усе́рдно рабо́тать (*impf*); ~ **luck!** не везёт!; **no** ~ **feelings!** не держи́те зла!; **I don't have any** ~ **feelings** я не держу́ зла; **he is** ~ **of hearing** он туг на́ ухо; **to think** ~ хорошо́ поду́мать (*perf*); **to try** ~ **to win** упо́рно добива́ться (*impf*) побе́ды; **to look** ~ **at** смотре́ть* (посмотре́ть* *perf*) при́стально на +*acc*; **I felt** ~ **done by** я почу́вствовал, что со мной обошли́сь несправедли́во; **I find it** ~ **to believe that ...** мне тру́дно пове́рить, что ....

hard-and-fast ['hɑ:dən'fɑ:st] *adj* неукосни́тельный*.

hardback ['hɑ:dbæk] *n* (*book*) кни́га в твёрдом переплёте.

hardboard ['hɑ:dbɔ:d] *n* древе́сно-стру́жечная плита́.

hard-boiled egg ['hɑ:d'bɔɪld-] *n* яйцо́*

вкрутую.
hard cash *n* наличные деньги* *pl*.
hard copy *n* (*COMPUT*) печатная копия, распечатка.
hard core *n* (*of group*) группа преданных сторонников.
hard-core ['hɑːd'kɔː'] *adj* (*pornography*) предельно откровенный*; (*supporters*) верный*.
hard court *n* (*TENNIS*) твёрдый корт.
hard disk *n* (*COMPUT*) жёсткий* диск.
harden ['hɑːdn] *vt* (*substance*) делать (сделать *perf*) твёрдым(-ой); (*attitude, person*) ожесточать (ожесточить *perf*) ♦ *vi* (*substance*) твердеть (затвердеть *perf*); (*attitude, person*) ожесточаться (ожесточиться *perf*).
hardened ['hɑːdnd] *adj* (*criminal*) закоренелый; **to be ~ to sth** быть* (*impf*) нечувствительным(-ой) к чему-н.
hardening ['hɑːdnɪŋ] *n* закаливание; (*of opposition*) усиление.
hard graft *n*: **by sheer ~ ~** только благодаря упорной работе.
hard-headed ['hɑːd'hɛdɪd] *adj* (*businessman*) расчётливый (расчётлив).
hardhearted ['hɑːd'hɑːtɪd] *adj* бессердечный* (бессердечен).
hard-hitting ['hɑːd'hɪtɪŋ] *adj* (*report, speech, article*) бьющий напрямик.
hard labour *n* (*punishment*) принудительные работы *fpl*.
hardliner [hɑːd'laɪnə'] *n* сторонник(-ица) жёсткой линии (*в политике*).
hard-luck story ['hɑːdlʌk-] *n* жалостливая история.
hardly ['hɑːdlɪ] *adv* (*scarcely*) едва; (*no sooner*) как только; (*harshly*) сурово; **~ anywhere/ ever** почти нигде/никогда; **it's ~ the case** это не тот случай; **I ~ think so** я так не думаю; **I can ~ believe it** я с трудом могу поверить в это.
hard-nosed [hɑːd'nəuzd] *adj* трёзвый.
hard-pressed [hɑːd'prɛst] *adj*: **I am ~ for time/ money** у меня туго со временем/деньгами.
hard sell *n* (*COMM*) усиленное рекламирование товаров.
hardship ['hɑːdʃɪp] *n* (*difficulty*) трудности *fpl*.
hard shoulder *n* (*BRIT*: *AUT*) обочина с *твёрдым покрытием, на которой разрешена остановка транспорта*.
hard up *adj* (*inf*) на мели.
hardware ['hɑːdwɛə'] *n* скобяные изделия *ntpl*; (*COMPUT*) оборудование, аппаратура; (*MIL*) военная техника.
hardware shop *n* магазин скобяных изделий.
hard-wearing [hɑːd'wɛərɪŋ] *adj* (*clothes, shoes*)

крепкий* (крепок).
hard-won [hɑːd'wʌn] *adj* с трудом завоёванный (завоёван); (*victory*) с трудом одержанный (одержан).
hard-working [hɑːd'wəːkɪŋ] *adj* (*employee, student*) усердный* (усерден).
hardy ['hɑːdɪ] *adj* (*animals, people*) выносливый (вынослив); (*plant*) морозо-устойчивый (морозоустойчив).
hare [hɛə'] *n* заяц*.
harebrained ['hɛəbreɪnd] *adj* (*scheme, idea*) несуразный* (несуразен).
harelip ['hɛəlɪp] *n* заячья губа*.
harem [hɑː'riːm] *n* гарем.
hark back [hɑːk-] *vi*: **to ~ ~ to** (*be reminiscent of*) напоминать (напомнить *perf*) о +*prp*; (*remember*) вспоминать (вспомнить *perf*) о +*prp*.
harm [hɑːm] *n* (*injury*) телесное повреждение; (*damage*) ущерб ♦ *vt* (*thing*) повреждать (повредить* *perf*); (*person*) наносить* (нанести* *perf*) вред +*dat*; **to mean no ~** не хотеть* (*impf*) обидеть; **to come to no ~** закончиться (*perf*) благополучно; **out of ~'s way** от греха подальше; **there's no ~ in trying** попытка – не пытка.
harmful ['hɑːmful] *adj* (*toxin, influence etc*) вредный* (вреден).
harmless [hɑːmlɪs] *adj* (*animal, person*) безобидный* (безобиден); (*joke, activity*) невинный* (невинен).
harmonic [hɑː'mɔnɪk] *adj* гармонический.
harmonica [hɑː'mɔnɪkə] *n* губная гармоника.
harmonics [hɑː'mɔnɪks] *npl* гармония *fsg*.
harmonious [hɑː'məunɪəs] *adj* гармоничный* (гармоничен).
harmonium [hɑː'məunɪəm] *n* фисгармония.
harmonize ['hɑːmənaɪz] *vi* (*MUS*) гармон-ировать (*impf*); (*colours, ideas*): **to ~ (with)** гармонировать (*impf*) (с +*instr*).
harmony ['hɑːmənɪ] *n* (*accord*) гармония; (*MUS*) созвучие.
harness ['hɑːnɪs] *n* (*for horse*) упряжь *f*; (*for child*) постромки* *fpl*; (*safety harness*) привязные ремни *mpl* ♦ *vt* (*horse, dog*) запрягать (запрячь* *perf*); (*resources, energy etc*) обуздывать (обуздать *perf*).
harp [hɑːp] *n* арфа ♦ *vi*: **to ~ on about** (*pej*) заводить* (завести* *perf*) волынку о +*prp*.
harpist ['hɑːpɪst] *n* арфист(ка*).
harpoon [hɑː'puːn] *n* гарпун*.
harpsichord [hɑː'psɪkɔːd] *n* клавесин.
harried ['hærɪd] *adj* замученный (замучен).
harrow ['hærəu] *n* (*AGR*) борона.
harrowing ['hærəuɪŋ] *adj* душераздирающий*.
harry ['hærɪ] *vt* изводить* (извести* *perf*).
harsh [hɑːʃ] *adj* (*sound, light, criticism*) резкий* (резок); (*person*) жёсткий* (жёсток);

---

* marks translations which have irregular inflections. The Russian-English side of the dictionary gives inflectional information.

(*remark*) стро́гий* (строг); (*life, winter*) суро́вый (суро́в).
harshly [ˈhɑːʃlɪ] *adv* (*criticize*) ре́зко; (*mark, speak*) стро́го; (*act*) жёстко.
harshness [ˈhɑːʃnɪs] *n* (*see adj*) ре́зкость *f*; жёсткость *f*; стро́гость *f*; суро́вость *f*.
harvest [ˈhɑːvɪst] *n* (*harvest time*) жа́тва; (*of barley, fruit etc*) урожа́й ♦ *vt* собира́ть (собра́ть *perf*) урожа́й.
harvester [ˈhɑːvɪstəʳ] *n* (*machine: also:* **combine** ~) комба́йн.
has [hæz] *vb see* **have.**
has-been [ˈhæzbiːn] *n* (*inf: person*): **he's/she's a** ~ его́/её вре́мя прошло́.
hash [hæʃ] *n* (*CULIN*) мясно́е рагу́ *nt ind*; (*fig: mess*): **to make a** ~ **of sth** запа́рывать (запоро́ть *perf*) что-н.
hash [hæʃ] *n abbr* (*inf*) = **hashish.**
hashish [ˈhæʃɪʃ] *n* гаши́ш.
hasn't [ˈhæznt] = **has not.**
hassle [ˈhæsl] (*inf*) *n* моро́ка ♦ *vt* надоеда́ть (*impf*) +*dat*.
haste [heɪst] *n* спе́шка; **in** ~ в спе́шке; **to make** ~ **(to do)** торопи́ться (поторопи́ться *perf*) (+*infin*).
hasten [ˈheɪsn] *vt* (*speed up*) торопи́ть* (поторопи́ть* *perf*) ♦ *vi* (*hurry*): **to** ~ **to do** торопи́ться* (поторопи́ться* *perf*) +*infin*; **I** ~ **to add** ... спешу́ доба́вить ...; **she** ~**ed back to the house** она́ поспеши́ла обра́тно к до́му.
hastily [ˈheɪstɪlɪ] *adv* (*hurriedly*) поспе́шно; (*rashly*) опроме́тчиво.
hasty [ˈheɪstɪ] *adj* (*hurried*) поспе́шный* (поспе́шен); (*rash*) опроме́тчивый (опроме́тчив).
hat [hæt] *n* шля́па; (*woolly, furry*) ша́пка*; **to keep sth under one's** ~ держа́ть* (*impf*) что-н в секре́те.
hatbox [ˈhætbɒks] *n* шля́пная коро́бка*.
hatch [hætʃ] *n* (*NAUT: also:* ~**way**) люк; (*also:* **service** ~) разда́точное *or* буфе́тное окно́* ♦ *vi* (*also:* ~ **out: chick, egg**) вылупля́ться (вы́лупиться* *perf*) ♦ *vt* (*egg, chick etc*) выси́живать (вы́сидеть* *perf*); (*plot*) вына́шивать (вы́носить* *perf*).
hatchback [ˈhætʃbæk] *n* (*AUT*) маши́на-пика́п *f*.
hatchet [ˈhætʃɪt] *n* (*axe*) топо́рик; **to bury the** ~ мири́ться (помири́ться *perf*).
hatchet job (*inf*) *n* напа́дки* *pl*; **to do a** ~ ~ **on sb** разноси́ть* (разнести́* *perf*) кого́-н в пух и прах.
hatchet man *n* (*US: inf*) наёмник.
hate [heɪt] *vt* ненави́деть* (*impf*) ♦ *n* не́нависть *f*; **to** ~ **to do** *or* **doing** ненави́деть* (*impf*) +*infin*; **I** ~ **to trouble you, but** ... мне о́чень не хо́чется беспоко́ить Вас, но ....
hateful [ˈheɪtful] *adj* ненави́стный* (ненави́стен).
hatred [ˈheɪtrɪd] *n* не́нависть *f*.
hat trick *n* (*SPORT, also fig*) побе́да три ра́за подря́д.

haughty [ˈhɔːtɪ] *adj* надме́нный*.
haul [hɔːl] *vt* (*pull*) таска́ть/тащи́ть* (*impf*); (*transport*) перевози́ть* (перевезти́* *perf*) ♦ *n* (*of stolen goods etc*) добы́ча; (*of fish*) уло́в; **he** ~**ed himself out of the pool** он с трудо́м вы́брался из бассе́йна.
haulage [ˈhɔːlɪdʒ] *n* перево́зка.
haulage contractor *n* (*BRIT: COMM: firm*) фи́рма, производя́щая перево́зки; (: *person*) руководи́тель *m* фи́рмы, производя́щей перево́зки.
hauler [ˈhɔːləʳ] *n* (*US*) = **haulage contractor.**
haulier [ˈhɔːlɪəʳ] *n* (*BRIT*) руководи́тель *m* фи́рмы, производя́щей перево́зки.
haunch [hɔːntʃ] *n* бедро́*; (*of meat*) бе́дренная часть* *f*.
haunt [hɔːnt] *n* (*of crooks*) прито́н; (*in childhood etc*) люби́мое ме́сто* ♦ *vt* (*subj: problem, memory, fear*) пресле́довать (*impf*); **to** ~ **sb/a house** явля́ться (яви́ться* *perf*) кому́-н/в до́ме.
haunted [ˈhɔːntɪd] *adj* (*expression, look*) встрево́женный* (встрево́жен); **a** ~ **house** дом* с привиде́ниями; **this house is** ~ в э́том до́ме есть привиде́ния.
haunting [ˈhɔːntɪŋ] *adj* (*sight, music*) пресле́дующий.
Havana [həˈvænə] *n* Гава́на.

KEYWORD
---

have [hæv] (*pt, pp* **had**) *aux vb*: **1: to have arrived** прие́хать (*perf*); **have you already eaten?** ты уже́ пое́л?; **he has been kind to me** он прояви́л доброту́ по отноше́нию ко мне; **he has been promoted** он получи́л повыше́ние по слу́жбе; **has he told you?** он Вам сказа́л?; **having finished** *or* **when he had finished, he went to bed** зако́нчив *or* когда́ он зако́нчил, он пошёл спать
2 (*in tag questions*): **you've done it, haven't you?** Вы сде́лали э́то, да?; **he hasn't done it, has he?** он ведь э́то не сде́лал, ве́рно?
3 (*in short answers and questions*): **you've made a mistake – no I haven't/so I have** Вы оши́блись – нет, не оши́бся/да, оши́бся; **we haven't paid – yes we have!** мы не заплати́ли – нет, заплати́ли!; **I've been there before, have you?** я там был, а Вы?
♦ *modal aux vb* (*be obliged*): **to have (got) to do** быть (*impf*) до́лжным(-ой) +*infin*; **I have (got) to finish this work** я до́лжен зако́нчить э́ту рабо́ту; **you haven't to tell her** Вы не должны́ говори́ть ей; **I haven't got** *or* **I don't have to wear glasses** я могу́ не носи́ть очки́; **this has to be a mistake** э́то, наверняка́, оши́бка
♦ *vt* **1** (*possess*): **I** *etc* **have** у меня́ *etc*; **he has (got) blue eyes/dark hair** у него́ голубы́е глаза́/тёмные во́лосы; **do you have** *or* **have you got a car/phone?** у Вас есть маши́на/телефо́н?
2 (*referring to meals etc*): **to have breakfast** за́втракать (поза́втракать *perf*); **to have**

dinner обéдать (пообéдать *perf*); **to have a cigarette** выкýривать (выкурить *perf*) сигарéту; **to have a glass of wine** выпивáть (выпить* *perf*) стакáн винá
3 (*receive, obtain etc*): **may I have your address?** Вы мне мóжете дать свой áдрес?; **you can have the book for £5** эта кнúга вáша за £5; **I must have it by tomorrow** это должнó быть у меня к зáвтрашнему дню; **she is having a baby in March** у неё в мáрте бýдет ребёнок
4 (*maintain, allow*): **he will have it that he is right** он настáивает на том, что он прав; **I won't have it!** я этого не допущý!
5: I am having my television repaired мне должны починúть телевúзор; **to have sb do** попросúть* (*perf*) когó-н +*infin*; **he soon had them all laughing/working** онú у негó все тут же стáли смеяться/рабóтать
6 (*experience, suffer*): **I have flu/a headache** у меня грипп/болúт головá; **to have a cold** простужáться (простудúться* *perf*); **she had her bag stolen** у неё укрáли сýмку; **he had an operation** емý сдéлали опéрацию
7 (+*n*): **to have a swim** плáвать (поплавáть *perf*); **to have a rest** отдыхáть (отдохнýть *perf*); **let's have a look** давáйте посмóтрим; **we are having a meeting/party tomorrow** зáвтра у нас бýдет собрáние/бýдут гóсти; **let me have a try** дáйте мнé попрóбовать
8 (*inf: dupe*) провестú* (*perf*); **he's been had** егó провелú; **to have sb on** (*BRIT: inf*) водúть* (*impf*) когó-н зá нос
▶ **have in** *vt* (*inf*): **he has got it in for me** у негó прóтив меня зуб
▶ **have on** *vt*: **have you anything on tomorrow?** у Вас есть на зáвтра какúе-нибудь плáны?; **I don't have any money on me** у меня нет при себé дéнег; **he had a black sweater on** на нём был чёрный свúтер
▶ **have out** *vt*: **to have it out with sb** объясняться (объяснúться *perf*) с кем-н; **she had her tooth out** ей удалúли зуб; **she had her tonsils/appendix out** ей вырезали глáнды/аппендицúт.

haven ['heivn] *n* гáвань *f*; (*fig*) убéжище.
haven't ['hævnt] = have not.
haversack ['hævəsæk] *n* (*of hiker*) рюкзáк*; (*of soldier*) рáнец*.
haves [hævz] *npl* (*inf*): **the ~ and have-nots** имýщие *pl adj* и неимýщие *pl adj*.
havoc ['hævək] *n* (*chaos*) хаóс; **to play ~ with** (*plans etc*) игрáть (*impf*) злые шýтки над +*instr*.
Hawaii [hə'waii:] *n* Гавáйи *m ind*.
Hawaiian [hə'waijən] *adj* гавáйский ◆ *n* гаваéц*(-áйка*); (*LING*) гавáйский язык*.

hawk [hɔ:k] *n* ястреб*.
hawker ['hɔ:kə'] *n* (*COMM*) ýличный(-ая) торгóвец*(-вка*).
hawkish ['hɔ:kiʃ] *adj* хúщный.
hawthorn ['hɔ:θɔ:n] *n* боярышник.
hay [hei] *n* сéно.
hay fever *n* сеннáя лихорáдка*.
haystack ['heistæk] *n* стог* сéна; **it's like looking for a needle in a ~** это как искáть игóлку в стóге сéна.
haywire ['heiwaiə'] (*inf*) *adj*: **to go ~** (*machine*) барахлúть (забарахлúть *perf*); (*plans*) нарушáться (нарýшиться *perf*).
hazard ['hæzəd] *n* (*danger*) опáсность *f* ◆ *vt* (*risk*): **to ~ a guess** осмéливаться (осмéлиться *perf*) предположúть; **it's a health ~** это опáсно для здорóвья; **smoking is a fire ~** курéние мóжет служúть причúной пожáра.
hazard lights *npl* = hazard warning lights.
hazardous ['hæzədəs] *adj* опáсный* (опáсен).
hazard pay *n* (*US*) дополнúтельная плáта за труд в опáсных услóвиях.
hazard warning lights *npl* (*AUT*) аварúйные огнú *mpl*.
haze [heiz] *n* дымка*; **heat ~** мáрево.
hazel ['heizl] *n* лещúна ◆ *adj* (*eyes*) зеленовáто-кáрий*.
hazelnut ['heizlnʌt] *n* леснóй орéх.
hazy ['heizi] *adj* тумáнный* (тумáнен); **I'm rather ~ about the details** у меня довóльно смýтное представлéние о подрóбностях.
H-bomb ['eitʃbɔm] *n* водорóдная бóмба.
HE *abbr* (*REL, DIPLOMACY*: = His/Her Excellency*) Егó/Её Превосходúтельство; = high explosive.
he [hi:] *pron* он.
head [hɛd] *n* (*ANAT*) головá*; (*mind*) ум*; (*of list, queue*) начáло; (*of table*) главá*; (*of company, organization*) руководúтель(ница) *m(f)*; (*of school*) дирéктор*; (*on tape recorder etc*) голóвка ◆ *vt* (*list, queue*) стоять (*impf*) пéрвым(-ой) в +*prp*; (*group, company*) возглавлять (возглáвить* *perf*); **~s or tails** ≈ орёл или рéшка; **~ over heels in love** влюблён пó уши; **to ~ a ball** забивáть (забúть* *perf*) мяч головóй; **£10 a** *or* **per ~** по £10 кáждому *or* на кáждого; **to sit at the ~ of the table** сидéть* (сесть* *perf*) во главé столá; **he has a ~ for business** у негó спосóбности к бúзнесу; **I have no ~ for heights** у меня крýжится головá от высоты; **to come to a ~** (*fig: situation etc*) доходúть (дойтú* *perf*) до критúческой тóчки; **let's put our ~s together** давáйте обсýдим это вмéсте; **to say sth off the top of one's ~** говорúть (сказáть *perf*) что-н не задýмываясь; **on your own ~ be it!** пусть это бýдет на Вáшей сóвести!; **to bite**

or **snap sb's ~ off** огрызáться (огрызнýться *perf*) комý-н, грýбо обрывáть (обры́ть* *perf*) когó-н; **to go to sb's ~** (*alcohol*) ударя́ть (удáрить *perf*) комý-н в гóлову; (*success, power*) кружи́ть (вскружи́ть* *perf*) комý-н гóлову; **to keep/lose one's ~** не теря́ть (потеря́ть *perf*)/теря́ть (потеря́ть *perf*) гóлову; **I can't make ~ nor tail of this** я ничегó не могý поня́ть в э́том; **he's off his ~!** (*inf*) он рехнýлся!

▸ **head for** *vt fus* (*place*) направля́ться (напрáвиться* *perf*) в/на +*acc or* к +*dat*; (*disaster*) обрекáть (обрéчь* *perf*) себя́ на +*acc*

▸ **head off** *vt* (*threat, danger*) отводи́ть* (отвести́* *perf*).

headache [ˈhɛdeɪk] *n* головнáя боль* *f*; (*fig: problem*) неприя́тность *f*; **I've got a ~** у меня́ боли́т головá.

headband [ˈhɛdbænd] *n* óбруч* для волóс.

headboard [ˈhɛdbɔːd] *n* спи́нка* кровáти.

head cold *n* нáсморк.

headdress [ˈhɛddrɛs] *n* головнóе украшéние.

headed notepaper [ˈhɛdɪd-] *n* бланк; (*personal*) *бланк для письмá со штáмпом отправи́теля.*

header [ˈhɛdə*ʳ*] *n* (*BRIT: inf: FOOTBALL*) удáр головóй.

headfirst [ˈhɛdˈfəːst] *adv* (*dive, fall*) головóй вниз; (*rush*) сломя́ гóлову.

headgear [ˈhɛdgɪə*ʳ*] *n* головнóй убóр.

head-hunt [ˈhɛdhʌnt] *vi* смáнивать (смани́ть* *perf*) лýчших специали́стов ◆ *vt* смáнивать (смани́ть *perf*).

head-hunter [ˈhɛdhʌntə*ʳ*] *n* (*COMM*) человéк, *котóрый перемáнивает сотрýдников из однóй фи́рмы в другýю.*

heading [ˈhɛdɪŋ] *n* (*of chapter, article*) заголóвок*.

headlamp [ˈhɛdlæmp] *n* (*BRIT*) = **headlight**.

headland [ˈhɛdlənd] *n* мыс*.

headlight [ˈhɛdlaɪt] *n* фáра.

headline [ˈhɛdlaɪn] *n* (*PRESS, TV, RADIO*) заголóвок*.

headlong [ˈhɛdlɔŋ] *adv* (*headfirst*) головóй вперёд; (*hastily*) опромéтчиво.

headmaster [hɛdˈmɑːstə*ʳ*] *n* дирéктор* шкóлы.

headmistress [hɛdˈmɪstrɪs] *n* дирéктор* шкóлы.

head office *n* (*of company etc*) дирéкция.

head of state (*pl* **~s ~~**) *n* главá* госудáрства.

head-on [hɛdˈɔn] *adj* (*collision, confrontation*) лобовóй ◆ *adv* нóсом к нóсу.

headphones [ˈhɛdfəunz] *npl* нáушники *mpl*.

headquarters [ˈhɛdkwɔːtəz] *npl* (*of company, organization*) глáвное управлéние *ntsg*; (*MIL*) штаб-кварти́ра *fsg*.

headrest [ˈhɛdrɛst] *n* подголóвник.

headroom [ˈhɛdrum] *n* (*in car*) внýтренняя высотá (*кýзова*); (*under bridge*) просвéт.

headscarf [ˈhɛdskɑːf] *n* косы́нка*; (*square*) головнóй платóк*.

headset [ˈhɛdsɛt] *n* = **headphones**.

head start *n*: **to have/get a ~~** имéть (*impf*)/получáть (получи́ть* *perf*) исхóдное преимýщество.

headstone [ˈhɛdstəun] *n* (*on grave*) надгрóбный кáмень* *m*.

headstrong [ˈhɛdstrɔŋ] *adj* упóрный* (упóрен).

head teacher *n* дирéктор* шкóлы.

head waiter *n* (*in restaurant*) глáвный официáнт.

headway [ˈhɛdweɪ] *n*: **to make ~** продвигáться (продви́нуться *perf*) вперёд.

headwind [ˈhɛdwɪnd] *n* встрéчный вéтер*.

heady [ˈhɛdɪ] *adj* (*experience, time*) головокружи́тельный; (*drink*) хмельнóй; (*atmosphere*) взбудорáженный.

heal [hiːl] *vt* (*patient*) излéчивать (излечи́ть* *perf*); (*injury*) заживля́ть (зажи́вить* *perf*); (*damage*) восстанáвливать (восстанови́ть* *perf*) ◆ *vi* (*injury*) заживáть (зажи́ть *perf*); (*damage*) восстанáвливаться (восстанови́ться* *perf*).

health [hɛlθ] *n* (*also MED*) здорóвье; **good ~** крéпкое здорóвье.

health care *n* здравоохранéние.

health centre *n* (*BRIT*) поликли́ника.

health food *n* здорóвая пи́ща.

health-food shop [ˈhɛlθfuːd-] *n* магази́н здорóвого питáния.

health hazard *n* опáсность *f* для здорóвья.

Health Service *n* (*BRIT*): **the ~~** слýжба здравоохранéния.

healthy [ˈhɛlθɪ] *adj* (*person*) здорóвый* (здорóв); (*economy, appetite*) здорóвый; (*pursuit, pastime*) полéзный* (полéзен); (*profit*) достáточно хорóший; **it's not ~ to drink too much** сли́шком мнóго пить – врéдно для здорóвья.

heap [hiːp] *n* (*small*) кýча; (*large*) грýда ◆ *vt* (*stones, sand*): **to ~ (up)** свáливать (свали́ть* *perf*) в кýчу; (*plate, sink*): **to ~ with sth** наполня́ть (напóлнить *perf*) чем-н; (*food, books*): **to ~ sth on** навáливать (навали́ть* *perf*) что-н на +*acc*; **~s of** (*inf*) кýча *fsg* +*gen*; **to ~ favours/praise/gifts on sb** осыпáть (осы́пать* *perf*) когó-н ми́лостями/похвалáми/подáрками.

hear [hɪə*ʳ*] (*pt, pp* **heard**) *vt* слы́шать (услы́шать *perf*); (*lecture, concert*) слýшать (*impf*); (*LAW: case*) слýшать (*impf*); **to ~ about** слы́шать (услы́шать *perf*) о +*prp*; **did you ~ about the move?** Вы слы́шали о переéзде?; **to ~ from sb** слы́шать (услы́шать *perf*) от когó-н; **I can't ~ you** Вас не слы́шно; **I've never ~d of that book** я никогдá не слы́шал об э́той кни́ге; **I wouldn't ~ of it!** я и слы́шать об э́том не хочý!

▸ **hear out** *vt* выслýшивать (вы́слушать *perf*).

heard [həːd] *pt, pp of* **hear**.

hearing ['hɪərɪŋ] *n* (*sense*) слух; (*LAW*, *POL*) слушание; **she is a bit hard of ~** она туговата на ухо; **within/out of ~ distance** в пределах/ за пределами слышимости; **to give sb a (fair) ~** (*BRIT*) дать* (*perf*) кому-н высказаться.
hearing aid *n* слуховой аппарат.
hearsay ['hɪəseɪ] *n* слух; **by ~** по слухам.
hearse [hə:s] *n* катафалк.
heart [hɑ:t] *n* сердце*; (*of lettuce*) сердцевина; (*of problem, matter*) суть *f*; **~s** *npl* (*CARDS*) черви *fpl*; **to lose/take ~** пасть* (*perf*)/не падать (*impf*) духом; **at ~** в глубине души; **(off) by ~** наизусть; **he has a weak ~** у него слабое сердце; **to set one's ~ on sth/on doing** стремиться* (*impf*) всей душой к чему-н/ +*infin*; **to pour one's ~ out to sb** изливать (излить* *perf*) кому-н душу; **he's a man after my own ~** он мне по сердцу; **the ~ of the matter** суть дела.
heartache ['hɑ:teɪk] *n* сердечная боль *f*.
heart attack *n* сердечный приступ.
heartbeat ['hɑ:tbi:t] *n* (*one pulsation*) сердечное сокращение; (*rhythm*) сердцебиение.
heartbreak ['hɑ:tbreɪk] *n* большое горе.
heartbreaking ['hɑ:tbreɪkɪŋ] *adj* душе- раздирающий* (душераздираюащ).
heartbroken ['hɑ:tbrəukən] *adj*: **he is ~** (*sad*) он убит горем.
heartburn ['hɑ:tbə:n] *n* изжога.
-hearted ['hɑ:tɪd] *suffix*: **kind-~** добро- сердечный.
hearten ['hɑ:tn] *vt* воодушевлять (воодушевить* *perf*).
heart failure *n* (*resulting in death*) остановка сердца.
heartfelt ['hɑ:tfɛlt] *adj* искренний*.
hearth [hɑ:θ] *n* очаг*.
heartily ['hɑ:tɪlɪ] *adv* (*thank, welcome*) сердечно; (*dislike*) всем сердцем; **to laugh ~** смеяться (*impf*) от души.
heartland ['hɑ:tlænd] *n* (*of country*) сердце; **Britain's industrial ~** промышленный центр Британии.
heartless ['hɑ:tlɪs] *adj* бессердечный* (бессердечен).
heartstrings ['hɑ:tstrɪŋz] *npl* душевные струны* *ntpl*; **the film really tugs at your ~** фильм берёт за душу.
heartthrob ['hɑ:tθrɔb] *n* сердцеед.
heart-to-heart ['hɑ:t'tə'hɑ:t] *adj* сердечный; **to have a ~** говорить (*impf*) по душам.
heart transplant *n* пересадка* сердца.
heartwarming ['hɑ:twɔ:mɪŋ] *adj* (*sight*) трогательный* (трогателен).
hearty ['hɑ:tɪ] *adj* (*person, laugh*) весёлый* (весел); (*welcome, support*) сердечный; (*appetite*) здоровый; (*dislike*) глубокий*.

heat [hi:t] *n* тепло; (*extreme*) жар; (*of weather*) жара; (*temperature*) температура; (*excitement*) пыл*; (*also*: **qualifying ~**: *in race etc*) забег; (: *in swimming*) заплыв; (*ZOOL*): **our dog is in** *or* (*US*) **on ~** у нашей собаки течка ◆ *vt* (*water, food*) греть *or* нагревать (нагреть *perf*); (*house*) отапливать (отопить* *perf*)
▶ **heat up** *vi* (*water, house*) согреваться (согреться *perf*) ◆ *vt* (*food, water*) подогревать (подогреть *perf*); (*room*) обогревать (обогреть *perf*); (*engine*) разогревать (разогреть *perf*).
heated ['hi:tɪd] *adj* отапливаемый; (*argument*) горячий*; (*pool*) обогреваемый.
heater ['hi:tə'] *n* обогреватель *m*.
heath [hi:θ] *n* (*BRIT*) (вересковая) пустошь *f*.
heathen ['hi:ðn] *n* язычник(-ица).
heather ['hɛðə'] *n* вереск.
heating ['hi:tɪŋ] *n* отопление.
heat-resistant ['hi:trɪzɪstənt] *adj* жаро- прочный* (жаропрочен), термостойкий* (термостоек).
heat-seeking ['hi:tsi:kɪŋ] *adj* тепло- улавливающий.
heatstroke ['hi:tstrəuk] *n* тепловой удар.
heatwave ['hi:tweɪv] *n* период сильной жары.
heave [hi:v] *vt* (*pull*) вытягивать (вытянуть *perf*); (*push*) толкать (толкнуть *perf*); (*lift*) взваливать (взвалить *perf*); (*throw*) швырять (швырнуть *perf*) ◆ *vi* (*chest*) вздыматься (*impf*); (*retch*) чувствовать (почувствовать *perf*) тошноту ◆ *n* (*upwards*) подъём; (*sideways*) рывок; **to ~ a sigh** глубоко вздохнуть (*perf*)
▶ **heave to** ◆ (*pt, pp* **hove**) *vi* (*NAUT*) ложиться (лечь* *perf*) в дрейф.
heaven ['hɛvn] *n* (*also fig*) рай*; **thank ~(s)!** слава Богу!; **~ forbid! Боже** упаси!; **for ~'s sake! ради** Бога!
heavenly ['hɛvnlɪ] *adj* небесный; (*fig*) райский*.
heaven-sent ['hɛvn'sɛnt] *adj* благодатный* (благодатен).
heavily ['hɛvɪlɪ] *adv* (*fall, sigh*) тяжело*; (*drink, smoke, depend*) сильно; (*sleep*) крепко; (*say*) весомый (весом).
heavy ['hɛvɪ] *adj* тяжёлый* (тяжёл); (*rain, blow, fall*) сильный* (силен); (*breathing, sleep*) тяжёлый*; (*build: of person*) грузный; (*sea*) бурный* (бурен); **he is a ~ drinker/ smoker** он много пьёт/курит; **the work is ~ going** работа идёт тяжело; **he is ~ going** с ним трудно иметь дело.
heavy cream *n* (*US*) жирные сливки* *pl*.
heavy-duty ['hɛvɪ'dju:tɪ] *adj* сверхпрочный.
heavy goods vehicle *n* (*BRIT*) грузовик, перевозящий тяжёлые грузы.

---

* marks translations which have irregular inflections. The Russian-English side of the dictionary gives inflectional information.

heavy-handed ['hɛvɪ'hændɪd] *adj* вла́стный* (вла́стен).
heavy industry *n* тяжёлая промы́шленность *f*.
heavy metal *n* (*MUS*) хэ́ви ме́тал, (тяжёлый) мета́лл.
heavy-set ['hɛvɪ'sɛt] *adj* (*esp US*) корена́стый (коре́наст), пло́тный* (пло́тен).
heavy user *n* лицо́/компа́ния, покупа́ющее/-ая больши́е па́ртии определённого това́ра.
heavyweight ['hɛvɪweɪt] *n* боксёр тяжёлого ве́са.
Hebrew ['hi:bru:] *adj* древнееврейский ◆ *n* (*LING: ancient*) древнееврейский язы́к*; (*modern*) иври́т.
Hebrides ['hɛbrɪdi:z] *npl*: **the ~** Гебри́дские острова́* *mpl*.
heck [hɛk] *excl* (*inf*) чёрт.
heckle ['hɛkl] *vt* перебива́ть (переби́ть* *perf*).
heckler ['hɛklə'] *n*: **there were several ~s in the audience** не́которые лю́ди в за́ле перебива́ли.
hectare ['hɛktɑ:'] *n* (*BRIT*) гекта́р.
hectic ['hɛktɪk] *adj* (*day*) сумато́шный* (сумато́шен); (*actions, activities*) лихора́дочный* (лихора́дочен).
hector ['hɛktə'] *vt* запу́гивать (запуга́ть *perf*).
he'd [hi:d] = **he would, he had**.
hedge [hɛdʒ] *n* жива́я и́згородь *f* ◆ *vi* (*stall*) уви́ливать (увильну́ть *perf*) ◆ *vt*: **to ~ one's bets** подстрахо́вываться (подстрахова́ться *perf*); **as a ~ against inflation** как страхо́вка от инфля́ции
▸ **hedge in** *vt* ограни́чивать (ограни́чить *perf*).
hedgehog ['hɛdʒhɔg] *n* ёж*.
hedgerow ['hɛdʒrəu] *n* жива́я и́згородь *f*.
hedonism ['hi:dənɪzm] *n* гедони́зм.
heed [hi:d] *vt* (*also:* **take ~ of**) принима́ть (приня́ть* *perf*) во внима́ние ◆ *n*: **to pay (no) ~ to, take (no) ~ of** (не) принима́ть (приня́ть* *perf*) во внима́ние.
heedless ['hi:dlɪs] *adj*: **~ of** не обраща́я внима́ния на +*acc*.
heel [hi:l] *n* (*of foot*) пя́тка*; (*of shoe*) каблу́к* ◆ *vt* (*shoe*) подбива́ть (подби́ть* *perf*); **to bring to ~** (*dog*) заставля́ть (заста́вить* *perf*) идти́ *or* стоя́ть ря́дом; (*person*) подчиня́ть (подчини́ть *perf*); **to take to one's ~s** (*inf*) пуска́ться (пусти́ться* *perf*) наутёк.
hefty ['hɛftɪ] *adj* (*person, object*) здорове́нный; (*profit, fine*) изря́дный*.
heifer ['hɛfə'] *n* тёлка*.
height [haɪt] *n* (*of tree, of plane*) высота́*; (*of person*) рост; (*of power*) верши́на; (*of mountain*) возвы́шенность *f*; (*of season*) разга́р; (*of luxury, taste*) верх; **what ~ are you?** како́й у Вас рост?; **of average ~** сре́днего ро́ста; **to be afraid of ~s** боя́ться (*impf*) высоты́; **it's the ~ of fashion** э́то верх мо́ды; **at the ~ of the tourist season** в разга́р туристи́ческого сезо́на.

heighten ['haɪtn] *vt* уси́ливать (уси́лить *perf*).
heinous ['heɪnəs] *adj* (*crime*) чудо́вищный.
heir [ɛə'] *n* насле́дник.
heir apparent *n* прямо́й насле́дник.
heiress ['ɛərɛs] *n* насле́дница.
heirloom ['ɛəlu:m] *n* семе́йная рели́квия.
heist [haɪst] *n* (*US: inf*) грабёж*.
held [hɛld] *pt, pp of* **hold**.
helicopter ['hɛlɪkɔptə'] *n* вертолёт.
heliport ['hɛlɪpɔ:t] *n* вертодро́м.
helium ['hi:lɪəm] *n* ге́лий.
hell [hɛl] *n* (*also fig*) ад*; **~!** (*inf*) чёрт!; **a** *or* **one ~ of a mess** (*inf*) кошма́рный беспоря́док*; **a** *or* **one ~ of a party** (*inf*) кла́сссная вечери́нка.
he'll [hi:l] = **he will, he shall**; *see* **will**.
hellish ['hɛlɪʃ] *adj* (*inf: awful*) кошма́рный* (кошма́рен).
hello [hə'ləu] *excl* здра́вствуйте; (*informal*) приве́т; (*TEL: on answering*) алло́; (*to attract attention*) эй; (*in surprise*): **~(, what's this!)** эй (что э́то!).
helm [hɛlm] *n* (*NAUT*) руль* *m*; **man at the ~** (*fig*) рулево́й *m adj*; **at the ~** of у корми́ла +*gen*.
helmet ['hɛlmɪt] *n* (*of policeman, miner*) ка́ска*; (*also:* **crash ~**) шлем.
helmsman ['hɛlmzmən] *n* рулево́й *m adj*.
help [hɛlp] *n* по́мощь *f*; (*charwoman*) прислу́га ◆ *vt* помога́ть (помо́чь* *perf*) +*dat*; **with the ~ of** (*person*) с по́мощью +*gen*; (*tool*) при по́мощи +*gen*; **can I be of (any) ~?** я могу́ Вам чем-нибу́дь помо́чь?; **~!** помоги́те!; **can I ~ you?** (*in shop*) чем могу́ быть поле́зен?; **~ yourself** угоща́йтесь; **he can't ~ it** он ничего́ не мо́жет поде́лать с э́тим; **I can't ~ thinking that ...** я не могу́ не ду́мать, что ....
helper ['hɛlpə'] *n* помо́щник(-ица).
helpful ['hɛlpful] *adj* поле́зный* (поле́зен).
helping ['hɛlpɪŋ] *n* по́рция.
helping hand *n*: **to lend a ~ ~** протя́гивать (протяну́ть *perf*) ру́ку по́мощи.
helpless ['hɛlplɪs] *adj* беспо́мощный* (беспо́мощен).
helplessly ['hɛlplɪslɪ] *adv* беспо́мощно.
helpline ['hɛlplaɪn] *n* телефо́н дове́рия.
Helsinki ['hɛlsɪŋkɪ] *n* Хе́льсинки *m ind*.
helter-skelter ['hɛltə'skɛltə'] *n* (*BRIT*) спира́льная го́рка (*аттракцио́н*).
hem [hɛm] *n* (*of dress*) подо́л; (*of curtains*) низ ◆ *vt* подшива́ть (подши́ть* *perf*)
▸ **hem in** *vt* пло́тно окружа́ть (окружи́ть *perf*); **city life made him feel ~med in** жизнь в го́роде стесня́ла его́.
hematology ['hi:mə'tɔlədʒɪ] *n* (*US*) = **haematology**.
hemisphere ['hɛmɪsfɪə'] *n* полуша́рие.
hemlock ['hɛmlɔk] *n* (*BOT*) болиголо́в.
hemoglobin ['hi:mə'gləubɪn] *n* (*US*) = **haemoglobin**.
hemophilia ['hi:mə'fɪlɪə] *n* (*US*) = **haemophilia**.
hemorrhage ['hɛmərɪdʒ] *n* (*US*) = **haemorrhage**.
hemorrhoids ['hɛmərɔɪdz] *npl* (*US*) =

haemorrhoids.
hemp [hɛmp] *n* конопля́.
hen [hɛn] *n* (*chicken*) ку́рица*; (*female bird*) са́мка*.
hence [hɛns] *adv* (*therefore*) сле́довательно; (*from now*): **2 years ~** (*formal*) по истече́нии двух лет.
henceforth [hɛns'fɔ:θ] *adv* впредь.
henchman ['hɛntʃmən] *irreg n* приспе́шник.
henna ['hɛnə] *n* хна.
hen party *n* (*inf*) деви́чник.
henpecked ['hɛnpɛkt] *adj* (*husband*) поко́рный* (поко́рен).
hepatitis [hɛpə'taɪtɪs] *n* гепати́т.
her [hə:ʳ] *pron* (*direct*) её; (*indirect*) ей; (*after prep: +gen, +dat, +prp*) ней; (: *+instr*) неё; *see also* **me** ♦ *adj* её; (*referring to subject of sentence*) свой; *see also* **my**.
herald ['hɛrəld] *n* (*precursor*) предве́стник ♦ *vt* (*event*) предвеща́ть (*impf*).
heraldic [hɛ'rældɪk] *adj* геральди́ческий.
heraldry ['hɛrəldrɪ] *n* (*study*) гера́льдика; (*coat of arms*) герб.
herb [hə:b] *n* (BOT, CULIN) трава́*; (MED) лека́рственная трава́; **~s** *npl* (CULIN) зе́лень *fsg*.
herbaceous [hə:'beɪʃəs] *adj*: **~ plant** цвето́чное расте́ние; **~ border** клу́мба.
herbal ['hə:bl] *adj*: **~ medicine** лече́ние тра́вами; **~ remedy** лека́рство из трав; **~ tea** чай* из трав.
herbicide ['hə:bɪsaɪd] *n* гербици́д.
herd [hə:d] *n* ста́до* ♦ *vt* (*drive: animals, people*) гнать (*impf*); (*gather*) сгоня́ть (согна́ть* *perf*).
here [hɪəʳ] *adv* (*location*) здесь; (*destination*) сюда́; (*departure point*): **from ~** отсю́да; (*at this point: in past*) тут; "**here!**" (*present*) „здесь!"; **~ is ...**, **~ are ...** вот ...; **~ you are** (*giving*) вот, пожа́луйста; **where are my keys? ~ we are!** (*finding sth*) где мои ключи? вот они́!; **~'s my sister** вот моя́ сестра́; **~ she comes** вот она́ идёт; **come ~!** иди́те сюда́!; **she left ~ yesterday** она́ уе́хала отсю́да вчера́; **~ and there** (*location*) там и сям; (*motion*) туда́ и сюда́; "**here's to ...!**" (*toast*) „за +*acc* ...!".
hereabouts ['hɪərə'bauts] *adv* побли́зости.
hereafter [hɪər'ɑ:ftəʳ] *adv* в дальне́йшем.
hereby [hɪə'baɪ] *adv* (*formal: in letter*): **we ~ acknowledge ...** настоя́щим подтвержда́ем ....
hereditary [hɪ'rɛdɪtrɪ] *adj* насле́дственный.
heredity [hɪ'rɛdɪtɪ] *n* насле́дственность *f*.
heresy ['hɛrəsɪ] *n* е́ресь *f*.
heretic ['hɛrətɪk] *n* ерети́к*(-и́чка*).
heretical [hɪ'rɛtɪkl] *adj* ерети́ческий*.
herewith [hɪə'wɪð] *adv* (*formal: letter*): **please find enclosed ~ ...** при сём прилага́ется ....
heritage ['hɛrɪtɪdʒ] *n* насле́дие; **our national ~**

на́ше национа́льное бога́тство.
hermetically [hə:'mɛtɪklɪ] *adv*: **~ sealed** гермети́чески закры́тый.
hermit ['hə:mɪt] *n* отше́льник(-ица).
hernia ['hə:nɪə] *n* гры́жа.
hero ['hɪərəu] *n* (*pl* **~es**) *n* геро́й.
heroic [hɪ'rəuɪk] *adj* геро́ический*.
heroin ['hɛrəuɪn] *n* геро́ин.
heroin addict *n* наркома́н (*принима́ющий геро́ин*).
heroine ['hɛrəuɪn] *n* геро́иня.
heroism ['hɛrəuɪzəm] *n* геро́изм.
heron ['hɛrən] *n* ца́пля*.
hero worship *n* культ геро́я.
herring ['hɛrɪŋ] *n* (ZOOL) сельдь* *f*; (CULIN) селёдка.
hers [hə:z] *pron* её; (*referring to subject of sentence*) свой; *see also* **mine**[1].
herself [hə:'sɛlf] *pron* (*reflexive, after prep: +acc, +gen*) себя́; (: *+dat, +prp*) себе́; (: *+instr*) собо́й; (*emphatic*) сама́; (*alone*): **by ~** одна́; *see also* **myself**.
Herts *abbr* (BRIT: POST) = Hertfordshire.
he's [hi:z] = **he is**, **he has**; *see* **be**, **have**.
hesitant ['hɛzɪtənt] *adj* нереши́тельный* (нереши́телен); **to be ~ about doing** не реша́ться (*impf*) *или* колеба́ться* (*impf*) +*infin*.
hesitate ['hɛzɪteɪt] *vi* (*pause*) колеба́ться* (поколеба́ться* *perf*); (*be unwilling*) не реша́ться (*impf*); **to ~ (about/to do)** не реша́ться (*impf*) (на +*acc*/+*infin*); **don't ~ to see a doctor if you are worried** е́сли Вы обеспоко́ены (э́тим), без колеба́ний обрати́тесь к врачу́.
hesitation [hɛzɪ'teɪʃən] *n* (*pause*) колеба́ние; **I have no ~ in saying (that)** ... я говорю́ не коле́блясь(, что) ....
hessian ['hɛsɪən] *n* мешкови́на.
heterogeneous ['hɛtərə'dʒi:nɪəs] *adj* разноро́дный* (разноро́ден).
heterosexual ['hɛtərəu'sɛksjuəl] *adj* гетеросексуа́льный ♦ *n* гетеросексуа́льный челове́к*.
het up [hɛt-] *adj* (*inf*): **to get ~ ~ (about)** заводи́ться* (завести́сь* *perf*) (из-за +*gen*).
HEW *n abbr* (US) = **Department of Health, Education and Welfare**.
hew [hju:] (*pp* **hewed** *or* **hewn**) *vt* (*stone*) выда́лбливать (вы́долбить* *perf*); (*wood*) выруба́ть (вы́рубить* *perf*).
hewn [hju:n] *pp of* **hew**.
hex [hɛks] (US) *n* колдунья*, ве́дьма ♦ *vt* завора́живать (заворожи́ть *perf*).
hexagon ['hɛksəgən] *n* шестиуго́льник.
hexagonal [hɛk'sægənl] *adj* шестиуго́льный.
hey [heɪ] *excl* эй.
heyday ['heɪdeɪ] *n*: **the ~ of** расцве́т +*gen*.
HF *n abbr* (= *high frequency*) ВЧ= *высо́кая*

---

* marks translations which have irregular inflections. The Russian-English side of the dictionary gives inflectional information.

частота.

HGV *n abbr* (*BRIT*: = *heavy goods vehicle*) грузовой автомобиль *m*.

HI *abbr* (*US*: *POST*) = *Hawaii*.

hi [haɪ] *excl* (*as greeting*) привет; (*to attract attention*) эй.

hiatus [haɪˈeɪtəs] *n* (*in activity*) пробел; (*in conversation*) пауза.

hibernate [ˈhaɪbəneɪt] *vi* впадать (впасть* *perf*) в зимнюю спячку.

hibernation [haɪbəˈneɪʃən] *n* зимняя спячка.

hick [hɪk] *n* (*US*: *inf*: *pej*) деревенщина *m/f*.

hiccough *etc* = **hiccup** *etc*.

hiccup [ˈhɪkʌp] *vi* икать (*impf*).

hiccups [ˈhɪkʌps] *npl* икота *fsg*; **she's got (the)** ~ у неё икота.

hid [hɪd] *pt of* **hide**.

hidden [ˈhɪdn] *pp of* **hide** ♦ *adj*: **there are no** ~ **extras** здесь нет скрытых добавочных расходов; **there is a** ~ **agenda** за этим что-то кроется.

hide [haɪd] (*pt* **hid**, *pp* **hidden**) *n* (*skin*) шкура; (*of birdwatcher*) укрытие ♦ *vt* (*object, person*) прятать* (спрятать* *perf*); (*feeling, information*) скрывать (скрыть* *perf*); (*sun, view*) закрывать (закрыть* *perf*) ♦ *vi*: **to** ~ **(from sb)** прятаться* (спрятаться* *perf*) (от кого-н); **to** ~ **sth (from sb)** (*object, person*) прятать* (спрятать* *perf*) что-н (от кого-н); (*information*) скрывать (скрыть* *perf*) что-н (от кого-н).

hide-and-seek [ˈhaɪdənˈsiːk] *n* прятки* *fpl*.

hideaway [ˈhaɪdəweɪ] *n* убежище.

hideous [ˈhɪdɪəs] *adj* (*painting, conditions*) жуткий* (жуток); (*face*) омерзительный* (омерзителен).

hideously [ˈhɪdɪəslɪ] *adv* (*ugly*) омерзительно; (*difficult*) жутко.

hide-out [ˈhaɪdaut] *n* укрытие; (*of criminals*) логовище.

hiding [ˈhaɪdɪŋ] *n* (*beating*) порка*; (*concealed*): **to be in** ~ скрываться (*impf*).

hiding place *n* (*for person*) укрытие; (*for money etc*) тайник*, потайное место*.

hierarchy [ˈhaɪərɑːkɪ] *n* иерархия.

hieroglyphic [haɪərəˈɡlɪfɪk] *adj* иероглифический.

hieroglyphics [haɪərəˈɡlɪfɪks] *npl* иероглифы *mpl*.

hi-fi [ˈhaɪfaɪ] *n abbr* (= *high fidelity*) высокая верность звуковоспроизведения ♦ *adj* (*equipment, system*): ~ **equipment** аппаратура с высокой верностью звуковоспроизведения.

higgledy-piggledy [ˈhɪɡldɪˈpɪɡldɪ] (*inf*) *adj* беспорядочный* (беспорядочен) ♦ *adv* кое-как, беспорядочно.

high [haɪ] *adj* высокий* (высок); (*wind*) сильный*; (*BRIT*: *meat*) выдержанный (выдержан) ♦ *adv* (*climb, aim etc*) высоко ♦ *n*: **exports have reached a new** ~ экспорт достиг

новой высоты; **the building is 20 m** ~ высота здания – 20 м; **to be** ~ (*inf*: *on drugs, drink*) кайфовать (*impf*); ~ **risk** высокая степень *f* риска; ~ **in the air** (*position*) высоко в воздухе; (*motion*) высоко в воздух; **to pay a** ~ **price for sth** платить* (заплатить* *perf*) высокую цену за что-н; **it's** ~ **time you learned how to do it** Вам давно пора научиться делать это.

highball [ˈhaɪbɔːl] *n* (*US*) виски с содовой и льдом (*в высоком стакане*).

highboy [ˈhaɪbɔɪ] *n* (*US*) высокий комод.

highbrow [ˈhaɪbrau] *adj* (*subjects*) учёный; (*person*) интеллектуальный* (интеллектуален).

highchair [ˈhaɪtʃɛəʳ] *n* высокий* стульчик (*для маленьких детей*).

high-class [ˈhaɪklɑːs] *adj* (*hotel, performance*) первоклассный, высокого класса; (*neighbourhood*) престижный* (престижен).

High Court *n* (*BRIT*): **the** ~ ~ ≈ Верховный суд*.

higher [ˈhaɪəʳ] *adj* высший* ♦ *adv* выше.

higher education *n* высшее образование.

highfalutin [haɪfəˈluːtɪn] *adj* (*inf*) высокопарный* (высокопарен).

high finance *n*: **the world of** ~ ~ мир высших финансовых кругов.

high-five [ˈhaɪfaɪv] *n* пятерня (*хлопок ладонью по чьей-нибудь ладони*).

high-flier [ˈhaɪflaɪəʳ] *n* птица высокого полёта.

high-flying [ˈhaɪflaɪɪŋ] *adj* (*person*) честолюбивый; (*lifestyle*) шикарный.

high-handed [ˈhaɪˈhændɪd] *adj* (*decision, person*) своевольный* (своеволен).

high-heeled [ˈhaɪˈhiːld] *adj* на высоком каблуке.

high heels *npl* туфли* *fpl* на высоком каблуке.

high jump *n* прыжок* в высоту.

Highlands [ˈhaɪləndz] *npl*: **the** ~ Высокогорья* *ntpl* (*Шотландии*).

high-level [ˈhaɪlɛvl] *adj* (*talks etc*) на высшем уровне; ~ **language** (*COMPUT*) язык* высокого уровня.

highlight [ˈhaɪlaɪt] *n* (*of event*) кульминация ♦ *vt* (*problem, need*) выявлять (выявить* *perf*); ~**s** *npl* (*in hair*) пряди *fpl*; **the match** ~**s were shown on TV** кульминационные моменты матча были показаны по телевидению.

highlighter [ˈhaɪlaɪtəʳ] *n* (*also*: ~ **pen**) фломастер (*для выделения частей текста*).

highly [ˈhaɪlɪ] *adv* очень; (*paid*) высоко; **to speak** ~ **of** быть* отзываться* (отозваться* *perf*) о +*prp*; **to think** ~ **of** быть* (*impf*) высокого мнения о +*prp*.

highly strung *adj* нервозный* (нервозен).

High Mass *n* торжественная месса.

highness [ˈhaɪnɪs] *n*: **Her/His H**~ Её/Его Высочество.

high-pitched [ˈhaɪˈpɪtʃt] *adj* пронзительный* (пронзителен).

high point *n* кульминация.

high-powered ['haɪ'pauəd] *adj* (*engine*) мо́щный*; (*job*) отве́тственный; (*course, person*) высо́кого у́ровня.
high-pressure ['haɪprɛʃə'] *adj* высо́кого давле́ния.
high-rise ['haɪraɪz] *adj* (*buildings, flats*) высо́тный.
high school *n* (*BRIT*) сре́дняя шко́ла (*для 11-18ти ле́тних*); (*US*) сре́дняя шко́ла (*для 15-18ти летних*).
high season *n* (*BRIT*) разга́р сезо́на.
high spirits *npl* припо́днятое настрое́ние *ntsg*.
high street *n* (*BRIT*) центра́льная у́лица.
high-strung ['haɪ'strʌŋ] *adj* (*US*) = **highly strung**.
high tide *n* прили́в.
highway ['haɪweɪ] *n* (*US: between towns, states*) шоссе́ *nt ind*, автостра́да; (*main road*) автостра́да.
Highway Code *n* (*BRIT*) ≈ пра́вила *ntpl* доро́жного движе́ния.
highwayman ['haɪweɪmən] *irreg n* разбо́йник с большо́й доро́ги.
hijack ['haɪdʒæk] *vt* угоня́ть (угна́ть* *perf*); (*fig*) перехва́тывать (перехвати́ть* *perf*) ♦ *n* (*also:* ~**ing**) уго́н.
hijacker ['haɪdʒækə'] *n* уго́нщик.
hike [haɪk] *vi* ходи́ть*/идти́* (*impf*) в похо́д ♦ *vt* (*inf: prices*) взви́нчивать (взвинти́ть* *perf*) ♦ *n:* **to go for a** ~ идти́* (пойти́* *perf*) на дли́тельную прогу́лку; (*inf*): **a** ~ **in prices** скачо́к* цен.
hiker ['haɪkə'] *n* тури́ст(ка).
hiking ['haɪkɪŋ] *n:* **to go** ~ ходи́ть*/идти́* (*impf*) в похо́д.
hilarious [hɪ'lɛərɪəs] *adj* чрезвыча́йно смешно́й* (смешо́н).
hilarity [hɪ'lærɪtɪ] *n* бу́йное весе́лье.
hill [hɪl] *n* (*small*) холм*; (*fairly high*) (небольша́я) гора́*; (*slope*) склон; (*on road*) подъём.
hillbilly ['hɪlbɪlɪ] *n* (*US*) го́рец*; (: *pej*) дереве́нщина *m/f*.
hillock ['hɪlək] *n* приго́рок*.
hillside ['hɪlsaɪd] *n* склон.
hill start *n* (*AUT*) заво́д и управле́ние автомоби́лей на подъёме.
hilltop ['hɪltɔp] *n* верши́на (*холма́, горы́*).
hilly ['hɪlɪ] *adj* холми́стый (холми́ст).
hilt [hɪlt] *n* рукоя́тка*; **to back sb to the** ~ подде́рживать (*impf*) кого́-н по́лностью.
him [hɪm] *pron* (*direct*) его́; (*indirect*) ему́; (*after prep: +gen*) него́; (: +*dat*) нему́; (: +*instr*) ним; (: +*prp*) нём; *see also* **me**.
Himalayas [hɪmə'leɪəz] *npl:* **the** ~ Гимала́и* *pl*.
himself [hɪm'sɛlf] *pron* (*reflexive, after prep: +acc, +gen*) себя́; (: +*dat, +prp*) себе́; (: +*instr*) собо́й; (*emphatic*) сам; (*alone*): **by** ~ оди́н; *see*

also **myself**.
hind [haɪnd] *adj* за́дний* ♦ *n* са́мка* оле́ня.
hinder ['hɪndə'] *vt* (*progress, movement*) препя́тствовать (воспрепя́тствовать *perf*) *or* меша́ть (помеша́ть *perf*) +*dat*; **to** ~ **sb from doing** меша́ть (помеша́ть *perf*) кому́-н +*infin*.
hindquarters ['haɪnd'kwɔ:təz] *npl* (*of animal*) зад *msg*.
hindrance ['hɪndrəns] *n* (*nuisance, interruption*) поме́ха.
hindsight ['haɪndsaɪt] *n:* **with** ~ ретроспекти́вным взгля́дом.
Hindu ['hɪndu:] *adj* инду́сский.
hinge [hɪndʒ] *n* (*on door*) петля́* ♦ *vi* (*fig*): **to** ~ **on** зави́сеть (*impf*) от +*gen*.
hint [hɪnt] *n* (*suggestion*) намёк; (*tip*) сове́т; (*sign, glimmer*) подо́бие ♦ *vt:* **to** ~ **that** намека́ть (намекну́ть *perf*) что ♦ *vi:* **to** ~ **at** намека́ть (намекну́ть *perf*) на +*acc*; **to drop a** ~ оброни́ть* (*perf*) намёк; **to give sb a** ~ подска́зывать (подсказа́ть* *perf*) кому́-н; **white with a** ~ **of pink** бе́лый с намёком на ро́зовый.
hip [hɪp] *n* бедро́*.
hip flask *n* набе́дренная фля́га.
hip hop *n* стиль поп-му́зыки.
hippie ['hɪpɪ] *n* хи́ппи *m/f ind*.
hippo ['hɪpəu] *n* гиппопота́м.
hip pocket *n* за́дний карма́н.
hippopotami [hɪpə'pɔtəmaɪ] *npl of* **hippopotamus**.
hippopotamus [hɪpə'pɔtəməs] (*pl* ~**es** *or* **hippopotami**) *n* гиппопота́м.
hippy ['hɪpɪ] *n* = **hippie**.
hire ['haɪə'] *vt* (*BRIT: car, equipment*) брать* (взять* *perf*) напрока́т; (*venue*) снима́ть (снять* *perf*), арендова́ть (*impf/perf*); (*worker*) нанима́ть (наня́ть* *perf*) ♦ *n* (*BRIT: of car*) прока́т; (*venue*) аре́нда; **for** ~ напрока́т; **on** ~ взя́тый напрока́т
▶ **hire out** *vt* (*car, equipment*) дава́ть* (дать* *perf*) напрока́т; (*venue*) сдава́ть* (сдать* *perf*) внаём.
hire(d) car *n* (*BRIT*) маши́на, взя́тая напрока́т.
hire-purchase [haɪə'pə:tʃɪs] *n* (*BRIT*): **to buy sth on** ~ покупа́ть (купи́ть* *perf*) что-н в рассро́чку.
Hiroshima [hɪ'rɔʃɪmə] *n* Хироси́ма.
his [hɪz] *adj* его́; (*referring to subject of sentence*) свой; *see also* **my** ♦ *pron* его́; *see also* **mine**[1].
hiss [hɪs] *vi* (*snake, gas, fat*) шипе́ть* (*impf*); (*person, audience*) осви́стывать* (освиста́ть* *perf*), ши́кать (оши́кать *perf*) ♦ *n* (*see vb*) шипе́ние; свист, ши́кание.
histogram ['hɪstəgræm] *n* гистогра́мма.
historian [hɪ'stɔ:rɪən] *n* исто́рик.
historic [hɪ'stɔrɪk] *adj* (*agreement, achievement*)

истори́ческий*.
historical [hɪ'stɔrɪkl] *adj* (*event, film*)
истори́ческий*.
history ['hɪstərɪ] *n* исто́рия; **medical** ~ (*of
patient*) исто́рия боле́зни; **there's a long** ~ **of
illness in his family** боле́знь передава́лась в
его́ семье́ по насле́дству.
hit [hɪt] (*pt* **hit**) *vt* ударя́ть (уда́рить *perf*);
(*reach: target*) попада́ть (попа́сть* *perf*) в
+*acc*; (*collide with: car*) ста́лкиваться
(столкну́ться *perf*) с +*instr*; (*affect: person,
services*) ударя́ть (уда́рить *perf*) по +*dat* ♦ *n*
(*knock*) уда́р; (*success*): **the play was a big** ~
пье́са по́льзовалась больши́м успе́хом; **to** ~
it off (with sb) (*inf*) найти́* (*perf*) о́бщий язы́к
(с кем-н); **to** ~ **the headlines** попа́сть* (*perf*) на
пе́рвые страни́цы газе́т; **to** ~ **the road** (*inf*)
отправля́ться (отпра́виться* *perf*) в путь;
he'll ~ **the roof when he finds out about it** (*inf*)
он всё здесь разнесёт, когда́ узна́ет об э́том
▸ **hit back** *vi*: **to** ~ **back at sb** (*in fight, argument*)
наноси́ть* (нанести́* *perf*) отве́тный уда́р на
кого́-н
▸ **hit out at** *vt fus* (*also fig*) набра́сываться
(набро́ситься* *perf*) на +*acc*
▸ **hit (up)on** *vt fus* (*answer, solution etc*)
оты́скивать (отыска́ть* *perf*).
hit and miss *adj* (*unpredictable*) непред-
сказу́емый (непредсказу́ем).
hit-and-run driver ['hɪtən'rʌn-] *n* води́тель,
кото́рый, сбив пешехо́да, уезжа́ет с ме́ста
происше́ствия.
hitch [hɪtʃ] *vt* (*also*: ~ **up**: *trousers, skirt*)
подтя́гивать (подтяну́ть* *perf*) ♦ *n* (*difficulty*)
поме́ха; **to** ~ **sth to** (*fasten*) привя́зывать
(привяза́ть* *perf*) что-н к +*dat*; (*hook*)
прицепля́ть (прицепи́ть* *perf*) что-н к +*dat*; **to**
~ **a lift** лови́ть* (пойма́ть *perf*) попу́тку;
technical ~ техни́ческая неувя́зка*
▸ **hitch up** *vt* (*horse, cart*) запряга́ть (запря́чь*
perf); *see also* **hitch**.
hitchhike ['hɪtʃhaɪk] *vi* е́здить*/е́хать*
(пое́хать* *perf*) автосто́пом.
hitchhiker ['hɪtʃhaɪkə*] *n* путеше́ственник
(-ица) автосто́пом.
hi-tech ['haɪ'tɛk] *adj* высокотехни́ческий.
hitherto [hɪðə'tu:] *adv* (*formal*) до настоя́щего
вре́мени.
hit list *n* спи́сок* наме́ченных жертв.
hit man *irreg n* наёмный уби́йца *m*.
hit-or-miss ['hɪtə'mɪs] *adj* сде́ланный (сде́лан)
науга́д; (*casual*) сде́ланный как попа́ло *or*
ко́е-как; (*unpredictable*) непредсказу́емый
(непредсказу́ем); **it's** ~ **whether I'll be able to
come** тру́дно предсказа́ть, смогу́ ли я
прийти́.
hit parade *n* (*formerly*) хит-пара́да.
HIV *n abbr* (= *human immunodeficiency virus*)
ВИЧ= *ви́рус иммунодефици́та челове́ка*;
~**-negative** с отрица́тельной реа́кцией на
ВИЧ; ~**-positive** с положи́тельной реа́кцией

на ВИЧ.
hive [haɪv] *n* (*of bees*) у́лей*; (*fig*): **Moscow is a**
~ **of activity** жизнь в Москве́ кипи́т
▸ **hive off** *vt* отделя́ть (отдели́ть* *perf*).
hl *abbr* (= *hectolitre*) гектоли́тр.
HM *abbr* (= *His/Her Majesty*) Его́/Её
Вели́чество.
HMG *abbr* (*BRIT*) = *His (or Her) Majesty's
Government*.
HMI *n abbr* (*BRIT: SCOL*) = *His (or Her) Majesty's
Inspector*.
HMO *n abbr* (*US*) = *health maintenance
organization*.
HMS *abbr* (*BRIT*) = *His (or Her) Majesty's Ship*.
HMSO *n abbr* (*BRIT*) = *His (or Her) Majesty's
Stationery Office*.
HNC *n abbr* (*BRIT*: = *Higher National Certificate*)
свиде́тельство о сре́днем техни́ческом
образова́нии.
HND *n abbr* (*BRIT*: = *Higher National Diploma*)
дипло́м о сре́днем техни́ческом
образова́нии.
hoard [hɔ:d] *n* (*of food*) (та́йный) запа́с; (*of
treasure*) клад ♦ *vt* (*provisions*) запаса́ть
(запасти́* *perf*); (*money*) копи́ть* (скопи́ть*
perf).
hoarding ['hɔ:dɪŋ] *n* (*BRIT*) рекла́мный щит*.
hoarfrost ['hɔ:frɔst] *n* и́ней.
hoarse [hɔ:s] *adj* (*voice*) хри́плый* (хрипл).
hoax [həuks] *n* (*trick*) мистифика́ция; (*false
alarm*) ло́жная трево́га.
hob [hɔb] *n* ве́рхняя часть плиты́ с
конфо́рками.
hobble ['hɔbl] *vi* ковыля́ть (*impf*).
hobby ['hɔbɪ] *n* хо́бби *nt ind*.
hobbyhorse ['hɔbɪhɔ:s] *n* (*fig*) люби́мый
конёк*; **he is on his** ~ он сел на своего́
люби́мого конька́.
hobnail boot ['hɔbneɪl-] *n* подко́ванный
сапо́г.
hobnob ['hɔbnɔb] *vi* (*inf*): **to** ~ **with** води́ться
(*impf*) с +*instr*.
hobo ['həubəu] *n* (*US*) бродя́га *m/f*.
hock [hɔk] *n* (*BRIT: wine*) рейнве́йн; (*of horse*)
скака́тельный суста́в ♦ *vt* (*inf*) закла́дывать
(заложи́ть* *perf*); **to be in** ~ (*inf: person*) быть*
(*impf*) в долга́х; (: *object*) быть* (*impf*) в
закла́де.
hockey ['hɔkɪ] *n* хокке́й (на траве́).
hocus-pocus ['həukəs'pəukəs] *n* (*trickery*)
очковтира́тельство; (*words: of magician*)
фо́кус-по́кус; (*jargon*) белиберда́.
hod [hɔd] *n* лото́к* (*для перено́ски кирпиче́й*).
hodgepodge ['hɔdʒpɔdʒ] *n* (*US*) = **hotchpotch**.
hoe [həu] *n* моты́га, тя́пка* ♦ *vt* моты́жить
(*impf*).
hog [hɔg] *n* бо́ров ♦ *vt* (*inf: road, telephone*)
завладева́ть (завладе́ть *perf*) +*instr*; **to go the
whole** ~ (*inf*) гуля́ть (*impf*) на всю кату́шку.
Hogmanay [hɔgmə'neɪ] *n* (*SCOTTISH*) кану́н
Но́вого го́да.

hogwash ['hɒgwɒʃ] *n* (*inf*) чушь *f*.

hoist [hɔɪst] *n* подъёмник, лебёдка* ◆ *vt* поднима́ть (подня́ть* *perf*); **to ~ sth on to one's shoulders** взва́ливать (взвали́ть* *perf*) что-н на плечи́.

hoity-toity [hɔɪtɪ'tɔɪtɪ] *adj* (*inf: pej*) кичли́вый (кичли́в).

hold [həʊld] (*pt, pp* **held**) *vt* (*grip*) держа́ть* (*impf*); (*contain*) вмеща́ть (вмести́ть* *perf*); (*power, qualification*) облада́ть (*impf*) +*instr*; (*opinion*) приде́рживаться (*impf*) +*gen*; (*post*) занима́ть (заня́ть* *perf*); (*conversation, meeting*) вести́* (провести́* *perf*); (*party*) устра́ивать (устро́ить* *perf*); (*detain*) держа́ть* (*impf*) ◆ *vi* (*withstand pressure*) выде́рживать (вы́держать *perf*); (*be valid*) остава́ться (оста́ться* *perf*) в си́ле; (*weather*) держа́ться* (продержа́ться* *perf*) ◆ *n* (*grasp*) захва́т; (*NAUT*) трюм; (*AVIAT*) грузово́й отсе́к; **to ~ one's head up** высоко́ держа́ть* (*impf*) го́лову; **to ~ sb hostage** держа́ть* (*impf*) кого́-н в ка́честве зало́жника(-ицы); **~ the line!** (*TEL*) не кладите трубку!; **to ~ one's own** не ударя́ть (уда́рить *perf*) лицо́м в грязь; **he ~s you responsible for her death** он счита́ет тебя́ вино́вным в её сме́рти; **~ it!** подожди́те!; **he ~s the view that ...** он приде́рживается того́ мне́ния, что ...; **to ~ firm** *or* **fast** кре́пко держа́ться* (*impf*); **~ still, ~ steady** не дви́гайтесь; **if my luck ~s ...** е́сли мне бу́дет продолжа́ть везти́ ...; **I don't ~ with ...** я не одобря́ю ...; **to get ~ of** (*obtain*) достава́ть* (доста́ть* *perf*); **to get ~ of o.s.** сде́рживать (сдержа́ть *perf*) себя́, сде́рживаться (сдержа́ться* *perf*); **to catch** *or* **grab ~ of** хвата́ться (схвати́ться* *perf*) за +*acc*; **to have a ~ over sb** держа́ть (*impf*) кого́-н в рука́х

▸ **hold back** *vt* (*thing*) приде́рживать (придержа́ть* *perf*); (*person*) уде́рживать (удержа́ть* *perf*); (*information*) скрыва́ть (скрыть* *perf*)

▸ **hold down** *vt* (*person*) уде́рживать (удержа́ть* *perf*); **to ~ down a job** уде́рживаться (удержа́ться* *perf*) не рабо́те

▸ **hold forth** *vi*: **to ~ forth** (**on** *or* **about**) увлечённо говори́ть (*impf*) (о +*prp*)

▸ **hold off** *vt* (*enemy*) сде́рживать (сдержа́ть* *perf*) ◆ *vi* (*weather*): **if the rain ~s off** е́сли не пойдёт дождь

▸ **hold on** *vi* (*hang on*) держа́ться* (*impf*); (*wait*) ждать* (подожда́ть* *perf*); **~ on!** (*TEL*) не ве́шайте тру́бку!

▸ **hold on to** *vt fus* (*for support*) держа́ться* (*impf*) за +*acc*; (*keep: an object*) приде́рживать (придержа́ть* *perf*); (: *beliefs*) сохраня́ть (сохрани́ть* *perf*)

▸ **hold out** *vt* (*hand*) протя́гивать (протяну́ть* *perf*); (*hope, prospect*) сохраня́ть (сохрани́ть* *perf*) ◆ *vi* (*resist*) держа́ться (продержа́ться* *perf*)

▸ **hold over** *vt* (*meeting*) откла́дывать (отложи́ть* *perf*)

▸ **hold up** *vt* (*raise*) поднима́ть (подня́ть* *perf*); (*support*) подде́рживать (поддержа́ть* *perf*); (*delay*) заде́рживать (задержа́ть* *perf*); (*rob*) гра́бить* (огра́бить* *perf*).

holdall ['həʊldɔːl] *n* (*BRIT*) доро́жная су́мка*.

holder ['həʊldə'] *n* (*container*) держа́тель *m*; (*of ticket, record*) облада́тель(ница) *m(f)*; **post ~** занима́ющий(-ая) *m(f) adj* пост; **title ~** нося́щий(-ая) *m(f) adj* ти́тул.

holding ['həʊldɪŋ] *n* (*share*) вклад; (*farm*) уча́сток* земли́ ◆ *adj*: **~ operation/tactic** опера́ция/та́ктика сде́рживания.

holding company *n* хо́лдинг-компа́ния.

hold-up ['həʊldʌp] *n* (*robbery*) ограбле́ние; (*delay*) заде́ржка*; (*BRIT: in traffic*) про́бка*.

hole [həʊl] *n* (*in wall*) дыра́*; (*in road*) я́ма; (*burrow*) нора́*; (*in clothing*) ды́рка*; (*in argument*) брешь *f*; (*inf: place*) дыра́* ◆ *vt* (*ship, building*) пробива́ть (проби́ть* *perf*); **~ in the heart** поро́к се́рдца; **to pick ~s (in)** находи́ть* (найти́* *perf*) сла́бое ме́сто (в +*prp*)

▸ **hole up** *vi* уединя́ться (уедини́ться *perf*).

holiday ['hɒlɪdeɪ] *n* (*BRIT: from school*) кани́кулы *mpl*; (: *from work*) о́тпуск*; (*day off*) выходно́й день* *m*; (*also*: **public ~**) пра́здник; **on ~** (*from school*) на кани́кулах; (*from work*) в о́тпуске; **tomorrow is a (public) ~** за́втра – пра́здник.

holiday camp *n* (*for children*) молодёжный ла́герь *m*; (*BRIT: also*: **holiday centre**) ба́за о́тдыха.

holiday-maker ['hɒlɪdɪmeɪkə'] *n* (*BRIT*) отпускни́к(-и́ца), отдыха́ющий*(-ая) *m(f) adj*.

holiday pay *n* отпускны́е *pl adj*.

holiday resort *n* куро́рт.

holiday season *n* куро́ртный сезо́н.

holiness ['həʊlɪnɪs] *n* свято́сть *f*.

holistic [həʊ'lɪstɪk] *adj* це́лостный.

Holland ['hɒlənd] *n* Голла́ндия.

holler ['hɒlə'] *vt* (*inf*) ора́ть (заора́ть *perf*).

hollow ['hɒləʊ] *adj* (*container*) по́лый; (*log, tree*) дупли́стый; (*cheeks*) впа́лый (впал*); (*eyes*) ввали́вшийся; (*laugh*) неи́скренний (неи́скренен); (*claim, sound*) пусто́й* (пуст*); (*doctrine, opinion*) пове́рхностный (пове́рхностен) ◆ *n* (*in ground*) впа́дина; (*in tree*) дупло́* ◆ *vt*: **to ~ out** выка́пывать (вы́копать *perf*).

holly ['hɒlɪ] *n* остроли́ст.

hollyhock ['hɒlɪhɒk] *n* алте́й ро́зовый.

Hollywood ['hɒlɪwʊd] *n* Голливу́д.

holocaust ['hɒləkɔːst] *n* (*nuclear*) истребле́ние;

---

* marks translations which have irregular inflections. The Russian-English side of the dictionary gives inflectional information.

(*Jewish*) холокост.

hologram ['hɔləgræm] *n* голограмма.

hols [hɔlz] (*inf*) *npl* (*for students, pupils etc*) каникулы *pl*; (*for working people*) отпуск* *msg*.

holster ['həulstə] *n* кобура*.

holy ['həulɪ] *adj* святой* (свят).

Holy Communion *n* Святое Причастие.

Holy Father *n* Его святейшество *m* (*пана римский*).

Holy Ghost *n* святой дух.

Holy Land *n*: the ~~ святая земля*.

holy orders *npl* духовный сан *msg*.

Holy Spirit *n* = Holy Ghost.

homage ['hɔmɪdʒ] *n* почтение; **to pay ~ to** воздавать* (воздать* *perf*) почести +*dat*.

home [həum] *n* (*house, institution, family*) дом*; (*area, country*) родина ♦ *cpd* (*domestic*) домашний*; (*ECON, POL*) внутренний; (*SPORT*): ~ **team** хозяева* *mpl* поля ♦ *adv* (*go, come*) домой; (*right in*) в цель *or* точку; **at ~** (*house*) дома; (*country*) на родине; (*in situation*) как у себя дома; **make yourself at ~** чувствуйте себя как дома; **to make one's ~ somewhere** поселяться (поселиться *perf*) где-то; **the ~ of free enterprise/jazz** *etc* родина свободного предпринимательства/джаза *etc*; **a ~ from ~** второй дом; **~ match/win** матч/выигрыш на своём поле; **~ and dry** цел и невредим; **to bring sth ~ to sb** доводить* (довести* *perf*) что-н до чьего-н сознания

▶ **home in on** *vt fus* (*subj: missile*) осуществлять (осуществить* *perf*) самонаведение на +*acc*.

home address *n* домашний* адрес*.

home-brew [həum'bru:] *n* домашнее пиво.

homecoming ['həumkʌmɪŋ] *n* возвращение домой.

home computer *n* домашний компьютер.

Home Counties *npl* (*BRIT*): **the ~~** графства прилегающие к Лондону.

home economics *n* домоводство.

home ground *n*: **to be ~~** (*in place*) чувствовать (*impf*) себя дома.

home-grown ['həumgrəun] *adj* (*from garden*) домашний*; (*not foreign*) отечественный.

home help *n* работник собеса оказывающий помощь по дому больным и престарелым.

homeland ['həumlænd] *n* родина.

homeless ['həumlɪs] *adj* (*family, refugee*) бездомный* (бездомен) ♦ *npl*: **the ~** бездомные *pl adj*.

home loan *n* банковская ссуда на покупку дома.

homely ['həumlɪ] *adj* простой* (прост), уютный* (уютен).

home-made [həum'meɪd] *adj* (*food*) домашний*; (*bomb*) самодельный.

Home Office *n* (*BRIT*): **the ~~** ≈ Министерство внутренних дел.

homeopathy *etc* (*US*) = **homoeopathy** *etc*.

home rule *n* самоуправление.

Home Secretary *n* (*BRIT*) ≈ министр внутренних дел.

homesick ['həumsɪk] *adj*: **to be ~** (*for family*) скучать (*impf*) по дому; (*for country*) скучать по родине.

homestead ['həumstɛd] *n* усадьба.

home stretch *n* (*of race*) финишная прямая.

home town *n* родной город*.

home truth *n*: **he needs to learn some ~ ~s** ему пора объяснить, что к чему.

homeward ['həumwəd] *adj* (*journey*) обратный ♦ *adv*: **~(s)** домой.

homework ['həumwə:k] *n* домашняя работа, домашнее задание.

homicidal [hɔmɪ'saɪdl] *adj* предрасположенный к убийству.

homicide ['hɔmɪsaɪd] *n* (*esp US*) убийство.

homily ['hɔmɪlɪ] *n* (*tirade*) тирада; (*sermon*) нравоучение.

homing ['həumɪŋ] *adj*: **~ device** головка* самонаведения; **~ pigeon** почтовый голубь* *m*.

homoeopath ['həumɪəupæθ] (*US* **homeopath**) *n* гомеопат.

homoeopathy [həumɪ'ɔpəθɪ] (*US* **homeopathy**) *n* гомеопатия.

homogeneous [hɔməu'dʒi:nɪəs] *adj* однородный* (однороден).

homogenize [hə'mɔdʒənaɪz] *vt* гомогенизировать (*impf/perf*).

homosexual [hɔməu'sɛksjuəl] *adj* гомосексуальный ♦ *n* гомосексуалист(ка*).

Hon. *abbr* = **honorary**, **honourable**.

Honduras [hɔn'djuərəs] *n* Гондурас.

hone [həun] *n* точильный камень* *m* ♦ *vt* точить (наточить *perf*); (*TECH*) хонинговать (*impf/perf*); (*fig*) оттачивать (отточить* *perf*).

honest ['ɔnɪst] *adj* честный* (честен); **to be quite ~ (with you)** ... честно говоря, ...

honestly ['ɔnɪstlɪ] *adv* честно.

honesty ['ɔnɪstɪ] *n* честность *f*.

honey ['hʌnɪ] *n* мёд*; (*esp US: inf: darling*) милый(-ая) *m(f) adj*, голубчик.

honeycomb ['hʌnɪkəum] *n* (пчелиные) соты *fpl*; (*pattern*) шестиугольный мозаичный узор ♦ *vt*: **to ~ with** кишеть (*impf*) +*instr*.

honeymoon ['hʌnɪmu:n] *n* медовый месяц.

honeysuckle ['hʌnɪsʌkl] *n* жимолость *f*.

Hong Kong ['hɔŋ'kɔŋ] *n* Гонконг.

honk [hɔŋk] *vi* (*AUT*) гудеть* (прогудеть* *perf*).

Honolulu [hɔnə'lu:lu:] *n* Гонолулу *m ind*.

honor *etc* (*US*) = **honour** *etc*.

honorary ['ɔnərərɪ] *adj* почётный* (почётен).

honour ['ɔnə] (*US* **honor**) *vt* (*person*) почитать (*impf*), чтить* (*impf*); (*commitment*) выполнять (выполнить *perf*) ♦ *n* (*pride*) честь *f*; (*tribute, distinction*) почесть *f*; **in ~ of** в честь +*gen*.

honourable ['ɔnərəbl] *adj* благородный* (благороден); (*BRIT: POL*) уважаемый (*о* членах парла́мента).

honour-bound [ˈɔnəˈbaund] *adj*: **he is ~ to keep his word** сдержа́ть сло́во явля́ется для него́ де́лом че́сти.

honours degree [ˈɔnəz-] *n* учёная сте́пень *f* (обы́чно бакала́вра).

honours list *n* (*BRIT*) спи́сок* предста́вленных к награ́де.

Hons. *abbr* (*SCOL*) = **honours degree**.

hood [hud] *n* капюшо́н; (*AUT*: *BRIT*: *folding roof*) откидно́й верх*; (: *US*: *bonnet*) капо́т; (*of cooker*) вытяжно́й колпа́к.

hooded [ˈhudɪd] *adj* (*robber*) в ма́ске; (*jacket*) с капюшо́ном.

hoodlum [ˈhuːdləm] *n* (*inf*) громи́ла *m*.

hoodwink [ˈhudwɪŋk] *vt* (*inf*) одура́чивать (одура́чить *perf*).

hoof [huːf] (*pl* **hooves**) *n* копы́то.

hook [huk] *n* крючо́к* ♦ *vt* прицепля́ть (прицепи́ть* *perf*); (*fish*) пойма́ть (*perf*) (на крючо́к); **by ~ or by crook** все́ми пра́вдами и непра́вдами; **he is ~ed on her/sweets** (*inf*) он поме́шан на ней/конфе́тах; **to get ~ed (on)** (*on drugs*) пристрасти́ться* *perf* (к +*dat*)

▸ **hook up** *vt* (*dress*) застёгивать (застегну́ть *perf*) на крючо́к; (*COMPUT, TV*): **to ~ up to the main network** подключа́ть (подключи́ть* *perf*) к центра́льной сети́.

hook and eye (*pl* ~**s** ~ ~**s**) *n* крючо́к* и петля́* (на оде́жде).

hooligan [ˈhuːlɪɡən] *n* хулига́н.

hooliganism [ˈhuːlɪɡənɪzəm] *n* хулига́нство.

hoop [huːp] *n* о́бруч*; (*for croquet*) воро́та *pl*.

hooray [huːˈreɪ] *excl* = **hurrah**.

hoot [huːt] *vi* (*AUT*: *horn*) гуде́ть* (прогуде́ть* *perf*); (*siren*) выть (*impf*); (*owl*) у́хать (*impf*); (*laugh, jeer*) улюлю́кать (*impf*) ♦ *vt* (*horn*) гуде́ть* (прогуде́ть* *perf*) в +*acc* ♦ *n* (*see vi*) гудо́к*; вой; у́ханье; улюлю́канье; **to ~ with laughter** разража́ться (разрази́ться* *perf*) оглуши́тельным сме́хом.

hooter [ˈhuːtəʳ] *n* (*BRIT*) гудо́к*.

hoover® [ˈhuːvəʳ] (*BRIT*) *n* пылесо́с ♦ *vt* пылесо́сить (пропылесо́сить *perf*).

hooves [huːvz] *npl of* **hoof**.

hop [hɔp] *vi* скака́ть* (*impf*) на одно́й ноге́; (*bird*) скака́ть (*impf*) ♦ *n* скачо́к*.

hope [həup] *vti* наде́яться (*impf*) ♦ *n* наде́жда; **to ~ that/to do** наде́яться (*impf*), что/+*infin*; **I ~ so/not** наде́юсь, что да́/нет; **to ~ for the best** наде́яться (*impf*) на лу́чшее; **I have no ~ of sth/doing** у меня́ нет никако́й наде́жды на что-н/+*infin*; **in the ~ of/that** в наде́жде на +*acc*/что.

hopeful [ˈhəupful] *adj* (*person*) по́лный* (по́лон) наде́жд; (*situation etc*) обнадёживающий; **to be ~ of sth** наде́яться (*impf*) на что-н; **I'm ~ that she'll manage to**

come я наде́юсь, что она́ смо́жет прийти́.

hopefully [ˈhəupfulɪ] *adv* (*expectantly*) с наде́ждой; (*one hopes*): ~, **he'll come back** бу́дем наде́яться, что он вернётся.

hopeless [ˈhəuplɪs] *adj* (*situation, person*) безнадёжный* (безнадёжен); (*incorrigible*) неисправи́мый (неисправи́м); **I'm ~ at names** я не в состоя́нии запомина́ть имена́.

hopper [ˈhɔpəʳ] *n* бу́нкер*.

hops [hɔps] *npl* хмель *msg*.

horde [hɔːd] *n* по́лчище.

horizon [həˈraɪzn] *n* горизо́нт.

horizontal [hɔrɪˈzɔntl] *adj* горизонта́льный* (горизонта́лен).

hormone [ˈhɔːməun] *n* гормо́н.

hormone replacement therapy *n* гормона́льная терапи́я.

horn [hɔːn] *n* (*of animal*) рог*; (*also*: **French ~**) валто́рна; (*AUT*) гудо́к*.

horned [hɔːnd] *adj* рога́тый.

hornet [ˈhɔːnɪt] *n* (*insect*) ше́ршень* *m*.

horn-rimmed [ˈhɔːnˈrɪmd] *adj*: ~ **spectacles** очки́ в рогово́й опра́ве.

horny [ˈhɔːnɪ] *adj* (*inf*: *aroused*) (сексуа́льно) возбуждённый* (возбуждён).

horoscope [ˈhɔrəskəup] *n* гороско́п.

horrendous [həˈrɛndəs] *adj* ужаса́ющий*.

horrible [ˈhɔrɪbl] *adj* ужа́сный* (ужа́сен).

horrid [ˈhɔrɪd] *adj* проти́вный* (проти́вен), ме́рзкий* (ме́рзок).

horrific [həˈrɪfɪk] *adj* ужа́сный* (ужа́сен); **it was simply ~** э́то бы́ло про́сто ужа́сно.

horrify [ˈhɔrɪfaɪ] *vt* ужаса́ть (ужасну́ть *perf*).

horrifying [ˈhɔrɪfaɪɪŋ] *adj* ужаса́ющий*.

horror [ˈhɔrəʳ] *n* (*alarm*) у́жас; (*abhorrence*) отвраще́ние; (*of war*) у́жасы *mpl*.

horror film *n* фильм у́жасов.

horror-stricken [ˈhɔrəstrɪkn] *adj* = **horror-struck**.

horror-struck [ˈhɔrəstrʌk] *adj* объя́тый (объя́т) у́жасом.

hors d'oeuvre [ɔːˈdəːvrə] *n* заку́ска*.

horse [hɔːs] *n* ло́шадь* *f*; (*male*) конь* *m*.

horseback [ˈhɔːsbæk] *adj* верхово́й ♦ *adv*: **on ~** верхо́м; **police on ~** ко́нная поли́ция.

horsebox [ˈhɔːsbɔks] *n* (*BRIT*) ваго́н для лошаде́й.

horse chestnut *n* ко́нский* кашта́н.

horse-drawn [ˈhɔːsdrɔːn] *adj* ко́нный; (*transport*) гужево́й.

horsefly [ˈhɔːsflaɪ] *n* слепе́нь* *m*.

horseman [ˈhɔːsmən] *irreg n* вса́дник.

horsemanship [ˈhɔːsmənʃɪp] *n* иску́сство верхово́й езды́.

horseplay [ˈhɔːspleɪ] *n* возня́.

horsepower [ˈhɔːspauəʳ] *n* лошади́ная си́ла; **a 30 ~ engine** дви́гатель *m* мо́щностью в 30 лошади́ных сил.

---

* marks translations which have irregular inflections. The Russian-English side of the dictionary gives inflectional information.

horse racing *n* скáчки* *fpl*.
horseradish ['hɔ:srædɪʃ] *n* хрен*.
horseshoe ['hɔ:sʃu:] *n* подкóва.
horse show *n* соревновáния по выездке.
horse trading *n* закулисные сдéлки *fpl*.
horse trials *npl* = **horse show**.
horsewhip ['hɔ:swɪp] *n* хлыст* ♦ *vt* хлестáть* (отхлестáть* *perf*).
horsewoman ['hɔ:swumən] *irreg n* всáдница.
horsey ['hɔ:sɪ] *adj* (*person*) увлекáющийся* лошадьми; (*features*) лошадиный.
horticulture ['hɔ:tɪkʌltʃə'] *n* садовóдство.
hose [həuz] *n* (*also:~pipe*) шланг
► **hose down** *vt* поливáть (полить *perf*) из шлáнга.
hosepipe ['həuzpaɪp] *n* шланг.
hosiery ['həuzɪərɪ] *n* чулóчные издéлия *ntpl*.
hospice ['hɔspɪs] *n* больница (*для безнадёжно больных*).
hospitable ['hɔspɪtəbl] *adj* (*person, behaviour*) гостеприимный* (гостеприимен); (*climate*) благоприятный* (благоприятен).
hospital ['hɔspɪtl] *n* больница; **to be in ~** *or* (*US*) **in the ~** лежáть* (*impf*) в больнице.
hospitality [hɔspɪ'tælɪtɪ] *n* гостеприимство.
hospitalize ['hɔspɪtəlaɪz] *vt* госпитализировать (*impf/perf*).
host [həust] *n* (*at party, dinner*) хозяин*; (*TV, RADIO*) ведущий* *m adj* ♦ *adj* (*country, organization*) принимáющий ♦ *vt* (*programme*) вести* (*impf*); (*event*) проводить* (провести* *perf*); **the H~** (*REL*) просвирá*; **a ~ of** мáсса +*gen*, мнóжество +*gen*.
hostage ['hɔstɪdʒ] *n* залóжник(-ица); **he was taken/held ~** егó взяли/держáли в кáчестве залóжника.
hostel ['hɔstl] *n* общежитие; (*for homeless*) приют; (*also:* **youth ~**) молодёжная гостиница.
hostelling ['hɔstlɪŋ] *n*: **to go (youth) ~** путешéствовать (*impf*), останáвливаясь в молодёжных гостиницах.
hostess ['həustɪs] *n* (*at party, dinner etc*) хозяйка*; (*BRIT: also:* **air ~**) стюардéсса; (*TV, RADIO*) ведущая *f adj*; (*in club, restaurant*) жéнщина, развлекáющая посетителей нóчного клýба, ресторáна *итп*.
hostile ['hɔstaɪl] *adj* (*person, attitude*) враждéбный* (враждéбен); (*conditions, environment*) неблагоприятный* (неблагоприятен); (*troops*) врáжеский; **~ to** *or* **towards** враждéбный* (враждéбен) по отношéнию к +*dat*.
hostility [hɔ'stɪlɪtɪ] *n* враждéбность *f*; **hostilities** *npl* (*fighting*) воéнные дéйствия *ntpl*.
hot [hɔt] *adj* (*object, temper, argument etc*) горячий* (горяч); (*weather*) жáркий*; (*spicy: food*) óстрый* (остр); **she is ~** ей жáрко; **it's ~** (*weather*) жáрко; **I'm not too ~ on**

mathematics я не óчень разбирáюсь в матемáтике
► **hot up** *vi* (*BRIT: inf: situation*) накаляться (накалиться *perf*); (: *party*) разгорáться (разгорéться *perf*) ♦ *vt* (*engine*) разогревáть (разогрéть* *perf*); (*pace*) ускорять (ускорить *perf*).
hot air *n* (*fig*) пустословие, болтовня.
hot-air balloon [hɔt'ɛə-] *n* воздушный шар*.
hotbed ['hɔtbɛd] *n* (*fig*) рассáдник.
hot-blooded [hɔt'blʌdɪd] *adj* пылкий* (пылок).
hotchpotch ['hɔtʃpɔtʃ] *n* (*BRIT*) сбóрная солянка (*также перен*).
hot dog *n* ≈ сосиска* в бýлке.
hotel [həu'tɛl] *n* гостиница, отéль *m*.
hotelier [həu'tɛlɪə'] *n* (*owner*) владéлец* (-élица) гостиницы; (*manager*) администрáтор гостиницы.
hot flush *n* (*esp BRIT*) прилив.
hotel industry *n* гостиничный бизнес.
hotel room *n* гостиничный нóмер*.
hotfoot ['hɔtfut] *adv* (*inf*) стремглáв.
hothead ['hɔthɛd] *n* (*inf*) горячая головá*.
hot-headed [hɔt'hɛdɪd] *adj* (*person*) порывистый (порывист); (*remark*) необдýманный (необдýман).
hothouse ['hɔthaus] *n* оранжерéя, теплица.
hot line *n* (*POL*) *прямáя телефóнная связь мéжду прáвительствами рáзных стран*.
hotly ['hɔtlɪ] *adv* горячó.
hotplate ['hɔtpleɪt] *n* конфóрка*.
hotpot ['hɔtpɔt] *n* (*BRIT*) жаркóе *nt adj*.
hot potato *n* (*inf*) больнóй вопрóс.
hot seat *n* (*inf*): **to be in the ~~** занимáть (заня́ть* *perf*) отвéтственный пост.
hot spot *n* (*war zone*) горячая тóчка*.
hot spring *n* горячий* истóчник.
hot stuff *n* (*inf: woman*) красóтка*; (: *film, book*) клáссная вещь *f*.
hot-tempered ['hɔt'tɛmpəd] *adj* вспыльчивый (вспыльчив).
hot-water bottle [hɔt'wɔ:tə-] *n* грéлка*.
hound [haund] *vt* травить* (затравить* *perf*) ♦ *n* (*dog*) гончая *f adj*.
hour ['auə'] *n* час*; **at 60 miles an** *or* **per ~** со скóростью 60 миль в час; **24 ~ job** круглосýточная рабóта; **I am paid by the ~** я получáю почасовýю оплáту.
hourly ['auəlɪ] *adj* (*rate*) почасовóй; (*service*) ежечáсный ♦ *adv* (*each hour*) ежечáсно; (*soon*) с чáсу на час.
house [*n* haus, *vt* hauz] *n* дом*; (*company*) фирма; (*THEAT*) зал ♦ *vt* (*person*) селить (поселить *perf*); (*collection*) размещáть (разместить* *perf*); **at my ~** у меня дóма; **to my ~** ко мне домóй; **the H~ of Commons/Lords** (*BRIT*) палáта óбщин/лóрдов; **the H~ (of Representatives)** (*US*) палáта представителей; **the H~s of Parliament** здáние *ntsg* парлáмента; **on the ~** (*inf*) бесплáтно.
house arrest *n* домáшний* арéст.

houseboat ['hausbəut] *n* плаву́чий* дом*.
housebound ['hausbaund] *adj*: **she is** ~ она́ не
мо́жет выходи́ть из до́ма.
housebreaking ['hausbreikɪŋ] *n* грабёж со
взло́мом.
house-broken ['hausbrəukn] *adj* (*US*) = **house-
trained**.
housecoat ['hauskəut] *n* дома́шний* хала́т.
household ['haushəuld] *n* (*home, inhabitants*)
дом*; ~ **name** (*brand*) изве́стная ма́рка*;
(*person*) широко́ изве́стная ли́чность *f*.
householder ['haushəuldə] *n* домовладе́лец*.
house-hunting ['haushʌntɪŋ] *n*: **to go** ~
занима́ться (заня́ться* *perf*) по́исками до́ма.
housekeeper ['hauski:pə] *n* эконо́мка*.
housekeeping ['hauski:pɪŋ] *n* (*work*)
дома́шние дела́ *ntpl*; (*also*: ~ **money**) де́ньги*
pl на хозя́йственные ну́жды.
houseman ['hausmən] *irreg n* (*BRIT*) врач-
стажёр, инте́рн.
house-owner ['hausəunə] *n* домовладе́лец*
(-лица).
house-party ['hauspɑ:tɪ] *n* приглаше́ние люде́й
в го́сти с ночёвкой.
house plant *n* ко́мнатное расте́ние.
house-proud ['hauspraud] *adj* домови́тый
(домови́т).
house-to-house ['haustə'haus] *adj*: **to make** ~
enquiries проводи́ть* (провести́* *perf*)
покварти́рный опро́с.
house-train ['haustreɪn] *vt*: **to** ~ **a pet** приуча́ть
(приучи́ть* *perf*) дома́шнего живо́тного не
га́дить в до́ме.
house-trained ['haustreɪnd] *adj* (*BRIT*): **our dog
is fully** ~ на́ша соба́ка приу́чена к туале́ту.
house-warming ['hauswɔ:mɪŋ] *n* (*also*: ~
party) новосе́лье*.
housewife ['hauswaɪf] *irreg n* дома́шняя
хозя́йка*, домохозя́йка.
housework ['hauswə:k] *n* дома́шнее
хозя́йство.
housing ['hauzɪŋ] *n* жили́ще, жильё;
(*provision*) жили́щное снабже́ние; (*TECH*)
ко́рпус, кожу́х* ♦ *cpd* жили́щный; ~ **shortage**
недоста́ток жилья́.
housing association *n* (*BRIT*) ассоциа́ция
домовладе́льцев (*предоставля́ющая жильё
по бо́лее вы́годным це́нам*).
housing benefit *n* де́нежное посо́бие не-
иму́щим се́мьям по вы́плате квартпла́ты.
housing conditions *npl* жили́щные усло́вия
ntpl.
housing development *n* = **housing estate**.
housing estate (*US* **housing project**) *n*
жили́щный ко́мплекс; (*larger*) жило́й
масси́в.
housing project *n* (*US*) = **housing estate**.
hove [həuv] *pt, pp of* **heave**.

hovel ['hɔvl] *n* лачу́га.
hover ['hɔvə] *vi* (*bird, insect*) пари́ть (*impf*);
(*person*) мя́ться (*impf*); **to** ~ **round sb**
увива́ться (*impf*) вокру́г кого́-н.
hovercraft ['hɔvəkrɑ:ft] *n* су́дно на возду́шной
поду́шке.
hoverport ['hɔvəpɔ:t] *n* порт для су́ден на
возду́шной поду́шке.

KEYWORD
---

how [hau] *adv* **1** (*in what way*) как; **to know how
to do** знать *perf*, как +*infin*, уме́ть (*impf*) +*infin*;
how did you like the film? как Вам
понра́вился фильм?; **how are you?** как дела́?
2 ско́лько; **how much milk/many people?**
ско́лько молока́/челове́к?; **how long have
you been here?** ско́лько Вы уже́ здесь?; **how
old are you?** ско́лько Вам лет?; **how tall is he?**
како́го он ро́ста?; **how lovely/awful!** как
чуде́сно/ужа́сно!

---

however [hau'ɛvə] *conj* одна́ко ♦ *adv* (*no
matter how*) как бы ... ни; (*in questions*) как
же; ~ **did you find me?** как же Вы меня́
нашли́?
howl [haul] *vi* (*animal, wind*) выть* (*impf*); (*baby,
person*) реве́ть* (*impf*) ♦ *n* (*see vb*) вой; рёв.
howler ['haulə] *n* (*inf: mistake*) ля́псус.
howling ['haulɪŋ] *adj* невероя́тный*
(невероя́тен), фантасти́ческий*.
HP *n abbr* (*BRIT*) = **hire-purchase**.
h.p. *abbr* (*AUT*) (= **horsepower**) л.с.=
лошади́ная си́ла.
HQ *abbr* = **headquarters**.
HR *n abbr* (*US: POL: = House of Representatives*)
пала́та представи́телей.
HRH *abbr* (*BRIT*: = *His/Her Royal Highness*) Его́/
Её Короле́вское Высо́чество.
hr(s) *abbr* = **hour(s)**.
HS *abbr* (*US*) = **high school**.
HST *abbr* (*US*) = *Hawaiian Standard Time*.
hub [hʌb] *n* (*of wheel*) ступи́ца; (*fig*)
средото́чие.
hubbub ['hʌbʌb] *n* гам, го́мон.
hubcap ['hʌbkæp] *n* (*AUT*) покры́шка.
HUD *n abbr* (*US*) = *Department of Housing and
Urban Development*.
huddle ['hʌdl] *vi*: **to** ~ **together** прижима́ться
(прижа́ться* *perf*) друг к дру́гу ♦ *n*: **to lie in a**
~ лежа́ть* (*impf*) в ку́че.
hue [hju:] *n* тон, отте́нок*.
hue and cry *n* шум; (*pej*) шумми́ха.
huff [hʌf] *n*: **he's in a** ~ он оби́жен ♦ *vi*: **to** ~ **and
puff** (*also fig*) пыхте́ть* (*impf*).
huffy ['hʌfɪ] *adj* (*inf*) наду́тый (наду́т).
hug [hʌg] *vt* (*person*) обнима́ть (обня́ть* *perf*);
(*thing*) обхва́тывать (обхвати́ть* *perf*) ♦ *n*
объя́тие; **to give sb a** ~ обнима́ть (обня́ть*
perf) кого́-н.

---

* marks translations which have irregular inflections. The Russian-English side of the dictionary gives inflectional information.

huge [hju:dʒ] *adj* огро́мный* (огро́мен), грома́дный* (грома́ден).

hugely [ˈhju:dʒlɪ] *adv* чрезвыча́йно.

hulk [hʌlk] *n* (*NAUT*) ко́рпус* (*затону́вшего корабля́*); (*building, person*) грома́дина.

hulking [ˈhʌlkɪŋ] *adj* здорове́нный; **a ~ great oaf** у́валень *m*.

hull [hʌl] *n* (*NAUT*) корпу́с; (*of seeds*) шелуха́; (*of strawberries*) ча́шечка ◆ *vt* (*fruit*) лущи́ть (облущи́ть *perf*).

hullaba(l)loo [ˈhʌləbəˈlu:] *n* (*inf*) шуми́ха.

hullo [həˈləu] *excl* = **hello**.

hum [hʌm] *vt* напева́ть (*impf*) (*без слов*) ◆ *vi* (*person*) напева́ть (*impf*); (*machine*) гуде́ть* (прогуде́ть* *perf*); (*insect*) жужжа́ть (*impf*) ◆ *n* (*of wires*) гуде́ние; (*of voices, machines*) гул.

human [ˈhju:mən] *adj* челове́ческий* ◆ *n* (*also:* **~ being**) челове́к*.

humane [hju:ˈmeɪn] *adj* (*treatment*) челове́чный* (челове́чен); (*slaughter*) гума́нный* (гума́нен).

humanely [hju:ˈmeɪnlɪ] *adv* по-челове́чески, гума́нно.

humanism [ˈhju:mənɪzəm] *n* гумани́зм.

humanitarian [hju:mænɪˈteərɪən] *adj* (*aid*) гуманита́рный; (*principles*) гума́нный*.

humanity [hju:ˈmænɪtɪ] *n* (*mankind*) челове́чество; (*humaneness*) челове́чность *f*, гума́нность *f*; (*human nature*) челове́ческая суть *f*; **the humanities** *npl* гума́нитарные нау́ки *fpl*.

humanly [ˈhju:mənlɪ] *adv*: **it's not ~ possible** э́то вне челове́ческих возмо́жностей; **it is ~ possible** э́то в преде́лах челове́ческих возмо́жностей.

humanoid [ˈhju:mənɔɪd] *adj* человеко-подо́бный* ◆ *n* гумано́ид.

human relations *npl* (*COMM*) обще́ственные отноше́ния *ntpl*.

human rights *npl* права́ *ntpl* челове́ка.

humble [ˈhʌmbl] *adj* (*modest, simple*) скро́мный* (скро́мен) ◆ *vt* сбива́ть (сбить* *perf*) спесь с +*gen*.

humbly [ˈhʌmblɪ] *adv* скро́мно, смире́нно.

humbug [ˈhʌmbʌg] *n* (*of statement*) надува́тельство; (*BRIT: sweet*) чёрно-бе́лый мя́тный ледене́ц.

humdrum [ˈhʌmdrʌm] *adj* ну́дный* (ну́ден).

humid [ˈhju:mɪd] *adj* вла́жный* (вла́жен).

humidifier [hju:ˈmɪdɪfaɪəʳ] *n* увлажни́тель *m* во́здуха.

humidity [hju:ˈmɪdɪtɪ] *n* вла́жность *f*.

humiliate [hju:ˈmɪlɪeɪt] *vt* унижа́ть (уни́зить* *perf*).

humiliating [hju:ˈmɪlɪeɪtɪŋ] *adj* унизи́тельный* (унизи́телен).

humiliation [hju:mɪlɪˈeɪʃən] *n* униже́ние.

humility [hju:ˈmɪlɪtɪ] *n* (*modesty*) скро́мность *f*; (*humbleness*) смире́ние.

humming bird [ˈhʌmɪŋ-] *n* коли́бри *m/f ind*.

humor *etc* (*US*) = **humour** *etc*.

humorist [ˈhju:mərɪst] *n* юмори́ст(ка*).

humorous [ˈhju:mərəs] *adj* (*book*) юмористи́ческий*; (*remark*) шутли́вый (шутли́в); (*person*) с ю́мором.

humour [ˈhju:məʳ] (*US* **humor**) *n* ю́мор; (*mood*) настрое́ние ◆ *vt* ублажа́ть (ублажи́ть *perf*); **sense of ~** чу́вство ю́мора; **to be in good/ bad ~** быть* (*impf*) в хоро́шем/плохо́м настрое́нии.

humourless [ˈhju:məlɪs] *adj* лишённый (лишён) чу́вства ю́мора.

hump [hʌmp] *n* (*in ground*) буго́р*; (*on back*) горб*.

humpbacked [ˈhʌmpbækt] *adj*: **~ bridge** горба́тый мост.

humus [ˈhju:məs] *n* перегно́й.

hunch [hʌntʃ] *n* (*premonition*) дога́дка*; **I have a ~ that** ... я предчу́вствую, что ....

hunchback [ˈhʌntʃbæk] *n* горбу́н*(ья*).

hunched [hʌntʃt] *adj* суту́лый (суту́л).

hundred [ˈhʌndrəd] *n* сто*; **a** *or* **one ~ books/ people/dollars** сто* книг/люде́й/до́лларов; **about a ~** о́коло ста; **~ and first** сто* пе́рвый; **to live to be a ~** жить* (дожи́ть* *perf*) до ста лет; **~s of** со́тни* +*gen pl*; **people came in their ~s** *or* **by the ~** пришли́ со́тни люде́й; **I'm a ~ per cent sure** я уве́рен на сто проце́нтов.

hundredth [ˈhʌndrədθ] *adj* со́тый ◆ *n* (*fraction*) одна́ со́тая *f adj*.

hundredweight [ˈhʌndrɪdweɪt] *n* (*BRIT* ме́ра ве́са, равня́ющаяся 50.8 килогра́ммов; (*US*) ме́ра ве́са, равня́ющаяся 45.3 килогра́ммов.

hung [hʌŋ] *pt, pp of* **hang**.

Hungarian [hʌŋˈgeərɪən] *adj* венге́рский* ◆ *n* венгр(-ге́рка*); (*LING*) венге́рский* язы́к*.

Hungary [ˈhʌŋgərɪ] *n* Ве́нгрия.

hunger [ˈhʌŋgəʳ] *n* го́лод ◆ *vi*: **to ~ for** жа́ждать* (*impf*) +*gen*.

hunger strike *n* голодо́вка*.

hung over *adj* (*inf*): **I'm feeling ~ ~** у меня́ похме́лье.

hungrily [ˈhʌŋgrəlɪ] *adv* (*also fig*) жа́дно.

hungry [ˈhʌŋgrɪ] *adj* голо́дный* (го́лоден); (*keen*): **~ for** жа́ждущий +*gen*; **he is ~** он го́лоден; **to go ~** голода́ть (*impf*).

hung up *adj* (*inf*): **to be ~ ~ about** *or* **on** зацикливаться (заци́клиться *perf*) на +*prp*.

hunk [hʌŋk] *n* (*большо́й*) кусо́к*; (*of bread*) ломо́ть* *m*; (*inf: man*) краса́вчик.

hunt [hʌnt] *vt* (*animal*) охо́титься* (*impf*) на +*acc*; (*criminal*) охо́титься* (*impf*) за +*instr* ◆ *vi* (*SPORT*) охо́титься* (*impf*) ◆ *n* охо́та; (*for criminal*) ро́зыск; **to ~ (for)** (*search*) иска́ть* (*impf*)

► **hunt down** *vt* высле́живать (вы́следить* *perf*).

hunter [ˈhʌntəʳ] *n* охо́тник(-ица).

hunting [ˈhʌntɪŋ] *n* охо́та.

hurdle [ˈhə:dl] *n* (*difficulty*) препя́тствие; (*SPORT*) препя́тствие, барье́р.

hurl [hə:l] *vt* (*object*) швыря́ть (швырну́ть *perf*);

to ~ abuse *or* **insults at sb** осыпа́ть (осы́пать *perf*) кого́-н ру́ганью.

hurling ['hɜ:lɪŋ] *n* (*SPORT*) ирла́ндский* хокке́й на траве́.

hurly-burly ['hɜ:lɪ'bɜ:lɪ] *n* сумато́ха.

hurrah [hu'rɑ] *excl* ypá.

hurray [hu'reɪ] *excl* = **hurrah**.

hurricane ['hʌrɪkən] *n* урага́н.

hurried ['hʌrɪd] *adj* поспе́шный* (поспе́шен).

hurriedly ['hʌrɪdlɪ] *adv* поспе́шно.

hurry ['hʌrɪ] *n* спе́шка ◆ *vi* спеши́ть (поспеши́ть *perf*), торопи́ться* (поторопи́ться* *perf*) ◆ *vt* (*person*) подгоня́ть (подогна́ть* *perf*), торопи́ть* (поторопи́ть* *perf*); (*work*) ускоря́ть (ускори́ть *perf*); **to be in a ~** спеши́ть (*impf*); **to do sth in a ~** де́лать (сде́лать *perf*) что-н в спе́шке; **there's no ~** нет никако́й спе́шки; **what's the ~?** почему́ така́я спе́шка?; **to ~ in/out** поспе́шно входи́ть* (войти́* *perf*)/выходи́ть* (вы́йти* *perf*); **they hurried to help him** они́ поспеши́ли ему́ на по́мощь; **to ~ home** спеши́ть (поспеши́ть *perf*) домо́й

▸ **hurry along** *vi* поспе́шно проходи́ть* (пройти́* *perf*)

▸ **hurry away** *vi* поспе́шно уходи́ть* (уйти́* *perf*)

▸ **hurry off** *vi* = **hurry away**

▸ **hurry up** *vt* (*person*) подгоня́ть (подогна́ть* *perf*), торопи́ть* (поторопи́ть* *perf*); (*process*) ускоря́ть (ускори́ть *perf*) ◆ *vi* торопи́ться* (поторопи́ться* *perf*); **up!** поторопи́сь!

hurt [hɜ:t] (*pt, pp* **hurt**) *vt* (*also fig*) причиня́ть (причини́ть *perf*) боль +*dat*; (*injure*) ушиба́ть (ушиби́ть* *perf*); (*offend*) обижа́ть (оби́деть* *perf*); (*chances, reputation*) поврежда́ть (повреди́ть *perf*) ◆ *vi* (*be painful*) боле́ть (*impf*) ◆ *adj* (*offended*) оби́женный* (оби́жен); (*injured*) уши́бленный (уши́блен); **to ~ o.s.** ушиба́ться (ушиби́ться *perf*); **I've ~ my arm** я ушиб ру́ку; **where does it ~?** где боли́т?; **nobody was ~ in the crash** в ава́рии никто́ не пострада́л.

hurtful ['hɜ:tful] *adj* оби́дный* (оби́ден).

hurtle ['hɜ:tl] *vi*: **to ~ past** проноси́ться* (пронести́сь* *perf*); **to ~ down** ска́тываться (скати́ться* *perf*).

husband ['hʌzbənd] *n* муж*.

hush [hʌʃ] *n* тишина́ ◆ *vt* заставля́ть (заста́вить* *perf*) замолча́ть; **~!** ти́хо!, ти́ше!

▸ **hush up** *vt* (*scandal*) замина́ть (замя́ть* *perf*).

hushed [hʌʃt] *adj* (*place*) ти́хий* (тих); (*voice*) приглушённый (приглушён).

hush-hush [hʌʃ'hʌʃ] *adj* (*inf*) сугу́бо секре́тный* (секре́тен).

husk [hʌsk] *n* шелуха́.

husky ['hʌskɪ] *adj* (*voice*) хри́плый* (хрипл) ◆ *n* ездова́я соба́ка.

hustings ['hʌstɪŋz] *npl* (*BRIT: POL*) пред-вы́борные собра́ния *ntpl*.

hustle ['hʌsl] *vt* (*hurry*) подта́лкивать (подтолкну́ть *perf*) ◆ *n*: **~ and bustle** сумато́ха.

hut [hʌt] *n* (*house*) избу́шка*, хи́жина; (*shed*) сара́й.

hutch [hʌtʃ] *n* кле́тка* (*для кро́ликов итп*).

hyacinth ['haɪəsɪnθ] *n* гиаци́нт.

hybrid ['haɪbrɪd] *n* (*BIO*) гибри́д; (*fig*) смесь *f* ◆ *adj* (*see n*) гибри́дный; сме́шанный.

hydrant ['haɪdrənt] *n* (*also:* **fire ~**) ≈ пожа́рный кран.

hydraulic [haɪ'drɔ:lɪk] *adj* гидравли́ческий*.

hydraulics [haɪ'drɔ:lɪks] *n* гидра́влика.

hydrochloric acid ['haɪdrəu'klɔrɪk-] *n* соля́ная кислота́.

hydroelectric ['haɪdrəu'lɛktrɪk] *adj* гидро-электри́ческий.

hydrofoil ['haɪdrəfɔɪl] *n* су́дно на подво́дных кры́льях.

hydrogen ['haɪdrədʒən] *n* водоро́д.

hydrogen bomb *n* водоро́дная бо́мба.

hydrophobia ['haɪdrə'fəubɪə] *n* водобоя́знь *f*.

hydroplane ['haɪdrəpleɪn] *n* (*boat*) гли́ссер; (*plane*) гидросамолёт ◆ *vi* (*boat*) глисси́ровать (*impf*).

hyena [haɪ'i:nə] *n* гие́на.

hygiene ['haɪdʒi:n] *n* гигие́на.

hygienic [haɪ'dʒi:nɪk] *adj* (*product*) гигиени́ческий*; (*habits*) гигиени́чный (гигиени́чен).

hymn [hɪm] *n* церко́вный гимн.

hype [haɪp] *n* (*inf*) ажиота́ж.

hyperactive ['haɪpər'æktɪv] *adj* (*MED*) гиперакти́вный.

hyper-inflation ['haɪpərɪn'fleɪʃən] *n* гипер-инфля́ция.

hypermarket ['haɪpəmɑ:kɪt] *n* (*BRIT*) кру́пный универса́м.

hypertension ['haɪpə'tɛnʃən] *n* гипертони́я.

hyphen ['haɪfn] *n* дефи́с.

hyphenated ['haɪfəneɪtɪd] *adj*: **this word is ~** э́то сло́во пи́шется че́рез дефи́с.

hypnosis [hɪp'nəusɪs] *n* гипно́з.

hypnotic [hɪp'nɔtɪk] *adj* (*trance etc*) гипноти́ческий.

hypnotism ['hɪpnətɪzəm] *n* гипноти́зм.

hypnotist ['hɪpnətɪst] *n* гипноти́зёр.

hypnotize ['hɪpnətaɪz] *vt* (*also fig*) гипнотизи́ровать (загипнотизи́ровать *perf*).

hypoallergenic ['haɪpəuælə'dʒɛnɪk] *adj* не вызыва́ющий* алле́ргической реа́кции.

hypochondriac [haɪpə'kɔndrɪæk] *n* ипохо́ндрик.

hypocrisy [hɪ'pɔkrɪsɪ] *n* лицеме́рие.

hypocrite ['hɪpəkrɪt] *n* лицеме́р(ка*).

hypocritical [hɪpə'krɪtɪkl] *adj* лицеме́рный*

---

* marks translations which have irregular inflections. The Russian-English side of the dictionary gives inflectional information.

(лицемéрен).

hypodermic [haɪpə'də:mɪk] *adj* подкóжный ◆ *n* (*also:* ~ **syringe**) шприц для подкóжных инъéкций.

hypotenuse [haɪ'pɔtɪnju:z] *n* гипотенýза.

hypothermia [haɪpə'θə:mɪə] *n* гипотермия.

hypotheses [haɪ'pɔθɪsi:z] *npl of* **hypothesis**.

hypothesis [haɪ'pɔθɪsɪs] (*pl* **hypotheses**) *n* гипóтеза.

hypothesize [haɪ'pɔθɪsaɪz] *vi* предполагáть (предположи́ть* *perf*).

hypothetic(al) [haɪpəu'θɛtɪk(l)] *adj* гипотети́ческий*.

hysterectomy [hɪstə'rɛktəmɪ] *n* удалéние мáтки.

hysteria [hɪ'stɪərɪə] *n* истери́я.

hysterical [hɪ'stɛrɪkl] *adj* (*uncontrolled*) истери́ческий*; (*funny*) умори́тельный* (умори́телен); **to become** ~ впадáть (впасть* *perf*) в истéрику.

hysterically [hɪ'stɛrɪklɪ] *adv* истери́чески; ~ **funny** óчень смешнóй* (смешóн).

hysterics [hɪ'stɛrɪks] *npl:* **to be in** *or* **have** ~ быть* (*impf*) в истéрике.

Hz *abbr* (= *hertz*) Гц= *герц*.

I, i [aɪ] *n* (*letter*) 9-ая бу́ква англи́йского
алфави́та.

I [aɪ] *pron* я.

I *abbr* (= **island, isle**) о.= о́стров.

IA *abbr* (*US: POST*) = *Iowa*.

IAEA *n abbr* = **International Atomic Energy
Agency.**

IBA *n abbr* (*BRIT*) = *Independent Broadcasting
Authority.*

Iberian [aɪˈbɪərɪən] *adj:* **the ~ Peninsula**
Пирене́йский полуо́стров.

IBEW *n abbr* (*US*) = *International Brotherhood of
Electrical Workers.*

ib(id) *abbr* (*from the same source:* = *ibidem*) там
же.

i/c *abbr* (*BRIT*) = **in charge.**

ICBM *n abbr* (= *intercontinental ballistic missile*)
МБР= *межконтинента́льная
баллисти́ческая раке́та.*

ICC *n abbr* = **International Chamber of
Commerce;** (*US:* = *Interstate Commerce
Commission*) Коми́ссия по торго́вле ме́жду
шта́тами.

ice [aɪs] *n* лёд*; (*portion of ice cream*)
моро́женое *nt adj* ◆ *vt* (*cake*) покрыва́ть
(покры́ть* *perf*) глазу́рью; **to put sth on ~**
(*fig*) заморо́зить* (*perf*) что-н
► **ice over** *vi* (*road, window etc*) обледене́ть
(*perf*), покрыва́ться (покры́ться* *perf*) льдом
► **ice up** *vi* = **ice over.**

Ice Age *n* леднико́вый пери́од.

ice axe *n* ледору́б.

iceberg [ˈaɪsbəːg] *n* а́йсберг; **the tip of the ~**
(*fig*) верху́шка а́йсберга.

icebox [ˈaɪsbɔks] *n* (*US: fridge*) холоди́льник;
(*BRIT: compartment*) морози́льник; (*insulated
box*) су́мка-холоди́льник *f*.

ice breaker *n* ледоко́л.

ice bucket *n* ведёрко* со льдом.

ice-cap [ˈaɪskæp] *n* леднико́вый покро́в.

ice-cold [aɪsˈkəuld] *adj* ледяно́й.

ice cream *n* моро́женое *nt adj*.

ice-cream soda [ˈaɪskriːm-] *n* со́довая вода́ с
моро́женым.

ice cube *n* ку́бик льда.

iced [aɪst] *adj* (*cake*) покры́тый глазу́рью; ~

tea холо́дный чай со льдом; **~ beer**
холо́дное пи́во.

ice hockey *n* (*SPORT*) хокке́й (на льду́).

Iceland [ˈaɪslənd] *n* Исла́ндия.

Icelander [ˈaɪsləndəʳ] *n* исла́ндец*(-дка*).

Icelandic [aɪsˈlændɪk] *adj* исла́ндский* ◆ *n*
(*LING*) исла́ндский* язы́к*.

ice lolly *n* (*BRIT*) фрукто́вое моро́женое на
па́лочке.

ice pick *n* топо́рик для льда.

ice rink *n* като́к*.

ice-skate [ˈaɪsskeit] *n* конёк* ◆ *vi* ката́ться (*impf*)
на конька́х.

ice-skating [ˈaɪsskeitɪŋ] *n* (*SPORT*) ката́ние на
конька́х.

icicle [ˈaɪsɪkl] *n* сосу́лька*.

icing [ˈaɪsɪŋ] *n* (*on cake*) глазу́рь *f*; (*on window
etc*) обледене́ние.

icing sugar *n* (*BRIT*) са́харная пу́дра для
приготовле́ния глазу́ри.

ICJ *n abbr* = **International Court of Justice.**

icon [ˈaɪkɔn] *n* (*REL*) ико́на.

ICR *n abbr* (*US*) = *Institute for Cancer Research.*

ICU *n abbr* (*MED:* = *intensive care unit*)
отделе́ние интенси́вной терапи́и.

icy [ˈaɪsɪ] *adj* (*cold*) ледяно́й; (*covered in ice*)
покры́тый (покры́т) льдом.

ID *abbr* (*US: POST*) = *Idaho.*

I'd [aɪd] = **I would, I had.**

ID card *n* = **identity card.**

IDD *n abbr* (*BRIT: TEL:* = *international direct
dialling*) пряма́я междунаро́дная связь *f*.

idea [aɪˈdɪə] *n* (*scheme, opinion*) иде́я; (*notion*)
представле́ние; (*objective*) зада́ча; **good ~**!
прекра́сная иде́я!; **to have an ~ that**
подозрева́ть (*impf*) что; **I haven't the least ~** я
не име́ю ни мале́йшего представле́ния.

ideal [aɪˈdɪəl] *n* иде́ал ◆ *adj* идеа́льный*
(идеа́лен).

idealist [aɪˈdɪəlɪst] *n* идеали́ст(ка*).

ideally [aɪˈdɪəlɪ] *adv* идеа́льно; **~ the work
should be done by tomorrow** в иде́але,
рабо́та должна́ бы́ть зако́нчена к
за́втрашнему дню; **she's ~ suited for the job**
она́ идеа́льно похо́дит для э́той рабо́ты.

identical [aɪˈdɛntɪkl] *adj* одина́ковый

(одина́ков), иденти́чный* (иденти́чен).

identification [aɪdɛntɪfɪ'keɪʃən] *n* определе́ние; (*process*) выявле́ние; (*of person, dead body*) опозна́ние; **(means of)** ~ удостовере́ние ли́чности.

identify [aɪ'dɛntɪfaɪ] *vt* (*recognize*) определя́ть (определи́ть *perf*); (: *person*) узнава́ть* (узна́ть* *perf*); (: *body*) опознава́ть* (опозна́ть* *perf*); (*distinguish*) отлича́ть (отличи́ть *perf*); **he is identified with radical politics** он отлича́ется радика́льными полити́ческими взгля́дами.

Identikit® [aɪ'dɛntɪkɪt] *n*: ~ **(picture)** портре́т-ро́бот престу́пника, соста́вленный по описа́нию свиде́телей.

identity [aɪ'dɛntɪtɪ] *n* (*of person, suspect etc*) ли́чность *f*; (*of group, culture, nation etc*) самосозна́ние.

identity card *n* удостовере́ние ли́чности.

identity papers *npl* докуме́нты *mpl*, удостоверя́ющие ли́чности.

identity parade *n* (*BRIT*) процеду́ра опозна́ния подозрева́емого в гру́ппе люде́й.

ideological [aɪdɪə'lɔdʒɪkl] *adj* идеологи́ческий*.

ideology [aɪdɪ'ɔlədʒɪ] *n* идеоло́гия.

idiocy [ˈɪdɪəsɪ] *n* идиоти́зм.

idiom [ˈɪdɪəm] *n* (*style*) стиль *m*; (*phrase*) идио́ма.

idiomatic [ɪdɪə'mætɪk] *adj* идиомати́чный* (идиомати́чен).

idiosyncrasy [ɪdɪəu'sɪŋkrəsɪ] *n* (*foible*) осо́бенность *f*, характе́рная черта́.

idiosyncratic [ɪdɪəusɪŋ'krætɪk] *adj* индивидуа́льный* (индивидуа́лен), осо́бенный.

idiot [ˈɪdɪət] *n* идио́т(ка*).

idiotic [ɪdɪ'ɔtɪk] *adj* идио́тский*.

idle [ˈaɪdl] *adj* пра́здный; (*lazy*) лени́вый (лени́в); (*unemployed*) безрабо́тный; (*machinery, factory*) безде́йствующий ♦ *vi* (*machine*) проста́ивать (*impf*); (*engine*) рабо́тать (*impf*) на холосто́м ходу́; **to be ~** безде́йствовать (*impf*); **to lie ~** быть* (*impf*) неиспо́льзованным(-ой); **an ~ hour** час досу́га

▸ **idle away** *vt*: **to ~ away the time** корота́ть (*impf*) вре́мя.

idle capacity *n* неиспо́льзуемая произво́дственная мо́щность *f*.

idle money *n* неинвести́рованные де́ньги* *pl*.

idleness [ˈaɪdlnɪs] *n* (*inactivity*) безде́лье; (*laziness*) лень *f*.

idler [ˈaɪdlə] *n* безде́льник(-ица), лентя́й(ка*).

idle time *n* (*COMM*) просто́й.

idly [ˈaɪdlɪ] *adv* пра́здно, лени́во.

idol [ˈaɪdl] *n* (*hero*) куми́р; (*REL*) йдол.

idolize [ˈaɪdəlaɪz] *vt* боготвори́ть (*impf*).

idyllic [ɪ'dɪlɪk] *adj* (*place, holiday*) идилли́ческий*.

i.e. *abbr* (*that is*: = *id est*) т.е.= *то есть*.

if [ɪf] *conj* **1** (*conditional use*) е́сли; **if I finish early today, I will ring you** е́сли я зако́нчу ра́но сего́дня, я тебе́ позвоню́; **if I were you (I would ...)** на Ва́шем ме́сте (я бы ...)
2 (*whenever*) когда́
3 (*although*): **(even) if** (да́же) е́сли; **I'll get it done, even if it takes all night** я сде́лаю э́то, е́сли да́же э́то займёт у меня́ всю ночь; **I like it, (even) if you don't** хоть Вам и не нра́вится э́то, а мне (всё равно́) нра́вится
4 (*whether*) ли; **I don't know if he is here** я не зна́ю, здесь ли он; **ask him if he can stay** спроси́те, смо́жет ли он оста́ться
5: **if so/not** е́сли да/нет; **if only** е́сли то́лько; **if only I could** е́сли бы я то́лько мог; *see also* **as.**

iffy [ˈɪfɪ] *adj* (*inf: scheme, suggestion*) подозри́тельный; **I'm feeling a bit ~ today** я сего́дня фиго́во себя́ чу́вствую.

igloo [ˈɪgluː] *n* и́глу *nt ind* (*жили́ще эскимо́сов*).

ignite [ɪg'naɪt] *vt* (*set fire to*) зажига́ть (заже́чь* *perf*) ♦ *vi* воспламеня́ться (воспламени́ться *perf*), загора́ться (загоре́ться *perf*).

ignition [ɪg'nɪʃən] *n* (*AUT*) зажига́ние; **to switch on/off the ~** включа́ть (включи́ть *perf*)/ выключа́ть (вы́ключить *perf*) зажига́ние.

ignition key *n* (*AUT*) ключ* зажига́ния.

ignoble [ɪg'nəubl] *adj* недосто́йный* (недосто́ен).

ignominious [ɪgnə'mɪnɪəs] *adj* позо́рный* (позо́рен).

ignoramus [ɪgnə'reɪməs] *n* неве́жда *m/f*.

ignorance [ˈɪgnərəns] *n* неве́жество; ~ **of the facts** незна́ние фа́ктов; **to keep sb in ~ of sth** держа́ть* (*impf*) кого́-н в неве́дении по по́воду чего́-н.

ignorant [ˈɪgnərənt] *adj* (*uninformed, unaware*) несве́дущий* (несве́дущ); (*badly educated*) неве́жественный* (неве́жествен); **to be ~ of** (*subject, events etc*) быть* (*impf*) неосведомлённым(-ой) относи́тельно +*gen*.

ignore [ɪg'nɔː] *vt* (*pay no attention to*) игнори́ровать* (*impf/perf*); (*fail to take into account*) упуска́ть (упусти́ть* *perf*) из ви́ду.

ikon [ˈaɪkɔn] *n* = **icon**.

IL *abbr* (*US: POST*) = *Illinois*.

ILA *n abbr* (*US*) = *International Longshore Association*.

I'll [aɪl] = **I will, I shall**.

ill [ɪl] *adj* (*child etc*) больно́й*; (*harmful: effects*) дурно́й ♦ *n* (*evil*) зло; (*trouble*) беда́ ♦ *adv*: **to speak/think ~ (of sb)** пло́хо говори́ть (*impf*)/ ду́мать (*impf*) (о ком-н); **he is ~** он бо́лен; **to be taken ~** заболева́ть (заболе́ть *perf*).

ill-advised [ɪləd'vaɪzd] *adj* опроме́тчивый (опроме́тчив).

ill-at-ease [ɪlət'iːz] *adj* (*awkward, uncomfortable*) нело́вкий*.

ill-considered [ɪlkən'sɪdəd] *adj* необду́манный* (необду́ман).

ill-disposed [ˌɪldɪs'pəuzd] *adj*: **to be ~ towards
sb/sth** недоброжелательно относиться*
(impf) к кому-н/чему-н.
illegal [ɪ'liːgl] *adj* нелегальный* (нелегален),
незаконный* (незаконен).
illegally [ɪ'liːgəlɪ] *adv* нелегально, незаконно.
illegible [ɪ'lɛdʒɪbl] *adj* неразборчивый
(неразборчив).
illegitimate [ˌɪlɪ'dʒɪtɪmət] *adj* (*child*)
внебрачный; (*activity, treaty*) незаконный*
(незаконен).
ill-fated [ɪl'feɪtɪd] *adj* (*doomed*) злополучный*
(злополучен).
ill-favoured [ɪl'feɪvəd] (*US* **ill-favored**) *adj*
некрасивый (некрасив).
ill feeling *n* неприязнь *f.*
ill-gotten [ˈɪlgɔtn] *adj*: **~ gains** добытый
нечестным путём доход.
ill-health [ɪl'hɛlθ] *n* плохое здоровье.
illicit [ɪ'lɪsɪt] *adj* незаконный* (незаконен).
ill-informed [ɪlɪn'fɔːmd] *adj* неосведомлённый*
(неосведомлён).
illiterate [ɪ'lɪtərət] *adj* неграмотный*
(неграмотен).
ill-mannered [ɪl'mænəd] *adj* невоспитанный*
(невоспитан), невежливый (невежлив).
illness [ˈɪlnɪs] *n* болезнь *f.*
illogical [ɪ'lɔdʒɪkl] *adj* нелогичный*
(нелогичен).
ill-suited [ɪl'suːtɪd] *adj*: **they are ~** они не
подходят друг к другу; **he is ~ to the job** он
не годится для этой работы.
ill-timed [ɪl'taɪmd] *adj* несвоевременный*
(несвоевремен); **her comments were ~** её
замечания были не к месту.
ill-treat [ɪl'triːt] *vt* плохо обращаться *(impf)* с
+*instr.*
ill-treatment [ɪl'triːtmənt] *n* жестокость *f.*
illuminate [ɪ'luːmɪneɪt] *vt* (*light up*) освещать
(осветить* *perf*).
illuminated sign [ɪ'luːmɪneɪtɪd-] *n* освещённая
вывеска*.
illuminating [ɪ'luːmɪneɪtɪŋ] *adj* (*report, book etc*)
разъясняющий; (*person*) просвещённый*
(просвещён), познавательный*
(познавателен).
illumination [ɪluːmɪ'neɪʃən] *n* (*lighting*)
освещение; **~s** *npl* (*decorative lights*)
иллюминация *fsg.*
illusion [ɪ'luːʒən] *n* (*false idea*) иллюзия; (*trick*)
фокус; **to be under the ~ that ...** находиться
(impf) под впечатлением, что ....
illusive [ɪ'luːsɪv] *adj* = **illusory**.
illusory [ɪ'luːsərɪ] *adj* иллюзорный*
(иллюзорен), обманчивый (обманчив).
illustrate [ˈɪləstreɪt] *vt* иллюстрировать
(проиллюстрировать *perf*).
illustration [ɪlə'streɪʃən] *n* (*example, picture*)

иллюстрация; (*act*) иллюстрирование.
illustrator [ˈɪləstreɪtə'] *n* иллюстратор.
illustrious [ɪ'lʌstrɪəs] *adj* (*career*) блестящий*
(блестящ); (*predecessor, partner*)
прославленный* (прославлен).
ill will *n* неприязнь *f.*
ILO *n abbr* = **International Labour Organization**.
ILWU *n abbr* (*US*) = **International
Longshoremen's and Warehousemen's Union**.
I'm [aɪm] = **I am**.
image [ˈɪmɪdʒ] *n* (*picture*) образ; (*public face*)
имидж; (*reflection*) отражение.
imagery [ˈɪmɪdʒərɪ] *n* (*ART, LITERATURE*)
образность *f*, образный мир.
imaginable [ɪ'mædʒɪnəbl] *adj* вообразимый;
we've tried every ~ solution мы
перепробовали все вообразимые решения;
she had the prettiest hair ~ у неё были
невообразимо красивые волосы.
imaginary [ɪ'mædʒɪnərɪ] *adj* (*creature, land*)
воображаемый; (*danger, illness*) мнимый.
imagination [ɪmædʒɪ'neɪʃən] *n* воображение;
(*illusion*) фантазия; **it's just your ~** это
просто плод Вашего воображения.
imaginative [ɪ'mædʒɪnətɪv] *adj* (*person*)
обладающий богатым *or* творческим
воображением; (*solution*) хитроумный*
(хитроумен).
imagine [ɪ'mædʒɪn] *vt* (*visualize*) представлять
(представить* *perf*) (себе), воображать
(вообразить* *perf*); (*dream*) воображать
(вообразить* *perf*); (*suppose*) полагать *(impf)*.
imbalance [ɪm'bæləns] *n* несоответствие,
неравновесие.
imbecile [ˈɪmbəsiːl] *n* ненормальный(-ая) *m(f)
adj.*
imbue [ɪm'bjuː] *vt*: **to ~ sb with sth**
вдохновлять (вдохновить* *perf*) кого-н
чем-н; **to ~ sth with sth** наполнять
(наполнить *perf*) что-н чем-н.
IMF *n abbr* (= *International Monetary Fund*)
МВФ= *Международный валютный фонд.*
imitate [ˈɪmɪteɪt] *vt* (*copy*) копировать
(скопировать *perf*); (*mimic*) подражать *(impf)*
+*dat*, имитировать *(impf)*.
imitation [ɪmɪ'teɪʃən] *n* (*see vb*) копирование;
подражание; (*instance*) имитация.
imitator [ˈɪmɪteɪtə'] *n* подражатель(ница) *m(f).*
immaculate [ɪ'mækjulət] *adj* безупречный*
(безупречен); (*REL*) непорочный.
immaterial [ɪmə'tɪərɪəl] *adj* (*unimportant*)
несущественный* (несуществен).
immature [ɪmə'tjuə'] *adj* (*fruit*) неспелый
(неспел); (*cheese*) незрелый; (*organism*)
недоразвившийся; (*person*) незрелый
(незрел).
immaturity [ɪmə'tjuərɪtɪ] *n* незрелость *f.*
immeasurable [ɪ'mɛʒrəbl] *adj* неизмеримый

---

* marks translations which have irregular inflections. The Russian-English side of the dictionary gives inflectional information.

(неизмери́м).

immediacy [ı'mi:dɪəsı] *n* (*of events etc*) непосре́дственность *f*; (*of needs*) безотлага́тельность *f*.

immediate [ı'mi:dɪət] *adj* (*reaction, answer*) неме́дленный, мгнове́нный; (*pressing: need*) безотлага́тельный* (безотлага́телен); (*nearest: neighbourhood, family etc*) ближа́йший*.

immediately [ı'mi:dɪətlı] *adv* (*at once*) неме́дленно; (*directly*) непосре́дственно; ~ **next to** непосре́дственно ря́дом с +*instr*.

immense [ı'mɛns] *adj* (*huge: size*) необъя́тный* (необъя́тен); (: *progress, importance*) огро́мный* (огро́мен).

immensely [ı'mɛnslı] *adv* (*grateful etc*) бесконе́чно; (*difficult*) необыча́йно; **I enjoyed it** ~ мне э́то о́чень понра́вилось.

immensity [ı'mɛnsıtı] *n* необъя́тность *f*.

immerse [ı'mə:s] *vt* (*submerge*) погружа́ть (погрузи́ть* *perf*); **to** ~ **sth in** погружа́ть (погрузи́ть* *perf*) что-н в +*acc*; **to be** ~**d in** (*fig*) быть* (*impf*) погружённым(-ой) в +*acc*.

immersion heater [ı'mə:ʃən-] *n* (*BRIT*) бо́йлер.

immigrant ['ımıgrənt] *n* иммигра́нт(ка*).

immigration [ımı'greıʃən] *n* (*process*) иммигра́ция; (*also:* ~ **control**: *at airport etc*) пограни́чный контро́ль *m* ♦ *cpd:* ~ **laws** зако́ны *mpl* об иммигра́ции; ~ **authorities** пограни́чная слу́жба.

imminent ['ımınənt] *adj* (*arrival, departure*) немину́емый (немину́ем).

immobile [ı'məubaıl] *adj* неподви́жный* (неподви́жен).

immobilize [ı'məubılaız] *vt* (*person, machine*) остана́вливать (останови́ть* *perf*), свя́зывать (связа́ть* *perf*).

immoderate [ı'mɔdərət] *adj* неуме́ренный* (неуме́рен).

immodest [ı'mɔdıst] *adj* нескро́мный* (нескро́мен).

immoral [ı'mɔrl] *adj* амора́льный* (амора́лен), безнра́вственный* (безнра́вственен).

immorality [ımɔ'rælıtı] *n* амора́льность *f*, безнра́вственность *f*.

immortal [ı'mɔ:tl] *adj* (*also fig*) бессме́ртный* (бессме́ртен).

immortality [ımɔ:'tælıtı] *n* бессме́ртие.

immortalize [ı'mɔ:tlaız] *vt* увекове́чивать (увекове́чить *perf*).

immovable [ı'mu:vəbl] *adj* (*object*) неподви́жный* (неподви́жен); (*opinion*) неизме́нный* (неизме́нен).

immune [ı'mju:n] *adj:* ~ (**to**) (*disease*) облада́ющий иммуните́том (к +*dat*); **he is** ~ **to** ... (*flattery, criticism etc*) он неподве́ржен влия́нию +*gen* ....

immune system *n* имму́нная систе́ма.

immunity [ı'mju:nıtı] *n* (*to disease*) иммуните́т; (*to criticism*) невос-

прии́мчивость *f*; (*of diplomat, from prosecution*) неприкоснове́нность *f*.

immunization [ımjunaı'zeıʃən] *n* иммуниза́ция, приви́вка*.

immunize ['ımjunaız] *vt* (*MED*): **to** ~ (**against**) привива́ть (приви́ть* *perf*) (про́тив +*gen*).

imp [ımp] *n* бесёнок*.

impact ['ımpækt] *n* (*of bullet*) моме́нт попада́ния; (*of crash*) уда́р; (*of law, measure*) возде́йствие.

impair [ım'pɛəʳ] *vt* (*vision, judgement*) ослабля́ть (осла́бить* *perf*).

impaired [ım'pɛəd] *adj* осла́бленный (осла́блен).

impale [ım'peıl] *vt* нака́лывать (наколо́ть* *perf*); **to** ~ **sth on** наса́живать (насади́ть* *perf*) что-н на +*acc*.

impart [ım'pɑ:t] *vt:* **to** ~ (**to**) (*information*) передава́ть (переда́ть* *perf*) (+*dat*); (*flavour*) придава́ть* (прида́ть* *perf*) (+*dat*).

impartial [ım'pɑ:ʃl] *adj* беспристра́стный* (беспристра́стен).

impartiality [ımpɑ:ʃı'ælıtı] *n* беспристра́стие.

impassable [ım'pɑ:səbl] *adj* непроходи́мый (непроходи́м).

impasse [æm'pɑ:s] *n* тупи́к*; **to reach an** ~ зайти́* (*perf*) в тупи́к.

impassive [ım'pæsıv] *adj* бесстра́стный* (бесстра́стен).

impatience [ım'peıʃəns] *n* нетерпели́вость *f*.

impatient [ım'peıʃənt] *adj* нетерпели́вый (нетерпели́в); **to get** *or* **grow** ~ начина́ть (нача́ть* *perf*) теря́ть терпе́ние; **she was** ~ **to leave** ей не терпе́лось уйти́.

impatiently [ım'peıʃəntlı] *adv* нетерпели́во.

impeach [ım'pi:tʃ] *vt* привлека́ть (привле́чь* *perf*) к отве́тственности.

impeachment [ım'pi:tʃmənt] *n* привлече́ние к отве́тственности.

impeccable [ım'pɛkəbl] *adj* безупре́чный* (безупре́чен).

impecunious [ımpı'kju:nıəs] *adj* (*formal*) нужда́ющийся.

impede [ım'pi:d] *vt* затрудня́ть (затрудни́ть *perf*).

impediment [ım'pɛdımənt] *n* (*obstacle*) препя́тствие; **speech** ~ дефе́кт ре́чи.

impel [ım'pɛl] *vt:* **to** ~ **sb to do** вынужда́ть (вы́нудить* *perf*) кого́-н +*infin*.

impending [ım'pɛndıŋ] *adj* надвига́ющийся.

impenetrable [ım'pɛnıtrəbl] *adj* (*jungle, fortress*) непроходи́мый (непроходи́м); (*look, expression*) непроница́емый (непроница́ем); (*darkness, fog*) непрогля́дный* (непрогля́ден); (*fig: law, text*) недосту́пный* (недосту́пен) (для понима́ния).

imperative [ım'pɛrətıv] *adj* (*tone*) вла́стный* (вла́стен); (*need etc*) настоя́тельный* (настоя́телен) ♦ *n* (*LING*) повели́тельное наклоне́ние; **it is** ~ **that** ... необходи́мо, чтобы ....

imperceptible [ɪmpə'sɛptɪbl] *adj* незаме́тный*
(назаме́тен).

imperfect [ɪm'pə:fɪkt] *adj* (*system etc*)
несовершённый* (несоверше́нен); (*goods*)
дефе́ктный ♦ *n* (*LING: also:* ~ **tense**)
имперфе́кт.

imperfection [ɪmpə:'fɛkʃən] *n* (*failing*)
недоста́ток*; (*blemish*) изъя́н.

imperial [ɪm'pɪərɪəl] *adj* (*history, power*)
импе́рский*; (*BRIT: measure*): ~ **system**
брита́нская систе́ма ме́ры и ве́са.

imperialism [ɪm'pɪərɪəlɪzəm] *n* империали́зм.

imperil [ɪm'pɛrɪl] *vt* подверга́ть (подве́ргнуть*
perf) опа́сности.

imperious [ɪm'pɪərɪəs] *adj* (*person*) вла́стный*
(вла́стен).

impersonal [ɪm'pə:sənl] *adj* (*organization,
place*) безли́кий*.

impersonate [ɪm'pə:səneɪt] *vt* (*pass o.s. off as*)
выдава́ть* (вы́дать *perf*) себя́ за +*acc*; (*THEAT*)
изобража́ть (изобрази́ть* *perf*).

impersonation [ɪmpə:sə'neɪʃən] *n*
изображе́ние; (*LAW*) самозва́нство; (*THEAT*)
исполне́ние ро́ли.

impertinent [ɪm'pə:tɪnənt] *adj* (*pupil, question*)
де́рзкий* (де́рзок), наха́льный* (наха́лен).

imperturbable [ɪmpə'tə:bəbl] *adj* невоз-
мути́мый (невозмути́м).

impervious [ɪm'pə:vɪəs] *adj* (*fig*): **he is** ~ **to** ... на
него́ не де́йствует ....

impetuous [ɪm'pɛtjuəs] *adj* поры́вистый
(поры́вист).

impetus ['ɪmpətəs] *n* (*momentum*) ине́рция;
(*fig*) сти́мул.

impinge [ɪm'pɪndʒ]: **to** ~ **on** *vt fus* (*person*)
посяга́ть (посягну́ть *perf*) на +*acc*; (*rights*)
попира́ть (попра́ть* *perf*).

impish ['ɪmpɪʃ] *adj* озорно́й.

implacable [ɪm'plækəbl] *adj* непримири́мый
(непримири́м).

implant [ɪm'plɑ:nt] *vt* (*MED*) переса́живать
(пересади́ть* *perf*); (*fig: idea, principle*)
внуша́ть (внуши́ть* *perf*).

implausible [ɪm'plɔ:zɪbl] *adj* неправдо-
подо́бный* (неправдоподо́бен).

implement [*vt* 'ɪmplɪmɛnt, *n* 'ɪmplɪmənt] *vt* (*plan,
regulation*) проводи́ть* (провести́* *perf*) в
жизнь ♦ *n*: **gardening** ~ садо́вый
инструме́нт; **farming** ~**s** сельско-
хозя́йственные ору́дия; **cooking** ~**s**
ку́хонные принадле́жности.

implicate ['ɪmplɪkeɪt] *vt* (*in crime, error*)
вовлека́ть (вовле́чь* *perf*).

implication [ɪmplɪ'keɪʃən] *n* (*inference*) вы́вод;
(*involvement*) прича́стность *f*; **by** ~ су́дя по
всему́.

implicit [ɪm'plɪsɪt] *adj* (*inferred*) подраз-

умева́ющийся; (*unquestioning*)
безогово́рочный.

implicitly [ɪm'plɪsɪtlɪ] *adv* (*totally*)
безогово́рочно.

implore [ɪm'plɔ:'] *vt* (*beg*) умоля́ть (*impf*); **to** ~
sb to do умоля́ть (*impf*) кого́-н +*infin*.

imply [ɪm'plaɪ] *vt* (*hint*) намека́ть (намекну́ть
perf) на +*acc*; (*mean*) подразумева́ть (*impf*).

impolite [ɪmpə'laɪt] *adj* (*rude, offensive*)
неве́жливый (неве́жлив).

imponderable [ɪm'pɒndərəbl] *adj* неулови́мый
(неулови́м) ♦ *n* вещь, *не поддаю́щаяся
определе́нию.*

import [*vb* ɪm'pɔ:t, *n, cpd* 'ɪmpɔ:t] *vt*
импорти́ровать (*impf/perf*), ввози́ть* (ввезти́*
perf) ♦ *n* (*article*) импорти́руемый това́р;
(*importation*) и́мпорт ♦ *cpd*: ~ **duty** по́шлина
на ввоз; ~ **licence** лице́нзия на ввоз; ~ **quota**
и́мпортная кво́та.

importance [ɪm'pɔ:tns] *n* ва́жность *f*; **it is of
great/little** ~ э́то о́чень/не о́чень ва́жно.

important [ɪm'pɔ:tnt] *adj* ва́жный* (ва́жен);
(*influential: person*) ва́жный*; **it's not** ~ э́то
нева́жно.

importantly [ɪm'pɔ:tntlɪ] *adv* ва́жно; **but more**
~ ... но ещё важне́е ..., но са́мое гла́вное ....

importation [ɪmpɔ:'teɪʃən] *n* и́мпорт.

imported [ɪm'pɔ:tɪd] *adj* и́мпортный.

importer [ɪm'pɔ:tə'] *n* импортёр.

impose [ɪm'pəuz] *vt* (*sanctions, restrictions,
discipline etc*) налага́ть (наложи́ть* *perf*) ♦ *vi*:
to ~ **on sb** навя́зываться (навяза́ться* *perf*)
кому́-н.

imposing [ɪm'pəuzɪŋ] *adj* (*building*) внуши́тельный*
(внуши́телен), вели́чественный*
(вели́чествен).

imposition [ɪmpə'zɪʃən] *n* (*of tax etc*)
обложе́ние; **to be an** ~ **on sb** быть* (*impf*)
обу́зой кому́-н.

impossibility [ɪmpɒsə'bɪlɪtɪ] *n* невозмо́жность
f.

impossible [ɪm'pɒsɪbl] *adj* (*task, demand,
person*) невозмо́жный* (невозмо́жен);
(*situation*) невероя́тный* (невероя́тен); **it's** ~
for me to leave now я не могу́ сейча́с уйти́.

impossibly [ɪm'pɒsɪblɪ] *adv* невозмо́жно.

imposter [ɪm'pɒstə'] *n* = **impostor**.

impostor [ɪm'pɒstə'] *n* самозва́нец*(-нка*).

impotence ['ɪmpɒtns] *n* бесси́лие; (*MED*)
импоте́нция.

impotent ['ɪmpɒtnt] *adj* бесси́льный*
(бесси́лен); (*MED*) импоте́нтный*
(импоте́нтен).

impound [ɪm'paund] *vt* конфиско́вывать
(конфискова́ть* *perf*).

impoverished [ɪm'pɒvərɪʃt] *adj* (*country*)
обедне́вший*.

impracticable [ɪm'præktɪkəbl] *adj*

---

* marks translations which have irregular inflections. The Russian-English side of the dictionary gives inflectional information.

неосуществи́мый (неосуществи́м).
impractical [ɪmˈpræktɪkl] *adj* (*plan etc*)
нереа́льный* (нереа́лен); (*person*)
непракти́чный* (непракти́чен).
imprecise [ɪmprɪˈsaɪs] *adj* нето́чный*
(нето́чен).
impregnable [ɪmˈprɛgnəbl] *adj* (*castle, fortress*)
непристу́пный* (непристу́пен); (*fig: person*)
неуязви́мый (неуязви́м).
impregnate [ˈɪmprɛgneɪt] *vt* (*saturate*)
пропи́тывать (пропита́ть *perf*); (*fertilize*)
оплодотворя́ть (оплодотвори́ть *perf*).
impresario [ɪmprɪˈsɑːrɪəu] *n* импреса́рио *m ind*.
impress [ɪmˈprɛs] *vt* (*person*) производи́ть*
(произвести́* *perf*) впечатле́ние на +*acc*;
(*mark*) отпеча́тывать (отпеча́тать *perf*); **to ~
sth on sb** внуша́ть (внуши́ть *perf*) что-н
кому́-н.
impression [ɪmˈprɛʃən] *n* впечатле́ние; (*of
stamp, seal*) отпеча́ток*; (*imitation*)
имита́ция; **to make a good/bad ~ on sb**
производи́ть* (произвести́* *perf*) хоро́шее/
плохо́е впечатле́ние на кого́-н; **he is under
the ~ that ...** у него́ создало́сь впечатле́ние,
что ....
impressionable [ɪmˈprɛʃnəbl] *adj*
впечатли́тельный* (впечатли́телен).
impressionist [ɪmˈprɛʃənɪst] *n* (*ART*)
импрессиони́ст; (*entertainer*) имита́тор.
impressive [ɪmˈprɛsɪv] *adj* впечатля́ющий.
imprest system [ˈɪmprɛst-] *n* систе́ма
де́нежного ава́нса.
imprint [ˈɪmprɪnt] *n* отпеча́ток*; (*PUBLISHING*)
выходны́е да́нные *pl adj*; (: *label*) печа́ть на
переплёте с и́менем владе́льца и́ли
изда́теля.
imprinted [ɪmˈprɪntɪd] *adj*: **~ on** (*surface*)
отпеча́тавшийся в/на +*prp*; (*memory*)
запечатлённый (запечатлён) в +*prp*.
imprison [ɪmˈprɪzn] *vt* (*criminal*) заключа́ть
(заключи́ть *perf*) в тюрьму́.
imprisonment [ɪmˈprɪznmənt] *n* (тюре́мное)
заключе́ние.
improbable [ɪmˈprɔbəbl] *adj* (*outcome*)
маловероя́тный* (маловероя́тен); (*story*)
неправдоподо́бный* (неправдоподо́бен).
impromptu [ɪmˈprɔmptjuː] *adj* (*celebration,
party*) импровизи́рованный
(импровизи́рован); (*tactics*) непла́новый.
improper [ɪmˈprɔpəʳ] *adj* (*unsuitable: conduct*)
неуме́стный* (неуме́стен); (: *procedure*)
непра́вильный* (непра́вилен); (*dishonest*:
activities) незако́нный* (незако́нен).
impropriety [ɪmprəˈpraɪətɪ] *n* (*indecency*)
неприли́чие; **the ~ of his conduct**
непристо́йность *f* его́ поведе́ния.
improve [ɪmˈpruːv] *vt* улучша́ть (улу́чшить
perf) ◆ *vi* улучша́ться (улу́чшиться *perf*);
(*pupil*) станови́ться* (стать* *perf*) лу́чше;
(*patient*) начина́ть (нача́ть *perf*)
выздора́вливать

► **improve (up)on** *vt fus* (*work, achievement etc*)
де́лать (сде́лать *perf*) лу́чше.
improvement [ɪmˈpruːvmənt] *n*: **~ (in)**
улучше́ние (+*gen*); **to make ~s to** вноси́ть*
(внести́* *perf*) улучше́ния в +*acc*.
improvisation [ɪmprəvaɪˈzeɪʃən] *n* (*THEAT*)
импровиза́ция.
improvise [ˈɪmprəvaɪz] *vt* (*meal*) на́скоро
гото́вить* (пригото́вить* *perf*); (*bed, shelter*)
на́скоро устра́ивать (устро́ить *perf*) ◆ *vi*
(*THEAT, MUS*) импровизи́ровать
(сымпровизи́ровать *perf*).
imprudence [ɪmˈpruːdns] *n* неблагоразу́мное
поведе́ние.
imprudent [ɪmˈpruːdnt] *adj* неблагоразу́мный*
(неблагоразу́мен); **it would be ~ of you to
insult him** оскорби́ть его́ бу́дет
неблагоразу́мием с Ва́шей стороны́.
impudent [ˈɪmpjudnt] *adj* на́глый* (нагл).
impugn [ɪmˈpjuːn] *vt* подверга́ть
(подве́ргнуть* *perf*) сомне́нию.
impulse [ˈɪmpʌls] *n* (*urge*) поры́в; (*ELEC*)
и́мпульс; **to act on ~** поддава́ться*
(подда́ться* *perf*) поры́ву.
impulse buy *n* случа́йная поку́пка*.
impulsive [ɪmˈpʌlsɪv] *adj* (*purchase*) случа́й-
ный* (случа́ен); (*person*) импульси́вный*
(импульси́вен); (*gesture*) поры́вистый
(поры́вист).
impunity [ɪmˈpjuːnɪtɪ] *n*: **with ~** безнака́занно.
impure [ɪmˈpjuəʳ] *adj* нечи́стый (нечи́ст);
(*sinful*) непристо́йный* (непристо́ен).
impurity [ɪmˈpjuərɪtɪ] *n* (*foreign substance*)
при́месь *f*.
IN *abbr* (*US: POST*) = Indiana.

in [ɪn] *prep* **1** (*indicating place, position*) в/на
+*prp*; **in the house/garden** в до́ме/саду́; **in the
street/Ukraine/north** на у́лице/Украи́не/
се́вере; **in London/Canada** в Ло́ндоне/
Кана́де; **in the country** за́городом; **in town** в
го́роде; **in here** здесь; **in there** там
2 (*indicating motion*) в +*acc*; **in the house/
room** в дом/ко́мнату
3 (*indicating time: during*) в +*prp*; **in spring/
summer/autumn/winter** весно́й/ле́том/
о́сенью/зимо́й; **in the morning/afternoon/
evening** у́тром/днём/ве́чером; **they often
play cards in the evening** они́ ча́сто игра́ют в
ка́рты по вечера́м; **at 4 o'clock in the
afternoon** в 4 часа́ дня
4 (*indicating time: in the space of*) за +*acc*; (:
after a period of) че́рез +*acc*; **I did it in 3 hours** я
сде́лал э́то за 3 часа́; **I'll see you in 2 weeks**
уви́димся че́рез 2 неде́ли
5 (*indicating manner etc*): **in a loud/quiet voice**
гро́мким/ти́хим го́лосом; **in English/Russian**
по-англи́йски/по-ру́сски, на англи́йском/
ру́сском языке́; **the boy in the blue shirt**
ма́льчик в голубо́й руба́шке
6 (*indicating circumstances*): **in the sun** на

со́лнце; **in the rain** под дождём; **in the shade** в
тени́; **there has been a change in public
opinion** обще́ственное мне́ние
перемени́лось; **a rise in prices** повыше́ние
цен
7 (*indicating mood, state*) в +*prp*
8 (*with ratios, numbers*): **one in ten households
have a second car** одна́ из десяти́ семе́й
име́ет втору́ю маши́ну; **20 pence in the
pound** 20 пе́нсов с фу́нта; **they lined up in
twos** они́ вы́строились по́ дво́е; **a gradient of
one in five** укло́н оди́н к пяти́
9 (*referring to people, works*): **the disease is
common in children** э́то заболева́ние ча́сто
встреча́ется у дете́й; **in Dickens** у Ди́ккенса;
you have a good friend in him он тебе́
хоро́ший друг
10 (*indicating profession etc*): **to be in teaching**
рабо́тать (*impf*) учи́телем; **to be in publishing**
занима́ться (*impf*) изда́тельским де́лом; **to
be in the army** быть* (*impf*) в а́рмии
11 (*after superlative*) в +*prp*; **the best doctor in
the city** лу́чший* врач в го́роде
12 (*with present participle*): **in saying this**
говоря́ э́то; **in behaving like this, she ...**
поступа́я таки́м о́бразом, она́ ...
♦ *adv*: **to be in** (*train, ship, plane*) прибы́ть*
(*perf*); (*in fashion*) быть* (*impf*) в мо́де; **is he in
today? – yes, he's in/no, he's not in** (*at work*)
он сего́дня на рабо́те? – да, он на рабо́те/
нет, его́ сего́дня нет; (*at home*) он сего́дня
до́ма? – да, он до́ма/нет, его́ сего́дня нет; **he
wasn't in yesterday** его́ вчера́ не́ было; **he'll
be in later today** он бу́дет сего́дня по́зже; **to
ask sb in** предложи́ть* (*perf*) кому́-н зайти́; **to
run/walk** *etc* **in** вбега́ть (вбежа́ть* *perf*)/
входи́ть* (войти́* *perf*) *etc*
♦ *n*: **to know all the ins and outs** знать (*impf*)
все ходы́.

in. *abbr* = **inch**.
inability [ɪnə'bɪlɪtɪ] *n* (*incapacity*): ~ **(to do)**
неспосо́бность *f* (+*infin*).
inaccessible [ɪnæk'sɛsɪbl] *adj* (*also fig*)
недосту́пный* (недосту́пен).
inaccuracy [ɪn'ækjʊrəsɪ] *n* (*quality*) нето́чность
f; (*mistake*) оши́бка*.
inaccurate [ɪn'ækjʊrət] *adj* нето́чный*
(нето́чен).
inaction [ɪn'ækʃən] *n* безде́йствие.
inactive [ɪn'æktɪv] *adj* (*person*) безде́ятельный*
(безде́ятелен), пасси́вный* (пасси́вен);
(*animal*) пасси́вный* (пасси́вен); (*volcano*)
поту́хший.
inactivity [ɪnæk'tɪvɪtɪ] *n* (*idleness*) без-
де́ятельность *f*.
inadequacy [ɪn'ædɪkwəsɪ] *n* недоста́точность
f; (*of person*) неполноце́нность *f*.

inadequate [ɪn'ædɪkwət] *adj* (*income, amount,
preparation*) недоста́точный*
(недоста́точен); (*reply*) неадеква́тный*
(неадеква́тен); (*work, result*) неудовле-
твори́тельный* (неудовлетвори́телен);
(*person*) неполноце́нный (неполноце́н).
inadmissible [ɪnəd'mɪsəbl] *adj* недопусти́мый
(недопусти́м); (*LAW: evidence*) неприе́м-
лемый (неприе́млем).
inadvertently [ɪnəd'və:tntlɪ] *adv*
неумы́шленно.
inadvisable [ɪnəd'vaɪzəbl] *adj* (*course of action*)
нецелесообра́зный* (нецелесообра́зен); **it is
~ to ...** не рекоменду́ется +*infin* ....
inane [ɪ'neɪn] *adj* (*smile*) глу́пый* (глуп);
(*remark etc*) бессмы́сленный* (бессмы́слен).
inanimate [ɪn'ænɪmət] *adj* (*object*)
неодушевлённый* (неодушевлён).
inapplicable [ɪn'æplɪkəbl] *adj* (*description,
comment*) неподходя́щий*; (*rule*)
неприменимый (неприменим).
inappropriate [ɪnə'prəʊprɪət] *adj* (*unsuitable*)
неподходя́щий*; (*improper*) неуме́стный*
(неуме́стен).
inapt [ɪn'æpt] *adj* неуме́стный* (неуме́стен).
inarticulate [ɪnɑː'tɪkjʊlət] *adj* (*person*)
косноязы́чный* (косноязы́чен); (*speech*)
невня́тный* (невня́тен).
inasmuch as [ɪnəz'mʌtʃ-] *adv* (*in that*)
посто́льку поско́льку; (*insofar as*) насто́лько
наско́лько.
inattention [ɪnə'tɛnʃən] *n* невнима́ние.
inattentive [ɪnə'tɛntɪv] *adj* невнима́тельный*
(невнима́телен).
inaudible [ɪn'ɔːdɪbl] *adj* неслы́шный*
(неслы́шен).
inaugural [ɪ'nɔːgjʊrəl] *adj* (*speech*)
вступи́тельный; (*meeting*) пе́рвый.
inaugurate [ɪ'nɔːgjʊreɪt] *vt* (*president, official*)
вводи́ть* (ввести́* *perf*) в до́лжность;
(*system, measure*) вводи́ть* (ввести́* *perf*);
(*organization*) открыва́ть (откры́ть* *perf*).
inauguration [ɪnɔːgjʊ'reɪʃən] *n* (*see vb*)
вступле́ние в до́лжность; введе́ние;
откры́тие.
inauspicious [ɪnɔːs'pɪʃəs] *adj* (*occasion*)
неблагоприя́тный* (неблагоприя́тен).
in-between [ɪnbɪ'twiːn] *adj* (*intermediate*)
промежу́точный; ~ **stage** промежу́точная
ста́дия.
inborn [ɪn'bɔːn] *adj* врождённый, приро́дный.
inbred [ɪn'brɛd] *adj* (*quality*) врождённый,
приро́дный; **an ~ family** семья́, *в кото́рой
де́ти рождены́ от роди́телей, состоя́щих в
кро́вном родстве́*.
inbreeding [ɪn'briːdɪŋ] *n* (*among animals*)
ро́дственное спа́ривание; (*among people*)
узкоро́дственные бра́чные отноше́ния *ntpl*.

---

* marks translations which have irregular inflections. The Russian-English side of the dictionary gives inflectional information.

inbuilt [ɪn'bɪlt] adj (quality, feeling etc) врождённый.

Inc. abbr = **incorporated**.

Inca ['ɪŋkə] adj: **the ~** or **~n civilization** инки fpl.

incalculable [ɪn'kælkjuləbl] adj (effect) огро́мный* (огро́мен); (loss) неисчисли́мый (неисчисли́м); (consequences) непред-ви́денный.

incapable [ɪn'keɪpəbl] adj (helpless) бес-по́мощный* (беспо́мощен); (unable to): **~ of sth/doing** неспосо́бный* (неспосо́бен) на что-н/+infin.

incapacitate [ɪnkə'pæsɪteɪt] vt: **to ~ sb** выводи́ть* (вы́вести* perf) кого́-н из стро́я; **to ~ sb for work** де́лать (сде́лать perf) кого́-н нетрудоспосо́бным(-ой).

incapacitated [ɪnkə'pæsɪteɪtɪd] adj (LAW) лишённый (лишён) пра́ва.

incapacity [ɪnkə'pæsɪtɪ] n (weakness) беспо́мощность f; (inability) неспосо́бность f.

incarcerate [ɪn'kɑ:səreɪt] vt заключа́ть (заключи́ть perf) в тюрьму́.

incarnate [ɪn'kɑ:nɪt] adj воплощённый (воплощён), олицетворённый (олицетворён); **evil ~** воплоще́ние or олицетворе́ние зла.

incarnation [ɪnkɑ:'neɪʃən] n воплоще́ние, олицетворе́ние; (REL) инкарна́ция.

incendiary [ɪn'sɛndɪərɪ] adj (device, bomb) зажига́тельный.

incense [n 'ɪnsɛns, vt ɪn'sɛns] n (also REL) ла́дан ♦ vt (anger) приводи́ть* (привести́* perf) в я́рость.

incense burner n кури́льница.

incentive [ɪn'sɛntɪv] n (inducement) сти́мул ♦ cpd: **~ scheme** систе́ма поощре́ния; **~ bonus** материа́льное поощре́ние.

inception [ɪn'sɛpʃən] n (of institution) откры́тие, основа́ние; (of activity) нача́ло.

incessant [ɪn'sɛsnt] adj бесконе́чный* (бесконе́чен), постоя́нный* (постоя́нен).

incessantly [ɪn'sɛsntlɪ] adv бесконе́чно, постоя́нно.

incest ['ɪnsɛst] n кровосмеше́ние.

inch [ɪntʃ] n (measurement) дюйм; **he was within an ~ of succeeding** он был уже́ бли́зок к успе́ху; **to be within an ~ of one's life** быть* (impf) на волоско́к от сме́рти; **he didn't give an ~** (fig: back down, yield) он не уступи́л ни на йо́ту.

▶ **inch forward** vi ме́дленно тро́гаться (тро́нуться perf) с ме́ста.

incidence ['ɪnsɪdns] n (of crime, disease) чи́сленность f.

incident ['ɪnsɪdnt] n (event) слу́чай; (MIL) инциде́нт; **without ~** без происше́ствий.

incidental [ɪnsɪ'dɛntl] adj (additional, supplementary) дополни́тельный*; **these duties are ~ to the job** э́ти обя́занности сопряжены́ с рабо́той; **ills ~ to old age**

неду́ги, прису́щие ста́рости; **~ expenses** побо́чные расхо́ды.

incidentally [ɪnsɪ'dɛntəlɪ] adv (by the way) кста́ти, ме́жду про́чим.

incidental music n (CINEMA) му́зыка к кинофи́льму.

incident room n диспе́тчерская f adj (в полице́йском управле́нии).

incinerate [ɪn'sɪnəreɪt] vt (rubbish, paper etc) сжига́ть (сжечь* perf).

incinerator [ɪn'sɪnəreɪtəʳ] n мусоросжига́тель m.

incipient [ɪn'sɪpɪənt] adj (baldness) начина́ющийся*; (madness) в нача́льной ста́дии.

incision [ɪn'sɪʒən] n (also MED) разре́з.

incisive [ɪn'saɪsɪv] adj (comment) о́стрый* (остёр), ре́зкий* (ре́зок); (criticism) ре́зкий* (ре́зок).

incisor [ɪn'saɪzəʳ] n резе́ц*.

incite [ɪn'saɪt] vt (rioters) подстрека́ть (подстрекну́ть perf); (violence, hatred) вызыва́ть (вы́звать* perf).

incl. abbr = **including, inclusive (of)**.

inclement [ɪn'klɛmənt] adj (weather) нена́стный* (нена́стен).

inclination [ɪnklɪ'neɪʃən] n (tendency) скло́нность f; (disposition, desire) жела́ние.

incline [n 'ɪnklaɪn, vb ɪn'klaɪn] n (slope) укло́н, накло́н ♦ vt (bend: head) наклоня́ть (наклони́ть* perf) ♦ vi (surface) наклоня́ться (наклони́ться* perf); **to be ~d to sth/to do** быть* (impf) скло́нным(-ой) к чему́-н/+infin; **to be well ~d towards sb** быть* (impf) благоскло́нным(-ой) к кому́-н.

include [ɪn'klu:d] vt включа́ть (включи́ть perf); **to be ~d (in)** быть* (impf) включённым(-ой) (в +acc); **to ~ sth in the price** включа́ть (включи́ть perf) в це́ну.

including [ɪn'klu:dɪŋ] prep включа́я +acc; **~ service charge** включа́я пла́ту за обслу́живание.

inclusion [ɪn'klu:ʒən] n включе́ние.

inclusive [ɪn'klu:sɪv] adj (price, terms) включа́ющий в себя́ все услу́ги; **~ of** включа́я +acc; **from March 1st to 5th ~** с 1-ого до 5-ое ма́рта включи́тельно.

incognito [ɪnkɔg'ni:təu] adv инко́гнито.

incoherent [ɪnkəu'hɪərənt] adj (argument) непосле́довательный* (непосле́дователен); (speech) несвя́зный* (несвя́зен); (person) косноязы́чный* (косноязы́чен).

income ['ɪnkʌm] n (earned) за́работок*; (from property, investment) дохо́д; **gross/net ~** валово́й/чи́стый дохо́д; **~ and expenditure account** прихо́дно-расхо́дный счёт*; **high/low ~ bracket** гру́ппа населе́ния с высо́ким/ни́зким у́ровнем дохо́да.

income support n де́нежное посо́бие.

income tax n подохо́дный нало́г ♦ cpd (COMM) нало́говый.

incoming ['ɪnkʌmɪŋ] *adj* (*flight, passenger*) прибыва́ющий; (*call*) поступа́ющий; (*mail*) входя́щий; (*government*) новои́збранный; (*official*) вступа́ющий* в до́лжность; ~ **tide** прили́в.

incommunicado ['ɪnkəmjunɪ'kɑːdəu] *adj*: **to hold sb** ~ держа́ть* (*impf*) кого́-н взаперти́.

incomparable [ɪn'kɔmpərəbl] *adj* несравне́нный*.

incompatible [ɪnkəm'pætɪbl] *adj* (*lifestyles*) соверше́нно ра́зный; (*systems, aims*) несовмести́мый (несовмести́м); **they are** ~ они́ соверше́нно ра́зные.

incompetence [ɪn'kɔmpɪtns] *n* некомпете́нтность *f*.

incompetent [ɪn'kɔmpɪtnt] *adj* (*person*) некомпете́нтный* (некомпете́нтен); (*work*) неуме́лый (неуме́л).

incomplete [ɪnkəm'pliːt] *adj* (*unfinished*) незако́нченный* (незако́нчен); (*partial*) непо́лный* (непо́лон).

incomprehensible [ɪnkɔmprɪ'hɛnsɪbl] *adj* непоня́тный* (непоня́тен).

inconceivable [ɪnkən'siːvəbl] *adj* немы́слимый (немы́слим); **it is** ~ **that ...** немы́слимо, что ....

inconclusive [ɪnkən'kluːsɪv] *adj* (*evidence*) недоста́точный* (недоста́точен); (*result*) неоконча́тельный* (неоконча́телен); (*argument*) неубеди́тельный* (неубеди́телен); **the experiment was** ~ экспериме́нт не дал определённых результа́тов; **the discussion was** ~ диску́ссия зако́нчилась ниче́м.

incongruous [ɪn'kɔŋgruəs] *adj* (*strange*) неле́пый (неле́п); (*inappropriate*) неуме́стный* (неуме́стен).

inconsequential [ɪnkɔnsɪ'kwɛnʃl] *adj* несуще́ственный* (несуще́ственен), незначи́тельный* (незначи́телен).

inconsiderable [ɪnkən'sɪdərəbl] *adj*: **not** ~ значи́тельный* (значи́телен).

inconsiderate [ɪnkən'sɪdərət] *adj* (*person*) не счита́ющийся ни с ке́м; (*action*) безду́мный* (безду́мен); ~ **towards** невнима́тельный к +*dat*.

inconsistency [ɪnkən'sɪstənsɪ] *n* (*of behaviour*) непосле́довательность *f*; (*of statement*) противоречи́вость *f*.

inconsistent [ɪnkən'sɪstnt] *adj* (*behaviour, person*) непосле́довательный* (непосле́дователен); (*work*) неро́вный* (неро́вен); (*statement*) противоречи́вый (противоречи́в); ~ **with** (*beliefs, values*) несовмести́мый (несовмести́м) с +*instr*.

inconsolable [ɪnkən'səuləbl] *adj* безуте́шный* (безуте́шен).

inconspicuous [ɪnkən'spɪkjuəs] *adj* незаме́т-ный* (незаме́тен), непримéтный* (непримéтен); **to make o.s.** ~ стара́ться (постара́ться *perf*) не привлека́ть к себе́ внима́ния.

incontinence [ɪn'kɔntɪnəns] *n* (*MED*) недержа́ние (*мочи́ или ка́ла*).

incontinent [ɪn'kɔntɪnənt] *adj* (*MED*) страда́ющий недержа́нием (*мочи́ или ка́ла*).

inconvenience [ɪnkən'viːnjəns] *n* (*problem*) неудо́бство; (*trouble*) беспоко́йство ♦ *vt* причиня́ть (причини́ть *perf*) неудо́бство +*dat*; **don't** ~ **yourself** не утружда́йте себя́; **sorry about the** ~ извини́те за причинённое неудо́бство.

inconvenient [ɪnkən'viːnjənt] *adj* неудо́бный* (неудо́бен); (*visitor*) прише́дший не ко вре́мени; **that time is very** ~ **for me** э́то о́чень неудо́бное для меня́ вре́мя.

incorporate [ɪn'kɔːpəreɪt] *vt* (*contain*) содержа́ть* (*impf*); **to** ~ (**into**) включа́ть (включи́ть *perf*) (в +*acc*); **safety features have been** ~**d in the design** предохрани́тельные устро́йства бы́ли внесены́ в прое́кт; **the coat of arms** ~**s three lions** на гербе́ изображены́ три льва́.

incorporated company [ɪn'kɔːpəreɪtɪd-] *n* (*US*) компа́ния, зарегистри́рованная как корпора́ция.

incorrect [ɪnkə'rɛkt] *adj* неве́рный* (неве́рен), непра́вильный* (непра́вилен).

incorrigible [ɪn'kɔrɪdʒɪbl] *adj* (*liar, crook*) неисправи́мый (неисправи́м).

incorruptible [ɪnkə'rʌptɪbl] *adj* (*not open to bribes*) неподку́пный* (неподку́пен).

increase [*n* 'ɪnkriːs, *vb* ɪn'kriːs] *n*: ~ (**in**), ~ (**of**) увеличе́ние (+*gen*) ♦ *vi* увели́чиваться (увели́читься *perf*) ♦ *vt* увели́чивать (увели́чить *perf*); (*price*) поднима́ть (подня́ть* *perf*); (*knowledge*) расширя́ть (расши́рить *perf*); **an** ~ **of 5%** увеличе́ние на 5%; **to be on the** ~ увели́чиваться (*impf*), расти́* (*impf*).

increasing [ɪn'kriːsɪŋ] *adj* увели́чивающийся, возраста́ющий.

increasingly [ɪn'kriːsɪŋlɪ] *adv* (*more intensely*) всё бо́лее; (*more often*) всё ча́ще.

incredible [ɪn'krɛdɪbl] *adj* (*unbelievable*) неправдоподо́бный* (неправдоподо́бен), невероя́тный* (невероя́тен); (*enormous*) невероя́тный* (невероя́тен); (*amazing, wonderful*) потряса́ющий* (потряса́ющ); **it was an** ~ **experience** э́то бы́ло потряса́юще.

incredulity [ɪnkrɪ'djuːlɪtɪ] *n* недове́рие.

incredulous [ɪn'krɛdjuləs] *adj* недове́рчивый (недове́рчив).

increment ['ɪnkrɪmənt] *n* (*in salary*) приба́вка*.

incriminate [ɪn'krɪmɪneɪt] *vt* изоблича́ть (изобличи́ть *perf*).

---

* marks translations which have irregular inflections. The Russian-English side of the dictionary gives inflectional information.

incriminating [ɪn'krɪmɪneɪtɪŋ] *adj* изоблич-
а́ющий.
incrusted [ɪn'krʌstɪd] *adj* = **encrusted**.
incubate ['ɪnkjubeɪt] *vt* (*egg*) выси́живать
(вы́сидеть* *perf*) ♦ *vi* (*chickens*) вылупля́ться
(вы́лупиться *perf*); (*disease*) развива́ться
(разви́ться* *perf*).
incubation [ɪnkju'beɪʃən] *n* (*by bird*) выведе́ние
цыпля́т; (*of illness*) инкубацио́нный пери́од.
incubation period *n* инкубацио́нный пери́од.
incubator ['ɪnkjubeɪtə'] *n* (*for babies*)
инкуба́тор.
inculcate ['ɪnkʌlkeɪt] *vt*: **to ~ sth in sb** внуша́ть
(внуши́ть *perf*) что-н кому́-н.
incumbent [ɪn'kʌmbənt] *n* (*official*)
отве́тственное лицо́* ♦ *adj*: **it is ~ on him to ...**
он обя́зан +*infin* ....
incur [ɪn'kə:'] *vt* (*expenses, loss*) нести́*
(понести́ *perf*); (*debt*) наде́лать (*perf*) +*gen*;
(*disapproval, anger*) навлека́ть (навле́чь* *perf*)
на себя́.
incurable [ɪn'kjuərəbl] *adj* (*disease*)
неизлечи́мый (неизлечи́м).
incursion [ɪn'kə:ʃən] *n* (*MIL*) вторже́ние.
indebted [ɪn'dɛtɪd] *adj*: **to be ~ to sb** (*grateful*)
быть* (*impf*) обя́занным(-ой) кому́-н.
indecency [ɪn'di:snsɪ] *n* непристо́йность *f*.
indecent [ɪn'di:snt] *adj* непристо́йный*
(непристо́ен); (*haste*) неприли́чный*
(неприли́чен).
indecent assault *n* (*BRIT*) (сексуа́льное)
оскорбле́ние де́йствием.
indecent exposure *n* обнаже́ние половы́х
о́рганов.
indecipherable [ɪndɪ'saɪfərəbl] *adj* (*writing*)
неразбо́рчивый (неразбо́рчив); (*expression,
glance etc*) зага́дочный* (зага́дочен).
indecision [ɪndɪ'sɪʒən] *n* нереши́тельность *f*.
indecisive [ɪndɪ'saɪsɪv] *adj* нереши́тельный*
(нереши́телен).
indeed [ɪn'di:d] *adv* (*certainly*) коне́чно,
безусло́вно; (*in fact, furthermore*) в са́мом
де́ле; (*rather*) скоре́е да́же; **I'm upset, ~
shocked** я расстро́ен, пожа́луй да́же
шоки́рован; **this book is very interesting ~**
э́та кни́га чрезвыча́йно интере́сна; **thank
you very much ~** большо́е Вам спаси́бо; **he
was ~ very talented** он и впра́вду *or* в са́мом
де́ле о́чень тала́нтлив; **yes ~!** ну коне́чно!
indefatigable [ɪndɪ'fætɪgəbl] *adj* (*person*)
неутоми́мый (неутоми́м); (*rhythm, pulse etc*)
неослабева́ющий.
indefensible [ɪndɪ'fɛnsɪbl] *adj* (*conduct*)
непрости́тельный* (непрости́телен).
indefinable [ɪndɪ'faɪnəbl] *adj* (*quality*) не
поддаю́щийся определе́нию.
indefinite [ɪn'dɛfɪnɪt] *adj* (*answer, view*)
неопределённый* (неопределён); (*period,
number*) неограни́ченный* (неограни́чен).
indefinite article *n* (*LING*) неопределённый
арти́кль *m*.

indefinitely [ɪn'dɛfɪnɪtlɪ] *adv* (*continue, wait*)
бесконе́чно; (*be closed, postponed*) на
неопределённое вре́мя.
indelible [ɪn'dɛlɪbl] *adj* (*mark, stain: on clothes*)
неотсти́рывающийся; (: *on hands, furniture*)
несмыва́емый; (*fig: memory, impact*)
неизглади́мый.
indelicate [ɪn'dɛlɪkɪt] *adj* нетакти́чный*
(нетакти́чен).
indemnify [ɪn'dɛmnɪfaɪ] *vt* (*COMM*) гаранти́-
ровать (*impf*) возмеще́ние убы́тков +*dat*.
indemnity [ɪn'dɛmnɪtɪ] *n* (*insurance*) гара́нтия
возмеще́ния убы́тков; (*compensation*)
возмеще́ние.
indent [ɪn'dɛnt] *vt* (*line of text*) писа́ть*
(написа́ть* *perf*) с кра́сной строки́.
indentation [ɪndɛn'teɪʃən] *n* углубле́ние; (*TYP*)
абза́ц; (*on metal*) зазу́брина.
indenture [ɪn'dɛntʃə'] *n* догово́р* (*ме́жду
подмасте́рьем и́ли ученико́м и хозя́ином*).
independence [ɪndɪ'pɛndns] *n* незави́симость
f.
independent [ɪndɪ'pɛndnt] *adj* незави́симый
(незави́сим).
independently [ɪndɪ'pɛndntlɪ] *adv* незави́симо;
~ of незави́симо от +*gen*.
in-depth ['ɪndɛpθ] *adj* дета́льный, глубо́кий*.
indescribable [ɪndɪs'kraɪbəbl] *adj* неописуемый
(неопису́ем).
indestructible [ɪndɪs'trʌktəbl] *adj* (*object*)
неразруши́мый (неразруши́м); (*friendship,
alliance*) неруши́мый (неруши́м); (*army*)
непобеди́мый (непобеди́м).
indeterminate [ɪndɪ'tə:mɪnɪt] *adj* неопределённый* (неопределён).
index ['ɪndɛks] (*pl ~es*) *n* (*in book*)
(слова́рь*-)указа́тель *m*; (*in library etc*)
катало́г; (*pl indices*; *MATH*) показа́тель* *msg*.
index card *n* (картоте́чная) ка́рточка*.
indexed ['ɪndɛkst] *adj* (*US*) = **index-linked**.
index finger *n* указа́тельный па́лец*.
index-linked ['ɪndɛks'lɪŋkt] *adj* (*income,
payment*) изменя́ющийся в соотве́тствии с
и́ндексом инфля́ции.
India ['ɪndɪə] *n* И́ндия.
Indian ['ɪndɪən] *adj* инди́йский* ♦ *n* инди́ец*
(инди́анка*); **Red ~** инде́ец* (индиа́нка*).
Indian Ocean *n*: **the ~ ~** Инди́йский океа́н.
Indian Summer *n* инде́йское *or* ба́бье ле́то.
India paper *n* кита́йская бума́га.
India rubber *n* рези́на, каучу́к.
indicate ['ɪndɪkeɪt] *vt* (*point to: also fig*)
ука́зывать (указа́ть* *perf*) на +*acc*; (*mention*)
дава́ть* (дать* *perf*) знать о +*prp* ♦ *vi*: **to ~
that** (*show*) пока́зывать (показа́ть* *perf*), что;
(*BRIT: AUT*): **to ~ left/right** включа́ть
(включи́ть *perf*) ле́вый/пра́вый указа́тель
поворо́та.
indication [ɪndɪ'keɪʃən] *n* знак; **all the ~s are
that ...** всё ука́зывает на то, что ....
indicative [ɪn'dɪkətɪv] *n* (*LING*) изъяви́тельное

наклоне́ние ♦ *adj*: **to be ~ of**
свиде́тельствовать *(impf)* о +*prp*, ука́зывать
(impf) на +*acc*.

indicator ['ɪndɪkeɪtə'] *n* (*marker, signal*)
указа́тель *m*; (*AUT*) указа́тель поворо́та; (*fig*)
показа́тель *m*.

indices ['ɪndɪsiːz] *npl of* **index**.

indict [ɪn'daɪt] *vt* (*LAW*) предъявля́ть
(предъяви́ть* *perf*) обвине́ние +*dat*.

indictable [ɪn'daɪtəbl] *adj* подлежа́щий
уголо́вному рассмотре́нию; ~ **offence**
уголо́вное преступле́ние.

indictment [ɪn'daɪtmənt] *n* (*denunciation*)
осужде́ние; (*charge*) обвини́тельный акт.

indie ['ɪndɪ] *adj* (*music, chart etc*) *вы́пущенный*
ма́ленькой незави́симой сту́дией
звукоза́писи.

indifference [ɪn'dɪfrəns] *n* (*lack of interest*)
безразли́чие, равноду́шие.

indifferent [ɪn'dɪfrənt] *adj* безразли́чный*
(безразли́чен), равноду́шный*
(равноду́шен); (*mediocre*) посре́дственный*
(посре́дствен).

indigenous [ɪn'dɪdʒɪnəs] *adj* (*wildlife,*
population) коренно́й; (*culture*) ме́стный.

indigestible [ɪndɪ'dʒɛstɪbl] *adj* тру́дно
перева́риваемый (перева́риваем).

indigestion [ɪndɪ'dʒɛstʃən] *n* расстро́йство
желу́дка.

indignant [ɪn'dɪgnənt] *adj* возмущённый*
(возмущён); **to be ~ at sth/with sb** быть*
(impf) возмущённым(-ой) чем-н/кем-н.

indignation [ɪndɪg'neɪʃən] *n* возмуще́ние,
негодова́ние.

indignity [ɪn'dɪgnɪtɪ] *n* униже́ние.

indigo ['ɪndɪgəʊ] *n* (*colour*) инди́го *nt ind*.

indirect [ɪndɪ'rɛkt] *adj* (*way, route*) око́льный,
обхо́дный; (*answer*) укло́нчивый
(укло́нчив); (*effect*) побо́чный; (*LING*): ~
object ко́свенное дополне́ние.

indirectly [ɪndɪ'rɛktlɪ] *adv* ко́свенно.

indiscreet [ɪndɪs'kriːt] *adj* неосмотри́тельный*
(неосмотри́телен), неблагоразу́мный*
(неблагоразу́мен).

indiscretion [ɪndɪs'krɛʃən] *n* неосмотри́тель-
ность *f*; (*indiscreet act*) неблагоразу́мный
посту́пок*.

indiscriminate [ɪndɪs'krɪmɪnət] *adj* (*bombing*)
беспоря́дочный* (беспоря́дочен); (*taste,*
reader, love) неразбо́рчивый (неразбо́рчив);
(*criticism*) огу́льный.

indispensable [ɪndɪs'pɛnsəbl] *adj* (*object*)
необходи́мый (необходи́м); (*person*)
незамени́мый (незамени́м).

indisposed [ɪndɪs'pəʊzd] *adj* (*unwell*)
нездоро́вый (нездоро́в).

indisputable [ɪndɪs'pjuːtəbl] *adj* (*undeniable*)
неоспори́мый (неоспори́м).

indistinct [ɪndɪs'tɪŋkt] *adj* (*image, noise*)
нея́сный* (нея́сен); (*memory*) сму́тный*
(сму́тен).

indistinguishable [ɪndɪs'tɪŋgwɪʃəbl] *adj*: ~ **from**
неотличи́мый (неотличи́м) от +*gen*.

individual [ɪndɪ'vɪdjuəl] *n* (*person*) ли́чность *f*,
индиви́дуум ♦ *adj* (*personal*) индивид-
уа́льный* (индивидуа́лен), ли́чный; (*single*)
отде́льный; (*particular: characteristic*)
своеобра́зный* (своеобра́зен),
индивидуа́льный* (индивидуа́лен); **certain**
~**s** не́которые лю́ди.

individualist [ɪndɪ'vɪdjuəlɪst] *n* индивид-
уали́ст(ка*).

individuality [ɪndɪvɪdju'ælɪtɪ] *n* индивид-
уа́льность *f*.

individually [ɪndɪ'vɪdjuəlɪ] *adv* отде́льно; **he is**
~ **responsible** он несёт ли́чную
отве́тственность; **we'll help each of you** ~ мы
помо́жем ка́ждому из Вас.

indivisible [ɪndɪ'vɪzɪbl] *adj* недели́мый
(недели́м).

Indo-China ['ɪndəu'tʃaɪnə] *n* Индокита́й.

indoctrinate [ɪn'dɔktrɪneɪt] *vt* подверга́ть
(подве́ргнуть* *perf*) идеологи́ческой
обрабо́тке.

indoctrination [ɪndɔktrɪ'neɪʃən] *n* идеолог-
и́ческая обрабо́тка.

indolence ['ɪndələns] *n* ле́ность *f*.

indolent ['ɪndələnt] *adj* лени́вый (лени́в).

Indonesia [ɪndə'niːzɪə] *n* Индоне́зия.

Indonesian [ɪndə'niːzɪən] *adj* индонези́йский* ♦
n индонези́ец*(-и́йка*).

indoor ['ɪndɔː'] *adj* (*plant, games for children*)
ко́мнатный; (*swimming pool*) закры́тый; ~
games спорти́вные и́гры в закры́том
помеще́нии.

indoors [ɪn'dɔːz] *adv* (*go*) в помеще́ние; (*be*) в
помеще́нии; **he stayed ~ all morning** он
проси́дел до́ма всё у́тро.

indubitable [ɪn'djuːbɪtəbl] *adj* несомне́нный*
(несомне́нен).

indubitably [ɪn'djuːbɪtəblɪ] *adv* несомне́нно.

induce [ɪn'djuːs] *vt* (*bring about*) вызыва́ть
(вы́звать* *perf*); (*persuade*) побужда́ть
(побуди́ть* *perf*); (*MED: birth*) стимули́ровать
(impf/perf); **to ~ sb to do** побужда́ть
(побуди́ть* *perf*) кого́-н +*infin*.

inducement [ɪn'djuːsmənt] *n* (*incentive*)
сти́мул; (*pej: bribe*) по́дкуп.

induct [ɪn'dʌkt] *vt* назнача́ть (назна́чить *perf*)
на до́лжность; (*fig*) посвяща́ть (посвяти́ть*
perf) в(о) +*acc*.

induction [ɪn'dʌkʃən] *n* (*MED: of birth*)
стимуля́ция.

induction course *n* (*BRIT*) вво́дный курс.

indulge [ɪn'dʌldʒ] *vt* (*desire, whim etc*)
потво́рствовать *(impf)* +*dat*, потака́ть *(impf)*

---

* marks translations which have irregular inflections. The Russian-English side of the dictionary gives inflectional information.

+*dat*; (*person, child*) баловáть (избаловáть *perf*) ◆ *vi*: **to ~ in** баловáться (побаловáться *perf*) +*instr*.

indulgence [ɪn'dʌldʒəns] *n* (*pleasure*) прихоть *f*; (*leniency*) потвóрство.

indulgent [ɪn'dʌldʒənt] *adj* (*smile*) снис-ходи́тельный* (снисходи́телен); **he has very ~ parents** егó роди́тели (во всём) ему́ потакáют.

industrial [ɪn'dʌstrɪəl] *adj* индустриáльный, промы́шленный; **~ accident** несчáстный слýчай на произвóдстве.

industrial action *n* забастóвка.

industrial design *n* промы́шленный дизáйн.

industrial estate *n* (*BRIT*) промы́шленный кóмплекс.

industrialist [ɪn'dʌstrɪəlɪst] *n* промы́шленник.

industrialize [ɪn'dʌstrɪəlaɪz] *vt* (*country*) индустриализи́ровать (*impf/perf*).

industrial park *n* (*US*) = **industrial estate**.

industrial relations *npl* произвóдственные отношéния *ntpl*.

industrial tribunal *n* (*BRIT*) суд, занимáющийся рассмотрéнием произ-вóдственных конфли́ктов.

industrial unrest *n* (*BRIT*) рабóчие волнéния *ntpl*.

industrious [ɪn'dʌstrɪəs] *adj* трудолюби́вый (трудолюби́в).

industry ['ɪndəstrɪ] *n* (*manufacturing*) индустри́я, промы́шленность *f no pl*; (*diligence*) трудолю́бие; **industries** óтрасли *pl* промы́шленности; **the oil/textile ~** нефтянáя/тексти́льная промы́шленность.

inebriated [ɪ'niːbrɪeɪtɪd] *adj* нетрéзвый (нетрéзв).

inedible [ɪn'ɛdɪbl] *adj* несъедóбный* (несъедóбен).

ineffective [ɪnɪ'fɛktɪv] *adj* неэффекти́вный* (неэффекти́вен).

ineffectual [ɪnɪ'fɛktʃuəl] *adj* = **ineffective**.

inefficiency [ɪnɪ'fɪʃənsɪ] *n* неэффекти́вность *f*; непроизводи́тельность *f*.

inefficient [ɪnɪ'fɪʃənt] *adj* неэффекти́вный* (неэффекти́вен); (*machine*) непроиз-води́тельный* (непроизводи́телен).

inelegant [ɪn'ɛlɪɡənt] *adj* неэлегáнтный* (неэлегáнтен).

ineligible [ɪn'ɛlɪdʒɪbl] *adj* (*candidate*) неподходя́щий*; **to be ~ for sth** не имéть (*impf*) прáво на что-н.

inept [ɪ'nɛpt] *adj* (*management etc*) неумéлый (неумéл).

ineptitude [ɪ'nɛptɪtjuːd] *n* неумéние, неумéлость *f*.

inequality [ɪnɪ'kwɔlɪtɪ] *n* (*of system*) нерáвенство; (*of amount, share*) рáзница.

inequitable [ɪn'ɛkwɪtəbl] *adj* несправедли́вый (несправедли́в).

inert [ɪ'nəːt] *adj* (*immobile*) неподви́жный* (неподви́жен); (*gas*) инéртный.

inertia [ɪ'nəːʃə] *n* (*laziness*) инéртность *f*; (*PHYS*) инéрция.

inertia-reel seat belt [ɪ'nəːʃə'riːl-] *n* инерциóнный ремéнь* *m* безопáсности.

inescapable [ɪnɪ'skeɪpəbl] *adj* неизбéжный* (неизбéжен).

inessential [ɪnɪ'sɛnʃl] *adj* несущéственный* (несущéственен).

inessentials [ɪnɪ'sɛnʃlz] *npl* рóскошь *fsg*.

inestimable [ɪn'ɛstɪməbl] *adj* (*value*) неоцени́мый (неоцéним); (*cost*) неподдаю́щийся* оцéнке.

inevitability [ɪnɛvɪtə'bɪlɪtɪ] *n* неизбéжность *f*; **the ~ of change** неизбéжность изменéний; **it is an ~** э́то неизбéжность.

inevitable [ɪn'ɛvɪtəbl] *adj* неизбéжный* (неизбéжен).

inevitably [ɪn'ɛvɪtəblɪ] *adv* неизбéжно; **as ~ happens, ...** как э́то неизбéжно случáется, ...

inexact [ɪnɪɡ'zækt] *adj* нетóчный* (нетóчен).

inexcusable [ɪnɪks'kjuːzəbl] *adj* непрости́тельный* (непрости́телен).

inexhaustible [ɪnɪɡ'zɔːstɪbl] *adj* (*wealth, resources*) неисчерпáемый (неисчерпáем).

inexorable [ɪn'ɛksərəbl] *adj* (*progress*) неотврати́мый (неотврати́м); (*decline*) неумоли́мый (неумоли́м).

inexpensive [ɪnɪk'spɛnsɪv] *adj* недорогóй* (недóрог).

inexperience [ɪnɪk'spɪərɪəns] *n* неóпытность *f*.

inexperienced [ɪnɪk'spɪərɪənst] *adj* неóпытный* (неóпытен); **to be ~ in sth** не имéть (*impf*) óпыта в чём-н.

inexplicable [ɪnɪk'splɪkəbl] *adj* необъясни́мый (необъясни́м).

inexpressible [ɪnɪk'sprɛsɪbl] *adj* невырази́мый (невырази́м).

inextricable [ɪnɪk'strɪkəbl] *adj* (*union, knot, tangle*) неразры́вный* (неразры́вен); (*dilemma*) безвы́ходный* (безвы́ходен).

inextricably [ɪnɪk'strɪkəblɪ] *adv* неразры́вно.

infallibility [ɪnfælə'bɪlɪtɪ] *n* непогреши́мость *f*.

infallible [ɪn'fælɪbl] *adj* (*person*) непогреши́мый (непогреши́м); (*guide*) надёжный* (надёжен).

infamous ['ɪnfəməs] *adj* бесчéстный* (бесчéстен).

infamy ['ɪnfəmɪ] *n* бесчéстие.

infancy ['ɪnfənsɪ] *n* (*of person*) млáденчество; (*of movement, firm*) перио́д становлéния.

infant ['ɪnfənt] *n* (*baby*) младéнец*; (*young child*) ребёнок* ◆ *cpd* дéтский*.

infantile ['ɪnfəntaɪl] *adj* (*disease*) дéтский*; (*childish*) инфанти́льный* (инфанти́лен).

infantry ['ɪnfəntrɪ] *n* пехóта.

infantryman ['ɪnfəntrɪmən] *irreg n* пехоти́нец*.

infant school *n* (*BRIT*) ≈ начáльная шкóла (*для детéй от 5-и до 7-и лет*).

infatuated [ɪn'fætjueɪtɪd] *adj*: **~ with** увлечённый (увлечён) +*instr*; **to become ~ with** увлекáться (увлéчься* *perf*) +*instr*.

infatuation [ɪnfætju'eɪʃən] *n* увлечéние*.
infect [ɪn'fɛkt] *vt* (*also fig*) заражáть (зарази́ть*
perf); **to become ~ed** (*wound*) заражáться
(зарази́ться* *perf*).
infection [ɪn'fɛkʃən] *n* инфéкция.
infectious [ɪn'fɛkʃəs] *adj* (*person, animal*)
зарáзный* (зарáзен); (*disease*)
инфекциóнный; (*fig*) зарази́тельный*
(зарази́телен).
infer [ɪn'fəː'] *vt* (*deduce*) заключáть
(заключи́ть* *perf*); (*imply*) подразумевáть
(*impf*).
inference ['ɪnfərəns] *n* (*deduction*) заключéние;
(*implication*) вы́вод.
inferior [ɪn'fɪərɪə'] *adj* (*position, status*)
подчинённый; (*goods*) ни́зкого кáчества ◆ *n*
(*subordinate*) подчинённый(-ая) *m(f) adj*;
(*junior*) млáдший* по чи́ну; **to feel ~ (to)**
ощущáть (ощути́ть* *perf*) свою́ неполно-
цéнность (по сравнéнию с +*instr*); **he is ~ to
me in rank** он ни́же меня́ по дóлжности; **the
second model is ~ to the first** вторáя модéль
уступáет пéрвой в кáчестве.
inferiority [ɪnfɪərɪ'ɔrətɪ] *n* (*of position, status*)
подчинённое положéние; (*of goods*)
низкосóртность *f*.
inferiority complex *n* кóмплекс неполноцéнности.
infernal [ɪn'fəːnl] *adj* áдский*.
inferno [ɪn'fəːnəu] *n* (*also fig*) ад.
infertile [ɪn'fəːtaɪl] *adj* (*soil*) неплодорóдный*
(неплодорóден); (*person, animal*) бес-
плóдный* (бесплóден).
infertility [ɪnfəː'tɪlɪtɪ] *n* (*see adj*)
неплодорóдность *f*; бесплóдие.
infested [ɪn'fɛstɪd] *adj*: **the house is ~ with rats**
дом киши́т кры́сами.
infidelity [ɪnfɪ'dɛlɪtɪ] *n* невéрность *f*.
infighting ['ɪnfaɪtɪŋ] *n* внýтренний* конфли́кт.
infiltrate ['ɪnfɪltreɪt] *vt* проникáть
(прони́кнуть* *perf*) в +*acc*.
infinite ['ɪnfɪnɪt] *adj* бесконéчный* (бесконéч-
ен); (*resources*) несмéтный* (несмéтен).
infinitely ['ɪnfɪnɪtlɪ] *adv* бесконéчно.
infinitesimal [ɪnfɪnɪ'tɛsɪməl] *adj* бесконéчно
мáлый* (мал).
infinitive [ɪn'fɪnɪtɪv] *n* инфинити́в,
неопределённая фóрма глагóла.
infinity [ɪn'fɪnɪtɪ] *n* бесконéчность *f*.
infirm [ɪn'fəːm] *adj* нéмощный* (нéмощен).
infirmary [ɪn'fəːmərɪ] *n* больни́ца.
infirmity [ɪn'fəːmɪtɪ] *n* нéмощь *f*.
inflame [ɪn'fleɪm] *vt* (*person, crowd*) распаля́ть
(распали́ть* *perf*); (*situation, emotions*)
накаля́ть (накали́ть* *perf*).
inflamed [ɪn'fleɪmd] *adj* (*throat, appendix*)
воспалённый (воспалён).
inflammable [ɪn'flæməbl] *adj* (*fabric*) легкó

воспламеня́ющийся; (*chemical*) горю́чий*
(горю́ч).
inflammation [ɪnflə'meɪʃən] *n* воспалéние.
inflammatory [ɪn'flæmətərɪ] *adj* (*speech*)
подстрекáтельский.
inflatable [ɪn'fleɪtəbl] *adj* надувнóй.
inflate [ɪn'fleɪt] *vt* (*tyre*) накáчивать (накачáть
perf); (*balloon*) надувáть (надýть *perf*); (*price*)
вздувáть (вздуть *perf*); (*expectation, position,
ideas*) раздувáть (разду́ть *perf*).
inflated [ɪn'fleɪtɪd] *adj* (*style*) напы́щенный*
(напы́щен); (*prices*) вздýтый (вздут).
inflation [ɪn'fleɪʃən] *n* (*ECON*) инфля́ция.
inflationary [ɪn'fleɪʃənərɪ] *adj* инфляциóнный.
inflationist [ɪn'fleɪʃənɪst] *n* сторóнник(-ица)
поли́тики инфля́ции.
inflexible [ɪn'flɛksɪbl] *adj* (*rule, timetable*)
жёсткий* (жёсток); (*person*) неги́бкий*
(неги́бок).
inflict [ɪn'flɪkt] *vt*: **to ~ sth on sb** причиня́ть
(причини́ть *perf*) что-н комý-н; (*penalty*)
налагáть (наложи́ть *perf*) что-н на когó-н.
infliction [ɪn'flɪkʃən] *n* (*of pain*) причинéние; (*of
penalty*) наложéние.
in-flight ['ɪnflaɪt] *adj* (*meal, entertainment*) на
бортý самолёта; **~ refuelling** дозапрáвка в
полёте.
inflow ['ɪnfləu] *n* прито́к.
influence ['ɪnfluəns] *n* (*power*) влия́ние; (*effect*)
воздéйствие ◆ *vt* (*person, situation, choice etc*)
влия́ть (повлия́ть *perf*) на +*acc*, оказывать
(оказáть *perf*) влия́ние на +*acc*; **under the ~
of alcohol** под воздéйствием алкогóля.
influential [ɪnflu'ɛnʃl] *adj* влия́тельный*
(влия́телен).
influenza [ɪnflu'ɛnzə] *n* грипп.
influx ['ɪnflʌks] *n* (*of people, funds*) прито́к.
inform [ɪn'fɔːm] *vt*: **to ~ sb of sth** (*tell*)
сообщáть (сообщи́ть *perf*) комý-н о чём-н,
информи́ровать (проинформи́ровать *perf*)
когó-н о чём-н ◆ *vi*: **to ~ on sb** доноси́ть*
(донести́* *perf*) на когó-н.
informal [ɪn'fɔːml] *adj* (*visit, meeting, invitation*)
неофициáльный* (неофициáлен); (*manner,
discussion*) непринуждённый*
(непринуждён); (*clothes*) бýдничный,
повседнéвный* (повседнéвен); (*language*)
разговóрный.
informality [ɪnfɔː'mælɪtɪ] *n* непринуждённость
f.
informally [ɪn'fɔːməlɪ] *adv* неофициáльно;
(*discuss*) непринуждённо; (*dress*) бýднично;
(*invite*) без церемóний.
informant [ɪn'fɔːmənt] *n* (*source*) информáнт.
information [ɪnfə'meɪʃən] *n* информáция; **to
get ~ on** получáть (получи́ть *perf*)
информáцию о +*prp*; **a piece of ~**
сообщéние; **for your ~** к Вáшему свéдению.

---

* marks translations which have irregular inflections. The Russian-English side of the dictionary gives inflectional information.

information bureau *n* = **information office**.
information office *n* спра́вочное бюро́ *nt ind*.
information processing *n* обрабо́тка
информа́ции.
information retrieval *n* (*COMPUT*) по́иск
информа́ции, информацио́нный по́иск.
information science *n* информа́тика.
information technology *n* информацио́нная
техноло́гия.
informative [ɪnˈfɔːmətɪv] *adj* содержа́тельный*
(содержа́телен).
informed [ɪnˈfɔːmd] *adj* осведомлённый*
(осведомлён), информи́рованный*
(информи́рован); **well/ill** ~ хорошо́/пло́хо
информи́рованный (информи́рован); **an** ~
guess обосно́ванная дога́дка*.
informer [ɪnˈfɔːmə*] *n* (*also*: **police** ~)
осведоми́тель(ница) *m(f)*.
infra dig [ˈɪnfrəˈdɪg] *adj abbr* (*inf*. = *beneath one's
dignity*. = *infra dignitatem*) ни́же чьего́-н
досто́инства.
infrared [ɪnfrəˈrɛd] *adj* инфракра́сный.
infrastructure [ˈɪnfrəstrʌktʃə*] *n*
инфраструкту́ра.
infrequent [ɪnˈfriːkwənt] *adj* ре́дкий* (ре́док).
infringe [ɪnˈfrɪndʒ] *vt* (*law*) преступа́ть
(преступи́ть *perf*) ♦ *vi*: **to** ~ **on** (*rights*)
ущемля́ть (ущеми́ть* *perf*), посяга́ть
(посягну́ть *perf*) на +*acc*.
infringement [ɪnˈfrɪndʒmənt] *n* (*see vb*)
наруше́ние; ущемле́ние, посяга́тельство.
infuriate [ɪnˈfjuərɪeɪt] *vt* (*person*) приводи́ть*
(привести́* *perf*) в я́рость *or* бе́шенство,
беси́ть* (взбеси́ть* *perf*).
infuriating [ɪnˈfjuərɪeɪtɪŋ] *adj* приводя́щий в
я́рость *or* бе́шенство; **the noise is** ~ шум
приво́дит меня́ *etc* в я́рость.
infuse [ɪnˈfjuːz] *vt* (*tea, herbs*) наста́ивать
(настоя́ть *perf*); (*person*): **to** ~ **sb with sth**
вселя́ть (всели́ть *perf*) что-н в кого́-н.
infusion [ɪnˈfjuːʒən] *n* (*tea*) насто́йка*.
ingenious [ɪnˈdʒiːnjəs] *adj* хитроу́мный*
(хитроу́мен); (*person*) изобрета́тельный*
(изобрета́телен).
ingenuity [ɪndʒɪˈnjuːɪtɪ] *n* хитроу́мность *f*; (*of
person*) изобрета́тельность *f*.
ingenuous [ɪnˈdʒɛnjuəs] *adj* бесхи́тростный*
(бесхи́тростен).
ingot [ˈɪŋgət] *n* сли́ток*.
ingrained [ɪnˈgreɪnd] *adj* закорене́лый.
ingratiate [ɪnˈgreɪʃɪeɪt] *vt*: **to** ~ **o.s. with**
заи́скивать (*impf*) пе́ред +*instr*.
ingratiating [ɪnˈgreɪʃɪeɪtɪŋ] *adj* (*smile, speech*)
заи́скивающий*; (*person*) льсти́вый
(льстив).
ingratitude [ɪnˈgrætɪtjuːd] *n* неблагода́р-
ность *f*.
ingredient [ɪnˈgriːdɪənt] *n* (*CULIN*) ингредие́нт;
(*of situation*) составна́я часть* *f*.
ingrowing [ˈɪngrəuɪŋ] *adj*: ~ **toenail**
враста́ющий но́готь* *m* (*на па́льце ноги́*).

inhabit [ɪnˈhæbɪt] *vt* населя́ть (*impf*).
inhabitant [ɪnˈhæbɪtnt] *n* жи́тель(ница) *m(f)*.
inhale [ɪnˈheɪl] *vt* вдыха́ть (вдохну́ть* *perf*) ♦ *vi*
вдыха́ть (вдо́хнуть* *perf*); (*when smoking*)
затя́гиваться (затяну́ться* *perf*).
inhaler [ɪnˈheɪlə*] *n* ингаля́тор.
inherent [ɪnˈhɪərənt] *adj* (*laziness*)
прирождённый; ~ **in** *or* **to** сво́йственный*
(сво́йствен) +*dat*, прису́щий* (прису́щ) +*dat*.
inherently [ɪnˈhɪərəntlɪ] *adv* (*easy, difficult*) по
приро́де; (*lazy*) по нату́ре.
inherit [ɪnˈhɛrɪt] *vt* насле́довать (*impf/perf*),
унасле́довать (*perf*).
inheritance [ɪnˈhɛrɪtəns] *n* насле́дство;
(*cultural, political etc*) насле́дие; **right of** ~
пра́во насле́дования.
inhibit [ɪnˈhɪbɪt] *vt* (*impulse*) ско́вывать
(скова́ть *perf*); (*growth*) заде́рживать
(задержа́ть* *perf*).
inhibited [ɪnˈhɪbɪtɪd] *adj* (*see vb*) ско́ванный*
(ско́ван); заде́ржанный.
inhibiting [ɪnˈhɪbɪtɪŋ] *adj* (*situation*)
ско́вывающий; (*factor*) препя́тствующий.
inhibition [ɪnhɪˈbɪʃən] *n* (*see vb*) ско́ванность *f*
no pl; заде́ржка*.
inhospitable [ɪnhɔsˈpɪtəbl] *adj* (*person*)
негостеприи́мный* (негостеприи́мен);
(*place*) неприве́тливый (неприве́тлив).
inhuman [ɪnˈhjuːmən] *adj* (*behaviour*)
бесчелове́чный* (бесчелове́чен);
(*appearance*) нечелове́ческий*.
inhumane [ɪnhjuːˈmeɪn] *adj* негума́нный*
(негума́нен).
inimitable [ɪˈnɪmɪtəbl] *adj* неподража́емый
(неподража́ем).
iniquitous [ɪˈnɪkwɪtəs] *adj* (*see n*) чудо́вищный
(чудо́вищен); чудо́вищно несправедли́вый
(несправедли́в).
iniquity [ɪˈnɪkwɪtɪ] *n* (*wickedness*) чудо́вищ-
ность *f*; (*injustice*) несправедли́вость *f*.
initial [ɪˈnɪʃl] *adj* первонача́льный, нача́льный
♦ *n* (*also*: ~ **letter**) нача́льная бу́ква ♦ *vt*
ста́вить* (поста́вить* *perf*) инициа́лы на
+*prep*; ~**s** *npl* инициа́лы *mpl*.
initialize [ɪˈnɪʃəlaɪz] *vt* (*COMPUT*) инициализ-
и́ровать (*impf/perf*).
initially [ɪˈnɪʃəlɪ] *adv* (*at first*) внача́ле, снача́ла;
(*first*) первонача́льно.
initiate [ɪˈnɪʃɪeɪt] *vt* (*talks, process*) класть*
(положи́ть *perf*) нача́ло +*dat*; (*new member*)
посвяща́ть (посвяти́ть* *perf*); **to** ~ **sb into a
secret** посвяща́ть (посвяти́ть* *perf*) кого́-н в
та́йну; **to** ~ **proceedings against sb**
возбужда́ть (возбуди́ть* *perf*) де́ло про́тив
кого́-н.
initiation [ɪnɪʃɪˈeɪʃən] *n* (*beginning*) основа́ние;
(*into secret etc*) посвяще́ние; ~ **ceremony**
церемо́ния посвяще́ния.
initiative [ɪˈnɪʃətɪv] *n* (*move*) инициати́ва,
начина́ние; (*enterprise*) инициати́вность *f*; **to
take the** ~ брать* (взять* *perf*) на себя́

инициати́ву.

inject [ɪn'dʒɛkt] *vt* (*drugs, poison*) вводи́ть*
(ввести́* *perf*); (*patient*): **to ~ sb with sth**
де́лать (сде́лать *perf*) уко́л *or* инъе́кцию
чего-н кому́-н; (*money*): **to ~ into** влива́ть
(влить* *perf*) в +*acc*.

injection [ɪn'dʒɛkʃən] *n* уко́л, инъе́кция; (*of
money*) влива́ние; **to give an ~** де́лать
(сде́лать *perf*) уко́л *or* инъе́кцию; **I had an ~**
мне сде́лали уко́л.

injudicious [ɪndʒu'dɪʃəs] *adj* неразу́мный*
(неразу́мен).

injunction [ɪn'dʒʌŋkʃən] *n* (*LAW*) (суде́бный)
запре́т.

injure ['ɪndʒəʳ] *vt* (*person, limb, feelings*) ра́нить
(*impf/perf*); (*reputation*) поврежда́ть
(поврреди́ть* *perf*); **to ~ o.s.** порани́ться
(*perf*), ушиба́ться (ушиби́ться* *perf*).

injured ['ɪndʒəd] *adj* (*see vb*) ра́неный;
повреждённый (поврежде́н); ушибленный
(уши́блен); **~ party** (*LAW*) потерпе́вшая
сторона́.

injurious [ɪn'dʒuəriəs] *adj*: **~ to** вре́дный*
(вре́ден) для +*gen*, губи́тельный*
(губи́телен) для +*gen*.

injury ['ɪndʒəri] *n* повреждёние; (*more serious*)
ране́ние; (*industrial, sports*) тра́вма; (*to
reputation, feelings*) оскорбле́ние; **to escape
without ~** избега́ть (избежа́ть* *perf*)
ране́ний.

injury time *n* (*SPORT*) доба́вочное вре́мя* *nt*.

injustice [ɪn'dʒʌstɪs] *n* несправедли́вость *f*; **you
do me an ~** Вы ко мне несправедли́вы.

ink [ɪŋk] *n* (*in pen*) черни́ла *pl*; (*for printing*)
типогра́фская кра́ска*.

ink-jet printer ['ɪŋkdʒɛt-] *n* (*COMPUT*)
стру́йный при́нтер.

inkling ['ɪŋklɪŋ] *n* (*idea, clue*): **to have an ~ of**
име́ть (*impf*) поня́тие о +*prp*.

ink pad *n* штёмпельная поду́шечка*.

inky ['ɪŋkɪ] *adj* (*blackness, sky*) черни́льный;
(*fingers*) запа́чканный (запа́чкан)
черни́лами.

inlaid ['ɪnleɪd] *adj*: **~ (with)** инкрусти́рованный
(инкрусти́рован) (+*instr*).

inland ['ɪnlənd] *adj* вну́тренний* ♦ *adv* (*travel*)
вглубь.

Inland Revenue *n* (*BRIT*) ≈ Гла́вное нало́говое
управле́ние.

in-laws ['ɪnlɔːz] *npl* родня́ со стороны́ му́жа
и́ли жены́.

inlet ['ɪnlet] *n* (у́зкий*) зали́в.

inlet pipe *n* впускна́я труба́*.

inmate ['ɪnmeɪt] *n* (*of prison*)
заключённый(-ая) *m(f) adj*; (*of asylum*)
пацие́нт(ка*).

inmost ['ɪnməust] *adj* сокрове́ннейший.

inn [ɪn] *n* тракти́р.

innards ['ɪnədz] *npl* (*inf*) вну́тренности *fpl*.

innate [ɪ'neɪt] *adj* врождённый.

inner ['ɪnəʳ] *adj* вну́тренний*.

inner city *n* центра́льная часть* *f* го́рода.

innermost ['ɪnəməust] *adj* = **inmost**.

inner tube *n* ка́мера (ши́ны).

innings ['ɪnɪŋz] *n* се́рия атаку́ющих уда́ров в
кри́кете; **he's had a good ~** (*BRIT*: *inf*) он
прожи́л до́лгую и счастли́вую жизнь.

innocence ['ɪnəsns] *n* (*LAW*) невино́вность *f*;
(*naivety*) неви́нность *f*.

innocent ['ɪnəsnt] *adj* (*also LAW*) невино́вный*
(невино́вен); (*naive*) неви́нный* (неви́нен).

innocuous [ɪ'nɔkjuəs] *adj* (*substance*)
безвре́дный* (безвре́ден); (*remarks*)
безоби́дный* (безоби́ден).

innovation [ɪnəu'veɪʃən] *n* но́вшество.

innuendo [ɪnju'ɛndəu] (*pl* **~es**) *n* инсинуа́ция.

innumerable [ɪ'njuːmrəbl] *adj* бесчи́сленный*
(бесчи́слен).

inoculate [ɪ'nɔkjuleɪt] *vt*: **to ~ sb against sth**
де́лать (сде́лать *perf*) кому́-н приви́вку
про́тив чего́-н; **to ~ sb with sth** привива́ть
(приви́ть* *perf*) кому́-н что-н.

inoculation [ɪnɔkju'leɪʃən] *n* приви́вка*.

inoffensive [ɪnə'fɛnsɪv] *adj* безоби́дный*
(безоби́ден).

inopportune [ɪn'ɔpətjuːn] *adj* (*moment*)
неподходя́щий*; (*event*) несвоевре́менный*
(несвоевре́мен).

inordinate [ɪ'nɔːdɪnət] *adj* необыча́йный*
(необыча́ен).

inordinately [ɪ'nɔːdɪnətlɪ] *adv* необыча́йно.

inorganic [ɪnɔː'gænɪk] *adj* неоргани́ческий*.

inpatient ['ɪnpeɪʃnt] *n* стациона́рный(-ая)
больно́й(-а́я) *m(f) adj*.

input ['ɪnput] *n* (*resources, money*) вложе́ние;
(*COMPUT*) ввод ♦ *vt* (*COMPUT*): **to ~ (into)**
вводи́ть* (ввести́* *perf*) (в +*acc*).

inquest ['ɪnkwɛst] *n* (*on sb's death*) (суде́бное)
рассле́дование.

inquire [ɪn'kwaɪəʳ] *vt* спра́шивать (спроси́ть*
perf) ♦ *vi*: **to ~ (about)** справля́ться
(спра́виться* *perf*) (о +*prp*); **to ~ when/where**
справля́ться (спра́виться* *perf*) когда/где; **he
~d whether he could go** он спра́вился мо́жет
ли он идти́

► **inquire after** *vt fus* спра́шивать (спроси́ть*
perf) о +*prp*

► **inquire into** *vt fus* рассле́довать (*impf/perf*).

inquiring [ɪn'kwaɪərɪŋ] *adj* пытли́вый.

inquiry [ɪn'kwaɪəri] *n* (*question*) вопро́с; (: *more
official*) запро́с; (*investigation*)
рассле́дование; (: *LAW*) сле́дствие; **to make
inquiries about sth** наводи́ть* (навести́* *perf*)
спра́вки о чём-н; **to hold an ~ into sth** вести́*
(*impf*) рассле́дование чего́-н.

inquiry desk *n* (*BRIT*) спра́вочный стол*.

inquiry office n (BRIT) спра́вочное бюро́ nt ind.
inquisition [ɪnkwɪ'zɪʃən] n сле́дствие no pl; (REL): **the I~** Инквизи́ция.
inquisitive [ɪn'kwɪzɪtɪv] adj любопы́тный* (любопы́тен).
inroads ['ɪnrəudz] npl: **to make ~ into** (savings, resources) тра́тить* (потра́тить* perf).
ins abbr = **inches**.
ins and outs ['ɪnzən'auts] npl: **to know all the ~ ~~** знать (impf) все ходы́.
insane [ɪn'seɪn] adj (foolish, crazy) безу́мный* (безу́мен); (PSYCH) душевнобольно́й.
insanitary [ɪn'sænɪtərɪ] adj антисанита́рный* (антисанита́рен).
insanity [ɪn'sænɪtɪ] n (also fig) безу́мие, сумасше́ствие.
insatiable [ɪn'seɪʃəbl] adj ненасы́тный* (ненасы́тен).
inscribe [ɪn'skraɪb] vt надпи́сывать (надписа́ть* perf).
inscription [ɪn'skrɪpʃən] n на́дпись f.
inscrutable [ɪn'skru:təbl] adj зага́дочный* (зага́дочен).
inseam measurement ['ɪnsi:m-] n (US) = **inside leg measurement**.
insect ['ɪnsɛkt] n насеко́мое nt adj.
insect bite n уку́с насеко́мого.
insecticide [ɪn'sɛktɪsaɪd] n инсектици́д.
insect repellent n сре́дство от насеко́мых.
insecure [ɪnsɪ'kjuər] adj (structure, border) ненадёжный* (ненадёжен); (person) неуве́ренный* (неуве́рен) в себе́.
insecurity [ɪnsɪ'kjuərɪtɪ] n (see adj) ненадёжность f; неуве́ренность f в себе́.
insemination [ɪnsɛmɪ'neɪʃən] n: **artificial ~** иску́сственное оплодотворе́ние.
insensible [ɪn'sɛnsɪbl] adj (unconscious) без созна́ния; (unable to feel): **~ to** нечувстви́тельный* (нечувстви́телен) к +dat; (unaware): **~ of** не сознаю́щий +gen.
insensitive [ɪn'sɛnsɪtɪv] adj бесчу́вственный* (бесчу́вствен).
insensitivity [ɪnsɛnsɪ'tɪvɪtɪ] n (of person) бесчу́вственность f.
inseparable [ɪn'sɛprəbl] adj (ideas, elements) нераздели́мый (нераздели́м); (friends) неразлу́чный* (неразлу́чен).
insert [vt ɪn'sə:t, n 'ɪnsə:t] vt: **to ~ (into)** вставля́ть (вста́вить* perf) (в +acc); (piece of paper) вкла́дывать (вложи́ть* perf) ♦ n вкла́дыш, вкла́дка.
insertion [ɪn'sə:ʃən] n (in book, file) вста́вка*; (of needle) введе́ние; (of peg) вбива́ние.
in-service ['ɪn'sə:vɪs] adj: **~ training** произво́дственное обуче́ние.
inshore [ɪn'ʃɔ:'] adj (fishing, waters) при-бре́жный ♦ adv (be) у бе́рега; (go) к бе́регу.
inside ['ɪn'saɪd] n вну́тренняя часть* f; (of coat etc) изна́нка; (of road: BRIT) ле́вая сорона́; (: US, Europe etc) пра́вая сторона́ ♦ adj вну́тренний* ♦ adv (go) внутрь; (be) внутри́ ♦

prep (position) внутри́ +gen; (motion) внутрь +gen; (of time): **~ ten minutes** в преде́лах деся́ти мину́т; **~s** npl (inf: stomach) вну́тренности fpl.
inside forward n (FOOTBALL) полусре́дний напада́ющий* m adj.
inside information n информа́ция, полу́ченная из вну́тренних исто́чников.
inside lane n (AUT: BRIT) ле́вый ряд*; (: US, Europe etc) пра́вый ряд*.
inside leg measurement n (BRIT) вну́тренняя* длина́ ноги́.
inside out adv (be, wear, turn) наизна́нку; (know) вдоль и поперёк.
insider [ɪn'saɪdə'] n свой челове́к; (COMM) инса́йдер.
insider dealing n (STOCK EXCHANGE) незако́нное испо́льзование делово́й информа́ции при сде́лках на би́рже.
insider trading n = **insider dealing**.
inside story n информа́ция из пе́рвых рук.
insidious [ɪn'sɪdɪəs] adj кова́рный* (кова́рен).
insight ['ɪnsaɪt] n: **~ (into)** понима́ние no pl (+gen); **to gain (an) ~ into sth** вника́ть (вни́кнуть perf) в что-н.
insignia [ɪn'sɪgnɪə] n inv зна́ки mpl отли́чия.
insignificant [ɪnsɪg'nɪfɪknt] adj незначи́тельный* (незначи́телен).
insincere [ɪnsɪn'sɪə'] adj неи́скренний* (неи́скренен).
insincerity [ɪnsɪn'sɛrɪtɪ] n неи́скренность f.
insinuate [ɪn'sɪnjueɪt] vt намека́ть (намекну́ть* perf) на +acc.
insinuation [ɪnsɪnju'eɪʃən] n инсинуа́ция.
insipid [ɪn'sɪpɪd] adj (person) бесцве́тный* (бесцве́тен); (colour) блёклый; (food, drink) пре́сный* (пре́сен).
insist [ɪn'sɪst] vi: **to ~ (on)** наста́ивать (настоя́ть perf) (на +prp); **to ~ that** (demand) наста́ивать (настоя́ть perf) на том, что́бы +past tense; (claim) наста́ивать (настоя́ть perf) на том, что.
insistence [ɪn'sɪstəns] n настоя́ние; **at his ~** по его́ настоя́нию.
insistent [ɪn'sɪstənt] adj насто́йчивый (насто́йчив).
insofar as [ɪnsəu'fɑ:'-] adv тоско́льку.
insole ['ɪnsəul] n стелька*.
insolence ['ɪnsələns] n на́глость f.
insolent ['ɪnsələnt] adj (attitude, remark) на́глый* (нагл).
insoluble [ɪn'sɔljubl] adj неразреши́мый (неразреши́м).
insolvency [ɪn'sɔlvənsɪ] n неплатёже-спосо́бность f.
insolvent [ɪn'sɔlvənt] adj неплатёже-спосо́бный* (неплатёжеспосо́бен).
insomnia [ɪn'sɔmnɪə] n бессо́нница.
insomniac [ɪn'sɔmnɪæk] n страда́ющий(-ая) m(f) adj бессо́нницей.
inspect [ɪn'spɛkt] vt (premises, equipment)

осма́тривать (осмотре́ть* *perf*); (*BRIT*: *ticket, luggage*) проверя́ть (прове́рить *perf*).

inspection [ɪnˈspɛkʃən] *n* (*see vb*) осмо́тр; прове́рка*.

inspector [ɪnˈspɛktəʳ] *n* (*ADMIN, POLICE*) инспе́ктор*; (*BRIT*: *on buses, trains*) контролёр.

inspiration [ɪnspəˈreɪʃən] *n* вдохнове́ние.

inspire [ɪnˈspaɪəʳ] *vt* (*workers, troops*) вдохновля́ть (вдохнови́ть* *perf*); **to ~ sth (in sb)** внуша́ть (внуши́ть *perf*) что-н (кому́-н).

inspired [ɪnˈspaɪəd] *adj* (*writer etc*) вдохновлённый (вдохновлён); (*book*) вдохнове́нный (вдохнове́нен); **in an ~ moment** в моме́нт вдохнове́ния.

inspiring [ɪnˈspaɪərɪŋ] *adj* вдохновля́ющий*.

inst. *abbr* (*BRIT*: *COMM*: = *instant*) с.м.= *сего́ ме́сяца*.

instability [ɪnstəˈbɪlɪtɪ] *n* нестаби́льность *f*.

install [ɪnˈstɔːl] *vt* (*machine*) устана́вливать (установи́ть* *perf*); (*official*) ста́вить* (поста́вить* *perf*).

installation [ɪnstəˈleɪʃən] *n* (*of machine, plant*) устано́вка; (*MIL*) объе́кт.

installment plan *n* (*US*) рассро́чка.

instalment [ɪnˈstɔːlmənt] (*US* **installment**) *n* (*of payment*) взнос; (*of story, TV serial*) часть* *f*; **to pay in ~s** плати́ть* (заплати́ть* *perf*) в рассро́чку.

instance [ˈɪnstəns] *n* (*example*) приме́р; **for ~** наприме́р; **in this** *or* **that ~** в да́нном слу́чае; **in many ~s** во мно́гих слу́чаях; **in the first ~** в пе́рвую о́чередь.

instant [ˈɪnstənt] *n* мгнове́ние, миг ◆ *adj* (*reaction, success*) мгнове́нный* (мгнове́нен); **come here this ~!** иди́ сюда́ сию́ мину́ту!; **the 10th ~** (*COMM, ADMIN*) 10-ое число́ сего́ ме́сяца; **~ coffee** раствори́мый ко́фе; **~ food** пищево́й концентра́т.

instantaneous [ɪnstənˈteɪnɪəs] *adj* (*immediate*) мгнове́нный* (мгнове́нен).

instantly [ˈɪnstəntlɪ] *adv* неме́дленно, сра́зу.

instant replay *n* (*TV*) повто́р.

instead [ɪnˈstɛd] *adv* взаме́н ◆ *prep*: **~ of** вме́сто +*gen*, взаме́н +*gen*; **~ of sb** вме́сто кого́-н.

instep [ˈɪnstɛp] *n* подъём (*ноги́, ту́фли*).

instigate [ˈɪnstɪgeɪt] *vt* (*rebellion, strike etc*) подстрека́ть (*impf*) к +*dat*; (*talks*) дава́ть* (дать* *perf*) толчо́к перегово́рам.

instigation [ɪnstɪˈgeɪʃən] *n* подстрека́тельство; **at my ~** по мое́й инициати́ве.

instil [ɪnˈstɪl] *vt*: **to ~ sth in(to) sb** (*confidence, fear etc*) вселя́ть (всели́ть *perf*) что-н в кого́-н.

instinct [ˈɪnstɪŋkt] *n* инсти́нкт; **by ~** инстинкти́вно; **maternal ~** матери́нский инсти́нкт.

instinctive [ɪnˈstɪŋktɪv] *adj* инстинкти́вный*

(инстинкти́вен).

instinctively [ɪnˈstɪŋktɪvlɪ] *adv* инстинкти́вно.

institute [ˈɪnstɪtjuːt] *n* (*for research, teaching*) институ́т; (*professional body*) ассоциа́ция ◆ *vt* (*system, rule*) учрежда́ть (учреди́ть* *perf*); (*inquiry*) назнача́ть (назна́чить *perf*); **to ~ proceedings (against)** возбужда́ть (возбуди́ть* *perf*) суде́бное де́ло (про́тив +*gen*).

institution [ɪnstɪˈtjuːʃən] *n* учрежде́ние; (*custom, tradition*) институ́т.

institutional [ɪnstɪˈtjuːʃənl] *adj* (*value, quality etc*) закреплённый (закреплён); (*education*) осуществля́емый кру́пными учрежде́ниями; **~ care** попече́ние (*осуществля́емое учрежде́ниями*); **~ reform** рефо́рма социа́льных учрежде́ний.

instruct [ɪnˈstrʌkt] *vt*: **to ~ sb in sth** обуча́ть (обучи́ть* *perf*) кого́-н чему́-н; **to ~ sb to do** поруча́ть (поручи́ть* *perf*) кому́-н +*infin*.

instruction [ɪnˈstrʌkʃən] *n* (*teaching*) обуче́ние ◆ *cpd*: **~ manual**, **~ leaflet** инстру́кция; **~s** *npl* (*orders*) указа́ния *ntpl*; **~s (for use)** инстру́кция *or* руково́дство (по примене́нию).

instructive [ɪnˈstrʌktɪv] *adj* поучи́тельный* (поучи́телен).

instructor [ɪnˈstrʌktəʳ] *n* преподава́тель(ница) *m(f)*; (*for skiing, driving etc*) инстру́ктор*.

instrument [ˈɪnstrumənt] *n* инструме́нт.

instrumental [ɪnstruˈmɛntl] *adj* (*MUS*) инструмента́льный; (*important*): **to be ~ in** игра́ть (сыгра́ть *perf*) суще́ственную роль в +*prp*.

instrumentalist [ɪnstruˈmɛntəlɪst] *n* инструментали́ст.

instrument panel *n* прибо́рная пане́ль *f*.

insubordination [ɪnsəbɔːˈdeɪʃən] *n* неповинове́ние.

insufferable [ɪnˈsʌfrəbl] *adj* невыноси́мый (невыноси́м).

insufficient [ɪnsəˈfɪʃənt] *adj* недоста́точный* (недоста́точен).

insufficiently [ɪnsəˈfɪʃəntlɪ] *adv* недоста́точно.

insular [ˈɪnsjuləʳ] *adj* ограни́ченный* (ограни́чен).

insulate [ˈɪnsjuleɪt] *vt* (*protect*: *person, group, also ELEC*) изоли́ровать (*impf/perf*); (*against cold*) утепля́ть (утепли́ть *perf*); (*against sound*) (звуко)изоли́ровать (*impf/perf*).

insulating tape [ˈɪnsjuleɪtɪŋ-] *n* (*BRIT*) изоляцио́нная ле́нта.

insulation [ɪnsjuˈleɪʃən] *n* (*see vb*) изоля́ция; (тепло)изоля́ция; (звуко)изоля́ция.

insulator [ˈɪnsjuleɪtəʳ] *n* (*material*) изоля́тор.

insulin [ˈɪnsjulɪn] *n* инсули́н.

insult [*vt* ɪnˈsʌlt, *n* ˈɪnsʌlt] *vt* оскорбля́ть (оскорби́ть* *perf*) ◆ *n* оскорбле́ние.

---

insulting [ɪn'sʌltɪŋ] *adj* оскорби́тельный*
(оскорби́телен).
insuperable [ɪn'sjuːprəbl] *adj* непреодоли́мый
(непреодоли́м).
insurance [ɪn'ʃuərəns] *n* страхова́ние; **life/fire
~** страхова́ние жи́зни/на слу́чай пожа́ра; **to
take out ~ (against)** брать* (взять* *perf*)
страхо́вку (от +*gen*).
insurance agent *n* страхово́й аге́нт.
insurance broker *n* страхово́й бро́кер.
insurance policy *n* страхово́й по́лис.
insurance premium *n* страхова́я пре́мия.
insure [ɪn'ʃuə'] *vt*: **to ~ (against)** страхова́ть
(застрахова́ть *perf*) (от +*gen*); **to ~ (o.s.)
against** страхова́ться (застрахова́ться *perf*)
от +*gen*; **the car is ~d for £5,000** маши́на
застрахо́вана на су́мму в £5.000.
insured [ɪn'ʃuəd] *n*: **the ~** страхова́тель(ница)
m(f).
insurer [ɪn'ʃuərə'] *n* (*insurance company*)
страхо́вщик.
insurgent [ɪn'səːdʒənt] *adj* восста́вший ♦ *n*
повста́нец*.
insurmountable [ɪnsə'mauntəbl] *adj*
непреодоли́мый (непреодоли́м).
insurrection [ɪnsə'rɛkʃən] *n* восста́ние.
intact [ɪn'tækt] *adj* (*whole*) нетро́нутый
(нетро́нут); (*unharmed*) неповреждённый
(неповреждён).
intake ['ɪnteɪk] *n* (*of food, drink*) потребле́ние;
(*of air*) поглоще́ние; (*BRIT: of pupils, recruits*)
набо́р.
intangible [ɪn'tændʒɪbl] *adj* неощути́мый
(неощути́м).
integer ['ɪntɪdʒə'] *n* це́лое число́*.
integral ['ɪntɪgrəl] *adj* (*feature, element*)
неотъе́млемый (неотъе́млем) ♦ *n* (*MATH*)
интегра́л.
integrate ['ɪntɪgreɪt] *vt* интегри́ровать (*impf/
perf*) ♦ *vi* (*groups, individuals*) объединя́ться
(объедини́ться *perf*).
integrated circuit ['ɪntɪgreɪtɪd-] *n* (*COMPUT*)
интегра́льная схе́ма.
integration [ɪntɪ'greɪʃən] *n* интегра́ция; **racial ~**
ра́совая интегра́ция.
integrity [ɪn'tɛgrɪtɪ] *n* (*morality*) че́стность *f*,
поря́дочность *f*; (*wholeness*) це́лостность *f*.
intellect ['ɪntəlɛkt] *n* интелле́кт.
intellectual [ɪntə'lɛktjuəl] *adj*
интеллектуа́льный* (интеллектуа́лен) ♦ *n*
интеллектуа́л.
intelligence [ɪn'tɛlɪdʒəns] *n* (*cleverness*) ум*;
(*thinking power*) у́мственные спосо́бности
fpl; (*MIL etc*) разве́дка.
intelligence quotient *n* коэффицие́нт
у́мственного разви́тия.
intelligence service *n* разве́дывательная
слу́жба.
intelligence test *n* тест, определя́ющий
у́ровень у́мственных спосо́бностей.
intelligent [ɪn'tɛlɪdʒənt] *adj* у́мный* (умён);

(*animal*) разу́мный* (разу́мен).
intelligently [ɪn'tɛlɪdʒəntlɪ] *adv* умно́.
intelligentsia [ɪntɛlɪ'dʒɛntsɪə] *n*: **the ~**
интеллиге́нция.
intelligible [ɪn'tɛlɪdʒɪbl] *adj* поня́тный*
(поня́тен).
intemperate [ɪn'tɛmpərət] *adj* несде́ржанный*
(несде́ржан).
intend [ɪn'tɛnd] *vt*: **to ~ sth for** предназнача́ть
(предназна́чить *perf*) что-н для +*gen*; **to ~ to
do** намерева́ться (*impf*) +*infin*.
intended [ɪn'tɛndɪd] *adj* (*effect, route*)
заплани́рованный (заплани́рован); (*victim*)
предполага́емый (предполага́ем); (*insult*)
преднаме́ренный* (преднаме́рен).
intense [ɪn'tɛns] *adj* (*heat, emotion*) си́льный*
(силён); (*look*) напряжённый; (*noise, activity*)
интенси́вный* (интенси́вен); **she is very ~**
она́ всё о́чень серьёзно воспринима́ет.
intensely [ɪn'tɛnslɪ] *adv* (*see adj*) си́льно;
напряжённо.
intensify [ɪn'tɛnsɪfaɪ] *vt* уси́ливать (уси́лить
perf).
intensity [ɪn'tɛnsɪtɪ] *n* (*of effort, sun*)
интенси́вность *f*; (*of look*) напряжённость *f*.
intensive [ɪn'tɛnsɪv] *adj* интенси́вный*
(интенси́вен).
intensive care *n* интенси́вная терапи́я.
intensive care unit *n* отделе́ние интенси́вной
терапи́и.
intent [ɪn'tɛnt] *n* (*also LAW*) наме́рение ♦ *adj*:
(on) сосредото́ченный* (сосредото́чен) (на
+*prp*); **to all ~s and purposes** что бы там ни́
бы́ло; **to be ~ on doing** (*determined*)
стреми́ться* (*impf*) +*infin*.
intention [ɪn'tɛnʃən] *n* наме́рение.
intentional [ɪn'tɛnʃənl] *adj* наме́ренный
(наме́рен); (*LAW*) преднаме́ренный*
(преднаме́рен).
intentionally [ɪn'tɛnʃnəlɪ] *adv* (*see adj*)
наме́ренно; преднаме́ренно.
intently [ɪn'tɛntlɪ] *adv* при́стально.
inter [ɪn'təː'] *vt* погреба́ть (погрести́* *perf*).
interact [ɪntər'ækt] *vi*: **to ~ (with)**
взаимоде́йствовать (*impf*) (с +*instr*).
interaction [ɪntər'ækʃən] *n* взаимоде́йствие.
interactive [ɪntər'æktɪv] *adj* взаимо-
де́йствующий; (*COMPUT*) интеракти́вный,
диало́говый.
intercede [ɪntə'siːd] *vi*: **to ~ (with sb/on behalf
of sb)** хода́тайствовать (*impf*) (пе́ред кем-н/
за кого́-н).
intercept [ɪntə'sɛpt] *vt* перехва́тывать
(перехвати́ть* *perf*).
interception [ɪntə'sɛpʃən] *n* перехва́т.
interchange ['ɪntətʃeɪndʒ] *n* (*on motorway*)
тра́нспортная развя́зка*; **~ (of)** (*exchange*)
обме́н (+*instr*).
interchangeable [ɪntə'tʃeɪndʒəbl] *adj*
взаимозаменя́емый (взаимозаменя́ем).
intercity [ɪntə'sɪtɪ] *adj* междугоро́дный.

intercom ['ɪntəkəm] n селе́ктор.
interconnect [ɪntəkə'nɛkt] vi соединя́ться (impf) (ме́жду собо́й).
intercontinental ['ɪntəkɒntɪ'nɛntl] adj межконтинента́льный.
intercourse ['ɪntəkɔːs] n (sexual) половое сноше́ние; (social, verbal) обще́ние.
interdependence [ɪntədɪ'pɛndəns] n взаимозави́симость f.
interdependent [ɪntədɪ'pɛndənt] adj взаимозави́симый (взаимозави́сим).
interest ['ɪntrɪst] n: ~ (in) интере́с (к +dat); (COMM: in company) до́ля*; (: sum of money) проце́нты mpl ♦ vt интересова́ть (impf); **compound/simple** ~ сло́жные/просты́е проце́нты mpl; **it is in our** ~**s** (to our advantage) э́то в на́ших интере́сах; **British** ~**s in the Middle East** брита́нские интере́сы на Бли́жнем Восто́ке; **his main** ~ **is history** его́ основно́й интере́с – э́то исто́рия.
interested ['ɪntrɪstɪd] adj заинтересо́ванный (заинтересо́ван); **to be** ~ **(in sth)** (music etc) интересова́ться (impf) (чем-н); **they are** ~ **in increasing production** они́ заинтересо́ваны в увеличе́нии производи́тельности; **she is** ~ **in becoming a nurse** она́ хо́чет стать медсестро́й.
interest-free ['ɪntrɪst'friː] adj беспроце́нтный ♦ adv без упла́ты проце́нтов.
interesting ['ɪntrɪstɪŋ] adj интере́сный* (интере́сен).
interest rate n проце́нтная ста́вка*.
interface ['ɪntəfeɪs] n (COMPUT) интерфе́йс; (area of contact): ~ **between technology and design** соприкоснове́ние техноло́гии с диза́йном.
interfere [ɪntə'fɪəʳ] vi: **to** ~ **in** вме́шиваться (вмеша́ться perf) в +acc; **to** ~ **with** (object) тро́гать (impf); (plans, career, duty, decision) меша́ть (помеша́ть perf) +dat; **don't** ~ не вме́шивайтесь.
interference [ɪntə'fɪərəns] n вмеша́тельство; (RADIO, TV) поме́хи fpl.
interfering [ɪntə'fɪərɪŋ] adj назо́йливый (назо́йлив).
interim ['ɪntərɪm] adj (government) вре́менный; (report) промежу́точный ♦ n: **in the** ~ тем вре́менем.
interim dividend n промежу́точный дивиде́нд.
interior [ɪn'tɪərɪəʳ] n (of building) интерье́р; (of car, box etc) вну́тренность f; (of country) глуби́нные райо́ны mpl ♦ adj (door, room etc) вну́тренний*; ~ **minister/department** мини́стр/департа́мент вну́тренних дел.
interior decorator n худо́жник(-ица) по интерье́ру.
interior designer n диза́йнер интерье́ра.

interjection [ɪntə'dʒɛkʃən] n перебива́ющий во́зглас; (LING) междоме́тие.
interlock [ɪntə'lɔk] vi сцепля́ться (сцепи́ться* perf).
interloper ['ɪntələupəʳ] n наруши́тель m.
interlude ['ɪntəluːd] n переры́в; (THEAT) антра́кт.
intermarry [ɪntə'mærɪ] vi вступа́ть (вступи́ть* perf) в сме́шанный брак.
intermediary [ɪntə'miːdɪərɪ] n посре́дник (-ица).
intermediate [ɪntə'miːdɪət] adj (stage) промежу́точный; ~ **student** студе́нт сре́дней ступе́ни обуче́ния.
interment [ɪn'təːmənt] n погребе́ние.
interminable [ɪn'təːmɪnəbl] adj бесконе́чный* (бесконе́чен).
intermission [ɪntə'mɪʃən] n переры́в.
intermittent [ɪntə'mɪtnt] adj периоди́ческий*.
intermittently [ɪntə'mɪtntlɪ] adv периоди́чески.
intern [vt ɪn'təːn, n 'ɪntəːn] vt интерни́ровать (impf/perf) ♦ n (US: MED) врач-стажёр.
internal [ɪn'təːnl] adj вну́тренний*.
internally [ɪn'təːnəlɪ] adv: "**not to be taken** ~" „внутрь не принима́ть".
Internal Revenue Service n (US) ≈ Гла́вное нало́говое управле́ние.
international [ɪntə'næʃənl] adj междунаро́дный ♦ n (BRIT: SPORT: also: ~ **match**) междунаро́дная встре́ча.
International Atomic Energy Agency n Междунаро́дное аге́нтство по а́томной эне́ргии.
International Chamber of Commerce n Междунаро́дная торго́вая пала́та.
International Court of Justice n Междунаро́дный суд*.
International Date Line n ли́ния переме́ны дат.
International Labour Organization n Междунаро́дная организа́ция труда́.
internationally [ɪntə'næʃnəlɪ] adv в междунаро́дном масшта́бе.
International Monetary Fund n Междунаро́дный валю́тный фонд.
international relations npl междунаро́дные отноше́ния ntpl.
internecine [ɪntə'niːsaɪn] adj междоусо́бный.
internee [ɪntəː'niː] n интерни́рованный(-ая) m(f) adj.
internment [ɪn'təːnmənt] n интерни́рование.
interplay ['ɪntəpleɪ] n: ~ **(of** or **between)** взаимоде́йствие (+gen).
Interpol ['ɪntəpɔl] n интерпо́л.
interpret [ɪn'təːprɪt] vt (explain) интерпрети́ровать (impf/perf), толкова́ть (impf); (translate) переводи́ть* (перевести́* perf) ♦ vi (у́стно) переводи́ть* (перевести́* perf)

---

* marks translations which have irregular inflections. The Russian-English side of the dictionary gives inflectional information.

(у́стно).
interpretation [ɪntəːprɪˈteɪʃən] *n* интерпрета́ция, толкова́ние.
interpreter [ɪnˈtəːprɪtəʳ] *n* перево́дчик(-ица).
interpreting [ɪnˈtəːprɪtɪŋ] *n* (у́стный) перево́д.
interrelated [ɪntərɪˈleɪtɪd] *adj* взаимо-свя́занный (взаимосвя́зан).
interrogate [ɪnˈtɛrəʊgeɪt] *vt* допра́шивать (допроси́ть* *perf*).
interrogation [ɪntɛrəʊˈgeɪʃən] *n* допро́с.
interrogative [ɪntəˈrɔgətɪv] *adj* (*LING*) вопроси́тельный.
interrogator [ɪnˈtɛrəgeɪtəʳ] *n* сле́дователь *m*.
interrupt [ɪntəˈrʌpt] *vti* прерыва́ть (прерва́ть* *perf*).
interruption [ɪntəˈrʌpʃən] *n* (*act*) прерыва́ние; **I hate ~s when I'm working** я ненави́жу, когда́ меня́ прерыва́ют во вре́мя рабо́ты.
intersect [ɪntəˈsɛkt] *vi* пересека́ться (пересе́чься* *perf*) ◆ *vt* пересека́ть (пересе́чь* *perf*).
intersection [ɪntəˈsɛkʃən] *n* (*of roads*) пересече́ние; (*MATH*) то́чка* пересече́ния.
intersperse [ɪntəˈspəːs] *vt*: **to ~ with** перемежа́ть (*impf*) с +*instr*.
intertwine [ɪntəˈtwaɪn] *vi* переплета́ться (переплести́сь* *perf*).
interval [ˈɪntəvl] *n* (*also MUS*) интерва́л; (*BRIT: SPORT*) переры́в; (: *THEAT*) антра́кт; **bright ~s** (*in weather*) проясне́ния *ntpl*; **at ~s** вре́мя от вре́мени.
intervene [ɪntəˈviːn] *vi* (*in conversation, situation*) вме́шиваться (вмеша́ться *perf*); (*event*) меша́ть (помеша́ть *perf*); (*time*) проходи́ть* (пройти́* *perf*).
intervening [ɪntəˈviːnɪŋ] *adj* (*period*) про-межу́точный.
intervention [ɪntəˈvɛnʃən] *n* (*interference*) вмеша́тельство; (*mediation*) посре́дничество; **military ~** вое́нная интерве́нция.
interview [ˈɪntəvjuː] *n* (*for job*) собесе́дование; (*RADIO, TV etc*) интервью́ *nt ind* ◆ *vt* (*see n*) проводи́ть* (провести́* *perf*) собесе́дование с +*instr*; интервьюи́ровать (*impf/perf*), брать* (взять* *perf*) интервью́ у +*gen*; **to give an ~** дава́ть* (дать* *perf*) интервью́.
interviewee [ɪntəvjuːˈiː] *n* интервьюи́руемый (-ая) *m(f) adj*.
interviewer [ˈɪntəvjuəʳ] *n* (*of candidate*) проводя́щий(-ая) *m(f) adj* собесе́дование; (*RADIO, TV etc*) интервью́ер.
intestate [ɪnˈtɛsteɪt] *adj*: **to die ~** сконча́ться (*perf*), не оста́вив завеща́ния.
intestinal [ɪnˈtɛstɪnl] *adj* кише́чный.
intestine [ɪnˈtɛstɪn] *n* кишка́*; **large/small ~** то́лстая/то́нкая кишка́; **~s** кише́чник *msg*.
intimacy [ˈɪntɪməsɪ] *n* инти́мность *f*.
intimate [*adj* ˈɪntɪmət, *vt* ˈɪntɪmeɪt] *adj* (*very close*) бли́зкий* (бли́зок); (*relationship, conversation, atmosphere*) инти́мный*

(инти́мен); (*knowledge*) глубо́кий* (глубо́к) ◆ *vt* намека́ть (намекну́ть *perf*) на +*acc*; **to ~ that** намека́ть (намекну́ть *perf*), что.
intimately [ˈɪntɪmətlɪ] *adv* (*see adj*) инти́мно; глубоко́.
intimation [ɪntɪˈmeɪʃən] *n* намёк.
intimidate [ɪnˈtɪmɪdeɪt] *vt* запу́гивать (запуга́ть *perf*).
intimidation [ɪntɪmɪˈdeɪʃən] *n* запу́гивание.

KEYWORD

into [ˈɪntu] *prep* **1** (*indicating motion or direction*) в/на +*acc*; **into the house/garden** в дом/сад; **into the post office/factory** на по́чту/фа́брику; **research into cancer** иссле́дования *ntpl* в о́бласти ра́ковых заболева́ний; **he worked late into the night** он рабо́тал до по́здней но́чи
2 (*indicating change of condition, result*): **she has translated the letter into Russian** она́ перевела́ письмо́ на ру́сский язы́к; **the vase broke into pieces** ва́за разби́лась вдре́безги *or* на кусо́чки; **they got into trouble for it** им попа́ло за э́то; **he lapsed into silence** он погрузи́лся в молча́ние; **to burst into tears** распла́каться* (*perf*); **to burst into flames** загоре́ться (загоре́ться *perf*).

---

intolerable [ɪnˈtɔlərəbl] *adj* нетерпи́мый (нетерпи́м), невыноси́мый (невыноси́м).
intolerance [ɪnˈtɔlərns] *n* нетерпи́мость *f*.
intolerant [ɪnˈtɔlərnt] *adj*: **~ (of)** нетерпи́мый (нетерпи́м) (к +*dat*).
intonation [ɪntəʊˈneɪʃən] *n* интона́ция.
intoxicated [ɪnˈtɔksɪkeɪtɪd] *adj* (*drunk*) опьяне́вший; (*fig*) опьянённый (опьянён).
intoxication [ɪntɔksɪˈkeɪʃən] *n* (*also fig*) опьяне́ние.
intractable [ɪnˈtræktəbl] *adj* (*person, temper*) неподатли́вый (неподатли́в); (*problem*) трудноразреши́мый (трудноразреши́м); (*illness*) трудноизлечи́мый (трудно-излечи́м).
intransigence [ɪnˈtrænsɪdʒəns] *n* упо́рство.
intransigent [ɪnˈtrænsɪdʒənt] *adj* упо́рный* (упо́рен).
intransitive [ɪnˈtrænsɪtɪv] *adj* (*LING*) непереходный.
intrauterine device [ˈɪntrəˈjuːtərəm-] *n* внутрима́точное противозача́точное сре́дство.
intravenous [ɪntrəˈviːnəs] *adj* внутриве́нный.
in-tray [ˈɪntreɪ] *n* (*in office*) корзи́на для входя́щих бума́г.
intrepid [ɪnˈtrɛpɪd] *adj* неустраши́мый (неустраши́м).
intricacy [ˈɪntrɪkəsɪ] *n* (*of situation*) сло́жность *f*; (*of pattern, design*) замыслова́тость *f*.
intricate [ˈɪntrɪkət] *adj* замыслова́тый (замыслова́т).
intrigue [ɪnˈtriːg] *n* интри́га ◆ *vt* интригова́ть (заинтригова́ть *perf*).

.**intriguing** [ɪn'tri:gɪŋ] *adj* (*fascinating*)
интригу́ющий.
intrinsic [ɪn'trɪnsɪk] *adj* неотъе́млемый
(неотъе́млем).
introduce [ɪntrə'dju:s] *vt* (*new idea, measure
etc*) вводи́ть* (ввести́* *perf*); (*speaker, TV show
etc*) представля́ть (предста́вить* *perf*); **to ~
sb (to sb)** представля́ть (предста́вить* *perf*)
кого́-н (кому́-н); **to ~ sb to** (*pastime,
technique*) знако́мить* (познако́мить* *perf*)
кого́-н с +*instr*; **may I ~ ...?** разреши́те Вам
предста́вить ....
introduction [ɪntrə'dʌkʃən] *n* введе́ние; (*to
person, new experience*) знако́мство; **a letter
of ~** рекоменда́тельное письмо́*.
introductory [ɪntrə'dʌktərɪ] *adj* (*lesson*)
вступи́тельный; **~ remarks** вступи́тельные
замеча́ния; **an ~ offer** предвари́тельная
цена́*.
introspection [ɪntrəu'spɛkʃən] *n* самоана́лиз.
introspective [ɪntrəu'spɛktɪv] *adj*
самосозерца́тельный.
introvert ['ɪntrəuvə:t] *n* интрове́рт.
introverted ['ɪntrəuvə:tɪd] *adj* само-
углублённый (самоуглублён).
intrude [ɪn'tru:d] *vi*: **to ~ (on)** вторга́ться
(вто́ргнуться* *perf*) (в/на +*acc*); **am I
intruding?** я не помеша́ю?
intruder [ɪn'tru:də^r] *n*: **there is an ~ in our house**
к нам в дом кто-то вто́ргся.
intrusion [ɪn'tru:ʒən] *n* вторже́ние.
intrusive [ɪn'tru:sɪv] *adj* назо́йливый
(назо́йлив).
intuition [ɪntju:'ɪʃən] *n* интуи́ция.
intuitive [ɪn'tju:ɪtɪv] *adj* интуити́вный*
(интуити́вен).
inundate ['ɪnʌndeɪt] *vt*: **to ~ with** (*calls, letters
etc*) зава́ливать (завали́ть* *perf*) +*instr*;
Moscow is ~d with visitors Москва́
наводнена́ прие́зжими.
inure [ɪn'juə^r] *vt*: **to ~ o.s. to** приуча́ть
(приучи́ть* *perf*) себя́ к +*dat*.
invade [ɪn'veɪd] *vt* (*MIL*) вторга́ться
(вто́ргнуться* *perf*) в +*acc*; (*fig: subj: people,
animals etc*) наводня́ть (наводни́ть* *perf*).
invader [ɪn'veɪdə^r] *n* (*MIL*) захва́тчик.
invalid [*n* 'ɪnvəlɪd, *adj* ɪn'vælɪd] *n* (*MED*) инвали́д
◆ *adj* (*not valid*) недействи́тельный*
(недействи́телен).
invalidate [ɪn'vælɪdeɪt] *vt* (*argument, result etc*)
дока́зывать (доказа́ть* *perf*) несостоя́тель-
ность *f* +*gen*; (*law, marriage, election*) де́лать
(сде́лать *perf*) недействи́тельным.
invaluable [ɪn'væljuəbl] *adj* (*person, thing*)
неоцени́мый (неоцени́м).
invariable [ɪn'vɛərɪəbl] *adj* (*amount, result,
routine*) неизме́нный* (неизме́нен).
invariably [ɪn'vɛərɪəblɪ] *adv* неизме́нно; **she is**

~ late она́ неизме́нно опа́здывает.
invasion [ɪn'veɪʒən] *n* (*MIL*) вторже́ние; (*fig*)
посяга́тельство; **an ~ of privacy** вторже́ние в
ли́чную жизнь.
invective [ɪn'vɛktɪv] *n* оскорбле́ние.
inveigle [ɪn'vi:gl] *vt*: **to ~ sb into sth** вовлека́ть
(вовле́чь* *perf*) кого́-н во что́-н.
invent [ɪn'vɛnt] *vt* (*machine, game, phrase etc*)
изобрета́ть (изобрести́* *perf*); (*fabricate: lie,
excuse*) выду́мывать (вы́думать *perf*).
invention [ɪn'vɛnʃən] *n* изобрете́ние; (*untrue
story*) вы́думка.
inventive [ɪn'vɛntɪv] *adj* (*person*)
изобрета́тельный* (изобрета́телен).
inventiveness [ɪn'vɛntɪvnɪs] *n*
изобрета́тельность *f*.
inventor [ɪn'vɛntə^r] *n* (*of machines, systems*)
изобрета́тель *m*.
inventory ['ɪnvəntrɪ] *n* (*of house, ship etc*)
(инвентаризацио́нная) о́пись.
inventory control *n* (*COMM*) управле́ние
запа́сами.
inverse [ɪn'və:s] *adj* (*relationship*) обра́тный; **in
~ proportion to** в обра́тной пропорциона́ль-
ности к +*dat*.
invert [ɪn'və:t] *vt* (*turn upside down*)
перевора́чивать (переверну́ть *perf*).
invertebrate [ɪn'və:tɪbrət] *n* беспозвоно́чное *nt*
adj.
inverted commas [ɪn'və:tɪd-] *npl* (*BRIT: LING*)
кавы́чки *fpl*.
invest [ɪn'vɛst] *vt* (*money*) инвести́ровать*
(*impf/perf*) в(о) +*acc*; (*fig: time, energy*)
вкла́дывать (вложи́ть* *perf*) ◆ *vi*: **~ in** (*COMM*)
помеща́ть (помести́ть* *perf*) капита́л в +*acc*;
(*fig: sth useful*) вкла́дывать (вложи́ть* *perf*)
де́ньги в +*acc*; **to ~ sb with sth** облека́ть
(обле́чь* *perf*) кого́-н чем-н.
investigate [ɪn'vɛstɪgeɪt] *vt* (*accident, crime*)
рассле́довать* (*impf/perf*); (*person*)
иссле́довать* (*impf/perf*).
investigation [ɪnvɛstɪ'geɪʃən] *n* рассле́дование.
investigative [ɪn'vɛstɪgeɪtɪv] *adj*: **~ journalism**
журнали́стское рассле́дование.
investigator [ɪn'vɛstɪgeɪtə^r] *n* (*of events, people
etc*) иссле́дователь(ница) *m(f)*; **private ~**
ча́стный сле́дователь *m*.
investiture [ɪn'vɛstɪtʃə^r] *n* (*of chancellor*)
введе́ние в до́лжность *f*; (*of prince*)
пожа́лование зва́ния.
investment [ɪn'vɛstmənt] *n* (*activity*)
инвести́рование; (*amount of money*)
инвести́ция, вклад.
investment grant *n* (*COMM*) инвестицио́нные
субси́дии *fpl*.
investment income *n* (*COMM*) дохо́д с
инвести́ций.
investment portfolio *n* (*COMM*) портфе́ль *m*

---

* marks translations which have irregular inflections. The Russian-English side of the dictionary gives inflectional information.

це́нных бума́г.
investment trust *n* (COMM) инвестицио́нный
трест.
investor [ɪn'vɛstəʳ] *n* (COMM) инве́стор,
вкла́дчик.
inveterate [ɪn'vɛtərət] *adj* (*liar, cheat etc*)
неисправи́мый (неисправи́м); (*smoker*)
зая́длый; (*dislike etc*) да́вний*.
invidious [ɪn'vɪdɪəs] *adj* (*task, job*) неприя́тный*
(неприя́тен); (*comparison, decision*)
несправедли́вый (несправедли́в).
invigilator [ɪn'vɪdʒɪleɪtəʳ] *n* (*in exam*)
экзамⁱна́тор, следя́щий за тем, что́бы
студе́нты не спи́сывали во вре́мя экза́менов.
invigorating [ɪn'vɪgəreɪtɪŋ] *adj* (*air*) бодря́щий
(бодря́щ); (*experience*) воодушевля́ющий.
invincible [ɪn'vɪnsɪbl] *adj* (*army, team*)
непобеди́мый (непобеди́м); (*belief,
conviction*) неукроти́мый (неукроти́м).
inviolate [ɪn'vaɪələt] *adj* ненару́шенный
(ненару́шен).
invisible [ɪn'vɪzɪbl] *adj* неви́димый (неви́дим)
♦ *cpd* (COMM: *exports, earnings, assets*)
неви́димый.
invisible mending *n* худо́жественная
што́пка.
invitation [ɪnvɪ'teɪʃən] *n* приглаше́ние; **by ~
only** то́лько по приглаше́нию; **at sb's ~** по
приглаше́нию кого́-н.
invite [ɪn'vaɪt] *vt* (*to party, meal, meeting etc*)
приглаша́ть (пригласи́ть* *perf*); (*discussion,
criticism*) побужда́ть (побуди́ть* *perf*) к +*dat*;
to ~ sb to do предлага́ть (предложи́ть* *perf*)
кому́-н +*infin*; **to ~ sb to dinner** приглаша́ть
(пригласи́ть* *perf*) кого́-н на обе́д
▸ **invite out** *vt* приглаша́ть (пригласи́ть* *perf*).
inviting [ɪn'vaɪtɪŋ] *adj* (*attractive, desirable*)
соблазни́тельный* (соблазни́телен).
invoice ['ɪnvɔɪs] *n* (COMM) счёт, факту́ра ♦ *vt*
выпи́сывать (вы́писать* *perf*) счёт *or*
факту́ру; **to ~ sb for goods** выпи́сывать
(вы́писать* *perf*) счёт *or* факту́ру кому́-н за
това́ры.
invoke [ɪn'vəuk] *vt* (*law, principle*) обраща́ться
(обрати́ться* *perf*) к +*dat*; (*feelings, memories
etc*) взыва́ть (воззва́ть* *perf*) к +*dat*.
involuntary [ɪn'vɔləntrɪ] *adj* (*action, reflex etc*)
непроизво́льный* (непроизво́лен).
involve [ɪn'vɔlv] *vt* (*person, thing: include, use*)
вовлека́ть (вовле́чь* *perf*) в +*acc*; (: *concern,
affect*) включа́ть (включи́ть* *perf*); **to ~ sb (in
sth)** вовлека́ть (вовле́чь* *perf*) кого́-н (во
что-н).
involved [ɪn'vɔlvd] *adj* (*complicated*)
запу́танный* (запу́тан); (*thing required: in
task, situation etc*) включённый (включён); **to
be ~ in** (*in activity etc*) быть* (*impf*)
вовлечённым(-ой) в(о) +*acc*; **to feel ~** быть*
(*impf*) вовлечённым; **to become ~ with sb**
(*socially*) свя́зываться (связа́ться *perf*) с
кем-н; (*emotionally*) увлека́ться (увле́чься*

perf) кем-н.
involvement [ɪn'vɔlvmənt] *n* (*participation*)
прича́стность *f*; (*concern, enthusiasm*)
вовлечённость *f*; (*relationship*) связь *f*.
invulnerable [ɪn'vʌlnərəbl] *adj* (*person, ship,
building etc*) неуязви́мый (неуязви́м).
inward ['ɪnwəd] *adj* (*thought, feeling*)
вну́тренний*; (*movement*) напра́вленный
внутрь ♦ *adv* = **inwards**.
inwardly ['ɪnwədlɪ] *adv* внутри́.
inwards ['ɪnwədz] *adv* (*move, face*) внутрь.
I/O *abbr* (COMPUT: = *input/output*) ввод-вы́вод.
IOC *n abbr* = *International Olympic Committee*.
iodine ['aɪəudiːn] *n* йод.
IOM *abbr* (BRIT: POST) = *Isle of Man*.
ion ['aɪən] *n* (ELEC) ио́н.
Ionian Sea [aɪ'əunɪən-] *n*: **the ~ ~** Иони́ческое
мо́ре.
ioniser ['aɪənaɪzəʳ] *n* ионизи́рующая
устано́вка*.
iota [aɪ'əutə] *n* йо́та.
IOU *n abbr* (= *I owe you*) *просте́йший долгово́й
докуме́нт*.
IOW *abbr* (BRIT: POST) = *Isle of Wight*.
IPA *n abbr* (= *International Phonetic Alphabet*)
Междунаро́дная систе́ма транскри́пции.
IQ *n abbr* (= *intelligence quotient*) коэффицие́нт
у́мственного разви́тия.
IRA *n abbr* (= *Irish Republican Army*) ИРА=
Ирла́ндская респу́бликанская а́рмия; (US) =
individual retirement account.
Iran [ɪ'rɑːn] *n* Ира́н.
Iranian [ɪ'reɪnɪən] *adj* ира́нский* ♦ *n*
ира́нец(-нка).
Iraq [ɪ'rɑːk] *n* Ира́к.
Iraqi [ɪ'rɑːkɪ] *adj* ира́кский* ♦ *n* жи́тель(ница)
m(f) Ира́ка.
irascible [ɪ'ræsɪbl] *adj* (*person*) вспы́льчивый
(вспы́льчив).
irate [aɪ'reɪt] *adj* (*person, letter etc*)
разгне́ванный* (разгне́ван).
Ireland ['aɪələnd] *n* Ирла́ндия; **the Republic of
~** Ирла́ндская Респу́блика.
iris ['aɪrɪs] (*pl* **~es**) *n* (ANAT) ра́дужная
оболо́чка* (гла́за); (BOT) и́рис.
Irish ['aɪrɪʃ] *adj* ирла́ндский*; **the ~** ирла́ндцы.
Irishman ['aɪrɪʃmən] *irreg n* ирла́ндец*.
Irish Sea *n*: **the ~ ~** Ирла́ндское мо́ре.
Irishwoman ['aɪrɪʃwumən] *irreg n* ирла́ндка.
irk [əːk] *vt* (*person*) раздража́ть (*impf*).
irksome ['əːksəm] *adj* надое́дливый
(надое́длив).
IRN *n abbr* = *Independent Radio News*.
IRO *n abbr* (US) = *International Refugee
Organization*.
iron ['aɪən] *n* (*metal*) желе́зо *no pl*; (*for clothes*)
утю́г ♦ *cpd* желе́зный ♦ *vt* (*clothes*) гла́дить*
(погла́дить* *perf*)
▸ **iron out** *vt* (*fig: problems*) ула́живать
(ула́дить* *perf*).
Iron Curtain *n* (POL: *formerly*): **the ~ ~**

желе́зный за́навес.
iron foundry *n* чугунолите́йный цех.
ironic(al) [aɪˈrɒnɪk(l)] *adj* ирони́ческий.
ironically [aɪˈrɒnɪklɪ] *adv* (*say, enquire etc*) ирони́чно; ~, **the intelligence chief was the last to find out** иро́ния в том, что шеф разве́дки узна́л после́дним.
ironing [ˈaɪənɪŋ] *n* (*activity*) гла́женье; (*clothes*) бельё для гла́женья.
ironing board *n* глади́льная доска́.
iron lung *n* (*MED*) аппара́т (для) иску́сственного дыха́ния.
ironmonger [ˈaɪənmʌŋɡəʳ] *n* (*BRIT*) торго́вец скобяны́ми изде́лиями.
ironmonger's (shop) [ˈaɪənmʌŋɡəz-] *n* магази́н скобяны́х изде́лий.
iron ore *n* желе́зная руда́.
irons [ˈaɪəns] *npl* (*chains*) кандалы́ *pl*; **to clap sb in** ~ зако́вывать (закова́ть *perf*) кого́-н в кандалы́.
ironworks [ˈaɪənwəːks] *n* чугунолите́йный заво́д.
irony [ˈaɪrənɪ] *n* иро́ния.
irrational [ɪˈræʃənl] *adj* (*feelings, behaviour*) нерациона́льный* (нерациона́лен), неразу́мный* (неразу́мен).
irreconcilable [ɪrɛkənˈsaɪləbl] *adj* (*ideas, conflict*) непримири́мый (непримири́м).
irredeemable [ɪrɪˈdiːməbl] *adj* (*COMM*) не подлежа́щий погаше́нию *or* вы́купу; (*fault, character*) неисправи́мый (неисправи́м).
irrefutable [ɪrɪˈfjuːtəbl] *adj* (*fact, argument*) неопровержи́мый (неопровержи́м).
irregular [ɪˈrɛɡjuləʳ] *adj* (*surface*) неро́вный* (неро́вен); (*pattern*) непра́вильной фо́рмы; (*action, event*) нерегуля́рный* (нерегуля́рен); (*behaviour*) распу́щенный; (*LING: verb etc*) непра́вильный.
irregularity [ɪrɛɡjuˈlærɪtɪ] *n* (*see adj*) неро́вность *f*; непра́вильность *f*; нерегуля́рность *f*; распу́щенность *f*.
irrelevance [ɪˈrɛləvəns] *n* неуме́стность *f*.
irrelevant [ɪˈrɛləvənt] *adj* (*fact, information*) неуме́стный.
irreligious [ɪrɪˈlɪdʒəs] *adj* неве́рующий*.
irreparable [ɪˈrɛprəbl] *adj* (*harm, damage etc*) непоправи́мый (непоправи́м).
irreplaceable [ɪrɪˈpleɪsəbl] *adj* (*antique, wedding ring etc*) незамени́мый (незамени́м).
irrepressible [ɪrɪˈprɛsəbl] *adj* (*person, good humour, enthusiasm etc*) неудержи́мый (неудержи́м).
irreproachable [ɪrɪˈprəutʃəbl] *adj* (*behaviour, character*) безупре́чный* (безупре́чен).
irresistible [ɪrɪˈzɪstɪbl] *adj* (*urge, desire*) непреодоли́мый (непреодоли́м); (*person, thing*) неотрази́мый (неотрази́м).
irresolute [ɪˈrɛzəluːt] *adj* (*person*)

нереши́тельный* (нереши́телен).
irrespective [ɪrɪˈspɛktɪv] *prep*: ~ **of** незави́симо от +*gen*.
irresponsible [ɪrɪˈspɒnsɪbl] *adj* (*person, action*) безотве́тственный* (безотве́тствен).
irretrievable [ɪrɪˈtriːvəbl] *adj* (*object*) безвозвра́тный* (безвозвра́тен); (*loss, damage*) непоправи́мый (непоправи́м).
irreverent [ɪˈrɛvərnt] *adj* (*person, behaviour, comment etc*) непочти́тельный* (непочти́телен).
irrevocable [ɪˈrɛvəkəbl] *adj* (*action, decision*) бесповоро́тный* (бесповоро́тен).
irrigate [ˈɪrɪɡeɪt] *vt* (*AGR: land*) ороша́ть (ороси́ть* *perf*).
irrigation [ɪrɪˈɡeɪʃən] *n* (*AGR*) ороше́ние, иррига́ция.
irritable [ˈɪrɪtəbl] *adj* раздражи́тельный* (раздражи́телен).
irritant [ˈɪrɪtənt] *n* раздражи́тель *m*.
irritate [ˈɪrɪteɪt] *vt* (*also MED*) раздража́ть (раздражи́ть *perf*).
irritating [ˈɪrɪteɪtɪŋ] *adj* (*person, sound etc*) раздража́ющий.
irritation [ɪrɪˈteɪʃən] *n* (*also MED*) раздраже́ние; (*annoying thing*) раздража́ющий фа́ктор.
IRS *n abbr* (*US*) = **Internal Revenue Service**.
is [ɪz] *vb see* **be**.
ISBN *n abbr* (= *International Standard Book Number*) ISBN.
Islam [ˈɪzlɑːm] *n* (*REL*) исла́м; (*Islamic countries*) мусульма́нские стра́ны *fpl*.
Islamic [ɪzˈlæmɪk] *adj* мусульма́нский*.
island [ˈaɪlənd] *n* о́стров*; (*also*: **traffic** ~) острово́к безопа́сности.
islander [ˈaɪləndəʳ] *n* островитя́нин*(-нка).
isle [aɪl] *n* о́стров*.
isn't [ˈɪznt] = **is not**.
isobar [ˈaɪsəubɑːʳ] *n* изоба́ра.
isolate [ˈaɪsəleɪt] *vt* (*set apart*) изоли́ровать* (*impf/perf*); (*substance*) выделя́ть (вы́делить* *perf*).
isolated [ˈaɪsəleɪtɪd] *adj* (*place, person*) изоли́рованный* (изоли́рован); (*incident*) отде́льный.
isolation [aɪsəˈleɪʃən] *n* изоля́ция.
isolationism [aɪsəˈleɪʃənɪzəm] *n* изоляциони́зм.
isotope [ˈaɪsəutəup] *n* (*PHYS*) изото́п.
Israel [ˈɪzreɪl] *n* Изра́иль *m*.
Israeli [ɪzˈreɪlɪ] *adj* изра́ильский* ♦ *n* (*person*) израильтя́нин*(-нка).
issue [ˈɪʃuː] *n* (*problem, subject*) вопро́с; (*most important part*) суть *f*; (*of book, stamps etc*) вы́пуск; (*LAW, old: offspring*) пото́мок* ♦ *vt* (*statement, newspaper*) издава́ть* (изда́ть* *perf*); (*rations, equipment, documents*) выдава́ть* (вы́дать* *perf*) ♦ *vi*: **to** ~ **from**

---

* marks translations which have irregular inflections. The Russian-English side of the dictionary gives inflectional information.

(*liquid, gas*) вытека́ть (вы́течь* *perf*) из +*gen*; (*sound, smell*) исходи́ть* (*impf*) из/от +*gen*; **to be at** ~ быть* (*impf*) предме́том обсужде́ния; **to avoid the** ~ обходи́ть* (обойти́* *perf*) суть де́ла; **to confuse** *or* **obscure the** ~ затемня́ть (затемни́ть *perf*) суть вопро́са; **to** ~ **sth to sb** выдава́ть* (вы́дать* *perf*) что-н кому́-н; **to** ~ **sb with sth** снабжа́ть (снабди́ть* *perf*) кого́-н чем-н; **to take** ~ **with sb (over)** начина́ть (нача́ть* *perf*) спо́рить с кем-н (о +*prp*); **to make an** ~ **of sth** де́лать (сде́лать *perf*) исто́рию из чего́-н.

issued capital [ˈɪʃuːd-] *n* (*COMM*) вы́пущенный акционе́рный капита́л.

Istanbul [ɪstænˈbuːl] *n* Стамбу́л.

isthmus [ˈɪsməs] *n* переше́ек.

IT *n abbr* = **information technology**.

KEYWORD
---

it [ɪt] *pron* **1** (*specific subject*) он (*f* она́, *nt* оно́); (*direct object*) его́ (*f* её); (*indirect object*) ему́ (*f* ей); (*after prep: +gen*) его́ (*f* её); (: +*dat*) ему́ (*f* ей); (: +*instr*) им (*f* ей); (: +*prp*) нём (*f* ней); **where is your car? – it's in the garage** где Ва́ша маши́на? – она́ в гараже́; **I like this hat, whose it it?** мне нра́вится э́та шля́па, чья она́?; **have you got the dictionary with you? – no, I gave it to Mary** у Вас с собо́й слова́рь? – нет, я дал его́ Мэ́ри; **this pen is fine, I wrote with it yesterday** э́та ру́чка рабо́тает, я писа́л е́ю вчера́
2 э́то; (: *indirect object*) э́тому; **what kind of car is it? – it's a Lada** кака́я э́то маши́на? – э́то Ла́да; **who is it? – it's me** кто э́то? – э́то я
3 (*after prep: +gen*) э́того; (: +*dat*) э́тому; (: +*instr*) э́тим; (: +*prp*) э́том; **I spoke to him about it** я говори́л с ним об э́том; **that's just it!** вот име́нно!; **why is it that ...** почему́ же тогда́ ...; **what is it?** (*what's wrong*) что тако́е?; **that's it for today** на сего́дня всё
4 (*impersonal*): **it's raining** идёт дождь; **it's cold today** сего́дня хо́лодно; **it's interesting that ...** интере́сно, что ...; **it's 6 o'clock** сейча́с 6 часо́в; **it's the 10th of August** сего́дня 10-ое а́вгуста.

ITA *n abbr* (*BRIT*: = **initial teaching alphabet**)

алфави́т, испо́льзуемый при обуче́нии чте́нию.

Italian [ɪˈtæljən] *adj* италья́нский* ♦ *n* (*person*) италья́нец(-нка); (*LING*) италья́нский* язы́к*; **the** ~**s** италья́нцы.

italics [ɪˈtælɪks] *npl* (*TYP*) курси́в *msg*.

Italy [ˈɪtəlɪ] *n* Ита́лия.

itch [ɪtʃ] *n* (*irritation*) зуд ♦ *vi* (*part of body*) чеса́ться* (*impf*); **I am** ~**ing all over** у меня́ всё че́шется; **he was** ~**ing to know our secret** ему́ не терпе́лось узна́ть наш секре́т.

itchy [ˈɪtʃɪ] *adj* (*skin*) зудя́щий; **I feel all** ~ у меня́ всё че́шется; **my back is** ~ у меня́ че́шется спина́.

it'd [ˈɪtd] = **it had**, **it would**.

item [ˈaɪtəm] *n* (*one thing: of list, collection*) предме́т; (*on agenda*) пункт; (*also*: **news** ~) сообще́ние; ~**s of clothing** предме́ты оде́жды.

itemize [ˈaɪtəmaɪz] *vt* (*list*) составля́ть (соста́вить* *perf*) спи́сок +*gen*.

itemized bill [ˈaɪtəmaɪzd-] *n* счёт с указа́нием сто́имости ка́ждой ве́щи и́ли ка́ждого ви́да услу́г.

itinerant [ɪˈtɪnərənt] *adj* (*labourer, salesman, priest etc*) стра́нствующий.

itinerary [aɪˈtɪnərərɪ] *n* маршру́т.

it'll [ˈɪtl] = **it shall**, **it will**.

ITN *n abbr* (*BRIT*: *TV*) = **Independent Television News**.

its [ɪts] *adj* его́/её; **свой/своя́/своё**; *see also* **my** ♦ *pron* его́/её; **свой/своя́/своё**; *see also* **mine**[1].

it's [ɪts] = **it has**, **it is**.

itself [ɪtˈself] *pron* (*reflexive*) себя́*; (*emphatic*) он сам/она́ сама́/оно́ само́.

ITV *n abbr* (*BRIT*: *TV*) = **Independent Television**.

IUD *n abbr* (= **intrauterine device**) внутри-ма́точное противозача́точное сре́дство.

I've [aɪv] = **I have**.

ivory [ˈaɪvərɪ] *n* (*substance*) слоно́вая кость* *f*; (*colour*) цвет слоно́вой ко́сти.

Ivory Coast *n* Бе́рег Слоно́вой Ко́сти.

ivory tower *n* (*fig*) ба́шня из слоно́вой ко́сти.

ivy [ˈaɪvɪ] *n* (*BOT*) плющ*.

Ivy League *n* (*US*: *SCOL*) гру́ппа старе́йших университе́тов США.

~ J, j ~

J, j [dʒeɪ] n (letter) 10-ая бу́ква англи́йского
алфави́та.
JA n abbr = **judge advocate**.
J/A abbr = **joint account**.
jab [dʒæb] vt (with finger, stick etc) ты́кать*
(ткну́ть perf) ♦ n (BRIT: inf: MED) уко́л ♦ vi: **to ~
at** стуча́ть (impf) по +dat; **to ~ sth into sth**
втыка́ть* (воткну́ть perf) что-н в что-н.
jack [dʒæk] n (AUT) домкра́т; (SPORT) ма́лый
шар, слу́жащий мише́нью для игро́ков в
шары́; (CARDS) вале́т
▶ **jack in** vt (inf) завя́зывать (завяза́ть* perf) с
+instr
▶ **jack up** vt (AUT) поднима́ть (подня́ть* perf)
домкра́том.
jackal ['dʒækl] n шака́л.
jackass ['dʒækæs] n (also fig) осёл*.
jackdaw ['dʒækdɔ:] n га́лка*.
jacket ['dʒækɪt] n (of suit) пиджа́к*; (casual)
ку́ртка*; (of book) суперобло́жка; **potatoes in
their ~s, jacket potatoes** карто́шка в
мунди́ре.
jack-in-the-box ['dʒækɪnðəbɔks] n чёртик в
табаке́рке.
jackknife ['dʒæknaɪf] n складно́й нож* ♦ vi: **the
lorry ~d** грузови́к заноси́ло.
jack of all trades n: **he's a ~ ~ ~ ~** он ма́стер
на все ру́ки.
jack plug n штéккер.
jackpot ['dʒækpɔt] n куш; **to hit the ~** (fig)
срыва́ть (сорва́ть perf) куш.
jacuzzi [dʒə'ku:zɪ] n „джаку́зи" m ind (ва́нна, в
кото́рой под напо́ром циркули́рует водо́й).
jade [dʒeɪd] n нефри́т.
jaded ['dʒeɪdɪd] adj утомлённый (утомлён) и
равноду́шный (равноду́шен).
JAG n abbr (= Judge Advocate General) гла́вный
прави́тельственный сове́тник по вое́нно-
юриди́ческим вопро́сам.
jagged ['dʒægɪd] adj зу́бчатый.
jaguar ['dʒægjuə] n ягуа́р.
jail [dʒeɪl] n тюрьма́* ♦ vt заключа́ть
(заключи́ть perf) в тюрьму́.
jailbird ['dʒeɪlbə:d] n (inf) уголо́вник.
jailbreak ['dʒeɪlbreɪk] n побе́г из тюрьмы́.
jalopy [dʒə'lɔpɪ] n (inf) драндуле́т.

jam [dʒæm] n (preserve) джем; (conserve)
варе́нье; (also: traffic ~) про́бка* ♦ vt
(passage) забива́ть (заби́ть* perf);
(mechanism) закли́нивать (закли́нить perf);
(RADIO) глуши́ть (заглуши́ть perf) ♦ vi
(drawer) застрева́ть (застря́ть* perf);
(mechanism): **the engine/rifle has ~med** заéло
or закли́нило мото́р/ружьё; **I'm in a real ~**
(inf: difficulty) я (здо́рово) влип; **to get sb out
of a ~** (inf) помога́ть (помо́чь perf) кому́-н
вы́браться из переде́лки; **to ~ sth into sth**
запи́хивать (запихну́ть perf) что-н во что-н;
the telephone lines are ~med все ли́нии
(свя́зи) перегру́жены.
Jamaica [dʒə'meɪkə] n Яма́йка.
Jamaican [dʒə'meɪkən] adj яма́йский* ♦ n
жи́тель(ница) m(f) Яма́йки.
jamb ['dʒæm] n кося́к*.
jamboree [dʒæmbə'ri:] n гуля́нье*.
jam-packed [dʒæm'pækt] adj: ~ **(with)** битко́м
наби́тый (наби́т) (+instr).
jam session n джем-сéйшен.
Jan. abbr = **January**.
jangle ['dʒæŋgl] vi (keys, bracelets etc)
бренча́ть (impf).
janitor ['dʒænɪtə] n (caretaker) вахтёр(ша).
January ['dʒænjuərɪ] n янва́рь m; see also **July**.
Japan [dʒə'pæn] n Япо́ния.
Japanese [dʒæpə'ni:z] adj япо́нский* ♦ n inv
(person) япо́нец*(-нка*); (LING) япо́нский*
язы́к*.
jar [dʒɑ:] n ба́нка* ♦ vi (sound) ре́зать* (impf)
слух; (colours) ре́зать* (impf) глаза́ ♦ vt (fig)
потряса́ть (потрясти́* perf).
jargon ['dʒɑ:gən] n жарго́н.
jarring ['dʒɑ:rɪŋ] adj (sound) ре́жущий у́хо;
(colour) ре́жущий глаз.
Jas. abbr = **James**.
jasmine ['dʒæzmɪn] n жасми́н.
jaundice ['dʒɔ:ndɪs] n желтуха́.
jaundiced ['dʒɔ:ndɪst] adj: **he has a very ~ view
of politics** он смо́трит на поли́тику весьма́
пессимисти́чески.
jaunt [dʒɔ:nt] n вы́лазка*.
jaunty ['dʒɔ:ntɪ] adj (tone, step) бо́йкий*.
Java ['dʒɑ:və] n Я́ва.

---

* marks translations which have irregular inflections. The Russian-English side of the dictionary gives inflectional information.

javelin ['dʒævlɪn] *n* копьё*.
jaw [dʒɔ:] *n* чéлюсть* *f*.
jawbone ['dʒɔ:bəun] *n* челюстнáя кость* *f*.
jay [dʒeɪ] *n* сóйка*.
jaywalker ['dʒeɪwɔ:kə'] *n* недисциплини́рованный пешехóд.
jazz [dʒæz] *n* джаз
▶ **jazz up** (*inf*) ◆ *vt* (*party, image etc*) оживля́ть (ожи́вить* *perf*); (*food*) придавáть* (придáть* *perf*) пикáнтность.
jazz band *n* джáзовый оркéстр, джаз-бáнд.
JCB® *n* (колёсный) экскавáтор.
JCS *n abbr* (*US: = Joint Chiefs of Staff*) Комитéт начáльников штабóв.
JD *n abbr* (*US: = Doctor of Laws*) доктóр правовéдения; (*= Justice Department*) Министéрство юсти́ции.
jealous ['dʒeləs] *adj* ревни́вый (ревни́в); **to be ~ of** (*possessive*) ревновáть (*impf*) к +*dat*; (*envious*) зави́довать (*impf*) +*dat*.
jealously ['dʒeləslɪ] *adv* (*enviously*) ревни́во; (*watchfully*) рéвностно.
jealousy ['dʒeləsɪ] *n* (*resentment*) рéвность *f*; (*envy*) зáвисть *f*.
jeans [dʒi:nz] *npl* джи́нсы *pl*.
jeep [dʒi:p] *n* джип.
jeer [dʒɪə'] *vi*: **to ~ (at)** (*mock, scoff*) насмехáться (*impf*) (над +*instr*), высмéивать (вы́смеять *perf*).
jeering ['dʒɪərɪŋ] *adj* насмéшливый ◆ *n* насмéшки* *fpl*.
jeers ['dʒɪəz] *npl* улюлю́канье *ntsg*.
jelly ['dʒelɪ] *n* желé *nt ind*; (*US*) джем.
jellyfish ['dʒelɪfɪʃ] *n* медýза.
jeopardize ['dʒepədaɪz] *vt* подвергáть (подвéргнуть* *perf*) опáсности, стáвить* (постáвить* *perf*) под угрóзу.
jeopardy ['dʒepədɪ] *n*: **to be in ~** быть* (*impf*) в опáсности.
jerk [dʒə:k] *n* (*jolt*) толчóк*, рывóк*; (*inf: idiot*) болвáн ◆ *vt* дёргать (дёрнуть *perf*), рванýть (*perf*) ◆ *vi* дёргаться (дёрнуться *perf*); **the car ~ed to a halt** маши́на рéзко затормози́ла.
jerkin ['dʒə:kɪn] *n* безрукáвка.
jerky ['dʒə:kɪ] *adj* судорожный (судорожен).
jerry-built ['dʒerɪbɪlt] *adj* пострóенный (пострóен) кóе-как *or* на скóрую рýку.
jerry can ['dʒerɪ-] *n* кани́стра.
Jersey ['dʒə:zɪ] *n* Джéрси *nt ind*.
jersey ['dʒə:zɪ] *n* (*pullover*) сви́тер; (*fabric*) джéрси *nt ind*.
Jerusalem [dʒə'ru:sləm] *n* Иерусали́м.
jest [dʒest] *n* шýтка.
jester ['dʒestə'] *n* (*HISTORY*) шут*.
Jesus ['dʒi:zəs] *n* (*REL*) Иисýс; **~ Christ** Иисýс Христóс.
jet [dʒet] *n* (*of gas, liquid*) струя́*; (*AVIAT*) реакти́вный самолёт*; (*MINERALOGY*) гагáт.
jet-black ['dʒet'blæk] *adj* (*hair*) чёрный как смоль; (*eyes*) агáтовый.
jet engine *n* реакти́вный дви́гатель *m*.

jet lag *n* наруше́ние сýточного режи́ма органи́зма пóсле дли́тельного полёта.
jet-propelled ['dʒetprəpeld] *adj* реакти́вный.
jetsam ['dʒetsəm] *n* плавни́к.
jet-setter ['dʒetsetə'] *n* человéк, разъезжáющий по свéту.
jettison ['dʒetɪsn] *vt* выбрáсывать (вы́бросить* *perf*) за борт.
jetty ['dʒetɪ] *n* причáл.
Jew [dʒu:] *n* еврéй(ка*).
jewel ['dʒu:əl] *n* (*also fig*) драгоцéнный кáмень* *m*; (*in watch*) кáмень.
jeweller ['dʒu:ələ'] (*US* **jeweler**) *n* ювели́р.
jeweller's (shop) *n* ювели́рный магази́н.
jewellery ['dʒu:əlrɪ] (*US* **jewelry**) *n* драгоцéнности *fpl*.
Jewess ['dʒu:ɪs] *n* еврéйка, жидóвка (*пренебр*).
Jewish ['dʒu:ɪʃ] *adj* еврéйский*.
JFK *n abbr* (*US*) = *John Fitzgerald Kennedy International Airport*.
jib [dʒɪb] *n* (*NAUT*) кли́вер*; (*of crane*) стрелá* ◆ *vi* (*horse*) упирáться (упере́ться* *perf*), артáчиться (*impf*); **to ~ at doing** наотрéз отказáться (*perf*) +*infin*.
jibe [dʒaɪb] *n* = **gibe**.
jiffy ['dʒɪfɪ] *n* (*inf*): **in a ~** ми́гом.
jig [dʒɪg] *n* джи́га.
jigsaw ['dʒɪgsɔ:] *n* (*also:* **~ puzzle**) головолóмка (*в ви́де карти́ны, кусóчки котóрой нýжно сложи́ть вмéсте*); (*tool*) ажýрная пилá*.
jilt [dʒɪlt] *vt* (*person*) бросáть (брóсить* *perf*).
jingle ['dʒɪŋgl] *n* (*for advert*) корóткая незамыслóватая мелóдия в реклáме ◆ *vi* звенéть (*impf*).
jingoism ['dʒɪŋgəuɪzəm] *n* ура-патриоти́зм.
jinx [dʒɪŋks] *n* (*inf*): **he is a ~** у негó дурнóй глаз.
jitters ['dʒɪtəz] *npl* (*inf*): **she's got the ~** её трясёт.
jittery ['dʒɪtərɪ] *adj* (*inf*) нéрвный (нéрвен).
jiujitsu [dʒu:'dʒɪtsu:] *n* джи́у-джи́тсу *nt ind*.
job [dʒɔb] *n* (*employment*) рабóта; (*task*) дéло*; (*inf: difficulty*): **I had a ~ getting here!** я с трудóм добрáлся сюдá!; **it's not my ~** это не моё дéло; **a part-time/full-time ~** рабóта на почасовóй/пóлной стáвке; **he's only doing his ~** он всегó-нáвсего выполня́ет свои́ обя́занности; **it's a good ~ that ...** хорошó ещё, что ...; **just the ~!** сáмое то!
jobber ['dʒɔbə'] *n* (*BRIT*) джóббер.
jobbing ['dʒɔbɪŋ] *adj* (*BRIT*): **~ workman** шабáшник.
Jobcentre ['dʒɔbsentə'] *n* (*BRIT*) бюрó *nt ind* по трудоустрóйству.
job creation scheme *n* прогрáмма заня́тости.
job description *n* описáние служéбных обя́занностей.
jobless ['dʒɔblɪs] *adj* безрабóтный*; **the ~** *npl* безрабóтные *pl adj*.

job lot *n* па́ртия деше́вых това́ров, продаю́щихся о́птом.
job satisfaction *n* удовлетворённость *f* рабо́той.
job security *n* гара́нтия рабо́ты.
job sharing *n* ситуа́ция, когда́ два челове́ка де́лят рабо́чее ме́сто.
job specification *n* пе́речень *m* служе́бных обя́занностей.
jock [dʒɔk] *n* (*US: inf*) спортсме́н.
jockey ['dʒɔkɪ] *n* жоке́й ♦ *vi*: **to ~ for position** сопе́рничать (*impf*).
jockey box *n* (*US: AUT*) перча́точный я́щик, бардачо́к (*разг*).
jocular ['dʒɔkjuləʳ] *adj* (*person*) весёлый* (ве́сел); (*remark*) шутли́вый (шутли́в).
jog [dʒɔg] *vt* толка́ть (толкну́ть *perf*) ♦ *vi* бе́гать (*impf*) трусцо́й; **to ~ sb's memory** подстёгивать (подстегну́ть *perf*) чью-н па́мять
▶ **jog along** *vi* ме́дленно продвига́ться (*impf*).
jogger ['dʒɔgəʳ] *n* бегу́н* (*трусцо́й*).
jogging ['dʒɔgɪŋ] *n* бег трусцо́й.
Johannesburg [dʒəu'hænɪsbə:g] *n* Йоха́ннесбург.
john [dʒɔn] *n* (*inf: US*) туале́т.
join [dʒɔɪn] *vt* (*queue*) вставля́ть* (встать* *perf*) в +*acc*; (*organization*) вступа́ть (вступи́ть* *perf*) в +*acc*; (*put together: things, places*) соединя́ть (соедини́ть *perf*); (*meet: group of people*) присоединя́ться (присоедини́ться *perf*) к +*dat* ♦ *vi* (*rivers*) слива́ться (сли́ться* *perf*); (*roads*) сходи́ться (сойти́сь* *perf*) ♦ *n* сочлене́ние; **to ~ forces (with)** (*fig*) объединя́ть (объедини́ть *perf*) уси́лия (с +*instr*); **will you ~ us for dinner?** не хоти́те с на́ми поу́жинать?; **I'll ~ you later** я присоединю́сь к Вам по́зже
▶ **join in** *vi* присоединя́ться (присоедини́ться *perf*) ♦ *vt fus* (*work, discussion etc*) принима́ть (приня́ть* *perf*) уча́стие в +*prp*
▶ **join up** *vi* (*meet*) соединя́ться (соедини́ться *perf*); (*MIL*) поступа́ть (поступи́ть* *perf*) на вое́нную слу́жбу.
joiner ['dʒɔɪnəʳ] *n* (*BRIT*) столя́р*.
joinery ['dʒɔɪnərɪ] *n* (*BRIT*) столя́рное ремесло́*.
joint [dʒɔɪnt] *n* (*TECH*) сочлене́ние, стык; (*ANAT*) суста́в; (*BRIT: CULIN*) кусо́к* (*мя́са*); (*inf: place*) прито́н; (: *of cannabis*) скру́тка с марихуа́ной ♦ *adj* совме́стный.
joint account *n* совме́стный счёт (*в ба́нке*).
jointly ['dʒɔɪntlɪ] *adv* совме́стно.
joint owners *npl* совладе́льцы *mpl*.
joint ownership *n* совме́стное владе́ние.
joint-stock bank ['dʒɔɪntstɔk-] *n* акционе́рный банк.
joint-stock company *n* акционе́рная компа́ния.

joint venture *n* совме́стное предприя́тие.
joist [dʒɔɪst] *n* ба́лка*.
joke [dʒəuk] *n* (*gag*) шу́тка*, анекдо́т; (*also*: **practical ~**) ро́зыгрыш ♦ *vi* шути́ть* (пошути́ть* *perf*); **to play a ~ on** шути́ть* (пошути́ть* *perf*) над +*instr*, сыгра́ть (*perf*) шу́тку с +*instr*.
joker ['dʒəukəʳ] *n* (*person*) шу́тник; (*CARDS*) джо́кер.
joking ['dʒəukɪŋ] *adj* (*remark*) шу́точный.
jokingly ['dʒəukɪŋlɪ] *adv* в шу́тку.
jollity ['dʒɔlɪtɪ] *n* жизнера́достность *f*.
jolly ['dʒɔlɪ] *adj* (*merry*) весёлый* (ве́сел) ♦ *adv* (*BRIT: inf*) о́чень ♦ *vt* (*BRIT*): **to ~ sb along** ободря́ть (*impf*) кого́-н; **~ good!** о́чень хорошо́!, здо́рово!
jolt [dʒəult] *n* (*jerk*) толчо́к*; (*shock*) потрясе́ние ♦ *vt* (*physically*) тряхну́ть *or* встря́хивать (встряхну́ть *perf*); (*emotionally*) потряса́ть (потрясти́* *perf*).
Jordan [dʒɔ:dən] *n* (*country*) Иорда́ния; (*river*) Иорда́н.
Jordanian [dʒɔ:'deɪmɪən] *adj* иорда́нский* ♦ *n* иорда́нец*(-нка*).
joss stick ['dʒɔs-] *n* 735 аромати́ческая па́лочка*.
jostle ['dʒɔsl] *vt* (*subj: passers-by etc*) толка́ть (толкну́ть *perf*), раста́лкивать (растолка́ть *perf*) ♦ *vi* толка́ться (*impf*).
jot [dʒɔt] *n*: **not one ~** ни ка́пли, ниско́лько
▶ **jot down** *vt* помеча́ть (поме́тить* *perf*).
jotter ['dʒɔtəʳ] *n* (*BRIT*) блокно́т.
journal ['dʒə:nl] *n* (*periodical*) журна́л; (*diary*) дне́вник*.
journalese [dʒə:nə'li:z] *n* (*pej*) газе́тный штамп.
journalism ['dʒə:nəlɪzəm] *n* журнали́стика.
journalist ['dʒə:nəlɪst] *n* журнали́ст(ка*).
journey ['dʒə:nɪ] *n* (*trip, route*) пое́здка*; (*distance covered*) путь* *m*, доро́га ♦ *vi* путеше́ствовать (*impf*); **a five-hour ~** пятичасова́я пое́здка; **return ~** обра́тный путь*, обра́тная доро́га.
jovial ['dʒəuvɪəl] *adj* бо́дрый, жизнера́достный.
jowl [dʒaul] *n* че́люсть* *f*.
joy [dʒɔɪ] *n* ра́дость *f*.
joyful ['dʒɔɪful] *adj* ра́достный* (ра́достен).
joyride ['dʒɔɪraɪd] *n* ката́ние на укра́денной маши́не.
joyrider ['dʒɔɪraɪdəʳ] *n* челове́к, кото́рый угоня́ет маши́ны и ката́ется на них.
joyriding ['dʒɔɪraɪdɪŋ] *n* езда́ (*обы́чно на у́гнанном автомоби́ле*).
joystick ['dʒɔɪstɪk] *n* (*AVIAT*) рыча́г* управле́ния; (*COMPUT*) джо́йстик.
JP *n abbr* = **Justice of the Peace**.
Jr. *abbr* (*in names*) = **junior**.
JTPA *n abbr* (*US*) = **Job Training Partnership Act**.

---

* marks translations which have irregular inflections. The Russian-English side of the dictionary gives inflectional information.

jubilant ['dʒu:bɪlnt] *adj* лику́ющий.
jubilation [dʒu:bɪ'leɪʃən] *n* ликова́ние.
jubilee ['dʒu:bɪli:] *n* (*anniversary*) юбиле́й;
silver/golden ~ 25-ле́тний/50-ле́тний
юбиле́й.
judge [dʒʌdʒ] *n* судья́* *m* ♦ *vt* (*LAW*) выноси́ть*
(вы́нести* *perf*) пригово́р; (*competition,*
person etc) суди́ть* (*impf*); (*consider, estimate*)
оце́нивать (оцени́ть* *perf*) ♦ *vi*: **judging** *or* **to ~**
by his expression су́дя по его́ выраже́нию;
she's a good ~ of character она́ хорошо́
разбира́ется в лю́дях; **I'll be the ~ of that** ну
э́то уж мне суди́ть; **I ~d it necessary to inform**
him я посчита́л ну́жным сообщи́ть ему́ об
э́том; **as far as I can ~** наско́лько я могу́
суди́ть.
judge advocate *n* (*MIL*) вое́нный прокуро́р.
judg(e)ment ['dʒʌdʒmənt] *n* (*LAW*) пригово́р,
реше́ние суда́; (*view*) сужде́ние;
(*discernment*) рассуди́тельность *f*; **in my ~**
по моему́ мне́нию; **to pass ~ (on)** (*LAW*)
выноси́ть* (вы́нести* *perf*) реше́ние (на +*acc*);
(*fig*) суди́ть* (*impf*).
judicial [dʒu:'dɪʃl] *adj* (*LAW*) суде́бный; (*fig*)
рассуди́тельный* (рассуди́телен); **~ review**
суде́бное разбира́тельство.
judiciary [dʒu:'dɪʃɪərɪ] *n*: **the ~** суде́бные
о́рганы *mpl*.
judicious [dʒu:'dɪʃəs] *adj* благоразу́мный*
(благоразу́мен).
judo ['dʒu:dəu] *n* дзюдо́ *nt ind*.
jug [dʒʌg] *n* кувши́н.
jugged hare ['dʒʌgd-] *n* (*BRIT*) ≈ жарко́е *nt adj*
из за́йца.
juggernaut ['dʒʌgənɔ:t] *n* (*BRIT*) многото́нный
грузови́к*.
juggle ['dʒʌgl] *vi* (*also fig*) жонгли́ровать (*impf*)
♦ *vt* (*fig*) жонгли́ровать (*impf*) +*instr*; **to ~ with**
sth жонгли́ровать (*impf*) чем-н.
juggler ['dʒʌglə'] *n* жонглёр.
Jugoslav *etc* ['ju:gəu'slɑ:v] = **Yugoslav** *etc*.
jugular ['dʒʌgjulə'] *n* (*also:* **~ vein**) яре́мная
ве́на.
juice [dʒu:s] *n* сок*; (*inf: petrol*) бензи́н.
juicy ['dʒu:sɪ] *adj* со́чный* (со́чен).
jukebox ['dʒu:kbɔks] *n* музыка́льный
автома́т.
Jul. *abbr* = **July**.
July [dʒu:'laɪ] *n* ию́ль *m*; **the first of ~** пе́рвое
ию́ля; **on the eleventh of ~** оди́ннадцатого
ию́ля; **in the month of ~** в ию́ле ме́сяце; **at**
the beginning/end of ~ в нача́ле/конце́ ию́ля;
in the middle of ~ в середи́не ию́ля; **during ~**
в тече́ние ию́ля; **in ~** в ию́ле; **in ~ of next year**
в ию́ле сле́дующего го́да; **each** *or* **every ~**
ка́ждый ию́ль; **~ was wet this year** в э́том
году́ ию́ль был дождли́вым.
jumble ['dʒʌmbl] *n* нагроможде́ние; (*BRIT:*
items for sale) старьё ♦ *vt* (*also:* **~ up**)
переме́шивать (перемеша́ть *perf*).
jumble sale *n* (*BRIT*) *благотвори́тельная*

распрода́жа поде́ржанных веще́й.
jumbo ['dʒʌmbəu] *n* (*also:* **~ jet**) реакти́вный
аэро́бус.
jumbo-size ['dʒʌmbəusaɪz] *adj* гига́нтский*.
jump [dʒʌmp] *vi* пры́гать (пры́гнуть *perf*);
(*start*) подпры́гивать (подпры́гнуть *perf*);
(*increase*) подска́кивать (подскочи́ть* *perf*) ♦
vt (*fence*) перепры́гивать (перепры́гнуть
perf), переска́кивать (перескочи́ть* *perf*) ♦ *n*
прыжо́к*; (*increase*) скачо́к*; **to ~ the queue**
(*BRIT*) идти́* (пойти́* *perf*) без о́череди
▸ **jump about** *vi* суети́ться* (*impf*)
▸ **jump at** *vt fus* (*seize*) ухва́тываться
(ухвати́ться *perf*) за +*acc*
▸ **jump down** *vi* спры́гивать (спры́гнуть *perf*)
▸ **jump up** *vi* (*from a seat*) вска́кивать
(вскочи́ть* *perf*); (*into the air*) подпры́гивать
(подпры́гнуть *perf*).
jumped-up ['dʒʌmptʌp] *adj* (*BRIT: pej*): **~ office**
boy вы́скочка *m*.
jumper ['dʒʌmpə'] *n* (*BRIT: pullover*) сви́тер,
джемпер; (*US: dress*) сарафа́н; (*SPORT*)
прыгу́н*(ья*).
jumper cables *npl* (*US*) = **jump leads**.
jump leads *npl* (*BRIT*) про́вод большо́го
сече́ния (*для пу́ска двига́теля*).
jump-start ['dʒʌmpstɑ:t] *vt*: **to ~ a car**
подта́лкивать (подтолкну́ть *perf*) маши́ну,
что́бы завести́ её.
jump suit *n* комбинезо́н.
jumpy ['dʒʌmpɪ] *adj* не́рвный.
Jun. *abbr* = **June**.
junction ['dʒʌŋkʃən] *n* (*BRIT: of roads*)
пересече́ние; (*RAIL*) у́зел*.
juncture ['dʒʌŋktʃə'] *n*: **at this ~** в да́нный
моме́нт.
June [dʒu:n] *n* ию́нь *m*; *see also* **July**.
jungle ['dʒʌŋgl] *n* (*also fig*) джу́нгли *pl*.
junior ['dʒu:nɪə'] *adj* мла́дший* ♦ *n*
мла́дший*(-ая) *m(f) adj*; **he's ~ to me (by 2**
years), **he's my ~ (by 2 years)** он мла́дше
меня́ (на 2 го́да); **he's ~ to me** (*seniority*) он
мой подчинённый.
junior executive *n* мла́дший* руководя́щий*
рабо́тник.
junior high school *n* (*US*) ≈ непо́лная сре́дняя
шко́ла.
junior minister *n* (*BRIT*) мла́дший* мини́стр.
junior partner *n* мла́дший* партнёр.
junior school *n* (*BRIT*) *шко́ла для дете́й в*
во́зрасте от 7 до 11 лет.
junior sizes *npl* де́тские разме́ры *mpl*.
juniper ['dʒu:nɪpə'] *n*: **~ berry** можжеве́льник.
junk [dʒʌŋk] *n* барахло́, хлам; (*ship*) джо́нка*
♦ *vt* (*inf*) выки́дывать (вы́кинуть *perf*).
junk bond *n* *облига́ции, обеща́ющие высо́кие*
проце́нты, но не даю́щие гара́нтий.
junket ['dʒʌŋkɪt] *n* (*CULIN*) *сла́дкое моло́чное*
блю́до; (*US: inf: pej*): **to go on a ~**
прокати́ться* (*perf*) за казённый счёт.
junk food *n* *еда́, содержа́щая ма́ло*

junkie ['dʒʌŋkɪ] n (*inf*) наркома́н.
junk mail n *незапро́шенная рекла́ма, доставля́емая по по́чте.*
junk room n чула́н.
junk shop n ла́вка* старьёвщика.
Junr *abbr* (*in names*) = **junior**.
junta ['dʒʌntə] n ху́нта.
Jupiter ['dʒu:pɪtə'] n Юпи́тер.
jurisdiction [dʒuərɪs'dɪkʃən] n (*LAW*)
юрисди́кция; (*ADMIN*) сфе́ра полномо́чий; **it is within/outside my** ~ э́то вхо́дит/не вхо́дит в мои́ полномо́чия.
jurisprudence [dʒuərɪs'pru:dəns] n
юриспруде́нция.
juror ['dʒuərə'] n прися́жный заседа́тель m.
jury ['dʒuərɪ] n прися́жные pl adj (заседа́тели).
jury box n ска́мья* прися́жных.
juryman ['dʒuərɪmən] *irreg* n = **juror**.
just [dʒʌst] adj справедли́вый (справедли́в) ♦
adv (*exactly*) как раз, и́менно; (*only*) то́лько;
(*barely*) едва́; **he's** ~ **left/done it** он то́лько
что ушёл/э́то сде́лал; ~ **as I expected** как я и
ожида́л; **it's** ~ **right** э́то как раз то, что на́до;
~ **two o'clock** ро́вно два часа́; **we were** ~
going or **about to go** мы как раз собира́лись
уходи́ть; **I was** ~ **about to phone** я уже́
собра́лся позвони́ть; **she's** ~ **as clever as you**
она́ столь же умна́, как и ты; **it's** ~ **as well**
(that) ... даже́ и хорошо́, (что) ...; ~ **as he was**
leaving как раз когда́ он собра́лся уходи́ть;
~ **before Christmas** пе́ред са́мым
Рождество́м; **there was** ~ **enough petrol** едва́
хвати́ло бензи́на; ~ **here** вот здесь; **he (only)**
~ **missed** он чуть не попа́л; **it's** ~ **me** э́то
(то́лько) я; **it's** ~ **a mistake** э́то про́сто
оши́бка; ~ **listen!** ты то́лько послу́шай!; ~
ask someone the way про́сто спроси́ у кого́-
нибудь доро́гу; **not** ~ **now** то́лько не сейча́с;

~ **a minute!,** ~ **one moment!** подожди́те!,
(одну́) мину́ту!
justice ['dʒʌstɪs] n (*LAW: system*) правосу́дие;
(*rightness*) справедли́вость f; (*US: judge*)
судья́* m; **Lord Chief J**~ (*BRIT*) *второ́й по*
значе́нию судья́ в брита́нской систе́ме
правосу́дия; **to do** ~ **to** (*fig: task, meal, person*)
отдава́ть* (отда́ть* *perf*) до́лжное +dat.
Justice of the Peace n (*BRIT*) мирово́й судья́*
m.
justifiable [dʒʌstɪ'faɪəbl] adj опра́вданный*
(опра́вдан), обосно́ванный (обосно́ван).
justifiably [dʒʌstɪ'faɪəblɪ] adv опра́вданно,
обосно́ванно.
justification [dʒʌstɪfɪ'keɪʃən] n (*of action*)
оправда́ние; (*reason*) основа́ние; (*TYP*)
выра́внивание строки́.
justify ['dʒʌstɪfaɪ] vt опра́вдывать (оправда́ть
perf); (*text*) выра́внивать (вы́ровнять *perf*); **to**
~ **o.s.** опра́вдываться (оправда́ться *perf*); **to**
be justified in doing име́ть (*impf*) все
основа́ния +infin.
justly ['dʒʌstlɪ] adv справедли́во.
jut [dʒʌt] vi (*also:* ~ **out**) выступа́ть (*impf*).
jute [dʒu:t] n джут.
juvenile ['dʒu:vənaɪl] n (*LAW, ADMIN*)
подро́сток*, несовершенноле́тний*(-яя) m(f)
adj ♦ adj (*humour, mentality*) де́тский*.
juvenile court n суд для несовершенно-
ле́тних.
juvenile delinquency n престу́пность f среди́
несовершенноле́тних.
juvenile delinquent n несовершенно-
ле́тний(-яя) правонаруши́тель(-ница) m(f).
juxtapose [dʒʌkstəpəuz] vt сопоставля́ть
(сопоста́вить* *perf*).
juxtaposition ['dʒʌkstəpə'zɪʃən] n
сопоставле́ние.

---

* marks translations which have irregular inflections. The Russian-English side of the dictionary gives inflectional information.

~ K, k ~

K, k [keɪ] *n* (*letter*) 11-ая бу́ква англи́йского алфави́та.

K *abbr* = *one thousand*; (*COMPUT*) (= **kilobyte**) К= килоба́йт; (*BRIT: in titles*) = **knight.**

Kabul [ˈkɑːbul] *n* Кабу́л.

kaftan [ˈkæftæn] *n* кафта́н.

Kalahari Desert [kæləˈhɑːrɪ-] *n*: **the ~ ~** пусты́ня Калаха́ри.

kale [keɪl] *n* капу́ста кормова́я.

kaleidoscope [kəˈlaɪdəskəup] *n* калейдоско́п.

kamikaze [kæmɪˈkɑːzɪ] *n* камика́дзе *m ind*, лётчик-сме́ртник.

Kampala [kæmˈpɑːlə] *n* Кампа́ла.

Kampuchea [kæmpuˈtʃɪə] *n* Кампучи́я.

Kampuchean [kæmpuˈtʃɪən] *adj* кампучи́йский*.

kangaroo [kæŋgəˈruː] *n* кенгуру́ *m ind*.

kaput [kəˈput] (*inf*) *adj*: **the TV is ~!** телеви́зору капу́т!

karaoke [kɑːrəˈəukɪ] *n* карио́ки *ind* (*самоде́ятельное пе́ние под за́пись профессиона́льного анса́мбла*).

karate [kəˈrɑːtɪ] *n* карате́ *nt ind*.

Kashmir [kæʃˈmɪəʳ] *n* Кашми́р.

kayak [ˈkaɪæk] *n* кая́к*.

Kazakh [ˈkæzæk] *n* (*person*) каза́х(-а́шка*); (*LING*) каза́хский* язы́к* ♦ *adj* каза́хский*.

Kazakhstan [kæzækˈstɑːn] *n* Казахста́н.

KC *n abbr* (*BRIT: LAW*: = *King's Counsel*) короле́вский* адвока́т (*адвока́тский ранг*).

kd *abbr* (*US: COMM*: = *knocked down*) в разо́бранном ви́де.

kebab [kəˈbæb] *n* шашлы́к*.

keel [kiːl] *n* киль *m*; **on an even ~** (*fig*) в состоя́нии стаби́льности

▸ **keel over** *vi* опроки́дываться (опроки́нуться *perf*).

keen [kiːn] *adj* о́стрый; (*eager*) стра́стный* (стра́стен), увлечённый; **to be ~ to do** *or* **on doing** о́чень хоте́ть* (*impf*) +*infin*; **to be ~ on sth** увлека́ться (*impf*) чем-н; **he is ~ on her** увлечён е́ю; **I'm not ~ on going** мне не о́чень хо́чется идти́; **~ competition** напряжённая конкуре́нтая борьба́.

keenly [ˈkiːnlɪ] *adv* (*enthusiastically*) увлечённо; (*intently*) при́стально; **to feel sth ~** глубоко́ пережива́ть (*impf*) что-н.

keenness [ˈkiːnnɪs] *n* (*eagerness*) увлечённость *f*; **~ to do** стремле́ние +*infin*.

keep [kiːp] (*pt, pp* **kept**) *vt* (*receipt, money*) оставля́ть (оста́вить* *perf*) себе́; (*store*) храни́ть (*impf*); (*preserve*) сохраня́ть (сохрани́ть* *perf*); (*house, garden, shop, family*) содержа́ть (*impf*); (*prisoner, chickens, bees*) держа́ть* (*impf*); (*accounts, diary*) вести́* (*impf*); (*promise*) сде́рживать (сдержа́ть* *perf*) ♦ *vi* (*in a certain state or place*) остава́ться* (оста́ться* *perf*); (*food*) сохраня́ться (*impf*); (*continue*): **to ~ doing** продолжа́ть (*impf*) +*impf infin* ♦ *n* (*of castle*) центра́льная ба́шня*; (*food etc*): **he has enough for his ~** ему́ доста́точно на прожи́тие; **he kept the job** он сохрани́л э́ту рабо́ту; **where do you ~ the salt?** где у Вас соль?; **he tries to ~ her happy** он де́лает всё для того́, что́бы она́ была́ дово́льна; **to ~ the house tidy** содержа́ть* (*impf*) дом в поря́дке; **to ~ sb waiting** заставля́ть (заста́вить* *perf*) кого́-н ждать; **to ~ sb from doing** не дава́ть* (дать* *perf*) кому́-н +*infin*; **to ~ an appointment** прийти́* (*perf*) в назна́ченное вре́мя; **to ~ a record** вести́* (*impf*) учёт; **to ~ sth to o.s.** держа́ть (*impf*) что-н при себе́; **to ~ sth (back) from sb** скрыва́ть (скрыть* *perf*) что-н от кого́-н; **to ~ sth from happening** не дава́ть* (дать* *perf*) чему́-н случи́ться; **to ~ time** (*clock*) идти́* (*impf*) то́чно

▸ **keep away** *vi*: **to ~ sth/sb away from sb/sth** держа́ть (*impf*) что-н/кого́-н пода́льше от кого́-н/чего́-н ♦ *vi*: **to ~ away (from)** держа́ться* (*impf*) пода́льше (от +*gen*)

▸ **keep back** *vt* (*crowds, tears*) сде́рживать (сдержа́ть* *perf*); (*money*) уде́рживать (удержа́ть* *perf*) ♦ *vi* держа́ться* (*impf*) на расстоя́нии

▸ **keep down** *vt* (*prices, spending*) сде́рживать (сдержа́ть* *perf*); (*retain*): **she can't ~ her food down** что бы она́ ни съе́ла, её всё вре́мя рвёт ♦ *vi*: **~ down!** ложи́сь!

▸ **keep in** *vt* (*person*) держа́ть (*impf*) до́ма ♦ *vi* (*inf*): **to ~ in with sb** подде́рживать (*impf*) хоро́шие отноше́ния с кем-н

▸ **keep off** *vt* (*hold back*) не подпуска́ть (подпусти́ть* *perf*); (*abstain*) избега́ть (*impf*) +*gen* +*infin*; **to ~ off sth** избега́ть (*impf*); "**keep off the grass**" „по газо́нам не ходи́ть"; **~ your hands off** рука́ми не тро́гать

▸ **keep on** *vi*: **to ~ on doing** продолжа́ть (*impf*)

+*impf infin*; **to ~ on (about sth)** не переставáя
говорúть *(impf)* (о чём-н)
▶ **keep out** *vt* не впускáть (впустúть* *perf)*;
"**keep out**" „посторóнним вход воспрещён"
▶ **keep up** *vt (payments, standards)*
поддéрживать *(impf)* ◆ *vi*: **to ~ up (with)** *(pace)*
поспевáть (поспéть *perf)* (за +*instr)*; *(level)*
идтú* *(impf)* в нóгу (с +*instr)*.
keeper ['ki:pə'] *n (of zoo, park)* смотрúтель
(ница) *m(f)*.
keep fit *n* аэрóбика.
keeping ['ki:pɪŋ] *n (care)* присмóтр; **I'll leave
this in your ~** оставля́ю э́то под Вáшим
присмóтром; **in ~ with** в соотвéтствии с
+*instr*; **out of ~ with** несовместúмый
(несовместúм) с +*instr*.
keeps [ki:ps] *n*: **for ~** *(inf)* на совсéм.
keepsake ['ki:pseɪk] *n* пáмятный подáрок.
keg [kɛg] *n* бочóнок*; **~ beer** бочковóе пúво.
kennel ['kɛnl] *n* конурá*.
kennels ['kɛnlz] *npl* гостúница *fsg or* плáтный
прию́т *msg* для собáк.
Kenya ['kɛnjə] *n* Кéния.
Kenyan ['kɛnjən] *adj* кенúйский* ◆ *n*
кенúец*(-úйка*).
kept [kɛpt] *pt, pp of* **keep.**
kerb [kə:b] *n (BRIT)* бордю́р.
kerb crawler [-'krɔ:lə'] *n шофёр, выбирáющий
себé проститу́ток из окнá мéдленно
ползу́щего автомобúля.*
kernel ['kə:nl] *n (of nut)* ядрó*; *(of idea)* суть *f*.
kerosene ['kɛrəsi:n] *n* кероси́н.
kestrel ['kɛstrəl] *n* пустельгá*.
ketchup ['kɛtʃəp] *n* кéтчуп.
kettle ['kɛtl] *n* чáйник.
kettledrum ['kɛtldrʌm] *n* литáвра.
key [ki:] *n* ключ*; *(MUS)* тонáльность *f*; *(of
piano, computer)* клáвиш(а) ◆ *cpd (issue etc)*
ключевóй ◆ *vt (also: ~ in)* набирáть
(набрáть* *perf)* на клавиату́ре.
keyboard ['ki:bɔ:d] *n* клавиату́ра.
keyboarder ['ki:bɔ:də'] *n* машинúст(ка),
опе́ратор клавиату́ры.
keyed up [ki:d'] *adj*: **he was all ~ ~** он был
óчень взвúнчен.
keyhole ['ki:həul] *n* замóчная сквáжина.
keyhole surgery *n полостнáя опера́ция,
осуществля́емая через минимáльный
разрéз.*
keynote ['ki:nəut] *n (MUS)* тóника; *(of speech)*
лейтмотúв.
keypad ['ki:pæd] *n (COMPUT)* (мáлая)
клавиату́ра, клáвишная панéль *f*.
keyring ['ki:rɪŋ] *n* брелóк*.
keystroke ['ki:strəuk] *n (COMPUT)* нажáтие
клáвиши.
kg *abbr (=* **kilogram(me))** кг= *килогрáмм*.
KGB *n abbr (POL: formerly)* КГБ.

khaki ['kɑ:kɪ] *n, adj* хáки *nt, adj ind.*
kHz *abbr (= kilohertz)* кГц= *килогéрц*.
kibbutz ['kɪ'buts] *n* киббу́ц.
kick [kɪk] *vt (person, table)* ударя́ть (удáрить
perf) ногóй; *(ball)* ударя́ть (удáрить *perf)*
ногóй по +*dat*; *(inf: habit, addiction)* поборóть
(perf) ◆ *vi (horse)* ляга́ться *(impf)* ◆ *n* удáр; *(of
rifle)* отдáча; *(thrill: inf)*: **he does it for ~s** он
дéлает э́то, чтóбы пощекотáть себé нéрвы
▶ **kick around** *vi (inf)* валя́ться *(impf)*
▶ **kick off** *vi*: **the match ~s off at 3pm** матч
начинáется в 3 часá *(в футбóле)*.
kickoff ['kɪkɔf] *n* начáло (футбóльного)
мáтча.
kick-start ['kɪksta:t] *n (also: ~er: BRIT)* ножнóй
стартёр.
kid [kɪd] *n (inf: child)* ребёнок*; *(goat)*
козлёнок*; *(leather)* лáйка ◆ *vt (inf)* водúть*
(impf) за нос, дура́чить *(impf)*; **~ brother**
млáдший* брáтишка* *m*; **~ sister** млáдшая
сестрёнка*; **you're ~ding!** ты шу́тишь!
kid gloves *n*: **to handle sb with ~ ~** бéрежно
обраща́ться *(impf)* с кем-н.
kidnap ['kɪdnæp] *vt* похища́ть (похúтить* *perf)*.
kidnapper ['kɪdnæpə'] *n* похитúтель(ница)
m(f).
kidnapping ['kɪdnæpɪŋ] *n* похищéние.
kidney ['kɪdnɪ] *n (MED)* пóчка*; *(CULIN)* пóчки
fpl.
kidney bean *n* крáсная фасóль *f no pl*.
kidney machine *n* искýсственная пóчка*.
Kiev ['ki:ɛf] *n* Кúев.
Kilimanjaro [kɪlɪmən'dʒa:rəu] *n*: **Mount ~**
Килиманджáро *nt ind.*
kill [kɪl] *vt* убивáть (убúть* *perf)*; *(proposal)*
губúть (загубúть *perf)*; *(rumour)* пресекáть
(пресéчь* *perf)* ◆ *n (prey)* добы́ча; **to ~ time**
(inf) убивáть (убúть* *perf)* врéмя; **to ~ o.s.**
покóнчить *(perf)* с собóй; **to be ~ed** *(in war,
accident)* погибáть (погúбнуть* *perf)*; **to ~
o.s. to do** *(fig)* надрывáться *(impf)*, чтóбы
+*perf infin*; **to ~ o.s. (laughing)** помирáть *(impf)*
(сó смеху)
▶ **kill off** *vt (also fig)* уничтожáть (уничтóжить
perf).
killer ['kɪlə'] *n* убúйца *m/f*.
killer instinct *n* смертéльная *or* мёртвая
хвáтка.
killing ['kɪlɪŋ] *n* убúйство; *(profit)*: **to make a ~**
(inf) срывáть (сорвáть* *perf)* куш.
killjoy ['kɪldʒɔɪ] *n*: **don't be such a ~!** не
отравля́й другúм удовóльствие!
kiln [kɪln] *n* печь* *f (для обжúга)*.
kilo ['ki:ləu] *n* килó *nt ind.*
kilobyte ['ki:ləubaɪt] *n* килобáйт.
kilogram(me) ['kɪləugræm] *n* килогрáмм.
kilohertz ['kɪləuhə:ts] *n inv* килогéрц.
kilometre ['kɪləmi:tə'] *(US* **kilometer)** *n*

---

* marks translations which have irregular inflections. The Russian-English side of the dictionary gives inflectional information.

километр.
kilowatt ['kɪləuwɔt] *n* киловатт.
kilt [kɪlt] *n* шотландская юбка*.
kilter ['kɪltə*] *n*: out of ~ в беспорядке.
kimono [kɪ'məunəu] *n* кимоно *nt ind*.
kin [kɪn] *n see* kith, next.
kind [kaɪnd] *adj* добрый* (добр) ♦ *n* род*; would you be ~ enough *or* so ~ as to ...? не будете ли Вы так добры́ *or* любезны +*perf infin* ...?; it's very ~ of you to help me о́чень любезно с Вашей стороны́, что Вы мне помогли́; he seemed ~ of unhappy он был вро́де бы недово́лен; in ~ (*COMM*) товарами и услугами; a ~ of род +*gen*; two of a ~ две ве́щи одного́ ти́па; what ~ of person is he? что он за челове́к?; she has a strange ~ of smile у неё стра́нная улы́бка.
kindergarten ['kɪndəgɑːtn] *n* де́тский сад*.
kind-hearted [kaɪnd'hɑːtɪd] *adj* до́брый* (добр), добросерде́чный* (добросерде́чен).
kindle ['kɪndl] *vt* (*also fig*) разжига́ть (разже́чь* *perf*).
kindling ['kɪndlɪŋ] *n* ще́пки* *fpl*, расто́пка.
kindly ['kaɪndlɪ] *adj* (*smile*) до́брый* (добр); (*person, tone*) доброжела́тельный* (доброжела́телен) ♦ *adv* (*smile, behave*) любе́зно, доброжела́тельно; will you ~ ... бу́дьте добры́ ...; he didn't take it ~ он был далеко́ не рад э́тому.
kindness ['kaɪndnɪs] *n* (*quality*) доброта́; (*act*) любе́зность *f*.
kindred ['kɪndrɪd] *adj*: ~ spirit ро́дственная душа́*.
kinetic [kɪ'netɪk] *adj* кинети́ческий*.
king [kɪŋ] *n* коро́ль* *m*.
kingdom ['kɪŋdəm] *n* короле́вство; the animal/ plant ~ живо́тное/расти́тельное ца́рство.
kingfisher ['kɪŋfɪʃə*] *n* зиморо́док*.
kingpin ['kɪŋpɪn] *n* (*TECH*) шкво́рень* *m*; (*fig*) ва́жная ши́шка*.
king-size(d) ['kɪŋsaɪz(d)] *adj* са́мого большо́го разме́ра.
kink [kɪŋk] *n* (*in rope*) у́зел; (*in hair*) завито́к*; (*in character*) причу́да, стра́нность *f*.
kinky ['kɪŋkɪ] *adj* (*inf*) поро́чный* (поро́чен).
kinship ['kɪnʃɪp] *n* родство́.
kinsman ['kɪnzmən] *irreg n* ро́дич.
kinswoman ['kɪnzwumən] *irreg n* кро́вная ро́дственница.
kiosk ['kiːɔsk] *n* кио́ск*; (*BRIT*: *TEL*) телефо́нная бу́дка*; (*also*: newspaper ~) газе́тный кио́ск.
kipper ['kɪpə*] *n* ≈ копчёная селёдка*.
Kirghiz ['kəːgɪz] *n* (*person*) кирги́з(ка*); (*LING*) кирги́зский* язы́к* ♦ *adj* кирги́зский*.
Kirghizia [kəː'gɪzɪə] *n* Кирги́зия.
Kishinev [kiʃi'njɔf] *n* Кишинёв.
kiss [kɪs] *n* поцелу́й ♦ *vt* целова́ть (поцелова́ть *perf*) ♦ *vi* целова́ться (поцелова́ться *perf*); to ~ sb goodbye целова́ть (поцелова́ть *perf*) кого́-н на проща́ние.
kissagram ['kɪsəgr[+e]m] *n* сюрпри́зная

доста́вка поздравле́ний, сопровожда́ющаяся поцелу́ем доста́вщика и́ли доста́вщицы.
kiss of life *n* (*BRIT*): the ~ ~ ~ иску́сственное дыха́ние.
kit [kɪt] *n* (*also*: sports ~) костю́м; (*equipment*) снаряже́ние; (*set of tools*) набо́р; (*for assembly*) компле́кт.
► **kit out** *vt* (*BRIT*) снаряжа́ть (снаряди́ть* *perf*).
kitbag ['kɪtbæg] *n* вещмешо́к* = вещево́й мешо́к.
kitchen ['kɪtʃɪn] *n* ку́хня*.
kitchen garden *n* огоро́д.
kitchen sink *n* (ку́хонная) мо́йка* *or* ра́ковина.
kitchen unit *n* (*BRIT*) ку́хонный шкаф.
kitchenware ['kɪtʃɪnwɛə*] *n* ку́хонные принадле́жности *fpl*, (ку́хонная) у́тварь *f*.
kite [kaɪt] *n* (*toy*) возду́шный змей*; (*ZOOL*) ко́ршун.
kith [kɪθ] *n*: ~ and kin родны́е *pl adj* и бли́зкие *pl adj*.
kitten ['kɪtn] *n* котёнок*.
kitty ['kɪtɪ] *n* (*pool of money*) о́бщая ка́сса.
kiwi ['kiːwiː] *n* ки́ви *f ind*.
KKK *n abbr* (*US*: = Ku Klux Klan) ку-клукс-кла́н.
Kleenex® ['kliːnɛks] *n inv* бума́жный носово́й плато́к*.
kleptomaniac [klɛptəu'meɪnɪæk] *n* клептома́н(ка*).
km *abbr* (= kilometre) км = киломе́тр.
km/h *abbr* (= kilometres per hour) км/ч = киломе́тров в час.
knack [næk] *n*: he has the ~ of imitating other people он о́чень ло́вко имити́рует други́х люде́й; there's a ~ to doing this тут есть оди́н секре́т *or* осо́бая хи́трость.
knackered ['nækəd] *adj* (*inf*: *tired*) вы́мотанный (вы́мотан).
knapsack ['næpsæk] *n* (небольшо́й) рюкза́к.
knead [niːd] *vt* меси́ть* (смеси́ть* *perf*).
knee [niː] *n* коле́но*.
kneecap ['niːkæp] *n* коле́нная ча́шечка*.
kneecapping ['niːkæpɪŋ] *n* вы́стрел по коле́нной ча́шечке (фо́рма ме́сти, применя́емой террори́стами).
knee-deep ['niː'diːp] *adj*, *adv* по коле́но.
knee-jerk ['niːdʒəːk] *n* коле́нный рефле́кс ♦ *adj*: ~ reaction (*fig*) рефле́кс.
kneel [niːl] (*pt*, *pp* knelt) *vi* (*also*: ~ down: action) встава́ть* (встать* *perf*) на коле́ни; (: state) стоя́ть (*impf*) на коле́нях.
kneepad ['niːpæd] *n* наколе́нник.
knell [nɛl] *n* погреба́льный звон; (*fig*) коне́ц*.
knelt [nɛlt] *pt*, *pp of* kneel.
knew [njuː] *pt of* know.
knickers ['nɪkəz] *npl* (*BRIT*) (же́нские) тру́сики *mpl*.
knick-knacks ['nɪknæks] *npl* безделу́шки* *fpl*.
knife [naɪf] (*pl* knives) *n* нож* ♦ *vt* ра́нить (*impf*) ножо́м.

knight [naɪt] *n* ры́царь *m*; (*CHESS*) конь* *m*.
knighthood ['naɪthud] *n* (*BRIT*) ры́царство
(*полученное от монарха за заслуги перед
страной*).
knit [nɪt] *vt* (*garment*) вяза́ть (связа́ть *perf*) ◆ *vi*
(*with wool etc*) вяза́ть (*impf*); (*bones*)
сраста́ться (срасти́сь* *perf*); **to ~ one's brows**
хму́рить (нахму́рить *perf*) бро́ви.
knitted ['nɪtɪd] *adj* (*garment*) вя́заный.
knitting ['nɪtɪŋ] *n* вяза́нье.
knitting machine *n* вяза́льная маши́на.
knitting needle *n* вяза́льная спи́ца.
knitting pattern *n* вя́зка*.
knitwear ['nɪtwɛəʳ] *n* трикота́ж.
knives [naɪvz] *npl of* **knife**.
knob [nɔb] *n* (*of door*) ру́чка*; (*on radio etc*)
кно́пка*; (*of stick*) набалда́шник; **a ~ of butter**
(*BRIT*) кусо́чек (сли́вочного) ма́сла.
knobbly ['nɔblɪ] (*US* **knobby**) *adj* (*surface*)
бугри́стый (бугри́ст); (*hand*) узлова́тый
(узлова́т); (*knee*) шишкова́тый.
knobby ['nɔbɪ] *adj* (*US*) = **knobbly**.
knock [nɔk] *vt* (*strike*) ударя́ть (уда́рить *perf*);
(*bump into*) ста́лкиваться (столкну́ться *perf*)
с +*instr*; (*inf: criticize*) критикова́ть (*impf*) ◆ *vi*
(*engine*) стуча́ть (*impf*) ◆ *n* (*blow, bump*) уда́р,
толчо́к*; (*on door*) стук; **to ~ a nail into sth**
вбива́ть (вбить* *perf*) гвоздь во что-н; **to ~
some sense into sb** учи́ть (научи́ть* *perf*)
кого́-н уму́-ра́зуму; **he ~ed at** *or* **on the door**
он постуча́л в дверь
► **knock about** (*inf*) ◆ *vt* (*hit*) колоти́ть*
(поколоти́ть* *perf*) ◆ *vi* (*travel*) шата́ться
(*impf*) по све́ту; (*hang out*): **~ about (with)**
води́ться (*impf*) (с +*instr*)
► **knock around** *vti* = **knock about**
► **knock back** *vt* (*inf: drink*) пропуска́ть
(пропусти́ть* *perf*)
► **knock down** *vt* (*person, price*) сбива́ть
(сбить* *perf*); (*building*) сноси́ть (снести́* *perf*)
► **knock off** *vi* (*inf: finish*) закругля́ться
(закругли́ться *perf*) ◆ *vt* (*from price*) сба́влять
(сба́вить* *perf*); (*inf: steal*) стяну́ть* (*perf*)
► **knock out** *vt* (*subj: person, drug*) оглуша́ть
(оглуши́ть *perf*); (*BOXING*) нокаути́ровать
(*perf*); (*defeat*) выбива́ть (вы́бить* *perf*)
► **knock over** *vt* (*person, object*) сбива́ть
(сбить* *perf*).
knockdown ['nɔkdaun] *adj*: **~ price** сни́женная
цена́.
knocker ['nɔkəʳ] *n* дверно́й молото́к*.
knocking ['nɔkɪŋ] *n* стук.
knock-kneed [nɔk'niːd] *adj* с вы́вернутыми
внутрь коле́нями.
knockout ['nɔkaut] *n* (*BOXING*) нока́ут ◆ *cpd*
(*competition*) отбо́рочный.
knock-up ['nɔkʌp] *n* (*TENNIS*): **to have a ~**
размина́ться (размя́ться* *perf*).

knot [nɔt] *n* (*also NAUT*) у́зел*; (*in wood*) сучо́к*
◆ *vt* завя́зывать (завяза́ть* *perf*) узло́м; **to
tie/untie a ~** завя́зывать (завяза́ть* *perf*)/
развя́зывать (развяза́ть* *perf*) у́зел.
knotty ['nɔtɪ] *adj* (*fig*) запу́танный.
know [nəu] (*pt* **knew**, *pp* **known**) *vt* (*facts,
people*) знать (*impf*); **to ~ how to do** уме́ть
(*impf*) +*infin*; **to ~ about** *or* **of sth/sb** знать (*impf*)
о чём-н/ком-н; **to get to ~ sth** (*news*)
узнава́ть* (узна́ть* *perf*) что-н; **to get to ~ sb**
(*more intimately*) узнава́ть* (узна́ть* *perf*)
кого́-н побли́же; (*get acquainted*)
знако́миться* (познако́миться* *perf*) с кем-н;
to get to ~ about узна́ть (*perf*) о +*prp*; **as far as
I ~** наско́лько мне изве́стно; **yes, I ~** да,
зна́ю; **I don't ~** не зна́ю.
know-all ['nəuɔːl] *n* (*BRIT: inf: pej*) всезна́йка*
m/f.
know-how ['nəuhau] *n* но́у-ха́у *nt ind*.
knowing ['nəuɪŋ] *adj* (*look*) понима́ющий.
knowingly ['nəuɪŋlɪ] *adv* (*purposely*)
созна́тельно; (*smile, look*) понима́юще.
know-it-all ['nəuɪtɔːl] *n* (*US*) = **know-all**.
knowledge ['nɔlɪdʒ] *n* (*abstract concept*)
зна́ние; (*things learnt*) зна́ния *ntpl*;
(*awareness*) представле́ние; **to have no ~ of**
не име́ть (*impf*) никако́го представле́ния о
+*prp*; **not to my ~** наско́лько мне изве́стно –
нет; **without my ~** без моего́ ве́дома; **to have
a working ~ of Russian** непло́хо владе́ть
(*impf*) ру́сским (языко́м); **it is common ~ that
... общеизве́стно, что ...; **it has come to my ~
that ...** мне ста́ло изве́стно, что ....
knowledgeable ['nɔlɪdʒəbl] *adj* зна́ющий*; **he
is very ~ about art** он большо́й знато́к
иссќуства.
known [nəun] *pp of* **know** ◆ *adj* (*thief, facts*)
изве́стный* (изве́стен).
knuckle ['nʌkl] *n* костя́шка*
► **knuckle down** *vi* бра́ться* (взя́ться* *perf*) за
де́ло
► **knuckle under** *vi* (*inf*) подчиня́ться
(подчини́ться *perf*).
knuckleduster ['nʌkldʌstəʳ] *n* касте́т.
KO *n abbr* (= **knockout**) нока́ут ◆ *vt*
нокаути́ровать (*impf/perf*).
koala [kəu'ɑːlə] *n* (*also: ~ **bear**) коа́ла *f ind*.
kook [kuːk] *n* (*US: inf*) поме́шанный(-ая) *m(f)*
adj.
Koran [kɔ'rɑːn] *n*: **the ~** Кора́н.
Korea [kə'rɪə] *n* Коре́я; **North/South ~**
Се́верная/Ю́жная Коре́я.
Korean [kə'rɪən] *adj* коре́йский* ◆ *n*
коре́ец*(-е́янка*).
kosher ['kəuʃəʳ] *adj* (*food*) коше́рный.
kowtow ['kau'tau] *vi*: **to ~ to sb** заи́скивать
(*impf*) *or* уго́дничать (*impf*) пе́ред кем-н.
Kremlin ['krɛmlɪn] *n*: **the ~** Кремль* *m*.

---

* marks translations which have irregular inflections. The Russian-English side of the dictionary gives inflectional information.

KS *abbr* (*US*: *POST*) = Kansas.
Kt *abbr* (*BRIT*: *in titles*) = **knight**.
Kuala Lumpur [ˈkwɑːləˈlumpuəʳ] *n*
 Куала-Лумпу́р.
kudos [ˈkjuːdɔs] *n* прести́жность *f*.
Kurd [kəːd] *n* курд(ка*).

Kuwait [kuˈweɪt] *n* Куве́йт.
Kuwaiti [kuˈweɪtɪ] *adj* куве́йтский ◆ *n*
 жи́тель(ница) *m(f)* Куве́йта.
kW *abbr* (= **kilowatt**) кВт= *килова́тт*.
KY *abbr* (*US*: *POST*) = Kentucky.

~ L, l ~

L, l [ɛl] *n* (*letter*) 12-ая бу́ква англи́йского
алфави́та.
L *abbr* (*BRIT*: *AUT*: = *learner*) учебная *f adj*; (=
lake) о.= о́зеро; = **large**, **left**.
l. *abbr* (= **litre**) л= *литр*.
LA *n abbr* (*US*) = *Los Angeles* ♦ *abbr* (*POST*) =
Louisiana.
lab [læb] *n abbr* = **laboratory**.
label ['leɪbl] *n* этике́тка*, ярлы́к; (*on suitcase*)
би́рка*; (*also*: **record** ~) знак фи́рмы
грамза́писи ♦ *vt* (*suitcase*) прикрепля́ть
(прикрепи́ть* *perf*) би́рку к +*dat*;
(*merchandise*) прикрепля́ть (прикрепи́ть*
perf) ярлы́к на +*acc*; (*fig*) накле́ивать
(накле́ить *perf*) ярлы́к на +*acc*.
labor *etc* ['leɪbəˈ] *n* (*US*) = **labour** *etc*.
laboratory [ləˈbɒrətərɪ] *n* лаборато́рия.
Labor Day *n* (*US*) День* *m* Труда́.
laborious [ləˈbɔːrɪəs] *adj* трудоёмкий*
(трудоёмок).
labor union *n* (*US*) профсою́з.
labour ['leɪbəˈ] (*US* **labor**) *n* (*work*) труд*;
(*workforce*) рабо́чая си́ла; (*MED*): **to be in** ~
рожа́ть (*impf*) ♦ *vi*: **to** ~ (**at sth**) труди́ться*
(*impf*) (над чем-н) ♦ *vt*: **to** ~ **the point** входи́ть*
(*impf*) в изли́шние подро́бности; **L**~, **the L**~
Party (*BRIT*) лейбори́сты *mpl*, Лейбори́стская
Па́ртия; **hard** ~ ка́торжные рабо́ты *pl*.
labour camp *n* исправи́тельно-трудово́й
ла́герь* *m*.
labour cost *n* сто́имость *f* рабо́чей си́лы.
labour dispute *n* трудово́й конфли́кт.
laboured ['leɪbəd] *adj* (*breathing, movement*)
затруднённый (затруднён); (*style, joke*)
вы́мученный (вы́мучен).
labourer ['leɪbərəˈ] *n* (неквалифици́рованный)
рабо́чий *m adj*; **farm** ~ се́льско-
хозя́йственный рабо́чий.
labour force *n* рабо́чая си́ла.
labour-intensive [leɪbərɪnˈtɛnsɪv] *adj*
трудоёмкий* (трудоёмок).
labour market *n* ры́нок* труда́.
labour pains *npl* родовы́е схва́тки *fpl*.
labour relations *npl* трудовы́е отноше́ния
ntpl.
labour-saving ['leɪbəseɪvɪŋ] *adj* облегча́ющий

труд.
labour unrest *n* рабо́чие волне́ния *ntpl*.
laburnum [ləˈbəːnəm] *n* (*BOT*) золото́й дождь*
m.
labyrinth ['læbɪrɪnθ] *n* лабири́нт.
lace [leɪs] *n* (*fabric*) кру́жево*; (*of shoe*)
шнуро́к* ♦ *vt* (*shoe*: *also*: ~ **up**) шнурова́ть
(зашнурова́ть *perf*); **I** ~**d his coffee with**
arsenic я подмеша́л в его́ ко́фе мышья́к.
lacemaking ['leɪsmeɪkɪŋ] *n* плете́ние кру́жев.
lacerate ['læsəreɪt] *vt* раздира́ть (разодра́ть*
perf).
laceration [læsəˈreɪʃən] *n* рва́ная ра́на.
lace-up ['leɪsʌp] *adj* шнуро́ванный.
lack [læk] *n* (*absence*) отсу́тствие; (*shortage*)
недоста́ток*, нехва́тка ♦ *vt*: **she** ~**ed self-**
confidence ей не хвата́ло *or* не достава́ло
уве́ренности в себе́; **he is** ~**ing in experience**
ему́ не хвата́ет *or* не достаёт о́пыта; **through**
or **for** ~ **of** из-за недоста́тка +*gen*.
lackadaisical [lækəˈdeɪzɪkl] *adj* вя́лый (вял).
lackey ['lækɪ] *n* (*pej*) лаке́й.
lacklustre ['læklʌstəˈ] (*US* **lackluster**) *adj*
ту́склый* (тускл).
laconic [ləˈkɒnɪk] *adj* лакони́чный*
(лакони́чен).
lacquer ['lækəˈ] *n* лак*.
lacrosse [ləˈkrɒs] *n* (*SPORT*) лакро́сс.
lacy ['leɪsɪ] *adj* кружевно́й.
lad [læd] *n* па́рень* *m*.
ladder ['lædəˈ] *n* (*also fig*) ле́стница; (*BRIT*: *in*
tights) спусти́вшиеся пе́тли *fpl* ♦ *vti*: **I've** ~**ed**
my tights, my tights have ~**ed** у меня́ пе́тли
на колго́тках спусти́лись.
laden ['leɪdn] *adj*: **to be** ~ (**with**) ломи́ться (*impf*)
от +*gen*; (*person*): ~ (**with**) нагру́женный
(нагру́жен) (+*instr*); **fully** ~ по́лностью
загру́женный; **the trees were** ~ **with fruit**
дере́вья ломи́лись от плодо́в.
ladle ['leɪdl] *n* поло́вник ♦ *vt* (*soup, stew*)
разлива́ть (разли́ть* *perf*)
▶ **ladle out** *vt* (*advice, money*) раздава́ть*
(разда́ть* *perf*) напра́во и нале́во.
Ladoga ['lædəgə] *n*: **Lake** ~ Ла́дожское о́зеро.
lady ['leɪdɪ] *n* да́ма; (*BRIT*: *title*) ле́ди *f ind*; **ladies**
and gentlemen ... да́мы и господа́ ...; **young** ~

молода́я же́нщина; (*younger*) де́вушка*; **old ~** пожила́я же́нщина; **the ladies' (room)** же́нский туале́т.

ladybird [ˈleɪdɪbəːd] *n* бо́жья коро́вка.

ladybug [ˈleɪdɪbʌg] *n* (*US*) = **ladybird**.

lady-in-waiting [ˈleɪdɪɪnˈweɪtɪŋ] *n* фре́йлина.

lady-killer [ˈleɪdɪkɪlə*] *n* (*fig*) сердцее́д.

ladylike [ˈleɪdɪlaɪk] *adj* элега́нтный* (элега́нтен).

ladyship [ˈleɪdɪʃɪp] *n*: **your ~** Ва́ша ми́лость *f*.

lag [læg] *n* (*period of time*) заде́ржка ◆ *vi* (*also*: **~ behind**: *person*) тащи́ться* (*impf*) (позади́); (: *trade, investment*) отстава́ть* (отста́ть* *perf*) ◆ *vt* (*pipes etc*) покрыва́ть (покры́ть* *perf*) теплоизоля́цией; **old ~** (*inf*: *prisoner*) рецидиви́ст; **to ~ behind** (*trade, development*) отстава́ть (отста́ть* *perf*) от +*gen*.

lager [ˈlɑːgə*] *n* све́тлое пи́во.

lager lout *n* (*inf*) пья́ная шпана́ *f no pl*.

lagging [ˈlægɪŋ] *n* (*for pipes*) теплоизоля́ция.

lagoon [ləˈguːn] *n* лагу́на.

Lagos [ˈleɪgɔs] *n* Ла́гос.

laid [leɪd] *pt, pp of* **lay**.

laid-back [leɪdˈbæk] *adj* (*inf*) споко́йный* (споко́ен).

laid up *adj*: **~ ~ (with)** прико́ванный (прико́ван) к посте́ли (+*instr*).

lain [leɪn] *pp of* **lie**.

lair [lɛə*] *n* ло́гово, ло́говище.

laissez faire [lɛseɪˈfɛə*] *n* (*ECON*) экономи́ческое невмеша́тельство.

laity [ˈleɪətɪ] *n or npl* (*REL*) миря́не *mpl*; (*non-professionals*) не профессиона́лы *mpl*.

lake [leɪk] *n* о́зеро*.

Lake District *n* (*BRIT*): **the ~ ~** Озёрный край.

lamb [læm] *n* (*ZOOL*) ягнёнок*; (*CULIN*) (молода́я) бара́нина.

lambada [læmˈbɑːdə] *n* ламба́да.

lamb chop *n* бара́нья котле́та.

lambskin [ˈlæmskɪn] *n* овчи́на.

lambswool [ˈlæmzwul] *n* поя́рок* ◆ *cpd* поя́рковый.

lame [leɪm] *adj* (*person, animal*) хромо́й* (хром); (*excuse, argument*) сла́бый* (слаб).

lame duck *n* неуда́чник(-ица).

lamely [ˈleɪmlɪ] *adv* неубеди́тельно.

lament [ləˈmɛnt] *n* плач ◆ *vt* опла́кивать (опла́кать* *perf*).

lamentable [ˈlæməntəbl] *adj* плаче́вный* (плаче́вен).

laminated [ˈlæmɪneɪtɪd] *adj* (*layered*) сло́истый; (*plastic coated*) с пла́стиковым покры́тием.

lamp [læmp] *n* (*electric, gas, oil*) ла́мпа; (*street lamp*) фона́рь* *m*.

lamplight [ˈlæmplaɪt] *n*: **by ~** (*indoors*) при све́те ла́мпы.

lampoon [læmˈpuːn] *n* па́сквиль *m* ◆ *vt* писа́ть* (написа́ть* *perf*) па́сквиль на +*acc*.

lamppost [ˈlæmppəust] *n* (*BRIT*) фона́рный столб*.

lampshade [ˈlæmpʃeɪd] *n* абажу́р.

lance [lɑːns] *n* пи́ка ◆ *vt* (*MED*) вскрыва́ть (вскрыть* *perf*).

lance corporal *n* (*BRIT*) мла́дший* капра́л.

lancet [ˈlɑːnsɪt] *n* ланце́т.

Lancs [læŋks] *abbr* (*BRIT*: *POST*) = **Lancashire**.

land [lænd] *n* земля́*; (*not sea*) су́ша; (*country*) страна́* ◆ *vi* (*from ship*) выса́живаться (вы́садиться* *perf*); (*AVIAT*) приземля́ться (приземли́ться* *perf*); (*fig*: *arrive unexpectedly*) очути́ться* (*perf*) ◆ *vt* (*plane*) посади́ть* (*perf*); (*passengers*) выса́живать (вы́садить* *perf*); (*goods*) выгружа́ть (вы́грузить* *perf*); **to own ~** владе́ть (*impf*) землёй; **to go by ~** е́хать*/е́здить* (*impf*) по су́ше; **he always ~s on his feet** (*fig*) в конце́ концо́в везёт; **she ~ed (herself) a good job** (*inf*) она́ доби́лась хоро́шей рабо́ты; **to ~ sb with sth** (*inf*) нава́ливать (навали́ть* *perf*) что-н на кого́-н

▸ **land up** *vi*: **to ~ up (in/at)** очути́ться* (*perf*) (в/ на +*prp*).

landed gentry [ˈlændɪd-] *n* землевладе́льческая аристокра́тия.

landfill site [ˈlændfɪl-] *n* ме́сто захороне́ния отхо́дов.

landing [ˈlændɪŋ] *n* (*of house*) ле́стничная площа́дка*; (*of plane*) поса́дка*, приземле́ние.

landing card *n* ка́рта, заполня́емая прибыва́ющими в страну́ иностра́нцами.

landing craft *n inv* деса́нтное су́дно*.

landing gear *n* (*AVIAT*) шасси́ *nt ind*.

landing stage *n* при́стань* *f*.

landing strip *n* взлётно-поса́дочная полоса́*.

landlady [ˈlændleɪdɪ] *n* (*of house, flat*) домовладе́лица, хозя́йка*; (*of pub*) хозя́йка*.

landlocked [ˈlændlɔkt] *adj* без вы́хода к мо́рю.

landlord [ˈlændlɔːd] *n* (*of house, flat*) домовладе́лец*, хозя́ин*; (*of pub*) хозя́ин*.

landlubber [ˈlændlʌbə*] *n*: **to be a ~** не люби́ть (*impf*) путеше́ствовать мо́рем.

landmark [ˈlændmɑːk] *n* (*landmark*) ориенти́р; (*fig*) ве́ха.

landowner [ˈlændəunə*] *n* землевладе́лец (-лица).

landscape [ˈlænskeɪp] *n* (*view, painting*) пейза́ж; (*terrain*) ландша́фт ◆ *vt*: **to ~ an area** (иску́сственно) создава́ть* (созда́ть* *perf*) ландша́фт.

landscape architect *n* = **landscape gardener**.

landscape gardener *n* ландша́фтный архите́ктор.

landscape painting *n* (*picture*) пейза́ж; (*art*) пейза́жная жи́вопись *f*.

landslide [ˈlændslaɪd] *n* (*GEO*) о́ползень* *m*; (*POL*: *also*: **~ victory**) реши́тельная побе́да.

lane [leɪn] *n* (*in country*) тропи́нка*; (*in town*) переу́лок*; (*of carriageway*) полоса́; (*SPORT*) доро́жка*; **shipping ~** морска́я тра́сса.

language [ˈlæŋgwɪdʒ] *n* язы́к*; **bad ~** скверносло́вие.

language laboratory *n* лингафо́нный кабине́т.
languid [ˈlæŋgwɪd] *adj* то́мный* (то́мен).
languish [ˈlæŋgwɪʃ] *vi* (*person*) томи́ться* (истоми́ться* *perf*); (*project, case*) тяну́ться* (*impf*).
lank [læŋk] *adj* (*hair*) дли́нный* и са́льный*.
lanky [ˈlæŋkɪ] *adj* долговя́зый (долговя́з).
lanolin(e) [ˈlænəlɪn] *n* ланоли́н.
lantern [ˈlæntən] *n* фона́рь* *m*.
Laos [laus] *n* Лао́с.
lap [læp] *n* коле́ни* *ntpl*; (*SPORT*) круг* ◆ *vt* (*also:* ~ **up**) лака́ть (вы́лакать *perf*) ◆ *vi* (*water*) плеска́ться* (*impf*); **in his/my** ~ у него́/меня́ на коле́нях
▶ **lap up** *vt* (*fig: flattery*) упива́ться (упи́ться* *perf*) +*instr*.
La Paz [læˈpæz] *n* Ла-Па́с.
lapdog [ˈlæpdɔg] *n* боло́нка*.
lapel [ləˈpɛl] *n* ла́цкан.
Lapland [ˈlæplænd] *n* Лапла́ндия.
Lapp [læp] *adj* лапла́ндский ◆ *n* (*person*) лапла́ндец*(-дка), саа́м(ка); (*LING*) саа́мский язы́к*.
lapse [læps] *n* (*bad behaviour*) про́мах*; (*of time*) промежу́ток*; (*of concentration*) потеря ◆ *vi* (*law, membership*) теря́ть (потеря́ть *perf*) си́лу; **memory** ~ прова́л в па́мяти; **to** ~ **into bad habits** усва́ивать (усво́ить *perf*) дурны́е привы́чки.
lap-top [ˈlæptɔp] *n*: ~ **computer** портати́вный компью́тер.
larceny [ˈlɑːsənɪ] *n* (*esp US*) воровство́.
larch [lɑːtʃ] *n* ли́ственница.
lard [lɑːd] *n* свино́й жир*.
larder [ˈlɑːdəʳ] *n* кладова́я *f adj*.
large [lɑːdʒ] *adj* большо́й; (*major*) кру́пный*; **to make** ~**r** увели́чивать (увели́чить *perf*); **this coat is too** ~ **for me** э́то пальто́ мне велико́; **a** ~ **number of people** большо́е число́ люде́й; **on a** ~ **scale** в кру́пном масшта́бе; **at** ~ (*as a whole*) в цело́м; (*at liberty*) на во́ле; **by and** ~ вообще́.
largely [ˈlɑːdʒlɪ] *adv* по бо́льшей ча́сти; ~ **because** ... в осново́м, потому́ что ....
large-scale [ˈlɑːdʒˈskeɪl] *adj* крупномасшта́бный.
largesse [lɑːˈʒɛs] *n* ще́дрость* *f*.
lark [lɑːk] *n* (*bird*) жа́воронок*; (*BRIT: inf: joke*) прока́за
▶ **lark about** *vi* (*BRIT: inf*) прока́зничать (напрока́зничать *perf*).
larva [ˈlɑːvə] (*pl* ~**e**) *n* личи́нка.
larvae [ˈlɑːviː] *npl of* **larva**.
laryngitis [lærɪnˈdʒaɪtɪs] *n* ларинги́т.
larynx [ˈlærɪŋks] *n* горта́нь *f*.
lasagne [ləˈzænjə] *n* лаза́нья (*италья́нское блю́до*).

lascivious [ləˈsɪvɪəs] *adj* похотли́вый (похотли́в).
laser [ˈleɪzəʳ] *n* ла́зер.
laser beam *n* ла́зерный луч*.
laser printer *n* ла́зерный при́нтер.
lash [læʃ] *n* (*eyelash*) ресни́ца; (*of whip*) уда́р (хлыста́) ◆ *vt* (*whip*) хлеста́ть* (*impf*), стега́ть (*impf*); (*also:* ~ **against**: *subj*: *rain, wind*) хлеста́ть* (*impf*) о +*acc*; (*tie*): **to** ~ **to** привя́зывать (привяза́ть* *perf*) к +*dat*; **to** ~ **together** свя́зывать (связа́ть* *perf*)
▶ **lash down** *vt* привя́зывать (привяза́ть* *perf*) ◆ *vi* (*rain*) хлеста́ть* (*impf*)
▶ **lash out** *vi*: **to** ~ **out at** (*also fig*) наки́дываться (наки́нуться *perf*) на +*acc*; **to** ~ **out** (**on sth**) (*inf*) разоря́ться (разори́ться *perf*) (на что-н).
lashing [ˈlæʃɪŋ] *n*: ~**s of** (*BRIT: inf: cream etc*) ку́ча +*gen*.
lass [læs] *n* (*BRIT: girl*) де́вочка*; (: *young woman*) де́вушка*.
lasso [læˈsuː] *n* лассо́ *nt ind*, арка́н ◆ *vt* арка́нить (заарка́нить *perf*).
last [lɑːst] *adj* (*most recent*) про́шлый; (*final*) после́дний* ◆ *adv* в после́дний раз; (*finally*) в конце́ ◆ *vi* (*continue*) дли́ться (продли́ться *perf*), продолжа́ться (продо́лжиться* *perf*); (*keep: thing*) сохраня́ться (сохрани́ться *perf*); (: *person*) держа́ться (продержа́ться *perf*); (*suffice*): **we had enough money to** ~ **us** нам хвати́ло де́нег; ~ **year** в про́шлом году́; ~ **week** в про́шлой неде́ле; ~ **night** (*early*) вчера́ ве́чером; (*late*) про́шлой но́чью; **at** ~ наконе́ц; ~ **but one** предпосле́дний*; **the** ~ **time** в после́дний раз; **the film** ~**s (for) 2 hours** фильм дли́тся 2 часа́.
last-ditch [ˈlɑːstˈdɪtʃ] *adj* (*attempt*) отча́янный.
lasting [ˈlɑːstɪŋ] *adj* (*friendship*) продолжи́тельный* (продолжи́телен), дли́тельный* (дли́телен); (*solution*) долговре́менный* (долговре́менен).
lastly [ˈlɑːstlɪ] *adv* наконе́ц.
last-minute [ˈlɑːstmɪnɪt] *adj* (*attempt*) сде́ланный в после́днюю мину́ту; (*details, meeting*) после́дний*.
latch [lætʃ] *n* (*on gate*) задви́жка*; (*on front door*) замо́к* *m*; **to leave the door on the** ~ оставля́ть (оста́вить* *perf*) замо́к на предохрани́тель
▶ **latch on to** *vt fus* (*person*) прилипа́ть (прили́пнуть *perf*) к +*dat*; (*idea*) привя́зываться (привяза́ться* *perf*) к +*dat*.
latchkey [ˈlætʃkiː] *n* ключ от замка́ (*к входно́й две́ри*).
latchkey child *n* ребёнок, *находя́щий до́ма в то вре́мя когда́ роди́тели рабо́тают*.
late [leɪt] *adj* (*far on in time, process, work etc*) по́здний*; (*former*) бы́вший*; (*dead*)

---

* marks translations which have irregular inflections. The Russian-English side of the dictionary gives inflectional information.

поко́йный ♦ *adv* по́здно; (*behind time*) с опозда́нием; **to be** ~ опа́здывать (опозда́ть *perf*); **I was 10 minutes** ~ я опозда́л на 10 мину́т; **in the** ~ **1970s** к концу́ семидеся́тых годо́в; **he is in his** ~ **thirties** ему́ далеко́ за три́дцать; **in** ~ **May** в конце́ ма́я; **to work** ~ рабо́тать (*impf*) допоздна́; ~ **in life** в пожило́м во́зрасте; **of** ~ в после́днее вре́мя.

latecomer ['leɪtkʌmə'] *n* опозда́вший(-ая)*m(f) adj.*

lately ['leɪtlɪ] *adv* в после́днее вре́мя.

lateness ['leɪtnɪs] *n* опозда́ние; **owing to the** ~ **of the hour** из-за по́зднего ча́са.

latent ['leɪtnt] *adj* скры́тый (скрыт); ~ **defect** скры́тый дефе́кт.

later ['leɪtə'] *adj* (*time, date*) бо́лее по́здний*; (*meeting, version*) после́дующий* ♦ *adv* по́зже, поздне́е; ~ **on** в после́дствии, пото́м; **he arrived** ~ **than me** он пришёл по́зже меня́.

lateral ['lætərl] *adj* боково́й; ~ **thinking** нестанда́ртное мы́шление.

latest ['leɪtɪst] *adj* са́мый по́здний*; (*most recent*) (са́мый) но́вый *or* после́дний*; (*news*) после́дний*; **at the** ~ са́мое по́зднее.

latex ['leɪtɛks] *n* ла́текс.

lathe [leɪð] *n* тока́рный стано́к*.

lather ['lɑːðə'] *n* (мы́льная) пе́на ♦ *vt* мы́лить (намы́лить *perf*).

Latin ['lætɪn] *n* (*LING*) лати́нский* язы́к; (*person*) жи́тель(ница) *m(f)* ю́жной Евро́пы ♦ *adj:* ~ **languages** рома́нские языки́; ~ **countries** стра́ны ю́жной Евро́пы.

Latin America *n* Лати́нская Аме́рика.

Latin American *adj* латиноамерика́нский ♦ *n* латиноамерика́нец*(-а́нка*).

latitude ['lætɪtjuːd] *n* (*GEO*) широта́*; (*fig*) свобо́да.

latrine [lə'triːn] *n* отхо́жее ме́сто*.

latter ['lætə'] *adj* после́дний* ♦ *n:* **the** ~ после́дний*(-яя) *m(f) adj;* **the** ~ **part of the week** втора́я полови́на неде́ли.

latter-day ['lætədeɪ] *adj* совреме́нный.

latterly ['lætəlɪ] *adv* неда́вно, в после́днее вре́мя.

lattice ['lætɪs] *n* решётка*.

lattice window *n* решётчатое окно́*.

Latvia ['lætvɪə] *n* Ла́твия.

Latvian ['lætvɪən] *adj* латви́йский ♦ *n* латы́ш(ка); (*LING*) латы́шский язы́к*.

laudable ['lɔːdəbl] *adj* похва́льный* (похва́лен).

laudatory ['lɔːdətrɪ] *adj* хвале́бный* (хвале́бен).

laugh [lɑːf] *n* смех* ♦ *vi* смея́ться* (*impf*); (**to do sth) for a** ~ (*inf*) (де́лать (*impf*) что-н) для сме́ха.

► **laugh at** *vt fus* смея́ться* (посмея́ться *perf*) над +*instr*

► **laugh off** *vt:* **to** ~ **sth off** отде́лываться (отде́латься *perf*) от чего́-н шу́ткой.

laughable ['lɑːfəbl] *adj* смехотво́рный*

(смехотво́рен).

laughing gas ['lɑːfɪŋ-] *n* веселя́щий газ*.

laughing matter *n:* **this is no** ~ ~ э́то де́ло нешу́точное.

laughing stock *n* посме́шище; **to be the** ~ ~ **of** служи́ть (*impf*) посме́шищем для +*gen*.

laughter ['lɑːftə'] *n* смех*.

launch [lɔːntʃ] *n* (*of rocket, product*) за́пуск; (*motorboat*) мото́рный ка́тер* ♦ *vt* (*ship*) спуска́ть (спусти́ть* *perf*) на́ воду; (*rocket*) запуска́ть (запусти́ть* *perf*); (*campaign, attack*) начина́ть (нача́ть* *perf*); (*product*) пуска́ть (пусти́ть* *perf*) в прода́жу

► **launch into** *vt fus* (*speech, activity*) пуска́ться (пусти́ться* *perf*) в +*acc*

► **launch out** *vi:* **to** ~ **out into** бра́ться* (взя́ться* *perf*) за +*acc*.

launching ['lɔːntʃɪŋ] *n* (*of ship*) спуск (на́ воду); (*of rocket, product*) за́пуск; (*of campaign, attack*) нача́ло.

launch(ing) pad *n* ста́ртовая площа́дка*.

launder ['lɔːndə'] *vt* (*clothes, sheets*) стира́ть (вы́стирать *perf*); (*money*) отмыва́ть (отмы́ть *perf*).

laundrette [lɔːn'drɛt] *n* (*BRIT*) пра́чечная *f adj* самообслу́живания.

Laundromat® ['lɔːndrəmæt] *n* (*US*) = **laundrette**.

laundry ['lɔːndrɪ] *n* (*washing*) сти́рка; (*place*) пра́чечная *f adj;* **to do the** ~ стира́ть (вы́стирать *perf*).

laureate ['lɔːrɪət] *adj see* **poet laureate**.

laurel ['lɔrl] *n* (*tree*) лавр, ла́вровое де́рево; **to rest on one's** ~**s** почива́ть (почи́ть* *perf*) на ла́врах.

Lausanne [ləu'zæn] *n* Лоза́нна.

lava ['lɑːvə] *n* ла́ва.

lavatory ['lævətərɪ] *n* туале́т.

lavatory paper *n* туале́тная бума́га.

lavender ['lævəndə'] *n* лава́нда.

lavish ['lævɪʃ] *adj* (*amount, hospitality*) ще́дрый* (щедр); (*meal*) оби́льный* (оби́лен); (*surroundings*) пы́шный* (пы́шен); (*person*): ~ **with** ще́дрый* (щедр) на +*acc* ♦ *vt:* **to** ~ **sth on sb** осыпа́ть (осы́пать* *perf*) кого́-н чем-н.

lavishly ['lævɪʃlɪ] *adv* (*generously*) ще́дро; (*sumptuously*) пы́шно.

law [lɔː] *n* зако́н; (*professions*): **(the)** ~ юриспруде́нция; (*SCOL*) пра́во; **it's against the** ~ э́то противозако́нно; **to study** ~ изуча́ть (*impf*) пра́во; **to go to** ~ обраща́ться (обрати́ться* *perf*) в суд; **to break the** ~ наруша́ть (наруши́ть *perf*) зако́н.

law-abiding ['lɔːəbaɪdɪŋ] *adj* законопослу́шный.

Law Lord *n* (*BRIT*) судья́, назнача́емый в *аппеляцио́нный суд пала́ты Ло́рдов*.

law and order *n* правопоря́док*.

lawbreaker ['lɔːbreɪkə'] *n* правонаруши́тель-(ница) *m(f).*

law court *n* суд*.
lawful ['lɔ:ful] *adj* зако́нный.
lawfully ['lɔ:fəlɪ] *adv* зако́нно.
lawless ['lɔ:lɪs] *adj* (*action*) беззако́нный.
lawmaker ['lɔ:meɪkəʳ] *n* законода́тель(ница) *m(f)*.
lawn [lɔ:n] *n* газо́н.
lawnmower ['lɔ:nməuəʳ] *n* газонокоси́лка*.
lawn tennis *n* те́ннис (*на травяно́м ко́рте*).
law school *n* (*US*) юриди́ческий институ́т.
law student *n* студе́нт(ка) юриди́ческого факульте́та.
lawsuit ['lɔ:su:t] *n* суде́бный иск.
lawyer ['lɔ:jəʳ] *n* (*solicitor, barrister*) адвока́т; (*legal specialist*) юри́ст.
lax [læks] *adj* (*discipline, standards*) нестро́гий (нестро́г); (*morals, behaviour*) распу́щенный (распу́щен).
laxative ['læksətɪv] *n* слаби́тельное *nt adj*.
laxity ['læksɪtɪ] *n* небре́жность *f*; (*moral*) распу́щенность *f*.
lay [leɪ] (*pt, pp* **laid**) *pt of* **lie** ♦ *adj* (*REL*) мирско́й; (*not expert*) непрофессиона́льный ♦ *vt* (*place*) класть* (положи́ть* *perf*); (*table*) накрыва́ть (накры́ть* *perf*) (на +*acc*); (*carpet*) стлать (настла́ть *or* настели́ть* *perf*); (*cable*) прокла́дывать (проложи́ть* *perf*); (*plans*) составля́ть (соста́вить* *perf*); (*trap*) ста́вить* (поста́вить* *perf*); (: *fig*) подстра́ивать (подстро́ить *perf*); (*egg*) откла́дывать (отложи́ть *perf*); **to ~ facts/proposals before sb** излага́ть (изложи́ть* *perf*) фа́кты/предложе́ния пе́ред кем-н; **to ~ one's hands on sth** (*inf*) достава́ть* (доста́ть* *perf*) что-н; **to get laid** (*inf!*) тра́хаться (трахну́ться *perf*) (*!*)
► **lay aside** *vt* откла́дывать (отложи́ть* *perf*)
► **lay by** *vt* = **lay aside**
► **lay down** *vt* (*object*) класть* (положи́ть* *perf*); (*rules, laws*) устана́вливать (установи́ть* *perf*); (*weapons*) скла́дывать (сложи́ть* *perf*); **to ~ down the law** прика́зывать (*impf*); **to ~ down one's life** положи́ть* (*perf*) жизнь
► **lay in** *vt* (*supplies*) запаса́ть (запасти́* *perf*)
► **lay into** *vt fus* (*also fig*) набра́сываться (набро́ситься* *perf*) на +*acc*
► **lay off** *vt* (*workers*) увольня́ть (уво́лить *perf*)
► **lay on** *vt* (*meal, entertainment*) устра́ивать (устро́ить *perf*); (*water, gas*) прокла́дывать (проложи́ть* *perf*); (*paint*) наноси́ть* (нанести́* *perf*)
► **lay out** *vt* раскла́дывать (разложи́ть* *perf*); (*inf*): **to ~ out money on sth** выкла́дывать (вы́ложить* *perf*) де́ньги на что-н
► **lay up** *vt* (*ship*) ста́вить* (поста́вить* *perf*) на прико́л; (*sick person*): **to be laid up with** валя́ться (*impf*) с +*instr*; **the car was laid up all**

year маши́на простоя́ла весь год.
layabout ['leɪəbaut] *n* (*inf*) безде́льник(-ица).
lay-by ['leɪbaɪ] *n* (*BRIT*) площа́дка для вре́менной стоя́нки (*на автодоро́ге*).
lay days *npl* (*NAUT*) стали́йное вре́мя* *ntsg*.
layer ['leɪəʳ] *n* слой*.
layette [leɪˈet] *n* прида́ное *nt adj* (*для новорождённого*).
layman ['leɪmən] *irreg n* (*non-expert*) неспециали́ст.
lay-off ['leɪɔf] *n* увольне́ние.
layout ['leɪaut] *n* (*of garden, building*) плани́ровка*; (*of page*) компано́вка*.
laze [leɪz] *vi* (*also:* **~ about**) безде́льничать (*impf*); **to ~ about in bed/the sun** не́житься (*impf*) в посте́ли/на со́лнце.
laziness ['leɪzɪnɪs] *n* лень *f*.
lazy ['leɪzɪ] *adj* лени́вый (лени́в).
LB *abbr* (*CANADA*) = **Labrador**.
lb. *abbr* (= *pound (weight)*) фунт.
lbw *abbr* (*CRICKET*) = **leg before wicket**.
LC *n abbr* (*US*) = **Library of Congress**.
lc *abbr* (*TYP*: = *lower case*) строчна́я бу́ква.
L/C *abbr* (= *letter of credit*) аккредити́в.
LCD *n abbr* = **liquid crystal display**.
Ld *abbr* (*BRIT*: *in titles*) = **lord**.
LDS *n abbr* (*BRIT*: = *Licentiate in Dental Surgery*) лице́нзия на стоматологи́ческую пра́ктику ♦ *abbr* (= *Latter-day Saints*) „Святы́е после́днего дня" (*официа́льное назва́ние се́кты мормо́нов*).
LEA *n abbr* (*BRIT*: = *Local Education Authority*) ме́стное управле́ние по дела́м просвеще́ния.
lead¹ [li:d] (*pt, pp* **led**) *n* (*front position*) пе́рвенство, ли́дерство; (*clue*) нить *f*; (*in play, film*) гла́вная роль *f*; (*for dog*) поводо́к*; (*ELEC*) про́вод* ♦ *vt* (*competition, market*) лиди́ровать (*impf*) в +*prp*; (*opponent*) опережа́ть (*impf*); (*person, group: guide*) вести́* (повести́* *perf*); (*activity, organization etc*) руководи́ть* (*impf*) +*instr*, возглавля́ть (возгла́вить* *perf*) ♦ *vi* (*road, pipe etc*) вести́* (*impf*); (*SPORT*) лиди́ровать (*impf*); **to take the ~** (*SPORT*) выходи́ть* (вы́йти* *perf*) вперёд; (*fig*) брать* (взять* *perf*) на себя́ веду́щую роль; **to ~ the way** (*also fig*) ука́зывать (указа́ть* *perf*) путь; **to ~ sb astray** вводи́ть* (ввести́* *perf*) кого́-н в заблужде́ние; **to ~ sb to do** приводи́ть* (привести́* *perf*) кого́-н к чему́-н; **to ~ sb to believe that …** дава́ть* (дать* *perf*) кому́-н поня́ть, что …; **to ~ an interesting life** вести́* (*impf*) интере́сную жизнь; **to ~ an orchestra** (*BRIT*) исполня́ть (испо́лнить *perf*) пе́рвую скри́пку
► **lead away** *vt* уводи́ть* (увести́* *perf*)
► **lead back** *vt* приводи́ть* (привести́* *perf*) обра́тно
► **lead into** *vt fus* вводи́ть* (ввести́* *perf*) в +*acc*

* marks translations which have irregular inflections. The Russian-English side of the dictionary gives inflectional information.

▶ **lead off** *vi* (*in game, conversation*) начина́ть
(нача́ть* *perf*); (*road, corridor*) отходи́ть*
(*impf*) ◆ *vt fus* отходи́ть* (*impf*) от +*gen*
▶ **lead on** *vt* (*tease*) води́ть* (*impf*) за́ нос
▶ **lead out of** *vt fus* выводи́ть* (вы́вести* *perf*)
из +*gen*
▶ **lead to** *vt fus* вести́* (привести́* *perf*) к +*dat*
▶ **lead up to** *vt fus* (*events*) приводи́ть*
(привести́* *perf*) к +*dat*; (*topic*) подводи́ть*
(подвести́* *perf*) к +*dat*.
lead² [lɛd] *n* (*metal*) свине́ц*; (*in pencil*) графи́т.
leaded [ˈlɛdɪd] *adj* (*window, glass*) со
свинцо́выми крепле́ниями; (*petrol*)
содержа́щий свине́ц.
leaden [ˈlɛdn] *adj* (*sky, sea*) свинцо́вый;
(*movements*) ско́ванный (ско́ван).
leader [ˈliːdə*ˈ*] *n* (*of group, SPORT*) ли́дер; (*in
newspaper*) передова́я статья́; **the L~ of the
House (of Commons/Lords)** (*BRIT*)
*представи́тель пра́вящей па́ртии в Пала́те
Общи́н/Ло́рдов, наделённый осо́быми
полномо́чиями.*
leadership [ˈliːdəʃɪp] *n* (*position, process*)
руково́дство; (*quality*) ли́дерские ка́чества
ntpl.
lead-free [ˈlɛdfriː] *adj* (*petrol*) не содержа́щий
свине́ц.
leading [ˈliːdɪŋ] *adj* (*most important*) веду́щий*;
(*first, front*) пере́дний*; (*winning*)
лиди́рующий; **~ role** (*in film, play*) гла́вная
роль *f*.
leading lady *n* (*THEAT*) исполни́тельница
гла́вной ро́ли.
leading light *n* (*person*) свети́ло.
leading man *irreg n* (*THEAT*) исполни́тель *m*
гла́вной ро́ли.
leading question *n* наводя́щий* вопро́с.
lead pencil [lɛd-] *n* гри́фельный каранда́ш*.
lead poisoning [lɛd-] *n* отравле́ние свинцо́м.
lead singer [liːd-] *n* соли́ст(ка).
lead time [liːd-] *n* (*COMM*) вре́мя* *ntsg*
реализа́ции зака́за.
lead-up [ˈliːdʌp] *n*: **in the ~ to** незадо́лго до
+*gen*.
leaf [liːf] (*pl* **leaves**) *n* (*BOT, of book*) лист*; (*of
table*) откидна́я доска́* ◆ *vi*: **to ~ through**
листа́ть (пролиста́ть *perf*); **to turn over a new
~** нача́ть* (*perf*) но́вую жизнь; **to take a ~ out
of sb's book** сле́довать (после́довать *perf*)
приме́ру кого́-н.
leaflet [ˈliːflɪt] *n* листо́вка*.
leafy [ˈliːfɪ] *adj* (*trees, vegetables*) покры́тый
(покры́т) листво́й; (*place*) зелёный* (зе́лен).
league [liːg] *n* ли́га; **to be in ~ with sb** быть*
(*impf*) в сго́воре с кем-н.
league table *n* (*BRIT: SPORT*) табли́ца
результа́тов спортклу́бов одно́й из лиг;
(*fig: of wages, prices*) сравни́тельная
табли́ца.
leak [liːk] *n* (*hole*) течь *f*; (*seepage*) уте́чка*;
(*fig*): (**information**) **~** уте́чка* информа́ции ◆

vi (*pipe, roof, shoes*) протека́ть (проте́чь*
perf); (*ship*) дава́ть* (дать* *perf*) течь; (*liquid,
gas*) проса́чиваться (просочи́ться *perf*) ◆ *vt*
(*information*) разглаша́ть (разгласи́ть* *perf*)
▶ **leak out** *vi* (*liquid*) вытека́ть (вы́течь* *perf*);
(*information*) проса́чиваться (просочи́ться
perf).
leakage [ˈliːkɪdʒ] *n* уте́чка*.
leaky [ˈliːkɪ] *adj* (*roof etc*) дыря́вый,
проходи́вшийся.
lean [liːn] (*pt, pp* **leaned** *or* **leant**) *adj* (*person*)
поджа́рый (поджа́р); (*meat*) по́стный
(*period*) ску́дный* (ску́ден) ◆ *vt*: **to ~ sth on** *or*
against sth прислоня́ть (прислони́ть *perf*)
что-н к чему́-н ◆ *vi*: **to ~ (forward/back)**
наклоня́ться (наклони́ться* *perf*) (вперёд/
наза́д); **to ~ against** (*wall*) прислоня́ться
(прислони́ться *perf*) к +*dat*; (*person*)
опира́ться (опере́ться* *perf*) на +*acc*; **to ~ on**
(*chair*) опира́ться (опере́ться* *perf*) о +*acc*;
(*rely on*) опира́ться (опере́ться* *perf*) на +*acc*;
(*pressurize*) нажима́ть (нажа́ть* *perf*) на +*acc*;
to ~ towards (*idea, belief*) склоня́ться
(склони́ться* *perf*) к +*dat*
▶ **lean out** *vi*: **to ~ out (of)** высо́вываться
(вы́сунуться *perf*) (из +*gen*)
▶ **lean over** *vi* наклоня́ться (наклони́ться*
perf).
leaning [ˈliːnɪŋ] *n*: **~ (towards)** скло́нность *f* (к
+*dat*).
leant [lɛnt] *pt, pp of* **lean**.
lean-to [ˈliːntuː] *n* пристро́йка*.
leap [liːp] (*pt, pp* **leaped** *or* **leapt**) *n* прыжо́к*,
скачо́к*; (*increase*) скачо́к* ◆ *vi* пры́гать
(пры́гнуть *perf*); (*price, number*)
подска́кивать (подскочи́ть *perf*); **to ~ at**
(*offer, opportunity*) ухвати́ться* (*perf*) за +*acc*;
to ~ to one's feet вска́кивать (вскочи́ть *perf*)
на́ ноги
▶ **leap up** *vi* подпры́гивать (подпры́гнуть
perf).
leapfrog [ˈliːpfrɔg] *n* чехарда́.
leapt [lɛpt] *pt, pp of* **leap**.
leap year *n* високо́сный год*.
learn [ləːn] (*pt, pp* **learned** *or* **learnt**) *vt* (*skill*)
учи́ться* (научи́ться* *perf*) +*dat*; (*facts, poem*)
учи́ть* (вы́учить* *perf*) ◆ *vi* учи́ться* (*impf*); **to
~ about** *or* **of/that ...** (*hear, read*) узнава́ть*
(узна́ть* *perf*) о +*prp*/, что ...; **to ~ about sth**
(*study*) изуча́ть (изучи́ть* *perf*) что-н; **to ~
(how) to do** учи́ться* (научи́ться* *perf*) +*impf
infin*.
learned [ˈləːnɪd] *adj* учёный.
learner [ˈləːnə*ˈ*] *n* учени́к*(-и́ца*).
learning [ˈləːnɪŋ] *n* учёность *f*; **person of ~**
учёный челове́к.
learnt [ləːnt] *pt, pp of* **learn**.
lease [liːs] *n* аре́ндный догово́р ◆ *vt*: **to ~ sth
(to sb)** сдава́ть* (сдать* *perf*) что-н в аре́нду
(кому́-н); **to ~ sth from sb** арендова́ть (*impf/
perf*) *or* брать* (взять* *perf*) в аре́нду у кого́-н;

on ~ (to sb) сда́нный (сдан) в аре́нду
(кому́-н)
► **lease back** vt сдава́ть* (сдать* perf) в аре́нду
пре́жнему владе́льцу (*для мобилиза́ции
де́нежных средств*).
leaseback ['liːsbæk] n сда́ча со́бственность в
аре́нду её пре́жнему владе́льцу.
leasehold ['liːshəuld] n (also:~ **property**)
арендо́ванная со́бственность f ◆ adj
арендо́ванный (аре́ндо́ван).
leash [liːʃ] n поводо́к*.
least [liːst] adj: **the** ~ (+noun: *smallest*)
наиме́ньший*; (: *slightest*) мале́йший* ◆ adv
(+vb) ме́ньше всего́; (+adj): **the** ~ наиме́нее;
the ~ possible effort наиме́ньшее уси́лие; **I
don't have the ~ idea about it** я не име́ю ни
мале́йшего представле́ния об э́том; **at** ~ по
кра́йней ме́ре; **you could at ~ have written**
Вы могли́ бы по кра́йней ме́ре написа́ть;
not in the ~ совсе́м нет; (+vb, +adj) совсе́м *or*
во́все не.
leather ['lɛðə^r] n ко́жа.
leather goods npl ко́жаные изде́лия ntpl.
leave [liːv] (pt, pp **left**) vt оставля́ть (оста́вить*
perf); (*go away from: on foot*) уходи́ть* (уйти́*
perf) из +gen; (: *by transport*) уезжа́ть (уе́хать*
perf) из +gen; (*party, committee*) выходи́ть*
(вы́йти* perf) из +gen ◆ vi (*on foot*) уходи́ть*
(уйти́* perf); (*by transport*) уезжа́ть (уе́хать*
perf); (*bus, train*) уходи́ть* (уйти́* perf) ◆ n
о́тпуск*; **to** ~ **sth to sb** (*money, property*)
оставля́ть (оста́вить* perf) что-н кому́-н;
(*responsibility*) оставля́ть (оста́вить* perf)
что-н под чью-н отве́тственность; **to be left
(over)** остава́ться* (оста́ться* perf); **to take
one's** ~ **of sb** проща́ться (попроща́ться perf)
с кем-н; **on** ~ в о́тпуске
► **leave behind** vt оставля́ть (оста́вить* perf)
► **leave off** vt (*heating, light*) не включа́ть
(включи́ть perf) ◆ vi (*stop: inf*) отстава́ть*
(отста́ть* perf); **he left the lid off** он не
положи́л кры́шку
► **leave on** vt (*coat*) не снима́ть (снять* perf);
(*light, heating*) оставля́ть (оста́вить* perf)
► **leave out** vt (*omit*) пропуска́ть (пропусти́ть*
perf); **he was left out** его́ пропусти́ли.
leave of absence n о́тпуск без содержа́ния.
leaves [liːvz] npl of **leaf**.
Lebanese [lɛbə'niːz] adj лива́нский* ◆ n inv
лива́нец(-нка).
Lebanon ['lɛbənən] n Лива́н.
lecherous ['lɛtʃərəs] adj развра́тный*
(развра́тен).
lectern ['lɛktəːn] n ка́федра.
lecture ['lɛktʃə^r] n ле́кция ◆ vi чита́ть (impf)
ле́кции ◆ vt (*scold*): **to** ~ **sb on** *or* **about sth**
чита́ть (impf) кому́-н ле́кции по по́воду
чего́-н; **to give a** ~ **on** чита́ть (прочита́ть perf)

ле́кцию о +prp.
lecture hall n аудито́рия, лекцио́нный зал.
lecturer ['lɛktʃərə^r] n (BRIT: *at university*)
преподава́тель(ница) m(f); (*speaker*) ле́ктор.
LED n abbr (ELEC: = *light-emitting diode*) СИД=
светоизлуча́ющий дио́д.
led [lɛd] pt, pp of **lead**[1].
ledge [lɛdʒ] n (*of mountain*) вы́ступ; (*of
window*) подоко́нник; (*on wall*) по́лка*.
ledger ['lɛdʒə^r] n расхо́дно-прихо́дная кни́га.
lee [liː] n (*shelter*) покро́в.
leech [liːtʃ] n (also fig) пия́вка*.
leek [liːk] n лук-поре́й no pl.
leer [lɪə^r] vi: **to** ~ **at sb** похотли́во смотре́ть
(посмотре́ть perf) на кого́-н.
leeward ['liːwəd] (NAUT) adj подве́тренный ◆
adv с подве́тренной стороны́ ◆ n под-
ве́тренная сторона́*; **to** ~ на подве́тренную
сто́рону.
leeway ['liːweɪ] n (fig): **to allow o.s. some** ~
дава́ть* (дать* perf) себе́ свобо́ду; **we have a
lot of** ~ **to make up** нам ну́жно мно́гое
наверста́ть.
left [lɛft] pt, pp of **leave** ◆ adj (*remaining*)
оста́вшийся; (*of direction, position*) ле́вый ◆ n
ле́вая сторона́* ◆ adv (*motion*): **(to the)** ~
нале́во; (*position*): **(on the)** ~ сле́ва; **the L~**
(POL) ле́вые pl adj.
left-hand drive ['lɛfthænd-] adj (AUT) с руле́м
на ле́вой стороне́.
left-handed [lɛft'hændɪd] adj: **he/she is** ~ он/
она́ левша́.
left-hand side n: **the** ~ ~ ле́вая сторона́.
leftie ['lɛftɪ] n (inf. pej: BRIT: *left winger*)
ле́вый(-ая) m/f adj.
leftist ['lɛftɪst] n ле́вый(-ая) m(f) adj ◆ adj ле́вый.
left-luggage (office) [lɛft'lʌgɪdʒ(-)] n (BRIT)
ка́мера хране́ния.
leftovers ['lɛftəuvəz] npl оста́тки mpl.
left-wing ['lɛft'wɪŋ] adj (POL) ле́вый.
left-winger ['lɛft'wɪŋgə^r] n (BRIT: POL)
ле́вый(-ая) m(f) adj, представи́тель m ле́вого
крыла́.
lefty ['lɛftɪ] n = **leftie**.
leg [lɛg] n (ANAT, also CULIN: *of lamb*) нога́*; (*of
insect, furniture, also CULIN: of chicken*) но́жка*;
(*also: trouser ~*) штани́на; (*of journey, race*)
эта́п; **to stretch one's** ~**s** размина́ть
(размя́ть* perf) но́ги.
legacy ['lɛgəsɪ] n (*in will*) насле́дство; (*fig*)
насле́дие.
legal ['liːgl] adj (*advice, requirement*)
юриди́ческий*; (*system, action*) суде́бный;
(*lawful*) зако́нный* (зако́нен); **to take** ~
action *or* **proceedings against sb** возбужда́ть
(возбуди́ть* perf) суде́бное де́ло про́тив
кого́-н.
legal adviser n юрисконсу́льт.

---

legal holiday *n* (*US*) непрису́тственный день*
m.
legality [lɪˈgælɪtɪ] *n* зако́нность *f.*
legalize [ˈliːgəlaɪz] *vt* узако́нивать (узако́нить*
perf); (*party, group*) легализова́ть (*impf/perf*).
legally [ˈliːgəlɪ] *adv* юриди́чески; (*act*)
зако́нно; (*by law*) по зако́ну; ~ **binding**
юриди́чески обяза́тельный* (обяза́телен).
legal tender *n* зако́нное сре́дство платежа́
(*обы́чно о бума́жных и металли́ческих*
деньга́х).
legatee [lɛgəˈtiː] *n* насле́дник.
legation [lɪˈgeɪʃən] *n* ми́ссия,
представи́тельство.
legend [ˈlɛdʒənd] *n* (*story*) леге́нда; (*person*)
легенда́рная ли́чность *f.*
legendary [ˈlɛdʒəndərɪ] *adj* легенда́рный*
(легенда́рен).
-legged [ˈlɛgɪd] *suffix* -но́гий*.
leggy [ˈlɛgɪ] *adj* длинноно́гий* (длинноно́г).
leggings [ˈlɛgɪŋz] *npl* лоси́ны *fpl.*
legibility [lɛdʒɪˈbɪlɪtɪ] *n* разбо́рчивость *f.*
legible [ˈlɛdʒəbl] *adj* разбо́рчивый
(разбо́рчив).
legibly [ˈlɛdʒəblɪ] *adv* разбо́рчиво.
legion [ˈliːdʒən] *n* легио́н ♦ *adj* (*numerous*):
their problems are ~ у них легио́н пробле́м.
legionnaire [liːdʒəˈnɛəʳ] *n* легионе́р.
legionnaire's disease *n* боле́знь *f*
„легионе́ров".
legislate [ˈlɛdʒɪsleɪt] *vi* издава́ть* (изда́ть* *perf*)
зако́н(ы).
legislation [lɛdʒɪsˈleɪʃən] *n* законода́тельство.
legislative [ˈlɛdʒɪslətɪv] *adj* (*POL*)
законода́тельный.
legislator [ˈlɛdʒɪsleɪtəʳ] *n* (*POL*) законода́тель *m.*
legislature [ˈlɛdʒɪslətʃəʳ] *n* законода́тельные
о́рганы *mpl.*
legitimacy [lɪˈdʒɪtɪməsɪ] *n* зако́нность *f.*
legitimate [lɪˈdʒɪtɪmət] *adj* зако́нный*
(зако́нен).
legitimize [lɪˈdʒɪtɪmaɪz] *vt* узако́нивать
(узако́нить *perf*).
legless [ˈlɛglɪs] *adj* (*without legs*) безно́гий*
(безно́г); (*very drunk: inf: BRIT*) пья́ный в
сте́льку.
legroom [ˈlɛgruːm] *n* (*in car etc*) простра́нство
для ног.
Leics *abbr* (*BRIT: POST*) = **Leicestershire.**
Leipzig [ˈlaɪpsɪg] *n* Ле́йпциг.
leisure [ˈlɛʒəʳ] *n* (*also:* ~ **time**) досу́г,
свобо́дное вре́мя* *nt*; **to do sth at (one's)** ~
де́лать (сде́лать *perf*) что-н не спеша́.
leisure centre *n* спорти́вно-
оздорови́тельный ко́мплекс.
leisurely [ˈlɛʒəlɪ] *adj* неторопли́вый
(неторопли́в).
leisure suit *n* спорти́вный костю́м.
lemon [ˈlɛmən] *n* лимо́н ♦ *adj* лимо́нный.
lemonade [lɛməˈneɪd] *n* лимона́д.
lemon cheese *n* = **lemon curd.**

lemon curd *n* (*CULIN*) сла́дкое лимо́нное
пови́дло.
lemon juice *n* лимо́нный сок*.
lemon squeezer *n* (ручна́я) соковыжима́лка*.
lemon tea *n* чай* с лимо́ном.
lend [lɛnd] (*pt, pp* lent) *vt*: **to** ~ **sth to sb**, ~ **sb sth**
ода́лживать (одолжи́ть *perf*) что-н кому́-н;
it ~**s itself to** ... э́то поддаётся +*dat* ...; **to** ~ **sb**
a hand выруча́ть (вы́ручить *perf*) кого́-н.
lender [ˈlɛndəʳ] *n* кредито́р.
lending library [ˈlɛndɪŋ-] *n* библиоте́ка,
выдаю́щая кни́ги на́ дом.
length [lɛŋθ] *n* (*measurement*) длина́;
(*distance*) протяжённость *f*; (*piece: of wood,*
cloth etc) кусо́к*; (*duration*)
продолжи́тельность *f*; (*of book*) объём; **2**
metres in ~ длино́й в 2 ме́тра; **he walked the**
(**whole**) ~ **of the island** он прошёл че́рез весь
о́стров; **I swam three** ~**s** я проплы́л три
длины́ пла́вательного бассе́йна; **at** ~ (*at*
last) наконе́ц; (*for a long time*) до́лго; **to lie**
full ~ растя́гиваться (растяну́ться* *perf*) во
весь рост; **to go to any** ~(**s**) **to do**
прикла́дывать (приложи́ть* *perf*) все уси́лия
что́бы +*perf infin*.
lengthen [ˈlɛŋθn] *vt* удлиня́ть (удлини́ть *perf*)
♦ *vi* удлиня́ться (удлини́ться *perf*).
lengthways [ˈlɛŋθweɪz] *adv* вдоль.
lengthy [ˈlɛŋθɪ] *adj* (*text*) дли́нный* (дли́нен);
(*meeting*) продолжи́тельный*
(продолжи́телен); (*explanation*) до́лгий*.
leniency [ˈliːnɪənsɪ] *n* мя́гкость *f.*
lenient [ˈliːnɪənt] *adj* мя́гкий* (мя́гок).
leniently [ˈliːnɪəntlɪ] *adv* мя́гко.
Leningrad [ˈlɛnɪngræd] *n* Ленингра́д.
lens [lɛnz] *n* (*of spectacles, camera*) ли́нза; (*of*
telescope) объекти́в.
Lent [lɛnt] *n* Вели́кий* пост*.
lent [lɛnt] *pt, pp of* **lend.**
lentil [ˈlɛntl] *n* чечеви́ца *no pl.*
Leo [ˈliːəu] *n* Лев*; **he is** ~ он – Лев.
leopard [ˈlɛpəd] *n* леопа́рд.
leotard [ˈliːətɑːd] *n* трико́ *nt ind.*
leper [ˈlɛpəʳ] *n* прокажённый(-ая) *m(f) adj.*
leper colony *n* лепрозо́рий.
leprosy [ˈlɛprəsɪ] *n* прока́за.
lesbian [ˈlɛzbɪən] *adj* лесби́йский ♦ *n*
лесбия́нка*.
lesion [ˈliːʒən] *n* поврежде́ние.
Lesotho [lɪˈsuːtuː] *n* Лесо́то.
less [lɛs] *adj* (*in size, degree, amount*) ме́ньше;
(*in quality*) ме́нее ♦ *adv* ме́ньше ♦ *prep*: ~
tax/10% discount ми́нус нало́г/ски́дка на
10%; ~ **than half** ме́ньше полови́ны; ~ **than**
ever ме́ньше, чем когда́-либо; ~ **and** ~ всё
ме́ньше и ме́ньше; **the** ~ ... **the more** ... чем
ме́ньше ..., тем бо́льше ...; **the Prime**
Minister, no ~ никто́ ино́й как
премье́р-мини́стр.
lessee [lɛˈsiː] *n* (*of premises*) съёмщик; (*of*
land) аренда́тор.

lessen ['lɛsn] *vt* уменьша́ть (уме́ньшить *perf*)
♦ *vi* уменьша́ться (уме́ньшиться *perf*).
lesser ['lɛsə'] *adj* ме́ньший*; **to a ~ extent** в
ме́ньшей сте́пени.
lesson ['lɛsn] *n* (*also fig*) уро́к; **to teach sb a ~**
(*fig*) проучи́ть* (*perf*) кого́-н.
lessor ['lɛsə'] *n* лицо́*, сдаю́щее со́бствен-
ность в аре́нду.
lest [lɛst] *conj*: **~ you (should) forget** чтобы Вы
не забы́ли.
let [lɛt] (*pt, pp* **let**) *vt* (*BRIT: lease*) сдава́ть*
(сдать* *perf*) (внаём); (*allow*): **to ~ sb do**
разреша́ть (разреши́ть *perf*) *or* позволя́ть
(позво́лить *perf*) кому́-н +*infin*; **~ me try**
да́йте я попро́бую; **~ him come** пусть он
придёт; **to ~ sb know about ...** дава́ть* (дать*
perf) кому́-н знать о +*prp* ...; **~'s go** пошли́,
пойдёмте; **"to ~"** „сдаётся внаём"; **to ~ go of**
отпуска́ть (отпусти́ть* *perf*); **~ go!** (от)пусти́!;
to ~ sth drop роня́ть (урони́ть* *perf*) что-н; **to
~ o.s. go** (*relax*) расслабля́ться
(рассла́биться* *perf*); (*neglect o.s.*)
опуска́ться (опусти́ться* *perf*)
▶ **let down** *vt* (*tyre etc*) спуска́ть (спусти́ть*
perf); (*fig: person*) подводи́ть* (подвести́*
perf); (*hair*) распуска́ть (распусти́ть* *perf*);
(*dress, hem*) отпуска́ть (отпусти́ть* *perf*)
▶ **let in** *vt* (*water, air*) пропуска́ть (пропусти́ть*
perf); (*person*) впуска́ть (впусти́ть* *perf*)
▶ **let off** *vt* (*culprit, schoolchildren*) отпуска́ть
(отпусти́ть* *perf*); (*bomb*) взрыва́ть
(взорва́ть* *perf*); (*gun*) выстре́ливать
(вы́стрелить *perf*) из +*gen*; (*smell*) испуска́ть
(испусти́ть* *perf*); **to ~ off steam** (*inf*)
выпуска́ть (вы́пустить* *perf*) пар
▶ **let on** *vi* проговори́ваться (проговори́ться
perf)
▶ **let out** *vt* (*person, dog, water, air*) выпуска́ть
(вы́пустить* *perf*); (*passenger*) выса́живать
(вы́садить* *perf*); (*sound*) издава́ть* (изда́ть*
perf); (*house, room*) сдава́ть* (сдать* *perf*).
▶ **let up** *vi* (*cease*) перестава́ть* (переста́ть*
perf); (*diminish*) ослабева́ть (ослабе́ть *perf*).
letdown ['lɛtdaun] *n* разочарова́ние.
lethal ['li:θl] *adj* (*weapon, chemical*)
смертоно́сный* (смертоно́сен); (*dose*)
смерте́льный* (смерте́лен).
lethargic [lɛ'θɑ:dʒɪk] *adj* вя́лый* (вял),
со́нный* (со́нен).
lethargy ['lɛθədʒɪ] *n* вя́лость *f*.
letter ['lɛtə'] *n* (*correspondence*) письмо́*; (*of
alphabet*) бу́ква; **small/capital ~** строчна́я/
прописна́я бу́ква.
letter bomb *n* бо́мба, при́сланная по по́чте.
letter box *n* (*BRIT*) почто́вый я́щик.
letterhead ['lɛtəhɛd] *n* ша́пка (*в письме́*).
lettering ['lɛtərɪŋ] *n* шрифт.
letter of credit *n* аккредити́в.

letter opener *n* нож для разреза́ния бума́ги.
letterpress ['lɛtəprɛs] *n* (*method*) высо́кая
печа́ть *f*.
letter quality *n* (*of printer*) ка́чество печа́ти.
letters patent *npl* пате́нт.
lettuce ['lɛtɪs] *n* сала́т* лату́к.
let-up ['lɛtʌp] *n* ослабле́ние.
leukaemia [lu:'ki:mɪə] (*US* **leukemia**) *n*
белокро́вие, лейкеми́я.
level ['lɛvl] *adj* (*flat*) ро́вный* (ро́вен) ♦ *n*
у́ровень* *m*; (*also:* **spirit ~**) ватерпа́с ♦ *vt*
(*land*) ровня́ть (сровня́ть *perf*); (*building*)
сровня́ть* (*perf*) с землёй ♦ *vi* (*inf*): **to ~ with
sb** объясня́ться (объясни́ться *perf*) с кем-н
начистоту́ ♦ *adv*: **to draw ~ with** (*person,
vehicle*) поравня́ться (*perf*) с +*instr*; **to be ~
with** быть* (*impf*) на одно́м у́ровне с +*instr*;
"A" ~s (*BRIT: exams*) выпускны́е экза́мены (*в
сре́дней шко́ле*); (: *qualification*)
квалифика́ция, получа́емая при успе́шной
сда́че выпускно́го экза́мена; **on the ~** (*inf*)
че́стный* (че́стен); **to ~ a gun at sb** наводи́ть*
(навести́* *perf*) ружьё на кого́-н; **to ~ an
accusation/a criticism at** *or* **against sb**
направля́ть (напра́вить *perf*) обвине́ние/
кри́тику про́тив кого́-н
▶ **level off** *vi* (*prices etc*) выра́вниваться
(вы́ровняться *perf*)
▶ **level out** *vi* = **level off**.
level crossing *n* (*BRIT*) железнодоро́жный
перее́зд.
level-headed [lɛvl'hɛdɪd] *adj* уравнове́шенный
(уравнове́шен).
levelling ['lɛvlɪŋ] *n* выра́внивание.
level playing field *n* ра́вные пози́ции *fpl*.
lever ['li:və'] *n* (*also fig*) рыча́г*; (*bar*) лом ♦ *vt*:
to ~ up/out поднима́ть (подня́ть *perf*)/
тащи́ть (вы́тащить *perf*) с уси́лием.
leverage ['li:vərɪdʒ] *n* рыча́жная си́ла; (*fig:
influence*) влия́ние.
levity ['lɛvɪtɪ] *n* легкомы́слие.
levy ['lɛvɪ] *n* нало́г ♦ *vt* взима́ть (*impf*).
lewd [lu:d] *adj* (*look*) похотли́вый (похотли́в);
(*remark*) непристо́йный* (непристо́ен).
LI *abbr* (*US*) = **Long Island**.
liability [laɪə'bɪlətɪ] *n* (*LAW: responsibility*)
отве́тственность *f*; (*person, thing*) обу́за *m/f*;
liabilities *npl* (*COMM*) обяза́тельства *ntpl*.
liable ['laɪəbl] (*LAW*) *adj* (*responsible*): **~ for** (*for
actions*) отве́тственный (отве́тствен) за
+*acc*; (*legally responsible*) подсу́дный*
(подсу́ден) за +*acc*; (*subject*): **~ to**
подлежа́щий +*dat*; **to be ~ for** нести́* (*impf*)
отве́тственность за +*acc*; **to be ~ to**
подлежа́ть (*impf*) +*dat*; **he's ~ to take offence**
возмо́жно, что он оби́дется.

---

* marks translations which have irregular inflections. The Russian-English side of the dictionary gives inflectional information.

liaise [liː'eɪz] *vi*: **to ~ (with)** коопери́роваться (скоопери́роваться *perf*) (с +*instr*).

liaison [liː'eɪzən] *n* (*cooperation*) коопера́ция; (*sexual*) связь *f*.

liar ['laɪə] *n* лжец*, лгун*(ья).

libel ['laɪbl] *n* клевета́ ♦ *vt* клевета́ть* (оклевета́ть* *perf*).

libellous ['laɪbləs] (*US* **libelous**) *adj* (*comment etc*) клеветни́ческий*.

liberal ['lɪbərl] *adj* (*tolerant, also POL*) либера́льный* (либера́лен); (*large, generous*) ще́дрый; **~ with** ще́дрый* (щедр) на +*acc* ♦ *n* (*tolerant person*) либера́л; (*POL*): **L~** либера́л.

liberalize ['lɪbərəlaɪz] *vt* либерализова́ть (*impf/perf*).

liberally ['lɪbrəlɪ] *adv* (*see adj*) либера́льно; ще́дро.

Liberal Democrat *n* либера́л-демокра́т; **the ~ ~s** (*party*) па́ртия Либера́л-демокра́тов.

liberal-minded ['lɪbərl'maɪndɪd] *adj* либера́льно-настро́енный (либера́льно-настро́ен).

liberate ['lɪbəreɪt] *vt* освобожда́ть (освободи́ть* *perf*).

liberation [lɪbə'reɪʃən] *n* освобожде́ние.

Liberia [laɪ'bɪərɪə] *n* Либе́рия.

Liberian [laɪ'bɪərɪən] *adj* либери́йский ♦ *n* либери́ец*(-и́йка*).

liberty ['lɪbətɪ] *n* свобо́да; **to be at ~** (*criminal*) быть* (*impf*) на свобо́де; **I'm not at ~ to comment** я не во́лен комменти́ровать; **to take the ~ of doing** позволя́ть (позво́лить* *perf*) себе́ +*infin*.

libido [lɪ'biːdəu] *n* либи́до *nt ind*.

Libra ['liːbrə] *n* Весы́ *pl*; **he is ~** он – Весы́.

librarian [laɪ'brɛərɪən] *n* библиоте́карь *m*.

library ['laɪbrərɪ] *n* библиоте́ка.

library book *n* библиоте́чная кни́га.

libretto [lɪ'brɛtəu] *n* либре́тто *nt ind*.

Libya ['lɪbɪə] *n* Ли́вия.

Libyan ['lɪbɪən] *adj* ливи́йский ♦ *n* ливи́ец*(-и́йка*).

lice [laɪs] *npl of* **louse**.

licence ['laɪsns] (*US* **license**) *n* (*permit*) лице́нзия; (*AUT: also: driving ~*) (води́тельские) права́ *ntpl*; (*freedom*) во́льность *f*; **under ~** (*COMM*) по лице́нзии.

license ['laɪsns] *n* (*US*) = **licence** ♦ *vt* выдава́ть* (вы́дать* *perf*) лице́нзию на +*acc*.

licensed ['laɪsnst] *adj* (*car etc*) зарегистри́рованный (зарегистри́рован); (*restaurant*) с лице́нзией на прода́жу спиртны́х напи́тков.

licensed trade *n* организа́ции, торгу́ющие алкого́льными напи́тками.

licensee [laɪsən'siː] *n* держа́тель *m* лице́нзии.

license plate *n* (*US*) номерно́й знак (*на автомоби́ле*).

licensing hours ['laɪsnsɪŋ] *npl* (*BRIT*) часы́, в кото́рые разрешена́ торго́вля спиртны́ми напи́тками.

licentious [laɪ'sɛnʃəs] *adj* распу́щенный (распу́щен).

lichen ['laɪkən] *n* лиша́йник.

lick [lɪk] *vt* (*stamp, fingers etc*) лиза́ть* (*impf*), обли́зывать (облиза́ть* *perf*); (*inf: defeat*) положи́ть* (*perf*) на лопа́тки ♦ *n*: **to give sth a ~** лизну́ть (*perf*) что-н; **to give sth a ~ of paint** подкра́шивать (подкра́сить* *perf*) что-н; **to ~ one's lips** обли́зываться (облиза́ться* *perf*); (*fig*) обли́зываться (*impf*).

licorice ['lɪkərɪs] *n* (*US*) = **liquorice**.

lid [lɪd] *n* кры́шка*; (*also: eyelid*) ве́ко; **to take the ~ off sth** (*fig*) выта́скивать (вы́тащить *perf*) что-н на свет бо́жий.

lido ['laɪdəu] *n* (*BRIT: pool*) бассе́йн на откры́том во́здухе.

lie [laɪ] (*pt* **lay**, *pp* **lain**) *vi* (*be horizontal*) лежа́ть* (*impf*); (*be situated*) лежа́ть* (*impf*), находи́ться* (*impf*); (*problem, cause*) заключа́ться (*impf*); (*be untruthful*) (*pt, pp* **lied**) лгать* (солга́ть* *perf*), врать* (совра́ть* *perf*) ♦ *n* (*untrue statement*) ложь *f no pl*; **to ~** *or* **be lying in first/last place** быть* (*impf*) на пе́рвом/после́днем ме́сте; **to ~ low** (*fig*) пережида́ть (пережда́ть* *perf*); **to tell ~s** говори́ть (*impf*) непра́вду

► **lie about** *vi* валя́ться (*impf*)
► **lie around** *vi* = **lie about**
► **lie back** *vi* отки́дываться (отки́нуться *perf*); (*fig*) успока́иваться (успоко́иться *perf*)
► **lie down** *vi* ложи́ться (лечь* *perf*); **to be lying down** лежа́ть* (*impf*)
► **lie up** *vi* (*hide*) скрыва́ться (скры́ться* *perf*).

Liechtenstein ['lɪktənstaɪn] *n* Лихтенште́йн.

lie detector *n* дете́ктор лжи.

lie-down ['laɪdaun] *n* (*BRIT*): **to have a ~** полежа́ть* (*perf*).

lie-in ['laɪn] *n* (*BRIT*): **to have a ~** встава́ть* (встать* *perf*) попо́зже.

lieu [luː]: **in ~ of** *prep* вме́сто +*gen*.

Lieut. *abbr* (*MIL*) = **lieutenant**.

lieutenant [lɛf'tɛnənt, (*US*) luː'tɛnənt] *n* лейтена́нт.

lieutenant colonel *n* подполко́вник.

life [laɪf] (*pl* **lives**) *n* жизнь *f no pl*; **true to ~** правдоподо́бный* (правдоподо́бен); **to paint from ~** писа́ть* (написа́ть* *perf*) с нату́ры; **to be sent to prison for ~** получа́ть (получи́ть* *perf*) пожи́зненное заключе́ние; **to come to ~** (*fig: person*) ожива́ть (ожи́ть* *perf*); (*: party*) оживля́ться (оживи́ться* *perf*).

life annuity *n* пожи́зненный аннуите́т.

life assurance *n* (*BRIT*) = **life insurance**.

life belt *n* (*BRIT*) спаса́тельный круг*.

lifeblood ['laɪfblʌd] *n* (*fig*) жи́зненная осно́ва.

lifeboat ['laɪfbəut] *n* (*rescue launch*) спаса́тельное су́дно*; (*on ship*) спаса́тельная шлю́пка.

life buoy *n* = **life belt**.

life expectancy *n* продолжи́тельность *f* жи́зни.

lifeguard ['laɪfgɑːd] *n* спаса́тель(ница) *m(f)*.
life imprisonment *n* пожи́зненное заключе́ние.
life insurance *n* страхова́ние жи́зни.
life jacket *n* спаса́тельный жиле́т.
lifeless ['laɪflɪs] *adj* (*also fig*) безжи́зненный (безжи́знен).
lifelike ['laɪflaɪk] *adj* (*model, robot*) как живо́й; (*performance*) реалисти́чный* (реалисти́чен).
lifeline ['laɪflaɪn] *n* (*fig*) сре́дство вы́живания; (*rope*) спаса́тельный кана́т.
lifelong ['laɪflɔŋ] *adj* (*friend, habit*) неизме́нный; **it was a ~ ambition of his** э́то бы́ло мечто́й всей его́ жи́зни.
life preserver *n* (*US*) = **life belt, life jacket.**
lifer ['laɪfə°] *n* бессро́чник(-ица).
life raft *n* спаса́тельный плот*.
life-saver ['laɪfseɪvə°] *n* спасе́ние.
life science *n* есте́ственные нау́ки *fpl*.
life sentence *n* пригово́р к пожи́зненному заключе́нию.
life-size(d) ['laɪfsaɪz(d)] *adj* в натура́льную величину́.
life span *n* (*of living thing*) продолж-и́тельность *f* жи́зни; (*of product*) срок* слу́жбы; (*of idea, organization*) долгове́чность *f*.
lifestyle ['laɪfstaɪl] *n* о́браз жи́зни.
life-support system ['laɪfsəpɔːt-] *n* систе́ма жизнеобеспече́ния.
lifetime ['laɪftaɪm] *n* (*of person*) жизнь *f*; (*of institution*) вре́мя* *nt* существова́ния; **the chance of a ~** уника́льный шанс.
lift [lɪft] *vt* поднима́ть (подня́ть* *perf*); (*ban, sanctions*) снима́ть (снять* *perf*); (*inf: steal*) тащи́ть (стащи́ть* *perf*) ♦ *vi* (*fog*) рассе́иваться (рассе́яться *perf*) ♦ *n* (*BRIT*) лифт; **to give sb a ~** (*BRIT: AUT*) подвози́ть* (подвезти́* *perf*) кого́-н
▶ **lift in** *vt* (*goods, people*) ввози́ть* (ввезти́* *perf*) самолётом
▶ **lift off** *vi* (*rocket*) отрыва́ться (оторва́ться* *perf*) от земли́, стартова́ть (*impf/perf*)
▶ **lift out** *vt* (*goods, people*) вывози́ть* (вы́везти* *perf*) самолётом
▶ **lift up** *vt* (*object, person*) поднима́ть (подня́ть* *perf*).
liftoff ['lɪftɔf] *n* старт.
ligament ['lɪgəmənt] *n* (*ANAT*) свя́зка*.
light [laɪt] (*pt, pp* **lit**) *n* свет*; (*AUT*) фа́ра ♦ *vt* (*candle, cigarette, fire*) зажига́ть (заже́чь* *perf*); (*place*) освеща́ть (освети́ть* *perf*) ♦ *adj* (*pale, bright*) све́тлый* (све́тел); (*not heavy*) лёгкий* (лёгок) ♦ *adv* (*travel*) налегке́; **~s** *npl* (*also: traffic ~s*) светофо́р *msg*; **to turn the ~ on/off** включа́ть (включи́ть *perf*)/выключа́ть (вы́ключить *perf*) свет; **have you got a ~?** (*for

cigarette) мо́жно у Вас прикури́ть?; **to come to ~** выясня́ться (вы́ясниться *perf*); **to cast or shed** *or* **throw ~ on** пролива́ть (проли́ть* *perf*) свет на +*acc*; **in the ~ of** (*discussions, new evidence*) в све́те +*gen*; **to make ~ of** не заостря́ть (*impf*) внима́ние на +*acc*; **the house is lit by electricity** дом освещён электри́чеством
▶ **light up** *vi* (*face*) светле́ть (просветле́ть *perf*) ♦ *vt* (*illuminate*) освеща́ть (освети́ть* *perf*).
light bulb *n* ла́мпочка*.
lighten ['laɪtn] *vi* (*become less dark*) светле́ть (посветле́ть *perf*) ♦ *vt* (*make less heavy*) облегча́ть (облегчи́ть *perf*).
lighter ['laɪtə°] *n* (*also: cigarette ~*) зажига́лка*; (*boat*) ли́хтер.
light-fingered [laɪt'fɪŋgəd] *adj* нечи́стый* (нечи́ст) на́ руку.
light-headed [laɪt'hɛdɪd] *adj*: **she felt ~** у неё кружи́лась голова́.
light-hearted [laɪt'hɑːtɪd] *adj* (*person*) беспе́чный* (беспе́чен); (*question, remark*) несерьёзный* (несерьёзен).
lighthouse ['laɪthaus] *n* мая́к*.
lighting ['laɪtɪŋ] *n* освеще́ние.
lighting-up time [laɪtɪŋ'ʌp-] *n* вре́мя* *nt* включе́ния у́личного освеще́ния.
lightly ['laɪtlɪ] *adv* (*touch, kiss*) слегка́; (*eat, treat*) легко́; (*sleep*) неглубоко́; **to get off ~** легко́ отде́лываться (отде́латься *perf*).
light meter *n* экспоно́метр.
lightness ['laɪtnɪs] *n* (*in weight*) лёгкость *f*.
lightning ['laɪtnɪŋ] *n* мо́лния ♦ *adj* (*rapid*) молниено́сный* (молниено́сен).
lightning conductor *n* (*BRIT*) громоотво́д.
lightning rod *n* (*US*) = **lightning conductor.**
light pen *n* прибо́р, счи́тывающий штрихово́й код.
lightship ['laɪtʃɪp] *n* плаву́чий мая́к*.
lightweight ['laɪtweɪt] *adj* (*suit*) лёгкий* ♦ *n* (*BOXING*) бо́ксер лёгкого ве́са.
light year *n* светово́й год*.
like [laɪk] *prep* как +*acc*; (*similar to*) похо́жий на +*acc* ♦ *adj* подо́бный (подо́бен) ♦ *vt* (*sweets, reading*) люби́ть* (*impf*); (*find attractive, acceptable*): **I ~ him** он мне нра́вится ♦ *n*: **and the ~** тому́ подо́бное; **to be** *or* **look ~** походи́ть* (*impf*) на +*acc*; **he looks ~ his father** он похо́ж на своего́ отца́; **what does she look ~?** как она́ вы́глядит?; **what's he ~?** что он за челове́к?; **what's the weather ~?** кака́я сего́дня пого́да?; **something ~ that** что́-то в э́том ро́де; **I feel ~ a drink** я хочу́ что́-нибудь вы́пить; **there's nothing ~ ...** ничто́ не мо́жет сравни́ться с +*instr* ...; **do it ~ this** де́лайте (сде́лайте *perf*) э́то так; **that's just ~ him** (*typical*) э́то на него́ похо́же; **it is nothing ~ ...** э́то совсе́м не то, что ...; **I would ~, I'd ~** мне

---

* marks translations which have irregular inflections. The Russian-English side of the dictionary gives inflectional information.

хоте́лось бы, я бы хоте́л; **would you ~ a coffee?** хоти́те ко́фе?; **I ~d him** он мне понра́вилось; **I don't ~ his behaviour** мне не нра́вится его́ поведе́ние; **if you ~** е́сли хоти́те; **his ~s and dislikes** его́ вку́сы.

likeable ['laɪkəbl] *adj* симпати́чный* (симпати́чен).

likelihood ['laɪklɪhud] *n* вероя́тность *f*; **in all ~** по все́й вероя́тности; **there is every ~ that ...** о́чень вероя́тно, что ....

likely ['laɪklɪ] *adj* вероя́тный* (вероя́тен); **she is ~ to agree** она́ вероя́тно согласи́тся; **not ~!** (*inf*) ни за что!

like-minded ['laɪk'maɪndɪd] *adj*: **a ~ person** единомы́шленник; **~ friends/colleagues** друзья́/колле́ги – единомы́шленники.

liken ['laɪkən] *vt*: **to ~ sth/sb to** уподобля́ть (уподо́бить* *perf*) что-н/кого́-н +*dat*.

likeness ['laɪknɪs] *n* схо́дство; **the portrait is a good ~ of her** портре́т обнару́живает большо́е схо́дство с ней.

likewise ['laɪkwaɪz] *adv* та́кже; **to do ~** поступа́ть (поступи́ть* *perf*) таки́м же о́бразом.

liking ['laɪkɪŋ] *n*: **~ (for)** (*person*) симпа́тия (к +*dat*); (*thing*) вкус (к +*dat*); **to be to sb's ~** быть* (*impf*) *or* приходи́ться* (прийти́сь* *perf*) кому́-н по вку́су; **I took an instant ~ to him** он мне сра́зу понра́вился.

lilac ['laɪlək] *n* сире́нь *f no pl* ♦ *adj* сире́невый.

Lilo® ['laɪləu] *n* надувно́й рези́новый матра́ц.

lilt [lɪlt] *n* (*in voice*) переливы *mpl*.

lilting ['lɪltɪŋ] *adj* (*voice*) мелоди́чный* (мелоди́чен).

lily ['lɪlɪ] *n* ли́лия.

lily of the valley *n* ла́ндыш.

Lima ['liːmə] *n* Ли́ма.

limb [lɪm] *n* (*ANAT*) коне́чность *f*; (*of tree*) ветвь* *f*; **to be out on a ~** быть* (*impf*) *or* находи́ться* (*impf*) в крити́ческом положе́нии.

limber up ['lɪmbə'-] *vi* размина́ться (размя́ться* *perf*).

limbo ['lɪmbəu] *n*: **to be in ~** (*fig*) находи́ться* (*impf*) в состоя́нии неопределённости.

lime [laɪm] *n* (*fruit*) лайм; (*tree*) ли́па*; (*also*: ~ **juice**) сок ла́йма; (*chemical*) и́звесть *f*; (*rock*) известня́к*.

limelight ['laɪmlaɪt] *n*: **to be in the ~** быть* (*impf*) в це́нтре внима́ния.

limerick ['lɪmərɪk] *n* лиме́рик (*юмористи́ческое пятистро́чное стихотворе́ние*).

limestone ['laɪmstəun] *n* известня́к*.

limit ['lɪmɪt] *n* преде́л; (*restriction*) лими́т, ограниче́ние ♦ *vt* (*production, expense etc*) лимити́ровать (*impf/perf*), ограни́чивать (ограни́чить *perf*); **speed ~** преде́льная ско́рость *f*; **within ~s** в преде́лах допусти́мого; **that's the ~!** э́то перехо́дит все грани́цы!

limitation [lɪmɪ'teɪʃən] *n* ограниче́ние; **~s** *npl* недоста́тки *mpl*.

limited ['lɪmɪtɪd] *adj* ограни́ченный (ограни́чен); **to be ~ to** ограни́чиваться (ограни́читься *perf*) +*instr*.

limited edition *n* малотира́жное изда́ние.

limited (liability) company *n* (*BRIT*) компа́ния с ограни́ченной отве́тственностью.

limitless ['lɪmɪtlɪs] *adj* беспреде́льный* (беспреде́лен).

limousine ['lɪməziːn] *n* лимузи́н.

limp [lɪmp] *vi* хрома́ть (*impf*) ♦ *adj* (*person, limb*) бесси́льный* (бесси́лен); (*material*) мя́гкий* (мя́гок) ♦ *n*: **to have a ~** хрома́ть (*impf*).

limpet ['lɪmpɪt] *n* блю́дечко* (*моллю́ск*).

limpid ['lɪmpɪd] *adj* прозра́чный* (прозра́чен).

limply ['lɪmplɪ] *adv* (*lie*) бесси́льно; (*fall*) мя́гко.

linchpin ['lɪntʃpɪn] *n* опо́ра.

Lincs [lɪŋks] *abbr* (*BRIT. POST*) = **Lincolnshire**.

line [laɪn] *n* (*also TEL, RAIL*) ли́ния; (*row*) ряд*; (*US: queue*) о́чередь *f*; (*of writing, song*) строка́*, стро́чка*; (*wrinkle*) морщи́на; (*rope*) верёвка*; (*for fishing*) леска́*; (*wire*) про́вод; (*route*) маршру́т*; (*fig: attitude, policy*) ли́ния; (*: of thought, reasoning*) ход; (*of business, work*) о́бласть *f*; (*of product(s)*) моде́ль *f*, тип ♦ *vt* (*stand along*) выстра́иваться (вы́строиться *perf*) вдоль +*gen*; (*clothing*) подбива́ть (подби́ть* *perf*); (*container*) выкла́дывать (вы́ложить* *perf*) изнутри́; **hold the ~ please!** (*TEL*) пожа́луйста, не клади́те тру́бку!; **to cut in ~** (*US*) идти́* (пойти́* *perf*) без о́череди; **to stand in ~** (*in a row*) стоя́ть (*impf*) в шере́нге *or* ряд; **in ~ with** (*in keeping with*) в соотве́тствии с +*instr*; **to bring sth into ~ with sth** приводи́ть* (привести́* *perf*) что-н в соотве́тствие с чем-н; **on the right ~s** на ве́рном пути́; **to draw the ~ at sth** ограни́чиваться (ограни́читься *perf*) чем-н; **he is in ~ for a pay rise** он ско́ро до́лжен получи́ть повыше́ние зарпла́ты; **the streets are ~d with trees** у́лицы обса́жены дере́вьями; **the walls were ~d with pictures** сте́ны бы́ли заве́шены карти́нами

▶ **line up** *vi* выстра́иваться (вы́строиться *perf*) ♦ *vt* (*place in order*) выстра́ивать (вы́строить *perf*); (*prepare*) подгота́вливать (подгото́вить* *perf*); **she has a new job ~d up** она́ устро́илась на но́вую рабо́ту.

linear ['lɪnɪə'] *adj* лине́йный*.

lined [laɪnd] *adj* (*paper*) лино́ванный; (*face*) морщи́нистый (морщи́нист); (*skirt, jacket*) на подкла́дке, с подкла́дкой.

line editing *n* (*COMPUT*) постро́чное редакти́рование.

line feed *n* (*COMPUT*) перево́д *or* прого́н строки́.

lineman ['laɪnmən] *n* (*US: workman*) инжене́р телефо́нной свя́зи; (*: SPORT*) боково́й судья́.

linen ['lɪnɪn] *n* (*material*) лён*; (*sheets etc*)

бельё.
line printer *n* (*COMPUT*) постро́чно-
печата́ющее устро́йство, устро́йство
постро́чной печа́ти.
liner ['laɪnə'] *n* (*ship*) ла́йнер; (*also:* **bin** ~)
целофа́новый мешо́к для му́сорного ведра́.
linesman ['laɪnzmən] *irreg n* судья́* *m* на ли́нии.
line-up ['laɪnʌp] *n* (*also:* **team** ~) соста́в
кома́нды; (*at event*) соста́в уча́стников; (*US:*
queue) о́чередь* *f*; (*identity parade*)
опозна́ние (*престу́пника*).
linger ['lɪŋgə'] *vi* (*smell, tradition*)
уде́рживаться (удержа́ться* *perf*); (*person*)
заде́рживаться (задержа́ться* *perf*).
lingerie ['lænʒəriː] *n* же́нское ни́жнее бельё.
lingering ['lɪŋgərɪŋ] *adj* (*sense, feeling, doubt*)
усто́йчивый.
lingo ['lɪŋgəu] (*pl* ~**es**) *n* (*inf: language*)
(иностра́нный) язы́к.
linguist ['lɪŋgwɪst] *n* (*language specialist*)
лингви́ст; **he is a good** ~ (*speaks several
languages*) он спосо́бен к языка́м.
linguistic [lɪŋ'gwɪstɪk] *adj* лингвисти́ческий*.
linguistics [lɪŋ'gwɪstɪks] *n* языкозна́ние,
лингви́стика.
liniment ['lɪnɪmənt] *n* жи́дкая мазь *f*.
lining ['laɪnɪŋ] *n* (*cloth*) подкла́дка*; (*TECH*)
прокла́дка*; (*of stomach etc*) вы́стилка.
link [lɪŋk] *n* связь *f*; (*of a chain*) звено́* ◆ *vt* (*join*)
соединя́ть (соедини́ть *perf*); (*associate*): **to** ~
with *or* **to** свя́зывать (связа́ть* *perf*) с +*instr*;
~**s** *npl* (*GOLF*) по́ле для игры́ в гольф; **rail** ~
железнодоро́жная связь
▶ **link up** *vt* (*machines, systems*) соединя́ть
(соедини́ть *perf*) ◆ *vi* соединя́ться
(соедини́ться *perf*).
linkup ['lɪŋkʌp] *n* соедине́ние; (*of spaceships*)
стыко́вка*; (*RADIO, TV*) свя́зка*, связна́я
часть *f*; (*between studios: RADIO*) радиомо́ст;
(*: TV*) телемо́ст.
lino ['laɪnəu] *n* = **linoleum**.
linoleum [lɪ'nəuliəm] *n* лино́леум.
linseed oil ['lɪnsiːd-] *n* льняно́е ма́сло.
lint [lɪnt] *n* ма́рля.
lintel ['lɪntl] *n* при́толока.
lion ['laɪən] *n* лев*.
lion cub *n* львёнок*.
lioness ['laɪənɪs] *n* льви́ца.
lip [lɪp] *n* (*ANAT*) губа́*; (*of container*) край*; (*inf:
insolence*) гру́бости *fpl*.
liposome ['lɪpəusəum] *n* липосо́ма.
liposuction ['lɪpəusʌkʃən] *n* липоса́кция,
отса́сывание жирово́й тка́ни.
lip-read ['lɪpriːd] *vi* чита́ть (*impf*) с губ.
lip salve *n* мазь *f* для смягче́ния губ.
lip service *n*: **to pay** ~ ~ **to sth** признава́ть*
(призна́ть *perf*) что-н то́лько на слова́х.
lipstick ['lɪpstɪk] *n* губна́я пома́да.

liquefy ['lɪkwɪfaɪ] *vt* превраща́ть (преврати́ть*
perf) в жи́дкость ◆ *vi* переходи́ть* (перейти́*
perf) в жи́дкое состоя́ние.
liqueur [lɪ'kjuə'] *n* ликёр.
liquid ['lɪkwɪd] *n* жи́дкость *f* ◆ *adj* жи́дкий*
(жи́док).
liquid assets *npl* ликви́дные акти́вы *mpl*.
liquidate ['lɪkwɪdeɪt] *vt* ликвиди́ровать (*impf/
perf*).
liquidation [lɪkwɪ'deɪʃən] *n* ликвида́ция; **to go
into** ~ ликвиди́роваться (*impf*).
liquidation sale *n* (*US*) распрода́жа
иму́щества ликви́дированного предприя́тия.
liquidator ['lɪkwɪdeɪtə'] *n* ликвида́тор.
liquid crystal display *n*
жидкокристалли́ческий индика́тор.
liquidity [lɪ'kwɪdɪtɪ] *n* ликви́дность *f*.
liquidize ['lɪkwɪdaɪz] *vt* пропуска́ть
(пропусти́ть* *perf*) че́рез ми́ксер.
liquidizer ['lɪkwɪdaɪzə'] *n* ми́ксер, смеси́тель *m*.
liquor ['lɪkə'] *n* (*esp US*) спиртно́е *nt adj*,
спиртно́й напи́ток*.
liquorice ['lɪkərɪs] *n* (*BRIT: sweet*) лакри́ца.
liquor store *n* (*US*) магази́н спиртны́х
напи́тков.
Lisbon ['lɪzbən] *n* Лиссабо́н.
lisp [lɪsp] *n* шепеля́вость *f* ◆ *vi* шепеля́вить*
(*impf*).
lissom(e) ['lɪsəm] *adj* изя́щный* (изя́щен).
list [lɪst] *n* (*also COMPUT*) спи́сок* ◆ *vt*
(*enumerate*) перечисля́ть (перечи́слить *perf*);
(*write down*) составля́ть (соста́вить* *perf*)
спи́сок +*gen*; (*put on list*) включа́ть
(включи́ть* *perf*) в спи́сок ◆ *vi* (*ship*)
крени́ться (накрени́ться *perf*).
listed building *n* (*BRIT*) зда́ние, охраня́емое
госуда́рством.
listed company *n* официа́льно
зарегистри́рованная компа́ния.
listen ['lɪsn] *vi*: **to** ~ (**to sb/sth**) слу́шать (*impf*)
(кого́-н/что́-н); **to** ~ **to sb** *or* **sb's advice**
слу́шать (послу́шать *perf*) кого́-н; **I'm** ~**ing
out for him** я прислу́шиваюсь, не идёт ли он;
~! послу́шайте!
listener ['lɪsnə'] *n* слу́шатель(ница) *m(f)*;
(*RADIO*) радиослу́шатель(ница) *m(f)*.
listeria [lɪs'tɪərɪə] *n* листе́рия.
listing [lɪstɪŋ] *n* (*COMPUT*) распеча́тка, ли́стинг.
listless ['lɪstlɪs] *adj* вя́лый (вял).
listlessly ['lɪstlɪslɪ] *adv* вя́ло.
list price *n* прейскура́нтная цена́*.
lit [lɪt] *pt, pp of* **light**.
litany ['lɪtənɪ] *n* (*REL: Catholic*) лита́ния;
(*: Orthodox*) ектенья́; (*list*) моното́нное
перечисле́ние.
liter ['liːtə'] *n* (*US*) = **litre**.
literacy ['lɪtərəsɪ] *n* гра́мотность *f*.
literacy campaign *n* борьба́ с

неграмотностью.
literal [ˈlɪtərl] *adj* буквальный* (буквален).
literally [ˈlɪtrəlɪ] *adv* буквально.
literary [ˈlɪtərərɪ] *adj* литературный*.
literate [ˈlɪtərət] *adj* (*able to read and write*) грамотный* (грамотен); (*educated*) образованный (образован).
literature [ˈlɪtrɪtʃəʳ] *n* литература.
lithe [laɪð] *adj* гибкий* (гибок).
lithograph [ˈlɪθəgrɑ:f] *n* литография.
lithography [lɪˈθɔgrəfɪ] *n* литография.
Lithuania [lɪθjuˈeɪnɪə] *n* Литва.
Lithuanian [lɪθjuˈeɪnɪən] *adj* литовский* ♦ *n* (*person*) литовец*(-вка*); (*LING*) литовский язык.
litigation [lɪtɪˈgeɪʃən] *n* тяжба.
litmus paper [ˈlɪtməs-] *n* лакмусовая бумага.
litre [ˈliːtəʳ] (*US* **liter**) *n* литр.
litter [ˈlɪtəʳ] *n* (*rubbish*) мусор; (*young animals*) помёт.
litter bin *n* (*BRIT*) урна (*для мусора*).
litterbug [ˈlɪtəbʌg] *n* (*inf*) человек, который сорит в общественных местах.
littered [ˈlɪtəd] *adj*: ~ **with** заваленный (завален) +*instr*.
litter lout *n* (*inf*) = **litterbug**.
little [ˈlɪtl] *adj* (*small, young*) маленький*; (*younger*) младший*; (*short*) короткий* ♦ *adv* мало; **a** ~ (**bit**) немного; **I have** ~ **time/money** у меня мало времени/денег; **to make** ~ **of** не заострять (*impf*) внимание на +*prp*; ~ **by** ~ мало-помалу, понемногу.
little finger *n* мизинец* (*на руке*).
little-known [ˈlɪtlˈnəun] *adj* малоизвестный* (малоизвестен).
liturgy [ˈlɪtədʒɪ] *n* литургия.
live [*vb* lɪv, *adj* laɪv] *vi* жить* (*impf*) ♦ *adj* (*animal, plant*) живой*; (*broadcast*) прямой; (*performance*) перед публикой; (*ELEC*) под напряжением; (*bullet*) боевой; (*bomb*) не взорвавшийся; **to** ~ **with sb** жить* (*impf*) с кем-н; **he** ~**d to** (**be**) **a hundred** он прожил до ста лет
▶ **live down** *vt* заглаживать (загладить* *perf*)
▶ **live for** *vi* жить* (*impf*) для +*gen*
▶ **live in** *vi*: **most students** ~ **in** большинство студентов живёт в общежитии
▶ **live off** *vt fus* (*survive on*): **we** ~**d off fish** мы жили на одной рыбе; (*pej: parents etc*) жить* (*impf*) за счёт +*gen*
▶ **live on** *vt fus* (*food*) жить* (*impf*) на одном(-ой) +*prp*; (*salary*) жить* (*impf*) на +*acc*
▶ **live out** *vi*: **postgraduates usually** ~ **out** аспиранты обычно не живут в общежитии ♦ *vt*: **to** ~ **out one's days** *or* **life** проживать (прожить* *perf*) остаток своей жизни
▶ **live together** *vi* жить* (*impf*) вместе
▶ **live up** *vt*: **to** ~ **it up** (*inf*) жить* (*impf*) широко
▶ **live up to** *vt fus* оправдывать (оправдать* *perf*).
live-in [ˈlɪvɪn] *adj*: ~ **lover** сожитель(ница) *m(f)*;

they have a ~ **nanny** с ними живёт няня.
livelihood [ˈlaɪvlɪhud] *n* средства *ntpl* к существованию.
liveliness [ˈlaɪvlɪnɪs] *n* живость *f*.
lively [ˈlaɪvlɪ] *adj* (*person, book, interest, mind*) живой*; (*place, event*) оживлённый (оживлён).
liven up [ˈlaɪvn-] *vt* (*person*) ободрять (ободрить* *perf*); (*discussion, evening*) оживлять (оживить* *perf*) ♦ *vi* оживляться (оживиться* *perf*).
liver [ˈlɪvəʳ] *n* (*ANAT*) печень *f*; (*CULIN*) печёнка.
liverish [ˈlɪvərɪʃ] *adj*: **he is feeling** ~ его подташнивает.
Liverpool [ˈlɪvəpuːl] *n* Ливерпуль *m*.
Liverpudlian [lɪvəˈpʌdlɪən] *adj* ливерпульский ♦ *n* ливерпулец*(-лька*).
livery [ˈlɪvərɪ] *n* (*of servant*) ливрея.
lives [laɪvz] *npl of* **life**.
livestock [ˈlaɪvstɔk] *n* скот*.
live wire *n* (*inf*): **he's a real** ~ ~ он ужасно заводной.
livid [ˈlɪvɪd] *adj* (*colour*) серовато-синий*; (*inf: furious*): **she was** ~ она была в ярости.
living [ˈlɪvɪŋ] *adj* живой* ♦ *n*: **to earn** *or* **make a** ~ зарабатывать (заработать* *perf*) на жизнь; **within** ~ **memory** на памяти живущих; **the cost of** ~ стоимость *f* жизни.
living conditions *npl* условия *ntpl* жизни.
living expenses *npl* расходы *mpl* на жизнь.
living room *n* гостиная *f adj*.
living standards *npl* жизненный уровень* *msg*.
living wage *n* прожиточный минимум.
lizard [ˈlɪzəd] *n* ящерица.
Ljubljana [luːˈbljɑːnə] *n* Любляна.
llama [ˈlɑːmə] *n* лама (*ЗООЛ*).
LLB *n abbr* (= *Bachelor of Laws*) ≈ бакалавр правоведения.
LLD *n abbr* (= *Doctor of Laws*) ≈ доктор правоведения.
LMT *abbr* (*US*) = *Local Mean Time*.
load [ləud] *n* (*of person, animal*) ноша; (*of vehicle*) груз; (*weight, also ELEC, TECH*) нагрузка* ♦ *vt* (*also:* ~ **up**: *cargo, goods*) грузить (погрузить* *perf*); (*COMPUT*) загружать (загрузить* *perf*); (*gun, camera*) заряжать (зарядить* *perf*); (*tape recorder*) ставить* (поставить* *perf*) кассету в +*prp*; **to** ~ (**with**) (*also:* ~ **up**: *vehicle, ship*) нагружать (нагрузить* *perf*) (+*instr*); ~**s of, a** ~ **of** (*inf*) куча +*gen*; **a** ~ **of rubbish** (*inf*) сплошная чепуха.
loaded [ˈləudɪd] *adj* (*gun*) заряженный (заряжен); (*dice*) утяжелённый (утяжелён); (*vehicle*): ~ (**with**) нагруженный (нагружен) (+*instr*); (*inf*): **he's** ~ у него куча денег; ~ **question** вопрос с подвохом.
loading bay [ˈləudɪŋ-] *n* погрузочная площадка*.
loaf [ləuf] (*pl* **loaves**) *n* буханка* ♦ *vi* (*also:* ~ **about** *or* **around**: *inf*) болтаться (*impf*) без

де́ла; **use your ~!** (*inf*) шевели́те мозга́ми!
loam [ləum] *n* сугли́нок*.
loan [ləun] *n* заём*; (*money*) ссу́да* ♦ *vt* дава́ть*
(дать* *perf*) взаймы́; (*money*) ссужа́ть
(ссуди́ть* *perf*); **to take sth on ~** брать*
(взять* *perf*) что́-н на вре́мя.
loan account *n* ссу́дный счёт*.
loan capital *n* заёмный *or* ссу́дный капита́л.
loan shark *n* (*inf: pej*) ростовщи́к
(*ссужа́ющий де́ньги под о́чень высо́кие
проце́нты*).
loath [ləuθ] *adj*: **he is ~ to ...** ему́ о́чень не
хо́чется +*infin* ....
loathe [ləuð] *vt* ненави́деть* (*impf*).
loathing ['ləuðɪŋ] *n* отвраще́ние, омерзе́ние.
loathsome ['ləuðsəm] *adj* отврати́тельный*
(отврати́телен), омерзи́тельный*
(омерзи́телен).
loaves [ləuvz] *npl of* **loaf**.
lob [lɔb] *vt* (*ball*) переба́сывать (переба́сить*
perf).
lobby ['lɔbɪ] *n* (*of building*) вестибю́ль *m*;
(*pressure group*) ло́бби *nt ind* ♦ *vt* (*politician*)
склоня́ть (склони́ть *perf*) на свою́ сто́рону.
lobbyist ['lɔbɪɪst] *n* лобби́ст.
lobe [ləub] *n* (*of ear*) мо́чка*.
lobster ['lɔbstə'] *n* ома́р.
lobster pot *n* ве́рша* для ома́ров.
local ['ləukl] *adj* ме́стный* ♦ *n* (*BRIT: inf*): **this is
my ~** э́то мой люби́мый ме́стный паб; **the
~s** *npl* ме́стные жи́тели *mpl*.
local anaesthetic *n* ме́стный нарко́з.
local authority *n* ме́стные вла́сти* *fpl*.
local call *n* (*TEL*) ме́стный (телефо́нный)
разгово́р.
locale [ləu'kɑ:l] *n* ме́сто*.
local government *n* ме́стные вла́сти* *fpl*.
locality [ləu'kælɪtɪ] *n* ме́стность *f*.
localize ['ləukəlaɪz] *vt* (*limit*) локализова́ть
(*impf/perf*).
locally ['ləukəlɪ] *adv* (*live*) побли́зости; (*solve
problems*) на места́х.
locate [ləu'keɪt] *vt* определя́ть (определи́ть
perf) местонахожде́ние +*gen*; (*situate*): **to be
~d in** находи́ться* (*impf*) в *or* на +*prp*.
location [ləu'keɪʃən] *n* (*place*)
местонахожде́ние; (*finding*): **~ (of)** лока́ция
(+*gen*); **on ~** (*CINEMA*) на нату́ре.
loch [lɔx] *n* (*SCOTTISH*) о́зеро*.
lock [lɔk] *n* (*on door etc*) замо́к*; (*on canal*)
шлюз; (*of hair*) ло́кон ♦ *vt* запира́ть
(запере́ть* *perf*); (*immobilize*) фикси́ровать
(зафикси́ровать *perf*) ♦ *vi* (*door*) запира́ться
(запере́ться* *perf*); (*jaw, mechanism*)
смыка́ться (сомкну́ться *perf*); (*wheels*)
тормози́ть (затормози́ть *perf*); **the steering
wheel was on full ~** (*AUT*) руль был повёрнут
до отка́за; **~, stock and barrel** всё целико́м

▶ **lock away** *vt* (*valuables*) пря́тать* (спря́тать*
perf) под замо́к; (*criminal*) заключа́ть
(заключи́ть *perf*) под стра́жу
▶ **lock in** *vt*: **to ~ sb in** запира́ть (запере́ть* *perf*)
кого́-н
▶ **lock out** *vt* (*person*) запира́ть (запере́ть* *perf*)
дверь и не впуска́ть (впусти́ть* *perf*);
(*INDUSTRY*) объявля́ть (объяви́ть* *perf*)
лока́ут +*dat*
▶ **lock up** *vt* (*criminal, mental patient*)
упря́тывать (упря́тать* *perf*); (*house*)
запира́ть (запере́ть* *perf*) ♦ *vi* запира́ться
(запере́ться* *perf*).
locker ['lɔkə'] *n* шка́фчик.
locker room *n* раздева́лка*.
locket ['lɔkɪt] *n* медальо́н.
lockjaw ['lɔkdʒɔ:] *n* (*trismus*) тризм; (*tetanus*)
столбня́к.
lockout ['lɔkaut] *n* (*INDUSTRY*) лока́ут.
locksmith ['lɔksmɪθ] *n* сле́сарь* *m*.
lockup ['lɔkʌp] *n* (*jail*) куту́зка*; (*BRIT: also:
lock-up garage) гара́ж.
locomotive [ləukə'məutɪv] *n* локомоти́в.
locum ['ləukəm] *n* (*MED*) врач, вре́менно
замеща́ющий друго́го врача́.
locust ['ləukəst] *n* саранча́* *f no pl*.
lodge [lɔdʒ] *n* привра́тницкая *f adj*; (*also:
hunting ~) охо́тничий* дом*; (*also:* **masonic
~**) масо́нская ло́жа ♦ *vt* (*complaint*)
подава́ть* (пода́ть* *perf*) ♦ *vi* (*bullet*)
застрева́ть (застря́ть* *perf*); (*person*): **to ~
(with)** (вре́менно) жить* (*impf*) на кварти́ре (у
+*gen*).
lodger ['lɔdʒə'] *n* квартира́нт(ка).
lodging ['lɔdʒɪŋ] *n* (вре́менное) жильё.
lodging house *n* мебелиро́ванные комнаты
fpl.
lodgings ['lɔdʒɪŋz] *npl* кварти́ра *fsg*.
loft [lɔft] *n* черда́к*.
lofty ['lɔftɪ] *adj* (*high*) высо́кий* (высо́к);
(*noble*) возвы́шенный (возвы́шен); (*self-
important*) высокоме́рный* (высокоме́рен).
log [lɔg] *n abbr* = **logarithm**.
log [lɔg] *n* (*piece of wood*) бревно́*; (: *for fire*)
поле́но*; (*account*) журна́л ♦ *vt* (*event, fact*)
регистри́ровать (зарегистри́ровать *perf*)
▶ **log in** *vi* (*COMPUT*) входи́ть* (войти́* *perf*) в
систе́му
▶ **log into** *vt fus* (*COMPUT*) входи́ть* (войти́* *perf*)
в +*acc*
▶ **log off** *vi* (*COMPUT*) выходи́ть* (вы́йти* *perf*)
из систе́мы
▶ **log on** *vi* = **log in**
▶ **log out** *vi* = **log off**.
logarithm ['lɔgərɪðm] *n* логари́фм.
logbook ['lɔgbuk] *n* (*NAUT*) ва́хтенный
журна́л; (*AVIAT*) бортово́й журна́л; (*of car,
lorry*) формуля́р; (*of events, movement of*

---

goods) журна́л.
log fire *n* дровяно́й ками́н.
logger ['lɔgə'] *n* лесору́б.
loggerheads ['lɔgəhɛdz] *npl*: **to be at ~ (with)** конфликтова́ть *(impf)* (с +*instr*).
logic ['lɔdʒɪk] *n* ло́гика.
logical ['lɔdʒɪkl] *adj (based on logic)* логи́ческий*; *(reasonable)* логи́чный* (логи́чен).
logically ['lɔdʒɪkəlɪ] *adv (see adj)* логи́чески; логи́чно.
logistics [lɔ'dʒɪstɪks] *npl* организа́ция *fsg*.
logjam ['lɔgdʒæm] *n (fig)* зато́р.
logo ['ləugəu] *n* эмбле́ма.
loin [lɔɪn] *n (of meat)* филе́йная часть* *f*; **~s** *npl* (ANAT) чре́сла *pl*.
loincloth ['lɔɪnklɔθ] *n* набе́дренная повя́зка*.
Loire [lwɑ:] *n*: **the ~** Луа́ра.
loiter ['lɔɪtə'] *vi* сло́няться *(impf)*.
loll [lɔl] *vi (person: also: ~ about)* разва́ливаться (развали́ться* *perf*); *(head, tongue)* све́шиваться (све́ситься* *perf*).
lollipop ['lɔlɪpɔp] *n* ледене́ц* на па́лочке ♦ *cpd*: **~ man/lady** *(BRIT)* регулиро́вщик/ регулиро́вщица движе́ния, кото́рый обеспе́чивает безопа́сный перехо́д у́лицы шко́льниками.
lollop ['lɔləp] *vi* бе́гать/бежа́ть* *(impf)* вперева́лку.
lolly ['lɔlɪ] *n (inf: lollipop)* ледене́ц на па́лочке; (: *also*: **ice ~**) моро́женое на па́лочке; (: *money*) деньжа́та *pl*.
London ['lʌndən] *n* Ло́ндон.
Londoner ['lʌndənə'] *n* лондоне́ц*(-до́нка).
lone [ləun] *adj (person, parent)* одино́кий*; *(thing)* еди́нственный.
loneliness ['ləunlɪnɪs] *n* одино́чество.
lonely ['ləunlɪ] *adj (person, childhood)* одино́кий* (одино́к); *(place)* уединённый (уединён).
lonely hearts *n* одино́кие сердца́ *nt pl*.
lone parent *n (father)* оте́ц*-одино́чка; *(mother)* мать* *f*-одино́чка.
loner ['ləunə'] *n* одино́чка* *m/f*.
long [lɔŋ] *adj (in time)* до́лгий* (до́лог); *(road, book)* дли́нный* (дли́нен); *(clothes)* дли́нен ♦ *adv (see adj)* до́лго; дли́нно ♦ *vi*: **to ~ for sth/to do** жа́ждать *(impf)* чего-н/+*infin*; **in the ~ run** в коне́чном ито́ге; **so** *or* **as ~ as you don't mind** е́сли то́лько Вы не возража́ете; **don't be ~!** не заде́рживайтесь!; **how ~ is the street?** какова́ длина́ э́той у́лицы?; **how ~ is the lesson?** ско́лько дли́тся уро́к?; **6 metres ~** длино́й в 6 ме́тров; **6 months ~** продолжи́тельностью в 6 ме́сяцев; **all night (long)** всю ночь (напролёт); **he no ~er comes** он бо́льше не прихо́дит; **~ ago** давно́; **~ before** задо́лго до +*gen*; **~ after** до́лгое вре́мя по́сле +*gen*; **before ~** вско́ре; **at ~ last** наконе́ц; **the ~ and the short of it is that ...** коро́че говоря́ ....

long-distance [lɔŋ'dɪstəns] *adj (travel)* да́льний* (да́лен); **~ race** забе́г на дли́нную диста́нцию; **~ runner** бегу́н на дли́нные диста́нции.
long-distance call *n (within same country)* междугоро́дный (телефо́нный) разгово́р; *(international)* междунаро́дный (телефо́нный) разгово́р.
longevity [lɔn'dʒevɪtɪ] *n (of person)* долголе́тие; *(of scheme, marriage etc)* долгове́чность *f*.
long-haired ['lɔŋ'hɛəd] *adj (person)* длинноволо́сый (длинноволо́с); *(animal)* длинношёрстый.
longhand ['lɔŋhænd] *n*: **in ~** *(write)* от руки́.
longing ['lɔŋɪŋ] *n*: **~ (for)** тоска́ (по +*dat*).
longingly ['lɔŋɪŋlɪ] *adv* с тоско́й.
longitude ['lɔŋgɪtju:d] *n* долгота́*.
long johns [-dʒɔnz] *npl* кальсо́ны* *pl*.
long jump *n* прыжо́к* в длину́.
long-life ['lɔŋlaɪf] *adj (milk etc)* консерви́рованный; *(battery)* продлённого де́йствия.
long-lost ['lɔŋlɔst] *adj (relative etc)* давно́ утра́ченный (утра́чен) *or* поте́рянный (поте́рян).
long-playing record ['lɔŋpleɪŋ-] *n* долгоигра́ющая пласти́нка*.
long-range ['lɔŋ'reɪndʒ] *adj (plan, forecast)* долгосро́чный* (долгосро́чен); *(missile)* дальнобо́йный.
longshoreman ['lɔŋʃɔːmən] *n (US)* порто́вый гру́зчик.
long-sighted ['lɔŋ'saɪtɪd] *adj* дальнозо́ркий* (дальнозо́рок).
long-standing ['lɔŋ'stændɪŋ] *adj* долголе́тний.
long-suffering [lɔŋ'sʌfərɪŋ] *adj* много-страда́льный* (многострада́лен).
long-term ['lɔŋtə:m] *adj* долгосро́чный* (долгосро́чен).
long wave *n (RADIO)* дли́нные во́лны *fpl*.
long-winded [lɔŋ'wɪndɪd] *adj* многосло́вный* (многосло́вен).
loo [lu:] *n (BRIT: inf)* туале́т.
loofah ['lu:fə] *n* люфа́ *(гу́бка)*.
look [luk] *vi (see)* смотре́ть* (посмотре́ть* *perf*); *(glance)* взгляну́ть *(perf)*; *(seem, appear)* вы́глядеть* *(impf)* ♦ *n (glance)* взгляд; *(appearance)* вид; *(expression)* выраже́ние; **~s** *npl*: **good ~s** краси́вая вне́шность *fsg*; **to ~ south/(out) onto the sea** *(face)* выходи́ть* *(impf)* на юг/на мо́ре; **~!** *(expressing annoyance)* послу́шайте!; **~!** *(expressing surprise)* смотри́те!; **to ~ like sb/sth** походи́ть* *(impf)* на кого-н/что-н; **the wall ~s about 4 metres long** похо́же, что длина́ э́той стены́ 4 ме́тра; **everything ~s all right to me** мне ка́жется, что всё в поря́дке; **it ~s as if he's not coming** похо́же, что он не придёт; **to ~ ahead** смотре́ть* (посмотре́ть* *perf*) вперёд; **to have a ~** посмотре́ть* *(perf)*,

взгляну́ть *(perf)*; **to ~ around** осма́триваться (осмотре́ться* *perf)*; **to have a ~ at sth** *(glance at)* взгляну́ть* *(perf)* на что-н; *(study)* рассма́тривать (рассмотре́ть* *(perf))* что-н; **to have a ~ for sth** иска́ть* (поиска́ть* *perf)* что-н; **you can't tell by ~s alone** нельзя́ суди́ть то́лько по вне́шности

▶ **look after** *vt fus (care for)* уха́живать *(impf)* за +*instr*; *(deal with)* забо́титься* *(impf)* о +*prp*
▶ **look around** *vt fus (castle, museum etc)* осма́тривать (осмотре́ть* *perf)*
▶ **look at** *vt fus (see)* смотре́ть* (посмотре́ть* *perf)* на +*acc*; *(study)* рассма́тривать (рассмотре́ть* *perf)*; *(read quickly)* просма́тривать (просморе́ть* *perf)*
▶ **look back** *vi (turn around)*: **to ~ back (at sth/ sb)** огля́дываться (огляну́ться* *perf)* (на что-н/кого́-н); **to ~ back (at** *or* **on the past)** огля́дываться (огляну́ться* *perf)* (на про́шлое)
▶ **look down on** *vt fus (fig)* смотре́ть* *(impf)* свысока́ на +*acc*
▶ **look for** *vt fus* иска́ть* (поиска́ть* *perf)*
▶ **look forward to** *vt fus*: **to ~ forward to sth** ждать* *(impf)* чего́-н с нетерпе́нием; *(in letters)*: **we ~ forward to hearing from you** (с нетерпе́нием) ждём Ва́шего отве́та
▶ **look in** *vi*: **to ~ in on sb** загля́дывать (загляну́ть* *perf)* к кому́-н
▶ **look into** *vt fus* рассле́довать *(impf/perf)*
▶ **look on** *vi (watch)* наблюда́ть *(impf)*
▶ **look out** *vi (beware)*: **to ~ out (for)** острега́ться *(impf)* (+*gen)*; *(glance out)*: **to ~ out (of)** выгля́дывать (вы́глянуть *perf)* (в +*acc*)
▶ **look out for** *vt fus (search for)* стара́ться (постара́ться *perf)* найти́
▶ **look over** *vt (essay)* просма́тривать (просмотре́ть* *perf)*; *(town, building)* осма́тривать (осмотре́ть* *perf)*; *(person)* проверя́ть (прове́рить *perf)*
▶ **look round** *vi* осма́триваться (осмотре́ться* *perf)*
▶ **look through** *vt fus (papers)* просма́тривать (просмотре́ть* *perf)*; *(window)* смотре́ть* (посмотре́ть* *perf)* в +*acc*
▶ **look to** *vt fus (rely on)* ждать* *(impf)* от +*gen*
▶ **look up** *vi (with eyes)* поднима́ть (подня́ть* *perf)* глаза́; *(situation)* идти́* *(impf)* к лу́чшему ◆ *vt (piece of information)* посмотре́ть* *(perf)*
▶ **look up to** *vt fus* почита́ть *(impf)*.
lookalike ['lukəlaik] *n* двойни́к*.
look-in ['lukın] *n*: **to get a ~** *(inf)* получи́ть* *(perf)* свой кусо́к пирога́; **I couldn't get a ~** *(in conversation)* я не мог вста́вить сло́во.
lookout ['lukaut] *n (person)* наблюда́тель (ница) *m(f)*; *(point)* наблюда́тельный пункт; **to be on the ~** быть* *(impf)* начеку́ *or*

насторо́же; **to be on the ~ for sth** присма́тривать *(impf)* что-н.
LOOM *n abbr* (*US*: = *Loyal Order of Moose*) *та́йное о́бщество*.
loom [lu:m] *vi (also: ~ up: object)* нея́сно вырисо́вываться *(impf)*; *(event)* надвига́ться *(impf)* ◆ *n* тка́цкий* стано́к*.
loony ['lu:nı] *(inf) adj* чо́кнутый ◆ *n* чо́кнутый(-ая) *m(f) adj*.
loop [lu:p] *n (also COMPUT)* пе́тля*; *(contraceptive)* спира́ль *f* ◆ *vt*: **to ~ sth round sth** завя́зывать (завяза́ть* *perf)* что-н пе́тлей вокру́г чего́-н.
loophole ['lu:phəul] *n* лазе́йка*.
loose [lu:s] *adj* свобо́дный* (свобо́ден); *(knot, grip)* сла́бый (слаб); *(hair)* распу́щенный (распу́щен); *(definition, translation)* приблизи́тельный* (приблизи́телен); *(weave)* непло́тный* (непло́тен); *(promiscuous)* распу́щенный; *(ELEC)*: **~ connection** сла́бый конта́кт ◆ *n*: **to be on the ~** быть* *(impf)* в бега́х; **the handle is ~** ру́чка расшата́лась; **to set ~** *(prisoner)* освобожда́ть (освободи́ть* *perf)*; *(unleash)* высвобожда́ть (вы́свободить* *perf)*; **to come ~** расша́тываться (расшата́ться *perf)*.
loose change *n* ме́лочь *f*.
loose chippings *npl (on road)* щебёнка *fsg*.
loose end *n*: **to be at a ~ ~** *or (US)* **at ~ ~s** шата́ться *(impf)* без де́ла; **to tie up (the) ~ ~s** заверши́ть* (заверши́ть *perf)* все ме́лочи.
loose-fitting ['lu:sfıtıŋ] *adj* просто́рный* (просто́рен).
loose-leaf ['lu:sli:f] *adj* отрывно́й.
loose-limbed [lu:s'lımd] *adj* ги́бкий* (ги́бок).
loosely ['lu:slı] *adv (freely)* свобо́дно; *(vaguely)* приблизи́тельно.
loosely-knit ['lu:slı'nıt] *adj* ре́дко свя́занный*.
loosen ['lu:sn] *vt (belt, screw, grip)* ослабля́ть (осла́бить* *perf)*; *(by shaking)* расша́тывать (расшата́ть *perf)*
▶ **loosen up** *vi (before game)* разогрева́ться (разогре́ться *perf)*; *(inf: relax)* расслабля́ться (рассла́биться* *perf)*.
loot [lu:t] *n (inf)* награ́бленное *nt adj* ◆ *vt (shops, homes)* разграбля́ть (разгра́бить* *perf)*.
looter ['lu:tə'] *n (during riot)* граби́тель(ница) *m(f)*; *(during war)* мародёр.
looting ['lu:tıŋ] *n* разграбле́ние; *(during war)* мародёрство.
lop off [lɔp-] *vt (branches etc)* отреза́ть (отре́зать* *perf)*.
lopsided ['lɔp'saıdıd] *adj* кривобо́кий (кривобо́к); *(smile)* криво́й* (крив).
lord [lɔ:d] *n (BRIT: peer)* лорд; *(REL)*: **the L~** Госпо́дь* *m*; **my L~** *(to bishop, noble, judge)* мило́рд; **good L~!** Бо́же мой!; **the (House of) L~s** *(BRIT)* пала́та ло́рдов.

---

lordly ['lɔ:dlɪ] *adj* ба́рственный.
lordship ['lɔ:dʃɪp] *n*: **your L~** Ва́ша све́тлость *f*.
lore [lɔ:ʳ] *n* преда́ния *ntpl*.
lorry ['lɒrɪ] *n* (*BRIT*) грузови́к*.
lorry driver *n* (*BRIT*) води́тель *m* грузовика́.
Los Angeles [lɒs 'ændʒɪli:z] *n* Лос-␣́нджелес.
lose [lu:z] (*pt, pp* **lost**) *vt* теря́ть (потеря́ть *perf*); (*contest, argument*) прои́грывать (проигра́ть *perf*); (*pursuers*) избавля́ться (изба́виться* *perf*) от +*gen* ♦ *vi* (*in contest, argument*) прои́грывать (проигра́ть *perf*); **to ~ (time)** (*clock*) отстава́ть* (отста́ть* *perf*); **to ~ sight of sth** теря́ть (потеря́ть *perf*) из ви́ду что-н; (*fig*) упуска́ть (упусти́ть* *perf*) из ви́ду что-н.
loser ['lu:zəʳ] *n* (*in contest*) проигра́вший(-ая) *m(f) adj*; (*inf: failure*) неуда́чник(-ица); **to be a good/bad ~** уме́ть (*impf*)/не уме́ть досто́йно прои́грывать (*impf*).
loss [lɒs] *n* поте́ря; (*sense of bereavement*) утра́та; (*COMM*): **to make a ~** терпе́ть* (потерпе́ть* *perf*) убы́ток; **to sell sth at a ~** продава́ть* (прода́ть* *perf*) что-н в убы́ток; **heavy ~es** тяжёлые поте́ри *fpl*; **to cut one's ~es** сокраща́ть (сократи́ть* *perf*) поте́ри; **to be at a ~** теря́ться (растеря́ться *perf*); **to be at a ~ for words** не найти́сь* (*perf*), что сказа́ть.
loss adjuster *n* специали́ст по оце́нке убы́тков.
loss leader *n товáр, продавáемый в убы́ток для привлечéния покупáтелей.*
lost [lɒst] *pt, pp of* **lose** ♦ *adj* пропа́вший; (*object*) потéрянный (потéрян); **to get ~** заблуди́ться* (*perf*); **get ~!** (*inf*) прова́ливай!; **he was ~ in thought** он был погружён в свои́ мы́сли.
lost and found *n* (*US*) стол *or* бюро́ *nt ind* нахо́док.
lost cause *n* про́игранное де́ло*.
lost property *n* потéрянные вéщи *fpl*; (*BRIT: also:* **~ ~ office**) стол *or* бюро́ *nt ind* нахо́док.
lot [lɒt] *n* (*of people, goods*) па́ртия; (*at auction*) лот; (*destiny*) у́часть *f*; (*esp US: ground*) (земéльный) участ́ок*; (*large number, amount*): **a ~ (of)** мно́го; **the ~** (*everything*) всё; **~s of ...** мно́го +*gen* ...; **I see a ~ of him** мы с ним ча́сто ви́димся; **I read/ don't read a ~** я мно́го/ма́ло чита́ю; **a ~ bigger/louder/more expensive** намно́го *or* гора́здо бо́льше/гро́мче/доро́же; **to draw ~s (for sth)** тяну́ть* (*impf*) жре́бий (для чего́-н).
lotion ['ləuʃən] *n* (*for skin, hair*) лосьо́н.
lottery ['lɒtərɪ] *n* лотере́я.
loud [laud] *adj* (*noise, voice, laugh*) гро́мкий* (гро́мок); (*support, condemnation*) шу́мный* (шу́мен); (*clothes*) крича́щий* ♦ *adv* гро́мко; **out ~** вслух.
loud-hailer [laud'heɪləʳ] *n* (*BRIT*) ру́пор.
loudly ['laudlɪ] *adv* (*see adj*) гро́мко; шу́мно.
loudmouthed ['laudmauθt] *adj* горла́стый (горла́ст).
loudspeaker [laud'spi:kəʳ] *n* громко-

говори́тель *m*.
lounge [laundʒ] *n* (*in house, hotel*) гости́ная *f adj*; (*at airport*) зал ожида́ния; (*BRIT: also:* **~ bar**) *часть бáра, где посетúтели сидя́т* ♦ *vi* (*in chair*) развали́ться (*perf*)
► **lounge about** *vi* болта́ться (*impf*) (без де́ла)
► **lounge around** *vi* = **lounge about**.
lounge suit *n* (*BRIT*) пиджа́чный костю́м.
louse [laus] (*pl* **lice**) *n* (*insect*) вошь* *f*
► **louse up** *vt* (*inf*) напо́ртить* (*perf*) +*dat*.
lousy ['lauzɪ] *adj* (*inf: bad quality*) парши́вый; (*: ill*): **to feel ~** чу́вствовать (*impf*) себя́ парши́во.
lout [laut] *n* (*inf*) хам.
louvre ['lu:vəʳ] (*US* **louver**) *n* жалюзи́ *nt ind*.
lovable ['lʌvəbl] *adj* ми́лый* (мил).
love [lʌv] *vt* люби́ть* (*impf*) ♦ *n*: **~ (for)** любо́вь* *f* (к +*dat*); **to ~ to do** люби́ть* (*impf*) +*infin*; **I ~ chocolate** я люблю́ шокола́д; **I'd ~ to come** я с удово́льствием пришёл бы; **"love (from) Anne"** (*in letter*) „люби́щая Вас Ա́нна"; **to fall in ~ with** влюбля́ться (влюби́ться* *perf*) в +*acc*; **he is in ~ with her** он в неё влюблён; **to make ~** занима́ться (заня́ться* *perf*) любо́вью; **~ at first sight** любо́вь* с пе́рвого взгля́да; **to send one's ~ to sb** передава́ть* (переда́ть* *perf*) приве́т кому́-н; **"fifteen ~"** (*TENNIS*) „пятна́дцать – ноль".
love affair *n* рома́н.
love child *n* дитя́* *nt* любви́.
loved ones ['lʌvdwʌnz] *npl* люби́мые *pl adj*.
love-hate relationship ['lʌvheɪt-] *n* любо́вь *f*-не́нависть *f*.
love letter *n* любо́вное письмо́*.
love life *n* инти́мная жизнь *f*.
lovely ['lʌvlɪ] *adj* (*beautiful*) краси́вый (краси́в); (*delightful*) чуде́сный* (чуде́сен).
lover ['lʌvəʳ] *n* (*sexual partner*) любо́вник (-ица); (*person in love*) влюблённый(-ая)*m(f) adj*; **a ~ of art/music** люби́тель(ница) *m(f)* иску́сства/му́зыки.
lovesick ['lʌvsɪk] *adj* томи́мый любо́вью; **to be ~** томи́ться* (*impf*) от любви́.
love song *n* любо́вная пе́сня*.
loving ['lʌvɪŋ] *adj* (*person*) лю́бящий*, не́жный* (не́жен); (*actions*) не́жный* (не́жен).
low [ləu] *adj* ни́зкий* (ни́зок); (*sound: quiet*) ти́хий* (тих); (*depressed*) пода́вленный (пода́влен); (*ill*) нездоро́вый (нездоро́в) ♦ *adv* (*sing: deeply*) ни́зким го́лосом; (*: quietly*) ти́хо; (*fly*) ни́зко ♦ *n* (*METEOROLOGY*) ни́зкое давле́ние; **we are (running) ~ on milk** у нас остаётся ма́ло молока́; **to reach a new** *or* **an all-time ~** (*morale, profits*) опуска́ться (опусти́ться* *perf*) на небыва́ло ни́зкий у́ровень.
low-alcohol ['ləu'ælkəhɒl] *adj*: **~ wine/beer** вино́/пи́во с ни́зким содержа́нием алкого́ля.
lowbrow ['ləubrau] *adj* низкопро́бный.
low-calorie ['ləu'kælərɪ] *adj* низко-

калори́йный* (низкокалори́ен).

low-cut ['ləukʌt] *adj* с глубо́ким вы́резом.

lowdown ['ləudaun] *n* (*inf*): **to give sb the ~ on sth** расскрыва́ть (расскры́ть* *perf*) кому́-н всю подного́тную чего́-н.

lower ['ləuə] *adj* (*bottom: of two things*) ни́жний*; (*less important*) ни́зший* ♦ *vt* (*object*) спуска́ть (спусти́ть* *perf*); (*level, price*) снижа́ть (сни́зить* *perf*); (*voice*) понижа́ть (пони́зить* *perf*); (*eyes*) опуска́ть (опусти́ть* *perf*).

low-fat ['ləu'fæt] *adj* обезжи́ренный (обезжи́рен).

low-key ['ləu'ki:] *adj* сде́ржанный (сде́ржан).

lowlands ['ləuləndz] *npl* ни́зменность *fsg*.

low-level language ['ləulɛvl-] *n* (*COMPUT*) язы́к* программи́рования ни́зкого у́ровня.

low-loader ['ləuləudə] *n* автомоби́ль *m* с погру́зочным приспособле́нием.

lowly ['ləulɪ] *adj* (*position, origin*) ни́зкий* (ни́зок).

low-lying [ləu'laɪŋ] *adj* ни́зменный.

low-paid [ləu'peɪd] *adj* низкоопла́чиваемый (низкоопла́чиваем).

low-rise ['ləuraɪz] *adj* ни́зкий* (ни́зок).

low-tech ['ləutɛk] *adj*: **their office is very ~** у них в о́фисе техноло́гия на о́чень ни́зком у́ровне.

loyal ['lɔɪəl] *adj* ве́рный* (ве́рен); (*POL*) лоя́льный* (лоя́лен).

loyalist ['lɔɪəlɪst] *n* лоя́лист(ка).

loyalty ['lɔɪəltɪ] *n* ве́рность *f*; (*POL*) лоя́льность *f*.

lozenge ['lɔzɪndʒ] *n* (*shape*) ромб; (*pastille*): **throat ~** табле́тка* от ка́шля.

LP *n abbr* = **long-playing record**.

L-plate ['ɛlpleɪt] *n* (*BRIT*) *знак на маши́не, обознача́ющий "учени́к"*.

LPN *n abbr* (*US*) = **Licensed Practical Nurse**.

LRAM *n abbr* (*BRIT*) = **Licentiate of the Royal Academy of Music**.

LSAT *n abbr* (*US*) = **Law School Admissions Test**.

LSD *n abbr* (= *lysergic acid diethylamide*) ЛСД; (*BRIT*: = *pounds, shillings and pence*) *фу́нты, ши́ллинги и пе́нсы*.

LSE *n abbr* (*BRIT*) = **London School of Economics**.

LT *abbr* (*ELEC*: = *low tension*) ни́зкое напряже́ние.

Lt *abbr* (*MIL*) = **lieutenant**.

Ltd *abbr* (*COMM*) = **limited (liability) company**.

lubricant ['lu:brɪkənt] *n* сма́зка, лубрика́тор.

lubricate ['lu:brɪkeɪt] *vt* сма́зывать (сма́зать* *perf*).

lucid ['lu:sɪd] *adj* (*writing, speech*) я́сный* (я́сен); (*thinking*): **I'm not feeling very ~ today** я сего́дня пло́хо сообража́ю.

lucidity [lu:'sɪdɪtɪ] *n* я́сность *f*.

luck [lʌk] *n* (*also: good ~*) уда́ча; **bad ~** неуда́ча; **good ~!** уда́чи (Вам)!; **bad** *or* **hard** *or* **tough ~!** не повезло́!; **we are in ~/out of ~** нам везёт/не везёт; **to push one's ~** искуша́ть (*impf*) судьбу́.

luckily ['lʌkɪlɪ] *adv* к сча́стью.

luckless ['lʌklɪs] *adj* невезу́чий (невезу́ч).

lucky ['lʌkɪ] *adj* (*situation, event, object*) счастли́вый; (*person*) уда́чливый (уда́члив); **he is ~ at cards/in love** ему́ везёт в ка́ртах/любви́; **how did you manage it? – I was ~** как Вас э́то удало́сь? – мне повезло́.

lucrative ['lu:krətɪv] *adj* (*profitable*) при́быльный* (при́былен), дохо́дный* (дохо́ден); (*job*) высокоопла́чиваемый.

ludicrous ['lu:dɪkrəs] *adj* смехотво́рный* (смехотво́рен).

ludo ['lu:dəu] *n* насто́льная игра́ с фи́шками и броса́нием косте́й.

lug [lʌg] *vt* (*inf*) воло́чь* (*impf*).

luggage ['lʌgɪdʒ] *n* бага́ж*.

luggage car *n* = **luggage van**.

luggage rack *n* (*in train*) бага́жная по́лка.

luggage van *n* (*BRIT*) бага́жный ваго́н.

lugubrious [lu'gu:brɪəs] *adj* скорбный* (ско́рбен).

lukewarm ['lu:kwɔ:m] *adj* (*liquid*) слегка́ тёплый; (*reaction*) прохла́дный* (прохла́ден).

lull [lʌl] *n* зати́шье ♦ *vt*: **to ~ sb to sleep** убаю́кивать (убаю́кать *perf*) кого́-н; **to ~ sb into a false sense of security** усыпля́ть (усыпи́ть* *perf*) чью-н бди́тельность.

lullaby ['lʌləbaɪ] *n* колыбе́льная *f adj*.

lumbago [lʌm'beɪgəu] *n* люмба́го *nt ind*.

lumber ['lʌmbə] *n* (*esp US: wood*) лесоматериа́лы *mpl*; (*junk*) ру́хлядь *f* ♦ *vi*: **to ~ about/along** *etc* тащи́ться (*impf*)

▸ **lumber with** *vt*: **to ~ sb with sth** навя́зывать (навяза́ть* *perf*) кому́-н что-н; **he was ~ed with all the work** ему́ навяза́ли всю рабо́ту.

lumberjack ['lʌmbədʒæk] *n* лесору́б.

lumber room *n* (*BRIT*) чула́н.

lumberyard ['lʌmbəjɑːd] *n* (*US*) склад лесоматериа́лов.

luminous ['lu:mɪnəs] *adj* (*fabric, colour*) блестя́щий*; (*digit, star*) светя́щийся.

lump [lʌmp] *n* (*of clay, snow*) ком; (*of butter, sugar etc*) кусо́к*; (*swelling*) ши́шка; (*growth*) о́пухоль *f* ♦ *vt*: **to ~ together** меша́ть (смеша́ть *perf*) в (одну́) ку́чу; **a ~ sum** единовре́менно выпла́чиваемая су́мма.

lumpy ['lʌmpɪ] *adj* (*sauce*) комкова́тый; (*bed*) бугри́стый (бугри́ст).

lunacy ['lu:nəsɪ] *n* (*fig*) безу́мие; (*mental illness*) помеша́тельство.

lunar ['lu:nə] *adj* лу́нный.

lunatic ['lu:nətɪk] *adj* (*behaviour*) безу́мный* (безу́мен) ♦ *n* (*also fig*) сумасше́дший*(-ая)

---

m(f) adj.

lunatic asylum *n* сумасше́дший* дом*.

lunatic fringe *n*: **the ~~** ку́чка фана́тиков.

lunch [lʌntʃ] *n* обе́д ♦ *vi* обе́дать (пообе́дать *perf*).

lunch break *n* переры́в на обе́д, обе́денный переры́в.

luncheon ['lʌntʃən] *n* (*formal meal*) за́втрак.

luncheon meat *n* свина́я тушёнка.

luncheon voucher *n* (*BRIT*) тало́н на обе́д.

lunch hour *n* = **lunch break.**

lunch time *n* обе́денное вре́мя* *nt*.

lung [lʌŋ] *n* лёгкое *nt adj*; **~ cancer** рак лёгких.

lunge [lʌndʒ] *vi* (*also*: **~ forward**) рвану́ться (*perf*); (*SPORT*) де́лать (сде́лать *perf*) вы́пад; **to ~ at** ри́нуться (*perf*) на +*acc*; (*SPORT*) де́лать (сде́лать *perf*) вы́пад про́тив +*gen*.

lupin ['lu:pɪn] *n* (*BOT*) люпи́н.

lurch [lɜːtʃ] *vi* (*person*) покачну́ться (*perf*); (*vehicle*) рвану́ть (*perf*); (*ship*): **to ~ sideways** крени́ться* (накрени́ться* *perf*) ♦ *n* (*of ship*) крен; (*of vehicle*) бросо́к*; **the car ~ed forward** маши́ну бро́сило вперёд; **to leave sb in the ~** (*inf*) броса́ть (бро́сить* *perf*) кого́-н в беде́.

lure [luə] *n* прима́нка ♦ *vt* зама́нивать (замани́ть* *perf*); **to ~ sb away from** отвлека́ть (отвле́чь* *perf*) кого́-н от +*gen*.

lurid ['luərɪd] *adj* (*garish*) аляпова́тый (аляпова́т).

lurk [lɜːk] *vi* (*animal, person, also fig*) таи́ться (*impf*).

luscious ['lʌʃəs] *adj* (*person, thing*) притяга́тельный* (притяга́телен); (*food*) со́чный* (со́чен).

lush [lʌʃ] *adj* (*fields, gardens*) пы́шный* (пы́шен); (*restaurant, lifestyle*) роско́шный* (роско́шен).

lust [lʌst] *n* (*sexual desire*) по́хоть *f*; (*greed*): **~ (for)** жа́жда (к +*dat*)

▶ **lust after** *vt fus* (*desire sexually*) испы́тывать (испыта́ть *perf*) вожделе́ние к +*dat*; (*crave*) жа́ждать* (*impf*) +*gen*

▶ **lust for** *vt fus* = **lust after.**

lustful ['lʌstful] *adj* похотли́вый (похотли́в).

lustre ['lʌstə*] (*US* **luster**) *n* блеск.

lusty ['lʌstɪ] *adj* по́лный* (по́лон) жи́зни и здоро́вья.

lute [lu:t] *n* лю́тня*.

luvvie ['lʌvɪ] *n* (*inf*) дорогу́ша *m/f.*

luvvy ['lʌvɪ] *n* = **luvvie.**

Luxembourg ['lʌksəmbɜːg] *n* Люксембу́рг.

luxuriant [lʌg'zjuərɪənt] *adj* (*plants, gardens*) бу́йный* (бу́ен); (*hair*) пы́шный* (пы́шен).

luxuriate [lʌg'zjuərɪeɪt] *vi*: **to ~ in** наслажда́ться (наслади́ться* *perf*) +*instr*.

luxurious [lʌg'zjuərɪəs] *adj* роско́шный* (роско́шен).

luxury ['lʌkʃərɪ] *n* (*great comfort*) ро́скошь *f*; (*treat*) роско́шество ♦ *cpd* роско́шный.

luxury tax *n* нало́г на предме́ты ро́скоши.

LV *n abbr* = **luncheon voucher.**

Lvov ['ljvɔf] *n* Львов.

LW *abbr* (*RADIO*) (= **long wave**) ДВ= *дли́нные во́лны.*

lycra® ['laɪkrə] *n* синтети́ческий эласти́чный материа́л, испо́льзуемый при изготовле́нии трикота́жной оде́жды.

lying ['laɪŋ] *n* ложь *f* ♦ *adj* лжи́вый.

lynch [lɪntʃ] *vt* линчева́ть* (*impf/perf*).

lynx [lɪŋks] *n* (*ZOOL*) рысь *f.*

Lyon ['liː3] *n* Лион.

lyric ['lɪrɪk] *adj*: **~ poetry** ли́рика, лири́ческая поэ́зия.

lyrical ['lɪrɪkl] *adj* (*poem*) лири́ческий*; (*fig: praise, comment*) восто́рженный (восто́ржен).

lyricism ['lɪrɪsɪzəm] *n* лири́зм.

lyrics ['lɪrɪks] *npl* слова́ *ntpl or* текст *msg* (*пе́сни*).

~ M, m ~

M, m [ɛm] *n* (*letter*) 13-ая буква английского алфавита.

M *n abbr* (*BRIT*: = *motorway*) автомагистраль *f* ♦ *abbr* = **medium**.

m. *abbr* (= **metre**) м= *метр*; = **mile, million**.

MA *n abbr* (= *Master of Arts*) = магистр гуманитарных наук; (= *military academy*) Военная академия ♦ *abbr* (*US*: *POST*) = *Massachusetts*.

mac [mæk] *n* (*BRIT*: *inf*) макинтош.

macabre [mə'kɑ:brə] *adj* жуткий* (жуток).

macaroni [mækə'rəʊnɪ] *n* макароны* *pl*.

macaroon [mækə'ru:n] *n* миндальное безе *nt ind*.

mace [meɪs] *n* (*weapon*) булава*; (*ceremonial*) жезл*; (*spice*) мускат.

Macedonia [mæsɪ'dəʊnɪə] *n* Македония.

Macedonian [mæsɪ'dəʊnɪən] *adj* македонский*.

machinations [mækɪ'neɪʃənz] *npl* (*plot*) козни* *pl*; (*scheme*) махинация *fsg*.

machine [mə'ʃi:n] *n* (*also fig*) машина ♦ *vt* (*TECH*) подвергать (подвергнуть* *perf*) машинной обработке; (*dress etc*) шить* (сшить* *perf*) на машине.

machine code *n* (*COMPUT*) машинный код.

machine gun *n* пулемёт.

machine language *n* (*COMPUT*) машинный язык*.

machine readable *adj* (*COMPUT*) машиночитаемый.

machinery [mə'ʃi:nərɪ] *n* оборудование; (*of government*) механизм.

machine shop *n* механический* цех*.

machine tool *n* станок*.

machine washable *adj* (*garment*) пригодный к машинной стирке.

machinist [mə'ʃi:nɪst] *n* станочник(-ица).

macho ['mætʃəʊ] *adj* мужицкий.

mackerel ['mækrl] *n inv* скумбрия.

mackintosh ['mækɪntɔʃ] *n* (*BRIT*) макинтош.

macro... ['mækrəʊ] *prefix* макро....

macroeconomics ['mækrəʊi:kə'nɔmɪks] *npl* макроэкономика *fsg*.

mad [mæd] *adj* (*also fig*) сумасшедший*, помешанный (помешан); (*angry*) бешеный; (*keen*): **he is ~ about** он помешан на +*prp*; **to**

go ~ (*insane*) сходить* (сойти* *perf*) с ума; (*angry*) беситься* (взбеситься* *perf*).

Madagascar [mædə'gæskə] *n* Мадагаскар.

madam ['mædəm] *n* (*form of address*) мадам *f ind*, госпожа; **yes, ~** да, мадам; **Dear M~** (*in formal letter*) уважаемая госпожа; **M~ Chairman** госпожа председатель.

madcap ['mædkæp] *adj* сумасбродный*.

mad cow disease *n* (*inf*) энцефалопатия крупного рогатого скота.

madden ['mædn] *vt* (*make angry*) бесить* (взбесить* *perf*).

maddening ['mædnɪŋ] *adj* невыносимый (невыносим).

made [meɪd] *pt, pp of* **make**.

Madeira [mə'dɪərə] *n* (*GEO*) Мадейра; (*wine*) мадера.

made-to-measure ['meɪdtə'mɛʒə'] *adj* (*BRIT*) индивидуального пошива.

madhouse ['mædhaʊs] *n* (*inf*: *asylum*) сумасшедший* дом*, психушка*; (*state of uproar*) сумасшедший дом.

madly ['mædlɪ] *adv* безумно; **she is ~ in love with him** она безумно влюблена в него; **to fall ~ in love with sb** безумно влюбиться* (*perf*) в кого-н.

madman ['mædmən] *irreg n* сумасшедший* *m adj*.

madness ['mædnɪs] *n* (*insanity*) безумие, сумасшествие; (*foolishness*) безумие.

Madrid [mə'drɪd] *n* Мадрид.

madwoman ['mædwʊmən] *irreg n* сумасшедшая* *f adj*.

Mafia ['mæfɪə] *n*: **the ~** мафия.

mag [mæg] *n abbr* (*BRIT*: *inf*) = **magazine**.

magazine [mægə'zi:n] *n* журнал; (*RADIO*) радиожурнал; (*TV*) тележурнал; (*MIL*: *store*) склад боеприпасов; (: *of firearm*) магазин.

maggot ['mægət] *n* личинка* мухи.

magic ['mædʒɪk] *n* магия; (*conjuring*) фокусы *mpl* ♦ *adj* (*powers, ritual*) магический*; (*fig*: *place, moment, experience*) волшебный* (волшебен); **~ wand** волшебная палочка*.

magical ['mædʒɪkl] *adj* (*powers, ritual*) магический*; (*experience, evening*) волшебный* (волшебен).

---

* marks translations which have irregular inflections. The Russian-English side of the dictionary gives inflectional information.

magician [mə'dʒɪʃən] *n* (*wizard*) маг; (*conjurer*) фо́кусник.
magistrate ['mædʒɪstreɪt] *n* (*LAW*) мирово́й судья́* *m.*
magistrates' court *n* магистрату́ра.
magnanimous [mæg'nænɪməs] *adj* великоду́шный* (великоду́шен).
magnate ['mægneɪt] *n* магна́т.
magnesium [mæg'ni:zɪəm] *n* ма́гний.
magnet ['mægnɪt] *n* магни́т.
magnetic [mæg'nɛtɪk] *adj* магни́тный; (*personality*) притяга́тельный* (притяга́телен).
magnetic disk *n* (*COMPUT*) магни́тный диск.
magnetic tape *n* магни́тная плёнка*.
magnetism ['mægnɪtɪzəm] *n* магнети́зм.
magnetize ['mægnɪtaɪz] *vt* намагни́чивать (намагни́тить* *perf*).
magnification [mægnɪfɪ'keɪʃən] *n* увеличе́ние.
magnificence [mæg'nɪfɪsns] *n* великоле́пие.
magnificent [mæg'nɪfɪsnt] *adj* великоле́пный* (великоле́пен).
magnify ['mægnɪfaɪ] *vt* увели́чивать (увели́чить *perf*); (*sound*) уси́ливать (уси́лить *perf*); (*exaggerate*) преувели́чивать (преувели́чить *perf*).
magnifying glass ['mægnɪfaɪɪŋ-] *n* увеличи́тельное стекло́*, лу́па.
magnitude ['mægnɪtju:d] *n* (*size*) величина́; (*importance*) масшта́б.
magnolia [mæg'nəʊlɪə] *n* магно́лия.
magpie ['mægpaɪ] *n* соро́ка.
mahogany [mə'hɒgənɪ] *n* кра́сное де́рево ◆ *cpd* кра́сного де́рева.
maid [meɪd] *n* (*in private house*) служа́нка*; (*in hotel*) го́рничная *f adj*; **old ~** (*pej*) ста́рая де́ва.
maiden ['meɪdn] *n* (*literary*) де́ва ◆ *adj* (*aunt etc*) незаму́жняя; (*speech, voyage*) пе́рвый.
maiden name *n* де́вичья фами́лия.
mail [meɪl] *n* по́чта ◆ *vt* отправля́ть (отпра́вить* *perf*) по по́чте; **by ~** по по́чте.
mailbox ['meɪlbɒks] *n* (*US*: *letter box, also COMPUT*) почто́вый я́щик.
mailing list ['meɪlɪŋ-] *n* спи́сок* адреса́тов.
mailman ['meɪlmæn] *irreg n* (*US*) почтальо́н.
mail order *n* систе́ма зака́за това́ров по по́чте ◆ *cpd*: **~~ catalogue** катало́г „Това́ры по́чтой"; **~~ firm** *фи́рма, продаю́щая това́ры по по́чте.*
mailshot ['meɪlʃɒt] *n* рассы́лка объявле́ний по по́чте.
mail train *n* почто́вый по́езд*.
mail truck *n* (*US*) почто́вый фурго́н.
mail van *n* (*BRIT*: *AUT*) почто́вый фурго́н; (: *RAIL*) почто́вый ваго́н.
maim [meɪm] *vt* кале́чить (искале́чить *perf*).
main [meɪn] *adj* (*reason, point, door*) гла́вный ◆ *n* (*pipe*): **gas/water ~** газопрово́дная/водопрово́дная магистра́ль *f*; **the ~s** *npl* сеть *fsg*; **~ meal** обе́д; **in the ~** в основно́м.

main course *n* основно́е *or* второ́е блю́до.
mainframe ['meɪnfreɪm] *n* (*COMPUT*) (универса́льная) вычисли́тельная маши́на.
mainland ['meɪnlənd] *n*: **the ~** матери́к, больша́я земля́*.
main line *n* (*RAIL*) железнодоро́жная магистра́ль *f*.
mainline ['meɪnlaɪn] *adj* (*RAIL*: *station*) магистра́льный ◆ *vt* (*DRUGS*) вка́лывать (вколо́ть* *perf*) ◆ *vi* (*DRUGS*) коло́ться* (*impf*).
mainly ['meɪnlɪ] *adv* гла́вным о́бразом.
main road *n* шоссе́ *nt ind*; (*in town, village*) гла́вная у́лица.
mainstay ['meɪnsteɪ] *n* гла́вная опо́ра.
mainstream ['meɪnstri:m] *n* госпо́дствующая тенде́нция ◆ *adj* госпо́дствующий*.
maintain [meɪn'teɪn] *vt* (*friendship, system, momentum*) подде́рживать (поддержа́ть* *perf*); (*dependant*) содержа́ть* (*impf*); (*building*) обслу́живать (*impf*); (*affirm: belief, opinion*) утвержда́ть (*impf*); **to ~** (**that ...**) утвержда́ть (*impf*) (, что ...).
maintenance ['meɪntənəns] *n* (*see vb*) поддержа́ние; содержа́ние; обслу́живание; утвержде́ние; (*LAW: alimony*) алиме́нты* *pl.*
maintenance contract *n* контра́кт по обслу́живанию.
maintenance grant *n* стипе́ндия.
maintenance order *n* (*LAW*) постановле́ние о вы́плате алиме́нтов.
maisonette [meɪzə'nɛt] *n* (*BRIT*) двухэта́жная кварти́ра.
maize [meɪz] *n* кукуру́за, маи́с.
Maj. *abbr* (*MIL*) = **major.**
majestic [mə'dʒɛstɪk] *adj* вели́чественный* (вели́чествен).
majesty ['mædʒɪstɪ] *n* (*sovereignty*) короле́в-ская власть *f*; (*splendour*) вели́чественность *f*; (*form of address*): **Your M~** Ва́ше Вели́чество.
major ['meɪdʒə] *n* (*MIL*) майо́р ◆ *adj* (*important*) гла́вный; (*MUS*) мажо́рный ◆ *vi* (*US: SCOL*): **to ~ in** специализи́роваться (*impf/perf*) в +*prp*; **a ~ operation** (*also fig*) кру́пная опера́ция.
Majorca [mə'jɔ:kə] *n* Майо́рка, Майо́рка.
major general *n* генера́л-майо́р.
majority [mə'dʒɒrɪtɪ] *n* большинство́ ◆ *cpd*: **~ verdict** пригово́р, вы́несенный большинство́м (голосо́в); **~ (share)holding** контро́льный паке́т а́кций.
make [meɪk] (*pt, pp* **made**) *vt* де́лать (сде́лать *perf*); (*clothes*) шить* (сшить* *perf*); (*manufacture*) изготовля́ть (изгото́вить* *perf*); (*meal*) гото́вить (пригото́вить* *perf*); (*money*) зараба́тывать (зарабо́тать *perf*) ◆ *n* (*brand*) ма́рка*; **to ~ sb do** (*force*) заставля́ть (заста́вить* *perf*) кого́-н +*infin*; **two and two ~ four** (*equal*) два плюс два – четы́ре; **to ~ sb unhappy** расстра́ивать (расстро́ить *perf*) кого́-н; **to ~ a noise** шуме́ть* (*impf*); **to ~ the bed** стели́ть* (постели́ть* *perf*) посте́ль; **to ~**

a fool of sb де́лать (сде́лать *perf*) из кого́-н дурака́; to ~ a profit получа́ть (получи́ть* *perf*) при́быль; to ~ a loss нести́* (понести́* *perf*) убы́ток; to ~ it (*succeed*) преуспева́ть (преуспе́ть* *perf*); (*arrive*) успева́ть (успе́ть* *perf*); what time do you ~ it? ско́лько на ва́ших (часа́х)?; let's ~ it Monday дава́йте договори́мся на поне́дельник; to ~ good ♦ *vi* (*succeed*) преуспева́ть (преуспе́ть* *perf*) ♦ *vt* (*deficit*) возмеща́ть (возмести́ть* *perf*); (*damage*) исправля́ть (испра́вить* *perf*); to ~ do with/without обходи́ться* (обойти́сь* *perf*) +*instr*/без +*gen*

► make for *vt fus* (*place*) направля́ться (напра́виться* *perf*) к +*dat*/в +*acc*

► make off *vi* (*escape*) скрыва́ться (скры́ться* *perf*)

► make out *vt* (*decipher*) разбира́ть (разобра́ть* *perf*); (*see*) различа́ть (различи́ть *perf*); (*write out*) выпи́сывать (вы́писать* *perf*); (*claim*) утвержда́ть (*impf*); (*understand*) разбира́ться (разобра́ться* *perf*) в +*prp*; (*claim, imply*) де́лать (сде́лать *perf*) вид; to ~ out a case for sth обосно́вывать (обоснова́ть *perf*) что-н

► make over *vt* (*assign*): to ~ over (to) передава́ть (переда́ть* *perf*) (+*dat*)

► make up *vt fus* (*constitute*) составля́ть (соста́вить* *perf*) ♦ *vt* (*invent*) выду́мывать (вы́думать *perf*); (*prepare: bed, parcel*) гото́вить (пригото́вить* *perf*); (*with cosmetics*) де́лать (сде́лать *perf*) макия́ж +*dat* ♦ *vi* (*after quarrel*) мири́ться (помири́ться *perf*); (*with cosmetics*): to ~ (o.s.) up де́лать (сде́лать *perf*) макия́ж; to be made up of состоя́ть (*impf*) из +*gen*

► make up for *vt fus* (*mistake, misdemeanour*) загла́живать (загла́дить* *perf*); (*loss*) восполня́ть (воспо́лнить *perf*); to ~ up for lost time навёрстывать (наверста́ть *perf*) упу́щенное вре́мя.

make-believe ['meɪkbɪliːv] *n* фанта́зии *fpl*; a world of ~ мир фанта́зий; it's just ~ э́то – про́сто фанта́зия.

maker ['meɪkəʳ] *n* (*of programme, film*) созда́тель(ница) *m(f)*; (*of goods*) изготови́тель *m*.

makeshift ['meɪkʃɪft] *adj* (*temporary*) вре́менный.

make-up ['meɪkʌp] *n* косме́тика, макия́ж; (*THEAT*) грим.

make-up bag *n* косме́тичка*.

make-up remover *n* сре́дство для сня́тия макия́жа.

making ['meɪkɪŋ] *n* (*of programme*) созда́ние; (*of goods*) изготовле́ние; (*fig*): in the ~ в проце́ссе созда́ния; to have the ~s of име́ть (*impf*) зада́тки +*gen*; the problem is of your

own ~ пробле́ма Ва́ми же и со́здана.

maladjusted [mælə'dʒʌstɪd] *adj* (*child*) трудновоспиту́емый.

maladroit [mælə'drɔɪt] *adj* (*behaviour*) неуме́лый (неуме́л); (*comment*) беста́ктный* (беста́ктен).

malaise [mæ'leɪz] *n* (*of society*) неду́г.

malaria [mə'lɛərɪə] *n* маляри́я.

Malawi [mə'lɑːwɪ] *n* Мала́ви *nt ind*.

Malay [mə'leɪ] *adj* мала́йский* ♦ *n* (*person*) мала́ец*(-а́йка*); (*LING*) мала́йский* язы́к*.

Malaya [mə'leɪə] *n* Мала́йя.

Malayan [mə'leɪən] *adj, n* = **Malay**.

Malaysia [mə'leɪzɪə] *n* Мала́йзия.

Malaysian [mə'leɪzɪən] *adj* малайзи́йский ♦ *n* малайзи́ец*(-и́йка*).

Maldives ['mɔːldaɪvz] *npl*: the ~ Мальди́вские острова́* *mpl*.

male [meɪl] *n* (*human*) мужчи́на *m*; (*animal*) саме́ц* ♦ *adj* (*sex, attitude*) мужско́й; (*child etc*) мужско́го по́ла; (*ELEC*) охва́тываемый; ~ and female students студе́нты: ю́ноши и де́вушки*.

male chauvinist *n*: he's a ~~ он о́чень пренебрежи́тельно отно́сится к же́нщинам.

male nurse *n* медбра́т*.

malevolence [mə'lɛvələns] *n* (*act*) злодея́ние; (*feeling*) зло́ба.

malevolent [mə'lɛvələnt] *adj* зло́бный* (зло́бен).

malformed [mæl'fɔːmd] *adj* непра́вильно сформирова́вшийся.

malfunction [mæl'fʌŋkʃən] *n* неиспра́вность *f*.

Mali ['mɑːli] *n* Мали́ *nt ind*.

Malian ['mɑːlɪən] *adj* мали́йский ♦ *n* мали́ец*(-и́йка*).

malice ['mælɪs] *n* зло́ба.

malicious [mə'lɪʃəs] *adj* (*person, gossip*) зло́бный* (зло́бен), злой* (зол); (*LAW*) злонаме́ренный (злонаме́рен).

malign [mə'laɪn] *vt* клевета́ть* (оклевета́ть* *perf*) ♦ *adj* па́губный* (па́губен).

malignant [mə'lɪɡnənt] *adj* (*MED*) злока́чественный*; (*behaviour, intention*) зло́стный* (зло́стен).

malingerer [mə'lɪŋɡərəʳ] *n* симуля́нт(ка*).

mall [mɔːl] *n* (*also*: shopping ~) ≈ торго́вая у́лица.

malleable ['mælɪəbl] *adj* (*clay, substance*) пода́тливый (пода́тлив); (*person*) поко́рный* (поко́рен).

mallet ['mælɪt] *n* деревя́нный молото́к*.

malnutrition [mælnju:'trɪʃən] *n* недоеда́ние.

malpractice [mæl'præktɪs] *n* злоупотребле́ние служе́бным положе́нием.

malt [mɔːlt] *n* (*grain*) со́лод*; (*also*: ~ whisky) солодо́вое ви́ски *nt ind*.

Malta ['mɔːltə] *n* Ма́льта.

---

* marks translations which have irregular inflections. The Russian-English side of the dictionary gives inflectional information.

Maltese [mɔ:l'ti:z] *adj* мальти́йский* ◆ *n inv*
мальти́ец*(-и́йка*); (*LING*) мальти́йский*
язы́к*.
maltreat [mæl'tri:t] *vt* пло́хо обраща́ться (*impf*)
с +*instr*.
mammal ['mæml] *n* млекопита́ющее *nt adj*.
mammoth ['mæməθ] *n* ма́монт ◆ *adj* (*task*)
колосса́льный* (колосса́лен).
man [mæn] (*pl* **men**) *n* (*adult male*) мужчи́на *m*;
(*person, mankind*) челове́к*; (*CHESS*) фигу́ра ◆
vt (*machine*) обслу́живать (*impf*); (*post*)
занима́ть (заня́ть* *perf*); (*NAUT*): **to ~ a ship**
набира́ть (набра́ть* *perf*) кома́нду корабля́;
an old ~ стари́к*; **~ and wife** муж и жена́.
manage ['mænɪdʒ] *vi* (*get by*) обходи́ться*
(обойти́сь* *perf*) ◆ *vt* (*business, organization*)
руководи́ть* (*impf*) +*instr*, управля́ть (*impf*)
+*instr*; (*shop, restaurant*) заве́довать (*impf*)
+*instr*; (*economy*) управля́ть (*impf*) +*instr*;
(*control*) кома́ндовать (*impf*) +*instr*; (*workload,
task*) справля́ться (*impf*) с +*instr*; **to ~ without
sb/sth** обходи́ться* (обойти́сь* *perf*) без
кого́-н/чего́-н; **I ~d to convince him** мне
удало́сь убеди́ть его́; **I ~d to finish in time** я
успе́л зако́нчить во́время.
manageable ['mænɪdʒəbl] *adj* (*task*)
выполни́мый (выполни́м); (*number, size*)
удо́бный.
management ['mænɪdʒmənt] *n* (*body*)
руково́дство; (*act*): **~ (of)** управле́ние
(+*instr*); **"under new ~"** "под но́вым
руково́дством".
management accounting *n* управле́нческий*
учёт.
management consultant *n* консульта́нт по
вопро́сам ме́неджмента.
manager ['mænɪdʒə'] *n* (*of business,
organization*) управля́ющий* *m adj*,
ме́неджер; (*of estate*) управля́ющий; (*of
shop*) заве́дующий*(-ая) *m(f) adj*; (*of pop star*)
ме́неджер; (*SPORT*) гла́вный тре́нер; **sales ~**
нача́льник по сбы́ту.
manageress [mænɪdʒə'rɛs] *n* (*of shop*)
заве́дующая *f adj*.
managerial [mænɪ'dʒɪərɪəl] *adj* (*role*)
управле́нческий*; **~ staff** управле́нческий*
аппара́т; **~ decisions** реше́ния, при́нятые
руково́дством.
managing director ['mænɪdʒɪŋ-] *n*
дире́ктор*-распоряди́тель *m*.
Managua [mə'nægwə] *n* Мана́гуа.
Manchester ['mæntʃɪstə'] *n* Манче́стер.
Manchuria [mæn'tʃuərɪə] *n* Маньчжу́рия.
Mancunian [mæn'kju:nɪən] *n* жи́тель(ница)
m(f) Манче́стера.
mandarin ['mændərɪn] *n* (*also*: **~ orange**)
мандари́н; (*BRIT: POL*) кру́пный чино́вник;
(*LING*): **M~ (Chinese)** мандари́нское наре́чие
кита́йского языка́.
mandate ['mændeɪt] *n* (*POL: from electorate*)
полномо́чие; (: *from UN etc*) манда́т; (*task*)

поруче́ние.
mandatory ['mændətərɪ] *adj* обяза́тельный*
(обяза́телен).
mandolin(e) ['mændəlɪn] *n* мандоли́на.
mane [meɪn] *n* гри́ва.
maneuver *etc* (*US*) = **manoeuvre** *etc*.
manfully ['mænfəlɪ] *adv* му́жественно.
manganese [mæŋgə'ni:z] *n* ма́рганец*.
mangetout ['mɔnʒ'tu:] *n* стручко́вый горо́х
(*со съедо́бными стру́чками*).
mangle ['mæŋgl] *vt* корёжить (искорёжить
perf) ◆ *n* пресс для отжима́ния белья́.
mango ['mæŋgəu] (*pl* **~es**) *n* ма́нго *nt ind*.
mangrove ['mæŋgrəuv] *n* ма́нгровое де́рево*.
mangy ['meɪndʒɪ] *adj* (*diseased*) парши́вый
(парши́в); (*scruffy*) обле́злый (обле́зл).
manhandle ['mænhændl] *vt* (*mistreat*) гру́бо
обраща́ться (*impf*) с +*instr*; (*move by hand*)
приводи́ть* (привести́* *perf*) в де́йствие
вручну́ю.
manhole ['mænhəul] *n* люк.
manhood ['mænhud] *n* (*state*) возмужа́лость *f*;
(*age*) зре́лость *f*.
man-hour ['mænauə'] *n* челове́ко-час*.
manhunt ['mænhʌnt] *n* ро́зыск.
mania ['meɪnɪə] *n* (*also PSYCH*) ма́ния.
maniac ['meɪnɪæk] *n* (*also fig*) манья́к; **he's a
football ~** он стра́стный люби́тель футбо́ла.
manic ['mænɪk] *adj* безу́мный* (безу́мен).
manic-depressive ['mænɪkdɪ'prɛsɪv] *adj*
маниака́льно-депресси́вный* ◆ *n* челове́к,
*страда́ющий маниака́льно-депресси́вным
психо́зом*.
manicure ['mænɪkjuə'] *n* маникю́р ◆ *vt* (*person*)
де́лать (сде́лать *perf*) маникю́р +*dat*.
manicure set *n* маникю́рный набо́р.
manifest ['mænɪfɛst] *vt* проявля́ть (прояви́ть*
perf) ◆ *adj* очеви́дный* (очеви́ден), я́вный*
(я́вен) ◆ *n* (*NAUT*) деклара́ция (судово́го
гру́за); (*AVIAT*) манифе́ст.
manifestation [mænɪfɛs'teɪʃən] *n*: **a ~ of**
проявле́ние +*gen*.
manifesto [mænɪ'fɛstəu] *n* манифе́ст.
manifold ['mænɪfəuld] *adj* многообра́зный*
(многообра́зен) ◆ *n* (*AUT*): **exhaust ~**
выхлопно́й колле́ктор.
Manila [mə'nɪlə] *n* Мани́ла.
manila [mə'nɪlə] *adj*: **~ paper** пло́тная
кори́чневая бума́га.
manipulate [mə'nɪpjuleɪt] *vt* манипули́ровать
(*impf*) +*instr*.
manipulation [mənɪpju'leɪʃən] *n* манипуля́ция.
mankind [mæn'kaɪnd] *n* челове́чество.
manliness ['mænlɪnɪs] *n* му́жественность *f*.
manly ['mænlɪ] *adj* му́жественный*
(му́жествен).
man-made ['mæn'meɪd] *adj* иску́сственный.
manna ['mænə] *n* ма́нна небе́сная.
mannequin ['mænɪkɪn] *n* (*dummy*) манеке́н;
(*fashion model*) манеке́нщица.
manner ['mænə'] *n* (*way*) о́браз; (*behaviour*)

манéра; ~s *npl* манéры *fpl*; **bad** ~s плохи́е манéры; **all** ~ **of things/people** всевозмóжные вéщи/лю́ди; **in a** ~ **of speaking** в некотóром рóде.

mannerism ['mænərɪzəm] *n* осóбенность *f* манéра.

mannerly ['mænəlɪ] *adj* учти́вый (учти́в).

manning ['mænɪŋ] *n* набóр рабóчей си́лы.

manoeuvrable [mə'nu:vrəbl] (*US* **maneuvrable**) *adj* манёвренный.

manoeuvre [mə'nu:vəʳ] (*US* **maneuver**) *vt* (*move*) умéло передвигáть (передви́нуть *perf*); (*manipulate*) маневри́ровать (*impf*) +*instr* ♦ *vi* маневри́ровать (*impf*) ♦ *n* манёвр; ~s *npl* (*MIL*) манёвры *mpl*; **to** ~ **sb into doing** подводи́ть* (подвести́* *perf*) когó-н к томý, чтóбы сдéлал чтó-н.

manor ['mænəʳ] *n* (*also*: ~ **house**) усáдебный дом*.

manpower ['mænpauəʳ] *n* рабóчая си́ла.

manservant ['mænsə:vənt] (*pl* **menservants**) *n* слугá* *m*.

mansion ['mænʃən] *n* особня́к*.

manslaughter ['mænslɔ:təʳ] *n* непредумы́шленное уби́йство.

mantelpiece ['mæntlpi:s] *n*ками́нная доскá*.

mantle ['mæntl] *n* (*cloak*) мáнтия; (*fig: covering*) покрóв.

man-to-man ['mæntə'mæn] *adj* мужскóй ♦ *adv* по-мужски́, как мужчи́на с мужчи́ной.

manual ['mænjuəl] *adj* ручнóй ♦ *n* (*book*) посóбие; ~ **worker** чернорабóчий*(-ая) *m(f)* *adj*.

manufacture [mænju'fæktʃəʳ] *vt* (*goods*) изготовля́ть (изготóвить* *perf*), производи́ть* (произвести́* *perf*) ♦ *n* изготовлéние, произвóдство.

manufactured goods *npl* промы́шленные товáры *mpl*.

manufacturer [mænju'fæktʃərəʳ] *n* изготови́тель *m*, производи́тель *m*.

manufacturing [mænju'fæktʃərɪŋ] *n* изготовлéние, произвóдство.

manure [mə'njuəʳ] *n* навóз.

manuscript ['mænjuskrɪpt] *n* (*author's draft*) рýкопись *f*; (*old document*) манускри́пт, рýкопись.

many ['mɛnɪ] *adj* (*a lot of*) мнóго +*gen* ♦ *pron* (*several*) мнóгие; **a great** ~ óчень мнóго +*gen*, мнóжество +*gen*; **how** ~? скóлько?; **how people/times?** скóлько людéй/раз?; **too** ~ **difficulties** сли́шком мнóго трýдностей; **twice as** ~ вдвóе бóльше, в два рáза бóльше; ~ **a time** мнóго раз; **in** ~ **cases** во мнóгих слýчаях; ~ **of us** мнóгие из нас.

Maori ['mauri] *n* мáори *m/f ind*.

map [mæp] *n* кáрта; (*of town*) план ♦ *vt* составля́ть (состáвить* *perf*) кáрту +*gen*

▶ **map out** *vt* (*plan*) составля́ть (состáвить* *perf*); (*task, holiday, career*) плани́ровать (*impf*).

maple ['meɪpl] *n* клён ♦ *cpd* кленóвый.

mar [mɑ:ʳ] *vt* пóртить* (испóртить* *perf*).

Mar. *abbr* = **March**.

marathon ['mærəθən] *n* марафóн ♦ *adj* (*fig*) марафóнский.

marathon runner *n* марафóнец*.

marauder [mə'rɔ:dəʳ] *n* мародёр.

marble ['mɑ:bl] *n* (*stone*) мрáмор; (*toy*) стекля́нный шáрик ♦ *adj* мрáморный.

marbles ['mɑ:blz] *n* (*game*) дéтская игрá* в стекля́ные шáрики.

March [mɑ:tʃ] *n* март; *see also* **July**.

march [mɑ:tʃ] *vi* маршир[овáть] (промарширов[áть] *perf*); (*protesters*) проходи́ть* (пройти́* *perf*) мáршем ♦ *n* марш ♦ *vt*: **to** ~ **sb out of** выдворя́ть (вы́дворить *perf*) когó-н из +*gen*; **to** ~ **out of** демонстрати́вно выходи́ть* (вы́йти* *perf*) из +*gen*; **to** ~ **into** реши́тельно входи́ть* (войти́* *perf*) в +*acc*.

marcher ['mɑ:tʃəʳ] *n* (*demonstrator*) учáстник(-ица) мáрша.

marching orders ['mɑ:tʃɪŋ-] *npl*: **to give sb his** ~~ увольня́ть (уволить *perf*) когó-н.

march past *n* (*MIL*) строевóй смотр.

mare [mɛəʳ] *n* кобы́ла.

marge [mɑ:dʒ] *n abbr* (*BRIT*: *inf*) = **margarine**.

margarine [mɑ:dʒə'ri:n] *n* маргари́н.

margin ['mɑ:dʒɪn] *n* (*on page*) поля́ *ntpl*; (*of group*) перифери́я; (*of area*) край*; (*difference: of victory*) преимýщество; (*: of defeat*) мéньшинство; (*also*: **profit** ~) чи́стая при́быль *f no pl*; **safety** ~ предéл прóчности; ~ **of error** предéл допусти́мой погрéшности; **they won by a** ~ **of five votes** они́ победи́ли с большинствóм в пять голосóв.

marginal ['mɑ:dʒɪnl] *adj* незначи́тельный* (незначи́телен) ♦ *n* (*also*: ~ **seat** *or* **constituency**: *BRIT*: *POL*) избирáтельный учáсток где правя́щая пáртия имéет незначи́тельное большинствó голосóв.

marginally ['mɑ:dʒɪnəlɪ] *adv* незначи́тельно.

marigold ['mærɪɡəuld] *n* (*BOT*) ноготки́ *mpl*.

marijuana [mærɪ'wɑ:nə] *n* марихуáна.

marina [mə'ri:nə] *n* мари́на *or* при́стань* *f* для яхт.

marinade [mærɪ'neɪd] *n* маринáд ♦ *vt* = **marinate**.

marinate ['mærɪneɪt] *vt* маринов[áть] (замаринов[áть] *perf*).

marine [mə'ri:n] *adj* морскóй; (*engineer*) судовóй ♦ *n* (*BRIT*) служáщий* *m adj* воéнно-морскóго флóта; (*US*) морскóй пехоти́нец*.

marine insurance *n* морскóе страховáние.

---

marital ['mærɪtl] *adj* супру́жеский*; ~ **status** семе́йное положе́ние.
maritime ['mærɪtaɪm] *adj* морско́й; ~ **law** морско́е пра́во.
Mariupol [mari'upəlj] *n* Мариу́поль *m*.
marjoram ['mɑːdʒərəm] *n* души́ца, майора́н.
mark [mɑːk] *n* (*written symbol*) значо́к*, поме́тка*; (*stain*) пятно́*; (*trace*) след*; (*of friendship, respect*) знак; (*BRIT: SCOL*) отме́тка*, оце́нка*; (*level*) отме́тка*; (*currency*) ма́рка* ♦ *vt* (*with pen*) помеча́ть (поме́тить* *perf*); (*subj: shoes, tyres*) оставля́ть (оста́вить* *perf*) след на +*prp*; (*furniture etc*) повряжда́ть (повреди́ть* *perf*); (*clothes, carpet*) ста́вить* (поста́вить* *perf*) пятно́ на +*prp*; (*place, time*) ука́зывать (указа́ть* *perf*); (*characterize*) отмеча́ть (отме́тить* *perf*); (*BRIT: SCOL*) проверя́ть (прове́рить* *perf*); (*SPORT: player*) блоки́ровать (*impf*); **punctuation** ~ знак препина́ния; **M~ 2/3** (*BRIT: TECH*) второ́го/ тре́тьего вы́пуска; **up to the** ~ на высоте́; **to be quick off the** ~ **to do** (*fig*) не заме́длить (*perf*) +*infin*; **to** ~ **the price on sth** ста́вить* (поста́вить* *perf*) це́ну на чём-н; **to** ~ **time** (*MIL*) марширова́ть (*impf*) на ме́сте; (*fig*) топта́ться* (*impf*)
▸ **mark down** *vt* (*price*) снижа́ть (сни́зить* *perf*); (*goods*) уце́нивать (уцени́ть* *perf*)
▸ **mark off** *vt* (*tick off*) отмеча́ть (отме́тить* *perf*)
▸ **mark out** *vt* (*area, road*) размеча́ть (разме́тить* *perf*); (*person*) выделя́ть (вы́делить *perf*)
▸ **mark up** *vt* (*price*) повыша́ть (повы́сить* *perf*).
marked [mɑːkt] *adj* заме́тный* (заме́тен).
markedly ['mɑːkɪdlɪ] *adv* заме́тно.
marker ['mɑːkə] *n* (*sign*) знак; (*bookmark*) закла́дка*; (*pen*) флома́стер.
market ['mɑːkɪt] *n* (*also COMM*) ры́нок* ♦ *vt* выпуска́ть (вы́пустить* *perf*) в прода́жу; **to be on the** ~ быть* (*impf*) в прода́же; **on the open** ~ в свобо́дной прода́же; **to play the** ~ игра́ть (*impf*) на би́рже.
marketable ['mɑːkɪtəbl] *adj* по́льзующийся спро́сом; **to be** ~ по́льзоваться (*impf*) спро́сом.
market analysis *n* ана́лиз ры́нка.
market day *n* база́рный день* *m*.
market demand *n* ры́ночный спрос.
market economy *n* ры́ночная эконо́мика.
market forces *npl* ры́ночные си́лы *fpl*.
market garden *n* (*BRIT*) огоро́д (*для выра́щивания овоще́й на прода́жу*).
marketing ['mɑːkɪtɪŋ] *n* ма́ркетинг.
marketing manager *n* ме́неджер по ма́ркетингу.
marketplace ['mɑːkɪtpleɪs] *n* ры́ночная *or* база́рная пло́щадь* *f*; (*COMM*) ры́нок*.
market price *n* ры́ночная цена́.

market research *n* иссле́дование ры́нка.
market value *n* ры́ночная сто́имость *f*.
marking ['mɑːkɪŋ] *n* (*on animal*) расцве́тка; (*on road*) разме́тка.
marksman ['mɑːksmən] *irreg n* ме́ткий* стрело́к*.
marksmanship ['mɑːksmənʃɪp] *n* ме́ткая стрельба́.
mark-up ['mɑːkʌp] *n* (*margin*) ра́зница (*ме́жду себесто́имостью и прода́жной цено́й*); (*increase*) наце́нка*.
marmalade ['mɑːməleɪd] *n* джем (*ци́трусовый*).
maroon [mə'ruːn] *adj* бордо́вый ♦ *vt*: **we were** ~**ed** мы бы́ли отре́заны от вне́шнего ми́ра; (*fig*) мы бы́ли в изоля́ции.
marquee [mɑː'kiː] *n* марки́за, пала́точный павильо́н, шатёр.
marquess ['mɑːkwɪs] *n* (*BRIT*) марки́з.
marquis ['mɑːkwɪs] *n* = **marquess**.
Marrakech [mærə'kɛʃ] *n* = **Marrakesh**.
Marrakesh [mærə'kɛʃ] *n* Марраке́ш.
marriage ['mærɪdʒ] *n* брак; (*wedding*) сва́дьба*.
marriage bureau *n* бюро́ *nt ind* знако́мств.
marriage certificate *n* свиде́тельство о бра́ке.
marriage guidance (*US* **marriage counselling**) *n* консульта́ция по вопро́сам семьи́ и бра́ка.
marriage of convenience *n* фикти́вный брак.
married ['mærɪd] *adj* (*man*) жена́тый (жена́т); (*woman*) заму́жняя; (*couple*) жена́тые (жена́ты); (*life*) супру́жеский*; **he is** ~ **to** он жена́т на +*prp*; **she is** ~ **to** она́ за́мужем за +*instr*; **they are** ~ они́ жена́ты.
marrow ['mærəu] *n* (*vegetable*) кабачо́к*; (*also:* **bone** ~) ко́стный мозг.
marry ['mærɪ] *vt* (*subj: man*) жени́ться* (*impf/ perf*) на +*prp*; (*: woman*) выходи́ть* (вы́йти* *perf*) за́муж за +*acc*; (*also:* ~ **off: son**) жени́ть (*impf/perf*); (*: daughter*) выдава́ть* (вы́дать* *perf*) за́муж; (*priest*) венча́ть (обвенча́ть *perf*) ♦ *vi* (*get married: man*) жени́ться (*impf*); (*: woman*) выходи́ть* (вы́йти* *perf*) за́муж; (*: couple*) жени́ться (пожени́ться *perf*).
Mars [mɑːz] *n* Марс.
Marseilles [mɑː'seɪlz] *n* Марсе́ль *m*.
marsh [mɑːʃ] *n* боло́то; **salt** ~ солонча́ковое боло́то.
marshal ['mɑːʃl] *n* (*MIL*) ма́ршал; (*at public event*) распоряди́тель(ница) *m(f)* ♦ *vt* (*thoughts, support*) упоря́дочить (*perf*); (*soldiers*) выстра́ивать (вы́строить *perf*); **police/fire** ~ (*US*) нача́льник полице́йского уча́стка/пожа́рной ча́сти.
marshalling yard ['mɑːʃlɪŋ-] *n* (*RAIL*) сортиро́вочная ста́нция.
marshmallow [mɑːʃ'mæləu] *n* (*BOT*) мушмула́; (*sweet*) ≈ зефи́р.
marshy ['mɑːʃɪ] *adj* боло́тистый (боло́тист).
marsupial [mɑː'suːpɪəl] *n* су́мчатое *nt adj*

(живо́тное) ♦ *adj* су́мчатый.
marten ['mɑːtɪn] *n* куни́ца.
martial ['mɑːʃl] *adj* вое́нный.
martial art *n* восто́чное единобо́рство.
martial law *n* вое́нное положе́ние.
Martian ['mɑːʃən] *n* марсиа́нин*(-а́нка*).
martin ['mɑːtɪn] *n*: **house/sand** ~ городска́я/
берегова́я ла́сточка*.
martyr ['mɑːtə^r] *n* му́ченик(-ица) ♦ *vt* му́чить
(замучить *perf*).
martyrdom ['mɑːtədəm] *n* му́ченичество.
marvel ['mɑːvl] *n* чу́до* ♦ *vi*: **to ~ (at)**
восхища́ться (восхити́ться* *perf*) (+*instr*).
marvellous ['mɑːvləs] (*US* **marvelous**) *adj*
восхити́тельный* (восхити́телен),
изуми́тельный* (изуми́телен).
Marxism ['mɑːksɪzəm] *n* маркси́зм.
Marxist ['mɑːksɪst] *adj* маркси́стский ♦ *n*
маркси́ст(ка*).
marzipan ['mɑːzɪpæn] *n* марципа́н.
mascara [mæs'kɑːrə] *n* тушь *f* для ресни́ц.
mascot ['mæskət] *n* талисма́н.
masculine ['mæskjulɪn] *adj* мужско́й; (*woman*)
мужеподо́бный* (мужеподо́бен); **~ noun/
pronoun** существи́тельное/местоиме́ние
мужско́го ро́да.
masculinity [mæskju'lɪnɪtɪ] *n* му́жественность
f.
MASH [mæʃ] *n abbr* (*US*: = *mobile army surgical
hospital*) ≈ ППГ= *полевой подви́жный
го́спиталь*.
mash [mæʃ] *vt* де́лать (сде́лать *perf*) пюре́ из
+*gen*.
mashed potatoes [mæʃt-] *npl* карто́фельное
пюре́ *nt ind*.
mask [mɑːsk] *n* ма́ска* ♦ *vt* (*face*) закрыва́ть
(закры́ть* *perf*); (*feelings*) маскирова́ть (*impf*).
masking tape ['mɑːskɪŋ-] *n* кле́йкая ле́нта.
masochism ['mæsəukɪzəm] *n* мазохи́зм.
masochist ['mæsəukɪst] *n* мазохи́ст(ка*).
mason ['meɪsn] *n* (*also:* **stone** ~) ка́менщик;
(*also:* **freemason**) масо́н.
masonic [mə'sɔnɪk] *adj* масо́нский*.
masonry ['meɪsnrɪ] *n* (*stonework*) (ка́менная)
кла́дка.
masquerade [mæskə'reɪd] *n* маскара́д ♦ *vi*: **to
~ as** выдава́ть* (*impf*) себя́ за +*acc*.
mass [mæs] *n* (*also PHYS*) ма́сса; (*REL*:
Orthodox) обе́дня*; (: *Catholic*) ме́сса ♦ *cpd*
ма́ссовый ♦ *vi* сосредото́чиваться
(сосредото́читься *perf*); **the ~es** (*inf*)
(наро́дные) ма́ссы *fpl*; **to go to M~** идти́*
(пойти́* *perf*) к обе́дне/ме́ссе; **~es of** (*inf*)
ма́сса *fsg* +*gen*, у́йма *fsg* +*gen*.
massacre ['mæsəkə] *n* ма́ссовое уби́йство ♦ *vt*
зве́рски убива́ть (уби́ть* *perf*).
massage ['mæsɑːʒ] *n* масса́ж ♦ *vt* (*rub*)
масси́ровать (*impf*).

masseur [mæ'sə:^r] *n* массажи́ст.
masseuse [mæ'sə:z] *n* массажи́стка*.
massive ['mæsɪv] *adj* (*furniture, person*)
масси́вный* (масси́вен); (*support, changes*)
огро́мный* (огро́мен).
mass market *n* массо́вый спрос.
mass media *n inv* сре́дства *ntpl* ма́ссовой
информа́ции.
mass meeting *n* ма́ссовый ми́тинг.
mass-produce ['mæsprə'djuːs] *vt* ма́ссово
производи́ть* (произвести́* *perf*).
mass production *n* ма́ссовое произво́дство.
mast [mɑːst] *n* ма́чта.
mastectomy [mæs'tɛktəmɪ] *n* мастэктоми́я.
master ['mɑːstə^r] *n* (*also fig*) хозя́ин*; (*BRIT:
SCOL*) учи́тель* *m*; (*expert*) ма́стер ♦ *cpd*
(*baker, craftsman*) уме́лый ♦ *vt* (*control*)
владе́ть (овладе́ть *perf*) +*instr*; (*learn,
understand*) овладева́ть (овладе́ть *perf*)
+*instr*; **M~ Smith** (*title for boys*) господи́н *or*
ма́стер Смит; **M~'s degree** сте́пень *f*
маги́стра; **M~ of Arts/Science** маги́стр
гуманита́рных/есте́ственных нау́к; **M~ of
Ceremonies** церемониймейстер.
master disk *n* (*COMPUT*) оригина́л ди́ска.
masterful ['mɑːstəful] *adj* вла́стный*
(вла́стен).
master key *n* универса́льный ключ
(*подходя́щий ко всем дверя́м зда́ния*).
masterly ['mɑːstəlɪ] *adj* ма́стерский.
mastermind ['mɑːstəmaɪnd] *n* (*of plan*)
созда́тель(ница) *m(f)* ♦ *vt* разраба́тывать
(разрабо́тать *perf*).
masterpiece ['mɑːstəpiːs] *n* шеде́вр.
master plan *n* гениа́льный план.
masterstroke ['mɑːstəstrəuk] *n* гениа́льный
ход*.
mastery ['mɑːstərɪ] *n* (*excellence: skill*)
мастерство́; **~ of** (*skill, language*) владе́ние
+*instr*.
mastiff ['mæstɪf] *n* (*dog*) ма́стифф.
masturbate ['mæstəbeɪt] *vi* мастурби́ровать
(*impf*).
masturbation [mæstə'beɪʃən] *n* мастурба́ция.
mat [mæt] *n* ко́врик; (*also:* **doormat**) дверно́й
ко́врик; (*also:* **table** ~) подста́вка* ♦ *adj* =
matt.
match [mætʃ] *n* спи́чка; (*SPORT*) матч; (*equal*)
ро́вня *m/f* ♦ *vt* (*subj: colours*) сочета́ться (*impf*)
с +*instr*; (*equal*) сравня́ться (*perf*) с +*instr*;
(*correspond to*) соотве́тствовать (*impf*) +*dat* ♦
vi (*colours, materials*) сочета́ться (*impf*); **to be
a good ~** (*colours, clothes*) сочета́ться (*impf*);
they make *or* **are a good ~** они́ хоро́шая па́ра;
I'm no ~ for him я ему́ не ро́вня; **to ~ sth (up)
with sth** (*pair*) подбира́ть (подобра́ть* *perf*)
что-н к чему́-н
▶ **match up** *vi* совпада́ть (совпа́сть* *perf*).

---

* marks translations which have irregular inflections. The Russian-English side of the dictionary gives inflectional information.

matchbox ['mætʃbɒks] *n* спи́чечная коро́бка*.
matching ['mætʃɪŋ] *adj* (*clothes, colours*)
сочета́ющийся.
matchless ['mætʃlɪs] *adj* несравне́нный*
(несравне́нен).
mate [meɪt] *n* (*inf: friend*) друг* (подру́га);
(*animal*) саме́ц*(-мка*); (*workman's assistant*)
подру́чный *m adj*; (*NAUT*) помо́щник
(*капита́на*) ◆ *vi* спа́риваться (спа́риться
perf).
material [mə'tɪərɪəl] *n* (*substance, information*)
материа́л; (*cloth*) материа́л, ткань *f* ◆ *adj*
(*possessions, existence*) материа́льный*;
(*evidence*) веще́ственный*; ~**s** *npl*
принадле́жности *fpl*; **building** ~**s**
строи́тельные материа́лы; **reading** ~
материа́л для чте́ния.
materialistic [mətɪərɪə'lɪstɪk] *adj* (*person etc*)
материалисти́ческий.
materialize [mə'tɪərɪəlaɪz] *vi*
материализова́ться (*impf/perf*),
осуществля́ться (осуществи́ться* *perf*).
maternal [mə'tə:nl] *adj* матери́нский*.
maternity [mə'tə:nɪtɪ] *n* матери́нство ◆ *cpd*
(*hospital, ward*) роди́льный; ~ **care** ухо́д за
роже́ницами.
maternity benefit *n* декре́тные *pl adj*.
maternity dress *n* пла́тье* для бере́менной
(же́нщины).
maternity hospital *n* роди́льный дом*,
роддо́м*.
maternity leave *n* декре́тный о́тпуск.
matey ['meɪtɪ] *adj* (*BRIT: inf*) дружелю́бный*
(дружелю́бен).
math [mæθ] *n abbr* (*US*) = **mathematics**.
mathematical [mæθə'mætɪkl] *adj*
математи́ческий*.
mathematician [mæθəmə'tɪʃən] *n* матема́тик.
mathematics [mæθə'mætɪks] *n* матема́тика.
maths [mæθs] *n abbr* (*BRIT*) = **mathematics**.
matinée ['mætɪneɪ] *n* (*CINEMA*) дневно́й сеа́нс;
(*THEAT*) дневно́й спекта́кль *m*.
mating ['meɪtɪŋ] *n* спа́ривание, слу́чка.
mating call *n* бра́чный призы́в.
mating season *n* бра́чный сезо́н.
matriarchal [meɪtrɪ'ɑ:kl] *adj* матриарха́льный.
matrices ['meɪtrɪsi:z] *npl of* **matrix**.
matriculation [mətrɪkju'leɪʃən] *n* (*enrolment*)
зачисле́ние в университе́т.
matrimonial [mætrɪ'məunɪəl] *adj*
матримониа́льный, бра́чный.
matrimony ['mætrɪmənɪ] *n* супру́жество.
matrix ['meɪtrɪks] *n* (*pl* **matrices**) *n* ма́трица.
matron ['meɪtrən] *n* (*in hospital*) ста́ршая
медсестра́*; (*in school*) (шко́льная)
медсестра́*.
matronly ['meɪtrənlɪ] *adj* пы́шный* (пы́шен).
matt [mæt] *adj* ма́товый.
matted ['mætɪd] *adj* (*hair*) спу́танный (спу́тан).
matter ['mætə] *n* де́ло*, вопро́с; (*PHYS*)
мате́рия; (*substance, material*) вещество́*;

(*MED: pus*) гной ◆ *vi* име́ть (*impf*) значе́ние; ~**s**
npl (*affairs, situation*) дела́ *ntpl*; **printed** ~
печа́тный материа́л; **reading** ~ (*BRIT*)
материа́л для чте́ния; **what's the** ~? в чём
де́ло?; **no** ~ **what** несмотря́ ни на что́, что́
бы то ни бы́ло; **that's another** ~ э́то друго́е
де́ло; **as a** ~ **of course** как само́ собо́й
разуме́ющееся; **as a** ~ **of fact** со́бственно
говоря́; **it's a** ~ **of habit** э́то де́ло привы́чки; **it**
doesn't ~ э́то не ва́жно.
matter-of-fact ['mætərəv'fækt] *adj*
безразли́чный* (безразли́чен).
matting ['mætɪŋ] *n* цино́вка; **rush** ~
камышо́вая цино́вка.
mattress ['mætrɪs] *n* матра́с, матра́ц.
mature [mə'tjuə] *adj* (*person*) зре́лый* (зрел);
(*cheese, wine*) вы́держанный* (вы́держан) ◆
vi (*develop*) развива́ться (разви́ться* *perf*);
(*grow up*) взросле́ть (повзросле́ть *perf*);
(*cheese*) зреть *or* созрева́ть (созре́ть *perf*);
(*wine*) выста́иваться (вы́стояться *perf*);
(*COMM*): **this policy is due to** ~ **next year** в
сле́дующем году́ начина́ются вы́платы по
э́тому по́лису.
mature student *n* студе́нт, начина́ющий
вы́сшее образова́ние в во́зрасте 23 лет и́ли
ста́рше.
maturity [mə'tjuərɪtɪ] *n* зре́лость *f*.
maudlin ['mɔ:dlɪn] *adj* плакси́вый (плакси́в),
слезли́вый (слезли́в).
maul [mɔ:l] *vt* (*physically*) терза́ть (растерза́ть
perf).
Mauritania [mɔ:rɪ'teɪnɪə] *n* Маврита́ния.
Mauritius [mə'rɪʃəs] *n* Маври́кий.
mausoleum [mɔ:sə'lɪəm] *n* мавзоле́й.
mauve [məuv] *adj* сире́невый.
maverick ['mævrɪk] *n* индивидуали́ст.
mawkish ['mɔ:kɪʃ] *adj* слаща́вый (слаща́в).
max. *abbr* (= **maximum**) макс(им).,
масима́льно.
maxim ['mæksɪm] *n* ма́ксима.
maxima ['mæksɪmə] *npl of* **maximum**.
maximize ['mæksɪmaɪz] *vt* максима́льно
увели́чивать (увели́чить *perf*).
maximum ['mæksɪməm] (*pl* **maxima** *or* ~**s**) *adj*
максима́льный* (максима́лен) ◆ *n*
ма́ксимум.
May [meɪ] *n* май; *see also* **July**.
may [meɪ] (*conditional* **might**) *vi* (*indicating*
possibility): **I** ~ **go to Russia** я, мо́жет быть,
пое́ду в Росси́ю; (*indicating permission*): ~ **I**
smoke/sit here мо́жно закури́ть/здесь
присе́сть; (*indicating wishes*): ~ **God bless**
you! да благослови́т Вас Бог!; **it** ~ *or* **might**
rain мо́жет пойти́ дождь; **he might be there**
возмо́жно, что он там; **you might like to try**
мо́жет быть, Вы хоти́те попро́бовать; **you**
~ *or* **might as well go now** Вы, пожа́луй,
мо́жете уйти́ сейча́с; **come what** ~ будь что
бу́дет.
maybe ['meɪbi:] *adv* мо́жет быть; ~ **he'll** ...

мо́жет быть, он +*infin* ...; ~ **not** мо́жет быть, нет.
mayday ['meɪdeɪ] *n* сигна́л бе́дствия.
May Day *n* Пе́рвое Ма́я.
mayhem ['meɪhɛm] *n* погро́м.
mayonnaise [meɪə'neɪz] *n* майоне́з.
mayor [mɛə'] *n* мэр.
mayoress ['mɛərɛs] *n* (*partner*) жена́* мэ́ра.
maypole ['meɪpəul] *n* укра́шенный цвета́ми столб.
maze [meɪz] *n* (*labyrinth*) лабири́нт; (*puzzle*) головоло́мка*; (*of ideas*) пу́таница.
MB *abbr* (*COMPUT*) (= **megabyte**) M= мегаба́йт; (*CANADA*) = Manitoba.
MBA *n abbr* (= *Master of Business Administration*) маги́стрская сте́пень по менеджме́нту.
MBBS *n abbr* (*BRIT*: = *Bachelor of Medicine and Surgery*) бакала́вр медици́нских нау́к и хирурги́и.
MBChB *n abbr* (*BRIT*: = *Bachelor of Medicine and Surgery*) бакала́вр медици́нских нау́к и хирурги́и.
MBE *n abbr* (*BRIT*) = *Member of the Order of the British Empire*.
MC *n abbr* = **Master of Ceremonies**.
MCAT *n abbr* (*US*) = *Medical College Admissions Test*.
MCP *n abbr* (*BRIT*: *inf*) = *male chauvinist pig*.
MD *n abbr* (= *Doctor of Medicine*) до́ктор медици́ны *or* медици́нских нау́к; (*COMM*) = **managing director** ◆ *abbr* (*US*: *POST*) = Maryland.
MDT *abbr* (*US*) = *Mountain Daylight Time*.
ME *n abbr* (*US*: = *medical examiner*) суде́бно-медици́нский экспе́рт; (*MED*: = *myalgic encephalomyelitis*) миалги́ческий энцефаломиели́т ◆ *abbr* (*US*: *POST*) = Maine.

KEYWORD

me [mi:] *pron* **1** (*direct*) меня́; **he loves me** он лю́бит меня́; **it's me** э́то я
2 (*indirect*) мне; **give me them** *or* **them to me** да́йте их мне
3 (*after prep*: +*gen*) меня́; (: +*dat*, +*prp*) мне; (: +*instr*) мной; **it's for me** (*on answering phone*) э́то мне *or* для меня́; **this kind of work is not for me** э́та рабо́та не для меня́
4 (*referring to subject of sentence*: *after prep*: +*gen*) себя́; (: +*dat*) себе́; (: +*instr*) собо́й; (: +*prp*) себе́; **I took him with me** я взял его́ с собо́й.

meadow ['mɛdəu] *n* луг*.
meagre ['mi:gə'] (*US* **meager**) *adj* ску́дный* (ску́ден).
meal [mi:l] *n* еда́ *no pl*; (*afternoon*) обе́д; (*evening*) у́жин; (*flour*) мука́ гру́бого помо́ла; **during** ~**s** во вре́мя еды́; **to go out**

for a ~ (*in the evening*) у́жинать (поу́жинать *perf*) в рестора́не; **to eat 3** ~**s a day** есть* (*impf*) 3 ра́за в день; **to make a** ~ **of sth** безоснова́тельно усложня́ть (усложни́ть *perf*) что-л.
meals on wheels *npl* доста́вка обе́дов на́ дом инвали́дам и престаре́лым.
meal time *n* вре́мя* *nt* еды́; **during** ~~**s** во вре́мя еды́, за едо́й.
mealy-mouthed ['mi:lɪmauðd] *adj* чрезме́рно делика́тный* (делика́тен) в вы́боре слов.
mean [mi:n] (*pt, pp* **meant**) *adj* (*miserly*) скупо́й* (скуп); (*unkind*) по́длый* (подл); (*US*: *inf*: *animal*) зло́бный* (зло́бен); (*shabby*) убо́гий* (убо́г); (*average*) сре́дний ◆ *vt* (*signify*) зна́чить (*impf*), означа́ть (*impf*); (*refer to*) име́ть (*impf*) в виду́ ◆ *n* (*average*) середи́на; ~**s** *npl* (*way*) спо́соб *msg*, сре́дство *ntsg*; (*money*) сре́дства *ntpl*; **by** ~**s of** посре́дством +*gen*, с по́мощью +*gen*; **by all** ~**s!** пожа́луйста!; **do you** ~ **it?** Вы говори́те об э́том всерьёз?, Вы э́то серьёзно?; **what do you** ~? что Вы име́ете в виду́?; **to** ~ **to do** (*intend*) намерева́ться (*impf*) +*infin*; **to be** ~**t for sb/sth** предназнача́ться (*impf*) кому́-н/ чему́-н.
meander [mɪ'ændə'] *vi* (*river*) извива́ться (*impf*); (*person*) броди́ть* (*impf*).
meaning ['mi:nɪŋ] *n* (*purpose, value*) смысл; (*definition*) значе́ние; **this word has two** ~**s** э́то сло́во име́ет два значе́ния; **his words have no** ~ его́ слова́ не име́ют смы́сла.
meaningful ['mi:nɪŋful] *adj* (*result, occasion*) значи́тельный* (значи́телен); (*explanation*) вразуми́тельный* (вразуми́телен); (*glance, remark*) многозначи́тельный* (многозначи́телен); (*relationship*) серьёзный* (серьёзен).
meaningless ['mi:nɪŋlɪs] *adj* бессмы́сленный (бессмы́слен).
meanness ['mi:nnɪs] *n* (*with money*) ску́пость *f*; (*unkindness*) по́длость *f*; (*shabbiness*) убо́гость *f*.
means test [mi:nz-] *n* (*ADMIN*) прове́рка* дохо́дов (*при получе́нии социа́льного посо́бия*).
meant [mɛnt] *pt, pp of* **mean**.
meantime ['mi:ntaɪm] *adv* (*also*: **in the** ~) тем вре́менем, ме́жду тем.
meanwhile ['mi:nwaɪl] *adv* = **meantime**.
measles ['mi:zlz] *n* корь *f*.
measly ['mi:zlɪ] *adj* (*inf*) жа́лкий*.
measurable ['mɛʒərəbl] *adj* измери́мый (измери́м).
measure ['mɛʒə'] *vt* измеря́ть (изме́рить *perf*) ◆ *n* (*action, amount*) ме́ра; (*of whisky etc*) по́рция; (*also*: **tape** ~) руле́тка*, сантиме́тр; (*of achievement*) мери́ло; (*of performance*)

---

* marks translations which have irregular inflections. The Russian-English side of the dictionary gives inflectional information.

крите́рий ♦ *vi*: **the room** ~**s 10 feet by 20** пло́щадь э́той ко́мнаты 10 фу́тов на 20; **in some/great** ~ (*extent*) в како́й-то/ значи́тельной ме́ре; **a litre** ~ (*vessel*) литро́вый сосу́д; **to take** ~**s (to do)** принима́ть (приня́ть* *perf*) ме́ры (что́бы +*infin*)

▶ **measure up** *vi*: **to** ~ **up to** (*to standard*) отвеча́ть (*impf*) +*dat*; (*to expectations*) опра́вдывать (оправда́ть* *perf*).

measured ['mɛʒəd] *adj* (*tone*) сде́ржанный* (сде́ржан); (*step*) разме́ренный* (разме́рен); (*opinion*) взве́шенный (взве́шен).

measurement ['mɛʒəmənt] *n* разме́р; (*process*) измере́ние; **chest/hip** ~ объём груди́/бёдер.

measurements ['mɛʒəmənts] *npl* разме́ры *mpl*; **to take sb's** ~ снима́ть (сня́ть* *perf*) с кого́-н ме́рки.

meat [mi:t] *n* мя́со; **cold** ~**s** (*BRIT*) холо́дные мясны́е заку́ски* *fpl*; **crab** ~ мя́со кра́ба.

meatball ['mi:tbɔ:l] *n* фрикаде́лька*.

meat pie *n* пиро́г* с мя́сом.

meaty ['mi:tɪ] *adj* (*hand, face*) мяси́стый (мяси́ст); (*stew*) мясно́й; (*discussion*) содержа́тельный* (содержа́телен).

Mecca ['mɛkə] *n* (*also fig*) Ме́кка.

mechanic [mɪ'kænɪk] *n* меха́ник.

mechanical [mɪ'kænɪkl] *adj* механи́ческий*.

mechanical engineering *n* машинострое́ние.

mechanics [mɪ'kænɪks] *n* (*PHYS*) меха́ника ♦ *npl* (*of reading, government*) меха́ника *fsg*.

mechanism ['mɛkənɪzəm] *n* механи́зм.

mechanization [mɛkənaɪ'zeɪʃən] *n* механиза́ция.

mechanize ['mɛkənaɪz] *vt* механизи́ровать (*impf/perf*) ♦ *vi* проводи́ть* (провести́* *perf*) механиза́цию.

MEd *n abbr* (= *Master of Education*) маги́стр педагоги́ческих нау́к.

medal ['mɛdl] *n* меда́ль *f*.

medalist ['mɛdlɪst] *n* (*US*) = **medallist**.

medallion [mɪ'dælɪən] *n* медальо́н.

medallist ['mɛdlɪst] (*US* **medalist**) *n* медали́ст(ка*).

meddle ['mɛdl] *vi*: **to** ~ **in** вме́шиваться (вмеша́ться *perf*) в +*acc*; **to** ~ **with sth** вторга́ться (вто́ргнуться *perf*) в что-н.

meddlesome ['mɛdlsəm] *adj* назо́йливый (назо́йлив).

media ['mi:dɪə] *n or npl*: **the** ~ сре́дства *ntpl* ма́ссовой информа́ции ♦ *npl see* **medium**.

mediaeval [mɛdɪ'i:vl] *adj* = **medieval**.

median ['mi:dɪən] *n* медиа́на.

median strip ['mi:dɪən-] *n* (*US*) раздели́тельная полоса́* (*автостра́ды*).

media research *n* иссле́дование *or* опро́с сре́дствами ма́ссовой информа́ции.

mediate ['mi:dɪeɪt] *vi* (*arbitrate*) посре́дничать (*impf*).

mediation [mi:dɪ'eɪʃən] *n* посре́дничество.

mediator ['mi:dɪeɪtə'] *n* посре́дник(-ица).

Medicaid ['mɛdɪkeɪd] *n* (*US*) госуда́рственная програ́мма, субсиди́рующая медици́нское обслу́живание малоиму́щей ча́сти населе́ния.

medical ['mɛdɪkl] *adj* медици́нский* ♦ *n* (*examination*) медосмо́тр= *медици́нский* осмо́тр*.

medical certificate *n* медици́нская спра́вка*.

medical examiner *n* (*US*) суде́бно-медици́нский* экспе́рт.

medical student *n* студе́нт – ме́дик.

Medicare ['mɛdɪkɛə'] *n* (*US*) госуда́рственная програ́мма медици́нского страхова́ния для люде́й в во́зрасте от 65 лет и ста́рше.

medicated ['mɛdɪkeɪtɪd] *adj* содержа́щий лека́рственное вещество́.

medication [mɛdɪ'keɪʃən] *n* лека́рство, лека́рственный препара́т; **to be on** ~ проходи́ть* (пройти́* *perf*) лека́рственную терапи́ю.

medicinal [mɛ'dɪsɪnl] *adj* (*substance, qualities*) лека́рственный; (*purposes, reasons*) лече́бный.

medicine ['mɛdsɪn] *n* (*science*) медици́на; (*drug*) лека́рство.

medicine ball *n* (*SPORT*) ≈ ги́ря.

medicine chest *n* апте́чка*.

medicine man *n* зна́харь *m*.

medieval [mɛdɪ'i:vl] *adj* средневеко́вый.

mediocre [mi:dɪ'əukə'] *adj* заря́дный* (заря́ден), посре́дственный* (посре́дствен).

mediocrity [mi:dɪ'ɔkrɪtɪ] *n* заря́дность *f*, посре́дственность *f*.

meditate ['mɛdɪteɪt] *vi* размышля́ть (*impf*); (*REL*) занима́ться (заня́ться* *perf*) медита́цией.

meditation [mɛdɪ'teɪʃən] *n* (*see vb*) размышле́ние; медита́ция.

Mediterranean [mɛdɪtə'reɪnɪən] *adj* средиземномо́рский; **the** ~ **(Sea)** Средизе́мное мо́ре.

medium ['mi:dɪəm] (*pl* **media** *or* ~**s**) *adj* сре́дний* ♦ *n* (*means*) сре́дство; (*substance*) материа́л; (*environment*) среда́; (*pl* ~**s**; *person*) ме́диум; **a happy** ~ золота́я середи́на.

medium-dry ['mi:dɪəm'draɪ] *adj* полусухо́й.

medium-sized ['mi:dɪəm'saɪzd] *adj* (*tin etc*) сре́дней величины́.

medium wave *n* (*RADIO*) сре́дние во́лны *fpl*.

medley ['mɛdlɪ] *n* (*mixture*) смесь *f*; (*MUS*) попурри́ *n. ind*.

meek [mi:k] *adj* кро́ткий* (кро́ток).

meet [mi:t] (*pt, pp* **met**) *vt* (*friend, opponent etc*) встреча́ть (встре́тить* *perf*); (*obligations*) выполня́ть (вы́полнить *perf*); (*problem*) ста́лкиваться (столкну́ться *perf*) с +*instr*; (*need*) удовлетворя́ть (удовлетвори́ть *perf*); (*expenses, bill*) опла́чивать (оплати́ть* *perf*) ♦ *vi* (*people*) встреча́ться (встре́титься* *perf*);

(*lines, roads*) пересека́ться (пересе́чься* *perf*)
♦ *n* (*BRIT: hunting*) сбор; (*US: SPORT*) встре́ча;
pleased to ~ you! рад (с Ва́ми)
познако́миться!, о́чень прия́тно!
▶ **meet up** *vi*: **to ~ up with sb** сходи́ться*
(сойти́сь* *perf*) с кем-н
▶ **meet with** *vt fus* (*difficulty*) ста́лкиваться
(столкну́ться *perf*) с +*instr*; (*success*)
по́льзоваться (*impf*) +*instr*; (*approval*)
находи́ть* (найти́* *perf*).
meeting ['mi:tɪŋ] *n* встре́ча; (*of club,
committee etc*) собра́ние; (*POL: also: mass ~*)
ми́тинг; **she's at a ~** она́ на заседа́нии; **to call
a ~** созыва́ть (созва́ть* *perf*) собра́ние.
meeting place *n* ме́сто* встре́чи.
megabyte ['mɛɡəbaɪt] *n* мегаба́йт.
megadrive ['mɛɡədraɪv] *n* ме́гадрайв (*игрова́я
систе́ма*).
megalomania [mɛɡələ'meɪnɪə] *n* ма́ния
вели́чия.
megaphone ['mɛɡəfəʊn] *n* мегафо́н.
megawatt ['mɛɡəwɔt] *n* мегава́тт.
melancholy ['mɛlənkəlɪ] *n* меланхо́лия ♦ *adj*
(*smile*) меланхоли́ческий; (*person*)
меланхоли́чный* (меланхоли́чен).
Melbourne ['mɛlbən] *n* Ме́льбурн.
mellow ['mɛləʊ] *adj* (*sound, colour, light*)
бархати́стый (бархати́ст); (*taste*) мя́гкий*
(мя́гок); (*stone, building*) *приобре́тший с
года́ми гла́дкую пове́рхность и мя́гкий цвет*
♦ *vi* (*person*) смягча́ться (смягчи́ться *perf*).
melodious [mɪ'ləʊdɪəs] *adj* мелоди́чный*
(мелоди́чен).
melodrama ['mɛləʊdrɑːmə] *n* мелодра́ма.
melodramatic [mɛlədrə'mætɪk] *adj* (*situation*)
мелодрамати́ческий; (*behaviour, person*)
мелодрамати́чный* (мелодрамати́чен).
melody ['mɛlədɪ] *n* мело́дия.
melon ['mɛlən] *n* ды́ня.
melt [mɛlt] *vi* (*metal*) пла́виться* (рас-
пла́виться* *perf*); (*snow, butter, also fig*) та́ять
(раста́ять *perf*) ♦ *vt* (*metal*) пла́вить*
(распла́вить* *perf*); (*snow, butter*) топи́ть*
(растопи́ть* *perf*)
▶ **melt down** *vt* (*metal*) расплавля́ть
(распла́вить* *perf*).
meltdown ['mɛltdaʊn] *n* (*in nuclear reactor*)
расплавле́ние сте́ржня (*в а́томном
реа́кторе*).
melting point ['mɛltɪŋ-] *n* то́чка* пла́вле́ния.
melting pot *n* (*fig*) смеше́ние; **to be in the ~ ~**
вари́ться* (*impf*) в одно́м котле́.
member ['mɛmbə'] *n* (*also ANAT*) член ♦ *cpd*: **~
country** *or* **state** госуда́рство-член; **M~ of
Parliament** (*BRIT*) член парла́мента.
membership ['mɛmbəʃɪp] *n* (*members*) чле́ны
mpl; (*status*) чле́нство; (*number of members*)
число́* чле́нов.

membership card *n* чле́нский* биле́т.
membrane ['mɛmbreɪn] *n* мембра́на.
memento [mə'mɛntəʊ] *n* сувени́р.
memo ['mɛməʊ] *n* (*ADMIN: report*) докладна́я
запи́ска; (: *instruction*) отноше́ние, запи́ска.
memoir ['mɛmwɑː'] *n* биографи́ческий о́черк.
memoirs ['mɛmwɑːz] *npl* мемуа́ры *pl*.
memo pad *n* записна́я кни́жка*.
memorable ['mɛmərəbl] *adj* па́мятный*
(па́мятен).
memoranda [mɛmə'rændə] *npl of*
memorandum.
memorandum [mɛmə'rændəm] (*pl
memoranda) *n* мемора́ндум.
memorial [mɪ'mɔːrɪəl] *n* па́мятник ♦ *cpd*
(*service*) мемориа́льный; ... **M~ Prize** пре́мия
и́мени +*gen* ....
Memorial Day *n* (*US*) *30 ма́я – день па́мяти
поги́бших*.
memorize ['mɛməraɪz] *vt* зау́чивать (зауч́ить
perf) (наизу́сть).
memory ['mɛmərɪ] *n* (*ability to remember*)
па́мять *f no pl*; (*COMPUT*) па́мять *f*,
запомина́ющее устро́йство; (*recollection*)
воспомина́ние; **in ~ of** в па́мять +*gen*; **I have a
good/bad ~** у меня́ хоро́шая/плоха́я
па́мять; **loss of ~** поте́ря па́мяти.
men [mɛn] *npl of* **man**.
menace ['mɛnɪs] *n* (*threat*) угро́за; (*nuisance*)
наказа́ние ♦ *vt* угрожа́ть (*impf*) +*dat*, грози́ть*
(*impf*) +*dat*; **a public ~** угро́за о́бществу.
menacing ['mɛnɪsɪŋ] *adj* угрожа́ющий*
(угрожа́ющ).
menagerie [mɪ'nædʒərɪ] *n* звери́нец*.
mend [mɛnd] *vt* ремонти́ровать
(отремонти́ровать *perf*), чини́ть* (почини́ть*
perf); (*clothes*) чини́ть* (почини́ть* *perf*) ♦ *n*: **to
be on the ~** идти́* (*impf*) на попра́вку; **to ~
one's ways** исправля́ться (испра́виться*
perf).
mending ['mɛndɪŋ] *n* (*of machine etc*) ремо́нт;
(*of clothes*) почи́нка.
menial ['mi:nɪəl] *adj* (*work, tasks*) чёрный*
meningitis [mɛnɪn'dʒaɪtɪs] *n* менинги́т.
menopause ['mɛnəʊpɔːz] *n*: **the ~**
климактери́ческий пери́од, кли́макс.
menservants ['mɛnsəːvənts] *npl of* **manservant**.
men's room *n* (*US*): **the ~ ~** мужска́я
раздева́лка.
menstrual ['mɛnstruəl] *adj* менструа́льный.
menstruate ['mɛnstrueɪt] *vi* менструи́ровать
(*impf*).
menstruation [mɛnstru'eɪʃən] *n* менструа́ция.
menswear ['mɛnzwɛə'] *n* мужска́я оде́жда.
mental ['mɛntl] *adj* (*ability, exhaustion*)
у́мственный; (*image*) мы́сленный; (*illness*)
душе́вный, психи́ческий; (*arithmetic,
calculation*) в уме́; **~ healthcare** забо́та о

душевнобольны́х.
mental hospital *n* психиатри́ческая
больни́ца.
mentality [mɛn'tælɪtɪ] *n* менталите́т,
умонастрое́ние; (*way of thinking*) склад ума́.
mentally ['mɛntlɪ] *adv* (*see adj*) у́мственно;
мы́сленно; ~ **ill** душевнобольно́й.
mentally handicapped *adj* у́мственно
отста́лый.
menthol ['mɛnθɔl] *n* менто́л.
mention ['mɛnʃən] *n* упомина́ние ♦ *vt*
упомина́ть (упомяну́ть* *perf*); **don't ~ it!**
ничего́!, не́ за что!; **I need hardly ~ that ...**
вряд ли сто́ит упомина́ть, что ...; **not to ~ ...,**
without ~ing ... не говоря́ уж о +*prp* ....
mentor ['mɛntɔː'] *n* наста́вник.
menu ['mɛnjuː] *n* (*also COMPUT*) меню́ *nt ind*.
menu-driven ['mɛnjuːdrɪvn] *adj* (*COMPUT*)
управля́емый меню́.
MEP *n abbr* (*BRIT* = Member of the European
Parliament) член Европе́йского парла́мента.
mercantile ['məːkəntaɪl] *adj* (*society, law*)
торго́вый.
mercenary ['məːsɪnərɪ] *adj* коры́стный*
(коры́стен) ♦ *n* (*soldier*) наёмник.
merchandise ['məːtʃəndaɪz] *n* това́ры *mpl*.
merchandiser ['məːtʃəndaɪzəʳ] *n* торго́вец*.
merchant ['məːtʃənt] *n* (*trader*) торго́вец*,
купе́ц* (*ИСТ*); **timber/wine ~** торго́вец*
ле́сом/вино́м.
merchant bank *n* (*BRIT*) торго́вый банк.
merchantman ['məːtʃəntmən] *irreg n* торго́вое
су́дно*.
Merchant Navy (*US* **merchant marine**) *n*
торго́вый флот.
merciful ['məːsɪful] *adj* (*person*) милосе́рдный*
(милосе́рден); (*fortunate*) благо́й.
mercifully ['məːsɪflɪ] *adv* милосе́рдно;
(*fortunately*) к сча́стью.
merciless ['məːsɪlɪs] *adj* беспоща́дный*
(беспоща́ден).
mercurial [məːˈkjuərɪəl] *adj* изме́нчивый
(изме́нчив).
mercury ['məːkjurɪ] *n* ртуть *f*; (*planet*): **M~**
Мерку́рий.
mercy ['məːsɪ] *n* милосе́рдие; **to have ~ on sb**
проявля́ть (прояви́ть* *perf*) милосе́рдие к
кому́-н; **to be at sb's ~** быть* (*impf*) или
находи́ться* (*impf*) во вла́сти кого́-н.
mercy killing *n* уби́йство из милосе́рдия.
mere [mɪəʳ] *adj*: **she's a ~ child** она́ всего́ лишь
ребёнок; **his ~ presence irritates her** само́ его́
прису́тствие раздража́ет её; **by a ~ chance**
по чи́стой случа́йности.
merely ['mɪəlɪ] *adv* (*simply*) про́сто; (*just*)
то́лько.
merge [məːdʒ] *vt* (*also COMPUT*) слива́ть
(слить* *perf*), объединя́ть (объедини́ть *perf*)
♦ *vi* (*also COMM*) слива́ться (сли́ться* *perf*);
(*roads*) сходи́ться* (сойти́сь* *perf*).
merger ['məːdʒəʳ] *n* (*COMM*) слия́ние.

meridian [məˈrɪdɪən] *n* меридиа́н.
meringue [məˈræŋ] *n* безе́ *nt ind*.
merit ['mɛrɪt] *n* (*worth, value*) досто́инство ♦ *vt*
заслу́живать (заслужи́ть* *perf*); **to judge sth**
on its ~s оце́нивать (оцени́ть *perf*) что-н по
досто́инству.
meritocracy [mɛrɪˈtɔkrəsɪ] *n* о́бщество, в
кото́ром положе́ние челове́ка определя́ется
его́ спосо́бностями.
mermaid ['məːmeɪd] *n* руса́лка*.
merrily ['mɛrɪlɪ] *adv* ве́село.
merriment ['mɛrɪmənt] *n* весе́лье.
merry ['mɛrɪ] *adj* весёлый* (ве́сел); **M~**
Christmas! С Рождество́м!
merry-go-round ['mɛrɪɡəuraund] *n* карусе́ль *f*.
mesh [mɛʃ] *n* (*net*) сеть *f*; **wire ~** про́волочная
се́тка.
mesmerize ['mɛzməraɪz] *vt* гипнотизи́ровать
(загипнотизи́ровать *perf*).
mess [mɛs] *n* (*muddle: in room*) беспоря́док*; (:
of situation) неразбери́ха; (*dirt*) грязь* *f*; (*MIL*)
столо́вая *f adj*; **to be in a ~** (*untidy*) быть*
(*impf*) в беспоря́дке; **to get o.s. into a ~** (*inf*)
влипа́ть (вли́пнуть* *perf*); **my life is in a real ~**
(*inf*) у меня́ в жи́зни всё идёт вверх дном
▸ **mess about** *vi* (*inf: fool around*) дура́читься
(*impf*), валя́ть (*impf*) дурака́
▸ **mess about with** *vt fus* (*inf: play around with*)
вози́ться* (*impf*) с +*instr*
▸ **mess around** *vi* (*inf*) = **mess about**
▸ **mess around with** *vt fus* (*inf*) = **mess about**
with
▸ **mess up** *vt* (*spoil*) по́ртить* (испо́ртить*
perf); (*dirty*) па́чкать (испа́чкать *perf*).
message ['mɛsɪdʒ] *n* (*piece of information*)
сообще́ние; (*note*) запи́ска*; (*of play, book*)
иде́я; **to leave sb a ~** (*note*) оставля́ть
(оста́вить* *perf*) кому́-н запи́ску; **can I give**
him a ~? ему́ что́-нибудь переда́ть?; **he got**
the ~ (*fig: inf*) до него́ дошло́.
message switching [-'swɪtʃɪŋ] *n* (*COMPUT*)
коммута́ция сообще́ний.
messenger ['mɛsɪndʒəʳ] *n* курье́р, посы́льный
m adj.
Messiah [mɪˈsaɪə] *n* Месси́я *m*.
Messrs *abbr* (*on letters*: = *messieurs*) гг.=
господа́.
Messrs. *abbr* = **Messrs**.
messy ['mɛsɪ] *adj* (*untidy*) неу́бранный
(неу́бран); (*dirty*) гря́зный* (гря́зен).
Met [mɛt] *n abbr* (*US*) = Metropolitan Opera.
met [mɛt] *pt, pp of* **meet**.
met *adj abbr* = *meteorological*: **the M~ Office**
метеоце́нтр.
metabolism [mɛˈtæbəlɪzəm] *n* метаболи́зм,
обме́н веще́ств.
metal ['mɛtl] *n* мета́лл.
metal fatigue *n* уста́лость *f* мета́лла.
metalled ['mɛtld] *adj*: **~ road** доро́га, с
щебёночным покры́тием.
metallic [mɪˈtælɪk] *adj* металли́ческий*.

metallurgy [mɛ'tælədʒɪ] n металлурги́я.
metalwork ['mɛtlwəːk] n рабо́та по мета́ллу.
metamorphoses [mɛtə'mɔːfəsiːz] npl of
metamorphosis.
metamorphosis [mɛtə'mɔːfəsɪs] (pl
metamorphoses) n метаморфо́за.
metaphor ['mɛtəfəʳ] n мета́фора.
metaphorical [mɛtə'fɔrɪkl] adj
метафори́ческий.
metaphysics [mɛtə'fɪzɪks] n метафи́зика.
meteor ['miːtɪəʳ] n метео́р.
meteoric [miːtɪ'ɒrɪk] adj (fig) метеори́ческий.
meteorite ['miːtɪəraɪt] n метеори́т.
meteorological [miːtɪərə'lɒdʒɪkl] adj
метеорологи́ческий.
meteorology [miːtɪə'rɒlədʒɪ] n метеороло́гия.
mete out [miːt-] vt отмеря́ть (отме́рить perf).
meter ['miːtəʳ] n (instrument) счётчик; (US: unit)
= **metre**.
methane ['miːθeɪn] n мета́н.
method ['mɛθəd] n (way) ме́тод, спо́соб; ~ **of**
payment спо́соб опла́ты.
methodical [mɪ'θɒdɪkl] adj методи́чный*
(методи́чен).
Methodist ['mɛθədɪst] n (REL) методи́ст(ка*).
methodology [mɛθə'dɒlədʒɪ] n методоло́гия.
meths [mɛθs] n (BRIT: inf) = **methylated spirit**.
methylated spirit ['mɛθɪleɪtɪd-] n (BRIT)
денатура́т.
meticulous [mɪ'tɪkjuləs] adj тща́тельный*
(тща́телен).
metre ['miːtəʳ] (US **meter**) n метр.
metric ['mɛtrɪk] adj метри́ческий*; **to go** ~
переходи́ть* (перейти́* perf) на метри́ческую
систе́му мер.
metrical ['mɛtrɪkl] adj метри́ческий*.
metrication [mɛtrɪ'keɪʃən] n введе́ние
метри́ческой систе́мы мер.
metric system n метри́ческая систе́ма мер.
metric ton n (метри́ческая) то́нна.
metronome ['mɛtrənəum] n метроно́м.
metropolis [mɪ'trɒpəlɪs] n столи́ца.
metropolitan [mɛtrə'pɒlɪtn] adj столи́чный.
Metropolitan Police n (BRIT): **the** ~ ~
Ло́ндонская поли́ция.
mettle ['mɛtl] n: **to show one's** ~ проявля́ть
(прояви́ть* perf) (свой) хара́ктер.
mew [mjuː] vi мяу́кать (impf).
mews [mjuːz] n (BRIT) переу́лок в жило́е
помеще́ние.
Mexican ['mɛksɪkən] adj мексика́нский* ◆ n
мексика́нец*(-нка*).
Mexico ['mɛksɪkəu] n Ме́ксика.
Mexico City n Ме́хико m ind.
mezzanine ['mɛtsəniːn] n (also: ~ **floor**)
мезони́н, полуэта́ж.
MFA n abbr (US: = Master of Fine Arts) маги́стр
иску́сств.
mfr abbr = **manufacture, manufacturer**.

mg abbr (= milligram(me)) мг.= миллигра́мм.
Mgr abbr (= Monseigneur, Monsignor)
монсеньёр; (COMM) = **manager**.
MHR n abbr (US: = Member of the House of
Representatives) член пала́ты
представи́телей.
MHz abbr (= megahertz) МГц= мегаге́рц.
MI abbr (US: POST) = Michigan.
MI5 n abbr (BRIT: = Military Intelligence 5)
вне́шняя разве́дка Великобрита́нии.
MI6 n abbr (BRIT: = Military Intelligence 6)
вну́тренняя разве́дка Великобрита́нии.
MIA abbr (MIL: = missing in action) пропа́вший
бе́з вести.
miaow [miː'au] vi мяу́кать (impf).
mice [maɪs] npl of **mouse**.
micro... ['maɪkrəu] prefix микро....
microbe ['maɪkrəub] n микро́б.
microbiology [maɪkrəbaɪ'ɔlədʒɪ] n микро-
биоло́гия.
microchip ['maɪkrəutʃɪp] n микрочи́п.
micro(computer) ['maɪkrəu(kəm'pjuːtəʳ)] n
микрокомпью́тер.
microcosm ['maɪkrəukɔzəm] n микроко́смос,
микроко́см.
microeconomics ['maɪkrəuiːkə'nɔmɪks] n
микроэконо́мика.
microelectronics ['maɪkrəuɪlɛk'trɒnɪks] n
микроэлектро́ника.
microfiche ['maɪkrəufiːʃ] n микрофи́ша.
microfilm ['maɪkrəufɪlm] n микрофи́льм,
микроплёнка*.
microlight ['maɪkrəulaɪt] n сверхлёгкий
самолёт.
micrometer [maɪ'krɔmɪtəʳ] n микро́метр.
microphone ['maɪkrəfəun] n микрофо́н.
microprocessor ['maɪkrəu'prəusɛsəʳ] n
микропроце́ссор.
microscope ['maɪkrəskəup] n микроско́п;
under the ~ под микроско́пом.
microscopic [maɪkrə'skɔpɪk] adj микро-
скопи́ческий*.
microsurgery [maɪkrəusəːdʒərɪ] n микро-
хирурги́я.
microwave ['maɪkrəuweɪv] n (also: ~ **oven**)
микроволно́вая печь* f.
mid [mɪd] adj: **in** ~ **May/afternoon** в середи́не
ма́я/дня; **in** ~ **air** в во́здухе; **he's in his** ~
thirties ему́ за три́дцать.
midday [mɪd'deɪ] n по́лдень* m.
middle ['mɪdl] n середи́на; (waist) по́яс* ◆ adj
сре́дний*; **in the** ~ **of the night** посреди́ но́чи;
I'm in the ~ **of reading it** я как раз сейча́с э́то
чита́ю.
middle age n сре́дний* во́зраст.
middle-aged [mɪdl'eɪdʒd] adj сре́дних лет.
Middle Ages npl: **the** ~ ~ сре́дние века́* mpl.
middle class n: **the** ~ ~ сре́дний* класс.

---

* marks translations which have irregular inflections. The Russian-English side of the dictionary gives inflectional information.

middle-class [mɪdl'klɑːs] *adj* принадлежа́щий к сре́днему кла́ссу.

middle classes *npl* = **middle class**.

Middle East *n*: the ~ ~ Бли́жний* Восто́к.

middleman [ˈmɪdlmæn] *irreg n* посре́дник.

middle management *n* сре́днее руководя́щее звено́.

middle name *n* второ́е и́мя* *nt*.

middle-of-the-road [ˈmɪdləvðəˈrəud] *adj* (*politician*) уме́ренный; (*music*) лёгкий*.

middleweight [ˈmɪdlweɪt] *n* (*BOXING*) боксёр сре́днего ве́са.

middling [ˈmɪdlɪŋ] *adj* сре́дний*.

Middx *abbr* (*BRIT: POST*) = **Middlesex**.

midge [mɪdʒ] *n* мо́шка*.

midget [ˈmɪdʒɪt] *n* ка́рлик(-ица).

midi system [ˈmɪdɪ-] *n* МИ́ДИ (*электро́нный контро́ль для синтеза́торов*).

Midlands [ˈmɪdləndz] *npl*: the ~ Центра́льные райо́ны *mpl* А́нглии.

midnight [ˈmɪdnaɪt] *n* по́лночь* *f* ♦ *cpd* (*party, feast*) полно́чный; **at** ~ в по́лночь.

midriff [ˈmɪdrɪf] *n* живо́т.

midst [mɪdst] *n*: **in the** ~ **of** посреди́ +*gen*.

midsummer [mɪdˈsʌmə'] *n* середи́на ле́та; **M~'s Day** *m* ле́тнего солнцестоя́ния.

midway [mɪdˈweɪ] *adv*: ~ (**between**) на полпути́ (ме́жду +*instr*); ~ **through** в середи́не +*gen*; **to turn back** ~ верну́ться (*perf*) с полпути́.

midweek [mɪdˈwiːk] *adj, adv* в середи́не неде́ли.

midwife [ˈmɪdwaɪf] (*pl* **midwives**) *n* акуше́рка*.

midwifery [ˈmɪdwɪfərɪ] *n* акуше́рство.

midwinter [mɪdˈwɪntə'] *n* середи́на зимы́.

midwives [ˈmɪdwaɪvz] *npl of* **midwife**.

miffed [mɪft] *adj* (*inf*) оби́женный (оби́жен).

might [maɪt] *vb see* **may** ♦ *n* (*power*) мощь *f*.

mighty [ˈmaɪtɪ] *adj* мо́щный* (мо́щен).

migraine [ˈmiːɡreɪn] *n* мигре́нь *f*.

migrant [ˈmaɪɡrənt] *adj* (*bird*) перелётный ♦ *n* (*bird*) перелётная пти́ца; (*animal*) мигри́рующее живо́тное *nt adj*; (*person*) переселе́нец*(-нка*); ~ **worker** рабо́чий*-мигра́нт.

migrate [maɪˈɡreɪt] *vi* мигри́ровать (*impf/perf*).

migration [maɪˈɡreɪʃən] *n* мигра́ция.

mike [maɪk] *n abbr* = **microphone**.

Milan [mɪˈlæn] *n* Мила́н.

mild [maɪld] *adj* (*character, climate, taste, reproach*) мя́гкий* (мя́гок); (*infection, illness*) лёгкий* (лёгок); (*interest*) незначи́тельный* (незначи́телен).

mildew [ˈmɪldjuː] *n* пле́сень *f*.

mildly [ˈmaɪldlɪ] *adv* (*see adj*) мя́гко; легко́; слегка́; **to put it** ~ мя́гко говоря́.

mildness [ˈmaɪldnɪs] *n* (*see adj*) мя́гкость *f*; лёгкость *f*; незначи́тельность *f*.

mile [maɪl] *n* ми́ля*; **this car does 30** ~**s to the gallon** э́тот автомоби́ль затра́чивает галло́н бензи́на ка́ждые 30 миль; ~**s better**

(*inf*) намно́го лу́чше.

mileage [ˈmaɪlɪdʒ] *n* (*number of miles*) пробе́г ми́лях; (*distance*) расстоя́ние в ми́лях.

mileage allowance *n* покры́тие доро́жных расхо́дов (*в расчёте на ка́ждую ми́лю*).

mileometer [maɪˈlɔmɪtə'] *n* счётчик (*про́йденных миль*).

milestone [ˈmaɪlstəun] *n* ≈ киломе́тровый столб; (*fig*) ве́ха.

milieu [ˈmiːljəː] *n* среда́*.

militant [ˈmɪlɪtnt] *adj* во́инствующий ♦ *n* радика́л.

militarism [ˈmɪlɪtərɪzəm] *n* милитари́зм.

militaristic [mɪlɪtəˈrɪstɪk] *adj* милитаристи́ческий.

military [ˈmɪlɪtərɪ] *adj* вое́нный ♦ *n*: the ~ вое́нные *pl adj*.

military police *n* вое́нная поли́ция.

military service *n* вое́нная слу́жба.

militate [ˈmɪlɪteɪt] *vi*: **to** ~ **against** препя́тствовать (*impf*) +*dat*.

militia [mɪˈlɪʃə] *n* (*MIL*) (наро́дное) ополче́ние.

milk [mɪlk] *n* молоко́ ♦ *vt* (*cow*) дои́ть* (подои́ть* *perf*); (*fig: situation, person*) эксплуати́ровать (*impf*).

milk chocolate *n* моло́чный шокола́д.

milk float *n* (*BRIT*) моло́чный фурго́н.

milking [ˈmɪlkɪŋ] *n* дое́ние.

milkman [ˈmɪlkmən] *irreg n* разно́счик молока́.

milk shake *n* моло́чный кокте́йль *m*.

milk tooth *n* моло́чный зуб*.

milk truck *n* (*US*) = **milk float**.

milky [ˈmɪlkɪ] *adj* моло́чный.

Milky Way *n*: the ~ ~ Мле́чный путь* *m*.

mill [mɪl] *n* (*windmill*) ме́льница; (*factory: making cloth*) фа́брика; (: *making steel*) заво́д; (*also: coffee* ~) кофемо́лка* ♦ *vt* моло́ть* (смоло́ть* *perf*) ♦ *vi* (*also:* ~ **about**) толо́чься* (*impf*).

millennia [mɪˈlɛnɪə] *npl of* **millennium**.

millennium [mɪˈlɛnɪəm] (*pl* ~**s** *or* **millennia**) *n* тысячеле́тие.

miller [ˈmɪlə'] *n* ме́льник.

millet [ˈmɪlɪt] *n* пшено́.

milli... [ˈmɪlɪ] *prefix* милли....

milligram(me) [ˈmɪlɪɡræm] (*US* **milligram**) *n* миллигра́м.

millilitre [ˈmɪlɪliːtə'] (*US* **milliliter**) *n* миллили́тр.

millimetre [ˈmɪlɪmiːtə'] (*US* **millimeter**) *n* миллиме́тр.

millinery [ˈmɪlɪnərɪ] *n* да́мские шля́пы *fpl*.

million [ˈmɪljən] *n* миллио́н.

millionaire [mɪljəˈnɛə'] *n* миллионе́р.

millipede [ˈmɪlɪpiːd] *n* тысячено́жка*.

millstone [ˈmɪlstəun] *n* (*fig*): **a** ~ **around one's neck** ка́мень *m* на шее.

millwheel [ˈmɪlwiːl] *n* ме́льничное колесо́*.

milometer [maɪˈlɔmɪtə'] *n* = **mileometer**.

mime [maɪm] *n* (*art*) пантоми́ма; (*also:* ~ **artist**) мим ♦ *vt* изобража́ть (изобрази́ть* *perf*) же́стами.

mimic ['mɪmɪk] *n* пароди́ст ◆ *vt* (*subj: comedian*) пароди́ровать (*impf/perf*); (*animal, person*) имити́ровать (*impf*).

mimicry ['mɪmɪkrɪ] *n* имита́ция.

Min. *abbr* (*BRIT: POL*) = **ministry**.

min. *abbr* (= **minute**) мин(.); (= **minimum**) мин.= минама́льный.

minaret [mɪnə'rɛt] *n* минаре́т.

mince [mɪns] *vt* (*meat*) пропуска́ть (пропусти́ть* *perf*) че́рез мясору́бку ◆ *vi* (*in walking*) семени́ть (*impf*) ◆ *n* (*BRIT*) (мясно́й) фарш; **he doesn't ~ (his) words** он не выбира́ет выраже́ний.

mincemeat ['mɪnsmiːt] *n* (*BRIT: fruit*) начи́нка из сухофру́ктов (*для пирожко́в*); (*US: meat*) (мясно́й) фарш; **to make ~ of sb** разбива́ть (разби́ть* *perf*) кого́-н в пух и прах.

mince pie *n* (*BRIT: sweet*) пирожо́к* с начи́нкой из сухофру́ктов.

mincer ['mɪnsə'] *n* мясору́бка*.

mincing ['mɪnsɪŋ] *adj* (*walk*) семеня́щий; (*voice*) жема́нный* (жема́нен).

mind [maɪnd] *n* (*intellect*) ум*; (*thoughts*) голова́* ◆ *vt* (*look after*) смотре́ть (*impf*) за +*instr*; (*object to*): **I don't ~ the noise** меня́ не беспоко́ит шум; **to be out of one's ~** быть* (*impf*) не в своём уме́; **it's constantly on my ~** э́то не выхо́дит у меня́ из головы́; **to keep** *or* **bear sth in ~** по́мнить (*impf*) что-н, име́ть (*impf*) что-н в виду́; **to make up one's ~** реша́ться (реши́ться *perf*); **to change one's ~** переду́мывать (переду́мать *perf*); **to my ~ ...** (*opinion*) по моему́ мне́нию ...; **to be in two ~s about sth** сомнева́ться (*impf*) в чём-н; **to have in ~ to do** намерева́ться (*impf*) +*infin*; **I have somebody in ~** у меня́ есть ко́е-кто на приме́те; **it went right out of my ~** э́то совсе́м вы́летело у меня́ из головы́; **to bring** *or* **call to ~** напомина́ть (напо́мнить *perf*) о +*prp*; **she doesn't ~ the cold** она́ не бои́тся хо́лода; **do you ~ if ...?** Вы не возража́ете, е́сли ...?; **I don't ~** мне всё равно́; **~ you, ...** име́йте в виду́ ...; **never ~!** ничего́!; **"mind the step"** "осторо́жно, не споткни́тесь".

mind-boggling ['maɪndbɔglɪŋ] *adj* (*inf*) уму́ непостижи́мый.

-minded ['maɪndɪd] *adj*: **fair-~** справедли́вый (справедли́в); **an industrially-~ nation** наро́д, скло́нный к индустриа́льной де́ятельности.

minder ['maɪndə'] *n* (*childminder*) ня́ня*; (*inf: bodyguard*) телохрани́тель *m*.

mindful ['maɪndful] *adj*: **to be ~ of** име́ть (*impf*) в виду́.

mindless ['maɪndlɪs] *adj* (*violence*) безду́мный* (безду́мен); (*job*) механи́ческий*.

| KEYWORD |

mine¹ [maɪn] *pron* **1** мой; **that book is mine** э́та кни́га моя́, э́то моя́ кни́га; **this is mine** э́то моё; **an uncle of mine** мой дя́дя
2 (*referring back to subject*) свой; **may I borrow your pen? I have forgotten mine** мо́жно взять Ва́шу ру́чку? я забы́л свою́.

mine² [maɪn] *n* (*coal*) ша́хта; (*gold, diamonds*) при́иск; (*copper, tin*) рудни́к; (*explosive*) ми́на ◆ *vt* (*coal*) добыва́ть (добы́ть* *perf*); (*beach*) мини́ровать (замини́ровать *perf*).

mine detector *n* миноиска́тель *m*.

minefield ['maɪnfiːld] *n* (*also fig*) ми́нное по́ле*.

miner ['maɪnə'] *n* шахтёр.

mineral ['mɪnərəl] *n* (*crystalline*) минера́л; (*ore*) поле́зное ископа́емое *nt adj* ◆ *adj* минера́льный; **~s** *npl* (*BRIT: soft drinks*) прохлади́тельные напи́тки *mpl*.

mineralogy [mɪnə'rælədʒɪ] *n* минерало́гия.

mineral water *n* минера́льная вода́.

minesweeper ['maɪnswiːpə'] *n* ми́нный тра́льщик.

mingle ['mɪŋgl] *vi*: **to ~ with** сме́шиваться (смеша́ться *perf*) с +*instr*.

mingy ['mɪndʒɪ] *adj* (*inf: person*) прижи́мистый (прижи́мист); (: *amount*) ми́зерный* (ми́зерен).

mini... ['mɪnɪ] *prefix* мини....

miniature ['mɪnətʃə'] *adj* миниатю́рный* (миниатю́рен) ◆ *n* миниатю́ра.

minibus ['mɪnɪbʌs] *n* микроавто́бус.

minicab ['mɪnɪkæb] *n* (*BRIT*) такси́ *nt ind*.

minicomputer ['mɪnɪkəm'pjuːtə'] *n* мини-компью́тер.

minim ['mɪnɪm] *n* полови́нная но́та.

minima ['mɪnɪmə] *npl of* **minimum**.

minimal ['mɪnɪml] *adj* минима́льный* (минима́лен).

minimalist ['mɪnɪməlɪst] *adj* минимали́ст(-ка).

minimize ['mɪnɪmaɪz] *vt* (*reduce*) своди́ть* (свести́* *perf*) к ми́нимуму; (*play down*) преуменьша́ть (преуме́ньшить *perf*).

minimum ['mɪnɪməm] (*pl* **minima**) *n* ми́нимум ◆ *adj* минима́льный; **to reduce to a ~** своди́ть* (свести́* *perf*) к ми́нимуму; **~ wage** минима́льная зарпла́та.

minimum lending rate *n* минима́льная ссу́дная ста́вка.

mining ['maɪnɪŋ] *n* (*process*) добы́ча; (*science*) го́рное де́ло; (*industry*) у́гольная промы́шленность *f* ◆ *cpd* (*industry*) горнодобыва́ющий*; (*region*) шахтёрский.

minion ['mɪnjən] *n* (*pej*) подчинённый *m adj*.

mini-series ['mɪnɪsɪərɪːz] *n* минисериа́л.

miniskirt ['mɪnɪskəːt] *n* ми́ни ю́бка*.

minister ['mɪnɪstə'] *n* (*BRIT: POL*) мини́стр; (*REL*) свяще́нник ◆ *vi*: **to ~ to** (*people, needs*) служи́ть (*impf*) +*dat*.

ministerial [mɪnɪs'tɪərɪəl] *adj* (*BRIT: POL*) министе́рский*; **~ post** пост мини́стра.

---

* marks translations which have irregular inflections. The Russian-English side of the dictionary gives inflectional information.

ministry ['mɪnɪstrɪ] *n* (*BRIT: POL*) министе́рство;
(*REL*): **to go into the** ~ принима́ть (приня́ть*
perf) духо́вный сан.
Ministry of Defence *n* Министе́рство
оборо́ны.
mink [mɪŋk] *n* но́рка*.
mink coat *n* но́рковая шу́ба.
minnow ['mɪnəu] *n* пескарь *m*.
minor ['maɪnə'] *adj* (*injuries, poet*)
незначи́тельный; (*repairs*) ме́лкий*; (*MUS*)
мино́рный ♦ *n* (*LAW*) несовершенноле́тний*
(-яя) *m(f) adj*.
Minorca [mɪ'nɔ:kə] *n* Мино́рка.
minority [maɪ'nɔrɪtɪ] *n* меньшинство́*; **to be in
a** ~ быть* (*impf*) в меньшинстве́; ~ **interest**
(*COMM*) неконтро́льный паке́т а́кций.
Minsk [mɪnsk] *n* Минск.
minster ['mɪnstə'] *n* собо́р.
minstrel ['mɪnstrəl] *n* менестре́ль *m*.
mint [mɪnt] *n* (*BOT*) мя́та; (*sweet*) мя́тная
конфе́та ♦ *vt* (*coins*) чека́нить (отчека́нить
perf); **the (Royal) M**~, *(US)* **the (US) M**~ ≈
Моне́тный двор; **in** ~ **condition** как
но́венький*.
mint sauce *n* со́ус из мя́ты.
minuet [mɪnju'ɛt] *n* менуэ́т.
minus ['maɪnəs] *n* (*also:* ~ **sign**) ми́нус ♦ *prep*:
12 ~ **6 equals 6** 12 ми́нус 6 равня́ется 6;
(*temperature*): ~ **24 (degrees)** ми́нус 24
гра́дуса.
minuscule ['mɪnəskju:l] *adj* кро́хотный*
(кро́хотен), кро́шечный* (кро́шечен).
minute¹ [maɪ'nju:t] *adj* (*search*) тща́тельный; **in**
~ **detail** до мале́йших подро́бностей.
minute² ['mɪnɪt] *n* (*also fig*) мину́та; (*official
record*) за́пись *f*; ~**s** *npl* (*of meeting*) протоко́л
msg; **it's five** ~**s past three** сейча́с пять мину́т
четвёртого ...; **wait a** ~!, **just a** ~! подожди́те
мину́точку!; **up to the** ~ (*fashion, news*)
са́мый после́дний*; (*technology*) нове́йший;
at the last ~ в после́днюю мину́ту.
minute book *n* кни́га протоко́лов.
minute hand *n* мину́тная стре́лка*.
minutely [maɪ'nju:tlɪ] *adv* (*by a small amount*)
едва́ заме́тно; (*in detail*) подро́бно,
подро́бнейшим о́бразом.
minutiae [mɪ'nju:ʃɪi:] *npl* мельча́йшие дета́ли
fpl.
miracle ['mɪrəkl] *n* чу́до*.
miraculous [mɪ'rækjuləs] *adj* чуде́сный*
(чуде́сен).
mirage ['mɪrɑ:ʒ] *n* мира́ж.
mire ['maɪə'] *n* тряси́на.
mirror ['mɪrə'] *n* зе́ркало*; (*also:* **hand-**~)
зе́ркальце ♦ *vt* отража́ть (отрази́ть* *perf*).
mirror image *n* зерка́льное отраже́ние.
mirth [mə:θ] *n* весе́лье.
misadventure [mɪsəd'vɛntʃə'] *n* злоключе́ние;
death by ~ (*BRIT*) смерть* *f* в результа́те
несча́стного слу́чая.
misanthropist [mɪ'zænθrəpɪst] *n* мизантро́п.

misapply [mɪsə'plaɪ] *vt* непра́вильно
применя́ть (примени́ть *perf*).
misapprehension ['mɪsæprɪ'hɛnʃən] *n* ло́жное
представле́ние.
misappropriate [mɪsə'prəuprɪeɪt] *vt* незако́нно
присва́ивать (присво́ить *perf*).
misappropriation ['mɪsəprəuprɪ'eɪʃən] *n*
назако́нное присвое́ние.
misbehave [mɪsbɪ'heɪv] *vi* пло́хо себя́ вести́*
(*impf*).
misbehaviour [mɪsbɪ'heɪvjə'] (*US* **misbehavior**)
n плохо́е поведе́ние.
misc. *abbr* = **miscellaneous**.
miscalculate [mɪs'kælkjuleɪt] *vt* неве́рно
оце́нивать (оцени́ть *perf*) ♦ *vi*
просчи́тываться (просчита́ться *perf*).
miscalculation ['mɪskælkju'leɪʃən] *n* просчёт.
miscarriage ['mɪskærɪdʒ] *n* (*MED*) вы́кидыш;
(*LAW*): ~ **of justice** суде́бная оши́бка.
miscarry [mɪs'kærɪ] *vi* (*plans*) не удава́ться*
(уда́ться* *perf*); **she miscarried** у неё был
вы́кидыш.
miscellaneous [mɪsɪ'leɪnɪəs] *adj* (*collection,
group*) разноро́дный* (разноро́ден);
(*subjects, items*) разнообра́зный*
(разнообра́зен); ~ **expenses** ме́лкие
расхо́ды; ~ **files** ра́зное *nt adj*.
mischance [mɪs'tʃɑ:ns] *n* (*misfortune*)
невезе́ние; **by (some)** ~ по несча́стной
случа́йности.
mischief ['mɪstʃɪf] *n* (*naughtiness, playfulness*)
озорство́; (*maliciousness*) зло; **to get into** ~
прока́зничать (напрока́зничать *perf*); **to do
sb a** ~ причиня́ть (причини́ть *perf*) кому́-н
зло.
mischievous ['mɪstʃɪvəs] *adj* (*naughty, playful*)
озорно́й; (*malicious*) зло́бный.
misconception ['mɪskən'sɛpʃən] *n* ло́жное
представле́ние.
misconduct [mɪs'kɔndʌkt] *n* дурно́е
поведе́ние; **professional** ~ наруше́ние
профессиона́льной э́тики.
misconstrue [mɪskən'stru:] *vt* неве́рно
истолко́вывать (истолкова́ть* *perf*).
miscount [mɪs'kaunt] *vt* неве́рно счита́ть
(сосчита́ть *perf*) ♦ *vi* ошиба́ться (ошиби́ться*
perf) в подсчётах.
misdemeanour [mɪsdɪ'mi:nə'] (*US*
misdemeanor) *n* просту́пок*.
misdirect [mɪsdɪ'rɛkt] *vt* (*person*) оши́бочно
направля́ть (напра́вить* *perf*); (*letter*)
непра́вильно адресова́ть (*impf/perf*).
miser ['maɪzə'] *n* скря́га *m/f*.
miserable ['mɪzərəbl] *adj* (*unhappy: person,
expression*) несча́стный* (несча́стен);
(*unpleasant: weather, person*) скве́рный*
(скве́рен); (*donation, conditions*) жа́лкий*
(жа́лок); (*failure*) позо́рный; **to feel** ~
чу́вствовать (*impf*) себя́ о́чень пло́хо; **she
looked** ~ у неё был несча́стный вид.
miserably ['mɪzərəblɪ] *adv* (*live, pay*) ску́дно;

(*smile*) жа́лко; (*small*) ничто́жно; (*fail*) позо́рно.

miserly ['maɪzəlɪ] *adj* (*person*) скупо́й* (скуп); (*amount*) ми́зерный* (ми́зерен).

misery ['mɪzərɪ] *n* (*unhappiness*) невзго́да; (*pain*) страда́ние; (*wretchedness*) бе́дственное положе́ние.

misfire [mɪs'faɪə] *vi* (*plan*) прова́ливаться (провали́ться *perf*); (*car engine*) пропуска́ть (пропусти́ть* *perf*) вспы́шку.

misfit ['mɪsfɪt] *n* (*person*): **he was a ~ in our community** он не подходи́л к на́шему о́бществу.

misfortune [mɪs'fɔ:tʃən] *n* несча́стье*.

misgiving [mɪs'ɡɪvɪŋ] *n* опасе́ния *ntpl*; **I have ~s about it** у меня́ есть опасе́ния на э́тот счёт.

misguided [mɪs'ɡaɪdɪd] *adj* (*person*) неве́рно ориенти́рованный (ориенти́рован); (*ideas*) оши́бочный* (оши́бочен).

mishandle [mɪs'hændl] *vt* (*problem, situation*) не справля́ться (спра́виться* *perf*) с +*instr*.

mishap ['mɪshæp] *n* неприя́тность *f*.

mishear [mɪs'hɪə] (*irreg: like* **hear**) *vt* не расслы́шать (*perf*) ◆ *vi* ослы́шаться (*perf*).

misheard [mɪs'hɜːd] *pt, pp of* **mishear**.

mishmash ['mɪʃmæʃ] *n* (*inf*) неразбери́ха.

misinform [mɪsɪn'fɔːm] *vt* неве́рно информи́ровать (проинформи́ровать *perf*); (*deliberately*) дезинформи́ровать (*impf/perf*).

misinterpret [mɪsɪn'tə:prɪt] *vt* неве́рно интерпрети́ровать (*impf/perf*) *or* истолко́вывать (истолкова́ть *perf*).

misinterpretation ['mɪsɪntə:prɪ'teɪʃən] *n* неве́рная интерпрета́ция.

misjudge [mɪs'dʒʌdʒ] *vt* неве́рно оце́нивать (оцени́ть *perf*).

mislay [mɪs'leɪ] *irreg vt* (*lose*) дева́ть (подева́ть *perf*).

mislead [mɪs'liːd] (*irreg: like* **lead**[1]) *vt* вводи́ть* (ввести́* *perf*) в заблужде́ние.

misleading [mɪs'liːdɪŋ] *adj* обма́нчивый (обма́нчив).

misled [mɪs'lɛd] *pt, pp of* **mislead**.

mismanage [mɪs'mænɪdʒ] *vt* (*business, institution*) неуме́ло руководи́ть* (*impf*) +*instr*; (*problem, situation*) неуме́ло справля́ться (спра́виться* *perf*) с +*instr*.

mismanagement [mɪs'mænɪdʒmənt] *n* (*of company*) неуме́лое руково́дство; (*of situation*) неуме́лое реше́ние.

misnomer [mɪs'nəumə] *n* непра́вильное назва́ние.

misogynist [mɪ'sɔdʒɪnɪst] *n* женоненави́стник.

misplace [mɪs'pleɪs] *vt* (*lose*) дева́ть (подева́ть *perf*).

misplaced [mɪs'pleɪst] *adj* (*unwarranted*) неуме́стный* (неуме́стен).

misprint ['mɪsprɪnt] *n* опеча́тка*.

mispronounce [mɪsprə'nauns] *vt* непра́вильно произноси́ть* (произнести́* *perf*).

misquote ['mɪs'kwəut] *vt* неве́рно цити́ровать (процити́ровать *perf*).

misread [mɪs'riːd] *irreg vt* непра́вильно чита́ть (прочита́ть *or* проче́сть* *perf*).

misrepresent [mɪsrɛprɪ'zent] *vt* преподноси́ть* (преподнести́* *perf*) в ло́жном све́те.

misrepresentation [mɪsrɛprɪzen'teɪʃən] *n* искаже́ние; (*LAW*) умы́шленный обма́н.

Miss [mɪs] *n* мисс *f ind*; **Dear ~ Smith** (*formal*) Госпожа́ Смит; (*informal*) Мисс Смит.

miss [mɪs] *vt* (*train, bus, class etc*) пропуска́ть (пропусти́ть* *perf*); (*fail to hit*) не попада́ть (попа́сть* *perf*) в +*acc*; (*notice loss of: money etc*) обнару́живать (обнару́жить *perf*) пропа́жу +*gen*; (*pine for*) скуча́ть (*impf*) по +*dat*; (*chance, opportunity*) упуска́ть (упусти́ть* *perf*) ◆ *vi* (*subj: person*) прома́хиваться (промахну́ться* *perf*); (: *missile, object*) не достига́ть (дости́чь* *or* дости́гнуть* *perf*) це́ли ◆ *n* (*failure to hit*) про́мах; **you can't ~ my house** мой дом невозмо́жно не заме́тить; **the bus just ~ed the wall** авто́бус чуть не вре́зался в сте́ну; **I ~ him** я скуча́ю по нему́; **nobody will ~ us** никто́ не заме́тит, что нас нет; **you're ~ing the point** Вы не понима́ете су́ти де́ла

▶ **miss out** *vt* (*BRIT*) пропуска́ть (пропусти́ть* *perf*)

▶ **miss out on** *vt fus* (*fun, party*) пропуска́ть (пропусти́ть* *perf*); (*chance, bargain*) упуска́ть (упусти́ть* *perf*).

missal ['mɪsl] *n* моли́твенник.

misshapen [mɪs'ʃeɪpən] *adj* деформи́рованный (деформи́рован).

missile ['mɪsaɪl] *n* (*MIL*) раке́та; (*projectile*): **demonstrators threw ~s at the police** демонстра́нты забра́сывали поли́цию разли́чными предме́тами.

missile base *n* раке́тная ба́за.

missile launcher [-'lɔ:ntʃə] *n* раке́тная пускова́я устано́вка*.

missing ['mɪsɪŋ] *adj* (*lost*) пропа́вший; (*removed: tooth, wheel*) недостаю́щий*; (*absent*): **who is ~ today?** кто сего́дня отсу́тствует?; **to be ~**, **go ~** пропада́ть (пропа́сть* *perf*) бе́з вести; **~ person** пропа́вший(-ая) *m(f) adj* бе́з вести.

mission ['mɪʃən] *n* (*also POL, REL*) ми́ссия; (*MIL*) зада́ние; **on a ~ to sb** с ми́ссией к кому́-н.

missionary ['mɪʃənrɪ] *n* миссионе́р(ка*).

Mississippi [mɪsɪ'sɪpɪ] *n*: **the ~** Миссиси́пи *f ind*.

missive ['mɪsɪv] *n* посла́ние.

misspell ['mɪs'spɛl] (*irreg: like* **spell**) *vt* писа́ть* (написа́ть* *perf*) с оши́бками.

misspent ['mɪs'spɛnt] *adj*: **a ~ youth**

---

* marks translations which have irregular inflections. The Russian-English side of the dictionary gives inflectional information.

расстра́ченная ю́ность *f*.

mist [mɪst] *n* (*heavy*) тума́н; (*light*) ды́мка ◆ *vi* (*also:* ~ **over**: *eyes*) затума́ниваться (затума́ниться *perf*); (*BRIT: also:* ~ **over** *or* **up**: *windows*) запотева́ть (запоте́ть *perf*).

mistake [mɪs'teɪk] (*irreg: like* **take**) *n* оши́бка* ◆ *vt* (*be wrong about*) ошиба́ться (ошиби́ться* *perf*) в +*prp*; (*intentions*) непра́вильно понима́ть (поня́ть* *perf*); **by** ~ по оши́бке; **to make a** ~ ошиба́ться (ошиби́ться* *perf*), де́лать (сде́лать *perf*) оши́бку; **to make a** ~ **about sb/sth** ошиба́ться (ошиби́ться* *perf*) в ком-н/чём-н; **to** ~ **A for B** принима́ть (приня́ть* *perf*) А за Б.

mistaken [mɪs'teɪkən] *pp of* **mistake** ◆ *adj* оши́бочный* (оши́бочен); **to be** ~ ошиба́ться (ошиби́ться* *perf*).

mistaken identity *n*: **a case of** ~ ~ слу́чай оши́бочного опозна́ния.

mistakenly [mɪs'teɪkənlɪ] *adv* оши́бочно.

mister ['mɪstə'] *n* (*inf*) дя́дя *m* (*обраще́ние*); *see* **Mr**.

mistletoe ['mɪsltəu] *n* (*BOT*) оме́ла.

mistook [mɪs'tuk] *pt of* **mistake**.

mistranslation [mɪstræns'leɪʃən] *n* непра́вильный перево́д.

mistreat [mɪs'triːt] *vt* пло́хо обраща́ться (*impf*) с +*instr*.

mistress ['mɪstrɪs] *n* (*lover*) любо́вница; (*also fig*) хозя́йка*; (*BRIT: SCOL*) учи́тельница.

mistrust [mɪs'trʌst] *vt* не доверя́ть (*impf*) +*dat*, испы́тывать (испыта́ть *perf*) недове́рие к +*dat* ◆ *n*: ~ (**of**) недове́рие (к +*dat*).

mistrustful [mɪs'trʌstful] *adj* недове́рчивый (недове́рчив); **to be** ~ **of** не доверя́ть (*impf*) +*dat*.

misty ['mɪstɪ] *adj* (*day*) тума́нный* (тума́нен); (*eyes*) затума́ненный (затума́нен); (*glasses, window*) запоте́вший*.

misty-eyed ['mɪstɪ'aɪd] *adj* (*girl*) с глаза́ми по́лными слёз; (*fig: girl*) с затума́ненным взгля́дом.

misunderstand [mɪsʌndə'stænd] (*irreg: like* **understand**) *vt* непра́вильно понима́ть (поня́ть* *perf*) ◆ *vi* не понима́ть (поня́ть* *perf*).

misunderstanding ['mɪsʌndə'stændɪŋ] *n* недоразуме́ние.

misunderstood [mɪsʌndə'stud] *pt, pp of* **misunderstand**.

misuse [*n* mɪs'juːs, *vb* mɪs'juːz] *n* (*of power, funds*) злоупотребле́ние; (*of word*) непра́вильное употребле́ние ◆ *vt* (*see n*) злоупотребля́ть (злоупотреби́ть* *perf*) +*instr*; непра́вильно употребля́ть (употреби́ть* *perf*).

MIT *n abbr* (*US*) = *Massachusetts Institute of Technology*.

mite [maɪt] *n* (*small quantity*) ка́пля*; (*BRIT: small child*) кро́шка* *m/f*.

miter ['maɪtə'] *n* (*US*) = **mitre**.

mitigate ['mɪtɪgeɪt] *vt* смягча́ть (смягчи́ть

perf); **mitigating circumstances** смягча́ющие обстоя́тельства.

mitigation [mɪtɪ'geɪʃən] *n* смягче́ние; **in** ~ (*LAW*) в оправда́ние.

mitre ['maɪtə'] (*US* **miter**) *n* ми́тра; (*also:* ~ **joint**) соедине́ние в ус.

mitt [mɪt] *n* (*inf*) = **mitten**.

mitten ['mɪtn] *n* ва́режка*, рукави́ца.

mix [mɪks] *vt* (*cake, cement*) заме́шивать (замеси́ть* *perf*) ◆ *n* смесь *f* ◆ *vi* (*people*): **to** ~ (**with**) обща́ться (*impf*) (с +*instr*); **to** ~ **sth (with sth)** сме́шивать (смеша́ть *perf*) что-н (с чем-н); **to** ~ **business with pleasure** сочета́ть (*impf*) прия́тное с поле́зным; **cake** ~ гото́вая смесь для то́рта.

▶ **mix in** *vt* (*eggs etc*) вме́шивать (вмеша́ть *perf*)

▶ **mix up** *vt* (*combine*) переме́шивать (перемеша́ть *perf*); (*confuse: people*) пу́тать (спу́тать *perf*); (: *things*) пу́тать (перепу́тать *perf*); **to get** ~**ed up in sth** впу́тываться (впу́таться *perf*) во что-н; **he's** ~**ed up in this business too** он то́же заме́шан в э́том де́ле.

mixed [mɪkst] *adj* сме́шанный.

mixed-ability ['mɪkstə'bɪlɪtɪ] *adj* с ра́зными спосо́бностями.

mixed bag *n* (*of people*) разноше́рстная гру́ппа; (*of activities*) всего́ понемно́жку.

mixed blessing *n*: **it was a** ~ ~ э́то бы́ло ба́бушка на́двое сказа́ла.

mixed doubles *npl* (*TENNIS etc*) игра́ *fsg* сме́шанных пар.

mixed economy *n* сме́шанная эконо́мика.

mixed grill *n* (*BRIT*) ассорти́ из жа́реного мя́са и овоще́й.

mixed marriage *n* сме́шанный брак.

mixed-up [mɪkst'ʌp] *adj* (*confused*) сби́тый (сбит) с то́лку.

mixer ['mɪksə'] *n* (*for food*) ми́ксер; (*for drinks*) смеси́тель *m*; (*person*): **she is a good** ~ она́ о́чень общи́тельна.

mixer tap *n* кран со смеси́телем.

mixture ['mɪkstʃə'] *n* смесь *f*; (*MED*) миксту́ра.

mix-up ['mɪksʌp] *n* пу́таница.

Mk *abbr* (*BRIT: TECH*) = **mark**.

mk *abbr* (*COMM*) = **mark**.

mkt *abbr* = **market**.

MLitt *n abbr* (= *Master of Literature, Master of Letters*) ≈ маги́стр литературове́дения.

MLR *n abbr* (*BRIT*: = *minimum lending rate*) минима́льная ссу́дная ста́вка.

mm *abbr* (= *millimetre*) мм= *миллиме́тр*.

MN *abbr* (*BRIT*) = **Merchant Navy**; (*US: POST*) = *Minnesota*.

MO *n abbr* = *medical officer*; (*US: inf*. = *modus operandi*) при́нцип рабо́ты ◆ *abbr* (*US: POST*) = *Missouri*.

m.o. *abbr* = **money order**.

moan [məun] *n* (*cry*) стон ◆ *vi* (*inf: complain*): **to** ~ (**about**) ныть* (*impf*) (о +*prp*).

moaner ['məunə'] *n* (*inf: pej*) ны́тик.

moat [məut] *n* ров*.

mob [mɔb] *n* толпа*; (*inf: group of friends*) компа́ния ♦ *vt* осажда́ть (осади́ть* *perf*).

mobile ['məubaɪl] *adj* подви́жный* (подви́жен); (*population, forces*) моби́льный* (моби́лен) ♦ *n* (*decoration*) подвесно́е декорати́вное украше́ние; **applicants must be** ~ кандида́ты должны́ бы́ть гото́вы к сме́не местожи́тельства.

mobile home *n* дом* на колёсах.

mobile phone *n* портати́вный телефо́н.

mobile shop *n* (*BRIT*) автола́вка*.

mobility [məu'bɪlɪtɪ] *n* (*see adj*) подви́жность *f*; моби́льность *f*; (*of applicant*) гото́вность *f* меня́ть местожи́тельство.

mobility allowance *n* (*BRIT*) *посо́бие, выпла́чиваемое инвали́дам для покры́тия дополни́тльных доро́жных расхо́дов.*

mobilize ['məubɪlaɪz] *vt* мобилизова́ть (*impf/ perf*) ♦ *vi* мобилизова́ться (*impf/perf*).

moccasin ['mɔkəsɪn] *n* мокаси́н.

mock [mɔk] *vt* (*ridicule*) издева́ться (*impf*) над +*instr*; (*laugh at*) насмеха́ться (*impf*) над +*instr* ♦ *adj* (*fake*) ло́жный* (ло́жен); (: *emotion*) притво́рный; ~ (**exam**) (*BRIT*) про́бный экза́мен (*для подгото́вки к основно́му*); ~ **battle** инсцениро́вка бо́я.

mockery ['mɔkərɪ] *n* издева́тельство; **to make a ~ of sb/sth** выставля́ть (вы́ставить* *perf*) кого́-н/что-н на посме́шище.

mocking ['mɔkɪŋ] *adj* издева́тельский*.

mockingbird ['mɔkɪŋbəːd] *n* пересме́шник.

mock-up ['mɔkʌp] *n* маке́т.

MOD *n abbr* (*BRIT*: = *Ministry of Defence*) Министе́рство оборо́ны.

mod cons ['mɔd'kɔnz] *npl abbr* (*BRIT*: = *modern conveniences*) совреме́нные удо́бства *ntpl*.

mode [məud] *n* (*form: of life*) о́браз; (: *of transport*) вид; (*COMPUT*) режи́м.

model ['mɔdl] *n* моде́ль *f*, маке́т; (*also:* **fashion** ~) манеке́нщик(-ица); (*also:* **artist's** ~) нату́рщик(-ица) ♦ *adj* (*small scale*) моде́льный; (*ideal*) образцо́вый ♦ *vt* (*clothes*) демонстри́ровать (*impf/perf*); (*with clay etc*) лепи́ть* (вы́лепить* *perf*) ♦ *vi* (*for designer, photographer*) пози́ровать (*impf*); **to ~ o.s. on** (*copy*) копи́ровать (*impf*).

modeller ['mɔdlə'] (*US* **modeler**) *n* (*model maker*) модели́ст(ка*).

model railway *n* маке́т желе́зной доро́ги.

modem ['məudɛm] *n* (*COMPUT*) моде́м.

moderate [*adj, n* 'mɔdərət, *vb* 'mɔdəreɪt] *adj* (*views, amount*) уме́ренный* (уме́рен); (*change*) незначи́тельный* ♦ *n* челове́к* уме́ренных взгля́дов ♦ *vt* умеря́ть (уме́рить* *perf*) ♦ *vi* (*storm, wind etc*) утиха́ть (ути́хнуть* *perf*).

moderately ['mɔdərətlɪ] *adv* (*act*) уме́ренно; ~

expensive/pleased дово́льно до́рого/рад; ~ **priced** по уме́ренной цене́.

moderation [mɔdə'reɪʃən] *n* уме́ренность *f*; **in** ~ в уме́ренных коли́чествах.

moderator ['mɔdəreɪtə'] *n* (*mediator*) посре́дник; (*chairman*) председа́тель *m*.

modern ['mɔdən] *adj* совреме́нный; ~ **languages** совреме́нные языки́ *mpl*.

modernization [mɔdənaɪ'zeɪʃən] *n* модерниза́ция.

modernize ['mɔdənaɪz] *vt* модернизи́ровать (*impf/perf*).

modest ['mɔdɪst] *adj* скро́мный* (скро́мен).

modestly ['mɔdɪstlɪ] *adv* скро́мно.

modesty ['mɔdɪstɪ] *n* скро́мность *f*.

modicum ['mɔdɪkəm] *n*: **a** ~ **of** то́лика +*gen*.

modification [mɔdɪfɪ'keɪʃən] *n* (*of vehicle, engine*) модифика́ция; (*of plan*) видоизмене́ние; **to make ~s to** вноси́ть* (внести́* *perf*) видоизмене́ния в +*acc*.

modify ['mɔdɪfaɪ] *vt* (*see n*) модифици́ровать (*impf/perf*); видоизменя́ть (видоизмени́ть* *perf*).

modish ['məudɪʃ] *adj* мо́дный* (мо́ден).

Mods [mɔdz] *n abbr* (*BRIT: SCOL:* = (*Honour*) *Moderations*) экза́мен, позволя́ющий перейти́ на ку́рс, необходи́мый для получе́ния сте́пени бакала́вра в О́ксфордском университе́те.

modular ['mɔdjulə'] *adj* (*filing, unit*) мо́дульный.

modulate ['mɔdjuleɪt] *vt* (*voice*) модули́ровать (*impf*).

modulation [mɔdju'leɪʃən] *n* (*MUS, RADIO*) модуля́ция.

module ['mɔdju:l] *n* мо́дуль *m*; (*SPACE*) отсе́к; (*BRIT: SCOL*) курс.

modus operandi ['məudəsɔpə'rændi:] *n* при́нцип рабо́ты.

Mogadishu [mɔgə'dɪʃu:] *n* Могади́шу *m ind*.

mogul ['məugl] *n* (*fig*) магна́т.

MOH *n abbr* (*BRIT*) = *Medical Officer of Health*.

mohair ['məuhɛə'] *n* мохе́р.

Mohammed [mə'hæmɛd] *n* Магоме́т.

moist [mɔɪst] *adj* вла́жный* (вла́жен).

moisten ['mɔɪsn] *vt* (*lips*) увлажня́ть (увлажни́ть* *perf*); (: *with tongue*) обли́зывать (облиза́ть* *perf*); (*sponge*) мочи́ть* (намочи́ть* *perf*).

moisture ['mɔɪstʃə'] *n* вла́га.

moisturize ['mɔɪstʃəraɪz] *vt* увлажня́ть (увлажни́ть* *perf*).

moisturizer ['mɔɪstʃəraɪzə'] *n* увлажня́ющий крем.

molar ['məulə'] *n* коренно́й зуб*.

molasses [məu'læsɪz] *n* па́тока.

mold *etc* [məuld] (*US*) = **mould** *etc*.

Moldavian [mɔl'deɪvɪən] *n* (*person*)

молдова́нин*(-а́нка*) ◆ *adj* молдо́вский.
Moldova [mɔl'dəuvə] *n* Молдо́ва.
mole [məul] *n* (*spot*) ро́динка*; (*ZOOL*) крот*; (*spy*) доно́счик(-ица), стука́ч*(ка).
molecular [məu'lɛkjulə*] *adj* молекуля́рный.
molecule ['mɔlɪkjuːl] *n* моле́кула.
molehill ['məulhɪl] *n* крото́вая нора́*.
molest [mə'lɛst] *vt* (*assault sexually*) надруга́ться (*perf*) над +*instr*; (*harass*) трави́ть* (затрави́ть* *perf*).
mollusc ['mɔləsk] *n* моллю́ск.
mollycoddle ['mɔlɪkɔdl] *vt* трясти́сь* (*impf*) над +*instr*.
Molotov cocktail ['mɔlətɔf-] *n* коктейль *m* Мо́лотова (*буты́лка с зажига́тельной сме́сью*).
molt [məult] *vi* (*US*) = moult.
molten ['məultən] *adj* распла́вленный.
mom [mɔm] *n* (*US*) = mum.
moment ['məumənt] *n* моме́нт, мгнове́ние; (*PHYS*) моме́нт; **for a** ~ на мгнове́ние *or* мину́ту; **at that** ~ в э́тот моме́нт; **at the** ~ в настоя́щий* моме́нт; **for the** ~ пока́; **in a** ~ че́рез мину́ту; **(at) any** ~ (**now**) в любо́й моме́нт; **"one – please"** „одну́ мину́точку".
momentarily ['məuməntrɪlɪ] *adv* на мгнове́ние; (*US: very soon*) в любо́й моме́нт.
momentary ['məuməntərɪ] *adj* (*brief*) мгнове́нный.
momentous [məu'mɛntəs] *adj* важне́йший.
momentum [məu'mɛntəm] *n* (*PHYS*) и́мпульс; (*fig*) дви́жущая си́ла; **to gather** *or* **gain** ~ набира́ть (набра́ть* *perf*) си́лу.
mommy ['mɔmɪ] *n* (*US: mother*) = mummy.
Mon. *abbr* = Monday.
Monaco ['mɔnəkəu] *n* Мона́ко *nt ind*.
monarch ['mɔnək] *n* мона́рх.
monarchist ['mɔnəkɪst] *n* монархи́ст(ка*).
monarchy ['mɔnəkɪ] *n* мона́рхия.
monastery ['mɔnəstərɪ] *n* монасты́рь* *m*.
monastic [mə'næstɪk] *adj* (*vows, order, also fig*) мона́шеский*; (*building*) монасты́рский.
Monday ['mʌndɪ] *n* понеде́льник; *see also* Tuesday.
Monegasque [mɔnə'gæsk] *adj* мона́кский ◆ *n* жи́тель(ница) *m(f)* Мона́ко.
monetarist ['mʌnɪtərɪst] *n* монетари́ст ◆ *adj* монетари́стский.
monetary ['mʌnɪtərɪ] *adj* де́нежный.
money ['mʌnɪ] *n* де́ньги* *pl*; **to make** ~ (*person*) зараба́тывать (зарабо́тать *perf*); (*business*) приноси́ть* (принести́* *perf*) дохо́д; **danger** ~ (*BRIT*) надба́вка за вре́дность*; **I've got no** ~ **left** у меня́ совсе́м не оста́лось де́нег.
moneyed ['mʌnɪd] *adj* де́нежный.
moneylender ['mʌnɪlɛndə*] *n* ростовщи́к*.
money-maker ['mʌnɪmeɪkə*] *n* (*person*) кру́пный деле́ц*; (*project, investment*) при́быльное де́ло.
moneymaking ['mʌnɪmeɪkɪŋ] *adj* при́быльный.

money market *n* де́нежный ры́нок*.
money order *n* де́нежный перево́д.
money-spinner ['mʌnɪspɪnə*] *n* (*inf*): **this business/idea will be a real** ~ э́тот би́знес/э́та иде́я бу́дет де́лать больши́е де́ньги.
money supply *n* де́нежная ма́сса.
Mongol ['mɔŋgəl] *n* (*LING*) монго́льский* язы́к*; (*HISTORY*): **the** ~**s** монго́ло-тата́ры.
mongol ['mɔŋgəl] *n* (*pej*) челове́к, страда́ющий боле́знью Да́уна.
Mongolia [mɔŋ'gəulɪə] *n* Монго́лия.
Mongolian [mɔŋ'gəulɪən] *adj* монго́льский ◆ *n* (*person*) монго́л(ка*); (*LING*) монго́льский* язы́к*.
mongoose ['mɔŋguːs] *n* мангу́ст.
mongrel ['mʌŋgrəl] *n* дворня́га.
monitor ['mɔnɪtə*] *n* монито́р ◆ *vt* (*broadcasts*) контроли́ровать (*impf*); (*heartbeat, pulse*) наблюда́ть (*impf*) за +*instr*; (*progress*) следи́ть* (*impf*) за +*instr*; (*foreign station*) прослу́шивать (*impf*).
monk [mʌŋk] *n* мона́х.
monkey ['mʌŋkɪ] *n* обезья́на.
monkey business *n* (*inf*) проде́лки* *fpl*.
monkey nut *n* (*BRIT*) ара́хис *no pl*.
monkey tricks *npl* = monkey business.
monkey wrench *n* разводно́й га́ечный ключ*.
mono ['mɔnəu] *adj* (*recording*) мо́но *ind*.
monochrome ['mɔnəkrəum] *adj* черно-бе́лый; (*COMPUT*) монохро́мный.
monogamous [mɔ'nɔgəməs] *adj* монога́мный* (монога́мен).
monogamy [mə'nɔgəmɪ] *n* монога́мия, единобра́чие.
monogram ['mɔnəgræm] *n* моногра́мма.
monolith ['mɔnəlɪθ] *n* моноли́т.
monolithic [mɔnə'lɪθɪk] *adj* моноли́тный.
monologue ['mɔnəlɔg] *n* моноло́г.
monoplane ['mɔnəpleɪn] *n* монопла́н.
monopolist [mə'nɔpəlɪst] *n* монополи́ст.
monopolize [mə'nɔpəlaɪz] *vt* (*ECON*) монополизи́ровать (*impf/perf*); (*place, conversation*) завладева́ть (завладе́ть *perf*) +*instr*; (*person*) захва́тывать (захвати́ть* *perf*).
monopoly [mə'nɔpəlɪ] *n* (*also ECON*) монопо́лия; **Monopolies and Mergers Commission** (*BRIT*) Коми́ссия по монопо́лиям и слия́ниям.
monorail ['mɔnəureɪl] *n* моноре́льсовая доро́га.
monosodium glutamate [mɔnə'səudɪəm 'gluːtəmeɪt] *n* глутамина́т на́трия.
monosyllabic [mɔnəsɪ'læbɪk] *adj* (*word*) односло́жный; (*person*) немногосло́вный*.
monosyllable ['mɔnəsɪləbl] *n* односло́жное сло́во*.
monotone ['mɔnətəun] *n*: **to speak in a** ~ говори́ть (*impf*) моното́нно.
monotonous [mə'nɔtənəs] *adj* (*life, job etc*)

однообра́зный* (однообра́зен); (*voice, sound*) моното́нный* (моното́нен).

monotony [mə'nɒtənɪ] *n* (*see adj*) однообра́зие; моното́нность *f*.

monsoon [mɒn'su:n] *n* муссо́н.

monster ['mɒnstə^r] *n* (*also fig*) чудо́вище, монстр.

monstrosity [mɒn'strɒsɪtɪ] *n* (*object, building*) чу́дище, монстр.

monstrous ['mɒnstrəs] *adj* чудо́вищный* (чудо́вищен).

montage [mɒn'tɑːʒ] *n* монта́ж*.

Mont Blanc [mɔ̃ blɑ̃] *n* Монбла́н.

Montenegrin [mɒntə'niːgrɪn] *n* черного́рец*(-о́рка*) ♦ *adj* черного́рский*.

Montenegro [mɒntə'niːgrəʊ] *n* Черного́рия.

month [mʌnθ] *n* ме́сяц; **every ~** ка́ждый ме́сяц; **300 dollars a ~** 300 до́лларов в ме́сяц.

monthly ['mʌnθlɪ] *adj* ежеме́сячный; (*ticket*) ме́сячный ♦ *adv* ежеме́сячно; **twice ~** два́жды в ме́сяц.

Montreal [mɒntrɪ'ɔːl] *n* Монреа́ль *m*.

monument ['mɒnjumənt] *n* (*memorial*) па́мятник, монуме́нт; (*historical building*) па́мятник.

monumental [mɒnju'mɛntl] *adj* (*building, book*) монумента́льный* (монумента́лен); (*storm, row*) колосса́льный.

moo [mu:] *vi* мыча́ть* (*impf*).

mood [mu:d] *n* настрое́ние; (*of group, crowd*) настро́й; **to be in a good/bad ~** быть* (*impf*) в хоро́шем/плохо́м настрое́нии; **I'm in the ~ for a drink/to watch TV** у меня́ есть настрое́ние вы́пить/смотре́ть телеви́зор.

moodily ['mu:dɪlɪ] *adv* мра́чно, угрю́мо.

moody ['mu:dɪ] *adj* (*sullen*) угрю́мый (угрю́м); (*temperamental*): **she is a very ~ person** у неё о́чень переме́нчивое настрое́ние.

moon [mu:n] *n* луна́*.

moonlight ['mu:nlaɪt] *n* лу́нный свет ♦ *vi* (*inf*) рабо́тать (*impf*) на стороне́.

moonlighting ['mu:nlaɪtɪŋ] *n* (*inf*) рабо́та по совмести́тельству.

moonlit ['mu:nlɪt] *adj*: **a ~ night** лу́нная ночь*.

moonshot ['mu:nʃɒt] *n* полёт на Луну́.

moor [muə^r] *n* ве́ресковая пу́стошь *f* ♦ *vt* (*ship*) пришварто́вывать (пришвартова́ть *perf*) ♦ *vi* пришварто́вываться (пришвартова́ться *perf*).

mooring ['muərɪŋ] *n* прича́л; **~s** *npl* (*chains*) швартовые це́пи* *fpl*.

Moorish ['muərɪʃ] *adj* маврита́нский.

moorland ['muələnd] *n* ве́ресковая пу́стошь *f*.

moose [mu:s] *n inv* лось* *m*.

moot [mu:t] *vt*: **it was ~ed that ...** бы́ло предло́жено, что ... ♦ *adj*: **~ point** спо́рный вопро́с.

mop [mɒp] *n* (*for floor*) шва́бра; (*for dishes*)

щётка*; (*of hair*) копна́ ♦ *vt* (*floor*) мыть* (вы́мыть* *or* помы́ть* *perf*) (шва́брой); (*eyes, face*) вытира́ть (вы́тереть* *perf*).

► **mop up** *vt* (*liquid*) вытира́ть (вы́тереть* *perf*).

mope [məup] *vi* хандри́ть (*impf*)

► **mope about** *vi* слоня́ться (*impf*)

► **mope around** *vi* = **mope about**.

moped ['məupɛd] *n* мопе́д.

moquette [mɒ'kɛt] *n* ≈ плюш.

MOR *adj abbr* (*MUS*: = middle-of-the-road) лёгкий*.

moral ['mɒrl] *adj* нра́вственный, мора́льный; (*person*) нра́вственный* (нра́вственен) ♦ *n* (*of story*) мора́ль *f*; **~s** *npl* нра́вы *mpl*; **~ support/dilemma/victory** мора́льная подде́ржка/диле́мма/побе́да; **~ courage** душе́вное му́жество.

morale [mɒ'rɑːl] *n* мора́льный дух.

morality [mə'rælɪtɪ] *n* нра́вственность *f*.

moralize ['mɒrəlaɪz] *vi*: **to ~ (about)** морализи́ровать (*impf*) (о +*prp*).

morally ['mɒrəlɪ] *adv* (*wrong, responsible*) мора́льно; (*live, behave*) нра́вственно.

moral victory *n* мора́льная побе́да.

morass [mə'ræs] *n* (*also fig*) тряси́на.

moratorium [mɒrə'tɔːrɪəm] *n* морато́рий.

morbid ['mɔːbɪd] *adj* (*imagination*) ненорма́льный; (*ideas*) жу́ткий*.

KEYWORD
---

more [mɔː^r] *adj* **1** (*greater in number etc*) бо́льше +*gen*; **I have more friends than enemies** у меня́ бо́льше друзе́й, чем враго́в **2** (*additional*) ещё; **do you want (some) more tea?** хоти́те ещё ча́ю?; **is there any more wine?** ещё есть вино́?; **I have no** *or* **I don't have any more money** у меня́ бо́льше нет де́нег; **it'll take a few more weeks** э́то займёт ещё не́сколько неде́ль

♦ *pron* **1** (*greater amount*): **more than ten** бо́льше десяти́; **we've sold more than a hundred tickets** мы про́дали бо́лее ста биле́тов; **it cost more than we expected** э́то сто́ит бо́льше, чем мы ожида́ли **2** (*further or additional amount*): **is there any more?** ещё есть?; **there's no more** бо́льше ничего́ нет; **a little more** ещё немно́го *or* чуть-чу́ть; **many/much more** намно́го/гора́здо бо́льше

♦ *adv* **1** (+*vb*) бо́льше; **I like this one more** мне э́то бо́льше нра́вится **2** (+*adj*): **more dangerous/difficult** *etc* (**than**) бо́лее опа́сный/тру́дный *etc*, (чем) **3** (+*adv*): **more economically** (**than**) бо́лее эконо́мично (чем); **more easily/quickly** (**than**) ле́гче/быстре́е (чем); **he became more and more excited/friendly** он станови́лся всё бо́лее и бо́лее возбуждённым/дружелю́бным; **he grew to like her more and**

more она нравилась ему всё больше и больше; **more or less** более или менее; **it should cost £500, more or less** это должно стоить приблизительно £500; **she is more beautiful than ever** она прекраснее, чем когда-либо; **he loved her more than ever** он любил её больше, чем когда-либо; **the more ..., the better** чем больше ..., чем лучше; **once more** ещё раз; **I'd like to see more of you** хотелось бы почаще Вас видеть.

moreover [mɔːˈrəuvəʳ] *adv* более того.
morgue [mɔːg] *n* морг.
MORI [ˈmɔːrɪ] *n abbr* (*BRIT.* = *Market & Opinion Research Institute*) научно-исследовательский институт изучения рынка и общественного мнения.
moribund [ˈmɔrɪbʌnd] *adj* (*industry*) отживший своё.
Mormon [ˈmɔːmən] *n* мормон(ка*).
morning [ˈmɔːnɪŋ] *n* утро*; (*between midnight and 3 a.m.*) ночь *f* ♦ *cpd* (*paper, sun, walk*) утренний*; **in the ~** утром; **3 o'clock in the ~** 3 часа ночи; **7 o'clock in the ~** 7 часов утра; **this ~** сегодня утром.
morning-after pill [ˈmɔːnɪŋˈɑːftə-] *n* противозачаточная таблетка с высоким содержанием гормональных препаратов (*обычно принимается в экстренных случаях после полового акта*).
morning sickness *n* утренняя тошнота (*у беременных*).
Moroccan [məˈrɔkən] *adj* марокканский ♦ *n* марокканец*(-нка*).
Morocco [məˈrɔkəu] *n* Морокко *nt ind*.
moron [ˈmɔːrɔn] *n* (*inf*) кретин(ка*).
moronic [məˈrɔnɪk] *adj* (*inf*) кретинский.
morose [məˈrəus] *adj* (*miserable*) угрюмый (угрюм).
morphine [ˈmɔːfiːn] *n* морфий.
morris dancing [ˈmɔrɪs-] *n* (*BRIT*) моррис (*народный английский танец*).
Morse [mɔːs] *n* (*also*: **~ code**) азбука Морзе.
morsel [ˈmɔːsl] *n* (*of food*) кусочек*.
mortal [ˈmɔːtl] *adj* (*human*) смертный* (смертен); (*deadly*) смертельный* (смертелен); (*sin*) смертный* ♦ *n*: **mere ~** простой(-ая) смертный(-ая) *m(f) adj*; **~ remains** бренные останки.
mortality [mɔːˈtælɪtɪ] *n* (*death*) смертность *f*.
mortality rate *n* смертность *f*.
mortar [ˈmɔːtəʳ] *n* (*cannon*) миномёт; (*cement*) цементный раствор; (*bowl*) ступка*.
mortgage [ˈmɔːgɪdʒ] *n* ипотечная ссуда ♦ *vt* закладывать (заложить* *perf*); **to take out a ~** брать* (взять* *perf*) ссуду (*для покупки дома*).
mortgage company *n* (*US*) ипотечная компания.
mortgagee [mɔːgəˈdʒiː] *n* кредитор (*при ипотечном кредите*).
mortgagor [ˈmɔːgədʒəʳ] *n* заёмщик (*при ипотечном кредите*).

mortician [mɔːˈtɪʃən] *n* (*US*) работник похоронного бюро.
mortified [ˈmɔːtɪfaɪd] *adj*: **to be ~** быть* (*impf*) в смертельном ужасе.
mortify [ˈmɔːtɪfaɪ] *vt* приводить* (привести* *perf*) в полный ужас.
mortise lock [ˈmɔːtɪs-] *n* врезной замок*.
mortuary [ˈmɔːtjuərɪ] *n* морг (*при больнице*), покойницкая *f adj*.
mosaic [məuˈzeɪɪk] *n* мозаика.
Moscow [ˈmɔskəu] *n* Москва.
Moslem [ˈmɔzləm] *adj, n* = **Muslim**.
mosque [mɔsk] *n* мечеть *f*.
mosquito [mɔsˈkiːtəu] (*pl* **~es**) *n* комар*.
mosquito net *n* москитная сетка*.
moss [mɔs] *n* мох*.
mossy [ˈmɔsɪ] *adj* поросший мхом.

KEYWORD

most [məust] *adj* **1** (*almost all: countable nouns*) большинство +*gen*; (: *uncountable and collective nouns*) по большей части; **most people/cars** большинство людей/машин; **most milk** молоко, по большей части; **in most cases** в большинстве случаев
2 (*largest, greatest*): **who has the most money?** у кого больше всего денег?; **this book has attracted the most interest among the critics** эта книга вызвала наибольший интерес у критиков
♦ *pron* (*greatest quantity, number: countable nouns*) большинство; (: *uncountable and collective nouns*) большая часть *f*; **most of the houses/her friends** большинство из домов/её друзей; **most of the cake** большая часть торта; **do the most you can** делайте всё, что можете; **I ate the most** я съел больше всех; **to make the most of sth** максимально использовать (*impf*) что-н; **at the (very) most** самое большее
♦ *adv* (+*vb*) больше всего; (+*adv*) исключительно; **the most interesting/expensive** наиболее *or* самый интересный/дорогой; **I liked him the most** он понравился мне больше всех; **what do you value most, wealth or health?** что Вы больше цените, богатство или здоровье?

---

mostly [ˈməustlɪ] *adv* в основном, главным образом.
MOT *n abbr* (*BRIT.* = *Ministry of Transport*) Министерство транспорта; **~ (test)** техосмотр = технический осмотр.
motel [məuˈtɛl] *n* мотель *m*.
moth [mɔθ] *n* мотылёк*; (*also*: **clothes ~**) моль *f no pl*.
mothballs [ˈmɔθbɔːlz] *npl* нафталиновые шарики *mpl*.
moth-eaten [ˈmɔθiːtn] *adj* (*also fig*) изъеденный (изъеден).
mother [ˈmʌðəʳ] *n* мать* *f* ♦ *vt* (*raise*)

выра́щивать (вы́растить* *perf*); (*pamper*) ня́нчиться (*impf*) с +*instr* ♦ *adj*: ~ **country** ро́дина; ~ **company** матери́нская компа́ния.
motherboard ['mʌðəbɔ:d] *n* (*COMPUT*) объедини́тельная пла́та.
motherhood ['mʌðəhud] *n* матери́нство.
mother-in-law ['mʌðərɪnlɔ:] *n* (*wife's mother*) тёща; (*husband's mother*) свекро́вь *f*.
motherly ['mʌðəlɪ] *adj* матери́нский*.
mother-of-pearl ['mʌðərəv'pɜ:l] *n* перламу́тр ♦ *adj* перламу́тровый.
Mother's Day *n пра́здник посвящённый матеря́м.*
mother's help *n* ня́ня.
mother-to-be ['mʌðətə'bi:] *n* бу́дущая мать* *f*.
mother tongue *n* родно́й язы́к*.
mothproof ['mɔθpru:f] *adj* (*fabric etc*) молесто́йкий.
motif [məu'ti:f] *n* (*design*) орна́мент; (*theme*) моти́в.
motion ['məuʃən] *n* (*movement, gesture*) движе́ние; (*proposal*) предложе́ние; (*BRIT*: *bowel movement*) стул *no pl* ♦ *vti*: **he ~ed (to) her to sit down** он жёстом предложи́л ей сесть; **to be in ~** быть* (*impf*) в движе́нии; **to set in ~** приводи́ть* (привести́* *perf*) в де́йствие; **to go through the ~s** (*fig*: *formalities*) исполня́ть (испо́лнить *perf*) форма́льности.
motionless ['məuʃənlɪs] *adj* неподви́жный* (неподви́жен).
motion picture *n* кинокарти́на.
motivate ['məutɪveɪt] *vt* (*act, decision*) мотиви́ровать (*impf*); (*person*) заинтересо́вывать (заинтересови́ть *perf*); **he is ~d by ambition** им дви́жет честолю́бие.
motivated ['məutɪveɪtɪd] *adj* (*enthusiastic*) заинтересо́ванный (заинтересо́ван); (*impelled*): ~ **by envy/greed** движи́мый чу́вством за́висти/жа́дности.
motivation [məutɪ'veɪʃən] *n* (*drive*) целеустремлённость *f*.
motivational research *n* иссле́дование мотива́ций.
motive ['məutɪv] *n* моти́в, побужде́ние ♦ *adj*: ~ **power** *or* **force** дви́жущая си́ла; **from the best (of) ~s** из лу́чших побужде́ний.
motley ['mɔtlɪ] *adj* пёстрый* (пёстр).
motor ['məutə] *n* (*also BRIT*: *inf*) мото́р ♦ *cpd* (*industry, trade*) автомоби́льный.
motorbike ['məutəbaɪk] *n* мотоци́кл.
motorboat ['məutəbəut] *n* мото́рная ло́дка*.
motorcade ['məutəkeɪd] *n* корте́ж автомоби́лей.
motorcar ['məutəkɑ:] *n* (*BRIT*) автомоби́ль *m*.
motorcoach ['məutəkəutʃ] *n* (*BRIT*) авто́бус.
motorcycle ['məutəsaɪkl] *n* мотоци́кл.
motorcycle racing *n* мотого́нки* *fpl*.

motorcyclist ['məutəsaɪklɪst] *n* мотоцикли́ст(ка*).
motoring ['məutərɪŋ] (*BRIT*) *n* е́зда на автомоби́ле ♦ *cpd*: ~ **accident** автомоби́льная ава́рия; ~ **offence** наруше́ние пра́вил доро́жного движе́ния; **we went on a ~ holiday in France** мы провели́ о́тпуск путеше́ствуя по Фра́нции на маши́не.
motorist ['məutərɪst] *n* автомобили́ст.
motorized ['məutəraɪzd] *adj*: ~ **transport** автотра́нспорт; ~ **vehicle** автомаши́на; ~ **regiment** моторизо́ванный полк*.
motor oil *n* мото́рное ма́сло.
motor racing *n* (*BRIT*) автого́нки* *fpl= автомоби́льные го́нки*.*
motor scooter *n* моторо́ллер.
motor vehicle *n* автомаши́на.
motorway ['məutəweɪ] *n* (*BRIT*) автомагистра́ль *f*, автостра́да.
mottled ['mɔtld] *adj* пятни́стый.
motto ['mɔtəu] (*pl ~es*) *n* деви́з.
mould [məuld] (*US mold*) *n* (*cast*) фо́рма; (*mildew*) пле́сень *f* ♦ *vt* (*substance*) лепи́ть* (слепи́ть* *or* вы́лепить* *perf*); (*fig*: *opinion, character*) формирова́ть (сформирова́ть *perf*).
moulder ['məuldə] *vi* разлага́ться (разложи́ться* *perf*).
moulding ['məuldɪŋ] *n* (*ARCHIT*) лепно́е украше́ние.
mouldy ['məuldɪ] *adj* (*food*) заплесневе́лый; (*smell*) за́тхлый (за́тхл).
moult [məult] (*US molt*) *vi* линя́ть (*impf*).
mound [maund] *n* (*hillock*) холм, приго́рок*; (*heap*) ку́ча.
mount [maunt] *n* (*horse*) ло́шадь* *f*; (*for picture, photograph*) паспарту́ *nt ind* ♦ *vt* (*horse*) сади́ться* (сесть* *perf*) на +*acc*; (*exhibition, display*) устра́ивать (устро́ить *perf*); (*jewel*) оправля́ть (опра́вить* *perf*); (*picture*) обрамля́ть (обрами́ть* *perf*; (*staircase*) всходи́ть* (взойти́* *perf*) по +*dat*; (*attack*) предпринима́ть (предприня́ть* *perf*) ♦ *vi* (*increase*) расти́* (*impf*); (*on a horse*) сади́ться* (сесть* *perf*) на ло́шадь; **M~ Ararat/Kilimanjaro** гора́ Арара́т/Килиманджа́ро
▸ **mount up** *vi* (*bills, costs*) нака́пливаться (накопи́ться* *perf*).
mountain ['mauntɪn] *n* (*also fig*) гора́* ♦ *cpd* го́рный; **to make a ~ out of a molehill** де́лать (сде́лать *perf*) из му́хи слона́.
mountain bike *n велосипе́д, приспосо́бленный для испо́льзования на пересечённой ме́стности.*
mountaineer [mauntɪ'nɪə] *n* альпини́ст(ка*).
mountaineering [mauntɪ'nɪərɪŋ] *n* альпини́зм;

to go ~ ходи́ть* (impf) в го́ры.
mountainous ['mauntɪnəs] adj гори́стый
(гори́ст).
mountain range n го́рная цепь* f.
mountain rescue team n
горноспаса́тельный отря́д.
mountainside ['mauntɪnsaɪd] n склон горы́.
mounted ['mauntɪd] adj (on horseback)
ко́нный.
Mount Everest n гора́ Эвере́ст.
mourn [mɔːn] vt опла́кивать (impf) ♦ vi: **to** ~ **for**
скорбе́ть (impf) по +dat or о +prp.
mourner ['mɔːnəʳ] n прису́тствующий(-ая) m(f)
adj на похорона́х.
mournful ['mɔːnful] adj (sad) ско́рбный*
(ско́рбен).
mourning ['mɔːnɪŋ] n тра́ур; **in** ~ в тра́уре.
mouse [maus] (pl **mice**) n (also fig, COMPUT)
мышь* f.
mousetrap ['maustræp] n мышело́вка*.
moussaka [muːˈsɑːkə] n мусса́ка (гре́ческое
блю́до).
mousse [muːs] n мусс.
moustache [məsˈtɑːʃ] (US **mustache**) n усы́ mpl.
mousy ['mausɪ] adj (hair) мыши́ного цве́та.
mouth [mauθ] (pl ~**s**) n рот*; (of cave, hole)
вход; (of river) у́стье*; (of bottle) го́рлышко*.
mouthful ['mauθful] n (of food) кусо́чек*; (of
drink) глото́к*.
mouth organ n губна́я гармо́шка*.
mouthpiece ['mauθpiːs] n (of musical
instrument) мундшту́к*; (of telephone)
микрофо́н; (spokesman, newspaper)
глаша́тай.
mouth-to-mouth ['mauθtəˈmauθ] adj: ~
resuscitation иску́сственное дыха́ние.
mouthwash ['mauθwɔʃ] n жи́дкость f для
полоска́ния рта.
mouthwatering ['mauθwɔːtərɪŋ] adj о́чень
аппети́тный* (аппети́тен).
movable ['muːvəbl] adj подвижно́й; **Easter is a**
~ **feast** в ра́зные го́ды Па́сха прихо́дится на
ра́зные чи́сла.
move [muːv] n (movement) движе́ние; (in
game) ход; (change: of house) перее́зд; (: of
job) перехо́д (на другу́ю рабо́ту) ♦ vt
передвига́ть (передви́нуть perf); (piece: in
game) ходи́ть* (пойти́* perf) +instr; (part of
body) дви́гать (дви́нуть perf) +instr; (person:
emotionally) тро́гать (тро́нуть perf),
растро́гать (perf); (resolution etc) предлага́ть
(предложи́ть* perf) ♦ vi дви́гаться
(дви́нуться perf); (in game) де́лать (сде́лать
perf) ход; (of things) дви́гаться (impf); (also: ~
house) переезжа́ть (перее́хать* perf); **get a** ~
on! потора́пливайтесь!; **to** ~ **to a new job**
переходи́ть* (перейти́* perf) на но́вую
рабо́ту; **to** ~ **sb to sth** подвига́ть* (perf)
кого́-н на что-н; **to** ~ **towards** дви́гаться
(дви́нуться perf) к +dat
▶ **move about** vi (change position)

передвига́ться (передви́нуться perf); (travel,
change residence) переезжа́ть (impf) с ме́ста
на ме́сто; (change job) переходи́ть* (impf) с
рабо́ты на рабо́ту
▶ **move along** vi проходи́ть* (пройти́* perf)
▶ **move around** vi = **move about**
▶ **move away** vi: **to** ~ **away (from)** (leave)
уезжа́ть (уе́хать* perf) (из +gen); (step away)
отходи́ть* (отойти́* perf) (от +gen)
▶ **move back** vi переезжа́ть (перее́хать* perf)
обра́тно
▶ **move forward** vi продвига́ться
(продви́нуться perf)
▶ **move in** vi (police, soldiers) входи́ть* (войти́*
perf); **to** ~ **in(to)** (house) въезжа́ть (въе́хать*
perf) (в +acc)
▶ **move off** vi отъезжа́ть (отъе́хать* perf)
▶ **move on** vi (leave) направля́ться
(напра́виться* perf) да́льше ♦ vt (onlookers)
продвига́ть (продви́нуть perf)
▶ **move out** vi (of house) выезжа́ть (вы́ехать*
perf)
▶ **move over** vi (to make room) подвига́ться
(подви́нуться perf)
▶ **move up** vi (be promoted) продвига́ться
(продви́нуться perf).
moveable ['muːvəbl] adj = **movable**.
movement ['muːvmənt] n (action, also POL, REL)
движе́ние; (between two fixed points)
передвиже́ние; (transportation: of goods etc)
перево́зка*; (shift: in attitude, policy) сдвиг;
(MUS) часть f.
mover ['muːvəʳ] n (of proposal) инициа́тор.
movie ['muːvɪ] n фильм, кинофи́льм; **to go to
the** ~**s** ходи́ть*/идти́* (пойти́* perf) в кино́.
movie camera n кинока́мера.
moviegoer ['muːvɪgəuəʳ] n (US) кинолюби́тель
m.
moving ['muːvɪŋ] adj (emotional)
тро́гательный* (тро́гателен); (mobile)
подвижно́й* (подви́жен); (spirit, force)
дви́жущий ♦ n (US) перее́зд.
mow [mau] (pt **mowed**, pp **mowed** or **mown**) vt
(grass) подстрига́ть (подстри́чь* perf); (hay)
коси́ть* (скоси́ть* perf)
▶ **mow down** vt (kill) коси́ть* (скоси́ть* perf).
mower ['məuəʳ] n коси́лка*.
mown [məun] pp of **mow**.
Mozambique [məuzəmˈbiːk] n Мозамби́к.
MP n abbr (= Member of Parliament) член
парла́мента; (= Military Police) вое́нная
поли́ция; (CANADA: = Mounted Police) ко́нная
поли́ция.
mpg n abbr = miles per gallon.
mph abbr = miles per hour.
MPhil n abbr (= Master of Philosophy) ≈ маги́стр
филосо́фии.
MPS n abbr (BRIT) = Member of the
Pharmaceutical Society.
Mr ['mɪstəʳ] (US **Mr.**) n: ~ **Smith** (informal)
ми́стер Смит; (formal) г-н Смит= господи́н

Смит.

MRC *n abbr* (*BRIT*) = Medical Research Council.
MRCP *n abbr* (*BRIT*) = Member of the Royal College of Physicians.
MRCS *n abbr* (*BRIT*) = Member of the Royal College of Surgeons.
MRCVS *n abbr* (*BRIT*) = Member of the Royal College of Veterinary Surgeons.
Mrs ['mɪsɪz] (*US* **Mrs.**) *n*: ~ **Smith** (*informal*) миссис Смит; (*formal*) г-жа Смит= *госпожá Смит*.
Ms [mɪz] (*US* **Ms.**) *n* (= Miss or Mrs): ~ **Smith** г-жа Смит= *госпожá Смит*.
MS *n abbr* = **multiple sclerosis**; (*US*: = Master of Science) ≈ магистр естественных наук ♦ *abbr* (*US*: *POST*) = Mississippi.
MS. *n abbr* = **manuscript**.
MSA *n abbr* (*US*: = Master of Science in Agriculture) ≈ магистр сельско-хозяйственных наук.
MSc *n abbr* (= Master of Science) ≈ магистр естественных наук.
MSG *n abbr* = monosodium glutamate.
MST *abbr* (*US*) = Mountain Standard Time.
MSW *n abbr* (*US*: = Master of Social Work) ≈ магистр социологии.
MT *n abbr* (*COMPUT, LING*: = machine translation) МП= *машúнный перевóд* ♦ *abbr* (*US*: *POST*) = Montana.
Mt *abbr* (*GEO*) = **mount**.
MTV *n abbr* (*US*) = music television.

KEYWORD

much [mʌtʃ] *adj* (*time, money, effort*) мнóго +*gen*; **we haven't got much time/money** у нас не так мнóго врéмени/дéнег; **how much money/time do you need?** скóлько дéнег/врéмени Вам нýжно?; **he's spent so much money today** он сегóдня потрáтил стóлько дéнег; **I have as much money as you (do)** у меня стóлько же дéнег, скóлько у Вас; **I don't have as much time as you do** у меня нет стóлько врéмени, скóлько у Вас
♦ *pron*: **there isn't much to do here** здесь нéчего дéлать; **much is still unclear** мнóгое ещё неясно; **much has been gained from our discussions** нáша дискýссия дáла большúе результáты *or* мнóгое; **how much does it cost? - too much** скóлько это стóит? - слúшком дóрого; **how much is it?** почём это?
♦ *adv* **1** (*greatly, a great deal*): **thank you very much** большóе спасúбо; **we are very much looking forward to your visit** мы óчень ждём Вáшего приéзда; **he is very much a gentleman/politician** он настоящий джентльмéн/полúтик; **however much he tries** скóлько бы он ни старáлся; **I try to help**

as much as possible *or* **as much as I can** я старáюсь помогáть как мóжно бóльше *or* скóлько могý; **I read as much as ever** я читáю стóлько же, скóлько прéжде; **he is as much a member of the family as you** он такóй же член семьú, как и Вы
2 (*by far*) намнóго, горáздо; **I'm much better now** мне намнóго *or* горáздо лýчше; **it's much the biggest publishing company in Europe** это сáмое крýпное издáтельство в Еврóпе
3 (*almost*) почтú; **the view from my window today is much as it was 10 years ago** вид из моегó окнá сегóдня сейчáс почтú такóй же, как и 10 лет назáд; **how are you feeling? - much the same** как Вы себя чýвствуете? - всё тáк же.

---

muck [mʌk] *n* (*dirt*) грязь* *f*; (*manure*) навóз
► **muck about** *vi* (*inf*) валять (*impf*) дуракá; (*tinker*): **to ~ about with** возúться* (*impf*) с +*instr*
► **muck around** *vi* = **muck about**
► **muck in** *vi* (*inf*) впрягáться (впрячься* *perf*)
► **muck out** *vt* (*stable*) выгребáть (выгрести* *perf*) навóз из +*gen*
► **muck up** *vt* (*inf*) завáливать (завалúть* *perf*).
muckraking ['mʌkreɪkɪŋ] *n* (*fig: inf*) копáние в грязном бельé.
mucky ['mʌkɪ] *adj* грязный* (грязен).
mucus ['mju:kəs] *n* слизь *f*.
mud [mʌd] *n* грязь* *f*.
muddle ['mʌdl] *n* (*mess*) беспорядок*; (*mix-up*) неразберúха, пýтаница ♦ *vt* (*also*: ~ **up**: *person*) запýтывать (запýтать *perf*); (: *things*) перемéшивать (перемешáть *perf*); (: *story, names*) пýтать (перепýтать *perf*); **to get in(to) a ~** (*while explaining etc*) запýтываться (запýтаться *perf*); **I'm in a real ~** я совершéнно запýтался
► **muddle along** *vi* справляться (*impf*) кóе-как
► **muddle through** *vi* выкарáбкиваться (выкарабкаться *perf*).
muddleheaded [mʌdl'hɛdɪd] *adj* бестолкóвый (бестолкóв).
muddy ['mʌdɪ] *adj* грязный* (грязен).
mud flats *npl* úлистые учáстки *mpl* (*вскрывáющиеся во врéмя отлúва*).
mudguard ['mʌdgɑ:d] *n* (*on vehicle*) крылó*.
mudpack ['mʌdpæk] *n* грязевáя мáска*.
mudslinging ['mʌdslɪŋɪŋ] *n* (*fig*) поливáние грязью.
muesli ['mju:zlɪ] *n* смесь *f* овсяных хлóпьев и сухофрýктов.
muffin ['mʌfɪn] *n* (*BRIT*) (сдóбная) бýлочка; (*US*) кекс.
muffle ['mʌfl] *vt* (*sound*) приглушáть (приглушúть *perf*); (*against cold*: *also*: ~ **up**)

закýтывать (закýтать *perf*).
muffled ['mʌfld] *adj* (*see vb*) приглушённый (приглушён); (*also:* ~ **up**) закýтанный.
muffler ['mʌflə'] *n* (*US: AUT*) глушúтель *m*; (*scarf*) шарф.
mufti ['mʌftɪ] *n*: **in** ~ в штáтском.
mug [mʌg] *n* крýжка*; (*inf: face*) мóрда; (: *fool*) дурáк* (дýра) ♦ *vt* (*assault*) грáбить* (ограбить* *perf*) (*на ýлице*); **it's a ~'s game** (*BRIT: inf*) э́то никчёмное дéло
▶ **mug up** *vt* (*BRIT: inf: also:* ~ **up on**) зубрúть* (вы́зубрить *perf*).
mugger ['mʌgə'] *n* ýличный грабúтель *m*.
mugging ['mʌgɪŋ] *n* грабёж* (*на ýлице*).
muggins ['mʌgɪnz] *n* (*inf*) простáк*.
muggy ['mʌgɪ] *adj* дýшный* (дýшен).
mug shot *n* (*inf*) фотогрáфия подозревáемого в приступлéние.
mulatto [mju:'lætəu] (*pl* ~**es**) *n* мулáт(ка*).
mulberry ['mʌlbrɪ] *n* (*fruit*) тýтовая я́года; (*tree*) тýтовое дéрево*, шелковúца.
mule [mju:l] *n* (*ZOOL*) мул.
mulled wine [mʌld-] *n* глинтвéйн.
mullioned ['mʌlɪənd] *adj* (*ARCHIT*): ~ **window** окнó сп срéдником.
mull over [mʌl-] *vt* размышля́ть (*impf*) над +*instr*.
multi... [['mʌltɪ]] *prefix* мнóго..., мýльти....
multiaccess ['mʌltɪ'æksɛs] *adj* (*COMPUT*) многопóльзовательский*.
multicoloured ['mʌltɪkʌləd] (*US* **multicolored**) *adj* многоцвéтный* (многоцвéтен).
multifarious [mʌltɪ'fɛərɪəs] *adj* многообрáзный (многообрáзен).
multilateral [mʌltɪ'lætərl] *adj* многосторо́нний*.
multilevel ['mʌltɪlɛvl] *adj* (*US*) = **multistorey**.
multimillionaire [mʌltɪmɪljə'nɛə'] *n* мультимиллионéр.
multinational [mʌltɪ'næʃənl] *adj* междунарóдный ♦ *n* междунарóдная корпорáция.
multiple ['mʌltɪpl] *adj* (*injuries*) мнóго-чúсленный; (*interests*) разнообрáзный* (разнообрáзен) ♦ *n* (*MATH*) крáтное числó*; (*BRIT: also:* ~ **store**) филиáл сéти (*магазúнов*); ~ **collision** столкновéние нéскольких автомобúлей.
multiple-choice ['mʌltɪpltʃɔɪs] *adj*: ~ (**exam**) *тест на вы́бор, прáвильного отвéта из нéскольких предлóженных вариáнтов*.
multiple sclerosis *n* рассéянный склерóз.
multiplication [mʌltɪplɪ'keɪʃən] *n* умножéние.
multiplication table *n* таблúца умножéния.
multiplicity [mʌltɪ'plɪsɪtɪ] *n*: **a** ~ **of** мнóжество +*gen*.
multiply ['mʌltɪplaɪ] *vt* умножáть (умнóжить *perf*) ♦ *vi* размножáться (размнóжиться *perf*).
multiracial [mʌltɪ'reɪʃl] *adj* мнóго-национáльный* (многонационáлен).
multistorey ['mʌltɪ'stɔ:rɪ] *adj* (*BRIT*)

многоэтáжный.
multitude ['mʌltɪtju:d] *n* (*crowd*) мáссы *fpl*; (*large number*): **a** ~ **of** мнóжество +*gen*.
mum [mʌm] (*BRIT: inf*) *n* мáма ♦ *adj*: **to keep** ~ **about sth** помáлкивать (*impf*) о чём-н; **"mum's the word!"** „молчý!".
mumble ['mʌmbl] *vt* бормотáть* (пробормотáть* *perf*) ♦ *vi* бормотáть (*impf*).
mumbo jumbo ['mʌmbəu-] *n* (*inf*) тарабáрщина.
mummify ['mʌmɪfaɪ] *vt* мумифицúровать (*impf/perf*).
mummy ['mʌmɪ] *n* (*BRIT: inf: mother*) мáма; (*embalmed corpse*) мýмия.
mumps [mʌmps] *n* свúнка.
munch [mʌntʃ] *vti* (*chew*) жевáть (*impf*).
mundane [mʌn'deɪn] *adj* обы́денный (обы́ден).
Munich ['mju:nɪk] *n* Мю́нхен.
municipal [mju:'nɪsɪpl] *adj* муниципáльный.
municipality [mju:nɪsɪ'pælɪtɪ] *n* гóрод*; (*authority*) муниципалитéт.
munitions [mju:'nɪʃənz] *npl* боеприпáсы *mpl*.
mural ['mjuərl] *n* настéнная рóспись *f*, фрéска.
murder ['mə:də'] *n* убúйство (*умы́шленное*) ♦ *vt* (*kill*) убивáть (убúть* *perf*) (*умы́шленно*); (*fig: inf*) угрóбить* (*perf*); **to commit** ~ совершúть (совершúть *perf*) убúйство.
murderer ['mə:dərə'] *n* убúйца *m/f*.
murderess ['mə:dərɪs] *n* убúйца *m/f*.
murderous ['mə:dərəs] *adj* (*dictator, regime*) кровáвый; (*look*) убúйственный; (*attack*) смертонóсный* (смертонóсен); ~ **tendencies** склóнность *f* к убúйству.
murk [mə:k] *n* мгла.
murky ['mə:kɪ] *adj* (*street, night*) мрáчный* (мрáчен); (*water*) мýтный* (мýтен).
murmur ['mə:mə'] *n* (*of voices, waves*) рóпот; (*of wind*) шéлест ♦ *vti* шептáть* (*impf*); **heart** ~ шумы́ *mpl* в сéрдце.
MusB(ac) *n abbr* (= *Bachelor of Music*) бакалáвр музыковéдения.
muscle ['mʌsl] *n* (*ANAT*) мы́шца, мýскул; (*fig: strength*) сúла.
▶ **muscle in** *vi* пролезáть (пролéзть* *perf*).
Muscovite ['mʌskəvaɪt] *n* москвúч*(ка*).
muscular ['mʌskjulə'] *adj* (*pain, injury*) мы́шечный; (*person, build*) мýскулистый (мýскулист).
muscular dystrophy *adj* мýскульная дистрофúя.
MusD(oc) *n abbr* (= *Doctor of Music*) дóктор музыковéдения.
muse [mju:z] *vi* размышля́ть (*impf*) ♦ *n* мýза.
museum [mju:'zɪəm] *n* музéй.
mush [mʌʃ] *n* мéсиво; (*pej*) мáсса.
mushroom ['mʌʃrum] *n* гриб* ♦ *vi* (*fig*) бы́стро разрастáться (разрастúсь* *perf*).
mushroom cloud *n* áтомный гриб*.
mushy ['mʌʃɪ] *adj* разварúвшийся, как кáша; (*inf. pej: story, fiction*) слащáвый (слащáв); ~

music ~ mysteriously

peas горо́шек.

music ['mju:zɪk] *n* му́зыка; **sheet** ~ но́ты *fpl*.

musical ['mju:zɪkl] *adj* (*career, skills*) музыка́льный; (*person*) музыка́льный* (музыка́лен); (*sound, tune*) мелоди́чный* (мелоди́чен) ◆ *n* (*show, film*) мю́зикл.

music(al) box *n* музыка́льная шкату́лка*.

musical chairs *n* ≈ тре́тий* ли́шний* *m adj* (игра́).

musical instrument *n* музыка́льный инструме́нт.

music centre *n* де́ка с прои́грывателем и магнитофо́ном.

music hall *n* (*BRIT*: *vaudeville*) мю́зик-холл.

musician [mju:'zɪʃən] *n* музыка́нт.

music stand *n* пюпи́тр.

musk [mʌsk] *n* му́скус.

musket ['mʌskɪt] *n* мушке́т.

muskrat ['mʌskræt] *n* онда́тра.

musk rose *n* му́скусная ро́за.

Muslim ['mʌzlɪm] *n* мусульма́нин*(-нка*) ◆ *adj* мусульма́нский*.

muslin ['mʌzlɪn] *n* ма́рля.

musquash ['mʌskwɔʃ] *n* = **muskrat**.

mussel ['mʌsl] *n* ми́дия.

must [mʌst] *n* (*necessity*) необходи́мость *f* ◆ *aux vb* (*necessity*): **I** ~ **do it** я до́лжен э́то сде́лать; (*probability*): **he** ~ **be there by now** он до́лжен уже́ там быть; **it's (simply) a** ~ э́то про́сто необходи́мость; **you** ~ **come and see me soon** Вы обяза́тельно должны́ ско́ро ко мне зайти́; **why** ~ **he behave so badly?** отчего́ он так пло́хо себя́ ведёт?; **I** ~ **have made a mistake** я, должно́ быть, оши́бся.

mustache ['mʌstæʃ] *n* (*US*) = **moustache**.

mustard ['mʌstəd] *n* горчи́ца.

mustard gas *n* ипри́т, горчи́чный газ.

muster ['mʌstə'] *vt* (*support, energy*) собира́ть (собра́ть* *perf*); (*troops*) набира́ть (набра́ть* *perf*); (*also*: ~ **up**: *strength, courage*) набира́ться (набра́ться* *perf*) +*gen*.

mustiness ['mʌstɪnɪs] *n* за́тхлость *f*.

mustn't ['mʌsnt] = **must not**.

musty ['mʌstɪ] *adj* (*smell*) за́тхлый (за́тхл).

mutant ['mju:tənt] *n* мута́нт.

mutate [mju:'teɪt] *vi* (*BIO*) мути́ровать (*impf*).

mutation [mju:'teɪʃən] *n* (*BIO*) мута́ция; (*change*) преобразова́ние *ntpl*.

mute [mju:t] *adj* (*silent*) безмо́лвный* (безмо́лвен) ◆ *n* (*MUS*) сурди́нка.

muted ['mju:tɪd] *adj* (*reaction, criticism*) сде́ржанный* (сде́ржан); (*colour, noise*) приглушённый (приглушён); ~ **strings** стру́ны под сурди́нкой.

mutilate ['mju:tɪleɪt] *vt* (*person*) уве́чить (изуве́чить *perf*); (*thing*) уро́довать (изуро́довать *perf*).

mutilation [mju:tɪ'leɪʃən] *n* (*injury*) уве́чье*;

(*maiming*) нанесе́ние уве́чья.

mutinous ['mju:tɪnəs] *adj* (*troops, attitude*) мяте́жный*.

mutiny ['mju:tɪnɪ] *n* мяте́ж*, бунт ◆ *vi* бунтова́ть (*impf*).

mutter ['mʌtə'] *vti* бормота́ть* (*impf*).

mutton ['mʌtn] *n* бара́нина.

mutual ['mju:tʃuəl] *adj* (*feeling*) взаи́мный* (взаи́мен); (*help*) взаи́мный; (*friend, interest*) о́бщий*; ~ **understanding** взаимо-понима́ние; ~ **aid** взаимопо́мощь *f*.

mutually ['mju:tʃuəlɪ] *adv* взаи́мно; ~ **beneficial** взаимовы́годный* (взаимовы́годен).

Muzak® ['mju:zæk] *n* бессодержа́тельная лёгкая му́зыка, испо́льзуемая в магази́нах и рестора́нах как фон.

muzzle ['mʌzl] *n* (*mouth: of dog*) мо́рда; (: *of gun*) ду́ло; (*guard: for dog*) намо́рдник ◆ *vt* (*dog*) надева́ть (наде́ть* *perf*) намо́рдник на +*acc*; (*fig: press, person*) затыка́ть (заткну́ть *perf*) рот +*dat*.

MV *n abbr* = **motor vessel**.

MVP *n abbr* (*US*: *SPORT*: = **most valuable player**) са́мый це́нный игро́к.

MW *abbr* (*RADIO*) (= **medium wave**) СВ= сре́дние во́лны.

━━━━━━━━━━━━━━━━━━━━━━
KEYWORD
━━━━━━━━━━━━━━━━━━━━━━

my [maɪ] *adj* **1** (*with objects, possessions*) мой; **this is my house/car** э́то мой дом/моя́ маши́на; **is this my pen or yours?** э́то моя́ ру́чка и́ли ва́ша?

2 (*with parts of the body etc*): **I've washed my hair/cut my finger** я помы́л го́лову/поре́зал па́лец

3 (*referring to subject of sentence*) свой; **I've lost my key** я потеря́л свой ключ.

myopic [maɪ'ɔpɪk] *adj* (*also fig*) близору́кий* (близору́к).

myriad ['mɪrɪəd] *n* мириа́ды *mpl*.

myrrh [mə:'] *n* ми́рра.

━━━━━━━━━━━━━━━━━━━━━━
KEYWORD
━━━━━━━━━━━━━━━━━━━━━━

myself [maɪ'sɛlf] *pron* **1** (*reflexive*): **I've hurt myself** я уши́бся; **I consider myself clever** я счита́ю себя́ у́мным

2 (*complement*): **she's the same age as myself** она́ одного́ во́зраста со мной

3 (*after prep: +gen*) себя́; (: +*dat, +prp*) себе́; (: +*instr*) собо́й; **I wanted to keep the book for myself** я хоте́л оста́вить кни́гу для себя́; **I sometimes talk to myself** иногда́ я сам с собо́й разгова́риваю; **(all) by myself** (*alone*) сам; **I made it all by myself** я всё э́то сде́лал сам; **I myself chose the flowers** я сам выбира́л цветы́.

━━━━━━━━━━━━━━━━━━━━━━

mysterious [mɪs'tɪərɪəs] *adj* таи́нственный* (таи́нствен).

mysteriously [mɪs'tɪərɪəslɪ] *adv* (*disappear, die*)

━━━━━━━━━━━━━━━━━━━━━━

* marks translations which have irregular inflections. The Russian-English side of the dictionary gives inflectional information.

тайнственно; (*smile*) зага́дочно.
mystery ['mɪstərɪ] *n* (*strangeness*) та́йна;
(*puzzle*) зага́дка* ♦ *cpd* (*tour, guest, voice*)
зага́дочный.
mystery story *n* детекти́в.
mystic ['mɪstɪk] *n* ми́стик ♦ *adj* мисти́ческий.
mystical ['mɪstɪkl] *adj* = mystic.
mystify ['mɪstɪfaɪ] *vt* (*perplex*) озада́чивать

(озада́чить *perf*).
mystique [mɪs'tiːk] *n* ми́стика.
myth [mɪθ] *n* миф.
mythical ['mɪθɪkl] *adj* (*also fig*) мифи́ческий*.
mythological [mɪθə'lɔdʒɪkl] *adj*
мифологи́ческий.
mythology [mɪ'θɔlədʒɪ] *n* мифоло́гия.

~ *N, n* ~

N, n [ɛn] *n* (*letter*) 14-ая бу́ква англи́йского алфави́та.

N *abbr* (= **north**) C= *се́вер*.

NA *n abbr* (*US*: = *Narcotics Anonymous*) о́бщество анони́много излече́ния от наркома́нии; = *National Academy*.

n/a *abbr* (= *not applicable*) не применя́ется; (*COMM etc*: = *no account*) счёт отсу́тствует.

NAACP *n abbr* (*US*) = *National Association for the Advancement of Colored People*.

NAAFI ['næfɪ] *n abbr* (*BRIT*: = *Navy, Army & Air Force Institute*) Институ́т а́рмии, вое́нно-морско́го и вое́нно-возду́шного фло́та.

NACU *n abbr* (*US*) = *National Association of Colleges and Universities*.

nadir ['neɪdɪəʳ] *n* (*ASTRONOMY*) нади́р; (*fig*) ни́зшая то́чка.

nag [næg] *vt* (*scold*) пили́ть* (*impf*) ♦ *vi*: **to ~ at** ныть (*impf*) (из-за +*gen*) ♦ *n* (*pej: horse*) кля́ча; (*: person*): **she's an awful ~** она́ жу́ткая зану́да.

nagging ['nægɪŋ] *adj* (*pain*) но́ющий; (*suspicion, doubt*) неотвя́зный.

nail [neɪl] *n* (*on finger etc*) но́готь* *m*; (*metal*) гвоздь* *m* ♦ *vt* (*inf: catch*) засту́кивать (засту́кать *perf*); **to ~ sth to sth** прибива́ть (приби́ть* *perf*) что-н к чему́-н; **to ~ sb down to doing** (*inf*) прижима́ть (прижа́ть* *perf*) кого́-н к сте́нке и заста́вить +*infin*.

nailbrush ['neɪlbrʌʃ] *n* щёточка* для ногте́й.

nailfile ['neɪlfaɪl] *n* пи́лка* (*для ногте́й*).

nail polish *n* лак для ногте́й.

nail polish remover *n* жи́дкость *f* для сня́тия ла́ка.

nail scissors *npl* маникю́рные но́жницы *pl*.

nail varnish *n* (*BRIT*) = **nail polish**.

Nairobi [naɪˈrəubɪ] *n* Найро́би *m ind*.

naive [naɪˈiːv] *adj* наи́вный* (наи́вен).

naiveté [naɪˈiːvteɪ] *n* = **naivety**.

naivety [naɪˈiːvteɪ] *n* наи́вность *f*.

naked ['neɪkɪd] *adj* (*also fig*) го́лый* (гол); (*anger*) не скрыва́емый; **with the ~ eye** невооружённым гла́зом.

nakedness ['neɪkɪdnɪs] *n* нагота́.

NAM *n abbr* (*US*) = *National Association of Manufacturers*.

name [neɪm] *n* (*of person*) и́мя* *nt*; (*of place, object, species*) назва́ние; (*of pet*) кли́чка* ♦ *vt* называ́ть (назва́ть* *perf*); **what's your ~?** как Вас зову́т?; **my ~ is Peter** меня́ зову́т Пи́тер; **what's the ~ of this place?** как называ́ется э́то ме́сто?; **by ~** по и́мени; **in the ~ of** во и́мя +*gen*; **to give one's ~ and address** (*to police etc*) дава́ть* (дать* *perf*) своё и́мя и а́дрес; **to make a ~ for o.s.** создава́ть* (созда́ть* *perf*) себе́ и́мя; **to get (o.s.) a bad ~** зараба́тывать (зарабо́тать (*perf*)) себе́ дурну́ю репута́цию; **to call sb ~s** обзыва́ть (обозва́ть* *perf*) кого́-н.

name-dropping ['neɪmdrɔpɪŋ] *n* упомина́ние изве́стных имён.

nameless ['neɪmlɪs] *adj* (*unknown*) безымя́нный* (безымя́нен); (*anonymous*) неизве́стный* (неизве́стен).

namely ['neɪmlɪ] *adv* а и́менно.

nameplate ['neɪmpleɪt] *n* табли́чка* (с и́менем).

namesake ['neɪmseɪk] *n* тёзка* *m/f*.

Namibia [nəˈmɪbɪə] *n* Нами́бия.

nan bread [nɑːn-] *n* инди́йский* хлеб в фо́рме лепёшки.

nanny ['nænɪ] *n* ня́ня.

nanny goat *n* коза́.

nap [næp] *n* коро́ткий* сон; (*of fabric*) ворс ♦ *vi*: **he was caught ~ping** (*fig*) его́ заста́ли враспло́х; **to have** *or* **take a ~** вздремну́ть (*perf*).

NAPA *n abbr* (*US*) = *National Association of Performing Artists*.

napalm ['neɪpɑːm] *n* напа́лм.

nape [neɪp] *n*: **~ of the neck** за́дняя часть *f* ше́и.

napkin ['næpkɪn] *n* (*also: table ~*) салфе́тка*.

Naples ['neɪplz] *n* Неа́поль *m*.

Napoleonic [nəpəulɪˈɔnɪk] *adj* наполео́новский.

nappy ['næpɪ] *n* (*BRIT*) подгу́зник.

nappy liner *n* (*BRIT*) прокла́дка для подгу́зника.

nappy rash *n* (*BRIT*) потни́ца.

narcissi [nɑːˈsɪsaɪ] *npl of* **narcissus**.

narcissistic [nɑːsɪˈsɪstɪk] *adj* самовлюблённый.

---

* marks translations which have irregular inflections. The Russian-English side of the dictionary gives inflectional information.

narcissus [nɑ:'sɪsəs] (*pl* **narcissi**) *n* (*BOT*) нарци́сс.

narcotic [nɑ:'kɔtɪk] *adj* наркоти́ческий ◆ *n* (*MED*) снотво́рное *nt adj*; **~s** *npl* (*drugs*) нарко́тики *mpl*.

nark [nɑ:k] *vt* (*BRIT: inf*) раздража́ть (раздражи́ть *perf*).

narrate [nə'reɪt] *vt* (*story, novel*) расска́зывать (рассказа́ть* *perf*); **to ~ a film/programme** чита́ть (*impf*) текст фи́льма/переда́чи.

narration [nə'reɪʃən] *n* повествова́ние.

narrative ['nærətɪv] *n* исто́рия.

narrator [nə'reɪtə'] *n* (*in book*) расска́зчик(-ица); (*in film*) ди́ктор.

narrow ['nærəu] *adj* (*also fig*) у́зкий* (у́зок); (*majority, advantage*) незначи́тельный* (незначи́телен) ◆ *vi* (*road*) сужа́ться (су́зиться* *perf*); (*gap, difference*) уменьша́ться (уме́ньшиться *perf*) ◆ *vt*: **to ~ sth down to** своди́ть* (свести́* *perf*) что-н к +*dat*; **to have a ~ escape** едва́ спасти́сь* (*perf*).

narrow-gauge ['nærəugeuɪdʒ] *adj* (*RAIL*) узкоколе́йный.

narrowly ['nærəulɪ] *adv* (*miss*) чуть не; (*interpret*) у́зко; **he only ~ avoided injury/ defeat** он чуть не покале́чился/проигра́л; **he only ~ missed the target** он почти́ попа́л в цель.

narrow-minded [nærəu'maɪndɪd] *adj* ограни́ченный (ограни́чен).

narrowness ['nærəunɪs] *n* у́зость *f*.

NAS *n abbr* (*US*) = *National Academy of Sciences*.

NASA ['næsə] *n abbr* (*US*: = *National Aeronautics and Space Administration*) НАСА.

nasal ['neɪzl] *adj* (*ANAT*) носово́й; (*tone, voice*) гнуса́вый.

Nassau ['næsɔ:] *n* Нассау *m ind*.

nastily ['nɑ:stɪlɪ] *adv* зло́бно.

nastiness ['nɑ:stɪnɪs] *n* (*unpleasantness*) проти́вность *f*; (*spitefulness*) зло́бность *f*.

nasturtium [nəs'tə:ʃəm] *n* насту́рция.

nasty ['nɑ:stɪ] *adj* (*unpleasant*) проти́вный* (проти́вен); (*malicious*) зло́бный* (зло́бен); (*situation, wound*) скве́рный* (скве́рен); **to say ~ things about sb** говори́ть (*impf*) га́дости о ком-н; **to turn ~** (*situation*) принима́ть (приня́ть* *perf*) скве́рный оборо́т; (*weather*) де́латься (сде́латься *perf*) скве́рным; (*person*) озлобля́ться (озло́биться* *perf*); **it's a ~ business** э́то ме́рзкое де́ло.

NAS/UWT *n abbr* (*BRIT*) = *National Association of Schoolmasters/Union of Women Teachers*.

nation ['neɪʃən] *n* (*POL*) на́ция; (*people*) наро́д; (*state*) страна́, госуда́рство.

national ['næʃənl] *adj* национа́льный ◆ *n* граждани́н*(-да́нка*).

national anthem *n* госуда́рственный гимн.

national curriculum *n* (*BRIT*) всео́бщая програ́мма (обуче́ния) (*в шко́лах*).

national debt *n* госуда́рственный долг*.

national dress *n* национа́льная оде́жда.

National Guard *n* (*US*) Национа́льная гва́рдия.

National Health Service *n* (*BRIT*) Госуда́рственная слу́жба здравоохране́ния.

National Insurance *n* (*BRIT*) госуда́рственное страхова́ние.

nationalism ['næʃnəlɪzəm] *n* национали́зм.

nationalist ['næʃnəlɪst] *adj* националисти́ческий ◆ *n* националист(ка*).

nationality [næʃə'nælɪtɪ] *n* (*status*) гражда́нство; (*ethnic group*) наро́дность *f*.

nationalization [næʃnəlaɪ'zeɪʃən] *n* национализа́ция.

nationalize ['næʃnəlaɪz] *vt* национализи́ровать (*impf/perf*).

nationalized industry ['næʃnəlaɪzd-] *n* национализи́рованная промы́шленность *f*.

nationally ['næʃnəlɪ] *adv* (*nationwide*) в национа́льном всей страны́.

national park *n* национа́льный па́рк.

national press *n* национа́льная пре́сса.

National Security Council *n* (*US*) Сове́т национа́льной безопа́сности.

national service *n* (*MIL: esp BRIT*) во́инская пови́нность *f*.

National Trust *n* (*BRIT*) *организа́ция, занима́ющаяся охра́ной архитекту́рных па́мятников и приро́дных запове́дников*.

nationwide ['neɪʃənwaɪd] *adj* общенаро́дный ◆ *adv* по всей стране́.

native ['neɪtɪv] *n* (*local inhabitant*) ме́стный(-ая) жи́тель(ница) *m(f)* ◆ *adj* (*indigenous*) коренно́й, исконный; (*of one's birth*) родно́й; (*innate*) врождённый; **a ~ of Russia** уроже́нец(-нка*) Росси́и; **a ~ speaker of Russian** носи́тель(ница) *m(f)* ру́сского языка́.

Native American *n* *пото́мок коренно́го населе́ния Се́веро-Америка́нского контине́нта*.

native language *n* родно́й язы́к*.

Nativity [nə'tɪvɪtɪ] *n*: **the ~** Рождество́ Христо́во.

nativity play *n* Рождественская мисте́рия (*обы́чно разы́грываемая детьми́*).

NATO ['neɪtəu] *n abbr* (= *North Atlantic Treaty Organization*) НАТО.

natter ['nætə'] (*BRIT*) *vi* трепа́ться* (*impf*) ◆ *n*: **to have a ~** трепа́ться* (потрепа́ться* *perf*).

natural ['nætʃrəl] *adj* (*behaviour*) есте́ственный (есте́ствен); (*aptitude, materials*) приро́дный; (*foods*) натура́льный; (*disaster*) стихи́йный; **to die of ~ causes** умира́ть (умере́ть* *perf*) есте́ственной сме́ртью.

natural childbirth *n* есте́ственные ро́ды *pl*.

natural gas *n* приро́дный газ.

natural history *n* естествозна́ние.

naturalist ['nætʃrəlɪst] *n* натурали́ст.

naturalize ['nætʃrəlaɪz] *vt*: **to become ~d** (*person*) получа́ть (получи́ть* *perf*) гражда́нство; (*plant*) акклиматизи́роваться *(impf/perf).*

naturally ['nætʃrəlɪ] *adv* естéственно; (*innately*) от прирóды; (*in nature*) в прирóде; ~, **I refused** естéственно, я отказáлся.

naturalness ['nætʃrəlnɪs] *n* естéственность *f*.

natural resources *npl* прирóдные ресýрсы *mpl*.

natural selection *n* (*BIO*) естéственный отбóр.

natural wastage *n* (*INDUSTRY*) естéственная ýбыль* *f* (*рабóчей сѝлы*).

nature ['neɪtʃə'] *n* (*also*: **N~**) прирóда; (*character*) натýра; (*sort*) харáктер; **by** ~ (*person*) по натýре; (*event, thing*) по прирóде; **documents of a confidential** ~ докумéнты конфиденциáльного харáктера.

-natured ['neɪtʃəd] *suffix*: **ill-~** злóбный по натýре.

nature reserve *n* (*BRIT*) заповéдник.

nature trail *n размéченная трóпа, проходящая чéрез сéльскую мéстность, заповéдник итп.*

naturist ['neɪtʃərɪst] *n* нудѝст(ка*).

naught [nɔːt] *n* = **nought.**

naughtiness ['nɔːtɪnɪs] *n* (*see adj*) непослушáние, озорствó; пикáнтность *f*.

naughty ['nɔːtɪ] *adj* (*child*) непослýшный* (непослýшен), озорнóй; (*story, film*) пикáнтный* (пикáнтен).

nausea ['nɔːsɪə] *n* тошнотá.

nauseate ['nɔːsɪeɪt] *vt* (*also fig*) вызывáть (вызвать* *perf*) тошнотý в +*prp* or у +*gen*.

nauseating ['nɔːsɪeɪtɪŋ] *adj* (*also fig*) тошнотвóрный* (тошнотвóрен).

nauseous ['nɔːsɪəs] *adj* тошнотвóрный* (тошнотвóрен); **he's feeling** ~ егó тошнѝт.

nautical ['nɔːtɪkl] *adj* морскóй.

naval ['neɪvl] *adj* воéнно-морскóй; (*battle, power*) морскóй.

naval officer *n* морскóй офицéр.

nave [neɪv] *n* неф.

navel ['neɪvl] *n* пупóк*.

navigable ['nævɪɡəbl] *adj* судохóдный* (судохóден).

navigate ['nævɪɡeɪt] *vt* (*NAUT, AVIAT*) управлять (*impf*) +*instr* ♦ *vi* определять (определѝть* *perf*) маршрýт; **to** ~ **a ship through/around** вестѝ* (провестѝ* *perf*) корáбль чéрез +*acc*/вокрýг +*gen.*

navigation [nævɪˈɡeɪʃən] *n* (*science*) навигáция; (*action*): ~ (**of**) управлéние (+*instr*).

navigator ['nævɪɡeɪtə'] *n* штýрман.

navvy ['nævɪ] *n* (*BRIT*) чернорабóчий* *m adj.*

navy ['neɪvɪ] *n* воéнно-морскóй флот; **Department of the N~** (*US*) ≈ Министéрство воéнно-морскóго флóта.

navy(-blue) ['neɪvɪ('bluː)] *adj* тёмно-сѝний*.

Nazareth ['næzərɪθ] *n* Назарéт.

Nazi ['nɑːtsɪ] *n* нацѝст(ка*).

NB *abbr* = *nota bene*; (*note well*) NB, нотабéне; (*CANADA*) = New Brunswick.

NBA *n abbr* (*US*) = National Basketball Association; National Boxing Association.

NBC *n abbr* (*US*) = National Broadcasting Company.

NBS *n abbr* (*US*) = National Bureau of Standards.

NC *abbr* (*COMM etc*: = *no charge*) беспláтно; (*US*: *POST*) = North Carolina.

NCC *n abbr* (*BRIT*) = Nature Conservancy Council; (*US*) National Council of Churches.

NCCL *n abbr* (*BRIT*: = National Council for Civil Liberties*) Национáльный совéт по граждáнским правáм.

NCO *n abbr* (*MIL*) = **noncommissioned officer.**

ND *abbr* (*US*: *POST*) = North Dakota.

NE *abbr* (*US*: *POST*) = New England; Nebraska.

NEA *n abbr* (*US*) = National Education Association.

neap [niːp] *n* (*also*: ~ **tide**) квадратýрный прилѝв.

Neapolitan [nɪəˈpɒlɪtən] *adj* неаполитáнский* ♦ *n* неаполитáнец(-нка*).

near [nɪə'] *adj* блѝзкий* (блѝзок) ♦ *adv* блѝзко ♦ *prep* (*also*: ~ **to**: *space*) вóзле +*gen*, óколо +*gen*; (: *time*) к +*dat*, óколо +*gen* ♦ *vt* приближáться (приблѝзиться* *perf*) к +*dat*; ~ **here/there** недалекó отсюда/оттýда; **£25,000 or ~est offer** (*BRIT*) ценá £25.000 йли по договорённости; **in the** ~ **future** в ближáйшем бýдущем; ~**er (to) the time** óколо положéнной дáты; **to come** ~ (**to**) (*also fig*) приближáться (приблѝзиться* *perf*) (к +*dat*); **he was** ~ **to despair/victory** он был блѝзок к отчáянию/побéде; **the building is** ~**ing completion** строѝтельство приближáется к завершéнию.

nearby [nɪəˈbaɪ] *adj* близлежáщий ♦ *adv* поблѝзости.

Near East *n*: **the** ~ ~ Блѝжний* Востóк.

nearer ['nɪərə'] *adj*, *adv* блѝже.

nearly ['nɪəlɪ] *adv* почтѝ; **I** ~ **fell** я чуть (бѝло) не упáл; **she was** ~ **crying** онá почтѝ плáкала; **it's not** ~ **as easy as it looks** это отнюдь не так прóсто, как кáжется; **the house is not** ~ **big enough** дом совсéм мал.

near miss *n* (*failed attempt*): **that was a** ~ ~! промахнýлся!; **we had a** ~ ~ **in the car today** мы сегóдня чуть не попáли в авáрию.

nearness ['nɪənɪs] *n* блѝзость *f*.

nearside ['nɪəsaɪd] *n* (*AUT*: *in Britain*) лéвая сторонá; (: *in US, Europe etc*) прáвая сторонá.

near-sighted [nɪəˈsaɪtɪd] *adj* близорýкий* (близорýк).

neat [niːt] *adj* (*person, place*) опрятный* (опрятен); (*work*) аккурáтный* (аккурáтен);

(*clear. categories*) чёткий* (чёток); (*esp US: inf*) кла́ссный* (кла́ссен); (*alcohol*) неразба́вленный.

neatly ['ni:tlɪ] *adv* (*dress*) опря́тно; (*work*) аккура́тно; (*sum up*) чётко.

neatness ['ni:tnɪs] *n* (*see adv*) опря́тность *f*; аккура́тность *f*; чёткость *f*.

nebulous ['nɛbjuləs] *adj* (*concept, proposal*) тума́нный* (тума́нен).

necessarily ['nɛsɪsrɪlɪ] *adv* неизбе́жно; **not** ~ не обяза́тельно.

necessary ['nɛsɪsrɪ] *adj* необходи́мый (необходи́м); (*inevitable*) обяза́тельный, неизбе́жный; **if** ~ е́сли необходи́мо; **it's not** ~ э́то не обяза́тельно; **it is** ~ **to/that** ... необходи́мо +*infin*/что́бы ....

necessitate [nɪ'sɛsɪteɪt] *vt* обусло́вливать (обусло́вить* *perf*).

necessity [nɪ'sɛsɪtɪ] *n* необходи́мость *f*; **necessities** *npl* (*essentials*) предме́ты *mpl* пе́рвой необходи́мости; **in case of** ~ в слу́чае необходи́мости.

neck [nɛk] *n* (*ANAT*) ше́я; (*of garment*) во́рот; (*of bottle*) го́рлышко* ◆ *vi* (*inf*) милова́ться (*impf*); ~ **and** ~ вро́вень; **to stick one's** ~ **out** (*inf*) лезть* (*impf*) на рожо́н; **to risk one's** ~ (*inf*) рискова́ть (рискну́ть *perf*) голово́й.

necklace ['nɛklɪs] *n* ожере́лье.

neckline ['nɛklaɪn] *n* вы́рез.

necktie ['nɛktaɪ] *n* (*US*) га́лстук.

nectar ['nɛktə*] *n* некта́р.

nectarine ['nɛktərɪn] *n* нектари́н.

NEDC *n abbr* (*BRIT*: = *National Economic Development Council*) Национа́льный сове́т экономи́ческого разви́тия.

Neddy ['nɛdɪ] *n abbr* (*BRIT*: *inf*) = **NEDC.**

née [neɪ] *adj*: ~ **Scott** урождённая Скотт.

need [ni:d] *n* (*thing needed*) потре́бность *f*; (*deprivation*) нужда́; (*necessity*): ~ (**for**) нужда́ (в +*prp*) ◆ *vt*: **I** ~ **time/money** мне ну́жно вре́мя/нужны́ де́ньги; **there's no** ~ **to worry** неза́чем волнова́ться; **to be in** ~ **of, have** ~ **of** нужда́ться (*impf*) в +*prp*; **in case of** ~ в слу́чае необходи́мости; **the** ~**s of industry** потре́бности промы́шленности; **£10 will meet my immediate** ~**s** £10 удовлетворя́т мои́ ну́жды на да́нный моме́нт; **I** ~ **to see him** мне на́до *or* ну́жно с ним уви́деться; **you don't** ~ **to leave yet** Вам ещё не пора́ идти́; **a signature is** ~**ed** тре́буется по́дпись.

needle ['ni:dl] *n* игла́, иго́лка*; (*for knitting*) спи́ца ◆ *vt* (*fig: inf*) подка́лывать (подколо́ть *perf*).

needlecord ['ni:dlkɔ:d] *n* (*BRIT*) то́нкий* вельве́т.

needless ['ni:dlɪs] *adj* изли́шний* (изли́шен); ~ **to say** само́ собо́й разуме́ется.

needlessly ['ni:dlɪslɪ] *adv* напра́сно.

needlework ['ni:dlwə:k] *n* рукоде́лие.

needn't ['ni:dnt] = **need not;** *see* **need.**

needy ['ni:dɪ] *adj* нужда́ющийся; **the** ~ *npl*

нужда́ющиеся *pl adj*.

negation [nɪ'geɪʃ/ən] *n* отрица́ние.

negative ['nɛɡətɪv] *adj* (*also ELEC*) отрица́тельный ◆ *n* (*LING*) отрица́ние; (*PHOT*) негати́в; **to answer in the** ~ дава́ть* (дать* *perf*) отрица́тельный отве́т.

negative cash flow *n* отрица́тельный пото́к нали́чности.

negative equity *n* (*COMM*) отрица́тельная *or* негати́вная ма́ржа.

neglect [nɪ'glɛkt] *vt* (*child, work*) забра́сывать (забро́сить* *perf*); (*garden, area, health*) запуска́ть (запусти́ть* *perf*); (*duty*) пренебрега́ть (пренебре́чь* *perf*) ◆ *n*: ~ (**of**) невнима́ние (к +*dat*); (*duty*) пренебреже́ние (+*instr*); **in a state of** ~ в запусте́нии.

neglected [nɪ'glɛktɪd] *adj* (*animal, child*) забро́шенный (забро́шен).

neglectful [nɪ'glɛktful] *adj* небре́жный* (небре́жен); **to be** ~ **of sb** невнима́тельно* относи́ться* к кому́-н без внима́ния; **to be** ~ **of sth** пренебрега́ть (пренебре́чь* *perf*) чем-н.

negligee ['nɛglɪʒeɪ] *n* пеньюа́р.

negligence ['nɛglɪdʒəns] *n* хала́тность *f*.

negligent ['nɛglɪdʒənt] *adj* хала́тный* (хала́тен); **to be** ~ **in** хала́тно относи́ться* (*impf*) к +*dat*.

negligently ['nɛglɪdʒəntlɪ] *adv* (*irresponsibly*) хала́тно; (*offhandedly*) небре́жно.

negligible ['nɛglɪdʒɪbl] *adj* ничто́жный* (ничто́жен).

negotiable [nɪ'gəuʃɪəbl] *adj*: **the price/contract is** ~ це́ну/контра́кт мо́жно обсуди́ть; (*road*) проходи́мый (проходи́м); (*cheque, assets*): ~/**not negotiable** с пра́вом/без пра́ва переда́чи.

negotiate [nɪ'gəuʃɪeɪt] *vt* (*treaty, transaction*) заключа́ть (заключи́ть* *perf*); (*obstacle*) преодолева́ть (преодоле́ть* *perf*); (*bend in road*) огиба́ть (обогну́ть* *perf*) ◆ *vi*: **to** ~ (**with sb for sth**) вести́* (*impf*) перегово́ры (с кем-н о чём-н).

negotiating table [nɪ'gəuʃɪeɪtɪŋ-] *n* стол* перегово́ров.

negotiation [nɪgəuʃɪ'eɪʃən] *n* (*see vb*) заключе́ние; преодоле́ние; перегово́ры *mpl*; **to enter into** ~**s with sb** вступа́ть (вступи́ть* *perf*) в перегово́ры с кем-н.

negotiator [nɪ'gəuʃɪeɪtə*] *n* уча́стник перегово́ров.

Negress ['ni:grɪs] *n* негритя́нка*.

Negro ['ni:grəu] (*pl* ~**es**) *adj* негритя́нский* ◆ *n* (*old-fashioned*) негр(итя́нка*); (*pej*) чёрный(-ая) *m(f) adj*.

neigh [neɪ] *vi* ржать* (*impf*).

neighbor *etc* (*US*) = **neighbour** *etc.*

neighbour ['neɪbə*] (*US* **neighbor**) *n* сосе́д*(ка*).

neighbourhood ['neɪbəhud] *n* (*place*) райо́н; (*people*) сосе́ди *mpl*.

neighbourhood watch *n систе́ма, при кото́рой сосе́ди догова́риваются смотре́ть*

за домáми друг друга.
neighbouring ['neɪbərɪŋ] *adj* сосéдний*.
neighbourly ['neɪbəlɪ] *adj* добрососéдский.
neither ['naɪðə] *adj* ни тот, ни другóй ♦ *conj*: **I didn't move and ~ did John** ни я, ни Джон не двúнулись с мéста ♦ *pron*: **~ of them came** ни одúн из них не пришёл, ни тот, ни другóй не пришлú; **~ version is true** ни та, ни другáя вéрсия не вернá; **~ ... nor ...** ни ..., ни ...; **~ good nor bad** ни хорошó, ни плóхо.
neo... ['niːəu] *prefix* нео....
neolithic [niːəu'lɪθɪk] *adj* неолитúческий.
neologism [nɪ'ɔlədʒɪzəm] *n* неологúзм.
neon ['niːɔn] *n* неóн.
neon light *n* неóновый свет.
neon sign *n* неóновая вúвеска.
Nepal [nɪ'pɔːl] *n* Непáл.
Nepalese [nɛpə'liːz] *adj* непáльский*.
nephew ['nɛvjuː] *n* племя́нник.
nepotism ['nɛpətɪzəm] *n* непотúзм, кумовствó.
Neptune ['nɛptjuːn] *n* (*planet*) Нептýн.
nerd [nəːd] *n* (*inf*) придýрок*.
nerve [nəːv] *n* (*ANAT*) нерв; (*courage*) вúдержка; (*impudence*) нáглость *f*; **to have a fit of ~s** перенéрвничать (*perf*); **he gets on my ~s** он дéйствует мне на нéрвы; **she lost her ~** у неё сдáли нéрвы.
nerve centre *n* (*ANAT*) нéрвный центр; (*fig*) мозговóй центр.
nerve gas *n* нéрвный газ.
nerve-racking ['nəːvrækɪŋ] *adj* (*period*) нéрвный; (*situation*) нервóзный* (нервóзен).
nervous ['nəːvəs] *adj* нéрвный* (нéрвен); (*ANAT*) нéрвный; **to be** *or* **feel ~** нéрвничать (*impf*).
nervous breakdown *n* нéрвный срыв.
nervously ['nəːvəslɪ] *adv* нéрвно.
nervousness ['nəːvəsnɪs] *n* нéрвность *f*.
nervous wreck *n* (*inf*) комóк нéрвов.
nervy ['nəːvɪ] *adj* нéрвный*.
nest [nɛst] *n* гнездó* ♦ *vi* гнездúться* (*impf*); **~ of tables** комплéкт стóликов (*вставляющихся один в другóй*).
nest egg *n* занáчка*.
nestle ['nɛsl] *vi* (*snuggle*) приютúться (*perf*).
nestling ['nɛstlɪŋ] *n* птенéц*.
net [nɛt] *n* (*fabric*) тюль *m*; (*netting, also SPORT*) сéтка*; (*for fish, game: also fig*) сеть* *f* ♦ *adj* (*COMM*) чúстый ♦ *vt* (*fish*) ловúть* (поймáть* *perf*) в сеть; (*profit*) приносúть* (принестú* *perf*); (*deal, sale*) провора́чивать (проверну́ть *perf*); **~ of tax** пóсле вúчета налóгов*; **~ assets** нéтто-актúвы; **he earns ten thousand ~ per year** он зараба́тывает чúстыми дéсять тúсяч в год.
netball ['nɛtbɔːl] *n* нетбóл.
net curtains *npl* тюлевые занавéски *fpl*.

Netherlands ['nɛðələndz] *npl*: **the ~** Нидерлáнды *pl*.
nett [nɛt] *adj* = **net**.
netting ['nɛtɪŋ] *n* сéтка*.
nettle ['nɛtl] *n* крапúва; **to grasp the ~** (*fig*) без промедлéния взя́ться (*perf*) за дéло.
network ['nɛtwəːk] *n* сеть* *f* ♦ *vt* (*RADIO, TV*) транслúровать (*impf/perf*) по разлúчным канáлам; (*COMPUT*) подключáть (подключúть* *perf*) к систéме.
neuralgia [njuə'rældʒə] *n* невралгúя.
neurosis [njuə'rəusɪs] *n* неврóз.
neurological [njuərə'lɔdʒɪkl] *n* невролог-úческий.
neurotic [njuə'rɔtɪk] *adj* неврастенúчный* (неврастенúчен) ♦ *n* неврастéник.
neuter ['njuːtə] *vt* (*cat etc*) кастрúровать (*impf/perf*) ♦ *adj* (*LING*): **~ noun** существúтельное *nt* *adj* срéднего рóда.
neutral ['njuːtrəl] *adj* нейтрáльный* (нейтрáлен) ♦ *n* (*AUT*) холостóй ход*.
neutrality [njuː'trælɪtɪ] *n* нейтралитéт.
neutralize ['njuːtrəlaɪz] *vt* нейтрализовáть (*impf/perf*).
neutron ['njuːtrɔn] *n* нейтрóн.
neutron bomb *n* нейтрóнная бóмба.
Neva ['niːvə] *n*: **the ~** Невá.
never ['nɛvə] *adv* никогдá; **~ in my life** никогдá в жúзни; **~ again** бóльше никогдá; **I ~ went** я не ходúл; *see also* **mind**.
never-ending [nɛvər'ɛndɪŋ] *adj* нескончáемый (нескончáем).
nevertheless [nɛvəðə'lɛs] *adv* тем не мéнее.
new [njuː] *adj* (*brand new*) нóвый* (нов); (*recent*) недáвний*; **I'm ~ to this business** я в этом дéле новичóк; **as good as ~** совсéм как нóвый.
New Age *adj* (*PHILOSOPHY*) филосóфская систéма, базúрующаяся на вéре в альтернатúвную медицúну, астролóгию *итп*; **~ ~** (*music*) тип мýзыки, включáющий элемéнты джáза, нарóдной и классúческой мýзыки.
newborn ['njuːbɔːn] *adj* новорóжденный.
newcomer ['njuːkʌmə] *n* новичóк*.
newfangled ['njuːfæŋgld] *adj* (*pej*) новомóдный* (новомóден).
new-found ['njuːfaund] *adj* недáвно обретённый.
Newfoundland ['njuːfənlənd] *n* Нью-фáундлéнд.
New Guinea *n* Нóвая Гвинéя.
newly ['njuːlɪ] *adv* недáвно.
newlyweds ['njuːlɪwɛdz] *npl* новобрáчные *pl* *adj*.
new moon *n* молодóй мéсяц; (*time*) новолýние.
newness ['njuːnɪs] *n* новизнá.

New Orleans [-'ɔ:li:ənz] *n* Но́вый Орлеа́н.
news [nju:z] *n* (*good, bad*) но́вость* *f*,
изве́стие; **a piece of** ~ но́вость*; **the** ~ (*RADIO*,
TV) но́вости *fpl*; **what's the** ~? каки́е
но́вости?; **financial** ~ фина́нсовые но́вости*.
news agency *n* информацио́нное аге́нтство.
newsagent ['nju:zeɪdʒənt] *n* (*BRIT: also:* ~'s) ≈
газе́тный кио́ск; (*person*) владе́лец*(-лица)
газе́тного кио́ска.
news bulletin *n* сво́дка* новосте́й.
newscaster ['nju:zkɑːstəʳ] *n* ди́ктор
(*програ́ммы новосте́й*).
newsdealer ['nju:zdi:ləʳ] *n* (*US*) = **newsagent**.
newsflash ['nju:zflæʃ] *n* э́кстренное
сообще́ние.
newsletter ['nju:zlɛtəʳ] *n* информацио́нный
бюллете́нь *m*.
newspaper ['nju:zpeɪpəʳ] *n* газе́та; **daily/
weekly** ~ ежедне́вная/еженеде́льная газе́та.
newsprint ['nju:zprɪnt] *n* (*paper*) газе́тная
бума́га.
newsreader ['nju:zri:dəʳ] *n* = **newscaster**.
newsreel ['nju:zri:l] *n* информацио́нный
киножурна́л.
newsroom ['nju:zru:m] *n* (*PRESS*) отде́л
новосте́й; (*RADIO, TV*) сту́дия новосте́й.
newsstand ['nju:zstænd] *n* газе́тный кио́ск.
newsworthy ['nju:zwɜːðɪ] *adj* досто́йный*
(досто́ен) интере́са.
newt [nju:t] *n* трито́н.
new town *n* но́вый го́род*.
New Year *n* Но́вый год*; **Happy** ~~! С
Но́вым го́дом!; **to wish sb a Happy** ~ ~ (*for
the festive season*) поздравля́ть
(поздра́вить* *perf*) кого́-н с Но́вым го́дом;
(*for the coming year*) жела́ть (пожела́ть *perf*)
кому́-н счастли́вого но́вого го́да.
New Year's Day *n* пе́рвое января́.
New Year's Eve *n* кану́н Но́вого го́да.
New York [-'jɔ:k] *n* Нью-Йо́рк.
New Zealand [-'zi:lənd] *n* Но́вая Зела́ндия ♦
adj новозела́ндский*.
New Zealander [-'zi:ləndəʳ] *n*
новозела́ндец*(-дка*).
next [nɛkst] *adj* сле́дующий*; (*neighbouring*)
сосе́дний ♦ *adv* пото́м, зате́м ♦ *prep*: ~ **to**
ря́дом с +*instr*, во́зле +*gen*; ~ **time** в
сле́дующий* раз; **the** ~ **day** на сле́дующий*
день; **the** ~ **week** на сле́дующей неде́ле; **the
week after** ~ че́рез неде́лю; ~ **year** в
бу́дущем *or* сле́дующем году́; **in the** ~ **15
minutes** в ближа́йшие 15 мину́т; ~ **to
nothing** почти́ ничего́; ~ **please!** сле́дующий,
пожа́луйста!; **who's** ~? кто сле́дующий?;
"turn to the ~ **page"** "переверни́те
страни́цу"; **when do we meet** ~? когда́ мы
сно́ва встре́тимся?
next door *adv* по сосе́дству, ря́дом ♦ *adj* (*flat,
house*) сосе́дний*; ~~ **neighbour**
ближа́йший* сосе́д*.
next of kin *n* ближа́йший* ро́дственник.

NF *n abbr* (*BRIT: POL: = National Front*) НФ=
Национа́льный фронт ♦ *abbr* (*CANADA*) =
Newfoundland.
NFL *n abbr* (*US*) = *National Football League*.
NG *abbr* (*US*) = **National Guard**.
NGO *n abbr* (*US: = non-governmental
organization*) неправи́тельственная
организа́ция.
NH *abbr* (*US: POST*) = *New Hampshire*.
NHL *n abbr* (*US: = National Hockey League*)
НХЛ= *Национа́льная хокке́йная ли́га*.
NHS *n abbr* (*BRIT*) = **National Health Service**.
NI *abbr* = **Northern Ireland**; (*BRIT*) = **National
Insurance**.
Niagara Falls [naɪ'æɡərə-] *npl*: **the** ~ ~
Ниага́рский водопа́д *msg*.
nib [nɪb] *n* перо́*.
nibble ['nɪbl] *vt* надку́сывать (надкуси́ть* *perf*)
♦ *vi*: **to** ~ **at** (*mice*) грызть* (*impf*); (*at grass*)
щипа́ть* (*impf*).
NICAM *n abbr* = *near-instantaneous companding
system*: ~ **stereo** систе́ма стереозвуча́ния.
Nicaragua [nɪkə'ræɡjuə] *n* Никара́гуа *f ind*.
Nicaraguan [nɪkə'ræɡjuən] *adj*
никарагуа́нский* ♦ *n* никарагуа́нец*(-нка*).
Nice [ni:s] *n* Ни́цца.
nice [naɪs] *adj* прия́тный* (прия́тен), хоро́ший*
(хоро́ш); (*attractive*) симпати́чный*
(симпати́чен); **to look** ~ хорошо́ вы́глядеть*
(*impf*); **that's very** ~ **of you** о́чень ми́ло с
ва́шей стороны́.
nicely ['naɪslɪ] *adv* прия́тно, хорошо́; **that will
do** ~ э́то вполне́ подойдёт.
niceties ['naɪsɪtɪz] *npl* то́нкости *fpl*.
niche [ni:ʃ] *n* (*also fig*) ни́ша.
nick [nɪk] *n* (*in skin*) поре́з; (*in surface*) зару́бка*
♦ *vt* (*inf: steal*) пере́ть* (спере́ть* *perf*); (: *BRIT:
arrest*) ца́пать (сца́пать *perf*); (*cut*): **to** ~ **o.s.**
поре́заться* (*perf*); **in the** ~ **of time** как раз
во́время; **in good** ~ (: *BRIT: inf: condition*) в
хоро́шем состоя́нии.
nickel ['nɪkl] *n* ни́кель *m*; (*US: coin*) моне́та в 5
це́нтов.
nickname ['nɪkneɪm] *n* кли́чка*, про́звище ♦ *vt*
прозыва́ть (прозва́ть* *perf*).
Nicosia [nɪkə'si:ə] *n* Никоси́я.
nicotine ['nɪkəti:n] *n* никоти́н.
niece [ni:s] *n* племя́нница.
nifty ['nɪftɪ] *adj* (*inf: car, jacket*) сти́льный*
(сти́лен); (: *gadget, tool*) ло́вко
приду́манный (приду́ман).
Niger ['naɪdʒəʳ] *n* Ни́гер.
Nigeria [naɪ'dʒɪərɪə] *n* Ниге́рия.
Nigerian [naɪ'dʒɪərɪən] *adj* нигери́йский* ♦ *n*
нигери́ец(-и́йка).
niggardly ['nɪɡədlɪ] *adj* (*person*) ска́редный;
(*amount*) ску́дный.
nigger ['nɪɡəʳ] *n* (*infl!*) черномá́зый(-ая) *m(f) adj*
(!)
niggle ['nɪɡl] *vt* задева́ть (заде́ть* *perf*) ♦ *vi* (*find
fault*) придира́ться (придра́ться* *perf*).

niggling ['nɪglɪŋ] *adj* (*trifling*) придирчивый (придирчив); (*annoying*) навязчивый (навязчив).

night [naɪt] *n* ночь* *f*; (*evening*) вечер*; **at ~**, **by ~** ночью; **all ~ long** всю ночь напролёт; **in** *or* **during the ~** ночью; **last ~** вчера ночью; (*evening*) вчера вечером; **the ~ before last** позапрошлой ночью; (*evening*) позавчера вечером.

nightcap ['naɪtkæp] *n* (*drink*) стаканчик на ночь.

nightclub ['naɪtklʌb] *n* ночной клуб.

nightdress ['naɪtdrɛs] *n* ночная рубашка*.

nightfall ['naɪtfɔːl] *n* сумерки* *pl*.

nightgown ['naɪtgaʊn] *n* = **nightdress**.

nightie ['naɪtɪ] *n* (*inf*) = **nightdress**.

nightingale ['naɪtɪŋgeɪl] *n* соловей*.

nightlife ['naɪtlaɪf] *n* ночная жизнь *f*.

nightly ['naɪtlɪ] *adj* (*every night*) еженощный; (*by night*) ночной ♦ *adv* еженощно.

nightmare ['naɪtmɛə'] *n* (*also fig*) кошмар.

nightmarish ['naɪtmɛərɪʃ] *adj* кошмарный*.

night porter *n* ночной портье *m ind*.

night safe *n* ночной сейф (*в банке*).

night school *n* вечерняя школа.

nightshade ['naɪtʃeɪd] *n*: **deadly ~** белладонна, красавка.

night shift *n* ночная смена.

night-time ['naɪttaɪm] *n* ночное время* *nt*.

night watchman *n* ночной сторож*.

nihilism ['naɪlɪzəm] *n* нигилизм.

nil [nɪl] *n* нуль* *m*; (*BRIT: SPORT*) ноль* *m* ♦ *cpd* нулевой.

Nile [naɪl] *n*: **the ~** Нил.

nimble ['nɪmbl] *adj* (*agile*) проворный* (проворен); (*alert*) сообразительный* (сообразителен).

nine [naɪn] *n* девять*; *see also* **five**.

nineteen ['naɪn'tiːn] *n* девятнадцать*; *see also* **five**.

nineteenth ['naɪn'tiːnθ] *adj* девятнадцатый; *see also* **fifth**.

ninetieth ['naɪntɪɪθ] *adj* девяностый; *see also* **fifth**.

ninety ['naɪntɪ] *n* девяносто*; *see also* **fifty**.

ninth [naɪnθ] *adj* девятый; *see also* **fifth**.

nip [nɪp] *vt* (*pinch*) щипать* (ущипнуть *perf*); (*bite*) кусать (*impf*) ♦ *n* (*pinch*) щипок*; (*bite*) укус; (*drink*) рюмочка* ♦ *vi* (*BRIT: inf*): **to ~ out** выскакивать (выскочить *perf*); **to ~ into a shop** заскакивать (заскочить* *perf*) в магазин.

nipple ['nɪpl] *n* (*ANAT*) сосок*; (*TECH*) ниппель* *m*.

nippy ['nɪpɪ] *adj* (*BRIT: inf*) проворный* (проворен); (: *weather*) холодноватый (холодноват).

nit [nɪt] *n* (*in hair*) гнида; (*BRIT: inf: idiot*) олух.

nit-pick ['nɪtpɪk] *vi* (*inf*) придираться (придраться* *perf*).

nitrogen ['naɪtrədʒən] *n* азот.

nitroglycerin(e) ['naɪtrəʊ'glɪsəriːn] *n* нитроглицерин.

nitty-gritty ['nɪtɪ'grɪtɪ] *n* (*inf*): **to get down to the ~** переходить* (перейти* *perf*) к сути дела.

nitwit ['nɪtwɪt] *n* (*inf*) олух.

Nizhni Novgorod ['nɪʒnɪj 'nɔvgərət] *n* Нижний Новгород.

NJ *abbr* (*US: POST*) = **New Jersey**.

NLF *n abbr* (= *National Liberation Front*) ФНО= *Фронт национального освобождения*.

NLQ *abbr* (*COMPUT, TYP*: = *near letter quality*) *повышенное качество печати*.

NLRB *n abbr* (*US*) = *National Labor Relations Board*.

NM *abbr* (*US: POST*) = **New Mexico**.

KEYWORD

no [nəʊ] (*pl* **noes**) *adv* (*opposite of "yes"*) нет; **are you coming? – no (I'm not)** Вы придёте? -нет(, не приду); **no thank you** нет, спасибо

♦ *adj* (*not any*): **I have no money/time/books** у меня нет денег/времени/книг; **there is no bread left** хлеб кончился; **there is no one here** здесь никого нет; **it is of no importance at all** это не имеет никакого значения; **no system is totally fair** ни одна система не бывает полностью справедливо; **"no entry"** "вход воспрещён"; **"no smoking"** "не курить"

♦ *n*: **there were twenty noes** двадцать (человек) были "против".

---

no. *abbr* = **number**.

nobble ['nɔbl] *vt* (*BRIT: inf: bribe*) покупать (купить* *perf*); (: *to speak to*) подлавливать (подловить* *perf*); (: *RACING*) портить* (испортить* *perf*).

Nobel Prize [nəʊ'bɛl-] *n* Нобелевская премия.

nobility [nəʊ'bɪlɪtɪ] *n* (*social class*) знать *f*, дворянство; (*quality*) благородство.

noble ['nəʊbl] *adj* (*aristocratic*) дворянский; (*high-minded*) благородный* (благороден); (*impressive*) величавый (величав).

nobleman ['nəʊblmən] *irreg n* дворянин*.

noblewoman ['nəʊblwʊmən] *irreg n* дворянка*.

nobly ['nəʊblɪ] *adv* (*behave, act*) благородно.

nobody ['nəʊbədɪ] *pron* никто*.

no-claim(s) bonus ['nəʊkleɪmz-] *n* (*INSURANCE*) скидка со следующей страховой премии (*предоставляется страхователю в случае отсутствия страховых претензий в предыдущем году*).

nocturnal [nɔk'təːnl] *adj* ночной.

nod [nɔd] *vi* (*gesture*) кивать (*impf*); (*doze*) клевать* (*impf*) носом ♦ *n* кивок* ♦ *vt*: **to ~ one's head** кивать (*impf*) головой; **they ~ded their agreement** они кивнули в знак

согла́сия
▶ **nod off** *vi* задрема́ть* *(perf)*.
no-fly zone [nəʊ'flaɪ-] *n* запре́тная возду́шная зо́на.
noise [nɔɪz] *n* шум.
noiseless ['nɔɪzlɪs] *adj* бесшу́мный* (бесшу́мен).
noisily ['nɔɪzɪlɪ] *adv* шу́мно.
noisy ['nɔɪzɪ] *adj* шу́мный* (шу́мен).
nomad ['nəʊmæd] *n* коче́вник(-ица).
nomadic [nəʊ'mædɪk] *adj* кочево́й.
no-man's-land ['nəʊmænzlænd] *n* (MIL) ниче́йная полоса́; *(fig)* тума́нность *f*.
nominal ['nɒmɪnl] *adj* номина́льный* (номина́лен); *(value)* номина́льный.
nominate ['nɒmɪneɪt] *vt* *(propose)*: **to ~ sb (for)** выставля́ть (вы́ставить* *perf)* кандидату́ру кого́-н (на +*acc*); *(appoint)*: **to ~ sb (to/as)** назнача́ть (назна́чить *perf)* кого́-н (на +*acc*/ +*instr*).
nomination [nɒmɪ'neɪʃən] *n* *(see vb)* выставле́ние; назначе́ние.
nominee [nɒmɪ'niː] *n* кандида́т.
non... [nɒn] *prefix* не....
nonalcoholic [nɒnælkə'hɒlɪk] *adj* *(drink)* безалкого́льный* (безалкого́лен).
nonaligned *adj* неприсоедини́вшийся.
nonbreakable [nɒn'breɪkəbl] *adj* небью́щийся.
nonce word ['nɒns-] *n* окказионали́зм.
nonchalant ['nɒnʃələnt] *adj* беспе́чный* (беспе́чен).
noncommissioned officer [nɒnkə'mɪʃənd-] *n* у́нтер-офице́р.
noncommittal [nɒnkə'mɪtl] *adj* укло́нчивый (укло́нчив).
nonconformist [nɒnkən'fɔːmɪst] *n* нонконформи́ст(ка*); *(BRIT: REL)*: **N~** нонконформи́ст(ка ◆ *adj* нонконформи́стский.
non-contributory pension scheme *n* пенсио́нные схе́мы, по кото́рым рабо́тники не должны́ де́лать регуля́рных взно́сов.
noncooperation ['nɒnkəʊɔpə'reɪʃən] *n* отка́з в сотру́дничестве.
nondescript ['nɒndɪskrɪpt] *adj* *(person, clothing)* невзра́чный* (невзра́чен); *(colour)* небро́ский*.
none [nʌn] *pron* *(person)* никто́*, ни оди́н*; *(thing)* ничто́*, ни оди́н*; **~ of you** никто́ *or* ни оди́н из Вас; **I've ~ left** у меня́ ничего́ не оста́лось; **~ at all** совсе́м ничего́; **he's ~ the worse for it** ему́ от э́того отню́дь не ху́же.
nonentity [nɒ'nɛntɪtɪ] *n* ничто́жество.
nonessential [nɒnɪ'sɛnʃl] *adj* *(items)* несуще́ственный (несуще́ствен) ◆ *n*: **~s** несуще́ственные ве́щи *fpl*.
nonetheless ['nʌnðə'lɛs] *adv* тем не ме́нее, всё же.
non-event [nɒnɪ'vɛnt] *n* бессмы́сленное мероприя́тие.
nonexecutive [nɒnɪg'zɛkjutɪv] *adj*: **~ director** дире́ктор* без распоряди́тельных

полномо́чий.
nonexistent [nɒnɪg'zɪstənt] *adj* несущест- ву́ющий.
nonfiction [nɒn'fɪkʃən] *n* документа́льная литерату́ра.
nonflammable [nɒn'flæməbl] *adj* невоспламеня́ющийся*.
nonintervention ['nɒnɪntə'vɛnʃən] *n* невмеша́тельство.
no-no ['nəʊnəʊ] *n* *(inf)* запре́тная те́ма.
non obst. *abbr* *(notwithstanding*: = *non obstante)* несмотря́ на +*acc*.
no-nonsense [nəʊ'nɒnsəns] *adj* делово́й.
nonpayment [nɒn'peɪmənt] *n* неупла́та.
nonplussed [nɒn'plʌst] *adj* ошеломлённый (ошеломлён).
non-profit-making [nɒn'prɒfɪtmeɪkɪŋ] *adj*: **~ organization** некомме́рческая организа́ция.
nonsense ['nɒnsəns] *n* *(rubbish)* ерунда́, чепуха́; **it is ~ to say that ...** говори́ть (сказа́ть* *perf)*, что ... -- про́сто глу́пость.
nonsensical [nɒn'sɛnsɪkl] *adj* бессмы́сленный* (бессмы́слен).
nonshrink [nɒn'ʃrɪŋk] *adj* *(BRIT)*: **nylon is (a) ~ (fabric)** нейло́н не сади́тся.
nonskid [nɒn'skɪd] *adj* нескользя́щий.
nonsmoker ['nɒn'sməʊkəʳ] *n* некуря́щий*(-ая) *m(f) adj*.
nonstarter [nɒn'stɑːtəʳ] *n* мёртвый но́мер *no pl*.
nonstick ['nɒn'stɪk] *adj* непригора́ющий.
nonstop ['nɒn'stɒp] *adj* *(conversation)* беспреры́вный* (беспреры́вен); *(flight)* беспоса́дочный; *(train, bus)* иду́щий без остано́вок ◆ *adv* *(see adj)* беспреры́вно; без поса́док; без остано́вок.
nontaxable [nɒn'tæksəbl] *adj* необлага́емый (необлага́ем) нало́гом.
non-U *adj abbr* *(BRIT: inf.*: = *non-upper class)* не принадлежа́щий к вы́сшему (социа́льному) кла́ссу.
nonvolatile [nɒn'vɒlətaɪl] *adj*: **~ memory** *(COMPUT)* энергонезави́симая па́мять *f*.
nonvoting [nɒn'vəʊtɪŋ] *adj*: **~ shares/member** а́кции/член без пра́ва голосова́ния.
non-white [nɒn'waɪt] *adj* *(person)* цветно́й ◆ *n*: **non-White** цветно́й(-а́я) *m(f) adj*.
noodles ['nuːdlz] *npl* вермише́ль *fsg*.
nook [nuk] *n*: **in every ~ and cranny** во всех угла́х.
noon [nuːn] *n* по́лдень* *m*.
no-one ['nəʊwʌn] *pron* = **nobody**.
noose [nuːs] *n* пе́тля*.
nor [nɔːʳ] *conj* = **neither** ◆ *adv see* **neither**.
Norf *abbr* *(BRIT: POST)* = **Norfolk**.
norm [nɔːm] *n* но́рма.
normal ['nɔːml] *adj* норма́льный* (норма́лен) ◆ *n*: **to return to ~** возвраща́ться (верну́ться *perf)* в норма́льное состоя́ние.
normality [nɔː'mælɪtɪ] *n* норма́льность *f*.
normally ['nɔːməlɪ] *adv* *(usually)* обы́чно; *(properly)* норма́льно.

Normandy ['nɔ:məndɪ] *n* Нормандия.
north [nɔ:θ] *n* север ◆ *adj* северный ◆ *adv* (*go*) на север; (*be*) к северу.
North Africa *n* Северная Африка.
North African *adj* североафриканский ◆ *n* житель(ница) *m(f)* Северной Африки.
North America *n* Северная Америка.
North American *adj* североамериканский ◆ *n* североамериканец*(-нка*).
Northants [nɔ:'θænts] *abbr* (*BRIT: POST*) = *Northamptonshire*.
northbound ['nɔ:θbaund] *adj* (*traffic, carriageway*) на север; (*platform*) северного направления.
Northd *abbr* (*BRIT: POST*) = *Northumberland*.
northeast [nɔ:θ'i:st] *n* северо-восток.
northerly ['nɔ:ðəlɪ] *adj* северный.
northern ['nɔ:ðən] *adj* северный.
northerner ['nɔ:ðənəʳ] *n* северянин*(-янка*).
Northern Ireland *n* Северная Ирландия.
North Korea *n* Северная Корея.
North Pole *n* Северный полюс.
North Sea *n* Северное море.
North-Sea oil ['nɔ:θsi:-] *n* нефть *f* Северного моря.
northward(s) ['nɔ:θwəd(z)] *adv* к северу.
northwest [nɔ:θ'wɛst] *n* северо-запад.
Norway ['nɔ:weɪ] *n* Норвегия.
Norwegian [nɔ:'wi:dʒən] *adj* норвежский* ◆ *n* норвежец*(-жка*); (*LING*) норвежский* язык*.
nos. *abbr* = *numbers*.
nose [nəuz] *n* нос*; (*sense of smell*) нюх, чутьё ◆ *vi*: to ~ **forward** осторожно пробираться (пробраться* *perf*) вперёд; **he has a ~ for danger/scandal** у него нюх на опасность/скандал; **to pay through the ~** (**for sth**) (*inf*) платить* (заплатить* *perf*) втридорога (за что-н)
▶ **nose about** *vi* вынюхивать (вынюхать *perf*)
▶ **nose around** *vi* = **nose about**.
nosebleed ['nəuzbli:d] *n* носовое кровотечение.
nose dive *n* (крутое) пикирование.
nose drops *npl* капли *fpl* для носа.
nosey ['nəuzɪ] *adj* (*inf*) = **nosy**.
nostalgia [nɔs'tældʒɪə] *n* ностальгия.
nostalgic [nɔs'tældʒɪk] *adj* (*film, memory*) ностальгический*; (*person*): **to be ~** (**for**) испытывать (*impf*) ностальгию (по +*dat*).
nostril ['nɔstrɪl] *n* ноздря*.
nosy ['nəuzɪ] *adj* (*inf*): **to be ~** совать* (*impf*) нос в чужие дела.

━━━ **KEYWORD** ━━━━━━━━━━━━━━━━

not [nɔt] *adv* нет; (*before verbs*) не; **he is not** *or* **isn't at home** его нет дома; **he asked me not to do it** он попросил меня не делать этого; **you must not** *or* **you mustn't do that** (*forbidden*) этого нельзя делать; (*should not*)

Вы не должны это делать; **it's too late, isn't it?** уже слишком поздно, да?; **not that ...** не то, чтобы ...; **not yet** нет ещё, ещё нет; **not now** не сейчас; *see also* **all, only**.

━━━━━━━━━━━━━━━━━━━━━━━━━━

notable ['nəutəbl] *adj* примечательный* (примечателен).
notably ['nəutəblɪ] *adv* (*particularly*) особенно; (*markedly*) заметно.
notary ['nəutərɪ] *n* (*also*: ~ **public**) нотариус.
notation [nəu'teɪʃən] *n* (*MUS etc*) нотация.
notch [nɔtʃ] *n* (*on the edge*) зазубрина; (*on the surface*) выемка*
▶ **notch up** *vt* (*victory*) добиваться (добиться* *perf*) +*instr*; (*score*) набирать (набрать* *perf*).
note [nəut] *n* (*record*) запись *f*; (*letter*) записка*; (*also*: **footnote**) примечание; (*also*: **banknote**) банкнота; (*MUS*) нота; (*tone*) тон ◆ *vt* (*observe*) замечать (заметить* *perf*); (*also*: ~ **down**) записывать (записать* *perf*); **of** ~ примечательный (примечателен).
notebook ['nəutbuk] *n* записная книжка; (*exercise book*) тетрадь *f*.
notecase ['nəutkeɪs] *n* (*BRIT*) бумажник.
noted ['nəutɪd] *adj* известный (известен).
notepad ['nəutpæd] *n* блокнот.
notepaper ['nəutpeɪpəʳ] *n* писчая бумага.
noteworthy ['nəutwə:ðɪ] *adj* достойный* (достоен) внимания; **it is ~ that ...** достойно внимания что ....
nothing ['nʌθɪŋ] *n* ничто*; (*zero*) ноль *m*; **he does ~** он ничего не делает; **there is ~ to do/be said** делать/сказать нечего; (~/ **new/ much/of the sort** ничего нового/особенного/ подобного; **for ~** даром; **think ~ of it!**, **it was ~!** не за что!; ~ **like as ... as ...** совсем не так ..., как ...; **to say ~ of ...** не говоря уже о +*prp* ...; **it has ~ to do with you** это Вас не касается.
notice ['nəutɪs] *n* (*announcement*) объявление; (*official letter, circular*) уведомление, извещение; (*warning*) предупреждение; (*BRIT: review*) отзыв ◆ *vt* замечать (заметить* *perf*); **to take ~ of** обращать (обратить* *perf*) внимание на +*acc*; **to bring sth to sb's ~** (*attention*) обращать (обратить* *perf*) внимание кого-н на что-н; **to escape** *or* **avoid** ~ оставаться* (остаться* *perf*) незамеченным; **it has come to my ~ that ...** мне стало известно, что ...; **to hand in one's** ~ подавать* (подать* *perf*) заявление об уходе с работы; **he was given 2 weeks** ~ его предупредили, что он будет уволен через 2 недели; **advance** ~ заблаговременное предупреждение; **without** ~ без предупреждения; **at short** ~ без предупреждения; **until further** ~ впредь до дальнейшего уведомления.

---

* marks translations which have irregular inflections. The Russian-English side of the dictionary gives inflectional information.

noticeable ['nəutɪsəbl] *adj* заме́тный* (заме́тен).
notice board *n* (*BRIT*) доска́* объявле́ний.
notification [nəutɪfɪ'keɪʃən] *n* уведомле́ние.
notify ['nəutɪfaɪ] *vt*: **to ~ sb (of sth)** уведомля́ть (уве́домить* *perf*) кого́-н (о чём-н).
notion ['nəuʃən] *n* (*idea*) поня́тие; (*opinion*) представле́ние; **~s** *npl* (*US*: *haberdashery*) галантере́я *fsg*.
notoriety [nəutə'raɪətɪ] *n* дурна́я сла́ва.
notorious [nəu'tɔ:rɪəs] *adj* (*criminal, liar*) изве́стный* (изве́стен); (*place*) печа́льно изве́стный* (изве́стен).
notoriously [nəu'tɔ:rɪəslɪ] *adv*: **she is ~ unreliable** у неё дурна́я сла́ва ненадёжного челове́ка; **this word is ~ difficult to translate** э́то сло́во изве́стно тем, что его́ тру́дно перевести́.
Notts [nɔts] *abbr* (*BRIT*: *POST*) = **Nottinghamshire**.
notwithstanding [nɔtwɪθ'stændɪŋ] *adv* тем не ме́нее ♦ *prep* несмотря́ на +*acc*.
nougat ['nu:gɑ:] *n* нуга́.
nought [nɔ:t] *n* ноль* *m*.
noun [naun] *n* (и́мя* *nt*) существи́тельное *nt adj*.
nourish ['nʌrɪʃ] *vt* (*feed*) пита́ть (*impf*); (*fig*: *foster*) взра́щивать (взрасти́ть* *perf*).
nourishing ['nʌrɪʃɪŋ] *adj* пита́тельный* (пита́телен).
nourishment ['nʌrɪʃmənt] *n* (*food*) пита́ние.
Nov. *abbr* = **November**.
Nova Scotia ['nəuvə'skəuʃə] *n* Но́вая Шотла́ндия.
Novaya Zemlya ['nɔvəjə zɪm'lja] *n* Но́вая Земля́.
novel ['nɔvl] *n* рома́н ♦ *adj* оригина́льный* (оригина́лен).
novelist ['nɔvəlɪst] *n* романи́ст(ка*).
novelty ['nɔvəltɪ] *n* (*newness*) новизна́; (*object*) нови́нка*.
November [nəu'vɛmbə^r] *n* ноя́брь* *m*; *see also* **July**.
novice ['nɔvɪs] *n* новичо́к*; (*REL*) послу́шник(-ица).
Novosibirsk [nəvəsi'birsk] *n* Новосиби́рск.
NOW [nau] *n abbr* (*US*) = **National Organization for Women**.
now [nau] *adv* тепе́рь, сейча́с ♦ *conj*: **~ (that)** ... тепе́рь, когда́ ...; **right ~** пря́мо сейча́с; **by ~** к настоя́щему вре́мени; **~ and then** *or* **again** вре́мя от вре́мени; **from ~ on** впредь; **until ~** до сих пор; **that's the fashion just ~** э́то сейча́с в мо́де; **I saw her just ~** я то́лько что её ви́дел; **in 3 days from ~** че́рез 3 дня; **between ~ and Monday** ме́жду сего́дняшним днём и понеде́льником; **that's all for ~** пока́ всё.
nowadays ['nauədeɪz] *adv* в на́ши дни.
nowhere ['nəuwɛə^r] *adv* (*be*) нигде́; (*go*) никуда́; **~ else** (*be*) бо́льше нигде́; (*go*) бо́льше никуда́; **I have ~ else to go** мне бо́льше не́куда идти́.

no-win situation [nəu'wɪn-] *n* безвы́игрышное положе́ние.
noxious ['nɔkʃəs] *adj* вредоно́сный; (*smell*) проти́вный* (проти́вен).
nozzle ['nɔzl] *n* (*TECH*) сопло́*; (*of hose, vacuum cleaner*) наса́дка*; (*of fire extinguisher*) брандспо́йт.
NP *n abbr* (*LAW*) = **notary public**.
NS *abbr* (*CANADA*) = **Nova Scotia**.
NSC *n abbr* (*US*: = **National Security Council**) Сове́т национа́льной безопа́сности.
NSF *n abbr* (*US*) = **National Science Foundation**.
NSPCC *n abbr* (*BRIT*) = **National Society for the Prevention of Cruelty to Children**.
NSW *abbr* (*AUSTRALIA*) = **New South Wales**.
NT *n abbr* (*BIBLE*: = **New Testament**) Но́вый заве́т.
nth [enθ] *adj*: **for the ~ time** (*inf*) в э́нный раз.
nuance ['nju:ɑ̃:ns] *n* нюа́нс.
nubile ['nju:baɪl] *adj* (*woman*) зре́лый; (*attractive*) прельсти́тельный.
nuclear ['nju:klɪə^r] *adj* я́дерный.
nuclear disarmament *n* я́дерное разоруже́ние.
nuclear-free zone ['nju:klɪə'fri:-] *n* внея́дерная зо́на.
nuclear reactor *n* я́дерный реа́ктор.
nuclei ['nju:klɪaɪ] *npl of* **nucleus**.
nucleus ['nju:klɪəs] *n* (*pl* **nuclei**) *n* (*also fig*) ядро́*.
NUCPS *n abbr* (*BRIT*) = **National Union of Civil and Public Servants**.
nude [nju:d] *adj* обнажённый (обнажён), наго́й* (наг) ♦ *n* обнажённая фигу́ра; **in the ~** в обнажённом ви́де.
nudge [nʌdʒ] *vt* подта́лкивать (подтолкну́ть* *perf*).
nudist ['nju:dɪst] *n* нуди́ст(ка*).
nudist colony *n* коло́ния нуди́стов.
nudity ['nju:dɪtɪ] *n* нагота́.
nugget ['nʌgɪt] *n* (*of gold*) саморо́док*; **~ of information** це́нная информа́ция.
nuisance ['nju:sns] *n* (*state of affairs, thing*) доса́да; (*person*) доку́чливый челове́к*; **what a ~!** кака́я доса́да!; **that noise is a real ~** э́тот шум си́льно раздража́ет; **he is a real ~** он о́чень надое́дливый.
NUJ *n abbr* (*BRIT*) = **National Union of Journalists**.
nuke [nju:k] *n* (*inf*) я́дерное ору́жие.
null [nʌl] *adj*: **to be ~ and void** потеря́ть (*perf*) зако́нную си́лу.
nullify ['nʌlɪfaɪ] *vt* (*efforts*) своди́ть* (свести́* *perf*) к нулю́; (*LAW*) аннули́ровать (*impf/perf*).
NUM *n abbr* (*BRIT*) = **National Union of Mineworkers**.
numb [nʌm] *adj*: **~ (with)** онеме́вший (от +*gen*) ♦ *vt*: **the cold ~ed his fingers** его́ па́льцы онеме́ли от хо́лода; **to go ~** онеме́ть (*perf*).
number ['nʌmbə^r] *n* но́мер*; (*MATH*) число́*; (*written figure*) ци́фра; (*quantity*) коли́чество ♦ *vt* (*pages etc*) нумерова́ть (пронумерова́ть

perf); (*amount to*) насчи́тывать (*impf*); **a ~ of** не́сколько +*gen*; **in a ~ of cases** в ря́де слу́чаев; **they were ten in ~** их бы́ло де́сять; **you've got the wrong ~** (*TEL*) Вы не туда́ попа́ли; **he is ~ed among ...** его́ причисля́ют к +*dat* ...; **~ed (bank) account** номерно́й счёт в ба́нке.

numberplate ['nʌmbəpleɪt] *n* (*BRIT*: *AUT*) номерно́й знак.

Number Ten *n* (*BRIT*: *also:* ~ ~ **Downing Street**) но́мер 10 по Да́унинг Стри́т (*резиде́нция премье́р-мини́стра*).

numbness ['nʌmnɪs] *n* (*due to cold*) онеме́ние; (*due to fear, shock*) оцепене́ние.

numbskull ['nʌmskʌl] *n* (*inf*) тупи́ца *m/f*.

numeral ['nju:mərəl] *n* ци́фра.

numerate ['nju:mərɪt] *adj* (*BRIT*): **to be ~** знать (*impf*) арифме́тику.

numerical [nju:'mɛrɪkl] *adj* (*value*) числово́й; (*superiority*) чи́сленный; (*data*) цифрово́й; **in ~ order** по номера́м.

numerous ['nju:mərəs] *adj* многочи́сленный (многочи́слен); **on ~ occasions** многокра́тно.

nun [nʌn] *n* мона́хиня.

nunnery ['nʌnərɪ] *n* же́нский* монасты́рь *m*.

nuptial ['nʌpʃəl] *adj* бра́чный.

nurse [nə:s] *n* медсестра́*; (*also: male* ~) медбра́т; (*also:* ~**maid**) ня́ня ◆ *vt* (*patient*) уха́живать (*impf*) за +*instr*, (*desire, also BRIT*: *cuddle*) леле́ять (взлеле́ять *perf*); (*grudge*) тайть (*impf*); (*US: suckle*) корми́ть* (*impf*) гру́дью; **to ~ a cold** сиде́ть* (*impf*) до́ма с просту́дой.

nursery ['nə:sərɪ] *n* (*institution*) я́сли* *pl*; (*room*) де́тская *f adj*; (*for plants*) пито́мник.

nursery rhyme *n* пе́сенка для дете́й.

nursery school *n* де́тский* сад*.

nursery slope *n* (*BRIT*) спуск для начина́ющих лы́жников.

nursing ['nə:sɪŋ] *n* (*profession*) профе́ссия

медсестры́; (*care*) ухо́д.

nursing home *n* ча́стный дом* (*для престаре́лых*).

nursing mother *n* кормя́щая мать* *f*.

nurture ['nə:tʃəˈ] *vt* (*child, plant*) выра́щивать (вы́растить* *perf*).

NUS *n abbr* (*BRIT*) = National Union of Students.

NUT *n abbr* (*BRIT*) = National Union of Teachers.

nut [nʌt] *n* (*BOT*) оре́х; (*TECH*) га́йка; (*inf*) = **nutcase**.

nutcase ['nʌtkeɪs] *n* (*inf*) псих.

nutcrackers ['nʌtkrækəz] *npl* щипцы́* *pl* для оре́хов.

nutmeg ['nʌtmɛg] *n* муска́тный оре́х.

nutrient ['nju:trɪənt] *n* пита́тельное вещество́.

nutrition [nju:'trɪʃən] *n* (*diet*) пита́ние; (*nourishment*) пита́тельность *f*.

nutritionist [nju:'trɪʃənɪst] *n* дието́лог.

nutritious [nju:'trɪʃəs] *adj* пита́тельный* (пита́телен).

nuts [nʌts] (*inf*) *adj*: **he's ~** он чо́кнутый; **to be ~ about sb** с ума́ сходи́ть* (*impf*) по кому́-н.

nutshell ['nʌtʃɛl] *n* оре́ховая скорлупа́*; **in a ~** (*fig*) в двух слова́х.

nutty ['nʌtɪ] *adj* (*flavour*) похо́жий* (по вку́су) на оре́хи; (*inf: person*) чо́кнутый (чо́кнут); (*idea*) бредо́вый.

nuzzle ['nʌzl] *vi*: **to ~ up to** тере́ться* (потере́ться* *perf*) но́сом о +*acc*.

NV *abbr* (*US*: *POST*) = Nevada.

NWT *abbr* (*CANADA*) = Northwest Territories.

NY *abbr* (*US*: *POST*) = New York.

NYC *abbr* (*US*: *POST*) = New York City.

nylon ['naɪlən] *n* нейло́н ◆ *adj* нейло́новый; **~s** *npl* нейло́новые чулки́* *mpl*.

nymph [nɪmf] *n* (*MYTHOLOGY*) ни́мфа; (*ZOOL*) личи́нка*.

nymphomaniac ['nɪmfəuˈmeɪnɪæk] *n* нимфома́нка*.

NYSE *n abbr* (*US*) = New York Stock Exchange.

NZ *abbr* = New Zealand.

---

* marks translations which have irregular inflections. The Russian-English side of the dictionary gives inflectional information.

~ O, o ~

O, o [əu] *n* (*letter*) 15-ая бу́ква англи́йского алфави́та; (*number*: *TEL etc*) ноль* *m*.

O *abbr* = outstanding; (*US*: *SCOL*) ≈ отл.= отли́чно.

oaf [əuf] *n* чурба́н, дуби́на *m*/*f*.

oak [əuk] *n* дуб* ♦ *adj* дубо́вый.

O & M *n abbr* = organization and method.

OAP *n abbr* (*BRIT*) = old age pensioner.

oar [ɔ:'] *n* весло́*; **to put** *or* **shove one's** ~ **in** (*fig*: *inf*) встрева́ть (встрять* *perf*).

oarsman ['ɔ:zmən] *n* гребе́ц*.

OAS *n abbr* = Organization of American States.

oases [əu'eɪsi:z] *npl of* oasis.

oasis [əu'eɪsɪs] (*pl* **oases**) *n* (*also fig*) оа́зис.

oath [əuθ] *n* (*promise*) кля́тва; (: *LAW*) прися́га; (*swear word*) прокля́тие; **on** (*BRIT*) **or under** ~ под прися́гой; **to take the** ~ принима́ть (приня́ть* *perf*) прися́гу.

oatmeal ['əutmi:l] *n* овся́ная мука́.

oats [əuts] *npl* овёс*.

OAU *n abbr* = Organization of African Unity.

obdurate ['ɔbdjurɪt] *adj* непрекло́нный* (непрекло́нен).

OBE *n abbr* (*BRIT*: = Order of the British Empire) о́рден Брита́нской импе́рии.

obedience [ə'bi:dɪəns] *n* повинове́ние, послуша́ние; **in** ~ **to** повину́ясь +*dat*.

obedient [ə'bi:dɪənt] *adj* послу́шный* (послу́шен); **to be** ~ **to sb/sth** слу́шаться (послу́шаться *perf*) кого́-н/чего́-н.

obelisk ['ɔbɪlɪsk] *n* обели́ск.

obese [əu'bi:s] *adj* ту́чный* (ту́чен).

obesity [əu'bi:sɪtɪ] *n* ожире́ние, ту́чность *f*.

obey [ə'beɪ] *vt* подчиня́ться (подчини́ться *perf*) +*dat*, повинова́ться (*impf*/*perf*) +*dat* ♦ *vi* подчиня́ться (подчини́ться *perf*), повинова́ться (*impf*).

obituary [ə'bɪtjuərɪ] *n* некроло́г.

object [*n* 'ɔbdʒɪkt, *vi* əb'dʒɛkt] *n* (*thing*) предме́т; (*aim, purpose*) цель *f*; (*of affection, desires*) объе́кт; (*LING*) дополне́ние ♦ *vi*: **to** ~ (**to**) возража́ть (возрази́ть* *perf*) (про́тив +*gen*); **expense is no** ~ де́ньги – не пробле́ма; **what's the** ~ **of doing that?** для чего́ де́лать э́то?; **he** ~**ed that ...** он возрази́л, что ...; **I** ~**!** я возража́ю!; **do you** ~ **to my smoking?** Вы не возража́ете если я бу́ду кури́ть?

objection [əb'dʒɛkʃən] *n* возраже́ние; **I have no** ~ **to ...** я не име́ю никаки́х возраже́ний про́тив +*gen* ...; **if you have no** ~ е́сли Вы не возража́ете; **to make** *or* **raise an** ~ выдвига́ть (вы́двинуть *perf*) возраже́ние.

objectionable [əb'dʒɛkʃənəbl] *adj* (*language, conduct*) возмути́тельный* (возмути́телен); (*person*) неприя́тный* (неприя́тен).

objective [əb'dʒɛktɪv] *adj* объекти́вный* (объекти́вен) ♦ *n* (*aim, purpose*) цель *f*.

objectively [əb'dʒɛktɪvlɪ] *adv* объекти́вно.

objectivity [ɔbdʒɪk'tɪvɪtɪ] *n* объекти́вность *f*.

object lesson *n*: **an** ~ ~ **in** нагля́дный приме́р +*gen*.

objector [əb'dʒɛktə'] *n* протесту́ющий*(-ая) *m*(*f*) *adj*.

obligation [ɔblɪ'geɪʃən] *n* обяза́тельство; **we are under no** ~ **to them** мы им ниче́м не обя́заны; **we are under (an)** ~ **to give him what he needs** мы обя́заны дать ему́ всё, что потре́буется; "**without** ~" (*COMM*) „без обяза́тельств".

obligatory [ə'blɪgətərɪ] *adj* обяза́тельный* (обяза́телен).

oblige [ə'blaɪdʒ] *vt* (*do a favour for*) обя́зывать (обяза́ть *perf*); (*force*): **to** ~ **sb to do** обя́зывать (обяза́ть* *perf*) кого́-н +*infin*; **I'm much** ~**d to you for your help** (*grateful*) я о́чень обя́зан Вам за ва́шу по́мощь; **anything to** ~**!** (*inf*) (я весь) к ва́шим услу́гам!

obliging [ə'blaɪdʒɪŋ] *adj* (*helpful*) любе́зный* (любе́зен).

oblique [ə'bli:k] *adj* (*line*) накло́нный; (*comment, reference*) ко́свенный ♦ *n* (*BRIT*: *TYP*): ~ (**stroke**) накло́нная черта́.

obliterate [ə'blɪtəreɪt] *vt* (*destroy*) уничтожа́ть (уничто́жить *perf*); (*from mind*) стира́ть (стере́ть* *perf*).

oblivion [ə'blɪvɪən] *n* забве́ние; **these events have sunk into** ~ э́ти собы́тия пре́даны забве́нию.

oblivious [ə'blɪvɪəs] *adj*: **to be** ~ **of** *or* **to** не сознава́ть* (*impf*) +*gen*.

oblong ['ɔblɔŋ] *adj* продолгова́тый ♦ *n* продолгова́тый предме́т.

obnoxious [əb'nɔkʃəs] *adj* отврати́тельный* (отврати́телен).

o.b.o. *abbr* (*US*: *in classified ads*: = or best offer) и́ли по договорённости.

oboe ['əubəu] *n* гобо́й.

obscene [əbˈsiːn] *adj* непристо́йный*
(непристо́ен).
obscenity [əbˈsɛnɪtɪ] *n* непристо́йность *f*.
obscure [əbˈskjuə] *adj* (*little known*) мало-
изве́стный* (малоизве́стен); (*difficult to
understand*) нея́сный* (нея́сен), сму́тный*
(сму́тен) ♦ *vt* (*view, sun etc*) загора́живать
(загороди́ть* *perf*); (*truth, meaning etc*)
затемня́ть (затемни́ть *perf*).
obscurity [əbˈskjuərɪtɪ] *n* (*see adj*) безве́стность
f; нея́сность *f*.
obsequious [əbˈsiːkwɪəs] *adj* подобо-
стра́стный* (подобостра́стен).
observable [əbˈzɜːvəbl] *adj* наблюда́емый;
(*appreciable*) заме́тный* (заме́тен).
observance [əbˈzɜːvns] *n* (*of law, custom*)
соблюде́ние; **religious ~s** религио́зные
обря́ды.
observant [əbˈzɜːvnt] *adj* наблюда́тельный*
(наблюда́телен).
observation [ɔbzəˈveɪʃən] *n* (*remark*)
замеча́ние; (*surveillance, also MED*)
наблюде́ние.
observation post *n* наблюда́тельный пост* *or*
пункт.
observatory [əbˈzɜːvətrɪ] *n* обсервато́рия.
observe [əbˈzɜːv] *vt* (*watch*) наблюда́ть (*impf*)
за +*instr*; (*comment*) замеча́ть (заме́тить*
perf); (*abide by*) соблюда́ть (соблюсти́* *perf*).
observer [əbˈzɜːvə] *n* наблюда́тель *m*.
obsess [əbˈsɛs] *vt* владева́ть (владе́ть *perf*);
you are ~ed by the idea Вы одержи́мы э́той
иде́ей; **he is totally ~ed with this woman** он
соверше́нно поме́шан на э́той же́нщине.
obsession [əbˈsɛʃən] *n* навя́зчивая иде́я; **she
has an ~ for cats** она́ поме́шана на ко́шках.
obsessive [əbˈsɛsɪv] *adj* одержи́мый
(одержи́м).
obsolescence [ɔbsəˈlɛsns] *n* устаре́лость *f*.
obsolete [ˈɔbsəliːt] *adj* (*words*) устаре́вший;
(*technology*) устаре́лый.
obstacle [ˈɔbstəkl] *n* (*also fig*) препя́тствие.
obstacle race *n* бег с препя́тствиями.
obstetrician [ɔbstəˈtrɪʃən] *n* врач-акуше́р.
obstetrics [ɔbˈstɛtrɪks] *n* акуше́рство.
obstinacy [ˈɔbstɪnəsɪ] *n* (*of person*) упря́мство.
obstinate [ˈɔbstɪnɪt] *adj* (*person, behaviour*)
упря́мый (упря́м); (*cold, pain*) упо́рный.
obstruct [əbˈstrʌkt] *vt* (*road, path*)
загора́живать (загороди́ть* *perf*); (*traffic,
progress*) препя́тствовать
(воспрепя́тствовать *perf*).
obstruction [əbˈstrʌkʃən] *n* (*action*)
препя́тствование; (: *of law*) обстру́кция;
(*object*) препя́тствие.
obstructive [əbˈstrʌktɪv] *adj* (*behaviour*)
обструкцио́нный; **he is ~** он чи́нит
препя́тствия.

obtain [əbˈteɪn] *vt* (*get hold of*) достава́ть*
(доста́ть* *perf*); (*gain*) получа́ть (получи́ть*
perf) ♦ *vi* (*formal: exist*) существова́ть (*impf*); **to
~ sth (for o.s.)** добива́ться (доби́ться* *perf*)
чего́-н (для себя́).
obtainable [əbˈteɪnəbl] *adj* достижи́мый
(достижи́м).
obtrusive [əbˈtruːsɪv] *adj* навя́зчивый
(навя́зчив).
obtuse [əbˈtjuːs] *adj* (*person, remark*)
бестолко́вый (бестолко́в); (*MATH*) тупо́й.
obverse [ˈɔbvəːs] *n*: **the ~** обра́тное *nt adj*.
obviate [ˈɔbvɪeɪt] *vt* устраня́ть (устрани́ть
perf).
obvious [ˈɔbvɪəs] *adj* очеви́дный* (очеви́ден).
obviously [ˈɔbvɪəslɪ] *adv* очеви́дно; (*of course*)
разуме́ется; **he was ~ not drunk** бы́ло
очеви́дно, что он не пьян; **he was not ~
drunk** он не был очеви́дным о́бразом пьян;
~ not разуме́ется, нет.
OCAS *n abbr* = **Organization of Central American
States**.
occasion [əˈkeɪʒən] *n* (*time*) раз*; (*case*)
слу́чай; (*event*) собы́тие; (*opportunity*)
возмо́жность *f* ♦ *vt* (*cause*) вызыва́ть
(вы́звать* *perf*); **on this ~** на э́тот раз; **on that
~** в тот раз; **to rise to the ~** ока́зываться
(оказа́ться* *perf*) на высоте́.
occasional [əˈkeɪʒənl] *adj* ре́дкий*, неча́стый.
occasionally [əˈkeɪʒənəlɪ] *adv* вре́мя от
вре́мени, и́зредка; **very ~** о́чень ре́дко.
occasional table *n* запасно́й сто́лик.
occult [ɔˈkʌlt] *n*: **the ~** окку́льтные нау́ки *fpl*.
occupancy [ˈɔkjupənsɪ] *n* пребыва́ние.
occupant [ˈɔkjupənt] *n* (*long-term*)
обита́тель(ница) *m(f)*; (*temporary*): **the ~s of
the car/room** находя́щиеся *pl adj* в маши́не/
ко́мнате.
occupation [ɔkjuˈpeɪʃən] *n* заня́тие;
(*occupancy*) пребыва́ние; (*MIL*) оккупа́ция;
unfit for ~ (*house*) неприго́дный*
(неприго́ден) для жилья́.
occupational accident [ɔkjuˈpeɪʃənl-] *n*
произво́дственный несча́стный слу́чай.
occupational guidance (*BRIT*) консульта́ция
по по́иску ме́ста рабо́ты.
occupational hazard *n* произво́дственный
риск.
occupational pension scheme *n* пенсио́нный
план, по кото́рому пенсио́нный фонд
форми́руется за счёт взно́сов рабо́тника и
его́ работода́теля.
occupational therapy *n* трудотерапи́я.
occupier [ˈɔkjupaɪə] *n* прожива́ющий(-ая) *m(f)*
adj; "**to the ~**" „прожива́ющему" (*обраще́ние
в письме́*).
occupy [ˈɔkjupaɪ] *vt* занима́ть (заня́ть* *perf*);
(*country, attention*) захва́тывать (захвати́ть*

---

perf); **to ~ o.s. (with sth)** занима́ться (заня́ться *perf*) (чем-н); **all of the rooms are occupied** все ко́мнаты за́няты; **he was occupied with his work** он был за́нят рабо́той.

occur [ə'kəː'] *vi* (*take place*) происходи́ть* (произойти́* *perf*), случа́ться (случи́ться *perf*); (*exist*) встреча́ться (встре́титься *perf*); **to ~ to sb** приходи́ть* (прийти́* *perf*) кому́-н в го́лову.

occurrence [ə'kʌrəns] *n* (*event*) происше́ствие; (*existence*) слу́чай.

ocean ['əuʃən] *n* океа́н; **~s of** (*fig: inf*) мо́ре +*gen*.

ocean bed *n* дно* океа́на.

ocean-going ['əuʃəngəuɪŋ] *adj* (*ship etc*) океа́нский.

Oceania [əuʃɪ'eɪnɪə] *n* Океа́ния.

ocean liner *n* океа́нский ла́йнер.

ochre ['əukə'] (*US* **ocher**) *adj* (*colour*) о́хровый.

o'clock [ə'klɔk] *adv*: **it is five ~** сейча́с пять часо́в.

OCR *n abbr* (*COMPUT*) = **optical character recognition, optical character reader**.

Oct. *abbr* = **October**.

octagonal [ɔk'tægənl] *adj* восьмиуго́льный.

octane ['ɔkteɪn] *n* окта́н; **high-~ petrol** *or* (*US*) **gas** бензи́н с высо́ким окта́новым число́м.

octave ['ɔktɪv] *n* окта́ва.

October [ɔk'təubə'] *n* октя́брь* *m*; *see also* **July**.

octogenarian ['ɔktəudʒɪ'nɛərɪən] *n*: **he is an ~** ему́ за во́семьдесят.

octopus ['ɔktəpəs] *n* осьмино́г.

odd [ɔd] *adj* (*strange*) стра́нный* (стра́нен), необы́чный* (необы́чен); (*uneven*) нечётный; (*not paired*) непа́рный; (*rare*) ре́дкий*; **60-~** шестьдеся́т с ли́шним; **at ~ times** вре́мя от вре́мени; **I was the ~ one out** я был ли́шний.

oddball ['ɔdbɔːl] *n* (*inf*) чуда́к*.

oddity ['ɔdɪtɪ] *n* (*thing*) дико́винка; (*person*) ре́дкость *f*; (*characteristic*) стра́нность *f*.

odd-job man [ɔd'dʒɔb-] *n* разнорабо́чий* *m adj*.

odd jobs *npl* случа́йные рабо́ты *fpl*.

oddly ['ɔdlɪ] *adv* (*strangely: behave, dress*) стра́нно; *see also* **enough**.

oddments ['ɔdmənts] *npl* оста́тки *mpl*.

odds [ɔdz] *npl* (*in betting*) ста́вки* *fpl*; **the ~ are against him** обстоя́тельства про́тив него́; **to succeed against all the ~** добива́ться (доби́ться* *perf*) успе́ха напереко́р всему́; **it makes no ~** всё равно́; **to be at ~ (with)** быть* (*impf*) не в лада́х (с +*instr*).

odds and ends *npl* ме́лочи* *fpl*.

odds-on [ɔdz'ɔn] *adj* (*inf: favourite*) абсолю́тный; **he is ~ to win the election** он наверняка́ победи́т на вы́борах.

ode [əud] *n* о́да.

Odessa [əu'dɛsə] *n* Оде́сса.

odious ['əudɪəs] *adj* одио́зный* (одио́зен).

odometer [ɔ'dɔmɪtə'] *n* одо́метр.

odour ['əudə'] (*US* **odor**) *n* за́пах.

odourless ['əudəlɪs] *adj* без за́паха.

OECD *n abbr* = **Organization for Economic Cooperation and Development**.

oesophagus [iː'sɔfəgəs] (*US* **esophagus**) *n* пищево́д.

oestrogen ['iːstrəudʒən] (*US* **estrogen**) *n* эстроге́н.

KEYWORD

of [ɔv] *prep*: **1: the history of Russia** исто́рия Росси́и; **a friend of ours** наш друг*; **a boy of 10** ма́льчик десяти́ лет; **that was kind of you** э́то бы́ло о́чень любе́зно с ва́шей стороны́; **a man of great ability** челове́к больши́х спосо́бностей; **the city of New York** го́род Нью-Йо́рк; **south of London** к ю́гу от Ло́ндона

2 (*expressing quantity, amount, dates etc*): **a kilo of flour** килогра́мм муки́; **how much of this material do you need?** ско́лько тако́й тка́ни Вам ну́жно?; **there were three of them** (*people*) их бы́ло тро́е; (*objects*) их бы́ло три; **3 of us stayed** тро́е из нас оста́лись; **the 5th of July** 5-ое ию́ля; **on the 5th of July** 5-ого ию́ля

3 (*from, out of*) из +*gen*; **the house is made of wood** дом* сде́лан из де́рева.

KEYWORD

off [ɔf] *adv* **1** (*referring to distance, time*): **it's a long way off** э́то далеко́ отсю́да; **the city is five miles off** до го́рода пять миль; **the game is 3 days off** до игры́ оста́лось 3 дня

2 (*departure*): **to go off to Paris/Italy** уезжа́ть (уе́хать* *perf*) в Пари́ж/Ита́лию; **I must be off** мне пора́ идти́*

3 (*removal*): **to take off one's hat/coat/clothes** снима́ть (снять* *perf*) шля́пу/пальто́/оде́жду; **the button came off** пу́говица оторвала́сь; **10% off** (*COMM*) ски́дка 10%

4: **I'm off on Fridays** у меня́ выходно́й по пя́тницам; **he was off on Friday** в пя́тницу его́ не́ было на рабо́те; **I have a day off** у меня́ отгу́л; **to be off sick** не рабо́тать (*impf*) по боле́зни

♦ *adj* **1** (*not turned on*) вы́ключенный (вы́ключен); (: *tap*) закры́тый (закры́т); (*disconnected*) отключённый (отключён)

2 (*cancelled: meeting, match*) отменённый (отменён); (*agreement*) расто́ргнутый (расто́ргнут)

3 (*BRIT*): **to go off** (*milk*) прокиса́ть (проки́снуть* *perf*); (*cheese, meat*) по́ртиться (испо́ртиться *perf*); **the milk has gone off** молоко́ проки́сло:

4: **on the off chance** на вся́кий* слу́чай; **to have an off day** встава́ть (встать* *perf*) с ле́вой ноги́

♦ *prep* **1** (*indicating motion, removal etc*) с +*gen*; **to fall off a cliff** упа́сть (*perf*) со скалы́

2 (*distant from*) от +*gen*; **it's just off the M1** это недалеко от автострады M1; **it's five km off the main road** это в пяти км от шоссе; **to be off meat** (*no longer eat it*) не есть* (*impf*) мясо; (*no longer like it*) разлюбить* (*perf*) мясо.

offal ['ɔfl] *n* потроха* *pl*.
offbeat ['ɔfbi:t] *adj* нетривиальный* (нетривиален).
off-centre [ɔf'sɛntəʳ] (*US* **off-center**) *adj* смещённый* (смещён) ♦ *adv* не по центру.
off colour *adj* (*BRIT*: *inf*): **I feel ~ ~** мне нездоровится.
offence [ə'fɛns] (*US* **offense**) *n* (*crime*) правонарушение; (*insult*) оскорбление; **to commit an ~** совершать (совершить *perf*) правонарушение; **to take ~ at** обижаться (обидеться* *perf*) на +*acc*; **to give ~ to** обижать (обидеть* *perf*), оскорблять (оскорбить* *perf*); "**no ~, but ...**" „не в обиду будет сказано, но ...".
offend [ə'fɛnd] *vt* (*person*) обижать (обидеть* *perf*); (*feelings*) оскорблять (оскорбить* *perf*) ♦ *vi*: **to ~ against** (*law, rule*) нарушать (нарушить *perf*).
offender [ə'fɛndəʳ] *n* правонарушитель(ница) *m(f)*.
offending [ə'fɛndɪŋ] *adj* соответствующий*.
offense [ə'fɛns] *n* (*US*) = **offence**.
offensive [ə'fɛnsɪv] *adj* (*remark, behaviour*) оскорбительный* (оскорбителен); (*smell etc*) отвратительный* (отвратителен) ♦ *n* (*MIL*) наступление; **~ weapon** орудие нападения.
offer ['ɔfəʳ] *n* предложение ♦ *vt* предлагать (предложить* *perf*); **to make an ~ for sth** предлагать (предложить* *perf*) цену за что-н; **to ~ sth to sb** предлагать (предложить* *perf*) кому-н что-н; **to ~ to do** предлагать (предложить* *perf*) +*infin*; "**on ~**" (*COMM*) „продаётся со скидкой".
offering ['ɔfərɪŋ] *n* (*also REL*) подношение.
offer price *n* цена продавца.
offhand [ɔf'hænd] *adj* (*unfriendly*) пренебрежительный* (пренебрежителен); (*easy-going*) непринуждённый* (непринуждён) ♦ *adv* сразу, не думая; **I can't tell you ~** я не могу Вам сказать сразу.
office ['ɔfɪs] *n* офис; (*room*) кабинет; (*position*) пост, должность *f*; **doctor's ~** (*US*) кабинет врача; **to take ~** (*person*) вступать (вступить* *perf*) в должность; (*political party*) приходить* (прийти* *perf*) к власти; **through his good ~s** (*fig*) благодаря его услугам; **the O~ of Fair Trading** (*BRIT*) Управление добросовестной конкуренции.
office automation *n* автоматизация делопроизводства.

office bearer *n* должностное лицо*.
office block (*US* **office building**) *n* административное здание.
office boy *n* посыльный *m adj*.
office hours *npl* часы* *mpl* работы; (*US*: *MED*) приёмные часы* *mpl*.
office manager *n* начальник конторы.
officer ['ɔfɪsəʳ] *n* (*MIL*) офицер; (*also*: **police ~**) полицейский* *m adj*; (: *in Russia*) милиционер; (*of organization*) заведующий* *m adj*.
office work *n* канцелярская работа.
office worker *n* канцелярский*(-ая) *or* конторский*(-ая) служащий*(-ая) *m(f) adj*.
official [ə'fɪʃl] *adj* официальный* ♦ *n* должностное лицо*; **government ~** официальное лицо*.
officialdom [ə'fɪʃldəm] *n* (*pej*) бюрократия.
officially [ə'fɪʃəlɪ] *adv* официально.
Official Receiver *n* (*COMM*) официальное лицо, назначенное для проведения ликвидации неплатёжеспособной компании.
official strike *n* официальная забастовка.
officiate [ə'fɪʃɪeɪt] *vi* распоряжаться (*impf*); (*REL*) совершать (совершить *perf*) богослужение; **to ~ as Mayor** исполнять (*impf*) обязанности мэра; **to ~ at a marriage** совершать (совершить *perf*) бракосочетание.
officious [ə'fɪʃəs] *adj* придирчивый.
offing ['ɔfɪŋ] *n*: **war is in the ~** война грядёт.
off-key [ɔf'ki:] *adj* (*MUS*) фальшивый.
off-licence [ɔf'laɪsns] *n* (*BRIT*) винный магазин.
off-limits [ɔf'lɪmɪts] *adj* (*esp US*) закрытый (закрыт).
off-line [ɔf'laɪn] *adj* (*COMPUT*) автономный, независимый ♦ *adv* (*COMPUT*) автономно, независимо; (: *switched off*) отключено.
off-load [ɔf'ləud] *vt* сваливать (свалить* *perf*).
off-peak ['ɔf'pi:k] *adj* (*heating, electricity*) непиковый; (*train, ticket*) со скидкой.
off-putting ['ɔfputɪŋ] *adj* (*BRIT*) неприятный.
off-season ['ɔf'si:zn] *adj* (*booking etc*) несезонный ♦ *adv* не в сезон.
offset ['ɔfsɛt] *irreg vt* уравновешивать (*impf*).
offshoot ['ɔfʃu:t] *n* (*fig*) ответвление; (: *of discussion*) последствие.
offshore [ɔf'ʃɔ:ʳ] *adj* (*oilrig, fishing*) морской; **there was a gentle ~ breeze** на море дул лёгкий бриз.
offside [ɔf'saɪd] *n* (*AUT*: *in Britain*) правая сторона ♦ *adj* (*SPORT*): **to be ~** быть* (*impf*) в офсайде.
offspring ['ɔfsprɪŋ] *n inv* отпрыск.
offstage [ɔf'steɪdʒ] *adv* (*sounds*) за сценой.
off-the-cuff [ɔfðə'kʌf] *adj* импровизированный.

---

* marks translations which have irregular inflections. The Russian-English side of the dictionary gives inflectional information.

off-the-job ['ɔfðə'dʒɔb] *adj*: ~ **training**
обучéние с отры́вом от произвóдства.
off-the-peg ['ɔfðə'pɛg] (*US* **off-the-rack**) *adj*: ~
clothing готóвая одéжда.
off-the-rack ['ɔfðə'ræk] *adj* (*US*) = **off-the-peg**.
off-the-record ['ɔfðə'rɛkɔːd] *adj*
неофициáльный* (неофициáлен) ♦ *adv*
неофициáльно.
off-white ['ɔfwaɪt] *adj* белова́тый.
Ofgas ['ɔfgæs] *n* (*BRIT*) управлéние по
контрóлю за газоснабжéнием.
Oftel ['ɔftɛl] *n* (*BRIT*) управлéние по контрóлю
за телефóнной сéтью.
Ofwat ['ɔfwɔt] *n* (*BRIT*) управлéние по
контрóлю за водоснабжéнием.
often ['ɔfn] *adv* чáсто; **how** ~ ...? как чáсто ...?;
more ~ **than not** чáще всегó; **as** ~ **as not**
довóльно чáсто; **every so** ~ врéмя от
врéмени.
ogle ['əugl] *vt* глазéть *(impf)* на +*acc*.
ogre ['əugəʳ] *n* великáн-людоéд.
OH *abbr* (*US*: *POST*) = *Ohio*.
oh [əu] *excl* о, а; ~ **really!** да!; ~ **no!** (о) нет!
ohm [əum] *n* (*ELEC*) ом.
OHMS *abbr* (*BRIT*: = *On His/Her Majesty's*
Service) на слýжбе у Егó/Её Королéвского
Вели́чества.
oil [ɔɪl] *n* (*CULIN*) мáсло; (*petroleum*) нефть *f*;
(*for heating*) печнóе тóпливо ♦ *vt* (*engine, gun*
etc) смáзывать (смáзать* *perf*); ~**s** *npl* (*ART*)
мáсляные крáски *fpl*.
oilcan ['ɔɪlkæn] *n* маслёнка*.
oil change *n* (*AUT*) смéна мáсла (*в мотóре*).
oilcloth ['ɔɪlklɔθ] *n* клеёнка*.
oilfield ['ɔɪlfiːld] *n* месторождéние нéфти.
oil filter *n* (*AUT*) мáсляный фильтр.
oilfired ['ɔɪlfaɪəd] *adj* мáсляный.
oil gauge *n* (*AUT*) индикáтор ýровня мáсла.
oil industry *n* нефтянáя промы́шленность *f*.
oil painting *n* карти́на, напи́санная мáслом.
oil refinery *n* нефтеперерабáтывающий
завóд.
oil rig *n* нефтянáя платфóрма.
oilseed rape ['ɔɪlsiːd-] *n* рáпс, сурéпка.
oilskins ['ɔɪlskɪnz] *npl* водонепроницáемая
одéжда *fsg*.
oil slick *n* нефтянóе пятнó*.
oil tanker *n* (*ship*) тáнкер; (*truck*) нефтевóз.
oil well *n* нефтянáя сквáжина.
oily ['ɔɪlɪ] *adj* (*rag*) промáсленный
(промáслен); (*substance*) маслян́истый;
(*food*) жи́рный* (жи́рен).
ointment ['ɔɪntmənt] *n* мазь *f*.
OK *abbr* (*US*: *POST*) = *Oklahoma*.
O.K. ['əu'keɪ] *excl* (*inf*) хорошó, лáдно ♦ *adj*
(*film, meal etc*) срéдний* ♦ *vt* (*approve*)
одобря́ть (одóбрить *perf*) ♦ *n*: **to give sth the**
~ давáть* (дать* *perf*) добрó на что-н; **is it** ~?
(э́то) нормáльно?; **is everything** ~? всё в
поря́дке?; **are you (feeling)** ~? Вы себя́
нормáльно чýвствуете?; **are you** ~ **for**

money? у Вас нет проблéм с деньгáми?; **it's**
~ **with** *or* **by me** я не прóтив.
okay ['əu'keɪ] *excl* = **O.K.**.
old [əuld] *adj* (*aged*) стáрый* (стар); (*former*)
стáрый; **how** ~ **are you?** скóлько Вам лет?;
he's 10 years ~ емý 10 лет; ~ **man** стари́к; ~
woman старýха; ~**er brother** стáрший*
брат*; **any** ~ **rag will do** сойдёт любáя
тря́пка.
old age *n* стáрость *f*.
old age pension *n* пéнсия по стáрости.
old age pensioner *n* (*BRIT*) пенсионéр(ка*).
old-fashioned ['əuld'fæʃnd] *adj* старомóдный*
(старомóден).
old hand *n* óпытный человéк.
old hat *adj* (*inf*): **this is very** ~ ~ э́то ужáсно
ненóво.
old maid *n* стáрая дéва.
old people's home *n* дом* для престарéлых.
old-style ['əuldstaɪl] *adj* в стари́нном сти́ле.
old-time ['əuld'taɪm] *adj* (*dancing*)
старомóдный.
old-timer [əuld'taɪməʳ] *n* (*inf*) старожи́л(ка*).
old wives' tale *n* бáбушкины скáзки* *fpl*.
oleander [əulɪ'ændəʳ] *n* олеáндр.
O-level [əulɛvl] *n* (*formerly*) ≈ экзáмены в
8-ом клáссе срéдней шкóлы.
olive ['ɔlɪv] *n* (*fruit*) масли́на, оли́вка* ♦ *adj*
(*also*: ~**-green**) оли́вковый; ~ **tree** оли́вковое
дéрево*; **to offer an** ~ **branch** (*fig*) предлагáть
(предложи́ть* *perf*) переми́рие.
olive oil *n* оли́вковое мáсло.
Olympic [əu'lɪmpɪk] *adj* олимпи́йский*.
Olympic Games *npl*: **the** ~ (*also*: **the**
Olympics) Олимпи́йские и́гры *fpl*.
OM *n abbr* (*BRIT*: = *Order of Merit*) óрден "За
заслýги".
Oman [əu'mɑːn] *n* Омáн.
OMB *n abbr* (*US*) = *Office of Management and*
Budget.
ombudsman ['ɔmbudzmən] *n* официáльное
лицó, рассмáтривающее жáлобы чáстных
лиц на госудáрственные учреждéния.
omelet(te) ['ɔmlɪt] *n* омлéт; **ham/cheese** ~
омлéт с ветчинóй/сы́ром.
omen ['əumən] *n* предзнаменовáние.
ominous ['ɔmɪnəs] *adj* злове́щий* (злове́щ).
omission [əu'mɪʃən] *n* прóпуск.
omit [əu'mɪt] *vt* пропускáть (пропусти́ть* *perf*)
♦ *vi*: **he** ~**ted to inform me of this** он не
проинформи́ровал меня́ об э́том.
omnipotent [ɔm'nɪpətnt] *adj* всемогýщий*
(всемогýщ).
omnivorous [ɔm'nɪvrəs] *adj* всея́дный*
(всея́ден).
ON *abbr* (*CANADA*) = *Ontario*.

KEYWORD
---

on [ɔn] *prep* **1** (*position*) на +*prp*; (*motion*) на
+*acc*; **the book is on the table** кни́га на столé;
to put the book on the table класть*
(положи́ть* *perf*) кни́гу на стол; **on the left**

слёва; **the house is on the main road** дом
стоит у шоссе

2 (*indicating means, method, condition etc*): **on
foot** пешком; **on the train/plane** (*go*) на поезде/
самолёте; (*be*) в поезде/самолёте; **on the
telephone/radio/television** по телефону/
радио/телевизору; **she's on the telephone**
она разговаривает по телефону; **to be on
drugs** принимать (*impf*) лекарства; **to be on
holiday/business** быть (*impf*) в отпуске/
командировке

3 (*referring to time*): **on Friday** в пятницу; **on
Fridays** по пятницам; **on June 20th** 20-ого
июня; **a week on Friday** через неделю, считая
с пятницы; **on arrival** по приезде; **on seeing
this** увидев это

4 (*about, concerning*) о +*prp*, по +*dat*;
information on train services информация о
расписании поездов; **a book on physics**
книга по физике

♦ *adv* **1** (*referring to dress*) в +*prp*; **to have
one's coat on** быть (*impf*) в пальто; **what's she
got on?** во что она была одета?; **she put her
boots/gloves/hat on** она надела сапоги/
перчатки/шляпу

2 (*further, continuously*) дальше, далее; **to
walk on** идти* (*impf*) дальше

♦ *adj* **1** (*functioning, in operation*)
включённый (включён); (: *tap*) открытый
(открыт); **is the meeting still on?** (*in progress*)
собрание ещё идёт?; (*not cancelled*)
собрание не отменили?; **there's a good film
on at the cinema** в кинотеатре идёт хороший
фильм

2: **that's not on!** (*inf: of behaviour*) так не
пойдёт *or* не годится!

ONC *n abbr* (*BRIT*: = *Ordinary National Certificate*)
≈ свидетельство об окончании начальной
школы.
once [wʌns] *adv* (*on one occasion*) (один) раз;
(*formerly*) когда-то, однажды ♦ *conj*
(*immediately afterwards*) как только; ~ **he
had left** как только он ушёл; **at** ~
(*immediately*) сразу же; (*simultaneously*)
вместе; **come here at** ~! сейчас же подойди
сюда!; (**all**) **at** ~ все вместе; ~ **a week** (один)
раз в неделю; ~ **more** ещё раз; ~ **and for all**
раз и навсегда; **I knew him** ~ я когда-то был
знаком с ним; ~ **upon a time there lived** ...
жил-был ....
oncoming [ˈɔnkʌmɪŋ] *adj* (*traffic etc*)
встречный.
OND *n abbr* (*BRIT*: = *Ordinary National Diploma*)
диплом о среднем техническом
образовании.

KEYWORD

one [wʌn] *n* один* (*f* одна*, *nt* одно*, *pl* одни*);
one hundred and fifty сто пятьдесят; **one day
there was a sudden knock at the door**
однажды неожиданно раздался стук в
дверь; **one by one** по одному, один за
другим; *see also* **five**

♦ *adj* **1** (*sole*) единственный; **the one book
which** единственная книга, которая
2 (*same*) один; **they all belong to the one
family** они все из одной семьи

♦ *pron*: **1**: **I'm the one who did it** это я сделал;
this one этот (*f* эта, *nt* это); **that one** тот (*f* та,
nt то); **I've already got one** у меня уже есть:
2: **one another** друг друга; **do you two ever
see one another?** Вы когда-нибудь
видитесь?; **the boys didn't dare look at one
another** мальчики не смели взглянуть друг
на друга
3 (*impersonal*): **one never knows** никогда не
знаешь; **to cut one's finger** порезать (*perf*)
(себе) палец; **one needs to eat** надо *or* нужно
есть.

one-day excursion [ˈwʌndeɪ-] *n* (*US*)
обратный билет (*действительный в
течение одного дня*).
One-hundred share index [ˈwʌnhʌndrəd-] *n*
индекс ста акций (*публикуемый ежедневно
и показывающий состояние фондовой
биржи*).
one-man [ˈwʌnˈmæn] *adj* (*business*)
индивидуальный; (*canoe*) одноместный.
one-man band *n* человек-оркестр.
one-off [wʌnˈɔf] *n* (*BRIT: inf*) единичный
случай.
one-parent family [ˈwʌnpɛərənt-] *n* неполная
семья*.
one-piece [ˈwʌnpiːs] *adj*: ~ **bathing suit**
цельный купальник.
onerous [ˈɔnərəs] *adj* тягостный* (тягостен),
обременительный* (обременителен).
one's [wʌnz] *adj*: **to dry** ~ **hands** вытирать
(вытереть* *perf*) руки; *see also* **my**.
oneself [wʌnˈsɛlf] *pron* (*reflexive*) себя;
(*emphatic*) сам; (*after prep: +acc, +gen*)
самого себя; (: +*dat*) самому себе; (: +*instr*)
самим собой; (: +*prp*) самом себе; **to hurt** ~
ушибаться (ушибиться *perf*); **to keep sth for**
~ держать* (*impf*) что-н при себе; **to talk to** ~
разговаривать (*impf*) с самим собой.
one-shot [ˈwʌnʃɔt] *n* (*US*) = **one-off**.
one-sided [wʌnˈsaɪdɪd] *adj* односторонний
(односторонен); (*contest*) неравный*
(неравен).
one-time [ˈwʌntaɪm] *adj* бывший*.
one-to-one [ˈwʌntəwʌn] *adj* (*tuition etc*)
индивидуальный ♦ *adv* один на один.

---

one-upmanship [wʌn'ʌrmənʃɪp] *n*: **the art of ~** умéние вы́делиться и показáть своё превосхóдство.

one-way ['wʌnweɪ] *adj* (*traffic*) одно-стóрóнний*; **~ street** у́лица с одностóрóнним движéнием.

ongoing ['ɒngəʊɪŋ] *adj* продолжáющийся.

onion ['ʌnjən] *n* лук*.

on-line ['ɒnlaɪn] (*COMPUT*) *adj* неавтонóмный; (*switched on*) подключённый ♦ *adv* неавтонóмно.

onlooker ['ɒnlukəʳ] *n* зри́тель(ница) *m(f)*.

only ['əʊnlɪ] *adv* тóлько ♦ *adj* еди́нственный ♦ *conj* (*but*) тóлько; **an ~ child** еди́нственный ребёнок*; **I ~ bought one bottle** я купи́л тóлько одну́ буты́лку; **I saw her ~ yesterday** я тóлько вчерá ви́дел её; **I'd be ~ too pleased to help** я был бы óчень рад помóчь; **I would come, ~ I'm too busy** я бы пришёл, тóлько я сли́шком зáнят; **not ~ ... but also ...** не тóлько ..., но и ....

o.n.o. *abbr* (*BRIT*: *in classified ads*) **= or near(est) offer**.

onset ['ɒnsɛt] *n* наступлéние.

onshore ['ɒnʃɔːʳ] *adj*: **~ wind** вéтер с мóря; (*oil rig, drilling*) назéмный.

onslaught ['ɒnslɔːt] *n* нападéние.

on-the-job ['ɒnðə'dʒɒb] *adj*: **~ training** обучéние без отры́ва от произвóдства.

onto ['ɒntu] *prep* = **on to**.

onus ['əʊnəs] *n*: **the ~ is on him to prove it** егó долг – доказáть э́то.

onward(s) ['ɒnwəd(z)] *adv* вперёд, дáльше; **from that time ~** с тех пор.

onyx ['ɒnɪks] *n* óникс.

oops [ups] *excl* (*inf*) ой!

ooze [uːz] *vi* сочи́ться (*impf*) ♦ *vt*: **to ~ confidence** излучáть (*impf*) увéренность.

opacity [əʊ'pæsɪtɪ] *n* непрозрáчность *f*.

opal ['əʊpl] *n* опáл.

opaque [əʊ'peɪk] *adj* непрозрáчный* (непрозрáчен).

OPEC ['əʊpɛk] *n abbr* (= *Organization of Petroleum-Exporting Countries*) ОПÉК.

open ['əʊpn] *adj* (*also fig*) откры́тый; (*enemy, hostility*) откровéнный; (*vacancy*) свобóдный* ♦ *vt* открывáть (откры́ть* *perf*) ♦ *vi* открывáться (откры́ться* *perf*); (*flower*) раскрывáться (раскры́ться* *perf*); (*book, debate etc: commence*) начинáться (начáться* *perf*); **in the ~ (air)** на откры́том вóздухе; **the ~ sea** откры́тое мóре; **~ ground** (*among trees*) поля́на; (*waste ground*) пусты́рь* *m*; **to have an ~ mind on sth** подходи́ть* (*impf*) к чему́-н без предубеждéния

▶ **open on to** *vt fus* (*subj: room, door*) выходи́ть* (*impf*) в/на +*acc*

▶ **open out** *vt* раскрывáть (раскры́ть* *perf*) ♦ *vi* раскрывáться (раскры́ться* *perf*)

▶ **open up** *vt* открывáть (откры́ть* *perf*) ♦ *vi* открывáться (откры́ться* *perf*).

open-air [əʊpn'ɛəʳ] *adj* (*concert*) на откры́том вóздухе; (*swimming pool*) откры́тый.

open-and-shut ['əʊpnən'ʃʌt] *adj*: **~ case** элементáрное дéло.

open day *n* день* *m* откры́тых дверéй.

open-ended [əʊpn'ɛndɪd] *adj* (*fig: question*) откры́тый; (: *discussion*) незавершённый.

opener ['əʊpnəʳ] *n* (*also: tin or can ~*) открывáлка*.

open-heart [əʊpn'hɑːt] *adj*: **~ surgery** откры́тая опéрáция на сéрдце.

opening ['əʊpnɪŋ] *adj* (*speech, remarks etc*) вступи́тельный ♦ *n* (*gap, hole*) отвéрстие; (*start*) начáло; (*opportunity*) возмóжность *f*; (*job*) вакáнсия.

opening night *n* (*THEAT*) премьéра.

open learning *n* самообучéние (*по подготóвленным посóбиям*).

openly ['əʊpnlɪ] *adv* откры́то.

open-minded [əʊpn'maɪndɪd] *adj* (*person*) откры́тый; (*approach*) непредвзя́тый.

open-necked ['əʊpnnɛkt] *adj* расстёгнутый.

openness ['əʊpnnɪs] *n* (*frankness*) откры́тость *f*.

open-plan ['əʊpn'plæn] *adj*: **~ office** óфис с откры́той планирóвкой.

open prison *n* тюрьмá свобóдного режи́ма.

open sandwich *n* бутербрóд.

open shop *n* (*TRADE UNIONS*) *предприя́тие, на котóрое нанимáют рабóчих независимо от члéнства в профсою́зе.*

Open University *n* (*BRIT*): **the ~ ~** Откры́тый университéт.

open verdict *n* (*LAW*): **an ~ ~ was passed** объяви́ли, что причи́на смéрти неустанóвлена.

opera ['ɒpərə] *n* óпера.

opera glasses *npl* театрáльный бинóкль *msg*.

opera house *n* óперный теáтр.

opera singer *n* óперный(-ая) певéц*(-ви́ца).

operate ['ɒpəreɪt] *vt* управля́ть (*impf*) +*instr* ♦ *vi* дéйствовать (*impf*); (*drug*) дéйствовать (подéйствовать *perf*); (*MED*): **to ~ (on sb)** опери́ровать (прооперировáть *perf*) (когó-н).

operatic [ɒpə'rætɪk] *adj* óперный.

operating costs *n* эксплуатациóнные затрáты *fpl*.

operating profit *n* при́быль *f* от произ-вóдственной дéятельности.

operating room ['ɒpəreɪtɪŋ-] *n* (*US*) операциóнная *f adj*.

operating statement *n* отчёт о при́были и убы́тках; (*esp US*) теку́щий балáнс.

operating system *n* (*COMPUT*) операциóнная систéма.

operating table *n* операциóнный стол*.

operating theatre *n* операциóнная *f adj*.

operation [ɒpə'reɪʃən] *n* (*of machine: functioning*) рабóта; (: *controlling*) управле́ние; (*MED, MIL, COMM*) опера́ция; **to be in ~** де́йствовать *(impf)*; **he had an ~** (*MED*) ему́ сде́лали опера́цию; **to perform an ~** (*MED*) де́лать (сде́лать *perf*) опера́цию.

operational [ɔpə'reɪʃənl] *adj* (*working*) функциони́рующий; **the machine was ~** маши́на функциони́ровала.

operative ['ɔpərətɪv] *adj* (*law etc*) де́йствующий*; (*position*) операти́вный ♦ *n* (*in factory*) опера́тор; **the ~ word** ключево́е сло́во*.

operator ['ɔpəreɪtə'] *n* (*TEL*) телефони́ст(ка*); (*of machine*) опера́тор.

operetta [ɔpə'rɛtə] *n* опере́тта.

ophthalmic [ɔf'θælmɪk] *adj* офтальмолог-и́ческий.

ophthalmic optician *n* окули́ст.

ophthalmologist [ɔfθæl'mɔlədʒɪst] *n* офталь-мо́лог.

opinion [ə'pɪnjən] *n* мне́ние; **in my ~** по-мо́ему, по моему́ мне́нию; **to seek a second ~** запра́шивать (запроси́ть* *perf*) дополни́тельное мне́ние.

opinionated [ə'pɪnjəneɪtɪd] *adj* само-уве́ренный.

opinion poll *n* опро́с обще́ственного мне́ния.

opium ['əupɪəm] *n* о́пиум.

opponent [ə'pəunənt] *n* оппоне́нт, проти́вник(-ница); (*MIL, SPORT*) проти́вник.

opportune ['ɔpətju:n] *adj* подходя́щий*.

opportunism [ɔpə'tju:nɪsəm] *n* оппортуни́зм.

opportunist [ɔpə'tju:nɪst] *n* оппортуни́ст.

opportunity [ɔpə'tju:nɪtɪ] *n* возмо́жность *f*; **to take the ~ of doing** по́льзоваться (воспо́льзоваться *perf*) слу́чаем чтобы +*infin*.

oppose [ə'pəuz] *vt* проти́виться* (воспроти́виться* *perf*) +*dat*; **to be ~d to sth** проти́виться *(impf)* чему́-н; **as ~d to** в противополо́жность +*dat*.

opposing [ə'pəuzɪŋ] *adj* (*ideas, forces*) противополо́жный; **the ~ team** кома́нда проти́вника.

opposite ['ɔpəzɪt] *adj* противополо́жный ♦ *adv* напро́тив ♦ *prep* напро́тив +*gen* ♦ *n*: **the ~** (*say, think, do etc*) противополо́жное *nt adj*; **the ~ sex** противополо́жный пол; **"see ~ page"** „см. на противополо́жной страни́це".

opposite number *n* (*person*) лицо́, занима́ющее соотве́тствующую до́лжность в друго́й организа́ции.

opposition [ɔpə'zɪʃən] *n* оппози́ция; **the O~** (*POL*) оппозицио́нная па́ртия.

oppress [ə'prɛs] *vt* угнета́ть *(impf)*.

oppression [ə'prɛʃən] *n* угнете́ние.

oppressive [ə'prɛsɪv] *adj* (*régime*) угнета́тельский; (*weather, heat*) гнету́щий*.

opprobrium [ə'prəubrɪəm] *n* (*formal*) осужде́ние.

opt [ɔpt] *vi*: **to ~ for** избира́ть (избра́ть* *perf*); **to ~ to do** реша́ть (реши́ть *perf*) +*infin*
▶ **opt out** *vi* (*school, hospital etc*) выходи́ть* (вы́йти* *perf*) из-под госуда́рственного контро́ля; **to ~ out of sth** выходи́ть* (вы́йти* *perf*) из чего́-н.

optical ['ɔptɪkl] *adj* опти́ческий*.

optical character reader *n* (*COMPUT*) устро́йство опти́ческого считыва́ния си́мволов.

optical character recognition *n* (*COMPUT*) опти́ческое распознава́ние си́мволов.

optical fibre *n* опти́ческое волокно́.

optical illusion *n* опти́ческий* обма́н.

optician [ɔp'tɪʃən] *n* окули́ст.

optics ['ɔptɪks] *n* (*PHYS*) о́птика.

optimism ['ɔptɪmɪzəm] *n* оптими́зм.

optimist ['ɔptɪmɪst] *n* оптими́ст(ка*).

optimistic [ɔptɪ'mɪstɪk] *adj* оптимисти́чный* (оптимисти́чен).

optimum ['ɔptɪməm] *adj* оптима́льный.

option ['ɔpʃən] *n* (*choice*) вариа́нт; (*SCOL*) предме́т по вы́бору; (*COMM*) опцио́н; **to keep one's ~s open** оставля́ть (оста́вить* *perf*) за собо́й пра́во вы́бора; **I have no ~** у меня́ нет вы́бора.

optional ['ɔpʃənl] *adj* (*also COMM*) необяза́тельный*; **~ extras** дополни́тельные, но необяза́тельные това́ры и́ли услу́ги.

opulence ['ɔpjuləns] *n* бога́тство.

opulent ['ɔpjulənt] *adj* (*person, society etc*) бога́тый.

OR *abbr* (*US: POST*) = Oregon.

or [ɔː'] *conj* и́ли; (*otherwise*): **~ (else)** а то, ина́че; (*with negative*): **he hasn't seen ~ heard anything** он ничего́ не ви́дел и не слы́шал.

oracle ['ɔrəkl] *n* (*prophet*) ора́кул; (*prophecy*) прорица́ние.

oral ['ɔːrəl] *adj* (*test, report*) у́стный; (*vaccine, medicine*) ора́льный ♦ *n* (*exam*) у́стный экза́мен.

orange ['ɔrɪndʒ] *n* апельси́н ♦ *adj* (*colour*) ора́нжевый.

orangeade [ɔrɪndʒ'eɪd] *n* апельси́новый напи́ток*.

oration [ɔː'reɪʃən] *n* торже́ственная речь *f*.

orator ['ɔrətə'] *n* ора́тор.

oratorio [ɔrə'tɔːrɪəu] *n* орато́рия.

orb [ɔːb] *n* шар*.

orbit ['ɔːbɪt] *n* орби́та ♦ *vt* обраща́ться *(impf)* вокру́г +*gen*.

orchard ['ɔːtʃəd] *n* сад* (*фрукто́вый*); **apple ~** я́блоневый сад*.

orchestra ['ɔːkɪstrə] *n* орке́стр; (*US: seating*) парте́р.

orchestral [ɔː'kɛstrəl] *adj* оркестро́вый; **~ musician** оркестра́нт(ка*).

---

* marks translations which have irregular inflections. The Russian-English side of the dictionary gives inflectional information.

orchestrate [ˈɔːkɪstreɪt] *vt* (*stage-manage*)
организо́вывать (организова́ть *perf*); (*MUS*)
оркестрова́ть (*impf/perf*).
orchid [ˈɔːkɪd] *n* орхиде́я.
ordain [ɔːˈdeɪn] *vt* (*REL*) посвяща́ть (посвяти́ть*
perf) в сан; (*decide*) предпи́сывать
(предписа́ть* *perf*).
ordeal [ɔːˈdiːl] *n* испыта́ние.
order [ˈɔːdəʳ] *n* (*command*) прика́з; (*from shop,
company, in restaurant*) зака́з; (*sequence,
discipline*) поря́док* ◆ *vt* (*command*)
прика́зывать (приказа́ть* *perf*) +*dat*; (*from
shop, company, in restaurant*) зака́зывать
(заказа́ть* *perf*); (*also:* **put in** ~) располага́ть
(расположи́ть* *perf*) по поря́дку; **in** ~ в
поря́дке; **in (working)** ~ испра́вный*
(испра́вен); **in** ~ **to do** для того́ что́бы +*infin*;
in ~ **of size** по разме́ру; **it is already on** ~
(*COMM*) э́то уже́ зака́зано; **out of** ~ (*not in
sequence*) не по поря́дку; (*not working*)
неиспра́вный* (неиспра́вен); **to place an** ~ **for
sth with sb** зака́зывать (заказа́ть* *perf*) что-н
кому́-н; **made to** ~ сде́лан на зака́з; **she is
under** ~**s to remain silent** ей прика́зано
молча́ть; **a point of** ~ вопро́с о наруше́нии
регла́мента; **to the** ~ **of** (*BANKING*)
опла́чиваемый по ве́кселю на и́мя +*gen*; **to** ~
sb to do прика́зывать (приказа́ть* *perf*)
кому́-н +*infin*.
order book *n* кни́га зака́зов.
order form *n* бланк зака́за.
orderly [ˈɔːdəlɪ] *n* (*MIL*) ордина́рец*; (*MED*)
санита́р ◆ *adj* (*room*) опря́тный* (опря́тен);
(*person*) организо́ванный* (организо́ван);
(*system*) упоря́доченный* (упоря́дочен).
order number *n* но́мер* зака́за.
ordinal [ˈɔːdɪnl] *adj*: ~ **number** поря́дковое
числи́тельное *nt adj*.
ordinarily [ˈɔːdnrɪlɪ] *adv* обы́чно.
ordinary [ˈɔːdnrɪ] *adj* (*everyday, usual*)
обыкнове́нный* (обыкнове́нен), обы́чный*
(обы́чен); (*mediocre*) зауря́дный*
(зауря́ден); **out of the** ~ (*exceptional*)
необыкнове́нный* (необыкнове́нен).
ordinary seaman *n* (*BRIT*) мла́дший* матро́с.
ordinary shares *npl* обыкнове́нные а́кции *fpl*.
ordination [ɔːdɪˈneɪʃən] *n* (*REL*) посвяще́ние в
духо́вный сан.
ordnance [ˈɔːdnəns] *n* (*MIL*) ору́дие ◆ *adj*
(*factory, supplies*) оруже́йный.
Ordnance Survey *n* (*BRIT*) ≈ Госуда́рственное
Управле́ние по геоде́зии и картогра́фии.
ore [ɔːʳ] *n* руда́*.
Orenburg [ˈɔrənbɜːg] *n* Оренбу́рг.
organ [ˈɔːgən] *n* (*ANAT*) о́рган; (*MUS*) орга́н.
organic [ɔːˈgænɪk] *adj* (*fertilizer*)
органи́ческий*; (*food*) вы́ращенный без
примене́ния химика́тов.
organism [ˈɔːgənɪzəm] *n* органи́зм.
organist [ˈɔːgənɪst] *n* органи́ст(ка*).
organization [ɔːgənaɪˈzeɪʃən] *n* организа́ция.

organization chart *n* организацио́нная
структу́ра.
organize [ˈɔːgənaɪz] *vt* организо́вывать
(организова́ть *perf*), устра́ивать (устро́ить
perf); **to get** ~**d** организо́вываться
(организова́ться *perf*).
organized crime *n* организо́ванная
престу́пность *f*.
organized labour *n* чле́ны *mpl* профсою́зов.
organizer [ˈɔːgənaɪzəʳ] *n* организа́тор,
устро́итель(ница) *m(f)*.
orgasm [ˈɔːgæzəm] *n* орга́зм.
orgy [ˈɔːdʒɪ] *n* о́ргия, разгу́л.
Orient [ˈɔːrɪənt] *n*: **the** ~ Восто́к.
orient [ˈɔːrɪənt] *vt* ориенти́ровать
(сориенти́ровать *perf*).
oriental [ɔːrɪˈɛntl] *adj* восто́чный.
orientate [ˈɔːrɪənteɪt] *vt*: **to** ~ **o.s.** ориент-
и́роваться (сориенти́роваться *perf*).
orifice [ˈɔrɪfɪs] *n* отве́рстие.
origin [ˈɔrɪdʒɪn] *n* происхожде́ние; **country of** ~
ме́сто* рожде́ния.
original [əˈrɪdʒɪnl] *adj* (*new*) оригина́льный*
(оригина́лен); (*genuine*) по́длинный*
(по́длинен); (*imaginative: writer, artist etc*)
самобы́тный* (самобы́тен) ◆ *n* по́длинник,
оригина́л.
originality [ərɪdʒɪˈnælɪtɪ] *n* (*of artist etc*)
самобы́тность *f*, оригина́льность *f*.
originally [əˈrɪdʒɪnəlɪ] *adv* первонача́льно.
originate [əˈrɪdʒɪneɪt] *vi*: **to** ~ **from**
происходи́ть* (произойти́* *perf*) от/из +*gen*;
to ~ **in** зарожда́ться (зароди́ться* *perf*) в
+*prp*.
originator [əˈrɪdʒɪneɪtəʳ] *n* созда́тель *m*.
Orkneys [ˈɔːknɪz] *npl*: **the** ~ (*also:* **the Orkney
Islands**) Оркне́йские острова́* *mpl*.
ornament [ˈɔːnəmənt] *n* (*decorative object*)
украше́ние; (*on building, dress etc*)
орна́мент.
ornamental [ɔːnəˈmɛntl] *adj* (*decorative:
garden, pond*) декорати́вный.
ornamentation [ɔːnəmɛnˈteɪʃən] *n* украше́ние.
ornate [ɔːˈneɪt] *adj* декорати́вный.
ornithologist [ɔːnɪˈθɔlədʒɪst] *n* орнито́лог.
ornithology [ɔːnɪˈθɔlədʒɪ] *n* орнитоло́гия.
orphan [ˈɔːfn] *n* сирота́* *m/f* ◆ *vt*: **to be** ~**ed**
оста́ться* (*perf*) сирото́й, осироте́ть (*perf*).
orphanage [ˈɔːfənɪdʒ] *n* де́тский* дом*.
orthodox [ˈɔːθədɔks] *adj* (*also fig*)
ортодокса́льный* (ортодокса́лен); **the
Russian O**~ **Church** Ру́сская Правосла́вная
це́рковь.
orthodoxy [ˈɔːθədɔksɪ] *n* ортодокса́льные
воззре́ния *ntpl*.
orthopaedic [ɔːθəˈpiːdɪk] (*US* **orthopedic**) *adj*
ортопеди́ческий*.
OS *abbr* (*BRIT*) = **Ordnance Survey**; (*NAUT*) =
ordinary seaman; (*DRESS*) = **outsize**.
O/S *abbr* (*COMM*: = *out of stock*) нет в прода́же.
Oscar [ˈɔskəʳ] *n* О́скар (*приз*).

oscillate ['ɒsɪleɪt] *vi* (*ELEC*, *PHYS*) колеба́ться* (*impf*), осцилли́ровать (*impf*); (*fig*) колеба́ться* (*impf*).

OSHA *n abbr* (*US*) = *Occupational Safety and Health Administration*.

Oslo ['ɒzləu] *n* О́сло *nt ind*.

ostensible [ɒs'tɛnsɪbl] *adj* мни́мый.

ostensibly [ɒs'tɛnsɪblɪ] *adv* я́кобы.

ostentation [ɒstɛn'teɪʃən] *n* показна́я ро́скошь *f*.

ostentatious [ɒstɛn'teɪʃəs] *adj* (*building, car*) бро́ский*; (*behaviour*) показно́й; **he is very ~** он выставля́ет себя́ напока́з.

osteopath ['ɒstɪəpæθ] *n* остеопа́т.

ostracize ['ɒstrəsaɪz] *vt* подверга́ть (подве́ргнуть* *perf*) остраки́зму.

ostrich ['ɒstrɪtʃ] *n* стра́ус.

OT *abbr* (*BIBLE*: = *Old Testament*) Ве́тхий* заве́т.

OTB *n abbr* (*US*: = *off-track betting*) внеиппод́ромный тотализа́тор.

OTE *abbr* (*COMM*: = *on-target earnings*) предполага́емый дохо́д.

other ['ʌðə⁷] *adj* друго́й ♦ *pron*: **the ~ (one)** друго́й(-а́я) *m(f) adj*, тот (*f* та) ♦ *adv*: **~ than** кро́ме +*gen*; **~s** (*other people*) други́е *pl adj*; **the ~s** остальны́е *pl adj*; **the ~ day** на днях; **some ~ people have still to arrive** прие́дет ещё не́сколько челове́к; **some actor or ~** како́й-то из актёров; **somebody or ~** кто-нибу́дь, кто-то; **it was none ~ than the prime minister** э́то был ни кто ино́й как премье́р-мини́стр.

otherwise ['ʌðəwaɪz] *adv* (*differently*) ина́че, по-друго́му; (*apart from that*) в остально́м ♦ *conj* а то, ина́че; **it is an ~ good piece of work** в остально́м э́то о́чень хоро́шая рабо́та.

OTT *abbr* (*inf*) = *over the top see* **top**.

Ottawa ['ɒtəwə] *n* Отта́ва.

otter ['ɒtə⁷] *n* вы́дра.

OU *n abbr* (*BRIT*) = *Open University*.

ouch [autʃ] *excl* ай, ой.

ought [ɔ:t] (*pt* **ought**) *aux vb*: **I ~ to do it** мне сле́довало бы э́то сде́лать; **this ~ to have been corrected** э́то сле́довало испра́вить; **he ~ to win** он до́лжен вы́играть; **you ~ to go and see this film** Вы обяза́тельно должны́ посмотре́ть э́тот фильм.

ounce [auns] *n* у́нция.

our ['auə⁷] *adj* наш; *see also* **my**.

ours [auəz] *pron* наш; (*referring to subject of sentence*) свой; *see also* **mine**[1].

ourselves [auə'sɛlvz] *pl pron* (*reflexive*) себя́; (*complement*) себя́; (*after prep*: +*acc*, +*gen*) себя́; (: +*dat*) себе́; (: +*instr*) собо́й; (: +*prp*) себе́; (*emphatic*) са́ми; (*alone*): **(all) by ~** са́ми; **let's keep it between ~** дава́йте оста́вим э́то ме́жду на́ми; *see also* **myself**.

oust [aust] *vt* изгоня́ть (изгна́ть* *perf*).

┌─────────────┐
│ **KEYWORD** │
└─────────────┘

out [aut] *adv* **1** (*not in*): **they're out in the garden** они́ в саду́; **out in the rain/snow** под дождём/сне́гом; **out here** здесь; **out there** там; **to go out** выходи́ть* (вы́йти* *perf*); **out loud** гро́мко **2** (*not at home, absent*): **he is out at the moment** его́ сейча́с нет (до́ма); **let's have a night out on Friday!** дава́йте пойдём куда́-нибудь в пя́тницу ве́чером! **3** (*indicating distance*) в +*prp*; **the boat was 10 km out (from the shore)** кора́бль находи́лся в 10 км от бе́рега; **three days out from Plymouth** в трёх днях пла́вания от Пли́мута **4** (*SPORT*): **the ball is out** мяч за преде́лами по́ля; **out!** (*TENNIS etc*) а́ут!
♦ *adj*: **1**: **to be out** (*unconscious*) быть (*impf*) без созна́ния; (*out of game*) быть (*impf*) удалённым(-ой) с по́ля; (*have appeared: flowers*) распуска́ться (распусти́ться* *perf*); (: *news, secret*) станови́ться* (стать* *perf*) изве́стным(-ой); (*extinguished: fire, light, gas*) ту́хнуть* (поту́хнуть* *perf*), га́снуть* (пога́снуть* *perf*); (*fashion*): **to be out** выходи́ть* (вы́йти* *perf*) из мо́ды **2** (*finished*): **before the week was out** до оконча́ния неде́ли; **3**: **to be out to do** (*intend*) намерева́ться (*impf*) +*infin*; **to be out in one's calculations** (*wrong*) ошиба́ться (ошиби́ться* *perf*) в расчётах
♦ *prep* **1** (*outside, beyond*) из +*gen*; **to go out of the house** выходи́ть* (вы́йти* *perf*) из до́ма; **to be out of danger** (*safe*) быть (*impf*) вне опа́сности **2** (*cause, motive*): **out of curiosity** из любопы́тства; **out of fear** от стра́ха; **out of boredom** от *or* со ску́ки; **out of grief/joy** с го́ря/ра́дости; **out of necessity** по необходи́мости **3** (*from, from among*) из +*gen* **4** (*without*): **we are out of sugar/petrol** *etc* у нас ко́нчился са́хар/бензи́н *etc*.

---

outage ['autɪdʒ] *n* (*esp US: power failure*) отключе́ние электри́чества.

out-and-out ['autəndaut] *adj* отъя́вленный.

outback ['autbæk] *n* (*in Australia*): **the ~** необжиты́е райо́ны *mpl*.

outbid [aut'bɪd] *vt*: **to ~ sb** перебива́ть (переби́ть* *perf*) чью-н це́ну.

outboard ['autbɔ:d] *n* (*also*: **~ motor**) подвесно́й мото́р.

outbreak ['autbreɪk] *n* (*of disease, violence*) вспы́шка*; (*of war*) нача́ло.

outbuilding ['autbɪldɪŋ] *n* надво́рная постро́йка*.

outburst ['autbə:st] *n* вспы́шка*, взрыв.

outcast ['autkɑ:st] *n* изго́й.

outclass [aut'klɑ:s] *vt* превосходи́ть*

---

* marks translations which have irregular inflections. The Russian-English side of the dictionary gives inflectional information.

(превзойти* *perf*).

outcome ['autkʌm] *n* исхо́д, результа́т.

outcrop ['autkrɔp] *n* (*of rock*) обнаже́ние.

outcry ['autkraɪ] *n* негодова́ние, проте́ст.

outdated [aut'deɪtɪd] *adj* (*customs, ideas*) отжи́вший; (*clothes*) старомо́дный*; (*technology*) устаре́лый.

outdo [aut'du:] *irreg vt* превосходи́ть* (превзойти́* *perf*).

outdoor [aut'dɔ:ʳ] *adj* на откры́том во́здухе; (*swimming pool*) откры́тый; ~ **clothes** ве́рхняя оде́жда.

outdoors [aut'dɔ:z] *adv* на у́лице, на откры́том во́здухе.

outer ['autəʳ] *adj* нару́жный; ~ **suburbs** да́льние предме́стья; **the** ~ **office** кра́йний* кабине́т.

outer space *n* косми́ческое простра́нство.

outfit ['autfɪt] *n* (*set of clothes*) компле́кт (оде́жды); (*inf: organization*) компа́ния.

outfitter's ['autfɪtəz] *n* (*BRIT*) торго́вец* мужско́й оде́ждой.

outgoing ['autɡəuɪŋ] *adj* (*extrovert*) общи́тельный* (общи́телен); (*president, mayor etc*) уходя́щий; (*mail etc*) исходя́щий*.

outgoings ['autɡəuɪŋz] *npl* (*BRIT*) расхо́ды *mpl*.

outgrow [aut'ɡrəu] *irreg vt* (*one's clothes*) выраста́ть (вы́расти* *perf*) из +*gen*; (*friends, habits*) перераста́ть (перерасти́* *perf*).

outhouse ['authaus] *n* надво́рная постро́йка*.

outing ['autɪŋ] *n* похо́д.

outlandish [aut'lændɪʃ] *adj* дико́винный.

outlast [aut'lɑ:st] *vt* пережива́ть (пережи́ть* *perf*).

outlaw ['autlɔ:] *n* челове́к вне зако́на ♦ *vt* объявля́ть (объяви́ть* *perf*) вне зако́на.

outlay ['autleɪ] *n* (*expenditure*) затра́ты *fpl*; (*investment*) вложе́ния *ntpl*.

outlet ['autlɛt] *n* (*hole*) выходно́е отве́рстие; (*pipe*) сток; (*US: ELEC*) розе́тка*; (*COMM: also:* **retail** ~) торго́вая то́чка*; (*for emotions*) вы́ход.

outline ['autlaɪn] *n* (*shape*) очерта́ния *ntpl*; (*sketch, explanation*) набро́сок* ♦ *vt* (*fig: theory, plan etc*) набра́сывать (наброса́ть* *perf*).

outlive [aut'lɪv] *vt* пережива́ть (пережи́ть* *perf*).

outlook ['autluk] *n* (*attitude*) взгля́ды *mpl*, воззре́ния *ntpl*; (*prospects*) перспекти́вы *fpl*; (: *for weather*) прогно́з.

outlying ['autlaɪŋ] *adj* отдалённый.

outmanoeuvre [autmə'nu:vəʳ] (*US* **outmaneuver**) *vt* перехитри́ть (*perf*).

outmoded [aut'məudɪd] *adj* устаре́вший.

outnumber [aut'nʌmbəʳ] *vt* превосходи́ть* (превзойти́* *perf*) чи́сленно; **they were ~ed by 5 to 1** их бы́ло в пять раз ме́ньше.

out of bounds *adj*: **this area is** ~ ~ ~ э́та ме́сто явля́ется запре́тным.

out-of-court [autəv'kɔ:t] *adv*: **to settle** ~

приходи́ть* (прийти́* *perf*) к соглаше́нию без обраще́ния в суд.

out-of-date [autəv'deɪt] *adj* (*clothes etc*) немо́дный; (*dictionary*) устаре́вший; (*equipment*) устаре́лый; (*passport*) просро́ченный.

out-of-doors [autəv'dɔ:z] *adv* на у́лице, на откры́том во́здухе.

out-of-the-way ['autəvðə'weɪ] *adj* (*place*) глуби́нный; (*fig*) глухо́й.

out of touch *adj*: **to be** ~ ~ ~ отстава́ть* (отста́ть* *perf*) от вре́мени.

out-of-work ['autəvwə:k] *adj* безрабо́тный.

outpatient ['autpeɪʃənt] *n* амбулато́рный(-ая) больно́й(-а́я) *m(f) adj*.

outpouring ['autpɔ:rɪŋ] *n* (*of emotions*) излия́ние.

outpost ['autpəust] *n* аванпо́ст.

output ['autput] *n* (*production*) вы́работка; (*COMPUT*) выходны́е да́нные *pl adj* ♦ *vt* (*COMPUT*) выводи́ть* (вы́вести* *perf*) (*да́нные*).

outrage ['autreɪdʒ] *n* (*action: scandalous*) возмути́тельный посту́пок*; (: *violent*) акт наси́лия; (*emotion*) возмуще́ние ♦ *vt* (*shock, anger*) возмуща́ть (возмути́ть* *perf*); **his behaviour is an** ~ его́ поведе́ние про́сто возмути́тельно.

outrageous [aut'reɪdʒəs] *adj* возмути́тельный* (возмути́телен).

outrider ['autraɪdəʳ] *n* (*on motorcycle, horse*) эско́рт.

outright [aut'raɪt] *adv* (*win, own*) абсолю́тно; (*refuse, deny*) наотре́з; (*ask*) пря́мо; (*kill*) напова́л ♦ *adj* (*winner, victory*) абсолю́тный; (*refusal, hostility*) откры́тый; **to be killed** ~ погиба́ть (поги́бнуть *perf*) сра́зу.

outrun [aut'rʌn] *irreg vt* обгоня́ть (обогна́ть* *perf*), опережа́ть (опереди́ть* *perf*).

outset ['autsɛt] *n* нача́ло; **from the** ~ с са́мого нача́ла; **at the** ~ внача́ле.

outshine [aut'ʃaɪn] *irreg vt* (*fig*) затмева́ть (затми́ть *perf*).

outside [aut'saɪd] *n* нару́жная сторона́* ♦ *adj* нару́жный, вне́шний* ♦ *adv* (*be*) снару́жи; (*go*) нару́жу ♦ *prep* вне +*gen*, за преде́лами +*gen*; (*next to: building*) у +*gen*; (: *London etc*) под +*gen*; **at the** ~ (*with times*) са́мое по́зднее; (*of size*) са́мое бо́льшее; **an** ~ **chance** ничто́жный шанс; **it's cold** ~ на у́лице хо́лодно.

outside broadcast *n* (*RADIO, TV*) репорта́ж *or* трансля́ция с ме́ста собы́тий.

outside lane *n* (*AUT: in Britain*) пра́вый ряд; (: *in US, Europe*) ле́вый ряд.

outside left *n* (*FOOTBALL*) ле́вый кра́йний* напада́ющий* *m adj*.

outside line *n* (*TEL*) городско́й телефо́н; **dial "9" for an** ~ ~ го́род – че́рез девя́тку.

outsider [aut'saɪdəʳ] *n* (*person not involved*) посторо́нний*(-яя) *m(f) adj*; (*in race etc*) аутса́йдер.

outside right n (FOOTBALL) пра́вый кра́йний*
напада́ющий* m adj.
outsize ['autsaiz] adj: ~ **clothes** оде́жда fsg
больши́х разме́ров.
outskirts ['autskə:ts] npl окра́ины fpl.
outsmart [aut'smɑːt] vt перехитри́ть (perf).
outspoken [aut'spəukən] adj открове́нный*
(открове́нен).
outspread [aut'sprɛd] adj (wings) распростёртый (распростёрт).
outstanding [aut'stændiŋ] adj (exceptional)
выдаю́щийся*; (unfinished) незако́нченный
(незако́нчен); (unpaid) неопла́ченный
(неопла́чен); **your account is still** ~ Вы до сих
пор не уплати́ли по счёту.
outstay [aut'stei] vt: **to** ~ **one's welcome**
заси́живаться (засиде́ться* perf) в гостя́х.
outstretched [aut'strɛtʃt] adj (hand)
протя́нутый; (arms) вы́тянутый; (body)
вы́тянувшийся.
outstrip [aut'strip] vt превосходи́ть*
(превзойти́* perf).
out tray n корзи́на для исходя́щих
докуме́нтов.
outvote [aut'vəut] vt: **to** ~ **sb by 3 votes**
победи́ть (perf) кого́-н с переве́сом в 3
го́лоса.
outward ['autwəd] adj (sign, appearances)
вне́шний*, нару́жный; **the** ~ **journey was
much quicker** пое́здка туда́ намно́го
быстре́е, чем пое́здка обра́тно.
outwardly ['autwədlı] adv вне́шне.
outweigh [aut'wei] vt переве́шивать
(переве́сить* perf).
outwit [aut'wit] vt перехитри́ть (perf).
ova ['əuvə] npl of **ovum**.
oval ['əuvl] adj ова́льный ♦ n ова́л.
ovarian [əu'vɛərıən] adj: ~ **cyst** киста́ яи́чника;
~ **cancer** рак яи́чника.
ovary ['əuvərı] n яи́чник.
ovation [əu'veıʃən] n ова́ция.
oven ['ʌvn] n (domestic) духо́вка*; (baker's,
industrial) печь* f.
ovenproof ['ʌvnpru:f] adj жаросто́йкий,
жаропро́чный*.
oven-ready ['ʌvnrɛdı] adj (chicken, chips etc)
гото́вый для жа́рения в духо́вке.
ovenware ['ʌvnwɛə'] n жаросто́йкая or
жаропро́чная посу́да.

KEYWORD

over ['əuvə'] adv **1** (across): **to cross over (to the
other side of the road)** переходи́ть* (перейти́*
perf) (на другу́ю сто́рону доро́ги); **over here**
здесь; **over there** там; **to ask sb over** (to one's
house) приглаша́ть (пригласи́ть* perf)
кого́-н в го́сти or к себе́
2 (indicating movement from upright): **to
knock/turn sth over** сбива́ть (сбить* perf)/

перевора́чивать (переверну́ть perf) что-н; **to
fall over** па́дать (упа́сть* perf); **to bend over**
нагиба́ться (нагну́ться perf)
3 (finished): **the game is over** игра́ око́нчена;
his life is over его́ жизнь ко́нчена
4 (excessively) сли́шком, чересчу́р
5 (remaining: money, food etc): **there are 3
over** 3 оста́лось:
6: **all over** (everywhere) везде́, повсю́ду; **over
and over** (again) сно́ва и сно́ва
♦ prep **1** (on top of) на +prp; (above) над +instr
2 (on the other side of) че́рез +acc; **the pub
over the road** паб че́рез доро́гу; **he jumped
over the wall** он перепры́гнул че́рез сте́ну
3 (more than) свы́ше +gen; **over and above**
бо́льше (чем); **this is over and above what we
have already ordered** э́то бо́льше, чем мы
уже́ заказа́ли
4 (in the course of) в тече́ние +gen, за +acc;
over the winter за зи́му, в тече́ние зи́мы; **let's
discuss it over dinner** дава́йте обсу́дим э́то за
обе́дом; **the work is spread over two weeks**
рабо́та рассчи́тана на две неде́ли.

over... ['əuvə'] prefix пере....
overact [əuvər'ækt] vi переи́грывать
(переигра́ть perf).
overall ['əuvərɔːl] adj о́бщий* ♦ adv (in general)
в це́лом or о́бщем; (entirely) целико́м ♦ n
(BRIT: child's, painter's etc) хала́т; ~**s** npl
(clothing) комбинезо́н msg.
overall majority n большинство́.
overanxious [əuvər'æŋkʃəs] adj весьма́
встрево́женный* (встрево́жен).
overawe [əuvər'ɔː] vt вызыва́ть (вы́звать* perf)
благогове́ние в +prp.
overbalance [əuvə'bæləns] vi теря́ть (потеря́ть
perf) равнове́сие.
overbearing [əuvə'bɛərıŋ] adj вла́стный
(вла́стен).
overboard ['əuvəbɔːd] adv: **to fall** ~ па́дать
(упа́сть* perf) за борт; **man** ~! челове́к за
бо́ртом!; **to go** ~ (fig) перебо́рщивать
(переборщи́ть perf).
overbook [əuvə'buk] vt продава́ть* (прода́ть*
perf) бо́льше биле́тов, чем име́ется мест; **the
hotel is** ~**ed** гости́ница перепо́лнена.
overcame [əuvə'keim] pt of **overcome**.
overcapitalize [əuvə'kæpıtəlaız] vt: **to** ~ **a
project** вкла́дывать (вложи́ть* perf) в прое́кт
неопра́вданно большо́й капита́л.
overcast ['əuvəkɑːst] adj па́смурный
(па́смурен), хму́рый (хмур).
overcharge [əuvə'tʃɑːdʒ] vt обсчи́тывать
(обсчита́ть perf).
overcoat ['əuvəkəut] n пальто́ nt ind.
overcome [əuvə'kʌm] irreg vt (opponent,
enemy) одолева́ть (одоле́ть perf);

---

* marks translations which have irregular inflections. The Russian-English side of the dictionary gives inflectional information.

(*difficulties, problems*) преодолева́ть (преодоле́ть *perf*) ♦ *adj*: ~ **by** (*fear, suspicion*) одолева́емый (одолева́ем) +*instr*; ~ **with** (*joy*) охва́ченный (охва́чен) +*instr*; **he was** ~ **with grief** он был уби́т го́рем.

overconfident [əuvə'kɒnfɪdənt] *adj* (*person*) самонаде́янный (самонаде́ян).

overcrowded [əuvə'kraudɪd] *adj* перепо́лненный (перепо́лнен).

overcrowding [əuvə'kraudɪŋ] *n* перенаселённость *f*; (*in bus*) теснота́.

overdo [əuvə'du:] *irreg vt* (*work, exercise*) перестара́ться (*perf*) в +*prp*; (*interest, concern*) утри́ровать (*impf*); (*overcook: boil*) перева́ривать (перевари́ть* *perf*); (: *fry, bake*) пережа́ривать (пережа́рить *perf*); **don't** ~ **it!** (*compliments etc*) не переусе́рдствуйте!; (*work etc*) не перестара́йтесь!

overdose ['əuvədəus] *n* передозиро́вка*.

overdraft ['əuvədrɑ:ft] *n* (*COMM*) овердра́фт.

overdrawn [əuvə'drɔ:n] *adj*: **he is** *or* **his account is** ~ он превы́сил креди́т своего́ теку́щего счёта.

overdrive ['əuvədraɪv] *n* (*AUT*) ускоря́ющая переда́ча.

overdue [əuvə'dju:] *adj* (*change, reform etc*) запозда́лый; (*account*) просро́ченный (просро́чен); **he/the bus is an hour** ~ он/ авто́бус опа́здывает на час; **these changes were long** ~ э́тих переме́н давно́ жда́ли.

overemphasis [əuvər'ɛmfəsɪs] *n*: ~ **on** изли́шнее ударе́ние на +*prp*.

overestimate [əuvər'ɛstɪmeɪt] *vt* переоце́нивать (переоцени́ть* *perf*).

overexcited [əuvərɪk'saɪtɪd] *adj* чрезме́рно возбуждённый* (возбуждён).

overexertion [əuvərɪg'zə:ʃən] *n* перенапряже́ние.

overexpose [əuvərɪk'spəuz] *vt* (*PHOT*) переде́рживать (передержа́ть* *perf*).

overflow [əuvə'fləu] *vi* (*river*) разлива́ться (разли́ться* *perf*); (*sink, vase etc*) перепо́лня́ться (перепо́лниться *perf*) ♦ *n* (*also:* ~ **pipe**) сливна́я труба́.

overfly [əuvə'flaɪ] *irreg vt* (*fly past*) пролета́ть (пролете́ть* *perf*).

overgenerous [əuvə'dʒɛnərəs] *adj* сли́шком ще́дрый* (щедр).

overgrown [əuvə'grəun] *adj* (*garden*) заро́сший; **he's just an** ~ **schoolboy** он про́сто перепо́росток.

overhang ['əuvə'hæŋ] *irreg vt* нависа́ть (нави́снуть* *perf*) над +*instr* ♦ *vi* нависа́ть (нави́снуть* *perf*) ♦ *n* наве́с.

overhaul [əuvə'hɔ:l] *vt* (*engine, equipment*) производи́ть* (произвести́* *perf*) по́лную прове́рку и ремо́нт +*gen* ♦ *n* по́лная прове́рка и ремо́нт.

overhead [*adv* əuvə'hɛd, *adj, n* 'əuvəhɛd] *adv* (*above*) наверху́, над голово́й; (*in the sky*) в не́бе ♦ *adj* (*lighting*) ве́рхний*; (*cable, railway*)

надзе́мный ♦ *n* (*US*) = **overheads**; ~**s** *npl* (*expenses*) накладны́е расхо́ды *mpl*.

overhear [əuvə'hɪə'] *irreg vt* (*случа́йно*) подслу́шать* (*perf*).

overheat [əuvə'hi:t] *vi* перегрева́ться (перегре́ться *perf*).

overjoyed [əuvə'dʒɔɪd] *adj*: **to be** ~ (**at**) о́чень ра́доваться (обра́доваться *perf*) (+*dat*); **she was** ~ **to see him** она́ была́ о́чень ра́да его́ ви́деть.

overkill ['əuvəkɪl] *n* (*fig*): **it would be** ~ э́то бу́дет я́вный перебо́р.

overland ['əuvəlænd] *adj* сухопу́тный ♦ *adv* (*travel*) по су́ше.

overlap [əuvə'læp] *vi* (*edges*) находи́ть* (*impf*) оди́н на друго́й; (*fig: ideas, activities etc*) части́чно совпада́ть (совпа́сть* *perf*).

overleaf [əuvə'li:f] *adv* на оборо́те.

overload [əuvə'ləud] *vt* (*also ELEC, fig*) перегружа́ть (перегрузи́ть* *perf*); **to** ~ **with work/problems** перегружа́ть (перегрузи́ть* *perf*) рабо́той/пробле́мами.

overlook [əuvə'luk] *vt* (*have view into*) выходи́ть* (*impf*) на +*acc*; (*fail to consider*) упуска́ть (упусти́ть* *perf*) из ви́ду; (*excuse*) закрыва́ть (закры́ть* *perf*) глаза́ на +*acc*.

overlord ['əuvəlɔ:d] *n* повели́тель *m*.

overmanning [əuvə'mænɪŋ] *n* (*INDUSTRY*) избы́ток* рабо́чей си́лы.

overnight [əuvə'naɪt] *adv* (*for the night*) на ночь; (*during the night*) за́ ночь; (*fig: suddenly*) за́ день, сра́зу же ♦ *adj* (*train, journey*) ночно́й; **to travel** ~ путеше́ствовать (*impf*) но́чью; **to stay** ~ ночева́ть (переночева́ть *perf*); **he'll be away** ~ он е́дет с ночёвкой.

overpass ['əuvəpɑ:s] *n* (*esp US*) путепрово́д.

overpay [əuvə'peɪ] *vt*: **to** ~ **sb by £50** перепла́чивать (переплати́ть* *perf*) кому́-н £50.

overplay [əuvə'pleɪ] *vt* преувели́чивать (преувели́чить *perf*) значе́ние +*gen*.

overpower [əuvə'pauə'] *vt* переси́ливать (переси́лить *perf*).

overpowering [əuvə'pauərɪŋ] *adj* (*heat, stench*) невыноси́мый (невыноси́м).

overproduction ['əuvəprə'dʌkʃən] *n* перепроизво́дство.

overrate [əuvə'reɪt] *vt* переоце́нивать (переоцени́ть* *perf*).

overreach [əuvə'ri:tʃ] *vt*: **to** ~ **o.s.** перенапряга́ться (перенапря́чься* *perf*).

overreact [əuvəri:'ækt] *vi* горячи́ться (погорячи́ться *perf*).

override [əuvə'raɪd] *irreg vt* (*order, objection*) отверга́ть (отве́ргнуть* *perf*).

overriding [əuvə'raɪdɪŋ] *adj* (*importance*) первостепе́нный; (*factor, consideration*) реша́ющий*.

overrule [əuvə'ru:l] *vt* (*decision*) отменя́ть (отмени́ть* *perf*); (*objection*) отверга́ть

(отве́ргнуть* *perf*); **the judge ~d the defence** судья́ отклони́л тре́бования защи́тника.
overrun [əuvə'rʌn] *irreg vt* (*country*) бы́стро овладева́ть (овладе́ть *perf*) +*instr*; (*time limit*) превыша́ть (превы́сить* *perf*) ♦ *vi* дли́ться* (*impf*) до́льше поло́женного (вре́мени); **the town is ~ with tourists** го́род наводнён тури́стами.
overseas [əuvə'si:z] *adv* (*live, travel, work*) за рубежо́м *or* грани́цей; (*to go*) за рубе́ж *or* грани́цу ♦ *adj* (*market, trade*) вне́шний*; (*student, visitor*) иностра́нный; **to trade ~** торгова́ть (*impf*) с иностра́нными госуда́рствами.
oversee [əuvə'si:] *vt* следи́ть* (*impf*) за +*instr*.
overseer ['əuvəsiə'] *n* (*in factory*) контролёр.
overshadow [əuvə'ʃædəu] *vt* (*place, building etc*) возвыша́ться (*impf*) над +*instr*; (*fig*) затмева́ть (затми́ть* *perf*).
overshoot [əuvə'ʃu:t] *irreg vt* проезжа́ть (прое́хать* *perf*).
oversight ['əuvəsaɪt] *n* недосмо́тр; **due to an ~** по недосмо́тру.
oversimplify [əuvə'sɪmplɪfaɪ] *vt* сли́шком упроща́ть (упрости́ть* *perf*).
oversleep [əuvə'sli:p] *irreg vi* просыпа́ть (проспа́ть* *perf*).
overspend [əuvə'spɛnd] *irreg vi* перерасхо́довать (*impf/perf*); **we have overspent by 5,000 dollars** наш перерасхо́д соста́вил 5,000 до́лларов.
overspill ['əuvəspɪl] *n* (*excess population*) избы́точное населе́ние.
overstaffed [əuvə'stɑ:ft] *adj*: **this office is ~** в э́том отде́ле сли́шком мно́го рабо́тников.
overstate [əuvə'steɪt] *vt* преувели́чивать (преувели́чить *perf*).
overstatement [əuvə'steɪtmənt] *n* преувеличе́ние.
overstay [əuvə'steɪ] *vt*: **to ~ one's welcome** загости́ться* (*perf*).
overstep [əuvə'stɛp] *vt*: **to ~ the mark** переходи́ть* (перейти́* *perf*) грани́цы.
overstock [əuvə'stɔk] *vt* затова́ривать (затова́рить *perf*).
overstretched [əuvə'strɛtʃt] *adj* (*at work*) перегру́женный (перегру́жен); (*funds*) переизрасхо́дованный (переизрасхо́дован).
overstrike ['əuvəstraɪk] *irreg n* (*on printer*) набо́р ли́шних си́мволов ♦ *vt* набира́ть (набра́ть* *perf*) (*на клавиату́ре*).
oversubscribed [əuvəsəb'skraɪbd] *adj*: **this product is ~** коли́чество зая́вок на э́тот това́р превы́шает предложе́ние.
overt [əu'və:t] *adj* открове́нный* (открове́нен).
overtake [əuvə'teɪk] *irreg vt* (*AUT*) обгоня́ть (обогна́ть* *perf*); (*subj: event, change*)

застига́ть (засти́гнуть* *perf*) враспло́х; (: *emotion, weakness*) овладева́ть (овладе́ть *perf*) +*instr*.
overtaking [əuvə'teɪkɪŋ] *n* (*AUT*) обго́н.
overtax [əuvə'tæks] *vt* (*ECON*) облага́ть (обложи́ть* *perf*) сли́шком высо́ким нало́гом; (*strength, patience*) истоща́ть (истощи́ть *perf*); **to ~ o.s.** перенапряга́ться (перенапря́чься* *perf*).
overthrow [əuvə'θrəu] *irreg vt* сверга́ть (све́ргнуть* *perf*).
overtime ['əuvətaɪm] *n* сверхуро́чное вре́мя* *nt*; **to do** *or* **work ~** рабо́тать (*impf*) в сверхуро́чное вре́мя.
overtime ban *n* запре́т на сверхуро́чную рабо́ту.
overtone ['əuvətəun] *n* (*also*: **~s**): **~ of** намёк на +*acc*.
overture ['əuvətʃuə'] *n* (*MUS*) увертю́ра; (*fig*) подгото́вка*.
overturn [əuvə'tə:n] *vt* (*car, chair*) перевора́чивать (переверну́ть *perf*); (*decision, plan*) отверга́ть (отве́ргнуть *perf*); (*government, system*) сверга́ть (све́ргнуть *perf*) ♦ *vi* перевора́чиваться (переверну́ться *perf*).
overview ['əuvəvju:] *n* (*summary*) обзо́р; (*general understanding*) о́бщее представле́ние.
overweight [əuvə'weɪt] *adj* (*person*) ту́чный* (ту́чен); **your luggage is ~** у Вас переве́с.
overwhelm [əuvə'wɛlm] *vt* (*opponent, enemy etc*) оде́рживать (одержа́ть *perf*) верх над +*instr*; (*subj: feelings, emotions*) переполня́ть (перепо́лнить *perf*).
overwhelming [əuvə'wɛlmɪŋ] *adj* (*victory, defeat*) по́лный; (*majority*) подавля́ющий; (*feeling, desire*) всепобежда́ющий*; (*heat*) невыноси́мый (невыноси́м); **~ impression** о́бщее впечатле́ние.
overwhelmingly [əuvə'wɛlmɪŋlɪ] *adv* (*vote, win*) по́лностью; (*appreciative, generous etc*) безграни́чно; (*predominantly: opposed etc*) в основно́м.
overwork [əuvə'wə:k] *n* перегру́зка ♦ *vt* (*person*) перегружа́ть (перегрузи́ть* *perf*); (*cliché etc*) зата́скивать (затаска́ть *perf*) ♦ *vi* (*person*) переутомля́ться (переутоми́ться* *perf*).
overwrite [əuvə'raɪt] *vt* (*COMPUT*) переписа́ть (переписа́ть* *perf*).
overwrought [əuvə'rɔ:t] *adj* (*person*) переутомлённый (переутомлён).
ovulate ['ɔvjuleɪt] *vi* овули́ровать (*impf/perf*).
ovulation [ɔvju'leɪʃən] *n* овуля́ция.
ovum ['əuvəm] (*pl* **ova**) *n* яйцо́* (*АНАТ*).
owe [əu] *vt*: **she ~s me £500** она́ мне должна́ £500; **we ~ him our gratitude** мы должны́

быть* благода́рны ему́; **he ~s his talent/life to that man** он обя́зан свои́м тала́нтом/ свое́й жи́знью э́тому челове́ку.
owing to [ˈəuɪŋ-] *prep* всле́дствие +*gen*.
owl [aul] *n* сова́*.
own [əun] *vt* владе́ть *(impf)* +*instr* ♦ *vi* (*BRIT*): **to ~ to sth** признава́ться* (призна́ться *perf*) в чём-н ♦ *adj* (*house, work, style etc*) со́бственный; **a room of one's ~** своя́ со́бственная ко́мната; **he lives on his ~** он живёт оди́н; **to come into one's ~** быть* *(impf)* в свое́й стихи́и; **to get one's ~ back** отьи́грываться (отьигра́ться *perf*)
▶ **own up** *vi*: **to ~ up to sth** признава́ться* (призна́ться *perf*) в чём-н.
own brand *n* (*COMM*) това́р с ма́ркой продаю́щей его́ торго́вой компа́нии.
owner [ˈəunəʳ] *n* владе́лец*(-лица).
owner-occupier [ˈəunəʳˈɔkjupaɪəʳ] *n* домовладе́лец(-лица).
ownership [ˈəunəʃɪp] *n*: **~ (of)** владе́ние (+*instr*); **under new ~** в но́вом владе́нии.
own goal *n* (*SPORT*): **to score an ~ ~** забива́ть (заби́ть* *perf*) гол в свои́ воро́та.

ox [ɔks] (*pl* **~en**) *n* бык*.
oxen [ˈɔksn] *npl of* **ox**.
Oxfam [ˈɔksfæm] *n abbr* (*BRIT*: = *Oxford Committee for Famine Relief*) О́ксфордский комите́т по́мощи голода́ющим.
Oxford [ˈɔksfəd] *n* О́ксфорд.
oxide [ˈɔksaɪd] *n* о́кись *f*, окси́д.
oxidize [ˈɔksɪdaɪz] *vi* окисля́ться (окисли́ться *perf*).
Oxon. [ˈɔksn] *abbr* (*BRIT*: *POST*) = *Oxfordshire*; (*in degree titles*) *Oxoniensis*.
oxtail [ˈɔksteɪl] *n*: **~ soup** суп из бы́чьего хвоста́.
oxyacetylene [ˈɔksɪəˈsɛtɪliːn] *adj* (*flame*) ацетиле́новый.
oxygen [ˈɔksɪdʒən] *n* кислоро́д.
oxygen mask *n* кислоро́дная ма́ска*.
oxygen tent *n* кислоро́дная пала́тка*.
oyster [ˈɔɪstəʳ] *n* у́стрица.
oz. *abbr* = **ounce**.
ozone [ˈəuzəun] *n* озо́н.
ozone layer *n* озо́новый слой*.
ozonosphere [əuˈzəunəsfɪəʳ] *n* озо́нный слой.

~ *P, p* ~

P, p [pi:] *n* (*letter*) 16-ая бу́ква англи́йского
алфави́та.
P. *abbr* = **president, prince.**
p *abbr* (*BRIT*) = **penny, pence.**
p. *abbr* (= **page**) стр.= *страни́ца.*
PA *n abbr* = **personal assistant, public-address
system ◆** *abbr* (*US: POST*) = **Pennsylvania.**
pa [pɑ:] *n* (*inf*) па́па.
p.a. *abbr* (= *per annum*) в год.
PAC *n abbr* (*US*) = *political action committee.*
pace [peɪs] *n* (*step*) шаг*; (*speed*) темп ◆ *vi*: **to ~
up and down** ходи́ть* (*impf*) взад вперёд; **to
keep ~ with** (*person, events*) идти́* (*impf*) в
но́гу с +*instr*; **to set the ~** (*also fig*)
определя́ть (определи́ть *perf*); **I put him
through his ~s** (*fig*) я посмотре́л, на что он
спосо́бен.
pacemaker [ˈpeɪsmeɪkəʳ] *n* (*MED*) ритмиза́тор
се́рдца; (*SPORT*) ли́дер.
Pacific [pəˈsɪfɪk] *n*: **the ~ (Ocean)** Ти́хий* океа́н.
pacific [pəˈsɪfɪk] *adj* (*intentions etc*)
миролюби́вый.
pacifier [ˈpæsɪfaɪəʳ] *n* (*US: dummy*)
со́ска*(-пусты́шка*).
pacifist [ˈpæsɪfɪst] *n* пацифи́ст(ка*).
pacify [ˈpæsɪfaɪ] *vt* умиротворя́ть
(умиротвори́ть *perf*).
pack [pæk] *n* (*packet*) па́чка*; (*of hounds*)
сво́ра; (*of wolves*) ста́я; (*of people*)
компа́ния; (*also: backpack*) рюкза́к*; (*of
cards*) коло́да ◆ *vt* (*fill*) пакова́ть *or*
упако́вывать (упакова́ть *perf*); (*press down*)
уплотня́ть (уплотни́ть *perf*); (*COMPUT*)
упако́вывать (упакова́ть *perf*); (*cram*): **to ~
into** набива́ть (набить* *perf*) в +*acc* ◆ *vi*: **to ~
(one's bags)** пакова́ть *or* упако́вывать
(упакова́ть *perf*) чемода́ны; **to ~ sb off**
отправля́ть (отпра́вить* *perf*) кого́-н; **to send
sb ~ing** (*inf*) посыла́ть (посла́ть* *perf*) кого́-н
пода́льше
▸ **pack in** (*BRIT: inf*) ◆ *vi* (*machine*)
разва́ливаться (разва́литься *perf*) ◆ *vt*
(*boyfriend*) завя́зывать (завяза́ть* *perf*) с
+*instr*; **~ it in!** прекрати́!
▸ **pack off** *vt* отправля́ть (отпра́вить* *perf*)
▸ **pack up** *vi* (*BRIT: inf: machine*) разва́ливаться

(разва́литься *perf*); (: *person*) закругля́ться
(закругли́ться *perf*) ◆ *vt* пакова́ть *or*
упако́вывать (упакова́ть *perf*).
package [ˈpækɪdʒ] *n* (*parcel, also COMPUT*)
паке́т; (*also: ~ deal*) (туристи́ческая) путёвка
◆ *vt* (*goods*) пакова́ть *or* упако́вывать
(упакова́ть *perf*).
package holiday *n* (*BRIT*) организо́ванный
о́тдых по путёвке.
package tour *n* (*BRIT*) туристи́ческая пое́здка*
по путёвке.
packaging [ˈpækɪdʒɪŋ] *n* упако́вка.
packed [pækt] *adj* (*crowded*) наби́тый (наби́т).
packed lunch *n* (*BRIT*) за́втрак в паке́те.
packer [ˈpækəʳ] *n* упако́вщик(-ица).
packet [ˈpækɪt] *n* (*of cigarettes, washing powder
etc*) па́чка*; (*of crisps*) паке́т.
packet switching *n* (*COMPUT*) коммута́ция
паке́тов, паке́тная коммута́ция.
pack ice [ˈpækaɪs] *n* пак, па́ковый лёд*.
packing [ˈpækɪŋ] *n* (*act*) упако́вка; (*material*)
прокла́дочный материа́л.
packing case *n* упако́вочный я́щик.
pact [pækt] *n* пакт.
pad [pæd] *n* (*of paper*) блокно́т; (*soft material*)
прокла́дка*; (*for inking*) поду́шечка*; (*inf:
home*) (свой) у́гол* ◆ *vt* (*cushion, soft toy etc*)
набива́ть (наби́ть* *perf*); (*shoulder, suit*)
подбива́ть (подби́ть* *perf*) ◆ *vi*: **to ~ about**
ступа́ть (*impf*).
padded cell [ˈpædɪd-] *n* пала́та, оби́тая
во́йлоком (*в психиатри́ческой больни́це*).
padding [ˈpædɪŋ] *n* (*material*) наби́вочный
материа́л, наби́вка; (*in speech*) вода́*.
paddle [ˈpædl] *n* (*oar*) байда́рочное весло́*;
(*US: for table tennis*) раке́тка* ◆ *vt* (*boat, canoe
etc*) грести́* (*impf*) ◆ *vi* (*with feet*) шлёпать
(*impf*).
paddle steamer *n* колёсный парохо́д.
paddling pool [ˈpædlɪŋ-] *n* (*BRIT*) лягуша́тник.
paddock [ˈpædək] *n* (*field*) вы́гон; (*at
racecourse*) заго́н.
paddy field [ˈpædɪ-] *n* ри́совое по́ле*.
padlock [ˈpædlɔk] *n* (вися́чий*) замо́к* ◆ *vt*
запира́ть (запере́ть* *perf*) на вися́чий замо́к.
padre [ˈpɑ:drɪ] *n* (*REL*) па́дре *m ind*.

---

* marks translations which have irregular inflections. The Russian-English side of the dictionary gives inflectional information.

paediatrician [piːdɪə'trɪʃən] (*US* **pediatrician**) *n* педиа́тр, де́тский* врач.

paediatrics [piːdɪ'ætrɪks] (*US* **pediatrics**) *n* педиатри́я.

paedophile ['piːdəufaɪl] (*US* **pedophile**) *n* педофи́л.

paedophilia [piːdəu'fɪlɪə] (*US* **pedophilia**) *n* педофили́я.

pagan ['peɪɡən] *adj* язы́ческий* ♦ *n* язы́чник(-ица).

page [peɪdʒ] *n* страни́ца; (*also:*~**boy**) паж*; (: *at wedding*) ма́льчик, несу́щий шлейф неве́сты ♦ *vt* (*in hotel etc*) вызыва́ть (вы́звать* *perf*).

pageant ['pædʒənt] *n* театрализо́ванное представле́ние.

pageantry ['pædʒəntrɪ] *n* пы́шное зре́лище.

pageboy ['peɪdʒbɔɪ] *n see* **page**.

pager ['peɪdʒə'] *n* портати́вное электро́нное устро́йство для вы́зова полице́йского, врача́ итп.

page three girl *n* де́вушка, снима́ющаяся в полуобнажённом ви́де для фотогра́фий в бульва́рных газе́тах.

paginate ['pædʒɪneɪt] *vt* нумерова́ть (пронумерова́ть* *perf*) страни́цы +*gen*.

pagination [pædʒɪ'neɪʃən] *n* нумера́ция страни́ц, пагина́ция.

pagoda [pə'ɡəudə] *n* па́года.

paid [peɪd] *pt, pp of* **pay** ♦ *adj* опла́чиваемый; **to put ~ to** (*BRIT*) класть* (положи́ть* *perf*) коне́ц +*dat*.

paid-in ['peɪdɪn] *adj* (*US*) = **paid-up**.

paid-up ['peɪdʌp] (*US* **paid-in**) *adj* (*COMM: shares*) опла́ченный; **he is a ~ member** он уплати́л чле́нский* взнос; **~ capital** (*COMM*) опла́ченная часть объя́вленного акционе́рного капита́ла.

pail [peɪl] *n* ведро́*.

pain [peɪn] *n* (*also fig*) боль *f*; **to be in ~** страда́ть (*impf*) от бо́ли; **to have a ~ in** чу́вствовать (*impf*) боль в +*prp*; **to take ~s to do** стара́ться (постара́ться *perf*) изо всех сил, что́бы +*infin*; **on ~ of death** под стра́хом сме́рти.

pained [peɪnd] *adj* оби́женный (оби́жен).

painful ['peɪnful] *adj* (*upsetting, unpleasant, laborious*) мучи́тельный* (мучи́телен); (*sore*): **my back is ~** спина́ причиня́ет мне боль.

painfully ['peɪnfəlɪ] *adv* (*fig: very*) глубоко́; (: *aware, familiar*) до бо́ли; (: *dull, obvious*) мучи́тельно.

painkiller ['peɪnkɪlə'] *n* болеутоля́ющее *nt adj* (сре́дство).

painless ['peɪnlɪs] *adj* безболе́зненный* (безболе́знен).

painstaking ['peɪnzteɪkɪŋ] *adj* кропотли́вый (кропотли́в).

paint [peɪnt] *n* кра́ска* ♦ *vt* (*wall, door, house etc*) кра́сить* (вы́красить* *or* покра́сить*

perf); (*picture, portrait*) рисова́ть (нарисова́ть *perf*); (*about artists*) писа́ть* (написа́ть* *perf*); (*fig*) изобража́ть (изобрази́ть* *perf*); **a tin of ~** ба́нка* кра́ски; **to ~ the door blue** кра́сить* (вы́красить* *or* покра́сить* *perf*) дверь в голубо́й цвет; **to ~ in oils** писа́ть* (написа́ть* *perf*) ма́слом.

paintbox ['peɪntbɔks] *n* набо́р кра́сок.

paintbrush ['peɪntbrʌʃ] *n* кисть* *f*.

painter ['peɪntə'] *n* (*artist*) худо́жник(-ица); (*decorator*) маля́р*.

painting ['peɪntɪŋ] *n* (*activity: of artist*) жи́вопись *f*; (: *of decorator*) маля́рное де́ло; (*picture*) карти́на.

paint stripper *n* сре́дство для сня́тия кра́ски.

paintwork ['peɪntwəːk] *n* кра́ска.

pair [pɛə'] *n* па́ра; **a ~ of scissors** но́жницы *pl*; **a ~ of trousers** па́ра брюк

▶ **pair off** *vi*: **to ~ off with sb** объединя́ться (объедини́ться* *perf*) в па́ре с кем-н.

pajamas [pə'dʒɑːməz] *npl* (*US*) пижа́ма *fsg*.

Pakistan [pɑːkɪ'stɑːn] *n* Пакиста́н.

Pakistani [pɑːkɪ'stɑːnɪ] *adj* пакиста́нский* ♦ *n* пакиста́нец*(-нка*).

PAL *n abbr* (*TV:* = phase alternation line) ПАЛ.

pal [pæl] *n* (*inf*) ко́реш.

palace ['pæləs] *n* дворе́ц*.

palaeontology [pælɪɔn'tɔlədʒɪ] *n* палеонтоло́гия.

palatable ['pælɪtəbl] *adj* (*food, drink*) вку́сный* (вку́сен); (*idea, fact*) прие́млемый.

palate ['pælɪt] *n* (*ANAT*) нёбо; (*fig*) вкус.

palatial [pə'leɪʃəl] *adj* роско́шный* (роско́шен).

palaver [pə'lɑːvə'] *n* (*inf*) суетня́.

pale [peɪl] *adj* бле́дный* (бле́ден) ♦ *vi* бледне́ть (побледне́ть *perf*) ♦ *n*: **his behaviour is beyond the ~** (*unacceptable*) его́ поведе́ние перехо́дит все грани́цы; **to grow** *or* **turn ~** бледне́ть (побледне́ть *perf*); **~ blue** бле́дно-голубо́й; **to ~ into insignificance beside** бледне́ть (побледне́ть *perf*) пе́ред +*instr*.

paleness ['peɪlnɪs] *n* бле́дность *f*.

Palestine ['pælɪstaɪn] *n* Палести́на.

Palestinian [pælɪs'tɪnɪən] *adj* палести́нский* ♦ *n* палести́нец*(-нка*).

palette ['pælɪt] *n* (*ART*) пали́тра.

palings ['peɪlɪŋz] *npl* частоко́л *msg*.

palisade [pælɪ'seɪd] *n* крепостна́я огра́да.

pall [pɔːl] *n* (*cloud of smoke*) покро́в ♦ *vi* приеда́ться (прие́сться* *perf*).

pallet ['pælɪt] *n* (*for goods*) поддо́н.

palliative ['pælɪətɪv] *n* (*MED*) паллиати́вное сре́дство; (*fig*) полуме́ра.

pallid ['pælɪd] *adj* бле́дный* (бле́ден).

pallor ['pælə'] *n* бле́дность *f*.

pally ['pælɪ] *adj* (*inf*) сво́йский*.

palm [pɑːm] *n* (*also:*~ **tree**) па́льма; (*of hand*) ладо́нь *f* ♦ *vt*: **to ~ sth off on sb** (*inf*) подсо́вывать (подсу́нуть *perf*) что-н кому́-н.

palmist ['pɑːmɪst] *n* хирома́нт(ка*).
Palm Sunday *n* ≈ Ве́рбное воскресе́нье.
palpable ['pælpəbl] *adj* ощути́мый (ощути́м).
palpitations [pælpɪ'teɪʃənz] *npl* (учащённое) сердцебие́ние *ntsg*.
paltry ['pɔːltrɪ] *adj* (*amount*) ничто́жный* (ничто́жен).
pamper ['pæmpə*ʳ*] *vt* балова́ть (избалова́ть *perf*).
pamphlet ['pæmflət] *n* (*leaflet*) брошю́ра; (: *political, literary etc*) памфле́т.
pan [pæn] *n* (*also*: **saucepan**) кастрю́ля; (*also*: **frying** ~) сковорода́ ◆ *vi* (*CINEMA, TV*) панорами́ровать (*impf/perf*) ◆ *vt* (*inf*: *book, film*) разноси́ть* (разнести́* *perf*); **to** ~ **for gold** намыва́ть (намы́ть* *perf*) зо́лото.
panacea [pænə'sɪə] *n* панаце́я.
panache [pə'næʃ] *n* щегольство́.
Panama ['pænəmɑː] *n* Пана́ма.
panama *n* (*also*: ~ **hat**) пана́ма.
Panama Canal *n*: **the** ~ ~ Пана́мский* кана́л.
Panamanian [pænə'meɪnɪən] *adj* пана́мский* ◆ *n* пана́мец*(-мка).
pancake ['pænkeɪk] *n* (*thin*) блин*; (*thick*) ола́дья.
Pancake Day *n* (*BRIT*) вто́рник во вре́мя ма́сленицы, в кото́рый пеку́т блины́.
pancake roll *n* бли́нчик с начи́нкой (*свёрнутый в тру́бочку*).
pancreas ['pæŋkrɪəs] *n* поджелу́дочная железа́*.
panda ['pændə] *n* бамбу́ковый медве́дь *m*.
panda car *n* (*BRIT*) полице́йская маши́на.
pandemonium [pændɪ'məunɪəm] *n* столпотворе́ние.
pander ['pændə*ʳ*] *vi*: **to** ~ **to** потво́рствовать (*impf*) +*dat*.
p & h *abbr* (*US*: = *postage and handling*) почто́вые расхо́ды *pl*.
P & L *abbr* (= *profit and loss*) при́быль *f* и убы́ток.
p & p *abbr* (*BRIT*: = *postage and packing*) почто́вые расхо́ды и упако́вка.
pane [peɪn] *n*: ~ (**of glass**) (*in window*) око́нное стекло́*.
panel ['pænl] *n* (*of wood, metal, glass*) пане́ль *f*; (*of judges, experts*) коми́ссия.
panel game *n* (*BRIT*: *TV, RADIO*) виктори́на.
panelling ['pænəlɪŋ] (*US* **paneling**) *n* деревя́нная обши́вка.
panellist ['pænəlɪst] (*US* **panelist**) *n* (*TV, RADIO*) уча́стник(-ица) програ́ммы.
pang [pæŋ] *n*: ~ **of jealousy** уко́л ре́вности; ~**s of conscience** уко́ры со́вести; ~ **of regret** му́ки сожале́ния; **hunger** ~**s** голо́дные бо́ли.
panhandler ['pænhændlə*ʳ*] *n* (*US*: *inf*) ни́щий* *m adj*.
panic ['pænɪk] *n* па́ника ◆ *vi* паникова́ть (*impf*).

panic buying [-baɪɪŋ] *n* ску́пка дефици́тных това́ров.
panicky ['pænɪkɪ] *adj* (*feeling, reaction*) пани́ческий*; (*person*): **he is very** ~ он панику́ет.
panic-stricken ['pænɪkstrɪkən] *adj* (*person, crowd*) охва́ченный (охва́чен) па́никой.
pannier ['pænɪə*ʳ*] *n* (*on bicycle*) корзи́нка*-бага́жник; (*on animal*) корзи́на.
panorama [pænə'rɑːmə] *n* панора́ма.
panoramic [pænə'ræmɪk] *adj* панора́мный.
pansy ['pænzɪ] *n* аню́тины гла́зки *mpl*; (*inf*: *pej*) флунтя́й.
pant [pænt] *vi* задыха́ться (задохну́ться *perf*).
pantechnicon [pæn'tɛknɪkən] *n* (*BRIT*: *AUT*) автофурго́н для перево́зки ме́бели *or* обору́дования.
panther ['pænθə*ʳ*] *n* панте́ра.
panties ['pæntɪz] *npl* тру́сики *pl*.
pantihose ['pæntɪhəuz] *npl* (*US*) колго́тки* *pl*.
panto ['pæntəu] *n* = **pantomime**.
pantomime ['pæntəmaɪm] *n* (*BRIT*) рожде́ственское представле́ние для дете́й; (: *fig*) фарс.
pantry ['pæntrɪ] *n* кладова́я *f adj*, кладо́вка; (*room*) буфе́тная *f adj*.
pants [pænts] *npl* (*BRIT*: *underwear*) трусы́ *pl*; (*US*: *trousers*) брю́ки *pl*.
pantsuit ['pæntsuːt] *n* (*US*) брю́чный костю́м.
papacy ['peɪpəsɪ] *n* па́пство.
papal ['peɪpl] *adj* па́пский.
paparazzi [pæpə'rætsiː] *npl* фото́графы, гоня́ющиеся за знамени́тостями и фотографи́рующие их для бульва́рной пре́ссы.
paper ['peɪpə*ʳ*] *n* бума́га; (*also*: **newspaper**) газе́та; (*exam*) пи́сьменный экза́мен; (*academic essay*: *at conference*) докла́д; (: *in journal*) статья́*; (*also*: **wallpaper**) обо́и *pl* ◆ *adj* бума́жный ◆ *vt* (*room*) окле́ивать (окле́ить* *perf*) обо́ями; ~**s** *npl* (*also*: **identity** ~**s**) докуме́нты *mpl*; **a piece of** ~ (*odd bit*) клочо́к бума́ги, бума́жка; (*sheet*) лист* бума́ги; **to put** *or* **get sth down on** ~ запи́сывать (записа́ть* *perf*) что-н на бума́ге.
paper advance *n* (*on printer*) продвиже́ние бума́ги.
paperback ['peɪpəbæk] *n* кни́га в мя́гкой обло́жке ◆ *adj*: ~ **edition** изда́ние в мя́гкой обло́жке.
paper bag *n* бума́жный паке́т.
paperboy ['peɪpəbɔɪ] *n* ма́льчик-разно́счик газе́т.
paperclip ['peɪpəklɪp] *n* (канцеля́рская) скре́пка.
papergirl ['peɪpəgəːl] *n* де́вочка-разно́счица газе́т.

---

* marks translations which have irregular inflections. The Russian-English side of the dictionary gives inflectional information.

paper hankie n бума́жный носово́й плато́к*.
paper mill n бума́жная фа́брика.
paper profit n бума́жная or нереализо́ванная при́быль f.
paper shop n ≈ газе́тный кио́ск.
paperweight ['peɪpəweɪt] n пресс-папье́ nt ind.
paperwork ['peɪpəwə:k] n канцеля́рская рабо́та.
papier-mâché ['pæpɪeɪ'mæʃeɪ] n папье́-маше́ nt ind.
paprika ['pæprɪkə] n кра́сный мо́лотый пе́рец*.
Pap smear ['pæp-] n мазо́к* с ше́йки ма́тки.
Pap test n = Pap smear.
par [pɑ:ʳ] n (equality of value) ра́венство; (GOLF) коли́чество уда́ров, допусти́мое для ка́ждой лу́нки и́ли для всего́ по́ля; **to be on a ~ with** быть* (impf) на одно́м у́ровне с +instr; **at ~** (COMM) по номина́лу; **to feel below** or **under ~** чу́вствовать (impf) себя́ нева́жно.
parable ['pærəbl] n при́тча.
parabola [pə'ræbələ] n пара́бола.
parachute ['pærəʃu:t] n парашю́т.
parachute jump n прыжо́к* с парашю́том.
parachutist ['pærəʃu:tɪst] n парашюти́ст(ка).
parade [pə'reɪd] n (public procession) ше́ствие; (MIL) пара́д ♦ vt (troops etc) выстра́ивать (вы́строить perf); (show off: wealth, knowledge etc) выставля́ть (вы́ставить* perf) напока́з ♦ vi (MIL) идти́* (impf) стро́ем; **fashion ~** пока́з мод.
parade ground n (уче́бный) плац*.
paradise ['pærədaɪs] n (also fig) рай*.
paradox ['pærədɔks] n парадо́кс.
paradoxical [pærə'dɔksɪkl] adj парадокса́льный* (парадокса́лен).
paradoxically [pærə'dɔksɪklɪ] adv как э́то ни парадокса́льно.
paraffin ['pærəfɪn] n (BRIT: also: ~ oil) кероси́н; **liquid ~** (BRIT) вазели́новое ма́сло.
paraffin heater n (BRIT) обогрева́тель m на твёрдом парафи́не.
paraffin lamp n (BRIT) кероси́новая ла́мпа.
paragon ['pærəgən] n (of honesty, virtue etc) образе́ц*.
paragraph ['pærəgrɑ:f] n абза́ц; (of document) пара́граф; **to begin a new ~** начина́ть (нача́ть* perf) писа́ть с абза́ца.
Paraguay ['pærəgwaɪ] n Парагва́й.
Paraguayan [pærə'gwaɪən] adj парагва́йский ♦ n парагва́ец*(-а́йка*).
parallel ['pærəlɛl] adj паралле́льный* (паралле́лен); (fig: similar) аналоги́чный* (аналоги́чен); (COMPUT) паралле́льный ♦ n (GEO, fig) паралле́ль f; **to draw ~s between/ with** проводи́ть* (провести́* perf) паралле́ль ме́жду +instr/с +instr; **~ (with** or **to)** паралле́льно (с +instr); **in ~** (ELEC) паралле́льно.
paralyse ['pærəlaɪz] vt (BRIT: also fig) парализова́ть (impf/perf); **he is ~d** (BRIT) он парализо́ван.

paralyses [pə'rælɪsi:z] npl of **paralysis**.
paralysis [pə'rælɪsɪs] (pl **paralyses**) n (MED) парали́ч*.
paralytic [pærə'lɪtɪk] adj (MED) парализо́ванный (парализо́ван); (BRIT: inf: drunk) упи́вшийся.
paralyze ['pærəlaɪz] vt (US) = **paralyse**.
paramedic [pærə'mɛdɪk] n парамéдик; **~s** кома́нда ско́рой по́мощи.
parameter [pə'ræmɪtəʳ] n пара́метр.
paramilitary [pærə'mɪlɪtərɪ] adj военизи́рованный.
paramount ['pærəmaunt] adj первостепе́нный.
paranoia [pærə'nɔɪə] n парано́йя.
paranoid ['pærənɔɪd] adj (person) парано́идный; (feeling) параной́ческий.
paranormal [pærə'nɔ:ml] adj не поддаю́щийся объясне́нию ♦ n: **the ~** явле́ния ntpl, не поддаю́щиеся объясне́нию.
parapet ['pærəpɪt] n парапе́т.
paraphernalia [pærəfə'neɪlɪə] n (gear) принадле́жности fpl.
paraphrase ['pærəfreɪz] vt перефрази́ровать (impf/perf).
paraplegic [pærə'pli:dʒɪk] n страда́ющий(-ая) m(f) adj параличо́м ни́жней ча́сти те́ла.
parapsychology [pærəsaɪ'kɔlədʒɪ] n парапсихоло́гия.
parasite ['pærəsaɪt] n (also fig) парази́т.
parasol ['pærəsɔl] n зо́нтик (защища́ющий от со́лнца); (at café etc) тент.
paratrooper ['pærətru:pəʳ] n деса́нтник.
parcel ['pɑ:sl] n (package) свёрток*; (sent by post) посы́лка* ♦ vt (also: ~ up) завёртывать (заверну́ть perf).
▸ **parcel out** vt раздава́ть* (разда́ть* perf).
parcel bomb n (BRIT) бо́мба, спря́танная в паке́т.
parcel post n почто́во-посы́лочная слу́жба.
parch [pɑ:tʃ] vt (crops, land) выжига́ть (вы́жечь* perf).
parched [pɑ:tʃt] adj: **I'm ~** у меня́ пересо́хло в го́рле.
parchment ['pɑ:tʃmənt] n перга́мент.
pardon ['pɑ:dn] n (LAW) поми́лование ♦ vt проща́ть (прости́ть* perf); (LAW) поми́ловать (perf); **~ me!, I beg your ~!** прошу́ проще́ния!; **(I beg your) ~?**, (US) **~ me?** (what did you say?) прости́те, не расслы́шал.
pare [pɛəʳ] vt (BRIT: nails) стричь* (остри́чь* perf); (fruit) чи́стить* (очи́стить* perf); (costs) урéзывать or урезáть (урéзать* perf).
parent [ˈpɛərənt] n роди́тель(ница) m(f); **~s** npl (mother and father) роди́тели mpl.
parentage ['pɛərəntɪdʒ] n происхожде́ние; **she is of unknown ~** её происхожде́ние неизве́стно.
parental [pə'rɛntl] adj роди́тельский*.
parent company n (COMM) матери́нская компа́ния.
parentheses [pə'rɛnθɪsi:z] npl of **parenthesis**.

parenthesis [pə'rɛnθɪsɪs] (*pl* **parentheses**) *n*
(*word*) вво́дное сло́во*; (*phrase*) вво́дное
предложе́ние; **in ~** в ско́бках.
parenthood ['pɛərənthud] *n* (*motherhood*)
матери́нство; (*fatherhood*) отцо́вство.
parenting ['pɛərəntɪŋ] *n* воспита́ние.
Paris ['pærɪs] *n* Пари́ж.
parish ['pærɪʃ] *n* (*REL*) прихо́д; (*BRIT*: *civil*)
о́круг*.
parish council *n* (*BRIT*) прихо́дский* сове́т.
parishioner [pə'rɪʃənə'] *n* (*REL*)
прихожа́нин*(-а́нка*).
Parisian [pə'rɪzɪən] *adj* пари́жский* ◆ *n*
парижа́нин*(-нка*).
parity ['pærɪtɪ] *n* (*equality: of pay, conditions etc*)
парите́т.
park [pɑːk] *n* парк ◆ *vt* (*AUT*) ста́вить*
(поста́вить* *perf*), паркова́ть (припаркова́ть
perf) ◆ *vi* (*AUT*) паркова́ться (припаркова́ться
perf).
parka ['pɑːkə] *n* *стёганная ку́ртка на меху́.*
parking ['pɑːkɪŋ] *n* (*of vehicle*) паркова́ние;
(*space to park*) стоя́нка*; ″**no ~**″ ,,стоя́нка
запрещена́″.
parking lights *npl* подфа́рники *mpl*.
parking lot *n* (*US*) (авто)стоя́нка.
parking meter *n* счётчик на (авто)стоя́нке.
parking offence *n* (*BRIT*) наруше́ние пра́вил
стоя́нки.
parking place *n* ме́сто* на автостоя́нке.
parking ticket *n* штраф за наруше́ние пра́вил
паркова́ния.
parking violation *n* (*US*) = **parking offence**.
Parkinson's ['pɑːkɪnsənz] *n* (*also*: **~ disease**)
боле́знь *f* Паркинсона.
parkway ['pɑːkweɪ] *n* (*US*) *доро́га, обса́женная*
дере́вьями.
parlance ['pɑːləns] *n*: **in common/modern ~**
говоря́ обы́чным/совреме́нным языко́м.
parliament ['pɑːləmənt] *n* парла́мент.
parliamentary [pɑːlə'mɛntərɪ] *adj* парла́мент-
ский*.
parlour ['pɑːlə'] (*US* **parlor**) *n* гости́ная *f adj*.
parlous ['pɑːləs] *adj* бе́дственный.
Parmesan [pɑːmɪ'zæn] *n* (*also*: **~ cheese**) сыр
пармеза́н.
parochial [pə'rəukɪəl] *adj* (*pej*) ограни́ченный*
(ограни́чен).
parody ['pærədɪ] *n* паро́дия ◆ *vt* пароди́ровать
(*impf/perf*).
parole [pə'rəul] *n*: **he is/was released on ~** (*LAW*)
он освобождён/был освобождён под
че́стное сло́во.
paroxysm ['pærəksɪzəm] *n* (*also MED*)
парокси́зм.
parquet ['pɑːkeɪ] *n*: **~ floor(ing)** парке́тный
пол*.
parrot ['pærət] *n* попуга́й.

parrot-fashion ['pærətfæʃən] *adv* как попуга́й.
parry ['pærɪ] *vt* (*blow*) отража́ть (отрази́ть*
perf); (*question*) пари́ровать (*impf/perf*).
parsimonious [pɑːsɪ'məunɪəs] *adj* (*person*)
скупо́й* (скуп).
parsley ['pɑːslɪ] *n* петру́шка.
parsnip ['pɑːsnɪp] *n* пастерна́к (посевно́й).
parson ['pɑːsn] *n* прихо́дский* свяще́нник;
(*Church of England*) па́стор.
part [pɑːt] *n* (*section, division*) часть *f*;
(*component*) дета́ль *f*; (*role*) роль* *f*; (*episode*)
се́рия; (*MUS*) па́ртия; (*US*: *in hair*) пробо́р ◆
adv = **partly** ◆ *vt* разделя́ть (раздели́ть* *perf*);
(*hair*) расчёсывать (расчеса́ть* *perf*) на
пробо́р ◆ *vi* (*people*) расстава́ться*
(расста́ться* *perf*); (*crowd*) расступа́ться
(расступи́ться *perf*); (*roads*) расходи́ться*
(разойти́сь* *perf*); **to take ~ in** принима́ть
(приня́ть* *perf*) уча́стие в +*prp*; **to take sth in**
good ~ не обижа́ться (оби́деться* *perf*)
что-н; **to take sb's ~** (*support*) станови́ться*
(стать* *perf*) на чью-н сто́рону; **on his/for my**
~ с его́/мое́й стороны́; **for the most**
~ бо́льшей ча́стью; **for the better ~ of the day**
бо́льшую часть дня; **to be ~ and parcel of**
явля́ться (*impf*) неотъе́млемой ча́стью +*gen*;
~ of speech (*LING*) часть ре́чи
▶ **part with** *vt fus* (*money, possessions*)
расстава́ться* (расста́ться* *perf*) с +*infin*.
partake [pɑː'teɪk] *irreg vi* (*formal*): **to ~ of sth**
отве́дывать (отве́дать *perf*) чего́-н.
part exchange *n* (*BRIT*: *COMM*) *рассчёт, при*
кото́ром де́нежный взнос сочета́ется с
обме́ном ста́рого това́ра на но́вый.
partial ['pɑːʃl] *adj* (*not complete*) части́чный*;
(*biased*) пристра́стный* (пристра́стен); **I am**
~ to chocolate (*like*) я пристра́стен к
шокола́ду.
partially ['pɑːʃəlɪ] *adv* части́чно.
participant [pɑː'tɪsɪpənt] *n* уча́стник(-ица).
participate [pɑː'tɪsɪpeɪt] *vi*: **to ~ in** уча́ствовать
(*impf*) в +*prp*.
participation [pɑːtɪsɪ'peɪʃən] *n* уча́стие.
participle ['pɑːtɪsɪpl] *n* прича́стие.
particle ['pɑːtɪkl] *n* (*also PHYS*) части́ца.
particular [pə'tɪkjulə'] *adj* (*distinct, special*)
осо́бый*; (*demanding*) привере́дливый
(привере́длив); **~s** *npl* (*specifics*) ча́стности
fpl; (*personal details*) да́нные *pl adj*; **he is very**
~ about what he eats он о́чень привере́длив
в еде́; **in ~** в ча́стности.
particularly [pə'tɪkjuləlɪ] *adv* осо́бенно.
parting ['pɑːtɪŋ] *n* (*action*) разделе́ние;
(*farewell*) проща́ние; (*BRIT*: *in hair*) пробо́р ◆
adj (*words, gift etc*) проща́льный; **~ shot**
проща́льное замеча́ние.
partisan [pɑːtɪ'zæn] *adj* (*politics, views*)
пристра́стный* (пристра́стен) ◆ *n* (*supporter*)

---

* marks translations which have irregular inflections. The Russian-English side of the dictionary gives inflectional information.

приве́рженец*; (*resistance fighter*) партиза́н(ка*).

partition [pɑ:'tɪʃən] *n* (*wall, screen*) перегоро́дка*; (*of country*) разде́л ♦ *vt* разделя́ть (раздели́ть* *perf*).

partly ['pɑ:tlɪ] *adv* части́чно.

partner ['pɑ:tnəʳ] *n* (*spouse*) супру́г(а); (*girlfriend*) де́вушка*; (*boyfriend*) па́рень* *m*; (*COMM, SPORT, CARDS*) партнёр ♦ *vt*: **I used to ~ him** я был его́ партнёром.

partnership ['pɑ:tnəʃɪp] *n* (*COMM: company*) това́рищество; (: *with person*) партнёрство; (*POL*) сою́з; **to go into** *or* **form a ~ (with)** устана́вливать (установи́ть* *perf*) партнёрство (с +*instr*).

part payment *n* части́чная опла́та.

partridge ['pɑ:trɪdʒ] *n* (се́рая) куропа́тка*.

part-time ['pɑ:t'taɪm] *adj* (*work*) почасово́й*; (*staff*) за́нятый* (за́нят) непо́лный рабо́чий* день* ♦ *adv*: **to work ~** быть* (*impf*) на почасово́й ста́вке; **to study ~** обуча́ться (*impf*) по непо́лной програ́мме.

part-timer [pɑ:t'taɪməʳ] *n* (*also*: **part-time worker**) рабо́тник-(ица) на почасово́й ста́вке, почасови́к.

party ['pɑ:tɪ] *n* (*POL*) па́ртия; (*celebration: formal*) ве́чер*; (: *informal*) вечери́нка*; (*group of people: surveying etc*) па́ртия; (: *rescue etc*) отря́д; (: *tourists etc*) гру́ппа; (*LAW*) сторона́* ♦ *cpd* (*POL*) парти́йный; **dinner ~** зва́нный обе́д; **to give** *or* **throw a ~** (*official*) устра́ивать (устро́ить* *perf*) ве́чер; **we're having a ~ next Saturday** в сле́дующую суббо́ту у нас вечери́нка; **birthday ~** пра́зднование дня рожде́ния; **he was (a) ~ to the crime** он явля́лся соуча́стником преступле́ния.

party dress *n* вече́рнее пла́тье*.

party line *n* (*TEL*) о́бщая телефо́нная ли́ния; (*POL*) парти́йная ли́ния.

party piece *n* коро́нный но́мер*.

party-political ['pɑ:tɪpə'lɪtɪkl] *adj* парти́йный полити́ческий*.

party-political broadcast *n* рекла́ма *полити́ческой па́ртии по ра́дио и телеви́дению.*

pass [pɑ:s] *vt* (*spend: time*) проводи́ть* (провести́* *perf*); (*hand over*) передава́ть* (переда́ть* *perf*); (*go past: on foot*) проходи́ть* (пройти́* *perf*); (: *by transport*) проезжа́ть (прое́хать* *perf*); (*overtake: vehicle*) обгоня́ть (обогна́ть* *perf*); (*fig: surpass*) превосходи́ть* (превзойти́* *perf*); (*exam*) сдава́ть* (сдать* *perf*); (*approve: law, proposal*) принима́ть (приня́ть* *perf*) ♦ *vi* (*go past: on foot*) проходи́ть* (пройти́* *perf*); (: *by transport*) проезжа́ть (прое́хать* *perf*); (*in exam*) сдава́ть* (сдать* *perf*) ♦ *n* (*permit*) про́пуск*; (*membership card*) чле́нский* биле́т; (*GEO*) перева́л; (*SPORT*) пас, переда́ча; (*SCOL: also*: **~ mark**): **to get a ~** получа́ть (получи́ть *perf*)

зачёт; **to ~ sth through sth** просо́вывать (просу́нуть *perf*) что-н че́рез что-н; **could you ~ the vegetables round?** переда́йте, пожа́луйста, о́вощи всем; **she could ~ for 25** она́ могла́ бы сойти́ за 25-ле́тнюю; **things have come to a pretty ~** дела́ пло́хи; **to make a ~ at sb** (*inf*) пристава́ть* (приста́ть* *perf*) к кому́-н

▶ **pass away** *vi* (*die*) сконча́ться (*perf*)

▶ **pass by** *vi* (*on foot*) проходи́ть* (пройти́* *perf*); (*by transport*) проезжа́ть (прое́хать* *perf*) ♦ *vt* (*ignore*) не обраща́ть (обрати́ть* *perf*) внима́ния на +*acc*

▶ **pass down** *vt* (*customs, inheritance*) передава́ть* (переда́ть* *perf*)

▶ **pass on** *vt* передава́ть* (переда́ть* *perf*); (*price rises*) перекла́дывать (переложи́ть* *perf*) ♦ *vi* (*die*) сконча́ться (*perf*)

▶ **pass out** *vi* (*faint*) теря́ть (потеря́ть *perf*) созна́ние; (*BRIT: MIL*) успе́шно проходи́ть* (пройти́* *perf*) подгото́вку

▶ **pass over** *vt* (*ignore*) не оставля́ть (оста́вить* *perf*) без внима́ния ♦ *vi* (*die*) сконча́ться (*perf*)

▶ **pass up** *vt* (*opportunity*) упуска́ть (упусти́ть* *perf*).

passable ['pɑ:səbl] *adj* (*road*) проходи́мый (проходи́м); (*acceptable: work*) сно́сный* (сно́сен).

passage ['pæsɪdʒ] *n* (*also ANAT*) прохо́д; (*in book*) отры́вок*; (*act of passing*) прохожде́ние; (*journey: on boat*) путеше́ствие.

passenger ['pæsɪndʒəʳ] *n* пассажи́р(ка*).

passer-by [pɑ:sə'baɪ] (*pl* **passers-by**) *n* прохо́жий*(-ая) *m(f) adj*.

passers-by [pɑ:səz'baɪ] *npl of* **passer-by**.

passing ['pɑ:sɪŋ] *adj* мимолётный* (мимолётен) ♦ *n*: **in ~** мимохо́дом; **to mention sth in ~** замеча́ть (заме́тить* *perf*) что-н мимохо́дом.

passing place *n* (*AUT*) расшире́ние на доро́ге.

passion ['pæʃən] *n* (*also fig*) страсть* *f*; **she has a ~ for history** у неё страсть к исто́рии.

passionate ['pæʃənɪt] *adj* стра́стный* (стра́стен).

passion fruit *n* плод* страстоцве́та.

Passion play *n* мисте́рия, *в кото́рой представля́ются стра́сти Госпо́дни.*

passive ['pæsɪv] *adj* пасси́вный* (пасси́вен); (*LING*) пасси́вный, страда́тельный ♦ *n* (*LING*): **the ~** страда́тельный зало́г.

passive smoking *n* пасси́вное куре́ние.

passkey ['pɑ:ski:] *n* отмы́чка*.

Passover ['pɑ:səuvəʳ] *n* евре́йская Па́сха.

passport ['pɑ:spɔ:t] *n* (*official document*) па́спорт*; (*fig*) ключ*.

passport control *n* па́спортный контро́ль *m*.

password ['pɑ:swə:d] *n* паро́ль *m*.

past [pɑ:st] *prep* (*in front of*) ми́мо +*gen*; (*beyond*) за +*instr*; (*later than*) по́сле +*gen* ♦ *adj* (*previous: government etc*) бы́вший*; (: *week,*

month etc) про́шлый ♦ n про́шлое nt adj;
(LING): **the ~ (tense)** проше́дшее вре́мя* nt ♦
adv: **to run ~** пробега́ть (пробежа́ть* perf)
ми́мо; **he's ~ forty** (older than) ему́ за со́рок;
it's ~ midnight уже́ за́ по́лночь; **ten/quarter ~
eight** де́сять мину́т/че́тверть девя́того; **he
ran ~ me** он пробежа́л ми́мо меня́; **I'm ~
caring** мне у́же всё равно́; **he's ~ it** (BRIT: inf)
он вы́дохнулся; **for the ~ few/3 days** за
после́дние не́сколько дней/3 дня; **in the ~** в
про́шлом; (LING) в проше́дшем вре́мени.
pasta ['pæstə] n макаро́нные изде́лия ntpl.
paste [peɪst] n (wet mixture) па́ста; (glue)
кле́йстер; (jewellery) страз; (fish, meat paste)
паштет ♦ vt (paper etc) наноси́ть* (нанести́*
perf) клей на +acc; **tomato ~** тома́тная па́ста;
to ~ sth onto sth наноси́ть* (нанести́* perf)
что-н на что-н.
pastel ['pæstl] adj (colour) пасте́льный.
pasteurized ['pæstʃəraɪzd] adj (milk etc)
пастеризо́ванный.
pastille ['pæstl] n пасти́ла́.
pastime ['pɑːstaɪm] n (hobby) время-
препровожде́ние.
past master n (BRIT) непревзойдённый
ма́стер.
pastor ['pɑːstə] n па́стор.
pastoral ['pɑːstərl] adj (REL) па́сторский.
pastry ['peɪstrɪ] n (dough) те́сто; (cake)
пиро́жное nt adj.
pasture ['pɑːstʃə] n па́стбище.
pasty [adj 'peɪstɪ, n 'pæstɪ] adj (complexion, face)
бле́дный* (бле́ден) ♦ n пирожо́к*.
pat [pæt] adj (answer, remark) станда́ртный*
(станда́ртен) ♦ vt (dog) ласка́ть (приласка́ть
perf) ♦ n: **to give sb/o.s. a ~ on the back** (fig)
хвали́ть* (похвали́ть* perf) кого́-н/себя́ ♦ adv:
to know sth off ~, (US) **have sth down ~** знать
(impf) что-н назубо́к; **to ~ sb's back**
похло́пывать (похло́пать perf) кого́-н по
спине́.
patch [pætʃ] n (piece of material) запла́та; (also:
eye ~) повя́зка*; (area: damp, black etc)
пятно́*; (repair: on tyre etc) запла́та,
запла́тка*; (of land) уча́сток* ♦ vt (clothes)
лата́ть (залата́ть perf); **to go through a bad ~**
попада́ть (попа́сть* perf) в полосу́
невезе́ния; **bald ~** лы́сина
▸ **patch up** vt (mend temporarily) заде́лывать
(заде́лать perf); (quarrel) ула́живать
(ула́дить* perf).
patchwork ['pætʃwəːk] n (SEWING) лоску́тная
рабо́та.
patchy ['pætʃɪ] adj (uneven: colour) пятни́стый
(пятни́ст); (incomplete: information,
knowledge etc) отры́вочный* (отры́вочен).
pate [peɪt] n: **a bald ~** лы́сина на маку́ше.
pâté ['pæteɪ] n (CULIN) паштет.

patent ['peɪtnt] n (COMM) пате́нт ♦ vt (COMM)
патентова́ть* (запатентова́ть* perf) ♦ adj
(obvious) я́вный* (я́вен).
patent leather n лакиро́ванная ко́жа.
patently ['peɪtntlɪ] adv (obvious, wrong)
очеви́дно.
patent medicine n патенто́ванное лека́рство.
Patent Office n пате́нтное бюро́ nt ind.
patent rights npl пате́нтное пра́во ntsg.
paternal [pə'təːnl] adj (love, duty) отцо́вский*;
(grandmother etc) по отцу́.
paternalistic [pətə:nə'lɪstɪk] adj (society,
attitudes) патерналисти́ческий.
paternity [pə'təːnɪtɪ] n отцо́вство.
paternity leave n о́тпуск отца́ по ухо́ду за
ребёнком.
paternity suit n (LAW) установле́ние
отцо́вства.
path [pɑːθ] n (trail, track) тропа́*, тропи́нка*;
(concrete path, gravel path etc) доро́жка*;
(trajectory) путь* m движе́ния; (fig) путь*.
pathetic [pə'θetɪk] adj (pitiful: sight, cries)
жа́лостный* (жа́лостен); (very bad) жа́лкий*
(жа́лок).
pathological [pæθə'lɔdʒɪkl] adj (liar, hatred)
патологи́ческий*; (MED: work) в о́бласти
патоло́гии.
pathologist [pə'θɔlədʒɪst] n (MED) пато́лог.
pathology [pə'θɔlədʒɪ] n (MED) патоло́гия.
pathos ['peɪθɔs] n па́фос.
pathway ['pɑːθweɪ] n (path) тропа́; (route, fig)
путь* m.
patience ['peɪʃns] n (personal quality)
терпе́ние; (BRIT: CARDS) пасья́нс; **to lose one's
~** теря́ть (потеря́ть perf) терпе́ние.
patient ['peɪʃnt] n (MED) пацие́нт(ка) ♦ adj
(person) терпели́вый (терпели́в); **he is ~ with
me** он терпели́в со мной.
patiently ['peɪʃntlɪ] adv терпели́во.
patio ['pætɪəu] n па́тио m ind, вну́тренний
дво́рик.
patriot ['peɪtrɪət] n патрио́т(ка).
patriotic [pætrɪ'ɔtɪk] adj (person) патрио-
ти́чный* (патриоти́чен); (song, speech etc)
патриоти́ческий, патриоти́чный*
(патриоти́чен).
patriotism ['pætrɪətɪzəm] n патриоти́зм.
patrol [pə'trəul] n (MIL, POLICE) патру́ль m ♦ vt
(MIL, POLICE: city, streets etc) патрули́ровать*
(impf); **to be on ~** быть* (impf) в дозо́ре;
(POLICE) быть* (impf) на дежу́рстве.
patrol boat n (NAUT, MIL, CUSTOMS etc)
сторожево́й ка́тер.
patrol car n (POLICE) полице́йская патру́льная
маши́на.
patrolman [pə'trəulmən] irreg n (US: POLICE)
дежу́рный полице́йский m adj.
patron ['peɪtrən] n (customer, client)

---

* marks translations which have irregular inflections. The Russian-English side of the dictionary gives inflectional information.

(постоя́нный) клие́нт; (*benefactor: of charity*) спо́нсор, шеф; ~ **of the arts** покрови́тель (ница) *m(f)* иску́сств.

patronage ['pætrənɪdʒ] *n* (*of artist etc*) покрови́тельство; (*of charity*) спо́нсорство, шефство.

patronize ['pætrənaɪz] *vt* (*pej: look down on*) относи́ться* (отнести́сь* *perf*) свысока́; (*artist, writer etc*) покрови́тельствовать (*impf*); (*shop, club, firm*) постоя́нно посеща́ть (*impf*).

patronizing ['pætrənaɪzɪŋ] *adj* (*pej: person, tone, comment etc*) снисходи́тельный* (снисходи́телен).

patron saint *n* (*REL*) засту́пник(-ица).

patter ['pætə] *n* (*sound: of feet, rain*) топота́ние; (*of rain*) стук; (*sales talk etc*) речитати́в ♦ *vi* (*footsteps*) топота́ть (*impf*); (*rain*) бараба́нить (*impf*).

pattern ['pætən] *n* (*design*) узо́р; (*SEWING*) вы́кройка*; (*sample*) образе́ц*; **behaviour** ~**s** мане́ры *fpl* поведе́ния.

patterned ['pætənd] *adj* (*fabric, wallpaper, carpet etc*) узо́рчатый; ~ **with flowers** с узо́ром из цвето́в.

paucity ['pɔːsɪtɪ] *n* недоста́ток*.

paunch [pɔːntʃ] *n* брюшко́*.

pauper ['pɔːpə] *n* ни́щий*(-ая) *m(f) adj*; ~**'s grave** бедня́цкая моги́ла.

pause [pɔːz] *n* (*temporary halt*) па́уза ♦ *vi* (*stop temporarily*) де́лать (сде́лать *perf*) переры́в; (*: while speaking*) де́лать (сде́лать *perf*) па́узу; **to** ~ **for breath** переводи́ть* (перевести́* *perf*) дыха́ние; (*fig*) передохну́ть (*perf*).

pave [peɪv] *vt* (*street, yard etc*) мости́ть* (вы́мостить* *perf*); **to** ~ **the way for** (*fig*) прокла́дывать (проложи́ть* *perf*) путь к +*dat*.

pavement ['peɪvmənt] *n* (*BRIT: for pedestrians*) тротуа́р; (*US: roadway*) доро́жное покры́тие.

pavilion [pə'vɪlɪən] *n* (*SPORT*) павильо́н.

paving ['peɪvɪŋ] *n* (*material*) доро́жное покры́тие.

paving stone *n* брусча́тка*.

paw [pɔː] *n* (*of animal*) ла́па* ♦ *vt* (*animal*) тро́гать (потро́гать *perf*) ла́пой *or* ла́пами; (*horse, bull*) бить* (*impf*) копы́том *or* копы́тами; (*pej: touch*) ла́пать (*impf*).

pawn [pɔːn] *n* (*CHESS, fig*) пе́шка ♦ *vt* закла́дывать (заложи́ть* *perf*).

pawnbroker ['pɔːnbrəukə] *n* ростовщи́к(-и́ца), слу́жащий(-ая) *m(f) adj*.

pawnshop ['pɔːnʃɔp] *n* ломба́рд.

pay [peɪ] (*pt, pp* **paid**) *n* (*wage, salary etc*) зарпла́та ♦ *vt* (*sum of money, wage*) плати́ть* (заплати́ть* *perf*); (*debt, bill*) плати́ть* (уплати́ть* *perf*); (*be profitable to: also fig*) окупа́ть (окупи́ть* *perf*) ♦ *vi* (*be profitable*) окупа́ться (окупи́ться* *perf*); **how much did you** ~ **for it?** ско́лько Вы за него́/неё/э́то заплати́ли?; **I paid £5 for that record** я

заплати́л £5 за ту пласти́нку; **to** ~ **one's way** обеспе́чивать (обеспе́чить *perf*) себя́; **to** ~ **dividends** (*fig*) вознагражда́ться (вознагради́ться* *perf*); **it won't** ~ **you to do that** э́то де́ло не принесёт вам успе́ха; **to** ~ **attention (to)** обраща́ть (обрати́ть* *perf*) внима́ние (на +*acc*); **to** ~ **sb a visit** наноси́ть* (нанести́* *perf*) кому́-н визи́т; **to** ~ **one's respects to sb** свиде́тельствовать* (засвиде́тельствовать* *perf*) кому́-н (своё) почте́ние

▸ **pay back** *vt* (*money*) возвраща́ть (возврати́ть* *or* верну́ть *perf*); (*person*) отплати́ть* (*perf*)

▸ **pay for** *vt fus* (*purchases*) опла́чивать (оплати́ть* *perf*); (*fig*) поплати́ться* (*perf*)

▸ **pay in** *vt* (*money, cheque etc*) вноси́ть* (внести́* *perf*)

▸ **pay off** *vt* (*debt, creditor, mortgage*) распла́чиваться (расплати́ться* *perf*) с +*instr*; (*person*) рассчи́тывать (рассчита́ть *perf*) ♦ *vi* (*also fig*) окупа́ться (окупи́ться* *perf*); **to** ~ **sth off in instalments** расплачи́ваться (расплати́ться* *perf*) за что-н в рассро́чку

▸ **pay out** *vt* (*money*) выпла́чивать (вы́платить* *perf*); (*rope*) трави́ть* (потрави́ть* *perf*)

▸ **pay up** *vt* (*money*) выпла́чивать (вы́платить* *perf*) ♦ *vi* (*person, company etc*) рассчи́тываться (рассчита́ться *perf*) (сполна́).

payable ['peɪəbl] *adj* (*sum of money*) подлежа́щий упла́те; (*cheque*): ~ **to** подлежа́щий упла́те на имя +*gen*.

pay award *n* повыше́ние зарпла́ты.

payday ['peɪdeɪ] *n* день* *m* зарпла́ты.

PAYE *n abbr* (*BRIT*: = *pay as you earn*) *отчисле́ние подохо́дного нало́га из зарпла́ты.*

payee [peɪ'iː] *n* (*of cheque, postal order*) получа́тель(ница) *m(f)*.

pay envelope *n* (*US*) = **pay packet**.

paying guest ['peɪŋ-] *n* постоя́лец(-лица).

payload ['peɪləud] *n* (*COMM*) поле́зная нагру́зка*.

payment ['peɪmənt] *n* (*act*) платёж*, упла́та; (*of bill*) опла́та; (*amount of money*) вы́плата; **advance** ~ (*part sum*) внесе́ние ава́нса; (*total sum*) платёж ава́нсом; **deferred** ~ отсро́ченный платёж; ~ **by instalments** платёж в рассро́чку; **monthly** ~ ме́сячный платёж; **in** ~ **for, in** ~ **of** в опла́ту за +*acc*; **on** ~ **of five pounds** по упла́те пяти́ фу́нтов.

pay packet *n* (*BRIT*) паке́т с зарпла́той.

payphone ['peɪfəun] *n* (*TEL*) телефо́н-автома́т.

payroll ['peɪrəul] *n* платёжная ве́домость *f*; **to be on a firm's** ~ быть* (*impf*) в спи́сочном соста́ве фи́рмы.

pay slip *n* (*BRIT*) извеще́ние о зарпла́те.

pay station *n* (*US*) телефо́н-автома́т.

PBS *n abbr* (*US*: = *Public Broadcasting Service*)

Госуда́рственная слу́жба радиовеща́ния.
PC *n abbr* (= **personal computer**) ПК=
персона́льный компью́тер; (*BRIT*) = **police
constable** ◆ *adj abbr* = **politically correct** ◆ *abbr*
(*BRIT*) = **Privy Councillor**.
pc *abbr* = **per cent, postcard**.
p/c *abbr* = **petty cash**.
PCB *n abbr* (*ELEC, COMPUT*: = *printed circuit
board*) печа́тная пла́та; (= *polychlorinated
biphenyl*) полихлори́рованный дифени́л.
pcm *abbr* (= *per calendar month*) в ме́сяц.
PD *n abbr* (*US*) = **police department**.
pd *abbr* = **paid**.
PDQ *adv abbr* (*inf*: = *pretty damn quick*)
черто́вски бы́стро.
PDSA *n abbr* (*BRIT*: = *People's Dispensary for Sick
Animals*) благотвори́тельное о́бщество,
организу́ющее ветерина́рную по́мощь
живо́тным.
PDT *abbr* (*US*) = *Pacific Daylight Time*.
PE *n abbr* (*SCOL*) (= **physical education**)
физкульту́ра= физи́ческая культу́ра ◆ *abbr*
(*CANADA*) = *Prince Edward Island*.
pea [pi:] *n* (*BOT, CULIN*) горо́х *no pl*.
peace [pi:s] *n* (*not war*) мир; (*calm: of place,
surroundings*) поко́й, споко́йствие;
(: *personal*) поко́й; **to be at ~ with sb** быть*
(*impf*) в ми́ре с ке́м-н; **to be at ~ with sth**
смиря́ться (смири́ться* *perf*) с чем-н; **to keep
the ~** (*policeman*) подде́рживать
(поддержа́ть* *perf*) споко́йствие; (*citizen*)
соблюда́ть (*impf*) споко́йствие.
peaceable ['pi:səbl] *adj* миролюби́вый
(миролюби́в).
peaceful ['pi:sful] *adj* (*calm*) ми́рный* (ми́рен).
peacekeeper ['pi:ski:pəʳ] *n* член ми́рных
во́йск.
peacekeeping force ['pi:ski:piŋ-] *n* миро-
тво́рческие си́лы *fpl*.
peace offering *n* задабривание.
peach [pi:tʃ] *n* пе́рсик.
peacock ['pi:kɔk] *n* павли́н.
peak [pi:k] *n* верши́на, пик; (*of cap*) козырёк*.
peak hours *npl* часы́ *mpl* пик.
peak period *n* пи́ковый пери́од.
peak rate *n* (*TEL*) расце́нки, применя́емые в
пи́ковый пери́од.
peaky ['pi:kɪ] *adj* (*BRIT: inf*) до́хлый.
peal [pi:l] *n* (*of bells*) перезво́н; **~ of laughter**
раска́т сме́ха.
peanut ['pi:nʌt] *n* ара́хис.
peanut butter *n* ара́хисовая па́ста.
pear [pɛəʳ] *n* гру́ша.
pearl [pə:l] *n* жемчу́жина; **~s** же́мчуг.
peasant ['pɛznt] *n* крестья́нин*(-нка*).
peat [pi:t] *n* торф.
pebble ['pɛbl] *n* га́лька* *no pl*.
peck [pɛk] *vt* (*subj: bird*) клева́ть* (*impf*); (: *once*)

клю́нуть (*perf*); (*also: ~* **at:** *food*) поклева́ть*
(*impf*) ◆ *n* (*of bird*) клево́к*; (*kiss*) чмо́канье.
pecking order ['pɛkɪŋ-] *n* старшинство́.
peckish ['pɛkɪʃ] *adj* (*BRIT: inf*): **I'm feeling ~** мне
хо́чется пожева́ть.
peculiar [pɪ'kju:lɪəʳ] *adj* (*strange*) свое-
обра́зный* (своеобра́зен); (*belonging
exclusively*): **~ to** сво́йственный* (сво́йствен)
+*dat*.
peculiarity [pɪkju:lɪ'ærɪtɪ] *n* (*strange habit*)
стра́нность *f*; (*distinctive feature*)
осо́бенность *f*.
peculiarly [pɪ'kju:lɪəlɪ] *adv* (*oddly*) стра́нно;
(*distinctively*) осо́бенно.
pecuniary [pɪ'kju:nɪərɪ] *adj* де́нежный.
pedal ['pɛdl] *n* педа́ль *f* ◆ *vi* крути́ть* (*impf*)
педа́ли.
pedal bin *n* (*BRIT*) му́сорное ведро́* с педа́лью.
pedant ['pɛdənt] *n* педа́нт(ка*).
pedantic [pɪ'dæntɪk] *adj* педанти́чный*
(педанти́чен).
peddle ['pɛdl] *vt* (*goods, drugs*) торгова́ть
(*impf*) +*instr*; (*gossip*) разноси́ть* (разнести́*
perf).
peddler ['pɛdləʳ] *n*: (*drug*) **~** торго́вец*
нарко́тиками.
pedestal ['pɛdəstl] *n* пьедеста́л.
pedestrian [pɪ'dɛstrɪən] *n* пешехо́д ◆ *adj*
пешехо́дный; (*fig*) ску́чный.
pedestrian crossing *n* (*BRIT*) пешехо́дный
перехо́д.
pedestrian precinct *n* (*BRIT*) пешехо́дная
зо́на.
pediatrics [pi:dɪ'ætrɪks] *n* (*US*) = **paediatrics**.
pedigree ['pɛdɪgri:] *n* (*also fig*) родосло́вная *f*
adj ◆ *cpd* (*animal*) поро́дистый (поро́дист).
pee [pi:] *vi* (*inf*) пи́сать (попи́сать *perf*).
peek [pi:k] *vi*: **to ~ at/over** взгля́дывать
(взгляну́ть* *perf*) на +*acc*/пове́рх +*gen* ◆ *n*: **to
have** *or* **take a ~ (at)** взгля́дывать (взгляну́ть*
perf) (на +*acc*); **to ~ into** загля́дывать
(загляну́ть* *perf*) в +*acc*.
peel [pi:l] *n* кожура́ ◆ *vt* (*vegetables, fruit*)
чи́стить* (почи́стить* *perf*), очища́ть
(очи́стить* *perf*) ◆ *vi* (*paint*) лупи́ться*
(облупи́ться* *perf*); (*wallpaper*) отстава́ть*
(отста́ть* *perf*); (*skin*) шелуши́ться (*impf*)
▶ **peel back** *vt* оття́гивать (оттяну́ть* *perf*).
peeler ['pi:ləʳ] *n* (*for potatoes etc*) нож для
очи́стки ово́щей и фру́ктов.
peelings ['pi:lɪŋz] *npl* очи́стки *pl*.
peep [pi:p] *n* (*look*) взгляд укра́дкой; (*sound*)
писк ◆ *vi* взгля́дывать (взгляну́ть* *perf*); **to
have** *or* **take a ~ (at)** взгля́дывать (взгляну́ть*
perf) (на +*acc*)
▶ **peep out** *vi* (*be visible*) пока́зываться
(показа́ться* *perf*), выгля́дывать (вы́глянуть*
perf).

---

* marks translations which have irregular inflections. The Russian-English side of the dictionary gives inflectional information.

peephole ['piːphəul] *n* глазо́к*.
peer [pɪə'] *n* (*BRIT: noble*) пэр; (*equal*) ро́вня *m/f*; (*contemporary*) рове́сник(-ица) ♦ *vi*: **to ~ at** всма́триваться (всмотре́ться* *perf*) в +*acc*.
peerage ['pɪərɪdʒ] *n* (*title, position*) пэ́рство; **the ~** пэ́ры.
peerless ['pɪəlɪs] *adj* несравне́нный* (несравне́нен).
peeved [piːvd] *adj* (*inf*) злой* (зол).
peevish ['piːvɪʃ] *adj* капри́зный* (капри́зен), сварли́вый (сварли́в).
peg [pɛg] *n* (*for coat etc*) крючо́к*; (*BRIT: also*: **clothes ~**) прище́пка*; (*also*: **tent ~**) ко́лышек* (*для натя́гивания пала́тки*) ♦ *vt* (*clothes: on line*) прикрепля́ть (прикрепи́ть* *perf*) прище́пками; (*prices*) замора́живать (заморо́зить* *perf*); **off the ~ clothing** гото́вая оде́жда.
pejorative [pɪ'dʒɔrətɪv] *adj* уничижи́тельный* (уничижи́телен).
Pekin [piː'kɪn] *n* = **Peking**.
Pekinese [piːkɪ'niːz] *n* = **Pekingese**.
Peking [piː'kɪn] *n* Пеки́н.
Pekingese [piːkɪ'niːz] *n* (*dog*) кита́йский* мопс.
pelican ['pɛlɪkən] *n* пелика́н.
pelican crossing *n* (*BRIT*) пешехо́дный перехо́д, на кото́ром переключе́ние светофо́ра регули́руется нажа́тием кно́пки.
pellet ['pɛlɪt] *n* (*of paper, mud*) ша́рик, ка́тышек*; (*for shotgun*) дроби́на.
pell-mell ['pɛl'mɛl] *adv* очертя́ го́лову.
pelmet ['pɛlmɪt] *n* ламбреке́н.
pelt [pɛlt] *n* (*animal skin*) шку́ра ♦ *vi* (*rain: also*: **~ down**) лить* (*impf*) как из ведра́; (*inf: run*) проноси́ться* (пронести́сь* *perf*) ♦ *vt*: **to ~ sb with sth** забра́сывать (заброса́ть *perf*) кого́-н чем-н.
pelvis ['pɛlvɪs] *n* таз* *no pl*.
pen [pɛn] *n* ру́чка*; (*felt-tip*) флома́стер; (*enclosure*) заго́н; (*US: inf: prison*) тюрьма́*; **to put ~ to paper** бра́ться* (взя́ться* *perf*) за перо́.
penal ['piːnl] *adj* (*colony, institution*) испра́вительный*; (*system*) кара́тельный; **~ code** уголо́вный ко́декс.
penalize ['piːnəlaɪz] *vt* (*also fig*) нака́зывать (наказа́ть* *perf*); (*SPORT*) штрафова́ть (оштрафова́ть *perf*).
penal servitude [-'səːvɪtjuːd] *n* ка́торжные рабо́ты *fpl*.
penalty ['pɛnltɪ] *n* (*punishment*) наказа́ние; (*fine*) штраф; (*RUGBY*) штрафно́й *m adj* (уда́р); (*FOOTBALL*) штрафно́й (уда́р), пена́льти *m ind*.
penalty area *n* (*BRIT: SPORT*) штрафна́я *f adj* (площа́дка*).
penalty clause *n* (*COMM*) пункт, предусма́тривающий вид и разме́р штра́фа за наруше́ние усло́вий контра́кта.

penalty kick *n* (*RUGBY*) штрафно́й *m adj* (уда́р); (*FOOTBALL*) штрафно́й (уда́р), пена́льти *m ind*.
penalty shoot-out [-'ʃuːtaut] *n* определе́ние кома́нды-победи́теля путём забива́ния се́рии штрафны́х уда́ров по́сле ма́тча око́нчившегося ничье́й.
penance ['pɛnəns] *n* ка́ра.
pence [pɛns] *npl of* **penny**.
penchant ['pɑ̃ːʃɑ̃ːŋ] *n* скло́нность *f*; **to have a ~ for** име́ть (*impf*) скло́нность к +*dat*.
pencil ['pɛnsl] *n* каранда́ш* ♦ *vt*: **to ~ sth in** впи́сывать (вписа́ть* *perf*) что-н карандашо́м; (*fig*) помеча́ть (поме́тить* *perf*) что-н.
pencil case *n* пена́л.
pencil sharpener *n* точи́лка.
pendant ['pɛndnt] *n* куло́н.
pending ['pɛndɪŋ] *prep* вредь до +*gen*, в ожида́нии +*gen* ♦ *adj* (*lawsuit, exam etc*) предстоя́щий*.
pendulum ['pɛndjuləm] *n* ма́ятник.
penetrate ['pɛnɪtreɪt] *vt* (*subj: person, light*) проника́ть (прони́кнуть* *perf*) в/на +*acc*.
penetrating ['pɛnɪtreɪtɪŋ] *adj* (*sound, glance*) пронзи́тельный* (пронзи́телен); (*mind*) проница́тельный* (проница́телен); (*observation*) глубо́кий*.
penetration [pɛnɪ'treɪʃən] *n* проникнове́ние.
pen friend *n* (*BRIT*) друг* (подру́га) по перепи́ске.
penguin ['pɛŋgwɪn] *n* пингви́н.
penicillin [pɛnɪ'sɪlɪn] *n* пеницилли́н.
peninsula [pə'nɪnsjulə] *n* полуо́стров*.
penis ['piːnɪs] *n* пе́нис, мужско́й полово́й член.
penitence ['pɛnɪtns] *n* раска́яние.
penitent ['pɛnɪtnt] *adj* ка́ющийся.
penitentiary [pɛnɪ'tɛnʃərɪ] *n* (*US*) тюрьма́*.
penknife ['pɛnnaɪf] *n* перочи́нный нож*.
pen name *n* (литерату́рный) псевдони́м.
pennant ['pɛnənt] *n* (*NAUT*) сигна́льный флажо́к*.
penniless ['pɛnɪlɪs] *adj* без гроша́; **she is ~** у неё нет ни гроша́.
Pennines ['pɛnaɪnz] *npl*: **the ~** Пени́нские го́ры* *fpl*.
penny ['pɛnɪ] (*pl* **pennies** *or* (*BRIT*) **pence**) *n* пе́нни *nt ind*, пенс; (*US*) цент.
pen pal *n* = **pen friend**.
penpusher ['pɛnpuʃə'] *n* занима́ющийся ну́днок пи́сьменной рабо́той/пи́сарь *m*.
pension ['pɛnʃən] *n* пе́нсия
► **pension off** *vt* отправля́ть (отпра́вить* *perf*) на пе́нсию.
pensionable ['pɛnʃnəbl] *adj* (*age*) пенсио́нный; (*job*) даю́щий пра́во на пе́нсию.
pensioner ['pɛnʃənə'] *n* (*BRIT: also*: **old age ~**) пенсионе́р(ка*).
pension fund *n* пенсио́нный фонд.
pensive ['pɛnsɪv] *adj* заду́мчивый (заду́мчив).

pentagon ['pɛntəgən] n пятиугóльник; (US): **the P~** Пентагóн.

Pentecost ['pɛntɪkɔst] n (Jewish) пятидесятница; (Christian) Трóицый день* m.

penthouse ['pɛnthaus] n (flat) „пéнтхаус" (фешенéбельная кварти́ра, располóженная на кры́ше).

pent-up ['pɛntʌp] adj (feelings) сдéрживаемый.

penultimate [pɛ'nʌltɪmət] adj предпослéдний*.

penury ['pɛnjurɪ] n нуждá, бéдность f.

people ['pi:pl] npl (persons) лю́ди* pl; (nation, race) нарóд; **old ~** старики́ mpl; **young ~** молодёжь fsg; **the ~** (POL) нарóд; **~ at large** лю́ди в мáссе своéй; **a man of the ~** человéк из нарóда; **several ~ came** пришлó нéсколько человéк; **the room was full of ~** в кóмнате бы́ло полнó нарóду; **~ say that ...** говоря́т, что ....

pep [pɛp] (inf) n бóдрость f
▸ **pep up** vt (enliven) оживи́ть* (perf); (food) дéлать (сдéлать perf) острéе.

pepper ['pɛpə'] n пéрец* ◆ vt (fig): **to ~ with** забрáсывать (заброcáть perf) +instr.

peppercorn ['pɛpəkɔ:n] n перчи́нка*.

pepper mill n мéльница для пéрца.

peppermint ['pɛpəmɪnt] n (sweet) мя́тная конфéта; (plant) мя́та пéречная.

pepperoni [pɛpə'rəunɪ] n пеперóни f ind (италья́нская колбасá).

pepper pot n пéречница.

pep talk n (inf) накáчка*.

per [pə:'] prep (for each: of amounts) на +acc; (: of price) за +acc; (: of charge) c +gen; **~ annum/day/hour** в год/день/час; **~ person** на человéка; **~ kilo** за килогрáмм; **as ~ your instructions** соглáсно вáшим инстрýкциям; **as ~ usual** по обыкновéнию.

per capita adj, adv (income) на дýшу населéния.

perceive [pə'si:v] vt (sound, light, idea) воспринимáть (восприня́ть* perf); (realize) понимáть (поня́ть* perf).

per cent n процéнт; **a twenty ~ ~ discount** двадцатипроцéнтная ски́дка.

percentage [pə'sɛntɪdʒ] n (of income) процéнт; (of immigrants etc) дóля; (of substances) (процéнтное) содержáние; **on a ~ basis** на основáнии процéнтного отчислéния.

percentage point n процéнт.

perceptible [pə'sɛptɪbl] adj ощути́мый (ощути́м).

perception [pə'sɛpʃən] n (faculty) восприя́тие; (insight) понимáние no pl; (opinion, understanding) ощущéние.

perceptive [pə'sɛptɪv] adj проницáтельный* (проницáтелен).

perch [pə:tʃ] n (for bird) насéст ◆ n inv (fish)

óкунь* m ◆ vi: **to ~ (on)** (bird) сади́ться* (сесть* perf) (на +acc); (person) присáживаться (присéсть* perf) (на +acc).

percolate ['pə:kəleɪt] vt (coffee) вари́ть* (свари́ть* perf) в кофевáрке ◆ vi (coffee) вари́ться (свари́ться perf) в кофевáрке; (idea, information, light etc): **to ~ through/into** просáчиваться (просочи́ться perf) сквозь +acc/в +acc.

percolator ['pə:kəleɪtə'] n (also: **coffee ~**) кофевáрка.

percussion [pə'kʌʃən] n удáрные инструмéнты mpl.

peremptory [pə'rɛmptərɪ] adj (pej: person) влáстный* (влáстен), категори́чный* (категори́чен); (: order, instruction) категори́ческий*.

perennial [pə'rɛnɪəl] adj (plant) многолéтний*; (fig: problem, feature etc) вéчный* (вéчен) ◆ n (BOT) многолéтнее nt adj (растéние).

perfect [adj, n 'pə:fɪkt, vt pə'fɛkt] adj (person, behaviour etc) безупрéчный* (безупрéчен); (weather) прекрáсный* (прекрáсен); (: utter: nonsense etc) совершéнный ◆ n (also: **~ tense**) перфéкт ◆ vt (technique) совершéнствовать (усовершéнствовать perf); **he's a ~ stranger to me** он мне совершéнно незнакóм.

perfection [pə'fɛkʃən] n совершéнство.

perfectionist [pə'fɛkʃənɪst] n взыскáтельный* человéк*.

perfective [pə'fɛktɪv] n (also: **~ aspect**) совершéнный вид.

perfectly ['pə:fɪktlɪ] adv (emphatic) вполнé, совершéнно; (faultlessly) безупрéчно; (completely) вполнé, прекрáсно; **I'm ~ happy with the situation** я вполнé довóлен положéнием дел; **you know ~ well** Вы прекрáсно знáете.

perforate ['pə:fəreɪt] vt перфори́ровать (impf/perf).

perforated ulcer ['pə:fəreɪtəd-] n перфорати́вная я́зва желýдка.

perforation [pə:fə'reɪʃən] n перфорáция.

perform [pə'fɔ:m] vt (task, operation) выполня́ть (вы́полнить perf); (ceremony, experiment) проводи́ть* (провести́* perf); (piece of music) исполня́ть (исполнить perf); (play) игрáть (сыгрáть perf); (subj: mechanism) рабóтать (impf) ◆ vi (well, badly) спрáвиться* (perf).

performance [pə'fɔ:məns] n (of actor, athlete etc) выступлéние; (of musical work) исполнéние; (of play, show) представлéние; (of car, engine, company) рабóта; (of economy) эффекти́вность f; **the team put up a good ~** комáнда хорошó вы́ступила.

performer [pə'fɔ:mə'] n исполни́тель(ница)

---

* marks translations which have irregular inflections. The Russian-English side of the dictionary gives inflectional information.

m(f).

performing [pə'fɔ:mɪŋ] *adj* (*animal*) дрессир-
о́ванный.

perfume ['pə:fju:m] *n* духи́ *pl*; (*aroma*) арома́т
◆ *vt* (*air, room etc*) ароматизи́ровать (*impf/
perf*).

perfunctory [pə'fʌŋktərɪ] *adj* (*kiss, remark etc*)
небре́жный* (небре́жен).

perhaps [pə'hæps] *adv* мо́жет бы́ть,
возмо́жно; ~ **he'll come** мо́жет бы́ть, *or*
возмо́жно он придёт; ~ **so** мо́жет бы́ть; ~
not мо́жет бы́ть* и нет.

peril ['pɛrɪl] *n* опа́сность *f*.

perilous ['pɛrɪləs] *adj* опа́сный* (опа́сен).

perilously ['pɛrɪləslɪ] *adv*: **they came ~ close to
being caught** они́ находи́лись на гра́ни
разоблаче́ния.

perimeter [pə'rɪmɪtə'] *n* пери́метр.

perimeter wall *n* стена́ по пери́метру.

period ['pɪərɪəd] *n* (*length of time*) пери́од;
(*SCOL*) уро́к; (*esp US: full stop*) то́чка*; (*MED*)
менструа́ция ◆ *adj* (*costume, furniture*)
стари́нный*; ~ **of validity** срок де́йствия; **for a
~ of three weeks** (*go*) на три неде́ли; (*be*) три
неде́ли; **the holiday ~** (*BRIT*) вре́мя* *or* пери́од
о́тпускóв.

periodic [pɪərɪ'ɔdɪk] *adj* периоди́ческий*.

periodical [pɪərɪ'ɔdɪkl] *n* (*magazine*)
периоди́ческое изда́ние ◆ *adj*
периоди́ческий*.

periodically [pɪərɪ'ɔdɪklɪ] *adv* периоди́чески.

period pains *npl* (*BRIT: MED*) менструа́льные
бо́ли *fpl*.

peripatetic [pɛrɪpə'tɛtɪk] *adj* (*salesman*)
бродя́чий; (*BRIT: teacher*) приходя́щий*.

peripheral [pə'rɪfərəl] *adj* (*also COMPUT*)
перифери́йный ◆ *n* (*COMPUT*) перифери́я.

periphery [pə'rɪfərɪ] *n* перифери́я.

periscope ['pɛrɪskəup] *n* периско́п.

perish ['pɛrɪʃ] *vi* (*person*) погиба́ть
(поги́бнуть* *perf*); (*fabric*) приходи́ть*
(прийти́* *perf*) в него́дность.

perishable ['pɛrɪʃəbl] *adj* (*food, goods*)
скоропо́ртящийся*.

perishables ['pɛrɪʃəblz] *npl* (*food*)
скоропо́ртящиеся проду́кты *mpl*.

perishing ['pɛrɪʃɪŋ] *adj* (*BRIT: inf*): **it's ~** (**cold**)
ужа́сно хо́лодно.

peritonitis [pɛrɪtə'naɪtɪs] *n* перитони́т.

perjure ['pə:dʒə'] *vt*: **to ~ o.s.** дава́ть* (дать*
perf) ло́жные показа́ния.

perjury ['pə:dʒərɪ] *n* (*LAW*) лжесвиде́тельство.

perk [pə:k] *n* (*inf*) льго́та.

perk up *vi* (*inf*) оживля́ться (ожи́виться* *perf*).

perky ['pə:kɪ] *adj* (*cheerful*) весёлый* (ве́сел),
бо́йкий* (бо́ек).

perm [pə:m] *n* (*for hair*) пермане́нт,
хими́ческая зави́вка ◆ *vt*: **to have one's hair
~ed** де́лать (сде́лать *perf*) себе́ хими́ческую
зави́вку *or* хи́мию.

permanence ['pə:mənəns] *n* постоя́нство.

permanent ['pə:mənənt] *adj* постоя́нный*
(постоя́нен); (*job, position*) постоя́нный;
(*dye, ink*) сто́йкий*; ~ **address** постоя́нное
местожи́тельство; **I'm not ~ here** я нахожу́сь
здесь вре́менно.

permanently ['pə:mənəntlɪ] *adv* постоя́нно.

permeable ['pə:mɪəbl] *adj* водопроница́емый
(водопроница́ем).

permeate ['pə:mɪeɪt] *vt* (*subj: liquid*)
пропи́тывать (пропита́ть *perf*); (: *idea*)
прони́зывать (прониза́ть *perf*) ◆ *vi*: **to ~ into/
through** проника́ть (прони́кнуть* *perf*) в +*acc/
сквозь* +*acc*.

permissible [pə'mɪsɪbl] *adj* (*action, behaviour*)
допусти́мый (допусти́м), позволи́тельный*
(позволи́телен).

permission [pə'mɪʃən] *n* (*consent*) позволе́ние;
(*official authorization*) разреше́ние; **to give sb
~ to do** разреша́ть (разреши́ть *perf*) кому́-н
+*infin*.

permissive [pə'mɪsɪv] *adj* (*person*) терпи́мый
(терпи́м); (*behaviour*) во́льный* (во́лен); **the
~ society** о́бщество вседозво́ленности.

permit [*vt* pə'mɪt, *n* 'pə:mɪt] *vt* (*allow*) позволя́ть
(позво́лить *perf*), разреша́ть (разреши́ть
perf); (*make possible*) дава́ть* (дать* *perf*)
возмо́жность +*dat* ◆ *n* (*official authorization*)
разреше́ние; (*entrance pass*) про́пуск*; **to ~
sb to do** разреша́ть (разреши́ть *perf*) кому́-н
+*infin*; **weather ~ting** е́сли пого́да позволя́ет;
fishing ~ разреше́ние на ры́бную ло́влю.

permutation [pə:mju'teɪʃən] *n* (*MATH*)
перестано́вка*; (*fig*) перемеще́ние.

pernicious [pə:'nɪʃəs] *adj* (*attitude, influence
etc*) па́губный* (па́губен); (*MED*)
перницио́зный.

pernickety [pə'nɪkɪtɪ] *adj* (*inf*) привере́дливый
(привере́длив).

perpendicular [pə:pən'dɪkjulə'] *adj* (*line,
surface*) перпендикуля́рный*
(перпендилуля́рен); (*cliff, slope*) отве́сный*
(отве́сен).

perpetrate ['pə:pɪtreɪt] *vt* соверша́ть
(соверши́ть *perf*).

perpetual [pə'pɛtjuəl] *adj* (*motion, questions*)
ве́чный* (ве́чен); (*darkness, noise*)
постоя́нный* (постоя́нен).

perpetuate [pə'pɛtjueɪt] *vt* увекове́чивать
(увекове́чить *perf*).

perpetuity [pə:pɪ'tju:ɪtɪ] *n*: **in ~** навсегда́,
наве́чно.

perplex [pə'plɛks] *vt* озада́чивать (озада́чить
perf).

perplexing [pə'plɛksɪŋ] *adj* запу́танный*
(запу́тан), сло́жный* (сло́жен).

perquisites ['pə:kwɪzɪts] *npl* (*formal*) льго́ты
fpl.

per se [-seɪ] *adv* (*as such*) как таково́й; (*in
itself*) само́ по себе́.

persecute ['pə:sɪkju:t] *vt* пресле́довать (*impf*),
подверга́ть (подве́ргнуть* *perf*) гоне́ниям

+*dat.*

persecution [pə:sɪ'kju:ʃən] *n* преслéдование.

perseverance [pə:sɪ'vɪərns] *n* настóйчивость *f.*

persevere [pə:sɪ'vɪəʳ] *vi* упóрно добивáться (*impf*).

Persia ['pə:ʃə] *n* Пéрсия.

Persian ['pə:ʃən] *adj:* **the (Persian) Gulf** Персúдский* залúв.

Persian cat *n* персúдский*(-ая) кот* (кóшка).

persist [pə'sɪst] *vi:* **to ~ (in doing)** настáивать (настоя́ть *perf*) (на том, чтóбы +*infin*).

persistence [pə'sɪstəns] *n* упóрство.

persistent [pə'sɪstənt] *adj* (*noise*) непрекращáющийся*; (*smell*) стóйкий* (стóек); (*cough*) непроходя́щий; (*person*) упóрный* (упóрен); (*lateness*) постоя́нный* (постоя́нен); (*rain*) непрерывный* (непрерывен); **~ offender** рецидивúст(ка*).

persnickety [pə'snɪkɪtɪ] *adj* (*US: inf*) = **pernickety**.

person ['pə:sn] *n* человéк*; **in ~** лúчно; **to have sth on** *or* **about one's ~** (*weapon*) носúть* (*impf*) что-н при себé; **~ to ~ call** (*TEL*) *междугорóдный телефóнный разговóр с вызовом абонéнта.*

personable ['pə:snəbl] *adj* (*adult*) представúтельный* (представúтелен).

personal ['pə:snl] *adj* лúчный; (*car*) персонáльный.

personal allowance *n* (*COMM*) лúчные скúдки *fpl* с подохóдного налóга.

personal assistant *n* лúчный секретáрь* *m.*

personal column *n* колóнка* для чáстных объявлéний.

personal computer *n* персонáльный компьютер.

personal details *npl* биографúческие дáнные *pl adj.*

personal effects *npl* лúчные вéщи *fpl or* принадлéжности *fpl.*

personal hygiene *n* лúчная гигиéна.

personal identification number *n* (*BANKING*) лúчный идентификацióнный нóмер* (*владéльца плáстиковой кáрточки*); (*COMPUT*) персонáльный *or* лúчный идентификацióнный нóмер*.

personality [pə:sə'nælɪtɪ] *n* харáктер; (*famous person*) знаменúтость *f.*

personal loan *n* (*COMM*) лúчная ссýда.

personally ['pə:snəlɪ] *adv* лúчно; **to take sth ~** принимáть (приня́ть* *perf*) что-н на свой счёт.

personal organizer *n* ежеднéвник.

personal property *n* лúчное имýщество.

personal stereo *n* персонáльное стéрео *nt ind.*

personify [pə:'sɔnɪfaɪ] *vt* олицетворя́ть (олицетворúть* *perf*), воплощáть (воплотúть* *perf*).

personnel [pə:sə'nɛl] *n* персонáл, штáт; (*MIL*) лúчный состáв.

personnel department *n* отдéл кáдров.

personnel management *n* руковóдство кáдрами.

personnel manager *n* начáльник отдéла кáдров.

perspective [pə'spɛktɪv] *n* (*ARCHIT, ART*) перспектúва; (*way of thinking*) вúдение; **to get sth into ~** (*fig*) смотрéть* (посмотрéть* *perf*) на что-н в úстинном свéте.

Perspex® ['pə:spɛks] *n* плексиглáс.

perspicacity [pə:spɪ'kæsɪtɪ] *n* проницáтельность *f.*

perspiration [pə:spɪ'reɪʃən] *n* пот*.

perspire [pə'spaɪəʳ] *vi* потéть (вспотéть *perf*).

persuade [pə'sweɪd] *vt:* **to ~ sb to do** убеждáть (убедúть* *perf*) *or* угова́ривать (уговорúть *perf*) когó- н +*infin*; **to ~ sb of/that** убеждáть (убедúть* *perf*) когó-н в +*prp/*, что.

persuasion [pə'sweɪʒən] *n* убеждéние; (*religious*) вероисповéдание.

persuasive [pə'sweɪsɪv] *adj* (*argument*) убедúтельный* (убедúтелен); (*person*) настóйчивый (настóйчив).

pert [pə:t] *adj* (*impudent*) дéрзкий* (дéрзок); (*jaunty: hat etc*) кокéтливый.

pertaining [pə:'teɪnɪŋ]: **~ to** *prep* относя́щийся к +*dat*, касáющийся +*gen.*

pertinent ['pə:tɪnənt] *adj* умéстный* (умéстен).

perturb [pə'tə:b] *vt* тревóжить (встревóжить *perf*).

Peru [pə'ru:] *n* Перý *f ind.*

perusal [pə'ru:zl] *n* прочтéние.

peruse [pə'ru:z] *vt* просмáтривать (просмотрéть* *perf*).

Peruvian [pə'ru:vjən] *adj* перуáнский* ◆ *n* перуáнец*(-нка*).

pervade [pə'veɪd] *vt* (*subj: smell, feeling*) наполня́ть (напóлнить *perf*).

pervasive [pə'veɪzɪv] *adj* (*smell, influence, ideas*) всепроникáющий; (*gloom*) проницáющий.

perverse [pə'və:s] *adj* (*contrary*) врéдный* (врéден).

perversion [pə'və:ʃən] *n* извращéние.

perversity [pə'və:sɪtɪ] *n* врéдность *f.*

pervert [*vt* pə'və:t, *n* 'pə:və:t] *vt* (*person, mind*) развращáть (развратúть* *perf*), растлевáть (растлúть *perf*); (*truth, sb's words*) извращáть (изврати́ть* *perf*) ◆ *n* (*also:* **sexual ~**) (половóй) извращéнец.

pessimism ['pɛsɪmɪzəm] *n* пессимúзм.

pessimist ['pɛsɪmɪst] *n* пессимúст(ка*).

pessimistic [pɛsɪ'mɪstɪk] *adj* пессимистúчный* (пессимистúчен).

pest [pɛst] *n* (*insect*) вредúтель *m*; (*fig: nuisance*) занýда *m/f.*

---

* marks translations which have irregular inflections. The Russian-English side of the dictionary gives inflectional information.

pest control *n* борьба́ с вреди́телями.
pester ['pɛstə'] *vt* приставать* (пристать* *perf*)
к +*dat*.
pesticide ['pɛstɪsaɪd] *n* пестици́д.
pestilence ['pɛstɪləns] *n* мор.
pestle ['pɛsl] *n* пе́стик.
pet [pɛt] *n* дома́шнее живо́тное *nt adj* ◆ *cpd*
излю́бленный ◆ *vt* (*stroke*) ласка́ть (*impf*) ◆ *vi*
(*inf: sexually*) обнима́ться (*impf*), целова́ться
(*impf*); ~ **lion** *etc* ручно́й лев *etc*; **teacher's** ~
люби́мчик.
petal ['pɛtl] *n* лепесто́к*.
peter out ['pi:tə-] *vi* (*road*) исчеза́ть
(исче́знуть* *perf*); (*stream, conversation*)
иссяка́ть (исся́кнуть* *perf*); (*meeting*)
зака́нчиваться (зако́нчиться *perf*).
petite [pə'ti:t] *adj* миниатю́рный*
(миниатю́рен).
petition [pə'tɪʃən] *n* (*signed document*)
пети́ция; (*LAW*) хода́тайство ◆ *vt*
обраща́ться (обрати́ться* *perf*) с пети́цией к
+*dat* ◆ *vi*: **to** ~ **for divorce** подава́ть* (пода́ть*
perf) заявле́ние о разво́де.
pet name *n* (*BRIT*) ласка́тельное и́мя* *nt*.
petrified ['pɛtrɪfaɪd] *adj* (*fig*) оцепене́вший.
petrify ['pɛtrɪfaɪ] (*fig*) *vt* приводи́ть* (привести́*
perf) в оцепене́ние.
petrochemical [pɛtrə'kɛmɪkl] *adj*
нефтехими́ческий.
petrodollars ['pɛtrəudɔləz] *npl* (*COMM*)
нефтедо́ллары *mpl*.
petrol ['pɛtrəl] (*BRIT*) *n* бензи́н; **two/four-star** ~
ни́зкоокта́новый/высо́коокта́новый
бензи́н; **unleaded** ~ бензи́н не содержа́щий
свинца́.
petrol bomb *n* ба́нка со взрывча́той сме́сью.
petrol can *n* (*BRIT*) кани́стра для бензи́на.
petrol engine *n* (*BRIT*) бензи́новый дви́гатель
m.
petroleum [pə'trəuliəm] *n* нефть *f*.
petroleum jelly *n* вазели́н*.
petrol pump *n* (*BRIT: in garage*) бензо-
коло́нка*; (: *in engine*) бензонасо́с.
petrol station *n* (*BRIT*) бензозапра́вочная
ста́нция.
petrol tank *n* (*BRIT*) бензоба́к.
petticoat ['pɛtɪkəut] *n* (*full-length*)
комбина́ция; (*waist slip*) ни́жняя ю́бка*.
pettifogging ['pɛtɪfɔgɪŋ] *adj* ме́лочный*
(ме́лочен).
pettiness ['pɛtɪnɪs] *n* (*of actions*) ме́лочность *f*;
(*of mind*) ограни́ченность *f*.
petty ['pɛtɪ] *adj* (*small, unimportant*) ме́лкий*
(ме́лок); (*small-minded*) ограни́ченный*
(ограни́чен).
petty cash *n* (*in office*) де́ньги *pl* на ме́лкие
расхо́ды.
petty officer *n* старшина́ *m* (*во фло́те*).
petulant ['pɛtjulənt] *adj* оби́дчивый (оби́дчив).
pew [pju:] *n* скамья́* (*в це́ркви*).
pewter ['pju:tə'] *n* сплав о́лова со свинцо́м.

Pfc *abbr* (*US: MIL*: = *private first class*) рядово́й
1-го кла́сса.
PG *n abbr* (*CINEMA*: = *parental guidance*) *фильм
до 16-ти лет.*
PGA *n abbr* = *Professional Golfers Association*.
PH *n abbr* (*US: MIL*: = *Purple Heart*) ≈ меда́ль *f*
„За отва́гу".
pH *n abbr* (= *potential of hydrogen*) pH
(*водоро́дный показа́тель*).
PHA *n abbr* (*US*) = *Public Housing Administration*.
phallic ['fælɪk] *adj* фалли́ческий.
phantom ['fæntəm] *n* фанто́м ◆ *adj* (*fig*)
при́зрачный* (при́зрачен).
Pharaoh ['fɛərəu] *n* фарао́н.
pharmaceutical [fɑ:mə'sju:tɪkl] *adj*
фармацевти́ческий ◆ *n*: ~**s** медикаме́нты
mpl.
pharmacist ['fɑ:məsɪst] *n* фармаце́вт.
pharmacy ['fɑ:məsɪ] *n* (*profession*)
фармаце́втика; (*shop*) апте́ка.
phase [feɪz] *n* фа́за ◆ *vt*: **to** ~ **sth in** поэта́пно
вводи́ть* (ввести́* *perf*) что-н; **to** ~ **sth out**
ликвиди́ровать (*impf/perf*) что-н.
PhD *n abbr* (= *Doctor of Philosophy*) до́ктор
филосо́фии.
pheasant ['fɛznt] *n* фаза́н.
phenomena [fə'nɔmɪnə] *npl of* **phenomenon**.
phenomenal [fə'nɔmɪnl] *adj* феномена́льный*
(феномена́лен).
phenomenon [fə'nɔmɪnən] (*pl* **phenomena**) *n*
явле́ние, фено́мен.
phew [fju:] *excl* уф.
phial ['faɪəl] *n* скля́нка*.
philanderer [fɪ'lændərə'] *n* волоки́та *m*.
philanthropic [fɪlən'θrɔpɪk] *adj* филантроп-
и́ческий.
philanthropist [fɪ'lænθrəpɪst] *n* филантро́п
(ка*).
philatelist [fɪ'lætəlɪst] *n* филатели́ст(ка*).
philately [fɪ'lætəlɪ] *n* филатели́я.
Philippines ['fɪlɪpi:nz] *npl*: **the** ~ Филиппи́ны
pl, Филиппи́нские острова́* *mpl*.
philosopher [fɪ'lɔsəfə'] *n* фило́соф.
philosophical [fɪlə'sɔfɪkl] *adj* филосо́фский.
philosophize [fɪ'lɔsəfaɪz] *vi* филосо́фствовать
(*impf*).
philosophy [fɪ'lɔsəfɪ] *n* филосо́фия.
phlegm [flɛm] *n* (*MED*) мокро́та.
phlegmatic [flɛg'mætɪk] *adj* флегмати́чный*
(флегмати́чен).
phobia ['fəubjə] *n* (*MED*) фо́бия, страх.
phone [fəun] *n* телефо́н ◆ *vt* звони́ть
(позвони́ть *perf*) (по телефо́ну) +*dat*; **to be on
the** ~ (*possess a phone*) име́ть (*impf*) телефо́н;
(*be calling*) говори́ть (*impf*) по телефо́ну
▸ **phone back** *vt* перезва́нивать (перезвони́ть
perf) +*dat* ◆ *vi* перезва́нивать (перезвони́ть
perf)
▸ **phone up** *vt* звони́ть (позвони́ть *perf*) +*dat* ◆
vi звони́ть (позвони́ть *perf*).
phone book *n* телефо́нная кни́га.

phone booth *n* телефóн-автомáт.
phone box *n* (*BRIT*) телефóнная бýдка*,
телефóн-автомáт.
phone call *n* телефóнный звонóк*.
phone-card [ˈfəunkɑːd] *n* телефóнная
кáрточка (*испóльзуется в автомáтах для
безналúчной оплáты переговóров*).
phone-in [ˈfəunɪn] *n* (*BRIT*: *RADIO, TV*)
прогрáмма „звонúте-отвечáем".
phone tapping [-tæpɪŋ] *n* прослýшивание
телефóнных разговóров.
phonetics [fəˈnɛtɪks] *n* фонéтика.
phoney [ˈfəunɪ] *adj* фальшúвый (фальшúв).
phonograph [ˈfəunəgrɑːf] *n* (*US*) про-
úгрыватель *m*.
phony [ˈfəunɪ] *adj* = **phoney**.
phosphate [ˈfɔsfeɪt] *n* фосфáт.
phosphorus [ˈfɔsfərəs] *n* фóсфор.
photo [ˈfəutəu] *n* фотогрáфия.
photo... [ˈfəutəu] *prefix* фóто....
photocopier [ˈfəutəukɔpɪəʳ] *n* (*machine*)
ксéрокс, копировáльная машúна.
photocopy [ˈfəutəukɔpɪ] *n* ксерокóпия,
фотокóпия ◆ *vt* фотокопúровать
(сфотокопúровать *perf*), ксерокопúровать
(*impf/perf*).
photoelectric [fəutəuɪˈlɛktrɪk] *adj* фото-
электрúческий; ~ **cell** фотоэлемéнт.
photo finish *n* фотофúниш.
Photofit® [ˈfəutəufɪt] *n* фотореконстрýкция.
photogenic [fəutəuˈdʒɛnɪk] *adj* фотогенúчный*
(фотогенúчен).
photograph [ˈfəutəgrɑːf] *n* фотогрáфия ◆ *vt*
фотографúровать (сфотографúровать *perf*);
to take a ~ **of sb** фотографúровать
(сфотографúровать *perf*) когó-н.
photographer [fəˈtɔgrəfəʳ] *n* фотóграф.
photographic [fəutəˈgræfɪk] *adj* фото-
графúческий.
photography [fəˈtɔgrəfɪ] *n* фотогрáфия.
photo opportunity *n* ситуáция, дáющая
возмóжность знаменúтостям быть
представленным в выгодном свете на
фотогрáфии.
Photostat® [ˈfəutəustæt] *n* фотокóпия.
photosynthesis [fəutəuˈsɪnθəsɪs] *n* (*BIO*)
фотосúнтез.
phrase [freɪz] *n* (*also LING, MUS*) фрáза ◆ *vt*
формулúровать (сформулúровать *perf*);
(*letter*) составлять (состáвить* *perf*).
phrase book *n* разговóрник.
physical [ˈfɪzɪkl] *adj* физúческий*; (*world,
universe, object*) материáльный*
(материáлен); ~ **examination** медосмóтр=
медицúнский* осмóтр; ~ **exercises**
физúческие упряжнéния.
physical education *n* физúческое
воспитáние, физкультýра.

physically [ˈfɪzɪklɪ] *adv* физúчески.
physician [fɪˈzɪʃən] *n* (*esp US*) врач*.
physicist [ˈfɪzɪsɪst] *n* фúзик.
physics [ˈfɪzɪks] *n* фúзика.
physiological [ˈfɪzɪəˈlɔdʒɪkl] *adj* физиолог-
úческий*.
physiology [fɪzɪˈɔlədʒɪ] *n* физиолóгия.
physiotherapist [fɪzɪəuˈθɛrəpɪst] *n* физио-
терапéвт.
physiotherapy [fɪzɪəuˈθɛrəpɪ] *n* физиотерапúя.
physique [fɪˈziːk] *n* (*build*) телосложéние;
(*health*) физúческие дáнные *pl adj*.
pianist [ˈpiːənɪst] *n* пианúст(ка*).
piano [pɪˈænəu] *n* пианúно, фортепьяно *nt ind*;
grand ~ рояль *m*.
piano accordion *n* (*BRIT*) аккордеóн.
piccolo [ˈpɪkələu] *n* пúкколо *nt ind.*
pick [pɪk] *n* (*also:* ~**axe**) киркá* ◆ *vt* (*select*)
выбирáть (выбрать* *perf*); (*gather: fruit,
flowers*) собирáть (собрáть* *perf*); (*pluck*)
рвать* (*impf*); (*lock*) взлáмывать (взломáть
perf); (*scab, spot*) сковыривать (сковырнýть
perf); **take your** ~ выбирáйте; **the** ~ **of the
bunch** (*best*) сáмое лýчшее; **to** ~ **one's nose/
teeth** ковырять (*impf*) в носý/зубáх; **to** ~ **sb's
brains** обращáться (обратúться* *perf*) к
комý-н с совéтом; **to** ~ **pockets** лáзать
(*impf*) кармáнам; **to** ~ **a quarrel (with sb)**
искáть* (*impf*) пóвод для ссóры (с кем-н)
▶ **pick at** *vt fus* (*food*) ковырять (*impf*)
▶ **pick off** *vt* (*planes*) методúчно сбивáть
(сбить* *perf*); (*people*) методúчно стреля́ть
(*impf*) по +*dat*
▶ **pick on** *vt fus* (*criticize*) придирáться
(придрáться* *perf*) к +*dat*; (*treat badly*)
цепля́ться (*impf*) к +*dat*
▶ **pick out** *vt* (*distinguish*) разглядéть (*perf*);
(*select*) выбирáть (выбрать* *perf*)
▶ **pick up** *vi* (*improve: health, economy*)
улучшáться (улýчшиться *perf*) ◆ *vt* (*lift*)
поднимáть (поднять* *perf*); (*POLICE: arrest*)
забирáть (забрáть* *perf*); (*collect: person: on
foot*) заходúть* (зайтú* *perf*) за +*instr*; (: *with
transport*) заезжáть (заéхать* *perf*) за +*instr*;
(: *parcel*) забирáть (забрáть* *perf*); (*AUT:
passenger*) подбирáть (подобрáть* *perf*); (*inf:
person: for sexual encounter*) подцепúть*
(*perf*); (*language, skill etc*) усвáивать (усвóить
perf); (*RADIO*) ловúть* (поймáть* *perf*); **to** ~ **up
speed** набирáть (набрáть* *perf*) скóрость; **to**
~ **o.s. up** (*after falling etc*) поднимáться
(подня́ться* *perf*); **we** ~**ed up where we left off**
мы нáчали с тогó мéста, где остановúлись.
pickaxe [ˈpɪkæks] (*US* **pickax**) *n* киркá*.
picket [ˈpɪkɪt] *n* (*in strike*) пикéт ◆ *vt*
пикетúровать (*impf*).
picketing [ˈpɪkɪtɪŋ] *n* пикетúрование.
picket line *n* лúния пикéтов.

---

* marks translations which have irregular inflections. The Russian-English side of the dictionary gives inflectional information.

pickings ['pɪkɪŋz] *npl*: **there are good ~ to be had here** на э́том мо́жно хорошо́ нажи́ться.

pickle ['pɪkl] *n* (*marinade*) марина́д; (*also*:~**s**) соле́нья *ntpl*; (*fig*: *inf*) переде́лка* ♦ *vt* (*in vinegar*) маринова́ть (замаринова́ть *perf*); (*in salt water*) соли́ть* (засоли́ть* *perf*); **to be in a** ~ (*fig*: *inf*) попада́ть (попа́сть* *perf*) в переде́лку.

pick-me-up ['pɪkmiːʌp] *n* тонизи́рующий* напи́ток*.

pickpocket ['pɪkpɔkɪt] *n* вор*-карма́нник.

pick-up ['pɪkʌp] *n* (*also*: ~ **truck** *or* **van**) пика́п; (*BRIT*: *on record player*) звукоснима́тель *m*.

picnic ['pɪknɪk] *n* пикни́к* ♦ *vi* устра́ивать (устро́ить *perf*) пикни́к.

picnicker ['pɪknɪkəʳ] *n* уча́стник(-ица) пикника́.

pictorial [pɪk'tɔːrɪəl] *adj* иллюстри́рованный (иллюстри́рован).

picture ['pɪktʃəʳ] *n* (*also fig*) карти́на; (*photograph*) фотогра́фия; (*TV*) изображе́ние; (*film*) (кино)карти́на ♦ *vt* (*imagine*) рисова́ть (нарисова́ть *perf*) карти́ну +*gen*; **the ~s** *npl* (*BRIT*: *inf*) кино́ *nt ind*; **to take a ~ of sb/sth** фотографи́ровать (сфотографи́ровать *perf*) кого́-н/что-н; **the overall ~** о́бщая карти́на; **to put sb in the ~** вводи́ть* (ввести́* *perf*) кого́-н в курс де́ла.

picture book *n* кни́га* с карти́нками.

picturesque [pɪktʃə'rɛsk] *adj* живопи́сный* (живопи́сен).

picture window *n* (*ARCHIT*) большо́е окно́, из кото́рого открыва́ется краси́вый вид.

piddling ['pɪdlɪŋ] *adj* (*inf*) пустя́чный*.

pidgin ['pɪdʒɪn] *adj*: ~ **English** пи́джин-и́нглиш.

pie [paɪ] *n* пиро́г*; (*small*) пирожо́к*.

piebald ['paɪbɔːld] *adj* пе́гий* (пег).

piece [piːs] *n* (*portion, part*) кусо́к*; (*component*) дета́ль *f*; (*CHESS*) фигу́ра; (*DRAUGHTS*) ша́шка* ♦ *vt*: **to ~ together** (*information*) свя́зывать (связа́ть* *perf*); (*parts of a whole*) соединя́ть (соедини́ть *perf*); **a ~ of clothing** вещь* *f*; **a ~ of advice** сове́т; **in ~s** (*broken*) вдре́безги; (*not yet assembled*) разо́бранный (разо́бран); **to take to ~s** (*dismantle*) разбира́ть (разобра́ть* *perf*); **in one ~** в це́лости и сохра́нности; **to get back all in one ~** возвраща́ться (верну́ться *perf*) це́лым и невреди́мым; **a 10p ~** (*BRIT*) моне́та в 10 пе́нсов; ~ **by ~** по частя́м; **a six-~ band** анса́мбль *m* из шести́ музыка́льных инструме́нтов; **to say one's ~** выска́зывать (вы́сказать* *perf*) своё мне́ние.

piecemeal ['piːsmiːl] *adv* понемно́гу.

piece rate *n* тари́ф *or* ста́вка за едини́цу вы́полненных рабо́т.

piecework ['piːswəːk] *n* сде́льная рабо́та.

pie chart *n* се́кторная диагра́мма.

pier [pɪəʳ] *n* пирс.

pierce [pɪəs] *vt* протыка́ть (проткну́ть *perf*), прока́лывать (проколо́ть* *perf*); **to have one's ears ~d** прока́лывать (проколо́ть* *perf*) у́ши.

piercing ['pɪəsɪŋ] *adj* (*cry, eyes, stare*) пронзи́тельный* (пронзи́телен); (*wind*) прони́зывающий.

piety ['paɪətɪ] *n* на́божность *f*.

piffling ['pɪflɪŋ] *adj* (*inf*) никчёмный* (никчёмен).

pig [pɪg] *n* (*also fig*) свинья́*.

pigeon ['pɪdʒən] *n* го́лубь* *m*.

pigeonhole ['pɪdʒənhəul] *n* (*in office, bureau*) яче́йка (*для корреспонде́нции*); (*fig*) ни́ша ♦ *vt* (*person*) накле́ивать (накле́ить *perf*) ярлыки́ на +*acc*.

pigeon-toed ['pɪdʒəntəud] *adj* косола́пый (косола́п).

piggy bank ['pɪgɪ-] *n* копи́лка*.

pig-headed ['pɪg'hɛdɪd] *adj* (*inf*) упря́мый (упря́м).

piglet ['pɪglɪt] *n* поросёнок*.

pigment ['pɪgmənt] *n* пигме́нт.

pigmentation [pɪgmən'teɪʃən] *n* пигмента́ция.

pigmy ['pɪgmɪ] *n* = **pygmy**

pigskin ['pɪgskɪn] *n* свина́я ко́жа.

pigsty ['pɪgstaɪ] *n* (*also fig*) свина́рник.

pigtail ['pɪgteɪl] *n* коси́чка*.

pike [paɪk] *n inv* (*fish*) щу́ка ♦ *n* (*spear*) пи́ка.

pilchard ['pɪltʃəd] *n* сарди́на.

pile [paɪl] *n* (*large heap*) ку́ча, гру́да; (*neat stack*) сто́пка*; (*pillar*) сва́я; (*of carpet, cloth*) ворс ♦ *vi*: **to ~ into** (*vehicle*) набива́ться (наби́ться* *perf*) в +*acc*; **in a ~** в ку́че; **to ~ out of** (*vehicle*) выва́ливаться (вы́валиться *perf*) из +*gen*

▶ **pile on** *vt*: **to ~ it on** (*inf*) перебо́рщивать (переборщи́ть* *perf*)

▶ **pile up** *vt* (*objects*) сва́ливать (свали́ть* *perf*) в ку́чу ♦ *vi* громозди́ться* (*impf*); (*problems, work*) нака́пливаться (накопи́ться* *perf*).

piles [paɪlz] *npl* (*MED*) геморро́й *msg*.

pile-up ['paɪlʌp] *n* (*AUT*) столкнове́ние не́скольких маши́н.

pilfer ['pɪlfəʳ] *vti* ворова́ть (*impf*).

pilfering ['pɪlfərɪŋ] *n* ме́лкое воровство́.

pilgrim ['pɪlgrɪm] *n* пало́мник(-ица), пилигри́м.

pilgrimage ['pɪlgrɪmɪdʒ] *n* пало́мничество.

pill [pɪl] *n* табле́тка*; **the ~** (*contraceptive*) противозача́точные *pl adj* (табле́тки); **to be on the ~** принима́ть (*impf*) противозача́точ-ные табле́тки.

pillage ['pɪlɪdʒ] *n* грабёж*.

pillar ['pɪləʳ] *n* (*ARCHIT*) столб*, коло́нна; **a ~ of society** (*fig*) столп о́бщества.

pillar box *n* (*BRIT*) почто́вый я́щик*.

pillion ['pɪljən] *n*: **to ride ~** (*on motorcycle*) е́хать*/е́здить* (*impf*) на за́днем сиде́нье мотоци́кла; (*on horse*) е́хать*/е́здить* (*impf*) верхо́м на ло́шади сза́ди вса́дника.

pillory ['pɪlərɪ] *vt* выставля́ть (вы́ставить* *perf*) на осмея́ние ♦ *n* позо́рный столб*.

pillow ['pɪləu] *n* поду́шка*.

pillowcase ['pɪləukeɪs] *n* наволочка*.
pillowslip ['pɪləuslɪp] *n* = **pillowcase**.
pilot ['paɪlət] *n* (AVIAT) пилот, лётчик; (NAUT) лоцман ♦ *cpd* (scheme, study etc) экспериментальный ♦ *vt* (aircraft) управлять (impf) +instr; (fig: new law, scheme) апробировать (impf/perf).
pilot boat *n* лоцманский катер*.
pilot light *n* запальник.
pimento [pɪ'mɛntəu] *n* душистый перец.
pimp [pɪmp] *n* сутенёр.
pimple ['pɪmpl] *n* прыщ*, прыщик.
pimply ['pɪmplɪ] *adj* прыщавый (прыщав).
PIN *n abbr* = **personal identification number**.
pin [pɪn] *n* булавка*; (TECH) штифт*; (BRIT: also: **drawing** ~) кнопка*; (of grenade) чека*; (BRIT: ELEC: of plug) штырь* *m* ♦ *vt* прикалывать (приколоть* perf); ~**s and needles** (fig) колоть; **to** ~ **sb against** *or* **to** прижимать (прижать* perf) кого-н к +dat; **to** ~ **sth on sb** (fig) возлагать (возложить* perf) на кого-н вину за что-н
▶ **pin down** *vt* (fig): **to** ~ **sb down** припирать (припереть* perf) кого-н к стенке; **there's something strange here but I can't quite** ~ **it down** что-то здесь не так, но не пойму что.
pinafore ['pɪnəfɔ:'] *n* (also: ~ **dress**) сарафан.
pinball ['pɪnbɔ:l] *n* китайский* бильярд.
pincers ['pɪnsəz] *npl* (TECH) клещи* *pl*; (of crab etc) клешни *fpl*.
pinch [pɪntʃ] *n* (small amount) щепотка* ♦ *vt* щипать* (ущипнуть* perf); (inf: steal) стащить* (perf) ♦ *vi* (shoe) жать* (impf); **at a** ~ в крайнем случае; **to feel the** ~ (fig) оказываться (оказаться* perf) в стеснённых обстоятельствах.
pinched [pɪntʃt] *adj* (drawn) осунувшийся; ~ **with cold** съёжившийся от холода; **I am** ~ **for money** у меня туго с деньгами; **we're** ~ **for space here** у нас здесь мало места.
pincushion ['pɪnkuʃən] *n* игольник.
pine [paɪn] *n* (tree, wood) сосна* ♦ *vi*: **to** ~ **for** тосковать (impf) по +dat
▶ **pine away** *vi* (gradually die) чахнуть* (зачахнуть* perf).
pineapple ['paɪnæpl] *n* ананас *m no pl*.
pine cone *n* сосновая шишка.
pine needles *npl* сосновые иголки *fpl*.
ping [pɪŋ] *n* (noise) звон.
Ping-Pong® ['pɪŋpɔŋ] *n* настольный теннис, пинг-понг.
pink [pɪŋk] *adj* розовый ♦ *n* (colour) розовый цвет*; (BOT) гвоздика.
pinking shears *npl* зубчатые ножницы *pl*.
pin money *n* (BRIT) деньги* *pl* на булавки.
pinnacle ['pɪnəkl] *n* (of building) шпиц; (of mountain, also fig) вершина.
pinpoint ['pɪnpɔɪnt] *vt* (discover) точно

определять (определить* perf); (explain) точно объяснять (объяснить* perf); (position of sth) точно указывать (указать* perf).
pinstripe ['pɪnstraɪp] *n* полоска*; ~ **suit** костюм в полоску.
pint [paɪnt] *n* пинта.
pin-up ['pɪnʌp] *n* (picture) журнальная вырезка с изображением красивых девушек.
pioneer [paɪə'nɪə'] *n* (initiator: of scheme, science, method) первооткрыватель *m*, новатор; (early settler, also fig) первопроходец*, пионер ♦ *vt* (initiate) прокладывать (проложить* perf) путь к +dat.
pious ['paɪəs] *adj* набожный* (набожен).
pip [pɪp] *n* (of grape, melon) косточка*; (of apple, orange) зёрнышко; **the** ~**s** *npl* (BRIT: RADIO) сигнал *msg* (точного времени).
pipe [paɪp] *n* (for water, gas) труба*; (for smoking) трубка*; (MUS) дудка* ♦ *vt* (water, gas, oil) подавать* (подать* perf); ~**s** *npl* (also: **bagpipes**) волынка* *fsg*
▶ **pipe down** *vi* (inf: be quiet) затыкаться (заткнуться perf).
pipe cleaner *n* ёршик (для трубки).
piped music [paɪpt-] *n* музыка из громкоговорителя.
pipe dream *n* пустые мечты *fpl*.
pipeline ['paɪplaɪn] *n* трубопровод; **oil** ~ нефтепровод; **gas** ~ газопровод; **a new project is in the** ~ (fig) дан ход новому проекту.
piper ['paɪpə'] *n* (bagpipe player) волынщик.
pipe tobacco *n* трубочный табак*.
piping ['paɪpɪŋ] *adv*: ~ **hot** очень горячий*.
piquant ['pi:kənt] *adj* (also fig) пикантный* (пикантен).
pique ['pi:k] *n* задетое самолюбие.
piracy ['paɪərəsɪ] *n* пиратство.
pirate ['paɪərət] *n* (sailor) пират* ♦ *vt* (video tape, cassette) незаконно распространять (распространить* perf); (book) незаконно переиздавать* (переиздать* perf).
pirate radio *n* (BRIT): ~ ~ **station** пиратская радиостанция.
pirouette [pɪru'ɛt] *n* пируэт.
Pisces ['paɪsi:z] *n* (ASTROLOGY) Рыбы; **he is** ~ он – Рыба.
piss [pɪs] (infl) *vi* писать (пописать perf) (!); ~ **off!** пошёл ты! (!)
pissed [pɪst] *adj* (infl: drunk) пьяный* (пьян) в стельку (!)
pistol ['pɪstl] *n* пистолет.
piston ['pɪstən] *n* поршень* *m*.
pit [pɪt] *n* (in ground) яма; (in surface of sth) ямка*; (also: **coal** ~) шахта; (also: **orchestra** ~) оркестровая яма; (quarry) карьер ♦ *vt*: **to** ~ **one's wits against sb** состязаться (impf) в эрудиции с чем-н; ~**s** *npl* (in motor racing)

пункт *msg* ремо́нта и запра́вки; **to ~ sb against sb** направля́ть (напра́вить* *perf*) кого́-н на кого́-н.

pitapat ['pɪtə'pæt] *adv* (*BRIT: of heart*) тук-ту́к; (: *of rain*) кап-ка́п.

pitch [pɪtʃ] *n* (*BRIT: SPORT*) по́ле*; (*MUS*) высота́; (*fig: level, degree*) у́ровень *m*; (*tar*) смола́; (*also: sales ~*) рула́да; (*NAUT*) килева́я ка́чка ♦ *vt* (*throw*) подава́ть* (пода́ть* *perf*), гнать* (погна́ть* *perf*); (*set: price*) устана́вливать (установи́ть* *perf*); (: *message*) подстра́ивать (подстро́ить *perf*) ♦ *vi* (*fall*) па́дать (упа́сть* *perf*); (*NAUT*) испы́тывать (испыта́ть *perf*) килеву́ю ка́чку; **at this ~** (*fig*) на тако́м у́ровне; **to ~ a tent** ста́вить* (поста́вить* *perf*) пала́тку; **he was ~ed forward** его́ бро́сило вперёд.

pitch-black ['pɪtʃ'blæk] *adj* о́чень тёмный.

pitched battle [pɪtʃt-] *n* ожесточённая схва́тка*.

pitcher ['pɪtʃə'] *n* (*jug*) кувши́н; (*US: BASEBALL*) подаю́щий *m adj*.

pitchfork ['pɪtʃfɔ:k] *n* ви́лы *pl*.

piteous ['pɪtɪəs] *adj* (*sound etc*) жа́лобный* (жа́лобен); (*sight*) несча́стный* (несча́стен).

pitfall ['pɪtfɔ:l] *n* (*difficulty, danger*) лову́шка, подво́дные ка́мни *mpl*.

pith [pɪθ] *n* (*of orange, lemon etc*) паренхи́ма; (*of plant*) сердцеви́на; (*fig*) суть *f*.

pithead ['pɪthɛd] *n* (*BRIT*) копёр (*над ша́хтой*).

pithy ['pɪθɪ] *adj* (*saying etc*) содержа́тельный* (содержа́телен).

pitiable ['pɪtɪəbl] *adj* (*sight, person*) жа́лкий* (жа́лок).

pitiful ['pɪtɪful] *adj* жа́лкий* (жа́лок).

pitifully ['pɪtɪfəlɪ] *adv* жа́лобно; **it's ~ obvious** к несча́стью, э́то очеви́дно.

pitiless ['pɪtɪlɪs] *adj* безжа́лостный* (безжа́лостен).

pittance ['pɪtns] *n* гроши́ *mpl*.

pitted ['pɪtɪd] *adj*: **~ with** (*holes, acne*) изры́тый (изры́т) +*instr*; (*rust*) изъе́денный (изъе́ден) +*instr*.

pity ['pɪtɪ] *n* жа́лость *f* ♦ *vt* жале́ть (пожале́ть* *perf*); **what a ~!** кака́я жа́лость!; **it is a ~ that you can't come** жа́лко, что Вы не смо́жете прийти́; **to have** *or* **take ~ on sb** сжа́литься (*perf*) над кем-н.

pitying ['pɪtɪɪŋ] *adj* жа́лостливый (жа́лостлив).

pivot ['pɪvət] *n* (*TECH: pin*) ось *f*; (: *point*) то́чка* враще́ния; (*fig*) центр ♦ *vi*: **to ~ on** (*balance*) держа́ться* (*perf*) на +*prp*; (*turn*) враща́ться (*impf*) вокру́г +*gen*; (*fig: depend on*) зави́сеть* (*impf*) от +*gen*.

pixel ['pɪksl] *n* (*COMPUT*) пи́ксель *m*, элеме́нт изображе́ния.

pixie ['pɪksɪ] *n* эльф.

pizza ['pi:tsə] *n* пи́цца.

placard ['plækɑ:d] *n* плака́т.

placate [plə'keɪt] *vt* (*person*) умиротворя́ть (умиротвори́ть *perf*); (*anger*) усмиря́ть (усмири́ть *perf*).

placatory [plə'keɪtərɪ] *adj* примири́тельный* (примири́телен).

place [pleɪs] *vt* (*put*) помеща́ть (помести́ть* *perf*); (*identify: person*) вспомина́ть (вспо́мнить *perf*) ♦ *n* ме́сто*; (*home*): **at his ~** у него́; (*in street names*): **Laurel P~** Ло́рел Плейс; **to ~ an order with sb for sth** (*COMM*) зака́зывать (заказа́ть* *perf*) что-н у кого́-н; **to be ~d** (*in race, exam*) быть* (*impf*) на како́м-н ме́сте; **how are you ~d next week?** как у Вас со сле́дующей неде́лей?; **to take ~** происходи́ть* (произойти́* *perf*); **from ~ to ~** с ме́ста на ме́сто; **all over the ~** повсю́ду; **out of ~** (*not suitable*) неуме́стный* (неуме́стен); **I feel out of ~ here** я чу́вствую себя́ не в свое́й таре́лке/не на ме́сте здесь; **in the first ~** (*first of all*) во-пе́рвых; **to put sb in his ~** (*fig*) ста́вить* (поста́вить* *perf*) кого́-н на ме́сто; **he's going ~s** он далеко́ пойдёт; **it's not my ~** э́то не моё де́ло; **to change ~s with sb** меня́ться (поменя́ться *perf*) места́ми с кем-н.

placebo [plə'si:bəu] *n* (*MED*) плаце́бо *nt ind*; (*fig*) успокои́тельное сре́дство.

place mat *n* подста́вка* (*для столо́вых прибо́ров*); (*in linen etc*) салфе́тка*.

placement ['pleɪsmənt] *n* (*action*) размеще́ние*; (*job*) ме́сто*.

place name *n* географи́ческое назва́ние, топони́м.

placenta [plə'sɛntə] *n* плаце́нта.

place of birth *n* ме́сто* рожде́ния.

place setting *n* столо́вый прибо́р.

placid ['plæsɪd] *adj* (*person*) споко́йный* (споко́ен); (*place*) ти́хий* (тих).

plagiarism ['pleɪdʒərɪzəm] *n* плагиа́т.

plagiarist ['pleɪdʒərɪst] *n* плагиа́тор.

plagiarize ['pleɪdʒəraɪz] *vt* красть* (укра́сть* *perf*), спи́сывать (списа́ть* *perf*).

plague [pleɪg] *n* (*MED*) чума́; (*fig: of locusts etc*) наше́ствие ♦ *vt* (*fig: subj: problems, difficulties*) осажда́ть (осади́ть* *perf*); **to ~ sb with questions** донима́ть (*impf*) кого́-н вопро́сами.

plaice [pleɪs] *n inv* ка́мбала.

plaid [plæd] *n* шотла́ндка* (*ткань*).

plain [pleɪn] *adj* (*simple, not beautiful*) просто́й* (прост); (*unpatterned*) гла́дкий* (гла́док); (*clear, easily understood*) я́сный* (я́сен), поня́тный* (поня́тен); (*frank*) прямо́й* (прям) ♦ *adv* (*wrong, stupid etc*) я́вно ♦ *n* (*GEO*) равни́на; (*KNITTING*) чуло́чная вя́зка; **to make sth ~ to sb** разъясня́ть (разъясни́ть *perf*) что-н кому́-н.

plain chocolate *n* го́рький* шокола́д.

plain-clothes ['pleɪnkləuðz] *adj*: **~ policeman** полице́йский* *m adj* в шта́тском.

plain flour *n* мука́ без дрожжевы́х доба́вок.

plainly ['pleɪnlɪ] *adv* я́сно.

plainness ['pleɪnnɪs] n (*simplicity*) простота́; (*clarity*) я́сность f.
plaintiff ['pleɪntɪf] n исте́ц*(-ти́ца).
plain speaking n прямота́.
plaintive ['pleɪntɪv] adj (*voice, look, song*) жа́лобный* (жа́лобен).
plait [plæt] n (*of hair*) коса́* ♦ vt (*hair*) заплета́ть (заплести́* perf); (*rope*) плести́* (сплести́* perf).
plan [plæn] n план ♦ vt плани́ровать (запланı́ровать perf); (*draw up plans for*) плани́ровать (*impf*) ♦ vi плани́ровать (*impf*); **to ~ to do** плани́ровать (заплани́ровать perf) +infin; **how long do you ~ to stay?** как до́лго Вы плани́руете пробы́ть здесь?; **to ~ for sth** (*anticipate*) рассчи́тывать (*impf*) на что-н.
plane [pleɪn] n (*AVIAT*) самолёт; (*MATH*) пло́скость f; (*fig: level*) план; (*tool*) руба́нок*; (*BOT*) плата́н ♦ vt (*wood*) строга́ть (вы́строгать perf) ♦ vi (*NAUT, AUT*): **to ~ across** скользи́ть* (*impf*) по +dat.
planet ['plænɪt] n плане́та.
planetarium [plænɪ'tɛərɪəm] n планета́рий.
plank [plæŋk] n доска́*; (*fig: of policy etc*) при́нцип.
plankton ['plæŋktən] n планкто́н.
planned economy ['plænd-] n пла́новая эконо́мика.
planner ['plænə'] n (*of towns*) планиро́вщик; (*of TV programme, project*) состави́тель m.
planning ['plænɪŋ] n (*of future, event*) плани́рование; (*of programme etc*) составле́ние; (*also: town ~*) планоро́вка.
planning permission n (*BRIT*) разреше́ние на строи́тельство.
plant [plɑːnt] n (*BOT*) расте́ние; (*factory*) заво́д; (*machinery*) устано́вка* ♦ vt (*seed, plant, garden*) сажа́ть (посади́ть* perf); (*field*) засе́ивать (засе́ять perf); (*bomb, evidence*) подкла́дывать (подложи́ть* perf); (*fig: kiss*) запечатлева́ть (запечатле́ть perf).
plantation [plæn'teɪʃən] n (*of tea, rubber, sugar etc*) планта́ция; (*of trees*) лесонасажде́ние.
plant pot n (*BRIT*) цвето́чный горшо́к*.
plaque [plæk] n (*on building etc*) мемориа́льная доска́*; (*on teeth*) налёт.
plasma ['plæzmə] n пла́зма.
plaster ['plɑːstə'] n (*for walls*) штукату́рка*; (*also: ~ of Paris*) гипс; (*BRIT: also: sticking ~*) пла́стырь m ♦ vt (*wall, ceiling*) штукату́рить (оштукату́рить perf); (*cover*): **to ~ with** залепля́ть (залепи́ть* perf) +instr; **in ~** (*BRIT*) в ги́псе.
plasterboard ['plɑːstəbɔːd] n ги́псовые щиты́ (*для обши́вки стен и потолка́*).
plaster cast n (*MED*) гипс; (*model, statue*) ги́псовый слепо́к*.
plastered ['plɑːstəd] adj (*inf: drunk*): **he is ~** он

нажра́лся.
plasterer ['plɑːstərə'] n штукату́р.
plastic ['plæstɪk] n пластма́сса ♦ adj (*made of plastic*) пластма́ссовый; (*flexible*) пласти́чный*; (*art*) пласти́ческий*.
plastic bag n полиэтиле́новый мешо́к*.
plastic bullet n пластма́ссовая пу́ля*.
plastic explosive n синтети́ческая взрывча́тка консисте́нции пластили́на.
Plasticine® ['plæstɪsiːn] n пластили́н.
plastic surgery n (*science*) пласти́ческая хирурги́я; (*operation*) пласти́ческая опера́ция.
plate [pleɪt] n (*dish*) таре́лка*; (*metal cover: on building, machinery*) пласти́на; (*TYP*) печа́тная фо́рма; (*PHOT*) фотопласти́нка*; (*AUT: number plate*) но́мер*; (*in book*) вкладна́я иллюстра́ция; (*also: dental ~*) вставна́я че́люсть* f; (*on door*) табли́чка*; **gold ~** позоло́та; **silver ~** серебре́ние.
plateau ['plætəʊ] (*pl ~s or ~x*) n (*GEO, also fig*) плато́ nt ind.
plateaux ['plætəʊz] npl of **plateau**.
plateful ['pleɪtful] n: **a ~ of** таре́лка* +gen.
plate glass n (*for window, door*) зерка́льное стекло́.
platen ['plætən] n (*TYP*) ва́лик.
plate rack n суши́лка* (*для посу́ды*).
platform ['plætfɔːm] n (*at meeting*) трибу́на; (*at concert*) помо́ст; (*for landing, loading on etc*) площа́дка; (*RAIL, POL*) платфо́рма; (*BRIT: of bus*) подно́жка*; **the train leaves from ~ seven** по́езд отправля́ется с седьмо́го пути́.
platform ticket n (*BRIT: RAIL*) перро́нный биле́т.
platinum ['plætɪnəm] n пла́тина.
platitude ['plætɪtjuːd] n пло́скость f, бана́льность f.
platonic [plə'tɔnɪk] adj платони́ческий.
platoon [plə'tuːn] n взвод.
platter ['plætə'] n блю́до.
plaudits ['plɔːdɪts] npl похвала́ fsg.
plausible ['plɔːzɪbl] adj (*theory, excuse etc*) правдоподо́бный* (правдоподо́бен); (*person*) убеди́тельный*.
play [pleɪ] n пье́са ♦ vt (*subj: children: game*) игра́ть (*impf*) в +acc; (*sport, cards*) игра́ть (сыгра́ть perf) в +acc; (*opponent*) игра́ть (сыгра́ть perf) с +instr; (*part, role, piece of music*) игра́ть (сыгра́ть perf); (*instrument*) игра́ть (*impf*) на +prp; (*listen to: tape, record*) ста́вить* (поста́вить* perf) ♦ vi игра́ть (*impf*); **a ~ on words** игра́* слов; **to bring** or **call into ~** вводи́ть* (ввести́* perf) в де́йствие; **to ~ a trick on sb** сыгра́ть (perf) шу́тку над кем-н; **they're ~ing at soldiers** они игра́ют в солда́тики; **to ~ for time** тяну́ть (*impf*) вре́мя; **to ~ safe** де́йствовать (*impf*) осторо́жно; **to ~**

into sb's hands игра́ть (сыгра́ть *perf*) кому́-н
на́ руку
▶ **play about** *vi*: **to ~ about with** (*feelings*)
игра́ть (*impf*) +*instr*; (*object*) вози́ться (*impf*) с
+*instr*
▶ **play along** *vi* (*fig*): **to ~ along with** (*person,
plan, idea*) подыгрывать (подыгра́ть *perf*)
+*dat* ♦ *vt* (*fig*): **to ~ sb along** испо́льзовать
(*impf*) кого́-н в свои́х це́лях
▶ **play around** *vi* = **play about**
▶ **play back** *vt* (*recording*) прои́грывать
(проигра́ть *perf*) (*повто́рно*)
▶ **play down** *vt* не заостря́ть (*impf*) внима́ние
на +*prp*
▶ **play on** *vt fus* (*sb's feelings etc*) игра́ть (*impf*)
на +*prp*; **to ~ on sb's nerves** де́йствовать
(*impf*) кому́-н на не́рвы
▶ **play up** *vi* (*machine*) барахли́ть* (*impf*);
(*children*) шали́ть (*impf*), прики́дываться
(*impf*).
play-act ['pleɪækt] *vi* де́лать (сде́лать *perf*) вид.
playboy ['pleɪbɔɪ] *n* хлыщ.
player ['pleɪə'] *n* (*SPORT*) игро́к*; (*MUS, THEAT*)
исполни́тель(ница) *m(f)*.
playful ['pleɪful] *adj* (*person*) игри́вый (игри́в).
playgoer ['pleɪgəuə'] *n* театра́л.
playground ['pleɪgraund] *n* (*in park*) (де́тская)
площа́дка*; (*in school*) (игрова́я) площа́дка*.
playgroup ['pleɪgru:p] *n* де́тская гру́ппа.
playing card ['pleɪɪŋ-] *n* игра́льная ка́рта.
playing field *n* игрово́е по́ле*.
playmate ['pleɪmeɪt] *n* прия́тель(ница) *m(f)*.
play-off ['pleɪɔf] *n* (*SPORT*) игра́ за призово́е
ме́сто.
playpen ['pleɪpɛn] *n* (де́тский*) мане́ж.
playroom ['pleɪru:m] *n* де́тская *f adj*.
playschool ['pleɪsku:l] *n* = **playgroup**.
plaything ['pleɪθɪŋ] *n* игру́шка*.
playtime ['pleɪtaɪm] *n* (*SCOL*) переме́на.
playwright ['pleɪraɪt] *n* драмату́рг.
plc *abbr* (*BRIT*: = *public limited company*)
публи́чная компа́ния с ограни́ченной
отве́тственностью.
plea [pli:] *n* (*personal request*) мольба́; (*public
request*) призы́в; (*LAW*) заявле́ние; (*excuse*)
предло́г.
plea bargaining *n* призна́ние вино́вности в
обме́н на бо́лее коро́ткое тюре́мное
заключе́ние.
plead [pli:d] *vt* (*ignorance, ill health etc*)
ссыла́ться (сосла́ться* *perf*) на +*acc* ♦ *vi* (*LAW*)
признава́ть (призна́ть* *perf*) себя́; (*beg*): **to ~
with sb** умоля́ть (*impf*) кого́-н, моли́ть* (*impf*)
кого́-н; **to ~ sb's case** (*LAW*) защища́ть (*impf*)
кого́-н (*в суде́*); **to ~ for sth** призыва́ть
(призва́ть* *perf*) к чему́-н; **to ~ guilty/not
guilty** признава́ть* (призна́ть* *perf*) себя́
вино́вным(-ой)/невино́вным(-ой).
pleasant ['plɛznt] *adj* прия́тный* (прия́тен).
pleasantly ['plɛzntlɪ] *adv* прия́тно.
pleasantries ['plɛzntrɪz] *npl* любе́зности *fpl*.

please [pli:z] *excl* пожа́луйста ♦ *vt* угожда́ть
(угоди́ть* *perf*) +*dat* ♦ *vi* (*give pleasure,
satisfaction*) угожда́ть (угоди́ть* *perf*); **yes, ~**
да, спаси́бо; **my bill, ~** получи́те (с меня́),
пожа́луйста; **~ don't cry!** не пла́чь,
пожа́луйста!; **~ yourself!** (*inf*) как Вам
уго́дно!; **do as you ~** де́лайте как хоти́те; **he
is difficult/easy to ~** ему́ тру́дно/легко́
угоди́ть (*perf*).
pleased [pli:zd] *adj*: **~ (with)** дово́льный*
(дово́лен) (+*instr*); **~ to meet you** о́чень
прия́тно; **we are ~ to inform you that ...** мы
ра́ды сообщи́ть Вам, что ....
pleasing ['pli:zɪŋ] *adj* прия́тный* (прия́тен).
pleasurable ['plɛʒərəbl] *adj* ра́достный*
(ра́достен).
pleasure ['plɛʒə'] *n* удово́льствие; **it's a ~** не
сто́ит; **with ~** с удово́льствием; **to take ~ in**
получа́ть (получи́ть *perf*) удово́льствие от
+*gen*; **is this trip for business or ~?** э́та пое́здка
делова́я и́ли развлека́тельная?
pleasure boat *n* прогу́лочный ка́тер.
pleasure cruise *n* круи́з.
pleat [pli:t] *n* скла́дка*.
plebiscite ['plɛbɪsɪt] *n* плебисци́т.
plebs [plɛbz] *npl* (*pej*) плебе́и *mpl*, плебс *msg*.
plectrum ['plɛktrəm] *n* плектр.
pledge [plɛdʒ] *n* (*promise*) обяза́тельство ♦ *vt*
(*promise*: *money, support, help*) обяза́ться
(*perf*); **to ~ sb to secrecy** брать* (взять* *perf*) с
кого́-н сло́во молча́ть.
plenary ['pli:nərɪ] *adj*: **in ~ session** на
плена́рном заседа́нии.
plentiful ['plɛntɪful] *adj* оби́льный* (оби́лен).
plenty ['plɛntɪ] *n* (*sufficient*) доста́точное
коли́чество; **~ of** (*food, money etc*) мно́го
+*gen*; (*jobs, people, houses etc*) мно́жество
+*gen*; **we've got ~ of time to get there** у нас
дово́льно вре́мени, чтобы туда́ добра́ться.
plethora ['plɛθərə] *n*: **a ~ of** вели́кое
мно́жество +*gen*.
pleurisy ['pluərɪsɪ] *n* плеври́т.
Plexiglas® ['plɛksɪglɑ:s] *n* (*US*) плексигла́с.
pliable ['plaɪəbl] *adj* (*material*) ги́бкий* (ги́бок);
(*fig*: *person*) усту́пчивый (усту́пчив),
пода́тливый (пода́тлив).
pliant ['plaɪənt] *adj* = **pliable**.
pliers ['plaɪəz] *npl* плоскогу́бцы* *pl*.
plight [plaɪt] *n* мучи́тельное положе́ние.
plimsolls ['plɪmsəlz] *npl* (*BRIT*) паруси́новые
ту́фли *pl*, ке́ды *fpl*.
plinth [plɪnθ] *n* постаме́нт.
PLO *n abbr* (= *Palestine Liberation Organization*)
ООП= *Организа́ция освобожде́ния
Палести́ны*.
plod [plɔd] *vi* (*walk, also fig*) тащи́ться* (*impf*).
plodder ['plɔdə'] *n* (*pej*: *slow worker*)
болоки́тчик; **he is a real ~** (*pej*) он тако́й
медли́тельный.
plonk [plɔŋk] *n* (*inf*: *BRIT*: *wine*) дешёвое вино́ ♦
vt (*inf*): **to ~ sth down** бу́хать (бу́хнуть *perf*)

что-н.

plot [plɔt] *n* (*conspiracy*) за́говор; (*of story*) сюже́т; (*of land*) уча́сток* ◆ *vt* (*sb's downfall etc*) замышля́ть (*impf*); (*AVIAT, NAUT*) прокла́дывать (проложи́ть *perf*); (*MATH*) наноси́ть* (нанести́* *perf*) ◆ *vi* (*conspire*) составля́ть (соста́вить* *perf*) за́говор; **a vegetable** ~ (*BRIT*) садо́вый уча́сток*, огоро́д.

plotter ['plɔtəʳ] *n* (*instrument*) графо-постро́итель *m*; (: *AVIAT, NAUT*) курсопрокла́дчик; (*COMPUT*) пло́ттер, графопостро́итель *m*.

plough [plau] (*US* **plow**) *n* плуг* ◆ *vt* паха́ть* (вспаха́ть* *perf*); **to** ~ **money into** вкла́дывать (вложи́ть *perf*) де́ньги в +*acc*
▸ **plough back** *vt* (*COMM*) реинвести́ровать (*impf/perf*)
▸ **plough through** *vt fus* (*crowd*) продира́ться (продра́ться* *perf*) сквозь +*acc*; (*snow etc*) пробира́ться (пробра́ться* *perf*) че́рез +*acc*.

ploughman ['plaumən] (*US* **plowman**) *irreg n* па́харь *m*.

ploughman's lunch ['plaumənz-] *n* (*BRIT*) ≈ крестья́нский* обе́д.

plow *etc* (*US*) = **plough** *etc*.

ploy [plɔɪ] *n* уло́вка*.

pluck [plʌk] *n* (*courage*) му́жество ◆ *vt* (*fruit, flower*) срыва́ть (сорва́ть *perf*); (*bird*) ощи́пывать (ощипа́ть* *perf*); (*eyebrows*) выщи́пывать (вы́щипать* *perf*); (*string instrument*): **to** ~ (**the strings of**) **sth** перебира́ть (*impf*) стру́ны чего́-н; **to** ~ **up courage** набира́ться (набра́ться* *perf*) хра́брости *or* му́жества.

plucky ['plʌkɪ] *adj* му́жественный* (му́жествен), отва́жный* (отва́жен).

plug [plʌg] *n* (*ELEC*) ви́лка*; (*in sink, bath*) про́бка*; (*AUT: also:* **spark(ing)** ~) свеча́ (зажига́ния) ◆ *vt* (*hole*) затыка́ть (заткну́ть *perf*); (*inf: advertise*) реклами́ровать (разреклами́ровать *perf*); **to give sb/sth a** ~ реклами́ровать (разреклами́ровать *perf*) кого́-н/что-н
▸ **plug in** *vt* (*ELEC*) включа́ть (включи́ть *perf*) в розе́тку ◆ *vi* включа́ться (включи́ться *perf*).

plughole ['plʌghəul] *n* (*BRIT*) сток.

plum [plʌm] *n* сли́ва ◆ *cpd* (*inf*): ~ **job** мирова́я рабо́та.

plumage ['plu:mɪdʒ] *n* опере́ние.

plumb [plʌm] *vt*: **to** ~ **the depths of** (*fig*) достига́ть (дости́чь* *perf*) глуби́н +*gen*
▸ **plumb in** *vt* (*washing machine*) подключа́ть (подключи́ть* *perf*), подсоединя́ть (подсоедини́ть *perf*).

plumber ['plʌməʳ] *n* водопрово́дчик.

plumbing ['plʌmɪŋ] *n* (*piping*) водопрово́д и канализа́ция; (*trade, work*) слеса́рное де́ло.

plumb line *n* отве́с.

plume [plu:m] *n* (*of bird*) перо́*; (*on helmet, horse's head*) плюма́ж; (*fig*): ~ **of smoke** струя́* ды́ма.

plummet ['plʌmɪt] *vi*: **to** ~ (**down**) (*bird, aircraft*) ру́хнуть (*perf*); (*price, amount*) ре́зко па́дать (упа́сть* *perf*).

plump [plʌmp] *adj* (*adult*) по́лный*; (*child*) пу́хлый* (пухл) ◆ *vi*: **to** ~ **for** (*inf*) выбира́ть (вы́брать* *perf*)
▸ **plump up** *vt* взбива́ть (взбить* *perf*).

plunder ['plʌndəʳ] *n* (*activity*) грабёж*; (*stolen things*) награ́бленное *nt adj* ◆ *vt* гра́бить* (разгра́бить* *perf*).

plunge [plʌndʒ] *n* (*dive: of bird, person*) бросо́к*; (*fig: of prices, rates etc*) ре́зкое паде́ние ◆ *vt* (*knife*) мета́ть (метну́ть *perf*); (*hand*) выбра́сывать (вы́бросить* *perf*) ◆ *vi* (*fall: person, thing*) ру́хнуть (*perf*); (*dive: bird, person*) броса́ться (бро́ситься* *perf*); (*fig: prices, rates etc*) ре́зко па́дать (упа́сть* *perf*); **to take the** ~ (*fig*) отва́живаться (отва́житься *perf*); **the room was** ~**d into darkness** ко́мната погрузи́лась во тьму.

plunger ['plʌndʒəʳ] *n* (*for sink*) плу́нжер.

plunging ['plʌndʒɪŋ] *adj*: ~ **neckline** декольте́ *nt ind*.

pluperfect [plu:'pə:fɪkt] *n* плюсквамперфе́кт.

plural ['pluərl] *adj* мно́жественный ◆ *n* мно́жественное число́*.

plus [plʌs] *n, adj* плюс *ind* ◆ *prep*: **ten** ~ **ten is twenty** де́сять плюс де́сять – два́дцать; **ten/ twenty** ~ (*more than*) де́сять/два́дцать с ли́шним; **we discussed the** ~**es of the plan** (*fig*) мы обсужда́ли плю́сы прое́кта.

plus fours *npl* бри́джи *pl*.

plush [plʌʃ] *adj* шика́рный* (шика́рен), роско́шный* (роско́шен) ◆ *n* (*fabric*) плюш.

Pluto ['plu:təu] *n* (*planet*) Плуто́н.

plutonium [plu:'təunɪəm] *n* плуто́ний.

ply [plaɪ] *vt* (*a trade*) занима́ться (заня́ться* *perf*) +*instr*; (*tool*) ору́довать (*impf*) +*instr* ◆ *vi* (*ship*) курси́ровать (*impf*) ◆ *n* (*of wool, rope*) нить *f*; (*of wood*) слой*; **to** ~ **sb with sth** (*food, drink*) подчива́ть (*perf*) кого́-н чем-н; **to** ~ **sb with questions** засыпа́ть (засы́пать* *perf*) кого́-н вопро́сами; **two/three** ~ двойна́я/тройна́я нить.

Plymouth ['plɪməθ] *n* Пли́мут.

plywood ['plaɪwud] *n* фане́ра.

PM *abbr* (*BRIT*) = **Prime Minister**.

p.m. *adv abbr* (= *post meridiem*) по́сле полу́дня.

PMT *abbr* = **premenstrual tension**.

pneumatic [nju:'mætɪk] *adj* пневмати́ческий*.

pneumatic drill *n* пневмати́ческая дрель *f*.

pneumonia [nju:'məunɪə] *n* воспале́ние лёгких, пневмони́я.

Pnomh Penh [nɔm pɛn] *n* Пномпе́нь *m*.

PO *n abbr* = **Post Office**; (*MIL*) = **petty officer**.

---

p.o. *abbr* = **postal order.**

POA *n abbr* (*BRIT*) = *Prison Officers' Association.*

poach [pəutʃ] *vt* (*steal: fish etc*) охо́титься (*impf*) без лице́нзии на +*acc*; (*cook: fish*) вари́ть* (свари́ть* *perf*) ♦ *vi* (*steal*) охо́титься (*impf*) без лице́нзии; **to ~ an egg** вари́ть* (свари́ть* *perf*) яйцо́-пашо́т.

poached [pəutʃt] *adj*: **~ egg** яйцо́-пашо́т *ind.*

poacher ['pəutʃə'] *n* браконье́р.

PO Box *n abbr* = **Post Office Box.**

pocket ['pɔkɪt] *n* (*on clothes*) карма́н; (*on suitcase, car door*) отделе́ние; (*fig: small area*) уголо́к* ♦ *vt* класть* (положи́ть* *perf*) себе́ в карма́н; **to be out of ~** (*BRIT*) быть* (*impf*) в убы́тке на чём-н.

pocketbook ['pɔkɪtbuk] *n* (*US: wallet*) бума́жник; (*handbag*) (да́мская) су́мочка*; (*notebook*) записна́я кни́жка*.

pocket calculator *n* карма́нный калькуля́тор.

pocketknife ['pɔkɪtnaɪf] *n* перочи́нный нож*.

pocket money *n* карма́нные де́ньги* *pl.*

pocket-sized ['pɔkɪtsaɪzd] *adj* (*book*) карма́нный; (*nation*) крохотный.

pockmarked ['pɔkmɑːkt] *adj* рябо́й* (ряб).

pod [pɔd] *n* (*BOT*) стручо́к*.

podgy ['pɔdʒɪ] *adj* (*inf*) то́лстый* (толст).

podiatrist [pɔ'di:ətrɪst] *n* (*US*) ортопе́д.

podiatry [pɔ'di:ətrɪ] *n* (*US*) ортопеди́я.

podium ['pəudɪəm] *n* по́диум.

POE *n abbr* (= *port of embarkation*) порт вы́садки; (= *port of entry*) порт захо́да.

poem ['pəuɪm] *n* (*short*) стихотворе́ние; (*long*) поэ́ма.

poet ['pəuɪt] *n* (*male*) поэ́т; (*female*) поэте́сса.

poetic [pəu'etɪk] *adj* (*also fig*) поэти́ческий*.

poetic justice *n* воздая́ние.

poetic licence *n* поэти́ческая во́льность *f.*

poet laureate *n* придво́рный поэ́т.

poetry ['pəuɪtrɪ] *n* поэ́зия.

poignant ['pɔɪnjənt] *adj* жа́лостный* (жа́лостен).

point [pɔɪnt] *n* (*of needle, knife etc*) острие́*, ко́нчик; (*purpose*) цель *f*; (*significant part*) смысл; (*subject, idea*) предме́т; (*detail, aspect, quality*) аспе́кт; (*particular place or position*) то́чка*, ме́сто*; (*moment*) моме́нт; (*stage in development*) ста́дия; (*score: in competition, game, sport*) очко́*; (*ELEC: also:* **power ~**) розе́тка* ♦ *vt* (*show, mark*) ука́зывать (указа́ть* *perf*); (*gun etc*): **to ~ sth at sb** наце́ливать (наце́лить *perf*) что-н на кого́-н ♦ *vi*: **to ~ at** ука́зывать (указа́ть* *perf*) на +*acc*; **~s** *npl* (*AUT*) конта́кт *msg* (зажига́ния); (*RAIL*) стре́лка* *fsg*; **good ~s** (*of person, plan*) досто́инства; **2 ~ 3 (2.3)** 2 и 3 деся́тых; **to be on the ~ of doing** собира́ться (*impf*) +*infin*; **I made a ~ of visiting him** я счёл необходи́мым посети́ть его́; **to get/miss the ~** понима́ (поня́ть* *perf*)/не понима́ть (поня́ть* *perf*) суть; **to come to the ~**

доходи́ть* (дойти́* *perf*) до су́ти; **when it comes to the ~** когда́ дохо́дит до де́ла; **that's the whole ~!** в э́том-то и де́ло!; **that's beside the ~** не в э́том де́ло; **there's no ~ in doing** нет смы́сла +*infin*; **you've got a ~ there!** в э́том Вы пра́вы!; **in ~ of fact** на де́ле; **~ of departure** (*also fig*) отправно́й пункт; **~ of sale** (*COMM*) торго́вая то́чка*

► **point out** *vt* ука́зывать (указа́ть* *perf*) на +*acc*

► **point to** *vt fus* (*also fig*) ука́зывать (указа́ть* *perf*) на +*acc.*

point-blank ['pɔɪnt'blæŋk] *adv* (*refuse*) наотре́з; (*say, ask*) напрями́к ♦ *adj*: **at ~ range** в упо́р.

point duty *n* (*BRIT*): **to be on ~** ~ находи́ться* (*impf*) на посту́ регулиро́вщика.

pointed ['pɔɪntɪd] *adj* о́стрый* (остёр); (*fig: remark*) язви́тельный.

pointedly ['pɔɪntɪdlɪ] *adv* язви́тельно.

pointer ['pɔɪntə] *n* (*on chart, machine*) стре́лка*; (*stick*) указка*; (*fig*) намёк; (*dog*) по́йнтер.

pointing ['pɔɪntɪŋ] *n* (*CONSTR*) заме́на раство́ра в швах.

pointless ['pɔɪntlɪs] *adj* бессмы́сленный* (бессмы́слен).

point of order *n* вопро́с по поря́дку веде́ния.

point-of-sale advertising ['pɔɪntəv'seɪl-] *n* рекла́ма в места́х соверше́ния поку́пок.

point of view *n* то́чка* зре́ния.

poise [pɔɪz] *n* (*composure, balance*) равнове́сие; (*of head, body*) оса́нка* ♦ *vt*: **to be ~d for** (*fig*) наце́ливаться (наце́литься *perf*) на +*acc.*

poison ['pɔɪzn] *n* яд, отра́ва ♦ *vt* отравля́ть (отрави́ть* *perf*).

poisoning ['pɔɪznɪŋ] *n* отравле́ние.

poisonous ['pɔɪznəs] *adj* ядови́тый (ядови́т); (*fig*) гну́сный* (гну́сен).

poison-pen letter [pɔɪzn'pɛn] *n* анони́мка*.

poke [pəuk] *vt* (*with finger, stick etc*) ты́кать* (ткнуть *perf*); (*fire*) вороши́ть (*impf*), меша́ть (*impf*) ♦ *n* (*jab*) толчо́к*; (*to fire*) помеши́вание; **to ~ sth in(to)** (*put*) втыка́ть (воткну́ть *perf*) что-н в +*acc*; **to ~ one's head out of the window** высо́вываться (вы́сунуться *perf*) из окна́; **to ~ fun at sb** подка́лывать (подколо́ть* *perf*) кого́-н

► **poke about** *vi* ша́рить (поша́рить *perf*)

► **poke out** *vi* высо́вывать (вы́сунуть *perf*).

poker ['pəukə'] *n* кочерга́*; (*CARDS*) по́кер.

poker-faced ['pəukə'feɪst] *adj* невозмути́мый (невозмути́м).

poky ['pəukɪ] *adj* (*room, house*) убо́гий* (убо́г).

Poland ['pəulənd] *n* По́льша.

polar ['pəulə'] *adj* поля́рный.

polar bear *n* бе́лый медве́дь* *m.*

polarize ['pəuləraɪz] *vt* раска́лывать (расколо́ть* *perf*), поляризи́ровать (*impf/perf*).

Pole [pəul] *n* поля́к(-лька*).

pole [pəul] *n* (*stick, staff*) шест*; (*for flag*) дре́вко; (*telegraph pole*) столб; (*GEO, ELEC*) по́люс.

poleaxe ['pəulæks] *n* (*butcher's*) топо́р; (*HISTORY*) секи́ра ♦ *vt* (*hit*) тре́снуть (*perf*); (*surprise*) ошеломля́ть (ошеломи́ть* *perf*).

pole bean *n* (*US*) стручко́вая фасо́ль *f*.

polecat ['pəulkæt] *n* (чёрный) хорёк*.

Pol. Econ. ['pɔlɪkən] *n abbr* (= *political economy*) политэконо́мия= *полити́ческая эконо́мия.*

polemic [pɔ'lɛmɪk] *n* поле́мика.

Pole Star *n* поля́рная звезда́*.

pole vault ['pəulvɔ:lt] *n* прыжо́к* с шесто́м.

police [pə'li:s] *npl* поли́ция *fsg*; (*in Russia*) мили́ция *fsg* ♦ *vt* следи́ть* (*impf*) за поря́дком; **a large number of ~ were hurt** бы́ло ра́нено мно́го полице́йских.

police car *n* полице́йская маши́на.

police constable *n* (*BRIT*) полице́йский* *m adj*.

police department *n* (*US*) полице́йский* уча́сток*.

police force *n* поли́ция.

policeman [pə'li:smən] *irreg n* полице́йский* *m adj*.

police officer *n* = police constable.

police record *n*: **to have a ~** ~ состоя́ть (*impf*) на учёте в поли́ции.

police state *n* (*POL*) полице́йское госуда́рство.

police station *n* полице́йский* уча́сток*; (*in Russia*) отделе́ние мили́ции.

policewoman [pə'li:swumən] *irreg n* (же́нщина-) полице́йский* *m adj*.

policy ['pɔlɪsɪ] *n* поли́тика; (*also*: **insurance ~**) по́лис; **to take out a ~** (*INSURANCE*) застрахо́вываться (застрахова́ться *perf*).

policyholder ['pɔlɪsɪ'həuldə'] *n* (*INSURANCE*) держа́тель *m* страхово́го по́лиса.

policymaking ['pɔlɪsɪmeɪkɪŋ] *n* разрабо́тка страте́гии.

polio ['pəulɪəu] *n* полиомиели́т.

Polish ['pəulɪʃ] *adj* по́льский* ♦ *n* (*LING*) по́льский* язы́к*.

polish ['pɔlɪʃ] *n* (*for shoes*) гутали́н; (*for furniture*) лак*; (*for floors*) масти́ка; (*shine, also fig*) лоск ♦ *vt* (*shoes*) вычища́ть (вы́чистить* *perf*); (*floors*) натира́ть (натере́ть *perf*); (*furniture etc*) полирова́ть (отполирова́ть *perf*); (*fig: improve*) шлифова́ть (отшлифова́ть *perf*)

▶ **polish off** *vt fus* (*work, food*) поко́нчить (*perf*).

polished ['pɔlɪʃt] *adj* (*person*) изы́сканный* (изы́скан); (*style*) отто́ченный (отто́чен).

polite [pə'laɪt] *adj* (*well-mannered*) ве́жливый (ве́жлив); (*socially superior: company, society*) све́тский; **it's not ~ to do that** так де́лать не при́нято.

politely [pə'laɪtlɪ] *adv* ве́жливо.

politeness [pə'laɪtnɪs] *n* ве́жливость *f*.

politic ['pɔlɪtɪk] *adj*: **it would be ~ to** ... бы́ло бы благоразу́мно +*infin* ....

political [pə'lɪtɪkl] *adj* полити́ческий*; (*person*) полити́чески акти́вный, политизи́рованный (политизи́рован).

political asylum *n* полити́ческое убе́жище.

politically [pə'lɪtɪklɪ] *adv* полити́чески; **~ correct** полити́чески прави́льный.

politician [pɔlɪ'tɪʃən] *n* поли́тик, полити́ческий* де́ятель *m*.

politics ['pɔlɪtɪks] *n* поли́тика; (*subject*) политоло́гия ♦ *npl* (*beliefs, opinions*) полити́ческие убежде́ния *ntpl*.

polka ['pɔlkə] *n* по́лька*.

poll [pəul] *n* (*also*: **opinion ~**) опро́с; (*election*) вы́боры *mpl* ♦ *vt* (*in opinion poll*) опра́шивать (опроси́ть* *perf*); (*number of votes*) набира́ть (набра́ть* *perf*); **to go to the ~s** (*voters*) голосова́ть (проголосова́ть *perf*) (*на вы́борах*); (*government*) объявля́ть (объяви́ть* *perf*) вы́боры.

pollen ['pɔlən] *n* пыльца́.

pollen count *n* содержа́ние пыльцы́ в во́здухе.

pollinate ['pɔlɪneɪt] *vt* (*BOT*) опыля́ть (опыли́ть *perf*).

polling booth ['pəulɪŋ-] *n* (*BRIT*) каби́на для голосова́ния.

polling day *n* (*BRIT*) день* *m* вы́боров.

polling station *n* (*BRIT*) избира́тельный уча́сток*.

pollster ['pəulstə'] *n* челове́к, производя́щий* опро́с обще́ственного мне́ния.

poll tax *n* (*BRIT: formerly*) поду́шный нало́г.

pollutant [pə'lu:tənt] *n* загрязня́ющий аге́нт.

pollute [pə'lu:t] *vt* загрязня́ть (загрязни́ть *perf*).

pollution [pə'lu:ʃən] *n* загрязне́ние; (*substances*) загрязни́тель *m*.

polo ['pəuləu] *n* по́ло *nt ind*.

polo neck *n* (*also*: **~ ~ sweater** *or* **jumper**) сви́тер с кру́глым воротнико́м.

polo-necked ['pəuləunɛkt] *adj*: **~ sweater** *or* **jumper** сви́тер с кру́глым воротнико́м.

poltergeist ['pɔːltəgaɪst] *n* полтерге́йст.

poly ['pɔlɪ] *n abbr* (*BRIT*) = **polytechnic**.

poly... ['pɔlɪ] *prefix* мно́го..., поли....

poly bag *n* полиэтиле́новый мешо́к* *or* паке́т.

polyester [pɔlɪ'ɛstə'] *n* (*CHEM*) сло́жный полиэфи́р; (*fabric*) полиэфи́рное волокно́.

polygamy [pə'lɪgəmɪ] *n* многобра́чие, полига́мия.

polygraph ['pɔlɪgrɑːf] *n* дете́ктор лжи.

Polynesia [pɔlɪ'niːzɪə] *n* Полине́зия.

Polynesian [pɔlɪ'niːzɪən] *adj* полинези́йский ♦ *n* полинези́ец*(-и́йка*).

polyp ['pɔlɪp] *n* (*MED*) поли́п.

---

* marks translations which have irregular inflections. The Russian-English side of the dictionary gives inflectional information.

polystyrene [pɔlɪ'staɪriːn] *n* пенопла́ст.
polytechnic [pɔlɪ'tɛknɪk] *n* (*college*) ≈ политехни́ческий* институ́т.
polythene ['pɔlɪθiːn] *n* полиэтиле́н.
polythene bag *n* полиэтиле́новый мешо́к* *or* паке́т.
polyurethane [pɔlɪ'juərɪθeɪn] *n* полиурета́н.
pomegranate ['pɔmɪgrænɪt] *n* (*BOT*) грана́т.
pommel ['pɔml] *n* (*of saddle*) лука́; (*of sword*) голо́вка* ♦ *vt* = **pummel.**
pomp [pɔmp] *n* пы́шность *f*.
pompom ['pɔmpɔm] *n* помпо́н.
pompous ['pɔmpəs] *adj* (*pej: person, style*) напы́щенный* (напы́щен).
pond [pɔnd] *n* пруд*; (*stagnant*) за́водь *f*.
ponder ['pɔndə'] *vt* обду́мывать (обду́мать *perf*) ♦ *vi* размышля́ть (*impf*).
ponderous ['pɔndərəs] *adj* (*style*) тяжело-ве́сный* (тяжелове́сен); (*person*) неповоро́тливый (неповоро́тлив).
pong [pɔŋ] (*BRIT*: *inf*) *n* вонь *f* ♦ *vi* воня́ть (*impf*).
pontiff ['pɔntɪf] *n* (*REL*) Па́па *m* ри́мский*.
pontificate [pɔn'tɪfɪkeɪt] *vi* (*fig*): **to ~ (about)** разглаго́льствовать (*impf*) (о +*prp*).
pontoon [pɔn'tuːn] *n* (*floating platform*) понто́н; (*CARDS*) два́дцать одно́.
pony ['pəunɪ] *n* по́ни *m ind*.
ponytail ['pəunɪteɪl] *n* (*hairstyle*) хвост*, хво́стик; **to have one's hair in a ~** носи́ть* (*impf*) хво́стик.
pony trekking *n* (*BRIT*) ко́нный похо́д.
poodle ['puːdl] *n* пу́дель* *m*.
pooh-pooh [puː'puː] *vt* заши́кивать (заши́кать *perf*).
pool [puːl] *n* (*puddle*) лу́жа; (*pond*) пруд*; (*also:* **swimming ~**) бассе́йн; (*fig: of light, paint*) пятно́; (*SPORT, COMM*) пул; (*money at cards*) банк ♦ *vt* (*money, knowledge, resources*) объединя́ть (объедини́ть *perf*); **~s** *npl* (*also:* **football ~s**) тотализа́тор; **typing ~,** *(US)* **secretary ~** машинопи́сное бюро́ *nt ind*; **to do the (football) ~s** игра́ть (сыгра́ть *perf*) в тотализа́тор.
poor [puə'] *adj* (*not rich*) бе́дный* (бе́ден); (*bad*) плохо́й* (плох); **the ~** *npl* (*people*) беднота́ *fsg*; **~ in** (*resources etc*) бе́дный* (бе́ден) +*instr*.
poorly ['puəlɪ] *adv* пло́хо ♦ *adj*: **she is feeling ~** она́ пло́хо себя́ чу́вствует.
pop [pɔp] *n* (*also:* **~ music**) поп-му́зыка; (*inf: fizzy drink*) лимона́д*; (: *US: father*) па́па, оте́ц; (*sound*) хлопо́к* ♦ *vi* (*balloon*) ло́паться (ло́пнуть *perf*); (*cork*) выстре́ливать (вы́стрелить *perf*); (*fig: eyes*) тара́щиться (вы́тараращиться *perf*) ♦ *vt* (*put quickly*): **to ~ sth into/onto** *etc* забра́сывать (забро́сить* *perf*) в +*acc*/на +*acc etc*; **she ~ped her head out of the window** она́ вы́сунула го́лову из окна́
▸ **pop in** *vi* загля́дывать (загляну́ть* *perf*), заска́кивать (заскочи́ть *perf*)
▸ **pop out** *vi* выска́кивать (вы́скочить *perf*)
▸ **pop up** *vi* вылеза́ть (вы́лезти *perf*).

popcorn ['pɔpkɔːn] *n* возду́шная кукуру́за, попко́рн.
pope [pəup] *n*: **the P~** Па́па *m* ри́мский*.
poplar ['pɔplə'] *n* то́поль* *m*.
poplin ['pɔplɪn] *n* попли́н.
popper ['pɔpə'] *n* (*BRIT: fastener*) кно́пка*.
poppy ['pɔpɪ] *n* мак.
poppycock ['pɔpɪkɔk] *n* (*inf*) вздор.
Popsicle® ['pɔpsɪkl] *n* (*US*) ≈ фрукто́вое моро́женое *nt adj*.
pop star *n* поп-звезда́* *m/f*.
populace ['pɔpjuləs] *n*: **the ~** наро́д*.
popular ['pɔpjulə'] *adj* популя́рный* (популя́рен); (*POL*) наро́дный; **to be ~ (with)** (*person, belief*) по́льзоваться (*impf*) популя́рностью (среди́ +*gen*); (*decision*) по́льзоваться (*impf*) подде́ржкой (+*gen*); **a ~ song** популя́рная пе́сня*.
popularity [pɔpju'lærɪtɪ] *n* популя́рность *f*.
popularize ['pɔpjuləraɪz] *vt* (*pastime, fashion*) де́лать (сде́лать *perf*) популя́рным; (*science, ideas*) популяризи́ровать (*impf/perf*).
popularly ['pɔpjuləlɪ] *adv* (*generally*) обы́чно; **it is ~ believed that ...** мно́гие полага́ют, что ....
population [pɔpju'leɪʃən] *n* населе́ние; (*of a species*) популя́ция; **the civilian ~s** гражда́нское населе́ние; **Britain has a prison ~ of 44 thousand** о́бщее коли́чество заключённых в тю́рмах Великобрита́нии составля́ет 44 ты́сячи.
population explosion *n* демографи́ческий* взрыв.
populous ['pɔpjuləs] *adj* густонаселённый*.
porcelain ['pɔːslɪn] *n* фарфо́р.
porch [pɔːtʃ] *n* крыльцо́*; (*US*) вера́нда.
porcupine ['pɔːkjupaɪn] *n* дикообра́з.
pore [pɔː'] *n* по́ра ♦ *vi*: **to ~ over** погружа́ться (погрузи́ться* *perf*) в +*acc*.
pork [pɔːk] *n* свини́на.
pork chop *n* свина́я отбивна́я *f adj*.
porn [pɔːn] *n* (*inf*) порногра́фия.
pornographic [pɔːnə'græfɪk] *adj* порно-графи́ческий*.
pornography [pɔː'nɔgrəfɪ] *n* порногра́фия.
porous ['pɔːrəs] *adj* по́ристый (по́рист).
porpoise ['pɔːpəs] *n* бу́рый дельфи́н.
porridge ['pɔrɪdʒ] *n* овся́ная ка́ша.
port [pɔːt] *n* (*harbour, also COMPUT*) порт*; (*opening in ship*) люк; (*NAUT*) ле́вый борт*; (*wine*) портве́йн ♦ *cpd* (*NAUT*) ле́вый; **to ~** (*NAUT*) нале́во; **~ of call** порт* захо́да.
portable ['pɔːtəbl] *adj* порта́тивный.
portal ['pɔːtl] *n* порта́л.
portcullis [pɔː'tkʌlɪs] *n* (*опускна́я*) решётка* (*в воро́тах*).
portend [pɔː'tɛnd] *vt* предвеща́ть (*impf*).
portent ['pɔːtɛnt] *n* предзнаменова́ние, предве́стник.
porter ['pɔːtə'] *n* (*for luggage*) носи́льщик; (*doorkeeper*) швейца́р, портье́ *m ind*; (: *in offices*) вахтёр; (*US: RAIL*) проводни́к*(-ица).

portfolio [pɔːt'fəulɪəu] *n* (*also POL*) портфе́ль *m*; (*FINANCE*) портфе́ль це́нных бума́г; (*of artist*) па́пка*.
porthole ['pɔːthəul] *n* иллюмина́тор.
portico ['pɔːtɪkəu] *n* по́ртик.
portion ['pɔːʃən] *n* (*part*) часть* *f*; (*equal part*) до́ля*; (*helping of food*) по́рция.
portly ['pɔːtlɪ] *adj* доро́дный* (доро́ден).
portrait ['pɔːtreɪt] *n* портре́т.
portray [pɔː'treɪ] *vt* изобража́ть (изобрази́ть* *perf*).
portrayal [pɔː'treɪəl] *n* изображе́ние; (*representation*) о́браз.
Portsmouth ['pɔːtsməθ] *n* По́ртсмут.
Portugal ['pɔːtjugl] *n* Португа́лия.
Portuguese [pɔːtju'giːz] *adj* португа́льский* ♦ *n inv* португа́лец*(-лка*); (*LING*) португа́льский* язы́к*.
Portuguese man-of-war [-mænəv'wɔːʳ] *n* (*ZOOL*) португа́льский* вое́нный кора́бль *m*.
pose [pəuz] *n* по́за ♦ *vt* (*question*) ста́вить* (поста́вить* *perf*); (*problem, danger*) создава́ть* (созда́ть* *perf*) ♦ *vi* (*pretend*): **to ~ as** выдава́ть* (вы́дать* *perf*) себя́ за +*acc*; **to strike a ~** принима́ть (приня́ть* *perf*) по́зу; **to ~ for** пози́ровать (*impf*) для +*gen*.
poser ['pəuzəʳ] *n* (*puzzle*) головоло́мка*; (*person*) = **poseur**.
poseur [pəu'zəːʳ] *n* (*pej*) позёр(ка*).
posh [pɔʃ] *adj* (*inf*: *hotel, restaurant etc*) фешене́бельный* (фешене́белен); (: *person, behaviour*) великосве́тский; **to talk ~** (*inf*) мане́рничать (*impf*).
position [pə'zɪʃən] *n* положе́ние; (*of house, thing*) расположе́ние, ме́сто*; (*job*) до́лжность *f*; (*in race, competition*) ме́сто*; (*attitude*) пози́ция ♦ *vt* располага́ть (расположи́ть* *perf*); **to be in a ~ to do** име́ть (*impf*) возмо́жность +*infin*.
positive ['pɔzɪtɪv] *adj* (*affirmative*) положи́тельный* (положи́телен); (*certain*) уве́ренный* (уве́рен), убеждённый* (убеждён); (*definite: decision, action, policy*) несомне́нный* (несомне́нен), определённый* (определён); (*MATH, ELEC*) положи́тельный.
positive cash flow *n* положи́тельный пото́к нали́чности.
positively ['pɔzɪtɪvlɪ] *adv* (*for emphasis*) положи́тельно; (*definitely*) несомне́нно.
posse ['pɔsɪ] *n* (*US*) ко́нный отря́д доброво́льных помо́щников шери́фа при ло́вле престу́пника.
possess [pə'zɛs] *vt* владе́ть (*impf*) +*instr*; (*quality, ability*) облада́ть (*impf*) +*instr*; (*subj: feeling, belief*) овладева́ть (овладе́ть *perf*); **like one ~ed** как одержи́мый*(-ая) *m(f) adj*; **whatever can have ~ed you?** и какой чёрт

тебя́ попу́тал?
possession [pə'zɛʃən] *n* (*state*) владе́ние; **~s** *npl* (*belongings*) принадле́жности *fpl*; **to take ~ of** вступа́ть (вступи́ть* *perf*) во владе́ние +*instr*.
possessive [pə'zɛsɪv] *adj* со́бственнический*; (*LING*) притяжа́тельный.
possessiveness [pə'zɛsɪvnɪs] *n* (*of another person*) со́бственничество; **~ towards sb/sth** ревни́вое отноше́ние к кому́-н/чему́-н.
possessor [pə'zɛsəʳ] *n* (*of property*) владе́лец*(-е́лица); (*of quality*) облада́тель(ница) *m(f)*.
possibility [pɔsɪ'bɪlɪtɪ] *n* возмо́жность *f*; **he's a ~ (for the part)** он возмо́жный кандида́т (на роль).
possible ['pɔsɪbl] *adj* возмо́жный* (возмо́жен); **it's ~** э́то не исключено́; **it is ~ to do it** э́то осуществи́мо; **as far as ~** наско́лько возмо́жно; **if ~** е́сли (э́то) возмо́жно; **as big as ~** са́мый большо́й.
possibly ['pɔsɪblɪ] *adv* (*perhaps*) возмо́жно; **if you ~ can** е́сли то́лько Вы мо́жете; **I cannot ~ come** я ника́к не смогу́.
post [pəust] *n* (*BRIT*: *mail*) по́чта; (*pole*) столб*; (*job, situation, also MIL*) пост* ♦ *vt* (*BRIT*: *mail*) посыла́ть (посла́ть* *perf*), отправля́ть (отпра́вить* *perf*) (по по́чте); (: *MIL*) выставля́ть (вы́ставить* *perf*); (: *appoint*) откомандиро́вывать (откомандирова́ть *perf*); **by ~** (*BRIT*) по по́чте; **by return of ~** (*BRIT*) с обра́тной по́чтой; **trading ~** фракто́рия; **to keep sb ~ed** держа́ть* (*impf*) кого́-н в ку́рсе (дел).
post... [pəust] *prefix* пост..., по́сле...; **~-1990** (*as adj*) в 90-е го́ды; (*as adv*) как 90-е го́ды.
postage ['pəustɪdʒ] *n* (*charge*) почто́вые расхо́ды *mpl*; **~ paid, (*US*) ~ prepaid** с предвари́тельно опла́ченными почто́выми расхо́дами.
postage stamp *n* почто́вая ма́рка*.
postal ['pəustl] *adj* почто́вый.
postal order *n* (де́нежный) почто́вый перево́д.
postbag ['pəustbæg] *n* (*BRIT*: *letters received*) по́чта, корреспонде́нция; (: *postman's*) су́мка* (*почтальо́на*).
postbox ['pəustbɔks] *n* (*BRIT*) почто́вый я́щик.
postcard ['pəustkɑːd] *n* (почто́вая) откры́тка*.
postcode ['pəustkəud] *n* (*BRIT*) почто́вый и́ндекс.
postdate ['pəust'deɪt] *vt* дати́ровать (*impf/perf*) бо́лее по́здним число́м.
poster ['pəustəʳ] *n* афи́ша, плака́т; (*for advertising*) по́стер.
poste restante [pəust'rɛstɑ̃ːnt] *adv* (*BRIT*) до востре́бования.
posterior [pɔs'tɪərɪəʳ] *n* зад.

---

* marks translations which have irregular inflections. The Russian-English side of the dictionary gives inflectional information.

posterity [pɔs'tɛrɪtɪ] *n* после́дующие поколе́ния *ntpl*, пото́мство.

poster paint *n* плака́тная тушь *f*.

post exchange *n* (*US: MIL*) военто́рг, гарнизо́нный магази́н.

post-free [pəust'fri:] *adj, adv* (*BRIT*) с предвари́тельно опла́ченными почто́выми расхо́дами.

postgraduate ['pəust'grædjuət] *n* аспира́нт(ка*) ◆ *adj*: ~ **study** аспиранту́ра.

posthumous ['pɔstjuməs] *adj* посме́ртный.

posthumously ['pɔstjuməslɪ] *adv* посме́ртно.

posting ['pəustɪŋ] *n* (*job*) командиро́вка.

postman ['pəustmən] *irreg n* почтальо́н.

postmark ['pəustma:k] *n* почто́вый штémпель* *m*.

postmaster ['pəustma:stə*] *n* нача́льник по́чты *or* почто́вого отделе́ния.

postmaster general *n* ≈ мини́стр свя́зи.

postmistress ['pəustmɪstrɪs] *n* нача́льник по́чты *or* почто́вого отделе́ния (*же́нщина*).

postmortem [pəust'mɔ:təm] *n* (*MED*) вскры́тие, аутопси́я.

postnatal ['pəust'neɪtl] *adj* послеродово́й.

post office *n* почто́вое отделе́ние, отделе́ние свя́зи; (*organization*): **the P~ O~** ≈ Министе́рство свя́зи.

Post Office Box *n* абоне́нтский я́щик.

post-paid ['pəust'peɪd] *adj* (*BRIT*) с опла́ченными почто́выми расхо́дами.

postpone [pəus'pəun] *vt* откла́дывать (отложи́ть* *perf*).

postponement [pəus'pəunmənt] *n* отсро́чка.

postscript ['pəustskrɪpt] *n* (*in letter*) постскри́птум.

postulate ['pɔstjuleɪt] *vt* постули́ровать (*impf/ perf*).

posture ['pɔstʃə*] *n* (*of body*) оса́нка; (*fig*) положе́ние ◆ *vi* (*pej*) пози́ровать (*impf*).

postwar [pəust'wɔ:*] *adj* послевое́нный.

posy ['pəuzɪ] *n* буке́тик.

pot [pɔt] *n* (*for cooking, flowers*) горшо́к*; (*also:* **teapot**) (зава́рочный) ча́йник; (*also:* **coffeepot**) кофе́йник; (*bowl, container*) ба́нка; (*inf: marijuana*) план ◆ *vt* (*plant*) сажа́ть (посади́ть* *perf*); **a ~ of tea** ча́йник ча́я; **to go to ~** (*inf: work, performance*) разва́ливаться (развали́ться* *perf*); **~s of** (*BRIT: inf*) ку́ча +*gen*, у́йма +*gen*.

potash ['pɔtæʃ] *n* пота́ш.

potassium [pə'tæsɪəm] *n* ка́лий.

potato [pə'teɪtəu] (*pl* ~**es**) *n* карто́фель *m no pl*, карто́шка *f no pl* (*разг*); (*single potato*) карто́фелина.

potato chips *npl* (*US*) = **potato crisps**.

potato crisps *npl* (*BRIT*) чи́псы *pl*.

potato flour *n* карто́фельная мука́.

potato peeler *n* картофелечи́стка.

potbellied ['pɔtbɛlɪd] *adj* (*from overeating*) пуза́тый (пуза́т); (*from malnutrition*) со взду́тым живото́м.

potency ['pəutnsɪ] *n* си́ла; (*of drink*) кре́пость *f*.

potent ['pəutnt] *adj* (*weapon*) мо́щный; (*argument*) убеди́тельный* (убеди́телен); (*drink*) кре́пкий* (кре́пок); (*man*) облада́ющий сексуа́льной поте́нцией.

potentate ['pəutnteɪt] *n* властели́н, повели́тель *m*.

potential [pə'tɛnʃl] *adj* потенциа́льный, возмо́жный ◆ *n* потенциа́л; **to have ~** облада́ть (*impf*) (доста́точным) потенциа́лом.

potentially [pə'tɛnʃəlɪ] *adv* потенциа́льно; **it's ~ dangerous** э́то в при́нципе опа́сно.

pothole ['pɔthəul] *n* (*in road*) вы́боина; (*BRIT: underground*) прова́л.

potholing ['pɔthəulɪŋ] (*BRIT*) *n* спелеоло́гия; **to go ~** отправля́ться (отпра́виться *perf*) обсле́довать пеще́ры.

potion ['pəuʃən] *n* насто́йка; (*poison*) зе́лье.

potluck [pɔt'lʌk] *n*: **to take ~** обе́дать (пообе́дать *perf*) чем Бог посла́л.

potpourri [pəu'purɪ:] *n* ароматúческая смесь из сухúх лепесткóв; (*fig*) попурри́ *nt ind*.

pot roast *n* тушёное мя́со.

pot shot *n*: **to take ~~s at** стреля́ть (вы́стрелить *perf*) навски́дку в +*acc*.

potted ['pɔtɪd] *adj* (*food*) консерви́рованный; (*plant*) ко́мнатный; (*account, biography*) кра́ткий*.

potter ['pɔtə*] *n* (*pottery maker*) гонча́р* ◆ *vi*: **to ~ around, ~ about** (*BRIT*) вози́ться* (*impf*); **to ~ about (in) the garden** вози́ться* (*impf*) в саду́.

potter's wheel *n* гонча́рный круг*.

pottery ['pɔtərɪ] *n* кера́мика; (*factory*) заво́д керами́ческих изде́лий; (*workshop*) гонча́рная мастерска́я *f adj*; **a piece of ~** керами́ческое изде́лие.

potty ['pɔtɪ] *adj* (*inf: mad*) чо́кнутый ◆ *n* (*for child*) горшо́к* (*ночно́й*).

potty-training ['pɔtɪtreɪnɪŋ] *n* приуче́ние ребёнка к горшку́.

pouch [pautʃ] *n* (*for tobacco*) кисе́т; (*for coins*) кошелёк*; (*ZOOL*) су́мка*.

pouf(fe) [pu:f] *n* пуф.

poultice ['pəultɪs] *n* припа́рка*.

poultry ['pəultrɪ] *n* (*birds*) дома́шняя пти́ца; (*meat*) пти́ца.

poultry farm *n* птицефе́рма.

poultry farmer *n* птицево́д.

pounce [pauns] *vi*: **to ~ on** набра́сываться (набро́ситься* *perf*) на +*acc*.

pound [paund] *n* (*money, weight*) фунт; (*for dogs*) живодёрня; (*for cars*) стоя́нка для непра́вильно припарко́ванных автомаши́н, увезённых поли́цией ◆ *vt* (*beat*) колоти́ть* (*impf*) по +*dat*; (*crush*) толо́чь* (растоло́чь* *perf*); (*with guns*) обстре́ливать (обстреля́ть *perf*) ◆ *vi* (*heart*) колоти́ться* (*impf*); **half a ~ of** полфу́нта +*gen*; **a five-~ note** банкно́та в пять фу́нтов; **my car has been taken to the ~** мою́ маши́ну арестова́ли.

pounding ['paundıŋ] n: **we took a ~** (SPORT) нас поби́ли; (fig) нас разнесли́.
pound sterling n фунт сте́рлингов.
pour [pɔː'] vt (liquid) налива́ть (нали́ть* perf); (dry substance) насыпа́ть (насы́пать* perf) ◆ vi (water, blood, sweat etc) ли́ться* (impf); (rain) лить* (impf); **to ~ sb some tea** налива́ть (нали́ть* perf) кому́-н чай; **it's ~ing with rain** льёт дождь
▸ **pour away** vt вылива́ть (вы́лить* perf)
▸ **pour in** vi (people) вали́ть* (повали́ть* perf); (news, letters etc) сы́паться* (impf)
▸ **pour into** vt fus устремля́ться (устреми́ться* perf) в +acc
▸ **pour off** vt слива́ть (слить* perf)
▸ **pour out** vi (people) вали́ть* (повали́ть* perf) ◆ vt (drink) налива́ть (нали́ть* perf); (fig: thoughts, feelings, etc) излива́ть (изли́ть* perf).
pouring ['pɔːrıŋ] adj: **~ rain** проливно́й дождь m.
pout [paut] vi надува́ть (наду́ть perf) гу́бы, ду́ться (наду́ться perf).
poverty ['pɔvətı] n бе́дность f, нищета́.
poverty line n черта́ бе́дности.
poverty-stricken ['pɔvətıstrıkn] adj впа́вший в нищету́, обнища́вший.
poverty trap n (BRIT) тиски́ pl бе́дности.
POW n abbr = **prisoner of war**.
powder ['paudə'] n порошо́к*; (also: **face ~**) пу́дра ◆ vt: **to ~ one's face** пу́дрить (напу́дрить perf) лицо́; **to ~ one's nose** (euphemism) помы́ть* (perf) ру́ки.
powder compact n пу́дреница.
powdered milk ['paudəd-] n сухо́е молоко́.
powder keg n порохова́я бо́чка.
powder puff n пухо́вка.
powder room n да́мская ко́мната.
power ['pauə'] n (authority) власть f; (ability, opportunity) возмо́жность f; (legal right) полномо́чие; (strength: of person, speech, thought) мощь f; (of explosion, engine) мо́щность f; (electricity) электроэне́ргия; (MATH) сте́пень f; **to do all in one's ~ to help** де́лать (сде́лать perf) всё что в свои́х си́лах, чтобы помога́ть (помо́чь* perf); **the world ~s** мировы́е держа́вы; **to be in ~** находи́ться* (impf) у вла́сти.
powerboat ['pauəbəut] n мото́рный ка́тер*.
power cut n (BRIT) отключе́ние электро-эне́ргии.
powered ['pauəd] adj: **~ by** рабо́тающий на +prp; **nuclear-~ submarine** а́томная подво́дная ло́дка*.
power failure n остано́вка* пода́чи электроэне́ргии.
powerful ['pauəful] adj могу́чий* (могу́ч); (person, organization) могу́щественный*

(могу́ществен); (engine, argument) мо́щный; (smell, voice, emotion) си́льный* (си́лен); (evidence) ве́ский* (ве́сок).
powerhouse ['pauəhaus] n (person): **a ~ of ideas** генера́тор иде́й.
powerless ['pauəlıs] adj бесси́льный* (бесси́лен).
power line n ли́ния электропереда́чи.
power of attorney n (LAW) дове́ренность f.
power point n (BRIT) (штéпсельная) розе́тка*.
power station n электроста́нция.
power steering n (AUT) рулево́й приво́д с усили́телем.
powwow ['pauwau] n сове́т.
pp abbr = **per procurationem**; (by proxy) по дове́ренности.
pp. abbr = **pages**.
PPE n abbr (BRIT: SCOL) = **philosophy, politics and economics**.
PPS n abbr (= **post postscriptum**) второ́й постскри́птум; (BRIT: = **parliamentary private secretary**) ли́чный парла́ментский секрета́рь мини́стра.
PQ abbr (CANADA) = **Province of Quebec**.
PR n abbr = **public relations**; (POL) = **proportional representation** ◆ abbr (US: POST) = **Puerto Rico**.
Pr. abbr = **prince**.
practicability [præktıkə'bılıtı] n осуществи́мость f.
practicable ['præktıkəbl] adj осуществи́мый (осуществи́м).
practical ['præktıkl] adj (not theoretical) практи́ческий*; (sensible, viable) практи́чный* (практи́чен); (good with hands) уме́лый (уме́л).
practicality [præktı'kælıtı] n практи́чность f; **practicalities** npl (of situation etc) практи́ческая сторона́ fsg.
practical joke n ро́зыгрыш.
practically ['præktıklı] adv практи́чески.
practice ['præktıs] n (habit) привы́чка*; (of profession) пра́ктика; (REL) обы́чай; (exercise, training) пра́ктика, трениро́вка ◆ vti (US) = **practise**; **in ~** я давно́ э́того не де́лал; **it's common ~** э́то распространено́; **to put sth into ~** осуществля́ть (осуществи́ть* perf) что-н на пра́ктике; **target ~** уче́бная стрельба́.
practice match n трениро́вочный матч.
practise ['præktıs] (US **practice**) vt (musical instrument) упражня́ться (impf) на +acc; (SPORT, piece of music, language) отраба́тывать (отрабо́тать perf); (custom) выполня́ть (вы́полнить perf); (craft) занима́ться (impf) +instr; (religion) испове́дывать (impf) ◆ vi (on instrument) упражня́ться (impf); (SPORT) трениров́аться (impf); (lawyer, doctor) практикова́ть (impf); **to**

---

* marks translations which have irregular inflections. The Russian-English side of the dictionary gives inflectional information.

(impf) важнее, чем.

practised ['præktɪst] *adj* (*BRIT*: *person*)
опытный; (: *performance*) искусный; (: *liar*)
закоренелый; **with a** ~ **eye** (*BRIT*)
намётанным глазом.

practising ['præktɪsɪŋ] *adj* (*Christian etc*)
верующий*; (*doctor, lawyer*) практикующий;
(*homosexual*) ведущий* активную половую
жизнь.

practitioner [præk'tɪʃənəʳ] *n* (*MED*) терапевт.

pragmatic [præg'mætɪk] *adj* (*reason etc*)
прагматический; (*person*) прагматичный*
(прагматичен).

pragmatism ['prægmətɪzəm] *n* прагматизм.

Prague [prɑ:g] *n* Прага.

prairie ['prɛərɪ] *n* прерия; (*US*): **the** ~**s** прерии
fpl.

praise [preɪz] *n* (*approval*) похвала;
(*admiration*) восхваление ◆ *vt* (*see n*)
хвалить* (похвалить* *perf*); восхвалять
(impf).

praiseworthy ['preɪzwə:ðɪ] *adj* достойный*
(достоен) похвалы.

pram [præm] *n* (*BRIT*) детская коляска.

prance [prɑ:ns] *vi* (*horse*) гарцевать *(impf)*;
(*person*): **to** ~ **about** красоваться *(impf)*.

prank [præŋk] *n* (*practical joke*) розыгрыш;
(*tomfoolery*) проделка*.

prat [præt] *n* (*inf. pej*: *BRIT*) идиот.

prattle ['prætl] *vi*: **to** ~ **on (about)** трепаться
(impf) (о +*prp*).

prawn [prɔ:n] *n* креветка*.

pray [preɪ] *vi* молиться* (помолиться* *perf*); **to**
~ **for** молиться* *(impf)* за +*acc*; **to** ~ **that**
молиться* *(impf)*, чтобы.

prayer [prɛəʳ] *n* (*activity*) молитва, моление;
(*words*) молитва.

prayer book *n* молитвенник.

pre... ['pri:...] *prefix* до..., пред...; ~**-1970** до
1970-го года.

preach [pri:tʃ] *vi* (*also fig*) проповедовать *(impf)*
◆ *vt*: **to** ~ **a sermon** (*also fig*) произносить*
(произнести* *perf*) проповедь; **to** ~ **at sb**
читать *(impf)* проповеди кому-н.

preacher ['pri:tʃəʳ] *n* проповедник(-ица).

preamble [prɪ'æmbl] *n* преамбула.

prearranged [pri:ə'reɪndʒd] *adj* (*заранее*)
подготовленный (подготовлен).

precarious [prɪ'kɛərɪəs] *adj* рискованный*
(рискован).

precaution [prɪ'kɔ:ʃən] *n* предосторожность *f*;
to take ~**s** принимать (принять* *perf*) меры
предосторожности.

precautionary [prɪ'kɔ:ʃənrɪ] *adj* (*measure*)
предупредительный.

precede [prɪ'si:d] *vt* предшествовать *(impf)*
+*dat*; (*person*) быть* *(impf)* впереди +*gen*.

precedence ['prɛsɪdəns] *n* (*priority*)
первоочерёдность *f*; **to take** ~ **over** быть*

(impf) важнее, чем.

precedent ['prɛsɪdənt] *n* прецедент; **to
establish** *or* **set a** ~ создавать* (создать* *perf*)
прецедент.

preceding [prɪ'si:dɪŋ] *adj* предыдущий*,
предшествующий*.

precept ['pri:sɛpt] *n* правило.

precinct ['pri:sɪŋkt] *n* (*US*: *part of city*) район,
префектура; (*round cathedral*) двор*; ~**s** *npl*
(*of large building*) территория *fsg*; **pedestrian**
~ (*BRIT*) пешеходная зона; **shopping** ~ (*BRIT*)
торговый центр.

precious ['prɛʃəs] *adj* (*commodity, object*)
ценный* (ценен); (*stone*) драгоценный; (*pej:
person, behaviour*) манерный ◆ *adv* (*inf*): ~
little *or* **few** очень мало; **your** ~ **dog** (*ironic*)
Ваша драгоценная собака.

precious stone *n* (*GEO*) драгоценный камень*
m.

precipice ['prɛsɪpɪs] *n* обрыв.

precipitate [*vb* prɪ'sɪpɪteɪt, *adj* prɪ'sɪpɪtɪt] *vt*
(*hasten*) ускорять (ускорить* *perf*) ◆ *adj*
скоропалительный* (скоропалителен).

precipitation [prɪsɪpɪ'teɪʃən] *n* (*rain*) осадки
mpl.

precipitous [prɪ'sɪpɪtəs] *adj* (*steep*) крутой*
(крут), обрывистый (обрывист); (*hasty*)
поспешный* (поспешен).

précis ['preɪsɪ] (*pl* ~) *n* конспект.

precise [prɪ'saɪs] *adj* точный* (точен).

precisely [prɪ'saɪslɪ] *adv* (*accurately*) точно;
(*exactly*) ровно; ~! вот именно!,
совершенно верно!

precision [prɪ'sɪʒən] *n* точность *f*.

preclude [prɪ'klu:d] *vt* предотвращать
(предотвратить* *perf*); **to** ~ **sb from doing**
мешать (помешать* *perf*) кому-н +*infin*.

precocious [prɪ'kəuʃəs] *adj* (*talent*) рано
развившийся; **a** ~ **child** не по годам
развитой ребёнок.

preconceived [pri:kən'si:vd] *adj* предвзятый
(предвзят).

preconception ['pri:kən'sɛpʃən] *n* предвзятое
мнение.

precondition ['pri:kən'dɪʃən] *n* непременное
условие, предпосылка*.

precursor [pri:'kə:səʳ] *n* (*person, thing*)
предтеча *m/f*.

predate ['pri:'deɪt] *vt* предшествовать *(impf)*
+*dat*.

predator ['prɛdətəʳ] *n* (*also fig*) хищник.

predatory ['prɛdətərɪ] *adj* (*animal*) хищный;
(*fig*) хищный* (хищен).

predecessor ['pri:dɪsɛsəʳ] *n* предшественник
(-ица).

predestination [pri:dɛstɪ'neɪʃən] *n* предо-
пределение.

predetermine [pri:dɪ'tə:mɪn] *vt*
предопределять (предопределить* *perf*).

predicament [prɪ'dɪkəmənt] *n* затруднение; **to
be in a** ~ быть* *(impf)* в затруднении.

predicate [ˈprɛdɪkɪt] *n* (*LING*) сказу́емое *nt adj*.
predict [prɪˈdɪkt] *vt* предска́зывать
(предсказа́ть* *perf*).
predictable [prɪˈdɪktəbl] *adj* предсказу́емый
(предсказу́ем).
predictably [prɪˈdɪktəblɪ] *adv* как и ожида́лось;
~ **she didn't arrive** как и ожида́лось, она́ не
пришла́.
prediction [prɪˈdɪkʃən] *n* предсказа́ние.
predispose [ˈpriːdɪsˈpəuz] *vt* предрасполага́ть
(предрасположи́ть* *perf*).
predominance [prɪˈdɔmɪnəns] *n* пре-
облада́ние; (*dominance*) госпо́дство.
predominant [prɪˈdɔmɪnənt] *adj*
домини́рующий, преоблада́ющий
(преоблада́ющ); **to become** ~ станови́ться*
(стать* *perf*) преоблада́ющим(-ей).
predominantly [prɪˈdɔmɪnəntlɪ] *adv*
преиму́щественно.
predominate [prɪˈdɔmɪneɪt] *vi* преоблада́ть
(*impf*).
pre-eminent [priːˈɛmɪnənt] *adj* выдаю́щийся*.
pre-empt [priːˈɛmt] *vt* предупрежда́ть
(предупреди́ть* *perf*); **to** ~ **the issue**
предупрежда́ть (предупреди́ть* *perf*)
собы́тия.
pre-emptive [priːˈɛmtɪv] *adj*: ~ **strike**
упрежда́ющий уда́р.
preen [priːn] *vt*: **to** ~ **itself** (*bird*) чи́стить*
(почи́стить* *perf*) пёрышки; **to** ~ **o.s.**
прихора́шиваться (*impf*).
prefab [ˈpriːfæb] *n* сбо́рный дом*.
prefabricated [priːˈfæbrɪkeɪtɪd] *adj* сбо́рный.
preface [ˈprɛfəs] *n* (*in book*) предисло́вие ♦ *vt*:
to ~ **sth with** предпосыла́ть (предпосла́ть*
perf) чему́-н +*acc*.
prefect [ˈpriːfɛkt] *n* (*BRIT*: *SCOL*) ста́роста *m/f*.
prefer [prɪˈfəːʳ] *vt* предпочита́ть (предпоче́сть*
perf); (*LAW*): **to** ~ **charges against** выдвига́ть
(вы́двинуть *perf*) обвине́ние про́тив +*gen*; **to**
~ **doing** *or* **to do** предпочита́ть (предпоче́сть*
perf) +*infin*; **I** ~ **coffee to tea** я предпочита́ю
ко́фе ча́ю.
preferable [ˈprɛfrəbl] *adj* предпочти́тельный*
(предпочти́телен).
preferably [ˈprɛfrəblɪ] *adv* предпочти́тельно.
preference [ˈprɛfrəns] *n* (*liking*): **to have a** ~ **for**
предпочита́ть (*impf*); (*priority*): **to give** ~ **to**
отдава́ть* (отда́ть* *perf*) предпочте́ние +*dat*;
in ~ **to sth** вме́сто чего́-н.
preference shares *npl* (*BRIT*: *COMM*)
привилегиро́ванные а́кции *fpl*.
preferential [prɛfəˈrɛnʃəl] *adj*: ~ **treatment**
осо́бое отноше́ние.
preferred stock [prɪˈfəd-] *npl* (*US*) = **preference
shares.**
prefix [ˈpriːfɪks] *n* приста́вка*, префикс.
pregnancy [ˈprɛgnənsɪ] *n* бере́менность *f*.

pregnancy test *n* ана́лиз на бере́менность.
pregnant [ˈprɛgnənt] *adj* бере́менная
(бере́менна); (*remark, pause*)
многозначи́тельный* (многозначи́телен);
she is 3 months ~ она́ на четвёртом ме́сяце
(бере́менности).
prehistoric [ˈpriːhɪsˈtɔrɪk] *adj* доистори́ческий*.
prehistory [priːˈhɪstərɪ] *n* первобы́тная
исто́рия.
prejudge [priːˈdʒʌdʒ] *vt* предреша́ть
(предреши́ть* *perf*).
prejudice [ˈprɛdʒudɪs] *n* (*unreasonable dislike*)
предрассу́док*; (*bias in favour*) предвзя́тость
f, предубежде́ние ♦ *vt* (*harm*) вреди́ть*
(повреди́ть* *perf*) +*dat*; **without** ~ **to** без
уще́рба для +*gen*; **to** ~ **sb in favour of**
располага́ть (расположи́ть* *perf*) кого́-н в
по́льзу +*gen*; **to** ~ **sb against** настра́ивать
(настро́ить *perf*) кого́-н про́тив +*gen*.
prejudiced [ˈprɛdʒudɪst] *adj* (*biased against*)
предубеждённый (предубеждён); (*in favour*)
располо́женный* (располо́жен); (*view*)
предвзя́тый (предвзя́т).
prelate [ˈprɛlət] *n* (*REL*) прела́т.
preliminaries [prɪˈlɪmɪnərɪz] *npl*
предвари́тельные мероприя́тия *ntpl*; (*in
competition*) предвари́тельный отбо́р *msg*.
preliminary [prɪˈlɪmɪnərɪ] *adj*
предвари́тельный.
prelude [ˈprɛljuːd] *n* (*MUS, fig*) прелю́дия.
premarital [ˈpriːˈmærɪtl] *adj* добра́чный.
premature [ˈprɛmətʃuəʳ] *adj*
преждевре́менный* (преждевре́мен); (*baby*)
недоно́шенный* (недоно́шен); **you are being
a little** ~ Вы не́сколько поторопи́лись.
premeditated [priːˈmɛdɪteɪtɪd] *adj*
преднаме́ренный* (преднаме́рен).
premeditation [priːmɛdɪˈteɪʃən] *n* разду́мье.
premenstrual tension [priːˈmɛnstruəl-] *n*
предменструа́льный синдро́м.
premier [ˈprɛmɪəʳ] *adj* (*best*) лу́чший* ♦ *n* (*POL*)
премье́р-мини́стр.
première [ˈprɛmɪɛəʳ] *n* премье́ра.
premise [ˈprɛmɪs] *n* предпосы́лка*; ~**s** *npl* (*of
business*) помеще́ние *ntsg*; **on the** ~**s** в
помеще́нии.
premium [ˈpriːmɪəm] *n* (*COMM, INSURANCE*)
пре́мия; **to be at a** ~ (*expensive*) сто́ить (*impf*)
вы́ше номина́ла; (*hard to get*) по́льзоваться
(*impf*) больши́м спро́сом; **to sell at a** ~
(*shares*) продава́ть* (прода́ть* *perf*) по цене́
вы́ше номина́ла.
premium bond *n* (*BRIT*) премиа́льная
(сберега́тельная) облига́ция.
premium deal *n* (*COMM*) премиа́льная
сде́лка*.
premium gasoline *n* (*US*) высокоокта́новый
бензи́н.

---

* marks translations which have irregular inflections. The Russian-English side of the dictionary gives inflectional information.

premonition [prɛmə'nɪʃən] *n* предчу́вствие.
preoccupation [pri:ɔkju'peɪʃən] *n*: ~ **with** озабо́ченность *f* +*instr*.
preoccupied [pri:'ɔkjupaɪd] *adj* озабо́ченный* (озабо́чен).
prep [prɛp] *adj abbr*: ~ **school** = *preparatory school*; (*BRIT*) ча́стная нача́льная шко́ла; (*US*) сре́дняя шко́ла ♦ *n abbr* = *preparation*.
prep *n* (*homework*) дома́шнее зада́ние.
prepaid [pri:'peɪd] *adj* зара́нее опла́ченный (опла́чен); (*envelope*) с зара́нее опла́ченными почто́выми расхо́дами.
preparation [prɛpə'reɪʃən] *n* (*activity*) подгото́вка*; (*of food*) приготовле́ние; (*medicine, cosmetic*) препара́т; ~**s** *npl* (*arrangements*) приготовле́ния *ntpl*; **in** ~ **for sth** гото́вясь к чему́-н.
preparatory [prɪ'pærətərɪ] *adj* подготови́тельный; ~ **to doing** пре́жде чем +*infin*.
preparatory school *n* (*BRIT*) ча́стная нача́льная шко́ла; (*US*) сре́дняя шко́ла.
prepare [prɪ'pɛə'] *vt* (*plan, speech, room etc*) подгота́вливать (подгото́вить* *perf*); (*CULIN*) гото́вить* (*impf*), пригота́вливать (пригото́вить* *perf*) ♦ *vi*: **to** ~ **for** (*event, action etc*) гото́виться* (*impf*) *or* подгота́вливаться (подгото́виться* *perf*) к +*dat*.
prepared [prɪ'pɛəd] *adj* гото́вый (гото́в); **I am** ~ **to help you** (*willing*) я гото́в помо́чь Вам; ~ **for** (*ready*) гото́вый (гото́в) к +*dat*.
preponderance [prɪ'pɔndərns] *n* (*of people, things*) преоблада́ние.
preposition [prɛpə'zɪʃən] *n* (*LING*) предло́г.
prepossessing [pri:pə'zɛsɪŋ] *adj* привлека́тельный* (привлека́телен).
preposterous [prɪ'pɔstərəs] *adj* (*outrageous*) ди́кий*.
prep school *n* = *preparatory school*.
prerecorded ['pri:rɪ'kɔ:dɪd] *adj* предвари́тельно запи́санный.
prerequisite [pri:'rɛkwɪzɪt] *n* предпосы́лка*, непреме́нное усло́вие.
prerogative [prɪ'rɔgətɪv] *n* прерогати́ва.
Presbyterian [prɛzbɪ'tɪərɪən] *n* (*REL*) пресвитериа́нин*(-а́нка*) ♦ *adj* пресвитериа́нский.
presbytery ['prɛzbɪtərɪ] *n* пресвите́рия.
preschool ['pri:'sku:l] *adj* (*age, education*) дошко́льный; ~ **child** ребёнок дошко́льного во́зраста.
prescribe [prɪ'skraɪb] *vt* (*MED*) пропи́сывать (прописа́ть* *perf*); (*action, duty*) предпи́сывать (предписа́ть* *perf*); ~**d books** (*BRIT*: *SCOL*) рекомендо́ванные уче́бники.
prescription [prɪ'skrɪpʃən] *n* (*MED*: *slip of paper*) реце́пт; (: *medicine*) лека́рство (назна́ченное врачо́м); **to make up** *or* (*US*) **fill a** ~ приготовля́ть (пригото́вить* *perf*) лека́рство по реце́пту; **"only available on** ~**"** „прода́жа лека́рства то́лько по реце́птам".

prescription charges *npl* (*BRIT*) минима́льная цена́ за лека́рства, отпуска́емые по реце́пту.
prescriptive [prɪ'skrɪptɪv] *adj* нормати́вный* (нормати́вен).
presence ['prɛzns] *n* прису́тствие; (*fig*) нару́жность *f*; **in sb's** ~ в кого́-н прису́тствии.
presence of mind *n* прису́тствие ду́ха.
present [*adj, n* 'prɛznt, *vt* 'prɛznt] *adj* (*current*) ны́нешний*, настоя́щий*; (*in attendance*) прису́тствующий ♦ *n* (*gift*) пода́рок*; (*LING*: *also*: ~ **tense**) настоя́щее вре́мя* *nt* ♦ *vt* представля́ть (предста́вить* *perf*); (*threat*) представля́ть (предста́вить* *perf*) собо́й; (*RADIO, TV*) вести́* (*impf*); (*give*): **to** ~ **sth to sb,** ~ **sb with sth** (*prize, award etc*) вруча́ть (вручи́ть* *perf*) что-н кому́-н; (*gift*) преподноси́ть* (преподнести́* *perf*) что-н кому́-н; (*formally introduce*): **to** ~ **sb (to)** представля́ть (предста́вить* *perf*) кого́-н (+*dat*); **to be** ~ **at** прису́тствовать (*impf*) на +*prp*; **those** ~ прису́тствующие; **the** ~ (*time*) настоя́щее *nt adj*; **at** ~ в настоя́щее вре́мя; **to give sb a** ~ дари́ть* (подари́ть* *perf*) кому́-н пода́рок.
presentable [prɪ'zɛntəbl] *adj* представи́тельный* (представи́телен), презента́бельный* (презента́белен).
presentation [prɛzn'teɪʃən] *n* (*of plan, report etc*) изложе́ние; (*appearance*) вне́шний* вид; (*also*: ~ **ceremony**) представле́ние, презента́ция; (*lecture, talk*) выступле́ние; **on** ~ **of** (*voucher etc*) по предъявле́нии +*gen*.
present-day ['prɛzntdeɪ] *adj* совреме́нный, ны́нешний*.
presenter [prɪ'zɛntə'] *n* (*RADIO, TV*) ди́ктор; (: *of news*) веду́щий*(-ая) *m(f) adj*.
presently ['prɛzntlɪ] *adv* вско́ре; (*now*) в да́нный моме́нт, в настоя́щее вре́мя.
present participle *n* прича́стие настоя́щего вре́мени.
preservation [prɛzə'veɪʃən] *n* (*act: of building, democracy*) сохране́ние; (: *of food*) хране́ние; (*state*) сохра́нность *f*.
preservative [prɪ'zə:vətɪv] *n* (*for food*) консерва́нт; (*for wood*) пропи́точный соста́в; (*for metal*) защи́тное сре́дство.
preserve [prɪ'zə:v] *vt* сохраня́ть (сохрани́ть* *perf*); (*food*) консерви́ровать (законсерви́ровать *perf*); (*keep safe*) оберега́ть (*impf*), охраня́ть (*impf*) ♦ *n* (*often pl*: *jam*) варе́нье; (*for game, fish*) запове́дник; **a working class** ~ стихи́я рабо́чего кла́сса; **a male** ~ чи́сто мужско́е заня́тие.
preshrunk ['pri:'ʃrʌŋk] *adj*: ~ **fabric** ткань, проше́дшая предвари́тельную уса́дку.
preside [prɪ'zaɪd] *vi*: **to** ~ **(over)** председа́тельствовать (*impf*) (на +*prp*).
presidency ['prɛzɪdənsɪ] *n* президе́нтство.
president ['prɛzɪdənt] *n* (*POL, COMM*) президе́нт;

(*US: SCOL*) ре́ктор.

presidential [prɛzɪ'dɛnʃl] *adj* (*election, campaign etc*) президе́нтский; ~ **candidate** кандида́т в президе́нты; ~ **adviser** сове́тник президе́нта.

press [prɛs] *n* (*also*: **printing** ~) печа́тный стано́к*; (*of switch, button, bell*) кно́пка*; (*for wine*) пресс для виногра́да; (*crowd*) да́вка ◆ *vt* (*hold together*) прижима́ть (прижа́ть* *perf*); (*push*) нажима́ть (нажа́ть* *perf*); (*iron*) гла́дить* (погла́дить* *perf*); (*put pressure on: person*) наста́ивать (настоя́ть *perf*); (*squeeze*) выжима́ть (вы́жать* *perf*); (*pursue*) добива́ться (доби́ться* *perf*) +*gen* ◆ *vi* (*squeeze*) жать* (*impf*), дави́ть* (*impf*); **the** ~ (*newspapers, journalists*) пре́сса; **to go to** ~ идти́* (*impf*) в печа́ть; **to be in the** ~ (*being printed*) находи́ться* (*impf*) в печа́ти; (*in the newspapers*) быть* (*impf*) в газе́тах; **we are** ~**ed for time/money** у нас ма́ло вре́мени/ де́нег; **to** ~ **sth on sb** (*insist*) навя́зывать (навяза́ть* *perf*) что-н кому́-н; **to** ~ **sb to do** *or* **into doing** вынужда́ть (вы́нудить *perf*) кого́-н +*infin*; **to** ~ **sb for an answer** торопи́ть* (поторопи́ть* *perf*) кого́-н с отве́том; **to** ~ **charges against sb** выдвига́ть (вы́двинуть *perf*) обвине́ния про́тив кого́-н; **to** ~ **for** (*improvement, change etc*) наста́ивать (настоя́ть *perf*) на +*prp*

▸ **press ahead** *vi* приступа́ть (приступи́ть* *perf*) к де́лу

▸ **press on** *vi* продолжа́ть (*impf*).

press agency *n* аге́нтство печа́ти.

press clipping *n* газе́тная вы́резка.

press conference *n* пресс-конфере́нция.

press cutting *n* = **press clipping**.

press-gang ['prɛsgæŋ] *vt*: **to** ~ **sb into doing** наси́льно заставля́ть (заста́вить* *perf*) кого́-н +*infin*.

pressing ['prɛsɪŋ] *adj* (*urgent*) сро́чный* (сро́чен), неотло́жный* (неотло́жен).

press officer *n* сотру́дник(-ица) отде́ла информа́ции.

press release *n* сообще́ние для печа́ти.

press stud *n* (*BRIT*) одёжная кно́пка*.

press-up ['prɛsʌp] *n* (*BRIT: SPORT*) отжима́ние, отжи́м.

pressure ['prɛʃə'] *n* давле́ние; (*stress*) напряже́ние ◆ *vt*: **to** ~ **sb (to do)** принужда́ть (прину́дить* *perf*) кого́-н (+*infin*); **to put** ~ **on sb (to do)** ока́зывать (оказа́ть* *perf*) давле́ние *or* нажи́м на кого́-н (+*infin*); **high/low** ~ высо́кое/ни́зкое давле́ние.

pressure cooker *n* скорова́рка*.

pressure gauge *n* мано́метр.

pressure group *n* инициати́вная гру́ппа.

pressurize ['prɛʃəraɪz] *vt*: **to** ~ **sb (to do** *or* **into doing)** ока́зывать (оказа́ть* *perf*) давле́ние на

кого́-н (+*infin*).

pressurized ['prɛʃəraɪzd] *adj* (*cabin, container, spacesuit*) гермети́чный.

Prestel® ['prɛstɛl] *n* Пре́стел.

prestige [prɛs'tiːʒ] *n* прести́ж.

prestigious [prɛs'tɪdʒəs] *adj* прести́жный* (прести́жен).

presumably [prɪ'zjuːməblɪ] *adv* наве́рно; ~ **he did it** наве́рно, э́то сде́лал он.

presume [prɪ'zjuːm] *vt*: **to** ~ **(that)** (*suppose*) предполага́ть (предположи́ть* *perf*)(, что); **to** ~ **to do** (*dare*) реша́ться (реши́ться *perf*) +*infin*.

presumption [prɪ'zʌmpʃən] *n* предположе́ние.

presumptuous [prɪ'zʌmpʃəs] *adj* самонаде́янный* (самонаде́ян).

presuppose [priːsə'pəuz] *vt* прелpolaга́ть (предположи́ть* *perf*).

presupposition [priːsʌpə'zɪʃən] *n* предположе́ние.

pretax [priː'tæks] *adj* (*profit*) до вы́чета нало́гов.

pretence [prɪ'tɛns] (*US* **pretense**) *n* (*false appearance*) притво́рство; (*excuse*) предло́г; **under false** ~**s** под ло́жным предло́гом; **she is devoid of all** ~ она́ соверше́нно лишена́ притво́рства; **he is making a** ~ **of helping** он де́лает вид, что помога́ет.

pretend [prɪ'tɛnd] *vi*: **to** ~ **that** притворя́ться (притвори́ться *perf*), что; **he** ~**ed to help** он притвори́лся, что помога́ет; **to** ~ **to sth** (*make claim*) претендова́ть (*impf*) на что-н.

pretense [prɪ'tɛns] *n* (*US*) = **pretence**.

pretentious [prɪ'tɛnʃəs] *adj* претенцио́зный* (претенцио́зен).

preterite ['prɛtərɪt] *n* прете́рит.

pretext ['priːtɛkst] *n* предло́г; **on** *or* **under the** ~ **of being busy/tired** под предло́гом за́нятости/уста́лости.

Pretoria [prɪ'tɔːrɪə] *n* Прето́рия.

pretty ['prɪtɪ] *adj* (*person*) хоро́шенький*; (*thing*) краси́вый (краси́в) ◆ *adv* (*quite*) дово́льно.

prevail [prɪ'veɪl] *vi* (*be current*) преоблада́ть (*impf*), превали́ровать (*impf*); (*gain influence*) оде́рживать (одержа́ть *perf*) верх; (*persuade*): **to** ~ **(up)on sb to do** убежда́ть (убеди́ть* *perf*) кого́-н +*infin*.

prevailing [prɪ'veɪlɪŋ] *adj* (*wind*) преоблада́ющий; (*fashion, attitude*) превали́рующий.

prevalent ['prɛvələnt] *adj* (*belief, custom*) преоблада́ющий; (*fashion*) превали́рующий; (*disease*) распространённый* (распростране́н).

prevaricate [prɪ'værɪkeɪt] *vi* извора́чиваться (*impf*).

prevarication [prɪværɪ'keɪʃən] *n* виля́ние.

---

* marks translations which have irregular inflections. The Russian-English side of the dictionary gives inflectional information.

prevent [prɪ'vɛnt] *vt* (*accident etc*) предотвращать (предотвратить* *perf*); **to ~ sb from doing** мешать (помешать *perf*) кому́-н +*infin*; **this policy ~s inflation from rising** эта поли́тика препя́тствует ро́сту инфля́ции.

preventable [prɪ'vɛntəbl] *adj* предотврати́мый (предотврати́м).

preventative [prɪ'vɛntətɪv] *adj* = **preventive**.

prevention [prɪ'vɛnʃən] *n* предотвраще́ние, предупрежде́ние.

preventive [prɪ'vɛntɪv] *adj* (*measures*) предупреди́тельный; (: *POL*) превенти́вный; (*medicine*) профилакти́ческий*.

preview ['priːvjuː] *n* (*of film*) (закры́тый) просмо́тр; (*fig*) предвари́тельная карти́на.

previous ['priːvɪəs] *adj* предыду́щий*; **I have a ~ engagement** э́то вре́мя у меня́ уже́ за́нято; **~ to** до +*gen*.

previously ['priːvɪəslɪ] *adv* (*before*) ра́нее; (*in the past*) пре́жде; **I retired two years ~** я ушёл на пе́нсию двумя́ года́ми ра́нее.

prewar [priː'wɔːʳ] *adj* довое́нный, предвое́нный.

prey [preɪ] *n* добы́ча ♦ *vi*: **to ~ on** (*animal: feed on*) охо́титься* (*impf*) на +*acc*; **it was ~ing on his mind** э́то терза́ло его́.

price [praɪs] *n* (*also fig*) цена́* ♦ *vt* (*goods*) оце́нивать (оцени́ть* *perf*); **what is the ~ of ...?** ско́лько сто́ит ...?; **to go up** *or* **rise in ~** дорожа́ть (вздорожа́ть *or* подорожа́ть *perf*); **to put a ~ on sth** назнача́ть (назна́чить *perf*) це́ну чему́-н; **Britain has been out of the market** Великобрита́ния была́ вы́теснена из ры́нка из-за завыше́ния цен; **what ~ his promises now?** (*BRIT*) что сто́ят все его́ обеща́ния сейча́с?; **he regained his freedom, but at a ~** он получи́л свобо́ду, но дорого́й цено́й.

price control *n* контро́ль *m* за це́нами.

price cutting *n* сниже́ние цен.

priceless ['praɪslɪs] *adj* бесце́нный* (бесце́нен); (*inf: amusing*) бесподо́бный* (бесподо́бен).

price list *n* прейскура́нт.

price range *n* диапазо́н цен; **it's within my ~ ~** э́то мне по карма́ну.

price tag *n* це́нник; (*fig*) цена́*.

price war *n* война́ цен.

pricey ['praɪsɪ] *adj* (*inf*) дорого́й.

prick [prɪk] *n* (*short, sharp pain*) уко́л; (*ANAT: infl*) хуй (*!*) ♦ *vt* (*make hole in*) прока́лывать (проколо́ть* *perf*); (*cause pain to*) уколо́ть* (*perf*); **to ~ up one's ears** (*listen eagerly*) навостри́ть (*perf*) у́ши.

prickle ['prɪkl] *n* (*of plant*) шип*, коло́чка*; (*sensation*) пока́лывание.

prickly ['prɪklɪ] *adj* колю́чий* (колю́ч).

prickly heat *n* потни́ца.

prickly pear *n* (*BOT*) опу́нция.

pride [praɪd] *n* го́рдость *f*; (*pej: feeling of superiority*) горды́ня ♦ *vt*: **to ~ o.s. on** горди́ться* (*impf*) +*instr*; **to take (a) ~ in**

горди́ться* (*impf*) +*instr*; **I take (a) ~ in working well** я горжу́сь тем что я рабо́таю хорошо́; **to have ~ of place** (*BRIT*) занима́ть (заня́ть* *perf*) почётное ме́сто.

priest [priːst] *n* свяще́нник; (*non-Christian*) жрец*.

priestess ['priːstɪs] *n* (*non-Christian*) жри́ца.

priesthood ['priːsthud] *n* свяще́нство.

prig [prɪg] *n*: **he's a ~** он така́я ца́ца.

prim [prɪm] *adj* чо́порный* (чо́порен).

primacy ['praɪməsɪ] *n* пе́рвенство.

prima-facie ['praɪmə'feɪʃɪ] *adj*: **to have a ~ case** (*LAW*) разбира́ть (*impf*) я́сное суде́бное де́ло*.

primal ['praɪməl] *adj* (*instinct*) перви́чный; (*cause*) изнача́льный; **~ scream** пе́рвый крик (младе́нца).

primarily ['praɪmərɪlɪ] *adv* в пе́рвую о́чередь.

primary ['praɪmərɪ] *adj* (*first in importance*) первостепе́нный* (первостепе́нен), первоочередно́й ♦ *n* (*US: POL*) предвари́тельные вы́боры *mpl*; **~ education** нача́льное образова́ние; **~ teacher** учи́тель(ница) *m(f)* нача́льных кла́ссов.

primary colour *n* основно́й цвет*.

primary school *n* (*BRIT*) нача́льная шко́ла.

primate ['praɪmɪt] *n* (*ZOOL*) прима́т; (*REL*) при́мас.

prime [praɪm] *adj* (*most important*) гла́вный, основно́й; (*best quality*) первосо́ртный ♦ *n* (*of person's life*) расцве́т ♦ *vt* (*wood, canvas*) грунтова́ть (загрунтова́ть *perf*); (*fig: person*) подгота́вливать (подгото́вить* *perf*); (*gun*) заряжа́ть (заряди́ть *perf*); (*pump*) залива́ть (зали́ть* *perf*); **in the ~ of life** в расцве́те сил, во цве́те лет; **~ example** (*typical*) я́ркий* приме́р.

Prime Minister *n* премье́р-мини́стр.

primer ['praɪməʳ] *n* (*paint*) грунто́вка; (*book*) уче́бник-введе́ние.

prime time *n* (*RADIO, TV*) лу́чшее эфи́рное вре́мя* *nt*.

primeval [praɪ'miːvl] *adj* первобы́тный.

primitive ['prɪmɪtɪv] *adj* (*early*) первобы́тный; (*unsophisticated: way of life, tool etc*) примити́вный* (примити́вен).

primrose ['prɪmrəuz] *n* первоцве́т.

primula ['prɪmjulə] *n* при́мула.

Primus® ['praɪməs] *n* (*BRIT: also: p~ stove*) при́мус.

prince [prɪns] *n* принц; (*Russian*) князь* *m*.

prince charming *n* прекра́сный принц.

princess [prɪn'sɛs] *n* принце́сса; (*Russian*) княги́ня, княжна́*.

principal ['prɪnsɪpl] *adj* гла́вный, основно́й ♦ *n* (*of school, college*) дире́ктор*; (*of university*) ре́ктор; (*in play*) веду́щий*(-ая) актёр (-три́са); (*money*) капита́л.

principality [prɪnsɪ'pælɪtɪ] *n* кня́жество.

principally ['prɪnsɪplɪ] *adv* преиму́щественно, гла́вным о́бразом.

principle ['prɪnsɪpl] *n* при́нцип; (*scientific law*)

закóн; **in** ~ в при́нципе; **on** ~ из при́нципа.
print [print] *n* (*TYP*) шрифт*; (*ART*)
гравю́ра; (*PHOT, fingerprint*) отпеча́ток*;
(*footprint*) след*; (*fabric*) си́тец* ◆ *vt* (*book etc*)
печа́тать (напеча́тать *perf*); (*cloth*) набива́ть
(наби́ть* *perf*); (*write in capitals*) писа́ть*
(написа́ть* *perf*) печа́тными бу́квами; **this
book is out of** ~ э́та кни́га распро́дана
▸ **print out** *vt* (*COMPUT*) распеча́тывать
(распеча́тать *perf*), выводи́ть* (вы́йти* *perf*)
на печа́ть.
printed circuit board ['printid-] *n* (*ELEC*)
печа́тная схе́ма *or* пла́та.
printed matter *n* печа́тные материа́лы *mpl*.
printer ['printə'] *n* (*person*) печа́тник;
(*machine*) при́нтер; (*firm: also:* ~'s)
типогра́фия.
printhead ['printhɛd] *n* (*COMPUT*) печа́тающая
голо́вка.
printing ['printiŋ] *n* (*act*) печа́тание; (*art*)
печа́тное де́ло.
printing press *n* печа́тный стано́к*.
print-out ['printaut] *n* (*COMPUT*) распеча́тка*.
print wheel *n* (*COMPUT*) печа́тающее колесо́*.
prior ['praiə'] *adj* (*previous*) пре́жний*; (*more
important*) первоочередно́й ◆ *n* (*REL*)
настоя́тель *m*, прио́р; **without** ~ **notice** без
предвари́тельного предупрежде́ния; **to have**
~ **knowledge of sth** знать* (*impf*) о чём-н
зара́нее; **to have a** ~ **claim to sth** име́ть (*impf*)
первоочередно́е *or* преиму́щественное
пра́во на что-н; ~ **to** до +*gen*.
priority [prai'ɔriti] *n* (*most urgent task*)
первоочередна́я зада́ча; (*most important
thing, task*) приорите́т; **to have** ~ **(over)**
име́ть (*impf*) преиму́щество (пе́ред +*instr*).
priory ['praiəri] *n* монасты́рь* *m*.
prise [praiz] *vt*: **to** ~ **open** взла́мывать
(взлома́ть *perf*).
prism ['prizəm] *n* при́зма.
prison ['prizn] *n* тюрьма́* ◆ *cpd* тюре́мный.
prison camp *n* исправи́тельно-трудово́й
ла́герь* *m*.
prisoner ['priznə'] *n* (*in prison*) заключённый
(-ая) *m(f) adj*; (*captured person*) пле́нный(-ая)
m(f) adj; **the** ~ **at the bar** подсуди́мый(-ая) *m(f)
adj*; **to take sb** ~ брать* (взять* *perf*) кого́-н в
плен.
prisoner of war *n* военнопле́нный *m adj*.
prissy ['prisi] *adj* (*pej*) чо́порный.
pristine ['pristi:n] *adj* безупре́чный*
(безупре́чен).
privacy ['privəsi] *n* уедине́ние; **invasion of sb's**
~ вторже́ние в чью-н ча́стную жизнь.
private ['praivit] *adj* (*not public: property,
industry*) ча́стный; (: *discussion, club*)
закры́тый; (*personal, confidential*:
belongings, life) ли́чный; (: *thoughts, plans*)

скры́тый; (*secluded*: *place*) уединённый
(уединён); (*secretive, reserved*) за́мкнутый
(за́мкнут); (*confidential*)
конфиденциа́льный* (конфиденциа́лен) ◆ *n*
(*MIL*) рядово́й *m adj*; *"private"* (*on envelope*)
„ли́чно"; (*on door*) „посторо́нним вход
воспрещён"; в ~ конфиденциа́льно; **in** (**his**)
~ **life** в (его́) ли́чной жи́зни; **he is a very** ~
person он о́чень за́мкнутый челове́к; **to be in**
~ **practice** име́ть (*impf*) ча́стную пра́ктику; ~
hearing (*LAW*) закры́тое слу́шание.
private enterprise *n* (*economic activity*)
ча́стное предпринима́тельство.
private eye *n* ча́стный сы́щик.
private limited company *n* (*BRIT*) ча́стная
акционе́рная компа́ния.
privately ['praivitli] *adv* (*discuss*) конфиденци-
а́льно; (*act*) в ча́стном поря́дке; (*within o.s.*)
в душе́.
private parts *npl* (*ANAT*) (нару́жные) половы́е
о́рганы *mpl*.
private property *n* ча́стная со́бственность *f*.
private school *n* ча́стная шко́ла.
privation [prai'veiʃən] *n* (*state*) лише́ния *ntpl*.
privatize ['praivitaiz] *vt* приватизи́ровать (*impf/
perf*).
privet ['privit] *n* (*BOT*) бирючи́на.
privilege ['privilidʒ] *n* привиле́гия.
privileged ['privilidʒd] *adj*
привилегиро́ванный; **to be** ~ **to do** име́ть
(*impf*) честь +*infin*.
privy ['privi] *adj*: ~ **to** поцвещённый в +*acc*.
Privy Council *n* (*BRIT*) Та́йный Сове́т.
Privy Councillor *n* (*BRIT*) Та́йный Сове́тник.
prize [praiz] *n* приз*; (*money*) пре́мия ◆ *adj*
(*first-class*) первокла́ссный; (*example, idiot*)
класси́ческий* ◆ *vt* (*высоко*) цени́ть (*impf*).
prizefighter ['praizfaitə'] *n* профессиона́льный
боксёр.
prize-giving ['praizgiviŋ] *n* церемо́ния
вруче́ния награ́д за хоро́шую успева́емость.
prize money *n* призовы́е де́ньги* *pl*.
prizewinner ['praizwinə'] *n* призёр, лауреа́т.
prizewinning ['praizwiniŋ] *adj* (*person*)
удосто́енный награ́ды; (*animal*) призово́й;
(*novel, essay etc*) удосто́енный пре́мии.
PRO *n abbr* = **public relations officer**.
pro [prəu] *n* (*SPORT: inf*) профессиона́л ◆ *prep*
(*in favour of*) за +*acc*; **the** ~**s and cons**
(до́воды) „за" и „про́тив".
pro- [prəu] *prefix* про-.
proactive [prəu'æktiv] *adj* де́йственный.
probability [prɔbə'biliti] *n*: ~ **of/that**
вероя́тность *f* +*gen*/что; **in all** ~ по всей
вероя́тности.
probable ['prɔbəbl] *adj* вероя́тный*
(вероя́тен); **it seems** ~ **that** ...
представля́ется вероя́тным, что ....

---

probably ['prɔbəblɪ] *adv* вероя́тно.

probate ['prəubɪt] *n* утвержде́ние завеща́ния.

probation [prə'beɪʃən] *n*: **he is on ~** (*LAW*) он осуждён усло́вно; (*employee*) он прохо́дит испыта́тельный срок; (*REL*) он отбыва́ет по́слух.

probationary [prə'beɪʃənrɪ] *adj* (*period*) испыта́тельный.

probationer [prə'beɪʃənəʳ] *n* (*LAW*) усло́вно осуждённый.

probation officer *n должностно́е лицо́, осуществля́ющее надзо́р за усло́вно осуждёнными.*

probe [prəub] *n* (*MED, SPACE*) зонд; (*enquiry*) рассле́дование ♦ *vt* (*investigate*) рассле́довать (*impf/perf*); (*poke*) прощу́пывать (*impf*).

probity ['prəubɪtɪ] *n* че́стность *f*.

problem ['prɔbləm] *n* пробле́ма; **we are having ~s with the car** у нас непола́дки с маши́ной; **what's the ~?** в чём де́ло?; **I had no ~ in finding her** я нашёл её без труда́; **no ~!** нет пробле́м!

problematic(al) [prɔblə'mætɪk(l)] *adj* проблемати́чный* (проблемати́чен).

problem-solving ['prɔbləmsɔlvɪŋ] *n уме́ние находи́ть вы́ход из тру́дного положе́ния.*

procedural [prə'si:djurəl] *adj* процеду́рный.

procedure [prə'si:dʒəʳ] *n* процеду́ра.

proceed [prə'si:d] *vi* (*subj: activity, event, process: carry on*) продолжа́ться (продо́лжиться *perf*); (*person: go*) дви́гаться (дви́нуться *perf*); (*continue*): **to ~ (with)** продолжа́ть (продо́лжить *perf*); **to ~ to do** продолжа́ть (продо́лжить *perf*) +*infin*; **to ~ against sb** (*LAW*) возбужда́ть (возбуди́ть* *perf*) де́ло про́тив кого́-н.

proceedings [prə'si:dɪŋz] *npl* (*organized events*) собы́тия *ntpl*; (*LAW*) суде́бное разбира́тельство *ntsg*; (*minutes*) протоко́л *msg*.

proceeds ['prəusi:dz] *npl* поступле́ния *ntpl*.

process ['prəusɛs] *n* проце́сс ♦ *vt* (*also COMPUT*) обраба́тывать (обрабо́тать *perf*) ♦ *vi* (*BRIT: go in procession*) уча́ствовать (*impf*) в проце́ссии; **in ~** в проце́ссе; **we are in the ~ of moving house** сейча́с мы переезжа́ем.

processed cheese ['prəusɛst-] (*US* **process cheese**) *n* пла́вленый сыр*.

processing ['prəusɛsɪŋ] *n* (*PHOT*) обрабо́тка*.

procession [prə'sɛʃən] *n* проце́ссия.

pro-choice [prəu'tʃɔɪs] *adj защища́ющий пра́во же́нщины на або́рт.*

proclaim [prə'kleɪm] *vt* провозглаша́ть (провозгласи́ть* *perf*).

proclamation [prɔklə'meɪʃən] *n* провоз-глаше́ние.

proclivity [prə'klɪvɪtɪ] *n* накло́нность *f*.

procrastinate [prəu'kræstɪneɪt] *vi* оття́гивать (оттяну́ть* *perf*).

procrastination [prəukræstɪ'neɪʃən] *n*

оття́гивание.

procreation [prəukrɪ'eɪʃən] *n* размноже́ние.

procurator fiscal ['prɔkjureɪtə-] *n* (*SCOTTISH: LAW*) прокуро́р.

procure [prə'kjuəʳ] *vt* приобрета́ть (приобрести́* *perf*).

procurement [prə'kjuəmənt] *n* приобрете́ние.

prod [prɔd] *vt* ты́кать* (ткнуть *perf*); (*fig: remind*) подстёгивать (подстегну́ть *perf*) ♦ *n* (*see vb*) тычо́к*; (*fig*) напомина́ние.

prodigal ['prɔdɪgl] *adj* блу́дный.

prodigious [prə'dɪdʒəs] *adj* огро́мный* (огро́мен).

prodigy ['prɔdɪdʒɪ] *n* (*person*) тала́нт; (*achievement*) успе́хи *mpl*; **child ~** вундерки́нд.

produce [*vt* prə'dju:s, *n* 'prɔdju:s] *vt* (*object, offspring, effect*) производи́ть* (произвести́* *perf*); (*BIO, CHEM*) выраба́тывать (вы́работать *perf*); (*evidence, argument*) представля́ть (предста́вить* *perf*); (*bring or take out*) предъявля́ть (предъяви́ть* *perf*); (*play, film*) ста́вить* (поста́вить* *perf*) ♦ *n* (*AGR*) проду́кция.

producer [prə'dju:səʳ] *n* (*of film, play*) режиссёр-постано́вщик, проддю́сер; (*of record*) проддю́сер; (*country, company*) производи́тель *m*.

product ['prɔdʌkt] *n* (*thing*) изде́лие; (*food, result*) проду́кт.

production [prə'dʌkʃən] *n* (*process*) произво́дство; (*amount produced*) проду́кция; (*of electricity etc*) вы́работка*; (*THEAT*) постано́вка*; **to put into ~** (*goods*) запуска́ть (запусти́ть* *perf*) в произво́дство.

production agreement *n* (*US*) соглаше́ние о долево́м распределе́нии проду́кции.

production line *n* пото́чная ли́ния.

production manager *n* руководи́тель *m* произво́дством.

productive [prə'dʌktɪv] *adj* (*also fig*) производи́тельный* (производи́телен), продукти́вный* (продукти́вен).

productivity [prɔdʌk'tɪvɪtɪ] *n* произ-води́тельность *f*, продукти́вность *f*.

productivity agreement *n* (*BRIT*) догово́р о производи́тельности труда́.

productivity bonus *n* пре́мия за высо́кую производи́тельность труда́.

Prof. *n abbr* = professor.

profane [prə'feɪn] *adj* (*secular*) све́тский*; (*language etc*) богоху́льный* (богоху́лен).

profess [prə'fɛs] *vt* (*claim*) претендова́ть (*impf*) на +*acc*; (*express*) заявля́ть (заяви́ть* *perf*) о +*prp*; (*REL*) испове́довать (*impf/perf*); **I do not ~ to be an expert** я не претенду́ю на роль специали́ста.

professed [prə'fɛst] *adj* (*self-declared*) открове́нный.

profession [prə'fɛʃən] *n* профе́ссия; **the ~s** „профе́ссии с большо́й бу́квы" (*ЮР, МЕД*,

РЕЛ).

professional [prə'fɛʃənl] *adj* профессиона́льный ◆ *n* (*doctor, lawyer, teacher etc*) специали́ст; (*skilled person, also SPORT*) профессиона́л; **he's a ~ man** он – челове́к с образова́нием; **to take ~ advice** получа́ть (получи́ть* *perf*) профессиона́льный сове́т.

professionalism [prə'fɛʃnəlɪzəm] *n* профессионали́зм.

professionally [prə'fɛʃnəlɪ] *adv* (*also SPORT, MUS*) профессиона́льно; **I only know him ~** я зна́ю его́ то́лько по рабо́те.

professor [prə'fɛsə'] *n* (*BRIT*) профе́ссор; (*US*) преподава́тель(ница) *m(f)*.

professorship [prə'fɛsəʃɪp] *n* профе́ссорство.

proffer ['prɔfə'] *vt* (*remark*) выска́зывать (вы́сказать* *perf*); (*apologies*) приноси́ть* (принести́* *perf*); (*one's hand*) протя́гивать (протяну́ть* *perf*).

proficiency [prə'fɪʃənsɪ] *n* квалифика́ция, уме́ние.

proficient [prə'fɪʃənt] *adj* уме́лый; **to be ~ at sth** (*at sth mental*) быть* (*impf*) знатоко́м чем-н; **he is ~ at swimming** он ма́стерски пла́вает.

profile ['prəufaɪl] *n* (*of face*) про́филь *m*; (*article*) о́черк; **to keep a high ~** (*fig*) находи́ться* (*impf*) в це́нтре (обще́ственного) внима́ния; **to keep a low ~** (*fig*) стара́ться (*impf*) не выделя́ться.

profit ['prɔfɪt] *n* при́быль *f*, дохо́д ◆ *vi*: **to ~ by** *or* **from** (*fig*) извлека́ть (извле́чь* *perf*) вы́году из +*gen*; **~ and loss account** счёт при́былей и убы́тков; **to make a ~** получа́ть (получи́ть* *perf*) при́быль; **to sell (sth) at a ~** продава́ть* (прода́ть* *perf*) (что-н) с вы́годой.

profitability [prɔfɪtə'bɪlɪtɪ] *n* при́быльность *f*.

profitable ['prɔfɪtəbl] *adj* при́быльный* (при́былен); (*fig*) вы́годный* (вы́годен).

profit centre *n* (*COMM*) „центр получе́ния при́были".

profiteering [prɔfɪ'tɪərɪŋ] *n* (*pej*) спекуля́ция.

profitmaking ['prɔfɪtmeɪkɪŋ] *adj* при́быльный* (при́былен).

profit margin *n* ма́ржа при́быльности.

profit-sharing ['prɔfɪtʃɛərɪŋ] *n* уча́стие (слу́жащих) в при́былях.

profits tax *n* (*BRIT*) нало́г с при́были.

profligate ['prɔflɪgɪt] *adj*: **~ (with)** расточи́тельный* (расточи́телен) (в +*prp*).

pro forma ['prəu'fɔ:mə] *adj*: **~ ~ invoice** предвари́тельный счёт-факту́ра.

profound [prə'faund] *adj* глубо́кий* (глубо́к).

profuse [prə'fju:s] *adj* оби́льный* (оби́лен).

profusely [prə'fju:slɪ] *adv* оби́льно; (*apologize*) горячо́.

profusion [prə'fju:зən] *n* оби́льность *f*.

progeny ['prɔdʒɪnɪ] *n* пото́мство.

prognoses [prɔg'nəusi:z] *npl of* **prognosis**.

prognosis [prɔg'nəusɪs] (*pl* **prognoses**) *n* прогно́з.

program ['prəugræm] *n* (*COMPUT*) програ́мма ◆ *vt* (*COMPUT*) программиова́ть (запрограмми́ровать *perf*).

programme ['prəugræm] (*US* **program**) *n* програ́мма ◆ *vt* программи́ровать (запрограмми́ровать *perf*).

programmer ['prəugræmə'] *n* (*COMPUT*) программи́ст(ка*).

programming ['prəugræmɪŋ] (*US* **programing**) *n* (*COMPUT*) программи́рование.

programming language *n* (*COMPUT*) язы́к* программи́рования.

progress [*n* 'prəugrɛs, *vi* prə'grɛs] *n* (*advances, changes*) прогре́сс; (*development*) разви́тие ◆ *vi* прогресси́ровать (*impf*); (*move up in rank*) продвига́ться (продви́нуться *perf*) (по слу́жбе); (*continue*) продолжа́ться (продо́лжиться* *perf*); **the meeting/match is in ~** сейча́с идёт собра́ние/матч; **to make ~** де́лать (сде́лать *perf*) успе́хи; **as the match ~ed** по хо́ду ма́тча.

progression [prə'grɛʃən] *n* (*gradual development*) продвиже́ние; (*series*) череда́; (*MATH*) прогре́ссия.

progressive [prə'grɛsɪv] *adj* прогресси́вный* (прогресси́вен); (*gradual*) постепе́нный.

progressively [prə'grɛsɪvlɪ] *adv*: **the work became ~ harder** рабо́та станови́лась всё трудне́е.

progress report *n* (*MED*) протоко́л о хо́де боле́зни; (*ADMIN*) докла́д о хо́де дел.

prohibit [prə'hɪbɪt] *vt* запреща́ть (запрети́ть* *perf*); **to ~ sb from doing** запреща́ть (запрети́ть* *perf*) кому́-н +*infin*; **"smoking ~ed"** „кури́ть воспреща́ется".

prohibition [prəuɪ'bɪʃən] *n* запреще́ние, запре́т; **P~** сухо́й зако́н.

prohibitive [prə'hɪbɪtɪv] *adj* (*price etc*) недосту́пный* (недосту́пен).

project [*n* 'prɔdʒɛkt, *vb* prə'dʒɛkt] *n* (*large-scale plan, scheme*) прое́кт; (*SCOL*) рабо́та ◆ *vt* (*plan, estimate*) проекти́ровать (*impf*); (*film*) демонстри́ровать (продемонстри́ровать *perf*); (*light, picture*) проеци́ровать (спроеци́ровать *perf*) ◆ *vi* (*stick out*) выступа́ть (вы́ступить* *perf*).

projectile [prə'dʒɛktaɪl] *n* снаря́д.

projection [prə'dʒɛkʃən] *n* (*estimate*) перспекти́вная оце́нка*; (*overhang*) вы́ступ; (*CINEMA*) прое́кция.

projectionist [prə'dʒɛkʃənɪst] *n* (*CINEMA*) киномеха́ник.

projection room *n* бу́дка киномеха́ника, проекцио́нная каби́на.

projector [prə'dʒɛktə'] *n* (*CINEMA*)

кинопроéктор; (*also*: **slide** ~) проéктор.

proletarian [prəʊlɪˈtɛərɪən] *adj* пролетáрский*.

proletariat [prəʊlɪˈtɛərɪət] *n*: **the** ~
пролетариáт.

pro-life [prəʊˈlaɪf] *adj выступáющий прóтив
абóртов.*

proliferate [prəˈlɪfəreɪt] *vi* распространя́ться
(распространи́ться *perf*).

proliferation [prəlɪfəˈreɪʃən] *n* рас-
пространéние.

prolific [prəˈlɪfɪk] *adj* плодови́тый (плодови́т).

prologue [ˈprəʊlɒg] (*US* **prolog**) *n* прологг.

prolong [prəˈlɒŋ] *vt* продлевáть (продли́ть
perf).

prom [prɒm] *n abbr* = **promenade**; (*MUS*) =
promenade concert; (*US*: *college ball*)
студéнческий* бал.

promenade [prɒməˈnɑːd] *n* променáд, мéсто*
для прогýлок.

promenade concert *n* (*BRIT*) променáдный
концéрт (*на котóром часть пýблики
стои́т*).

promenade deck *n* вéрхняя пáлуба.

prominence [ˈprɒmɪnəns] *n* (*of person*) ви́дное
положéние; (*of issue*) ви́дное мéсто.

prominent [ˈprɒmɪnənt] *adj* (*important, very
noticeable*) выдаю́щийся*; **he is** ~ **in the field
of** ... он извéстен в о́бласти +*gen* ....

prominently [ˈprɒmɪnəntlɪ] *adv* замéтно; **he
figured** ~ **in the case** он игрáл замéтную
роль в э́том дéле.

promiscuity [prɒmɪsˈkjuːɪtɪ] *n* распýщенность
f.

promiscuous [prəˈmɪskjuəs] *adj* распýщенный.

promise [ˈprɒmɪs] *n* (*vow*) обещáние; (*talent*)
потенциáл; (*hope*) надéжда ♦ *vi* (*vow*)
давáть* (дать* *perf*) обещáние ♦ *vt*: **to** ~ **sb
sth,** ~ **sth to sb** обещáть (пообещáть *perf*)
что-н комý-н; **a young man of** ~ мно́го-
обещáющий* молодóй человéк*; **she shows**
~ **она́** подаёт надéжды; **to** ~ **(sb) to do/that**
обещáть (пообещáть *perf*) (комý-н) +*infin*/
что; **to** ~ **well** подавáть* (*impf*) больши́е
надéжды.

promising [ˈprɒmɪsɪŋ] *adj* многообещáющий*.

promissory note [ˈprɒmɪsərɪ-] *n* (просто́й)
вéксель* *m*.

promontory [ˈprɒməntrɪ] *n* мыс*.

promote [prəˈməʊt] *vt* (*employee*) повышáть
(повы́сить* *perf*) (в дóлжности); (*product,
pop star*) реклами́ровать (*impf/perf*); (*ideas*)
поддéрживать (поддержáть* *perf*); (*venture,
event*) содéйствовать (поддержáть* *perf*) +*dat*; **the team
was** ~**d to the second division** (*BRIT*) комáнда
былá переведенá во вторýю ли́гу.

promoter [prəˈməʊtə^] *n* (*of event*) агéнт; (*of
cause, idea*) пропаганди́ст(ка*).

promotion [prəˈməʊʃən] *n* (*at work*)
повышéние (в дóлжности); (*of product,
event, idea*) реклами́рование; (*publicity
campaign*) реклáма.

prompt [prɒmpt] *adj* незамедли́тельный*
(незамедли́телен) ♦ *n* (*COMPUT*)
приглашéние ♦ *vt* (*cause*) побуждáть
(побуди́ть* *perf*); (*sb talking*) подскáзывать
(подсказáть* *perf*); (*THEAT*) суфли́ровать
(*impf*) +*dat* ♦ *adv*: **at 8 o'clock** ~ рóвно в 8
часóв; **they're very** ~ они́ óчень
пунктуáльны; **he was** ~ **to accept** он
немéдленно согласи́лся; **to** ~ **sb to do**
побуждáть (побуди́ть* *perf*) когó-н +*infin*.

prompter [ˈprɒmptə^] *n* (*THEAT*) суфлёр.

promptly [ˈprɒmptlɪ] *adv* (*immediately*)
незамедли́тельно; (*exactly*) тóчно.

promptness [ˈprɒmptnɪs] *n* незамедли́тель-
ность *f*.

promulgate [ˈprɒməlgeɪt] *vt* обнарóдовать
(*impf*).

prone [prəʊn] *adj*: **to lie** ~ лежáть (*impf*)
ничкóм; ~ **to** (*inclined to*) склóнный*
(склóнен) к +*dat*; **I am** ~ **to illness** у меня́
слáбое здорóвье; **he is** ~ **to colds** он
подвéржен простýдам; **she is** ~ **to burst into
tears if you shout at her** éсли на неё кричáть,
онá мóжет легкó разрыдáться.

prong [prɒŋ] *n* (*of fork*) зубéц*.

pronoun [ˈprəʊnaʊn] *n* местоимéние.

pronounce [prəˈnaʊns] *vt* (*word*) произноси́ть*
(произнести́* *perf*); (*declaration, verdict*)
объявля́ть (объяви́ть* *perf*); (*opinion*)
выскáзывать (вы́сказать* *perf*) ♦ *vi*: **to** ~
(up)on выскáзываться (вы́сказаться* *perf*)
относи́тельно +*gen*; **they** ~**d him unfit to drive**
егó объяви́ли неприго́дным к вождéнию
автомоби́ля.

pronounced [prəˈnaʊnst] *adj* отчётливый
(отчётлив).

pronouncement [prəˈnaʊnsmənt] *n*
объявлéние.

pronto [ˈprɒntəʊ] *adv* (*inf*) жи́во.

pronunciation [prənʌnsɪˈeɪʃən] *n* (*of word*)
произношéние; (*by person*) вы́говор.

proof [pruːf] *n* (*evidence*) доказáтельство;
(*TYP*) корректýра; (*test, PHOT*) прóбный
отпечáток*; (*of alcohol*) крéпость *f* ♦ *vt* (*BRIT*:
tent, anorak) дéлать (сдéлать *perf*)
водонепроницáемым ♦ *adj*: **this material is** ~
against water э́тот материáл не пропускáет
вóду; **this vodka is 70%** ~ э́то – семи́десяти-
процéнтная вóдка.

proofreader [ˈpruːfriːdə^] *n* корréктор.

prop [prɒp] *n* (*support*) подпóрка*; (*fig*: *person*)
опóра ♦ *vt* (*also*: ~ **up**) подпирáть
(подперéть* *perf*); (*lean*): **to** ~ **sth against**
прислоня́ть (прислони́ть* *perf*) что-н к +*dat*;
~**s** *npl* (*THEAT*) реквизи́т *msg*.

Prop. *abbr* (*COMM*) = **proprietor**.

propaganda [prɒpəˈgændə] *n* пропагáнда.

propagate [ˈprɒpəgeɪt] *vt* (*idea, information*)
распространя́ть (распространи́ть *perf*);
(*plant*) разводи́ть* (развести́* *perf*).

propagation [prɒpəˈgeɪʃən] *n* (*see vt*)

распростране́ние; разведе́ние.
propel [prə'pɛl] *vt* (*vehicle, machine*)
приводи́ть* (привести́* *perf*) в движе́ние; (*fig*:
person) толка́ть (толкну́ть *perf*).
propeller [prə'pɛlə'] *n* пропе́ллер.
propelling pencil [prə'pɛlɪŋ-] *n* (*BRIT*) авто-
мати́ческий* каранда́ш*.
propensity [prə'pɛnsɪtɪ] *n*: **a ~ for/to do**
расположе́нность *f* к +*dat*/+*infin*.
proper ['prɔpə'] *adj* (*real*) настоя́щий*; (*correct*)
подходя́щий*, надлежа́щий*; (*socially
acceptable*) прили́чный* (прили́чен); **he
looked a ~ fool** (*inf*) он вы́глядел настоя́щим
дурако́м; **the village ~** со́бственно дере́вня*;
to go through the ~ channels проходи́ть*
(пройти́* *perf*) че́рез надлежа́щие кана́лы.
properly ['prɔpəlɪ] *adv* (*eat, study*) как сле́дует;
(*behave*) прили́чно, до́лжным о́бразом.
proper noun *n* и́мя* *nt* со́бственное.
property ['prɔpətɪ] *n* (*possessions*)
со́бственность *f*; (*building and its land*)
недви́жимость *f*; (*quality*) сво́йство
♦ *cpd*: ~ **developer** застро́йщик; **it's their ~**
э́то их со́бственность; ~ **market** ры́нок
недви́жимости; ~ **tax** нало́г на
со́бственность.
prophecy ['prɔfɪsɪ] *n* проро́чество.
prophesy ['prɔfɪsaɪ] *vti* проро́чить
(напроро́чить *perf*).
prophet ['prɔfɪt] *n* проро́к.
prophetic [prə'fɛtɪk] *adj* проро́ческий*.
proportion [prə'pɔ:ʃən] *n* (*part*) часть* *f*, до́ля;
(*ratio*) пропо́рция, соотноше́ние; **his head is
in perfect ~ to his body** голова́ его́
абсолю́тно пропорциона́льна его́ те́лу; **to
be out of all ~ to** ника́к не соотве́тствовать
(*impf*) +*dat*; **to get sth in(to) ~** соизмеря́ть
(соизме́рить *perf*) что-н; **to get sth out of ~** не
соизмеря́ть (соизме́рить *perf*) что-н; **a sense
of ~** чу́вство ме́ры.
proportional [prə'pɔ:ʃənl] *adj*: ~ **(to)**
пропорциона́льный* (пропорциона́лен)
(+*dat*).
proportional representation *n* (*POL*)
пропорциона́льное представи́тельство.
proportionate [prə'pɔ:ʃənɪt] *adj*: ~ **(to)**
пропорциона́льный* (пропорциона́лен)
(+*dat*).
proposal [prə'pəuzl] *n* предложе́ние.
propose [prə'pəuz] *vt* (*plan, toast*) предлага́ть
(предложи́ть* *perf*); (*motion*) выдвига́ть
(вы́двинуть *perf*) ♦ *vi* (*offer marriage*): **to ~ (to
sb)** де́лать (сде́лать *perf*) предложе́ние
(кому́-н); **to ~ sth/to do** *or* **doing** (*have in
mind*) предполага́ть (*impf*) что-н/+*infin*.
proposer [prə'pəuzə'] *n* (*BRIT*): **the ~ of the
motion** внося́щий(-ая) *m(f)* *adj* предложе́ние.
proposition [prɔpə'zɪʃən] *n* (*statement*)

утвержде́ние; (*offer*) предложе́ние; **to make
sb a ~** де́лать (сде́лать *perf*) предложе́ние
кому́-н.
propound [prə'paund] *vt* (*idea, argument*)
выдвига́ть (вы́двинуть *perf*).
proprietary [prə'praɪətərɪ] *adj* (*medicine*)
патенто́ванный; (*brand*) фи́рменный;
(*behaviour*) со́бственнический*.
proprietor [prə'praɪətə'] *n* (*of hotel, shop,
newspaper etc*) владе́лец(-лица).
propriety [prə'praɪətɪ] *n* присто́йность *f*.
propulsion [prə'pʌlʃən] *n* дви́жущая си́ла.
pro rata [prəu'rɑ:tə] *adv* пропорциона́льно ♦
adj пропорциона́льный* (пропорциона́лен);
on a ~ ~ basis на пропорциона́льной
осно́ве.
prosaic [prəu'zeɪk] *adj* (*person*) прозаи́чный*
(прозаи́чен); (*piece of writing*)
прозаи́ческий*.
Pros. Atty. *abbr* (*US*) = **prosecuting attorney**.
proscribe [prə'skraɪb] *vt* воспреща́ть
(воспрети́ть* *perf*).
prose [prəuz] *n* (*not poetry*) про́за; (*SCOL*)
отры́вок* для перево́да.
prosecute ['prɔsɪkju:t] *vt* (*case*) вести́* (*impf*); **to
~ sb** подава́ть* (пода́ть* *perf*) на кого́-н в
суд.
prosecuting attorney ['prɔsɪkju:tɪŋ-] *n* (*US*)
обвини́тель *m*.
prosecution [prɔsɪ'kju:ʃən] *n* (*LAW: action*)
суде́бное пресле́дование; (: *accusing side*)
обвине́ние.
prosecutor ['prɔsɪkju:tə'] *n* обвини́тель *m*;
(*also*: **public ~**) прокуро́р.
prospect ['prɔspɛkt] *n* перспекти́ва ♦ *vi*: **to ~
for** разве́дывать (разве́дать *perf*) на +*acc*; **~s**
npl (*for work etc*) перспекти́вы *fpl*; **we are
faced with the ~ of leaving** нас ожида́ет
перспекти́ва отъе́зда; **there's every ~ of an
early victory** есть перспекти́ва ско́рой
побе́ды.
prospecting ['prɔspɛktɪŋ] *n* разве́дка,
изыска́ние.
prospective [prə'spɛktɪv] *adj* (*son-in-law*)
бу́дущий*; (*customer, candidate*)
возмо́жный.
prospectus [prə'spɛktəs] *n* проспе́кт.
prosper ['prɔspə'] *vi* преуспева́ть (преуспе́ть
perf).
prosperity [prɔ'spɛrɪtɪ] *n* преуспева́ние.
prosperous ['prɔspərəs] *adj* преуспева́ющий.
prostate ['prɔsteɪt] *n* (*also*: ~ **gland**)
предста́тельная железа́*.
prostitute ['prɔstɪtju:t] *n* проститу́тка*.
prostitution [prɔstɪ'tju:ʃən] *n* проститу́ция.
prostrate [*vt* prɔ'streɪt, *adj* 'prɔstreɪt] *vt*: **to ~ o.s.
before** па́дать (упа́сть* *perf*) ниц пе́ред +*instr*
♦ *adj* (*fig*) уби́тый; **to lie ~** лежа́ть (*impf*)

---

* marks translations which have irregular inflections. The Russian-English side of the dictionary gives inflectional information.

ничко́м.

protagonist [prə'tægənɪst] *n* (*supporter*) сторо́нник(-ица); (*leading participant*) де́ятель *m*; (*THEAT*) (гла́вный) геро́й.

protect [prə'tɛkt] *vt* защища́ть (защити́ть* *perf*).

protection [prə'tɛkʃən] *n* защи́та; **to be under sb's ~** находи́ться* (*impf*) под защи́той кого́-н.

protectionism [prə'tɛkʃənɪzəm] *n* протекциони́зм.

protection racket *n* рэ́кет.

protective [prə'tɛktɪv] *adj* (*clothing, layer, gesture etc*) защи́тный; (*person*) покрови́тельственный; **~ custody** (*LAW*) опе́ка.

protector [prə'tɛktə'] *n* (*person*) защи́тник(-ница); (*device*) защи́тное устро́йство.

protégé ['prəutɛʒeɪ] *n* протеже́ *m ind*.

protégée ['prəutɛʒeɪ] *n* протеже́ *f ind*.

protein ['prəuti:n] *n* бело́к*, протеи́н.

pro tem [prəu'tɛm] *adv abbr* = **pro tempore**; (*for the time being*) вре́менно.

protest [*n* 'prəutɛst, *vb* prə'tɛst] *n* проте́ст ◆ *vi*: **to ~ about/against** протестова́ть (*impf*) по по́воду +*gen*/про́тив +*gen* ◆ *vt* (*insist*): **to ~ that** заявля́ть (заяви́ть* *perf*), что.

Protestant ['prɔtɪstənt] *n* протеста́нт(ка*) ◆ *adj* протеста́нтский*.

protester [prə'tɛstə'] *n* протесту́ющий*(-ая) *m(f) adj*.

protest march *n* марш проте́ста.

protestor [prə'tɛstə'] *n* = **protester**.

protocol ['prəutəkɔl] *n* протоко́л.

prototype ['prəutətaɪp] *n* прототи́п.

protracted [prə'træktɪd] *adj* затяну́вшийся.

protractor [prə'træktə'] *n* (*GEOM*) транспорти́р.

protrude [prə'tru:d] *vi* выдава́ться* (*impf*).

protuberance [prə'tju:bərəns] *n* вы́пуклость *f*.

proud [praud] *adj*: **~ (of)** го́рдый* (горд) (+*instr*); **I am ~ to know him** я горжу́сь знако́мством с ним *or* тем, что я знако́м с ним; **to do sb ~** (*inf*) принима́ть (приня́ть* *perf*) кого́-н на сла́ву; **to do o.s. ~** (*inf*) име́ть (*impf*) основа́ния горди́ться.

proudly ['praudlɪ] *adv* (*say, smile*) го́рдо; (*show*) с го́рдостью.

prove [pru:v] *vt* дока́зывать (доказа́ть* *perf*) ◆ *vi*: **to ~ (to be)** оказа́ться (*impf*/*perf*) +*instr*; **to ~ o.s.** проявля́ть (прояви́ть* *perf*) себя́; **he was ~d right in the end** в конце́ (концо́в) бы́ло дока́зано, что он прав.

Provençal [prɔvɔn'sɑ:l] *adj* прованса́льский.

Provence [prɔ'vɑ̃:s] *n* Прова́нс.

proverb ['prɔvə:b] *n* посло́вица.

proverbial [prə'və:bɪəl] *adj* знамени́тый.

provide [prə'vaɪd] *vt* обеспе́чивать (обеспе́чить *perf*) +*instr*; **to ~ sb with sth** обеспе́чивать (обеспе́чить *perf*) кого́-н чем-н; **to be ~d with** (*person*) быть* (*impf*)

обеспе́ченным(-ой); (*thing*) быть* (*impf*) снабжённым(-ой)

▶ **provide for** *vt fus* (*person*) обеспе́чивать (обеспе́чить *perf*); (*future event*) предусма́тривать (предусмотре́ть* *perf*); (*emergency*) забо́титься (позабо́титься *perf*) о +*prp*.

provided (that) [prə'vaɪdɪd-] *conj* при усло́вии, что.

Providence ['prɔvɪdəns] *n* провиде́ние.

providing [prə'vaɪdɪŋ] *conj* = **provided (that)**.

province ['prɔvɪns] *n* (*of country*) о́бласть *f*; (*of person*) о́бласть *f*; **the ~s** *npl*: **in the ~s** (*regions*) в прови́нции.

provincial [prə'vɪnʃəl] *adj* провинциа́льный*.

provision [prə'vɪʒən] *n* (*supplying*) обеспе́чение; (*supply*) снабже́ние; (*stipulation*) усло́вие; (*of contract, agreement*) положе́ние; **~s** *npl* (*food*) прови́зия *fsg*; **to make ~s for** забо́титься (позабо́титься *perf*) о +*prp*; **there's no ~ for this in the contract** в контра́кте э́то не предусмо́трено.

provisional [prə'vɪʒənl] *adj* вре́менный ◆ *n*: **P~** (*IRISH: POL*) член Ирла́ндской Республика́нской А́рмии.

provisional licence *n* (*BRIT: AUT*) предвари́тельные води́тельские права́ *ntpl*.

provisionally [prə'vɪʒnəlɪ] *adv* вре́менно.

proviso [prə'vaɪzəu] *n* усло́вие; **with the ~ that ...** с усло́вием, что ....

Provo ['prɔvəu] *n abbr* (*IRISH: POL: inf*) = **Provisional**.

provocation [prɔvə'keɪʃən] *n* провока́ция; **under ~** бу́дучи спровоци́рован.

provocative [prə'vɔkətɪv] *adj* (*remark, article, gesture*) провокацио́нный* (провокацио́нен), вызыва́ющий* (вызыва́ющ); (*intellectually or sexually stimulating*) возбужда́ющий*.

provoke [prə'vəuk] *vt* (*person*) задира́ть (*impf*); (*fight, argument etc*) провоци́ровать (спровоци́ровать *perf*); **to ~ sb to sth/to do** *or* **into doing** провоци́ровать (спровоци́ровать *perf*) кого́-н на что-н/+*infin*.

provost ['prɔvəst] *n* (*BRIT: of university*) ре́ктор; (*SCOTTISH: POL*) мэр.

prow [prau] *n* (*NAUT*) нос*.

prowess ['prauɪs] *n* мастерство́; **his ~ as a footballer** его́ мастерство́ футболи́ста.

prowl [praul] *vi* (*also:* **~ about**, **~ around**) кра́сться* (*impf*) ◆ *n*: **to be on the ~ for** охо́титься* (*impf*) на +*acc*.

prowler ['praulə'] *n* подозри́тельный тип.

proximity [prɔk'sɪmɪtɪ] *n* бли́зость *f*.

proxy ['prɔksɪ] *n*: **by ~** по дове́ренности.

PRP *abbr* (= *performance related pay*) опла́та по результа́там рабо́ты.

prude [pru:d] *n* ханжа́* *m/f*.

prudence ['pru:dns] *n* благоразу́мие.

prudent ['pru:dnt] *adj* благоразу́мный* (благоразу́мен).

prudish ['pru:dɪʃ] *adj* ханжеский.
prune [pru:n] *n* чернослив* *m no pl* ♦ *vt*
подрезать (подрезать* *perf*).
pry [praɪ] *vi*: **to ~ (into)** совать* (сунуть *perf*)
нос (в +*acc*).
PS *abbr* = **postscript**.
psalm [sɑ:m] *n* псалом*.
PSAT *n abbr* (*US*) = **Preliminary Scholastic
Aptitude Test.**
PSBR *n abbr* (*BRIT*: *ECON*: = **public sector
borrowing requirement**) потребность
государственного сектора в заёмных
средствах.
pseud [sju:d] (*BRIT*: *inf*) *n* (*intellectually*)
псевдоинтеллектуал(ка*); (*socially*)
позёр(ша).
pseudo- ['sju:dəu] *prefix* псевдо-.
pseudonym ['sju:dənɪm] *n* псевдоним.
PST *abbr* (*US*) = **Pacific Standard Time.**
PSV *n abbr* (*BRIT*) = **public-service vehicle.**
psyche ['saɪkɪ] *n* психика.
psychedelic [saɪkɪ'dɛlɪk] *adj* психо-
делический.
psychiatric [saɪkɪ'ætrɪk] *adj* психиатрический*.
psychiatrist [saɪ'kaɪətrɪst] *n* психиатр.
psychiatry [saɪ'kaɪətrɪ] *n* психиатрия.
psychic ['saɪkɪk] *adj* (*person: also:~al*)
ясновидящий*; (*of the mind*) психический*.
psycho ['saɪkəu] *n* (*inf*) псих.
psychoanalyse [saɪkəu'ænəlaɪz] *vt* подвергать
(подвергнуть *perf*) психоанализу.
psychoanalysis [saɪkəuə'nælɪsɪs] *n* психо-
анализ.
psychoanalyst [saɪkəu'ænəlɪst] *n* психо-
аналитик.
psychological [saɪkə'lɔdʒɪkl] *adj* психо-
логический*.
psychologist [saɪ'kɔlədʒɪst] *n* психолог.
psychology [saɪ'kɔlədʒɪ] *n* психология.
psychopath ['saɪkəupæθ] *n* психопат(ка*).
psychoses [saɪ'kəusi:z] *npl of* **psychosis**.
psychosis [saɪ'kəusɪs] (*pl* **psychoses**) *n* психоз.
psychosomatic ['saɪkəusə'mætɪk] *adj* психо-
соматический.
psychotherapy [saɪkəu'θɛrəpɪ] *n* психо-
терапия.
psychotic [saɪ'kɔtɪk] *adj* психически больной.
PT *n abbr* (*BRIT*: *SCOL*: = **physical training**)
физкультура= *физическая культура.*
Pt *abbr* (*in place names*) = **Point.**
pt *abbr* = **pint, point.**
PTA *n abbr* (= **Parent-Teacher Association**)
*общество, деятельность которого
направлена на объединение усилий школы и
родителей.*
Pte *abbr* (*BRIT*: *MIL*) = **private.**
PTO *abbr* (= **please turn over**) смотри на
обороте.

PTV *n abbr* (*US*: = **pay television**) коммерческое
телевидение; (= **public television**)
некоммерческое (общеобразовательное)
телевидение.
pub [pʌb] *n* = **public house.**
pub crawl *n* (*inf*) поход по пабам *or* барам.
puberty ['pju:bətɪ] *n* половая зрелость *f*.
pubic ['pju:bɪk] *adj* лобковый.
public ['pʌblɪk] *adj* общественный; (*statement,
action etc*) публичный ♦ *n*: **the ~** (*all people of
country*) народ; (*particular set of people*)
публика; **the general ~** общественность *f*;
this is ~ knowledge это широко известно; **to
make ~** предавать* (предать* *perf*)
гласности; **to go ~** (*COMM*) выпускать
(выпустить* *perf*) акции на продажу через
биржу; **in ~** публично.
public-address system [pʌblɪkə'drɛs-] *n*
(радио)трансляция.
publican ['pʌblɪkən] *n* содержатель(ница) *m(f)*
пивного бара *or* паба.
publication [pʌblɪ'keɪʃən] *n* публикация,
издание.
public company *n* (*COMM*) публичная
компания, компания открытого типа.
public convenience *n* (*BRIT*) общественный
туалет.
public holiday *n* общенародный праздник.
public house *n* (*BRIT*) паб, пивная *f adj*, пивной
бар.
publicity [pʌb'lɪsɪtɪ] *n* (*information*) реклама,
паблисити *nt ind*; (*attention*) шумиха.
publicize ['pʌblɪsaɪz] *vt* (*fact, event*) предавать*
(предать* *perf*) гласности.
public limited company *n* (*COMM*) публичная
компания с ограниченной ответствен-
ностью.
publicly ['pʌblɪklɪ] *adv* публично; (*COMM*): **~
owned** государственный.
public opinion *n* общественное мнение.
public ownership *n*: **to be taken into ~ ~**
(*COMM*) переходить* (перейти* *perf*) в
государственную *or* общенародную
собственность.
Public Prosecutor *n* ≈ генеральный
поркурор.
public relations *npl* внешние связи *fpl*.
public relations officer *n* сотрудник отдела
внешних связей.
public school *n* (*BRIT*) частная школа; (*US*)
государственная школа.
public sector *n*: **the ~ ~** государственный
сектор.
public-service vehicle [pʌblɪk'sə:vɪs-] *n* (*BRIT*)
общественное транспортное средство.
public-spirited [pʌblɪk'spɪrɪtɪd] *adj*
заботящийся об общественных интересах.
public transport *n* общественный транспорт.

---

* marks translations which have irregular inflections. The Russian-English side of the dictionary gives inflectional information.

public utility *n* компа́ния, обеспе́чивающая каки́й-либо вид коммуна́льных услу́г.
public works *npl* обще́ственные сооруже́ния *ntpl.*
publish ['pʌblɪʃ] *vt (book, magazine)* издава́ть* (изда́ть* *perf); (letter, article)* публикова́ть (опубликова́ть *perf).*
publisher ['pʌblɪʃə'] *n (person)* изда́тель *m; (company)* изда́тельство.
publishing ['pʌblɪʃɪŋ] *n (profession)* изда́тельское де́ло; *(of a book)* изда́ние, публика́ция.
publishing company *n* изда́тельство.
puce [pju:s] *adj* краснова́то-кори́чневый.
puck [pʌk] *n (ICE HOCKEY)* ша́йба.
pucker ['pʌkə'] *vt* мо́рщить (намо́рщить *or* смо́рщить *perf).*
pudding ['pudɪŋ] *n* пу́динг; *(BRIT: dessert)* сла́дкое *nt adj; rice* ~ ри́совый пу́динг; **black** ~, *(US)* **blood** ~ кровяна́я колбаса́*.
puddle ['pʌdl] *n* лу́жа.
puerile ['pjuəraɪl] *adj* ребя́ческий*.
Puerto Rico ['pwə:təu'ri:kəu] *n* Пуэ́рто-Ри́ко *f ind.*
puff [pʌf] *n (of cigarette, pipe)* затя́жка*; *(gasp)* пыхте́ние; *(of wind)* дунове́ние; *(of smoke)* клуб ♦ *vi (breathe loudly)* пыхте́ть* *(impf)* ♦ *vt:* **to ~ one's pipe** затя́гиваться (затяну́ться* *perf)*
▶ **puff out** *vt (chest, cheeks)* раздува́ть (разду́ть* *perf); (smoke)* выпуска́ть (вы́пустить* *perf).*
puffed [pʌft] *adj (inf: out of breath)* запыха́вшийся.
puffin ['pʌfɪn] *n (ZOOL)* ту́пик.
puff pastry *(US* **puff paste)** *n* слоёное те́сто.
puffy ['pʌfɪ] *adj* опу́хший*.
pugnacious [pʌg'neɪʃəs] *adj* зади́ристый (зади́рист).
pull [pul] *n (of moon, magnet, the sea etc)* притяже́ние; *(fig)* тя́га ♦ *vt* тяну́ть* (потяну́ть* *perf); (trigger)* нажима́ть (нажа́ть *perf)* на +*acc; (close: curtains, blind)* заде́ргивать (задёрнуть *perf); (inf: people)* привлека́ть (привле́чь* *impf); (pint of beer)* нака́чивать (накача́ть *perf)* ♦ *vi (tug)* тяну́ть* *(impf);* **to give sth a ~** *(tug)* тяну́ть* (потяну́ть* *perf);* **to ~ a face** крои́ть (скрои́ть *perf)* грима́су; **to ~ to pieces** разрыва́ть (разорва́ть* *perf)* на ча́сти; **to ~ one's punches** дра́ться* *(impf)* вполси́лы; **he doesn't ~ his punches** *(fig)* он дерётся всерьёз; **to ~ one's weight** выполня́ть (вы́полнить *perf)* свою́ часть рабо́ты; **to ~ o.s. together** взять* *(perf)* себя́ в ру́ки; **to ~ sb's leg** *(fig)* разы́грывать (разыгра́ть *perf)* кого́-н; **to ~ strings (for sb)** пуска́ть (пусти́ть* *perf)* в ход все свя́зи *(для кого́-н)*
▶ **pull about** *vt (BRIT: object, person)* трепа́ть *(impf)*
▶ **pull apart** *vt* разрыва́ть (разорва́ть* *perf)* на куски́

▶ **pull back** *vi* отступа́ть (отступи́ть* *perf)*
▶ **pull down** *vt (building)* сноси́ть* (снести́* *perf); (tree)* сруба́ть (сруби́ть* *perf)*
▶ **pull in** *vt (money)* загреба́ть (загрести́* *perf); (crowds, people)* привлека́ть (привле́чь* *perf); (subj: police: suspect)* сца́пать *(perf)*
▶ **pull into** *vt (AUT)* подъезжа́ть (подъе́хать* *perf)* к +dat
▶ **pull off** *vt (clothes etc)* стя́гивать (стяну́ть* *perf); (fig):* **he managed to ~ it off** ему́ удало́сь ски́нуть э́то с себя́
▶ **pull out** *vt (extract)* выта́скивать (вы́тащить *perf)* ♦ *vi:* **to ~ out (from)** *(AUT: from kerb)* отъезжа́ть (отъе́хать* *perf)* (от +gen); *(RAIL)* отходи́ть* (отойти́* *perf)* (от +gen); *(withdraw):* **to ~ out (of)** выходи́ть* (вы́йти* *perf)* (из +gen)
▶ **pull over** *vi (AUT)* подъезжа́ть (подъе́хать* *perf)* к кра́ю доро́ги
▶ **pull round** *vi (unconscious person)* приходи́ть* (прийти́* *perf)* в себя́; *(sick person)* поправля́ться (попра́виться* *perf)*
▶ **pull through** *vi (MED)* выкара́бкиваться (вы́карабкаться *perf)*
▶ **pull up** *vi (stop)* остана́вливаться (останови́ться* *perf)* ♦ *vt (object, clothing)* подтя́гивать (подтяну́ть* *perf); (plant)* вырыва́ть (вы́рвать* *perf)* (с ко́рнем); *(chair)* пододвига́ть (пододви́нуть *perf).*
pullback ['pulbæk] *n* отступле́ние.
pulley ['pulɪ] *n* шкив*.
pull-out ['pulaut] *n (of forces etc)* отхо́д ♦ *cpd (pages)* вкладно́й; ~ **magazine** журна́л с вкла́дками.
pullover ['puləuvə'] *n* пуло́вер.
pulp [pʌlp] *n (of fruit)* мя́коть *f; (for paper)* бума́жная ма́сса; *(pej: magazines, fiction)* чти́во; **to reduce sth to a ~** превраща́ть (преврати́ть* *perf)* что-н в мя́гкую ма́ссу *or* пу́льпу.
pulpit ['pulpɪt] *n* ка́федра.
pulsate [pʌl'seɪt] *vi* пульси́ровать *(impf); (music)* вибри́ровать *(impf)*
pulse [pʌls] *n (ANAT)* пульс; *(of blood)* пульси́рование; *(of heart)* бие́ние; *(rhythm)* такт ♦ *vi* пульси́ровать* *(impf);* ~**s** *npl (BOT)* семена́ бобо́вых, употребля́емые в пи́щу; *(CULIN)* бобо́вые *pl adj;* **to take** *or* **feel sb's ~** нащу́пывать (нащу́пать *perf)* чей-н пульс.
pulverize ['pʌlvəraɪz] *vt* размельча́ть (размельчи́ть* *perf); (fig: destroy)* сокруша́ть (сокруши́ть *perf).*
puma ['pju:mə] *n* пу́ма.
pumice ['pʌmɪs] *n (also:* ~ **stone)** пе́мза.
pummel ['pʌml] *vt* колоти́ть* *(impf).*
pump [pʌmp] *n* насо́с; *(also:* **petrol** ~) бензоколо́нка*; *(shoe)* паруси́новая ту́фля* ♦ *vt* кача́ть* *(impf); (extract: oil, water, gas)* выка́чивать (вы́качать *perf);* **to ~ sb for information** выка́чивать *(impf)* из кого́-н

информа́цию
▶ **pump up** *vt* нака́чивать (накача́ть *perf*).
pumpkin ['pʌmpkɪn] *n* ты́ква.
pun [pʌn] *n* каламбу́р.
punch [pʌntʃ] *n* (*blow*) уда́р; (*fig: force*) заря́д; (*for making holes*) дырокол; (*drink*) пунш ♦ *vt* (*make a hole in*) пробива́ть (проби́ть* *perf*); (*hit*): **to ~ sb/sth** ударя́ть (уда́рить *perf*) кого́-н/что-н кулако́м; **to ~ a hole (in)** пробива́ть (проби́ть* *perf*) отве́рстие (в +*prp*)
▶ **punch in** *vi* (*US*) отмеча́ться (отме́титься* *perf*) (*приходя́ на рабо́ту*)
▶ **punch out** *vi* (*US*) отмеча́ться (отме́титься* *perf*) (*уходя́ с рабо́ты*).
Punch and Judy show *n* Панч и Джу́ди (*ку́кольное представле́ние*).
punch-drunk ['pʌntʃdrʌŋk] (*BRIT*) *adj* (*confused*) со сму́тным; **~ boxer** боксёр с травматологи́ческой энцералопа́телей.
punch(ed) card *n* (*COMPUT*) перфока́рта.
punch line *n* изю́минка.
punch-up ['pʌntʃʌp] *n* (*BRIT: inf*) потасо́вка*.
punctual ['pʌŋktjuəl] *adj* пунктуа́льный* (пункту́ален).
punctuality [pʌŋktjuˈælɪti] *n* пунктуа́льность *f*.
punctually ['pʌŋktjuəlɪ] *adv* (*arrive, leave, deliver*) пунктуа́льно; **the film will start ~ at 6** фильм начнётся ро́вно в 6 часо́в.
punctuation [pʌŋktjuˈeɪʃən] *n* пунктуа́ция.
punctuation mark *n* знак препина́ния.
puncture ['pʌŋktʃəʳ] *n* (*AUT*) проко́л ♦ *vt* прока́лывать (проколо́ть* *perf*); **I have a ~** у меня́ проко́лота ши́на.
pundit ['pʌndɪt] *n* до́ка *m/f*.
pungent ['pʌndʒənt] *adj* е́дкий* (е́док).
punish ['pʌnɪʃ] *vt* (*person*) нака́зывать (наказа́ть* *perf*); **to ~ sb for sth** нака́зывать (наказа́ть* *perf*) кого́-н за что-н; **this crime must be ~ed** э́то преступле́ние должно́ быть* нака́зано.
punishable ['pʌnɪʃəbl] *adj* наказу́емый (наказу́ем).
punishing ['pʌnɪʃɪŋ] *adj* (*fig: defeat, exercise*) изма́тывающий.
punishment ['pʌnɪʃmənt] *n* наказа́ние; **he took a lot of ~** (*inf: boxer*) ему́ си́льно доста́лось.
punitive ['pjuːnɪtɪv] *adj* кара́тельный.
Punjab [pʌnˈdʒɑːb] *n* Пенджа́б.
Punjabi [pʌnˈdʒɑːbɪ] *n* пенджа́бец*(-бка*); (*LING*) пенджа́бский* язы́к* ♦ *adj* пенджа́бский*.
punk [pʌŋk] *n* (*also: ~* **rocker**) панк; (*also: ~* **rock**) панк-рок; (*US: inf: thug*) громи́ла *m*.
punnet ['pʌnɪt] *n* корзи́ночка*.
punt [pʌnt] *n* (*boat*) плоскодо́нка* ♦ *vi* пла́вать/ плыть* (*impf*) на плоскодо́нке.
punter ['pʌntəʳ] *n* (*BRIT: gambler*) (профессиона́льный) игро́к*; (*inf: customer*)

кли́ент(ка*); **the ~s** (*inf*) клиенту́ра *fsg*.
puny ['pjuːnɪ] *adj* хи́лый (хил).
pup [pʌp] *n* (*young dog, seal etc*) щено́к*.
pupil ['pjuːpl] *n* (*SCOL*) учени́к*(-и́ца); (*of eye*) зрачо́к*.
puppet ['pʌpɪt] *n* (*also fig*) марионе́тка*.
puppet government *n* марионе́точное прави́тельство.
puppy ['pʌpɪ] *n* (*young dog*) щено́к*.
purchase ['pəːtʃɪs] *n* поку́пка*; (*grip etc*) захва́т ♦ *vt* покупа́ть (купи́ть* *perf*); **to get a ~ on** ухва́тываться (ухвати́ться* *perf*) за +*acc*.
purchase order *n* зака́з на това́ры.
purchase price *n* заку́почная цена́*.
purchaser ['pəːtʃɪsəʳ] *n* покупа́тель *m*.
purchase tax *n* нало́г на поку́пку.
purchasing power ['pəːtʃɪsɪŋ-] *n* покупа́тельная спосо́бность *f*.
pure [pjuəʳ] *adj* чи́стый; (*water, air, woman*) чи́стый* (чист); **a ~ wool jumper** сви́тер из чи́стой шерсти; **~ and simple** про́сто-на́просто; **it's laziness ~ and simple** э́то про́сто-на́просто лень.
purebred ['pjuəbrɛd] *adj* чистопоро́дный, чистокро́вный.
purée ['pjuəreɪ] *n* пюре́ *nt ind*.
purely ['pjuəlɪ] *adv* чи́сто.
purgatory ['pəːgətərɪ] *n* (*REL*) чисти́лище; (*fig*) муче́ние.
purge [pəːdʒ] *n* (*POL*) чи́стка*; (*MED*) слаби́тельное *nt adj* ♦ *vt* (*thoughts, mind etc*) очища́ть (очи́стить* *perf*); (*organization*): **to (of)** чи́стить* (очи́стить* *perf*) (от +*gen*); (*extremists etc*): **to ~ from** вычища́ть (вы́чистить* *perf*) от +*gen*.
purification [pjuərɪfɪˈkeɪʃən] *n* очи́стка*.
purify ['pjuərɪfaɪ] *vt* очища́ть (очи́стить* *perf*).
purist ['pjuərɪst] *n* пури́ст.
puritan ['pjuərɪtən] *n* пурита́нин*(-а́нка*).
puritanical [pjuərɪˈtænɪkl] *adj* пурита́нский*.
purity ['pjuərɪtɪ] *n* чистота́.
purl [pəːl] *n* изна́ночная вя́зка ♦ *vt* провя́зывать (провяза́ть *perf*) изна́ночной вязк.
purloin [pəːˈlɔɪn] *vt* присва́ивать (присво́ить *perf*).
purple ['pəːpl] *adj* фиоле́товый.
purport [pəːˈpɔːt] *vi*: **he ~s to be an objective party** он притяза́ет на роль объекти́вных наблюда́телей; **he ~s to care about this** он притяза́ет на то, что он обеспоко́ен э́той.
purpose ['pəːpəs] *n* цель *f*; **on ~** наме́ренно; **for illustrative ~s** в ка́честве иллюстра́ции; **for the ~s of this meeting** пресле́дуя це́ли да́нного собра́ния; **to no ~** напра́сно.
purpose-built ['pəːpəsˈbɪlt] *adj* (*BRIT*): **~ school** шко́ла целево́го назначе́ния.
purposeful ['pəːpəsful] *adj* целеустремлённый*

---

* marks translations which have irregular inflections. The Russian-English side of the dictionary gives inflectional information.

(целеустремлён).
purposely ['pɜ:pəslɪ] *adv* преднаме́ренно.
purr [pɜ:'] *vi* мурлы́кать* (*impf*).
purse [pɜ:s] *n* (*BRIT*) кошелёк*; (*US*: handbag)
су́мка* ◆ *vt*: **to ~ one's lips** поджима́ть
(поджа́ть* *perf*) гу́бы.
purser ['pɜ:sə'] *n* (*NAUT*) (судово́й) казначе́й.
purse-snatcher ['pɜ:ssnætʃə'] *n* (*US*) вор,
краду́щий су́мки.
pursue [pə'sju:] *vt* (*person, thing, aim*)
пресле́довать (*impf*); (*fig*: *activity*)
осуществля́ть (*impf*); (: *interest*) занима́ться
(*impf*) +*instr*; (: *plan*) сле́довать (*impf*) +*dat*.
pursuer [pə'sju:ə'] *n* пресле́дователь(ница) *m(f)*.
pursuit [pə'sju:t] *n* (*of person, thing*)
пресле́дование; (*of happiness, wealth etc*)
по́иски *mpl*; (*pastime*) заня́тие; **scientific ~s**
нау́чные по́иски; **in (the) ~ of sth** (*of wealth,
fame*) в пого́не за чем-н; (*of truth, knowledge*)
в по́исках чего́-н.
purveyor [pə'veɪə'] *n* поставщи́к(-и́ца).
pus [pʌs] *n* гной.
push [puʃ] *n* (*of button etc*) нажа́тие; (*of car,
door, person etc*) толчо́к*; (*fig*: *urgent
demand*) тре́бование ◆ *vt* (*press*) нажима́ть
(нажа́ть* *perf*); (*shove*) толка́ть (толкну́ть
perf); (*promote*) прота́лкивать (протолкну́ть
perf) ◆ *vi* (*press*) нажима́ть (нажа́ть* *perf*);
(*shove*) толка́ться (*impf*); (*fig*): **to ~ for**
тре́бование (потре́бовать *perf*) +*acc or* +gen; **at
a ~** (*BRIT*: *inf*) при жела́нии; **to ~ a door open**
распа́хивать (распахну́ть *perf*) дверь; **to ~ a
door shut** захло́пывать (захло́пнуть *perf*)
дверь; **"push"** (*on door*) „от себя́"; (*on bell*)
„нажми́те"; **to be ~ed for time/money** име́ть
(*impf*) ма́ло вре́мени/
де́нег; **she is ~ing fifty** (*inf*) ей под пятьдеся́т
▸ **push aside** *vt* (*person, object*) отта́лкивать
(оттолкну́ть *perf*); (*issue*) отмета́ть
(отмести́* *perf*)
▸ **push in** *vi* влеза́ть (влезть* *perf*)
▸ **push off** *vi* (*inf*) убира́ться (убра́ться* *perf*)
▸ **push on** *vi* (*continue*) дви́гаться (*impf*)
да́льше *or* вперёд
▸ **push over** *vt* опроки́дывать (опроки́нуть
perf)
▸ **push through** *vi* (*crowd etc*) прота́лкиваться
(протолкну́ться *perf*) ◆ *vt* (*measure, scheme*)
прота́лкивать (протолкну́ть *perf*)
▸ **push up** *vt* (*prices*) повыша́ть (повы́сить*
perf).
push-bike ['puʃbaɪk] *n* (*BRIT*) велосипе́д.
push-button ['puʃbʌtn] *adj* кно́пка*.
pushchair ['puʃtʃɛə'] *n* (*BRIT*) (складна́я)
коля́ска*.
pusher ['puʃə'] *n* (*drug pusher*) торго́вец*
(-вка*) нарко́тиками.
pushover ['puʃəuvə'] *n* (*inf*): **it's a ~** э́то па́ра
пустяко́в *or* пустяко́вое де́ло.
push-up ['puʃʌp] *n* (*US*: *press-up*) отжима́ние.
pushy ['puʃɪ] *adj* (*pej*: *person*) насты́рный*

(насты́рен).
puss [pus] *n* (*inf*) ки́ска*.
pussy(cat) ['pusɪ(kæt)] *n* (*inf*: *female*) ки́ска*;
(: *male*) ко́тик.
put [put] (*pt, pp* put) *vt* (*thing: horizontally*)
класть* (положи́ть *perf*); (: *vertically*)
ста́вить* (поста́вить* *perf*); (*person: in
institution*) помеща́ть (помести́ть* *perf*); (: *in
prison, in situation*) сажа́ть (посади́ть* *perf*);
(*idea, remark etc*) говори́ть (сказа́ть* *perf*);
(*case, view*) излага́ть (изложи́ть* *perf*);
(*question, word, sentence*) ста́вить*
(поста́вить* *perf*); (*estimate*) относи́ть*
(отнести́* *perf*), ста́вить* (поста́вить* *perf*); **to
~ sb in a good mood** приводи́ть* (привести́*
perf) кого́-н в хоро́шее настрое́ние; **to ~ sb in
a bad mood** по́ртить* (испо́ртить* *perf*)
кому́-н настрое́ние; **to ~ sb to bed**
укла́дывать (уложи́ть* *perf*) кого́-н спать *or*
в крова́ть; **to ~ sb to a lot of trouble**
доставля́ть (доста́вить* *perf*) кому́-н мно́го
хлопо́т; **how shall I ~ it?** как бы э́то сказа́ть?;
to ~ a lot of time into sth уделя́ть (удели́ть
perf) мно́го вре́мени чему́-н; **to ~ money on a
horse** ста́вить* (поста́вить* *perf*) на ло́шадь;
the cost is now ~ at 2 billion pounds сейча́с
сто́имость оце́нивается в 2 миллиа́рда
фу́нта; **I ~ it to you that ...** я говорю́ Вам, что
...; **to stay ~** остава́ться* (оста́ться* *perf*)
▸ **put about** *vi* (*NAUT*) развора́чиваться
(разверну́ться *perf*) ◆ *vt* (*rumour*) пуска́ть
(пусти́ть* *perf*)
▸ **put across** *vt* (*ideas etc*) объясня́ть
(объясни́ть* *perf*)
▸ **put around** *vt* = put about
▸ **put aside** *vt* откла́дывать (отложи́ть* *perf*);
(*idea*) отгоня́ть (отогна́ть* *perf*)
▸ **put away** *vt* (*store*) убира́ть (убра́ть* *perf*);
(*eat*) умина́ть (умя́ть* *perf*); (*save*)
откла́дывать (отложи́ть* *perf*); (*imprison*)
упря́тать* (*perf*)
▸ **put back** *vt* (*replace*) класть* (положи́ть*
perf) на ме́сто; (*postpone*) откла́дывать
(отложи́ть* *perf*); (*delay*) заде́рживать
(задержа́ть* *perf*); **this will ~ us back 10 years**
э́то отбро́сит нас на 10 лет наза́д
▸ **put by** *vt* откла́дывать (отложи́ть* *perf*)
▸ **put down** *vt* (*place*) класть* (положи́ть* *perf*),
ста́вить* (поста́вить* *perf*); (*note down*)
запи́сывать (записа́ть* *perf*); (*suppress,
humiliate*) подавля́ть (подави́ть* *perf*);
(*animal: kill*) умерщвля́ть (умертви́ть* *perf*);
(*attribute*): **to ~ sth down to** объясня́ть
(объясни́ть *perf*) что-н +*instr*
▸ **put forth** *vt* объявля́ть (объяви́ть* *perf*)
▸ **put forward** *vt* (*ideas, proposal*) выдвига́ть
(вы́двинуть *perf*); (*date*) переноси́ть*
(перенести́* *perf*); (*watch, clock*) переводи́ть*
(перевести́* *perf*) вперёд
▸ **put in** *vt* (*application, complaint*) подава́ть*
(пода́ть* *perf*); (*time, effort*) вкла́дывать

(вложи́ть *perf*); (*gas, electricity*) проводи́ть*
(провести́* *perf*) ♦ *vi* (*NAUT*) заходи́ть* (зайти́*
perf) в порт; **the ship ~ in at Plymouth**
кора́бль* зашёл в Пли́мут
▶ **put in for** *vt fus* (*job, promotion*) подава́ть*
(пода́ть* *perf*) заявле́ние на +*acc*
▶ **put off** *vt* (*delay*) откла́дывать (отложи́ть*
perf); (*discourage*) отта́лкивать (оттолкну́ть
perf); (*switch off*) выключа́ть (вы́ключить *perf*)
▶ **put on** *vt* (*clothes*) надева́ть (наде́ть* *perf*);
(*make-up, ointment etc*) накла́дывать
(наложи́ть* *perf*); (*light etc*) включа́ть
(включи́ть* *perf*); (*play, kettle, record, dinner*)
ста́вить* (поста́вить* *perf*); (*brake*) жать*
(нажа́ть* *perf*) на +*acc*; (*extra bus, train etc*)
пуска́ть (пусти́ть* *perf*); (*assume: look*)
напуска́ть (напусти́ть* *perf*) на себя́;
(*behaviour*) принима́ть (приня́ть* *perf*); (*inf:
tease*) разы́грывать (разыгра́ть *perf*);
(*inform, indicate*): **to ~ sb on to sb** связа́ть*
(*perf*) кого́-н с кем-н; **to ~ sb on to sth**
выводи́ть* (вы́вести* *perf*) кого́-н на что-н;
to ~ on weight поправля́ться (попра́виться*
perf); **to ~ on airs** ва́жничать (*impf*)
▶ **put out** *vt* (*fire*) туши́ть* (потуши́ть* *perf*);
(*candle, cigarette*) гаси́ть* (погаси́ть* *perf*);
(*electric light*) выключа́ть (вы́ключить *perf*);
(*rubbish*) выноси́ть* (вы́нести* *perf*); (*cat*)
выпуска́ть (вы́пустить* *perf*); (*one's hand*)
вытя́гивать (вы́тянуть *perf*); (*story*)
выду́мывать (вы́думать *perf*), пуска́ть
(пусти́ть* *perf*); (*BRIT: dislocate*) выви́хивать
(вы́вихнуть *perf*); (*inf*): **he was rather ~ out** он
был вы́бит из колеи́ ♦ *vi* (*NAUT*): **to ~ out to
sea** выходи́ть* (вы́йти* *perf*) в мо́ре; **to ~ out
from Plymouth** выходи́ть* (вы́йти* *perf*) из
Пли́мута
▶ **put through** *vt* (*person, call*) соединя́ть
(соедини́ть *perf*); (*plan, agreement*)
выполня́ть (вы́полнить *perf*); **~ me through
to Miss Blair** соедини́те меня́ с мисс Блэр
▶ **put together** *vt* соединя́ть (соедини́ть *perf*);
(*furniture, toys etc*) собира́ть (собра́ть* *perf*);
(*meal*) гото́вить* (пригото́вить* *perf*); (*plan,
campaign*) организова́ть (*impf/perf*)
▶ **put up** *vt* (*building, tent*) ста́вить*
(поста́вить* *perf*); (*umbrella*) раскрыва́ть
(раскры́ть* *perf*); (*hood*) надева́ть (наде́ть*
perf); (*poster, sign etc*) выве́шивать

(вы́весить* *perf*); (*price, cost*) поднима́ть
(подня́ть* *perf*); (*guest, visitor*) размеща́ть
(размести́ть* *perf*); (*opposition, resistance*)
подавля́ть (подави́ть* *perf*); (*incite*): **to ~ sb
up to sth** толка́ть (толкну́ть *perf*) кого́-н на
что-н; **to ~ sth up for sale** выставля́ть
(вы́ставить* *perf*) что-н на прода́жу
▶ **put upon** *vt fus*: **to be ~ upon: we are not
prepared to be ~ upon** мы не привы́кли,
чтобы на нас е́здили
▶ **put up with** *vt fus* терпе́ть (*impf*), мири́ться
(*impf*) с +*instr*.
putative ['pjuːtətɪv] *adj* предполага́емый.
putrid ['pjuːtrɪd] *adj* гнило́й.
putt [pʌt] *n* (*GOLF*) уда́р, загоня́ющий мяч в
лу́нку (в го́льфе).
putter ['pʌtə'] *n* (*GOLF*) коро́ткая клю́шка для
го́льфа ♦ *vi* (*US*) = **potter**.
putting green ['pʌtɪŋ-] *n* по́ле для го́льфа, на
кото́ром мяч прогоня́ется к лу́нками а не
поддаётся уда́рами.
putty ['pʌtɪ] *n* зама́зка.
put-up ['putʌp] *n*: **~ job** (*BRIT: inf*) под-
стро́енное де́ло*.
puzzle ['pʌzl] *n* (*question, mystery*) зага́дка;
(*game, toy*) головоло́мка*; (*also:* **crossword
~**) кроссво́рд ♦ *vt* озада́чивать (озада́чить
perf) ♦ *vi*: **to ~ over sth** лома́ть (*impf*) го́лову
над чем-н; **to be ~d about sth** пребыва́ть
(*impf*) в недоуме́нии по по́воду чего́-н.
puzzling ['pʌzlɪŋ] *adj* запу́танный* (запу́тан).
PVC *n abbr* (= *polyvinyl chloride*) поливинил-
хлори́д.
Pvt. *abbr* (*US: MIL*) = **private**.
PW *n abbr* (*US*) = **prisoner of war**.
p.w. *abbr* = **per week**.
PX *n abbr* (*US: MIL*) = **post exchange**.
pygmy ['pɪgmɪ] *n* пигме́й.
pyjamas [pɪ'dʒɑːməz] (*US* **pajamas**) *npl*: **(a pair
of)** ~ пижа́ма *fsg*.
pylon ['paɪlən] *n* пило́н, опо́ра.
Pyongyang ['pjɒŋ'jæŋ] *n* Пхенья́н.
pyramid ['pɪrəmɪd] *n* (*ARCHIT, GEOM*) пирами́да;
(*pile*) гру́да.
Pyrenean [pɪrə'niːən] *adj* пирене́йский.
Pyrenees [pɪrə'niːz] *npl*: **the ~** Пирене́и *pl*.
Pyrex® ['paɪrɛks] *n* пи́рекс ♦ *cpd*: **~ dish**
таре́лка пи́рекс.
python ['paɪθən] *n* пито́н.

---

* marks translations which have irregular inflections. The Russian-English side of the dictionary gives inflectional information.

~ Q, q ~

Q, q [kju:] *n* (*letter*) 17-ая бу́ква англи́йского алфави́та.

Qatar [kæ'tɑ:'] *n* Ка́тар.

QC *n abbr* (*BRIT: LAW:* = *Queen's Counsel*) короле́вский* адвока́т (*адвока́тский ранг*).

QED *abbr* (= *quod erat demonstrandum*) что и тре́бовалось доказа́ть.

QM *n abbr* (*MIL*) = **quartermaster**.

q.t. *n abbr* (*inf*) = *quiet*: **on the ~**. тишко́м.

qty *abbr* (= **quantity**) коли́чество.

quack [kwæk] *n* кря́канье; (*doctor*) шарлата́н ◆ *vi* кря́кать (*impf*).

quad [kwɔd] *abbr* = **quadrangle, quadruplet**.

quadrangle ['kwɔdræŋgl] *n* (*courtyard*) двор*; (*MATH*) четырёхуго́льник.

quadrilateral [kwɔdrɪ'lætərəl] *n* четырёху-го́льник.

quadruped ['kwɔdrupɛd] *n* четвероно́гое *nt adj*.

quadruple [kwɔ'dru:pl] *vt* увели́чивать (увели́чить *perf*) в четы́ре ра́за ◆ *vi* увели́чиваться (увели́читься *perf*) в четы́ре ра́за.

quadruplets [kwɔ'dru:plɪts] *npl* четы́ре близнеца́.

quagmire ['kwægmaɪə'] *n* (*also fig*) тряси́на.

quail [kweɪl] *n* (*bird*) пе́репел(-пёлка*) ◆ *vi*: **to ~ at the thought of** содрага́ться (содрогну́ться *perf*) при мы́сли об +*prp*.

quaint [kweɪnt] *adj* (*house, village*) причу́д-ливый (причу́длив); (*ideas, customs*) своеобра́зный* (своеобра́зен).

quake [kweɪk] *vi* трепета́ть* (*impf*) ◆ *n abbr*.

Quaker ['kweɪkə'] *n* ква́кер.

qualification [kwɔlɪfɪ'keɪʃən] *n* (*usu pl*: *academic, vocational*) квалифика́ция *no pl*; (*skill, quality*) ка́чество; (*reservation*) огово́рка*; **what are your ~s?** кака́я у Вас квалифика́ция?

qualified ['kwɔlɪfaɪd] *adj* (*trained*: *person*) квалифици́рованный (квалифици́рован); (*limited*: *approval etc*) небезусло́вный; **I'm not ~ to discuss/judge that** я не компете́нтен обсужда́ть/суди́ть об э́том; **the show was a ~ success** спекта́кль не по́льзовался осо́бым успе́хом; **he's not ~ for the job** у него́ нет необходи́мой квалифика́ции для э́той рабо́ты.

qualify ['kwɔlɪfaɪ] *vt* (*modify*: *make more specific*) уточня́ть (уточни́ть *perf*); (: *express*

reservation) огова́ривать (оговори́ть *perf*); (*make competent*): **to ~ sb to do** позволя́ть (позво́лить *perf*) кому́-н +*infin* ◆ *vi*: **to ~ as an engineer** получа́ть (получи́ть* *perf*) квалифика́цию инжене́ра; (*be eligible: for benefit, grant*): **to ~ (for)** име́ть (*impf*) пра́во (на +*acc*); (*in competition*): **to ~ (for)** выходи́ть* (вы́йти* *perf*) (в +*acc*).

qualifying ['kwɔlɪfaɪŋ] *adj*: **~ exam** квалификацио́нный экза́мен; **~ round** отбо́рочное соревнова́ние.

qualitative ['kwɔlɪtətɪv] *adj* ка́чественный.

quality ['kwɔlɪtɪ] *n* (*standard, characteristic*) ка́чество; (*property: of wood, stone etc*) сво́йство ◆ *cpd* ка́чественный; **of good/poor ~** хоро́шего/плохо́го ка́чества.

quality control *n* контро́ль *m* ка́чества.

quality of life *n* у́ровень* *m* жи́зни.

quality papers *npl* (*BRIT*): **the ~ ~** серьёзные газе́ты *fpl*.

qualm [kwɑ:m] *n* сомне́ние; **to have ~s about** сомнева́ться (*impf*) в +*prp*.

quandary ['kwɔndrɪ] *n*: **to be in a ~** быть* (*impf*) в затрудне́нии.

quango ['kwæŋgəu] *n abbr* (*BRIT*: = *quasi-autonomous non-governmental organization*) *организа́ция, име́ющая распоряди́тельные и координацио́нные фу́нкции*.

quantifiable ['kwɔntɪfaɪəbl] *adj* измери́мый (измери́м).

quantitative ['kwɔntɪtətɪv] *adj* коли́чественный.

quantity ['kwɔntɪtɪ] *n* коли́чество; (*large amount*): **in ~** в большо́м коли́честве; **an unknown ~** зага́дка.

quantity surveyor *n* инжене́р-планови́к* (*на строи́тельных рабо́тах*).

quantum leap ['kwɔntəm-] *n* скачо́к*.

quarantine ['kwɔrntiːn] *n* каранти́н.

quark [kwɑːk] *n* кварк.

quarrel ['kwɔrl] *n* ссо́ра ◆ *vi*: **to ~ (with)** ссо́риться (поссо́риться *perf*) (с +*instr*); **to have a ~ with sb** поссо́риться (*perf*) с кем-н; **I've no ~ with him** у меня́ нет прете́нзий к нему́; **I can't ~ with that** я не могу́ не согласи́ться с э́тим.

quarrelsome ['kwɔrəlsəm] *adj* вздо́рный* (вздо́рен).

quarry ['kwɔrɪ] *n* карье́р; (*for stone*)

каменоло́мня; (*hunted animal*) добы́ча ◆ *vt* добыва́ть (добы́ть* *perf*).

quart [kwɔːt] *n* ква́рта.

quarter ['kwɔːtəʳ] *n* че́тверть* *f*; (*of year, town*) кварта́л; (*US: coin*) два́дцать пять це́нтов ◆ *vt* дели́ть* (раздели́ть* *perf*) на четы́ре ча́сти; (*MIL: lodge*) квартирова́ть (расквартирова́ть *perf*); ~s *npl* (*living quarters*) помеще́ние *ntsg*; (: *MIL*) каза́рмы *fpl*; **a ~ of an hour** че́тверть* *f* ча́са; **it's a ~ to three**, *or* (*US*) **of three** сейча́с без че́тверти три; **it's a ~ past three**, *or* (*US*) **after three** сейча́с че́тверть четвёртого; **from all ~s** отовсю́ду; **at close ~s** вблизи́.

quarterback ['kwɔːtəbæk] *n* (*SPORT*) гла́вный напада́ющий* (*в америка́нском футбо́ле*).

quarterdeck ['kwɔːtədɛk] *n* (*NAUT*) квартерде́к.

quarterfinal ['kwɔːtə'faɪnl] *n* четвертьфина́л.

quarterly ['kwɔːtəlɪ] *adj* (*meeting*) (по)кварта́льный; (*payment*) (по)кварта́льный ◆ *adv* (*meet*) ежекварта́льно; (*pay*) покварта́льно ◆ *n* кварта́льный журна́л.

quartermaster ['kwɔːtəmɑːstəʳ] *n* (*MIL*) квартирме́йстер.

quartet(te) [kwɔː'tɛt] *n* (*group*) кварте́т.

quarto ['kwɔːtəu] *n* (*book*) кни́га форма́та ин-ква́рто.

quartz [kwɔːts] *n* кварц ◆ *cpd* ква́рцевый.

quash [kwɔʃ] *vt* (*verdict, judgement*) отменя́ть (отмени́ть* *perf*).

quasi- ['kweɪzaɪ] *prefix* ква́зи-.

quaver ['kweɪvəʳ] *n* (*BRIT: MUS*) восьма́я *f adj* ◆ *vi* дрожа́ть (*impf*).

quay [kiː] *n* (*also:* ~**side**) при́стань* *f*.

quayside ['kiːsaɪd] *n* при́стань* *f*.

queasiness ['kwiːzɪnɪs] *n* тошнота́.

queasy ['kwiːzɪ] *adj*: **I feel a bit ~** меня́ немно́го мути́т.

Quebec [kwɪ'bɛk] *n* Квебе́к.

queen [kwiːn] *n* короле́ва; (*also:* ~ **bee**) пчели́ная ма́тка*; (*CARDS*) да́ма; (*CHESS*) ферзь* *m*, короле́ва.

queen mother *n* короле́ва-мать* *f*.

Queen's speech *n* (*at Christmas*) обраще́ние (короле́вы) к по́дданым; (*at opening of parliament*) тро́нная речь *f* (короле́вы).

queer [kwɪəʳ] *adj* стра́нный* (стра́нен); (*BRIT*): **I feel ~** мне ду́рно ◆ *n* (*pej: homosexual*) го́мик.

quell [kwɛl] *vt* подавля́ть (подави́ть* *perf*).

quench [kwɛntʃ] *vt*: **to ~ one's thirst** утоля́ть (утоли́ть* *perf*) жа́жду.

querulous ['kwɛruləs] *adj* (*voice*) жа́лобный* (жа́лобен); (*child*) хны́кающий.

query ['kwɪərɪ] *n* вопро́с ◆ *vt* подверга́ть (подве́ргнуть *perf*) сомне́нию.

quest [kwɛst] *n* по́иск.

question ['kwɛstʃən] *n* вопро́с; (*doubt*) сомне́ние ◆ *vt* (*interrogate*) допра́шивать (допроси́ть* *perf*); (*doubt*) сомнева́ться (*impf*) в +*prp*; **to ask sb a ~**, **put a ~ to sb** задава́ть* (зада́ть* *perf*) кому́-н вопро́с; **to bring** *or* **call sth into ~** ста́вить* (поста́вить* *perf*) что-н под вопро́с *or* сомне́ние; **the ~ is ...** вопро́с в том, ...; **it's (just) a ~ of finding out** де́ло (то́лько) за тем, что́бы узна́ть; **there's some ~ as to whether** существу́ют не́которые сомне́ния в том, что; **beyond ~** беспо́рно; **that's out of the ~** об э́том не мо́жет быть* и ре́чи.

questionable ['kwɛstʃənəbl] *adj* сомни́тельный* (сомни́телен).

questioner ['kwɛstʃənəʳ] *n* зада́вший(-ая) *m(f)* *adj* вопро́с.

questioning ['kwɛstʃənɪŋ] *adj* (*expression*) вопроси́тельный* (вопроси́телен); (*mind*) пытли́вый (пытли́в) ◆ *n* (*POLICE*) допро́с.

question mark *n* вопроси́тельный знак.

questionnaire [kwɛstʃə'nɛəʳ] *n* анке́та.

queue [kjuː] *n* (*BRIT*) о́чередь* *f* ◆ *vi* (*also:* ~ **up**) стоя́ть (*impf*) в о́череди; **to jump the ~** проходи́ть* (пройти́* *perf*) без о́череди.

quibble ['kwɪbl] *vi*: **to ~ about** *or* **over** спо́рить (поспо́рить *perf*) о +*prp*.

quiche [kiːʃ] *n* киш (*откры́тый пиро́г с овощно́й итп начи́нкой*).

quick [kwɪk] *adj* бы́стрый* (быстр); (*clever: person*) сообрази́тельный* (сообрази́телен); (: *mind*; *brief*) коро́ткий* (коро́ток) ◆ *adv* бы́стро ◆ *n*: **to cut to the ~** задева́ть (заде́ть* *perf*) за живо́е; **be ~!** бы́стро!, побыстре́е!; **to be ~ to act** бы́стро реаги́ровать (отреаги́ровать *perf*); **she was ~ to see that ...** она́ сра́зу заме́тила, что ...; **to have a ~ look** взгляну́ть (*perf*); **she has a ~ temper** она́ вспы́льчива.

quicken ['kwɪkən] *vt* ускоря́ть (ускори́ть *perf*) ◆ *vi* ускоря́ться (ускори́ться *perf*).

quick-fire ['kwɪkfaɪəʳ] *adj*: ~ **questions** град *msg* вопро́сов.

quicklime ['kwɪklaɪm] *n* негашёная и́звесть *f*.

quickly ['kwɪklɪ] *adv* бы́стро.

quickness ['kwɪknɪs] *n* быстрота́; (*of mind*) жи́вость *f*.

quicksand ['kwɪksænd] *n* зыбу́чий* песо́к*.

quickstep ['kwɪkstɛp] *n* куи́к-сте́п.

quick-tempered [kwɪk'tɛmpəd] *adj* вспы́льчивый (вспы́льчив).

quick-witted [kwɪk'wɪtɪd] *adj* сообрази́тельный* (сообрази́телен).

quid [kwɪd] *n inv* (*BRIT: inf*) фунт (сте́рлингов).

quid pro quo ['kwɪdprəu'kwəu] *n* услу́га за услу́гу.

quiet ['kwaɪət] *adj* (*not loud or noisy*) ти́хий* (тих); (: *engine*) бесшу́мный* (бесшу́мен); (*peaceful, not busy*) споко́йный* (споко́ен); (*without fuss: wedding etc*) скро́мный*

---

* marks translations which have irregular inflections. The Russian-English side of the dictionary gives inflectional information.

(скро́мен) ♦ *n* (*silence*) тишина́; (*peace*) поко́й ♦ *vti* (*US*) = **quieten**; **be** ~! ти́хо!; **I'll have a ~ word with him** я поговорю́ с ним наедине́; **business is ~ at this time of year** в э́то вре́мя го́да в дела́х зати́шье; **on the ~** тайко́м.

quieten ['kwaɪətn] *vi* (*also:* ~ **down**) затиха́ть (зати́хнуть *perf*) ♦ *vt* (*also:* ~ **down**) успока́ивать (успоко́ить *perf*).

quietly ['kwaɪətlɪ] *adv* (*not loudly*) ти́хо; (*calmly*) споко́йно.

quietness ['kwaɪətnɪs] *n* (*silence*) тишина́; (*peacefulness*) поко́й.

quill [kwɪl] *n* перо́*; (*of porcupine*) игла́*.

quilt [kwɪlt] *n* (*covering*) стёганое покрыва́ло; (*also:* **continental** ~) стёганое одея́ло.

quilting ['kwɪltɪŋ] *n* (*quilt-making*) стёжка; (*material*) стёганая ткань *f*.

quin [kwɪn] *n abbr* (*BRIT*) = **quintuplet**.

quince [kwɪns] *n* айва́.

quinine [kwɪ'ni:n] *n* хини́н.

quintessential [kwɪntɪ'senʃəl] *adj* показа́тельный.

quintet(te) [kwɪn'tɛt] *n* (*group*) квинте́т.

quintuplets [kwɪn'tju:plɪts] *npl* пя́теро* близнецо́в.

quip [kwɪp] *n* остро́та ♦ *vt* остри́ть (состри́ть *perf*); ... **he ~ped** ... состри́л он.

quire ['kwaɪə'] *n* (*of paper*) десть *f*.

quirk [kwə:k] *n* причу́да, при́хоть *f*; **by some ~ of fate** по при́хоти судьбы́.

quit [kwɪt] (*pt, pp* **quit** *or* **quitted**) *vt* броса́ть (бро́сить* *perf*); (*premises*) съезжа́ть (съе́хать* *perf*) с +*gen* ♦ *vi* (*give up*) сдава́ться* (сда́ться* *perf*); (*resign*) увольня́ться (уво́литься* *perf*); **to ~ smoking** броса́ть (бро́сить* *perf*) кури́ть*; ~ **stalling!** (*US: inf*) переста́ньте ходи́ть вокру́г да о́коло!; **they were given 3 months notice to ~** (*BRIT*) их предупреди́ли, что они́ должны́ освобо- ди́ть помеще́ние в трёхме́сячный срок.

quite [kwaɪt] *adv* (*rather*) дово́льно; (*entirely*) соверше́нно; (*following negative: almost*): **the flat's not ~ big enough** кварти́ра недоста́точно больша́я; **he's ~ right** он соверше́нно прав; **she's ~ pretty** она́ дово́льно симпати́чная; **I ~ understand** я вполне́ понима́ю; **I'm not ~ sure** я не совсе́м уве́рен; **not ~ as many as the last time** не так мно́го, как в про́шлый раз; **that lunch was ~ something!** вот э́то был обе́д!; ~ **a few** дово́льно мно́го; ~ **(so)!** ве́рно!

Quito ['ki:təu] *n* Ки́то *m ind*.

quits [kwɪts] *adj*: **to be ~ (with)** быть* (*impf*) в расчёте (с +*instr*); **let's call it ~** бу́дем кви́ты.

quiver ['kwɪvə'] *vi* трепета́ть (*impf*).

quiz [kwɪz] *n* (*game*) викто́рина ♦ *vt* расспра́шивать (расспроси́ть* *perf*).

quizzical ['kwɪzɪkl] *adj*: **a ~ look** понима́ющий и насме́шливый взгляд.

quoits [kwɔɪts] *npl игра́, заключа́ющаяся в мета́нии коле́ц в цель.*

quorum ['kwɔ:rəm] *n* кво́рум.

quota ['kwəutə] *n* кво́та.

quotation [kwəu'teɪʃən] *n* цита́та; (*estimate*) цена́ (продавца́); (*of shares etc*) котиро́вка*.

quotation marks *npl* кавы́чки *fpl*.

quote [kwəut] *n* (*from book, play etc*) цита́та; (*estimate*) цена́ ♦ *vt* цити́ровать (процити́ровать *perf*); (*figure, example*) приводи́ть* (привести́* *perf*); (*price*) назнача́ть (назна́чить *perf*); ~**s** *npl* (*quotation marks*) кавы́чки *fpl*; **to ~ for a job** устана́вливать (установи́ть* *perf*) сто́имость *f* рабо́ты; **in ~s** в кавы́чках; ~ ... **unquote** ... в кавы́чках.

quotient ['kwəuʃənt] *n* (*factor*) фа́ктор.

qv *abbr* = *quod vide*; (*which see*) см.= *смотри́*.

qwerty keyboard ['kwə:tɪ-] *n типи́чная англи́йская клавиату́ра печа́тной маши́нки и́ли компью́тера.*

~ R, r ~

R, r [ɑ:ʳ] *n* (*letter*) 18-ая бу́ква англи́йского алфави́та.

R. *abbr* = **right**;(= **river**) р.= *река́*; (= *Réaumur (scale)*) по шкале́ Реомю́ра; (*US: CINEMA*: = **restricted**) ≈ до 18-ти лет; (*US: POL*) = **republican**; (*BRIT*) = **Rex**, (*BRIT*) = **Regina**.

RA *abbr* (*MIL*) = **rear admiral** ♦ *n abbr* (*BRIT*) = *Royal Academy*; (*BRIT*) = *Royal Academician*.

RAAF *n abbr* (*MIL*) = *Royal Australian Air Force*.

Rabat [rə'bɑ:t] *n* Раба́т.

rabbi ['ræbaɪ] *n* равви́н.

rabbit ['ræbɪt] *n* (*male*) кро́лик; (*female*) крольчи́ха ♦ *vi*: **to ~ (on)** (*BRIT*: *inf*) треща́ть (*impf*).

rabbit hole *n* кро́личья нора́*.

rabbit hutch *n* кро́личья кле́тка*.

rabble ['ræbl] *n* (*pej*) чернь *f*.

rabid ['ræbɪd] *adj* (*also fig*) бе́шеный.

rabies ['reɪbi:z] *n* бе́шенство, водобоя́знь *f*.

RAC *n abbr* (*BRIT*: = *Royal Automobile Club*) Короле́вский автомоби́льный клуб (*крупне́йшая автомоби́льная ассоциа́ция*).

raccoon [rə'ku:n] *n* ено́т.

race [reɪs] *n* (*species*) ра́са; (*competition*: *NAUT, AUT, SKIING etc*) го́ньки* *fpl*; (: *running*) забе́г; (: *swimming*) заплы́в; (: *horse race*) ска́чки* *fpl*; (*for power, control*) борьба́ ♦ *vt* (*horse*) гнать* (*impf*); (*pigeon*) гоня́ть (*impf*); (*car etc*) вести́* (*impf*); (*person*) бежа́ть* (*impf*) напереги́нки с +*instr* ♦ *vi* (*compete*) принима́ть (приня́ть* *perf*) уча́стие в го́нках/ забе́ге/заплы́ве/ска́чках; (*hurry*) мча́ться (*impf*); (*pulse*) учаща́ться (участи́ться* *perf*); (*engine*) увели́чивать (увели́чить *perf*) оборо́ты; **the human ~** челове́чество, челове́ческий* род; **the arms ~** го́нка вооруже́ний; **he ~d across the road** он бы́стро перебежа́л че́рез доро́гу; **to ~ in(to)** влета́ть (влете́ть* *perf*) (в +*acc*); **to ~ out (of)** выска́кивать (вы́скочить *perf*) (из +*gen*).

race car *n* (*US*) = **racing car**.

race car driver *n* (*US*) = **racing driver**.

racecourse ['reɪskɔ:s] *n* ипподро́м.

racehorse ['reɪshɔ:s] *n* скакова́я ло́шадь* *f*.

race meeting *n* день* *m* ска́чек.

race relations *npl* ра́совые отноше́ния *ntpl*.

racetrack ['reɪstræk] *n* (*for people*) бегова́я доро́жка*; (*for cars*) трек; (*US*) = **racecourse**.

racial ['reɪʃl] *adj* (*discrimination, prejudice*) ра́совый; **~ equality** ра́совое ра́венство.

racialism ['reɪʃlɪzm] *n* раси́зм.

racialist ['reɪʃlɪst] *adj* (*beliefs, attitudes*) раси́стский* ♦ *n* раси́ст(ка*).

racing ['reɪsɪŋ] *n* (*horse racing*) ска́чки* *fpl*; (*motor racing*) го́нки* *fpl*.

racing car *n* (*BRIT*) го́ночный автомоби́ль *m*.

racing driver *n* (*BRIT*) го́нщик.

racism ['reɪsɪzəm] *n* раси́зм.

racist ['reɪsɪst] *adj* (*statement, policy*) раси́стский* ♦ *n* раси́ст(ка*).

rack [ræk] *n* (*shelf*) по́лка*; (*also*: **luggage ~**) бага́жная по́лка*; (*also*: **roof ~**) бага́жник (*на кры́ше автомоби́ля*); (*also*: **dish ~**) суши́лка* для посу́ды ♦ *vt*: **she was ~ed by pain** её терза́ла боль; **to ~ one's brains** лома́ть (*impf*) го́лову; **magazine ~** журна́льная по́лка; **toast ~** подста́вка для то́стов; **shoe ~** по́лка* для о́буви; **to go to ~ and ruin** (*building*) ветша́ть (обветша́ть *perf*); (*business*) разоря́ться (разори́ться *perf*).

racket ['rækɪt] *n* (*SPORT*) раке́тка*; (*noise*) шум; (*swindle*) жу́льничество; (*organized crime*) рэ́кет.

racketeer [rækɪ'tɪə*] *n* (*esp US*) рэкети́р.

racoon [rə'ku:n] *n* = **raccoon**.

racquet ['rækɪt] *n* (*SPORT*) раке́тка*.

racy ['reɪsɪ] *adj* (*book*) пика́нтный* (пика́нтен); (*behaviour etc*) экстравага́нтный* (экстравага́нтен).

RADA [rɑ:də] (*BRIT*) *n abbr* = *Royal Academy of Dramatic Art*.

radar ['reɪdɑ:*] *n* рада́р, радиолока́тор ♦ *cpd* рада́рный, радиолокацио́нный.

radar trap *n* (*AUT*) радиолокацио́нная лову́шка.

radial ['reɪdɪəl] *adj* (*also*: **~~-ply**: *tyre*) радиа́льный.

radiance ['reɪdɪəns] *n* (*glow*) сия́ние.

radiant ['reɪdɪənt] *adj* (*smile, person*) сия́ющий*; (*PHYS*) лучи́стый.

radiate ['reɪdɪeɪt] *vt* (*also fig*) излуча́ть (*impf*) ♦ *vi* (*lines*) радиа́льно расходи́ться* (разойти́сь* *perf*).

---

* marks translations which have irregular inflections. The Russian-English side of the dictionary gives inflectional information.

radiation [reɪdɪ'eɪʃən] n (*radioactive*) радиа́ция, радиоакти́вное излуче́ние; (*of heat, light*) излуче́ние.

radiation sickness n лучева́я боле́знь f.

radiator ['reɪdɪeɪtə'] n (*heater*) радиа́тор, батаре́я; (*AUT*) радиа́тор.

radiator cap n кры́шка* радиа́тора.

radiator grill n (*AUT*) решётка* радиа́тора.

radical ['rædɪkl] adj (*extreme*) радика́льный* (радика́лен) ◆ n (*person*) радика́л.

radii ['reɪdɪaɪ] npl of **radius**.

radio ['reɪdɪəu] n (*broadcasting*) ра́дио nt ind; (*device: for receiving broadcasts*) радио-приёмник; (: *for transmitting and receiving*) радиопереда́тчик ◆ vt (*person*) свя́зываться (связа́ться* perf) по ра́дио с +instr; (*information*) передава́ть* (переда́ть* perf) по ра́дио ◆ vi: **to ~ to sb** ради́ровать (*impf/perf*) кому́-н; **on the ~** по ра́дио.

radio... ['reɪdɪəu] prefix ра́дио....

radioactive ['reɪdɪəu'æktɪv] adj радио-акти́вный* (радиоакти́вен).

radioactivity ['reɪdɪəuæk'tɪvɪtɪ] n радио-акти́вность f.

radio announcer n ди́ктор ра́дио.

radio-controlled ['reɪdɪəukən'trəuld] adj управля́емый при по́мощи радиосигна́лов.

radiographer [reɪdɪ'ɔgrəfə'] n рентгено́лог.

radiography [reɪdɪ'ɔgrəfɪ] n рентгеногра́фия, радиогра́фия.

radiologist [reɪdɪ'ɔlədʒɪst] n рентгено́лог, радио́лог.

radiology [reɪdɪ'ɔlədʒɪ] n рентгеноло́гия, радиоло́гия.

radio station n радиоста́нция.

radio taxi n радиофици́рованное такси́ nt ind.

radiotelephone ['reɪdɪəu'tɛlɪfəun] n радио-телефо́н.

radio telescope n радиотелеско́п.

radiotherapist ['reɪdɪəu'θɛrəpɪst] n радио-терапе́вт.

radiotherapy ['reɪdɪəu'θɛrəpɪ] n радиотерапи́я, рентгенотерапи́я.

radish ['rædɪʃ] n (*one radish*) реди́ска*; ~**es** реди́с msg, реди́ска fsg (*разг*).

radium ['reɪdɪəm] n ра́дий.

radius ['reɪdɪəs] (pl **radii**) n ра́диус; (*ANAT*) лучева́я кость* f; **within a ~ of 50 miles** в ра́диусе 50-ти миль.

RAF n abbr (*BRIT*) (= **Royal Air Force**) ≈ ВВС= вое́нно-возду́шные си́лы.

raffia ['ræfɪə] n ра́фия.

raffish ['ræfɪʃ] adj разгу́льный* (разгу́лен).

raffle ['ræfl] n (*вещева́я*) лотере́я ◆ vt (*prize*) разы́грывать (разыгра́ть perf) в лотере́е.

raft [rɑːft] n плот*.

rafter ['rɑːftə'] n (*CONSTR*) стропи́ло.

rag [ræg] n тря́пка*; (*pej: newspaper*) газете́нка*; (*SCOL: for charity*) благотвор-и́тельное шу́точное студе́нческое представле́ние ◆ vt (*BRIT: tease*) те́шиться

(поте́шиться perf) над +instr; ~**s** npl (*torn clothes*) лохмо́тья* pl; **in ~s** (*person*) в лохмо́тьях; (*clothes*) изно́шенный* (изно́шен) до дыр.

rag-and-bone man [rægən'bəun-] irreg n (*BRIT*) старьёвщик.

ragbag ['rægbæg] n (*fig: inf*) вся́кая вся́чина.

rag doll n тряпи́чная ку́кла*.

rage [reɪdʒ] n (*fury*) я́рость f, бе́шенство ◆ vi (*person*) свире́пствовать (impf); (*storm, debate*) бушева́ть (impf); **it's all the ~** (*very fashionable*) все помеша́лись на э́том; **to fly into a ~** приходи́ть* (прийти́* perf) в я́рость, свирепе́ть (рассвирепе́ть perf).

ragged ['rægɪd] adj (*edge*) зазу́бренный* (зазу́брен); (*clothes*) потрёпанный* (потрёпан), изо́рванный (изо́рван); (*appearance*) обо́рванный* (обо́рван).

raging ['reɪdʒɪŋ] adj (*sea, storm*) бушу́ющий; (*pain, fever*) свире́пый; ~ **toothache** свире́пая зубна́я боль; **in a ~ temper** в я́рости.

rag trade n (*inf*): **the ~ ~** инду́стрия оде́жды.

raid [reɪd] n (*MIL*) рейд; (*criminal*) налёт; (*by police*) обла́ва, рейд ◆ vt (*see n*) соверша́ть (соверши́ть perf) рейд; соверша́ть (соверши́ть perf) налёт; устра́ивать (устро́ить perf) обла́ву or рейд.

rail [reɪl] n (*on stairs, bridge etc*) пери́ла pl; (*of ship*) борт*; ~**s** npl (*RAIL*) ре́льсы mpl; **by ~** по́ездом.

railing(s) ['reɪlɪŋ(z)] n(pl) (*iron fence*) решётка fsg.

railroad ['reɪlrəud] n (*US*) = **railway**.

railway ['reɪlweɪ] n (*BRIT*) желе́зная доро́га ◆ cpd железнодоро́жный.

railway engine n локомоти́в.

railway line n (*BRIT*) железнодоро́жная ли́ния.

railwayman ['reɪlweɪmən] irreg n (*BRIT*) железнодоро́жник.

railway station n (*BRIT: large*) железно-доро́жный вокза́л; (: *small*) железнодоро́жная ста́нция.

rain [reɪn] n дождь* m ◆ vi: **it's ~ing** идёт дождь ◆ vt: **it's ~ing cats and dogs** льёт как из ведра́; **in the ~** под дождём, в дождь; **it ~ed a lot last night** вчера́ но́чью шёл си́льный дождь.

rainbow ['reɪnbəu] n ра́дуга.

rain check n (*US*): **I'll take a ~ ~** я ещё немно́го поду́маю.

raincoat ['reɪnkəut] n плащ*.

raindrop ['reɪndrɔp] n дождева́я ка́пля*.

rainfall ['reɪnfɔːl] n оса́дки mpl; (*measurement*) коли́чество оса́дков.

rainforest ['reɪnfɔrɪst] n тропи́ческий* лес.

rainproof ['reɪnpruːf] adj непромока́емый (непромока́ем).

rainstorm ['reɪnstɔːm] n ли́вень* m.

rainwater ['reɪnwɔːtə'] n дождева́я вода́*.

rainy ['reɪnɪ] adj (*day*) дождли́вый (дождли́в); **Manchester is a ~ place** в Манче́стере ча́сто иду́т дожди́; **to save sth for a ~ day**

откла́дывать (отложи́ть* *perf*) что-н на
чёрный день.
raise [reɪz] *n* (*esp US: pay rise*) повыше́ние ◆ *vt*
(*lift, produce*) поднима́ть (подня́ть* *perf*);
(*end: siege, embargo*) снима́ть (снять* *perf*);
(*increase, improve*) повыша́ть (повы́сить*
perf); (*doubts*) выска́зывать (вы́сказать* *perf*);
(*rear: cattle*) разводи́ть* (развести́* *perf*);
(: *family*) воспи́тывать (воспита́ть* *perf*);
(*cultivate: crop*) выра́щивать (вы́растить*
perf); (*get together: army, funds*) собира́ть
(собра́ть* *perf*); (: *loan*) достава́ть (доста́ть*
perf); **to ~ a glass to sb/sth** поднима́ть
(подня́ть* *perf*) бока́л за кого́-н/что-н; **to ~
one's voice** повыша́ть (повы́сить* *perf*)
го́лос; **to ~ one's hopes** обнадёживать
(обнадёжить *perf*); **to ~ a laugh/smile**
вызыва́ть (вы́звать* *perf*) смех/улы́бку.
raisin [ˈreɪzn] *n* (*one raisin*) изю́минка*; **~s**
изю́м* *m no pl.*
Raj [rɑːdʒ] *n*: **the ~** *пери́од брита́нского
правле́ния в Инди́и.*
rajah [ˈrɑːdʒə] *n* ра́джа.
rake [reɪk] *n* (*tool*) гра́бли* *pl*; (*person*) пове́са *m*
◆ *vt* (*garden*) разра́внивать (разровня́ть *perf*)
(гра́блями); (*leaves, hay*) сгреба́ть (сгрести́*
perf); (*with machine gun*) обстре́ливать
(обстреля́ть *perf*) ◆ *vi*: **to ~ through** (*search*)
ры́ться* (*impf*) в +*prp.*
rake-off [ˈreɪkɔf] *n* (*inf*) до́ля* при́были.
rally [ˈrælɪ] *n* (*POL etc*) ми́тинг; (*AUT*)
авторалли *nt ind*; (*TENNIS*) ра́лли *nt ind* ◆ *vt*
(*support*) спла́чивать (сплоти́ть* *perf*) ◆ *vi*
(*sick person*) оправля́ться (опра́виться* *perf*);
(*Stock Exchange*) оживля́ться (оживи́ться*
perf)
▸ **rally round** *vt fus* (*fig: give support to*)
спла́чиваться (сплоти́ться* *perf*) вокру́г +*gen*
◆ *vi* бра́ться* (взя́ться* *perf*) за де́ло вме́сте.
rallying point [ˈrælɪŋ-] *n* (*idea*) объедин-
я́ющая иде́я.
RAM [ræm] *n abbr* (*COMPUT*) (= **random access
memory**) ЗУПВ= *запомина́ющее
устро́йство с произво́льной вы́боркой.*
ram [ræm] *n* бара́н ◆ *vt* (*crash into*) тара́нить
(протара́нить *perf*); (*push: bolt*) задвига́ть
(задви́нуть *perf*); (: *fist*) дви́нуть (*perf*) +*instr.*
ramble [ˈræmbl] *n* прогу́лка* ◆ *vi* (*walk*)
броди́ть* (*impf*); (*talk: also: ~ on*) болта́ть
(*impf*).
rambler [ˈræmblə] *n* (*walker*) тури́ст(ка)
(*уча́стник пешехо́дной прогу́лки и́ли
похо́да*); (*BOT*) вью́щееся расте́ние.
rambling [ˈræmblɪŋ] *adj* (*speech*) несвя́зный*
(несвя́зен); (*house*) беспоря́дочно
вы́строенный (вы́строен); (*BOT*) вью́щийся.
rambunctious [ræmˈbʌŋkʃəs] *adj* (*US*) =
rumbustious.

RAMC *n abbr* (*BRIT*) = *Royal Army Medical Corps.*
ramification [ræmɪfɪˈkeɪʃən] *n* сле́дствие.
ramp [ræmp] *n* (*incline*) скат, укло́н; (*in garage*)
па́ндус; **on ~** (*US: AUT*) въезд на автостра́ду;
off ~ (*US: AUT*) съезд с автостра́ды.
rampage [ræmˈpeɪdʒ] *n*: **to be on the ~**
бу́йствовать (*impf*) ◆ *vi*: **they went rampaging
through the town** они́ бу́йствовали по всему́
го́роду.
rampant [ˈræmpənt] *adj*: **to be ~** (*crime*)
свире́пствовать (*impf*).
rampart [ˈræmpɑːt] *n* крепостно́й вал*.
ram raid *n* *ограбле́ние, совершённое при
по́мощи автотара́на.*
ramshackle [ˈræmʃækl] *adj* ве́тхий* (ветх).
RAN *n abbr* = *Royal Australian Navy.*
ran [ræn] *pt of* **run.**
ranch [rɑːntʃ] *n* ра́нчо *nt ind.*
rancher [ˈrɑːntʃə] *n* (*owner*) владе́лец*(-лица)
ра́нчо; (*ranch hand*) рабо́тник на ра́нчо.
rancid [ˈrænsɪd] *adj* (*butter*) прого́рклый;
(*bacon*) ту́хлый*.
rancour [ˈræŋkə] (*US* **rancor**) *n* зло́ба.
R & B *n abbr* (= *rhythm and blues*) ритм и блюз.
R & D *n abbr* (= *research and development*)
нау́чно-иссле́довательские и о́пытно-
констру́кторские рабо́ты.
random [ˈrændəm] *adj* (*arrangement, selection*)
случа́йный*; (*COMPUT, MATH*) случа́йный,
произво́льный ◆ *n*: **at ~** науга́д.
random access *n* (*COMPUT*) прямо́й *or*
произво́льный до́ступ.
random access memory *n* (*COMPUT*)
запомина́ющее устро́йство с произво́льной
вы́боркой.
R & R *n abbr* (*US: MIL*) = *rest and recreation.*
randy [ˈrændɪ] *adj* (*BRIT: inf*) похотли́вый
(похотли́в).
rang [ræŋ] *pt of* **ring.**
range [reɪndʒ] *n* (*series: of proposals, offers*)
ряд*; (: *of products*) ассортиме́нт *no pl*,
вы́бор *no pl*; (: *of colours*) га́мма; (*of
mountains*) цепь* *f*; (*of missile*) да́льность *f*,
ра́диус де́йствия; (*of voice*) диапазо́н; (*MIL:
also: shooting ~*) стре́льбище; (: *indoor*) тир;
(*also: kitchen ~*) ку́хонная плита́* ◆ *vt* (*place
in a line*) выстра́ивать (вы́строить *perf*) ◆ *vi*:
to ~ over (*extend*) простира́ться (*impf*); **price
~** диапазо́н цен; **do you have anything else in
this price ~?** у Вас есть что́-нибудь ещё в
преде́лах э́той цены́?; **within** (*firing*) **~** на
расстоя́нии вы́стрела; **~d right/left** (*text*) с
поля́ми спра́ва/сле́ва; **to ~ from ... to ...**
колеба́ться* (*impf*) от +*gen* ... до +*gen* ....
ranger [ˈreɪndʒə] *n* (*in forest*) лесни́чий* *m adj*,
лесни́к*; (*in park*) смотри́тель(ница) *m(f).*
Rangoon [ræŋˈguːn] *n* Рангу́н.
rank [ræŋk] *n* (*row*) ряд*; (*MIL*) шере́нга;

---

* marks translations which have irregular inflections. The Russian-English side of the dictionary gives inflectional information.

(*status*) чин*, ранг; (*BRIT: also:* taxi ~) стоя́нка* такси́ ♦ *adj* (*stinking*) злово́нный* (злово́нен); (*injustice*) вопию́щий*; (*hypocrisy*) я́вный* (я́вен) ♦ *vi:* to ~ among чи́слиться (*impf*) среди́ +*gen* ♦ *vt:* I ~ him sixth я ста́влю его́ на шесто́е ме́сто; the ~s *npl* (*MIL*) рядовы́е *pl adj*, рядово́й соста́в *msg*; the ~ and file (*fig*) рядовы́е чле́ны *mpl*; to close ~s (*MIL, also fig*) смыка́ть (сомкну́ть *perf*) ряды́.

rankle ['ræŋkl] *vi:* to ~ with sb терза́ть (*impf*) кого́-н.

rank outsider *n* соверше́нно безнадёжный кандида́т, кандида́т без ша́нсов на успе́х.

ransack ['rænsæk] *vt* (*search*) переры́ть* (*perf*); (*plunder*) гра́бить* (разгра́бить* *perf*).

ransom ['rænsəm] *n* вы́куп; to hold to ~ (*fig: nation, company, individual*) держа́ть (*impf*) в зало́жниках.

rant [rænt] *vi:* to ~ and rave рвать* (*impf*) и мета́ть (*impf*).

ranting ['ræntɪŋ] *n* разглаго́льствование.

rap [ræp] *n* стук; (*POETRY, MUS*) стиль в му́зыке и́ли поэ́зии, характеризу́ющийся отры́вистым ри́тмом, испо́льзованием речитати́ва ♦ *vi:* to ~ on a door/table стуча́ть (постуча́ть *perf*) в дверь/по столу́.

rape [reɪp] *n* изнаси́лование; (*BOT*) рапс ♦ *vt* (*woman*) наси́ловать (изнаси́ловать *perf*).

rape(seed) oil ['reɪp(si:d)-] *n* ра́псовое ма́сло.

rapid ['ræpɪd] *adj* стреми́тельный* (стреми́телен).

rapidity [rə'pɪdɪtɪ] *n* стреми́тельность *f*.

rapidly ['ræpɪdlɪ] *adv* стреми́тельно.

rapids ['ræpɪdz] *npl* (*GEO*) стремни́на *fsg*.

rapist ['reɪpɪst] *n* наси́льник.

rapport [ræ'pɔ:'] *n* взаимопонима́ние.

rapprochement [ræ'prɒʃmã:ŋ] *n* сближе́ние.

rapt [ræpt] *adj* (*attention*) сосредото́ченный* (сосредото́чен); he was ~ in contemplation он был погружён в разду́мья.

rapture ['ræptʃə'] *n* (*delight*) восто́рг; to go into ~s over приходи́ть* (прийти́* *perf*) в восто́рг от +*gen.*

rapturous ['ræptʃərəs] *adj* (*applause*) восто́рженный* (восто́ржен).

rare [rɛə'] *adj* ре́дкий* (ре́док); (*rare steak*) крова́вый; it is ~ to find ... ре́дко удаётся найти́ ....

rarebit ['rɛəbɪt] *n see* Welsh rarebit.

rarefied ['rɛərɪfaɪd] *adj* разрежённый* (разрежён).

rarely ['rɛəlɪ] *adv* ре́дко, нечасто.

raring ['rɛərɪŋ] *adj:* he is ~ to go (*inf: keen*) ему́ не те́рпится приступи́ть к де́лу.

rarity ['rɛərɪtɪ] *n* ре́дкость *f.*

rascal ['rɑ:skl] *n* негодя́й(ка*).

rash [ræʃ] *adj* опроме́тчивый (опроме́тчив) ♦ *n* (*MED*) сыпь *f no pl*; (*spate: of events, robberies*) ряд*, волна́*; he came out in a ~ у него́ вы́ступила сыпь.

rasher ['ræʃə'] *n* (*of bacon*) ло́мтик.

rashly ['ræʃlɪ] *adv* опроме́тчиво.

rasp [rɑ:sp] *n* (*tool*) ра́шпиль *m* ♦ *vt* (*speak: also:* ~ out) хрипе́ть* (прохрипе́ть* *perf*).

raspberry ['rɑ:zbərɪ] *n* мали́на *f no pl.*

rasping ['rɑ:spɪŋ] *adj:* a ~ noise скреже́щущий звук; a ~ voice скрипу́чий го́лос.

rat [ræt] *n* (*also fig*) кры́са.

ratable ['reɪtəbl] *adj* = rateable.

ratchet ['rætʃɪt] *n* храпови́к; ~ wheel храпово́е колесо́*.

rate [reɪt] *n* (*speed*) ско́рость *f*; (: *of change, inflation*) темп; (*of interest*) ста́вка; (*ratio*) у́ровень *m*; (*price: at hotel etc*) расце́нка ♦ *vt* (*value*) оце́нивать (оцени́ть* *perf*); (*estimate*) расце́нивать (расцени́ть* *perf*); ~s *npl* (*BRIT: property tax*) нало́г *msg* на недви́жимость; (*fees*) расце́нки *fpl*; at a ~ of 60 kilometres an hour со ско́ростью 60 киломе́тров в час; ~ of flow ско́рость пото́ка; ~ of growth те́мпы ро́ста; ~ of return ста́вка дохо́да (*от вложе́ния капита́ла*); pulse ~ частота́ пу́льса; to ~ sb as счита́ть (*impf*) кого́-н +*instr*; to ~ sth as расце́нивать (расцени́ть (*perf*)) что-н как; to ~ sb/sth among относи́ть* (отнести́* *perf*) кого́-н/что-н к +*dat*; to ~ sb/sth highly высоко́ цени́ть* (*impf*) кого́-н/что-н.

rateable value ['reɪtəbl-] *n* (*BRIT: formerly*) сто́имость до́ма на осно́ве кото́рой рассчи́тывается нало́г на недви́жимость.

ratepayer ['reɪtpeɪə'] *n* (*BRIT: formerly*) лицо́, выпла́чивающее нало́г на недви́жимость.

rather ['rɑ:ðə'] *adv* (*quite, somewhat*) дово́льно; (*to some extent*) не́сколько; (*more accurately*): or ~ верне́е сказа́ть; it's ~ expensive (*quite*) э́то дово́льно до́рого; (*too*) э́то сли́шком до́рого; there's ~ a lot сли́шком мно́го; I would ~ go я, пожа́луй, пойду́; I'd ~ not leave я бы не хоте́л уходи́ть; I ~ think he won't come я ду́маю, что, пожа́луй, он не придёт.

ratification [rætɪfɪ'keɪʃən] *n* ратифика́ция.

ratify ['rætɪfaɪ] *vt* ратифици́ровать (*impf/perf*).

rating ['reɪtɪŋ] *n* (*assessment*) оце́нка*, ре́йтинг; (*NAUT: BRIT*) матро́с; ~s *npl* (*RADIO, TV*) ре́йтинг *msg.*

ratio ['reɪʃɪəu] *n* отноше́ние, соотноше́ние; in the ~ of one hundred to one в отноше́нии сто к одному́.

ration ['ræʃən] *n* (*allowance: of food*) рацио́н, паёк*; (: *of petrol*) но́рма ♦ *vt* норми́ровать (*impf/perf*); ~s *npl* (*MIL*) рацио́н *msg*; to be on ~s быть* (*impf*) на дово́льствии.

rational ['ræʃənl] *adj* (*solution, reasoning*) рациона́льный* (рациона́лен); (*person*) разу́мный* (разу́мен).

rationale [ræʃə'nɑ:l] *n* рациона́льное *or* разу́мное обоснова́ние.

rationalization [ræʃnəlaɪ'zeɪʃən] *n* рационализа́ция.

rationalize ['ræʃnəlaɪz] *vt* (*justify*) дава́ть*

(дать* *perf*) рациона́льное объясне́ние.

rationally ['ræʃnəlɪ] *adv* рациона́льно.

rationing ['ræʃnɪŋ] *n* нормирова́ние.

rat poison *n* крыси́ный яд.

rat race *n*: **the ~~** грызня́ за власть.

rattan [ræ'tæn] *n* рота́нг.

rattle ['rætl] *n* дребезжа́ние; (*of train, car*) громыха́ние; (*baby's toy*) погрему́шка* ♦ *vi* (*small objects*) дребезжа́ть (*impf*) ♦ *vt* (*shake noisily*) греме́ть (прогреме́ть *perf*); (*fig: unsettle*) нерви́ровать (*impf*), выводи́ть* (вы́вести* *perf*) из себя́; **to ~ along** (*car, bus*) прогромыха́ть (*impf*); **a cold November wind ~d the windows** от холо́дного ноя́брьского ве́тра дребезжа́ли о́кна.

rattlesnake ['rætlsneɪk] *n* грему́щая змея́*.

ratty ['rætɪ] *adj* (*inf: person*) издёрганный* (издёрган).

raucous ['rɔːkəs] *adj* оглуши́тельный* (оглуши́телен).

raucously ['rɔːkəslɪ] *adv* оглуши́тельно.

raunchy ['rɔːntʃɪ] *adj* (*song*) распу́тный* (распу́тен).

ravage ['rævɪdʒ] *vt* разоря́ть (разори́ть *perf*).

ravages ['rævɪdʒɪz] *npl* (*of time, weather*) разруши́тельные после́дствия *ntpl*.

rave [reɪv] *vi* (*in anger*) беснова́ться (*impf*), бушева́ть (*impf*); (*MED*) бре́дить* (*impf*); (*with enthusiasm*): **to ~ about** восторга́ться (*impf*) +*instr* ♦ *cpd* (*inf*) восто́рженный.

raven ['reɪvən] *n* во́рон.

ravenous ['rævənəs] *adj* (*person*) голо́дный* (го́лоден) как волк.

ravine [rə'viːn] *n* уще́лье*.

raving ['reɪvɪŋ] *adj*: **~ lunatic** бу́йно поме́шанный(-ая) *m(f) adj*.

ravings ['reɪvɪŋz] *npl* бред *msg*.

ravioli [rævɪ'əʊlɪ] *n* равио́ли *ind* (*итальянское блюдо, напоминающее пельмени*).

ravishing ['rævɪʃɪŋ] *adj* (*beautiful*) восхити́тельный* (восхити́телен).

raw [rɔː] *adj* (*uncooked*) сыро́й*; (*not processed: cotton*) необрабо́танный* (необрабо́тан); (: *unrefined sugar*) нерафини́рованный (нерафини́рован); (*sore*) све́жий* (свеж); (*inexperienced*) зелёный* (зе́лен); (*weather, day*) промо́зглый.

raw deal *n* (*inf: bad bargain*) неуда́чная сде́лка*; (: *unfair treatment*): **he got a ~~** с ним пло́хо обошли́сь.

raw material *n* сырьё *nt no pl*.

ray [reɪ] *n* (*of light, sunshine*) луч*; (*of heat*) пото́к*; **~ of hope** луч* наде́жды.

rayon ['reɪɒn] *n* иску́сственный шёлк.

raze [reɪz] *vt* (*building, forest: also:* **~ to the ground**) сровня́ть (*perf*) с землёй.

razor ['reɪzəʳ] *n* бри́тва; **safety ~** безопа́сная бри́тва; **electric ~** электробри́тва.

razor blade *n* ле́звие (бри́твы).

razzle(-dazzle) ['ræzl('dæzl)] *n* (*BRIT: inf*): **to go on the ~** идти́* (*impf*) кути́ть.

razzmatazz ['ræzmə'tæz] *n* (*inf*) буффона́да.

RC *abbr* = **Roman Catholic.**

RCAF *n abbr* = *Royal Canadian Air Force.*

RCMP *n abbr* = *Royal Canadian Mounted Police.*

RCN *n abbr* = *Royal Canadian Navy.*

RD *abbr* (*US: POST.* = *rural delivery*) *доста́вка по́чты в се́льскую ме́стность.*

Rd *abbr* = **road.**

RDC *n abbr* (*BRIT.* = *rural district council*) райо́нный сове́т (*в се́льской ме́стности*).

RE *n abbr* (*BRIT: SCOL:* = *religious education*) религио́зное воспита́ние; (*MIL:* = *Royal Engineers*) ≈ инжене́рные войска́.

re [riː] *prep* (*with regard to*) относи́тельно +*gen*.

reach [riːtʃ] *n* (*scope: of imagination*) разма́х ♦ *vt* (*place, end, agreement*) достига́ть (дости́гнуть* *or* дости́чь* *perf*) +*gen*; (: *conclusion, decision*) приходи́ть* (прийти́* *perf*) к +*dat*; (*be able to touch*) достава́ть* (доста́ть* *perf*); (*by telephone*) свя́зываться (связа́ться* *perf*) с +*instr* ♦ *vi*: **to ~ into** сова́ть (су́нуть *perf*) в +*acc*; **within ~** в преде́лах досяга́емости; **out of ~** вне досяга́емости; **within ~ of the shops/station** недалеко́ от магази́нов/вокза́ла; **within easy ~ of** (*place*) недалеко́ от +*gen*; **"keep out of the ~ of children"** „бере́чь от дете́й"; **upper ~es** (*of river*) верхо́вья *ntpl*; **lower ~es** (*of river*) низо́вья *ntpl*; **can I ~ you at your hotel?** мо́жно ли связа́ться с Ва́ми в гости́нице?; **to ~ for** протя́гивать (протяну́ть* *perf*) ру́ку к +*dat*; **to ~ up** протя́гивать (протяну́ть* *perf*) ру́ку вверх

▸ **reach out** *vt* протя́гивать (протяну́ть* *perf*) ♦ *vi* вытя́гиваться (вы́тянуться *perf*); **to ~ out for sth** протя́гивать (протяну́ть* *perf*) ру́ку за чем-н.

react [riː'ækt] *vi* (*CHEM*): **to ~ (with)** вступа́ть (вступи́ть* *perf*) в реа́кцию (с +*instr*); (*MED*): **to ~ (to)** реаги́ровать (*impf*) (на +*acc*); (*respond*) реаги́ровать (отреаги́ровать *perf*) (на +*acc*); (*rebel*): **to ~ (against)** восстава́ть* (восста́ть* *perf*) (про́тив +*gen*).

reaction [riː'ækʃən] *n* (*CHEM*) реа́кция; (*also MED, POL*): **~ (to/against)** реа́кция (на +*acc*/ про́тив +*gen*); **~s** *npl* (*reflexes*) реа́кция *fsg*.

reactionary [riː'ækʃənrɪ] *adj* реакцио́нный* (реакцио́нен).

reactor [riː'æktəʳ] *n* (*also: nuclear ~*) реа́ктор.

read[1] [red] *pt, pp of* **read**[2].

read[2] [riːd] (*pt, pp* **read**) *vt* чита́ть (прочита́ть *or* проче́сть* *perf*); (*mood*) определя́ть (определи́ть* *perf*); (*meter, thermometer etc*) снима́ть (снять* *perf*) показа́ния +*gen*; (*subj: instrument etc*) пока́зывать (*impf*); (*study: at*

---

university) изуча́ть (*impf*) ♦ *vi* (*person*) чита́ть (*impf*); (*text etc*) чита́ться (*impf*); **the notice ~s ...** в объявле́нии говори́тся ...; **it can be taken as ~ that ...** (*fig*) само́ собо́й разуме́ется, что ...; **do you ~ me?** (*TEL*) Вы слы́шите меня́?

▶ **read out** *vt* зачи́тывать (зачита́ть *perf*)

▶ **read over** *vt* перечи́тывать (перечита́ть *perf*)

▶ **read through** *vt* (*quickly*) проли́стывать (пролиста́ть *perf*); (*thoroughly*) прочи́тывать (прочита́ть *perf*)

▶ **read up** *vt* мно́го чита́ть (*impf*)

▶ **read up on** *vt fus* мно́го чита́ть (*impf*) по +*dat*.

readable ['riːdəbl] *adj* (*handwriting*) разбо́рчивый (разбо́рчив); (*book, author*) хорошо́ чита́ющийся; **this book is very ~** э́та кни́га хорошо́ чита́ется.

reader ['riːdə'] *n* (*of book, newspaper etc*) чита́тель(ница) *m(f)*; (*book*) кни́га для чте́ния, хрестома́тия; (*BRIT: at university*) ≈ доце́нт.

readership ['riːdəʃɪp] *n* (*of newspaper etc*) круг чита́телей.

readily ['rɛdɪlɪ] *adv* (*willingly*) с гото́вностью; (*easily*) легко́; (*quickly*) охо́тно.

readiness ['rɛdɪnɪs] *n* гото́вность *f*; **in ~** нагото́ве, в состоя́нии гото́вности.

reading ['riːdɪŋ] *n* (*of books, newspapers etc*) чте́ние; (*understanding*) толкова́ние; (*as entertainment*) чте́ния *ntpl*; (*on meter, thermometer etc*) показа́ние.

reading lamp *n* насто́льная ла́мпа.

reading matter *n* материа́л для чте́ния.

reading room *n* чита́льный зал.

readjust [riːə'dʒʌst] *vt* (*alter: position*) переменя́ть (*impf*); (: *knob, mirror*) повора́чивать (поверну́ть *perf*); (*instrument*) подрегули́ровать (*perf*) ♦ *vi* (*adapt*): **to ~ (to)** приспоса́бливаться (приспосо́биться* *perf*) (к +*dat*).

readjustment [riːə'dʒʌstmənt] *n* (*adapting*) приспособле́ние; (*alteration*) регулиро́вка*.

ready ['rɛdɪ] *adj* гото́вый (гото́в); (*available*) гото́вый ♦ *n*: **at the ~** (*MIL*) в положе́нии для стрельбы́; (*fig*) нагото́ве; **~ for use** гото́вый (гото́в) к употребле́нию; **I am ~ to help** я гото́в помо́чь; **to get ~** приготавливаться (пригото́виться* *perf*); **to get sb/sth ~** подгота́вливать (подгото́вить* *perf*) кого́-н/ что-н.

ready cash *n* нали́чные де́ньги* *pl*.

ready-cooked ['rɛdɪkukt] *adj* гото́вый.

ready-made ['rɛdɪ'meɪd] *adj* гото́вый.

ready-mix ['rɛdɪmɪks] *n* (*for cakes etc*) полуфабрика́т; (*concrete*) това́рный бето́н.

ready money *n* нали́чные де́ньги* *pl*.

ready reckoner [-'rɛkənə'] *n* (*BRIT*) арифмети́ческие табли́цы *fpl* гото́вых расчётов.

ready-to-wear ['rɛdɪtə'wɛə'] *adj* (*dress etc*) гото́вый.

reaffirm [riːə'fəːm] *vt* вновь подтвержда́ть

(подтверди́ть* *perf*).

reagent [riː'eɪdʒənt] *n*: **chemical ~** хими́ческий* реакти́в.

real [rɪəl] *adj* (*reason, interest, result etc*) настоя́щий*, реа́льный* (реа́лен); (*leather*) натура́льный*; (*gold, feeling*) настоя́щий* ♦ *adv* (*US: inf: very*) о́чень; **in ~ life** в действи́тельности; **in ~ terms** реа́льно; **a ~ idiot** (*for emphasis*) настоя́щий* идио́т.

real estate *n* недви́жимость *f* ♦ *cpd* (*US*): **~-~ agency** аге́нтство по прода́же недви́жимости.

realign [riːə'laɪn] *vt* перестра́ивать (перестро́ить *perf*).

realism ['rɪəlɪzəm] *n* реали́зм.

realist ['rɪəlɪst] *n* реали́ст(ка*).

realistic [rɪə'lɪstɪk] *adj* (*practical*) реалисти́чный* (реалисти́чен); (*true to life*) реалисти́ческий.

reality [riː'ælɪtɪ] *n* реа́льность *f*, действи́тельность *f*; **in ~** на са́мом де́ле, в реа́льности.

realization [rɪəlaɪ'zeɪʃən] *n* (*understanding*) осозна́ние; (*fulfilment: of hopes*) осуществле́ние; (*of asset*) реализа́ция.

realize ['rɪəlaɪz] *vt* (*understand*) осознава́ть* (осозна́ть* *perf*); (*fulfil*) осуществля́ть (осуществи́ть* *perf*); (*COMM: asset*) реализова́ть (*impf/perf*); **I ~ that ...** я осозна́ю, что ....

reallocate [riː'æləkeɪt] *vt* перераспределя́ть (перераспредели́ть *perf*).

really ['rɪəlɪ] *adv* (*very*) о́чень; (*actually*): **what ~ happened?** что произошло́ на са́мом де́ле?; **~?** (*indicating interest*) пра́вда?, да?; (*expressing surprise*) неуже́ли?, серьёзно?; **~!** (*indicating annoyance*) ну, зна́ете!

realm [rɛlm] *n* (*of monarch*) короле́вство; (*fig: area of activity or study*) о́бласть* *f*, сфе́ра.

real-time ['riːltaɪm] *adj* (*COMPUT*) в реа́льном вре́мени.

realtor ['rɪəltɔː'] *n* (*US*) аге́нт по прода́же недви́жимости.

ream [riːm] *n* (*of paper*) стопа́*; **~s of** (*fig: inf*) ку́ча, ма́сса; **she's written ~s!** у неё ма́сса *or* ку́ча напи́санного!

reap [riːp] *vt* (*crop*) жать* (сжать* *perf*); (*fig: benefits, rewards*) пожина́ть (пожа́ть* *perf*).

reaper ['riːpə'] *n* (*machine*) жа́тка*.

reappear [riːə'pɪə'] *vi* сно́ва появля́ться (появи́ться* *perf*).

reappearance [riːə'pɪərəns] *n* но́вое появле́ние.

reapply [riːə'plaɪ] *vi*: **to ~ for** повто́рно обраща́ться (обрати́ться* *perf*) за +*instr*.

reappoint [riːə'pɔɪnt] *vt* повто́рно назнача́ть (назна́чить* *perf*).

reappraisal [riːə'preɪzl] *n* переоце́нка*.

rear [rɪə'] *adj* за́дний ♦ *n* (*back*) за́дняя часть* *f*; (*buttocks*) зад; (*MIL*) тыл* ♦ *vt* (*cattle, family*) выра́щивать (вы́растить* *perf*) ♦ *vi* (*also: ~*

up) станови́ться* (стать* *perf*) на дыбы́.

rear admiral *n* контр-адмира́л.

rear-engined ['rɪər'ɛndʒɪnd] *adj* (*AUT*) с мото́ром в за́дней ча́сти.

rearguard ['rɪɡɑːd] *n* (*MIL*) арьерга́рд.

rearm [riː'ɑːm] *vi* перевооружа́ться (перевооружи́ться *perf*) ♦ *vt* перевооружа́ть (перевооружи́ть *perf*).

rearmament [riː'ɑːməmənt] *n* перевооруже́ние.

rearrange [riːə'reɪndʒ] *vt* (*objects*) переставля́ть (переста́вить* *perf*); (*order*) изменя́ть (измени́ть* *perf*).

rear-view mirror ['rɪəvjuː-] *n* (*AUT*) зе́ркало* за́днего ви́да *or* обзо́ра.

reason ['riːzn] *n* (*cause*) причи́на; (*ability to think*) ра́зум, рассу́док*; (*sense*) смысл ♦ *vi*: **to ~ with sb** убежда́ть (*impf*) кого́-н; **the ~ for/why** причи́на для +*gen*/по кото́рой; **to have ~ to think that** ... име́ть (*impf*) основа́ние ду́мать; **it stands to ~ that** ... разуме́ется, что ...; **she claims with good ~ that** ... она́ не без причи́ны счита́ет, что ...; **all the more ~ why** ... тем бо́лее ....

reasonable ['riːznəbl] *adj* разу́мный* (разу́мен); (*quality*) неплохо́й* (непло́х); (*price*) прие́млемый (прие́млем), уме́ренный* (уме́рен); (*not bad*) сно́сный* (сно́сен); **be ~!** бу́дьте благоразу́мны!

reasonably ['riːznəblɪ] *adv* (*sensibly*) разу́мно; (*fairly*) дово́льно; **one can ~ assume that** ... мо́жно справедли́во предположи́ть, что ....

reasoned ['riːznd] *adj* (*argument*) обосно́ванный* (обосно́ван).

reasoning ['riːznɪŋ] *n* рассужде́ние.

reassemble [riːə'sɛmbl] *vt* (сно́ва) собира́ть (собра́ть* *perf*).

reassert [riːə'səːt] *vt* (*authority, oneself*) сно́ва утвержда́ть (утверди́ть* *perf*).

reassurance [riːə'ʃuərəns] *n* подтвержде́ние; (*comfort*) подде́ржка.

reassure [riːə'ʃuə'] *vt* (*comfort*) утеша́ть (уте́шить *perf*); **to ~ sb of** заверя́ть (заве́рить *perf*) кого́-н в +*prp*.

reassuring [riːə'ʃuərɪŋ] *adj* (*smile, manner*) ободря́ющий.

reawakening [riːə'weɪknɪŋ] *n* пробужде́ние.

rebate ['riːbeɪt] *n* обра́тная вы́плата.

rebel [*n* 'rɛbl, *vi* rɪ'bɛl] *n* бунта́рь*(-рка*) *m(f)* ♦ *vi* восстава́ть* (восста́ть* *perf*).

rebellion [rɪ'bɛljən] *n* восста́ние.

rebellious [rɪ'bɛljəs] *adj* (*child, behaviour*) стропти́вый (стропти́в); (*troops*) мяте́жный*; (*factions*) бунту́ющий.

rebirth [riː'bəːθ] *n* возрожде́ние.

rebound [*vi* rɪ'baund, *n* 'riːbaund] *vi*: **to ~ (off)** отска́кивать (отскочи́ть* *perf*) (от +*gen*) ♦ *n*: **on the ~** (*ball*) на отско́ке; **he married her on**

the ~ он жени́лся на ней по́сле разочарова́ния в любви́ к друго́й.

rebuff [rɪ'bʌf] *n* отпо́р ♦ *vt* (*suggestion*) ре́зко отклоня́ть (отклони́ть *perf*); (*person*) дава́ть* (дать* *perf*) отпо́р +*dat*.

rebuild [riː'bɪld] *irreg vt* (*town, building etc*) перестра́ивать (перестро́ить *perf*); (*economy, confidence*) восстана́вливать (восстанови́ть* *perf*).

rebuke [rɪ'bjuːk] *vt* упрека́ть (упрекну́ть *perf*), де́лать (сде́лать *perf*) вы́говор +*dat* ♦ *n* упрёк, вы́говор.

rebut [rɪ'bʌt] *vt* опроверга́ть (опрове́ргнуть* *perf*).

rebuttal [rɪ'bʌtl] *n* опроверже́ние.

recalcitrant [rɪ'kælsɪtrənt] *adj* непоко́рный* (непоко́рен).

recall [*vb* rɪ'kɔːl, *n* 'riːkɔːl] *vt* вспомина́ть (вспо́мнить *perf*); (*parliament, ambassador etc*) отзыва́ть (отозва́ть* *perf*); (*COMPUT*) перевызыва́ть (перевы́звать *perf*), вызыва́ть (вы́звать *perf*) повто́рно ♦ *n* (*ability to remember*) па́мять *f*; (*of ambassador etc*) о́тзыв; **the event is beyond ~** собы́тие безвозвра́тно исче́зло из па́мяти.

recant [rɪ'kænt] *vi* отрека́ться (отре́чься* *perf*).

recap ['riːkæp] *vt* (*summarize*) резюми́ровать (*impf/perf*) ♦ *vi* де́лать (сде́лать *perf*) резюме́ ♦ *n* резюме́ *nt ind*.

recapitulate [riːkə'pɪtjuleɪt] *vti* = **recap**.

recapture [riː'kæptʃə'] *vt* (*town, territory etc*) сно́ва захва́тывать (захвати́ть* *perf*); (*atmosphere, mood etc*) воссоздава́ть* (воссозда́ть* *perf*).

rec'd *abbr* (*COMM*) = received.

recede [rɪ'siːd] *vi* (*tide*) спада́ть (спасть* *perf*); (*lights*) угаса́ть* (уга́снуть* *perf*); (*memory*) слабе́ть (ослабе́ть *perf*); (*hair*) реде́ть* (пореде́ть *perf*).

receding [rɪ'siːdɪŋ] *adj* (*hair*) реде́ющий; (*chin*) сре́занный (сре́зан).

receipt [rɪ'siːt] *n* (*document*) квита́нция; (*act of receiving*) получе́ние; **~s** *npl* (*COMM*) де́нежные поступле́ния *ntpl*, платежи́ *mpl*; **to acknowledge ~ of** подтвержда́ть (подтверди́ть* *perf*) получе́ние +*gen*; **on ~ of** по получе́нии; **we are in ~ of** ... (*COMM*) мы получи́ли ....

receivable [rɪ'siːvəbl] *adj* (*COMM*) подлежа́щий получе́нию; (: *bill, account*) надлежа́щий упла́те.

receive [rɪ'siːv] *vt* получа́ть (получи́ть* *perf*); (*criticism*) встреча́ть (встре́тить* *perf*); (*visitor, guest*) принима́ть (приня́ть* *perf*); **"received with thanks"** (*formal*) „полу́чено с благода́рностью".

receiver [rɪ'siːvə'] *n* (*TEL*) (телефо́нная трубка*; (*RADIO*) (радио-)прие́мник; (*TV*)

---

* marks translations which have irregular inflections. The Russian-English side of the dictionary gives inflectional information.

телеви́зор; (*COMM*) ликвида́тор (*неплатёжеспосо́бной компа́нии*); ~ **of stolen goods** укрыва́тель(ница) *m(f)* кра́деного.

receivership [rɪ'siːvəʃɪp] *n конфиска́ция иму́щества обанкро́тившейся компа́нии суде́бными исполни́телями в це́лях вы́платы долго́в кредито́рам.

recent ['riːsnt] *adj* (*event, times*) неда́вний*; **in ~ years** в *or* за после́дние го́ды.

recently ['riːsntlɪ] *adv* неда́вно; **until ~** до неда́внего вре́мени; **as ~ as last year** ещё в про́шлом году́.

receptacle [rɪ'sɛptɪkl] *n* сосу́д.

reception [rɪ'sɛpʃən] *n* (*in hotel*) регистра́ция; (*in office*) приёмная *f adj*; (*in hospital*) регистрату́ра; (*party, also RADIO, TV*) приём; **we got a warm ~** нам был ока́зан тёплый приём.

reception centre *n* (*BRIT*) *приёмный пункт для размеще́ния бе́женцев, бездо́мных итп.*

reception desk *n* (*in hotel*) стол регистра́ции; (*in hospital, at doctor's*) регистрату́ра; (*in large building, offices*) отде́л приёма посети́телей.

receptionist [rɪ'sɛpʃənɪst] *n* (*in hotel, hospital*) регистра́тор; (*in firm*) секрета́рь* *m* по приёму посети́телей.

receptive [rɪ'sɛptɪv] *adj* восприи́мчивый (восприи́мчив).

recess [rɪ'sɛs] *n* (*in room*) ни́ша; (*secret place*) тайни́к*; (*POL etc*: *holiday*) кани́кулы *pl*; (*US: LAW: short break*) переры́в; (: *SCOL*) больша́я переме́на.

recession [rɪ'sɛʃən] *n* (*ECON*) спад.

recharge [riː'tʃɑːdʒ] *vt* (*battery*) перезаряжа́ть (перезаряди́ть* *perf*).

rechargeable [riː'tʃɑːdʒəbl] *adj* перезаряжа́ющийся.

recipe ['rɛsɪpɪ] *n* (*also fig*) реце́пт.

recipient [rɪ'sɪpɪənt] *n* получа́тель *m*.

reciprocal [rɪ'sɪprəkl] *adj* взаи́мный* (взаи́мен), обою́дный* (обою́ден).

reciprocate [rɪ'sɪprəkeɪt] *vt* отвеча́ть (отве́тить* *perf*) на +*acc* ♦ *vi* (*favour*) отпла́чивать (отплати́ть* *perf*); (*feeling*) отвеча́ть (отве́тить* *perf*) взаи́мностью.

recital [rɪ'saɪtl] *n* (*concert*) со́льный конце́рт.

recitation [rɛsɪ'teɪʃən] *n* (*of poetry*) деклама́ция; (*of prose*) чте́ние.

recite [rɪ'saɪt] *vt* (*poem*) деклами́ровать (продеклами́ровать *perf*); (*prose*) чита́ть (*impf*) (вслух); (*complaints, grievances etc*) произноси́ть* (произнести́* *perf*).

reckless ['rɛkləs] *adj* безрассу́дный* (безрассу́ден).

recklessly ['rɛkləslɪ] *adv* безрассу́дно.

reckon ['rɛkən] *vt* (*calculate*) счита́ть (посчита́ть *or* сосчита́ть *perf*); (*think*): **I ~ that ...** я счита́ю, что ... ♦ *vi*: **he is somebody to be ~ed with** с таки́м челове́ком, как он, ну́жно счита́ться; **to ~ without sb** не счита́ться

(посчита́ться *perf*) с кем-н; **to ~ without sth** не учи́тывать (уче́сть* *perf*) чего́-н

▶ **reckon on** *vt fus* рассчи́тывать (*impf*) на +*acc*.

reckoning ['rɛknɪŋ] *n* (*calculation*) подсчёт, расчёт; **the day of ~** час распла́ты.

reclaim [rɪ'kleɪm] *vt* (*demand back*) тре́бовать (потре́бовать *perf*) обра́тно; (*land: from sea*) отвоёвывать (отвоева́ть* *perf*); (: *from forest etc*) осва́ивать (осво́ить *perf*); (*waste materials*) перераба́тывать (перерабо́тать *perf*).

reclamation [rɛklə'meɪʃən] *n* (*of land*) освое́ние.

recline [rɪ'klaɪn] *vi* отки́дываться (откину́ться *perf*).

reclining [rɪ'klaɪnɪŋ] *adj* (*seat*) отки́дывающийся.

recluse [rɪ'kluːs] *n* затво́рник(-ица).

recognition [rɛkəg'nɪʃən] *n* призна́ние; (*of person, place*) узнава́ние; **in ~ of** в знак призна́ния +*gen*; **to gain ~** получа́ть (получи́ть* *perf*) призна́ние; **he has changed beyond ~** он измени́лся до неузнава́емости.

recognizable ['rɛkəgnaɪzəbl] *adj*: ~ **(by)** узнава́емый (по +*dat*).

recognize ['rɛkəgnaɪz] *vt* признава́ть* (призна́ть* *perf*); (*person, place*) узнава́ть* (узна́ть *perf*); (*attitude, illness*) распознава́ть* (распозна́ть* *perf*); **to ~ by** узнава́ть* (узна́ть* *perf*) по +*dat*.

recoil [*n* 'riːkɔɪl, *vb* rɪ'kɔɪl] *n* (*of gun*) отда́ча ♦ *vi* (*person*): **to ~ from doing** в у́жасе отказа́ться (*perf*) +*infin*.

recollect [rɛkə'lɛkt] *vt* припомина́ть (припо́мнить *perf*), вспомина́ть (вспо́мнить *perf*).

recollection [rɛkə'lɛkʃən] *n* воспомина́ние, па́мять *f*; **to the best of my ~** наско́лько мне по́мнится.

recommend [rɛkə'mɛnd] *vt* рекомендова́ть (порекомендова́ть *perf*); **she has a lot to ~ her** мно́гое говори́т в её по́льзу.

recommendation [rɛkəmɛn'deɪʃən] *n* рекоменда́ция; **on the ~ of** по рекоменда́ции +*gen*.

recommended retail price *n* (*BRIT*) рекоменду́емая ро́зничная цена́*.

recompense ['rɛkəmpɛns] *n* компенса́ция.

reconcilable ['rɛkənsaɪləbl] *adj* (*ideas*) совмести́мый (совмести́м).

reconcile ['rɛkənsaɪl] *vt* (*people*) мири́ть (помири́ть *perf*); (*facts, beliefs*) примиря́ть (примири́ть *perf*); **to ~ o.s. to sth** смиря́ться (смири́ться *perf*) с чем-н.

reconciliation [rɛkənsɪlɪ'eɪʃən] *n* примире́ние.

recondite [rɪ'kɔndaɪt] *adj* зау́мный* (зау́мен).

recondition [riːkən'dɪʃən] *vt* (*machine*) ремонти́ровать (отремонти́ровать *perf*).

reconditioned [riːkən'dɪʃənd] *adj* отремонти́рованный (отремонти́рован).

reconnaissance [rɪ'kɔnɪsns] *n* (*MIL*) разве́дка,

рекогносциро́вка.

reconnoitre [rɛkə'nɔɪtə^r] (US **reconnoiter**) vt (MIL: enemy territory) разве́дывать (разве́дать perf).

reconsider [ri:kən'sɪdə^r] vt пересма́тривать (пересмотре́ть* perf) ♦ vi переду́мать (perf).

reconstitute [ri:'kɔnstɪtju:t] vt (organization) реорганизова́ть (impf/perf); (food) восстана́вливать (восстанови́ть* perf).

reconstruct [ri:kən'strʌkt] vt перестра́ивать (перестро́ить perf); (event, crime) воспроизводи́ть* (воспроизвести́* perf), реконструи́ровать (impf/perf).

reconstruction [ri:kən'strʌkʃən] n (of building) реконстру́кция; (of country) перестро́йка; (of crime) воспроизведе́ние.

reconvene [ri:kən'vi:n] vi возобновля́ть (возобнови́ть* perf) рабо́ту.

record [vb rɪ'kɔ:d, n, adj 'rɛkɔ:d] vt (in writing, on tape) запи́сывать (записа́ть* perf); (register: temperature, speed etc) регистри́ровать (зарегистри́ровать perf) ♦ n (written account, also COMPUT) за́пись f; (of meeting) протоко́л; (of attendance) учёт; (file) де́ло*; (MUS) пласти́нка*; (history: of person, company) репута́ция; (also: criminal ~) суди́мость f; (SPORT) реко́рд ♦ adj: in ~ time в реко́рдное вре́мя; **public ~ s** архи́вные за́писи; **to keep a ~ of** вести́* (impf) учёт +gen; **to put the ~ straight** (fig) пока́зывать (показа́ть* perf) и́стинное положе́ние веще́й; **he is on ~ as saying that** ... изве́стно, что он сказа́л, что ...; **off the ~** (statement) неофициа́льный; (speak) неофициа́льно.

recorded delivery [rɪ'kɔ:dɪd-] n (BRIT) доста́вка с уведомле́нием (о вруче́нии).

recorder [rɪ'kɔ:də^r] n (MUS) англи́йская фле́йта; (LAW) реко́рдер.

record holder (SPORT) n рекордсме́н(ка).

recording [rɪ'kɔ:dɪŋ] n за́пись f.

recording studio n сту́дия звукоза́писи.

record library n фоноте́ка.

record player n прои́грыватель m.

recount [rɪ'kaunt] vt (story) передава́ть* (переда́ть* perf); (event) пове́дать (perf) о +prp.

re-count ['ri:kaunt] n (of votes) пересчёт ♦ vt пересчи́тывать (пересчита́ть perf).

recoup [rɪ'ku:p] vt: **to ~ one's losses** возвраща́ть (верну́ть perf) поте́рянное.

recourse [rɪ'kɔ:s] n: **to have ~ to** прибега́ть (прибе́гнуть* perf) к +dat.

recover [rɪ'kʌvə^r] vt (lost or stolen items) получа́ть (получи́ть* perf) обра́тно; (financial loss) возмеща́ть (возмести́ть* perf) ♦ vi (subj: country) встава́ть* (встать* perf) на́ ноги; (: economy) улучша́ться (улу́чшиться perf); (get better): **to ~ (from)** оправля́ться

(опра́виться* perf) (от +gen).

re-cover [ri:'kʌvə^r] vt (chair etc) перебива́ть (переби́ть* perf) (оби́вку).

recovery [rɪ'kʌvərɪ] n (from illness, operation) выздоровле́ние; (in economy, finances) подъём; (of stolen items) возвраще́ние; (of lost items) обнаруже́ние.

re-create [ri:krɪ'eɪt] vt воссоздава́ть* (воссозда́ть* perf).

recreation [rɛkrɪ'eɪʃən] n (free time) о́тдых; (leisure activities) развлече́ние.

recreational [rɛkrɪ'eɪʃənl] adj: ~ **facilities** усло́вия ntpl для о́тдыха и развлече́ния.

recreational drug n нарко́тик, принима́емый для удово́льствия и не предполага́ющий наркоти́ческой зави́симости.

recrimination [rɪkrɪmɪ'neɪʃən] n взаи́мные обвине́ния ntpl.

recruit [rɪ'kru:t] n (MIL) новобра́нец*, призывни́к*; (in company) но́вый сотру́дник; (in organization) но́вый член ♦ vt (into army, organization) вербова́ть (завербова́ть perf); (into comany) нанима́ть (наня́ть* perf).

recruiting office [rɪ'kru:tɪŋ-] n (MIL) вербо́вочный пункт.

recruitment [rɪ'kru:tmənt] n (MIL) вербо́вка; (by company) набо́р (на рабо́ту).

rectangle ['rɛktæŋgl] n прямоуго́льник.

rectangular [rɛk'tæŋgjulə^r] adj прямоуго́льный.

rectify ['rɛktɪfaɪ] vt исправля́ть (испра́вить* perf).

rector ['rɛktə^r] n (REL) прихо́дский* свяще́нник.

rectory ['rɛktərɪ] n (house) дом* прихо́дского свяще́нника.

rectum ['rɛktəm] n прямая кишка́*.

recuperate [rɪ'kju:pəreɪt] vi оправля́ться (опра́виться* perf).

recur [rɪ'kɔ:^r] vi повторя́ться (повтори́ться perf).

recurrence [rɪ'kɔ:rns] n повторе́ние.

recurrent [rɪ'kɔ:rnt] adj повторя́ющийся.

recurring [rɪ'kɔ:rɪŋ] adj (problem) постоя́нно возника́ющий; (dream) повторя́ющийся.

recycle [ri:'saɪkl] vt перераба́тывать (перерабо́тать perf).

red [rɛd] n кра́сный цвет; (pej: POL) кра́сный (-ая) m(f) adj ♦ adj кра́сный* (кра́сен); (hair) ры́жий*; (wine) кра́сный; **she was dressed in ~** она́ была́ в кра́сном; **to be in the ~** име́ть (impf) задо́лженность.

red alert n состоя́ние боево́й гото́вности.

red-blooded ['rɛd'blʌdɪd] adj: ~ **male** саме́ц* (перен).

red-carpet treatment [rɛd'ka:pɪt-] n торже́ственный приём.

Red Cross n Кра́сный Крест*.

redcurrant ['rɛdkʌrənt] n кра́сная сморо́дина f

---

* marks translations which have irregular inflections. The Russian-English side of the dictionary gives inflectional information.

no pl.
redden ['rɛdn] *vi* красне́ть (покрасне́ть *perf*) ♦
vt окра́шивать (окра́сить* *perf*) в кра́сный
цвет.
reddish ['rɛdɪʃ] *adj* краснова́тый (краснова́т);
(*hair*) рыжева́тый (рыжева́т).
redecorate [ri:'dɛkəreɪt] *vt* ремонти́ровать
(отремонти́ровать *perf*) ♦ *vi* де́лать (сде́лать
perf) ремо́нт.
redecoration [ri:dɛkə'reɪʃən] *n* ремо́нт.
redeem [rɪ'di:m] *vt* (*situation, reputation*)
спаса́ть (спасти́* *perf*); (*pawned item*)
выкупа́ть (вы́купить* *perf*); (*debt*)
выпла́чивать (вы́платить* *perf*); (*REL*)
искупа́ть (искупи́ть* *perf*); **to ~ o.s.** искупа́ть
(искупи́ть* *perf*) свою́ вину́.
redeemable [rɪ'di:məbl] *adj* подлежа́щий
вы́купу.
redeeming [rɪ'di:mɪŋ] *adj*: **~ feature**
подкупа́ющее ка́чество.
redefine [ri:dɪ'faɪn] *vt* (*position, theory*) пере-
сма́тривать (пересмотре́ть* *perf*); (*word,
concept*) дава́ть* (дать* *perf*) но́вое
определе́ние +*dat*.
redemption [rɪ'dɛmʃən] *n* (*REL*) искупле́ние
грехо́в; **past** *or* **beyond ~** (*fig*) безнаде́жный*
(безнаде́жен), без наде́жды на спасе́ние.
redeploy [ri:dɪ'plɔɪ] *vt* (*resources*) перерас-
пределя́ть (перераспредели́ть *perf*); (*MIL*)
передислоци́ровать (*impf/perf*).
redeployment [ri:dɪ'plɔɪmənt] *n* (*see vb*)
перераспределе́ние; передислока́ция.
redevelop [ri:dɪ'vɛləp] *vt* (*area*) перестра́ивать
(перестро́ить *perf*).
redevelopment [ri:dɪ'vɛləpmənt] *n*
перестро́йка.
red-handed [rɛd'hændɪd] *adj*: **he was caught ~**
его́ пойма́ли с поли́чным.
redhead ['rɛdhɛd] *n* ры́жий*(-ая) *m(f) adj.*
red herring *n* (*fig*) отвлека́ющий манёвр.
red-hot [rɛd'hɔt] *adj* (*metal*) раскалённый*
(раскалён) докрасна́.
redirect [ri:daɪ'rɛkt] *vt* (*mail*) переадресо́в-
ывать (переадресова́ть *perf*).
rediscover [ri:dɪs'kʌvə'] *vt* за́ново открыва́ть
(откры́ть* *perf*).
redistribute [ri:dɪs'trɪbju:t] *vt* перерас-
пределя́ть (перераспредели́ть *perf*).
red-letter day ['rɛdlɛtə-] *n* пра́здничный день*
m.
red light *n*: **to go through a ~ ~** (*AUT*) е́хать*
(пое́хать* *perf*) на кра́сный свет.
red-light district ['rɛdlaɪt-] *n* кварта́л
публи́чных домо́в.
red meat *n* тёмное мя́со (*осо́бенно говя́дина и
бара́нина*).
redness ['rɛdnɪs] *n* краснота́; (*of hair*)
рыжина́*.
redo [ri:'du:] *irreg vt* переде́лывать
(переде́лать *perf*).
redolent ['rɛdələnt] *adj* (*fig*) напомина́ющий;

(*smell*): **~ of** (*unpleasant*) отдаю́щий +*instr*;
(*pleasant*) па́нущий +*gen*.
redouble [ri:'dʌbl] *vt*: **to ~ one's efforts**
удва́ивать (удво́ить *perf*) свои́ уси́лия.
redraft [ri:'drɑ:ft] *vt* перепи́сывать
(переписа́ть* *perf*).
redraw [ri:'drɔ:] *vt* изменя́ть (измени́ть* *perf*).
redress [rɪ'drɛs] *n* (*compensation*) возмеще́ние
♦ *vt* (*error, wrong*) исправля́ть (испра́вить*
perf); **to ~ the balance** восстана́вливать
(восстанови́ть* *perf*) равнове́сие сил.
Red Sea *n*: **the ~ ~** Кра́сное мо́ре.
red tape *n* (*fig*) волоки́та.
reduce [rɪ'dju:s] *vt* сокраща́ть (сократи́ть*
perf); **to ~ sth by/to** сокраща́ть (сократи́ть*
perf) что-н на +*acc*/до +*gen*; **to ~ sb to** (*tears*)
доводи́ть* (довести́* *perf*) кого́-н до +*gen*; **to
~ sb to silence** заставля́ть (заста́вить* *perf*)
кого́-н замолча́ть; **he was ~d to stealing** он
дошёл до того́, что стал ворова́ть; **"reduce
speed now"** (*AUT*) "сба́вьте ско́рость".
reduced [rɪ'dju:st] *adj* (*goods*) по сни́женным
це́нам; (*ticket*) со ски́дкой; **at a ~ price**
(*goods*) по сни́женной цене́; (*ticket*) со
ски́дкой.
reduction [rɪ'dʌkʃən] *n* (*in price*) ски́дка; (*in
numbers*) сокраще́ние.
redundancy [rɪ'dʌndənsɪ] (*BRIT*) *n* (*dismissal*)
увольне́ние (*при сокраще́нии шта́тов*);
(*unemployment*) сокраще́ние шта́тов;
compulsory ~ вы́нужденное увольне́ние;
voluntary ~ увольне́ние по со́бственному
жела́нию.
redundancy payment *n* (*BRIT*) выходно́е
посо́бие (*при сокраще́нии шта́тов*).
redundant [rɪ'dʌndnt] *adj* (*BRIT: unemployed*)
уво́ленный (уво́лен); (*useless*) изли́шний*
(изли́шен); **he was made ~** его́ сократи́ли.
reed [ri:d] *n* (*BOT*) тростни́к*; (*MUS*) язычо́к*.
re-educate [ri:'ɛdjukeɪt] *vt* перевоспи́тывать
(перевоспита́ть *perf*).
reedy ['ri:dɪ] *adj* (*voice*) пронзи́тельный*
(пронзи́телен).
reef [ri:f] *n* риф.
reek [ri:k] *vi*: **to ~ (of)** си́льно па́хнуть* (*impf*)
(+*instr*).
reel [ri:l] *n* кату́шка*; (*of film, tape*) боби́на;
(*dance*) рил (*наро́дный хорово́дный та́нец*) ♦
vi (*sway*) кача́ться (*impf*), шата́ться (*impf*); **my
head is ~ing** у меня́ кру́жится голова́
▸ **reel in** *vt* (*line*) сма́тывать (смота́ть *perf*);
(*fish*) выта́скивать (вы́тащить *perf*) (*при
по́мощи спи́ннинга*)
▸ **reel off** *vt* (*say*) вы́палить (*perf*).
re-election [ri:ɪ'lɛkʃən] *n* (*event*) перевы́боры
pl; (*of person*) переизбра́ние.
re-enter [ri:'ɛntə'] *vt* вновь входи́ть* (войти́*
perf).
re-entry [ri:'ɛntrɪ] *n* повто́рный вход.
re-examine [ri:ɪg'zæmɪn] *vt* пересма́тривать
(пересмотре́ть* *perf*).

re-export ['riːɪks'pɔːt] vt реэкспортировать (impf/perf) ◆ n реэкспорт.

ref [rɛf] n abbr (SPORT: inf) = **referee**.

ref. abbr (COMM: = with reference to) ссылаясь на +acc.

refectory [rɪ'fɛktərɪ] n столовая f adj.

refer [rɪ'fɜː'] vt: **to ~ sb to** (book, source) отсылать (отослать* perf) кого-н к +dat; (doctor) направлять (направить* perf) кого-н к +dat; **to ~ sth to** (pass on) передавать* (передать* perf) что-н к +dat; **he ~red me to the manager** он направил меня к управляющему

▸ **refer to** vt fus (mention) упоминать (упомянуть* perf) о +prp; (relate to) относиться* (impf) к +dat; (consult) обращаться (обратиться* perf) к +dat; **~ring to your letter** ссылаясь на Ваше письмо.

referee [rɛfə'riː] n (SPORT) рефери m ind, судья* m; (BRIT: for job application) лицо, дающее рекомендацию ◆ vt судить* (impf).

reference ['rɛfrəns] n (mention) упоминание; (in book, paper) ссылка*; (for job application: letter) рекомендация; (: person) лицо, дающее рекомендацию; **with ~ to** (in letter) ссылаясь на +acc; **"please quote this ~"** (COMM) "сошлитесь на этот справочный номер".

reference book n справочник.

reference library n справочная библиотека.

reference number n справочный номер*.

referenda [rɛfə'rɛndə] npl of **referendum**.

referendum [rɛfə'rɛndəm] (pl **referenda**) n референдум.

referral [rɪ'fɜːrəl] n направление.

refill [vb riː'fɪl, n 'riːfɪl] vt (glass) снова наполнять (наполнить perf); (pen) заправлять (заправить* perf) ◆ n (for pen) запасной стержень* m.

refine [rɪ'faɪn] vt (sugar) рафинировать (impf/perf); (oil) очищать (очистить* perf); (theory, idea, task) совершенствовать (усовершенствовать perf).

refined [rɪ'faɪnd] adj (person, taste) утончённый* (утончён); (sugar) рафинированный*; (oil) очищенный*.

refinement [rɪ'faɪnmənt] n (of person) утончённость f; (of system) усовершенствование.

refinery [rɪ'faɪnərɪ] n (for oil) нефтеперерабатывающий завод.

refit [riː'fɪt] n (NAUT) переоборудование ◆ vt (ship) переоборудовать (impf/perf).

reflate [riː'fleɪt] vt: **to ~ the economy** проводить* (провести* perf) рефляцию.

reflation [riː'fleɪʃən] n рефляция.

reflationary [riː'fleɪʃənrɪ] adj рефляционный.

reflect [rɪ'flɛkt] vt (also fig) отражать

(отразить* perf) ◆ vi (think) размышлять (impf)

▸ **reflect on** vt (discredit) бросать (бросить* perf) тень на +acc.

reflection [rɪ'flɛkʃən] n (also fig) отражение; (thought) размышление; (criticism): **~ on** осуждение +gen; **on ~** по размышлении.

reflector [rɪ'flɛktə'] n (on car, bicycle) отражатель m; (for light, heat) рефлектор.

reflex ['riːflɛks] adj (action, gesture) рефлекторный ◆ n рефлекс.

reflexive [rɪ'flɛksɪv] adj (LING) возвратный.

reform [rɪ'fɔːm] n (of law, system) реформа; (of sinner, character) преобразование ◆ vt (character) преобразовать (impf/perf); (system) реформировать (impf/perf).

reformat [riː'fɔːmæt] vt (COMPUT) переформатировать (impf/perf).

Reformation [rɛfə'meɪʃən] n: **the ~** Реформация.

reformatory [rɪ'fɔːmətərɪ] n (US) исправительное заведение.

reformed [rɪ'fɔːmd] adj (character, alcoholic) исправившийся.

refrain [rɪ'freɪn] n (of song) припев ◆ vi: **to ~ from commenting/visiting** воздерживаться (воздержаться* perf) от комментариев/визита.

refresh [rɪ'frɛʃ] vt освежать (освежить perf).

refresher course [rɪ'frɛʃə-] n (BRIT) курс повышения квалификации.

refreshing [rɪ'frɛʃɪŋ] adj (drink, sleep) освежающий (освежающ); (change, idea) свежий.

refreshment [rɪ'frɛʃmənt] n (food) закуска*; (drink) напиток*; **I am in need of (some) ~** мне надо закусить.

refreshments [rɪ'frɛʃmənts] npl закуски fpl и напитки mpl.

refrigeration [rɪfrɪdʒə'reɪʃən] n (low temperature) охлаждение; (in deep freeze) замораживание.

refrigerator [rɪ'frɪdʒəreɪtə'] n холодильник.

refuel [riː'fjuəl] vi заправляться (заправиться* perf) ◆ vt заправлять (заправить* perf).

refuelling [riː'fjuəlɪŋ] n заправка*.

refuge ['rɛfjuːdʒ] n (shelter) убежище; **to take ~ in** укрываться (укрыться* perf) в +prp.

refugee [rɛfjuː'dʒiː] n беженец*(-нка*); **a political ~** политический*(-ая) беженец (-нка*).

refugee camp n лагерь* m беженцев.

refund [n 'riːfʌnd, vb rɪ'fʌnd] n возмещение ◆ vt (money) возмещать (возместить* perf).

refurbish [riː'fəːbɪʃ] vt заново отделывать (отделать perf).

refurbishment [riː'fəːbɪʃmənt] n ремонт.

refurnish [riː'fəːnɪʃ] vt заново обставлять (обставить* perf).

---

refusal [rɪ'fjuːzəl] n отка́з; **first ~** (*option*)
пра́во пе́рвого вы́бора.
refuse¹ [rɪ'fjuːz] vt (*offer, gift*) отка́зываться
(отказа́ться* perf) от +gen; (*permission,
consent*) отка́зывать (отказа́ть* perf) в +prp ◆
vi отка́зываться (отказа́ться* perf); (*horse*)
упря́миться (заупря́миться perf); **to ~ to do**
отка́зываться (отказа́ться* perf) +infin.
refuse² ['rɛfjuːs] n му́сор*.
refuse collection n убо́рка му́сора.
refuse disposal n (*by carting away*) вы́воз
му́сора.
refusenik [rɪ'fjuːznɪk] n отка́зник.
refute [rɪ'fjuːt] vt опроверга́ть (опрове́ргнуть*
perf).
regain [rɪ'geɪn] vt (*power, position*) вновь
обрета́ть (обрести́* perf).
regal ['riːgl] adj короле́вский*.
regale [rɪ'geɪl] vt: **to ~ sb with sth** развлека́ть
(развле́чь* perf) кого́-н чем-н.
regalia [rɪ'geɪlɪə] n рега́лии fpl.
regard [rɪ'gɑːd] n (*esteem*) уваже́ние ◆ vt
(*consider*) счита́ть (*impf*); (*view, look on*): **to ~
with** относи́ться (*impf*) or рассма́триваться
(*impf*) с +instr; **to give one's ~s to** передава́ть*
(переда́ть* perf) приве́т +dat; **"with kindest
~s"** „с наилу́чшими пожела́ниями"; (*more
formal*) „с уваже́нием"; **as ~s, with ~ to** что
каса́ется +gen, относи́тельно +gen.
regarding [rɪ'gɑːdɪŋ] prep относи́тельно +gen.
regardless [rɪ'gɑːdlɪs] adv (*carry on, continue*)
несмотря́ ни на что́; **~ of** не счита́ясь с
+instr.
regatta [rɪ'gætə] n рега́та.
regency ['riːdʒənsɪ] n ре́генство ◆ adj: **R~**
(*furniture, style*) эпо́хи ре́гентства.
regenerate [rɪ'dʒɛnəreɪt] vt возрожда́ть
(возроди́ть* perf) ◆ vi возрожда́ться
(возроди́ться* perf).
regent ['riːdʒənt] n ре́гент.
reggae ['rɛgeɪ] n рэ́гги m ind.
regime [reɪ'ʒiːm] n (*system of government*)
режи́м.
regiment ['rɛdʒɪmənt] n полк* ◆ vt подчиня́ть
(подчини́ть perf) жёсткому контро́лю.
regimental [rɛdʒɪ'mɛntl] adj полково́й.
regimentation [rɛdʒɪmɛn'teɪʃən] n жёсткий*
контро́ль m.
region ['riːdʒən] n (*area: of country*) райо́н,
регио́н; (*ADMIN, ANAT*) о́бласть* f; **in the ~ of**
(*fig: approximately*) в райо́не +gen.
regional ['riːdʒənl] adj (*organization,
committee*) областно́й, региона́льный;
(*characteristic of region*) ме́стный.
regional development n региона́льное
разви́тие.
register ['rɛdʒɪstəʳ] n (*census, record*) за́пись f;
(*SCOL*) журна́л; (*also:* **electoral ~**) спи́сок*
избира́телей; (*MUS*) реги́стр ◆ vt
регистри́ровать (зарегистри́ровать perf);
(*subj: meter, gauge*) пока́зывать (показа́ть*

perf) ◆ vi регистри́роваться
(зарегистри́роваться perf); (*as student*)
запи́сываться (записа́ться* perf); (*make
impression*) запечатлева́ться (запечатле́ться
perf) в па́мяти; **to ~ for a course**
запи́сываться (записа́ться* perf) на курс; **to
~ a protest** выража́ть (вы́разить* perf)
проте́ст.
registered ['rɛdʒɪstəd] adj (*letter*) заказно́й;
(*nurse, addict*) зарегистри́рованный*.
registered company n зарегистри́рованная
компа́ния.
registered nurse n (*US*) зарегистри́рованная
медсестра́*.
registered office n зарегистри́рованный
о́фис.
Registered Trademark n зарегистри́р-
ованный това́рный знак.
registrar ['rɛdʒɪstrɑː'] n регистра́тор; (*BRIT: in
hospital*) гла́вный врач*.
registration [rɛdʒɪs'treɪʃən] n регистра́ция;
(*AUT: also:* **~ number**) (регистрацио́нный)
но́мер* маши́ны.
registry ['rɛdʒɪstrɪ] n регистрату́ра.
registry office n (*BRIT*) ≈ ЗАГС (*отде́л за́писей
гражда́нского состоя́ния*).
regret [rɪ'grɛt] n (*sorrow*) сожале́ние ◆ vt
сожале́ть (*impf*) о +prp; (*death*) опла́кивать
(опла́кать* perf); **to ~ that** ... сожале́ть (*impf*),
что ...; **we ~ to inform you that** ... мы с
сожале́нием сообща́ем Вам, что ....
regretfully [rɪ'grɛtfəlɪ] adv (*unfortunately*) к
сожале́нию.
regrettable [rɪ'grɛtəbl] adj (*unfortunate*)
приско́рбный* (приско́рбен), досто́йный*
(досто́ин) сожале́ния.
regrettably [rɪ'grɛtəblɪ] adv (*drunk, late*)
огорчи́тельным о́бразом; **~, he** ... к
сожале́нию, он ....
Regt abbr (*MIL*) = **regiment**.
regular ['rɛgjuləʳ] adj регуля́рный*
(регуля́рен); (*even*) ро́вный* (ро́вен);
(*symmetrical*) пра́вильный* (пра́вилен); (:
usual: time) определённый; (: *doctor,
customer*) регуля́рный; (*LING*) пра́вильный;
(*COMM: size*) сре́дний* ◆ n (*in cafe, restaurnat*)
завсегда́тай; (*in shop*) клие́нт; **~ soldier**
солда́т регуля́рной а́рмии.
regularity [rɛgju'lærɪtɪ] n (*frequency*)
регуля́рность f.
regularly ['rɛgjuləlɪ] adv регуля́рно;
(*symmetrically: shaped etc*) пра́вильно.
regulate ['rɛgjuleɪt] vt (*control, adjust*)
регули́ровать (*impf*).
regulation [rɛgju'leɪʃən] n регули́рование;
(*rule*) пра́вило.
regulatory [rɛgju'leɪtrɪ] adj регули́рующий.
rehabilitate [riːə'bɪlɪteɪt] vt (*criminal*)
интегри́ровать (*impf/perf*); (*invalid, addict*)
реабилити́ровать (*impf/perf*).
rehabilitation ['riːəbɪlɪ'teɪʃən] n (*of criminal*)

интегра́ция; (*of disabled, addict*)
реабилита́ция.
rehash [riːˈhæʃ] *vt* (*inf*) преподноси́ть*
(преподнести́* *perf*) в но́вом све́те.
rehearsal [rɪˈhəːsəl] *n* репети́ция; **dress ~**
генера́льная репети́ция.
rehearse [rɪˈhəːs] *vt* репети́ровать
(отрепети́ровать *perf*).
rehouse [riːˈhauz] *vt* (*person*) переселя́ть
(пересели́ть *perf*).
reign [reɪn] *n* ца́рствование; (*fig*) госпо́дство ◆
vi (*monarch*) ца́рствовать (*impf*); (*fig*) цари́ть
(*impf*).
reigning [ˈreɪnɪŋ] *adj* (*monarch*) ца́рствующий;
(*champion*) ны́нешний*.
reimburse [riːɪmˈbəːs] *vt* возмеща́ть
(возмести́ть* *perf*).
rein [reɪn] *n* (*for horse*) вожжа́*; **to give sb free ~**
(*fig*) дава́ть* (дать* *perf*) кому́-н свобо́ду
де́йствий.
reincarnation [riːɪnkɑːˈneɪʃən] *n* (*belief*)
переселе́ние душ*.
reindeer [ˈreɪndɪəʳ] *n inv* се́верный оле́нь *m*.
reinforce [riːɪnˈfɔːs] *vt* (*strengthen*) укрепля́ть
(укрепи́ть* *perf*); (*back up*) подкрепля́ть
(подкрепи́ть* *perf*).
reinforced concrete *n* железобето́н.
reinforcement [riːɪnˈfɔːsmənt] *n* (*strengthening*)
укрепле́ние; (*action*) усиле́ние; **~s** *npl* (*MIL*)
подкрепле́ние *ntsg*.
reinstate [riːɪnˈsteɪt] *vt* восстана́вливать
(восстанови́ть* *perf*) в пре́жнем положе́нии.
reinstatement [riːɪnˈsteɪtmənt] *n*
восстановле́ние в пре́жнем положе́нии.
reissue [riːˈɪʃjuː] *vt* (*book*) переиздава́ть*
(переизда́ть* *perf*); (*film*) сно́ва выпуска́ть
(вы́пустить* *perf*).
reiterate [riːˈɪtəreɪt] *vt* повторя́ть (повтори́ть
perf).
reject [*vt* rɪˈdʒɛkt, *n* ˈriːdʒɛkt] *vt* отклоня́ть
(отклони́ть* *perf*), отверга́ть (отве́ргнуть*
perf); (*political system*) отверга́ть
(отве́ргнуть* *perf*); (*candidate*) отклоня́ть
(отклони́ть* *perf*); (*coin*) не принима́ть
(приня́ть* *perf*); (*goods, fruit etc*) бракова́ть
(забракова́ть *perf*) ◆ *n* (*COMM: single item*)
бако́ванное изде́лие; **~s** брак.
rejection [rɪˈdʒɛkʃən] *n* отклоне́ние; (*of
candidate*) отклоне́ние.
rejoice [rɪˈdʒɔɪs] *vi*: **to ~ at** *or* **over** ликова́ть
(*impf*) по по́воду +*gen*.
rejoinder [rɪˈdʒɔɪndəʳ] *n* (*retort*) возраже́ние,
отве́т.
rejuvenate [rɪˈdʒuːvəneɪt] *vt* (*person*)
омола́живать (омолоди́ть* *perf*);
(*organization, system etc*) обновля́ть
(обнови́ть* *perf*).
rekindle [riːˈkɪndl] *vt* разжига́ть (разже́чь*

perf).
relapse [rɪˈlæps] *n* (*MED*) рециди́в ◆ *vi*: **to ~ into**
(*depression*) (сно́ва) впада́ть (впасть* *perf*) в
+*acc*.
relate [rɪˈleɪt] *vt* (*tell*) переска́зывать
(пересказа́ть* *perf*); (*connect*): **to ~ sth to**
относи́ть* (отнести́* *perf*) что-н к +*dat* ◆ *vi*: **to
~ to** (*person*) сходи́ться* (*impf*) с +*instr*;
(*subject, thing*) относи́ться* (*impf*) к +*dat*.
related [rɪˈleɪtɪd] *adj*: **~ (to)** (*person*) свя́занный
роство́м (с +*instr*); (*animal, language*)
ро́дственный* (ро́дствен) (с +*instr*); **they are
~** они́ состоя́т в родстве́.
relating to [rɪˈleɪtɪŋ-] *prep* относи́тельно +*gen*.
relation [rɪˈleɪʃən] *n* (*member of family*)
ро́дственник(-ица); (*connection*) отноше́ние;
~s *npl* (*dealings*) сноше́ния *ntpl*; (*relatives*)
родня́ *fsg*; **diplomatic/international ~s**
дипломати́ческие/междунаро́дные
отноше́ния; **in ~ to** относи́тельно +*gen*; **to
bear no ~ to** не име́ть (*impf*) никако́го
отноше́ния к +*dat*.
relationship [rɪˈleɪʃənʃɪp] *n* (*between two
people, countries*) (взаимо-)отноше́ния *ntpl*;
(*between two things*) связь *f*; (*also:* **family ~**)
родство́; (*affair*) связь; **they have a good ~** у
них хоро́шие (взаимо-)отноше́ния.
relative [ˈrɛlətɪv] *n* (*member of family*)
ро́дственник(-ица) ◆ *adj* (*comparative*)
относи́тельный* (относи́телен); (*connected*):
~ to относя́щийся к +*dat*.
relatively [ˈrɛlətɪvlɪ] *adv* относи́тельно.
relative pronoun *n* (*LING*) относи́тельное
местоиме́ние.
relax [rɪˈlæks] *vi* (*person: unwind*) расслаб-
ля́ться (рассла́биться* *perf*); (: *calm down*)
успока́иваться (успоко́иться *perf*); (*muscle*)
расслабля́ться (рассла́биться* *perf*) ◆ *vt*
(*one's grip, rule*) ослабля́ть (осла́бить* *perf*);
(*mind, person*) расслабля́ть (рассла́бить*
perf); (*control*) ослабля́ть (осла́бить* *perf*).
relaxation [riːlækˈseɪʃən] *n* (*rest*) о́тдых; (*of
muscle*) расслабле́ние; (*of grip, rule, control
etc*) ослабле́ние; (*recreation*) о́тдых,
развлече́ние.
relaxed [rɪˈlækst] *adj* (*person, atmosphere*)
споко́йный*.
relaxing [rɪˈlæksɪŋ] *adj* (*holiday, afternoon*)
расслабля́ющий*.
relay [*n* ˈriːleɪ, *vt* rɪˈleɪ] *n* (*race*) эстафе́та ◆ *vt*
(*pass on: message etc*) передава́ть*
(переда́ть* *perf*); (*transmit*) трансли́ровать
(*impf/perf*).
release [rɪˈliːs] *n* (*from prison, obligation*)
освобожде́ние; (*of gas, water etc*) вы́пуск; (*of
film, book, record*) вы́пуск; (*device*) спусково́е
устро́йство, спуск ◆ *vt* (*prisoner*)
освобожда́ть (освободи́ть* *perf*); (*gas etc*)

---

* marks translations which have irregular inflections. The Russian-English side of the dictionary gives inflectional information.

выпуска́ть (вы́пустить* *perf*); (*free: from wreckage etc*) высвобожда́ть (вы́свободить* *perf*); (*TECH: catch, spring etc*) отпуска́ть (отпусти́ть* *perf*); (*book, film*) выпуска́ть (вы́пустить* *perf*); (*report, news*) передава́ть* (переда́ть* *perf*); **to ~ the clutch** (*AUT*) отпуска́ть (отпусти́ть* *perf*) сцепле́ние; *see also* **press release**.

relegate ['rɛləgeɪt] *vt* понижа́ть (пони́зить* *perf*); (*BRIT: SPORT*): **to be ~d** переводи́ть* (перевести́* *perf*) в ни́зшую ли́гу.

relent [rɪ'lɛnt] *vi* (*give in*) уступа́ть (уступи́ть* *perf*).

relentless [rɪ'lɛntlɪs] *adj* (*effort*) неосла́бный; (*rain*) продолжи́тельный* (продолжи́телен); (*determined*) неуста́нный* (неуста́нен).

relevance ['rɛləvəns] *n* (*of remarks*) уме́стность *f*, релева́нтность *f*; (*of information*) актуа́льность *f*; (*of question*) уме́стность; **~ of sth to sth** уме́стность чего́-н по отноше́нию к чему́-н.

relevant ['rɛləvənt] *adj* (*pertinent*) актуа́льный* (актуа́лен), релева́нтный* (релева́нтен); (*corresponding*) соотве́тствующий*; **~ to** относя́щийся* к +*dat*.

reliability [rɪlaɪə'bɪlɪtɪ] *n* (*see adj*) надёжность *f*; достове́рность *f*.

reliable [rɪ'laɪəbl] *adj* надёжный* (надёжен); (*news, information*) достове́рный* (достове́рен).

reliably [rɪ'laɪəblɪ] *adv*: **to be ~ informed that** ... име́ть (*impf*) достове́рную информа́цию о том, что ....

reliance [rɪ'laɪəns] *n*: **~ (on)** (*person, drugs*) зави́симость *f* (от +*gen*).

reliant [rɪ'laɪənt] *adj*: **to be ~ on sth/sb** полага́ться (положи́ться* *perf*) на кого́-н/что-н.

relic ['rɛlɪk] *n* (*REL*) мо́щи *pl*; (*of the past etc*) рели́квия.

relief [rɪ'liːf] *n* облегче́ние; (*aid*) по́мощь *f*; (*ART, GEO*) релье́ф; **by way of light ~** для разря́дки напряжённости.

relief map *n* релье́фная ка́рта.

relief road *n* объе́зд (*доро́га, отводя́щая тра́нспорт*).

relieve [rɪ'liːv] *vt* (*pain, sufferings*) облегча́ть (облегчи́ть *perf*); (*fear, worry*) уменьша́ть (уме́ньшить *perf*); (*patient*) освобожда́ть (освободи́ть* *perf*); (*victims, refugees etc*) ока́зывать (оказа́ть* *perf*) по́мощь +*dat*; (*colleague, guard*) сменя́ть (смени́ть* *perf*); **to ~ sb of sth** освобожда́ть (освободи́ть* *perf*) кого́-н от чего́-н; **to ~ o.s.** облегча́ться (облегчи́ться *perf*).

relieved [rɪ'liːvd] *adj*: **to feel ~** почу́вствовать (*perf*) облегче́ние; **he is ~ that** ... он рад, что ...; **I'm ~ to hear it** я рад э́то слы́шать.

religion [rɪ'lɪdʒən] *n* рели́гия.

religious [rɪ'lɪdʒəs] *adj* религио́зный* (религио́зен).

religious education *n* религио́зное воспита́ние.

religiously [rɪ'lɪdʒəslɪ] *adv* (*scrupulously*) неукосни́тельно.

relinquish [rɪ'lɪŋkwɪʃ] *vt* (*authority*) отка́зываться (отказа́ться* *perf*) от +*gen*; (*plan, habit*) оставля́ть (оста́вить* *perf*).

relish ['rɛlɪʃ] *n* (*CULIN*) припра́ва; (*enjoyment*) наслажде́ние ♦ *vt* (*food, drink*) наслажда́ться (наслади́ться* *perf*) +*instr*; (*idea, thought, prospect etc*) наслажда́ться (*impf*).

relive [riː'lɪv] *vt* (*memory, pleasure, visit etc*) вновь пережива́ть (пережи́ть* *perf*).

reload [riː'ləud] *vt* (*gun*) перезаряжа́ть (перезаряди́ть* *perf*).

relocate [riː'ləu'keɪt] *vt* перемеща́ть (перемести́ть* *perf*) ♦ *vi*: **to ~ (in)** перемеща́ться (перемести́ться* *perf*) (в +*acc*).

reluctance [rɪ'lʌktəns] *n* неохо́та, нежела́ние.

reluctant [rɪ'lʌktənt] *adj* (*acceptance*) неохо́тный* (неохо́тен); (*person*): **he is ~ to go there** он идёт туда́ неохо́тно.

reluctantly [rɪ'lʌktəntlɪ] *adv* неохо́тно.

rely on [rɪ'laɪ-] *vt fus* (*be dependent on*) полага́ться (*impf*) на +*acc*; (*trust*) полага́ться (положи́ться* *perf*) на +*acc*.

remain [rɪ'meɪn] *vi* оставаться́ (оста́ться* *perf*); (*survive*) сохраня́ться (сохрани́ться *perf*); **to ~ silent** храни́ть (*impf*) молча́ние; **I ~, yours faithfully** (*BRIT: in letters*) остаю́сь, и́скренно Ваш.

remainder [rɪ'meɪndə*] *n* оста́ток*.

remaining [rɪ'meɪnɪŋ] *adj* сохрани́вшийся; (*surviving*) оста́вшийся.

remains [rɪ'meɪnz] *npl* (*of meal*) оста́тки *mpl*; (*of building*) разва́лины *fpl*; (*of corpse*) оста́нки *mpl*.

remand [rɪ'mɑːnd] *n*: **on ~** взя́тый под стра́жей ♦ *vt*: **he was ~ed in custody** он был взят под стра́жу.

remand home *n* (*BRIT*) исправи́тельная коло́ния для несовершеннолетних.

remark [rɪ'mɑːk] *n* замеча́ние ♦ *vt* замеча́ть (заме́тить* *perf*) ♦ *vi*: **to ~ on sth** де́лать (сде́лать *perf*) замеча́ние относи́тельно +*gen*; **to ~ that** замеча́ть (заме́тить* *perf*), что.

remarkable [rɪ'mɑːkəbl] *adj* замеча́тельный* (замеча́телен).

remarry [riː'mærɪ] *vi* вступа́ть (вступи́ть* *perf*) в повто́рный брак.

remedial [rɪ'miːdɪəl] *adj* (*tuition, classes*) исправи́тельный* (исправи́телен), корректи́вный; (*exercise*) лече́бный.

remedy ['rɛmədɪ] *n* (*cure*) сре́дство ♦ *vt* исправля́ть (испра́вить* *perf*).

remember [rɪ'mɛmbə*] *vt* (*call back to mind*) вспомина́ть (вспо́мнить *perf*); (*bear in mind*) по́мнить (*impf*); (*send greetings*): **~ me to him** переда́йте ему́ от меня́ приве́т; **I ~ seeing her, I ~ having seen her** я по́мню, что я её ви́дел; **she ~ed to call me** она́ не забы́ла позвони́ть мне.

remembrance [rɪ'mɛmbrəns] *n* па́мять *f*.

remind [rɪ'maɪnd] *vt*: **to ~ sb to do** напомина́ть (напо́мнить *perf*) кому́-н +*infin*; **to ~ sb of sth/sb** напомина́ть (напо́мнить *perf*) кому́-н о чём-н/ком-н; **that ~s me!** кста́ти!; **she ~s me of her mother** она́ напомина́ет мне свою́ мать.

reminder [rɪ'maɪndə'] *n* напомина́ние.

reminisce [rɛmɪ'nɪs] *vi* вспомина́ть (вспо́мнить *perf*).

reminiscences [rɛmɪ'nɪsnsɪz] *npl* воспомина́ния *ntpl*.

reminiscent [rɛmɪ'nɪsnt] *adj*: **to be ~ of sth** напомина́ть (напо́мнить *perf*) что-н.

remiss [rɪ'mɪs] *adj* (*careless*) небре́жный* (небре́жен); **it was ~ of him** с его́ стороны́ э́то бы́ло небре́жностью.

remission [rɪ'mɪʃən] *n* (*cancelling: of debt, fee*) освобожде́ние; (*reduction: of prison sentence*) сокраще́ние; (*MED*) реми́ссия; (*REL*) отпуще́ние.

remit [rɪ'mɪt] *vt* (*send*) пересыла́ть (пересла́ть* *perf*).

remittance [rɪ'mɪtns] *n* (*payment*) де́нежный перево́д (*для опла́ты чего́-н*).

remnant ['rɛmnənt] *n* оста́ток*; **~s** *npl* (*COMM*) оста́тки *mpl*.

remonstrate ['rɛmənstreɪt] *vi*: **to ~ (with sb about sth)** выража́ть (вы́разить* *perf*) проте́ст (кому́-н по по́воду чего́-н).

remorse [rɪ'mɔ:s] *n* раска́яние.

remorseful [rɪ'mɔ:sful] *adj* по́лный* (по́лон) раска́яния.

remorseless [rɪ'mɔ:slɪs] *adj* (*person*) нещáдный* (нещáден); (*noise, pain*) невыноси́мый (невыноси́м).

remote [rɪ'məut] *adj* (*place, time*) отдалённый* (отдалён); (*person*) за́мкнутый (за́мкнут); (*possibility, chance*) незначи́тельный* (незначи́телен); **there is a ~ possibility that ...** существу́ет маловероя́тная возмо́жность, что ....

remote control *n* дистанцио́нное управле́ние.

remote-controlled [rɪ'məutkən'trəuld] *adj* с дистанцио́нным управле́нием.

remotely [rɪ'məutlɪ] *adv* отдалённо; **I'm not ~ interested** я ниско́лько не заинтересо́ван.

remoteness [rɪ'məutnɪs] *n* (*of place*) отдалённость *f*; (*of person*) за́мкнутость *f*.

remould ['ri:məuld] *n* (*BRIT: tyre*) ши́на с восстано́вленным проте́ктором.

removable [rɪ'mu:vəbl] *adj* (*detachable*) съёмный.

removal [rɪ'mu:vəl] *n* (*also MED*) удале́ние; (*BRIT: of furniture*) перево́зка; (*dismissal*) отстране́ние.

removal man *irreg n* (*BRIT*) перево́зчик ме́бели.

removal van *n* (*BRIT*) автофурго́н для перево́зки ме́бели.

remove [rɪ'mu:v] *vt* (*take away*) убира́ть (убра́ть* *perf*); (*clothing, bandage, employee*) снима́ть (снять* *perf*); (*stain, also MED*) удаля́ть (удали́ть *perf*); (*problem, doubt*) устраня́ть (устрани́ть *perf*); **first cousin once ~d** двою́родный(-ая) племя́нник(-ица).

remover [rɪ'mu:və'] *n* (*for paint, varnish*) сре́дство для сня́тия; **stain ~** пятно-выводи́тель *m*; **paint/make-up ~** сре́дство для сня́тия кра́ски/макия́жа.

remunerate [rɪ'mju:nəreɪt] *vt* вознагражда́ть (вознаргради́ть* *perf*).

remuneration [rɪmju:nə'reɪʃən] *n* вознагражде́ние.

Renaissance [rɪ'neɪsɑ:s] *n*: **the ~** (*HISTORY*) Возрожде́ние.

renal ['ri:nl] *adj* по́чечный.

renal failure *n* по́чечная недоста́точность *f*.

rename [ri:'neɪm] *vt* переимено́вывать (переименова́ть *perf*).

rend [rɛnd] (*pt, pp* **rent**) *vt* (*subj: society*) раздира́ть (*impf*); **a whistle rent the air** свист рассёк во́здух.

render ['rɛndə'] *vt* (*give: assistance*) ока́зывать (оказа́ть* *perf*); (*cause to become: harmless, useless*) де́лать (сде́лать *perf*) +*instr*; (*submit: account*) представля́ть (предъяви́ть* *perf*); **the blow ~ed him unconscious** уда́р привёл его́ в бессозна́тельное состоя́нию.

rendering ['rɛndərɪŋ] *n* (*MUS etc*) исполне́ние; (*CONSTR*) штукату́рка.

rendezvous ['rɔndɪvu:] *n* (*meeting*) свида́ние, рандеву́ *nt ind*; (*place*) ме́сто свида́ния ♦ *vi* встреча́ться (встре́титься* *perf*); **to ~ with sb** встреча́ться (встре́титься* *perf*) с кем-н.

rendition [rɛn'dɪʃən] *n* (*MUS*) исполне́ние.

renegade ['rɛnɪgeɪd] *n* ренега́т.

renew [rɪ'nju:] *vt* возобновля́ть (возобнови́ть* *perf*).

renewal [rɪ'nju:əl] *n* возобновле́ние.

renounce [rɪ'nauns] *vt* отка́зываться (отказа́ться* *perf*) от +*gen*; (*belief, throne*) отрека́ться (отре́чься* *perf*) от +*gen*; (*holy orders*) отверга́ть (отве́ргнуть *perf*).

renovate ['rɛnəveɪt] *vt* (*building, machine*) ремонти́ровать (отремонти́ровать *perf*); (*painting*) реставри́ровать (отреставри́ровать *perf*).

renovation [rɛnə'veɪʃən] *n* ремо́нт; (*of work of art*) реставра́ция.

renown [rɪ'naun] *n* сла́ва.

renowned [rɪ'naund] *adj* просла́вленный.

rent [rɛnt] *pt, pp of* **rend** ♦ *n* кварти́рная пла́та ♦ *vt* (*take for rent: house*) снима́ть (снять* *perf*);

---

* marks translations which have irregular inflections. The Russian-English side of the dictionary gives inflectional information.

(: *television, car*) брать* (взять* *perf*)
напрока́т; (*also:* ~ **out**: *house*) сдава́ть*
(сдать* *perf*) (внаём); (: *television, car*)
дава́ть* (дать* *perf*) напрока́т.
rental ['rɛntl] *n* (*for television, car*) пла́та за
прока́т.
rent strike *n* неупла́та жильца́ми аре́ндной
пла́ты с це́лью выраже́ния проте́ста.
renunciation [rɪnʌnsɪ'eɪʃən] *n* отка́з; (*of belief,*
throne) отрече́ние.
reopen [riː'əupən] *vt* (*shop, restaurant etc*)
сно́ва открыва́ть (откры́ть* *perf*);
(*discussion, legal case etc*) возобновля́ть
(возобнови́ть* *perf*).
reopening [riː'əupnɪŋ] *n* (*see vb*) откры́тие
(*по́сле ремо́нта итп*); возобновле́ние.
reorder [riː'ɔːdəʳ] *vt* возобновля́ть
(возобнови́ть* *perf*) зака́з на +*acc*; (*rearrange*)
перестра́ивать (перестро́ить *perf*).
reorganization ['riːɔːgənaɪ'zeɪʃən] *n*
реорганиза́ция.
reorganize [riː'ɔːgənaɪz] *vt* реорганизо́вывать
(реорганизова́ть *perf*).
rep [rɛp] *n abbr* (*COMM*) = **representative**; (*THEAT*)
= **repertory**.
Rep. *abbr* (*US: POL*) = **representative, republican**.
repair [rɪ'pɛəʳ] *n* ремо́нт ♦ *vt* (*clothes, shoes*)
чини́ть* (почини́ть* *perf*); (*car, engine*)
ремонти́ровать (отремонти́ровать *perf*); **in**
good/bad ~ в хоро́шем/плохо́м состоя́нии;
under ~ в ремо́нте.
repair kit *n* ремо́нтный компле́кт.
repairman [rɪ'pɛəmæn] *irreg n* ма́стер* по
ремо́нту.
repair shop *n* ремо́нтная мастерска́я *f adj*.
repartee [rɛpɑː'tiː] *n* (*conversation*)
остроу́мная бесе́да; (*riposte*) остро́та.
repast [rɪ'pɑːst] *n* тра́пеза.
repatriate [riː'pætrɪeɪt] *vt* репатрии́ровать
(*impf/perf*).
repay [riː'peɪ] *irreg vt* (*money, debt*)
выпла́чивать (вы́платить* *perf*); (*person*)
упла́чивать (уплати́ть* *perf*) +*dat*; (: *reward*)
вознаграждА́ть (вознаградИ́ть* *perf*);
(*efforts*) возмеща́ть (возмести́ть* *perf*); **to** ~
sb (for sth) (*favour*) отпла́чивать (отплати́ть*
perf) кому́-н (за что-н).
repayment [riː'peɪmənt] *n* вы́плата.
repeal [rɪ'piːl] *n* отме́на ♦ *vt* отменя́ть
(отмени́ть* *perf*).
repeat [rɪ'piːt] *vt* повторя́ть (повтори́ть *perf*) ♦
vi повторя́ться (повтори́ться *perf*) ♦ *n* (*RADIO,*
TV) повторе́ние ♦ *cpd* (*performance, order etc*)
повто́рный; **to** ~ **a class** (*SCOL*) остава́ться*
(оста́ться* *perf*) на второ́й год.
repeatedly [rɪ'piːtɪdlɪ] *adv* неоднокра́тно.
repel [rɪ'pɛl] *vt* (*drive away*) отбива́ть (отби́ть*
perf); (*disgust*) отта́лкивать (оттолкну́ть
perf).
repellent [rɪ'pɛlənt] *adj* (*appearance, smell*)
отта́лкивающий*; (*idea, thought*) отврат-

и́тельный* (отврати́телен) ♦ *n*: **insect** ~
репелле́нт.
repent [rɪ'pɛnt] *vi*: **to** ~ **(of)** ка́яться (пока́яться
perf) (в +*prp*).
repentance [rɪ'pɛntəns] *n* покая́ние.
repercussions [riːpəˈkʌʃənz] *npl* после́дствия
ntpl.
repertoire ['rɛpətwɑː'] *n* репертуа́р.
repertory ['rɛpətərɪ] *n* (*also:* ~ **theatre**)
репертуа́рный теа́тр.
repertory company *n* постоя́нная тру́ппа.
repetition [rɛpɪ'tɪʃən] *n* повторе́ние; (*of order,*
in text) повто́р.
repetitious [rɛpɪ'tɪʃəs] *adj* изоби́лующий
повто́рами.
repetitive [rɪ'pɛtɪtɪv] *adj* повторя́ющийся.
replace [rɪ'pleɪs] *vt* (*put back: vertically*) класть*
(положи́ть* *perf*) обра́тно; (: *horizontally*)
ста́вить* (поста́вить* *perf*) обра́тно; (*take the*
place of) заменя́ть (замени́ть* *perf*); **to** ~ **sth**
with sth заменя́ть (замени́ть* *perf*) что-н
чем-н; "**replace the receiver**" (*TEL*) „положи́те
тру́бку".
replacement [rɪ'pleɪsmənt] *n* заме́на.
replacement cost *n* изде́ржки* *pl*
возмеще́ния.
replacement part *n* запасна́я часть* *f*.
replacement value *n* (*INSURANCE*) сто́имость *f*
страхово́го возмеще́ния.
replay [*n* 'riːpleɪ, *vb* riː'pleɪ] *n* (*of match*)
переигро́вка*; (*of tape*) повто́рное
прои́грывание; (*of film*) повто́рный пока́з ♦
vt (*match, game*) переи́грывать (переигра́ть
perf); (*part of tape*) повто́рно прои́грывать
(проигра́ть *perf*).
replenish [rɪ'plɛnɪʃ] *vt* (*glass*) сно́ва наполня́ть
(напо́лнить *perf*); (*stock etc*) пополня́ть
(попо́лнить *perf*).
replete [rɪ'pliːt] *adj* (*well-fed*) насы́тившийся; ~
with загру́женный (загру́жен) +*instr*; **I'm**
quite ~ я впо́лне насы́тился.
replica ['rɛplɪkə] *n* (*copy*) ко́пия.
reply [rɪ'plaɪ] *n* отве́т ♦ *vi* отвеча́ть (отве́тить*
perf); **in** ~ **to** в отве́т на +*acc*; **there's no** ~ (*TEL*)
не отвеча́ет.
reply coupon *n* бланк для отве́та.
reply-paid postcard *n* откры́тка* с
опла́ченным отве́том.
report [rɪ'pɔːt] *n* (*account*) докла́д; (*PRESS, TV*
etc: statement) репорта́ж; (: *information*)
сообще́ние; (*BRIT. also:* **school** ~) отчёт об
успева́емости; (*of gun*) вы́стрел ♦ *vt*
сообща́ть (сообщи́ть *perf*) о +*prp*; (*event,*
meeting) докла́дывать (доложи́ть* *perf*) о
+*prp*; (*person*) доноси́ть* (донести́* *perf*) на
+*acc* ♦ *vi* (*make a report*) докла́дывать
(доложи́ть* *perf*); (*present o.s.*): **to** ~ **(to sb)**
явля́ться (яви́ться* *perf*) (к кому́-н); (*be*
responsible to): **to** ~ **to sb** быть* (*impf*) под
нача́лом кого́-н; **to** ~ **that** сообща́ть
(сообщи́ть *perf*), что; **to** ~ **on** представля́ть

(предста́вить* *perf*) докла́д о +*prp*; **it is ~ed that** ... сообща́ется, что ....

report card *n* (*US, SCOTTISH*) та́бель *m* успева́емости.

reportedly [rɪ'pɔːtɪdlɪ] *adv*: **she is ~ living in Spain** по сообще́ниям, она́ живёт в Испа́нии; **he ~ ordered them to** ... сообща́ют, что он приказа́л им +*infin* ....

reported speech *n* (*LING*) ко́свенная речь *f*.

reporter [rɪ'pɔːtə*ʳ*] *n* репортёр.

repose [rɪ'pəuz] *n*: **in ~** (*face*) в поко́е.

repository [rɪ'pɔzɪtərɪ] *n* (*place*) храни́лище; (*person*) храни́тель *m*.

repossess ['riːpə'zɛs] *vt* (*goods, building*) изыма́ть (изъя́ть* *perf*) (*за неплатёж*).

reprehensible [rɛprɪ'hɛnsɪbl] *adj* (*behaviour*) предосуди́тельный* (предосуди́телен).

represent [rɛprɪ'zɛnt] *vt* (*person, nation*) представля́ть (предста́вить* *perf*); (*view, belief*) излага́ть (изложи́ть* *perf*); (*constitute*) представля́ть (*impf*) собо́й; (*idea, emotion*) символизи́ровать* (*impf/perf*); (*describe*): **to ~ sth as** изобража́ть (изобрази́ть* *perf*) что-н как; (*explain*): **to ~ to sb that** объясня́ть (объясни́ть* *perf*) кому́-н, что.

representation [rɛprɪzɛn'teɪʃən] *n* (*state*) представи́тельство; (*picture, statue*) изображе́ние; (*petition*) заявле́ние; **~s** *npl* (*protest*) представле́ния *ntpl*.

representative [rɛprɪ'zɛntətɪv] *n* представи́тель(ница) *m(f)*; (*of belief, also COMM, POL*) представи́тель *m* ♦ *adj* (*group, survey, cross-section*) представи́тельный* (представи́телен); **~ of** характе́рный* (характе́рен) для +*gen*.

repress [rɪ'prɛs] *vt* подавля́ть (подави́ть* *perf*).

repression [rɪ'prɛʃən] *n* подавле́ние.

repressive [rɪ'prɛsɪv] *adj* (*society, measures*) репресси́вный* (репресси́вен).

reprieve [rɪ'priːv] *n* (*LAW*) отсро́чка (*в исполне́нии пригово́ра*); (*fig: delay*) переды́шка* ♦ *vt* (*LAW*): **he was ~d** он получи́л отсро́чку.

reprimand ['rɛprɪmɑːnd] *n* вы́говор ♦ *vt* де́лать (сде́лать *perf*) вы́говор +*dat*.

reprint [*n* 'riːprɪnt, *vb* riː'prɪnt] *n* перепеча́тка ♦ *vt* перепеча́тывать (перепеча́тать *perf*).

reprisal [rɪ'praɪzl] *n* отве́тное де́йствие; **~s** *npl* (*acts of revenge*) отве́тные де́йствия *ntpl*; **to take ~s** мстить* (отомсти́ть* *perf*).

reproach [rɪ'prəutʃ] *n* упрёк ♦ *vt*: **to ~ sb for sth/with sth** упрека́ть (упрекну́ть *perf*) кого́-н за что-н/в чём-н; **his behaviour was beyond ~** его́ поведе́ние бы́ло безупре́чно.

reproachful [rɪ'prəutʃful] *adj* (*look, remark*) укори́зненный* (укори́знен).

reproduce [riːprə'djuːs] *vt* воспроизводи́ть* (воспроизвести́* *perf*) ♦ *vi* размножа́ться

(размножи́ться *perf*).

reproduction [riːprə'dʌkʃən] *n* воспроизведе́ние; (*ART*) репроду́кция; (*breeding*) воспроизведе́ние.

reproductive [riːprə'dʌktɪv] *adj* (*process*) репродукти́вный; (*system*) половой.

reproof [rɪ'pruːf] *n* (*rebuke*) порица́ние; (*disapproval*): **with ~** с уко́ром.

reprove [rɪ'pruːv] *vt* (*person*): **to ~ sb for sth** осужда́ть (осуди́ть* *perf*) кого́-н за что-н.

reproving [rɪ'pruːvɪŋ] *adj* осужда́ющий.

reptile ['rɛptaɪl] *n* пресмыка́ющееся *nt adj* (живо́тное).

Repub. *abbr* (*US: POL*) = **republican**.

republic [rɪ'pʌblɪk] *n* респу́блика.

republican [rɪ'pʌblɪkən] *adj* республика́нский* ♦ *n* (*US: POL*): **R~** республика́нец*(-нка*).

repudiate [rɪ'pjuːdɪeɪt] *vt* отверга́ть (отве́ргнуть* *perf*).

repudiation [rɪpjuːdɪ'eɪʃən] *n* отрица́ние, отрече́ние; (*COMM*) отка́з от до́лга *or* выполне́ния контра́кта.

repugnance [rɪ'pʌgnəns] *n* отвраще́ние.

repugnant [rɪ'pʌgnənt] *adj* отврати́тельный* (отврати́телен).

repulse [rɪ'pʌls] *vt* (*drive back*) отража́ть (отрази́ть* *perf*); (: *enemy*) отбра́сывать (отбро́сить* *perf*); (*disgust*) отта́лкивать (оттолкну́ть* *perf*).

repulsion [rɪ'pʌlʃən] *n* отвраще́ние.

repulsive [rɪ'pʌlsɪv] *adj* отврати́тельный* (отврати́телен).

reputable ['rɛpjutəbl] *adj* (*person*) уважа́емый; **~ company etc** компа́ния с хоро́шей репута́цией.

reputation [rɛpju'teɪʃən] *n* репута́ция; **to have a ~ for** име́ть (*impf*) репута́цию +*gen*; **he has a ~ for being tactless** он изве́стен свое́й беста́ктностью.

repute [rɪ'pjuːt] *n* до́брая сла́ва.

reputed [rɪ'pjuːtɪd] *adj* (*rumoured*) предполага́емый; **he is ~ to be intelligent/rich** счита́ется, что он умён/бога́т.

reputedly [rɪ'pjuːtɪdlɪ] *adv* по о́бщему мне́нию.

request [rɪ'kwɛst] *n* (*polite demand*) про́сьба; (*formal demand*) зая́вка* ♦ *vt*: **to ~ sth of** *or* **from sb** проси́ть* (попроси́ть* *perf*) что-н у кого́-н; **at the ~ of** по про́сьбе +*gen*; (*formal*) по зая́вке +*gen*; "**you are ~ed not to smoke**" „про́сим не кури́ть".

request stop *n* (*BRIT*) остано́вка* по тре́бованию.

requiem ['rɛkwɪəm] *n* (*REL*) панихи́да; (*MUS*) ре́квием.

require [rɪ'kwaɪə*ʳ*] *vt* (*person*) нужда́ться (*impf*) в +*prp*; (*thing, situation*) тре́бовать (*impf*); (*order*): **to ~ sth of sb** тре́бовать (потре́бовать *perf*) что-н от кого́-н; **we ~ you**

---

* marks translations which have irregular inflections. The Russian-English side of the dictionary gives inflectional information.

to complete the task мы требуем, чтобы Вы
завершили работу; **if ~d** если требуется;
what documents are ~d? какие документы
требуются?; **~d by law** требуется по закону.

required [rɪ'kwaɪəd] *adj* необходимый.

requirement [rɪ'kwaɪəmənt] *n* (*need, want*)
потребность *f*; (*condition*) требование; **to
meet sb's ~s** удовлетворять (удовлетвор-
ить *perf*) чьим-н требованиям.

requisite ['rɛkwɪzɪt] *n* требование ♦ *adj*
необходимый.

requisition [rɛkwɪ'zɪʃən] *vt* (*MIL*) реквиз-
ировать (*impf/perf*) ♦ *n*: ~ **(for)** заявка (на
+*acc*)

reroute [ri:'ru:t] *vt* (*train etc*) изменять
(изменить* *perf*) маршрут +*gen*.

resale [ri:'seɪl] *n* перепродажа; "**not for ~**"
„перепродажа запрещена".

resale price maintenance *n* поддержание
цен при перепродаже товаров.

reschedule [ri:'ʃɛdjuːl] *vt*: ~ **(for)** переносить*
(перенести* *perf*) (на +*acc*).

rescind [rɪ'sɪnd] *vt* (*law, judgement*) отменять
(отменить* *perf*); (*contract, order etc*)
аннулировать (*impf/perf*).

rescue ['rɛskjuː] *n* спасение ♦ *vt*: **to ~ (from)**
спасать (спасти* *perf*) (от +*gen*); **to come to
sb's ~** приходить* (прийти* *perf*) кому-н на
помощь.

rescue party *n* спасательный отряд,
спасательная партия.

rescuer ['rɛskjuə'] *n* спасатель(ница) *m(f)*.

research [rɪ'səːtʃ] *n* исследование ♦ *vt*
исследовать (*impf/perf*) ♦ *vi* проводить*
(провести* *perf*) исследования; **a piece of ~** (научное)
исследование; **~ and development**
научно-исследовательские и
опытно-конструкторские работы.

researcher [rɪ'səːtʃə'] *n* исследователь(ница)
m(f).

research work *n* научно-исследовательская
работа.

research worker *n* научный работник.

resell [ri:'sɛl] *irreg vt* перепродавать*
(перепродать* *perf*).

resemblance [rɪ'zɛmbləns] *n* сходство; **he
bears a strong ~ to his father** он сильно
походит на отца; **this bears no ~ to ...** это не
имеет никакого сходства на +*acc* ....

resemble [rɪ'zɛmbl] *vt* походить* (*impf*) на +*acc*;
he very much ~s his father он очень походит
на отца.

resent [rɪ'zɛnt] *vt* (*situation*) негодовать (*impf*)
против +*gen*; (*person*) негодовать (*impf*) на
+*acc*.

resentful [rɪ'zɛntful] *adj* негодующий*.

resentment [rɪ'zɛntmənt] *n* негодование.

reservation [rɛzə'veɪʃən] *n* (*booking*) предварительный заказ; (*doubt*) сомнение; (*for tribe*)
резервация; **to make a ~ (in an hotel/on a**

plane) бронировать* (забронировать* *perf*)
(место в гостинице/на самолёте); **with ~s**
(*doubts*) с оговорками.

reservation desk *n* (*US: in hotel*) стол*
администратора.

reserve [rɪ'zəːv] *n* (*store*) резерв, запас; (*also:
nature ~*) заповедник; (*SPORT*) запасной
игрок*; (*restraint*) сдержанность *f* ♦ *vt* (*keep:
money, food*) приберегать (приберечь* *perf*);
(*: energy*) беречь* (сберечь* *perf*); (*seats, table
etc*) бронировать (забронировать *perf*); **~s**
npl (*MIL*) запас *msg*; (*COMM*) резервы *mpl*; **in ~** в
резерве *or* запасе.

reserve currency *n* резервная валюта.

reserved [rɪ'zəːvd] *adj* (*restrained*)
сдержанный* (сдержан); (*seat*)
забронированный* (забронирован).

reserve price *n* (*BRIT*) отправная *or*
резервированная цена*.

reserve team *n* (*BRIT: SPORT*) запасная
команда.

reservist [rɪ'zəːvɪst] *n* резервист.

reservoir ['rɛzəvwɑː'] *n* (*of water*)
водохранилище; (*small: of ink etc*) резерву-
ар; (*fig: of talent, strength*)
хранилище.

reset [ri:'sɛt] *irreg vt* вновь устанавливать
(установить* *perf*); (*clock, watch*) переводить*
(перевести* *perf*); (*COMPUT*) сбрасывать
(сбросить* *perf*), возвращать (возвратить*
perf) в исходное положение.

reshape [ri:'ʃeɪp] *vt* (*policy*) изменять
(изменить* *perf*).

reshuffle [ri:'ʃʌfl] *n*: **Cabinet ~** перестановки
fpl в кабинете министров.

reside [rɪ'zaɪd] *vi* (*live*) проживать (*impf*).

residence ['rɛzɪdəns] *n* (*home*) резиденция;
(*length of stay*) пребывание; **to take up ~**
поселяться (поселиться *perf*); **to be in ~**
(*queen etc*) пребывать (*impf*); (*artist*)
проживать (*impf*) по месту службы.

residence permit *n* (*BRIT*) вид на жительство.

resident ['rɛzɪdənt] *n* (*of country, town*)
(постоянный(-ая)) житель(ница) *m(f)*; (*in
hotel*) проживающий(-ая) *m(f) adj* ♦ *adj*: **~
population** постоянное население; **~ doctor**
врач*, живущий при больнице.

residential [rɛzɪ'dɛnʃəl] *adj* (*area*) жилой*;
(*course, college*) с проживанием.

residue ['rɛzɪdjuː] *n* остаток*; (*CHEM, PHYS*)
осадок*.

resign [rɪ'zaɪn] *vi* (*from post*) оставлять
(оставить* *perf*) ♦ *vt* (*one's post*) уходить*
(уйти* *perf*) в отставку с +*gen*; **to ~ o.s. to**
смиряться (смириться *perf*) с +*instr*.

resignation [rɛzɪg'neɪʃən] *n* отставка*;
(*acceptance*) покорность *f*; **to tender one's ~**
подавать* (подать* *perf*) в отставку.

resigned [rɪ'zaɪnd] *adj* (*to situation etc*)
смирившийся.

resilience [rɪ'zɪlɪəns] *n* (*of material*) упругость *f*;

(*of person*) стойкость *f*.

resilient [rɪ'zɪlɪənt] *adj* (*material*) упругий*
(упруг); (*person*) стойкий* (стоек).

resin ['rɛzɪn] *n* смола*.

resist [rɪ'zɪst] *vt* сопротивляться (*impf*) +*dat*;
(*temptation*) не поддаваться* (поддаться*
perf) +*dat*.

resistance [rɪ'zɪstəns] *n* (*opposition*)
сопротивление; (*to illness, infection*)
сопротивляемость *f*.

resistant [rɪ'zɪstənt] *adj*: **to be ~ to** (*opposing*)
сопротивляться (*impf*) +*dat*; (*immune*)
обладать (*impf*) устойчивостью к +*dat*.

resolute ['rɛzəlu:t] *adj* твёрдый* (твёрд).

resolution [rɛzə'lu:ʃən] *n* (*decision*) решение;
(: *formal*) резолюция; (*determination*)
решимость *f*; (*of problem, difficulty*)
разрешение; **to make a ~** принимать
(принять* *perf*) решение.

resolve [rɪ'zɔlv] *n* решительность *f* ◆ *vt*
(*problem, difficulty*) разрешать (разрешить*
perf) ◆ *vi*: **to ~ to do** решать (решить *perf*)
+*infin*.

resolved [rɪ'zɔlvd] *adj* (*determined*)
решительный* (решителен).

resonance ['rɛzənəns] *n* (*TECH*) резонанс.

resonant ['rɛzənənt] *adj* (*voice*) звучный*
(звучен); (*place*) резонирующий.

resort [rɪ'zɔ:t] *n* (*town*) курорт; (*recourse*)
прибегание ◆ *vi*: **to ~ to** прибегать
(прибегнуть *perf*) к +*dat*; **seaside/winter
sports ~** морской/зимний* спортивный
курорт; **the last/only ~** последняя/
единственная надежда; **in the last ~** в
крайнем случае.

resound [rɪ'zaund] *vi*: **to ~ with** наполняться
(наполниться *perf*) +*instr*.

resounding [rɪ'zaundɪŋ] *adj* (*noise*) звучный*
(звучен); (*fig: success*) громкий*.

resource [rɪ'zɔ:s] *n* (*raw material*) ресурс; **~s** *npl*
(*money, energy, coal etc*) ресурсы *mpl*; **natural
~s** природные ресурсы; **he was left to his
own ~s** (*fig*) он мог положиться только на
самого себя.

resourceful [rɪ'zɔ:sful] *adj* изобретательный*
(изобретателен).

resourcefulness [rɪ'zɔ:sfəlnɪs] *n*
изобретательность *f*.

respect [rɪs'pɛkt] *n* уважение ◆ *vt* уважать
(*impf*); **~s** *npl* (*greetings*) почтение *ntsg*; **to have
or show ~ for sb/sth** относиться* (*impf*) к
кому-н/чему-н с уважением; **out of ~ for** из
уважения к +*dat*; **with ~ to, in ~ of** в
отношении +*gen*; **in this ~** в этом
отношении; **in some ~s** в некоторых
отношениях; **with (all) due ~ ...** при всём
уважении ....

respectability [rɪspɛktə'bɪlɪtɪ] *n* респекта-

бельность *f*.

respectable [rɪs'pɛktəbl] *adj* приличный*
(приличен); (*morally correct*) респекта-
бельный.

respected [rɪs'pɛktɪd] *adj* (*scholar, actor etc*)
признанный (признан).

respectful [rɪs'pɛktful] *adj* почтительный*
(почтителен).

respectfully [rɪs'pɛktfəlɪ] *adv* почтительно.

respective [rɪs'pɛktɪv] *adj* (*policies, measures*)
соответствующий*; **he drove them to their ~
homes** он отвёз их обоих по домам.

respectively [rɪs'pɛktɪvlɪ] *adv* соответственно;
France and Britain were 3rd and 4th ~
Франция и Великобритания были на 3-ем и
4-ом месте соответственно.

respiration [rɛspɪ'reɪʃən] *n* дыхание.

respirator ['rɛspɪreɪtə] *n* (*MED*) аппарат
искусственного дыхания.

respiratory ['rɛspərətərɪ] *adj* (*ANAT, MED*)
дыхательный, респираторный.

respite ['rɛspaɪt] *n* (*rest*) передышка*.

resplendent [rɪs'plɛndənt] *adj* блистательный*
(блистателен).

respond [rɪs'pɔnd] *vi* (*answer*) отвечать
(ответить* *perf*); (*react*): **to ~ (to)** (*to pressure,
criticism*) реагировать (отреагировать *perf*)
(на +*acc*); (*to treatment*) поддаваться*
(поддаться* *perf*) (+*dat*).

respondent [rɪs'pɔndənt] *n* (*LAW*) ответчик
(-ица).

response [rɪs'pɔns] *n* (*answer*) ответ; (*reaction*)
реакция; **in ~ to** (*your letter*) в ответ на
(Ваше письмо).

responsibility [rɪspɔnsɪ'bɪlɪtɪ] *n* (*liability*)
ответственность *f*; (*duty*) обязанность *f*; **to
take ~ for sth/sb** принимать (принять* *perf*)
(на себя) ответственность за что-н/кого-н.

responsible [rɪs'pɔnsɪbl] *adj* ответственный*
(ответствен); **~ for** ответственный*
(ответствен) за +*acc*; **to be ~ to sb (for sth)**
отвечать (ответить* *perf*) перед кем-н (за
что-н).

responsibly [rɪs'pɔnsɪblɪ] *adv* ответственно.

responsive [rɪs'pɔnsɪv] *adj* (*child, nature*)
отзывчивый (отзывчив); (*gesture*)
ответный; **~ to demand/treatment**
восприимчивый (восприимчив) к
требованиям/лечению.

rest [rɛst] *n* (*relaxation, pause*) отдых; (*MUS*)
пауза; (*stand, support*) подставка* ◆ *vi* (*relax,
stop*) отдыхать (отдохнуть *perf*) ◆ *vt* (*head,
eyes etc*) давать* (дать* *perf*) отдых +*dat*;
(*lean*): **to ~ sth against** прислонять
(прислонить *perf*) что-н к +*dat*; **the ~**
(*remainder of sth*) остальное *nt adj*; **the ~ of
them** остальные из них; **to set sb's mind at ~**
утешать (утешить *perf*) кого-н; **to ~ one's**

---

arms on облокáчивать (облокотúть* *perf*) на +*acc*; **to ~ sth on** (*object*) опускáть (опустúть* *perf*) на +*acc*; **to ~ on** (*weight*) опирáться (оперéться* *perf*) на +*acc*; (*idea*) опирáться (*impf*) на +*acc*; (*object*) лежáть (*impf*) на +*prp*; (*hope*) надéяться (*impf*) на +*acc*; **~ assured that** ... бýдьте увéрены, что ...; **it ~s with him to** ... на нём лежúт +*infin* ...; **to ~ one's eyes** *or* **gaze on** останáвливать (остановúть* *perf*) (свой) взгляд на +*acc*.

restart [riː'stɑːt] *vt* (*engine*) вновь запускáть (запустúть* *perf*); (*work*) возобновлять (возобновúть* *perf*).

restaurant ['rɛstərɔŋ] *n* ресторáн.

restaurant car *n* (*BRIT*) вагóн-ресторáн.

rest-cure ['rɛstkjuə] *n* лечéние покóем.

restful ['rɛstful] *adj* успокáивающий.

rest-home ['rɛsthəum] *n* дом для престарéлых.

restitution [rɛstɪ'tjuːʃən] *n*: **to make ~ to sb for sth** (*compensate*) возмещáть (возместúть* *perf*) комý-н что-н.

restive ['rɛstɪv] *adj* неспокóйный* (неспокóен); (*horse*) норовúстый (норовúст).

restless ['rɛstlɪs] *adj* (*person, audience*) беспокóйный* (беспокóен); **to get ~** проявлять (проявúть* *perf*) нетерпéние.

restlessly ['rɛstlɪslɪ] *adv* беспокóйно.

restock [riː'stɔk] *vt* пополнять (пополнить *perf*) запáсы в +*prp*; **to ~ a lake/river (with fish)** пополнять (пополнить *perf*) óзеру/рéку рыбой.

restoration [rɛstə'reɪʃən] *n* (*of building etc*) реставрáция; (*of order, health*) восстановлéние; (*of stolen property*) возвращéние.

restorative [rɪ'stɔrətɪv] *adj* укрепляющий* ◆ *n* укрепляющее срéдство.

restore [rɪ'stɔː'] *vt* (*building, painting*) реставрúровать (отреставрúровать *perf*); (*order, health etc*) восстанáвливать (восстановúть* *perf*); (*stolen property*) возвращáть (возвратúть* *perf*); (*to power*) возвращáть (вернýть *perf*).

restorer [rɪ'stɔːrə'] *n* (*ART etc*) реставрáтор; **hair ~** восстановúтель *m* для волóс.

restrain [rɪs'treɪn] *vt* сдéрживать (сдержáть* *perf*); (*person*): **to ~ sb from doing** не давáть* (дать* *perf*) комý-н +*infin*.

restrained [rɪs'treɪnd] *adj* сдéржанный* (сдéржан).

restraint [rɪs'treɪnt] *n* (*moderation*) сдéржанность *f*; (*restriction*) ограничéние; **wage ~** сдéрживание рóста зáработной плáты.

restrict [rɪs'trɪkt] *vt* ограничивать (ограничить *perf*).

restricted area *n* (*AUT*) райóн ограниченной скóрости движéния.

restriction [rɪs'trɪkʃən] *n*: **~ (on)** ограничéние (на +*acc*).

restrictive [rɪs'trɪktɪv] *adj* ограничúтельный; (*clothing*) стесняющий.

restrictive practices *npl* (*INDUSTRY*) ограничúтельная деловáя прáктика *fsg*.

rest room *n* (*US*) туалéт.

restructure [riː'strʌktʃə'] *vt* (*business, economy*) перестрáивать (перестрóить *perf*).

result [rɪ'zʌlt] *n* результáт ◆ *vi*: **to ~ in** закáнчиваться (закóнчиться *perf*) +*instr*; **as a ~ of** в результáте +*gen*; **as a ~ it is too expensive** в результáте э́то слúшком дóрого; **the fire ~ed from bombing** пожáр вознúк вслéдствие бомбёжки.

resultant [rɪ'zʌltənt] *adj*: **~ saving/problem** вытекáющая из э́того экономúя/проблéма.

resume [rɪ'zjuːm] *vt* (*work, journey*) возобновлять (возобновúть* *perf*) ◆ *vi* продолжáть (продóлжить *perf*); **to ~ one's seat** возвращáться (вернýться* *perf*) на (своё) мéсто.

résumé ['reɪzjuːmeɪ] *n* резюмé *nt ind*; (*US: curriculum vitae*) автобиогрáфия (*обычно пúшущаяся при поступлéнии на учёбу úли рабóту*).

resumption [rɪ'zʌmpʃən] *n* возобновлéние.

resurgence [rɪ'səːdʒəns] *n* (*of energy, activity*) всплеск.

resurrection [rɛzə'rɛkʃən] *n* (*of hopes, fears*) возрождéние; (*REL*): **the R~** Воскресéние.

resuscitate [rɪ'sʌsɪteɪt] *vt* (*MED*) приводúть* (привестú* *perf*) в сознáние; (*fig*) возвращáть (возвратúть* *perf*) к жúзни.

resuscitation [rɪsʌsɪ'teɪʃən] *n* (*MED*) приведéние в сознáние; (*fig*) возвращéние к жúзни.

retail ['riːteɪl] *adj* рóзничный ◆ *adv* в рóзницу ◆ *vt* продавáть* (продáть* *perf*) ь рóзницу ◆ *vi*: **to ~ at £5** продавáться* (*impf*) по рóзничной цене £5; **~ shop** магазúн рóзничной торгóвли.

retailer ['riːteɪlə'] *n* рóзничный торгóвец*.

retail outlet *n* рóзничная торгóвая тóчка.

retail price *n* рóзничная ценá*.

retail price index *n* (*BRIT*) úндекс рóзничных цен.

retain [rɪ'teɪn] *vt* (*keep*) сохранять (сохранúть *perf*), удéрживать (удержáть *perf*).

retainer [rɪ'teɪnə'] *n* (*fee*) предварúтельный гонорáр.

retaliate [rɪ'tælɪeɪt] *vi*: **to ~ (against)** (*attack*) наносúть* (нанестú* *perf*) отвéтный удáр (+*dat*); (*ill-treatment*) отплáчивать (отплатúть* *perf*) (+*dat*); **to ~ (on sb)** предъявлять (предъявúть* *perf*) встрéчный иск (комý-н).

retaliation [rɪtælɪ'eɪʃən] *n* (*against attack*) отвéтный удáр; (*against ill-treatment*) возмéздие; **in ~ for** в отвéт на +*acc*.

retaliatory [rɪ'tælɪətərɪ] *adj* отвéтный.

retarded [rɪ'tɑːdɪd] *adj* (*development, growth*) замéдленный* (замéдлен); (*also*: **mentally ~**:

person) у́мственно отста́лый.

retch [rɛtʃ] *vi*: **the thought made him ~** от э́той мы́сли его́ затошни́ло.

retention [rɪ'tɛnʃən] *n* удержа́ние; (*of tradition, rights*) сохране́ние; (*MED: of fluid*) заде́ржка.

retentive [rɪ'tɛntɪv] *adj*: **a ~ memory** це́пкая па́мять *f*.

rethink ['riː'θɪŋk] *vt* (*proposal, policy*) пересма́тривать (пересмотре́ть* *perf*).

reticence ['rɛtɪsns] *n* скры́тность *f*.

reticent ['rɛtɪsnt] *adj* сде́ржанный* (сде́ржан).

retina ['rɛtɪnə] *n* сетча́тка.

retinue ['rɛtɪnjuː] *n* сви́та.

retire [rɪ'taɪə'] *vi* (*give up work*) уходи́ть* (уйти́* *perf*) на пе́нсию; (*withdraw*) удаля́ться (удали́ться *perf*); (*go to bed*) удаля́ться (удали́ться *perf*) на поко́й.

retired [rɪ'taɪəd] *adj*: **he is ~** он на пе́нсии.

retirement [rɪ'taɪəmənt] *n* вы́ход *or* ухо́д на пе́нсию; **we hope to enjoy a long and happy ~** мы наде́емся жить до́лго и сча́стливо, вы́йдя на пе́нсию.

retirement age *n* пенсио́нный во́зраст.

retiring [rɪ'taɪərɪŋ] *adj* (*leaving*) уходя́щий на пе́нсию; (*shy*) засте́нчивый (засте́нчив).

retort [rɪ'tɔːt] *vi* ре́зко отвеча́ть (отве́тить* *perf*) ♦ *n* ре́зкий* отве́т.

retrace [riː'treɪs] *vt*: **to ~ one's steps** возвраща́ться (верну́ться *perf*) тем же путём; (*fig*) восстана́вливать (восстанови́ть* *perf*).

retract [rɪ'trækt] *vt* (*statement, offer*) забира́ть (забра́ть* *perf*) наза́д; (*claws*) втя́гивать (втяну́ть* *perf*); (*undercarriage, aerial*) убира́ть (убра́ть* *perf*).

retractable [rɪ'træktəbl] *adj* (*TECH*) убира́ющийся.

retrain [riː'treɪn] *vt* переподгота́вливать (переподгото́вить* *perf*), переквали-фици́ровать (*impf/perf*) ♦ *vi* (*see vt*) пройти́* (*perf*) переподгото́вку; переквали-фици́роваться (*impf/perf*).

retraining [riː'treɪnɪŋ] *n* (*see vb*) переподгото́вка*; переквалифика́ция.

retread ['riː'trɛd] *n* (*tyre*) ши́на с восстановле́нным проте́ктором.

retreat [rɪ'triːt] *n* (*place*) убе́жище; (*withdrawal*) ухо́д; (*MIL*) отступле́ние ♦ *vi* отступа́ть (отступи́ть* *perf*); **to go into ~** (*withdraw*) уйти́* (*perf*) от ми́ра; **to beat a hasty ~** поспе́шно отступа́ть (отступи́ть* *perf*).

retrial [riː'traɪəl] *n* (*LAW*) повто́рное слу́шание де́ла.

retribution [rɛtrɪ'bjuːʃən] *n* возме́здие.

retrieval [rɪ'triːvəl] *n* восстановле́ние; (*of error*) исправле́ние; (*COMPUT*) по́иск; (*by dog*) по́иск (ди́чи).

retrieve [rɪ'triːv] *vt* (*object*) брать* (взять* *perf*)

обра́тно; (*situation, honour, loss*) восстана́вливать (восстанови́ть* *perf*); (*error*) исправля́ть (испра́вить* *perf*); (*COMPUT*) оты́скивать (отыска́ть* *perf*); (*subj: dog*) приноси́ть* (принести́* *perf*) (уби́тую ди́чь).

retriever [rɪ'triːvə'] *n* (*dog*) охо́тничья соба́ка.

retroactive [rɛtrəu'æktɪv] *adj* име́ющий обра́тное де́йствие.

retrograde ['rɛtrəugreɪd] *adj* реакцио́нный* (реакцио́нен).

retrospect ['rɛtrəspɛkt] *n*: **in ~** ретроспе́кция.

retrospective [rɛtrə'spɛktɪv] *adj* (*exhibition, view*) ретроспекти́вный* (ретроспекти́вен); (*law, tax*) име́ющий обра́тную си́лу ♦ *n* (*ART*) ретроспекти́вная вы́ставка*.

return [rɪ'təːn] *n* (*going or coming back*) возвраще́ние; (*of sth stolen, borrowed, bought*) возвра́т; (*FINANCE: from land, shares etc*) дохо́д; (*official report*) отчёт ♦ *cpd* (*journey, ticket*) обра́тный; (*match*) отве́тный ♦ *vi* возвраща́ться (верну́ться *perf*) ♦ *vt* возвраща́ть (верну́ть *perf*); (*LAW: verdict*) выноси́ть* (вы́нести* *perf*); (*POL: candidate*) избира́ть (избра́ть* *perf*); (*ball*) отбива́ть (отби́ть* *perf*); **~s** *npl* (*COMM*) дохо́ды *mpl*; **in ~ (for)** в отве́т (на *+acc*); **by ~ of post** обра́тной по́чтой; **many happy ~s (of the day)!** с днём рожде́ния!; **to ~ to** (*consciousness*) приходи́ть (прийти́* *perf*) в *+acc*; (*power*) возвраща́ться (верну́ться *perf*) к *+dat*.

returnable [rɪ'təːnəbl] *adj* (*bottle etc*) подлежа́щий возвра́ту *or* обме́ну.

returning officer [rɪ'təːnɪŋ-] *n* председа́тель *m* окружно́й коми́ссии.

return key *n* (*COMPUT*) кла́виша ''возвра́т каре́тки''.

reunion [riː'juːnɪən] *n* (*reuniting*) воссоедине́ние; (*party*) встре́ча.

reunite [riːju:'naɪt] *vt* воссоединя́ть (воссоедини́ть *perf*).

rev [rɛv] *n abbr* (*AUT*: = *revolution*) оборо́т.

Rev. *abbr* (*REL*) = **Reverend**.

revaluation [riːvæljuː'eɪʃən] *n* (*of property, attitudes*) переоце́нка*; (*of currency*) ревальва́ция.

revamp [riː'væmp] *vt* (*organization, system*) обновля́ть (обнови́ть* *perf*).

rev counter *n* (*BRIT: AUT*) счётчик оборо́тов.

Revd. *abbr* (*REL*) = **Reverend**.

reveal [rɪ'viːl] *vt* (*make known*) обнару́живать (обнару́жить* *perf*); (*make visible*) открыва́ть (откры́ть* *perf*).

revealing [rɪ'viːlɪŋ] *adj* (*action, statement*) показа́тельный* (показа́телен); (*dress*) откры́тый.

reveille [rɪ'vælɪ] *n* (*MIL*) побу́дка*.

revel ['rɛvl] *vi*: **to ~ in sth** упива́ться (*impf*)

---

* marks translations which have irregular inflections. The Russian-English side of the dictionary gives inflectional information.

чем-н; **to ~ in doing** обожа́ть *(impf)* *+infin*.
revelation [rɛvə'leɪʃən] *n (fact)* откры́тие;
(experience) открове́ние.
reveller ['rɛvlə'] *n* гуля́ка *m/f*.
revelry ['rɛvlrɪ] *n* кутёж.
revenge [rɪ'vɛndʒ] *n* месть *f* ◆ *vt (also:* **get one's
~ for)** мстить* (отомсти́ть* *perf)* за *+acc*; **to
take ~ on, ~ o.s. on** мстить* (отомсти́ть* *perf)*
+dat.
revengeful [rɪ'vɛndʒful] *adj* мсти́тельный*
(мсти́телен).
revenue ['rɛvənju:] *n* дохо́ды *mpl*; **~ account**
счёт поступле́ний.
reverberate [rɪ'və:bəreɪt] *vi (also fig)*
отдава́ться* (отда́ть* *perf)* э́хом.
reverberation [rɪvə:bə'reɪʃən] *n (of thunder)*
раска́т; *(shock)* резона́нс.
revere [rɪ'vɪə'] *vt (person)* почита́ть *(impf)*,
чтить* *(impf)*.
reverence ['rɛvərəns] *n (feeling)* почте́ние.
Reverend ['rɛvərənd] *adj:* **the ~** его́
преподо́бие; **the ~ John Smith** его́
преподо́бие Джон Смит.
reverent ['rɛvərənt] *adj (behaviour etc)*
почти́тельный* (почти́телен).
reverie ['rɛvərɪ] *n* мечта́ние.
reversal [rɪ'və:sl] *n* радика́льное измене́ние;
(of roles) переме́на.
reverse [rɪ'və:s] *n (opposite)*
противополо́жность *f*; *(back: of cloth)*
обра́тная сторона́*; *(: of coin, medal)*
оборо́тная сторона́*; *(: of paper)* оборо́т;
(AUT: also: **~ gear)** обра́тный ход*; *(setback,
defeat)* неуда́ча ◆ *adj (opposite)* обра́тный* ◆
vt (order, position) по́лностью изменя́ть
(измени́ть* *perf)*; *(direction)* изменя́ть
(измени́ть *perf)*; *(process, policy, decision)*
кру́то изменя́ть (измени́ть* *perf)*; *(LAW:
judgement)* отменя́ть (отмени́ть *perf)* ◆ *vi
(BRIT: AUT)* дава́ть* (дать* *perf)* за́дний ход;
their fortunes went into ~ уда́ча отверну́лась
от них; **in ~ order** в обра́тном поря́дке; **to ~
direction** изменя́ть (измени́ть *perf)*
направле́ние на обра́тное; **to ~ a car** дава́ть*
(дать* *perf)* за́дний ход; **to ~ roles** меня́ться
(поменя́ться *perf)* места́ми.
reverse-charge call [rɪ'və:stʃɑ:dʒ-] *n (BRIT: TEL)*
*телефо́нный разгово́р за счёт принима́ющ-
его абоне́нта*.
reverse video *n* негати́вное изображе́ние на
экра́не диспле́я.
reversible [rɪ'və:səbl] *adj (garment, material)*
двусторо́нний*; *(procedure)* обрати́мый
(обрати́м).
reversing lights [rɪ'və:sɪŋ-] *npl (BRIT: AUT)*
фона́рь *msg* за́днего.
reversion [rɪ'və:ʃən] *n (ZOOL)* проявле́ние
атави́зма; **~ to** возвраще́ние к *+dat*.
revert [rɪ'və:t] *vi:* **to ~ to** *(to former state)*
возвраща́ться (возврати́ться* *perf)* к *+dat*;
(LAW: money, property) переходи́ть*

(перейти́* *perf)* к *+dat*.
review [rɪ'vju:] *n (of situation, policy etc)*
пересмо́тр; *(MIL)* смотр*; *(of book, film etc)*
реце́нзия; *(magazine)* обозре́ние ◆ *vt
(situation, policy etc)* пересма́тривать
(пересмотре́ть* *perf)*; *(MIL)* проводи́ть*
(провести́* *perf)* смотр *+gen*; *(book, film etc)*
рецензи́ровать (отрецензи́ровать *perf)*; **to
come under ~** рассма́триваться *(impf)*.
reviewer [rɪ'vju:ə'] *n (of book, film etc)*
рецензе́нт.
revile [rɪ'vaɪl] *vt* поноси́ть* *(impf)*.
revise [rɪ'vaɪz] *vt (manuscript)* перераба́тывать
(перерабо́тать *perf)*; *(opinion)* пересма́-
тривать (пересмотре́ть* *perf)*; *(price,
procedure)* изменя́ть (измени́ть* *perf)*; *(SCOL:
lesson, maths)* повторя́ть (повтори́ть *perf)*;
~d edition пересмо́тренное изда́ние.
revision [rɪ'vɪʒən] *n (amendment)* измене́ние;
(for exam) повторе́ние.
revitalize [ri:'vaɪtəlaɪz] *vt* оживля́ть (оживи́ть*
perf).
revival [rɪ'vaɪvəl] *n (recovery)* оживле́ние; *(of
interest, faith)* возрожде́ние; *(THEAT)*
возобновле́ние.
revive [rɪ'vaɪv] *vt (person)* возвраща́ть
(возврати́ть* *perf)* к жи́зни; *(economy,
industry)* оживля́ть (оживи́ть* *perf)*;
(tradition, hope, interest etc) возрожда́ть
(возроди́ть* *perf)*; *(play)* восстана́вливать
(восстанови́ть* *perf)* ◆ *vi (person: from faint)*
приходи́ть* (прийти́* *perf)* в созна́ние;
(activity, economy etc) оживля́ться
(оживи́ться* *perf)*; *(faith, hope, interest etc)*
возрожда́ться (возроди́ться* *perf)*.
revoke [rɪ'vəuk] *vt (treaty, law, title etc)*
отменя́ть (отмени́ть *perf)*; *(promise,
decision)* брать* (взять* *perf)* наза́д.
revolt [rɪ'vəult] *n (rebellion)* восста́ние ◆ *vi
(rebel)* восстава́ть* (восста́ть* *perf)* ◆ *vt*
вызыва́ть (вы́звать* *perf)* отвраще́ние у
+gen; **to ~ against sb/sth** восстава́ть*
(восста́ть* *perf)* про́тив кого́-н/чего́-н.
revolting [rɪ'vəultɪŋ] *adj (disgusting)*
отврати́тельный* (отврати́телен).
revolution [rɛvə'lu:ʃən] *n* револю́ция; *(of
wheel, earth etc)* оборо́т.
revolutionary [rɛvə'lu:ʃənrɪ] *adj*
революцио́нный* (революцио́нен) ◆ *n*
революционе́р(ка*).
revolutionize [rɛvə'lu:ʃənaɪz] *vt (industry,
society etc)* революционизи́ровать *(impf/perf)*.
revolve [rɪ'vɔlv] *vi (turn)* враща́ться *(impf)*; *(fig)*:
to ~ (a)round враща́ться *(impf)* вокру́г *+gen*.
revolver [rɪ'vɔlvə'] *n (gun)* револьве́р.
revolving [rɪ'vɔlvɪŋ] *adj (chair etc)*
враща́ющийся.
revolving door *n* враща́ющаяся дверь* *f*.
revue [rɪ'vju:] *n* реви́ю *nt ind*.
revulsion [rɪ'vʌlʃən] *n (disgust)* отвраще́ние.
reward [rɪ'wɔ:d] *n (recompense: for work,*

service, merit) награ́да; (*sum of money*)
пре́мия; (: *for capture of criminal, information
etc*) вознагражде́ние ♦ *vt*: **to ~ (for)** (*effort*)
вознагражда́ть (вознагради́ть* *perf*) (за
+*acc*).
rewarding [rɪ'wɔːdɪŋ] *adj* (*fig*): **this work is very
~** э́та рабо́та прино́сит удовлеторе́ние;
financially ~ хорошо́ опла́чиваемый.
rewind [riː'waɪnd] *irreg vt* (*cassette*)
перема́тывать (перемота́ть* *perf*) (*наза́д*).
rewire [riː'waɪə'] *vt*: **to ~ a house** заменя́ть
(замени́ть *perf*) прово́дку в до́ме.
reword [riː'wɔːd] *vt* перефрази́ровать (*impf/
perf*).
rework [riː'wɔːk] *vt* переде́лывать (переде́лать
perf).
rewrite [riː'raɪt] *irreg vt* (*rework*) перепи́сывать
(переписа́ть* *perf*).
Reykjavik ['reɪkjəviːk] *n* Рейкья́вик.
RFD *abbr* (*US: POST.* = *rural free delivery*)
беспла́тная доста́вка по́чты в се́льской
ме́стности.
Rh *abbr* (*MED.* = *rhesus*) ре́зус.
rhapsody ['ræpsədɪ] *n* (*MUS*) рапсо́дия.
rhesus negative *adj* (*MED*) с отрица́тельным
ре́зусом.
rhesus positive *adj* (*MED*) с положи́тельным
ре́зусом.
rhetoric ['rɛtərɪk] *n* рито́рика.
rhetorical [rɪ'tɔrɪkl] *adj* ритори́ческий.
rheumatic [ruː'mætɪk] *adj* ревмати́ческий*.
rheumatism ['ruːmətɪzəm] *n* ревмати́зм.
rheumatoid arthritis ['ruːmətɔɪd-] *n*
ревмато́идный артри́т.
Rhine [raɪn] *n*: **the ~** Рейн.
rhinestone ['raɪnstəun] *n* фальши́вый
бриллиа́нт.
rhinoceros [raɪ'nɔsərəs] *n* носоро́г.
Rhodes [rəudz] *n* Ро́дос.
Rhodesia [rəu'diːʒə] *n* Роде́зия.
Rhodesian [rəu'diːʒən] *adj* родези́йский ♦ *n*
родези́ец*(-и́йка*).
rhododendron [rəudə'dɛndrn] *n* рододе́ндрон.
Rhone [rəun] *n*: **the ~** Ро́на.
rhubarb ['ruːbɑːb] *n* реве́нь* *m*.
rhyme [raɪm] *n* ри́фма; (*verse*) стихотворе́ние;
(*in poetry*) разме́р ♦ *vi*: **to ~ (with)**
рифмова́ться (*impf*) (с +*instr*); **without ~ or
reason** ни с того́ ни с сего́.
rhythm ['rɪðm] *n* ритм.
rhythmic(al) ['rɪðmɪk(l)] *adj* (*sound*)
ритми́ческий*, ритми́чный* (ритми́чен).
rhythmically ['rɪðmɪklɪ] *adv* ритми́чно.
rhythm method *n* есте́ственный *or*
натура́льный ме́тод контраце́пции.
RI *n abbr* (*BRIT: SCOL.* = *religious instruction*)
религио́зное воспита́ние ♦ *abbr* (*US: POST.*) =
Rhode Island.

rib [rɪb] *n* (*ANAT*) ребро́* ♦ *vt* (*inf: mock*)
подшу́чивать (подшути́ть* *perf*) над +*instr*.
ribald ['rɪbəld] *adj* (*laughter, jokes*) непри-
сто́йный* (непристо́ен), скабрёзный*
(скабрёзен); (*person*) гру́бый* (груб).
ribbed [rɪbd] *adj* (*shell*) ребри́стый (ребри́ст);
~ knitting вяза́ние рези́нкой.
ribbon ['rɪbən] *n* ле́нта; **in ~s** (*torn*) в клочья.
rice [raɪs] *n* рис.
rice field *n* ри́совое по́ле*.
rice pudding *n* ри́совый пу́динг.
rich [rɪtʃ] *adj* бога́тый (бога́т); (*clothes, jewels*)
роско́шный* (роско́шен); (*soil*) бога́тый;
(*food, colour, life*) насы́щенный* (*voice*)
густо́й (густ); (*abundant*): **~ in** бога́тый
(бога́т) +*instr*; **the ~** *npl* (*rich people*) бога́тые
pl adj.
riches ['rɪtʃɪz] *npl* (*wealth*) бога́тство *ntsg*.
richly ['rɪtʃlɪ] *adv* (*dressed, decorated*)
роско́шно, бога́то; (*rewarded*) ще́дро;
(*deserved, earned*) вполне́.
richness ['rɪtʃnɪs] *n* бога́тство.
rickets ['rɪkɪts] *n* (*MED*) рахи́т.
rickety ['rɪkɪtɪ] *adj* (*furniture etc*) ша́ткий*
(ша́ток).
rickshaw ['rɪkʃɔ:] *n* ри́кша.
ricochet ['rɪkəʃeɪ] *vi* (*bullet, stone*)
рикошети́ровать (*impf*) ♦ *n* рикоше́т.
rid [rɪd] (*pt, pp* **rid**) *vt*: **to ~ sb of sth** избавля́ть
(изба́вить* *perf*) кого́-н от чего́-н; **to get ~ of**
избавля́ться (изба́виться* *perf*) *or*
отде́лываться (отде́латься *perf*) от +*gen*.
riddance ['rɪdns] *n*: **good ~!** ска́тертью
доро́га!
ridden ['rɪdn] *pp of* ride.
riddle ['rɪdl] *n* (*conundrum*) зага́дка*; (*mystery*)
та́йна ♦ *vt*: **~d with** (*holes, bullets*)
изрешечённый (изрешечён) +*instr*; (*guilt,
doubts*) по́лный* (по́лон) +*gen*; (*corruption*)
прони́занный (прони́зан) +*instr*.
ride [raɪd] (*pt* **rode**, *pp* **ridden**) *n* пое́здка*; (*track,
path*) лесна́я доро́га, тропа́* ♦ *vi* (*as sport*)
е́здить* (*impf*) верхо́м; (*go somewhere, travel*)
е́хать/е́здить* (*impf*) ♦ *vt* (*horse*) е́хать*/
е́здить* (*impf*) верхо́м на +*prp*; (*bicycle,
motorcycle*) е́хать*/е́здить* (*impf*) на +*prp*;
(*distance*) проезжа́ть (прое́хать* *perf*); **a 5
mile ~** пое́здка в 5 миль; **horse/car ~**
пое́здка* верхо́м/на маши́не; **to go for a ~**
пойти́* (*perf*) поката́ться; **to take sb for a ~**
(*fig*) прокати́ть* (*perf*) кого́-н; **we rode all
day/all the way** мы е́хали весь день/всю
доро́гу; **to ~ at anchor** (*NAUT*) стоя́ть (*impf*) на
я́коре; **can you ~ a bike?** Вы уме́ете е́здить
на велосипе́де?
▶ **ride out** *vt*: **to ~ out the storm** (*fig*)
выде́рживать (вы́держать *perf*) тру́дности.
rider ['raɪdə'] *n* (*on horse*) нае́здник(-ица),

---

* marks translations which have irregular inflections. The Russian-English side of the dictionary gives inflectional information.

всáдник(-ица); (*on bicycle*)
велосипедúст(ка*); (*on motorcycle*)
мотоциклúст(ка*); (*in document*)
дополнéние.
ridge [rɪdʒ] *n* (*of hill*) грéбень *m*; (*of roof*) конёк*
(*крыши*); (*on material*) вы́ступ.
ridicule ['rɪdɪkjuːl] *n* насмéшка* ◆ *vt*
высмéивать (вы́смеять *perf*); **an object of** ~
предмéт насмéшек.
ridiculous [rɪ'dɪkjuləs] *adj* смехотвóрный*
(смехотвóрен); **it's** ~ э́то смешнó.
riding ['raɪdɪŋ] *n* верховáя езда́.
riding school *n* шкóла верховóй езды́.
rife [raɪf] *adj*: **to be** ~ (*bribery, corruption*)
процветáть (*impf*); **to be** ~ **with** (*rumours,
fears*) изобúловать (*impf*) +*instr*.
riffraff ['rɪfræf] *n* шу́шера.
rifle ['raɪfl] *n* (*MIL*) винтóвка*; (*for hunting*)
ружьё* ◆ *vt* (*steal from: pockets etc*) очи́стить*
(*perf*)
► **rifle through** *vt fus* (*papers, belongings*)
бы́стро перебирáть (перебрáть* *perf*).
rifle range *n* (*outdoor*) стрéльбище; (*indoor, at
fair*) тир.
rift [rɪft] *n* (*also fig*) трéщина; (*in clouds*)
просвéт.
rig [rɪg] *n* (*also: oil* ~) бурова́я устанóвка; (: *on
land*) бурова́я вы́шка* ◆ *vt* (*election etc*)
подтасóвывать (подтасовáть *perf*)
результáты +*gen*
► **rig out** *vt* (*BRIT*): **to** ~ **out as/in** наряжáть
(наряди́ть *perf*) как/в +*acc*
► **rig up** *vt* нáскоро сооружáть (сооруди́ть*
perf).
Riga [rɪ'gə] *n* Ри́га.
rigging ['rɪgɪŋ] *n* (*NAUT*) такелáж.
right [raɪt] *adj* (*answer, solution, decision etc*)
прáвильный* (прáвилен); (*size*) ну́жный;
(*person, clothes, time*) подходя́щий*; (*morally
good, fair, just*) справедли́вый (справедли́в),
прáвильный* (прáвилен); (*not left*) прáвый ◆
n справедли́вость *f*; (*entitlement*) прáво*; (*not
left*) прáвая сторонá ◆ *adv* (*correctly*)
прáвильно; (*properly, fairly*) справедли́во;
(*not on the left*) спрáва; (*to the left*)
напрáво ◆ *vt* (*ship*) выра́внивать (вы́ровнять
perf); (*car*) стáвить* (постáвить* *perf*) на
колёса; (*fault, situation*) исправля́ть
(испрáвить* *perf*); (*wrong*) устраня́ть
(устрани́ть *perf*) ◆ *excl* так, хорошó; **the** ~
time (*precise*) тóчное врéмя; (*not wrong*)
ну́жный *or* подходя́щий* момéнт; **she's** ~
онá прáва; **that's** ~**!** прáвильно!; **is
that clock** ~**?** э́то тóчные часы́?; **to get sth** ~
дéлать (сдéлать *perf*) что-н как слéдует; **let's
get it** ~ **this time!** давáйте сдéлаем э́то как
слéдует на э́тот раз; **you did the** ~ **thing** Вы
поступи́ли прáвильно; **to put a mistake** ~
(*BRIT*) исправля́ть (испрáвить* *perf*) оши́бку;
on the ~ спрáва; **you are in the** ~ прáвда за
Вáми; **by** ~**s** по справедли́вости; ~ **and**

wrong прáвильное и непрáвильное; **he
doesn't know the difference between** ~ **and
wrong** он не знáет рáзницы мéжду
прáвильным и непрáвильным; **film** ~**s**
прáво на экраниза́цию; ~ **now** сейча́с же; ~
away сра́зу же; ~ **before/after** как ра́з пéред
+*instr*/пóсле +*gen*; ~ **against the wall** пря́мо у
стены́; ~ **ahead** пря́мо вперёд; ~ **in the
middle** пря́мо посереди́не; ~ **to the end of sth**
до сáмого концá чего-н.
right angle *n* прямóй у́гол*.
righteous ['raɪtʃəs] *adj* прáведный* (прáведен).
righteousness ['raɪtʃəsnɪs] *n* прáведность *f*.
rightful ['raɪtful] *adj* закóнный.
rightfully ['raɪtfəlɪ] *adv* (*yours etc*) закóнно.
right-hand drive ['raɪthænd-] *n* право-
стóроннее управлéние ◆ *adj* (*vehicle*) с
правостóронним управлéнием.
right-handed [raɪt'hændɪd] *adj*: **he is** ~ он
правшá.
right-hand man *n* прáвая рука́* (*перен*).
right-hand side *n* прáвая сторонá*.
rightly ['raɪtlɪ] *adv* (*with reason*) справедли́во; **if
I remember** ~ (*BRIT*) éсли я прáвильно
пóмню.
right-minded [raɪt'maɪndɪd] *adj*
благоразу́мный* (благоразу́мен).
right of way *n* (*path etc*) прáво* прохóда;
(*AUT*) прáво* проéзда.
rights issue *n* (*STOCK EXCHANGE*) вы́пуск áкции
*для продáжи ужé существу́ющим
акционéрам по льгóтным цéнам.*
right wing *n* (*POL*) прáвое крылó; (*MIL, SPORT*)
прáвый фланг.
right-wing [raɪt'wɪŋ] *adj* (*POL*) прáвый.
right-winger [raɪt'wɪŋə] *n* (*POL*) человéк
прáвых взгля́дов, прáвый(-ая) *m(f) adj*;
(*SPORT*) прáвый нападáющий* *m adj*.
rigid ['rɪdʒɪd] *adj* (*structure, principle*) жёсткий*
(жёсток); (*fig: attitude, views etc*) кóсный*
(кóсен); (: *principle, control etc*) стрóгий*
(строг).
rigidity [rɪ'dʒɪdɪtɪ] *n* (*of structure*) жёсткость *f*;
(*of attitude etc*) кóсность *f*.
rigidly ['rɪdʒɪdlɪ] *adv* (*hold, fix etc*) прóчно;
(*control*) жёстко; (*behave*) скóванно.
rigmarole ['rɪgmərəul] *n* (*procedure*) кани́тель
f.
rigor ['rɪgə] *n* (*US*) = **rigour**.
rigor mortis ['rɪgə'mɔːtɪs] *n* тру́пное
окоченéние.
rigorous ['rɪgərəs] *adj* стрóгий* (строг);
(*training*) серьёзный.
rigorously ['rɪgərəslɪ] *adv* (*test, assess etc*)
стрóго.
rigour ['rɪgə] (*US* **rigor**) *n* (*strictness*) стрóгость
f; (*severity*) ~**s of life/winter** трýдности *fpl*
жи́зни/зимы́.
rigout ['rɪgaut] *n* (*BRIT: inf: clothes*) одея́ние.
rile [raɪl] *vt* раздражáть (раздражи́ть *perf*).
rim [rɪm] *n* (*of glass, dish*) край*; (*of spectacles*)

ободо́к*; (*of wheel*) о́бод*.
rimless ['rɪmlɪs] *adj* (*spectacles*) без ободка́.
rimmed [rɪmd] *adj*: ~ **with** окаймлённый
(окаймлён) +*instr*.
rind [raɪnd] *n* (*of bacon, cheese*) ко́рка; (*of
lemon, orange etc*) кожура́.
ring [rɪŋ] (*pt* **rang**, *pp* **rung**) *n* (*of metal, smoke*)
кольцо́*; (*of people, objects, light*) круг*; (*of
spies, drug dealers etc*) сеть* *f*; (*for boxing*)
ринг; (*bullring, also of circus*) аре́на; (*of
doorbell, telephone*) звоно́к* ♦ *vi* звони́ть
(позвони́ть *perf*); (*doorbell*) звони́ть
(зазвони́ть *perf*); (*also:* ~ **out**: *voice, shot*)
раздава́ться* (разда́ться* *perf*) ♦ *vt* (*BRIT: TEL*)
звони́ть (позвони́ть *perf*) +*dat*; (*bell etc*)
звони́ть (позвони́ть *perf*) в +*acc*; **to give sb a**
~ (*BRIT: TEL*) звони́ть (позвони́ть *perf*)
кому́-н; **that has a** ~ **of truth about it** э́то
звучи́т правдоподо́бно; **my ears are** ~**ing** у
меня́ звени́т в уша́х; **to** ~ **the bell** звони́ть
(*impf*) в звоно́к; (*doorbell*) звони́ть
(позвони́ть *perf*) в дверь; **the name doesn't** ~
a bell (with me) э́то и́мя мне ни о чём не
говори́т
▶ **ring back** (*BRIT*) ♦ *vt* перезва́нивать
(перезвони́ть *perf*) +*dat* ♦ *vi* звони́ть
(позвони́ть *perf*) (в отве́т)
▶ **ring off** *vi* (*BRIT*) ве́шать (пове́сить* *perf*)
тру́бку
▶ **ring up** *vt* (*BRIT*) звони́ть (позвони́ть *perf*)
+*dat*.
ring binder *n* скоросшива́тель *m*.
ring finger *n* безымя́нный па́лец*.
ringing ['rɪŋɪŋ] *n* (*of telephone, doorbell*)
звоно́к*; (*of church bell, in ears*) звон.
ringing tone *n* (*BRIT: TEL*) дли́нные гудки́ *pl*.
ringleader ['rɪŋliːdə'] *n* (*of gang*) глава́рь* *m*.
ringlets ['rɪŋlɪts] *npl* ло́коны *mpl*.
ring road *n* (*BRIT*) кольцева́я доро́га.
rink [rɪŋk] *n* (*also:* **ice** ~, **roller skating** ~) като́к*.
rinse [rɪns] *n* (*process*) полоска́ние; (*dye: for
hair*) кра́ска* для воло́с ♦ *vt* полоска́ть*
(прополоска́ть* *perf*); (*clothes*) полоска́ть
(вы́полоскать *perf*); **to give sth a** ~
опола́скивать (ополосну́ть *perf*) что-н.
Rio (de Janeiro) ['riːəʊ(dədʒə'nɪərəʊ)] *n*
Ри́о-де-Жане́йро *m ind*.
riot ['raɪət] *n* (*disturbance*) беспоря́дки *mpl*,
бесчи́нства *ntpl*; (*of colours, flowers*) бу́йство
♦ *vi* бесчи́нствовать (*impf*); **to run** ~
бу́йствовать* (*impf*).
rioter ['raɪətə'] *n* наруши́тель *m* поря́дка.
riot gear *n* защи́тное снаряже́ние поли́ции.
riotous ['raɪətəs] *adj* (*mob, behaviour, party*)
бесчи́нствующий; (*living*) разгу́льный*
(разгу́лен); (*welcome*) бу́рный* (бу́рен).
riotously ['raɪətəslɪ] *adv*: ~ **funny** неимове́рно
смешно́й.

riot police *n* спецподразделе́ние поли́ции для
подавле́ния беспоря́дков.
RIP *abbr* (= *rest in peace*) мир пра́ху твоему́.
rip [rɪp] *n* (*tear*) разры́в ♦ *vt* (*paper, cloth*)
разрыва́ть* (разорва́ть* *perf*) ♦ *vi* (*see vt*)
разрыва́ться* (разорва́ться* *perf*)
▶ **rip up** *vt* разрыва́ть (разорва́ть* *perf*).
ripcord ['rɪpkɔːd] *n* (*on parachute*) вытяжно́й
трос.
ripe [raɪp] *adj* спе́лый* (спел), зре́лый* (зрел);
(*cheese*) вы́держанный* (вы́держан).
ripen ['raɪpn] *vi* спеть* (поспе́ть* *perf*), зреть *or*
созрева́ть (созре́ть *perf*) ♦ *vt*: **the sun will** ~
them soon они́ ско́ро созре́ют на со́лнце.
ripeness ['raɪpnɪs] *n* спе́лость *f*, зре́лость *f*.
rip-off ['rɪpɔf] *n* (*inf*): **it's a** ~! э́то
обдира́ловка!
riposte [rɪ'pɔst] *n* нахо́дчивый отве́т.
ripple ['rɪpl] *n* (*wave: caused by wind, rain etc*)
рябь *f no pl*; (: *caused by stone etc*) зыбь *f no pl*;
(*of laughter, applause*) волна́*, гул *m no pl* ♦ *vt*
(*water, sand*) поднима́ть (подня́ть* *perf*)
зыбь на +*prp* ♦ *vi* (*water*) покрыва́ться
(покры́ться* *perf*) ря́бью.
rise [raɪz] (*pt* **rose**, *pp* **risen**) *n* (*slope*) подъём;
(*increase*) повыше́ние; (*fig: of state, leader*)
возвыше́ние ♦ *vi* поднима́ться (подня́ться*
perf); (*prices, numbers, voice*) повыша́ться
(повы́ситься* *perf*); (*sun, moon*) всходи́ть*
(взойти́* *perf*); (*sound*) нараста́ть (*impf*); (*also:*
~ **up**: *building*) возвыша́ться (*impf*); (: *rebels*)
восстава́ть* (восста́ть* *perf*); (*in rank*)
продвига́ться (продви́нуться *perf*); ~ **to**
power прихо́д к вла́сти; **to give** ~ **to**
вызыва́ть (вы́звать* *perf*); **to** ~ **to the**
occasion ока́зываться (оказа́ться* *perf*) на
высоте́ положе́ния.
risen [rɪzn] *pp of* **rise**.
rising ['raɪzɪŋ] *adj* (*number, prices*) расту́щий;
(*tide*) нараста́ющий; (*sun, moon*) восход-
я́щий.
rising damp *n* засоле́ние (*поднима́ющаяся
вверх сы́рость*).
rising star *n* (*fig*) восходя́щая звезда́*.
risk [rɪsk] *n* риск ♦ *vt* (*endanger*) рискова́ть
(*impf*) +*instr*; (*chance*) рискова́ть* (рискну́ть
perf) +*instr*; **to take a** ~ рискова́ть (рискну́ть
perf), идти́* (*impf*) на риск; **to run the** ~ **of**
doing рискова́ть (*impf*) +*infin*; **at** ~ в опа́сной
ситуа́ции; **to put sb/sth at** ~ подверга́ть
(подве́ргнуть *perf*) кого́-н/что-н ри́ску; **at**
one's own ~ на свой (страх и) риск; **at the** ~
of sounding rude ... рискуя́ показа́ться
гру́бым(-ой) ...; **it's a fire** ~ с противо-
пожа́рной то́чки зре́ния э́то опа́сно; **it's a**
health ~ э́то опа́сно для здоро́вья; **I'll** ~ **it** я
рискну́.
risk capital *n* „ри́сковый" *or* ве́нчурный

---

* marks translations which have irregular inflections. The Russian-English side of the dictionary gives inflectional information.

капита́л.

risky ['rɪskɪ] *adj* риско́ванный* (риско́ван).

risqué ['riːskeɪ] *adj* (*joke*) сомни́тельный* (сомни́телен).

rissole ['rɪsəul] *n* биток*.

rite [raɪt] *n* обря́д; **last ~s** после́днее прича́стие.

ritual ['rɪtjuəl] *adj* ритуа́льный ♦ *n* (*of religion*) обря́д; (*of procedure*) ритуа́л.

rival ['raɪvl] *n* сопе́рник(-ица); (*in business*) конкуре́нт ♦ *adj* (*competing: business*) конкури́рующий; (*competition*) сопе́рничающий ♦ *vt* сопе́рничать (*impf*) с +*instr*; **to ~ sb/sth in** сопе́рничать (*impf*) с кем-н/с чем-н в +*prp*; **~ team** кома́нда сопе́рника.

rivalry ['raɪvlrɪ] *n* (*in sport, love*) сопе́рничество; (*in business*) конкуре́нция.

river ['rɪvə'] *n* река́* ♦ *cpd* (*port, traffic*) речно́й; **up/down** ~ вверх/вниз по реке́.

riverbank ['rɪvəbæŋk] *n* бе́рег* реки́.

riverbed ['rɪvəbed] *n* ру́сло реки́.

riverside ['rɪvəsaɪd] *n* бе́рег* реки́.

rivet ['rɪvɪt] *n* заклёпка* ♦ *vt* (*fig*) прико́вывать (прикова́ть *perf*).

riveting ['rɪvɪtɪŋ] *adj* (*fig*) захва́тывающий*.

Riviera [rɪvɪ'eərə] *n*: **the (French) ~** (францу́зская) Ривье́ра; **the Italian ~** италья́нская Ривье́ра.

Riyadh [rɪ'jɑːd] *n* Эр-Рия́д.

RN *n abbr* (*BRIT*) **= Royal Navy**; (*US*: = *registered nurse*) ≈ медсестра́= *медици́нская сестра́*.

RNA *n abbr* (= *ribonucleic acid*) РНК= *рибонуклеи́новая кислота́*.

RNLI *n abbr* (*BRIT*) = *Royal National Lifeboat Institution*.

RNZAF *n abbr* = *Royal New Zealand Air Force*.

RNZN *n abbr* = *Royal New Zealand Navy*.

road [rəud] *n* (*also fig*) путь* *m*, доро́га; (*in town*) доро́га; (*motorway etc*) шоссе́ *nt ind*; **~ accident** доро́жная ава́рия; **main ~** гла́вная доро́га; **major/minor ~** гла́вная/второстепе́нная доро́га; **it takes 4 hours by ~** э́то 4 часа́ по доро́ге; **let's hit the ~** дава́йте вы́едем на доро́гу; **to be on the ~** (*tramp*) бродя́жничать (*impf*); (*salesman*) быть* (*impf*) в разъе́здах; (*pop group*) быть* (*impf*) на гастро́лях, гастроли́ровать* (*impf*); **on the ~ to success** на пути́ к успе́ху; **~ sense** чу́вство доро́ги; **~ junction** пересече́ние доро́г, перекрёсток*.

roadblock ['rəudblɔk] *n* доро́жное загражде́ние.

road haulage *n* доро́жная перево́зка.

road hog *n* лиха́ч.

road map *n* доро́жная ка́рта.

road safety *n* доро́жная безопа́сность *f*.

roadside ['rəudsaɪd] *n* обо́чина ♦ *cpd* придоро́жный; **~ verge** обо́чина; **by the ~** у обо́чины.

road sign *n* доро́жный знак.

road sweeper *n* (*BRIT*: *person*) дво́рник; (*vehicle*) подмета́льная маши́на.

road user *n* (*driver*) води́тель *m*.

roadway ['rəudweɪ] *n* (*central part of road*) прое́зжая часть* *f* (доро́ги).

road works *npl* доро́жно-ремо́нтные рабо́ты *fpl*.

roadworthy ['rəudwə:ðɪ] *adj* (*car*) приго́дный* (приго́ден) к эксплуата́ции.

roam [rəum] *vi* броди́ть* (*impf*), скита́ться (*impf*) ♦ *vt* броди́ть* (*impf*) по +*dat*.

roar [rɔː'] *n* (*of animal*) рёв *m no pl*; (*of crowd, engine, wind*) рёв; (*of laughter*) взрыв ♦ *vi* (*animal, person*) реве́ть (*impf*); (*crowd, engine, wind*) реве́ть (*impf*); **to ~ with laughter** хохота́ть (*impf*).

roaring ['rɔːrɪŋ] *adj*: **a ~ fire** я́рко пыла́ющий ками́н; **a ~ success** гро́мкий успе́х; **to do a ~ trade** вести́* (*impf*) бо́йкую торго́влю.

roast [rəust] *n* (*of meat*) жарко́е *nt adj* ♦ *vt* (*meat, potatoes*) жа́рить (зажа́рить *perf*); (*coffee*) жа́рить (поджа́рить *perf*).

roast beef *n* ро́стбиф, жа́реная говя́дина.

roasting ['rəustɪŋ] *n* (*inf*): **to give sb a ~** устра́ивать (устро́ить *perf*) кому́-н разно́с.

rob [rɔb] *vt* (*person, house, bank*) обкра́дывать (обокра́сть* *perf*); **to ~ sb of sth** красть* (укра́сть* *perf*) что-н у кого́-н; (*fig*) лиша́ть (лиши́ть *perf*) кого́-н чего́-н.

robber ['rɔbə'] *n* граби́тель *m*.

robbery ['rɔbərɪ] *n* (*theft*) ограбле́ние, грабёж.

robe [rəub] *n* (*for ceremony etc*) ма́нтия; (*also*: **bath ~**) ба́нный хала́т; (*US*) плед ♦ *vt* облача́ть (облачи́ть *perf*).

robin ['rɔbɪn] *n* (*also*: **~ redbreast**) заря́нка*.

robot ['rəubɔt] *n* ро́бот.

robotics [rə'bɔtɪks] *n* (*ELEC, COMPUT*) робототе́хника.

robust [rəu'bʌst] *adj* кре́пкий* (кре́пок).

rock [rɔk] *n* (*substance*) (го́рная) поро́да; (*boulder*) валу́н*; (*cliff*) скала́*; (*US*: *small stone*) ка́мешек*; (*BRIT*: *sweet*) леденцо́вая караме́ль в фо́рме дли́нных па́лочек; (*MUS*: *also*: **~ music**) рок ♦ *vt* (*swing gently*) кача́ть (*impf*); (*shake*) шата́ть (*impf*) ♦ *vi* (*object*) кача́ться (*impf*), шата́ться (*impf*); (*person*) кача́ться (*impf*); **on the ~s** (*drink*) со льдо́м; (*marriage etc*) на гра́ни распа́да; **the ship was smashed on the ~s** кора́бль разби́лся о ска́лы; **to ~ the boat** (*fig*) наруши́ть (*perf*) поко́й.

rock and roll *n* рок-н-ро́лл.

rock bottom *n* (*fig*) преде́льная ни́зкая черта́; **to reach** *or* **touch** *or* **hit ~ ~** (*price*) достига́ть (дости́чь* *perf*) преде́льно ни́зкой черты́; (*person*) доходи́ть* (дойти́* *perf*) до крити́ческой то́чки.

rock-bottom ['rɔk'bɔtəm] *adj* (*fig*: *prices*) преде́льно ни́зкий*.

rock cake *n* ко́ржик с изю́мом.

rock climber *n* скалола́з.

rock climbing n скалолазание.
rockery ['rɔkərɪ] n альпийский* сад*.
rocket ['rɔkɪt] n ракета ♦ vi (prices)
подскакивать (подскочить* perf).
rocket launcher n (MIL) пусковая ракетная
установка*.
rock face n поверхность f скалы.
rock fall n камнепад.
rocking chair ['rɔkɪŋ-] n (кресло-)качалка*.
rocking horse n конь-качалка*.
rocky ['rɔkɪ] adj (mountain) скалистый
(скалист); (path, soil) каменистый
(каменист); (unsteady, unstable) шаткий*
(шаток).
Rocky Mountains npl: the ~ ~ Скалистые
горы* fpl.
rod [rɔd] n прут*; (TECH) стержень* m; (also:
fishing ~) удочка*.
rode [rəud] pt of **ride**.
rodent ['rəudnt] n грызун*.
rodeo ['rəudɪəu] n (US) родео nt ind.
roe [rəu] n (also: ~ deer) косуля; (of fish): **hard**
~ икра; **soft** ~ молоки fpl.
roe deer n inv косуля.
rogue [rəug] n (dishonest person) мошенник,
жулик.
roguish ['rəugɪʃ] adj (mischevious) плутоватый
(плутоват).
role [rəul] n (THEAT, fig) роль* f.
role model n пример.
role play n ролевые игры fpl.
roll [rəul] n (of paper, cloth etc) рулон; (of
banknotes) свиток*; (also: **bread** ~) булочка*;
(register, list) список*; (sound: of drums) бой*;
(: of thunder) раскат ♦ vt (ball, stone etc)
катать/катить* (impf); (also: ~ **up**: string)
скручивать (скрутить* perf); (: sleeves)
закатывать (закатать perf); (cigarette)
свёртывать (свернуть perf); (eyes)
закатывать (закатить* perf); (also: ~ **out**:
pastry) раскатывать (раскатать perf); (lawn,
road etc) укатывать (укатать perf) ♦ vi (ball,
stone etc) катиться* (impf); (drum) греметь
(impf); (car. also: ~ **along**) катиться* (impf);
(ship) качаться (impf); **cheese/ham** ~
булочка* с сыром/с ветчиной
► **roll about** vi перекатываться
(перекатиться* perf)
► **roll around** vi = **roll about**
► **roll by** vi (time) протекать (протечь* perf)
► **roll in** vi (orders) сыпаться* (impf); (cash)
течь* (потечь* perf)
► **roll over** vi переворачиваться
(перевернуться perf)
► **roll up** vi (inf: arrive) подкатывать
(подкатить* perf) ♦ vt (carpet, newspaper)
сворачивать (свернуть perf); (umbrella)
складывать (сложить* perf); **to** ~ **o.s. up into**

a ball сворачиваться (свернуться perf)
калачиком.
roll call n перекличка*.
roller ['rəulə'] n (in machine) валик; (wheel)
ролик; (for lawn, road) каток*; (for hair)
бигуди pl ind.
roller blind n штора на роликах.
roller coaster n аттракцион "американские
горы" fpl.
roller skates npl ролики mpl, роликовые
коньки mpl.
rollicking ['rɔlɪkɪŋ] adj потрясающий*
(потрясающ); **to have a** ~ **time** веселиться
(повеселиться perf).
rolling ['rəulɪŋ] adj (landscape) холмистый
(холмист).
rolling mill n прокатный стан.
rolling pin n скалка*.
rolling stock n (RAIL) подвижной состав.
roll-on/roll-off ferry adj (BRIT) паром,
приспособленный для въезда и выезда
автомобилей.
roly-poly ['rəulɪ'pəulɪ] n (BRIT: CULIN) рулет с
вареньем.
ROM [rɔm] n abbr (COMPUT: = read-only
memory) ПЗУ = постоянное запоминающее
устройство.
Roman ['rəumən] adj римский* ♦ n (person)
римлянин(-нка).
Roman Catholic adj (римско-)католический*
♦ n католик(-ичка*).
romance [rə'mæns] n (love affair, novel) роман;
(charm) романтика; (MUS) романс.
Romanesque [rəumə'nɛsk] adj романский*.
Romania [rəu'meɪnɪə] n Румыния.
Romanian [rəu'meɪnɪən] adj румынский* ♦ n
(person) румын(ка*); (LING) румынский*
язык*.
Roman numeral n римская цифра.
romantic [rə'mæntɪk] adj романтичный*
(романтичен); (play, story etc)
романтический.
romanticism [rə'mæntɪsɪzəm] n романтизм.
Romany ['rɔmənɪ] adj цыганский* ♦ n
цыган(ка*); (LING) цыганский* язык*.
Rome [rəum] n Рим.
romp [rɔmp] n возня ♦ vi (also: ~ **about**)
возиться* (impf); **to** ~ **home** (horse)
выигрывать (выиграть perf) скачки.
rompers ['rɔmpəz] npl ползунки mpl.
rondo ['rɔndəu] n рондо nt ind.
roof [ru:f] (pl ~s) n крыша ♦ vt (house)
настилать (настлать* perf) крышу +gen or на
+prp; **the** ~ **of the mouth** нёбо.
roof garden n сад* на крыше.
roofing ['ru:fɪŋ] n кровельный материал; ~
felt рулонный кровельный материал.
roof rack n (AUT) багажник (на крыше

---

* marks translations which have irregular inflections. The Russian-English side of the dictionary gives inflectional information.

автомоби́ля).

rook [ruk] *n* (*bird*) грач*; (*CHESS*) ладья́*, тура́* ♦ *vt* (*inf*: *cheat*) надува́ть (наду́ть *perf*).

rookie ['ruki:] *n* (*US*: *inf*) новичо́к.

room [ru:m] *n* (*in house*) ко́мната; (*in school*) класс; (*in hotel*) но́мер*; (*space*) ме́сто*; ~s *npl* (*lodging*) кварти́ра *fsg*; **"rooms to let"**, (*US*) **"rooms for rent"** „сдаю́тся ко́мнаты"; **single/double ~** (*in hotel*) одноме́стный/двухме́стный но́мер*; **is there ~ for this?** э́то здесь поме́стится?; **to make ~ for sb** дава́ть* (дать* *perf*) ме́сто кому́-н; **there is ~ for improvement** ко́е-что мо́жно улу́чшить; **there is still ~ for doubt** ещё есть основа́ния сомнева́ться.

rooming house ['ru:mɪŋ-] *n* (*US*) меблиро́ванные ко́мнаты *fpl*.

roommate ['ru:mmeɪt] *n* сосе́д*(ка*) по ко́мнате.

room service *n* обслу́живание в но́мере.

room temperature *n* ко́мнатная температу́ра.

roomy ['ru:mɪ] *adj* (*building, car, garment*) просто́рный* (просто́рен); (*bag*) вмести́тельный* (вмести́телен).

roost [ru:st] *vi* уса́живаться (усе́сться* *perf*) на ночле́г.

rooster ['ru:stə] *n* (*esp US*) пету́х*.

root [ru:t] *n* ко́рень* *m* ♦ *vi* (*plant, belief*: *also*: **take ~**) укореня́ться (укорени́ться *perf*); ~s *npl* (*family origins*) ко́рни* *mpl*; **the ~ of the problem is that ...** ко́рень пробле́мы в том ...
▶ **root about** *vi* (*fig*) ры́ться* (*impf*)
▶ **root for** *vt fus* (*inf*: *support*) боле́ть (*impf*) за +*acc*
▶ **root out** *vt* откопа́ть (*perf*).

root beer *n* безалкого́льный напи́ток из корне́й трав.

rope [rəup] *n* верёвка*, кана́т; (*NAUT*) трос ♦ *vt* (*area*: *also*: ~ **off**) отгора́живать (отгороди́ть* *perf*) верёвкой; (*tie on*): **to ~ to** привя́зывать (привяза́ть* *perf*) верёвкой к +*dat*; (*join*): **to ~ together** свя́зывать (связа́ть* *perf*) верёвкой; **to know the ~s** (*fig*) знать (*impf*), что к чему́
▶ **rope in** *vt* (*fig*) втя́гивать (втяну́ть* *perf*).

rope ladder *n* верёвочная ле́стница.

ropey ['rəupɪ] *adj* (*inf*) дрянно́й.

rosary ['rəuzərɪ] *n* чётки* *pl*.

rose [rəuz] *pt of* **rise** ♦ *n* ро́за; (*on watering can*) наса́дка ♦ *adj* (*colour*) ро́зовый* (ро́зов).

rosé ['rəuzeɪ] *n* (*wine*) ро́зовое вино́*.

rosebed ['rəuzbɛd] *n* клу́мба с ро́зами.

rosebud ['rəuzbʌd] *n* буто́н ро́зы.

rosebush ['rəuzbuʃ] *n* ро́зовый куст*.

rosemary ['rəuzmərɪ] *n* розмари́н.

rosette [rəu'zɛt] *n* (*decoration*) розе́тка*.

ROSPA ['rɔspə] *n abbr* (*BRIT*) = *Royal Society for the Prevention of Accidents*.

roster ['rɔstə] *n*: **duty ~** расписа́ние дежу́рств.

rostrum ['rɔstrəm] *n* (*POL*) трибу́на.

rosy ['rəuzɪ] *adj* (*colour*) ро́зовый (ро́зов); (*face, cheeks*) румя́ный (румя́н); (*situation*) ра́достный* (ра́достен); **a ~ future** ра́дужное бу́дущее.

rot [rɔt] *n* (*process*) гние́ние; (*result*) гниль *f*; (*fig*: *nonsense*) чушь *f* ♦ *vt* (*wood, fruit*) гнои́ть (сгнои́ть *perf*); (*teeth*) по́ртить* (испо́ртить* *perf*) ♦ *vi* гнить* (сгни́ть* *perf*); **to stop the ~** (*BRIT*: *fig*) навести́* (*perf*) поря́док; **dry/wet ~** суха́я/мо́края гниль.

rota ['rəutə] *n* чередова́ние; **on a ~ basis** череду́ясь, поочерёдно.

rotary ['rəutərɪ] *adj* (*motion*) враща́тельный; (*machine*) ротацио́нный, враща́ющийся; **~ engine** ро́торно-поршнево́й дви́гатель.

rotate [rəu'teɪt] *vt* враща́ть (*impf*); (*change round*: *crops, jobs*) чередова́ть (*impf*) ♦ *vi* враща́ться (*impf*).

rotating [rəu'teɪtɪŋ] *adj* (*movement*) враща́тельный.

rotation [rəu'teɪʃən] *n* враще́ние; (*of crops*) севооборо́т; **in ~** поочерёдно.

rote [rəut] *n*: **to learn by ~** учи́ть (*impf*) наизу́сть.

rotor ['rəutə] *n* (*also*: ~ **blade**) (несу́щий) винт* (вертолёта).

rotten ['rɔtn] *adj* (*fruit, wood, teeth*) гнило́й*; (*meat, eggs*) ту́хлый; (*fig*: *unpleasant*) ме́рзкий* (ме́рзок), отврати́тельный* (отврати́телен); (*dishonest*) прода́жный* (прода́жен); (*inf*: *bad*) пога́ный; **to feel ~** (*ill*) чу́вствовать (*impf*) себя́ пло́хо.

Rotterdam ['rɔtədæm] *n* Ро́ттердам.

rotund [rəu'tʌnd] *adj* (*person*) по́лный.

rouble ['ru:bl] (*US* **ruble**) *n* рубль* *m*.

rouge [ru:ʒ] *n* румя́на *pl*.

rough [rʌf] *adj* гру́бый (груб); (*surface*) шерохова́тый (шерохова́т); (*terrain*) пересечённый; (*road*) уха́бистый (уха́бист); (*brusque*: *person, manner*) ре́зкий* (ре́зок); (*weather*) нена́стный* (нена́стен); (*sea*) бу́рный* (бу́рен); (*town, area*) опа́сный* (опа́сен); (*plan, sketch, work*) черново́й; (*guess*) приблизи́тельный* (приблизи́телен) ♦ *n* (*GOLF*): **in the ~** на нестри́женой ча́сти по́ля ♦ *vt*: **to ~ it** обходи́ться* (обойти́сь* *perf*) без удо́бств ♦ *adv*: **to play ~** вести́* (*impf*) жёсткую игру́; **the sea is ~ today** мо́ре сего́дня штормит/неспоко́йно; **we had a ~ time (of it)** нам пришло́сь ту́го; **~ estimate** гру́бая оце́нка* *or* сме́та; **to sleep ~** (*BRIT*) ночева́ть* (*impf*), где придётся; **to feel ~** (*BRIT*: *ill*) чу́вствовать (*impf*) себя́ пло́хо
▶ **rough out** *vt* (*draft*) набра́сывать (наброса́ть *perf*).

roughage ['rʌfɪdʒ] *n* гру́бая пи́ща.

rough-and-ready ['rʌfən'rɛdɪ] *adj* дряно́й.

rough-and-tumble ['rʌfən'tʌmbl] *n* потасо́вка.

roughcast ['rʌfkɑːst] *n* (*for wall*) га́лечная штукату́рка.

rough copy *n* чернови́к*.

rough draft *n* чернови́к*.
rough justice *n* жёсткий* суд.
roughly [ˈrʌflɪ] *adv* гру́бо; (*approximately*) приблизи́тельно; ~ **speaking** гру́бо говоря́.
roughness [ˈrʌfnɪs] *n* (*of surface*) шерохова́тость *f*; (*of manner*) гру́бость *f*.
roughshod [ˈrʌfʃɔd] *adv*: **to ride ~ over** не счита́ться (*impf*) с +*instr*.
roulette [ruːˈlɛt] *n* руле́тка*.
Roumania *etc* = **Romania** *etc*.
round [raund] *adj* кру́глый* (кругл); (*figures, sum*) кру́глый ♦ *n* (*BRIT*: *of toast*) ло́мтик; (*duty*: *of policeman, doctor*) обхо́д; (: *of milkman*) маршру́т; (*game*: *of cards, golf*) па́ртия; (*in competition*) тур; (*of ammunition*) патро́н, компле́кт вы́стрела; (*of talks, also BOXING*) ра́унд ♦ *vt* огиба́ть (обогну́ть *perf*) ♦ *prep* (*surrounding*): ~ **his neck/the table** вокру́г его́ ше́и/стола́; (*approximately*): ~ **about three hundred** (приблизи́тельно) о́коло трёхсот ♦ *adv*: **all** ~ круго́м, вокру́г; **in** ~ **figures** в кру́глых ци́фрах; **a** ~ **of applause** взрыв аплодисме́нтов; **a** ~ **of drinks** по бока́лу для всех; **the daily** ~ (*fig*) повседне́вные дела́; **it's just** ~ **the corner** (*fig*) э́то как раз за угло́м; ~ **the clock** кру́глые су́тки, круглосу́точно; **to go** ~ **the back** обходи́ть* (обойти́* *perf*) сза́ди; **to walk** ~ **the room** ходи́ть* (*impf*) по ко́мнате; **to go** ~ **an obstacle** огиба́ть (обогну́ть *perf*) *or* обходи́ть* (обойти́* *perf*) препя́тствие; **the long way** ~ кру́жным путём; **all the year** ~ кру́глый год; **to ask sb** ~ приглаша́ть (пригласи́ть* *perf*) кого́-н в го́сти; **I'll be** ~ **at 6 o'clock** я приду́ в 6 часо́в; **to go** ~ **to sb's (house)** идти́*/ходи́ть* (*impf*) к кому́-н; **there's enough to go** ~ хва́тит на всех
▸ **round off** *vt* (*speech etc*) заверша́ть (заверши́ть *perf*)
▸ **round up** *vt* (*cattle, people*) сгоня́ть (согна́ть* *perf*); (*price, figure*) округля́ть (округли́ть *perf*).
roundabout [ˈraundəbaut] *n* (*BRIT*: *AUT*) кольцева́я тра́нспортная развя́зка*; (: *at fair*) карусе́ль *f* ♦ *adj* око́льным путём.
rounded [ˈraundɪd] *adj* окру́глый (окру́гл).
rounders [ˈraundəz] *n* англи́йская лапта́.
roundly [ˈraundlɪ] *adv* (*fig*: *criticize*) ре́зко.
round robin *n* (*letter*) коллекти́вное письмо́*.
round-shouldered [ˈraundˈʃəuldəd] *adj* суту́лый (суту́л).
round trip *n* пое́здка* туда́-обра́тно.
roundup [ˈraundʌp] *n* (*information*) сво́дка*; (*of animals*) заго́н; (*of criminals*) обла́ва; **a** ~ **of the latest news** сво́дка после́дних новосте́й.
rouse [rauz] *vt* (*wake up*) буди́ть* (разбуди́ть* *perf*); (*stir up*) возбужда́ть (возбуди́ть* *perf*).
rousing [ˈrauzɪŋ] *adj* (*cheer, welcome*) бу́рный*

(бу́рен).
rout [raut] *n* (*MIL*) разгро́м ♦ *vt* (*defeat*) громи́ть* (разгроми́ть* *perf*).
route [ruːt] *n* (*way*) путь* *m*, доро́га; (*of bus, train, shipping*) маршру́т; **the best** ~ **to London** лу́чший* путь в Ло́ндон; **en** ~ **for** по пути́ в +*acc*; **en** ~ **from ... to ...** по пути́ из +*gen* ... в +*acc* ....
route map *n* (*BRIT*) маршру́тная ка́рта.
routine [ruːˈtiːn] *adj* (*work*) повседне́вный* (повседне́вен); (*procedure*) обы́чный* (обы́чен) ♦ *n* (*habits*) распоря́док*; (*drudgery*) рути́на; (*THEAT*) но́мер*; **daily** ~ распоря́док* дня.
rove [rəuv] *vt* (*streets*) броди́ть* (*impf*) по +*dat*, скита́ться (*impf*) по +*dat*.
roving reporter *n* разъездно́й репортёр.
row[1] [rəu] *n* ряд* ♦ *vi* (*in boat*) грести́* (*impf*) ♦ *vt* (*boat*) управля́ть (*impf*) +*instr*; **in a** ~ (*fig*) подря́д.
row[2] [rau] *n* (*noise*) шум; (*dispute*) сканда́л, ссо́ра; (*inf*: *scolding*) нагоня́й ♦ *vi* (*argue*) сканда́лить (посканда́лить *perf*); **to have a** ~ ссо́риться (поссо́риться *perf*), посканда́лить (*perf*).
rowboat [ˈrəubəut] *n* (*US*) гребна́я шлю́пка*.
rowdiness [ˈraudɪnɪs] *n* бу́йство.
rowdy [ˈraudɪ] *adj* бу́йный* (бу́ен).
rowdyism [ˈraudɪzəm] *n* бу́йство.
rowing [ˈrəuɪŋ] *n* гре́бля.
rowing boat *n* (*BRIT*) гребна́я шлю́пка*.
rowlock [ˈrɔlək] *n* (*BRIT*) уклю́чина.
royal [ˈrɔɪəl] *adj* короле́вский*.
Royal Air Force *n* (*BRIT*) Брита́нские вое́нно-возду́шные си́лы.
royal-blue [ˈrɔɪəlbluː] *adj* я́рко-си́ний*.
royalist [ˈrɔɪəlɪst] *adj* роя́листский* ♦ *n* рояли́ст(ка*).
Royal Navy *n* (*BRIT*) Брита́нский вое́нно-морско́й флот.
royalty [ˈrɔɪəltɪ] *n* (*royal persons*) чле́ны *mpl* короле́вской семьи́; (*payment*) (а́вторский*) гонора́р.
RP *n abbr* (*BRIT*: = *received pronunciation*) станда́ртное произноше́ние.
rpm *abbr* (= *revolutions per minute*) оборо́тов в мину́ту.
RR *abbr* (*US*) (= *railroad*) ж.д., ж/д = желе́зная доро́га.
RRP *n abbr* (*BRIT*) (= *recommended retail price*) рекомендо́ванная ро́зничная цена́.
RSA *n abbr* (*BRIT*) = *Royal Society of Arts*; *Royal Scottish Academy*.
RSI *n abbr* (*MED*: = *repetitive strain injury*) произво́дственная тра́вма, вы́званная напряже́нием одно́й и той же гру́ппы мышц (*у машини́сток итп*).
RSPB *n abbr* (*BRIT*) = *Royal Society for the*

Protection of Birds.
RSPCA n abbr (BRIT) = Royal Society for the Prevention of Cruelty to Animals.
RSVP abbr (= répondez s'il vous plaît) про́сьба отве́тить на приглаше́ние.
RTA n abbr = road traffic accident.
Rt Hon. abbr (BRIT: = Right Honourable) высокочти́мый.
Rt Rev. abbr (REL: = Right Reverend) высокопреподо́бный.
rub [rʌb] vt (part of body) тере́ть* (потере́ть* perf); (object: to clean) тере́ть* (impf); (: to polish) натира́ть (натере́ть* perf); (: to dry) вытира́ть (вы́тереть* perf); (hands: also: ~ together) потира́ть (потере́ть* perf) ♦ n: to give sth a ~ (polish) натира́ть (натере́ть* perf) что-н; to ~ one's hands (together) тере́ть* (потере́ть* perf) ру́ки; to ~ sb up or (US) ~ sb the wrong way раздража́ть (impf) кого́-н
▸ **rub down** vt обтира́ть (обтере́ть* perf)
▸ **rub in** vt (ointment) втира́ть (втере́ть* perf); don't ~ it in! (fig: inf) не ка́пай!
▸ **rub off** vi (paint) стира́ться (стере́ться* perf)
▸ **rub off on** vt fus передава́ться* (переда́ться* perf) +dat
▸ **rub out** vt стира́ть (стере́ть* perf).
rubber ['rʌbə'] n (substance) рези́на, каучу́к; (BRIT: eraser) рези́нка, ла́стик; (US: inf. condom) презервати́в.
rubber band n (кру́глая) рези́нка*.
rubber bullet n рези́новая пу́ля.
rubber plant n каучуконо́с, (каучуконо́сный) фи́кус.
rubber ring n надувно́й рези́новый круг*.
rubber stamp n штамп; (POST) штёмпель m.
rubber-stamp [rʌbə'stæmp] vt (fig) штампова́ть (проштампова́ть perf).
rubbery ['rʌbərɪ] adj (material, substance) похо́жий на рези́ну; (meat, food) жёсткий* как рези́на.
rubbish ['rʌbɪʃ] n му́сор; (waste food) отбро́сы mpl; (junk) хлам; (fig: pej: nonsense) ерунда́, чушь f; (: junk) дрянь f ♦ vt (BRIT: inf) критикова́ть (impf); what you've just said is ~ то, что Вы то́лько что сказа́ли – ерунда́ or чепуха́ or чушь.
rubbish bin n (BRIT) му́сорное ведро́*.
rubbish dump n сва́лка*.
rubbishy ['rʌbɪʃɪ] adj (BRIT: inf) дрянно́й.
rubble ['rʌbl] n обло́мки mpl; (building material) бут.
ruble ['ru:bl] n (US) = rouble.
ruby ['ru:bɪ] n руби́н.
RUC n abbr (BRIT: = Royal Ulster Constabulary) североирла́ндская поли́ция.
rucksack ['rʌksæk] n рюкза́к*.
ructions ['rʌkʃənz] npl (protest) возмуще́ние ntsg; (quarrel) сканда́л msg.
rudder ['rʌdə'] n руль* m.
ruddy ['rʌdɪ] adj (face, complexion) румя́ный (румя́н); (glow) краснова́тый; (inf: damned)

прокля́тый.
rude [ru:d] adj (impolite) гру́бый* (груб); (shocking) непристо́йный* (непристо́ен); (crudely made) гру́бо сде́ланный (сде́лан); he was ~ to me он был груб со мной; a ~ awakening глубо́кое разочарова́ние, неприя́тное откры́тие.
rudely ['ru:dlɪ] adv гру́бо.
rudeness ['ru:dnɪs] n (impoliteness) гру́бость f.
rudimentary [ru:dɪ'mɛntərɪ] adj (equipment, knowledge) элемента́рный* (элемента́рен).
rudiments ['ru:dɪmənts] npl осно́вы fpl.
rue [ru:] vt (action, decision) жале́ть (пожале́ть perf) о +prp; (day, hour etc) проклина́ть (прокля́сть* perf).
rueful ['ru:ful] adj (expression, person etc) печа́льный* (печа́лен).
ruffian ['rʌfiən] n банди́т.
ruffle ['rʌfl] vt (hair) еро́шить (взъеро́шить perf); (clothes) гофрирова́ть (impf/perf); (water) ряби́ть* (impf); (fig: person) раздража́ть (impf).
rug [rʌg] n ко́врик; (BRIT: blanket) плед.
rugby ['rʌgbɪ] n (also: ~ football) ре́гби nt ind.
rugged ['rʌgɪd] adj (landscape) скали́стый (скали́ст); (features) гру́бый* (груб); (character) прямо́й (прям); (determination) непрекло́нный* (непрекло́нен), твёрдый* (твёрд).
rugger ['rʌgə'] n (BRIT: inf) ре́гби nt ind.
ruin ['ru:ɪn] n (destruction: of building, hopes, plans) разруше́ние; (: of hopes, plans) круше́ние; (downfall) ги́бель f; (bankruptcy) разоре́ние; (remains: of building) разва́лины fpl ♦ vt (building, hopes, plans) разруша́ть (разру́шить perf); (future, health, reputation) губи́ть* (погуби́ть* perf); (person: financially) разоря́ть (разори́ть perf); (spoil: clothes) по́ртить* (испо́ртить* perf); ~s npl (of building, castle etc) разва́лины fpl, руи́ны fpl; in ~s (building) в разва́линах or руи́нах; my life is in ~s моя́ жизнь загу́блена.
ruination [ru:ɪ'neɪʃən] n уничтоже́ние.
ruinous ['ru:ɪnəs] adj (interest) губи́тельный* (губи́телен); (expense) разори́тельный* (разори́телен).
rule [ru:l] n (norm, regulation) пра́вило; (government) правле́ние, власть f; (ruler) лине́йка ♦ vt (country, people) управля́ть (impf) +instr ♦ vi (leader, monarch etc) пра́вить* (impf), управля́ть (impf); (LAW): to ~ in favour of/against выноси́ть* (вы́нести perf) реше́ние в по́льзу +gen/про́тив +gen; under British ~ (dominion) под брита́нским правле́нием; it's against the ~s э́то про́тив пра́вил; by ~ of thumb наугля́д; as a ~ как пра́вило; to ~ that (umpire, judge etc) постановля́ть (постанови́ть* perf), что ...
▸ **rule out** vt (exclude) исключа́ть (исключи́ть perf); **murder cannot be ~d out** уби́йство не мо́жет быть* исключено́.

ruled [ru:ld] *adj* (*paper*) линóваный.
ruler ['ru:lǝ³] *n* прави́тель(ница) *m(f)*; (*for measuring*) линéйка.
ruling ['ru:lɪŋ] *adj* (*party*) пра́вящий*; (*class*) госпóдствующий* ◆ *n* (*LAW*) постановлéние.
rum [rʌm] *n* ром ◆ *adj* (*BRIT*: *inf*) чуднóй.
Rumania *etc* = **Romania** *etc*.
rumble ['rʌmbl] *n* (*of traffic, thunder*) гул ◆ *vi* бубни́ть (*impf*); (*also:* ~ **along**) с гýлом проезжáть (проéхать* *perf*); (*stomach, pipe*) бурчáть (*impf*); (*thunder*) грохотáть* (прогрохотáть* *perf*).
rumbustious [rʌm'bʌstʃǝs] *adj* бóйкий* (бóек).
ruminate ['ru:mɪneɪt] *vi* жевáть* (*impf*) жвáчку; (*fig*) размышлять (*impf*).
rummage ['rʌmɪdʒ] *vi* (*search*) ры́ться (*impf*).
rummage sale *n* (*US*) благотвори́тельная распродáжа подéржанных вещéй.
rumour ['ru:mǝ³] (*US* **rumor**) *n* слух ◆ *vt*: **it is ~ed that** ... хóдят слýхи, что ....
rump [rʌmp] *n* (*of horse*) круп; (*of cow*) зáдняя часть *f*; (*of group, political party*) остáтки *mpl*.
rumple ['rʌmpl] *vt* (*clothes*) мять* (помять* *or* измя́ть* *perf*).
rump steak *n* вы́резка* (*из зáдней частéй*).
rumpus ['rʌmpǝs] *n* шум; **to kick up a ~** поднимáть (поднять* *perf*) шум.
run [rʌn] (*pt* **ran**, *pp* **run**) *n* (*fast pace*) бег*; (*journey*) поéздка; (*distance travelled*) пробéг; (*SKIING*) трáсса; (*CRICKET, BASEBALL*) очкó*; (*in tights, stockings*) спусти́вшиеся пéтли *fpl* ◆ *vt* (*race, distance*) пробегáть (пробежáть* *perf*); (*operate: business, hotel*) управля́ть (*impf*) +*instr*; (: *competition, course*) устрáивать (устрóить *perf*); (: *house*) вести́* (*impf*); (*COMPUT*: *program*) выполня́ть (вы́полнить *perf*); (*pass: hand, fingers*): **to ~ along** *or* **over** проводи́ть* (провести́* *perf*) +*instr* по +*dat*; (*water*) пускáть (пусти́ть* *perf*); (*bath*) наполня́ть (напóлнить *perf*); (*PRESS: feature*) печáтать (напечáтать *perf*) ◆ *vi* бéгать/бежáть* (*impf*); (*flee*) бежáть* (*impf/ perf*), сбегáть (сбежáть* *perf*); (*work: machine*) рабóтать (*impf*); (*bus, train*) ходи́ть* (*impf*); (*continue: play, show*) идти́* (*impf*); (: *contract*) дли́ться (*impf*); (*in election*) баллоти́роваться (*perf*); (*river*) течь* (*impf*), протекáть (*impf*); (*bath*) наполня́ться (напóлниться *perf*); (*colours, washing*) линя́ть (полиня́ть *perf*); (*nose*) течь* (*impf*); **to go for a ~** (*for exercise*) идти́* (пойти́* *perf*) побéгать; **to break into a ~** пускáться (пусти́ться* *perf*) бежáть; **a ~ of luck** перóд удáч; **the play had a 6 week** пьéса шла 6 недéль; **to have the ~ of sb's house** имéть (*impf*) разрешéние пóльзоваться чьим-н дóмом; **there was a ~ on tickets** на билéты был большóй спрос; **in the long ~** в конéчном итóге; **in the short ~** на

какóе-то врéмя; **to make a ~ for it** убежáть* (убегáть *perf*) со всех ног; **to be on the ~** скрывáться (*impf*); (*inf: to be busy*) быть* (*impf*) в бегáх; **I'll ~ you to the station** я подвезý Вас до стáнции; **to ~ a risk** подвергáться (подвéргнуться *perf*) ри́ску; **to ~ errands for sb** выполня́ть (*impf*) мéлкие поручéния для когó-н; **my car is very cheap to ~** моя́ маши́на экономи́чна; **to be ~ off one's feet** (*BRIT*) сби́ться* (*perf*) с ног; **the train ~s between Gatwick and Victoria** пóезд хóдит мéжду Гáтвиком и Виктóрией; **the bus ~s every 20 minutes** автóбус хóдит кáждые 20 минýт; **to ~ on petrol** *or* (*US*) **gas/on diesel/off batteries** рабóтать (*impf*) на бензи́не/на ди́зеле/на батарéйках; **to ~ for president** баллоти́роваться (*perf*) в президéнти; **their losses ran into millions** их потéри исчисля́лись миллиóнами
▶ **run about** *vi* бéгать (*impf*)
▶ **run across** *vt fus* (*find*) натыкáться (наткнýться *perf*) на +*acc*
▶ **run around** *vi* = **run about**
▶ **run away** *vi* убегáть (убежáть* *perf*)
▶ **run down** *vt* (*production, industry*) сокращáть (сократи́ть* *perf*); (*AUT: hit*) сбивáть (сбить* *perf*); (*criticize*) поноси́ть* (*impf*); **to be ~ down** (*person*) выбивáться (вы́биться* *perf*) из сил; (*battery*) кончáться (*impf*), иссякáть (*impf*)
▶ **run in** *vt* (*BRIT: car*) обкáтывать (обкатáть *perf*)
▶ **run into** *vt fus* (*meet: person*) стáлкиваться (столкнýться *perf*) с +*instr*; (: *trouble*) натáлкиваться (натолкнýться *perf*) на +*acc*; (*collide with*) врезáться (врéзаться* *perf*) в +*acc*; **to ~ into debt** залезáть (залéзть* *perf*) в долги́
▶ **run off** *vt* (*subj: water*) спускáть (спусти́ть* *perf*); (*copies*) дéлать (сдéлать *perf*), отсня́ть* (*perf*) ◆ *vi* (*person, animal*) сбегáть (сбежáть* *perf*), убегáть (убежáть* *perf*)
▶ **run out** *vi* (*person*) выбегáть (вы́бежать* *perf*); (*liquid*) вытекáть (вы́течь* *perf*); (*lease, visa*) истекáть (истéчь* *perf*); (*money*) закáнчиваться (закóнчиться *perf*); **my passport ~s out in July** срок дéйствия мосгó пáспорта истекáет в июле
▶ **run out of** *vt fus*: **I've ~ out of money/time/ petrol** *or* (*US*) **gas** у меня́ кóнчились дéньги/ кóнчилось врéмя/кóнчился бензи́н
▶ **run over** *vt* (*AUT*) задави́ть* (*perf*) ◆ *vt fus* (*revise*) пробегáть (пробежáть *perf*)
▶ **run through** *vt fus* пробегáть (пробежáть *perf*); (*rehearse*) прогоня́ть (прогонáть *perf*)
▶ **run up** *vt*: **to ~ up a debt** влезáть (влезть* *perf*) в долги́; **to ~ up against** (*difficulties*)

---

* marks translations which have irregular inflections. The Russian-English side of the dictionary gives inflectional information.

ста́лкиваться (столкну́ться *perf*) с +*instr*.
runabout ['rʌnəbaut] *n* (*AUT*) малолитра́жка*.
run around *n* (*inf*): **to give sb the** ~~ води́ть*
(*impf*) кого́-н за нос.
runaway ['rʌnəweɪ] *adj* (*truck, horse etc*)
потеря́вший управле́ние; (*person*) бе́глый;
(*inflation*) неуправля́емый.
rundown ['rʌndaun] *n* (*BRIT: of industry etc*)
сокраще́ние.
run-down [rʌn'daun] *adj* (*tired, ill*)
изможде́нный* (изможде́н).
rung [rʌŋ] *pp of* **ring** ◆ *n* (*of ladder*) ступе́нька*;
(*in organization*) ступе́нь *m*.
run-in ['rʌnɪn] *n* (*inf*) сты́чка*.
runner ['rʌnəʳ] *n* (*in race: person*) бегу́н*(ья);
(: *horse*) скаку́н*; (*on sledge, for drawer etc*)
по́лоз*; (*carpet: in hall etc*) доро́жка*.
runner bean *n* (*BRIT*) стручко́вая фасо́ль *f no pl*.
runner-up [rʌnərʌp] *n* финали́ст (*заня́вший
второ́е ме́сто*).
running ['rʌnɪŋ] *n* (*sport*) бег*; (*of business,
organization*) руково́дство; (*of event*)
организа́ция; (*of machine etc*) эксплуата́ция
◆ *adj* (*water*) теку́щий*; (: *to house*)
водопрово́дный; **he is in/out of the** ~ **for sth**
ему́ сули́т/не сули́т что-н; **6 days** ~ 6 дней
подря́д.
running commentary *n* (*TV, RADIO*) прямо́й
репорта́ж.
running costs *npl* (*of business*) операцио́нные
изде́ржки *fpl*; (*of car*) содержа́ние *ntsg*.
running head *n* колонти́тул (*заголо́вок,
печа́таемый на верху́ ка́ждой страни́цы*).
running mate *n* (*US: POL*) кандида́т на
до́лжность вице-президе́нта.
runny ['rʌnɪ] *adj* (*honey, egg*) жи́дкий*
(жи́док); (*nose*) сопли́вый (сопли́в); (*eyes*)
слезя́щийся.
runoff ['rʌnɔf] *n* (*in contest, election*)
повто́рные вы́боры *mpl*; (*extra race*)
повто́рный забе́г.
run-of-the-mill [rʌnəvðə'mɪl] *adj* сре́дний*.
runt [rʌnt] *n* (*animal*) недоме́рок*; (*pej: person*)
сморчо́к*.
run-through ['rʌnθruː] *n* (*rehearsal*) прого́н.
run-up ['rʌnʌp] *n* пери́од, предше́ствующий
како́му-нибудь собы́тию.
runway ['rʌnweɪ] *n* взлётно-поса́дочная
полоса́*.
rupee [ruː'piː] *n* ру́пия.
rupture ['rʌptʃəʳ] *n* (*MED: hernia*) гры́жа;
(*between people, groups*) разры́в ◆ *vt*: **to** ~
o.s. (*MED*) получа́ть (получи́ть *perf*) гры́жу.
rural ['ruərl] *adj* се́льский*; (*accent*)
дереве́нский*.
rural district council *n* (*BRIT*) се́льский*
райо́нный сове́т.
ruse [ruːz] *n* уло́вка*, ухищре́ние.

rush [rʌʃ] *n* (*hurry*) спе́шка; (*COMM: sudden
demand*) большо́й спрос; (*of water, current*)
пото́к; (*of emotion*) прили́в; (*plant*) камы́ш*
◆ *vt* (*BRIT: inf: overcharge*) обсчи́тывать
(обсчита́ть *perf*) ◆ *vi* (*person*) бежа́ть* (*impf*);
(*air, water*) хлы́нуть (*perf*); **is there any** ~ **for
this?** э́то спе́шно?; **a** ~ **of orders** напль́в
зака́зов; **I'm in a** ~ (**to do**) я спешу́ (+*infin*);
gold ~ золота́я лихора́дка; **to** ~ **one's meal/
work** второпя́х есть (*impf*)/де́лать (*impf*)
рабо́ту; **don't** ~ **me!** не подгоня́йте от
торопи́те меня́!; **to** ~ **sth off** (*do*) спе́шно
де́лать (сде́лать *perf*) что-н; (*send*) спе́шно
отправля́ть (отпра́вить* *perf*) что-н; **she** ~**ed
to the door** она́ бро́силась к две́ри
▶ **rush through** *vt fus* де́лать (сде́лать *perf*) в
спе́шке; (*meal*) прогла́тывать (проглоти́ть*
perf); (*town*) носи́ться* (нести́сь* *perf*) по +*dat*.
rush hour *n* час пик.
rush job *n* рабо́та, сде́ланная на́спех.
rush matting *n* цино́вка*.
rusk [rʌsk] *n* (*biscuit*) ≈ суха́рь *m*.
Russia ['rʌʃə] *n* Росси́я.
Russian ['rʌʃən] *adj* (*native Russian*) ру́сский*;
(*belonging to Russian Federation*)
росси́йский* ◆ *n* ру́сский(-ая) *m(f) adj*; (*LING*)
ру́сский* язы́к*.
rust [rʌst] *n* (*also BOT*) ржа́вчина ◆ *vi* ржаве́ть
(заржаве́ть *perf*).
rustic ['rʌstɪk] *adj* дереве́нский* ◆ *n* (*pej*)
дереве́нщина *m/f no pl*.
rustle ['rʌsl] *vi* шурша́ть (*impf*), шелесте́ть*
(*impf*) ◆ *vt* шелесте́ть* (*impf*) +*instr*; (*US: steal*)
угоня́ть (угна́ть* *perf*).
rustproof ['rʌstpruːf] *adj* (*metal*) нержаве́ющ-
ий; (*car*) сде́ланный (сде́лан) из
нержаве́ющего материа́ла.
rustproofing ['rʌstpruːfɪŋ] *n* обрабо́тка
про́тив ржа́вчины.
rusty ['rʌstɪ] *adj* ржа́вый* (*fig: skill*)
подзабы́тый.
rut [rʌt] *n* (*groove*) колея́, борозда́*; (*ZOOL:
season*) полова́я охо́та; **to get into a** ~ (*fig*)
заходи́ть* (зайти́* *perf*) в тупи́к, застрева́ть
(застря́ть* *perf*).
rutabaga [ruːtə'beɪgə] *n* (*US*) ре́па.
ruthless ['ruːθlɪs] *adj* (*person, action*)
беспоща́дный* (беспоща́ден),
безжа́лостный* (безжа́лостен).
ruthlessness ['ruːθlɪsnɪs] *n* беспоща́дность *f*,
безжа́лостность *f*.
RV *abbr* (*BIBLE:* = revised version) испра́вленное
изда́ние Би́блии ◆ *n abbr* (*US*) = recreational
vehicle.
Ryazan [rɪ'zanj] *n* Ряза́нь *f*.
rye [raɪ] *n* рожь* *f*.
rye bread *n* ржано́й хлеб.

~ S, s ~

S, s [ɛs] *n* (*letter*) 19-ая бу́ква англи́йского алфави́та; (*US: SCOL*: = *satisfactory*) ≈ удовлетвори́тельно.

S *abbr* (= **south**) Ю= *юг*; = **small**; (= **saint**) св= *свято́й*.

SA *abbr* = **South Africa, South America.**

Sabbath ['sæbəθ] *n* (*Jewish*) суббо́та; (*Christian*) воскресе́нье.

sabbatical [sə'bætɪkl] *n* (*also:* ~ **year**) тво́рческий* о́тпуск*.

sabotage ['sæbətɑːʒ] *n* сабота́ж ♦ *vt* (*machine, building*) выводи́ть* (вы́вести* *perf*) из стро́я; (*plan, meeting*) саботи́ровать (*impf/perf*).

sabre ['seɪbə'] *n* са́бля*.

sabre-rattling ['seɪbərætlɪŋ] *n* бряца́ние ору́жием (*перен*).

saccharin(e) ['sækərɪn] *n* сахари́н.

sachet ['sæʃeɪ] *n* (*of shampoo, sugar etc*) паке́тик.

sack [sæk] *n* (*bag*) мешо́к* ♦ *vt* (*dismiss*) выгоня́ть (вы́гнать* *perf*) с рабо́ты; (*plunder*) опустоша́ть (опустоши́ть *perf*); **to give sb the** ~ выгоня́ть (вы́гнать* *perf*) кого́-н (с рабо́ты); **I got the** ~ меня́ вы́гнали (с рабо́ты).

sackful ['sækful] *n*: **a** ~ **of** мешо́к* +*gen*.

sacking ['sækɪŋ] *n* (*dismissal*) увольне́ние; (*material*) мешкови́на.

sacrament ['sækrəmənt] *n* (*rite*) та́инство.

sacred ['seɪkrɪd] *adj* свяще́нный; (*place*) свято́й; (*music*) духо́вный.

sacred cow *n* (*fig*) святы́ня.

sacrifice ['sækrɪfaɪs] *n* (*offering*) жертвоприноше́ние; (*thing or person offered*) же́ртва ♦ *vt* (*animal*) приноси́ть* (принести́* *perf*) в же́ртву +*dat*; (*fig*) же́ртвовать (поже́ртвовать *perf*) +*instr*; **to make** ~**s (for sb)** же́ртвовать (поже́ртвовать *perf*) собо́й (ра́ди кого́-н).

sacrilege ['sækrɪlɪdʒ] *n* святота́тство.

sacrosanct ['sækrəusæŋkt] *adj* (*also fig*) свяще́нный.

sad [sæd] *adj* печа́льный* (печа́лен).

sadden ['sædn] *vt* печа́лить (опеча́лить *perf*).

saddle ['sædl] *n* седло́* ♦ *vt* (*horse*) седла́ть (оседла́ть *perf*); **to** ~ **sb with sth** (*inf*)

навешивать (навесить* *perf*) что-н на кого́-н.

saddlebag ['sædlbæg] *n* (*on bicycle*) седе́льная су́мка.

sadism ['seɪdɪzəm] *n* сади́зм.

sadist ['seɪdɪst] *n* сади́ст(ка*).

sadistic [sə'dɪstɪk] *adj* (*person, behaviour*) сади́стский.

sadly ['sædlɪ] *adv* (*unhappily*) печа́льно, гру́стно; (*unfortunately*) к сожале́нию; (*seriously: mistaken, neglected*) серьёзно; **the school is** ~ **lacking in equipment** шко́ла испы́тывает серьёзный недоста́ток в обору́довании.

sadness ['sædnɪs] *n* печа́ль *f*, грусть *f*.

sadomasochism [seɪdəu'mæsəkɪzəm] *n* са́до-мазохи́зм.

sae *abbr* (*BRIT*) = **stamped addressed envelope**; *see* **stamp**.

safari [sə'fɑːrɪ] *n* сафа́ри *nt ind*; **to go on** ~ проводи́ть* (провести́* *perf*) о́тпуск в сафа́ри.

safari park *n* парк сафа́ри.

safe [seɪf] *adj* (*place, subject*) безопа́сный* (безопа́сен); (*return, journey*) благополу́чный* (благополу́чен); (*bet, appointment*) надёжный* (надёжен) ♦ *n* сейф; **to be** ~ находи́ться* (*impf*) в безопа́сности; ~ **from** (*attack*) защищённый (защищён) от +*gen*; ~ **and sound** цел и невреди́м; (**just**) **to be on the** ~ **side** на вся́кий слу́чай; **to play** ~ де́йствовать (*impf*) осторо́жно; **it is** ~ **to say that** ... мо́жно с уве́ренностью сказа́ть, что ...; ~ **journey!** счастли́вого пути́! ♦ **seat** (*POL*) парла́ментское ме́сто с гаранти́рованной подде́ржкой избира́телей.

safe bet *n* ве́рное де́ло; **he is a** ~ ~ на него́ мо́жно положи́ться.

safe-breaker ['seɪfbreɪkə'] *n* (*BRIT*) взло́мщик сейфо́в.

safe-conduct [seɪf'kɔndʌkt] *n* неприкоснове́нность *f*.

safe-cracker ['seɪfkrækə'] *n* = **safe-breaker.**

safe-deposit ['seɪfdɪpɔzɪt] *n* сейф.

safeguard ['seɪfgɑːd] *n* гара́нтия ♦ *vt* (*life, interests*) охраня́ть (*impf*); (*future*) гаранти́ровать (*impf/perf*).

---

* marks translations which have irregular inflections. The Russian-English side of the dictionary gives inflectional information.

safe haven *n* зо́на безопа́сности.
safe house *n* конспирати́вная кварти́ра.
safekeeping ['seif'ki:piŋ] *n* сохра́нность *f*.
safely ['seifli] *adv* (*assume, say*) с
уве́ренностью; (*drive, arrive*) благополу́чно;
I can ~ say ... я могу́ с уве́ренностью сказа́ть
....
safe passage *n* безопа́сный путь* *m*.
safe sex *n* безопа́сный секс; **to practise ~ ~**
испо́льзовать (*impf*) презервати́вы во вре́мя
се́кса.
safety ['seifti] *n* безопа́сность *f*; **~ first!**
соблюда́йте осторо́жность!
safety belt *n* привязно́й реме́нь *m*.
safety catch *n* (*on gun*) замо́к*; (*on window*)
защёлка*.
safety net *n* (*also fig*) сеть *f* безопа́сности.
safety pin *n* англи́йская була́вка*.
safety valve *n* предохрани́тельный кла́пан.
saffron ['sæfrən] *n* шафра́н.
sag [sæg] *vi* (*breasts*) отвиса́ть (отви́снуть
perf); (*roof, hem*) провиса́ть (прови́снуть
perf); (*spirits, prices*) па́дать (упа́сть* *perf*).
saga ['sɑːgə] *n* са́га.
sage [seidʒ] *n* (*herb*) шалфе́й; (*wise man*)
мудре́ц*.
Sagittarius [sædʒi'tɛəriəs] *n* Стреле́ц*; **he is ~**
он – Стреле́ц.
sago ['seigəu] *n* са́го *nt ind*.
Sahara [sə'hɑːrə] *n*: **the ~ (Desert)** Саха́ра.
Sahel [sæ'hɛl] *n* Сахе́ль *f*.
said [sɛd] *pt, pp of* **say**.
Saigon [sai'gɔn] *n* Сайго́н.
sail [seil] *n* па́рус* ♦ *vt* (*boat*) пла́вать/плыть*
(*impf*) на +*prp* ♦ *vi* (*ship, passenger*) пла́вать/
плыть* (*impf*); (*SPORT*) занима́ться (*impf*)
па́русным спо́ртом; (*also:* **set ~**) отплыва́ть
(отплы́ть* *perf*); **to go for a ~** е́хать* (пое́хать*
perf) ката́ться на ло́дке; **they ~ed into
Copenhagen** они́ приплы́ли в Копенга́ген
▶ **sail through** *vt fus* (*fig*) с лёгкостью сдава́ть*
exam/interview (сдать* *perf*) экза́мен/проходи́ть* (пройти́*
perf) собесе́дование.
sailboat ['seilbəut] *n* (*US*) = **sailing boat**.
sailing ['seiliŋ] *n* (*SPORT*) па́русный спорт; **to
go ~** занима́ться (*impf*) па́русным спо́ртом.
sailing boat *n* па́русная ло́дка*.
sailing ship *n* па́русное су́дно*.
sailor ['seilə'] *n* моря́к*, матро́с.
saint [seint] *n* (*also fig*) свято́й(-а́я) *m(f) adj*.
saintly ['seintli] *adj* свято́й*.
sake [seik] *n*: **for the ~ of sb/sth, for sb's/sth's ~**
ра́ди кого́-н/чего́-н; **arguing for arguing's ~**
спор ра́ди спо́ра; **for the ~ of argument** в
ка́честве предположе́ния; **for heaven's ~!**
ра́ди Бо́га!
Sakhalin [səxa'lin] *n* Сахали́н.
salad ['sæləd] *n* сала́т; **tomato ~** сала́т из
помидо́ров; **green ~** зелёный сала́т.
salad bowl *n* сала́тница.

salad cream *n* (*BRIT*) сала́тный со́ус.
salad dressing *n* припра́ва к сала́ту.
salami [sə'lɑːmi] *n* саля́ми *f ind*.
salaried ['sælərid] *adj* (*staff*) получа́ющий
зарпла́ту.
salary ['sæləri] *n* зарпла́та (= *за́работная
пла́та*).
salary scale *n* шкала́* за́работной пла́ты.
sale [seil] *n* (*act of selling*) прода́жа; (*at reduced
prices*) распрода́жа; (*auction*) то́рги *mpl*; **~s**
npl (*total amount sold*) объём прода́жи ♦ *cpd*
(*campaign, conference*) рекла́мный; (*figures,
target*) прода́жный; **"for ~"** „продаётся"; **on
~** в прода́же; **these goods are on ~ or return**
е́сли э́ти това́ры не бу́дут про́даны, они́
бу́дут возвращены́ владе́льцу; **closing-down**
or (*US*) **liquidation ~** ликвидацио́нная
распрода́жа.
sale and lease back *n* (*COMM*) *прода́жа
со́бственности с усло́вием получе́ния её
обра́тно в аре́нду на оговорённый срок.*
saleroom ['seilru:m] *n* торго́вый зал.
sales assistant [seilz-] (*US* **salesclerk**) *n* (*BRIT*)
продаве́ц*(-вщи́ца).
salesclerk ['seilzklə:rk] *n* (*US*) = **sales assistant**.
sales force *n* торго́вые аге́нты *mpl*.
salesman ['seilzmən] *irreg n* (*in shop*)
продаве́ц*; (*also:* **travelling ~**) торго́вый
аге́нт.
sales manager *n* (*in company*) нача́льник
отде́ла сбы́та; (*in shop*) ста́рший*(-ая)
продаве́ц*(-вщи́ца).
salesmanship ['seilzmənʃip] *n* уме́ние
продава́ть.
sales tax *n* (*US*) нало́г на прода́жи
(*упла́чивается потреби́телем при поку́пке
определённых това́ров*).
saleswoman ['seilzwumən] *irreg n* (*in shop*)
продавщи́ца; (*representative*) торго́вый
аге́нт.
salient ['seiliənt] *adj* суще́ственный.
saline ['seilain] *adj* соляно́й.
saliva [sə'laivə] *n* слюна́.
sallow ['sæləu] *adj* (*complexion*) желту́шный.
sally forth ['sæli-] *vi* отправля́ться
(отпра́виться* *perf*).
sally out *vi* = **sally forth**.
salmon ['sæmən] *n inv* (*ZOOL*) ло́сось* *m*; (*CULIN*)
лососи́на.
salmon trout *n* тайме́нь *m*.
salon ['sælɔn] *n* сало́н; **beauty ~**
космети́ческий* сало́н.
saloon [sə'lu:n] *n* (*US: bar*) бар; (*BRIT: AUT*)
"седа́н" (*тип автомоби́ля*); (*ship's lounge*)
сало́н.
SALT [sɔ:lt] *n abbr* (= *Strategic Arms Limitation
Talks/Treaty*) перегово́ры *pl*/догово́р ОСВ
= *об ограниче́нии стратеги́ческих
наступа́тельных вооруже́ний.*
salt [sɔ:lt] *n* соль *f* ♦ *vt* (*preserve*) заса́ливать
(засоли́ть* *perf*); (*season*) соли́ть* (посоли́ть*

perf) ♦ *cpd* солёный; **the ~ of the earth** соль земли́.

saltcellar ['sɔːltsɛlə'] *n* соло́нка*.

salt-free ['sɔːlt'friː] *adj* не содержа́щий со́ли.

salt mine *n* соляна́я ша́хта.

saltwater ['sɔːlt'wɔːtə'] *adj* живу́щий в солёных во́дах.

salty ['sɔːltɪ] *adj* солёный* (солён).

salubrious [sə'luːbrɪəs] *adj* целе́бный* (целе́бен); (*fig: district etc*) благода́тный* (благода́тен).

salutary ['sæljutərɪ] *adj* поле́зный* (поле́зен).

salute [sə'luːt] *n* (MIL) салю́т; (*greeting*) приве́тствие ♦ *vt* (MIL) отдава́ть (отда́ть* *perf*) честь +*dat*; (*fig*) приве́тствовать (*impf*).

salvage ['sælvɪdʒ] *n* (*saving*) спасе́ние; (*things saved*) спасённые ве́щи *fpl* ♦ *vt* (*also fig*) спаса́ть (спасти́* *perf*).

salvage vessel *n* спаса́тельное су́дно*.

salvation [sæl'veɪʃən] *n* спасе́ние.

Salvation Army *n* А́рмия Спасе́ния.

salver ['sælvə'] *n* подно́с.

salvo ['sælvəu] (*pl* ~**es**) *n* залп.

Samaritans [sə'mærɪtənz] *npl*: **the ~** Самаритя́не* *mpl*.

same [seɪm] *adj* тако́й же; (*identical*) одина́ковый ♦ *pron*: **the ~** тот же (са́мый) (*f* та же (са́мая), *nt* то же (са́мое), *pl* те же (са́мые)); **the ~ book as** та же (са́мая) кни́га, что и; **on the ~ day** в тот же день; **at the ~ time** (*simultaneously*) в э́то же вре́мя; (*yet*) в то же вре́мя; **all** *or* **just the ~** всё равно́; **to do the ~ (as sb)** де́лать (сде́лать *perf*) то же (са́мое) (что и кто-н); **Happy New Year! – the ~ to you!** С Но́вым Го́дом! – Вас та́кже!; **you're a fool! – the ~ to you!** ты дура́к! – сам (ты) дура́к!; **I hate him – ~ here!** я ненави́жу его́ – и я то́же!; **the company director and Mr Smith are one and the ~** дире́ктор компа́нии и Ми́стер Смит одно́ лицо́; **the books we're talking about are one and the ~** мы говори́ли об одно́й и то́же кни́ге; **~ again!** (*in bar etc*) повтори́те!

sample ['sɑːmpl] *n* (*of water*) про́ба; (*of work, merchandise*) образе́ц* ♦ *vt* (*food, wine*) про́бовать (попро́бовать *perf*); **to take a ~** брать* (взять* *perf*) про́бу; **to take a blood/urine ~** брать* (взять* *perf*) кровь/мочу́ для ана́лиза; **free ~** беспла́тный образе́ц*.

sanatoria [sænə'tɔːrɪə] *npl of* **sanatorium**.

sanatorium [sænə'tɔːrɪəm] (*pl* **sanatoria** *or* ~**s**) *n* (MED) санато́рий.

sanctify ['sæŋktɪfaɪ] *vt* освяща́ть (освяти́ть* *perf*).

sanctimonious [sæŋktɪ'məunɪəs] *adj* благочи́нный* (благочи́нен).

sanction ['sæŋkʃən] *n* (*approval*) са́нкция ♦ *vt* (*give approval to*) санкциони́ровать (*impf/*

perf); ~**s** *npl* (*severe measures*) са́нкции *fpl*; **to impose economic ~s on** *or* **against** применя́ть (примени́ть* *perf*) экономи́ческие са́нкции про́тив +*gen*.

sanctity ['sæŋktɪtɪ] *n* свя́тость *f*.

sanctuary ['sæŋktjuərɪ] *n* (*for animals*) запове́дник; (*for people*) убе́жище; (*in church*) алта́рная часть *f*.

sand [sænd] *n* песо́к* ♦ *vt* (*also:* ~ **down**) ошку́ривать (ошку́рить *perf*); *see also* **sands**.

sandal ['sændl] *n* санда́лия.

sandbag ['sændbæg] *n* мешо́к* с песко́м.

sandblast ['sændblɑːst] *vt* подверга́ть (подве́ргнуть *perf*) пескостру́йной обрабо́тке.

sandbox ['sændbɔks] *n* (US) песо́чница.

sand castle *n* песча́ный за́мок*.

sand dune *n* (песча́ная) дю́на.

sander ['sændə'] *n* ручно́й шлифова́льный стано́к.

S & M *n abbr* (= *sadomasochism*) садомазохи́зм.

sandpaper ['sændpeɪpə'] *n* нажда́чная бума́га, шку́рка.

sandpit ['sændpɪt] *n* песо́чница.

sands [sændz] *npl* пески́ *mpl*.

sandstone ['sændstəun] *n* песча́ник.

sandstorm ['sændstɔːm] *n* песча́ная бу́ря.

sandwich ['sændwɪtʃ] *n* бутербро́д ♦ *vt*: ~**ed between** зажа́тый ме́жду +*instr*; **cheese/ham ~** бутербро́д с сы́ром/ветчино́й.

sandwich board *n* (*notice*) рекла́мный щит*.

sandwich course *n* (BRIT) курс обуче́ния, сочета́ющий тео́рию с пра́ктикой.

sandwich man *n irreg* челове́к, несу́щий на себе́ рекла́мный щит.

sandy ['sændɪ] *adj* песча́ный; (*hair*) песо́чный.

sane [seɪn] *adj* разу́мный* (разу́мен).

San Francisco [sæn fræn'sɪskəu] *n* Сан-Франци́ско *m ind*.

sang [sæŋ] *pt of* **sing**.

sanguine ['sæŋgwɪn] *adj* оптимисти́чный* (оптимисти́чен).

sanitaria [sænɪ'tɛərɪə] *npl* (US) *of* **sanitarium**.

sanitarium [sænɪ'tɛərɪəm] (*pl* **sanitaria** *or* ~**s**) (US) = **sanatorium**.

sanitary ['sænɪtərɪ] *adj* (*system, arrangements, inspector*) санита́рный; (*clean*) гигиени́чный* (гигиени́чен).

sanitary towel (US **sanitary napkin**) *n* гигиени́ческий* паке́т.

sanitation [sænɪ'teɪʃən] *n* санитари́я.

sanitation department *n* (US) санита́рное управле́ние.

sanity ['sænɪtɪ] *n* (*of person*) рассу́док*; (*of suggestion etc*) разу́мность *f*.

sank [sæŋk] *pt of* **sink**.

San Marino ['sænmə'riːnəu] *n* Сан-Мари́но *nt*

ind.

Santa Claus [sæntə'klɔːz] *n* (*in Britain, US etc*) Cа́нта-Кла́ус; (*in Russia*) ≈ Дед Моро́з.

Santiago [sæntɪ'ɑːgəu] *n* (*also:* ~ **de Chile**) Санть́яго *m ind.*

sap [sæp] *n* (*BOT*) сок* ◆ *vt* (*strength, confidence*) выса́сывать (вы́сосать *perf*).

sapling ['sæplɪŋ] *n* молодо́е де́ревце*, побе́г.

sapper ['sæpə^r] *n* сапёр.

sapphire ['sæfaɪə^r] *n* сапфи́р.

Sarajevo [særə'jeɪvəu] *n* Сара́ево.

sarcasm ['sɑːkæzm] *n* сарка́зм.

sarcastic [sɑː'kæstɪk] *adj* саркасти́чный* (саркасти́чен).

sarcophagi [sɑː'kɔfəgaɪ] *npl of* **sarcophagus.**

sarcophagus [sɑː'kɔfəgəs] (*pl* **sarcophagi**) *n* саркофа́г.

sardine [sɑː'diːn] *n* сарди́на.

Sardinia [sɑː'dɪnɪə] *n* Сарди́ния.

Sardinian [sɑː'dɪnɪən] *adj* сарди́нский ◆ *n* сарди́нец*(-нка*); (*LING*) сарди́нский диале́кт*.

sardonic [sɑː'dɔnɪk] *adj* сардони́ческий.

sari ['sɑːrɪ] *n* са́ри *nt ind.*

sartorial [sɑː'tɔːrɪəl] *adj:* ~ **elegance** уме́ние одева́ться.

SAS *n abbr* (*BRIT. MIL:* = Special Air Service) осо́бые возду́шно-деса́нтные войска́.

SASE *n abbr* (*US*) = self-addressed stamped envelope.

sash [sæʃ] *n* (*around waist*) куша́к*; (*over shoulder*) ле́нта; (*of window*) подъёмная ра́ма.

sash window *n* окно́* с подъёмной ра́мой.

SAT *n abbr* (*US*) = Scholastic Aptitude Test.

sat [sæt] *pt, pp of* **sit.**

Sat. *abbr* = **Saturday.**

Satan ['seɪtn] *n* Сатана́ *m.*

satanic [sə'tænɪk] *adj* сатани́нский.

satanism ['seɪtnɪzəm] *n* сатани́зм.

satchel ['sætʃl] *n* ра́нец*.

sated ['seɪtɪd] *adj* (*person*): **to be** ~ **(with)** пресыща́ться (пресы́титься* *perf*) (+*instr*).

satellite ['sætəlaɪt] *n* спу́тник*; (*POL: country*) сателли́т; ~ **town** го́род-спу́тник.

satellite dish *n* спу́тниковая анте́нна.

satellite television *n* спу́тниковое телеви́дение.

satiate ['seɪʃɪeɪt] *vt* насыща́ть (насы́тить* *perf*).

satin ['sætɪn] *n* атла́с ◆ *adj* атла́сный; **with a** ~ **finish** с атла́сным отли́вом.

satire ['sætaɪə^r] *n* сати́ра.

satirical [sə'tɪrɪkl] *adj* сатири́ческий*.

satirist ['sætɪrɪst] *n* сати́рик.

satirize ['sætɪraɪz] *vt* высме́ивать (вы́смеять *perf*).

satisfaction [sætɪs'fækʃən] *n* (*pleasure*) удовлетворе́ние; (*refund, apology etc*) возмеще́ние; **has it been done to your** ~**?** Вы удовлетворе́ны тем, как э́то сде́лано?

satisfactorily [sætɪs'fæktərɪlɪ] *adv* удовле-

твори́тельно.

satisfactory [sætɪs'fæktərɪ] *adj* удовлетвори́тельный* (удовлетвори́телен).

satisfied ['sætɪsfaɪd] *adj* (*customer*) дово́льный* (дово́лен), удовлетворённый* (удовлетворён); **he is/was** ~ **(with sth)** он дово́лен/был дово́лен *or* удовлетворён/был удовлетворён (чем-н).

satisfy ['sætɪsfaɪ] *vt* (*please, fulfil*) удовлетворя́ть (удовлетвори́ть *perf*); (*convince*) убежда́ть (убеди́ть* *perf*); **to** ~ **the requirements** удовлетворя́ть (удовлетвори́ть *perf*) тре́бованиям; **to** ~ **sb (that)** убежда́ть (убеди́ть* *perf*) кого́-н (в том, что); **to** ~ **o.s. of sth** удостоверя́ться (удостове́риться *perf*) в чём-н.

satisfying ['sætɪsfaɪɪŋ] *adj* прия́тный* (прия́тен).

satsuma [sæt'suːmə] *n* мандари́н.

saturate ['sætʃəreɪt] *vt:* **to** ~ **(with)** (*also fig*) насыща́ть (насы́тить* *perf*) (+*instr*).

saturated fat ['sætʃəreɪtɪd-] *n* насы́щенные жиры́ *mpl.*

saturation [sætʃə'reɪʃən] *n* (*process*) насыще́ние; (*CHEM, fig*) насы́щенность *f.*

Saturday ['sætədɪ] *n* суббо́та; *see also* **Tuesday.**

Saturn ['sætən] *n* Сату́рн.

sauce [sɔːs] *n* со́ус.

saucepan ['sɔːspən] *n* кастрю́ля.

saucer ['sɔːsə^r] *n* блю́дце*.

saucy ['sɔːsɪ] *adj* (*inf*) по́шлый (пошл).

Saudi Arabia ['saudɪ-] *n* Сау́довская Ара́вия.

Saudi (Arabian) *adj* сау́довский*.

sauna ['sɔːnə] *n* са́уна, фи́нская ба́ня.

saunter ['sɔːntə^r] *vi* прогу́ливаться (*impf*).

sausage ['sɔsɪdʒ] *n* (*for cooking*) сарде́лька*, соси́ска*; (*cold meat*) колбаса́*.

sausage roll *n* (*BRIT*) пирожо́к* с соси́ской.

sauté ['səuteɪ] *adj* жа́реный ◆ *vt* жа́рить (пожа́рить *perf*).

savage ['sævɪdʒ] *adj* (*attack*) зве́рский*; (*voice*) я́ростный* (я́ростен); (*dog, criticism*) свире́пый (свире́п); (*primitive: tribe*) ди́кий ◆ *n* дика́рь*(-рка*) *m(f)* ◆ *vt* (*attack, also fig*) разрыва́ть (разорва́ть* *perf*) на ча́сти.

savagely ['sævɪdʒlɪ] *adv* (*attack, pull*) я́ростно; (*criticize*) свире́по.

savagery ['sævɪdʒrɪ] *n* свире́пость *f.*

save [seɪv] *vt* (*rescue*) спаса́ть (спасти́* *perf*); (*economize on: money, time*) эконо́мить* (сэконо́мить* *perf*); (*put by: food, money*) откла́дывать (отложи́ть* *perf*); (*receipts, also COMPUT*) сохраня́ть (сохрани́ть *perf*); (*avoid: work, trouble*) избавля́ть (изба́вить* *perf*) от +*gen*; (*keep: seat, place*) занима́ть (заня́ть* *perf*); (*SPORT: shot, ball*) отбива́ть (отби́ть* *perf*), отража́ть (отрази́ть* *perf*) ◆ *vi* (*also:* ~ **up**) копи́ть* (скопи́ть* *perf*) де́ньги* ◆ *prep* (*except*) поми́мо +*gen*; **it will** ~ **me an hour** я сэконо́млю на э́том час; **to** ~ **face** спасти́* (*perf*) свою́ репута́цию; **God** ~ **the Queen!**

Бóже храни́ короле́ву!; **that was a brilliant ~ (by the goalkeeper)** врата́рь прекра́сно отрази́л уда́р.

saving ['seɪvɪŋ] *n* (*on price etc*) эконо́мия ◆ *adj*: **the ~ grace of** спасе́ние +*gen*; **~s** *npl* (*money*) сбереже́ния *ntpl*; **to make ~s** откла́дывать (отложи́ть* *perf*).

savings account *n* сберега́тельный счёт*.

savings bank *n* сберега́тельный банк.

saviour ['seɪvjəʳ] (*US* **savior**) *n* спаси́тель(ница) *m(f)*; (*REL*) Спаси́тель *m*.

savoir-faire ['sævwɑːfɛəʳ] *n* све́тскость *f*.

savour ['seɪvəʳ] (*US* **savor**) *vt* (*food, drink*) смакова́ть (*impf*); (*experience*) наслажда́ться (наслади́ться* *perf*) +*instr* ◆ *n* (*of food*) арома́т.

savoury ['seɪvərɪ] (*US* **savory**) *adj* (*dish*) несла́дкий* (несла́док).

savvy ['sævɪ] *n* (*inf*) понима́ние.

saw [sɔː] (*pt* **sawed**, *pp* **sawed** *or* **sawn**) *vt* пили́ть* (*impf*) ◆ *n* пила́* ◆ *pt of* **see**; **to ~ sth up** распи́ливать (распили́ть* *perf*) что-н.

sawdust ['sɔːdʌst] *n* опи́лки* *pl*.

sawed-off ['sɔːdɔf] *adj* (*US*) = **sawn-off**.

sawmill ['sɔːmɪl] *n* лесопи́льный заво́д.

sawn [[sɔːn]] *pp of* **saw**.

sawn-off ['sɔːnɔf] (*US* **sawed-off**) *adj*: **~ shotgun** обре́з.

saxophone ['sæksəfəun] *n* саксофо́н.

say [seɪ] (*pt, pp* **said**) *vt* говори́ть (сказа́ть* *perf*) ◆ *n*: **to have one's ~** выража́ть (вы́разить* *perf*) своё мне́ние; **to ~ yes** соглаша́ться (согласи́ться* *perf*); **to ~ no** отка́зываться (отказа́ться* *perf*); **could you ~ that again?** повтори́те, пожа́луйста; **she said (that) I was to give you this** она́ сказа́ла, что я до́лжен отда́ть э́то Вам; **my watch ~s 3 o'clock** мои́ часы́ пока́зывают 3 часа́; **shall we ~ Tuesday?** ну, ска́жем, во вто́рник?; **that doesn't ~ much for him** э́то не говори́т в его́ по́льзу; **when all is said and done** когда́ всё (бу́дет) огово́рено; **there is a lot to be said for ...** мно́гое мо́жно сказа́ть в по́льзу +*gen* ...; **that is to ~** то есть; **that goes without ~ing** э́то само́ собо́й разуме́ется; **to ~ nothing of** не говоря́ уже́ о +*prp*; **~ (that) you ...** ну, ска́жем, Вы ...; **to have a** *or* **some ~ in sth** име́ть (*impf*) пра́во го́лоса в чём-н.

saying ['seɪŋ] *n* погово́рка*.

say-so ['seɪsəu] *n*: **to do sth on sb's ~** де́лать (сде́лать* *perf*) что-н с чьего́-н согла́сия.

SBA (*US*) *n abbr* = **Small Business Administration**.

SC *n abbr* (*US*) = **Supreme Court** ◆ *abbr* (*POST*) = **South Carolina**.

s/c *abbr* = **self-contained**.

scab [skæb] *n* (*on wound*) струп*; (*inf: pej*) штрейкбре́хер.

scabby ['skæbɪ] *adj* (*pej: hands, skin*) покры́тый

(покры́т) стру́пьями.

scaffold ['skæfəld] *n* (*for execution*) эшафо́т.

scaffolding ['skæfəldɪŋ] *n* леса́* *pl*.

scald [skɔːld] *n* ожо́г ◆ *vt* (*burn*) ошпа́ривать (ошпа́рить* *perf*).

scalding ['skɔːldɪŋ] *adj* (*also*: **~ hot**) о́чень горя́чий*.

scale [skeɪl] *n* шкала́*; (*usu pl: of fish*) чешуя́ *f no pl*; (*MUS*) га́мма; (*of map, model, project etc*) масшта́б ◆ *vt* (*mountain, tree*) взбира́ться (взобра́ться* *perf*) на +*acc*; **~s** *npl* (*for weighing*) весы́ *pl*; **to draw sth to ~** черти́ть* (начерти́ть* *perf*) что-н по масшта́бу; **a small-~ model** уме́ньшенная моде́ль; **on a large ~** в широ́ком масшта́бе; **pay ~** тари́фная се́тка* зарпла́ты; **~ of charges** шкала́* расце́нок

▶ **scale down** *vt* сокраща́ть (сократи́ть* *perf*).

scaled down [skeɪld-] *adj* в уме́ньшенном масшта́бе.

scale drawing *n* масшта́бный рису́нок* *or* чертёж*.

scallion ['skæljən] *n* (*shallot*) зелёный лук *m no pl*; (*US: leek*) лук-поре́й *m no pl*.

scallop ['skɔləp] *n* (*ZOOL*) (морско́й) гребешо́к*; (*in sewing etc*) фесто́н.

scalp [skælp] *n* скальп ◆ *vt* скальпи́ровать (*impf/perf*); **I have an itchy ~** у меня́ че́шется голова́.

scalpel ['skælpl] *n* ска́льпель *m*.

scalper ['skælpə] *n* (*US: inf: ticket tout*) спекуля́нт(ка*).

scam [skæm] *n* (*inf*) жу́льничество *nt no pl*.

scamp [skæmp] *n* (*inf*) безобра́зник(-ица).

scamper ['skæmpə] *vi*: **to ~ away** *or* **off** уска́кать* (*impf*).

scampi ['skæmpɪ] *npl* (*BRIT*) паниро́ванные креве́тки* *fpl*.

scan [skæn] *vt* (*examine*) обсле́довать (*perf*); (*read quickly*) просма́тривать (просмотре́ть* *perf*); (*TV*) разлага́ть (*impf*) изображе́ние; (*RADAR*) скани́ровать (*impf*) ◆ *vi* (*poetry*) рифмова́ться (*impf*) ◆ *n* (*MED*) скани́рование; **ultrasound ~** ультразву́к.

scandal ['skændl] *n* (*shocking event*) сканда́л; (*gossip*) спле́тни* *fpl*; (*fig: disgrace*) позо́р.

scandalize ['skændəlaɪz] *vt* скандализи́ровать (*impf/perf*).

scandalous ['skændələs] *adj* сканда́льный* (сканда́лен); (*waste*) возмути́тельный* (возмути́телен).

Scandinavia [skændɪ'neɪvɪə] *n* Скандина́вия.

Scandinavian [skændɪ'neɪvɪən] *adj* скандина́вский ◆ *n* скандина́в(ка*).

scanner ['skænə] *n* (*RADAR, MED*) ска́нер.

scant [skænt] *adj* (*attention*) пове́рхностный; (*reward*) незначи́тельный*.

scantily ['skæntɪlɪ] *adv*: **she was ~ clad** *or*

dressed она́ была́ едва́ оде́та.
· **scanty** ['skæntı] adj (meal) ску́дный* (ску́ден); **her underwear was** ~ бельё едва́ прикрыва́ло её те́ло.
scapegoat ['skeıpgəut] n козёл* отпуще́ния.
scar [skɑ:] n (on skin) шрам; (fig) тра́вма ♦ vt (also fig) травми́ровать (impf/perf); **his face is** ~**red** у него́ на лице́ шрам.
scarce [skɛəs] adj ре́дкий* (ре́док); **to make o.s.** ~ (inf) улизну́ть (perf).
scarcely ['skɛəslı] adv (hardly) едва́; (with numbers: barely) то́лько; ~ **anybody** едва́ ли кто́-нибудь; **I can** ~ **believe it** я едва́ могу́ э́тому пове́рить; **that is** ~ **the point** едва́ ли в э́том де́ло.
scarcity ['skɛəsıtı] n нехва́тка*, недоста́ток*; ~ **value** (COMM) це́нность това́ра, определя́емая его́ дефици́тностью.
scare [skɛəʳ] n (fright) испу́г; (public fear) трево́га ♦ vt (frighten) пуга́ть (испуга́ть or напуга́ть perf); **to** ~ **sb stiff** (inf) пуга́ть (напуга́ть perf) кого́-н до́ смерти; **there was a bomb** ~ **at the station** опаса́лись, что на ста́нции подло́жена бо́мба
▸ **scare away** vt отпу́гивать (отпугну́ть perf)
▸ **scare off** vt = scare away.
scarecrow ['skɛəkrəu] n (огоро́дное) чу́чело.
scared ['skɛəd] adj испу́ганный (испу́ган), напу́ганный (напу́ган); **he was** ~ он испуга́лся or был напу́ган.
scaremonger ['skɛəmʌŋgəʳ] n паникёр.
scarf [skɑ:f] (pl ~**s** or **scarves**) n шарф; (also: **headscarf**) плато́к*.
scarlet ['skɑ:lıt] adj а́лый (ал).
scarlet fever n скарлати́на.
scarper ['skɑ:pəʳ] vi (inf) смыва́ться (смы́ться* perf).
scarred [skɑ:d] adj (fig: person) травми́рованный (травми́рован); ~ **face** лицо́ с шра́мом.
scarves [skɑ:vz] npl of scarf.
scary ['skɛərı] adj стра́шный* (стра́шен).
scathing ['skeıðıŋ] adj уничтожа́ющий*; **to be** ~ **about sth** относи́ться* (отнести́сь* perf) к чему́-н с презре́нием.
scatter ['skætəʳ] vt (papers, seeds) разбра́сывать (разброса́ть perf); (flock of birds, crowd) разгоня́ть (разогна́ть* perf) ♦ vi (crowd) рассыпа́ться (рассы́паться* perf).
scatterbrained ['skætəbreınd] adj (inf) рассе́янный* (рассе́ян).
scattered ['skætəd] adj разбро́санный; ~ **showers** преры́вистие ли́вни.
scatty ['skætı] adj (BRIT: inf) несобранный (несо́бран).
scavenge ['skævəndʒ] vi: **to** ~ **for food** ры́скать* (impf) в по́исках пи́щи.
scavenger ['skævəndʒəʳ] n (person) старьёвщик; (animal, bird) живо́тное nt adj, пита́ющееся па́далью.
SCE n abbr = Scottish Certificate of Education.

scenario [sı'nɑ:rıəu] n (also fig) сцена́рий.
scene [si:n] n (THEAT, fig) сце́на; (of crime, accident) ме́сто*; (sight, view) карти́на; **behind the** ~**s** (also fig) за кули́сами; **to make a** ~ (inf: fuss) устра́ивать (устро́ить perf) сце́ну; **to appear on the** ~ появля́ться (появи́ться* perf) на сце́не; **the political** ~ полити́ческая аре́на.
scenery ['si:nərı] n (THEAT) декора́ции fpl; (landscape) пейза́ж.
scenic ['si:nık] adj живопи́сный* (живопи́сен).
scent [sɛnt] n (smell) за́пах; (track, also fig) след; (perfume) духи́* pl; **to put** or **throw sb off the** ~ (fig) сбива́ть (сбить* perf) кого́-н со сле́да.
sceptic ['skɛptık] (US **skeptic**) n ске́птик.
sceptical ['skɛptıkl] (US **skeptical**) adj (person) скепти́чный* (скепти́чен); (remarks) скепти́ческий*.
scepticism ['skɛptısızəm] (US **skepticism**) n скептици́зм.
sceptre ['sɛptəʳ] (US **scepter**) n ски́петр.
schedule ['ʃɛdju:l, (US) 'skɛdju:l] n (timetable) расписа́ние, гра́фик; (list of prices, details etc) пе́речень* m ♦ vt (timetable) распи́сывать (расписа́ть* perf); (visit) назнача́ть (назна́чить perf); **on** ~ по расписа́нию or гра́фику; **as** ~**d** как (бы́ло) заплани́ровано; **we are working to a very tight** ~ мы рабо́таем по пло́тному гра́фику; **everything went according to** ~ всё прошло́ по гра́фику or расписа́нию; **to be ahead of** ~ опережа́ть (опереди́ть* perf) гра́фик; **to be behind** ~ отстава́ть (impf) от гра́фика.
scheduled ['ʃɛdju:ld, (US) 'skɛdju:ld] adj (time, event) заплани́рованный (заплани́рован); (train, bus, stop) обозна́ченный (обозна́чен) в расписа́нии.
scheduled flight n регуля́рный рейс.
schematic [skı'mætık] adj схемати́ческий*.
scheme [ski:m] n (plan, idea) за́мысел*; (plot) про́иски pl, ко́зни pl; (pension plan etc) програ́мма; (arrangement) план, схе́ма ♦ vi стро́ить (impf) ко́зни; **colour** or (US) **color** ~ цветова́я га́мма.
scheming ['ski:mıŋ] adj кова́рный ♦ n ко́зни pl, про́иски pl.
schism ['skızəm] n раско́л.
schizophrenia [skıtsə'fri:nıə] n шизофрени́я.
schizophrenic [skıtsə'frɛnık] adj шизофрени́ческий ♦ n шизофре́ник(-и́чка*).
scholar ['skɔləʳ] n (scholarship holder) стипендиа́т; (learned person) учёный m adj.
scholarly ['skɔlərı] adj (text, approach) академи́ческий*; (person) учёный.
scholarship ['skɔləʃıp] n (academic knowledge) учёность f; (grant) стипе́ндия.
school [sku:l] n шко́ла; (US: inf) университе́т; (BRIT) институ́т; (of fish, whales) ста́я ♦ cpd шко́льный.
school age n шко́льный во́зраст.

schoolbook [ˈskuːlbuk] n (шко́льный) уче́бник.
schoolboy [ˈskuːlbɔɪ] n шко́льник.
schoolchildren [ˈskuːltʃɪldrən] npl шко́льники mpl.
school days npl шко́льные дни mpl.
schooled [skuːld] adj: ~ (in) обу́ченный (обу́чен) (+dat).
schoolgirl [ˈskuːlgəːl] n шко́льница.
schooling [ˈskuːlɪŋ] n шко́льное образова́ние.
school-leaver [skuːlˈliːvəʳ] n (BRIT) выпускни́к(-и́ца) шко́лы.
schoolmaster [ˈskuːlmɑːstəʳ] n учи́тель* m.
schoolmistress [ˈskuːlmɪstrɪs] n учи́тельница.
school report n (BRIT) та́бель m успева́емости.
schoolroom [ˈskuːlruːm] n класс, кла́ссная ко́мната.
schoolteacher [ˈskuːltiːtʃəʳ] n (шко́льный(-ая)) учи́тель*(ница) m(f).
schoolyard [ˈskuːljɑːd] n (US) шко́льный двор*.
schooner [ˈskuːnəʳ] n (ship) шху́на; (BRIT: for sherry) фуже́р (для хе́реса); (US: for beer) кру́жка* (для пи́ва).
sciatica [saɪˈætɪkə] n и́шиас.
science [ˈsaɪəns] n (study of natural things) нау́ка; (in school) есте́ственные нау́ки fpl; **the ~s** есте́ственные и то́чные нау́ки.
science fiction n нау́чная фанта́стика.
scientific [saɪənˈtɪfɪk] adj нау́чный.
scientist [ˈsaɪəntɪst] n учёный m adj.
sci-fi [ˈsaɪfaɪ] n abbr (inf) (= **science fiction**) НФ= нау́чная фанта́стика.
Scillies [ˈsɪlɪz] npl = **Scilly Isles**.
Scilly Isles [ˈsɪlɪˈaɪlz] npl: **the ~ ~** острова́ mpl Си́лли.
scintillating [ˈsɪntɪleɪtɪŋ] adj (fig: conversation, wit) блестя́щий*; (smile) сия́ющий*.
scissors [ˈsɪzəz] npl: **(a pair of)** ~ но́жницы pl.
sclerosis [sklɪˈrəusɪs] n склеро́з.
scoff [skɔf] vt (BRIT: inf: eat) жрать* (сожра́ть* perf) ♦ vi: **to ~ (at)** (mock) насмеха́ться (impf) (над +instr).
scold [skəuld] vt брани́ть (вы́бранить perf), руга́ть (отруга́ть perf).
scolding [ˈskəuldɪŋ] n вы́говор.
scone [skɔn] n (CULIN) кекс.
scoop [skuːp] n (measuring scoop: for flour etc) сово́к*; (: for ice-cream) черпа́к; (PRESS) сенсацио́нное сообще́ние.
▶ **scoop out** vt выскреба́ть (вы́скрести* perf)
▶ **scoop up** vt зачёрпывать (зачерпну́ть perf).
scooter [ˈskuːtəʳ] n (also: **motor ~**) мопе́д; (toy) самока́т.
scope [skəup] n (opportunity) просто́р; (of plan, undertaking) масшта́б; (of person) компете́нция; **within the ~ of** в ра́мках +gen;

there is plenty of ~ for improvement (BRIT) есть просто́р для совершенствова́ния; **it is well within his ~ to ... ...** в его́ компете́нции.
scorch [skɔːtʃ] vt (clothes) сжига́ть (сжечь* perf); (earth, grass) выжига́ть (вы́жечь* perf).
scorched-earth policy [skɔːtʃtˈəːθ-] n (MIL) поли́тика or та́ктика вы́жженой земли́.
scorcher [ˈskɔːtʃəʳ] n (inf: hot day) жари́ща.
scorching [ˈskɔːtʃɪŋ] adj (day, weather) паля́щий.
score [skɔːʳ] n (number of points etc) счёт; (MUS) партиту́ра; (twenty) два́дцать ♦ vt (goal) забива́ть (заби́ть* perf); (point) набира́ть (набра́ть* perf); (mark) получа́ть (получи́ть* perf); (cut: leather, wood etc) цара́пать (поцара́пать perf); (achieve: success) завоёвывать (завоева́ть perf) ♦ vi (in game) набира́ть (набра́ть* perf) очки́; (FOOTBALL etc) забива́ть (заби́ть* perf) гол; (keep score) вести́* (perf) счёт; **to settle an old ~ with sb** (fig) своди́ть (свести́* perf) с кем-н ста́рые счёты; **~s of** деся́тки +gen; **on that ~** на э́тот счёт; **to ~ well** набира́ть (набра́ть* perf) мно́го очко́в; **to ~ 6 out of 10** набира́ть (perf) 6 ба́ллов из 10; **to ~ (a point) over sb** превосходи́ть* (превзойти́* perf) кого́-н
▶ **score out** vt вычёркивать (вы́черкнуть perf).
scoreboard [ˈskɔːbɔːd] n табло́ nt ind.
scorecard [ˈskɔːkɑːd] n (SPORT) ка́рта, на кото́рую зано́сится счёт.
scoreline [ˈskɔːlaɪn] n счёт* на да́нный моме́нт.
scorer [ˈskɔːrəʳ] n (FOOTBALL) игро́к*, заби́вший гол; (scorekeeper) судья́*.
scorn [skɔːn] n презре́ние ♦ vt презира́ть (impf).
scornful [ˈskɔːnful] adj презри́тельный* (презри́телен).
Scorpio [ˈskɔːpɪəu] n Скорпио́н; **he is ~** он – Скорпио́н.
scorpion [ˈskɔːpɪən] n скорпио́н.
Scot [skɔt] n шотла́ндец*(-дка*).
Scotch [skɔtʃ] n (whisky) (шотла́ндское) ви́ски nt ind.
scotch [skɔtʃ] vt (end: rumour, plan) пресека́ть (пресе́чь* perf).
Scotch tape® n кле́йкая ле́нта, "скотч" (разг).
scot-free [ˈskɔtˈfriː] adv: **to get off ~** легко́ отде́лываться (отде́латься perf).
Scotland [ˈskɔtlənd] n Шотла́ндия.
Scots [skɔts] adj шотла́ндский*.
Scotsman [ˈskɔtsmən] irreg n шотла́ндец*.
Scotswoman [ˈskɔtswumən] irreg n шотла́ндка*.
Scottish [ˈskɔtɪʃ] adj шотла́ндский*; **the ~ National Party** Шотла́ндская национа́льная па́ртия.
scoundrel [ˈskaundrl] n негодя́й.
scour [ˈskauəʳ] vt (search) обы́скивать

---

* marks translations which have irregular inflections. The Russian-English side of the dictionary gives inflectional information.

(обыска́ть* *perf*); (*clean*) выска́бливать (вы́скоблить* *perf*).

scourer ['skauərə'] *n* жёсткая моча́лка*.

scourge [skə:dʒ] *n* (*cause of trouble*) бич.

scout [skaut] *n* (*MIL*) разве́дчик; (*also:* **boy** ~) (бой)ска́ут; **girl** ~ (*US*) (де́вочка*-)ска́ут
▶ **scout around** *vi* ры́скать* (*impf*) в по́исках +*gen*.

scowl [skaul] *vi* хму́риться (нахму́риться *perf*); **to** ~ **at sb** хму́ро смотре́ть* (посмотре́ть* *perf*) на кого́-н.

scrabble ['skræbl] *vi* (*also:* ~ **around**: *search*) ша́рить (поша́рить *perf*); (*claw*): **to** ~ **at** цепля́ться (*impf*) (за +*acc*) ♦ *n*: **S~**® (игра́) Скрэбл *ind*; **to** ~ **about** *or* **around for sth** ша́рить (поша́рить *perf*) в по́исках чего́-н.

scraggy ['skrægɪ] *adj* то́щий* (тощ).

scram [skræm] *vi* (*inf*) смыва́ться (смы́ться* *perf*); ~! убира́йся!

scramble ['skræmbl] *n* (*climb: using hands*) кара́банье; (*struggle, rush*) сва́лка* ♦ *vi*: **to** ~ **out** выкара́бкиваться (вы́карабкаться *perf*) из +*gen*; **to** ~ **for** дра́ться* (подра́ться* *perf*) за +*acc*.

scrambled eggs ['skræmbld-] *n* яи́чница болту́нья.

scrambling ['skræmblɪŋ] *n* (*SPORT*) мотокро́сс.

scrap [skræp] *n* (*of paper*) клочо́к*; (*of information*) обры́вок*; (*of material etc*) лоску́т*; (*fig: of truth*) крупи́ца; (*inf: fight*) потасо́вка; (*also:* ~ **metal**) металли́ческий* лом, металлоло́м ♦ *vt* (*discard: machines etc*) отдава́ть* (отда́ть* *perf*) на слом; (*fig: plans etc*) отка́зываться (отказа́ться* *perf*) от +*gen* ♦ *vi* (*fight*) дра́ться* (подра́ться* *perf*); ~**s** *npl* (*of food*) объе́дки *mpl*; (*of material*) обре́зки *mpl*; **to sell sth for** ~ сдава́ть* (сдать* *perf*) в ути́ль.

scrapbook ['skræpbuk] *n* альбо́м для вы́резок.

scrap dealer *n* ути́льщик.

scrape [skreɪp] *vt* (*scrape off*) очища́ть (очи́стить* *perf*); (*scrape against*) цара́пать (поцара́пать *perf*), обдира́ть (ободра́ть* *perf*) ♦ *vi*: **to** ~ **through** (*exam etc*) пролеза́ть (проле́зть* *perf*) на +*prp* ♦ *n* (*fig*): **to get into a** ~ попада́ть (попа́сть* *perf*) в переде́лку
▶ **scrape together** *vt* (*money*) наскреба́ть (наскрести́* *perf*).

scraper ['skreɪpə'] *n* скребо́к*.

scrapheap ['skræphi:p] *n*: **on the** ~ (*fig*) на сва́лку.

scrap merchant *n* (*BRIT*) ути́льщик.

scrap metal *n* металлоло́м.

scrap paper *n* макулату́ра.

scrappy ['skræpɪ] *adj* (*piece of work*) дрянно́й.

scrap yard *n* сва́лка.

scratch [skrætʃ] *n* цара́пина ♦ *cpd* импровизи́рованный ♦ *vt* цара́пать (поцара́пать *perf*); (*an itch*) чеса́ть* (почеса́ть* *perf*); (*COMPUT*) стира́ть (стере́ть* *perf*) ♦ *vi* чеса́ться* (почеса́ться* *perf*); **to start**

from ~ начина́ть (нача́ть* *perf*) с нуля́; **to be up to** ~ (*person, conditions, standard*) быть* (*impf*) на вы́сшем у́ровне.

scratch pad *n* (*US*) блокно́т.

scrawl [skrɔ:l] *n* кара́кули *fpl* ♦ *vi* цара́пать (нацара́пать *perf*).

scrawny ['skrɔ:nɪ] *adj* то́щий* (тощ).

scream [skri:m] *n* вопль *m*, крик ♦ *vi* крича́ть (*impf*); **it's a real** ~ (*inf*) э́то пря́мо умо́ра; **to** ~ **at sb** крича́ть (*impf*) на кого́-н.

scree [skri:] *n* камени́стая о́сыпь *f*.

screech [skri:tʃ] *vi* визжа́ть (*impf*) ♦ *n* визг.

screen [skri:n] *n* (*CINEMA, TV, COMPUT*) экра́н; (*barrier, also fig: cover*) ши́рма; (*also:* **windscreen**) ветрово́е стекло́* ♦ *vt* (*protect, conceal*) заслоня́ть (заслони́ть* *perf*); (*show: film, programme*) выпуска́ть (вы́пустить* *perf*) на экра́н; (*check: candidates etc*) проверя́ть (прове́рить *perf*); **to** ~ **sb for sth** (*for illness*) проверя́ть (прове́рить *perf*) кого́-н на что-н.

screen editing *n* (*COMPUT*) экра́нное редакти́рование.

screening ['skri:nɪŋ] *n* (*MED*) профилакти́ческий* осмо́тр; (*of film*) вы́пуск на экра́н; (*for security*) прове́рка*.

screen memory *n* (*COMPUT*) экра́нная па́мять *f*, видеопа́мять *f*.

screenplay ['skri:npleɪ] *n* сцена́рий.

screen test *n* кинопро́ба.

screw [skru:] *n* винт* ♦ *vt* (*fasten*) приви́нчивать (привинти́ть* *perf*); (*inf!: have sex with*) тра́хать (тра́хнуть *perf*) (*!*); **to** ~ **sth in** зави́нчивать (завинти́ть* *perf*) что-н; **to** ~ **sth to the wall** приви́нчивать (привинти́ть* *perf*) что-н к стене́; **he's got his head** ~**ed on** (*inf*) у него́ есть голова́ на плеча́х
▶ **screw up** *vt* (*paper etc*) ко́мкать (ско́мкать *perf*); (*inf: ruin*) порта́чить (напорта́чить *perf*); **to** ~ **up one's eyes** прищу́ривать (прищу́рить *perf*) глаза́.

screwdriver ['skru:draɪvə'] *n* отвёртка*.

screwed-up ['skru:d'ʌp] *adj* (*paper*) ско́мканный (ско́мкан); (*inf: person*) закомплексо́ванный (закомплексо́ван).

screwy ['skru:ɪ] *adj* (*inf*) с завихре́нием.

scribble ['skrɪbl] *n* кара́кули *mpl* ♦ *vt* черкну́ть (*perf*) ♦ *vi* исчёркивать (исче́ркать *perf*); **to** ~ **sth down** запи́сывать (записа́ть* *perf*) что-н на́скоро.

scribe [skraɪb] *n* писе́ц*.

script [skrɪpt] *n* (*CINEMA etc*) сцена́рий; (*system of writing*) шрифт*; (*in exam*) конспе́кт.

scripted ['skrɪptɪd] *adj* (*RADIO, TV*) зара́нее подгото́вленный.

Scripture(s) ['skrɪptʃə'(-əz)] *n(pl)* Свяще́нное писа́ние.

scriptwriter ['skrɪptraɪtə'] *n* сценари́ст.

scroll [skrəul] *n* сви́ток* ♦ *vt* (*COMPUT*) прокру́чивать (прокрути́ть* *perf*), перемеща́ть (перемести́ть* *perf*).

scrotum ['skrəʊtəm] *n* (*ANAT*) мошо́нка*.
scrounge [skraundʒ] (*inf*) *vt*: **to ~ sth off** *or* **from sb** кля́нчить (вы́клянчить *perf*) что-н у кого́-н ♦ *vi* попроша́йничать (*impf*) ♦ *n*: **to be on the ~** бы́ть* (*impf*) на ме́ли.
scrounger ['skraundʒə'] *n* (*inf*) попроша́йка* *m/f*.
scrub [skrʌb] *n* (*land*) куста́рник ♦ *vt* скрести́* (*impf*); (*inf*: *reject*) отбра́сывать (отбро́сить* *perf*).
scrubbing brush ['skrʌbɪŋ-] *n* жёсткая щётка*.
scruff [skrʌf] *n*: **by the ~ of the neck** за ши́ворот.
scruffy ['skrʌfɪ] *adj* потрёпанный*.
scrum(mage) ['skrʌm(ɪdʒ)] *n* (*RUGBY*) разы́грывание мяча́.
scruple ['skru:pl] *n* (*usu pl*) терза́ние; **to have no ~s about doing sth** де́лать (сде́лать *perf*) что-н без угрызе́ний со́вести.
scrupulous ['skru:pjuləs] *adj* (*painstaking*) тща́тельный* (тща́телен), скрупулёзный* (скрупулёзен); (*fair-minded*) щепети́льный* (щепети́лен).
scrupulously ['skru:pjuləslɪ] *adv* (*behave, act*) добросо́вестно; **he is ~ honest/fair/clean** он преде́льно че́стен/справедли́в/чистопло́тен.
scrutinize ['skru:tɪnaɪz] *vt* тща́тельно изуча́ть (изучи́ть *perf*) *or* рассма́тривать (рассмотре́ть* *perf*).
scrutiny ['skru:tɪnɪ] *n* тща́тельно изуче́ние *or* рассмотре́ние; **under sb's ~** под чьим-н наблюде́нием.
scuba ['sku:bə] *n* акввала́нг.
scuba diving *n* подво́дное пла́вание.
scuff [skʌf] *vt* (*feet*) волочи́ть (*impf*); (*mark*: *shoes*) ста́птывать (стопта́ть *perf*).
scuffle ['skʌfl] *n* потасо́вка*.
scull [skʌl] *n* (*on rowing boat*) весло́*.
scullery ['skʌlərɪ] *n* (*old*) подсо́бное помеще́ние (*при ку́хне*).
sculptor ['skʌlptə'] *n* ску́льптор.
sculpture ['skʌlptʃə'] *n* скульпту́ра.
scum [skʌm] *n* пе́на; (*inf*: *pej*: *people*) подо́нки *mpl*; **the ~ of society** отбро́сы о́бщества.
scupper ['skʌpə'] *vt* (*BRIT*: *inf*: *plan*) срыва́ть (сорва́ть* *perf*).
scurrilous ['skʌrɪləs] *adj* (*accusation, gossip etc*) оскорби́тельный* (оскорби́телен).
scurry ['skʌrɪ] *vi* юркну́ть (*perf*)
▶ **scurry off** *vi* ры́сью убега́ть (убежа́ть *perf*).
scurvy ['skə:vɪ] *n* цинга́.
scuttle ['skʌtl] *n* (*also*: **coal ~**) ведро́* для угля́ ♦ *vt* (*ship*) топи́ть* (затопи́ть* *or* потопи́ть* *perf*) ♦ *vi*: **to ~ away** *or* **off** ры́сью убега́ть (убежа́ть *perf*).
scythe [saɪð] *n* серп*.
SD *abbr* (*US*: *POST*) = South Dakota.
SDI *n abbr* (*US*: *MIL*: = Strategic Defense Initiative) СОИ = *стратеги́ческая оборо́нная*

инициати́ва.
SDLP *n abbr* (*BRIT*: *POL*) = Social Democratic and Labour Party.
SDP *n abbr* (*BRIT*: *POL*: *formerly*) = Social Democratic Party.
sea [si:] *n* мо́ре* ♦ *cpd* морско́й; **by ~** (*travel*) мо́рем; **beside the ~** у мо́ря; **on the ~** (*boat*) в мо́ре; (*town*) на мо́ре; **to be all at ~** (*fig*) быть* (*impf*) в расте́рянности; **out to ~**, **out at ~** в мо́ре; **to look out to ~** смотре́ть* (*impf*) на мо́ре; **heavy** *or* **rough ~(s)** бу́рное мо́ре; **a ~ of faces** мо́ре лиц.
sea anemone *n* морско́й анемо́н.
sea bed *n* морско́е дно.
seaboard ['si:bɔ:d] *n* побере́жье*.
seafarer ['si:fɛərə'] *n* морепла́ватель *m*.
seafaring ['si:fɛərɪŋ] *adj* морско́й; **~ people** морехо́ды *mpl*.
seafood ['si:fu:d] *n* ры́бные блю́да *ntpl*.
seafront ['si:frʌnt] *n* на́бережная *f adj*.
seagoing ['si:gəʊɪŋ] *adj* морско́й.
seagull ['si:gʌl] *n* ча́йка*.
seal [si:l] *n* (*ZOOL*) тюле́нь *m*; (*stamp*) печа́ть *f* ♦ *vt* (*close*: *envelope*) запеча́тывать (запеча́тать *perf*); (: *opening*) заде́лывать (заде́лать *perf*); (*decide*: *sb's fate*) предреша́ть (предреши́ть* *perf*); (*deal*) заключа́ть (заключи́ть *perf*); **to give sth one's ~ of approval** официа́льно одо́брить (*perf*) что-н
▶ **seal off** *vt* (*area, street*) огора́живать (огороди́ть* *perf*); (*building*) опеча́тывать (опеча́тать *perf*).
sea level *n* у́ровень* *m* мо́ря; **2,000 feet above/below ~ ~** 2000 фу́тов над у́ровнем мо́ря/ ни́же у́ровня мо́ря.
sealing wax ['si:lɪŋ-] *n* сургу́ч*.
sea lion *n* морско́й лев*.
sealskin ['si:lskɪn] *n* ко́тик (*мех*).
seam [si:m] *n* (*of garment*) шов*; (*of coal*) слой*; **the hall was bursting at the ~s** зал треща́л по швам.
seaman ['si:mən] *irreg n* матро́с, моря́к.
seamanship ['si:mənʃɪp] *n* судовожде́ние.
seamless ['si:mlɪs] *adj* без шва; (*fig*) це́лостный.
seamy ['si:mɪ] *adj* тёмный* (тёмен).
seance ['seɪɒns] *n* спирити́ческий сеа́нс.
seaplane ['si:pleɪn] *n* гидросамолёт*.
seaport ['si:pɔ:t] *n* (морско́й) порт*.
search [sə:tʃ] *n* (*for person*) ро́зыск; (*for thing*) по́иски *mpl*; (*COMPUT*) по́иск; (*inspection: of sb's home etc*) о́быск ♦ *vt* (*place, person*) обы́скивать (обыска́ть* *perf*); (*memory*) ры́ться* (*impf*) в +*prp* ♦ *vi*: **to ~ for** иска́ть* (*impf*); **in ~ of** в по́исках +*gen*; **"search and replace"** (*COMPUT*) "по́иск и заме́на".
▶ **search through** *vt fus* переры́ть (*perf*).
searcher ['sə:tʃə'] *n* иска́тель(ница) *m(f)*.

---

* marks translations which have irregular inflections. The Russian-English side of the dictionary gives inflectional information.

searching ['sə:tʃɪŋ] *adj* (*look*) пытли́вый
(пытли́в); (*question*) наводя́щий*;
(*examination*) тща́тельный* (тща́телен).
searchlight ['sə:tʃlaɪt] *n* проже́ктор*.
search party *n* поиско́вая гру́ппа; **to send out
a ~ ~** посыла́ть (посла́ть* *perf*) поиско́вую
гру́ппу.
search warrant *n* о́рдер на о́быск.
searing ['sɪərɪŋ] *adj* (*heat, pain*) жгу́чий* (жгуч).
seashore ['si:ʃɔ:'] *n* бе́рег* мо́ря; **on the ~** на
берегу́ мо́ря.
seasick ['si:sɪk] *adj*: **to be ~** страда́ть (*impf*)
морско́й боле́знью.
seasickness ['si:sɪknɪs] *n* морска́я боле́знь *f*.
seaside ['si:saɪd] *n* взмо́рье, примо́рье; **to go
to the ~** е́здить*/е́хать* (пое́хать* *perf*) на
взмо́рье; **at the ~** на взмо́рье.
seaside resort *n* примо́рский* куро́рт.
season ['si:zn] *n* (*of year*) вре́мя* *nt* го́да; (*for
football, of films etc*) сезо́н ◆ *vt* (*food*)
заправля́ть (запра́вить* *perf*); **the busy ~**
акти́вный сезо́н; **the open ~** (*HUNTING*)
охо́тничий* сезо́н; **tomatoes are in ~** сейча́с
сезо́н помидо́ров.
seasonal ['si:znl] *adj* сезо́нный.
seasoned ['si:znd] *adj* (*fig: traveller*)
закалённый; (*wood*) вы́держанный; **a ~
campaigner** о́пытный агита́тор.
seasoning ['si:znɪŋ] *n* припра́ва.
season ticket *n* (*RAIL*) сезо́нный (проездно́й)
биле́т; (*THEAT, SPORT*) абонеме́нт.
seat [si:t] *n* (*chair, place*) сиде́нье; (*in theatre, in
parliament*) ме́сто*; (*of trousers*) зад; (*of
government*) резиде́нция; (*of learning etc*)
центр ◆ *vt* (*place: guests etc*) расса́живать
(рассади́ть* *perf*), уса́живать (усади́ть* *perf*);
(*subj: venue*) вмеща́ть (вмести́ть* *perf*); **are
there any ~s left?** есть ещё места́?; **to take
one's ~** сади́ться* (сесть* *perf*); **please be ~ed**
пожа́луйста, сади́тесь; **to be ~ed** сиде́ть
(*impf*); **this table ~s 10 people** за э́тим столо́м
умеща́ется 10 челове́к.
seat belt *n* привязно́й ремёнь* *m*.
seating arrangements ['si:tɪŋ-] *npl*
распределе́ние *ntsg* мест.
seating capacity *n* сидя́чие места́ *ntpl*; **the hall
has a ~ ~ of 100** зал рассчи́тан на 100 сидя́чих
мест.
SEATO ['si:təu] *n abbr* (= *Southeast Asia Treaty
Organization*) СЕАТО.
sea urchin *n* морско́й ёж.
sea water *n* морска́я вода́.
seaweed ['si:wi:d] *n* во́доросли *fpl*.
seaworthy ['si:wə:ðɪ] *adj* мореходный.
Sebastopol [sɪ'bæstəpəl] *n* Севасто́поль *m*.
SEC *n abbr* (*US*: = *Securities and Exchange
Commission*) Коми́ссия по це́нным бума́гам
и би́ржам.
sec. *abbr* = **second**.
secateurs [sɛkə'tə:z] *npl* садо́вые но́жницы *pl*,
сека́тор *msg*.

secede [sɪ'si:d] *vi*: **to ~ (from)** отделя́ться
(отдели́ться* *perf*) (от +*gen*).
secluded [sɪ'klu:dɪd] *adj* уединённый.
seclusion [sɪ'klu:ʒən] *n* уедине́ние; **in ~** в
уедине́нии.
second[1] [sɪ'kɔnd] *vt* (*BRIT: employee*)
командирова́ть* (*impf*).
second[2] ['sɛkənd] *adj* второ́й ◆ *adv* (*come, be
placed*) вторы́м; (*when listing*) во-вторы́х ◆ *n*
(*unit of time*) секу́нда; (*AUT: also:* ~ **gear**)
втора́я ско́рость *f*; (*COMM: imperfect*)
дефе́ктное изде́лие; (*BRIT: SCOL: degree*)
дипло́м второ́го кла́сса ◆ *vt* (*motion*)
подде́рживать (поддержа́ть* *perf*); **Charles
the S~** Карл Второ́й; ~ **floor** (*BRIT*) тре́тий*
эта́ж; (*US*) второ́й эта́ж; **just a ~!**
секу́ндочку!; *see also* **fifth**.
secondary ['sɛkəndərɪ] *adj* втори́чный.
secondary education *n* сре́днее
образова́ние.
secondary picketing [-'pɪkɪtɪŋ] *n* втори́чное
пикети́рование.
secondary school *n* сре́дняя шко́ла.
second-best [sɛkənd'bɛst] *n* не са́мом лу́чшее
nt adj ◆ *adj* (*hotel, room*) второ́й по ка́честву;
(*pupil*) второ́й (по успева́емости); **as a ~** за
неиме́нием лу́чшего.
second-class ['sɛkənd'klɑ:s] *adj* (*citizen,
standard etc*) второразря́дный; (*POST, RAIL*)
второ́го кла́сса ◆ *adv* вторы́м кла́ссом.
second cousin *n* (*male*) трою́родный брат*;
(*female*) трою́родная сестра́*.
seconder ['sɛkəndə'] *n*: **he is the ~ of the
proposal** он поддержа́л предложе́ние.
second-guess ['sɛkənd'gɛs] *vt* предска́зывать
(предсказа́ть* *perf*).
second hand *n* (*on clock*) секу́ндная стре́лка*.
second-hand ['sɛkənd'hænd] *adj* поде́ржанный
◆ *adv* (*buy*) с рук; **to hear sth ~** узнава́ть*
(узна́ть* *perf*) что-н из вторы́х рук.
second in command *n* (*MIL*) второ́й *m adj* по
зва́нию; (*ADMIN*) второ́й *m adj* по до́лжности.
secondly ['sɛkəndlɪ] *adv* во-вторы́х.
secondment [sɪ'kɔndmənt] *n* (*BRIT*)
командиро́вка*.
second-rate ['sɛkənd'reɪt] *adj* (*film etc*)
посре́дственный* (посре́дствен); (*restaurant*)
второразря́дный.
second thoughts *npl*: **to have ~ ~ (about
doing)** начина́ть (нача́ть* *perf*) сомнева́ться
(сле́дует ли +*infin*); **on ~ ~** *or* (*US*) **thought** по
зре́лом размышле́нии.
Second World War *n*: **the ~ ~ ~** Втора́я
мирова́я война́.
secrecy ['si:krəsɪ] *n* секре́тность *f*; **in ~** в та́йне.
secret ['si:krɪt] *adj* секре́тный* (секре́тен),
та́йный; (*admirer*) та́йный ◆ *n* секре́т, та́йна;
to keep sth ~ from sb держа́ть* (*impf*) что-н в
секре́те *or* та́йне от кого́-н; **keep it ~**
держи́те э́то в секре́те *or* в та́йне; **in ~** (*say,
give*) по секре́ту; (*do, meet*) секре́тно; **to**

make no ~ of sth не де́лать *(impf)* секре́та из
чего́-н.
secret agent *n* секре́тный *or* та́йный аге́нт.
secretarial [sɛkrɪ'tɛərɪəl] *adj* секрета́рский; **~**
course ку́рсы *mpl* секретаре́й.
secretariat [sɛkrɪ'tɛərɪət] *n* секретариа́т.
secretary ['sɛkrətərɪ] *n* секрета́рь *m*; **S~ of**
State (for) (*BRIT*) ≈ мини́стр (+*gen*); **S~ of**
State (*US*) Госуда́рственный секрета́рь* *m*.
secretary-general ['sɛkrətərɪ'dʒɛnərl] *n*
генера́льный секрета́рь *m*.
secrete [sɪ'kriːt] *vt* (*BIO*) выделя́ть (вы́делить
perf); (*hide*) пря́тать* (спря́тать* *perf*).
secretion [sɪ'kriːʃən] *n* (*substance*) выделе́ние,
секре́ция.
secretive ['siːkrətɪv] *adj* (*pej: person*)
скры́тный* (скры́тен); **he is ~ about his plans**
он де́ржит свои́ пла́ны в секре́те.
secretly ['siːkrɪtlɪ] *adv* (*do, meet*) секре́тно;
(*marry*) та́йно.
secret police *n* секре́тная поли́ция.
secret service *n* секре́тная слу́жба.
sect [sɛkt] *n* се́кта.
sectarian [sɛk'tɛərɪən] *adj* секта́нтский*.
section ['sɛkʃən] *n* (*part*) часть* *f*; (*of*
population, company) се́ктор; (*in shop*)
се́кция; (*of document, book*) разде́л; (*cross-*
section) сече́ние, разре́з ◆ *vt* рассека́ть
(рассе́чь* *perf*); **the business** *etc* **~** (*PRESS*)
разде́л би́знеса *etc*.
sectional ['sɛkʃənl] *adj*: **~ drawing** рису́нок в
разре́зе, разре́з.
sector ['sɛktə'] *n* (*part, also MIL*) се́ктор.
secular ['sɛkjulə'] *adj* (*music, society*)
све́тский*; (*priest*) мирско́й.
secure [sɪ'kjuə'] *adj* (*safe: person, money, job*)
надёжный* (надёжен); (: *building*)
безопа́сный* (безопа́сен); (*firmly fixed,*
strong: rope, shelf) про́чный* (про́чен); (*free*
from anxiety: person) уве́ренный ◆ *vt* (*fix:*
rope, shelf etc) (про́чно) закрепля́ть
(закрепи́ть* *perf*); (*get: job, contract etc*)
обеспе́чивать (обеспе́чить *perf*); (*COMM: loan*)
обеспе́чивать (обеспе́чить *perf*); **to make sth**
~ про́чно *or* надёжно закрепля́ть
(закрепи́ть* *perf*) что-н; **to ~ sth for sb**
обеспе́чивать (обеспе́чить *perf*) для кого́-н
что-н.
secured creditor [sɪ'kjuəd-] *n* кредито́р,
получи́вший обеспече́ние.
securely [sɪ'kjuəlɪ] *adv* (*fasten*) про́чно; (*keep*) в
надёжном ме́сте.
security [sɪ'kjuərɪtɪ] *n* (*protection*) безопа́с-
ность *f*; (*for one's future*) обеспе́ченность *f*;
(*FINANCE*) зало́г; **securities** *npl* (*COMM*) це́нные
бума́ги *fpl*; **to increase** *or* **tighten ~** повыша́ть
(повы́сить* *perf*) безопа́сность; **~ of tenure**
гаранти́рованное пра́во.

Security Council *n*: **the ~ ~** Сове́т
безопа́сности.
security forces *npl* си́лы *fpl* безопа́сности.
security guard *n* охра́нник.
security risk *n*: **it's a ~ ~** (*for country*) э́то
представля́ет угро́зу для безопа́сности
страны́.
secy. *abbr* = **secretary**.
sedan [sə'dæn] *n* (*US: AUT*) седа́н.
sedate [sɪ'deɪt] *adj* (*person*) степе́нный*
(степе́нен); (*pace*) разме́ренный* (разме́рен)
◆ *vt* (*MED*) дава́ть* (дать* *perf*) седати́вное *or*
успокои́тельное сре́дство.
sedation [sɪ'deɪʃən] *n*: **to be under ~**
находи́ться* (*impf*) под возде́йствием
седати́вных *or* успокои́тельных сре́дствах.
sedative ['sɛdɪtɪv] *n* седати́вное *or*
успокои́тельное сре́дство.
sedentary ['sɛdntrɪ] *adj* сидя́чий*.
sediment ['sɛdɪmənt] *n* оса́док*.
sedimentary [sɛdɪ'mɛntərɪ] *adj* оса́дочный.
sedition [sɪ'dɪʃən] *n* антиправи́тельственная
пропага́нда.
seduce [sɪ'djuːs] *vt* соблазня́ть (соблазни́ть
perf).
seduction [sɪ'dʌkʃən] *n* (*attraction*) собла́зн;
(*act of seducing*) обольще́ние.
seductive [sɪ'dʌktɪv] *adj* (*look, voice*)
обольсти́тельный* (обольсти́телен); (*offer*)
соблазни́тельный* (соблазни́телен).
see [siː] (*pt* **saw**, *pp* **seen**) *vt* ви́деть* (*impf*);
(*understand*) понима́ть (поня́ть* *perf*) ◆ *vi*
ви́деть* (*impf*); (*find out*) выясня́ть (вы́яснить
perf) ◆ *n* епа́рхия; **to ~ sb to the door**
(*accompany*) провожа́ть (проводи́ть* *perf*)
кого́-н до две́ри; **to ~ that** (*ensure*) следи́ть*
(проследи́ть* *perf*), чтобы; **there was nobody**
to be ~n никого́ не́ было ви́дно; **let me ~**
(*show me*) да́йте мне посмотре́ть; (*let me*
think) да́йте мне поду́мать; **to go and ~ sb**
навеща́ть (навести́ть* *perf*) кого́-н; **~ for**
yourself (*suggestion*) убеди́тесь са́ми; **I don't**
know what she saw in him я не зна́ю, что она́
в нём нашла́; **as far as I can ~** наско́лько я
понима́ю; **~ you!** пока́!; **~ you soon!** до
ско́рого!, пока́!
▶ **see about** *vt fus* (*deal with*) занима́ться
(заня́ться* *perf*) +*instr*
▶ **see off** *vt* провожа́ть (проводи́ть* *perf*)
▶ **see through** *vt* доводи́ть* (довести́* *perf*) до
конца́ ◆ *vt fus* ви́деть* (*impf*) наскво́зь
▶ **see to** *vt fus* забо́титься* (позабо́титься* *perf*)
о +*prp*.
seed [siːd] *n* се́мя* *nt*; **~s** (*fig*) семена́* *ntpl*; **he is**
the number 2 ~ (*SPORT*) в ранжиро́вке
спортсме́нов он второ́й; **to go to ~** (*plant*)
пойти́* (*perf*) в семена́; (*fig*) сдать* (*perf*).
seedless ['siːdlɪs] *adj* без ко́сточек.

---

* marks translations which have irregular inflections. The Russian-English side of the dictionary gives inflectional information.

seedling ['si:dlɪŋ] *n* расса́да *no pl.*
seedy ['si:dɪ] *adj* (*person*) потрёпанный*
(потрёпан); (*place*) захуда́лый.
seeing ['si:ɪŋ] *conj*: ~ **(that)** поско́льку, так как.
seek [si:k] (*pt, pp* **sought**) *vt* иска́ть* (*impf*); **to ~**
advice/help from sb обраща́ться
(обрати́ться* *perf*) за сове́том/по́мощью к
кому́-н
▸ **seek out** *vt* (*person*) разы́скивать
(разыска́ть* *perf*).
seem [si:m] *vi* каза́ться* (показа́ться* *perf*);
there ~s to be ... ка́жется, что име́ется ...; **it**
~s (that) ка́жется, (что); **what ~s to be the**
trouble? что у Вас за пробле́ма?
seemingly ['si:mɪŋlɪ] *adv* по-ви́димому.
seemly ['si:mlɪ] *adj* (*behaviour*) подоба́ющий*;
(*dress*) надлежа́щий*.
seen [si:n] *pp of* **see**.
seep [si:p] *vi* проса́чиваться (просочи́ться
perf).
seersucker ['sɪəsʌkə'] *n* (*fabric*) марлёвка.
seesaw ['si:sɔ:] *n* каче́ли *pl.*
seethe [si:ð] *vi* (*place*) кише́ть* (*impf*); **to ~ with**
anger кипе́ть* (*impf*) от гне́ва.
see-through ['si:θru:] *adj* прозра́чный*
(прозра́чен).
segment ['sɛgmənt] *n* (*of circle*) сегме́нт; (*of*
population) се́ктор; (*of orange*) до́лька*.
segregate ['sɛgrɪgeɪt] *vt* разделя́ть
(раздели́ть* *perf*).
segregation [sɛgrɪ'geɪʃən] *n* (*racial*)
сегрега́ция; (*SCOL*) разде́льное обуче́ние.
seismic ['saɪzmɪk] *adj* сейсми́ческий*.
seize [si:z] *vt* хвата́ть (схвати́ть* *perf*); (*power,*
hostage, territory) захва́тывать (захвати́ть*
perf); (*opportunity*) по́льзоваться
(воспо́льзоваться *perf*) +*instr*; (*LAW*)
конфискова́ть (*impf/perf*)
▸ **seize up** *vi* (*TECH: engine*) гло́хнуть*
(загло́хнуть* *perf*)
▸ **seize (up)on** *vt fus* ухва́тываться
(ухвати́ться* *perf*) за +*instr*.
seizure ['si:ʒə'] *n* (*MED*) при́ступ; (*of power*)
захва́т; (*of goods*) конфиска́ция.
seldom ['sɛldəm] *adv* ре́дко.
select [sɪ'lɛkt] *adj* (*school, area*) элита́рный;
(*pupils*) и́збранный; (*goods*) отбо́рный ♦ *vt*
(*choose*) выбира́ть (вы́брать* *perf*); (*SPORT*)
отбира́ть (отобра́ть* *perf*); **a ~ few** немно́гие
и́збранные *pl adj.*
selection [sɪ'lɛkʃən] *n* (*process*) отбо́р; (*COMM:*
range available) вы́бор; (*medley*) подбо́рка.
selection committee *n* отбо́рочная
коми́ссия.
selective [sɪ'lɛktɪv] *adj* (*careful in choosing*)
разбо́рчивый (разбо́рчив); (*not general*)
избира́тельный.
selector [sɪ'lɛktə'] *n* (*person*) член отбо́рочной
коми́ссии; (*TECH*) селе́ктор.
self [sɛlf] (*pl* **selves**) *n*: **he became his usual ~**
again он стал опя́ть сами́м собо́й; **my own ~**

моё со́бственное "я".
self... [sɛlf] *prefix* са́мо..., себя́....
self-addressed ['sɛlfə'drɛst] *adj*: ~ **envelope**
конве́рт, адресо́ванный на со́бственное
и́мя.
self-adhesive [sɛlfəd'hi:zɪv] *adj* само-
прикле́ивающийся.
self-appointed [sɛlfə'pɔɪntɪd] *adj* самозва́ный.
self-assertive [sɛlfə'sə:tɪv] *adj* уве́ренный*
(уве́рен).
self-assurance [sɛlfə'ʃuərəns] *n* само-
уве́ренность *f.*
self-assured [sɛlfə'ʃuəd] *adj* самоуве́ренный*
(самоуве́рен).
self-catering [sɛlf'keɪtərɪŋ] *adj* (*BRIT*): ~ **holiday**
путёвка, в кото́рую включа́ется прое́зд и
жильё с самообслу́живанием.
self-centred [sɛlf'sɛntəd] (*US* **self-centered**) *adj*
эгоцентри́чный* (эгоцентри́чен).
self-cleaning [sɛlf'kli:nɪŋ] *adj* само-
очища́ющийся.
self-confessed [sɛlfkən'fɛst] *adj* (*alcoholic etc*)
созна́вшийся.
self-confidence [sɛlf'kɔnfɪdns] *n* уве́ренность *f*
в себе́.
self-confident [sɛlf'kɔnfɪdənt] *adj* уве́ренный*
(уве́рен) в себе́.
self-conscious [sɛlf'kɔnʃəs] *adj* (*nervous*)
засте́нчивый (засте́нчив).
self-contained [sɛlfkən'teɪnd] *adj* (*BRIT: flat*)
отде́льный, изоли́рованный; (*society,*
person) незави́симый.
self-control [sɛlfkən'trəul] *n* самооблада́ние.
self-defeating [sɛlfdɪ'fi:tɪŋ] *adj* (*plan, action*)
па́губный* (па́губен).
self-defence [sɛlfdɪ'fɛns] (*US* **self-defense**) *n*
самозащи́та, самооборо́на; **in ~** защища́я
себя́.
self-discipline [sɛlf'dɪsɪplɪn] *n* само-
дисципли́на.
self-employed [sɛlfɪm'plɔɪd] *adj* рабо́тающий
на себя́.
self-esteem [sɛlfɪs'ti:m] *n* чу́вство
со́бственного досто́инства.
self-evident [sɛlf'ɛvɪdnt] *adj* самоочеви́дный*
(самоочеви́ден).
self-explanatory [sɛlfɪks'plænətrɪ] *adj*: **this**
phrase is ~ э́та фра́за не тре́бует
разъясне́ний.
self-financing [sɛlffaɪ'nænsɪŋ] *n*
самофинанси́рование.
self-governing [sɛlf'gʌvənɪŋ] *adj* (*organization,*
group) рабо́тающий по при́нципу
самоуправле́ния.
self-help ['sɛlf'hɛlp] *n* самопо́мощь *f.*
self-importance [sɛlfɪm'pɔːtns] *n* самомне́ние.
self-indulgent [sɛlfɪn'dʌldʒənt] *adj*: **he is being**
~ он потво́рствует свои́м сла́бостям.
self-inflicted [sɛlfɪn'flɪktɪd] *adj* (*injury*)
нанесённый (нанесён) самому́ себе́;
(*problems*) причинённый самому́ себе́.

self-interest [sɛlf'ɪntrɪst] *n* коры́сть *f*.
selfish ['sɛlfɪʃ] *adj* (*behaviour, attitude*) эгоисти́ческий*; (*person*) эгоисти́чный* (эгоисти́чен).
selfishly ['sɛlfɪʃlɪ] *adv* эгоисти́чно.
selfishness ['sɛlfɪʃnɪs] *n* (*of behaviour*) эгоисти́чность *f*; (*of person*) эгои́зм.
selfless ['sɛlflɪs] *adj* самоотве́рженный* (самоотве́ржен).
selflessly ['sɛlflɪslɪ] *adv* самоотве́рженно.
selflessness ['sɛlflɪsnɪs] *n* самоотве́рженность *f*.
self-made ['sɛlfmeɪd] *adj*: he's a ~ man он доби́лся всего́ свои́ми си́лами.
self-perpetuating [sɛlfpə'pɛtʃueɪtɪŋ] *adj* несконча́емый.
self-pity [sɛlf'pɪtɪ] *n* жа́лость *f* к (самому́) себе́.
self-portrait [sɛlf'pɔ:treɪt] *n* автопортре́т.
self-possessed [sɛlfpə'zɛst] *adj* хладнокро́вный* (хладнокро́вен).
self-preservation ['sɛlfprɛzə'veɪʃən] *n* самосохране́ние.
self-raising [sɛlf'reɪzɪŋ] (*US* **self-rising**) *adj* (*BRIT*): ~ **flour** мука́ с разрыхли́телем.
self-reliant [sɛlfrɪ'laɪənt] *adj* (*person*) самостоя́тельный* (самостоя́телен).
self-respect [sɛlfrɪs'pɛkt] *n* самоуваже́ние.
self-respecting [sɛlfrɪs'pɛktɪŋ] *adj* уважа́ющий себя́.
self-righteous [sɛlf'raɪtʃəs] *adj* (*person*) убеждённый* в свое́й правоте́.
self-rising [sɛlf'raɪzɪŋ] *adj* (*US*) = **self-raising**.
self-sacrifice [sɛlf'sækrɪfaɪs] *n* самопоже́ртвование.
selfsame ['sɛlfseɪm] *adj* тот же са́мый.
self-satisfied [sɛlf'sætɪsfaɪd] *adj* самодово́льный* (самодово́лен).
self-sealing [sɛlf'si:lɪŋ] *adj* (*envelope*) самозакле́ивающийся.
self-service [sɛlf'sə:vɪs] *adj*: ~ **restaurant/shop** рестора́н/магази́н самообслу́живания.
self-styled ['sɛlfstaɪld] *adj* самозва́ный.
self-sufficient [sɛlfsə'fɪʃənt] *adj* самостоя́тельный* (самостоя́телен); **to be ~ in sth** по́лностью обеспе́чивать (*impf*) себя́ чем-н.
self-supporting [sɛlfsə'pɔ:tɪŋ] *adj* само-окупа́ющийся.
self-taught [sɛlf'tɔ:t] *adj*: ~ **artist/pianist** худо́жник-/пиани́ст-самоу́чка.
self-test ['sɛlftɛst] *n* (*COMPUT*) самопрове́рка*.
sell [sɛl] (*pt, pp* **sold**) *vt* продава́ть* (прода́ть* *perf*) ♦ *vi* продава́ться* (прода́ться* *perf*); **to ~ at** *or* **for 10 pounds** продава́ться* (прода́ться* *perf*) по 10 фу́нтов; **to ~ sb sth, ~ sth to sb** продава́ть* (прода́ть* *perf*) что-н кому́-н; **to ~ sb an idea** (*fig*) убежда́ть (убеди́ть* *perf*) кого́-н в иде́е

▶ **sell off** *vt* распродава́ть* (распрода́ть* *perf*)
▶ **sell out** *vi* (*book etc*) расходи́ться* (разойти́сь* *perf*); (*shop*): **to ~ out of sth** распродава́ть* (распрода́ть* *perf*) что-н; **the tickets are sold out** все биле́ты про́даны
▶ **sell up** *vi* продава́ть* (прода́ть* *perf*) всё иму́щество.
sell-by date ['sɛlbaɪ-] *n* срок го́дности.
seller ['sɛlə'] *n* продаве́ц*(-вщи́ца); ~**'s market** "ры́нок продавцо́в" (*на кото́ром усло́вия дикту́ют продавцы́*).
selling price ['sɛlɪŋ-] *n* прода́жная цена́*.
Sellotape® ['sɛləuteɪp] *n* (*BRIT*) кле́йкая ле́нта.
sellout ['sɛlaut] *n* (*inf*: *betrayal*) преда́тельство; (*of tickets*): **the match was a ~** все биле́ты на матч бы́ли распро́даны.
selves [sɛlvz] *pl of* **self**.
semantic [sɪ'mæntɪk] *adj* семанти́ческий*.
semantics [sɪ'mæntɪks] *n* сема́нтика.
semaphore ['sɛməfɔ:'] *n* семафо́р.
semblance ['sɛmblns] *n* ви́димость *f*.
semen ['si:mən] *n* се́мя* *nt*, спе́рма.
semester [sɪ'mɛstə'] *n* (*esp US*) семе́стр.
semi ['sɛmɪ] *n* = **semidetached (house)**.
semi... ['sɛmɪ] *prefix* полу....
semibreve ['sɛmɪbri:v] *n* (*BRIT*) це́лая но́та.
semicircle ['sɛmɪsə:kl] *n* полукру́г.
semicircular ['sɛmɪ'sə:kjulə'] *adj* полукру́глый.
semicolon [sɛmɪ'kəulən] *n* то́чка* с запято́й.
semiconductor [sɛmɪkən'dʌktə'] *n* полу-прово́дник*.
semiconscious [sɛmɪ'kɔnʃəs] *adj* в полу-забытьи́.
semidetached [sɛmɪdɪ'tætʃt-] *n* (*BRIT*: *also:* ~ **house**) дом, примыка́ющий к сосе́днему.
semifinal [sɛmɪ'faɪnl] *n* полуфина́л.
seminar ['sɛmɪnɑ:'] *n* семина́р.
seminary ['sɛmɪnərɪ] *n* семина́рия.
semiprecious [sɛmɪ'prɛʃəs] *adj*: ~ **stone** полудрагоце́нный ка́мень* *m*, самоцве́т.
semiquaver ['sɛmɪkweɪvə'] *n* (*BRIT*) шестна́дцатая но́та.
semiskilled [sɛmɪ'skɪld] *adj* (*work, worker*) полуквалифици́рованный.
semiskimmed [sɛmɪ'skɪmd] *adj* полужи́рный, полуобезжи́ренный.
semitone ['sɛmɪtəun] *n* полуто́н*.
semolina [sɛmə'li:nə] *n* ма́нная крупа́, ма́нка (*inf*).
SEN *n abbr* (*BRIT*: = *State Enrolled Nurse*) медсестра́= *меди́цинская сестра́*.
Sen. *abbr* (*US*) = *senator*; (*in names*) = *senior*.
sen. *abbr* = **Sen**.
senate ['sɛnɪt] *n* сена́т.
senator ['sɛnɪtə'] *n* (*US etc*) сена́тор.
send [sɛnd] (*pt, pp* **sent**) *vt* (*dispatch*) посыла́ть (посла́ть* *perf*), отправля́ть (отпра́вить* *perf*); (*transmit*) посыла́ть (посла́ть* *perf*); **to**

---

* marks translations which have irregular inflections. The Russian-English side of the dictionary gives inflectional information.

~ by post *or (US)* **mail** посыла́ть (посла́ть*
perf) or отправля́ть (отпра́вить* *perf)* по
по́чте; **to ~ sb for sth** посыла́ть (посла́ть*
perf) кого́-н за чем-н; **to ~ word that ...**
передава́ть (переда́ть* *perf),* что ...; **she ~s
(you) her love** она́ передаёт Вам приве́т; **to ~
sb to Coventry** (*BRIT*) объявля́ть (объяви́ть*
perf) кому́-н бойко́т; **to ~ sb to sleep**
нагоня́ть (нагна́ть* *perf)* на кого́-н сон; **to ~
sb into fits of laughter** смеши́ть (рассмеши́ть
perf) кого́-н; **to ~ sth flying** рассе́ивать
(рассе́ять *perf)* что-н в во́здухе
▸ **send away** *vt (letter, goods)* отправля́ть
(отпра́вить* *perf),* отсыла́ть (отосла́ть* *perf);*
(unwelcome visitor) прогоня́ть (прогна́ть*
perf)
▸ **send away for** *vt fus* зака́зывать (заказа́ть*
perf)
▸ **send back** *vt* посыла́ть (посла́ть* *perf)*
обра́тно
▸ **send for** *vt fus (by post)* зака́зывать
(заказа́ть* *perf); (person)* посыла́ть (посла́ть*
perf) за +*instr*
▸ **send in** *vt (report)* представля́ть
(предста́вить* *perf); (resignation, application)*
подава́ть (пода́ть* *perf)* заявле́ние о +*prp*
▸ **send off** *vt (goods)* отправля́ть (отпра́вить*
perf); (BRIT: SPORT: player) удаля́ть (удали́ть*
perf)
▸ **send on** *vt (BRIT: letter)* пересыла́ть
(пересла́ть* *perf); (: luggage etc: in advance)*
переправля́ть (перепра́вить* *perf)*
▸ **send out** *vt (invitation)* рассыла́ть
(разосла́ть* *perf); (heat, smell, light)*
распространя́ть (распространи́ть *perf);*
(signal) посыла́ть (посла́ть* *perf)*
▸ **send round** *vt (letter, document etc)*
рассыла́ть (разосла́ть* *perf)*
▸ **send up** *vt (price, blood pressure)* поднима́ть
(подня́ть* *perf); (astronaut)* запуска́ть
(запусти́ть* *perf); (BRIT: parody)* высме́ивать
(вы́смеять *perf).*
sender ['sɛndə] *n* отправи́тель(ница) *m(f).*
sending-off ['sɛndɪŋɒf] *n* удале́ние с по́ля.
sendoff ['sɛndɒf] *n:* **a good send-off** хоро́шие
про́воды *pl.*
send-up ['sɛndʌp] *n* паро́дия.
Senegal [sɛnɪ'gɔːl] *n* Сенега́л.
Senegalese ['sɛnɪgə'liːz] *adj* сенега́льский ◆ *n
inv* сенега́лец*(-лка*).
senile ['siːnaɪl] *adj* маразмати́ческий.
senility [sɪ'nɪlɪtɪ] *n* ста́рческий* мара́зм.
senior ['siːnɪə] *adj (staff, officer)* ста́рший*;
(manager, consultant) гла́вный; *(of higher
rank):* **to be ~ to sb** быть* *(impf)* вы́ше кого́-н
по до́лжности; **the ~s** *npl (SCOL: at school)*
старшекла́ссники *mpl; (: at college, university)*
старшеку́рсники *mpl;* **she is 15 years his ~** она́
ста́рше его́ на 15 лет; **P. Jones ~** П. Джоунз
ста́рший*.
senior citizen *n (esp BRIT)* пожило́й челове́к*,

челове́к* пенсио́нного во́зраста.
senior high school *n (US)* ≈ ста́ршие ку́рсы
ко́лледжа.
seniority [siːnɪ'ɔrɪtɪ] *n* старшинство́.
sensation [sɛn'seɪʃən] *n (ability to feel)*
чувстви́тельность *f; (feeling)* ощуще́ние;
(great success) сенса́ция; **to cause a ~**
вызыва́ть (вы́звать* *perf)* сенса́цию.
sensational [sɛn'seɪʃənl] *adj (wonderful)*
потряса́ющий* (потряса́ющ); *(causing much
interest)* сенсацио́нный* (сенсацио́нен).
sensationalize [sɛn'seɪʃnəlaɪz] *vt* де́лать
(сде́лать *perf)* сенса́цию из +*gen.*
sense [sɛns] *vt (become aware of)* чу́вствовать
(почу́вствовать *perf),* ощуща́ть (ощути́ть*
perf) ◆ *n (feeling)* чу́вство, ощуще́ние;
(meaning of word) смысл; *(also: good ~):* **it
makes ~** в э́том есть смысл; **~s** *npl (sanity)*
рассу́док* *msg;* **the ~s** пять чувств; **there is no
~ in that/in doing that** нет смы́сла в э́том/
де́лать э́то; **to come to one's ~s**
образу́миться *(perf);* **to take leave of one's ~s**
теря́ть (потеря́ть *perf)* рассу́док.
senseless ['sɛnslɪs] *adj (pointless)*
бессмы́сленный* (бессмы́слен); *
(unconscious) без чувств.
sense of humour *(US* **sense of humor***) n*
чу́вство ю́мора.
sensibility [sɛnsɪ'bɪlɪtɪ] *n* чувстви́тельность *f.*
sensible ['sɛnsɪbl] *adj* разу́мный* (разу́мен); *
(shoes) практи́чный.
sensitive ['sɛnsɪtɪv] *adj* чувстви́тельный*
(чувстви́телен); *(understanding)* чу́ткий*
(чу́ток); *(issue)* щекотли́вый (щекотли́в); **~
to** чувстви́тельный* (чувстви́телен) к +*dat;*
he is very ~ about it он отно́сится к э́тому
о́чень боле́зненно.
sensitivity [sɛnsɪ'tɪvɪtɪ] *n (responsiveness)*
чувстви́тельность *f; (understanding)*
чу́ткость *f; (delicate nature: of issue etc)*
щекотли́вость *f.*
sensual ['sɛnsjuəl] *adj (of the senses)*
чу́вственный; *(sexual)* чу́вственный*
(чу́вствен).
sensuous ['sɛnsjuəs] *adj (lips)* чу́вственный*
(чу́вствен); *(material)* не́жный* (не́жен).
sent [sɛnt] *pt, pp of* **send.**
sentence ['sɛntns] *n (LING)* предложе́ние; *(LAW)*
пригово́р ◆ *vt:* **to ~ sb to death/to five years in
prison** пригова́ривать (приговори́ть *perf)*
кого́-н к сме́рти/к пяти́ года́м тюре́много
заключе́ния; **to pass ~ on sb** выноси́ть*
(вы́нести* *perf)* кому́-н пригово́р.
sentiment ['sɛntɪmənt] *n (tender feelings)*
чу́вство; *(opinion)* мне́ние, настрое́ние.
sentimental [sɛntɪ'mɛntl] *adj*
сентимента́льный* (сентимента́лен).
sentimentality ['sɛntɪmɛn'tælɪtɪ] *n*
сентимента́льность *f.*
sentry ['sɛntrɪ] *n* часово́й *m adj,* карау́льный *m
adj.*

sentry duty *n*: **to be on** ~ ~ нести* *(impf)* караýльную слýжбу.

Seoul [səul] *n* Сеýл.

separable ['sɛprəbl] *adj*: ~ **(from)** отделúмый (отделúм) (от +*gen*).

separate [*adj* 'sɛprɪt, *vb* 'sɛpəreɪt] *adj* отдéльный; (*ways*) рáзный ♦ *vt* (*split up: people*) разлучáть (разлучúть *perf*); (: *things*) разделять (разделúть* *perf*); (*make a distinction between*) различáть (различúть *perf*) ♦ *vi* расходúться* (разойтúсь* *perf*); ~ **from** отдéльно от +*gen*; **to** ~ **into** разделять (разделúть* *perf*) на +*acc*; *see also* **separates**.

separately ['sɛprɪtlɪ] *adv* отдéльно.

separates ['sɛprɪts] *npl* (*clothes*) предмéты жéнской одéжды, не входящие в комплéкт.

separation [sɛpə'reɪʃən] *n* (*being apart*) разлýка; (*LAW*) раздéльное прожива́ние.

sepia ['si:pjə] *adj*: ~ **photograph** фотогрáфия, вы́полненная в тéхнике сéпии.

Sept. *abbr* = **September.**

September [sɛp'tɛmbə'] *n* сентябрь* *m*; *see also* **July.**

septic ['sɛptɪk] *adj* заражённый* (заражён); **to go** ~ заражáться (заразúться* *perf*).

septicaemia [sɛptɪ'si:mɪə] (*US* **septicemia**) *n* сéпсис, септицемúя.

septic tank *n* ≈ выгребнáя яма.

sequel ['si:kwl] *n* продолжéние.

sequence ['si:kwəns] *n* послéдовательность *f*; (*dance sequence*) комбинáция; (*CINEMA*) эпизóд; **in the correct** ~ в прáвильной послéдовательности; ~ **of tenses** согласовáние времён.

sequential [sɪ'kwɛnʃəl] *adj* (*process, link etc*) послéдовательный* (послéдователен); ~ **access** (*COMPUT*) послéдовательный дóступ.

sequestrate [sɪ'kwɛstreɪt] *vt* конфисковáть (*impf/perf*).

sequin ['si:kwɪn] *n* блёстка*.

Serbia ['sə:bɪə] *n* Сéрбия.

Serbian ['sə:bɪən] *n* серб(ка) ♦ *adj* сéрбский*.

Serbo-Croat ['sə:bəu'krəuæt] *n* (*LING*) сербскохорвáтский язы́к*.

serenade [sɛrə'neɪd] *n* серенáда ♦ *vt* петь* (спеть* *perf*) серенáду +*dat*.

serene [sɪ'ri:n] *adj* безмятéжный* (безмятéжен).

serenity [sə'rɛnɪtɪ] *n* безмятéжность *f*.

sergeant ['sɑ:dʒənt] *n* сержáнт.

sergeant major *n* ≈ стáрший сержáнт.

serial ['sɪərɪəl] *n* (*TV, RADIO*) сериáл; (*in magazine*) ромáн, печáтающийся в нéскольких частях ♦ *adj* (*COMPUT*) послéдовательный; ~ **printer** посимвóльно печáтающее устрóйство.

serialize ['sɪərɪəlaɪz] *vt* (*story, book: in print*) тиражúровать (*impf*) частями; (: *on TV, RADIO*)

стáвить* (постáвить* *perf*) сериáл по +*prp*.

serial killer *n* маньяк (*совершúвший многочúсленные убúйства*).

serial number *n* серúйный нóмер*.

series ['sɪərɪz] *n inv* сéрия.

serious ['sɪərɪəs] *adj* серьёзный* (серьёзен); **are you** ~ **(about it)?** Вы (э́то) серьёзно?

seriously ['sɪərɪəslɪ] *adv* серьёзно; **to take sb/ sth** ~ принимáть (воспринимáть *perf*) когó-н/что-н серьёзно.

seriousness ['sɪərɪəsnɪs] *n* серьёзность *f*.

sermon ['sə:mən] *n* (*also fig*) прóповедь *f*.

serrated [sɪ'reɪtɪd] *adj* зазýбренный*.

serum ['sɪərəm] *n* сы́воротка.

servant ['sə:vənt] *n* (*male*) слугá* *m*; (*female*) служáнка; (*fig*) слугá*.

serve [sə:v] *vt* (*company, country*) служúть* (*impf*) +*dat*; (*customer: in shop, restaurant*) обслýживать (обслужúть* *perf*); (*purpose*) служúть* (послужúть (*impf*)) +*dat*; (*food, goods: to sb*) подавáть* (подáть* *perf*); (*subj: train etc*) обслýживать (*impf*); (*apprenticeship*) проходúть (пройтú* *perf*); (*prison term*) отбывáть (отбы́ть* *perf*) ♦ *vi* (*at table*) прислýживать (*impf*); (*TENNIS*) подавáть* (подáть* *perf*); (*soldier etc*) служúть* (*impf*) ♦ *n* (*TENNIS*) подáча; **are you being** ~**d?** Вас ужé обслýживают?; **it** ~**s my purpose** э́то мне подхóдит; **it** ~**s him right** подéлом емý; **to** ~ **on a committee/jury** состоя́ть (*impf*) в комитéте/жюрú; **to** ~ **as/for** служúть* (послужúть *perf*) +*instr*/вмéсто +*gen*

▶ **serve out** *vt* (*food*) расклáдывать (разложúть* *perf*)

▶ **serve up** *vt* = **serve out.**

service ['sə:vɪs] *n* (*help*) услýга; (*in hotel*) обслýживание, сéрвис; (*REL*) слýжба; (*AUT*) техобслýживание; (*TENNIS*) подáча; (*dinner set etc*) сервúз ♦ *vt* (*car, washing machine*) проводúть* (провестú* *perf*) техоб- слýживание +*gen*; **the S**~**s** *npl* (*army, navy etc*) Вооружённые сúлы *fpl*; **military** *or* **national** ~ воéнная слýжба; **train** ~ железнодорóжное сообщéние; **postal** ~ почтóвая связь; **how can I be of** ~ **(to you)?** чем могý быть* полéзен?; **to do sb a** ~ окáзывать (оказáть* *perf*) комý-н услýгу; **to put one's car in for** ~ отдавáть* (отдáть* *perf*) машúну на техобслýживание.

serviceable ['sə:vɪsəbl] *adj* прóчный* (прóчен).

service area *n* (*on motorway*) сéрвисная стáнция.

service charge *n* (*BRIT*) (*рестора́нная*) нацéнка.

service industry *n* сфéра услýг.

serviceman ['sə:vɪsmən] *irreg n* военно- слýжащий* *m adj*.

service station *n* (*AUT*) стáнция

---

* marks translations which have irregular inflections. The Russian-English side of the dictionary gives inflectional information.

техобслу́живания.
serviette [sə:vɪ'ɛt] *n* (*BRIT*) салфе́тка*.
servile ['sə:vaɪl] *adj* подобостра́стный*
(подобостра́стен).
session ['sɛʃən] *n* (*sitting*) се́ссия; (*SCOL*:
academic year) уче́бный год*; **recording** ~
за́пись *f*; **drinking** ~ запо́й; **to be in** ~ (*court
etc*) заседа́ть (*impf*).
session musician *n* музыка́нт, кото́рого
приглаша́ют на за́писи в ра́зные анса́мбли.
set [sɛt] (*pt, pp* **set**) *n* (*collection*) набо́р; (*of
saucepans, clothes*) компле́кт; (*of books*)
многото́мник; (*also:* **radio** ~)
радиоприёмник; (*also:* **television** ~)
телеви́зор; (*TENNIS*) сет; (*group of people*)
круг*, о́бщество; (*MATH*) мно́жество;
(*CINEMA, THEAT: stage*) сце́на; (: *scenery*)
(худо́жественное) оформле́ние; (*hairdo*)
укла́дка ♦ *adj* (*fixed*) устано́вленный; (*ready*)
гото́вый (гото́в) ♦ *vt* (*place: vertically*)
ста́вить* (поста́вить* *perf*); (: *horizontally*)
класть* (положи́ть* *perf*); (*table*) накрыва́ть
(накры́ть* *perf*); (*time*) назнача́ть (назна́чить
perf); (*price, rule, record*) устана́вливать
(установи́ть* *perf*); (*alarm, watch, task*)
ста́вить* (поста́вить* *perf*); (*exam*)
составля́ть (соста́вить* *perf*); (*TYP*) набира́ть
(набра́ть* *perf*) ♦ *vi* (*sun*) сади́ться* (сесть*
perf), заходи́ть* (зайти́* *perf*); (*jam*) густе́ть
(загусте́ть *perf*); (*jelly, concrete*) застыва́ть
(засты́ть* *perf*); (*bone*) сраста́ться (впра́вить*
perf); **a** ~ **of false teeth** вставны́е зу́бы* *mpl*; **a**
~ **of dining-room furniture** столо́вый
гарниту́р; **a chess** ~ ша́хматы *pl*; **to be** ~ **on
doing** настра́иваться (настро́иться *perf*)
+*infin*; **to be all** ~ **to do** собира́ться (*impf*) +*infin*;
to be (dead) ~ **against** быть* (*impf*)
(категори́чески) про́тив +*gen*; **he's** ~ **in his
ways** у него́ устоя́вшиеся привы́чки; **the
novel is** ~ **in Rome** де́йствие рома́на
происхо́дит в Ри́ме; **a** ~ **phrase** усто́йчивое
словосочета́ние; **to** ~ **to music** класть*
(положи́ть* *perf*) на му́зыку; **to** ~ **on fire**
поджига́ть (подже́чь* *perf*); **to** ~ **free**
освобожда́ть (освободи́ть* *perf*); **to** ~ **sth
going** приводи́ть* (привести́* *perf*) что-н в
де́йствие; **to** ~ **sail** отплыва́ть (отплы́ть*
perf)
▶ **set about** *vt fus* (*task*) приступа́ть
(приступи́ть* *perf*) к +*dat*; **to** ~ **about doing**
принима́ться (приня́ться* *perf*) +*infin*
▶ **set aside** *vt* (*money*) откла́дывать
(отложи́ть* *perf*); (*time*) выделя́ть (вы́делить
perf)
▶ **set back** *vt* (*progress*) заде́рживать
(задержа́ть* *perf*); (*cost*): **to** ~ **sb back £5**
обходи́ться* (обойти́сь* *perf*) кому́-н в £5; (*in
time*): **to** ~ **sb back (by)** заде́рживать
(задержа́ть* *perf*) кого́-н (на +*acc*); (*place*):
the house is ~ **back from the road** дом
нахо́дится в стороне́ от доро́ги

▶ **set in** *vi* (*infection*) внедря́ться (внедри́ться
perf); (*bad weather*) устана́вливаться
(установи́ться* *perf*); (*complications*)
начина́ться (нача́ться* *perf*); **the rain has** ~ **in
for the day** дождь заряди́л на весь день
▶ **set off** *vi* отправля́ться (отпра́виться* *perf*) ♦
vt (*bomb*) взрыва́ть (взорва́ть* *perf*); (*alarm*)
приводи́ть* (привести́* *perf*) в де́йствие;
(*chain of events*) вызыва́ть (вы́звать* *perf*);
(*show up well*) подчёркивать (*impf*)
▶ **set out** *vt* (*goods etc*) расставля́ть
(расста́вить* *perf*); (*arguments*) излага́ть
(изложи́ть* *perf*) ♦ *vi* (*depart*): **to** ~ **out (from)**
отправля́ться (отпра́виться* *perf*) (из +*gen*);
to ~ **out to do** намерева́ться (*impf*) +*infin*
▶ **set up** *vt* (*organization*) учрежда́ть
(учреди́ть* *perf*); (*monument*) устана́вливать
(установи́ть* *perf*); **to** ~ **up shop** (*fig*)
открыва́ть (откры́ть* *perf*) своё де́ло.
setback ['sɛtbæk] *n* (*hitch*) неуда́ча; (*in health*)
ухудше́ние.
set menu *n* ко́мплексное меню́ *nt ind*.
set square *n* уго́льник.
settee [sɛ'ti:] *n* дива́н.
setting ['sɛtɪŋ] *n* (*background*) обстано́вка*;
(*position: of controls*) положе́ние; (*of sun*)
зака́т, захо́д; (*of jewel*) опра́ва.
setting lotion *n* (*for hair*) лосьо́н для укла́дки
воло́с.
settle ['sɛtl] *vt* (*argument, problem*) разреша́ть
(разреши́ть *perf*); (*matter*) ула́живать
(ула́дить* *perf*); (*accounts*) рассчи́тываться
(рассчита́ться *perf*) с +*instr*; (*colonize: land*)
заселя́ть (засели́ть *perf*) ♦ *vi* (*also:* ~ **down**:
somewhere) обосно́вываться (*perf*); (: *live
sensibly*) остепеня́ться (*perf*); (*bird*) сади́ться*
(сесть* *perf*); (*dust, sediment*) оседа́ть
(осе́сть* *perf*); (*calm down*) успока́иваться
(успоко́иться* *perf*); **to** ~ **one's stomach**
успока́ивать (успоко́ить *perf*) желу́док; **to** ~
down to sth уса́живаться (усе́сться* *perf*) за
что-н; **to** ~ **for sth** соглаша́ться
(согласи́ться* *perf*) на что-н; **to** ~ **on sth**
остана́вливаться (останови́ться* *perf*) на
чём-н
▶ **settle in** *vi* осва́иваться (осво́иться *perf*)
▶ **settle up** *vi*: **to** ~ **up with sb** рассчи́тываться
(рассчита́ться *perf*) с кем-н.
settlement ['sɛtlmənt] *n* (*payment*) упла́та;
(*agreement*) соглаше́ние; (*village, colony*)
поселе́ние; (*of conflict*) урегули́рование; **in** ~
of our account (*COMM*) для опла́ты на́шего
счёта.
settler ['sɛtlə'] *n* поселе́нец*(-нка*).
setup ['sɛtʌp] *n* (*organization*) устро́йство;
(*situation*) положе́ние дел.
seven ['sɛvn] *n* семь*; *see also* **five**.
seventeen [sɛvn'ti:n] *n* семна́дцать*; *see also*
five.
seventeenth [sɛvn'ti:nθ] *adj* семна́дцатый; *see
also* **fifth**.

seventh ['sεvnθ] *adj* седьмо́й; *see also* **fifth**.
seventieth ['sεvntɪɪθ] *adj* семидеся́тый; *see also* **fifth**.
seventy ['sεvntɪ] *n* се́мьдесят*; *see also* **fifty**.
sever ['sεvə'] *vt* (*artery, pipe*) перереза́ть (перере́зать* *perf*); (*relations*) прерыва́ть (прерва́ть* *perf*); (*ties, connections*) обрыва́ть (оборва́ть* *perf*).
several ['sεvərl] *adj* не́сколько +*gen* ◆ *pron* не́которые *pl adj*; ~ **of us** не́которые из нас; ~ **times** не́сколько раз.
severance ['sεvərəns] *n* разры́в.
severance pay *n* выходно́е посо́бие (*при сокраще́нии шта́тов*).
severe [sɪ'vɪə'] *adj* (*shortage, pain, winter*) жесто́кий* (жесто́к); (*damage*) серьёзный (серьёзен); (*stern*) жёсткий* (жёсток); (*plain: dress*) стро́гий* (строг).
severely [sɪ'vɪəlɪ] *adv* (*punish*) жесто́ко; (*look*) жёстко; (*damaged*) серьёзно; (*wounded, ill*) тяжело́.
severity [sɪ'vεrɪtɪ] *n* жёсткость *f*; (*of damage*) серьёзность *f*; (*of illness*) тя́жесть *f*.
sew [səu] (*pt* **sewed**, *pp* **sewn**) *vti* шить* (*impf*)
▶ **sew up** *vt* (*clothes*) зашива́ть (заши́ть* *perf*); **it is all ~n up** (*fig*) де́ло на мази́.
sewage ['su:ɪdʒ] *n* (*waste*) сто́чные во́ды* *fpl*; ~ **system** канализа́ция.
sewage works *n* канализацио́нные очисти́тельные сооруже́ния *ntpl*.
sewer ['su:ə'] *n* канализацио́нная труба́*.
sewing ['səuɪŋ] *n* шитьё.
sewing machine *n* шве́йная маши́на.
sewn [səun] *pp of* **sew**.
sex [sεks] *n* (*gender*) пол; (*lovemaking*) секс; **both ~es** о́ба по́ла; **to have ~ with sb** переспа́ть* (*perf*) с кем-н.
sex act *n* сексуа́льный акт.
sex appeal *n* сексопи́льность *f*, сексуа́льная привлека́тельность *f*; **he's got a lot of ~ ~** он о́чень сексопи́льный.
sex education *n* сексуа́льное воспита́ние.
sexism ['sεksɪzəm] *n* предубежде́ние к ли́цам противополо́жного по́ла.
sexist ['sεksɪst] *adj* характе́ризующийся предубежде́нием к мужчи́нам и́ли же́нщинам.
sex life *n* полова́я *or* сексуа́льная жизнь *f*.
sex object *n* сексуа́льный объе́кт.
sextet [sεks'tεt] *n* (*group*) сексте́т.
sexual ['sεksjuəl] *adj* (*reproduction, equality*) полово́й; (*attraction, relationship*) сексуа́льный* (сексуа́лен), полово́й; ~ **equality** ра́венство поло́в.
sexual assault *n* нападе́ние с сексуа́льным моти́вом.
sexual harassment *n* нежела́тельное проявле́ние полово́го интере́са, а та́кже нетакти́чные замеча́ния, намёки и т.п. со стороны́ представи́теля противополо́жного по́ла.
sexual intercourse *n* полово́й акт.
sexually ['sεksjuəlɪ] *adv* (*attractive, attract*) сексуа́льно; (*segregated*) в зави́симости от по́ла; (*discriminate*) по полово́му при́знаку; (*reproduce*) половы́м путём.
sexual orientation *n* сексуа́льная ориента́ция.
sexy ['sεksɪ] *adj* сексуа́льный* (сексуа́лен).
Seychelles [seɪ'ʃεl(z)] *npl*: **the ~** Сейше́льские острова́ *mpl*.
SF *n abbr* (= **science fiction**) НФ= *нау́чная фанта́стика*.
SG *n abbr* (*US*: MIL, MED: = **Surgeon General**) ≈ начмед= *нача́льник медици́нской слу́жбы*.
Sgt *abbr* (*POLICE, MIL*) = **sergeant**.
shabbiness ['ʃæbɪnɪs] *n* запу́щенность *f*.
shabby ['ʃæbɪ] *adj* (*person*) обтрёпанный; (*clothes*) потрёпанный (потрёпан); (*treatment, behaviour*) недосто́йный* (недосто́ен); (*building*) ве́тхий* (ветх).
shack [ʃæk] *n* лачу́га
▶ **shack up** *vi* (*inf*): **to ~ up (with sb)** нача́ть* (*perf*) сожи́тельствовать (с +*instr*).
shackles ['ʃæklz] *npl* (*also fig*) око́вы *pl*.
shade [ʃeɪd] *n* (*shelter*) тень *f*; (*for lamp*) абажу́р; (*of colour*) оттéнок*; (*US: also*: **window ~**) што́ра ◆ *vt* (*shelter*) затеня́ть (затени́ть* *perf*); (*eyes*) заслоня́ть (заслони́ть* *perf*); ~**s** *npl* (*inf: sunglasses*) тёмные очки́ *pl*; **in the ~** в тени́; **a ~ (more/too large)** чу́точку (бо́льше/великова́т).
shadow ['ʃædəu] *n* тень* *f* ◆ *vt* (*follow*) ходи́ть* (*impf*) как тень за +*instr*; **without** *or* **beyond a ~ of a doubt** без те́ни сомне́ния.
shadow cabinet *n* (*BRIT: POL*) тенево́й кабине́т.
shadowy ['ʃædəuɪ] *adj* (*place*) тени́стый (тени́ст); (*figure, shape*) сму́тный* (сму́тен).
shady ['ʃeɪdɪ] *adj* (*place, trees*) тени́стый (тени́ст); (*fig: dishonest*) тёмный* (тёмен).
shaft [ʃɑ:ft] *n* (*of arrow, spear*) дре́вко; (*AUT, TECH*) вал; (*of mine, lift*) ша́хта; (*of light*) сноп; **ventilation ~** вентиляцио́нная труба́*.
shag [ʃæg] *vt* (*inf!*) тра́хать (тра́хнуть *perf*) (!) ◆ *vi* (*inf!*) тра́хаться (тра́хнуться *perf*) (!) ◆ *n* (*also*: ~ **tobacco**) махо́рка; (*ZOOL*) длиннохво́стый бакла́н; (*inf!*): **to have a ~** тра́хнуться (*perf*).
shaggy ['ʃægɪ] *adj* лохма́тый (лохма́т).
shake [ʃeɪk] (*pt* **shook**, *pp* **shaken**) *vt* трясти́* (*impf*); (*bottle*) взба́лтывать (взболта́ть *perf*); (*building*) сотряса́ть (сотрясти́* *perf*); (*weaken: beliefs, resolve*) пошатну́ть* (*perf*); (*upset, surprise*) потряса́ть (потрясти́* *perf*) ◆ *vi* (*voice*) дрожа́ть (*impf*) ◆ *n* (*movement*)

---

* marks translations which have irregular inflections. The Russian-English side of the dictionary gives inflectional information.

дрожа́ние; **to ~ one's head** кача́ть (покача́ть *perf*) голово́й; **to ~ hands with sb** жать* (пожа́ть* *perf*) кому́-н ру́ку; **to ~ with** трясти́сь* (*impf*) от +*gen*; **give the bottle a good ~** хорошо́ взболта́йте буты́лку

▶ **shake off** *vt* стря́хивать (стряхну́ть *perf*); (*fig: pursuer*) избавля́ться (изба́виться* *perf*) от +*gen*

▶ **shake up** *vt* (*ingredients*) взба́лтывать (взболта́ть *perf*); (*fig: organization*) встря́хивать (встряхну́ть *perf*).

shaken ['ʃeɪkn] *pp of* **shake**.

shake-out ['ʃeɪkaut] *n* перетря́ска.

shake-up ['ʃeɪkʌp] *n* встря́ска*.

shakily ['ʃeɪkɪlɪ] *adv* (*reply*) с дро́жью в го́лосе; (*walk*) шата́ясь; (*write*) дрожа́щей руко́й.

shaky ['ʃeɪkɪ] *adj* (*hand, voice*) дрожа́щий; (*table, knowledge*) ша́ткий* (ша́ток); (*memory*) непро́чный* (непро́чен); (*prospects, future*) неопределённый*; (*start*) неуве́ренный*; **his voice was ~** го́лос его́ дрожа́л.

shale [ʃeɪl] *n* сла́нец*.

shall [ʃæl] *aux vb*: **I ~ go** я пойду́; **~ I open the door?** (мне) откры́ть дверь?; **I'll get some, ~ I?** я принесу́ немно́го, да?

shallot [ʃə'lɔt] *n* (*BRIT*) лук-шало́т *no pl*.

shallow ['ʃæləu] *adj* (*water*) ме́лкий*; (*box*) неглубо́кий*; (*breathing, also fig*) пове́рхностный* (пове́рхностен).

sham [ʃæm] *n* притво́рство; (*jewellery, furniture*) подде́лка* ♦ *vt* притворя́ться (притвори́ться *perf*) +*instr*.

shambles ['ʃæmblz] *n* неразбери́ха; **the economy is (in) a complete ~** в эконо́мике цари́т по́лная неразбери́ха.

shambolic [ʃæm'bɔlɪk] *adj* (*inf*) хаоти́чный* (хаоти́чен).

shame [ʃeɪm] *n* (*embarrassment*) стыд*; (*disgrace*) позо́р ♦ *vt* позо́рить (опозо́рить *perf*); **it is a ~ that/to do** жаль, что/+*infin*; **what a ~!** кака́я жа́лость!, как жаль!; **to put sb to ~** (*fig*) заставля́ть (заста́вить* *perf*) кого́-н устыди́ться; **your work puts mine to ~** моя́ рабо́та бледне́ет в сравне́нии с Ва́шей.

shamefaced ['ʃeɪmfeɪst] *adj* устыжённый.

shameful ['ʃeɪmful] *adj* позо́рный* (позо́рен).

shameless ['ʃeɪmlɪs] *adj* бессты́дный* (бессты́ден).

shampoo [ʃæm'pu:] *n* шампу́нь *m* ♦ *vt* мыть* (помы́ть* *or* вы́мыть* *perf*) шампу́нем.

shampoo and set *n* мытьё и укла́дка воло́с.

shamrock ['ʃæmrɔk] *n* трили́стник, кисли́ца.

shandy ['ʃændɪ] *n смесь пи́ва с лимона́дом*.

shan't [ʃɑːnt] = **shall not**.

shanty town ['ʃæntɪ-] *n* трущо́бы *fpl*.

SHAPE [ʃeɪp] *n abbr* (*MIL*: = *Supreme Headquarters Allied Powers, Europe*) Штаб верхо́вного главнокома́ндующего НАТО в Евро́пе.

shape [ʃeɪp] *n* фо́рма ♦ *vt* (*fashion, ideas,*

events) формирова́ть (сформирова́ть *perf*); (*clay*) лепи́ть* (слепи́ть* *perf*); (*statement*) оформля́ть (офо́рмить* *perf*); **to take ~** (*painting, plan etc*) обрета́ть (обрести́* *perf*) фо́рму; **in the ~ of a heart** в фо́рме серде́чка; **I can't bear gardening in any ~ or form** я не выношу́ садово́дства ни в како́й фо́рме; **to get o.s. into ~** приводи́ть (привести́* *perf*) себя́, входи́ть* (войти́* *perf*) в фо́рму

▶ **shape up** *vi* (*events*) скла́дываться (сложи́ться* *perf*); (*person*) формирова́ться (сформирова́ться *perf*).

-shaped [ʃeɪpt] *suffix*: **heart-~** сердцеви́дный*.

shapeless ['ʃeɪplɪs] *adj* бесфо́рменный (бесфо́рмен).

shapely ['ʃeɪplɪ] *adj* (*woman*) хорошо́ сло́женный (сло́жен); (*legs*) краси́вый (краси́в).

share [ʃeə˧] *n* до́ля*; (*COMM*) а́кция ♦ *vt* (*books, cost*) дели́ть* (раздели́ть* *or* подели́ть* *perf*); (*toys*) дели́ться* (подели́ться* *perf*) +*instr*; (*features, qualities etc*) разделя́ться (*impf*); (*opinion, concern*) разделя́ть (раздели́ть* *perf*); **to ~ in** (*joy, sorrow*) дели́ться* (раздели́ться* *perf*); (*profits*) дели́ться* (подели́ться* *perf*); (*work*) уча́ствовать (*impf*) в +*prp*

▶ **share out** *vt* дели́ть* (раздели́ть* *perf*).

share capital *n* акционе́рный капита́л.

share certificate *n* сертифика́т а́кции.

shareholder ['ʃeəhəuldə˧] *n* акционе́р.

share index *n* (*COMM*) фо́ндовый и́ндекс.

share issue *n* (*COMM*) вы́пуск а́кции.

shareware ['ʃeəwɛə˧] *n* програ́ммное обеспе́чение о́бщего по́льзования.

shark [ʃɑːk] *n* аку́ла.

sharp [ʃɑːp] *adj* ре́зкий* (ре́зок); (*knife, teeth, nose*) о́стрый* (остр); (*curve, bend*) круто́й* (крут); (*MUS*) дие́з; (*dishonest: practice etc*) ло́вкий* (ло́вок) ♦ *n* (*MUS*) дие́з ♦ *adv* (*precisely*): **at 2 o'clock ~** ро́вно в два часа́; **he is very ~** у него́ о́чень о́стрый ум; **he was rather ~ with her** он был дово́льно ре́зок с ней; **look ~!** поторопи́тесь!; **C ~** (*MUS*) до-дие́з.

sharpen ['ʃɑːpn] *vt* (*stick etc*) заостря́ть (заостри́ть *perf*); (*pencil, knife*) точи́ть* (поточи́ть* *perf*); (*fig: appetite*) уси́ливать (уси́лить *perf*).

sharpener ['ʃɑːpnə˧] *n* (*also*: **pencil ~**) точи́лка*; (*also*: **knife ~**) точи́ло.

sharp-eyed [ʃɑːp'aɪd] *adj* (*person*) зо́ркий* (зо́рок).

sharpish ['ʃɑːpɪʃ] *adj* (*inf*) бы́стренько.

sharply ['ʃɑːplɪ] *adv* ре́зко.

sharp-tempered [ʃɑːp'tɛmpəd] *adj* (*person*) вспы́льчивый (вспы́льчив).

sharp-witted [ʃɑːp'wɪtɪd] *adj* (*person*) сообрази́тельный* (сообрази́телен).

shatter ['ʃætə˧] *vt* (*vase, hopes*) разбива́ть (разби́ть* *perf*); (*fig: nerves*) надрыва́ть (надорва́ть* *perf*); (: *person*) потряса́ть (потрясти́* *perf*) ♦ *vi* би́ться* (разби́ться* *perf*).

shattered ['ʃætəd] *adj* (*overwhelmed, grief-stricken*) потрясённый (потрясён); (*inf: exhausted*) разби́тый (разби́т).

shattering ['ʃætərɪŋ] *adj* (*experience*) тя́жкий*; (*day*) утоми́тельный* (утоми́телен).

shatterproof ['ʃætəpruːf] *adj* небью́щийся.

shave [ʃeɪv] *vt* брить* (побри́ть* *perf*) ♦ *vi* бри́ться* (побри́ться* *perf*) ♦ *n*: **to have a ~** бри́ться* (побри́ться* *perf*).

shaven ['ʃeɪvn] *adj* бри́тый (брит).

shaver ['ʃeɪvəʳ] *n* (*also:* **electric ~**) (электри́ческая) бри́тва.

shaver point *n* розе́тка* для бри́твы.

shaving ['ʃeɪvɪŋ] *n* бритьё; **~s** *npl* (*of wood etc*) стру́жки* *fpl*.

shaving brush *n* ки́сточка* для бритья́, помазо́к*.

shaving cream *n* крем для бритья́.

shaving foam *n* крем для бритья́.

shaving soap *n* крем для бритья́.

shawl [ʃɔːl] *n* шаль *f*.

she [ʃiː] *pron* она́.

sheaf [ʃiːf] (*pl* **sheaves**) *n* (*of corn*) сноп*; (*of papers*) сто́пка*.

shear [ʃɪəʳ] (*pt* **sheared**, *pp* **shorn**) *vt* (*sheep*) стричь* (постри́чь* *or* остри́чь* *perf*)

▶ **shear off** *vi* (*bolt etc*) надла́мываться (надломи́ться* *perf*).

shears ['ʃɪəz] *npl* (*for hedge*) садо́вые но́жницы *pl*.

sheath [ʃiːθ] *n* (*of knife*) но́жны* *pl*; (*contraceptive*) презервати́в.

sheathe [ʃiːð] *vt* (*sword, knife etc*) вкла́дывать (вложи́ть* *perf*) в но́жны.

sheaves [ʃiːvz] *npl of* **sheaf**.

shed [ʃed] (*pt, pp* **shed**) *n* сара́й; (*INDUSTRY, RAIL*) наве́с ♦ *vt* (*skin, load*) сбра́сывать (сбро́сить* *perf*); (*tears*) лить* (*impf*); (*blood*) пролива́ть (проли́ть* *perf*); (*workers*) увольня́ть (уво́лить *perf*); **to ~ light on** пролива́ть (проли́ть* *perf*) свет на +*acc*.

she'd [ʃiːd] = **she had**, **she would**.

sheen [ʃiːn] *n* лоск.

sheep [ʃiːp] *n inv* овца́*; (*male*) бара́н.

sheepdog ['ʃiːpdɔg] *n* овча́рка*.

sheep farmer *n* овцево́д.

sheepish ['ʃiːpɪʃ] *adj* ро́бкий* (ро́бок).

sheepskin ['ʃiːpskɪn] *n* овчи́на ♦ *cpd* (*jacket, mittens*) овчи́нный; **~ coat** (*short*) дублёный полушу́бок; (*long*) дублёная шу́ба, дублёнка (*разг*).

sheer [ʃɪəʳ] *adj* (*utter*) су́щий*; (*steep*) отве́сный; (*almost transparent*) сквозно́й ♦ *adv* (*straight up or down*) отве́сно; **by ~ chance** по чи́стой случа́йности.

sheet [ʃiːt] *n* (*on bed*) простыня́*; (*of paper, metal, glass*) лист*; (*of ice*) полоса́*.

sheet feed *n* (*on printer*) автопода́ча бума́ги.

sheet lightning *n* зарни́ца.

sheet metal *n* листово́й мета́лл.

sheet music *n* но́ты *fpl*.

sheik(h) [ʃeɪk] *n* шейх.

shelf [ʃelf] (*pl* **shelves**) *n* по́лка*.

shelf life *n* срок го́дности.

shell [ʃel] *n* (*of mollusc*) ра́ковина; (*of egg, nut*) скорлупа́; (*explosive*) снаря́д; (*of building*) карка́с; (*of ship*) ко́рпус ♦ *vt* (*peas*) лущи́ть (облущи́ть *perf*); (*MIL: fire on*) обстре́ливать (обстреля́ть *perf*)

▶ **shell out** *vt* (*inf*): **to ~ out (for)** выкла́дывать (вы́ложить *perf*) (на +*acc*).

she'll [ʃiːl] = **she will**, **she shall**.

shellfish ['ʃelfɪʃ] *n inv* (*crab etc*) рачки́ *pl*; (*scallop etc*) моллю́ски *mpl*.

shellsuit ['ʃelsuːt] *n* спорти́вный костю́м (*капро́новый на покла́дке*).

shelter ['ʃeltəʳ] *n* (*refuge*) прию́т; (*protection*) укры́тие; (*also:* **air-raid ~**) бомбоубе́жище ♦ *vt* (*protect*) укрыва́ть (укры́ть* *perf*); (*give lodging to*) дава́ть* (дать* *perf*) прию́т +*dat* ♦ *vi* укрыва́ться (укры́ться* *perf*); **to take ~ (from)** приюти́ться* (*perf*) (от +*gen*).

sheltered ['ʃeltəd] *adj* (*life*) беззабо́тный; (*spot*) защищённый (защищён).

sheltered housing *n* жили́щный ко́мплекс, специа́льно приспосо́бленный для нужд престаре́лых, инвали́дов *итп*.

shelve [ʃelv] *vt* (*fig: plan*) класть* (положи́ть *perf*) под сукно́.

shelves [ʃelvz] *npl of* **shelf**.

shelving ['ʃelvɪŋ] *n* (*shelves*) стелла́ж*.

shepherd ['ʃepəd] *n* пасту́х* ♦ *vt* (*guide*) направля́ть (напра́вить* *perf*).

shepherdess ['ʃepədɪs] *n* пасту́шка*.

shepherd's pie *n* (*BRIT*) ≈ запека́нка* из мя́са и карто́феля.

sherbet ['ʃəːbət] *n* щербе́т; (*US: water ice*) фрукто́вое моро́женое *nt adj*.

sheriff ['ʃerɪf] *n* (*US*) шери́ф.

sherry ['ʃerɪ] *n* хе́рес*.

she's [ʃiːz] = **she is**, **she has**.

Shetland ['ʃetlənd] *n* (*also:* **the ~ Islands**) Шетла́ндские острова́* *mpl*.

Shetland pony *n* шетла́ндский* по́ни *m ind*.

shield [ʃiːld] *n* (*protection, also MIL*) щит*; (*trophy*) трофе́й ♦ *vt*: **to ~ (from)** заслоня́ть (заслони́ть* *perf*) (от +*gen*).

shift [ʃɪft] *n* (*in direction, conversation*) переме́на; (*in policy, emphasis*) сдвиг; (*at work*) сме́на ♦ *vt* сдвига́ть (передви́нуть *perf*), перемеща́ть (перемести́ть* *perf*); (*stain*) выводи́ть* (вы́вести* *perf*) ♦ *vi* перемеща́ться

(перемести́ться* *perf*); **a ~ in demand**
измене́ние в спро́се; **the wind has ~ed to the**
south ве́тер перемени́лся к ю́гу.
shift key *n* реги́стровая кла́виша.
shiftless [ˈʃɪftlɪs] *adj* (*person*) безде́йственный.
shiftwork [ˈʃɪftwɜːk] *n* сме́нная рабо́та; **to do**
~ рабо́тать (*impf*) посме́нно.
shifty [ˈʃɪftɪ] *adj* (*person*) уве́ртливый
(уве́ртлив); (*eyes*) бе́гающий.
Shiite [ˈʃiːaɪt] *n* шии́т ♦ *adj* шии́тский.
shilling [ˈʃɪlɪŋ] *n* (*BRIT*) ши́ллинг.
shillyshally [ˈʃɪlɪʃælɪ] *vi* тяну́ть* (*impf*).
shimmer [ˈʃɪmə'] *vi* мерца́ть (*impf*).
shimmering [ˈʃɪmərɪŋ] *adj* мерца́ющий; (*satin*
etc) перелива́ющийся.
shin [ʃɪn] *n* го́лень *f* ♦ *vi:* **to ~ up a tree** влеза́ть
(влезть* *perf*) на де́рево; **to ~ down a tree**
слеза́ть (слезть* *perf*) с де́рева.
shindig [ˈʃɪndɪg] *n* (*inf*) сабанту́й.
shine [ʃaɪn] (*pt, pp* **shone**) *n* блеск ♦ *vi* (*sun,*
light) свети́ть* (*impf*); (*eyes, hair*) блесте́ть*
(*impf*); (*fig: person*) сия́ть (*impf*), свети́ться*
(*impf*) ♦ *vt* (*polish*) (*pt, pp* **shined**) натира́ть
(натере́ть* *perf*); **to ~ a torch on sth** свети́ть*
(посвети́ть* *perf*) фонарём на что-н.
shingle [ˈʃɪŋgl] *n* (*on beach*) га́лька; (*on roof*)
кро́вельная дра́нка.
shingles [ˈʃɪŋglz] *n* опоя́сывающий лиша́й*.
shining [ˈʃaɪnɪŋ] *adj* блестя́щий*.
shiny [ˈʃaɪnɪ] *adj* блестя́щий*.
ship [ʃɪp] *n* кора́бль* *m* ♦ *vt* (*transport*)
перевози́ть* (перевезти́* *perf*) по мо́рю;
(*send*) экспеди́ровать (*impf/perf*); (*water*)
забира́ть (забра́ть* *perf*); **on board ~** на
борту́ корабля́.
shipbuilder [ˈʃɪpbɪldə'] *n* кораблестрои́тель *m*,
судострои́тель *m*.
shipbuilding [ˈʃɪpbɪldɪŋ] *n* кораблестрое́ние,
судострое́ние.
ship canal *n* судохо́дный кана́л.
ship chandler [-ˈtʃɑːndlə'] *n* поставщи́к
корабе́льного обору́дования.
shipment [ˈʃɪpmənt] *n* (*goods*) па́ртия.
shipowner [ˈʃɪpəunə'] *n* судовладе́лец*.
shipper [ˈʃɪpə'] *n* отправи́тель *m*.
shipping [ˈʃɪpɪŋ] *n* (*transport of cargo*)
перево́зка; (*ships*) судохо́дство.
shipping agent *n* экспеди́тор.
shipping company *n* судохо́дная компа́ния.
shipping lane *n* морска́я тра́сса.
shipping line *n* = **shipping company**.
shipshape [ˈʃɪpʃeɪp] *adj* (*house, boat etc*)
ла́дный.
ship's manifest *n* деклара́ция судово́го
гру́за.
shipwreck [ˈʃɪprɛk] *n* (*event*) корабле-
круше́ние; (*ship*) потерпе́вшее круше́ние
су́дно ♦ *vt:* **to be ~ed** терпе́ть (потерпе́ть*
perf) кораблекруше́ние.
shipyard [ˈʃɪpjɑːd] *n* (судострои́тельная)
верфь *f*.

shire [ˈʃaɪə'] *n* (*BRIT*) гра́фство.
shirk [ʃɜːk] *vt* уви́ливать (увильну́ть *perf*) от
+*gen*.
shirt [ʃɜːt] *n* (*man's*) руба́шка*; (*woman's*)
блу́зка*; **in (one's) ~ sleeves** в одно́й
руба́шке.
shirty [ˈʃɜːtɪ] *adj* (*BRIT: inf: person*) наду́тый
(наду́т).
shit [ʃɪt] *excl* (*inf!*) чёрт.
shiver [ˈʃɪvə'] *n* дрожь *f* ♦ *vi* дрожа́ть (*impf*).
shoal [ʃəul] *n* (*of fish*) коса́к*; (*fig: also:* **~s**)
то́лпы *fpl*.
shock [ʃɔk] *n* (*start, impact*) толчо́к*; (*ELEC,*
MED) шок; (*emotional*) потрясе́ние ♦ *vt*
(*upset*) потряса́ть (потрясти́* *perf*); (*offend*)
возмуща́ть (возмути́ть* *perf*), шоки́ровать
(*impf/perf*); **to be suffering from ~** (*MED*)
находи́ться* (*impf*) в состоя́нии шо́ка; **the**
news gave us a ~ э́та но́вость нас потрясла́;
it came as a ~ to hear that ... мы бы́ли
потрясены́, когда́ услы́шали, что ....
shock absorber *n* амортиза́тор.
shocker [ˈʃɔkə'] *n* (*inf: film*) ужа́сник; (: *news*)
ужаса́ющая но́вость *f*.
shocking [ˈʃɔkɪŋ] *adj* (*outrageous*)
возмути́тельный* (возмути́телен); (*dreadful*) кошма́рный* (кошма́рен).
shockproof [ˈʃɔkpruːf] *adj* противоуда́рный.
shock therapy *n* шокотерапи́я.
shock treatment *n* = **shock therapy**.
shock wave *n* уда́рная волна́; (*fig*) чу́вство
потрясе́ния.
shod [ʃɔd] *pt, pp of* **shoe** ♦ *adj:* **well-~** хорошо́
обу́тый (обу́т).
shoddy [ˈʃɔdɪ] *adj* (*goods*) дрянно́й;
(*workmanship*) куста́рный.
shoe [ʃuː] (*pt, pp* **shod**) *n* (*for person*) ту́фля*;
(*for horse*) подко́ва; (*AUT: also:* **brake ~**)
коло́дка ♦ *vt* (*horse*) подко́вывать
(подкова́ть* *perf*); **~s** (*footwear*) о́бувь *fsg*.
shoebrush [ˈʃuːbrʌʃ] *n* обувна́я щётка*.
shoehorn [ˈʃuːhɔːn] *n* рожо́к* (*для о́буви*).
shoelace [ˈʃuːleɪs] *n* шнуро́к*.
shoemaker [ˈʃuːmeɪkə'] *n* сапо́жник.
shoe polish *n* гутали́н.
shoe shop *n* обувно́й магази́н.
shoestring [ˈʃuːstrɪŋ] *n* (*fig*): **on a ~** на гроши́.
shoetree [ˈʃuːtriː] *n* распо́рка* для о́буви.
shone [ʃɔn] *pt, pp of* **shine**.
shoo [ʃuː] *excl* вон; (*to cats*) брысь ♦ *vt* (*also:* **~**
away, ~ off) отгоня́ть (отогна́ть* *perf*).
shook [ʃuk] *pt of* **shake**.
shoot [ʃuːt] (*pt, pp* **shot**) *n* (*BOT*) росто́к*, побе́г;
(*SPORT: event*) охо́та; (*CINEMA*) съёмка ♦ *vt*
(*gun, arrow*) стреля́ть (*impf*) из +*gen*; (*kill: bird,*
robber etc) застре́ливать (застрели́ть* *perf*);
(*BRIT: game*) стреля́ть (*impf*); (*wound*)
вы́стрелить (*perf*) в +*acc*; (*execute*)
расстре́ливать (расстреля́ть *perf*); (*film*)
снима́ть (снять* *perf*) ♦ *vi:* **to ~ (at)** стреля́ть
(вы́стрелить *perf*) (в +*acc*); (*FOOTBALL etc*)

бить* *(impf)* (по +*dat*); **to ~ past** *(move)*
проноси́ться* (пронести́сь* *perf*); **he shot
through the door** он влете́л в дверь
▶ **shoot down** *vt (plane)* сбива́ть (сбить* *perf*)
▶ **shoot in** *vi (rush in)* стремгла́в вбега́ть
(вбежа́ть* *perf*)
▶ **shoot out** *vi (rush out)* стремгла́в выбега́ть
(вы́бежать* *perf*)
▶ **shoot up** *vi (fig: prices)* подска́кивать
(подскочи́ть* *perf*); *(child)* вытя́гиваться
(вы́тянуться *perf*).
shooting [ˈʃuːtɪŋ] *n (shots, attack)* стрельба́;
(murder) уби́йство; *(CINEMA)* съёмки* *fpl*;
(HUNTING) охо́та.
shooting range *n* стре́льбище.
shooting star *n* па́дающая звезда́*.
shop [ʃɔp] *n* магази́н; *(also: workshop)*
мастерска́я *f adj* ♦ *vi (also: **go ~ping**)* ходи́ть*
(impf) по магази́нам, де́лать *(impf)* поку́пки;
repair ~ (ремо́нтная) мастерска́я; **to talk ~**
(fig) говори́ть *(impf)* *or* разгова́ривать *(impf)* о
рабо́те
▶ **shop around** *vi (also fig)* прице́ниваться
(прицени́ться* *perf*).
shopaholic [ˌʃɔpəˈhɔlɪk] *n (inf)* челове́к,
поме́шанный на магази́нах.
shop assistant *n (BRIT)* продаве́ц*(-вщи́ца).
shop floor *n (BRIT: INDUSTRY)* цех*.
shopkeeper [ˈʃɔpkiːpəʳ] *n* владе́лец*(-лица)
магази́на.
shoplifter [ˈʃɔplɪftəʳ] *n* вор*(о́вка*) *(краду́щий в
магази́нах)*.
shoplifting [ˈʃɔplɪftɪŋ] *n* кра́жа това́ров *(из
магази́нов)*.
shopper [ˈʃɔpəʳ] *n* покупа́тель(ница) *m(f)*.
shopping [ˈʃɔpɪŋ] *n (goods)* поку́пки* *fpl*.
shopping bag *n* хозя́йственная су́мка*.
shopping centre (*US* **shopping center**) *n*
торго́вый центр.
shopping mall *n (esp US)* торго́вый центр.
shopsoiled [ˈʃɔpsɔɪld] *adj (goods)* лежа́лый.
shop steward *n (BRIT: INDUSTRY)* цехово́й
ста́роста *m*.
shop window *n (also fig)* витри́на.
shore [ʃɔːʳ] *n* бе́рег* ♦ *vt:* **to ~ (up)** подпира́ть
(подпере́ть* *perf*); **on ~** на берегу́.
shore leave *n (NAUT)* увольне́ние на бе́рег.
shorn [ʃɔːn] *pp of* **shear** ♦ *adj:* **~ of** *(power,
protection etc)* лишённый (лишён) +*gen*.
short [ʃɔːt] *adj (in length, time)* коро́ткий*
(ко́роток); *(in height)* невысо́кий* (невысо́к);
(curt) ре́зкий* (ре́зок); *(insufficient)* ску́дный
♦ *n (also: **~ film**)* короткометра́жный фильм;
we are ~ of milk у нас ма́ло молока́; **I'm ten
pence ~** мне не хвата́ет десяти́ пе́нсов; **in ~**
коро́че говоря́; **water is in ~ supply** э́тот
райо́н испы́тывает нехва́тку воды́; **it is ~ for
...** э́то сокраще́ние от +*gen* ...; **a ~ time ago**

неда́вно; **in the ~ term** в настоя́щее вре́мя;
to cut ~ *(speech, visit)* сокраща́ть
(сократи́ть* *perf*); **everything ~ of ...** всё,
кро́ме +*gen* ...; **~ of doing** остаётся то́лько
+*infin* ...; **to fall ~ of** не выполня́ть
(вы́полнить *perf*); **we're running ~ of time** у
нас зака́нчивается вре́мя; **to stop ~**
застыва́ть (засты́ть* *perf*) на ме́сте; **to stop ~
of doing** не осме́ливаться (осме́литься *perf*)
+*infin*; *see also* **shorts**.
shortage [ˈʃɔːtɪdʒ] *n:* **a ~ of** нехва́тка +*gen*,
дефици́т +*gen*.
shortbread [ˈʃɔːtbrɛd] *n* ≈ песо́чное пече́нье.
short-change [ʃɔːtˈtʃeɪndʒ] *vt:* **to ~ sb**
обсчи́тывать (обсчита́ть *perf*) кого́-н.
short circuit *n* коро́ткое замыка́ние.
shortcoming [ˈʃɔːtkʌmɪŋ] *n* недоста́ток*.
short(crust) pastry [ˈʃɔːt(krʌst)-] *n (BRIT)*
песо́чное те́сто.
short cut *n* коро́ткий* путь* *m no pl*; *(fig)*
эконо́мный путь*.
shorten [ˈʃɔːtn] *vt (clothes)* укора́чивать
(укороти́ть* *perf*); *(visit)* сокраща́ть
(сократи́ть* *perf*).
shortening [ˈʃɔːtnɪŋ] *n (CULIN)* жир*.
shortfall [ˈʃɔːtfɔːl] *n* недоста́ток*.
shorthand [ˈʃɔːthænd] *n (BRIT)* стеногра́фия;
(fig) сокраще́ние; **to take sth down in ~**
стенографи́ровать (застенографи́ровать
(impf)) что-н.
shorthand notebook *n (BRIT)* стеногра́ф-
и́ческая тетра́дь *f*.
shorthand typist *n (BRIT)* стенографи́ст(ка*).
short list *n (BRIT)* спи́сок* оконча́тельных
кандида́тов.
short-lived [ʃɔːtˈlɪvd] *adj* кратковре́менный*
(кратковре́мен), недо́лгий* (недо́лог).
shortly [ˈʃɔːtlɪ] *adv* вско́ре.
shorts [ʃɔːts] *npl:* **(a pair of) ~** шо́рты *pl*.
short-sighted [ʃɔːtˈsaɪtɪd] *adj (BRIT: also fig)*
близору́кий* (близору́к).
short-sightedness [ʃɔːtˈsaɪtɪdnɪs] *n*
близору́кость *f*.
short-staffed [ʃɔːtˈstɑːft] *adj:* **to be ~**
испы́тывать *(impf)* нехва́тку персона́ла.
short story *n* расска́з.
short-tempered [ʃɔːtˈtɛmpəd] *adj*
вспы́льчивый (вспы́льчив).
short-term [ˈʃɔːttəːm] *adj (effect)* кратко-
вре́менный; *(borrowing)* краткосро́чный.
short time *n:* **to be on ~ ~** *(INDUSTRY)* быть*
(impf) на сокращённой рабо́чей неде́ле.
short wave *n (RADIO)* коро́ткие во́лны* *fpl* ♦ *adj*
(RADIO): **~ ~** коротково́лновый.
shot [ʃɔt] *pt, pp of* **shoot** ♦ *n (of gun)* вы́стрел*;
(shotgun pellets) дробь *f*; *(injection)* уко́л; *(PHOT)* сни́мок*; **to fire a ~ at
sb/sth** вы́стрелить *(perf)* в кого́-н/что-н; **to**

---

have a ~ at sth попытáть (*perf*) удáчи в чём-н;
to have a ~ at doing (*try*) пробовать
(попробовать *perf*) +*infin*; **to get ~ of sb/sth**
(*inf*) распространиться* (*perf*) с кем-н/чем-н; **a**
big ~ (*inf*) большáя шишка* *m/f*; **a good/poor**
~ (*person*) мéткий*/плохой стрелок*; **like a ~**
мигом.

shotgun ['ʃɔtɡʌn] *n* дробовик*.

should [ʃud] *aux vb*: **I ~ go now** я должен идти
тепéрь; **he ~ be there now** сейчáс он должен
быть там; **I ~ go if I were you** на Вáшем
мéсте я бы пошёл; **I ~ like to** я бы хотéл; **~**
he phone ... éсли он позвонит ....

shoulder ['ʃəuldə'] *n* (*ANAT*) плечо* ♦ *vt* (*fig*:
responsibility, blame) принимáть (принять*
perf) на себя; **to look over one's ~** смотрéть*
(посмотрéть* *perf*) чéрез плечо; **to rub ~'s**
with sb (*fig*) вращáться (*impf*) с кем-н в одних
кругáх; **to give sb the cold ~** обходиться*
(обойтись* *perf*) с кем-н прохлáдно.

shoulder bag *n* сýмка* на длинном ремнé.
shoulder blade *n* лопáтка*.
shoulder strap *n* бретéлька*; (*on dungarees*)
лямка*; (*on bag*) ремéнь* *m*.
shouldn't ['ʃudnt] = **should not**.
shout [ʃaut] *n* крик ♦ *vt* выкрикивать
(выкрикнуть *perf*) ♦ *vi* (*also: ~* **out**) кричáть
(*impf*); **to give sb a ~** крикнуть (*perf*) комý-н.
▶ **shout down** *vt* заглушáть (заглушить *perf*)
криками.

shouting ['ʃautɪŋ] *n* крик.
shouting match *n* (*inf*) крик, скандáл.
shove [ʃʌv] *vt* толкáть (*impf*); (*inf*: *put*): **to ~ sth**
in затáлкивать (затолкáть *perf*) что-н,
запихивать (запихáть *or* запихнýть *perf*)
что-н ♦ *n*: **to give sb/sth a ~** пихáть (пихнýть
perf) кого-н/что-н; **he ~d me out of the way**
он отпихнýл меня.
▶ **shove off** (*inf*) ♦ *vi* отвáливать (отвалить*
perf).

shovel ['ʃʌvl] *n* лопáта; (*mechanical*) ковш ♦ *vt*
(*snow, coal, earth*) грести* (сгрести* *perf*)
(*лопáтой*).

show [ʃəu] (*pt* **showed**, *pp* **shown**) *n* (*of emotion*)
покáз; (*semblance*) подобие; (*exhibition*)
выставка*; (*THEAT*) спектáкль *m*; (*TV*)
прогрáмма, шоу *nt ind*; (*CINEMA*) сеáнс ♦ *vt*
покáзывать (показáть* *perf*); (*courage etc*)
проявлять (проявить* *perf*) ♦ *vi* (*be evident*)
проявляться (проявиться* *perf*),
обнарýживать (обнарýжиться *perf*); (*inf*:
also: ~ **up**) являться (явиться* *perf*); **to ~ sb to**
his seat проводить* (провести* *perf*) кого-н
на мéсто; **to ~ sb to the door** укáзывать
(указáть* *perf*) комý-н на дверь; **to ~ a profit/**
loss (*COMM*) демонстрировать (*impf/perf*)
прибыль/убытки; **it just goes to ~ that ...** это
просто покáзывает, что, ...; **to ask for a ~ of**
hands просить* (попросить* *perf*) поднять
рýки (*при голосовáнии*); **for ~** для виду; **on ~**
(*exhibits etc*) на выставке; **who's running the**

~ here? (*inf*) кто здесь заправляет?
▶ **show in** *vt* (*person*) проводить* (провести*
perf)
▶ **show off** *vi* хвáстаться (похвáстаться *perf*) ♦
vt (*display*) хвáстаться (похвáстаться *perf*)
+*instr*
▶ **show out** *vt* (*person*) провожáть
(проводить* *perf*) к выходу
▶ **show up** *vi* (*stand out: against background*)
виднéться (*impf*); (: *fig*) обнарýживаться
(обнарýжиться *perf*); (*inf*: *turn up*) являться
(явиться* *perf*) ♦ *vt* (*uncover: imperfections*
etc) выявлять (выявить* *perf*).

showbiz ['ʃəubɪz] *n* (*inf*) = **show business**.
show business *n* шоу бизнес.
showcase ['ʃəukeɪs] *n* витрина; (*fig*)
показáтельный примéр.
showdown ['ʃəudaun] *n*: **to have a ~ (with)**
раскрывáть (раскрыть* *perf*) кáрты (+*dat*)
shower ['ʃauə'] *n* (*also: ~* **bath**) душ; (*of rain*)
ливень* *m*; (*of stones etc*) град; (*US*: *party*)
звáный вéчер ♦ *vi* принимáть (принять*
perf) душ ♦ *vt*: **to ~ sb with** (*gifts, abuse etc*)
осыпáть (осыпать* *perf*) кого-н +*instr*;
(*missiles*) забрáсывать (забросáть* *perf*); **to**
have *or* **take a ~** принимáть (принять* *perf*)
душ.
showercap ['ʃauəkæp] *n* шáпочка* (*для дýша*).
showerproof ['ʃauəpru:f] *adj* (*clothing*)
непромокáемый.
showery ['ʃauərɪ] *adj* дождливый.
showground ['ʃəugraund] *n* выставка* (*на*
открытом воздухе).
showing ['ʃəuɪŋ] *n* (*of film*) покáз.
show jumping *n* конкýр.
showman ['ʃəumən] *irreg n* (*at fair, circus*)
ведýщий* *m adj*, конферансьé *m ind*; (*owner of*
circus) хозяин цирка; (*fig*) позёр.
showmanship ['ʃəumənʃɪp] *n* талáнт.
shown [ʃəun] *pp of* **show**.
show-off ['ʃəuɔf] *n* (*inf*) хвастýн(ья).
showpiece ['ʃəupi:s] *n* (*of exhibition etc*)
центрáльный экспонáт; **this is a ~ of ...** это
является блестящим образом +*gen* ....
showroom ['ʃəurum] *n* демонстрационный
зал.
show trial *n* показáтельный процéсс.
showy ['ʃəuɪ] *adj* броский*.
shrank [ʃræŋk] *pt of* **shrink**.
shrapnel ['ʃræpnl] *n* шрапнéль *f*.
shred [ʃrɛd] *n* (*usu pl*) клочок*; (*fig*: *of truth,*
evidence) крупица ♦ *vt* крошить*
(накрошить* *perf*); (*CULIN*) шинковáть
(нашинковáть *perf*).
shredder ['ʃrɛdə'] *n* (*also*: **vegetable ~**)
шинковка; (*also*: **document ~**) машина для
дезинтегрáции докумéнтов.
shrew [ʃru:] *n* (*ZOOL*) землеройка*; (*pej*:
woman) змея.
shrewd [ʃru:d] *adj* проницáтельный*
(проницáтелен).

shrewdness ['ʃru:dnɪs] *n* проница́тельность *f*.
shriek [ʃri:k] *n* визг ♦ *vi* визжа́ть* *(impf)*.
shrift [ʃrɪft] *n*: **to give sb short ~** бы́стро отде́лываться (отде́латься *perf*) от кого́-н.
shrill [ʃrɪl] *adj* визгли́вый (визгли́в).
shrimp [ʃrɪmp] *n* (ме́лкая) креве́тка*.
shrimping ['ʃrɪmpɪŋ] *n* ло́вля креве́ток.
shrine [ʃraɪn] *n* (*tomb*) ра́ка; (*place of worship, also fig*) святы́ня.
shrink [ʃrɪŋk] (*pt* **shrank**, *pp* **shrunk**) *vi* (*cloth*) сади́ться* (сесть* *perf*); (*profits, audiences*) сокраща́ться (сократи́ться* *perf*); (*also:* **~ away**) отпря́нуть *(perf)* ♦ *vt*: **washing will ~ the dress** от сти́рки пла́тье сади́тся ♦ *n* (*inf: psychiatrist*) психиа́тор; **to ~ from sth** ускольза́ть (ускользну́ть *perf*) от +*gen*.
shrinkage ['ʃrɪŋkɪdʒ] *n* уса́дка.
shrink-wrap ['ʃrɪŋkræp] *vt* (*goods etc*) упако́вывать (упакова́ть *perf*) в уса́дочную плёнку.
shrivel ['ʃrɪvl] (*also:* **~ up**) *vt* высу́шивать (вы́сушить *perf*) ♦ *vi* высыха́ть (вы́сохнуть *perf*).
shroud [ʃraud] *n* са́ван ♦ *vt*: **~ed in mystery** оку́танный (оку́тан) в та́йну.
Shrove Tuesday ['ʃrəuv-] *n вто́рник на ма́сленой неде́ле*.
shrub [ʃrʌb] *n* куст*.
shrubbery ['ʃrʌbərɪ] *n* куста́рник.
shrug [ʃrʌg] *n* пожима́ние (*плеча́ми*) ♦ *vb*: **to ~ (one's shoulders)** пожима́ть (пожа́ть* *perf*) плеча́ми
▶ **shrug off** *vt* отма́хиваться (отмахну́ться *perf*) от +*gen*.
shrunk [ʃrʌŋk] *pp of* **shrink**.
shrunken ['ʃrʌŋkn] *adj* (*material*) се́вший; (*person, figure*) съёженный.
shudder ['ʃʌdəʳ] *n* дрожь *f* ♦ *vi* содрога́ться (содрогну́ться *perf*).
shuffle ['ʃʌfl] *vt* тасова́ть (стасова́ть *perf*) ♦ *vi*: **to ~ (one's feet)** волочи́ть *(impf)* но́ги.
shun [ʃʌn] *vt* избега́ть *(impf)* +*gen*.
shunt [ʃʌnt] *vt* (*train*) переводи́ть* (перевести́* *perf*) на друго́й путь ♦ *vi* (*RAIL*): **to ~ (to and fro)** маневри́ровать *(impf/perf)*.
shunting yard ['ʃʌntɪŋ-] *n* сортиро́вочная ста́нция.
shush [ʃuʃ] *excl* ш-ш.
shut [ʃʌt] (*pt, pp* **shut**) *vt* закрыва́ть (закры́ть* *perf*) ♦ *vi* закрыва́ться (закры́ться* *perf*)
▶ **shut down** *vt* закрыва́ть (закры́ть* *perf*); (*machine*) отключа́ть (отключи́ть* *perf*) ♦ *vi* закрыва́ться (закры́ться* *perf*); (*machine*) отключа́ться (отключи́ться *perf*)
▶ **shut off** *vt* (*supply etc*) отключа́ть (отключи́ть *perf*)
▶ **shut out** *vt* (*person, cold, noise*) не проупска́ть (пропусти́ть* *perf*); (*view,*

memory) заслоня́ть (заслони́ть *perf*)
▶ **shut up** *vi* (*inf: keep quiet*) заткну́ться *(perf)* ♦ *vt* (*close*) запира́ть (запере́ть* *perf*); (*silence*) затыка́ть (заткну́ть *perf*) рот +*dat*; **~ up!** заткни́сь!
shutdown ['ʃʌtdaun] *n* (*temporary*) приостановле́ние; (*permanent*) закры́тие.
shutter ['ʃʌtəʳ] *n* (*on window*) ста́вень* *m*; (*PHOT*) затво́р.
shuttle ['ʃʌtl] *n*: **~ plane** самолёт-челно́к; (*also:* **space ~**) шатл; (*also:* **~ service**) челно́чный маршру́т; (*for weaving*) челно́к ♦ *vi*: **to ~ between** соверша́ть *(impf)* челно́чные ре́йсы ме́жду +*instr* ♦ *vt* (*passengers*) вози́ть* *(impf)* туда́ и обра́тно.
shuttlecock ['ʃʌtlkɔk] *n* (*SPORT*) вола́н.
shuttle diplomacy *n* челно́чная диплома́тия.
shy [ʃaɪ] *adj* (*timid*) засте́нчивый (засте́нчив), стесни́тельный* (стесни́телен); (*reserved*) осторо́жный* (осторо́жен) ♦ *vi*: **to ~ away from doing** (*fig*) чужда́ться *(impf)* +*infin*; **to fight ~ of** избега́ть *(impf)* +*gen*; **to be ~ of doing** стесня́ться (постесня́ться *perf*) +*infin*.
shyly ['ʃaɪlɪ] *adv* засте́нчиво.
shyness ['ʃaɪnɪs] *n* (*see adj*) засте́нчивость *f*, стесни́тельность *f*; осторо́жность *f*.
Siamese [saɪə'mi:z] *adj*: **~ cat** сиа́мская ко́шка*; **~ twins** сиа́мские близнецы́ *mpl*.
Siberia [saɪ'bɪərɪə] *n* Сиби́рь *f*.
sibling ['sɪblɪŋ] *n* (*brother*) родно́й брат; (*sister*) родна́я сестра́.
Sicilian [sɪ'sɪlɪən] *adj* сицили́йский ♦ *n* сицили́ец*(-и́йка*).
Sicily ['sɪsɪlɪ] *n* Сици́лия.
sick [sɪk] *adj* (*ill*) больно́й* (бо́лен); (*humour*) пога́ный, скве́рный* (скве́рен); (*vomiting*): **he is/was ~** его́ рвёт/вы́рвало; (*nauseated*): **I feel ~** меня́ тошни́т; **to fall ~** заболева́ть (заболе́ть *perf*); **to be (off) ~** быть* *(impf)* на больни́чном; **a ~ person** больно́й челове́к*; **to be ~ of** (*of war etc*) смерте́льно уста́ть* *(perf)* от +*gen*; **I'm ~ of arguing/school** меня́ тошни́т от спо́ров/шко́лы.
sickbag ['sɪkbæg] *n* (*on airplane*) санита́рный паке́т.
sickbay ['sɪkbeɪ] *n* изоля́тор.
sickbed ['sɪkbed] *n* посте́ль *f* больно́го.
sick building *n* помеще́ние с нездоро́вым *микрокли́матом*.
sicken ['sɪkn] *vt* (*disgust*) вызыва́ть (вы́звать* *perf*) отвраще́ние у +*gen* ♦ *vi*: **to be ~ing for sth** заболева́ть *(impf)* чем-н.
sickening ['sɪknɪŋ] *adj* (*fig*) проти́вный (проти́вен).
sickle ['sɪkl] *n* серп*.
sick leave *n* о́тпуск по боле́зни.
sick list *n*: **to be on the ~ ~** быть* *(impf)* на бюллете́не *or* больни́чном.

---

sickly ['sɪklɪ] *adj* (*child, plant*) хи́лый* (хил); (*smell*) тошнотво́рный* (тошнотво́рен).

sickness ['sɪknɪs] *n* (*illness*) боле́знь *f*; (*vomiting*) рво́та.

sickness benefit *n* посо́бие по боле́зни.

sick note *n* бюллете́нь *m*, больни́чный лист*.

sick pay *n* опла́та по бюллете́ню *or* больни́чному листу́.

sickroom ['sɪkru:m] *n* ко́мната больно́го.

side [saɪd] *n* сторона́*; (*of body*) бок*; (*of paper*) страни́ца; (*team*) кома́нда; (*of hill*) склон ♦ *adj* (*door etc*) боково́й ♦ *vi*: **to ~ with sb** вставать* (встать* *perf*) на сто́рону кого́-н; **by the ~ of** у +*gen*; **by her ~** во́зле неё; **by ~** (*to walk*) ря́дом; (*to work*) бок о́ бок; **the right ~** (*of material*) лицо́; **the wrong ~** (*of material*) изна́нка; **we're on the wrong ~ of the road/river** мы не на то́й стороне́ доро́ги/реки́; **they are on our ~** они́ на на́шей стороне́; **from ~ to ~** с бо́ку на́ бок; **from all ~s** со всех сторо́н; **to take ~s (with sb)** принима́ть (приня́ть* *perf*) (чью-н) сто́рону; **a ~ of beef** полови́на говя́жьей ту́ши.

sideboard ['saɪdbɔ:d] *n* буфе́т; **~s** *npl* (*BRIT*) = **sideburns**.

sideburns ['saɪdbə:nz] *npl* бакенба́рды *pl*.

sidecar ['saɪdkɑ:ʳ] *n* (*AUT*) коля́ска* (*мотоци́кла*).

side dish *n* гарни́р.

side drum *n* ма́лый бараба́н.

side effect *n* побо́чное де́йствие.

sidekick ['saɪdkɪk] *n* (*inf*) подру́чный *m adj*.

sidelight ['saɪdlaɪt] *n* (*AUT*) боково́е освеще́ние.

sideline ['saɪdlaɪn] *n* (*SPORT*) боковая ли́ния; (*fig: supplementary job*) побо́чная рабо́та; **to stand on the ~s** стоя́ть* (*impf*) в стороне́.

sidelong ['saɪdlɔŋ] *adj* косо́й; **to give sb a ~ glance** смотре́ть* (посмотре́ть* *perf*) на кого́-н и́скоса.

side plate *n* десе́ртная таре́лка.

side road *n* просёлочная доро́га.

side-saddle ['saɪdsædl] *adv*: **to ride ~** е́хать* (*impf*) в да́мском седле́.

sideshow ['saɪdʃəu] *n* аттракцио́н.

sidestep ['saɪdstɛp] *vt* (*fig*) обходи́ть* (обойти́* *perf*) ♦ *vi* отступа́ть (отступи́ть* *perf*).

side street *n* переу́лок*.

sidetrack ['saɪdtræk] *vt* уводи́ть* (увести́* *perf*) в сто́рону.

sidewalk ['saɪdwɔ:k] *n* (*US*) тротуа́р.

sideways ['saɪdweɪz] *adv* (*go in, lean*) бо́ком; (*look*) и́скоса.

siding ['saɪdɪŋ] *n* (*RAIL*) запасно́й путь* *m*.

sidle ['saɪdl] *vi*: **to ~ up (to)** подходи́ть* (подойти́* *perf*) бочко́м (к +*dat*).

SIDS *n abbr* (*MED*: = *sudden infant death syndrome*) синдро́м внеза́пной сме́рти вне́шне здоро́вого младе́нца.

siege [si:dʒ] *n* оса́да; **to be under ~** быть* (*impf*) в оса́де; **to lay ~ to** осажда́ть (осади́ть* *perf*).

siege economy *n* засто́йная эконо́мика.

siege mentality *n* психоло́гия люде́й в оса́дном положе́нии.

Sierra Leone [sɪˈɛrəlɪˈəun] *n* Сье́рра-Лео́не.

siesta [sɪˈɛstə] *n* сие́ста.

sieve [sɪv] *n* (*CULIN*) си́то*; (*for garden*) решето́* ♦ *vt* просе́ивать (просе́ять *perf*).

sift [sɪft] *vt* (*flour, sand*) просе́ивать (просе́ять *perf*); (*also*: ~ **through**: *evidence etc*) просе́ивать (просе́ять *perf*).

sigh [saɪ] *n* вздох ♦ *vi* вздыха́ть (вздохну́ть *perf*).

sight [saɪt] *n* (*faculty*) зре́ние; (*spectacle*) вид; (*on gun*) прице́л ♦ *vt* замеча́ть (заме́тить* *perf*); **in ~** в по́ле зре́ния; **out of ~** из ви́да; **at ~** (*COMM*) по предъявле́нию; **at first ~** с пе́рвого взгля́да; **I know her by ~** я зна́ю её в лицо́; **to catch ~ of** замеча́ть (заме́тить* *perf*); **to lose ~ of sb/sth** теря́ть (потеря́ть *perf*) кого́-н/что-н из ви́ду; **to set one's ~s on sth** положи́ть* (*perf*) глаз на что-н; **to shoot sb on ~** стреля́ть (*impf*) в кого́-н на ме́сте.

sighted ['saɪtɪd] *adj* (*person*) зря́чий* (зряч); **partially ~** слабовидящий.

sightseeing ['saɪtsi:ɪŋ] *n* осмо́тр достопримеча́тельностей; **to go ~** осма́тривать (осмотре́ть* *perf*) достопримеча́тельности.

sightseer ['saɪtsi:əʳ] *n* тури́ст(ка*).

sign [saɪn] *n* (*notice*) вы́веска*; (*with hand*) знак; (*indication, evidence*) при́знак; (*also*: **road ~**) доро́жный знак ♦ *vt* (*document*) подпи́сывать (подписа́ть* *perf*); (*player*) нанима́ть (наня́ть* *perf*); **as a ~ of** в знак +*gen*; **it's a good/bad ~** э́то хоро́ший/плохо́й знак; **plus/minus ~** знак "плюс"/"ми́нус"; **there's no ~ of her changing her mind** нет никаки́х при́знаков того́, что она́ переду́мала; **he is showing ~s of improvement** у него́ видны́ при́знаки улучше́ния; **to ~ one's name** распи́сываться (расписа́ться* *perf*); **to ~ sth over to sb** передава́ть* (переда́ть* *perf*) что-н в дар кому́-н

▶ **sign away** *vt* (*rights etc*) передава́ть* (переда́ть* *perf*)

▶ **sign in** *vi* регистри́роваться (зарегистри́роваться *perf*)

▶ **sign off** *vi* зака́нчивать (зако́нчить *perf*)

▶ **sign on** *vi* (*MIL*) нанима́ться (наня́ться* *perf*); (*BRIT: as unemployed*) отмеча́ться (отме́титься* *perf*) как безрабо́тный; (*for course*) регистри́роваться (зарегистри́роваться *perf*) ♦ *vt* (*MIL: recruits*) набира́ть (набра́ть* *perf*); (*employee*) нанима́ть (наня́ть* *perf*)

▶ **sign out** *vi* выпи́сываться (вы́писаться* *perf*)

▶ **sign up** *vi* (*MIL*) нанима́ться (наня́ться* *perf*); (*for course*) регистри́роваться (зарегистри́роваться *perf*) ♦ *vt* (*player, recruit*) нанима́ть (наня́ть* *perf*)

signal ['sɪgnl] *n* сигна́л ♦ *vi* сигнализи́ровать

(*impf/perf*) ♦ *vt* (*person*) подавáть* (подáть*
perf) знак +*dat*; (*message*) передавáть*
(передáть* *perf*); **to ~ a right/left turn** (*AUT*)
давáть* (дать* *perf*) сигнáл прáвого/лéвого
поворóта; **to ~ to sb (to do)** подавáть*
(подáть* *perf*) знак комý-н (+*infin*).
signal box *n* сигнáльная бýдка*.
signalman [sɪgnlmən] *irreg n* стрéлочник.
signatory ['sɪgnətərɪ] *n* подписáвшая
сторонá*.
signature ['sɪgnətʃə'] *n* пóдпись *f*.
signature tune *n* музыкáльная шáпка*.
signet ring ['sɪgnət-] *n* кольцó* с печáткой.
significance [sɪg'nɪfɪkəns] *n* значéние; **that is of
no ~** это не имéет значéния.
significant [sɪg'nɪfɪkənt] *adj* (*amount, discovery
etc*) значи́тельный* (значи́телен); (*look,
smile*) многозначи́тельный*
(многозначи́телен); **it is ~ that** ... вáжно,
что ....
significantly [sɪg'nɪfɪkəntlɪ] *adv* (*see adj*)
значи́тельно; многозначи́тельно.
signify ['sɪgnɪfaɪ] *vt* (*subj: sign, gesture etc*)
означáть (*impf*); (: *person*) выражáть
(вы́разить* *perf*).
sign language *n* язы́к* знáков.
sign post *n* (*also fig*) указáтель *m*.
Sikh [si:k] *n* сикх ♦ *adj* си́кхский.
silage ['saɪlɪdʒ] *n* (*fodder*) си́лос; (*method*)
силосовáние.
silence ['saɪləns] *n* тишинá ♦ *vt* заставля́ть
(застáвить* *perf*) замолчáть.
silencer ['saɪlənsə'] *n* (*BRIT*) глуши́тель *m*.
silent ['saɪlənt] *adj* (*place, person, prayer*)
безмóлвный* (безмóлвен); (*machine*)
бесшýмный* (бесшýмен); (*taciturn*)
молчали́вый (молчали́в); (*film*) немóй; **to
remain ~** молчáть* (*impf*).
silently ['saɪləntlɪ] *adv* мóлча.
silent partner *n* (*COMM*) пасси́вный партнёр.
silhouette [sɪlu:'ɛt] *n* силуэ́т ♦ *vt*: **to be ~d
against** вырисóвываться (*impf*) на фóне +*gen*.
silicon ['sɪlɪkən] *n* крéмний.
silicon chip *n* крéмниевый кристáлл,
крéмниевая микропласти́нка.
silicone ['sɪlɪkəun] *n* силокóн.
Silicon Valley *n* зóна скоплéния предприя́тий,
занимáющихся вы́пуском вычисли́тельной
тéхники.
silk [sɪlk] *n* шёлк* ♦ *adj* шёлковый.
silky ['sɪlkɪ] *adj* шелкови́стый (шелкови́ст).
sill [sɪl] *n* (*also*: **window ~**) подокóнник; (*of
door*) порóг; (*AUT*) карни́з.
silly ['sɪlɪ] *adj* глу́пый* (глуп); **to do something
~** де́лать (сде́лать *perf*) глу́пость.
silo ['saɪləu] *n* (*on farm*) си́лосная бáшня*; (*for
missile*) стáртовая шáхта.
silt [sɪlt] *n* ил

► **silt up** *vi* заи́ливаться (заи́литься* *perf*) ♦ *vt*
засоря́ть (засори́ть *perf*).
silver ['sɪlvə'] *n* серебрó ♦ *adj* серéбряный.
silver foil *n* (*BRIT*) = **silver paper**.
silver paper *n* (*BRIT*) фольгá.
silver-plated [sɪlvə'pleɪtɪd] *adj* серебрёный.
silversmith ['sɪlvəsmɪθ] *n* серéбряных дел
мáстер.
silverware ['sɪlvəwɛə'] *n* серебрó.
silver wedding (anniversary) *n* серéбряная
свáдьба*.
silvery ['sɪlvrɪ] *adj* серебри́стый (серебри́ст);
(*sound*) серебри́стый, серéбряный.
similar ['sɪmɪlə'] *adj*: ~ **(to)** схóдный* (схóден)
(с +*instr*), подóбный* (подóбен) (+*dat*).
similarity [sɪmɪ'lærɪtɪ] *n* схóдство.
similarly ['sɪmɪləlɪ] *adv* (*in a similar way*)
подóбным óбразом; (*likewise*) таки́м же
óбразом.
simile ['sɪmɪlɪ] *n* сравнéние.
simmer ['sɪmə'] *vi* (*CULIN*) кипéть* (*impf*) на
мéдленном огнé

► **simmer down** *vi* (*fig: inf*) остывáть (осты́ть*
perf).
simper ['sɪmpə'] *vi* жемáнничать (*impf*).
simpering ['sɪmprɪŋ] *adj* (*person, smile*)
жемáнный* (жемáнен).
simple ['sɪmpl] *adj* (*easy, plain*) простóй*
(прост); (*foolish*) недалёкий* (недалёк); **the
~ truth** очеви́дная и́стина.
simple interest *n* просты́е процéнты *mpl*.
simple-minded [sɪmpl'maɪndɪd] *adj*
простодýшный* (простодýшен).
simpleton ['sɪmpltən] *n* простáк.
simplicity [sɪm'plɪsɪtɪ] *n* (*see adj*) простотá;
недалёкость *f*.
simplification [sɪmplɪfɪ'keɪʃən] *n* упрощéние.
simplify ['sɪmplɪfaɪ] *vt* упрощáть (упрости́ть*
perf).
simply ['sɪmplɪ] *adv* прóсто.
simulate ['sɪmjuleɪt] *vt* (*enthusiasm*)
симули́ровать (*impf/perf*); (*innocence*)
изображáть (изобрази́ть* *perf*).
simulated ['sɪmjuleɪtɪd] *adj* (*hair, fur*)
поддéльный; (*nuclear explosion*)
имити́рованный.
simulation [sɪmju'leɪʃən] *n* притвóрство.
simultaneous [sɪməl'teɪnɪəs] *adj*
одноврéменный.
simultaneously [sɪməl'teɪnɪəslɪ] *adv*
одноврéменно.
sin [sɪn] *n* грех* ♦ *vi* греши́ть (согреши́ть *perf*).
Sinai ['saɪneɪaɪ] *n* Синáйский полуóстров.
since [sɪns] *adv* с тех пор ♦ *conj* (*time*) с тех пор,
как; (*because*) так как ♦ *prep*: ~ **July** с ию́ля;
~ **then, ever** ~ с тех пор; **it's two weeks ~ I
wrote** ужé две недéли с тех пор, как я
написáл; ~ **our last meeting** со врéмени

---

* marks translations which have irregular inflections. The Russian-English side of the dictionary gives inflectional information.

нашей последней встречи.

sincere [sɪn'sɪəʳ] *adj* искренний* (искренен).

sincerely [sɪn'sɪəlɪ] *adv* искренне; **Yours ~** искренне Вам.

sincerity [sɪn'sɛrɪtɪ] *n* искренность *f*.

sine [saɪn] *n* (MATH) синус.

sine qua non [sɪnɪkwɑ:'nɔn] *n* необходимое условие.

sinew ['sɪnju:] *n* сухожилие.

sinful ['sɪnful] *adj* грешный* (грешен).

sing [sɪŋ] (*pt* **sang**, *pp* **sung**) *vti* петь* (спеть* *perf*).

Singapore [sɪŋə'pɔ:'] *n* Сингапур.

singe [sɪndʒ] *vt* палить (опалить *perf*); (*clothes*) подпаливать (подпалить *perf*).

singer ['sɪŋəʳ] *n* певец*(-вица).

Singhalese [sɪŋə'li:z] *adj* = **Sinhalese**.

singing ['sɪŋɪŋ] *n* пение; (*in the ears*) звон.

single ['sɪŋgl] *adj* (*individual*) одинокий*; (*man*) холостой* (холост); (*woman*) незамужняя; (*not double*) одинарный* (одинарен) ◆ *n* (BRIT: *also:* ~ **ticket**) билет в один конец; (*record*) сорокопятка*; **not a** ~ **one was left** ни одного не осталось; **every ~ day** каждый божий день; ~ **spacing** одинарное расстояние

▶ **single out** *vt* (*choose*) отбирать (отобрать* *perf*); (*distinguish*) выделять (выделить *perf*).

single bed *n* односпальная кровать *f*.

single-breasted ['sɪŋglbrɛstɪd] *adj* однобортный.

Single European Market *n*: **the ~ ~ ~** Единый европейский* рынок*.

single file *n*: **in ~ ~** в колонку.

single-handed [sɪŋgl'hændɪd] *adv* без посторонней помощи.

single-minded [sɪŋgl'maɪndɪd] *adj* целеустремлённый* (целеустремлён).

single parent *n* (*mother*) мать-одиночка*; (*father*) отец-одиночка*.

single room *n* комната на одного.

singles ['sɪŋglz] *n* (TENNIS) один на один ◆ *npl* (*single people*) несемейные *pl adj*.

singles bar *n* бар для несемейных.

single-sex [sɪŋgl'sɛks] *adj* раздельный.

singly ['sɪŋglɪ] *adv* (*alone, one by one*) врозь, в отдельности.

singsong ['sɪŋsɔŋ] *adj* (*tone*) монотонно идущий то вверх, то вниз ◆ *n*: **to have a ~** попеть* (*perf*) хором.

singular ['sɪŋgjuləʳ] *adj* необычайный* (необычаен); (LING) единственный ◆ *n* (LING) единственное число; **in the feminine ~** женского рода единственного числа.

singularly ['sɪŋgjuləlɪ] *adv* необычайно.

Sinhalese [sɪnhə'li:z] *adj* сингальский* ◆ *n inv* сингалец*(-ка*); (LING) сингальский язык*.

sinister ['sɪnɪstəʳ] *adj* зловещий* (зловещ).

sink [sɪŋk] (*pt* **sank**, *pp* **sunk**) *n* раковина ◆ *vt* (*ship*) топить* (потопить* *perf*); (*well*) рыть* (вырыть* *perf*); (*foundations*) врывать

(врыть* *perf*) ◆ *vi* (*ship*) тонуть* (потонуть* *perf*); (*heart, spirits*) падать (упасть* *perf*); (*ground*) оседать (осесть* *perf*); (*also:* ~ **back**, ~ **down**) откидываться (откинуться *perf*); **to ~ sth into** (*teeth, claws etc*) вонзать (вонзить* *perf*) что-н в +*acc*; **he sank into a chair/the mud** он опустился на стул/провалился в грязь

▶ **sink in** *vi* (*fig*): **it took a long time for her words to ~ in** потребовалось долгое время чтобы до меня дошли её слова.

sinking ['sɪŋkɪŋ] *adj* (*sun*) опускающийся; (*ship*) тонущий; **I had a ~ feeling** у меня всё опустилось.

sinking fund *n* (COMM) фонд погашения.

sink unit *n* комбинированная *or* встроенная раковина.

sinner ['sɪnəʳ] *n* грешник(-ица).

Sinn Féin *n* Шинн Фейн (*ирландская политическая партия*).

Sino- ['saɪnəu] *prefix* сино-, китае-.

sinuous ['sɪnjuəs] *adj* извивающийся.

sinus ['saɪnəs] *n* пазуха.

SIPS *n abbr* (= *side impact protection system*) система защиты автомобилей от боковых ударов.

sip [sɪp] *n* маленький* глоток* ◆ *vt* пить* (выпить* *perf*) маленькими глотками.

siphon ['saɪfən] *n* сифон

▶ **siphon off** *vt* выкачивать (выкачать *perf*).

sir [sə'] *n* сэр, господин; **S~ John Smith** Сэр Джон Смит; **yes ~** да, сэр; **Dear S~** (*in letter*) Уважаемый господин.

siren ['saɪərn] *n* сирена.

sirloin ['sə:lɔɪn] *n* (*also:* ~ **steak**) говяжье филе *nt ind*.

sirocco [sɪ'rɔkəu] *n* сирокко *m ind*.

sisal ['saɪsəl] *n* сизаль *m*.

sissy ['sɪsɪ] *n* (*inf*) неженка* *m/f*.

sister ['sɪstəʳ] *n* (*also* REL) сестра*; (BRIT: MED) (медицинская *or* мед-) сестра* ◆ *cpd*: ~ **organization** параллельная организация; ~ **ship** однотипное судно*.

sister-in-law ['sɪstərɪnlɔ:] *n* (*brother's wife*) невестка*; (*husband's sister*) золовка*; (*wife's sister*) своячeница.

sit [sɪt] (*pt, pp* **sat**) *vi* (*sit down*) садиться* (сесть* *perf*); (*be sitting*) сидеть* (*impf*); (*assembly*) заседать (*impf*); (*for painter*) позировать (*impf*) ◆ *vt* (*exam*) сдавать* (сдать* *perf*) экзамен; **to ~ on a committee** входить* (*impf*) в комитет; **to ~ tight** не принимать (*impf*) никаких действий

▶ **sit about** *vi* сидеть* (*impf*)

▶ **sit around** *vi* = **sit about**

▶ **sit back** *vi* (*in seat*) сидеть* (*impf*)

▶ **sit down** *vi* садиться* (сесть* *perf*); **to be ~ting down** сидеть* (*impf*)

▶ **sit in on** *vt fus* (*meeting*) присутствовать (*impf*) в/на +*prp*

▶ **sit up** *vi* (*after lying*) приподниматься (приподняться* *perf*); (*straight*)

выпрямля́ться (вы́прямиться* *perf*); (*not go to bed*) заси́живаться (засиде́ться* *perf*).

sitcom ['sɪtkɔm] *n abbr* (*TV*) = **situation comedy**.

sit-down ['sɪtdaun] *adj*: **a ~ strike** сидя́чая забасто́вка*; **a ~ meal** приём пи́щи, си́дя.

site [saɪt] *n* (*place*) ме́сто*; (*also:* **building ~**) строи́тельная площа́дка* ◆ *vt* (*factory, missiles*) помеща́ть (помести́ть* *perf*).

sit-in ['sɪtɪn] *n* демонстрати́вное заня́тие помеще́ния.

siting ['saɪtɪŋ] *n* (*location*) расположе́ние.

sitter ['sɪtə'] *n* (*for painter*) нату́рщик(-ица); (*also:* **baby-~**) приходя́щая ня́ня.

sitting ['sɪtɪŋ] *n* (*of assembly etc*) заседа́ние; (*in canteen*) сме́на.

sitting member *n* (*POL*) де́йствующий* депута́т парла́мента.

sitting room *n* гости́ная *f adj*.

sitting tenant *n* (*BRIT*) квартиросъёмщик (-ица).

situate ['sɪtjueɪt] *vt* располага́ть (расположи́ть* *perf*).

situated ['sɪtjueɪtɪd] *adj* располо́женный* (располо́жен); **to be ~** находи́ться* (*impf*).

situation [sɪtju'eɪʃən] *n* (*state*) ситуа́ция, положе́ние; (*job*) ме́сто*; (*location*) ме́сто*, положе́ние; "**situations vacant**" (*BRIT*) "вака́нтные места́".

situation comedy *n* коме́дия положе́ний.

six [sɪks] *n* шесть*; *see also* **five**.

six-pack ['sɪkspæk] *n шестибуты́лочная упако́вка пи́ва*.

sixteen [sɪks'ti:n] *n* шестна́дцать*; *see also* **five**.

sixteenth [sɪks'ti:nθ] *adj* шестна́дцатый; *see also* **fifth**.

sixth ['sɪksθ] *adj* шесто́й ◆ *n* (*fraction*) одна́ шеста́я *f adj*, шеста́я часть *f*; **the upper/lower ~** (*BRIT: SCOL*) пе́рвая/ста́рая ступе́нь вы́пускно́го кла́сса; *see also* **fifth**.

sixtieth ['sɪkstɪθ] *adj* шестидеся́тый; *see also* **fifth**.

sixty ['sɪkstɪ] *n* шестьдеся́т*; *see also* **fifty**.

size [saɪz] *n* разме́р; (*extent*) величина́, масшта́б; (*glue*) клей*; **I take ~ 14** я ношу́ четы́рнадцатый разме́р; **the small/large ~** ма́ленького/большо́го разме́ра; **it's the ~ of** ... э́то разме́ром с +*acc* ...; **cut to ~** обре́занный согла́сно разме́рам +*gen*.

▶ **size up** *vt* оце́нивать (оцени́ть* *perf*).

sizeable ['saɪzəbl] *adj* поря́дочный.

sizzle ['sɪzl] *vi* шипе́ть* (*impf*).

SK *abbr* (*CANADA*) = Saskatchewan.

skate [skeɪt] *n* (*also:* **ice ~**) конёк*; (*also:* **roller ~**) ро́ликовый конёк*, ро́лик; (*fish: pl inv*) скат ◆ *vi* ката́ться (*impf*) на конька́х

▶ **skate around** *vt fus* (*problem, issue*) обходи́ть* (обойти́* *perf*)

▶ **skate over** *vt fus* (*problem, issue*)

игнори́ровать (*impf/perf*).

skateboard ['skeɪtbɔ:d] *n* ро́ликовая доска́*.

skater ['skeɪtə'] *n* конькобе́жец*(-жка*).

skating ['skeɪtɪŋ] *n* (*for pleasure*) ката́ние на конька́х; (*SPORT*) конькобе́жный спорт.

skating rink *n* като́к*.

skeleton ['skɛlɪtn] *n* (*ANAT*) скеле́т*; (*TECH*) карка́с*; (*outline*) набро́сок*, схе́ма.

skeleton key *n* отмы́чка*.

skeleton staff *n* минима́льный персона́л.

skeptic *etc* ['skɛptɪk] (*US*) = **sceptic** *etc*.

sketch [skɛtʃ] *n* (*drawing*) эски́з, набро́сок*; (*outline*) набро́сок*; (*THEAT, TV*) скетч ◆ *vt* (*drawing*) наброса́ть (*impf*); (*also:* **~ out**) обрисо́вывать (обрисова́ть* *perf*) в о́бщих черта́х.

sketchbook ['skɛtʃbuk] *n* альбо́м для зарисо́вок.

sketchpad ['skɛtʃpæd] *n* блокно́т для зарисо́вок.

sketchy ['skɛtʃɪ] *adj* пове́рхностный* (пове́рхностен).

skew [skju:] *n*: **on the ~** (*BRIT*) ко́со, кри́во.

skewed [skju:d] *adj* (*idea, outlook*) искажённый (искажён).

skewer ['skju:ə'] *n* ве́ртел.

ski [ski:] *n* лы́жа ◆ *vi* ката́ться (*impf*) на лы́жах.

ski boot *n* лы́жный боти́нок*.

skid [skɪd] *n* (*AUT*) зано́с, юз ◆ *vi* скользи́ть* (*impf*); (*AUT*) идти́* (пойти́* *perf*) ю́зом; **the car went into a ~** маши́ну занесло́.

skid mark *n* тормозно́й след*.

skier ['ski:ə'] *n* лы́жник(-ица).

skiing ['ski:ɪŋ] *n* (*for pleasure*) ката́ние на лы́жах; (*SPORT*) лы́жный спорт; **to go ~** идти́* (пойти́* *perf*) *or* éхать* (поéхать* *perf*) ката́ться на лы́жах.

ski instructor *n* инстру́ктор по лы́жному спо́рту.

ski jump *n* (*ramp*) лы́жный трампли́н; (*event*) прыжки́ *mpl* на лы́жах с трампли́на.

skilful ['skɪlful] (*US* **skillful**) *adj* иску́сный* (иску́сен), уме́лый (умёл).

ski lift *n* (лы́жный) подъёмник.

skill [skɪl] *n* (*ability, dexterity*) мастерство́; (*computer skill etc*) на́вык.

skilled [skɪld] *adj* (*able*) иску́сный* (иску́сен), уме́лый (умёл); (*worker*) квалифиц-и́рованный.

skillet ['skɪlɪt] *n* (*CULIN*) неглубо́кая сковорода́*.

skillful ['skɪlful] *adj* (*US*) = **skilful**.

skil(l)fully ['skɪlfəlɪ] *adv* иску́сно, уме́ло.

skim [skɪm] *vt* (*milk*) снима́ть (снять* *perf*) сли́вки с +*gen*; (*soup*) снима́ть (снять* *perf*) на́кипь с +*gen*; (*glide over*) скользи́ть* (*impf*) над +*instr* ◆ *vi*: **to ~ through** пробежа́ть* (*perf*).

skimmed milk [skɪmd-] *n* обезжи́ренное

молоко́.

skimp [skɪmp] *vt* (*also*: ~ **on**: *work*)
манки́ровать (*impf/perf*) +*instr*; (: *cloth etc*)
эконо́мить* (*impf*) на +*prp*.

skimpy ['skɪmpɪ] *adj* ску́дный* (ску́ден); (*skirt*)
те́сный* (те́сен).

skin [skɪn] *n* (*of person*) ко́жа; (*of animal*)
шку́ра; (*of fruit, vegetable*) кожура́; (*of
grapes, tomatoes*) ко́жица ♦ *vt* (*fruit etc*)
снима́ть (снять* *perf*) кожуру́ с +*gen*,
чи́стить (очи́стить* *perf*); (*animal*) снима́ть
(снять* *perf*) шку́ру с +*gen*, свежева́ть
(освежева́ть *perf*); **she is soaked to the** ~ она́
промо́кла до ни́тки.

skin cancer *n* рак ко́жи.

skin-deep ['skɪn'diːp] *adj* пове́рхностный*
(пове́рхностен).

skin-diver ['skɪndaɪvə'] *n* аквалангист(ка*).

skin diving *n* подво́дное пла́ванье.

skinflint ['skɪnflɪnt] *n* (*inf*) скря́га *m/f*.

skin graft *n* ко́жный трансплантáт.

skinhead ['skɪnhɛd] *n* бритоголо́вый(-ая) *m(f)*
adj.

skinny ['skɪnɪ] *adj* то́щий* (тощ).

skin test *n* ана́лиз ко́жи.

skintight ['skɪntaɪt] *adj* в обтя́жку.

skip [skɪp] *n* прыжо́к*, скачо́к*; (*BRIT: container*)
скип ♦ *vi* подпры́гивать (подпры́гнуть *perf*);
(*with rope*) скака́ть* (*impf*) ♦ *vt* (*miss out*)
пропуска́ть (пропусти́ть* *perf*); **to** ~ **school**
(*esp US*) прогу́ливать (прогуля́ть *perf*)
уро́ки.

ski pants *npl* лы́жные брю́ки *pl*.

ski pole *n* лы́жная па́лка*.

skipper ['skɪpə'] *n* (*NAUT*) шки́пер, капита́н;
(*SPORT*) капита́н ♦ *vt* быть* (*impf*) капита́ном
+*gen*.

skipping rope ['skɪpɪŋ-] *n* (*BRIT*) скака́лка*.

ski resort *n* лы́жная ба́за.

skirmish ['skə:mɪʃ] *n* сты́чка*.

skirt [skə:t] *n* ю́бка* ♦ *vt* обходи́ть* (обойти́*
perf).

skirting board ['skə:tɪŋ-] *n* (*BRIT*) пли́нтус.

ski run *n* лыжня́.

ski slope *n* лы́жный спуск.

ski suit *n* лы́жный костю́м.

skit [skɪt] *n* паро́дия.

ski tow *n* букси́рный подъёмник.

skittle ['skɪtl] *n* ке́гля*; ~**s** *npl* (*game*) ке́гли* *fpl*.

skive [skaɪv] *vi* (*BRIT: inf*) сачкова́ть (*impf*).

skulk [skʌlk] *vi* (*hide*) пря́таться* (*impf*); (*prowl
about*) кра́сться* (*impf*).

skull [skʌl] *n* че́реп*.

skullcap ['skʌlkæp] *n* ермо́лка*.

skunk [skʌŋk] *n* (*animal*) скунс*; (*fur*)
ску́нсовый мех*.

sky [skaɪ] *n* не́бо*; **to praise sb to the skies**
превозноси́ть* (превознести́* *perf*) кого́-н до
небе́с.

sky-blue [skaɪ'bluː] *adj* небе́сно-голубо́й,
лазу́рный.

skydiving ['skaɪdaɪvɪŋ] *n* свобо́дное паде́ние
(*при прыжка́х с парашю́та*).

sky-high ['skaɪ'haɪ] *adj* (*prices*) сумасше́дший*;
(*structure*) до небе́с; **to blow** ~ разноси́ть*
(разнести́* *perf*) вчисту́ю.

skylark ['skaɪlɑːk] *n* жа́воронок*.

skylight ['skaɪlaɪt] *n* окно́* в кры́ше.

skyline ['skaɪlaɪn] *n* горизо́нт; (*of city*) силуэ́т.

skyscraper ['skaɪskreɪpə'] *n* небоскрёб.

slab [slæb] *n* (*of stone*) плита́*; (*of wood*)
пласти́на; (*of cake, cheese*) кусо́к*.

slack [slæk] *adj* (*rope*) прови́сший; (*trousers*)
вися́щий; (*discipline*) сла́бый* (слаб);
(*security*) плохо́й* (плох); (*market*) вя́лый;
(*demand*) небольшо́й ♦ *n* (*in rope etc*)
слабина́; ~**s** *npl* (*trousers*) брю́ки *pl*; **business
is** ~ в дела́х засто́й.

slacken ['slækn] *vi* (*also*: ~ **off**: *demand, speed*)
па́дать (упа́сть* *perf*), (*rain*) перестава́ть*
(переста́ть* *perf*) ♦ *vt* (*grip, clothing etc*)
ослабля́ть (осла́бить* *perf*); (*speed*) снижа́ть
(сни́зить* *perf*).

slacker ['slækə'] *n* (*inf*) ло́дырь *m*.

slag heap [slæg-] *n* шла́ковая гора́*.

slag off *vt* (*BRIT: inf*): **to slag sb off** перемыва́ть
(перемы́ть* *perf*) кому́-н ко́сточки.

slain [sleɪn] *pp of* **slay**.

slake [sleɪk] *vt*: **to** ~ **one's thirst** утоля́ть
(утоли́ть *perf*) жа́жду.

slalom ['slɑːləm] *n* сла́лом.

slam [slæm] *vt* (*door*) хло́пать (хло́пнуть *perf*)
+*instr*; (*throw*) швыря́ть (швырну́ть *perf*);
(*criticize*) раскритикова́ть (*perf*) ♦ *vi* (*door*)
захло́пываться (захло́пнуться *perf*); **to** ~ **on
the brakes** ре́зко тормози́ть* (затормози́ть*
perf).

slammer ['slæmə'] *n* (*inf*) кутузка.

slander ['slɑːndə'] *n* клевета́ ♦ *vt* клевета́ть*
(наклевета́ть* *perf*) на +*acc*.

slanderous ['slɑːndrəs] *adj* клеветни́ческий*.

slang [slæŋ] *n* (*informal language*) сленг;
(*jargon*) жарго́н.

slanging match ['slæŋɪŋ-] *n* перебра́нка*.

slant [slɑːnt] *n* накло́н; (*fig: approach*) укло́н.

slanted ['slɑːntɪd] *adj* (*roof*) накло́нный,
пока́тый; (*eyes*) раско́сый.

slanting ['slɑːntɪŋ] *adj* = **slanted**.

slap [slæp] *n* шлепо́к* ♦ *vt* шлёпать (шлёпнуть
perf) ♦ *adv* (*directly*) пря́мо; **to** ~ **sb in the face**
дать* (*perf*) кому́-н пощёчину; **to** ~ **sth on sth**
(*paint etc*) ля́пать (наля́пать *perf*) что-н на
что-н; **it fell** ~ **in the middle** оно́ упа́ло пря́мо
посереди́не.

slapdash ['slæpdæʃ] *adj* небре́жный*
(небре́жен).

slapstick ['slæpstɪk] *n* фарс.

slap-up ['slæpʌp] *adj*: **a** ~ **meal** (*BRIT*)
роско́шный обе́д.

slash [slæʃ] *vt* ре́зать* (поре́зать* *perf*); (*fig:
prices*) ре́зко снижа́ть (сни́зить* *perf*).

slat [slæt] *n* пла́нка*.

slate [sleɪt] *n* (*material*) сла́нец*; (*tile*)
ши́ферная пли́тка* ♦ *vt* (*fig*) разноси́ть*
(разнести́* *perf*) в пух и прах.

slaughter ['slɔ:təʳ] *n* (*of animals*) убо́й; (*of
people*) резня́ ♦ *vt* (*animals*) забива́ть
(заби́ть* *perf*); (*people*) ре́зать* (*impf*).

slaughterhouse ['slɔ:təhaus] *n* скотобо́йня.

Slav [slɑ:v] *adj* славя́нский* ♦ *n* славяни́н
(-я́нка).

slave [sleɪv] *n* раб*(ы́ня) ♦ *vi* (*also:* ~ **away**)
рабо́тать (*impf*) как раб; **to** ~ (**away**) **at sth**
рабо́тать (*impf*) над чем-н как про́клятый.

slave-driver ['sleɪvdraɪvəʳ] *n* (*inf*) де́спот.

slave labour *n* (*also fig*) ра́бский* труд*.

slaver ['slævəʳ] *vi* пуска́ть (*impf*) слюну́.

slavery ['sleɪvərɪ] *n* ра́бство.

Slavic ['slævɪk] *adj* славя́нский*.

slavish ['sleɪvɪʃ] *adj* ра́бский*; (*copy*) слепо́й.

slavishly ['sleɪvɪʃlɪ] *adv* по-ра́бски.

Slavonic [slə'vɔnɪk] *adj* славя́нский*.

slay [sleɪ] (*pt* **slew**, *pp* **slain**) *vt* поража́ть
(порази́ть* *perf*).

SLD *n abbr* (*BRIT: POL*) = Social and Liberal
Democratic Party.

sleazy ['sli:zɪ] *adj* (*place*) запу́щенный*
(запу́щен).

sled [slɛd] *n* (*esp US*) = **sledge**.

sledge [slɛdʒ] *n* са́ни* *pl*; (*for children*) са́нки *pl*.

sledgehammer ['slɛdʒhæməʳ] *n* кува́лда.

sleek [sli:k] *adj* (*shiny, smooth: fur*)
лосня́щийся; (: *hair*) блестя́щий* и гла́дкий*;
(*car, boat etc*) аэродинами́чный.

sleep [sli:p] (*pt, pp* **slept**) *n* сон* ♦ *vi* спать* (*impf*);
(*spend night*) ночева́ть* (переночева́ть* *perf*)
♦ *vt*: **the house can** ~ **four** в до́ме мо́жно
размести́ть четверы́х; **to go to** ~ засыпа́ть
(засну́ть *perf*); **to have a good night's** ~
(хорошо́) вы́спаться* (*perf*); **to put to** ~
(*animal*) усыпля́ть (усыпи́ть* *perf*); **to** ~
lightly спать* (*impf*) чу́тко; **to** ~ **with sb** спать*
(*impf*) с кем-н

▸ **sleep around** *vi* спать* (*impf*) с кем попа́ло

▸ **sleep in** *vi* (*oversleep*) просыпа́ть (проспа́ть*
perf); (*lie late*) отсыпа́ться (отоспа́ться* *perf*).

sleeper ['sli:pəʳ] *n* (*RAIL: train*) по́езд* со
спа́льными ваго́нами; (: *carriage*) спа́льный
ваго́н; (: *berth*) спа́льное ме́сто*; (: *BRIT: on
track*) шпа́ла; (*person*) спя́щий(-ая) *m(f) adj*.

sleepily ['sli:pɪlɪ] *adv* со́нно.

sleeping ['sli:pɪŋ] *adj* (*person*) спя́щий.

sleeping bag *n* спа́льный мешо́к*.

sleeping car *n* спа́льный ваго́н.

sleeping partner *n* (*BRIT: COMM*) = **silent
partner**.

sleeping pill *n* снотво́рное *nt adj*, снотво́рная
табле́тка*.

sleeping sickness *n* со́нная боле́знь *f*.

sleepless ['sli:plɪs] *adj* (*night*) бессо́нный.

sleeplessness ['sli:plɪsnɪs] *n* бессо́нница.

sleepwalk ['sli:pwɔ:k] *vi* ходи́ть* (*impf*) во сне.

sleepwalker ['sli:pwɔ:kəʳ] *n* луна́тик.

sleepy ['sli:pɪ] *adj* со́нный; **I feel** *or* **am** ~ мне
хо́чется спать.

sleet [sli:t] *n* дождь *m* со сне́гом.

sleeve [sli:v] *n* (*of jacket etc*) рука́в*; (*of record*)
конве́рт; **to have sth up one's** ~ име́ть (*impf*)
ко́е-что на уме́.

sleeveless ['sli:vlɪs] *adj* без рукаво́в.

sleigh [sleɪ] *n* са́ни* *pl*.

sleight [slaɪt] *n*: ~ **of hand** ло́вкость *f* рук.

slender ['slɛndəʳ] *adj* (*figure*) стро́йный*
(стро́ен); (*means*) ску́дный* (ску́ден);
(*majority*) небольшо́й.

slept [slɛpt] *pt, pp of* **sleep**.

sleuth [slu:θ] *n* сы́щик.

slew [slu:] *vi* (*BRIT: also:* ~ **round**) кру́то
повора́чивать (поверну́ть *perf*) ♦ *pt of* **slay**.

slice [slaɪs] *n* (*of meat*) кусо́к*; (*of bread, lemon*)
ло́мтик; (*also:* **fish** ~) ры́бный нож; (*also:*
cake ~) лопа́тка* для то́рта ♦ *vt* (*bread, meat
etc*) нареза́ть (наре́зать* *perf*), ре́зать*
(наре́зать* *perf*); ~**d bread** наре́занный хлеб.

slick [slɪk] *adj* (*performance*) гла́дкий*;
(*salesman, answer*) бо́йкий* (бо́ек) ♦ *n* (*also:*
oil ~) плёнка не́фти.

slid [slɪd] *pt, pp of* **slide**.

slide [slaɪd] (*pt, pp* **slid**) *n* (*downward movement*)
скольже́ние; (*in playground*) де́тская го́рка*;
(*PHOT*) слайд; (*BRIT: also:* **hair** ~) зако́лка*;
(*also:* **microscope** ~) предме́тное стекло́*; (*in
prices*) сниже́ние ♦ *vi* задвига́ть (задви́нуть
perf), сова́ть* (су́нуть *perf*) ♦ *vi* скользи́ть*
(скользну́ть *perf*); **to let things** ~ (*fig*)
запуска́ть (запусти́ть* *perf*) дела́, пусти́ть*
(*perf*) дела́ самотёком.

slide projector *n* диапрое́ктор.

slide rule *n* логарифми́ческая лине́йка.

sliding door ['slaɪdɪŋ-] *n* задвижна́я дверь *f*.

sliding roof *n* (*AUT*) сдвига́ющийся верх.

sliding scale *n* скользя́щий* тари́ф.

slight [slaɪt] *adj* (*slim: figure*) то́нкий* (то́нок);
(*frail*) хру́пкий* (хру́пок); (*small, trivial*)
незначи́тельный; (*error*) небольшо́й;
(*accent*) сла́бый*; (*pain*) неси́льный ♦ *n* (*insult*)
униже́ние; **the** ~**est noise** мале́йший* шум; **I
haven't the** ~**est idea** я поня́тия не име́ю; **not
in the** ~**est** ниско́лько.

slightly ['slaɪtlɪ] *adv* немно́го, слегка́; ~ **built**
хру́пкого сложе́ния.

slim [slɪm] *adj* (*figure*) стро́йный* (стро́ен);
(*chance*) небольшо́й ♦ *vi* худе́ть (похуде́ть
perf).

slime [slaɪm] *n* слизь *f*.

slimming [slɪmɪŋ] *n* (*losing weight*) похуде́ние.

slimy ['slaɪmɪ] *adj* (*pond*) и́листый (и́лист);
(*covered with mud*) ско́льзкий* и ли́пкий*;

(*fig: person*) гну́сный.
sling [slɪŋ] (*pt, pp* **slung**) *n* (*MED*) пе́ревязь *f*; (*for baby*) *приспособле́ние, позволя́ющее носи́ть ребёнка на спине́ и́ли груди́*; (*weapon*) праща́, рога́тка* ♦ *vt* (*throw*) швыря́ть (швырну́ть *perf*); **his arm is in a ~** у него́ рука́ на пе́ревязи.
slingshot [ˈslɪŋʃɔt] *n* рога́тка*.
slink [slɪŋk] (*pt, pp* **slunk**) *vi*: **to ~ away** *or* **off** уходи́ть* (уйти́* *perf*) подджа́вши хвост*.
slinky [ˈslɪŋkɪ] *adj* в обтя́жку.
slip [slɪp] *n* (*fall*) обва́л; (*mistake*) про́мах; (*underskirt*) подъю́бник; (*of paper*) поло́ска* ♦ *vt* сова́ть* (су́нуть *perf*) ♦ *vi* (*slide*) скользи́ть* (скользну́ть *f*); (*lose balance*) поскользну́ться (*perf*); (*decline*) снижа́ться (сни́зиться* *perf*); (*move smoothly*): **to ~ into** (*room etc*) скользну́ть (*perf*) в +*acc*; **to give sb the ~** ускольза́ть (ускользну́ть *perf*) от кого́-н; **a ~ of the tongue** сгово́рка*; **to ~ sth on** надева́ть (наде́ть* *perf*) что-н; **to ~ sth off** сбра́сывать (сбро́сить* *perf*) что-н; **to ~ out of** (*room etc*) выска́льзывать (*perf*) из +*gen*; **to let a chance ~ by** упуска́ть (упусти́ть* *perf*) возмо́жность; **the cup ~ped from her hand** ча́шка вы́скользнула из её рук
▶ **slip away** *vi* улизну́ть (*perf*)
▶ **slip in** *vt* сова́ть* (су́нуть *perf*) ♦ *vi* (*errors*) закра́сться* (*perf*)
▶ **slip out** *vi* (*go out*) выска́кивать (вы́скочить *perf*)
▶ **slip up** *vi* (*make mistake*) ошиба́ться (ошиби́ться* *perf*).
slip-on [ˈslɪpɔn] *adj* без пу́говиц и застёжек; **~ shoes** ту́фли без шнурко́в и застёжек.
slipped disc [slɪpt-] *n* смещённый позвоно́к.
slipper [ˈslɪpəʳ] *n* та́почка*.
slippery [ˈslɪpərɪ] *adj* (*also fig*) ско́льзкий*.
slippy [ˈslɪpɪ] *adj* (*inf*) ско́льзкий* (ско́льзок).
slip road *n* (*BRIT: on to*) въезд на автостра́ду; (*off from*) съезд с автостра́ды.
slipshod [ˈslɪpʃɔd] *adj* небре́жный* (небре́жен).
slipstream [ˈslɪpstriːm] *n* возду́шный пото́к.
slip-up [ˈslɪpʌp] *n* оши́бка*.
slipway [ˈslɪpweɪ] *n* (*NAUT*) ста́пель* *m*.
slit [slɪt] (*pt, pp* **slit**) *n* (*cut*) разре́з; (*opening*) щель* *f*; (*tear*) разры́в ♦ *vt* разреза́ть (разре́зать* *perf*); (*tear*) разрыва́ть (разорва́ть* *perf*); **to ~ sb's throat** перере́зать* (*perf*) кому́-н го́рло.
slither [ˈslɪðəʳ] *vi* (*person*) скользи́ть* (*impf*); (*snake*) извива́ться (*impf*).
sliver [ˈslɪvəʳ] *n* (*of glass*) оско́лок*; (*of wood*) ще́пка*; (*of cheese etc*) кусо́чек*.
slob [slɔb] *n* (*inf*) о́лух*.
slog [slɔg] *vi* (*BRIT: work hard*) корпе́ть* (*impf*) ♦ *n*: **it was a hard ~** э́то была́ тяжёлая рабо́та.
slogan [ˈsləugən] *n* ло́зунг.
slop [slɔp] *vi* (*also: ~ over*) выплёскиваться (вы́плеснуться *perf*) ♦ *vt* выплёскивать (вы́плеснуть *perf*)

▶ **slop out** *vi* (*in prison etc*) выноси́ть* (вы́нести* *perf*) пара́шу.
slope [sləup] *n* (*gentle hill*) укло́н; (*side of mountain*) склон; (*ski slope*) спуск; (*slant*) накло́н ♦ *vi*: **to ~ down** спуска́ться (*impf*); **to ~ up** поднима́ться (*impf*) под укло́ном.
sloping [ˈsləupɪŋ] *adj* (*ground, roof*) пока́тый (пока́т); (*handwriting*) накло́нный.
sloppy [ˈslɔpɪ] *adj* (*work*) небре́жный* (небре́жен), халту́рный; (*appearance*) неря́шливый (неря́шлив); (*pej: film etc*) сентимента́льный* (сентимента́лен).
slops [slɔps] *npl* помо́и *pl*.
slosh [slɔʃ] (*inf*) *vi*: **to ~ around** *or* **about** плеска́ться* (*impf*).
sloshed [slɔʃt] *adj* (*inf: drunk*) пья́ный в дыми́ну.
slot [slɔt] *n* (*in machine*) про́резь *f*, паз*; (*fig: in timetable*) окно́*; (*RADIO, TV*) ме́сто* ♦ *vt*: **to ~ sth into** опуска́ть (опусти́ть* *perf*) что-н в +*acc* ♦ *vi*: **to ~ into** входи́ть* (войти́* *perf*) в +*acc*.
sloth [sləuθ] *n* (*laziness*) лень *f*; (*ZOOL*) лени́вец*.
slot machine *n* (*BRIT: vending machine*) торго́вый автома́т; (: *fruit machine*) игра́льный автома́т.
slot meter *n* (*BRIT*) счётчик.
slouch [slautʃ] *vi* суту́литься (ссуту́литься *perf*); **she was ~ed in a chair** она́ сиде́ла на сту́ле, сго́рбившись.
Slovakia [sləuˈvækɪə] *n* Слова́кия.
Slovakian [sləuˈvækɪən] *adj* слова́цкий* ♦ *n* (*person*) слова́к(-а́чка).
Slovenia [sləuˈviːnɪə] *n* Слове́ния.
Slovenian [sləuˈviːnɪən] *adj* слове́нский* ♦ *n* (*person*) слове́нец*(-нка); (*LING*) слове́нский* язы́к*.
slovenly [ˈslʌvənlɪ] *adj* неря́шливый (неря́шлив).
slow [sləu] *adj* ме́дленный; (*not clever*) тупо́й* (туп) ♦ *adv* ме́дленно ♦ *vt* (*also: ~ down, ~ up*: *vehicle*) приторма́живать (притормози́ть* *perf*); (: *business*) приостана́вливать (приостанови́ть* *perf*) ♦ *vi* (*traffic*) замедля́ться (заме́длиться *perf*); (*car, train etc*) сбавля́ть (сба́вить* *perf*) ход; **at a ~ speed** на ни́зкой ско́рости; **to be ~ to act/ decide** быть ~ (*impf*) медли́тельным(-ой) в дела́х/в реше́ниях; **my watch is (20 minutes) ~** мои́ часы́ отстаю́т (на 20 мину́т); **business is ~** дела́ иду́т нева́жно; **"slow"** (*road sign*) "ме́дленно"; **to go ~** (*driver*) дви́гаться (*impf*) ме́дленно; (*BRIT: workers*) снижа́ть (сни́зить* *perf*) темп рабо́ты.
slow-acting [sləuˈæktɪŋ] *adj* заме́дленного де́йствия.
slowly [ˈsləulɪ] *adv* ме́дленно; **to drive ~** води́ть*/вести́* (*impf*) маши́ну ме́дленно.
slow motion *n*: **in ~** в заме́дленном де́йствии.

slow-moving [sləu'muːvɪŋ] *adj* ме́дленно дви́жущийся, ме́дленный.

slowness ['sləunɪs] *n* ме́дленность *f*.

sludge [slʌdʒ] *n* грязь *f*.

slue [sluː] *vi* (*US*) = **slew**.

slug [slʌg] *n* (*ZOOL*) слизня́к*; (*bullet*) пу́ля.

sluggish ['slʌgɪʃ] *adj* (*stream*) ме́дленно теку́щий*; (*engine*) пло́хо рабо́тающий; (*person*) медли́тельный* (медли́телен); (*trading*) вя́лый.

sluice [sluːs] *n* (*gate*) шлюз; (*channel*) жёлоб* ♦ *vt*: **to ~ down** *or* **out** промыва́ть (промы́ть* *perf*), ока́тывать (окати́ть* *perf*).

slum [slʌm] *n* трущо́ба.

slumber ['slʌmbə] *n* сон*.

slump [slʌmp] *n* (*economic*) спад; (*in profits, sales*) ре́зкое паде́ние ♦ *vi* (*person*) вали́ться* (повали́ться* *perf*); (*prices*) ре́зко па́дать (упа́сть* *perf*); **he was ~ed over the wheel** он сиде́л, упа́в на руль.

slung [slʌŋ] *pt, pp of* **sling**.

slunk [slʌŋk] *pt, pp of* **slink**.

slur [sləː] *vt* (*words*) произноси́ть* (произнести́* *perf*) нечленоразде́льно ♦ *n* (*MUS*) ли́га; (*fig*): **~ (on)** пятно́ (на +*prp*); **to cast a ~ on** поро́чить (*impf*).

slurp [sləːp] *vt* (гро́мко) хлеба́ть (хлебну́ть* *perf*).

slurred [sləːd] *adj* (*speech, voice*) невня́тный* (невня́тен).

slush [slʌʃ] *n* сля́коть *f*.

slush fund *n* (*POL*) *фонд для по́дкупа госуда́рственных лиц.*

slushy ['slʌʃɪ] *adj* (*snow*) мо́крый; (*street*) покры́тый сля́котью; (*BRIT*: *fig*) сентимента́льный* (сентимента́лен).

slut [slʌt] *n* (*inf. pej*) потаску́ха.

sly [slaɪ] *adj* хи́трый* (хитёр) ♦ *n*: **on the ~** тайко́м.

smack [smæk] *n* (*slap*) шлепо́к*; (*on face*) пощёчина; (*inf: heroin*) герои́н ♦ *vt* хло́пать (хло́пнуть* *perf*); (*child*) шлёпать (отшлёпать* *perf*); (*on face*) дава́ть* (дать* *perf*) пощёчину +*dat* ♦ *vi*: **to ~ of** попа́хивать (*impf*) +*instr* ♦ *adv* (*inf*): **the ball fell ~ in the middle** мяч упа́л пря́мо посереди́не; **to ~ one's lips** чмо́кать (чмо́кнуть *perf*) губа́ми.

smacker ['smækə] *n* (*inf: kiss*) поцелу́й; (: *BRIT: pound note*) бума́жный фунт; (: *US: dollar bill*) бума́жный до́ллар.

small [smɔːl] *adj* ма́ленький*; (*quantity, amount*) небольшо́й ♦ *n*: **the ~ of the back** поясни́ца; **to get** *or* **grow ~er** уменьша́ться (уме́ньшиться *perf*); **to make ~er** (*amount, income*) снижа́ть (сни́зить* *perf*); (*object, garment*) уменьша́ть (уме́ньшить *perf*); **a ~ shopkeeper** ме́лкий(-ая) ла́вочник(-ица).

small ads *npl* (*BRIT*) ма́ленькие объявле́ния

ntpl (*в газе́те о ку́пле-прода́же*).

small arms *npl* (*MIL*) стрелко́вое ору́жие *ntsg*.

small business *n* ма́лое предприя́тие.

small change *n* ме́лочь* *f*.

small fry *npl* (*fig*) ме́лкая со́шка *fsg*.

smallholder ['smɔːlhəuldə'] *n* (*BRIT*) *владе́лец небольшо́го земе́льного уча́стка.*

smallholding ['smɔːlhəuldɪŋ] *n* (*BRIT*) *небольшо́е земе́льное владе́ние.*

small hours *npl*: **in the ~** ~ в предрассве́тные часы́*.

smallish ['smɔːlɪʃ] *adj* небольшо́й, дово́льно ма́ленький*.

small-minded [smɔːl'maɪndɪd] *adj* ограни́ченный.

smallpox ['smɔːlpɔks] *n* о́спа.

small print *n* ме́лкий* шрифт.

small-scale ['smɔːlskeɪl] *adj* (*map, model*) ма́ленького масшта́ба; (*business, farming*) ме́лкий*.

small screen *n*: **the ~ ~** телеви́дение, ма́лый экра́н.

small talk *n* све́тская бесе́да.

small-time ['smɔːltaɪm] *adj* (*farmer etc*) ме́лький.

small-town ['smɔːltaun] *adj* провинциа́льный* (провинциа́лен).

smarmy ['smɑːmɪ] *adj* (*BRIT: pej*) вкра́дчивый (вкра́дчив).

smart [smɑːt] *adj* (*neat, tidy*) опря́тный* (опря́тен); (*fashionable*) мо́дный* (мо́ден); (*clever*) толко́вый (толко́в); (*quick*) бы́стрый* (быстр); (*pej*) наха́льный* (наха́лен) ♦ *vi* (*also fig*) жечь* (*impf*); **the ~ set** фешене́бельное о́бщество; **to look ~** вы́глядеть* (*impf*) элега́нтно; **my eyes are ~ing** у меня́ глаза́ щи́плет.

smart card *n* (*for transactions*) *вид креди́тной ка́рточки с микропроце́ссором, испо́льзуемой в платёжных опера́циях.*

smarten up ['smɑːtn-] *vi* приоде́ться* (*perf*), принаряди́ться (*perf*) ♦ *vt* (*place*) приводи́ть* (привести́* *perf*) в поря́док; (*person*) принаряжа́ть (принаряди́ть* *perf*).

smash [smæʃ] *n* (*collision: also: ~-up*) ава́рия; (*sound*) гро́хот; (*TENNIS*) смэш ♦ *vt* разбива́ть (разби́ть* *perf*); (*SPORT: record*) поби́ть* (*perf*) ♦ *vi* (*break*) разбива́ться (разби́ться* *perf*); (*collide*): **to ~ against** *or* **into** вреза́ться (вре́заться* *perf*) в +*acc*

▶ **smash up** *vt* (*car*) разбива́ть (разби́ть* *perf*); (*room*) громи́ть* (разгроми́ть* *perf*).

smash hit *n* шля́гер.

smashing ['smæʃɪŋ] *adj* (*inf*) потряса́ющий*.

smattering ['smætərɪŋ] *n*: **a ~ of** пове́рхностное зна́ние +*gen*.

smear [smɪə'] *n* (*trace*) след*; (*insult*) клевета́; (*MED*) мазо́к* ♦ *vt* (*spread*) ма́зать*

---

* marks translations which have irregular inflections. The Russian-English side of the dictionary gives inflectional information.

(нама́зать* *perf*); (*make dirty*) па́чкать (испа́чкать *perf*); **his hands were ~ed with oil/ink** его́ ру́ки бы́ли испа́чканы ма́слом/ черни́лами.

smear campaign *n* клеветни́ческая кампа́ния.

smear test *n* (*BRIT: MED*) мазо́к* для ана́лиза.

smell [smɛl] (*pt, pp* **smelt** *or* **smelled**) *n* за́пах; (*sense*) обоня́ние ♦ *vt* чу́вствовать (почу́вствовать *perf*) за́пах +*gen* ♦ *vi:* **to ~ (of)** (*unpleasant*) воня́ть (*impf*) (+*instr*); (*food etc*) па́хнуть (*impf*) (+*instr*).

smelly ['smɛlɪ] *adj* воню́чий* (воню́ч).

smelt [smɛlt] *pt, pp of* **smell** ♦ *vt* (*ore*) пла́вить* (распла́вить* *perf*).

smile [smaɪl] *n* улы́бка* ♦ *vi* улыба́ться (улыбну́ться *perf*).

smiling ['smaɪlɪŋ] *adj* улыба́ющийся.

smirk [smə:k] *n* (*pej*) ухмы́лка*.

smithy ['smɪðɪ] *n* ку́зница.

smitten ['smɪtn] *adj:* **he is ~ with her** он от неё без ума́.

smock [smɔk] *n* блу́за; (*children's*) де́тское пла́тье в сбо́рочку; (*US: overall*) комбинезо́н.

smog [smɔg] *n* смог.

smoke [sməuk] *n* дым ♦ *vi* (*person*) кури́ть* (*impf*); (*chimney*) дыми́ться (*impf*) ♦ *vt* (*cigarettes*) кури́ть* (вы́курить *perf*); **to have a ~** кури́ть* (покури́ть* *perf*); **to go up in ~** сгоре́ть (*perf*); (*fig*) пойти́* (*perf*) пра́хом; **do you ~?** Вы ку́рите?

smoked ['sməukt] *adj* (*bacon, fish*) копчёный; (*glass*) ды́мчатый.

smokeless fuel ['sməuklɪs-] *n* безды́мное то́пливо.

smokeless zone *n* (*BRIT*) безды́мная городска́я зо́на.

smoker ['sməukə^r] *n* (*person*) кури́льщик(-щица); (*RAIL*) ваго́н для куря́щих.

smoke screen *n* (*also fig*) дымова́я заве́са.

smoke shop *n* (*US*) копти́льня.

smoking ['sməukɪŋ] *n* (*act*) куре́ние; **"no ~"** "не кури́ть".

smoking compartment (*US* **smoking car**) *n* ваго́н для куря́щих.

smoking room *n* кури́тельная ко́мната.

smoky ['sməukɪ] *adj* (*atmosphere, room*) зады́мленный (зады́млен); (*taste*) с при́вкусом ды́ма.

smolder ['sməuldə^r] *vi* (*US*) = **smoulder**.

smoochy ['smu:tʃɪ] *adj* (*inf*) ме́дленный и романти́чный (*о му́зыке, под кото́рую легко́ целова́ться*).

smooth [smu:ð] *adj* гла́дкий* (гла́док); (*sauce*) без комко́в; (*sea*) споко́йный* (споко́ен); (*flavour*) мя́гкий* (мя́гок); (*movement*) пла́вный* (пла́вен); (*flight*) ро́вный*; (*pej: person*) ло́вкий* (ло́вок) ♦ *vt* (*also: ~* **out**) разгла́живать (разгла́дить* *perf*); (:

difficulties) устраня́ть (устрани́ть *perf*)

▶ **smooth over** *vt:* **to ~ things over** (*fig*) ула́живать (ула́дить* *perf*) дела́.

smoothly ['smu:ðlɪ] *adv* (*easily*) без труда́; **everything went ~** всё прошло́ гла́дко.

smoothness ['smu:ðnɪs] *n* гла́дкость *f*; (*flavour*) мя́гкость *f*; (*movement*) пла́вность *f*.

smother ['smʌðə^r] *vt* (*fire*) туши́ть* (потуши́ть* *perf*); (*person*) души́ть* (задуши́ть* *perf*); (*emotions*) подавля́ть (подави́ть* *perf*).

smoulder [sməuldə^r] (*US* **smolder**) *vi* (*fire*) тлеть* (*impf*); (*fig: anger, hatred*) зреть (*impf*).

smudge [smʌdʒ] *n* пятно́* ♦ *vt* разма́зывать (разма́зать* *perf*).

smug [smʌg] *adj* самодово́льный* (самодово́лен).

smuggle ['smʌgl] *vt* (*goods*) провози́ть* (провезти́* *perf*) контраба́ндой; (*refugees*) переправля́ть (перепра́вить* *perf*) та́йно; **to ~ in/out** (*goods etc*) ввози́ть* (ввезти́* *perf*)/ вывози́ть* (вы́везти* *perf*) контраба́ндой.

smuggler ['smʌglə^r] *n* контрабанди́ст(ка*).

smuggling ['smʌglɪŋ] *n* контраба́нда.

smut [smʌt] *n* (*soot*) са́жа *no pl*; (*in conversation etc*) поха́бщина.

smutty ['smʌtɪ] *adj* (*joke, book*) поха́бный* (поха́бен).

snack [snæk] *n* заку́ска*; **to have a ~** заку́сывать (закуси́ть* *perf*), переку́сывать (перекуси́ть* *perf*).

snack bar *n* заку́сочная *f adj*.

snag [snæg] *n* (*problem*) загво́здка*, затрудне́ние.

snail [sneɪl] *n* ули́тка*.

snake [sneɪk] *n* змея́*.

snap [snæp] *n* (*sound*) треск; (*photograph*) сни́мок*; (*game*) снэп ♦ *adj* (*decision etc*) необду́манный* (необду́ман) ♦ *vt* (*break*) разла́мывать (разлома́ть *perf*); (*fingers*) щёлкать (щёлкнуть *perf*) +*instr* ♦ *vi* (*break*) разла́мываться (разлома́ться *or* разломи́ться* *perf*); (*fig: lose control*) слома́ться (*perf*); (: *speak sharply*) крича́ть* (*impf*); **to ~ at sb** (*subj: person*) крича́ть* (*impf*) на кого́-н; **to ~ one's fingers at** (*fig*) отма́хиваться (отмахну́ться *perf*) от +*gen*; **a cold ~** (*weather*) внеза́пное ре́зкое похолода́ние; **to ~ shut** (*trap, jaws etc*) защёлкивать (защёлкнуть *perf*)

▶ **snap at** *vt fus* огрыза́ться (огрызну́ться *perf*) на +*acc*

▶ **snap off** *vi* отла́мывать (отлома́ть *or* отломи́ть* *perf*)

▶ **snap up** *vt* (*bargains*) расхва́тывать (расхвата́ть *perf*)

snap fastener *n* кно́пка*.

snappy ['snæpɪ] (*inf*) *adj* (*slogan*) бро́ский*; (*answer*) бы́стрый; **make it ~!** потора́пливайся!

snapshot ['snæpʃɒt] *n* сни́мок*.
snare [snɛəʳ] *n* лову́шка*, капка́н ♦ *vt* (*also fig*) зама́нивать (замани́ть* *perf*) в лову́шку.
snarl [snɑ:l] *vi* (*animal, person*) рыча́ть (*impf*), ворча́ть (*impf*) ♦ *vt*: **to get ~ed up** (*plans*) пу́таться (запу́таться *perf*); **the traffic was ~ed up** произошёл зато́р в ули́чном движе́нии.
snarl-up ['snɑ:lʌp] *n* пу́таница.
snatch [snætʃ] *n* (*of conversation, song etc*) обры́вок* ♦ *vt* (*grab*) хвата́ть (схвати́ть* *perf*); (*handbag*) вырыва́ть (вы́рвать* *perf*); (*child etc*) красть* (укра́сть* *perf*); (*opportunity, look etc*) урыва́ть (урва́ть* *perf*) ♦ *vi*: **don't ~!** не хвата́й!; **to ~ a sandwich** перехва́тывать (перехвати́ть* *perf*) бутербро́д; **I managed to ~ some sleep** мне удало́сь немно́го поспа́ть
▸ **snatch up** *vt* схва́тывать (схвати́ть* *perf*).
snazzy ['snæzi] *adj* (*inf*) шика́рный* (шика́рен).
sneak [sni:k] *n* (*inf: informer*) я́беда *m/f* ♦ *vi*: **to ~ into/out of** незаме́тно проска́льзывать (проскользну́ть *perf*) в +*acc*/из +*gen* ♦ *vt*: **to ~ a look at sth** взгля́дывать (взгляну́ть* *perf*) укра́дкой на что-н; **to ~ up on sb** я́бедничать (ная́бедничать *perf*) на кого́-н.
sneakers ['sni:kəz] *npl* красо́вки* *fpl*.
sneaking ['sni:kɪŋ] *adj*: **I have a ~ feeling** *or* **suspicion that ...** у меня́ закра́лось подозре́ние, что ....
sneaky ['sni:kɪ] *adj* (*pej: person*) хи́трый* (хитёр); (*advantage, look*) незаме́тный* (незаме́тен).
sneer [snɪəʳ] *vi* (*laugh*) посме́иваться (*impf*); (*mock*): **to ~ at** глуми́ться* (*impf*) над +*instr*.
sneeze [sni:z] *n* чиха́ние ♦ *vi* чиха́ть (чихну́ть *perf*)
▸ **sneeze at** *vt fus*: **such things are not to be ~d at** таки́ми веща́ми не броса́ются.
snide [snaɪd] *adj* (*pej*) ехи́дный* (ехи́ден).
sniff [snɪf] *n* (*sound*) сопе́ние; (*smell: by dog, person*) обню́хивание ♦ *vi* шмы́гать (шмы́гнуть *perf*) но́сом; (*when crying*) всхли́пывать (*impf*) ♦ *vt* ню́хать (*impf*); (*glue, drugs*) вдыха́ть (*impf*), ню́хать (*impf*)
▸ **sniff at** *vt fus*: **such things are not to be ~ed at** таки́ми веща́ми не броса́ются.
sniffer dog ['snɪfə-] *n* (*POLICE*) соба́ка-ище́йка (*для обнаруже́ния нарко́тиков и взры́вчатых веще́ств*).
snigger ['snɪgəʳ] *vi* хихика́ть (хихи́кнуть *perf*).
snip [snɪp] *n* (*cut*) надре́з; (*BRIT: inf: bargain*) нахо́дка* ♦ *vt* (*cut*) ре́зать* (*impf*).
sniper ['snaɪpəʳ] *n* сна́йпер.
snippet ['snɪpɪt] *n* обры́вок*.
snivel ['snɪvl] *vi* хны́кать (*impf*).
snob [snɒb] *n* сноб.
snobbery ['snɒbəri] *n* сноби́зм.
snobbish ['snɒbɪʃ] *adj* сноби́стский*.

snog [snɒg] *vi* лиза́ться (*impf*) ♦ *n*: **to have a ~** лиза́ться (*impf*).
snooker ['snu:kəʳ] *n* сну́кер (*игра́ в билья́рд*) ♦ *vt* (*BRIT: inf: fig*): **we're completely ~ed** мы соверше́нно за́гнаны в у́гол.
snoop ['snu:p] *vi*: **to ~ about** шпио́нить (*impf*); **to ~ on sb** подгля́дывать (*impf*) за кем-н (в щёлочку).
snooper ['snu:pəʳ] *n* шпио́н.
snooty ['snu:tɪ] *adj* задири́стый.
snooze [snu:z] *vi* прикорну́ть (*perf*), вздремну́ть (*perf*) ♦ *n*: **to have a ~** вздремну́ть (*perf*).
snore [snɔ:ʳ] *n* храп ♦ *vi* храпе́ть* (*impf*).
snoring ['snɔ:rɪŋ] *n* храп.
snorkel ['snɔ:kl] *n* тру́бка*.
snort [snɔ:t] *n* фы́рканье ♦ *vi* (*animal*) фаркну́ть (*perf*); (*horse*) всхра́пывать (*impf*) ♦ *vt* (*inf: drugs*) ню́хать (*impf*).
snotty ['snɒtɪ] *adj* (*inf: handkerchief, nose*) сопли́вый; (: *pej: snobbish*) на́глый.
snout [snaut] *n* (*of pig*) ры́ло; (*of dog etc*) мо́рда.
snow [snəu] *n* снег* ♦ *vi*: **it's ~ing** идёт снег ♦ *vt*: **she is ~ed under with work** она́ зава́лена рабо́той.
snowball ['snəubɔ:l] *n* снежо́к* ♦ *vi* (*fig: problem, campaign*) нараста́ть (*impf*) как сне́жный ком.
snowbound ['snəubaund] *adj* засы́панный сне́гом.
snowcapped ['snəukæpt] *adj* сне́жный.
snowdrift ['snəudrɪft] *n* мете́ль *f*, бура́н.
snowdrop ['snəudrɒp] *n* (*BOT*) подсне́жник.
snowfall ['snəufɔ:l] *n* снегопа́д.
snowflake ['snəufleɪk] *n* снежи́нка*.
snow line *n* снегова́я ли́ния.
snowman ['snəumæn] *n irreg* сне́жная ба́ба, снегови́к.
snowplough ['snəuplau] (*US* **snowplow**) *n* снегоубо́рочный комба́йн.
snowshoes ['snəuʃu:z] *npl* снегосту́пы *mpl*.
snowstorm ['snəustɔ:m] *n* бура́н, вьюга.
snowy ['snəuɪ] *adj* сне́жный; (*covered with snow*) засне́женный.
SNP *n abbr* (*BRIT: POL*) = **Scottish National Party**.
snub [snʌb] *vt* (*person*) пренебрежи́тельно обходи́ться* (обойти́сь* *perf*) с +*instr* ♦ *n* вы́зов.
snub-nosed [snʌb'nəuzd] *adj* курно́сый.
snuff [snʌf] *n* ню́хательный таба́к* ♦ *vt* (*also: ~ out*) туши́ть* (потуши́ть* *perf*).
snuff movie *n* порнографи́ческий фильм, в кото́ром засня́то настоя́щее уби́йство.
snug [snʌg] *adj* (*place*) ую́тный* (ую́тен); (*well-fitting*) пло́тно облега́ющий*; **I'm very ~ here** мне здесь о́чень ую́тно; **the sweater is a ~ fit** сви́тер хорошо́ прилега́ет.

---

* marks translations which have irregular inflections. The Russian-English side of the dictionary gives inflectional information.

snuggle ['snʌgl] *vi*: **to ~ up to sb** прижима́ться (прижа́ться* *perf*) к кому́-н; **to ~ down in bed** забива́ться (заби́ться* *perf*) под одея́ло.

snugly ['snʌglɪ] *adv* ую́тно; **to fit ~** (*object in pocket etc*) удо́бно помеща́ться (*impf*); **the sweater fits ~** сви́тер хорошо́ прилега́ет.

SO *n abbr* (*COMM*) = **standing order.**

KEYWORD
---

so [səu] *adv* **1** (*thus, likewise*): **so saying he walked away** с э́тими слова́ми, он ушёл; **while she was so doing, he ...** пока́ она́ э́то де́лала, он ...; **if so** е́сли да; **if this is so** е́сли э́то так; **I didn't do it – you did so!** э́то не я (сде́лал) – нет, ты!; **I like him – so do I** мне он нра́вится – мне то́же; **I'm still at school – so am I** я ещё учу́сь в шко́ле – я то́же; **he has a brother – so has David** у него́ есть брат – у Дави́да то́же; **so it is!** да, действи́тельно!; **I hope/think so** наде́юсь/ду́маю, что да; **so far I haven't had any problems** пока́ что у меня́ не́ было пробле́м; **how do you like the book so far?** ну как, нра́вится Вам кни́га?
2 (*in comparisons etc: +adv*) насто́лько, так; (*+adj*) насто́лько, тако́й; **so quickly (that)** насто́лько *or* так бы́стро(, что); **the house is so big (that)** дом насто́лько *or* тако́й большо́й(, что); **she's not so clever as her brother** она́ не так умна́, как её брат; **I'm so glad to see you** я так рад Вас ви́деть;
3: **I've got so much work** у меня́ так мно́го рабо́ты; **I love you so much** я Вас так люблю́; **thank you so much** спаси́бо Вам большо́е; **there are so many books I would like to read** сто́лько есть книг, кото́рые я бы хоте́л проче́сть
4 (*phrases*): **ten or so** о́коло десяти́; **so long!** (*inf: goodbye*) пока́!

♦ *conj* **1** (*expressing purpose*): **so as to do** что́бы сде́лать (*perf*); **I brought this wine so that you could try it** я принёс э́то вино́, что́бы Вы могли́ его́ попро́бовать
2 (*expressing result*) так что; **so I was right after all** так что, я был всё-таки прав; **so you see, I could have stayed** так что ви́дите, я мог бы оста́ться; **so, what shall we do now** так, что тепе́рь бу́дем де́лать.

soak [səuk] *vt* (*drench*) промочи́ть* (*perf*); (*steep in water*) зама́чивать (замочи́ть* *perf*) ♦ *vi* (*washing, dishes*) отмока́ть (*impf*); **to be ~ed through** промо́кнуть (*perf*) наскво́зь
▶ **soak in** *vi* впи́тываться (впита́ться *perf*)
▶ **soak up** *vt* впи́тывать (впита́ть *perf*) (в себя́).

soaking ['səukɪŋ] *adj* (*also: ~ wet*) мо́крый наскво́зь.

so-and-so ['səuənsəu] *n* (*somebody*) не́кто*; **Mr ~** Господи́н тако́й-то; **you little ~!** (*pej*) ах ты э́дакий!

soap [səup] *n* мы́ло*; (*TV: also: ~ opera*) мы́льная о́пера.

soapbox ['səupbɔks] *n* (*container*) я́щик из-под

мы́ла; (*platform*) импровизи́рованная трибу́на.

soap flakes *npl* мы́льная хло́пья *pl*.

soap opera *n* (*TV*) мы́льная о́пера.

soap powder *n* мы́льный порошо́к*.

soapsuds ['səupsʌds] *npl* мы́льная пе́на *fsg*.

soapy ['səupɪ] *adj* мы́льный.

soar [sɔː] *vi* (*bird, rocket*) взвива́ться (взви́ться* *perf*) в во́здух; (*price, production, temperature*) ре́зко подска́кивать (подскочи́ть* *perf*); (*building etc*) возвыша́ться (*impf*).

soaring ['sɔːrɪŋ] *adj* (*prices, inflation*) неуправля́емый.

sob [sɔb] *n* рыда́ние ♦ *vi* рыда́ть (*impf*), всхли́пывать (*impf*).

s.o.b. *n abbr* (*US: infl:* = *son of a bitch*) су́кин сын* (*!*)

sober ['səubə] *adj* тре́звый* (трезв); (*colour, style*) небро́ский*
▶ **sober up** *vt* протрезви́ть* (*perf*) ♦ *vi* трезве́ть (*impf*), протрезвля́ться (протрезви́ться* *perf*).

sobriety [sə'braɪətɪ] *n* тре́звость *f*.

sobriquet ['səubrɪkeɪ] *n* (*nickname*) про́звище.

sob story *n* душещипа́тельная исто́рия.

Soc. *abbr* = **society.**

so-called ['səu'kɔːld] *adj* так называ́емый.

soccer ['sɔkə] *n* футбо́л.

soccer pitch *n* футбо́льное по́ле*.

soccer player *n* футболи́ст.

sociable ['səuʃəbl] *adj* (*person*) общи́тельный* (общи́телен); (*behaviour*) све́тский*.

social ['səuʃl] *adj* (*history, structure etc*) обще́ственный, социа́льный; (*event*) све́тский*; (*sociable: animal*) ста́дный ♦ *n* (*party*) встре́ча, ве́чер*; **he has a good ~ life** он мно́го обща́ется с людьми́.

social class *n* социа́льный класс.

social climber *n* челове́к, стремя́щийся заня́ть бо́лее высо́кое социа́льное положе́ние.

social club *n* клуб обще́ния.

social democrat *n* (*POL*) социа́л-демокра́т.

social insurance *n* (*US*) социа́льное обеспече́ние *or* страхова́ние.

socialism ['səuʃəlɪzəm] *n* социали́зм.

socialist ['səuʃəlɪst] *n* социали́ст ♦ *adj* социалисти́ческий*.

socialite ['səuʃəlaɪt] *n* све́тский челове́к*.

socialize ['səuʃəlaɪz] *vi*: **to ~ (with)** обща́ться (пообща́ться *perf*) (с *+instr*).

socially ['səuʃəlɪ] *adv*: **to visit sb ~** зайти́* (*perf*) к кому́-н по-дру́жески; **~ acceptable** социа́льно прие́млемый.

social science *n* (*SCOL*) обще́ственные нау́ки *fpl*.

social security *n* (*BRIT*) социа́льное обеспече́ние; **Department of S~ S~** Министе́рство социа́льного обеспече́ния.

social services *npl* систе́ма *fsg* социа́льного обслу́живания.

social welfare *n* социа́льное обеспече́ние.

social work *n* рабо́та по социа́льному обеспече́нию.
social worker *n* рабо́тник систе́мы социа́льного обеспече́ния.
society [sə'saɪətɪ] *n* о́бщество ◆ *cpd* (*party*) све́тский*.
socioeconomic ['səusɪəui:kə'nɒmɪk] *adj* (*group, factor*) социа́льно-экономи́ческий*.
sociological [səusɪə'lɒdʒɪkl] *adj* (*study*) социологи́ческий.
sociologist [səusɪ'ɒlədʒɪst] *n* социо́лог.
sociology [səusɪ'ɒlədʒɪ] *n* социоло́гия.
sock [sɒk] *n* носо́к* ◆ *vt* (*inf*): **to ~ sb in the face** дава́ть* (дать* *perf*) кому́-н по физионо́мии; **to pull one's ~s up** (*fig*) подтяну́ться* (*perf*).
socket ['sɒkɪt] *n* глазни́ца; (*BRIT: ELEC: in wall*) розе́тка*; (: *for light bulb*) патро́н.
sod [sɒd] *n* (*of earth*) дёрн; (*BRIT: inf!*) дрянь *f* така́я (*!*)
▶ **sod off** *vi* (*inf!*): **~ off** убира́йсь отсю́да! (*!*), прова́ливай! (*!*)
soda ['səudə] *n* (*CHEM*) со́да; (*also*: ~ **water**) со́довая *f adj*; (*US: also*: ~ **pop**) газиро́вка*.
sodden ['sɒdn] *adj* прокля́тый.
sodium ['səudɪəm] *n* на́трий.
sodium chloride *n* хлори́д на́трия.
sofa ['səufə] *n* дива́н.
Sofia ['səufɪə] *n* Софи́я.
soft [sɒft] *adj* мя́гкий* (мя́гок); (*music*) негро́мкий* (негро́мок); **don't be ~!** (*inf: stupid*) не будь дурако́м!
soft-boiled ['sɒftbɔɪld] *adj*: ~ **egg** яйцо́* всмя́тку.
soft currency *n* неконверти́руемая валю́та.
soft drink *n* безалкого́льный напи́ток*, сок*.
soft drugs *npl* мя́гкие нарко́тики *mpl*.
soften ['sɒfn] *vt* смягча́ть (смягчи́ть *perf*) ◆ *vi* смягча́ться (смягчи́ться *perf*).
softener ['sɒfnə'] *n* (*also*: **water ~**) хими́ческое сре́дство, смягча́ющее во́ду; (*also*: **fabric ~**) смягча́ющее сре́дство для сти́рки.
soft fruit *n* (*BRIT*) я́годы *fpl*.
soft furnishings *npl* мя́гкая оби́вка *fsg*.
softhearted [sɒft'hɑːtɪd] *adj* мягкосерде́чный* (мягкосерде́чен).
softly ['sɒftlɪ] *adv* (*gently*) мя́гко; (*quietly*) ти́хо.
softness ['sɒftnɪs] *n* мя́гкость *f*.
soft option *n* лёгкий путь* *m*.
soft sell *n* (*COMM*) мя́гкая та́ктика сбы́та проду́кции.
soft spot *n*: **to have a ~ ~ for sb** пита́ть (*impf*) к кому́-н сла́бость.
soft target *n* лёгкая добы́ча.
soft toy *n* мя́гкая игру́шка*.
software ['sɒftwɛə'] *n* (*COMPUT*) програ́ммное обеспече́ние.
software package *n* (*COMPUT*) паке́т програ́мм.

soft water *n* мя́гкая вода́.
soggy ['sɒgɪ] *adj* (*ground*) сыро́й; (*sandwiches*) размо́кший.
soil [sɔɪl] *n* (*earth*) по́чва; (*territory*) земля́* ◆ *vt* па́чкать (запа́чкать *or* испа́чкать *perf*); (*fig*) мара́ть (замара́ть *perf*).
soiled [sɔɪld] *adj* испа́чканный (испа́чкан); (*COMM*) повреждённый.
sojourn ['sɒdʒəːn] *n* пребыва́ние.
solace ['sɒlɪs] *n* утеше́ние.
solar ['səulə'] *adj* со́лнечный.
solaria [sə'lɛərɪə] *npl of* **solarium**.
solarium [sə'lɛərɪəm] (*pl* **solaria**) *n* соля́рий.
solar panel *n* со́лнечная батаре́я.
solar plexus [-'plɛksəs] *n* со́лнечное сплете́ние.
solar power *n* со́лнечная эне́ргия.
solar system *n* со́лнечная систе́ма.
solar wind *n* со́лнечная бу́ря.
sold [səuld] *pt, pp of* **sell**.
solder ['səuldə'] *vt* пая́ть (*impf*), спа́ивать (спая́ть *perf*) ◆ *n* припо́й.
soldier ['səuldʒə'] *n* (*not officer*) солда́т*; (*in army*) вое́нный *m adj* ◆ *vi*: **to ~ on** не сдава́ться* (*impf*); **toy ~** солда́тик.
sold out *adj* распро́данный (распро́дан).
sole [səul] *n* (*of foot*) подо́шва; (*of shoe*) подо́шва, подмётка* ◆ *n inv* (*fish*) па́лтус ◆ *adj* (*unique*) еди́нственный; (*exclusive*) исключи́тельный; **the ~ reason** еди́нственная причи́на.
solely ['səullɪ] *adv* то́лько; **I will hold you ~ responsible** вся отве́тственность лежи́т то́лько на Вас.
solemn ['sɒləm] *adj* торже́ственный* (торже́ствен).
sole trader *n* (*COMM*) единоли́чный торго́вец*.
solicit [sə'lɪsɪt] *vt* (*request*) обраща́ться (обрати́ться* *perf*) с про́сьбой за +*instr* ◆ *vi* (*prostitute*) предлага́ть (*impf*) себя́.
solicitor [sə'lɪsɪtə'] *n* (*BRIT*) адвока́т.
solid ['sɒlɪd] *adj* (*not hollow*) це́льный; (*not liquid*) твёрдый; (*reliable*) непоколеби́мый (непоколеби́м); (*meal*) пло́тный; (*entire*) це́лый; (*gold*) чи́стый ◆ *n* (*solid object*) твёрдое те́ло*; ~**s** *npl* (*food*) твёрдая пи́ща *fsg*; (*for babies*) прико́рм *msg*); **to be on ~ ground** (*fig*) твёрдо стоя́ть (*impf*) на нога́х; **we waited two ~ hours** мы прожда́ли це́лых два часа́.
solidarity [sɒlɪ'dærɪtɪ] *n* солида́рность *f*.
solid fuel *n* твёрдое то́пливо.
solidify [sə'lɪdɪfaɪ] *vi* (*fat etc*) застыва́ть (засты́ть* *perf*); (*metal*) затвердева́ть (затверде́ть *perf*) ◆ *vt* де́лать (*impf*) твёрдым.
solidity [sə'lɪdɪtɪ] *n* твёрдость *f*.
solidly ['sɒlɪdlɪ] *adv* (*built*) кре́пко; (*respectable*) соли́дно; (*in favour*) по́лностью.

---

solid-state ['sɔlɪdsteɪt] *adj* (*ELEC*) твёрдый, в твёрдым состоянии.

soliloquy [sə'lɪləkwɪ] *n* монолог.

solitaire [sɔlɪ'tɛəʳ] *n* (*gem*) солитёр; (*game*) пасьянс.

solitary ['sɔlɪtərɪ] *adj* одинокий* (одинок); (*isolated*) уединённый; (*single*) единичный.

solitary confinement *n* одиночное заключение; **to be in ~ ~** находиться* (*impf*) в одиночном заключении.

solitude ['sɔlɪtjuːd] *n* одиночество, уединение; **to live in ~** жить* (*impf*) в уединении.

solo ['səuləu] *n* соло *nt ind* ♦ *adv* (*fly*) в одиночку; (*play*) соло.

soloist ['səuləuɪst] *n* солист*(а).

Solomon Islands ['sɔləmən-] *npl*: **the ~ ~** Соломоновы острова *mpl*.

solstice ['sɔlstɪs] *n* солнцестояние.

soluble ['sɔljubl] *adj* растворимый.

solution [sə'luːʃən] *n* (*answer*) решение; (*liquid*) раствор.

solve [sɔlv] *vt* (*puzzle*) решать (решить *perf*); (*problem*) разрешать (разрешить *perf*); (*mystery*) раскрывать (раскрыть* *perf*).

solvency ['sɔlvənsɪ] *n* платёжеспособность *f*.

solvent ['sɔlvənt] *adj* (*COMM*) платёжеспособный ♦ *n* (*CHEM*) растворитель *m*.

solvent abuse *n* злоупотребление химическими веществами с наркотическим действием.

Som. *abbr* (*BRIT*: *POST*) = **Somerset**.

Somali [sə'mɑːlɪ] *adj* сомалийский ♦ *n* сомалиец*(-ийка*).

Somalia [sə'mɑːlɪə] *n* Сомали *nt ind*.

sombre ['sɔmbəʳ] (*US* **somber**) *adj* мрачный* (мрачен).

KEYWORD

some [sʌm] *adj* **1** (*a certain amount or number of*): **would you like some tea/biscuits?** хотите чая/печенья?; **there's some milk in the fridge** в холодильнике есть молоко; **he asked me some questions** он задал мне несколько вопросов; **there are some people waiting to see you** Вас ждут какие-то люди; **I've got some money, but not much** у меня есть деньги, но немного

2 (*certain: in contrasts*) некоторый; **some people say that …** некоторые говорят, что …

3 (*unspecified*) какой-то; **some woman phoned you this afternoon** Вам сегодня днём звонила какая-то женщина; **we'll meet again some day** мы когда-нибудь опять встретимся; **shall we meet some day next week?** встретимся как-нибудь на той *or* следующей неделе?

♦ *pron* (*a certain number*: *people*) одни; **I've got some** у меня есть; **some took the bus, and some walked** одни поехали на автобусе, а другие пошли пешком; кто-то поехал на автобусе, кто-то пошёл пешком; **who would like a piece of cake? – I'd like some** кто хочет

кусок торта? – я с удовольствием; **I've read some of the book** я прочёл часть книги

♦ *adv*: **some ten people** человек десять.

somebody ['sʌmbədɪ] *pron* = **someone**.

someday ['sʌmdeɪ] *adv* когда-нибудь.

somehow ['sʌmhau] *adv* (*in some way*) как-нибудь; (*for some reason*) почему-то, каким-то образом.

someone ['sʌmwʌn] *pron* (*specific person*) кто-то; (*unspecified person*) кто-нибудь; **I saw ~ in the garden** я видел кого-то в саду; **~ will help you** Вам кто-нибудь поможет.

someplace ['sʌmpleɪs] *adv* (*US*) = **somewhere**.

somersault ['sʌməsɔːlt] *n* (*in the air*) сальто *nt ind*; (*on the ground*) кувырок* ♦ *vi* кувыркаться (*impf*), перекувырнуться (*perf*).

something ['sʌmθɪŋ] *pron* (*something specific*) что-то; (*something unspecified*) что-нибудь; **there's ~ wrong with my car** у меня что-то случилось с машиной; **would you like ~ to eat/drink?** хотите чего-нибудь поесть/выпить?; **I have ~ for you** у меня кое-что для Вас есть.

sometime ['sʌmtaɪm] *adv* (*in future*) когда-нибудь; (*in past*): **~ last month** где-то в прошлом месяце; **I'll finish it ~** когда-нибудь я это закончу.

sometimes ['sʌmtaɪmz] *adv* иногда.

somewhat ['sʌmwɔt] *adv* несколько.

somewhere ['sʌmwɛəʳ] *adv* (*be: somewhere specific*) где-то; (: *anywhere*) где-нибудь; (*go: somewhere specific*) куда-то; (: *anywhere*) куда-нибудь; (*come from*) откуда-то; **it's ~ or other in Scotland** это где-то в Шотландии; **is there a post office ~ around here?** здесь где-нибудь есть почта?; **let's go ~ else** давайте поедем куда-нибудь в другое место.

son [sʌn] *n* сын*.

sonar ['səunɑːʳ] *n* (*NAUT*) гидролокатор, эхолот.

sonata [sə'nɑːtə] *n* соната.

song [sɔŋ] *n* песня*.

song book *n* сборник песен, песенник.

songwriter ['sɔŋraɪtəʳ] *n* (композитор-) песенник, (поэт-)песенник.

sonic ['sɔnɪk] *adj* звуковой.

son-in-law ['sʌnɪnlɔː] *n* зять* *m*.

sonnet ['sɔnɪt] *n* сонет.

sonny ['sʌnɪ] *n* (*inf*) сынок*.

soon [suːn] *adv* (*in a short time*) скоро; (*early*) рано; **~ (afterwards)** вскоре; **quite ~** довольно скоро; **how ~ can you do it/come back?** когда Вы сможете это сделать/вернуться?; **see you ~!** до скорого!; *see also* **as**.

sooner ['suːnəʳ] *adv* (*time*) скорее; (*preference*): **I would ~ do that** я бы скорее сделал это; **~ or later** рано или поздно; **the ~ the better** чем скорее, тем лучше; **no ~ said than done** сказано-сделано; **no ~ had we left than … не**

успе́ли мы уйти́, как ....

soot [sut] *n* са́жа.

soothe [su:ð] *vt* успока́ивать (успоко́ить *perf*).

soothing ['su:ðɪŋ] *adj* (*ointment, drink, bath*) успокои́тельный; (*tone, words etc*) утеши́тельный* (утеши́телен).

SOP *n abbr* (= standard operating procedure) станда́ртная рабо́чая процеду́ра.

sop [sɔp] *n*: **that's only a ~** э́то то́лько пода́чка.

sophisticated [sə'fɪstɪkeɪtɪd] *adj* изощрённый* (изощрён); (*woman*) изы́сканная (изы́скана).

sophistication [səfɪstɪ'keɪʃən] *n* (see adj) изощрённость *f*; изы́сканность *f*.

sophomore ['sɔfəmɔːʳ] *n* (*US: SCOL*) второку́рсник(-ица).

soporific [sɔpə'rɪfɪk] *adj* (*speech*) усыпля́ющий; (*drug*) снотво́рный ♦ *n* снотво́рное *nt adj*.

sopping ['sɔpɪŋ] *adj*: ~ **(wet)** (*hair, clothes etc*) промо́кший насквозь.

soppy ['sɔpɪ] *adj* (*pej*) душещипа́тельный, сентимента́льный.

soprano [sə'prɑːnəu] *n* сопра́но *f ind*.

sorbet ['sɔːbeɪ] *n* (*CULIN*) фрукто́вое моро́женое *nt adj*.

sorcerer ['sɔːsərəʳ] *n* колду́н*.

sordid ['sɔːdɪd] *adj* (*place*) зага́женный (зага́жен); (*story etc*) гну́сный* (гну́сен).

sore [sɔː] *n* я́зва, боля́чка* ♦ *adj* (*esp US: offended*) оби́женный* (оби́жен); (*painful*): **my arm is ~, I've got a ~ arm** у меня́ боли́т рука́; **it's a ~ point** (*fig*) э́то боле́зненный предме́т.

sorely ['sɔːlɪ] *adv*: **I am ~ tempted (to)** у меня́ большо́й собла́зн (+*infin*).

soreness ['sɔːnɪs] *n* боль *f*.

sorrel ['sɔrəl] *n* щаве́ль* *m*.

sorrow ['sɔrəu] *n* (*regret*) печа́ль* *f*, грусть *f*; **~s** *npl* (*troubles*) печа́ли *fpl*.

sorrowful ['sɔrəuful] *adj* печа́льный* (печа́лен).

sorry ['sɔrɪ] *adj* (*condition, excuse, sight*) плаче́вный* (плаче́вен); (*regretful*): **I'm ~** мне жаль; **~!** (*apology*) извини́те, пожа́луйста!; **~?** (*pardon*) прости́те?; **I feel ~ for him** мне его́ жа́лко; **I'm ~ to hear that ...** мне гру́стно слы́шать, что ...; **to be ~ about sth** сожале́ть (*impf*) о чём-н.

sort [sɔːt] *n* сорт*; (*of car etc*) тип ♦ *vt* (*also: ~ out: papers, mail, belongings*) разбира́ть (разобра́ть* *perf*); (: *problems*) разбира́ться (разобра́ться* *perf*) в +*prp*; (*COMPUT*) сортирова́ть (*impf*); **what ~ do you want?** како́й сорт Вы хоти́те?; **what ~ of car?** кака́я маши́на?; **I'll do nothing of the ~!** я не собира́юсь де́лать ничего́ подо́бного!; **it's ~ of awkward** (*inf*) э́то как-то неудо́бно.

sortie ['sɔːtɪ] *n* (*MIL: on the ground*) вы́лазка*; (: *by air*) вы́лет; (*fig*) вы́лазка*.

sorting office ['sɔːtɪŋ-] *n* (*POST*) сортиро́вочное отделе́ние.

SOS *n abbr* (= save our souls) SOS.

so-so ['səusəu] *adv* так себе́.

soufflé ['su:fleɪ] *n* суфле́ *nt ind*.

sought [sɔːt] *pt, pp of* **seek**.

sought-after ['sɔːtɑːftəʳ] *adj* (*person, thing*) по́льзующийся спро́сом; **a much ~ item** вещь, по́льзующаяся больши́м спро́сом.

soul [səul] *n* душа́*; (*music*) (му́зыка) "со́ул"; **the poor ~ had nowhere to sleep** несча́стному не́где бы́ло спать; **I didn't see a ~** я не ви́дел ни души́.

soul-destroying ['səuldɪstrɔɪŋ] *adj*: **this work is ~** э́та рабо́та выма́тывает ду́шу.

soulful ['səulful] *adj* проникнове́нный*.

soulless ['səullɪs] *adj* (*place*) мёртвый (мёртв); **this is a ~ task** э́то иссуша́ет ду́шу.

soul mate *n* родна́я душа́*.

soul-searching ['səulsɑːtʃɪŋ] *n*: **after much ~, I decided ...** по́сле дли́тельного копа́ния в себе́ я реши́л ....

sound [saund] *adj* (*healthy*) здоро́вый; (*safe, not damaged*) про́чный* (про́чен), це́лый (цел); (*secure: investment*) надёжный* (надё жен); (*reliable, thorough*) соли́дный* (соли́ден); (*sensible: advice*) разу́мный* (разу́мен); (*valid: argument*) ве́ский*; (: *policy*) здравомы́слящий*; (: *claim*) основа́тельный* ♦ *n* звук; (*GEO*) зонд ♦ *vt* (*alarm*) поднима́ть (подня́ть* *perf*) ♦ *vi* звуча́ть (прозвуча́ть *perf*) ♦ *adv*: **he is ~ asleep** он кре́пко спит; **to be of ~ mind** быть* (*impf*) в здра́вом уме́; **I don't like the ~ of it** э́то мне не нра́вится; **to ~ one's horn** (*AUT*) сигна́лить (*impf*); **to ~ like** звуча́ть (прозвуча́ть *perf*) как (бу́дто); **it ~s like Russian** похо́же на ру́сский; **that ~s like them arriving** слы́шится, похо́же они́ прие́хали; **it ~s as if ...** похо́же, что ...;, похо́же как бу́дто ...

▸ **sound off** *vi* (*inf*): **to ~ off (about)** вы́сказаться* (*perf*) (о +*prp*).

▸ **sound out** *vt* (*person, opinion*) зонди́ровать (прозонди́ровать *perf*).

sound barrier *n* звуково́й барье́р.

sound effects *npl* звуковы́е эффе́кты *mpl*.

sound engineer *n* звукорежиссёр.

sounding ['saundɪŋ] *n* (*NAUT etc*) проме́р глубины́.

sounding board *n* (*MUS*) де́ка; **to use sb as a ~ for one's ideas** проверя́ть (прове́рить *perf*) свои́ иде́и на ком-н.

soundly ['saundlɪ] *adv* (*sleep*) кре́пко; (*beat etc*) здо́рово.

soundproof ['saundpru:f] *adj* звуконепроница́емый (звуконепроница́ем)

---

* marks translations which have irregular inflections. The Russian-English side of the dictionary gives inflectional information.

боб/со́ус.

sound system n (*TECH*) (звукова́я) систе́ма.

sozzled ['sɔzld] adj (*inf*) под му́хой.

soundtrack ['saundtræk] n му́зыка (*из кинофи́льма*).

spa [spɑː] n (*town*) куро́ртный го́род*; (*US: also*: **health** ~) лече́бно-оздорови́тельный куро́рт.

sound wave n звукова́я волна́*.

soup [suːp] n суп*; **to be in the ~** (*fig*) попада́ть (попа́сть* *perf*) в передря́гу.

space [speɪs] n (*gap*) простра́нство; (*place: small*) ме́сто*; (: *large*) простра́нство; (*room*) ме́сто*; (*beyond Earth*) ко́смос; (*interval, period*) промежу́ток* ◆ *cpd* косми́ческий* ◆ *vt* (*also*: ~ **out**: *text*) разбива́ть (разби́ть* *perf*); (: *payments, visits*) распределя́ть (распредели́ть* *perf*); **to clear a ~ for sth** расчища́ть (расчи́стить* *perf*) ме́сто для чего́-н; **in a confined ~** в ограни́ченном простра́нстве; **in a short ~ of time** в коро́ткий промежу́ток вре́мени; **(with)in the ~ of an hour** в тече́ние ча́са.

soup course n пе́рвое nt adj.

soup kitchen n столо́вая f adj для бе́дных, супова́я ку́хня.

soup plate n глубо́кая таре́лка*.

soupspoon ['suːpspuːn] n столо́вая ло́жка*.

sour ['sauə'] adj ки́слый; (*fig: bad-tempered*) неприя́зненный* (неприя́знен); **to go** or **turn ~** скиса́ть (ски́снуть* *perf*); (*fig*) по́ртиться* (испо́ртиться* *perf*); **it's ~ grapes** (*fig*) э́то за́висть.

space-bar ['speɪsbɑː'] n (*TYP*) интерва́л.

spacecraft ['speɪskrɑːft] n косми́ческий* кора́бль* m.

source [sɔːs] n (*also fig*) исто́чник; **I have it from a reliable ~ that** ... у меня́ есть све́дения из надёжного исто́чника, что ....

spaceman ['speɪsmæn] irreg n космона́вт.

spaceship ['speɪsʃɪp] n = **spacecraft**.

south [sauθ] n юг m ◆ adj ю́жный ◆ adv (*go*) на юг; (*be*) на ю́ге; **(to the) ~ of** к ю́гу от +gen; **to travel** ~ е́хать*/е́здить* (*impf*) на юг; **the S~ of France** Юг Фра́нции.

space shuttle n косми́ческий кора́бль ти́па "шатл".

spacesuit ['speɪssuːt] n скафа́ндр.

spacewoman ['speɪswumən] irreg n же́нщина-космона́вт.

South Africa n Ю́жная А́фрика.

South African adj южноафрика́нский ◆ n южноафрика́нец*(-нка*).

spacing ['speɪsɪŋ] n (*TYP*) промежу́тки mpl; интерва́лы mpl; **single/double ~** (*TYP*) с одни́м/двойны́м интерва́лом.

South America n Ю́жная Аме́рика.

South American adj южноамерика́нский ◆ n южноамерика́нец*(-нка*).

spacious ['speɪʃəs] adj просто́рный* (просто́рен).

spade [speɪd] n (*tool*) лопа́та; (*child's*) лопа́тка*; **~s** npl (*CARDS*) пи́ки fpl.

southbound ['sauθbaund] adj (*traffic*) дви́жущийся в ю́жном направле́нии; (*train, carriageway*) ю́жного направле́ния.

spadework ['speɪdwəːk] n (*fig*) чернова́я рабо́та.

spaghetti [spə'gɛtɪ] n спаге́тти pl ind.

southeast [sauθ'iːst] n юго-восто́к.

Southeast Asia n Ю́го-восто́чная А́зия.

Spain [speɪn] n Испа́ния.

southerly ['sʌðəlɪ] adj обращённый к ю́гу; (*wind*) ю́жный.

span [spæn] pt of **spin** ◆ n (*of hand, wings*) разма́х; (*of bridge*) пролёт; (*of time*) промежу́ток* ◆ vt (*river*) переки́нуть (*perf*) че́рез +acc; (*fig: time*) охва́тывать (охвати́ть* *perf*).

southern ['sʌðən] adj ю́жный; **a room with a ~ aspect** ко́мната, выходя́щая на юг; **the ~ hemisphere** ю́жное полуша́рие.

Spaniard ['spænjəd] n испа́нец*(-нка*).

spaniel ['spænjəl] n спание́ль m.

South Korea n Ю́жная Коре́я.

South Pole n: **the ~ ~** Ю́жный по́люс.

Spanish ['spænɪʃ] adj испа́нский* ◆ n (*LING*) испа́нский* язы́к*; **the ~** npl испа́нцы mpl; **~ omelette** омле́т по-испа́нски.

South Sea Islands npl: **the ~ ~ ~** острова́ mpl ю́жной ча́сти Ти́хого Океа́на.

South Seas npl: **the ~ ~** ю́жная часть f Ти́хого Океа́на.

spank [spæŋk] vt шлёпать (отшлёпать* *perf*).

spanner ['spænə'] n (*BRIT*) га́ечный ключ*.

southward(s) ['sauθwəd(z)] adv на юг, в ю́жном направле́нии.

spar [spɑː'] n (*pole*) шта́нга ◆ vi (*BOXING*) спари́нговать (*impf*).

southwest [sauθ'wɛst] n юго-за́пад.

souvenir [suːvə'nɪə'] n сувени́р.

sovereign ['sɔvrɪn] n (*ruler*) госуда́рь(-рыня) m(f).

spare [spɛə'] adj (*free: time, seat*) свобо́дный* (свобо́ден); (*surplus*) ли́шний; (*reserve*) запасно́й ◆ n = **spare part** ◆ vt (*trouble, expense, effort*) избавля́ть (изба́вить* *perf*) от +gen; (*refrain from using: energy, water etc*) бере́чь* (сбере́чь* *perf*); (*make available: person, time, money*) выделя́ть (вы́делить* *perf*); (*afford to give: money*) дава́ть* (дать* *perf*); (*refrain from hurting: person, city etc*)

sovereignty ['sɔvrɪntɪ] n суверените́т.

Soviet ['səuvɪət] adj сове́тский* ◆ n (*person*) сове́тский*(-ая) граждани́н*(-а́нка*); **the ~ Union** Сове́тский* Сою́з.

sow[1] [sau] n (*pig*) свинья́*, свинома́тка*.

sow[2] [səu] (*pt* **sowed**, *pp* **sown**) vt (*also fig*) се́ять (посе́ять *perf*).

sown [səun] pp of **sow**[2].

soya ['sɔɪə] (*US* **soy**) n: ~ **bean/sauce** со́евый

щади́ть* (пощади́ть* perf); **I have some time to** ~ име́ть (impf) свобо́дное вре́мя; **to have money to** ~ име́ть (impf) ли́шние де́ньги; **these 2 are going** ~ э́ти два – ли́шние; **to** ~ **no expense** не жале́ть (пожале́ть perf) средств; **can you** ~ **the time?** у Вас найдётся вре́мя?; **I've a few minutes to** ~ у меня́ есть не́сколько мину́т; **there is no time to** ~ у нас нет ли́шнего вре́мени; **can you** ~ **ten pounds?** у Вас не найдётся десяти́ фу́нтов?

spare part n запча́сть f= запасна́я часть.
spare room n свобо́дная ко́мната.
spare time n свобо́дное вре́мя* nt.
spare tyre n запасна́я ши́на.
spare wheel n запасно́е колесо́*.
sparing ['spɛərɪŋ] adj: **he is** ~ **with his money** он эконо́мен с деньга́ми; **he was** ~ **with his praise** он был ску́пен на похвалу́.
sparingly ['spɛərɪŋlɪ] adv эконо́мно.
spark [spɑːk] n (also fig) и́скра.
spark(ing) plug ['spɑːk(ɪŋ)-] n запа́льная свеча́*.
sparkle ['spɑːkl] n блеск ♦ vi (diamonds, water) сверка́ть (сверкну́ть perf); (eyes) блесте́ть* (impf); (bubble) шипе́ть* (impf).
sparkler ['spɑːklər] n (firework) бенга́льский ого́нь* m.
sparkling ['spɑːklɪŋ] adj (wine) игри́стый; (conversation, performance) блестя́щий*.
sparring partner ['spɑːrɪŋ-] n (BOXING) партнёр для трениро́вок в бо́ксе.
sparrow ['spærəu] n воробе́й*.
sparse [spɑːs] adj ре́дкий* (ре́док).
spartan ['spɑːtən] adj спарта́нский.
spasm ['spæzəm] n (MED) спазм; (of anger etc) при́ступ.
spasmodic [spæz'mɔdɪk] adj (fig) спазмати́ческий.
spastic ['spæstɪk] n (MED) парали́тик ♦ adj (MED) спасти́ческий.
spat [spæt] pt, pp of **spit** ♦ n (US: quarrel) размо́лвка*.
spate [speɪt] n (fig): **a** ~ **of** пото́к* +gen; **the river is in** ~ река́ вздула́сь.
spatial ['speɪʃl] adj простра́нственный.
spatter ['spætər] vt бры́згать (бры́знуть perf) ♦ vi обры́згаться (обры́знуться perf).
spatula ['spætjulə] n (MED) шпа́тель m; (CULIN) лопа́тка*.
spawn [spɔːn] vi (fish etc) мета́ть* (impf) икру́ ♦ vt (fig) порожда́ть (породи́ть* perf) ♦ n икра́.
SPCA n abbr (US) = Society for the Prevention of Cruelty to Animals.
SPCC n abbr (US) = Society for the Prevention of Cruelty to Children.
speak [spiːk] (pt **spoke**, pp **spoken**) vi (use voice) говори́ть (impf); (make a speech) выступа́ть (вы́ступить* perf) ♦ vt (truth) говори́ть

(сказа́ть* perf); **to** ~ **to sb** разгова́ривать (impf) с кем-н; **to** ~ **of** or **about** говори́ть (impf) о +prp; **he has no money to** ~ **of** у него́ о́чень немно́го де́нег; ~ **up!** говори́те гро́мче!; **to** ~ **at a conference/in a debate** выступа́ть (вы́ступить* perf) на конфере́нции/в деба́тах; **to** ~ **Russian/several languages** говори́ть (impf) по-ру́сски/на не́скольких языка́х; **to** ~ **one's mind** выска́зывать (вы́сказать* perf) своё мне́ние
▶ **speak for** vt fus: **to** ~ **for sb** говори́ть (impf) за кого́-н; **that picture is already spoken for** (already sold) э́ту карти́ну уже́ сторгова́ли.
speaker ['spiːkər] n (in public) ора́тор; (also: **loudspeaker**) громкоговори́тель m; (POL): **the S**~ спи́кер; **are you a Welsh** ~? Вы говори́те по-уэ́льски?
speaking ['spiːkɪŋ] adj говоря́щий; **Italian**-~ **people** италогово́рящие pl adj; **we are no longer on** ~ **terms** мы бо́льше не обща́емся.
spear [spɪər] n копьё* ♦ vt пронза́ть (пронзи́ть* perf) копьём.
spearhead ['spɪəhɛd] vt возглавля́ть (возгла́вить* perf).
spearmint ['spɪəmɪnt] n мя́та колосова́я.
spec [spɛk] n (inf): **on** ~ (buy, go etc) науда́чу.
spec. n abbr (TECH: = specification) специфика́ция.
special ['spɛʃl] adj (important) осо́бый, осо́бенный; (edition, adviser, school etc) специа́льный; (RAIL) по́езд* специа́льного назначе́ния; **take** ~ **care** прояви́те осо́бенную забо́ту; **nothing** ~ ничего́ осо́бенного; **today's** ~ (at restaurant) сего́дняшнее фи́рменное блю́до.
special agent n аге́нт по осо́бым поруче́ниям.
special correspondent n специа́льный корреспонде́нт.
special delivery n (POST): **by** ~ ~ сро́чной доста́вкой.
special effects npl (CINEMA) специа́льные съёмочные эффе́кты mpl.
specialist ['spɛʃəlɪst] n специали́ст; **heart** ~ специали́ст-кардио́лог.
speciality [spɛʃɪ'ælɪtɪ] n (dish) фи́рменное блю́до; (subject) специализа́ция.
specialize ['spɛʃəlaɪz] vi: **to** ~ **(in)** специализи́роваться (impf/perf) (в +prp).
specially ['spɛʃlɪ] adv (especially) осо́бенно; (on purpose) специа́льно.
special offer n: **the book is on** ~ ~ кни́гу продаю́т по сни́женной цене́.
specialty ['spɛʃəltɪ] n (esp US) = speciality.
species ['spiːʃiːz] n inv вид.
specific [spə'sɪfɪk] adj определённый; ~ **to** характе́рно для +gen.
specifically [spə'sɪfɪklɪ] adv (exactly)

---

* marks translations which have irregular inflections. The Russian-English side of the dictionary gives inflectional information.

определённо; (*specially*) специа́льно.
specification [spɛsɪfɪ'keɪʃən] *n* (*TECH*)
специфика́ция; (*requirement*) тре́бование;
~s *npl* (*TECH*) техни́ческие усло́вия *ntpl*.
specify ['spɛsɪfaɪ] *vt* (*time, place, colour etc*)
уточня́ть (уточни́ть *perf*); **unless otherwise
specified** е́сли нет други́х указа́ний.
specimen ['spɛsɪmən] *n* (*example*) экземпля́р;
(*sample for testing*) образе́ц*; **a ~ of urine**
моча́ для ана́лиза.
specimen copy *n* образцо́вый экземпля́р.
specimen signature *n* образе́ц* по́дписи.
speck [spɛk] *n* (*of dirt*) пя́тнышко; (*of dust*)
кра́пинка*.
speckled ['spɛkld] *adj* (*hen, eggs*) пёстрый
(пёстр).
specs [spɛks] *npl* (*inf: glasses*) очки́ *pl*.
spectacle ['spɛktəkl] *n* (*scene, event*) зре́лище;
~s *npl* (*glasses*) очки́ *pl*.
spectacle case *n* (*BRIT*) футля́р для очко́в.
spectacular [spɛk'tækjulə'] *adj* впечатля́ющий
(впечатля́ющ) ♦ *n* (*THEAT etc*) впечатля́ющее
зре́лище.
spectator [spɛk'teɪtə'] *n* зри́тель(ница) *m(f)* ♦
cpd: **a ~ sport** зре́лищный спорт.
spectra ['spɛktrə] *npl of* **spectrum**.
spectre ['spɛktə'] (*US* **specter**) *n* (*also fig*)
при́зрак.
spectrum ['spɛktrəm] (*pl* **spectra**) *n* спектр.
speculate ['spɛkjuleɪt] *vi* (*COMM*) игра́ть (*impf*)
на би́рже; (*guess*): **to ~ about** стро́ить (*impf*)
дога́дки *or* размышля́ть (*impf*) о +*prp*.
speculation [spɛkju'leɪʃən] *n* (*see vb*) биржева́я
игра́; дога́дка, предположе́ние.
sped [spɛd] *pt, pp of* **speed**.
speech [spi:tʃ] *n* речь *f*; (*THEAT*) моноло́г, речь.
speech day *n* (*BRIT: SCOL*) а́ктовый день* *m*.
speech impediment *n* дефе́кт ре́чи.
speechless ['spi:tʃlɪs] *adj* безмо́лвный*
(безмо́лвен).
speech therapist *n* логопе́д.
speech therapy *n* логопе́дия.
speed [spi:d] (*pt, pp* **sped**) *n* (*rate*) ско́рость* *f*;
(*promptness*) быстрота́ ♦ *vi* (*AUT: exceed
speed limit*) превыша́ть (превы́сить* *perf*)
ско́рость; (*move*): **to ~ along/by** *etc* мча́ться*
(промча́ться* *perf*) по +*dat*/ми́мо +*gen etc*; **at ~**
(*BRIT*) на большо́й ско́рости; **at full** *or* **top ~**
на по́лной *or* преде́ле ско́рости; **at a ~ of
70km/h** со ско́ростью 70км в час; **shorthand/
typing ~** ско́рость* маши́нописы/
стеногра́фи́рования; **a five-~ gearbox**
коро́бка* переда́ч с пятью́ скоростя́ми
▶ **speed up** (*pt, pp* **speeded up**) *vi* (*also fig*)
ускоря́ться (уско́риться* *perf*) ♦ *vt* (*also fig*)
ускоря́ть (уско́рить *perf*).
speedboat ['spi:dbəut] *n* быстрохо́дный
ка́тер*.
speedily ['spi:dɪlɪ] *adv* ско́ро.
speeding ['spi:dɪŋ] *n* (*AUT*) превыше́ние
ско́рости.

speed limit *n* (*AUT*) ограниче́ние ско́рости.
speedometer [spɪ'dɔmɪtə'] *n* (*AUT*) спидо́метр.
speed trap *n* (*AUT*) пост доро́жной поли́ции по
контро́лю за ско́ростью.
speedway ['spi:dweɪ] *n* (*sport: also:~ racing*)
спидве́й; (*track*) го́ночный трек.
speedy [spi:dɪ] *adj* (*fast: car*) бы́стрый (быстр);
(*prompt: reply, recovery, settlement*) ско́рый
(скор).
speleologist [spɛlɪ'ɔlədʒɪst] *n* спелео́лог.
spell [spɛl] (*pt, pp* **spelt** (*BRIT*) *or* **spelled**) *n* (*also:*
magic ~) колдовство́; (*period of time*)
пери́од ♦ *vt* (*in writing*) объясня́ть
(объясни́ть *perf*) в деталя́х; (*also:~ out*)
произноси́ть* (произнести́* *perf*) по бу́квам;
(*fig: advantages, difficulties*) разъясня́ть
(разъясни́ть *perf*) ♦ *vi*: **he can't ~** он не уме́ет
писа́ть без оши́бок; **to cast a ~ on sb**
околдо́вывать (околдова́ть *perf*) кого́-н;
how do you ~ your surname? как пи́шется
Ва́ша фами́лия?; **can you ~ it for me?** Вы
мо́жете произнести́ э́то по бу́квам?
spellbound ['spɛlbaund] *adj* зачаро́ванный
(зачаро́ван).
spelling ['spɛlɪŋ] *n* правописа́ние.
spelt [spɛlt] *pt, pp of* **spell**.
spend [spɛnd] (*pt, pp* **spent**) *vt* (*money*) тра́тить*
(истра́тить* *perf*); (*time, life*) проводи́ть*
(провести́* *perf*); (*devote*): **to ~ time/effort on
sth** тра́тить (потра́тить *perf*) вре́мя/си́лы на
что-н.
spending ['spɛndɪŋ] *n* расхо́ды *mpl*;
government ~ госуда́рственные расхо́ды
mpl.
spending money *n* карма́нные де́ньги* *pl*.
spending power *n* покупа́тельная
спосо́бность *f*.
spendthrift ['spɛndθrɪft] *n* расточи́тель(ница)
m(f).
spent [spɛnt] *pt, pp of* **spend** ♦ *adj* (*cartridge*)
пусто́й (пуст); (*bullets*) израсхо́дованный; **~
matches** испо́льзованные *or* израсхо́до-
ванные спи́чки; **my patience is ~** у меня́
терпе́ние кончи́лось.
sperm [spə:m] *n* спе́рма.
sperm bank *n* храни́лище до́норской
спе́рмы.
sperm whale *n* кашало́т.
spew [spju:] *vt* изрыга́ть (изрыгну́ть *perf*) ♦ *vi*
(*inf: vomit*) рвать (вы́рвать *perf*); **he ~ed** его́
вы́рвало.
sphere [sfɪə'] *n* сфе́ра.
spherical ['sfɛrɪkl] *adj* сфери́ческий*,
шарообра́зный* (шарообра́зен).
sphinx [sfɪŋks] *n* сфинкс.
spice [spaɪs] *n* спе́ция, пря́ность *f* ♦ *vt* (*food*)
приправля́ть (припра́вить* *perf*) спе́циями.
spick-and-span ['spɪkən'spæn] *adj*: **to be ~**
сверка́ть (*impf*).
spicy ['spaɪsɪ] *adj* (*food*) о́стрый (остр).
spider ['spaɪdə'] *n* пау́к*; **~'s web** паути́на.

spidery ['spaɪdərɪ] *adj* (*handwriting*) то́нкий*
(то́нок) и небре́жный* (небре́жен).
spiel [spiːl] *n* (*inf*) говори́льня.
spike [spaɪk] *n* (*point*) остриё; (*BOT: of flower*)
соцве́тие; (: *of corn*) ко́лос; (*ELEC*) штырь *m*;
~**s** *npl* (*SPORT*) шипы́ *mpl*.
spike heel *n* (*US*) шпи́лька*.
spiky ['spaɪkɪ] *adj* (*plant, animal*) колю́чий*
(колю́ч).
spill [spɪl] (*pt, pp* **spilt** *or* **spilled**) *vt* (*liquid*)
пролива́ть (проли́ть* *perf*), разлива́ть
(разли́ть* *perf*) ◆ *vi* (*liquid*) пролива́ться
(проли́ться* *perf*), разлива́ться (разли́ться*
perf); **to** ~ **the beans** (*inf*) проба́лтываться
(проболта́ться *perf*)
▶ **spill out** *vi* вылива́ться (вы́литься* *perf*)
▶ **spill over** *vi* (*liquid*) перелива́ться
(перели́ться* *perf*) (че́рез край); (*fig: crowd,
conflict*) вылива́ться (вы́литься* *perf*).
spillage ['spɪlɪdʒ] *n* (*of oil*) разли́в.
spilt [spɪlt] *pt, pp of* **spill**.
spin [spɪn] (*pt* **spun** *or* **span**, *pp* **spun**) *n* (*trip in
car*) ката́ние; (*revolution of wheel*) поворо́т,
враще́ние; (*AVIAT*) што́пор ◆ *vt* (*wool etc*)
прясть* (спрясть* *perf*); (*top*) крути́ть*
(закрути́ть* *perf*); (*wheel*) враща́ть (верте́ть*
perf); **to** ~ **a yarn** (*inf: story*)
плести́* (наплести́* *perf*) небыли́цы; **to** ~ **a
coin** (*BRIT*) подбра́сывать (подбро́сить* *perf*)
моне́ту
▶ **spin out** *vt* растя́гивать (растяну́ть* *perf*).
spina bifida ['spaɪnə'bɪfɪdə] *n* расщепле́ние
оста́тых отро́стков позвоно́чника.
spinach ['spɪnɪtʃ] *n* шпина́т.
spinal ['spaɪnl] *adj* спинно́й; ~ **injury**
поврежде́ние позвоно́чника.
spinal column *n* позвоно́чный столб*.
spinal cord *n* спинно́й мозг*.
spindly ['spɪndlɪ] *adj* дли́нный* (дли́нен) и
то́нкий* (то́нок).
spin doctor *n* (*inf*) *челове́к, роль кото́рого –
влия́ть на обще́ственное восприя́тие
полити́ческих програ́мм, и́миджа па́ртии
итп.*
spin-dry ['spɪn'draɪ] *vt* (*clothes, washing*)
выжима́ть (вы́жать* *perf*) до́суха (*в
центрифу́ге*).
spin-dryer [spɪn'draɪə'] *n* (*BRIT*)
центрифу́га-суши́лка*.
spine [spaɪn] *n* (*ANAT*) позвоно́чник; (*thorn*)
колю́чка*, игла́*.
spine-chilling ['spaɪntʃɪlɪŋ] *adj* (*story, film*)

жу́ткий* (жу́ток).
spineless ['spaɪnlɪs] *adj* (*fig*) бесхребе́тный*
(бесхребе́тен).
spinner ['spɪnə'] *n* (*of thread*) пряди́ль-
щик(-щица), пря́ха *m/f*.
spinning ['spɪnɪŋ] *n* (*craft*) пряде́ние.
spinning top *n* волчо́к*.
spinning wheel *n* пря́лка*.
spin-off ['spɪnɔf] *n* (*fig: by-product*) побо́чный
результа́т.
spinster ['spɪnstə'] *n* (*unmarried woman*)
незаму́жняя же́нщина.
spiral ['spaɪərl] *n* спира́ль *f* ◆ *vi* (*fig: prices etc*)
ре́зко возраста́ть (возрасти́* *perf*); **the
inflationary** ~ спира́ль инфля́ции.
spiral staircase *n* винтова́я ле́стница.
spire ['spaɪə'] *n* шпиль *m*.
spirit ['spɪrɪt] *n* дух; (*soul*) душа́*; ~**s** *npl* (*drink*)
спиртно́е *ntsg adj*; **in good/low** ~ в хоро́шем/
пода́вленном настрое́нии; **community** ~,
public ~ обще́ственный дух.
spirited ['spɪrɪtɪd] *adj* энерги́чный*
(энерги́чен); (*performance*) воодушевл-
ённый (воодушевлён); (*horse*) горя́чий*
(горя́ч).
spirit level *n* ватерпа́с.
spiritual ['spɪrɪtjuəl] *adj* духо́вный* (духо́вен) ◆
n (*also:* **Negro** ~) спи́ричуал.
spiritualism ['spɪrɪtjuəlɪzəm] *n* спирити́зм.
spit [spɪt] (*pt, pp* **spat**) *n* (*for roasting*) ве́ртел;
(*saliva*) слюна́ ◆ *vi* (*person*) плева́ть*
(плю́нуть* *perf*); (*fire, hot oil*) шипе́ть* (*impf*);
(*inf: rain*) мороси́ть* (*impf*).
spite [spaɪt] *n* зло́ба, злость *f* ◆ *vt* досажда́ть
(досади́ть* *perf*); **in** ~ **of** несмотря́ на +*acc*.
spiteful ['spaɪtful] *adj* зло́бный* (зло́бен).
spit roast *n* мя́со, зажа́ренное на ве́ртеле.
spitting ['spɪtɪŋ] *n*: "**spitting prohibited**"
"плева́ть воспреща́ется" ◆ *adj*: **he is the** ~
image of his father он вы́литый оте́ц.
spittle ['spɪtl] *n* слюна́.
spiv [spɪv] *n* (*BRIT: inf: pej*) жу́лик.
splash [splæʃ] *n* (*sound*) всплеск ◆ *excl*: ~!
плюх! ◆ *vt* брызга́ть* (бры́знуть *perf*) ◆ *vi*
(*also:* ~ **about**) плеска́ться* (*impf*); **a** ~ **of
colour** цветово́е пятно́; **to** ~ **paint on the floor**
забры́згивать (забры́згать* *perf*) пол
кра́ской.
splashdown ['splæʃdaun] *n* (*SPACE*)
приводне́ние.
splayfooted ['spleɪfutɪd] *adj* ступа́ющий
пя́тками внутрь, носка́ми врозь.
spleen [spliːn] *n* (*ANAT*) селезёнка*.
splendid ['splɛndɪd] *adj* великоле́пный*
(великоле́пен).
splendour ['splɛndə'] *n* (*US* **splendor**) *n*
великоле́пие; ~**s** *npl* (*features*) великоле́пие
ntsg.

---

* marks translations which have irregular inflections. The Russian-English side of the dictionary gives inflectional information.

splice [splaɪs] *vt* соединя́ть (соедини́ть *perf*); (*tape, film*) скле́ивать (скле́ить *perf*).

splint [splɪnt] *n* ши́на.

splinter ['splɪntə] *n* (*of wood*) ще́пка*; (*of glass*) оско́лок*; (*in finger*) зано́за ♦ *vi* (*bone, wood, glass etc*) расщепля́ться (расщепи́ться* *perf*).

splinter group *n* отколо́вшаяся фра́кция.

split [splɪt] (*pt, pp* **split**) *n* (*crack, tear*) тре́щина; (*POL, fig*) раско́л ♦ *vt* (*divide*) расщепля́ть (расщепи́ть* *perf*); (*POL*) раска́лывать (расколо́ть* *perf*); (*share equally: work, profits*) разделя́ть (раздели́ть* *perf*) ♦ *vi* (*divide*) расщепля́ться (расщепи́ться* *perf*), разделя́ться (раздели́ться* *perf*); (*glass, wood*) раска́лываться (расколо́ться* *perf*); (*cloth*) разрыва́ться (разорва́ться* *perf*); **let's ~ the difference** дава́йте сойдёмся на сре́дней ци́фре; **to do the ~s** де́лать (сде́лать *perf*) шпага́т
▸ **split up** *vi* (*couple*) расходи́ться* (разойти́сь* *perf*); (*group*) разделя́ться (раздели́ться* *perf*); (*meeting*) зака́нчиваться (зако́нчиться *perf*).

split-level ['splɪtlɛvl] *adj*: **~ house** дом, постро́енный на ра́зных у́ровнях.

split peas *npl* лущёный горо́х *msg*.

split personality *n* раздвое́ние ли́чности.

split second *n* до́ля* секу́нды.

splitting ['splɪtɪŋ] *adj*: **I've got a ~ headache** у меня́ голова́ раска́лывается.

splutter ['splʌtə'] *vi* (*engine etc*) треща́ть* (*impf*); (*person*) бры́згать* (*impf*) слюно́й.

spoil [spɔɪl] (*pt, pp* **spoilt** *or* **spoiled**) *vt* (*damage, mar*) по́ртить* (испо́ртить* *perf*); (*indulge*) балова́ть (избалова́ть *perf*) ♦ *vi*: **he's ~ing for a fight** он так и ле́зет в дра́ку.

spoils [spɔɪlz] *npl* (*also fig*) трофе́и *mpl*.

spoilsport ['spɔɪlspɔ:t] *n* (*pej: person*): **don't be a ~** не отравля́й лю́дям настрое́ние.

spoilt [spɔɪlt] *pt, pp of* **spoil** ♦ *adj* испо́рченный* (испо́рчен); (*child*) избало́ванный* (избало́ван).

spoke [spəʊk] *pt of* **speak** ♦ *n* (*of wheel*) спи́ца.

spoken ['spəʊkn] *pp of* **speak**.

spokesman ['spəʊksmən] *irreg n* представи́тель *m*.

spokesperson ['spəʊkspə:sn] *irreg n* представи́тель(ница) *m(f)* по свя́зам с пре́ссой.

spokeswoman ['spəʊkswumən] *irreg n* представи́тельница.

sponge [spʌndʒ] *n* гу́бка*; (*also:* **cake**) бискви́т ♦ *vt* (*wash*) обтира́ть (обтере́ть* *perf*) гу́бкой ♦ *vi*: **to ~ off** *or* **on sb** сиде́ть* (*impf*) на ше́е у кого́-н.

sponge bag *n* (*BRIT*) су́мочка* для туале́тных принадле́жностей.

sponger ['spʌndʒə'] *n* (*pej*) парази́т.

spongy ['spʌndʒɪ] *adj* гу́бчатый.

sponsor ['spɔnsə'] *n* спо́нсор; (*for application*) поручи́тель *m* ♦ *vt* финанси́ровать (*impf/perf*);

(*applicant*) поруча́ться (поручи́ться *perf*) за +*acc*; (*proposal, bill etc*) вноси́ть* (внести́* *perf*) на рассмотре́ние; **I ~ed him at twenty pence a mile** я пож́ертвовал ему́ два́дцать пе́нса за ми́лю.

sponsorship ['spɔnsəʃɪp] *n* спо́нсорство.

spontaneity [spɔntə'neɪtɪ] *n* спонта́нность *f*.

spontaneous [spɔn'teɪnɪəs] *adj* (*gesture*) спонта́нный* (спонта́нен); (*demonstration*) стихи́йный; **~ combustion** самовозгора́ние, самовоспламене́ние.

spoof [spu:f] (*inf*) *n* (*imitation*) паро́дия; (*joke*) ро́зыгрыш ♦ *vt* (*imitate*) передра́знивать (*impf*).

spooky ['spu:kɪ] *adj* (*inf: place, atmosphere*) злове́щий*, жу́ткий*.

spool [spu:l] *n* (*for thread*) кату́шка*; (*for film, tape etc*) боби́на.

spoon [spu:n] *n* ло́жка*.

spoon-feed ['spu:nfi:d] *vt* (*baby, patient*) корми́ть* (*impf*) с ло́жки; (*fig: students*) всё разжёвывать (*impf*) +*dat*.

spoonful ['spu:nful] *n* (*по́лная ло́жка*).

sporadic [spə'rædɪk] *adj* споради́ческий*.

sport [spɔ:t] *n* (*game*) спорт *m no pl*; (*person: also:* **good ~**) молодчи́на *m* ♦ *vt* (*wear*) щеголя́ть (щегольну́ть *perf*) +*instr*; **indoor/ outdoor ~s** ви́ды спо́рта для закры́тых помеще́ний/на откры́том во́здухе.

sporting ['spɔ:tɪŋ] *adj* (*event etc*) спорти́вный; (*generous*) ры́царский*; **to give sb a ~ chance** дава́ть* (дать* *perf*) кому́-н не́который шанс.

sport jacket *n* (*US*) = **sports jacket**.

sports car *n* спорти́вная маши́на.

sports centre *n* спорти́вный центр.

sports ground *n* спорти́вная площа́дка*.

sports jacket *n* (*BRIT*) спорти́вная ку́ртка* из тви́да.

sportsman ['spɔ:tsmən] *irreg n* спортсме́н.

sportsmanship ['spɔ:tsmənʃɪp] *n* спорти́вный дух; **he showed real ~** он показа́л себя́ настоя́щим спортсме́ном.

sports page *n* спорти́вная страни́ца.

sportswear ['spɔ:tswɛə'] *n* спорти́вная оде́жда.

sportswoman ['spɔ:tswumən] *irreg n* спортсме́нка*.

sporty ['spɔ:tɪ] *adj* спорти́вный* (спорти́вен).

spot [spɔt] *n* (*mark*) пятно́*; (*dot: on pattern*) кра́пинка*; (*on skin*) пры́щик; (*place*) ме́сто*; (*RADIO, TV*) рекла́мный переры́в; **~ advertisement** рекла́мная ру́брика ♦ *vt* (*notice*) замеча́ть (заме́тить* *perf*); **a ~ of bother** ма́ленькая неприя́тность *f*; **shall we have a ~ of lunch?** не перекуси́ть ли нам?; **~s of rain** ка́пли дождя́; **on the ~** (*in that place*) на ме́сте; (*immediately*) в тот же моме́нт; **to put sb on the ~** ста́вить* (поста́вить* *perf*) кого́-н в затрудни́тельное положе́ние; **in a ~** (*in difficulty*) в затрудни́тельном

положе́нии; **to come out in** ~**s** (*rash*)
покрыва́ться (покры́ться* *perf*) сы́пью;
(*blemishes*) покрыва́ться (покры́ться* *perf*)
прыща́ми.
spot check *n* вы́борочная прове́рка*.
spotless ['spɔtlɪs] *adj* (*shirt, kitchen etc*) без
пя́тнышка.
spotlight ['spɔtlaɪt] *n* (освети́тельный)
проже́ктор; **to be in the** ~ (*fig*) быть* (*impf*) в
це́нтре внима́ния.
spot-on [spɔt'ɔn] *adj* (*BRIT*: *inf*): **to be** ~
попа́сть* (*perf*) в са́мую то́чку.
spot price *n* (*COMM*) цена́ при усло́вии
неме́дленной опла́ты (нали́чными).
spotted ['spɔtɪd] *adj* (*pattern*) пятни́стый
(пятни́ст); ~ **with** запя́тнанный (запя́тнан)
+*instr*.
spotty ['spɔtɪ] *adj* (*face, youth*) прыща́вый
(прыща́в).
spouse [spaus] *n* супру́г(а).
spout [spaut] *n* (*of jug*) но́сик; (*of pipe*)
выпускно́е отве́рстие; (*of liquid*) струя́* ♦ *vi*
(*water etc*) бить* (*impf*) струёй; (*volcano*)
изверга́ться (изве́ргнуться *perf*).
sprain [spreɪn] *n* (*MED*) растяже́ние ♦ *vt*: **to** ~
one's ankle/wrist растя́гивать (растяну́ть*
perf) щи́колотку/запя́стье.
sprang [spræŋ] *pt of* **spring**.
sprawl [sprɔ:l] *vi* (*person*) разва́ливаться
(развали́ться* *perf*); (*place*) раски́дываться
(раски́нуться *perf*) ♦ *n*: **urban** ~ разраста́ние
го́рода; **to send sb** ~**ing** сбива́ть (сбить* *perf*)
кого́-н с ног.
spray [spreɪ] *n* (*drops of water*) бры́зги *pl*; (*hair
spray*) аэрозо́ль *m*; (*garden spray*)
разбры́згиватель *m*; (: *chemicals*)
ядохимика́ты *mpl*; (*of flowers*) ве́точка* ♦ *vt*
(*sprinkle*) обры́згивать (обры́згать *perf*);
(*crops*) опры́скивать (опры́скать *perf*) ♦ *cpd*:
~ **deodorant** дезодора́нт в аэрозо́льной
упако́вке.
spread [sprɛd] (*pt, pp* **spread**) *n* (*range*) спектр;
(*distribution*) распростране́ние; (*CULIN*: *paste*)
па́ста; (: *margarine etc*) бутербро́дный
маргари́н; (*inf: food*) оби́льное угаще́ние;
(*PRESS, TYP*: *two pages*) разворо́т ♦ *vt* (*lay out*)
расстила́ть (расстели́ть* *perf*); (*scatter*)
разбра́сывать (разброса́ть* *perf*); (*butter,
paste*) нама́зывать (нама́зать* *perf*); (*wings*)
расправля́ть (распра́вить* *perf*); (*arms*)
раскрыва́ть (раскры́ть* *perf*); (*sail*)
развёртывать (разверну́ть* *perf*); (*workload,
wealth*) распределя́ть (распредели́ть* *perf*);
(*rumour, disease*) распространя́ть
(распространи́ть* *perf*); (*repayments*)
отсро́чивать (отсро́чить *perf*) ♦ *vi* (*disease,
news*) распространя́ться (распростр-
ани́ться *perf*); (*also:* ~ **out**) расширя́ться

(расши́риться *perf*); **middle-age** ~
возрастна́я полнота́
▶ **spread out** *vi* (*move apart*) раздвига́ть
(раздви́нуть *perf*).
spread-eagled ['sprɛdi:gld] *adj*
распла́станный (распла́стан); **to be** *or* **lie** ~
лежа́ть* (*impf*) плашмя́.
spreadsheet ['sprɛdʃi:t] *n* (*COMPUT*)
электро́нная табли́ца.
spree [spri:] *n*: **to go on a** ~ кути́ть* (покути́ть*
perf).
sprig [sprɪg] *n* (*BOT*) ве́точка*.
sprightly ['spraɪtlɪ] *adj* (*old person*) бо́дрый
(бодр).
spring [sprɪŋ] (*pt* **sprang**, *pp* **sprung**) *n* (*coiled
metal*) пружи́на; (*season*) весна́*; (*of water*)
исто́чник, родни́к*; (*leap*) прыжо́к*;
(*bounciness*) упру́гость *f* ♦ *vi* (*leap*) пры́гать
(пры́гнуть *perf*) ♦ *vt*: **to** ~ **a leak** (*pipe etc*)
дава́ть* (дать* *perf*) течь; **in** ~ весно́й; **to walk
with a** ~ **in one's step** ходи́ть*/идти́* (*impf*)
упру́гой *or* пружи́нистой похо́дной; **to** ~
from sth (*be the result of*) быть* (*impf*)
вы́званным(-ой) чем-н; **he sprang the news
on me** он вы́валил на меня́ э́ту но́вость; **to** ~
into action ри́нуться (*perf*) в де́ло
▶ **spring up** *vi* (*building, plant*) выраста́ть
(вы́расти* *perf*).
springboard ['sprɪŋbɔ:d] *n* (*SPORT*) трампли́н;
(*fig*): **to be the** ~ **for** быть* (*impf*) трампли́ном
для +*gen*.
spring-clean(ing) [sprɪŋ'kli:n(ɪŋ)] *n*
генера́льная убо́рка*.
spring onion *n* (*BRIT*: *BOT*) лук-бату́н *no pl*;
(: *CULIN*) зелёный лук *no pl*.
spring roll *n* бли́нчик с начи́нкой, свёрнутый в
тру́бочку.
springtime ['sprɪŋtaɪm] *n* весна́я пора́.
springy ['sprɪŋɪ] *adj* упру́гий*.
sprinkle ['sprɪŋkl] *vt* (*salt, sugar*) посыпа́ть
(посы́пать* *perf*) +*instr*; **to** ~ **water on sth**, ~
sth with water бры́згать (побры́згать *perf*)
водо́й на что-н; **to** ~ **sugar on sth**, ~ **sth with
sugar** посыпа́ть (посы́пать* *perf*) что-н
са́харом; ~**d with** (*fig*) усы́панный (усы́пан)
+*instr*.
sprinkler ['sprɪŋklə'] *n* (*for lawn*)
разбры́згиватель *m*; (*to put out fire*)
спри́нклер.
sprinkling ['sprɪŋklɪŋ] *n* небольшо́е
коли́чество; (*of salt, sugar*) небольшо́е
го́рстка.
sprint [sprɪnt] *n* (*race*) спринт ♦ *vi* (*run fast*)
стреми́тельно бе́гать/бежа́ть* (*impf*); (*SPORT*)
спринтова́ть (*impf*); **the 200 metres** ~ спринт
на 200-ме́тровую диста́нцию.
sprinter ['sprɪntə'] *n* спри́нтер.
sprite [spraɪt] *n* эльф, фе́я.

---

* marks translations which have irregular inflections. The Russian-English side of the dictionary gives inflectional information.

spritzer ['sprɪtsəʳ] *n* бéлое винó с сóдовой (водóй).

sprocket ['sprɔkɪt] *n* (*TECH*) (цепнáя) звёздочка*.

sprout [spraut] *vi* (*BOT*) пускáть (пустúть* *perf*) ростки.

sprouts [sprauts] *npl* (*also:* **Brussels** ~) брюссéльская капýста *fsg*.

spruce [spru:s] *n inv* (*BOT*) ель *f* ♦ *adj* (*neat*) опрятный* (опрятен); (*smart*) нарядный* (наряжен)

▸ **spruce up** *vt* (*smarten up: room etc*) наводúть* (навести* *perf*) глянец на +*acc*; **to** ~ **o.s. up** наводúть* (навести* *perf*) на себя глянец.

sprung [sprʌŋ] *pp of* **spring**.

spry [spraɪ] *adj* (*old person*) бóдрый (бодр).

SPUC *n abbr* (= *Society for the Protection of Unborn Children*) *óбщество, бóрющееся прóтив дозволúтельности абóртов.*

spud [spʌd] *n* (*inf: potato*) картóшка*.

spun [spʌn] *pt, pp of* **spin**.

spur [spə:ʳ] *n* шпóра; (*fig*) стúмул ♦ *vt* (*also:* ~ **on**) подстёгивать (постегнýть* *perf*); **to** ~ **sb on to** побуждáть (побудúть* *perf*) когó-н к +*dat*; **on the** ~ **of the moment** под влиянием минýты.

spurious ['spjuərɪəs] *adj* поддéльный.

spurn [spə:n] *vt* (*reject*) отвергáть (отвéргнуть* *perf*).

spurt [spə:t] *n* (*of blood etc*) струя; (*of energy*) порыв ♦ *vi* хлынуть (*perf*); **to put on a** ~ дéлать (сдéлать *perf*) рывóк.

sputter ['spʌtəʳ] *vi* = **splutter**.

spy [spaɪ] *n* шпиóн ♦ *vi*: **to** ~ **on** шпиóнить (*impf*) за +*instr* ♦ *vt* (*see*) замечáть (замéтить* *perf*) ♦ *cpd* (*film, story*) шпиóнский.

spying ['spaɪɪŋ] *n* шпионáж.

Sq. *abbr* (*in address*) (= **square**) пл.= *плóщадь*.

sq. *abbr* = **square**.

squabble ['skwɔbl] *vi* вздóрить (повздóрить *perf*) ♦ *n* перебрáнка*.

squad [skwɔd] *n* (*MIL, POLICE*) комáнда; (*SPORT*) комáнда; **flying** ~ (*POLICE*) летýчий* полицéйский* отряд.

squad car *n* (*BRIT: POLICE*) дежýрная полицéйская машúна.

squaddie ['skwɔdɪ] *n* (*inf*) солдатня *f no pl*.

squadron ['skwɔdrn] *n* (*MIL*) эскадрóн; (*AVIAT*) эскадрúлья; (*NAUT*) эскáдра.

squalid ['skwɔlɪd] *adj* (*conditions, room*) убóгий (убóг); (*story etc*) грязный (грязен).

squall [skwɔ:l] *n* (*stormy wind*) шквал.

squalor ['skwɔləʳ] *n* убóгость *f*.

squander ['skwɔndəʳ] *vt* (*money*) промáтывать (промотáть *perf*); (*chances*) растрáчивать (растрáтить* *perf*).

square [skwɛəʳ] *n* (*shape*) квадрáт; (*in town*) плóщадь *f*; (*US: block of houses*) квартáл; (*also:* **set** ~) угóльник; (*inf: person*) немóдный, сéрый человéк* ♦ *adj*

квадрáтный; (*inf: ideas, tastes*) немóдный, сéрый ♦ *vt* (*reconcile, settle*) улáживать (улáдить* *perf*); (*MATH*) возводúть* (возвести* *perf*) в квадрáт ♦ *vi* (*agree*) согласóвываться (согласовáться *perf*); **we are all** ~ мы квúты; **a** ~ **meal** плóтная трапéза; **2 metres** ~ 2 мéтра длинóй и 2 мéтра ширинóй; **2** ~ **metres** 2 квадрáтных мéтра; **I'll** ~ **it with him** (*inf*) я с ним э́то улáжу; **can you** ~ **it with your conscience?** (*reconcile*) э́то согласýется с Вáшей сóвестью?; **we're back to** ~ **one** мы вернýлись тудá, откýда начáли

▸ **square up** *vi* (*BRIT*): **to** ~ **up with sb** поквитáться (*perf*) с кем-н.

square bracket *n* (*TYP*) квадрáтная скóбка*.

squarely ['skwɛəlɪ] *adv* прямо.

square root *n* квадрáтный кóрень* *m*.

squash [skwɔʃ] *n* (*BRIT: drink*): **lemon/orange** ~ лимóнный/апельсúновой напúток* (*приготóвленный из концентрáта*); (*US*) тыква; (*SPORT*) ракетбóл ♦ *vt* давúть* (раздавúть* *perf*).

squat [skwɔt] *adj* призéмистый (призéмист) ♦ *vi* (*also:* ~ **down: position**) сидéть* (*impf*) на кóрточках; (: *motion*) сесть* (*perf*) на кóрточки; (*on property*) незакóнно поселяться (поселúться *perf*) в дом.

squatter ['skwɔtəʳ] *n* (*in house*) *лицó, самовóльно поселяющееся в чужóм дóме*; (*on land*) сквáттер.

squawk [skwɔ:k] *vi* (*bird*) клекотáть* (*impf*).

squeak [skwi:k] *vi* (*door*) скрипéть* (скрúпнуть *perf*); (*mouse*) пищáть* (пúскнуть *perf*) ♦ *n* (*of hinge, wheel etc*) скрип.

squeaky-clean [skwi:kɪ'kli:n] *adj* (*surface etc*) чúстый (чист) до скрúпа; (*fig*) без пятнышка.

squeal [skwi:l] *vi* визжáть* (*impf*), взвúзгивать (взвúзгнуть *perf*).

squeamish ['skwi:mɪʃ] *adj* (*person*) брезглúвый (брезглúв).

squeeze [skwi:z] *n* (*of hand*) сжáтие; (*ECON*) ограничéние; (*also:* **credit** ~) ограничéние кредúта ♦ *vt* сжимáть (сжать* *perf*); (*juice*) выжимáть (выжать* *perf*) ♦ *vi*: **to** ~ **past/ under sth** протúскиваться (протúснуться *perf*) чéрез что-н/под чем-н; **a** ~ **of lemon** нéсколько капéль лимóнного сóка

▸ **squeeze out** *vt* (*juice etc*) выжимáть (выжать* *perf*); (*fig: money etc*) выжимáть (выжать* *perf*).

squelch [skwɛltʃ] *vi* (*mud etc*) хлюпать (хлюпнуть *perf*).

squib [skwɪb] *n* (*firework*) петáрда.

squid [skwɪd] *n* кальмáр.

squiggle ['skwɪgl] *n* загогýлина.

squint [skwɪnt] *vi* (*permanently*) косúть* (*impf*); (*in sunlight*) щýриться (*impf*), прищýриваться (прищýриться *perf*) ♦ *n* (*MED*) косоглáзие; **he has a** ~ у негó косоглáзие, он косúт.

squire ['skwaɪə^r] *n* (*BRIT*) поме́щик; (*inf*) нача́льник.

squirm [skwə:m] *vi* выгиба́ться (вы́гнуться *perf*); (*with embarrassment or shame*) поёживаться (поёжиться *perf*).

squirrel ['skwɪrəl] *n* бе́лка*.

squirt [skwə:t] *vi* бры́згать* (бры́знуть *perf*) ♦ *vt* бры́згать* (бры́знуть *perf*) +*instr*.

Sr *abbr* (*in names*) = **senior**; (*REL*) = **sister**.

SRC *n abbr* (*BRIT*) = **Students' Representative Council**.

Sri Lanka [srɪ'læŋkə] *n* Шри-Ла́нка.

SRN *n abbr* (*BRIT*: = **State Registered Nurse**) медсестра́= *медици́нская сестра́*.

SRO *abbr* (*US*: = **standing room only**) то́лько стоя́чие места́ *ntpl*.

SS *abbr* = **steamship**.

SSA *n abbr* (*US*: = **Social Security Administration**) ≈ департа́мент социа́льного обеспе́чения.

SST *n abbr* (*US*: = **supersonic transport**) сверхзвуково́й реакти́вный самолёт.

ST *abbr* (*US*) = **Standard Time**.

St *abbr* = **saint**; (= **street**) ул.= *у́лица*.

stab [stæb] *n* (*with knife etc*) уда́р (*чем-н о́стрым*); (*of pain*) уко́л; (*inf: try*): **to have a ~ at doing** пыта́ться (попыта́ться *perf*) +*infin* ♦ *vt* наноси́ть* (нанести́* *perf*) уда́р +*dat*; **to ~ sb to death** зака́лывать (заколо́ть* *perf*) кого́-н.

stabbing ['stæbɪŋ] *n*: **there's been a ~** здесь была́ поножо́вщина ♦ *adj* (*pain, ache*) ре́зкий*.

stability [stə'bɪlɪtɪ] *n* (*of object*) усто́йчивость *f*; (*of government, economy etc*) стаби́льность *f*.

stabilization [steɪbəlaɪ'zeɪʃən] *n* стабилиза́ция.

stabilize ['steɪbəlaɪz] *vt* (*prices*) стабилизи́ровать (*impf/perf*) ♦ *vi* стабилизи́роваться (*impf/ perf*).

stabilizer ['steɪbəlaɪzə^r] *n* стабилиза́тор.

stable ['steɪbl] *adj* стаби́льный* (стаби́лен), усто́йчивый (усто́йчив) ♦ *n* (*for horse*) коню́шня*, сто́йло; (*for cattle*) хлев*, сто́йло; **riding ~s** (*school*) ко́нно-спорти́вная шко́ла.

staccato [stə'kɑ:təu] *adv* (*MUS*) стакка́то ♦ *adj* отры́вистый (отры́вист).

stack [stæk] *n* (*pile: of hay*) стог*, скирда́*; (*of wood*) шта́бель *m*, поле́нница; (*of papers*) ки́па, сто́пка; (*of plates*) стопа́* ♦ *vt* (*also: ~ up: chairs etc*) скла́дывать (сложи́ть* *perf*) в ку́чу; (: *books, plates*) скла́дывать (сложи́ть* *perf*) в сто́пку; (*room, table etc*): **to ~ (with)** уставля́ть (уста́вить* *perf*) сто́пками; **there's ~s of time** (*BRIT: inf*) ещё есть ку́ча вре́мени.

stadia ['steɪdɪə] *npl* **of stadium**.

stadium ['steɪdɪəm] (*pl* **stadia** *or* **~s**) *n* (*SPORT*) стадио́н.

staff [stɑ:f] *n* (*workforce*) рабо́тники *pl*, штат; (*BRIT: SCOL: also:* **teaching ~**) штат учителе́й, преподава́тельский соста́в; (*servants*) штат;

(*MIL*) ли́чный соста́в; (*stick*) по́сох ♦ *vt* укомплекто́вывать (укомплектова́ть *perf*).

staffroom ['stɑ:fru:m] *n* (*SCOL*) учи́тельская *f adj*.

Staffs *abbr* (*BRIT: POST*) = **Staffordshire**.

stag [stæg] *n* саме́ц* оле́ня; (*BRIT: STOCK EXCHANGE*) спекуля́нт це́нными бума́гами.

stage [steɪdʒ] *n* (*in theatre*) сце́на; (*platform*) подмо́стки *pl*; (*profession*): **the ~** сце́на; (*point, period*) ста́дия ♦ *vt* (*play*) ста́вить* (поста́вить* *perf*); (*demonstration*) устра́ивать (устро́ить *perf*); (*fig: recovery etc*) осуществля́ть (осуществи́ть* *perf*); **in ~s** поэта́пно, по эта́пам; **he is going through a difficult ~** он пережива́ет тру́дный пери́од; **in the early/final ~s** на ра́нних/после́дних ста́диях *or* эта́пах.

stagecoach ['steɪdʒkəutʃ] *n* почто́вый дилижа́нс.

stage door *n* (*THEAT*) служе́бный вход (*в теа́тр*).

stage fright *n* волне́ние пе́ред выступле́нием.

stagehand ['steɪdʒhænd] *n* рабо́чий*(-ая) *m(f) adj* сце́ны.

stage-manage ['steɪdʒmænɪdʒ] *vt* (*fig*) закули́сно руководи́ть* (*impf*) +*instr*.

stage manager *n* дире́ктор сце́ны.

stagger ['stægə^r] *vi* (*amaze*) потряса́ть (потрясти́* *perf*) ♦ *vi*: **he ~ed along the road** он шёл по доро́ге, пошатываясь; **the management has ~ed the workers' leave** администра́ция соста́вила гра́фик о́тпусков.

staggering ['stægərɪŋ] *adj* потряса́ющий*.

staging post ['steɪdʒɪŋ-] *n* (*on flight*) промежу́точный аэродро́м.

stagnant ['stægnənt] *adj* (*water*) стоя́чий*; (*economy*) засто́йный.

stagnate [stæg'neɪt] *vi* (*person*) засижива́ться (засиде́ться* *perf*); (*economy, business*) быть* (*impf*) в засто́е.

stagnation [stæg'neɪʃən] *n* засто́й; (*ECON*) стагна́ция, засто́й.

stag party *n* ма́льчишник.

staid [steɪd] *adj* (*person, attitudes*) степе́нный* (степе́нен).

stain [steɪn] *n* пятно́*; (*for wood*) мори́лка* ♦ *vt* (*mark*) пятна́ть (запятна́ть *perf*), па́чкать (запа́чкать *perf*); (*wood*) мори́ть (замори́ть *perf*).

stained glass window [steɪnd-] *n* витра́ж.

stainless steel ['steɪnlɪs-] *n* нержаве́ющая сталь *f*.

stain remover *n* пятновыводи́тель *m*.

stair [steə^r] *n* (*step*) ступе́нь *f*, ступе́нька*; **~s** *npl* (*steps*) ле́стница *fsg*; **on the ~s** на ле́стнице.

staircase ['steəkeɪs] *n* ле́стница.

---

* marks translations which have irregular inflections. The Russian-English side of the dictionary gives inflectional information.

stairway ['stɛəweɪ] = **staircase.**

stairwell ['stɛəwɛl] *n* лéстничная клéтка*.

stake [steɪk] *n* (*post*) кол*; (*investment*) дóля*; (*wager*) стáвка*; (*horse race: usu pl*) скáчки* *fpl* ◆ *vt* (*wager: money, life, reputation*) стáвить* (постáвить* *perf*); (*also: ~ out: area*) огорáживать (огородить* *perf*); (*fig*) очéрчивать (очертить* *perf*) грани́цы +*gen*; **his reputation was at ~** егó репутáция былá постáвлена на кáрту; **he has a ~ in this business** он крóвно заинтересóван в э́том би́знесе; **to ~ a claim (to sth)** притязáть (*impf*) (на что-н).

stake out *n* (*US: inf*) засáда.

stalactite ['stæləktaɪt] *n* сталакти́т.

stalagmite ['stæləgmaɪt] *n* сталагми́т.

stale [steɪl] *adj* (*bread*) чёрствый (чёрств); (*food, beer*) несвéжий* (несвéж); (*air, smell*) зáтхлый.

stalemate ['steɪlmeɪt] *n* (*CHESS*) пат; (*fig*) тупи́к.

stalk [stɔ:k] *n* (*of flower*) стéбель *m*; (*of fruit*) черенóк* ◆ *vt* (*person, animal*) крáсться* (подкрáсться* *perf*) к +*dat* ◆ *vi*: **to ~ out/off** удаля́ться (удали́ться *perf*).

stall [stɔ:l] *n* (*BRIT: in street*) ларёк*, киóск; (*in market*) прилáвок*; (*in stable*) стóйло ◆ *vt* (*fig: delay*) задéрживать (задержáть* *perf*) ◆ *vi* (*AUT*) глóхнуть* (заглóхнуть* *perf*); (*fig: person*) мéшкать (помéшкать *perf*); **~s** *npl* (*BRIT: THEAT*) партéр *msg*; **watch you don't ~ the engine** смотри́, чтóбы мотóр не заглóх; **a seat in the ~s** мéсто* *or* крéсло* в партéре; **a newspaper/flower ~** газéтный/цветóчный ларёк.

stallholder ['stɔ:lhəʊldə'] *n* (*BRIT*) владéлец* ларькá.

stallion ['stæljən] *n* жеребéц*.

stalwart ['stɔ:lwət] *adj* (*worker, supporter, party member*) стóйкий*.

stamen ['steɪmɛn] *n* тычи́нка*.

stamina ['stæmɪnə] *n* вынóсливость *f*.

stammer ['stæmə'] *n* заикáние ◆ *vi* заикáться.

stamp [stæmp] *n* (*postage stamp*) мáрка*; (*rubber stamp*) печáть *f*, штамп; (*mark, also fig*) печáть *f* ◆ *vi* (*also: ~ one's foot*) тóптать* (тóпнуть *perf*) ногóй ◆ *vt* (*letter*) наклéивать (наклéить *perf*) мáрку на +*acc*; (*mark*) опи́скивать (описну́ть *perf*); (*with rubber stamp*) стáвить* (постáвить* *perf*) печáть *or* штамп на +*acc*; **~ed addressed envelope** надпи́санный конвéрт с мáркой

▶ **stamp out** *vt* (*fire*) затáптывать (затоптáть* *perf*); (*crime*) уничтожáть (уничтóжить *perf*); (*opposition*) подавля́ть (подави́ть* *perf*).

stamp album *n* альбóм для мáрок.

stamp collecting *n* филатели́я.

stamp duty *n* (*BRIT*) гéрбовый сбор.

stampede [stæm'pi:d] *n* (*also fig*) мáссовое бéгство.

stamp machine *n* автомáт по продáже

почтóвых мáрок.

stance [stæns] *n* (*also fig*) пози́ция.

stand [stænd] (*pt, pp* **stood**) *n* (*stall*) ларёк*, киóск; (*at exhibition*) стенд; (*SPORT*) трибу́на; (*piece of furniture: for umbrellas*) подстáвка*; (*: for coats, hats*) вéшалка* ◆ *vi* (*be upright*) стоя́ть* (*impf*); (*rise*) вставáть* (встать* *perf*); (*remain: decision, offer*) оставáться* (остáться* *perf*) в си́ле; (*in election etc*) выставля́ть (вы́ставить* *perf*) свою́ кандидату́ру, баллоти́роваться (*impf*); (*value, level, score etc*): **to ~ at** оставáться* (остáться* *perf*) на +*prp* ◆ *vt* (*place: object*) стáвить* (постáвить* *perf*); (*tolerate, withstand*) терпéть* (*impf*), выноси́ть* (вы́нести* *perf*); **to make a ~ against sth** окáзывать (оказáть* *perf*) сопротивлéние чему́-н; **to take a ~ on sth** занимáть (заня́ть* *perf*) пози́цию по пóводу чегó-н; **to take the ~** (*US: LAW*) занимáть (заня́ть* *perf*) мéсто свидéтеля; **to ~ for parliament** (*BRIT*) баллоти́роваться (*impf*) в парлáмент; **to ~ to gain/lose sth** имéть (*impf*) шанс обрести́/потеря́ть что-н; **to ~ sb dinner** угощáть (угости́ть* *perf*) когó-н обéдом; **to ~ sb a drink** стáвить* (постáвить* *perf*) кому́-н вы́пивку; **it ~s to reason** самó собóй разумéется; **as things ~** в э́той ситуáции; **I can't ~ him** я егó терпéть не могу́

▶ **stand aside** *vi* (*fig*) стоя́ть (*impf*) в сторонé

▶ **stand by** *vi* (*be ready*) быть* (*impf*) наготóве ◆ *vt fus* (*opinion, decision*) не отступáть (не отступи́ть* *perf*) от +*gen*; (*person*) поддéрживать (поддержáть* *perf*)

▶ **stand down** *vi* (*withdraw*) уступáть (уступи́ть* *perf*) мéсто +*dat*, уходи́ть* (уйти́* *perf*); (*LAW*) покидáть (покину́ть *perf*) мéсто свидéтеля

▶ **stand for** *vt fus* (*signify*) обозначáть (*impf*); (*represent*) представля́ть (*impf*); **I won't ~ for it** я э́того не потéрплю

▶ **stand in for** *vt fus* (*replace*) замещáть (замести́ть* *perf*) +*acc*

▶ **stand out** *vi* (*be prominent*) выделя́ться (вы́делиться *perf*)

▶ **stand up** *vi* (*rise*) вставáть* (встать* *perf*)

▶ **stand up for** *vt fus* (*defend: rights etc*) отстáивать (отстоя́ть* *perf*); (*: person*) стоя́ть* (постоя́ть* *perf*) за +*acc*

▶ **stand up to** *vt fus* (*withstand: also fig*) выдéрживать (вы́держать* *perf*).

stand-alone ['stændələʊn] *adj* (*COMPUT*) автонóмный.

standard ['stændəd] *n* (*level*) у́ровень* *m*; (*norm, criterion*) стандáрт; (*flag*) знáмя* *nt* ◆ *adj* (*normal: size etc*) стандáртный (стандáртен); (*text*) основнóй; (*practice*) общепри́нятый (общепри́нят); (*model, feature*) типи́чный* (типи́чен); **~s** *npl* (*morals*) нрáвы *mpl*; **to be** *or* **come up to ~** быть* (*impf*) на соотвéтствующем у́ровне; **to apply**

a double ~ испо́льзовать *(impf/perf)* двойну́ю мора́ль.
standardization [stændədaɪ'zeɪʃən] *n* стандартиза́ция.
standardize ['stændədaɪz] *vt* стандартизи́ровать *(impf/perf)*.
standard lamp *n (BRIT)* торше́р.
standard of living *n* у́ровень* *m* жи́зни.
standard time *n* станда́ртное вре́мя* *nt*.
stand-by ['stændbaɪ] *n (reserve)* резе́рв, подмо́га ♦ *adj* запасно́й, резе́рвный; **to be on ~** *(doctor, crew, firemen etc)* быть* *(impf)* наготове.
stand-by ticket *n (THEAT etc)* биле́т, ку́пленный пе́ред нача́лом представле́ния.
stand-in ['stændɪn] *n* замести́тель(ница) *m(f)*.
standing ['stændɪŋ] *adj (permanent)* постоя́нный; *(ovation)* стоя́чий* ♦ *n (status)* положе́ние; *(duration)* of 6 months' ~ 6-ти ме́сячной да́вности; **he received/was given a ~ ovation** ему́ устро́или стоя́чую ова́цию; **he gave me a ~ invitation** он сказа́л, что́бы я приходи́л в любо́е вре́мя; **a man of some ~** челове́к с положе́нием; **promises of many years ~** многоле́тние обеща́ния.
standing committee *n* постоя́нный комите́т.
standing joke *n* дежу́рная шу́тка*.
standing order *n (BRIT: at bank)* прика́з о регуля́рных платежа́х.
standing room *n* стоя́чие места́ *ntpl*.
standoffish [stænd'ɒfɪʃ] *adj* спеси́вый (спеси́в).
standpat ['stændpæt] *adj (US: person)* консервати́вный.
standpipe ['stændpaɪp] *n* напо́рная труба́*.
standpoint ['stændpɔɪnt] *n* то́чка* зре́ния.
standstill ['stændstɪl] *n*: **to be at a ~** *(also fig)* проста́ивать *(impf)*; **to come to a ~** остана́вливаться (останови́ться* *perf)*.
stank [stæŋk] *pt of* **stink**.
stanza ['stænzə] *n (of poem)* строфа́*.
staple ['steɪpl] *n (for papers)* ско́бка*; *(chief product)* основно́й проду́кт ♦ *adj (food etc)* основно́й ♦ *vt (fasten)* сшива́ть (сшить* *perf)* сте́плером.
stapler ['steɪplə] *n* сшива́тель *m*, сте́плер.
star [stɑ:] *n (also fig)* звезда́ ♦ *vi*: **to ~ in** игра́ть (сыгра́ть *perf)* гла́вную роль в +*prp* ♦ *vt (THEAT, CINEMA)*: **the film ~s my brother** гла́вную роль игра́ет в фи́льме мой брат; **the ~s** *npl (horoscope)* звёзды *fpl*; **4-~ hotel** четырёхзвёздочная гости́ница; **2-~/4-~ petrol** *(BRIT)* бензи́н с ни́зким/высо́ким окта́новым число́м.
star attraction *n* гвоздь* *m* програ́ммы.
starboard ['stɑ:bəd] *n (NAUT)* пра́вый борт*; **to ~** пра́во руля́.
starch [stɑ:tʃ] *n (also CULIN)* крахма́л.
starched ['stɑ:tʃt] *adj (collar)* накрахма́ленный

(накрахма́лен).
starchy ['stɑ:tʃɪ] *adj (food)* содержа́щий крахма́л; *(pej: person)* чо́порный* (чо́порен).
stardom ['stɑ:dəm] *n* сла́ва.
stare [steəˈ] *n* при́стальный взгляд ♦ *vi*: **to ~ at** при́стально смотре́ть* *(impf)* на +*acc*.
starfish ['stɑ:fɪʃ] *n* морска́я звезда́*.
stark [stɑ:k] *adj (bleak)* го́лый* (гол); *(facts, reality)* го́лый; *(poverty)* соверше́нный; *(colour, contrast)* я́вный* (я́вен) ♦ *adv*: **~ naked** соверше́нно го́лый.
starkers ['stɑ:kəz] *adj, adv* без всего́*.
starlet ['stɑ:lɪt] *n (CINEMA)* молода́я актри́са.
starlight ['stɑ:laɪt] *n*: **by ~** при све́те звёзд.
starling ['stɑ:lɪŋ] *n* скворе́ц*.
starlit ['stɑ:lɪt] *adj (night)* звёздный.
starry ['stɑ:rɪ] *adj (night, sky)* звёздный.
starry-eyed [stɑ:rɪ'aɪd] *adj (innocent)* наи́вный* (наи́вен); *(from wonder)* она́ очаро́ванна.
Stars and Stripes *n*: **the ~ ~ ~** звёздно-полоса́тый *m adj (флаг США)*.
star sign *n* знак зодиа́ка.
star-studded ['stɑ:stʌdɪd] *adj*: **this film has a ~ cast** в э́том фи́льме снима́ются мно́гие знамени́тые актёры.
START *n abbr (MIL*: = *Strategic Arms Reduction Talks)* перегово́ры *pl* о сокраще́нии стратеги́ческих вооруже́ний.
start [stɑ:t] *n* нача́ло; *(SPORT)* старт; *(departure)* отправле́ние; *(sudden movement)* вздра́гивание; *(advantage)* преиму́щество ♦ *vt (begin)* начина́ть (нача́ть* *perf)*; *(cause)* вызыва́ть (вы́звать* *perf)*; *(found: business etc)* осно́вывать (основа́ть* *perf)*; *(engine)* заводи́ть (завести́* *perf)*, запуска́ть (запусти́ть* *perf)* ♦ *vi (begin)* начина́ться (нача́ться* *perf)*; *(begin moving)* отправля́ться (отпра́виться* *perf)*; *(engine, car)* заводи́ться* (завести́сь* *perf)*; *(jump: with fright)* вздра́гивать (вздро́гнуть* *perf)*; **to ~ doing** *or* **to do** начина́ть (нача́ть* *perf)* +*impf infin*; **at the ~** в нача́ле; **for a ~** для нача́ла; **to make an early ~** ра́но начина́ть (нача́ть* *perf)*; **to ~ (off) with ...** *(firstly)* во-пе́рвых ...; *(at the beginning)* снача́ла
▸ **start off** *vi (begin)* начина́ться (нача́ться* *perf)*; *(begin moving, leave)* отправля́ться (отпра́виться* *perf)*
▸ **start out** *vi (leave)* отправля́ться (отпра́виться* *perf)*
▸ **start over** *vi (US)* начина́ть (нача́ть* *perf)* сно́ва
▸ **start up** *vi (business etc)* открыва́ться (откры́ться* *perf)*; *(engine, car)* заводи́ться* (завести́сь* *perf)* ♦ *vt (business etc)* осно́вывать (основа́ть* *perf)*; *(engine, car)* заводи́ть* (завести́* *perf)*, запуска́ть (запусти́ть* *perf)*.

---

* marks translations which have irregular inflections. The Russian-English side of the dictionary gives inflectional information.

starter ['stɑːtəʳ] *n* (*AUT, SPORT*) ста́ртер; (*runner, horse*) уча́стник(-ица) забе́га; (*BRIT: CULIN*) заку́ска.
starting point ['stɑːtɪŋ-] *n* (*for journey*) отправно́й пункт; (*for discussion, idea etc*) отправна́я то́чка*.
starting price *n* (*at auction*) нача́льная *or* отправна́я цена́*.
startle ['stɑːtl] *vt* вспу́гивать (вспугну́ть *perf*).
startling ['stɑːtlɪŋ] *adj* порази́тельный* (порази́телен).
star turn *n* (*BRIT*) коро́нный но́мер*.
starvation [stɑːˈveɪʃən] *n* го́лод; **to die of** *or* **from ~** умира́ть (умере́ть* *perf*) от го́лода.
starve [stɑːv] *vi* (*to death*) умира́ть (умере́ть* *perf*) с го́лоду; (*be very hungry*) проголода́ться (*perf*) ♦ *vt* (*person, animal*) мори́ть (замори́ть *perf*) го́лодом; (*fig: deprive*): **to ~ sb of sth** лиша́ть (лиши́ть *perf*) кого́-н чего́-н; **I'm starving** (*inf*) я голо́дный как волк.
Star Wars *n* „Звёздные во́йны" *fpl*.
stash [stæʃ] *vt* (*inf*) припря́тывать (припря́тать *perf*), запаса́ться (запасти́сь* *perf*) +*instr*.
state [steɪt] *n* (*condition*) состоя́ние; (*government*) госуда́рство ♦ *vt* (*say, declare*) констати́ровать (*impf/perf*); **the S~s** *npl* (*GEO*) Шта́ты *mpl*; **to be in a ~** быть* (*impf*) в па́нике; **~ of emergency** чрезвыча́йное положе́ние; **~ of mind** душе́вное состоя́ние.
state control *n* госуда́рственный контро́ль *m*.
stated ['steɪtɪd] *adj* (*aims, beliefs etc*) устано́вленный.
State Department *n* (*US*) Госуда́рственный департа́мент.
state education *n* (*BRIT*) госуда́рственное образова́ние.
stateless ['steɪtlɪs] *adj* (*person*) не име́ющий гражда́нства.
stately ['steɪtlɪ] *adj* вели́чественный* (вели́чествен); **~ home** дом-уса́дьба.
statement ['steɪtmənt] *n* (*declaration*) заявле́ние; (*FINANCE*) отчёт, счёт; **official ~** официа́льное заявле́ние; **bank ~** вы́писка* с ба́нковского счёта.
state of the art *n* после́днее сло́во те́хники ♦ *adj*: ~~~~~ ультрасовреме́нный.
state-owned ['steɪtəund] *adj* (*industry etc*) госуда́рственный.
state school *n* (*BRIT*) госуда́рственная шко́ла.
state secret *n* госуда́рственная та́йна.
statesman ['steɪtsmən] *irreg n* госуда́рственный де́ятель *m*.
statesmanship ['steɪtsmənʃɪp] *n* госуда́рственная де́ятельность *f*.
static ['stætɪk] *n* (*RADIO, TV*) (атмосфе́рные) поме́хи *fpl* ♦ *adj* (*not moving*) стати́чный* (стати́чен), неподви́жный* (неподви́жен).
static electricity *n* стати́ческое электри́чество.

station ['steɪʃən] *n* ста́нция; (*larger railway station*) вокза́л; (*also*: **police ~**) полице́йский* уча́сток* ♦ *vt* (*position: guards etc*) выставля́ть (вы́ставить* *perf*); (*base: soldiers etc*) дислоци́ровать (*impf/perf*), размеща́ть (размести́ть* *perf*); **action ~s** сигна́л "все по места́м!"; **to get above one's ~** сади́ться* (сесть* *perf*) не в свои́ са́ни.
stationary ['steɪʃnərɪ] *adj* (*vehicle*) неподви́жный.
stationer ['steɪʃənəʳ] *n* торго́вец* канцеля́рскими това́рами.
stationer's (shop) *n* магази́н канцеля́рских това́ров.
stationery ['steɪʃnərɪ] *n* канцеля́рские принадле́жности *fpl*.
stationmaster ['steɪʃənmɑːstəʳ] *n* нача́льник ста́нции.
station wagon *n* (*US*) автомоби́ль-фурго́н, пика́п.
statistic [stəˈtɪstɪk] *n* стати́стик.
statistical [stəˈtɪstɪkl] *adj* (*evidence, techniques*) статисти́ческий*.
statistics [stəˈtɪstɪks] *n* (*science*) стати́стика.
statue ['stætjuː] *n* ста́туя.
statuesque [stætjuˈɛsk] *adj* (*woman*) ста́тная (ста́тна).
statuette [stætjuˈɛt] *n* статуэ́тка*.
stature ['stætʃəʳ] *n* рост; (*fig: reputation*) положе́ние.
status ['steɪtəs] *n* ста́тус; (*importance*) значе́ние; **the ~ quo** ста́тус-кво *m ind*.
status line *n* (*COMPUT*) строка́* состоя́ния.
status symbol *n* си́мвол положе́ния в о́бществе.
statute ['stætjuːt] *n* стату́т, законода́тельный акт; **~s** *npl* (*of club etc*) уста́в *msg*.
statute book *n* (*LAW, POL*): **the ~~** свод зако́нов.
statutory ['stætjutrɪ] *adj* (*powers, rights etc*) устано́вленный зако́ном; **~ meeting** учреди́тельное собра́ние.
staunch [stɔːntʃ] *adj* (*ally etc*) пре́данный ♦ *vt* остана́вливать (останови́ть* *perf*).
stave [steɪv] *n* (*MUS*) но́тный стан
▶ **stave off** *vt* (*attack*) отсро́чивать (отсро́чить *perf*); (*threat*) отводи́ть* (отвести́* *perf*).
stay [steɪ] *n* пребыва́ние ♦ *vi* (*remain*) остава́ться (оста́ться* *perf*); (*with sb, as guest*) гости́ть* (*impf*); (*in place: spend some time*) остана́вливаться (останови́ться* *perf*); **~ of execution** (*LAW*) отсро́чка* исполне́ния; **to ~ at home** сиде́ть* (*impf*) до́ма; **to ~ in bed** лежа́ть* (*impf*) в посте́ли; **to ~ put** не дви́гаться (дви́нуться *perf*) с ме́ста; **to ~ with friends** остана́вливаться (останови́ться* *perf*) *or* гости́ть* (*impf*) у друзе́й; **to ~ the night** (*in a place*) ночева́ть (заночева́ть* *perf*); (*with sb*) проводи́ть* (провести́* *perf*) ночь
▶ **stay behind** *vi* остава́ться (оста́ться* *perf*)
▶ **stay in** *vi* (*at home*) остава́ться* (оста́ться*

perf) до́ма
▶ **stay on** *vi* остава́ться* (оста́ться* *perf*)
▶ **stay out** *vi* (*of house*) отсу́тствовать (*impf*);
(*remain on strike*) продолжа́ть (*impf*)
бастова́ть
▶ **stay up** *vi* (*at night*) не ложи́ться (*impf*) спать.
staying power ['steɪŋ-] *n* выно́сливость *f*.
STD *n abbr* (*BRIT*: *TEL*: = *subscriber trunk dialling*)
≈ АМТС= *автомати́ческая междугоро́д-*
ная телефо́нная связь; (*MED*: = *sexually*
transmitted disease) *заболева́ние,*
передава́емое половы́м путём.
stead [stɛd] *n*: **in sb's ~** вме́сто кого́-н; **to stand**
sb in good ~ пригожда́ться (пригоди́ться*
perf) кому́-н.
steadfast ['stɛdfɑːst] *adj* (*person*) сто́йкий*
(сто́ек); (*refusal, support*) твёрдый.
steadily ['stɛdɪlɪ] *adv* (*firmly*) про́чно;
(*constantly, fixedly*) постоя́нно; (*walk:*
decisively) реши́тельно; (: *without stumbling*)
твёрдо.
steady ['stɛdɪ] *adj* (*constant*) стаби́льный*
(стаби́лен); (: *boyfriend, speed*) постоя́нный;
(*person, character*) уравнове́шенный*
(уравнове́шен); (*firm: hand etc*) твёрдый*
(твёрд); (*calm: look, voice*) ро́вный* (ро́вен) ♦
vt (*object*) придава́ть* (прида́ть* *perf*)
усто́йчивость; (*nerves, person*) успока́ивать
(успоко́ить *perf*); (*voice*) придава́ть*
(прида́ть* *perf*) ро́вность +*dat*; **to ~ o.s. on** *or*
against sth опира́ться (опере́ться* *perf*) о(бо)
что-н.
steak [steɪk] *n* (*beef*) бифште́кс; (*fish*) филе́ *nt*
ind; (*pork*) вы́резка*.
steakhouse ['steɪkhaus] *n* бифште́ксная *f adj*.
steal [stiːl] (*pt* **stole**, *pp* **stolen**) *vt* ворова́ть
(свороба́ть *perf*), красть* (укра́сть* *perf*) ♦ *vi*
(*thieve*) ворова́ть (*impf*); (*move secretly*)
кра́сться* (*impf*)
▶ **steal away** *vi* незаме́тно ускольза́ть
(ускользну́ть *perf*)
▶ **steal off** *vi* = **steal away**.
stealth [stɛlθ] *n*: **by ~** укра́дкой.
stealthy ['stɛlθɪ] *adj* (*movements, actions*)
та́йный.
steam [stiːm] *n* пар* ♦ *vt* (*CULIN*) вари́ть*
(свари́ть* *perf*) на пару́, па́рить (*impf*) ♦ *vi*
(*give off steam*) испуска́ть (испусти́ть* *perf*)
пар; **under one's own ~** (*fig*) свои́ми си́лами;
to run out of ~ (*fig: person*) выдыха́ться
(вы́дохнуться *perf*); **to let off ~** (*fig: inf*)
выпуска́ть (вы́пустить* *perf*) пар
▶ **steam up** *vi* (*window*) запотева́ть (запоте́ть
perf); **to get ~ed up about sth** (*fig: inf*)
кипяти́ться* (раскипяти́ться* *perf*) из-за
чего́-н.
steam engine *n* (*RAIL*) парово́з.
steamer ['stiːmər] *n* парохо́д; (*CULIN*)

парова́рка*.
steam iron *n* утю́г* с отпа́ривателем.
steamroller ['stiːmrəulə'] *n* парово́й като́к*.
steamship ['stiːmʃɪp] *n* = **steamer**.
steamy ['stiːmɪ] *adj* (*room*) по́лный* (по́лон)
па́ра; (*window*) запоте́вший*.
steed [stiːd] *n* конь *m*.
steel [stiːl] *n* сталь *f* ♦ *adj* стально́й.
steel band *n* (*MUS*) кари́бский уда́рный
орке́стр.
steel industry *n* сталелите́йная
промы́шленность *f*.
steel mill *n* сталелите́йный заво́д.
steelworks ['stiːlwəːks] *n* сталелите́йный
заво́д.
steely ['stiːlɪ] *adj* (*eyes, gaze*) стально́й;
(*determination*) непрекло́нный*.
steep [stiːp] *adj* круто́й* (крут); (*price*)
высо́кий* (высо́к) ♦ *vt* (*soak: food*)
выма́чивать (вы́мочить *perf*); (: *clothes*)
зама́чивать (замочи́ть* *perf*); **a house ~ed in**
history (*fig*) дом* с истори́ческим про́шлым
ове́янный исто́рией.
steeple ['stiːpl] *n* шпиль *m*; (*belltower*)
колоко́льня*.
steeplechase ['stiːpltʃeɪs] *n* стипль-че́з.
steeplejack ['stiːpldʒæk] *n* верхола́з.
steeply ['stiːplɪ] *adv* кру́то.
steer [stɪə'] *vt* (*vehicle, person*) води́ть*/вести́*
(*impf*) ♦ *vi* (*manoeuvre*) маневри́ровать (*impf*)
♦ *n* кастри́рованный бык*; **to ~ clear of sb/**
sth (*fig*) избега́ть (*impf*) кого́-н/чего́-н.
steering ['stɪərɪŋ] *n* (*AUT*) управле́ние.
steering column *n* рулева́я коло́нна.
steering committee *n* коми́ссия по
вы́работке регла́мента.
steering wheel *n* руль* *m*.
stellar ['stɛlə'] *adj* (*of stars*) звёздный.
stem [stɛm] *n* (*BOT: of plant*) ствол*, сте́бель* *m*;
(*of leaf, fruit*) черешо́к*; (*of glass*) но́жка*; (*of*
pipe) черено́к* ♦ *vt* (*stop*) остана́вливать
(останови́ть* *perf*)
▶ **stem from** *vt fus* (*subj: condition, problem*)
происходи́ть* (произойти́* *perf*) от +*gen*; **their**
agressiveness ~med from fear их
агресси́вность порождена́ стра́хом.
stench [stɛntʃ] *n* (*pej*) вонь *f*.
stencil ['stɛnsl] *n* трафаре́т ♦ *vt* (*letters, designs*
etc) де́лать (сде́лать *perf*) по трафаре́ту.
stenographer [stɛ'nɔgrəfə'] *n* (*US*)
стенографи́ст(ка*).
stenography [stɛ'nɔgrəfɪ] *n* (*US*) стеногра́фия.
step [stɛp] *n* (*also fig*) шаг*; (*of stairs*) ступе́нь *f*
♦ *vi*: **to ~ forward/back** ступа́ть (ступи́ть*
perf) вперёд/наза́д; **~s** *npl* (*BRIT*) = **stepladder**;
~ by ~ (*also fig*) шаг за ша́гом; **to be in/out of**
~ (with) идти́* (*impf*) в но́гу/не в но́гу (с
+*instr*); (*fig*) соотве́тствовать (*impf*)/не

---

* marks translations which have irregular inflections. The Russian-English side of the dictionary gives inflectional information.

соответствовать *(impf)* *(+dat)*
▶ **step down** *vi* (*fig: resign*) уходи́ть* (уйти́* *perf*) в отста́вку
▶ **step in** *vi* (*fig*) вме́шиваться (вмеша́ться *perf*)
▶ **step off** *vt fus* сходи́ть* (сойти́* *perf*) с +*gen*
▶ **step on** *vt fus* (*walk on*) наступа́ть (наступи́ть* *perf*) на +*acc*
▶ **step over** *vt fus* переступа́ть (переступи́ть* *perf*) че́рез +*acc*
▶ **step up** *vt* (*increase*) усилива́ть (уси́лить *perf*).

step aerobics *n* степ-аэро́бика (*с использованием особой ступеньки*).

stepbrother ['stɛpbrʌðə^r] *n* сво́дный брат*.

stepchild ['stɛptʃaɪld] *n* (*boy*) па́сынок*; (*girl*) па́дчерица.

stepdaughter ['stɛpdɔ:tə^r] *n* па́дчерица.

stepfather ['stɛpfɑ:ðə^r] *n* о́тчим.

stepladder ['stɛplædə^r] *n* (*BRIT*) стремя́нка*.

stepmother ['stɛpmʌðə^r] *n* ма́чеха.

stepping stone ['stɛpɪŋ-] *n* (*in river*) опо́рный ка́мень *m*; (*fig*) ступе́нька.

step-reebok® [stɛp'ri:bɔk] *n* ступе́нька, *используемая при степ-аэробике.*

stepsister ['stɛpsɪstə^r] *n* сво́дная сестра́*.

stepson ['stɛpsʌn] *n* па́сынок*.

stereo ['stɛrɪəu] *n* (*system*) стереосисте́ма; (*record player*) стереопройгрыватель *m* ♦ *adj* (*also:*~**phonic**) стереофони́ческий; **in** ~ сте́рео.

stereotype ['stɪərɪətaɪp] *n* стереоти́п ♦ *vt* воспринима́ть *(impf)* по стереоти́пу.

sterile ['stɛraɪl] *adj* (*also fig*) беспло́дный* (беспло́ден); (*free from germs*) стери́льный* (стери́лен).

sterility [stɛ'rɪlɪtɪ] *n* (*infertility*) беспло́дие.

sterilization [stɛrɪlaɪ'zeɪʃən] *n* стерилиза́ция.

sterilize ['stɛrɪlaɪz] *vt* стерилизова́ть *(impf)*.

sterling ['stə:lɪŋ] *adj* (*efforts: noble*) благоро́дный*; (: *excellent*) отме́нный ♦ *n* (*ECON*) фунт сте́рлингов; ~ **silver** серебро́ 925-ой про́бы; **one pound** ~ оди́н фунт сте́рлингов.

sterling area *n* сте́рлинговая зо́на.

stern [stə:n] *adj* стро́гий* (строг) ♦ *n* (*of boat*) корма́.

sternum ['stə:nəm] *n* груди́на.

steroid ['stɪərɔɪd] *n* стеро́ид.

stet [stɛt] *n корректи́рующий знак, отменя́ющий попра́вки* ♦ *vt* оста́вить *(perf)* как бы́ло.

stethoscope ['stɛθəskəup] *n* стетоско́п.

stevedore ['sti:vədɔ:^r] *n* порто́вый гру́зчик.

stew [stju:] *n* (*meat*) туше́ное мя́со ♦ *vt* (*meat*) туши́ть* (потуши́ть* *perf*); (*fruit*) вари́ть (свари́ть *perf*) ♦ *vi* (*meat*) туши́ться* (потуши́ться* *perf*); (*fruit*) вари́ться (свари́ться *perf*); **vegetable** ~ тушёные о́вощи; ~**ed tea** перестоя́вшийся чай; ~**ed fruit** варёные фру́кты.

steward ['stju:əd] *n* (*on ship, train*) стюа́рд; (*on plane*) бортпроводни́к*; (*in club etc*) распоряди́тель *m*; (*also:* **shop** ~) уехово́й ста́роста.

stewardess ['stju:ədɛs] *n* (*on plane*) стюарде́сса, бортпроводни́ца.

stewardship ['stju:ədʃɪp] *n* управле́ние.

stewing steak ['stju:ɪŋ-] (*US* **stew meat**) *n* говя́дина для туше́ния.

St. Ex. *abbr* = **stock exchange**.

stg *abbr* = **sterling**.

stick [stɪk] (*pt, pp* **stuck**) *n* (*of wood*) па́лка*; (*of dynamite, chalk etc*) па́лочка*; (*walking stick*) трость *f* ♦ *vt* (*with glue etc*) кле́ить (прикле́ить *perf*); (*inf: put*) сова́ть* (су́нуть *perf*); (: *tolerate*) терпе́ть (вы́терпеть *perf*); (*thrust*) втыка́ть (воткну́ть *perf*) ♦ *vi* (*become attached*) прикле́иваться (прикле́иться *perf*); (*be unmoveable*) застрева́ть (застря́ть* *perf*); (*in mind etc*) засе́сть* (*perf*); (*get jammed: door*) заеда́ть (зае́сть* *perf*); (: *lift*) застрева́ть (застря́ть* *perf*); **to get hold of the wrong end of the** ~ (*BRIT: fig*) совсе́м не так понима́ть (поня́ть* *perf*); **he stuck a cigar in his mouth** он засу́нул сига́ру в рот; **to** ~ **to** (*become attached*) прикле́иваться (прикле́иться *perf*) к +*dat*; (*one's word, promise*) держа́ть* (сдержа́ть *perf*); (*principles*) остава́ться* (оста́ться* *perf*) ве́рным(-ой) +*dat*
▶ **stick around** *vi* (*inf*) торча́ть *(impf)*
▶ **stick out** *vi* (*ears etc*) торча́ть *(impf)* ♦ *vt*: **to** ~ **it out** (*inf*) терпе́ть* (вы́терпеть* *perf*)
▶ **stick up** *vi* (*hair etc*) торча́ть *(impf)*
▶ **stick up for** *vt fus* (*person*) заступа́ться (заступи́ться* *perf*) за +*acc*; (*principle*) отста́ивать (отстоя́ть *perf*).

sticker ['stɪkə^r] *n* накле́йка.

sticking plaster ['stɪkɪŋ-] *n* лейкопла́стырь *m*.

sticking point *n* (*in relationship*) то́чка преткнове́ния.

stickleback ['stɪklbæk] *n* ко́люшка.

stickler ['stɪklə^r] *n*: **to be a** ~ **for** наста́ивать *(impf)* на +*prp*.

stick shift *n* (*US: AUT*) переключа́тель *m* скоросте́й.

stick-up ['stɪkʌp] *n* (*inf*) вооружённое ограбле́ние.

sticky ['stɪkɪ] *adj* (*hands etc*) ли́пкий*; (*label*) кле́йкий*; (*fig: situation*) щекотли́вый (щекотли́в).

stiff [stɪf] *adj* (*brush*) жёсткий* (жёсток); (*paste*) густо́й; (*egg-white*) круто́й; (*person*) деревя́нный; (*door, zip*) туго́й* (туг); (*manner, smile*) натя́нутый (натя́нут); (*competition*) ожесточённый; (*severe: sentence*) суро́вый (суро́в); (: *high: price*) высо́кий* (высо́к); (: *strong: drink*) кре́пкий*; (: *breeze*) си́льный* (силён) ♦ *adv* (*bored, worried, scared*) до́ смерти; **I am** *or* **feel** ~ у меня́ всё те́ло но́ет; **I have a** ~ **neck** у меня́ свело́ ше́ю; **to keep a** ~ **upper lip** (*BRIT: fig*) сохраня́ть (сохрани́ть *perf*) хладнокро́вие.

stiffen ['stɪfn] *vi* (*body*) напряга́ться (напря́чься* *perf*); (*joints, neck*) не сгиба́ться (*impf*); **my muscles have ~ed** у меня́ свело́ мы́шцы.

stiffness ['stɪfnɪs] *n* (*of joints*) неподви́жность *f*; (*of paper, cloth*) жёсткость *f*; (*in consistency*) густота́ *f*; (*in behaviour etc*) натя́нутость *f*.

stifle ['staɪfl] *vt* (*yawn*) подавля́ть (подави́ть* *perf*); (*opposition*) души́ть (задуши́ть *perf*); (*subj: heat*) души́ть (*impf*).

stifling ['staɪflɪŋ] *adj* (*heat*) уду́шливый (уду́шлив).

stigma ['stɪgmə] *n* (*of failure, defeat etc*) клеймо́; (*BOT*) ры́льце; (*MED*) сти́гма.

stile [staɪl] *n* перела́з.

stiletto [stɪ'lɛtəu] *n* (*BRIT: also: ~ heel*) шпи́лька.

still [stɪl] *adj* ти́хий* (тих); (*BRIT: not fizzy*) негазиро́ванный ♦ *adv* (*up to this time*) всё ещё; (*even, yet*) ещё; (*nonetheless*) всё-таки, тем не ме́нее ♦ *n* (*CINEMA*) рекла́мный фотока́др; **to stand ~** стоя́ть* (*impf*) неподви́жно; **keep ~!** не шевели́тесь!; **he ~ hasn't arrived** он всё ещё не пришёл.

stillborn ['stɪlbɔːn] *adj* (*baby*) мертворождённый.

still life *n* (*ART*) натюрмо́рт.

stilt [stɪlt] *n* (*pile*) сва́я; (*for walking on*) ходуля́*.

stilted ['stɪltɪd] *adj* (*behaviour, conversation*) высокопа́рный* (высокопа́рен).

stimulant ['stɪmjulənt] *n* стимули́рующее *or* возбужда́ющее сре́дство.

stimulate ['stɪmjuleɪt] *vt* стимули́ровать (*impf/perf*).

stimulating ['stɪmjuleɪtɪŋ] *adj* вдохновля́ющий.

stimulation [stɪmju'leɪʃən] *n* стимули́рование.

stimuli ['stɪmjulaɪ] *npl of* **stimulus**.

stimulus ['stɪmjuləs] (*pl* **stimuli**) *n* (*encouragement*) сти́мул; (*MED*) стимуля́тор; (*BIO, PSYCH*) раздражи́тель *m*.

sting [stɪŋ] (*pt, pp* **stung**) *n* (*from insect*) уку́с; (*from plant*) ожо́г; (*organ: of wasp etc*) жа́ло; (*inf: confidence trick*) моше́нничество ♦ *vt* (*also fig*) уязвля́ть (уязви́ть* *perf*) ♦ *vi* (*insect, animal*) жа́литься (*impf*); (*plant*) же́чься* (*impf*); (*eyes, ointment etc*) жечь* (*impf*); **my eyes are ~ing** мне жжёт глаза́.

stingy ['stɪndʒɪ] *adj* (*pej: person*) ска́редный* (ска́реден).

stink [stɪŋk] (*pt* **stank**, *pp* **stunk**) *n* смрад, вонь *f* ♦ *vi* смерде́ть (*impf*).

stinker ['stɪŋkəʳ] (*inf*) *n* (*person*) мерза́вец*(-вка*); **it's a real ~ of a problem/ exam** э́то жу́ткая пробле́ма/ужа́сный

stinking ['stɪŋkɪŋ] (*inf*) *adj* (*inf*) воню́чий* (воню́ч); **a ~ cold** жу́ткая просту́да; **~ rich** жу́тко бога́тый.

stint [stɪnt] *n* пери́од рабо́ты ♦ *vi*: **to ~ on** (*work*) халту́рить (*impf*) в +*prp*; (*ingredients*) зажима́ть (зажа́ть* *perf*).

stipend ['staɪpɛnd] *n* (*of vicar etc*) жа́лованье; (*of student*) стипе́ндия.

stipendiary [staɪ'pɛndɪərɪ] *adj*: **~ magistrate** пла́тный магистра́т.

stipulate ['stɪpjuleɪt] *vt* (*condition, amount etc*) определя́ть (определи́ть *perf*).

stipulation [stɪpju'leɪʃən] *n* усло́вие.

stir [stəːʳ] *n* (*fig: agitation*) шум, сенса́ция ♦ *vt* (*tea etc*) меша́ть (помеша́ть *perf*); (*fig: emotions*) волнова́ть (взволнова́ть *perf*) ♦ *vi* (*move slightly*) шевели́ться (пошевели́ться *perf*); **to give sth a ~** разме́шивать (размеша́ть *perf*) что-н; **to cause a ~** вызыва́ть (вы́звать* *perf*) сенса́цию

▶ **stir up** *vt* (*trouble*) вызыва́ть (вы́звать* *perf*).

stir-fry ['stəː'fraɪ] *vt* бы́стро обжа́ривать (обжа́рить *perf*).

stirring ['stəːrɪŋ] *adj* (*speech, occasion*) волну́ющий.

stirrup ['stɪrəp] *n* стре́мя* *nt*.

stitch [stɪtʃ] *n* (*SEWING*) стежо́к*; (*KNITTING*) петля́*; (*MED*) шов* ♦ *vt* (*sew*) шить* (сшить* *perf*); (*MED: wound*) зашива́ть (заши́ть* *perf*); **I have a ~ in my side** у меня́ ко́лет в боку́.

stock [stɔk] *n* (*supply*) запа́с; (*AGR*) поголо́вье; (*CULIN*) бульо́н; (*descent, origin*) происхожде́ние; (*FINANCE*) це́нные бума́ги *fpl*; (*COMM: of company*) акционе́рный капита́л; (*RAIL: also:* **rolling ~**) (подвижно́й) соста́в ♦ *adj* (*fig: reply, excuse etc*) шабло́нный ♦ *vt* (*have in stock*) име́ть (*impf*) в нали́чии; **~s and shares** а́кции и це́нные бума́ги; **to be in/out of ~** име́ться (*impf*)/не име́ться (*impf*) в нали́чии; **a well-~ed shop** магази́н с больши́м ассортиме́нтом това́ров; **to take ~ of** (*fig*) оце́нивать (оцени́ть* *perf*); **government ~** прави́тельственные а́кции

▶ **stock up** *vi*: **to ~ up with** запаса́ться (запасти́сь* *perf*) +*instr*.

stockade [stɔ'keɪd] *n* частоко́л.

stockbroker ['stɔkbrəukəʳ] *n* (*COMM*) фо́ндовый бро́кер.

stock control *n* (*COMM*) управле́ние запа́сами.

stock cube *n* (*BRIT: CULIN*) бульо́нный ку́бик.

stock exchange *n* фо́ндовая би́ржа.

stockholder ['stɔkhəuldəʳ] *n* (*COMM*) акционе́р.

Stockholm ['stɔkhəum] *n* Стокго́льм.

stocking ['stɔkɪŋ] *n* чуло́к*.

stock in trade *n* (*COMM*) *запа́сы име́ющиеся в*

---

* marks translations which have irregular inflections. The Russian-English side of the dictionary gives inflectional information.

налі́чии и предназна́ченные для прода́жи; (*fig*): **it's his ~ ~ ~** э́то его́ обы́чное заня́тие.

stockist ['stɒkɪst] *n* (*BRIT*) сто́кист (*фи́рма, име́ющая запа́с како́й-нибудь проду́кции*).

stock market *n* (*BRIT*) фо́ндовая би́ржа.

stock phrase *n* клише́ *nt ind*.

stockpile ['stɒkpaɪl] *n* (*of weapons, food*) запа́с ◆ *vt* запаса́ть (запасти́* *perf*).

stockroom ['stɒkruːm] *n* (*COMM*) склад.

stocktaking ['stɒkteɪkɪŋ] *n* (*BRIT*: *COMM*) инвентариза́ция.

stocky ['stɒkɪ] *adj* корена́стый (корена́ст).

stodgy ['stɒdʒɪ] *adj* (*food*) тяжёлый.

stoic ['stəʊɪk] *n* сто́ик.

stoical ['stəʊɪkl] *adj* (*person, behaviour*) сто́йческий*.

stoke [stəʊk] *vt* (*fire*) подде́рживать (*impf*); (*boiler, furnace*) подде́рживать (*impf*) ого́нь в +*prp*.

stoker ['stəʊkə'] *n* (*RAIL, NAUT etc*) кочега́р.

stole [stəʊl] *pt of* **steal** ◆ *n* паланти́н.

stolen ['stəʊln] *pp of* **steal**.

stolid ['stɒlɪd] *adj* (*person, behaviour*) бесстра́стный* (бесстра́стен).

stomach ['stʌmək] *n* (*ANAT*) желу́док*; (*belly*) живо́т* ◆ *vt* (*fig*) переноси́ть* (*impf*).

stomachache ['stʌməkeɪk] *n* желу́дочные бо́ли *fpl*.

stomach pump *n* желу́дочный зонд.

stomach ulcer *n* я́зва желу́дка.

stomp [stɒmp] *vi*: **to ~ in/out** входи́ть* (войти́* *perf*)/уходи́ть* (уйти́* *perf*) тяжёлыми шага́ми.

stone [stəʊn] *n* (*also MED*) ка́мень* *m*; (*pebble*) ка́мешек*; (*in fruit*) ко́сточка*; (*BRIT*: *weight*) сто́ун (*14 фу́нтов*) ◆ *adj* ка́менный ◆ *vt* (*person*) заки́дывать (закида́ть *perf*) камня́ми в +*acc*; (*fruit*) вынима́ть (вы́нуть *perf*) ко́сточки из +*gen*; **within a ~'s throw of the school** в двух шага́х от шко́лы.

Stone Age *n*: **the ~ ~** ка́менный век.

stone-cold ['stəʊn'kəʊld] *adj* холо́дный* как лёд.

stoned [stəʊnd] *adj* (*inf*: *drunk*) мертве́цки пья́ный* (пьян); (: *on drugs*) обкури́вшийся.

stone-deaf ['stəʊn'dɛf] *adj* соверше́нно глухо́й.

stonemason ['stəʊnmeɪsn] *n* ка́менщик.

stonewall [stəʊn'wɔːl] *vti* занима́ться (*impf*) процеду́рными заде́ржками (*в парла́менте*).

stonework ['stəʊnwəːk] *n* (ка́менная) кла́дка.

stony ['stəʊnɪ] *adj* (*ground*) камени́стый (камени́ст); (*fig: glance, silence etc*) холо́дный.

stood [stud] *pt, pp of* **stand**.

stooge [stuːdʒ] *n* (*inf*) подставно́е лицо́*; (: *THEAT*) партнёр ко́мика.

stool [stuːl] *n* табуре́тка*.

stoop [stuːp] *vi* (*also*: **~ down**: *bend*) наклоня́ться (наклони́ться* *perf*),

нагиба́ться (нагну́ться *perf*); (*also*: **have a ~**) суту́литься (*impf*); (*fig*): **to ~ to sth/doing** унижа́ться (уни́зиться* *perf*) до чего́-н/до того́, что́бы +*infin*.

stop [stɒp] *n* остано́вка*; (*in punctuation*: *also*: **full ~**) то́чка* ◆ *vt* остана́вливать (останови́ть* *perf*); (*prevent*: *also*: **put a ~ to**) прекраща́ть (прекрати́ть* *perf*) ◆ *vi* (*person, clock*) остана́вливаться (останови́ться* *perf*); (*rain, noise etc*) прекраща́ться (прекрати́ться* *perf*); **to ~ sb (from) doing** уде́рживать (удержа́ть *perf*) кого́-н от того́, что́бы +*infin*; **~ it!** прекрати́те!; **to ~ doing** перестава́ть* (переста́ть* *perf*) +*infin*; **the car ~ped dead** маши́на останови́лась как вко́панная

▶ **stop by** *vi* заходи́ть* (зайти́* *perf*)

▶ **stop off** *vi* остана́вливаться (останови́ться* *perf*)

▶ **stop up** *vt* (*hole*) заде́лывать (заде́лать *perf*).

stopcock ['stɒpkɔk] *n* запо́рный кран.

stopgap ['stɒpgæp] *n* (*person, thing*) вре́менная заме́на; (*also*: **~ measure**) вре́менная ме́ра.

stop-go [stɒp'gəʊ] *adj* (*BRIT*: *ECON*): **~ policy** экономи́ческая поли́тика, череду́ющая.

stoplights ['stɒplaɪts] *npl* (*AUT*) стоп-сигна́л *msg*.

stopover ['stɒpəʊvə'] *n* остано́вка*; (*AVIAT*) поса́дка.

stoppage ['stɒpɪdʒ] *n* (*strike*) забасто́вка*; (*blockage*) остано́вка*; (*of pay*) прекраще́ние.

stopper ['stɒpə'] *n* про́бка*.

stop press *n* экстренное сообще́ние.

stopwatch ['stɒpwɔtʃ] *n* секундоме́р.

storage ['stɔːrɪdʒ] *n* хране́ние; (*in house*) кладо́вка*; (*COMPUT*) па́мять *f*, накопи́тель *m*.

storage capacity *n* ёмкость *f*.

storage heater *n* (*BRIT*) аккумули́рующий электрообогрева́тель *m*.

store [stɔː'] *n* (*stock, reserve*) запа́с; (*depot*) склад; (*BRIT*: *large shop*) универма́г; (*esp US*) магази́н ◆ *vt* храни́ть (*impf*); **~s** *npl* (*provisions*) запа́сы *mpl*; **in ~** в бу́дущем; **who knows what's in ~ for us?** кто зна́ет, что нас ждёт в бу́дущем?; **to set great/little ~ by sth** придава́ть* (прида́ть* *perf*) большо́е/ма́ленькое значе́ние чему́-н

▶ **store up** *vt* (*food*) запаса́ть (запасти́* *perf*); (*memories*) храни́ть (*impf*).

storehouse ['stɔːhaus] *n* (*US*: *COMM*) склад; (*fig*) кладова́я *f adj*.

storekeeper ['stɔːkiːpə'] *n* (*US*: *manager*) управля́ющий*(-ая) *m(f) adj* магази́ном; (*owner*) владе́лец*(-лица) магази́на.

storeroom ['stɔːruːm] *n* кладова́я *f adj*.

storey ['stɔːrɪ] (*US* **story**) *n* этаж*.

stork [stɔːk] *n* а́ист.

storm [stɔːm] *n* (*also fig*) бу́ря*; (*of criticism*) волна́*; (*of laughter*) взрыв; (*also*: **electric ~**)

гроза́* ♦ *vi* (*fig*: *speak angrily*) крича́ть* (*impf*)
♦ *vt* (*attack*: *place*) штурмова́ть (*impf*).
storm cloud *n* грозова́я ту́ча.
storm door *n* нару́жная дверь* *f*.
stormy ['stɔːmɪ] *adj* штормово́й; (*fig*: *debate,
relations*) бу́рный; ~ **weather** нена́стье.
story ['stɔːrɪ] *n* исто́рия; (*PRESS*: *article*)
статья́*; (: *subject*) газе́тный материа́л; (*lie*)
вы́думка*; (*US*) = **storey**; **short** ~ расска́з.
storybook ['stɔːrɪbuk] *n* сбо́рник расска́зов *or*
ска́зок (*для дете́й*).
storyteller ['stɔːrɪtɛləʳ] *n* расска́зчик(-ица); (*inf*:
liar) врун(ья).
stout [staut] *adj* (*strong: branch etc*) кре́пкий*
(кре́пок); (*fat*) доро́дный* (доро́ден);
(*resolute: friend, supporter*) надёжный*
(надёжен) ♦ *n* (*beer*) кре́пкий* по́ртер.
stove [stəuv] *n* (*for cooking*) плита́*; (: *small*)
пли́тка*; (*for heating*) печь* *f*; **gas/electric** ~
(*cooker*) га́зовая/электри́ческая плита́.
stow [stəu] *vt* (*also*: ~ **away**) убира́ть (убра́ть*
perf).
stowaway ['stəuəweɪ] *n* безбиле́тник(-ница).
St Petersburg [sənt'piːtəzbəːg] *n*
Санкт-Петербу́рг ♦ *adj* (санкт-)
петербу́ргский*.
straddle ['strædl] *vt* (*chair, fence etc*) оседла́ть
(*perf*); (*fig*) охва́тывать (охвати́ть* *perf*).
strafe [strɑːf] *vt* (*MIL: with bullets*)
обстре́ливать (обстреля́ть *perf*); (*with
bombs*) бомби́ть (*impf*), сбра́сывать
(сбро́сить* *perf*).
straggle ['strægl] *vi* (*houses etc*)
раски́дываться (раски́нуться *perf*); (*people*)
разбреда́ться (разбрести́сь* *perf*).
straggler ['stræɡləʳ] *n* (*person*) отста́вший(-ая)
m(f) adj.
straggly ['stræɡlɪ] *adj* (*hair*) беспоря́дочно
торча́щий.
straight [streɪt] *adj* прямо́й* (прям); (*simple:
choice*) я́сный* (я́сен); (*THEAT: part, play*)
серьёзный; (*inf: heterosexual*)
гетеросексуа́льный* ♦ *adv* прямо́ ♦ *n*: **the** ~
(*SPORT*) пряма́я *f adj*; **to put** *or* **get sth** ~ (*make
clear*) вноси́ть* (внести́* *perf*) я́сность во
что-н; **let's get this** ~ дава́йте внесём
я́сность *or* определённость в э́то; **to be (all)**
~ (*tidy*) быть* (*impf*) в (по́лном) поря́дке;
(*clarified*) быть* (*impf*) я́сным(-ой); **10** ~ **wins**
10 побе́д подря́д; **to go** ~ **home** идти́*
(пойти́* *perf*) сра́зу домо́й; **to tell sb** ~ **out**
говори́ть (сказа́ть* *perf*) кому́-н пря́мо; **to
drink vodka** ~ пить* (*impf*) неразба́вленную
во́дку; ~ **away**, ~ **off** (*at once*) сра́зу.
straighten ['streɪtn] *vt* (*skirt, tie etc*)
поправля́ть (попра́вить* *perf*); (*bed*)
заправля́ть (запра́вить* *perf*)
▶ **straighten out** *vt* (*fig: problem etc*)

ула́живать (ула́дить* *perf*).
straight-faced [streɪt'feɪst] *adj, adv* с серьёзным
ви́дом; **to be** ~ сохраня́ть (*impf*) серьёзный
вид.
straightforward [streɪt'fɔːwəd] *adj* (*simple*)
просто́й* (прост); (*honest*) прямо́й.
straight sets *n*: **to win in** ~ ~ (*men*) побежда́ть
(победи́ть* *perf*) в трёх па́ртиях подря́д;
(*women*) побежда́ть (победи́ть* *perf*) в двух
па́ртиях подря́д.
strain [streɪn] *n* (*TECH*) натяже́ние; (*pressure*)
нагру́зка*; (*MED: physical*) растяже́ние;
(: *mental*) напряже́ние; (*of virus*) вид; (*breed*)
поро́да ♦ *vt* (*back etc*) растя́гивать
(растяну́ть* *perf*); (*friendship, marriage*)
испы́тывать (*impf*); (*stretch: resources*)
удаля́ть (уда́рить *perf*) по +*dat*; (*CULIN*)
проце́живать (процеди́ть* *perf*); ~**s** *npl* (*MUS*)
зву́ки *mpl*; **he's been under a lot of** ~ у него́
был о́чень напряжённый пери́од.
strained [streɪnd] *adj* (*back, muscle*)
растя́нутый (растя́нут); (*laugh, relations*)
натя́нутый (натя́нут).
strainer ['streɪnəʳ] *n* (*for vegetables*) си́то; (*for
tea*) си́течко.
strait [streɪt] *n* (*GEO*) проли́в; ~**s** *npl* (*fig*):**to be in
dire** ~**s** находи́ться* (*impf*) *or* быть* (*impf*) в
бе́дственном положе́нии.
straitjacket ['streɪtdʒækɪt] *n* смири́тельная
руба́шка*.
strait-laced [streɪt'leɪst] *adj* (*person*)
пурита́нский*.
strand [strænd] *n* (*of thread*) ни́тка*; (*of wool*)
волокно́*, нить *f*; (*of hair*) прядь *f*; (*fig:
element of whole*) часть *f*.
stranded ['strændɪd] *adj* (*ship, sea creature etc*)
вы́брошенный на бе́рег *or* мель; (*traveller,
holidaymaker etc*): **to be** ~ быть* (*impf*) на
мели́.
strange [streɪndʒ] *adj* (*not known*) незнако́мый
(незнако́м); (*foreign*) чужо́й; (*odd*)
стра́нный* (стра́нен).
strangely ['streɪndʒlɪ] *adv* (*act, laugh*) стра́нно;
see also **enough**.
stranger ['streɪndʒəʳ] *n* (*unknown person*)
незнако́мый челове́к*, посторо́нний(-ая)
m(f) adj; **I'm a** ~ **here** я здесь чужо́й.
strangle ['stræŋgl] *vt* (*also fig*) души́ть*
(задуши́ть* *perf*).
stranglehold ['stræŋglhəuld] *n* (*SPORT*)
мёртвая хва́тка; (*fig*) заси́лье.
strangulation [stræŋgju'leɪʃən] *n* удуше́ние.
strap [stræp] *n* реме́нь* *m*; (*of slip, dress*)
брете́лька*; (*of watch, on shoes*) ремешо́к*
♦ *vt* (*also:* ~ **on**) пристёгивать (пристегну́ть*
perf).
straphanging ['stræphæŋɪŋ] *n*: **I hate** ~ я
ненави́жу стоя́ть в трансо́рте.

---

* marks translations which have irregular inflections. The Russian-English side of the dictionary gives inflectional information.

strapless ['stræplɪs] *adj* (*bra, dress*) без
бретéлек.
strapped [stræpt] *adj* (*inf*): **to be ~ for cash**
сидéть* (*impf*) на мели́ с деньга́ми.
strapping ['stræpɪŋ] *adj* ро́слый.
Strasbourg ['stræzbə:g] *n* Стра́сбург.
strata ['strɑ:tə] *npl of* **stratum**.
stratagem ['strætɪdʒəm] *n* хи́трость *f*.
strategic [strə'ti:dʒɪk] *adj* стратеги́ческий*.
strategist ['strætɪdʒɪst] *n* страте́г.
strategy ['strætɪdʒɪ] *n* (*plan, also* MIL)
страте́гия.
stratosphere ['strætəsfɪəʳ] *n* стратосфéра.
stratum ['strɑ:təm] (*pl* **strata**) *n* слой*.
straw [strɔ:] *n* соло́ма; (*drinking straw*)
соло́минка*; **that's the last ~!** э́то после́дняя
ка́пля!
strawberry ['strɔ:bərɪ] *n* (*cultivated*) клубни́ка *f*
no pl; (*wild*) земляни́ка *f no pl*.
stray [streɪ] *adj* (*animal*) бездо́мный,
бродя́чий; (*bullet*) шально́й; (*scattered*)
отде́льный ♦ *vi* заблуди́ться* (*perf*);
(*thoughts*) блужда́ть (*impf*).
streak [stri:k] *n* (*stripe*) полоса́*; (*in hair*) прядь
f; (*fig: of madness etc*) черта́, скло́нность *f* ♦
vt прони́зывать (прониза́ть* *perf*) ♦ *vi*: **to ~
past** мча́ться* (промча́ться* *perf*) ми́мо; **to
have ~s in one's hair** имéть (*impf*)
окра́шенные пря́ди воло́с; **a winning/losing
~** полоса́ уда́ч/неуда́ч; **~ed with ... с ...
поло́сками.
streaker ['stri:kəʳ] *n* человéк, появля́ющийся
го́лым пéред толпо́й.
streaky ['stri:kɪ] *adj*: **~ bacon** беко́н с
прожи́лками жи́ра.
stream [stri:m] *n* (*small river*) ручéй*; (*current*)
течéние; (*of people, vehicles, questions*)
пото́к; (*of smoke*) струя́* ♦ *vt* (SCOL) дели́ть*
(раздели́ть* *perf*) на гру́ппы ♦ *vi* (*liquid*) течь*
(*impf*), ли́ться* (*impf*); **to ~ in/out** (*people*)
вали́ть* (повали́ть* *perf*) толпо́й в +*acc*/из
+*gen*; **against the ~** про́тив течéния; **to come
on ~** (*new power plant etc*) вступа́ть
(вступи́ть* *perf*) в строй.
streamer ['stri:məʳ] *n* (*paper decoration*)
серпанти́н.
stream feed *n* (*on photocopier etc*) пода́ча
(страни́ц) пото́ком.
streamline ['stri:mlaɪn] *vt* придава́ть*
(прида́ть* *perf*) обтека́емую фо́рму +*dat*; (*fig*)
упроща́ть (упрости́ть* *perf*).
streamlined ['stri:mlaɪnd] *adj* обтека́емый;
(AVIAT, AUT) обтека́емой фо́рмы; (*fig*)
упрощённый.
street [stri:t] *n* у́лица; **the back ~s** переу́лки
mpl; **to be on the ~s** (*homeless*) быть* (*impf*)
бездо́мным(-ой); (*as prostitute*) занима́ться
(*impf*) проститу́цией.
streetcar ['stri:tkɑ:ʳ] *n* (US) трамва́й.
street cred [-krɛd] *n* (*inf*) и́мидж.
streetlamp ['stri:tlæmp] *n* у́личный фона́рь* *m*.

street lighting *n* у́личное освещéние.
street map *n* план у́лиц.
street market *n* у́личный ры́нок*.
street plan *n* план у́лиц.
streetwise ['stri:twaɪz] *adj* (*inf*) у́шлый.
strength [strɛŋθ] *n* си́ла; (*of girder, knot etc*)
про́чность *f*, крéпость *f*; (*of chemical solution,
wine*) крéпость; **on the ~ of** на основа́нии
+*gen*; **at full ~** во всём соста́ве; **below ~** (*not
enough people*) недоукомплекто́ванный
(недоукомплекто́ван); (*not all members
present*) не в по́лном соста́ве.
strengthen ['strɛŋθn] *vt* укрепля́ть (укрепи́ть*
perf); (*muscle*) развива́ть (*impf*); (*fig: group*)
пополня́ть (попо́лнить *perf*); (: *argument*)
подкрепля́ть (подкрепи́ть* *perf*).
strenuous ['strɛnjuəs] *adj* (*exercise*)
энерги́чный* (энерги́чен); (*efforts*)
напряжённый; (*tiring*) утоми́тельный*
(утоми́телен).
strenuously ['strɛnjuəslɪ] *adv* напряжённо; **she
~ denied the rumour** она́ уси́ленно отрица́ла
слу́хи.
stress [strɛs] *n* (*pressure, also* TECH) давлéние;
(*mental strain*) стресс; (LING: *accent*)
ударéние; (*emphasis*) значéние ♦ *vt* (*point,
importance etc*) подчёркивать (подчеркну́ть
perf); (*syllable*) ста́вить* (поста́вить* *perf*)
ударéние на +*acc*; **to lay great ~ on sth**
придава́ть* (прида́ть* *perf*) осо́бое значéние
на что-н; **to be under ~** быть* (*impf*) под
напряжéнием.
stressful ['strɛsful] *adj* (*job*) напряжённый*
(напряжён); (*situation*) стрéссовый.
stretch [strɛtʃ] *n* (*area: of sand, water etc*)
простра́нство; (*of time*) промежу́ток* ♦ *vt*
(*pull*) натя́гивать (натяну́ть* *perf*); (*fig: subj:
job, task*) утомля́ть (утоми́ть* *perf*); (*spread:
resources*) растя́гивать (растяну́ть* *perf*) ♦ *vi*
(*person, animal*) потя́гиваться (потяну́ться*
perf); (*extend*): **to ~ to** *or* **as far as**
простира́ться (простерéться* *perf*) к +*dat*; (*be
enough*): **to ~ (to)** хвата́ть (хвати́ть* *perf*) (на
+*acc*); **at a ~** подря́д; **he's no hero by any ~ of
the imagination** как ни стара́йтесь, его́
нельзя́ вообрази́ть герóем; **to ~ one's legs**
размина́ть (размя́ть* *perf*) но́ги
▸ **stretch out** *vi* растя́гиваться (растяну́ться*
perf) ♦ *vt* (*arm etc*) протя́гивать (протяну́ть*
perf); (*spread*) растя́гивать (растяну́ть* *perf*);
to ~ out for sth тяну́ться* (потяну́ться* *perf*)
за чем-н.
stretcher ['strɛtʃəʳ] *n* (MED) носи́лки* *pl*.
stretcher-bearer ['strɛtʃəbɛərəʳ] *n*
санита́р-носи́льщик.
stretchmarks ['strɛtʃmɑ:ks] *npl* следы́
растя́гивания на кóже.
strewn [stru:n] *adj*: **~ with** усы́панный
(усы́пан) +*instr*.
stricken ['strɪkən] *adj* (*person*) сражённый;
(*city, industry etc*) пострада́вший; **~ with**

(*arthritis, disease*) поражённый +*instr.*

strict [strɪkt] *adj* (*severe, firm: person, rule*) стро́гий* (строг); (*precise: meaning*) то́чный* (то́чен); **in ~** *or* **in the ~est confidence** в строжа́йшей та́йне.

strictly ['strɪktlɪ] *adv* (*severely*) стро́го; (*exactly*) то́чно; **~ confidential** соверше́нно конфиденциа́льно *or* секре́тно; **~ speaking** стро́го говоря́; **~ between ourselves** то́лько ме́жду на́ми.

strictness ['strɪktnɪs] *n* стро́гость *f.*

stridden ['strɪdn] *pp of* **stride**.

stride [straɪd] (*pt* **strode**, *pp* **stridden**) *n* (*step*) широ́кий* шаг* ♦ *vi* шага́ть (*impf*); **to take sth in one's ~** (*fig: changes etc*) относи́ться* (*impf*) споко́йно к чему́-н.

strident ['straɪdnt] *adj* (*voice, sound*) пронзи́тельный* (пронзи́телен); (*demands*) шу́мный.

strife [straɪf] *n* борьба́.

strike [straɪk] (*pt, pp* **struck**) *n* (*of workers*) забасто́вка*; (*MIL: attack*) уда́р; (*of oil etc*) откры́тие месторожде́ния ♦ *vt* (*hit: person, thing*) ударя́ть (уда́рить *perf*); (*fig: subj: disease, disaster*) поража́ть (порази́ть* *perf*); (: *idea, thought*) осеня́ть (осени́ть *perf*); (*oil etc*) открыва́ть (откры́ть* *perf*) месторожде́ние +*gen*; (*bargain, deal*) заключа́ть (заключи́ть *perf*); (*make: coin, medal*) чека́нить (отчека́нить *perf*) ♦ *vi* (*workers*) бастова́ть (*impf*); (*attack: soldiers*) напада́ть (напа́сть* *perf*); (: *disaster, illness*) приходи́ть* (прийти́* *perf*); (*clock*) бить* (проби́ть* *perf*); **to be on ~** (*workers*) бастова́ть (*impf*); **to ~ a balance** соблюда́ть (*impf*) равнове́сие; **to ~ a match** зажига́ть (заже́чь* *perf*) спи́чку

► **strike back** *vi* (*MIL, fig*) наноси́ть* (нанести́* *perf*) отве́тный уда́р

► **strike down** *vt* сража́ть (срази́ть* *perf*)

► **strike off** *vt* (*name from list*) вычёркивать (вы́черкнуть *perf*); (: *doctor etc*) лиша́ть (лиши́ть *perf*) пра́ва практикова́ть

► **strike out** *vt* (*word, sentence*) вычёркивать (вы́черкнуть *perf*)

► **strike up** *vt* (*MUS*) заигра́ть (*impf*); (*conversation, friendship*) завя́зывать (завяза́ть* *perf*).

strikebreaker ['straɪkbreɪkə^r] *n* штрейкбре́хер.

strike pay *n* посо́бие басту́ющим.

striker ['straɪkə^r] *n* (*person on strike*) забасто́вщик(-ица); (*SPORT*) напада́ющий* (-ая) *m(f) adj.*

striking ['straɪkɪŋ] *adj* порази́тельный* (порази́телен).

strimmer ['strɪmə^r] *n* механи́ческое ручно́е приспособле́ние для стри́жки газо́нов в труднодосту́пных места́х.

string [strɪŋ] (*pt, pp* **strung**) *n* верёвка*; (*row: of*

onions*) свя́зка*; (: *of islands*) цепь *f*; (: *of cars, people*) верени́ца; (*series: of disasters*) се́рия; (: *of excuses*) пото́к; (*COMPUT*) строка́, цепо́чка; (*MUS: for guitar etc*) струна́* ♦ *vt*: **to ~ together** свя́зывать (связа́ть* *perf*); **the ~s** *npl* (*MUS: section of orchestra*) стру́нные инструме́нты *mpl*; **to ~ out** растя́гивать (растяну́ть* *perf*); **a ~ of beads** бу́сы; **to pull ~s** (*fig*) испо́льзовать (*impf/perf*) свя́зи; **with no ~s attached** (*fig*) без дополни́тельных усло́вий.

string bean *n* стручко́вая фасо́ль *f.*

string(ed) instrument *n* стру́нный инструме́нт.

stringent ['strɪndʒənt] *adj* (*rules, measures*) стро́гий* (строг).

string quartet *n* (*MUS*) стру́нный кварте́т.

strip [strɪp] *n* полоса́*; (*SPORT*): **the Rangers ~** фо́рма Ре́йнджерз ♦ *vt* (*undress*) раздева́ть (разде́ть* *perf*); (*paint*) обдира́ть (ободра́ть* *perf*), сдира́ть (содра́ть* *perf*); (*also: ~* **down**: *machine*) разбира́ть (разобра́ть* *perf*) ♦ *vi* (*undress*) раздева́ться (разде́ться* *perf*).

strip cartoon *n* исто́рия в карти́нках.

stripe [straɪp] *n* поло́ска*; (*MIL, POLICE*) петли́ца.

striped ['straɪpt] *adj* (*fabric, animal etc*) полоса́тый (полоса́т).

strip lighting *n* (*BRIT*) дневно́е освеще́ние.

stripper ['strɪpə^r] *n* уча́стница стрипти́за.

strip-search ['strɪpsɛtʃ] *n* ли́чный досмо́тр ♦ *vt* производи́ть* (произвести́* *perf*) ли́чный досмо́тр.

striptease ['strɪptiːz] *n* стрипти́з.

strive [straɪv] (*pt* **strove**, *pp* **striven**) *vi*: **to ~ for sth/to do** стреми́ться* (*impf*) к чему́-н/+*infin*.

striven ['strɪvn] *pp of* **strive**.

strobe [strəʊb] *n* (*also: ~* **light**) строб-и́мпульс, селе́кторный и́мпульс.

strode [strəʊd] *pt of* **stride**.

stroke [strəʊk] *n* (*also MED*) уда́р; (*SWIMMING*) стиль *m*; (*of piston*) ход, такт; (*of paintbrush*) мазо́к*; (*of pen etc*) штрих ♦ *vt* (*caress*) гла́дить (погла́дить* *perf*); **at a ~** одни́м ма́хом; **on the ~ of 5** ро́вно в 5; **a ~ of luck** уда́ча; **a 2-~ engine** двухта́ктный дви́гатель *m.*

stroll [strəʊl] *n* прогу́лка* ♦ *vi* прогу́ливаться (прогуля́ться *perf*), пройти́сь* (*perf*); **to go for a ~, have** *or* **take a ~** идти́* (пойти́* *perf*) прогуля́ться.

stroller ['strəʊlə^r] *n* (*US: pushchair*) (складна́я) коля́ска.

strong [strɒŋ] *adj* си́льный* (силён); (*healthy, powerful*) кре́пкий* (кре́пок); (*object, material*) про́чный* (про́чен); (*imagination*) большо́й; (*drugs, chemicals*) си́льный; (*letters, measures*) ре́зкий* (ре́зок) ♦ *adv*: **to be going ~** занима́ть (*impf*) про́чные пози́ции;

---

* marks translations which have irregular inflections. The Russian-English side of the dictionary gives inflectional information.

they are 50 ~ их 50.
strong-arm ['strɔŋɑːm] *adj*: ~ **methods** приёмы
mpl сильной руки.
strongbox ['strɔŋbɔks] *n* сейф.
stronghold ['strɔŋhəuld] *n* район
сопротивления; (*fig*) оплот, твердыня.
strongly ['strɔŋlɪ] *adv* (*construct*) крепко; (*push,
defend, believe*) сильно; **I feel ~ about it** во
мне это вызывает сильные эмоции.
strongman ['strɔŋmæn] *irreg n* силач,
богатырь* *m*; (*fig*) сильная личность *f*.
strongroom ['strɔŋruːm] *n* сейф.
stroppy ['strɔpɪ] *adj* (*inf*) строптивый
(строптив).
strove [strəuv] *pt of* **strive**.
struck [strʌk] *pt, pp of* **strike**.
structural ['strʌktʃrəl] *adj* структурный.
structurally ['strʌktʃrəlɪ] *adv* (*sound*) со
структурной точки зрения.
structure ['strʌktʃəʳ] *n* структура.
struggle ['strʌgl] *n* борьба; (*difficulty*) усилие
◆ *vi* (*try hard*) прилагать (*impf*) большие
усилия; (*fight*) бороться* (*impf*); (: to free o.s.)
сопротивляться (*impf*); **to have a ~ to do**
делать (сделать *perf*) усилие +*infin*.
strum [strʌm] *vt* (*guitar*) играть (*impf*) на +*prp*.
strung [strʌŋ] *pt, pp of* **string**.
strut [strʌt] *n* (*wood, metal*) распорка* ◆ *vi*
ходить*/идти* (пойти* *perf*) величественно.
strychnine ['strɪkniːn] *n* стрихнин.
stub [stʌb] *n* (*of cheque, ticket etc*) корешок*;
(*of cigarette*) окурок* ◆ *vt*: **to ~ one's toe**
больно спотыкаться (споткнуться *perf*)
▸ **stub out** *vt* (*cigarette*) гасить* (загасить*
perf).
stubble ['stʌbl] *n* (*AGR*) жнивьё; (*on chin*)
щетина.
stubborn ['stʌbən] *adj* (*child, determination*)
упрямый (упрям), упорный (упорен);
(*stain*) несмывающийся; (*illness*) плохо
поддающийся лечению.
stubby ['stʌbɪ] *adj* (*fingers, pencil*) короткий*.
stucco ['stʌkəu] *n* (*CONSTR*) декоративная
"каменная" штукатурка.
stuck [stʌk] *pt, pp of* **stick** ◆ *adj*: **to be ~**
застрять* (*perf*); **to get ~** застревать
(застрять* *perf*).
stuck-up [stʌk'ʌp] *adj* (*inf*) надутый (надут).
stud [stʌd] *n* (*on clothing etc*) кнопка*,
заклёпка*; (*collar stud*) запонка*; (*earring*)
серьга* со штифтом*; (*on sole of boot*) шип*;
(*also*: ~ **farm**) конный завод*; (*also*: ~ **horse**)
племенной конь* *m* ◆ *vt* (*fig*): ~**ded with**
усыпанный +*instr*.
student ['stjuːdənt] *n* (*at university*)
студент(ка*); (*at school*) учащийся*(-аяся)
m(f) ◆ *adj* (*life, union*) студенческий*;
(*nurse: female*) медсестра-практикантка*;
(: *male*) медбрат-пратикант; **law/medical ~**
студент(ка*) юридического/медицинского
факультета.

student driver *n* (*US*) ученик* автомобиля.
student loan *n* студенческий* заём.
students' union ['stjuːdənts-] *n* (*BRIT*:
association) студенческий* союз; (*building*)
здание студенческого союза.
studied ['stʌdɪd] *adj* (*expression, attitude*)
продуманный* (продуман).
studio ['stjuːdɪəu] *n* студия.
studio flat (*US* **studio apartment**) *n*
однокомнатная квартира.
studious ['stjuːdɪəs] *adj* (*person*) усердный*
(усерден); (*careful: attention*) тщательный*
(тщателен).
studiously ['stjuːdɪəslɪ] *adv* (*carefully*)
тщательно.
study ['stʌdɪ] *n* (*activity*) учёба; (*room*) кабинет
◆ *vt* (*learn about, examine*) изучать (изучить*
perf) ◆ *vi* учиться* (*perf*); **studies** *npl* (*subjects
studied*) курсы *pl*; **to make a ~ of sth**
исследовать (*impf/perf*) что-н; **to ~ for one's
exams** готовиться* (*impf*) к экзаменам.
stuff [stʌf] *n* (*things*) вещи *fpl*; (*substance*)
вещество ◆ *vt* набивать (набить* *perf*);
(*CULIN*) начинять (начинить* *perf*),
фаршировать (нафаршировать *perf*); (*inf*:
push: object) запихивать (запихать *perf*); **my
nose is ~ed up** у меня заложен нос; **get ~ed!**
(*inf!*) пошёл ты!
stuffed toy [stʌft-] *n* мягкая игрушка*.
stuffing ['stʌfɪŋ] *n* набивка; (*CULIN*) начинка,
фарш.
stuffy ['stʌfɪ] *adj* (*room*) душный* (душен);
(*person, ideas*) чопорный* (чопорен).
stumble ['stʌmbl] *vi* спотыкаться
(споткнуться *perf*); **to ~ across** *or* **on** (*fig*)
натыкаться (наткнуться *perf*) на +*acc*.
stumbling block ['stʌmblɪŋ-] *n* камень* *m*
преткновения.
stump [stʌmp] *n* (*of tree*) пень* *m*; (*of limb*)
обрубок* ◆ *vt* озадачивать (озадачить *perf*);
he is ~ed он озадачен.
stun [stʌn] *vt* (*subj: news*) ошеломлять
(ошеломить* *perf*); (: *blow on head*)
оглушать (оглушить* *perf*).
stung [stʌŋ] *pt, pp of* **sting**.
stunk [stʌŋk] *pp of* **stink**.
stunning ['stʌnɪŋ] *adj* (*fig: news, event*)
ошеломительный* (ошеломителен); (: *girl,
dress*) потрясающий* (потрясающ),
изумительный* (изумителен).
stunt [stʌnt] *n* трюк.
stunted ['stʌntɪd] *adj* (*trees*) подрубленный*;
(*growth*) замедленный* (замедлен).
stuntman ['stʌntmæn] *irreg n* каскадёр.
stupefaction [stjuːpɪ'fækʃən] *n* отупение;
(*surprise*) остолбенение; **to my ~** к моему
изумлению.
stupefy ['stjuːpɪfaɪ] *vt* приводить* (привести*
perf) в отупение; (*fig*) изумлять (изумить*
perf).
stupendous [stjuː'pɛndəs] *adj* (*large*)

колосса́льный* (колосса́лен); (*impressive*) изуми́тельный* (изуми́телен).

stupid ['stjuːpɪd] *adj* (*person, question etc*) глу́пый (глуп).

stupidity [stjuːˈpɪdɪtɪ] *n* глу́пость *f*.

stupidly ['stjuːpɪdlɪ] *adv* (*say, look*) глу́по.

stupor ['stjuːpəʳ] *n* сту́пор; **in a** ~ в сту́поре.

sturdily ['stəːdɪlɪ] *adv* (*built*) про́чно, кре́пко.

sturdy ['stəːdɪ] *adj* (*person, thing*) кре́пкий* (кре́пок).

sturgeon ['stəːdʒən] *n* (*ZOOL*) осётр*.

stutter ['stʌtəʳ] *n* заика́ние ♦ *vi* заика́ться (*impf*).

Stuttgart ['stutgɑːt] *n* Шту́тгарт.

sty [staɪ] *n* (*for pigs*) свина́рник.

stye [staɪ] *n* ячме́нь *m*.

style [staɪl] *n* стиль *m*; **in the latest** ~ по после́дней мо́де; **hair** ~ причёска*.

styli ['staɪlaɪ] *npl of* **stylus**.

stylish ['staɪlɪʃ] *adj* шика́рный* (шика́рен).

stylist ['staɪlɪst] *n* (*also:* **hair** ~) парикма́хер-модельёр; (*literary stylist*) стили́ст.

stylized ['staɪlaɪzd] *adj* (*picture, account*) стилизо́ванный* (стилизо́ван).

stylus ['staɪləs] (*pl* **styli** *or* ~**es**) *n* (*of record player*) игла́*, иго́лька*.

Styrofoam® ['staɪrəfəum] *n* (*US*) синтети́ческий упако́вочный материа́л.

suave [swɑːv] *adj* (*person, manners etc*) еле́йный* (еле́ен).

sub [sʌb] *n abbr* (*NAUT*) (= **submarine**) подло́дка= *подво́дная ло́дка*; (*ADMIN* = **subscription**; (*PRESS*: = **sub-editor**) помо́щник *or* замести́тель *m* реда́ктора.

sub... [sʌb] *prefix* суб..., под....

subcommittee ['sʌbkəmɪtɪ] *n* подкомите́т.

subconscious [sʌbˈkɔnʃəs] *adj* (*desire etc*) подсозна́тельный* (подсозна́телен).

subcontinent [sʌbˈkɔntɪnənt] *n*: **the (Indian)** ~ (инди́йский*) субконтине́нт.

subcontract [*vt* sʌbkənˈtrækt, *n* 'sʌbˈkɔntrækt] *vt* заключа́ть (заключи́ть *perf*) субподря́д с +*instr* ♦ *n* субподря́д.

subcontractor ['sʌbkənˈtræktəʳ] *n* субподря́дчик.

subdivide [sʌbdɪˈvaɪd] *vt* подразделя́ть (подраздели́ть *perf*).

subdivision ['sʌbdɪvɪʒən] *n* подразделе́ние.

subdue [səbˈdjuː] *vt* подавля́ть (подави́ть* *perf*).

subdued [səbˈdjuːd] *adj* (*light*) приглушённый (приглушён); (*person*) пода́вленный* (пода́влен).

sub-editor ['sʌbˈɛdɪtəʳ] *n* (*BRIT: PRESS*) помо́щник *or* замести́тель *m* реда́ктора.

subject [*n* 'sʌbdʒɪkt, *vt* səbˈdʒɛkt] *n* (*topic*) те́ма; (*SCOL*) предме́т; (*of kingdom*) по́данный(-ая) *m(f) adj*; (*LING*) подлежа́щее *nt adj* ♦ *vt*: **to** ~ **sb**

to sth подверга́ть (подве́ргнуть* *perf*) кого́-н чему́-н; **to be** ~ **to** (*tax*) подлежа́ть (*impf*) +*dat*; (*law*) подчиня́ться (*impf*) +*dat*; **he is** ~ **to heart attacks** он подве́ржен серде́чным при́ступам; **this is** ~ **to confirmation in writing** э́то подлежи́т пи́сьменному подтвержде́нию; **to change the** ~ меня́ть (поменя́ть *perf*) те́му (разгово́ра).

subjection [səbˈdʒɛkʃən] *n* (*of women, enemy etc*) подчине́ние.

subjective [səbˈdʒɛktɪv] *adj* субъекти́вный* (субъекти́вен).

subject matter *n* (*content*) те́ма.

sub judice [sʌbˈdjuːdɪsɪ] *adj*: **the case is** ~~ в да́нным моме́нт э́то де́ло рассма́тривается судо́м.

subjugate ['sʌbdʒugeɪt] *vt* (*people*) покоря́ть (покори́ть *perf*).

subjunctive [səbˈdʒʌŋktɪv] *n* сослага́тельное наклоне́ние.

sublet [sʌbˈlɛt] *vt* (*property*) передава́ть* (переда́ть* *perf*) в субаре́нду.

sublime [səˈblaɪm] *adj* возвы́шенный* ; **from the** ~ **to the ridiculous** от вели́кого до смешно́го.

subliminal [sʌbˈlɪmɪnl] *adj* (*memory*) подсозна́тельный; (*advertising*) де́йствующий* на подсозна́ние.

submachine gun ['sʌbməˈʃiːn-] *n* автома́т.

submarine [sʌbməˈriːn] *n* подво́дная ло́дка*.

submerge [səbˈməːdʒ] *vt* погружа́ть (погрузи́ть* *perf*) (в во́ду) ♦ *vi* (*submarine, sea creature*) погружа́ться (погрузи́ться* *perf*) (в во́ду).

submersion [səbˈməːʃən] *n* погруже́ние.

submission [səbˈmɪʃən] *n* (*state*) подчине́ние, повинове́ние; (*of plan etc*) пода́ча; (*to committee etc*) представле́ние.

submissive [səbˈmɪsɪv] *adj* поко́рный* (поко́рен).

submit [səbˈmɪt] *vt* (*proposal, application etc*) представля́ть (предста́вить* *perf*) на рассмотре́ние ♦ *vi*: **to** ~ **to sth** подчиня́ться (подчини́ться *perf*) чему́-н.

subnormal [sʌbˈnɔːml] *adj* (*backward: child etc*) отста́лый; ~ **temperatures** температу́ры *fpl* ни́же норма́льных.

subordinate [səˈbɔːdɪnət] *adj* (*position, rank*): **to be** ~ **to sb** подчиня́ться (*impf*) кому́-н; (*LING: clause*) прида́точный ♦ *n* подчинённый(-ая) *m(f) adj*.

subpoena [səbˈpiːnə] *n* (*LAW*) пове́стка* ♦ *vt* (*LAW: witness etc*) вызыва́ть (вы́звать* *perf*) в суд.

subroutine [sʌbruːˈtiːn] *n* (*COMPUT*) подпрогра́мма.

subscribe [səbˈskraɪb] *vi* подпи́сываться (подписа́ться* *perf*); **to** ~ **to** (*opinion, fund*)

поддержива́ть (поддержа́ть* *perf*); (*magazine etc*) подпи́сываться (подписа́ться* *perf*) на +*acc*; ~**d capital** подписно́й акционе́рный капита́л.
subscriber [səb'skraɪbə] *n* (*to periodical*) подпи́счик; (*to telephone*) абоне́нт.
subscript ['sʌbskrɪpt] *n* (*TYP*) подстро́чный знак.
subscription [səb'skrɪpʃən] *n* (*to magazine etc*) подпи́ска*; (*membership dues*) (чле́нский*) взнос; **to take out a ~ to** подпи́сываться (подписа́ться* *perf*) на +*acc*.
subsequent ['sʌbsɪkwənt] *adj* после́дующий*; ~ **to** всле́д +*dat*.
subsequently ['sʌbsɪkwəntlɪ] *adv* впосле́дствии.
subservient [səb'sə:vɪənt] *adj* (*person, behaviour*) подобостра́стный* (подобостра́стен); (*less important: policy etc*) подвла́стный* (подвла́стен); **he is ~ to ...** он подвла́стен +*dat* ....
subside [səb'saɪd] *vi* (*feeling, wind*) утиха́ть (ути́хнуть* *perf*); (*flood*) убыва́ть (убы́ть* *perf*).
subsidence [səb'saɪdns] *n* (*in road etc*) оседа́ние.
subsidiarity [səbsɪdɪ'ærɪtɪ] *n* (*POL*) у́ровень* *m* зави́симости.
subsidiary [səb'sɪdɪərɪ] *adj* (*question, details*) второстепе́нный* (второстепе́н); (*BRIT: SCOL: subject*) факультати́вный ◆ *n* (*also: ~ company*) доче́рняя компа́ния.
subsidize ['sʌbsɪdaɪz] *vt* (*education, industry etc*) субсиди́ровать (*impf/perf*).
subsidy ['sʌbsɪdɪ] *n* субси́дия, дота́ция.
subsist [səb'sɪst] *vi*: **to ~ on sth** существова́ть (*impf*) за счёт чего́-н.
subsistence [səb'sɪstəns] *n* (*ability to live*) существова́ние; (*food*) пропита́ние.
subsistence allowance *n* ава́нс (*пе́ред пе́рвой зарпла́той*).
subsistence level *n* прожи́точный ми́нимум.
substance ['sʌbstəns] *n* (*product, material*) вещество́; (*fig: essence*) суть* *f*; **a man of ~** соли́дный мужчи́на; **the essay lacks ~** в сочине́нии нет сте́ржня.
substance abuse *n* токсикома́ния.
substandard [sʌb'stændəd] *adj* (*goods*) нека́чественный; (*housing*) неприго́дный* (неприго́ден) для жилья́.
substantial [səb'stænʃl] *adj* (*solid*) про́чный* (про́чен), основа́тельный* (основа́телен); (*fig: reward, meal*) значи́тельный* (значи́телен), соли́дный* (соли́ден).
substantially [səb'stænʃəlɪ] *adv* (*by a large amount*) значи́тельно; (*in essence*) суще́ственно, основа́тельно; ~ **bigger** значи́тельно бо́льше.
substantiate [səb'stænʃɪeɪt] *vt* (*claim, story, statement etc*) обосно́вывать (обоснова́ть* *perf*).

substitute ['sʌbstɪtju:t] *n* (*person*) заме́на; (: *FOOTBALL etc*) запасно́й *m adj* (игро́к*); (*thing*) замени́тель *m* ◆ *vt*: **to ~ A for B** заменя́ть (замени́ть* *perf*) А на Б.
substitute teacher *n* (*US*) замеща́ющий(-ая) учи́тель(ница) *m(f)*.
substitution [sʌbstɪ'tju:ʃən] *n* (*act of substituting*) заме́на.
subterfuge ['sʌbtəfju:dʒ] *n* уло́вка*.
subterranean [sʌbtə'reɪnɪən] *adj* (*passage*) подзе́мный.
subtitle ['sʌbtaɪtl] *n* (*CINEMA*) субти́тр.
subtle ['sʌtl] *adj* (*change*) то́нкий*, едва́ улови́мый; (*person*) иску́сный* (иску́сен).
subtlety ['sʌtltɪ] *n* (*small detail*) то́нкость *f*; (*of person*) иску́сность *f*.
subtly ['sʌtlɪ] *adv* (*change, vary*) едва́ улови́мо; (*different*) слегка́; (*criticize, persuade*) иску́сно.
subtotal [sʌb'təutl] *n* сумма́рное число́*.
subtract [səb'trækt] *vt* вычита́ть (вы́честь* *perf*).
subtraction [səb'trækʃən] *n* вычита́ние.
subtropical [sʌb'trɔpɪkl] *adj* субтропи́ческий.
suburb ['sʌbə:b] *n* при́город; **the ~s** *npl* (*area*) при́город *msg*.
suburban [sə'bə:bən] *adj* при́городный.
suburbia [sə'bə:bɪə] *n* при́город.
subvention [səb'vɛnʃən] *n* (*subsidy*) дота́ция, субси́дия.
subversion [səb'və:ʃən] *n* подрывна́я де́ятельность *f*.
subversive [səb'və:sɪv] *adj* (*activities, literature*) подрывно́й.
subway ['sʌbweɪ] *n* (*US: underground railway*) метро́ *nt ind*, подзе́мка*; (*BRIT: underpass*) подзе́мный перехо́д.
sub-zero [sʌb'zɪərəu] *adj*: ~ **temperatures** температу́ры *fpl* ни́же нуля́.
succeed [sək'si:d] *vi* (*plan etc*) удава́ться* (уда́ться* *perf*), име́ть (*impf*) успе́х; (*person: in career etc*) преуспева́ть (преуспе́ть *perf*) ◆ *vt* (*in job, order*) сменя́ть (смени́ть* *perf*); **he ~ed in finishing the article** ему́ удало́сь зако́нчить статью́.
succeeding [sək'si:dɪŋ] *adj* (*following*) после́дующий*; ~ **generations** после́дующие поколе́ния.
success [sək'sɛs] *n* (*achievement*) успе́х, уда́ча; (*hit*): **the book was a ~** кни́га име́ла успе́х; **he was a ~** он доби́лся успе́ха.
successful [sək'sɛsful] *adj* (*venture*) успе́шный* (успе́шен); **he was ~ in convincing her** ему́ удало́сь убеди́ть её.
successfully [sək'sɛsfəlɪ] *adv* (*complete, do*) успе́шно.
succession [sək'sɛʃən] *n* (*series*) череда́, ряд*; (*to throne etc*) насле́дование; **in ~** подря́д; **3 years in ~** три го́да подря́д.
successive [sək'sɛsɪv] *adj* (*governments*) сле́дующий* оди́н за други́м; **3 ~ days/**

attempts три дня/попы́тки подря́д.
successor [sək'sɛsə'] n прее́мник(-ица); (*to throne*) насле́дник(-ица).
succinct [sək'sɪŋkt] adj (*explanation*) сжа́тый (сжат).
succulent ['sʌkjulənt] adj (*fruit, meat*) со́чный* (со́чен) ♦ n (BOT): **~s** суккуле́нты pl.
succumb [sə'kʌm] vi (*to temptation*) поддава́ться* (подда́ться* perf); **he ~ed to illness** боле́знь оконча́тельно его́ победи́ла.
such [sʌtʃ] adj тако́й; (*emphasizing similarity*) подо́бный, тако́й ♦ adv: **~ a long trip** така́я дли́нная пое́здка; **~ a book** така́я кни́га; **~ books** таки́е кни́ги; **~ a lot of** тако́е мно́жество +gen; **making ~ a noise that …** создава́я тако́й шум, что …; **~ as** (*like*) таки́е как; **~ books as I have** таки́е кни́ги, как у меня́; **I said no ~ thing** я ничего́ подо́бного or тако́го не говори́л; **as ~** как таково́й.
such-and-such ['sʌtʃənsʌtʃ] adj таки́е-то и таки́е-то.
suchlike ['sʌtʃlaɪk] pron (*inf*): **and ~** и им подо́бные.
suck [sʌk] vt соса́ть* (*impf*); (*subj: pump, machine*) вса́сывать (всоса́ть perf).
sucker ['sʌkə'] n присо́ска*; (BOT) корнево́й побе́г; (*inf*) о́лух.
suckle ['sʌkl] vt корми́ть* (*impf*) (гру́дью), дава́ть* (дать* perf) грудь +dat; (*subj: animal*) корми́ть* (*impf*).
sucrose ['su:krəuz] n сахаро́за.
suction ['sʌkʃən] n вса́сывание.
suction pump n вса́сывающий насо́с.
Sudan [su'dɑ:n] n Суда́н.
Sudanese [su:də'ni:z] adj суда́нский ♦ n inv суда́нец*(-ка*).
sudden ['sʌdn] adj внеза́пный* (внеза́пен); **all of a ~** (*unexpectedly*) внеза́пно, вдруг.
sudden death n (*in competition*) дополни́тельный матч (*по́сле ничьи́*).
suddenly ['sʌdnlɪ] adv (*unexpectedly*) внеза́пно, вдруг.
suds [sʌdz] npl (мы́льные) пузыри́ mpl.
sue [su:] vt предъявля́ть (предъяви́ть* perf) иск +dat, возбужда́ть (возбуди́ть* perf) де́ло про́тив +gen ♦ vi: **to ~ (for)** суди́ться (*impf*) (за +acc); **to ~ for divorce** возбужда́ть (возбуди́ть* perf) де́ло о разво́де; **to ~ sb for damages** предъявля́ть (предъяви́ть* perf) иск кому́-н о компенса́ции.
suede [sweɪd] n за́мша ♦ cpd за́мшевый.
suet ['suɪt] n жир.
Suez ['su:ɪz] n: **the ~ Canal** Суэ́цкий* кана́л.
Suff. abbr (BRIT: POST) = Suffolk.
suffer ['sʌfə'] vt (*hardship etc*) переноси́ть* (перенести́* perf); (*pain, rudeness*) страда́ть (*impf*) от +gen ♦ vi (*person, results etc*) страда́ть (пострада́ть perf); **to ~ from** (*illness*

etc) страда́ть (*impf*) +instr; **to ~ the effects of alcohol/a fall** страда́ть (пострада́ть perf) от возде́йствия алкого́ля/от после́дствий паде́ния.
sufferance ['sʌfərns] n: **she hadn't wanted him to go, so he was only there on ~** она́ не хоте́ла отпуска́ть его́, он был там, причиня́я ей страда́ния.
sufferer ['sʌfərə'] n (MED) страда́ющий(-ая) m(f) adj.
suffering ['sʌfərɪŋ] n (*hardship*) страда́ние.
suffice [sə'faɪs] vi (*be enough*): **this ~s …** э́того доста́точно, ….
sufficient [sə'fɪʃənt] adj доста́точный* (доста́точен); **~ money** доста́точное коли́чество де́нег.
sufficiently [sə'fɪʃəntlɪ] adv (*recover, provide*) доста́точно; (*powerful, enthusiastic*) в доста́точной ме́ре.
suffix ['sʌfɪks] n (LING) су́ффикс.
suffocate ['sʌfəkeɪt] vi задыха́ться (задохну́ться perf); (*have difficulty breathing*) задыха́ться (*impf*); (*die*) задохну́ться (*impf*) ♦ vt (*gas etc*) удуша́ть (удуши́ть perf).
suffocation [sʌfə'keɪʃən] n удушье.
suffrage ['sʌfrɪdʒ] n (*right to vote*) избира́тельное пра́во.
suffragette [sʌfrə'dʒɛt] n суфражи́стка*.
suffused [sə'fju:zd] adj: **~ with** (*light, colour*) погружённый (погружён) в +prp; (*tears*) зали́тый (зали́т) +instr.
sugar ['ʃugə'] n са́хар* ♦ vt (*tea etc*) сласти́ть* (посласти́ть* perf).
sugar beet n са́харная свёкла.
sugar bowl n са́харница.
sugar cane n са́харный тростни́к.
sugar-coated ['ʃugə'kəutɪd] adj (*sweet*) заса́харенный.
sugar lump n кусо́к* са́хара.
sugar refinery n сахарорафина́дный заво́д.
sugary ['ʃugərɪ] adj сла́дкий* (сла́док), сахари́стый (сахари́ст); (*fig*) слаща́вый (слаща́в).
suggest [sə'dʒɛst] vt (*propose*) предлага́ть (предложи́ть* perf); (*indicate*) предполага́ть (предположи́ть* perf); **what do you ~ I do?** что Вы предлага́ете мне де́лать?
suggestion [sə'dʒɛstʃən] n (*proposal*) предложе́ние; (*indication*) предположе́ние.
suggestive [sə'dʒɛstɪv] adj (pej: *remarks, looks*) неприли́чный* (неприли́чен).
suicidal [suɪ'saɪdl] adj (*person*) стоя́щий на гра́ни самоуби́йства; (*act*) само-уби́йственный.
suicide ['suɪsaɪd] n (*death*) самоуби́йство; (*person*) самоуби́йца m/f; see also **commit**.
suicide attempt n попы́тка* самоуби́йства.
suicide bid n попы́тка* самоуби́йства.

---

* marks translations which have irregular inflections. The Russian-English side of the dictionary gives inflectional information.

suit [su:t] *n* костюм; (*LAW*) иск; (*CARDS*) масть *f*
♦ *vt* (*be convenient, appropriate*) подходить*
(подойти* *perf*) +*dat*; (*colour, clothes*) идти*
(*impf*) +*dat*; (*adapt*): **to ~ sth to**
приспосабливать (приспособить* *perf*) что-н
к +*dat*; **he was ~ed to lead the party** он
хорошо подходил на роль лидера партии;
to bring a ~ against sb предъявлять
(предъявить* *perf*) иск кому-н; **to follow ~**
(*fig*) следовать (последовать *perf*) примеру;
they are well ~ed (*couple*) они хорошо друг
другу подходят.

suitability [su:tə'bɪlɪtɪ] *n* пригодность *f*.

suitable ['su:təbl] *adj* подходящий*; **would
tomorrow be ~?** завтра Вам подойдёт *or* Вас
устроит?; **we found somebody ~** мы нашли
подходящего человека.

suitably ['su:təblɪ] *adv* надлежащим образом.

suitcase ['su:tkeɪs] *n* чемодан.

suite [swi:t] *n* (*of rooms*) апартаменты *mpl*;
(*MUS*) сюита; (*furniture*): **bedroom/dining
room ~** спальный/столовый гарнитур; **a
three-piece ~** мягкая мебель *f*.

suitor ['su:tə'] *n*: **he is her ~** он ищет её руки.

sulfate ['sʌlfeɪt] *n* (*US*) = **sulphate**.

sulfur ['sʌlfə'] *n* (*US*) = **sulphur**.

sulfuric [sʌl'fjuərɪk] (*US*) = **sulphuric**.

sulk [sʌlk] *vi* быть* (*impf*) в дурном
настроении.

sulky ['sʌlkɪ] *adj* (*child, mood*) сумрачный*
(сумрачен).

sullen ['sʌlən] *adj* (*person, silence*) угрюмый
(угрюм).

sulphate ['sʌlfeɪt] (*US* **sulfate**) *n* сульфат.

sulphur ['sʌlfə'] (*US* **sulfur**) *n* сера.

sulphur dioxide (*US* **sulfur dioxide**) *n*
двуокись *f* серы, сернистый ангидрид.

sulphuric [sʌl'fjuərɪk] (*US* **sulfuric**) *adj*: **~ acid**
серная кислота.

sultan ['sʌltən] *n* султан.

sultana [sʌl'tɑ:nə] *n* (*CULIN*) кишмиш.

sultry ['sʌltrɪ] *adj* (*weather*) душный* (душен).

sum [sʌm] *n* (*calculation*) арифметика,
вычисление; (*amount*) сумма
▶ **sum up** *vt* (*describe*) суммировать (*impf/perf*);
(*evaluate rapidly*) вычислять (вычислить
perf) ♦ *vi* (*summarize*) подводить* (подвести*
perf) итог.

Sumatra [su'mɑ:trə] *n* Суматра.

summarize ['sʌməraɪz] *vt* суммировать (*impf/
perf*).

summary ['sʌmərɪ] *n* (*of essay etc*) краткое
изложение ♦ *adj* (*justice*) поспешный;
weather/news ~ сводка погоды/новостей.

summer ['sʌmə'] *n* (*season*) лето ♦ *adj* (*dress,
school*) летний*; **in ~** летом.

summer camp *n* (*US*) летний* лагерь* *m*.

summer holidays *npl* летние каникулы *pl*.

summerhouse ['sʌməhaus] *n* (*in garden*)
беседка*.

summertime ['sʌmətaɪm] *n* (*season*) лето,

летний* период.

summer time *n* летнее время* *nt*.

summery ['sʌmərɪ] *adj* (*day, dress*) летний*.

summing-up [sʌmɪŋ'ʌp] *n* (*LAW*) краткое
изложение дела (*обращённое к
присяжным*).

summit ['sʌmɪt] *n* (*of mountain*) вершина, пик;
(*also: ~* **conference**) конференция на
высшем уровне; (*also: ~* **meeting**) встреча
на высшем уровне.

summon ['sʌmən] *vt* вызывать (вызвать* *perf*);
(*help*) звать* (позвать* *perf*) на +*acc*
▶ **summon up** *vt* собирать (собрать* *perf*).

summons ['sʌmənz] *n* (*LAW*) повестка; (*fig*)
приказание ♦ *vt* (*LAW*) вызывать (вызвать*
perf); **to serve a ~ on sb** посылать (послать*
perf) кому-н повестку.

sumo ['su:məu] *n* (*also: ~* **wrestling**) сумо *ind*
(*японская борьба*).

sump [sʌmp] *n* (*BRIT: AUT*) масляный поддон.

sumptuous ['sʌmptjuəs] *adj* (*meal, costume*)
роскошный* (роскошен), великолепный*
(великолепен).

sun [sʌn] *n* солнце; **in the ~** на солнце; **to catch
the ~** слегка загореть (*perf*); **everything under
the ~** всё в мире.

Sun. *abbr* = **Sunday**.

sunbathe ['sʌnbeɪð] *vi* загорать (*impf*).

sunbeam ['sʌnbi:m] *n* солнечный луч*.

sunbed ['sʌnbed] *n* шезлонг; (*with sun lamp*)
устройство с кварцевой лампой для
получения искусственно загара.

sunburn ['sʌnbə:n] *n* (*painful*) солнечный
ожог.

sunburned ['sʌnbə:nd] *adj* = **sunburnt**.

sunburnt ['sʌnbə:nt] *adj* (*tanned*) загорелый;
(*painfully*) обожённый (*солнцем*).

sun-cream ['sʌnkri:m] *n* солнцезащитный
крем.

sundae ['sʌndeɪ] *n* мороженое *nt adj* с
фруктами.

Sunday ['sʌndɪ] *n* воскресенье; *see also*
Tuesday.

Sunday paper *n* воскресная газета.

Sunday school *n* воскресная школа.

sundial ['sʌndaɪəl] *n* солнечные часы *pl*.

sundown ['sʌndaun] *n* закат, заход (солнца).

sundries ['sʌndrɪz] *npl* (*miscellaneous items*)
разное *nt adj*.

sundry ['sʌndrɪ] *adj* (*various*) разного рода; **all
and ~** все подряд.

sunflower ['sʌnflauə'] *n* (*BOT*) подсолнечник.

sunflower oil *n* (*CULIN*) подсолнечное масло.

sung [sʌŋ] *pp of* **sing**.

sunglasses ['sʌnglɑ:sɪz] *npl* солнцезащитные
очки* *pl*.

sunk [sʌŋk] *pp of* **sink**.

sunken ['sʌŋkn] *adj* (*rock, ship*) затонувший;
(*cheeks*) впалый; (*eyes*) ввалившийся; (*bath*)
встроенный в углубление.

sunlamp ['sʌnlæmp] *n* ультрафиолетовая *or*

кварцевая лампа.
sunlight ['sʌnlaɪt] *n* солнечый свет.
sunlit ['sʌnlɪt] *adj* освещённый (освещён)
солнцем.
sunny ['sʌnɪ] *adj* (*weather, day, place*)
солнечный; (*fig*) светлый; **it is** ~ солнечно.
sunrise ['sʌnraɪz] *n* восход (солнца).
sun roof *n* (*AUT*) раздвижная панель *f* (*в*
крыше автомобиля).
sunscreen ['sʌnskriːn] *n* солнцезащитный
крем.
sunset ['sʌnsɛt] *n* заход (солнца), закат.
sunshade ['sʌnʃeɪd] *n* зонтик.
sunshine ['sʌnʃaɪn] *n* солнечный свет; **we sat**
in the ~ мы сидели на солнце.
sunspot ['sʌnspɒt] *n* (*ASTRONOMY*) солнечное
место*.
sunstroke ['sʌnstrəuk] *n* солнечный удар.
suntan ['sʌntæn] *n* загар.
suntan lotion *n* лосьон для загара.
suntanned ['sʌntænd] *adj* (*body, person*)
загорелый.
suntan oil *n* масло для загара.
suntrap ['sʌntræp] *n* солнечный островок*.
super ['suːpəʳ] *adj* (*inf*) потрясающий*.
superannuation [suːpərænjuˈeɪʃən] *n*
ежегодный пенсионный вклад.
superb [suːˈpəːb] *adj* великолепный*
(великолепен).
Super Bowl *n* (*US*) *финальный матч*
американского чемпионата по футболу.
supercilious [suːpəˈsɪlɪəs] *adj* (*disdainful,*
haughty) высокомерный (высокомерен).
superconductor [suːpəkənˈdʌktəʳ] *n*
сверхпроводник.
superficial [suːpəˈfɪʃəl] *adj* поверхностный*
(поверхностен); (*wound*) лёгкий* (лёгок).
superficially [suːpəˈfɪʃəlɪ] *adv* поверхностно.
superfluous [suːˈpəːfluəs] *adj* излишный,
ненужный.
superglue ['suːpəgluː] *n* суперклей.
superhuman [suːpəˈhjuːmən] *adj* (*effort,*
strength) сверхчеловеческий*.
superimpose ['suːpərɪmˈpəuz] *vt*: **to** ~ **(on)**
накладывать (наложить* *perf*) (на +*acc*).
superintend [suːpərɪnˈtɛnd] *vt* надзирать (*impf*)
за +*instr*; **to be** ~**ed by** быть* (*impf*) под
надзором +*gen*.
superintendent [suːpərɪnˈtɛndənt] *n* (*of place*)
заведующий*(-ая) *m(f)adj*; (*of activity*)
руководитель(ница) *m(f)*; (*POLICE*)
начальник, надзиратель *m*.
superior [suˈpɪərɪəʳ] *adj* (*better*)
превосходящий; (*more senior*) старший*;
(*smug*) высокомерный ♦ *n* начальник(-ица);
Mother S~ (*REL*) настоятельница.
superiority [supɪərɪˈɔrɪtɪ] *n* превосходство.
superlative [suˈpəːlətɪv] *n* прилагательное или

наречие превосходной степени.
superman ['suːpəmæn] *irreg n* супермен,
сверхчеловек *m no pl*.
supermarket ['suːpəmɑːkɪt] *n* универмаг,
универсам; (*in Europe, US etc*) супермаркет.
supermodel ['suːpəmɔdl] *n* супермодель *f*.
supernatural [suːpəˈnætʃərəl] *adj* (*creature,*
force etc) сверхъестественный ♦ *n*: **the** ~
сверхъестественные силы *fpl*.
supernova [suːpəˈnəuvə] *n* взрывающаяся
новая звезда.
superpower ['suːpəpauə] *n* (*POL*)
сверхдержава.
superscript ['suːpəskrɪpt] *n* (*TYP*) надстрочные
знаки *mpl*.
supersede [suːpəˈsiːd] *vt* сменять (сменить*
perf).
supersonic [suːpəˈsɔnɪk] *adj* (*flight, aircraft*)
сверхзвуковой.
superstar ['suːpəstɑːʳ] *n* (*CINEMA, SPORT etc*)
суперзвезда*.
superstition [suːpəˈstɪʃən] *n* суеверие.
superstitious [suːpəˈstɪʃəs] *adj* суеверный*
(суеверен).
superstore ['suːpəstɔːʳ] *n* (*BRIT: COMM*)
универмаг, супермаркет.
supertanker ['suːpətæŋkəʳ] *n* (*NAUT*)
супертанкер.
supertax ['suːpətæks] *n* дополнительный
подоходный налог.
supervise ['suːpəvaɪz] *vt* (*person, activity*)
следить* (*impf*) *or* наблюдать (*impf*) за +*instr*.
supervision [suːpəˈvɪʒən] *n* руководство,
надзор; **under medical** ~ под наблюдением
врача.
supervisor ['suːpəvaɪzəʳ] *n* (*of workers*)
начальник(-ица); (*of students*) научный(-ая)
руководитель(ница) *m(f)*.
supervisory ['suːpəvaɪzərɪ] *adj* (*role*)
руководящий*; (*staff*) контролирующий.
supine ['suːpaɪn] *adj* лежащий на спине ♦ *adv*
лёжа на спине.
supper ['sʌpəʳ] *n* ужин; **to have** ~ ужинать
(поужинать *perf*).
supplant [səˈplɑːnt] *vt* (*person, thing*)
приходить* (прийти* *perf*) на смену +*dat*.
supple ['sʌpl] *adj* (*person, body*) гибкий*
(гибок); (*leather*) мягкий* (мягок*).
supplement ['sʌplɪmənt] *n* (*vitamins etc*)
добавка*; (*of book, newspaper etc*)
приложение ♦ *vt* (*diet*) добавлять (*impf*) к
+*dat*; (*income*) подрабатывать (*impf*).
supplementary [sʌplɪˈmɛntərɪ] *adj* (*question*)
дополнительный.
supplementary benefit *n* (*BRIT: formerly*)
пособие для малоимущих в Велико-
британии.
supplier [səˈplaɪəʳ] *n* (*COMM: person, firm*)

---

* marks translations which have irregular inflections. The Russian-English side of the dictionary gives inflectional information.

поставщи́к*.

supply [sə'plaɪ] *n* (*stock*) запа́с, запа́сы *mpl*; (*supplying*) поста́вка*; (*TECH*) обеспе́чение ◆ *vt* (*need*) удовлетворя́ть (удовлетвори́ть *perf*); (*provide*): **to ~ sth (to sb)** поставля́ть (поста́вить* *perf*) что-н (кому́-н); **supplies** *npl* (*food*) запа́сы *mpl* (продово́льствия); (*MIL*) боеприпа́сы *mpl* (и продово́льствие); **office supplies** канто́рские принадле́жности; **water is in short ~** э́тот райо́н испы́тывает нехва́тку воды́; **the electricity ~** снабже́ние электроэне́ргии; **the water ~** водоснабже́ние; **the gas ~** снабже́ние га́зом; **~ and demand** спрос и предложе́ние; **to ~ sb with sth** снабжа́ть (снабди́ть* *perf*) кого́-н чем-н; (*system, machine*) обору́довать (*impf/ perf*) кого́-н чем-н; **it comes supplied with an adaptor** поставля́ется с ада́птером.

supply teacher *n* (*BRIT*) замеща́ющий(-ая) учи́тель(ница) *m(f)*.

support [sə'pɔːt] *n* (*moral, financial etc*) подде́ржка; (*TECH*) опо́ра, подпо́рка* ◆ *vt* (*football team etc*) боле́ть (*impf*) за +*acc*; (*financially: family etc*) содержа́ть (*impf*); (*TECH: hold up*) подде́рживать (*impf*); (*sustain: theory etc*) подтвержда́ть (подтверди́ть* *perf*); **they stopped work in ~ of** они́ прекрати́ли рабо́ту в подде́ржку +*gen*; **to ~ o.s.** (*financially*) зараба́тывать (*impf*) (самому́) себе́ на жизнь.

support buying *n* (*COMM*) *заку́пка в це́лях пониже́ния цен.*

supporter [sə'pɔːtəʳ] *n* (*POL etc*) сторо́нник(-ица); (*SPORT*) боле́льщик(-ица).

supporting [sə'pɔːtɪŋ] *adj* второстепе́нный; **~ actor** актёр второ́го пла́на.

supportive [sə'pɔːtɪv] *adj*: **to be ~ of sb** подде́рживать (поддержа́ть* *perf*) кого́-н.

suppose [sə'pəuz] *vt* полага́ть (*impf*); **he was ~d to do it** (*duty*) он до́лжен был э́то сде́лать; **it was worse than she'd ~d** э́то оказа́лось ху́же, чем она́ предполага́ла; **I don't ~ she'll come** я полага́ю, она́ не прийдёт; **he's about sixty, I ~** я полага́ю, ему́ лет шестьдеся́т; **he's ~d to be an expert** счита́ется, что он в э́том разбира́ется.

supposedly [sə'pəuzɪdlɪ] *adv* по иде́е.

supposing [sə'pəuzɪŋ] *conj* предположи́м, допу́стим.

supposition [sʌpə'zɪʃən] *n* предположе́ние, допуще́ние.

suppository [sə'pɔzɪtrɪ] *n* (*MED*) свеча́*.

suppress [sə'prɛs] *vt* подавля́ть (подави́ть* *perf*); (*scandal*) замя́ть* (*perf*); (*publication*) запреща́ть (запрети́ть* *perf*).

suppression [sə'prɛʃən] *n* подавле́ние.

suppressor [sə'prɛsəʳ] *n* (*ELEC etc*) глуши́тель *m*.

supremacy [su'prɛməsɪ] *n* (*MIL, POL etc*) госпо́дство.

supreme [su'priːm] *adj* (*in titles: court etc*)

Верхо́вный; (*effort, achievement*) велича́йший.

Supreme Court *n* (*US*) Верхо́вный Суд.

supremo [su'priːməu] *n* (*BRIT: inf*) верхо́вный *or* гла́вный нача́льник.

Supt. *abbr* (*POLICE*) = **superintendent**.

surcharge ['sɜːtʃɑːdʒ] *n* (*extra cost*) дополни́тельный сбор, дополни́тельная пла́та.

sure [ʃuəʳ] *adj* (*definite, convinced*) твёрдый* (твёрд); (*aim, friend, remedy*) ве́рный* (ве́рен) ◆ *adv* (*inf: esp US*): **that ~ is pretty, that's ~ pretty** э́то пра́вда ми́ло; **to make ~ of sth/that** удостоверя́ться (*perf*) в чём-н/что; **~!** (*of course*) безусло́вно!; **~ enough** и пра́вда *or* впра́вду; **I'm not ~ how/why/when** я не уве́рен, как/почему́/когда́; **to be ~ of o.s.** не сомнева́ться (*impf*) в себе́.

sure-fire ['ʃuəfaɪəʳ] *adj* (*inf*) ве́рный.

sure-footed [ʃuə'futɪd] *adj* (*animal, person*) твёрдо держа́щийся на нога́х.

surely ['ʃuəlɪ] *adv* (*certainly*) наверняка́; **~ you don't mean that!** наверняка, Вы э́то несерьёзно!

surety ['ʃuərətɪ] *n* (*money*) зало́г; **to go** *or* **stand ~ for sb** брать* (взять* *perf*) кого́-н на пору́ки.

surf [sɜːf] *n* (*waves*) прибо́й; (*foam*) бара́шки *mpl*.

surface ['sɜːfɪs] *n* пове́рхность *f* ◆ *vt* (*road*) покрыва́ть (покры́ть* *perf*) ◆ *vi* (*fish, person in water*) пока́зываться (показа́ться* *perf*) на пове́рхности; (*fig: news, feeling*) всплыва́ть (всплы́ть* *perf*); (: *person in bed*) объявля́ться (объяви́ться* *perf*); **on the ~** (*fig*) с ви́ду.

surface area *n* пло́щадь *f* пове́рхности.

surface mail *n* обы́чная по́чта.

surface-to-surface ['sɜːfɪstə'sɜːfɪs] *adj*: **~ missile** раке́та ти́па "земля́-земля́".

surfboard ['sɜːfbɔːd] *n* аквапла́н.

surfeit ['sɜːfɪt] *n*: **a ~ of** переизбы́ток* +*gen*.

surfer ['sɜːfəʳ] *n* челове́к* занима́ющийся сёрфингом.

surfing ['sɜːfɪŋ] *n* сёрфинг.

surge [sɜːdʒ] *n* (*increase*) прито́к*; (*fig: of emotion*) прили́в; (*ELEC*) и́мпульс ◆ *vi* (*water*) вздыма́ться (*impf*), нахлы́нуть (*perf*); (*people, vehicles*) ри́нуться (*perf*); (*ELEC: power*) ре́зко увели́чиваться (увели́читься *perf*); **to ~ forward** ри́нуться (*perf*) *or* броса́ться (бро́ситься* *perf*) вперёд; **relief ~d through her** она́ почу́вствовала прили́в облегче́ния.

surgeon ['sɜːdʒən] *n* (*MED*) хиру́рг.

Surgeon General *n* (*US: MED, MIL*) нача́льник медици́нского управле́ния.

surgery ['sɜːdʒərɪ] *n* (*treatment*) хирурги́ческое вмеша́тельство; (*BRIT: room*) кабине́т врача́; (: *of MP, doctor etc*) приём; **to undergo ~** переноси́ть* (перенести́* *perf*) опера́цию.

surgical ['sɜːdʒɪkl] *adj* хирурги́ческий*.

surgical spirit *n* (*BRIT*) медици́нский* спирт.

surly ['sə:lɪ] *adj* (*person, behaviour*)
неприве́тливый.
surmise [sə:'maɪz] *vt*: **to ~ that** выска́зывать
(вы́сказать* *perf*) предположе́ние, что.
surmount [sə:'maunt] *vt* (*fig: problem, difficulty*)
преодолева́ть (преодоле́ть *perf*).
surname ['sə:neɪm] *n* фами́лия.
surpass [sə:'pɑ:s] *vt* (*person, thing*)
превосходи́ть* (превзойти́* *perf*).
surplus ['sə:pləs] *n* избы́ток*, изли́шек*; (*of
trade, payments*) акти́вное са́льдо *nt ind* ♦ *adj*
(*stock, grain*) ли́шний*; **it is ~ to our
requirements** э́то превыша́ет на́ши
тре́бования.
surprise [sə'praɪz] *n* удивле́ние ♦ *vt* (*astonish*)
удивля́ть (удиви́ть* *perf*); (*catch unawares*)
застава́ть* (заста́ть* *perf*) враспло́х; **to take
by ~** застига́ть (засти́гнуть *perf*) враспло́х.
surprising [sə'praɪzɪŋ] *adj* (*situation,
announcement*) неожи́данный* (неожи́дан);
it is ~ how/that удиви́тельно как/что.
surprisingly [sə'praɪzɪŋlɪ] *adv* удиви́тельно;
(**somewhat**) **~, he agreed** как ни
удиви́тельно, он согласи́лся.
surrealism [sə'rɪəlɪzəm] *n* сюрреали́зм.
surrealist [sə'rɪəlɪst] *adj* сюрреалисти́ческий.
surrender [sə'rɛndə^r] *n* капитуля́ция ♦ *vi* (*army,
hijackers etc*) сдава́ться* (сда́ться* *perf*) ♦ *vt*
(*claim, right*) отка́зываться (отказа́ться* *perf*)
от +*gen*.
surrender value *n* (*INSURANCE*) *сто́имость
страхово́го по́лиса при возвра́те его́
страхово́му о́бществу.*
surreptitious [sʌrəp'tɪʃəs] *adj* скры́тый.
surrogate ['sʌrəgɪt] *n* (*substitute*) замени́тель
m ♦ *adj* замеща́ющий.
surrogate mother *n* суррога́тная мать* *f*.
surround [sə'raund] *vt* (*subj: walls, hedge etc*)
окружа́ть (*impf*); (*MIL, POLICE etc*) окружа́ть
(окружи́ть *perf*).
surrounding [sə'raundɪŋ] *adj* (*countryside*)
близлежа́щий.
surroundings [sə'raundɪŋz] *npl* окре́стности *fpl*.
surtax ['sə:tæks] *n* доба́вочный подохо́дный
нало́г.
surveillance [sə:'veɪləns] *n* патрули́рование.
survey [*vt* sə:'veɪ, *n* 'sə:veɪ] *vt* (*land*) де́лать
(сде́лать *perf*) топографи́ческие съёмки +*gen*;
(*house*) производи́ть* (произвести́* *perf*)
осмо́тр +*gen*; (*scene, work etc*) осма́тривать
(осмотре́ть* *perf*) ♦ *n* (*of land*)
топографи́ческая *or* геодези́ческая съёмка;
(*of house*) инспе́кция; (*of habits etc*)
иссле́дование; (*of situation etc*) оце́нка*.
surveying [sə:'veɪɪŋ] *n* (*of land*) геоде́зия,
топографи́ческие съёмки* *fpl*.
surveyor [sə:'veɪə^r] *n* (*of land*) топо́граф; (*of
house*) инспе́ктор.

survival [sə'vaɪvl] *n* (*continuation of life*)
выжива́ние; (*relic*) пережи́ток* ♦ *cpd* (*kit, bag*)
неприкоснове́нный запа́с; **~ course**
обуче́ние выжива́нию в экстрема́льных
усло́виях.
survive [sə'vaɪv] *vi* (*person, thing*) уцеле́ть
(*perf*), выжива́ть (вы́жить* *perf*); (*custom etc*)
сохраня́ться (сохрани́ться *perf*), уцеле́ть
(*perf*) ♦ *vt* (*person*) пережи́ть* (*perf*).
survivor [sə'vaɪvə^r] *n* (*of illness, accident*)
пережи́вший(-ая) *m(f) adj*; **~s of an accident**
оста́вшиеся в живы́х по́сле ава́рии.
susceptible [sə'sɛptəbl] *adj*: **~ (to)** (*heat*)
чувстви́тельный* (чувстви́телен) (к +*dat*);
(*injury*) подве́ржный* (подве́ржен) (+*dat*);
(*flattery, pressure*) подда́ющийся (на +*acc*).
suspect [*vb* səs'pɛkt, *n, adj* 'sʌspɛkt] *vt* (*person*)
подозрева́ть (*impf*), заподо́зрить (*perf*);
(*think*) подозрева́ть (*impf*); (*doubt*) не
доверя́ть (*impf*) ♦ *n* подозрева́емый(-ая) *m(f)
adj* ♦ *adj* подозри́тельный* (подозри́телен).
suspected [səs'pɛktɪd] *adj* подозрева́емый
(подозрева́ем).
suspend [səs'pɛnd] *vt* (*hang*) подве́шивать
(подве́сить* *perf*); (*delay, stop*)
приостана́вливать (приостанови́ть* *perf*);
(*from employment*) отстраня́ть (отстрани́ть
perf) от до́лжности.
suspended animation [səs'pɛndɪd-] *n*
вре́менное замора́живание (*живо́го
органи́зма*).
suspended sentence *n* усло́вный пригово́р.
suspender belt [səs'pɛndə^r-] *n* (же́нский*)
по́яс*.
suspenders [səs'pɛndəz] *npl* (*BRIT*) рези́нки* *fpl*;
(*US*) подтя́жки* *fpl*.
suspense [səs'pɛns] *n* (*uncertainty*) трево́га
ожида́ния; (*in film etc*) напряже́ние; **to keep
sb in ~** держа́ть* (*impf*) кого́-н в
подве́шенном состоя́нии.
suspension [səs'pɛnʃən] *n* (*from job, team*)
отстране́ние от до́лжности; (*AUT*)
амортиза́тор; (*of driving licence*) изъя́тие; (*of
payment*) прекраще́ние.
suspension bridge *n* подвесно́й *or* вися́чий*
мост*.
suspicion [səs'pɪʃən] *n* (*distrust*) подозре́ния
ntpl; (*bad feeling*) подозре́ние; (*trace*) намёк,
след; **to be under ~** находи́ться* (*impf*) под
подозре́нием; **arrested on ~ of murder**
аресто́ванный по подозре́нию в уби́йстве.
suspicious [səs'pɪʃəs] *adj* подозри́тельный*
(подозри́телен); **to be ~ of** *or* **about sb/sth**
относи́ться* (отнести́сь* *perf*)
подозри́тельно *or* с подозре́нием к кому́-н/
чему́-н.
suss out [sʌs-] (*BRIT: inf*) *vt* (*discover*)
разобра́ться* (*perf*) в +*prp*; (*understand*)

---

* marks translations which have irregular inflections. The Russian-English side of the dictionary gives inflectional information.

раскусить* (perf); **I've sussed him out** я его раскусил.

sustain [səs'teɪn] vt поддерживать (поддержать* perf); (injury) понести* (perf).

sustainable [səs'teɪnəbl] adj (economy, development) жизнеспособный.

sustained [səs'teɪnd] adj (effort, attack) неослабевающий.

sustenance ['sʌstɪnəns] n пропитание.

suture ['suːtʃə] n (MED) шов*.

SW abbr (RADIO) (= **short wave**) КВ= *короткие волны*.

swab [swɔb] n (MED) тампон ♦ vt (also: ~ **down**) мыть* (вымыть* perf) (шваброй).

swagger ['swægə] vi расхаживать (impf) с важным видом.

swallow ['swɔləu] n (ZOOL) (деревенская) ласточка*; (of food) кусочек*; (of drink) глоток* ♦ vt (food, pills, insult) глотать (impf), проглатывать (проглотить* perf); (fig: story) купиться* (perf) на +acc; (one's pride, one's words) подавлять (подавить* perf)
▶ **swallow up** vt (savings etc) съедать (съесть* perf).

swam [swæm] pt of **swim**.

swamp [swɔmp] n болото ♦ vt (with water etc) заливать (залить* perf); (fig: person) заваливать (завалить* perf).

swampy ['swɔmpɪ] adj (ground) болотистый.

swan [swɔn] n лебедь* m.

swank [swæŋk] vi (inf: talk boastfully) хвастать (impf); (: show off) рисоваться (impf).

swansong ['swɔnsɔŋ] n (fig) лебединая песнь f.

swap [swɔp] n обмен ♦ vt: **to** ~ **(for)** (exchange (for)) менять (обменять perf) (на +acc); (replace (with)) сменить (perf) (на +acc).

SWAPO n abbr (= South-West Africa People's Organization) СВАПО (*Народная организация Юго-Западной Африки*).

swarm [swɔːm] n (of bees) рой; (of people) тьма ♦ vi (bees) роиться (impf); (people) толочься* (impf); (place): **to be** ~**ing with** кишеть (impf) +instr.

swarthy ['swɔːðɪ] adj (person, complexion, face) смуглый, тёмный.

swashbuckling ['swɔʃbʌklɪŋ] adj (film) залихватский; (role, hero) удалой.

swastika ['swɔstɪkə] n свастика.

swat [swɔt] vt (insect) прихлопнуть (perf) ♦ n (BRIT: also: **fly** ~) хлопушка*.

swathe [sweɪð] vt: **to** ~ **in** (blankets) закутывать (закутать perf) в +acc; (bandages) обматывать (обмотать perf) +instr.

swatter ['swɔtə] n (also: **fly** ~) хлопушка*.

sway [sweɪ] vi (person, tree) качаться (качнуться perf) ♦ vt (influence) склонять (склонить* perf) ♦ n: **to hold** ~ **(over sb)** пользоваться* (impf) непререкаемым авторитетом (у кого-н).

Swaziland ['swɑːzɪlænd] n Свазиленд.

swear [swɛə] (pt **swore**, pp **sworn**) vi (curse) ругаться (выругаться perf) ♦ vt (promise) торжественно давать (дать* perf); **to** ~ **an oath** давать* (дать* perf) клятву
▶ **swear in** vt (person) приводить* (привести* perf) к присяге.

swearword ['swɛəwəːd] n ругательство.

sweat [swɛt] n пот* ♦ vi потеть (вспотеть perf), пропотеть (perf); **in a** ~ в поту.

sweatband ['swɛtbænd] n повязка*.

sweater ['swɛtə] n свитер*.

sweatshirt ['swɛtʃəːt] n хлопчатобумажный спортивный свитер*.

sweatshop ['swɛtʃɔp] n (pej) *предприятие, где существует потогонная система*.

sweaty ['swɛtɪ] adj (clothes) пропотевший; (hands) потный.

Swede [swiːd] n швед(ка*).

swede [swiːd] n (BRIT) брюква.

Sweden ['swiːdn] n Швеция.

Swedish ['swiːdɪʃ] adj шведский* ♦ n (LING) шведский* язык*; **the** ~ npl шведы.

sweep [swiːp] (pt, pp **swept**) n (act of sweeping) подметание; (curve) изгиб; (range) размах; (also: **chimney** ~) трубочист* ♦ vt (brush) мести* or подметать (подмести* perf); (with arm) смахивать (смахнуть perf); (subj: current) смывать (смыть* perf) ♦ vi (hand, arm) двигаться (impf); (wind) бушевать (impf)
▶ **sweep away** vt сметать (смести* perf), уносить* (унести* perf)
▶ **sweep past** vi проноситься* (пронестись* perf) мимо
▶ **sweep up** vi подметать (подмести* perf).

sweeper ['swiːpə] n (also: **carpet** ~) щётка для ковра; (FOOTBALL) либеро nt ind.

sweeping ['swiːpɪŋ] adj (gesture) широкий* (широк); (changes, reforms) всеобъемлющий*; (statement) огульный.

sweepstake ['swiːpsteɪk] n пари nt ind на скачках.

sweet [swiːt] n (candy) конфета; (BRIT: CULIN) сладкое nt adj no pl ♦ adj сладкий* (сладок); (kind, attractive) милый* (мил) ♦ adv: **to smell** ~ сладко пахнуть (impf); **to taste** ~ иметь (impf) сладкий вкус; ~ **and sour** кисло-сладкий*.

sweetbread ['swiːtbrɛd] n (CULIN) "сладкое мясо" (*поджелудочная железа*).

sweet corn n кукуруза.

sweeten ['swiːtn] vt добавлять (добавить* perf) сахар к +dat; (temper) смирять (смирить perf).

sweetener ['swiːtnə] n заменитель m сахара; (fig) подслащённая пилюля.

sweetheart ['swiːthɑːt] n возлюбленный(-ая) m(f) adj; (term of affection) дорогой(-ая) m(f) adj.

sweetness ['swiːtnɪs] n (amount of sugar) сладость f; (kindness) приятность f.

sweet pea n душистый горошек*.

sweet potato *n* ямс.
sweet shop *n* (*BRIT*) конди́терская ла́вка.
sweet tooth *n*: he/she has a ~ ~ он/она́ сласт́ёна.
swell [swɛl] (*pt* **swelled**, *pp* **swollen** *or* **swelled**) *n* (*of sea*) волне́ние ◆ *adj* (*US*: *inf*: *excellent*) мирово́й ◆ *vi* (*numbers*) расти́* (вы́расти* *perf*); (*sound*, *feeling*) расти́* (*impf*); (*also*: ~ **up**: *face*, *ankle etc*) опуха́ть (опу́хнуть *perf*).
swelling ['swɛlɪŋ] *n* (*MED*) о́пухоль *f*.
sweltering ['swɛltərɪŋ] *adj* ду́шный.
swept [swɛpt] *pt*, *pp of* **sweep**.
swerve [swəːv] *vi* ре́зко виля́ть (вильну́ть *perf*).
swift [swɪft] *n* (*bird*) стриж* ◆ *adj* стреми́тельный (стреми́телен).
swiftly ['swɪftlɪ] *adv* стреми́тельно.
swiftness ['swɪftnɪs] *n* стреми́тельность *f*.
swig [swɪg] *n* (*inf*: *drink*) глото́к*.
swill [swɪl] *vt* (*also*: ~ **out**, ~ **down**) спола́скивать (сполосну́ть *perf*) ◆ *n* (*for pigs*) по́йло.
swim [swɪm] (*pt* **swam**, *pp* **swum**) *vi* пла́вать/ плыть* (*impf*); (*as sport*) пла́вать (*impf*); (*head*) идти́* (пойти́* *perf*) кру́гом; (*room*) плыть* (поплы́ть* *perf*) ◆ *vt* (*the Channel*) переплыва́ть (переплы́ть* *perf*); (*a length*) проплыва́ть (проплы́ть* *perf*); **to go ~ming**, **go for a** ~ ходи́ть*/идти́* (пойти́* *perf*) пла́вать.
swimmer ['swɪmə'] *n* пловец́*(-вчи́ха).
swimming ['swɪmɪŋ] *n* пла́вание.
swimming baths *npl* (*BRIT*) пла́вательный бассе́йн *msg*.
swimming cap *n* рези́новая ша́почка* (*для пла́вания*).
swimming costume *n* (*BRIT*) купа́льный костю́м.
swimmingly ['swɪmɪŋlɪ] *adv* как по ма́слу; **everything's going** ~ всё идёт как по ма́слу.
swimming pool *n* пла́вательный бассе́йн.
swimming trunks *npl* пла́вки* *pl*.
swimsuit ['swɪmsuːt] *n* купа́льник.
swindle ['swɪndl] *n* моше́нничество ◆ *vt* надува́ть (наду́ть* *perf*).
swindler ['swɪndlə'] *n* жу́лик.
swine [swaɪn] *n* (*inf*!) свинья́* *m*/*f* (*!*)
swing [swɪŋ] (*pt*, *pp* **swung**) *n* (*in playground*) каче́ли *pl*; (*movement*) кача́ние; (*change: in opinions etc*) колеба́ние; (*MUS*, *rhythm*) свинг ◆ *vt* (*arms*) разма́хивать (*impf*) +*instr*; (*legs*) болта́ть (*impf*) +*instr*; (*also*: ~ **round**: *vehicle etc*) развора́чивать (разверну́ть *perf*) ◆ *vi* кача́ться (*impf*); (*also*: ~ **round**: *vehicle etc*) свора́чивать (сверну́ть *perf*); **a** ~ **to the left** (*POL*) крен вле́во; **to get into the** ~ **of things** входи́ть* (войти́* *perf*) в ритм; **to be in full** ~ (*party etc*) быть* (*impf*) в по́лном разга́ре; **the road ~s south** доро́га свора́чивает на юг.

swing bridge *n* разводно́й мост*.
swing door (*US* **swinging door**) *n* дверь, открыва́ющаяся в о́бе сто́роны.
swingeing ['swɪndʒɪŋ] *adj* (*BRIT*: *blow*, *attack*) сокруши́тельный* (сокруши́телен); (: *cuts*) беспоща́дный.
swinging ['swɪŋɪŋ] *adj* кача́ющийся; (*fig*) весёлый.
swipe [swaɪp] *vt* (*hit*) ударя́ть (уда́рить *perf*) с разма́ху; (*inf*: *steal*) тащи́ть (стащи́ть* *perf*).
swirl [swəːl] *vi* (*water*, *smoke*, *leaves*) кружи́ться (*impf*) ◆ *n* (*of water*) водоро́т; (*of leaves*) круже́ние.
swish [swɪʃ] *vi* (*tail*) маха́ть* (*impf*); (*clothes*) шелесте́ть* (*impf*), шурша́ть (*impf*) ◆ *n* свист ◆ *adj* (*inf*) шика́рный.
Swiss [swɪs] *adj* швейца́рский* ◆ *n inv* швейца́рец*(-рка*).
Swiss French *adj* фра́нко-швейца́рский* ◆ *n* (*person*) франкоговоря́щий(-ая) швейца́рец(-рка); (*LING*) швейца́рский* диале́кт францу́зского языка́.
Swiss German *adj* неме́цко-швейца́рский* ◆ *n* (*person*) немецкоговоря́щий(-ая) швейца́рец(-рка); (*LING*) швейца́рский* диале́кт неме́цкого языка́.
swiss roll *n* руле́т с варе́ньем.
switch [swɪtʃ] *n* (*for light*, *radio etc*) выключа́тель *m*; (*change*) переключе́ние ◆ *vt* (*change*) переключа́ть (переключи́ть *perf*); (*exchange*) переменя́ть* (*perf*); **to** ~ (**round** *or* **over**) меня́ть (поменя́ть *perf*) места́ми
▶ **switch off** *vt* выключа́ть (вы́ключить *perf*)
▶ **switch on** *vt* включа́ть (включи́ть *perf*).
switchback ['swɪtʃbæk] *n* (*BRIT*) доро́га иду́щая то вверх, то вниз.
switchblade ['swɪtʃbleɪd] *n* (*also*: ~ **knife**) нож с заменя́ющимися ле́звиями.
switchboard ['swɪtʃbɔːd] *n* (*TEL*) коммута́тор.
switchboard operator *n* (*TEL*) телефони́ст(ка*).
Switzerland ['swɪtsələnd] *n* Швейца́рия.
swivel ['swɪvl] *vi* (*also*: ~ **round**) верте́ться* (*impf*).
swollen ['swəulən] *pp of* **swell** ◆ *adj* (*ankle*) опу́хший*; (*lake*) перепо́лнившийся.
swoon [swuːn] *vi* замира́ть (замере́ть *perf*).
swoop [swuːp] *n* (*by police etc*) налёт; (*of bird etc*) стреми́тельное паде́ние ◆ *vi* (*also*: ~ **down**: *bird*, *plane*) стреми́тельно па́дать (*impf*).
swop [swɔp] = **swap**.
sword [sɔːd] *n* шпа́га, меч*.
swordfish ['sɔːdfɪʃ] *n* меч-ры́ба.
swore [swɔː'] *pt of* **swear**.
sworn [swɔːn] *pp of* **swear** ◆ *adj* (*statement*, *evidence*) под прися́гой; (*enemy*) закля́тый.
swot [swɔt] *vi* зубри́ть (*impf*) ◆ *n* (*pej*: *of person*)

---

* marks translations which have irregular inflections. The Russian-English side of the dictionary gives inflectional information.

зубри́ла *m/f*

▶ **swot up** *vt*: **to ~ up (on)** зазу́бривать (зазубри́ть *perf*).

swum [swʌm] *pp of* **swim**.

swung [swʌŋ] *pt, pp of* **swing**.

sycamore ['sɪkəmɔː'] *n* я́вор.

sycophant ['sɪkəfænt] *n* подхали́м.

sycophantic [sɪkə'fæntɪk] *adj* подхали́мский*.

Sydney ['sɪdnɪ] *n* Сидне́й.

syllable ['sɪləbl] *n* слог*.

syllabus ['sɪləbəs] *n* програ́мма; **on the ~** входя́щий* в програ́мму.

symbol ['sɪmbl] *n* (*sign, also* MATH) знак; (*representation*) си́мвол.

symbolic(al) [sɪm'bɔlɪk(l)] *adj* символи́ческий*; **to be symbolic of sth** символизи́ровать (*impf*) что-н.

symbolism ['sɪmbəlɪzəm] *n* символи́зм.

symbolize ['sɪmbəlaɪz] *vt* символизи́ровать (*impf*).

symmetrical [sɪ'mɛtrɪkl] *adj* симметри́чный* (симметри́чен).

symmetry ['sɪmɪtrɪ] *n* симметри́я.

sympathetic [sɪmpə'θɛtɪk] *adj* (*person*) сочу́вствующий*; (*remark*) сочу́вственный; (*likeable: character*) прия́тный* (прия́тен); (*showing support*): **~ to(wards)** благоскло́нно настро́енный по отноше́нию к +*dat*; **to be ~ to sth** (*well-disposed*) сочу́вственно относи́ться* (отнести́сь* *perf*) к чему́-н.

sympathetically [sɪmpə'θɛtɪklɪ] *adv* сочу́вственно.

sympathize ['sɪmpəθaɪz] *vi*: **to ~ with** (*person*) сочу́вствовать* (*impf*) +*dat*, проявля́ть (прояви́ть* *perf*) сочу́вствие к +*dat*; (*feelings, cause*) сочу́вственно относи́ться* (отнести́сь* *perf*) к +*dat*.

sympathizer ['sɪmpəθaɪzə'] *n* (POL) симпатизи́рующий(-ая) *m(f) adj*.

sympathy ['sɪmpəθɪ] *n* (*pity*) сочу́вствие; **sympathies** *npl* (*support, tendencies*) симпа́тии *fpl*; **with our deepest ~** прими́те на́ши глубоча́йшие соболе́знования; **to come out in ~** (*workers*) бастова́ть (*impf*) в знак солида́рности.

symphonic [sɪm'fɔnɪk] *adj* симфони́ческий*.

symphony ['sɪmfənɪ] *n* симфо́ния.

symphony orchestra *n* симфони́ческий* орке́стр.

symposia [sɪm'pəuzɪə] *npl of* **symposium**.

symposium [sɪm'pəuzɪəm] (*pl* **~s** *or* **symposia**) *n* симпо́зиум.

symptom ['sɪmptəm] *n* (MED) симпто́м; (*indicator*) при́знак.

symptomatic [sɪmptə'mætɪk] *adj*: **~ of**

sync [sɪŋk] *n* (*inf*: *watches etc*): **out of ~** в разнобо́й.

synagogue ['sɪnəgɔg] *n* синаго́га.

synchromesh [sɪŋkrəu'mɛʃ] *n* синхрониза́тор.

synchronize ['sɪŋkrənaɪz] *vt* (*watches*) сверя́ть (све́рить *perf*); (*sound, movements*) синхронизи́ровать (*impf/perf*) ◆ *vi*: **to ~ with** совпада́ть (совпа́сть* *perf*) (по вре́мени) с +*instr*.

synchronized swimming ['sɪŋkrənaɪzd-] *n* синхро́нное пла́вание.

syncopated ['sɪŋkəpeɪtɪd] *adj* (*rhythm, beat*) синкопи́рованный.

syndicate ['sɪndɪkɪt] *n* (*of people, businesses*) синдика́т; (*of newspapers*) аге́нтство печа́ти.

syndrome ['sɪndrəum] *n* (*also* MED) синдро́м.

synonym ['sɪnənɪm] *n* сино́ним.

synonymous [sɪ'nɔnɪməs] *adj* (*fig*): **~ (with)** равноси́льный* (равноси́лен) (+*dat*).

synopses [sɪ'nɔpsiːz] *npl of* **synopsis**.

synopsis [sɪ'nɔpsɪs] (*pl* **synopses**) *n* кра́ткое изложе́ние.

syntactic [sɪn'tæktɪk] *adj* синтакси́ческий*.

syntax ['sɪntæks] *n* си́нтаксис.

syntax error *n* (COMPUT) синтакси́ческий* оши́бка*.

syntheses ['sɪnθəsiːz] *npl of* **synthesis**.

synthesis ['sɪnθəsɪs] (*pl* **syntheses**) *n* (*of ideas, styles*) слия́ние, си́нтез.

synthesizer ['sɪnθəsaɪzə'] *n* синтеза́тор.

synthetic [sɪn'θɛtɪk] *adj* (*materials*) синтети́ческий*, иску́сственный ◆ *n* иску́сственный материа́л; (TEXTILES) синте́тика, иску́сственный материа́л; **~s** *npl* (*man-made fabrics*) синте́тика *fsg*; синтети́ческие тка́ни *fpl*.

syphilis ['sɪfɪlɪs] *n* си́филис.

syphon ['saɪfən] = **siphon**.

Syria ['sɪrɪə] *n* Си́рия.

Syrian ['sɪrɪən] *adj* сири́йский* ◆ *n* сири́ец*(-и́йка).

syringe [sɪ'rɪndʒ] *n* шприц*.

syrup ['sɪrəp] *n* (*juice*) сиро́п; (*also*: **golden ~**) (све́тлая ог жёлтая) па́тока.

syrupy ['sɪrəpɪ] *adj* (*liquid*) густо́й* (густ); (*pej*: *quality*) слаща́вый (слаща́в).

system ['sɪstəm] *n* систе́ма; **it was a shock to his ~** э́то яви́лось для него́ потрясе́нием.

systematic [sɪstə'mætɪk] *adj* (*methodical*) системати́ческий*.

systems analyst ['sɪstəmz-] *n* (COMPUT) систе́мный анали́тик, системоте́хник.

systems disk *n* (COMPUT) систе́мный диск.

~ T, t ~

T, t [ti:] *n* (*letter*) 20-ая бу́ква англи́йского алфави́та.

TA *n abbr* (*BRIT*: = *Territorial Army*) территориа́льная а́рмия.

ta [tɑ:] *excl* (*BRIT*: *inf*) спаси́бо.

tab [tæb] *n abbr* = **tabulator**.

tabby [ˈtæbɪ] *n* (*also*: ~ *cat*: *male*) полоса́тый кот; (*also*: *female*) полоса́тая ко́шка.

tabernacle [ˈtæbənækl] *n* (*REL*) ски́ния.

table [ˈteɪbl] *n* (*piece of furniture*) стол*; (*MATH, CHEM etc*) табли́ца ◆ *vt* (*BRIT*: *motion etc*) выноси́ть* (вы́нести* *perf*) на обсужде́ние; **to lay** *or* **set the** ~ накрыва́ть (накры́ть* *perf*) на стол; **to clear the** ~ убира́ть (убра́ть* *perf*) со стола́; **league** ~ (*BRIT*: *FOOTBALL, RUGBY*) табли́ца кома́нд 1-й, 2-й и т.д. ли́ги; ~ **of contents** оглавле́ние.

tablecloth [ˈteɪblklɔθ] *n* ска́терть *f*.

table d'hôte [[tɑːblˈdəut]] *adj*: ~ ~ **menu** табльдо́т.

table lamp *n* насто́льная ла́мпа.

tablemat [ˈteɪblmæt] *n* подста́вка.

table salt *n* столо́вая соль *f*.

tablespoon [ˈteɪblspuːn] *n* столо́вая ло́жка.

tablet [ˈtæblɪt] *n* (*MED*) табле́тка*; (*for writing*) доще́чка* (для письма́); (*of stone*) доска́*; ~ **of soap** (*BRIT*) кусо́к* мы́ла.

table tennis *n* насто́льный те́ннис.

table wine *n* столо́вое вино́.

tabloid [ˈtæblɔɪd] *n* (*newspaper*) малоформа́тная газе́та, табло́ид; **the** ~**s** жёлтая *or* бульва́рная пре́сса.

taboo [təˈbuː] *n* табу́ *nt ind* ◆ *adj* запрещённый.

tabulate [ˈtæbjuleɪt] *vt* (*data, figures*) своди́ть* (свести́* *perf*) в табли́цу.

tabulator [ˈtæbjuleɪtə'] *n* колонкоустанови́тель *m*; (*on typewriter*) табуля́тор.

tachograph [ˈtækəgrɑːf] *n* (*AUT*) тахо́граф (*для регистра́ции режи́ма движе́ния автомоби́ля*).

tachometer [tæˈkɔmɪtə'] *n* (*AUT*) тахо́метр, счётчик числа́ оборо́тов.

tacit [ˈtæsɪt] *adj* (*agreement, approval etc*) молчали́вый.

taciturn [ˈtæsɪtəːn] *adj* (*person*) молчали́вый

(молчали́в).

tack [tæk] *n* (*nail*) гвоздь *m* с широ́кой шля́пкой; (*fig*) путь *m* ◆ *vt* (*nail*) прибива́ть (приби́ть* *perf*); (*stitch*) смётывать (смета́ть *perf*) ◆ *vi* (*NAUT*) идти́* (пойти́* *perf*) га́лсами; **on the wrong** ~ (*fig*) на ло́жном пути́; **to** ~ **sth on to (the end of) sth** прикрепля́ть (прикрепи́ть* *perf*) что-н к чему́-н.

tackle [ˈtækl] *n* (*for fishing etc*) снасть *f*; (*for lifting*) сло́жный блок; (*FOOTBALL, RUGBY*) блокиро́вка ◆ *vt* (*difficulty*) справля́ться (спра́виться* *perf*); (*grapple with, challenge*) схвати́ться* (*perf*) с +*instr*; (*FOOTBALL, RUGBY*) блоки́ровать (*impf/perf*).

tacky [ˈtækɪ] *adj* (*sticky*) ли́пкий*; (*pej*: *of poor quality*) дешёвый.

tact [tækt] *n* такт, такти́чность *f*.

tactful [ˈtæktful] *adj* такти́чный* (такти́чен); **she is very** ~ она́ о́чень такти́чна.

tactfully [ˈtæktfəlɪ] *adv* такти́чно.

tactical [ˈtæktɪkl] *adj* (*also MIL*) такти́ческий*; ~ **error** такти́ческая оши́бка.

tactician [tækˈtɪʃən] *n* та́ктик.

tactics [ˈtæktɪks] *npl* та́ктика *fsg*.

tactless [ˈtæktlɪs] *adj* беста́ктный* (беста́ктен).

tactlessly [ˈtæktlɪslɪ] *adv* беста́ктно.

tadpole [ˈtædpəul] *n* голова́стик.

taffy [ˈtæfɪ] *n* (*US*: *toffee*) ири́ска*, тяну́чка*.

tag [tæg] *n* (*label*) этике́тка*, ярлы́к*; **price** ~ этике́тка*; **name** ~ би́рка*

▶ **tag along** *vi* сле́довать (*impf*) по пята́м.

Tahiti [tɑːˈhiːtɪ] *n* Таи́ти *m ind*.

tail [teɪl] *n* (*of animal, plane*) хвост*; (*of shirt*) коне́ц*; (*of coat*) пола́* ◆ *vt* (*follow*) сади́ться* (сесть* *perf*) на хвост +*dat*; ~**s** *npl* (*formal suit*) фрак *msg*; **to turn** ~ броса́ться (бро́ситься* *perf*) наутёк; *see also* **head**

▶ **tail away** *vi* (*voice, wind*) затиха́ть (зати́хнуть *perf*)

▶ **tail off** *vi* = **tail away**.

tailback [ˈteɪlbæk] *n* (*BRIT*: *AUT*) хвост.

tail coat *n* фрак.

tail end *n* (*of train etc*) хвост; (*of meeting etc*) коне́ц.

tailgate [ˈteɪlgeɪt] *n* (*AUT*) за́дняя дверь *f*.

taillight [ˈteɪllaɪt] *n* (*US*: *AUT*) за́дняя фа́ра.

---

* marks translations which have irregular inflections. The Russian-English side of the dictionary gives inflectional information.

tailor ['teɪlə'] n (мужской) портной m adj ♦ vt: **to ~ sth (to)** приспосабливать (приспособить perf) что-н (к +dat); **~'s shop** портняжная мастерская f adj.

tailoring ['teɪlərɪŋ] n (cut) покрой; (craft) портняжное дело.

tailor-made ['teɪlə'meɪd] adj (suit) сшитый на заказ; (fig): **she is ~ for the job** она идеально подходит для этой работы.

tailwind ['teɪlwɪnd] n хвостовой or попутный ветер.

taint [teɪnt] vt (meat, food) портить* (испортить* perf); (fig) пятнать (запятнать perf).

tainted ['teɪntɪd] adj (food) испорченный; (air, water) загрязнённый* (загрязнён); (fig) запятнанный.

Taiwan ['taɪ'wɑːn] n Тайвань m.

Tajik ['tɑːdʒɪk] n таджик(-ийчка*).

Tajiki [tɑː'dʒɪkɪ] adj таджикский* ♦ n таджикский* язык*.

Tajikistan [tɑːdʒɪkɪ'stɑːn] n Таджикистан.

take [teɪk] (pt **took**, pp **taken**) vt брать* (взять* perf); (photo, measures) снимать (снять* perf); (shower, decision, drug) принимать (принять* perf); (notes) делать (сделать perf); (grab: sb's arm etc) хватать (схватить* perf); (require: courage, time) требовать (потребовать perf); (pain etc) переносить* (перенести* perf); (hold: passengers etc) вмещать (вместить* perf); (person: on foot) отводить* (отвести* perf); (thing: on foot) относить* (отнести* perf); (person, thing: by transport) отвозить* (отвезти perf); (exam) сдавать* (сдать* perf); (conduct: meeting) вести* (impf) ♦ vi (fire) заниматься (заняться* perf); (dye) впитываться (впитаться perf); (plant, injection) приниматься (приняться* perf) ♦ n (CINEMA) дубль m; **to ~ sth from** (drawer etc) вынимать (вынуть* perf) что-н из +gen; (steal from: person) брать* (взять* perf) что-н у +gen; **I ~ it that ...** как я понимаю, ...; **I took him for a doctor** я принял его за врача; **to ~ sb's hand** брать* (взять* perf) кого-н за руку; **to ~ for a walk** (child, dog) брать* (взять* perf) на прогулку; **to be ~n ill** заболевать (заболеть perf); **to ~ it upon o.s. to do** браться* (взяться* perf) +infin; **~ the first (street) on the left** первый поворот налево; **to ~ Russian at university** изучать (impf) русский язык в университете; **it won't ~ long** это не займёт много времени; **I was quite ~n with her** (attracted) она произвела на меня большое впечатление

▶ **take after** vt fus (resemble) пойти* (perf) в +acc

▶ **take apart** vt разбирать (разобрать* perf)

▶ **take away** vt (remove) убирать (убрать* perf); (carry off) забирать (забрать* perf); (MATH) отнимать (отнять* perf) ♦ vi: **to ~ away from** отнимать (отнять* perf) от +gen

▶ **take back** vt (return: thing) относить*

(отнести* perf) обратно; (: person) отводить* (отвести* perf) обратно; (one's words) брать* (взять* perf) назад

▶ **take down** vt (building) сносить* (снести* perf); (scaffolding) разбирать (разобрать* perf); (picture) снимать (снять* perf); (write down: letter etc) записывать (записать* perf)

▶ **take in** vt (deceive) обманывать (обмануть perf); (understand) воспринимать (воспринять* perf); (include) включать (включить perf); (lodger, orphan) брать* (взять* perf); (dress, waistband) ушивать (ушить* perf)

▶ **take off** vi (AVIAT) взлетать (взлететь* perf); (go away) улетать (улететь* perf) ♦ vt (remove) снимать (снять* perf); (imitate) копировать (скопировать perf)

▶ **take on** vt (work, employee) брать* (взять* perf); (opponent) сражаться (сразиться* perf) с +instr

▶ **take out** vt (invite) водить* (повести* perf); (remove) вынимать (вынуть* perf); (licence) оформлять (оформить* perf); **to ~ sth out of sth** (drawer, pocket etc) вынимать (вынуть* perf) что-н из чего-н; **don't ~ it out on me!** не вымещай это на мне!

▶ **take over** vt (business, country) принимать (принять* perf) руководство ♦ vi: **to ~ over from sb** сменять (сменить perf) кого-н

▶ **take to** vt fus (activity) пристраститься* (perf) к +dat, заниматься (заняться* perf) +instr; (form habit of): **to ~ to doing** пристраститься* (perf) +infin; **she took to him at once** он ей сразу понравился

▶ **take up** vt (hobby, sport, job) заняться* (perf) +instr; (idea, suggestion, story) подхватывать (подхватить* perf); (time, space) занимать (занять* perf); (garment) подшивать (подшить* perf) ♦ vi: **to ~ up with sb** сходиться* (сойтись* perf) с кем-н; **to ~ sb up on sth** (offer, suggestion) воспользоваться (perf) +instr; **I'll ~ you up on that!** ловлю Вас на слове!

takeaway ['teɪkəweɪ] n (BRIT) магазин или ресторан, где продаётся горячая еда на вынос; (food) горячая еда на вынос.

take-home pay ['teɪkhəum-] n чистый заработок*.

taken ['teɪkən] pp of **take**.

takeoff ['teɪkɔf] n (AVIAT) взлёт.

takeout ['teɪkaut] (US) n = **takeaway**.

takeover ['teɪkəuvə'] n (COMM) поглощение; (of country) захват власти.

takeover bid n (COMM) попытка поглощения.

takings ['teɪkɪŋz] npl (COMM) выручка fsg.

talc [tælk] n тальк.

talcum powder ['tælkəm-] n = **talc**.

tale [teɪl] n (story, account) рассказ, сказание; **to tell ~s** (fig: to teacher, parents etc) ябедничать (наябедничать perf).

talent ['tælnt] n талант.

talented ['tæləntɪd] *adj* (*person, actor etc*) тала́нтливый (тала́нтлив).

talent scout *n* (*THEAT, SPORT*) челове́к, занима́ющийся по́иском молоды́х дарова́ний.

talisman ['tælɪzmən] *n* талисма́н.

talk [tɔːk] *n* (*a (prepared) speech*) докла́д; (*conversation, interview*) бесе́да; (*gossip*) слух ♦ *vi* (*speak*) разгова́ривать (*impf*); ~**s** *npl* (*POL etc*) перегово́ры *pl*; **to give a** ~ де́лать (сде́лать *perf*) докла́д; **to** ~ **about** расска́зывать (рассказа́ть *perf*) о +*prp*; ~**ing of films, have you seen ...?** кста́ти о фи́льмах, вы ви́дели ...?; **to** ~ **sb into doing** угова́ривать (уговори́ть *perf*) кого́-н +*infin*; **to** ~ **sb out of sth** отгова́ривать (отговори́ть *perf*) кого́-н от чего́-н; **to** ~ **shop** говори́ть (*impf*) о дела́х
▸ **talk over** *vt* (*problem etc*) обгова́ривать (обговори́ть *perf*).

talkative ['tɔːkətɪv] *adj* (*person*) разгово́рчивый (разгово́рчив).

talker ['tɔːkə'] *n*: **she is a good** ~ она́ хоро́ший ора́тор; (*pej*) болту́н(-у́шка); **he is a fast** ~ он красноречи́в.

talking point ['tɔːkɪŋ-] *n* те́ма для разгово́ра.

talking-to ['tɔːkɪŋtu] *n*: **to give sb a good** ~ отчи́тывать (отчита́ть *perf*) кого́-н как сле́дует.

talk show *n* (*TV, RADIO*) ток-шо́у *ind*.

tall [tɔːl] *adj* высо́кий* (высо́к); **he is 6 feet** ~ его́ рост – 6 фу́тов; **how** ~ **are you?** како́й у Вас рост?

tallboy ['tɔːlbɔɪ] *n* (*BRIT*) высо́кий* комо́д.

Tallin(n) ['tælɪn] *n* Та́ллин(н).

tallness ['tɔːlnɪs] *n* высота́.

tall story *n* небыли́ца.

tally ['tælɪ] *n* (*of marks, amounts of money etc*) счёт ♦ *vi*: **to** ~ (**with**) (*subj: figures, stories etc*) сходи́ться* (сойти́сь* *perf*) (с +*instr*); **to keep a** ~ **of sth** вести́* (*impf*) счёт чего́-н.

talon ['tælən] *n* (*of eagle, owl etc*) ко́готь* *m*.

tambourine [tæmbə'riːn] *n* (*MUS*) тамбури́н, бу́бен.

tame [teɪm] *adj* (*animal, bird*) ручно́й; (*fig: story, style*) вя́лый (вял).

tamper ['tæmpə'] *vi*: **to** ~ **with sth** пыта́ться (попыта́ться *perf*) измени́ть что-н.

tampon ['tæmpɔn] *n* тампо́н.

tan [tæn] *n* (*also*: **suntan**) зага́р ♦ *vi* (*person*) загора́ть (загоре́ть *perf*); (*skin*) загоре́ть (*perf*) ♦ *vt* дуби́ть* (вы́дубить* *perf*) ♦ *adj* (*colour*) рыжева́то-кори́чневый; **to get a** ~ загора́ть (загоре́ть *perf*).

tandem ['tændəm] *n* (*cycle*) танде́м; **in** ~ (*together*) совме́стно, вме́сте.

tandoori [tæn'duərɪ] *n* инди́йский ме́тод приготовле́ния мя́са и лепёшек в гли́няной печи́.

tang [tæŋ] *n* си́льный за́пах.

tangent ['tændʒənt] *n* (*MATH*) каса́тельная *f adj*; **to go off at a** ~ (*fig*) сбива́ться (сби́ться* *perf*).

tangerine [tændʒə'riːn] *n* (*fruit*) мандари́н; (*colour*) я́рко-ора́нжевый цвет.

tangible ['tændʒəbl] *adj* (*proof, benefits*) ощути́мый (ощути́м); ~ **assets** реа́льный акти́в.

Tangier [tæn'dʒɪə'] *n* Танже́р.

tangle ['tæŋgl] *n* пу́таница; **to get in(to) a** ~ (*also fig*) запу́тываться (запу́таться *perf*).

tango ['tæŋgəu] *n* та́нго *nt ind*.

tank [tæŋk] *n* (*water tank*) бак; (: *large*) цисте́рна; (*PHOT*) ва́нна; (*for fish*) аква́риум; (*MIL*) танк.

tankard ['tæŋkəd] *n* (*for beer*) пивна́я кру́жка.

tanker ['tæŋkə'] *n* (*ship*) та́нкер; (*truck, RAIL*) цисте́рна.

tanned [tænd] *adj* загоре́лый.

tannin ['tænɪn] *n* тани́н.

tanning ['tænɪŋ] *n* (*of leather*) дубле́ние.

Tannoy® ['tænɔɪ] *n* (*BRIT*) громкоговори́тель *m*; **over the** ~ по громкоговори́телю.

tantalizing ['tæntəlaɪzɪŋ] *adj* (*smell, possibility*) дразня́щий*.

tantamount ['tæntəmaunt] *adj*: ~ **to** равноси́льный* (равноси́лен) +*dat*.

tantrum ['tæntrəm] *n* исте́рика; **to throw a** ~ устра́ивать (устро́ить *perf*) исте́рику.

Tanzania [tænzə'nɪə] *n* Танза́ния.

Tanzanian [tænzə'nɪən] *adj* танзани́йский* ♦ *n* танзани́ец(-и́йка).

tap [tæp] *n* кран; (*gentle blow*) стук ♦ *vt* (*hit gently*) стуча́ть (постуча́ть *perf*) по +*dat*; (*resources*) испо́льзовать (*impf/perf*); (*telephone, conversation*) прослу́шивать (*impf*); **to be on** ~ (*fig: resources*) находи́ться* (*impf*) под руко́й; (*beer*) в разли́в.

tap-dancing ['tæpdɑːnsɪŋ] *n* чечётка.

tape [teɪp] *n* (*also*: **magnetic** ~) плёнка; (*cassette*) кассе́та; (*sticky tape*) кле́йкая ле́нта; (*for tying*) ле́нта ♦ *vt* (*record*) запи́сывать (записа́ть* *perf*); (*stick with tape*) закле́ивать (закле́ить *perf*) кле́йкой ле́нтой; **on** ~ (*song etc*) на кассе́те.

tape deck *n* кассе́тный магнитофо́н.

tape measure *n* санти́метр.

taper ['teɪpə'] *n* (*candle*) то́нкая восковая свеча́ ♦ *vi* (*narrow*) сужа́ться (су́зиться* *perf*).

tape recorder *n* магнитофо́н.

tape recording *n* магнитофо́нная за́пись *f*.

tapered ['teɪpəd] *adj* (*skirt*) сужа́ющийся.

tapering ['teɪpərɪŋ] *adj* (*fingers*) то́нкий*.

tapestry ['tæpɪstrɪ] *n* (*object*) гобеле́н; (*art*) иску́сство гобеле́на.

tapeworm ['teɪpwəːm] *n* лентéц*, лéнточный червь *m*.

---

* marks translations which have irregular inflections. The Russian-English side of the dictionary gives inflectional information.

tapioca [tæpɪ'əukə] n тапио́ка.
tappet ['tæpɪt] n (AUT) толка́тель m кла́пана.
tar [tɑ:] n дёготь m; **low/middle ~ cigarettes** сигаре́ты с ни́зким/сре́дним содержа́нием никоти́на.
tarantula [tə'ræntjulə] n тара́нтул.
tardy ['tɑ:dɪ] adj (reply, development) запозда́лый.
target ['tɑ:gɪt] n цель f; **to be on ~** (project) идти́* (impf) согла́сно пла́ну.
target audience n потенциа́льные клие́нты mpl.
target market n целево́й ры́нок*.
target practice n уче́бная стрельба́.
tariff ['tærɪf] n (tax on goods) тари́ф; (BRIT: in hotels, restaurants) прейскура́нт.
tariff barrier n (COMM) тари́фный барье́р.
tarmac ['tɑ:mæk] n (BRIT: on road) асфа́льт; (AVIAT) преданга́рная площа́дка ♦ vt (BRIT: road, drive etc) асфальти́ровать (заасфальти́ровать perf).
tarn [tɑ:n] n ка́ровое о́зеро.
tarnish ['tɑ:nɪʃ] vt (silver, brass etc) де́лать (сде́лать perf) ту́склым; (fig: reputation etc) броса́ть (бро́сить* perf) тень на +acc.
tarot ['tærəu] adj: **~ cards** гада́льные ка́рты fpl.
tarpaulin [tɑ:'pɔ:lɪn] n брезе́нт.
tarragon ['tærəgən] n (herb) эстраго́н.
tart [tɑ:t] n (CULIN: large) пиро́г; (: small) пиро́жное nt adj; (BRIT: inf: prostitute) шлю́ха ♦ adj (flavour) го́рький*
► **tart up** (BRIT: inf) ♦ vt (object etc) принаряжа́ть (принаряди́ть* perf); **to ~ o.s. up** принаряжа́ться (принаряди́ться* perf); (pej) нама́зываться (нама́заться* perf), выря́живаться (вы́рядиться* perf).
tartan ['tɑ:tn] n шотла́ндка (ткань) ♦ adj (rug, scarf etc) кле́тчатый.
tartar ['tɑ:tə'] n (on teeth) (зубно́й) ка́мень m; (pej: person) сте́рва.
tartar(e) sauce ['tɑ:tə-] n со́ус с лу́ком и ка́персами.
Tashkent [tæʃ'kɛnt] n Ташке́нт.
task [tɑ:sk] n зада́ча; **to take sb to ~** отчи́тывать (отчита́ть perf) кого́-н.
task force n (MIL, POLICE) операти́вная гру́ппа.
taskmaster ['tɑ:skmɑ:stə'] n: **he's a hard ~** он настоя́щий* надсмо́трщик.
Tasmania [tæz'meɪnɪə] n Тасма́ния.
tassel ['tæsl] n ки́сточка; **~s** бахрома́ fsg.
taste [teɪst] n вкус; (sample) про́ба; (fig: glimpse, idea) представле́ние ♦ vt про́бовать (попро́бовать perf) ♦ vi: **the fish ~s of** or **like** ры́ба име́ет вкус +gen; **what does the fish ~ like?** какова́ ры́ба на вкус?; **you can ~ the garlic (in the dish)** (в блю́де) чу́вствуется чесно́к; **to have a ~ of sth** про́бовать (попро́бовать perf) чего́-н; **to have a ~ for sth** име́ть (impf) вкус к чему́-н; **in good/bad ~** в хоро́шем/дурно́м вку́се.
taste bud n (ANAT) вкусово́й буго́р.

tasteful ['teɪstful] adj (furnishings) элега́нтный.
tastefully ['teɪstfəlɪ] adv (decorated, furnished etc) со вку́сом.
tasteless ['teɪstlɪs] adj безвку́сный* (безвку́сен).
tasty ['teɪstɪ] adj (food) вку́сный* (вку́сен).
tattered ['tætəd] adj (clothes, paper etc) изо́рванный (в кло́чья); (fig: hopes etc) разби́тый (разби́т).
tatters ['tætəz] npl: **in ~** (clothes) изо́рванный (изо́рван) в кло́чья.
tattoo [tə'tu:] n (on skin) татуиро́вка; (spectacle) вое́нный смотр ♦ vt (name, design) татуи́ровать (вы́татуировать perf).
tatty ['tætɪ] adj (BRIT: inf) потрёпанный.
taught [tɔ:t] pt, pp of **teach**.
taunt [tɔ:nt] n издева́тельство ♦ vt (person) издева́ться (impf) над +instr.
Taurus ['tɔ:rəs] n (ASTROLOGY) Теле́ц*; **he is ~** он – Теле́ц.
taut [tɔ:t] adj (thread etc) туго́й (туг); (skin) упру́гий* (упру́г).
tavern ['tævən] n (old) таве́рна.
tawdry ['tɔ:drɪ] adj (jewellery etc) безвку́сный* (безвку́сен).
tawny ['tɔ:nɪ] adj желтова́то-кори́чневый.
tawny owl n неясыть f.
tax [tæks] n нало́г ♦ vt (earnings, goods etc) облага́ть (обложи́ть perf) нало́гом; (fig: memory, patience) испы́тывать (испыта́ть perf); **before ~** до вы́чета нало́гов; **after ~** за вы́четом нало́гов; **free of ~** не облага́емый нало́гом.
taxable ['tæksəbl] adj (income) облага́емый (облага́ем) нало́гом.
tax allowance n нало́говая ски́дка.
taxation [tæk'seɪʃən] n (system) налогообложе́ние; (money paid) разме́р нало́га.
tax avoidance n оптимиза́ция нало́говой поли́тики.
tax collector n сбо́рщик нало́гов.
tax disc n (BRIT: AUT) свиде́тельство об упла́те подоро́жного нало́га, кото́рое прикрепля́ется к ветрово́му стеклу́.
tax evasion n уклоне́ние от нало́гов.
tax exemption n освобожде́ние от нало́гов.
tax exile n челове́к с высо́ким дохо́дом, кото́рый живёт за грани́цей с це́лью минимиза́ции свои́х нало́гов.
tax-free ['tæksfri:] adj (goods, services) необлага́емый нало́гом.
tax haven n нало́говое убе́жище (страна́ с ни́зкими нало́гами).
taxi ['tæksɪ] n такси́ nt ind ♦ vi (AVIAT: plane) выру́ливать (вы́рулить perf).
taxidermist ['tæksɪdə:mɪst] n наби́вщик чу́чел.
taxi driver n води́тель m такси́, такси́ст.
tax inspector n (BRIT) нало́говый инспе́ктор.
taxi rank n (BRIT) стоя́нка такси́.
taxi stand n = **taxi rank**.

taxpayer ['tækspeɪəʳ] *n* налогоплате́льщик (-щица).
tax rebate *n* возвра́т нало́га.
tax relief *n* ски́дка с нало́га.
tax return *n* поступле́ния *ntpl* от нало́гов.
tax shelter *n* нало́говая защи́та (*че́рез вложе́ния в це́нные бума́ги*).
tax year *n* нало́говый год*.
TB *n abbr* = **tuberculosis**.
Tbilisi [dbɪˈliːsɪ] *n* Тбили́си *m ind*.
TD *n abbr* (*US*) = **Treasury Department**; (:
FOOTBALL) = **touchdown**.
tea [tiː] *n* (*drink*) чай; (*BRIT*: *meal*) у́жин;
afternoon ~ чай (с бутербро́дами и пиро́жными); **high** ~ (*BRIT*) (по́здний*) обе́д.
tea bag *n* чай в паке́тике.
tea break *n* (*BRIT*) переры́в.
teacake ['tiːkeɪk] *n* (*BRIT*) сдо́бная бу́лка с излю́мом.
teach [tiːtʃ] (*pt,pp* **taught**) *vi* (*be a teacher*) преподава́ть* (*impf*) ♦ *vt*: **to** ~ **sb sth**, ~ **sth to sb** учи́ть (научи́ть *perf*) кого́-н чему́-н; (*in school*) преподава́ть* (*impf*) что-н; **it taught him a lesson** (*fig*) э́то послужи́ло ему́ хоро́шим уро́ком.
teacher ['tiːtʃəʳ] *n* (*in secondary school*) учи́тель(ница) *m(f)*, преподава́тель(ница) *m(f)*; (*in primary school*) учи́тель(ница); **Russian** ~ учи́тель(ница) *or* преподава́тель(ница) ру́сского.
teacher training college *n* (*for primary schools*) педагоги́ческое учи́лище; (*for secondary schools*) педагоги́ческий* институ́т.
teaching ['tiːtʃɪŋ] *n* (*work of teacher*) преподава́ние.
teaching aids *npl* уче́бные посо́бия *ntpl*.
teaching hospital *n* (*BRIT*: *MED*) ≈ клини́ческая больни́ца.
teaching staff *n* (*BRIT*) преподава́тельский соста́в.
tea cosy *n* ≈ "ба́ба" на ча́йник.
teacup ['tiːkʌp] *n* ча́йная ча́шка*.
teak [tiːk] *n* тик.
tea leaves *npl* зава́рка *fsg*.
team [tiːm] *n* (*of people*) кома́нда; (*of animals*) упря́жка
► **team up** *vi*: **to** ~ **up (with)** объединя́ть (объедини́ть *perf*) уси́лия (с +*instr*).
team games *npl* кома́ндные и́гры *fpl*.
team spirit *n* дух това́рищества, кома́ндный дух.
teamwork ['tiːmwəːk] *n* коллекти́вная рабо́та.
tea party *n* чаепи́тие, чай.
teapot ['tiːpɔt] *n* (зава́рочный) ча́йник.
tear¹ [tɛəʳ] (*pt* **tore**, *pp* **torn**) *n* (*hole*) дыра́*, ды́рка* ♦ *vt* (*rip*) рвать* (порва́ть* *perf*) ♦ *vi*

(*become torn*) рва́ться* (порва́ться* *perf*); **to** ~ **to pieces** *or* **to bits** *or* **to shreds** (*also fig*) разрыва́ть (разорва́ть* *perf*) на ме́лкие клочки́
► **tear along** *vi* (*rush*) нести́сь* (понести́сь* *perf*)
► **tear apart** *vt* (*also fig*) разрыва́ть (разорва́ть* *perf*) на ча́сти
► **tear away** *vt*: **to** ~ **o.s. away (from sth)** (*fig*) отрыва́ться (оторва́ться* *perf*) (от чего́-н)
► **tear out** *vt* (*sheet of paper, cheque*) вырыва́ть (вы́рвать* *perf*)
► **tear up** *vt* (*sheet of paper etc*) разрыва́ть (разорва́ть* *perf*).
tear² [tɪəʳ] *n* слеза́; **in** ~**s** в слеза́х; **to burst into** ~**s** распла́каться (*perf*), разрыда́ться (*perf*).
tearaway ['tɛərəweɪ] *n* (*inf*: *person*) сорвиголова́ *m/f*.
teardrop ['tɪədrɔp] *n* слези́нка*.
tearful ['tɪəful] *adj* запла́канный* (запла́кан).
tear gas *vt* слезоточи́вый газ.
tearing ['tɛərɪŋ] *adj*: **to be in a** ~ **hurry** быть* (*impf*) в безу́мной спе́шке.
tearoom ['tiːruːm] *n* ча́йная *f adj*.
tease [tiːz] *vt* дразни́ть (*impf*); (*unkindly*) дразни́ть (задразни́ть *perf*) ♦ *n* (*person*) насме́шник.
tea set *n* ча́йный серви́з.
teashop ['tiːʃɔp] *n* (*BRIT*) = **tearoom**.
Teasmade® ['tiːzmeɪd] *n* приспособле́ние для зава́ривания ча́я, приводи́мое в де́йствие буди́льником.
teaspoon ['tiːspuːn] *n* ча́йная ло́жка.
tea strainer *n* ча́йное си́течко.
teat [tiːt] *n* (*of bottle*) со́ска.
teatime ['tiːtaɪm] *n* у́жин.
tea towel *n* (*BRIT*) полоте́нце для посу́ды.
tea urn *n* тита́н с ча́ем.
tech [tɛk] *n abbr* (*inf*) = **technology, technical college**) ≈ ПТУ= *профессиона́льно-техни́ческое учи́лище*.
technical ['tɛknɪkl] *adj* (*terms, advances*) техни́ческий*.
technical college *n* (*BRIT*) техни́ческий* ко́лледж, те́хникум.
technicality [tɛknɪˈkælɪtɪ] *n* (*point of law*) техни́ческая то́нкость *f*; (*detail*) форма́льность *f*; **on a (legal)** ~ из-за юриди́ческой форма́льности.
technically ['tɛknɪklɪ] *adv* (*strictly speaking*) техни́чески, форма́льно; (*regarding technique*) с техни́ческой то́чки зре́ния.
technician [tɛkˈnɪʃən] *n* те́хник.
technique [tɛkˈniːk] *n* те́хника.
techno ['tɛknəu] *n* (*MUS*) стиль поп му́зыки.
technocrat ['tɛknəkræt] *n* технокра́т.
technological [tɛknəˈlɔdʒɪkl] *adj* (*development,*

---

knowledge) техни́ческий*.
technologist [tɛk'nɔlədʒɪst] *n* те́хник; (*in particular field*) техно́лог.
technology [tɛk'nɔlədʒɪ] *n* те́хника; (*in particular field*) техноло́гия.
teddy (bear) ['tɛdɪ(-)] *n* (плю́шевый *or* игру́шечный) ми́шка.
tedious ['tiːdɪəs] *adj* (*work, discussions etc*) ну́дный* (ну́ден), ску́чный.
tedium ['tiːdɪəm] *n* ску́ка.
tee [tiː] *n* ме́тка для мяча́
▶ **tee off** *vi* де́лать (сде́лать *perf*) пе́рвый уда́р.
teem [tiːm] *vi*: **the city is ~ing with** (*visitors, tourists etc*) го́род киши́т +*gen*; **it is ~ing (with rain)** льёт как ведра́.
teenage ['tiːneɪdʒ] *adj* (*fashions etc*) подростко́вый; ~ **children** подро́стки *mpl*.
teenager ['tiːneɪdʒə'] *n* подросто́к*.
teens [tiːnz] *npl*: **to be in one's ~** быть* (*impf*) подростко́вого во́зраста.
tee shirt *n* = **T-shirt**.
teeter ['tiːtə'] *vi* (*also fig*) колеба́ться (*impf*).
teeth [tiːθ] *npl of* **tooth**.
teethe [tiːð] *vi*: **she is teething** (*baby*) у неё ре́жутся зу́бы.
teething ring ['tiːðɪŋ-] *n* кольцо́.
teething troubles *npl* (*fig*) боле́зни *fpl* ро́ста.
teetotal ['tiː'təutl] *adj* тре́звый, не пью́щий*.
teetotaller ['tiː'təutlə'] (*US* **teetotaler**) *n* тре́звенник.
TEFL ['tɛfl] *n abbr* = *Teaching of English as a Foreign Language*.
Teflon® ['tɛflɔn] *n* Тефло́н.
Teheran [tɛə'rɑːn] *n* Тегера́н.
tel. *abbr* (= **telephone**) тел.= *телефо́н*.
Tel Aviv ['tɛlə'viːv] *n* Тель Ави́в.
telecast ['tɛlkɑːst] *vt* передава́ть* (переда́ть* *perf*) по телеви́дению.
telecommunications ['tɛlɪkəmjuːnɪ'keɪʃənz] *n* телекоммуника́ции *fpl*.
telegram ['tɛlɪgræm] *n* телегра́мма.
telegraph ['tɛlɪgrɑːf] *n* (*system*) телегра́ф.
telegraphic [tɛlɪ'græfɪk] *adj* (*equipment*) телеграфи́ческий.
telegraph pole *n* телегра́фный столб.
telegraph wire *n* телегра́фные провода́ *mpl*.
telepathic [tɛlɪ'pæθɪk] *adj* телепати́ческий.
telepathy [tə'lɛpəθɪ] *n* телепа́тия.
telephone ['tɛlɪfəun] *n* телефо́н ◆ *vt* (*person*) звони́ть (позвони́ть *perf*) +*dat*; (*message*) сообща́ть (сообщи́ть *perf*) (по телефо́ну); **on the ~** (*talking*) по телефо́ну; **are you on the ~?** (*possessing phone*) у Вас есть телефо́н?
telephone booth (*BRIT* **telephone box**) *n* телефо́нная бу́дка.
telephone call *n* телефо́нный звоно́к*; **there is a ~ ~ for Peter** Пи́тера про́сят к телефо́ну.
telephone directory *n* телефо́нный спра́вочник.
telephone exchange *n* телефо́нная ста́нция.
telephone number *n* но́мер* телефо́на.

telephone operator *n* телефони́ст(ка).
telephone tapping *n* прослу́шивание телефо́на.
telephonist [tə'lɛfənɪst] *n* (*BRIT*) телефони́ст(ка).
telephoto ['tɛlɪ'fəutəu] *adj*: ~ **lens** телефотообъекти́в.
teleprinter ['tɛlɪprɪntə'] *n* телета́йп.
Teleprompter® ['tɛlɪprɔmptə'] *n* (*US*) телесуфлёр, телете́кст.
telesales ['tɛlɪseɪlz] *n* прода́жа по телефо́ну.
telescope ['tɛlɪskəup] *n* телеско́п ◆ *vi* (*fig: vehicles*) ста́лкиваться (столкну́ться *perf*) ◆ *vt* раскла́дывать (расложи́ть* *perf*).
telescopic [tɛlɪ'skɔpɪk] *adj* (*lens*) телескопи́ческий*; (*legs, aerial*) складно́й.
Teletext® ['tɛlɪtɛkst] *n* телете́кст, веща́тельная видеогра́фия.
telethon ['tɛlɪθɔn] *n* благотвори́тельная телевизио́нная програ́мма (*продолжа́ющаяся мно́го часо́в подря́д*).
televangelist [tɛlɪ'vændʒəlɪst] *n* телепроповéдник(-ица).
televise ['tɛlɪvaɪz] *vt* передава́ть* (*impf*) по телеви́дению.
television ['tɛlɪvɪʒən] *n* телеви́дение; (*set*) телеви́зор; **on ~** по телеви́дению.
television licence *n* (*BRIT*) телевизио́нная лице́нзия.
television programme *n* телевизио́нная програ́мма.
television set *n* телеви́зор.
telex ['tɛlɛks] *n* те́лекс ◆ *vt* (*company*) свя́зываться (связа́ться* *perf*) по те́лексу с +*instr*; (*message*) передава́ть* (переда́ть* *perf*) по те́лексу ◆ *vi* посыла́ть (посла́ть* *perf*) те́лекс.
tell [tɛl] (*pt,pp* **told**) *vt* (*say*) говори́ть (сказа́ть* *perf*); (*relate*) расска́зывать (рассказа́ть* *perf*); (*distinguish*): **to ~ sth from** отлича́ть (отличи́ть *perf*) что-н от +*gen* ◆ *vi* (*talk*): **to ~ of** расска́зывать (рассказа́ть* *perf*) о +*prp*; (*have an effect*): **to ~ (on)** ска́зываться (сказа́ться* *perf*) (на +*prp*); **to ~ sb to do** говори́ть (сказа́ть* *perf*) кому́-н +*infin*; **to ~ sb about sth** расска́зывать (рассказа́ть* *perf*) кому́-н о чём-н; **he told me what happened** он рассказа́л мне, что случи́лось; **to ~ the time** (*know how to*) определя́ть (определи́ть *perf*), кото́рый час; **can you ~ me the time?** Вы не ска́жете, кото́рый час?; **(I) ~ you what** ... вот что: ...; **I can't ~ them apart** я не могу́ их различи́ть
▶ **tell off** *vt*: **to ~ sb off** отчи́тывать (отчита́ть *perf*) кого́-н
▶ **tell on** *vt fus* (*inform on*) жа́ловаться (нажа́ловаться *perf*) на +*acc*.
teller ['tɛlə'] *n* (*in bank*) касси́р.
telling ['tɛlɪŋ] *adj* (*remark, detail*) показа́тельный* (показа́телен).
telltale ['tɛlteɪl] *adj* (*sign*) преда́тельский* ◆ *n*

(*pej: child*) ябеда *m/f*.

telly ['tɛlɪ] *n abbr* (*BRIT: inf*) (= **television**) тéлик.

temerity [tə'mɛrɪtɪ] *n* смéлость *f*.

temp [tɛmp] *n abbr* (*BRIT: inf.* = *temporary office worker*) врéменный делопроизводúтель *m* ◆ *vi* врéменно рабóтать (*impf*) делопроизводúтелем.

temper ['tɛmpə'] *n* (*nature*) нрав; (*mood*) настроéние; (*fit of anger*) гнев ◆ *vt* (*moderate*) смягчáть (смягчúть *perf*); **to be in a ~** быть* (*impf*) в гнéве; **to lose one's ~** выходúть* (выйти* *perf*) из себя; **to keep one's ~** сдéрживаться (сдержáться* *perf*).

temperament ['tɛmprəmənt] *n* темперáмент.

temperamental [tɛmprə'mɛntl] *adj* темперáментный* (темперáментен); (*fig*) капрúзный.

temperate ['tɛmprət] *adj* (*climate, zone, behaviour*) умéренный* (умéрен); **~ country** странá с умéренным клúматом.

temperature ['tɛmprətʃə'] *n* температýра; **he has** *or* **is running a ~** у негó температýра.

temperature chart *n* температýрный грáфик.

tempered ['tɛmpəd] *adj* (*steel*) отпýщенный.

tempest ['tɛmpɪst] *n* бýря.

tempestuous [tɛm'pɛstjuəs] *adj* (*time, relationship*) бýрный* (бýрен); (*person*) бýйный* (бýен).

tempi ['tɛmpiː] *npl of* **tempo**.

template ['tɛmplɪt] *n* шаблóн.

temple ['tɛmpl] *n* (*REL*) храм; (*ANAT*) висóк*.

templet ['tɛmplɪt] *n* = **template**.

tempo ['tɛmpəu] (*pl* **~s** *or* **tempi**) *n* (*MUS, also fig*) темп.

temporal ['tɛmpərl] *adj* (*non-religious*) свéтский*; (*relating to time*) временнóй.

temporarily ['tɛmpərərɪlɪ] *adv* врéменно.

temporary ['tɛmpərərɪ] *adj* врéменный* (врéменен).

temporize ['tɛmpəraɪz] *vi* мéдлить (*impf*).

tempt [tɛmpt] *vt* соблазнять (соблазнúть *perf*), искушáть (искусúть* *perf*); **to ~ sb into doing** соблазнять (соблазнúть *perf*) *or* искушáть (искусúть* *perf*) когó-н +*infin*; **I was ~ed to call you** у меня бы́ло искушéние позвонúть Вам.

temptation [tɛmp'teɪʃən] *n* соблáзн, искушéние.

tempting ['tɛmptɪŋ] *adj* (*offer*) соблазнúтельный* (соблазнúтелен).

ten [tɛn] *n* дéсять*; **~s of thousands** десятки тысяч; *see also* **five**.

tenable ['tɛnəbl] *adj* здрáвый (здрав); **the position of Chairman is ~ for three years** пост председáтеля закреплён за ним на три гóда.

tenacious [tə'neɪʃəs] *adj* настóйчивый (настóйчив).

tenacity [tə'næsɪtɪ] *n* настóйчивость *f*.

tenancy ['tɛnənsɪ] *n* (*possession of room, land etc*) владéние на услóвиях арéнды; (*period of possession*) срок арéнды *or* нáйма.

tenant ['tɛnənt] *n* съёмщик(-мщица).

tend [tɛnd] *vt* (*crops, sick person*) ухáживать (*impf*) за +*instr* ◆ *vi*: **to ~ to do** имéть (*impf*) склóнность +*infin*; **he ~s to do everything in a hurry** он склóнен к томý, чтóбы дéлать всё в спéшке.

tendency ['tɛndənsɪ] *n* (*habit*) склóнность *f*; (*trend*) тенденция.

tender ['tɛndə'] *adj* нéжный* (нéжен); (*sore*) чувствúтельный* (чувствúтелен) ◆ *n* (*COMM: offer*) предложéние ◆ *vt* (*offer*) подавáть* (подáть* *perf*); (*apology*) приносúть* (принестú* *perf*); **to put in a ~ (for)** подавáть* (подáть* *perf*) заявку (на +*acc*); **to put sth out to ~** (*BRIT*) объявлять (объявúть* *perf*) тóрги на что-н; **legal ~** (*money*) закóнное платёжное срéдство; **to ~ one's resignation** подáть* (*perf*) в отстáвку.

tenderize ['tɛndəraɪz] *vt* (*meat*) отбивáть (отбúть* *perf*).

tenderly ['tɛndəlɪ] *adv* нéжно.

tenderness ['tɛndənɪs] *n* нéжность *f*.

tendon ['tɛndən] *n* сухожúлие.

tendril ['tɛndrɪl] *n* (*BOT*) ýсик; (*of hair*) прядь *f*.

tenement ['tɛnəmənt] *n* многоквартúрный дом* (*сдавáемый внаём*).

Tenerife [tɛnə'riːf] *n* Тенерúфе *m ind*.

tenet ['tɛnət] *n* основополагáющий прúнцип.

tenner ['tɛnə'] *n* (*BRIT: inf: ten pounds*) ≈ десятка*.

tennis ['tɛnɪs] *n* тéннис.

tennis ball *n* тéннисный мяч*.

tennis club *n* тéннисный клуб.

tennis court *n* тéннисный корт.

tennis elbow *n* (*MED*) тéннисный лóкоть *m*, лучеплечевóй бурсúт.

tennis match *n* тéннисный матч.

tennis player *n* тенннисúст(ка*).

tennis racket *n* тéннисная ракéтка*.

tennis shoes *npl* тéннисные тýфли* *fpl*.

tenor ['tɛnə'] *n* (*MUS*) тéнор*; (*of speech etc*) смысл.

tenpin bowling ['tɛnpɪn-] *n* (*BRIT*) кéгли *pl*.

tense [tɛns] *adj* (*person, muscle, period*) напряжённый* (напряжён); (*smile*) натя́нутый (натя́нут) ◆ *n* (*LING*) врéмя* *nt* ◆ *vt* напрягáть (напря́чь* *perf*).

tenseness ['tɛnsnɪs] *n* напряжённость *f*.

tension ['tɛnʃən] *n* (*nervousness*) напряжённость *f*; (*between ropes etc*) натя́нутость *f*.

tent [tɛnt] *n* палáтка*.

tentacle ['tɛntəkl] *n* щýпальце*.

tentative ['tɛntətɪv] *adj* (*person, smile*)

---

* marks translations which have irregular inflections. The Russian-English side of the dictionary gives inflectional information.

осторо́жный* (осторо́жен); (*conclusion, plans*) предвари́тельный* (предвари́телен).

tentatively [ˈtɛntətɪvlɪ] *adv* (*suggest*) предвари́тельно; (*wave*) осторо́жно.

tenterhooks [ˈtɛntəhuks] *npl*: **on ~** как на иго́лках.

tenth [tɛnθ] *adj* деся́тый ♦ *n* (*fraction*) деся́тая часть *f*, одна́ деся́тая *f adj*; *see also* **fifth**.

tent peg *n* ко́лышек* для пала́тки.

tent pole *n* столб* для пала́тки.

tenuous [ˈtɛnjuəs] *adj* (*hold, links etc*) сла́бый* (слаб).

tenure [ˈtɛnjuəʳ] *n* (*of land, buildings etc*) срок аре́нды; (*of office*) пребыва́ние в до́лжности; **to have ~** име́ть (*impf*) постоя́нную рабо́ту.

tepid [ˈtɛpɪd] *adj* (*tea, pool etc*) теплова́тый (теплова́т); (*reaction, applause*) прохла́дный* (прохла́ден).

Ter. *abbr* = **Terrace**.

term [tə:m] *n* (*word, expression*) те́рмин; (*period in power etc*) срок*; (*SCOL: in school*) че́тверть *f*; (: *at university*) триме́стр ♦ *vt* (*call*) называ́ть (назва́ть* *perf*); **~s** *npl* (*conditions*) усло́вия *ntpl*; **in abstract ~s** в абстра́ктных выраже́ниях; **~ of imprisonment** срок заключе́ния; **"easy ~s"** (*COMM*) "льго́тные усло́вия"; **in the short ~** в настоя́щее вре́мя; **in the long ~** в перспекти́ве; **to be on good ~s with sb** подде́рживать (*impf*) хоро́шие отноше́ния с кем-н; **to come to ~s with sth** примиря́ться (примири́ться *perf*) с +*instr*.

terminal [ˈtə:mɪnl] *adj* неизлечи́мый (неизлечи́м) ♦ *n* (*ELEC*) кле́мма, зажи́м; (*COMPUT, COMM*) термина́л; (*also*: **air ~**) аэровокза́л; (*BRIT*: *also*: **coach ~**) авто́бусный вокза́л.

terminate [ˈtə:mɪneɪt] *vt* прекраша́ть (прекрати́ть* *perf*) ♦ *vi*: **to ~ in** зака́нчиваться (зако́нчиться *perf*) +*instr*.

termination [tə:mɪˈneɪʃən] *n* прекраще́ние.

termini [ˈtə:mɪnaɪ] *npl of* **terminus**.

terminology [tə:mɪˈnɔlədʒɪ] *n* терминоло́гия.

term insurance *n* страхова́ние на определённый срок.

terminus [ˈtə:mɪnəs] (*pl* **termini**) *n* (*for buses*) коне́чная остано́вка*; (*for trains*) коне́чная ста́нция.

termite [ˈtə:maɪt] *n* терми́т.

term paper *n* (*US*: *at university*) ≈ курсова́я *f adj*.

Terr. *abbr* = **Terrace**.

terrace [ˈtɛrəs] *n* терра́са; (*BRIT*: *row of houses*) ряд примыка́ющих друг к дру́гу однотѝпных домо́в; (*in street names*): **Rose T~** Роу́з Те́ррес; **the ~s** *npl* (*BRIT*: *standing areas*) трибу́ны *fpl*.

terraced [ˈtɛrəst] *adj* (*garden*) терра́сный; **~ house** дом в ряду́ примыка́ющих друг к дру́гу однотѝпных домо́в.

terracotta [tɛrəˈkɔtə] *n* (*clay*) террако́та; (*colour*) террако́товый цвет ♦ *adj* террако́товый.

terrain [tɛˈreɪn] *n* ландша́фт.

terrible [ˈtɛrɪbl] *adj* ужа́сный* (ужа́сен).

terribly [ˈtɛrɪblɪ] *adv* ужа́сно.

terrier [ˈtɛrɪəʳ] *n* терье́р.

terrific [təˈrɪfɪk] *adj* (*thunderstorm, speed etc*) колосса́льный* (колосса́лен); (*time, party etc*) потряса́ющий*.

terrify [ˈtɛrɪfaɪ] *vt* ужаса́ть (ужасну́ть *perf*); **to be terrified** быть* (*impf*) в у́жасе.

terrifying [ˈtɛrɪfaɪɪŋ] *adj* ужаса́ющий*.

territorial [tɛrɪˈtɔ:rɪəl] *adj* территориа́льный ♦ *n* (*BRIT*: *MIL*) военнослу́жащий* *m adj* территориа́льной а́рмии.

Territorial Army *n* (*BRIT*: *MIL*): **the ~ ~** территориа́льная а́рмия.

territorial waters *npl* территориа́льные во́ды *fpl*.

territory [ˈtɛrɪtərɪ] *n* террито́рия; (*fig*) о́бласть *f*.

terror [ˈtɛrəʳ] *n* у́жас.

terrorism [ˈtɛrərɪzəm] *n* террори́зм.

terrorist [ˈtɛrərɪst] *n* террори́ст(ка*).

terrorize [ˈtɛrəraɪz] *vt* терроризи́ровать (*impf/perf*).

terse [tə:s] *adj* сжа́тый (сжат), кра́ткий* (кра́ток).

tertiary [ˈtə:ʃərɪ] *adj* (*system*) трети́чный; (*third in order, importance*) тре́тий*; **~ education** (*BRIT*) вы́сшее образова́ние.

Terylene® [ˈtɛrɪli:n] *n* териле́н.

TESSA [ˈtɛsə] *abbr* (*BRIT*: = *Tax Exempt Special Savings Account*) безнало́говый сберега́тельный счёт.

test [tɛst] *n* (*trial, check*) прове́рка, тест; (*of courage etc*) испыта́ние; (*MED*) ана́лиз; (*CHEM*) о́пыт; (*SCOL*) контро́льная рабо́та, тест; (*also*: **driving ~**) экза́мен на води́тельские права́ ♦ *vt* проверя́ть (прове́рить *perf*); (*courage*) испы́тывать (испыта́ть *perf*); (*MED*) анализи́ровать (*impf/perf*); **to put sth to the ~** подверга́ть (подве́ргнуть* *perf*) что-н прове́рке; **to ~ sth for sth** проверя́ть (прове́рить *perf*) что-н на что-н.

testament [ˈtɛstəmənt] *n* свиде́тельство; **the Old/New T~** Ве́тхий*/Но́вый заве́т.

test ban *n* (*also*: **nuclear ~ ~**) запреще́ние испыта́ний я́дерного ору́жия.

test card *n* (*TV*) телевизио́нная табли́ца.

test case *n* (*LAW, fig*) про́бное *or* прецеде́нтное де́ло.

testes [ˈtɛsti:z] *npl* (*ANAT*) яи́чки *ntpl*.

test flight *n* испыта́тельный полёт.

testicle [ˈtɛstɪkl] *n* яи́чко*.

testify [ˈtɛstɪfaɪ] *vi* (*LAW*) дава́ть* (дать* *perf*) показа́ния; **to ~ to sth** свиде́тельствовать (*impf*) о чём-н.

testimonial [tɛstɪˈməunɪəl] *n* (*BRIT*: *reference*) рекоменда́ция.

·testimony ['tɛstɪmənɪ] *n* (*LAW*: *statement*) показа́ние, свиде́тельство; (*clear proof*): **to be (a) ~ to** явля́ться (яви́ться* *perf*) свиде́тельством +*gen*.
testing ['tɛstɪŋ] *adj* (*situation, period*) испыта́тельный.
test match *n* (*CRICKET, RUGBY*) междунаро́дный матч.
testosterone [tɛs'tɔstərəun] *n* тестостеро́н.
test paper *n* (*SCOL*) экзаменацио́нный биле́т.
test pilot *n* лётчик-испыта́тель *m*.
test tube *n* проби́рка*.
test-tube baby ['tɛsttjuːb-] *n* ребёнок, зача́тый с по́мощью иску́сственного оплодотворе́ния в проби́рке.
testy ['tɛstɪ] *adj* (*person, comment*) невы́держанный* (невы́держан).
tetanus ['tɛtənəs] *n* столбня́к*.
tetchy ['tɛtʃɪ] *adj* (*person, behaviour*) раздражи́тельный* (раздражи́телен).
tether ['tɛðə'] *vt* (*animal*) привя́зывать (привяза́ть* *perf*) ◆ *n*: **at the end of one's ~** на гра́ни сры́ва.
Texas ['tɛksəs] *n* Теха́с.
text [tɛkst] *n* текст.
textbook ['tɛkstbuk] *n* уче́бник.
textiles ['tɛkstaɪlz] *npl* (*fabrics*) тексти́льные изде́лия *ntpl*; (*TECH*) тексти́ль *msg*; (*textile industry*) тексти́льная промы́шленность *fsg*.
textual ['tɛkstjuəl] *adj*: **~ analysis** ана́лиз те́кста.
texture ['tɛkstʃə'] *n* (*of cloth, soil*) строе́ние; (*feel: of cloth, silk*) факту́ра; (*of skin*) ка́чество.
TGWU *n abbr* (*BRIT*) = *Transport and General Workers' Union*.
Thai [taɪ] *adj* тайла́ндский ◆ *n* таила́ндец* (-дка*).
Thailand ['taɪlænd] *n* Таила́нд.
thalidomide [θə'lɪdəmaɪd] *n* талидоми́д.
Thames [tɛmz] *n*: **the ~** Те́мза.
than [ðæn] *conj* (*in comparisons*): **you have more ~ ten** у Вас бо́льше десяти́; **I have more/less work ~ you/Paul** у меня́ бо́льше/ме́ньше рабо́ты, чем у Вас/у Па́вла; **she is older ~ you think** она́ ста́рше, чем Вы ду́маете; **more ~ once** не раз; **more ~ three times** бо́лее *or* бо́льше трёх раз.
thank [θæŋk] *vt* благодари́ть (поблагодари́ть *perf*); **~ you (very much)** (большо́е) спаси́бо; **~ God!** сла́ва Бо́гу!
thankful ['θæŋkful] *adj*: **~ (for)** благода́рный* (благода́рен) (за +*acc*); **~ that** (*relieved*) благода́рный за то, что.
thankfully ['θæŋkfəlɪ] *adv* к сча́стью; **~ there were few victims** к сча́стью, жертв бы́ло ма́ло.
thankless ['θæŋklɪs] *adj* неблагода́рный*.

thanks [θæŋks] *npl* благода́рность *fsg* ◆ *excl* спаси́бо; **many ~, ~ a lot** большо́е спаси́бо; **~ to** благодаря́ +*dat*.
Thanksgiving (Day) ['θæŋksgɪvɪŋ(-)] *n* (*US*) День* *m* благодаре́ния.

KEYWORD

that [ðæt] (*pl* **those**) *adj* (*demonstrative*) тот*; **that man** тот мужчи́на; **which book would you like? – that one over there** каку́ю кни́гу Вы хоти́те? – вон ту, пожа́луйста; **I like this film better than that one** мне э́тот фильм нра́вится бо́льше, чем тот
◆ *pron* **1** (*demonstrative: in questions*): **who's/what's that?** кто/что э́то?; **is that you?** э́то Вы?; **we talked of this and that** мы говори́ли о том о сём; **that's how ...** вот так ...; **that's what he said** так он сказа́л; **what happened after that?** а что пото́м произошло́?; **that is (to say)** то есть
2 (*direct object*) кото́рый (*f* кото́рая, *nt* кото́рое, *pl* кото́рые); (*indirect object*) кото́рому (*f* кото́рой, *pl* кото́рым); (*after prep*: +*acc*) кото́рый (*f* кото́рую, *nt* кото́рое, *pl* кото́рые); (: +*gen*) кото́рого (*f* кото́рой, *pl* кото́рых); (: +*dat*) кото́рому (*f* кото́рой, *pl* кото́рым); (: +*instr*) кото́рым (*f* кото́рой, *pl* кото́рыми); (: +*prp*) кото́ром (*f* кото́рой, *pl* кото́рых); **the theory that we discussed last week** тео́рия, кото́рую мы обсужда́ли на про́шлом неде́ле; **all (that) I have** всё, что у меня́ есть
3 (*of time*) когда́; **the day (that) he died** день, когда́ он умер
◆ *conj* что; (*introducing purpose*) что́бы; **he thought that I was ill** он ду́мал, что я был бо́лен; **she suggested that I phone you** она́ предложи́ла, что́бы я Вам позвони́л
◆ *adv* (*demonstrative*): **I can't work that much** я не могу́ сто́лько мно́го рабо́тать; **it can't be that bad** ну не так уж всё пло́хо; **I have drunk that much** я вы́пил вот сто́лько; **the wall's about that high and that thick** стена́ приме́рно вот тако́й высоты́ и вот тако́й толщины́.

thatched [θætʃt] *adj* соло́менный.
Thatcherism ['θætʃərɪzəm] *n* тэтчери́зм.
Thatcherite ['θætʃəraɪt] *n* сторо́нник(-ица) поли́тики Тэ́тчер.
thaw [θɔː] *n* о́ттепель *f* ◆ *vi* (*ice*) та́ять (раста́ять *perf*); (*food*) отта́ять (отта́ять *perf*) ◆ *vt* (*food: also: ~ out*) отта́ивать (отта́ять *perf*); **it's ~ing** (*weather*) о́ттепель.

KEYWORD

the [ðiː] *def art*: **1: the books/children are in the library** кни́ги/де́ти в библиоте́ке; **the rich and the poor** бога́тые *pl adj* и бе́дные *pl adj*; **to attempt the impossible** пыта́ться

---

* marks translations which have irregular inflections. The Russian-English side of the dictionary gives inflectional information.

(попытаться *perf*) сделать невозможное
2 (*in titles*): **Elizabeth the First** Елизавета Первая
3 (*in comparisons*): **the more I think about it the more I like it** чем больше я думаю об этом, тем больше мне это нравится.

theatre ['θɪətəʳ] (*US* **theater**) *n* театр; (*also*: **lecture** ~) лекционный зал; (*MED*: *also*: **operating** ~) операционная *f adj*.

theatregoer ['θɪətəgəuəʳ] *n* театрал(ка*).

theatrical [θɪ'ætrɪkl] *adj* театральный; (*gestures*) театральный* (театрален); ~ **company** театральная труппа.

theft [θεft] *n* кража.

their [δεəʳ] *adj* их; (*referring to subject of sentence*) свой.

theirs [δεəz] *pron* (*see adj*) их; свой; *see also* **mine**[1].

them [δεm] *pron* (*direct*) их; (*indirect*) им; (*after prep*: +*gen*, +*prp*) их; (: +*dat*) им; (: +*instr*) ими; (*referring to subject of sentence*) свой; **a few of** ~ **are going to the cinema** некоторые из них идут в кино; **give me a few of** ~ дайте мне их немного; *see also* **me**.

theme [θiːm] *n* тема.

theme park *n парк, стилизованный под определённую эпоху или тему.*

theme song *n* песня из кинофильма.

theme tune *n* мелодия из кинофильма.

themselves [δəm'sɛlvz] *pl pron* (*reflexive*) себя; (*emphatic*) сами; (*after prep*: +*gen*) себя; (: +*dat*, +*prp*) себе; (: +*instr*) собой; (*alone*) (**all**) **by** ~ одни; **they shared the money between** ~ они разделили деньги между собой; *see also* **myself**.

then [δεn] *adv* потом; (*at that time*) тогда ◆ *conj* (*therefore*) тогда ◆ *adj*: **the** ~ **president** тогдашний* президент; **from** ~ **on** с тех пор; **by** ~ (*past*) к этому *or* тому времени; **we should know by** ~ к тому времени мы уже будем знать; **if** ... ~ ... если ... то ...; **before** ~ до этого *or* того времени; **until** ~ до тех пор; **and** ~ **what?** и что потом?; **what do you want me to do** ~? (*afterwards*) что Вы мне делать потом?; (*in that case*) что Вы мне делать тогда?

theologian [θɪə'ləudʒən] *n* богослов, теолог.

theological [θɪə'lɔdʒɪkl] *adj* теологический*, богословский.

theology [θɪ'ɔlədʒɪ] *n* теология, богословие.

theorem ['θɪərəm] *n* теорема.

theoretical [θɪə'rɛtɪkl] *adj* теоретический*.

theorize ['θɪəraɪz] *vi* теоретизировать (*impf*).

theory ['θɪərɪ] *n* теория; **in** ~ теоретически, в теории.

therapeutic(al) [θɛrə'pju:tɪk(l)] *adj* терапевтический.

therapist ['θɛrəpɪst] *n* врач.

therapy ['θɛrəpɪ] *n* терапия.

KEYWORD

there [δεəʳ] *adv*: **1**: **there is some milk in the fridge** молоко в холодильнике; **there is someone in the room** в комнате кто-то есть; **there will be a lot of people at the concert** на концерте будет много народу; **there was a book/there were flowers on the the table** на столе лежала книга/стояли цветы; **there has been an accident** произошла авария
2 (*referring to place*: *position*) там; (: *motion*) туда; **there he is!** вот он!:
3: **there, there** (*esp to child*) ну, ничего, ничего.

thereabouts ['δεərə'bauts] *adv* (*place*) поблизости; (*amount*) около этого.

thereafter [δεər'ɑ:ftəʳ] *adv* с того времени.

thereby ['δεəbaɪ] *adv* таким образом.

therefore ['δεəfɔ:ʳ] *adv* поэтому.

there's ['δεəz] = **there is, there has.**

thereupon [δεərə'pɔn] *adv* (*at that point*) вслед за тем; (*formal*: *on that subject*) в связи с этим.

thermal ['θə:ml] *adj* (*springs*) горячий*; (*energy*) термический*; (*underwear*) утеплённый*; (*paper, printer*) термографический.

thermodynamics ['θə:mədaɪ'næmɪks] *n* термодинамика.

thermometer [θə'mɔmɪtəʳ] *n* термометр, градусник.

thermonuclear ['θə:məu'nju:klɪəʳ] *adj* термоядерный.

Thermos® ['θə:məs] *n* (*also*: ~ **flask**) термос.

thermostat ['θə:məustæt] *n* термостат.

thesaurus [θɪ'sɔ:rəs] *n* тезаурус.

these [δi:z] *pl adj, pron* эти.

theses ['θi:si:z] *npl of* **thesis.**

thesis ['θi:sɪs] (*pl* **theses**) *n* (*SCOL*) диссертация; (*theory*) тезис.

they [δeɪ] *pron* они; ~ **say that ...** говорят, что ...

they'd [δeɪd] = **they had, they would.**

they'll [δeɪl] = **they shall, they will.**

they're [δεəʳ] = **they are.**

they've [δeɪv] = **they have.**

thick [θɪk] *adj* (*in shape*) толстый (толст); (*in consistency*) густой (густ); (*inf*: *stupid*) тупой (туп) ◆ *n*: **in the** ~ **of the battle** в самой гуще битвы; **the wall is 20 cm** ~ толщина стены – 20 см.

thicken ['θɪkn] *vi* (*fog etc*) сгущаться (сгуститься* *perf*); (*plot*) усложняться (усложниться *perf*) ◆ *vt* (*sauce etc*) делать (сделать *perf*) гуще.

thicket ['θɪkɪt] *n* заросли *fpl*.

thickly ['θɪklɪ] *adv* (*spread*) густо; (*cut*) толсто; ~ **populated** густонаселённый.

thickness ['θɪknɪs] *n* (*size*) толщина; (*layer*) слой*.

thickset [θɪk'sɛt] *adj* коренастый (коренаст).

thick-skinned [θɪk'skɪnd] *adj* (*fig*) толстокожий*.

thief [θi:f] (*pl* **thieves**) *n* вор(о́вка).

thieves [θi:vz] *npl of* **thief**.

thieving ['θi:vɪŋ] *n* воровство́.

thigh [θaɪ] *n* бедро́*.

thighbone ['θaɪbəun] *n* (*ANAT*) бе́дренная кость* *f*.

thimble ['θɪmbl] *n* напёрсток*.

thin [θɪn] *adj* то́нкий* (то́нок); (*person, animal*) худо́й (худ); (*soup, sauce*) жи́дкий* (жи́док); (*hair, crowd*) ре́дкий*; (*fog*) лёгкий* (лёгок) ◆ *vt*: **to ~ (down)** (*sauce, paint*) разбавля́ть (разба́вить* *perf*); (*hair. at hairdresser's*) разре́живать (*impf*) ◆ *vi* (*fog*) рассе́иваться (рассе́яться *perf*); (*also:* **~ out**: *crowd*) реде́ть (пореде́ть *perf*); **his hair is ~ning** у него́ реде́ют во́лосы.

thing [θɪŋ] *n* вещь* *f*; **~s** *npl* (*belongings*) ве́щи* *fpl*; **first ~ (in the morning)** пе́рвым де́лом (с утра́); **last ~ (at night), he ...** напосле́док (но́чью) он ...; **the ~ is ...** де́ло в том, что ...; **for one ~** во-пе́рвых; **she's got a ~ about mice** она́ не выно́сит мыше́й; **don't worry about a ~** ни о чём не беспоко́йтесь; **you'll do no such ~!** попро́буй то́лько!; **poor ~** бедня́жка* *m/f*; **the best ~ would be to ...** са́мое лу́чшее бы́ло бы +*infin* ...; **how are ~s?** как дела́?

think [θɪŋk] (*pt,pp* **thought**) *vt* (*reflect, believe*) ду́мать (*impf*); (*imagine*) предполага́ть (предположи́ть* *perf*); **to ~ of** ду́мать (поду́мать *perf*) о +*prp*; (*remember*) вспомина́ть (вспо́мнить *perf*); (*consider*) приводи́ть* (привести́* *perf*); **what did you ~ of them?** что Вы о них ду́маете?; **to ~ about sth/sb** ду́мать (поду́мать *perf*) о чём-н/ком-н; **I'll ~ about it** я поду́маю (об э́том); **I am ~ing of starting a business** я ду́маю нача́ть би́знес; **I ~ so/not** я ду́маю, что да/нет; **to ~ well of sb** хорошо́ о ком-н ду́мать (*impf*); **to ~ aloud** ду́мать (*impf*) вслух; **~ again!** поду́майте ещё раз!

▸ **think out** *vt* (*plan, solution*) обду́мывать (обду́мать *perf*), проду́мывать (проду́мать *perf*)

▸ **think over** *vt* обду́мывать (обду́мать *perf*); **I'd like to ~ things over** я хочу́ всё обду́мать

▸ **think through** *vt* проду́мывать (проду́мать *perf*) до конца́

▸ **think up** *vt* приду́мывать (приду́мать *perf*).

thinking ['θɪŋkɪŋ] *n* мышле́ние; **to my way of ~** на мой взгляд.

think-tank ['θɪŋktæŋk] *n* мозгово́й центр.

thinly ['θɪnlɪ] *adv* то́нко.

thinness ['θɪnnɪs] *n* то́нкость *f*.

third [θə:d] *adj* тре́тий* ◆ *n* (*fraction*) треть *f*, одна́ тре́тья *f adj*; (*AUT: also:* **~ gear**) тре́тья ско́рость *f*; (*BRIT: SCOL: degree*) *диплом*

тре́тьей и́ли ни́зшей сте́пени; **a ~ of** треть +*gen*, тре́тья часть +*gen*; *see also* **fifth**.

third-degree burns ['θə:ddɪgri:-] *npl* (*MED*) ожо́ги *mpl* тре́тьей сте́пени.

thirdly ['θə:dlɪ] *adv* в-тре́тьих.

third party insurance *n* (*BRIT*) страхова́ние в по́льзу тре́тьей стороны́.

third-rate ['θə:d'reɪt] *adj* (*pej: performance, actor etc*) третьесо́ртный* (третьесо́ртен).

Third World *n*: **the ~ ~** Тре́тий* мир.

thirst [θə:st] *n* (*also fig*) жа́жда.

thirsty ['θə:stɪ] *adj*: **to be ~** (*person, animal*) хоте́ть* (*impf*) пить; **I am ~** я хочу́ *or* мне хо́чется пить; **gardening is ~ work** рабо́та в саду́ вызыва́ет жа́жду.

thirteen [θə:'ti:n] *n* трина́дцать*; *see also* **five**.

thirteenth [θə:'ti:nθ] *adj* трина́дцатый; *see also* **fifth**.

thirtieth ['θə:tɪθ] *adj* тридца́тый; *see also* **fifth**.

thirty ['θə:tɪ] *n* три́дцать*; *see also* **fifty**.

KEYWORD
---

this [ðɪs] (*pl* **these**) *adj* (*demonstrative*) э́тот; **this man** э́тот мужчи́на; **which book would you like? – this one please** каку́ю кни́гу Вы хоти́те? – вот э́ту, пожа́луйста

◆ *pron* (*demonstrative*) э́тот (*f* э́та, *nt* э́то); **who/what is this?** кто/что э́то?; **this is where I live** вот здесь я живу́; **this is what he said** вот, что он сказа́л; **this is Mr Brown** э́то ми́стер Бра́ун

◆ *adv* (*demonstrative*): **this high/long** *etc* тако́й высоты́/длины́ *etc*; **the dog was about this big** соба́ка была́ приме́рно тако́го разме́ра *or* тако́й величины́; **we can't stop now we've gone this far** мы не мо́жет тепе́рь останови́ться, ведь мы так далеко́ ушли́.

thistle ['θɪsl] *n* чертополо́х.

thong [θɔŋ] *n* реме́нь* *m*.

thorn [θɔ:n] *n* шип, коло́чка*.

thorny ['θɔ:nɪ] *adj* (*plant, tree*) коло́чий* (коло́ч); (*problem*) нелёгкий*.

thorough ['θʌrə] *adj* (*search, wash*) тща́тельный* (тща́телен); (*knowledge, research*) основа́тельный* (основа́телен); (*person*) скрупулёзный* (скрупулёзен).

thoroughbred ['θʌrəbrɛd] *n* чистокро́вная *or* чистопоро́дная ло́шадь *f*.

thoroughfare ['θʌrəfɛə] *n* гла́вная арте́рия (го́рода), тра́нспортная магистра́ль *f*; **"no ~"** (*BRIT*) "Прое́зда нет".

thoroughgoing ['θʌrəgəuɪŋ] *adj* доскона́льный* (доскона́лен), тща́тельный* (тща́телен).

thoroughly ['θʌrəlɪ] *adv* (*fully*) тща́тельно; (*very*) вполне́; **he ~ agreed** он по́лностью согласи́лся.

thoroughness ['θʌrənɪs] *n* тща́тельность *f*.

---

* marks translations which have irregular inflections. The Russian-English side of the dictionary gives inflectional information.

those [ðəuz] *pl adj, pron* те.
though [ðəu] *conj* хотя́ ♦ *adv* в про́чем,
одна́ко; **even** ~ ... хотя́ и ...; **it's not easy,** ~ в
про́чем *or* одна́ко э́то не про́сто.
thought [θɔ:t] *pt, pp of* **think** ♦ *n* (*idea, intention*)
мысль *f*; (*reflection*) размышле́ние; (*opinion*)
соображе́ние; **after much** ~ по́сле до́лгих
размышле́ний; **I've just had a** ~ мне то́лько
что пришла́ в го́лову мысль; **to give sth**
some ~ обду́мывать (обду́мать *perf*) о
чём-н.
thoughtful ['θɔ:tful] *adj* (*deep in thought*)
заду́мчивый (заду́мчив); (*serious*)
глубо́кий*; (*considerate*) внима́тельный*
(внима́телен).
thoughtfully ['θɔ:tfəlɪ] *adv* (*pensively*)
заду́мчиво; (*considerately*) внима́тельно.
thoughtless ['θɔ:tlɪs] *adj* безду́мный*
(безду́мен), неосмотри́тельный*
(неосмотри́телен).
thoughtlessly ['θɔ:tlɪslɪ] *adv* безду́мно,
неосмотри́тельно.
thoughtlessness ['θɔ:tlɪsnɪs] *n* безду́мность *f*,
неосмотри́тельность *f*.
thought-out [θɔ:t'aut] *adj* проду́манный*
(проду́ман).
thought-provoking ['θɔ:tprəvəukɪŋ] *adj*
провоци́рующий на мы́сли.
thousand ['θauzənd] *n* ты́сяча*; **two** ~ две
ты́сячи; **five** ~ пять ты́сяч; **about a** ~ о́коло
ты́сячи; **people came in their** ~s *or* **by the** ~
пришли́ ты́сячи люде́й; ~s of ты́сячи +*gen*.
thousandth ['θauzəntθ] *adj* ты́сячный.
thrash [θræʃ] *vt* (*beat*) поро́ть* (вы́пороть*
perf); (*inf: defeat*) побива́ть (поби́ть* *perf*)
► **thrash about** *vi* мета́ться* (*impf*)
► **thrash around** *vi* = **thrash about**
► **thrash out** *vt* (*problem*) прораба́тывать
(прорабо́тать *perf*).
thrashing ['θræʃɪŋ] *n*: **to give sb a** ~ поро́ть*
(вы́пороть* *perf*) кого́-н.
thread [θrɛd] *n* (*yarn*) нить *f*, ни́тка*; (*of screw*)
резьба́ ♦ *vt* (*needle*) продева́ть (проде́ть*
perf) ни́тку в +*acc*; **to** ~ **one's way between**
пробира́ться (пробра́ться* *perf*) че́рез *or*
сквозь +*acc*.
threadbare ['θrɛdbɛəʳ] *adj* потёртый (потёрт),
потрёпанный* (потрёпан).
threat [θrɛt] *n* (*also fig*) угро́за; **to be under** ~ **of**
быть* (*impf*) под угро́зой +*gen*.
threaten ['θrɛtn] *vi* (*storm, danger*) грози́ть*
(*impf*) ♦ *vt*: **to** ~ **sb with** угрожа́ть (*impf*) *or*
грози́ть* (*impf*) кому́-н +*instr*; **to** ~ **to do**
угрожа́ть (*impf*) *or* грози́ть* (*impf*) +*infin*.
threatening ['θrɛtnɪŋ] *adj* угрожа́ющий*.
three [θri:] *n* три*; (*collective*) тро́е*; *see also*
five.
three-dimensional [θri:dɪ'mɛnʃənl] *adj* (*object*)
трёхме́рный; (*film, picture, image*)
стереоскопи́ческий.
threefold ['θri:fəuld] *adv*: **to increase** ~

увели́чиваться (увели́читься *perf*) в три
ра́за.
three-piece suit ['θri:pi:s-] *n* (костю́м)-тро́йка
m.
three-piece suite *n* мя́гкая ме́бель *f*.
three-ply [θri:'plaɪ] *adj* трехсло́йный.
three quarters *npl* три* че́тверти; ~ ~ **full**
по́лный* на три че́тверти.
three-wheeler (car) [θri:'wi:ləʳ(-)] *n*
трехколёсная маши́на.
thresh [θrɛʃ] *vt* молоти́ть* (*impf*).
threshing machine ['θrɛʃɪŋ-] *n* (*old*)
молоти́лка*.
threshold ['θrɛʃhəuld] *n* (*also fig*) поро́г; **to be**
on the ~ **of** (*fig*) быть* (*impf*) на поро́ге +*gen*.
threshold agreement *n* (*ECON*) спо́соб
приведе́ния в соотве́тствие за́работной
пла́ты рабо́тников со сто́имостью жи́зни.
threw [θru:] *pt of* **throw**.
thrift [θrɪft] *n* бережли́вость *f*.
thrifty ['θrɪftɪ] *adj* бережли́вый (бережли́в).
thrill [θrɪl] *n* тре́пет ♦ *vi* трепета́ть* (*impf*) ♦ *vt*
(*person, audience*) восхища́ть (восхити́ть*
perf); **to be** ~**ed** быть* (*impf*) в восто́рге; **I am**
~**ed** я восто́ржен.
thriller ['θrɪləʳ] *n* три́ллер.
thrilling ['θrɪlɪŋ] *adj* захва́тывающий*.
thrive [θraɪv] (*pt* **thrived** *or* **throve,** *pp* **thrived**) *vi*
(*child, animal, business*) процвета́ть (*impf*);
(*plant*) разраста́ться (разрасти́сь* *perf*); **to** ~
on sth процвета́ть (*impf*) на что-н.
thriving ['θraɪvɪŋ] *adj* процвета́ющий.
throat [θrəut] *n* го́рло; **I have a sore** ~ у меня́
боли́т го́рло.
throb [θrɔb] *n* (*of heart*) бие́ние; (*of wound*)
пульса́ция; (*of engine*) вибра́ция ♦ *vi* (*heart*)
би́ться* (*impf*); (*with pain: arm*) ныть* (*impf*);
(*machine: vibrate*) вибри́ровать* (*impf*); **my**
head is ~**ing** у меня́ гуди́т голова́.
throes [θrəuz] *npl*: **in the** ~ **of** (*war, moving*
house etc) в лихора́дке +*gen*; **death** ~
смерте́льные му́ки.
thrombosis [θrɔm'bəusɪs] *n* тромбо́з.
throne [θrəun] *n* трон.
throng ['θrɔŋ] *n* толпа́* ♦ *vt* заполня́ть
(запо́лнить *perf*).
throttle ['θrɔtl] *n* (*AUT*) дро́ссель *m* ♦ *vt*
(*strangle*) души́ть* (задуши́ть* *perf*).
through [θru:] *prep* (*space*) че́рез +*acc*; (*water*
etc) в +*acc*; (*time*) в тече́ние +*gen*; (*by means*
of) че́рез +*acc*, посре́дством +*gen*; (*owing to*)
из-за +*gen* ♦ *adj* (*ticket, train*) прямо́й ♦ *adv*
наскво́зь; **he is absent** ~ **illness** он
отсу́тствовал по боле́зни; **(from) Monday** ~
Friday (*US*) с понеде́льника по пя́тницу; **to**
put sb ~ **to sb** (*TEL*) соедини́ть (соедини́ть
perf) кого́-н с кем-н; **to be** ~ (*TEL*)
дозвони́ться (*perf*); **to be** ~ **with sb/sth**
поканчивать (поко́нчить *perf*) с кем-н/чем-н;
"no ~ **road"** (*BRIT*) "нет сквозно́го прое́зда";
"no ~ **traffic"** (*US*) "нет сквозно́го

движе́ния"; **to let sb ~** пропуска́ть (пропусти́ть* *perf*) кого́-н.

throughout [θruːˈaut] *prep* (*place*) по +*dat*; (*time*) в тече́ние +*gen* ♦ *adv* везде́, повсю́ду.

throughput [ˈθruːput] *n* пропускна́я спосо́бность *f*; (*COMPUT*) производи́тельность *f*.

throve [θrəuv] *pt of* **thrive**.

throw [θrəu] (*pt* **threw**, *pp* **thrown**) *n* бросо́к* ♦ *vt* (*object*) броса́ть (бро́сить* *perf*); (*rider*) сбра́сывать (сбро́сить* *perf*); (*fig: person*) сбива́ть (сбить* *perf*) с то́лку; (*pottery*) обраба́тывать (обрабо́тать *perf*) на гонча́рном кру́ге; **to ~ a party** устра́ивать (устро́ить *perf*) ве́чер; **to ~ open** (*doors, windows*) распа́хивать (распахну́ть *perf*); (*competition, race etc*) открыва́ть (откры́ть* *perf*)

▸ **throw about** *vt* (*litter etc*) разбра́сывать (разброса́ть *perf*)

▸ **throw around** *vt* = **throw about**

▸ **throw away** *vt* (*rubbish*) выбра́сывать (вы́бросить* *perf*); (*money*) броса́ть (*impf*) на ве́тер

▸ **throw off** *vt* сбра́сувать (сбро́сить* *perf*)

▸ **throw out** *vt* (*rubbish, person*) выбра́сывать (вы́бросить* *perf*); (*idea*) отверга́ть (отве́ргнуть* *perf*)

▸ **throw together** *vt* (*clothes, meal etc*) сооружа́ть (сооруди́ть* *perf*); (*essay*) набра́сывать (наброса́ть *perf*)

▸ **throw up** *vi* (*vomit*) рвать* (вы́рвать* *perf*); **he threw up** его́ вы́рвало.

throwaway [ˈθrəuəweɪ] *adj* (*toothbrush etc*) однора́зовый; (*line, remark*) ска́занный невзнача́й.

throwback [ˈθrəubæk] *n*: **it's a ~ to** э́то возвра́т к +*dat*.

throw-in [ˈθrəuɪn] *n* (*FOOTBALL*) вбра́сывание.

thrown [θrəun] *pp of* **throw**.

thru [θruː] (*US*) = **through**.

thrush [θrʌʃ] *n* (*ZOOL*) дрозд*; (*MED*) моло́чница.

thrust [θrʌst] (*pt, pp* **thrust**) *n* (*TECH*) дви́жущая си́ла; (*push*) толчо́к*; (*main idea*) направле́ние ♦ *vt* толка́ть (толкну́ть *perf*).

thud [θʌd] *n* глухо́й стук.

thug [θʌg] *n* (*criminal*) головоре́з; (*pej*) банди́т.

thumb [θʌm] *n* (*ANAT*) большо́й па́лец* (*руки́*) ♦ *vt*: **to ~ a lift** (*inf*) голосова́ть* (*impf*); **to give sb/sth the ~s up** (*approve*) одобря́ть (одо́брить *perf*) кого́-н/что-н; **to give sth the ~s down** отверга́ть (отве́ргнуть *perf*) что-н

▸ **thumb through** *vt fus* перели́стывать (перелиста́ть *perf*).

thumb index *n* бу́квенный указа́тель *m* (*на обре́зе кни́ги*).

thumbnail [ˈθʌmneɪl] *n* но́готь* *m* (*большо́го па́льца руки́*).

thumbnail sketch *n* набро́сок*.

thumbtack [ˈθʌmtæk] *n* (*US*) кно́пка*.

thump [θʌmp] *n* (*blow*) уда́р; (*sound*) глухо́й стук ♦ *vt* (*person*) сту́кнуть (*perf*) ♦ *vi* (*heart etc*) стуча́ть (*impf*).

thumping [ˈθʌmpɪŋ] *adj* (*inf: majority, victory etc*) грома́дный; (: *headache, cold*) жу́ткий*.

thunder [ˈθʌndə'] *n* гром ♦ *vi* (*shout*) реве́ть (*impf*); (*train etc*): **to ~ past** громыха́ть (прогромыха́ть *perf*) ми́мо; **it's ~ing** греми́т гром.

thunderbolt [ˈθʌndəbəult] *n* уда́р мо́лнии.

thunderclap [ˈθʌndəklæp] *n* раска́т гро́ма.

thunderous [ˈθʌndrəs] *adj* (*applause*) оглуши́тельный; (*crash*) громово́й.

thunderstorm [ˈθʌndəstɔːm] *n* гроза́*.

thunderstruck [ˈθʌndəstrʌk] *adj* (*fig*): **I was ~** я был потрясён.

thundery [ˈθʌndərɪ] *adj* грозово́й.

Thur(s). *abbr* = **Thursday**.

Thursday [ˈθəːzdɪ] *n* четве́рг*; *see also* **Tuesday**.

thus [ðʌs] *adv* таки́м о́бразом.

thwart [θwɔːt] *vt* (*person*) чини́ть (*impf*) препя́тствия +*dat*; (*plans*) расстра́ивать (расстро́ить *perf*).

thyme [taɪm] *n* тимья́н.

thyroid [ˈθaɪrɔɪd] *n* (*also:* **~ gland**) щитови́дная железа́.

tiara [tɪˈɑːrə] *n* тиа́ра.

Tiber [ˈtaɪbə'] *n*: **the ~** Тибр.

Tibet [tɪˈbɛt] *n* Тибе́т.

Tibetan [tɪˈbɛtən] *adj* тибе́тский* ♦ *n* тибе́тец(-е́тка*); (*LING*) тибе́тский язы́к*.

tibia [ˈtɪbɪə] *n* большеберцо́вая кость* *f*.

tic [tɪk] *n* тик.

tick [tɪk] *n* (*sound: of clock*) ти́канье; (*mark*) га́лочка*; (*ZOOL*) клещ* ♦ *vi* (*clock*) ти́кать (*impf*) ♦ *vt* отмеча́ть (отме́тить* *perf*) га́лочкой; **to put a ~ against sth** ста́вить* (поста́вить* *perf*) га́лочку ря́дом с +*instr*; **in a ~** (*BRIT: inf*) минут́очку; **to buy sth on ~** (*BRIT: inf*) покупа́ть (купи́ть* *perf*) что-н в креди́т

▸ **tick off** *vt* (*item on list*) отмеча́ть (отме́тить* *perf*) га́лочкой; (*person*) отчи́тывать (отчита́ть *perf*)

▸ **tick over** *vi* (*engine*) рабо́тать (*impf*) на холосто́м ходу́; (*fig: business*) идти́* (*impf*) свои́м чередо́м.

ticker tape [ˈtɪkəteɪp] *n* ти́керная ле́нта, ти́кер; (*US: in celebrations*) серпанти́н из ти́керной ле́нты.

ticket [ˈtɪkɪt] *n* биле́т; (*price tag*) этике́тка*; (*from cash register*) чек; (*also:* **parking ~**) штраф за наруше́ние пра́вил паркова́ния; (*US: POL*) спи́сок* кандида́тов па́ртии.

ticket agency *n* (*THEAT*) театра́льная ка́сса.

---

* marks translations which have irregular inflections. The Russian-English side of the dictionary gives inflectional information.

ticket collector *n* контролёр.
ticket holder *n* владе́лец(-лица) биле́та.
ticket inspector *n* контролёр.
ticket office *n* биле́тная ка́сса.
tickle ['tɪkl] *vt* щекота́ть* (пощекота́ть* *perf*) ♦ *vi* щекота́ть* (*impf*).
ticklish ['tɪklɪʃ] *adj* (*problem*) щекотли́вый (щекотли́в); (*blanket*) колю́чий* (колю́ч); (*cough*) перша́щий; (*person*): **to be ~** боя́ться* (*impf*) щеко́тки.
tidal ['taɪdl] *adj* (*force*) прили́вный; (*estuary*) прили́во-отли́вный.
tidal wave *n* прили́вная волна́*.
tidbit ['tɪdbɪt] *n* (*US*) = **titbit**.
tiddlywinks ['tɪdlɪwɪŋks] *n* бло́шки *pl*.
tide [taɪd] *n* прили́в и отли́в; (*fig: of events*) волна́; (*of fashion, opinion*) направле́ние; **high ~** по́лная вода́*, вы́сшая то́чка прили́ва; **low ~** ма́лая вода́*, ни́зшая то́чка отли́ва
▶ **tide over** *vt* (*help out*): **this money will ~ me over till Monday** на э́ти де́ньги я смогу́ продержа́ться до понеде́льника.
tidily ['taɪdɪlɪ] *adv* (*dress*) опря́тно; (*arrange*) аккура́тно.
tidiness ['taɪdɪnɪs] *n* опря́тность *f*; (*of person*) аккура́тность *f*.
tidy ['taɪdɪ] *adj* опря́тный* (опря́тен); (*person, mind*) аккура́тный* (аккура́тен) ♦ *vt* (*also: ~ up*) прибира́ть (прибра́ть* *perf*); **to ~ o.s. up** приводи́ть* (привести́* *perf*) себя́ в поря́док.
tie [taɪ] *n* (*string etc*) шнуро́к*; (*BRIT: also: necktie*) га́лстук; (*fig: link*) связь *f*; (*SPORT: game, match*) игра́ вничью́; (: *draw*) ничья́; (*US: RAIL*) шпа́ла ♦ *vt* завя́зывать (завяза́ть* *perf*) ♦ *vi* (*SPORT etc*) игра́ть (сыгра́ть *perf*) вничью́; "**black/white ~**" *пара́дный костю́м*; **family ~s** семе́йные у́зы; **to ~ sth in a bow** завя́зывать (завяза́ть* *perf*) что-н ба́нтом; **to ~ a knot in sth** завя́зывать (завяза́ть* *perf*) что-н узло́м
▶ **tie down** *vt* (*fig: person*) свя́зывать (связа́ть* *perf*)
▶ **tie in** *vi*: **to ~ in with** (*correspond*) увя́зываться (*impf*) с +*instr*
▶ **tie on** *vt* (*BRIT: label etc*) привя́зывать (привяза́ть* *perf*)
▶ **tie up** *vt* (*dog, boat*) привя́зывать (привяза́ть* *perf*); (*prisoner, parcel*) свя́зывать (связа́ть* *perf*); (*arrangements*) организова́ть (*impf/perf*); **I'm ~d up at the moment** (*busy*) я сейча́с о́чень за́нят.
tie-break ['taɪbreɪk] *n* (*TENNIS*) реша́ющий гейм *по́сле ничейного се́та*; (*in quiz*) дополни́тельный реша́ющий* вопро́с.
tiebreaker ['taɪbreɪkə'] *n* = **tie-break**.
tie-on ['taɪɔn] *adj* (*BRIT: label*) привязно́й.
tiepin ['taɪpɪn] *n* (*BRIT*) була́вка* для га́лстука.
tier [tɪə'] *n* (*of stadium etc*) я́рус; (*of cake*) слой*.
Tierra del Fuego [tɪ'ɛrədɛl'fweɪgəu] *n* Óгненная Земля́*.

tie tack *n* (*US*) = **tiepin**.
tiff [tɪf] *n* размо́лвка*.
tiger ['taɪgə'] *n* тигр.
tight [taɪt] *adj* (*firm: rope*) туго́й; (*narrow: shoes, bend, clothes*) у́зкий* (у́зок); (*strict: security*) стро́гий*; (*schedule, budget*) жёсткий* ♦ *adv* (*hold, squeeze*) кре́пко; (*shut*) пло́тно; **money is ~** у меня́ ту́го с деньга́ми; **he is ~** (*inf: drunk*) он навеселе́; **the suitcase is packed ~** чемода́н ту́го наби́т; **everybody hold ~!** все держи́тесь кре́пко!
tighten ['taɪtn] *vt* (*rope*) натя́гивать (натяну́ть* *perf*); (*screw*) подтя́гивать (подтяну́ть *perf*); (*grip*) кре́пче сжима́ть (сжать* *perf*); (*security*) уси́ливать (уси́лить *perf*) ♦ *vi* (*grip*) кре́пче сжима́ться (сжа́ться* *perf*); (*rope*) натя́гиваться (натяну́ться *perf*).
tightfisted [taɪt'fɪstɪd] *adj* прижи́мистый (прижи́мист).
tight-lipped ['taɪt'lɪpd] *adj* скры́тный* (скры́тен); (*fig: through anger*) с поджа́тыми губа́ми.
tightly ['taɪtlɪ] *adv* (*grasp*) кре́пко.
tightrope ['taɪtrəup] *n* натя́нутый кана́т; **to be on** *or* **walking a ~** (*fig*) ходи́ть* (*impf*) по острию́ ножа́.
tightrope walker *n* канатохо́дец*.
tights [taɪts] *npl* (*BRIT*) колго́тки* *pl*.
tigress ['taɪgrɪs] *n* тигри́ца.
tilde ['tɪldə] *n* (*LING*) ти́льда.
tile [taɪl] *n* (*on roof*) черепи́ца; (*on floor*) пли́тка*; (*on wall*) ка́фельная пли́тка* ♦ *vt*: **to ~ the floor/bathroom** выкла́дывать (вы́ложить* *perf*) пли́ткой/ка́фелем; **~s** (*on wall*) ка́фель *m*; **to ~ the roof** крыть* (покры́ть* *perf*) кры́шу черепи́цей.
tiled [taɪld] *adj* (*see n*) черепи́чный; пли́точный; ка́фельный.
till [tɪl] *n* (*in shop etc*) ка́сса ♦ *vt* (*land: cultivate*) возде́лывать (возде́лать *perf*) ♦ *prep, conj* = **until**.
tiller ['tɪlə'] *n* (*NAUT*) ру́мпель *m*.
tilt [tɪlt] *vt* наклоня́ть (наклони́ть* *perf*); (*head*) склоня́ть (склони́ть* *perf*) ♦ *vi* наклоня́ться (наклони́ться* *perf*) ♦ *n* (*slope*) накло́н; **to wear one's hat at a ~** носи́ть* (*impf*) шля́пу набекре́нь; (**at**) **full ~** во весь дух.
timber ['tɪmbə'] *n* (*material*) древеси́на; (*trees*) лес.
time [taɪm] *n* вре́мя* *nt*; (*epoch: often pl*) времена́* *pl*, вре́мя*; (*occasion, also MATH*) раз; (*MUS*) разме́р, темп ♦ *vt* (*measure time of: race etc*) засека́ть (засе́чь* *perf*) вре́мя; (*fix moment for: visit etc*) выбира́ть (вы́брать* *perf*) вре́мя; **a long ~** до́лго; **for the ~ being** пока́; **4 at a ~** по четы́ре; **from ~ to ~** вре́мя от вре́мени; **after ~**, **time and again** сно́ва и сно́ва; **at ~s** времена́ми; **in ~** (*soon enough*) во́время; (*after some time*) со вре́менем; (*MUS: be*) в та́кте; (: *play*) в такт; **in a week's ~** че́рез неде́лю; **in no ~** в два счёта; **any ~**

любо́е вре́мя; **on ~** во́время; **to be 30 mins behind/ahead of ~** опа́здывать (опозда́ть *perf*)/опережа́ть (опереди́ть* *perf*) на 30 мину́т; **by the ~ he arrived** к тому́ вре́мени, когда́ он пришёл; **five ~s five** пя́тью пять; **what ~ is it?** кото́рый час?; **to have a good ~** хорошо́ проводи́ть* (провести́* *perf*) вре́мя; **we had a hard ~** нам бы́ло о́чень тяжело́; **~'s up!** вре́мя истекло́!; **I've no ~ for it** (*fig*) мне э́то не интересу́ет; **he'll do it in his own** (**good**) **~** (*without being hurried*) он сде́лает э́то неторопя́сь; **he'll do it in** *or* (*US*) **on his own ~** (*out of working hours*) он сде́лает э́то в свобо́дное (в нерабо́чее) вре́мя*; **to be behind the ~s** отстава́ть* (отста́ть* *perf*) от вре́мени; **to ~ sth well/badly** выбира́ть (вы́брать* *perf*) подходя́щее/неподходя́щее вре́мя для чего́-н; **the bomb was ~d to go off 5 minutes later** часово́й механи́зм бо́мбы до́лжен был срабо́тать че́рез 5 мину́т.

time and motion study *n* ана́лиз эффекти́вности рабо́ты.

time bomb *n* бо́мба с часовы́м механи́змом; (*fig*) бо́мба заме́дленного де́йствия.

timecard ['taɪmkɑːd] *n* хронока́рта.

time clock *n* (*in factory etc*) часы́-та́бель *m*.

time-consuming ['taɪmkənsjuːmɪŋ] *adj* отнима́ющий мно́го вре́мени.

time difference *n* ра́зница во вре́мени.

time frame *n*: **within a broad/narrow ~ ~** в тече́ние продолжи́тельного/коро́ткого отре́зка вре́мени.

time-honoured ['taɪmɔnəd] (*US* **time-honored**) *adj* освящённый века́ми.

timekeeper ['taɪmkiːpəʳ] *n* судья́*-хронометри́ст; **she's a very good ~** она́ о́чень пунктуа́льная.

time-lag ['taɪmlæg] *n* (*BRIT*) (временно́й) промежу́ток вре́мени.

timeless ['taɪmlɪs] *adj* ве́чный* (ве́чен).

time limit *n* преде́льный срок.

timely ['taɪmlɪ] *adj* своевре́менный* (своевре́менен).

time off *n* свобо́дное вре́мя* *nt*.

timer ['taɪmə] *n* (*time switch*) та́ймер.

timesaving ['taɪmseɪvɪŋ] *adj* (*gadget, method etc*) эконо́мящий вре́мя.

timescale ['taɪmskeɪl] *n* (*BRIT*) вре́мя* *nt*, пери́од вре́мени.

time-share ['taɪmʃɛəʳ] *n* жильё в куро́ртной зо́не, находя́щееся в совме́стном владе́нии нескольких лиц.

time sharing *n* (*COMPUT*) разделе́ние вре́мени, режи́м разделе́ния вре́мени.

time sheet *n* = **timecard**.

time signal *n* (*RADIO*) сигна́л вре́мени.

time switch *n* та́ймер, выключа́тель *m* с часовы́м механи́змом.

timetable ['taɪmteɪbl] *n* расписа́ние.

time zone *n* часово́й по́яс*.

timid ['tɪmɪd] *adj* ро́бкий* (ро́бок).

timidity [tɪ'mɪdɪtɪ] *n* ро́бкость *f*.

timing ['taɪmɪŋ] *n* (*SPORT*) хронометра́ж; **the ~ of his resignation was unfortunate** вы́бор вре́мени для его́ отста́вки был неуда́чным.

timing device *n* (*on bomb*) часово́й механи́зм.

timpani ['tɪmpənɪ] *npl* лита́вры *fpl*.

tin [tɪn] *n* (*material*) о́лово; (*also*: **~ plate**) бе́лая жесть *f*; (*container*) (жестяна́я) ба́нка*; (: *for baking*) про́тивень* *m*; (: *BRIT*: *can*) консе́рвная ба́нка*; **we'll need 2 ~s of paint** (*quantity*) нам ну́жно бу́дет 2 ба́нки кра́ски.

tinfoil ['tɪnfɔɪl] *n* фо́льга.

tinge [tɪndʒ] *n* отте́нок* ◆ *vt*: **~d with** с отте́нком +*gen*.

tingle ['tɪŋgl] *vi* пока́лывать (*impf*); **I was tingling with excitement** я горе́л от возбужде́ния.

tinker ['tɪŋkəʳ] *n* (*gipsy*) бродя́чий луди́льщик
▸ **tinker with** *vt fus* вози́ться* (*impf*) с +*instr*.

tinkle ['tɪŋkl] *vi* звя́кать (звя́кнуть *perf*) ◆ *n* (*inf*): **to give sb a ~** (*TEL*) звя́кнуть (*perf*) кому́-н.

tin mine *n* оловя́нный рудни́к*.

tinned [tɪnd] *adj* (*BRIT*) консерви́рованный.

tinnitus ['tɪnɪtəs] *n* звон в уша́х.

tinny ['tɪnɪ] *adj* (*pej*: *sound*) металли́ческий*; (: *car etc*) как консе́рвная ба́нка.

tin-opener ['tɪnəupnəʳ] *n* (*BRIT*) консе́рвный нож*.

tinsel ['tɪnsl] *n* мишура́.

tint [tɪnt] *n* отте́нок*; (*for hair*) кра́ска ◆ *vt* (*hair*) кра́сить* (покра́сить* *perf*).

tinted ['tɪntɪd] *adj* (*hair*) кра́шеный; (*spectacles, glass*) ды́мчатый.

tiny ['taɪnɪ] *adj* кро́шечный* (кро́шечен).

tip [tɪp] *n* (*of pen etc*) ко́нчик; (*on umbrella etc*) наконе́чник; (*gratuity*) чаевы́е *pl adj*; (*BRIT*: *for rubbish*) сва́лка*; (: *for coal*) гора́*; (*advice*) сове́т ◆ *vt* (*waiter*) дава́ть* (дать* *perf*) на чай +*dat*; (*tilt*) наклоня́ть (наклони́ть* *perf*); (*also*: **~ over**) опроки́дывать (опроки́нуть *perf*); (*also*: **~ out**) выва́ливать (вы́валить *perf*); (*winner etc*) уга́дывать (угада́ть *perf*); (*for a job etc*) про́чить (*impf*); **he ~ped out the contents of the box** он вы́валил содержи́мое я́щика
▸ **tip off** *vt* предупрежда́ть (предупреди́ть* *perf*).

tip-off ['tɪpɔf] *n* предупрежде́ние.

tipped ['tɪpt] *adj* (*BRIT*: *cigarette*) с фи́льтром; **steel-~** со стальны́м наконе́чником.

Tipp-Ex® ['tɪpɛks] *n* ≈ штрих®, Ти́пекс.

tipple ['tɪpl] (*BRIT*) *vi* выпива́ть (*impf*) ◆ *n*: **to have a ~** выпива́ть (вы́пить* *perf*) по

---

* marks translations which have irregular inflections. The Russian-English side of the dictionary gives inflectional information.

ма́ленькой.

tipster ['tɪpstə^r] *n* жучо́к* *(на ска́чках)*.

tipsy ['tɪpsɪ] *adj* *(inf)* хмельно́й* (хмелён).

tiptoe ['tɪptəu] *n*: **on** ~ на цы́почках.

tiptop ['tɪptɔp] *adj*: **in** ~ **condition** в прекра́сном состоя́нии.

tirade [taɪ'reɪd] *n* тира́да.

Tirana [tɪ'rɑːnə] *n* Тира́на.

tire ['taɪə^r] *n* *(US)* = **tyre** ◆ *vt* *(make tired)* утомля́ть (утоми́ть* *perf*) ◆ *vi* устава́ть* (уста́ть* *perf*)

▸ **tire out** *vt* *(exhaust)* выма́тывать (вы́мотать *perf*).

tired ['taɪəd] *adj* уста́лый (уста́л); **I am** ~ я уста́л; **he feels** ~ он чу́вствует себя́ уста́вшим; **you look** ~ Вы вы́глядите уста́лым; **to be** ~ **of sth** устава́ть* (уста́ть* *perf*) от чего́-н.

tiredness ['taɪədnɪs] *n* уста́лость *f*.

tireless ['taɪəlɪs] *adj* *(worker, efforts)* неутоми́мый (неутоми́м).

tiresome ['taɪsəm] *adj* надое́дливый (надое́длив).

tiring ['taɪərɪŋ] *adj* утоми́тельный* (утоми́телен).

tissue ['tɪʃuː] *n* *(handkerchief)* бума́жная салфе́тка*; *(ANAT, BIO)* ткань *f*.

tissue paper *n* папиро́сная *or* то́нкая обёрточная бума́га.

tit [tɪt] *n* *(ZOOL)* сини́ца; *(inf: breast)* си́ська*; **to give** ~ **for tat** отпла́чивать (отплати́ть* *perf*) зуб за зуб.

titanium [tɪ'teɪnɪəm] *n* тита́н.

titbit ['tɪtbɪt] *(US* **tidbit**) *n* *(food)* ла́комый кусо́чек*; *(news)* пика́нтная но́вость* *f*.

titillate ['tɪtɪleɪt] *vt* *(person, senses)* возбужда́ть (возбуди́ть* *perf*).

titivate ['tɪtɪveɪt] *vt* *(oneself)* прихора́шиваться *(impf)*; *(place)* украша́ть (укра́сить* *perf*).

title ['taɪtl] *n* *(of book, play etc)* назва́ние; *(rank, BOXING etc)* ти́тул; *(LAW)*: ~ **to** пра́во* на +*acc*.

title deed *n* *(LAW)* докуме́нт, подтвержда́ющий пра́во со́бственности.

title page *n* ти́тульный лист*.

title role *n* *(in play, film)* гла́вная роль *f*.

title track *n* назва́ние пе́сни и́ли музыка́льной пье́сы, кото́рое та́кже явля́ется назва́нием пласти́нки, альбо́ма, плёнки *итп*.

titter ['tɪtə^r] *vi* хихи́кать (хихи́кнуть *perf*).

tittle-tattle ['tɪtltætl] *n* *(inf)* болтовня́.

tizzy ['tɪzɪ] *n*: **to be in a** ~ волнова́ться (разволнова́ться *perf*) по пустяка́м.

T-junction ['tiː'dʒʌŋkʃən] *n* *(AUT)* Т-обра́зный перекрёсток*.

TM *abbr* = **trademark, transcendental meditation**.

TN *abbr* *(US: POST)* = **Tennessee**.

TNT *n abbr* (= **trinitrotoluene**) троти́л.

┌─────────┐
│ **KEYWORD** │
└─────────┘

to [tuː] *prep* **1** *(direction)* в/на +*acc*; **to drive to school/the station** е́хать*/е́здить* (пое́хать*

perf) в шко́лу/на ста́нцию; **the road to Edinburgh** доро́га в Эдинбу́рг; **to the left** нале́во; **to the right** напра́во

2 *(as far as)* до +*gen*; **from Paris to London** от Пари́жа до Ло́ндона; **to count to ten** счита́ть (посчита́ть *perf*) до десяти́

3 *(with expressions of time)*: **a quarter to five** без че́тверти пять

4 *(for, of)*: **a letter to his wife** письмо́ жене́; **the key to the front door** ключ от входно́й две́ри; **she is secretary to the director** она́ секрета́рь дире́ктора

5 *(expressing indirect object)*: **to give sth to sb** дава́ть* (дать* *perf*) что-н кому́-н; **to talk to sb** разгова́ривать *(impf)* *or* говори́ть *(impf)* с кем-н; **what have you done to your hair?** что Вы сде́лали с свои́ми волоса́ми

6 *(in relation to)* к +*dat*; **A is to B as C is to D** "А" отно́сится к "Б", как "В" отно́сится к "Г"; **three goals to two** три два; **X miles to the gallon** Х ли́тров на киломе́тр; **1500 roubles to the dollar** 1500 рубле́й за до́ллар

7 *(purpose, result)* к +*dat*; **to my surprise** к моему́ удивле́нию; **to come to sb's aid** приходи́ть* (прийти́* *perf*) кому́-н на по́мощь

◆ *with vb* **1** перево́дится неопределённой фо́рмой глаго́ла; **to want/try to do** хоте́ть* (захоте́ть* *perf*)/пыта́ться (попыта́ться *perf*) +*infin*; **he has nothing to lose** ему́ не́чего теря́ть; **ready to use** гото́в к употребле́нию; **too old/young to ...** сли́шком стар/мо́лод, что́бы +*infin* ...

2 *(with vb omitted)*: **I don't want to** я не хочу́; **I don't feel like going – you really ought to** мне не хо́чется идти́ – нет, Вы должны́

3 *(purpose, result)* что́бы +*infin*; **I did it to help you** я сде́лал э́то, что́бы помо́чь Вам

◆ *adv*: **push/pull the door to** закрыва́ть (закры́ть* *perf*) дверь.

toad [təud] *n* *(ZOOL)* жа́ба.

toadstool ['təudstuːl] *n* *(BOT)* пога́нка*.

toady ['təudɪ] *vi* *(pej)*: **to** ~ **to sb** подхали́мничать *(impf)* пе́ред кем-н.

toast [təust] *n* *(CULIN)* тост; *(drink, speech)* тост ◆ *vt* *(CULIN: bread etc)* поджа́ривать (поджа́рить *perf*); *(drink to)* пить* (вы́пить* *perf*) за +*acc*; **a piece** *or* **slice of** ~ ло́мтик то́ста.

toaster ['təustə^r] *n* то́стер.

toastmaster ['təustmɑːstə^r] *n* тамада́ *m*.

toast rack *n* подста́вка для то́стов.

tobacco [tə'bækəu] *n* таба́к*; **pipe** ~ тру́бочный таба́к*.

tobacconist [tə'bækənɪst] *n* торго́вец*(-вка*) таба́чными изде́лиями.

tobacconist's (shop) [tə'bækənɪsts-] *n* таба́чная ла́вка.

Tobago [tə'beɪgəu] *n see* **Trinidad**.

toboggan [tə'bɔgən] *n* *(child's)* са́нки *pl*.

today [tə'deɪ] *adv, n* сего́дня; **what day is it ~?**
какóй сего́дня день?; **what date is it ~?** какóе
сего́дня числó?; ~ **is the 4th of March** сего́дня
4-ое ма́рта; **a week ago** ~ рóвно неде́лю
наза́д.

toddle ['tɔdl] (*inf*) *vi*: **to ~ in** проковыля́ть
(*impf*); **to ~ along** *or* **off** приковыля́ть (*impf*).

toddler ['tɔdlə'] *n* малы́ш*.

to-do [tə'du:] *n* (*fuss*) шум.

toe [təu] *n* (*of foot*) па́лец* (*ноги́*); (*of shoe, sock*)
носóк*; **to ~ the line** (*fig*) ходи́ть* (*impf*) по
стру́нке; **big ~** большóй па́лец* (*ноги́*); **little**
~ мизи́нец* (*ноги́*).

TOEFL *n abbr* = *Teaching of English as a Foreign*
Language.

toehold ['təuhəuld] *n* (*in climbing*) тóчка
опóры; (*fig*): **to get** *or* **gain a ~** находи́ть*
(найти́* *perf*) тóчку опóры.

toenail ['təuneɪl] *n* нóготь* *m* (*на па́льце ноги́*).

toffee ['tɔfɪ] *n* ири́ска*, тяну́чка*.

toffee apple *n* (*BRIT*) я́блоко на па́лочке,
глазирóванное ири́сом.

toga ['təugə] *n* тóга.

together [tə'gɛðə'] *adv* вме́сте; (*at same time*)
одновреме́нно; ~ **with** вме́сте с +*instr.*

togetherness [tə'gɛðənɪs] *n* бли́зость *f.*

toggle switch ['tɔgl-] *n* (*COMPUT*) ту́мблер,
переключа́тель *m.*

Togo ['təugəu] *n* Тóго *m ind.*

togs [tɔgz] *npl* (*inf: clothes*) одéжды *fpl.*

toil [tɔɪl] *n* тяжёлый труд* ◆ *vi* рабóтать (*impf*)
в пóте лица́.

toilet ['tɔɪlət] *n* унита́з; (*BRIT: room*) туале́т ◆
cpd (*kit, accessories etc*) туале́тный; **to go to**
the ~ ходи́ть* (сходи́ть* *perf*) в туале́т.

toilet bag *n* (*BRIT*) туале́тная су́мочка.

toilet bowl *n* унита́з.

toilet paper *n* туале́тная бума́га.

toiletries ['tɔɪlətrɪz] *npl* туале́тные
принадле́жности *fpl.*

toilet roll *n* рулóн туале́тной бума́ги.

toilet soap *n* туале́тное мы́ло.

toilet water *n* туале́тная водá.

toing and froing ['tu:ɪŋən'frəuɪŋ] *n* (*BRIT: on*
foot) ходьбá ту́да-обрáтно; (: *by transport*)
еэдá ту́да-обрáтно.

token ['təukən] *n* (*sign, souvenir*) знак;
(*substitute coin*) жетóн ◆ *adj* (*strike, payment*
etc) символи́ческий*; **by the same ~** (*fig*) по
той же причи́не; **book/gift ~** (*BRIT*) кни́жный/
пода́рочный талóн; **record ~** (*BRIT*) талóн на
пласти́нку.

tokenism ['təukənɪzəm] *n* ви́димость *f.*

Tokyo ['təukjəu] *n* Тóкио *m ind.*

told [təuld] *pt, pp of* **tell.**

tolerable ['tɔlərəbl] *adj* (*bearable*) терпи́мый
(терпи́м); (*fairly good*) снóсный* (снóсен).

tolerably ['tɔlərəblɪ] *adv*: ~ **good** довóльно

хорошó.

tolerance ['tɔlərns] *n* (*patience*) терпи́мость *f*;
(*also TECH*) дóпуск.

tolerant ['tɔlərnt] *adj*: ~ (**of**) терпи́мый
(терпи́м) (к +*dat*).

tolerate ['tɔləreɪt] *vt* терпе́ть* (*impf*).

toleration [tɔlə'reɪʃən] *n* терпи́мость *f.*

toll [təul] *n* (*of casualties, deaths*) числó; (*tax,*
charge) пла́та ◆ *vi* (*bell*) звони́ть (*impf*); **the**
accident ~ on the roads числó ава́рий на
дорóгах.

toll bridge *n* (*AUT*) пла́тный мост*.

toll call *n* (*US*) междугорóдный телефóнный
звонóк*.

toll-free ['təul'fri:] *adj* (*US*) беспла́тный.

toll road *n* (*AUT*) пла́тная дорóга.

tomato [tə'mɑ:təu] (*pl* ~**es**) *n* помидóр.

tomato purée *n* томáтная пáста.

tomb [tu:m] *n* моги́ла.

tombola [tɔm'bəulə] *n* лотере́я.

tomboy ['tɔmbɔɪ] *n* (*girl*) сорванéц*.

tombstone ['tu:mstəun] *n* надгрóбная плита́*.

tomcat ['tɔmkæt] *n* кот*.

tome [təum] *n* том*.

tomorrow [tə'mɔrəu] *adv, n* (*also fig*) за́втра;
the day after ~ послеза́втра; **a week ~/on**
Monday чéрез неде́лю, счита́я с
за́втрашнего дня/с понеде́льника; ~
morning за́втра у́тром.

ton [tʌn] *n* (*BRIT*) дли́нная тóнна; (*US: also:*
short ~) корóткая тóнна; (*also:* **metric ~**)
метри́ческая тóнна; (*NAUT: also:* **register ~**)
реги́стровая тóнна; ~**s of** (*inf*) тóнны +*gen.*

tonal ['təunl] *adj* тона́льный.

tone [təun] *n* тон*; (*TEL*) гудóк* ◆ *vi* (*colours:*
also: ~ **in**) сочета́ться (*impf*)

▶ **tone down** *vt* (*colour, criticism, demands*)
смягча́ть (смягчи́ть *perf*); (*sound*)
уменьша́ть (уме́ньшить *perf*)

▶ **tone up** *vt* (*muscles*) укрепля́ть (укрепи́ть*
perf).

tone-deaf [təun'dɛf] *adj* без слу́ха.

toner ['təunə'] *n* (*for photocopier*) черни́ла.

Tonga ['tɔŋgə] *n* Тóнга.

tongs [tɔŋz] *npl* щипцы́ *pl.*

tongue [tʌŋ] *n* язы́к*; ~ **in cheek** (*speak, say*) в
шу́тку.

tongue-tied ['tʌŋtaɪd] *adj* (*fig*): **he was ~** он
лиши́лся да́ра рéчи.

tongue twister [-twɪstə'] *n* скороговóрка.

tonic ['tɔnɪk] *n* (*MED*) тонизи́рующее срéдство;
(*also:* ~ **water**) тóник; (*MUS*) тóника.

tonight [tə'naɪt] *adv* (*this evening*) сего́дня
вéчером; (*this night*) сего́дня нóчью ◆ *n* (*see*
adv) сего́дняшний вéчер; сего́дняшняя ночь
f; (**I'll) see you ~!** до вéчера!

tonnage ['tʌnɪdʒ] *n* (*NAUT*) тоннáж.

tonne [tʌn] *n* (*BRIT: metric ton*) тóнна.

---

* marks translations which have irregular inflections. The Russian-English side of the dictionary gives inflectional information.

tonsil ['tɔnsl] *n* (*gen pl*) минда́лина; **to have one's ~s out** удаля́ть (удали́ть *perf*) минда́лины.

tonsillitis [tɔnsɪ'laɪtɪs] *n* тонзилли́т.

too [tu:] *adv* (*excessively*) сли́шком; (*also: referring to subject*) та́кже, то́же; (: *referring to object*) та́кже; **the tea is ~ sweet** чай сли́шком сла́дкий; **I went ~** я то́же пошёл; **~ much, ~ many** сли́шком мно́го; **~ bad!** о́чень жаль!

took [tuk] *pt of* **take**.

tool [tu:l] *n* инструме́нт; (*fig: person*) ору́дие.

tool box *n* я́щик для инструме́нтов.

tool kit *n* набо́р инструме́нтов.

toot [tu:t] *n* (*of horn*) гудо́к*; (*of whistle*) свисто́к* ◆ *vi* (*with car horn*) сигна́лить (посигна́лить *perf*).

tooth [tu:θ] (*pl* **teeth**) *n* (*ANAT*) зуб*; (*TECH*) зубе́ц*; **to have a ~ out** *or* (*US*) **pulled** удаля́ть (удали́ть *perf*) *or* вырыва́ть (вы́рвать* *perf*) зуб; **to brush one's teeth** чи́стить* (почи́стить* *perf*) зу́бы; **by the skin of one's teeth** (*fig*) чу́дом.

toothache ['tu:θeɪk] *n* зубна́я боль *f*; **I have ~** у меня́ боли́т зуб.

toothbrush ['tu:θbrʌʃ] *n* зубна́я щётка.

toothpaste ['tu:θpeɪst] *n* зубна́я па́ста.

toothpick ['tu:θpɪk] *n* зубочи́стка*.

tooth powder *n* зубно́й порошо́к*.

top [tɔp] *n* (*of mountain*) верши́на; (*of tree*) верху́шка*; (*of head*) маку́шка; (*of ladder*) верх; (*of page, list etc*) нача́ло; (*of cupboard, table, box*) ве́рхняя пове́рхность *f*; (*lid: of box, jar*) кры́шка*; (: *bottle*) про́бка*; (*AUT: also: ~* **gear**) са́мая вы́сшая ско́рость *f*; (*also: spinning ~*) юла́, волчо́к*; (*blouse etc*) верх ◆ *adj* (*shelf, step*) ве́рхний*; (*marks*) вы́сший*; (*salesman etc*) веду́щий*; (*best*) отме́нный ◆ *vt* (*poll, vote*) лиди́ровать (*impf*) в +*prp*; (*list*) возглавля́ть (возгла́вить* *perf*); (*exceed: estimate etc*) превыша́ть (превы́сить* *perf*); **the ~ of the milk** (*BRIT*) сли́вки* *pl* (на молоке́); **at the ~ of the stairs/page** на верху́ ле́стницы/страни́цы; **at the ~ of the street** в да́льнем конце́ у́лицы; **on ~ of** (*above: be*) на +*prp*; (: *put etc*) на +*acc*; (*in addition to*) сверх +*gen*; **put the book on ~ of the table** положи́те кни́гу на стол; **from ~ to bottom** све́рху до́низу; **from ~ to toe** (*BRIT*) с головы́ до ног *or* до пят; **at the ~ of the list** пе́рвый по спи́ску; **at the ~ of one's voice** во весь го́лос; **at ~ speed** на максима́льной ско́рости; **over the ~** (*inf: behaviour etc*) сверх ме́ры.

► **top up** (*US* **top off**) *vt* (*bottle*) долива́ть (доли́ть* *perf*); (*salary*) прибавля́ть (приба́вить* *perf*).

topaz ['təupæz] *n* топа́з.

top-class ['tɔp'klɑ:s] *adj* вы́сшего кла́сса.

topcoat ['tɔpkəut] *n* ве́рхний* слой*.

top floor *n* ве́рхний эта́ж*.

top hat *n* цили́ндр, котело́к*.

top-heavy [tɔp'hɛvɪ] *adj*: **~ object** предме́т с утяжелённым ве́рхом; **~ bureaucracy** бюрократи́ческий аппара́т с громо́здким ве́рхним эшело́ном.

topic ['tɔpɪk] *n* те́ма.

topical ['tɔpɪkl] *adj* актуа́льный* (актуа́лен).

topless ['tɔplɪs] *adj* обнажённый до по́яса.

top-level ['tɔplɛvl] *adj* на вы́сшем у́ровне.

topmost ['tɔpməust] *adj* (*branch etc*) са́мый ве́рхний *or* бли́жний к верху́шке.

topnotch ['tɔp'nɔtʃ] *adj* первосо́ртный.

topography [tə'pɔgrəfɪ] *n* топогра́фия.

topping ['tɔpɪŋ] *n* (*CULIN*): **with a ~ of** с ве́рхом из +*gen*.

topple ['tɔpl] *vt* (*government, leader*) ски́дывать (ски́нуть *perf*) ◆ *vi* (*person, object*) опроки́дываться (опроки́нуться *perf*).

top-ranking ['tɔpræŋkɪŋ] *adj* (*official*) высокопоста́вленный.

top-secret ['tɔp'si:krɪt] *adj* сверхсекре́тный* (сверхсекре́тен).

top-security ['tɔpsə'kjuərɪtɪ] *adj* (*BRIT*) под уси́ленной охра́ной.

topsy-turvy ['tɔpsɪ'tə:vɪ] *adj* перевёрнутый ◆ *adv* вверх нога́ми.

top-up ['tɔpʌp] *n*: **would you like a ~?** Вам ещё подли́ть?

top-up loan *n* (*BRIT*) доба́вочная ссу́да.

torch [tɔ:tʃ] *n* (*with flame*) фа́кел; (*BRIT: electric*) фона́рь* *m*.

tore [tɔ:ʳ] *pt of* **tear**.

torment [*n* 'tɔ:mɛnt, *vt* tɔ:'mɛnt] *n* муче́ние ◆ *vt* му́чить* (*impf*).

torn [tɔ:n] *pp of* **tear**[1] ◆ *adj*: **she is ~ between ...** она́ разрыва́ется ме́жду +*instr* ....

tornado [tɔ:'neɪdəu] (*pl* **~es**) *n* смерч.

torpedo [tɔ:'pi:dəu] (*pl* **~es**) *n* торпе́да.

torpedo boat *n* торпе́дный ка́тер.

torpor ['tɔ:pəʳ] *n* оцепене́ние.

torrent ['tɔrnt] *n* (*also fig*) пото́к.

torrential [tə'rɛnʃl] *adj* (*rain*) проливно́й.

torrid ['tɔrɪd] *adj* (*weather*) зно́йный* (зно́ен); (*love affair*) бу́рный.

torso ['tɔ:səu] *n* ту́ловище, торс.

tortoise ['tɔ:təs] *n* черепа́ха.

tortoiseshell ['tɔ:təʃɛl] *adj* черепа́ховый; (*cat*) с пёстрым окра́сом.

tortuous ['tɔ:tjuəs] *adj* (*path*) изви́листый (изви́лист); (*argument, mind*) зау́мный* (зау́мен).

torture ['tɔ:tʃəʳ] *n* (*also fig*) пы́тка* ◆ *vt* (*also fig*) пыта́ть (*impf*).

torturer ['tɔ:tʃərəʳ] *n* пала́ч*, мучи́тель *m*.

Tory ['tɔ:rɪ] (*BRIT: POL*) *adj* консервати́вный ◆ *n* (*POL*) то́ри *m/f ind*, консерва́тор.

toss [tɔs] *vt* (*throw*) подки́дывать (подкину́ть *perf*), подбра́сывать (подбро́сить* *perf*); (*one's head*) отки́дывать (отки́нуть *perf*); (*salad*) меша́ть (*impf*) ◆ *vi*: **to ~ and turn** (*in bed*) воро́чаться (*impf*) ◆ *n*: **with a ~ of her head, she...** отки́нув го́лову, она́ ...; **to ~ a**

coin подбра́сывать (подбро́сить* *perf*)
моне́ту; **to ~ up to do** подбра́сывать
(подбро́сить* *perf*) моне́ту, что́бы +*infin*; **to
win/lose the ~** выи́грывать (вы́играть *perf*)/
прои́грывать (проигра́ть *perf*) подбра́сы-
вание моне́ты.

tot [tɔt] *n* (*drink*) глото́к*; (*child*) малы́ш*
▶ **tot up** *vt* (*BRIT*: *figures*) подсчи́тывать
(подсчита́ть *perf*).

total ['təutl] *adj* (*number, workforce etc*)
о́бщий*; (*failure, wreck etc*) по́лный ♦ *n*
о́бщая су́мма ♦ *vt* (*add up*) скла́дывать
(сложи́ть *perf*); (*add up to*) составля́ть
(соста́вить* *perf*); **in ~** в о́бщей сло́жности.

totalitarian [təutælɪ'tɛərɪən] *adj* (*POL*)
тоталита́рный.

totality [təu'tælɪtɪ] *n* полнота́.

totally ['təutəlɪ] *adv* по́лностью; (*unprepared*)
соверше́нно.

tote bag [təut-] *n* сума́.

totem pole ['təutəm-] *n* тоте́мный столб*.

totter ['tɔtəʳ] *vi* (*person*) ходи́ть*/идти́*/ (*impf*)
шата́ясь *or* ша́ткой похо́дкой; (*fig*:
government) занима́ть (*impf*) ша́ткую
пози́цию.

touch [tʌtʃ] *n* осяза́ние; (*approach*) мане́ра;
(*detail*) штрих; (*contact*) прикоснове́ние ♦ *vt*
(*with hand, foot*) каса́ться (косну́ться *perf*),
тро́гать (тро́нуть *perf*); (*tamper with*)
тро́гать (*impf*); (*make contact with*)
прикаса́ться (прикосну́ться *perf*),
дотра́гиваться (дотро́нуться *perf*);
(*emotionally*) тро́гать (тро́нуть *perf*); **the
personal ~** индивидуа́льность *f*; **to put the
finishing ~es to sth** вноси́ть* (внести́* *perf*)
после́дние штрихи́ в что-н; **there's been a ~
of frost** подморо́зило; **in ~ with** в конта́кте с
+*instr*; **to get in ~ with sb** связа́ться* (*perf*) с
кем-н; **I'll be in ~ with you** я свяжу́сь с Ва́ми;
to lose ~ (*friends*) теря́ть (потеря́ть *perf*)
связь; **to be out of ~ with events** быть* (*impf*)
не в ку́рсе собы́тий
▶ **touch on** *vt fus* каса́ться (косну́ться *perf*)
▶ **touch up** *vt* (*paint*) подкра́шивать
(подкра́сить* *perf*).

touch-and-go ['tʌtʃən'gəu] *adj* нея́сный*
(нея́сен); **it was ~ whether we'd succeed**
бы́ло нея́сно, вы́шло ли э́то у нас.

touchdown ['tʌtʃdaun] *n* (*of rocket, plane*)
поса́дка*; (*US: FOOTBALL*) гол.

touched [tʌtʃt] *adj* тро́нутый (тро́нут).

touching ['tʌtʃɪŋ] *adj* (*scene, photograph etc*)
тро́гательный* (тро́гателен).

touchline ['tʌtʃlaɪn] *n* (*SPORT*) боковая́ ли́ния.

touch-sensitive ['tʌtʃ'sɛnsɪtɪv] *adj*
сраба́тывающий на прикоснове́ние.

touch-type ['tʌtʃtaɪp] *vi* печа́тать (*impf*)
слепы́м ме́тодом.

touchy ['tʌtʃɪ] *adj* (*person*) оби́дчивый
(оби́дчив); (*subject*) больно́й; **he is ~** его́
легко́ заде́ть.

tough [tʌf] *adj* (*strong, hard-wearing*: *material*)
кре́пкий* (кре́пок), про́чный* (про́чен);
(*meat, policies, negotiations*) жёсткий*;
(*person*: *physically*) выно́сливый
(выно́слив); (: *mentally*) сто́йкий* (сто́ек);
(*task, problem, journey*) тяжёлый (тяжёл);
(*rough*) опа́сный* (опа́сен); **~ luck!** не везёт!

toughen ['tʌfn] *vt* закаля́ть (закали́ть *perf*).

toughness ['tʌfnɪs] *n* про́чность *f*; (*of person*)
сто́йкость *f*.

toupee ['tu:peɪ] *n* (*wig*) пари́к*.

tour ['tuəʳ] *n* (*journey*) пое́здка*; (*also*: **package
~**) туристи́ческая пое́здка*; (*of town, factory,
museum*) экску́рсия; (*by pop group etc*)
гастро́ли *fpl* ♦ *vt* (*country, city*) объезжа́ть
(объе́хать* *perf*); (*factory*) обходи́ть*
(обойти́* *perf*); **to go on a ~ of** (*museum,
region*) осма́тривать (осмотре́ть* *perf*); **to go
on ~** (*band*) е́здить*/е́хать* (*impf*) на
гастро́ли.

touring ['tuərɪŋ] *n* гастроли́рование.

tourism ['tuərɪzm] *n* (*business*) тури́зм.

tourist ['tuərɪst] *n* тури́ст*(ка*) ♦ *cpd*
(*attractions, season*) тури́стский*; **the ~ trade**
инду́стрия тури́зма.

tourist class *n* (*NAUT, AVIAT*) второ́й класс.

tourist information centre *n* (*BRIT*)
туристи́ческое бюро́ *nt ind*.

tourist office *n* туристи́ческое бюро́ *nt ind*.

tournament ['tuənəmənt] *n* турни́р,
состяза́ние.

tourniquet ['tuənɪkeɪ] *n* жгут, турнике́т.

tour operator *n* (*BRIT*) рабо́тник
туристи́ческой фи́рмы.

tousled ['tauzld] *adj* (*hair*) взъеро́шенный
(взъеро́шен).

tout [taut] *n* (*also*: **ticket ~**) спекуля́нт(ка*) ♦ *vi*:
to ~ for (*business*) добива́ться (*impf*) +*gen*,
выбива́ть (*impf*) ♦ *vt*: **to ~ sth (around)** (*BRIT*)
спекули́ровать* (*impf*) чем-н.

tow [təu] *vt* (*vehicle, caravan, trailer*) везти́*/
вози́ть* (*impf*) на букси́ре ♦ *n*: **to give sb a ~**
(*AUT*) брать* (взять* *perf*) кого́-н на букси́р;
"on *or* (US) in ~" (*AUT*) "на букси́ре".

toward(s) [tə'wɔ:d(z)] *prep* к +*dat*; (*attitude*) по
отноше́нию к +*dat*; (*purpose*): **~ doing** с тем
что́бы +*infin*; **towards noon/the end of the
year** к полу́дню/концу́ го́да; **to feel friendly ~
sb** относи́ться* (*impf*) дружелю́бно к кому́-н.

towel ['tauəl] *n* (*also*: **hand ~**) полоте́нце* для
рук; (*also*: **bath ~**) ба́нное полоте́нце*; **to
throw in the ~** (*fig*) сдава́ться* (сда́ться* *perf*).

towelling ['tauəlɪŋ] *n* (*fabric*) махро́вая ткань
f.

towel rail (*US* **towel rack**) *n* ве́шалка* для

полотéнец.

tower ['tauə'] *n* бáшня* ♦ *vi* (*building, mountain*) возвышáться (*impf*); **to ~ above** *or* **over sb/sth** возвышáться (*impf*) над кем-н/чем-н.

tower block *n* (*BRIT*) бáшня*, высóтный дом*.

towering ['tauərɪŋ] *adj* возвышáющийся.

towline ['təulaɪn] *n* буксúрный трос.

town [taun] *n* гóрод*; **to go to ~** ходúть*/идтú* (*impf*) в гóрод; (*fig*) разоряться (разорúться *perf*); **in ~** в гóроде; **to be out of ~** (*person*) быть* (*impf*) в отъéзде.

town centre *n* центр (гóрода).

town clerk *n* глáвный делопроизводúтель *m* городскóго совéта.

town council *n* городскóй совéт.

town crier [-'kraɪə'] *n* глашáтай.

town hall *n* рáтуша.

townie ['tauni] *n* (*inf*) городскóй(-áя) *m(f) adj.*

town plan *n* план гóрода.

town planner *n* градострóитель *m*, планирóвщик.

town planning *n* городскóе планúрование, градострóительство.

township ['taunʃɪp] *n* (*in South Africa*) негритянский* прúгород; (*in America*) городскóй райóн.

townspeople ['taunzpi:pl] *npl* горожáне *mpl.*

towpath ['təupɑ:θ] *n* (*of canal*) тропúнка.

towrope ['təurəup] *n* буксúрный трос.

tow truck *n* (*US*) аварúйная машúна.

toxic ['tɔksɪk] *adj* токсúчный* (токсúчен).

toxic waste *n* ядовúтые отхóды *mpl.*

toxin ['tɔksɪn] *n* токсúн.

toy [tɔɪ] *n* игрýшка*

▶ **toy with** *vt fus* (*object*) игрáть (*impf*) +*instr*; (*food*) возúться* (*impf*) с +*instr*; (*idea*) игрáть (*impf*) с +*instr.*

toy shop *n* магазúн игрýшек.

trace [treɪs] *n* след* ♦ *vt* (*draw*) переводúть* (перевестú* *perf*); (*follow*) прослéживать (проследúть* *perf*); (*locate*) устанáвливать (установúть* *perf*); **without ~** (*disappear*) бесслéдно, без следá; **there was no ~ of him** он исчéз без следá.

trace element *n* микроэлемéнт.

tracer ['treɪsə'] *n* (*also*: **~ bullet**) трассúрующий снаряд.

trachea [trə'kɪə] *n* трахéя.

tracing paper ['treɪsɪŋ-] *n* кáлька.

track [træk] *n* след*; (*path*) тропá*; (*of bullet etc*) трактóрия; (*RAIL*) (железнодорóжный) путь* *m*; (*on tape, record, also SPORT*) дорóжка* ♦ *vt* (*follow: animal, person*) идтú* (*impf*) по слéду +*gen*; **to keep ~ of** следúть* (*impf*) за +*instr*; **to be on the right ~** (*fig*) быть* (*impf*) на вéрном путú

▶ **track down** *vt* (*prey*) выслéживать (вы́следить* *perf*); (*sth lost*) оты́скивать (отыскáть* *perf*).

tracked [trækt] *adj* (*AUT*) гýсеничный.

tracker dog ['trækə-] *n* собáка-ищéйка.

track events *npl* соревновáния *ntpl* по лёгкой атлéтике.

tracking station ['trækɪŋ-] *n* пульт управлéния полётом.

track meet *n* (*SPORT*) соревновáния *ntpl* по атлéтике.

track record *n*: **to have a good ~ ~** (*fig*) имéть (*impf*) хорóшую репутáцию.

tracksuit ['træksu:t] *n* тренирóвочный костю́м.

tract [trækt] *n* (*GEO*) прострáнство; (*pamphlet*) трактáт; **respiratory ~** (*ANAT*) дыхáтельные путú *mpl*; **digestive ~** желýдочно-кишéчный тракт.

traction ['trækʃən] *n* (*power*) тяга; (*AUT*: *grip*) сúла сцеплéния; (*MED*): **in ~** в вытяжéнии.

traction engine *n* тягáч*.

tractor ['træktə'] *n* трáктор.

trade [treɪd] *n* (*activity*) торгóвля; (*skill, job*) род занятий ♦ *vi* (*do business*) торговáть* (*impf*) ♦ *vt*: **to ~ sth (for sth)** обмéнивать (обменять *perf*) что-н (на что-н); **to ~ with/in** торговáть* (*impf*) с +*instr/*+*instr*; **foreign ~** внéшняя торгóвля; **Department of T~ and Industry** (*BRIT*) *Министéрство торгóвли и промы́шленности*

▶ **trade in** *vt* (*old car etc*) предлагáть (предложúть* *perf*) для встрéчной продáжи.

trade barrier *n* торгóвый барьéр.

trade deficit *n* торгóвый дефицúт.

Trade Descriptions Act *n* (*BRIT*: *LAW, COMM*) *положéние о торгóвле.*

trade discount *n* торгóвая скúдка (*óптовым торгóвцам*).

trade fair *n* торгóвая ярмарка*.

trade figures *npl* показáтель *msg* товарооборóта.

trade-in ['treɪdɪn] *n*: **to take as a ~** принимáть (принять *perf*) как встрéчную продáжу.

trade-in price *n* ценá* с учётом встрéчной продáжи.

trademark ['treɪdmɑ:k] *n* товáрный знак.

trade mission *n* торгóвое представúтельство.

trade name *n* торгóвое назвáние.

trade-off ['treɪdɔf] *n* компромúсс.

trade price *n* торгóвая ценá.

trader ['treɪdə'] *n* торгóвец*.

trade reference *n* информáция о состоянии дел фúрмы.

trade secret *n* промы́шленный секрéт.

tradesman ['treɪdzmən] *irreg n* рабóтник*; (*shopkeeper*) торгóвец*, лáвочник.

trade union *n* профсою́з= *профессионáльный сою́з.*

trade unionist [-'ju:njənɪst] *n* член профсою́за.

trade wind *n* (*GEO*) пассáт.

trading ['treɪdɪŋ] *n* торгóвля.

trading account *n* счёт расчётов.

trading estate *n* (*BRIT*) промы́шленная зóна.

trading stamps *npl* бумáжные мáрки с

объявленной стоимостью.
tradition [trə'dɪʃən] *n* традиция.
traditional [trə'dɪʃənl] *adj* (*also fig*)
традиционный*.
traditionally [trə'dɪʃnəlɪ] *adv* традиционно.
traffic ['træfɪk] *n* (*of people, vehicles*) движение;
(*of drugs etc*) нелегальная торговля ◆ *vi*: **to ~
in** (*liquor, drugs*) нелегально торговать*
(*impf*) +*instr*.
traffic circle *n* (*US*) кольцевая транспортная
развязка*.
traffic island *n* островок* безопасности.
traffic jam *n* пробка*.
trafficker ['træfɪkə'] *n* (*also*: **drug ~**) торговец*
наркотиками.
traffic lights *npl* светофор *msg*.
traffic offence *n* (*BRIT*) нарушение правил
дорожного движения.
traffic sign *n* дорожный знак.
traffic violation *n* (*US*) = **traffic offence**.
traffic warden *n* (*BRIT*) регулировщик
парковання машин на улицах города.
tragedy ['trædʒədɪ] *n* трагедия.
tragic ['trædʒɪk] *adj* трагический*.
tragically ['trædʒɪkəlɪ] *adv* трагически.
trail [treɪl] *n* (*path*) дорожка*, тропинка*;
(*track*) след; (*of smoke, dust*) хвост* ◆ *vt* (*drag*)
волочить* (*impf*); (*follow: person, animal*)
следовать (*impf*) по пятам за +*instr* ◆ *vi* (*hang
loosely*) волочиться* (*impf*); (*in game, contest*)
волочиться* (*impf*) в хвосте, оставать* (*impf*);
to be on sb's ~ устраивать (устроить *perf*)
слёжку за кем-н
▶ **trail away** *vi* (*sound, voice*) затихать
(затихнуть *perf*)
▶ **trail behind** *vi* (*lag*) волочиться* (*impf*) в
хвосте
▶ **trail off** *vi* = **trail away**.
trailer ['treɪlə'] *n* (*AUT*) прицеп; (*US: caravan*)
автоприцеп; (*CINEMA*) кинореклама, анонс.
trailer tent *n* прицеп с палаткой.
trailer truck *n* (*US*) грузовик* с прицепом.
train [treɪn] *n* поезд*; (*of dress*) шлейф ◆ *vt*
(*apprentice, doctor etc*) учить* (обучить* *perf*);
(*athlete, mind*) тренировать (*impf*); (*dog*)
дрессировать (выдрессировать *perf*); (*plant*)
приучать (приучить* *perf*) ◆ *vi* (*learn a skill*)
учиться* (обучиться* *perf*); (*SPORT*)
тренироваться (*impf*); **one's ~ of thought** ход
чьих-н мыслей; **~ of events** цепь *f* событий;
to go by ~ ездить*/ехать* (*impf*) поездом *or* на
поезде; **to ~ sb to do** обучать* (обучить* *perf*)
кого-н +*impf infin*; **to ~ sb as** учиться* (*impf*)
кого-н на +*acc*; **to ~ on** (*camera etc*)
направлять (направить* *perf*) на +*acc*.
train attendant *n* (*US*) проводник.
trained [treɪnd] *adj* (*worker, teacher*)
подготовленный; (*animal*) тренированный;

(*eye*) натренированный* (натренирован).
trainee [treɪ'niː] *n* (*hairdresser*) ученик*; ~
teacher студент(ка*) практикант.
trainer ['treɪnə'] *n* (*coach*) тренер; (*of animals*)
дрессировщик(-щица); ~**s** *npl* (*sports shoes*)
кроссовки *fpl*.
training ['treɪnɪŋ] *n* (*for occupation*) обучение,
подготовка*; (*SPORT*) тренировка; **to be in ~**
(*SPORT*) тренироваться (*impf*).
training college *n* (*for teachers*)
педагогический* институт.
training course *n* курс профессиональной
подготовки.
traipse [treɪps] *vi*: **to ~ through**
притаскиваться (притащиться* *perf*).
trait [treɪt] *n* черта.
traitor ['treɪtə'] *n* предатель(ница) *m(f)*.
trajectory [trə'dʒɛktərɪ] *n* траектория.
tram [træm] *n* (*BRIT*) трамвай.
tramcar ['træmkɑː'] *n* (*BRIT*) = **tram**.
tramline ['træmlaɪn] *n* трамвайная линия.
tramp [træmp] *n* (*person*) бродяга *m/f*; (*inf. pej:
woman*) шлюха ◆ *vi* бродить* (*impf*) ◆ *vt*
(*town, streets*) бродить*/брести* (*impf*) по
+*dat*.
trample ['træmpl] *vt*: **to ~ (underfoot)**
растаптывать (растоптать* *perf*) ◆ *vi* (*fig*): **to ~
on** растаптывать (растоптать* *perf*).
trampoline ['træmpəliːn] *n* трамплин.
trance [trɑːns] *n* (*also fig*) транс; **to go into a ~**
входить* (войти* *perf*) в транс.
tranquil ['træŋkwɪl] *adj* безмятежный*
(безмятежен).
tranquillity [træŋ'kwɪlɪtɪ] (*US* **tranquility**) *n*
безмятежность *f*.
tranquillizer ['træŋkwɪlaɪzə'] (*US* **tranquilizer**) *n*
(*MED*) транквилизатор.
transact [træn'zækt] *vt* (*business*) вести* (*impf*).
transaction [træn'zækʃən] *n* (*piece of business*)
операция; **cash ~** оплата наличными.
transatlantic ['trænzət'læntɪk] *adj*
трансатлантический.
transcend [træn'sɛnd] *vt* (*boundaries, loyalties
etc*) выходить* (выйти* *perf*) за пределы
+*gen*.
transcendental [trænsɛn'dɛntl] *adj*: ~
meditation трансцендентная медитация.
transcribe [træn'skraɪb] *vt* переписывать
(переписать* *perf*), транскрибировать (*impf/
perf*).
transcript ['trænskrɪpt] *n* (*typed*) печатная
копия; (*hand-written*) рукописная копия.
transcription [træn'skrɪpʃən] *n* транскрипция.
transept ['trænsɛpt] *n* трансепт.
transfer ['trænsfə'] *n* перевод; (*POL*) передача;
(*SPORT*) переход; (*picture etc*) переводная
картинка ◆ *vt* (*employees, money etc*)
переводить* (перевести* *perf*); (*POL, SPORT*)

передава́ть* (переда́ть* *perf*); **to ~ the charges** (*BRIT*: *TEL*) звони́ть (позвони́ть *perf*) по колле́кту; **by bank** ~ по ба́нковскому перево́ду.

transferable [træns'fə:rəbl] *adj* (*ticket*) перево́дный, с пре́вом переда́чи; "**not ~**" "без пра́ва переда́чи".

transfix [træns'fɪks] *vt* (*person, animal*) пронза́ть (пронзи́ть* *perf*); (*fig*): **~ed with fear** пронзённый стра́хом.

transform [træns'fɔ:m] *vt* (*person, situation etc*) преобража́ть (преобрази́ть* *perf*).

transformation [trænsfə'meɪʃən] *n* преобразова́ние, перевоплоще́ние.

transformer [træns'fɔ:məʳ] *n* трансформа́тор.

transfusion [træns'fju:ʒən] *n* (*also:* **blood ~**) перелива́ние кро́ви.

transgress [træns'grɛs] *vt* преступа́ть (преступи́ть* *perf*) грани́цы +*gen*.

transient ['trænzɪənt] *adj* мимолётный* (мимолётен).

transistor [træn'zɪstəʳ] *n* (*ELEC*) транзи́сторное устро́йство; (*also:* **~ radio**) транзи́стор.

transit ['trænzɪt] *n*: **in ~** (*people, things*) транзи́том.

transit camp *n* перева́лочный пункт.

transition [træn'zɪʃən] *n* перехо́д.

transitional [træn'zɪʃənl] *adj* перехо́дный.

transitive ['trænzɪtɪv] *adj* (*LING*) перехо́дный.

transit lounge *n* зал транзи́тных пассажи́ров.

transitory ['trænzɪtərɪ] *adj* преходя́щий*.

transit visa *n* транзи́тная ви́за.

translate [trænz'leɪt] *vt*: **to ~ (from/into)** переводи́ть* (перевести́* *perf*) (с +*gen*/на +*acc*).

translation [trænz'leɪʃən] *n* перево́д; (*SCOL: as opposed to prose*) перево́д на родно́й язы́к.

translator [trænz'leɪtəʳ] *n* перево́дчик(-ица).

translucent [trænz'lu:snt] *adj* (*object, quality*) прозра́чный* (прозра́чен), просве́чивающий.

transmission [trænz'mɪʃən] *n* переда́ча; (*AUT*) коро́бка переда́ч, приво́д.

transmit [trænz'mɪt] *vt* передава́ть* (переда́ть* *perf*).

transmitter [trænz'mitəʳ] *n* (*equipment*) переда́тчик.

transparency [træns'pɛərnsɪ] *n* (*of glass etc*) прозра́чность *f*; (*BRIT*: *PHOT*) диапозити́в.

transparent [træns'pærnt] *adj* прозра́чный* (прозра́чен).

transpire [træns'paɪəʳ] *vi* (*turn out*) выясня́ться (вы́ясниться *perf*); (*happen*) происходи́ть* (произойти́* *perf*); **it finally ~d that ...** наконе́ц вы́яснилось, что ....

transplant [*n* 'trænsplɑ:nt, *vt* træns'plɑ:nt] *n* переса́дка* ◆ *vt* (*MED, seedlings*) переса́живать (пересади́ть* *perf*); **he had a heart ~** ему́ сде́лали переса́дку се́рдца.

transport [*n* 'trænspɔ:t, *vt* træns'pɔ:t] *n*

тра́нспорт; (*moving people, goods*) перево́зка* ◆ *vt* (*carry*) перевози́ть* (перевезти́* *perf*); **public ~** обще́ственный тра́нспорт; **Department of T~** (*BRIT*) Министе́рство тра́нспорта.

transportation ['trænspɔ:'teɪʃən] *n* (*transport*) транспортиро́вка*, перево́зка*; (*means of transport*) тра́нспорт; **Department of T~** (*US*) Министе́рство тра́нспорта.

transport café *n* (*BRIT*) доро́жное кафе́ *nt ind*.

transpose [træns'pəuz] *vt* перемеща́ть (перемести́ть* *perf*).

transsexual [trænz'sɛksuəl] *n* транссексуа́л.

transverse ['trænzvə:s] *adj* (*beam etc*) попере́чный.

transvestite [trænz'vɛstaɪt] *n* трансвести́т.

trap [træp] *n* западня́, лову́шка; (*carriage*) двуко́лка* ◆ *vt* лови́ть* (пойма́ть *perf*) в лову́шку *or* западню́; (*confine*) запира́ть (запере́ть* *perf*); (*immobilize*) ско́вывать (скова́ть* *perf*); (*jam*) защемля́ть (защеми́ть* *perf*); **to set** *or* **lay a ~ (for sb)** расставля́ть (расста́вить* *perf*) лову́шку *or* западню́ (кому́-н); **to shut one's ~** (*inf*) затыка́ть (заткну́ть *perf*) свою́ гло́тку; **to ~ one's finger in the door** защемля́ть (защеми́ть* *perf*) себе́ па́лец.

trap door *n* люк.

trapeze [trə'pi:z] *n* трапе́ция.

trapper ['træpəʳ] *n* ловец*.

trappings ['træpɪŋz] *npl* атрибу́ты *mpl*.

trash [træʃ] *n* (*rubbish: also pej*) сор, му́сор; (: *nonsense*) чушь *f*.

trash can *n* (*US*) му́сорное ведро́*.

trashy ['træʃɪ] *adj* (*inf*) дрянно́й.

trauma ['trɔ:mə] *n* тра́вма.

traumatic [trɔ:'mætɪk] *adj* травмати́ческий.

traumatize ['trɔ:mətaɪz] *vt* травми́ровать* (*impf/perf*).

travel ['trævl] *n* (*travelling*) путеше́ствия *ntpl* ◆ *vi* (*for pleasure*) путеше́ствовать (*impf*); (*commute*) е́здить* (*impf*); (*move*) передвига́ться (*impf*); (*news, sound*) распространя́ться (распространи́ться *perf*); (*wine, food*) сохраня́ться (*impf*) при перево́зке ◆ *vt* (*distance: by transport*) проезжа́ть (прое́хать* *perf*); (: *on foot*) проходи́ть* (пройти́* *perf*); **~s** *npl* (*journeys*) путеше́ствия *ntpl*.

travel agency *n* туристи́ческое аге́нство.

travel agent *n* рабо́тник туристи́ческого аге́нства.

travel brochure *n* рекла́мная брошю́ра для тури́стов.

traveller ['trævləʳ] (*US* **traveler**) *n* путеше́ственник(-ица); (*COMM*) коммивояжёр.

traveller's cheque (*US* **traveler's check**) *n* доро́жный чек.

travelling ['trævlɪŋ] (*US* **traveling**) *n* (*for pleasure*) путеше́ствия *ntpl*; (*from necessity*) переéзды *mpl* ♦ *cpd* (*circus, exhibition*) передвижнóй; (*bag, clock, expenses*) дорóжный.

travel(l)ing salesman *irreg n* коммивояжёр.

travelogue ['trævəlɔg] *n* (*book*) кнйга о путешéствиях.

travel-sickness ['trævlsɪknɪs] *n* (*on ship*) морскáя болéзнь *f*; **he suffers from travel sickness** (*in car*) егó укáчивает в машйне.

traverse ['trævəs] *vt* пересекáть (пересéчь* *perf*).

travesty ['trævəstɪ] *n* парóдия.

trawler ['trɔ:lə^r] *n* трáулер.

tray [treɪ] *n* (*for carrying*) поднóс; (*on desk*) корзйнка.

treacherous ['trɛtʃərəs] *adj* (*person*) вероломный* (вероломен); (*look, action*) предáтельский*; (*ground, tide*) ковáрный* (ковáрен); **road conditions are ~** склáдывается слóжная дорóжная обстанóвка.

treachery ['trɛtʃərɪ] *n* предáтельство, вероломство.

treacle ['tri:kl] *n* (*black treacle*) пáтока; (*golden syrup*) свéтлая *or* очйщенная пáтока.

tread [trɛd] (*pt* **trod**, *pp* **trodden**) *n* (*step*) похóдка; (*sound*) пóступь *f*; (*of stair*) ступéнь *f*; (*of tyre*) протéктор ♦ *vi* ступáть (*impf*)

► **tread on** *vt fus* наступáть (наступйть* *perf*) на +*acc*.

treadle ['trɛdl] *n* (*on sewing machine etc*) педáль *f*.

treas. *abbr* = **treasurer**.

treason ['tri:zn] *n* измéна.

treasure ['trɛʒə^r] *n* сокрóвище ♦ *vt* (*object*) хранйть (*impf*) как зенйцу óка; (*friendship*) высóко ценйть* (*impf*); (*memory*) свято хранйть (*impf*); (*thought*) лелéять (*impf*); (*store*) хранйть (*impf*); **~s** *npl* (*art treasures etc*) сокрóвища *ntpl*.

treasure hunt *n* пóиски *mpl* сокрóвищ.

treasurer ['trɛʒərə^r] *n* казначéй.

treasury ['trɛʒərɪ] *n*: **the T~**, (*US*) **the T~ Department** Госудáрственное Казначéйство.

Treasury bill *n* (*BRIT*) казначéйский вéксель *m*.

treat [tri:t] *n* (*present*) удовóльствие ♦ *vt* (*person, object*) обращáться (*impf*) с +*instr*; (*patient, illness*) лечйть* (*impf*); (*TECH: coat*) обрабáтывать (обрабóтать *perf*); **it was a ~** это бýло наслаждéние; **to ~ sth as a joke** относйться* (отнестйсь *perf*) к чемý-н несерьёзно; **to ~ sb to sth** угощáть (угостйть* *perf*) когó-н чем-н.

treatment ['tri:tmənt] *n* (*attention, handling*) обращéние; (*MED*) лечéние; **to have ~ for sth** проходйть* (пройтй* *perf*) курс лечéния от чегó-н.

treaty ['tri:tɪ] *n* соглашéние.

treble ['trɛbl] *adj* (*triple*) тройнóй; (*MUS: voice, part*) дискáнтный, сопрáно *ind*; (: *instrument*) сопрáновый ♦ *n* (*MUS*) дискáнт, сопрáно *m ind*; (*on hi-fi, radio etc*) высóкие частóты *fpl* ♦ *vt* утрáивать (утрóить *perf*) ♦ *vi* утрáиваться (утрóиться *perf*); **to be ~ the size of sth** быть* (*impf*) бóльше чегó-н втрóе.

treble clef *n* скрипйчный ключ*.

tree [tri:] *n* дéрево*.

tree-lined ['tri:laɪnd] *adj* усáженный дерéвьями.

treetop ['tri:tɔp] *n* верхýшка дéрева.

tree trunk *n* ствол дéрева.

trek [trɛk] *n* (*long difficult journey*) похóд, перехóд ♦ *vi* (*as holiday*) идтй* (пойтй* *perf*) в похóд.

trellis ['trɛlɪs] *n* шпалéра.

tremble ['trɛmbl] *vi* дрожáть (*impf*).

trembling ['trɛmblɪŋ] *n* дрожáние ♦ *adj* (*hand, voice etc*) дрожáщий.

tremendous [trɪ'mɛndəs] *adj* (*enormous*) огрóмный* (огрóмен); (*excellent*) великолéпный* (великолéпен).

tremendously [trɪ'mɛndəslɪ] *adv* чрезвычáйно; **he enjoyed it ~** он получйл огрóмное удовóльствие от этого.

tremor ['trɛmə^r] *n* (*trembling*) дрожь *f*, содрогáние; (*also*: **earth ~**) толчóк* (землетрясéния).

trench [trɛntʃ] *n* канáва; (*MIL*) траншéя, окóп.

trench coat *n* тёплая полушинéль *f*.

trench warfare *n* окóпная войнá*.

trend [trɛnd] *n* (*tendency*) тендéнция; (*of events, fashion*) направлéние; **~ towards sth** тендéнция к чемý-н; **~ away from sth** отхóд от чегó-н; **to set the ~** задавáть* (задáть* *perf*) направлéнию; **to set a ~** задавáть* (задáть* *perf*) тон.

trendy ['trɛndɪ] *adj* мóдный* (мóден).

trepidation [trɛpɪ'deɪʃən] *n* (*apprehension*) трéпет; **in ~** в трéпете.

trespass ['trɛspəs] *vi*: **to ~ on** (*private property*) вторгáться (вторгнуться *perf*) в +*acc*; **"no ~ing"** "вход воспрещён".

trespasser ['trɛspəsə^r] *n* вторгáющийся(-ая) *m(f) adj* в чáстные владéния; **"trespassers will be prosecuted"** "лицá, вторгáющиеся на дáнную территóрию бýдут преслéдоваться закóном".

tress [trɛs] *n* (*of hair*) косá*.

trestle ['trɛsl] *n* кóзлы *pl*.

trestle table *n* стол* на кóзлах.

trial ['traɪəl] *n* (*LAW*) процéсс, суд*; (*test: of machine etc*) испытáние *ntpl*; (*worry*) переживáние; **~s** *npl* (*unpleasant experiences*) перипетйи *fpl*; **horse ~s** соревновáния *ntpl* по выéздка; **~ by jury** суд* присяжных; **to be**

---

* marks translations which have irregular inflections. The Russian-English side of the dictionary gives inflectional information.

sent for ~ предава́ть* (преда́ть* *perf*) суду́; on ~ (*LAW*) под судо́м; **by** ~ **and error** ме́тодом проб и оши́бок.

trial balance *n* (*COMM*) про́бный бала́нс.

trial basis *n*: **on a** ~ ~ на испыта́тельный срок.

trial period *n* испыта́тельный срок.

trial run *n* прого́н.

triangle ['traɪæŋgl] *n* (*MATH, MUS*) треуго́льник.

triangular [traɪ'æŋgjulə'] *adj* треуго́льный.

tribal ['traɪbl] *adj* (*warrior, warfare, dance*) племенно́й.

tribe [traɪb] *n* пле́мя* *nt*.

tribesman ['traɪbzmən] *irreg n* туземец*.

tribulations [trɪbju'leɪʃənz] *npl* злоключе́ния *ntpl*.

tribunal [traɪ'bjuːnl] *n* трибуна́л.

tributary ['trɪbjutərɪ] *n* (*of river*) прито́к*.

tribute ['trɪbjuːt] *n* (*compliment*) дань *f*; **to pay** ~ **to** отдава́ть* (отда́ть* *perf*) дань +*dat*.

trice [traɪs] *n*: **in a** ~ ми́гом.

trick [trɪk] *n* (*magic trick*) фо́кус; (*prank, joke*) подво́х; (*skill, knack*) прие́м; (*CARDS*) взя́тка* ◆ *vt* проводи́ть* (провести́* *perf*); **to play a** ~ **on sb** разы́грывать (разыгра́ть *perf*) кого́-н; **to** ~ **sb into doing** обма́ном заставля́ть (заста́вить* *perf*) кого́-н +*infin*; **to** ~ **sb out of sth** выма́нивать (вы́манить *perf*) что-н у кого́-н; **a** ~ **of the light** игра́* све́та, опти́ческий* обма́н; **that should do the** ~ э́то должно́ срабо́тать.

trickery ['trɪkərɪ] *n* моше́нничество.

trickle ['trɪkl] *n* (*of water etc*) стру́йка ◆ *vi* (*water, rain etc*) струи́ться (*impf*); (*people*) стека́ться (*impf*) потихо́ньку.

trick question *n* хи́трый вопро́с.

trickster ['trɪkstə'] *n* моше́нник.

tricky ['trɪkɪ] *adj* (*job*) непросто́й; (*business*) хи́трый; (*problem*) заковы́ристый.

tricycle ['traɪsɪkl] *n* трёхколёсный велосипе́д.

trifle ['traɪfl] *n* (*small detail*) пустя́к*; (*CULIN*) десе́рт из ке́кса, фрукто́вого желе́ и сли́вок ◆ *adv*: **a** ~ **long** чуть длиннова́т ◆ *vi*: **to** ~ **with sb/sth** шути́ть* (*impf*) с кем-н/чем-н.

trifling ['traɪflɪŋ] *adj* пустяко́вый.

trigger ['trɪgə'] *n* (*of gun*) куро́к*
  ► **trigger off** *vt* (*reaction, riot*) спровоци́ровать (*perf*), вызыва́ть (вы́звать* *perf*).

trigonometry [trɪgə'nɔmətrɪ] *n* тригономе́трия *f*.

trilby ['trɪlbɪ] *n* (*BRIT: also:* ~ **hat**) фе́тровая шля́па.

trill [trɪl] *vi* (*birds*) залива́ться (зали́ться *perf*) ◆ *n* (*MUS*) трель *f*.

trilogy ['trɪlədʒɪ] *n* трило́гия *f*.

trim [trɪm] *adj* (*house, garden*) ухо́женый; (*figure*) подтя́нутый ◆ *n* отде́лка ◆ *vt* (*cut*) подра́внивать (подравня́ть *perf*); (*NAUT*) ста́вить* (поста́вить* *perf*) по́ ветру; (*decorate*): **to** ~ **(with)** отде́лывать (отде́лать *perf*) (+*instr*); **to give sb a** ~ подра́внивать

(подравня́ть *perf*) во́лосы кому́-н; **to keep in (good)** ~ держа́ть* (*impf*) (в хоро́шей) фо́рме.

trimmings ['trɪmɪŋz] *npl* (*CULIN*) потроха́ *mpl*; (*cuttings*) обре́зки *mpl*.

Trinidad and Tobago ['trɪnɪdæd-] *n* Тринида́д и Тоба́го.

trinity ['trɪnɪtɪ] *n* (*group*) тро́йка; (*REL*): **the (Holy) T**~ Тро́ица.

trinket ['trɪŋkɪt] *n* (*ornament*) безделу́шка*; (*jewellery*) побряку́шка*.

trio ['triːəu] *n* тро́йка; (*MUS*) три́о *nt ind*.

trip [trɪp] *n* (*journey*) пое́здка*; (*outing*) прогу́лка* ◆ *vi* (*stumble*) спотыка́ться (споткну́ться *perf*); (*go lightly*) идти́* (*impf*) лёгкой похо́дкой; **on a** ~ на экску́рсии
  ► **trip up** *vi* (*stumble*) ста́вить* (поста́вить* *perf*) подно́жку ◆ *vt* (*person*) подставля́ть (подста́вить* *perf*) но́жку.

tripartite [traɪ'pɑːtaɪt] *adj* трёхсторо́нний*.

tripe [traɪp] *n* (*CULIN*) требуха́; (*pej: rubbish*) чушь *f*.

triple ['trɪpl] *adj* тройно́й ◆ *adv*: ~ **the distance/ the speed** тройно́е расстоя́ние/тройна́я ско́рость, в три ра́за да́льше/быстре́е.

triple jump *n* тройно́й прыжо́к (в длину́).

triplets ['trɪplɪts] *npl* тройня́шки* *fpl*.

triplicate ['trɪplɪkət] *n*: **in** ~ в трёх экземпля́рах.

tripod ['traɪpɔd] *n* трено́га.

Tripoli ['trɪpəlɪ] *n* Три́поли *m ind*.

tripper ['trɪpə'] *n* (*BRIT*) тури́ст(ка*).

tripwire ['trɪpwaɪə'] *n* замаскиро́ванная про́волока, свя́занная с капка́ном и́ли взрывча́ткой.

trite [traɪt] *adj* (*pej*) изби́тый.

triumph ['traɪʌmf] *n* (*satisfaction*) торжество́; (*great achievement*) триу́мф ◆ *vi*: **to** ~ **(over)** торжествова́ть (восторжествова́ть *perf*) (над +*instr*).

triumphal [traɪ'ʌmfl] *adj* (*arch, return*) триумфа́льный.

triumphant [traɪ'ʌmfənt] *adj* (*team, wave*) торжеству́ющий; (*return*) побе́дный.

triumphantly [traɪ'ʌmfəntlɪ] *adv* (*shout, look etc*) торжеству́юще.

trivia ['trɪvɪə] *npl* (*pej*) тривиа́льности *fpl*, тривиа́льные ве́щи *fpl*.

trivial ['trɪvɪəl] *adj* (*unimportant*) незначи́тельный* (незначи́телен); (*commonplace*) тривиа́льный* (тривиа́лен).

triviality [trɪvɪ'ælɪtɪ] *n* ме́лочи *fpl*.

trivialize ['trɪvɪəlaɪz] *vt* упроща́ть (упрости́ть* *perf*).

trod [trɔd] *pt of* tread.

trodden ['trɔdn] *pp of* tread.

trolley ['trɔlɪ] *n* теле́жка*; (*also:* ~ **bus**) тролле́йбус.

trollop ['trɔləp] *n* (*pej*) лаху́дра.

trombone [trɔm'bəun] *n* тромбо́н.

troop [truːp] *n* (*of people*) отря́д, гру́ппа; (*of monkeys*) ста́до ◆ *vi*: **to** ~ **in/out** входи́ть*

(войти* *perf*)/выходить* (выйти* *perf*)
строем; ~s *npl* (*MIL*) войска́ *ntpl*; **a ~ of
children** ста́йка ребяти́шек.
troop carrier *n* (*plane*) тра́нспортно-
деса́нтный самолёт; (*NAUT*: *also*: **troopship**)
тра́нспорт для перево́зки войск.
trooper ['tru:pə^r] *n* (*MIL*: *in cavalry*) кавалери́ст;
(: *in armoured regiment*) солда́т*; (*US*:
policeman) ко́нный полице́йский* *m adj.*
trooping the colour ['tru:pɪŋ-] *n* (*BRIT*:
ceremony) внос зна́мени.
troopship ['tru:pʃɪp] *n* тра́нспорт для
перево́зки войск.
trophy ['trəufɪ] *n* трофе́й.
tropic ['trɔpɪk] *n*: ~s тро́пики *mpl*; **in the ~s** в
тро́пиках; **T~ of Cancer/Capricorn** Тро́пик
Ра́ка/Козеро́га.
tropical ['trɔpɪkl] *adj* (*rain forest, climate etc*)
тропи́ческий*.
trot [trɔt] *n* рысь *f* ♦ *vi* (*horse*) идти́* (*impf*)
ры́сью; (*person*) плести́сь* (*impf*) рысцо́й; **on
the ~** (*BRIT*: *fig*) подря́д
▶ **trot out** *vt* (*excuse, reason*) приводи́ть*
(привести́* *perf*); (*names, facts*) сы́пать (*impf*)
+*instr*.
trouble ['trʌbl] *n* (*difficulty*) затрудне́ние;
(*worry, unrest*) беспоко́йство; (*bother, effort*)
хло́поты *pl* ♦ *vt* (*worry*) беспоко́ить (*impf*);
(*person: disturb*) беспоко́ить (побеспоко́ить
perf) ♦ *vi*: **to ~ to do** побеспоко́иться (*perf*)
+*infin*; ~s *npl* (*personal, POL etc*) бе́ды *fpl*; **to be
in ~** име́ть (*impf*) неприя́тности; (*ship,
climber etc*) быть* (*impf*) в беде́; **to have ~
doing** с трудо́м мочь (*impf*) +*infin*; **to go to the
~ of doing** заботи́ться* (позабо́титься* *perf*)
о том, что́бы +*infin*; **it's no ~!** э́то ника́к не
затрудни́т меня́!; **it's too much ~** сли́шком
мно́го хлопо́т; **please don't ~ yourself**
пожа́луйста, не беспоко́йтесь; **the ~ is ...**
беда́ в том, что ...; **what's the ~?** (*with broken
television etc*) где непола́дки?, в чём там
де́ло?; (*MED*) что Вас беспоко́ит?; **stomach ~**
больно́й желу́док.
troubled ['trʌbld] *adj* (*person*) в постоя́нной
трево́ге; (*country*) бе́дствующий; (*life, era*)
беспоко́йный.
trouble-free ['trʌblfri:] *adj* (*period, campaign
etc*) без происше́ствий.
troublemaker ['trʌblmeɪkə^r] *n* смутья́н.
troubleshooter ['trʌblʃu:tə^r] *n* (*in conflict*)
*специа́льный уполномо́ченный по
ула́живанию конфли́ктов*.
troublesome ['trʌblsəm] *adj* (*child*)
прока́зливый.
trouble spot *n* (*MIL*) горя́чая то́чка*.
troubling ['trʌblɪŋ] *adj* трево́жный.
trough [trɔf] *n* (*also*: **drinking ~**) коры́то; (*also*:
feeding ~) корму́шка*; (*channel*) жёлоб; (*low

point) впа́дина; **a ~ of low pressure**
(*METEOROLOGY*) фронт ни́зкого давле́ния.
trounce [trauns] *vt* (*defeat*) разбива́ть
(разби́ть* *perf*).
troupe [tru:p] *n* тру́ппа.
trouser press ['trauzə-] *n* приспособле́ние для
гла́жки брюк.
trousers ['trauzəz] *npl* брю́ки *mpl*; **short ~**
штаны́ *mpl*.
trouser suit *n* (*BRIT*: *for woman*) брю́чной
костю́м.
trousseau ['tru:səu] (*pl* ~**x** *or* ~**s**) *n* прида́ное *nt
adj.*
trousseaux ['tru:səuz] *npl of* **trousseau**.
trout [traut] *n inv* (*ZOOL*) форе́ль *f.*
trowel ['trauəl] *n* (*garden tool*) сово́к*; (*builder's
tool*) мастеро́к*.
truant ['truənt] *n* (*BRIT*): **to play ~** прогу́ливать
(прогуля́ть *perf*).
truce [tru:s] *n* переми́рие.
truck [trʌk] *n* (*lorry*) грузови́к; (*RAIL*) откры́тая
това́рная платфо́рма; (*for luggage*)
теле́жка*, вагоне́тка*.
truck driver *n* води́тель *m* грузовика́.
trucker ['trʌkə^r] *n* води́тель *m* грузовика́.
truck farm *n* (*US*) овощево́дческая фе́рма.
trucking ['trʌkɪŋ] *n* (*esp US*) грузова́я
транспортиро́вка*.
trucking company *n* (*US*) грузово́е
тра́нспортное аге́нтство.
truculent ['trʌkjulənt] *adj* (*person*) свире́пый
(свире́п).
trudge [trʌdʒ] *vi* (*also*: ~ **along**) плести́сь*
(*impf*), тащи́ться (*impf*).
true [tru:] *adj* (*real, genuine*) настоя́щий*,
и́стинный; (*accurate: likeness*) то́чный;
(*faithful: friend*) настоя́щий*; (*wall*) прямо́й;
(*beam, wheel*) центри́рованный; **to come ~**
сбыва́ться (сбы́ться* *perf*); ~ **to life**
жи́зненный.
truffle ['trʌfl] *n* трю́фель *m.*
truly ['tru:lɪ] *adv* (*really*) по-настоя́щему;
(*truthfully*) и́скренне; **yours ~** (*in letter*)
и́скренне Ваш.
trump [trʌmp] *n* (*also*: ~ **card**: *also fig*) ко́зырь
m; **to turn up ~s** (*fig*) подава́ть* (пода́ть* *perf*)
ру́ку по́мощи.
trumped-up [trʌmpt'ʌp] *adj* (*pej*)
сфабрико́ванный.
trumpet ['trʌmpɪt] *n* труба́.
truncated [trʌŋ'keɪtɪd] *adj* (*object*)
обре́занный; (*message*) сокращённый.
truncheon ['trʌntʃən] *n* (*BRIT*) дуби́нка*.
trundle ['trʌndl] *vt* (*push slowly: trolley etc*)
кати́ть* (*impf*) ♦ *vi*: **to ~ along** (*person*) брести́*
(*impf*); (*vehicle*) кати́ться* (*impf*).
trunk [trʌŋk] *n* (*of tree*) ствол*; (*of person*)
ту́ловище; (*of elephant*) хо́бот; (*case*)

доро́жный сунду́к; (*US: AUT*) бага́жник; **~s**
npl (*also:* **swimming ~s**) пла́вки* *pl.*
trunk call *n* (*BRIT: TEL*) междугоро́дные
переговоры *mpl,* междугоро́дный звоно́к*.
trunk road *n* (*BRIT*) магистра́ль *f.*
truss [trʌs] *n* (*MED*) грыжево́й банда́ж
▶ **truss (up)** *vt* (*CULIN*) перетя́гивать
(перетяну́ть* *perf*) бечёвкой; (*person*)
свя́зывать (связа́ть* *perf*).
trust [trʌst] *n* (*faith*) дове́рие; (*responsibility*)
долг*; (*LAW*) *управле́ние иму́ществом по
дове́ренности;* (*COMM*) трест ◆ *vt* (*rely on,
have faith in*) доверя́ть (*impf*) +*dat*; (*hope*): **to ~
(that)** полага́ть (*impf*)(, что); (*entrust*): **to ~ sth
to sb** доверя́ть (дове́рить *perf*) что-н кому́-н;
to take sth on ~ принима́ть (приня́ть* *perf*)
что-н на ве́ру; **in ~** (*LAW*) управля́емый по
дове́ренности.
trust company *n* (*COMM*) трест.
trusted ['trʌstɪd] *adj* (*friend, servant*)
пре́данный.
trustee [trʌs'tiː] *n* (*also LAW*) попечи́тель *m.*
trustful ['trʌstful] *adj* (*person, nature, smile*)
дове́рчивый (дове́рчив).
trust fund *n* (*COMM*) фонд тре́ста.
trusting ['trʌstɪŋ] *adj* (*person, nature*)
дове́рчивый (дове́рчив).
trustworthy ['trʌstwə:ðɪ] *adj* (*person, report*)
надёжный, заслу́живающий дове́рия.
trusty ['trʌstɪ] *adj* испы́танный.
truth [truːθ] (*pl* **~s**) *n* пра́вда; (*universal
principle*) и́стина.
truthful ['truːθful] *adj* правди́вый (правди́в).
truthfully ['truːθfəlɪ] *adv* (*answer*) правди́во.
truthfulness ['truːθfəlnɪs] *n* правди́вость *f.*
try [traɪ] *n* (*attempt*) попы́тка*; (*RUGBY*) прохо́д
с мячо́м ◆ *vt* (*test*) про́бовать (попро́бовать
perf); (*LAW: person*) суди́ть* (*impf*); (*strain:
patience*) испы́тывать (*impf*); (*attempt*): **to ~
to do** стара́ться (*impf*) *or* пыта́ться (*impf*) +*infin*
◆ *vi* (*make effort, attempt*) стара́ться (*impf*),
пыта́ться (*impf*); **to have a ~** про́бовать
(попро́бовать *perf*); **I tried a different key** я
пыта́лся откры́ть други́м ключо́м; **to ~
one's (very) best** *or* **one's (very) hardest**
стара́ться (постара́ться *perf*) изо́ всех сил
▶ **try on** *vt* (*dress etc*) ме́рить (поме́рить *perf*),
примеря́ть (приме́рить *perf*); **to ~ it on** (*fig*)
вести́* (*impf*) себя́ на́гло
▶ **try out** *vt* про́бовать (попро́бовать *perf*).
trying ['traɪɪŋ] *adj* (*person, experience*)
утоми́тельный* (утоми́телен).
tsar [zɑː] *n* царь* *m.*
T-shirt ['tiːʃəːt] *n* футбо́лка*.
T-square ['tiːskwɛə] *n* (*TECH*) рейсши́на.
TT *adj abbr* (*BRIT: inf*) = **teetotal** ◆ *abbr* (*US: POST*)
= *Trust Territory;* = *telegraphic transfer*
телегра́фный де́нежный перево́д.
tub [tʌb] *n* (*container*) бо́чка*; (*bath*) ва́нна.
tuba ['tjuːbə] *n* ту́ба.
tubby ['tʌbɪ] *adj* упи́танный.

tube [tjuːb] *n* (*pipe*) тру́бка*; (*container*)
тю́бик; (*BRIT: underground*) метро́ *nt ind*; (*for
tyre*) ка́мера; (*inf: television*): **the ~** те́лик.
tubeless ['tjuːblɪs] *adj* беска́мерный.
tuber ['tjuːbə] *n* клу́бень *m.*
tuberculosis [tjubəːkjuˈləusɪs] *n* туберкулёз.
tube station *n* (*BRIT*) ста́нция *f* метро́.
tubing ['tjuːbɪŋ] *n* шланг тру́бки; **a piece of ~**
тру́бка*.
tubular ['tjuːbjulə'] *adj* (*furniture, metal*)
тру́бчатый.
TUC *n abbr* (*BRIT:* = *Trades Union Congress*)
Конгре́сс (брита́нских) тред-юнио́нов.
tuck [tʌk] *vt* (*put*) запиха́ть (подобра́ть* *perf*)
◆ *n* (*SEWING*) вы́кладка
▶ **tuck away** *vt* (*money*) припря́тывать
(припря́тать* *perf*); (*building*): **to be ~ed away**
приткну́ться (*perf*)
▶ **tuck in** *vt* (*clothing*) заправля́ть (запра́вить*
perf); (*child*) укрыва́ть (укры́ть* *perf*) ◆ *vi* (*eat*)
умина́ть (умя́ть* *perf*)
▶ **tuck up** *vt* (*invalid, child*) укрыва́ть (укры́ть*
perf).
tuck shop *n* буфе́т.
Tue(s). *abbr* = **Tuesday.**
Tuesday ['tjuːzdɪ] *n* вто́рник; **it is ~ 23rd March**
(сего́дня) вто́рник 23-его ма́рта; **on ~** во
вто́рник; **on ~s** по вто́рникам; **every ~**
ка́ждый вто́рник; **every other ~** ка́ждый
второ́й вто́рник; **last/next ~** в про́шлый/
сле́дующий вто́рник; **the following ~** в
сле́дующий вто́рник; **~'s newspaper** газе́та
за вто́рник; **a week/fortnight on ~** во
вто́рник че́рез неде́лю/че́рез две неде́ли; **the
~ before last** позапро́шлый вто́рник; **the ~
after next** во вто́рник че́рез неде́лю; **we'll
spend ~ morning/lunchtime/afternoon/evening** во
вто́рник у́тром/в обе́д/днём/ве́чером; **we'll
spend ~ night in Rome** во вто́рник мы
проведём ночь в Ри́ме.
tuft [tʌft] *n* (*of hair*) пучо́к*.
tug [tʌg] *n* (*ship*) букси́р ◆ *vt* тяну́ть* (*impf*).
tug of war *n* перетя́гивание кана́та; (*fig*)
тя́жба.
tuition [tjuːˈɪʃən] *n* (*BRIT*) обуче́ние; (: *private
tuition*) ча́стные уро́ки *mpl,* дома́шнее
обуче́ние; (*US: school fees*) пла́та за
обуче́ние.
tulip ['tjuːlɪp] *n* тюльпа́н.
tumble ['tʌmbl] *n* (*fall*) паде́ние ◆ *vi* (*fall:
person*) па́дать (упа́сть* *perf*); (: *water*)
журча́ть (*impf*); (*somersault*) ска́тываться
(скати́ться* *perf*); **to ~ to sth** (*inf*) набрести́*
(*perf*) на что-н.
tumbledown ['tʌmbldaun] *adj* (*building*)
полуразру́шенный.
tumble dryer *n* (*BRIT*) суши́лка* для белья́.
tumbler ['tʌmblə'] *n* бока́л.
tummy ['tʌmɪ] *n* (*inf*) пу́зо *nt no pl.*
tummy tuck *n пласти́ческая опера́ция по
ушива́нию живота́.*

tumour ['tju:mə'] (*US* **tumor**) *n* (*MED*) о́пухоль *f.*
tumult ['tju:mʌlt] *n* шум, сумато́ха.
tumultuous [tju:'mʌltjuəs] *adj* бу́рный.
tuna ['tju:nə] *n inv* (*also:* ~ **fish**) туне́ц*.
tune [tju:n] *n* (*melody*) моти́в ♦ *vt* (*MUS, RADIO, TV*) настра́ивать (настро́ить *perf*); (*AUT*) нала́живать (нала́дить* *perf*); **the guitar is in/out of** ~ гита́ра настро́ена/расстро́ена; **to sing in** ~ петь* (*impf*) чи́сто; **to sing out of** ~ фальши́вить* (*impf*); **to be in/out of** ~ **with** (*fig*) быть* (*impf*) в ладу́/не в ладу́ с +*instr*; **she was robbed to the** ~ **of £10,000** (*fig*) её огра́били на це́лых £10 000
▶ **tune in** *vi* (*RADIO, TV*): **to** ~ **in (to)** настра́иваться (настро́иться *perf*) (на +*acc*)
▶ **tune up** *vi* (*musician*) настра́ивать (настро́ить *perf*) инструме́нт; (*orchestra*) настра́ивать (настро́ить *perf*) инструме́нты.
tuneful ['tju:nful] *adj* (*music*) мелоди́чный* (мелоди́чен).
tuner ['tju:nə'] *n* (*radio set*) блок настро́йки; **piano** ~ настро́йщик фортепья́но.
tuner amplifier *n* резона́нсный усили́тель *m.*
tungsten ['tʌŋstn] *n* вольфра́м.
tunic ['tju:nɪk] *n* ту́ника.
tuning fork ['tju:nɪŋ-] *n* камерто́н.
Tunis ['tju:nɪs] *n* Туни́с.
Tunisia [tju:'nɪzɪə] *n* Туни́с.
Tunisian [tju:'nɪzɪən] *adj* Туни́сский* ♦ *n* туни́сец*(-ска*).
tunnel ['tʌnl] *n* (*passage*) тунне́ль *m*; (*in mine*) што́льня ♦ *vi* прокла́дывать (проложи́ть* *perf*) тунне́ль.
tunnel vision *n* у́зость *f* зре́ния; (*fig*) тру́бочнее зре́ние.
tunny ['tʌnɪ] *n* туне́ц*.
turban ['tə:bən] *n* чалма́, тюрба́н.
turbid ['tə:bɪd] *adj* (*water*) му́тный* (му́тен); (*air*) пы́льный* (пы́лен).
turbine ['tə:baɪn] *n* (*TECH*) турби́на.
turbo ['tə:bəu] *n* турби́на.
turbojet [tə:bəu'dʒɛt] *n* (*AVIAT*) турбореакти́вный самолёт.
turboprop [tə:bəu'prɔp] *n* (*engine*) турбовинтово́й мото́р.
turbot ['tə:bət] *n inv* белоко́рый па́лтус.
turbulence ['tə:bjuləns] *n* встре́чные пото́ки *mpl* во́здуха.
turbulent ['tə:bjulənt] *adj* (*also fig*) бу́рный.
tureen [tə'ri:n] *n* (*for soup*) су́пница; (*for vegetables*) глубо́кое блю́до с кры́шкой.
turf [tə:f] *n* (*grass*) дёрн; (*clod*) торф ♦ *vt* (*area*) покрыва́ть (покры́ть* *perf*) дёрном; **the T~** (*course*) скакова́я доро́жка; (*horse-racing*) ска́чки *mpl*
▶ **turf out** *vt* (*inf: person*) выставля́ть (вы́ставить* *perf*).
turf accountant *n* (*BRIT*) букме́кер.

turgid ['tə:dʒɪd] *adj* (*speech*) напы́щенный.
Turin ['tjuə'rɪn] *n* Тури́н.
Turk [tə:k] *n* ту́рок* (турча́нка*).
Turkey ['tə:kɪ] *n* Ту́рция.
turkey ['tə:kɪ] *n* инде́йка.
Turkish ['tə:kɪʃ] *adj* туре́цкий* ♦ *n* (*LING*) туре́цкий* язы́к*.
Turkish bath *n* туре́цкие ба́ни *fpl.*
Turkish delight *n* рахат-луку́м.
Turkmen ['tə:kmɛn] *n,adj* туркме́нский*; (*person*) туркме́н(ка*); (*LING*) туркме́нский* язы́к*.
Turkmenia [tə:k'mi:nɪə] *n* Туркме́ния.
turmeric ['tə:mərɪk] *n* (*CULIN*) курку́ма.
turmoil ['tə:mɔɪl] *n* смяте́ние; **in** ~ в смяте́нии.
turn [tə:n] *n* поворо́т; (*performance*) но́мер*; (*chance*) о́чередь *f*; (*inf: MED*) вы́вих ♦ *vt* повора́чивать (поверну́ть *perf*); (*collar*) отвора́чивать (отверну́ть *perf*); (*change: wood, metal*) обта́чивать (обточи́ть* *perf*) ♦ *vi* (*object*) повора́чиваться (поверну́ться *perf*); (*person: look back*) обора́чиваться (оберну́ться *perf*); (*reverse direction: in car*) развора́чиваться (разверну́ться *perf*); (: *wind*) переменя́ться (перемени́ться *perf*); (*milk*) скиса́ть (ски́снуть *perf*); (*change*) изменя́ться (измени́ться *perf*); (*become*): **he's** ~**ed forty** ему́ испо́лнилось со́рок; **a good/ bad** ~ до́брая/плоха́я услу́га; **it gave me quite a** ~ э́то меня́ си́льно испуга́ло; **"no left** ~**"** (*AUT*) "нет ле́вого поворо́та"; **it's your** ~ твоя́ о́чередь; **in** ~ по о́череди; **to take** ~**s at sth** де́лать (*impf*) что-н по о́череди; **at the** ~ **of the century** на рубеже́ ве́ка; **at the** ~ **of the year** под коне́ц го́да; **to take a** ~ **for the worse** (*situations, events*) принима́ть (приня́ть* *perf*) дурно́й оборо́т; **his health** *or* **he has taken a** ~ **for the worse** ему́ сде́лалось ху́же; **to** ~ **sth into sth** (*change*) превраща́ть (преврати́ть* *perf*) что-н в что-н; **to** ~ **nasty** озлобля́ться (озлоби́ться* *perf*)
▶ **turn about** *vi* повора́чиваться (поверну́ться *perf*)
▶ **turn away** *vi* отвора́чиваться (отверну́ться *perf*) ♦ *vt* (*business, applicant*) отклоня́ть (отклони́ть* *perf*)
▶ **turn back** *vi* повора́чивать (поверну́ть *perf*) наза́д ♦ *vt* (*person*) верну́ть (*perf*); (*vehicle*) развора́чивать (разверну́ть *perf*); (*clock*) переводи́ть* (перевести́* *perf*) наза́д; **to** ~ **back the clock** (*fig*) поверну́ть (*perf*) вре́мя вспять
▶ **turn down** *vt* (*request*) отклоня́ть (отклони́ть* *perf*); (*heating*) уменьша́ть (уме́ньшить *perf*); (*bedclothes*) отвора́чивать (отверну́ть *perf*)
▶ **turn in** *vi* (*inf: go to bed*) идти́* (пойти́* *perf*) на боковую́ ♦ *vt* (*fold*) свора́чивать

---

* marks translations which have irregular inflections. The Russian-English side of the dictionary gives inflectional information.

(сверну́ть *perf*)
▶ **turn off** *vi* (*from road*) свора́чивать
(сверну́ть *perf*) ◆ *vt* выключа́ть (вы́ключить
perf)
▶ **turn on** *vt* включа́ть (включи́ть *perf*)
▶ **turn out** *vt* (*light, gas*) выключа́ть
(вы́ключить *perf*); (*produce*) выпуска́ть
(вы́пустить* *perf*) ◆ *vi* (*troops, doctor, voters*)
прибыва́ть (прибы́ть* *perf*); **to ~ out to be**
(*prove to be*) ока́зываться (оказа́ться* *perf*)
+*instr*
▶ **turn over** *vi* (*person*) перевора́чиваться
(переверну́ться *perf*) ◆ *vt* (*object, page*)
перевора́чивать (переверну́ть *perf*); (*funds,
production etc*): **to ~ over to** передава́ть*
(переда́ть* *perf*) +*dat*
▶ **turn round** *vi* (*person, vehicle*)
развора́чиваться (разверну́ться *perf*);
(*rotate*) повора́чиваться (*impf*)
▶ **turn up** *vi* (*person*) объявля́ться
(объяви́ться* *perf*); (*lost object*) находи́ться*
(найти́сь* *perf*) ◆ *vt* (*collar*) поднима́ть
(подня́ть* *perf*); (*radio*) де́лать (сде́лать *perf*)
гро́мче; (*heater*) де́лать (сде́лать *perf*) вы́ше.
turnabout ['tə:nəbaut] *n* (*fig*) поворо́т на 180
гра́дусов.
turnaround ['tə:nəraund] *n* (*fig*) = **turnabout**.
turncoat ['tə:nkəut] *n* ренега́т, отсту́пник.
turned-up ['tə:ndʌp] *adj* (*nose*) вздёрнутый,
курно́сый.
turning ['tə:nɪŋ] *n* (*in road*) поворо́т; **the first ~
on the right** пе́рвый поворо́т напра́во.
turning circle *n* (*BRIT: AUT*) окру́жность *f*
поворо́та.
turning point *n* (*fig*) поворо́тный пункт,
перело́мный моме́нт.
turning radius *n* (*US*) = **turning circle**.
turnip ['tə:nɪp] *n* (*BOT, CULIN*) ре́па.
turnout ['tə:naut] *n* (*of voters etc*) число́.
turnover ['tə:nəuvə'] *n* (*COMM*) оборо́т; (: *of
staff*) теку́честь *f*; (*CULIN*): **apple ~** я́блочная
сло́йка; **there is a rapid ~ in staff** больша́я
теку́честь ка́дров.
turnpike ['tə:npaik] *n* (*US*) магистра́ль *f*, шоссе́
nt ind.
turnstile ['tə:nstail] *n* турнике́т.
turntable ['tə:nteibl] *n* (*on record player*)
верту́шка*, прои́грыватель *m*.
turn-up ['tə:nʌp] *n* (*BRIT: on trousers*) манжéта,
отворо́т; **that's a ~ for the books!** вот
неожи́данность!
turpentine ['tə:pəntaɪn] *n* (*also:* **turps**)
скипида́р.
turquoise ['tə:kwɔɪz] *n* (*stone*) бирюза́ ◆ *adj*
(*colour*) бирюзо́вый.
turret ['tʌrɪt] *n* ба́шенка*.
turtle ['tə:tl] *n* черепа́ха.
turtleneck (sweater) ['tə:tlnɛk(-)] *n*
водола́зка*.
Tuscany ['tʌskənɪ] *n* Тоска́нь *f*.
tusk [tʌsk] *n* (*of elephant*) би́вень* *m*; (*of boar*)

клык*.
tussle ['tʌsl] *n* (*fight, scuffle*) схва́тка*.
tutor ['tju:tə'] *n* (*SCOL*) преподава́тель(ница)
m(f); (*private tutor*) репети́тор.
tutorial [tju:'tɔ:rɪəl] *n* (*SCOL*) семина́р.
tuxedo [tʌk'si:dəu] *n* (*US*) смо́кинг.
TV [ti:'vi:] *n abbr* (= **television**) ТВ=
телеви́дение; **~ dinner** *пищево́й
полуфабрика́т, го́дный к потребле́нию по́сле
разогре́ва*.
twaddle ['twɒdl] *n* (*inf*) чепуха́.
twang [twæŋ] *n* (*of instrument*) протя́жный
звук; (*of voice*) гну́сность *f* ◆ *vi* протя́жно
звенéть (зазвенéть *perf*) ◆ *vt* (*guitar*)
бренча́ть* (*impf*) на +*prp*.
tweak [twi:k] *vt* дёргать (дёрнуть *perf*) за +*acc*.
tweed [twi:d] *n* твид ◆ *adj* (*jacket, skirt*)
тви́довый.
tweezers ['twi:zəz] *npl* пинцéт *msg*.
twelfth [twɛlfθ] *adj* двена́дцатый; *see also* **fifth**.
Twelfth Night *n* Двена́дцатая ночь *f*.
twelve [twɛlv] *n* двена́дцать*; **at ~** (*o'clock*)
(*midday*) в двена́дцать (дня); (*midnight*) в
двена́дцать (но́чи); *see also* **five**.
twentieth ['twɛntɪɪθ] *adj* двадца́тый; *see also*
fifth.
twenty ['twɛntɪ] *n* два́дцать*; *see also* **fifty**.
twerp [twə:p] *n* (*inf*) крети́н.
twice [twaɪs] *adv* два́жды; **~ as much** вдво́е
бо́льше; **~ a week** два ра́за в неде́лю; **she is
~ your age** она́ вдво́е *or* в два ра́за ста́рше
Вас.
twiddle ['twɪdl] *vt* тереби́ть* (*impf*) ◆ *vi*: **to ~
with sth** тереби́ть* (*impf*) что-н; **to ~ one's
thumbs** (*fig*) бить* (*impf*) баклу́ши.
twig [twɪg] *n* ве́тка* ◆ *vi* (*inf*) стекну́ть (*perf*).
twilight ['twaɪlaɪt] *n* су́мерки *mpl*; (*morning*)
(предрассве́тные) су́мерки; **in the ~** в
су́мерках.
twill [twɪl] *n* (*cloth*) твил, са́ржа.
twin [twɪn] *adj* (*towers*) па́рный ◆ *n* близне́ц*,
двойня́*; (*room in hotel etc*) двойно́й но́мер*
◆ *vt* (*towns etc*) де́лать (сде́лать *perf*)
побрати́мами; **~ sister** сестра́-близне́ц*; **~
brother** брат-близне́ц*.
twin-bedded room ['twɪn'bɛdɪd-] *n* но́мер с
двумя́ односпа́льными крова́тями.
twin beds *npl* две односпа́льные крова́ти *fpl*.
twin-carburettor ['twɪnka:bju'rɛtə'] *adj*
двухкарбюра́торный.
twine [twaɪn] *n* бечёвка ◆ *vi* (*plant*) ви́ться*
(*impf*).
twin-engined [twɪn'ɛndʒɪnd] *adj* (*aircraft*) с
двумя́ дви́гателями.
twinge [twɪndʒ] *n* (*of pain*) при́ступ; (*of
conscience, regret*) уко́л.
twinkle ['twɪŋkl] *vi* (*star, light*) мéрцать (*impf*);
(*eyes*) мига́ть (*impf*), подми́гивать (*impf*) ◆ *n*
мерца́ние.
twin town *n* го́род-побрати́м.
twirl [twə:l] *vt* верте́ть* (*impf*) ◆ *vi* крути́ться*

(*impf*) ♦ *n* поворо́т.

twist [twɪst] *n* (*action*) закру́чивание; (*in road, coil, flex*) изги́б; (*in story*) поворо́т ♦ *vt* (*turn*) изгиба́ть (изогну́ть *perf*); (*injure: ankle etc*) выви́хивать (вы́вихнуть *perf*); (*weave*) сплета́ть (сплести́* *perf*); (*fig: meaning, words*) исказа́ть (исказа́ть* *perf*) ♦ *vi* (*road, river*) извива́ться (*impf*).

twisted ['twɪstɪd] *adj* (*wire, rope*) скру́ченный; (*ankle, wrist*) вы́вихнутый; (*fig: logic, mind*) извращённый.

twit [twɪt] *n* (*inf*) недоу́мок*.

twitch [twɪtʃ] *n* (*pull*) рыво́к*; (*nervous*) подёргивание ♦ *vi* (*muscle, body*) подёргиваться (*impf*).

two [tu:] *n* два* *m/nt* (*f* две*); ~ **by** ~, **in** ~**s** па́рами; **to put** ~ **and** ~ **together** (*fig*) сложи́ть (*perf*) два и два; *see also* **five.**

two-bit [tu:'bɪt] *adj* (*esp US: inf*) расхо́жий.

two-door [tu:'dɔ:'] *adj* (*AUT*) двухдве́рный.

two-faced [tu:'feɪst] *adj* (*pej: person*) двули́чный* (двули́чен).

twofold ['tu:fəuld] *adj* (*increase*) двойно́й; (*reply*) дво́йственный ♦ *adv*: **to increase** ~ вдво́е.

two-piece (suit) ['tu:pi:s-] *n* (костю́м) дво́йка.

two-piece swimsuit *n* разде́льный купа́льник.

two-ply ['tu:plaɪ] *adj* (*wool*) двойно́й; (*tissues*) двухсло́йный* (двухсло́ен).

two-seater car [tu:'si:tə-] *n* двухме́стный автомоби́ль *m*.

twosome ['tu:səm] *n* (*people*) па́ра.

two-stroke ['tu:strəuk] *n* (*also:* ~ **engine**) двухта́ктный дви́гатель *m* ♦ *adj* двухта́ктный.

two-tone ['tu:'təun] *adj* (*in colour*) двухцве́тный.

two-way ['tu:weɪ] *adj*: ~ **traffic** двусторо́ннее движе́ние; ~ **radio** приёмо-переда́ющая радиоста́нция.

TX *abbr* (*US: POST*) = *Texas.*

tycoon [taɪ'ku:n] *n*: (**business**) ~ магна́т.

type [taɪp] *n* (*category, model, example*) тип; (*TYP*) шрифт ♦ *vt* (*letter etc*) печа́тать (напеча́тать *perf*); **what** ~ **do you want?** како́й вид Вы бы хоте́ли?; **in bold** ~ жи́рным шри́фтом; **in italic** ~ курси́вом шри́фтом.

typecast ['taɪpkɑ:st] *adj* (*actor*) одноти́пных роле́й.

typeface ['taɪpfeɪs] *n* шрифт.

typescript ['taɪpskrɪpt] *n* машинопи́сный текст.

typeset ['taɪpset] *vt* набира́ть (набра́ть* *perf*).

typesetter ['taɪpsɛtə] *n* набо́рщик(-ица).

typewriter ['taɪpraɪtə'] *n* пи́шущая маши́нка*.

typewritten ['taɪprɪtn] *adj* машинопи́сный, напеча́танный (напеча́тан) (на маши́нке).

typhoid ['taɪfɔɪd] *n* брюшно́й тиф.

typhoon [taɪ'fu:n] *n* тайфу́н.

typhus ['taɪfəs] *n* сыпно́й тиф.

typical ['tɪpɪkl] *adj* (*behaviour, weather etc*): ~ (**of**) типи́чный* (типи́чен) (для +*gen*); **that's** ~! (*pej*) вот так всегда́!

typify ['tɪpɪfaɪ] *vt* явля́ться (яви́ться* *perf*) типи́чным приме́ром +*gen*.

typing ['taɪpɪŋ] *n* маши́нопись *f*.

typing error *n* опеча́тка*.

typing pool *n* (*BRIT*) машинопи́сное бюро́ *nt ind*.

typist ['taɪpɪst] *n* машини́стка*.

typo ['taɪpəu] *n abbr* (*inf.* = *typographical error*) типогра́фская опеча́тка*.

typography [tɪ'pɔɡrəfɪ] *n* типогра́фия.

tyranny ['tɪrənɪ] *n* тирани́я, деспоти́зм.

tyrant ['taɪərnt] *n* тира́н, де́спот.

tyre ['taɪə'] (*US* **tire**) *n* ши́на.

tyre pressure *n* давле́ние в ши́не.

Tyrol [tɪ'rəul] *n* Тиро́ль *m*.

Tyrolean [tɪrə'li:ən] *adj* тиро́льский ♦ *n* тиро́лец*.

Tyrolese [tɪrə'li:z] = **Tyrolean.**

Tyrrhenian Sea [tɪ'ri:nɪən-] *n*: **the** ~ ~ Тирре́нское мо́ре.

tzar [zɑ:'] *n* = **tsar.**

---

* marks translations which have irregular inflections. The Russian-English side of the dictionary gives inflectional information.

~ U, u ~

U, u [ju:] *n* (*letter*) 21-ая бу́ква англи́йского алфави́та.

U *n abbr* (*BRIT: CINEMA:* = *universal*) фильм, приго́дный для пока́за всем возрастны́м гру́ппам.

UAW *n abbr* (*US*) = United Automobile Workers.

UB40 *n abbr* (*BRIT:* = *unemployment benefit form 40*) бланк, заполня́емый при получе́нии посо́бия по безрабо́тице.

U-bend ['juːbend] *n* (*in pipe*) двойно́й изги́б.

ubiquitous [juːˈbɪkwɪtəs] *adj* вездесу́щий* (вездесу́щ).

UCCA [ˈʌkə] *n abbr* (*BRIT:* = *Universities Central Council on Admissions*) организа́ция, координи́рующая приём в университе́ты.

UDA *n abbr* (*BRIT:* = *Ulster Defence Association*) военизи́рованная организа́ция, борю́щаяся за сохране́ние Се́верой Ирла́ндии как ча́сти Великобрита́нии.

UDC *n abbr* (*BRIT*) = Urban District Council.

udder [ˈʌdə'] *n* вы́мя* *nt.

UDI *n abbr* (*BRIT: POL:* = *unilateral declaration of independence*) односторо́ннее провозглаше́ние незави́симости.

UDR *n abbr* (*BRIT:* = *Ulster Defence Regiment*) ча́сти брита́нской а́рмии, размещённые в Се́верной Ирла́ндии.

UEFA [juːˈeɪfə] *n abbr* (= *Union of European Football Associations*) УЕФА́.

UFO [ˈjuːfəu] *n abbr* (= *unidentified flying object*) НЛО= неопо́знанный лета́ющий объе́кт.

Uganda [juːˈɡændə] *n* Уга́нда.

Ugandan [juːˈɡændən] *adj* уга́ндский ♦ *n* уга́ндец*(-дка*).

UGC *n abbr* (*BRIT:* = *University Grants Committee*) комите́т, координи́рующий финанси́рование университе́тов.

ugh [əːh] *excl* фу.

ugliness [ˈʌɡlɪnɪs] *n* уро́дство.

ugly [ˈʌɡlɪ] *adj* (*person, dress etc*) уро́дливый (уро́длив), безобра́зный* (безобра́зен); (*dangerous: situation*) опа́сный* (опа́сен).

UHF *abbr* (= *ultra-high frequency*) УВЧ= ультравысо́кая частота́.

UHT *abbr* = *ultra heat treated* ♦ *adj abbr:* ~ **milk** молоко́, проше́дшее обрабо́тку сверх-высо́кой температу́рой.

UK *n abbr* = United Kingdom.

Ukraine [juːˈkreɪn] *n* Украи́на.

Ukrainian [juːˈkreɪnɪən] *adj* украи́нский* ♦ *n* украи́нец*(-нка); (*LING*) украи́нский* язы́к*.

Ulan Bator *n* [uˈlɑːnˈbɑːtɔːˈ] Ула́н-Ба́тор.

ulcer [ˈʌlsə'] *n* я́зва.

Ulster [ˈʌlstə'] *n* О́льстер.

ulterior [ʌlˈtɪərɪə'] *adj:* ~ **motive** скры́тый моти́в.

ultimata [ʌltɪˈmeɪtə] *npl of* **ultimatum.**

ultimate [ˈʌltɪmət] *adj* (*final*) оконча́тельный*, коне́чный*; (*greatest*) преде́льный* ♦ *n:* **the** ~ **in luxury** преде́л ро́скоши.

ultimately [ˈʌltɪmətlɪ] *adv* в конце́ концо́в.

ultimatum [ʌltɪˈmeɪtəm] (*pl* ~**s** *or* **ultimata**) *n* ультима́тум.

ultrasonic [ʌltrəˈsɔnɪk] *adj* (*sound*) сверхзвуково́й, ультразвуково́й.

ultrasound [ˈʌltrəsaund] *n* ультразву́к.

ultraviolet [ˈʌltrəˈvaɪəlɪt] *adj* (*light etc*) ультрафиоле́товый.

umbilical cord [ʌmˈbɪlɪkl-] *n* пупови́на.

umbrage [ˈʌmbrɪdʒ] *n:* **to take** ~ обижа́ться (оби́деться* *perf*).

umbrella [ʌmˈbrelə] *n* зо́нтик, зонт*; (*fig*): **under the** ~ **of** под защи́той +*gen*.

umlaut [ˈumlaut] *n* у́мляут.

umpire [ˈʌmpaɪə'] *n* (*TENNIS, CRICKET*) судья́* *m*, рефери́ *m ind* ♦ *vt* (*game*) суди́ть* (*impf*).

umpteen [ʌmpˈtiːn] *adj* (*inf*) бесчи́сленный; ~ **stories** бесконе́чное коли́чество исто́рии.

umpteenth [ʌmpˈtiːnθ] *adj* (*inf*): **for the** ~ **time** в э́нный *or* со́тый раз.

UMW *n abbr* = United Mineworkers of America.

UN *n abbr* = United Nations.

unabashed [ʌnəˈbæʃt] *adj:* **she seemed** ~ она́ каза́лась не возмути́мой.

unabated [ʌnəˈbeɪtɪd] *adj* (*enthusiasm, excitement*) неосла́бный* (неосла́бен) ♦ *adv:* **to continue** ~ продолжа́ться (продо́лжиться *perf*) с той же си́лой.

unable [ʌnˈeɪbl] *adj* неспосо́бный*; **he is** ~ **to pay** он не спосо́бен заплати́ть.

unabridged [ʌnəˈbrɪdʒd] *adj* (*novel etc*) несокращённый.

unacceptable [ʌnəkˈsɛptəbl] *adj* неприе́млемый (неприе́млем).

unaccompanied [ʌnəˈkʌmpənɪd] *adj* (*child, luggage*) не сопровожда́емый; (*song*) без аккомпанеме́нта.

unaccountably [ʌnəˈkauntəblɪ] *adv* необъяснймо.

unaccounted [ʌnə'kauntɪd] *adj*: **several people are still ~ for** нескольких людей недосчитались.

unaccustomed [ʌnə'kʌstəmd] *adj*: **he is ~ to ...** он не привычен к +*dat* ....

unacquainted [ʌnə'kweɪntɪd] *adj*: **he is ~ with these ideas** он не знаком с этими идеями.

unadulterated [ʌnə'dʌltəreɪtɪd] *adj* настоящий*; (*wine*) чистый*.

unaffected [ʌnə'fɛktɪd] *adj* (*person, behaviour*) естественный* (естествен); **~ by** (*emotionally*) безучастный (безучастен) к +*dat*.

unafraid [ʌnə'freɪd] *adj* незапуганный.

unaided [ʌn'eɪdɪd] *adv* без помощи.

unanimity [juːnə'nɪmɪtɪ] *n* единодушие, единогласие.

unanimous [juː'nænɪməs] *adj* единодушный* (единодушен), единогласный* (единогласен).

unanimously [juː'nænɪməslɪ] *adv* единодушно, единогласно.

unanswered [ʌn'ɑːnsəd] *adj* оставшийся без ответа.

unappetizing [ʌn'æpɪtaɪzɪŋ] *adj* (*food etc*) неаппетитный* (неаппетитен).

unappreciative [ʌnə'priːʃɪətɪv] *adj* неблагодарный* (неблагодарен).

unarmed [ʌn'ɑːmd] *adj* безоружный* (безоружен); (*combat*) без оружия.

unashamed [ʌnə'ʃeɪmd] *adj* бесстыдный* (бесстыден).

unassisted [ʌnə'sɪstɪd] *adj, adv* без посторонней помощи.

unassuming [ʌnə'sjuːmɪŋ] *adj* (*person, manner*) непритязательный* (непритязателен).

unattached [ʌnə'tætʃt] *adj* (*person*) одинокий* (одинок); (*part etc*) неприкреплённый.

unattended [ʌnə'tɛndɪd] *adj* оставленный (оставлен) без присмотра.

unattractive [ʌnə'træktɪv] *adj* непривлекательный* (непривлекателен).

unauthorized [ʌn'ɔːθəraɪzd] *adj* неразрешённый*.

unavailable [ʌnə'veɪləbl] *adj* (*article, room etc*) недоступный* (недоступен); (*person*) недосягаемый (недосягаем).

unavoidable [ʌnə'vɔɪdəbl] *adj* (*delay*) неизбежный* (неизбежен).

unavoidably [ʌnə'vɔɪdəblɪ] *adv* (*delayed etc*) неизбежно.

unaware [ʌnə'wɛə'] *adj*: **to be ~ of** не подозревать (*impf*) о +*prp*.

unawares [ʌnə'wɛəz] *adv* врасплох.

unbalanced [ʌn'bælənst] *adj* (*report*) односторонний*; (*mentally*) неуравновешенный* (неуравновешен).

unbearable [ʌn'bɛərəbl] *adj* невыносимый (невыносим).

unbeatable [ʌn'biːtəbl] *adj* (*team*) непобедимый (непобедим); (*price, quality*) непревзойдённый* (непревзойдён).

unbeaten [ʌn'biːtn] *adj* (*person*) непобедимый (непобедим); (*record*) непревзойдённый* (непревзойдён).

unbecoming [ʌnbɪ'kʌmɪŋ] *adj* (*language, behaviour*) неподобающий (неподобающ); (*garment*) не идущий к лицу; **that dress is ~ on you** Вам не идёт это платье.

unbeknown(st) [ʌnbɪ'nəun(st)] *adv*: **~ to me** без моего ведома.

unbelief [ʌnbɪ'liːf] *n* неверие.

unbelievable [ʌnbɪ'liːvəbl] *adj* невероятный* (невероятен).

unbelievably [ʌnbɪ'liːvəblɪ] *adv* невероятно.

unbend [ʌn'bɛnd] *irreg vi* (*relax*) расслабляться (расслабиться* *perf*) ◆ *vt* (*wire*) выпрямлять (выпрямить* *perf*).

unbending [ʌn'bɛndɪŋ] *adj* непреклонный* (непреклонен).

unbias(s)ed [ʌn'baɪəst] *adj* (*report*) непредвзятый (непредвзят); (*person*) беспристрастный* (беспристрастен).

unblemished [ʌn'blɛmɪʃt] *adj* незапятнанный (незапятнан).

unblock [ʌn'blɔk] *vt* (*pipe*) прочищать (прочистить* *perf*).

unborn [ʌn'bɔːn] *adj* (ещё) не рождённый.

unbounded [ʌn'baundɪd] *adj* безграничный* (безграничен).

unbreakable [ʌn'breɪkəbl] *adj* небьющийся.

unbridled [ʌn'braɪdld] *adj* необузданный* (необуздан).

unbroken [ʌn'brəukən] *adj* (*seal*) целый* (цел); (*silence, series*) непрерванный; (*window*) неразбитый, целый* (цел); (*SPORT: record*) непобитый.

unbuckle [ʌn'bʌkl] *vt* (*belt, shoe*) расстёгивать (расстегнуть* *perf*).

unburden [ʌn'bəːdn] *vt*: **to ~ o.s. (to sb)** изливать (излить* *perf*) душу (кому-н).

unbusinesslike [ʌn'bɪznɪslaɪk] *adj* неделовой.

unbutton [ʌn'bʌtn] *vt* расстёгивать (расстегнуть* *perf*).

uncalled-for [ʌn'kɔːldfɔː'] *adj* неуместный* (неуместен).

uncanny [ʌn'kænɪ] *adj* (*resemblance, knack*) необъяснимый (необъясним); (*silence*) жуткий* (жуток).

unceasing [ʌn'siːsɪŋ] *adj* (*misery, flow etc*) беспрерывный* (беспрерывен); (*search*) неустанный* (неустанен).

unceremonious [ʌnsɛrɪ'məunɪəs] *adj* (*abrupt, rude*) бесцеремонный* (бесцеремонен).

uncertain [ʌn'səːtn] *adj* (*hesitant*)

---

* marks translations which have irregular inflections. The Russian-English side of the dictionary gives inflectional information.

неуве́ренный* (неуве́рен), нереши́тельный* (нереши́телен); (*unsure*): ~ **about** неуве́ренный* (неуве́рен) относи́тельно +*gen*; **in no** ~ **terms** без обиняко́в.

uncertainty [ʌn'sɜ:tntɪ] *n* (*not knowing*) неопределённость *f*; (*often pl*: *doubt*) сомне́ние.

unchallenged [ʌn'tʃælɪndʒd] *adj* не вызыва́ющий* возраже́ний; **to go** ~ не вызыва́ть (вы́звать* *perf*) возраже́ний.

unchanged [ʌn'tʃeɪndʒd] *adj* (*condition*) неизмени́вшийся; **my orders remain** ~ мои́ прика́зы остаю́тся неизме́нными.

uncharitable [ʌn'tʃærɪtəbl] *adj* немилосе́рдный* (немилосе́рден).

uncharted [ʌn'tʃɑ:tɪd] *adj* (*land, sea*) не отме́ченный на ка́рте.

unchecked [ʌn'tʃɛkt] *adv* беспрепя́тственно.

uncivil [ʌn'sɪvɪl] *adj* гру́бый* (груб).

uncivilized [ʌn'sɪvɪlaɪzd] *adj* (*country, people*) нецивилизо́ванный (нецивилизо́ван); (*fig*: *behaviour etc*) ди́кий* (дик); **at an** ~ **hour** ни свет, ни заря́.

uncle ['ʌŋkl] *n* дя́дя* *m*.

unclear [ʌn'klɪəʳ] *adj* нея́сный* (нея́сен); **I'm still** ~ **about what I'm supposed to do** мне всё ещё нея́сно, что мне на́до де́лать.

uncoil [ʌn'kɔɪl] *vt* разма́тывать (размота́ть *perf*) ◆ *vi* разма́тываться (размота́ться *perf*).

uncomfortable [ʌn'kʌmfətəbl] *adj* (*physically*) неудо́бный* (неудо́бен); (*uneasy*) неудо́бный* (неудо́бен), нело́вкий* (нело́вок); (*unpleasant*) трево́жный* (трево́жен).

uncomfortably [ʌn'kʌmfətəblɪ] *adv* (*sit*) неудо́бно; (*smile*) нело́вко; (*tall, shy*) до нело́вкого.

uncommitted [ʌnkə'mɪtɪd] *adj* нейтра́льный* (нейтра́лен).

uncommon [ʌn'kɔmən] *adj* (*rare, unusual*) необы́чный* (необы́чен).

uncommunicative [ʌnkə'mju:nɪkətɪv] *adj* необщи́тельный* (необщи́телен).

uncomplicated [ʌn'kɔmplɪkeɪtɪd] *adj* несло́жный* (несло́жен).

uncompromising [ʌn'kɔmprəmaɪzɪŋ] *adj* бескомпроми́ссный.

unconcerned [ʌnkən'sɜ:nd] *adj* (*person*) беззабо́тный* (беззабо́тен); ~ **about** равноду́шный* (равноду́шен) к +*dat*.

unconditional [ʌnkən'dɪʃənl] *adj* (*acceptance, obedience*) безусло́вный* (безусло́вен); (*discharge, surrender*) безогово́рочный* (безогово́рочен).

uncongenial [ʌnkən'dʒi:nɪəl] *adj* (*surroundings*) чу́ждый* (чужд), неприя́тный* (неприя́тен).

unconnected [ʌnkə'nɛktɪd] *adj* (*unrelated*): ~ **(with)** несвя́занный (с +*instr*).

unconscious [ʌn'kɔnʃəs] *adj* без созна́ния; (*unaware*): ~ **of** не сознаю́щий* +*gen* ◆ *n*: **the** ~ подсозна́ние; **he was knocked** ~ он упа́л без созна́ния.

unconsciously [ʌn'kɔnʃəslɪ] *adv* (*unawares*) подсозна́тельно.

unconsciousness [ʌn'kɔnʃəsnɪs] *n* бессозна́тельное состоя́ние.

unconstitutional ['ʌnkɔnstɪ'tju:ʃənl] *adj* неконституцио́нный* (неконституцио́нен).

uncontested [ʌnkən'tɛstɪd] *adj* (*champion*) неоспори́мый* (неоспори́м); ~ **election** вы́боры, на кото́рых баллоти́руется (лишь) оди́н кандида́т.

uncontrollable [ʌnkən'trəuləbl] *adj* (*child, animal*) неуправля́емый (неуправля́ем); (*temper*) неукроти́мый* (неукроти́м); (*laughter*) неудержи́мый* (неудержи́м).

uncontrolled [ʌnkən'trəuld] *adj* безу́держный* (безу́держен).

unconventional [ʌnkən'vɛnʃənl] *adj* нетрадицио́нный* (нетрадицио́нен).

unconvinced [ʌnkən'vɪnst] *adj*: **to be** *or* **remain** ~ остава́ться* (оста́ться* *perf*) неубеждённым(-ой).

unconvincing [ʌnkən'vɪnsɪŋ] *adj* неубеди́тельный* (неубеди́телен).

uncork [ʌn'kɔ:k] *vt* (*bottle*) отку́поривать (отку́порить *perf*).

uncorroborated [ʌnkə'rɔbəreɪtɪd] *adj* неподтверждённый.

uncouth [ʌn'ku:θ] *adj* неотёсанный* (неотёсан).

uncover [ʌn'kʌvəʳ] *vt* открыва́ть (откры́ть* *perf*); (*plot, secret*) раскрыва́ть (раскры́ть* *perf*).

unctuous ['ʌŋktjuəs] *adj* еле́йный* (еле́ен).

undamaged [ʌn'dæmɪdʒd] *adj* (*goods*) неповреждённый* (*fig*: *reputation*) незапя́тнанный (незапя́тнан).

undaunted [ʌn'dɔ:ntɪd] *adj* (*person*) неустраши́мый* (неустраши́м); ~, **she struggled on** она́ неустраши́мо продолжа́ла свои́ стара́ния.

undecided [ʌndɪ'saɪdɪd] *adj* (*person*) нереши́тельный* (нереши́телен); (*question*) нерешённый.

undelivered [ʌndɪ'lɪvəd] *adj* (*goods, letters*) недоста́вленный; **if** ~ **return to sender** е́сли не доста́влено, верну́ть отправи́телю.

undeniable [ʌndɪ'naɪəbl] *adj* (*fact, evidence*) неоспори́мый* (неоспори́м).

undeniably [ʌndɪ'naɪəblɪ] *adv* несомне́нно.

under ['ʌndəʳ] *adv* (*go, fly etc*) вниз ◆ *prep* (*position*) под +*instr*; (*motion*) под +*acc*; (*less than: in price*) ни́же +*gen*; (*according to: law, agreement etc*) по +*dat*; (*during: sb's leadership*) при +*prp*; (*in age*): **children** ~ **16** де́ти до 16-ти лет; **from** ~ **sth** из-под чего́-л; ~ **there** там внизу́; **in** ~ **2 hours** ме́ньше, чем за 2 часа́; ~ **anaesthetic** под нарко́зом; ~ **discussion** в проце́ссе обсужде́ния; ~ **repair** в ремо́нте; ~ **the circumstances** при сложи́вшихся обстоя́тельствах.

under... ['ʌndə'] *prefix* недо....
underage [ʌndər'eɪdʒ] *adj* (*person*) несовершеннолétний*; ~ **smoking/drinking** курéние/потреблéние алкогóля несовершеннолéтними.
underarm ['ʌndərɑːm] *adv* (*bowl*) снúзу ♦ *adj* (*deodorant*) для подмýшек; ~ **throw** бросóк* снúзу.
undercapitalized ['ʌndə'kæpɪtəlaɪzd] *adj* (*project, industry*) недостáточно капитализúрованный.
undercarriage ['ʌndəkærɪdʒ] *n* (BRIT) шассú *nt ind*.
undercharge [ʌndə'tʃɑːdʒ] *vt* назначáть (назнáчить *perf*) слúшком нúзкую цéну.
underclass ['ʌndəklɑːs] *n* неимýщий* класс.
underclothes ['ʌndəkləuðz] *npl* нúжнее бельё *ntsg*.
undercoat ['ʌndəkəut] *n* (*paint*) грунтóвка*.
undercover [ʌndə'kʌvə'] *adj* тáйный.
undercurrent ['ʌndəkʌrnt] *n* (*fig*) затаённое чýвство.
undercut [ʌndə'kʌt] *irreg vt* (*prices*) сбивáть (сбúть* *perf*); **he can ~ his competitors** он мóжет продавáть по бóлее нúзкой ценé, чем егó конкурéнты.
underdeveloped ['ʌndədɪ'vɛləpt] *adj* (*country, region*) слаборáзвитый (слаборáзвит).
underdog ['ʌndədɔg] *n*: **the ~** (*in society*) обездóленный *m adj*; (*in team competition*) слáбая комáнда.
underdone [ʌndə'dʌn] *adj* (*fried, roasted food*) недожáренный; (*boiled food*) недовáр-енный.
underemployment ['ʌndərɪm'plɔɪmənt] *n* непóлная зáнятость *f*.
underestimate ['ʌndər'ɛstɪmeɪt] *vt* недооцéнивать (недооценúть* *perf*).
underexposed ['ʌndərɪks'pəuzd] *adj* (PHOT) недодéржанный.
underfed [ʌndə'fɛd] *adj* недокóрмленный.
underfoot [ʌndə'fut] *adv* (*crush, trample*) ногáми.
underfunded ['ʌndə'fʌndɪd] *adj* плóхо финансúруемый.
undergo [ʌndə'gəu] *irreg vt* (*repair*) проходúть* (пройтú* *perf*); (*operation*) переносúть* (перенестú* *perf*); (*change*) подвергáться (подвéргнуться* *perf*) +*dat*; **the car is ~ing repairs** машúна проходит ремóнт.
undergraduate [ʌndə'grædjuɪt] *n* студéнт(ка) ♦ *cpd*: ~ **courses** университéтские кýрсы *mpl*.
underground ['ʌndəgraund] *adv* (*work*) под землёй ♦ *adj* (*car park*) подзéмный; (*newspaper, activities*) подпóльный ♦ *n*: **the ~** (BRIT: *railway*) метрó *nt ind*; (POL) подпóлье; **to go ~** (*fig*) уходúть* (уйтú* *perf*) в подпóлье.
undergrowth ['ʌndəgrəuθ] *n*: **the ~** подлéсок*.

underhand(ed) [ʌndə'hænd(ɪd)] *adj* (*fig: behaviour, method etc*) закулúсный.
underinsured [ʌndərɪn'ʃuəd] *adj* непóлностью застрахóванный*.
underlay [ʌndə'leɪ] *n* подклáдка*.
underlie [ʌndə'laɪ] *irreg vt* (*fig*) лежáть (*impf*) в оснóве +*gen*; **the underlying cause** причúна, лежáщая в оснóве.
underline [ʌndə'laɪn] *vt* (*also fig*) подчёркивать (подчеркнýть *perf*).
underling ['ʌndəlɪŋ] *n* (*pej*) мéлкая сóшка*.
undermanning [ʌndə'mænɪŋ] *n* недостáток* в рабóчей сúле.
undermentioned [ʌndə'mɛnʃənd] *adj* нижеупомя́нутый.
undermine [ʌndə'maɪn] *vt* (*confidence, authority*) подрывáть (подорвáть* *perf*).
underneath [ʌndə'niːθ] *adv* внизý ♦ *prep* (*position*) под +*instr*; (*motion*) под +*acc*.
undernourished [ʌndə'nʌrɪʃt] *adj* недокóрмленный.
underpaid [ʌndə'peɪd] *adj* (*person*) не получáющий дóлжной оплáты, низкооплáчиваемый (низкооплáчиваем).
underpants ['ʌndəpænts] *npl* (*men's*) трусы́ *pl*.
underpass ['ʌndəpɑːs] *n* (BRIT) туннéль *m*, тоннéль *m*.
underpin [ʌndə'pɪn] *vt* (*argument, case*) подкреплять (подкрепúть* *perf*).
underplay [ʌndə'pleɪ] *vt* (BRIT) преуменьшáть (преумéньшить *perf*).
underpopulated [ʌndə'pɔpjuleɪtɪd] *adj* малонаселённый* (малонаселён).
underprice [ʌndə'praɪs] *vt* занижáть (занизúть* *perf*) слúшком нúзкую цéну на +*acc*.
underprivileged [ʌndə'prɪvɪlɪdʒd] *adj* (*family*) неимýщий*.
underrate [ʌndə'reɪt] *vt* недооцéнивать (недооценúть* *perf*).
underscore [ʌndə'skɔː'] *vt* (*word*) подчёркивать (подчеркнýть *perf*).
underseal [ʌndə'siːl] *vt* (BRIT: AUT) наносúть* (нанестú* *perf*) антикоррозúйное покрытие (*на днúще автомобúля*) ♦ *n* (AUT) антикоррозúйное покрытие (*днúща автомобúля*).
undersecretary ['ʌndə'sɛkrətərɪ] *n* (POL) заместúтель *m* минúстра.
undersell [ʌndə'sɛl] *irreg vt* (*competitors*) продавáть* (продáть* *perf*) дешéвле +*gen*.
undershirt ['ʌndəʃəːt] *n* (US) нúжняя рубáшка*.
undershorts ['ʌndəʃɔːts] *npl* (US) трусы́ *pl*.
underside ['ʌndəsaɪd] *n* нúжняя сторонá*.
undersigned ['ʌndə'saɪnd] *adj* (*document*) подпúсанный нúже ♦ *n* нижепод-писáвшийся*(-аяся) *m(f) adj*; **we the ~ agree**

that ... мы, нижеподписа́вшиеся,
догова́риваемся, что ....
underskirt [ˈʌndəskɔːt] n (BRIT) ни́жняя ю́бка*.
understaffed [ʌndəˈstɑːft] adj (project etc)
неукомплекто́ванный ка́драми.
understand [ʌndəˈstænd] (irreg: like **stand**) vt
понима́ть (поня́ть* perf); (believe): **to ~ that**
полага́ть (impf), что ...; **to make o.s.**
understood объясня́ться (объясни́ться perf).
understandable [ʌndəˈstændəbl] adj
поня́тный* (поня́тен).
understanding [ʌndəˈstændɪŋ] adj (kind)
понима́ющий ♦ n понима́ние; (agreement)
взаимопонима́ние; **to come to an ~ with sb**
достига́ть (дости́чь* perf) взаимопонима́ния
с кем-н; **on the ~ that** ... при усло́вии, что ....
understate [ʌndəˈsteɪt] vt преуменьша́ть
(преуме́ньшить perf).
understatement [ˈʌndəsteɪtmənt] n (quality)
преуменьше́ние; **that's an ~!** э́то сли́шком
мя́гко ска́зано!
understood [ʌndəˈstud] pt, pp of **understand** ♦
adj (agreed) согласо́ванный* (согласо́ван);
(implied) подразумева́емый
(подразумева́ем).
understudy [ˈʌndəstʌdɪ] n дублёр.
undertake [ʌndəˈteɪk] (irreg: like **take**) vt (task,
duty) брать* (взять* perf) на себя́; **to ~ to do**
обя́зываться (обяза́ться* perf) +infin.
undertaker [ˈʌndəteɪkəʳ] n владе́лец*
похоро́нного бюро́.
undertaking [ˈʌndəteɪkɪŋ] n (job) предприя́тие;
(promise) обяза́тельство.
undertone [ˈʌndətəun] n (of criticism etc)
отте́нок*; (speak): **in an ~** вполго́лоса.
undervalue [ʌndəˈvælju:] vt недооце́нивать
(недооцени́ть* perf).
underwater [ʌndəˈwɔːtəʳ] adv (use, swim etc)
под водо́й ♦ adj (exploration, camera etc)
подво́дный.
underwear [ˈʌndəwɛəʳ] n ни́жнее бельё.
underweight [ʌndəˈweɪt] adj вся́щий ни́же
но́рмы.
underworld [ˈʌndəwɔːld] n (of crime)
престу́пный мир.
underwrite [ʌndəˈraɪt] vt (FINANCE) гаран-
ти́ровать (impf/perf) размеще́ние +gen;
(COMM) брать* (взять* perf) на себя́
финанси́рование +gen; (INSURANCE)
принима́ть (приня́ть* perf) на себя́
страхово́й риск.
underwriter [ˈʌndəraɪtə] n (INSURANCE)
андерра́йтер, принима́ющий m adj на себя́
страхово́й риск.
undeserving [ʌndɪˈzɜːvɪŋ] adj: **to be ~ of** не
заслу́живать (impf) +gen.
undesirable [ʌndɪˈzaɪərəbl] adj нежела́тель-
ный* (нежела́телен).
undeveloped [ʌndɪˈvɛləpt] adj (land) незастро́-
енный; (resources) неразрабо́танный.
undies [ˈʌndɪz] npl (inf) (ни́жнее) бельё ntsg.

undiluted [ˈʌndaɪˈluːtɪd] adj (substance, liquid)
неразба́вленный; (emotion) чи́стый.
undiplomatic [ˈʌndɪpləˈmætɪk] adj
недипломати́чный* (недипломати́чен).
undischarged [ˈʌndɪsˈtʃɑːdʒd] adj: **~ bankrupt**
не восстано́вленный в права́х банкро́т.
undisciplined [ʌnˈdɪsɪplɪnd] adj недисциплин-
и́рованный (недисциплини́рован).
undiscovered [ˈʌndɪsˈkʌvəd] adj (island)
неоткры́тый; (fact) необнару́женный;
(situation) неиссле́дованный.
undisguised [ˈʌndɪsˈgaɪzd] adj я́вный* (я́вен).
undisputed [ˈʌndɪsˈpjuːtɪd] adj неоспори́мый
(неоспори́м).
undistinguished [ˈʌndɪsˈtɪŋgwɪʃt] adj
посре́дственный* (посре́дствен).
undisturbed [ˈʌndɪsˈtɜːbd] adj (uninterrupted)
безмяте́жный* (безмяте́жен); **to leave ~** не
волнова́ть (impf).
undivided [ʌndɪˈvaɪdɪd] adj: **can I have your ~**
attention? я прошу́ Ва́шего неразде́льного
внима́ния.
undo [ʌnˈduː] (irreg: like **do**) vt (unfasten: laces,
strings) развя́зывать (развяза́ть* perf);
(: buttons) расстёгивать (расстегну́ть perf);
(spoil) губи́ть* (погуби́ть* perf).
undoing [ʌnˈduːɪŋ] n (downfall) ги́бель f.
undone [ʌnˈdʌn] pp of **undo**; (unfastened): **my**
lace has come ~ у меня́ развяза́лся шнуро́к.
undoubted [ʌnˈdautɪd] adj несомне́нный*
(несомне́нен), беспо́рный* (беспо́рен).
undoubtedly [ʌnˈdautɪdlɪ] adv несомне́нно,
беспо́рно.
undress [ʌnˈdrɛs] vt раздева́ть (разде́ть* perf) ♦
vi раздева́ться (разде́ться* perf).
undrinkable [ʌnˈdrɪŋkəbl] adj (poisonous)
неприго́дный для питья́; (unpalatable): **this**
wine is ~ э́то вино́ невозмо́жно пить.
undue [ʌnˈdjuː] adj изли́шний*.
undulating [ˈʌndjuleɪtɪŋ] adj холми́стый*.
unduly [ʌnˈdjuːlɪ] adv изли́шне.
undying [ʌnˈdaɪɪŋ] adj бессме́ртный*.
unearned [ʌnˈɜːnd] adj незарабо́танный; **~**
income нетрудовы́е дохо́ды mpl.
unearth [ʌnˈɜːθ] vt выка́пывать (вы́копать
perf); (fig) раска́пывать (раскопа́ть perf).
unearthly [ʌnˈɜːθlɪ] adj: **at an ~ hour** ни свет,
ни заря́.
unease [ʌnˈiːz] n нело́вкость f.
uneasy [ʌnˈiːzɪ] adj (feeling) трево́жный*
(трево́жен); (peace, truce) напряжённый*;
(person): **he is** or **feels ~** он неспоко́ен; **I feel ~**
about taking his money я неспоко́ен, когда́
беру́ у него́ де́ньги.
uneconomic(al) [ˈʌniːkəˈnɔmɪk(l)] adj
неэконо́мный*.
uneducated [ʌnˈɛdjukeɪtɪd] adj (person)
необразо́ванный*.
unemployed [ʌnɪmˈplɔɪd] adj (worker)
безрабо́тный ♦ npl: **the ~** безрабо́тные pl adj.
unemployment [ʌnɪmˈplɔɪmənt] n

безрабо́тица.
unemployment benefit *n* посо́бие по
безрабо́тице.
unemployment compensation *n* (*US*) =
unemployment benefit.
unending [ʌnˈɛndɪŋ] *adj* несконча́емый.
unenviable [ʌnˈɛnvɪəbl] *adj* незави́дный*
(незави́ден).
unequal [ʌnˈiːkwəl] *adj* нера́вный* (нера́вен);
to feel ~ to чу́вствовать (*impf*) себя́
неспосо́бным отвеча́ть тре́бованиям +*gen*.
unequalled [ʌnˈiːkwəld] (*US* **unequaled**) *adj*
несравни́мый (несравни́м).
unequivocal [ʌnɪˈkwɪvəkl] *adj* (*answer, person*)
недвусмы́сленный*.
unerring [ʌnˈəːrɪŋ] *adj* безоши́бочный*
(безоши́бочен).
UNESCO [juːˈnɛskəu] *n abbr* (= *United Nations
Educational, Scientific and Cultural
Organization*) ЮНЕ́СКО.
unethical [ʌnˈɛθɪkl] *adj* неэти́чный*
(неэти́чен).
uneven [ʌnˈiːvn] *adj* неро́вный*.
uneventful [ʌnɪˈvɛntful] *adj* без осо́бых
собы́тий.
unexceptional [ʌnɪkˈsɛpʃənl] *adj* заурядный*
(заурядн).
unexciting [ʌnɪkˈsaɪtɪŋ] *adj* (*news, film*)
неинтере́сный* (неинтере́сен).
unexpected [ʌnɪksˈpɛktɪd] *adj* неожи́данный*
(неожи́дан).
unexpectedly [ʌnɪksˈpɛktɪdlɪ] *adv* неожи́данно.
unexplained [ʌnɪksˈpleɪnd] *adj* необъясн-
ённый.
unexploded [ʌnɪksˈpləudɪd] *adj* (*bomb*)
невзорва́вшийся.
unfailing [ʌnˈfeɪlɪŋ] *adj* неизме́нный*
(неизме́нен).
unfair [ʌnˈfɛəʳ] *adj*: ~ (**to**) несправедли́вый (к
+*dat*); **it's ~ that** ... несправедли́во, что ....
unfair dismissal *n* незако́нное увольне́ние.
unfairly [ʌnˈfɛəlɪ] *adv* (*treat*) несправедли́во;
(*dismiss*) незако́нно.
unfaithful [ʌnˈfeɪθful] *adj* неве́рный* (неве́рен).
unfamiliar [ʌnfəˈmɪlɪəʳ] *adj* незнако́мый
(незнако́м); **he is ~ with the accent** он
незнако́м с акце́нтом.
unfashionable [ʌnˈfæʃnəbl] *adj* немо́дный*
(немо́ден).
unfasten [ʌnˈfɑːsn] *vt* (*undo*) расстёгивать
(расстегну́ть *perf*); (*open*) открыва́ть
(откры́ть *perf*).
unfathomable [ʌnˈfæðəməbl] *adj* (*mystery*)
непостижи́мый (непостижи́м).
unfavourable [ʌnˈfeɪvrəbl] (*US* **unfavorable**) *adj*
неблагоприя́тный* (неблагоприя́тен).
unfavourably [ʌnˈfeɪvrəblɪ] (*US* **unfavorably**)
adv (*compare, review*) неблагоприя́тно; **to**

look ~ on (*suggestion etc*) смотре́ть* (*impf*)
неблагоскло́нно на +*acc*.
unfeeling [ʌnˈfiːlɪŋ] *adj* бесчу́вственный*
(бесчу́вствен).
unfinished [ʌnˈfɪnɪʃt] *adj* незако́нченный.
unfit [ʌnˈfɪt] *adj* (*physically*): **she is ~** она́ в
плохо́й спорти́вной фо́рме; **he is ~ for the
job** он неприго́ден к рабо́те.
unflagging [ʌnˈflægɪŋ] *adj* неосла́бный*
(неосла́бен).
unflappable [ʌnˈflæpəbl] *adj* невозмути́мый
(невозмути́м).
unflattering [ʌnˈflætərɪŋ] *adj* (*remark*)
нелéстный* (нелéстен); (*garment*) не иду́щий
к лицу́; **that dress is ~ on you** Вам не идёт
э́то пла́тье.
unflinching [ʌnˈflɪntʃɪŋ] *adj* неустраши́мый
(неустраши́м).
unfold [ʌnˈfəuld] *vt* (*sheets, map*)
развора́чивать *or* развёртывать
(разверну́ть *perf*) ♦ *vi* (*situation*)
развора́чиваться (разверну́ться *perf*).
unforeseeable [ʌnfɔːˈsiːəbl] *adj*
непредви́денный* (непредви́ден).
unforeseen [ˈʌnfɔːˈsiːn] *adj* непредви́денный.
unforgettable [ʌnfəˈgɛtəbl] *adj* незабыва́емый
(незабыва́ем).
unforgivable [ʌnfəˈgɪvəbl] *adj*
непрости́тельный* (непрости́телен).
unformatted [ʌnˈfɔːmætɪd] *adj* (*COMPUT*)
бесформа́тный, неформати́рованный.
unfortunate [ʌnˈfɔːtʃənət] *adj* (*person, event*)
несча́стный*; (*remark*) неуда́чный*; **he's been
very ~** ему́ о́чень не повезло́; **it is ~ that ...**
как неуда́чно, что ....
unfortunately [ʌnˈfɔːtʃənətlɪ] *adv* к
сожале́нию.
unfounded [ʌnˈfaundɪd] *adj* необосно́ванный*.
unfriendly [ʌnˈfrɛndlɪ] *adj* недружелю́бный*
(недружелю́бен).
unfulfilled [ʌnfulˈfɪld] *adj* (*ambition, prophecy,
desire*) неосуществлённый; (*promise,
terms*) неиспо́лненный; (*person*)
нереализова́вшийся.
unfurl [ʌnˈfɔːl] *vt* развора́чивать *or*
развёртывать (разверну́ть *perf*).
unfurnished [ʌnˈfɔːnɪʃt] *adj*
немеблиро́ванный.
ungainly [ʌnˈgeɪnlɪ] *adj* нело́вкий*.
ungodly [ʌnˈgɔdlɪ] *adj*: **at an ~ hour** не свет, ни
заря́.
ungrateful [ʌnˈgreɪtful] *adj* неблагода́рный*
(неблагода́рен).
unguarded [ʌnˈgɑːdɪd] *adj*: **in an ~ moment** в
моме́нт неосторо́жности.
UNHCR *n abbr* (= *United Nations High
Commission for Refugees*) *управле́ние
верхо́вного комисса́ра ООН по дела́м*

бе́женцев.

unhappily [ʌnˈhæpɪlɪ] *adv* несчастли́во;
(*unfortunately*) к несча́стью *or* сожале́нию.

unhappiness [ʌnˈhæpɪnɪs] *n* несча́стье.

unhappy [ʌnˈhæpɪ] *adj* (*sad*) гру́стный*
(гру́стен); (*unfortunate*) несча́стный*
(несча́стен); **I am ~ with** (*dissatisfied*) я
недово́лен +*instr*.

unharmed [ʌnˈhɑːmd] *adj* неповреждённый.

unhealthy [ʌnˈhɛlθɪ] *adj* (*also fig*) нездоро́вый
(нездоро́в).

unheard-of [ʌnˈhəːdɒv] *adj* (*event, situation*)
неслы́ханный* (неслы́хан); (*person*)
неизве́стный*.

unhelpful [ʌnˈhɛlpful] *adj* бесполе́зный*.

unhesitating [ʌnˈhɛzɪteɪtɪŋ] *adj* (*loyalty*)
непоколеби́мый (непоколеби́м); (*reply,
offer*) реши́тельный* (реши́телен).

unholy [ʌnˈhəulɪ] *adj* поро́чный* (поро́чен);
(*dreadful*) безобра́зный.

unhook [ʌnˈhuk] *vt* расстёгивать (расстегну́ть
perf) крючки́ +*gen*.

unhurt [ʌnˈhəːt] *adj* невреди́мый (невреди́м).

unhygienic [ˈʌnhaɪˈdʒiːnɪk] *adj*
негигиени́чный* (негигиени́чен).

UNICEF [ˈjuːnɪsɛf] *n abbr* (= *United Nations
International Children's Emergency Fund*)
ЮНИСЕ́Ф.

unicorn [ˈjuːnɪkɔːn] *n* единоро́г.

unidentified [ʌnaɪˈdɛntɪfaɪd] *adj* (*body*)
неопо́знанный* (*source, person*) анони́мный;
see also **UFO**.

unification [juːnɪfɪˈkeɪʃən] *n* (*POL etc*)
объедине́ние, унифика́ция.

uniform [ˈjuːnɪfɔːm] *n* фо́рма ◆ *adj* (*length,
width etc*) единообра́зный* (единообра́зен);
(*temperature*) постоя́нный* (постоя́нен).

uniformity [juːnɪˈfɔːmɪtɪ] *n* единообра́зие.

unify [ˈjuːnɪfaɪ] *vt* объединя́ть (объедини́ть
perf).

unilateral [juːnɪˈlætərəl] *adj* (*disarmament etc*)
односторо́нний* (односторо́нен).

unimaginable [ʌnɪˈmædʒɪnəbl] *adj*
невообрази́мый (невообрази́м).

unimaginative [ʌnɪˈmædʒɪnətɪv] *adj* (*person*)
лишённый воображе́ния; (*design*)
проза́ичный* (проза́ичен).

unimpaired [ʌnɪmˈpɛəd] *adj* непострада́вший.

unimportant [ʌnɪmˈpɔːtənt] *adj* нева́жный*
(нева́жен).

unimpressed [ʌnɪmˈprɛst] *adj*: **I was ~ by his
explanation** его́ объясне́ние меня́ не
убеди́ло.

uninhabited [ʌnɪnˈhæbɪtɪd] *adj* необита́емый
(необита́ем).

uninhibited [ʌnɪnˈhɪbɪtɪd] *adj* раско́ванный*
(раско́ван).

uninjured [ʌnˈɪndʒəd] *adj* непострада́вший.

uninspiring [ʌnɪnˈspaɪərɪŋ] *adj* не
вдохновля́ющий.

unintelligent [ʌnɪnˈtɛlɪdʒənt] *adj* (*person*)

неве́жественный* (неве́жествен).

unintentional [ʌnɪnˈtɛnʃənəl] *adj* неумы́шл-
енный* (неумы́шлен).

unintentionally [ʌnɪnˈtɛnʃnəlɪ] *adv* неумы́шл-
енно.

uninvited [ʌnɪnˈvaɪtɪd] *adj* незва́ный.

uninviting [ʌnɪnˈvaɪtɪŋ] *adj* (*food*)
неаппети́тный* (неаппети́тен),
несоблазни́тельный* (несоблазни́телен);
(*place*) непривлека́тельный*
(непривлека́телен).

union [ˈjuːnjən] *n* (*unification*) объедине́ние;
(*also: trade* ~) профсою́з ◆ *cpd* (*activities,
leader etc*) профсою́зный; **the U~** (*US*)
Соединённые Шта́ты *mpl*.

unionize [ˈjuːnjənaɪz] *vt* (*employees, industry*)
объединя́ть (объедини́ть *perf*) в
профсою́зы.

Union Jack *n* (*BRIT*) *госуда́рственный флаг
Соединённого Короле́вства.*

Union of Soviet Socialist Republics *n*
(*formerly*) Сою́з Сове́тских
Социалисти́ческих Респу́блик.

union shop *n предприя́тие, на кото́ром
мо́гут рабо́тать то́лько чле́ны профсою́за.*

unique [juːˈniːk] *adj* (*object etc*) уника́льный*
(уника́лен); (*ability, performance etc*)
исключи́тельный* (исключи́телен); **these
problems are not ~ to** ... э́ти пробле́мы
каса́ются не то́лько +*gen* ....

unisex [ˈjuːnɪsɛks] *adj* для обо́их поло́в.

unison [ˈjuːnɪsn] *n*: **in ~** (*say*) в оди́н го́лос;
(*sing*) в унисо́н.

unissued capital [ʌnˈɪʃuːd-] *n* невы́пущенный
акционе́рный капита́л.

unit [ˈjuːnɪt] *n* (*single whole*) це́лое *nt adj*;
(*measurement*) едини́ца; (*section: of furniture
etc*) се́кция; (*team, squad*) подразделе́ние;
production ~ едини́ца проду́кции; **kitchen ~**
ку́хонная се́кция.

unitary [ˈjuːnɪtrɪ] *adj* едини́чный* (едини́чен).

unite [juːˈnaɪt] *vt* объединя́ть (объедини́ть
perf) ◆ *vi* объединя́ться (объедини́ться *perf*).

united [juːˈnaɪtɪd] *adj* объединённый*; (*effort*)
совме́стный.

United Arab Emirates *npl*: **the ~ ~ ~**
Объединённые Ара́бские эмира́ты *mpl*.

United Kingdom *n* Соединённое
Короле́вство.

United Nations (Organization) *n*
Организа́ция Объединённых На́ций.

United States (of America) *n* Соединённые
Шта́ты *mpl* Аме́рики.

unit price *n* (*COMM*) цена́* за едини́цу,
шту́чная цена́*.

unit trust *n* (*BRIT: COMM*) (довери́тельный)
паево́й трест.

unity [ˈjuːnɪtɪ] *n* еди́нство.

Univ. *abbr* = **university**.

universal [juːnɪˈvɜːsl] adj универсáльный* (универсáлен).
universe [ˈjuːnɪvɜːs] n вселéнная f adj.
university [juːnɪˈvɜːsɪtɪ] n университéт ◆ cpd (education, year) университéтский*; ~ **student/professor** студéнт(ка*)/профéссор университéта.
university degree n университéтская стéпень* f.
unjust [ʌnˈdʒʌst] adj несправедлúвый (несправедлúв).
unjustifiable [ʌndʒʌstɪˈfaɪəbl] adj неоправданный* (неоправдан).
unjustified [ʌnˈdʒʌstɪfaɪd] adj (belief, action) неоправданный* (неоправдан); (text) невыравненный.
unkempt [ʌnˈkɛmpt] adj (appearance) неопрятный* (неопрятен); (hair, beard) растрёпанный* (растрёпан).
unkind [ʌnˈkaɪnd] adj (person, comment etc) злой; (behaviour) злóбный* (злóбен).
unkindly [ʌnˈkaɪndlɪ] adv недоброжелáтельно.
unknown [ʌnˈnəʊn] adj неизвéстный* (неизвéстен); ~ **to me** без моегó вéдома; ~ **quantity** (MATH) неизвéстная величинá; (fig) загáдка.
unladen [ʌnˈleɪdn] adj (ship) порóжний*; ~ **weight** вес порожнякóм.
unlawful [ʌnˈlɔːful] adj незакóнный* (незакóнен).
unleaded petrol [ˈʌnˈlɛdɪd-] n бензúн не содержáщий свинцá.
unleash [ʌnˈliːʃ] vt (fig) давáть* (дать* perf) вóлю +dat.
unleavened [ʌnˈlɛvnd] adj прéсный*.
unless [ʌnˈlɛs] conj éсли не; ~ **he comes** éсли он не придёт; ~ **otherwise stated** éсли не бýдут даны другúе указáния; ~ **I am mistaken** éсли я не ошибáюсь.
unlicensed [ʌnˈlaɪsnst] adj (BRIT: restaurant) не имéющий лицéнзии на продáжу спиртных напúтков.
unlike [ʌnˈlaɪk] adj (not alike) непохóжий* (непохóж) ◆ prep (different from) в отлúчие от +gen; **Russian is grammatically ~ English** с граммати́ческой тóчки зрéния рýсский не похóж на англúйский.
unlikelihood [ʌnˈlaɪklɪhud] n неправдо-подóбие.
unlikely [ʌnˈlaɪklɪ] adj (not likely) мало-верóятный* (маловерóятен); (unexpected) неверóятный* (неверóятен); **in the ~ event of** при маловерóятном слýчае +gen; **in the ~ event that ...** в том маловерóятном слýчае, когдá ....
unlimited [ʌnˈlɪmɪtɪd] adj (travel, wine etc) неограни́ченный.
unlisted [ˈʌnˈlɪstɪd] adj (US: TEL) не

включённый (включён) в телефóнный спрáвочник; (STOCK EXCHANGE) не коти́рующийся.
unlit [ʌnˈlɪt] adj (room) неосвещённый.
unload [ʌnˈləud] vt (box, car) разгружáть (разгрузúть* perf).
unlock [ʌnˈlɔk] vt отпирáть (отперéть* perf).
unlucky [ʌnˈlʌkɪ] adj (person) невезýчий (невезýч); (object, number) несчастлúвый; **he is ~** ему́ не везёт.
unmanageable [ʌnˈmænɪdʒəbl] adj (tool, vehicle) трудноконтролúруемый; (situation) неуправляемый (неуправляем).
unmanned [ʌnˈmænd] adj (spacecraft etc) автомати́чески управляемый.
unmarked [ʌnˈmɑːkt] adj (unstained) чúстый* (чист); ~ **police car** полицéйская маши́на без опознавáтельных знáков.
unmarried [ʌnˈmærɪd] adj (man) нежена́тый (нежена́т), холостóй* (хóлост); (woman) незамýжняя.
unmarried mother n мать* f-одинóчка.
unmask [ʌnˈmɑːsk] vt (thief etc) разоблачáть (разоблачúть perf).
unmatched [ʌnˈmætʃt] adj непревзойдённый* (непревзойдён).
unmentionable [ʌnˈmɛnʃnəbl] adj (topic) запрéтный* (запрéтен); (word) неприлúчный* (неприлúчен).
unmerciful [ʌnˈmɜːsɪful] adj безжáлостный* (безжáлостен).
unmistak(e)able [ʌnmɪsˈteɪkəbl] adj (voice, sound) характéрный*.
unmistak(e)ably [ʌnmɪsˈteɪkəblɪ] adv я́вно.
unmitigated [ʌnˈmɪtɪɡeɪtɪd] adj пóлный.
unnamed [ʌnˈneɪmd] adj (nameless) безымя́нный; (anonymous) не назвáвший себя́.
unnatural [ʌnˈnætʃrəl] adj неестéственный* (неестéственен); (against nature) противоестéственный* (противоестéственен).
unnecessarily [ʌnˈnɛsəsərɪlɪ] adv излúшне.
unnecessary [ʌnˈnɛsəsərɪ] adj излúшний* (излúшен).
unnerve [ʌnˈnɜːv] vt тревóжить (встревóжить perf).
unnoticed [ʌnˈnəʊtɪst] adj незамéченный.
UNO [ˈjuːnəʊ] n abbr (= United Nations Organization) ООН= Организáция Объединённых Нáций.
unobservant [ʌnəbˈzɜːvnt] adj (person) ненаблюдáтельный* (ненаблюдáтелен).
unobtainable [ʌnəbˈteɪnəbl] adj: **this book is ~** эту кни́гу нельзя́ достáть; **this number is ~** э́тот нóмер не функционúрует.
unobtrusive [ʌnəbˈtruːsɪv] adj (person) ненавя́зчивый (ненавя́зчив); (engine) бесшýмный* (бесшýмен).

---

* marks translations which have irregular inflections. The Russian-English side of the dictionary gives inflectional information.

unoccupied [ʌnˈɔkjupaɪd] *adj* (*also MIL*) незанятый.

unofficial [ʌnəˈfɪʃl] *adj* неофициальный* (неофициален).

unopened [ʌnˈəupənd] *adj* (*letter*) нераспечатанный; (*tin, bottle etc*) неоткрытый.

unopposed [ʌnəˈpəuzd] *adj* не встретивший сопротивления.

unorthodox [ʌnˈɔ:θədɔks] *adj* (*treatment*) неортодоксальный* (неортодоксален); (*REL*) неортодоксальный.

unpack [ʌnˈpæk] *vi* распаковываться (распаковаться *perf*) ◆ *vt* распаковывать (распаковать *perf*).

unpaid [ʌnˈpeɪd] *adj* (*bill*) неоплаченный; (*time off*) неоплачиваемый; (*work*) неоплачиваемый; (*worker*) бесплатный.

unpalatable [ʌnˈpælətəbl] *adj* (*meal*) невкусный* (невкусен); (*truth*) горький* (горек).

unparalleled [ʌnˈpærəlɛld] *adj* несравнимый (несравним).

unpatriotic [ˈʌnpætrɪˈɔtɪk] *adj* (*person*) непатриотически настроенный; (*speech, attitude*) непатриотичный* (непатриотичен).

unplanned [ʌnˈplænd] *adj* (*visit, baby*) незапланированный.

unpleasant [ʌnˈplɛznt] *adj* неприятный* (неприятен).

unplug [ʌnˈplʌg] *vt* отключать (отключить* *perf*) от сети.

unpolluted [ʌnpəˈlu:tɪd] *adj* (*river, water etc*) незагрязнённый.

unpopular [ʌnˈpɔpjulə^r] *adj* (*person, decision etc*) непопулярный* (непопулярен); **to make o.s. ~ (with)** терять (потерять *perf*) популярность (у +*gen*).

unprecedented [ʌnˈprɛsɪdəntɪd] *adj* беспрецедентный* (беспрецедентен).

unpredictable [ʌnprɪˈdɪktəbl] *adj* непредсказуемый (непредсказуем).

unprejudiced [ʌnˈprɛdʒudɪst] *adj* (*not biased*) непредвзятый; (*having no prejudices*) непредубеждённый*.

unprepared [ʌnprɪˈpɛəd] *adj* (*person, speech*) неподготовленный.

unprepossessing [ˈʌnpri:pəˈzɛsɪŋ] *adj* нерасполагающий.

unpretentious [ʌnprɪˈtɛnʃəs] *adj* непретенциоз|ный* (непретенциозен).

unprincipled [ʌnˈprɪnsɪpld] *adj* (*person*) беспринципный* (беспринципен).

unproductive [ʌnprəˈdʌktɪv] *adj* (*land*) неплодородный* (неплодороден); (*discussion*) непродуктивный* (непродуктивен); (*labour*) непроизводительный* (непроизводителен).

unprofessional [ʌnprəˈfɛʃənl] *adj* непрофессиональный (непрофессионален)*.

unprofitable [ʌnˈprɔfɪtəbl] *adj* невыгодный* (невыгоден).

unprotected [ˈʌnprəˈtɛktɪd] *adj* незащищённый; **~ sex** секс без контрацептивов.

unprovoked [ʌnprəˈvəukt] *adj* (*attack*) неспровоцированный.

unpunished [ʌnˈpʌnɪʃt] *adj*: **to go ~** оставаться* (остаться* *perf*) безнаказанным(-ой).

unqualified [ʌnˈkwɔlɪfaɪd] *adj* (*teacher, nurse etc*) неквалифицированный; (*disaster, success*) совершённый.

unquestionably [ʌnˈkwɛstʃənəblɪ] *adv* бесспорно.

unquestioning [ʌnˈkwɛstʃənɪŋ] *adj* беспрекословный* (беспрекословен).

unravel [ʌnˈrævl] *vt* (*ball of string*) распутывать (распутать *perf*); (*mystery*) разгадывать (разгадать *perf*).

unreal [ʌnˈrɪəl] *adj* (*not real*) нереальный* (нереален); (*peculiar*) фантастический.

unrealistic [ˈʌnrɪəˈlɪstɪk] *adj* (*person, project*) нереалистичный* (нереалистичен).

unreasonable [ʌnˈri:znəbl] *adj* (*person, attitude, demand*) неразумный* (неразумен); (*length of time*) нереальный* (нереален).

unrecognizable [ʌnˈrɛkəgnaɪzəbl] *adj* неузнаваемый (неузнаваем).

unrecognized [ʌnˈrɛkəgnaɪzd] *adj* (*also POL*) непризнанный*.

unreconstructed [ˈʌnri:kənˈstrʌktɪd] *adj* (*US*) неисправимый (неисправим).

unrecorded [ʌnrɪˈkɔ:dɪd] *adj* (*piece of music etc*) незаписанный; (*incident, statement*) незафиксированный.

unrefined [ʌnrɪˈfaɪnd] *adj* (*petroleum*) неочищенный; (*sugar*) нерафинированный.

unrehearsed [ʌnrɪˈhə:st] *adj* (*THEAT*) неотрепетированный; (*spontaneous*) неподготовленный.

unrelated [ʌnrɪˈleɪtɪd] *adj* (*incident*) отдельный; **to be ~** (*people*) не состоять (*impf*) в родстве.

unrelenting [ʌnrɪˈlɛntɪŋ] *adj* неумолимый (неумолим).

unreliable [ʌnrɪˈlaɪəbl] *adj* ненадёжный* (ненадёжен).

unrelieved [ʌnrɪˈli:vd] *adj* (*monotony*) невыносимый (невыносим).

unremitting [ʌnrɪˈmɪtɪŋ] *adj* неослабный* (неослабен).

unrepeatable [ʌnrɪˈpi:təbl] *adj* (*offer*) неповторимый; (*comment*) неприличный* (неприличен).

unrepentant [ʌnrɪˈpɛntənt] *adj* нераскаявшийся.

unrepresentative [ˈʌnrɛprɪˈzɛntətɪv] *adj*: **~ (of)** нетипичный* (нетипичен) (для +*acc*).

unreserved [ʌnrɪˈzə:vd] *adj* (*seat*) незабронированный; (*approval, admiration*) полный*.

unreservedly [ʌnrɪˈzə:vɪdlɪ] *adv* полностью.

unresponsive [ʌnrɪsˈpɔnsɪv] *adj* без-

разли́чный* (безразли́чен).
unrest [ʌn'rɛst] *n* волне́ние *ntpl*.
unrestricted [ʌnrɪ'strɪktɪd] *adj* (*power, time*)
неограни́ченный*; **to have ~ access to** име́ть
(*impf*) неограни́ченный до́ступ к +*dat*.
unrewarded [ʌnrɪ'wɔ:dɪd] *adj* (*efforts*)
безуспе́шный* (безуспе́шен).
unripe [ʌn'raɪp] *adj* незре́лый (незре́л).
unrivalled [ʌn'raɪvəld] (*US* **unrivaled**) *adj*
непревзойдённый* (непревзойдён).
unroll [ʌn'rəul] *vt* развёртывать (разверну́ть
perf).
unruffled [ʌn'rʌfld] *adj* (*person*) невоз-
мути́мый (невозмути́м); (*hair*) гла́дкий*.
unruly [ʌn'ru:lɪ] *adj* непослу́шный*
(непослу́шен).
unsafe [ʌn'seɪf] *adj* опа́сный* (опа́сен);
(*machine, bridge, car etc*) ненадёжный*
(ненадёжен); (*method*) риско́ванный; **~ to
eat/drink** неприго́дный* (неприго́ден) для
еды́/питья́.
unsaid [ʌn'sɛd] *adj*: **to leave sth ~** не
упомина́ть (*impf*) о чём-н.
unsaleable [ʌn'seɪləbl] (*US* **unsalable**) *adj*
неходово́й.
unsatisfactory ['ʌnsætɪs'fæktərɪ] *adj* неудовле-
твори́тельный* (неудовлетвори́телен).
unsatisfied [ʌn'sætɪsfaɪd] *adj*
неудовлетворённый.
unsavoury [ʌn'seɪvərɪ] (*US* **unsavory**) *adj* (*fig*)
сомни́тельный* (сомни́телен).
unscathed [ʌn'skeɪðd] *adj* невреди́мый
(невреди́м).
unscientific ['ʌnsaɪən'tɪfɪk] *adj* ненау́чный*
(ненау́чен).
unscrew [ʌn'skru:] *vt* отви́нчивать
(отвинти́ть* *perf*).
unscrupulous [ʌn'skru:pjuləs] *adj*
бессо́вестный*.
unseat [ʌn'si:t] *vt* (*from office*) смеща́ть
(смести́ть* *perf*).
unsecured ['ʌnsɪ'kjuəd] *adj*: **~ creditor**
незастрахо́ванный кредито́р; **~ loan**
необеспе́ченный заём*.
unseemly [ʌn'si:mlɪ] *adj* непристо́йный*
(непристо́ен).
unseen [ʌn'si:n] *adj* (*person*) невиди́мый
(неви́дим); (*danger*) скры́тый (скрыт).
unselfish [ʌn'sɛlfɪʃ] *adj* бескоры́стный*
(бескоры́стен).
unsettled [ʌn'sɛtld] *adj* (*person*) беспоко́йный*
(беспоко́ен); (*future*) нея́сный* (нея́сен);
(*question*) нерешённый; (*weather*)
неусто́йчивый (неусто́йчив).
unsettling [ʌn'sɛtlɪŋ] *adj* трево́жный*
(трево́жен).
unshak(e)able [ʌn'ʃeɪkəbl] *adj*
непоколеби́мый (непоколеби́м).

unshaven [ʌn'ʃeɪvn] *adj* небри́тый (небри́т).
unsightly [ʌn'saɪtlɪ] *adj* непригля́дный*
(непригля́ден).
unskilled [ʌn'skɪld] *adj* (*worker, work*)
неквалифици́рованный*.
unsociable [ʌn'səuʃəbl] *adj* (*person*)
необщи́тельный* (необщи́телен); (*way of
life*) за́мкнутый (за́мкнут).
unsocial [ʌn'səuʃl] *adj*: **~ hours** сверхуро́чные
часы́.
unsold [ʌn'səuld] *adj* (*goods*) непро́данный.
unsolicited [ʌnsə'lɪsɪtd] *adj* (*advice*)
непро́шенный; (*goods*) незатре́бованный.
unsophisticated [ʌnsə'fɪstɪkeɪtɪd] *adj*
бесхи́тростный* (бесхи́тростен); (*method,
device*) просто́й* (прост).
unsound [ʌn'saund] *adj* (*health*) сла́бый*
(слаб); (*floor, foundations*) непро́чный*
(непро́чен); (*policy*) ша́ткий* (ша́ток);
(*advice*) ненадёжный* (ненадёжен).
unspeakable [ʌn'spi:kəbl] *adj*
отврати́тельный (отврати́телен).
unspoken [ʌn'spəukn] *adj* (*word*)
невы́сказанный; (*agreement, approval*)
молчали́вый.
unstable [ʌn'steɪbl] *adj* (*piece of furniture*)
неусто́йчивый (неусто́йчив); (*government*)
нестаби́льный* (нестаби́лен); (*person:
mentally*) неуравнове́шенный*
(неуравнове́шен).
unsteady [ʌn'stɛdɪ] *adj* (*step*) нетвёрдый
(нетвёрд); (*voice, hands, legs*) дрожа́щий;
(*ladder*) неусто́йчивый (неусто́йчив),
ша́ткий* (ша́ток).
unstinting [ʌn'stɪntɪŋ] *adj* (*support*) огро́мный*
(огро́мен); (*generosity*) бесконе́чный*
(бесконе́чен).
unstuck [ʌn'stʌk] *adj*: **to come ~** (*label etc*)
откле́иваться (откле́иться *perf*); (*plan, idea
etc*) расстра́иваться (расстро́иться *perf*).
unsubstantiated ['ʌnsəb'stænʃɪeɪtɪd] *adj*
(*rumour*) неподтверждённый; (*accusation*)
необосно́ванный.
unsuccessful [ʌnsək'sɛsful] *adj* (*attempt*)
безуспе́шный* (безуспе́шен); (*writer*)
посре́дственный* (посре́дствен); (*proposal,
marriage*) неуда́чный* (неуда́чен); **to be ~ in
sth** терпе́ть* (потерпе́ть* *perf*) неуда́чу в +*prp*;
your application was ~ Ва́ше заявле́ние не
при́нято.
unsuccessfully [ʌnsək'sɛsfəlɪ] *adv* безуспе́шно.
unsuitable [ʌn'su:təbl] *adj* неподходя́щий*.
unsuited [ʌn'su:tɪd] *adj*: **to be ~ for** *or* **to** не
подходи́ть* (*impf*) для +*gen*.
unsung ['ʌnsʌŋ] *adj* незаме́ченный.
unsure [ʌn'ʃuə'] *adj* (*uncertain*) неуве́ренный*
(неуве́рен); **he is ~ of himself** он неуве́рен в
себе́.

---

* marks translations which have irregular inflections. The Russian-English side of the dictionary gives inflectional information.

unsuspecting [ʌnsəs'pɛktɪŋ] *adj* ничего́ не
подозрева́ющий.
unsweetened [ʌn'swi:tnd] *adj*
неподслащённый.
unswerving [ʌn'swə:vɪŋ] *adj* непоколеби́мый
(непоколеби́м).
unsympathetic ['ʌnsɪmpə'θɛtɪk] *adj*
равноду́шный* (равноду́шен); (*unlikeable*)
несимпати́чный* (несимпати́чен); ~ **to** *or*
towards равноду́шный +*dat*.
untangle [ʌn'tæŋgl] *vt* распу́тывать
(распу́тать *perf*).
untapped [ʌn'tæpt] *adj* (*resources*)
неиспо́льзованный.
untaxed [ʌn'tækst] *adj* не облага́емый
(облага́ем) нало́гом.
unthinkable [ʌn'θɪŋkəbl] *adj* немы́слимый
(немы́слим).
unthinking [ʌn'θɪŋkɪŋ] *adj* безду́мный*
(безду́мен).
untidy [ʌn'taɪdɪ] *adj* неопря́тный* (неопря́тен);
(*work, writing*) неаккура́тный*
(неаккура́тен).
untie [ʌn'taɪ] *vt* (*lace, person*) развя́зывать
(развяза́ть* *perf*); (*dog, horse etc*) отвя́зывать
(отвяза́ть* *perf*).
until [ən'tɪl] *prep* до +*gen*; (*after negative*) пока́ ♦
conj пока́ не; ~ **he comes** пока́ он не придёт;
~ **now/then** до сих/тех пор; **from morning** ~
night с утра́ до́ ночи.
untimely [ʌn'taɪmlɪ] *adj* (*inopportune: moment*)
неподходя́щий*; (: *arrival*) несвое-
вре́менный* (несвоевре́менен); (*death*)
безвре́менный.
untold [ʌn'təʊld] *adj* (*story*) нерасска́занный;
(*joy, suffering*) невырази́мый; (*wealth*)
несме́тный.
untouched [ʌn'tʌtʃt] *adj* (*not used etc*)
нетро́нутый (нетро́нут); (*safe*) невреди́мый
(невреди́м); ~ **by** (*unaffected*) нетро́нутый
(нетро́нут) +*instr*.
untoward [ʌntə'wɔ:d] *adj* (*events*) скве́рный*
(скве́рен); (*effects*) отрица́тельный*
(отрица́телен).
untrained ['ʌn'treɪnd] *adj* нетрениро́ванный.
untrammelled [ʌn'træmld] *adj* раско́ванный*
(раско́ван).
untranslatable [ʌntrænz'leɪtəbl] *adj*
непереводи́мый.
untried [ʌn'traɪd] *adj* (*policy, remedy*)
неиспы́танный; (*prisoner*) не
подверга́вшийся суду́.
untrue [ʌn'tru:] *adj* ло́жный* (ло́жен).
untrustworthy [ʌn'trʌstwə:ðɪ] *adj*
ненадёжный* (ненадёжен).
unusable [ʌn'ju:zəbl] *adj* непригодный*
(неприго́ден).
unused[1] [ʌn'ju:zd] *adj* (*not used*)
неиспо́льзованный.
unused[2] [ʌn'ju:st] *adj*: **he is** ~ **to it** он к э́тому
не привы́к; **she is** ~ **to flying** она́ не

привы́кла лета́ть.
unusual [ʌn'ju:ʒuəl] *adj* (*strange*) необы́чный*
(необы́чен); (*rare*) ре́дкий* (ре́док);
(*exceptional, distinctive*) необыкнове́нный*
(необыкнове́нен).
unusually [ʌn'ju:ʒuəlɪ] *adv* (*large, high etc*)
необыкнове́нно.
unveil [ʌn'veɪl] *vt* (*statue*) открыва́ть
(откры́ть* *perf*).
unwanted [ʌn'wɒntɪd] *adj* (*clothing etc*)
нену́жный; (*child, pregnancy*) нежела́нный.
unwarranted [ʌn'wɒrəntɪd] *adj* необосно́в-
анный*.
unwary [ʌn'wɛərɪ] *adj* неосторо́жный*
(неосторо́жен).
unwavering [ʌn'weɪvərɪŋ] *adj* (*faith*) твёрдый*
(твёрд), непоколеби́мый (непоколеби́м);
(*gaze*) при́стальный* (при́стален).
unwelcome [ʌn'wɛlkəm] *adj* (*guest*)
непро́шенный; (*news*) неприя́тный*
(неприя́тен); **to feel** ~ чу́вствовать (*impf*) себя́
ли́шним.
unwell [ʌn'wɛl] *adj*: **to feel** ~ чу́вствовать (*impf*)
себя́ пло́хо; **he is** ~ ему́ нездоро́вится, он
нездоро́в.
unwieldy [ʌn'wi:ldɪ] *adj* громо́здкий*
(громо́здок).
unwilling [ʌn'wɪlɪŋ] *adj*: **to be** ~ **to do** не
хоте́ть* (*impf*) +*infin*.
unwillingly [ʌn'wɪlɪŋlɪ] *adv* неохо́тно.
unwind [ʌn'waɪnd] *irreg vt* (*undo*) разма́тывать
(размота́ть *perf*) ♦ *vi* (*relax*) расслабля́ться
(рассла́биться* *perf*).
unwise [ʌn'waɪz] *adj* неблагоразу́мный*
(неблагоразу́мен).
unwitting [ʌn'wɪtɪŋ] *adj* нево́льный.
unworkable [ʌn'wə:kəbl] *adj* неосуществи́мый
(неосуществи́м).
unworthy [ʌn'wə:ðɪ] *adj* недосто́йный*
(недосто́ен); **to be** ~ **of sth/to do** быть* (*impf*)
недосто́йным(-ой) чего́-н/+*infin*; **that remark
is** ~ **of you** Вам не приста́ло э́то говори́ть.
unwrap [ʌn'ræp] *vt* развора́чивать
(разверну́ть *perf*).
unwritten [ʌn'rɪtn] *adj* (*law, agreement*)
непи́саный.
unzip [ʌn'zɪp] *vt* расстёгивать (расстегну́ть
perf) на мо́лнию.

KEYWORD

up [ʌp] *prep*: **he went up the stairs/the hill** он
подня́лся по ле́стнице/на́ гору; **the cat was
up a tree** ко́шка была́ на де́реве; **they live
further up the street** они́ живу́т да́льше на
э́той у́лице; **he has gone up to Scotland** он
пое́хал в Шотла́ндию
　♦ *adv* **1** (*upwards, higher*): **up in the sky/the
mountains** высоко́ в не́бе/в гора́х; **put the
picture a bit higher up** пове́сьте карти́ну
немно́го повы́ше; **up there** (*up above*) там
наверху́; **there's a village and up above, on the
hill, a monastery** там есть дере́вня, а над ней,

2: **to be up** (*out of bed*) вставать* (встать* *perf*); (*prices, level*) подниматься (подняться* *perf*); **the tent is up** палатка поставлена
3: **up to** (*as far as*) до +*gen*; **I've read up to page five** я дочитал до пятой страницы; **up to now** до сих пор
4: **to be up to** (*depending on*) зависеть* (*impf*) от +*gen*; **it's not up to me to decide** не мне решать; **it's up to you** это ваше дело
5: **to be up to** (*inf: be doing*) затевать (*impf*); **he's not up to the job** он не тянет на эту работу; **his work is not up to the required standard** его работа не соответствует требуемым стандартам; **what is he up to?** что он затевает?; **what's she up to these days?** а что она теперь поделывает?
♦ *n*: **ups and downs** (*in life, career*) взлёты *mpl* и падения *ntpl*.

up-and-coming [ʌpənd'kʌmɪŋ] *adj* перспективный* (перспективен).
upbeat ['ʌpbiːt] *n* (*MUS*) слабая доля такта; (*ECON*) подъём ♦ *adj* (*optimistic*) оживлённый* (оживлён).
upbraid [ʌp'breɪd] *vt* упрекать (упрекнуть *perf*).
upbringing ['ʌpbrɪŋɪŋ] *n* воспитание.
upcoming ['ʌpkʌmɪŋ] *adj* (*forthcoming*) предстоящий*, грядущий.
update [ʌp'deɪt] *vt* (*records, information*) вносить* (внести* *perf*) изменения и дополнения.
upend [ʌp'ɛnd] *vt* переворачивать (перевернуть *perf*) (вверх ногами).
upfront [ʌp'frʌnt] *adj* (*inf: frank*) открытый (открыт) ♦ *adv* (*pay*) вперёд.
upgrade [ʌp'greɪd] *vt* (*improve: house*) модернизировать (*impf/perf*); (: *job*) усложнять (усложнить *perf*); (*employee*) повышать (повысить* *perf*) в должности; (*COMPUT*) наращивать (*impf*) вычислительные возможности, модернизировать (*impf/perf*).
upheaval [ʌp'hiːvl] *n* переворот.
uphill [ʌp'hɪl] *adj* (*fig: task*) тяжёлый* (тяжёл) ♦ *adv* (*face, look*) вверх; (*go, move*) в гору; **to go ~** подниматься (*impf*) в гору.
uphold [ʌp'həuld] (*irreg: like* hold) *vt* поддерживать (поддержать* *perf*).
upholstery [ʌp'həulstərɪ] *n* обивка.
upkeep ['ʌpkiːp] *n* содержание.
up-market [ʌp'mɑːkɪt] *adj* (*product*) дорогой; (*area*) элитарный.
upon [ə'pɔn] *prep* (*position*) на +*prp*; (*motion*) на +*acc*.
upper ['ʌpə] *adj* верхний* ♦ *n* (*of shoe*) верх.
upper class *n*: **the ~ ~** высший* класс.
upper-class ['ʌpə'klɑːs] *adj* (*families, accent*)

аристократический*; (*district*) элитарный.
uppercut ['ʌpəkʌt] *n* (*BOXING*) апперкот.
upper hand *n*: **to have the ~ ~** контролировать (*impf*).
Upper House *n* (*BRIT*) Палата Лордов.
uppermost ['ʌpəməust] *adj* высший*; **what was ~ in my mind** что больше всего занимало мои мысли.
Upper Volta [-'vɔltə] *n* Верхняя Вольта, Буркина-Фасо *f ind*.
upright ['ʌpraɪt] *adj* (*straight, honest*) прямой* (прям); (*vertical*) вертикальный* (вертикален) ♦ *n* (*CONSTR*) вертикальная стойка*.
uprising ['ʌpraɪzɪŋ] *n* восстание.
uproar ['ʌprɔː'] *n* (*protests*) возмущение; (*shouts*) шум.
uproarious [ʌp'rɔːrɪəs] *adj* (*people*) хохочущий; (*play etc*) ужасно смешной (смешон).
uproot [ʌp'ruːt] *vt* (*tree*) вырывать (вырвать *perf*) с корнем; (*fig: people*) снимать (снять* *perf*) с места.
upset [*vb, adj* ʌp'sɛt, *n* 'ʌpsɛt] (*irreg: like* set) *vt* (*glass etc*) опрокидывать (опрокинуть* *perf*); (*routine*) нарушать (нарушить *perf*); (*plan, person*) расстраивать (расстроить *perf*); (*person: offend*) оскорблять (оскорбить* *perf*) ♦ *adj* расстроенный* (расстроен) ♦ *n* (*to plan etc*) нарушение; **to get ~** (*sad*) расстраиваться (расстроиться *perf*); (*offended*) оскорбляться (оскорбиться* *perf*); **to have a stomach ~** (*BRIT*) страдать (*impf*) расстройством желудка.
upset price ['ʌpsɛt-] *n* (*US, SCOTTISH*) низшая отправная цена на аукционе.
upsetting [ʌp'sɛtɪŋ] *adj* (*annoying*) досадный.
upshot ['ʌpʃɔt] *n* результат; **the ~ of it all was that ...** кончилось всё тем, что ....
upside down ['ʌpsaɪd-] *adv* (*hang, hold*) вверх ногами; (*turn*) вверх дном; **to turn a place ~ ~** (*fig*) перевернуть (*perf*) всё вверх дном.
upstairs [ʌp'stɛəz] *adv* (*be*) наверху; (*go*) наверх ♦ *adj* (*window, room*) верхний* ♦ *n* верхний* этаж*; **there's no ~** здесь нет верхнего этажа.
upstage [ʌp'steɪdʒ] *vt* затмевать (затмить* *perf*).
upstart ['ʌpstɑːt] *n* (*pej: person*) выскочка* *m/f*.
upstream [ʌp'striːm] *adv* против течения ♦ *adj* вверх по течению.
upsurge ['ʌpsəːdʒ] *n* (*of enthusiasm etc*) подъём.
uptake ['ʌpteɪk] *n*: **to be quick/slow on the ~** быстро/медленно соображать (*impf*).
uptight [ʌp'taɪt] *adj* (*inf*) натянутый (натянут).
up-to-date ['ʌptə'deɪt] *adj* (*information*) последний*; (*person*) современный*

(совреме́нен).

upturn [' ʌptə:n] *n* (*in economy*) подъём.

upturned ['ʌptə:nd] *adj* (*nose*) курно́сый (курно́с), вздёрнутый (вздёрнут).

upward ['ʌpwəd] *adj*: **~ movement/glance** движе́ние/взгляд вверх ♦ *adv* = **upwards**.

upwardly mobile ['ʌpwədlɪ-] *adj* преуспева́ющий; **a new ~ ~ generation** но́вое поколе́ние преуспева́ющих люде́й.

upwards ['ʌpwədz] *adv* (*move, glance*) вверх; (*more than*): **~ of** свы́ше +*gen*.

URA *n abbr* (*US*: = **Urban Renewal Administration**) прави́тельственная организа́ция, координи́рующая рабо́ты по обновле́нию и улучше́нию устро́йства городо́в.

Ural Mountains ['juərəl-] *npl*: **the ~ ~** (*also*: **the Urals**) Ура́л *msg*, Ура́льские го́ры *fpl*.

uranium [juə'reɪnɪəm] *n* ура́н.

Uranus [juə'reɪnəs] *n* Ура́н.

urban ['ə:bən] *adj* городско́й.

urbane [ə:'beɪn] *adj* учти́вый (учти́в).

urbanization ['ə:bənaɪ'zeɪʃən] *n* урбаниза́ция.

urchin ['ə:tʃɪn] *n* (*pej*) беспризо́рник(-ица).

Urdu ['uədu:] *n* язы́к урду́.

urge [ə:dʒ] *n* (*need, desire*) потре́бность *f* ♦ *vt*: **to ~ sb to do** наста́ительно сове́товать (*impf*) кому́-н +*infin*; **to ~ caution** сове́товать (посове́товать *perf*) быть* осторо́жным(-ой) (*impf*).

▶ **urge on** *vt* подгоня́ть (*impf*).

urgency ['ə:dʒənsɪ] *n* (*of task etc*) неотло́жность *f*, безотлага́тельность *f*; (*of tone*) насто́йчивость *f*.

urgent ['ə:dʒənt] *adj* (*need, message*) сро́чный* (сро́чен); (*voice*) насто́йчивый (насто́йчив).

urgently ['ə:dʒəntlɪ] *adv* сро́чно.

urinal ['juərɪnl] *n* (*building*) мужско́й туале́т; (*vessel*) писсуа́р.

urinate ['juərɪneɪt] *vi* мочи́ться* (помочи́ться* *perf*).

urine ['juərɪn] *n* моча́.

urn [ə:n] *n* (*container*) у́рна; (*also*: **tea ~**) бак.

Uruguay ['juərəgwaɪ] *n* Уругва́й.

Uruguayan [juərə'gwaɪən] *adj* уругва́йский* ♦ *n* уругва́ец*(-а́йка*).

US *n abbr* = **United States**.

us [ʌs] *pron* (*direct*) нас; (*indirect*) нам; (*after prep*: +*gen*, +*prp*) нас; (: +*dat*) нам; (: +*instr*) на́ми; (*referring to subject of sentence*) свой; **a few of ~ are going to the cinema** не́которые из нас иду́т в кино́; *see also* **me**.

USA *n abbr* (= **United States of America**) США= *Соединённые Шта́ты Аме́рики*; (*MIL*) = **United States Army**.

usable ['ju:zəbl] *adj* приго́дный* (приго́ден).

USAF *n abbr* = **United States Air Force**.

usage ['ju:zɪdʒ] *n* (*LING*) употребле́ние.

USCG *n abbr* = **United States Coast Guard**.

USDA *n abbr* = **United States Department of Agriculture**.

USDAW ['ʌzdɔ:] *n abbr* (*BRIT*) = **Union of Shop,** Distributive and Allied Workers.

USDI *n abbr* (= **United States Department of the Interior**) ≈ Министе́рство вну́тренних дел.

use [*vt* ju:z, *n* ju:s] *vt* (*object, tool*) испо́льзовать (*impf/perf*); (*phrase*) употребля́ть (употреби́ть* *perf*) ♦ *n* (*using*) испо́льзование, употребле́ние; (*usefulness*) по́льза; (*purpose*) примене́ние; **she ~d to do it** она́ когда́-то занима́лась э́тим; **what's this ~d for?** для чего́ э́то употребля́ется?; **to be ~d to** быть* привы́чным(-ой) к +*dat*; **to get ~d to** привыка́ть (привы́кнуть* *perf*) к +*dat*; **to be in ~** употребля́ться (*impf*), быть* (*impf*) в употребле́нии; **to be out of ~** не употребля́ться (*impf*); **to be of ~** быть* (*impf*) поле́зным(-ой); **to make ~ of sth** испо́льзовать (*impf/perf*) что-н; **it's no ~** э́то бесполе́зно; **to have the ~ of** по́льзоваться (*impf*) +*instr*.

▶ **use up** *vt* (*food, leftovers*) испо́льзовать (*impf/perf*); (*money*) расхо́довать (израсхо́довать *perf*).

used [ju:zd] *adj* (*object*) бы́вший* в употребле́нии; (*car*) поде́ржанный.

useful ['ju:sful] *adj* поле́зный* (поле́зен); **to come in ~** пригоди́ться* (*perf*).

usefulness ['ju:sfəlnɪs] *n* по́льза.

useless ['ju:slɪs] *adj* (*unusable*) непри́го́дный* (неприго́ден); (*pointless, hopeless*) бесполе́зный* (бесполе́зен).

user ['ju:zə'] *n* по́льзователь *f*; (*of petrol, gas etc*) потреби́тель *m*.

user-friendliness ['ju:zə'frendlɪnɪs] *n* простота́ в испо́льзовании.

user-friendly ['ju:zə'frendlɪ] *adj* просто́й (прост) в испо́льзовании.

USES *n abbr* (= **United States Employment Service**) управле́ние по размеще́нию и регули́рованию рабо́чей си́лы.

usher ['ʌʃə'] *n* (*at wedding*) распоряди́тель *m* ♦ *vt*: **to ~ sb into** проводи́ть* (провести́* *perf*) кого́-н в +*acc*.

usherette [ʌʃə'rɛt] *n* билетёрша.

USIA *n abbr* (= **United States Information Agency**) ЮСИА (*Информацио́нное аге́нтство США*).

USM *n abbr* (= **United States Mint**) Моне́тный двор США; (= **United States Mail**) По́чта США.

USN *n abbr* = **United States Navy**.

USPHS *n abbr* = **United States Public Health Service**.

USPO *n abbr* = **United States Post Office**.

USS *abbr* = **United States Ship**.

USSR *n abbr* (*formerly*: = **Union of Soviet Socialist Republics**) СССР= *Сою́з Сове́тских Социалисти́ческих Респу́блик*.

usu. *abbr* = **usually**.

usual ['ju:ʒuəl] *adj* (*time, place etc*) обы́чный; **as ~** как обы́чно.

usually ['ju:ʒuəlɪ] *adv* обы́чно.

usurer [ˈjuːʒərəˀ] *n* ростовщи́к*.
usurp [juːˈzəːp] *vt* узурпи́ровать *(impf/perf)*.
usury [ˈjuːʒʊrɪ] *n* ростовщи́чество.
UT (*US: POST*) *abbr* = *Utah*.
utensil [juːˈtɛnsl] *n* инструме́нт; **kitchen** ~s ку́хонные принадле́жности.
uterus [ˈjuːtərəs] *n* ма́тка*.
utilitarian [juːtɪlɪˈtɛərɪən] *adj* утилита́рный* (утилита́рен).
utility [juːˈtɪlɪtɪ] *n* (*usefulness*) поле́зность *f*; **public utilities** коммуна́льные услу́ги *fpl*.
utility room *n* подсо́бная ко́мната, подсо́бка* (*разг*).
utilization [juːtɪlaɪˈzeɪʃən] *n* утилиза́ция.
utilize [ˈjuːtɪlaɪz] *vt* утилизи́ровать *(impf/perf)*; (*information*) находи́ть (найти́* *perf*) примене́ние +*dat*.

utmost [ˈʌtməust] *adj* велича́йший ♦ *n*: **to do one's** ~ де́лать (сде́лать *perf*) всё возмо́жное; **of the** ~ **importance** велича́йшей ва́жности.
utter [ˈʌtəˀ] *adj* (*amazement*) по́лный; (*conviction*) глубо́кий*; (*rubbish*) соверше́нный ♦ *vt* (*sounds*) издава́ть* (изда́ть* *perf*); (*words*) произноси́ть* (произнести́* *perf*).
utterance [ˈʌtrns] *n* выска́зывание.
utterly [ˈʌtəlɪ] *adv* соверше́нно.
U-turn [ˈjuːˈtəːn] *n* (*AUT*) разворо́т на 180 гра́дусов; (*fig*) коренно́е измене́ние.
Uzbek [ˈʌzbɛk] *n* (*person*) узбе́к(-е́чка*); (*LING*) узбе́кский* язы́к* ♦ *adj* узбе́кский*.
Uzbekistan [ʌzbɛkɪˈstɑːn] *n* Узбекиста́н.

---

* marks translations which have irregular inflections. The Russian-English side of the dictionary gives inflectional information.

~ V, v ~

V, v [vi:] *n* (*letter*) 22-ая бу́ква англи́йского
алфави́та.
v. *abbr* = **verse, versus**; (= **volt**) В= *вольт*; (*see*: =
vide) см. *смотри́*.
VA (*US*: *POST*) *abbr* = *Virginia*.
vac [væk] *n abbr* (*BRIT*: *inf*) = **vacation**.
vacancy ['veɪkənsɪ] *n* (*BRIT*: *job*) вака́нсия;
(*room in hotel etc*) свобо́дный но́мер*; "no
vacancies" „мест нет"; **have you any
vacancies?** (*hotel*) у Вас есть свобо́дные
номера́?; (*office*) у Вас есть вака́нсии?
vacant ['veɪkənt] *adj* (*room, seat, toilet*)
свобо́дный* (свобо́ден); (*look, expression*)
отсу́тствующий*; (*job*) вака́нтный.
vacant lot *n* (*US*) пусты́рь* *m*; (: *for sale*)
уча́сток*.
vacate [vəˈkeɪt] *vt* освобожда́ть (освободи́ть*
perf).
vacation [vəˈkeɪʃən] *n* (*esp US*: *holiday*) о́тпуск*;
(*BRIT*: *SCOL*) кани́кулы *pl*; **to take a ~** брать*
(взять* *perf*) о́тпуск; **on ~** в о́тпуске.
vacation course *n* ле́тние ку́рсы *mpl*.
vaccinate ['væksɪneɪt] *vt*: **to ~ sb (against sth)**
де́лать (сде́лать *perf*) приви́вку кому́-н (от
чего́-н).
vaccination [væksɪˈneɪʃən] *n* приви́вка*.
vaccine ['væksi:n] *n* вакци́на.
vacuum ['vækjum] *n* (*empty space*) ва́куум ◆ *vt*
пылесо́сить (пропылесо́сить *perf*).
vacuum cleaner *n* пылесо́с.
vacuum flask *n* (*BRIT*) те́рмос.
vacuum-packed ['vækjumˈpækt] *adj*
гермети́чно упако́ванный (упако́ван).
Vaduz [faˈduts] *n*Ваду́ц.
vagabond ['vægəbɔnd] *n* бродя́га *m/f*.
vagary ['veɪgərɪ] *n*: **the vagaries of the weather**
капри́зы *mpl* пого́ды.
vagina [vəˈdʒaɪnə] *n* влага́лище.
vagrancy ['veɪgrənsɪ] *n* бродя́жничество.
vagrant ['veɪgrənt] *n* бродя́га *m/f*.
vague [veɪg] *adj* (*blurred*: *memory, outline*)
сму́тный* (сму́тен); (*uncertain*)
неопределённый; (*look*) рассе́янный; (*idea,
instructions*) расплы́вчатый (расплы́вчат);
(*evasive*: *answer*) укло́нчивый (укло́нчив);
he was ~ about it (*evasive*) он не сказа́л
ничего́ определённого об э́том; **I haven't the
~st idea** я не име́ю ни мале́йшего
представле́ния.

vaguely ['veɪglɪ] *adv* (*promise, say, plan*)
неопределённо; (*look*) рассе́янно; (*suspect*)
сму́тно; **they were ~ amused** они́ слегка́
развесели́лись; **it looks ~ like yours** э́то
немно́жко напомина́ет Ваш.
vagueness ['veɪgnɪs] *n* неопределённость *f*.
vain [veɪn] *adj* (*conceited*) тщесла́вный*
(тщесла́вен); (*useless*: *attempt, action*)
тще́тный* (тще́тен); **in ~** напра́сно.
vainly ['veɪnlɪ] *adv* тще́тно.
valance ['væləns] *n* (*for bed*) подзо́р.
valedictorian [vælɪdɪkˈtɔ:rɪən] *n* (*US*: *SCOL*)
"лу́чший" выпускни́к" (*в двена́дцатом кла́ссе
сре́дней шко́лы*).
valedictory [vælɪˈdɪktərɪ] *adj* (*speech, remarks*)
проща́льный.
valentine ['væləntaɪn] *n* (*also*: **~ card**)
(*анони́мное*) любо́вное посла́ние в день Св.
Валенти́на (*14 февраля́*).
valet ['vælɪt] *n* камерди́нер.
valet parking *n* припарко́вка автомоби́лей
клие́нтов, наприме́р в гости́ницах.
valet service *n* (*for clothes*) слу́жба по ухо́ду
за оде́ждой клие́нтов; (*for car*)
обслу́живание автомоби́лей – мо́йка,
запра́вка итп.
valiant ['vælɪənt] *adj* (*attempt, effort*)
отва́жный* (отва́жен).
valid ['vælɪd] *adj* (*ticket, document*)
действи́тельный* (действи́телен); (*reason*)
ве́ский* (ве́сок); (*argument*) убеди́тельный*
(убеди́телен).
validate ['vælɪdeɪt] *vt* (*contract, document*)
утвержда́ть (утверди́ть* *perf*); (*argument,
claim*) подтвержда́ть (подтверди́ть* *perf*).
validity [vəˈlɪdɪtɪ] *n* (*see adj*) действи́тельность
f; ве́скость *f*; убеди́тельность *f*.
valise [vəˈli:z] *n* саквоя́ж.
Valletta [vəˈletə] *n* Валле́тта.
valley ['vælɪ] *n* доли́на.
valour ['vælə] (*US* **valor**) *n* до́блесть *f*.
valuable ['væljuəbl] *adj* це́нный; (*time*)
драгоце́нный.
valuables ['væljuəblz] *npl* (*jewellery etc*)
це́нности *fpl*.
valuation [væljuˈeɪʃən] *n* оце́нка*.
value ['vælju:] *n* це́нность *f* ◆ *vt* (*fix price or
worth of*) оце́нивать (оцени́ть* *perf*);
(*appreciate*) цени́ть* (*impf*); **~s** *npl* (*principles,*

beliefs) це́нности *fpl*; **you get good ~ (for money) in that shop** в э́том магази́не вы́годно покупа́ть; **to lose (in) ~** па́дать (упа́сть* *perf*) в цене́; **to gain (in) ~** поднима́ться (подня́ться* *perf*) в цене́; **to be of great ~ to sb** (*fig*) представля́ть (*impf*) для кого́-н большу́ю це́нность.

value-added tax [vælju:'ædɪd-] *n* (*BRIT*) нало́г на доба́вленную сто́имость.

valued ['vælju:d] *adj* (*customer, advice*) це́нный.

valuer ['væljuəʳ] *n* оце́нщик.

valve [vælv] *n* (*also MED*) кла́пан.

vampire ['væmpaɪəʳ] *n* вампи́р.

van [væn] *n* (*AUT*) фурго́н; (*BRIT: RAIL*) бага́жный ваго́н.

V and A *n abbr* (*BRIT*) = **Victoria and Albert Museum.**

vandal ['vændl] *n* ванда́л.

vandalism ['vændəlɪzəm] *n* вандали́зм.

vandalize ['vændəlaɪz] *vt* (*damage*) бессмы́сленно уро́довать (изуро́довать *perf*); (*destroy*) бессмы́сленно разруша́ть (разру́шить *perf*).

vanguard ['vængɑːd] *n* (*fig*): **in the ~ of** в аванга́рде +*gen*.

vanilla [və'nɪlə] *n* вани́ль *f*.

vanilla ice cream *n* ≈ сли́вочное моро́женое *nt adj*.

vanish ['vænɪʃ] *vi* исчеза́ть (исче́знуть *perf*).

vanity ['vænɪtɪ] *n* (*of person*) тщесла́вие.

vanity case *n* косме́тичка*.

vantage point ['vɑːntɪdʒ-] *n* наблюда́тельный пункт; **from our 20th century ~ ~** (*fig*) с пози́ции на́шего 20-го ве́ка.

vapor *etc* (*US*) = **vapour** *etc*.

vaporize ['veɪpəraɪz] *vt* (*liquid*) выпа́ривать (вы́парить *perf*) ◆ *vi* испаря́ться (испари́ться *perf*).

vapour ['veɪpəʳ] (*US* **vapor**) *n* (*gas, mist, steam*) пар*.

vapour trail *n* (*AVIAT*) след* самолёта.

variable ['vɛərɪəbl] *adj* (*likely to change: mood, quality, weather*) изме́нчивый (изме́нчив); (*able to be changed: temperature, height, speed*) переме́нный ◆ *n* фа́ктор; (*MATH*) переме́нная *f adj*.

variance ['vɛərɪəns] *n*: **to be at ~ with** расходи́ться* (*impf*) (с +*instr*); (*facts*) противоре́чить (*impf*) +*dat*.

variant ['vɛərɪənt] *n* вариа́нт.

variation [vɛərɪ'eɪʃən] *n* (*in level, amount, quantity*) измене́ние; (*of plot, musical theme etc*) вариа́ция.

varicose veins ['værɪkəus-] *npl* (*MED*) варико́зное расшире́ние *ntsg* вен.

varied ['vɛərɪd] *adj* разнообра́зный* (разнообра́зен).

variety [və'raɪətɪ] *n* разнообра́зие; (*type*) разнови́дность *f*; **a wide ~ of** ... большо́е разнообра́зие +*gen* ...; **for a ~ of reasons** по ря́ду причи́н.

variety show *n* (*THEAT*) варьете́ *nt ind*.

various ['vɛərɪəs] *adj* (*different*) разли́чный; (*several*) ра́зный; **at ~ times** в ра́зное вре́мя.

varnish ['vɑːnɪʃ] *n* (*product*) лак; (*also: nail ~*) лак для ногте́й ◆ *vt* (*wood, piece of furniture etc*) покрыва́ть (покры́ть* *perf*) ла́ком; (*nails*) кра́сить* (накра́сить* *perf*).

vary ['vɛərɪ] *vt* (*routine, diet*) вноси́ть* (внести́* *perf*) разнообра́зие в +*acc* ◆ *vi* (*be different: sizes, colours*) различа́ться (*impf*); (*become different*): **to ~ with** (*weather, season etc*) меня́ться (*impf*) в зави́симости от +*gen*; **to ~ (according to or with)** меня́ться (*impf*) (в соотве́тствии с +*instr*).

varying ['vɛərɪɪŋ] *adj* (*amount, opinions etc*) разли́чный* (разли́чен).

vase [vɑːz] *n* ва́за.

vasectomy [væ'sɛktəmɪ] *n* (*MED*) вазектоми́я.

Vaseline® ['væsɪliːn] *n* вазели́н.

vast [vɑːst] *adj* (*knowledge*) обши́рный* (обши́рен); (*expense*) грома́дный* (грома́ден); (*area*) необъя́тный* (необъя́тен).

vastly ['vɑːstlɪ] *adv* кра́йне.

vastness ['vɑːstnɪs] *n* необъя́тность *f*.

VAT [væt] *n abbr* (*BRIT*) (= **value-added tax**) НДС= *нало́г на доба́вленную сто́имость.*

vat [væt] *n* ка́дка.

Vatican ['vætɪkən] *n*: **the ~** Ватика́н.

vatman ['vætmæn] *n* (*BRIT: inf*) чино́вник, *собира́ющий нало́г на доба́вочную сто́имость.*

vaudeville ['vəudəvɪl] *n* (*THEAT*) водеви́ль *m*.

vault [vɔːlt] *n* (*of roof*) свод; (*tomb*) склеп; (*in bank*) храни́лище; (*jump*) (опо́рный) прыжо́к ◆ *vt* (*also: ~ over*) перепры́гивать (перепры́гнуть *perf*) (че́рез +*acc*).

vaunted ['vɔːntɪd] *adj*: **much-~** восхваля́емый.

VC *n abbr* = **vice-chairman**; (*BRIT*: = **Victoria Cross**) "Крест Викто́рии" (*вы́сшая вое́нная награ́да*).

VCR *n abbr* = **video cassette recorder**.

VD *n abbr* = **venereal disease**.

VDU *n abbr* (*COMPUT*) = **visual display unit**.

veal [viːl] *n* (*CULIN*) теля́тина.

veer [vɪəʳ] *vi* (*vehicle*) свора́чивать (сверну́ть *perf*); (*wind*) меня́ть (применя́ть *perf*) направле́ние.

veg. [vɛdʒ] *n abbr* (*BRIT: inf*) = **vegetable(s)**.

vegan ['viːgən] *n* вегетариа́нец, *не употребля́ющий моло́чных проду́ктов* ◆ *adj* расти́тельный.

vegeburger ['vɛdʒɪbəːgəʳ] *n* вегетариа́нская котле́та.

---

* marks translations which have irregular inflections. The Russian-English side of the dictionary gives inflectional information.

vegetable ['vɛdʒtəbl] n (BOT) о́вощ ♦ adj (oil etc) расти́тельный; (dish) овощно́й; ~ **garden** огоро́д.

vegetarian [vɛdʒɪ'tɛərɪən] n (person) вегетариа́нец*(-а́нка*) ♦ adj (diet, restaurant etc) вегетариа́нский*.

vegetate ['vɛdʒɪteɪt] vi (person) прозяба́ть (impf).

vegetation [vɛdʒɪ'teɪʃən] n (plants) расти́тельность f.

vegetative ['vɛdʒɪtətɪv] adj (BIO) вегетати́вный; (fig) расти́тельный.

veggieburger ['vɛdʒɪbə:gəʳ] n = vegeburger.

vehemence ['vi:ɪməns] n я́рость f.

vehement ['vi:ɪmənt] adj (attack, denial) я́ростный* (я́ростен); (passions) нейстовый (нейстов).

vehicle ['vi:ɪkl] n автотра́нспортное сре́дство; (fig: means of expressing) сре́дство.

vehicular [vɪ'hɪkjuləʳ] adj (AUT): **"no ~ traffic"** „движе́ние автотра́нспорта запрещено́".

veil [veɪl] n вуа́ль f ♦ vt скрыва́ть (скрыть* perf); **under a ~ of secrecy** (fig) под покро́вом та́йны.

veiled [veɪld] adj (fig: threat) скры́тый.

vein [veɪn] n (of leaf) жи́лка*; (ANAT) ве́на; (of ore) жи́ла; (fig: of mood, style) тон.

Velcro® ['vɛlkrəu] n липу́чка.

vellum ['vɛləm] n (writing paper) веле́невая бума́га.

velocity [vɪ'lɔsɪtɪ] n ско́рость f.

velour [və'luəʳ] n велю́р.

velvet ['vɛlvɪt] n ба́рхат ♦ adj ба́рхатный.

vendetta [vɛn'dɛtə] n венде́тта.

vending machine ['vɛndɪŋ-] n автома́т по прода́же сигаре́т, шокола́да итп.

vendor ['vɛndəʳ] n (of house, land) продаве́ц; **street ~** у́личный(-ая) торго́вец(-вка).

veneer [və'nɪəʳ] n (on furniture) фанеро́вка; (fig: of person, place) личи́на.

venerable ['vɛnərəbl] adj (person) почте́нный; (building etc) дре́вний*; (REL) преподо́бный.

venereal disease [vɪ'nɪərɪəl-] n венери́ческое заболева́ние.

Venetian [vɪ'ni:ʃən] adj венециа́нский* ♦ n венециа́нец(-а́нка*).

Venetian blind n жалюзи́ pl.

Venezuela [vɛnɛ'zweɪlə] n Венесуэ́ла.

Venezuelan [vɛnɛ'zweɪlən] adj венесуэ́льский* ♦ n венесуэ́лец*(-лка).

vengeance ['vɛndʒəns] n возме́здие; **with a ~** (fig) с лихво́й.

vengeful ['vɛndʒful] adj мсти́тельный* (мсти́телен).

Venice ['vɛnɪs] n Вене́ция.

venison ['vɛnɪsn] n олени́на.

venom ['vɛnəm] n (of snake, insect) яд; (bitterness, anger) зло́ба.

venomous ['vɛnəməs] adj (snake, insect) ядови́тый (ядови́т); (look, stare) зло́бный* (зло́бен).

vent [vɛnt] n (also: **air ~**) вентиляцио́нное отве́рстие; (in jacket) разре́з ♦ vt (fig) дава́ть* (дать* perf) вы́ход +dat.

ventilate ['vɛntɪleɪt] vt (room, building) прове́тривать (прове́трить perf).

ventilation [vɛntɪ'leɪʃən] n вентиля́ция.

ventilation shaft n вентиляцио́нная ша́хта.

ventilator ['vɛntɪleɪtəʳ] n (TECH, MED) вентиля́тор.

ventriloquist [vɛn'trɪləkwɪst] n чревовеща́тель(ница) m(f).

venture ['vɛntʃəʳ] n (risky undertaking) сме́лое предприя́тие ♦ vt (opinion) осме́литься (осме́литься perf) вы́сказать ♦ vi (dare to go) осме́ливаться (осме́литься perf); **business ~** предприя́тие; **to ~ to do** отва́живаться (отва́житься perf) +infin.

venture capital n (COMM) ве́нчурный капита́л.

venue ['vɛnju:] n (place fixed for sth) ме́сто* проведе́ния.

Venus ['vi:nəs] n (planet) Вене́ра.

veracity [və'ræsɪtɪ] n правди́вость f.

veranda(h) [və'rændə] n вера́нда.

verb [və:b] n глаго́л.

verbal ['və:bl] adj (spoken: skills, translation etc) у́стный; (of a verb) глаго́льный.

verbally ['və:bəlɪ] adv (communicate, transmit) на слова́х.

verbatim [və:'beɪtɪm] adj досло́вный ♦ adv досло́вно.

verbose [və:'bəus] adj (person, writing) многосло́вный.

verdict ['və:dɪkt] n (LAW) пригово́р; (fig: opinion) заключе́ние; **to bring in a ~ of guilty/ not guilty** выноси́ть* (вы́нести* perf) обвини́тельный/оправда́тельный прогово́р.

verge [və:dʒ] n (BRIT: of road) обо́чина; **"soft ~s"** (BRIT: AUT) незаасфальти́рованная. грунто́вая обо́чина; **to be on the ~ of sth** быть* (impf) на гра́ни чего́-н

▸ **verge on** vt fus (panic etc) грани́чить (impf) с +instr.

verger ['və:dʒəʳ] n (REL) церко́вный служи́тель m.

verification [vɛrɪfɪ'keɪʃən] n (see vb) подтвержде́ние; прове́рка.

verify ['vɛrɪfaɪ] vt (confirm) подтвержда́ть (подтверди́ть* perf); (check) проверя́ть (прове́рить perf).

veritable ['vɛrɪtəbl] adj (for emphasis: real) настоя́щий*.

vermin ['və:mɪn] npl (animals) вреди́тели mpl; (fleas, lice etc) парази́ты mpl.

vermouth ['və:məθ] n ве́рмут.

vernacular [və'nækjuləʳ] n (language) национа́льный язы́к*; (local language) ме́стный диале́кт.

versatile ['və:sətaɪl] adj (person) разносторо́нний*; (substance, machine, tool etc) универса́льный* (универса́лен).

versatility [vəːsəˈtɪlɪtɪ] n (see adj) разно-сторóнность f; универсáльность f.

verse [vəːs] n (poetry, in Bible) стих; (one part of a poem) строфá*; **in ~** в стихáх.

versed [vəːst] adj: **(well-)~ in** свéдущий* (свéдущ) в +prp.

version [ˈvəːʃən] n (form: of design, production) вариáнт; (account: of events, accident etc) вéрсия.

versus [ˈvəːsəs] prep прóтив +gen.

vertebra [ˈvəːtɪbrə] (pl ~e) n (ANAT) позвонóк*.

vertebrae [ˈvəːtɪbriː] npl of **vertebra**.

vertebrate [ˈvəːtɪbrɪt] n позвонóчное nt adj (живóтное).

vertical [ˈvəːtɪkl] adj вертикáльный* (вертикáлен) ♦ n вертикáль f.

vertically [ˈvəːtɪklɪ] adv вертикáльно.

vertigo [ˈvəːtɪgəu] n головокружéние; **to suffer from ~** страдáть (impf) от головокружéний.

verve [vəːv] n (vivacity) воодушевлéние.

very [ˈvɛrɪ] adv óчень ♦ adj: **the ~ book which** тá сáмая кнúга, котóрая; **~ well/little** óчень хорошó/мáло; **thank you ~ much** большóе спасúбо; **~ much better** горáздо лýчше; **I ~ much hope so** я óчень надéюсь на э́то; **the ~ thought (of it) alarms me** самá мысль (об э́том) пугáет меня́; **at the ~ end** в сáмом концé; **the ~ last** сáмый послéдний*; **at the ~ least** как мúнимум.

vespers [ˈvɛspəz] npl (REL) вечéрня fsg.

vessel [ˈvɛsl] n (NAUT) сýдно*; (container) сосýд; see also **blood**.

vest [vɛst] n (BRIT: underwear) мáйка; (US: waistcoat) жилéт ♦ vt: **to ~ sb with sth, ~ sth in sb** наделя́ть (наделúть perf) когó-н чем-н.

vested interest [ˈvɛstɪd-] n (COMM) заинтересóванность f; **to have a ~ ~ in sth** быть* (impf) заинтересóванным(-ой) в чём-н.

vestibule [ˈvɛstɪbjuːl] n (in building) вестибю́ль m.

vestige [ˈvɛstɪdʒ] n остáток*.

vestment [ˈvɛstmənt] n (REL) рúза.

vestry [ˈvɛstrɪ] n (of church) рúзница.

Vesuvius [vɪˈsuːvɪəs] n Везýвий.

vet [vɛt] n abbr (BRIT) = **veterinary surgeon**.

veteran [ˈvɛtərn] n (of war) ветерáн ♦ adj: **she's a ~ campaigner for ...** онá стáрый ветерáн движéния за +acc ....

veteran car n (BRIT) машúна стáрой мáрки.

veterinarian [vɛtrɪˈnɛərɪən] n (US) ветеринáр.

veterinary [ˈvɛtrɪnərɪ] adj (practice, care etc) ветеринáрный.

veterinary surgeon n (BRIT) ветеринáр.

veto [ˈviːtəu] (pl ~es) n вéто nt ind ♦ vt (proposal etc) налагáть (наложúть* perf) вéто на +acc; **to put a ~ on** налагáть (наложúть* perf) вéто на +acc.

vetting [ˈvɛtɪŋ] n (of person) провéрка (на

благонадёжность).

vex [vɛks] vt (irritate, upset) досаждáть (досадúть* perf).

vexed [vɛkst] adj (question) досаждáющий.

VFD n abbr (US) = volunteer fire department.

VG n abbr (BRIT: SCOL etc) = very good.

VHF abbr (RADIO: = very high frequency) ОВЧ= óчень высóкая частотá.

VI abbr (US: POST) = Virgin Islands.

via [ˈvaɪə] prep (through, by way of) чéрез +acc.

viability [vaɪəˈbɪlɪtɪ] n жизнеспосóбность f; (of product) конкурентоспосóбность f.

viable [ˈvaɪəbl] adj (company) конкуренто-спосóбный; (project) осуществúмый.

viaduct [ˈvaɪədʌkt] n виадýк.

vial [ˈvaɪəl] n (for medicine) пузырёк; (for perfume) флакóн.

vibes [vaɪbz] npl (inf: atmosphere) флюúды mpl.

vibrant [ˈvaɪbrnt] adj (lively) пóлный* (пóлон) жúзни; (light) я́ркий* (я́рок); (colour) сóчный* (сóчен); (full of emotion: voice) насы́щенный.

vibraphone [ˈvaɪbrəfəun] n вибрафóн.

vibrate [vaɪˈbreɪt] vi (house, machine etc) вибрúровать* (impf); (resound) отдавáться* (impf).

vibration [vaɪˈbreɪʃən] n вибрáция.

vibrator [vaɪˈbreɪtə] n вибрáтор.

vicar [ˈvɪkə] n (REL) свящéнник.

vicarage [ˈvɪkərɪdʒ] n дом* свящéнника.

vicarious [vɪˈkɛərɪəs] adj (pleasure, experience) опосрéдованный (опосрéдован).

vice [vaɪs] n (moral fault) порóк; (TECH) тискú pl.

vice- [vaɪs] prefix (president) вице-.

vice-chairman [vaɪsˈtʃɛəmən] irreg n заместúтель m председáтеля.

vice chancellor n (BRIT: of university) вúце-кáнцлер.

vice president n вúце-президéнт.

viceroy [ˈvaɪsrɔɪ] n королéвский* намéстник.

vice squad n (POLICE) отдéл в полúции, котóрый имéет дéло с преступлéниями, свя́занными с порногрáфией, проститýцией, наркóтиками итп.

vice versa [ˈvaɪsɪˈvəːsə] adv наоборóт.

vicinity [vɪˈsɪnɪtɪ] n (area): **in the ~ (of)** в окрéстностях (+gen).

vicious [ˈvɪʃəs] adj (attack, blow) жестóкий* (жестóк); (words, look, dog) злой* (зол); (horse) норовúстый (норовúст).

vicious circle n порóчный круг.

viciousness [ˈvɪʃəsnɪs] n злóба.

vicissitudes [vɪˈsɪsɪtjuːdz] npl преврáтности fpl.

victim [ˈvɪktɪm] n (of) жéртва; **to be the ~ of** быть* (impf) жéртвой +gen.

victimization [ˈvɪktɪmaɪˈzeɪʃən] n преслéдование.

---

victimize ['vıktımaız] *vt* (*strikers etc*)
пресле́довать* (*impf/perf*).
victor ['vıktə^r] *n* победи́тель(ница) *m(f)*.
Victorian [vık'tɔ:rıən] *adj* викториа́нский.
victorious [vık'tɔ:rıəs] *adj* (*team*)
победоно́сный; (*shout*) побе́дный.
victory ['vıktərı] *n* побе́да; **to win a ~ over sb**
одержа́ть* (*perf*) побе́ду над кем-н.
video ['vıdıəu] *cpd* ви́део *ind* ♦ *n* (*also: ~ film*)
видеофи́льм; (*also: ~ cassette*)
видеокассе́та; (*also: ~ cassette recorder*)
видеомагнитофо́н; (*also: ~ camera*)
видеока́мера.
videodisc ['vıdıəudısk] *n* ви́деодиск.
video game *n* видеоигра́.
video nasty *n* видеофи́льм со сце́нами
наси́лия.
videophone ['vıdıəufəun] *n* видеотелефо́н.
video recorder *n* видеомагнитофо́н.
video recording *n* видеоза́пись *f*.
video tape *n* видеоле́нта.
vie [vaı] *vi*: **to ~ with sb/for sth** сопе́рничать
(*impf*) с кем-н/в чем-н.
Vienna [vı'ɛnə] *n* Ве́на.
Viennese [vıə'ni:z] *adj* ве́нский ♦ *n inv*
жи́тель(ница) *m(f)* Ве́ны.
Vietnam ['vjɛt'næm] *n* Вьетна́м.
Viet Nam ['vjɛt'næm] *n* = **Vietnam**.
Vietnamese [vjɛtnə'mi:z] *adj* вьетна́мский* ♦ *n*
inv (*person*) вьетна́мец*(-мка*); (*LING*)
вьетна́мский* язы́к*.
view [vju:] *n* (*sight, outlook*) вид; (*opinion*)
взгляд ♦ *vt* (*look at: also fig*) рассма́тривать
(рассмотре́ть *perf*); (*situation*) оце́нивать
(оцени́ть *perf*); (*house*) осма́тривать
(осмотре́ть *perf*); **to be on ~** (*in museum etc*)
выставля́ться (*impf*); **in full ~ (of)** на виду́ (у
+*gen*); **in ~ of the weather/the fact that** в виду́
плохо́й пого́ды/того́, что; **in my ~** на мой
взгляд; **an overall ~ of the situation** о́бщая
карти́на положе́ния; **with a ~ to doing** с тем,
что́бы +*infin*.
Viewdata® ['vju:deıtə] *n* (*BRIT: COMPUT*)
видеоте́кс; (*TEL*) *телекоммуникацио́нная*
систе́ма, позволя́ющая клие́нтам де́лать
зака́зы на това́ры и́ли услу́ги пря́мо из
до́ма.
viewer ['vju:ə^r] *n* (*person*) зри́тель *m*.
viewfinder ['vju:faındə^r] *n* (*PHOT*) видо-
иска́тель *m*.
viewpoint ['vju:pɔınt] *n* (*attitude*) то́чка
зре́ния; (*place*) ме́сто* обозре́ния.
vigil ['vıdʒıl] *n* бде́ние; **to keep ~** дежу́рить
(подежу́рить *perf*).
vigilance ['vıdʒıləns] *n* бди́тельность *f*.
vigilance committee *n* (*US*) "комите́т
бди́тельности" (*организа́ция линчева́телей*).
vigilant ['vıdʒılənt] *adj* бди́тельный.
vigilante [vıdʒı'læntı] *n самоде́ятельный*
блюсти́тель поря́дка, счита́ющий де́йствия
поли́ции недоста́точными.

vigor ['vıgə^r] (*US*) *n* = **vigour**.
vigorous ['vıgərəs] *adj* (*action, campaign*)
мо́щный; (*plant*) си́льный.
vigour ['vıgə^r] (*US* **vigor**) *n* (*energy: of person*)
си́ла; (: *of campaign*) мощь *f*.
vile [vaıl] *adj* (*evil*) гну́сный; (*unpleasant*)
ме́рзкий; **~ language** скверносло́вие.
vilify ['vılıfaı] *vt* (*person*) поноси́ть* (*impf*).
villa ['vılə] *n* ви́лла.
village ['vılıdʒ] *n* дере́вня.
villager ['vılıdʒə^r] *n* дереве́нский*(-ая)
жи́тель(ница) *m(f)*.
villain ['vılən] *n* (*scoundrel*) негодя́й; (*in novel*
etc) злоде́й; (*BRIT: criminal*) престу́пник.
Vilnius ['vılnıəs] *n* Ви́льнюс.
VIN *n abbr* (*US*) = *vehicle identification number*.
vinaigrette [vıneı'grɛt] *n* (*salad dressing*)
запра́вка для сала́та (*из у́ксуса и*
расти́тельного ма́сла).
vindicate ['vındıkeıt] *vt* (*person: free from*
blame) дока́зывать (доказа́ть* *perf*) правоту́
+*gen*; (*action: justify*) опра́вдывать
(оправда́ть *perf*).
vindication [vındı'keıʃən] *n*: **in ~ of sb/sth** в
оправда́ние кого́-н/чего́-н.
vindictive [vın'dıktıv] *adj* мсти́тельный*
(мсти́телен).
vine [vaın] *n* (*BOT: with grapes*) виногра́дная
лоза́*; (: *climbing plant*) вью́щееся расте́ние;
(: *in jungle*) лиа́на.
vinegar ['vınıgə^r] *n* у́ксус.
vineyard ['vınja:d] *n* виногра́дник.
vintage ['vıntıdʒ] *n* (*year*) *год изготовле́ния*
вина́ ♦ *cpd* (*classic: comedy, performance etc*)
класси́ческий*; **the 1970 ~** (*of wine*) урожа́я
1970 го́да.
vintage car *n* маши́на ста́рой ма́рки.
vintage wine *n* вы́держанное вино́.
vinyl ['vaınl] *n* вини́л.
viola [vı'əulə] *n* (*MUS*) альт*.
violate ['vaıəleıt] *vt* наруша́ть (нару́шить *perf*);
(*graveyard*) оскверня́ть (оскверни́ть *perf*).
violation [vaıə'leıʃən] *n* (*of agreement etc*)
наруше́ние; **in ~ of** в наруше́ние +*gen*.
violence ['vaıələns] *n* (*brutality*) наси́лие;
(*strength*) си́ла.
violent ['vaıələnt] *adj* (*behaviour*) жесто́кий*;
(*death*) наси́льственный; (*debate, criticism*)
я́ростный; **a ~ dislike of sb/sth** ре́зкая
неприя́знь к кому́-н/чему́-н.
violently ['vaıələntlı] *adv* (*dislike*) си́льно; (*ill,*
angry) о́чень.
violet ['vaıələt] *adj* фиоле́товый ♦ *n* (*colour*)
фиоле́товый цвет; (*plant*) фиа́лка*.
violin [vaıə'lın] *n* (*MUS*) скри́пка*.
violinist [vaıə'lınıst] *n* скрипа́ч*(ка*).
VIP *n abbr* (= *very important person*) о́чень
ва́жное лицо́.
viper ['vaıpə^r] *n* гадю́ка.
viral ['vaıərəl] *adj* ви́русный.
virgin ['və:dʒın] *n* (*person*) де́вственница;

(: *religious etc*) де́ва ♦ *adj* (*snow, forest etc*) де́вственный; **the Blessed V~** пресвята́я де́ва Мари́я; (*in Orthodox Church*) Богоро́дица.
virgin birth *n* рожде́ние от де́вственницы.
virginity [vəˈdʒɪnɪtɪ] *n* (*of person*) де́вственность *f*.
Virgo [ˈvəːgəu] *n* Де́ва; **he is ~** он – Де́ва.
virile [ˈvɪraɪl] *adj* облада́ющий мужско́й си́лой.
virility [vɪˈrɪlɪtɪ] *n* (*sexual power*) мужска́я си́ла; (*fig: masculine qualities*) му́жественность *f*.
virtual [ˈvəːtjuəl] *adj* факти́ческий*; (*COMPUT, PHYS*) виртуа́льный; (*in effect*): **it's a ~ impossibility** э́то практи́чески *or* факти́чески невозмо́жно.
virtually [ˈvəːtjuəlɪ] *adv* (*almost*) факти́чески, практи́чески; **it is ~ impossible** э́то факти́чески *or* практи́чески невозмо́жно.
virtual reality *n* систе́ма трёхме́рного телеви́дения.
virtue [ˈvəːtjuː] *n* (*moral correctness*) доброде́тель *f*; (*advantage*) преиму́щество; (*merit*) досто́инство; **by ~ of** благодаря́ +*dat*.
virtuosi [vəːtjuˈəuzɪ] *npl of* **virtuoso**.
virtuosity [vəːtjuˈɒsɪtɪ] *n* виртуо́зность *f*.
virtuoso [vəːtjuˈəuzəu] (*pl* **~s** *or* **virtuosi**) *n* виртуо́з.
virtuous [ˈvəːtjuəs] *adj* (*displaying virtue*) доброде́тельный.
virulence [ˈvɪruləns] *n* (*see adj*) ядови́тость *f*; смерте́льность *f*; не́нависть *f*.
virulent [ˈvɪrulənt] *adj* (*poison*) ядови́тый; (*disease*) смерте́льный; (*actions, feelings*) по́лный* (по́лон) не́нависти.
virus [ˈvaɪərəs] *n* (*MED*) ви́рус.
visa [ˈviːzə] *n* (*for travel*) ви́за.
vis-à-vis [viːzəˈviː] *prep* по отноше́нию к +*dat*.
viscose [ˈvɪskəus] *n* виско́за.
viscount [ˈvaɪkaunt] *n* вико́нт.
viscous [ˈvɪskəs] *adj* (*liquid, substance*) вя́зкий* (вя́зок).
vise [vaɪs] *n* (*US: TECH*) = **vice**.
visibility [vɪzɪˈbɪlɪtɪ] *n* ви́димость *f*.
visible [ˈvɪzəbl] *adj* (*able to be seen or recognized*) ви́димый (ви́дим); (*results, growth*) очеви́дный (очеви́ден); **~ exports/ imports** (*ECON*) ви́димый э́кспорт/и́мпорт.
visibly [ˈvɪzəblɪ] *adv* (*upset, nervous, damaged*) я́вно.
vision [ˈvɪʒən] *n* (*sight*) зре́ние; (*foresight*) предви́дение; (*in dream*) виде́ние.
visionary [ˈvɪʒənrɪ] *n* (*person*) прови́дец.
visit [ˈvɪzɪt] *n* (*to person, place*) посеще́ние; (*stay*) пребыва́ние ♦ *vt* (*person*) идти́ (прийти́* *perf*) *or* ходи́ть* (приходи́ть* *perf*) в го́сти к +*dat*; (*elderly, disabled person*) навеща́ть (навести́ть* *perf*); (*place*) посеща́ть (посети́ть* *perf*); **on a private/official ~** с

ча́стным/официа́льным визи́том.
visiting [ˈvɪzɪtɪŋ] *adj* (*speaker*) прие́хавший по приглаше́нию; **~ team** кома́нда госте́й.
visiting card *n* визи́тная ка́рточка*.
visiting hours *npl* (*in hospital etc*) часы́ *mpl* посеще́ния.
visiting professor *n* профе́ссор, прие́хавший по приглаше́нию.
visitor [ˈvɪzɪtə] *n* (*person visiting*) гость(я) *m(f)*; (*in public place, museum etc*) посети́тель(ница) *m(f)*; (*tourist: in town etc*) прие́зжий*(-ая) *m(f) adj*.
visitors' book [ˈvɪzɪtəz-] *n* кни́га посети́телей.
visor [ˈvaɪzə] *n* (*of helmet etc*) щито́к.
VISTA [ˈvɪstə] *n abbr* (= *Volunteers in Service to America*) доброво́льная организа́ция по оказа́нию по́мощи бе́дным.
vista [ˈvɪstə] *n* (*view*) перспекти́ва.
Vistula [ˈvɪstjulə] *n*: **the ~** Ви́сла.
visual [ˈvɪzjuəl] *adj* (*image*) зри́тельный.
visual aid *n* (*SCOL*) нагля́дное посо́бие.
visual arts *npl* изобрази́тельное иску́сство и кино́.
visual display unit *n* (*COMPUT*) устро́йство визуа́льного изображе́ния *or* диспле́й.
visualize [ˈvɪzjuəlaɪz] *vt* (*picture, imagine*) представля́ть (предста́вить* *perf*) мы́сленно; (*foresee*) представля́ть (предста́вить* *perf*) себе́.
visually [ˈvɪzjuəlɪ] *adv*: **~ appealing** привлека́тельный на вид; **~ handicapped** со зри́тельным дефе́ктом.
vital [ˈvaɪtl] *adj* (*essential, important, crucial*) жи́зненно необходи́мый (необходи́м); (*full of life: person*) живо́й, жизнеспосо́бный* (жизнеспосо́бен); (*necessary for life: organ*) жи́зненно ва́жный* (ва́жен); **of ~ importance (to sb/sth)** жи́зненно ва́жно (для кого́-н/ чего́-н).
vitality [vaɪˈtælɪtɪ] *n* (*liveliness*) жи́вость *f*.
vitally [ˈvaɪtəlɪ] *adv*: **~ important** жи́зненно ва́жный* (ва́жен).
vital statistics *npl* (*of woman*) габари́ты *mpl*; (*of population*) демографи́ческая стати́стика *fsg*.
vitamin [ˈvɪtəmɪn] *n* витами́н.
vitiate [ˈvɪʃɪeɪt] *vt* (*spoil*) по́ртить (испо́ртить* *perf*); **to ~ sb's efforts** своди́ть* (свести́* *perf*) на нет чьи-н уси́лия.
vitreous [ˈvɪtrɪəs] *adj* стеклови́дный.
vitriolic [vɪtrɪˈɒlɪk] *adj* (*fig: language*) ядови́тый (ядови́т); (: *behaviour*) зло́бный* (зло́бен).
viva (voce) [ˈvaɪvə(ˈvəutʃɪ)] *n* (*SCOL*) у́стный экза́мен.
vivacious [vɪˈveɪʃəs] *adj* (*person*) живо́й.
vivacity [vɪˈvæsɪtɪ] *n* жи́вость *f*.
vivid [ˈvɪvɪd] *adj* (*description, colour, light*) я́ркий*; (*memory*) отчётливый; (*imagination*)

живо́й.
vividly ['vɪvɪdlɪ] *adv* (*describe*) в живы́х
дета́лях; (*remember*) отчётливо.
vivisection [vɪvɪ'sɛkʃən] *n* вивисе́кция.
vixen ['vɪksn] *n* са́мка* лиси́цы; (*pej: woman*)
меге́ра.
viz [vɪz] *abbr* (*namely*: = *videlicet*) а и́менно.
Vladivostok [vlædɪ'vɒstɒk] *n* Владивосто́к.
VLF *abbr* (*RADIO*: = *very low frequency*) ОНЧ=
о́чень ни́зкая частота́.
V-neck ['vi:nɛk] *n* (*also:* ~ **jumper** *or* **pullover**)
джéмпер *or* пуло́вер с вы́резом.
VOA *n abbr* (= *Voice of America*) ″Го́лос
Аме́рики″.
vocabulary [vəu'kæbjulərɪ] *n* (*words known*)
слова́рный запа́с.
vocal ['vəukl] *adj* (*of the voice: in singing*)
вока́льный; (*articulate*) зву́чный* (зву́чен); **to
be ~ for/against** подня́ть (*perf*) го́лос в
по́льзу +*gen*/про́тив +*gen*.
vocal cords *npl* голосовы́е свя́зки *fpl*.
vocalist ['vəukəlɪst] *n* вокали́ст(ка*).
vocals ['vəuklz] *npl* (*MUS*) вока́льная па́ртия
fsg.
vocation [vəu'keɪʃən] *n* призва́ние.
vocational [vəu'keɪʃənl] *adj* (*training, guidance
etc*) профессиона́льный.
vociferous [və'sɪfərəs] *adj* (*protesters,
demands*) громогла́сный.
vodka ['vɒdkə] *n* во́дка.
vogue [vəug] *n* мо́да; **in ~** в мо́де.
voice [vɔɪs] *n* го́лос ♦ *vt* (*opinion*) выска́зывать
(вы́сказать* *perf*); **in a loud/soft ~** гро́мким/
ти́хим го́лосом; **to give ~ to sth** выража́ть
(вы́разить* *perf*) что-н.
voice-over ['vɔɪsəuvə'] *n* го́лос за ка́дром.
void [vɔɪd] *n* (*emptiness*) пустота́; (*hole*)
пробе́л ♦ *adj* (*invalid*) недействи́тельный*
(недействи́телен); **~ of** (*empty*) лишённый
(лишён) +*gen*.
voile [vɔɪl] *n* (*fabric*) вуа́ль *f*.
vol. *abbr* (= **volume**) т.= *том*.
volatile ['vɒlətaɪl] *adj* (*situation, person*)
изме́нчивый (изме́нчив); (*liquid*) лету́чий*.
volcanic [vɒl'kænɪk] *adj* (*rock, eruption*)
вулкани́ческий.
volcano [vɒl'keɪnəu] (*pl* **-es**) *n* вулка́н.
Volga ['vɒlgə] *n*: **the ~** Во́лга.
Volgograd ['vɒlgəgræd] *n* Волгогра́д.
volition [və'lɪʃən] *n*: **of one's own ~** по свое́й
во́ле.
volley ['vɒlɪ] *n* (*of gunfire*) залп; (*of stones etc*)
град; (*of questions etc*) пото́к; (*TENNIS etc*)
уда́р с лёта.
volleyball ['vɒlɪbɔ:l] *n* (*SPORT*) волейбо́л.
volt [vəult] *n* (*ELEC*) вольт.
voltage ['vəultɪdʒ] *n* (*ELEC*) напряже́ние; **high/
low ~** высо́кое/ни́зкое напряже́ние.
volte-face ['vɒlt'fɑːs] *n inv* ре́зкая переме́на.
voluble ['vɒljubl] *adj* (*person, speech*)
многосло́вный.

volume ['vɒljuːm] *n* (*space*) объём; (*amount*)
коли́чество; (*book*) том; (*sound level*)
гро́мкость *f*; **~ one/two** (*book*) том пе́рвый/
второ́й; **his expression spoke ~s** выраже́ние
его́ лица́ говори́т красноречи́вее вся́ких
слов.
volume control *n* (*RADIO, TV*) гро́мкость *f*.
volume discount *n* (*COMM*) ски́дка за поку́пку
кру́пной па́ртии това́ра.
voluminous [və'luːmɪnəs] *adj* (*clothes*)
просто́рный; (*correspondence, notes*)
простра́нный.
voluntarily ['vɒləntrɪlɪ] *adv* (*willingly*) добро-
во́льно.
voluntary ['vɒləntərɪ] *adj* (*willing: exile*)
доброво́льный*; (*unpaid: work, worker*)
обще́ственный.
voluntary liquidation *n* (*COMM*)
доброво́льная ликвида́ция.
voluntary redundancy *n* (*BRIT*) увольне́ние по
со́бственному жела́нию.
volunteer [vɒlən'tɪə'] *n* (*unpaid helper*)
доброво́льный(-ая) помо́щник(-ица); (*to
army etc*) доброво́лец ♦ *vt* (*information*)
предлага́ть (предложи́ть* *perf*) ♦ *vi* (*for army
etc*) идти́* (пойти́* *perf*) доброво́льцем; **to ~
to do** вызыва́ться (вы́зваться* *perf*) +*infin*.
voluptuous [və'lʌptjuəs] *adj* (*movement, body,
feeling*) сладостра́стный*.
vomit ['vɒmɪt] *n* рво́та ♦ *vi*: **he ~ed** его́
вы́рвало; **she began to ~** её начало рвать.
voracious [və'reɪʃəs] *adj* жа́дный* (жа́ден); **he
is a ~ reader** он с жа́дностью чита́ет.
vote [vəut] *n* (*indication of choice, opinion*)
голосова́ние; (*votes cast*) го́лос; (*right to
vote*) пра́во го́лоса ♦ *vi* (*in election etc*)
голосова́ть* (проголосова́ть* *perf*) ♦ *vt
(elect*): **he was ~d chairman** он был и́збран
председа́телем; (*propose*): **to ~ that**
предлага́ть (предложи́ть *perf*), что́бы; **to put
sth to the ~, take a ~ on sth** ста́вить*
(поста́вить* *perf*) что-н на голосова́ние; **~ of
censure** выраже́ние порица́ния; **~ of thanks**
благода́рственная речь *f*; **to pass a ~ of
confidence/no confidence** выража́ть
(вы́разить* *perf*) во́тум дове́рия/недове́рия;
to ~ for *or* **in favour of/against** голосова́ть*
(проголосова́ть* *perf*) за +*acc*/про́тив +*gen*; **to
~ Labour** голосова́ть* (проголосова́ть* *perf*)
за Лейбори́стскую па́ртию.
voter ['vəutə'] *n* избира́тель *m*.
voting ['vəutɪŋ] *n* голосова́ние.
voting paper *n* (*BRIT*) избира́тельный
бюллете́нь *m*.
voting right *n* пра́во го́лоса.
vouch [vautʃ] *vt fus*: **to ~ for** (*person, quality etc*)
руча́ться (поручи́ться* *perf*) за +*acc*.
voucher ['vautʃə'] *n* (*for meal: also:* **luncheon ~**)
тало́н на обе́д; (*with petrol, cigarettes etc*)
ва́учер; (*receipt*) распи́ска.
vow [vau] *n* кля́тва ♦ *vt*: **to ~ to do/that**

кля́сться* (покля́сться* *perf*) +*infin*/, что; **to take** *or* **make a ~ to do** дава́ть* (дать* *perf*) обе́т +*infin*.
vowel ['vauəl] *n* (*LING*) гла́сный *m adj*.
voyage ['vɔɪdʒ] *n* (*by ship*) пла́вание; (*by spacecraft*) полёт.
voyeur [vwɑː'jəːʳ] *n* челове́к, получа́ющий сексуа́льное удово́льствие от та́йного созерца́ния люде́й во вре́мя полово́го а́кта.
voyeurism [vwɑː'jəːrɪzəm] *n* проце́сс созерца́ния други́х люде́й во вре́мя полово́го а́кта.
VP *n abbr* = **vice president**.
vs *abbr* = **versus**.
V-sign ['viːsaɪn] *n* (*BRIT*: *as insult*) гру́бый жест; (*in victory*) знак побе́ды.

VSO *n abbr* (*BRIT*: = *Voluntary Service Overseas*) благотвори́тельное о́бщество,ока́зывающее по́мощь нужда́ющимся за рубежо́м.
VT *abbr* (*US*: *POST*) = *Vermont*.
vulgar ['vʌlgəʳ] *adj* (*remarks, gestures, graffiti*) вульга́рный; (*decor, ostentation*) по́шлый*.
vulgarity [vʌl'gærɪtɪ] *n* (*rudeness*) вульга́рность *f*; (*ostentation*) по́шлость *f*.
vulnerability [vʌlnərə'bɪlɪtɪ] *n* (*see adj*) уязви́мость *f*; рани́мость *f*.
vulnerable ['vʌlnərəbl] *adj* (*position*) уязви́мый*; (*person*) рани́мый*; **to be ~ to sth** (*person*) быть* (*impf*) подве́ржным(-ой) чему́-н.
vulture ['vʌltʃəʳ] *n* гриф; (*fig*: *pej*) стервя́тник.
vulva ['vʌlvə] *n* ву́льва.

---

* marks translations which have irregular inflections. The Russian-English side of the dictionary gives inflectional information.

~ W, w ~

W, w [ˈdʌblju:] n (letter) 23-ая буква
английского алфавита.
W abbr (= west) З= запад; (ELEC: = watt) Вт=
ватт.
WA abbr (US: POST) = Washington.
wad [wɔd] n (of cotton wool) комок*; (of
banknotes, paper) пачка*.
wadding [ˈwɔdɪŋ] n упаковочный материал.
waddle [ˈwɔdl] vi ходить*/идти* (impf)
вперевалку.
wade [weɪd] vi: **to ~ through** (water)
пробираться (пробраться* perf) через +acc;
(book) одолевать (одолеть perf).
wafer [ˈweɪfəˈ] n (biscuit) вафля*.
wafer-thin [ˈweɪfəˈθɪn] adj тончайший.
waffle [ˈwɔfl] n (CULIN) вафля*; (empty talk)
трёп ♦ vi (in speech, writing) трепаться (impf).
waffle iron n вафельница.
waft [wɔft] vt доносить* (донести* perf) ♦ vi
доноситься (донестись* perf).
wag [wæg] vt (head) качать (impf) +instr ♦ vi
(tail) вилять (impf); **the dog ~ged its tail**
собака виляла хвостом; **to ~ one's finger at
sb** грозить* (погрозить* perf) кому-н
пальцем.
wage [weɪdʒ] n (also: ~s) зарплата=
заработная плата ♦ vt: **to ~ war** вести* (impf)
войну; **a day's ~s** дневной заработок*.
wage claim n требование увеличения
заработной платы.
wage differential n дифференциальные
ставки* fpl заработной платы.
wage earner [-əːnəˈ] n лицо*, работающее по
найму; (in the family) кормилец*(-лица).
wage freeze n замораживание заработной
платы.
wage packet n конверт с зарплатой.
wager [ˈweɪdʒəˈ] n пари* nt ind ♦ vt ставить*
(поставить* perf); (reputation) ставить*
(поставить* perf) на карту.
waggle [ˈwægl] vt (ears, eyebrows etc)
шевелить (пошевелить perf) +instr ♦ vi (head)
покачиваться (impf).
wag(g)on [ˈwægən] n (horse-drawn) повозка*;
(BRIT: RAIL) товарный вагон.
wail [weɪl] n вопль m; (of siren) вой ♦ vi
(person) вопить* (impf); (siren) выть* (impf).
waist [weɪst] n талия.
waistcoat [ˈweɪskəut] n (BRIT) жилет.

waistline [ˈweɪstlaɪn] n линия талии.
wait [weɪt] vi ждать* (подождать* perf) ♦ n: **we
had a long ~ for the bus** мы долго ждали
автобуса; **to keep sb ~ing** заставлять
(заставить* perf) кого-н ждать; **I can't ~ to go
home/meet my new boss** (fig) мне не
терпится пойти домой/встретиться с моим
новым начальником; **to ~ for sb/sth** ждать*
(подождать* perf) кого-н/чего-н; **~ a minute!**
подождите минутку!; **"repairs while you ~"**
„ремонт в присутствии заказчика"; **to lie in
~ for** поджидать (impf) +gen
► **wait behind** vi задерживаться
(задержаться* perf)
► **wait on** vt fus (serve) обслуживать
(обслужить* perf)
► **wait up** vi: **don't ~ up for me** не ждите меня,
ложитесь спать.
waiter [ˈweɪtəˈ] n официант.
waiting [ˈweɪtɪŋ] n: **"no ~"** (BRIT: AUT)
„остановка запрещена".
waiting list n список* очередников.
waiting room n (in surgery) приёмная f adj; (in
station) зал ожидания.
waitress [ˈweɪtrɪs] n официантка*.
waive [weɪv] vt (rule) отменять (отменить
perf).
waiver [ˈweɪvəˈ] n отказ.
wake [weɪk] (pt **woke** or **waked**, pp **woken** or
waked) vt (also: ~ **up**) будить* (разбудить*
perf) ♦ vi (also: ~ **up**) просыпаться
(проснуться perf) ♦ n бдение у гроба; (NAUT)
кильватер; **to ~ up to danger/threat**
осознавать* (perf) опасность/угрозу; **in the ~ of**
(fig) вследствие +gen; **he followed in his
father's ~** (fig) он пошёл по стопам отца.
waken [ˈweɪkn] vti = **wake**.
Wales [weɪlz] n Уэльс; **the Prince of ~** принц
Уэльский.
walk [wɔːk] n (hike) поход*; (shorter)
прогулка*; (gait) походка*; (path) дорожка*,
тропа* ♦ vi (go on foot) ходить*/идти* (impf)
(пешком); (baby) ходить* (impf); (for pleasure,
exercise) гулять (impf) ♦ vt (distance)
проходить* (пройти* perf); (dog) выгуливать
(выгулять perf); **10 minutes' ~ from here** в
10-ти минутах ходьбы отсюда; **to go for a ~**
ходить*/идти* (impf) гулять or на прогулку;
at a quick ~ быстрым шагом; **to ~ in one's**

sleep ходи́ть* (*impf*) во сне́; **I'll ~ you home** я провожу́ Вас домо́й; **people from all ~s of life** лю́ди из всех слоёв о́бщества

▶ **walk out** *vi* (*audience*) демонстрати́вно покида́ть (поки́нуть *perf*) зал; (*workers*) бастова́ть (*impf*)

▶ **walk out on** *vt fus* (*inf: family etc*) броса́ть (бро́сить* *perf*).

walkabout ['wɔːkəbaut] *n* (*queen, politician etc*): **to go (on a) ~** проха́живаться (пройти́сь* *perf*) ми́мо толпы́.

walker ['wɔːkəʳ] *n* (*hiker*) тури́ст(ка).

walkie-talkie ['wɔːkɪ'tɔːkɪ] *n* переносна́я ра́ция.

walking ['wɔːkɪŋ] *n* ходьба́; **to be fond of ~** люби́ть* (*impf*) ходи́ть (пешко́м); **the university is within ~ distance** до университе́та мо́жно дойти́ пешко́м.

walking boots *npl* боти́нки *mpl* для ходьбы́.

walking holiday *n* похо́д.

walking stick *n* трость *f*.

Walkman® ['wɔːkmən] *n* пле́йер.

walk-on ['wɔːkɔn] *adj*: **~ part** второстепе́нная роль* *f*.

walkout ['wɔːkaut] *n* забасто́вка*.

walkover ['wɔːkəuvəʳ] *n* (*inf*) лёгкая побе́да.

walkway ['wɔːkweɪ] *n* пешехо́дная доро́жка*.

wall [wɔːl] *n* стена́*; **to go to the ~** (*fig*) терпе́ть (потерпе́ть *perf*) крах

▶ **wall in** *vt* обноси́ть* (обнести́* *perf*) стено́й.

wall cupboard *n* встро́енный шкаф*.

walled [wɔːld] *adj* (*city*) окружённый крепостно́й стено́й; (*garden*) обнесённый стено́й.

wallet ['wɔlɪt] *n* бума́жник.

wallflower ['wɔːlflauəʳ] *n* желтофио́ль *f*; **to be a ~** (*fig*) быть* (*impf*) незаме́тным(-ой).

wall hanging *n* насте́нный ковёр*.

wallop ['wɔləp] *vt* (*BRIT: inf*) дуба́сить* (отдуба́сить* *perf*).

wallow ['wɔləu] *vi* (*in mud*) валя́ться (*impf*); (*in water*) бара́хтаться (*impf*); (*in guilt, sentiment*) упива́ться (*impf*); **to ~ in one's grief** упива́ться (*impf*) свои́м го́рем.

wallpaper ['wɔːlpeɪpəʳ] *n* обо́и *pl* ♦ *vt* (*room*) окле́ивать (окле́ить *perf*) обо́ями.

wall-to-wall ['wɔːltə'wɔːl] *adj*: **~ carpeting** ковро́вое покры́тие для всей пло́щади по́ла.

wally ['wɔlɪ] *n* (*inf*) дурачо́к*.

walnut ['wɔːlnʌt] *n* (*nut*) гре́цкий* оре́х; (*tree*) оре́ховое де́рево*; (*wood*) оре́х.

walrus ['wɔːlrəs] (*pl ~ or ~es*) *n* морж*.

waltz [wɔːlts] *n* вальс ♦ *vi* (*dancers*) вальси́ровать (*impf*), танцева́ть (*impf*) вальс.

wan [wɔn] *adj* изнурённый* (изнурён); **~ complexion** боле́зненная бле́дность *f*.

wand [wɔnd] *n* (*also*: **magic ~**) волше́бная па́лочка*.

wander ['wɔndəʳ] *vi* (*person*) броди́ть* (*impf*); (*mind, thoughts*) блужда́ть (*impf*); (*river*) извива́ться (*impf*) ♦ *vt* броди́ть* (*impf*) по +*dat*.

wanderer ['wɔndərəʳ] *n* стра́нник(-ица), скита́лец*(-лица).

wandering ['wɔndrɪŋ] *adj* (*tribe*) кочево́й; (*minstrel, actor*) бродя́чий; (*path, river*) изви́листый; (*glance, mind*) блужда́ющий.

wane [weɪn] *vi* (*moon*) убыва́ть (убы́ть* *perf*); (*enthusiasm, influence etc*) ослабева́ть (ослабе́ть* *or* осла́бнуть *perf*).

wangle ['wæŋgl] *vt* (*BRIT: inf*) пробива́ть (проби́ть* *perf*), добива́ться (доби́ться* *perf*) +*gen*.

wanker ['wæŋkəʳ] *n* (*BRIT: inf!*) муда́к (*!*)

want [wɔnt] *vt* (*wish for*) хоте́ть* (*impf*) +*gen*; (*need*) нужда́ться (*impf*) в +*prp* ♦ *n*: **for ~ of** за недоста́тком +*gen*; **~s** *npl* (*needs*) ну́жды *fpl*; **to ~ to do** хоте́ть* (*impf*) +*infin*; **I ~ you to apologize** я хочу́, что́бы Вы извини́лись; **you're ~ed on the phone** Вас к телефо́ну; **a ~ of foresight** отсу́тствие предви́дения.

want ads *npl* (*US*) объявле́ния под ру́брикой "Куплю́", "Ищу́ рабо́ту" *umn*.

wanted ['wɔntɪd] *adj* (*criminal etc*) разы́скиваемый; **"cook ~"** "тре́буется по́вар".

wanting ['wɔntɪŋ] *adj*: **he was found ~** он оказа́лся не на высоте́ положе́ния; **he is ~ in common sense** ему́ недостаёт здра́вого смы́сла.

wanton ['wɔntn] *adj* (*gratuitous*) беспричи́нный* (беспричи́нен); (*promiscuous*) распу́тный* (распу́тен).

war [wɔːʳ] *n* война́*; **to go to ~** вступа́ть (вступи́ть* *perf*) в войну́; **to be at ~ with** воева́ть* (*impf*) с +*instr*; **to declare ~ (on)** (*also fig*) объявля́ть (объяви́ть* *perf*) войну́ (+*dat*).

warble ['wɔːbl] *n* (*of bird*) трель *f* ♦ *vi* издава́ть* (*impf*) тре́ли.

war crime *n* вое́нное преступле́ние.

war cry *n* боево́й клич.

ward [wɔːd] *n* (*MED*) пала́та; (*BRIT: POL*) о́круг; (*LAW*) ребёнок, *находя́щийся под опе́кой*

▶ **ward off** *vt* (*attack, enemy*) отража́ть (отрази́ть* *perf*); (*danger, illness*) отвраща́ть (отврати́ть* *perf*).

warden ['wɔːdn] *n* (*of park, game reserve*) смотри́тель(ница) *m(f)*; (*of prison*) нача́льник; (*of youth hostel*) коменда́нт; (*BRIT: of college*) ре́ктор; (*: also*: **traffic ~**) ≈ инспе́ктор* ГАИ́.

warder ['wɔːdəʳ] *n* (*BRIT*) надзира́тель(ница) *m(f)*, тюре́мщик(-ица).

wardrobe ['wɔːdrəub] *n* платяно́й шкаф, (*clothes*) гардеро́б; (*CINEMA, THEAT*) костюме́рная *f adj*.

---

* marks translations which have irregular inflections. The Russian-English side of the dictionary gives inflectional information.

warehouse ['wɛəhaus] *n* склад.
wares [wɛəz] *npl* това́ры *mpl*.
warfare ['wɔːfɛəʳ] *n* вое́нные *или* боевы́е
де́йствия *ntpl*.
war game *n* вое́нная игра́*.
warhead ['wɔːhɛd] *n* боеголо́вка*.
warily ['wɛərɪlɪ] *adv* осторо́жно,
насторо́женно.
Warks *abbr* (*BRIT: POST*) = *Warwickshire*.
warlike ['wɔːlaɪk] *adj* вои́нственный*
(вои́нствен).
warm [wɔːm] *adj* тёплый; (*thanks, supporter,
heart*) горя́чий*; (*person*) серде́чный; **it's ~
today** сего́дня тепло́; **I'm ~** мне тепло́; **to
keep sth ~** (*hands, feet etc*) держа́ть (*impf*)
что-н в тепле́; (*soup etc*) держа́ть (*impf*) что-н
тёплым(-ой); **with my ~est thanks** с горя́чей
or серде́чной благода́рностью; **please accept
my ~est congratulations** прими́те мои́
серде́чные поздравле́ния
▶ **warm up** *vi* (*person, room*) согрева́ться
(согре́ться *perf*); (*water*) нагрева́ться
(нагре́ться *perf*); (*athlete*) размина́ться
(размя́ться *perf*) ♦ *vt* (*food*) разогрева́ть
(разогре́ть *perf*), подогрева́ть (подогре́ть
perf); (*engine*) разогрева́ть (разогре́ть *perf*);
the weather ~ed up на у́лице потепле́ло.
warm-blooded ['wɔːm'blʌdɪd] *adj* тепло-
кро́вный* (теплокро́вен).
war memorial *n* вое́нный обели́ск.
warm-hearted [wɔːm'hɑːtɪd] *adj* серде́чный*
(серде́чен).
warmly ['wɔːmlɪ] *adv* (*applaud*) горячо́; (*dress,
welcome*) тепло́.
warmonger ['wɔːmʌŋgəʳ] *n* (*pej*) поджига́тель
(ница) *m(f)* войны́.
warmongering ['wɔːmʌŋgrɪŋ] *n* (*pej*)
разжига́ние войны́.
warmth [wɔːmθ] *n* тепло́.
warm-up ['wɔːmʌp] *n* разми́нка*.
warn [wɔːn] *vt:* **to ~ sb (not) to do/of/that**
предупрежда́ть (предупреди́ть* *perf*) кого́-н
(не) +*infin*/о +*prp*/, что.
warning ['wɔːnɪŋ] *n* предупрежде́ние; **without
(any) ~** (*suddenly*) неожи́данно; (*without
notifying*) без предупрежде́ния; **gale ~**
штормово́е предупрежде́ние.
warning light *n* предупреди́тельный
светово́й сигна́л.
warning triangle *n* авари́йный треуго́льник
(*знак, предупрежда́ющий о том, что
стоя́щая на доро́ге маши́на сло́мана*).
warp [wɔːp] *vi* (*wood etc*) коро́биться*
(покоро́биться* *perf*) ♦ *vt* (*fig*) коверка́ть
(исковерка́ть *perf*) ♦ *n* (*TEXTILES*) осно́ва.
warpath ['wɔːpɑːθ] *n:* **he is on the ~** (*fig*) он
настро́ен вои́нственно.
warped [wɔːpt] *adj* (*wood*) покоро́бленный
(покоро́блен); (*fig*) искове́рканный
(искове́ркан).
warrant ['wɔrnt] *n* (*document*) гара́нтия; (*LAW*)

о́рдер ♦ *vt* (*justify*) опра́вдывать (оправда́ть
perf); (*merit*) гаранти́ровать (*impf/perf*); **search
~** о́рдер на о́быск.
warrant officer *n* (*MIL*) ≈ старшина́* *m*; (*NAUT*)
ми́чман.
warranty ['wɔrəntɪ] *n* гара́нтия; **under ~** с
гара́нтией; **the car was still under ~** у
маши́ны ещё не истёк гаранти́йный срок.
warren ['wɔrən] *n* (*of rabbits*) ме́сто, где
во́дятся кро́лики; (*fig*) лабири́нт.
warring ['wɔrɪŋ] *adj* вою́щий; (*interests etc*)
непримири́мый (непримири́м).
warrior ['wɔrɪəʳ] *n* во́ин.
Warsaw ['wɔːsɔː] *n* Варша́ва.
warship ['wɔːʃɪp] *n* вое́нный кора́бль* *m*.
wart [wɔːt] *n* борода́вка*.
wartime ['wɔːtaɪm] *n:* **in ~** в вое́нное вре́мя.
wary ['wɛərɪ] *adj* (*person*) осторо́жный*
(осторо́жен), насторо́женный*
(насторо́жен); **to be ~ about** *or* **of sth**
относи́ться* (*impf*) к чему́-н насторо́женно;
to be ~ about doing остерега́ться (*impf*) +*infin*.
was [wɔz] *pt of* **be**.
wash [wɔʃ] *n* мытьё; (*clothes etc*) сти́рка;
(*washing programme*) режи́м сти́рки (*в
стира́льной маши́не*); (*of ship*) пе́нистый
след ♦ *vt* (*hands, body*) мыть* (помы́ть* *perf*);
(*clothes*) стира́ть (постира́ть *perf*); (*face*)
умыва́ть (умы́ть* *perf*); (*sweep away*)
смыва́ть (смыть* *perf*) ♦ *vi* (*person*) мы́ться*
(помы́ться* *perf*); (*sea etc*) перека́тываться (*impf*) че́рез что-н; **to have a
~** помы́ться* (*perf*); **to give sth a ~** помы́ть*
(*perf*) что-н; (*clothes*) постира́ть (*perf*) что-н;
the sea ~ed the body ashore мо́ре вы́несло
те́ло на бе́рег; **he was ~ed overboard** его́
смы́ло волно́й за́ борт
▶ **wash away** *vt* смыва́ть (смыть* *perf*)
▶ **wash down** *vt* (*wall, path, car*) мыть*
(вы́мыть* *perf*); (*food*) запива́ть (запи́ть* *perf*)
▶ **wash off** *vi* отмыва́ться (отмы́ться* *perf*);
(*out of clothes*) отсти́рываться (отстира́ться
perf)
▶ **wash up** *vi* (*BRIT*) мыть* (вы́мыть* *perf*)
посу́ду; (*US*) мы́ться* (помы́ться* *perf*).
washable ['wɔʃəbl] *adj* (*wallpaper etc*)
мо́ющийся; **acrylic blankets are ~** акри́ловые
одея́ла мо́жно стира́ть.
washbasin ['wɔʃbeɪsn] *n* (умыва́льная)
ра́ковина.
washbowl ['wɔʃbəul] *n* (*US*) (умыва́льная)
ра́ковина.
washcloth ['wɔʃklɔθ] *n* (*US: face cloth*)
салфе́тка для лица́ (*из махро́вой тка́ни*).
washer ['wɔʃəʳ] *n* (*TECH*) ша́йба.
washing ['wɔʃɪŋ] *n* (*dirty*) сти́рка; (*clean*)
сти́раные ве́щи *fpl*.
washing line *n* (*BRIT*) бельева́я верёвка*.
washing machine *n* стира́льная маши́на.
washing powder *n* (*BRIT*) стира́льный
порошо́к.

Washington ['wɔʃɪŋtən] n Вашингто́н.
washing-up [wɔʃɪŋ'ʌp] n (гря́зная) посу́да; **to do the ~** мыть* (вы́мыть* perf) посу́ду.
washing-up liquid n (BRIT) жи́дкое сре́дство для мытья́ посу́ды.
wash-out ['wɔʃaut] n (inf) прова́л.
washroom ['wɔʃrum] n (US) убо́рная f adj.
wasn't ['wɔznt] = was not.
WASP [wɔsp] n abbr (US: inf: = White Anglo-Saxon Protestant) америка́нец англо-саксо́нского происхожде́ния и протеста́нтского испове́дания.
Wasp [wɔsp] n abbr = **WASP**.
wasp [wɔsp] n оса́*.
waspish ['wɔspɪʃ] adj (person) раздражи́тельный* (раздражи́телен).
wastage ['weɪstɪdʒ] n (waste) растра́та; (ECON: loss) убы́ток*; **natural ~** есте́ственная у́быль f.
waste [weɪst] n (act) растра́та; (rubbish) отхо́ды mpl; (also: **household ~**) дома́шние отбро́сы mpl; (unwanted: energy, heat) изли́шек* ♦ adj (material: rejected, damaged) брако́ванный* (брако́ван); (unwanted: energy, heat) изли́шный* (изли́шен); (left over) отрабо́танный* (отрабо́тан); (also: **~ land**: in city) пусты́рь* m ♦ vt растра́чивать (растра́тить* perf); (opportunity) упуска́ть (упусти́ть* perf); **~s** npl (area of land) пусты́ня fsg; **it's a ~ of money/time** э́то пуста́я тра́та де́нег/вре́мени; **to go to ~** пропада́ть (пропа́сть* perf); **to lay ~** (destroy) уничтожа́ть (уничто́жить perf); **~ paper** испо́льзованная бума́га
▸ **waste away** vi (person) истоща́ть (истоща́ть себя́.
wastebasket ['weɪstbɑːskɪt] n (US) = **wastepaper basket**.
waste disposal unit n (BRIT) устро́йство для удале́ния отхо́дов (в ку́хонной ра́ковине).
wasteful ['weɪstful] adj (person) расточи́тельный* (расточи́телен); (process) неэконо́мный* (неэконо́мен).
waste ground n (BRIT) пусты́рь* m.
wasteland ['weɪstlənd] n пу́стошь f; (in town) пусты́рь* m; (fig) пусты́ня.
wastepaper basket ['weɪstpeɪpə-] n корзи́на для (нену́жных) бума́г.
waste pipe n сливна́я труба́*.
waste products npl отхо́ды pl произво́дства.
waster ['weɪstə'] n (inf) безде́льник(-ица).
watch [wɔtʃ] n (also: **wristwatch**) (нару́чные) часы́ pl; (act of watching) наблюде́ние; (MIL, NAUT: group of guards) патру́ль* m; (NAUT: spell of duty) ва́хта ♦ vt (look at) наблюда́ть (impf) за +instr; (match, programme) смотре́ть* (посмотре́ть* perf); (events, weight, language) следи́ть* (impf) за +instr; (be careful of: person)

остерега́ться (impf) +gen; (look after) смотре́ть (impf) за +instr ♦ vi (take care) смотре́ть (impf); (keep guard) дежу́рить (impf); **to keep a close ~ on sb/sth** внима́тельно следи́ть* (impf) за кем-н/чем-н; **~ what you're doing** смотри́, что ты де́лаешь; **~ how you drive** внима́тельно веди́те маши́ну
▸ **watch out** vi остерега́ться (остере́чься* perf).
watchband ['wɔtʃbænd] n (US) ремешо́к* для часо́в.
watchdog ['wɔtʃdɔg] n сторожева́я соба́ка; (fig) наблюда́тель m.
watchful ['wɔtʃful] adj бди́тельный* (бди́телен).
watchmaker ['wɔtʃmeɪkə'] n часовщи́к*.
watchman ['wɔtʃmən] irreg n see **night watchman**.
watchstrap ['wɔtʃstræp] n ремешо́к* для часо́в.
watchword ['wɔtʃwə:d] n ло́зунг.
water ['wɔ:tə'] n вода́* ♦ vt (plant, garden) полива́ть (поли́ть* perf) ♦ vi (eyes) слези́ться (impf); **a glass of ~** стака́н воды́; **in British ~s** в брита́нских во́дах; **to pass ~** (urinate) мочи́ться* (помочи́ться* perf); **my mouth is ~ing** у меня́ теку́т слю́нки
▸ **water down** vt разбавля́ть (разба́вить* perf) (водо́й); (fig) смягча́ть (смягчи́ть perf).
water biscuit n ≈ гале́та.
water cannon n брандспо́йт.
water closet n (BRIT) туале́т.
watercolour ['wɔ:təkʌlə'] (US **watercolor**) n (picture) акваре́ль f; **~s** npl (paints) акваре́льные кра́ски* fpl.
water-cooled ['wɔ:təku:ld] adj (engine) с водяны́м охлажде́нием.
watercress ['wɔ:təkrɛs] n кресс водяно́й.
waterfall ['wɔ:təfɔ:l] n водопа́д.
waterfront ['wɔ:təfrʌnt] n (seafront: street) на́бережная f adj; (: piece of land) берегова́я ли́ния; (at docks) райо́н по́рта.
water heater n кипяти́льник.
water hole n исто́чник (для водопо́я в пусты́не).
water ice n фрукто́вое моро́женое nt adj.
watering can ['wɔ:tərɪŋ-] n ле́йка*.
water level n у́ровень* m воды́.
water lily n кувши́нка*.
waterline ['wɔ:təlaɪn] n (NAUT) ватерли́ния.
waterlogged ['wɔ:təlɔgd] adj (ground) заболо́ченный* (заболо́чен), зато́пленный (зато́плен).
water main n водопрово́дная магистра́ль m.
watermark ['wɔ:təmɑːk] n (on paper) водяно́й знак; (level of water) отме́тка у́ровня воды́.
watermelon ['wɔ:təmɛlən] n арбу́з.
waterproof ['wɔ:təpru:f] adj непромока́емый

(непромокáем).
water-repellent ['wɔ:təri'pɛlnt] *adj* (*cloth etc*)
водооттáлкивающий*.
watershed ['wɔ:təʃɛd] *n* (*also fig*) водораздéл.
water-skiing ['wɔ:təski:ɪŋ] *n* воднолы́жный
спорт.
water softener *n* срéдство для смягчéния
воды́.
water tank *n* резервуáр для воды́; (*smaller*)
бак для воды́.
watertight ['wɔ:tətaɪt] *adj*
водонепроницáемый (водонепроницáем);
(*fig: argument*) неопроверж́имый
(неопроверж́им); (: *excuse*) вéский* (я́сен); (: *case,
agreement*) я́сный* (я́сен); (: *story*)
правдоподóбный* (правдоподóбен).
water vapour *n* (водянóй) пар*.
waterway ['wɔ:təweɪ] *n* (*canal, river*) вóдный
путь* *m*; (*at sea*) ватервéйс.
waterworks ['wɔ:təwə:ks] *n* (*building*)
гидротехни́ческое сооружéние; (*inf: ANAT*)
пóчки* *fpl*.
watery ['wɔ:təri] *adj* (*coffee, soup etc*)
водяни́стый (водяни́ст); (*eyes*) слезя́щийся.
watt [wɔt] *n* ватт.
wattage ['wɔtɪdʒ] *n* мóщность *f* в вáттах.
wattle ['wɔtl] *n* (*CONSTR*) плетéнь* *m*.
wattle and daub *n* прýтья и гли́на (*материáл
для пострóйки мáзанки*).
wave [weɪv] *n* волнá*; (*of hand*) взмах; (*in hair*)
зави́вка ♦ *vi* (*signal*) махáть* (*impf*); (*branches*)
качáться (*impf*); (*grass*) волновáться (*impf*);
(*flag*) развевáться (*impf*) ♦ *vt* махáть* (*impf*)
+*instr*; (*stick, gun, sword*) размáхивать (*impf*)
+*instr*; (*hair*) завивáть (зави́ть* *perf*); **short/
medium/long ~** корóткие/срéдние/дли́нные
вóлны *fpl*; **the new ~** (*CINEMA, MUS*) нóвая
волнá; **he ~d us over to his table** он знакóм
подозвáл нас к своемý столý; **to ~ goodbye
to sb** махáть* (помахáть* *perf*) комý-н на
прощáние
▸ **wave aside** *vt* (*person*) отстраня́ть
(отстрани́ть *perf*); (*fig*) отмáхиваться
(отмахнýться *perf*) от +*gen*
▸ **wave away** *vt* = **wave aside.**
waveband ['weɪvbænd] *n* диапазóн волн.
wavelength ['weɪvlɛŋθ] *n* (*RADIO*) длинá
волны́; **they are on the same ~** (*fig*) они́
одинáково смóтрят на вéщи.
waver ['weɪvəʳ] *vi* (*voice*) дрóгнуть (*perf*);
(*person, faith*) колебáться* (поколебáться*
perf).
wavy ['weɪvi] *adj* волни́стый (волни́ст).
wax [wæks] *n* (*polish*) воск; (*for skis*) мазь *f*;
(*for sealing*) сургýч*; (*in ear*) сéра ♦ *vt* (*floor*)
вощи́ть (навощи́ть *perf*), натирáть
(натерéть* *perf*) вóском; (*car*) натирáть
(натерéть* *perf*) вóском; (*skis*) мáзать
(намáзать* *perf*) мáзью ♦ *vi* (*moon*)
прибывáть (*impf*).
waxed [wækst] *adj* вощёный.

waxen [wæksn] *adj* (*face*) восковóй; **~
complexion** восковóй цвет лицá.
waxworks ['wækswə:ks] *npl* (*models*)
восковы́е фигýры *fpl* ♦ *n* (*place*) галерéя
восковы́х фигýр.
way [weɪ] *n* (*route*) путь* *m*, дорóга; (*path,
access*) путь*; (*manner, method*) спóсоб; (*usu
pl: habit*) привы́чка; **which ~? - this ~** кудá? -
сюдá; **is it a long ~ from here?** э́то далекó
отсю́да?; **which ~ do we go now?** кудá нам
тепéрь идти́?; **on the ~** (*en route*) по пути́ *or*
дорóге; **to be on one's ~** быть* (*impf*) в пути́;
I'd better be on my ~ мне ужé порá идти́; **to
fight one's ~ through a crowd** продирáться
(продрáться* *perf*) сквозь толпý; **to lie one's
~ out of the situation** выходи́ть* (вы́йти* *perf*)
из положéния за счёт лжи; **to keep out of sb's
~** держáться* (*impf*) от когó-н подáльше; **it's
a very long ~ away** э́то óчень далекó; **the
village is rather out of the ~** дерéвня
нахóдится довóльно далекó в сторонé; **to
go out of one's ~ to do** старáться
(постарáться *perf*) изо всех сил +*infin*; **to be in
sb's ~** (*also fig*) стоя́ть (*impf*) на чьей-н
дорóге; **to be in the ~** мешáть (помешáть
perf); **to lose one's ~** заблуди́ться* (*perf*); **the
plan is under ~** план осуществля́ется; **to
make ~ (for sb/sth)** уступáть (уступи́ть* *perf*)
мéсто (комý-н/чемý-н); **to get one's own ~**
дéлать (сдéлать *perf*) по-своéму; **to put sth
the right ~ up** (*BRIT*) стáвить* (постáвить*
perf) что-н как нáдо *or* прáвильно; **to be the
wrong ~ round** быть* (*impf*) задóм напéред;
he's in a bad ~ его́ делá плóхи; **that's a funny
~ to show your affection** э́то стрáнная
манéра выражáть свою́ привя́занность; **in a
~** в извéстном смы́сле; **in some ~s** в
нéкоторых отношéниях; **no ~!** (*inf*) ни в
кóем случáе!; **by the ~ ...** мéжду прóчим ...;
"way in" (*BRIT*) "вход"; **"way out"** (*BRIT*)
„вы́ход"; **the ~ back** обрáтный путь*,
обрáтная дорóга; **this ~ and that** тудá-сюдá;
"give ~" (*BRIT: AUT*) „уступи́те дорóгу".
waybill ['weɪbɪl] *n* накладнáя *f adj*.
waylay [weɪ'leɪ] (*irreg: like* **lay**) *vt* подстерегáть
(подстерéчь* *perf*); **I got waylaid** (*fig*) меня́
перехвати́ли по пути́.
wayside ['weɪsaɪd] *adj* придорóжный ♦ *n*
обóчина; **to fall by the ~** (*fig*) выбывáть
(вы́быть* *perf*) из стрóя.
way station *n* (*US: RAIL*) полустáнок*; (: *fig*)
промежýточный этáп.
wayward ['weɪwəd] *adj* своенрáвный*
(своенрáвен).
WC *n abbr* (*BRIT*) = **water closet.**
WCC *n abbr* = *World Council of Churches.*
we [wi:] *pron* мы.
weak [wi:k] *adj* слáбый* (слаб); (*morally*)
слабохарáктерный* (слабохарáктерен); **to
grow ~** ослабевáть *or* слабéть (ослабéть
perf).

weaken ['wi:kn] *vi* ослабева́ть *or* слабе́ть
(ослабе́ть *perf*); (*resolve, person*) смягча́ться
(смягчи́ться *perf*) ◆ *vt* (*person, government*)
ослабля́ть (осла́бить* *perf*).
weak-kneed ['wi:k'ni:d] *adj* (*fig*) мало-
ду́шный* (малоду́шен).
weakling ['wi:klɪŋ] *n* слаба́к*.
weakly ['wi:klɪ] *adv* сла́бо.
weakness ['wi:knɪs] *n* сла́бость *f*; **to have a ~
for** име́ть (*impf*) сла́бость к +*dat*.
wealth [wɛlθ] *n* (*money, resources*) бога́тство;
(*of details, knowledge etc*) оби́лие.
wealth tax *n* иму́щественный нало́г.
wealthy ['wɛlθɪ] *adj* состоя́тельный*
(состоя́телен).
wean [wi:n] *vt* (*baby*) отнима́ть (отня́ть* *perf*)
от гру́ди.
weapon ['wɛpən] *n* ору́жие*.
wear [wɛəʳ] (*pt* wore, *pp* worn) *n* (*use*) изно́с;
(*damage*) изно́шенность *f*; (*clothing*) оде́жда
◆ *vi* (*last*) носи́ться* (*impf*); (*rub through*)
изна́шиваться (износи́ться* *perf*) ◆ *vt* (*put on*)
надева́ть (наде́ть* *perf*); (*beard*) носи́ть*
(*impf*); (*damage*) изна́шивать (износи́ть* *perf*);
(*clothes*): **he was ~ing his new shirt** на нём
была́ его́ но́вая руба́шка; **evening ~** (*for
ladies*) вече́рнее пла́тье*; (*for men*) вече́рний*
костю́м; **to ~ a hole in sth** протира́ть
(протере́ть* *perf*) дыру́ в чём-н
▶ **wear away** *vt* стира́ть (стере́ть* *perf*) ◆ *vi*
стира́ться (стере́ться* *perf*)
▶ **wear down** *vt* (*heels*) сна́шивать (сноси́ть*
perf); (*resistance, strength*) сломи́ть (*perf*)
▶ **wear off** *vi* (*pain etc*) постепе́нно проходи́ть*
(пройти́* *perf*)
▶ **wear on** *vi* тяну́ться* (*impf*)
▶ **wear out** *vt* (*shoes, clothing*) изна́шиваться
(износи́ться* *perf*); (*person, strength*)
изма́тывать (измота́ть *perf*).
wearable ['wɛərəbl] *adj* приго́дный*
(приго́ден) для но́ски.
wear and tear [-tɛəʳ] *n* изно́с.
wearer ['wɛərəʳ] *n* владе́лец*(-лица).
wearily ['wɪərɪlɪ] *adv* уста́ло.
weariness ['wɪərɪnɪs] *n* утомле́ние.
wearisome ['wɪərɪsəm] *adj* (*tiring*)
утоми́тельный* (утоми́телен); (*boring*)
надое́дливый (надое́длив).
weary ['wɪərɪ] *adj* (*tired*) утомлённый
(утомлён); (*dispirited*) уста́лый ◆ *vi*: **to ~ of**
утомля́ться (утоми́ться* *perf*) от +*gen*.
weasel ['wi:zl] *n* (*ZOOL*) ла́ска*.
weather ['wɛðəʳ] *n* пого́да ◆ *vt* (*storm, crisis*)
переноси́ть* (перенести́* *perf*), выде́рживать
(вы́держать *perf*) ◆ *vi* (*wood*) подверга́ться
(подве́ргнуться* *perf*) атмосфе́рным
влия́ниям; **what's the ~ like today?** кака́я
сего́дня пого́да?; **I am under the ~** мне

нездоро́вится.
weather-beaten ['wɛðəbi:tn] *adj* (*face, skin*)
обве́тренный* (обве́трен); (*building, stone*)
повреждённый непого́дой.
weathercock ['wɛðəkɔk] *n* флю́гер*.
weather forecast *n* прогно́з пого́ды.
weatherman ['wɛðəmæn] *irreg n* (*inf*)
сино́птик.
weatherproof ['wɛðəpru:f] *adj* (*garment*)
защища́ющий от непого́ды; (*building*)
погодоусто́йчивый (погодоусто́йчив),
утеплённый* (утеплён).
weather report *n* сообще́ние о пого́де.
weather vane [-veɪn] *n* = **weathercock**.
weave [wi:v] (*pt* wove, *pp* woven) *vt* (*cloth*)
ткать* (сотка́ть* *perf*); (*basket*) плести́*
(сплести́* *perf*) ◆ *vi* (*pt, pp* weaved; *fig*)
лави́ровать (*impf*).
weaver ['wi:vəʳ] *n* ткач*(и́ха).
weaving ['wi:vɪŋ] *n* (*craft*) тка́чество; (*of
baskets*) плете́ние.
web [wɛb] *n* (*of spider*) паути́на; (*on duck's
foot*) перепо́нка*; (*also fig*) сеть* *f*.
webbed ['wɛbd] *adj* перепо́нчатый.
webbing ['wɛbɪŋ] *n* (*on chair*) тка́ный реме́нь
m.
wed [wɛd] (*pt,pp* wedded) *vt* (*marry*) венча́ться
(обвенча́ться *perf*) с +*instr* ◆ *vi* венча́ться
(обвенча́ться *perf*) ◆ *n*: **the newly-~s**
новобра́чные *pl adj*.
Wed. *abbr* = **Wednesday**.
we'd [wi:d] = **we had, we would**.
wedded ['wɛdɪd] *pt, pp of* **wed** ◆ *adj*: **he is ~ to**
(*idea, policy etc*) он пре́дан +*dat*.
wedding [wɛdɪŋ] *n* сва́дьба*; (*in church*)
венча́ние; **silver/golden ~** сере́бряная/
золота́я сва́дьба.
wedding day *n* день* *m* сва́дьбы.
wedding dress *n* сва́дебное *or* подвене́чное
пла́тье*.
wedding present *n* сва́дебный пода́рок*.
wedding ring *n* обруча́льное кольцо́*.
wedge [wɛdʒ] *n* клин*; (*of cake*) кусо́к* ◆ *vt*
закрепля́ть (закрепи́ть* *perf*) кли́ном; (*pack
tightly*): **to ~ in** вти́скивать (вти́снуть *perf*) в
+*acc*.
wedge-heeled shoes ['wɛdʒhi:ld-] *npl* ту́фли*
pl на танке́тке.
wedlock ['wɛdlɔk] *n* супру́жество.
Wednesday ['wɛdnzdɪ] *n* среда́*; *see also*
Tuesday.
wee [wi:] *adj* (*SCOTTISH: little*) кро́шечный*.
weed [wi:d] *n* сорня́к* ◆ *vt* (*garden*) поло́ть*
(вы́полоть *perf*)
▶ **weed out** *vt* устраня́ть (устрани́ть *perf*).
weedkiller ['wi:dkɪləʳ] *n* сре́дство от
сорняко́в.
weedy ['wi:dɪ] *adj* (*man*) худосо́чный*

---

* marks translations which have irregular inflections. The Russian-English side of the dictionary gives inflectional information.

(худосо́чен).

week [wiːk] *n* неде́ля; **once/twice a** ~ раз/два
ра́за в неде́лю; **in two** ~**s' time** че́рез две
неде́ли; **a** ~ **today** че́рез неде́лю, a week on
Friday, в сле́дующую пя́тницу.

weekday [ˈwiːkdeɪ] *n* (*Monday to Friday*)
бу́дний *or* рабо́чий* день* *m*; **on** ~**s** в бу́дни.

weekend [wiːkˈɛnd] *n* выходны́е *pl adj* (дни),
суббо́та и воскресе́нье, уик-э́нд; **this/next/
last** ~ в э́ти/сле́дующие/про́шлые выходны́е
(дни); **what are you doing at the** ~? что Вы
де́лаете в выходны́е?; **open at** ~**s** откры́то
по суббо́там и воскресе́ньям *or* по
выходны́м дням.

weekly [ˈwiːklɪ] *adv* еженеде́льно ◆ *adj*
еженеде́льный ◆ *n* еженеде́льник.

weep [wiːp] (*pt,pp* **wept**) *vi* (*person*) пла́кать*
(*impf*); (*wound*) сочи́ться (*impf*).

weeping willow [ˈwiːpɪŋ-] *n* плаку́чая и́ва.

weepy [ˈwiːpɪ] *adj* слезли́вый (слезли́в),
плакси́вый (плакси́в) ◆ *n* (*inf: film*)
душещипа́тельный фильм.

weft [wɛft] *n* уто́к*.

weigh [weɪ] *vt* взве́шивать (взве́сить* *perf*) ◆ *vi*
ве́сить* (*impf*); **to** ~ **anchor** поднима́ть
(подня́ть* *perf*) я́корь

▶ **weigh down** *vt* отягоща́ть (отяготи́ть* *perf*);
(*fig*) тяготи́ть* (*impf*), отягоща́ть (*impf*)

▶ **weigh out** *vt* отве́шивать (отве́сить* *perf*)

▶ **weigh up** *vt* взве́шивать (взве́сить* *perf*); **to**
~ **up all the pros and cons** взве́шивать
(взве́сить* *perf*) все „за“ и „про́тив“.

weighbridge [ˈweɪbrɪdʒ] *n* мостовы́е весы́ *pl*.

weighing machine [ˈweɪɪŋ-] *n* автомат-
и́ческие весы́ *pl*.

weight [weɪt] *n* (*for scales*) ги́ря; (*heaviness*)
вес* ◆ *vt*: **to be** ~**ed in favour of**
предоставля́ть (предоста́вить* *perf*)
преиму́щество +*dat*; **sold by** ~ продаётся на
вес; **to lose** ~ худе́ть (похуде́ть* *perf*); **to put
on** ~ поправля́ться (попра́виться* *perf*); **W**~**s
and Measures Office** Пала́та мер и весо́в.

weighting [ˈweɪtɪŋ] *n* (*allowance*) надба́вка.

weightlessness [ˈweɪtlɪsnɪs] *n* невесо́мость *f*.

weightlifter [ˈweɪtlɪftəʳ] *n* штанги́ст.

weight limit *n* преде́л ве́са.

weight training *n* силова́я гимна́стика.

weighty [ˈweɪtɪ] *adj* (*heavy: object*) тяжёлый
(тяжёл); (: *person*) гру́зный* (гру́зен);
(*important*) весо́мый (весо́м).

weir [wɪəʳ] *n* (*in river*) запру́да.

weird [wɪəd] *adj* (*strange*) стра́нный*
(стра́нен); (*eerie*) таи́нственный*
(таи́нствен).

weirdo [ˈwɪədəu] *n* (*inf*) чуда́к.

welcome [ˈwɛlkəm] *adj* жела́нный* (жела́нен)
◆ *n* (*hospitality*) приём; (*greeting*)
приве́тствие ◆ *vt* (*also: bid* ~)
приве́тствовать (*impf*); **to make sb** ~
ока́зывать (оказа́ть* *perf*) кому́-н ра́душный
приём; **you're** ~ **to try** пожа́луйста,

попро́буйте; **thank you – you're** ~! спаси́бо –
пожа́луйста!

welcoming [ˈwɛlkəmɪŋ] *adj* (*person, smile etc*)
ра́душный (ра́душен); (*room*) прия́тный*
(прия́тен); (*speech*) приве́тственный.

weld [wɛld] *n* сварно́й шов ◆ *vt* сва́ривать
(свари́ть* *perf*).

welder [ˈwɛldəʳ] *n* сва́рщик.

welding [ˈwɛldɪŋ] *n* сва́рка*.

welfare [ˈwɛlfɛəʳ] *n* (*well-being*) благополу́чие;
(*US: social aid*) социа́льное посо́бие.

welfare state *n* госуда́рство всео́бщего
благосостоя́ния.

welfare work *n* благотвори́тельность *f*.

well [wɛl] *n* (*for water*) коло́дец*; (*also: oil* ~)
(нефтяна́я) сква́жина ◆ *adv* хорошо́ ◆ *excl*
(*anyway*) ну; (*so*) ну вот ◆ *adj*: **he is** ~ он
здоро́в; **I don't feel** ~ я пло́хо себя́ чу́вствую;
to think ~ **of sb** быть* (*impf*) хоро́шего
мне́ния о ком-н; **as** ~ та́кже; **oh** ~ ... ну что
же ...; **you might as** ~ **tell me** уж лу́чше ты
скажи́ мне; **he played as** ~ **as he could** он
сыгра́л как смог; **I woke** ~ **before dawn** я
просну́лся задо́лго до рассве́та; **I've brought
my anorak as** ~ **as a jumper** кро́ме пуло́вера я
привёз ещё и анора́к; ~, **as I was saying** ... ну,
как я уже́ говори́л ...; ~ **done!** молоде́ц!; **get**
~ **soon!** поправля́йтесь скоре́е; **he is doing** ~
at school в шко́ле он успева́ет; **the business is
doing** ~ би́знес процвета́ет

▶ **well up** *vi* (*tears*) наверну́ться (*perf*).

we'll [wiːl] = **we will, we shall**.

well-behaved [ˈwɛlbɪˈheɪvd] *adj* воспи́танный
(воспи́тан).

well-being [ˈwɛlˈbiːɪŋ] *n* благополу́чие.

well-bred [ˈwɛlˈbrɛd] *adj* (*person*)
воспи́танный* (воспи́тан),
благовоспи́танный (благовоспи́тан).

well-built [ˈwɛlˈbɪlt] *adj* хорошо́ сложённый
(сложён), кре́пкий* (кре́пок).

well-chosen [ˈwɛlˈtʃəuzn] *adj* (*remarks, words*)
хорошо́ подо́бранный (подо́бран).

well-deserved [ˈwɛldɪˈzəːvd] *adj* заслу́ж-
енный* (заслу́жен).

well-developed [ˈwɛldɪˈvɛləpt] *adj* с
ра́звитыми фо́рмами.

well-disposed [ˈwɛlˈdɪspəuzd] *adj*: ~ **to(wards)**
благожела́тельный* (благожела́телен) к
+*dat*.

well-dressed [ˈwɛlˈdrɛst] *adj* хорошо́ оде́тый
(оде́т).

well-earned [ˈwɛlˈəːnd] *adj* заслу́женный*
(заслу́жен).

well-groomed [ˈwɛlˈgruːmd] *adj* (*person*)
ухо́женный* (ухо́жен).

well-heeled [ˈwɛlˈhiːld] *adj* (*inf*) де́нежный*.

well-informed [ˈwɛlɪnˈfɔːmd] *adj* (*about
something*) хорошо́ информи́рованный*
(информи́рован); (*in general*) зна́ющий*.

Wellington [ˈwɛlɪŋtən] *n* Веллингто́н.

wellingtons [ˈwɛlɪŋtənz] *npl* (*also: wellington

boots) рези́новые сапоги́* *mpl*.

well-kept ['wɛl'kɛpt] *adj* (*house, grounds*) ухо́женный (ухо́жен); (*secret*) по́лный.

well-known ['wɛl'nəun] *adj* (*famous*) изве́стный* (изве́стен).

well-mannered ['wɛl'mænəd] *adj* воспи́танный* (воспи́тан).

well-meaning ['wɛl'miːnɪŋ] *adj*: **he is very ~** он де́йствует из наилу́чших побужде́ний.

well-nigh ['wɛl'naɪ] *adv*: **~ impossible** почти́ невозмо́жно.

well-off ['wɛl'ɔf] *adj* состоя́тельный* (состоя́телен).

well-read ['wɛl'rɛd] *adj* начи́танный* (начи́тан).

well-spoken ['wɛl'spəukn] *adj* (*words*) учти́вый (учти́в); **she was ~** она́ говори́ла пра́вильным языко́м.

well-stocked ['wɛl'stɔkt] *adj* (*shop*) хорошо́ снабжа́емый.

well-timed ['wɛl'taɪmd] *adj* своевре́менный* (своевре́менен).

well-to-do ['wɛltə'duː] *adj* обеспе́ченный (обеспе́чен), состоя́тельный* (состоя́телен).

well-wisher ['wɛlwɪʃəʳ] *n* (*friend, admirer*) доброжела́тель(ница) *m(f)*; **scores of ~s had gathered** собрали́сь деся́тки доброжела́телей; **letters from ~s** пи́сьма от доброжела́телей.

well-woman clinic ['wɛlwumən-] *n* ≈ же́нская консульта́ция.

Welsh [wɛlʃ] *adj* уэ́льский* ♦ *n* (*LING*) уэ́льский* *or* валли́йский язы́к*; **the ~** *npl* (*people*) уэ́льсцы *mpl*, валли́йцы *mpl*.

Welshman ['wɛlʃmən] *irreg n* уэ́льсец*, валли́ец*.

Welsh rarebit *n* грено́к* с сы́ром.

Welshwoman ['wɛlʃwumən] *n irreg* валли́йка*, жи́тельница Уэ́льса.

welter ['wɛltəʳ] *n*: **a ~ of** ха́ос +*gen*.

went [wɛnt] *pt of* **go**.

wept [wɛpt] *pt, pp of* **weep**.

were [wəː] *pt of* **be**.

we're [wɪəʳ] = **we are**.

weren't [wəːnt] = **were not**.

werewolf ['wɪəwulf] (*pl* **werewolves**) *n* челове́к-волк.

werewolves ['wɪəwulvz] *npl of* **werewolf**.

west [wɛst] *n* за́пад ♦ *adj* за́падный ♦ *adv* на за́пад; **the W~** (*POL*) За́пад.

westbound ['wɛstbaund] *adj* (*carriageway, traffic*) за́падного направле́ния.

West Country *n*: **the ~ ~** (*BRIT*) за́падная А́нглия.

westerly ['wɛstəlɪ] *adj* за́падный.

western ['wɛstən] *adj* (*also POL*) за́падный ♦ *n* (*CINEMA*) ве́стерн.

westerner ['wɛstənəʳ] *n* за́падный челове́к*.

westernized ['wɛstənaɪzd] *adj* ориенти́рованный (ориенти́рован) на За́пад.

West German *adj* (*formerly*) западногерма́нский ♦ *n* жи́тель(ница) *m(f)* За́падной Герма́нии.

West Germany *n* (*formerly*) За́падная Герма́ния.

West Indian *adj* вест-инди́йский* ♦ *n* жи́тель(ница) *m(f)* Вест-И́ндии.

West Indies [-'ɪndɪz] *npl*: **the ~ ~** Вест-И́ндия *fsg*.

Westminster ['wɛstmɪnstəʳ] *n* Вестми́нстер.

westward(s) ['wɛstwəd(z)] *adv* на за́пад, к за́паду.

wet [wɛt] *adj* (*damp, rainy*) вла́жный* (вла́жен), сыро́й* (сыр); (*soaking*) мо́крый* (мокр) ♦ *n* (*BRIT: POL*) "уме́ренный(-ая)" *m(f)* *adj* ♦ *vt*: **to ~ one's pants** *or* **o.s.** мочи́ть (намочи́ть *perf*) штаны́; **to get ~** промока́ть (промо́кнуть* *perf*); **"~ paint!"** "осторо́жно, окра́шено!"; **he is a ~ blanket** (*fig*: *pej*) он – зану́да.

wetness ['wɛtnɪs] *n* вла́жность *f*, сы́рость *f*.

wetsuit ['wɛtsuːt] *n* гидрокостю́м.

we've [wiːv] = **we have**.

whack [wæk] *vt* дава́ть* (дать* *perf*) затре́щину +*dat*.

whacked [wækt] *adj* (*BRIT: inf*) разби́тый (разби́т).

whale [weɪl] *n* кит*.

whaler ['weɪləʳ] *n* (*ship*) китобо́йное су́дно.

whaling ['weɪlɪŋ] *n* китобо́йный про́мысел.

wharf [wɔːf] (*pl* **wharves**) *n* при́стань* *f*.

wharves [wɔːvz] *npl of* **wharf**.

KEYWORD

what [wɔt] *adj* **1** (*interrogative: direct, indirect*) како́й; **what size is the dress?** како́го разме́ра э́то пла́тье?; **what books do you need?** каки́е кни́ги Вам нужны́?

2 како́й; **what a lovely day!** како́й чуде́сный день!; **what a mess!** (*room etc*) ну и беспоря́док!; (*fig*) что за неразбери́ха!; **what a fool I am!** како́й же я дура́к!

♦ *pron* **1** (*interrogative*) что; **what are you doing?** что Вы де́лаете?; **what are you talking about?** о чём Вы говори́те?; **what is it called?** как э́то называ́ется?; **what about me?** а (как же) я?; **what about doing ...?** как насчёт того́, что́бы +*infin* ...?

2 (*relative*) что; **I saw what you did/was on the table** я ви́дел, что Вы де́лали/бы́ло на столе́; **is that what happened?** так э́то то, что случи́лось?; **tell me what you're thinking about** скажи́те мне, о чём Вы ду́маете; **what you say is wrong** то, что Вы говори́те, неве́рно

♦ *excl* (*disbelieving*) что; **I've crashed the car – what!** я разби́л маши́ну – что!

---

* marks translations which have irregular inflections. The Russian-English side of the dictionary gives inflectional information.

whatever [wɔt'ɛvə^r] *adj:* ~ **book** любáя кни́га ♦ *pron:* **do** ~ **is necessary/you want** дéлайте всё, что необходи́мо/хоти́те; ~ **happens** что бы ни случи́лось; **no reason** ~ *or* **whatsoever** нет никакóй причи́ны; **nothing** ~ совсéм ничегó.

whatsoever [wɔtsəu'ɛvə^r] *adj see* **whatever**.

wheat [wi:t] *n* пшени́ца.

wheatgerm ['wi:tdʒə:m] *n* зарóдыш пшени́чного зернá.

wheatmeal ['wi:tmi:l] *n* пшени́чная мукá грýбого помóла.

wheedle ['wi:dl] *vt:* **to** ~ **sb into doing** угова́ривать (уговори́ть *perf*) когó-н лéстью +*infin;* **to** ~ **sth out of sb** выма́нивать (вы́манить *perf*) что-н у когó-н.

wheel [wi:l] *n* (*of vehicle etc*) колесó*; (*also:* **steering** ~) руль* *m;* (*NAUT*) штурвáл ♦ *vt* (*pram etc*) катáть/кати́ть* (*impf*) ♦ *vi* (*birds*) кружи́ться (*impf*); (*also:* ~ **round**: *person*) крýто повора́чиваться (поверну́ться *perf*).

wheelbarrow ['wi:lbærəu] *n* тáчка*.

wheelbase ['wi:lbeis] *n* колёсная бáза.

wheelchair ['wi:ltʃeə^r] *n* инвали́дное крéсло*.

wheel clamp *n* (*AUT*) блокирáтор (*для блокирóвки рулевóго колесá*).

wheeler-dealer ['wi:lə'di:lə^r] *n* (*pej*) махинáтор.

wheelie-bin ['wi:lıbın] *n* мýсорное ведрó на колёсиках.

wheeling ['wi:lıŋ] *n:* ~ **and dealing** (*pej*) махинáции *fpl*.

wheeze [wi:z] *vi* (*person*) хрипéть* (*impf*) ♦ *n* (*idea, joke etc*) остроýмная идéя, затéя.

wheezy ['wi:zı] *adj* хрипя́щий, сипя́щий.

when [wɛn] *adv, conj* когдá; ~ **you've read the book, tell me what you think** когдá Вы прочитáете кни́гу, скажи́те мне что Вы дýмаете; **you said I was wrong** ~ **in fact I was right** Вы сказáли, что я был непрáв, когдá на сáмом дéле я был прав.

whenever [wɛn'ɛvə^r] *adv* в любóе врéмя ♦ *conj* (*any time*) когдá тóлько; (*every time that*) кáждый раз, когдá; **I go** ~ **I can** я пойдý, как тóлько смогý.

where [wɛə^r] *adv* (*place*) где; (*direction*) кудá; (*from where*) откýда ♦ *conj* где; **this is** ~ ... э́то там, где ...; ~ **possible** где возмóжно; ~ **have you come from?** откýда Вы прие́хали?

whereabouts [*adv* wɛərə'bauts, *n* 'wɛərəbauts] *adv* где; (*motion*) кудá ♦ *n:* **nobody knows his** ~ никтó не знáет его местонахождéния.

whereas [wɛər'æz] *conj* тогдá *or* в то врéмя как.

whereby [wɛə'baı] *adv* (*formal*) посрéдством чего.

whereupon [wɛərə'pɔn] *adv* пóсле *or* вслéдствие чего.

wherever [wɛər'ɛvə^r] *conj* (*no matter where:* *position*): ~ **he was** где бы он ни́ был; (: *motion*): ~ **he goes** кудá бы он ни шёл; (*not knowing where*): ~ **that is** где бы то ни́ было

♦ *adv* (*interrogative*): ~ **have you been?** где же Вы бы́ли?; **let's go away** ~ ~ **to?** давáйте уйдём отсю́да – кудá же?; **sit** ~ **you like** сади́тесь, где хоти́те.

wherewithal ['wɛəwıðɔ:l] *n:* **the** ~ **(to do)** срéдства *ntpl* (+*infin*).

whet [wɛt] *vt* (*appetite*) возбуждáть (возбуди́ть* *perf*); (*tool*) точи́ть* (наточи́ть* *perf*).

whether ['wɛðə^r] *conj:* **I doubt** ~ **she loves me** я сомневáюсь, лю́бит ли онá меня́; **I don't know** ~ **to accept this proposal or not** я не знáю, приня́ть э́то предложéние и́ли нет; ~ **you go or not** пойдёте Вы и́ли нет.

whey ['weı] *n* сы́воротка.

KEYWORD

which [wıtʃ] *adj* **1** (*interrogative: direct, indirect*) какóй; **which picture would you like?** какýю карти́ну Вы хоти́те?; **which books are yours?** каки́е кни́ги Вáши?; **which one?** какóй? (*f* какáя?, *nt* какóе?); **I've got two pens, which one do you want?** у меня́ есть две рýчки, какýю Вы хоти́те?; **which one of you did it?** кто из вас э́то сдéлал?

2: **in which case** в таком слýчае; **by which time** к томý врéмени

♦ *pron* **1** (*interrogative*) какóй (*f* какáя, *nt* какóе, *pl* каки́е); **there are several museums, which shall we visit first?** здесь есть нéсколько музéев, в какóй мы пойдём сначáла?; **which do you want, the apple or the banana?** что Вы хоти́те – я́блоко и́ли банáн?; **which of you are staying?** кто из вас остаётся?

2 (*relative*) котóрый (*f* котóрая, *nt* котóрое, *pl* котóрые); **the apple which you ate/which is on the table** я́блоко, котóрое Вы съéли/котóрое лежи́т на столé; **the news was bad, which is what I had feared** вéсти бы́ли плохи́е, как я и боя́лся; **I had lunch, after which I decided to go home** я пообéдал, пóсле чегó я реши́л пойти́ домóй; **I made a speech, after which nobody spoke** я вы́ступил с рéчью, пóсле котóрой никтó не произнёс ни слóва.

whichever [wıtʃ'ɛvə^r] *adj:* **take** ~ **book you prefer** возьми́те любýю кни́гу, какýю предпочтёте; ~ **book you take** какýю бы кни́гу Вы ни взя́ли.

whiff [wıf] *n* дуновéние; **to catch a** ~ **of sth** ула́вливать (улови́ть *perf*) почýять зáпах чегó-н.

while [waıl] *n* (*period of time*) врéмя* *nt* ♦ *conj* покá, в то врéмя как; (*although*) хотя́, несмотря́ на то, что; **for a** ~ ненадóлго; **in a** ~ скóро; **all the** ~ всё врéмя; **we promise to make it worth your** ~ мы обещáем, что Вы не остáнетесь в прóигрыше

▸ **while away** *vt:* **to** ~ **away the time** коротáть (скоротáть *perf*) врéмя.

whilst [waılst] *conj* = **while**.

whim [wɪm] n при́хоть f.
whimper ['wɪmpə'] n хны́канье ♦ vi хны́кать* (impf); (dog) скули́ть (impf).
whimsical ['wɪmzɪkl] adj причу́дливый (причу́длив).
whine [waɪn] n вой ♦ vi (person, animal) скули́ть (impf); (engine, siren) выть* (impf).
whip [wɪp] n кнут*, хлыст*; (POL: person) организа́тор парла́ментской фра́кции ♦ vt (person, animal) хлеста́ть* (impf); (cream, eggs) взбива́ть (взбить* perf); (move quickly): **to ~ sth out** выхва́тывать (вы́хватить* perf) что-н; **to ~ sth away** вырыва́ть (вы́рвать* perf) что-н
▸ **whip up** vt (cream) взбива́ть (взбить* perf); (inf: meal) де́лать (сде́лать perf) на ско́рую ру́ку; (support, emotion) возбужда́ть (возбуди́ть* perf).
whiplash ['wɪplæʃ] n (also: ~ injury) поврежде́ние ше́и, вы́званное ре́зким движе́нием головы́ вперёд и наза́д, наприме́р, при автомоби́льной ава́рии.
whipped cream [wɪpt-] n взби́тые сли́вки* pl.
whipping boy ['wɪpɪŋ-] n (fig) ≈ козёл отпуще́ния.
whip-round ['wɪpraund] n (BRIT) скла́дчина.
whirl [wə:l] vt враща́ть (impf), верте́ть* (impf) ♦ vi кружи́ться* (impf), враща́ться (impf) ♦ n круже́ние; **my mind is in a ~** у меня́ голова́ идёт кру́гом; **~ of social engagements** водоворо́т or вихрь све́тской жи́зни.
whirlpool ['wə:lpu:l] n водоворо́т.
whirlwind ['wə:lwɪnd] n вихрь m.
whirr [wə:'] vi (insects) стрекота́ть (impf); (motor etc) треща́ть (impf).
whisk [wɪsk] n (CULIN) ве́нчик ♦ vt (cream, eggs) взбива́ть (взбить* perf); **to ~ sb away** or **off** отгоня́ть (отогна́ть* perf).
whiskers ['wɪskəz] npl (of animal) усы́ mpl; (of man) бакенба́рды fpl.
whisky ['wɪskɪ] (US, IRELAND **whiskey**) n ви́ски nt ind.
whisper ['wɪspə'] n шёпот ♦ vi шепта́ться* (impf) ♦ vt шепта́ть* (impf); **to ~ sth to sb** шепта́ть* (impf) что-н кому́-н.
whispering ['wɪspərɪŋ] n перешёптывание.
whist [wɪst] n (BRIT) вист.
whistle ['wɪsl] n (sound) свист; (object) свисто́к* ♦ vi свисте́ть* (impf), сви́стнуть (perf) ♦ vt: **to ~ a tune** насви́стывать (impf) мело́дию.
whistle-stop ['wɪslstɔp] adj: **to make a ~ tour of** (POL) объезжа́ть (объе́хать* perf) с агитацио́нными це́лями.
Whit [wɪt] n Тро́ицын день* m.
white [waɪt] adj бе́лый* (бел) ♦ n (colour) бе́лый цвет; (person) бе́лый(-ая) m(f) adj; (of egg, eye) бело́к*; **to turn** or **go ~** беле́ть

(побеле́ть perf); **the ~s** (washing) бе́лое бельё; **tennis/cricket ~s** те́ннисная/кри́кетная фо́рма.
whitebait ['waɪtbeɪt] n снето́к*.
white coffee n (BRIT) ко́фе m ind с молоко́м.
white-collar worker ['waɪtkɔlə-] n слу́жащий*(-ая) m(f) adj.
white elephant n (fig) изли́шняя ро́скошь f.
white goods npl (appliances) бытовы́е электротова́ры mpl; (linen etc) белошве́йные това́ры mpl.
white-hot [waɪt'hɔt] adj раскалённый* (раскалён) добела́.
white lie n безоби́дная ложь* f.
whiteness ['waɪtnɪs] n белизна́.
white noise n (RADIO, ELEC etc) „бе́лый шум" (поме́хи в радиоэфи́ре).
whiteout ['waɪtaut] n бе́лая мгла.
white paper n (POL) „Бе́лая кни́га" (докуме́нт, излага́ющий поли́тику прави́тельства по тем и́ли ины́м вопро́сам).
whitewash ['waɪtwɔʃ] n (paint) известко́вый раство́р (для побе́лки); (inf: SPORT) „суха́я" ♦ vt (building) бели́ть* (побели́ть* perf); (fig: incident, reputation) обеля́ть (обели́ть perf).
white water n: **~~ rafting** пла́вание на плота́х по го́рным ре́кам.
whiting ['waɪtɪŋ] n inv хек.
Whit Monday n ≈ Ду́хов день* m.
Whitsun ['wɪtsn] n ≈ Тро́ицын день* m, Тро́ица.
whittle ['wɪtl] vt: **to ~ away** or **down** (costs) уменьша́ть (уменьши́ть perf).
whizz [wɪz] vi: **to ~ past** or **by** проноси́ться* (пронести́сь* perf) ми́мо.
whizz kid n (inf) вундерки́нд.
WHO n abbr (= World Health Organization) ВОЗ= Всеми́рная организа́ция здравоохране́ния.

KEYWORD

who [hu:] pron **1** (interrogative) кто*; **who is it?**, **who's there?** кто э́то or там?; **who did you see there?** кого́ Вы там ви́дели?
2 (relative) кото́рый (f кото́рая, nt кото́рое); **the woman who spoke to me** же́нщина, кото́рая говори́ла со мно́й; **those who can swim** те, кто уме́ют пла́вать.

whodunit [hu:'dʌnɪt] n (inf) детекти́в.
whoever [hu:'ɛvə'] pron: **~ finds him** ... тот, кто найдёт его́ ..., кто бы ни нашёл его́ ...; **ask ~ you like** спроси́те, кого́ хоти́те; **~ told you that?** кто Вам э́то сказа́л?; **come out, ~ you are!** выходи́, кто бы ты ни́ был!
whole [həul] adj це́лый (цел) ♦ n (entire unit) це́лое nt adj; (all): **the ~ of Europe** вся Евро́па; **the ~ lot (of it)** всё (э́то); **the ~ lot (of them)** все pl (они́); **the ~ of the time** всё вре́мя; **~**

---

* marks translations which have irregular inflections. The Russian-English side of the dictionary gives inflectional information.

villages were destroyed це́лые дере́вни бы́ли разру́шены; **the ~ of the town** весь го́род; **on the ~, as a ~** в це́лом.

wholefood(s) [ˈhəulfuːd(z)] *n(pl)* натура́льные проду́кты *mpl*.

wholefood shop *n* магази́н натура́льных проду́ктов.

wholehearted [həulˈhɑːtɪd] *adj* (*agreement etc*) и́скренний*; (*support*) горя́чий*.

wholeheartedly [həulˈhɑːtɪdlɪ] *adv* (*see adj*) и́скренне; горячо́.

wholemeal [ˈhəulmiːl] *adj* (*BRIT*): ~ **flour** мука́ гру́бого помо́ла; ~ **bread** хлеб из муки́ гру́бого помо́ла.

whole note *n* (*US*) це́лая но́та.

wholesale [ˈhəulseɪl] *n* опто́вая торго́вля ◆ *adj* (*price*) опто́вый; (*destruction*) ма́ссовый ◆ *adv* (*buy, sell*) о́птом.

wholesaler [ˈhəulseɪləʳ] *n* оптови́к*; (*insitution*) опто́вое предприя́тие.

wholesome [ˈhəulsəm] *adj* здоро́вый.

wholewheat [ˈhəulwiːt] *adj* = **wholemeal**.

wholly [ˈhəulɪ] *adv* по́лностью, целико́м.

KEYWORD

whom [huːm] *pron* **1** (*interrogative: +acc, +gen*) кого́; (: *+dat*) кому́; (: *+instr*) кем; (: *+prp*) ком; **whom did you see there?** кого́ Вы там ви́дели?; **to whom did you give the book?** кому́ Вы кни́гу отда́ли?

2 (*relative: +acc*) кото́рого (*f* кото́рую, *pl* кото́рых); (: *+gen*) кото́рого (*f* кото́рой, *pl* кото́рых); (: *+dat*) кото́рому (*f* кото́рой, *pl* кото́рым); (: *+instr*) кото́рым (*f* кото́рой, *pl* кото́рыми); (: *+prp*) кото́ром (*f* кото́рой, *pl* кото́рых); **the man whom I saw/to whom I spoke** челове́к, кото́рого я ви́дел/с кото́рым я говори́л.

---

whooping cough [ˈhuːpɪŋ-] *n* коклю́ш.

whoosh [wuʃ] *n* свист ◆ *vi*: **to ~ past** *etc* просвисте́ть* (*perf*) ми́мо *etc*; **the skiers ~ed past, skiers came by with a ~** лы́жники со сви́стом пронесли́сь ми́мо.

whopper [ˈwɔpəʳ] *n* (*inf: lie*) чудо́вищная ложь* *f*; (*large thing*) грома́дина.

whopping [ˈwɔpɪŋ] *adj* (*inf: big*) грома́дный* (грома́ден).

whore [hɔːʳ] *n* (*inf: pej*) шлю́ха.

KEYWORD

whose [huːz] *adj* **1** (*possessive: interrogative*) чей*; **whose book is this?, whose is this book?** чья э́то кни́га?

2 (*possessive: relative*) кото́рый; **the woman whose son you rescued** же́нщина, сы́на кото́рой Вы спасли́

◆ *pron* чей (*f* чья, *nt* чьё, *pl* чьи); **whose is this?** э́то чьё?; **I know whose it is** я зна́ю, чьё э́то.

Who's Who [ˈhuːzˈhuː] *n* Кто есть кто (*спра́вочник*).

KEYWORD

why [waɪ] *adv, conj* почему́; **why is he always late?** почему́ он всегда́ опа́здывает?; **why not?** почему́?; **why not do it now?** почему́ бы не сде́лать э́то сейча́с?; **I wonder why he said that** интере́сно, почему́ он э́то сказа́л; **that's not why I'm here** я здесь во́все не поэ́тому; **that's why** вот почему́; **there is a reason why I want to see him** у меня́ есть причи́ны для встре́чи с ним

◆ *excl*: **why, it's you!** о, неуже́ли э́то Вы?; **why, it's obvious/that's impossible!** но ведь э́то же очеви́дно/невозмо́жно!

WI *n abbr* (*BRIT*: = *Women's Institute*) ассоциа́ция же́нщин, интересу́ющихся вопро́сами домово́дства ◆ *abbr* = *West Indies*; (*US*: *POST*) Wisconsin.

wick [wɪk] *n* фити́ль* *m*; **he gets on my ~** (*inf*) он де́йствует мне на не́рвы.

wicked [ˈwɪkɪd] *adj* зло́бный* (зло́бен), злой*; (*mischievous: smile*) лука́вый, плутовско́й; (*terrible: prices, weather*) жу́ткий*.

wicker [ˈwɪkə] *adj* плетёный.

wickerwork [ˈwɪkəˈwəːk] *adj* плетёный ◆ *n* плете́ние.

wicket [ˈwɪkɪt] *n* (*CRICKET: stumps*) воро́тца* *pl*; (: *grass area*) кон ме́жду двумя́ воро́тцами.

wicket-keeper [ˈwɪkɪtkiːpəʳ] *n* игро́к, охраня́ющий воро́тца.

wide [waɪd] *adj* широ́кий* (широ́к) ◆ *adv*: **to open ~** широ́ко открыва́ть (откры́ть* *perf*); **to shoot ~** стреля́ть (*impf*) ми́мо це́ли; **the bridge is 3 metres ~** ширина́ моста́ – 3 ме́тра.

wide-angle lens [ˈwaɪdæŋgl-] *n* (*PHOT*) широкоуго́льная ли́нза.

wide-awake [waɪdəˈweɪk] *adj*: **I feel ~** у меня́ сна ни в одно́м глазу́.

wide-eyed [waɪdˈaɪd] *adj* (*fig*) наи́вный* (наи́вен); **she sat there ~** она́ сиде́ла с широ́ко раскры́тыми глаза́ми.

widely [ˈwaɪdlɪ] *adv* (*believed, known*) широко́; (*travelled*) мно́го; (*differing*) значи́тельно; **he is ~ read** (*author*) его́ мно́го чита́ют; (*reader*) он о́чень начи́тан.

widen [ˈwaɪdn] *vt* расширя́ть (расши́рить *perf*) ◆ *vi* расширя́ться (расши́риться *perf*).

wideness [ˈwaɪdnɪs] *n* широта́.

wide open *adj* широко́ раскры́тый (раскры́т).

wide-ranging [waɪdˈreɪndʒɪŋ] *adj* (*survey, report*) всесторо́нний* (всесторо́нен); (*interests*) широ́кий*.

widespread [ˈwaɪdsprɛd] *adj* (*belief etc*) распространённый* (распространён).

widow [ˈwɪdəu] *n* вдова́*.

widowed [ˈwɪdəud] *adj* овдове́вший.

widower [ˈwɪdəuəʳ] *n* вдове́ц*.

width [wɪdθ] *n* ширина́; **the street is 7 metres in ~** ширина́ у́лицы – 7 ме́тров.

widthways [ˈwɪdθweɪz] *adv* в ширину́.

wield [wiːld] *vt* (*sword*) владе́ть (*impf*) +*instr*;

(*power*) по́льзоваться* (*impf*) +*instr*.
wife [waɪf] (*pl* **wives**) *n* жена́*.
wig [wɪg] *n* пари́к*.
wigging ['wɪgɪŋ] *n* (*BRIT: inf*) разно́с.
wiggle ['wɪgl] *vt* (*hips*) пока́чивать (*impf*) +*instr*; (*ears*) шевели́ть (*impf*) +*instr*.
wiggly ['wɪglɪ] *adj* волни́стый* (волни́ст).
wigwam ['wɪgwæm] *n* вигва́м.
wild [waɪld] *adj* (*animal, plant*) ди́кий*; (*weather, sea*) бу́рный* (бу́рен); (*person, behaviour*) бу́йный* (бу́ен); (*idea, guess*) ди́кий; (*enthusiastic: applause*) бу́рный ♦ *n*: **the ~** (*natural surroundings*) ло́но приро́ды *ntpl*; **the ~s** *npl* (*remote area*) ди́кие места́ *ntpl*; **in the ~s of Taiga** в де́брях тайги́; **I am ~ about her/this film** я без ума́ от неё/э́того фи́льма.
wild card *n* (*COMPUT*) универса́льный си́мвол.
wildcat ['waɪldkæt] *n* ди́кая ко́шка*.
wildcat strike *n* неофициа́льная забасто́вка*.
wilderness ['wɪldənɪs] *n* ди́кая ме́стность *f*; (*desert*) пусты́ня.
wildfire ['waɪldfaɪə'] *n*: **to spread like ~** распространя́ться (распространи́ться *perf*) с быстрото́й огня́.
wild-goose chase [waɪld'gu:s-] *n* (*fig*) бессмы́сленная зате́я.
wildlife ['waɪldlaɪf] *n* ди́кая приро́да.
wildly ['waɪldlɪ] *adv* (*behave*) бу́йно, ди́ко; (*applaud*) бу́рно; (*hit, happy*) нейстово; (*guess*) наобу́м.
wiles [waɪlz] *npl* уло́вки* *fpl*.
wilful ['wɪlful] (*US* **willful**) *adj* (*obstinate*) своенра́вный* (своенра́вен); (*deliberate*) умы́шленный*.

KEYWORD

will [wɪl] *aux vb* **1** (*forming future tense*): **I will finish it tomorrow** я зако́нчу э́то за́втра; **I will be working all morning** я бу́ду рабо́тать всё у́тро; **I will have finished it by tomorrow** к за́втрашнему дню я э́то зако́нчу; **I will always remember you** я бу́ду по́мнить тебя́ всегда́; **will you do it? - yes, I will/no, I won't** Вы сде́лаете э́то? - да, сде́лаю/нет, не сде́лаю; **the car won't start** маши́на ника́к не заво́дится
2 (*in conjectures, predictions*): **he will** *or* **he'll be there by now** он, наве́рное, уже́ там; **mistakes will happen** оши́бки неизбе́жны
3 (*in commands, requests, offers*): **will you be quiet!** а ну́-ка поти́ше!; **will you help me?** Вы мне не помо́жете?; **will you have a cup of tea?** не хоти́те ли ча́шку ча́я?; **I won't put up with it!** я э́того не потерплю́!;
♦ (*pt,pp* **willed**) *vt*: **I willed him to win** я хоте́л всели́ть в него́ дух побе́ды
♦ *n* (*volition*) во́ля; (*testament*) завеща́ние.

willful ['wɪlful] *adj* (*US*) = **wilful**.
willing ['wɪlɪŋ] *adj* (*agreed*) согла́сный* (согла́сен); (*enthusiastic*) усе́рдный* (усе́рден); **he's ~ to do it** он гото́в э́то сде́лать; **to show ~** проявля́ть (прояви́ть* *perf*) гото́вность.
willingly ['wɪlɪŋlɪ] *adv* охо́тно.
willingness ['wɪlɪŋnɪs] *n* гото́вность *f*.
will-o'-the wisp ['wɪləðə'wɪsp] *n* (*also fig*) неулови́мое *nt adj*.
willow ['wɪləu] *n* (*tree*) и́ва; (*wood*) ивня́к.
willpower ['wɪl'pauə'] *n* си́ла во́ли.
willy-nilly ['wɪlɪ'nɪlɪ] *adv* во́лей-нево́лей.
wilt [wɪlt] *vi* поника́ть (пони́кнуть* *perf*).
Wilts [wɪlts] *abbr* (*BRIT: POST*) = **Wiltshire**.
wily ['waɪlɪ] *adj* хи́трый* (хитёр).
wimp [wɪmp] (*inf: pej*) *n* хлю́пик ♦ *vi*: **to ~ out** стру́сить* (*perf*).
wimpish ['wɪmpɪʃ] *adj* (*inf: pej*) хли́пкий* (хли́пок).
win [wɪn] (*pt,pp* **won**) *n* побе́да ♦ *vt* выи́грывать (вы́играть *perf*); (*support, popularity*) завоёвывать (завоева́ть* *perf*) ♦ *vi* побежда́ть (победи́ть* *perf*), выи́грывать (вы́играть *perf*)
▶ **win over** *vt* (*person*) покоря́ть (покори́ть *perf*)
▶ **win round** *vt* (*BRIT*) = **win over**.
wince [wɪns] *vi* мо́рщиться (помо́рщиться *perf*).
winch [wɪntʃ] *n* лебёдка*, во́рот.
Winchester disk ['wɪntʃɪstə-] *n* (*COMPUT*) винче́стерский диск.
wind¹ [wɪnd] *n* ве́тер*; (*MED*) га́зы *mpl*; (*breath*) дыха́ние ♦ *vt*: **the blow ~ed him** от уда́ра у него́ захвати́ло дух; **the ~s** *npl* (*MUS*) духовы́е инструме́нты *mpl*; **into** *or* **against the ~** про́тив ве́тра; **he got the ~ of the news** (*fig*) до него́ дошла́ но́вость; **to break ~** де́лать (сде́лать *perf*) отры́жку.
wind² [waɪnd] (*pt,pp* **wound**) *vt* (*roll: thread, rope*) мота́ть (смота́ть *perf*); (*rotate*) верте́ть* (*impf*), крути́ть* (*perf*); (*bandage*) зава́чивать (заверну́ть *perf*); (*clock, toy*) заводи́ть* (завести́* *perf*) ♦ *vi* (*road, river*) ви́ться* (*impf*)
▶ **wind down** *vt* (*car window*) опуска́ть (опусти́ть* *perf*); (*production, business*) свора́чивать (сверну́ть* *perf*)
▶ **wind up** *vt* (*clock, toy*) заводи́ть* (завести́* *perf*); (*debate*) заверша́ть (заверши́ть *perf*).
windbreak ['wɪndbreɪk] *n* бурело́м; (*plants*) ветрозащи́тная лесополоса́.
windbreaker ['wɪndbreɪkə'] *n* (*US*) = **windcheater**.
windcheater ['wɪndtʃi:tə'] *n* штормо́вка*.
winder ['waɪndə'] *n* (*BRIT: on watch*) (заводно́й) ключ*.

---

* marks translations which have irregular inflections. The Russian-English side of the dictionary gives inflectional information.

windfall [ˈwɪndfɔːl] *n* (*money*) неожи́данные
де́ньги *pl*; (*apple etc*) па́данец*.
winding [ˈwaɪndɪŋ] *adj* изви́листый
(изви́лист); ~ **staircase** вита́я ле́стница.
wind instrument [ˈwɪnd-] *n* духово́й
инструме́нт.
windmill [ˈwɪndmɪl] *n* ветряна́я ме́льница.
window [ˈwɪndəu] *n* (*in house, vehicle*) окно́*;
(*in shop*) витри́на; (*also:* ~ **pane**) око́нное
стекло́*.
window box *n* нару́жный я́щик для цвето́в.
window cleaner *n* мо́йщик(-ица) о́кон.
window dresser *n* оформи́тель(ница) *m(f)*
витри́н.
window envelope *n* конве́рт с прозра́чным
прямоуго́льником, че́рез кото́рый ви́ден
а́дрес, напеча́танный на письме́.
window frame *n* око́нная ра́ма.
window ledge *n* нару́жный подоко́нник.
window pane *n* око́нное стекло́*.
window-shopping [ˈwɪndəuʃɔpɪŋ] *n*: **to go** ~
рассма́тривать (*impf*) витри́ны.
windowsill [ˈwɪndəusɪl] *n* подоко́нник.
windpipe [ˈwɪndpaɪp] *n* (*ANAT*) трахе́я.
wind power [ˈwɪnd-] *n* си́ла ве́тра.
windscreen [ˈwɪndskriːn] *n* ветрово́е стекло́*.
windscreen washer *n* стеклоомыва́тель *m*.
windscreen wiper [-waɪpəʳ] *n* дво́рник,
стеклоочисти́тель *m*.
windshield [ˈwɪndʃiːld] *n* (*US*) = **windscreen**.
wind surfing [ˈwɪnd-] *n* виндсёрфинг.
windswept [ˈwɪndswɛpt] *adj* (*place*)
незащищённый от ве́тра; (*person, hair*)
растрёпанный* (растрёпан).
wind tunnel [ˈwɪnd-] *n* аэродинами́ческая
труба́*.
windy [ˈwɪndɪ] *adj* ве́треный* (ве́трен); **it's** ~
сего́дня ве́трено.
wine [waɪn] *n* вино́* ♦ *vt*: **to** ~ **and dine sb**
пойть*-корми́ть* (*impf*) кого́-н.
wine bar *n* ви́нный бар.
wine cellar *n* ви́нный по́греб*.
wine glass *n* бока́л.
wine grower *n* виногра́дарь *m*.
wine growing *n* виногра́дарство ♦ *adj*: ~~
region виногра́дарский райо́н.
wine list *n* ка́рта вин.
wine merchant *n* виноторго́вец*.
wine tasting [-teɪstɪŋ] *n* дегуста́ция вин.
wine waiter *n* официа́нт, ве́дающий ви́нами.
wing [wɪŋ] *n* (*also AUT*) крыло́*; ~**s** *npl* (*THEAT*)
кули́сы *fpl*.
winger [ˈwɪŋəʳ] *n* (*FOOTBALL, RUGBY*) кра́йний*
напада́ющий* *m adj*.
wing mirror *n* (*BRIT*) боково́е зе́ркало*.
wing nut *n* кры́льчатая га́йка*.
wingspan [ˈwɪŋspæn] *n* разма́х крыла́.
wingspread [ˈwɪŋsprɛd] *n* разма́х крыла́.
wink [wɪŋk] *n* подми́гивание ♦ *vi* (*with eye*)
подми́гивать (подмигну́ть *perf*); (*light etc*)
мига́ть (мигну́ть *perf*).
winkle [wɪŋkl] *n* берегова́я *or* морска́я

ули́тка*.
winner [ˈwɪnəʳ] *n* победи́тель(ница) *m(f)*.
winning [ˈwɪnɪŋ] *adj* (*team, competitor*)
победи́вший, вы́игравший; (*shot, goal*)
реша́ющий; (*smile*) обая́тельный*
(обая́телен), покоря́ющий; *see also* **winnings**.
winning post *n* фи́нишный столб*.
winnings [ˈwɪnɪŋz] *npl* вы́игрыш *msg*.
winsome [ˈwɪnsəm] *adj* привлека́тельный*
(привлека́телен).
winter [ˈwɪntəʳ] *n* (*season*) зима́* ♦ *vi* (*birds*)
зимова́ть (перезимова́ть *perf*); **in** ~ зимо́й.
winter sports *npl* зи́мние ви́ды *mpl* спо́рта.
wintry [ˈwɪntrɪ] *adj* зи́мний*.
wipe [waɪp] *n*: **to give sth a** ~ протира́ть
(протере́ть* *perf*) что-н ♦ *vt* (*rub*) вытира́ть
(вы́тереть* *perf*); (*erase*) стира́ть (стере́ть*
perf); **to** ~ **one's nose** вытира́ть (вы́тереть*
perf) нос
► **wipe off** *vt* стира́ть (стере́ть* *perf*)
► **wipe out** *vt* (*debt*) ликвиди́ровать (*impf/perf*);
(*memory*) стира́ть (стере́ть* *perf*); (*city,
population*) стира́ть (стере́ть* *perf*) с лица́
земли́
► **wipe up** *vt* (*mess*) подтира́ть (подтере́ть*
perf).
wire [ˈwaɪəʳ] *n* про́волока; (*ELEC*) про́вод*;
(*telegram*) телегра́мма ♦ *vt* (*fence*) скрепля́ть
(скрепи́ть* *perf*) про́волокой; (*ELEC: also:* ~
up) подключа́ть (подключи́ть* *perf*); **to** ~ **a
house** де́лать (сде́лать *perf*) прово́дку в
до́ме; **to** ~ **sb** телеграфи́ровать (*impf/perf*)
кому́-н.
wire brush *n* про́волочная щётка*.
wire cutters *npl* куса́чки* *pl*.
wireless [ˈwaɪəlɪs] *n* (*BRIT*) ра́дио *nt ind*.
wire netting *n* про́волочная сеть *f*.
wire service *n* (*US*) аге́нтство новосте́й.
wire-tapping [ˈwaɪətæpɪŋ] *n* подслу́шивание
телефо́нных разгово́ров.
wiring [ˈwaɪərɪŋ] *n* (*ELEC*) электропрово́дка.
wiry [ˈwaɪərɪ] *adj* (*person*) жи́листый (жи́лист);
(*hair*) жёсткий* (жёсток).
wisdom [ˈwɪzdəm] *n* му́дрость *f*.
wisdom tooth *n* зуб* му́дрости.
wise [waɪz] *adj* му́дрый* (мудр); **I'm none the**
~ **I** я всё равно́ ничего́ не понима́ю
► **wise up** *vi* (*inf*): **to** ~ **up to sth** осознава́ть*
(осозна́ть* *perf*) что-н.
...wise [waɪz] *suffix*: **timewise** *etc* в отноше́нии
вре́мени *etc*.
wisecrack [ˈwaɪzkræk] *n* шпи́лька*.
wisely [ˈwaɪzlɪ] *adv* му́дро.
wish [wɪʃ] *n* жела́ние ♦ *vt* жела́ть (пожела́ть
perf); **best** ~**es** (*for birthday etc*) всего́
наилу́чшего; **with best** ~**es** (*in letter*) с
наилу́чшими пожела́ниями; **give her my best**
~**es** переда́йте ей мои́ наилу́чшие
пожела́ния; **to** ~ **sb goodbye** проща́ться
(попроща́ться *perf*) с кем-н; **he** ~**ed me well**
он пожела́л мне всего́ хоро́шего; **to** ~ **to do**

хотеть* (*impf*) +*infin*; **I ~ him to come** я хочу, чтобы он пришёл; **to ~ for** желать (пожелать *perf*) +*acc or* +*gen*; **to ~ sth on sb** навязывать (навязать* *perf*) что-н кому-н.

wishbone ['wɪʃbəʊn] *n* счастливая дужка (*грудная кость птицы, разламывая которую, загадывают желание*).

wishful ['wɪʃful] *adj*: **it's ~ thinking** это – принятие желаемого за действительное.

wishy-washy ['wɪʃɪ'wɔʃɪ] *adj* (*inf*: *colour*) мутный; (*ideas, person*) вялый (вял).

wisp [wɪsp] *n* (*of grass, hair*) клочок*; (*of smoke*) струйка*.

wistful ['wɪstful] *adj* тоскливый (тоскли́в).

wit [wɪt] *n* (*wittiness*) остроумие; (*intelligence*: *also*: **~s**) ум*, разум; (*person*) остряк* (-ячка*); (*presence of mind*) сообразительность *f*; **to be at one's ~s' end** (*fig*) быть* (*impf*) в отчаянии; **to have one's ~s about one** не теряться (растеряться *perf*); **to ~ а** именно.

witch [wɪtʃ] *n* ведьма.

witchcraft ['wɪtʃkrɑ:ft] *n* колдовство.

witch doctor *n* знахарь(-рка*) *m(f)*.

witch-hunt ['wɪtʃhʌnt] *n* (*fig*) охота за ведьмами.

KEYWORD
---

with [wɪð] *prep* **1** (*accompanying, in the company of*) с +*instr*; **I spent the day with him** я провела с ним день; **we stayed with friends** мы останавливались у друзей; **I'll be with you in a minute** я освобожусь через минуту; **would you like chips with your steak?** Вы хотите жареную картошку к бифштексу?; **I'm with you** (*I understand*) я Вас понимаю; **she is really with it** (*inf*: *fashionable*) она очень современная девица; (: *aware*) она всё соображает

2 (*descriptive*) с +*instr*; **a girl with blue eyes** девушка с голубыми глазами; **a skirt with a silk lining** юбка на шёлковой подкладке

3 (*indicating manner*) с +*instr*; (*indicating cause*) от +*gen*; (*indicating means*): **to write with a pencil** писать* (*impf*) карандашом; **with tears in her eyes** со слезами на глазах; **red with anger** красный от гнева; **you can open the door with this key** Вы можете открыть дверь этим ключом; **to fill sth with water** наполнять (наполнить *perf*) что-н водой.

withdraw [wɪθ'drɔ:] (*irreg: like draw*) *vt* (*object*) извлекать (извлечь* *perf*); (*offer, remark*) брать* (взять* *perf*) назад ◆ *vi* (*troops, person*) уходить* (уйти* *perf*); **to ~ into o.s.** уходить* (уйти* *perf*) в себя; **to ~ money from an account** снимать (снять* *perf*) деньги со счёта.

withdrawal [wɪθ'drɔ:əl] *n* (*of offer, remark,*

participation) отказ; (*of troops*) вывод; (*of services*) отмена; (*of money*) снятие.

withdrawal symptoms *npl* (*MED*) синдром *msg* отмены *or* абстинентный синдром *msg* (*при отвыкании от лекарств, наркотиков итп*).

withdrawn [wɪθ'drɔ:n] *pp of* **withdraw** ◆ *adj* замкнутый (замкнут).

wither ['wɪðər] *vi* (*plant*) вянуть (завянуть *perf*), сохнуть (засохнуть *perf*).

withered ['wɪðəd] *adj* (*plant*) увядший*, засохший; (*limb*) высохший*.

withhold [wɪθ'həʊld] (*irreg: like hold*) *vt* (*money*) удерживать (удержать* *perf*); (*permission*) не давать* (дать* *perf*); (*information*) утаивать (утаить *perf*).

within [wɪð'ɪn] *prep* (*inside: of place, time, distance*) внутри +*gen*, в пределах +*gen* ◆ *adv* внутри; **~ reach** в пределах досягаемости; **~ sight (of)** в поле зрения (+*gen*); **the finish is ~ sight** конец не за горами; **~ the week** в пределах недели; **~ a mile of** в пределах мили от +*gen*; **~ an hour of** через час после +*gen*; **~ the law** в рамках закона.

without [wɪð'aʊt] *prep* без +*gen*; **~ a coat** без пальто; **~ saying a word** не говоря ни слова; **~ looking** не глядя; **to go ~ sth** обходиться* (обойтись* *perf*) без чего-н.

withstand [wɪθ'stænd] (*irreg: like stand*) *vt* выдерживать (выдержать* *perf*).

witness ['wɪtnɪs] *n* (*person, also LAW*) свидетель(ница) *m(f)* ◆ *vt* (*event*) быть* (*impf*) свидетелем(-льницей) +*gen*; (*document*) заверять (заверить *perf*); **to bear ~ to** (*fig*) свидетельствовать (*impf*) о +*prp*; **~ for the prosecution/defence** свидетель обвинения/ защиты; **to ~ to sth** засвидетельствовать (*perf*) факт чего-н; **I can ~ to having seen ...** я могу засвидетельствовать, что я видел ....

witness box *n* свидетельское место*.

witness stand (*US*) = **witness box**.

witticism ['wɪtɪsɪzəm] *n* острота.

witty ['wɪtɪ] *adj* остроумный* (остроумен).

wives [waɪvz] *npl of* **wife**.

wizard ['wɪzəd] *n* волшебник.

wizened ['wɪznd] *adj* (*person*) морщинистый (морщинист); (*fruit, vegetable*) сморщен-ный* (сморщен).

wk *abbr* = **week**.

Wm. *abbr* = **William**.

WO *n abbr* (*MIL*: = *warrant officer*) ≈ прапорщик.

wobble ['wɔbl] *vi* (*legs*) трястись* (*impf*); (*jelly*) колыхаться* (*impf*); (*chair*) шататься* (*impf*).

wobbly ['wɔblɪ] *adj* (*hand, voice*) дрожащий; (*table, chair*) шаткий* (шаток).

woe [wəʊ] *n* горе.

woeful ['wəʊful] *adj* (*sad*) печальный* (печален); (*awful*) вопиющий.

---

* marks translations which have irregular inflections. The Russian-English side of the dictionary gives inflectional information.

wok [wɔk] *n* глубо́кая сковорода́ (*в китáйской кýхне*).
woke [wəuk] *pt of* **wake**.
woken ['wəukn] *pp of* **wake**.
wolf [wulf] (*pl* **wolves**) *n* волк.
wolves [wulvz] *npl of* **wolf**.
woman ['wumən] (*pl* **women**) *n* же́нщина; ~ **friend** подрýга; ~ **teacher** учи́тельница; **young** ~ молодáя же́нщина; **women's page** (*PRESS*) страни́ца для же́нщин.
woman doctor *n* же́нщина-врач.
womanize ['wumənaɪz] *vi* (*pej*) вести́* (*impf*) распýтну жизнь.
womanizer ['wumənaɪzə'] *n* женолю́б, бáбник (*разг*).
womanly ['wumənlɪ] *adj* (*virtues etc*) же́нский*; (*figure*) же́нственный.
womb [wu:m] *n* мáтка*.
women ['wɪmɪn] *npl of* **woman**.
women's lib ['wɪmɪnz-] *n* (*inf*) эмансипáция же́нщин.
Women's (Liberation) Movement *n* движе́ние за эмансипáцию же́нщин.
won [wʌn] *pt, pp of* **win**.
wonder ['wʌndə'] *n* (*miracle*) чýдо; (*feeling*) изумле́ние ♦ *vi*: **I ~ whether you could tell me** ... не мо́жете ли Вы сказáть мне ...; **I ~ why he is late** интере́сно, почемý он опоздáл; **to ~ at** (*marvel at*) удивля́ться (*impf*) +*dat*; **to ~ about** раздýмывать* (*impf*) о +*prp*; **it's no ~ (that)** не удиви́тельно(, что).
wonderful ['wʌndəful] *adj* (*excellent*) замечáтельный* (замечáтелен); (*astonishing*) удиви́тельный (удиви́телен).
wonderfully ['wʌndəfəlɪ] *adv* (*see adj*) замечáтельно; удиви́тельно.
wonky ['wɔŋkɪ] *adj* (*BRIT*: *inf*) шáткий* (шáток).
wont [wəunt] *adj*: **he is ~ to** ... он имéет обыкнове́ние +*infin* ...; **as is my ~** по обыкнове́нию.
won't [wəunt] = **will not**.
woo [wu:] *vt* (*woman*) добивáться (доби́ться *perf*) расположе́ния +*gen*; (*audience etc*) зайгрывать* (*impf*) c +*instr*.
wood [wud] *n* (*timber*) де́рево; (*forest*) лес ♦ *cpd* (*house*) деревя́нный; (*shed*) дровяно́й; **~pile** штáбель *m* дров.
wood carving *n* (*act*) резьбá по де́реву; (*object*) резьбá (по де́реву).
wooded ['wudɪd] *adj* (*slopes, area*) леси́стый.
wooden ['wudn] *adj* (*object*) деревя́нный; (*fig*: *performance, actor*) дубо́вый.
woodland ['wudlənd] *n* леси́стая ме́стность *f*.
woodpecker ['wudpɛkə'] *n* дя́тел*.
wood pigeon *n* лесно́й го́лубь *m*.
woodwind ['wudwɪnd] *n* деревя́нный духово́й инструме́нт; **the ~** деревя́нные духовы́е *pl adj* инструме́нты.
woodwork ['wudwə:k] *n* (*skill*) столя́рное де́ло.
woodworm ['wudwə:m] *n* (*larvae*) личи́нка древото́чца.
woof [wuf] *n* лай ♦ *vi* лáять (*impf*); ~, ~! гав, гав!
wool [wul] *n* (*material, yarn*) шерсть *f*; **to pull the ~ over sb's eyes** (*fig*) ве́шать (*impf*) лапшý нá уши.
woollen ['wulən] (*US* **woolen**) *adj* шерстяно́й.
woollens ['wulənz] *npl* шерстяны́е ве́щи *fpl*.
woolly ['wulɪ] (*US* **wooly**) *adj* шерстяно́й; (*fig*: *ideas*) расплы́вчатый (расплы́вчат); (: *person*) вя́лый (вял) ♦ *n* шерстяно́й сви́тер* *m*.
woozy ['wu:zɪ] *adj* (*inf*) окосе́вший.
Worcs *abbr* (*BRIT*: *POST*) = **Worcestershire**.
word [wə:d] *n* сло́во; (*news*) слух ♦ *vt* (*letter, message*) формули́ровать* (сформули́ровать* *perf*); ~ **for** ~ (*repeat*) сло́во в сло́во; (*translate*) досло́вно; **what's the ~ for "pen" in French?** как (бýдет) по-францýзски (сло́во) "рýчка"?; **to put sth into ~s** выражáть (вы́разить* *perf*) что-н словáми; **in other ~s** другúми словáми; **to break/keep one's ~** нарушáть (нарýшить *perf*)/держáть (сдержáть *perf*) своё сло́во; **to have ~s with sb** имéть (*impf*) крýпный разгово́р с кем-н; **to have a ~ with sb** поговорúть (*perf*) с кем-н; **I'll take your ~ for it** я пове́рю Вам нá слово; **to send** ~ **of** извещáть (извести́ть* *perf*) о +*prp*; **to leave** ~ **(with sb/for sb) that** ... передавáть* (передáть* *perf*) (че́рез кого́-н/комý-н), что ....
wording ['wə:dɪŋ] *n* формулиро́вка*; (*in card*) поздрави́тельный текст.
word of mouth *n*: **by** *or* **through ~~~** из уст в устá; **I found out about it by ~~~** я об э́том услы́шал от кого́-то.
word-perfect ['wə:d'pə:fɪkt] *adj*: **to be ~** (*person*) знать (*impf*) кáждое сло́во; **the speech was ~** речь былá прекрáсно подгото́влена.
word processing *n* обрабо́тка *or* подгото́вка те́кстов.
word processor [-prəusɛsə'] *n* те́кстовый проце́ссор.
wordwrap ['wə:dræp] *n* (автомати́ческий*) перехо́д (*на но́вую стро́ку*).
wordy ['wə:dɪ] *adj* многосло́вный* (многосло́вен).
wore [wɔ:'] *pt of* **wear**.
work [wə:k] *n* рабо́та; (*ART, LITERATURE*) произведе́ние ♦ *vi* рабо́тать (*impf*); (*medicine etc*) де́йствовать (подде́йствовать *perf*) ♦ *vt* (*clay*) рабо́тать (*impf*) с +*instr*; (*wood, metal, land*) обрабáтывать (обрабо́тать *perf*); (*mine*) разрабáтывать (разрабо́тать *perf*); (*machine*) управля́ть (*impf*) +*instr*; (*effect, miracle*) производи́ть* (произвести́* *perf*); **go to** ~ ходи́ть*/идти́* (*impf*) на рабо́ту; **to start** *or* **set to** ~ принимáться (приня́ться* *perf*) за рабо́ту; **to be at** ~ **(on sth)** рабо́тать

(impf) (над чем-н); **he has been out of ~ for three months** у него уже три месяца нет работы; **to ~ hard** много работать *(impf)*; **to ~ loose** *(part)* расшатываться (расшататься *perf)*; *(knot)* слабнуть (ослабнуть *perf)*

▶ **work on** *vt fus (task)* работать *(impf)* над +*instr*; *(person)* работать *(impf)* с +*instr*; *(principle)* опираться *(impf)* на +*acc*; **he's ~ing on his car** *(repairing)* он чинит машину; *(doing up)* он работает над своей машиной

▶ **work out** *vi (plans etc)* удаваться* (удаться* *perf)*; *(SPORT)* заниматься *(impf)* физическими упражнениями ♦ *vt (problem)* решать (решить *perf)*; *(plan)* разрабатывать (разработать *perf)*; **it ~s out at £100** *(cost)* получается £100

▶ **work up** *vt*: **to get ~ed up (about sth)** разнервничаться *(perf)* (из-за чего-н).

workable ['wəːkəbl] *adj (solution)* осуществимый (осуществим), выполнимый (выполним).

workaholic [wəːkə'hɔlɪk] *n*: **he is a ~** он не может жить без работы.

workbench ['wəːkbɛntʃ] *n* верстак*.

worker ['wəːkə'] *n (in factory)* рабочий*(-ая) *m(f) adj*; *(in community etc)* работник(-ница); **office ~** конторский* служащий*(-ая) *m(f) adj*.

workforce ['wəːkfɔːs] *n* рабочая сила.

work-in ['wəːkɪn] *n (BRIT)* "уорк-ин" *(вид забастовки)*.

working ['wəːkɪŋ] *adj (day, tools etc)* рабочий*; **~ conditions** условия *ntpl* работы; **~ partner** деловой партнёр; **~ population** занятая часть населения; **a ~ knowledge of English** практическое знание английского языка.

working capital *n* оборотный капитал.

working class *n* рабочий* класс.

working-class ['wəːkɪŋ'klɑːs] *adj* рабочий*.

working man *n* работающий мужчина.

working order *n*: **in ~ ~** в рабочем состоянии.

working party *n (BRIT)* рабочая группа.

working relationship *n* деловые отношения *ntpl*.

working week *n* рабочая неделя.

work-in-progress ['wəːkɪn'prəugrɛs] *n (COMM: products)* объём продукции, выпущенной к настоящему моменту; (: *value)* стоимость продукции, выпущенной к настоящему моменту.

workload ['wəːkləud] *n* нагрузка*.

workman ['wəːkmən] *irreg n* (квалифиц-ированный) рабочий* *m adj*.

workmanship ['wəːkmənʃɪp] *n (skill)* мастерство; *(quality)* качество работы; **good/poor ~** тонкая/грубая работа.

workmate ['wəːkmeɪt] *n* товарищ по работе.

workout ['wəːkaut] *n* разминка.

work permit *n* разрешение на работу.

works [wəːks] *n (BRIT: factory)* завод, фабрика ♦ *npl (of clock, machine)* механизм *msg*.

worksheet ['wəːkʃiːt] *n* рабочая карта.

workshop ['wəːkʃɔp] *n (at home, in factory)* мастерская *f adj*, цех; *(practical session)* семинар, практические занятия *ntpl*; *(THEAT, MUS)* студия.

work station *n часть большого офиса, отделённая для работы одного служащего*; *(COMPUT)* рабочая станция.

work study *n* ≈ научная организация труда.

worktop ['wəːktɔp] *n* рабочая поверхность *f*.

work-to-rule ['wəːktə'ruːl] *n (BRIT)* "работа по правилам" *(вид забастовочной борьбы)*.

world [wəːld] *n* мир ♦ *cpd (tour)* кругосветный; *(war, record)* мировой; **~ champion** мировой чемпион, чемпион мира; **~ power** мировая держава; **all over the ~** во всём мире; **to think the ~ of sb** быть* *(impf)* очень высокого мнения о ком-н; **what in the ~ are you doing?** ты соображаешь, что ты делаешь?; **to do sb a ~ of good** приносить* (принести* *perf)* кому-н огромную пользу; **W~ War One/Two** первая/вторая мировая война; **out of this ~** неземной.

World Cup *n*: **the ~ ~** *(FOOTBALL)* Кубок *or* чемпионат мира.

world-famous [wəːld'feɪməs] *adj* всемирно известный* (известен).

worldly ['wəːldlɪ] *adj (not spiritual)* земной; *(knowledgeable)* искушённый.

world music *n* музыка народов мира.

World Series *n*: **the ~ ~** *(US: BASEBALL)* кубоковые соревнования *ntpl*.

worldwide ['wəːld'waɪd] *n* всемирный ♦ *adv* повсеместно.

worm [wəːm] *n (ZOOL)* червь *m*

▶ **worm out** *vt*: **to ~ sth out of sb** вытягивать (вытянуть *perf)* что-н из кого-н.

worn [wɔːn] *pp of* **wear** ♦ *adj (carpet)* потёртый (потёрт); *(shoe)* поношенный* (поношен).

worn-out ['wɔːnaut] *adj (object)* изношенный* (изношен); *(teddy)* потрёпанный* (потрёпан); *(person)* измотанный (измотан).

worried ['wʌrɪd] *adj* обеспокоенный (обеспокоен), встревоженный (встревожен); **she is ~ about it** она обеспокоена этим.

worrier ['wʌrɪə'] *n* человек, мучимый сомнениями, опасениями; **she is a natural ~** она всегда чем-то обеспокоена.

worrisome ['wʌrɪsəm] *adj* вызывающий беспокойство, тревожный.

worry ['wʌrɪ] *n (anxiety)* беспокойство, волнение ♦ *vi (person)* беспокоиться *(impf)*, волноваться *(impf)* ♦ *vt (person)* беспокоить *(impf)*, волновать (взволновать *perf)*; **to ~**

about *or* **over sth/sb** беспоко́иться *(impf)* за
что-н/кого́-н.

worrying [ˈwʌrɪŋ] *adj* трево́жный*
(трево́жен).

worse [wəːs] *adj* ху́дший* ♦ *adv* ху́же ♦ *n*
ху́дшее *nt adj*; **to get ~** ухудша́ться
(уху́дшиться *perf*); **a change for the ~**
ухудше́ние; **he is none the ~ for it** ему́ не
ста́ло от э́того ху́же; **so much the ~ for you!**
тем ху́же для Вас!

worsen [ˈwəːsn] *vt* ухудша́ть (уху́дшить *perf*) ♦
vi ухудша́ться (уху́дшиться *perf*).

worse off *adj* *(financially)* бедне́е; *(fig)*: **you'll be
~~ this way** Вам так бу́дет ху́же; **he is now
~~ than before** его́ положе́ние тепе́рь ху́же,
чем ра́ньше.

worship [ˈwəːʃɪp] *n* поклоне́ние, преклоне́ние
♦ *vt* поклоня́ться *(impf)* +*dat*, преклоня́ться
(impf) пе́ред +*instr*; **Your W~** *(BRIT: to mayor,
judge)* Ва́ша ми́лость.

worshipper [ˈwəːʃɪpəʳ] *n* *(REL)* моля́щийся
(-аяся) *m(f) adj*, прихожа́нин*(-нка); *(fig)*
поклóнник(-ница).

worst [wəːst] *adj* наиху́дший* ♦ *adv* ху́же всего́
♦ *n* наиху́дшее *nt adj*; **at ~** в ху́дшем слу́чае; **if
the ~ comes to the ~** на худо́й коне́ц, в
са́мом ху́дшем слу́чае.

worst-case scenario [ˈwəːstkeɪs-] *n* ху́дший*
вариа́нт.

worsted [ˈwustɪd] *n*: **(wool)** ~ гребенна́я
шерсть *f*.

worth [wəːθ] *n* *(value)* сто́имость *f* ♦ *adj*: **to be
~** сто́ить *(impf)*; **how much is it ~?** ско́лько
э́то сто́ит?; **50 pence ~ of apples** я́блок на 50
пе́нсов; **an hour's ~ of work** рабо́та на час;
it's ~ it э́то того́ сто́ит.

worthless [ˈwəːθlɪs] *adj* никчёмный* (никчё
мен).

worthwhile [ˈwəːθˈwaɪl] *adj* сто́ящий*; **a ~
book** сто́ящая кни́га.

worthy [wəːðɪ] *adj* досто́йный; **~ of**
досто́йный* (досто́ин) +*gen*.

KEYWORD
---

would [wud] *aux vb* **1** *(conditional tense)*: **I
would tell you if I could** я бы сказа́л Вам, е́сли
бы мог; **if you asked him he would do it** е́сли
Вы его́ попро́сите, (то) он э́то сде́лает; **if
you had asked him he would have done it** е́сли
бы Вы попроси́ли его́, (то) он бы э́то
сде́лал
2 *(in offers, invitations, requests)*: **would you
like a biscuit?** не хоти́те (ли) пече́нья?; **would
you ask him to come in?** пригласи́те его́
войти́?; **would you open the window please?**
откро́йте, пожа́луйста, окно́
3 *(in indirect speech)*: **I said I would do it** я
сказа́л, что сде́лаю э́то; **he asked me if I
would stay with him** он попроси́л меня́
оста́ться с ним; **he asked me if I would resit
the exam if I failed** он спроси́л меня́, бу́ду ли
я пересдава́ть экза́мен, е́сли я провалю́сь

4 *(emphatic)*: **it WOULD have to snow today!**
и́менно сего́дня до́лжен был пойти́ снег!;
you WOULD say that, wouldn't you! Вы,
коне́чно, э́то ска́жете!
5 *(insistence)*: **she wouldn't behave** она́ ника́к
не хоте́ла хорошо́ себя́ вести́
6 *(conjecture)*: **it would have been midnight**
должно́ быть, была́ по́лночь; **it would seem
so** должно́ быть, так; **it would seem that ...**
похо́же, что ...
7 *(indicating habit)*: **he would always come
here on Mondays** он всегда́ приходи́л сюда́
по понеде́льникам; **he would spend every day
on the beach** он проводи́л ка́ждый день на
пля́же.

---

would-be [ˈwudbiː] *adj* *(pej)*: **~ writer** челове́к*,
вообража́ющий себя́ писа́телем.

wouldn't [ˈwudnt] = **would not**.

wound¹ [waund] *pt, pp of* **wind²**.

wound² [wuːnd] *n* ра́на ♦ *vt* ра́нить *(impf/perf)*;
~ed in the leg ра́неный в но́гу.

wove [wəuv] *pt of* **weave**.

woven [ˈwəuvn] *pp of* **weave**.

WP *n abbr* = **word processing**, **word processor** ♦
abbr *(BRIT: inf: = weather permitting)* е́сли
позво́лит пого́да.

WPC *(BRIT)* *n abbr* = **woman police constable**.

wpm *abbr* = **words per minute**.

WRAC *n abbr* *(BRIT)* = **Women's Royal Army
Corps**.

WRAF *n abbr* *(BRIT)* = **Women's Royal Air Force**.

wrangle [ˈræŋgl] *n* пререка́ние ♦ *vi*: **to ~ with
sb over sth** пререка́ться *(impf)* с кем-н по
по́воду чего́-н.

wrap [ræp] *n* *(shawl)* широ́кий* шарф; *(cape)*
наки́дка* ♦ *vt* *(also: ~ up)* завора́чивать
(заверну́ть *perf*); *(wind)*: **to ~ sth round sth**
(tape etc) обора́чивать (оберну́ть *perf*) что-н
вокру́г чего́-н; **to keep sth under ~s** *(fig)*
скрыва́ть *(impf)* что-н.

wrapper [ˈræpəʳ] *n* *(on chocolate)* обёртка;
(BRIT: of book) обло́жка*.

wrapping paper [ˈræpɪŋ-] *n* обёрточная
бума́га.

wrath [rɔθ] *n* гнев.

wreak [riːk] *vt*: **to ~ havoc (on)** наноси́ть*
(нанести́* *perf*) уще́рб (+*dat*); **to ~ vengeance
or revenge on sb** отомсти́ть* *(perf)* кому́-н.

wreath [riːθ] *(pl ~s)* *n* *(at funeral)* вено́к*.

wreck [rɛk] *n* *(vehicle)* ава́рия; *(ship)*
круше́ние; *(sea disaster)* кораблекруше́ние;
(pej: person) развали́на ♦ *vt* *(car etc)*
разбива́ть (разби́ть* *perf*); *(stereo)* лома́ть
(слома́ть* *perf*); *(fig: weekend, relationship)*
по́ртить* (испо́ртить* *perf*); (: *life, health*)
губи́ть* (погуби́ть* *perf*).

wreckage [ˈrɛkɪdʒ] *n* обло́мки *pl*; *(of building)*
разва́лины *fpl*.

wrecker [ˈrɛkəʳ] *n* *(US: breakdown van)*
авари́йная маши́на.

Wren [rɛn] *n* (*BRIT: MIL*) жéнщина, слýжащая в
воéнно-морскóм флóте.
wren [rɛn] *n* крапи́вник.
wrench [rɛntʃ] *n* (*TECH*) гáечный ключ*; (*tug*)
рывóк*; (*fig*) щемя́щая тоскá ♦ *vt* (*twist*)
вывёртывать (вы́вернуть *perf*); **to ~ sth from
sb** вырывáть (вы́рвать *perf*) что-н у когó-н.
wrest [rɛst] *vt*: **to ~ sth from sb** вырывáть
(вы́рвать *perf*) что-н у когó-н.
wrestle ['rɛsl] *vi*: **to ~ (with sb)** борóться* (*impf*)
(с кем-н); **to ~ with a problem** мýчиться (*impf*)
над проблéмой.
wrestler ['rɛslə'] *n* борéц*.
wrestling ['rɛslɪŋ] *n* борьбá; (*also*: **all-in ~**)
кетч (*вид борьбы́*).
wrestling match *n* соревновáния *ntpl* по
борьбé.
wretch [rɛtʃ] *n* негодя́й; **little ~!** негóдник!
wretched ['rɛtʃɪd] *adj* несчáстный*
(несчáстен).
wriggle ['rɪgl] *vi* (*also*: ~ **about**: *person, snake
etc*) извивáться (*impf*) ♦ *n* выгибáние.
wring [rɪŋ] (*pt,pp* **wrung**) *vt* (*wet clothes*)
выжимáть (вы́жать* *perf*); (*hands*) ломáть
(*impf*); (*bird's neck*) свóрачивать (свернýть
perf); (*fig*): **to ~ sth out of sb** выжимáть
(вы́жать* *perf*) что-н из когó-н.
wringer ['rɪŋə'] *n* пресс для отжимáния белья́.
wringing ['rɪŋɪŋ] *adj* (*also*: ~ **wet**): **he is ~ (wet)**
с негó течёт (водá).
wrinkle ['rɪŋkl] *n* (*on skin*) морщи́на; (*on paper
etc*) склáдка* ♦ *vt* (*nose, forehead etc*)
мóрщить (смóрщить *perf*) ♦ *vi* (*skin etc*)
мóрщиться (смóрщиться *perf*); (*paint*)
покрывáться (покры́ться* *perf*) трéщинами.
wrinkled ['rɪŋkld] *adj* (*fabric, paper*) мя́тый;
(*surface*) смóрщенный* (смóрщен); (*skin*)
морщи́нистый (морщи́нист).
wrinkly ['rɪŋklɪ] *adj* = **wrinkled**.
wrist [rɪst] *n* (*ANAT*) запя́стье.
wristband ['rɪstbænd] *n* (*BRIT: of shirt*)
манжéта; (*of watch: leather*) ремешóк*;
(: *metal*) браслéт.
wristwatch ['rɪstwɔtʃ] *n* нарýчные часы́ *pl*.
writ [rɪt] *n* (*LAW*) óрдер; **to issue a ~ against sb**
выдавáть* (вы́дать* *perf*) óрдер на чей-н
арéст; **to serve a ~ on sb** посылáть (послáть*
perf) комý-н повéстку в суд.
write [raɪt] (*pt* **wrote**, *pp* **written**) *vt* (*letter, novel
etc*) писáть* (написáть* *perf*); (*cheque, receipt,
prescription*) выпи́сывать (вы́писать* *perf*) ♦
vi писáть* (*impf*); **to ~ to sb** писáть*
(написáть* *perf*) комý-н
▶ **write away** *vi*: **to ~ away for** (*information*)
запрáшивать (запроси́ть* *perf*) о(б) +*prp*;
(*goods*) посылáть (послáть* *perf*)
пи́сьменный закáз на +*acc*

▶ **write off** *vt* (*debt*) спи́сывать (списáть* *perf*);
(*plan, project*) аннули́ровать (*impf/perf*); (*car
etc*) спи́сывать (списáть* *perf*) ♦ *vi* = **write
away**
▶ **write out** *vt* (*put in writing*) излагáть
(изложи́ть *perf*) пи́сьменно; (*cheque, receipt
etc*) выпи́сывать (вы́писать* *perf*); (*copy:
address etc*) спи́сывать (списáть* *perf*)
▶ **write up** *vt* приводи́ть* (привести́* *perf*) в
поря́док.
write-off ['raɪtɔf] *n* (*inf*): **the car is a ~** маши́не
конéц.
write-protect ['raɪtprə'tɛkt] *vt* (*COMPUT*)
защищáть (защити́ть* *perf*) от зáписи.
writer ['raɪtə'] *n* писáтель *m*.
write-up ['raɪtʌp] *n* (*review*) рецéнзия.
writhe [raɪð] *vi* извивáться (*impf*).
writing ['raɪtɪŋ] *n* (*words written*) нáдпись *f*;
(*also*: **handwriting**) пóчерк; (*of author*)
рабóта, произведéние; **~ is his favourite
occupation** бóльше всегó он лю́бит писáть;
in ~ в пи́сьменном ви́де; **in my own ~**
напи́санный моéй рукóй.
writing case *n* пенáл.
writing desk *n* пи́сьменный стол*.
writing paper *n* пи́счая бумáга.
written ['rɪtn] *pp of* **write**.
WRNS *n abbr* (*BRIT*) = **Women's Royal Naval
Service**.
wrong [rɔŋ] *adj* непрáвильный* (непрáвилен);
(*information*) невéрный; (*immoral*) дурнóй ♦
adv непрáвильно; (*informed*) невéрно ♦ *n*
(*injustice*) несправедли́вость *f*; (*evil*) зло ♦ *vt*
(*treat unfairly*) нехорошó поступáть
(поступи́ть* *perf*) с +*instr*; **the answer was ~**
отвéт был непрáвильный *or* оши́бочный; **he
is ~ in saying that ...** он непрáв, когдá он
говори́т, что ...; **you are ~ to do it** э́то
нехорошó с Вáшей сторóны́; **it's ~ to steal,
stealing is ~** воровáть – нехорошó; **you are ~
about that, you've got it ~** Вы непрáвы; **who
is in the ~?** чья э́то винá?; **what's ~?** в чём
дéло?; **there's nothing ~** всё в поря́дке; **to go
~** (*plan*) не удавáться* (удáться* *perf*);
(*machine*) ломáться (сломáться *perf*); **right
and ~** хорóшее и дурнóе.
wrong-doer ['rɔŋduːə'] *n* правонаруши́тель *m*.
wrong-foot [rɔŋ'fut] *vt* (*SPORT*) застигáть
(засти́гнуть *perf*) врасплóх; (*fight*) лови́ть*
(пойма́ть* *perf*) когó-н на слóве.
wrongful ['rɔŋful] *adj* (*imprisonment,
dismissal*) несправедли́вый (несправедли́в).
wrongly ['rɔŋlɪ] *adv* непрáвильно; (*unjustly*)
несправедли́во.
wrong number *n*: **you have a ~~** (*TEL*) Вы не
тудá попáли.

---

* marks translations which have irregular inflections. The Russian-English side of the dictionary gives inflectional information.

wrong side *n*: the ~~ (*of material*) изна́нка*.
wrote [rəut] *pt of* **write**.
wrought [rɔːt] *adj*: ~ **iron** сва́рочная *or* ко́вкая сталь *f*.
wrung [rʌŋ] *pt, pp of* **wring**.
WRVS *n abbr* (*BRIT*) = Women's Royal Voluntary Service.
wry [raɪ] *adj* (*humour, expression*) лука́вый

(лука́в); (*smile*) криво́й* (крив).
wt. *abbr* = **weight**.
WV *abbr* (*US: POST*) = West Virginia.
WY *abbr* (*US: POST*) = Wyoming.
WYSIWYG ['wɪzɪwɪg] *abbr* (*COMPUT*: = what you see is what you get*) режи́м по́лного соотве́тствия (*в те́кстовых проце́ссорах и изда́тельских систе́мах*).

~ X, x ~

X, x [ɛks] n (letter) 24-ая бу́ква англи́йского алфави́та; (BRIT: CINEMA: formerly) свиде́тельство " X ", кото́рое разреша́ет пока́з кинофи́льма с элеме́нтами эро́тики йли карти́нами наси́лия.

Xerox® [ˈzɪərɔks] n (also: ~ **machine**) ксе́рокс; (photocopy) ксероко́пия ♦ vt де́лать (сде́лать perf) ко́пию +gen, ксерокопи́ровать (отксерокопи́ровать perf).

XL abbr = extra large.

Xmas [ˈɛksməs] n abbr = **Christmas**.

X-rated [ˈɛksˈreɪtɪd] adj (US: film) для взро́слых.

X-ray [ɛksˈreɪ] n (ray) рентге́новские лучи́ mpl; (photo) рентге́новский сни́мок* ♦ vt просве́чивать (просвети́ть* perf) (рентге́новскими луча́ми); to have an ~ де́лать (сде́лать perf) рентге́н.

xylophone [ˈzaɪləfəun] n ксилофо́н.

~ Y, y ~

Y, y [waɪ] n (letter) 25-ая бу́ква англи́йского алфави́та.
yacht [jɔt] n я́хта.
yachting [ˈjɔtɪŋ] n па́русный спорт.
yachtsman [ˈjɔtsmən] irreg n яхтсме́н.
yam [jæm] n (vegetable) ямс, бата́т.
Yank [jæŋk] n (pej) я́нки m ind.
yank [jæŋk] vt дёргать (дёрнуть perf) ♦ n рыво́к*.
Yankee [ˈjæŋkɪ] n (pej) = **Yank**.
yap [jæp] vi (dog) тя́вкать (impf).
yard [jɑːd] n (of house etc) двор; (US: garden) сад*; (measure) ярд; **builder's ~** строи́тельная площа́дка.
yardstick [ˈjɑːdstɪk] n (fig) мери́ло, крите́рий.
yarn [jɑːn] n (thread) пря́жа; (tale) ба́йка.
yawn [jɔːn] n зево́к* ♦ vi зева́ть (зевну́ть perf).
yawning [ˈjɔːnɪŋ] adj (gap) зия́ющий.
yd abbr = **yard**.
yeah [jɛə] adv (inf) да, ага́.
year [jɪəʳ] n год*; (at school) класс; (at university) курс; **every ~** ка́ждый год; **this ~** в э́том году́; **a** or **per ~** в год; **~ in, ~ out** из го́да в год; **school/academic ~** уче́бный/академи́ческий год; **he is eight ~s old** ему́ во́семь лет; **an eight-~-old child** восьмиле́тний* ребёнок*.
yearbook [ˈjɪəbuk] n ежего́дник.
yearling [ˈjɪəlɪŋ] n годова́лое живо́тное nt adj; (racehorse) стригуно́к*.
yearly [ˈjɪəlɪ] adj ежего́дный ♦ adv ежего́дно; **twice ~** два ра́за в год.
yearn [jəːn] vi: **to ~ for sth** тоскова́ть (impf) по чему́-н; **to ~ to do** жа́ждать (impf) +infin.
yearning [ˈjəːnɪŋ] n: **to have a ~ to do** име́ть (impf) стра́стное жела́ние +infin; **to have a ~ for** жа́ждать (impf) +gen.
yeast [jiːst] n дро́жжи pl.
yell [jɛl] n вопль m ♦ vi вопи́ть* (impf).
yellow [ˈjɛləu] adj жёлтый (жёлт) ♦ n (colour) жёлтый цвет.
yellow fever n жёлтая лихора́дка.
yellowish [ˈjɛləuɪʃ] adj желтова́тый (желтова́т).
Yellow Pages® n „Жёлтые страни́цы" fpl (телефо́нный спра́вочник).
Yellow Sea n: **the ~ ~** Жёлтое мо́ре.
yelp [jɛlp] n визг ♦ vi (person, animal) взви́згнуть (perf).

Yemen [ˈjɛmən] n Йе́мен.
Yemeni [ˈjɛmənɪ] adj йе́менский ♦ n (person) йе́менец*(-нка*).
yen [jɛn] n (currency) иена; (craving): **~ for** страсть f к +dat; **~ to do** стра́стное жела́ние +infin.
yeoman [ˈjəumən] irreg n (BRIT): **~ of the guard** лейб-гварде́ец* (короле́вской стра́жи).
yes [jɛs] particle да; (in reply to negative) нет ♦ n (in voting) проголосо́вавший(-ая) m(f) adj; **to say ~** говори́ть (сказа́ть* perf) да; **to answer ~** отвеча́ть (отве́тить* perf) согла́сием.
yes man irreg n (pej) подпева́ла m/f.
yesterday [ˈjɛstədɪ] adv вчера́ ♦ n вчера́шний* день m; **~ morning/evening** вчера́ у́тром/ве́чером; **the day before ~** позавчера́; **all day ~** вчера́ весь день.
yet [jɛt] adv ещё, до сих пор ♦ conj одна́ко, и всё же; **the work is not finished ~** рабо́та ещё не око́нчена; **must you go just ~?** Вам уже́ пора́ идти́?; **the best ~** са́мый лу́чший на сего́дняшний день; **as ~** ещё, до настоя́щего моме́нта; **a few days ~** ещё не́сколько дней; **~ again** ещё раз.
yew [juː] n (tree) ти́совое де́рево*; (wood) тис.
Y-fronts® [ˈwaɪfrʌnts] npl мужски́е трусы́* pl (с ширинко́й).
YHA n abbr (BRIT: = Youth Hostels Association) Ассоциа́ция молодёжных гости́ниц.
Yiddish [ˈjɪdɪʃ] n и́диш.
yield [jiːld] n (AGR) урожа́й m; (COMM) дохо́д ♦ vt (surrender) сдава́ться* (сда́ться* perf); (produce) приноси́ть* (принести́* perf) ♦ vi (surrender) отступа́ть (отступи́ть* perf); (US: AUT) уступа́ть (уступи́ть* perf) доро́гу; **a ~ of five percent** пятипроце́нтный дохо́д.
YMCA n abbr = Young Men's Christian Association; (organization) ИМКА; (hostel) общежи́тие ИМКА.
yob(bo) [ˈjɔb(əu)] n (BRIT: inf: pej) шпана́.
yodel [ˈjəudl] vi петь* (impf) и йо́длером.
yoga [ˈjəugə] n йо́га.
yog(h)ourt [ˈjəugət] n йо́гурт.
yog(h)urt [ˈjəugət] n = **yog(h)ourt**.
yoke [jəuk] n (also fig) ярмо́ ♦ vt (also: ~ together: oxen etc) запряга́ть (запря́чь* perf).
yolk [jəuk] n желто́к*.
yonder [ˈjɔndəʳ] adv вон там.
yonks [jɔŋks] n (inf): **for ~** давны́м-давно́.

Yorks [jɔːks] *abbr* (*BRIT: POST*) = *Yorkshire.*

KEYWORD

you [juː] *pron* **1** (*subject: familiar*) ты; (: *polite*) Вы; (: *2nd person pl*) вы; **you French enjoy your food** вы, французы, знáете толк в едé; **you and I will stay here** мы с тобóй/Вáми остáнется здесь
2 (*direct: familiar*) тебя́; (: *polite*) Вас; (: *2nd person pl*) вас
3 (*indirect: familiar*) тебé; (: *polite*) Вам; (: *2nd person pl*) вам; **I love you** я тебя́/Вас люблю́; **I'll give you a present** я тебé/Вам чтó-нибудь подарю́
4 (*after prep: +gen: familiar*) тебя́; (: *polite*) Вас; (: *2nd person pl*) вас; (: *+dat: familiar*) тебé; (: *polite*) Вам; (: *2nd person pl*) вам; (: *+instr: familiar*) тобóй; (: *2nd person pl*) вáми; (: *+prp: familiar*) тебé; (: *polite*) Вас; (: *2nd person pl*) вас; **they've been talking about you** они́ говори́ли о тебé/Вас
5 (*after prep: referring to subject of sentence*: *+gen*) себя́; (: *+dat, +prp*) себé; (: *+instr*) собóй; **will you take the children with you?** Вы возьмёте детéй с собóй?; **close the door behind you** закрóйте за собóй дверь; **she's younger than you** онá молóже Вас *or* молóже, чем Вы
6 (*impersonal: one*): **you never know what can happen** никогдá не знáешь, что мóжет случи́ться; **you never know!** трýдно предсказáть!; **you can't do that!** так нельзя́ (дéлать)!; **fresh air does you good** свéжий вóздух полéзен (для здорóвья).

you'd [juːd] = **you had, you would.**
you'll [juːl] = **you shall, you will.**
young [jʌŋ] *adj* молодóй (мóлод); (*child*) мáленький ◆ *npl* (*of animal*) молодня́к *msg*; (*people*): **the ~** молодёжь *f*; **a ~ man** молодóй человéк*; **a ~ lady** дéвушка*.
younger [ˈjʌŋɡəʳ] *adj* млáдший*; **the ~ generation** млáдшее поколéние.
youngish [ˈjʌŋɪʃ] *adj* моложáвый (моложáв).
youngster [ˈjʌŋstəʳ] *n* молодóй человéк*; (*child*) ребёнок*; **the ~s of today**

сегóдняшняя молодёжь.
your [jɔːʳ] *adj* (*polite*) Ваш; (*familiar*) твой; (*2nd person pl*) ваш; *see also* **my.**
you're [juəʳ] = **you are.**
yours [jɔːz] *pron* (*familiar*) твой; (*polite*) Ваш; (*2nd person pl*) ваш; (*referring to subject of sentence*) свой; **is this ~?** это твоё/Вáше?; **~ sincerely**, **~ faithfully** и́скренне Ваш; *see also* **mine¹.**
yourself [jɔːˈsɛlf] *pron* (*reflexive*) себя́; (*after prep: +gen*) себя́; (: *+dat, +prp*) себé; (: *+instr*) собóй; (*emphatic*) сам (*f* самá, *pl* сáми); (*alone*): **(all) by ~** оди́н; **you ~ told me** Вы сáми говори́ли мне; *see also* **myself.**
yourselves [jɔːˈsɛlvz] *pl pron* (*reflexive*) себя́; (*after prep: +gen*) себя́; (: *+dat, +prp*) себé; (: *+instr*) собóй; (*emphatic*) сáми; (*alone*): **(all) by ~** одни́; **talk amongst ~ for a moment** посовещáйтесь мéжду собóй покá; *see also* **myself.**
youth [juːθ] *n* (*young days*) мóлодость *f*, ю́ность *f*; (*pl* **~s**; *young man*) ю́ноша *m*; **in my ~** в мóлодости *or* ю́ности.
youth club *n* молодёжный клуб.
youthful [ˈjuːθful] *adj* ю́ношеский*; (*person, looks*) ю́ный.
youthfulness [ˈjuːθfəlnɪs] *n* мóлодость *f*.
youth hostel *n* молодёжная гости́ница.
youth movement *n* молодёжное движéние.
you've [juːv] = **you have.**
yowl [jaul] *n* (*of person, animal*) вой.
yr *abbr* = **year.**
Yugoslav [ˈjuːɡəuslɑːv] *adj* югослáвский ◆ *n* югослáв(ка*).
Yugoslavia [ˈjuːɡəuˈslɑːvɪə] *n* Югослáвия.
Yugoslavian [ˈjuːɡəuˈslɑːvɪən] *adj* югослáвский.
yule log [juːl-] *n большóе полéно, сжигáемое в сочéльник.*
yuppie [ˈjʌpɪ] *n* (*inf*) *молодóй человéк из срéднего клáсса, сдéлавший карьéру.*
YWCA *n abbr* = *Young Women's Christian Association*; (*organization*) жéнский христиáнский сою́з молодёжи; (*hostel*) общежи́тие жéнского христиáнского сою́за молодёжи.

~ Z, z ~

Z, z [zɛd, (US) zi:] n (letter) 26-ая бу́ква
англи́йского алфави́та.
Zagreb [ˈzɑːgrɛb] n За́греб.
Zaire [zɑːˈiːəʳ] n Заи́р.
Zambia [ˈzæmbɪə] n За́мбия.
Zambian [ˈzæmbɪən] adj замби́йский* ♦ n
замби́ец(-и́йка).
zany [ˈzeɪnɪ] adj (ideas, sense of humour)
заба́вный* (заба́вен).
zap [zæp] vt (COMPUT) стира́ть (стере́ть* perf).
zeal [ziːl] n рве́ние.
zealot [ˈzɛlət] n фана́тик.
zealous [ˈzɛləs] adj ре́вностный* (ре́вностен).
zebra [ˈziːbrə] n зе́бра.
zebra crossing n (BRIT) „зе́бра", пешехо́дный
перехо́д.
zenith [ˈzɛnɪθ] n (also fig) зени́т.
zero [ˈzɪərəu] n ноль m, нуль m ♦ vi: **to ~ in on**
(target) пристре́ливаться (пристреля́ться
perf); **5 degrees below** ~ 5 гра́дусов ни́же
нуля́ or ноля́.
zero hour n (fig) реши́тельный час.
zero option n нулево́й вариа́нт.
zero-rated [ˈziːrəureɪtɪd] adj (BRIT)
освобождённый от упла́ты нало́гов.
zest [zɛst] n (for life) вкус; (of orange) це́дра.
zigzag [ˈzɪgzæg] n зигза́г ♦ vi де́лать (impf)
зигза́ги.
Zimbabwe [zɪmˈbɑːbwɪ] n Зимба́бве ind.
Zimbabwean [zɪmˈbɑːbwɪən] adj: ~
government/people прави́тельство/наро́д

Зимба́бве.
zimmer frame® [ˈzɪmə-] n ходунки́ mpl
Зи́ммера.
zinc [zɪŋk] n цинк.
Zionism [ˈzaɪənɪzəm] n сиони́зм.
Zionist [ˈzaɪənɪst] adj сиони́стский ♦ n сиони́ст.
zip [zɪp] n (also: ~ **fastener**) мо́лния ♦ vt (also: ~
up) застёгивать (застегну́ть perf) на
мо́лнию.
zip code n (US) почто́вый и́ндекс.
zipper [ˈzɪpəʳ] n (US) = zip.
zither [ˈzɪðəʳ] n ци́тра.
zodiac [ˈzəudɪæk] n зодиа́к.
zombie [ˈzɔmbɪ] n (fig) зо́мби ind.
zone [zəun] n зо́на.
zonked [zɔŋkt] adj (inf): **I'm completely ~**
(exhausted) я соверше́нно одуре́вший.
zoo [zu:] n зоопа́рк.
zoological [zuəˈlɔdʒɪkl] adj зоологи́ческий*.
zoologist [zuˈɔlədʒɪst] n зоо́лог.
zoology [zuːˈɔlədʒɪ] n зооло́гия.
zoom [zu:m] vi: **to ~ past** промелькну́ть (perf)
ми́мо; **to ~ in (on sth/sb)** (PHOT, CINEMA)
дава́ть* (дать* perf) кру́пный план (чего́-н/
кого́-н).
zoom lens n объекти́в с переме́нным
фо́кусным расстоя́нием.
zucchini [zuːˈkiːnɪ] n(pl) (US: courgette(s))
кабачо́к*.
Zulu [ˈzuːluː] adj зулу́сский ♦ n зулу́с(ка).
Zürich [ˈzjuərɪk] n Цю́рих.

ПРИЛОЖЕНИЯ

APPENDICES

Английские Неправильные Глаголы

present	pt	pp	present	pt	pp
arise	arose	arisen	**dwell**	dwelt	dwelt
awake	awoke	awaked	**eat**	ate	eaten
be (am, is,	was,	been	**fall**	fell	fallen
are; being)	were		**feed**	fed	fed
bear	bore	born(e)	**feel**	felt	felt
beat	beat	beaten	**fight**	fought	fought
become	became	become	**find**	found	found
begin	began	begun	**flee**	fled	fled
behold	beheld	beheld	**fling**	flung	flung
bend	bent	bent	**fly (flies)**	flew	flown
beseech	besought	besought	**forbid**	forbade	forbidden
beset	beset	beset	**forecast**	forecast	forecast
bet	bet, betted	bet, betted	**forget**	forgot	forgotten
bid	bid, bade	bid, bidden	**forgive**	forgave	forgiven
bind	bound	bound	**forsake**	forsook	forsaken
bite	bit	bitten	**freeze**	froze	frozen
bleed	bled	bled	**get**	got	got, (*US*)
blow	blew	blown			gotten
break	broke	broken	**give**	gave	given
breed	bred	bred	**go (goes)**	went	gone
bring	brought	brought	**grind**	ground	ground
build	built	built	**grow**	grew	grown
burn	burnt, burned	burnt, burned	**hang**	hung, hanged	hung, hanged
burst	burst	burst	**have (has;**	had	had
buy	bought	bought	**having)**		
can	could	(been able)	**hear**	heard	heard
cast	cast	cast	**hide**	hid	hidden
catch	caught	caught	**hit**	hit	hit
choose	chose	chosen	**hold**	held	held
cling	clung	clung	**hurt**	hurt	hurt
come	came	come	**keep**	kept	kept
cost	cost	cost	**kneel**	knelt, kneeled	knelt, kneeled
creep	crept	crept	**know**	knew	known
cut	cut	cut	**lay**	laid	laid
deal	dealt	dealt	**lead**	led	led
dig	dug	dug	**lean**	leant, leaned	leant, leaned
do (*3rd*	did	done	**leap**	leapt, leaped	leapt, leaped
person: **he/**			**learn**	learnt, learned	learnt, learned
she/it/does)			**leave**	left	left
draw	drew	drawn	**lend**	lent	lent
dream	dreamed,	dreamed,	**let**	let	let
	dreamt	dreamt	**lie (lying)**	lay	lain
drink	drank	drunk	**light**	lit, lighted	lit, lighted
drive	drove	driven	**lose**	lost	lost

present	pt	pp	present	pt	pp
make	made	made	**speed**	sped, speeded	sped, speeded
may	might	—	**spell**	spelt, spelled	spelt, spelled
mean	meant	meant	**spend**	spent	spent
meet	met	met	**spill**	spilt, spilled	spilt, spilled
mistake	mistook	mistaken	**spin**	spun	spun
mow	mowed	mown, mowed	**spit**	spat	spat
must	(had to)	(had to)	**split**	split	split
pay	paid	paid	**spoil**	spoiled, spoilt	spoiled, spoilt
put	put	put	**spread**	spread	spread
quit	quit, quitted	quit, quitted	**spring**	sprang	sprung
read	read	read	**stand**	stood	stood
rid	rid	rid	**steal**	stole	stolen
ride	rode	ridden	**stick**	stuck	stuck
ring	rang	rung	**sting**	stung	stung
rise	rose	risen	**stink**	stank	stunk
run	ran	run	**stride**	strode	stridden
saw	sawed	sawn	**strike**	struck	struck, stricken
say	said	said			
see	saw	seen	**strive**	strove	striven
seek	sought	sought	**swear**	swore	sworn
sell	sold	sold	**sweep**	swept	swept
send	sent	sent	**swell**	swelled	swollen, swelled
set	set	set			
shake	shook	shaken	**swim**	swam	swum
shall	should	—	**swing**	swung	swung
shear	sheared	shorn, sheared	**take**	took	taken
shed	shed	shed	**teach**	taught	taught
shine	shone	shone	**tear**	tore	torn
shoot	shot	shot	**tell**	told	told
show	showed	shown	**think**	thought	thought
shrink	shrank	shrunk	**throw**	threw	thrown
shut	shut	shut	**thrust**	thrust	thrust
sing	sang	sung	**tread**	trod	trodden
sink	sank	sunk	**wake**	woke, waked	woken, waked
sit	sat	sat	**wear**	wore	worn
slay	slew	slain	**weave**	wove, weaved	woven, weaved
sleep	slept	slept			
slide	slid	slid	**wed**	wedded, wed	wedded, wed
sling	slung	slung	**weep**	wept	wept
slit	slit	slit	**win**	won	won
smell	smelt, smelled	smelt, smelled	**wind**	wound	wound
sow	sowed	sown, sowed	**wring**	wrung	wrung
speak	spoke	spoken	**write**	wrote	written

TABLES OF RUSSIAN IRREGULAR FORMS

Nouns

Table 1		мать	
		Singular	*Plural*
Nom		мать	ма́тери
Acc		мать	матере́й
Gen		ма́тери	матере́й
Dat		ма́тери	матеря́м
Instr		ма́терью	матеря́ми
Prp		о ма́тери	о матеря́х

Table 2		дочь	
		Singular	*Plural*
Nom		дочь	до́чери
Acc		до́чь	дочере́й
Gen		до́чери	дочере́й
Dat		до́чери	дочеря́м
Instr		до́черью	дочерьми́
Prp		о до́чери	о дочеря́х

Table 3		путь	
		Singular	*Plural*
Nom		путь	пути́
Acc		путь	пути́
Gen		пути́	путе́й
Dat		пути́	путя́м
Instr		путём	путя́ми
Prp		о пути́	о путя́х

Table 4		время	
		Singular	*Plural*
Nom		вре́мя	времена́
Acc		вре́мя	времена́
Gen		вре́мени	времён
Dat		вре́мени	времена́м
Instr		вре́менем	времена́ми
Prp		о вре́мени	о времена́х

(NB. Similarly with nouns like и́мя, пле́мя etc)

Pronouns

Personal Pronouns

Table 5a

Nom	я	ты	он	она́	оно́
Acc/Gen	меня́	тебя́	его́	её	его́
Dat	мне	тебе́	ему́	ей	ему́
Instr	мной	тобо́й	им	ей	им
Prp	обо мне	о тебе́	о нём	о ней	о нём

Table 5b

Nom	мы	вы	они́
Acc/Gen	нас	вас	их
Dat	нам	вам	им
Instr	на́ми	ва́ми	и́ми
Prp	о нас	о вас	о них

(NB. The instrumental forms мной, тобо́й, ей have alternatives мно́ю, тобо́ю and е́ю respectively. The reflexive personal pronoun себя́ declines like тебя́)

Interrogative Pronouns

(The alternatives given at the accusative are animate forms which are identical with the genitive.)

Table 6

Nom	кто	что
Acc	кого́	что
Gen	кого́	чего́
Dat	кому́	чему́
Instr	кем	чем
Prp	о ком	о чём

(NB. Similarly with никто́, ничто́ etc)

Table 7

	m	*f*	*nt*	*pl*
Nom	чей	чья	чьё	чьи
Acc	чей/чьего́	чью	чьё	чьи/чьих
Gen	чьего́	чьей	чьего́	чьих
Dat	чьему́	чьей	чьему́	чьим
Instr	чьим	чьей	чьим	чьи́ми
Prp	о чьём	о чьей	о чьём	о чьих

(NB. The instrumental form чьей has the alternative чье́ю.)

Possessive Pronouns

Table 8

	m	*f*	*nt*	*pl*
Nom	мой	моя́	моё	мои́
Acc	мой/моего́	мою́	моё	мои́/мои́х
Gen	моего́	мое́й	моего́	мои́х
Dat	моему́	мое́й	моему́	мои́м
Instr	мои́м	мое́й	мои́м	мои́ми
Prp	о моём	о мое́й	о моём	о мои́х

(NB. твой declines like мой, as does the reflexive possessive pronoun свой. The instrumental form мое́й has the alternative мое́ю)

Table 9

	m	*f*	*nt*	*pl*
Nom	наш	на́ша	на́ше	на́ши
Acc	наш/на́шего	на́шу	на́ше	на́ши/на́ших
Gen	на́шего	на́шей	на́шего	на́ших
Dat	на́шему	на́шей	на́шему	на́шим
Instr	на́шим	на́шей	на́шим	на́шими
Prp	о на́шем	о на́шей	о на́шем	о на́ших

(NB. ваш declines like наш. The instrumental form на́шей has the alternative на́шею. The possessive pronouns его́, её and их are invariable)

Demonstrative Pronouns

Table 10

	m	*f*	*nt*	*pl*
Nom	э́тот	э́та	э́то	э́ти
Acc	э́тот/э́того	э́ту	э́то	э́ти/э́тих
Gen	э́того	э́той	э́того	э́тих
Dat	э́тому	э́той	э́тому	э́тим
Instr	э́тим	э́той	э́тим	э́тими
Prp	об э́том	об э́той	об э́том	об э́тих

(NB. the instrumental form э́той has the alternative э́тою)

Table 11

	m	f	nt	pl
Nom	тот	та	то	те
Acc	тот/того́	ту	то	те/тех
Gen	того́	той	того́	тех
Dat	тому́	той	тому́	тем
Instr	тем	той	тем	те́ми
Prp	о том	о той	о том	о тех

(NB. The instrumental form той has the alternative то́ю)

Table 12

	m	f	nt	pl
Nom	сей	сия́	сие́	сий
Acc	сей/сего́	сию́	сие́	сий/сих
Gen	сего́	сей	сего́	сих
Dat	сему́	сей	сему́	сим
Instr	сим	сей	сим	си́ми
Prp	о сём	о сей	о сём	о сих

(NB. The instrumental form сей has the alternative се́ю)

Table 13

	m	f	nt	pl
Nom	весь	вся	всё	все
Acc	весь/всего́	всю	всё	все/всех
Gen	всего́	всей	всего́	всех
Dat	всему́	всей	всему́	всем
Instr	всем	всей	всем	все́ми
Prp	обо всём	обо всей	обо всём	обо всех

(NB. The instrumental form всей has the alternative все́ю)

Verbs

Table 14		дать		
		Present	*Past*	*Imperative*
	я	дам	дал/дала́	
	ты	дашь	дал/дала́	
	он	даст	дал	
	она́	даст	дала́	
	оно́	даст	да́ло	
	мы	дади́м	да́ли	
	вы	дади́те	да́ли	
	они́	даду́т	да́ли	
				да́й(те)

(NB. Similarly with verbs such as переда́ть, изда́ть, отда́ть, разда́ть etc)

Table 15		есть		
		Present	*Past*	*Imperative*
	я	ем	ел/е́ла	
	ты	ешь	ел/е́ла	
	он	ест	ел	
	она́	ест	е́ла	
	оно́	ест	е́ло	
	мы	еди́м	е́ли	
	вы	еди́те	е́ли	
	они́	едя́т	е́ли	
				е́шь(те)

(NB. Similarly with verbs such as съесть, пое́сть, перее́сть etc)

Table 16		хоте́ть	
		Present	*Past*
	я	хочу́	хоте́л/хоте́ла
	ты	хо́чешь	хоте́л/хоте́ла
	он	хо́чет	хоте́л
	она́	хо́чет	хоте́ла
	оно́	хо́чет	хоте́ло
	мы	хоти́м	хоте́ли
	вы	хоти́те	хоте́ли
	они́	хотя́т	хоте́ли

(NB. Similarly with verbs such as расхоте́ть, захоте́ть etc)

Table 17			чтить		
		Present	*Past*	*Imperative*	
	я	чту	чтил/чти́ла		
	ты	чтишь	чтил/чти́ла		
	он	чтит	чтил		
	она́	чтит	чти́ла		
	оно́	чтит	чти́ло		
	мы	чтим	чти́ли		
	вы	чти́те	чти́ли		
	они́	чтут/чтят	чти́ли		
				чти́(те)	

(NB. Similarly with verbs such as почти́ть etc)

Table 18			идти́		
		Present	*Past*	*Imperative*	
	я	иду́	шёл/шла		
	ты	идёшь	шёл/шла		
	он	идёт	шёл		
	она́	идёт	шла		
	оно́	идёт	шло		
	мы	идём	шли		
	вы	идёте	шли		
	они́	иду́т	шли		
				иди́(те)	

(NB. Similarly with verbs such as прийти́, уйти́, отойти́, зайти́ etc)

Table 19			е́хать		
		Present	*Past*	*Imperative*	
	я	е́ду	е́хал/е́хала		
	ты	едешь	е́хал/е́хала		
	он	е́дет	е́хал		
	она́	е́дет	е́хала		
	оно́	е́дет	е́хало		
	мы	е́дем	е́хали		
	вы	е́дете	е́хали		
	они́	е́дут	е́хали		
				поезжа́й(те)	

(NB. Similarly with verbs such as прие́хать, перее́хать, уе́хать, въе́хать)

Table 20		бежа́ть		
		Present	*Past*	*Imperative*
	я	бегу́	бежа́л/бежа́ла	
	ты	бежи́шь	бежа́л/бежа́ла	
	он	бежи́т	бежа́л	
	она́	бежи́т	бежа́ла	
	оно́	бежи́т	бежа́ло	
	мы	бежи́м	бежа́ли	
	вы	бежи́те	бежа́ли	
	они́	бегу́т	бежа́ли	
				беги́(те)

(NB. Similarly with verbs such as побежа́ть, убежа́ть, прибежа́ть etc)

Table 21		быть		
		Future	*Past*	*Imperative*
	я	бу́ду	был/была́	
	ты	бу́дешь	был/была́	
	он	бу́дет	был	
	она́	бу́дет	была́	
	оно́	бу́дет	бы́ло	
	мы	бу́дем	бы́ли	
	вы	бу́дете	бы́ли	
	они́	бу́дут	бы́ли	
				бу́дь(те)

(NB. Not used in present tense, except есть in certain cases)

Numerals

Cardinal Numbers

(NB. The alternatives given at the accusative are animate forms which are identical with the genitive)

Table 22

	m	f	nt	pl
Nom	оди́н	одна́	одно́	одни́
Acc	оди́н/одного́	одну́	одно́	одни́/одни́х
Gen	одного́	одно́й	одного́	одни́х
Dat	одному́	одно́й	одному́	одни́м
Instr	одни́м	одно́й	одни́м	одни́ми
Prp	об одно́м	об одно́й	об одно́м	об одни́х

(NB. The instrumental form одно́й has the alternative одно́ю)

Table 23

	m	f	nt
Nom	два	две	два
Acc	два/двух	две/двух	два/двух
Gen	двух	двух	двух
Dat	двум	двум	двум
Instr	двумя́	двумя́	двумя́
Prp	о двух	о двух	о двух

Table 24	три	
	Nom	три
	Acc	три/трёх
	Gen	трёх
	Dat	трём
	Instr	тремя́
	Prp	о трёх

Table 25	четы́ре	
	Nom	четы́ре
	Acc	четы́ре/четырёх
	Gen	четырёх
	Dat	четырём
	Instr	четырьмя́
	Prp	о четырёх

Table 26		о́ба	о́бе
		m/nt	f
	Nom	о́ба	о́бе
	Acc	о́ба/обо́их	о́бе/обе́их
	Gen	обо́их	обе́их
	Dat	обо́им	обе́им
	Instr	обо́ими	обе́ими
	Prp	об обо́их	об обе́их

Table 27		пять
	Nom	пять
	Acc	пять
	Gen	пяти́
	Dat	пяти́
	Instr	пятью́
	Prp	о пяти́

(NB. The numerals шесть to два́дцать plus три́дцать decline like пять)

Table 28		со́рок
	Nom	со́рок
	Acc	со́рок
	Gen	сорока́
	Dat	сорока́
	Instr	сорока́
	Prp	о сорока́

Table 29		пятьдеся́т
	Nom	пятьдеся́т
	Acc	пятьдеся́т
	Gen	пяти́десяти
	Dat	пяти́десяти
	Instr	пятью́десятью
	Prp	о пяти́десяти

(NB. Similarly with шестьдеся́т and семьдеся́т)

Table 30		сто
	Nom	сто
	Acc	сто
	Gen	ста
	Dat	ста
	Instr	ста
	Prp	о ста

(NB. Similarly with деьяно́сто)

Table 31		две́сти
	Nom	две́сти
	Acc	две́сти
	Gen	двухсо́т
	Dat	двумста́м
	Instr	двумяста́ми
	Prp	о двухста́х

Table 32		три́ста
	Nom	три́ста
	Acc	три́ста
	Gen	трёхсо́т
	Dat	трёмста́м
	Instr	тремяста́ми
	Prp	о трёхста́х

Table 33		четы́реста
	Nom	четы́реста
	Acc	четы́реста
	Gen	четырёхсо́т
	Dat	четырёмста́м
	Instr	четырьмяста́ми
	Prp	о четырёхста́х

Table 34		пятьсо́т
	Nom	пятьсо́т
	Acc	пятьсо́т
	Gen	пятисо́т
	Dat	пятиста́м
	Instr	пятьюста́ми
	Prp	о пятиста́х

(NB. Similarly with шестьсо́т, семьсо́т, восемьсо́т and девятьсо́т)

Table 35		ты́сяча	
		Singular	*Plural*
	Nom	ты́сяча	ты́сячи
	Acc	ты́сячу	ты́сячи
	Gen	ты́сячи	ты́сяч
	Dat	ты́сяче	ты́сячам
	Instr	ты́сячей	ты́сячами
	Prp	о ты́сяче	о ты́сячах

(NB. The instrumental singular form ты́сячью also exists)

Collective Numerals

The following tables shows how collective numerals 2-7 decline:

Table 36a

Nom	дво́е	тро́е	че́тверо
Acc	дво́е/двои́х	тро́е/трои́х	че́тверо/четверы́х
Gen	двои́х	трои́х	четверы́х
Dat	двои́м	трои́м	четверы́м
Instr	двои́ми	трои́ми	четверы́ми
Prp	о двои́х	о трои́х	о четверы́х

Table 36b

Nom	пя́теро	ше́стеро	се́меро
Acc	пя́теро/пятеры́х	ше́стеро/шестеры́х	се́меро/семеры́х
Gen	пятеры́х	шестеры́х	семеры́х
Dat	пяртеры́м	шестеры́м	семеры́м
Instr	пятеры́ми	шестеры́ми	семеры́ми
Prp	о пятеры́х	о шестеры́х	о семеры́х

(NB. The alternatives given at the accusative are animate forms and identical with the genitive. Other collective numerals decline like че́тверо)

NUMBERS

КОЛИЧЕСТВЕННЫЕ ЧИСЛИТЕЛЬНЫЕ

CARDINAL NUMBERS

оди́н (одна́, одно́, одни́)	1	one
два (две)	2	two
три	3	three
четы́ре	4	four
пять	5	five
шесть	6	six
семь	7	seven
во́семь	8	eight
де́вять	9	nine
де́сять	10	ten
оди́ннадцать	11	eleven
двена́дцать	12	twelve
трина́дцать	13	thirteen
четы́рнадцать	14	fourteen
пятна́дцать	15	fifteen
шестна́дцать	16	sixteen
семна́дцать	17	seventeen
восемна́дцать	18	eighteen
девятна́дцать	19	nineteen
два́дцать	20	twenty
два́дцать оди́н (одна́, одно́ одни́)	21	twenty-one
два́дцать два (две)	22	twenty-two
три́дцать	30	thirty
со́рок	40	forty
пятьдеся́т	50	fifty
шестьдеся́т	60	sixty
се́мьдесят	70	seventy
во́семьдесят	80	eighty
девяно́сто	90	ninety
сто	100	a hundred
сто оди́н (одна́, одно́, одни́)	101	a hundred and one
две́сти	200	two hundred
две́сти оди́н (одна́, одно́, одни́)	201	two hundred and one
три́ста	300	three hundred
четы́реста	400	four hundred
пятьсо́т	500	five hundred
ты́сяча	1 000	a thousand
миллио́н	1 000 000	a million

СОБИРАТЕЛЬНЫЕ ЧИСЛИТЕЛЬНЫЕ

COLLECTIVE NUMERALS

дво́е
тро́е
че́тверо
пя́теро
ше́стеро
се́меро

ПОРЯДКОВЫЕ ЧИСЛИТЕЛЬНЫЕ

ORDINAL NUMBERS

пе́рвый	**1-ый**	first	**1st**
второ́й	**2-ой**	second	**2nd**
тре́тий	**3-ий**	third	**3rd**
четвёртый	**4-ый**	fourth	**4th**
пя́тый	**5-ый**	fifth	**5th**
шесто́й	**6-ой**	sixth	**6th**
седьмо́й	**7-ой**	seventh	**7th**
восьмо́й	**8-ой**	eighth	**8th**
девя́тый	**9-ый**	ninth	**9th**
деся́тый	**10-ый**	tenth	**10th**
оди́ннадцатый		eleventh	
двена́дцатый		twelfth	
трина́дцатый		thirteenth	
четы́рнадцатый		fourteenth	
пятна́дцатый		fifteenth	
шестна́дцатый		sixteenth	
семна́дцатый		seventeenth	
восемна́дцатый		eighteenth	
девятна́дцатый		nineteenth	
двадца́тый		twentieth	
два́дцать пе́рвый		twenty-first	
два́дцать второ́й		twenty-second	
тридца́тый		thirtieth	
сороково́й		fortieth	
пятидеся́тый		fiftieth	
восьмидеся́тый		eightieth	
девяно́стый		ninetieth	
со́тый		hundredth	
сто пе́рвый		hundred-and-first	
ты́сячный		thousandth	
миллио́нный		millionth	

ДРОБИ

полови́на	½
треть (f)	⅓
че́тверть (f)	¼
одна́ пя́тая	⅕
три че́тверти	¾
две тре́ти	⅔
полтора́ (полторы́)	1½
ноль це́лых (и) пять деся́тых	0·5
три це́лых (и) четы́ре деся́тых	3·4
шесть це́лых (и) во́семьдесят де́вять со́тых	6·89
де́сять проце́нтов	10%
сто проце́нтов	100%

FRACTIONS

a half	½
a third	⅓
a quarter	¼
a fifth	⅕
three quarters	¾
two thirds	⅔
one and a half	1½
(nought) point five	0·5
three point four	3·4
six point eight nine	6·89
ten per cent	10%
a hundred per cent	100%

TIME AND DATE

ВРЕМЯ

который час?
сейчас 5 часов
в какое время?
в +*асс* ...
в час дня

полночь (*f*)
десять минут первого

десять минут второго, час десять
четверть второго, час пятнадцать
полвторого, половина второго, час
тридцать
без четверти два, час сорок пять
без десяти два, час пятьдесят
полдень (*m*)
полпервого, половина первого,
двенадцать тридцать
час дня

семь часов вечера

девять тридцать вечера
без четверти двенадцать, одиннадцать
сорок пять

через двадцать минут
двадцать минут назад
в ближайшие двадцать минут
за двадцать минут
спустя двадцать минут
сейчас двадцать минут четвёртого

полчаса
четверть часа
полтора часа
час с четвертью

через час
каждый час
через час, каждый час
через час

разбудите меня в семь часов
уже начало пятого
с девяти до пяти

TIME

what time is it?
it is *or* it's 5 o'clock
at what time?
at ...
at one p.m.

00.00 midnight
00.10, ten past midnight, ten past twelve
a.m.
01.10, ten past one, one ten
01.15, a quarter past one, one fifteen
01.30, half past one, one thirty

01.45, a quarter to two, one forty-five
01.50, ten to two, one fifty
12.00, midday
12.30, half past twelve, twelve thirty p.m.

13.00, one (o'clock) (in the afternoon), one
p.m.
19.00, seven (o'clock) (in the evening),
seven p.m.
21.30, nine thirty (p.m. *or* at night)
23.45, a quarter to twelve, eleven forty-five
p.m.

in twenty minutes
twenty minutes ago
in the next twenty minutes
within twenty minutes
after twenty minutes
it's twenty after three (*US*)

half an hour
quarter of an hour
an hour and a half
an hour and a quarter

in an hour's time
every hour, on the hour
hourly
in an hour from now

wake me up at seven
it's just gone four
from nine to five

с двух до трех (часо́в)   between two and three (o'clock)
сего́дня с девяти́ утра́   since nine o'clock this morning
до десяти́ часо́в ве́чера   till ten o'clock tonight
о́коло трёх часо́в дня   at about three o'clock in the afternoon
три часа́ по Гри́нвичу   three o'clock GMT

ДАТЫ

DATE

сего́дня   today
за́втра   tomorrow
вчера́   yesterday
сего́дня у́тром   this morning
за́втра днём/ве́чером   tomorrow afternoon/night
позавчера́ ве́чером, позапро́шлой   the night before last
но́чью
позавчера́   the day before yesterday
вчера́ ве́чером, прошлой но́чью   last night
послеза́втра   the day after tomorrow
два дня́/шесть лет наза́д   two days/six years ago
ка́ждый день/вто́рник   every day/Tuesday

в сре́ду   on Wednesday
он хо́дит туда́ по сре́дам   he goes there on Wednesdays
"закры́то по пя́тницам"   "closed on Fridays"
с понеде́льника до пя́тницы   from Monday to Friday
к четвергу́   by Thursday
как-то в ма́рте, в суббо́ту   one Saturday in March

че́рез неде́лю   in a week's time
во вто́рник на сле́дующей неде́ле   a week on *or* next Tuesday
в воскресе́нье на про́шлой неде́ле   a week last Sunday
че́рез понеде́льник   Monday week
на э́той/сле́дующей/про́шлой неде́ле   this/next/last week
че́рез две неде́ли   in two weeks *or* a fortnight
в понеде́льник че́рез две неде́ли   two weeks on Monday

в э́тот день шесть лет наза́д   six years to the day
пе́рвая/после́дняя пя́тница ме́сяца   the first/last Friday of the month
сле́дующий ме́сяц   next month
про́шлый год   last year
в конце́ ме́сяца   at the end of the month
два ра́за в неде́лю/ме́сяц/год   twice a week/month/year

како́е сего́дня число́?   what's the date?, what date it it today?
сего́дня 28-ое   today's date is the 28th, today is the 28th
пе́рвое января́   the first of January, January the first
ты́сяча девятьсо́т шестьдеся́т пя́тый   1965, nineteen (hundred and) sixty-five
год
роди́лся в 1967-ом году́   I was born in 1967

у него́ день рожде́ния 5 ию́ня	his birthday is on June 5th (*BRIT*) *or* 5th June (*US*)
18-го авгу́ста 1992	on 18th August (*BRIT*) *or* August 18th 1992 (*US*)
с 19-го до 3-го	from the 19th to the 3rd
в 89-ом году́	in '89
весна́ 87-го го́да	the Spring of '87
в 1930-ых года́х	in (*or* during) the 1930s
в 1940-ьíх года́х	in 1940 something
в 2006-ом году́	in the year 2006
в 13-ом ве́ке	in the 13th century
4 год до н.э.	4 BC
70 год н.э.	70 AD

А, а	[ɑʒ]
Б, б	[be]
В, в	[ve]
Г, г	[ge]
Д, д	[de]
Е, е	[je]
Ё, ё	[jɔ]
Ж, ж	[ʒe]
З, з	[ze]
И, и	[i]
Й, й	[iˈkratkɔje]
К, к	[ka]
Л, л	[ɛl]
М, м	[ɛm]
Н, н	[ɛn]
О, о	[ɔ]
П, п	[pe]
Р, р	[ɛr]
С, с	[ɛs]
Т, т	[te]
У, у	[u]
Ф, ф	[ɛf]
Х, х	[xa]
Ц, ц	[tse]
Ч, ч	[tʃe]
Ш, ш	[ʃa]
Щ, щ	[ʃta]
Ъ, ъ	[ˈtyɔrd+ znak]
Ы, ы	[+]
Ь, ь	[ˈmakk+ znak]
Э, э	[ɛ]
Ю, ю	[ju]
Я, я	[ja]

[eɪ]	**A, a**
[bi:]	**B, b**
[si:]	**C, c**
[di:]	**D, d**
[i:]	**E, e**
[ɛf]	**F, f**
[dʒi:]	**G, g**
[eɪtʃ]	**H, h**
[aɪ]	**I, i**
[dʒeɪ]	**J, j**
[keɪ]	**K, k**
[ɛl]	**L, l**
[ɛm]	**M, m**
[ɛn]	**N, n**
[əu]	**O, o**
[pi:]	**P, p**
[kju:]	**Q, q**
[ɑ:*]	**R, r**
[ɛs]	**S, s**
[ti:]	**T, t**
[ju:]	**U, u**
[vi:]	**V, v**
['dʌblju]	**W, w**
[ɛks]	**X, x**
[waɪ]	**Y, y**
[zɛd, (US) zi:]	**Z, z**